6/92

LAST LINES
An Index to the Last Lines of Poetry

LAST LINES
An Index to the Last Lines of Poetry

Volume 1
Last Line Index • Title Index

Victoria Kline

Facts On File
New York • Oxford

Last Lines: An Index to the Last Lines of Poetry

Copyright © 1991 by Victoria Kline

Facts On File, Inc.   Facts On File Limited
460 Park Avenue South   Collins Street
New York NY 10016   Oxford OX4 1XJ
USA   United Kingdom

Library of Congress Cataloging-in-Publication Data
Kline, Victoria K.
      Last lines.
        1. Poetry—Indexes. 2. English poetry—Indexes
3. Closure (Rhetoric)—Indexes. I. Title.
PN1022.K55   1989   016.80881   88-30948
ISBN 0-8160-1265-2 (set)
ISBN 0-8160-2763-3 (Vol. 1)
ISBN 0-8160-2764-1 (Vol. 2)

A British CIP catalogue record for this book is available from the British Library.

Facts On File books are available at special discounts when purchased in bulk quantities for businesses, associations, institutions or sales promotions. Please contact our Special Sales Department in New York at 212/683-2244 (dial 800/322- 8755 except in NY, AK, or HI) or in Oxford at 865/728399.

Composition by Logidec
Manufactured by Arcata Graphics/Kingsport Press
Printed in the United States of America

10 9 8 7 6 5 4 3 2 1

This book is printed on acid-free paper.

CONTENTS

PREFACE

The purpose of *Last Lines: An Index to Last Lines of Poetry* is to assist the reader in identifying and locating poems when only the last line of the poem is known. The index will also be useful to scholars studying thematic and structural elements of anthologies of poetry published between 1900 and 1987. The index covers approximately 171,000 poems originally written in English or translated into English. Coverage extends from Egyptian verses written as early as 2600 B.C. through contemporary poetry written as recently as 1987.

Granger's Index to Poetry, the classic reference tool that indexes poetry by first lines, was the inspiration for this book. Since *Last Lines* will often be used in conjunction with *Granger's*, the same 405 anthologies (394 titles) indexed in *Granger's* Eighth Edition by first lines are indexed by last lines in this book. In addition, 74 classic anthologies indexed in *Granger's* Sixth Edition but not included in *Granger's* Eighth Edition are covered in *Last Lines*. Five of the titles indexed are newer editions of the same anthologies indexed in the Eighth Edition of *Granger's*. Eighteen significant new anthologies published between 1985 and 1987, and not covered by *Granger's*, are indexed in *Last Lines*.

Last Lines is composed of the following five sections:

I. **Key to Symbols**. This section contains a complete listing of the alphabetical symbols used to represent the 497 anthologies indexed in *Last Lines*. Each symbol is followed by the full anthology title it represents as well as complete bibliographic information on the anthology. With only a few exceptions, *Last Lines* uses the same alphabetical location symbols to identify indexed anthologies as those used in *Granger's*.

II. **Last Line Index**. This is in alphabetical order by the first word in the last line. Entries include the last line of the poem, the poem title, the author's name, and a list of alphabetical location symbols that represent the anthologies in which the complete poem appears. The location symbols are in alphabetical order.

III. **Title Index**. This section is in alphabetical order by the first word in the poem title. Entries include the poem title, the author's name, the last line, and a list of alphabetical location symbols.

IV. **Author Index**. This section includes an entry for each poet whose work is indexed in the Title and Last Line Index. Authors' full names are given in inverted form and are listed alphabetically by surname. Titles of poems that appear in the Title Index and the Last Line Index are listed in alphabetical order under the name of the author in the Author Index.

V. **Key Word Index**. This section is an alphabetical list of significant words in the last lines and titles of all indexed poems. Each indexed poem is listed alphabetically by title under the key words in its last line and title. The last name of the author is also included. The Key Word Index is an excellent way to identify a poem when the reader remembers a significant word in the last line or title rather than the initial word in the last line or title. The Key Word Index also provides thematic access to all poetry covered in the index.

ACKNOWLEDGMENTS

In acknowledging my debts I must begin with Edith Granger. Her classic index to first lines of poetry, known to all librarians as *Granger's*, was an amazing accomplishment and I was inspired by her success. I am grateful to everyone who encouraged me to follow in her footsteps.

I would like to thank several institutions and innumerable librarians for their help. I am especially grateful to Jack Ramsey and the staff of the Glendale Public Library for their friendship as well as their professional assistance. The excellent poetry collection at the University of California, Santa Barbara was a valuable resource. The Huntington Library generously provided me with a desk in the General Reading Room where I worked and enjoyed the companionship of other "readers."

I could never have completed *Last Lines* without the help of my friend and assistant Pat Kelly. Even her insomnia helped.

I owe a special debt of love and gratitude to my dear friends Janet Jenks, Anna Raye Clarke, Elizabeth Turney Hanson, and Catherine Turney.

I can never adequately thank my husband, Charlie McBride. He knew all about my liaison with *Last Lines* and married me anyway. His love, and his unwavering support, optimism, and sense of humor, mean more to me than I can say.

Throughout the difficulties associated with the project, the poetry itself was always an inspiration. I hope this book is helpful to librarians and scholars, and especially to poetry lovers who are haunted by certain memorable but elusive last lines.

EXPLANATORY NOTES

Title Index and Last Line Index

1. **General Rules of Entry.** Titles and last lines are arranged in two separate alphabetical listings. All poems are indexed once under title in the Title Index and once under last line in the Last Line Index. All entries in the Title Index and the Last Line Index include last line, title, author, and location symbols.

   Punctuation of the title and the last line are generally faithful to the original, as is spacing of words within the last line. When inconsistencies occurred in the final punctuation of the same poem in different anthologies, a period is used as final punctuation.

   If any part of the last line is not included in its entirety, the last line entry begins with an ellipsis, e.g., "Out, Out" by Robert Frost: "... And they, since they/Were not the one dead, turned to their affairs."

2. **Titles.** Some poems, including nursery rhymes, limericks, and works by Emily Dickinson and several other poets, were not given titles by their authors or are known by various titles. In this index, the first lines of such poems are capitalized and used as titles.

3. **Poetic Forms.** Occasionally, the only title of a poem is the name of the poetic form in which it is written. In this case, the first line is given in quotes following the name of the form, e.g., Sonnet: "Oh, for some honest Lover's Ghost." The line is indexed under the name of the form and then under the initial word in the first line. Readers can use this feature to locate examples of the following poetic forms: ballad, canzone, clerihew, elegy, epigram, epitaph, haiku, limerick, lullaby, madrigal, nocturne, ode, riddle, song, and sonnet. Similarly, fragments of verse are listed under "Fragment" and then the first line as title.

4. **Foreign languages.** Words in non-English languages in titles or last lines of poems in English appear as written except for words or lines in a non-Latin alphabet, which are transliterated into English.

5. **Parodies.** If a poem is a parody it is identified as such, e.g., "Young Lochinvar (parody)."

6. **Shakespeare.** Since they have no titles, the sonnets are identified with Roman numerals and first lines.

7. **Song lyrics.** Songs are indexed on the last line of the chorus or refrain rather than on the last line of the last verse, e.g., "Where the skies are not cloudy all day."

Author Index

1. **General rules of entry.** Author's names appear in inverted form with last name first and are listed alphabetically by the author's surname. Authors who were better known by a pseudonym are listed under the pseudonym within quotation marks with the author's birth name shown in parentheses, e.g., "Carroll, Lewis" (Charles Dodgson). When an author is better known by his birth name than by his pseudonym, the pseudonym is given in parentheses, e.g., Russell, George ("AE"). Suitable cross-references are used in both cases. Poets commonly known by titles of nobility are listed under the title, e.g., "Byron, George Gordon, Lord." Monarchs and saints are listed in the Author Index alphabetically by first name, e.g., "Elizabeth I."

2. **Foreign names.**

Arabic—Modern Arabic surnames beginning with "al-" are generally alphabetized under the element following the particle. Surnames from earlier periods frequently have prefixes such as "ibn-," "bint-," "abu-." Such names are alphabetized under the prefix if that is how the poet is commonly known, e.g., "Abu Nuwas."

Asian—Chinese, Vietnamese, and Japanese family names generally come before given names. When the name is Westernized the order is reversed. Since it was impossible to tell which order was used in the various anthologies indexed, it is assumed that Asian names always appeared in Asian form and they are indexed as a unit with no inversions, e.g., "Li Po."

Dutch and German—Dutch "van," "van der," "van den," and German "von" are generally ignored in alphabetization, e.g., "Goethe" not "von Goethe." If the prefix is firmly established as an integral part of the last name, however, the name is alphabetized on the prefix, e.g., "Van Doren, Mark."

French—"de" is generally ignored unless firmly established by tradition. The preposition remains, however, when it elides with a surname beginning with a vowel, e.g., "D'Arcy, Jack" and when it takes the form of "Du," e.g., "Du Bois, William."

Italian—Many Italian poets who lived before the Renaissance are known by first names, e.g., "Dante Alighieri." Italian names beginning with "da," "de," "del," "della," and "di" are indexed under the particle, e.g., "D'Annunzio, Gabriele."

Roman—The forms most common in English are used, e.g., "Ovid" for "Publius Ovidius Neso."

Spanish—Spanish "de" is ignored in alphabetization. Spanish names sometimes include both paternal and maternal names. Poets commonly using both names are listed alphabetically by paternal name, e.g., "García Lorca, Federico."

KEY TO SYMBOLS

AA
American Anthology, An, 1787–1900.
Edmund Clarence Stedman, ed.
(1900)
Houghton Mifflin Company

AAS
Anchor Anthology of Sixteenth-Century Verse, The.
Richard S. Sylvester, ed.
(1974)
Doubleday Anchor Books

ABF
American Ballads and Folk Songs.
John A. Lomax and Alan Lomax, comps.
(1934, reissue, 1946)
The Macmillan Company

ACP
Anthology of Catholic Poets, An.
Shane Leslie, ed.
(Rev. ed., 1952)
The Macmillan Company, later pub. by the Newman Press

ACV
Anthology of Commonwealth Verse, An.
Margaret J. O'Donnell, ed.
(1963)
Blackie

AH
American Hymns Old and New.
Albert Christ-Janer, Charles W. Hughes, and Carleton Sprague Smith, eds.
(1980)
Columbia University Press (2 vols.; Vol I, with music; Vol. II, notes on the hymns and biographies of the authors and composers)

ALV
Anthology of Light Verse, An.
Louis Kronenberger, ed.
(1935)
The Modern Library

AMV–80
Anthology of Magazine Verse and Yearbook of American Poetry; 1980 Edition.
Alan F. Pater, ed.
(1980)
Monitor Book Company, Inc.

AMV–81
Anthology of Magazine Verse and Yearbook of American Poetry; 1981 Edition.
Alan F. Pater, ed.
(1981)
Monitor Book Company, Inc.

ANYP
Anthology of New York Poets, An.
Ron Padgett and David Shapiro, eds.
(1970)
Random House

AP
American Poetry.
Gay Wilson Allen, Walter B. Rideout, James K. Robinson, eds.
(1965)
Harper & Row

APA
American Poetry, 1671–1928.
Conrad Aiken, ed.
(1929)
The Modern Library

APAS
Anthology of Poems on Affairs of State; Augustan Satirical Verse, 1660–1714.
George deF. Lord, ed.
(1975)
Yale University Press

APU
American Poetry Since 1970: Up Late.
Andrei Codrescu, ed.
(1987)
Four Walls Eight Windows

AS
American Songbag, The.
Carl Sandburg, comp.
(1927)
Harcourt, Brace and Company

ATP
Approaches to Poetry.
Walter Blair and W.K. Chandler, eds.
(2nd ed., 1953)
Appleton-Century-Crofts

AWP
Anthology of World Poetry, An.
Mark Van Doren, ed.
(Rev. and enl. ed., 1936)
Harcourt Brace Jovanovich

AmC
American Classic; Car Poems for Collectors.
Mary Swope and Walter H. Kerr, eds.
(1985)
SCOP Publications

AmFN
America Forever New: a Book of Poems.
Sara Brewton and John E. Brewton, comps.
(1968)
Thomas Y. Crowell Company

AmFP
American Folk Poetry; an Anthology.
Duncan Emrich, ed.
(1974)
Little, Brown & Company

AmLP
American Lyric Poems; from Colonial Times to the Present.
Elder Olson, ed.
(1964)
Appleton-Century-Crofts

AmMo
Amazing Monsters; Verses to Thrill and Chill.
Robert Fisher, ed.
(1982)
Faber and Faber

AmNP
American Negro Poetry.
Arna Bontemps, ed.

(Rev. ed., 1974)
Hill and Wang

AmP
American Poetry (American Literary Forms).
Karl Shapiro, ed.
(1960)
Thomas Y. Crowell & Company

AmPA
American Poetry Anthology, The.
Daniel Halpern, ed.
(1975)
Westview

AmPC
American Poems; a Contemporary Collection.
Jascha Kessler, ed.
(1964)
Southern Illinois University Press

AmPP
American Poetry and Prose.
Norman Foerster, Norman S. Grabo, Russel B. Nye, E. Fred Carlisle, and Robert Falk, eds.
(5th ed., 1970)
Houghton Mifflin Company

AmSS
American Sea Songs and Chanteys.
Frank Shay, ed.
(1948)
W.W. Norton & Company. Edition of 1924, published by Doubleday, Doran & Company, had title Iron Men and Wooden Ships

AmePo
American Poets, The, 1800–1900.
Edwin H. Cady, ed.
(1966)
Scott, Foresman and Company

AnAmPo
Anthology of American Poetry, An.
Alfred Kreymborg, ed.
(2nd rev. ed., 1941)
Tudor

AnAnS 1–2
Anchor Anthology of Seventeenth-Century Verse, The.
Vol. I, Louis L. Martz, ed.; Vol. II, Richard Sylvester, ed.
(1963)
Doubleday Anchor Books

AnEnPo
Anthology for the Enjoyment of Poetry.
Max Eastman, ed.
(1951)
Charles Scribner's Sons

AnFe
Anthology of Famous English and American Poetry, An.
William Rose Benet and Conrad Aiken, eds.
(1945)
The Modern Library

AnIL
Anthology of Irish Literature, The
David H. Greene, ed.
(1954)
Modern Library

AnIV
Anthology of Irish Verse, An.
Padraic Colum, ed.
(Rev. ed., 1948)

Liveright Publishing Corporation

AnNE
Anthology of the New England Poets, An; from Colonial Times to the Present Day.
Louis Untermeyer, ed.
(1948)
Random House

AnNZ
Anthology of New Zealand Verse, An.
Robert Chapman and Jonathan Bennett, comps.
(1956)
Oxford University Press

AnOE
Anthology of Old English Poetry, An.
Charles W. Kennedy, tr.
(1960)
Oxford University Press

AtBAP
Atlantic Book of British and American Poetry, The.
Edith Sitwell, ed.
(1958)
Little, Brown & Company

BALP
Black American Literature: Poetry.
Darwin T. Turner, ed.
(1969)
Charles E. Merrill Publishing Company

BANP
Book of American Negro Poetry, The.
James Weldon Johnson, ed.
(Rev. ed., 1931)
Harcourt, Brace and Company

BBGG
Beastly Boys and Ghastly Girls.
William Cole, ed.
(1964)
World Publishing Company

BBV
Boy's Book of Verse, The.
Helen Dean Fish, comp.
(Rev. ed., 1951)
J.B. Lippincott Company

BFSS
Ballads and Folksongs of the Southwest.
Ethel Moore and Chauncey O. Moore, comps.
(1964)
University of Oklahoma Press

BIrV
Book of Irish Verse, The; an Anthology of Irish Poetry from the Sixth Century to the Present.
John Montague, ed.
(1974)
Macmillan Publishing Company (also published as the Faber Book of Irish Verse)

BLPA
Best Loved Poems of the American People, The.
Hazel Felleman, ed.
(1936)
Doubleday & Company

BLPL
Best-Loved Poems in Large Print.
Virginia S. Reiser, ed.
(1983)

G.K. Hall & Co.

BLRP
Best Loved Religious Poems, The.
James Gilchrist Lawson, comp.
(1933)
Fleming H. Revell Company

BLSo
Best Loved Songs of the American People. (With music.)
Denes Agay, ed.
(1975)
Doubleday & Company

BOLo
Black Out Loud: an Anthology of Modern Poems by Black Americans.
Arnold Adoff, ed.
(1970)
The Macmillan Company

BP
Black Poetry.
Dudley Randall, ed.
(1969)
Broadside Press

BPAW
Best Loved Poems of the American West.
John J. Gregg and Barbara T. Gregg, eds.
(1980)
Doubleday & Company

BPo
Black Poets, The.
Dudley Randall, ed.
(1971)
Bantam Books

BSV
Book of Scottish Verse, A.
Maurice Lindsay and R. L. Mackie, eds.
(3rd ed., 1983)
St. Martin's Press

BXAP
Brand-X Anthology of Poetry, The: Burnt Norton Edition.
William Zaranka, ed.
(1981)
Apple-Wood Books, Inc.

BaBo
Ballad Book, The.
MacEdward Leach, ed.
(1955)
Harper & Brothers

BeLS
Best Loved Story Poems.
Walter E. Thwing, ed.
(1949)
Garden City Publishing Company

BePJ
Beautiful Poems on Jesus.
Basil Miller, comp.
(1948)
Beacon Hill

BiCB
Birthday Candles Burning Bright; A Treasury of Birthday Poetry.
Sara Brewton and John E. Brewton, eds.
(1960)
The Macmillan Company

BiP
Beginnings in Poetry.

William J. Martz, ed.
(2nd ed., 1973)
Scott, Foresman and Company

BlSi
Black Sister; Poetry by Black American Women, 1746–1980.
Erlene Stetson, ed.
(1981)
Indiana University Press

BluL
Blues Line, The; a Collection of Blues Lyrics.
Eric Sackheim, comp.
(1969, paperback 1975)
Schirmer Books

BoAN 1–2
Books of American Negro Spirituals, The; including The Book of American Negro Spirituals and the Second Book of Negro Spirituals.
James Weldon Johnson, ed.
(1925, 1926, 2 vols. in 1, 1940)
The Viking Press

BoAV
Book of Australian Verse, A.
Judith Wright, ed.
(1956)
Oxford University Press

BoAnP
Book of Animal Poems, A.
William Cole, comp.
(1973)
The Viking Press

BoC
Book of Comfort, A; an Anthology.
Elizabeth Goudge, ed.
(1964)
Coward-McCann

BoLiVe
Book of Living Verse, The.
Louis Untermeyer, ed.
(New rev. ed., 1945)
Harcourt, Brace and Company

BoLoP
Book of Love Poetry, A.
Jon Stallworthy, ed.
(1974)
Oxford University Press. Published in England under the title The Penguin Book of Love Poetry

BoNaP
Book of Nature Poems, A.
William Cole, comp.
(1969)
The Viking Press

BoW
Book of Winter, A.
Edith Sitwell, comp.
(1951)
The Macmillan Company

BoWoP
Book of Women Poets from Antiquity to Now, A.
Aliki Barnstone and Willis Barnstone, eds.
(1969)
Schocken Books

BrPo
British Poetry 1880–1920; Edwardian Voices.
Paul L. Wiley and Harold Orel, eds.

(1969)
Appleton-Century-Crofts

BrR
Bridled with Rainbows.
Sara Brewton and John E. Brewton, eds.
(1949)
The Macmillan Company

BrRo
Bread and Roses; an Anthology of Nineteenth- and Twentieth-Century
    Poetry by Women Writers.
Diana Scott, comp.
(1982)
Virago Press

BrSi
Breaking Silence; an Anthology of Contemporary Asian American Poets.
Joseph Bruchac, ed.
(1983)
The Greenfield Review Press

BuBa
Bundle of Ballads, A.
Ruth Manning-Sanders, comp.
(1959)
J.B. Lippincott Company

CABA
College Anthology of British and American Poetry, The.
A. Kent Hieatt and William Park, eds.
(2nd ed.; 1972)
Allyn and Bacon

CABL
Collins Albatross Book of Longer Poems; English and American Poetry
    from the Fourteenth Century to the Present Day.
Edwin Morgan, ed.
(1963)
William Collins

CAD
City in All Directions; an Anthology of Modern Poems.
Arnold Adoff, ed.
(1969)
The Macmillan Company

CAPP
Contemporary American Poetry.
A. Poulin, Jr., ed
(1971)
Houghton Mifflin Company

CAW
Catholic Anthology, The.
Thomas Walsh, ed.
(1940)
The Macmillan Company

CBAP
Collins Book of Australian Poetry, The.
Rodney Hall, comp.
(1981, 1984)
Fontana Collins

CBEP
Cassell Book of English Poetry, The.
James Reeves, ed.
(1965)
Harper & Brothers

CDC
Caroling Dusk; an Anthology of Verse by Negro Poets.
Countee Cullen, ed.
(1927)

Harper & Brothers

CDW
Carriers of the Dream Wheel; Contemporary Native American Poetry.
Duane Niatum, ed.
(1975)
Harper & Row

CEP
Collection of English Poems, A., 1660–1800.
Ronald S. Crane, ed.
(1932)
Harper & Brothers

CH
Come Hither.
Walter de la Mare, comp.
(3rd ed., 1957)
Alfred A. Knopf

CIP
Contemporary Irish Poetry; an Anthology.
Anthony Bradley, ed.
(1980)
University of California Press

CMoP
Chief Modern Poets of Britain and America.
Gerald DeWitt Sanders, John Herbert Nelson, and M.L. Rosenthal, eds.
(1970)
Macmillan Publishing Company

CNA
Celebrations; a New Anthology of Black American Poetry.
Arnold Adoff, ed.
(1977)
Follett Publishing Company

CTBA
Crazy to Be Alive in Such a Strange World; Poems about People.
Nancy Larrick, comp.
(1977)
M. Evans and Company

CTC
Confucius to Cummings; an Anthology of Poetry.
Ezra Pound and Marcella Spann, eds.
(1964)
New Directions

CaP
Canadian Poetry in English (Canadian Literature Series).
Bliss Carmen, Loren Pierce, and V.B. Rhodenizer, eds.
(Rev. and enl. ed., 1954))
The Ryerson Press

CaPN
Canadian Poetry Now; 20 Poets of the 80's.
Ken Norris, ed.
(1984)
Anansi

CaPo
Cavalier Poets; Selected Poems.
Thomas Clayton, ed.
(1978)
Oxford University Press

CavP
Cavalier Poets; The.
Rogin Skelton, ed.
(1970)
Oxford University Press

CenHV
Century of Humorous Verse, A, 1850–1950 (Everyman's Library).

Roger Lancelyn Green, ed.
(1959)
E.P. Dutton & Company

ChBR
Christmas Bells Are Ringing; a Treasury of Christmas Poetry.
Sara Brewton and John E. Brewton, eds.
(1951)
The Macmillan Company

ChER
Choice of English Romantic Poetry, A.
Stephen Spender, ed.
(1947)
The Dial Press

ChMP
Chatto Book of Modern Poetry, The, 1915–1955.
C. Day-Lewis and John Lehmann, eds.
(New ed., 1959)
Chatto & Windus

ChTr
Cherry-Tree, The.
Geoffrey Grigson, comp.
(1959)
Phoenix House

CoAP
Contemporary American Poets, The; American Poetry since 1940.
Mark Strand, ed.
(1971)
World Publishing Company

CoAnAm
Comprehensive Anthology of American Poetry, A.
Conrad Aiken, ed.
(1944)
The Modern Library

CoBE
College Book of English Literature.
James Edward Tobin and others, comps.
(1949)
American Book Company

CoBMV
College Book of Modern Verse, A.
James K. Robinson and Walter B. Rideout, eds.
(1958)
Row, Peterson and Company

CoMu
Common Muse, The; an Anthology of Popular British Ballad Poetry, XVth–XXth Century.
Vivian De Sola Pinto and Allan Edwin Rodway, eds.
(1957)
Philosophical Library

CoPo
Controversy of Poets, A; an Anthology of Contemporary American Poetry.
Paris Leary and Robert Kelly, eds.
(1965)
Doubleday Anchor Books

CoSo
Cowboy Songs and Other Frontier Ballads.
John A. Lomax and Alan Lomax, eds.
(Rev. and enl. ed., 1938)
The Macmillan Company

ConAP
Contemporary American Poetry.
Donald Hall, ed.
(2nd ed., 1972)

Penguin Books

CrMA
Criterion Book of Modern American Verse, The.
W. H. Auden, ed.
(1956)
Criterion Books

DBV
Devil's Book of Verse, The; Masters of the Poison Pen from Ancient Times to the Present Day.
Richard Conniff, ed.
(1983)
Dodd, Mead & Company

DFF
Don't Forget to Fly; a Cycle of Modern Poems.
Paul B. Janeczko, comp.
(1981)
Bradbury Press

DFT
Disenchantments; an Anthology of Modern Fairy Tale Poetry.
Wolfgang Mieder, ed.
(1985)
Published for University of Vermont by University Press of New England

DL
Death in Literature.
Robert F. Weir, ed.
(1980)
Columbia University Press

DTC
Dylan Thomas's Choice; an Anthology of Verse Spoken by Dylan Thomas.
Ralph Maud and Aneirin Talfan Davies, eds.
(1963)
New Directions

DTo
Dark Tower, The; Nineteenth Century Narrative Poems.
Dairine Coffey, comp.
(1967)
Atheneum

DiL
Divided Light: Father and Son Poems; a Twentieth-Century American Anthology.
Jason Shinder, ed.
(1983)
The Sheep Meadow Press

DiPo
Dimensions of Poetry, The; a Critical Anthology.
James E. Miller, Jr., and Bernice Slote, eds.
(1962)
Dodd, Mead & Company

DuDa
Dusk to Dawn; Poems of Night.
Helen Hill, Agnes Perkins, and Alethea Helbig, comps.
(1981)
Thomas Y. Crowell Company

EAS
English and American Surrealist Poetry.
Edward B. Germain, ed.
(1978)
Penguin Books

EBCP
Eerdmans Book of Christian Poetry.
Pat Alexander, comp.
(1981)
William B. Eerdmans Publishing Company

EBEV
Everyman's Book of English Verse.
John Wain, ed.
(1981)
J.M. Dent & Sons Ltd.

EBVV
Everyman's Book of Victorian Verse.
J. R. Watson, ed.
(1982)
J.M. Dent & Sons Ltd.

EG
English Galaxy of Shorter Poems, The.
Gerald Bullett, ed.
(1939)
J.M. Dent & Sons Ltd.

ELP
English Lyric Poems, 1500–1900.
C. Day-Lewis, ed.
(1961)
Appleton-Century-Crofts

ELU
Eight Lines and Under; an Anthology of Short, Short Poems.
William Cole, ed.
(1967)
The Macmillan Company

ERoP 1-2
English Romantic Poetry.
Harold Bloom, ed.
(1961)
Doubleday

ESPB
English and Scottish Popular Ballads.
Helen Child Sargent and George Lyman Kittredge, eds, from the collection of Francis James Child.
(1904, 1932, reissue, 1947)
Houghton Mifflin Company

EaLo
Earth Is the Lord's, The; Poems of the Spirit.
Helen Plotz, comp.
(1965)
Thomas Y. Crowell Company

EiCP
Eighteenth-Century Poetry.
Patricia Meyer Spacks, ed.
(1964)
Prentice-Hall

EIL
Elizabethan Lyrics.
Norman Ault, ed.
(3rd ed., 1949)
William Sloane Associates. Paperback edition of 1960 published by G.P. Putnam's Sons.

EnL
English Literature; a College Anthology.
Donald B. Clark and others, eds.
(1960)
The Macmillan Company

EnLi 1–2
English Literature and Its Backgrounds, Vols. I–II.
Bernard D. N. Grebanier and Stith Thompson, eds.
(Rev. ed., c. 1949)
Dryden Press

EnLit
English Literature; a Period Anthology.
Albert C. Baugh and George William McClelland, eds.
(1954)
Appleton-Century-Crofts

EnLoPo
English Love Poems.
John Betjeman and Geoffrey Taylor, comps.
(1957; paperback 1964)
Faber and Faber

EnPE
English Poetry of the Mid and Late Eighteenth Century; an Historical Anthology.
Ricardo Quintana and Alvin Whitley, eds.
(1963)
Alfred A. Knopf

EnPo
English Poetry 1400–1580.
William Tydeman, ed.
(1970)
Barnes & Noble

EnRP
English Romantic Poetry and Prose.
Russell Noyes, ed.
(1956)
Oxford University Press

EnRePo
English Renaissance Poetry; a Collection of Shorter Poems from Skelton to Jonson.
John Williams, ed.
(1963)
Doubleday Anchor Books

EnSB
English and Scottish Ballads (The Poetry Bookshelf).
Robert Graves, ed.
(1957)
William Heinemann Ltd.

ErPo
Erotic Poetry; the Lyrics, Ballads, Idyls, and Epics of Love—Classical to Contemporary.
William Cole, ed.
(1963)
Random House

EtS
Eternal Sea, The; an Anthology of Sea Poetry (Granger Index Reprint Series).
W. M. Williamson, ed.
(1969)
Books for Libraries (Originally published in 1946 by Coward-McCann)

EvOK
Everybody Ought to Know.
Ogden Nash, ed.
(1961)
J.B. Lippincott Company

ExPo
Exploring Poetry.
M. L. Rosenthal and A. J. M. Smith, eds.
(1955)
The Macmillan Company

EyDe
Eye's Delight; Poems of Art and Architecture.
Helen Plotz, comp.
(1983)
Greenwillow Books

FAZ
From A to Z; 200 Contemporary American Poets.
David Ray, ed.
(1981)
Swallow Press/Ohio University Press

FB
Forerunners, The; Black Poets in America.
Woodie King, Jr., ed.
(1975)
Howard University Press

FCP
Five Courtier Poets of the English Renaissance.
Robert M. Bender, ed.
(1967)
Washington Square

FF
Fine Frenzy; Enduring Themes in Poetry.
Robert Baylor and Brenda Stokes, eds.
(2nd ed., 1978)
McGraw-Hill Book Company

FIA
Fiesta in Aztlan; Anthology of Chicano Poetry.
Toni Empringham, ed.
(1981)
Capra Press

FM
Fellow Mortals; an Anthology of Animal Verse.
Roy Fuller, comp.
(1981)
Macdonald and Evans Ltd.

FPL
Favorite Poems in Large Print.
Virginia S. Reiser, ed.
(1981)
G.K. Hall & Co.

FSN
Favorite Songs of the Nineties; Complete Original Sheet Music for 89
    Songs.
Robert A. Fremont, ed.
(1973)
Dover Publications

FSW
Folksinger's Wordbook.
Irwin Silber and Fred Silber, eds.
(1973)
Oak Publications

FYAP
Fifty Years of American Poetry; Anniversary Volume for the Academy of
    American Poets.
Introduction by Robert Penn Warren
(1984)
Harry N. Abrams, Inc.

FaBV
Family Book of Verse, The.
Lewis Gannett, ed.
(1961)
Harper & Row

FaBoBa
Faber Book of Ballads, The.
Matthew Hodgart, ed.
(1965; paperback 1971)
Faber and Faber

FaBoBe
Family Book of Best Loved Poems, The.
David L. George, ed.
(1952)
Doubleday & Company

FaBoCh
Faber Book of Children's Verse, The.
Janet Adam Smith, comp.
(1953; paperback 1963)
Faber and Faber

FaBoCo
Faber Book of Comic Verse, The.
Michael Roberts and Janet Adam Smith, eds.
(Rev. ed., 1974; paperback, 1978)
Faber and Faber

FaBoEE
Faber Book of Epigrams and Epitaphs, The.
Geoffrey Grigson, ed.
(1977)
Faber and Faber

FaBoEn
Faber Book of English Verse, The.
John Hayward, ed.
(1958)
Faber and Faber

FaBoIP
Faber Book of Contemporary Irish Poetry, The.
Paul Muldoon, ed.
(1986)
Faber and Faber

FaBoMo
Faber Book of Modern Verse, The.
Michael Roberts, ed.
(4th ed., revised by Peter Porter, 1982)
Faber and Faber

FaBoNo
Faber Book of Nonsense Verse, The.
Geoffrey Grigson, ed.
(1979)
Faber and Faber

FaBoPP
Faber Book of Poems and Places, The.
Geoffrey Grigson, ed.
(1980)
Faber and Faber

FaBoPV
Faber Book of Political Verse, The.
Tom Paulin, ed.
(1986)
Faber and Faber

FaBoPa
Faber Book of Parodies, The.
Simon Brett, ed.
(1984)
Faber and Faber

FaBoRV
Faber Book of Reflective Verse, The.
Geoffrey Grigson, ed.
(1984)
Faber and Faber

FaBoTw
Faber Book of Twentieth-Century Verse, The.
John Heath-Stubbs and David Wright, eds.

(1965)
Faber and Faber

FaBoUs
Faber Book of Useful Verse, The.
Simon Brett, ed.
(1981)
Faber and Faber

FaBoWP
Faber Book of 20th Century Women's Poetry, The.
Fleur Adcock, ed.
(1987)
Faber and Faber

FaFP
Family Album of Favorite Poems, The.
P. Edward Ernest, ed.
(1959)
Grosset & Dunlap

FaPON
Favorite Poems Old and New.
Helen Ferris, ed.
(1957)
Doubleday & Company

FaPo
Familiar Poems, Annotated.
Isaac Asimov
(1977)
Doubleday & Company

FaPoR
Faber Popular Reciter, The.
Kingsley Amis, ed.
(1978)
Faber and Faber

FiBHP
Fireside Book of Humorous Poetry, The.
William Cole, ed.
(1959)
Simon and Schuster

FiCP
Fifty Contemporary Poets; the Creative Process.
Alberta T. Turner, ed.
(1977)
David McKay Company

FiP
Fifteen Poets; Chaucer to Arnold.
(1941)
Oxford University Press

FiSC
Fire and Sleet and Candlelight.
August Derleth, ed.
(1961)
Arkham House

ForPo
Form of Poetry, The.
Thomas R. Arp, ed.
(1966)
The Macmillan Company

GBL
Gambit Book of Love Poems, The.
Geoffrey Grigson, ed.
(1975)
Gambit (Originally published in Great Britain by Faber and Faber as The Faber Book of Love Poems)

GBP
Gambit Book of Popular Verse, The.
Geoffrey Grigson, ed.
(1971)
Gambit (Also published as The Faber Book of Popular Verse)

GDP
Good Dog Poems.
William Cole, comp.
(1981)
Charles Scribner's Sons

GLGT
Gladly Learn and Gladly Teach; Poems of the School Experience.
Helen Plotz, comp.
(1981)
Greenwillow Books

GN
Golden Numbers
Kate Douglas Wiggin and Nora Archibald Smith, eds.
(1902)
Doubleday, Doran & Company

GOA
Gift Outright, The; America to Her Poets.
Helen Plotz, ed.
(1977)
Greenwillow Books

GOYP
Going Over to Your Place; Poems for Each Other.
Paul B. Janeczko, ed.
(1987)
Bradbury Press

GP
Geography of Poets, A; an Anthology of the New Poetry.
Edward Field, ed.
(1979)
Bantam Books

GTBS
Golden Treasury of the Best Songs and Lyrical Poems in the English Language.
Francis Palgrave, comp.
(1929)
Oxford University Press

GTBS-P
Golden Treasury of the Best Songs and Lyrical Poems in the English Language, The.
Francis Turner Palgrave, comp. with a fifth book selected by John Press.
(5th ed., 1964)
Oxford University Press

GeTw
Generation of 2000, The; Contemporary American Poets.
William Heyen, ed.
(1984)
Ontario Review Press

GoBC
Golden Book of Catholic Poetry, The.
Alfred Noyes, ed.
(1946)
J.B. Lippincott Company

GoJo
Golden Journey, The; Poems for Young People.
Louise Bogan and William Jay Smith, comps.
(1965)
Reilly & Lee Company

GoSl
Golden Slippers; an Anthology of Negro Poetry for Young Readers.
Arna Bontemps, comp.
(4th ed., 1941)
Harper & Brothers

GoTF
Golden Treasury of the Familiar, The.
Ralph L. Woods, ed.
(1980)
Macmillan Publishing Company

GoTL
Golden Treasury of Longer Poems, The (Everyman's Library).
Ernest Rhys, ed.
(1939)
J.M. Dent & Sons Ltd.

GoTS
Golden Treasury of Scottish Poetry, The.
Hugh MacDiarmid, ed.
(1946)
The Macmillan Company

GoYe
Golden Year, The; the Poetry Society of America Anthology, 1910–1960 (Granger Index Reprint Series).
Melville Cane, John Farrar, and Louise Townsend Nicholl, eds.
(1969)
Books for Libraries (Originally published in 1960 by Fine Editions Press)

GrPl
Green Place, A; Modern Poems.
William Jay Smith, comp.
(1982)
Delacorte Press/Seymour Lawrence

HAP
Harper Anthology of Poetry, The.
John Frederick Nims, ed.
(1981)
Harper & Row

HBMV
Home Book of Modern Verse, The.
Burton Egbert Stevenson, ed.
(2nd ed., 1953)
Henry Holt and Company

HBV 1–2
Home Book of Verse, The. Vols. I-II.
Burton Egbert Stevenson, ed.
(9th ed., 1953, 2 vols.)
Henry Holt and Company

HBVY
Home Book of Verse for Young Folks, The.
Burton Egbert Stevenson, ed.
(Rev. and enl. ed., 1929)
Henry Holt and Company

HW
High Wedlock Then Be Honoured.
Virginia Tufte, ed.
(1970)
The Viking Press

HaCAP
Harvard Book of Contemporary American Poetry, The.
Helen Vendler, ed.
(1985)
Belknap Press

HaMV
Harrap Book of Modern Verse, The.

Maurice Wollman and Kathleen B. Parker, comps.
Harrap's Modern English Series
(1958)
George G. Harrap

HeIP
Heath Introduction to Poetry, The.
Joseph de Roche, ed.
(2nd ed., 1984)
D.C. Heath and Company

HoAn
Hopwood Anthology, The; Five Decades of American Poetry.
Harry Thomas and Steven Lavine, eds.
(1981)
The University of Michigan Press

HoPM
How Does a Poem Mean?
John Ciardi and Miller Williams, eds.
(2nd ed., 1975)
Houghton Mifflin Company

IDB
I Am the Darker Brother; an Anthology of Modern Poems by Negro Americans.
Arnold Adoff, ed.
(1968)
The Macmillan Company

IHMS
I Hear My Sisters Saying; Poems by Twentieth-Century Women.
Carol Konek and Dorothy Walters, eds.
(1976)
Thomas Y. Crowell Company

ILwL
In Love with Love; 100 of the Greatest Mystical Poems.
Anne Freemantle and Christopher Freemantle, eds.
(1978)
Paulist Press

IPY
Irish Poets after Yeats; Seven Poets.
Maurice Harmon, ed.
(1979)
Little, Brown & Company

ISi
I Sing of a Maiden; the Mary Book of Verse.
Sister M. Thérèse, ed.
(1947)
The Macmillan Company

ImOP
Imagination's Other Place; Poems of Science and Mathematics.
Helen Plotz, comp.
(1955)
Thomas Y. Crowell Company

InMe
Innocent Merriment; an Anthology of Light Verse.
Franklin P. Adams, comp.
(1942)
McGraw-Hill Book Company

InPK
Introduction to Poetry, An.
X. J. Kennedy, ed.
(5th ed., 1982)
Little, Brown & Company

InPS
Introduction to Poetry, An.
Louis Simpson, ed.

(3rd ed., 1986)
St. Martin's Press

InPo
Introduction to Poetry.
Mark Van Doren, ed.
(1951)
Sloane

InW
Inventing a Word; an Anthology of Twentieth-Century Puerto Rican Poetry.
Julio Marzán, ed.
(1980)
Columbia University Press (in association with The Center for Inter-American Relations)

InvP
Invitation to Poetry; a Round of Poems from John Skelton to Dylan Thomas.
Lloyd Frankenberg, ed.
(1956)
Doubleday & Company

IrPN
Irish Poets of the Nineteenth Century.
Geoffrey Taylor, ed.
The Muses' Library
(1951)
Harvard University Press

JB
Jump Bad; a New Chicago Anthology.
Gwendolyn Brooks, ed.
(1971)
Broadside Press

JCP
Jacobean and Caroline Poetry; an Anthology.
T. G. S. Cain, ed.
(1981)
Methuen

Kal
Kaleidoscope; Poems by American Negro Poets.
Robert Hayden, ed.
(1967)
Harcourt, Brace and Company

KiLC
Kings, Lords, & Commons; an Anthology from the Irish (Granger Index Reprint Series).
Frank O'Connor, ed. and tr.
(1969)
Books for Libraries (Originally published in 1959 by Knopf)

LAuP
Late Augustan Poetry.
Patricia Meyer Spacks, ed.
(1973)
Prentice-Hall

LBN
Little Book of Necessary Nonsense, A (Granger Index Reprint Series).
Burges Johnson, comp.
(1970)
Books for Libraries (Originally published in 1929 by Harper & Brothers)

LCAP
Longman Anthology of Contemporary American Poetry, The, 1950–1980.
Stuart Friebert and David Young, eds.
(1983)
Longman

LFAC
Light from Another Country, The; Poetry from American Prisons.
Joseph Bruchac, ed.

(1984)
The Greenfield Review Press

LLLT
Love Is Like the Lion's Tooth; an Anthology of Love Poems.
Frances McCullough, ed.
(1984)
Harper & Row

LO
Love.
Walter de la Mare, ed.
(1946)
William Morrow & Company

LOW
Lean Out of the Window; an Anthology of Modern Poetry.
Sara Hannum and Gwendolyn E. Reed, comps.
(1965)
Atheneum

LTB
Leaving the Bough; 50 American Poets of the 80s.
Roger Gaess, ed.
(1982)
International Publishers

LaA
Late Augustans, The; Longer Poems of the Later Eighteenth Century (The Poetry Bookshelf).
Donald Davie, ed.
(1958)
The Macmillan Company

LaNeLa
Lays of the New Land; Stories of Some American Poets and Their Work.
Charlie May Simon, ed.
(1943)
E.P. Dutton & Company

LiBL
Little Book of Limericks, The (Granger Index Reprint Series).
H.I. Brock, comp.
(1969)
Books for Libraries (Originally published in 1947 by Duell, Sloan and Pearce)

LiSp
Literature of Sports, A.
Tom Dodge, ed.
(1980)
D.C. Heath and Company

LiTA
Little Treasury of American Poetry, A.
Oscar Williams, ed.
(1948)
Charles Scribner's Sons

LiTB
Little Treasury of British Poetry, A.
Oscar Williams, ed.
(1951)
Charles Scribner's Sons

LiTL
Little Treasury of Love Poems, A.
John Holmes, ed.
(1950)
Charles Scribner's Sons

LiTM
Little Treasury of Modern Poetry, A, English and American.
Oscar Williams, ed.
(3rd ed., 1970)

Charles Scribner's Sons

LiTW
Little Treasury of World Poetry, A.
Hubert Creekmore, ed.
(1952)
Charles Scribner's Sons

LoBV
London Book of English Verse, The.
Herbert Read and Bonamy Dobrée, comps.
(2d rev. ed., 1952)
The Macmillan Company

LoGBV
Looking Glass Book of Verse, The.
Janet Adam Smith, comp.
(1959)
Looking Glass Library

MAPA
Modern American Poets.
Conrad Aiken, ed.
(1927)
The Modern Library

MAT
Messages; a Thematic Anthology of Poetry.
X. J. Kennedy, ed.
(1973)
Little, Brown & Company

MAYP
Morrow Anthology of Younger American Poets, The.
Dave Smith and David Bottoms, eds.
(1985)
Quill (A Division of William Morrow & Company)

MAmP
Major American Poets to 1914.
Francis Murphy, ed.
(1967)
D.C. Heath and Company

MBW 1–2
Major British Writers; Shorter Edition.
G. B. Harrison, ed.
(1967)
Harcourt Brace & Company

MC
My Country (Granger Index Reprint Series).
Burton Egbert Stevenson, ed.
(1970)
Books for Libraries (Originally published in 1932 by Houghton Mifflin)

MCCG
Magic Casements.
George S. Carhart and Paul A. McGee, comps.
(c. 1926)
The Macmillan Company

MMA
Men Who March Away; Poems of the First World War.
I. M. Parsons, ed.
(1965)
The Viking Press

MOON
Noonstruck; an Anthology of Lunar Poetry.
Robert Phillips, ed.
(1974)
Vanguard

MOS
Moods of the Sea; Masterworks of Sea Poetry.

George C. Solley and Eric Steinbaugh, comps.
(1981)
Naval Institute Press

MP
Modern Poets, The; an American-British Anthology.
John Malcolm Brinnin and Bill Read, eds.
(1963)
McGraw-Hill Book Company

MaC
Magic Circle, The; Stories and People in Poetry.
Louis Untermeyer, ed.
(1952)
Harcourt, Brace & Company

MaVP
Major Victorian Poets.
William H. Marshall, ed.
(1966)
Washington Square

MasP
Master Poems of the English Language.
Oscar Williams, ed.
(1966)
Trident Press

MeEL
Medieval English Lyrics; a Critical Anthology.
R. T. Davies, ed.
(1964)
Northwestern University Press

MeEV
Medieval English Verse and Prose, in Modernized Versions.
Roger Sherman Loomis and Rudolph Willard, eds.
(1948)
Appleton-Century-Crofts

MeLP
Metaphysical Lyrics & Poems of the Seventeenth Century; Donne to Butler.
Herbert J. C. Grierson, ed.
(1925)
Oxford University Press

MePo
Metaphysical Poets, The.
Helen Gardner, ed.
(1957)
Penguin Books

MiAP
Mid-Century American Poets.
John Ciardi, ed.
(1950)
Twayne Publishers

MoAB
Modern American & Modern British Poetry.
Louis Untermeyer, ed., in consultation with Karl Shapiro and Richard Wilbur.
(Rev., shorter ed., 1955)
Harcourt, Brace & Company

MoAmPo
Modern American Poetry.
Louis Untermeyer, ed.
(8th rev. ed., 1962)
Harcourt, Brace & Company

MoBS
Modern Ballads and Story Poems.
Charles Causley, ed.
(1965)

Franklin Watts, Inc. English edition, published in 1964 by Brockhampton Press Ltd., had title Rising Early.

MoBrPo
Modern British Poetry.
Louis Untermeyer, ed.
(7th rev. ed., 1962)
Harcourt, Brace & Company

MoCV
Modern Canadian Verse.
A. J. M. Smith, ed.
(1967)
Oxford University Press

MoLP
Modern Love Poems.
D. J. Klemer, ed.
(1961)
Doubleday

MoPo
Modern Poetry, American and British.
Kimon Friar and John Malcolm Brinnin, eds.
(1951)
Appleton-Century-Crofts

MoRP
Modern Religious Poems; a Contemporary Anthology.
Jacop Trapp, ed.
(1964)
Harper & Row

MoShBr
Moon Is Shining Bright as Day, The; an Anthology of Good-humored Verse.
Ogden Nash, ed.
(1953)
J.B. Lippincott Company

MoVE
Modern Verse in English, 1900–1950.
David Cecil and Allen Tate, eds.
(1958)
The Macmillan Company

MyFE
My Favourite English Poems.
John Masefield, ed.
(1950)
William Heinemann Ltd.

NA
Nonsense Anthology, A.
Carolyn Wells, ed.
(1930)
Charles Scribner's Sons. Paperback edition published by Dover Publications

NAMP
New Anthology of Modern Poetry, A.
Selden Rodman, ed.
(1938)
Random House

NAWM 1–2
Norton Anthology of World Masterpieces, The, Vols. I–II.
Maynard Mack, general ed.
(5th ed., 1985)
W.W. Norton & Company

NAs
Naked Astronaut, The; Poems on Birth and Birthdays.
René Graziani, ed.
(1983)
Faber and Faber

NBM
19th Century British Minor Poets
W. H. Auden, ed.
(1966)
Delacorte Press

NBP
New Black Poetry, The.
Clarence Major, ed.
(1969)
International Publishing Company

NCEP
New Canon of English Poetry, A.
James Reeves and Martin Seymour-Smith, eds.
(1967)
Barnes & Noble

NCSH
New Coasts & Strange Harbors; Discovering Poems.
Helen Hill and Agnes Perkins, comps.
(1974)
Thomas Y. Crowell Company

NIP
Norton Introduction to Poetry, The.
J. Paul Hunter, ed.
(2nd ed., 1981)
W.W. Norton & Company. First edition had title The Norton Introduction to Literature: Poetry (NIL)

NLV
Norton Book of Light Verse, The.
Russell Baker, ed.
(1986)
W.W. Norton & Company

NMM
No More Masks! An Anthology of Poems by Women.
Florence Howe and Ellen Bass, eds.
(1973)
Doubleday Anchor Books

NMP
New Modern Poetry, The; British and American Poetry since World War II.
M. L. Rosenthal, ed.
(1967)
The Macmillan Company

NNP
New Negro Poets U.S.A.
Langston Hughes, ed.
(1964)
Indiana University Press

NOAV
New Oxford Book of Australian Verse.
Les Murray, ed.
(1986)
Oxford University Press

NOBA
New Oxford Book of American Verse, The.
Richard Ellmann, ed.
(1976)
Oxford University Press

NOBC
New Oxford Book of Canadian Verse in English, The.
Margaret Atwood, comp.
(1982)
Oxford University Press

NOBE
New Oxford Book of English Verse, The, 1250–1950.

Helen Gardner, ed.
(1972)
Oxford University Press

NOBI
New Oxford Book of Irish Verse, The.
Thomas Kinsella, ed.
(1986)
Oxford University Press

NOBL
New Oxford Book of English Light Verse, The.
Kingsley Amis, ed.
(1978)
Oxford University Press

NOBV
New Oxford Book of Victorian Verse, The.
Christopher Ricks, ed.
(1987)
Oxford University Press

NOCV
New Oxford Book of Christian Verse, The.
Donald Davie, ed.
(1981)
Oxford University Press

NOEC
New Oxford Book of Eighteenth Century Verse, The.
Roger Lonsdale, ed.
(1984)
Oxford University Press

NPAW
New Poetry of the American West.
Peter Wild and Frank Graziano, eds.
(1982)
Logbridge-Rhodes, Inc.

NPGG
19 New American Poets of the Golden Gate.
Philip Dow, ed.
(1984)
Harcourt Brace Jovanovich

NTCP
New Treasury of Children's Poetry, A; Old Favorites and New Discoveries.
Joanna Cole, comp.
(1984)
Doubleday & Company

NU
News of the Universe; Poems of Twofold Consciousness.
Robert Bly, comp.
(1980)
Sierra Club

NWHW
New Wind Has Wings, The; Poems from Canada.
Mary Alice Downie and Barbara Robertson, eds.
(1984)
Oxford University Press

NYBP
New Yorker Book of Poems, The.
(1969)
The Viking Press. Paperback edition of 1974 published by William Morrow & Company.

NYP
New York: Poems.
Howard Moss, ed.

(1980)
Avon Books

NNaP
New Naked Poetry, The; Recent American Poetry in Open Forms.
Stephen Berg and Robert Mezey, eds.
(1976)
Bobbs-Merrill

NaP
Naked Poetry; Recent American Poetry in Open Forms.
Stephen Berg and Robert Mezey, eds.
(1969)
Bobbs-Merrill

NeAC
New American and Canadian Poetry.
John Gill, ed.
(1971)
Beacon Press

NeAP
New American Poetry, The, 1945–1960.
Donald M. Allen, ed.
(1960)
Grove Press

NeBP
New British Poets, The.
Kenneth Rexroth, ed.
(1949)
New Directions

NeIP
New Irish Poets.
Devin A. Garrity, ed.
(1948)
The Devin-Adair Company

NePA
New Pocket Anthology of American Verse from Colonial Days to the Present, The.
Oscar Williams, ed.
(1955)
World Publishing Company

NePoAm
New Poems by American Poets.
Rolfe Humphries, ed.
(1953)
Ballantine Books

NePoAm–2
New Poems by American Poets #2.
Rolfe Humphries, ed.
(1957)
Ballantine Books

NePoEA
New Poets of England and America.
Donald Hall, Robert Pack, and Louis Simpson, eds.
(1957)
Meridian Books

NePoEA–2
New Poets of England and America; Second Selection.
Donald Hall and Robert Pack, eds.
(1962)
Meridian Books

NoAM
Norton Anthology of Modern Poetry, The.
Richard Ellman and Robert O'Clair, eds.
(1973)
W.W. Norton & Company

NoP
Norton Anthology of Poetry, The.
Alexander W. Allison and others, eds.
(3rd ed., 1983)
W.W. Norton & Company

OAEL 1–2
Oxford Anthology of English Literature, The, Vols. I–II.
Frank Kermode and John Hollander, general eds.
(1973)
Oxford University Press (also published as six paperback vols: Medieval English Literature, *J.B. Trapp, ed.*; The Literature of Renaissance England, *John Hollander and Frank Kermode, eds.*; The Restoration and the Eighteenth Century, *Martin Price, ed.*; Romantic Poetry and Prose, *Harold Bloom and Lionel Trilling, eds.*; Victorian Prose and Poetry, *Lionel Trilling and Harold Bloom, eds.*; Modern British Literature, *Frank Kermode and John Hollander, eds.*

OAEP
Oxford Anthology of English Poetry, An.
Howard Foster Lowry and Willard Thorp, eds.
(2nd ed., 1956)
Oxford University Press

OBAL
Oxford Book of American Light Verse, The.
William Harmon, ed.
(1979)
Oxford University Press

OBCA
Oxford Book of Children's Verse in America, The.
Donald Hall, ed.
(1985)
Oxford University Press

OBCP
Oxford Book of Christmas Poems, The.
Michael Harrison and Christopher Stuart-Clark, eds.
(1983)
Oxford University Press

OBCV
Oxford Book of Canadian Verse in English and French, The.
A. J. M. Smith, ed.
(1960)
Oxford University Press

OBEC
Oxford Book of Eighteenth Century Verse, The.
David Nichol Smith, ed.
(1926)
Oxford University Press

OBET
Oxford Book of English Traditional Verse, The.
Frederick Woods, ed.
(1983)
Oxford University Press

OBEV
Oxford Book of English Verse, The, 1250–1918.
Sir Arthur Quiller-Couch, ed.
(New ed., rev. and enl., 1939)
Oxford University Press

OBMV
Oxford Book of Modern Verse, The, 1892–1935.
William Butler Yeats, ed.
(1936)
Oxford University Press

OBNC
Oxford Book of Nineteenth-Century English Verse, The.
John Hayward, ed.

(1964)
Oxford University Press

OBNV
Oxford Book of Narrative Verse, The.
Iona Opie and Peter Opie, eds.
(1983)
Oxford University Press

OBRV
Oxford Book of Regency Verse, The, 1798–1837.
H. S. Milford, ed.
(1928)
Oxford University Press

OBS
Oxford Book of Seventeenth Century Verse, The.
H. J. C. Grierson and G. Bullough, eds.
(1934)
Oxford University Press

OBSC
Oxford Book of Sixteenth Century Verse, The.
E. K. Chambers, comp.
(1932)
Oxford University Press

OBSP
Oxford Book of Short Poems, The.
James Michie and P.J. Kavanagh, eds.
(1986)
Oxford University Press

OBSS
Oxford Book of Sea Songs, The.
Ray Palmer, ed.
(1986)
Oxford University Press

OBSV
Oxford Book of Satirical Verse, The.
Geoffrey Grigson, comp.
(1980)
Oxford University Press

OBTV
Oxford Book of Travel Verse, The.
Kevin Crossley-Holland, ed.
(1987)
Oxford University Press

OBVE
Oxford Book of Verse in English Translation, The.
Charles Tomlinson, ed.
(1980)
Oxford University Press

OBVV
Oxford Book of Victorian Verse, The.
Arthur Quiller-Couch, comp.
(1912)
Oxford University Press

OBWP
Oxford Book of War Poetry, The.
Jon Stallworthy, ed.
(1984)
Oxford University Press

OCNZ
Oxford Book of Contemporary New Zealand Poetry, The.
Fleur Adcock, comp.
(1982)
Oxford University Press

OFD
O Frabjous Day! Poetry for Holidays and Special Occasions.
Myra Cohn Livingston, ed.
(1977)
Atheneum

OHFP
One Hundred and One Famous Poems.
Roy R. Cook, comp.
(Rev. ed., 1958)
Reilly & Lee Company; reprinted 1981 by Contemporary Books

OHIP
Our Holidays in Poetry.
Mildred P. Harrington and Josephine H. Thomas, comps.
(1929)
The H.W. Wilson Company

OLR
One Little Room, an Everywhere; Poems of Love.
Myra Cohn Livingston, ed.
(1975)
Atheneum

OnMSP
100 More Story Poems.
Elinor Parker, comp.
(1960)
Thomas Y. Crowell Company

OnUR
Once Upon a Rhyme; 101 Poems for Young Children.
Sara Corrin and Stephen Corrin, eds.
(1982)
Faber and Faber

OnYI
1000 Years of Irish Poetry.
Kathleen Hoagland, ed.
(1947)
The Devin-Adair Company

OuSiCo
Our Singing Country; a Second Volume of American Ballads and Folk
  Songs.
John A. Lomax and Alan Lomax, comps.
(1941)
The Macmillan Company

OxBA
Oxford Book of American Verse, The.
F. O. Matthiessen, ed.
(1950)
Oxford University Press

OxBB
Oxford Book of Ballads, The.
James Kinsley, ed.
(1969)
Oxford University Press

OxBC
Oxford Book of Contemporary Verse, The, 1945–1980.
D. J. Enright, comp.
(1980)
Oxford University Press

OxBChV
Oxford Book of Children's Verse, The.
Iona Opie and Peter Opie, eds.
(1973)
Oxford University Press

OxBI
Oxford Book of Irish Verse, The; XVIIth Century-XXth Century.

Donagh MacDonagh and Lennox Robinson, comps.
(1958)
Oxford University Press

OxBM
Oxford Book of Medieval English Verse, The.
Celia Sisam and Kenneth Sisam, eds.
(1970)
Oxford University Press

OxBS
Oxford Book of Scottish Verse, The.
John MacQueen and Tom Scott, comps.
(1966)
Oxford University Press

OxBTC
Oxford Book of Twentieth-Century English Verse, The.
Philip Larkin, ed.
(1973)
Oxford University Press

OxBoCh
Oxford Book of Christian Verse, The.
Lord David Cecil, ed.
(1940)
Oxford University Press

OxBoLi
Oxford Book of Light Verse, The.
W. H. Auden, ed.
(1938)
Oxford University Press

OxNR
Oxford Nursery Rhyme Book, The.
Iona Opie and Peter Opie, comps.
(1955)
Oxford University Press

PAH
Poems of American History.
Burton Egbert Stevenson, ed.
(Rev. ed., 1936)
Houghton Mifflin Company

PAI
Poetry; an Introduction.
Ruth Miller and Robert A. Greenberg, eds.
(1981)
St. Martin's Press

PAL
Patriotic Poems America Loves.
Jean Anne Vincent, comp.
(1968)
Doubleday & Company

PB
Poetry of Birds, The.
Samuel Carr, ed.
(1976)
Taplinger Publishing Company

PBA
Poems from Black Africa.
Langston Hughes, ed.
(1963)
Indiana University Press

PBBP
Penguin Book of Bird Poetry, The.
Peggy Munsterberg, ed.
(1984)
Penguin Books

PBWP
Penguin Book of Women Poets, The.
Carol Cosman, Joan Keefe, and Kathleen Weaver, eds.
(1978)
Penguin Books

PCP
Postcard Poems; a Collection of Poetry for Sharing.
Paul B. Janeczko, ed.
(1979)
Bradbury Press

PCat
Poetry of Cats, The.
Samuel Carr, ed.
(1974)
The Viking Press

PChr
Poems of Christmas.
Myra Cohn Livingston, ed.
(1980)
Atheneum

PDV
Piping down the Valleys Wild; Poetry for the Young of All Ages.
Nancy Larrick, ed.
(1968)
Delacorte Press

PG
Poet's Gold
David Ross, ed.
(2nd rev. ed., 1956)
The Devin-Adair Company

PGD
Poems for the Great Days.
Thomas Curtis Clark and Robert Earle Clark, comps.
(1948)
Abingdon-Cokesbury Press

PH
Poetry of Horses, The.
William Cole, comp.
(1979)
Charles Scribner's Sons

POL
Poems One Line and Longer
William Cole, ed.
(1973)
Grossman

PP
Poems on Poetry; the Mirror's Garland.
Robert Wallace and James G. Taaffe, eds.
(1965)
E.P. Dutton & Company

PPJ
Pocket Poems; Selected for a Journey.
Paul B. Janeczko, ed.
(1985)
Bradbury Press

PPON
Poems of Protest Old and New.
Arnold Kenseth, ed.
(1968)
The Macmillan Company

PPP
Poetry: Past and Present.
Frank Brady and Martin Price, eds.

(1974)
Harcourt Brace Jovanovich

PPoe
Pleasures of Poetry, The.
Donald Hall, ed.
(1971)
Harper & Row

PSoN
Popular Songs of Nineteenth-Century America; Complete Original Sheet
    Music for 64 Songs.
Richard Jackson, ed.
(1976)
Dover Publications (Published in Great Britain by Constable and Company)

PV
Pith and Vinegar; an Anthology of Short Humorous Poetry.
William Cole, ed.
(1969)
Simon and Schuster

PaPo
Parlour Poetry; a Casquet of Gems.
Michael R. Turner, ed.
(1969)
The Viking Press

Par
Parodies; an Anthology from Chaucer to Beerbohm—and After.
Dwight Macdonald, ed.
(1960)
The Modern Library

PeCV
Penguin Book of Canadian Verse, The.
Ralph Gustafson, ed.
(Rev. ed., 1967)
Penguin Books

PeD
Pegasus Descending; a Book of the Best Bad Verse.
James Camp, X. J. Kennedy, and Keith Waldrop, eds.
(1971)
The Macmillan Company

PeHV
Penguin Book of Homosexual Verse, The.
Stephen Coote, ed.
(1983)
Penguin Books

PeSA
Penguin Book of South African Verse, The.
Jack Cope and Uys Krige, eds.
(1968)
Penguin Books

PoA
Poetry Anthology, The, 1912–1977.
Daryl Hine and Joseph Parisi, eds.
(1978)
Houghton Mifflin Company

PoAu 1–2
Poetry in Australia, Vols. I–II. Vol. I. From the Ballads to Brennan.
T. Inglis Moore, comp.
Vol. II: Modern Australian Verse.
Douglas Stewart, comp.
(1965)
University of California Press

PoBA
Poetry of Black America; The; Anthology of the 20th Century.
Arnold Adoff, ed.

(1973)
Harper & Row

PoCh
Poet's Choice.
Paul Engle and Joseph Langland, eds.
(1962)
The Dial Press

PoDr
Poet Dreaming in the Artist's House, The; Contemporary Poems about the
    Visual Arts.
Emilie Buchwald and Ruth Roston, eds.
(1984)
Milkweed Editions

PoEL 1–5
Poets of the English Language, Vols. I–V.
W. H. Auden and Norman Holmes Pearson, eds. Vol. I: Langland to
    Spenser; Vol. II: Marlowe to Marvel; Vol. III: Milton to Goldsmith; Vol.
    IV: Blake to Poe; Vol. V: Tennyson to Yeats
(1950)
The Viking Press

PoLF
Poems That Live Forever.
Hazel Felleman, ed.
(1965)
Doubleday & Company

PoM
Postmoderns, The; the New American Poetry Revised.
Donald Allen and George F. Butterick, eds.
(1982)
Grove Press

PoNE
Poetry of the Negro, The; 1746–1970.
Langston Hughes and Arna Bontemps, eds.
(Rev. ed., 1970)
Doubleday & Company

PoOW
Poems of the Old West; a Rocky Mountain Anthology.
Levette J. Davidson, ed.
(1951)
The University of Denver Press

PoPl
Poetry for Pleasure; the Hallmark Book of Poetry.
(1960)
Doubleday & Company

PoPle
Poetry for Pleasure; a Choice of Poetry and Verse on a Variety of Themes.
Ian Parsons, ed.
(1977)
W.W. Norton & Company

PoRA
Poems to Read Aloud.
Edward Hodnett, ed.
(Rev. ed., 1967)
W.W. Norton & Company

PoSC
Poems for Seasons and Celebrations.
William Cole, ed.
(1961)
World Publishing Company

PoSH
Poems of the Scottish Hills; an Anthology.
Hamish Brown, comp.
(1982)

Aberdeen University Press

PoToHe
Poems That Touch the Heart.
A.L. Alexander, comp.
(1956)
Garden City Publishing Company

PrIm
Practical Imagination, an Introduction to Poetry.
Northrop Frye, Sheridan Baker, and George Perkins.
(1983)
Harper & Row

Prf
Preferences; 51 American Poets Choose Poems from Their Own Work and
    from the Past.
Richard Howard, ed.
(1974)
The Viking Press

Psk
Poetspeak; in Their Work, about Their Work.
Paul B. Janeczko, comp.
(1983)
Bradbury Press

QFR
Quest for Reality; an Anthology of Short Poems in English.
Yvor Winters and Kenneth Fields, eds.
(1969)
The Swallow Press

QQQ
Of Quarks, Quasars, and Other Quirks; Quizzical Poems for the Supersonic
    Age.
Sara Brewton, John E. Brewton, and John Brewton Blackburn, eds.
(1977)
Thomas Y. Crowell Company

RFM
Room for Me and a Mountain Lion; Poetry of Open Space.
Nancy Larrick, comp.
(1974)
M. Evans and Company

RHPC
Random House Book of Poetry for Children, The.
Jack Prelutsky, ed.
(1983)
Random House

RoGo
Roofs of Gold; Poems to Read Aloud.
Padraic Colum, ed.
(1964)
The Macmillan Company

SBG
Salt and Bitter and Good; Three Centuries of English and American
    Women Poets.
Cora Kaplan, ed.
(1975)
Paddington Press Ltd.

SBVL
Shivering Babe, Victorious Lord; the Nativity in Poetry and Art.
Linda Ching Sledge.
(1981)
William B. Eerdmans Publishing Company

SCAP
Seventeenth-Century American Poetry.
Harrison T. Meserole, ed.
(1968)

Doubleday Anchor Books

SCV
Six Centuries of Verse.
Anthony Thwaite, comp.
1984
Thames Methuen

SD
Sprints and Distances; Sports in Poetry and the Poetry in Sport.
Lillian Morrison, comp.
(1965)
Thomas Y. Crowell Company

SM
Strong Measures; Contemporary American Poetry in Traditional Forms.
Philip Dacey, David Jauss, eds.
(1985)
Harper & Row

SO
Straight On Till Morning; Poems of the Imaginary World.
Helen Hill, Agnes Perkins, and Alethea Helbig, comps.
(1977)
Thomas Y. Crowell Company

SOTS
70 on the 70's; a Decade's History in Verse.
Richard Snyder and Robert McGovern, eds.
(1981)
The Ashland Poetry Press

SOTW
Sleeping on the Wing; an Anthology of Modern Poetry with Essays on
    Reading and Writing.
Kenneth Koch and Kate Farrell.
(1981)
Random House

STE
Songs from This Earth on Turtle's Back; Contemporary American Indian
    Poetry.
Joseph Bruchac, ed.
(1983)
The Greenfield Review Press

STF
Speaker's Treasury of 400 Quotable Poems, The.
Croft M. Pentz, comp.
(1963)
Zondervan Publishing House

SUMH
Scars Upon My Heart; Women's Poetry and Verse of the First World War.
Catherine W. Reilly, ed.
(1981)
Virago Press

SUS
Sung Under the Silver Umbrella.
Association for Childhood Education International.
(1935)
The Macmillan Company

SUW
Songs from Unsung Worlds; Science in Poetry.
Bonnie Bilyeu Gordon, ed.
(1985)
Birkhäuser

SV
Singular Voices; American Poetry Today.
Stephen Berg, ed.
(1985)
Avon Books

SaC
Saturday's Children; Poems of Work.
Helen Plotz, comp.
(1982)
Greenwillow Books

SeCP
Seventeenth Century Poetry; the Schools of Donne and Jonson.
Hugh Kenner, ed.
(1964)
Holt, Rinehart & Winston

SeCV 1–2
Seventeenth-Century Verse and Prose, Vols. I–II. Vol. I: 1600–1660; Vol.
    II: 1660–1700.
Helen C. White, Ruth C. Wallerstein, and Ricardo Quintana, eds.
(1951, 1952)
The Macmillan Company

SeCePo
Seven Centuries of Poetry; Chaucer to Dylan Thomas.
A. N. Jeffares, ed.
(1955)
Longmans, Green & Company

SeCeV
Seven Centuries of Verse, English and American.
A. J. M. Smith, ed.
(3rd ed., rev. and enl., 1967)
Charles Scribner's Sons

ShM
Shrieks at Midnight; Macabre Poems, Eerie and Humorous.
Sara Brewton and John E. Brewton, eds.
(1969)
Thomas Y. Crowell Company

ShS
Shantymen and Shantyboys; Songs of the Sailor and Lumberman.
William Main Doerflinger, comp.
(1951)
The Macmillan Company

SiPS
Silver Poets of the Sixteenth Century (Everyman's Library).
Gerald Bullett, ed.
(1947)
J.M. Dent & Sons Ltd.

SiSoSe
Sing a Song of Seasons; Poems about Holidays, Vacation Days, and Days
    to Go to School.
Sara Brewton and John E. Brewton, eds.
(1955)
The Macmillan Company

SoPo
Sound of Poetry, The.
Mary C. Austin and Queenie B. Mills, eds.
(1963)
Allyn & Bacon

SoSe
Sound and Sense; an Introduction to Poetry.
Laurence Perrine, ed., with the assistance of Thomas R. Arp.
(6th ed., 1982)
Harcourt Brace Jovanovich

SpRo
Speak Roughly to Your Little Boy; a Collection of Parodies and
    Burlesques, Together with the Original Poems, Chosen and Annotated
    for Young People.
Myra Cohn Livingston, ed.
(1971)
Harcourt Brace Jovanovich

StPo
Story Poems, New and Old.
William Cole, ed.
(1957)
World Publishing Company

Str
Strings; a Gathering of Family Poems.
Paul B. Janeczko, comp.
(1984)
Bradbury Press

SyP
Symbolist Poem, The.
Edward Engelberg, ed.
(1967)
E.P. Dutton & Company

TAP
Treasury of American Poetry, The.
Nancy Sullivan, ed.
(1978)
Doubleday & Company

TAT
Traveling America with Today's Poets.
David Kherdian, ed.
(1977)
Macmillan Publishing Company

TDH
They've Discovered a Head in the Box for the Bread and Other Laughable
    Limericks.
John E. Brewton and Lorraine A. Blackburn, comps.
(1978)
Thomas Y. Crowell Company

TEP
Treasury of English Poetry, The.
Mark Caldwell and Walter Kendrick, eds.
(1984)
Doubleday & Company

TRV
Treasury of Religious Verse, The.
Donald T. Kauffman, comp.
(1962)
Fleming H. Revell Company

TTY
3000 Years of Black Poetry.
Alan Lomax and Raoul Abdul, eds.
(1970)
Dodd, Mead & Company

TW
Tygers of Wrath; Poems of Hate, Anger, and Invective.
X. J. Kennedy, ed.
(1981)
The University of Georgia Press

TWSS
That's What She Said; Contemporary Poetry and Fiction by Native
    American Women.
Rayna Green, ed.
(1984)
Indiana University Press

TiPo
Time for Poetry.
May Hill Arbuthnot, comp.
(Rev. ed., 1959)
Scott, Foresman and Company

TrAS
Treasury of American Song, A.
Olin Downes and Elie Siegmeister, comps.
(2nd ed., rev. and enl., 1943)
Alfred A. Knopf

TrCP
Treasury of Christian Poetry, The.
*Lorraine Eitel, comp., with Jeannine Bohlmeyer, Lynn M. Faith, Gerald W.
    Healy, Daniel Taylor, and Christian Weintz.*
(1982)
Fleming H. Revell Company

TrGrPo
Treasury of Great Poems, English and American, A.
Louis Untermeyer, ed.
(Rev. and enl. ed., 1955)
Simon and Schuster

TrJP
Treasury of Jewish Poetry, A.
Nathan Ausubel and Marynn Ausubel, eds.
(1957)
Crown Publishers

TrPWD
Treasury of Poems for Worship and Devotion, A.
Charles L. Wallis, ed.
(1959)
Harper & Brothers

TreF
Treasury of the Familiar, A.
Ralph L. Woods, ed.
(1942)
The Macmillan Company

TreFS
Treasury of the Familiar, A Second.
Ralph L. Woods, ed.
(1950)
The Macmillan Company

TreFT
Treasury of the Familiar, A Third.
Ralph L. Woods, ed.
(1970)
The Macmillan Company

TwAmPo
Twentieth-Century American Poetry.
Conrad Aiken, ed.
(Rev. ed., 1963)
The Modern Library

TwCP
Twentieth Century Poetry; American and British (1900–1970).
John Malcolm Brinnin and Bill Read, eds.
(1963, rev. ed., 1970)
McGraw-Hill Book Company. Text edition entitled The Modern Poets; for
    the 1963 edition, *see* MP

UnPo
Understanding Poetry.
Cleanth Brooks and Robert Penn Warren, eds.
(4th ed., 1976)
Holt, Rinehart and Winston

UnS
Untune the Sky; Poems of Music and the Dance.
Helen Plotz, comp.
(1957)
Thomas Y. Crowell Company

UnTE
Uninhibited Treasury of Erotic Poetry, An.
Louis Untermeyer, ed.
(1963)
The Dial Press

VGW
Voice That Is Great Within Us, The; American Poetry of the Twentieth Century.
Hayden Carruth, ed.
(1970)
Bantam Books

VLP
Victorian Literature: Poetry.
Donald J. Gray and G. B. Tennyson, eds.
(1976)
Macmillan Publishing Company

VWA
Voices Within the Ark; the Modern Jewish Poets.
Howard Schwartz and Anthony Rudolf, eds.
(1980)
Avon Books

ViBoFo
Viking Book of Folk Ballads of the English-Speaking World, The. Vols. I–II.
Richard Aldington, ed.
(Rev., mid-century ed., 1958, in 2 vols.)
The Viking Press

ViBoPo
Viking Book of Poetry fo the English-Speaking World, The. Vols. I-II.
Richard Addington, ed.
(Rev., mid-century ed., 1958)
Viking

VoR
Voices of the Rainbow; Contemporary Poetry by American Indians.
Kenneth Rosen, ed.
(1975)
The Viking Press

WBLP
World's Best-Loved Poems, The.
James Gilchrist Lawson, comp.
(1927)
Harper & Brothers

WGRP
World's Great Religious Poetry, The.
Caroline Miles Hill, ed.
(1940)
The Macmillan Company

WHA
Winged Horse Anthology, The.
Joseph Auslander and Frank Ernest Hill, eds.
(1929)
Doubleday & Company

WOLT
Wetting Our Lines Together; an Anthology of Recent North American Fishing Poems.
Allen Hoey, ed., with Cynthia Hoey and Daniel J. Moriarty.
(1982)
Tamarack Editions

WPE
Women Poets in English, The; an Anthology.
Ann Stanford, ed.

(1972)
McGraw-Hill Book Company

WPOW
Women Poets of the World.
Joanna Bankier and Deirdre Lashgari, eds.
(1983)
Macmillan Publishing Company

WSC
Why Am I Grown So Cold? Poems of the Unknowable.
Myra Cohn Livingston, ed.
(1982)
Atheneum

WTO
World Treasury of Oral Poetry, A.
Ruth Finnegan, ed.
(1978)
Indiana University Press

WaP
War Poets, The; an Anthology of the War Poetry of the 20th Century.
Oscar Williams, ed.
(1945)
The John Day Company

WaaP
War and the Poet; an Anthology of Poetry Expressing Man's Attitudes to War from Ancient Times to the Present.
Richard Eberhart and Selden Rodman, eds.
(1945)
The Devin-Adair Company

WeW
Western Wind; an Introduction to Poetry.
John Frederick Nims, ed.
(2nd ed., 1983)
Random House

WhB
When My Brothers Come Home; Poems from Central and Southern Africa.
Frank M. Chipasula, ed.
(1985)
Wesleyan University Press

WhC
What Cheer; an Anthology of American and British Humorous and Witfy Verse.
David McCord, ed.
(1955)
The Modern Library

WiR
Wind and the Rain, The; an Anthology of Poems for Young People.
John Hollander and Harold Bloom, eds.
(1961)
Doubleday & Company

YaD
Yankee Doodles; a Book of American Verse.
Ted Malone, ed.
(1943)
McGraw-Hill Book Company. Edition of 1948, published by the Garden City Publishing Company, has title The All-American Book of Verse

YeAr
Year Around, The; Poems for Children.
Alice I. Hazeltine and Elva S. Smith, comps.
(1956)
Abingdon Press

LAST LINES
An Index to the Last Lines of Poetry

Volume 1

Last Line Index • Title Index

LAST LINE INDEX

A

A-a-all pewtrified, ladies and gentlemen,/Completely pewtrified. Away out Yonder in Arizony. *Anonymous.* OuSiCo

A. D. or B. C., ever can express. Aegean Islands 1940-41. Bernard Spencer. NeBP

An'–a Chola lay a-chokin', an' a buzzard cut the blue. Waring of Sonora-Town. Henry Herbert Knibbs. BPAW

An' a Hi, Hi, honey take a *! on me. Take a Whiff on Me. *Anonymous.* FSW; NOBA

An' a maid, wi' her head a-borne on in a proud/Gait o' walken, so smooth as an air-zwimmin cloud. Which Road? William Barnes. NOBV

An' a man will do you like Bill Martin done. Bill Martin and Ella Speed. *Anonymous.* ABF

An' a place where things come right. Just Keep On. Clifton Abbott. STF; WBLP

An' a rogue is married to, etc. The Sergeant's Weddin'. Rudyard Kipling. OxBTC

An' a voice drowns the hale o' the psalms an' the para-/phrases,/Cryin' "Jean, Jean, Jean!" Tam i' the Kirk. Violet Jacob. BSV; GBL; GoTS; HBMV

Aa gangs to grund and comes again in play. The Kirkyaird by the Sea (excerpt). Paul Valery. OBVE

Aa I can dae/is to pint in homage to the poem/as we drave by its theme and variations. Passin Ben Dorain. Alastair Mackie. PoSH

Aa was still an' saft an' silent in the smoky smirr o' rain. The Smoky Smirr o' Rain. George Campbell Hay. ACV

Aathing comes back–my heart is howe!–/Aathing but you, my dear. A New Spring. Albert D. Mackie. OxBS

Abandon the jig. On Hearing Prokofieff's Grotesque for Two Bassoons...(parody). Louis Untermeyer. BXAP

Abandon the whole township, and migrate. The Disused Temple. Norman Cameron. ChMP; OxBS; OxBTC

Abash'd before the perfect crowning sleep. Ode: "Sire of the rising day." John Byrne Leicester Warren, Lord De Tabley. OBVV

Abd-el-Fatteh./Servant/of the Open Door. Abdelfatteh. E. A. Lacey. PeHV

Abe will lead you through! Ballad of the Lincoln Penny. Alfred Kreymborg. YaD

Abelungu goddamn! The Work Song. Sipho Sepamla. WhB

Abide, and crowne thy Head with lasting glee. Oh King of Saints, How Great's Thy Work, Say We. Edward Johnson. SCAP

Abide with me and be my friend. Prayer of an Unemployed Man. W. C. Ackerly. PoToHe

The ability to love is the ability to leave/And move on. The Need to Love. Shlomo Vinner. VWA

Abject and lost, lay these, covering the flood,/Under amazement of their hideous change. Paradise Lost. John Milton. LiTB

Ablativo ab his, thus a gallant declined is. The Declining of a Gallant. *Anonymous.* FaBoUs

Ablaze to punish the presumptuous deed! Sonnets: A Sequence on Profane Love. George Henry Boker. AmePo

Ablaze, wondering how to throw the light in. Day of Atonement. Jack Myers. VWA

Able at last to give with an open hand. New Zealand. James Keir Baxter. NoP

Able to do these mortal miracles/In silence and solitude, without a word. Conversing with Paradise. Howard Nemerov. PoDr

Able to go/alone all the way. Love Comes Quietly. Robert Creeley. LLLT

Able to lull asleep a pensive heart/That of the round world's sorrows bears a part. Her Hair. Sir Robert Chester. EiL

Abnd lo! her blue eyes are now sealed in death. Blue Ey'd Mary. *Anonymous.* CoMu

Aboard the Victory, Victory O. A Ballad of the Good Lord Nelson. Lawrence Durrell. ErPo; LiTM

Abominable, inutterable, and worse/Than fables yet have feign'd, or fear conceiv'd. Paradise Lost. John Milton. MyFE

About a world so gentle– Metaphors. Sally McNall. FAZ

About heart,/By heart, for heart. For What As Easy. W. H. Auden. NoP

About love it has no right I Am with Those. Ingrid Jonker. BoWoP

About my yelling–"GraceAnAnne!" GraceAnAnne. Lysbeth Boyd Borie. BiCB

About our pines our sister, wind, is moving. Our Sunday morning when dawn-priests were applying. John Berryman. BoLoP

About that noisy nuisance, Gabriel. The Crusader. Dorothy Parker. ShM

About the blood-stained shrine of bygone wars! The Ancient Sacrifice. Mahlon Leonard Fisher. AnAmPo

About the child we saw pass by,/On Silent Hill. Silent Hill. Zilpha Keatley Snyder. WSC

About the cleft battlements of Can Grande's/castle... At the British Museum. Richard Aldington. MoBrPo

About the curious symbol of the cross. Two Poems on the Catholic Bavarians. Edgar Bowers. PoCh

About the gate, or labor at the oar. To His Friend in Elysium. Joachim Du Bellay. AWP

About the greatest plum-pudding for the greatest number? Christmas. [(James Henry(] Leigh Hunt. OBCP

About the lean hindquarters of my yelping, unpleasant guest. Entreaty. Robert Fitzgerald. OBSP

About the merry-ma-tanzie. Here We Go Dancing Jingo-Ring. *Anonymous.* OxNR

About the quarrels over water. Haiku: "Being newly-married before all the world." *Anonymous.* HW

About their spirits, as they mix and meet/In passion-lighted silence, 'tranced and/sweet. Speechless. Philip Bourke Marston. VLP

...About them watch/as through a mist, the pious prosperous ghosts. Indian Reservation: Caughnawaga. Abraham Moses Klein. LiTM; NOBC; NoP; OBCV

About thy caryan corps shall have, continuall debate. Invective against Ibis (excerpt). Ovid (Publius Ovidius Naso). OBVE

About to fall and crush them soon. Queen of Cheese. James McIntyre. FiBHP; PeD

About to tumble in snow. Two Mornings and Two Evenings. Elizabeth Bishop. PoA

About what they/believe/is/themselves. Oh--Yeah! Sharon Scott. JB

About which, conversation is not dull. Sestina. Donald Hall. NePoEA

Aboute midnight wente they to reste. The Canterbury Tales: The Mill at Trumpington. Geoffrey Chaucer. OxBM

Above all,/love ourselves. Mural (excerpt). Vicente Rodriguez Nietzche. InW

Above all other I love her best,/Until I die, what wald sho more? Welcome, Fortune. *Anonymous.* BSV

Above are restless motions, running lights,/Vast circling azure, giddy clouds, days, nights. Rules and Lessons. Henry Vaughan. TRV

Above beneath lit Gyre's Galax. Norman Henry Pritchard II. PoBA

Above bright Ophir and dark Gades sees. Dahlias. Padraic Colum. GoJo; NePoAm

Above curve the dark glittering twin suns. KRAA. William Pitt Root. SM

Above everything, and the sun/rising. The Crane's Ascent. Nick Bozanic. AMV-81

Above her body the thousand windows blur. Fifth & 94th. Stanley Plumly. NYP

...Above her,/the branches of the pines, their quilled expanse/blanketing the subtler vegetation. Why She Says No. Ellen Bryant Voigt. FaBoWP

Above me, a pair of/hawks hang like wet rags. Song: "Whipped by sorrow now." Miklos Radnoti. VWA

Above ourselves because we meant,/in time, to measure up. A Physics. Heather McHugh. MAYP

Above the ash and spittle croaks and leans. Aubade for Hope. Robert Penn Warren. MoAmPo

Above the children's street cries, a girl plays/A marching song not often sung these days. Tales of the Islands. Derek Walcott. OxBTC

Above the churned reeds, the leaves let go/a slow moan of silver. Lamentations. Louise Gluck. MAYP

Above the cloud, beneath the clod:/The Unknown God, The Unknown God. The Unknown God. William Watson. WGRP

Above the crowd he holds his breathing box/That only empties, fills, empties, fills. Wedding Party. Donald Hall. LCAP

Above the distant lonely road/Sails silently on wat'ry wings. Antique Glimpses (excerpt). Thomas Caulfield Irwin. IrPN

Above the eternal tide of tears? Agamemnon. Aeschylus. AWP; LiTW; PPON; WaaP

Acrobat, scavenger, mariner–and me. For My Twenty-Fifth Birthday in Nineteen Forty-One. John Ciardi. WaP

Across an autumn freezing everywhere. The Womanhood. Gwendolyn Brooks. BALP

Across angular bodies seeming thinner/and solid/as anvils. Chinese Camp, Kamloops (circa 1883). Andrew Suknaski. NOBC

Across from the muddy town square in Milano. Pisanello's Studies of Men Hanging on Gallows. John Wheatcroft. FAZ

Across my eyelids, and my soul recall/From worlds of sleeping pain. To a Linnet in a Cage. Francis Ledwidge. OnYI; RoGo

Across old peach cans and old jelly jars. The Birth in a Narrow Room. Gwendolyn Brooks. BlSi; NAs; PoNe

Across that fused Goliath's ring. Back Again from Yucca Flats. Reeve Spencer Kelley. AmFN

Across the broad-backed rollers in to shore. Tristram of Lyonesse. Algernon Charles Swinburne. GN

Across the carpets of my home, my own home. For No Good Reason. Peter Redgrove. NMP

Across the cottage pane. Interior. Padraic Colum. ACV; MoBrPo

Across the distance, in the same old way. The Mystic Borderland. Helen Field Fischer. WBLP

Across the expedient and wicked stones. Auto Wreck. Karl Shapiro. AmC; AmLP; BiP; CMoP; FF; LiTM; MiAP; MoVE; NIP; PoPl; VGW

Across the far and lonely place/That airplanes know. Threnody. John Farrar. BrR; SUS

Across the gardens of Life they go. Love and Time. Beatrix Demarest Lloyd. AA

Across the grass./Zwuzz, wisssh. Lawn-Mower. Dorothy Walter Baruch. SoPo; SUS

Across the grassy ranges of the world. The Last Whiskey Cup. Paul Engle. ATP; YaD

...Across/The hills to time's malignant sun. Blue Sleigh. Winfield Townley Scott. MP; NePoAm

Across the kindling skies/Takes over over our bodies. To My Father. W. S. Graham. FaBoTw

Across the meadows, we are one/Graceful movement. Haiku, for Cinnamon. Lillie D. Chaffin. PH

...Across the miles/Of the Atlantic, and the blinding/glitter/Of the sea. Bahamas. George Oppen. NYBP

Across the night-black templates/Of an open prairie. Marie Curie Contemplating the Role of Women Scientists... Robert Frazier. SUW

Across/The pane/In/Winter. The Frost Pane. David McCord. BrR

Across the phantom acres of the B-Bar-B. Riders. Linda Peavy. PH

Across the rug to the mouse hole The Silver Racer. Joseph Colin Murphey. AMV-80

Across the sands of Dee. The Sands of Dee. Charles Kingsley. BeLS; FaBoPP; FaPoR; GN; GTBS; HBV 1-2; MCCG; PoPle; TreF; VLP; WBLP

Across the sky/Rain turning to snow. Job Hunting. Tom Hennen. EaLo; GP; OuSiCo

Across the snow–in at the fox's death. The Seasons. Rolfe Humphries. NYBP

Across the spick torrent, ceaselessly,/Upon her irretrievable way. The Paltry Nude Starts on a Spring Voyage. Wallace Stevens. HaCAP

Across the sunset to their seaward isle/On solemn wings that wave but seldomwhile. The Story of Vinland. Sidney Lanier. PAH

Across the towering window fled/Disasters, victories, festivals. The Window. Edwin Muir. LiTM

Across the tremendous oceans of the Milky Way. Palm Trees. Rex Warner. OBTV

Across their shadowy forests into sleep. When from the Calyx-Canopy of Night. Freda Laughton. NeIP

Acting like Demons, that would All deprive/Of heav'n, to which themselves can ne'er arrive. The Envious Critick. William Wycherley. PV

Actions are authors, and of those in you/Your friends finde every day a mart of new. To Sir Edward Herbert at Julyers. John Donne. SeCV 1-2

"Actions of women, by affection led,/Must backward, like the sacred tongue, be read." Tell Me, O Love. William Hammond. CBEP

Active in's brain, and passive in his bones. On Playwright. Ben Jonson. NoP

Acts for a sanctuaryTo prevent a bird cemetery. Murdered Little Bird. Anonymous. FiBHP

The actual world in the heyday of the leaves. Contra Mortem. Hayden Carruth. PoA

"Actually, the universe is introspective." An Astronomer's Journal. Jane Shore. PoA

Ad I shall dever see her bore,/By beautiful! by owd!! Lay of the Deserted Influenzaed. Henry Cholmondeley-Pennell InMe

Ad wodt let be taste, shell or sig! Limerick: "A cold had a corpulent pig." Marnie and Harnie Wood. TDH

Adam after hundreds of years/laying him wantonly down to rest. Last Light. Robert Kelly. VGW

Adam come here for; and recites my motto.). Part of Mandevil's Travels. William Empson. AtBAP

Adam/Had 'em. Lines Written on the Antiquity of Microbes. Strickland Gillilan. AtBAP; GoTF; PoEL 1-5; TreFT

Adam in the garden pinning leaves. Adam in the Garden Pinning Leaves. Anonymous. FSW; NoP; OuSiCo

Adam is in this earth. So it begins. So It Begins. James Agee. ATP

Adam was/busy busy busy/dressing and keeping the garden/for God. An Old Story. Rena Lee. VWA

Adam was years four score. Riddle: "There was a thing a full month old." Anonymous. OxNR

Adam weeps... Written in Unbridled Repugnance near Sioux Falls, Alabama... A. K. Redwing. VoR

The Adamses have always been/Remarkably like that. John Quincy Adams 1767-1848. Stephen Vincent Benét. NAMP; OBCA

Add a picture of his factory. The Advertising Agency Song. Anonymous. FaBoUs; NLV; PV

Add gossip girls and western-throated boys. The End. Mark Van Doren. ViBoPo

Adding another painsong to the collection/dedicating it to this night To Night: To Judith. George, Jr Mosby. LFAC

...Adding/that for the tear she dropped/the man dies. It Says. Jon Silkin. VWA

Adequate as Drums/To enlist the Tomb. Some we see no more, tenements of wonder. Emily Dickinson. MoVE

Adequate for survival, withstanding all knocks. Chant Royal. Robert Morgan. SM

The Adequate of Hell– Remorse–is memory–awake. Emily Dickinson. NOBA; NOCV; NoP·

Adieu, Adieu! Faery Song. John Keats. CH

"Adieu, adieu" for evermore. In Memoriam A.H.H., LVII. Alfred, Lord Tennyson. VLP

Adieu, both! I shall see the shade you became. The Afternoon of a Faun: Eclogue. Stephane Mallarme. SyP

Adieu, dear Death–one kiss! We/part. My Enemy. Alice Williams Brotherton. AA

Adieu for ever now. Adieu. Thomas Carlyle. HBV 1-2; OBRV

Adieu, mine Host, Adieu,/Ile leave thy heart a dying. Anacreontea: The Cheat of Cupid. Anonymous. OBVE

Adieu, my goats; for ne'er shall rural muse/Your philosophic beards to stroke refuse. A Pastoral. In the Modern Style. Worcester". NOEC

"Adieu!" she cries; and waved her lily hand. Sweet William's Farewell to Black-Eyed Susan. John Gay. BeLS; BoLoP; CEP; NOEC; OBEC

Adieu the Birks of Endermay. The Birks of Endermay. David Mallet. OBEC

Adieu to all bad company! adieu to all bad rum! The Boston Burglar. Anonymous. AmFP; ViBoFo

...Adina in the breezes/Blazing effulgent in the Caribbean. Adina. Harold Milton Telemaque. TTY

"Adios, mi corazon!" Spanish Is the Loving Tongue. Anonymous. FSW

Administering to garrulous black ghetto residents. Missionaries in the Jungle. Linda Piper. BlSi

...Admire the Byzantine/monastery scene. Monastery on Athos. Richmond Lattimore. EyDe

Admiring it and adding noughts in vain. Star-Gazer. Louis MacNeice. NoP

Admiring the sun on Alcatraz. Weldon Kees. Larry Levis. FAZ

Admit no shade. Song: "When Love at first did move." Ben Jonson. GoBC

Admit that I have better taste. The Claim. Edith Nesbit. NOBV

Admit them, admit them. The Song of a Man Who Has Come Through. D. H. Lawrence. CMoP; CoBMV; FaBoMo; GTBS-P; InPS; LiTM; MoPo; NoAm; PAI

Admitted early into a house of light. Resurrection. Marie L. Kaschnitz. WPOW

Adonai Elohim! The Holy of Holies. Gilbert Keith Chesterton. MoRP; TRV; WGRP

Adorations of my rich escape. Morning in the Park. John Ciardi. MiAP

Adore the Son, and honour him as me. The Plan of Salvation. John Milton. WGRP

Adore the Wisdom, praise the Power,/That made and governs all. To God, Ye Choir above. Philip Skelton. OxBoCh

Adore thee present or lament thee lost. The Zucca (excerpt). Percy Bysshe Shelley. ERoP 1-2

Adore with stillness/in his mother's womb? The Visitation. Calvin Le Compte. ISi

Adored again with new apostasy. On the Death of Donne. Thomas Carew. NOBE

Adorned with violets. Night Singers. Sappho. HW

Adorning the head that destiny never worried. O Golden Fleece. George Barker. MoAB; MoBrPo

Adorns him, colour'd with the Florid hue/Of Rainbows and Starrie Eyes. Paradise Lost. John Milton. PB

Adread in that mere we drift toward map's end. Mappemounde. Earle Birney. OBCV; PeCV

Adreint al with shennesse, y-drawe down with shame.' Who Is This That Cometh from Edom? William Herebert. OxBM

Adrift in true night with the stars, the river winds and the abstract/faiths of October. The Cot. Grover Amen. NYBP; NYP

The Advance Prophet transcends the/Law concerning "A prophet." Primary Lesson: The Second Class Citizens. Sun-Ra. PoBA

Adventurous, it never will return. Marriage. Mark Van Doren. MoLP

...Advise/Forthwith how thou oughtst to receive him. Samson Agonistes. John Milton. OBS

...Advise if this be worth/Attempting, or to sit in darkness here/Hatching vain empires. Paradise Lost. John Milton. FaBoPV

Advise me well, but don't dissuade me! A Young Girl's Song. Paul Heyse. PoPl

"The ae best man about your house/Maun wait young Boonjie on." Young Benjie. Anonymous. ESPB

The ae in the mouth. Lines Inspired by the Controversy on the Value...of Old English... Anthony Burgess. FaBoCo

Aeneas still gazed after her in tears,/Shaken by her ill fate and pitying her. The Aeneid. Virgil (Publius Vergilius Maro). NAWM 1-2

...Aerates/the ground of his living. The Earth Worm. Denise Levertov. NOBA

Aeroplane/Aeroplane/Gone-by. Aeroplane. Mary McBride Green. SoPo; TiPo

AETATIS ANNO LXXVIII On Himself. Jonathan Swift. FaBoEE

Afar within its depths I too have seen/The star that glitters on the lilies there. After Reading Saint Teresa, Luis De Leon and Ramon Lull. Muna Lee. CAW

...The affair/Was opened, it is said, with prayer. Sheriff. Ambrose Bierce. DBV

Affirming it thy star, new-graven in heaven,/By which they knew thee King of Israel born. Paradise Regained. John Milton. PCh

Affliction shall advance the flight in me. Easter Wings. George Herbert. ATP; ExPo; HAP; HeIP; InPK; InPS; LiTB; MeLP; MePo; NIP; NoP; OAEL 1-2; OAEP; OBS; PAI; PoEL 1-5; PP; PPP; SeCP; TEP; TrCP

Afflictive is the Adjective/But affluent the doom— Birthday of but a single pang. Emily Dickinson. NAs; OFD

Afforded the men of Cohoes. Limerick: "There was a young man of Cohoes." Robert Jones Burdette. NA

Afield is no unpleasant place. Garden-Song. James Branch Cabell. HBMV

AFL, CIO/Callin' strike, out she go! Union Man. Anonymous. AmFP

Aflame with dreams/incredible is) 2 Little Whos. Edward Estlin Cummings. OLR

Afloat on that darkening, deepening sea,/helplessly, helplessly. Poem without a Main Verb. John Wain. NePoEA-2; NMP

Afore she see Sir Patrick Spens/Come drivin up the street. Sir Patrick Spens. Anonymous. BaBo

Afore they see Sir Patrick Spence/Come sailing to Leith Sands. Sir Patrick Spens. Anonymous. ESPB

Afraid of nothing. Nothing could frighten me. The Voice. Sister Maris Stella. GoBC

Afraid of the wrong goodbye, I stay too long. False Cadence. Bruce Berger. AMV-80

Africa called to her own again. The Zulu King: New Orleans. Josephine Copeland. GoSl

Africa is in your grave and may all the elements find peace/with you. For All Things Black and Beautiful. Conrad Kent Rivers. CNA

Africa is made of clay. Africa Is Made of Clay. Patu Simoko. WhB

African heaven! African Heaven. Frank Parkes. ACV

After a day and an hour/'Twill greet the sun a flower. Epitaph. Louise Driscoll. HBMV; WGRP

After a death in the house, mirrors be covered. Late Reflections. Babette Deutsch. NYBP

After a deepening Christmas. First Cold Night of Autumn. John Stupp. AMV-81

After a fall of rain. In Time of Grief. Lizette Woodworth Reese. AA; ATP

After a storm, I said, "She has shown to me/The deathless glory of the ageless sea." Of Little Faith. Harold Trowbridge Pulsifer. EtS

After a time the grave got up and went away. As He Came Near Death. Roy Fisher. FaBoMo

After a while it dies. The Couple Overhead. William Meredith. HoPM; NoAm; TW

After all/nothing causes death/and nothing/brings to life. Resurrection of the Dead. Aliza Shenhar. VWA

After all these years/Let sleeping beauty wake. After All These Years. May Sarton. AMV-81

After dark. Dive. Langston Hughes. CAD; NYP

After death the ghouls! Epitaph; "In my youth the growls!" Alfred, Lord Tennyson. FaBoEE

After death, when we are gone,/Joy and pleasure is there none. Carpe Diem. Thomas Lodge. OBSC

After dinner &/a Havatampa cigar. Revelation. David Meltzer. NeAP

& After fifty requests/you got your wish. Poem for Edie Sedgwick. Stewart Brisby. LFAC

After five, then you deserve to go without. A Song of the GPO. Gerry Hamill. NOBL

After hangin' Danny Deever in the mornin'. Danny Deever. Rudyard Kipling. AnFE; BrPo; DiPo; ExPo; FaBoBa; FaPoR; FPL; GoTF; GTBS; GTBS-P; HBV 1-2; InPS; LiTB; MaC; MCCG; MoBrPo; NOBE; NOBV; OAEP; OxBoLi; OxBTC; PAI; PoLf; SCV; SeCePo; TEP; TreFS; TrGrPo; UnPo; VLP; WaaP

After hatred's harvest joy will march, shrouded, to Finaghy. The Glorious Twelfth. Robert Greacen. NeIP

After her I sit on my laddered rain-bearing rug/and mend the tear with string. Grandmother. Paula Gunn Allen. STE; TWSS

After his head's pull'd off, to find it out. Epigram. Samuel (1612-80) Butler. FaBoEE

After I had broken a few/very fine mirrors/she said. I Have Come to the Conclusion. Nelle Fertig. FF

After, if you must,/you can talk of fate/and all that stuff. Helpmate. Henry Chapin. FAZ

After it, follow it,/Follow the Gleam. Follow the Gleam. Alfred, Lord Tennyson. BBV; GoTF; TreFT

After it was over everybody puked/And left. The Last Time. Tom Veitch. ANYP

After loving you so much, can I forget/you for eternity, and have no other choice? Obit. Robert Lowell. HaCAP

After many years this became clear to me/in the gardens of big cities/and in museums. Seeds of Lead. Amir Gilboa. VWA

After nine years, I sink my head abashed. The People. William Butler Yeats. CMoP

After noise, tranquillity. The Old. Roden and Wriothesley Berkeley Noel. OBVV

After one kiss, but still one kiss, my dear. Kisses Desired. William, of Hawthornden Drummond. EnLoPo

After our first tour by the Yangtze River. Tours. Stephen Shu Ning Liu. AMV-80

After our war, how will love speak? After Our War. John Balaban. FAZ

After our weary transit, find us rest. Lucifer in the Train. Adrienne Rich. EaLo; NePoEA-2

& After she dies, we will cry/& make her a saint. Alcestis on the Poetry Circuit. Erica Jong. AmPA

After she has asked me the way. Epitaph. Christopher Logue. OxBTC

...After short silence then/and summons read, the great consult began. Paradise Lost. John Milton. OAEL 1-2

After silence your legs/break open/the final measure Knee Lunes. Robert Kelly. CoPo

After 600 years/the ivory thought/is still warm. Lament for the Dorsets. Al Purdy. NoP

After six little spaces of chill, and six of burning. Here Lies a Lady. John Crowe Ransom. AnAmPo; AWP; CMoP; CoBMV; EvOK; ForPo; HAP; HBMV; InPo; InvP; LiTM; MoAB; MoAmPo; NAMP; NoAm; PoRA; TAP; VGW

After sleeping all night by the lake. Laziness and Silence. Robert Bly. PPP

After so foul a journey death is fair,/And but a chair. The Pilgrimage. George Herbert. AnAnS 1; FaBoRV

...After so many lessons/to laugh in garrulous Sabbath on this pavement? Survivors. Elaine Feinstein. VWA

After that alien, point-blank, green and actual Guatemala. Arrival at the Waldorf. Wallace Stevens. HaCAP; NYP; PP

After that,/he puts his red eyes out/under the extra blanket. The Appointment. Maxine W. Kumin. NMM

After that/I didn't see you anymore. The Door to the Future. Dick Gallup. ANYP

..."After that you're in the hands/of Herman Talmadge." Snapshot. George Garrett. NePoAm-2

After the air of summer. Roman Fountain. Louise Bogan. NoP; SBG; WPOW

After the day's great sun. At Nightfall. Charles Hanson Towne. BLPA; FaBoBe

After the dews of blood? Morning Light the Dew-Drier. Mary Effie Lee Newsome. AmNP; CDC; PoBA

After the dirigible comes the cow. Dear Country Cousin. E. G. Burrows. HoAn

After the first death, there is no other. A Refusal to Mourn the Death, by Fire, of a Child in London. Dylan Thomas. AtBAP; BLPL; CABA; ChMP; CMoP; CoBMV; DiPo; EBEV; FaBoMo; FaFP; FF; GTBS-P; HeIP; HoPM; InPo; LiTB; LiTM; MasP; MoAB; MoBrPo; MoPo; MoVE; MP;

NeBP; NoAm; NOBE; NoP; OAEL 1-2; OAEP; OxBTC; PoPl; SeCePo; TEP; TwCP; UnPo; WaaP; WaP

After the guns, when men smile in a street.   After Bombardment.   John Pudney.   WaP

After the long dark winter. After the night.   The Pelicans My Father Sees.   Sister Maris Stella.   GoBC

After the milk-white hounds of the moon.   Madman's Song.   Elinor Wylie.   LOW; MoAB; MoAmPo; MOON; PoRA

After the ploughshare and the stumbling team.   As the Team's Head-Brass.   Edward ("Edward Eastaway") Thomas.   ExPo; GTBS-P; MMM; OBWP; OxBTC; PoPle

After the prayer and the praise/Cometh His blessing again.   After.   Caroline Grayson.   BLRP

After the raven has died for the dove.   Prayer for Messiah.   Leonard Cohen.   OBCV

After the red rose bordered hem.   Apologia Addressed to Ireland in the Coming Days.   William Butler Yeats.   BrPo

After the searching share of pain/Has cut a furrow through my heart.   Process.   Charles L. O'Donnell.   TrPWD

After the silence of centuries?   The Man with the Hoe.   Edwin Markham.   AA; AmLP; AnAmPo; AnFE; APA; BLPA; BLPL; EaLo; FaFP; GoTF; HBV 1-2; LiTA; MCCG; MoAmPo; OHFP; PPON; PrIm; SaC; TreF; TrGrPo; TRV; WBLP; WGRP

After the sleeping–God!   Sequence.   Edgar Daniel Kramer.   BLRP

After their fall/leaves crumble/without explanation.   Auden.   Raymond F. Roseliep.   SOTS

After their life grant them/a place eternally to sing/Amen.   The Bailey Beareth the Bell Away.   Anonymous.   SeCePo

After ther liff grant them/A place eternally to sing. Amen.   The Maidens Came.   Anonymous.   PoEL 1-5

After these months of pain we begin/to admit our new lives have begun.   Libation.   Denise Levertov.   GP

After they hewed the love from it/as from a quarry/already abandoned.   I Am a Leaf.   Yehuda Amichai.   VWA

...After they're caught, fish keep/swimming.   A Fish Story.   Charles Fishman.   WOLT

After this interlude/He concentrates upon his food.   Table Talk.   Donald Mattam.   FiBHP

After 3 days the air/empty from the rain   That the Neighborhood Might Be Covered.   Larry Eigner.   PoM

After thy death me underfong/To ben forevermo. Amen.   Ler to Loven as I Love Thee.   Anonymous.   SBVL

After to scald him, until he fled despairing to his room–to the fist of/his cruel fate.   His Mother's Love.   Noah Stern.   VWA

After tomorrow–who can say?   To My Retired Friend Wei.   Tu Fu.   LiTW

After trying my animal noise/i break out with a man's cry   I Have Felt It as They've Said.   Larry Eigner.   PoM

After we have driven out of Troy the strong-greaved Achaians.'   The Iliad.   Homer.   NAWM 1-2

After what she gave me–/Rest her soul!   Godmother.   Dorothy Parker.   PoRA

–After which I'd not injure my spirit/standing guard for the rest of my life.'   A Magic Mist.   Eoghan Rua O Suilleabhain.   NOBI

After which I fancy we/Shall want a few bottles of Heidsieck or Roederer.   Salad.   Mortimer Collins.   Par

(After which the poet gets into his proper stride.)   Break, Break, Break (parody).   J. C. Squire.   BXAP

...After you, because of you,/all songs are possible.   Again for Hephaistos, the Last Time.   Richard Howard.   GP

After you Estella, Paella is my dish./(etc., ad naus.)   Song in Praise of Paella.   C. W. V. Wordsworth.   FiBHP

After you left that it was before you came.   The Dial Tone.   Howard Nemerov.   NYBP

After you're dead and gone,/In this poem you'll live on!   Shall I Compare Thee to a Summer's Day?   Howard Moss.   InPK

The afterimage/of this day on earth.   Blurry Cow.   Chase Twichell.   MAYP

Aftermath proof, extended radiance.   Reading Time: 1 Minute 26 Seconds.   Muriel Rukeyser.   MoPo; NePA; PBWP

The afternoon has gone to sleep/and the bells dream.   Poems.   Antonio Machado.   LiTW

...The afternoon sun/encircling her.   In Bed.   Myra Sklarew.   AMV-81

Afterward–day!   Our share of night to bear.   Emily Dickinson.   AA

Afterward I went past what you had passed/Before we met and you what I had passed.   Meeting and Passing.   Robert Frost.   OxBA

Afterward thanks, that the present yet knows/Not to ply!   The Conquerors.   Paul Laurence Dunbar.   AmePo

Afterwards I shall be ashes beneath the black earth.   Fleeting Restlessness.   Juana de Ibarbourou.   LiTW

Afterwards one guard said he didn't shoot/because he was afraid he would hit the mule.   Mule-Train.   John L. Sellers.   LFAC

Again a woman in her nakedness.   For Ruggiero and Angelica by Ingres.   Dante Gabriel Rossetti.   VLP

Again, again it would speak as it has spoken to me of things/That I shall not see!   Madeleine in Church (excerpt).   Charlotte Mew.   MoAB; MoBrPo; SBG

Again and again,/while History is unforgiven.   In the Naked Bed, in Plato's Cave.   Delmore Schwartz.   ExPo; LiTA; LiTM; MiAP; MoAB; MoAmPo; MoVE; NePA; NoAm; NOBA; PoA; VGW

Again, as someone lost in a quaint parable,/Comes up the Sun.   Break of Day.   John Shaw Neilson.   BoAV; PoAu 1-2

Again collect our jovial crew.   On the Ruins of a Country Inn.   Philip Freneau.   AA

Again forgetting/what I stood for.   Exercise.   Pat Nolan.   APU

Again he had come late to supper,/Then lied, to boot.   Penological Study: Southern Exposure, 3. Wet Hair...   Robert Penn Warren.   NoAm

Again, I/am the found one, intimate, returned/by all I touch on the way.   Under Stars.   Tess Gallagher.   GeTw; MAYP

Again I chant my refrain/Of long ago and a piano singing/Far into the night.   Piano at Evening.   Palea.   WTO

Again I'le put it in.   Have-at a Venture.   Anonymous.   CoMu; ErPo

Again I promise to try.   Manuelzinho.   Elizabeth Bishop.   FaBoWP; NYBP

Again I shake your hand,–friend Charles, good/night.   To Charles Cowden Clarke.   John Keats.   EnRP; PBBP

Again I spat up at the ceiling three times,/and missed all three times,/then I fell asleep.   Tuesday.   Ziche Landau.   VWA

Again in fleecy skies the lilies wave.   Lion, Leopard, Lady.   Douglas Le Pan.   OBCV

Again/inside/this small body.   After Your Death.   David James.   AMV-80

Again is hidden in the old embrace.   When She Comes Home.   James Whitcomb Riley.   AA; BLPL; FaBoBe; HBV 1-2

Again it will be grasped by thine, before/My steps can lose the way.   In the Dark.   Mary Thacher Higginson.   AA

Again on foot to rear her poulder'd corse.   Ruines of Rome.   Joachim Du Bellay.   FaBoPP

Again retreated–and a second time faced the screen.   The Silent One.   Ivor Gurney.   MMM; OBWP

...Again some writer/runs howling to his art.   Journey to Iceland.   W. H. Auden.   OBTV; PoA

Again stands superb as a temple.   An Incident.   Douglas LePan.   ACV; PeCV

Again the chirp of the stream running.   Lucina Schynning in Silence of the Night...   Eilean Ni Chuilleanain.   CIP

Again the Cousin's whistle! Go, my Love.   Andrea Del Sarto.   Robert Browning.   ATP; CTC; DiPo; EnL; HBV 1-2; MaVP; NOBV; NoP; OAEL 1-2; OAEP; PoEL 1-5; VLP; WHA

Again the dark Dove nestles in my breast.   Poem by the Clock Tower, Summer.   James Keir Baxter.   ACV

Again, the old dust-coated Jew, my father,/carries the ark of the Covenant on his way out of Cuba.   The Store in Havana.   Jose Kozer.   VWA

Again the stain has come/For thee.   To Dear Daniel.   Samuel Greenberg.   LiTA; MoPo

Again the wombs live.   Birthsong.   Jessica Scarbrough.   LFAC

"Again they come," and muttered as he died.   Peter Grimes.   George Crabbe.   OBNV; TEP

Again to feel the cold world's ruth and/wrong.   Bring Tem Not Back.   James Benjamin Kenyon.   AA

Again to Naucratis and to the Nile.   Doricha.   Edwin Arlington Robinson.   AWP; FaBoEE; OBVE

Again very queer but I'll go on looking   Wodwo.   Ted Hughes.   NoAm

Again you will dance and whisper in the wind.   Fatigues.   Richard Aldington.   BrPo

Against a shuddering wall of air/The strict head of his match.   One A. M.   X. J. Kennedy.   ELU

Against a whole world's pull.   The End of a Leave.   Roy Fuller.   NeBP

Against both bar and tower the black sea runs.   Point Shirley.   Sylvia Plath.   NIP; NoP

Against divine Light and the test/of transmitting the innermost Splendor.   Splendor.   Shin Shalom.   VWA

Against her breast:/propitiation.   Sibyl of the Waters.   Ruth Fainlight.   VWA

Against him, die, and find death good.   Love on the Farm.   D. H. Lawrence.   CMoP; ErPo; FaBV; FF; MoAB; MoBrPo; TrGrPo

Against my will, full pleased with my pain.   The Restless Heart.   Henry Howard, Earl of Surrey.   SiPS

Against the cars like young boys,/bored, waiting for the end of silence,/the guns lean.   South Dakota Refuge.   Lorna Crozier.   CaPN

Against the cool, reflective tiles.   My Six Toothbrushes.   Phyllis McGinley.   GoYe

Against the drift of the cold.   The Vision of Sir Launfal.   James Russell Lowell.   AnNE

Against the enemy before the gate.   No Season for Our Season.   Willard Maas. AnAmPo

Against the evidence, I live by choice.   Against the Evidence.   David Ignatow. NNaP

Against the foes of liberty and God!   One Country.   Frank Lebby Stanton. AA; PAL

Against the fortress of the Snow Princess.   The Heavenly Foreigner.   Denis Devlin. CIP

Against the knoll.   The Book of Wild Flowers.   Joseph Ceravolo. ANYP

Against the never-ending inroad/of North Atlantic weather.   Ironwood.   Don Domanski. CaPN

Against the paper sands of the paper shore!   The Katzenjammer Kids.   James Reaney. OBCV; PeCV

Against the pattern of the pillow,/sleeping.   Light.   Carol Coates. CaP

Against the poet and the legislator.   In Time of War.   W.H. Auden. CMoP

Against the potent poison of your hate.   The White House.   Claude McKay. AmNP; AmPP; NIP; PoBA; PoNe

Against the pre-cast forest of the city.   A Day in the City.   L. E. Sissman. NYBP

Against the sun, when they do stand?   Bird Riddle: "What is it more eyes doth wear."   Anonymous. GBP

Against the wide abyss, the gray waste nothingness of things.   They Sing.   Theodore Roethke. NYBP

Against thee, in thee I will overcome/The man who once against thee fought.   The Second Thanksgiving, or The Reprisal.   George Herbert. OAEP

Against their will Thou only hast the might!   Can I Believe.   Lodovico Ariosto. CAW

...Against what trembles/in my throat, a particular fear,/a word I have no words for.   Prison Letter.   Michael Knoll. LFAC

Agamemnon murdered;/And the mighty Twins?   Leda and the Swan.   Oliver St. John Gogarty. AnIL; HAP; OnYI

Agape we are & agape we'll be   After the Cries of the Birds.   Lawrence Ferlinghetti. CAPP

Age after age, the uninstructing dead.   The Gulf.   Derek Walcott. NoP

Age and need, those simple weeds,/were gathering around and taking you away.   I'm Just a Stranger Here, Heaven Is My Home.   Carole Gregory Clemmons. PoBA

Age, I do defy thee. O! sweet shepherd, hie thee,/For methinks thou stays too long.   Youth and Age.   William Shakespeare. OBSC

Age in woe and wisdom grey/Vainly mourns for them that play.   Anacreontic, On Parting with a little Child.   Samuel Wesley. NOEC

Age is no pain, and Youth no snare.   Happy Is the Country Life.   Anonymous. OBS

Age lights the candle and hobbles to/bed.   Points of View.   Amy Lowell. LOW

Age might but take the things Youth needed not!   The Small Celandine.   William Wordsworth. HBV 1-2; OBRV

–Age of Burroughs when we first met.   Aether.   Allen Ginsberg. CoPo

...Age that is bred/Of sights that no child should see.   Maturity.   J. Elgar Owen. WaP

Age then descends on us, calm, contented.   Evening Fantasy.   Friedrich Hoelderlin. LiTW

Agean, the pleace is ever dumb.   All Still.   William Barnes. NOBV

The ages of a putrefying corpse.   The Worms of History.   Robert Graves. MoPo

...Ages to come, may prove brethren and lovers, as/we are.   To Him That Was Crucified.   Walt Whitman. AnEnPo; MoRP

Aggrieving the sapless limbs, the shorn and shaken.   Dead Boy.   John Crowe Ransom. CMoP; FaBoMo; LiTA; MP; NoAm; NoP; OxBA; TwCP

Agh, did a word I said to her, and she said the same to me!   She Said the Same To Me (with music).   Anonymous. AS

Aghast at first, and stupid with Surprize.   The Iliad.   Homer. OBVE

Aghast I stood, a monument of woe!   The Odyssey.   Homer. LiTW

The agonising pincer-jaws of Heaven.   Sanctity.   Patrick Kavanagh. BIrV; ELU; NOBI

Agony, that pants for breath,/Despair and honourable Death.   The Triumphs of Owen.   Thomas Gray. CEP; PoEL 1-5

The agony we comprehend; of the rest, know nothing.   Crucifix.   Elder Olson. MoRP

Agree to form a Johnsonate of Briggs?   The Chemist to His Love.   Anonymous. InMe; QQQ

Agreeing with that Latin writer, Great is Truth and will prevail in/a bit.   Magna Est Veritas.   Stevie Smith. OxBC

Ah, all these works are thine!   Human Debasement. A Fragment.   Edward Rushton. NOEC

Ah, and had my song power, I too to Pluto had sung.   A Lament for Bion.   Moschus. AWP; EnLi 1-2

Ah! bitter word "Farewell."   The Parting Hour.   Olive Custance. HBV 1-2

Ah, bitterly I recall/the animals of last year.   The Temple of the Animals.   Robert Duncan. NOBA

Ah! breathe on it softly, it dies in an hour.   A Riddle: The Letter H.   Catherine Fanshawe. GN

Ah, but those tears are pearl which thy love sheds,/And they are rich, and ransom all ill deeds.   Sonnets, XXXIV: "Why didst thou promise such a beauteous day."   William Shakespeare. CBEP; OBSC

Ah! Chloe, when, my charming fair?   Epigram on the First of April.   John Winstanley. NOEC

Ah, curious friend!/Thou puzzlest me!   My friend must be a Bird.   Emily Dickinson. TAP

"Ah ddae-ken whu' the pplace is comin tae/wi aw thae, hechyuch! fforeign po'entates."   Heard in the Cougate.   Robert Garioch. OxBTC

Ah, dear Diana!   Diana.   Ernest Rhys. OBVV

Ah, dear Eurydice the echoing winds replied.   Thus Sung Orpheus to His Strings.   Anonymous. GBL; NCEP

Ah, do not let me fall in the abyss!   Prayer.   Gabrielle Coignard. WPOW

Ah, don't you hear the clinking of my chain?   The Convict.   Anonymous. CoSo

Ah! Druid, Druid, how great webs of sorrow/Lay hidden in the small slate-coloured thing!   Fergus and the Druid.   William Butler Yeats. CoBE; VLP

Ah! for the age when verse was clad,/Being godlike, to be bad and mad.   Impression.   Sir Edmund Gosse. HBV 1-2

Ah, for the face–the face of flowers–that blossoms on/earth no more.   A Dead March.   Cosmo Monkhouse. HBV 1-2; OBVV

Ah, friend, your memory is short as any woman's!   To a Faithless Friend.   Salaan Arrabey. WTO

(Ah, Gillyflower, ah Daisy!) with a grace/Like stars divine?   A Nosegay.   John Reynolds. OBEV

Ah God! Ah God! That dawn should come so soon!   Alba Innominata.   Anonymous. AWP; LiTW

Ah God, ah God, that day should be so soon.   In the Orchard.   Algernon Charles Swinburne. BoLoP; UnTE

Ah, God, ah God! 'tis food today/That feeds me and not kisses.   Retirement.   Anonymous. ErPo; KiLC

Ah! God, if it were really rain!   A Night in June.   Duncan Campbell Scott. OBCV

Ah, God! My God! Thou wilt not drift away.   Drifting away.   Charles Kingsley. OxBoCh

Ah, good Heaven, but I would I were out far away from the/pother!   Amours de Voyage.   Arthur Hugh Clough. FaBoPV

Ah, grey sacrament of the mundane!   The Zen of Housework.   Al Zolynas. LTB

"Ah ha, that is warm!" said Bryan O'Lin.   Bryan O'Lin Had No Breeches to Wear.   Mother Goose. BrR

Ah-hah, I'm bound away 'cross the wide Mizzoura.   The Wide Mizzoura (with music).   Anonymous. AS

Ah, hard Fate, that I must loose her.   A Song: "Boast no more fond Love, thy Power."   Thomas D'Urfey. CavP

Ah! he is not but gone to take his Right/Of Heritance among the Saints in Light.   A Brief Elegie on My Dear Son John the Second of That Name of Mine.   John Saffin. SCAP

Ah! he strikes all things, all alike,/But bargains: those he will not strike.   Age.   Walter Savage Landor. ELU; PoEL 1-5

Ah heart, heart, look! I throw myself at your feet.   Stormy Night.   W. R. Rodgers. OxBI

Ah heaven!–what truth to him.   The College Colonel.   Herman Melville. AA; AmePo; OBWP

Ah, heavy doubt! to doubt his dearest friend.   To L–.   D'Arcy Cresswell. AnNZ

Ah! here's the enemy with their powder and pills!"/Ri tu ral, lol, lu ral.   Brigham Young.   Anonymous. CoSo

Ah, how I shall miss you/When you have grown.   A Cradle Song.   William Butler Yeats. NOBV; PoPl

Ah, how poets sing and die!   Dunbar.   Anne Spencer. BANP; CDC

Ah, how the long, deep agony/Lasts here, under the sun.   Nor Will These Tears Be the Last.   Johann Wolfgang von Goethe. LiTW

Ah, joy! when with the closing street,/Forgivingly at last ye greet!   Sic Itur.   Arthur Hugh Clough. NCEP

Ah, Lenin, politics is bairns' play/To what this maun be!   Second Hymn to Lenin.   Hugh" (Christopher Murray Grieve) MacDiarmid. OAEL 1-2

Ah! let us carol and dance and be gay,/la-la-re-la-la.   Giovinette, Che Fate All'Amore.   Lorenzo Da Ponte. TrJP

Ah! linger in this lane,/Kissing each violet.   Morning.   Samuel Waddington. OBVV

Ah loiterer! I'll no more, no more I'll bring:/I did expect a ring.   Hope.   George Herbert. PoEL 1-5; WeW

Ah! Lord! and what a Purchase will that be/To take us sick, that sound would not take thee?   The Pursuite.   Henry Vaughan. SeCP

Ah love, in sorrow, thou abid'st with me.   The Spring.   John Francis O'Donnell. IrPN

(Ah, love is come indeed!)   Where Love Is King.   Hilda ("H. D.") Doolittle. HBMV

Ah, love, let us be true/To one another!   Dover Beach.   Matthew Arnold. ATP

Ah Love, my country in your arms–my home upon your/heart!   Where Love Is.   Amelia Josephine Burr.   HBV 1-2

Ah, love, thine eyes!–Nay, love–Thy/heart, thy heart!   A Woman's Pride. Helen Hay.   AA

Ah'm gonna send you off to school.   Paternal.   Ernest J. Wilson, Jr.   PoNe

Ah'm here in this unfriendly world/Don' know what to do.   Ah'm Broke an' Hungry.   Lawrence Gellert.   TrAS

Ah, Mary, Mary!   Lynton Verses.   Thomas Edward Brown.   PeD

Ah, may I stay forever blind/With lions, tigers, leopards, and their kind.   The Greater Cats.   Victoria Mary (Vita) Sackville-West.   OBMV; PoPle

Ah me, but where are now the songs I sang/When life was sweet because you called/them sweet?   Monna Innominata.   Christina Georgina Rossetti. VLP

Ah me, for Love–will Death my Love restore?   Love, Time and Death. Frederick Locker-Lampson.   HBV 1-2

Ah, me! I wish that I were quite/As young–as young as she!   The Chaperon. Henry Cuyler Bunner.   AA; HBV 1-2

Ah, me! it was he that won her/Because he dared to climb!   Nocturne. Thomas Bailey Aldrich.   HBV 1-2

Ah me, she sighs, ah me!   Spring Rain.   Harry Behn.   TiPo

Ah! my crop had better thriven/Had I sown and ploughed for heaven.   Hell. *Anonymous.*   WTO

Ah, my daughter, my grandchild!   All You Others, Eat.   Djurberaui. NOAV; WTO

Ah! my heart, ah! what aileth thee?   To His Heart.   Sir Thomas Wyatt. OBSC

Ah, my heart–my heart is yearning/Still to be by Mooni cool!   Mooni. Henry Clarence Kendall.   OBEV; OBVV

Ah! never have I seen so much light/Through thy father's doorway.   Song of Cradle-Making.   Constance Lindsay Skinner.   CaP

Ah never to escape from numbers and form!   The Abyss.   Charles Baudelaire.   SyP

Ah no, it's always just my luck to get/One perfect rose.   One Perfect Rose. Dorothy Parker.   ALV; FiBHP; NIP; NLV; NoP; OBAL; OLR

Ah, no Love, not while your hot kisses burn/Like a potato riding on the blast. Sonnet Found in a Deserted Mad-House.   *Anonymous.*   FaBoCo; FaBoNo; InvP; NA

Ah! no more: thou break'st my heart.   Dialogue.   George Herbert.   MePo; OBEV; OBS; SeCV 1-2

Ah, old man, do you serve me so?   Deceiver.   *Anonymous.*   OxNR

Ah! Once Upon!   Once and Upon.   Madeline Gleason.   NeAP

Ah, Padraic, I who tell the story/Cover my face and sigh.   The Waistcoat. Padraic Fallon.   OxBI

Ah poor Roger, flimsy Roger, ah poor Roger, hi ho.   Gee Ho, Dobin. *Anonymous.*   CoMu

Ah, Psyche, from the regions which/Are Holy Land!   To Helen.   Edgar Allan Poe.   AA; AP; APA; AtBAP; ATP; AWP; BoLoP; EG; ExPo; FaBoBe; FaBV; FaFP; FaPo; FPL; GBL; GoTF; HAP; HBV 1-2; HBVY; HeIP; HoPM; InPo; InPS; InvP; LaNeLa; LiTA; LiTL; LoBV; MAmP; MCCG; NePA; NIP; NOBA; NoP; OBEV; OBRV; OBVV; OxBA; PAI; PoEL 1-5; PoLf; PoRA; PrIm; SeCeV; TAP; TreF; TrGrPo; ViBoPo

–Ah, Puss, what a present/I'm giving to you!   Loulou and Her Cat. Frederick Locker-Lampson.   ALV

Ah! qu'elle est belle La Marguerite.   The Eve of Crecy.   William Morris. OBVV; VLP

...Ah, raccoon.   Lost Word.   Jean Burden.   AMV-80

Ah! Rubinstein only could make such an end!   The Rubinstein Staccato Etude.   R. Nathaniel Dett.   BANP

"Ah!" said mamma, "I knew he'd come/To naughty little Suck-a-Thumb." The Story of Little Suck-a-Thumb.   Heinrich Hoffmann.   EvOK; HBV 1-2; HBVY

(Ah, see), we truly die.   Walking Along the Hudson.   Donald Petersen. CoAP

Ah, she has such a beautiful soul!   Letters.   Charles Bukowski.   GP

Ah, Sidney! Sidney!   Tombstone Epitaphs.   *Anonymous.*   PeD

Ah, sing to him, nigger.   Night Song.   Wallace Gould.   AnAmPo

Ah, so my love and longing must be known, Dear Heart, to/you!   The Lover Thinks of His Lady in the North.   Shaemas O'Sheel.   HBV 1-2

Ah! still harp on what they heard.   Persistency of Poetry.   Matthew Arnold. VLP

Ah! Surely nothing dies but something mourns.   Don Juan.   George Gordon, Lord Byron.   BoLiVe; CoBE; MCCG; OAEP; TrGrPo

Ah! surely now the virgin year/Is in her blushing maidenhood.   Spring. Robert Loveman.   AA

Ah, sweet Camilla, thy songs for Felipe,/the fearless, are vain!   Camilla. Charles Augustus Keeler.   AA

Ah, sweet is Tipperary in the spring!   Ah, Sweet Is Tipperary.   Denis Aloysius McCarthy.   HBV 1-2

Ah! that alone is truly pain/Of which we never can complain.   Silent, You Say, I'm Grown of Late.   Walter Savage Landor.   GBL

Ah! that I were once more a careless child!   Sonnet: To the River Otter. Samuel Taylor Coleridge.   ChRP; OAEL 1-2

Ah, that moon of her brow shall be mighty/With mischief to her–and to me! Two Songs in Praise of Steingerd, 1.   Cormac Ogmundarson.   LiTW

Ah, that's better! cried one of the doctors.   The Death of an Angel.   Russell Edson.   LCAP

Ah! that thou couldst know thy joy,/Ere it passes, barefoot boy!   The Barefoot Boy.   John Greenleaf Whittier.   AA; AmePo; AnNE; FaBoBe; FPL; GN; GoTF; HBV 1-2; HBVY; LaNeLa; LiTA; OBAL; OBCA; OBVV; OHFP; PoLf; PoPl; TreF; WBLP

Ah, the heart's shivers–what life! what death!   Hungry China.   Cha Liang-cheng.   LiTW

Ah! the Rainbow's awake/and we will not fail!   The Ballad of Mrs. Noah. Robert Duncan.   NoAm; NOBA

Ah! then I knew;/Knew why it sang in my heart.   Homesick Song.   William Haskel Simpson.   BPAW

Ah, then watch him froth and gag, Earth./Watch him heave!   A Burnt Offering to Your Greenstone Eyes, Tangaroa.   Hone Tuwhare.   OCNZ

Ah, there are not many/Half so sly, or sad, or mad,/As my true-hearted Fannie.   Fannie.   Thomas Bailey Aldrich.   OBAL

Ah, there is lots of gold, oh, so I've been told,/Upon the banks of the Saccarimento!   Sacramento.   *Anonymous.*   FSW; ShS; TrAS

Ah! this miasma of a rotting God!   God.   Isaac Rosenberg.   MoPo; VWA

Ah, this thy emblem gives.   Unrest.   Richard Watson Dixon.   OBNC

Ah, to become nothing again, irrevocably spent!   Lightning of the Abyss. Jules Laforgue.   SyP

"Ah, tragic, tragic, tragic!"   Puerto Ricans in New York.   Charles Reznikoff. CTBA

Ah, turn it off.   Two Hangovers.   James Wright.   AmPC

Ah, vah, vack.   Ala, Mala, Mink, Monk.   *Anonymous.*   OxNR

Ah, warn some more ambitious heart,/And let the peaceful be!   Switzerland. Matthew Arnold.   OAEP; VLP

Ah, we are each at our station./Nothing is amiss.   Are the Sick in Their Beds as They Should Be?   Joan McIntosh.   AMV-80

Ah, we still have to live our lives/Till Thy tribunal turns to us.   The Trial. Gershom Scholem.   VWA

Ah! we've had many horses, but never a horse like her!   Kentucky Belle. Constance Fenimore Woolson.   BeLS; BLPA; FaBoBe; MaC; PAH; PH; StPo

Ah, well, its mission on earth is through./Adieu!   The Little Peach.   Eugene Field.   LBN; OBAL; ShM

Ah, well were I for ever,/Wouldst thou change lives with me.   To a Seamew. Algernon Charles Swinburne.   EtS; VLP

Ah, what a joy to hear, "Shall we again?"   Love's Fancy.   John Dryden. ErPo

Ah what a lovely voyage   The Staircase with a Hundred Steps.   Benjamin Peret.   EAS

"Ah, what a redoubtable god!"   A God in Wrath.   Stephen Crane.   OBSP; TAP

Ah! what is then this curious sky/But only my Corinna's eye?   The Eye. Robert Herrick.   CaPo

Ah, what is this? what wings unfold/In this miraculous rose of gold? Impression.   Arthur Symons.   SyP

...Ah! what leagues there are/Between our feet and day!   At last, to be identified!   Emily Dickinson.   WGRP

Ah, what sagacity perished here!   Safe in their Alabaster Chambers.   Emily Dickinson.   AmPP; CBEP; MasP; NAWM 1-2; NIP; NoP

–Ah, who among us all/Could say he had not erred as much, and more? Byron Recollected at Bologna.   Samuel Rogers.   OBNC

Ah, who can blame me, if I worship you?   Sweet mouth, that send'st a musky-rosed breath.   Joshua Sylvester.   EnLoPo

Ah! who can guess the rest?   The Willing Mistress.   Aphra Behn.   SBG; UnTE; ViBoPo

Ah, who will stand forever,/Out of this coil deliver.   Threnos.   J. R. Hervey. AnNZ

Ah! why has happiness–no second spring?   Sonnet Written at the Close of Spring.   Charlotte Smith.   OBEC

Ah, with what longing once again I turn!   Desire.   George William Russell. ILwL; OBMV; TrPWD

Ah, woeful lordship–alone to lead, no friend, no peer!   After the Plague. *Anonymous.*   LiTW

Ah! would but one might lay his lance in rest,/And charge in earnest–were it but a mill.   Don Quixote.   Henry Austin Dobson.   HBV 1-2; HBVY

Ah! would my tribe should chance/On such deliverance!   The Dove.   Judah Halevi.   TrJP

Ah! years may pass, and moons may fleet how many,/Ere we fond lovers meet again.   Parting.   *Anonymous.*   WTO

"Ah, yes, I crossed the plains with him!"   The Wagon Train.   Sam L. Simpson.   BPAW

Ah yes, Lucilla! and their fall/I still deplore.   In Clementina's Artless Mien. Walter Savage Landor.   ViBoPo

"Ah yes. Of course I need not remind you, we/Are an old family. It was our forebears speaking." Tongues. Philip Martin. NOAV

"Ah! you can love, true girl, and is your love for me?" Three Shadows. Dante Gabriel Rossetti. HBV 1-2; ViBoPo

Ah, you would understand these eyes,/Although with strange tears filled! Comrades. Lionel Pigot Johnson. HBV 1-2

Aha! a heigh-ho! The March Winds. George Washington Wright Houghton. YeAr

Aha, Johnie Blunt! ye hae spoke the first word,/Get up and bar the door, O. Johnie Blunt. Anonymous. OxBB

"Aha-there isn't any water!" Piano Practice. Ian Serraillier. BBGG

Ahead is the home light. Wise Owl. Patricia Goedicke. SM

Ahh–CHOO!–Ahh–CHOO! Sneezing. Marie Louise Allen. SoPo

Ahh what a thrill/is a god grope Holy Was Demeter Walking th' Corn Furrow. Edward Sanders. PoM

Ahmed was dead, and justice done. Ahmad. James Berry Bensel. AA

Ai! ai! the sleepers wake! Sleep Is a Suspension. Carl Sandburg. NAMP

Aid all this foolish people; let them take/Example, pattern: lead them to thy light. St. Simeon Stylites. Alfred, Lord Tennyson. NOBV; OAEL 1-2

Aided by Heaven, by earth unthwarted still. Substance and Shadow. John Henry, Cardinal Newman. GoBC

Aim their light shafts, and point their little stings. Vegetable Loves. Erasmus Darwin. OBEC; SeCePo

The aim was song–the wind could see. The Aim Was Song. Robert Frost. NoP; PP; SoSe

An aim whose center can be seen no more? Technique on the Firing Line. Turner Cassity. PoA

Aimed across Delos at a star. Delos. Lawrence Durrell. NeBP

An aimless unallay'd Desire. Destiny. Matthew Arnold. NOBV; OBSP

Ain' gonna worry my Lawd no mo'. Satan's a Liah (with music). Anonymous. AS

Ain't a-gonna grieve my Lord no more. Ain't Gonna Grieve My Lord No More. Anonymous. FSW

Ain't going nowhere/till you do Tambourine. James (Olumo) Cunningham. JB

Ain't going to study war no more. I'm Agoing to Lay Down My Sword. Anonymous. AH

Ain't got no home. Ballad of the Boll Weevil. Anonymous. FSW; TrAS

Ain't he cute? He's only six! Little Willie. Anonymous. GoTF; NA; TreFS

Ain't I been through it? Horace the Wise. Morrie Ryskind. HBMV

Ain't it a blooming shame? She Was Poor but She Was Honest. Anonymous. ErPo; FaBoCo; FiBHP; GBP; NOBL

Ain't it a shame. Ain't It a Shame. Anonymous. FSW

Ain't it fierce to be so brainy! Beautiful. Anonymous. ABF

Ain't it fine today? It's Fine Today. Douglas Malloch. BLPA

"Ain't it hard to see you in this lonesome place?" Shorty George. Anonymous. ABF; FSW

Ain't like they say/in the newspapers. Homecoming. Sonia Sanchez. PoBA

Ain't no grave can hold my body down. Ain't No Grave Can Hold My Body Down. Anonymous. AmFP

Ain't no tellen/where the jazz of yo/songs/wud have led us. For Our Lady. Sonia Sanchez. IHMS

Ain't no telling/what she might do Ain't No Tellin. Mississippi John Hurt. BluL

Ain't nothin' like river trout. Poem: "Disturbing to have a person." Barbara Guest. FaBoWP

Ain't shame all de debbil yit, outen de Boss! Brother Baptis' on Woman Suffrage. Rosalie Jonas. BlSi

Ain't singing for me/no more. The Blues Today. Mae Jackson. BOLo; PoBA

"Ain't this the stop where you get out?" Morning Bus. John Coulter. CaP

Ain't you heard? Lenox Avenue Mural. Langston Hughes. AmNP; HoPM

'Ain't you 'shamed, you sleepy-head? Time to Rise. Robert Louis Stevenson. OxBChV; SiSoSe

Aincha gwine, ancha gwine, boys, aincha gwine? Shack Bully Holler. Anonymous. ABF

Aint I glad I got out de wilderness,/Down in Alabam'. Down in Alabam'. J. Warner. PSoN

"Air..." Echo. Pamela Grey, Viscountess Grey of Falloden. CH

The air! and careless, far, far,/fly it. Fly. Bird Song. John Hay. NePoAm-2

Air and its light and scents are in my flesh. I Bring to You as Offering Tonight. Emile Verhaeren. AnEnPo

The air and the water go their ways. Terce. James McMichael. PoA

Air at a breath blown! Thistledown. James Merrill. UnPo

The air comes with us,/a warm halo of fog and icy water with no sense of motion. Poem. Tony Towle. ANYP

(The air commented in a whisper). Gallantry. Keith Douglas. OBWP

The air fills with delicate creatures/From the other world. Milkweed. James Wright. LCAP; NaP; NOBA; NU

The air full of bones. Cold Front. Peter Sharpe. AMV-80

The air is a bird. Everything in the Air Is a Bird. Barbara Guest. AmPC

The air is clear as though we should live forever Ballade of Sayings. William Stanley Merwin. NNaP

The air is not just air, it is an arctic/Confidence of flowers. Annunciation. D. G. Jones. PeCV

Air is woven by orchestral looms/into a robe of color, touch and scent. Symphony. Alfred Dorn. AMV-80

Air lifting the hair of one/Upside down in the reflecting pool. City Afternoon. John Ashbery. HeIP; InPK

...Air moves thru'/the quiet stream of my wrist, moths/strike the screen. Three Part Invention. Paul Blackburn. CoPo

Air on the way to Minneapolis. Daybreak. Tony Towle. ANYP

The air splotched with the gold,/Electric, coming day. This Shall Be Sufficient. Kenneth Rexroth. CAD

Air tasted good when I breathed the cold sun. The Ravine. James Applewhite. AMV-80

Air thickening in still streets and between brown walls. The Purpose of the Chesapeake & Ohio Canal. Dave Smith. GeTw

The air was colder, and grey. She stood alone. Mary and Gabriel. Rupert Brooke. ISi

The air will be sweet/as breath of new horses. Spring at Fort Okanogan. Ramona Wilson. VoR

Air, with dirt, with food/and with the sun's fire. With the Sun's Fire. David Ignatow. FAZ

An aircraft scribbles slogans on the sky. Beach Queen. David Campbell. BoAV

Airing the closet and/drawers of love. When You Are Gone. Nance Van Winckel. AMV-81

The airless secret I strangle not to share/With all the others as others share the air. Air. Edwin Denby. CrMA

Airplane,/Piloting you/Far in the blue? Up in the Air. James S. Tippett. SoPo; SUS; TiPo

Airships, reconnoitering,/All day, in the silent sky. Armistice. Elizabeth Daryush. AMV-81

Ajar to the still sky stripped bare of birds. Rabbit Cry. Edward Lucie-Smith. NePoEA-2

Al day yven agagement/To yiven us strokes grete. A Schoolboy's Lot. Anonymous. OxBM

Al stant on chaung like a mydsomyr rose. Lat Noman Booste of Konnyng Nor Vertu. John Lydgate. AtBAP

Al were his mytre, croune, or diademe. Gentilesse. Geoffrey Chaucer. AWP; CBEP; OAEL 1-2

Alack, and woe is me! The Bride's Tragedy: Poor Old Pilgrim Misery. Thomas Lovell Beddoes. EnRP

Alack, there's naething but the waukrife cheep/O' Smith, Ricardo, Bentham and their peers. On Glaister's Hill: Carlyle on Burns. William Jeffrey. OxBS

Aladdin's lamp is there. The Sorceress! Vachel Lindsay. WSC

Alang wi' the twenty candymen an' Johnny that carries the bell. The Oakey Street Evictions. Anonymous. OBET

Alarm clock bursts. Urban Dream. Victor Hernandez Cruz. NBP

Alas! alas! a devilish change indeed! Lines on the Author's Death. Robert Burns. PV

Alas, alas, in ever acre,/every one a ticket-taker. Crickets. David McCord. NTCP

Alas! Alas! the dawn–it comes too soon! Troubadour Alba. Anonymous. EnLi 1-2

Alas, alas, what a disaster has come upon me! As Camels Who Have Become Thirsty...The Poet's Lament. Ilmi Bowndheri. WTO

Alas! alike is punishment to me. With Two Fair Girls. Robert C. MacGregor. ALV

Alas! An age that honors clothes/Though worn by horse or ass! The Gentleman. Menahem Lonzano. TrJP

Alas! and not play too? Alciphron and Leucippe. Walter Savage Landor. OBEV; VLP

–"Alas, but must you take him again?'/Said the South to the North. The North and the South. Elizabeth Barrett Browning. OBVV

Alas, cling round me, for the day is done! Hope Overtaken. Dante Gabriel Rossetti. MaVP

Alas! Death mows down all with an impartial Hand. Odes. Horace. OBVE

Alas for love, if thou wert all,/And naught beyond, O Earth! The Graves of a Household. Felicia Dorothea Hemans. FaPoR; HBV 1-2; VLP; WBLP

Alas for me, that it is dead! I Doubt a Lovely Thing Is Dead. Neil Tracy. CaP

Alas for the unicorn! Dance Song. Anonymous. FaBoCh; LoGBV

Alas, for them, for me, for evermore! The Flight of the Earls, 1607 (excerpt). Fearghal Og MacWard. BIrV

Alas for youth, for youth gone by! Alas for Youth. Firdausi. AWP; LiTW

...Alas! how can I call her/well-beloved? Love. Pierre Louys. PeHV

Alas! how hurryingly the ebbing years/Then hasten to old age! The Ebb Tide. Robert Southey. OBNC

..."Alas! I did not know him at all." The U. S. Sailor with the Japanese Skull. Winfield Townley Scott. LiTM; MiAP; NMP; WaP

Alas! I found it not before/Three armored foemen burst the door. The Last Bowstrings. Edward Lucas White. AA

Alas, I go with child./Kyrie eleison. As I Went out on Christmas Day. Anonymous. CBEP

Alas! I go with child./Kyrieleison. Jolly Jankin. Anonymous. GBP; NoP; OxBM; OxBoLi

Alas! I'm told in no vicinity/Is such a thing as blessed twinnity! Oh, Noa, Noa! William Cole. NLV

Alas, is wiser far than I. The Bait. John Donne. AnEnPo; CABA; DiPo; ErPo; HoPM; InPK; InPS; LiTL; NIP; OAEL 1-2; OAEP; PAI; PoRA; SD; TEP

Alas, kind element! which comes to go. Alas, Kind Element. Léonie Adams. MoVE

Alas, my God, I know not what. The Thanksgiving. George Herbert. AnAnS 1

Alas, my God! Thy birth now here/Must not be numbred in the year. Silex Scintillans. Henry Vaughan. AnAnS 1

Alas! no eyebrows for tomorrow. Helen Was Just Slipped into Bed. Matthew Prior. EiCP

Alas! now consumed by the monster shark! Love Is a Shark. Anonymous. WTO

Alas, poor Love, then thou art woe-begone thee. Sweet Love, If Thou Wilt Gain a Monarch's Glory. Anonymous. EG

Alas! still faithful to his back./The pigtail hangs behind him. A Tragic Story. William Makepeace Thackeray. HBV 1-2; HBVY; MoShBr; OnMSP

Alas! that frowns could lie in wait/For such a foe as this! From all the jails the boys and girls. Emily Dickinson. GLGT

Alas, that I should die,/Who know so much. Song of a Woman Abandoned by the Tribe... Mary Austin. BPAW

Alas, that the torn heart can bleed but not for-/get. To Constantia Singing. Percy Bysshe Shelley. EnRP

Alas...the cold moon of spring... Old Scent of the Plum Tree. Fujiwara Ietaka. AWP

Alas! the gratitude of men/Hath oftener left me mourning. Simon Lee the Old Huntsman. William Wordsworth. EnRP; GTBS; GTBS-P

Alas the while! There was Never Nothing More Me Pained. Sir Thomas Wyatt. AAS; CBEP; FCP; GBL; SiPS

Alas, then, for the homeless beggar old! Summer and Winter. Percy Bysshe Shelley. BoNaP

Alas! They cannot be shaken! Government. Tuta Nihoniho. WTO

Alas, thou takest all my joy with thee! Parting at Morning. Sir Dietmar von Aist. AWP

Alas, Time stays,–we go. The Paradox of Time. Pierre Ronsard. AWP

Alas! 'Tis all too clear I'm not/In vein today. To Brander Matthews. Henry Austin Dobson. ALV

Alas! 'tis everywhere her grave. The Victories of Love. Coventry Patmore. FaBoRV

Alas! to know that the consuming mind/Shall leave its lamp cold, ere the sun appear. The Lamp. Charles Whitehead. OBEV; OBVV

Alas! too late–Entreaties are in vain!..... Of the Going Down of the Sun. John Bunyan. CH

Alas! 'twas not in them, but in thy power/To double even the sweetness of a flower. Don Juan. George Gordon, Lord Byron. FiP

Alas what hope is left, to quench his fire/That kindled is, by sight: blowne, by desire. Godfrey of Bulloigne: Armida...Sets out to undo the Crusaders. Torquato Tasso. OBVE

Alas, when Jews get together/they sigh. Diaspora Jews. Rachel Boimwall. VWA

(Alas! Where is there sport?) Puck Goes to Court. Fenton Johnson. CDC; GoSl

Alassen I mid want to stay/Behine' for thee, O flow'ry May! May. William Barnes. PoSC

Albeit felt of none/Save of him who, desiring, honors her. Ballata: He Will Gaze upon Beatrice. Dante Alighieri. AWP

Albeit thine ending be one wherein thou reactest to orange/hair. 10th Dance–Coming on As a Horn–20 February 1964. Jackson MacLow. CoPo

Albeit thy path is scarce above the mole's. Maggie's Star. Charles Tennyson Turner. FM

Alberta, don't you treat me unkind. Alberta. Anonymous. FSW

Alberto would have earned a hero's praise. Brother Astolfo Sated Appetite. Pietro Aretino. PeHV

Ali,/Is our prince Ali. Djangatolum. BOLo; CNA; PoBA

Alice, I know art thou! Alice, Where Art Thou? Wellington Guernsey. VLP

An alien and a vagabond. Envoy. Richard Hovey. AA

–Alien, determined/to make it out of this dreary household. Mythics. Helen Chasin. DFT

Aligned like pillars to shade what gods may yet arrive. The Pleasure of Ruins. J. D. McClatchy. PoA

Alike dissolving. Going and Staying. Thomas Hardy. CMoP; NoAm

Alike led lovers down the track/That knows no turning back. The Beaten Path. Anne Goodwin Winslow. HBMV

Alive, in a slippery grave. Weed Puller. Theodore Roethke. AmPP; HaCAP

Alive in the muscular sea. Returning to Store Bay. Barbara Howes. Psk

...Alive in this deep/Instinctive resistance to the perils of sleep. The Gunner. Francis Webb. BoAV; CBAP

ALIVE ON THIS AIR THESE LIVES ABIDE. Signature. Dorothy Livesay. OBCV

Alive or dead, take me,/Me too, my mother. Ex-Voto. Algernon Charles Swinburne. MOS

Alive ridiculous, and dead forgot. Moral Essays. Alexander Pope. ExPo

Alive under the wing of evening. A Bestiary of the Garden for Children Who Should Know Better. Phyllis Gotlieb. WHW

Alive we're alive)/we're wonderful one times one If Everything Happens That Can't Be Done. Edward Estlin Cummings. SoSe; WeW

Alkaline, so as not to destroy the spermatozoa. Sonnet. Tom Clark. ANYP; CoAP

All aboard all souls/half-mast aye aye/nay Malacoda. Samuel Beckett. CIP

All aboard for Bombay/On a floating cedar log! All Aboard for Bombay. Leroy F. Jackson. BrR

All above the wind-washed graves where dead seamen lie. The Lovers of Marchaid. Marjorie Pickthall. HBV 1-2

All acts in their secret core bear the violet jewel then. On Reading Gene Derwood's "The Innocent". Willard Maas. NePA; WaP

All admire my taste/Within thou mambo of much more haste. Anonymous. Victor Hernandez Cruz. APU

All after-life compressed within the span/Of that one year,–the year I met with/Rose! The World Well Lost. Edmund Clarence Stedman. AA

All afternoon, they cannot say why. Backwater Pond: The Canoeists. William Stanley Merwin. PoPl

All Aideen herself will own/Is that she will not sleep alone. Aideen. Anonymous. KiLC

All, all a-lonely,/Down in the green wood shady. All, All A-lonely. Anonymous. OxBoLi

All, all, all we did not know we meant. The British. Arthur Seymour John Tessimond. ChMP

All, all, and only, in my heart of hearts. Beauty. Joel Elias Spingarn. HBMV

All, all are gone, the old familiar faces. The Old Familiar Faces. Charles Lamb. AWP; BLPA; FaBoBe; FaBoRV; FaFP; FaPoR; FPL; GTBS; GTBS-P; HBV 1-2; NBM; NOBE; OBEV; OBRV; PG; PoPl; TreF; ViBoPo

All, all but Truth, drops dead-born from the Press,/Like the last Gazette, or the last Address. Satire. Alexander Pope. OBEC

All, all is fair; and gazing round, we feel/Over the yielding sense the torrid languor steal. Tropical Weather. Epes Sargent. EtS

All all is silent in the dark wood at night. I Rode with My Darling... Stevie Smith. BrRo

All, all is water!/Without which there is no living thing. Flood. Mary Grant Charles. GoYe

All, all, my joy, my grief, my love, are thine! Fulfilment. Robert Nichols. HBMV

All, all the stretch of these great green states–/And make America again! Let America Be America Again. Langston Hughes. PoNe

All alone, all alone, all alone!/It has such a wonderful sound. Alone. John Farrar. YeAr

All alone and unknown, at Edinbro' in an inn. Epitaph on Himself. Samuel Taylor Coleridge. FaBoEE

All alone as I am alone. The Traveling Out. Lucile Adler. IHMS

All alone on Airly Beacon,/With his baby on my knee! Airly Beacon. Charles Kingsley. GTBS; HBV 1-2; OBEV

All along, along, along/The Colorado Trail. The Colorado Trail. Anonymous. AS; CoSo; FSW

All along the Irish shore. On a Dead Scholar. Anonymous. AnIL

All among its petals, was his hairy face. Feri's Dream. Frances Cornford. BoC

All are compact of pity and of fear/As we are, only real. The Pool. E. L. Mayo. MiAP

All are fragments from His dish. Two Graces. Robert Herrick. PoPle

All are ghosts beside. Voluntaries. Ralph Waldo Emerson. AmePo; WGRP

All are gone, those damsels fair,/But you're here, so I don't care! Consolation (parody). Arthur Guiterman. BXAP

All are in thee; thou, in thyself alone. To Time. A. W. EiL

All are Stoics in the grave. The Epicure. Abraham Cowley. EG

All arise, arise, arise!/Rise! arise, arise! The Sunrise Call. *Anonymous.* WTO

All arms combined magnificently together. The Persian Version. Robert Graves. CMoP; FaBoCo; LiTB; LiTM; NoAm; NOBL; OBWP; WeW

All as to the benefit/Derived by the use of PAIN PAINT. Pain Paint. Peter Minck. FaBoUs

All ashes, all ashes again. On Neal's Ashes. Allen Ginsberg. CAPP; PoM

All, aswarm as bees, give ear,/Who by birth hold Athens dear. Delphic Hymn to Apollo. Algernon Charles Swinburne. VLP

All at one mark, all hitting: make-believes/For Edith and himself. Aylmer's Field. Alfred, Lord Tennyson. GN

All attend the steps of age. The Insatiate. Johannes Secundus. UnTE

All-beauteous Nature fears to be out-/done. The Seasons. James (1700-48) Thomson. OAEP

All beauty, and without a spot! The New Inn. Ben Jonson. TrGrPo

All because he wouldn't hoe corn. Young Man Who Wouldn't Hoe Corn. *Anonymous.* FSW

All behind her door is carefully concealed. Au Clair de la Lune. J. B. and Charles Fonteyn Manney Lully. FSW

All bent toward nourishing her children. Baking Day. Rosemary Joseph. Str

All Bologna's lore were vain,/To increase his mastery. The Highest Wisdom. Jacopone da Todi. CAW

All breathe, dance, skip, take breakfast, scamper about. The Last Bus (parody). E. V. Knox ("Evoe"). BXAP

All breeding places of the flesh we are. Island Dogs. Charles G. Bell. NePoAm-2

All but a few, mated, that lowered among the grasses/whom the gale, next morning, tried. Voyage. John Lyle Donaghy. OxBI

All but/Coyote. Myths and Texts. Gary Snyder. CAPP; NaP

All but the blithe/Hexameters. Verse. Oliver St.John Gogarty. AnIL; FaBoCh; HBV 1-2; LoGBV; OBEV; OBMV; PoRA

All by yourself, you can help her in childbirth! Djalbarmiwi's Song. *Anonymous.* CBAP

All came, all went; but never man/Knew whence they came, or where they went to! The World: a Ghazel. James Clarence Mangan. OBVV

All careless of thee too,/As I! Prometheus. Johann Wolfgang von Goethe. AWP

All causes end within the great Because. At Epidaurus. Lawrence Durrell. LiTB; MoPo; OBTV

All change, in thoughts/As well as things. Riprap. Gary Snyder. HaCAP; NeAP; NOBA; PoM

All chips of the old block from the stem to the starn. Cawsand Bay. *Anonymous.* PoPle

All Christly souls are one in Him,/Throughout the whole wide earth. No East or West. John Oxenham. TRV

All claims to the hour of death,/to be with you, Marban! The Hermit Marban. *Anonymous.* NOBI

All colors in a fountain changing. The Green and the Black. Anthony Bailey. NYBP

All combined in choired piety. View of the Cathedral. Raymond Henri. EyDe

All come to be Kings in their turn. The Chapter of Kings. John Collins. FaBoUs

All comes to nothing a hundred years hence. The Careless Gallant. Thomas Jordan. CoMu; HAP; OxBoLi

...All covering/His sad and usual heart, dry as a winter leaf. Aspects of Robinson. Weldon Kees. CoAP; NaP; NYBP; NYP

All crazy for my burning crown. The Poet. William Henry Davies. DTC

The all-creative Incorporeal Mouse,/Whose radiant doors warm this holy house. The Church Mouse. Gerald Bullett. BoAnP

All creatures knelt to worship the Child. Christmas Eve Legend. Frances Frost. BiCB

All Crete shall bless the marriage of tonight.' Ithocles, VI (excerpt). John Addington Symonds. PeHV

All crowded together, most of the pages/stuck like eyelids in the morning. Shadow of the Old City. Yehuda Amichai. VWA

All crueltyes which paper stain'd before/Are acted to the life here ore and ore. Seaconk or Rehoboths Fate. Benjamin Tompson. SCAP

All day, all night, I hear them flowing/To and fro. Chamber Music. James Joyce. FaBoCh

All day cheerily,/All night eerily! Voices from Things Growing in a Churchyard. Thomas Hardy. OxBTC

All day her hymns escape the house. Mrs. Macintosh. Rodney Hall. CBAP

All day it has been suspended there, above their heads. Suburban Lovers. Bruce Dawe. NOAV

All day long/Selling melons. Melons. Mary Mapes Dodge. TiPo

All day shall come the rushing rain. Yellow Butterflies. Koianimptiwa. WTO

All days are nights to see till I see thee,/And nights bright days when dreams do show thee/me. Sonnets, XLIII: "When most I wink, then do mine eyes best see." William Shakespeare. CBEP

All de horses in de stable/B'longs ter mammy's little baby. Go to Sleepy. *Anonymous.* AS; TrAS

All dice were cast. Late Light. Barbara Bellow Watson. NYBP

All difference with his fellow-mortal closed,/Shall be left standing face to face with God. To a Republican Friend. Matthew Arnold. VLP

...All difficulties postponed/because the weather is so good. I Come Home Wanting to Touch Everyone. Stephen P. Dunn. AMV-81

...All Divinity/Is built up from our good and evil luck. Bellerophon: There Are No Gods. Euripides. EaLo

All dream it, the dark wind crossing/The wide spaces between us. Poem about People. Robert Pinsky. NPGG

All eager-lipped I kissed the mouth of Death. Sonnet: "He came in silvern armor, trimmed with black." Gwendolyn B. Bennett. PoBA; PoNe

All eager to greet thee with praise and/with song. Thou Beautiful Sabbath. *Anonymous.* TrJP

All ears, all hearts but Death's could please and move. An Epitaph upon My Dear Brother, Francis Beaumont. Sir John Beaumont. JCP

All earth, all life, all else pass by. Silence. James Herbert Morse. AA

All earth and air seem only burning fire. Oenone. Alfred, Lord Tennyson. EnLi 1-2; MaVP; MBW 1-2; OAEP; OBRV; ViBoPo; VLP

All else, black water: and afloat,/One rood from shore, that single boat. The Hayeswater Boat (excerpt). Matthew Arnold. FaBoPP

All else is mortal but immortal–Love!' Malcolm's Katie. Isabella Valancy Crawford. OBCV

All else is vanished from my view/Like voices on the gale. Black Absence Hides upon the Past. John Clare. NOBV

The all-embracing bounteous bear/Dreams sweetly in his lowly lair. The little tigers are at rest. Tom (Thomas Hood, Jr.) Hood. CenHV

All ending in a sting. Epigram: "An epigram should be–if right." William Walsh. NIP

The all-endured this nothing-done costs me. The Last Wish. Edward Robert Bulwer, Earl of Lytton. OBSP; OBVV

All Europe is touched/With some of frigid York,/As York is now by Europe. The Coldness. Jon Silkin. VWA

All, except only Love, Love had died long ago. The Funeral of Youth: Threnody. Rupert Brooke. SeCeV

All/except the green ones Jake Hates All the Girls. Edward Estlin Cummings. CTBA

All fall down. Spoken through Glass. Eithne Wilkins. NeBP

All feather and fire. The Wing Factory. Dona Stein. AMV-80

All feeds on brimstone and is become one Gomorrah. Contempt for the World, III. Bernard de Morlas. PeHV

All follow and are standing by/On high, on high. Carol. W. R. Rodgers. ChMP; DTC; OBCP

All for her sake must the maiden die! Marriage. Mary Elizabeth Coleridge. PeHV

All for love I am so sick/That sleep I never may. Now Springs the Spray. *Anonymous.* MeEV; OAEL 1-2; OxBM

All for love–with a two-million dot! A Golden Sorrow. Martial (Marcus Valerius Martialis). LiTW

All for one and one for all! Brother, Lift Your Flag with Mine. Josephine Dodge Daskam Bacon. PoSC

All for Raffaella/Raffaella Flora. For the Fourth Birthday of My Daughter. George Barker. NAs

All for the good and honorable marriage/At Mary Kirk he gave me. Lord Ingram and Chiel Wyet. *Anonymous.* BaBo; ESPB

All for the love of a railroad man. Careless Love. *Anonymous.* TrAS

"All forms point to the formless/is itself a formal proposition. A Finger Points to the Moon. Ronald David Laing. MOON

All Four, in Consort join'd, shall Sing,/New Songs of Praise to Christ our King. Wednesday, January 1, 1701. Samuel Sewall. SCAP

All Frenchmen are of petit-maitre kind. Epistle to the Right Honourable William Pulteney, Esq. John Gay. OBTV

All Germany shall be the land! The German Fatherland. Ernst Moritz Arndt. HBV 1-2

All glorious, – yet forlorn. Columbus. Lydia Huntley Sigourney. AA; HBV1-2; MC; PAH

All Glory, glory, giv'n to Thee,/Thro' all the heav'nly height. The Shepherds Had an Angel. Christina Georgina Rossetti. OHIP

All glory with the Father be,/And Holy Ghost, eternally! Light of the Soul. Edward Caswall. BePJ

All god's SPADES got SHADES The Truth. Ted Joans. TTY

All goned afay mit de lager beer-/Afay in de ewigkeit! Hans Breitmann's Party. Charles Godfrey Leland. CenHV; FaBoCo; HBV 1-2; NOBL; OBAL

All good things go vanishing. Die Heimkehr (excerpt). Heinrich Heine. AWP

All good to kindred natures cleaveth soon. Sonnet: He Compares All Things with His Lady, and Finds Them Wanting. Guido Cavalcanti. AWP

All grief and ecstasy and pain/were they a phantom of the brain? Rontgen Photograph. Elisabeth Eybers. PeSA

All grief is done; and never more shall we/Make sail at dawning for the luring sea. Fiddler's Green. Theodore Goodridge Roberts. CaP

All hallelujah on my tongue,/All rapture in my heart. When Wild Confusion Wrecks the Air. Mather Byles. AH

"All hands go to sleep and I'll go to smoke." The Fishes' Lamentation. *Anonymous.* OBSS

All hands save ship! has startled dreamers. Old Counsel of the Young Master of a Wrecked California Clipper. Herman Melville. FaBoRV

All hangs together if you take it hard. What's Good for the Soul Is Good for Sales. Richard Wilbur. NLV

All haughty tyrants we disdain,/And shout "Long live America!" Ode on Science. Jezaniah Sumner. TrAS

All have been seized everywhere for the use of this dreadful/Mazzini. Amours de Voyage. Arthur Hugh Clough. FaBoPV

All have been vacuumed up. At 79th and Park. Barbara Howes. NYP

All he'll get is a kick in the arse. Dinky Di. *Anonymous.* NOAV

All he sought and gave/I am feeling. Song. John Boyle O'Reilly. ACP

All he want is boiler hot,/Run in there 'bout four o'clock. Joseph Mica. *Anonymous.* ViBoFo

All he wants/is for someone/to hold his hand The Cry of an Aged One. Ray Fraser. NeAC

All he was sorry for was one of the scabs bit him on the/knuckles of the right hand... Ice Handler. Carl Sandburg. OxBA

All heaven approves the sovereign choice. The Summer Harvest Spreads the Fields. Nathan Strong. AH

All heaven, meanwhile, condensed into one eye/Which fears to lose the wonder, should it wink. A Face. Robert Browning. CTC

...All her sweets convert to gall. Judah in Exile Wanders. George Sandys. AH

All her vows religious be,/And she vows her love to me. Castara. William Habington. HBV 1-2; LiTL

All her young admirers, whither/have they gone? The Young Acacia. Hayim Nahman Bialik. TrJP

All her young married life in one small dray. Auction Sale–Household Furnishings. Adele De Leeuw. PoToHe

All highest praise, all humblest thanks,/Now and for ever be! Fain Would My Thoughts. John Austin. OxBoCh

All highways make me think of you. For a Friend. Ted Kooser. GOYP

All his fellows lived, and waited. Shemuel. Edward Ernest Bowen. HBV 1-2

All his white beauty warm in the eye of the sun. The White Eagle. Nan McDonald. PoAu 1-2

All honor, as for trees/In the hot summer days. Song: "Now let us honor with violin and flute." May Sarton. MoRP

All honor to them/For what service I was to the people! Hamilton Greene. Edgar Lee Masters. NoAm; OxBA

All hope forsaking,/Died, swearing. The Starling. Robert Williams Buchanan. FM

All human reasons do rejoice and operate. Night Falls on China. W. H. Auden. CoBMV

All human tribes glad token see/In the close of the wars of Grant and/Lee. The Surrender at Appomattox. Herman Melville. MC; PAH

All hung with stars!), there still would be no bear. The Great Bear. John Hollander. LiTM; MP; NePoEA-2; NoAm; NYBP; TwCP

All I ask–all I wish–is a Tear. Hours of Idleness. George Gordon, Lord Byron. EvOK; Par

All I ask the heaven above,/And the road below me. The Vagabond. Robert Louis Stevenson. AnFE; BBV; BrPo; GTBS; HBV 1-2; HBVY; MCCG; TreFT; ViBoPo

All I can do, and this I do, is love, is pray. From St. Luke's Hospital. Madeleine L'Engle. CTBA

All I can give you is this description of my feelings. To His Wife. Ch'in Chia. LiTW

All I can say, and on a major note/Is–I am home again. The Return of the Native. Harley Matthews. PoAu 1-2

All I ever can be:/This I surrender, Oh, my Lord, to thee. All That I Am. Verna Arvey. VGW

An' all I ever done is kill my wife. Bad Man Ballad. *Anonymous.* ABF

...All I know/Is, there is not a word of fear. On Death. Walter Savage Landor. BoLiVe; TrGrPo

An' all I know is they was cried/In meetin' come nex' Sunday. The Biglow Papers. James Russell Lowell. AA; AnNE; NOBA; OBAL

All I need my little sweet woman/and to keep my company/hmmm hmmm hmmm hmmm/my company Hellhound on My Trail. Robert Johnson. BluL

"All,' I said, "all!" C Is for Charms. Eleanor Farjeon. WSC

All i want now is my woman back/so my soul can sing. Feeling Fucked/Up. Etheridge Knight. GP; NNaP

All ill come running in, all good keep out! The Witch, V, i. Thomas Middleton. WSC

All immersed and lost in love! Draw Me, Saviour, After Thee. Charles Wesley. BePJ

The All-in-All seems here a Greek. The Attic Landscape. Herman Melville. NOBA

All in gold, sir, all in gold. East Virginia. *Anonymous.* OuSiCo

All in magic murmurs she/Laps and lulls the wee one lying,/Pearl of twilight, on her knee. Dorothea. Sarah N. Cleghorn. HBMV

All in the Dark, He watches/And guards us while we rest. God's Dark. John Martin. PoLf

All in the diffidence that faltered. Canto LXXXI. Ezra Pound. CMoP; FaBoMo; HAP; MoAB; MoVE; NePA; NoAm; NOBA; OxBA; PAI; SeCeV; VGW; ViBoPo

All in the ecstasy of doing. On Fruition. Sir Charles Sedley. ErPo

All in the presence of the passinjare. Punch, Brothers, Punch! *Anonymous.* CBEP

All in white shall wait around. A Christmas Hymn. Cecil Frances Alexander. OHIP

All is, if I have grace to use it so,/As ever in my great task master's eye. Sonnet on His Having Arrived at the Age of Twenty-Three. John Milton. HBV 1-2; LoBV

All is less than/it is,/all is more. Cello Entry. Paul Celan. VWA

All is light and motion! Spring Song in the City. Robert Williams Buchanan. HBV 1-2

All is possible. Varium et Mutabile. Sir Thomas Wyatt. OBSC; QFR

All is rewarded on a breath/By an accident. Yeats in Dublin (excerpt). Vernon Watkins. PP

All its branches/which are/boards I know/soon enough. The City. Robert Creeley. LCAP

All its Field-floor shook. Death of Saint Guthlac. Cynewulf. ACP

All its indifference is a different rage. Codicil. Derek Walcott. NoAm

All join to chant the dirge of him/Who fell just now from Heaven. The Fallen Star. George Darley. AnFE; HBV 1-2; OBEV

All joy, all grief, all beauty to her lover. The Poet Describes His Love. Robert Nathan. HBMV

All knees shall bow to thee; all wits shall rise,/And praise him who did make and mend our eies. Love. George Herbert. AnAnS 1

All left in one small bottom swum imbark'd. The Ark. John Milton. EtS

All life is over, and all hope is dead. Man Is a Weaver. Moses Ibn Ezra. TrJP

All light is one. To My Son. *Anonymous.* PoLf

All looking down for the love of me. The Mermaid. Alfred, Lord Tennyson. GN; WSC

All losses are restored and sorrows end. Sonnets, XXX: "When to the sessions of sweet silent thought." William Shakespeare. ATP; AWP; BiP; BoLiVe; CTC; DiPo; EBEV; ExPo; FaBoRV; FaBV; FaFP; FF; FPL; GBL; GoTF; GTBS; GTBS-P; HAP; HBV 1-2; InPo; InPS; LiTB; LoBV; MasP; NOBE; NoP; OAEL 1-2; OBEV; OBSC; PAI; PoEL 1-5; PoLf; PoPle; PoRA; PPoe; PPP; PrIm; SeCeV; TEP; TreFS; TrGrPo; TRV; ViBoPo; WHA

All lost for nothing, and ourselves a ghost. One Star Fell and Another. Conrad Aiken. MoAmPo

All loth to part, but that the glooming skies/Warnd them to draw their bleating flocks to rest. Colin Clout's Come Home Again. Edmund Spenser. CABL; OAEL 1-2

All loved the strain, and all/Looked at the moon! The Flute of the Lonely. Vachel Lindsay. CrMA

All made out of nothing,/And so beautiful! Merchandise. Amy Lowell. LaNeLa; MAPA

All magic gifts of joy's simplicity. Idleness. Silas Weir Mitchell. AA

...All may move/Cheered with the prospect of a brighter day. Apology. William Wordsworth. VLP

All memory lost and forfeited all pride. The First Solitude. Luis de Gongora y Argote. OBVE

All men are bad and in their badness reign. Sonnets, CXXI: "'Tis better to be vile than vile esteemed." William Shakespeare. CBEP; InvP; OAEL 1-2; PoEL 1-5

All men are brothers or all my enemies. Five for the Grace. Winfield Townley Scott. VGW

All men are equal. Dupes of democracy! Bonfire of Kings. Donald Evans. AnAmPo

All men are Noah's sons. Still, Citizen Sparrow. Richard Wilbur. AmPP; AP; CMoP; HoPM; LiTM; MiAP; MoAB; MoPo; NePA; NoAm

"All men, to one so bound by such a vow,/And women were as phantoms...." Idylls of the King. Alfred, Lord Tennyson. OAEL 1-2

All Men wou'd wish to Live, and Dye like me. The Choice. John Pomfret. CEP; NOEC; OBEC

All might be seen beneath the waves to swim. Hero and Leander. George Chapman. EBEV

All mirth farewell, let me in sorrow live. Astrophel and Stella, C. Sir Philip Sidney. AAS; SiPS

All money ever saved by banking coal. Banking Coal. Jean Toomer. PoNe

All morning! All morning! All Morning. Theodore Roethke. NaP

All mourn the minstrel's harp unstrung,/Their name unknown, their praise unsung. The Minstrel Responds to Flattery. Sir Walter Scott. OBNC

All mouth that once had been all egg. The Little Birds. *Anonymous.* NTCP

All my castles, all, all, all,/They can never never fall! Castles. Glanz-Leyeles. A. TrJP; VWA

...All my desires ripen into fruits of love. Gitanjali. Rabindranath Tagore. WGRP

All my garden, banks and borders, up/into the gray rocks. I Planned to Have a Border of Lavender. Paul Goodman. VGW

All my legendary people, first of the brave. Legend. John Waller. NeBP

All my life I dream of dancers whirling/Through the trees like colorful wild beasts. Matisse. Edward Hirsch. PoDr

All my life I have wondered what he meant to tell me. The Hemingway House in Key West. Philip Schultz. MAYP

All my life I'll learn/How to love as long. When I Was Still a Child. Lesbia Harford. NOAV

All my love's in vain. Love in Vain. Robert Johnson. UnPo

All my perfumes, I give most willingly/To 'embalme thy fathers corse; What? will hee die? The Perfume. John Donne. AnAnS 1

All my sins been taken away, taken away. Mary Wore Three Links of Chain (with music). *Anonymous.* AS

All my trials, Lord, soon be over. All My Trials. *Anonymous.* FSW

All my twilen, wi' her ceare,/Did call me to my evenen feare. Day's Work A-Done. William Barnes. SaC

"All names mean God, perchance!" The Name. Don (Donald Robert Marquis) Marquis. HBV 1-2

All Nature's incense rise! The Universal Prayer. Alexander Pope. BLPA; CEP; EnLit; FaBoBe; FPL; GoBC; HBV 1-2; ILwL; NoP; OAEP; TreFT; WGRP

All nature to its God shall cry,/Who lives through vast eternity. To Thee, Then, Let All Beings Bend. Nathaniel Evans. AH

All never yielding/To a bulldozer approaching. Bulldozers. Frederick Dec. PCP

All night he shouts among the graves,/"Wake! Wake!–Wake! Wake!" The Corncrake. James H. Cousins. BoAnP; OnYI

All night I ask what time it is. A Night Vigil in the Left Court of the Palace. Tu Fu. LiTW

...All night I'm rocked beneath cold stars/to a destination too well known to fear. Amtrak. Elliot Fried. PPJ

All night, in a half dream, I have lain here listening. Night Thoughts in Age. John Hall Wheelock. MoVE; NYBP

All night long! Rambunctious Brook. Frances Frost. BrR

All night long, from midnight on. All Night Long. *Anonymous.* FSW

All night long he ploughed. The Vampire. Conrad Aiken. HBMV

...All night spilling into/the dark house, all night they are there. The Windows. Ron Loewinsohn. GP

All night the truth/of the frozen engine/burns in her eyes. Night Flight. Don Johnson. AMV-81

...All night, the world that lolled outside/Kept slipping newborn rats under his door. Artificer. X. J. Kennedy. TwCP

All night Thy dedicated lamp burns on. Uriel. William Force Stead. OxBoCh

All now at the center. Home. Hollis Summers. SOTS

All now seems possible. O let me nothing ask. Morning. Harry Fainlight. PoL

All of a summer's day. Milton by Firelight. Gary Snyder. CAPP; CoAP

All of her, but voice, is here. The Picture. Anacreon. UnTE

All of it gentle Plaza Real with Palmtrees. Paul Blackburn. NoAm

All of life and love my house shall know! Dream House. Catherine Parmenter Newell. PoToHe

All of my bones/remember Africa. Lucille Clifton. CNA

All of my enemies shall make a doomed journey. The Brut. Layamon. MeEV

& All of the blue-lipped/hills in their eyes. Weekend Sonnets. Cilla McQueen. OCNZ

All of the earth of love/And love's high heaven! Reparation. Helen Hoyt. HBMV

All of the olden time. The Fine Old English Gentleman. *Anonymous.* CH; HBV 1-2

All of them flow down into the sea. The Weepers Tower in Amsterdam. Paul Goodman. VGW

All of those Romanovs were a little bit crazy.' A Son of the Romanovs. Louis Simpson. OxBC

All of us/is tired. Mrs. Hamer. Jane Stembridge. NMM

All of us/shall/dance/within. The Liberator. Emily Holmes Coleman. EAS

All of you ba-bas/will hear of as a god. How We Heard the Name. Alan Dugan. CoAP; NMP; NoAm

All of you seem to make. Clerihew. Edmund Clerihew Bentley. NOBL

All on a Christmas day. I Wash My Face in a Golden Vase. *Anonymous.* ChBR

All on that day? Sinner Man. *Anonymous.* FSW

All on the threshold, yet all short of life. A Triad. Christina Georgina Rossetti. PBWP; VLP

...All one/odor and mortal taste. The Night-Apple. Allen Ginsberg. NoAm

All other blessings I resign/Make but the dear Amanda mine. For Ever, Fortune, Wilt Thou Prove. James (1700-48) Thomson. CBEP; GTBS; GTBS-P

All other fayre lyke flowres untymely fade. Amoretti, LXXIX. Edmund Spenser. AAS; AWP; EnLi 1-2; HBV 1-2; NoP

All other Love is to your sexe, not You. An Elegie. Thomas Randolph. MePo

All other women?–forgotten! I've/discovered Alison! Alison. *Anonymous.* HAP

All our hearts to thee incline. Sovereign and Transforming Grace. Frederic Henry Hedge. AH

All our high-toned questions/breed in a lively animal. Two Songs, 1. Adrienne Rich. NOBA; TAP

All our sorrow shall turn to game,/Verbum Caro factum est. Three Christmas Carols: III. *Anonymous.* ACP

...All our winter bears/toward its final overthrow. Lent Tending. J. Barrie Shepherd. AMV-80

All over dis worl',hanh, all over dis worl',hanh! Jumpin' Judy. *Anonymous.* ABF

...All over fashionable people,/comes the wide gray, forgiving rain. Whatever Comes. William Stafford. NPAW

All over the farm on a summer day! Follow the Leader. Harry Behn. SoPo

All over this world. Meeting at the Building. *Anonymous.* FSW

All owls are satisfactory;/Some excuses are unsatisfactory. Hit or Miss. Lewis (Charles Lutwidge Dodgson) Carroll. FaBoNo

All pain forgotten if only she comes back to me Souvenirs. Dudley Randall. BPo

All paine hath end and every war hath peace,/But mine no price nor prayer may surcease. Amoretti, XI. Edmund Spenser. AAS

All paines are nothing in respect of this,/All sorrowes short that gaine eternall blisse. Amoretti, LXIII. Edmund Spenser. AAS; EBEV; FaBoEn; OAEL 1-2; OAEP; OBSC

All partial evil, universal good. An Essay on Man. Alexander Pope. WGRP

All parts in place–/or nearly so. Cicada. Adrien Stoutenburg. NYBP

All peacefully from Bantry Bay. Bantry Bay. James Lyman Molloy. OnYI

All people weep. City-Storm. Harold Monro. MoBrPo

All Pillsbury were the Taystee loaves,/And in a Minute Maid. Jabber-Whacky. Isabelle Di Caprio. QQQ

All play and no work makes Jack a mere toy. All Work and No Play Makes Jack a Dull Boy. *Anonymous.* OxNR

All Plunky answered him was, Yes. Surprise. Harry Behn. BiCB; TiPo

All possible doubt whatever. The Grand Inquisitor's Song. Sir William Schwenck Gilbert. OnMSP

All praise to Jehovah, with gladness and singing! Floods Swell Around Me, Angry, Appalling. Zachary Eddy. AH

ALL PRAISES ARE DUE TO ALLAH FOR THE LAMB Hush, Honey. Ruby C. Saunders. BlSi

"All present, or accounted for!" Alma Mater's Roll. Edward Everett Hale. AA

All questions answered. Before the War. James Pendergast. AMV-81

All ranged in a ring, and dancing in delight. The Faerie Queene. Edmund Spenser. TrGrPo

All rapture through and through,/In God's most holy sight. Paradise. Frederick William Faber. HBV 1-2

All ravished with billing and dying with pleasure. Beneath a Cool Shade. Aphra Behn. UnTE

All remedie gone/except in Christ alone, alone. To Pass the Place where Pleasure Is. *Anonymous.* CoMu

...All, renewed assurance/And confirmation of the old despair. The City of Dreadful Night. James (1834-82) Thomson. GTBS-P; OAEP

All revelation has been ours. All Revelation. Robert Frost. CABA; MoPo; NePA

All right, go ahead and cry, damn it! Sales Talk for Annie. Morris Bishop. NLV

("–All right.")/"Good night!" Conversation. David McCord. GrPl; SO

"All right," he said, "he's guilty–let's go home." In the Jury Room. Hodding Carter. MAT

"All right! Lay down on deck!" Making Land. Thomas Fleming Day. EtS

All right. Once more, then. But just once. You hear? Romping. John Ciardi. CTBA; NCSH

"All right so far." The Optimist. *Anonymous.* BLPA; GoTF; TreFT; YaD

All roads and found them safe as far as they could see. Night Out. R. A. Simpson. PoAu 1-2

All roads descend toward town. Work to Do Toward Town. Gary Snyder. VGW

All round her galoshes! Galoshes. Rhoda Warner Bacmeister. BrR; NTCP; SoPo; TiPo

All round the valley?–Lost, O, lost! The Novice. Edward Davison. ErPo

All rudely and wildly dispelling/The love of the happiest home. Thou Hast Wounded the Spirit That Loved Thee. Mrs. David Porter. BLPA

All ruin is the same. All Ruin Is the Same. Emanuel Litvinoff. WaP

All's a scattering,/A shining. Meditation at Oyster River. Theodore Roethke. CAPP; CMoP; MoAmPo; NaP; NYBP

All's peace to-day at Beecher Isle. Beecher Island. Arthur Chapman. PoOW

All's right with the world! Pippa Passes. Robert Browning. ATP; BLPL; BrR; EBCP; FaFP; GoJo; GoTF; GTBS; LiTB; MCCG; NTCP; OBEV; OBVV; OHIP; PoPl; PoToHe; TEP; TrCP; TreF; TRV; UnPo; WGRP

"All's well! All's well!" All's Well! William Allen Butler. HBV 1-2

All's well, whichever side the grave for/me/The morning light may break. All's Well. Harriet McEwen Kimball. AA

All's well with the world! Madam Mouse Trots. Edith Sitwell. SyP

All's well with thee if thou art in just/hands. The Eternal Justice. Anne Reeve Aldrich. AA

All saner growth abhors it, and the bays/Wither, affronted, in the poisoned plot. The Life of Service. Donald Davie. NYBP

...All save a trusty band/Who keep strict watch along the northern heights. The Spanish Gypsy (excerpt). George Eliot. OBTV

All seas, all ships. Song for All Seas, All Ships. Walt Whitman. CH; FaBoBe; HBV 1-2; HBVY; MCCG; MoRP; MOS; NePA

All seem to know what is for heaven alone. Love in the Valley. George Meredith. AnEnPo; AWP; GTBS; HBV 1-2; InPo; LiTB; LiTL; NOBE; OAEL 1-2; OBEV; OBVV; ViBoPo; VLP; WHA

All sepulchers/Are sealed in vain! If a Man Die–. John Richard Moreland. PGD

All shadows dark and cause them slide,/According as his will is. The Spouse to the Beloved. William Baldwin. OBSC

All shadows procession in an acropolis of lights. Professor Kelleher and the Charles River. Desmond O'Grady. CIP; NoAm

All sick and sorrowing hearts to fold/In thy enfolding rest. A Prayer. Irene Rutherford McLeod. TrPWD

All sighing on, and will not hush,/Some pleasant tales of thee. To Mary: I Sleep with Thee, and Wake with Thee. John Clare. GBL

All signed–"Yours Gratefully, In Jesus Christ." Miss Marnell. Austin Clarke. IPY

All silken on one side,/all mud on the other one. For a Shetland Pony Brood Mare Who Died in Her Barren Year. Maxine W. Kumin. PH

All slightly disconnected in the head/and needing mercy. Loony, 29: The Good Folks at the Camp Meeting. William Kloefkorn. GP

...All so true/like a bit of yarrow and of rue. Bouquet in Dog Time. Hayden Carruth. GrPl

All sorrows in the loss of you, and turning/Your pretty head to me, set the old fires new burning. To L. C. Lucy Hawkins. HBMV

...All sorts of weather/Both cold, wet and snow. Country Hirings. *Anonymous.* OBET

All soulless now, yet merry with the Spring! The Sun's Shame. Dante Gabriel Rossetti. MaVP

All Souls will belong to me. On Sir William Anson, Fellow of All Souls. *Anonymous.* FaBoEE

All sounds to silence come. Faint Music. Walter De La Mare. FaBoCh; LoGBV

All spine and nerve. The Copperhead. David Bottoms. AMV-81; MAYP

All stars are angels; but the sun is God. William Shakespeare. Algernon Charles Swinburne. TrGrPo

All stars are hung so every Christmas tree/has one above it. Let's go out and see. Come Christmas. David McCord. PCh

All strikes like iron in the mind. The Birdsville Track. Douglas Stewart. CBAP

All sufficient is the glory/of the Lord's atoning Blood. The Precious Blood. *Anonymous.* STF

All summer go brown, go salt by the sea. January. Geoffrey Dutton. PoAu 1-2

All swelled up with scurvy so I really thought I'd die. Prospecting Dream. *Anonymous.* FSW

All Swindlers–be–infer– I meant to have but modest needs. Emily Dickinson. BiP

...All that ceases at hands that raise/through this wet nothingness of rain. Return of Autumn. Pablo Neruda. LiTW

All that he'd put into it. The Swimming Pool. Jonathan Holden. MAYP

All that he did not find, you have not found. Ode for the Burial of a Citizen. John Ciardi. LiTM; MiAP

All that her eyes could read in mine/Or mine in hers had read. During Music. Arthur Symons. NOBV

All that hilly sweetness wasting Lonesome in the Country. Al Young. MAT; NPGG

All that I ask–you keep the faith unbroken! The New Year. J. D. Templeton. PGD

"All that I axed vos, let me alone." The Old Cove. Henry Howard Brownell. PAH

All that I did has turned into this song. Drummer Boy. William Stafford. FAZ

All that I have–a humble gift/His evermore shall be. They Crucified My Lord. *Anonymous.* STF

All that I loved in all the world stands there,/And will not knock again. The Return. Arthur Symons. HBMV

All that I praise and bless. The Phoenix Answered. Anne Ridler. ChMP

All that I saw was China, China, China. Digging for China. Richard Wilbur. GoJo; GrPl; LOW; MP; NCSH; TwCP

All that I've never thought of–think of me! A Sick Child. Randall Jarrell. InPK; InvP; OxBC; SO; VGW

All that is beautiful and all divine/Is safe in thee. The Cloud of Carmel. Jessica Powers. ISi

All that is forever homeless/in this deep heavy darkness. In This Deep Darkness. Natan Zach. VWA

All that is lonely, and is beautiful! On a Lonely Spray. James Stephens. AnFE; OnYI

All that life can tell. A Cyprian Woman. Margaret Widdemer. AnAmPo; HBV 1-2

All that live upon the teeming earth his fame/Ever proclaim. Hail, Oh Hail to the King. Beatrice Quickenden. AH

All that man was and all he hopes to be. Portrait of a Child. Louis Untermeyer. HBMV

All that needs to be done, said he, shall be done, and/quickly. The Engagement. Arthur Hugh Clough. NBM

All that once done, Lal won the highest way. I Set Forth Hopeful. Lalleswari. WPOW

All that rigour gives me peace. Epigram: "Since first you knew my am'rous smart." Robert Nugent, Earl Nugent. NOEC

"All that's beautiful drifts away/Like the waters." The Old Men Admiring Themselves in the Water. William Butler Yeats. 06]CMoP; FaBoCh; GoJo; LoGBV; PCP

All that's sweet was made/But to be lost when sweetest. All That's Bright Must Fade. Thomas Moore. OxBI

...All that she knew/Of love and life and death and false and true. Tallahassee (excerpt). Andrew Merkel. CaP

All that the rain promised, and more. You Could Say. Robert Mezey. AmPC; NaP

All/that time for/Rhyme. The Aesthete Weasel. Christian Morgenstern. FaBoNo

All that time she thought she was nothing/But skin and bones. Trouble. James Wright. FF

All that was evil–to thy mother. Byron. J. Gordon Coogler. OBAL

All that was me is gone. Over the Sea to Skye. Robert Louis Stevenson. EtS; MOS

All that was promis'd by the Spring. To a Very Young Lady. Edmund Waller. AnAnS 2; OBS; SeCP; TrGrPo; ViBoPo

All that was told of her is true. The Girl in the Carriage. *Anonymous.* LiTW

All that we have is but deaths livery. Epigram: Fatum Supremum. *Anonymous.* OBS

All that we know in love is bitter./And it is not much. Annihilation. Conrad Aiken. CrMA; GBL; MoAB; MoAmPo

All that we learn we learn too late,/And it's not much. Sierra Kid. Philip Levine. AmPC

...All that we/may hope to be, locked in/our day-long longing for night. All Day We've Longed for Night. Sarah Webster Fabio. BlSi

"All that we saw/Was his shadow under his shield." The King of Connacht. *Anonymous.* KiLC

All that will remain/Is the love/That burns away the sun. The Crystal Skull. Kathleen Raine. NeBP

All that/Wrinkles like heat and disappears into thin air. April Fourth. Robert Mezey. NaP

All that you ever said/and for the worse,/an end. Pedlar. *Anonymous.* OBVE

All that you had I found. Exchanges. Ernest Christopher Dowson. OBMV

..."All that you missed/there/Has grown to be yours." The Album. Cecil Day Lewis. ChMP; EnLoPo; OxBI; OxBTC

All the air quivers, and the east sky glows. A Front. Randall Jarrell. OBWP; OxBC; VGW

All the art for Art's sake! Art for Art's Sake. Marc Blitzstein. TrJP

All the bats of Babel flap about/The rising sun of hell. The Slough of Despond. Robert Lowell. SyP

All things at rest, and imaged the still voice/Of Quiet whispering to the ear of Night. A Rhapsody, Written at the Lakes in Westmorland. John Brown. NOEC

All things bring me to love. Song: "Under a southern wind." Theodore Roethke. CrMA

All things burn with God's white fire. Revelation. Verne Bright. BLRP; WBLP

All things come to him who waits The Adorable Paratroopess. Michael Silverton. PoL

All things in this life that he could. The Performance. James Dickey. CAPP; CoAP; ConAP; LiTM; NePoEA-2; NoAm; NOBA

All things innocent, hapless, forsaken. The Meadow Mouse. Theodore Roethke. HeIP; NaP; PPoe

All things lustered/by the steady thoughtlessness/of human use. Songs to Survive the Summer. Robert Hass. AmPA

All things must end that have begun. Kyrielle. John Payne. HBV 1-2

All things remain in God. Words for Music Perhaps. William Butler Yeats. AtBAP

All things shall rise to you. Shut the Seven Seas against Us. George Barker. MoAB; MoBrPo

All things that fed luxurious sense/From appetite to innocence. October Poems: The Garden. Robert Penn Warren. PoA

All things were thus when Pym was King. Pyms Anarchy. Thomas Jordan. OBS

All things whisper in the blood,/Wondrous is God's sovereign will. Now Evening Puts Amen to Day. Paul Horgan. AH

All this, and so much more,/And so much more. A Life of T. S. Eliot (parody). Michael Frayn. FaBoPa

All this food is grown in the store. Picketing Supermarkets. Tom Wayman. NIP

All this happens, gentlemen, and I must say it. I Write Poems. Gloria Fuertes. WPOW

All this I'll do that men with praise may crown/My fame for turning the world upside-down. The Parliament of Bees. John Day. ViBoPo

All this I saw through my improved binoculars. The Improved Binoculars. Irving Layton. NOBC

All this is his/Who hath a book. Who Hath a Book. Wilbur D. Nesbit. BLPA; SiSoSe; TiPo; TreFS

All this is love; and all love is but this. Love. Rupert Brooke. MoLP

All this is true without deceit. Riddle: "Every lady in the land." *Anonymous.* OxNR; PoPle

...All this is what is not/For you, and the words rise outward toward your smile. Declension. Stephen Sandy. PoA

All this time–the Bugaboo! Journal (excerpt). Edna St. Vincent Millay. ImOP

All this will never be again. The Wheel Revolves. Kenneth Rexroth. NoAm

All this worlds glory seemeth vayne to me,/And all theyr shewes but shadowes saving she. Amoretti, LXXXIII. Edmund Spenser. AAS

...All those gentlemen. A Bird Sings to Establish Frontiers. Jack Gilbert. NPGG

All those years. For the West. Gary Snyder. NaP

All threaten the head that I love. The Pity of Love. William Butler Yeats. AnIV; CMoP; NOBV; VLP

All three/Were puffy as puffy can be. Three Little Puffins. Eleanor Farjeon. TiPo

All through/The voracity of that Emeu! The Ballad of the Emeu. Bret (Francis Bret Harte) Harte. NLV

All through the woods the trumpet called,/"Foul play, foul play, foul play." Kath'rine Jaffrey. *Anonymous.* BFSS

All thy attempts how can I blame/To work my Death? I seek the same. The Self-Deceaver. Juan de Montalvan. OBVE

All thy fellow birds do sing/Careless of thy sorrowing.... Philomel. Richard Barnfield. NOBE

All time shall hail thee, Europe's noblest Son! La Fayette. Dolly Madison. PAH; PAL

All to have a Kingsley/Swear it does him good! That English Weather: After Charles Kingsley (parody). *Anonymous.* Par

All to Mary Shepherdess they'd fold their hands and pray. Mary Shepherdess. Marjorie Pickthall. ISi

All to one common dissolution tends. Sentiment. Thomas Chatterton. NOEC

All, to the haven where each would be,/Fly. Envoi. Algernon Charles Swinburne. SUS; VLP

All to watch me while I sleep. God Bless This House from Thatch to Floor. *Anonymous.* OxNR

All tortured by choice with th' invisible nail. The Fakir. Richard Owen Cambridge. OBTV

...All true/silk purses are made of sows' ears./It's hard to do. Dislike of Tasks. Richmond Lattimore. SaC

All under the olive trees. A Stopwatch and an Ordanance Map. Stephen Spender. MoBS

All under the willow-tree.... O Sing unto my Roundelay. Thomas Chatterton. CH; LiTB

All upside-down, and try to doze. Bats. Mary Effie Lee Newsome. GoSl

All Venice is a falling of autumn leaves,/Brown, and yellow streaked with brown. The City of Falling Leaves. Amy Lowell. SUS; TiPo

All Virtue is to render good for ill. Sonnet: Of Virtue. Folgore da San Geminiano. AWP

All wan beneath the welkin. All creation wept. The Dream of the Rood. *Anonymous.* ACP

All was enjoyment. Not a cloud obscured/Present or future. Bologna, and Byron. Samuel Rogers. OBRV

...All was/Terribly silent where four people stood/Tall in the air, believing what they could. Burial. May Sarton. GP

All water without earth or sky a water all over water gone over for-/ever Who. Edwin Honig. TAP

All waters as the shore. Ave Atque Vale. Algernon Charles Swinburne. EnLi 1-2; MaVP; NOBE; OAEL 1-2; OAEP; OBNC; SyP; ViBoPo; VLP

All ways to enter/And no way to go. Prayer. Witter ("Emanuel Morgan") Bynner. EaLo

All we are sure of is goodbye, goodbye. Vale. John Ciardi. MiAP

...All we ask/Is the one gift you cannot give. At the British War Cemetery, Bayeux. Charles Causley. OBWP; OxBC

...All we can do is look/at each other and hum the music/that's there. Tractor Hour. Monty Reid. CaPN

All we can hope to leave them now is money. Homage to a Government. Philip Larkin. EBEV; FaBoPV

All we can wish is, may that earth lie light/Upon thy tender limbs! and so good night. To One Married to an Old Man. Edmund Waller. FaBoEE; OBSP; SeCP

All we have left, their pedagogues reply. The Celebration in the Plaza. Adrienne Rich. NePoEA

All welcome once more,"/Cried Dame Wiggins of Lee. Dame Wiggins of Lee. *Anonymous.* FaBoBe; OxBChV

All what I am, it is you. When To My Deadlie Pleasure. Sir Philip Sidney. AtBAP; EnLoPo; PoEL 1-5

All which, and thousands mo do make a loathsome life.' The Faerie Queene. Edmund Spenser. NOBE

All which are founded in desire,/As light in flame and heat in fire. Desire. Thomas Traherne. OxBoCh

All which happiness, he brags,/He doth owe unto his rags. Cast Our Caps and Cares Away. John Fletcher. ViBoPo

All who beheld it rejoiced, and praised the/Lord, and took courage. The Expedition to Wessagusset. Henry Wadsworth Longfellow. PAH

All who will closely look at once espy/A geometrical and insane eye. Pigeon. Roy Fuller. PB

All whose flowers are tears, and round his temples/Iron blossom of frost is bound for ever. Hendecasyllabics. Algernon Charles Swinburne. FaBoRV; SyP; VLP

All will grow white somehow,/Or bandage on a brow. Fresh Paint. Boris Pasternak. PoPl; TrJP

All winning, one after one. For the Running of the New York City Marathon. James Dickey. NYP

The All-wise no offering takes till man hath writ/The goal, the road, the yea and nay, on it. The Ampler Circumscription. William Baylebridge. BoAV

All with one deep voice exclaim,/"Watch and pray." Watch and Pray. Charlotte Elliott. STF

All wold zights welcomer than new,/A-look'd on as I look'd on you. The Vierzide Chairs. William Barnes. NOBV

All women born are so perverse/No man need boast their love possessing. Triolet. Robert Bridges. HBV 1-2; PV; TW

All women, O, are beautiful/When they are half-undressed. The Saginaw Song. Theodore Roethke. NLV

All words forgotten–/Thou, Lord, and I. The Scribe. Walter De La Mare. AnFE; AtBAP; CMoP; FaBoCh; LoGBV; MoRP; OBMV; TrCP; TrPWD

...All worldly joys go less/To the one joy of doing kindnesses. Be Useful. George Herbert. GN

All would be happy at the cheaper rate. The Churches of Rome and of England. John Dryden. ACP

All would have answered had you answered then/With even a sigh. Silences. Arthur William Edgar O'Shaughnessy. OBNC; VLP

All wrapped in white linen as cold as the clay. The Cowboy's Lament. *Anonymous.* BLSo

All wrath to power, all yearning/To truth, thy dwelling-place. The Hills. Julian Grenfell. HBV 1-2

All ye who do not love her–ye know where ye can go. Edna's Hymn. Barry Humphries. NOAV

All you have seen and heard. Ye Walls! Sole Witnesses of Happy Sighs. Walter Savage Landor. EnLoPo

All you have to do/is do it,/with your full being,/and know how to love, and eat, and laugh. Making Miso. Lawson Fusao Inada. GP

All you have to pay me is to take in my romanza. Home, Sweet Home. Henry Cuyler Bunner. CenHV

All you high power women, all got to bottle up and go. Bottle Up and Go. *Anonymous.* FSW

All you sinners gonna turn up missing,/One o' these days! God's Goin' to Set This World on Fire (A vers.) (with music). *Anonymous.* AS

—All/you would be doing is telling the difference/between a lie and the truth which is a story. The Difference between a Lie and the Truth. Ronald James Dessus. LFAC

All your hundred plans come to naught,/none matched my thought. Yung Wind. Confucius. CTC

...All your/imaginings/won't pull you out again from the waters. The Everlasting Forests. Dahlia Ravikovich. BoWoP

(All your life you wait around for some damn man!) Chant for Dark Hours. Dorothy Parker. SBG

Allah has given them rest. Arabia. John Meade Falkner. OxBTC

Allay the pangs of age, and smooth thy grave. Solitude. James Grainger. CEP

Alle him loveden that him sowe,/Bothen heye men and lowe. Havelok: Havelok at Grimsby and Lincoln. *Anonymous.* OxBM

Alleluia, alleluia, alleluia. Rejoice, Let Alleluias Ring. M. Cherubim Schaefer. AH

Alleluia, Alleluia, Alleluia, Amen. Alleluia! Christ Is Risen Today. John Henry Hopkins, Jr. AH

Alleluia–Amen–evermore with the Lord! I Would Not Live Alway. William Augustus Muhlenberg. AA; AH; HBV 1-2

Alleluia, Baby,/In the swaddling clothes! Carol: "When the herds were watching." William Canton. HBVY; OHIP

Alleluia, Great is God!/Alleluia, Alleluia! Praise Now Your God. H. P. Brucker. AH

Allons, from all bat-eyed formula. The Poets at Tea. Barry Pain. HBV 1-2; Par

Allow me this pleasure/in Bally-na-Lee. The Lass from Bally-Na-Lee. Anthony Raftery. BIrV

Allow me to tell you a couple!' Lewis Carroll. Eleanor Farjeon. OxBChV

Allow my prayer to reach you. To Eros. Anacreon. LiTW

Allow the country die for you. Heritage. Augustus Young. CIP

Allowed one to catch it with ease. Limerick: "There once were some learned MD's." Oliver Herford. LiBL

Allowing sleep to do our dreaming for us. Turn the Key Deftly. Edwin Brock. PoL

...Allows dispersion/to gather each molecule/in its vast uniting storm Energy. Judith Fitzgerald. CaPN

Allure us and reject us at thy will! Mona Lisa. Edward Dowden. OnYI

An allustion of degree to the wife of sudden passion. An Ancient Degree. Bernadette Mayer. ANYP

Almighty God suffered/Died and Rose/through the cross/Of glory.' The Dream of the Cross. *Anonymous.* EBEV

...The Almighty will/Aeons late stumble on it with surprise. Conclusion. John Frederick Nims. PoA

Almond and citron bloom quivering at start,/Ends in pure snows. In the Streets of Catania. Roger Casement. AnIV

Almond bloom, we greet thee well. Almond Blossom. Sir Edwin Arnold. GN; HBV 1-2

Almost an impertinence/To him embracing her. At a Loss. James L. Weil. GoYe

Almost as great as indigestion. Love's Torment. *Anonymous.* UnTE

Almost contented/I could be/'Mong such unique/Society. I Went to Heaven. Emily Dickinson. FaBV; NePA

Almost every working day. Song: "Sometimes in the fast food kitchen." Randy Lane. FAZ

Almost in space. The Man Awakened by a Song Above His Roof. Tomas Transtromer. EAS

Almost see the made souls, in their/Curious glory. If you are old. In Cemeteries. D. J. Enright. OxBC

Almost unconsciously they come/to change One should be to I am. Seminary. Constance Carrier. NePoAm

Almost walk air). now who stops. Smiles.he/stamps. What a Proud Dreamhorse. Edward Estlin Cummings. InvP; VGW

Aloft, the wild hawks clashed. A High Place. Eithne Wilkins. NeBP

Aloha means "I love you." So, I say "Aloha oe." Aloha Oe. Don Blanding. PoToHe

Alone am I, my love no longer living. Alone am I, and alone I wish to be. Christine de Pisan. BoWoP

Alone amid the rubble, amid the people/Who perish, being innocent. Birmingham 1963. Raymond Richard Patterson. CNA; GP; PoBA

Alone and bare, dynastic diagrams/Of their distinguished genealogies. Ginkgoes in Fall. Howard Nemerov. GP; HaCAP

Alone, and in a multitude. The Breastplate of Saint Patrick. *Anonymous.* BBV

Alone and merry at Forty Year,/Dipping my nose in the Gascon wine. The Age of Wisdom. William Makepeace Thackeray. ALV; HBV 1-2

Alone and pitched the desert path and gone. Rebuff. Samuel L. Albert. NePoAm-2

Alone and strong in my peace, I look upon you in yours. The Sleeping Fury. Louise Bogan. IHMS; LiTM

Alone and together on the way. Perpetual Motion. David Lehman. SUW

...Alone/as you are and as fearful/as some crab beneath some stone. By the Saltings. Ted Walker. NYBP

Alone below the stars. Tact. Edwin Arlington Robinson. NoAm

Alone, but equal to the morning. The Point. John Montague. IPY

Alone; for lo! our eyes see nought in heaven/Save what the living sun illumineth. Love, the Light-Giver. Buonarroti Michelangelo. AWP; LiTW

Alone God sufficeth. St. Theresa's Book Mark. Saint Theresa of Avila. BoC; GoTF; TreFT

Alone I'd rather go my way/Throughout eternity. Choice. Angela Morgan. PoLf

Alone I tow my death along. Hidesong. Aig Higo. TTY

Alone in the broom closet on the forty-third floor. Minnie and Mrs. Hoyne. Kenneth Fearing. AnEnPo; PoRA

...Alone,/in the clouds, he was humiliated. The Hunter. Frank O'Hara. NNaP

Alone, in the dusk, with the cleaning fluid. Tableau at Twilight. Ogden Nash. FiBHP

Alone, ironically enough, stands up for. A Healthy Spot. W. H. Auden. EnLit

...Alone/On the vast plains, with night and rain coming on. Independence. Nancy Cato. PoAu 1-2

Alone out there among the hireling men. The Muse to an Unknown Poet. Paul Potts. FaBoTw

Alone, set free, rejoicing,/With a green hill for his throne? I Heard Immanuel Singing. Vachel Lindsay. HAP

...Alone/this spray breaks from the stone. Rock-Lily. Roland Robinson. BoAV; PoAu 1-2

Alone through the woods and down to the frozen river. Stars. Alden Nowlan. PoL

Alone upon my couch I cannot stay. Epigram: "All through the night." Strato. PeHV

Alone upon the earth/to begin life. Always. Pablo Neruda. OLR

Alone with lost years. Rain. Vachel Lindsay. CMoP

Alone with the beloved dead found nothing to fear. I Who Had Been Afraid. Sister Maris Stella. GoBC

Along a Wichita tree avenue/traversed with streetlights on the plain. Chances "R". Allen Ginsberg. HaCAP

Along belly and thigh and breast,/Sinks in its long caress. When to My Serene Body. Freda Laughton. NeIP

Along came a blackbird and pecked off her nose. Sing a Song of Sixpence. Mother Goose. FaBoBe; HBVY; SoPo; TiPo

Along let them bring her. Shepheards Sirena: Song to Sirena. Michael Drayton. AtBAP; FaBoPP; PoEL 1-5

Along lines/they leave Artists East and West. Diana Chang. BrSi

Along that wild and lonely shore,/Such walks will be our ruin! Ode to Nea. Thomas Moore. OBNC

Along the banks of Acheron, river of Hell. Hermes came to me in a dream. Sappho. BoWoP

Along the boulevard laid with yellow evening. Encounter. Denis Devlin. BIrV; OnYI

Along the failing tightrope of the will. Reflections. Vivian Smith. CBAP

Along The Lincoln Highway of the dead. Elegy for Helen Trent. Paris Leary. CoPo

Along the Mekong Wonder Woman. Genny Lim. BrSi

Along the old deeps of being, the old/heights? The Inverted Torch. Edith Matilda Thomas. AA

Along the plains of Mexico! The Plains of Mexico; or, Santa Anna. *Anonymous.* AmSS

Along the rough and crooked lane he crept from Asaroe. Abbey Asaroe. William Allingham. OnYI; OxBI

Along the sidewalk over the cracks/The shadow bounces too. Kick a Little Stone. Dorothy Aldis. SoPo

Along the silent field of Asphodel. Demeter and Persephone. Alfred, Lord Tennyson. MBW 1-2; VLP

Along the soundless horizon. The Hawk. Raymond Knister. OBCV

Along the still and tilted track/That bears the zodiac. The Goose Fish. Howard Nemerov. CMoP; LiTM; NePoEA; NIP; NMP; NoAm; NoP; SM

...Along the windy Interstates,/where our shadows stretch for miles. Wild West. Mark Vinz. Psk

Along those roads we cannot hear him bark. The Dog from Malta. Tymnes. GDP

Along thy path the autumn flowers shall smile,/And to its close life's pilgrimage beguile. Autumn Flowers. Jones Very. MAmP

Along with being holy, life was hell. Whitebeard on Videotape. James Merrill. NoP

Along with Hogan's brindled bull/And Hogan's old grey mare!   The Road to Hogan's Gap.   Andrew Barton ("Banjo") Paterson.   CBAP

Along with the raggle-taggle gypsies, O!'   The Raggle Taggle Gypsies. *Anonymous.*   CBEP

Aloof from seasons, flowing.   In June and Gentle Oven.   Anne Wilkinson. NOBC; PeCV

Already becoming like the rest of us.   Back in the States.   Louis Simpson. AMV-81

Already fierce/at the trough.   Mother Cat.   John Montague.   NOBI

Already in a lost hub-cap is conceived/The ideal society which will replace our own.   The Mute Phenomena.   Derek Mahon.   FaBoIP

Already it is true.   Poop.   Gerald Locklin.   Str

Already it was too late: the bait swallowed,/The hook fast.   The Foreboding. Robert Graves.   ChMP; ELP; GBL; PoA

Already, masked, moving out.   Vanishing Point.   Peter Cooley.   AmPA

Already sacked by robbers,/Once, long ago.   Brooms.   Charles Simic. AmPA; LCAP; NNaP

Already showing the last light/in the grass long and nodding.   Eveningsong 1. Ramona Wilson.   VoR

Already sleek with narrow eyes.   Surfers at Santa Cruz.   Paul Goodman. FF; LiSp

Already the meter has ticked up an astronomical fare.   The Trip.   Emmett Jarrett.   NeAC

Already the sense/of the stone's inscription if final.   Wildfire.   Judit Toth. VWA

Already the spiders are hunched/and spinning new webs.   Moving.   Janet Reed McFatter.   GrPl

Already they have plans to grow/umbrellas under the side porch.   Probity. David Swanger.   FAZ

Also because of the hands of dew that lie on my burning cheeks/at night. Paris in the Snow.   L. Sedar-Senghor.   PBA

Also, he has the world at his command.   On a Picture by Michele da Verona, of Arion as a Boy Riding...   Anne Ridler.   PoA

The also imaginary/wafers of grace   A Coney Island of the Mind.   Lawrence Ferlinghetti.   PPP

Also the girls who break promises,/To marry a man for all his riches.   Early in One Spring.   *Anonymous.*   BFSS

–Also. What we say/Here is heard there.   Expounding the Torah.   Louis Zukofsky.   VWA

Alter or mend eternal Fact.   The Past.   Ralph Waldo Emerson.   AmePo; FaBoCh; FPL; LiTA; LoGBV; PoEL 1-5; TAP

Altered her substance, and made sport of death?   The Presence.   Robert Graves.   ChMP

Alternately they mount her back, and rest/Close by her mantling wings' embraces prest.   Swans.   William Wordsworth.   OBEC

Although at first she be not full so gay.   The Muse Reviving.   Sir John Davies.   SiPS

Although at Oxford long ago/We held that he was only clay.'   On the Safe Side.   Edward John, Lord Dunsany.   OxBI

Although but a ghost/With the ghosts of the year!   Ghost Night.   Lizette Woodworth Reese.   HBMV

Although corruption may our frame consume,/The immortal spirit in the skies may bloom!   Address to a Mummy.   Horace (or Horatio) Smith.   HBV 1-2; RoGo

Although her golden flowering lover/lies slain beside the winter sea. Casuarina.   Roland Robinson.   BoAV

Although I love you as I do the spring.   The Faithful Lover.   Robert Pack. NePoEA

Although I'm young and in my prime my courage is pull'd down.   The Little Farm; or, The Weary Ploughman.   *Anonymous.*   CoMu

Although I wear a proof/of the war's obscenity.   Fabrication of Ancestors. Alan Dugan.   NoAm

Although proclaimed aloud for evermore.   The City of Dreadful Night. James (1834-82) Thomson.   GoTS; CAEP

Although sad news to his beloved he bears.   Gentian.   Elizabeth Green Crane.   AA

...Although some boils,/God-given, might more surely make for laughs. From the Joke Shop.   Roy Fuller.   OxBC

Although the Prince is on the angels' side,/What got him there is wholesale homicide.   Elizabethan Tragedy: A Footnote.   Howard Moss.   NePoEA

Although the same deep force/buried deep in the stone/is poised for the pounce.   Burial in the Sand.   Nancy Sullivan.   NIP

Although the trumpet blew so loud.   In Memoriam A.H.H., XCVI.   Alfred, Lord Tennyson.   WGRP

Although the warmth on my back/flares from cities burning in the night. Watching Your Gray Eyes.   Morton Marcus.   GP

Although they're preserving the creases.   Limerick: "The bachelor growls when his peace is."   J. Adair Strawson.   TDH

Although they try and try!   Sky Pictures.   Mary Effie Lee Newsome. CDC; GoSl

Although we knew his death was near, we fought it hard.   Inevitable.   Sir John Betjeman.   MoBrPo

Although we say I love you no one cares.   Surprise.   Anthony Cronin. CIP

"Although you are but a maiden's child,/You are the King of Heaven!"   The Holy Well.   *Anonymous.*   NOCV; OxBoCh

Although you bore us all to tears.   Grandmamma's Birthday.   Hilaire Belloc.   DBV; ELU; FiBHP; PoPl

Although you're useless, our old West/Would not be West without you!   To a Jack Rabbit.   Squire Omar Barker.   BPAW

Although you try your best to please/Any man–on your hands and knees. Naso, You're All Men's Man.   Caius Valerius Catullus.   DBV

...Aluminum canoe/or weedless spoon–or whatever it is.   The Big One. Edward Morin.   WOLT

Always a ship...and pray the winds abate.   Tranquil Sea.   Claire Aven Thomson.   EtS

Always afraid to say more than it meant.   The Letter.   W. H. Auden. FaBoTw; NoAm

Always alone and always/the sun shining.   East Bronx.   David Ignatow. ConAP

Always and always ours, at Christmastide.   At Christmastide.   Laura Simmons.   PGD

Always and forever and forever moving,/in the wind.   I Love Old Women. William Kloefkorn.   AMV-80

Always and have no consolation from the ghosts?   Letter to My Wife.   Roy Fuller.   NeBP

Always aspiring, always low.   A Simile.   Matthew Prior.   CEP; CoBE; NOEC

Always chilled as snake or worm.   Thermometer Wine.   Robert Morgan. SUW

Always counting on the odds/that April may be kind.   Spring and All. Grace Bauer.   PPJ

Always do unto another/What you'd have him do to you.   The Golden Rule. James Wells.   STF

Always for there is small holiness/to be found in braver things.   Approach to a City.   William Carlos Williams.   CAD

Always for your never named sake   The Lost Baby Poem.   Lucille Clifton. BlSl

Always going somewhere/strongly.   Judy-One.   Don L. Lee.   TAP

Always health and joy undying,/To them every good supplying.   The Joys of Heaven.   Thomas a Kempis.   CAW

Always, I am left at home,/Sitting in my mind...   The Wanderer.   Amanda Benjamin Hall.   HBMV

Always I would acquire/its perfectly realized/experience.   My Definition of Poetry.   Douglas Blazek.   LTB

Always/Imamu Etheridge Knight Soa   A Poem to Galway Kinnell. Etheridge Knight.   NNaP

Always in/Superlative.   Petition.   Eleanor Slater.   TrPWD

...Always it's empty,/always it's filled to the brim.   An Abandoned, Overgrown Cemetery in the Pasture near Our House.   Gregory Orr. MAYP

Always just me.   Me.   Walter De la Mare.   FaPON

Always let some of my blond hair/be free   Love Me.   Maria Wine.   PBWP

Always like this, on the edge of/a safe sleep, lost in flight.   On the Edge of a Safe Sleep.   Teresa D. Cader.   AMV-81

Always lying/about who created death and light.   Saint Coyote.   Linda Hogan.   STE

Always seeking for a girl that is new.   Early One Morning.   *Anonymous.* FSW

"Always somebody goin' away,/Somebody gettin' home."   On the Quay. John Jay Bell.   HBV 1-2

Always summer for my mind.   Touring.   David Morton.   TrPWD

–Always the light within you hooded by/your own protecting fingers. Through All Your Abstract Reasoning.   Brian Patten.   FaBoTw

"Always the melting moon comes."   Always the Melting Moon Comes. Margot Osborn.   CaP

Always Thou lovedst me.   I Sought the Lord.   *Anonymous.*   TRV

Always thy honour, praise and name, shall last.   A Poem upon the Death of Oliver Cromwell (excerpt).   Andrew Marvell.   OBS; ViBoPo

Always thy honour, praise, and name shall last.   Upon the Death of His Late Highness the Lord Protector (excerpt).   Andrew Marvell.   JCP

Always used to say that stout and ale/Was good for a baby in a milking pail.   Under Milk Wood (excerpt).   Dylan Thomas.   GoJo; FiBHP; LOW

Always wanting what is not.   Man Is a Fool.   *Anonymous.*   FaFP

Always we couldn't do otherwise.   Prothalamion.   Michael Ryan.   AmPA

Always with love, with love.   The Letter.   Elizabeth Riddell.   NOAV

Always without words.   One Thought for My Lady.   Bloke Modisane. PBA

Alyssum and wild mint strain toward the weakening light.   Equinox.   Gary Young.   SUW

Am, by being dead, immortal. Can ghosts die?   The Computation.   John Donne.   DiPo; CAEP; OBSP

Am constant and invariant by night.   Motto for a Sun Dial.   J. V. Cunningham.   InPK

Am endlessly torn by dogs in my own flesh seeded.   Actaeon.   Rayner Heppenstall.   FaBoTw

Am I bringing you lilies to-day.   The Mystery.   Lilian Whiting.   AA

Am I freed or bound now/by a cry that dives/back into silence?/Both.   Encounter.   Geraldine Hammond.   IHMS

Am I happy? Totus in benigno positus!   A Bad Sleeper.   Paul Verlaine.   PeHV

Am I husband, wife, or chum.   The Oyster.   Ogden Nash.   PV

Am I it? I am./There is no time to explain.   The Last Ones.   Dan Pagis.   VWA

Am I lifted/To the porch of Aphrodite on your wings?   Hellenics: Blue Sleep.   Winifred Bryher.   PoA

Am I living or dead, am I leaves or grass?   Here, as in a Painting, Noon Burns Yellow.   Natalya Gorbanyevskaya.   BoWoP; PBWP

Am I not your quiet/older brother?   I Stood in Jerusalem.   Zelda.   VWA

Am I to turn for this unto thee, great Chapel of Sixtus?   Amours de Voyage.   Arthur Hugh Clough.   OBNC

...Am no longer/twenty-five am fat and/turning to stone.   Reflecting on the Aging-Process (parody).   Robert Peters.   BXAP

Am struck to the heart by the chiselled white/Of this handful of cyclamen.   Cyclamens.   Michael (Katherine Bradley and Edith Cooper) Field.   NOBV

Am, the world's my smilebutton.   What the Motorcycle Said.   Mona Van Duyn.   NIP

Am what I was no more, dear to another's eyes.   Spring.   Giovanni Battista Guarini.   AWP

Amang derk ghaists stravaigan sichtlesslie.   Deid Sall Ye Ligg, and Ne'er a Memorie.   Sappho.   OBVE

Amang the thummart dawlit wa'/To lilt your Johnnie.   Lilt Your Johnnie (parody).   Anonymous.   BXAP

Amazed, amazed, amazed, amazed.   Rhyme for a Child Viewing a Naked Venus in a Painting...   Robert Browning.   NOBV

Amazed, on Scylla's craggy dangers run.   Of Crossing the Street.   John Gay.   EnLi 1-2

Amazing eyes, and not/Acknowledge, but own?   Slave Quarters.   James Dickey.   CAPP; NYBP

Ambassador of God, great-hearted Jew!   Love's Cosmopolitan.   Annie Matheson.   OBVV

Amber and myrrh, benzoin and musk condense/To transports of the spirit and the sense!   Correspondences.   Charles Baudelaire.   AWP; LiTW

–The amber necklace then, and the grey dress.   Cressida.   James Keir Baxter.   AnNZ

Ambition should be made of much/sterner stuff./Q.E.D.   I Come to Bury Caesar.   Sydney Justin Harris.   PoA

Ambitionless as death, perfect, absorbed/Forever by her silent incantation.   Fire-Queen.   Ruth Fainlight.   PoA

Amen, dear God, I pray!/Amen!   Bruadar and Smith and Glinn.   Anonymous.   AnIV

Amen! even so let it be.   From Whence Doth This Union Arise?   Thomas Baldwin.   AH

Amen, Good Lord. Your charity/Is the ending of my song.   The Seven Virgins.   Anonymous.   GBP; OBET; OBEV; OxBoCh

Amen, Jesus and Mary:/Jesus, Mary and Joseph.   Alabado.   Anonymous.   TrAS

The amen of calm waters.   A Sea-Chantey (excerpt).   Derek Walcott.   TTY

Amen, pour saint charite.   Cokaygne.   Anonymous.   AnIL

Amen, say ye, for saint charity.   Everyman.   Anonymous.   EnLi 1-2; MeEV; PoEL 1-5

Amen, so let it be.   At Home in Heaven.   James Montgomery.   HBV 1-2; VLP

Amen, who scared off my girl.   The Rattle Bag.   Dafydd Ap Gwillym.   NLV; TW

Amende thee, and I forgif thee.   Christ Complains to Sinners.   Anonymous.   MeEL

Amends alike the arable and lawn.   How to Fertilize Soil.   John Scott.   FaBoUs

America I'm putting my queer shoulder to the wheel.   America.   Allen Ginsberg.   CAPP; CoAP; HaCAP; InPS; NaP; NMP; NoAm; PoM; PPoe; PPP

America's most profound and touching mystery.   Names From the War.   Bruce Catton.   AmFN

American ghosts running toward them/through the dark, with open hands.   Hallowe'en 1971.   Michael Dennis Browne.   AmPA

...The American/love song of the Mean Mary Jean Machine.   The Song of the Mean Mary Jean Machine.   James Baker Hall.   FiCP; TAT

American who would have preferred/to be merely an Indian.   Mr. Brodsky.   Charles Tomlinson.   NoAm; OxBC

Amid a blindly passing breed of men.   Bridge of the Carousel.   Rainer Maria Rilke.   AMV-80

Amid peach blossóms by the river.   Ryokan.   William Heyen.   AMV-81

Amid such unguessed glories–/That I am worse than blind.   Blind.   Harry Kemp.   HBMV

Amid the bitterness of things occult.   Sonnets for Pictures: Our Lady of the Rocks.   Dante Gabriel Rossetti.   EBEV

Amid the dragon's staring crew.   Clarel.   Herman Melville.   AmPP

Amid the garden gods, the marble fauns.   Moonlight.   Paul Verlaine.   SyP

Amid the jostled cries and laughter.   Aubade: Dick, the Donkey-Boy.   Osbert Sitwell.   HaMV

Amid the leafage of these breathless trees.   Variations on a Still Morning.   Thomas Cole.   NePoAm

Amid the lilies drowning all my care.   The Dark Night of the Soul.   Saint John of Damascus.   ErPo; LiTW; WeW

Amid the primary colors of the island, he will/become a fine thing, perhaps, but a different one.   The Revolution.   Jack Gilbert.   NPGG

Amid the sunny farms of Killingworth.   The Birds of Killingworth.   Henry Wadsworth Longfellow.   OnMSP; OxBA; WBLP

Amid tremendous history, new pity.   Tragic Guilt.   Keidrych Rhys.   WaP

Amid wind-swept wood/Now when dead he lieth.'   The Elder Edda: The First Lay of Gudrun.   Anonymous.   OBVE

Amidst the rage of murderous blows/They were in death to him restored.   The Harvesting of the Roses.   Menahem Ben Jacob.   TrJP

...Amnesia was the answer.   Grandmothers.   Adrienne Rich.   HaCAP

Among alarms, rust and the dead, waiting to be blest.   In Conjunction.   Charles Madge.   NeBP

Among almonds/a ploughman whistles.   Pastoral.   Robin Magowan.   PoDr

Among birch.   Seven Poems.   Lorine Niedecker.   VGW

Among bruised roses on the papered wall.   Paraphrase.   Hart Crane.   MoVE

Among clockwork robots/and malevolent puppets.   A Poem for Anton Schmidt.   [(or Pillin)] William Pillen.   VWA

Among dead statues in a frieze,/In the spectrum of his race.   The African Affair.   Bruce McM. Wright.   AmNP; NIP; PoBA; PoNe

Among green leaves and blossoms sweet.   The Birds.   William Blake.   CH; OBRV

Among her wildering whirls, forgetting him.   The Sad Shepherd.   William Butler Yeats.   MOS; PP

Among men waiting to be dead.   Officers' Mess.   Harold Monro.   BrPo

Among my flowers.   Friend Sparrow.   Basho (Matsuo Basho).   AWP

Among people sucked too dry/by their own all-day dying/to care about mine.   Town I Left.   Helen Sorrells.   IHMS

Among seven hills like broken/china in the sun.   Ibadan.   John Pepper Clark.   CAD

Among squat toad-leaves sprinkling the unborn/Erechtheion marbles.   Sicilian Cyclamens.   D. H. Lawrence.   ChMP; MoVE

Among the ash/you'll find my heart,/a peach stone.   Flower Song.   Diane Keating.   CaPN

Among the blessed who have Latin names.   The Rows of Cold Trees.   Yvor Winters.   NoAm; NOBA

Among the blest in endless joyes remain.   On My Dear Grand-Child Simon Bradstreet...   Anne Bradstreet.   SCAP

Among the clank of cans and the roistering files/Of steam the caterpillars wait for wings.   Perdita.   Louis MacNeice.   PoA

Among the coral crypts that hold the sea/Festoons of fishes weave insanity.   Festoons of Fishes.   Alfred Kreymborg.   HBMV

Among the dead men in the trench.   Battle: Hit.   Wilfred Wilson Gibson.   MCCG

Among the deepening shades.   The Tower.   William Butler Yeats.   CMoP; CoBMV

Among the flowers herself a flower,/A tiger-lily sheathed in white.   Intermezzo: At Glan-Y-Wern.   Arthur Symons.   VLP

Among the Furnaces of Los in the Valley of the Son of Hinnom.   In Deadly Fear.   William Blake.   SeCePo

Among the glittering stars your voices named.   Postscript: For Gweno.   Alun Lewis.   BoLoP; GTBS-P

Among the heathen live no more,/Come magnify thy God.   An Address to Miss Phillis Wheatley (excerpt).   Jupiter Hammon.   AmPP

Among the hills of St. Jerome/I would not fear to make my home.   At St. Jerome.   Frances Harrison.   WHW

...Among the last,/like the memory of a lovely fuck,/was: Do, ut des.   Dream Songs.   John Berryman.   CAPP; NaP

Among the leaves the small birds sing:/In solitude, for company.   Lauds.   W. H. Auden.   TrCP

Among the lilies, and forgetting them.   The Obscure Night of the Soul.   Saint John of Damascus.   AWP; CAW; OBMV

...Among the lonely mountains/At Roncesvalles, in one last prayer for me....   Under the Pyrenees.   Alfred Noyes.   GoBC

Among the noble host of those/Who perished in the cause of Right.   Abraham Lincoln.   William Cullen Bryant.   MC; PAH

Among the ransomed of Thy grace,/Forever I behold Thy face!   I Shall Be Satisfied.   M. Behemb.   BePJ

Among the resting deer, who/splash up away and vanish.   Beinn a' Ghlo.   Bill Tulloch.   PoSH

Among the rocks, the desert, and the waves.   The Eye.   Eithne Wilkins.   NeBP

And a faggot of useless memories.   Autumn Journal.   Louis MacNeice.
   AnIL; BIrV; FaBoIP

And a few dead men's thoughts have the same temper.   Wise Men in Their
   Bad Hours.   Robinson Jeffers.   AnAmPo

And a few of the nails.   Lullaby.   Sue Owen.   AMV-80

And a few plain household treasures are.   What Makes a Home?
   Anonymous.   PoToHe

...And a few reporters, if anything should break.   Love, 20c the First Quarter
   Mile.   Kenneth Fearing.   HAP; WeW

And a flunky thought she said the earl's room.   Goodbye Now, or, Pardon
   My Gauntlet.   Ogden Nash.   FiBHP

...And a fork to eat the fish/with some enchantment for the lake it had/crept
   in.   Accordance.   Henry Kanabus.   APU

And a friar shall sing for Barthram's soul,/While the Headless Cross shall
   bide.   Barthram's Dirge.   *Anonymous.*   FaBoRV

And a friend with whom/I can be silent.   A Prayer: "Give me work to do."
   Anonymous.   PGD

And a frightening clarity set in.   An Inscription.   Stanislav Vinaver.   VWA

And a gallant cock shall be/Offer'd up by her, to thee.   Upon Prudence
   Baldwin Her Sickness.   Robert Herrick.   JCP; OAEP; SeCV 1-2

And a girl of twenty/Who has loved no man, loves me.   Peggy.   Blanaid
   Salkeld.   OnYI

And a glass/of warm and oily/Cincinnati water.   L'Elisir d'Amore.   Dallas
   E. Wiebe.   MAT

And a Golden Lot is mine.   A Golden Lot.   Joseph Skipsey.   VLP

And a good little child will not play with him.   The Lion.   Hilaire Belloc.
   NLV

And a great, big puddle/Of blood on the ground.   Trail End.   *Anonymous.*
   CoSo

And a great pulse beating strong in towns like these.   Midwest Town.   Ruth
   Delong Peterson.   AmFN

...And a great/wind we ride.   A Gift of Great Value.   Robert Creeley.
   LCAP; NaP

And a green-and-yellow jumping jack.   Zebra.   William Jay Smith.   TiPo

And a green coat over me all.   Riddle: "As soft as silk, as white as milk."
   Anonymous.   GBP; HBV 1-2; HBVY; OxNR; PoPle

And a grey sky was drizzling down/Upon this sad, lethargic world.   Parisian
   Dream.   Charles Baudelaire.   NAWM 1-2

And a ha-ha-ha-ha and he hammers it through.   The Shoemaker.
   Anonymous.   SoPo

And a happier wedding scarce ever was seen,/Than a jolly young sailor to a
   beautiful queen.   The Jolly Young Sailor and the Beautiful Queen.
   Anonymous.   ShS

And a hateful wish to be empty and tall like you.   The Californians.
   Theodore Spencer.   NYBP; TW

And a health to thee, Tom Moore.   To Thomas Moore.   George Gordon,
   Lord Byron.   ATP; EnLit; EnRP; GoTF; MCCG; OAEP; TreFT

And a heart that begged to die/is keen again to face/A beckoning life.
   Rescue.   Olive Tilford Dargan.   GoYe

And a helmet full of Stars!   America Resurgent.   Wendell Phillips Stafford.
   MC

And-a home you go, the old last time,/And you know where.   Sally Goodin.
   Anonymous.   AmFP

And a horse that will not/obey.   The Man in the Dream Is Death.   Lynne
   Butler.   IHMS

And a housefly's panicked scribbling on the air.   Signs.   Gjertrud
   Schnackenberg.   PoA

And a hundred storks perch on the sun's right hand.   Among Those Killed in
   the Dawn Raid Was a Man Aged One Hundred.   Dylan Thomas.   InPo;
   MoPo

And a-hunting they did go.   The Three Huntsmen.   *Anonymous.*   OnMSP;
   OxBoLi

And a hush as if sparrows were listening.   Ghostly Story.   Milton Acorn.
   NeAC

And a jolly good bonfire to roast him.   The Gunpowder Plot.   *Anonymous.*
   FaBoUs

And a king in my small village.   The Vulture.   Israel Kafu Hoh.   ACV

...And a kiss better than all the/wild grapes that ever grew in Tuscany.   The
   Shovel Man.   Carl Sandburg.   HAP

And a lang lasting train o' peaceful' hours succeed!   The Farmer's Ingle.
   Robert Fergusson.   BSV; CEP

–And a last glance back at the sea/full   Poetry Is in the Darkness.   Aram
   Boyajian.   NeAC

And a lean christ lie back at ease/in the fat-rinded murderer.   The Girl Who
   Had Borne Too Much.   John Woods.   GP

And a little, falling on the leaves, becomes pearls waiting for the sun.   Rain.
   Haim Guri.   VWA

And a little handkerchief,/To wipe his pretty nose.   I Had a Little Husband.
   Mother Goose.   EvOK; ExPo; FaFP; HBV 1-2; HBVY

...And a little/nearer the vanishing point, thank you.   Gifts.   Leon
   Stokesbury.   GP

And a little peace.   Verona.   James Wright.   NNaP

And a little silk handkerchief/to wipe his pretty nose.   Little Husband.
   Anonymous.   OxNR

And a lone body lying in gentleness/silent as light. Afterwards the wind.
   Prelude.   D. Rosenmann-Taub.   VWA

And a lone rider sings to the moon?   The Night Herder.   Charles Badger
   Clark, Jr.   BPAW

And a lone ship that rides there with the moon.   Mariners.   David Morton.
   EtS

And a long ways from home.   Poor Lonesome Cowboy.   *Anonymous.*
   ABF; CoSo; TiPo

And a loving, sweet kiss will do her no harm.   Marching to Quebec.
   Anonymous.   AmFP

And a mad moon glared at Him.   The Lake.   James Stephens.   AnEnPo;
   MoBrPo

And a madder man than Matthew Mears/You would not wish to see.   The
   Sad Tale of Mr. Mears.   *Anonymous.*   GoTF; HBV 1-2; StPo; TreFS; YaD

And a man ploughs, a woman sews and/sings.   Beyond Wars.   David
   Morrow.   PAH

And a man with his back to the East.   Unwelcome.   Mary Elizabeth
   Coleridge.   CH; OBEV; OBNC; OBVV; PoPle

And a merry man is mine O.'   Seventeen Come Sunday.   *Anonymous.*
   OBET

And a million firs stand tipped with/lucent fire.   Moonrise in the Rockies.
   Ella Higginson.   AA

And a mouse is miracle enough to stagger sextillions of infidels.   I Believe a
   Leaf of Grass...   Walt Whitman.   TiPo

And a much fitter stone/To hide my dust then thee to hold.   Nature.
   George Herbert.   OAEP

And a neat little cottage that's ground for the floor.   Ground for the Floor.
   Anonymous.   OBET

And a new face at the door, my friend,/A new face at the door.   The Death
   of the Old Year.   Alfred, Lord Tennyson.   HBV 1-2; PoSC

And a nine-pound hammer in my hand.   If I Die a Railroad Man (with
   music).   *Anonymous.*   AS

And a painted rainbow/Shone above her there.   The Vestal.   Nathalia
   Crane.   AnAmPo; TrJP

And a party political man is the dregs!   Gilbertian Recipe for a Politician.
   J. A. Lindon.   DBV

And a patch of oats grew up out of his blood.   The Man Who Thought He
   Was a Horse.   Thomas Hornsby Ferril.   NePoAm-2

And a paying idea's afloat.   The Board Meeting.   John Gloag.   FiBHP

And a penchant for Brooks brothers suits.'   Limerick: "Two dykes went their
   separate routes."   *Anonymous.*   PeHV

And a person for work that is real.   To Be of Use.   Marge Piercy.   GeTw;
   HoAn

And a picture that is turned to the wall.   The Picture That Is Turned toward
   the Wall.   Charles Graham.   GoTF; TreF

And a poem full of ordinary words/about simple things/in the inconsolable
   rhythms of the heart.   The Heart's Location.   Peter Meinke.   GOYP

And a pond edged with grayish leaves.   Neutral Tones.   Thomas Hardy.
   BrPo; CABA; CMoP; CoBMV; HAP; HeIP; InPK; InPS; LiTL; MoBrPo;
   NoAm; NOBV; OAEL 1-2; PPP; SyP; TEP; UnPo; VLP

And a pretty maid's beauty it will soon fade away.   Molly of the North
   Country.   *Anonymous.*   OBET

...And a profound reactionary sorrow.   The Malefic Return.   Ramon Lopez
   Velarde.   OBVE

And a puma in very good huma.   Limerick: "A Boston boy went out to
   Yuma."   D. D..   ShM

And a purer love attaining,/May with Thee acceptance find.   Stabat Mater.
   Jacopone da Todi.   TreFS

And a pygmy pony-shoe.   A Circus Garland.   Rachel Field.   OBCA; SoPo

And a reason for putting forth flowers.   Houseplant.   Felicity Napier.
   BrRo

And a red, rousing light'ood fire.   The Light'ood Fire.   John Henry Boner.
   AA

And a rider and horse/the woods have laid siege to.   Woodcut.   R. N. D.
   Wilson.   OxBI

And a scarab aloft on the stem revelation had hollowed!   Late Dandelions.
   Ben Belitt.   NYBP

And a Sea whose menace leaves the quick/Colder than churchyard stone?
   The End.   Walter De La Mare.   OAEP

And a sexton in the churchyard/Digging in the cold.   A Song of the Seasons.
   Cosmo Monkhouse.   HBV 1-2

And a shaddaw for a windin' sheet/To row aboot his corse.   Under the
   Greenwood Tree.   *Anonymous.*   OBVE

And a sheet of paper, solid gray, floats/On the water, which is also gray.
   Water Color.   Stephen Mooney.   NYBP

And a simple, humble laugh fills his/mouth where he lies.   The Harp of
   David.   Jacob Cohen.   TrJP

And a singe runs through lace and feather.   A Utilitarian View of the
   Monitor's Fight.   Herman Melville.   AP; UnPo

And a single footprint/brother   Snowfall.   William Stanley Merwin.   NNaP

And a small bird singing on a mango tree. The Continent That Lies Within Us. Abioseh Nicol. ACV

And a small blue bubble of lead under the skin. Original Sin. Alexander Laing. NYBP

And a smile on the face of the tiger. Limerick: "There was a young lady of Riga." Anonymous. CenHV; FaBoCo

And a soft berth and a smooth course till the long trip's ended. Sea-Chill. Arthur Guiterman. BXAP; FaBoPa; MOS

And a sorrow that was to be! Prescience. Thomas Bailey Aldrich. AA; OBVV

And a spade will turn up trump at last/And dig each player's grave. Life's a Game. Anonymous. BLPA

And a sprig of the rosemary. The Rock. Anonymous. GBL

And a stamped, return envelope–/Too small to hold it. No Holes Marred. Suzanne Douglass. QQQ

And a star is his candle/to light him to bed. No Shop Does the Bird Use. Elizabeth Jane Coatsworth. OBCA

And a stench in the nose of piety. Rich and Poor; or, Saint and Sinner. Thomas Love Peacock. FaBoCo

And a still center. Prothalamium. May Sarton. HW; NePoAm

And a straight deep furrow! Student. Anonymous. AnIL; KiLC; OBMV

...And a stranger/leans listening on the gate, in all respect. Middle of the World. D. H. Lawrence. HAP

And a sullen glory pauses over them harmed,/incident to murder. Dream Song. John Berryman. CoAP

And a sweet orange lily for me. The Orange Lily. Anonymous. NOBI

And a swing in the walnut tree is why. The Walnut Tree. David McCord. OBCA

And a tall tree sprouted from his father's grave. The Truisms. Louis MacNeice. FaBoIP; NOBE; OBSV

And a ten-shilling tip to the driver. Limerick: "A taxi-cab whore out at Iver." Victor Gray. NOBL

And a tenderness too deep/To be gathered in a word. Appraisal. Sara Teasdale. MoAmPo

And a terrible business, McDowell, to you,/Was that pleasant excursion to Richmond. On to Richmond. John Reuben Thompson. PAH

And a' that ere the same did see/Knew they had true lovers been. Bonnie Annie Livieston. Anonymous. OxBB

And a' the birds that flew above,/They changed their notes and sang. Fair Janet. Anonymous. ESPB

And a' the glory shall be thine,/Amen, Amen! Holy Willie's Prayer. Robert Burns. BSV; CEP; EBEV; EnL; EnPE; EnRP; GoTS; InPS; LAuP; NOEC; NoP; OAEL 1-2; OBSV; OxBoLi; OxBS; PAI; PoEL 1-5; PPP; TW; ViBoPo

And a' the ladies who heard o it/Said she was a wise woman. The Twa Knights. Anonymous. ESPB

And a' the warld might ken right weel/They were twa lovers dear. The Douglas Tragedy. Anonymous. TrGrPo

And a thing of symmetry, seemly to view,/Brought to derision! On the Portrait of a Woman About to be Hanged. Thomas Hardy. CMoP

And a third in remembrance of Admiral Benbow. The Death of Admiral Benbow. Anonymous. OBSS

And a thought I can guess is underneath. Geraldine's Garden. John Francis O'Donnell. IrPN

And a tidy big cat she fetches back/To keep the mice from her kitchen. The Old Wife and the Ghost. James Reeves. ShM

And a tidy empty chair. The Cloak. Violet Anderson. CaP

And a toiler dies in a day. The Cry of a Dreamer. John Boyle O'Reilly. BLPA; GoTF; TreFS

...And a tortured Jew became God. The World's Wonders. Robinson Jeffers. NePA

And a traffic sign/that forbids/the passing of parades. The Death of a Warrior. Jenny Mastoraki. BoWoP

And a trail of gold weaves/away under weeds and thorns. Old Miniatures. Leo Vroman. VWA

And a two-penny apple pie. Ride a Cock-Horse. Anonymous. OxBoLi; OxNR

And a uniqueness is, that hasn't been. To Dorothy on Her Exclusion from the Guinness Book of World Records. X. J. Kennedy. Psk

And a vast army of granite-faced clowns. Sitting Bull's Will Versus the Sioux Treaty of 1868 and Monty Hall. A. K. Redwing. VoR

And a viewless rider swept the sky on the trail of a/shooting star? Riders of the Stars. Henry Herbert Knibbs. BPAW

And a voice in the void lamenting/and dying away. Apocalypse in Springtime. Lex Banning. NOAV

And a voice saying, not that case,/Take this. Womb Song. Susan Fromberg Schaeffer. IHMS

And a warm dog, snuggled by my feet Hometown. Luis Cabalquinto. BrSi

...And a waterfall/Unstitching itself down the front stairs. Venus and the Rain. Mebdh McGuckian. FaBoIP

And a wave fill'd it, as my sense was fill'd/With that new blissful golden melody. The Shell's Song. John Keats. EtS

...And a weak mailed fist/clenched ignorant against the sky! The Armadillo. Elizabeth Bishop. HaCAP; NoAm; NOBA; NoP; NYBP; SM; TAP; VGW

And a whole sky floods the pool of one mind. On the Third Day. Stephen Spender. NeBP

And a whore and a rogue may part when they please. Epigram: "Our fathers took oaths as of old they took wives." Thomas (Tom) Brown. FaBoEE

And a wife and baby at home? Soldier, Won't You Marry Me? Anonymous. AmFP; OLR; OxBoLi

And a wind to blaw owre the bonnie bare banes o' a man,/Ay, there for me! Faur Wid I Dee? J. C. Milne. PoSH

...And a winter tree/Golden with fruit of a man's body. In a Country Church. R. S. Thomas. FaBoMo

And a woe that no mortal can cure. My Love Is Like the Sun. Anonymous. AnIV

And a woman who ponders/On all these things. New Things and Old. Sister Mary Madeleva. GoBC

And a wooden leg Little Song of the Maimed. Benjamin Peret. OBWP

And a' ye lords o merry Scotland/Be kind to my ladie!' Lord Derwentwater (D version). Anonymous. ESPB

And a youthful measure tread. Roses. Thomas Stanley. AWP

And Abel wanes with the spent candle–/"Sweetheart, good-night!" The Bedpost. Robert Graves. SO

And able age, to do Thy holy will. On the Instability of Youth. Thomas, Lord Vaux. EnRePo

And abortions are hidden. Editor Whedon. Edgar Lee Masters. CMoP; CrMA; FaBoEE; NoAm; NOBA; OBSV; OxBA

And about go we, and about go wee. By the Moon. Thomas Ravenscroft. CH

And about the watered pastures/Sink to sleep the nomad years! Afoot. Sir Charles G. D. Roberts. CaP; HBV 1-2

And above all we have forgotten that this was supposed to/be/About tea... Teatime Variations. Peter Titheradge. FaBoPa

And above our waking limbs unfurl/Spirit-torsos of exquisite strength! The Blue Meridian. Jean Toomer. BALP; PoNe

And accept fully/all that was given Alone Is the Hunter. Harold Littlebird. VoR

And accepted life whose fragments I cast here. Burning the Letters. Randall Jarrell. MiAP; MoAB; MoAmPo

And according to the dark all wanderers are home. Shepherd. William Stafford. PoA

And achieved the miracle of one hundred and fifty-/five bales of cotton. Mamana Saquina. Jose Craveirinha. WhB

And across the darkness call. Verses at Night. Dannie Abse. MP

And Act your selves the Farce of your own Age. The Loyal General: Prologue. John Dryden. SeCV 1-2

And action must be learned from love of man. I Walked Out to the Graveyard to See the Dead. Richard Eberhart. MiAP; MoPo

And active to the Lord thy God,/Keep lust and conscience still. Hymns and Spiritual Songs. Christopher Smart. EiCP; LAuP

And Adam walks in the cold night/Wilderness, waste wood. Eve in Reflection. Jay Macpherson. OBCV

And add a perfume to our dust. The Reward of Innocent Love. William Habington. ACP

And, added to a myriad others,/Bring promised peace to all who live. The Paths of Prayer. Edouard Roditi. VWA

And adieu for evermore.' Song: "A weary lot is thine, fair maid." Sir Walter Scott. EnLoPo; OBNC

And adieu to my false love for ever. The False Bride. Anonymous. OBET

And adieu to you, my darlings. Three Knights from Spain. Anonymous. AtBAP; PoPle

And admit to himself and/the world that. It Is a Distinct Pleasure. Tom Veitch. ANYP

And affrights even fear. The Marionettes. Walter De La Mare. AtBAP; MMM

And, afore he fixed his error, Pete was dead beyond all/doubt. Pete's Error. Arthur Chapman. BPAW

And afraid of the dark,/As his fathers were. Nelly Trim. Sylvia Townsend Warner. ErPo; MoAB; MoBrPo

And, afraid of the gift of sudden blood,/beats back to his hand and melts once more to wood. Boomerang. William Hart-Smith. NOAV

And after all your trapesings, child, lie still! A St. Helena Lullaby. Rudyard Kipling. AtBAP; EBEV; FaBoCh; MoVE; OAEP; OBMV; PoEL 1-5

And after Amor vincit omnia. Madam Eglantine. Geoffrey Chaucer. NOBE

And after Charles, who wrongs you of your crown,/Shall cut a million of true English down. The Obscured Prince; or, the Black Box Boxed. Anonymous. APAS

And after death Thy boundless grace/Through everlasting years adore. Fillmore. Anonymous. AmFP

And after dinner there are lessons. A Roxbury Garden. Amy Lowell. LaNeLa

And after-glows that crown his labor done. The Guerdon of the Sun. George Sterling. HBMV

And after many years to have a blessed end. To Master Edward Cobham. Barnabe Googe. EnRePo

And after that, I always get them all mixed up. Pictures in the Smoke. Dorothy Parker. NLV

And after the killing/there will be peace. After the Killing. Dudley Randall. CNA; SoSe

And, after the subway, walk up to the night. The Report. Jon Swan. NYBP

And, after this life, to see thy glorious Face. Prayer to the Father in Heaven. John Skelton. HoPM; TrPWD

And after this shall things uprise/That men set now but at little price. Customs Change. Anonymous. OxBChV

And, after we've taken our doses,/Suppose we swear off, for a year. O, Be Not Too Hasty, My Dearest. Robert Henry Newell. OBAL

And afterwards death. First It Was Singing. Jon Silkin. NePoEA

And afterwards,/sat singing spirituals to sons. Ghetto Lovesong–Migration. Carole Gregory Clemmons. NBP; NMM

And afterwards,/sat singing spirituals to sons. Migration. Carole Gregory Clemmons. PoBA

And again and again and again. Limerick: "There was a young lady of Spain." Anonymous. FaBoCo

And again like a vein behind the iris leaping. The Cave-Drawing. Vernon Watkins. LiTB

And again the Spirit of Pity whispered, Why? And There Was a Great Calm. Thomas Hardy. CMoP; FaBoRV; LiTM; MoRP; OAEL 1-2

And again you'll come/forever... To Teresa. Ivan Silen. InW

And age, and then the only end of age. Dockery and Son. Philip Larkin. NoAm

And age on ages sing Amen. Prayer. Anonymous. CAW

And ages drop in it like rain. Two Rivers. Ralph Waldo Emerson. AnNE; AP; MAmP; NOBA; OxBA; TrGrPo

And agony is their making-kiss. The Word Made Flesh? Walter James Turner. OBMV

And ah! I cannot sleep at night. Foiled Sleep. Madelaine Marie. PeHV

And ah, the sweet sun! Epitaph of a Young Man. Anonymous. LiTW

And aim a telescope at the inviolate sun. A Letter. Ralph Waldo Emerson. OxBA

And al the erbes grouyng on the grounde. The Complaint of the Black Knight. John Lydgate. EnPo

And alas, alas, the drip-drop of the rain! Desolate. Sydney Thomas Dobell. CBEP; NBM; OBNC

And, alas, for the boasting, the vaunting, the/vain/Saint Leger! Saint Leger. Clinton Scollard. PAH

And Albion on the Appenines advance her conquering Crest. The Third Eclogue. Michael Drayton. AtBAP; PoEL 1-5

And ale make many a man to hang upon the galows./With doll! Doll Thy Ale. Anonymous. OxBM

And alien June; but thou art gone. A Far-Off Rose. Josephine Preston Peabody. AA

And all about were scatterd chips/Of pale cold light that was alive. The Signature of All Things. Kenneth Rexroth. BoNaP; NNaP; NU

And all, all except the black horseleech/let pass my entering pale enormous flesh. Creatures. Maxine W. Kumin. BoAnP

And all along the Western Front/The Christmas guns began to bark. Christmas 1914. Mike Harding. OBET

And all are ground to dust at last,/and trodden into clay! Keramos. Henry Wadsworth Longfellow. MAmP; PoEL 1-5

And all around me everywhere/A gentle sound like murmured prayer. Fir Forest. Ethel Romig Fuller. PGD

And all around where abouten it lay wharof men token/great game. Becket's Diadem. Anonymous. ACP

And all at length are gathered in. The Mark. Louise Bogan. MoPo; MoVE

And all at once caught sight of night. Ovedue Balance Sheet. Therese Plantier. BoWoP

And all because I did not hear the word/In English accents say, "It is the Lord." Omnipresence. Edward Everett Hale. TRV; WGRP

And all because I was brave, and tried." How the Little Kite Learned to Fly. Anonymous. HBV 1-2; HBVY

And all believe that his work is perfect. Whose Hand. Anonymous. TrJP

And all beyond is vast eternity. My Diet. Abraham Cowley. LiTL

And all beyond saving by children. Ethics. Linda Pastan. AMV-81

...And all bill said/was nerts insect nerts. Artists Shouldn't Have Offspring. Don (Donald Robert Marquis) Marquis. CrMA

...And all birds/have their voices, each means a different thing. Birds. D. H. Lawrence. BoAnP

And all but break under orchard bloom. Because I Live. Evelyn Ames. GoYe

And all but inmost faith is overthrown. Alone. Siegfried Sassoon. BoLiVe; MoBrPo

And all but thy government, Eire, have pleased me,/Thou waterful land. Colum-Cille's Farewell to Ireland. Anonymous. AnIV

And all come home/Some other day. Jump–Jump–Jump. Kate Greenaway. TiPo

And all did wishfully expect the silver-throned morne. The Iliad. Homer. OBVE

And all dishevelled wandering stars. Who Goes with Fergus? William Butler Yeats. CMoP; FaBoCh; GoJo; InPK; LoGBV; MBW 1-2; NoAm; NOBE; NOBV

And all familiar as a cup, a chair. Spicewood. Lizette Woodworth Reese. MoAmPo

And all fond love I will defy. Love. Anthony Munday. OBSC

And all for a farthing. A Farthing. Anonymous. OxNR

And all for love of one. I Must Go Walk the Wood. Anonymous. CBEP; MeEL; NCEP

And all for some strange name he read/In Purchas or in Holinshed. Thou Leanest to the Shell of Night. James Joyce. EBEV

And all for that my dear/Phillada flouts me. Phillada Flouts Me. Anonymous. HBV 1-2; OBEV; TrGrPo; ViBoPo

And all for the sake/Of my little nut tree. I Had a Little Nut Tree. Mother Goose. CBEP; CH; ExPo; OxBoLi; OxNR

And all for the want/Of a horse shoe nail. For Want of a Nail. Anonymous. FaBoBe; HBV 1-2; OxNR

And all for the want of a horseshoe nail. Cause and Effect. Anonymous. GoTF; TreFT

And all grace is the grace of God. The Joyful Wisdom. Coventry Patmore. HBV 1-2

And all he asked was kindness and food/From the parents of Amanda to the chief of the wood. Amanda. Anonymous. BFSS

And all He been to me. Under a Wiltshire Apple Tree. Anna De Bary. CH

And all her train were hurl'd. A Vision. Henry Vaughan. BBV; GTBS

And all his island shivered into flowers. Live Blindly. Trumbull Stickney. AmLP; APA; LiTA; NePA; TrGrPo

And all his labor now he laugh to scorne,/Mashed in the breers that erst was all to torne. Some Tyme I Fled the Fyre That Me Brent. Sir Thomas Wyatt. AAS

And all his laurels deepening but the shade. Orion. Richard Henry Horne. VLP

And all his life be always glad and well/As is a wanton woman in the spring. Sonnet: Of Love in Men and Devils. Cecco da Siena Angiolieri. AWP

And all his pictures faded. Sir Joshua Reynolds. William Blake. ELU; FaBoCo; FiBHP

And all his Righteousness devolv'd on thee. Religio Laici. John Dryden. NOCV; OBS

And all his sences were with deadly fit opprest. The Faerie Queene. Edmund Spenser. PoEL 1-5

And all his sorrows, till he reassumes his ancient bliss. Vala; or, The Four Zoas. William Blake. OBNC

And all humanity a jest. Museum-Piece. Audrey Alexandra Brown. CaP

And all I am living in hopes to see,/Is old Swansea Town once more, old girl, old girl. Swansea Town. Anonymous. ShS

And all I can grasp is an earlier, more haunted moment,/And a happier place. At a Concert of Music. Conrad Aiken. MoAB; MoAmPo; UnS

And all I could see/Was the green valley/Surrounding me. Green Valley. Dorothy Vena Johnson. PoNe

And all in a yere. Shepherd's Play,. Anonymous. FaBoUs

And all in all things with God's virtue filled. God's Virtue. Barnabe Barnes. NOCV; OBSC

And all into pieces she ought to be torn. The Nottinghamshire Poacher. Anonymous. OBET

And all is a tale for thee and me. Autumn on the Upper Thames. William Morris. FaBoPP

And all is done as I have told The Mental Traveler. William Blake. DiPo; EnRP; ERoP 1-2; LAuP; MasP; OAEL 1-2; PoEL 1-5

And all is family peace again. The Lion. Vachel Lindsay. HBMV; ShM

And all is hushed at Shiloh. Shiloh, A Requiem. Herman Melville. AmFN; AP; FF; LiTA; MAmP; NCEP; NOBA; NoP; OBWP; OxBA; PAL; SCV; ViBoPo; WiR

And all is made whole in the heart and time. Marrakech. Richard Eberhart. LiTM

And all is not pork that is pie. A Melton Mowbray Pork-Pie (parody). Richard Le Gallienne. BXAP; Par

And all is raked in ashy heaps of beastliness. The Malcontent. John Marston. TW

And all is rolled back in the book of days. The Alphabet. Karl Shapiro. MoRP; NoAm; PoA; VWA

And all is ruin, save one wrinkled gate/Whereon is written, "Only God is great." A Turkish Legend. Thomas Bailey Aldrich. GN; HBV 1-2; HBVY

And all is through thy negligence and rape. Unto Adam, His Own Scriveyn. Geoffrey Chaucer. OBSP

And all is what imagination dreams. How Great unto the Living Seem the Dead! Charles Heavysege. CaP

And all its charms, like death without its terrors. Don Juan". George Gordon, Lord Byron. ViBoPo

"And all its mystery," he said,/"Is clear as day to me!"... The Mad Gardener's Song. Lewis (Charles Lutwidge Dodgson) Carroll. OnUR

And all its sturdy everlasting foregrounds. Perspective. Margaret Avison. OBCV; PeCV

And all lies wrapt in silence, and unactive ease. Eclogue. William Diaper. SeCePo

And all life never has been, lives. I Look into the Stars. Jane Draper. HBMV

And all life that approaches I wait for in fear. The Wail of Prometheus Bound. Aeschylus. WGRP

And all lost, wild America/Is burning in their eyes. Daniel Boone, 1735-1820. Rosemary and Stephen Vincent Benét. AmFN; NAMP

And all love's wisdom that you left unsaid. The Train Butcher. Thomas Hornsby Ferril. GoYe

And all man's Babylons strive but to impart/The grandeurs of his Babylonian heart. The Heart. Francis Thompson. BoLiVe; OBMV

And all Mankind her Creatures are. Laura Sleeping. Charles Cotton. CavP; ELP; LoBV; OBS; ViBoPo

And all men are at home. The House of Christmas. Gilbert Keith Chesterton. GoBC; HBV 1-2; HBVY; MoBrPo; MoRP

And all men's God in every human soul. Harvest. Eva Gore Booth. HBMV; WGRP

And all men turn you from the door. Good Tradition. *Anonymous.* AnIL

And all my body's flight become a strange return. The Wind Was There. Bravig Imbs. EAS

And all my forces needs must be undone,/She having gained both the wind and sun. The Fair Singer. Andrew Marvell. CavP; CBEP; EG; EnLoPo; LiTL; MeLP; MePo; NOBE; NoP; PoEL 1-5; PoPle

And all my hearts in unison strike twelve. The Science of the Night. Stanley Jasspon Kunitz. MoAmPo; MP; TwCP; UnTE

And all my hopes must with my body soon/Be but as crouching dust and wind-blown sand. The Giant Puffball. Edmund Charles Blunden. FaBoTw

And all my life I'll mourn for young Sally Monroe! Sally Monroe. *Anonymous.* OBSS; ShS

And all my soul is a delight,/A swoon of shame. Alone. James Joyce. InvP

And all my sour-sweet days/I will lament, and love. Bitter-Sweet. George Herbert. NOBE; NoP; OBSP; OxBoCh; TrPWD

And all my spare time to God.' The Lay Preacher Ponders. Idris Davies. ACV; OxBTC

And all my thoughts are dashed into dust. Love and fortune and my mind... Sir Thomas Wyatt. FCP

And all my uncles wept. Grandpa Bear. Susan Eisenberg. AMV-81

And all my will was not enough/to hold the heavens out of me. In Heavy Mind I Strayed the Field. James Agee. MoAmPo

And all my work goes well. I Have Not Lingered in European Monasteries. Leonard Cohen. NOBC

And all needful blessing you surely will find. New England's Annoyances. *Anonymous.* AnAmPo; PAH

And all night in rainy weather,/I hear his gentle breathings by me. Sorrow. Aubrey Thomas De Vere. WiR

And all night the old man steers his room through the dark... The Pilot. Russell Edson. LCAP

And all of art contriving nature's charm/could never fill me with a wilder love. Sonnet XXI: "What grandeurs make a man seem venerable?" Louise Labe. BoWoP

And all of earth's dry murder thrown/overboard with ease. The Lighthouse Keeper's Offspring. James Richard Broughton. CrMA

And all of God, that bless Mankind or mend. An Essay on Man. Alexander Pope. ViBoPo

And all of their dancing was, "Life, thou art good!" The Daisies. Bliss Carman. BoNaP; HBV 1-2

And all of us are walking upon the waters under the earth. Sea-Grape Tree and the Miraculous. William Pitt Root. GeTw

And all of us harvesting still/that history. Arrowheads. Leona Gom. AMV-81

And all of us send our love to you, our friend. A Postcard. Edwin Denby. ANYP

And all of us will dance in a circle/And sing. The Eve. Howard Schwartz. VWA

And all old men/are hip to it. July 31. Norman Jordan. PoBA

And "All our days shall be as this," you said. Two Married. Helen Frazee-Bower. HBMV

And all our ease the emptied sands? Two Songs on the Economy of Abundance. James Agee. MoAmPo

And all our heavy heritage of grief. By the Potomac. Thomas Bailey Aldrich. PAH

And all our Knowledge, is OURSELVES TO KNOW. Essay on Man. Alexander Pope. ATP; CEP; MBW 1-2

And all our mourning should be to rejoice. Elegy on Gordon Barber. Gene Derwood. FaFP; NePA

And all our windows crack open/with the smell of lilacs. Night Flight. Ruth Daigon. AMV-81

And all poultry eaters are psychopaths. Annotations of Auschwitz. Peter Porter. NMP; OxBTC

And all preparation is for it–and identity is for it–and life/and materials are altogether for it To Think of Time. Walt Whitman. MAmP

And all's to do again. Yonder See the Morning Blink. Alfred Edward Housman. CMoP; EnLit; MoShBr; NOBV

And all sang Old Lang Syne. The Feast of the Monkeys. John Philip Sousa. OBAL

And all self-bruising heads loll into sleep. To Sleep. Robert Graves. MoVE

And all she takes she keeps. The Ant. Oliver Herford. LBN

And all so still, so still– Green Moth. Charles Simic. GeTw; TiPo

And all that belong to the jovial crew/On board of the Arethusa. The Arethusa. Prince Hoare. FaPoR

And all that day/Was a fairy tale/Told once in a while/To a good child. Song: "Morning opened." Donald Justice. DFF; NCSH

And all that lake a dewdrop on a rose. In Hospital. James Elroy Flecker. OxBTC

And all that matters is to live it well. All That Matters. Edgar A. Guest. ATP

And all that mighty heart is lying still! Sonnet Composed upon Westminster Bridge, September 3, 1802. William Wordsworth. FiP; HBV 1-2

And all that Misery's hand bestows,/To fill the catalogue of human woes. Retort on the Foregoing. John Scott. OBEV; PPON

And all that night...naked.../naked...naked. The Dance of Saul with the Prophets. Saul Tchernichovsky. TrJP

And all that once received the early rain/Declare to man it was not sent in vain. The Latter Rain. Jones Very. AmP; GN; OxBA

And all/that there is/Is/Between them. Love Poem. Judson Crews. UnTE

And all that vexes thy heart will they/put to flight. Rejoice, O Youth, in the Lovely Hind. Moses Ibn Ezra. TrJP

And all that view'd her were enamour'd on her... Hero and Leander. Christopher Marlowe. LoBV

...And all that we'll have/to love may be what's near/in the cold, even then. So Long. William Stafford. PPJ

And all that with hande-bowe shoteth,/That of heuen they may neuer mysse! Adam Bel, Clym of the Cloughe, and Wyllyam of Cloudesle. *Anonymous.* BuBa; ESPB; OxBB

And all the angels sat about/And praised my verses. Epigram: "I dreamt that I was God Himself." Ezra Pound. FaBoEE

And all the anger of the passionate heaven/Burst into tears. A Storm in Summer. Wilfrid Scawen Blunt. FaBoTw

And all the Aprils we assemble here. Miss Packard and Miss Giles. Owen Dodson. GLGT

And all the being is still to hear. The Livid Lightnings Flashed in the Clouds. Stephen Crane. AmePo

And all the bells in the city boomed out at once. Saint Erkenwald. *Anonymous.* MeEV

And all the berries now are gone! Birds at Winter Nightfall. Thomas Hardy. ELU; MoBrPo

...And all the big flower stooped/And stared upon the ground I Closed My Eyes Today and Saw. William Force Stead. OBMV

And all the birds are singing. All the Bells Were Ringing. Christina Georgina Rossetti. TiPo

And all the birds fly out of my scene. The Meeting. Muriel Rukeyser. MoAmPo; TrJP

And all the birds in the air/Couldn't catch me. The Nut Tree. Mother Goose. SoPo

And all the birds mourned that his blood was so spilled. The Courtship, Merry Marriage, and Picnic Dinner of Cock Robin... *Anonymous.* HBV 1-2

And all the books are twenty-seven. Old Testament Contents. *Anonymous.* BLPA

And all the city heard him moan. Heart-Hurt. *Anonymous.* TreFT

And all the comely Dress without the paint of Art. To the Royal Society. Abraham Cowley. AnAnS 2; JCP

And all the committee, all the one-man committee. The Committee. C. Day-Lewis. BiP; CMoP

And all the congregation sing/A Christian psalm for thee. Ruth; or, the Influences of Nature. William Wordsworth. ChRP; ERoP 1-2; GTBS; GTBS-P; PoEL 1-5

And all the courses of the suns. In Memoriam A.H.H., CXVII. Alfred, Lord Tennyson. VLP

And all the Day be Thine alone.   A Song: "If Wine and Musick have the Pow'r."   Matthew Prior.   LoBV

And all the deadly virtues plague my death!   Lament.   Dylan Thomas.   ErPo; MasP; PPP

And all the earth trembles when he rushes by.   A Modern Dragon.   Rowena Bastin Bennett.   SoPo; TiPo

And all the faults that you shall spy/Shall at your feet for pardon cry.   The Four Seasons of the Year.   Anne Bradstreet.   SCAP

And all the fell Society of Night.   The Seasons.   James (1700-48) Thomson.   AtBAP

And all the flowers wait for the moon's kiss/With endless longing.   The Moon.   Edith Sodergran.   LiTW

...And all the forest rocked and sang.   November: Epping Forest.   John Davidson.   GTBS

And all the fun was over.   Grig's Pig.   *Anonymous.*   OxNR

And all the gallant things there be.   To Patricia on Her Christening Day.   Edith Ballinger Price.   BiCB

And all the gilded tissues lost, unloosed.   At a Parade.   Frank Templeton Prince.   NeBP; WaP

And all the Golden Age, is but a Dream.   Letter to Viscount Cobham.   William Congreve.   LoBV

And all the great conclusions coming near.   Answers.   Elizabeth Jennings.   NePoEA; OBSP; OxBTC

And all the habits of it.   The Mountains in the Desert.   Robert Creeley.   CoPo

And all the Heav'n I hope above/Is but to see his face.   Felicity.   Isaac Watts.   OxBoCh

And all the hills echoed.   Nurse's Song.   William Blake.   AWP; BLPL; CEP; CH; EnRP; FaBoBe; FF; HBV 1-2; HBVY; InPo; OBEC; OxBChV

And all the horrors that the guilty feel/With anxious flutterings wake the guiltless breast.   The Art of Preserving Health (excerpt).   John Armstrong.   NOEC

And all the house is fast asleep.   Morning After.   Mark Vinz.   PPJ

And all the Hudson River/In which to wash my dishes.   My Plan.   Marchette Chute.   BiCB; BrR

And all the joyous scene revolves again.   The Bricklayer's Labours.   Robert Tatersal.   NOEC

And all the kinds of wood/Put forth/Fruit.   Iscah.   Howard Schwartz.   VWA

And all the king's horses can't fill it up.   Riddle: "As round as an apple, as deep as a cup."   Mother Goose.   TiPo

And all the kisses, to the last.   The Gifts Return'd.   Walter Savage Landor.   OBVV

And all the ladies swim through tears/Toward such a work of art.   The Choir Boys.   Heinrich Heine.   LiTW

And all the little children/That round the table go.   The Wassail Song.   *Anonymous.*   OHIP; PoSC

And all the little ladies/Are picking up their frocks.   It's Raining, It's Raining.   *Anonymous.*   OxNR

And all the little school children sat down   Slightly before the Middle of Congressman Pudd.   Edward Estlin Cummings.   OBAL

And all the little sparrows wonder why!   Georgian Spring.   Roy Campbell.   OBSV

And all the living landscape charms his eyes.'   The Action of Invisible Ink.   Erasmus Darwin.   FaBoUs

And all the living thoughts I had/Are like far ships at sea!   Garadh.   Padraic Colum.   OnYI

And all the living world and all the dead/Began a march which did not end at morn.   The Botanist's Vision.   Sydney Thomas Dobell.   VLP

And all the love he had.   Judas Iscariot.   Countee Cullen.   PoLf

And all the mighty ravishment of spring.   Sonnet: To the Lady Beaumont.   William Wordsworth.   ChRP

And all the mothers in the world today/hiding tactical weapons/in their babushkas!   Mother's Day.   Jerome Sala.   APU

And all the neighbors/Know you swear.   The Parrot.   Edward Lucie-Smith.   BoAnP; SO

And all the night in natural jubilee/Over a sea of blood rings the heart's revelry.   Invasion.   Hubert Witheford.   AnNZ

...And all the/olden golden men who rode horses in the rain.   Horses and Men in the Rain.   Carl Sandburg.   PoLf

And all the pageant scene expires.   Occasioned by General Washington's Arrival in Philadelphia...   Philip Freneau.   PAH

And all the people said: "Let's go/To see the bear and the circus show!"   The Three Wise Couples.   Elizabeth T. Corbett.   BLPA

And all the people that passed by/Thought the little boy was asleep.   Sir Hugh; or The Jew's Daughter (D vers.)   *Anonymous.*   BaBo

And all the playthings come alive.   Foreign Lands.   Robert Louis Stevenson.   HBV 1-2; HBVY; SUS

And all the poems that sang in my heart/Turned to the same white, bitter salt.   I Have Seen the Robins Fall.   Louis Dudek.   CaP

And all the rest, but vanity we find.   The Vanity of All Worldly Things.   Anne Bradstreet.   NoP; SCAP

And all the rest have thirty-one.   The Months of the Year.   Richard Grafton.   FaDoUs

And all the rest is literature.   The Art of Poetry.   Paul Verlaine.   SyP

And all the rest is only batter.   How Singular.   Tom (Thomas Hood, Jr.) Hood.   FaBoNo

And all the rings in which we're spun and swirled,/Whether around a clockface or a world.   A Clock in the Square.   Adrienne Rich.   HeIP; NIP

And all the rivers ran into my soul.   Sea-Monster.   Gertrud Kolmar.   VWA

And all the room is bathed in liquid amber.'   To Olive.   Lord Alfred Bruce Douglas.   OBEV; OBVV

And all the room with heavenly music float.   Preparation.   Thomas Edward Brown.   OBEV; OBVV

And all the saints come back for laughs.   The Only Bar in Dixon.   James Welch.   AmPA; FF

And all the sands where all the oceans flow!   The Easter Song.   Caelius Sedulius.   OnYI

And all the seas were running late.   Song: "The bells of Sunday rang us down."   John Ciardi.   WaP

And all the silly sightless people/Came and looked...and called it junk.   Hector the Collector.   Shel Silverstein.   CTBA

And all the song that he could sing/Was, "Carry me safe to Dover'.   As I Was Going up the Hill.   *Anonymous.*   OxNR

And all the sons of want are blest.   Jesus Shall Reign.   Isaac Watts.   BePJ; WGRP

And all the stars fall down.   Stone.   E. L. Mayo.   FAZ

And all the stars looked down.   A Christmas Carol.   Gilbert Keith Chesterton.   ChBR; FaFP; GoBC; HBV 1-2; HBVY; OBCP; OHIP; SUS

And all the stars that crowded the blue space/Saw nothing happier than her glowing face.   Don Juan.   George Gordon, Lord Byron.   ChRP

And all the Stars to follow!   Three Songs.   Francis Beaumont.   GoBC

And all the stones have wings.   The Small.   Theodore Roethke.   GrPl; SO

And all the storied, splendid sins.   Experience.   Lesbia Harford.   CBAP; PoAu 1-2

And all the streets with passing cries resound.   The Morning.   John Gay.   EnLi 1-2

And all the strings must sound/Which are strung in love.   Love Flows from God.   Mechtild of Magdeburg.   WPOW

And all the sulky fiends defy,/Is a most joyful thing.   Hymns for the Amusement of Chidlren.   Christopher Smart.   EiCP; LAuP

And all the summer through the water saunter.   Look, Stranger.   W. H. Auden.   CoBMV; InvP; MoAB; MoBrPo; OAEP; TrGrPo

And all the time God knew.   The Rebellious Vine.   Harold Monro.   BrPo

And all the time he wondered/What it was they could be saying.   The Death Bed.   Waring Cuney.   CDC

And all the Toms, though never so bold,/Quailed at the martial Marigold.   Marigold.   Richard Garnett.   PCat

And all the trees have silver skirts/And want to dance away.   Snow.   Dorothy Aldis.   TiPo

And all the waters of the world are vain/To put them out again.   The Thousand and One Nights: The Power of Love.   *Anonymous.*   LiTW

And all the waves toss wildly at the sight.   The Living Statue.   *Anonymous.*   UnTE

And all the way, to guide their chime,/With falling oars they kept the time.   Song of the Emigrants in Bermuda.   Andrew Marvell.   GTBS; GTBS-P; OxBoCh

And all the while, he knew there was no river.   Eli, Eli.   Judith Wright.   CBAP

And all the while, in perfect time,/His pendulous stomach hangs a-shaking.   Wagner.   Rupert Brooke.   FaBoTw; NAMP; NOBL

And all the while the sanded wind blew between us.   Watch Hill.   Winfield Townley Scott.   ErPo

And all the white doves kissing in its name.   In Assisi.   Michael C. Blumenthal.   MAYP

And all the wild sweetness I wak'd was thy own.   Dear Harp of My Country.   Thomas Moore.   AnIL; EnRP; NOBI; OAEP

And all the winters are hidden.   The Throstle.   Alfred, Lord Tennyson.   BoNaP; HBV 1-2; HBVY; MCCG; PBBP; PoSC

And all the woman glares in open day.   The Wife of Bath Her Prologue, from Chaucer (excerpt).   Alexander Pope.   OBSV

And all the wood was sick for song.   To Deck a Woman, XI (excerpt).   Ralph Hodgson.   LOW

And all the world a dream.   Belief in Plan of Thee.   Walt Whitman.   TRV

And all the world caroling/Songs of joy.   Christmas Is Remembering.   Elsie Binns.   BiCB; ChBR; SiSoSe

And all the world fall shadow/to the crumpling of that sheet.   Mythmaking.   Kathleen Spivack.   NMM

And all the world went wading towards the wave.   Abruptly All the Palm Trees.   William Jay Smith.   PoA

And all the world would be one dying swan,/To sing her funeral praise, and vanish then.   An Anatomy of the World. The First Anniversary.   John Donne.   JCP

And all the Xmas that she had/Was in her little head.   Xmas Time.   Walta Karsner.   ELU

And all the year have some green ears.   Love and Discipline.   Henry Vaughan.   TrPWD

And all their Brother Dunces lash,/Who crowd the press with hourly Trash.   On Poetry, A Rhapsody.   Jonathan Swift.   HAP; OBSV; PoEL 1-5; PP; SCV

And all their firing and their racket/Shot off the topmast of a packet.   The Bombardment of Bristol.   *Anonymous.*   PAH

And all their pilots fast asleep.   The River Boats.   Daniel Whitehead Hicky.   AmFN

And all their playthings crumble into light.   The City: Midnight.   Bruce Dawe.   PoAu 1-2

And all thensforth eternall peace shall see,/Betweene the Spyder and the gentle Bee.   Amoretti, LXXI.   Edmund Spenser.   AAS

And all there was between them then/was rain.   Party Piece.   Brian Patten.   BoLoP

And all these merry days mak'st merry men,/Thyself, and melancholy streams.   The Grasshopper.   Richard Lovelace.   OBEV

And all these through her eyes have stopped her ears.   My Picture Left in Scotland.   Ben Jonson.   AnAnS 2; EnRePo; ForPo; LiTL; MePo; PoEL 1-5; QFR; SeCP; SeCV 1-2

And all they had to strike now was the human face.   The Diaspora.   W. H. Auden.   LiTA

And all they see their vision sanctifies.   Miserere.   David Gascoyne.   NeBP

And all they will call you will be deportee.   Plane Wreck at Los Gatos.   Woody Guthrie.   InPK; PrIm; WTO

And all things are/and are not.   Song of Returnings.   William Pitt Root.   GeTw

And all things are because he willed them so.   Poet.   Peter Viereck.   HoPM; MiAP; MoAmPo

And all things fair and bright are Thine.   The Glory of God in Creation.   Thomas Moore.   OHIP

And all things flourish where you turn your eyes.   Sylvan Delights.   Alexander Pope.   NOBE

And all things seem only one/In the universal sun.   To Jane: The Invitation.   Percy Bysshe Shelley.   ERoP 1-2; HBV 1-2; OBRV; SeCeV

And all Things that go bump in the Night,/Good Lord deliver us.   From Ghoulies and Ghosties.   *Anonymous.*   OFD

And all this glory will not die.   Sic Transit Gloria Mundi.   James Wreford Watson.   CaP

And all this is folly to the world.   A Girl.   Ezra Pound.   MoAB; MoAmPo

And all this together is called love.   An Ancient Custom.   Anatoly Steiger.   VWA

And all those fringy leaves that flutter so.   Tree Feelings.   Charlotte Perkins Stetson Gilman.   PGD

And all those gems the ripening summer yields.   Song: "The fringed vallance of your eyes advance."   Thomas Shadwell.   ViBoPo

And all those other "I's who long for "We dying'.   An "I" Can Never Be a Great Man.   Stephen Spender.   OBMV

And all those weeping dewes which nightly fall,/Are but the tears shed for thy funerall.   My Midnight Meditation.   Henry, Bishop of Chichester King.   MePo; OBS

And all Thou hast, and all Thou art is mine!   Jesus Himself.   Henry K. Burton.   BLRP

And all three remained completely non-neurotic.   A Toast.   Charles Stetler.   GP

And all thuh host who rode thuh range/Now ride thuh Last Frontier.   Lay of the Last Frontier.   Harold Hersey.   PoOW

And all thy chosen race shall sing/Thy free, redeeming love.   The Time Will Surely Come.   Robert T. Daniel.   AH

And all thy fragrance saved for Love alone.   To a Mayflower.   William E. Marshall.   CaP

And all thy great Forefathers were from Homer down to Ben.   Destinie.   Abraham Cowley.   MeLP

And all thy paths are paths of peace.   Arise, My Soul! With Rapture Rise!   Samuel J. Smith.   AH

And all thy race (a num'rous seed)/Shall prove of caterpillar breed.   Fable XXIV: The Butterfly and the Snail.   John Gay.   FM

And all thy Sons, O Nature, learn my Tale.   Ode to Simplicity.   William Collins.   CEP; EiCP; EnLi 1-2; GTBS; LAuP; NOBE; OBEC; OBEV; TEP

And all thy thousand peaceful happy words.   The Earthly Paradise.   William Morris.   ViBoPo

And all to inform me so common a thing!   The Six Badgers.   Robert Graves.   GoJo; GrPl; WSC

And all true lovers that go thegither,/May they have mair luck than they.   The Douglas Tragedy.   *Anonymous.*   OxBB

And, all untroubled in her faith, she waits/The triumph or the tomb.   Charleston.   Henry Timrod.   AA; AP; MAmP; NOBA; OxBA; PAH; TAP

–And all was silent/as we resumed our memory of the present.   Castle Rock.   Frederick Morgan.   AMV-81

And all was still.   A Legend of Paul Bunyan.   Arthur Stanley Bourinot.   AmFN

And all watched over/by machines of loving grace.   All Watched over by Machines of Loving Grace.   Richard Brautigan.   MAT

And all we could do to be doing would be to be Wednes/day.   Summer Concert.   Reed Whittemore   AmFN

And all we have are bruised and bleeding hands.   The Deceptive Grin of the Gravel Porters.   Gavin Ewart.   FaBoMo

And all we velvet-jackets mourn his loss.   The Death of Puck.   Eugene Lee-Hamilton.   HBMV; OBVV

And all were as happy as happy could be,/With the Quangle Wangle Quee.   The Quangle Wangle's Hat.   Edward Lear.   AmMo; EBEV; OnUR

And all who in that following went with her.   On Knighthood.   Folgore da San Geminiano.   AWP

And all who know that love of Thine,/The joy of angels know.   For Perfect Peace.   Charles Wesley.   BePJ

And all who saw and heard him were amazed.   The Wind.   William Henry Davies.   SeCePo

And all winds go sighing/For sweet things dying.   A Dirge.   Christina Georgina Rossetti.   LoBV; NOBV; SBG; VLP

And all young men who get such wives/Should fight till you overcome them.   Locks and Bolts.   *Anonymous.*   TrAS

And all your wetness takes the form of tears.   Undine.   Irving Layton.   ErPo

And allow your breast to shelter my head,/The nest of my deepest prayers.   Place Me under Your Wing.   Hayim N. Bialik.   VWA

And almost as evil as I am.   Vinegaroon.   Witter ("Emanuel Morgan") Bynner.   BPAW

And almost breaks the bands/Which lock us in.   The Sprinters.   Lee Murchison.   SD

And almost gently asks: Are you a Jew?   The First Time.   Karl Shapiro.   ErPo; SM; VGW

And almost turned her brain to tinder.   The Thorn.   William Wordsworth.   EvOK; Par

And alone, on a tall stone, stood Grant.   Blocking the Pass.   Charles Madge.   FaBoMo

...And already begun to grow pale/green roots.   Roots.   Seymour Mayne.   NOBC

And also is fine for the liver.   Limerick: "There's a sensitive man in Toms River."   Morris Bishop.   TDH

And also much cattle?   Jonah.   Randall Jarrell.   MoRP

And also sweet potat-y.   A Negro Peddler's Song.   Fenton Johnson.   AmNP

And alswa litel thu gewurthe thet thu nawiht gewurthe!   Charm against Wens.   *Anonymous.*   OxBM

And alter with age.   The Lockless Door.   Robert Frost.   NOBA; WSC

And although we were both grown men/We had just been born   The Little Car.   Guillaume Apollinaire.   SOTW

...And alwayes praised be/for that abundant Love, which is in thee?   Brittan's Remembrancer (excerpt).   George Wither.   SeCV 1-2

And always hope the best.   A Poet's Wish: An Ode.   Allan Ramsay.   CEP

...And always, just there, is a shadow which the/firelight cannot cleave.   The Colors of Night.   N. Scott Momaday.   STE

And always keep a-hold of Nurse/For fear of finding something worse.   "Jim, Who Ran Away from His Nurse and Was Eaten by a Lion."   Hilaire Belloc.   EvOK; OxBChV; ShM

And always: man and branch.   Eden.   Lev Mak.   VWA

And always on the buttered side.   I never had a piece of toast.   James Payn.   CenHV; FaBoPa

And always remember to take the door-key.   The Willow-Tree.   William Makepeace Thackeray.   CenHV; HBV 1-2; InMe

And always said his prayers.   Little Fred.   *Anonymous.*   HBV 1-2; HBVY

And always the beautiful/trajectories.   In the Beginning Was the.   Lee Murchison.   SD

And always the room will throb quietly and slow.   A Man Walks in the Wind.   Maurice Lesemann.   AnAmPo; LiTL

And always there is some dam fool who writes them.   Reflection.   Kurt M. Stein.   InMe

And always, with a low despairful sound,/Tolls the disastrous bell of all our years!   Love.   James Clarence Mangan.   IrPN

And am amazed that Death, that tyrant grim,/Should think of me, who never thought of him.   An Epitaph.   *Anonymous.*   ExPo

And am at the end of soul's endless journey.   Seeing.   John Lyle Donaghy.   NeIP

"And am I glad I'm home? Ah, oui!"/Said Private Mike McCann.   Our Modest Doughboys.   Charlton Andrews.   PAH

And am not even sorry that I know nothing–/About fish. On His Queerness. Christopher Isherwood. OxBTC; PeHV

And am not sad, but feel her marvelous charm/As splendidly she plunges in the fight. Autumn. Edwin Curran. HBMV

And am only seeking one to receive it. Odes, XIII. Hafiz. AWP

And ambling through mirage/With the squatter's daughter. Song for the Cattle. David Campbell. NOAV

And America shall cease to be its name. Black Soul of the Land. Lance Jeffers. FB

And amid your naked vigor by the sky. The Body of Summer. Odysseus Elytis. LiTW

And among strictness sweetness grew,/mystery of flowering bars. The Flowering Bars. Charles Donnelly. CIP

And an address/forever unknown. The Final Cut. Vern Rutsala. AMV-81

And an altar of sacrifice, between the ocean/And the hidden quarry of the gods. Lost in Yucatan. Tom McKeown. HoAn

And an angel might direct us right, and where shall we go? The Streams of Lovely Nancy. *Anonymous.* FaBoBa; OBET; OxBoLi

And an elastic band, holding a bundle/of small white filing-cards/printed with important facts. Provisions. Margaret Atwood. IHMS

And an old fence post, and a little brown wren/That may any moment fly out again! Old Fence Post. Leigh Hanes. GoYe

And Ancus made the Ostian port,/Sublician bridge, and many a fort. Roman History in Rhyme (excerpt). Edward B. Goodwin. FaBoUs

And an is the rod without/Which no field. Risen Matters. Clark Coolidge. APU

And angels' hands thy body did entomb. To Saint Catherine. Henry Constable. GoBC

And angels point the way to peace. Solitude. Hannah More. WBLP

And angels' silver voices stir the air. A Doubting Heart. Adelaide Anne Procter. HBV 1-2

And Angels sound with endless Joy/The Saviour and the King. The Passion and Exaltation of Christ. Isaac Watts. NOCV

And angels will be born while thou dost sing. Upon Her Voice. Robert Herrick. CaPo

And anger to bloom green upon the trees. Citizen. Chris Wallace-Crabbe. CBAP

And angered, soul's harsh prize. Phoenix. W. H. Oliver. AnNZ

And another creature's belly forever. Pain. Robert Wrigley. AMV-81

And another Huzza for the U. S. A./Which produces so many heroes like they. Admiral Byrd. Ogden Nash. InMe; YaD

And another little drink wouldn't do us any harm. Another Little Drink. *Anonymous.* TrAS

And another time I think/you ought to be buried alive James Alley. Rabbit Brown. BluL

And another will take your place. You Will Die. *Anonymous.* AWP

And another with a submachine gun. Pacific Epitaphs. Dudley Randall. NoAm

And another wooden foot wouldn't do her any harm. There Was an Old Soldier. *Anonymous.* FSW; TrAS

And answer answer all–"Amen!" Stanzas Subjoined to the Yearly Bill of Mortality. William Cowper. NOCV

And answer, echoes, answer, dying, dying, dying. The Princess. Alfred, Lord Tennyson. AtBAP; AWP; BLPL; ELP; FiP; GN; GoJo; GTBS; GTBS-P; HBV 1-2; HeIP; InPo; LoBV; NoP; OAEL 1-2; OAEP; OBEV; OBNC; OBVV; PoEL 1-5; PoPl; PoPle; PrIm; RoGo; TreF; TrGrPo; UnS; ViBoPo; WSC

And answered thunder with his thunder back. Frederick Douglass. Paul Laurence Dunbar. BALP; PoBA

And answered with an echo/Like a resounding choir. I Hear a Voice. Halper Leivick. VWA

And answers not at all. Dwainie. James Whitcomb Riley. AA

And anthems in new tongues I hear saluting me. Prayer of Columbus. Walt Whitman. ATP; PGD; TrPWD; TRV; WGRP

And any bush becomes/our Bantu wonderland. Definition of Nature. Eugene B. Redmond. PoBA

And any thicket hide the unicorn. The Middle Ages: Two Views. Leah Bodine Drake. NePoAm-2

And anyhow you smell awful. To Noel Coward. Noel Coward. FaBoPa

And anyone who leaves my share/Of English fields and English air/May take the Alps for aught I care De Gustibus. St. John Emile Clavering Hankin. CenHV; LiSp

AND ANYTHING YOU SEE WILL BE USED/AGAINST YOU. Poem: "It doesn't look like a finger..." Hugh Sykes Davies. EAS

And apple trees/To scent the breeze/In blossom time. Johnny Appleseed. Arthur Stanley Bourinot. CaP

And April was german with his mating call. The Blizzard Ape. Kenneth Pitchford. CoPo

And April weeps–but, O, ye Hours,/Follow with May's fairest flowers. Dirge for the Year. Percy Bysshe Shelley. HBV 1-2; HBVY

And ar in mirth ay mair and mair/Thruch glaidnes of this lusty May. May Poems. *Anonymous.* OxBS

And Araby's or Eden's bowers/Were barren as this moorland hill. The Dreary Change. Sir Walter Scott. ERoP 1-2; FaBoPP; OAEL 1-2; OBNC

And archly looks to see if someone sees. The Young Bather. *Anonymous.* UnTE

And arcs out gracefully through air. Ed Shreckongost. Ed Ochester. TAT

And are astonisht when they view the same. Nosce Teipsum: An Acclamation. Sir John Davies. SiPS

And are content/With their poor frozen life and shallow banishment. Scotland's Winter. Edwin Muir. OxBS; OxBTC

And are dangerous, are bombs exploding/a long time, carrying bombs elsewhere to explode. Quiet Town. William Stafford. MAT

And are forced to sing lullaby/And like me wear the posy of thyme. The Posy of Thyme. *Anonymous.* OBET

And are hitched to the end of the wrist. Limerick: "The hands they were made to assist." Anthony Euwer. HBMV

And are if is a the this the the is it. High Pitched Whale. Clark Coolidge. ANYP

And are in mirth ay mair and mair/Through gladness of this lusty May. Lusty May. *Anonymous.* OBEV

And are returned upon your hand. Where Unimaginably Bright. Oliver Hale. GoYe

And are they dancing; or gazing at the earth? Are They Dancing. Edward Dorn. NeAP; PoM

And are waiting like me for the thaw. Before the Thaw. John Gill. NeAC

And are we not better than they? The Birds of the Air. Hollis Freeman. STF

And are we standing now, quietly, in the new life? Oceans. Juan Ramon Jimenez. NU

And–"Are we then so serious?" Conversation Galante. Thomas Stearns Eliot. HBMV

And are with gazing most content. The Phoenix. Arthur Christopher Benson. OBEV; OBVV

And are, without a beggar's blush, forgiven. Praise and Prayer. Sir William Davenant. GoBC; OBEV

And are you sure? Et Cetera. Dee Walker. GoYe

And are you sure where you will lie tonight, woman? Beggar's Serenade. John Heath-Stubbs. BoLoP; ErPo; NeBP

And argued city walls from uncut stone. Volubilis, North Africa. Ralph Nixon Currey. PeSA

And argues your wisdom down. After the Burial. James Russell Lowell AA; UnPo

And, armed like an archangel, returned. Death of an Aircraft. Charles Causley. MoBS

And armies shrink beneath the shadowy cloud. The Botanic Garden. Erasmus Darwin. NOEC

And around and over me/Winds and clouds for ever going. And There Will I Be Buried. Thomas Davidson. BSV

And arraign ye as our murderers, O spoilers of our land! The Famine Year. Lady Jane Francesca ("Speranza") Wilde. OnYI

And art delivered up/To nature and the wild again. An Open Air Performance of "As You Like It." E. J. Scovell. ChMP

And Art knew Titian and the tapestries. Renaissance. Robert Avrett. GoYe

And art, mine own unrivalled Fair! Carmina. Caius Valerius Catullus. OBVE

And art unfleshed desire. The Painter. Robert Fitzgerald. MoVE

And as a dying man to dying men. Love Breathing Thanks and Praise (excerpt). Richard Baxter. TRV

And as a rose in Venus' bosom worn,/So doth a bridegroom his bride's bed adorn. Roses. Thomas Campion. OBSC

And as a sign of his respect/said to the Great Shade: "same thing." Desert. Agnes Gergely. VWA

And, as always, the same folks/will go home emptyhanded. Building a Person. Stephen P. Dunn. FAZ

And, as anyone can see by reading this, he/also destroyed the meter. Limerick: "A decrepit old gas man named Peter." *Anonymous.* LiBL; SoSe

And, as at first, still lodge Him in the manger. The Guest. *Anonymous.* BoC; EaLo; EBCP; EvOK; GoBC; OBS; Oxboch; TrCP

And as clean and blue. Soeur Marie Emilie. Caryll Houselander. BoC

And as deep as the Kingdom of God. A New Patriotism. Chauncey R. Piety. PGD

And, as everyone who knows/anything about/poetry can tell you, he also/ruined the meter. A Decrepit Old Gasman. *Anonymous.* FaFP

And as far from home as kingdom come/I follow my mean desires. The Apostate. Alfred Edgar Coppard. OBMV

And as for his bed–he'll sleep alone in it. Boastful Husbandman. *Anonymous.* UnTE

And as for kissing, kiss my arse. On a Window at an Inn. *Anonymous.* FaBoEE

And as for the bucket Manhasset. Limerick: "Then the pair followed Pa to Manhasset." *Anonymous.* GoTF; LiBL

And as for the bucket, Nantucket. Limerick: "There was an old man of Nantucket." Dayton Voorhees. HBV 1-2; LiBL

And as he dropped his head the instant split/His startled life with lead, and all went out. A Working Party. Siegfried Sassoon. CMoP; MMM

And, as he goes, the transient vision mourns. To the Earl of Dorset. Ambrose Philips. LoBV

And as he spake,–all in a line, seaward the/ships set sail. The Legend of Walbach Tower. George Washington Houghton. PAH

And as he spake, upon the waves he springs. Hero and Leander. Christopher Marlowe. NOBE

And as he walked past me, I saw my face. A Second Birthday. Albert Kayper-Mensah ACV

And, as his lord, the lowly entreateth./Behold, love. Behold, Love, Thy Power How She Despiseth! Sir Thomas Wyatt. FCP; GBL

And as I did sing it you must learn it along. The Carter. *Anonymous.* OBET

And as I fall hear through the evening air/The distant horn of Roland, faintly blown. The Last Tourney. Frederic F. Van de Water. HBMV

And, as I gaze in the coals, I remember/Days long agone! Alone by the Hearth. George Arnold. HBV 1-2

And as I look around me, I'm very apt to smile,/To see so many people putting on the style. Putting on the Style. *Anonymous.* FSW

And as I'm told by men of sense,/He never has been living since! The Guinea Pig. *Anonymous.* NA; OxNR

...And as I/Once heard, hear the voice: It's late! Come home. What Voice at Moth-Hour. Robert Penn Warren. SM

And as I shall go from it. Desire for Hermitage. *Anonymous.* AnIL

And as I stooped, her own lips rising there/Bubbled with brimming kisses at my mouth. The House of Life. Dante Gabriel Rossetti. PoEL 1-5

And as I talked, I swam. With Kit, Age 7, at the Beach. William Stafford. RFM

And as I think of you I gather strength. Evening in the Walls. Jean Wahl. VWA

And as if I had lived all my life in arrears The Haunting. Irving Layton. NeAC

And (as if it had a meaning)/Views her sorrow. A Baroque Gravure. Thomas Merton. CoPo

And as if wanting griefe he must/Go take up sorrow upon trust. Humaine Cares. Nathaniel Wanley. OBS

And as in duty bound we all/Will ever pray. A Petition from the Chain Gang at Newcastle to Captain Furlong... Francis MacNamara. NOAV

And as it never shall remove,/So neither shall my praise. The Twenty-Third Psalm. George Herbert. EBCP

And as life is to the living, so death is to/the dead. The Two Mysteries. Mary Mapes Dodge. AA; HBV 1-2; TrCP; WGRP

And as merciless/as women. Crew-Cuts. Donald Hall. MAT

And as my love is now, it should remain. To Christ Crucified. *Anonymous.* CAW

And as my song beginning had/So must it have an end. The Praise of Sailors. *Anonymous.* OBSS

And as priests, His solemn praises/Each for a thank-offering brings. Glorious Things of Thee Are Spoken. John Newton. NOCV; WGRP

And as smart and as brave as can buay. Limerick: "The life boat that's kept at Torquay." *Anonymous.* LiBL

And, as soon as they start feeling no pain,/Write, in absentia, the music of Spain. Iberia. Leo Kirschenbaum. UnS

And as such I promote you to a saint. A Masque of Reason: God's Thanks to Job. Robert Frost. MoRP

And as the jeet hir yen glistren ay. Hoccleve's Humorous Praise of His Lady. Thomas Hoccleve. OAEP

And as the passes open, wind along. The Evening. John Gay. EnLi 1-2

And as the slave that is given in barter. Greek Epigram. Ezra Pound. MoAB; MoAmPo

And as the stream with murmur pass. Falsehood. William Cartwright. OBEV

...And as the weary amn/Stood up, coiled above his head, transforming all. A Tall Man Executes a Jig. Irving Layton. NOBC; PoCh

And as the wild rose, fair. Perdita. Florence Earle Coates. AA

And as their life's blood ebbed away it mingled in one stream. The Paisley Officer. *Anonymous.* ShS

And as these Excel in Beauty,/Those shall be Renown'd for Love. King Arthur. John Dryden. CEP

And, as they fleet,/Drop strength and riches at thy feet. Oh Mother of a Mighty Race. William Cullen Bryant. AP; FaBoBe; HBV 1-2; HBVY; PAH; PAL

And as they were thankful,/we're thankful today. The First Thanksgiving. Jack Prelutsky. NTCP

And as thou wound'st my Heart, inspire my Song. To Love A Sonnet. Philip Ayres. CEP

And as to the meaning, it's what you please. The Auld Wife. Charles Stuart Calverley. EnLi 1-2; NA; SpRo

And, as we gazed, our hearts, too full to speak,/Found in that vision all we sailed to seek. The Peak. Wilfrid Gibson. PoSH

And as well cry over a new-laid drain/As anything else, to ease your pain! In the Cemetery. Thomas Hardy. BrPo

And, as with us,/his warts are part of him. Toad. John Cotton. BoAnP

And ask her to permit me/To follow her to safety. Now the lotuses in the imperial lake. Wang Ch'ing-hui. BoWoP

And ask the fair creature herself if it's true,/Which I'm certain shee won't deny. Much Has Been Said... *Anonymous.* CoMu

And ask the gods to pardon this clear flame. Smoke. Henry David Thoreau. AA; AmPP; AnNE; APA; AWP; HeIP; InPo; NoP; OxBA

And ask the helping hospitable hand. The Seasons. James (1700-48) Thomson. FM

And ask within my whitened head/For wit that is not there. Self-Defense. Santob De Carrion. TrJP

And ask yourself if you care/about his cold or chain Cerberus. H. L. Van Brunt. FAZ

(And asking yawn'd) for what intent she came? Metamorphoses. Ovid (Publius Ovidius Naso). OBVE

And assemble the engine again. The Dying Airman. *Anonymous.* FaBoNo; FaFP; OxBoLi

And, at a flutter of wing,/Might vanish in song. The Linnet. Walter De La Mare. HBMV; LiTB; LoBV

And at bed, soft and sad. Demeanour. *Anonymous.* OxBChV

And at darky we waked him in clover,/And sent him to take a ground sweat. The Night before Larry Was Stretched. *Anonymous.* AnIV; BIrV; FaBoBa; GBP; IrPN; NOBI; NOBL; OnYI; OxBoLi

And at each shrine I bend my knee in turn. Epigram: "God scatters beauty as he scatters flowers." Walter Savage Landor. FaBoEE

And at her touch the dishes shine. Trim's Song: The Fair Kitchen-Maid. Sir Richard Steele. OBSP

And at his heart the strangling clasp of death. Haunted. Siegfried Sassoon. CMoP

And at his heels a stone. The Friar of Orders Grey. *Anonymous.* ACP; CAW; GoBC

And at His will my lyre grew audible. How My Songs of Her Began. Philip Bourke Marston. HBV 1-2

And at last, I'm told, his proprietors sacked him! The Editor's Tragedy. St. John Emile Clavering Hankin. CenHV

And at mankind rail with my parting breath. Farewell to the Court (excerpt). John Wilmot, Earl of Rochester. TrGrPo

And at morn I meet the Saviour,/In the glory of the dawn! Worship. Bob Jones, Jr. BePJ

And at my door the Pale Horse stands,/To bear me forth to unknown lands. The Stirrup Cup. John Milton Hay. AA; HBV 1-2

And at my feet the pale green Thames/Lies like a rod of rippled jade. Symphony in Yellow. Oscar Wilde. FaBoPP; MoBrPo; NOBV; OBSP; SyP

And at my gate despair shall linger still/To let in death when love and fortune will. The Hermit. Sir Walter Ralegh. OBSC

And at my table find himself at home. Blest Winter Nights. John Armstrong. OBEC

And at my work I'll think of them and holidays to come! The Little Factory Girl to a More Fortunate Playmate. *Anonymous.* SaC

And at night in the alehouse I'll stay and pay like a man. The Happy Beggarman. *Anonymous.* OnYI

And at night she'll return/To her nest back again. The Pretty Ploughboy. *Anonymous.* GBP

And at Night went away with a Green-Gown. The Green-Gown. *Anonymous.* CoMu

And at night you did not return. Fighting South of the Castle. *Anonymous.* AWP; WaaP

And at once the moving earth lay stretched abroad. Chant to Io. Tiwai Paraone. WTO

And at our Father's loved abode/Our souls arrive in peace. O God of Bethel. Doddridge. Philip Logan. John WTO

And at Our Lady that standeth in the Oak. The Play of the Four P.P.: The Palmer. John Heywood. ACP; CAW

And, at prime hour, behold!–He follows me/With golden shadows to my secret rooms! The Lattice at Sunrise. Charles Tennyson Turner. OBVV

And at the break of dawn, lead me/To work. Dress Me, Dear Mother. Avraham Shlonsky. VWA

And at the burial o' Willie Scott,/I wat was mony a weeping e'e. Jamie Telfer of the Fair Dodhead. *Anonymous.* BSV; OxBB

And at the centre of radiance the man's red smile Pauper Woodland. Ronald G. Everson. NOBC

And at the east gable/A corroded pipe—one in a hill of 500 acres—/Works   At a Ruined Croft.   John Manson.   PoSH

And at the end blessed them with dying grace   Advent.   Brian Coffey.   CIP

And at the end is a granite boulder with no name,/laid by the man for Dan, best loved of his horses   Horse Graveyard.   Fred Lape.   PH

And, at the end, need no Paradise.   Tell Me Now.   Wang Chi.   FaBoCh; LoGBV

And at the end of every day is night.   The Plains.   Roy Fuller.   MoPo

And at the end she didn't know a bit/What she'd been laughing at.   The Funny Old Man and His Wife.   *Anonymous.*   OnUR; SoPo; SUS

And at the Play-house Harry keeps her box.   The Toilette. A Town Eclogue.   John Gay.   CEP

And at the spiritual prime/Rewaken with the dawning soul.   In Memoriam A.H.H., XLIII.   Alfred, Lord Tennyson.   OBNC

And at the top twined in a lovers' knot/The red rose and the briar.   Barbara Allen.   *Anonymous.*   AS; FaBoBa; FSW; PrIm

And at this I was mildly abashed.   The Study in Aesthetics.   Ezra Pound.   CMoP; NOBA; NoP; PAI

And at this starting point of truth/Await a widening of the known.   Crossing the County Line.   Elizabeth Randall-Mills.   GoYe

And at thy call with burning lamps arise.   O King of Saints, We Give Thee Praise and Glory.   Mary A. Thomson.   AH

And at your lodging with their thanks appear.   The Rain.   George Herbert.   BoC

And at your marriage all its occasions shall dance for joy.   For The Time Being.   W. H. Auden.   AnFE; OAEP; SBVL

And at your voice Pride from his throne must/rise.'   Do You Remember Me?   Walter Savage Landor.   EnRP; OBNC; ViBoPo

And ate an egg.   In Some Seer's Cloud Car.   Christopher Middleton.   TwCP

And ate out twelve months' labour at a meal.   The Signal; or, A Satire against Modesty (excerpt).   Francis Hawling.   NOEC

And ate them thick with butter.   E, the Feasting Florentines.   Daniel Gerard Hoffman.   VGW

And Atlas blew his rustic rumbling horn.   Sonnet: Mockado, Fustian, and Motley.   John Taylor.   EIL

And attack me with swords/As ye have done.   Waldere 2.   *Anonymous.*   AnOE

,And attain thereafter/Bliss on high in the heavenly home.   The Phoenix.   *Anonymous.*   AnOE

And autumn leaves are selling at fifty cents a bunch.   The Complacent Cliff-Dweller.   Margaret Fishback.   PoLf

And autumn's golden sun beholds/A nation bowed, a world in tears.   On the Death of President Garfield.   Oliver Wendell Holmes.   PAH

And avarice be the only outcast thing.   Sonnets of the Months.   Folgore da San Geminiano.   AWP

And await some subtle invitation.   Waiting Carefully.   Nancy P. Kamm.   AMV-80

And awaits the fireball.   Exit, Pursued by a Bear.   Ogden Nash.   NYBP

And awake, my heart, to be loved, awake, awake!   Awake, My Heart.   Robert Bridges.   GTBS-P; HBV 1-2; MoAB; MoBrPo; NOBE; OBEV; OBVV

And away did hoppy-hop.   Nauty Pauty Jack-a-Dandy.   *Anonymous.*   OxNR

And away goes the mare.   One to Make Ready.   *Anonymous.*   OxNR

And away, my Johnnie boys,/We're bound to go!   We're All Bound to Go.   *Anonymous.*   AmSS

And away, my jolly boys, we're all bound to go!   Heave Away.   *Anonymous.*   ShS

And away the vapour flew.   Little Boy Lost.   William Blake.   CBEP; NoP

And away they all flew.   What's in the Cupboard.   *Anonymous.*   GBP; OxNR

And away to the meadows,/The meadows again!   Old Song.   Edward Fitzgerald.   GN; OBEV; OBVV

And away we went with our bonny grey.   The Bonny Grey.   *Anonymous.*   GBP

And away went the beggar-men all in a row.   Craigbilly Fair.   *Anonymous.*   GBP

And aye she loot the tears down fa/For John o Hazelgreen.   John of Hazelgreen (E version).   *Anonymous.*   BFSS; ESPB

And aye when you come into my sight/I'll wish you were away.   The Gardener.   *Anonymous.*   GBP

And azure water hoisting out of wells.   In the Elegy Season.   Richard Wilbur.   InPK; MoAB; NePoEA; NYBP

And b-b-b-b-b-butta.   Limerick: "There once was a man of Calcutta."   *Anonymous.*   LiBL

And Bacchus was out-done by me.   Epigram.   Thomas Moore.   ALV

And back it in care of/The Barbourville jail.   Down in the Valley.   *Anonymous.*   ABF; FaFP; FSW; WTO

And back through all that shining host/His mandate sends.   The Night-March.   Herman Melville   AnFE; CoAnAm; LiTA

And—backwards—is it thus the eagles fly?   The Urn.   Hart Crane.   PoA

And bade betwixt their shores to be/The unplumb'd, salt, estranging sea.   Switzerland.   Matthew Arnold.   GTBS P; OAEP; VLP

And bade him for Robin Hood to pray.   Robin Hood and the Bishop.   *Anonymous.*   BaBo; ESPB

And Bahram, that great Hunter—the Wild Ass/Stamps o'er his Head, but cannot break his Sleep.   The Rubaiyat: A book of verses underneath the bough.   Omar Khayyam.   EG

And bait his homilies with his brother worms?   The Moral Bully.   Oliver Wendell Holmes.   AnNE

And bake him in a pye.   The Lay of the Ettercap (parody).   John Leyden.   BXAP

And bales of fantasy from No-Man's Land.   The Wharf of Dreams.   Edwin Markham.   HBV 1-2

...And banks of cloud uptower/In bulging heads that crowd for miles the dazzling south.   April 1885.   Robert Bridges.   NBM; OBSP; OxBTC

And bar yourselves from heaven?   Amazing Sight! The Saviour Stands.   Henry Alline.   AH

...And bare I go/an armed Knight's captive and slave confessed.   To Tommaso de' Cavalieri.   Buonarroti Michelangelo.   PeHV

And barely can not hear them calling, "Here's one."   Memorial Service for the Invasion Beach Where the Vacation....   Alan Dugan.   MP; NMP; TwCP

And barely seen/On this shed wall.   Under the Woods.   Edward ("Edward Eastaway") Thomas.   CH; LoBV

And barked his "Yap...yap!"...   Conversation.   Anne Robinson.   SUS

And Barnaby's soul they bore aloft,/Singing with voices sweet and soft.   The Ballad of Barnaby.   W. H. Auden.   OBNV

And bask, a dreamer, in her dreamy smiles?   Spring Passion.   Joel Elias Spingarn.   HBV 1-2

And bask'd and batten'd in the woods.   In Memoriam A.H.H., XXXV.   Alfred, Lord Tennyson.   VLP

And be a friend to man.   The House by the Side of the Road.   Sam Walter Foss.   AmePo; BLPA; BLPL; FaBoBe; FaFP; GoTF; HBV 1-2; HBVY; OHFP; TreF; TRV; WBLP; WGRP

And be a good and faithful wife.   Marriage.   *Anonymous.*   AmFP

And be a man like other men.   Mortal Combat.   Mary Elizabeth Coleridge.   OBVV

And be a theme of elaboration in the deep, sweet singing.   Nemea 11 (excerpt).   Pindar.   SD

And be a true Whig, while I'm not in game.   An Excellent New Song, Being the Intended Speech of a Famous Orator...   Jonathan Swift.   APAS

And be able to finish/your poem.   The Long Word.   Deirdre Ballantyne.   AMV-80

And be among her cloudy trophies hung.   Ode on Melancholy.   John Keats.   AtBAP; BoLiVe; DiPo; ERoP 1-2; ExPo; FiP; ForPo; HAP; LiTB; MAT; MBW 1-2; NAWM 1-2; NIP; NOBE; NoP; OAEL 1-2; OAEP; OBEV; OBNC; PAI; PoEL 1-5; PoPle; PoRA; PPP; PrIm; SeCeV; TEP; TreFS; TrGrPo

And be as merciful as thou art chaste.   The Tempest.   Charles Cotton.   SeCePo

And be as wise as lilies of the field.   Second Wisdom.   Henry Morton Robinson   GoYe

And be buried in the dust of marching feet.   For Black Poets Who Think of Suicide.   Etheridge Knight.   BP; CNA; HeIP; PoBA

And be delivered, unafraid, from whatever I touched.   The Doctor Rebuilds a Hand.   Gary Young.   AMV-80; SUW

And be drunk on the wines of the postilion.   Song for "Buvez les Vins du Postillon"–Advt.   Jean Garrigue.   TAP

And be guid to beggar-bodies/When they come to your yett.   Supper.   William Soutar.   OxBS

And be (if God should please),/Almost as wise as geese.   The Wild Geese.   John Masefield.   NoAm

And be let in.   Glass.   Brendan Galvin.   LTB

And be like him, and he will then love me.   The Little Black Boy.   William Blake.   AtBAP; AWP; BiP; CABA; DiPo; EnPE; HBV 1-2; HeIP; InPo; LoGBV; MyFE; NAWM 1-2; NoP; OAEL 1-2; OBEC; OBEV; OxBChV; OxBoCh; PoNe; SeCeV; TreFS; TrGrPo

And be my night, my warmth, my wife.   The Passionate Shepherd to His Love.   Delmore Schwartz.   NIP

And be my own dear maid!   The Maple Hangs Its Green Bee Flowers.   John Clare.   AtBAP

And be my ugly pet/and sing me songs.   The Princess Addresses the Frog Prince.   Elizabeth Brewster.   DFT

And be not beaten with thine own rod.   Sources of Good Counsel.   Peter Idley.   OxBChV

And be ourselves, in turn, the brave!   Memorial Day.   Annette Wynne.   OHIP

And be refined with burning.   Of Astraea.   John Davies.   TrGrPo

And be struck dumb, if only for a time.   Out of a War of Wits.   Dylan Thomas.   PoA

And be sure that a "Luck" to our lot will fall/As it has to Edenhall.   Edenhall.   Susan (Sarah Chauncey Woolsey) Coolidge.   OBCA

And be the fate of all her foes/The same as here recorded.   The Fate of John Burgoyne.   *Anonymous.*   PAH

(And be the God that hears our prayers adored.)   Ye Scattered Nations.   Thomas Cradock.   AH

And be their wonder, as we were their scorn.   To His Late Majesty Concerning the True Form of English Poetry.   Sir John Beaumont.   JCP; OBS; PP

And be ye of good cheer–and go to the/devil!   The Dance of Despair.   Hayim Nahman Bialik.   TrJP

And beads in hand, I homeward/turned,/My thoughts all filled with wisdom/learned.   Confessio Amantis.   John Gower.   AtBAP; MeEV

And beaming, wrap the globe around.   To Thee the Tuneful Anthem Soars.   Mather Byles.   AH

And bear from hill and valley/The daffodil away/That dies on Easter day.   The Lent Lily.   Alfred Edward Housman.   OHIP; PoSC

And bear greetings from me/to the small shoots beneath the cold.   To My Child.   Abraham Sutzkever.   VWA

And bear sweet sunshine in the face.   A Little Word.   *Anonymous.*   STF

And bear the demon with his prey/From the forest to the sun.   The Waste Places.   James Stephens.   HBV 1-2

And bear the pain of silence/When my songs are old?   Foreboding.   Hazel Hall.   HBMV

And bear thee upwards to that blest abode,/Where, like the prophet, thou shalt find thy God.   To the Right Honourable William, Earl of Dartmouth.   Phillis Wheatley.   AmPP; SBG; WPOW

And bear with life, to love and pray for you!   Don Juan".   George Gordon, Lord Byron.   ViBoPo

And bearing brilliant and noble human beings.   How many wise men and heroes.   Ch'iu Chin.   BoWoP

And bears him as a courser bears a king.   The Diver.   John Frederic Herbin.   CaP

And bears no venture in impiety.   The High Mind.   Samuel Daniel.   AnEnPo

And bears the like antipathy to trees.   On Dr. Evans Cutting down a Row of Trees at St. John's College...   *Anonymous.*   FaBoEE

And beat back homeward in a shower of song!   Beethoven.   John Hall Wheelock.   PoA

And beat him soundly for the band.   The Drum.   John Farrar.   BrR

And beat my little drum.   A Starling's Spring Rondel.   James Cousins.   HBV 1-2; HBVY

And beat old Mr December,/Who seduced young Lady May.   The Naughty Lord & the Gay Young Lady.   *Anonymous.*   CoMu

And beat the Buckler's Verge, and bound the whole.   The Iliad.   Homer.   OBVE

And beat the cross to earth, and break the Kind/And all his Table'....   Idylls of the King.   Alfred, Lord Tennyson.   OAEL 1-2

And beat within his knotted, naked breast...   Malcolm's Katie.   Isabella Valancy Crawford.   OBCV

And beating the land's/Edge into a swoon.   Moonlight Night: Carmel.   Langston Hughes.   MOS

And beats the thin, tin sides of time/With hot and foggy hands.   Little Steamboat.   Oscar Williams.   PoPl

And Beaumonts and Bens be his Kellys above.   David Garrick.   Oliver Goldsmith.   CBEP; OBEC; SeCeV

And beauteous Emma ev'ry night my dream!   To Emma. Extempore. Hyaena, off Gambia, June 4, 1779.   Edward Thompson.   NOEC

And beautiful; and many a little child.   Death May Be Very Gentle.   Oliver St. John Gogarty.   PoRA

And beautiful young men died/all up and down the lines.   All Up and Down the Lines.   Robert Cooperman.   AMV-80

And beauty draws us with a single hair.   The Rape of the Lock.   Alexander Pope.   ACP; ViBoPo

And beauty glimpsed was swift withdrawn/As startled stag and soft-eyed fawn.   Caenlochan.   Helen B. Cruickshank.   PoSH

And beauty reared above her height.   On Sir Philip Sidney.   Matthew Royden.   EIL

And because it is my heart.   The Heart.   Stephen Crane.   HoPM; InPK; MoAmPo; TW

And because there is no other person, anywhere on earth, who remem-/bers these things as clearly...   Any Man's Advice to His Son.   Kenneth Fearing.   CMoP

And because they had/to sit up straight/so they could eat.   The Helmet.   Philip Levine.   LCAP

And beckoning signal of a sail unfurled!   Theocritus.   Annie Fields.   AA

...And become a poem.   Come, holy tortoise shell.   Sappho.   BoWoP

...And become confident/As the rock and ocean that we were made from.   Carmel Point.   Robinson Jeffers.   NoP

And becomes another star/in the distant night.   The Lone Biker.   R. Wayne Hardy.   LFAC

And becomes the third,/the knowing, between them.   Les Jours Gigantesques / The Titanic Days.   Kathleen Fraser.   NPGG

And Bedlington for nailers,/A, U, A.   A, U, Hinny Burd.   *Anonymous.*   GBP

And been left in the ocean to rot.   Limerick: "A Phoenician called Phlebas forgot."   Wendy Cope.   FaBoWP

And before I can count to ten she raises it high,/Slices it into my chest.   How to Murder Your Best Friend.   Diana O Hehir.   NPGG

And before it's all through,/I may be following you!   Award.   Ray Durem.   IDB; PoBA; PPON

And before we'll face for home, brave boys, we'll sing the lumbering theme.   Johnny Carroll's Camp.   *Anonymous.*   AmFP

And before you can wink/The tree stands bare!   The Christmas Tree in the Nursery.   Richard Watson Gilder.   HBVY; OHIP

And before you know there is war.   Big Dream, Little Dream.   Louis Simpson.   PoL

And beg for content at her feet!   Two Songs, II.   Abraham Reisen.   LiTW

And began making tortillas and Revolution.   About Women's Liberation.   Maria Saucedo.   FIA

And begat/and begat/and begat   Genealogy.   Donald Finkel.   VWA

And begun again to penetrate/into all crevices/of my world.   Coda.   William Carlos Williams.   NOBA

And behave mannerly at table;/At least as far as he is able.   Whole Duty of Children.   Robert Louis Stevenson.   EvOK; FaBoUs; GoTF; HBV 1-2; HBVY; NLV; OxBChV; TreFS

And behind her left ear was a wen.   Limerick: "H was an indigent Hen."   Bruce Porter.   NA

And behind her there were/flowers, and behind them/nothing.   The Rhyme.   Robert Creeley.   AmPC

And behind the curtain one marvelous belly/or else the wind is bringing the usual.   Flying Noises.   Thomas Lux.   LCAP

...And behind them/The eternal lightning of Lenin's bones.   The Skeleton of the Future.   Hugh" (Christopher Murray Grieve) MacDiarmid.   GoTS; MoBrPo; OBMV; OBTV

And, being forced, I cannot be myself.   My hated birthday is here, and I must go.   Sulpicia.   BoWoP

And being good for nothing else, be wise.   The Disabled Debauchee.   John Wilmot, Earl of Rochester.   BoLoP; HAP; NOBL; OBSV; PPP; WeW

And being neither part nor parcel of/Its tranquil beauty know herself in love.   Late Comer.   Fanny de Groot Hastings.   GoYe

And being one of them/leaves his shadow closer to the ground.   Guernica.   James Lewisohn.   LFAC

And beldams old my feats have told,/So vale, vale; ho, ho ho!   The Mad-Merry Pranks of Robin Good-Fellow.   *Anonymous.*   CBEP

And believe I'm still unique.   I Don't Want Any More Visitors.   Ingrid Jonker.   PeSA

And believe that beyond this flood a/kinder country lies.   Noah and the Waters: Chorus.   Cecil Day Lewis.   OAEP

And bellowed, with his best salute,/"A happy birthday, Father!"   The Ballad of Private Chadd.   A.(lan) A.(lexander) Milne.   CenHV

And bells beyond the sand.   Here We Come A-Piping.   *Anonymous.*   CH; ExPo; PoPle; SiSoSe; TiPo

And below the poppy flowers/Steals no dream.   After Summer.   Philip Bourke Marston.   HBV 1-2

And bend and kiss you, bid you follow me.   A Message.   George Ives.   PeHV

And bend and touch you on the cheek.   A Confession.   Robert Mezey.   AmPA; NaP

And bend with reverence where his ashes lie.   At Lulworth Cove a Century Back.   Thomas Hardy.   ChMP

And beneath its sway we decay apace.   The Midnight Court.   Brian Merriman.   BIrV

And benedictions on this hallowed/knife/Which pries the door to the eternal life.   Rabbi Yom-Tob of Mayence Petitions His God.   Abraham Moses Klein.   TrJP

And Benedictus sings my heart to Me.   Sheldonian Soliloquy.   Siegfried Sassoon.   UnS

...And besides, it wouldn't have been right.   Cora Punctuated with Strawberries.   George Starbuck.   NCSH; NMP

And best of all, along the way, friendship and mirth.   The Things I Prize.   Henry Van Dyke.   GoTF; TreFT

And, best of all, her little soul/Is, like a lily, white.   To a Little Girl.   Gustav Kobbe.   HBV 1-2

And, best of all, the eager silence there/When, swift from bat or hand, you hang in air.   To a Baseball.   *Anonymous.*   LiSp

And bethink thee thou art servant/To the same all-moving hand.   Think.   Charles Weekes.   AnIV; OnYI

And "better' "best".   Good, Better, Best.   *Anonymous.*   OxNR

And better fate, had perished alone.   Under a Lady's Picture.   Edmund Waller.   EnLoPo

...And better save/The rest, than all make offerings to the wave.   The Odyssey.   Homer.   OBS

And Betty's prais'd for Labours not her own.   The Rape of the Lock.   Alexander Pope.   AtBAP; CABA; CEP; CoBE; DiPo; NOBE

And bloody Faith the foulest birth of time. Feelings of a Republican on the Fall of Bonaparte. Percy Bysshe Shelley. AnEnPo

And blossom in purple and red. Come into the Garden, Maud. Alfred, Lord Tennyson. CBEP; ExPo; HBV 1-2; LiTL; NOBE; TreF

And blossoms and is you, when you are dead. Two Sonnets. Charles Hamilton Sorley. HBMV; MMM

And blot thy name from its place. The Church Walking with the World. Matilda C. Edwards. BLPA

And blots the foolish faces/Of my poor friends and me. On Forelands High in Heaven. Alfred Edward Housman. PAI

And blow his nails to warm them if he may. Old January. Edmund Spenser. YeAr

And blow like the wind away A Meditation. Richard Eberhart. LiTA

And blow you all a kiss from the tomb. A New England Bachelor. Richard Eberhart. MoAmPo; NoAm

And blowing on the fortunate face, reveals the man. Fortune. Charles Madge. FaBoMo

And blows good jazz/for the entire/human race Miles' Delight. Ted Joans. PoNe

And blows through the flint/Of an ox's horn. March. Anonymous. GBP

And blush'd, and ran away, and he ran after. Thyrsis and Milla, Arm in Arm Together. Anonymous. GBL

And blush to show their noses on a coin. Apple Dumplings and a King. John Wolcot. OBEC

And, blushing, smiled innocently. Pensionnaires. Paul Verlaine. PeHV

And blythe we'll sing, and hail the day/That gave us liberty, man. The Tree of Liberty. Robert Burns. FaBoPV

And bolts the door against her heart,/Out wailing in the rain. Interior. Dorothy Parker. SBG

And bones/of those I love. Hypodermic Release. Del Corey. AMV-81

And Bonne Sainte Anne not hunted down/by time. Sainte Anne de Beaupre. Richard Eberhart. NePoAm

And bore him joyous from his lonely isle. Cap'n. Arthur Wallace Peach. EtS

...And bore/where harmony, clear joy,/is enough, and nothing more is asked. For a Voice That Is Singing. Aldo Camerino. VWA

And, born of love, the vague desire/That spurs an imitative will. In Memoriam A.H.H., CX. Alfred, Lord Tennyson. VLP

And borrow ransom from this bowel of violence. Sunset Horn. Myron O'Higgins. AmNP; PoNe

And both, alas! take flight. To Youth. Walter Savage Landor. EnRP; HBV 1-2

And both for him, so tender-true,/Him that doth love me! Blue and White. Mary Elizabeth Coleridge. OBEV; OBVV

And both ride off together down his mind. Fairy Tale. John Frederick Nims. MiAP

...And both shall be/Jesu's eternally. The Spotless Maid. Vincent McNabb. ISi

And both thy servants be. Man. George Herbert. AnAnS 1; InPo; MePo; NoP; OAEP; PoEL 1-5; SeCP; TrGrPo; TrPWD

And both were hard as the nether stone. There Was a Strife 'Twixt Man and Maid. Rudyard Kipling. PV

And bouffants that bustle, and rustle. The Empty Woman. Gwendolyn Brooks. IHMS

And bought me/a 25c hamburger/out of $75.00 Old Man Con. Earl Gene Box. LFAC

And bought the New York Times, and went to bed. Hot Night on Water Street. Louis Simpson. MP; TwCP

And bound themselves by kisses twelve, to meet next/holiday. The Rural Dance about the Maypole. Anonymous. OxBoLi

And bound upon Parnassus' bi-cleft top. First Steps up Parnassus. Michael Drayton. NOBE

And bow before/They leave the school. The Wonder Clock. Katharine Pyle. OBCA

And bowed down/to worship/this perfection. The Gift. William Carlos Williams. MoRP; NePoAm-2; PoPl

And bowing not knowing to what For the Anniversary of My Death. William Stanley Merwin. CAPP; CoAP; HaCAP; InPK; NaP; NOBA

And bowing–with a Mighty look–/At me–The Sea withdrew– I started Early–Took my Dog. Emily Dickinson. AmPP; DiPo; HAP; InPK; LiTA; LiTM; MOS; NCEP; PoEL 1-5; SBG

And bowl the round nave down the hill of heaven,/As low as to the fiends! Hamlet. William Shakespeare. Par

And boys and girls are happy/And glad to have it so. January. Sylvia S. Lambdin. YeAr

And boys and kings thenceforth you'll see/Enjoy complete Equality. Maternal Despotism; or, The Rights of Infants. Richard Graves. NOEC

And boys like you are born. Manhattan Lullaby. Rachel Field. AmFN

And Bracelets or some toy/Snatcht from the willing Coy. Odes. Horace. OBVE

And braids her hair with the constellations. The Desert. Charles Erskine Scott Wood. AnAmPo

And brake her mould in great dispraise your like she could not frame. Tottel's Miscellany (excerpt). Anonymous. OAEL 1-2

And brandish vested rights to pillage and devour. The Poor of London. William Forster. CBAP

And brave Carnegie, wha but he,/The piper o' Dundee? The Piper o' Dundee. Anonymous. OxBS

And brave the wild winds and unhearing tide,/The World his country, and his GOD his guide. Sonnet at Dover Cliffs. William Lisle Bowles. OBEC

And bravery is set upon the mind/That man may act what truth he has divined. Alcestis. Euripides. LiTW

And braves as he may the night/Of darkness and tears. Winter Nightfall. Robert Bridges. MoAB; MoBrPo; OBEV

And bread shall be "a star upon the tongue." The Tomb of Honey Snaps Its Marble Chains. Derek Stanford. NeBP

And break 'em when she's kind. Song: "I lately vow'd, but 'twas in haste." John Oldmixon. PoL

And break my heart of stone. Break My Heart of Stone. Charles Wesley. BePJ

And break on the lips while meeting. Sparkling and Bright. Charles Fenno Hoffman AA; HBV 1-2

...And break/The low beginnings of content. In Memoriam A.H.H., LXXXIV. Alfred, Lord Tennyson. VLP

And break thy schemes of earthly joy,/That thou may'st seek thine all in Me. My Prayer. Anonymous. STF

And break thyself in shivers on her eye. The Bubble: A Song. Robert Herrick. CaPo

And breake before thee. On the Name of Jesus. Richard Crashaw. AnAnS 1

And breakers thundering upon a shore. Africa. Adele Naude. PeSA

And breaking hearts that hate the morning light! Sonnets. Frederick Goddard Tuckerman. AP

And breaks in hemispheres the obdurate shell. Reproduction of Life. Erasmus Darwin. PBBP

And breaks the glass of time. Waves. Ralph Waldo Emerson AA

And breath comes faster than the hounds/To sanction what remembered, what stuck. Baby's Awake Now. Bill Berkson. APU

And breath,/ribbed with mortality. Eve's Birth. Kim Chernin. VWA

...And breathe/Contentment, savouring wine and wreath. To a Friend on His Marriage. Frank Templeton Prince. LiTM

And breathed a gentle breath such as yellow/fruit or any sleeping beast may. In a Corner of Eden... Peter Levi. NePoEA-2

And breathed her fragrance on the lofty pines. John Smith's Approach to Jamestown. James Barron Hope. MC; PAH

And, breathing forth a pious wish,/Will cram his belly full of fish. The Careful Angler. Robert Louis Stevenson. LiSp; SD; SoSe

And brick upon grey brick. Dublin. Louis MacNeice. ACV; CIP; FaBoPP; OxBI; OxBTC

And bridal vines drink in his juices on each side. Pictures of the Rhine. George Meredith. OBTV

And bright on Bethlehem's joyous plains/Breaks the first Christmas morn. The Birth Song of Christ. Edward Hamilton Sears. BePJ

And brighter bliss of heaven. I Love Thy Kingdom, Lord. Timothy Dwight. AH

And brightest is their glory's sheen,/For greatest hath their labour been. Epilogue to Lessing's Laocoon. Matthew Arnold. VLP

And brilliant obscuring of the hole. Eclipse. Ed Roberson. PoNe

And bring about the collapse of the whole empire. Shame. Richard Wilbur. ConAP; FaBoMo; OxBC

And bring down eleven. The Ladybird. Anonymous. GBP

"And bring fresh wine for my friend and me." The Sunbeam. Anonymous. NA

And bring him home. But 'tis decreed/That I shall never find him. The Mad Maid's Song. Robert Herrick. AWP; BoLiVe; CaPo; EnLoPo; InPo; LoBV; OAEL 1-2; OBEV; SeCV 1-2; TrGrPo; ViBoPo; WiR

And bring my Soul to its desired place. October 14. 1644. Edward, Lord Herbert of Cherbury. AnAnS 2

And bring no book: for this one day/We'll give to idleness. To My Sister. William Wordsworth. EnRP; OAEL 1-2; OBRV

And bring seven other duties to your door. Duty. Edwin Markham. HBMV; HBVY

And bring the hour of thy conquering power/And the dawning of the day! Fainne Gael An Lae. Alice Milligan. HBV 1-2

And bring the promised day. Northfield. Anonymous. AmFP

And bring their tails behind them. Little Bo-Peep. Mother Goose. SoPo

And bring them all to heaven at last. O God, Great Father, Lord, and King. E. Embree Hoss. AH

And bring thy poor/commonwealth into decay. Bad Bishop Jegon. Anonymous. GBP

And bring Thy seed to flower. The Holy Spirit. Evelyn Underhill. BoC

And bring to my baby a fresh penny roll. The Mouse's Lullaby. Palmer Cox. OBCA

And bring us back the glory that hath been! Thou Shouldst Be Living at This Hour! Kenyon West. PGD

And bring us to blys that is abone./Amen, amen, amen, for charite. Mary Modyr, Cum and See. *Anonymous.* OxBoCh

And bring us to that haven of her breast. Rhodanthe. Agathias. AWP

And bring us wanderers home. Awake, My Soul! In Grateful Songs. Andrew Fowler. AH

And bringe us to his heighe blisse! Amen. The Canterbury Tales: The Nun's Priest's Tale. Geoffrey Chaucer. AtBAP; EnL; MBW 1-2; NAWM 1-2; NoP; OAEL 1-2; OAEP; PBBP; PoEL 1-5; SeCeV; TrGrPo

And brings the solemn, inward pain/Of truth into the heart again. In a Hard Intellectual Light. Richard Eberhart. CMoP; LiTM; MoVE

And brings the white money to me O. The Bonny Keel Laddie. *Anonymous.* GBP

And brings you a breath of sea, a/memory of stars. The Pear-Tree. Yvan Goll. TrJP

And Britain go on–to be damn'd if she will. Emancipation from British Dependence. Philip Freneau. PAH

And broad old cesspools glittered in the sun. Mouse's Nest. John Clare. ExPo; InPK; LiTB; LoBV; SeCeV; VLP

–And broke the useless knife across my knee. The Betrayal. Josephine Winslow Johnson. MoRP

And brook'st commandment from high Heaven alone/For marshalling thy waves. Mighty Sea! Cameleon-Like Thou Changest. Thomas Campbell. EtS

And, brother, for all time, hail and farewell. On the Burial of His Brother. Catallus. AWP; EnLi 1-2

And, brother,what shall you say? And What Shall You Say? Joseph Seamon, Jr. Cotter. BANP; CDC; PoBA; PoNe

And brotherhood like a coat of many colors/Cover the nakedness of man. Lenox Avenue. Sidney Alexander. PoNe

And brothers give you back the sword. Message to Siberia. Alexander Pushkin. AWP; TTY

And brothers in the young. Song. Richard Brinsley Sheridan. CEP

And brought forth music sweet and strong. The Master-Player. Paul Laurence Dunbar. TRV

And brought her home to merry England,/With her to lead his life. King Estmere. *Anonymous.* BuBa; ESPB; OBNV; OxBB

And brutal fact persuade us to/Adventure, Art, and Peace. Chorale. W. H. Auden. ILwL

And buck the odds, and hope, and give it my/Borrowed scratched-up happy hello-goodbye. The Universe Is Closed and Has REMs. George Starbuck. SUW

And buckle now and then, and that's enough. Song: "Chloris, forbear a while." Henry Bold. GBL

And buds and blossoms like the rest. In Memoriam A.H.H., CXV. Alfred, Lord Tennyson. GTBS-P; HBV 1-2; NOBE; OAEP; OBNC

..And build/A perfect freedom, though all else were foiled. The Vole. Marvin Solomon. NePoAm-2

And build his clay dungeons inside the roller blind. A Family Photograph 1939. James Keir Baxter. OxBC

And build my nest on the nearest tree! Rus in Urbe. Clement Scott. HBV 1-2

And build our crude villages under the frown/Of friendlier hills, where the vultures eat vegetables The Poets. David Wevill. PP

And build the new world in your eyes, Save it! Mantis. Louis Zukofsky. PoA

And build their anger, stone on stone–/Each silently, but not alone. In Time of Crisis. Raymond Richard Patterson. IDB

And build their secret nests/In his fluttering winding-sheet. Elegy. Leonard Cohen. HeIP

And builds a Hell in Heaven's despite. The Clod and the Pebble. William Blake. AWP; BoLiVe; CABA; EBCP; EnLoPo; FaBV; InPS; LoBV; NOBE; NoP; OBEC; OBNC; OBSP; PAI; PrIm; SCV; TEP; TrGrPo; ViBoPo

And builds the grudge of kinship/under quiet blue slopes. Brevard Fault. Robert Morgan. SUW

And built him a monument/When he was dead. Old Mother Hubbard. *Anonymous.* HBV 1-2; HBVY; OnMSP; OxNR

And built the nest in the rock! I Am the Mountainy Singer. Joseph Campbell. AnIL; GoBC; HBMV; MCCG; MoBrPo

And Buragh under Stanemiur there dwels Dickie. Dick O the Cow. *Anonymous.* BaBo; ESPB; OxBB

And buried him where he fell. Vigil Strange I Kept on the Field One Night. Walt Whitman. LoBV; MoAmPo; NOBA; NoP; OBWP; PeHV; TAP; WaaP; WHA

And burn me, O Lord, with a fiery zeal/Of Thee and Thy House, which doth in eating heal. Holy Sonnets, V. John Donne. MyFE; TEP

And burn men's hearts with this, my Word. The Prophet. Alexander Pushkin. AWP; EaLo; LiTW; WGRP

And burn thee' up, as well as I. To the Rose. Robert Herrick. HBV 1-2; OBS; SeCP

And burn with fire whose source I cannot trace. Sonnets: A Sequence on Profane Love. George Henry Boker. AmePo

And burn with fury through his age. Spring Burning. Patrick Roland. PeSA

And burned a doughnut/on my lawn. Four Translations from the English of Robert Hershon. Robert Hershon. NeAC

And burning with high hope, shall moulder cold and low. Childe Harold's Pilgrimage: Canto III, XXVII. George Gordon, Lord Byron. AnFE

And burnish gold each throat that pleads/For dawn's encomium. Nimbus. Douglas Le Pan. OBCV; PeCV

And burns a steadfast star to steadfast/eyes. On One Who Died in May. Clarence Chatham Cook. AA

And burnt a hole/In the child's new coat. I'll Tell. *Anonymous.* OxNR

And burnt by adequate objects of desire. The Higher Empiricism. Francis C. Golffing. PoA

And burnt his mouth/With supping cold plum porridge. The Man in the Moon. *Anonymous.* MOON; OxBoLi; OxNR

And burnt in the immortal tiles forever. Ku Li. Robin Hyde. AnNZ

And burst in music, and are seen no more. Coleridge. George Sidney Hellman. AA

And bursten figs won't keep? Figs. D. H. Lawrence. OAEL 1-2

And bury the statue of liberty/(because it begins to smell). Thanksgiving (1956). Edward Estlin Cummings. FaBoPV

And buses charge to the zoological gardens. The Gorilla. Baxter Hathaway. HoAn

And busy biting yet should never let/Thy wretched life, ne do thy death profet. If Thou Wilt Mighty Be. Sir Thomas Wyatt. EnRePo; FCP; SiPS

And but a body all, without a soul. On Writing for the Stage. John, Duke of Buckingham Sheffield. FaBoUs

And but in darkness is she visible. To an Old Lady. William Empson. AtBAP; CoBMV; FaBoTw; GTBS-P; MoAB; MOON; NoAm; NOBE

And but our selves can make us every thing. An Ode in the Praise of Sack. *Anonymous.* OBS

And buttoned her dress/afterwards. Miss Alderman. Robert Winner. GP

And buy molasses candy. Bluebird, Bluebird, Fly Through My Window. *Anonymous.* FSW

And buy our liberty with our last breath. But Two There Are... C. Day-Lewis. OxBI

And buzzings of the honied hours. In Memoriam A.H.H., LXXXIX. Alfred, Lord Tennyson. VLP

And by a chapel as I com. By a Chapel. *Anonymous.* GBP; OxBM

And, by a mighty hand, th' oppressed HE yet shall save! Liberty for All. William Lloyd Garrison. AA; AmePo

And by and by a cloud takes all away! The Two Gentlemen of Verona. William Shakespeare. GBL

And by came a greedy gled,/And snapt him a' away. Robin Redbreast's Testament. *Anonymous.* GBP

And, by God's help, I will. God Forward. A.R. G. BLRP

And by going to the zoo on a Greyhound bus with/Miss Foxx. Aquellos Vatos. Tino Villanueva. FIA

And by grace of "There is no god but God and Muhammad is/His Prophet." May I Be Beautiful. *Anonymous.* WTO

And by her oracles the world shall sway. Oceana and Britannia. John Ayloffe. APAS

And by his all subduing might/Make clay ascend more quick then light. Ascension-Hymn. Henry Vaughan. MeLP; NOCV; SeCeV; SeCV 1-2; TrCP

And by his going he may know his rider. Upon the Horse and Rider. John Bunyan. OxBChV

And, by Jup', you do–that's all. The Commission Man. Robert V. Carr. BPAW

And by misfortune cut them down,/Or they had now been there. Fair Margaret and Sweet William. *Anonymous.* ESPB; OxBB

And by morning the fields were new. Man and Machine. Robert Morgan. Str

And by my breast and brows the airs are riven. Nature. Alfred de Vigny. AWP

And, by my silence, I do prove/Wisdom and Love! Love's Wisdom. Margaret Deland. AA

And by noontide as by midnight make her mine, as hers she/makes me! Earl Mertoun's Song. Robert Browning. HBV 1-2; OBEV; PoPle

And, by one o'clock, he's gone. V. B. Nimble, V. B. Quick. John Updike. CTBA; NYBP

And by summer's end, perhaps ocher wind/Will keep these feathers for an open field. Digging Out the Roots. Duane Niatum. STE

And by swift currents throws off clean/Prolific particles of spleen. In Praise of Water-Gruel. Matthew Green. FaBoUs

And by that bede side there standeth a stone,/Corpus Christi wreten there on. Corpus Christie (A vers.). *Anonymous.* BaBo; EnPo; FaBoBa; GBP; MeEL; NOBE; NoP; OAEL 1-2; OxBM; SCV

And by that cry of her dear Lord obtain/That your sweet sap might come again. The Jews. George Herbert. JCP

And by that light found out. A Light Left On. May Sarton. MoLP

...And by that mean the city clearly freed. The Thirteenth Song. Michael Drayton. SeCePo

And by that ye may very weel ken/They were twa lovers dear. Prince Robert. *Anonymous.* ESPB; OxBB

And by the death within His bones/The dead became alive. Carol: "Mary laid her Child among." Norman Nicholson. NeBP

And by the discovery of His planting and by the thought of/His mind./ Hallelujah. Solomon: To Truth. *Anonymous.* WGRP

And, by the glow-worm's light well guided,/Goes to the feast that's now provided. The Fairy Temple; or, Oberon's Chapel.... Robert Herrick. CaPo

And, by the laws condemn'd ere long, most justly he will die. Tragic Verses. *Anonymous.* CoMu

And by these I lost my soul, as I sailed. Captain Kidd. *Anonymous.* FSW; MoShBr

And by this ye may ken right weil,/They ware twa luvers deare. Lord Thomas and Fair Annet. *Anonymous.* EnLit; ESPB; FaBoBa; OxBB; ViBoFo

And by thy Gold shew like some Copper-mine. La Gialletta Gallante. Edward, Lord Herbert of Cherbury. AtBAP

And by thy teeth we shall discern/what 'tis a clock, perhaps. Of One That Had a Great Nose. George Turberville. FaBoEE

And by what way shall I go back? L'an Trentiesme de Mon Eage. Archibald MacLeish. AmLP; APA; LiTM; MoVE; NePA; NoAm; NOBA

And C, B, A. And Backwards. *Anonymous.* OxNR

And ca'd it Andrew Turner. On Andrew Turner. Robert Burns. DBV; PV

And Caelia reign the Goddess of mankind. To Caelia. *Anonymous.* FaBoEE

And Cailte wept bitterly. The Place of the Fian Is Bare Tonight. *Anonymous.* NOBI

And Cain meets Abel in his book. Midrash on Hamlet. Francis Landy. VWA

And Caliban, and Lump and I are all agreed. On Two Ministers of State. Hilaire Belloc. PV

And call across the canyon on the trail to Lillooet. The Trail to Lillooet. [(Emily[) Pauline Johnson. CaP

And call across the years. The Welsh Sea. James Elroy Flecker. BrPo

And call her crazed with wrong. The Shadow of Night. Coventry Patmore. CH

And call me when the first birds stir/In the green wood to walk with her. The Old Love. Katharine Tynan Hinkson. HBMV

And call the man a liar who says I wrote/All that I wrote in love, for love of art. A Plea to Boys and Girls. Robert Graves. GTBS-P

And call this other thing, a/foxtail pine. Foxtail Pine. Gary Snyder. CoPo; NaP; NU

And call upon Dobbin with, "Hey, Gee, Ho!" The Brisk Girl. *Anonymous.* UnTE

And call your neighbours in. Crosspatch. *Anonymous.* GBP

And called for some hot buttered toast. Limerick: "There was an Old Man of the Coast." Edward Lear. CenHV; LiBL; MoShBr

And called her his bonny love, Lady Jane. Young Beichan and Susie Pye. *Anonymous.* OnMSP

And called it macaroni. Yankee Doodle. *Anonymous.* OxNR

And called their brother/A shocking bad name. Four Children. *Anonymous.* OxNR

And called their friend, my Father, God. The Cottage. Jones Very. OxBA

And calling Justice, all things burn. Decay. George Herbert. AnAnS 1; SeCP; SeCV 1-2

And calls her wanderd young, the call each banck replies. A Wild Romantic Dell. William Julius Mickle. OBEC

And calls the crows to peck his head. The Eye. Allen Tate. LiTA

And calm my transports with thy song! The Invitation. Thomas Godfrey. AnFE; APA

And calm of mind, all passion spent. Samson Agonistes. John Milton. BoC; EBEV; ExPo; FaBoRV; FiP; MBW 1-2; MyFE; NOBE; OAEL 1-2; OBEV; OBS; PoEL 1-5; SeCeV

...And calmed,/He sinks deep into innocent sleep. Isaac. Barry Holtz. VWA

And calmly responded, "Why, No!" Limerick: "There once was a man who said, 'Oh.'. Carolyn Wells. TDH

And came back/to your senses/like a recharged/robot Butch Is Back. Earl Gene Box. LFAC

And came from a solitary race. Jesse James. *Anonymous.* BeLS; UnPo

And came in laughing. This Morning. Javier Galvez. FF

And came my way no more. A Thought Went Up My Mind. Emily Dickinson. AmP; AnFE; APA; DiPo

And came roaring back down like a rocket! Limerick: "There was an Old Lady named Crockett." William Jay Smith. ShM

And came to burn Lawrence just over the line. Quantrell (I). *Anonymous.* ABF; CoSo

And came to shallow Jordan, where began/The matter of the platter and the sword. John the Baptist. Louis Simpson. NePoEA

And Camelot, and starlit Stonehenge. Channel Firing. Thomas Hardy. BiP; BrPo; CABA; CMoP; CoBMV; EBEV; ExPo; ForPo; HAP; HeIP; InPK; LiTB; MoPo; NIP; NoAm; NoP; OAEL 1-2; OAEP; OxBTC; PoEL 1-5; PoRA; PPON; PrIm; SeCeV; SoSe; UnPo; WaaP

And can be found in practically any magazine/You care to mention. Buy One Now. D. J. Enright. NOBL

And can/Be quite as unreliable/As Man. Experts on Woman. Arthur Guiterman. InMe

And can change/to an ugly stone/in the palm of your hand. Unusual Things. Tom Hennen. FAZ

And can Eternity belong to me,/Poor Pensioner on the bounties of an Hour? Night. Edward Hilton Young. OBEC; SeCePo

And can not see myself as once I was. Dedication of a Mirror. Plato. LiTW

...And/can think of nothing to say. Reaching the Horizon. Robert Mezey. NaP

And candles for a birthday's sake? A Birthday. Rachel Field. BiCB; SiSoSe; TiPo

And cannot drink or cannot rise. Epigram. Eugene Field. ALV

And cannot reach, a heart that hath got wings. Of Life and Death (excerpt). Henry Vaughan. FaBoRV

And capture another Dean of Jaen/And sell him in Algiers. A Dutch Picture. Henry Wadsworth Longfellow. EtS; ExPo; HBVV; MoShBr

And Cardiff cliffs obscured Ramillia's field. Abigail's Lamentation for the Loss of Mr. Harley... William Walsh. APAS

And cardinal flowers/Stand in their sylvan bowers. To the Maiden in the East. Henry David Thoreau. OxBA

And careless pass him by whose is the gift divine. Genius Loci. Margaret Louisa Woods. HBV 1-2; OBEV; OBVV

And caressing church tight breasts. Conversion. Geof Hewitt. NeAC

And Carol ran back to class/her underwear/lying on the pavement. Carol Took Her Clothes Off. Bill Messenger. CTBA

And carried 'em there in an after year. The Country Wedding. Thomas Hardy. UnPo

...And carrots/With the tops and mould still fresh on them. Triptych. Seamus Heaney. CIP

And carry away the song. The Unfailing One. Phillips Brooks. BLRP

And carry it all day, and sweeten it. The Close Clan. Mark Van Doren. GoYe

And carry that bread past your door,/Singing a sweet carol. In the Far Years. Wilson MacDonald. CaP

And carry the good king's daughter/Over the one-strand river. Grey Goose and Gander. *Anonymous.* GBP; PBBP

And carry the marks of the widow's old broom. The Widow's Old Broom. *Anonymous.* AmFP

And carrying always a private bucket of sand. Thank you. The Inflammable Woman. James Keir Baxter. OxBC

And carter-like comes whistling along/Our casual Anglian train. Departure. Edmund Charles Blunden. OBSP

And carved before his father when at table. The Canterbury Tales: A Squire. Geoffrey Chaucer. TrGrPo

And cases of green eye liner. From the Window of the Beverly Wilshire Hotel. Michael McClure. EAS

And, cast by conscience out, spendsavour salt? The Candle Indoors. Gerard Manley Hopkins. DiPo; FaBoMo; LiTB; LiTM; OxBoCh; PoEL 1-5

And cast her anchors in the pools of gold. The Ship. Lloyd Mifflin. AA

And cast her reeking fragments on the air. Fragment from the Elizabethans. W. Bridges-Adams. FaBoCo

And cast my selfe off, as I ne're had beene. Bussy d'Ambois. George Chapman. PoEL 1-5

And cast out the soul. Matrix (excerpt). Dorothy Wellesley. OBMV

And cattle stand and stare. Ducks. Phoebe Hesketh. BoAnP

And caught in the act. Meditation. Carl Rakosi. AMV-80

And caught/Its shadow/On the flypaper of my tongue. The Story. Charles Simic. NNaP

...And cause them slide/According as his will is. The Spouse to the Younglings. William Baldwin. OBSP

And ceases, in the heart, to be. The Panther. Rainer Maria Rilke. LiTW; NU; PoPl

And Cecily Roumeli came to this nation/With William the Norman, and laid its foundation. The Lay of St. Cuthbert (excerpt). Richard Harris Barham. NBM

And celestial flowes/Will follow after/On that water,/Which thy spirit blowes! Midnight. Henry Vaughan. OAEP

And cellophane shall wrap the heretic. Saturday Sundae. F. R. Scott. CaP

And center there, are better than gold. Better Than Gold. Abram Joseph Ryan. FaFP; PoToHe

And central peace, subsisting at the heart/Of endless agitation. The Excursion. William Wordsworth. GoTF; WGRP

And–certain keels for whose return the heathen look in vain. Epitaphs of the War, 1914-18. Rudyard Kipling. OBWP

And certainly she was not beautiful. In the Backs. James Kenneth Stephen. NOBV

And certes often like Sir Philip Francis. At the Gate of Heaven. George Gordon, Lord Byron. OBRV

And chairs of the office, should/It come between nine and five. Where I Am Now. Harvey Shapiro. GP

And challenge all the spaces of the sun. Out-of-Doors. Robert Whitaker. TrPWD

And chancellors, who nothing know at all. Against Education. Charles Churchill. TW

And change his soul for harmony. In Commendation of Music. William Strode. ELP; OBEV

And change the green lilacs to the red, white and blue. Green Grow the Lilacs. *Anonymous.* FSW

And changed in a moment go shouting away/To mansions of love in the skies. Death-Bed Song. *Anonymous.* AmFP

...And changeful Time/Sees him at will keep measure with his flight,/At will outstrip it. Poets. Mark Akenside. OBEC

And chant him a blessing, a sutra. What For. Garrett Kaoru Hongo. MAYP

And chants of victory amid the encircling hounds. Hound Voice. William Butler Yeats. SyP

And Chaos bids ten thousand spears/run to erase our straw-built folly. Our Love Was a Grim Citadel. R. A. K. Mason. AnNZ

And charge but a penny. Black Your Honour's Shoes? *Anonymous.* OxNR

And charge you not one shilling. The Five Best Doctors. O. S. Hoffman. PoToHe

And charged this very vital spark/To jump his mortal coil. Elegy on Thomas Hood (parody). Martin Fagg. FaBoPa

And charity our language prove/Derived from thee, O God of love? All-Knowing God, 'Tis Thine to Know. *Anonymous.* AH

And chase night's gloom, as thou the spirit's grief. Gracious Moonlight. Dante Gabriel Rossetti. MaVP

And chateau childhoods prisoned in the bell/of dark, held back excited by the urns. Sestina in Time of Winter. Patrick Anderson. PoA

And chatters wondrous things to me. My Little Neighbor. Mary Augusta Mason. AA

And cheat me with thy false delight,/Most Holy Night. The Night. Hilaire Belloc. HBV 1-2; OBEV; OBVV

And check the tear (if tear should start)/Too precious for dull clay. Fate! I Have Asked. Walter Savage Landor. ViBoPo

And cheer for him whose work is done. My Son. James D. Hughes. BLPA

And cheer his heart in many a lonely hour. Acadia (excerpt). Joseph Howe. CaP

And cheer my mind in sorrow. Yarrow Visited. William Wordsworth. EnLi 1-2; GTBS; GTBS-P; HBV 1-2

And cheer our hearts, Celestial Love! The Ransomed Spirit to Her Home. William B. Tappan. AH

And cherries overhead! Picnic Day. Rachel Field. SiSoSe; SoPo; TiPo

And Chesterfield the Elder. Anonymous Reply to the Above. *Anonymous.* FaBoEE

And chewed, and grinned quite amiably. Steam Shovel. Charles Malam. NTCP

And chews time like a white rabbit. Old Woman Awaiting the Greyhound Bus. Duane Niatum. CDW

And childhood's flower must waste its bloom/Beneath the shadow of the tomb. I Saw Thee, Child, One Summer's Day. Emily Bronte. VLP

And children at rest at their mothers' breast/Started, and scream'd with fear. The Old Woman of Berkeley. Robert Southey. OBRV

And children clap at the incense of small fires The Invention of Fire. Andrew Taylor. CBAP

And children must fear them–ahe, ahe, ee, ee, iee. The Wind Has Wings. *Anonymous.* GrPl; WHW

And children play in the street? The Cottage Hospital. Sir John Betjeman. GTBS-P; MoBrPo; MoVE; NOBE; UnPo

And children play with me. Riddle: "I come more softly than a bird." Mary Austin. SoPo; TiPo

And children swarmed to him like settlers. He became a land. Edward Lear. W. H. Auden. InvP

And chiseled generations/from ancient memories. Grandfathers. Dennis Shady. LFAC

And choked. What a sad afterMATH. Limerick: "A mathematician named Bath." J. F. Wilson. TDH

And choosing this, thou hast in fee/The peace of God. A Benedictine Garden. Alice Brown. HBV 1-2

And chopped off his head with a shubble. Limerick: "There was an old man said, 'I fear.'". Walter De la Mare. TDH

And Christ ain't a going to be too hard/On a man that died for men. Jim Bludso of the Prairie Belle. John Milton Hay. AA; AnAmPo; BBV; FaBoBe; FaFP; HBV 1-2; MaC; MCCG; PaPo; TreFS; YaD

And Christ be with me on the Judgment Day. Endpiece. *Anonymous.* KiLC

And Christ comes with a January flower. Advent. Patrick Kavanagh. FaBoIP

And Christ gave up the Ghost? The Bomber. Robert Lowell. WaaP

And Christ Himself doth rule. Resignation. Henry Wadsworth Longfellow. TRV

And Christ is risen to-day! Easter Carol. George Newell Lovejoy. OHIP; PGD

And Christ shall wield His sceptre,/Our Lord and God for aye. Great and Mighty Wonder. Saint Anatolius. CAW

And Christ, the flower of all. Noel. Richard Watson Gilder. AA

And Christian light, the Gothic thunder rolling. The Lunar Tides. Marya Zaturenska. MOON

And chuckled in his wooden heart, that ancient Willow tree. The Willow-Man. Juliana Horatia Ewing. OxBChV

And Cibber's Opera from Johnny Gay's. Time's Changes. James Bramston. OBEC

And Cinderella sleeps content beside/The kind and well-adjusted cobbler. Beth Appleyard's Verses. Peter DeVries. OBAL

And cipher verses on an abacus? The New Castalia. William Hayes Ward. AA

And cires, "It shall be done, sometime, somewhere!" Sometime–Somewhere. Ophelia Guyon Browning. BLRP; STF

And civilize it as well as they can. Body's Head: Head Itself. Laura Riding Gottschalk. PoA

And claim God's kiss. The Dead Heroes. Isaac Rosenberg. MoBrPo

And claim him as a trusted friend! The Sincere Man. Alfred Grant Walton. PoToHe

And claim the crown, through Christ, my own. Free Grace. Charles Wesley. NOCV

And claim we're charitable/And tax-exempt? M.A.P. Calvin Forbes. MAYP

And claimed it was mind/Over Matterhorn. High Brow. Robert Fitch. SD

And clangs the door upon the wolf outside. The Gulistan. Muslih-ud-Din Sa'di. AWP

And clap your PADLOCK–on her Mind. An English Padlock. Matthew Prior. CEP; OBEC

And clarity is but an edge/To the great weighted blade. Art and Civilization. Robert Conquest. NoAm

And clasp'd them sobbing, to his aching breast. Eliza. Erasmus Darwin. PaPo

And clasped their children in the shadowy rooms. Before Salamis. W. B. Stanford. NeIP

And classic bronze of Benin. A Different Image. Dudley Randall. BPo; CNA; FF; NoAm; TAP

And clerk and forcman, peddler and grocer, are in our/Family of God! Saturday Night. James Oppenheim. HBV 1-2

And clift his hart in sonder. O My Harte is Wo. *Anonymous.* AtBAP

And climb, to find,/Within, their nests. The Skull in the Desert. Alison A. Trimpi. AMV-81

And clip his wings, and break his glass,/And keep him ever by 'em. Three Songs. Francis Beaumont. GoBC

And close again the long unopened door. In a Garret. Elizabeth Akers Allen. AA

And, close confin'd to their own palace, sleep. Most Souls, 'Tis True, but Peep Out Once an Age. Alexander Pope. ELU

And close her fist. A Grief Ago. Dylan Thomas. AtBAP

And close his eyelids with thy silver wand! Ode to the Moon. Thomas Hood. OBVV

And close our eyes, still smiling, on the/dance. A Minuet on Reaching the Age of Fifty. George Santayana. BLPL; FaFP; HBMV

And close the evening of Life's wretched day. To Cordelia. Joseph Stansbury. CaP; NOBC

(And close your eyes) For Prodigal Read Generous. Edward Estlin Cummings. NoAm

And closed her up as in a tomb. The Funeral Rites of the Rose. Robert Herrick. AnAnS 2; CABA; CaPo; OBEV

And closed in with lisses of strong piles. A War Song. Bertrand. CTC

And clothe thee in a lion's skin. To a Gnat. *Anonymous.* UnTE

And clothe thee too in scarlet red,"/Said Dame Gunild. Ravngard and Memering. *Anonymous.* BaBo

And clothe us with the Spirit's might/For grander work below.   The Chosen Three, on Mountain Height.   David H. Ela.   AH

And clouded all the altar with soft smoke.   The Fall of Hyperion.   John Keats.   OBRV

And cloudless, soft, serene as May,/Opened the jocund day.   Lost in a Norther.   Hamlin Garland.   BPAW

And cluck your children in about your knee?   Sonnet to Gath.   Edna St. Vincent Millay.   BoWoP; CMoP; MoAB; MoAmPo

And clumsy sailors tumble in.   The Sea.   *Anonymous.*   NA

And clustering lilies spring up in His path.   The Christ-Child.   Saint Gregory of Narek.   CAW

And clutch at the bedclothes afraid to die?   Sonnet 21.   Paul Goodman.   VGW

And coach and wheelbarrow I carve in my stall,/Making things with no troubles in them.   The Toy-Maker.   Padraic Colum.   SaC

And, coarsely clad in Norwich drugget, came/To teach the nations in thy greater name...   MacFlecknoe, or a Satire upon the True-Blue Protestant Poet T.S.   John Dryden.   CoBE

And coaxed all growing things to greet/With gracious garb the May.   While April Rain Went By.   Shaemas O'Sheel.   HBMV

And cock-a-doo, a-doodle-doo!/Will be his epitaph for you.   Song for a Proud Relation.   Patrick MacDonogh.   OnYI

And cold as any icicle.   Parting, without a Sequel.   John Crowe Ransom.   DTC; LiTL; MoAB; MoAmPo; MoVE; OxBA; SoSe

...And coldy mounts the moon/Of thought, and rules among the quorum of the dead.   Song for War.   W. R. Rodgers.   NeBP

And collect the strange runes/that fall from their dreaming mouths.   The Collector.   Richard Behm.   AMV-81

And columbine.   And Can the Physician Make Sick Men Well.   *Anonymous.*   AtBAP; ELP

And Columbus and the two sons died.   The Experiment That Failed.   John Logan.   NU

And combining Stern Duty with Pleasure.   Two Smiles.   Oliver Herford.   PV

And come and be my guest,–for I am Love's.   Epipsychidion.   Percy Bysshe Shelley.   EnRP; ERoP 1-2

And come home to a woman saying honey.   Untitled Poem.   Alan Dugan.   GP

And come no more a wasselling/Until another year.   Wassail Song.   *Anonymous.*   GBP

And come out of my grave and bear the awful eyes.   He Loves and He Rides Away.   Sydney Thomas Dobell.   OBNC

And come unto my courtship as my prayer.   A Devout Lover.   Thomas Randolph.   EG; HBV 1-2; HoPM; LiTL; OBEV

And come, with terrible silence in your eyes,/To that dim monument where Tybalt lies.   In That Dim Monument Where Tybalt Lies.   Arthur Davison Ficke.   HBMV

And come–you will come? to Commem.   A Letter.   Sir Arthur Thomas ("Q") Quiller-Couch.   CenHV

And comes from a country far away as health.   Tulips.   Sylvia Plath.   HAP; NaP; NoP; NYBP; PPP

And comes to put my native fire to proof.   The Winter House.   Norman Cameron.   CBEP

And comfort us like the fingers of rain.   The Death Watchers.   Alice Ryerson.   AMV-80

And comfortless, and stormy round!   My Birth-Day.   Thomas Moore.   HBV 1-2

And coming the proud over all o' the birds o' the sea.   Sea-Change.   John Masefield.   AtBAP; FaBoTw; MOS; OBMV

And commerce fill our purses.   Convention Song.   *Anonymous.*   PAH

And complete the creation.   Our Lady.   Robert Bridges.   ISi

...And complex hungers/crashing on the high white beaches of the world.   Sea Things.   Gwendolyn MacEwen.   FaBoWP

And concluded the banquet by––   The Voice of the Lobster.   Lewis (Charles Lutwidge Dodgson) Carroll.   EvOK

And conferme fully up my choise ay from yere to/yere.   A Lover's New Year's Gift.   John Lydgate.   PoEL 1-5

And confident thou'lt raise me with the just.   His Metrical Prayer: Before Execution.   James Graham.   OxBS; PrIm

And conquer fortune, fate and destiny strange.   A Prayer Brings Rain.   Edward Fairfax.   OBSC

And conquer peace for Dixie!   Dixie.   Albert Pike   AA; MC

And consolation for their sorrow found.   The Parish Register.   George Crabbe.   EnPE; OAEL 1-2; OBRV

And consonance sublime amid confusion hears.   To Haydn.   Thomas Holcroft.   NOEC

And constantly a while must keepe his/bed.   Satire.   John Donne.   OAEP

And consummation comes, and jars two hemispheres.   The Convergence of the Twain.   Thomas Hardy.   BiP; BrPo; CoBMV; FaBoTw; HeIP; InPK; InPo; InPS; LiTB; LiTM; MoAB; MoBrPo; MoPo; MOS; MoVE; NoAm; NoP; OAEL 1-2; OAEP; OxBTC; PeD; PrIm; SeCeV; TEP

...And content/with the lilt of sunlight in their bones.   Hymn to the Sea.   Michael Roberts.   OxBTC

And contented with shellocks I live on half pay./With me kerry-ay-ay, fa la de ral lay.   The Kerry Recruit.   *Anonymous.*   FSW

And continued to knock him about.   Limerick: "There was an old man who screamed out."   Edward Lear.   EBEV; NOBV

And convenience such as ten poor Jewish mammas/could not hope to give him.   Ancestors.   Harold Schimmel.   VWA

And cool the black sun/Of a savage, insomniac, passion.   Phaedra.   Osip Mandelstam.   OBVE

And coolly then would flow through heart and brain/Respect for life again.   Eagles Over the Lambing Paddock.   Ernest G. Moll.   PoAu 1-2

And cope of stars re-echoed the same.   The Angels.   William, of Hawthornden Drummond.   HBV 1-2

And Corruption shrunk scorch'd from the glance of his/mind.   George the Fourth in Ireland.   George Gordon, Lord Byron.   OBRV

And cou'd not bear the Burd'n of a class.   The Hind and the Panther.   John Dryden.   OBS

And could have of a cat but her skin, skin, skin.   The Little Man and the Little Maid.   *Anonymous.*   OxNR

And could lift stones, and comprehend in the praises the cruelties of life.   Ante Mortem.   Robinson Jeffers.   MoAmPo; MoVE

And could no longer recollect my name.   Epigram: "Good Fortune, when I hailed her recently."   J. V. Cunningham.   PV

And could not should as he had broken the even tenour of her/ways.   Poems, XI.   Philip O'Connor.   EAS

And couldn't write.   A Bookshop Idyll.   Kingsley Amis.   NePoEA

And couldst not fall but with thy country's fate.   Upon the Death of the Earl of Dundee.   John Dryden.   ACP

And count the bell, and tremble lest I hear/(My work untrimmed) the sunset gun too soon.   The Morning Drum-Call on My Eager Ear.   Robert Louis Stevenson.   NOBV

And count the long night by the stroke of their hearts.   The Heroes.   Louis Simpson.   NePoAm; OBWP

And counterfeit mortality.   The Recurrence.   Edwin Muir.   MoPo

And countless butterfly!   A science–so the savans say.   Emily Dickinson.   ImOP

And countless fiends laughed loud and cried/"Amen!"   Im Traum Sah Ich Ein Mannchen Klein Und Putzig.   Heinrich Heine.   AWP

And counts it/as part of the/pattern of things.   The End Bit.   Jim Burns.   FF

And counts, perhaps, the days to Michaelmas.   Charles at the Siege.   George Hetherington.   AnIV

And court the vapoury God soft-breathing in the Wind.   The Sons of Indolence.   James (1700-48) Thomson.   OBEC

And cow pats–and inconsequent wild roses.   Woods.   Louis MacNeice.   FaBoIP

And cows awake.   To Myself, Late, in a Myrtle Grove.   Robert Peterson.   NeAC

And coy perdition every hour pursue.   The Dangers of Sexual Excess.   John Armstrong.   FaBoUs

And coyne to kepe as water in a syve.   A Spending Hand That Alway Powreth Owte.   Sir Thomas Wyatt.   AAS

And Coyote out collecting/dream chips along the shore.   Three Songs to Mark the Night.   Judith Mountain Leaf Volborth.   TWSS

And crack hazel-nuts/With a five-farthing beetle.   The People of Blakeney.   *Anonymous.*   GBP

And cradle me my Destiny.   You Masks of the Masquerade.   Gustave Kahn.   TrJP

And crashing spreads in ruin o'er the tides.   The Shipwreck.   William Falconer.   GoTL; MOS; OBEC

And craven White, to tell the wrong/A prudent nation bore.   The Gospel of Peace.   James Jeffrey Roche.   PAH

And crawled all the way back to El Paso   The Encounter.   Paul Blackburn.   NeAP

And creeps off into darkness,/smoking an orange.   The President Slumming.   James Tate.   OBAL

And crept into his grave when he was dead.   Saint.   Robert Graves.   CMoP

...And crews with/chain saws and representatives of the paper company.   Library.   Louis Jenkins.   NU

And crie, O Love, O death, O vaine desire,/When thou complainst the heate, and feeds the fire.   Feed Still Thyself.   Sir Walter Ralegh.   NCEP

And cried and cried No No No No/All day long.   Counting the Mad.   Donald Justice.   ConAP; FF; NePoEA; NIP; PPON; UnPo

And cried, "The expense is infolonel!"   Limerick: "A distinguished old one-legged colonel."   *Anonymous.*   TDH

And cries at the blood of his own life.   Three Prison Portraits: The Drug Addict.   Miriam Waddington.   ACV

And cries, "It shall be done sometime, somewhere."   Pray Without Ceasing.   Ophelia Guyon Browning.   BLPA; BLPL

And cries of love are cries of fear. Song for a Birth or a Death. Elizabeth Jennings. EBEV

And cries that Love is lovely–isn't it? Cobweb. Winifred Welles. AnAmPo

And cringe in the town. Lineage. Robert Farren. CoBE

And croodling shepherds bend along/Crouching to the whizzing storms The Shepherd's Calendar. John Clare. NCEP

And cross at Shawnee ferry/To the State of El-a-noy. El-A-Noy (with music). Anonymous. AS

And cross the world–/To see the cross at Christmas. To See the Cross at Christmas. Roger Cooper. TrCP

And crossed the threshold, and kindled the fire. Home. Wilfrid Gibson. HBMV

And crow, it's already/morning. Aube Provencale. Marilyn Hacker. AmPA

...And crowded with gesticulating poetesses. Poems, I. Philip O'Connor. EAS

And crown Him Lord of all! Coronation. Edward Perronet. BLSO; HBV 1-2; TreFs; WGRP

And crown my soul with the higher Trinity. Christmas Now Is Drawing Near. Anonymous. OBET

And crown my winding banks with many an anademe. Poly-Olbion. Michael Drayton. FaBoPP

And crown the fight. The Last Round. Anna Wickham. MoBrPo

And crown thy good with brotherhood/From sea to shining sea! America the Beautiful. Katharine Lee Bates. BLPA; EaLo; FaBoBe; FaBV; FaFP; FSW; GoTF; HBMV; HBVY; MC; MCCG; PAL; TAP; TreF; WBLP; WGRP; YaD

And crown with love my ever-during night. My Sweetest Lesbia. Thomas Campion. AAS; AtBAP; AWP; BiP; ElL; FF; GBL; HAP; HeIP; InPS; LoBV; NIP; NoP; OAEL 1-2; PoRA; PrIm; TEP; TrGrPo; UnTE

And crowned him with death's immortelles. Laurels and Immortelles. Anonymous. BLPA

And crush the spring leaf with your armies! In the Trenches. Richard Aldington. MMM

And crushed by feet in the yellow grass. Autobiography. Sonja Akesson. BoWoP

And crushed by remonstrance. Seven Stanzas at Easter. John Updike. EaLo; EBCP; TrCP

And crushed out Grendel's loathsome kin. Beowulf: The Fire-Dragon and the Treasure. Anonymous. AnOE

And crushed within a broken heart/That God bends low to hear. Praise. Edith Daley. TRV

And cry again melodious to the morn! Memnon. Clinton Scollard. AA

And cry against thee unto God. Aguinaldo. Bertrand Shadwell. PAH

And cry for love, and hear no answer. The Deaths at Paragon, Indiana. John Woods. CoPo

And cry, O hone! O hone!/For England hath its own. Lines on Swift's Ancestors. Alexander Pope. FaBoCo

And cry–"You stranger, you damned stranger!" For an Emigrant. Randall Jarrell. OxBA

And cuff the cliffs with Pinions not their own. The Aeneid. Virgil (Publius Vergilius Maro). OBVE

And cup my mouth on the gash of everything I craved,/And am ravaged with joy. The Gash. William Everson. GP

And Cupid's self about her fluttered all in green. May. Edmund Spenser. GN

And Cupids yoke the doves. Few Happy Matches. Isaac Watts. NOEC

And cure, and cure, all your ills, and cure your ills. Army Bugle Calls: Sick Call. Anonymous. TreF

And cured that Old Person of Prague. Limerick: "There was an old person of Prague." Edward Lear. EBEV

And cured the poor girl of her life. A Hawthorne Garland. Richard Harter Fogle. OBAL

And curl forever in some far-off farmyard flower. Beehive. Jean Toomer. IDB; PoBA; TTY

And curly cabbages, and add them too. Gourds. Nicander. FaBoUs

...And currents mark'd,/Which drive the heedless vessel from her course. British Commerce. John Dyer. OBEC

And curs'd for ever this victorious day. Ombre at Hampton Court. Alexander Pope. OBEC

And curse her yellow teeth with this. Zimmer's Head Thudding against the Blackboard. Paul Zimmer. PCP

And curse the heritage that we bequeath. The Dead. Mathilde Blind. OBVV; SBG; WGRP

And curse the moon and fear the rising of the sun. The Wheel. Robert Earl Hayden. BPo

And cursed th'access of that celestial thief. A Vision Upon This Conceipt of the Faerie Queene. Sir Walter Ralegh. CoBE; EnLi 1-2; EnLit; OBSC

And curses the old snagger with the blue-bellied "joe". Click Go the Shears, Boys. Anonymous. PoAu 1-2

And custom for the spreading laurel tree. A Prayer for My Daughter. William Butler Yeats. BLPL; CABA; CMoP; CoBMV; HAP; LiTB; LiTM; LoBV; MasP; MoAB; MoRP; NAs; NoAm; NoP; OxBTC; PoA; PoLf; PrIm; TEP; TW; ViBoPo

And cut them and gave them to me/in my hand. The Act. William Carlos Williams. ELU; SOTW; VGW

And cut thy heart in two,–/And then die, weeping you. Love-In-Idleness. Thomas Lovell Beddoes. LiTL; ViBoPo

And Cynthia gave what she for years/Had foolishly denied. Against Modesty in Love. Matthew Prior. ErPo

...And cypresses/From Ida waiting for dissever'd friends. Helen and Corythos. Walter Savage Landor. LoBV

And daily seek the hospitable feast,/Strewed to invite thee on the casement ledge. The Favourite Village (excerpt). James Hurdis. PBBP

And dainty dancing demoiselles/Above the dreamless dead. The Dancers. Wilfred Wilson Gibson. MMM

And daisies burn like stars on the darkened hill. Senlin. Conrad Aiken. LOW

...And Damballah, kind father,/sew up/her bleeding hole. Crow Jane. LeRoi (Imamu Amiri Baraka) Jones. PoM

And dammit, that's just what/I've gone and done.' Hay for the Horses. Gary Snyder. ConAP; CTBA; GrPl; InPS; NaP; PAI

...And damn/To tedious Hell this body with its muddy feet in my mind! Menses. Edna St. Vincent Millay. NMM

And damn your soul alive. The Song Against Songs. Gilbert Keith Chesterton. ALV

And damned be he who first cries "miracle." We Still Must Follow. E. L. Mayo. AMV-81

And dance again when trumpets blow. Epilogue for a Masque of Purcell. Adrienne Rich. NYBP

And dance and flute will cease. Song: "The gross sun squats above." Dom Moraes. NePoEA-2

And dance, and revell then, as we doe now. In Answer of an Elegiacall Letter upon the Death of the King of Sweden. Thomas Carew. AnAnS 2

And dance and sing all the night. Harry Parry. Anonymous. GBP; OxNR

And dance like a wave of the sea. The Fiddler of Dooney. William Butler Yeats. DiPo; FaBoCh; LoGBV; NLV; OBVV; PoPle; TiPo; UnS

And dance to th' music of your chains. The Vintage to the Dungeon. Richard Lovelace. CaPo; SeCV 1-2

And dance to the bag-pipes and beating of the drum. My Hobby Horse. Anonymous. OxNR

And dance with fire about the ships. Nude with Green Chair. Antony Oldknow. AMV-81

And dance with me in Ireland. I Am of Ireland. William Butler Yeats. LiTB; NAMP; OnYI

And danced on earth again, O! Us Idle Wenches. Anonymous. PoPle

And danced, unimagined and free,/Like the sun taking place on the sea. The Island. James Dickey. SM

And dances with the daffodils. Daffodils. William Wordsworth. AnFE; BLPA; FaBoBe; FaBV; FaFP; FiP; FPL; GN; GoJo; GoTF; GTBS; GTBS-P; LiTB; MCCG; NOBE; OBEV; OBNC; OHFP; PPoe; SCV; SeCeV; TreF; TrGrPo; WBLP

And dandelion-seed under the ground. The Moon in Your Hands. Hilda ("H. D.") Doolittle. BoWoP; NYBP

And dare I think it is absurd/If no such beast were, no such bird? Somewhere Is Such a Kingdom. John Crowe Ransom. CMoP; LiTA

And dare to take command. A Little Kingdom I Possess. Louisa May Alcott. AH

And dared not ask her why. The Flower of Flame (excerpt). Robert Nichols. OBMV

And dares not clutch what Love was half revealing. Revelation. Sir Edmund Gosse. OBEV; OBVV

And dark thrones totter in the baleful air! Sesostris. Lloyd Mifflin. AA; HBV 1-2

And darken'd sanctities with song. In Memoriam A.H.H., XXXVII. Alfred, Lord Tennyson. VLP

And darkening winter stars. Vain Advice at the Year's End. James Wright. NYBP

And darkness descends on the Department of Justice. Nocturne for the U.S. Congress. Victor Contoski. GP

And darkness everywhere I go. The Blind Man at the Fair. Joseph Campbell. AnIV; AWP

And darkness returns to our eyes. The Youth of Nature: Wordsworth's Country. Matthew Arnold. FaBoPP

And dash the gumlie jaups up to the pouring skies! The Brigs of Ayr. Robert Burns. MCCG

And dashed his beak through the rattlesnake. A California Idyl. Ernest McGaffey. BPAW

And dat'll pacify my min.' When a Woman Blue (with music). Anonymous. AS

And Dature starts her Highlad Flig. Kerchoo! Margaret Fishback. PoSC

And day and night yield one delight once more?   The House of Life.   Dante Gabriel Rossetti.   CTC

And day came crashing through pale judas-bud.   Apparition.   John Peale Bishop.   LiTA; MoVE

And day/Comes up on Rydal mere.   Sunrise on Rydal Water.   John Drinkwater.   HBV 1-2; LiTM

And day is brighter day.   The Stars Are with the Voyager.   Thomas Hood.   EnRP

And Day is More, I saw the melting Dark/Stir to the last, and know she laboured on.   Sonnet: The Common Grave.   Sydney Thomas Dobell.   NCEP

And daylight's seldom seen.   Greenland Whale Fishery.   *Anonymous.*   BaBo; OuSiCo; ViBoFo

..And daylight straddles the world.   Bread Is Born.   Anne Hebert.   BoWoP

And days are doubly full and rich/Since He's not crowded out.   Crowded Out.   Florence White Willett.   STF

And dazzled Reason yields as quite undone.   Your Beauty and My Reason.   *Anonymous.*   TrGrPo

And de bery nex President, will be Zip Coon.   Old Zip Coon (Turkey in the Straw).   Bob Farrell.   TrAS

An' de co'n pone's hot.   When de Co'n Pone's Hot.   Paul Laurence Dunbar.   BANP

An' de God dat lived in Daniel's time is jus' de same today.   He's Jus' de Same Today.   *Anonymous.*   BoAN 1-2

An' de good Lawd know my name.   De Good Lawd Know My Name.   Frank Lebby Stanton.   WBLP

An' de grave is nailed over yo' do'.   Good-By, Mother.   *Anonymous.*   ABF

An' de Hebrew chillum from de fiery furnace,/An' why not every man?   Didn' My Lord Deliver Daniel?   *Anonymous.*   TrAS

An' de lil' brack sheep—is me!   Poor Lil' Brack Sheep.   Ethel M. C. Brazelton.   BLPA

An' de one on de stick she didn't have no name.   Mule Skinner's Song (with music).   *Anonymous.*   AS

An' de slave'll be free/In dese hard times.   Black Soldier's Civil War Chant.   *Anonymous.*   TAP

An' de walls come tumblin' down.   Song: "Joshua fit de battle ob Jerico."   *Anonymous.*   NAMP

And de walls come tumbling down.   Joshua Fit de Battle of Jericho.   *Anonymous.*   BPo; MaC; TAP; TrGrPo

And dead calm in that noble breast/Which heaves but with the heaving deep.   Calm Is the Morn without a Sound.   Alfred, Lord Tennyson.   FaBoRV; ForPo

And dead, he builds it yet.   The Brigade Must Not Know, Sir!   *Anonymous.*   MC; PAH

And dead my life, that wants such lively bliss.   Amoretti, LXXXIX.   Edmund Spenser.   AAS; EG

And dead sea scrolls that were my heart attest/How once I visited your holy land.   The School of Night.   A. D. Hope.   PoA

And dead to hopes of future joy.   The River.   Matthew Arnold.   CBEP

And deal a death/That he nor it/(Nor I) have wit/To comprehend.   The Rabbit-Hunter.   Robert Frost.   GDP; LiSp

And dear I love the lady o' the west.   The Maid o' The West.   John Clare.   OAEL 1-2

And dear it is on summer days/To lie at rest among it.   The Broom Flower.   Mary Howitt.   HBV 1-2

And dear they are, but not so dear.   Shut Out.   Christina Georgina Rossetti.   VLP

And dearer still, as now I feel,/To memory's shadowy moonshine!   Yarrow Revisited.   William Wordsworth.   EnLi 1-2; VLP

And dearer was the mother for the child.   Sonnet to a Friend...   Samuel Taylor Coleridge.   EnRP

And, Dearest Friend, since we must part,/drown night/With hope of day; burdens well borne are/light   His Parting from Her.   John Donne.   CoBE

And death, after all, was only "another room'.   Resurrection of Arp.   A.J.M. Smith.   NOBC

...And death also/can still propose the old labors.   Heroes.   Robert Creeley.   NOBA; NoP; PPP

And death and all we came here to evade.   Obligations.   Jane Cooper.   AmPC; NePoEA-2

And death and torment, rightly understood.   Later Life, VII.   Christina Georgina Rossetti.   LO

And Death awaits us? Rest is but our due.   At the Worst.   Israel Zangwill.   TRV; WGRP

And death be strong, yet love is strong as/death.   Monna Innaminata.   Christina Georgina Rossetti.   VLP

And death beyond, and no hope of a man.   The Midnight Court.   Brian Merriman.   BIrV

And death draws nigh.   The Merchantman.   John Davidson.   OBVV

And death from out the grave replies Amen.   A Solemn Meditation.   Ruth Pitter.   OxBoCh

And death, I know is better than not-to-be.   Snap-Dragon.   D. H. Lawrence.   ErPo

And death i think is no parenthesis   Since Feeling Is First.   Edward Estlin Cummings.   BiP; MoAB; MoAmPo; NoP; PrIm

And Death, if Death must be my Doom,/Shall join my Soul to Thee!   Ode: "How are thy Servants blest, O Lord!"   Joseph Addison.   OBEC; TrPWD

And death is no evil.   Night.   Robinson Jeffers.   AP; AWP; CoBMV; InPo; LiTA; MoAmPo; MoPo; NOBA; OxBA; WHA

And death is no more dead than this/Flower-haunted haze.   What Is Winter?   Edmund Charles Blunden.   ChMP

And death looks like no look at all.   Death's the Classic Look.   John Ciardi.   PoA

And death may come, but loving is divine.   The Curtains Now Are Drawn.   Thomas Hardy.   CMoP

And Death must dig the level where these agree.   Sonnets from the Portuguese, III.   Elizabeth Barrett Browning.   GTBS; OAEP; OBEV; TrGrPo

And Death once dead, there's no more dying then.   Sonnets, CXLVI: "Poor soul, the centre of my sinful earth."   William Shakespeare.   AWP; CAW; DiPo; ExPo; GoBC; GoTF; GTBS; GTBS-P; HBV 1-2; InPo; LiTB; MasP; MyFE; NIP; NOBE; NOCV; OAEL 1-2; OBEV; OBSC; OxBoCh; PoEL 1-5; TreFS; ViBoPo; WHA

And death put an end to his growing.   Daily Growing.   *Anonymous.*   FSW

And, death resembling, equals all.   Song: "Say, lovely dream! where couldst thou find."   Edmund Waller.   CavP

And death shall be no more; death, thou shalt die.   Holy Sonnets, X.   John Donne.   AtBAP; BiP; DiPo; EnRePo; ForPo; HAP; HBV 1-2; HeIP; InPS; JCP; LoBV; MBW 1-2; MeLP; NAWM 1-2; NOBE; NoP; OAEP; OBS; PoEL 1-5; PPoe; PPP; SeCP; TrCP; TRV; ViBoPo

And death shall have no dominion.   And Death Shall Have No Dominion.   Dylan Thomas.   ACV; CMoP; EaLo; ExPo; LiTM; MoAB; MoBrPo; MoRP; MoVE; NeBP; NoAm; OAEP; PPoe; SeCePo

And death shall have no funeral/From shipless sea to sea.   Caged Rats.   Ebenezer Elliott.   EBEV; VLP

And death shall never approach us/In the bosom of the fragrant wood!   My Hope, My Love.   *Anonymous.*   BIrV

And death soon brings a swift relief!   The Yoke.   Ben Kalonymos.   TrJP

And Death takes all of us as one.   The Last Years.   William Henry Davies.   FM

And Death that robbed me of delight/Was but the radiant creature's flight.   A Chrysalis.   Mary Emily Bradley.   AA; HBV 1-2

And Death, the voluptuous, calling.   Prothalamium.   A. J. M. Smith.   CaP

And death this cold, black density of stone.   Rainy Mountain Cemetery.   N. Scott Momaday.   CDW

And Death to some more happy clime/Shall give his undivided time.   The Doomed City.   Edgar Allan Poe.   OBRV

And death was but the birthcry of/the morrow.   Genesis.   Jules Alan Wein.   TrJP

And death were ease to lay their ashes there.   What Was a Cure for Love?   Thomas Godfrey.   AnAmPo

And Death, whenever he comes to me,/Shall come on the wild, unbounded sea!   The Sea.   Barry (Bryan Waller Procter) Cornwall.   GN; GoTF; HBV 1-2; HBVY; TreFS

And death who had the soldier singled/has done the lover mortal hurt.   Vergissmeinicht.   Keith Douglas.   ChMP; FaBoMo; GTBS-P; InPS; NePoEA; OBWP; OxBTC; PAI; SoSe

...And death?/will be but a change of the weather.   Riding Song.   Isidor Schneider.   PG

And deck the broken stones like saxifrage.   She.   Richard Wilbur.   AmPP; ConAP; CoPo; NIP

And decked their lapis-lazuli/With crests as white as hawthorn spray.   May-Day at Sea.   John F. Finerty.   EtS

And decked with flowers from my/tomb,/Shall rise up newly-crowned.   I Believe.   Saul Tchernichovsky.   TrJP

And declare that rebellion no longer shall be!/Jefferson D.!   Jefferson D.   Henry Sylvester Cornwell.   PAH

And dedicate it/To this earth,/To Life.   O Master Masons.   Ernst Toller.   TrJP

And dedicated ourselves/to be unraveling.   The Rhetoric of Langston Hughes.   Margaret Danner.   BlSi; FB

And deep as the hunger/yet to come/of dark sons and daughters.   Answering Dance.   William Pitt Root.   MAYP

And deep repentance drown mine eyes/In undissembled woe.   Look on Him Whom They Pierced, and Mourn.   Isaac Watts.   NOCV

And deep the cavern of the fountain mutters.   A Sunset.   Samuel Taylor Coleridge.   ERoP 1-2; OBSP

And deeper grow the shadows of the hills.   Eclogues.   Virgil (Publius Vergilius Maro).   AWP

And deer bound through my hair.   Long Hair.   Gary Snyder.   NOBA

And defecar on dose goddam guidebook.   Sinaloa.   Earle Birney.   OxBC

And defeated by the raw land/and its wild secret.   October Hill.   R. Wayne Hardy.   LFAC

And deflowered a whole herd of cattle. Limerick: "The heavyweight champ of Seattle." *Anonymous.* OBAL

And Deianira, an imperfect shade,/Retreats in silence as my arc descends. Heracles. Yvor Winters. QFR

And deign to look upon me–/Then let the world end! First Love. *Anonymous.* OLR

...And delighted/by three shades of light/on the windowsill. Three Shades of Light on the Windowsill. Susan Griffin. NPGG

...And delivers/our unhaunted world to the Prince of Darkness! Papermill Graveyard. Ben Belitt. NYBP

And demolition workers putting back the sky. The Empty House. Max Williams. CBAP

And dense with happy blood, dark rainbow bliss in the sea. Whales Weep Not! D. H. Lawrence. CMoP; MOS; NU; PPoe

And depart the chilled island. Thirsty Island. Jim Tollerud. VoR

And despairs day, but for thy volume's light. To the Memory of My Beloved the Author Mr. William Shakespeare... Ben Jonson. AnAnS 2; BoLiVe; EnRePo; GoTL; HAP; HBV 1-2; HeIP; JCP; LiTB; NOBE; NoP; OAEL 1-2; OAEP; OBS; PoEL 1-5; PP; SeCeV; SeCP; SeCV 1-2; TreFS; TrGrPo; ViBoPo; WHA

And detect why the horde we are destroys itself. A Walk in Wurzburg. William Plomer. NYBP

And devil a cat for Monday./Oh Monday, oh Monday.' A Bold Dragoon. *Anonymous.* OBET

And devoured the Father Superior. Limerick: "There was a young monk of Siberia." *Anonymous.* TreFT

And dew-drops glisten,/Laughing on every spray. The Little Red Lark. Alfred Perceval Graves. HBV 1-2

And dewed with dream, her silence flower in song. The Bush (excerpt). Bernard O'Dowd. CBAP; PoAu 1-2

And diamonds and pieces of a hundred rainbows are strown/around. Lake Harvest. Raymond Knister. PeCV

And Dickens doling out the derring-do. Owed to Dickens, 1956. Jan Burroway. NePoAm-2

And did a full somersault. An Historic Moment. William J. Harris. BOLo

And did mischief enough to be called a great man. Lines from Crotchet Castle. Thomas Love Peacock. DBV; PV

And did not dye, but left her body dead. Epitaph. Caecil. Boulstr. Edward, Lord Herbert of Cherbury. SeCP

And did not mean to stay behind/Above an hour or so. A Ballad upon a Wedding. Sir John Suckling. HBV 1-2

And did not return with the birds. The Sisseton Indian Reservation. Richard Lyons. TAT

And did these die that thou mightst bear me Death? Newborn Death. Dante Gabriel Rossetti. MaVP

And did with soft attraction ever draw/Their spirits to the love of freedom's equal law. The Revolt of Islam. Percy Bysshe Shelley. ChRP

And didn't even/need a passport Rib Sandwich. William J. Harris. CNA

And die a martyr to thy love of light. Calvus to a Fly. Turner, Charles Tennyson. FM; NOBV

And die dumb-mad in the breaking-yard. Horses. Rudyard Kipling. BoAnP; PoL

And die ere man can say "Long live the Queen!" Ode to the Human Heart. Laman Blanchard. InMe; NA; NOBL

And die for love as Colin died, as Colin died. The Shepherd's Dirge. George Peele. OBSC

And die in flowers, stinking like a bear? A Night at the Napi in Browning. Richard Hugo. TAT

And die in love and rest. The Madman's Song. John Webster. EIL

And die in the evening/as a curfew breaker/is also for the love of life. The Curfew Breakers. Samuel Chimsoro. WhB

And die scratching it/with a coathanger. Warming Up for the Real Thing. Lee Rudolph. TW

And die unsatisfied–and this is Fate! Fate. Susan Marr Spalding. AA; BBV

...And die without grief or/fear knowing it survives us. Nova. Robinson Jeffers. HAP

And died. The Resurrection. William Edward Taylor. AMV-80

And died, a silent writing down. Dedication. Ralph Gustafson. CaP

And died, content. A Youth in Apparel That Glittered. Stephen Crane. LiTA; NePA

And died for them a martyr's death. A Martyr's Death. Menahem Ben Jacob. TrJP

And died in little swells. The Cherwell Water Lily. Frederick William Faber. CAW; GoBC

And died/in your place/so that you could. To a Christmas Two-Year-Old. Luci Shaw. TrCP

And died of drinking ardent spirits. Tammy Messer. *Anonymous.* FaBoEE

And died of the unworthiness of the world. Don Quixote. Arthur Davison Ficke. HBMV

And died regardless of his fate or fame. My Epitaph. H. J. Daniel. FaBoEE

And died the following June. Rhymes for a Modern Nursery. Paul Dehn. FiBHP

And died with a toothache in his heel. Sam, Sam the butcher man. *Anonymous.* FaFP

And dies a stranger to himself alone. The Choice. John Norris. CavP

And dies between three cannibals. The Fly. Karl Shapiro. MiAP; MoVE; NIP

And dieth towards thee with the dying day! Divided. David Gray. AA

And dig under the straws for a stone/To bruise himself on. The Cruel Falcon. Robinson Jeffers. BiP

And dimity petticoats over her knee. Did You See My Wife? *Anonymous.* OxNR

And dinner will be cold. A Shropshire Lad. Alfred Edward Housman. OAEP

And dip my coffee in bread, and eat some of it. You. Tom Clark. ANYP; EAS

And dip your club three times in fiery answer. Orion. Paul Engle. AnAmPo

And dipping swallows leave tight water rings/Which widen with a motion that is still. Refuge. Hervey Allen. HBMV

And disappeared among the greenery. The Satyr. James Stephens. OnYI

And disappeared/in silence/to the left. The Descent of Winter (Section 10/30). William Carlos Williams. InPK

And disappointed pedants stalk'd away. A Critical Fribble. Charles Churchill. OBEC

And discontent that casts a shadow gray/On all the brightness of the common day. These Are the Gifts I Ask. Henry Van Dyke. FaBoBe; TreFT

And disembodied bones. The Eagle and the Mole. Elinor Wylie. AnFE; APA; AWP; BoLiVe; BoWoP; HBMV; LiTA; LiTM; MoAB; MoAmPo; PG; TreFT; UnPo; ViBoPo; WHA

And dish water gives back no images. No Images. Waring Cuney. AmNP; BANP; CDC; GoSl; MAT; TTY

And disregard/of all commands. Every Day. Ingeborg Bachmann. BoWoP

And distant lands, as real and near to the inhabitants of them/as my land is to me. Salut Au Monde! Walt Whitman. AtBAP; SUS

And div'st, near drowning, for what's vanished. Satire. John Donne. OBSV

And dive off in my grave like the old swimmin'-hole. The Old Swimmin'-Hole. James Whitcomb Riley. BeLS; FaFP; HBV 1-2

And dizzy height/Of utmost worship, where it seems/Too still for dreams. Woodland Worship. Ethelwyn Wetherald. CaP

"And do fish bite? The horrid things! Indeed, I'll not catch/one!" Timid Hortense. Peter Newell. NA

And do not doubt, your friend/will come to claim it in the end. The Fisherman Writes a Letter to the Mermaid. Joan Aiken. WSC

And do not even know the places to fish? Photograph of My Father in His Twenty-Second Year. Raymond Carver. WOLT

And do not flow over like you or like me. The Jugs. Paul Celan. OBVE

And do not forget to scratch on them/The name of old Rosin, the Beau. Old Rosin the Beau. *Anonymous.* BLSo; CoSo; FSW

And do not know how far away you are. Suburban Wife's Song. Robert Hutchinson. NYBP

And do not make it strong. The Poets at Tea. Barry Pain. Par

And do not mind it if I cry/Passing my mother's bed. The Whisperer. Mark Van Doren. AnFE; CoAnAm; MoAmPo; UnTE

And do not shrink from sorrow's keenest wind. Weak Is the Will of Man, His Judgment Blind. William Wordsworth. EnRP

And do not weep a woodland-in-the-little. Wild Cherry. Louise Townsend Nicholl. NePoAm

And do the sort of things that I/Have read about in books. Adventures. Arthur Kramer. BiCB

And do their best to kill you. A Bestiary. Kenneth Rexroth. OBAL

And do to me as ye would be done to. Aeneid. Virgil (Publius Vergilius Maro). GoTS

And do we feel discouraged? We do not think we do! Manila. Eugene Fitch Ware. FiBHP; InMe; PV; YaD

And does another thousand start again? The Mahratta Ghats. Alun Lewis. OBTV

And does not care to learn the rest. Six Weeks Old. Christopher Morley. BiCB

And does not drift away. Medusa. Louise Bogan. AWP; BoWoP; HoPM; InPo; MoAB; MoAmPo; MoVE; NMM; NoP

And does not see me when I pass/And does not hear me when I call. She Is My Dear. *Anonymous.* KiLC

And does the miracles men say it does. Hospital Poems: Transfusion. Merrill Moore. PoA

And does...while we human beings lie cramped and fearful. Bagpipe Music. Hugh" (Christopher Murray Grieve) MacDiarmid. OAEL 1-2

And doing-down gets done in pious tones/Sam had tried to put on, but never could.   A Tribute to the Founder.   Kingsley Amis.   DBV; NePoEA-2

And don't be behind with the rent.   Pity the Down-Trodden Landlord.   Arnold Clayton.   FSW

And don't get any/Drink at all.   Drinking Fountain.   Marchette Chute.   TiPo

And don't go near the water.   Caution.   *Anonymous.*   OxNR

And don't leave them screaming and crying/on the graveyard ground   Fixing to Die.   Booker White.   BluL

And don't wait until you are dead.   Advice.   Ruth Stone.   NMM

And don't you remember/The babes in the wood?   My Dear, Do You Know.   *Anonymous.*   PBBP

And don't you want to hear him, Kate?   To Kate, Skating Better Than Her Date.   David Daiches.   CTBA; FiBHP; NYBP; SD

And doom this First, pioneering Genius.   Divine Poems.   Jose Garcia Villa.   MoRP

And doomed to know his aching heart alone.   I Would I Might Forget That I Am I.   George Santayana.   AWP

And Doric music make/To civilize with graver notes our wits again.   An Ode to Mr. Anthony Stafford to Hasten Him into the Country.   Thomas Randolph.   AnAnS 2; OBS; ViBoPo

And dost Thou not of pain a mingling pour,/To make the cup but overflow the more?   The Cup of Happiness.   Gilbert Thomas.   TrPWD

And doth again in seas his burden throw.   In This World's Raging Sea.   William, of Hawthornden Drummond.   CBEP

And doth consumer, waste, spoil, disorder all....   Who Doth Not See the Measure of the Moon?   Sir John Davies.   MOON

And doth flow deep the summer long.   The River Glideth in a Secret Tongue.   Anthony Ostroff.   NePoAm-2

And doth with his eternal motion make/A sound like thunder–everlastingly.   By the Sea.   William Wordsworth.   EtS

And double-crossed his friends, and died a peer.   Epitaph: "Tread softly; bid a solemn music sound."   J. B. Morton.   FaBoEE

And double its gladness so.   Nature's Easter Music.   Lucy Larcom.   OHIP

And down a thousand vales I dropped,/I flowed to Italy.   The Watershed.   Alice Meynell.   SBG

And down at one gulp house and old/woman went.   Nothing-At-All.   *Anonymous.*   OxNR

And down he lays his weary bones.   The Progress of Poesy.   Matthew Arnold.   EnL; NOBV; PP; VLP

And down her cheeks are cunning piles/Of little ripples when she smiles.   Growing Old.   Rose Henderson.   BiCB

And down his querulous challenge sent.   Snow-Bound.   John Greenleaf Whittier.   TrGrPo

And down the draughty/Passage-way nobody walks.   The Autumn House.   George M. Brady.   OnYI

And, down the heat, I heard a woman moaning.   Gamesters All.   DuBose Heyward.   HBMV

And down the sugar goes!   Tom's Little Dog.   Walter De la Mare.   GDP; TiPo

And down to make a bed for you.   Cackle, Cackle, Mother Goose.   *Anonymous.*   PBBP

(And down went/my Uncle/Sol/and started a worm farm)   Nobody Loses All the Time.   Edward Estlin Cummings.   AnNE; CMoP; DL; FaBoCo; FF; LiTM; MP; NLV; NOBA; TwCP

And down will come baby, cradle and all.   Rock-a-Bye Baby.   Mother Goose.   FaFP; TiPo

And dozens of other inspired phrases.   A Listener's Guide to the Birds.   E. B. White.   NYBP

And drag a long black trail across the light.   The Herring Weir.   Sir Charles G. D. Roberts.   NOBC; PeCV

And draged out the brains with my little black thing.   Black Thing.   *Anonymous.*   CoMu

And dragons in the crease!   I Had Not Minded Walls.   Emily Dickinson.   AWP; CABA; InPo

And drags her husband out to dinner.   Daily Paradox.   Sara Henderson Hay.   InMe

And drama enough, this time.   Together Again.   William Stafford.   LCAP

And drank Alph's sacred stream like one athirst.   Teatime Variations.   Peter Titheradge.   FaBoPa

And drank his blood and ate his heart.   The Rite.   Dudley Randall.   HoPM

And drank them both into the grave.   Twins.   Robert Graves.   FaBoEE; PV

And drave the first dart deeper more and more.   Epigram: "The enemy of life, decayer of all kind."   Sir Thomas Wyatt.   SiPS

And draw an adder or an eel.   Marriage.   *Anonymous.*   GBP

And draw away with me your every thought.   The Effigy.   Guido Cavalcanti.   LiTW

And draw me to her in the blessed place!   Go, Grieving Rimes of Mine.   Petrarch (Francesco Petrarca).   NAWM 1-2

And draw the sheet under my chin.   The Lonely Death.   Adelaide Crapsey.   AnFE; APA

And draw you up like a bucket/Of fresh water.   Fairy Tales.   Jane Flanders.   DFT

And dread once conquered means a victory won.   The Dreaded Task.   Margaret E. Bruner.   PoToHe

And dreaded him the least!   The Skeleton at the Feast.   James Jeffrey Roche.   AA

And dreads its captor and his handsel touch.   The Fireflies (excerpt).   Charles Mair.   OBCV

And dream and dream that I am home again!   Brumana.   James Elroy Flecker.   BrPo

And dream at dawn the idol in the stone.   Metaphysician.   Robert Fitzgerald.   PoA

And dream in the smoke, all alone.   Sorrow.   Chu Shu-chen.   BoWoP

And dream my time away.   Expostulation and Reply.   William Wordsworth.   BW 1-2; CBEP; EnL; EnLi 1-2; EnRP; ERoP 1-2; HBV 1-2; OAEP; OBRV

And dream of being men–and boys should dream.   A Boy's Need.   Herbert Clark Johnson.   PoNe

And dream of the birds and the hills of sheep.   The Sick Child.   Robert Louis Stevenson.   CH; PoSC

And dream sweet dreams of Mary Jane...   William Brown.   Joaquin Miller.   BPAW

And dream the next caress/of its devouring arms.   Curriculum Vitae.   Ingeborg Bachmann.   BoWoP

And dream visions of wa-na-bo-zho/thanking the Great One.   For the Children.   Thomas Love Peacock.   VoR

And dream your dream anew.   Trifle.   Georgia Douglas Johnson.   AmNP

And dreaming he's dead, he'll forget to awake.   Willie the Weeper.   *Anonymous.*   ABF; BeLS; BLPA; OBAL; TrAS; YaD

And dreams are what a dream should be, or true.   The Night Nurse Goes Her Round.   John Gray.   LoBV; OBNC

And dreams he is ringing a funeral knell!   The Windy Night.   Thomas Buchanan Read.   GN

And dreams 't is all to-day.   Her Answer.   John Bennett.   AA; BLPA

And dreamy lulla-lullaby, lullaby!   A Wand'ring Minstrel.   Sir William Schwenck Gilbert.   GoTF; TreFS

And dreamy scents of fragrance pass/That breathe of other years.   Mild the Mist upon the Hill.   Emily Bronte.   NOBV

And dress your hair for Judgment morn.   Night Song.   A. R. D. Fairburn.   AnNZ

And devine away the lange nightes blake.   Welcome, Summer.   Geoffrey Chaucer.   MeEL

And drew her backward home.   The Subverted Flower.   Robert Frost.   CMoP; HAP; NoAm; NOBA; OxBA; WeW

And dried in the air like the floor.   Note to the Previous Tenants.   John Updike.   GOYP

And dried to streaks of salt leaked white from the hair.   Silver.   Archie Randolph Ammons.   NoP

And drifted towards them and was land.   The Discovery.   Charles Brasch.   AnNZ

And drill ye tarriers drill,/And blast and fire.   Drill Ye Tarriers, Drill.   Thomas F. Casey.   FSW

And drink and drink old wine/At youth's eternal fount.   Under Leafy Bowers.   Judah Al-Harizi.   TrJP

And drink her in dew!   Wine and Dew.   Richard Henry Stoddard.   AA

And drink me at one draught!   The Kiss and the Cup.   *Anonymous.*   UnTE

And drink my lord's health in good wine.   Bold Reynard the Fox.   *Anonymous.*   OBET

And drink of the wine of the the vine benign/That sparkles warm in Sansovine.   Bacchus on Beverages.   Francesco Redi.   LiTW

And drink the floods of odour and of song.   The Loves of the Plants.   Erasmus Darwin.   PeD

And drink the small night chill like news of home.   Stars over the Dordogne.   Sylvia Plath.   PoA

And drink to days that yet may be.   Spring Flowers from Ireland.   Denis Florence McCarthy.   ACP; GoBC

...And drink your life very very slowly, without raising/my head.   Sylvius, your hands near my mouth are heady flowers.   Marguerite Burnat-Provins.   BoWoP

And drinking too much from the town well.   Incident at Imuris.   Alberto Rios.   APU

And drinks again.   Intersection.   Florence Dolgorukov.   AMV-80

And drinks, and stares, diversified with boggles?   Three Sonnets.   [James Henry] Leigh Hunt.   NOBL

And drinks from the rocky rills/The laughter of life.   A Hymn of Nature.   Robert Bridges.   YeAr

And drinks in skies serene the unsullied stream of day.   Aerophorion (excerpt).   Henry James Pye.   NOEC

And drive away the nights so long and black!   The Birds' Rondel (modern version).   Geoffrey Chaucer.   TrGrPo

And drive on summer evenings in my car/Around the courthouse of the living town. A Return from the Wars. Frederick Bock. SOTS

And drive them headlong in the waters/Oh, this is great Terrapin war! Terrapin War. *Anonymous.* PAH

And driven awey the longe nightes blake! Parlement of Foules. Geoffrey Chaucer. ATP; CTC; SeCePo

And drives him again and again on the same block. The World's Greatest Tricycle Rider. C. K. Williams. NYBP

And Dromio's denouement of tragic mirth. The Twins. Karl Shapiro. AnFE; MiAP; MoAmPo; TrJP

And drop a Regular tear! A Prayer. Berton Braley. BLPA

And drop for me the burning tear,"/She said, and sunk away. "Go Bring Me," Said the Dying Fair. William Hunter. AH

And drop her eyes, and turn home down the hill. Weeping Willow. Richard Aldridge. NePoAm-2

And dropped dead, which he's been ever since. Limerick: "A pointless old miser named Quince." John Ciardi. TDH

And dropped like firebrands on the fragrant hearth. Church Burning: Mississippi. James A. Emanuel. PoBA; PoNe

And drops a conscience-stricken tear in case he is found out. The Village Blacksmith. *Anonymous.* FiBHP

And drops down to earth by/a single strand. Tree Man. Rennie McQuilkin. AMV-81

And drops, ere he suspect the ill,/Into the inexorable sea. Birthday Verses Written in a Child's Album. James Russell Lowell. OxBChV

And drown all lesser cries/Your ears have known. The Eagle. James Daly. AnAmPo

And drowned it with my call. The Lighthouse. John Seller Anson. AMV-80

And drummed them out of town. Battle Royal. *Anonymous.* OxNR

And drunk and broke, alone, the game turned real. Five for the Grace. Winfield Townley Scott. VGW

And drunkenness grows sober as she reads. On the Translation of Anacreon. Horace Walpole. FaBoEE

And dry hearts smoked in its wake. The Maker. R. S. Thomas. ELU

And dry leaves churn in whirlwinds from their wings. California Quail in January. Will C. Jumper. GrPl

And dry the tears upon our face,/His deathless story. The Coplas on the Death of His Father, the Grandmaster of Santiago. Jorge Manrique. CAW

And dry their wings in the light of the beacon lamp. Shag Rookery. William Hart-Smith. AnNZ

And dub me knight/Domingo.' Mounsier Mingo. *Anonymous.* CBEP

And dulls to distance all we are. Ambulances. Philip Larkin. FaBoTw; OxBC

And duly seated on the Immortal Hill. Don Juan. George Gordon, Lord Byron. TrGrPo

And Dunderbeck was meat! Bang! Dunderbeck. *Anonymous.* FSW

And–during thunder-storms–the light comes shining/through. Precursors. Louis MacNeice. OBSP

And dusk with fire, and flames with shadows race. A Child's Winter Evening. Gwen John. CH

And dust implicit with lilies of His skull. Noah's Ark. Marguerite Young. MoPo

And dust that sifted toward the unseen, unmoved stars. Incident on a Front Not Far from Castel di Sangro. Harry Brown. NYBP

And, duty done, that rest shall be/Full of beatitudes to thee. Abide Not in the Realm of Dreams. William Henry Burleigh. AH

And Duty in the lofty ends of life. Sonnet: Of Beauty and Duty. Dante Alighieri. AWP

And dwell, like sleeping hermits, there. On a Watchman Asleep at Midnight. James Thomas Field. CenHV

And dwell with Thee in lasting bliss! Veni, Sancte Spiritus. King of France Robert II. HBV 1-2

And dwelleth now, that maiden's soul. On a Greek Vase. Frank Dempster Sherman. AA

And dwelling so, you may for ever be/The only Emblem of Tranquility. 'Tis Said the Gods Lower Down That Chain Above. George Alsop. SCAP

And dwindle away,/Never to reappear. Listen! Sacred Formula to Destroy Life. *Anonymous.* LiTA

And dying by its own excess of light,/Isabel. Isabel. Sydney Thomas Dobell. OBVV

And, dying, clasp Thee in my arms,/The antidote of death. Jesus, I Love Thy Charming Name. Philip Doddridge. BePJ

And dying in black and white we fight for what we love, not are Ode: Salute to the French Negro Poets. Frank O'Hara. NeAP; NNaP; PoM; PoNe

And e'en this endless faa'an that had caught me/wi ilka ither force was gether't in. Hurlygush. Maurice Lindsay. BSV; OxBS

And each a 2 pence, 2 pence, 2 pence gave him and went/away. The Rural Dance about the Maypole. *Anonymous.* GBP

And each anointed sense will see. Extreme Unction. Ernest Christopher Dowson. ACP; CAW; MoBrPo; OAEL 1-2; OBMV; VLP

And each as silent as a man being shaved. Prolonged Sonnet: When the Troops Were Returning from Milan. degli Albizzi, Niccolo. AWP; OBVE

And each book in my study your pleasure attends. Neither Blemish This Book, Nor the Leaves Double Down. *Anonymous.* FaBoUS

And each brave jolly tar/That boldly faced their enemies/In the time of the war. The Man-of-War's Garland. *Anonymous.* OBSS

And each consent a lucky gasp for life? Sonnet: "Is there a great green commonwealth of Thought." John Masefield. MoBrPo

And each day comes with its own/songs,/According to the day. The Heart of the World. Nahman of Bratzlav. TrJP

And each dew-note had a/lilac in it. The Lilac. Humbert Wolfe. HBVY

And each fowl that ledden makes/In this ship men may find. The Animals in the Ark. *Anonymous.* GBP

And each has his hour–to dwell in the sun! Hope. Georgia Douglas Johnson. CDC

And each heart which thus kindly dies,/Grows deathless by the sacrifice. Friendship's Mystery. Katherine ("Orinda") Philips. PeHV; ViBoPo

And each man has, at most, but a noble need. Tempora Acta. "Owen Meredith." OBVV

And each of them now is a mother. Limerick: "An amoeba named Sam and his brother." *Anonymous.* QQQ

(And each of us has leave to take/A ginger cookie, too.) Eunice in the Evening. Gwendolyn Brooks. TiPo

..;And each passing cloud/Expanded, whitening like the ocean foam. The Sun God. Aubrey Thomas De Vere. ACP; OBVV

And each should mete himself by his own measure. Epistles. Horace. OBVE

And each slow dusk a drawing-down of blinds. Anthem for Doomed Youth. Wilfred Owen. AnFE; BiP; BoLiVe; BrPo; CMoP; CoBMV; EBEV; EvOK; FaBoMo; FaBoRV; FaFP; GTBS; GTBS-P; HAP; HBMV; HeIP; HoPM; InPS; LiTM; MoAB; MoBrPo; MoVE; NoAm; NOBE; NoP; OAEL 1-2; OAEP; OBEV; OBWP; OxBTC; PPP; SCV; SeCePo; SoSe; TreFT; TrGrPo; ViBoPo; WaP; WeW; WHA

And Each the Bliss of all shall view/With infinite Delight. Hymn. Philip Doddridge. CEP; OBEC

And each will be home. Salmon Fly Hatch on Yankee Jim Canyon of the Yellowstone. Greg Keeler. WOLT

And each years Trafique to thy self get more. Trafique Is Earth's Great Atlas. George Alsop. SCAP

And earth, and air, and rain. Proud Songsters. Thomas Hardy. NoAm; PB

And earth and air come properly together. Quail in Autumn. William Jay Smith. Psk

And earth and air were shattered. Tohub. Jakov van Hoddis. VWA

And earth and all her fullness are forgotten... The Mathmid. Chaim Nachman Bialik. AWP

And earth bore East with all toward the new morning. Eye-Witness. Ridgely Torrence. HBMV

And Earth is but a star, that once had shone. The Golden Journey to Samarkand. James Elroy Flecker. BrPo; FaBoRV; FaPoR; GoJo; HBMV; NOBE; OBMV; OxBTC

And, earth, lie lightly on his little grave. Epitaph on an Infant. Crinagoras. AWP

And earth's foundations will depart/And all you folk will die. Good Creatures, Do You Love Your Lives. Alfred Edward Housman. TW

And Earth's old glooms and pains/Are still the same, and Life and Death are neighbors nigh Nature's Questioning. Thomas Hardy. CoBMV; InPo; MoPo; TEP; VLP

And Earth, Sea, Man, are all in each. The Sea-Limits. Dante Gabriel Rossetti. AnEnPo; EtS; MOS; NBM; OAEL 1-2; VLP

And earth shall eat the stones, and we/Shall be alone again. The Three Hills. J. C. Squire. HBMV

And earth sinks to rest/Until next spring. November. Elizabeth Jane Coatsworth. YeAr

And Earth, the ancient life-giver, increaseth/Joy among the meadows, like a tree. Hippolytus. Euripides. AWP

And earth, with all her millions, shout/Hosannas to the Lord. Christ, the Conqueror. Burder. BePJ

And earth with all her pleasant fruits and flowers/Fade, and participate in Man's decline. Sonnet: There Is a Bondage Worse. William Wordsworth. ChRP

And earthly Fires, within their ashes shrink. Upon the Author; by a Known Friend. Benjamin Woodbridge. SCAP

And Earthward he was gone! The Rahat. John Jerome Rooney. AA

And easy, quiet in the night, disturbing no one. Behind That Wall My Roommate Fucks His Girl. Geof Hewitt. NeAC; PoL

And eat him while he's hot. Davy Dumpling. *Anonymous.* OxNR

And eat, once again,/Of that forbidden fruit. Tree of Knowledge. Edward Lowbury. VWA

And eat our pot of honey on the grave. Modern Love, XXIX. George Meredith. OAEP; VLP

And eat the earth and drink the sea? Amber Beads. Audrey Alexandra Brown. CaP

And eate up those which now a while/Their fierce devourers be. What Habacuck Once Spake, Mine Eyes. Roger Williams. SCAP

And eating hoary grain and pulse the steeds,/Fixt by their cars, waited the golden dawn. The Iliad. Homer. RoGo

And eats its dead-dog off a golden dish. The Angel in the House. Coventry Patmore. VLP

And eats the meadow flowers. The Cow. Robert Louis Stevenson. BrPo; FM; NTCP; OxBCHV; SoPo; SUS; TiPo

And eats up her heart like two eggs. The Risk. Anne Sexton. BoWoP

And ebb-tide for ever and ever had passed. Assunpink and Princeton. Thomas Dunn English. MC; PAH

And Echo turns hunter and doubles the cry. Diana's Hunting-Song. John Dryden. SeCePo

And echoed with your crying/Your living paradox. At Birth. Anthony Thwaite. NePoEA-2

And echoes of the Harvest-home. Harvest Home. Frederick Tennyson. OBVV

And edge their love of freedom with contempt of/luxury. Shine, Republic. Robinson Jeffers. AmFN; FaBoPV; MoRP

And Edser, in bed sir, was dead sir. Limerick: "There was a young soldier called Edser." Spike Milligan. TDH

And Edwin wrapped up currants in a shop. Ed and Sid and Bernard. Edward MacDuff. QQQ

And eggs–boil 'em hard. Salad. Mortimer Collins. ALV; Par

And eke at last to scape and go so free. The Fruits of War (excerpt). George Gascoigne. OBWP

And eke the willow that stoopeth with the wind/Doth rise again, and greater wood doth bind. He is not dead that sometime hath a fall. Sir Thomas Wyatt. AAS; FCP; OBVE

And eke this battels end, will need an-/other place. The Faerie Queene. Edmund Spenser. OAEP

And Eliza worked hard, but could never obtain/The affection that freely was given to Jane. Jane and Eliza. Ann Taylor. HBV 1-2; HBVY

And eloped with the Mother Superior. Limerick: "There was an old monk of Siberia." Anonymous. LiBL

And eluding the dead hands, begging him to play. Foal. Vernon Watkins. OxBTC

And ELVIRA to her FERDINAND's irrevocably mated! Ferdinando and Elvira. Sir William Schwenck Gilbert. FaBoCo; FaBoNo; FiBHP; LBN

And embassies dissolve to molecules. The Potomac. Karl Shapiro. AP; CoBMV

And embrace this orphan over all/who never leaves me lonely. Company in Loneliness. Anonymous. NOBI

And embryo Good, to reach full stature,/Absorbs the Evil in its nature. Rev. Homer Wilbur's "Festina Lente." James Russell Lowell. OBAL

And empties a season of rain. The Sand Painters. Ben Belitt. EyDe

And emptiness where no life moves/beneath a stone. Bedlam Hills. Vivian Smith. PoAu 1-2

And empty all its store of rain/On me, our house, and you. Bouncing Ball. Sara Ruth Watson. SoPo

And empty when we go to rest. Riddle: "Two brothers we are." Anonymous. OxNR

And enchanted the city of Tyre. Limerick: "There was a young lady of Tyre." Edward Lear. TDH

And ended like the shining calm of rivers and the sea. A Song of Dagger-Dancing (excerpt). Tu Fu. UnS

And ends with sorrow and with sighs ere long. Popular Songs of Tuscany. Anonymous. AWP

And engines/that devour America In Goya's Greatest Scenes. Lawrence Ferlinghetti. HeIP; NMP; NoAm; TAP

And England's trousers falling down. Remember Suez? Adrian Mitchell. OxBTC

And engrossed, round-spectacled Chardin's/Passion for life. Still Life. Walter De la Mare. EyDe

And enter on the joys which are immortal. Hymn to the Holy Spirit. Richard Wilton. OxBoCh

And enter, with thine angel train,/Thy palace in the skies. Once More, O Lord. George Washington Doane. AH

And entertains the most exclusive worms. Tombstones in the Starlight. Dorothy Parker. NIP

And envied his few friends, and chose his love. In Time of War. W.H. Auden. CMoP

And envy more than they condemn/The rival who avenges them. La Promessa Sposa. Walter Savage Landor. NOBV

And envy times departed,–that knew a reign like his. The King of Brentford. William Makepeace Thackeray. HBV 1-2; OBNV

And Envy, watch the issue, while the lines,/By which thou shalt be judged, are written down. Earth. William Cullen Bryant. AmePo; AP

And Epicurus guessed as well as he. Religio Laici. John Dryden. ViBoPo

And equal Adoration be/Eternal Paraclete, to thee. Veni Crator Spiritus, Translated in Paraphrase. John Dryden. AWP; CAW; CEP; CoBE; FaPoR; GoBC; HBV 1-2; ILwL; SeCV 1-2; WGRP

And equal prowess still shall equal palms obtain. England, Unprepared for War. Mark Akenside. OBEC

And equally a miracle it were/That she could die, or that she could live here. On a Virtuous Young Gentlewoman That Died Suddenly. William Cartwright. CBEP; HAP; OBEV

And, ere dawning of the morning, I was/twenty miles away. The Sack of Deerfield. Thomas Dunn English. PAH

And ere I'm forced to break my troth/I'll lay me doun and dee. The Siller Croun. Susanna Blamire. HBV 1-2

And, ere that month was ended,/Was on her bier, and dead. Sir Ogey and Lady Elsey. Anonymous. BaBo

And ere the day of sorrow departed as he came. In Memoriam F. A. S. Robert Louis Stevenson. BrPo

And, ere the stars were visible, had reached/A village-inn,–our evening resting-place. The Excursion. William Wordsworth. EnRP

And ere the sun's set'll be in her own town. She Tied Up Her Few Things. John Clare. HAP

And, ere there comes a sunny hour/To cloud my heart, be gay! The Moon Is Up. Anonymous. NA

And ere thou change all human song shall die! Cheyenne Mountain. Helen Hunt Jackson. BPAW; PoOW

And Error loves and nourishes thy soul. Be Still. The Hanging Gardens Were a Dream. Trumbull Stickney. AmePo; AmLP; APA; LiTA; NCEP; NePA

And Esau's where it should be. On Miss Eleanor Ambrose, A Celebrated Beauty in Dublin. Philip Stanhope, Earl of Chesterfield. FaBoEE

And escaped from the people of Basing. Limerick: "There was an old person of Basing." Edward Lear. EBEV

And Eternity in an hour. Auguries of Innocence. William Blake. COBE; EnLit; GoTF; ImOP; TreFS; TRV; ViBoPo; WHA

...And eternity's strong mills grind out/vast paper of illusion! Death to Van Gogh's Ear. Allen Ginsberg. NaP; VGW

And eternity to sleep in. After. Philip Bourke Marston. HBV 1-2; NOBV

And Ettrick mourns with her their Poet dead. Extempore Effusion upon the Death of James Hogg. William Wordsworth. CBEP; EBEV; ERoP 1-2; FaBoRV; FiP; MyFE; NOBE; NoP; OAEL 1-2; OBRV; SCV

And Eugene Aram walked between,/With gyves upon his wrist. The Dream of Eugene Aram. Thomas Hood. BeLS; EnRP; HBV 1-2; StPo

And "Europe's Liberator"–still enslaved. Don Juan. George Gordon, Lord Byron. DBV

And ev'ry thing, save her, who all should grace. Phoebus, Arise. William, of Hawthornden Drummond. BSV; EIL; GoTS

And ev'rywhere he went he gave his war whoop. The Desperado. Anonymous. FSW

And Evan's, Donald's fame rings in each clansman's ears! Childe Harold's Pilgrimage: Canto III, XXVI. George Gordon, Lord Byron. AnFE

And Eve with cities tumbling from her flesh? Korea. Vincent Buckley. BoAV

And even as he goes his Friend/Is knocking at his heart. Quo Vadis? Myles Connolly. TRV

And even Boswell when we met,/Would not believe a word. Johnsonian Poem in Progress: "I put my hat upon my head." (parody). Peter Veale. BXAP

And even break his looking-glass. The World of Fools Has Such a Store. Anonymous. DBV

And even death must have been a little ashamed/At his eagerness! This Was My Brother. Mona Gould. CaP

And even in blind Chance's darkest crypt/The shrine-lamp of God's purposing is found. Accident in Art. Richard Hovey. HBV 1-2

And even in the fat domestic, something purely cat survives. On Sitting up Late, Watching Kittens. Eric W. Paff. AMV-81

And even in your grave, beauteous and free/From the cold grasp of mutability. Thysia. Morton Luce. HBV 1-2

And even into the belly of the land. The belly of the land. Luci Tapahonso. STE

And even its teeth fall out. Bald. Bill Zavatsky. APU

And, even more, protect the whites. In Westminster Abbey. Sir John Betjeman. ExPo

And even now I pose, so now go, for/I know you know. Carnal Knowledge. Thom Gunn. BoLoP

And even of man not a shadow remain/Of all he has done? The Corner Stone. Walter De la Mare. BrPo

And even our foemen cheer! The Victory Wreck. Will Carleton. PAH

And even princeton struts like one of god's betters? A Poem with Capital Letters. Jane Cooper. FaBoWP

And even the birds are singing the Lord God's praise! Prayer at Dawn. Diarmuid O'Shea. KiLC

And even the clock on the mantel/Moves its hands in a fierce delight/Of so, and so, and so. A Bright Day. John Montague. FaBoIP

And even the dream's confusion can/Sustain to-morrow's road. The Survival. Edmund Charles Blunden. OBEV; OBMV

And even the English–maybe they might die. Epigram: "The world laid low, and the wind blew like a dust." *Anonymous.* NOBI

And even the English, perchance their hour will come. Tara Is Grass. *Anonymous.* AnIL; AnIV; PoL

And even the greybeard will o'erlook/Connivingly my dreaming-book. Introduction.[To Poems, 1831]. Edgar Allan Poe. NOBA

And even the little vertical of man/is blocked out solid in a capital I. Lines on the Sea. Dilys Bennett Laing. NYBP

And even the sun, small as David the shepherd boy,/withholds its light from me. Like David. Gabriel Preil. VWA

And even the watchful hare stands not aloof. Immalee. Christina Georgina Rossetti. BoNaP

And even the writing of the rat footprints/tells us nothing, nothing at all Four Preludes on Playthings of the Wind. Carl Sandburg. MoAB

And even this is only half a revenge. Autobiography. Dan Pagis. VWA

And even though I was his eldest daughter/He cannot tell me one word of love. On the Road at Night There Stands the Man. Dahlia Ravikovich. WPOW

And even thus the Soul's/Dark hours are made. Earth's Night. William Allingham. IrPN; TRV

And evening come. Evening Songs. John Vance Cheney. AA

And evening finds you in a restless town/Where each has back his old restricted face. Versailles (Petit Trianon). Adrienne Rich. NePoEA

And evening tells us toil is o'er. Seneca Lake. James Gates Percival. AnNE

And evening/will camouflage the opening/to the bottomless pit. Swimmers. Paul D. Shiplett. LFAC

And eventually get around/to a better showing. Hooked on the Magic Muscle. Linda King. GP

And eventually send a telegram. How I Brought the Good News from Aix to Ghent or Vice Versa (parody). Robert J. and Walter Carruthers Sellar Yeatman. BXAP; FaBoPa; FiBHP; OnMSP; SpRo

And ever aloft on the palace roof the old banner of England blew. The Defense of Lucknow. Alfred, Lord Tennyson. BeLS

And ever among a Maiden sung,/"By by, Baby, lullay." This Other Night. *Anonymous.* ISi

And ever among thou thee en-nuye/Into this world and yesterday. All Turns into Yesterday. *Anonymous.* MeEL

And ever bereth the fox the box of all good/thewes. Snatches: "Winter alle etes." *Anonymous.* OxBM

And ever changing, like a joyless eye/That finds no object with its constancy? The Moon. Percy Bysshe Shelley. FaBoCh; LoGBV; OBEV

And ever deeper pleasures crowd/The long eternities! Home. Martha Snell Nicholson. STF

And ever for blossoming the first. The Last Day and the First. Theodore Weiss. TwCP; VGW

And ever for faint-heart scantest of hoards! Exeter Book: Maxims. *Anonymous.* AnOE

And ever fresh fire from its gazing caught. Divina Commedia: Paradiso. Dante Alighieri. ExPo; ILwL; ISi; LiTW; NAWM 1-2

And Ever is Now. A Pavane for the Nursery. William Jay Smith. DuDa; GoJo; MoAmPo; NePoAm-2; PoSC

And ever let his unrecalling crime/Have time to wail the abusing of his time. The Rape of Lucrece. William Shakespeare. OAEL 1-2

And ever let there rise to Thee/Glad hymns of praise from land and sea. Hymn: "Eternal Father, strong to save.". William Whiting. NBM

And ever-recurrent splendour of the eaglet. Shrouds and Away. Alfred Goldsworthy Bailey. PeCV

And ever round her shine the aureole/Of my sad verses, after I am dead! Sonnets. George Edward Woodberry. HBMV

And ever running, till we leave to fling/Dirt in her way, will keep above the skie. The Timber. Henry Vaughan. FaBoRV; NoP; OBEV; SeCP; SeCV 1-2

And ever rustles yearning to and fro... Souls. Paul Wertheimer. TrJP

And ever she sang: The Lily-White Rose. *Anonymous.* MeEL

And ever since then/she's been turning around. Anna Elise. *Anonymous.* OxNR

And ever the stars above look down/On the stars below in Frederick town. Barbara Frietchie. John Greenleaf Whittier. AmePo; AnNE; AP; BeLS; CTC; FaBoBe; FaBV; FaFP; FaPo; FaPoR; FPL; GN; GoTF; HBV 1-2; HBVY; MaC; MC; NOBA; OBAL; PAH; PAL; PoLf; PoSC; TreF; TrGrPo; WBLP; YaD

And ever the waste, and the dank mist, and night! Fog-Horn. George Herbert Clarke. CaP

And ever they stream in vain. I Wept as I Lay Dreaming. Heinrich Heine. AWP

And ever uplifting birds to wing! Grandma Fire. Charles G. Ballard. VoR

And ever was, and ever schall. There is a Floure Sprung of a Tree. *Anonymous.* AtBAP

And ever your own ye shall me find,/At all times redy to kiss you.' My Little Pretty Mopsy. *Anonymous.* OxBM

And evere he rode the hindreste of oure route. The Canterbury Tales: The Reeve. Geoffrey Chaucer. OxBM

And everilk grief is gane for evermair. Wha Is Perfyte. Alexander Scott. GoTS

And everlasting Canopy and starry Arch/and Shield of All. In State (excerpt). Forceythe Willson. AA

AND EVERLASTING GLORY UNTO BUENA/VISTA'S DEAD! Buena Vista. Albert Pike. PAH

And everlasting light shines here. Ivy Crest. *Anonymous.* AnIL

And evermore be merry! Our Joyful Feast. George Wither. ChBR; OHIP; SiSoSe

And evermore–I dance! I dance! The Spirit of the Birch. Arthur Ketchum. OHIP

And every billow was his mirror splendid! Sunrise at Sea. Epes Sargent. EtS

And every black he freed is now/His living monument. His Living Monument. Minna Irving. PGD

And every boy in secret anguish, worships/The hero of his sleepless, starlit hours. The Lyre Player. Stefan George. PeHV

And every breath of her's as full of ghosts/As a sunbeam with motes. Man's Anxious, but Ineffectual Guard Against Death. Thomas Lovell Beddoes. ChRP

And every bush an apocalypse of leaf. Emily Carr. Wilfred Watson. NOBC; OBCV

And every cat in the twilight's gray,/Every possible cat. The Tortoiseshell Cat. Patrick Reginald Chalmers. BoAnP; CenHV; PCat

And every changing season of the year/Stamps on the scene its English character. The Ancient Mansion. George Crabbe. FaBoPP

And every child who knew him, far or near,/Did love him faithfully. Uncle Ananias. Edwin Arlington Robinson. AnNE; LaNeLa; MoAmPo; NePA; NIP

And every cloud a solace and a balm. In the Woods. Frederick George Scott. ACV; CaP

And every customer takes two pair. Riddle: "A shoemaker makes shoes without leather." *Anonymous.* OxNR; SoPo

And every day be glad with joyful love. Sonnets of the Months. Folgore da San Geminiano. AWP

...And every fall/Is once for all. The View. Howard Nemerov. NYBP

And every five minutes he assured his public that he would/take up very little of their time. The God of War. Bertolt Brecht. FaBoPV

And every fraction/must be solved. The Ambition of Ghosts. Rosemarie Waldrop. APU

And every gate she bars to Hate shall open wide to Love! Brown of Ossawatomie. John Greenleaf Whittier. AmePo; HBV 1-2; MC; PAH

And every gazer applauds/The tremendous rubber tire. Hymn in Columbus Circle. Stephen Vincent Benét. OBAL

And every girl on Natchez bluff/Will cry as we go by-o! Western Star (excerpt). Stephen Vincent Benét. AmFN

And every hair a sheaf shall be,/And every sheaf a golden tree. Celanta at the Well of Life. George Peele. LoBV

And every heart think loathingly/Its dearest changed to bores. The Summer Malison. Gerard Manley Hopkins. CMoP; NoAm; PoEL 1-5

And every hope compassionately lives/Close to despair. Leaves Before the Wind. May Sarton. MoLP; NePoAm

And every hour be touched with grace and/light. The Pysidanthera. Augusta Cooper Bristol. AA

And every impulse from thy influence springs. I Mix in Life. Samuel Taylor Coleridge. CBEP

And every inch of him filled out with pride. Hound on the Church Porch. Robert P. Tristram Coffin. GDP

And every joy but as one kiss. Joy and Dream. Johann Wolfgang von Goethe. LiTW

And every lad his love can win,/For here is April weather. April Weather. Lizette Woodworth Reese. HBMV

And every lamb of Jesus/Shall then receive his crown. O Children, Would You Cherish? Christopher Dock. AH

And every leaf is exquisite with song. The Wind in the Elms. J. Corson Miller. HBMV

And every limb supplied, and t' every part/Had free access, but durst not touch her heart. Sonnet: "I saw the object of my pining thought." Thomas Watson. EiL

And every little buttercup/Looks down at me instead of up. Somersault. Dorothy Aldis. SoPo

And every little grass-blade/Wears a jewel all its own. Song: "The night is an ancient sorceress." Simeon S. Frug. LiTW

And every longing satisfied/With full salvation blest. Fulfillment. William Augustus Muhlenberg. WGRP

And every man decideth/The Way his soul shall go. The Ways. John Oxenham. HBMV; PoLf; TRV

And every man/who wants to die in peace in his bed/besides. Asphodel, That Greeny Flower. William Carlos Williams. CMoP; PP

And every Man within the Reach of Right. The Seasons. James (1700-48) Thomson. EnRP

And every moment blows blustrous wind. The Banks of Sweet Primroses. *Anonymous.* ELP

And every muse attend her on her way Fragment. William Cowper. WGRP

And every Muse in every tongue/Has heard and prais'd her nightly song. Parrot and Dove. Walter Savage Landor. PB

And every new day there is something new. Sonnets after the Italian. Richard Watson Gilder. HBV 1-2

And every night he percheth him/In my lady's chamber. I Have a Gentle Cock. *Anonymous.* CBEP; EBEV; EnPo; HAP; NCEP; NOBE; NoP; OxBM; PBBP; SeCePo; ViBoPo

And every one a fire bloom,/And every one a prayer. Candle-Lighting Song. Arthur Ketchum. HBMV

...And every one missed him. The People, Yes. Carl Sandburg. LiTA; MoAmPo

And every pool lies still as stone. Crumbs. Walter De la Mare. SoPo

And every rider caught outside/Must pray between his horse's knees. Landscape of Violence. Ralph Nixon Currey. PeSA

And every sheave a golden tree. The Old Wife's Tale. George Peele. OBSC

And every sickle-arm's left far,/far back to graze the crop. Harvest Time. G. A. Watermeyer. PeSA

"And–every–single–one–of–them–is–right!" In the Neolithic Age. Rudyard Kipling. NOBV

And every sort of walking man/Will stop to lift his hat to me! The Old Man at the Crossing. Leonard Alfred George Strong. OBMV

And every soul's a poet whose song/surmounts our height! Voice. Harriet Prescott Spofford. AA

And every sound that meets the ear is Love. A Spring Morning. John Clare. GBL

And every thought breaks out a rose. In Memoriam A.H.H., CXXII. Alfred, Lord Tennyson. VLP

And every time she gets the hiccups/I laugh Moochie. Eloise Greenfield. NTCP

And every tongue that wags will grace/Thy vertue with a story. Let Not Thy Beauty. Aurelian Townsend. AnAnS 2; JCP

And every treaty is erased by time. In Death's Field. Al-Khansa. BoWoP

And every turf beneath their feet/Shall be a soldier's sepulchre. Hohenlinden. Thomas Campbell. BeLS; CBEP; FaBoCh; FaBoRV; FaPoR; GN; GTBS; GTBS-P; HBV 1-2; NOBE; OBNC; OBRV; OBWP; OnMSP; RoGo; TreF; WaaP; WBLP; WHA

And every voice shall echo thine. The Country Clown. John Trumbull. AnAmPo

And every wanton willing kiss/Can season with a nay. She That Denies Me. Thomas Heywood. ErPo; UnTE

And every wave is charmed. Terminus. Ralph Waldo Emerson AA; AmePo; AmPP; AnNE; AP; AWP; FPL; HBV 1-2; InPo; NOBA; OxBA; PoEL 1-5; PoLf; TAP

And every world before silence begins a star. Amen. Purer Than Purest Pure. Edward Estlin Cummings. AH

And everybody said he was/A fine old gentleman. Old Grimes. Albert Gorton Greene. AnAmPo; GoTF; HBV 1-2; HBVY; InMe; TreFS

And everyone cuddles,/And everyone wins. Hug o' War. Shel Silverstein. NTCP

And everyone, everyone pointing up and shouting. Child on Top of a Greenhouse. Theodore Roethke. AtBAP; ELU; LCAP; LOW; MiAP; NCSH; PoPl

And everyone is happy,/Nor could be happier there. Above the Bright Blue Sky. Albert Midlane. OxBChV

And everyone now/Is a king in conceit. Now Thrice Welcome Christmas. *Anonymous.* OHIP

And everyone that comes by I'll cry: "Damn you, deliver your/purse".' Distressed Men of War. *Anonymous.* OBSS

And everyone thought it was me. Limerick: "I sat next the Duchess at tea." *Anonymous.* NIP; SoSe

And everyone will sing, even in the winter, even in the rain. Daydream. Arthur Seymour John Tessimond. SeCePo

And everything but Mira is forgot. In Praise of Laudanum. William Harrison. NOEC

And everything else is prose. Love and Poetry. Louis Simpson. PPoe

And everything he'd touched, an exposed nerve. The Empty House. Stephen Spender. PCP

And everything I felt in the world was love for her. My Dream by Henry James. Michael Ryan. SV

And everything is exactly as it should be. Subway Psalm. Alden Nowlan. Str

And "Everything is for a very short time." Response. Mary Ursula Bethell. FaBoWP

And everything, save Her, who all should grace. Summons to Love. William, of Hawthornden Drummond. GTBS

And everything that was/Hoisting water/Suddenly spilled over. Water Tap. Norman MacCaig. BSV

And everything we do is love. And This Is Love. Paula Reingold. IHMS

And everywhere, in every core, there's bitterness. Lord, Listen. E. Lasker-Schuler. VWA

And everywhere, on all of it, the brightness of the sun. Requiem. Kenneth Fearing. CMoP

And everywhere that man can be,/Thou, God, art present there. I Sing the Mighty Power of God. Isaac Watts. TRV

And everywhere the great green smell/Of grass the whole world over. Smells. Kathryn Worth. BrR

...And everywhere they seek/themselves formal forever, they reflect in codes. Snails. E. D. Blodgett. NOBC

And everywhere you looked was singing Hummingbird. Harold Littlebird. VoR

And evil-speaking shall part. April. Vidame de Chartres. AWP

And evirilk greif is gane/For evir mair. Quha Is Perfyte. Alexander Scott. OxBS

And exclaim: "It is biggish for King's!" Limerick: "There was a young critic of Kings." Arthur Clement Hilton. CenHV

And exclaimed, "I'll return to Dundee." Limerick: "There was an Old Man of Dundee." Edward Lear. FaBoNo

And exudes it again. Others May Praise What They Like. Walt Whitman. Par

And eyes, dimmed with losses, widening for losses. A Pause for Breath. Ted Hughes. NYBP

And eyes matted/with hyacinthine curls The Bull. William Carlos Williams. LiTM; MoVE; MP; NoP; TwCP

And eyther yeeld with me tin earth to lie,/Or else with thee to take me to the skie. Sinnes Heavie Loade. Robert Southwell. AnAnS 1

And F. P. A. ran a piece of mine in the New York Evening/Mail. Haec Olim Meminise Iuvabait. Deems Taylor. InMe

And fade into the light of common day. Our Birth Is but a Sleep and a Forgetting. William Wordsworth. EaLo

And fade/Like the luster of a pearl. Like a Pearl. Hayim Naggid. VWA

And fades away like the morning dew. The Water Is Wide. *Anonymous.* FSW; OBET

And failure, fear, disease, and death,/Love crowns with victory. Because He Lives. Adele Lathrop. BLRP

And fain to reap it with a scythe of fire. The Fox-Hunters. Ebenezer Elliott. TW

And fain would sin, but nature won't assist. Reformation of Manners. Daniel Defoe. OBSV

And faintly trust the larger hope. In Memoriam A.H.H., LV. Alfred, Lord Tennyson. HBV 1-2; LoBV; NAWM 1-2; OAEL 1-2; OAEP; OBNC

And faintly whisper, Lord deliver us. The Praying Mantis. Ogden Nash. PV

And Fair Ellen, she died also. Sweet William. *Anonymous.* OuSiCo

And fair Freedom is singing Sweet Home in the West. The Maryland Battalion. John Williamson Palmer. AA; HBV 1-2; MC; PAH

And, fair in sunset light, discern/Its mirage-lifted Isles of Peace. Burning Drift-Wood. John Greenleaf Whittier. MOS

And faith forbid to burn. The Eclipse of Faith. Theodore Dwight Woolsey. AA

And faith is sapped, and Heaven defied. Oedipus Rex: Chorus. Sophocles. WGRP

And, faith she thinks it very wrong/This jug should stand unfilled so long. Undying Thirst. Antipater of Sidon. AWP

And Faith their Consolation did afford,/Elijahs more Illustrious Second Coming with/his Lord. A Poem on Elijahs Translation.... Benjamin Colman. SCAP

And faithful Petrarch gloriously crown'd. Sonnet: "Keen, fitful gusts are whisp'ring here and there." John Keats. PoEL 1-5

And fall a-cursing, like a very drab,/A scullion! Hamlet. William Shakespeare. TreFT

And fall asleep/before I finish. Sheep. Rochelle Kraut. APU

And fall into my own backyard,/Clutching Long Island. Four Spacious Skies. Susan Astor. AMV-80

And fall into the ocean, ne'er be found! Faustus Faces His Doom. Christopher Marlowe. TreFT

And fall into the sky Sleep on the Fraser. Patrick Lane. NeAC

And fall on my knees then, womanly. III. Ted Berrigan. EAS

And fall these heavy tears. Votive Song. Edward Coate [(or Coote)] Pinkney. AA; APA

And fall upon mine sword, when I'm/not ready? The Lost History Plays: King Ethelred the Unready (parody). Bill Greenwell. BXAP

And falling down and down again/The ground it touch until. Slaves to the World. *Anonymous.* CBEP

And falling leaves saw old unhappy loves. O Amber Day, Amid the Autumn Gloom. William Talbot Allison. CaP

And falling on him brings up much black bile. Beware of Figs. Nicophon. FaBoUs

And, falling on the unholy beast,/Dispatched him with a pick and spade. The Devil's Dictionary: Body-Snatcher. Ambrose Bierce. OBAL

And falls, alas! unpitied, as he lived before. The Country Curate. Henry Taylor. NOEC

And falls into his empty bucket. August Evenings in Hatteras. Gabriele Glang. WOLT

And fame, this lord of useless thousands ends. Moral Essays. Alexander Pope. ExPo; FiP

And fame to shout with immortal voice/Dead on the field of Glory! Zollicoffer. Henry Lynden Flash. PAH

And fancied we were queens. One Saturday. Annie Douglas Robinson. AA

And fancy then the Lord of Light is there/As he did once in Moses-bush appeare. Upon Christmas Eve. Sir John Suckling. NCEP

And far abroad the canvas wings extend. All Hands Unmoor! William Falconer. EtS

And far and farther from me/Ebbs the wave of the sea. The Woman of Beare. *Anonymous.* AnIV

...And far doors bang in mind, idly. The Party. W. R. Rodgers. BIrV

And far-off gulls like risen souls. The Coast: Norfolk. Frances Cornford. OxBTC

And far worse damage done to bigger boys. The Hero. Robert Graves. PCP

And fare ye weel, the bonny lass/That kindles my mother's fire! The Wife of Usher's Well. *Anonymous.* AWP; BoLiVe; BSV; CBEP; DiPo; EBEV; FaBoBa; GoTS; HBV 1-2; InPo; LiTB; NOBE; NoP; OAEL 1-2; OAEP; OBEV; OnMSP; OxBB; OxBS; PoEL 1-5; PrIm; TreF; TrGrPo

And fares into the Night. To the Leanan Shee. Thomas Boyd. OnYI

And farewel shrine of which the saint is oute!' Troilus and Criseyde. Geoffrey Chaucer. OxBM

And farewell, fancy, that first wrought my woe. Fancy, Farewell. Sir Edward Dyer. EnRePo

And faring out for regions unexplored,/Went singing down the River of the Dead. When I Am Dead and Sister to the Dust. Elsa Barker. HBV 1-2

And farted a forty-day blizzard. Limerick: "There once was a wonderful wizard." Conrad Aiken. FaBoNo

And farther he pursued them not/Into Egypt's land.' The Crow and the Crane. *Anonymous.* BuBa

And Fashion, in freedom, will die of the lie/in her face. Land of the Wilful Gospel. Sidney Lanier. PAH

And fashioned in the looms of Paradise. The Creation of My Lady. Francesco Redi. AWP

And fashions men with true nobility. Tamburlaine the Great. Christopher Marlowe. AtBAP; TrGrPo

And fastened the door with a skewer. A Little Maid. *Anonymous.* OxNR

And Father and the Paraclete,/The while the endless ages run! The Holy Innocents. Prudentius (Aurelius Clemens Prudentius). CAW

And Father seems to know the minute anything/is gone! The Workshop. Aileen Fisher. SoPo

And/fathers/and fathers to me Fire, Hair, Meat and Bone. Fred Johnson. PoBA

And fathomed every mystery but Man. Epitaph, Found Somewhere in Space. Hugh Wilgus Ramsaur. TRV

And favors that make folly bold/Banish the light from virtue's face. Preludes. Coventry Patmore. HBV 1-2

And fawn-like eyes still tremble as they glow. Woman. *Anonymous.* HBV 1-2

And fays, or suchlike friendly things,/Throw kisses through the glass. A Sense of Humour. Vachel Lindsay. MAPA

And fear has cast our love, for flesh is grass/And we are withered with the wrath of God. Fear Has Cast Out Love. Wilfrid Scawen Blunt. VLP

And fear lit by the breadth of such calmly turns to praise. The City Limits. Archie Randolph Ammons. HaCAP; NoAm; NOBA; NoP; NYP

And fear of death, like childish dream,/Will pass and flee, when thou art here. Mortem, Quae Violat Suavia, Pellit Amor. William Johnson Cory. NBM

And fear to join him there. Colin and Lucy. Thomas Tickell. CEP; OBEC

And feared to hurt the very dust. A Circus Garland. Rachel Field. OBCA; SoPo

And, fearless, trust our cause to God! Cast Down, but Not Destroyed. *Anonymous.* PAH

And fears not portly Azcan nor his hoos. Bantams in Pine-Woods. Wallace Stevens. AtBAP; CMoP; InPo; InPS; MoVE; NOBA; OxBA; PAI; SeCeV; UnPo

And fed into the mouth of a large cylinder/Labelled "Lufthansa." No Offence. D. J. Enright. OxBTC

And feed on bitter fruits without accusing Fate. Childe Harold's Pilgrimage: Canto III. George Gordon, Lord Byron. FiP

And feed on rubbish and remains. The Moon Bird. V. C. Vickers. AmMo

And feed upon strawberries/Sugar and cream. Curly Locks. Mother Goose. HBV 1-2; HBVY; OxNR; SoPo

And feeds itself alone. Nausea. Catherine Davis. NePoEA

And feel, for a moment, certain/that as you notice it/you are the only one. Full Moon, Rising. Jonathan Holden. GOYP

And feel his little silvery feet. Child's Song. Thomas Moore. GoBC; OxBI; SUS; ViBoPo

And feel how tears can run. To an Icicle. Blanche Taylor Dickinson. CDC

And feel, in the swing of dedicated will,/the infinity of its embrace. The Circle. Carol Coates. CaP

And feel like a fossil/in a burning museum. Wind Flowers. Margo Lockwood. DFF

And feel like flowers that fade. Elena's Song. Sir Henry Taylor. OBVV

And feel no alarm at His coming,/But hasten His heralds to greet. When Will He Come? *Anonymous.* STF

And feel the Flesh becoming Word. Now in the Time of This Mortal Life. Norman Nicholson. NeBP

And feel the wafting of Her wings. Peace in the World. John Galsworthy. PoLf

And feel the wind of tresses unbeholden. A South Coast Idyll. Rosamund Marriott Watson. OBVV

And feel this classic water's cruelness with my hand. Inside the Cave. Geoffrey Grigson. FaBoPP

And feel, thou Earth, for this afflicted Race! Sonnet: September 1, 1802. William Wordsworth. ChRP

And feel with torment that 'tis so. To Lesbia. Caius Valerius Catullus. PoPl

And feels the iron in his soul. Cleator Moor. Norman Nicholson. FaBoTw; NeBP

And feet that fly on feathers,/And serpent-circled wand. A Shropshire Lad. Alfred Edward Housman. OAEP

And fell asleep again. The Ballad of Hampstead Heath. James Elroy Flecker. MoBrPo

And fell asleep by a fire. Redwings. James Wright. NNaP

And fell back with a splash in the bay. Limerick: "A hippo decided one day." *Anonymous.* TDH

And fell in love with sin. Elegy for a Puritan Conscience. Alan Dugan. NoAm; SM

And fell in the grass and lay there overpowered. For Arthur Gregor. Edward Field. FAZ

And fell it on the start. Dream Songs. John Berryman. CAPP

And fellow patriots' whispered words by night. To A Polish Mother. Adam Mickiewicz. CAW; LiTW

And felt a grandeur that disdained a crown. Mount Vernon, the Home of Washington. William Day. OHIP

And felt as if someone/were there, waiting, alone. The Moon. Robert Creeley. VGW

And felt my heart forbear, my pulse grow still. Brown Boy to Brown Girl. Countee Cullen. PoBA

...And felt the night, tall, black,/Above tall roofs. And Mr. Cooper dead. Mr. Cooper. Anthony Thwaite. OxBTC

And felt the rock move beneath my hand. Butterfly on Rock. Irving Layton. NOBC

And felt the swiftly passing feet of men. Time. Thomas Stephen Collier. AA

And ferns that never fade. After the Winter. Claude McKay. BANP; GoSl; IDB; PoBA

And fertile by faithful toil/Throughout unnumbered years. The Star of Sangamon. Lyman Whitney Allen. PGD

And festering in the infamy of years. A Sketch. George Gordon, Lord Byron. ERoP 1-2; OBRV

And fetch him winter fuel. A Nightly Deed. Charles Madge. NeBP

And fetch my longing soul on high,/That I may sing eternally. Thrice Welcome First and Best of Days. Isaac Chanler. AH

And fetterless high morning dip/Her two cold sandals in the stream. Early Waking. Léonie Adams. LiTM; MoVE

And fewer on graves at the end of the strife. The World Needs. *Anonymous.* PoToHe

And fewer were shyer/than doll. doll A Pretty A Day. Edward Estlin Cummings. CMoP

And fierce as storms that bluster! Song: "O ruddier than the cherry!" John Gay. HBV 1-2; OBEC

And fiery billows roll below. Greenwich. *Anonymous.* AmFP

And fiery tempered steel. Not Honey. Hilda ("H. D.") Doolittle. AnFE; APA; CoAnAm; MoPo

And fiftene sonnes this ladye beere/To Sir Cawline the knight. Sir Cawline. *Anonymous.* ESPB

And fifty fathom deep/Your colours still shall fly. Man Sails the Deep a While. Robert Louis Stevenson. MOS

And fifty francs will earn a stranger right/To take the shuddering city in his arms. Brussels in Winter. W. H. Auden. OBTV

And fight and shout and shout and fight/for North Americay! Free America. Joseph Warren. FSW; PAH

And fill and overflow the heart. Pallid Cuckoo. David Campbell. CBAP; PoAu 1-2

And fill'd the fields of the Evangelist/With thoughts as sweet as flowers. The First Fathers. Robert Stephen Hawker. OBVV

And, fill'd with England's Glory, smiles in Death. Blenheim. Joseph Addison. OBEC

And fill me with Thy perfect peace. The Light Yoke and Easy Burden. Charles Wesley. BePJ

And fill their ears (by word of mouth) with lies. Taylor's Travels from London to Prague (excerpt). John Taylor. OBTV

And fill their mouths with good bread,/And his happy song. Poem for Marc Chagall. Leonard Cohen. OBCV

And fill them gracefully with sud-/den joy. Leave Krete and come to this holy temple. Sappho. BoWoP

And fill these lines with other praise than thine. Jerusalem Delivered (excerpt). Torquato Tasso. CAW

And fill your eyes with sleep! The Shadows. Frank Dempster Sherman. AA

And filled each pause the nightingale had made. The Deserted Village. Oliver Goldsmith. TreFS

And filled the neighbouring village with their praise. The Old Cottagers. John Clare. OBRV

And filled the silence, weeping bitterly. The Look. Elizabeth Barrett Browning. TrCP; TRV

And filled with joy, we'll ever praise. With Christ and All His Shining Train. Thomas Prince. AH

And finally go/out of print. Second Reading. Richard Beyer. AMV-81

And finally he took her. He Took Her. Tom (Thomas Lansing Masson) Masson. OBAL

And finally my face. Lesson for Dreamers. Paul B. Janeczko. PCP

And finally to voices/in the gates/of home. The Alchemical Cupboard. Asa Benveniste. VWA

And, finally, without warning or desire,/the lonely and the feckless end. The Late Hour. Mark Strand. HaCAP

And find a friend at court, I'll find a voice. Eclogues. Virgil (Publius Vergilius Maro). AWP

And find a harvest-home of light. He Liveth Long Who Liveth Well. Horatius Bonar. HBV 1-2; HBVY

And find a hundred Edens at our feet. Independence. Guy Mason. CaP

And find a life of equal bliss,/Or own the next begun in this. A Hymn to Contentment. Thomas Parnell. CEP; NOEC; OBEC

And find an easier Love, tho' not so fair. The Second Pastoral, or, Alexis: The Argument. Virgil (Publius Vergilius Maro). PeHV

And find another lover. Song in Spite of Myself. Countee Cullen. BALP

And find at last, beneath Thy trees of healing,/The life for which I long. At Last. John Greenleaf Whittier. TreFS; TrPWD

And find, beyond the precincts of the day,/The gates of an elysium which is ours. Dreamland (excerpt). Charles Mair. CaP

And find delight in what is truly precious. Radiant Is the World Soul. Rav Abraham I. Kook. VWA

And find holiness, love and the peace which passeth under/standing. It Was Not Fate. William H. A. Moore. BANP

And find Ianthe's name again. Ianthe. Walter Savage Landor. TrGrPo

And find it has snowed. A White City. James Schuyler. ANYP

And find just the sun on a dry, old head. The Old Wife. Rolly Kent. FF

And find my ship with sails all set/By the dim quayside, and embark. The Last Voyage. Katharine Tynan Hinkson. HBMV

And find my solace following the Master's way. Sorrow. Marie Tello Phillips. GoYe

And find myself with/my erector set. The Toy. Cid Corman. GP

And find some star within the blue,/To which I may lead others. Others. *Anonymous.* STF

And find th' effect, for I do burn in love. Astrophel and Stella, XXV. Sir Philip Sidney. AAS; NoP; OAEL 1-2; SiPS

And find that hilltop Hands/have filled your altar cup. New Hampshire Farm Woman. Rachel Graham. GoYe

And find the center rustating, malevolent. Dark Conclusions. Ruth Stone. BoWoP

And find the path/at your soft command. Walk. Frank Horne. BPo

And find the path that, piercing it,/Leads through to Peace again. My Peace I Give unto You. G. A. Studdert Kennedy. EBCP

And find the peace which we had lost before. To R.W.E. Ellen Hooper. AnAmPo

And find the total of their hopes and fears/Dreams, empty dreams.... The Task. William Cowper. CoBE; OAEP

And find thee changeless, Pont-y-wern. Ambarvalia. Arthur Hugh Clough. FaBoPP

And find unwithered on its curls/The garland briefer than a girl's. A Shropshire Lad. Alfred Edward Housman. OAEP

And find where Love's red embers glow/A home, who ne'er had home before. The Heart's Low Door. Susan Mitchell. HBMV

And find your way to the parlour of Government House. Invitation to Hsiao Ch'U-Shih. Po Chu-i. OBVE

And finding a thousand faces round your boots. A Drum for Ben Boyd. Francis Webb. ACV

And finds all fast asleep. The Wonder Clock. Katharine Pyle. OBCA

And finds it a little strange/Beginning with a miniature hell. Comrades As We Rest Within. Ronald Hambleton. CaP

And finds it empty, the purse full. Storm Over Rockefeller Center. Raymond Holden. AnAmPo

And finds its peace/in pain/and in the flow of peace/its dying. I Am a King. Rimon. I. Z. VWA

And finds them ragged babes that weep! The Poor Children. Victor Hugo. AWP

And fingers straying/Upon an instrument. Chamber Music. James Joyce. LOW

And finished knowing–then– I felt a Funeral, in my Brain. Emily Dickinson. AmPP; AnFE; APA; BoWoP; CABA; CMoP; DiPo; ExPo; ForPo; InPo; LiTA; MAmP; MAPA; MasP; NOBA; NoP; OxBA; PBWP; PoEL 1-5; PoRA; SCV; TAP

And fire and ice within me fight/Beneath the suffocating night. A Shropshire Lad. Alfred Edward Housman. NOBV

...And fire/consume the sickness of desire. Pauca Mea: I Said, This Misery Must End. Christopher John Brennan. PoAu 1-2

And fire off a salvo for wine-cups and wars. Song: "The pints and the pistols, the pike-staves and pottles." Winthrop Mackworth Praed. SoSe

And fire the souls that gather here! Through Willing Heart and Helping Hand. Frederick Lucian Hosmer. AH

And fire will presently split the air. At War. Charles Madge. FaBoMo

And fires fade out which were not cold,/Erewhile. Jadis. Ernest Christopher Dowson. VLP

And firesides buried under fallen thatch. Laurence Bloomfield in Ireland. William Allingham. BIrV

And fishermen they fled all day from/(As big as this) and got away from. Fish Story. Richard Armour. LiSp

And fit us, by Thy grace, to share/The triumphs of Thy conquering power. The Triumphs of Thy Conquering Power. William Hiley Bathurst. BePJ

And fit us for heaven to live with Thee there. Away in a Manger. Martin Luther. GoTF; TreFS

And five cards up. Newton's Third. Jake T. W. Hubbard. AMV-80

And five since we were two. Epigram. George Gordon, Lord Byron. FaBoEE

...And fix'd the color of my mind/For every future year. Early Influences. Mark Akenside. OBEC

And fix it deep on this eternal Base. Britannia's Empire. James (1700-48) Thomson. OBEC

And flailed the messsage without air. Breathe dust... Fred Wah. NOBC

And flames flared up in stubborn homage/to their fathering first desire. House of Fire. Theodore Weiss. CoPo

And flashes into false and true,/And mingles all without a plan? In Memoriam A.H.H., XVI. Alfred, Lord Tennyson. VLP

And fled in tears from King and Queen and all. A Forced Music. Robert Graves. MoBrPo

And flee at the very first note! The Musical Lion. Oliver Herford. OBCA

...And flee/Into the heart of terror, to find myself in thee. The Sparrow's Skull. Ruth Pitter. EaLo; FaBoWP

And fleeing fast from Hell! That Hill. Blanche Taylor Dickinson. CDC

And fleets of rich light-laden clouds at dawn. Sonnets, I: "The rough green wealth of wheaten fields that sway." Thomas Caulfield Irwin. IrPN

And flew, instinctively, toward the dawn. The Roc. Richard Eberhart. CMoP

And flew out over the river toward the island. On the Wings of a Dove. Jim Wayne Miller. AMV-80

And flicker in playful flight. Les Halles d'Ypres. Edmund Charles Blunden. MMM

And flies the glory that would not pursue/To yon small cot, a poorly jointured Blue. The Dean's Lady. George Crabbe. LoBV

And flies with the cloud. Chimes. Alice Meynell. AnFE; CH; MoBrPo; SBG; WHY

And flights of angels sing thee to thy rest! Hamlet. William Shakespeare. DL; FaBoRV; FiP

And fling thy wither'd Garlands down/The River.' Odes. Horace. OBVE

And flipped, past sparkling regions, underground. Crane. Joseph Langland. NYBP

And floated away. The Moon in the Water. Ryota. SoPo

And, floating, follow the lazy yachts of the sky. Bathing Song. Anne Ridler. NYBP

And flop to something flipper. Effervescence and Evanescence. Keith Preston. OBAL

And flower-light, precise, and arabesque/Let their praise be. Watching Gymnasts. Robert Francis. LiSp

And flowering springs that mock her empty years? Dirge. Sarojini Naidu. ACV

And flowers, I want flowers on my coffin/While my burial is carried on. When I Am Dead. *Anonymous.* OxBoLi

And flowers in the bud that will never bloom. The Dynasts. Thomas Hardy. CMoP; WaaP

And flowers perched birds. Mirrorment. Archie Randolph Ammons. PCP

And flowers that opened in a song. All Night I Heard. Gertrude MacGregor Moffat. CaP

And fluffy opinions, and no brains at all. I Like Them Fluffy. Sir Alan Patrick Herbert. NLV

And flung his useless pen into the sea. The Broken Oar. Henry Wadsworth Longfellow. AmePo

And flung their crowns at the rising moon. Jumbo Jee. Laura E. Richards. SUS

And flunkeys galore/Poll-powdered, receive them at Paradise door. Hansom Cabbies. Wilfrid Thorley. HBMV

And fluted to the morning sea. To E.L., on His Travels in Greece. Alfred, Lord Tennyson. SeCePo

And fly all alone through the night/toward being the person I am. School Days. William Stafford. LCAP

And fly from joy to dwell with woe. Madrigal: "Oft thou hast with greedy ear." John Cooper. EnRePo

And fly into battle with broken aeriels. Central Park West. Stanley Moss. PCP

And fly up to acknowledge him there! For His Wife, on Her Birthday. Charles Wesley. NOCV

And fold at need a straggling one. The Folded Flock. Wilfrid Meynell. CAW; GoBC; TrPWD

And fold within the wet wings of thy dove. Sonnets from the Portuguese, XXXV. Elizabeth Barrett Browning. EnLi 1-2; ViBoPo

And folded both sheepdog/And Shepherd in Sleep. Ned Vaughan. Walter De la Mare. FaBoEE

And folded to his heart his boy–/Then fainted on the deck. A Leap for Life. Walter Colton. PaPo

And folks who sleep here overnight/Wake up a few quarts lighter. Father and Mother. X. J. Kennedy. GrPl

And follow'd the army, and the Senate in peace sat beneath/morning's beam. The French Revolution. William Blake. ChRP

And follow in thy steps to heaven. Solitude. John Clare. EnRP

And follow on to the fife and drum. King William Was King George's Son. *Anonymous.* AmFP

And follow the cow trail till I die. Trail to Mexico. *Anonymous.* FSW

And followed fettered in the train of Fate! Eric. John Barford. PeHV

And followed Him quite to the cross. The Little Black Dog. Elizabeth Gardner Reynolds. PoLf

And followed it as far as I could/Knowing it would lead me/Out of Egypt. Abraham in Egypt. Howard Schwartz. VWA

And, following thee, in thy ovation splendid,/Thine almoner, the wind, scatters the golden leaves! Autumn. Henry Wadsworth Longfellow. OBVV

And folly cannot die, but cannot grow for ever. ·In Our Time. Michael Roberts. WaP

And folwe we this joyful birth:/Transeamus. The Rose That Bore Jesu. *Anonymous.* OxBM

And food and the simple act of breathing. Valentine. Hollis Summers. GoYe

And foolish Fame, deriv'd from thence, despises. Praise of Homer. George Chapman. OBS

And footsteps pause behind the door– The Coming Forth by Day of Osiris Jones: The Nursery. Conrad Aiken. LOW

And for a breath of ecstasy/Give all you have been, or could be. Barter. Sara Teasdale. FaBV; GoTF; MCCG; SoSe; TreFS

And for a father hear a child!/Ave Maria!' The Lady of the Lake. Sir Walter Scott. EnRP; ISi

And, for a moment or two, accentuate a thirst. Epitaph for Liberal Poets. Louis MacNeice. FaBoIP

And for a space again there was no voice in Heaven. Catherine Kinrade. Thomas Edward Brown. OBVV

And for a' that they did search and ca,/For a kiss o the knight they were striving. The Duke of Athole's Nurse. *Anonymous.* BaBo

And for a time be gaseous and great. The Star System. Richard Wilbur. NLV

And for a word too much men oft have/died. Ku Klux. Madison Cawein. AA; PAH

And for Alice, his wife, pray too. Shameful Death. William Morris. GTBS-P; HBV 1-2; MaC; OAEP; OBVV; VLP

And for all I know men playing billiards temperately in there. The Temperance Billiards Rooms. P. J. Kavanagh. OxBTC

And for alle that on erthe us feden and foster,/Saye we nu alle the haly Pater Noster. A Bidding Prayer. *Anonymous.* OxBM

And for an instant new resentments kill/The swollen wraiths of guiltand perfidy. Here Is Your Realism. Maxwell Bodenheim. AnAmPo

And for bonnie Annie Laurie,/I'd lay me doun and dee. Annie Laurie. William Douglas. FaBoBe; FaBV; FaFP; FSW; GN; HBV 1-2; LiTL; MCCG; PoPle; TreF; WBLP

And for Death's sake, I am in love with Death. His Lady's Death. Pierre Ronsard. AWP

And for each kiss I take would give her twain. Sonnet: "Then whilst that Latmos did contain her bliss." William Alexander, Earl of Stirling. ViBoPo

And for England bore away. The Greenland Whale Fishery. *Anonymous.* AmFP; OBET

And for every pound that you give her,/I'll give her ten thousand pounds. Willie of Winsbury. *Anonymous.* AmFP

And for fifty piastres I give you a past to belong to. Ali Ben Shufti. Anthony Thwaite. OxBTC

And for her sake trip up Death. Little Elegy. X. J. Kennedy. CoAP; ConAP; ELU; GoJo; HoPM; NCSH

And for heroes like Winslow is shouting,/"Thank God!" The Eagle and Vulture. Thomas Buchanan Read. PAH

And for his lufe that bocht us deir/Think on the BLUDY SERK! The Bludy Serk. Robert Henryson. OxBoCh

And for his own soul, that it be the better for them. Amen. The Brut. Layamon. MeEV

And for his sake may no girl win/A corner in my heart. Epigram: "Give me a boy whose tender skin." Martial (Marcus Valerius Martialis). PeHV

And for His service and his throne/Selects the pure in heart. Purity of Heart. John Keble. BLRP

And for hissing was thrown in the street. Limerick: "One evening a goose, for a treat." Oliver Herford. TDH

And for hours and hours, well, that brakeman waited/For a train that will never pull in. The Wreck on the Somerset Road. *Anonymous.* OuSiCo

And for ilk inch he will thee quit a span. Good Counsel. James I King of Scotland. ACP

And for Justice! what has she to do with the Bush? Bush Justice. Charles Harpur. CBAP

And for Lotos-lands I'll never yearn/Maugare Alfred Tennyson. Lotos Eating. Mortimer Collins. NOBV

And for love's sake by Love be granted it! Monna Innaminata. Christina Georgina Rossetti. VLP

And for many rings the might of the hammer. The Lay of Thrym. *Anonymous.* LiTW

And for me, all this is the teeth of the last days of the world. Our Country Is Divided. Faarah Nuur. WTO

And for me to be sitting for a while praying to God in every/place. Wish of Manchin of Liath. *Anonymous.* AnIL

And for my foes may this their blessing be,/To talk like Doeg, and to write like thee. The Second Part of Absalom and Achitophel. John Dryden. OBSV

And for my hunger, you will give me Bread. Ordination. Sister Mary Immaculate. GoBC

And for my mind my heart must give up hope. Sonnet: "My simple heart, bred in provincial tenderness." G. S. Fraser. NeBP

And, for my people's welfare, banish love. Tecumseh. Charles Mair. NOBC

And for neighs, the sable thunder. Clouds. James Reaney. WHW

And for our dubious value it will do./It always does. Making. Phyllis Webb. PoCh

And for sea they bore away. The Whale. *Anonymous.* AmSS

And for short time an endless monument. Epithalamion. Edmund Spenser. EIL; EnL; OBSC; WHA

And, for some fine piece to goggle at, forego/all hope of eating, if the hallmarks show. When You Send Out Invitations, Don't Ask Me. Palladas. OBVE

And for strength to climb, and for eyes to see/His perfect garden of flowers. The Perfect Garden. Winifred Robertson. PoSH

And for such forced iniquity we're damned. If Wishing for the Mystic Joys of Love. Thomas Chatterton. OBSP

And, for that mat-ter, nor does he. Child's Natural History. Oliver Herford. HBV 1-2

And for the dark sad waters where legends swim backward like/squid Song of Expectancy. George Hitchcock. EAS

And for the homestead law he made,/This noble Moses P. Kinkaid. The Kinkaiders (with music). AS

And for the lily's sake! A Cry to Arms. Henry Timrod. PAH

And for the non-observance/of every order. Every Day. Ingeborg Bachmann. PBWP

And for the secret Scripture of the poor. To My Daughter Betty, the Gift of God. Thomas Michael Kettle. CAW; HBMV; OnYI

And for the stone I threw at him/My heart must bear a stone. After the Martyrdom. Scharmel Iris. HBV 1-2

And for the tree that will spring up/Out of those waters/And bear fruit. Psalm. Howard Schwartz. VWA

And for the words the queen had spoke/Young Waters he did die. Young Waters. *Anonymous.* EnLit; ESPB; OxBB

And for the worse,/an end. Wei Wind. Confucius. CTC

And for this I am at your door, waiting. You Have What I Look For. Jaime Sabines. LLLT

And for this trouble of spirit to come to an end. To the River Beach: Stalks of Wild Hay. H. L. Davis. PoA

And for thy Truth the world endure. By Gentle Love. *Anonymous.* TRV

And for thy veil gave me thy FACE. The Hymn of Saint Thomas in Adoration of the Blessed Sacrament. Richard Crashaw. MeLP; OBS

And forced me to turn back. Bangkok. F. R. Scott. OBCV

And forced the underbrush–and that was all. The Most of It. Robert Frost. BiP; CABA; CrMA; HAP; MoPo; NePA; NoP; NU; PPoe

And forest burn in their own funeral. Desire. Kathleen Raine. MoPo

And forfeit his whole life/rabidly/companeros. Central Park Some People (3 P.M.). Nancy Morejo. PBWP

And forges fetters for the mind. Love to Faults Is Always Blind. William Blake. ViBoPo

And forget I ever had ambition Regressing. Franz Douskey. LTB

And forget Phelim Brady, the Bard of Armagh. The Bard of Armagh. *Anonymous.* FSW

And forget the shirt. A New Shirt! Why? Paul L. Grano. PoAu 1-2

And forget these bones all day. The Drowned. Stephen Spender. MOS

And forget your own dark house. An Interview. K. W. Gransden. OxBTC

And forgetful of Europe, walked to bed/In the warm wind from the mountain. And Forgetful of Europe. Geoffrey Grigson. OBTV

And forgive your sins for the honour of Muhammad the Chosen of/beautiful name, O my Khan! The Story of Bamsi Beyrek of the Grey Horse. Dede Korkut. WTO

And forgot every word I designed to have said. A Lover's Anger. Matthew Prior. ErPo; UnTE

And forgot that he was a slave! Breath in My Nostrils. Lance Jeffers. CNA

And forgot to sail back up/in the high open sunny air. Rooftop. Willis Barnstone. FAZ

And forgotten everything after/on our journey into the dark. Love at Roblin Lake. Al Purdy. NoP

And form to him the relish of their souls. Nature's Influence on Man. Mark Akenside. CEP; OBEC

And forms itself/into the letters of your name. Too Late. Rachel Korn. VWA

And forms more bright than diamond diadems. The Winter Galaxy. Charles Heavysege. NOBC; OBCV

And forsake the mother of paths? Words Wherein Stinging Bees Lurk. Judah Halevi. TrJP

And forth I stride. On the Doorstep. Thomas Hardy. MoVE

And forts and frontier settlements will all be scenes of blood. The Gathering on the Plains. William Allen Butler. PoOW

And Fortune captive at her feet, condemned and conquered lies! Time Stands Still, with Gazing on Her Face! *Anonymous.* EnLoPo

And fortune said it should be you. The Rose Is Red, the Violet's Blue. *Anonymous.* OxNR

And Fortune tarnish every gem/That glitters in your diadem. Advice to Julia. Henry Luttrell. OBRV

And forty times he kissed her ruby lips/And let his lady in. John of Hazelgreen (C vers.). *Anonymous.* BaBo

And forward still the boatman moved, and made no sound. Death of a Jazz Musician. William Jay Smith. NePoAm-2

And forward, tho' I canna see,/I guess and fear. To a Field Mouse. Robert Burns. CBEP; GTBS-P

And fought his battles with anointed spears. A Dead Soldier. George Edgar Montgomery. AA

And fought his last fight. Mustang Gray. *Anonymous.* ABF; BFSS; CoSo

And fought the British Lion to his knees? Salem. Robert Lowell. AnNE; NePoEA

And fought with the invulnerable tide. Cuchulains's Fight with the Sea. William Butler Yeats. AnIL

And found himself/smiling. Brass Tacks. Denise Levertov. InPS

And found his fingers grafted to their backs. Indian Love Song. Lew Blockcolski. VoR

And found it was perfectly true. An Old Man from Peru. *Anonymous.* FaFP

And found Life stepping on my feet! Esthete in Harlem. Langston Hughes. BANP; BPo

And found myself in Thee–the Father then/Will come with Thee, and will abide with me. Within and Without. George Macdonald. TRV; WGRP

And found your ain true love. Ballad. William Soutar. NeBP

And 4 police cars parked outside the painted/gate, red lights revolving in the leaves. First Party at Ken Keseys with Hell's Angels. Allen Ginsberg. ConAP

And four times he who gets his fist in/fust. Thrice Is He Armed That Hath His Quarrel Just. Josh Billings. GoTF; TreFT

And fourth on a pig. First in a Carriage. *Anonymous.* OxNR

And fourth, whom Canning and Sir Will/preserve. The Royal Line. [James Henry] Leigh Hunt. FaBoUs

And foxes stunk and littered in St. Paul's.' On Lord Holland's Seat near Margate, Kent. Thomas Gray. CABA; LAuP; NOEC; OAEL 1-2; SeCeV; TW

And frail-headed poppies. Acon. Hilda ("H. D.") Doolittle. VGW

And free'd his soul the nearest way. On the Death of Dr. Robert Levet. Samuel Johnson. CEP; EBEV; EiCP; HBV 1-2; HeIP; InPS; LAuP; NOBE; NOEC; NoP; OAEL 1-2; OBEC; OBEV; PAI; PoEL 1-5; PPP; SCV; TEP; ViBoPo

And free for aye from sin's foul tyranny./Erasmus, his vow. Votive Ode. Desiderius Erasmus. ISi

And free land of the grave. Crossing Alone the Nighted Ferry. Alfred Edward Housman. ChMP; FaBoRV; GTBS-P; NOBE; NoP; OBSP

And free us all the wandering winds that blow/across the ruined rooftops of the world. Climb in Torridon. Brenda G. Macrow. PoSH

And free us from all ills/In this world and the next. Now Thank We All Our God. Martin Rinkart. GoTF; TreFS

...And freedom from my facile fears. Spring Stops Me Suddenly. Valentin Iremonger. OnYI

And freedom from our vast ambitions' fears? Victory Parade. George Edward Hoffman. PGD

And Freedom's banner streaming o'er/us? The American Flag. Joseph Rodman Drake. AA; AmLP; FaBoBe; FaFP; GN; HBV 1-2; HBVY; MC; PAH; PAL; PaPo; PGD; TreF; WBLP

And Freedom shall awhile repair,/To dwell a weeping hermit there! How Sleep the Brave! William Collins. GN; GoTF; HBV 1-2; HBVY; NOBE; OBEV; TreF

And Freedom smiles, her fate secure,/Beneath its steadfast stars. The Flag. Harry Lyndon Flash. MC

And freely give her Love. The Sound Country Lass. *Anonymous.* CoMu; ErPo

And freer dreams of heaven. The Alpine Flowers. Lydia Huntley Sigourney. AnAmPo

And freeze you back with that one hope, disdain. The Zonnebeke Road. Edmund Charles Blunden. MMM; OBWP

And frequently walked about Ryde. Limerick: "There was a young lady of Ryde." Edward Lear. OxBoLi

And fresh joys, as never too/Have ending. The White Island. Robert Herrick. AnAnS 2; HBV 1-2; JCP; NoP; OAEL 1-2; OBS; OxBoCh; WiR

And fresh your garlands. The End of the Story. Terence Tiller. ChMP; NeBP

–And Friday, my dear Friday, died of measles/seventeen years ago come March. Crusoe in England. Elizabeth Bishop. HaCAP

And frightened him so he spilled it. The Man in the Moon. Mother Goose. SoPo

And frightened Miss Muffet away. Little Miss Muffet. Mother Goose. FaBoBe; FaFP; HBV 1-2; HBVY; SoPo; TiPo

And frightens all the people. A Bestiary. Kenneth Rexroth. OBAL

And frolicked when I was able to in the soggy Scottish air. The Soldier (parody). J. Y. Watson. BXAP

And from a dripping hemlock crest/Falls the cold remnant of a nest. Midwinter Thaw. Lenore Pratt. CaP

And from afar 'tis all Descry'd. Reason. The Use of It in Divine Matters. Abraham Cowley. AnAnS 2

And from Hell tempestuous under! Storm at Sea. *Anonymous.* AnIL

And from his Minch of sherries mumble laws. Culloden and After. Iain Crichton Smith. OxBS

And from his presence instantly withdrew. The Gascon Punished. Jean de La Fontaine. UnTE

And from his rocky rostrum the dipper bows, and blesses/Every river sound and sight. The Dipper. Phoebe Hesketh. PoSH

And from his wrists the flame/Thaws manacles of ice. Hugh Maguire. Eochy O'Hussey. KiLC

And from it blazes down/The light of thy renown! Custer. Edmund Clarence Stedman. BPAW; PAH

And from its tiny window/Peeps a maple-sugar child. This Little House Is Sugar. Langston Hughes. NTCP

And from louts to run away! Eleventh Song. Sir Philip Sidney. EG; EnLi 1-2; TEP

And from my bosom find a surer rest. The Earth. Jones Very. AmP; OxBA

And from my heart, Lord, I would rout/All bitterness. This is my prayer. Prayer for Strength. Margaret E. Bruner. PoToHe

And from my view all objects shutting out. Very Old Man. James Henry. NOBV

And from now on the Earth without doors is your home. To Silvestre Revueltas of Mexico, in His Death. Pablo Neruda. AMV-81

And from our earthly memory fade away. Sonnet: Composed after a Journey across the Hamilton Hill, Yorkshire. William Wordsworth. ChRP

And from seed to seed/will remain last/one soul alone. She. Manfred Winkler. VWA

And from sky headlands/The gods looking down. The Cities. George William Russell. OBMV

And from Spring's choirstalls Amens clear and loud/End Winter's prayer. The Tall Sky. Arthur Ball. PoSH

And from that flaccid bundle upward cast/the blank, constrictive shade in which he'd live. The Murderer. Paul Petrie. NYBP

And from that ground there blossoms red/Life that shall endless be. O Love, That Wilt Not Let Me Go. George Matheson. TreFS; TrPWD; TRV; WGRP

And from that hour those Bachelors were never heard of more. The Two Old Bachelors. Edward Lear. BeLS; FiBHP; ShM

And from that song-cloud shaped as a man's/hand/There comes the sound as of abundant rain. The House of Life. Dante Gabriel Rossetti. VLP

And from that to the deluge of waters/In bounty and peace remain. Kilcash. *Anonymous.* BIrV; KiLC; OBMV; OxBI

And from the Ancient Hills alone we catch the view. Epigram: "Save by the Old Road none attain the new." Coventry Patmore. FaBoEE

And from the bosom's handkerchief/Bloom as it ne'er had lost a leaf. The Shepherd's Calendar. John Clare. FaBoUs

And from the bridges dangle trains and trams. End of the World. Jakov van Hoddis. VWA

And from the craggy ledge the poppy hangs in sleep. There Is Sweet Music Here. Alfred, Lord Tennyson. FaBV

And from the crouded Fold, in Order, drives/His Flock, to taste the Verdure of the Morn. Summer Morning. James (1700-48) Thomson. OBEC

And from the edge/Come pull me away. Slender Maid. Joseph Eliyia. VWA

And from the everlasting hills,/A song of rapture pour'd. Request of a Dying Child. Lydia Huntley Sigourney. OBCA

And from the flame, or from offensive taints/Pernicious to thy cattle, saves their food. A Method of Preserving Hay from Being Mow-Burnt, or Taking Fire. Robert Dodsley. FaBoUs

And from the force that works within the stream/The hidden working of the "Truth" may learn. The Hidden Truth. Jami. LiTW

And from the fulness of his heart he fished/A dime for Jesus who had died for men. Karma. Edwin Arlington Robinson. AmPP; AnNE; CMoP; CoBMV; HeIP; MoAB; MoAmPo; NoAm; OFD; TrCP

And from the hands of those that kept/silent. From All Peoples (excerpt). Nathan Alterman. TrJP

...And from the heat/Thereof is hid nothing. The Heavens Do Declare. *Anonymous.* AH

And from the Heaven within the Heaven of Heavens. Perhaps. Sydney Thomas Dobell. NOBV

And from the house his mother called his name. Childhood. Edwin Muir. CMoP; HeIP; NoP; SeCePo

And from the soil great Troy, Neptunus' town. The Shield of War. Thomas, Earl of Dorset Sackville. NOBE

And from the Star Chamber in Westminster Hall,/Libera nos Domine. A New Litany in the Year 1684. *Anonymous.* APAS

And from the stars still falls the answering fire. Zarathustra. Thomas S. Jones, Jr. AnAmPo

And from the twentieth story hurls/To the pave the factory girls. Journal (excerpt). Edna St. Vincent Millay. SaC

And from the wood/The hoot came ghostly of the owl. Stone Trees. John Freeman. BoNaP

"And from the yellow sod/The bees return to God." The Bees. Monk Gibbon. OnYI

And from thee many a parent stem/Arise to deck our land. On the Birth of a Posthumous Child, Born in Peculiar Circumstances... Robert Burns. NAs

And from their holes black eagles flew/screaming through the streets Malcolm. Lucille Clifton. CNA

And from their nests of clay/Like disembodied spirits suddenly fly away. The Young Martins. Andrew Young. FM

And from their strength my bones will/sing, that pine/to greet the Messiah. Place Me in the Breach. Yehuda Karni. TrJP

And from this nothing seen, tells news of devils,/Which but expressions be of inward evils. Sonnet C. Fulke, Lord Brooke Greville. QFR

And from those pretty things you speak have told/How Pallas talked when she was seven years old. Upon a Girl of Seven Years Old. Alexander Pope. OBSP

And from thy darkened window fades the light. The Evening Star. Henry Wadsworth Longfellow. AnNE

And front the sun undaunted: Pope is dead! Spoken Extempore on the Death of Mr. Pope. *Anonymous.* NOEC

And frowzy pores that taint the ambient air. Jacob Tonson, His Publisher. John Dryden. ChTr

And fruit killed them. Three Friends. *Anonymous.* BoWoP; PBA

And full five and twenty hundred ships/Perish'd all on the coast of Spain. The Carpenter's Wife (The Daemon Lover). *Anonymous.* OAEL 1-2; OxBB

And full of burning, it will whistle on a brick. Mr. Edwards and the Spider. Robert Lowell. SM

And full of furie on their maister feede,/To hasten on my haplesse death with speede. Devoide of Reason, Thrale to Foolish Ire. Thomas Lodge. AAS

And full of peace and light as this southern land! Distant View. Uys Krige. PeSA

And full of peace he died. Epigram: "Paddy, I have but stol'n your living." Ebenezer Elliott. FaBoEE

And full of understanding as the stars/That shone in wonder over Galilee. Confession. Elsa Barker. HBMV

And furnish, what the heart with transport fills,/The finest fishing. The Praise of New Netherland. Jacob Steendam. PAH

And furthermore I do hereby pronounce/Divorce between the nightingale and thee. Malvolio (parody). Walter Savage Landor. Par

And g-rrr lumbered off to his eight o'clock/Gladly to teach. A Teacher. Reed Whittemore. NCSH

And gained in service of our fair/And universal Queen. Pangloss's Song. Richard Wilbur. AP; NePoAm-2; NLV; NoAm; OxBC

And gained sufficient power/For ten evangelists. Communal. Mary Elizabeth ("E") Fullerton. PoAu 1-2

And gains the glorious title of/"Most Timid in the Land." A Bunny Romance. Oliver Herford. OBCA

And gainst the morn at twelve o'clock./He dined with his kind Scottish men. Gude Wallace (A version). *Anonymous.* BaBo; ESPB

And Galahad to me. My Hero. Benjamin Brawley. BANP; PoNe

And gallop terribly against each other's bodies. Autumn Begins in Martins Ferry, Ohio. James Wright. CAPP; HaCAP; InPK; InPS; NaP; PAI; PoL

And galloped woodward in that guise. Metamorphosis. Sylvia Plath. PoA

And Ganymede gives notice in the skies. Familiar Faces, Long Departed. Robert Hillyer. NYBP

And garland-streams. The Starre. George Herbert. AnAnS 1; AtBAP

And gateways, to the river and the bridge/Under the city walls. The Light of Asia (excerpt). Mrs. Major Arnold. OBTV

And gather an image whole. Reading in War Time. Edwin Muir. WaP

And gather in their blushing prime/The roses of your youth! Ronsard to His Mistress. William Makepeace Thackeray. HBV 1-2

And gather in your brow and air/The stillness of antiquity. At Majority. Adrienne Rich. NePoEA-2

And gather roses, while 'tis called to-day. Of His Lady's Old Age. Pierre Ronsard. AWP; CTC

...And gathered the mouth of Thora/to his mouth. Old Fisherman with Guitar. George Mackay Brown. BSV

And gathered up to Heaven, leave here a Spring. To the Best and Most Accomplished Couple--. Henry Vaughan. HW

And gathering all the fruits of earth and/crown'd with all her flowers. Ode Sung at the Opening of the International Exhibition. Alfred, Lord Tennyson. VLP

And gathering swallows twitter in the skies. To Autumn. John Keats. AnEnPo; AtBAP; AWP; BiP; BoNaP; DiPo; EBEV; ERoP 1-2; FaBoRV; FF; FiP; ForPo; FPL; GoTF; HAP; HBV 1-2; HBVY; InPK; InPo; InPS; InvP; LiTB; MBW 1-2; MyFE; NAWM 1-2; NIP; NOBE; NoP; NU; OAEL 1-2; OAEP; OBEV; OBNC; OBRV; PoEL 1-5; PoLf; PoPle; PPoe; PPP; Prf; PrIm; RoGo; SCV; SeCeV; SoSe; TEP; TreFS; UnPo; ViBoPo; WHA

And gathering up for use his ill-aim'd cocoa-nuts. Epigram: "Science, the agile ape, may well." Coventry Patmore. FaBoEE

And gathers multitudes like game to be hunted when the season comes. A Little Scraping. Robinson Jeffers. NoAm

And gave him his job again. The Daniel Jazz. Vachel Lindsay. CBEP; TrGrPo

And gave him his Rabinical degree,/Unknown to Foreign University. Absalom and Achitophel. John Dryden. EBEV

And gave him just ten minutes to skedaddle. The Pike's Peakers. Lawrence N Greenleaf. PoOW

And gave him such a lesson as might well suffice for ten. The School-Master and the Truants. John Brownjohn. OBCA

And gave it up with the morning light. The Midnight Court. Brian Merriman. BIrV

And gave that strength of feeling, great/Above all human estimate! Fidelity. William Wordsworth. FM

And gave the merchants everything they wanted. Fable of the Water Merchants. Stephen P. Dunn. LTB

And gave the Prince of Orange her. What Is the Rhyme for Porringer? *Anonymous.* OxNR

And gave to worms his corpse–to fiends his soul.   On Ryneveld, an Unpopular Dutch Judge at the Cape of Good Hope.   *Anonymous.* FaBoEE

And gave up loving/and lived with her.   A Marriage.   Robert Creeley. LiTM; NeAP

And gaze, and gazing think, how base a thing am I.   Arcades Ambo (parody).   Charles Stuart Calverley.   BXAP

And gaze on earth with shy glad eyes.   Easter in the Woods.   Frances Frost. BrR; SiSoSe

And gaze on God, into His azure eyes   Sursum.   Guillermo Valencia. CAW

And gaze upon his own dear son, swinging on the gallows high.   Rose Connoley.   *Anonymous.*   AmFP

And gazed when she had gone.   The Viper.   Ruth Pitter.   FaBoTw

And generally our planet/is like a recruit/sweating on a march.   Verses on Accepting the World.   Joseph Brodsky.   VWA

And gentle Mary, mother mild,/Did comfort Christ, the blessed child.   In All the Magic of Christmas Time.   John Jacob Niles.   AH

And gently lay us on the Spicy shore.   The New London.   John Dryden. FaBoCh

And gently leads the yoes that are with young.   Shepherd.   Edmund Charles Blunden.   HBMV

And gently spak the howie hill/Cuckoo, cuckoo.   The Gowk.   William Soutar.   BSV; NeBP

And gently with thy Hand replace the Gut.   Infant Diseases and Their Treatment.   M. Saint-Marthe.   FaBoUs

And Germans with no envy in their souls.   The Eugenist.   Robert Graves. FaBoEE

And get a job with it–as thunder!   Dan Dunder.   John Ciardi.   BBGG

And get back/before dark.   Feeding the Lions.   Norman Jordan.   BOLo; CTBA; NBP; PoBA

And get me a place to sleep in the hay/At the end of a live-and-let-live day. From the Santa-Fe Trail.   Vachel Lindsay.   LaNeLa

And get me back to my burrow.   Elf Owl.   Mary Austin.   BPAW

And get my bloody old sins washed white!   Stand-To: Good Friday Morning. Siegfried Sassoon.   FaBoTw

And get you gone, you little old/man!   My Little Old Man and I Fell Out. *Anonymous.*   OxNR

And gets more prompt reply.   Dial Call.   Christopher Morley.   NLV

And, getting up, he said, "Ah, there you are!"   At the Algonquin.   Howard Moss.   Psk

And ghastly comets over the raised fists.   Why East Wind Chills.   Dylan Thomas.   AtBAP

And ghosts then keep their distance; and I know some liberty.   Wessex Heights.   Thomas Hardy.   CMoP; FaBoPP; OAEL 1-2; OBNC; PoEL 1-5

And giblet pie/Is cheap in Rome to-day.   Goosey Goosey Gander.   William Percy French.   CenHV

And gie ye frogs instead o fish,/And play ye foul, foul play.   Katharine Jaffray (A vers.).   *Anonymous.*   BaBo; ESPB; ViBoFo

And giggles the child awakened/into day.   Untitled.   Peter Blue Cloud. VoR

And gilded pills, though bitter, may delight/The liquorish lust of wav'ring appetite.   The Happy Pair (excerpt).   Sir Charles Sedley.   OBSV

And gin the next, I'm dull as you:/Mix a' thegither.   Burns at Tea.   Barry Pain.   HBV 1-2

And ginger-bread nuts are smallish.   Dawlish Fair.   John Keats.   PoPle

And gingling sashes on the pent-house sound.   The Dangers of Foot-Ball. John Gay.   EnLi 1-2; SD

And gird us for our duties.   A Reminiscence of 1820.   H. H. Dugmore. ACV

And give a sadness to serenity.   The Borough.   George Crabbe.   OBRV

And give all the babies the colic.   Limerick: "You remember that pastoral frolic."   R. K. B.   LiBL

And give all thy blushes/And sweets to thy God.   Written to a Young Lady. Jeremiah Joseph Callanan.   IrPN

And give each tyrant to his grave/And freedom to each lovely land.   My Political Faith.   George Frederick Cameron.   PeCV

And give her angel plumage there!   My Bird.   Emily Chubbuck Judson AA

And give her so much of that/she doesn't need any more.   The Chandler's Wife.   *Anonymous.*   FSW

And give her to the god of storms/The lightning and the gale!   Old Ironsides. Oliver Wendell Holmes.   AA; AmePo; AmLP; AnNE; AP; BLPA; EtS; FaBoBe; FaFP; FaPo; FPL; GN; GoTF; HBV 1-2; HBVY; MaC; MC; MCCG; MOS; PAH; PAL; PoPl; TAP; TreF; YaD

And give him a dip upon the lip,/and the blood run to his toes.   Little Phoebe.   *Anonymous.*   FSW

And give him the largest half!   Sambo's Right to be Kilt.   Charles Graham Halpine.   AA

And give hundreds of thousands for their daughter's return.   Polly Oliver's Rambles.   *Anonymous.*   OBET

And give it good thought/OK?   Please Say Something.   Tomioka Taeko. WPOW

And give me back my freedom once more.   Married and Single Life. *Anonymous.*   AmFP

And give me, in adversity,/The heart that still can trust and sing.   A Prayer. Marion Franklin Ham.   TrPWD

And give me keener eyes to mark/The moving of Thy hand.   Christ's Sympathy.   Edward Robert Bulwer, Earl of Lytton.   BePJ

And give me meat, or give me else thy plate.   Upon Showbread: Epigram. Robert Herrick.   CaPo

And give me strength to surrender my strength to thy will with love.   For Strength.   Rabindranath Tagore.   MoRP

And give me the Heath; it's flat!   A Roundabout Turn.   Robert E. Charles. MoShBr

And give my tongue the glory/To boast, though my unfaithful eyes/Betray a tender story.   Song: "Too late, alas! I must confess."   John Wilmot, Earl of Rochester.   HBV 1-2

And give resounding grace to all Heaven's harmonies!   A Masque Presented at Ludlow Castle (Comus).   John Milton.   BoLiVe; ExPo; NOBE; OBEV; SeCeV; TrGrPo

And give thanks it was not I, nor yet one close to me.   The Open Sea. William Meredith.   CoAP; GrPl; MOS; NePoEA; TAP; UnPo

...And give/The ill he cannot cure a name.   A Wish.   Matthew Arnold. DBV

And give the reason why 'tis so.   Charm for Corns.   *Anonymous.*   FaBoUs

...And give/the wind away.   Small Song.   Archie Randolph Ammons. NoP; PoL

And give Thee thanks.   Song of Thanksgiving.   John Richard Moreland. PGD

And give them back/their eyelessness.   America.   Wendy Rose.   CDW

And give to dust that is a little gilt/More laud than gilt o'er-dusted.   Troilus and Cressida.   William Shakespeare.   LiTB

And give us a better atmosphere!   Israel Freyer's Bid for Gold.   Edmund Clarence Stedman.   PAH

And give us giftes most of prize,/Heaven to be our heritage.   Service Is No Heritage.   *Anonymous.*   CBEP; OxBM

And give you, white-footed field mice, my fidelity.   To the Field Mice. Richard Eberhart.   BoAnP

And given me back to weary care.   A Little While, a Little While.   Emily Bronte.   OBNC; OxBI; ViBoPo

And giver of all good things.   At the Grave of Henry James.   W. H. Auden. LiTA; MoPo; NoP

And gives all her girlfriends surprises.   Limerick: "A Lesbian born under Pisces."   *Anonymous.*   PeHV

And gives at need (as one who understands)/Draft, counsel, diagnosis, exhortation.   Staff-Nurse: New Style.   William Ernest Henley.   NBM

And gives back an image, the image of music?   Recital (excerpt).   Louise Townsend Nicholl.   UnS

And gives me back my life.   The Lost Angel.   Philip Levine.   NOBA

And gives me outdoor shadows/To haunt my indoor house.   Sing a Song of Juniper.   Robert Francis.   LOW; NCSH

And gives to candor all the grace/The heart can in its temple trace.   Forcing a Way.   *Anonymous.*   NA

And giving in to nothing/is too simple a choice/for madmen and black wings Captured Bird.   George Rachow.   LFAC

And giving it a name: No No No   Settler.   Stewart Lindh.   PoA

And glaciers move through the great beast's heart.   Ariel.   David Campbell. CBAP; PoAu 1-2

And glad hearts welcome back again/Her white sails from the sea!   The Ship-Builders.   John Greenleaf Whittier.   AnNE; EtS

And, glad to behold her young, the bird gave thanks/to the morn.   Epilogue. Aubrey Thomas De Vere.   IrPN

And gladly drudge at the accustom'd plough.   Fair and Softly.   Philip Ayres.   FaBoEE

And, gladly, spring begins.   Rural Dumpheap.   Melville Cane.   AmFN

And gladly wolde he lerne, and gladly teche.   The Canterbury Tales: A Clerk. Geoffrey Chaucer.   MBW 1-2; TrGrPo; ViBoPo

And glass were the faces in the last looking-glass.   And the Seventh Dream in the Dream of Isis.   David Gascoyne.   EAS

And glittering eyelids of my soul's desire.   Love and Sleep.   Algernon Charles Swinburne.   BoLoP; UnTE; VLP

And glitters next/in the Eagle's twice born eyes...   Twoborn.   Rokwaho. STE

And gloom, the name alone survives, Bob's Lane.   Women He Liked. Edward ("Edward Eastaway") Thomas.   HaMV

And glorify His name.   Thanksgiving Hymn.   *Anonymous.*   PAH

And glorious must their triumph be.   Our Country's Call.   William Cullen Bryant.   AnNE; MC; PAH

And glory for all time/Keep the boy Tom who tending geese/First made the nursery rhyme.   Wild Strawberries.   Robert Graves.   FaBoCh; LoGBV

And glory, laud, and praise be ever thine.   God of Our Fathers, Whose Almighty Hand.   Daniel C. Roberts.   AH

And glory shone around. Sherburne. *Anonymous.* AmFP

And glory thus bloom o'er the tomb of the/brave. The Tomb of the Brave. Joseph Hutton. PAH

And glory to our Sovereign Lord, King Henry/of Navarre! Ivry. Thomas Babington, Lord Macaulay. FaBV; GN; HBV 1-2; HBVY; OBRV

And glory will our valor crown. A Song: "Smile, Massachusetts, smile." *Anonymous.* PAH

And glow, beyond all telling bright,/Each time a brave soul dares a flight. The Eyes of God. Hermann Hagedorn. HBMV

And glowed a long time before it went out. Looking West. William Stafford. NYBP

And glowrin wi her een! Cat at the Cream. *Anonymous.* GBP; PoL

And go and get my portrait done. Christmas Thoughts, by a Modern Thinker. William Hurrell Mallock. NOBV

And go and kiss within the hay. Ametas and Thestylis Making Hay-Ropes. Andrew Marvell. ALV; CavP; InvP; SeCP

...And go/back to work happy at the thought possibly so. Personal Poem. Frank O'Hara. CAPP; NYP

...And go, believing they find us in the well-staged/parks. Tourism. Lillie D. Chaffin. TAT

And go contented to their sheep. The Shepherd's Ode. Robert Greene. OBSC

And go find thee in the sphere. Odes, XII. Hafiz. AWP

And go home to my Lord/And be free. Oh Freedom. *Anonymous.* FSW

And go in hope from this to Thee,/The pupil of Thy country air. A Prayer. Norman Gale. TrPWD

And go in there. And sleep. John Carey's Second Song. Thomas McGrath. FAZ

And "go it for" Tyler and "Tippecanoe." Old Tippecanoe. *Anonymous.* PAH

And go on pulling at the long rope. The Lives of Famous Men. Jack Gilbert. NPGG

And go, one hand held out, to meet a friend? The Corridor. Thom Gunn. NePoEA; PPP

And go out by the terrible gate. Eden: Or One View of It. Theodore Spencer. NePA

And go, though our paths separate for good. Chinese Poems: Arthur Waley. C. A. Fair. PeSA

And go to bed with backward looks/At my dear Land of Story-books. The Land of Story-Books. Robert Louis Stevenson. FaBoBe; HBV 1-2; HBVY; TiPo; TreFS

And go to strike, each with his trenchant lance. The Song of Roland, CCXL. *Anonymous.* WaaP

And go to the tenys. Hayll, Comly and Clene. *Anonymous.* AtBAP; OxBoLi

And go undreaming to our paradise. Corliss Engine-Wheel. MacKnight Black. AnAmPo

And goal of its age-long pilgrimage. The Songs of the Birds. Edward Carpenter. WGRP

And God alone be Lord! To William Lloyd Garrison. John Greenleaf Whittier. PAH

And God alone has saved me from my sins. God's Gifts. Jakov De Haan. VWA

And God alone will know his sin upon the judgment day. The Bank Thief. J. R. Farrell. BeLS; BLPA

And God and Angels, guard his Tent and Throne. God Save the King, That King That Sav'd the Land. Benjamin Harris. SCAP

And God, and Truth, and Freedom die! Our Orders. Julia Ward Lowe AA

And God as well, or I'm much mistaken. Donal Ogue. *Anonymous.* KiLC

And God at every gate. Our Journey Had Advanced. Emily Dickinson. AtBAP; ILwL; LiTA; LiTM; MoAB; NOCV; PoEL 1-5; QFR

And God bless me. I See the Moon. *Anonymous.* GBP; NTCP; OxNR; SoPo; TiPo

And God Bless the Duke of York/Who chose you as his bride. For the Queen Mother. Sir John Betjeman. NAs

And God for a frontier. I am afraid to own a body. Emily Dickinson. LiTA

And God forbid I look behind/Since that appalling day! The only ghost I ever saw. Emily Dickinson. NePA; WSC

And God formed each, and formed their sphere,/And thus his goodness doth appear. The Mole and the Eagle. Sarah Josepha Hale. OBCA

And God, God sent him to sea for pearls To Christopher Smart. Joseph Stroud. NPGG

And God has crossed the Delaware! Across the Delaware. Will Carleton. MC; PAH

And God help the lover of snakeskin and stone. Snakeskin and Stone. Keith Douglas. NePoEA

And God Himself and the rebels God threw into hell. To the Ghost of John Milton. Carl Sandburg. PP

..And God is here again, and/all His angels. God Is Here Again. Charles Angoff. AMV-80

And God made the little boy/To holla off the crow./Holla, boys, holla, hip hip hurrah! Bee Wassail. *Anonymous.* OBET

And God may call...and call...and/call. Doomsday Morning. Genevieve Taggard. MoAmPo

And God's good blessing is the end. Hymns for the Amusement of Children. Christopher Smart. NOCV

And God's great brow, the heavens, enfold/Its ashes like an urn. Domestic Scenes. Miguel de Unamuno. LiTW

And God's high praise sung to us,/For ever and for aye. Blessed Be the Holy Will of God. *Anonymous.* OnYI

And God's name written there–"John Doe." God's Acre. Witter ("Emanuel Morgan") Bynner. AnEnPo

And God's sweet peace when every day is done. A Birthday Wish. Dorothy Nell Mcdonald. PoToHe

And God save al this fayre companye! Amen! The Canterbury Tales: The Knight's Tale. Geoffrey Chaucer. GoTL; OBWP

And god save noble/Kynge/Henry/the VIII. A Ballade of the Scottyshe Kynge. John Skelton. CoMu; FaBoBa

And "God Save the King!" all his subjects' hearts say. England's Sovereigns in Verse. *Anonymous.* BLPA

And God send you a Happy New Year. Here We Come A-Wassailing. *Anonymous.* PCh

And God shall give him gold for his hire–not coin, but a crown! The Tapestry Weaver. Anson G. Chester. BLPA; BLRP; WBLP

And God shall hear your words and make them true. Optimism. Ella Wheeler Wilcox. BLPA; BLPL; FaBoBe

And god shall sende luck, to kepe open thy doore. A Hundreth Good Poyntes of Husbandry. Thomas Tusser. FaBoUs

And God the Father be by all adored./Alleluia! All Praise to Thee. F. Bland Tucker. AH

And God, the soul's desire. The Hill. Horace Holley. WGRP

And God visited him every day out of pity/Till in the end he became a most noble saint. The Road to Hate. Patrick Kavanagh. TW

And God, who knows who are the heroes,/Will give you the strength for the strife. Our Heroes. Phoebe Cary. BLPA

And God, Who sometimes spits right in its face. Two Somewhat Different Epigrams. Langston Hughes. NePoAm-2

And God, your glorious grave, your home. Ah Dearest Love, for How Long. Mechtild of Magdeburg. ILwL

And Goddes son is maked our make. Hand by Hand We Shall Us Take. *Anonymous.* SBVL

And gods are not begot from devils' sperm. Begetting. Dorothea Spears. PeSA

...And gods/are silent. The Paradox. Francesca Yetunde Pereira. PBA

And gods are supposed/but flowers be The Plight. James W. Thompson. BPo

And goes through the shut iron gate/With a pansy in his buttonhole. Man into a Churchyard. Bernard Gutteridge. EAS

And goest on thy way. He Singeth in the Underworld. Book of the Dead. AWP

And Goethe who never thought of Thought. University Examinations in Egypt. D. J. Enright. MP; OxBTC; TwCP

And going on forever This Is Our Music. George Leong. BrSi

And going to the office in the train. Dreamers. Siegfried Sassoon. BrPo; HBMV; MCCG; MoBrPo; NoAm

And gold is strained like sunshine/Through the heath. Lord Fluting Dreams of America on the Eve of His Departure... Paul Zimmer. VGW

And gold on my neck the sun. The Collier. Vernon Watkins. DTC; FaBoTw; MoVE

And golden light, and Golden Light! Cathemerinon: O Noble Virgin. Prudentius (Aurelius Clemens Prudentius). ISi

And golden-sphered persimmons spread o'er all. Autumn in the West. William Davis Gallagher. AA; AnAmPo

And gone to ashes, cold and gray. But Then and There the Sun Bore Down. N. Scott Momaday. CDW

And good but wished with God is done! The Waiting. John Greenleaf Whittier. WGRP

And good-by to the bar and its moaning. The Three Fishers. Charles Kingsley. BBV; BeLS; EtS; FaPoR; HBV 1-2; MCCG; OnMSP; PoLf; TreF; WBLP

And good to love the race of men a little ere we go. A Song of Fleet Street. Alice Werner. HBV 1-2

And goodbye to the fragrant world. Buster Keaton & the Cops. George Keithley. NPGG

And goodly were the deeds it wrought. En Las Internas Entranas. Saint Theresa of Avila. WPOW

And–goodness gracious! The Merry Little Maid and Wicked Little Monk. *Anonymous.* ErPo

And goodness only knowses/The Noselessness of Man. The Song of Quoodle. Gilbert Keith Chesterton. GoJo

And got well, while the scorpion died of the bite.   On Fell.   Gotthold Lessing.   ShM

And gracious! how Lord Lundy cried!   Lord Lundy.   Hilaire Belloc.   FaBoCo; OBSV; OxBoLi

And grackles by the shadow of a fountain.   Dearest Reader.   Michael Palmer.   NPGG

And Grandma hums prays hums   Remedies.   Gary Soto.   Str

And granite in man's character.   New England Is New England Is New England.   Brenda Heloise Green.   GoYe

And grant, as Timon grows, his hate may grow/To the whole race of mankind, high and low!/Amen.   Timon of Athens.   William Shakespeare.   EBEV; TW

And grant each day that I shall live/Will be Thanksgiving Day.   Thankful Heart.   F. W. Davis.   STF

And grant, henceforth, that foul debate/'Twixt noblemen may cease!   Chevy-Chace.   *Anonymous.*   EnLi 1-2; FaBoBa; GN; HBV 1-2; OBET; ViBoFo

And grant his reign over the entire building.   Homage to the British Museum.   William Empson.   CMoP; FaBoMo; LiTM; MoAB; MoBrPo

And grant me grace, and make you hear!   My Garden Is a Pleasant Place.   Louise Driscoll.   BLPA; FaBoBe

And grant me my second/starless inscrutable hour.   Whoroscope.   Samuel Beckett.   NoAm

And grant my soul in after days/In clovered meadowlands to graze.   Psalm of the Fruitful Field.   Abraham Moses Klein.   WHW

And grant new scions from each friendly sky.   To the Federal Convention.   Timothy Dwight.   PAH

And grant that henceforth fool debate/'Twixt noble lords may cease.   The Hunting of the Cheviot (C vers.).   *Anonymous.*   BaBo; ESPB; OAEP

And grant that in the shades below/My ghost may land the ghosts of fish.   The Last Chance.   Andrew Lang.   NOBV; SD

And grant their dead shall not have died in vain.   Mary at the Cross.   Clyde McGee.   PGD

And grant us in the end/The gift of sleep. Amen.   The Day Returns.   Robert Louis Stevenson.   TRV

And grass and goose-grass seeds found soil and grew.   Birds' Nests.   Edward ("Edward Eastaway") Thomas.   HeIP

And grasses green of sweet content.   The Grasses Green of Sweet Content.   Arthur Hugh Clough.   VLP

And grateful too/For sunlight on the garden.   The.Sunlight on the Garden.   Louis MacNeice.   BiP; CMoP; CoBMV; EBEV; GTBS-P; HAP; InPS; LiTB; MoPo; MP; NoAm; NOBE; NOBI; NoP; OAEP; OxBI; OxBTC; PPoe; PrIm; TwCP

And graunted hym on to be God, and graythly non other.   Jonah Is Cast into the Sea.   *Anonymous.*   OxBM

And grave by grave we civilize the ground.   To the Western World.   Louis Simpson.   CAPP; CoAP; ConAP; LiTM; NePoAm-2; NePoEA-2; NOBA; PoPl; SM; TAP

And grave is never far away.   Death Walks through the Mind's Dark Woods.   Henry Treece.   NeBP

And grave thy name immortal.   The Death of Lyon.   Henry Peterson.   PAH

And, gravely acquiescent, bows his head.   Discourse Heard One Day.   Donald Campbell Babcock.   NePoAm-2

And graze upon the sky.   Silver Sheep.   Anne Blackwell Payne.   SiSoSe

And greased it nice/With camphor-ice.   Oh, No!   Mary Mapes Dodge.   BBGG

And great-grandfather will be one of those.   Great-Grandfather.   Freda Downie.   FaBoWP

And great kings turned to a little bitter mould.   One Day.   Rupert Brooke.   MoLP

And great souls, at one stroke, may do and doat.   Sonnets from the Portuguese, XXXII.   Elizabeth Barrett Browning.   ViBoPo

And great Thy Wisdom, VANDER BRUIN.   A Dutch Proverb.   Matthew Prior.   CEP; FaBoEE; NOEC; PoL

And Greece and Troy retreat on either side.   Of Ballad-Singers.   John Gay.   EnLi 1-2

And Greece indignant thro' her seas returns.   The Iliad.   Homer.   ATP

And green as a grasshopper's leg is the evening sky.   Persian Miniature.   William Jay Smith.   CoAP; MoVE

And green sage cheese.   Will You Be My Little Wife.   Kate Greenaway.   MoShBr

And green spreads everywhere.   As the Rains of Spring.   Izumi Shikibu.   PBWP

And greet each hour with gratitude.   Life Owes Me Nothing.   *Anonymous.*   PoToHe

And greet her glory's dawn.   Father! I Own Thy Voice.   Samuel Wolcott.   AH

And greet the Blood-besprinkled bands/On the eternal shore.   The Ever-Living Church.   Charles Wesley.   STF

And greeted each other with the word "Peace."   Our Flag Was Still There.   Richard Tillinghast.   MAYP

And greets her friends as deaths' new wife.   Memorial Service.   Ursula Vaughan Williams.   PoL

And Gretchen is holding it fast.   A Little Dutch Garden.   Hattie Whitney.   AA

And grew wiser and better as his strength wore away,/Without Gout or Stone, by a gentle Decay.   The Old Man's Wish.   Walter Pope.   CoMu; OBS

And grey hairs were on my head.   The Angel.   William Blake.   CH

And grief unto my darling joys dost bring.   To–.   John Keats.   SyP

And grinds your charcoal with its own sad dust.   The Pavement Artist.   James Kirkup.   HaMV

And grins, then wipes the sweat from his hair.   Boy's Will, Joyful Labor without Pay, and Harvest Home (excerpt).   Robert Penn Warren.   SaC

And grope, in the green wheat,/Toward the woodwinds of the Western freight.   Aubade: Lake Erie.   Thomas Merton.   NYBP

And grow like birds, from ugliness to wings.   And Grow.   John Hay.   WaP

And grow old faithfully/With my master/Whom I was predestined to find.   The "Word" of a Watch-Dog.   Sandag.   WTO

And grow rich toward your God.   Your Money and Mine.   *Anonymous.*   STF

And grows with its roots upward!   Riddle: "Lives in winter."   Mother Goose.   HBV 1-2; NTCP; SoPo; TiPo

And guard the wells of pity of the/heart.   These Are the Chosen People.   Robert Nathan.   TrJP

And guarded as my own,/All my life long.   Shadow-Evidence.   Mary Mapes Dodge.   AA

And guards with arm of superhuman might/This favour'd land of liberty and light.   The Electric Telegraph.   Thomas Baker.   FaBoUs

And guide thee at last to the heavenly/garden.   Meditations.   Solomon Ibn Gabirol.   TrJP

And guile is where it goes.   Sweet Is the Swamp with Its Secrets.   Emily Dickinson.   MAPA

And gulp from them the dailiness of life.   Well Water.   Randall Jarrell.   NOBA; NoP; OBSP; VGW

And gyve me grace and forgyvenes/Of my mys-dede.   Confiteor.   *Anonymous.*   CoBE

And H-U-S-H spells–hush!   Adam and Eve.   Itzik Manger.   TrJP

And habit builds the bridge at last!   A Builder's Lesson.   John Boyle O'Reilly.   PoLf; PoToHe

And had a chancre the size/Of a chrysalis on her crotch.   Kafka's Other Metamorphosis.   Len Gasparini.   NeAC

And had a friend/Named Mary Magdalene.   Irony of God.   Eva Warner.   TrCP

And had a story left out of their lives.   In an Old House.   Spencer Brown.   NYBP

And had again their own high wall and hard.   The Runaways.   Mark Van Doren.   PoRA

And had another lad concealed/Beneath the tablecloth.   Teatime Variations.   Peter Titheradge.   FaBoPa

And had been left in darkness forever to founder and/fail.   After the Publication of Under the Volcano.   Malcolm Lowry.   FaBoTw

And had good sense, good nature, and good looks.   On a Gentleman Marrying His Cook.   Colin Ellis.   FaBoEE

And had I but an hour to live,/That little hour to bliss I'd give.   Ode of Anacreon.   Thomas Moore.   LoBV

And had not been asleep at the switch.   Asleep at the Switch.   George Hoey.   BeLS

And had read all the sovran schemes and divine riddles there.   Lines on the Celebrated Picture by Leonardo Da Vinci...   Charles Lamb.   ISi

And had told all, but did refrain/Because his tongue was tied again.   Upon Julia's Fall.   Robert Herrick.   UnTE

And hadde a wyf that heeld for contenance/A shoppe, and swyved for hir sustenance.   The Murder in the Cathedral: The Cook's Tale (parody).   Geoffrey Chaucer.   BXAP

And hadn't the courage to follow.   Limerick: "He died in attempting to swallow."   Roy Campbell.   LiBL

And hail upon the vine!   Praise of Earth.   Elizabeth Barrett Browning.   OBVV

And half a ha'penny candle.   My Father Died.   *Anonymous.*   PoPle

And half a yard of parkin hanging down below his knee   The Highland Tinker.   *Anonymous.*   CoMu

And half awake, half dreaming I/Aspire through you to heaven high.   Mother Earth.   Anna Margolin.   VWA

And, half believing, only half deny.   The Breaking of the Day.   Peter Davison.   CoPo

And half dried up thy waters be.   Song of the Argonauts.   William Morris.   EtS

And half had stagger'd that stout Stagirite!   Written at Cambridge.   Charles Lamb.   EnRP; OBRV

And half her crew, slow stealing through the Golden Gate.   The Ballad of the Ivanhoe.   Bill Adams.   BBV

And half illume the long departed dead.   Aspiration.   William Drennan.   IrPN

And half of the biddies in Moultrie. Limerick: "A certain old party of Moultrie." Jr, Blount Roy. TDH

And half our Judges are our Rivals too. Books. George Crabbe. OBEC

And halt and hobbled dragged the cars. For the Bicentenary of Isaac Watts. Norman Nicholson. EaLo

And hamadryads, in God, and the proud enigmatic angels. The Proud Trees. Walter H. Kerr. NePoAm-2

And hammer it til cold and flat. To an Old Poet. Walter Savage Landor. DBV

And hammered stars into the unforgetting sky–like nails/I am Goya I Am Goya. Andrei Voznesensky. OBWP; WeW

And hand on heart/is hand on every heart. When You Touch. William Hart-Smith. BoAV

And hands reach out to drag us down below. Graves Are Made to Waltz On. Peter Viereck. PoA

And hands so often clasp'd in mine,/Should toss with tangle and with shells. In Memoriam A.H.H., X. Alfred, Lord Tennyson. VLP

And hang a pearl in every cowslip's ear. A Midsummer-Night's Dream. William Shakespeare. BoLiVe; BoNaP; EiL; GN; HBV 1-2; HBVY; InvP; NOBE; OBSC; PoPle; TrGrPo; ViBoPo

And hang from implacable boughs. Chagrin. Isaac Rosenberg. ChMP; MoBrPo; VWA

And hang it in the junior college. Digging for Indians. Gary Gildner. AmPA

And hang like dreams around his guilty bed. Sonnet: The French and the Spanish Guerillas. William Wordsworth. ChRP

And hang limp and clean, an empty dress– The Five-Day Rain. Denise Levertov. NeAP

And hang them to dry,/On a clear frosty night,/From the beams of the moon. Fairy Wings. Winifred Howard. SUS

And hang, to dry upon the shore,/My trowsers and my jacket. Ode to Popularity. Winthrop Mackworth Praed. VLP

And hapless Lovers constancy in Love. Gondibert. Sir William Davenant. OBS

And, haply, from the nectar-breathing Rose/Extract a Blush for Love! Songs of the Pixies. Samuel Taylor Coleridge. OBEC

And happier systems bring to view,/Than all the eastern sages knew. On the Emigration to America. Philip Freneau. PAH; TAP

And happily I move/Forgetting weariness. Song: "I was so chill, and overworn, and sad." Anna Wickham. MoBrPo

And happiness is love. I've Learned to Sing. Georgia Douglas Johnson. GoSl

And happiness will come to you again. For One Lately Bereft. Margaret E. Bruner. PoToHe

And happy am I. And Happy Am I. Syd Scroggie. PoSH

And happy be the lot o' a' that wish the boat to speed. The Boatie Rows. Anonymous. OBSS

And Happy Birthday, with twice my heart. One, Two, Buckle My Shoe. Ogden Nash. BiCB

And happy dreams, we'll meet again next year! The Last Violet. Oliver Herford. OHIP

And happy each at home enjoys his love. Cymon and Iphigenia. John Dryden. OBNV

And happy the man who seeketh for mercy/From his heavenly Father, our Fortress and Strength. The Wanderer. Anonymous. AnOE; LiTW; NAWM 1-2; OAEL 1-2

And happy to be alive meanwhile. The Firmament Displays on High. Barend Toerien. PeSA

And hard as winter dies. Winter: East Anglia. Edmund Charles Blunden. LiSp; OxBTC

And harden not your heart. The Hidden Line. Joseph Addison Alexander. BLPA

And hardens her to bear/Serene the ills of life. To an Early Primrose. Henry Kirke White. HBV 1-2; OBNC; OBRV

And hardly know, at the first view,/If I were here, or there. On His Portrait. William Cowper. EyDe

And hardly safe from brother traitors there. To Sir Toby. Philip Freneau. AP; NoP; TAP

And hardy fingers find an eagle's hold. A Happy View. C. Day-Lewis. CMoP

And hark, the happy shepherds cry,/'Tis Kate of Aberdeen. Kate of Aberdeen. John Cunningham. HBV 1-2

...And harness you/fast,/With a cobweb, to Oberon's car. To the Lady-Bird. Anonymous. PoPl

And harpers harping on a sea of glass. Speculative Evening. Marguerite Young. LiTA

And Harry (The Cat) Brecheen? Where, O Where? Milton Bracker. LiSp; SD

...And has fed/Ineffectual herds of vanished delights. The Gazelles. Thomas Sturge Moore. BrPo; OBMV

And hast but showed me how I may resign/Possession of those things are none of mine. The Lady A. L., My Asylum in a Great Extremity. Richard Lovelace. CaPo

And hast command of every part/To live and die for thee. To Anthea, Who May Command Him Anything. Robert Herrick. BoC; CaPo; CBEP; EnLit; GTBS; GTBS-P; HBV 1-2; JCP; LoBV; NOBE; OAEL 1-2; OAEP; OBEV; OBS; SeCP; SeCV 1-2; TrGrPo; ViBoPo

And haste away over the steppes. Gilgamesh Laments the Death of Engidu. Anonymous. LiTW

And haste to thy fast-anchored isle,/O Johnny Bull, my jo. Johnny Bull, My Jo, John. Anonymous. FSW

And hate my next-door neighbor. The World State. Gilbert Keith Chesterton. CoBE; DBV

And hated life with heart and soul. In Time of War. W.H. Auden. CMoP

And hated the moon, he said. Moonlight. Berta Hart Nance. AmFN

And hates that form She knows to be her own. Conscience. Charles Churchill. OBEC

...And hatred, hatred of all men/–and disgust. The Raper from Passenack. William Carlos Williams. TW

And haue saved my children thre,/All and my louesome wyffe.' Captain Car, or, Edom o Gordon (A version). Anonymous. BaBo; ESPB; OAEP; ViBoFo

And hauls me gasping sandwards through his sonnet. Rope's End. Peter F. Neumeyer. WOLT

And haunt the houses you never built? Bombers. C. Day-Lewis. CMoP; MoAB

And haunt the places where their honour died. On Certain Ladies. Alexander Pope. FaBoCo

And haunt them when you depart. Song for a Departure. Elizabeth Jennings. GOYP; NMP

And haunted by all mystery. Dust. George William Russell. WGRP

And haunted with the ghost of home. The Empty House. William Dean Howells. AmePo

And haunts my breast by absence made/The living tomb of love. The Mistress (excerpt). John Wilmot, Earl of Rochester. ViBoPo

And have assumed the throne. C. G. Jung's First Years. Thomas Kinsella. IPY

And have compassion as in days/gone by. Loved of My Soul. Israel Najara. TrJP

And have done what they have told themselves to do. Metaphor for My Son. John Holmes. MiAP

And have forgotten since their beauty passed. Tears. Edward ("Edward Eastaway") Thomas. CBEP; GTBS-P; LiTB; PoPle

And have His bliss and blessedness for ever! The Whale. Anonymous. AnOE

And have its will upon the extreme seas. On Leaving Bruges. Dante Gabriel Rossetti. CBEP

And have maintained your honor in the same,/Who herein holds an interest in my fame. To the Right Worthy Knight Sir Fulke Greville. Samuel Daniel. EnRePo

And have mercy/On all that trows that God was born of thee, levedy. The Five Joys. Anonymous. OxBM

And have more cause than e'er I had before,/To fear that I shall never see thee more. Orinda to Lucasia Parting, October, 1661, at London. Katherine ("Orinda") Philips. OBS

And have no skill in either mode of song,/the graver English, or lyric Irish tongue. Once Alien Here. John Hewitt. CIP; NeIP

And have not wavered wickedly/Against my Lord and God. The Lord Descended from Above. Thomas Sternhold. AH

And have one Titan at a time. The Master. Edwin Arlington Robinson. AmP; HBV 1-2; LiTA; MoAB; MoAmPo; OHIP

And have proved unto him far better than their word,/As they sailed... The Golden Vanity. Anonymous. ViBoFo

And have the time to sort things out and make up. Two. Margarita Aliger. VWA

...And have their audience in whatever/hearing the heart or the deep of the belly owns. Regent's Park Terrace. Bernard Spencer. FaBoPP

And have turned slowly away to watch the stars/without counting losses. Arm Wrestling with My Father. Jack Driscoll. GOYP

And have within our Selves possest/All Love's and Nature's store. The Match. Andrew Marvell. EBEV

And having done that, thou hast done;/I fear no more. A Hymn to God the Father. John Donne. AWP; BiP; DiPo; EBCP; EBEV; EnLit; EnRePo; ForPo; GoBC; HAP; HBV 1-2; InPo; JCP; LiTB; LoBV; NoP; OAEL 1-2; OBS; OxBoCh; PoRA; PPoe; SCV; SeCeV; TrCP; TrGrPo; ViBoPo

And, having gained truth, keep truth: that is all. A Death in the Desert. Robert Browning. TRV

And, having meanly lived, is grandly dead. T.A.H. Ambrose Bierce. AA; AnAmPo; YaD

And having no need to let myself be robbed/a second time. Nomen. Naomi Long Madgett. BlSi

And having nothing: yet hath all.   The Character of a Happy Life.   Sir Henry Wotton.   AnAnS 2; EiL; FaPoR; GTBS; GTBS-P; HBV 1-2; HBVY; LiTB; MCCG; NOBE; OBEV; OBS; TreF; TrGrPo; ViBoPo.

And having now no more to say, I think it fit to end.   The Suburbs Is a Fine Place.   *Anonymous*.   CoMu

And having pleas'd our art wee'll try/To make a new, and hang that by.   In the Person of Woman Kind.   Ben Jonson.   NIP; SeCP; SeCV 1-2

And, having swerved, no might or main/Can ever put her straight again.   Songs about Life and Brighter Things Yet.   Samuel Hoffenstein.   NLV

And having the knob come off/in your hand.   The Comedian Said It.   Duff Bigger.   FAZ

And having to understand/for real   Virginia.   Elouise Loftin.   PoBA

And hawks nested there.   Walking on Sunday.   Richard Murphy.   IPY

And haze, and vista, and the far horizon, fading away.   A Farm Picture.   Walt Whitman.   InPS; PAI; PPoe

And he a larger package:/a brand-new windowshade.   Puerto Ricans in New York.   Charles Reznikoff.   CTBA

And he and his eight hundred/Must plough the wave no more.   On the Loss of the "Royal George."   William Cowper.   AnFE; EBEV; EtS; FiP; GN; HBV 1-2; InPo; MyFE; NOBE; OAEP; OBEC; RoGo; TrGrPo

And he answered, "I'm very well-buttered."   A Baker's Dozen of Wild Beasts.   Carolyn Wells.   OBCA

And he answered: "It's just as I thunk."   Limerick: "There was an old man in a trunk."   Ogden Nash.   CenHV; FaBoCo

And he, as sovereign Lord and King/Forevermore shall reign.   The Majesty of God.   Thomas Sternhold.   WGRP

And he beams on them all, the Old Showman.   The Puppet Play.   Padraic Colum.   RoGo

And he bled at the nose.   Unfrocked Priest.   Joseph Campbell.   AnIL; OnYI

And he bought a wedding Ring-o!   Bingo.   *Anonymous*.   CH

And he brake that gallant ship in twain,/And sank her in the sea.   James Harris (C vers.).   *Anonymous*.   BaBo; ESPB; FaBoBa 10]

And he but a blacksmith's son./Ri fol diddle O day.   The Knight and the Shepherd's Daughter.   *Anonymous*.   AmFP; BaBo; ViBoFo

And he called for his fiddlers three.   Old King Cole Was a Merry Old Soul.   Mother Goose.   ExPo; FaBoBe; FaFP; HBV 1-2; HBVY; OxNR; SoPo

And he can take the food for his soul,/Through the grace of our dear Lord.   The Nature of the Eagle.   *Anonymous*.   PBBP

And he cheerfully answered her, "Nomb."   Limerick: "Bill learned to play tunes on a comb."   *Anonymous*.   TDH

And he cherish'd his heart with a cup of old sack,/Oh ho! Oh ho! Oh ho! did he so?   There Was a Maid Went to the Mill.   *Anonymous*.   GBP

And he couldn't do it.   Somebody Said That It Couldn't Be Done.   *Anonymous*.   FiBHP

And he couldna preach for thinkin' o't.   We're a' Dry wi' the Drinkin' o't.   *Anonymous*.   ELU; ErPo

And he'd go and fetch her the drake, drake, drake.   Sam, the Sportsman.   *Anonymous*.   OxNR

And he dances all day, and/He likes himself.   A Goblinade.   Florence Page Jaques.   TiPo

And He dare not be silent or send me away.   Creed.   Anne Spencer.   CDC

And he departed swiftly as he came.   The Celestial Pilot.   Dante Alighieri.   WGRP

And—he did it with a saw.   Similia Similibus.   John Hunt Morgan.   ShM

And he did—nine soliloquies later.   Hamlet.   Stanley J. Sharpless.   NLV

And he died in the chamber that Jeanie died in.   Lord Saltoun and Auchanachie.   *Anonymous*.   BaBo; ESPB

And he died on the waters, away, far away!   O Brazil, the Isle of the Blest.   Gerald Griffin.   ACP

And he dips it in the moisture/Till it crackles and is quenched.   Princess Sabbath.   Heinrich Heine.   TrJP

And he does not like to wait!   A Psalm of Life.   Andrew Lang.   CenHV

And he doth best, that passeth all the rest.   Poetry's a Gift Wherein but Few Excell.   Nathaniel Ward.   SCAP

And he drew one Leg after a great way behind.   A Shepherd Kept Sheep on a Hill So High.   Thomas D'Urfey.   CoMu; ErPo

And he drives us out of the city/To be stabbed on a lonely hill.   Prophets for a New Day.   Margaret Walker.   BPo

And he droops, and turns, and goes.   In the Servants' Quarters.   Thomas Hardy.   MoAB; MoBrPo; MoRP

And he drops off to sleep/With one paw on his nose.   A Kitten.   Eleanor Farjeon.   TiPo

And he drove me off without a rap–the stringybark cockatoo.   The Stringybark Cockatoo.   *Anonymous*.   NOAV

And he drowned in the low-down, lonesome low.   The Low-Down, Lonesome Low.   *Anonymous*.   OuSiCo

And he follows its Gleam from the dawn to the gloaming.   The Fiddler.   Edna Valentine Trapnell.   HBMV

And He gave that dear mother to me.   A Wonderful Mother.   Pat O'Reilly.   BLPA

And he got lucky/stoled her back again.   Devil Got My Woman.   Skip James.   BluL

...And he got up in the way, like an armed robber, with a pike in/his hand.   He Understands the Great Cruelty of Death.   John Millington Synge.   BIrV; OBMV

And he grinned and said, "You ought to see that gol-darned wheel."   The Gol-Darned Wheel.   *Anonymous*.   CoSo

And he had lived enough when he had dried her tear.   For an Epitaph at Fiesole.   Walter Savage Landor.   FaBoEE; OBNC; OBRV

...And he hangs with closed eyes/and the concentration of someone listening to music.   Three-Toed Sloth.   Dorothy Donnelly.   HoAn

And he has got my wishing/In an awful knot.   The Fisherman.   David McCord.   TiPo

And he has something to do and what's/to die from–who's close to many, closer.   Iowa Land.   Marvin Bell.   SaC

And he has yet to live.   Manifest Destiny.   Anita Endrezze Probst.   CDW

And He hath not forgotten my age.'   The Old Man's Comforts and How He Gained Them.   Robert Southey.   HBV 1-2; HoPM; OxBChV; PaPo; Par; SpRo; UnPo

And he held up in his hand/the key,/which blinded me.   The Illumination.   Stanley Jasspon Kunitz.   GP; TAP

And he in ruth of my distressed cry/Plants me a weeping star within mine eye.   Diana.   Henry Constable.   OBSC

And he is ever a sad disgrace/To Jewish creed and Jewish race.   The Hypocrite.   Ben Kalonymos.   TrJP

And he is happy now because the spectators only call him a/little bum.   Decline and Fall of a Roman Umpire.   Ogden Nash.   SD

...And he is laughing, laughing/Like a Spanish guitar.   Lines to Garcia Lorca.   LeRoi (Imamu Amiri Baraka) Jones.   NNP

And he is mindful of his garden,/which prepares to die.   The Mulch.   Stanley Jasspon Kunitz.   GP

And he is wrought of the anguish of them that have greatly/needed him.   The Awakening.   Don (Donald Robert Marquis) Marquis.   HBMV

And he laughs, ha ha!–who cares! who/cares!   The Cowboy.   John Antrobus.   AA; FaBoBe

And he lay alone on pieces of unbleached canvas,/violently breaking into sail.   The Poet at Seven.   Arthur Rimbaud.   NaP

And he learned of finalities/Besides the grave.   The Hill Wife.   Robert Frost.   CMoP; HAP; InPS; LiTM; NePA; NoAm; NoP

And He led me toward the hills and the breaking of day in the/lone East.   The Gate of the Year.   M. Louise Haskins.   TRV

And he lets his hair grow long and snarley.   Limerick: "C is for Curious Charlie."   Isabel Frances Bellows.   TDH

And he lived over nine hundred years.   Methuselah.   *Anonymous*.   BLPA; BLPL; FaBoBe; GoTF; QQQ; TreFS

And he lives happily up in his hills.   I Am Now So Weary with Waiting.   Gaspara Stampa.   WPOW

And He'll conquer every foe!   Room for Jesus.   Barbara H. Staples.   STF

And he'll fight till by death overpowered.   The Cowboy.   *Anonymous*.   MaC

And he'll give us all a share/I dreamed–   Someone Like No One Else.   Forugh Farrokhzad.   WPOW

And he'll help thee climb up Calvary.   Come, Precious Soul.   *Anonymous*.   AH

And he'll never come bathing with me any more.   Nursery Rhymes for the Tender-Hearted.   Christopher Morley.   HBMV; YaD

And he'll not see his mother/When the work is done this fall.   When the Work's All Done This Fall.   *Anonymous*.   AS; BFSS; BPAW; CoSo; FSW

And he'll pay you back when he hoists his jack for a pilot down to/Tiger Bay.   Tiger Bay.   *Anonymous*.   OBSS

And He'll soon come back to take me/Where with Him I'll always be.   He Never Will Forget.   M. G. H..   STF

And he looked me in the eye and he said, Alone.   Edgar's Story.   X. J. Kennedy.   OFD

And he lost his case.   Ballad of the Trial of Sodom.   Vernon Watkins.   MoRP

And he made answer on high, "Is any here/Of fuller being than I? I'll bow to him!"   The Book of God's Madness.   Ralph Chubb.   PeHV

And he made her queen of the broader lands/He held of his lute in fee.   The Singing Leaves.   James Russell Lowell.   GN

And he made little Mary his bride.   William and Mary.   *Anonymous*.   AmFP

–And he made such funny faces!   Some Ruthless Rhymes.   Harry Graham.   CenHV

And he made the Bishop to dance in his boots,/And glad he could get so away.   Robin Hood and the Bishop of Hereford.   *Anonymous*.   BaBo; BuBa; ESPB

And he must be hanged tomorrow.   A Song: "I'll sing you a song."   *Anonymous*.   OxNR

And he must fall a Prey to Time,/While she is blooming in her Prime.   Cadenus and Vanessa (excerpt).   Jonathan Swift.   OxBI

And he ne'er came home again. God bless the Queen.   Upon Sir Francis Drake's Return from his Voyage about the World...   *Anonymous.*   CoMu; EIL; FaBoCh; OBSS

And he never returned to stand trial/For the awful deed that he had done.   Lula Vires.   *Anonymous.*   AmFP

And he never saw his bonny lady!   Annan Water.   *Anonymous*   CH; HBV 1-2

And he, not I, is here immortalized.   The Statue of Lorenso de Medici.   James Ernest Nesmith.   AA

And he owre him.../Till day brak.   This Is Willy Walker, and That's Tam Sim.   *Anonymous.*   OxNR

And he pays all his debts with the roll of his drums.   How Happy the Soldier.   *Anonymous.*   LoGBV

And he perchance attempt to scale,/Discharge the Jordan at him.   Odes.   Horace.   OBVE

And he piped his eye like a fool, oh!   The Dunce.   *Anonymous.*   OxNR

And he played upon a razor,/and his name was Willy Wood.   Aiken Drum.   *Anonymous.*   FaBoCh; LoGBV

And he points the way politely/To the playground or the park.   P's the Proud Policeman.   Phyllis McGinley.   SoPo; TiPo

And he returned to the merry green-wood,/With great joy, mirth and pride.   Robin Hood and the Two Priests.   *Anonymous.*   BuBa

And he's awake who thinks himself asleep.   What the Thrush Said.   John Keats.   DiPo; EBEV; NIP

And he's buried in the Louisiana Country-o.   Peggy-o.   *Anonymous.*   FSW

And he's drowned in the sea.   The Lowlands O'Holland.   *Anonymous*   CH

And he's goin', "Quank, quink-quank,"/Lord, Lord, Lord.   The Gray Goose.   *Anonymous.*   FSW

And he's got the game fixed so he'll win it.   Limerick: "Should a plan we suggest, just that minute."   *Anonymous.*   LiBL

...And he's making sure no more extra branches getting in/the way.   The Mango Tree.   Eric Chock.   BrSi

–And he's out there mowin' now.   Medical Aid (parody).   Walter Hard.   BXAP

And he's probably laughing still at the sound that came out of its/bill.   Ducks.   Frederick William Harvey.   BoC; EBCP

And he's set her on ahin' her love/And she's gane singin' hame.   The Bents and Broom.   *Anonymous.*   OxBB

And he's the one who has made it all.   The Simple Purification.   *Anonymous.*   NU

And he's trying to breathe thro' but one!   On a Valetudinarian.   Ibn al-Rumi.   LiTW

And he's twyn'd himself o' his ain sweet life/On the bonnie banks o' Fordie.   Baby Lon; or, The Bonnie Banks o' Fordie.   *Anonymous.*   SeCePo

And he said, "Cheep, cheep, cheep."   Good Morning.   Muriel Sipe.   SoPo; SUS; TiPo

And he said, "I always did get/them two guys mixed up."   Religion Back Home.   William Stafford.   OBAL

And he said,"My love was weary–God/bless her! she's asleep."   Asleep.   William Winter.   AA

And he said so again and again.   Limerick: "There was a young man on a plain."   William Jay Smith.   TDH

And he said to Susan, "My dear, what next?"   Susan.   *Anonymous.*   NA

And he sailed, by Sirens and thence outward and away/And unto Circe.   The Odyssey.   Homer.   OBVE

And He shall redeem Israel from all his iniquities.   Psalm CXXX, De Profundis.   Bible, O.T.   BLRP

And He shall your establishment renew.   Psalm XXXI.   Sir Philip Sidney.   FCP

And he showed me–'twas a stone.   The Wanderer.   Yehoash.   TrJP

And he steals off, leaving his stick unclaimed.   Outside the Window.   Thomas Hardy.   BrPo

And he stitches, until he drops dead at/his work.   The Tailor.   Joseph Leftwich.   TrJP

And he supplied my want the more/As his unlikeness fitted mine.   In Memoriam A.H.H., LXXIX.   Alfred, Lord Tennyson.   OAEL 1-2; OAEP

And he takes aim. And fires.   On Teaching David to Shoot.   Walter McDonald.   AMV-80

And he that's in bed with another man's wife,/It's time to get him away.   The Hunt Is Up.   *Anonymous.*   GBP

And he that shrieks from pride.   A Man Young and Old: The Friends of his Youth.   William Butler Yeats.   AtBAP

And he that was sae true to me,/Lies in the greenwood slain.   The Unquiet Grave.   *Anonymous.*   CBEP

And he thats no Cuckold, in Countrey or City,/However lucke hold, will buy this our Ditty.   The Merry Cuckold.   *Anonymous.*   CoMu

And He, the bounteous Sire, has given/His peace on earth,–his hope of Heaven!   An Evening Walk in Bengal.   Reginald Heber.   OBTV

And he there takes no interest in them.   To Think of Time.   Walt Whitman.   AnFE; AP; APA; BLPL; CoAnAm; LiTA

And he thinks of that secret room, half-way.   The Jogger: Denver to Kansas City.   David Ray.   FAZ

And he throws her a stray glance yearningly.   At Tea.   Thomas Hardy.   BrPo

And he, "To begin with a swelled head and end with swelled feet."   Ezra Pound.   Robert Lowell.   NoAm; NOBA

And he, too, whom we have by heart.   Unto Us a Son Is Given.   Alice Meynell.   EBCP; MoRP

And he trembled like a heatwave and faded.   Station Island (excerpt).   Seamus Heaney.   FaBoIP; FaBoPV

...And he waits for the world to begin.   Leviathan.   William Stanley Merwin.   ConAP; NePoEA; NoAm; NOBA

And he wanders the woods and wonders where the warriors have gone.   Gadoshkibos.   Diane Burns.   STE

And he was himself, besides, symmetrical and beautiful/of form, without blemish or reproach.   Cormac Mac Airt Presiding at Tara.   *Anonymous.*   BIrV

And he was left lamenting.   Lord Ullin's Daughter.   Thomas Campbell.   BeLS; FaPoR; GN; GTBS; GTBS-P; HBVY; OBRV; RoGo; TreF; WBLP

And he was off before you could say Jack Robinson.   Jack Robinson.   *Anonymous.*   OBET

And he was running all the way to the door where my grandmother/stood.   We'll All Feel Gay.   Winfield Townley Scott.   MiAP

And he was strong–and I was half asleep.   Seduced Girl.   Hedylos.   BoLoP; ErPo

And he was sure to view them.   Corruption.   Henry Vaughan.   CAW

And he welcomed death/From his head to his feet.   The Tragedy of Pete.   Joseph Seamon, Jr Cotter.   CDC

And he went him into the holy land,/Wheras Christ was quicke and dead.   Old Robin of Portingale.   *Anonymous.*   ESPB

And he went to fix it right.   Fixer of Midnight.   Reuel Denney.   OBAL

And he went to the chase with a tear on his cheek.   The Childless Father.   William Wordsworth.   CH

And he wept with delight in attempting to say/He considered the Beaver his friend.   The Hunting of the Snark.   Lewis (Charles Lutwidge Dodgson) Carroll.   NA

And He who charmed the troubled waves to sleep/With deathless words, would kneel again and weep.   Christmas 1930.   Anderson M. Scruggs.   CAW

And he who fain would find it, first must die.   Love's Entreaty.   Buonarroti Michelangelo.   AWP

And he who gives a passion-flower/Always asks it back.   Tampico.   Grace Hazard Conkling.   HBMV

And he who has one enemy shall meet him everywhere.   Make Friends.   Ali Ben Abu Taleb.   TRV

...And he/Who holds me today will in the end/Love me in another's body.   Before Your Waking.   Anna Greki.   WPOW

And he who judges is always innocent.   Tuesday, 4 March (Morning) 1963.   Pier Paolo Pasolini.   AMV-81

And he who sees no longer fears to die!   India the Magic.   H. A. Jules-Bois.   CAW

And he, who shall embrace thee,/Is at hand, and so farewell.   Death's Jest-Book.   Thomas Lovell Beddoes.   NOBV

And he who such a boy would wish to screw/Would let the wild beasts shag him in the woods!   To Corydon.   Antonio Beccadelli.   PeHV

And he who waits to have his task marked out,/Shall die and leaves his errand unfulfilled.   Work.   James Russell Lowell.   PoSC

And he who wants each other blessing,/In these must ever find a foe.   Song: "O memory! thou fond deceiver."   Oliver Goldsmith.   ViBoPo

And he whom we had hated, waxen weak,/First in his weakness learns a little love.   Peer Gynt.   Charles Hamilton Sorley.   HBMV

And he whose soul is flat–the sky/Will cave in on him by and by.   Renascence.   Edna St. Vincent Millay.   FaFP; HBV 1-2; MAPA; MoAB; MoAmPo; NePA; OHFP

And He will answer, He will say,/"Forgiven."   His Sovereignty.   Kalonymos Ben Moses.   TrJP

And he will count me among the helpers of death:/The uncircumcised.   A Poor Christian Looks at the Ghetto.   Czeslaw Milosz.   NIP

And he will ensure thee/A Happy New Year.   New Time.   *Anonymous.*   BLRP

And he will go with another/through eternity.   Ballad: "He passed by with another."   Gabriela (Lucila Godoy Alcayaga) Mistral.   OLR

...And he will hear that scream/Until his judgment-time.   The Sacrilege.   Thomas Hardy.   DTo

And He will keep His word!   His Promises.   Martha Snell Nicholson.   BePJ

And he will make it plain.   Light Shining Out of Darkness.   William Cowper.   AtBAP; EaLo; SeCePo

And he will never thirst.   Psalter of the Blessed Virgin Mary.   Saint Bonaventure.   ISi

...And He/Will only laugh, remembering, once/He was a boy in Galilee!   A Phantasy of Heaven.   Harry Kemp.   HBMV

And He will smile, that children's tongue/Has not changed since Thou wast young! Ex Ore Infantium. Francis Thompson. FaBV; HBV 1-2; OBVV; OxBChV; SUS

And he with saddest circumstance doth part,/Who seals his farewell with a bleeding heart. The Departure. Henry, Bishop of Chichester King. SeCP

And he won't be coming here any more. To a Bull-Dog. J. C. Squire. FM

And he won the heart of a lady. The Gypsy Rover. *Anonymous.* FSW

And he wrote only on the sand! Only One King. John Richard Moreland. PGD

And head-winds right for royal sails. Heroism. Ralph Waldo Emerson. AtBAP; ViBoPo

And headed on mules for the mountains, that autumn of the glut. The Dustbowl. Kenward Elmslie. ANYP

And heal my troubled breast which cryes,/Which dyes. Longing. George Herbert. AnAnS 1

And heal with freedom what your slavery/cursed. The Proclamation. John Greenleaf Whittier. PAH

And healing upon this festering of blame. Invalid. Audrey McGaffin. NePoAm-2

And heals his spirit's weariness. The Pipe. Sir John Collings Squire. PoPl

And heals the land with one quick lover's kiss. Dakota Badlands. Elizabeth Landeweer. AmFN

And Heaps on Heaps in wild Disorder fall. Heaps on Heaps. Matthew Concanen. SD

And hear all day long the thrush repeat his song. The Green Roads. Edward ("Edward Eastaway") Thomas. FaBoPP; NoAm

And hear, as now, the voices of the sea. The Witch's Whelp. Richard Henry Stoddard. AA; AnAmPo

And hear it, "Fear not: it is I." Judge Not According to the Appearance. Christina Georgina Rossetti. TrPWD

And hear my senses clamor in their rout. Even as the Others Mock. Dante Alighieri. LiTW

And hear new stars come singing from God's hand. The Immortal. Marjorie Pickthall. CaP

And hear no more at all. Songs of Travel. Robert Louis Stevenson. OBNC

And hear such Bible stories as you never heard before. Darky Sunday School. *Anonymous.* ABF

And hear the mighty waters rolling evermore. Intimations of Immortality from Recollections of Early Childhood. William Wordsworth. BoC

And hear the sap leap in trees/Already marked out for death. The Secular. Chris Wallace-Crabbe. NOAV

...And hear the song/Of the last bird, and wash of the cool sea. Sonnets, V: "Into the wood at close of rainy day." Thomas Caulfield Irwin. IrPN

And hear the thunder cross the sky/With elephant tread. What Could Be Lovelier Than to Hear. Elizabeth Jane Coatsworth. BrR; SiSoSe

And hear them wheeze would make a fellow wise. Bliss. George Johnston. NOBC

And hear we the song of monken band. The Monks of Ely. *Anonymous.* ACP; CAW

And heard her say, kiss my ass. Glory. Harvey Shapiro. PoL

...And heard the sea far off/Washing its hands. At the Slackening of the Tide. James Wright. AmPC; MOS; UnPo; VGW

And heard the sound of rushing wind. The Coming of the Plague. Weldon Kees. NaP; VGW

And hearing a new music, miss the theme. Her Beauty. Max Plowman. HBMV

And hearing me might freeze/My five extremities. A Fear. Robert Francis. GP

And hearken to their humble prayer. Let the Deep Organ Swell. Charles Constantine Pise. AH

And hears, far off, her muted children cry. Milkmaid. Laurie Lee. BoLoP; ChMP; FaBoTw

And hears from that green tower intone/The eternal voice of Time. The Churchyard. Robert Williams Buchanan. HBV 1-2

And hears the blind sea chanting to the sun. Three Sonnets on Oblivion. George Sterling. HBV 1-2

And hears the knuckle-cracking in his brain/turning his hairs white. Judge Kroll. Barbara L. Greenberg. AMV-81

And hears the sound of lakewater/splashing–that is now stone. These. William Carlos Williams. AP; CoBMV; MoAB; MoAmPo; NoAm; NOBA; NoP; OxBA

And heart in heart we weep Love's body laid. Dusk. Archibald MacLeish. HBMV

And heart's incompetence. In the Dark Caverns of the Night. Henry Treece. NeBP

And heartier loves; that lamp is from the tomb. The Leaders of the Crowd. William Butler Yeats. EBEV; EnLit; MoAB; MoBrPo

And heartily thereto I pledged will be. The Cudgelled but Contented Cuckold. Jean de La Fontaine. UnTE

And hearts are made to be broken/And love is always woe. The Cause of This I Know Not. Haniel Long. HBMV

And hearts of holy stone. These Magicians. Sarah Provost. AMV-81

And hearts resolved and hands prepared/The blessings they enjoy to guard. To Leven Water. Tobias George Smollett. OBEV

And Heav'n is double Heav'n, if thou art there. Sigismonda and Guiscardo. John Dryden. OBS

And Heav'n is won by violence of Song. The Poet's Use. Alexander Pope. OBEC

And heav'n reflected in her face. Addressed to a Young Lady. William Cowper. EnRP

And heaven and earth through the spotless birth/Are at peace on this night so fair. Silver Lamps. W.C. Dix. BePJ

And Heaven and Hell may meet,–yet never we. Farewell to Juliet. Wilfrid Scawen Blunt. AnEnPo

And Heaven its dews be staying. As We Dance Round. *Anonymous.* CH

(And heaven on the long reach home.) The Watchers. William Stanley Braithwaite. PoNe

And Heaven reflected in her face. To a Young Lady. William Cowper. GTBS; GTBS-P; HBV 1-2

And heaven's blest mansion be your last! Verses Addressed to a Friend... Samuel Henley. NOEC

...And Heaven's Judea/Was folded in a pannier. Humble Beginnings. Thomas Lovell Beddoes. NOBV

And heaven will be a better place/For a friend or two. A Friend or Two. Wilbur D. Nesbit. PoLf

And heaven will be of thy rich life a part. If Christ Were Here To-Night. Margaret E. Sangster. TRV

And heavenly freedom spread her golden ray. Liberty and Peace. Phillis Wheatley. BlSi; SBG

And heavenly Una with her milk-white Lamb. Personal Talk. William Wordsworth. DiPo

And heavy loads rest lightly, too,/When we have learned to bear. Life's Joy. *Anonymous.* STF

And heavy shadow pile up flake by flake. A Time of Light, a Time of Shadow. Samuel Yellen. NePoAm-2

And heavy was the lowered sky/With sin and pain and loss. Gallows and Cross. J. E. H. MacDonald. CaP

And Heber's banks Eurydice returned. The Great Frost. John Gay. OBEC; SeCePo

And hee, in ruth of my distressed cry,/Plants mee a weeping starre within mine eye. Whilst Eccho Cryes, What Shall Become of Mee. Henry Constable. AAS

And hee returnd to the merry green-wood,/With great joy, mirth and pride. Robin Hood's Golden Prize. *Anonymous.* BaBo; ESPB

And heere, He cryes,/My lovely Spouses shall abide. Love. Joseph Beaumont. OBS

And heighten it with Heaven. The Pet Name. Elizabeth Barrett Browning. HBV 1-2

And held her in my arms! Politics. William Butler Yeats. CMoP; FF; HeIP; InPS; OxBTC; PAI; PoL; SCV

And held him true and steered him home. Dunkirk. Robert Nathan. MaC

And held it trembling there. Twilight at Sea. Amelia C. Welby. AA; HBV 1-2

And held my ears, and like a Thief/Fled gasping from the House– I Years Had Been from Home. Emily Dickinson. AmP; BLPL; CBEP; DiPo; NOBA; OxBA; PoRA

And held my heart up like a cup... The Edge. Lola Ridge. AnAmPo; OnYI

And, held one moment, burns the hand. August for the People. W. H. Auden. WaP

And Helen feeds the flames as long ago! Helen. Edward A.U. Valentine. AA

And hell and heaven are the scales of the balance of life/which swing against each other. When Satan Fell. D. H. Lawrence. MoRP

And help a little in a year when things were bad. Good-bye to the People of Hang-Chow. Po Chu-i. LiTW

And help me when I seek Thy grace/To mean the words I say. Do I Really Pray? John Burton. STF

And help the age of peace to come/From a Dreamer's martyrdom. Christmas Prayer. Madeline Morse. PGD

And help us, this and every day,/to live more nearly as we pray. Morning. John Keble. OBRV

And helped him on his way, what praise/And gratitude are due! Columbus at the Convent. John Townsend Trowbridge. MC; PAH

And helped us all stay home from school. George Washington. Shel Silverstein. PoSC

And helps us to make us drink on. She's Pretty to Walk With. Sir John Suckling. ALV

And helps you with your girdle when your hips stick. The Perfect Husband. Ogden Nash. DFF; FaBoUs

And hemleock-headed in the wood of weathers.   Altarwise by Owl-Light.
Dylan Thomas.   CMoP; NoAm

And hence could stem such strain and ache/As each year might assign.   He
Never Expected Much.   Thomas Hardy.   NAs; NoAm; OxBTC; SCV

And hence the proverb rose that Truth/Lies in the bottom of a well.   The
Maid of the Moor, or The Water-Fiends.   George the Younger Colman.
NOEC

And hence we stars are deathless.   When Young Hearts Break.   Heinrich
Heine.   AWP

And henceforth I will not deny them—for how can I/deny myself?   You
Felons on Trial in Courts.   Walt Whitman.   CBEP

And Henry, a stock-broker, doing well.   Sonnet Reversed.   Rupert Brooke.
NOBL

And her all naked to his sight display'd.   Hero and Leander.   Christopher
Marlowe.   UnTE

And her arms make the rim of his rainbow world.   The Shadow House of
Lugh.   Ethna (Anna Johnston MacManus) Carbery.   AnIV

And her body burst like a fountain of flowers.   Daisies.   Alden Nowlan.
NeAC

And her dead mouth sings/By its shape, like thrushes in clear evening.   The
Bride.   D. H. Lawrence.   NoAm; OxBTC

And her eyes are dark-dappled/Like trout in the brooks.   Mac Diarmod's
Daughter.   Francis Carlin.   HBMV

And her eyes lightnings and her shoulders wing   In Progress.   Christina
Georgina Rossetti.   BoWoP

And her eyes were like black pearls/Within their shells.   Mohammed Ibrahim
Speaks.   Martha Beidler.   FF

And her eyes would not stop shining   Her Application to Elysium.
Kathleen Norris.   IHMS

And her faint tears are red upon His face.   Two Poems on the Catholic
Bavarians.   Edgar Bowers.   PoCh

And her furniture's coverd with dust.   Clubwoman.   Mary Carter Smith.
PoNe

And her griefs dead-ahead, fallow for the light-foot years.   Nuit Blanche.
Katherine Hoskins.   NMP

And her grove glow with love-lit fires of Troy.   Venus.   Dante Gabriel
Rossetti.   MaVP

And her hands held on to herself.   All That Matters...   Waltler Sorell.
GoYe

And her head was on his flank.   Two Dogs Have I.   Ogden Nash.   GDP

And her I have reserved/Within my heart forever.   Perdy, I said it not.   Sir
Thomas Wyatt.   FCP; PoEL 1-5

And her kind eyes shall lead me to the end.   Since Thou Hast Given Me This
Good Hope, O God.   Robert Louis Stevenson.   TrPWD

And her last request was granted, to be buried by young Monroe.   The Jam
on Gerry's Rock (I).   Anonymous.   BaBo; FaBoBa; ShS; ViBoFo

And her long robe trails all about the south.   Sois Sage O Ma Douleur.
Charles Baudelaire.   AWP

And her love,/Born above,/Guides the little feet.   Baby-Land.   George
Cooper.   HBV 1-2; HBVY

And her love she vowes to me.   The Description of Castara.   William
Habington.   AnAnS 2

And her poor flesh awake, adoring him.   Et Sa Pauvre Chair.   Alec Brock
Stevenson.   HBMV

And her red, laughing mouth that were so sweet to kiss.   There Is a Lady.
Walther von der Vogelweide.   AWP

And her right home and her right passion.   Lady Lost.   John Crowe
Ransom.   AnFE; MoAB; MoAmPo; TrGrPo; UnPo

And her shoes were full of feet.   The Night Was Growing Old.   Anonymous.
FaBoNo; NLV

And her simplicity of face.   A Maiden and Her Hair.   William Henry
Davies.   BrPo

And her skirt was over her head/as he did the round once more   The Insect
Kitchen.   Nicki Jackowska.   BrRo

And her slim body, white as the ash/of black flesh after flame.   Portrait in
Georgia.   Jean Toomer.   NoP

And her son who walked around dead.   Madonna of the Hills.   Paula Gunn
Allen.   TWSS

And her soul had fled to that home above/Where there's bread and room for
the poor.   The Orphan Girl.   Anonymous.   AmFP; AS

And her steps were lost in the dew.   Beauty.   Laurence Binyon.   MoBrPo

And her sure revenge shall be that of/Tamar!"/Speak at last!   Cuba.
Edmund Clarence Stedman.   PAH

And her sweet syllables seemed to play/Like flute-notes softly blown.   The
Satin Shoes.   Thomas Hardy.   CoBMV

And her thorns were my only delight.   My Pretty Rose Tree.   William
Blake.   BoLoP

And her thoughts as still/As the waters/Under a ruined mill.   The Old
Woman.   Joseph Campbell.   ACV; AWP; GoBC; HBMV; MCCG;
MoBrPo; OnYI; OxBI; OxBTC; TreFT; ViBoPo

And her to love saunce variaunce.   A Love Letter.   Anonymous.   MeEL

And her tongue raced like a squirrel in the park.   How She Resolved to Act.
Merrill Moore.   MoAmPo

And her uncle she slew/On the banks of a-Dundee.   The Banks of Dundee.
Anonymous.   BaBo

And her voice coming softly over the meadow/Was the mist becoming rain.
The Lost Heifer.   Austin Clarke.   BIrV; OxBI

And her white breath clouds/the field which is growing smaller/smaller.   The
Field.   Douglas Lawder.   PH

And her wide lap shall still provide for/thee.   To a Crow.   Robert Burns
Wilson.   AA

And her wind, her wind in my branches.   Waiting.   Hilary Corke.   ErPo

And her Yankee thunders roar.   Yankee Thunders.   Anonymous.   PAH

And her yes, once said to you,/SHALL be yes for evermore.   The Lady's
Yes.   Elizabeth Barrett Browning.   HBV 1-2; LiTL

And here a group of women wanly quarrel/At a sale of Cupids. A hawk looks
at them.   The Token.   Frank Templeton Prince.   FaBoTw; OxBTC

And here am I looking wantonly at her/Over the kitchen sink.   Evening.
Richard Aldington.   MoBrPo; MOON; SeCePo

And here am/I/my Lord/alone with Thee.   Two Prayers.   Adawiyya. Rabi'a
al-.   WPOW

And here and there his body lies,/A-tumbling o'er and o'er.   James Whaland
(with music).   Anonymous.   AS

And here are men to know, women to love.   A Ballad in Blank Verse of the
Making of a Poet.   John Davidson.   BSV

And here be the house of the Lord!   The Neighbors Help Him Build His
House.   Anonymous.   LiTW

And here, by the campfire,/Am I.   Open Range.   Kathryn and Byron
Jackson.   TiPo

And here comes a chopper to chop off your head.   London Bells.
Anonymous.   LiTB; OxBoLi

And here hath Truth summ'd up thy vital rest.""   Ulysses Hears the
Prophecies of Tiresias.   Homer.   LoBV

And here he is a-saying his prayers.   Here Is the Church, and Here Is the
Steeple.   Anonymous.   OxNR

And here he lies, all bona fide.   Epitaph on William Jones.   Anonymous.
FaBoEE

And here he lies and still is Knott.   Epitaph on John Knott.   Anonymous.
FaBoEE; ShM

And here I beg/permission to close a chapter of still life.   In Memory of
Your Body.   David Shapiro.   ANYP

And here I drank well good beer.   Snatches: "Here I was and here I drank."
Anonymous.   OxBM

And here I lie a-bleeding on the deck/And it's all for her safety I shall die.
The Valiant Sailor.   Anonymous.   OBSS

And here I wait till someone stirs/his coffee with his thumb.   The Frozen
Logger.   James Stephens.   FSW; OBAL

And here in dust and dirt, oh, here/The lilies of His love appear!   Unfold!
Unfold!   Henry Vaughan.   ELP

And here is fire.   Elegy for 41 Whales Beached in Florence, Ore., June, 1979.
Linda Bierds.   AMV-81

And here is love/like a tinsmith's scoop/sunk past its gleam/in the meal-bin.
Sunlight.   Seamus Heaney.   NOBI; NoP

And here is no shore, no intimacy,/Only the start of space, the road to suns.
Trans Canada.   F. R. Scott.   PeCV

And here is the baby's cradle.   Here Are the Lady's Knives and Forks.
Anonymous.   OxNR

And here is the long white winter road/And the silent woods.   The
Snowstorm.   Frederick George Scott.   PeCV

—And here it comes dancing over the bridge!   The Bridge.   James (1834-82)
Thomson.   OBVV

And here my ship rides, having anchor cast.   The End of His Work.   Robert
Herrick.   CaPo

And here, O great Jehovah, fix/Thy pleasant, lasting rest.   Now Let Our
Hearts Their Glory Wake.   Elizabeth Scott.   AH

—And here's an egg this morning laid!   The Lark's Nest.   John Clare.
PBBP

And here's hoping for a jolly lot more/like the handsome cabin boy.   The
Handsome Cabin Boy.   Anonymous.   FSW

And here's my ain—Yours, Alexander Scott.   Letter to Robert Fergusson.
Alexander Scott.   OxBS

And here's my horse, my dog and I.   On Frosty Days.   David Campbell.
CBAP

And here's the house of Stuart.   The Battle of Sole Bay.   Anonymous.
GBP

And here's to all the captains' names,/And here's to the House of Stuart.   A
Song on the Duke's Late Glorious Success over the Dutch.   Anonymous.
OBSS

And here's to the friend/Of the journey's end/At the Inn of the Silver Moon.
The Good Inn.   Herman Knickerbocker Viele.   HBV 1-2

And here shall your bones lie beside Bath.   The Brut.   Layamon.   MeEV

...And here sleep/Tosses a little with dreams.   Sunsets.   Carl Sandburg.
MoAmPo

And here sleeps as soundly as he did/in court.　Epitaph for a Judge.
Benedict Jeitteles.　TrJP

And here stand I, a suppliant at the door.　At the Grave of Henry Vaughan.
Siegfried Sassoon.　CMoP; EaLo; GTBS-P; PoPle

And here the judgment of the wood.　Revenge of the Hunted.　R. A. D.
Ford.　LiSp

And here the poet, paradox his fee,/learns to cage his truth to keep it free.
Sonnet Sonnet.　John D. Engle, Jr.　AMV-81

And here they lies as dead as nits.　Epitaph: "Two sweeter babes you nare
did see."　Anonymous.　FaBoEE

And here was April come back again.　April.　Theodosia Garrison.
HBMV

And here we go round, round,/roundy.　Hey, My Kitten, My Kitten.
Anonymous.　OxNR

And here we thes muneches sang.　Merie Sungen the Muneches.
Anonymous.　AtBAP

And here with him entomb'd do lye/Honour, and Hospitalitie.　Epitaph on
Mr. Robert Port.　Charles Cotton.　CavP

And HERMAN's a German.　Porson on German Scholarship.　Richard
Porson.　FaBoCo

And Hero's name dies bubbling on her lips.　Hero and Leander.　Thomas
Hood.　EnRP

And Hero shall watch for Leander/In vain on those dark, bitter seas.　Across
the Straits.　Rosemary Dobson.　PoAu 1-2

And hertes it sweteth.　Snatches: "Loverd, thy passion."　Anonymous.
OxBM

...And hes not a marrying man so somebody better get it/out of him...
Ulysses (excerpt).　James Joyce.　FaBoPV

And hid, and all my dinner eat,/Till four o'clock was gone.　The Landrail.
John Clare.　PBBP

And hid his face amid a crowd of stars.　When You Are Old.　William
Butler Yeats.　AWP; BoLiVe; BoLoP; CMoP; CTC; DiPo; FaBV; FaFP;
FPL; GBL; GoJo; GoTF; GTBS; HBV 1-2; HeIP; InvP; LiTL; LiTM;
MoAB; MoBrPo; MoLP; NAWM 1-2; NoAm; NOBV; NoP; OBEV; OBVV;
OxBTC; PCP; PoLf; PoPl; PP; PrIm; TEP; TreFS

And hide a tumult never to be told.　Letter.　William Empson.　ChMP;
LiTB

And hide away in these beautiful jars.　Old Man Pot.　Lyon Sharman.
CaP

And hide Great Oak Hill from sight?　Snow.　John Kelleher.　ELU

And hide itself for shame of such a deed.　The Atheist's Tragedy.　Cyril
Tourneur.　ViBoPo; WaaP

And hide me from the sight of life.　The Winter's Walk.　Samuel Johnson.
CBEP; EiCP

And hide the thrush's skull away.　The Relic.　Robert Hillyer.　GoYe; UnS

And hide them in the hay.　The King of Yellow Butterflies.　Vachel
Lindsay.　OBCA

And hide thy shame beneath the ground.　In Memoriam A.H.H., LXXII.
Alfred, Lord Tennyson.　VLP

And hides it from the Sun, deep in his heart.　The Sadness of the Moon.
Charles Baudelaire.　MOON

And hiding their tossing manes and their tumultuous feet.　Michael Robartes
Bids His Beloved Be at Peace.　William Butler Yeats.　BrPo; NoAm

And high above the fight the lonely bugle grieves!　The Lonely Bugle Grieves.
Grenville Mellen.　AA

...And high above/the tiny gentle voices of the larks.　Skye Summer.　Islay
Murray Donaldson.　PoSH

And higher into the endless winds of the world.　A Walk in Kyoto.　Earle
Birney.　GoYe

And higher shapes reflect, as we do now,/Upon the structure of the Mastodon.
To a Skull.　Thomas Caulfield Irwin.　IrPN

And highly praise his humble pomp,/Which he from heaven doth bring.
New Prince, New Pomp.　Robert Southwell.　AnAnS 1; EG; ELP; GN;
NOBE; NOCV; OBSC; OHIP; SBVL; TrCP

And hills and vales rejoice and sing.　Thy Praise, O God, in Zion Waits.
Jacob Kimball.　AH

And him as for a map doth Nature store,/To show false Art what beauty was
of yore.　Sonnets, LXVIII: "Thus is his cheek the map of days outworn."
William Shakespeare.　OBSC

And him, dear doubtless to someone, worth her dear tears.　Foresight.
Lincoln Kirstein.　NoAm; OBWP

And him, Ophion, earliest of the gods?　Sonnets, First Series.　Frederick
Goddard Tuckerman.　MAmP

And him reads Reason at his heels,/If heels in air the last of him!
Empedocles.　George Meredith.　VLP

And him that tells a bigger tale/Would have to tell a lie./Sing taddle-o-day.
Little Brown Dog.　Anonymous.　FSW

And him who saddled it, were both in Hell!　The Superfluous Saddle.　Jean
de La Fontaine.　UnTE

And himself desiring The Hill!　Jonathan Houghton.　Edgar Lee Masters.
OxBA

And hire a sterner will to guard the gate.　Sonnet Sequence.　Darwin T.
Turner.　BALP

And his arm lay lightly around my breast-and that night I/was happy.　When
I Heard at the Close of the Day.　Walt Whitman.　AP; GBL; NePA;
OxBA

And his arrow is tipped with a jewel,/And shot from a silver string.　Love in
a Cottage.　Nathaniel Parker Willis.　HBV 1-2

And his beard growing grey.　The Three Jovial Welshmen.　Anonymous.
HBVY; OxNR

And his beautified feet on flowers may tread/To-day with his Lord in Paradise.
Thaddeus Stevens.　Phoebe Cary.　PAH

And his blood cried out of the ground.　My Brother Was Silent.　Amir
Gilboa.　VWA

And his bodie lies dead in Durrisdeer,/And his hunting it is done.　Johnie
Cock (B vers.).　Anonymous.　ViBoFo

And his body is bathed in grass and sun.　Mishka.　John Gray.　VLP

And his consort, the False Imogine!'　Alonzo the Brave and Fair Imogine.
Matthew Gregory Lewis.　OBEC

And his crutches procure him permission to beg.　The Volunteer.
Anonymous.　NOEC

...And his cup of/sad enchantments/hold out to me, and it thus far still/
sounds and is flowing.　In the Old City.　Jacob Fichman.　TrJP

And his dad'll bring him a partridge nest,/As soon as his dad comes back.
John Brown's Body.　Stephen Vincent Benét.　MoAmPo

And his dark secret love/Does thy life destroy.　The Sick Rose.　William
Blake.　AtBAP; AWP; BoLiVe; BoLoP; BoW; DiPo; EnLoPo; ExPo; HAP;
HeIP; InPK; InPo; InPS; LoBV; NAWM 1-2; NIP; NOBE; NoP; OBNC;
OBSP; PAI; PPoe; PPP; PrIm; SeCeV; SoSe; TrGrPo; ViBoPo; WeW

And his death/is your freedom.　By Day and by Night.　William Stanley
Merwin.　AmPC

And his deed the echoes fill/When the dawn is come.　Of a Poet Patriot.
Thomas Macdonagh.　CAW; HBMV; OnYI; OxBI

And his dull torment mottles like a fly's/The lying amber of the histories.　A
Lullaby.　Randall Jarrell.　HaCAP; OxBC

And his dying head he rested/On Jerusalem's fair knees.　By the Waters of
Babylon.　Heinrich Heine.　TrJP

And his enlarg'd Ideas found the Road,/Which Faith had dictated, and Angels
trod.　On Exodus, III, 14, I Am That I Am.　Matthew Prior.　CEP

And his eyes behold/Things that shall never, never be to mortal/hearers told.
The Discoverer.　Edmund Clarence Stedman.　AA; HBV 1-2

And his eyes on the world.　Stylite.　Louis MacNeice.　MoPo

...And his face/Shone in the glory compassing her head.　The Vision of St.
Bernard.　M. Whitcomb Hess.　ISi

And his first minute, after noon, is night.　A Lecture Upon the Shadow.
John Donne.　AnEnPo; AtBAP; AWP; CABA; DiPo; InPo; OBS; SeCP;
TEP; UnPo

And his gallant heart swells with the pride of the free.　The White Steed of
the Prairies.　J. Barber.　BPAW; CoSo

And his ghost is a-lyin' thirsty in the ditch where Ira died.　Ballad of Ira
Hayes.　Peter La Farge.　MAT

And his gifts of love and peace/To his people never cease.　Angels' Song.
Charles Causley.　BePJ; FaPo; OBCP

And His gold did not suffer a bit more heat/Than was needed to make it pure.
The Refiner's Fire.　Anonymous.　BLRP

And His grace is all sufficient/For the needs of you and me.　Hitherto and
Henceforth.　Annie Johnson Flint.　BLRP

And his great Head be hid, within an humble Tomb.　Cato's Address to His
Troops in Lybia.　Nicholas Rowe.　OBEC

And His great works applaud.　The Voice of God.　Katherine R. Barnard.
BLRP; WBLP

And his hands full of clay.　Clap Hands, Daddy's Coming.　Anonymous.
OxNR

And his heart blazed while his hand smote.　No Miracle.　Daniel Corkery.
AnII

"And his heart it is poison!" another replies.　On W. R–, Esq.　Robert
Burns.　FaBoEE

And his household crockery.　Company Cook.　Anonymous.　ABF

And his last breath, let it be/Taken in by none but thee.　To Julia.　Robert
Herrick.　CaPo

And his last triumphs more than damn the first.　The British Prison Ship:
Canto III. The Hospital Prison Ship.　Philip Freneau.　AmPP

And his last words were, Dem my blood!　Epitaph: "Here cursing swearing
Burton lies."　Robert Burns.　FaBoEE

And his last words were, "Poor Mary died on the silvery tide."　The Silvery
Tide.　Anonymous.　AmFP

–And his lips part/To greet the perfect stranger.　The Friend of the Fourth
Decade.　James Merrill.　NYBP

And his little son to rosier health.　Three Streets.　Umberto Saba.　VWA

...And his little wife/who baked for him ran out/and tore up the gooseberries.
Gooseberries.　Peter Wild.　DFF; GP

And his malignant growth shall be/Monstered by lucid violence.　Aix-la-
Chappelle, 1945.　Edgar Bowers.　NePoEA

And his man's friendliness so good to have, and lost so soon.   Tobacco Plant.
Ivor Gurney.   OBTV

And his message easy?   Prognosis.   Louis MacNeice.   CMoP; OxBI

And his name was Aiken Drum.   The Surprising History of Aiken Drum.
Anonymous.   OxNR

And his name will go down through the ages, as the bravest hero of them all.
Lindbergh.   *Anonymous.*   AmFP

...And his neck comes back/in indented satisfaction.   Blue Heron.   Don
Welch.   GP

And his offspring–och, och–hidden within me!   A Connacht Caoine.
Anonymous.   AnIV

And his old Father digging round a vine.   Odysseus Dying.   Sheila
Wingfield.   OxBI

And his old wives and children–and look, how they smile!   Two Families.
Charles G. Bell.   FAZ

And his overthrow, our chorus.   The Misfortunes of Elphin: The War-Song of
Dinas Vawr.   Thomas Love Peacock.   AWP; MyFE; WaaP

And His own face to see.   The Mystery.   Ralph Hodgson.   HBV 1-2;
MoAB; MoBrPo

And His own Mother as our nursing Mother.   A Thought from Cardinal
Newman.   Matthew Russell.   CAW

And his people will answer/"Amen, amen."   He Is Coming, Adzed-Head.
Anonymous.   NOBI

And his plump fingers trembled in her lap.   Love in Brooklyn.   John
Wakeman.   AMV-81; SoSe

And His Right Hand doth embrace me.')   The Beloved.   May Probyn.
GoBC

And his sepulchre shall not be whicted.   The Devil's Dictionary:
Orthography.   Ambrose Bierce.   OBAL

And his shadow walks alone.   The Whisperers.   Wilfred Wilson Gibson.
HBV 1-2

And his shout that gives a hissing sound.   On Shooting Particles beyond the
World.   Richard Eberhart.   LiTA; LiTM; TW

And his shovel was lashed to his pack.   In the Township.   Denis Glover.
AnNZ

And his slow-spoken word: Farewell for ever,/Farewell, farewell.   World
without End.   Caius Valerius Catullus.   LiTW

And his slow strut moves him on again.   Harlem Freeze Frame.   Lebert
Bethune.   PoBA

And his sorrow and sighing have pass'd away.   Love-Song.   *Anonymous.*
AWP

And his soul is bound up in the bundle/of life.   Epitaph.   *Anonymous.*
TrJP

And his staccato snores,/pounding against the walls/like jack-hammers.
Derelict.   Henry Johnson.   LFAC

And his tears were thicker than forty days of rain.   Return to Ararat.
Martyn Halsall.   TrCP

And his terrible eyes knew them.   Auf Dem Wasser Zu Singen.   Stephen
Spender.   EnLoPo

And his tete-a-tete ate at 8.08.   Limerick: "There was a young fellow named
Tait."   Carolyn Wells.   HBV 1-2; HBVY

And his the speculative gaze/Of someone learning.   Sleep-Learning.   Ruth
Fainlight.   NMM

And his thoughts turned back to the place where she said, "I'm growing/
warmer now."   Young Charlottie.   Seba ("Major Jack Downing") Smith.
AmFP

And his thunderous wings be furled,/In the gaze of a gladdened world,/On the
nation's loftiest dome   The Eagle of Corinth.   Henry Howard Brownell.
PAH

And his too early tomb will not be dumb/To point a moral for our youth to
come.   Tempora Mutantur.   James Russell Lowell.   HAP

And his triumph will be carved on the rock of Yen-jan/Mountain!   Spring
Thoughts.   Huang-fu Jan.   OFD

And His voice has talked to me/In the sunlit apple tree.   Where Is Heaven?
Bliss Carman.   TRV

And his voice lies buried in the amber glass.   Cry for a Disused Synagogue in
Booysens.   Mannie Hirsch.   VWA

And his weeping will at last calm down in the all-/combining old roots.
There Is No Nearer Nearness.   Cha Liang-cheng.   LiTW

And his work its own reward shall be.   Plant a Tree.   Lucy Larcom.
HBVY; OHFP; PGD; WBLP

And hit 'em up a tune called Turkey in the Straw.   Turkey in the Straw.
Anonymous.   AS; BLSo; FSW; TrAS; TreFS

And ho but I love thee dearly!   The Orphan's Song.   Sydney Thomas
Dobell.   CH; ELP; OBNC

And hoarse loud bellows puffing up the blaze.   Winter.   John Clare.   ATP

And hobbled off/on mean and crooked feet.   Poem for My Dead Husband.
Sheila Roberts.   AMV-80

And "Hoick! Hoick!" cried he.   Huntsman, What Quarry?   Edna St. Vincent
Millay.   LiSp

And hold in my arms a child/Of water, water, water.   The Lifeguard.
James Dickey.   CoPo; LiSp; NoP; NYBP

And hold on and hold on.   The Way Down.   Philip Levine.   NOBA

And/hold/their/hands.   Untitled (Hi Ronda).   Sharon Scott.   JB

And hold their manhoods cheap, whiles any speaks/That fought with us upon
Saint Crispin's day.   King Henry V.   William Shakespeare.   FaPoR

And hold us in derision.   Eyes That Last I Saw in Tears.   Thomas Stearns
Eliot.   InPo; NOBE; ViBoPo

And holdeth in the hollow of his hand/My day and night.   Rondeau
Redouble.   John Payne.   HBV 1-2

And, holding still the token, sunk to the sands/Of the deep river, and I
breathed alone.   The Suire.   Thomas Caulfield Irwin.   IrPN

And holds back, holds back, like a closed church door.   Surgery.   Carol
Burbank.   SUW

And holds his hand out for a franc.   Paris.   Jane Garnett.   AMV-80

And hollow./and Alone.   When I Was Lost.   Dorothy Aldis.   SoPo

And hollow fragile strands in twos/rayed like tendrils/out about a root.   All
That Is Left.   Michael Hartnett.   NOBI

And Holy Spirit–Three in One!   Glad Tidings from the King of Kings.
Charles Coffin.   BePJ

And home be led in peace.   From Battle Clamour.   Samuele Romanelli.
TrJP

And home-coming for weary men.   Victory Bells.   Grace Hazard Conkling.
HBV 1-2; MC; PAH

And home is silent, and love is clay.   Feathers and Moss.   Jean Ingelow.
SpRo

And home is something/I carry within me.   Much of Me.   Chuck Eggerth.
AMV-80

And home lies beyond the stars and the sea.   A Song of Flight.   Christina
Georgina Rossetti.   CAW

And, home returning, soothly swear,/Was never scene so sad and fair!   The
Lay of the Last Minstrel.   Sir Walter Scott.   FaBoPP; OBRV

And Homer's angry Ghost repine in vain.   Troilus and Cressida.   John
Dryden.   SeCV 1-2

And honkie plunk/in Preservation/Hall.   Preservation.   Alcide Pavageau.   Miller Williams.
TAT

And honor be from sea to sea to the deed of/Private Blair!   Private Blair of
the Regulars.   Clinton Scollard.   PAH

And honour, as long as waves shall break,/To Nelson's peerless name!
Admirals All.   Sir Henry Newbolt.   FaPoR; MOS

...And honour/due/Be given to such as honour him with fear and reverence
true.'   Philemon and Baucis.   Arthur Golding.   OBSC

And honour my death with a double encore.   The Broken-Hearted Gardener.
Anonymous.   GBP

And honour which they do not understand.   November, 1806.   William
Wordsworth.   OBRV; OBWP

And, hooded by a smile, commits/his private murder to the mind.   My
Many-Coated Man.   Laurie Lee.   NYBP

And hoods the flames that to their quarry strove.   Annus Mirabilis.   John
Dryden.   FiP

And–hop, he goes!   What Is It?   Marie Louise Allen.   TiPo

And hope felt strong and life itself not weak.   Aloof.   Christina Georgina
Rossetti.   BoLiVe; OBEV; OBVV; TrGrPo

And hope, impact of fathom, lucid suavity.   Life and Impellance.   William
Frederick Stevenson.   NOBV

And hope is less dear than the dew of the morn.   Into the Twilight.
William Butler Yeats.   HBV 1-2

...And hope/is like a tin-cup toppled into the straw.   The Desert of Love.
Janos Pilinszky.   OBVE

And hope the centuries of grass/Are far too wide to leap across.   Distance.
Anthony Delius.   PeSA

And Hope, the Cherub of unwearied wing.   Sonnet: "A plaintive Sonnet
flow'd from MILTON's pen."   William Mason.   OBEC

And hope, the good and evil that we found.   Apology of the Young
Scientists.   Celia Dimmette.   GoYe

And hope was false, but love was true.   Newark Abbey.   Thomas Love
Peacock.   NOBE; OBNC

And Hope without an object cannot live.   Work without Hope.   Samuel
Taylor Coleridge.   BiP; BoNaP; EnLi 1-2; ERoP 1-2; FiP; HBV 1-2; LoBV;
NOBE; NoP; OBEV; OBRV; PG; SaC; TEP

And hoped Joe'd come my Way–   Because I Could Not Dump (parody).
Andrea Paterson.   BXAP

And hoping a little, a little, that either may be.   Blackberry Winter.   John
Crowe Ransom.   OxBA; PoRA

And hopped away proper/As any grasshopper.   The Grasshopper.   David
McCord.   GrPl

And hops about like a filly-foal.   Riddle: "As black as ink and isn't ink."
Anonymous.   OxNR

And horns beat on/brightly you know for song.   Percussions.   Ron Welburn.
CNA

And horses' hoofs ring loud where once their oarsmen/plied.   Winter at
Tomi.   Ovid.   AWP

And hostile Troy was ever full in sight.   The Iliad.   Homer.   OBVE

And, hot against my finger-tips,/The pulses leaping in her throat. Bianca. Arthur Symons. UnTE; VLP

And hot throats roaring that the King is dead! French Clock. Hortense Flexner. HBMV

And how a dull and heavy weight/Will press the life-drops from the heart. The Slave Auction. Frances E. W. Harper. BPo; PoNe; TTY

And how a god flimsy as a baby's finger/Shall unhusk himself and steer into the air. Flute Notes from a Reedy Pond. Sylvia Plath. FaBoMo

And how Alfonso sued for a divorce,/Were in the English newspapers, of course. Don Juan. George Gordon, Lord Byron. BiP

And how birds dipped in chromium sang in the crevices of our deeds. The Leg in the Subway. Oscar Williams. AnFE; LiTM; NePA

And how closely looms our destination. Bury Our Faces. Bob Millard. AMV-80

And how did he get out of the pea? Ultimate Problems. William Stafford. NU

And How do you do again. The Beggar's Opera. John Gay. ErPo; PoEL 1-5

And how do you do again? One Misty, Moisty Morning. Mother Goose. FaBoBe; HBV 1-2; HBVY; TiPo

And how from the best bush to receive a flower. The Southerner. Karl Shapiro. NYBP; PoNe

And how he would like/All eternity to stare/It down. In These Dissenting Times. Alice Walker. PoBA

And how his heart contained its bitterness,/He will not tell us. John Brown's Body. Stephen Vincent Benét. AmFN

...And how hulking/you are, my dear, my sweet black bear! Planning the Perfect Evening. Rita Dove. MAYP

...And how I love/my black and white and the gray war they make. Drawing Wildflowers. Jorie Graham. NPGG

And how I sought her/Through a hazardous maze/By shafted water. The Frightened Man. Louise Bogan. FaBoWP; SBG

And how I used to walk amid my corn/And through my fields. Alas! What can I do? I Wonder How My Home Is. Anonymous. WTO

And how I wish the rain/Would come again, and again! The Rainbow. William Henry Davies. BrPo

And how is a soul to see? Death at Daybreak. Anne Reeve Aldrich. AA

And how it is here and how it was always here. Contra Mortem. Hayden Carruth. PoA

And how it may this fowler's net escape,/And not commit upon itself this rape. Upon the Lark and the Fowler. John Bunyan. PBBP

And how long they will run over hill and dell/Is really more than I can tell. The Redingote and the Vamoose. Richard Kendall Munkittrick. OBCA

And how, of all things vainest, he/Journeys above both land and sea. Song: "Spring lights her candles everywhere." Fredegond Shove. HBMV

And how our angels in the night-time/sing? Song, to the Gods, is Sweetest Sacrifice. Annie Fields. AA

And: How's that yellow rose? One Kingfisher and One Yellow Rose. Eileen Brennan. NeIP

And how should this waterman ever know care,/When he's married and never in want of a fare? The Jolly Young Waterman. Charles Dibdin. NOEC; PoPle

And how the moon trembles on the crag's brink. Conversation Piece. Robert Graves. GrPl

And how the same inexorable price must still be paid for the same great purchase. Beginners. Walt Whitman AA

And how the sunlight strikes us dumb! In Bohemia. Arthur Symons. BrPo; SyP

And how the white hand flicked away the ash. Cigar Smoke, Sunday, after Dinner. Louise Townsend Nicholl. FYAP; NePoAm

And how they burn with passion. Die Welt Ist Dumm, Die Welt Ist Blind. Heinrich Heine. AWP

And how we bear them, let those ask who care! To My Tortoise. Eugene Lee-Hamilton. FM; OBVV

And Hubert Howe Bancroft sent his regrets. The Convicts' Ball. Ambrose Bierce. BPAW

And hug our fathers, once,/before they die. Night Fishing. Michael Waters. WOLT

And, human, tell me, if you have neither/love nor wine—what are you? A stone. The Three Kingdoms of Nature. Gotthold Lessing. NU

And human too—for private man's promotion. Quatrain. Joshua Sylvester. FaBoEE

And humble as a wondering child/I watched her vanishing. Path Flower. Olive Dargan. HBMV

And humbled her pride who is queen of the main! The Battle of Plattsburg Bay. Clinton Scollard. MC; PAH

And humbly learn, like him, to give/Our powers, our wills, to thee. O God, Accept the Sacred Hour. Samuel Gilman. AH

And humbly, or most royally, adds her own. Kiltartan Legend. Padraic Fallon. NOBI

And hundreds more, as though they were alive. From a Printed Bill, Fixed in the Beak of One in a Group... Anonymous. FaBoUs

And hung on every Spray, on every Blade/of Grass, the myriad Dew-Drops twinkle round. Moonlight in Autumn. James (1700-48) Thomson. OBEC

And hunger cannot make its home with/death. Compensation. Thomas Stephen Collier. AA

And hurl me to the shark, I shall not die! The Leg. Karl Shapiro. DFF; HAP; MoAB; MoAmPo; TrGrPo; UnPo

And hurls for him, O half hurls earth for him off under his feet. Hurrahing in Harvest. Gerard Manley Hopkins. BiP; BoC; BoNaP; BrPo; CMoP; EBCP; FaBoPP; InvP; MoAB; MoBrPo; MoPo; MoVE; VLP

And hurls her sixteen summers through the gates. Printing Jenny. Matthew Mitchell. OxBTC

And hurries from the hill. Canticle. William Griffith. HBMV; HBVY

...And hurries/Home to the light that floods the open door. Shadows among the Ettrick Hills. William Addison. PoSH

And hurry along, Van Winkle–it's get-/ting late! Van Winkle. Hart Crane. AmP; CrMA

And hurtled him into space forever. One, Two, Three. Samuel L. Albert. NePoAm-2

And hurtles into the sun. August from My Desk. Roland Flint. AmFN

And, huzzah for King George and our coun-/try forever!/Derry down, down, hey derry down. The Liberty Pole. Anonymous. PAH

And hymn thy fav'rite name! Ode to Evening. William Collins. AnEnPo; AnFE; ATP; AWP; EBEV; EG; EiCP; EnPE; EnRP; ExPo; FaBoBe; GTBS; HAP; HBV 1-2; InPo; LAuP; LiTB; LoBV; MasP; NOBE; NOEC; NoP; OAEL 1-2; OAEP; OBEC; OBEV; PoEL 1-5; PPP; SeCePo; SeCeV; TreFT; TrGrPo; ViBoPo; WHA

And hymns in praise of boys like flames to heaven are/flung. Peace on Earth. Bacchylides. AWP

And hypocrisy never brought me pain before now. Textile Mills and Prison Reform. George Rachow. LFAC

And I a little child who stands/And gravely kisses both her hands. Idyll. Hugh Macnaghten. HBMV

And I a monarch–at thy feet! My Queen. William Winter. AA

And I, a ship melting in the night. With the Nuns at Cape May Point. David Earle Anderson. AMV-81

And I a woman clinging close to thee? Aidenn. Katrina Trask. AA

And I ain't did no man,/Great Godamighty, no crime. Go Down, You Little Red Rising Sun. Anonymous. OuSiCo

And I ain't going to cry any more. Free Little Bird. Anonymous. AmFP

And I ain't gonna be treated this a-way. I'm Going Down This Road Feeling Bad. Anonymous. FSW

And I ain't gonna see those pretty gals no more. It's Almost Done. Anonymous. FSW

And I ain't got no loving baby now. Lost Lover Blues. Blind Boy Fuller. BluL

And I, alas! for peace. Beggars. Ella Higginson. AA

And I almost missed the opening throw/(A perfect strike) at the Polo Grounds. The Inflamed Disciple. Arthur Kramer. InMe

And I alone/Hear candle-voices waver as they burn. At the Party. Freda Laughton. NeIP

And I alone of all mankind/Were left in loneliness behind. A Winter Night. William Barnes. FaBoRV; NOBE; OBNC

And I alone remember yet. Old Loves. Henri Murger. AWP

And I alone with no other one–/With no other one! Dirge of the Lone Woman. Mary M. Colum. AnIV

And I also know/they can't help it. Her Story. Monty Reid. CaPN

And I always plaints that pass thorough my throat. Like to These Unmeasurable Mountains. Sir Thomas Wyatt. AAS; CABA; FCP

(And I am a doggerel bard). Emily, John, James, and I. Sir William Schwenck Gilbert. InMe

And I am an ape in half the world. Note. Frank Lima. ANYP

And I am behaving/As calm as I can. Christmas. Marchette Chute. BrR; ChBR; SiSoSe

And I am but a sheep-girl and who can me blame? The North Country Collier. Anonymous. OBSS

And I am concerned with the blossom. Reflections in a Slum. Hugh" (Christopher Murray Grieve) MacDiarmid. FaBoTw; NMP

And I am debtor in His sight. His Gift and Mine. Edith B. Gurley. BLRP

And I am gone. Morning. Marjorie Saiser. AMV-80

And I am here alone! A Night in Lesbos. George Horton AA

And I am here to see the last rose fall! The Old Casa. Torrey Connor. BPAW

And I am in the wilderness alone. The Prairies. William Cullen Bryant. AP; MAmP; NOBA; OxBA; PoEL 1-5; TAP

And I am Irish, too! I'll Wear a Shamrock. Mary Carolyn Davies. BrR; SiSoSe; YeAr

And I am left/Trembling with joy. Ayii, Ayii. The Great Sea Has Set Me in Motion. Anonymous. RFM

And I am lonely. I Am Lonely. George Eliot. GN; HBV 1-2

And I am lonely, O my brother. Dimidium Animae Meae. Charles A. Brady. GoYe

And I am lost without you. They Dream Only of America. John Ashbery. CAPP; EAS

And I am Marie of Roumania. Comment. Dorothy Parker. ALV; InMe; NIP; NLV; OBAL

...And I am never/sure. And I am always here. Medium Poem. Eileen Myles. APU

...And I am not resigned. Dirge without Music. Edna St. Vincent Millay. AnNE; CMoP; DL; LiTA; MoRP; NePA; NoAm; PG; PPON; SBG; TrGrPo

...And I/am not to be enough for myself. Marches Now the War Is Over (excerpt). Walt Whitman. PAI

And I am not yet ready to go home. New Skills. Naomi Shihab Nye. PH

And I am rich who learned from her/How beautiful they are. A Song for My Mother–Her Words. Anna Hempstead Branch. OHIP; YeAr

And I am safe and always have been. Kaddish. David Ignatow. NU; VWA

And I am saying to the hand/turn/open the river. To the Hand. William Stanley Merwin. EAS

And I am scared for all of us. Robert Lowell Is Dead. Patrick Worth Gray. SOTS

And I am shaken; but not as a leaf. Agitato Ma Non Troppo. John Crowe Ransom. OxBA

And I am so tired–father. Father. Margit Kaffka. PBWP

And I am sure if there's a heaven/That the miners will be there. Girl of Constant Sorrow. Sara Ogan Gunning. FSW

And I am the wild bird/Tempted by the toothsome trap. Love Song. Anonymous. TTY

And I am thinking–it is a light rain, just after... Light Rain. Christopher Buckley. AMV-81

And I am thinking of Thoreau's dry cow,/of his cornstalks splintered by hail. Thoreau. Rodney Jones. AmC; MAYP

And I am turned to sleep. The Plum Tree by the House. Oliver St. John Gogarty. OBEV; PoRA

And I am two-and-twenty,/And oh, 'tis true, 'tis true. A Shropshire Lad. Alfred Edward Housman. AnFE; OAEP; PoPle

And I am undefeated still! The Fighter. S. E. Kiser. BLPA

And I am upstream among my sisters/spawning. Coming Out. Jacqueline Lapidus. IHMS

And I am very weary; so, good-night! Scorned. Alexander Smith. OBVV

And I am weary of the skies,/For her sake that died for me. Helen of Kirconnell. Anonymous. AnFE; AWP; BSV; CBEP; CH; ELP; GoTS; HBV 1-2; InPo; LiTB; LoBV; OBEV; PoPle; SeCeV; TreFT

And I am wild and wanton like to him. The Vision. Robert Herrick. CaPo; CBEP

And I am, with the sun, alone. Adare (excerpt). John Francis O'Donnell. IrPN

And I, and you. Where Runs the River? Francis William Bourdillon. HBV 1-2; WGRP

And I aske the noght elles. Lo! Leman Sweet. Anonymous. CoBE

And I at the oars, our course to hold. The Willis. Samuel Willoughby Duffield. AA

And I awoik as wy that wes in weir. Followis How Dumbar Wes Desyrd to Be Ane Freir. William Dunbar. OAEP

And I awoke, for lo! it was a dream. Yom Kippur. Israel Zangwill. TrJP

And I awoke on the starved pavements of no love. The Mirage. Oscar Williams. CrMA; LiTL; LiTM; NePA

And I be buried here. In a Staffordshire Churchyard. Anonymous. PoPle

And I be sailing, sailing from the County of Mao. The County of Mayo. Anonymous. AnIV; BIrV

And I bear witness–all praise is due Allah! Malcolm X–An Autobiography. Larry Neal. BPo

And I became alone. The wind tapped like a tired man. Emily Dickinson. MoAB; MoAmPo; NePA

And I began to play/The bird-sweet flute of May. The Flute of May. Harry Woodbourne. GoYe

And I begin to be afraid. Return to Dachau. B. Z. Niditch. AMV-81

And I believe he's dead and gone. Batson. Anonymous. OuSiCo

And I believed them again ere night. Woman's Faith. Sir Walter Scott. ViBoPo

And I bend to hear who is beating The Hands. William Stanley Merwin. CAPP

And I betray the loch for a white coin.' Trout Fisher. George Mackay Brown. OxBC

And I blow horns–and I can't hear. A Parable. George L. Kress. STF

And I, bursting with flowers. In the Half-Point Time of Night. Ann Menebroker. AMV-80

And I, but for because my prospect lies/Upon that coast, am giv'n up for a slave. Astrophel and Stella, XXIX. Sir Philip Sidney. AAS; SiPS

And I but pause and pass. Why She Moved House. Thomas Hardy. FM

And I call your name as loud I can/and give you all the light I am. Poem and Message. Dannie Abse. TEP

And I called it by its name. Signature. Hannah Kahn. IHMS

And I can do most anything that come my hand All Around Man. Bo Carter. BluL

And I can go and court some other! The Banks of the Roses. Anonymous. ShS

And I can kiss a bonny girl/At twelve o'clock at night. When I Was a Little Boy. Anonymous. OxNR

And I can never forget the one/Lady of My Delight. Carol. John McClure. HBMV

And I can no longer hide from death. Plain Song. Benjamin Fondane. VWA

And I can remember when there were trees. When There Were Trees. Nancy Willard. HoAn

And I can scarce kiss you goodbye/before you run out into the street and they shoot. At First I Was Given Centuries. Margaret Atwood. HAP; NMM; WPOW

...And I can see all/those teeth/from across the room. Refusing What Would Bind You to Me Irrevocably. Ronald Koertge. GP

And I can sit, and look upon the stones/That cover Hallam's grave. A Sermon at Clevedon. Thomas Edward Brown. NOBV

And I can speak a little then. In Memoriam A.H.H., XIX. Alfred, Lord Tennyson. GTBS-P; LoBV; NAWM 1-2; OAEP

And I can't feel at home in this world anymore. I Can't Feel at Home in This World Anymore. Anonymous. FSW

And "I can't find my left shoe!" Waking Time. Ivy O. Eastwick. SiSoSe; TiPo

And I can't help but wonder where I'm bound. I Can't Help but Wonder Where I'm Bound. Tom Paxton. FSW

...And I can't see/Out my window anymore. Song: Paper. Keith Waldrop. MAT

And I can't sleep for thinking on't. We're All Dry. Anonymous. NOBL

And I can't think or write. The Country House. Louis Simpson. NOBA

And I can't think why! The Disagreeable Man. Sir William Schwenck Gilbert. ALV; FiBHP

And I can whistle now! The Little Whistler. Frances Frost. SoPo; TiPo

And I cannot even buy a little bottle/of wine or raki. When I Came to London. Rachael Castelete. VWA

And I catch your eye/in the silver reflection/of my wine goblet. Past Love. Anne Keiter. GOYP

And I choose, just a Crown– I'm ceded–I've stopped being theirs. Emily Dickinson. SBG; ViBoPo; WPOW

And I come home to Ludlow/Amidst the moonlight pale. Friends. Alfred Edward Housman. SeCePo

And I confess it by adoring you. To...in Church. Alan Seeger. HBV 1-2

And I content me with my hire. A Promise. Sir Thomas Wyatt. OBSC

...And I,/Content with one such flower, will die. A Separation. William Johnson Cory. OBNC

And I converse with many a shipwrecked crew. The Fisher's Boy. Henry David Thoreau. AA; AnNE; MOS

And I copied all the answers too,/A quack, a honk, an oink, a moo. When Did the World Begin. Robert Clairmont. GrPl

And I could change it, nevermore. The Sculptor. Anonymous. PoToHe

And I could do for many days/Without eggs. Soft-Boiled Egg. Russell Hoban. NTCP

And I could fashion it no more! Sculpture. Anonymous. BLPL; PoLf

And I could only look at her–through/tears. Separation. Alice Learned Bunner. AA

And I could sleep to their musical threats and accusations. Clinton South of Polk. Carl Sandburg. AmFN

And I could wish my days to be/Bound each to each by natural piety. My Heart Leaps Up. William Wordsworth. AtBAP; BiP; BoLiVe; DiPo; ERoP 1-2; ExPo; FaBV; FaFP; GoTF; GTBS; GTBS-P; InPK; InPo; InPS; LoBV; MBW 1-2; MCCG; NOBE; NoP; OAEL 1-2; OAEP; OBNC; OBRV; OBSP; PoPl; SoPo; TEP; TiPo; TreF; TrGrPo; TRV; ViBoPo

And I couldn't find a mule/there, with his shoulder well Captain Captain. Mance Lipscomb. BluL

And I couldn't hear nobody pray. I Couldn't Hear Nobody Pray. Anonymous. BoAN 1-2; FSW

And I cried The Mask. Patty L. Harjo. VoR

And I cried tears down. Crazy Jane on the Mountain. William Butler Yeats. CMoP

...And I curse my ancestors for being chickens/rather than horses. The Prophylactic. Russell Edson. GP

And I'd a filthy job–to waste and die. Epigram: "I read about the Blaskets and Dunquin." John Millington Synge. FaBoEE

And I'd better tell you what remarks is passed. Coals of Fire. Sir Alan Patrick Herbert. ALV

...And I'd just as soon/You hadn't to do that. Lizard. Alan McLean. BoAnP

And I'd like to buy every damn case   The Sculptors.   Alfred W. Purdy.
PeCV

And I'd like to hear the pipers blow,/And shake a fut with Fanny there!   Mr.
Molony's Account of the Ball.   William Makepeace Thackeray.   HBV 1-2

And I'd praise God in his bright abode.   Ecstasy.   *Anonymous.*   AmFP

And I'd rather be bride to a lad gone down/Than widow to one safe home.
Keen.   Edna St. Vincent Millay.   HBMV

And I'd sing on as I fly.   Young Hunting.   *Anonymous.*   OxBoLi

And I daresay she will do.   The Chilterns.   Rupert Brooke.   MoBrPo

And i deserved something/better/for myself/now/or never   Now or Never.
Astra.   BrRo

And I do not stand alone!   The Living God.   Charlotte Perkins Stetson
Gilman.   WGRP

And I do swear, even by the same delight,/I will but kiss, I never more will
bite.   Nymph of the Garden where All Beauties Be.   Sir Philip Sidney.
InvP

And I don't ever have to go/To bed, to bed, to bed!   Fourth of July Night.
Dorothy Aldis.   SiSoSe; TiPo

And I don't feel so well myself.   On the Vanity of Earthly Greatness.
Arthur Guiterman.   BXAP; HeIP; HoPM; InPK; NAMP; NIP; NLV;
OBCA; PoPl; PV; TrJP

And I don't know what I mean.   Foreign Streets.   Mary Crow.   AMV-80

"And I don't like the way Windsor/Does,either."   The Great Lakes Suite.
James Reaney.   WHW

And I don't think they ought to say "Bah!"   Bah!   Walter De La Mare.
BoAnP

And I don't want it to leave me behind.   Good News.   *Anonymous.*   FSW

And I don't want one–now.   Tragedy.   Jill Spargur.   BLPA

And I done told you two or three times/I don't want no junk   Sweet Patuni.
Jesse James.   BluL

And I drank Life through God's own death.   The Strong City.   Alfred
Noyes.   GoBC

And I drank who now am here/Where my dust with dust confers.   Envoy.
Bliss Carman.   HBV 1-2

And I drown/in my own/juices/of/joy.   Knee Deep.   Ted Joans.   GP

And I eat.   Mushroom Hunting in Late August, Peterborough, N.H.
Michael C. Blumenthal.   MAYP

And I eat men like air.   Lady Lazarus.   Sylvia Plath.   CAPP; ConAP;
FaBoWP; HaCAP; MAT; NaP; NIP; NoAm; NOBA; NoP; PPoe; PrIm;
TAP; VGW

And i end with my favorite motto/toujours gai toujours gai   The Song of
Mehitabel.   Don (Donald Robert Marquis) Marquis.   FiBHP; NLV; TreFS

And I fade into a dream.   Clair de Lune.   Arthur Symons.   SyP

And I fall and die/Through a wile.   Fallen Rain.   Richard Watson Dixon.
NBM

...And I feared/that they'd beat me up/in the boys' room.   I Think the New
Teacher's a Queer.   Perry Brass.   PeHV

And I feast on fat bacon and charming grey peas.'   The Country Mouse and
the City Mouse.   Richard Scrafton Sharpe.   OxBChV

And I feel in my own breast/Tears withholden wildly burning.   In the Night
of the Full Moon.   Carl Busse.   AWP

And I feel larger, equalizing myself to the equal men!...   Aspiration.   Mario
De Andrade.   TTY

And I feel my life fleeing/hushed and gentle like the gazelle.   Dusk.
Gabriela (Lucila Godoy Alcayaga) Mistral.   BoWoP

And I feel so God damned proud/That I want to shout out loud, "Fuck 'em
all."   Samuel Hall.   *Anonymous.*   DBV

And I feel when in love with my fair,/Like a ship that is breasting the sea.
White as a Paper A-Sail in the Air.   *Anonymous.*   WTO

And I fell, like a body falling dead.   Divina Commedia: Inferno.   Dante
Alighieri.   EnLi 1-2; ExPo; NAWM 1-2; TreFT

And I felt as independent/As the queen upon her throne.   Learning to Read.
Frances E. W. Harper.   BlSi

...And I felt my hair/Put on a glory, and my soul expand.   Meeting.
Christina Georgina Rossetti.   HBV 1-2

...And I felt the beat/of the old neighborhood stop, on our street.   Letter
from Oregon.   William Stafford.   NaP

And I find 'em all peeping at me.   Limerick: "Said old Peeping Tom of Fort
Lee."   Morris Bishop.   LiBL

...And I find/in the flesh a little peace of mind.   Bordello.   Lewis Turco.
SM

And I find revelation, sweet indeed/In her dear treasures of sea shells and
weed.   Sea Lavender.   Louise Morey Bowman.   CaP

And I forgot, and wept.   The Messenger.   Alfred Noyes.   GoBC

And I fought to cut it out.   Hornpout.   Prescott, Jr Evarts.   WOLT

And I found that though no others had bid, a/prize had been won by me.
At Casterbridge Fair.   Thomas Hardy.   EnLi 1-2

And I give heart to you/your own pulsing ember in fluid.   Going Back.
George Rachow.   LFAC

And I give her all my roses.   Under My Window.   Thomas Westwood.
HBV 1-2; HBVY

And I glide ahead as a leaf/that knows where the gates will open.   A Speck
of Sand.   Paul Celan.   VWA

And I go at Midsummer, when the hay is down.   Four Years.   Dinah Maria
Mulock Craik.   HBV 1-2

...And I go on/living in the durable world.   Tornado Watch, Bloomington,
Indiana.   Gary Young.   SUW

And I go to sleep, dreaming.   Music.   Amy Lowell.   AnAmPo; YaD

And I got an egg that day for my tay.   When I Was a Lad.   *Anonymous.*
OxNR

And I got some rain in my hair.   Little Rain.   Elizabeth Madox Roberts.
SoPo; SUS

And i had a day of mine/that made me as happy/as yours did you   A
Certain Peace.   Nikki Giovanni.   CNA

And I had a prayer like a white rose pinned/On the Virgin Mary's blouse.   A
Christmas Childhood.   Patrick Kavanagh.   AnIL; DTC; FaBoIP; IPY;
OxBI

And I had died low when I was young.   Love Is Teasing.   *Anonymous.*
OBET

And I had my arms again.   Nuclear Wind, When Wilt Thou Blow.   Paul
Dehn.   FiBHP

And I had power to kill!   Come Love or Death.   Will Henry Thompson.
AA

And I had rather torture mine,/Than rob you of one minute's rest.   The
Innocent Gazer.   John, Lord Cutts.   CavP

And I had wished the sky to fall.   Lullabye.   Kathryn Stripling.   AMV-80

And I hadn't been.   Come In.   Robert Frost.   AnNE; BoNaP; DiPo;
FaBV; ForPo; LiTA; LiTM; MoAB; MoAmPo; NOBA; NoP; TrGrPo

And I hae tane awa' the bonniest lass/That is in a' the north countrie.   The
Laird o' Ochiltree Wa's.   *Anonymous.*   OxBB

And I hallede to the hokes and the hert smote.   The Poacher.   *Anonymous.*
OxBM

And I have a brother who, being alive/Does not need to be put in a poem.
Family Fortunes.   C. H. Sisson.   OxBC

And I have been waiting for days.   The Tunnel.   Mark Strand.   HeIP;
TwCP; WeW

And I have bent to throwe me downe withall.   When Windesor Walles
Sustain'd My Wearied Arme.   Henry Howard, Earl of Surrey.   AAS;
EnPo; FCP; SiPS

And I have broken down before the wind.   Nocturne of the Wharves.   Arna
Bontemps.   BANP; BPo; PoNe

And I have come away peeled to the bone,/having given away all my weapons.
Poetry Workshop in a Reform School.   Betty Adcock.   AMV-80

And I have come here, seeking mine,/Jerusalem, Jerusalem!   Gates.   Sister
Mary Madeleva.   GoBC

...And I have/Come with blood in my mouth, my hands sopped/With red
snow, to speak and save.   A Scientific Expedition in Siberia, 1913.   Kelly
Cherry.   SM

And I have cried in my heart, "The world is love!"   The Hate and the Love
of the World.   Max Ehrmann.   PoToHe

And I have gone upon my way/Sorrowful.   The Wayfarer.   Padraic Pearse.
OxBI

And I have gotten the bonniest lass/That is in this countrie.'   The Broom of
Cowdenknows (B version).   *Anonymous.*   ESPB

...And I have known/That what I will have surely spoken/Abides thus–may it
yet thus broken.   Prologue: Moments in a Glade.   Alan Stephens.   QFR

And I have lived and loved, and closed the door.   I Have Trod the Upward
and the Downward Slope.   Robert Louis Stevenson.   NOBV

And I have married a keelman,/And my good days are done.   The Sandgate
Girl's Lamentation.   *Anonymous.*   CoMu; ELP; TW

And I have mastered the speed and strength which is the armor of the/world.
Poem: "There I could never be a boy."   Frank O'Hara.   HoAn

...And I have murdered it in my early manhood.)   The Dirty Word.   Karl
Shapiro.   CoAP; InPK; MiAP; PoA; PoCh

And I have/never worried about those things.   After the First Frost.   Lew
Blockcolski.   VoR

...And I have no sons/to float in the space between.   The Idea of Ancestry.
Etheridge Knight.   BALP; BPo; CNA; ConAP; LFAC; NIP; NNaP; PoBA;
PPoe; SV

And I have no thoughts.   Four Haiku.   Richard Wright.   NoAm

...,And I/have no way of turning now, no door.   A Little Boy Lost.   Jerome
Rothenberg.   CoPo

And I have only set the same to pen.   To Oxford.   Gerard Manley Hopkins.
BrPo; FaBoPP

And I have painted Miyoko San.   Miyoko San.   Mary McNeil Fenollosa.
AA

And I have seen them merge in their leafy sky/Till they became the light of
the full moon.   The Lost Orchard.   Edgar Lee Masters.   LaNeLa; MoPo

And I have something to expiate;/A pettiness.   Snake.   D.H. Lawrence.
AtBAP; BBV; BrPo; CMoP; CoBMV; DiPo; FaBoMo; HeIP; HoPM; LiTB;
LiTM; LoBV; MoAB; MoPo; MoVE; NoAm; NOBE; NoP; NU; OAEL 1-2;
OAEP; PPP; PrIm; SeCeV; SOTW

And, I have to add, I hope those satraps/do not wake in time. Eugene Delacroix Says. Edward Dorn. NoAm

And I have told thee all thou mayest hear. Endymion. John Keats. ViBoPo

"And I have tried to keep from falling." Canto XIII. Ezra Pound. CMoP

...And I have wandered over/The expanse of these wide wildernesses/In this great ship-- The Demon Speaks. Pedro Calderon de la Barca. CAW

And I headed South for a breathin' spell. Indigo Pete's J. B. Henry "Harry" Kibbs. BPAW

And I hear in the chain a chuckle I like to hear. Maybe Alone on My Bike. William Stafford. NYBP

And I hear the steady ringing of the phone/into the long night. Letter to My Mother. Anita Skeen. IHMS

And I Hear voices from Hades like bells on the wind. Gone on the Wind. James Clarence Mangan. CBEP

And I heard from heaven today. Hurry On, My Weary Soul. Anonymous. AH

...And I heard/roosters and dogs, the very same/as if he had written them. The Birthplace. Seamus Heaney. FaBoIP

And I heard the trumpets blowing earthly sounds Airship. Hy Sobiloff. NePA

And I his adversary desire that he shall gain. The Mystery of the Innocent Saints (excerpt). Charles Peguy. CAW

And I hold in my hand a hemisphere/of limestone silence. Brain Coral. Lois Bassen. SUW

And I hope all men/Who think like this/Will soon lie/Underground. The Horrid Voice of Science. Vachel Lindsay. PoA

And I hope every couple that ever do love/May see more pleasure than they. Earl Brand. Anonymous. FSW

And I hope to see the hoodoos dead and damn them all in hell. The Rustler. Anonymous. CoSo

And I hope you'll like your baseball suit. Happy Lifetime to You. Franklin Pierce ("F.P.A.") Adams. InMe

And I imagine roses for a moment on the winter hills. A Knight of Ghosts and Shadows. Dunstan Thompson. NePA

And I in arms of thine, my friend,/In dying arms of thine! A Lady to a Lover. Roden and Wriothesley Berkeley Noel. OBVV

And I in my turn, may be taught to love too. Song the Ninth. Edward moore. CEP

And I, in thee, have uttered what I am! The Lonely-Bird. Harrison Smith Morris. AA

And I inherit Strength and Spirit. The Lay of the Captive Count. Johann Wolfgang von Goethe. AWP

And I its happy guest. A Holiday. Lizette Woodworth Reese. AA

And I join the procession,/And my child follows behind. Moods. Leib Kwitko. TrJP

And I just broke his window, I think. Limerick: "I must eat an apple," said Link." Lee Blair. TDH

And I kept saying, I've got to, Mama,/hug me again. Please don't go. She Didn't Even Wave. Ai. MAYP

And I kiss but a mouthful of sand Oh Beach Love Blossom. Judson Crews. UnTE

And I kissed her at the Zoo. The Prodigy. Sir Alan Patrick Herbert. EvOK

And I knew as I entered that I had come/Through fields that were part of no earthly estate. Tarry Flynn (excerpt). Patrick Kavanagh. FaBoIP; IPY

And I know how I know. The Redwing. Patric Dickinson. BoAnP; HaMV

And, I know it's very naughty, but I don't like Cook! I Don't Like Beetles. Rose Fyleman. OxBChV

And I know something of how he felt. Armageddon, Armageddon (excerpt). Paul Muldoon. CIP

And I know, that though dead, I have never died. She and He. Sir Edwin Arnold. HBV 1-2

And I know the amplitude of time. Leaves of Grass. Walt Whitman AA

...And I know/the angle of their shoulder fits my head/if I need it again. International Motherhood Assoc. M. L., Jr. Hester. AMV-81

And I know your love will answer: "Here's my laddie/home from play!" The Wastrel. Reginald Wright Kauffman. HBV 1-2

And I lay still to watch him play. I Was Lying Still in a Field One Day. Zhenya Gay. TiPo

And I left him layin' dead, blast his eyes! Sam Hall. Anonymous. ViBoFo

And I left that place full of/breed, and brood, and cross-hatching. Carved by Obadiah Verity. Don Welch. PoDr

And I left them there at their altars/Ringing their own dead knells. New Year's Eve. Alfred Edward Housman. VLP

And I let the fish go. The Fish. Elizabeth Bishop. ExPo; FaBoWP; GoJo; HAP; HeIP; HoPM; InPK; LiTM; MiAP; MoAB; MoAmPo; MOS; NePA; NoAm; NOBA; NoP; NU; PoPl; TrGrPo; ViBoPo; WeW

And I lie here alone. A Ballad for Katharine of Aragon. Charles Causley. FaBoTw; NePoEA

And I lie in the sand. Exile. George Rostrevor Hamilton. FaBoEE

And I lie listening awake? Fragment Thirty-Six. Hilda ("H. D.") Doolittle. CMoP; OxBA; VGW

And I lie silent--but my body shakes. The Black Panther. John Hall Wheelock. FF; HBMV; LiTM

And I, like Earth all budding out with love. My Lady. Philip James Bailey. OBVV

And I, like them, would be lost in time. A Revel. Donagh MacDonagh. NeIP

And i listen to their footsteps in the wind/the wind/that only dead men do not hear. This Wind. Tom Kryss. NeAC

And I'll be no longer a poor collier/lass. The Collier Lass. Frankie Armstrong. BrRo

And I'll be sad. Patty-Poem. Nick Kenny. PoToHe

And I'll be six in June! Six in June. Mary Carolyn Davies. BiCB

And I'll be true to my love if my love'll be true to me. The Two Sisters. Anonymous. AmFP

And I'll build a cot on a corner lot/And get rich as soon as I can. Westward Ho. Anonymous. CoSo

And I'll cry out,/Shoo over! Shoo over! Anonymous. PBBP

And I'll dance till you be done. Moon, Moon. Anonymous. OxNR

And I'll do all that ever I can/To follow my Bangalorey Man. My Bangalorey Man. Anonymous. OxNR

And I'll dream of pretty Saro wherever I go. Pretty Saro. Anonymous. AmFP; FSW

And I'll drink a health to Flora, although she answers no. The Stormy Scenes of Winter. Anonymous. AmFP

And I'll eat you too, good body. Mouse and Mouser. Anonymous. OxNR

And I'll envy no Rothschild his million. Martial in London. Mortimer Collins. ALV; InMe

And I'll ever after love thee. The Lover's Invitation. John Clare. VLP

And I'll find her a wholesome corrective in Birch.' An Old Buffer. Frederick Locker-Lampson. CenHV

And I'll forgive Thy great big one on me. Forgive, O Lord, My Little Jokes on Thee. Robert Frost. EaLo; LiTM

And I'll forsake both father, mother,/And with you I'll run away. Awake, Arise, You Drowsy Sleeper. Anonymous. AmFP

And I'll forsake, I'll forsake father and mother,/Forsake them all and go with you. The Drowsy Sleeper (A vers.). Anonymous. BaBo

And I'll gae to my Anna. Anna. Robert Burns. TrGrPo; UnTE

And I'll get/I bet-a pet. My House. Jane W. Krows. SoPo

And I'll get over the misty moor. Pick-A-Back. Anonymous. OxNR

And I'll give you a jug of the best of brown ale.' All Jolly Fellows That Follow the Plow. Anonymous. OBET

And I'll give you bread and barley/corns. To the Snail. Anonymous. OxNR

And I'll go far, very far, like a gypsy,/Into Nature–happy, as if with a woman. Sensation. Arthur Rimbaud. SOTW; SyP

And I'll go forth and live with that. Touching. Christopher Gilbert. MAYP

And I'll go marry the Turkish lady/That crossed the roaring sea for me. Lord Bateman. Anonymous. AmFP; FSW; OBET

And I'll go with you a-milking. The Milkmaid. William Allingham. IrPN

And I'll go wooing in my boys. Winifreda. Anonymous. HBV 1-2; OBEV

And I'll have mine old cloak about me. This Winter's Weather It Waxeth Cold. Anonymous. InvP

And I'll hunt the runt that stole my girl,/If it takes 'til judgment day. Down in Lehigh Valley. Anonymous. TreF

And I'll leave poor mossback stay at home his buckwheat for to sow. Shanty-Boy and the Farmer's Son. Anonymous. ABF

And I'll lie in the cold, cold grave,/For of single life I'm weary. Jimmy's Enlisted; or, The Recruited Collier. Anonymous. CoMu; EBEV

And I'll marry that lady to-morrow! The Rover's Apology. Sir William Schwenck Gilbert. ALV

And I'll never go there any more. It's Once I Courted as Pretty a Lass. Anonymous. OxNR

And I'll nevermore shovel manure. Lyric to Spring. Joseph W. Stilwell. DBV; OBAL

And I'll not marry you. Paper of Pins. Anonymous. ABF; AmFP; BFSS; BLSo; FSW

...And I'll oftentimes recall/That lively gaited sworray-"The Cowboys' Christmas/Ball." The Cowboys' Christmas Ball. William Lawrence Chittenden. BPAW; CoSo

And I'll play my old squeezebox as we sail along/With the wind in the rigging to sing me this song. 'Fiddler's Green. Anonymous. OBSS

And I'll rock you away to that Sugar-Plum Tree/In the garden of Shut-Eye Town. The Sugar-Plum Tree. Eugene Field. FaFP; GoTF; HBV 1-2; HBVY; NLV; OxBChV; SoPo; TreF

And I'll save not a halfpenny pay till the day I die! Seamas, Light-Hearted and Loving Friend of My Breast (excerpt). Eoghan Rua O Suilleabhain. NOBI

And I'll sing of the sea and of battle/And of men's might.   Song against Women.   Willard Huntington Wright.   HBV 1-2

And I'll sleep that long and lonely sleep/Called slumber in the tomb.   Peter Emberley (III).   *Anonymous.*   ShS

And I'll split with you my money/Every pay-day of my life.   Reuben, Reuben.   *Anonymous.*   FSW

And I'll still be the jolly, jolly soldier.   Jolly Soldier.   *Anonymous.*   AmFP; OFD

And I'll supply the boiling oil,/If someone has a dipper.   Advice to Worriers.   George S. Kaufman.   ALV

...And I'll swear there's nothing/low,/In the pride of Human Nature when its pants begin to go.   When Your Pants Begin to Go.   Henry Lawson.   NOAV

And I'll take my old cloak about me.   The Old Cloak.   *Anonymous.*   BuBa; OBEV; OBSC; TrGrPo

And I'll take the complete works of Shakespeare and a box of chocolas.   They Don't Speak English in Paris.   Ogden Nash.   OBAL

And I'll thereto compassionate my voice.   Madrigal: "Come, woeful Orpheus."   William Byrd.   EnRePo

And I'll think on her when she's dead and gone.   Picking Lilies.   *Anonymous.*   OBET

And I'll turn my back on her and court who I please.   Way down the Ohio.   *Anonymous.*   TrAS

And I'll walk as proud by him as he walks by me.   The Cuckoo.   *Anonymous.*   FSW

And I'll wear it for my dear Johnson's sake.   The Lamenting Maid.   *Anonymous.*   OBET

And I'll wheel you all day in this barrow!'   Limerick: "There was an old person of Harrow."   Edward Lear.   FaBoNo

And I'll zing Tally ho!   The Cheerful Horn.   *Anonymous*   CH

—And I lo'e Love/Wi' a scunner in't.   Scunner.   Hugh" (Christopher Murray Grieve) MacDiarmid.   BSV; FaBoTw

And I long to reach the crest/Of my earthly life, and gain/Schiehallion.   Schiehallion.   Helen B. Cruickshank.   PoSH

And I longed that my kiss should strike you dead at my feet.   Sonnets of a Portrait Painter.   Arthur Davison Ficke   AnAmPo

And I longed to take shelter/in the forest of your hair.   The Wedding Poem (excerpt).   Lawrence Russ.   AMV-80

And I looked back very hard at him.   The Rabbit.   Elizabeth Madox Roberts.   OBCA; SoPo; TiPo

And I love all other things/Her bright eye looks upon.   I saw her crop a rose.   John Clare.   EG

And I love my Daddy like he loves his Dollar.   American Primitive.   William Jay Smith.   FF; InPK; MoAmPo; MP; NePoAm; NePoEA; OBSP; PoPl; PPON; TwCP

And I love my Lord Jesus above anything.   Down in Yon Forest.   *Anonymous.*   FSW

And I love the lad would break my heart.   Must I Go Bound?   *Anonymous.*   WTO

And I love the rain.   April Rain Song.   Langston Hughes.   NTCP; OBCA; SUS; TiPo

And I love you!" You don't say. Well, I don't believe you.   Words Words Words.   Marilyn Krysl.   AMV-80

And I loved her the more when I heard/Such tenderness fall from her tongue.   The Shepherd's Home.   William Shenstone.   GN

And I'm a meek little child and as harmless as a lamb.   Buckskin Joe.   *Anonymous.*   CoSo

And I'm alone; and you have not awoken.   Success.   Rupert Brooke.   OxBTC

And I'm bigger than Bob-tail the puppy,/Who used to be bigger than me.   Growing Up.   *Anonymous.*   BiCB

And I'm bound to the Rio Grande!   Rio Grande.   *Anonymous.*   ShS

And I'm but a breath on the steps of Heaven—/If I'm at all!   On the Edge of the Copper Pit.   Pauline Henson.   GoYe

And I'm dashed if ever I do, sirs,/O! no I won't.   Neddy Nibble'm and Biddy Finn.   *Anonymous.*   GBP

...And I'm/driving away from the gates of/Paradise.'   Goethe's Blues.   Denise Levertov.   FaBoWP

And I'm four years old.   I Am the Little Irish Boy.   Henry David Thoreau.   NAs

And I'm going back south/To my used to be   Tired as I Can Be.   Bessie Jackson.   BluL

And I'm going to get there ahead of you!   The Message.   Meleager.   LiTW

And I'm here, sizing the dark, saving my mother's seat.   Sitting at Night on the Front Porch.   Charles Wright.   LCAP

And I'm no shair o' maist the sinners either.   Up to Date.   Hugh" (Christopher Murray Grieve) MacDiarmid.   FaBoCo

And I'm not sure who sleep away/their lives, what we are here for,/where they've gone.   New Graveyard: Jerusalem.   Shirley Kaufman.   VWA

And I'm ringing the blonde's/door bell my eyes are just right   In Blue (parody).   D. C. Berry.   BXAP

And I'm slowly making a pit/to fit the circumstances.   Housework.   Amanda Berenguer.   WPOW

And I'm sure I can never do better than he.   Contentment; or, The Happy Workman's Song.   John Byrom.   OBEC

And I'm the little hot dog/That runs around the street.   My father owns the butcher shop.   *Anonymous.*   FaFP

And I'm told that it is haunted/By the ghost of Might-Have-Been.   Mr. Meant-To.   *Anonymous.*   WBLP

And I'm wondering how they manage to know/The way to your tummy below.   Mr. Giraffe.   Geoffrey Lapage.   OnUR

And I'm your servant, J. M. Synge.   The Curse.   John Millington Synge.   ChTr; DBV; FaBoCo; FaBoEE; GoTF; NOBI; PV; TreFT; TW

And I made this praise to your nakedness in the sea.   That Summer's Shore.   John Ciardi.   ErPo

And I make mistakes.   Arachne.   Jody Aliesan.   LTB

And I, marrow and blood,/am consumed in the flame.   I Didn't Find Light by Accident.   Hayim Nahman Bialik.   VWA

And I marvel at men never gentle until they are old.   Letter from a State Hospital.   Frank Mundorf.   GoYe

And I may be, some time.   Snake.   Theodore Roethke.   NOBA; NYBP; PoPl; RFM

And I may dine at journey's end/With Landor and with Donne.   To a Young Beauty.   William Butler Yeats.   CMoP

And I may have to wait for years/Till either of them reappears.   Patience.   Harry Graham.   FiBHP; MoShBr

And I may laugh at them because I knew them.   Isaac and Archibald.   Edwin Arlington Robinson.   MAmP; OxBA

And I may move again/with the great tides of cloud and wind/that cover me.   When I Die.   Brenda G. Macrow.   PoSH

And I may return/If disssatisfied/With what I learn/From having died.   Away!   Robert Frost.   NOBA

And I mean she is/making me over,/again.   Frigga with Hela.   Judy Grahn.   APU

And I might be in Atlantis, or any haunted place/Out of time and space.   Sailor and Inland Flower.   Hamish Maclaren.   EtS

And I might have, but it doesn't seem as if.   The Pauper Witch of Grafton.   Robert Frost.   CMoP; CrMA

And I mine own and yours no more.   To a Lady To Answer Directly with Yea or Nay.   Sir Thomas Wyatt.   ElL; EnLoPo

And I more of this will say,/If thou come next Holy day.   The Shepheards Hunting:.   George Wither.   SeCV 1-2

And I mourn for the time gone long ago,/The time of the Barmacides.   The Time of the Barmacides.   James Clarence Mangan.   EnRP; RoGo

And I must dream what taught our dreamless dead/To save Man, by a thread.   What Bids Me Leave.   Herbert Trench.   HBMV

And I must get a London one.   From the Wash the Laundress Sends.   Alfred Edward Housman.   NoAm

And I must home gone.   The Lily-white Rose.   *Anonymous.*   EG

And I must know more than I know.   The Hand.   Howard Moss.   TAP

And I must maintain them.   Market Women's Cries.   Jonathan Swift.   AnIV

And I must pick a few.   Crocuses.   Josa.   TiPo

And I must prepare a fitting silence.   The Stones.   Wendell Berry.   GP

And I must rest at last, in Thee, my home.   The Quest.   Eliza Scudder.   TrPWD

And I must say, I am often worsted.   What Would You Fight For?   D. H. Lawrence.   OBSP

And I my sweet love-song.   He'd Nothing But His Violin.   Mary Kyle Dallas.   AA; HBV 1-2

And I myself, from every face,/Will wipe off every tear.   Hark! 'Tis the Saviour of Mankind.   John Murray.   AH

And I myself myself always to hate/Till dreadful death do cease my doleful state?   The Pillar Perished Is.   Sir Thomas Wyatt.   AAS; FaBoPV; FCP

And I name it Roses Island.   Adrian Block's Song.   Edward Everett Hale.   PAH

And I never did lose boys,/I always did gain.   Stewball.   *Anonymous.*   FSW

And I never learned to sing for rain.   For My Brother and Sister Southwestern Indian Poets.   Geary Hobson.   STE

And I never lie.   Oliphaunt.   J. R. R. Tolkien.   AmMo

And I never, never, never, never, never/meant to tell.   Robin's Secret.   Katharine Lee Bates.   AA

And I never seen a cabbage head with a mustache on before.   The Four Nights' Drunk.   *Anonymous.*   FSW; OBAL

And I never will go near my false Polly any more.   Pretty Polly of Topsham.   *Anonymous.*   AmFP

And I never will play the wild rover no more.   Wild Rover.   *Anonymous.*   FSW

And I no longer knew who or what I was/and I was no more   Nothingness.   Aharon Amir.   VWA

And I no more such torments of the heart/Feel as I do. This shalt thou gain thereby. Sufficed not, madam, tht you did tear. Sir Thomas Wyatt. FCP; SiPS

And I no more will stir this earthly dust/Wherein I lose my name to take on lust. Caelica, LXXI. Fulke, Lord Brooke Greville. FCP

And I, O Fear, will dwell with Thee! Ode to Fear. William Collins. CEP; EiCP; EnPE; LAuP; NOEC; OAEP; TrGrPo

And I–oh, the hopelessness–I can't write. Letter from a Contract Worker. Antonio Jacinto. WhB

And I, on Cowper's grave, should see his rapture in a vision. Cowper's Grave. Elizabeth Barrett Browning. HBV 1-2; OBVV

And I oompahed, oompahed, oompahpahed, oompahed up and down the square. Seventy Six Trombones. Meredith Wilson. BLSo

And I open my eyes: and the world looks in! The Kid: The Awakening (excerpt). Conrad Aiken. MoVE

And I paid them for laying me in Limbo. Limbo. Anonymous. OBET

And I pass all the time I can spare from my meals/In innocent slumber–like this. The Sleepy Giant. Charles Edward Carryl. OnUR

And I, perchance, may therein comfort you. Turn Again to Life. Mary Lee Hall. BLPL; PoLf

And I plucked her a handful of may. As I Walked through the Meadows. Anonymous. OBET

And I pour it on my own tears. Sad Love and Sad Song. Homei Iwano. LiTW

–And I pray God rest her soul. After the Flight of the Earls. Fear Flatha O Gnimh. NOBI

And I prayed to the Lord to deliver another one into my hand. Pagett, M. P. Rudyard Kipling. BrPo

And I pretty wench can get none. Plaint. Anonymous. OxNR

And I push my fingers into his skin/To make little dents in his big round face. Father's Story. Elizabeth Madox Roberts. PoSC

And I refuse to let my mother past. Whiteness. Yunna Moritz. VWA

And I, releasing, thee enlarged. To God Our Strength Shout Joyfully. Henry Ainsworth. AH

And I remain alive instead/Along the year. An Autumn Walk. Witter ("Emanuel Morgan") Bynner. GoYe

And I remain all comfortless. My hope, alas, hath me abused. Sir Thomas Wyatt. FCP; SiPS

And I remain despairing of the port. The Lover Compareth His State to a Ship in Perilous Storm... Petrarch (Francesco Petrarca). GBL

And I remain divided from my sin. If I Could Shut the Gate against My Thoughts. John Daniel. ElL; HBV 1-2; LoBV; NOCV; OxBoCh

And I remain gazing into them. Towards Democracy. Edward Carpenter. PeHV

And I remain in light and stare–/In light, and nothing else, awake. At the San Francisco Airport. Yvor Winters. ForPo; HeIP; InPK; NIP; NOBA; QFR

And I remember a sad breeze through the olive trees. Lament for Ignacio Sanchez Mejias. Federico Garcia Lorca. LiTW

And I remembered the cry of the peacocks. Domination of Black. Wallace Stevens. AP; CoBMV; MAPA; MoAB; MoAmPo; OxBA

...And I,/Remembering, can almost feel/The sea sand sucking at his heel. Son and Surf. Julia Hurd Strong. GoYe

And I returned/smiling and haunted, to a dark morning. To the Snake. Denise Levertov. AmPP; LiTM; NePoEA-2; NMM; PoA

And I ride and I rede/To Callice. D'Artagnan's Ride. Gouverneur Morris. AA

And I rinse him all off in the sinkie. Kindness to Animals. Laura E. Richards. NTCP; SoPo; TiPo

...And I rise. The Ring and the Book. Robert Browning. OAEP

And I rock you easier/than your straight chair ever done Ham Hound Crave. Rube Lacy. BluL

And I rumple on through sorrows. Moles. William Stafford. NYBP; RFM

And I rushed away, exclaiming, "I have found him! I have/found him!" Ferdinando and Elvira. Sir William Schwenck Gilbert. NA

And I sail in a boat named the Assembler of Souls. He Commandeth a Fair Wind. Book of the Dead. AWP

And I sailing, sailing swiftly from the county of Mayo. The County of Mayo. George Fox. IrPN; OBEV; OnYI; OxBI

...And I sang/aloud to honor them/and their nation. Last May. Carroll Arnett. STE

And I saw a crowd of Hungarians under the trees with/their women and children and a keg of beer... Happiness. Carl Sandburg. OxBA

And I saw her, at that moment,/in her own death, and I knew that she/knew. Pain for a Daughter. Anne Sexton. SoSe

And I saw Jenny, the villages of her peaceful words in flower. Words of Oblivion and Peace. Gabriel Preil. VWA

And I saw not. Oh! open Thou mine eyes. A Prayer. Lord Alfred Bruce Douglas. CAW; TrPWD

And I saw the crystal city/That's behind the waterfall. Behind the Waterfall. Winifred Welles. TiPo

And I say, "Cousin Harriet, here is the Boston Evening Transcript." The Boston Evening Transcript. Thomas Stearns Eliot. InPK; NePA

And I say it, and repeat it,/Immeasurable sadness! Sadness. Alfred, Lord Tennyson. FaBoEE

And I say, "Sure, just what we needed!" We're OK. Gloria Fuertes. WPOW

And I say, "Taking Humanities?" My Grandmother's Funeral. Jascha Kessler. AmPC

And I say, "YES, WE DID!!!" Afternoon with Grandmother. Barbara A. Huff. GeTw

And I scarcely think/We'll get a drink/Till we get to Buffalo,/Till we get to Buffalo. The E-RI-E. Anonymous. AS; FSW

And I seated somewhere/praying to God a while. Manchan's Prayer. Anonymous. NOBI

And I see it rising there/New York/greater than the Rocky Mountains. Walking. Frank O'Hara. TAT

And I see on the fourth day of July. Old Kimball. Anonymous. AmFP

...And I see/the coming time loose and dark/above me, with new strength After Hours. Robert Mezey. AmPC; NaP

...And I see/those lesser rivals flee. At Ithaca. Hilda ("H. D.") Doolittle. AnAmPo; VGW

And I send it out of fear. Money in the Bank. W. D. Ehrhart. FAZ

And I set forth upon the southern road. The Southern Road. Dudley Randall. CNA; NNP; PoBA; SM

And I shal sing/"Lullay, by-by, lullay".' This Endris Night. Anonymous. EBEV; NOCV; NoP

And I shall be in Hell. For All Blasphemers. Stephen Vincent Benét. AtBAP; OxBA

And I shall be more silent and cold-hearted/Than you are now. I Shall Not Care. Sara Teasdale. AnEnPo; HBV 1-2; MoAmPo; PoPl; TrGrPo; UnPo

And I shall begin when you've done. Limerick: "A father once said to his son." Anonymous. TDH

And I shall catch, ere you can pass,/That winged word. Poems, LVIII: "Twenty years hence my eyes may grow." Walter Savage Landor. PG

And I shall conquer any dread of night. Kitchen Window. Ruth N. Ebberts. AMV-80

And I shall die an old Parisian. Four Sheets to the Wind and a One-Way Ticket to France. Conrad Kent Rivers. AmNP; BPo; IDB; NNP; PoBA; PoNe

...And I shall entomb/What's cold by then in an adjoining room. Fatal Interview. Edna St. Vincent Millay. VGW

And I shall find my peace,/My All in All. Break Thou the Bread of Life. Mary Artemisia ("Aunt Mary") Lathbury. AH; TRV

And I shall go with Him to dwell/For all eternity! Yes, I Have Been to Calvary. Avis B. Christiansen. STF

And I shall have gone away. The Cage. David Gascoyne. EAS

And I shall laugh my turn. The Revenge. Pierre Ronsard. AWP

And I shall lie for seven long years/On the grass below the hawthorn tree. The Milk White Doe. Anonymous. AWP

And I shall love you, keeping/His word, and no more weeping. Love Song. Elinor Wylie. BLPL

And I shall muse above the little dust/that was the flesh that held my world in trust. Lilith on the Fate of Man. Christopher John Brennan. PoAu 1-2

And I shall ne'er be lonely/Asleep with these or those. Hughley Steeple. Alfred Edward Housman. FaBoPP

And I shall never come back. The Last Bus. Mark Strand. TwCP

And I shall never deceive you any more. John Riley. Anonymous. FSW

And I shall never see your Promised Land. Moses' Account. Milan Fuest. VWA

And I shall not be here when you are gone. Why He Was There. Edwin Arlington Robinson. CMoP; NOBA

And I shall not blush in knowing that men call him lowly born. Lady Geraldine's Courtship. Elizabeth Barrett Browning. DTo

And I shall not come to it The Elaboration. Bill Manhire. OCNZ

And I shall place you living in your land. The New Ezekial. Emma Lazarus. AA; AnAmPo

And I shall see by that one kiss/The water turned to wine. To the Water Nymphs, Drinking at the Fountain. Robert Herrick. AnAnS 2; CaPo; EG; ViBoPo

And I shall see the sunset and anon/Shall know the velvet kindness of the night/And see the stars. When I Am Dead. Hugh Barrie. PoSH

And I shall sell you sell you/sell you of course, my dear, and you'll sell me. Varick Street. Elizabeth Bishop. NYP

And I shall shortly be with them that rest. Samson Agonistes. John Milton. EBEV

And I shall smile, though under ground. 'Tis Late and Cold. John Fletcher. ViBoPo

And I shall syng:/"By-by, baby, lullay!" A Christmas Carol. Anonymous. TrGrPo

And i shall/travel with the wind/no more. Phoenix. Carolyn M. Rodgers. JB

And I shall traverse old love's domain/Never again. At Castle Boterel. Thomas Hardy. DTC; EBEV; GTBS-P; MoVE; NOBE; OBNC; SCV

And I shall walk on down the street, down the street... Fifteen Boys, or Perhaps Even More. Bella Akhmadulina. WPOW

And I shall watch thee with untroubled heart. Sonnets, I. Robert Silliman Hillyer. HBMV

And I shan't sleep so easy as the lads who march no more. Victory March. Michael Kennedy Joseph. AnNZ

And I shivered the whole night through. In the Pines. *Anonymous.* AmFP; FSW

And I should have to keep my foolish word! The Princess. Sara Henderson Hay. DFT

And I should like to know where in the world/(or rather, out of it) they expect to go. The Lost Mr. Blake. Sir William Schwenck Gilbert. EnLi 1-2; InMe

And I sing and I sing and I sing. Singing-Time. Rose Fyleman. SiSoSe; TiPo

And I sing as I follow Him on–my Guide. Christ. Robert Jones Burdette. BePJ

And I sing my song as we plunge along to the chatter of wheel and/steel. West of Alice. W. E. Harney. NOAV; PoAu 1-2

And I sing this for her. Songs My Mother Taught Me. David Wagoner. Str

And I sneered–softly–"small"! A Solemn Thing–It Was–I Said. Emily Dickinson. AmePo

And i sneeze. The big trimmer. Ronald P. Tanaka. BrSi

And I snuggled you tight in my arms. To a Child Who Inquires. Olga Petrova. BLPA

And I sometimes visualize in my gin/The Audubon that I audibin. Up from the Egg: The Confessions of a Nuthatch Avoider. Ogden Nash. BoAnP; FiBHP

And I sorrow in sackcloth and ashes,/Longing to see her again. Incognita. Henry Austin Dobson. CenHV

And I sort of like them for that. I Have a Place. Lily A. De Young. AMV-80

...And I spake–and lo! that sign/Awakened me from my slumber. A Second Review of the Grand Army. Bret (Francis Bret Harte) Harte. HBV 1-2; MC; PAH

And I sped to succour thee. Prometheus Unbound. Percy Bysshe Shelley. ChRP; FiP; LoBV

And i spring from the/Buddha's forehead/black as jesus. Satori. Gayl Jones. BlSi

And I stagger through the streets/Sleep-bound. Sleeping They Bear Me. Alfred Mombert. AWP

...And I stand down/on my knees to cry Who the hell are you, kid? The Roundhouse Voices. Dave Smith. AMV-80; GeTw; LiSp; MAYP

And I stand, straight as I can. Calvin in the Attic Cleans. Craig Weeden. AMV-81

And I started to give God His ticket back. Blues and Bitterness. Lerone, Jr. Bennett. FF; NNP; PoBA

And I stept out in flesh and bone/Manful like the man of stone. Loitering with a Vacant Eye. Alfred Edward Housman. WeW

And I still can't get a ride. Trailer Park. Lewis MacAdams. ANYP

And I still don't know if I am a falcon,/Or a storm, or a great song. I Live My Life. Rainer Maria Rilke. NU

And I stood on the awl-like pinnacle/And faltered,/And fell! I Should Be Ashamed. Uvlunuaq. WTO

And I stowed all the studs on the edge of my plate. Literary Dinner. Vladimir Nabokov. FiBHP; OBAL

And I, submissive, felt/Unwanted and went out? Dear, though the night is gone. W. H. Auden. BoLoP; InvP

And I swim raging/against the stream. Leah. Shirley Kaufman. VWA

And I swoop with it/In the blue/And in the nest/Of a cloud. The Bird. Max Michelson. TrJP

And I swung in ahead of him and landed fine/Behind 9W-7679. Ambition. Morris Bishop. AmFN

And I take in their iodine. Seaweeds. Sandra McPherson. AmPA; PoA

And I talk to them/in my secret mind/out of pure happiness. The Thinker. William Carlos Williams. MoLP

And I taste at the root of the tongue the unreal of what is real. Holiday in Reality. Wallace Stevens. NePA; OxBA

And I tasting of sediment. Sediment. David Ignatow. NYBP

And I tell you from experience you had better stay at home. Texas Rangers. *Anonymous.* OuSiCo

And I thank God this bed is narrow. Letter from Slough Pond. Isabella Gardner. ELU

And I thanked the God that made him and the land and sea and me. A Kodak; Tregantle. Horatio Brown. PeHV

And I, that noon in winter,/Forgot the cruel splinter. The Splinter. James Kenneth Stephen. CenHV

And I the day's. Lord–Thine the Day. Dag Hammarskjöld. EaLo

And I, the ghost of one you could not save,/May find you planting lentils on my grave. The Prodigal Son. Edwin Arlington Robinson. MoAmPo

And I, the meanest of them all,/That live to weep, and sing their fall. The Gododdin (excerpt). Aneirin [(or Aneurin)]. OBVE; OBWP

And I the noble cat am poor/And left to crouch beside the door! Where Is Justice? Eliezer Steinbarg. VWA

...(And I/the people am still parted in/two & would cry). I the People. Alice Notley. APU

And I the race might win. In My Place. Esther Archibald. STF

And I the soul of it, which he did miss. Sonnet: "I envy not Endymion now no more." William Alexander, Earl of Stirling. EIL

And I there all alone. All Alone in My Little Cell. *Anonymous.* NOBI

And I therefore/express regret. For an Officer. *Anonymous.* OBVE

And I think in my sleep it must be that I call to them. Thailand Railway. Randolph Stow. CBAP

And I think of my lover away down in the sea,/For he never, never more will come again to me. The Fisher Lad of Whitby. *Anonymous.* OBSS

And I think of the lucky break he got. Marriage Couplet. William Cole. OBAL

...And I think the soul of a man/Shall answer for yours in hell. Emmy. Arthur Symons. HBV 1-2; OBNC; OBVV; TreF

And I thought, O God, please. Please! Northwest Airlines. Fred Chappell. HoPM

And I thought: Still, it's good, though it has to end. Some Night Again. William Stafford. GOYP

And I thrilled as I thought of the fun and the joy such/trivial things could give to a boy. Treasures. Claire Richcreek Thomas. PoToHe

And I throw back the sheets. Absence. Edwin Morgan. BSV

And I/throwed the limb over my shoulder and/carried'em home. Second Carolina Said-Song. Archie Randolph Ammons. OBAL

And I thrust both my hands into a pair of gloves, tight. Private Pantomime. Ruth Stone. PoA

And I tighten the black leather brace/that keeps my knife hand steady. Our People. Diane Burns. TWSS

And I to be sitting for a while/Praying God in every place. The Hermit's Song. *Anonymous.* KiLC; OnYI

And I to live and die her slave. As You Like It. William Shakespeare. CTC; GBL; OBSC

And I, too, am in danger, sir. When I Consider. Margaret Griffith. AMV-80

And I too had a mind to let her. Commination. Walter Savage Landor. ALV

And I too late shall sorrow. Love in Thy Youth. *Anonymous.* EG; ViBoPo

And I took her charred contract/And signed in triplicate. The Witch of East Seventy-Second Street. Morris Bishop. NYBP; NYP

And I took it as good, and a happy omen to me. An Old Woman Speaks of the Moon. Ruth Pitter. BoC

And I took to my wings/And away I flew. Song of the Murdered Child Whose Bones Grew into a Milk-white Dove. *Anonymous.* GBP

And I took your hand, and we smiled. A Dream as Reported. Virginia Earle. GoYe

And I touch you again as you tick in the silence and settle in sleep. Buick. Karl Shapiro. AmC; BiP; CMoP; DFF; HoPM; MiAP; MoAB; TrGrPo; ViBoPo

And I touched your hand, and we kissed, without a word. The Quarrel. Conrad Aiken. LiTL; MoAB; MoAmPo; MoLP; PoPl

And I triumph, whirled in the vacuum bag/with my satellite heart, brain, bones and blood. In a Dream. David Ignatow. PoA

And I trow that another were fitter to sing you a song for a Queen. Jubilee before Revolution (parody). Andrew Lang. BXAP

And I trust myself, as from the grave I may,/To the enchanting miracles of change. Renewal. Michael (Katherine Bradley and Edith Cooper) Field. OBVV

And I tucked my head and cried. Ten Thousand Miles Away from Home (with music). *Anonymous.* AS

And I turn from the tactful friend to the candid sky. Autobiography. Charles Causley. LiTM

And I turned and fled, like a soul pursued,/From the white, inviolate solitude. The Skater. Sir Charles G. D. Roberts. NOBC

And I've a bonnie laddie noo/And breists for him to sook. The Robber. *Anonymous.* OBVE

And I've been doing some hard traveling, Lord. Hard Traveling. Woody Guthrie. FSW

And I've got plenty! Will you drink lager beer with me? The Happy Miner. *Anonymous.* CoSo

And I've got to be a-movin'–movin' on. The Old Cowboy's Lament. Robert V. Carr. BPAW; PoOW

And i've got to negotiate/for my people's freedom. Concerning One Responsible Negro with Too Much Power. Nikki Giovanni. BPo

And I've no plate–but that I'm used to.– Fragment: "Mary, I believ'd you quick." Thomas Hood. NBM

And I wait till morning for guests that I love,/and rattle the door in its chains. Leningrad. Osip Mandelstam. FaBoPV

And I wake from and into/dream. Poem Following Discussion of Brain. Stan Rice. NPGG

And I wake prisoner/In morning's branches. Cadenza. Miriam Waddington. CaP

And I wake saved.–And yet, it will not be! Any Wife to Any Husband. Robert Browning. OBNC; VLP

And I wake up kicking and screaming, Lemme go!/Lemme go! Assimilation. Irving Feldman. AmPC

And I walk in a light divine/The path I had feared to see. Obedience. George Macdonald. BePJ; BLRP; TreFT; TRV; WGRP

And I want an art/that is something/else, is an exciting sound–/like myself! Against Borders. Yevgeny Yevtushenko. CAD

And I want an Elephant/Can sit DOWN behind. For Christmas. Dorothy Aldis. ChBR

And I want/High on the Hog. High on the Hog. Julia Fields. CNA

And I want the ducts. The Greed Song. Albert Goldbarth. AMV-80

And I want to be wanted more than anything else in the world. Homosexuality. Frank O'Hara. NYP; PeHV; PoA; TAP

And I want to be/your final adventure. Love Poem. Rosemary Aubert. AMV-80

And I want to get started, at least. Limerick: "There once was a pious young priest." Anonymous. NIP; TDH

And I want to lie down–for ever.' Henry My Son. Anonymous. OBET

And I want to ride back by the strong man's track/That I see tonight through tears. The Covered Wagon. Lena Whittaker Blakeney. BPAW

...And I want you never to die. Reveille. John Godfrey. APU

And I wanted somewhere to save your blood. Physical for My Son. Barbara Smith. AMV-80

And I wanted to die, but they left me there. River Song. Weldon Kees. NoAm; PPP

And I was asking him/to forgive me too. Ten Years and More. Miriam Waddington. NOBC

And I was beautiful Sarai. Joseph Sherman. VWA

And I was blind to/her but O the night Loving She Stood Apart. Patrick Lane. NeAC

And I was calling on May Colven,/To take the Cat from me. May Colven. Anonymous. BuBa; MaC; OxBB; StPo; TrGrPo

And I was dazzled by a sunset glow,/And he was gone. To Rupert Brooke. Wilfred Wilson Gibson. GTBS

...And I was his wife. He loved three things in life. Anna Akhmatova. BoWoP

And I was lord of life and death. Summer Magic. Leslie Pinckney Hill. BANP

And I was on my way anywhere Fourth Dance Poem. Gerald William Barrax. PoBA

–And I was picked to kill/A man like that. Connolly. Liam MacGowan. OnYI

And I was riding hard/to pull Janie/out of the flames. Janie Swecker and Me and Gone with the Wind. David Huddle. GrPl

And I was shaken, shaken/like a mouse/between their jaws. Listening to Grownups Quarreling. Ruth Whitman. NTCP

And I was there, and I was there. Experts at Veneers. Kenward Elmslie. ANYP

And I was unaware. The Darkling Thrush. Thomas Hardy. AnFE; ATP; BoLiVe; BrPo; CMoP; CoBMV; DiPo; EvOK; ExPo; FaFP; ForPo; FPL; GTBS; HAP; HBMV; InPS; LiTB; LiTM; MasP; MoAB; MoBrPo; MoPo; NIP; NoAm; NOBE; NOBV; NoP; OAEL 1-2; OAEP; OBEV; OBNC; OBVV; PAI; PBBP; PPP; RoGo; SeCeV; SoSe; TEP; TreFT; TrGrPo; UnPo; VLP; WaP

And I was weeping in the Iron Age. Chivalry. George William Russell. MoRP; ViBoPo

And I wasn't, so didn't–till teeth crunched on my skull. Nightmare of Mouse. Robert Penn Warren. SO

And I watch her as the wheels spin her away. Her Birthday. Harold Witt. AMV-80

And I watched the tourist stand/Spitting in Niagara Falls. Public Aid for Niagara Falls. Morris Bishop. InMe; NLV

And I waters the workers' beer. The Man That Waters the Workers' Beer. Anonymous. FSW

...And I/waved back over the water/which darkened between us/with distance and tears. Going to Norway. Jack Anderson. GP

...And I weep. My Best Clothes. Eli Netser. AMV-81

And I went down. At Slim's River. John Haines. NPAW

And I went in the snow/That became mud/To the school/In the German Colony. A Snow in Jerusalem. Hayim Naggid. VWA

And I went off to college/With a Gasoline can. The Beginning of a Long Poem on Why I Burned the City. Lawrence Benford. NBP; TTY

And I went reading in that rune of roses/Which to her votaries the moon discloses. Sapientia Lunae. Ernest Christopher Dowson. EnLi 1-2; HBV 1-2

And I went to a real tea, and Dorothy to/bed. Small and Early. Tudor Jenks. AA

And I wept for the deed I had done! The Violet and the Rose. Joseph Skipsey. OBVV

And I wept there, alone. The Beast. Theodore Roethke. AmLP; SO

And I were king of pain. A Match. Algernon Charles Swinburne. ALV; ELP; EnLi 1-2; GTBS; HBV 1-2; LiTL; NOBV; OBVV

And I were pleased amid these bowers to stay/More than an evening's hour, or a long summer's day. Stanzas (excerpt). Charles Newton. NOEC

And I were to spend myself in his torn body/As morning gritted on his eyes. Guest. E. A. Lacey. PeHV

And I who fondly trusted to their truth/By suffering found that falsehood in them lies. In the Forest. Sandor Petofi. LiTW

And I will bind in dreams the wraiths/that pilfered last night's sleep. Insomnia. Ethna MacCarthy. NeIP

And I will come after, on little Jack Nag.' Robin and Richard. Anonymous. OxBoLi; OxNR

And I will come again, my Luve,/Tho' it were ten thousand mile! A Red Red Rose. Robert Burns. AtBAP; AWP; BiP; BoLoP; BSV; CABA; CBEP; CEP; DiPo; EiCP; EnL; EnLi 1-2; FaBV; FaFP; FF; ForPo; GBL; HAP; HBV 1-2; HeIP; InPo; InvP; LAuP; MCCG; NIP; NOBE; NOEC; NoP; OAEL 1-2; OBEC; OBEV; OLR; OxBS; PG; PoEL 1-5; PoLf; PrIm; SeCeV; SoSe; TEP; ViBoPo

And I will come and wake thee on the morrow. The Dream of Gerontius. John Henry, Cardinal Newman. CoBE; OxBoCh; VLP

And I will come out to meet you/As far as Cho-fu-Sa. The River Merchant's Wife. Li Po. AWP; BoLoP; FYAP; HAP; HeIP; InPK; InPS; LiPo; LiTA; LiTW; MoAmPo; MoPo; MP; NIP; NoAm; NOBA; NOBE; NoP; OBMV; OBVE; PAI; PG; PPoe; PrIm; SOTW; TAP; TwCP; UnPo

And I will drink of you, and live. The Sparkling Bowl. John Pierpont. AnAmPo

And I will emerge from the night breaking into song/Like the sun, blowing out these evil stars. A Love Poem for My Country. Frank Mkalawile Chipasula. WhB

And I will follow her away. August. Francis Ledwidge. OxBI

And I will follow thee, O Death. Strong as Death. Henry Cuyler Bunner. HBV 1-2

And I will give my days i' the sun/For that great song of thine. The Passionate Reader to His Poet. Richard Le Gallienne. HBV 1-2

And I will give thee rest. A New Year's Promise. Anonymous. BLRP

And I will go a-walking with you anywhere.' My Man John. Anonymous. OBET

And I will have a special Care,/Of the rumpling of my Gown a. There Was a Knight and He Was Young. Anonymous. CoMu

And I will hold you, roots and fruit and fallen leaf. A Betrothal. E. J. Scovell. GBL

And "I will if I must' on his can. Limerick: "There once was a Renaissance man." Anonymous. PeHV

...And I will invite you in as my first guest. Believe It. John Logan. LCAP

And I will join you there. Jardin des Fleurs. Charles David Webb. NePoAm-2

And I will kneel and kiss thine ivory hands/Beneath the flowered music of thy face. Sonnets. Robert Hillyer. HBMV

And I will live to tell my children these things. At Mexican Springs. Laura Tohe. STE

And I will look like Death when last we meet.' I Met My Solitude. Naomi Replansky. BrRo

And I will love thee forever, and aye. The Hostess' Daughter. Ludwig Uhland. AWP

And I will make offerings/To the Master of Destiny. To Destiny. Anonymous. EaLo

And I will never read what's written/In another's solid hands. A Long & Happy Life. Simon Schuchat. APU

And I will not be the old man in the park/Who talks to his neighbor on the bench. Small Quiet Song. Robert Paul Smith. CAD

And I will play as much as she'll desire. My Mistress Makes Music. Anonymous. UnTE

And I will ride her thighs' white horses. Love Poem. Alex Comfort. ErPo

And I will roar some more! Wild Beasts. Evaleen Stein. SoPo

And I will see before I die/The palms and temples of the South. You Ask Me, Why, Tho' Ill at Ease. Alfred, Lord Tennyson. CABA; OAEP; VLP

And I will slay this fearful brute/With stones and sticks and guns and slings. The Cameloaprd. Hilaire Belloc. FaBoNo

And I will triumph still amidst my woe/Till mrcy shall my sorrowes overflowe. Some in Their Harts Their Mistris Colours Bears. William Smith. AAS

And I will venture, though I fall or tire. Emblem. Francis Quarles. TrPWD

And I will watch from Everest/The long heave of the surging world. Shakespeare. William Watson. HBV 1-2

And I wipe away my tears with my sleeve.   Lost.   Chu Shu-chen.   BoWoP

And I wish he had landed there sooner.   Limerick: "There once was a popular crooner."   M. B. Thornton.   LiBL

And I wish I could stop the clock.   Four.   Elise Gibbs.   BiCB

And I wish I did not/feel like your mother.   Rendezvous.   Edna St. Vincent Millay.   NMM

And I wish I was a mole in the ground.   I Wish I Was a Mole in the Ground.   *Anonymous.*   ABF; AmFP

And I wish I was single again.   When I Was Single.   *Anonymous.*   ABF

And I wish somebody'd shoot him.   Love Song.   Dorothy Parker.   InMe

And I wish to state/That I'll always mate/With whatever drone I encounter.   Song of the Queen Bee.   E. B. White.   NYBP

And I wish you a joyful May.   May Carol.   *Anonymous.*   OBET

And I with a heart not softer than a stone!   At Saint Patrick's Purgatory.   Donnchadh mor O'Dala.   AnIL; LiTW; OnYI

And I won't be no trouble./Whoa!   Georgia Land.   *Anonymous.*   OuSiCo

And I wonder if I am wrong, or the world, whose/aspect/Is nowhere strange, but is nowhere home.   As a Boy with a Richness of Needs I Wandered.   Clifford Dyment.   HaMV; OxBTC

And I wonder: Why?   Spruce.   Phil George.   VoR

And I would always remember/Times.   Remember Times for Sandy.   Carolyn M. Rodgers.   JB

And I would be for ever where they were.   Ballata: His Talk with Certain Peasant-Girls.   Franco Sacchetti.   AWP

And I would cry—but some would hear, I fear me.   Sweet, Let Me Go.   William Corkine.   EiL; InvP; OBSP; PV; TrGrPo; UnTE; ViBoPo

And I would let him in.   At Arm's Length.   Shirley Bossert.   FAZ

And I would make the Supreme Court eat shit from/a spoon.   The Hustler.   *Anonymous.*   TW

And I would remember, now the world is less,/His gentleness.   The Gift to Be Simple.   Howard Moss.   ImOP; MoRP; MP; Psk; TwCP

And I would that my ship went down within sight of/the shore!   Amoris Exsul.   Arthur Symons.   OBNC; PBBP; VLP

And I wrote my happy songs/Every child may joy to hear.   Piping Down the Valleys Wild.   William Blake.   EnPE; FaBoCh; FaBV; GoTF; InvP; LoGBV; NOBE; OBEC; OnUR; PoPle; TreFS; UnS

...And I/Yield to the strait allure of simple things.   Poem: "Geranium, houseleek, laid in oblong beds."   John Gray.   SyP

And I yn my bed agayne.   Song: "Westron wynde when wyll thou blow."   *Anonymous.*   SeCePo

And I your censure cou'd with pleasure bear,/Wou'd you but soon return, and speak itt here.   A Letter to Dafnis April: 2d 1685.   Anne Finch, Countess of Winchilsea.   EnLoPo; SBG

And ices pass around, and beauty smiles/Upon the pigeontry of Guelpho's Knights.   The Coming K–.   *Anonymous.*   VLP

And ich with wel michel wrong/Sorow and murne and fast.   Winterfall.   *Anonymous..*   OxBM

And if a star were falling now/I'd wish for her again.   Beyond Rathkelly.   Francis Carlin.   HBMV

And if after this you lose her—why you're paid two hundred/pound.   Damages, Two Hundred Pounds.   William Makepeace Thackeray.   OBSV

And if again such time and place I lose/To close with thee, let mine eyes never close.   Sonnet: "So shoots a star as doth my mistress glide."   John, of Hereford Davies.   EiL

...And if all faces are your own/And places, then I worship you alone.   Invocation.   Chad Walsh.   TrCP

And if America ever ceases to be good,/America will cease to be great.   America Is Great Because...   de Tocqueville.   TreFT

And if any one hinders our coming you'll starve!   Big Steamers.   Rudyard Kipling.   Par

And, if Arbattle's not enough,/To it we'll Fordoun join.   Sir Aldingar.   *Anonymous.*   ESPB

And if Cabal thus serve us Englishmen,/'Tis ten to one but I shall dream again.   The Dream of the Cabal.   *Anonymous.*   APAS

And if contentment be a stranger, then/I'l nere look for it, but in heaven again.   Valediction to Life.   Ignoto.   MeLP

And if either may carry on some reward or/regret for it/Whither he fares.   Two Travelers.   Lewis, Cecil Day.   EnLit

And if ever I meet another maid,/I rede that maid beware.'   Blow the Winds, I-Ho.   *Anonymous.*   GBP; OxBoLi

And if ever I return again I will make you my bride.'   Pleasant and Delightful.   *Anonymous.*   OBET; OBSS

And if ever I should sin so, Lord, have mercy!   Ganymede and Helen.   *Anonymous.*   PeHV

And if fate smile, with that our temples bound,/If not, with this our hearses shall be crowned.   Mutual Love.   William Hammond.   JCP

And if God grant this, then, under God, to Thomas Davis/Let the greater praise belong!   Lament for the Death of Thomas Davis.   Sir Samuel Ferguson.   AnIV; BIrV; IrPN; NBM; NOBI; OnYI; OxBI

And if he a guest should wish,/LET HIM SEND FOR ME!   Roasted Sucking Pig (parody).   *Anonymous.*   BXAP

And if he come, I shall be watching found.   This Day Be with Me.   George Macdonald.   TrCP

...And if he dies, why, that was my Purpose.   Bragging Song.   *Anonymous.*   LiTW

And, if he humbly kneel with them,/May catch far trumpets blowing.   Far Trumpets Blowing.   Louis F. Benson.   TRV

And if I am forsaken/I know not for why.   The Cuckoo (A vers.).   *Anonymous.*   OBET

And if I be thine enemy I may thy life end.   Vulcan begat me...   Sir Thomas Wyatt.   FCP

And if I could read the future/I would ask you not to come.   First and Last Man.   Ralph McTell.   OBET

And if I die before I'll keep.   Hiding Place.   Richard Armour.   NIP

And if I die before I wake,/I pray that Christ my soul will take.   Before Sleeping.   *Anonymous.*   CAW; GoTF; TreF

And if I die tomorrow, will I be gone?   On the Pilgrim's Way in Kent, as It Leads to the Coldrum Stones.   Asphodel.   BrRo

And if I die, who will say, this was Immerito?   Iambicum Trimetrum.   Edmund Spenser.   BoLoP; EBEV; EiL; OBEV; PoEL 1-5

And if I do for his soule, smal mote I thrive!   Snatches: ""Ich'ill pray for his soule that God gif him rest.""   *Anonymous.*   OxBM

And if I ended up with raccoons every guest would/turn out to be a raccoonteur.   A Dog's Best Friend Is His Illiteracy.   Ogden Nash.   BoAnP

And if I ever tackle another of these, so am I.   From My Rural Pen.   T. S. Watt.   FiBHP

And if I find you I must stay here with the separate leaves   Hymn.   Archie Randolph Ammons.   ConAP

And if I gaz'd a thousand years/I could no deeper love.   Song: "Love still has something of the Sea."   Sir Charles Sedley.   GBL; HBV 1-2; NOBE; OBS; SeCV 1-2; ViBoPo

And if I live and brook my life/Ye'se never hae cause to rue.'   The New-Slain Knight.   *Anonymous.*   ESPB

And if I love today, tomorrow's light/Against our love will e'en forbear to fight.   Epigram: "How shall I know if my love lose his youth."   Strato.   PeHV

...And if I love you, we'll fight again.   Mulata–to Skinny.   Frank Lima.   ANYP

And if I'm worthy of such a young lady,/I care not if they sink or swim.   A Pretty Fair Maid (with music).   *Anonymous.*   AS

And if I never lay him low,/I'll never turn him loose!   The Glory Trail.   Badger Clark.   BPAW; PH; StPo

"And if I set my foot on land/I'll ask the fairest for her hand."   Seven Years at Sea.   *Anonymous.*   OuSiCo

And if I were a wave I'd raise a commotion.   Sally My Dear.   *Anonymous.*   FSW

And, if illusion, feel it true.   Solitude and the Lily.   Richard Henry Horne.   OBVV

And if it be death, I will die with thee,/Or for thee, as it may befall.'   The Man with Three Friends.   Dora Greenwell.   OBVV

And if it be not broken, break,/And heal it, if it be.   The Contrite Heart.   William Cowper.   EiCP; PoEL 1-5; TrPWD

And if it doesn't cure you/She will sell you six for three.   Lydia Pinkham (with music).   *Anonymous.*   AS

And if it's by missile,/Forget about three.   Early Warning.   Shirley Marks.   QQQ

And if love such a thing not be,/I loved not thee.   Rondo.   George Moore.   UnTE

And if moonshine don't kill me, I'll live till I die.   Moonshiner.   *Anonymous.*   FSW

And if my Love leaves me, what will I do?   I Know My Love.   *Anonymous.*   AnIV; FSW

...And if my own breasts be not generous, my son/will put his lips to hers, that are rich.   Sister.   Gabriela (Lucila Godoy Alcayaga) Mistral.   BoWoP

And if no bookstore has it—why,/You're welcome to the one that we have.   Lines to a Man Who Thinks That Apple Betty With Hard Sauce Is Food..   George S. Kaufman.   InMe

And, if not shot or hanged, you'll get knighted.   When a Man Hath No Freedom to Fight for at Home.   George Gordon, Lord Byron.   EnRP; NIP; NLV; PoLf; PPoe; TrGrPo

And if one turns to leave you/Or stab you—smile, lad, smile.   To an Old Tune.   William Alexander Percy.   HBMV

And if perchance this sely rhyme/Do make thee blush at any time,/Blame not my lute.   Blame Not My Lute, for He Must Sound.   Sir Thomas Wyatt.   AAS; FCP; SiPS

And if preserved in so great a contest,/Life is redoubled.   Why Should Vain Mortals Tremble.   Nathaniel Niles.   AH

And if she goes too far, explodes.   The Nonny.   James Reeves.   AmMo

And if she's not gone/She lives there still.   Under a Hill.   *Anonymous.*   OxNR

And if she succeeds in that then she succeeds.   Pandora and the Moon.   Merrill Moore.   MoAmPo

And if she won't, she won't–and there's an end on't.   Woman's Will. *Anonymous.*   HBV 1-2

And if so, who??   "Who can make a poem of the depths of weariness."   Carl Sandburg.   NAMP

And if such a verse as this,/May not claime another kisse.   A Celebration of Charis.   Ben Jonson.   AnAnS 2; SeCP

And if that isn't patriotism, America, what is?   To the National Arts Council. Peter Schjeldahl.   ANYP

And if that will not please you, you shall have half a score,/Derry down, down, down derry down.   You Simple Bostonians.   *Anonymous.*   TrAS

...And if the end comes here, let it come–let this be/my parting word.   Let This Be My Parting Word.   Rabindranath Tagore.   MoRP

And if the glass, only the glass,/Could be removed, the poem would remain. Glass.   Robert Francis.   DFF; PP

And if the Temple is to be cast down/We must first build the Temple.   Why Should Men Love the Church?   Thomas Stearns Eliot.   MoRP

And if there's something, I can still hope on.   Beauty as a Shield.   Elsie Robinson.   BLPA; PoToHe

And if these poor limbs die, safest of all.   Safety.   Rupert Brooke.   BrPo; EnLoPo

And if they be broken, be sure they are dead.   Two Figures.   Molly Peacock.   AMV-81

And if they think fit they will court them next tide.   The Ship Is All Laden. *Anonymous.*   OBSS

And if they think, they fasten/Their hands upon their hearts.   Could Man Be Drunk for Ever.   Alfred Edward Housman.   EnLi 1-2; InPo; LiTM; OBMV; PPP

And if those fayle, fall downe and dy before her,/So dying live, and living do adore her.   Amoretti, XIV.   Edmund Spenser.   AAS

And, if thou bearest it, he will hear it.   The Golden Legend: This Is Indeed the Blessed Mary's Land.   Henry Wadsworth Longfellow.   ISi

And if thou canst not realize the Ideal, thou shalt at/least idealize the Real. Proverbial Philosophy: Of Reading.   Charles Stuart Calverley.   FaBoCo

And if we live to tarry the town,/We'll call another year.   May Song. *Anonymous.*   OBET

And if we never meet, think I/Bequeath'd it as my Legacy.   Upon a Braid of Hair in a Heart.   Henry, Bishop of Chichester King.   EnLoPo

And if we really care enough/We'll stop to help our brother.   A Helping Hand.   Georgia B. Adams.   STF

And if you can't finish this picture in/the final solution, then, presto grace,/ yourselves jump.   Faces (parody).   D. C. Berry.   BXAP

And if you do it, do it today.   Lessons.   Louis Untermeyer.   TiPo

And, if you don't believe me, get shikarred yourself./That's all.   Municipal (parody).   Rudyard Kipling.   BrPo; BXAP

And if you don't harm her she'll tell you no lies.   The Dove.   Ewan MacColl.   OBET

And if you're humble in estate,/Dream splendidly, at any rate!   The Gardener's Cat.   Patrick Reginald Chalmers.   HBMV; HBVY

And, if you see a beauteous thing, just say, he is not here.   Remember. William Johnson Cory.   OBVV

And if you sing though as angels, and love not the singing,/you muffle man's ears to the voices...   The Prophet.   Kahlil Gibran.   PoToHe

And if you think proper, add to it another.   A Letter from School.   Thomas Love Peacock.   FaBoUs

And if you want to chance it, well, you can.   Nesting Time.   Douglas Stewart.   BoAnP; PoAu 1-2

And if you want to know my name/'Tis Bill the rambling soldier.   The Rambling Soldier.   *Anonymous.*   OBET

And if you want to know the way,/Be pleased to hear what He did say.   The Truth from Above.   *Anonymous.*   OBET

And if you were here, would you kiss me again?   You Kissed Me. Josephine Slocum Hunt.   BLPA; FaBoBe; FPL

And if you will not have him,/You may let him be.   Tommy Tacket. *Anonymous.*   OxNR

And if you won't love him, he'll call you a whore.   Hard Is the Fortune of All Womankind.   *Anonymous.*   FSW

And if you won't, you may be damn'd,/My Murray.   To Mr. Murray. George Gordon, Lord Byron.   FaBoCo

And if your mother slight me, her blood on the hearth-/stone!   The Orphan. *Anonymous.*   KiLC

And if yt be not as I think,/Lyke wyse to think yt is not.   Deme As Ye List uppon Goode Cause.   Sir Thomas Wyatt.   PoEL 1-5

...And imag'd the still voice/Of quiet whispering in the ear of Night.   Night. John Brown.   OBEC

And imagined that Wells was a place.   Limerick: "There was an old man of Cape Race."   *Anonymous.*   FaBoCo

And imminent glory breaking through Man's circumstance.   An Autumn Park.   David Gascoyne.   MoPo

And Impli, though one of my/Dearest friends, can never,/I have decided, become great.   History of a Literary Movement.   Howard Nemerov. NePoEA; PP

And in a corner find the toys/Of the old Egyptian boys.   Travel.   Robert Louis Stevenson.   BrPo; FaBoCh; MoShBr; TiPo

And in a flower white-frocked like my small daughter.   The Daisy.   Marya Zaturenska.   GrPl; MoAmPo

And in a minute wander centuries away/In the deep sky.   Heaven and Earth. Frederic Thompson.   CAW

And in a moment was a lonely man!   Montefiore.   Ambrose Bierce.   AA; AnAmPo

And, in a month, to be at peace again.!   Wisdom.   Frank Yerby.   AmNP

And in a nest of snakes he courted her.   Jason and Medea.   Alun Lewis. CBEP

And in a still place in the wind,/be what I have become.   Looking Both Ways before Crossing.   John Woods.   ConAP

And in a tide of tears grow old and die.   Juvenal's Tenth Satire Translated (excerpt).   Henry Vaughan.   OBSV

And in a vision I have seen/My brothers playing on the green.   The Brothers. Edwin Muir.   GTBS-P; HeIP; NoP; PrIm

And in a Wench be cald a Boyes.   Metamorphoses.   Ovid (Publius Ovidius Naso).   OBVE

And in a world at war, only the wars live on.   Voices of Heroes.   Horace Gregory.   OFD

And, in Africa, a carcass quick with flies.   Black Tambourine.   Hart Crane. AP; CoBMV; InPS; NAMP; NoAm; OBSP; OxBA; PPP; TAP

And in all that silence, neither of us/can imagine where he'd rather be.   Poet in Residence at a Country School.   Don Welch.   GOYP

And in all their looks and words.   I Dream'd in a Dream.   Walt Whitman. AP

...And in all those strange/And varied lands, men were her children, and men had her love.   Heart for All Her Children.   Albert J. Hebert, Jr.   ISi

And in all times a forward scribbling fop/Has found some greater fool to cry him up.   L'Art poetique.   Nicholas Boileau-Despreaux.   EnLi 1-2

And in an everlasting peace/We build their proud memorial.   In Memoriam. Ada Jackson.   PGD

And in an instant the doe-eyed girl/Was completely merged in my heart. Meeting after Separation.   Marula.   BoWoP

And in at a paper doorie.   Johnnie Norrie.   *Anonymous.*   OxNR

And in August the barley grew up out of the grave.   Requiem for the Croppies.   Seamus Heaney.   BIrV; CIP; FaBoIP; FaBoMo; OBWP

And in awe by the colossal beauty/of an empty room.   My Fault's Small, About the Size of a Pin Prick.   Jeffrey Miller.   APU

And in beauty we walk   Morning and Myself.   Nia Francisco.   STE

And in between are the people.   The People.   Elizabeth Madox Roberts. GoJo; SoPo; TiPo

And in blackness and ashes/Behind was St. John!   St. John.   John Greenleaf Whittier.   PAH

And in bright trophies cloath the twilight wall.   Sonnet Written after Seeing Wilton-House.   Thomas Warton, Jr..   OBEC

And, in cloud, and clod, to Sing/Of Everything, and Anything.   The Pit of Bliss.   James Stephens.   AnFE

And in content may turn them to their sleep.   The Anxious Dead.   John McCrae.   OHIP

And in dark hollow tresses, gold.   The Painter's Mistress.   James Elroy Flecker.   BrPo

And in darkness/nothing falls/staining her lap.   Late Moon.   Philip Levine. LCAP

And in deep memory his bent fingers play/Long after the sunset of his piping day.   The Musician.   R. P. Lister.   UnS

And in drab frock on monday/Goes milking the cows.   The Mist Rauk Is Hanging.   John Clare.   NOBV

And in each microscopic spore to see/the enormous pattern of eternity. Autumn Mushrooms.   Kenneth Mackenzie.   CBAP

And in each/see a naked man playing a violin   I Love You.   Endre Farkas. CaPN

And in fear for that one.   Invented a Person.   Lenore G. Marshall.   GoYe

And in forbearance love will prove/There is no force so strong.   Forbearance. Della Adams Leitner.   STF

And in freedom think of danger.   To Pyrrha.   William Browne.   OAEL 1-2

And in garment let each man/Be a Dionysian!   Invitation to the Dance. Sidonius Apollinaris.   AWP

And in glazed brightness the sun says, Live...   The Class.   Josephine Jacobsen.   GP

And in God's house are many scansions.   Poetry.   Mary Elizabeth ("E") Fullerton.   NOAV

And in God's house forevermore/My dwelling-place shall be.   The Lord's My Shepherd, I'll Not Want.   Francis Rous.   AH

And in gray evening's emerald sea/The beauteous Star of Love is born. Superior Nonsense Verses.   *Anonymous.*   NA

And in Havana under the Southern Cross, all that is his/is where his bones lie. And of Columbus.   Horace Gregory.   OFD

And in her eightieth year she saw the wave/Of Acheron,–old Platthis,–kind and brave.   The Spinning Woman.   of Tarentum Leonidas.   AWP

And in her eyes I saw a ring/Of heaven's angels, listening. Evening Prayer. Hermann Hagedorn. GoBC

And in her eyes the forest pool. In Phaeacia. James Elroy Flecker. HBMV

And in her Father's arms/Contented dies away. Fill High the Bowl. John Keble. NOCV; OxBoCh

And in her hand/the sinking sun... Light a Candle. Zelda. VWA

And in her heart a voice that sighs. Pantomime. Paul Verlaine. AWP; SyP

And in her language share/Her blind and trivial cries. Child Crying. Anthony Thwaite. NePoEA-2

And in her mirror was and in her. This Is the Non-Existent Beast. Cid Corman. GP

And in her morning I can see Thy face. And in Her Morning. Jessica Powers. ISi

And in her smile there is a blight. The White Witch. James Weldon Johnson. BANP; CDC

And, in his arms, we waken! Security. Margaret E. Sangster. BLRP

And in his depths the first Iberian stirs. On the Welsh Marches. Walter Stone. NYBP

And in his golden hair I enter'd in. Eden-Gate. Sydney Thomas Dobell. OBVV

And in His hold the cross lay cold/Between her heart and His! The Ballad of the Cross. Theodosia Garrison. HBMV; HBVY

And in his leisure moments potted pheasants/And perseveringly collected stamps. King George V. Charles W. Hayward. NOAV

And in his orchard talk with God. Of an Orchard. Katharine Tynan Hinkson. GoBC; HBV 1-2; OBVV; WGRP

And in his own vile tatters stinks again. The Play-House. Joseph Addison. APAS

And in his sandy mouth there bursts its melting flower. Drinker. Patrick Anderson. PeCV

...And in his shroud/Seated their fellow-traveller on a cloud. The Vision of Judgement. George Gordon, Lord Byron. OBSV

And in immense perdition sinks the soul. To the University of Cambridge, in New-England. Phillis Wheatley. BALP; SBG; TAP

And in its ashes plant the tree of peace! Worship. John Greenleaf Whittier. NOCV

And in its brotherly unrest/I'll range for evermore. The Full Sea Rolls and Thunders. William Ernest Henley. EtS

And, in its center, Alcatraz. Scenic. John Updike. CAD

And, in its gentle mother's arm,/The Baby fast asleep. Ballad of the Epiphany. Charles Dalmon. HBMV; OnMSP

And in its head set the heart's singing birds. Nativity. W. R. Rodgers. NeBP

And, in its marriage robe, the heavy body wound. Lamia. John Keats. CABL; ERoP 1-2; OAEP

And, in its middle space, a sky that never lowers. Morning. John Keats. GN

And in its mouth it carries death. The Snake. Kenneth MacKenzie. BoAV

...And in/Its own reticence rests. Paired Lives. W. R. Rodgers. CIP

And, in its stead, will come a strange new peace. Time's Hand is Kind. Margaret E. Bruner. PoToHe

And, in its watches, wearies every star! Freedom For the Mind. William Lloyd Garrison AA; FaBoBe

And in Light of life I'll walk/Till traveling days be done. The Voice from Galilee. Horatius Bonar. HBV 1-2

And in man's spirit, where she comes by night/And shall remain when the last gunfires roll. We Who Build Visions. Stanton A. Coblentz. PGD

...And in me an old woman/Rises toward her day after day, like a terrible fish. Mirror. Sylvia Plath. FaBoWP; HAP; NYBP; SoSe

And in me loosed the tide/Of pigeons and the light in which they flew. The Pilot's Day of Rest. Lee Gerlach. HoAn

And in meeting it be great. Let's Forget. Charles L. H. Wagner. PoToHe

And in mine arms, clasped, like a child in tears. A Poet of One Mood. Alice Meynell. HBMV; SBG

And in my dream I squatted down and pressed my face/between the great toe/and the next one. Learning to Count. Alberta Turner. LCAP

And in my fingers long and brown/The little pebbles lay. Preexistence. Frances Cornford. HBMV

And in my hand a forest lies asleep. The Seed Shop. Muriel Stuart. BoNaP; GoTS

And in my heart a sound, a voice, a name/Hangs, as above the lamp hangs the expiring flame. The Poetic Land. William Caldwell Roscoe. OBVV

And in my heart her name shall live. We Never Speak as We Pass By. *Anonymous.* GoTF; TreFS

And in my heart I heard the little click/Of a door that closes–quietly, forever. Parting after a Quarrel. Eunice Tietjens. HBMV

And in my heart make straight the/crooked way. Awake, My Soul. Moses Ibn Ezra. TrJP

And in my heart the bitter wind of memory blowing. Sand Dunes and Sea. John Richard Moreland. HBMV

And in my mercy have affiance,/And thou shall get my grace.' Abide, Good Men. *Anonymous.* OxBM

And in My pain's darkness/trample her glass. Reckoning. Fay Zwicky. NOAV

And in my spouses pallace gyve me place. To Saint Mary Magdalen. Henry Constable. ACP; PoEL 1-5

And in my thoughts with scarce a sigh/I take the pressure of thine hand. In Memoriam A.H.H., CXIX. Alfred, Lord Tennyson. OBNC; PoEL 1-5

And in my urne I shall rejoyce, that I/Am both Testatour thus and Legacie. The Legacy. Henry, Bishop of Chichester King. AnAnS 2

And in nightmares they see him pull/A rickshaw at the next World Fair. Upper Family. Maxwell Bodenheim. OBAL

And in one act two vices gratified. Reformation of Manners. Daniel Defoe. OBSV

And in one another's blameless eyes go blind. The Tally Stick. Jarold Ramsey. NIP

And in one glorious minute needs/More soapsuds and another bath. The Bath. Rudolph Chambers Lehmann. GDP

And in one image Life and Death reposed,/To make my love an Immortality. She Took the Dappled Partridge Fleckt with Blood. Alfred, Lord Tennyson. FM

,And in one's naked soul/Confronted the eternal Verity. Twelve P.M. William Dean Howells. AmePo

And in our castles others come and go,/Dreaming our dreams and watching from our towers. Youth. Preston Clark. HBMV

And in our flesh, the vanities' false glass,/We thus deceived, adore these calves of brass. Caelica, XCI. Fulke, Lord Brooke Greville. FCP

And in passion past the reach of the stairs/To the world's towers or stars. The Roads Also. Wilfred Owen. EBEV

And in plumped this son of a woman to follow his wig, cane,/and hat. The Elderly Gentleman. George Canning. NA

And in purity once again be meek,/and submissive,/As is a blade of grass, as is mere man? When You Will Walk in the Field. Leah Goldberg. TrJP

And in regenerate rapture turns my face/Upon the devious coverts of dismay? The Monochord. Dante Gabriel Rossetti. MaVP

And in retirement, I can bless the shade. On Myselfe. Anne Finch, Countess of Winchilsea. SBG

And in return of it will take/Some levity from you. The New Year's Gift to Phyllis. Matthew Prior. CBEP

And in short measures life may perfect be. The Noble Nature. Ben Jonson. GN; GoBC; GTBS; GTBS-P; HBV 1-2; HBVY; MCCG; PG; TreFT

And in sweet-vowelled English echo them along. To the Greek Anthologists. George Rostrevor Hamilton. FaBoEE

And in that chaos like a migrant eel/Will breed a new direction through the deep. Port of Call: Brazil. Alun Lewis. OBTV

And in that dark, dark box, there was a GHOST! The Dark House. *Anonymous.* NTCP

And in that enormous sense, merely enjoy. The Ultimate Poem is Abstract. Wallace Stevens. PoA

And in that glory of love to learn/Words of the dead through living lips a prayer. The Speech of the Dead. Anne Ridler. ChMP

And in that hollow mould she cast him/to be her clay in ideal conformation. Clouds and Clay. Valerie Gillies. PoSH

And in that hour so sore/Died thirty knights and more. Sir Peter's Leman. *Anonymous.* BaBo

And in that just dominion bred/In which the nobler is the she. A Lady with a Falcon on Her Fist. Richard Lovelace. CaPo

And in that lambent medium/tomorrows bite off yesterday. Between Two Worlds. Rosemary Thomas. NYBP

And in that light of life I'll walk,/Till traveling days are done. I Heard the Voice of Jesus Say. Horatius Bonar. BePJ

...And in that light we see/Our Leader and our Lord, what will it be? The Last Defile. Amy Carmichael. TrCP; TRV

And in that Shape her former Art retains. Metamorphoses. Ovid (Publius Ovidius Naso). OBVE

And in that way I sank. I Carried Statues. Agnes Nemes Nagy. BoWoP

And in the angles of the fences found. Sonnets. Frederick Goddard Tuckerman. AP

...And in the ascending scale/Of heaven the stars that usher evening rose. Paradise Lost. John Milton. NIP

...And in the black space/of the sky down twinkled the stars like a gentle loving face. Microcosmos. Nigel Heseltine. NeBP

And in the blest hereafter I shall know,/Why, in His wisdom, He hath led me so. On the Twenty-Third Psalm. *Anonymous.* TRV

And in the buried sound along the buried mouth of the creek. Tornado. William Stafford. NaP

And in the cry of the crucified. The Funeral. J. M. TrJP

And in the dark house was I loved. Thunder in the Garden. William Morris. VLP

...And in the darkness rises/the body-odour of race. Political Meeting. Abraham Moses Klein. OBCV

And in the darkness trample on my poem written in the sand. Verses Written on Sand. Melech, Ravitch. VWA

And in the day's young sunshine, seeking still/For earliest flowers and gathering to the east. Hast Thou Seen Reversed the Prophet's Miracle. Frederick Goddard Tuckerman. NOBA

And in the deep of time,/set the wide wind rolling. I Feel an Apparition. Jean Le Roy. OBVE

And in the ear, not conscience, ring. The Windows. George Herbert. AnAnS 1; CABA; MeLP; NOCV; NoP; OAEP; SeCP; SeCV 1-2; TrCP

And in the edges of the snow. Tattoo. Wallace Stevens. AnFE; APA; LiTA

And in the emerald gloom the morning star. I Dare Not Pray to Thee. Maurice Baring. TrPWD

And in the end account himself a bore. The Travelers. James Reeves. PoL

And in the end, beg of her modestly. La Vita Nuova. Dante Alighieri. AWP

And in the end—with time and luck—to dance. Autumn Journal. Louis MacNeice. CMoP

And in the evening there was light. What the Birds Said. John Greenleaf Whittier. NOBA

And in the evenings businessmen from Boston/Sit in the beautiful houses, mobbed by cars. Salem, Massachusetts. Edwin Muir. OBTV

And in the family the Nations plan/Forgets the boy and finds himself a man! The Family of Nations. Willard Wattles. PAH

And in the fields of Oregon,/Unmarked, leave Dempsey's grave. The Nonpareil's Grave. M. J. McMahon. SD

And in the first does always see the last. From the Night of Forebeing. Francis Thompson. OBVV

And in the garden, cries and colors. Last Month. John Ashbery. ANYP; CAPP; CoAP

And in the grave one may forget–forget. Love's Kiss. Helen Hay. AA

And in the Gulf-stream drown and disappear. Icebergs. William Prescott Foster. EtS

And in the heart of Earth, and night/Find Heaven, and thee. Silence and Stealth of Dayes! Henry Vaughan. JCP; MePo; SeCV 1-2; WHA

And, in the holding of my dear Love's hand,/Forget the grieving and the misery. A Song of Angiola in Heaven. Henry Austin Dobson. HBV 1-2

And in the hope of religion, immortality. Inscription at Mount Vernon. *Anonymous.* MC; OHIP

And in the Item loved the Whole. Herman Melville. Conrad Aiken. NoAm; NOBA; TAP

And in the joyous errand reach the spot/Where I made One–turn down an empty Glass! Rubaiyat of Omar Khayyam. Omar Khayyam. AnFE; AtBAP; AWP; EBEV; EnL; FaBoBe; FaFP; FaPoR; GoTF; GTBS; GTBS-P; HAP; HBV 1-2; HeIP; LiTB; MasP; NOBV; NoP; OBEV; OBVE; OBVV; PoEL 1-5; PrIm; SeCeV; TreF; TrGrPo; ViBoPo; VLP; WeW; WHA

And in the light of truth thy Bondman let me live! Ode to Duty. William Wordsworth. AWP; BiP; EnLit; ERoP 1-2; FPL; GoTF; GTBS; GTBS-P; HBV 1-2; HBVY; InPo; NoP; OAEL 1-2; OBEV; OBRV; TreFS; TRV; WGRP

And in the link-in-link, the iron,/The coming days he sees. Ezekiel. A. N. Stencl. VWA

And in the long run we are all dead. Forecasting the Economy. Edward Morin. SOTS

And in the midst my wife and me! A Popular Functionary. Charles Dibdin. NOEC

And in the midst,/the grave of a victim. Grave at Cassino. Noah Stern. VWA

And in the morning I'll give you/a big clean shirt. Song: "Kiss me and hug me." *Anonymous.* BoWoP

And in the name of/God–abandon hope. So Little Wanted. Cid Corman. GP

And in the orchard fruit begins to fall. An Old Habitant. Frank Oliver Call. CaP

And in the other corner were battalions forming fours. The Sailors' Wives. *Anonymous.* OBSS

And in the phlox, the courteous bees/Are paying duty calls. Song for a Little House. Christopher Morley. TreF

And in the pit of terror thrown/Shall bear the wrath alone. Poem: "O who can ever praise enough." W. H. Auden. PoA

And in the realms of Sorrow all are friends. Ode for Decoration Day (excerpt). Henry Peterson AA; FaBoBe

And in the rifts of blue above the trees/Pass the full sails of natural Odyssyes. Bleue Maison. Edmund Charles Blunden. BrPo

And in the secret of thy presence dwelleth/Fullness of joy, for ever and for ever. When Winds Are Raging. Harriet Beecher Stowe. AH

And in the shambles of his room/angels sang/of the Heavenly Jerusalem. With My Grandfather. Zelda. VWA

And in the shelter of Thy wing/Obtain Thy leave and grace to sing. Whit Sunday. Joseph Beaumont. OxBoCh

And in the silence here at last I feel/Thy hand upon me, as I kneel. Prayer. Margueritte Harmon Bro. TrPWD

And in the silence she tenderly delighted my dreaming/with a singular vision. The Complaisant Friend. Pierre Louys. PeHV

And in the song within his head/The thanks from earth to heaven is said. Thanks from Earth to Heaven. John Hall Wheelock. HBMV; TrPWD

And in the South a/black,/dead/corridor. Going to the North. Stanislaw Wygodski. VWA

And in the stillness after song,/There is a Sound! Answer. Leonora Speyer. PG

And in the suburbs Can't sat down and cried. Kilroy. Peter Viereck. MoAmPo; NIP; PoRA

And in the twilight let me in the smallest gate. The Little Searcher. Donna Bowen. AMV-80

And in the way her steps shall place. O Lord, Thou Hast Been to the Land. *Anonymous.* AH

And in the winged freedom of homing birds. Transmigration. Seth D. Cudjoe. ACV

And in their eyes the promise of delight/Round the warm ingle at the fall of night. Norse Sailor's Joy. Wilfrid Thorley. EtS

And in their mastery teach me to be wise. At Tide Water. Sir Charles G. D. Roberts. PeCV

And, in their quiet way, they enjoyed it. Domestic: Climax. Merrill Moore. ErPo

And in their tall/flight's my betrayal. My Bird-Wrung Youth. Patrick Anderson. PeCV

And in their working, took great care/That all was full, and round, and fair. Photogenes and Apelles. Matthew Prior. GoTL

And in thine heart, where love and song make/strife,/Fire everlasting of eternal life. On the Cliffs. Algernon Charles Swinburne. VLP

And in this faith I choose to live and die. His Mother's Service to Our Lady. Francois Villon. AWP; CAW; CTC; ISi; LiTW

And in this fleeting lifetime trust/To find the narrow way. We Love the Venerable House. Ralph Waldo Emerson. AH

And in this frail transparency/God moves essentially and whole. The Jelly Fish. Robert P. Tristram Coffin. CAW

And in this heavenly wife might deem himself/Not blest, but lonely. Sometimes I Wish That I Were Helen-Fair. Lesbia Harford. NOAV

And in this land we/are their people, come/back to life again. The Pride. John Newlove. NOBC

And in this love, more then in bed, I rest. Even-Song. George Herbert. AnAnS 1

And in this simple story lies concealed/The germ of half that's plucked in fiction's/field. Jack and Jill. Harriet S. Morgridge. AA

And in this way we'll singe his skin for him. Sonnet: He Rails Against Dante... Cecco da Siena Angiolieri. AWP

And in this wise, sooth to sein,/Homward a softe pas I wente. Confessio Amantis. John Gower. PoEL 1-5

And in this you'll find your own! Thinking Happiness. Robert E. Farley. PoToHe

And in those weaker glories spy/Some shadows of eternity. The Retreat. Henry Vaughan. CAW

And in thy borders take delight,/An unconquered Canaanite. Farewell to Tobacco. Charles Lamb. NBM; OBRV; OxBoLi

And in thy court to have a place,/That we may there sing noel./Noel! Out of Your Sleep Arise and Wake. *Anonymous.* NoP

And in Thy gracious love hast given/Light upon earth and light in heaven. Prayer before Sleep. Alice Lucas. TrJP

And in thy mighty will to find/The joy, the freedom of the mind. A Little Bird I Am. Jeanne Marie Guyon. WGRP

And in thy presence I would spend/A long eternity. See How the Rising Sun. Elizabeth Scott. AH

And in thy shades the storm shall calm,/With songs of Liberty! On Liberty and Slavery. George Moses Horton. PoNe

And in thy songs, find speech. The Blind Psalmist. Elizabeth Clementine Kinney. AA

And in thy soul the sense of all the sea. Thalassius. Algernon Charles Swinburne. VLP

And in Thy temple-pavement give it place. Life-Mosaic. Frances Ridley Havergal. TrPWD

And in thy wisdom make me wise. Strong Son of God. Alfred, Lord Tennyson. OxBoCh

And in time, in time, the doll–/like new, though ancient–will be found. How to Be Old. May Swenson. MAT; UnPo

And in tranquillity the vision knocks. A Vision. Michael (Katherine Bradley and Edith Cooper) Field. SyP

And in triumph Irish Molly/Stands beside her smoking gun. Captain Molly. William Collins. PAL

And in truth, we half expect to see Lord Mayor Howard. The Utopia of Lord Mayor Howard. Randolph Stow. PoAu 1-2

And in us, warmer-hearted and brisker-eyed/Since you have been.   Birthday Poem for Thomas Hardy.   C. Day-Lewis.   CoBMV

And in virtue.   A Moral Poem Freely Accepted from Sappho.   James Wright.   CAPP

And in which we don't figure at all.   All the Roary Night.   Kenneth Patchen.   LiTM

And in Winter quite naked appear.   Riddle: "In Spring I look gay."   *Anonymous.*   OxNR

And in your fragrant bosom dies.   Ask Me No More.   Thomas Carew.   AWP; ELP; HAP; PoRA; WHA

And in your loved one's arms, remember.   Grieve Not, Ladies.   Anna Hempstead Branch.   AnAmPo; FaFP; HBV 1-2

And in your pastoral still my life has rest.   Old Homes.   Edmund Charles Blunden.   MoVE

And in your seeds may live your name, and in each/A renewal be given to your life.   To the Father of the Bride.   Torquato Tasso.   HW

And in your spirit flames your body's pyre.   Weltschmerz.   Frank Yerby.   AmNP

And in your wings a light and wind/Shall move from the Maestro's soul.   In the Cathedral Close.   Edward Dowden.   NBM; OBVV; OxBI

And incarnate raptly, once again,/the Word.   Lady of Letters.   Raymond F. Roseliep.   ISi

And inconclusive the triumph of Good.   Dead Snake.   William Jay Smith.   NePoAm-2

...And indeed there is mercy to him,/Solace from his Father in heaven, where all stability stands.   The Wanderer.   *Anonymous.*   TEP

And Independence thunder'd from his tongue.   The First American Congress.   Joel Barlow.   PAH

And indifferent as they.   The Daemon.   Mikhail Yuryevich Lermontov.   AWP

And infant voices shall proclaim/Their early blessings on his name.   King Triumphant.   Isaac Watts.   BLRP

And infinite still the discourse of the night.   Souls Lake.   Robert Fitzgerald.   MoPo; MP; TwCP

And inly clad/With the bridal robes of ardour virginal.   Deliciae Sapientiae de Amore.   Coventry Patmore.   OxBoCh

And innocence doth slumber now/Upon her candid April brow.   Her Fairness, Wedded to a Star.   Edward J. O'Brien.   FaBoBe; HBMV

And inside, only my books.   Free Fantasia on Japanese Themes.   Amy Lowell.   MoAmPo

...And insisted I try on/The blue kid gloves to make sure they were the right/ size.   Accomplishments.   Cynthia MacDonald.   DFF; GP

...And instantly her repose/Be silent and final.   Blind Girl.   William Stanley Merwin.   NePoEA-2

And instead of his ain ten milk-kye/Jamie Telfer's gotten thirty and/three.   Jamie Telfer in the Fair Dodhead.   *Anonymous.*   ESPB

And instructions to Norwegian immigrants.   Afternoon Sleep.   Robert Bly.   NaP

And into a white cauldron dives.   Now He Is Dead.   Alistair Campbell.   AnNZ

And into glory peep.   Friends in Paradise.   Henry Vaughan.   GTBS

And into her eyes/fall the shining feathers/of shyness and pleasure.   The Grace of Cynthia's Maidenhood.   Vinnie-Marie D'Ambrosio.   IHMS

And into his dead mouth slip the set of teeth.   The Linen Workers.   Michael Longley.   FaBoIP

And into the ground.   October Dusk.   C. Stephen Finley.   AMV-80

And into the old crow's nest.   Eeny, Weeny, Winey, Wo.   *Anonymous.*   OxNR

And into the rest of darkness.   Ojisan after the Stroke: Three Notes to Himself.   Tina Koyama.   BrSi

And into time's enormous nought,/Sweet-fed, will flit away.   Titmouse.   Walter De la Mare.   BrPo

And invalid's puissancy.   A Planet of Descendance.   William Frederick Stevenson.   NOBV

And iron is blooded.   A Calder.   Karl Shapiro.   EyDe

And iron is rust.   Dead in the Sierras.   Joaquin Miller.   AA; BPAW

And is about to be snuffed back to the wick of her black shoes.   Berlin Interior with Jews, 1939.   Lynn Emanuel.   MAYP

And is almost afraid that I will commit that indiscretion.   The Garden.   Ezra Pound.   AWP; CABA 049; HeIP; InPo; LiTA; MoAB; MoAmPo; MP; NIP; NoP; OBSP; PPP; SOTW; TwCP

And is as hainless to our hands/As the wild bird's cry?   Owre the Hill.   William Soutar.   PoSH

And is at the same time/erased.   To the Divine Neighbor.   Teller. J. L.   VWA

And is cut down ere it be night/All withered, dead, and dry.   Thou, Lord, Hast Been Our Sure Defense.   John Hopkins.   AH

And is e'en woe that so sweet comedy/By such unsuited speech should hind'red be.   Astrophel and Stella, LI.   Sir Philip Sidney.   AAS; SiPS

...And is fast asleep,/a butterfly.   Spring Scene.   Buson (Taniguchi Buso).   PoPl

And is forgotten, save by thee alone.   Eliot's Oak.   Henry Wadsworth Longfellow.   AmePo

And is immortal, Time beguiling!   To the Most Beautiful Lady, the Lady Bridget Manners.   Barnabe Barnes.   EnLoPo

And is Jesus riding to raise your wage and to cut that cord?   Nigger.   Karl Shapiro.   OxBA

And is mine/and endures.   The Summons.   James Laughlin.   ExPo

And is more Maine/than Maine.   Marin.   Philip Booth.   NYBP

"And is my praise nought worth for all my life undone?"   Echoes of Love's House.   William Morris.   GTBS

And is not much transported, but still pleased.   Against Love.   Katherine ("Orinda") Philips.   BoWoP; SBG

And is not she the very she-thing?   On Seeing a Pigeon Make Love.   [James Henry] Leigh Hunt.   FM

And is ourselves, and is the one/Unbounded thing we know.   In the Field.   Richard Wilbur.   NYBP

And is pure, new, even lovely/and is you.   Effendi.   Michael S. Harper.   CNA; PoBA

And is she not my Japan niece?   Japanesque.   Oliver Herford.   FiBHP

And is Shi'b 'Amir prospering since we departed, and/will it one day bring the lovers together?   Remembrance.   Ibnu'l-Farid.   LiTW

And is the illusion no one?   Galente Garden.   Juan Ramon Jimenez.   WSC

And is the yellow Autumns Nightingall.   Euthymiae Raptus.   George Chapman.   PoEL 1-5

And is there honey still for tea?   The Old Vicarage, Grantchester.   Rupert Brooke.   BrPo; DBV; FaBoPP; FaBV; MoBrPo; MoVE; OBTV; OxBTC; PoRA

And is traveled by dark feet and dark wings.   To Know the Dark.   Wendell Berry.   GP

And is what history is not. O love, O human fears!   The Statue.   Roy Fuller.   NOBE

And Isabel calmly cured the doctor.   Adventures of Isabel.   Ogden Nash.   CenHV; MoAmPo; MoShBr; NTCP; OBAL; OnMSP; OnUR; ShM; TiPo

And isn't it a sweet to-do?   Christmas-Time.   Rose Fyleman.   ChBR

And isn't quite sure what it means.   The Smile of the Walrus.   Oliver Herford.   FiBHP

And Israel full of comfort?   Psalm XIV.   Sir Philip Sidney.   FCP

And Israel's body in the smoke through the air!   O the Chimneys.   Nelly Sachs.   VWA

...And it all dies/down, down into the great world's flowering.   The Gardener to His God.   Mona Van Duyn.   TrCP; UnPo

...And it came/long, red and clamorous.   Firetruck.   The World of Expectations.   Albert Goldbarth.   HaCAP

And it didn't mind the sun!   The Snowman's Resolution.   Aileen Fisher.   SoPo

And it does no good.   Witness to Death.   Richmond Lattimore.   VGW

And it fills my heart with song.   The Troubadour of God.   Charles Wharton Stork.   WGRP

And it fits me/well!   Monks.   John Henry, Cardinal Newman.   GoBC

And it gained the title of Yellow Bow.   Eulogy to the Bow and Arrow.   *Anonymous.*   WTO

And it gave her queer feelings inside her.   Limerick: "I is for Ignorant Ida."   Isabel Frances Bellows.   TDH

And it had bled freely.   Domestic Scenes, 2.   Charles Reznikoff.   WeW

And it is a peculiar feeling!'   Limerick: "There was a young lady of Ealing."   *Anonymous.*   CenHV; TDH

And it is all because/You're out of town.   Stand By.   *Anonymous.*   STF

And it is as though I held/In my arms the bird filled/Evening sky of summer.   About the Cool Water.   Kenneth Rexroth.   ErPo

And it is hard and eternal.   Finds Something in New Jersey (parody).   Carol Poster.   BXAP

And it is hot, hotter than ever/and I like it.   The Hit.   John Drinkwater.   FaPON

And it is in dying that we are born to eternal life.   Prayer of St. Francis of Assisi for Peace.   Pat Therese Francis.   FPL

And it is something like love.   We Meet in the Lives of Animals.   Peter Everwine.   NNaP

And it is the brusque inquiry/and threat/that I remember of that night/rather than the stars.   Letter #8.   Dennis Brutus.   WhB

And it is/The last time.   The Life.   James Wright.   LCAP; NaP

And it isn't for you.   Several Voices out of a Cloud.   Louise Bogan.   ExPo; MoVE

And it keeps Time for you/with all the impartiality of a judge or a good watch.   Heart.   Joan LaBombard.   PPJ

And it'll break that heart of yours some time.   Careless Love (with music).   *Anonymous.*   AS

And it looks like/I'm never gonna cease my wanderin'.   Wanderin'(with music).   *Anonymous.*   AS; FSW

And it meant nothing to him to be shot dead.   Crazed Man in Concentration Camp.   Agnes Gergely.   BoWoP

"And it might now, Michael, so it might!"   Are Ye Right There, Michael?   Percy French.   WTO

And it never makes a sound.   The White Window.   James Stephens.   TiPo

And it's all I can do to stop crying.   The Form and Function of the Novel.   Albert Goldbarth.   GeTw

And it's all in the writing/It's The Talk of the Town!   The Talk of The Town.   Ed Fisher.   FiBHP

And it's as tender and as innocent/as your lines, divine Verlaine!   The Little Pig.   Ziche Landau.   VWA

And it's Death and not the Fairies/Who is holding carnival.   Death and the Fairies.   Patrick MacGill.   HBMV

And it's down, down, down derry down.   Go to Old Ireland.   Anonymous.   AmFP

And it's easy to pretend you're screwing her brother.   Epigram: "Hetero-sex is best."   Marcus Argentarious.   PeHV

And it's for this/our eyes were made to see.   Made to See.   John Nist.   AMV-80

And it's full of holes, it's full of holes.   The Ballet of the Boll Weevil (A vers.).   Anonymous.   ViBoFo

And it's goodbye to Owen!   The Volatile Kerryman.   Owen Roe O'Sullivan.   BIrV

And it's hard, hard times.   Hard Times.   Anonymous.   ABF

And it's hard times, boys.   When Young Ladies Get Married.   Anonymous.   AmFP

And it's hark, hark, forward./Tanara, tanara, tanara!   Call John the Boatman.   Anonymous.   ShS

And it's he I embrace while embracing you!   In the Nuptial Chamber.   Thomas Hardy.   BrPo

And it's his turn/to tell a lie....   Lies and Gossip.   Raymond Ringo Fernandez.   LFAC

And it's Killarney shall ring with our mirth.   Come Back to Erin.   Charlotte Allington ("Claribel") Barnard.   TreFS

And it's love me/love me/love me.   French Desire.   Keith Abbott.   APU

And it's music we're going to sing/Where the rainbow ends.   Where the Rainbow Ends.   Richard Rive.   PBA; TTY

And it's O! sweet, sweet! and a lullaby.   Mother's Song.   Anonymous.   GN; HBV 1-2

And it's only pride that robs us/Of the fun the kid enjoys.   Honest, Wouldn't You?   Anonymous.   WBLP

And it's over the hilltop he'd surely be.   The Grey Horse.   James Reeves.   PH

And it's this we're after: without the risk/what would be possible?   Suckers for Truth.   Robyn Sarah.   CaPN

And it seems, it was always/autumn then.   First Love.   Mary Dorcey.   BrRo

And it shall never, never end/till I am dead.   The River.   Leo Vroman.   VWA

And it spread out an Empire before us.   Lewis and Clark.   Rosemary and Stephen Vincent Benét.   BPAW

And it stings on the way down.   The Bottle.   Al Levine.   GrPl

And it stood still, so beautiful it left me crazed.   Dawn.   Louis Dudek.   PeCV

And it sufficed that I was found of Thee.   Seeking God.   Edward Dowden.   WGRP

And it tastes like nobody but you.   Ragout (parody).   William Zaranka.   BXAP

And it thinks we're awfully slow/Coming with the milk.   White Cat.   Raymond Knister.   WHW

And it took seven stitches in the tomcat's toe.   Oh, the Funniest Thing...   Anonymous.   EvOK

And it walks on knives, on knives.   Almost Human.   C. Day-Lewis.   NoAm

And it was about airplane glue he was thinking/when he fell and died beneath the Brooklyn Bridge.   The Last Warmth of Arnold.   Gregory Corso.   CoPo; NoAm

And it was all our searching spirits lacked.   The Window.   Iain Crichton Smith.   NePoEA-2

And it was, as you may understand,/Written in blood by the lady's hand.   My True Sailor Boy.   Anonymous.   BFSS

And it was autumn, and the present/world.   Adam and Eve.   Karl Shapiro.   AmP

And it was still the fifth/of February, 1918.   In the Waiting Room.   Elizabeth Bishop.   FaBoWP; HeIP; InPS; LCAP; NOBA; Prf

And it was that very red blanket that brought him to his end.   Utah Carroll.   Anonymous.   CoSo

And it was wealth enough/To know he would come/With a new theory or a laugh.   The Contentment of Willoughby.   Frances Alexander.   GoYe

And it went very well!   The True Story of Mary and Her Little Lamb.   Anonymous.   DBV

And it will be hard to keep on living.   The Death of Lester Brown, House Painter.   Rod Taylor.   WeW

And it will be like a new childhood shining for everyone...   Poem of Distant Childhood.   Noemia da Sousa.   PBWP

And it will be so hereafter.   Concepts and Their Bodies (The Boy in the Field Alone).   Pattiann Rogers.   MAYP

And it will beat for an answer.   Story.   Dennis Saleh.   NeAC

And it will cause a man to drink/Till he neither can go nor stand.   Sir John Barleycorn.   Anonymous.   CBEP; FaBoBa

And it will do, do, do.   Coo-Pe-Coo.   Anonymous.   PBBP

And it will make our earth his heaven/To live to-day–to-day.   To-Day.   Lydia Avery Coonley Ward.   HBV 1-2

And it will never have been written.   On Arrival.   Richard Howard.   TAP

And it will rain on the warm earth.   Indulgences.   Michael Hogan.   AMV-80

And it will sound like mourning when he cries/And waits for no reply.   Creation.   Louise Townsend Nicholl.   GoYe

And it will weep about her wish/silent about the child.   At Dawn the Light Will Come.   N. P. Van Wyk Louw.   PeSA

And it without a soul but wind.   Praises of God.   Anonymous.   AnIL

And it would be relief–to die!   Stack Arms!   Joseph Blynth Alston.   PAH

And it wouldn't of hurt God/To give 'em all wings!   A Note on Lizards' Feet.   James Van Rensselaer.   BPAW

And Italians become lizards/and Diogenes goes sailing.   Young Couples Strolling By.   Carl Rakosi.   PAI

And its Bible old, and its creed grown cold,/And the letters brown.   A New England Church.   Wilton Agnew Barrett.   WGRP

And its bleak sacrifice?   The Islands.   Hilda ("H. D.") Doolittle.   MoAmPo; PG

And its deepest resort/Lies high in my thought.   It Is No Dream of Mine.   Henry David Thoreau.   MAmP

And its forlorn Hic jacet!   Ellen Irwin; or, The Braes of Kirtle.   William Wordsworth.   PeD

And its fruit immortality.   I Live Only to Do Thy Will.   Ansari of Herat.   ILwL

And its hero, the Conqueror Worm.   The Conqueror Worm.   Edgar Allan Poe   AA; AnAmPo; AP; APA; AWP; BLPL; HBV 1-2; InPo; LiTA; MAmP; NOBA

And its last sighs shall breathe to bless thee!   Ah! What Woes Are Mine.   Edmond O'Ryan.   OnYI

And its lord's fortune finish'd with the pile!   Epigrams in Distich: A Vain Man Ruining in Debt.   Anonymous.   FaBoEE

And its mother's poor body/Lying mouldering away.   The Death of Queen Jane.   Anonymous.   AmFP

And its multitudinous summer under the whispering corn.   Tree Felling.   George Woodcock.   NeBP

And its thunder surged like the cry of a woman that/gives birth!   I Went Out into the Garden.   Moses Ibn Ezra.   LiTW; TrJP

And Itzik Manger sleeps on the hard ground,/stripped of all his dreams.   Autumn.   Itzik Manger.   VWA

And Jack from Joan, and they shall never marry.   Another Song.   Donald Justice.   ConAP; NePoEA-2; VGW

And Jack jump over/the candlestick.   Jack Be Nimble.   Mother Goose.   OxNR; SoPo; TiPo

And Jack the Giant-killer's high renown.   Well, Honest John.   John Clare.   NCEP

And James is going in for his degree.   The End of April.   Robert Fuller Murray.   CenHV

And Jane Eliza, she still snores on.   Away with Bloodshed.   Alfred Edward Housman.   ShM

And jangling like a bell.   The Parrots.   Wilfred Wilson Gibson.   CH; RoGo

And Jermyn straight has leave to come again.   The Last Instructions to a Painter.   Andrew Marvell.   OBSV

And jest upon their blind forefathers' eyes.   Ignotum per Ignotius, or a Furious Hodge-Podge of Nonsense.   Anonymous.   NOEC

And Jesus call us to heaven's perfect peace.   Peace, Perfect Peace.   Edward Henry, Bishop of Exeter Bickersteth.   BePJ; BLRP; WGRP

And Jesus crouched against a wall and cried for Calvary.   Indifference.   G. Anketall "Woodbine Willie" Studdert-Kennedy.   EBCP; PGD; TrCP; TRV

And Jesus fell like silver/from their mouths.   Jesus Drum.   Pearl Cleage Lomax.   CNA

And Jesus is forever mine!   Trust in Jesus.   Josiah Conder.   BePJ

And Jesus says, "As you've done to them,/You've done it unto me."   God Pity Him.   Anonymous.   STF

And Jethro's daughter, how shall I/amaze/Her ears with homage of unshackled/days!   Burning Bush.   Martin Feinstein.   TrJP

And jettisoned our chicken bones en route.   The Ascension: 1925.   John Malcolm Brinnin.   Str

And Jill came tumbling after.   Jack and Jill.   Mother Goose.   SoPo

And Jock bring in the spirit!/Amen.   Grace after Dinner.   Robert Burns.   FaBoEE

And John kept going/Ruthlessly.   Ruth and Johnnie.   Anonymous.   ShM

And John's old cow/Did nothing but laugh.   Jonathan.   Rose Fyleman.   TiPo

And Johnny's a drummer and drums for the King.   Hush-A-Byes.   Anonymous.   HBVY

And Johnny shall ride/To see his grandmother.   Ride away, Ride away.
Mother Goose.   OxNR; TiPo

And join in our embraces/Under the holly bough.   The Holly Bough.
Charles Mackay.   OBVV

And join us together with the chord of light/That reaches beneath the painted
eaves of your home.   To a Traveler.   Su Tung-P'o.   HoPM

And joy and strength and courage are with Thee?   Prayer.   Richard
Chenevix Trench.   BLRP; TRV; WBLP; WGRP

And joy at last for thee and me.   The Voice of Toil.   William Morris.
AnFE; HBV 1-2

And joy in its throbs/With the heart of a child.   I Found Her Out There.
Thomas Hardy.   CH; CMoP; MoVE; NoAm; NOBE; OAEL 1-2; PoEL 1-5

And joy of sailors in their ships/When home's in sight at last.   Traveller's
Hope.   Charles Granville.   HBV 1-2; OBVV

And joy of snow and snow.   Annual Gaiety.   Wallace Stevens.   MoAB;
MoAmPo

And joy thereby shall like a river/Wander from deep to deep for ever.   Song.
Sir Henry Newbolt.   FaBoTw

And joy to see the crystal web/within its cave-like shell.   The Fossil.   John
Lyle Donaghy.   NeIP

...And joy which shall forever, ever last.   O Blest Estate, Blest from Above.
George Sandys.   AH

And Jude, now you're married, will stretch on the floor.   On an Island.
John Millington Synge.   BIrV; MoBrPo; OBSP; OBVV

And judge he read the verdict:/A life in the Frankfort pen.   The Death of
Samuel Adams.   *Anonymous.*   AmFP

And judge me, O Christ, as I ride my ride.   Epigram: "Though riders be
thrown in black disgrace."   *Anonymous.*   BIrV

And judge thee, witch, in thy owne flames to burne.   To a Wanton.   William
Habington.   AnAnS 2; SeCP

And Juliet answer gently, "I forget."   The Fragment.   Hilaire Belloc.   PoL

AND JUMP HAPPY ALL OVER PUSSY LOVING ME!!   Chickitten
Gitten!   Ted Joans.   GP

And Juno lay unheeded by his Side.   The Iliad.   Homer.   OBVE

And just a day on Nature's heart.   An Angler's Wish.   Henry Van Dyke.
AA

And just as our bliss we began with a kiss,/He laugh'd out with A ha ha ha
ha.   Calm Was the Even.   John Dryden.   OAEP

And just awash, the low reef lifts its line.   Sonnets.   Frederick Goddard
Tuckerman.   AP

And just become/a sweet inspiration   Dreams.   Nikki Giovanni.   PoBA

And just before the shining shore,/We may almost discover.   My Days Are
Gliding Swiftly By.   David Nelson.   AH

And just come back, a sleepy head,/Late at night to go to bed.   The Little
Land.   Robert Louis Stevenson.   SoPo

And just lately we've struck oil.   Texas.   James Daugherty.   TiPo

And just now I ain't gonna tell you any more.   Roy Bean.   *Anonymous.*
ABF; CoSo

And just outside the door/The swords.   Cromwell.   Robert Francis.   GP

And just sent me/a fiver/to spend.   Christmas Thank You's.   Mick Gowar.
OBCP

And just the beginning of liver spots./Oh God.   Mirror Images.   Laurel
Speer.   AMV-80

And just went arunning running on.   The Stream.   Lula Lowe Weeden.
CDC

...And just where/He praid, halfe drownd, entirely sav'd him there.   The
Odyssey.   Homer.   MOS

And justify the ways of God to men.   Paradise Lost.   John Milton.
FaBoRV; FiP; NAWM 1-2; PoEL 1-5

And justly set the Gem above the Flow'r.   The Gem and the Flower.
Alexander Pope.   OBEC

And keener still the unrest of my tread.   The Pyre of My Indian Summer.
Mani Leib.   VWA

And keep a little path open!   Grass on the Prayer Path.   *Anonymous.*   PeD

And keep as all my own this higher music.   My Dog Ponto.   Edgar Lee
Masters.   FM

And keep back the cold.   The Manichaeans.   Gary Snyder.   VGW

And keep Christ in remembrance/Till seed time comes again.   Joseph, Jesus
and Mary.   *Anonymous.*   OHIP

And keep eternal Christmas in the heart.   Eternal Christmas.   Elizabeth
Stuart Phelps.   PGD; TRV

And keep for lovers yet to be/All the enchantment of our hearts.   Winds of
Eros.   George William Russell.   HBMV

And keep for us, those of us who need it, sleep, and sleep.   Prayer on the
Night Before Easter.   John Holmes.   MoRP

And keep for you, though far from clever,/Your job—and what a job!—forever!
Flower for a Professor's Garden of Verses.   Irwin Edman.   DBV; InMe

And keep frae us when we are auld/An empty jar.   The Empty Jar.
William Stenhouse.   AnNZ

And keep him ever by 'em.   The Masque of the Inner-Temple and Gray's
Inne.   Francis Beaumont.   OBS; TrGrPo

And keep himself safe from the noise of gun.   The Unconcerned.   Thomas
Flatman.   CEP; FaBoCh

And keep his head and keep his heart,/And only lose his soul.   Fantasia.
Gilbert Keith Chesterton.   HBMV

And keep looking, until big letters appear on one side.   Big City.   Michael
Brownstein.   ANYP

And keep me a pilgrim forever/To the shrine at my mother's knee.   At My
Mother's Knee.   *Anonymous.*   STF

And keep me warm/Before we go plunging into the dark for ever.   Girls in
Their Seasons.   Derek Mahon.   BoLoP

And keep our hearts from growing cold.   A Grace.   Thomas Tiplady.
TrPWD; TRV

And keep the amulets/intact.   Sarah: Cherokee Doctor.   Wendy Rose.
STE

And keep the birthday of the Lord/With merriment and singing.   The
Birthday of the Lord.   Mary Jane Carr.   BiCB; ChBR

And keep the candle burning.   For Three Swift Days.   Gennady Trifonov.
PeHV

And keep the public memory short.   Election Reflection.   M. Keel Jones.
NLV; PV

And keep the watch for me.   To a Dog's Memory.   Louise Imogen Guiney.
AnAmPo

And keep them free from all such pain and care.   Lament my loss...   Sir
Thomas Wyatt.   AAS; FCP

And keep us from the sin of gluttony.'   The Monk of Casal-Maggiore.
Henry Wadsworth Longfellow.   OxBA

And keep us safe, whate'er befall./For Jesus' sake. Amen.   Table Graces, or
Prayers for Children.   *Anonymous.*   BLRP

And keep us through life's wintry days.   'Tis Winter Now.   Samuel
Longfellow.   AH

And keeps, abjuring rum and gin,/A Temperance inn.   Beware of Dogmas.
Ebenezer Elliott.   FaBoEE

And keeps her stubborn suitor, Death,/Moping upon the stair.   The Old
Beauty.   Phyllis McGinley.   FaBoEE

And keeps our sturdy boys to-day/The rivals of the ancient Greeks.   Baseball.
Frank Dempster Sherman.   OBCA

And kent the glorie and the gleen/Was but the waukenin o' her een?   Loch
Leven.   Sydney Goodsir Smith.   BSV

And kept his faith with God. And he will reign.   Ishmael.   Herbert Palmer.
OBEV

And kept his father's asses all the while.   Charles II.   *Anonymous.*
FaBoEE

And kept in silence the same place.   The Bride's Prelude.   Dante Gabriel
Rossetti.   SeCePo

And kept my spirit with the free.   I Lost the Love of Heaven.   John Clare.
CBEP; ELP; LoBV

And kick a hole in his hat.   The Moral Taxi Ride.   Erich Kastner.   ErPo

And kick their heels at heaven a hundred happy ways,/Sky-larking down the
days!   The Glorious Game.   Richard Burton.   HBMV

And kicked/their mothers with joy and/evangelical fervor.   The Meeting.
Kathleen Spivack.   NMM

And killed my youngest daughter.   Rhymes for a Modern Nursery.   Paul
Dehn.   FiBHP

And kills a bird yesterday.   Eshu, the God of Fate.   *Anonymous.*   WTO

And kind hearts tire/Too soon, too soon.   Requiem.   Martin T. O'Connor.
AMV-80

And, kind Heaven, grant that spirit rest!'   Stanzas to—.   Emily Bronte.
LoBV

And kind the voice and glad the eyes/That welcome my return at night.   The
Hunter of the Prairies.   William Cullen Bryant.   AA; LiSp

And kindle with thy own productive fire.   De Rerum Natura.   Lucretius
(Titus Lucretitus Carus).   OBVE

And kindles it further at the core of utter mystery.   New Heaven and Earth.
D. H. Lawrence.   CMoP

And kindly gives the nights still shades/For wearied man to rest.   Arise and
See the Glorious Sun.   Francis Hopkinson.   AH

And kindly, kindly spare me/All this insignifigancia.   Please Tell Me Just the
Fabuli.   Shel Silverstein.   ELU

And kindness dwell in human hearts,/And all the earth find peace!   Eternal
God, Whose Power Upholds.   Henry Hallam Tweedy.   AH

And King David wrote the Psalms.   King David and King Solomon.   James
Ball Naylor.   CenHV

And King of Glory, dry up the roadway/Till I find my posy at Ballylee!
Mary Hynes.   Anthony Raftery.   KiLC

And King Solomon was dead!   The Dead Solomon.   John Aylmer Dorgan.
AA

And kingdoms like the orchard/Flit russetly away.   It is an honorable
thought.   Emily Dickinson.   MAPA; NOCV

...And kings come/in thousand horsepower Bentleys/to cheer.   To a Race
Horse at Ascot.   Jennie M. Palen.   PH

And kings may call in vain for strength/When the dead men die.   When the
Dead Men Die.   Rose O'Neill.   HBMV

And Kingsley goes to Froude for history.   A Hymn on Froude and Kingsley. William Stubbs. FaBoEE

And kis the steppes where as thou seest pace/Virgile, Ovide, Omer, Lucan, and Stace. Troilus and Criseyde. Geoffrey Chaucer. OxBM

And kiss amongst the willows.   See Where My Love A-Maying Goes. *Anonymous.* ElL

And kiss and hug most decently.   To His Young Mistress. Anacreon. UnTE

And kiss her over/and over again. Sally Waters. *Anonymous.* OxNR

And kiss her to the world of Consciousness.   The Sleeping Beauty. Wilfred Owen. DFT

And kiss him into slumbers like a bride.   Into Slumbers. John Fletcher. SeCePo

And kiss his young mouth into wisdom/And healing.   Young Poet. Myron O'Higgins. PoBA; PoNe

And kiss/my small mouth of cherries. Jarcha: "If you really care for me." *Anonymous.* BoWoP

And kiss on a grass-green pillow.   Where Be You Going, You Devon Maid? John Keats. ErPo; HBV 1-2; LiTL; UnTE

And kiss the heart you once betrayed. Forsaken (He Once Did Love with Fond Affection). *Anonymous.* AmFP

And kiss thee with soft laughter on thine eyes,/Ballad, and on thy mouth. A Ballad of Life. Algernon Charles Swinburne. HBV 1-2; MaVP

And kiss with two guineas, and all's your own.   What's Your Fancy. *Anonymous.* UnTE

And kiss your eyes, old/from pain and from cold.   They Go By, Go By, Love, the Days and the Hours. Teresa de Jesus. WPOW

And kiss your love and latch the door/And let the world go by!   Wisdom. Daniel Whitehead Hicky. BiCB

And kissed and kissed, as though to escape on a kite.   Kite Poem. James Merrill. MP; TwCP

And kissed her from her eyelids to her feet.   I Sought with Eager Hand. Allan Dowling. ErPo

And kissed me with her lips.   A Masque of Life and Death. Witter ("Emanuel Morgan") Bynner. AnAmPo

And kissed my sister instead of me.   Trip upon Trenchers. *Anonymous.* NOBL

And kissed the stars good night.   Very Early. Karla Kuskin. SoPo

And kissed the Vowels, for, you see,/They couldn't do without them.   The Letters at School. Mary Mapes Dodge. OBCA

And kissed their motherhood into his mother's eyes.   Nativity. Gladys May Casely Hayford. CDC

And kisses for young lasses.   Wine and Cakes for Gentlemen. *Anonymous.* OxNR

And, kissing his wife abruptly at the door,/Stamps fiercely off to catch the 8:04. Daniel at Breakfast. Phyllis McGinley. OBSV

And kittens miaow in circles, stalking/With tail and hindleg one straight line. Byre. Norman MacCaig. BoAnP; BSV

And knaves of high and low degree/Be destined to the cord.   Bunker's Hill; or, the Soldier's Lamentation. John Freeth. NOEC

And, kneeling under the willow-trees,/Piously prayed for their souls' peace. The Aliscamp. Frederic Mistral. CAW

And knew by the cold touch that he was dead.   The Death of Ailill. Francis Ledwidge. OnYI

And knew himself as one of many men.   In Time of War. W.H. Auden. CMoP

And knew/It's time for humility.   Humility. Marie L. Kaschnitz. WPOW

And knew that he was dead.   He Did Not Know. Harry Kemp. WGRP

And knew the place to which we were sent.   The Voyage. Edwin Muir. LiTM

And knew the Universe of no such span/As the august infinitude of man.   In the Wide Awe and Wisdom of the Night. Sir Charles G. D. Roberts. CaP

And knew them all for liars, rogues and knaves.   Lighten Our Darkness. Lord Alfred Bruce Douglas. HBMV

And knit again the knot that should not slide.   Epigram: "A face that should content me wonders well." Sir Thomas Wyatt. OBSC

And knock, and knock, and knock–but none replies.   On a Nun. Jacopo Vittorelli. AWP; CAW

  And knock at the door of my grave/With a loving hand.   A Dying Wife to Her Husband. Moses Ibn Ezra. TrJP

And knocked it right off his head,/head, head.   There was a little man. Mother Goose. FaFP; HBV 1-2; HBVY

And knocked out all their/teeth.   Two Simpleton Songs, I. *Anonymous.* OxNR

And know a god/to dedicate it to.   The Problem. Paul Blackburn. NeAP

And know, except slow death, no certain cure.   Snail. Elisabeth Eybers. PeSA

And know he's the king of the North Eastern Line.   Cannily, Cannily. *Anonymous.* FSW

And know once more the name of rest.   Arthur. William Winter. AA

And know that death flies into rooms/On a bird's wings.   The Sacred Children. H. R. Hays. EAS

And know that dim, wronged pattern for Thine own.   Thou Knowest. Katharine Lee Bates. TrPWD

And know that neither fate, nor time, nor God,/Robs me of that first mastery of you. Retractions. James Branch Cabell. HBMV

And know that this too needs heroes, and endurance, and ardor.   The Unknown Soldier. Conrad Aiken. WaP

And know that, though dead, I have never died.   He and She. Mrs. Major Arnold. BLPA

And know that Time at last/Will crowne thy hope, or fix thy fear. Expectation. Thomas Stanley. AnAnS 2; OBS

And know the earth is smaller than a man.   Challengers. Alfred Dorn. GoYe

And know the names/of many of these/wild flowers.   No Regret. Rochelle Kraut. APU

And know the thoughts of men in other/lands.   The Ship and Her Makers. John Masefield. CoBE

And know that neither storm nor death/Christ from His people parts.   On Top of Troubled Waters. Dorothy J. Langford. BePJ

And know what the fish know.   Darkness. Greg Kuzma. WOLT

And know where the words came from.   The Dead Poet. Al Purdy. NOBC

And know who you mean, and each/day you mean one more.   The Low Road. Marge Piercy. LTB

And know you dead, yet cannot take death in.   And There shall Be No More Death (excerpt). Ruth Gilbert. AnNZ

And know you still the best.   And Already the Minutes. Conrad Aiken. InPo

And knowing, can we love and let them pass?   Before Dawn in the Woods. Marguerite Wilkinson. HBMV

And knowing it by heart.   Travelling Light. David Wagoner. NPAW

And knowing, we may sow the seed/That blossoms through eternity.   God of the Strong, God of the Weak. Richard Watson Gilder. AH

And, knowing yourself no sinner,/Will go in to bathe before dinner.   Old Inn on the Eastern Shore. William H. Matchett. NePoEA

And knowledge and tears and chance.   Alive Together. Lisel Mueller. IHMS

And knowledge, but by year and hour/In reverence and in charity.   In Memoriam A.H.H., CXIV. Alfred, Lord Tennyson. VLP

And knowledge in your sombre depth/Embraces your perfection and your sleep. Adam's Song to Heaven. Edgar Bowers. ConAP; QFR

And knowledge seems no less absurd/If of a mistress, or a bird.   The Redshanks. Julian Bell. OBMV

And knows its waning.   March. Hart Crane. BoNaP

And knows not whether he be first or last.   Time, Real and Imaginary. Samuel Taylor Coleridge. EnRP; ERoP 1-2; NOBE; OBEV; OBRV; OBSP

And knows this is the fount of learning.   A Learned Song. *Anonymous.* FaBoUs

And L for Fifty, I'll tell you.   Roman Numerals. *Anonymous.* FaBoUs

And labor with the faith/of desert blooms.   Dream Farmer. Jill Witherspoon Boyer. CNA

And lack myself, that which yourself supplies.   Love Sonnets. Zora Cross. CBAP

And laid by the side of the fair Fannie Moore.   Fair Fannie Moore. *Anonymous.* BFSS

And laid her on her bed with tapets spread.   Virgil's Aeneid, Book IV (excerpt). Henry Howard, Earl of Surrey. EnLit

And laid in his lonesome grave.   Wreck on the C. and O.(Or) Death of Jack Hinton. *Anonymous.* ABF

And laid Jesse James in his grave.   I Went Down to the Depot (with music). *Anonymous.* AS

And laid my hand upon thy mane–as I do here.   Childe Harold's Pilgrimage: Canto IV. George Gordon, Lord Byron. FaBV; FiP; GN; HBV 1-2; LiTB; PoEL 1-5; TrGrPo; WGRP

And laid to see upon.   The Grave. *Anonymous.* ACP

And Lambert Simnel stirs the under-footman's porridge.   The Wheel of Fortune. Thom Gunn. OxBC

And lament for my shepherd all the days of my life.'   The Wandering Shepherdess. *Anonymous.* OBET

And land in some Anthology!   A Grub Street Recessional. Christopher Morley. InMe

And landed ker-plunk on his skulligan.   Limerick: "A clumsy young laddie was Mulligan." J. B. Lee. TDH

And landward through the rains, the sea/unrolls a proud vast tragedy. Orpheus. J. F. Hendry. NeBP

And language not involved in dark!   The Hymn of Adam. Joost van den Vondel. CAW

And lassies laugh and women weep,/And God knows why.   God's Will. Robert Louis Munger. AA

And last he kissed her ruby lips,/There was no breath within.   The Lass of Roch Royal. *Anonymous.* FSW

...–And, last, its instruments. The Web. Theodore Weiss. CoAP; NoAm

And last night–I changed the lock! Constancy. John Boyle O'Reilly. OnYI

And, last of all, I'll give thee a little lamb/To play withal, new-weaned from her dam. Daphnis to Ganymede. Richard Barnfield. ElL

And last till the end of time. The First Time Ever I Saw Your Face. Ewan MacColl. FSW

And last, when Words are into Clouds devolv'd. Love's Witness. Aphra Behn. BoWoP

And last year's blue and bloated suicides. The Break-Up. Abraham Moses Klein. NOBC

And, lastly, that done, three large dashes by/I doubt would serve to paint your destiny. The Answer of Mr. Waller's Painter to His Many New Advisers. *Anonymous.* APAS

And lat her hang there for the poysoning o me. Lord Randal (B vers.). *Anonymous.* BaBo; ESPB

And laugh and quaff and drink old sherry. A Boat, a Boat. *Anonymous.* CBEP

And laugh at the shriek of the baffled Fiend as his sounding/wing goes by! The Frost Spirit. John Greenleaf Whittier. HBV 1-2

And laugh–but smile no more. The Fall of the House of Usher: The Haunted Palace. Edgar Allan Poe. TrGrPo

And laugh - but smile no more. Israfel. Edgar Allan Poe AA

And laugh to see you run! Pirate Wind. Mary Jane Carr. BrR; SiSoSe

And laugh when I see her hiding/From my mocking eyes all day. Love Medicine. Eda Lou Walton. BPAW

And laughed and kissed his hand to me and died. I Did Not Lose My Heart in Summer's Even. Alfred Edward Housman. LiTM

And laughed at the sky through the sticks of her fan. Full Moon. Victoria Mary (Vita) Sackville-West. MoShBr

And laughed back/until my mind cracked. The Saints. Robert Creeley. NMP

And laughed like murmurs of the sea. The Wanderings of Oisin. William Butler Yeats. SeCePo

And laughed that pleasant sight to see. Cupid's Pastime. Francis Davison. UnTE

And laughing Ceres reassume the land. An Epistle to Richard Boyle, Earl of Burlington (excerpt). Alexander Pope. NOEC

And laughing hurry in to keep them dry. Signs of Winter. John Clare. BoNaP; ERoP 1-2; OAEL 1-2; PoSC; WiR

And laughing with work, living their work like a game. Morning Work. D. H. Lawrence. MoAB; MoBrPo

And laughs, not tears, will start. Life. Grace Treasone. PeD

And laught out with a ha, ha, ha, ha, ha, ha,/ha, ha, ha, ha, ha, ha. Amintas and Claudia. *Anonymous.* CoMu

And launched in space another, wilder song. Oystercatchers. Christopher Middleton. FaBoTw

And Laura had measles/And wanted to die! Old Bill's Memory Book. William Rose Benet. InMe

And Laura's are the lips I sing. The Shaded Pool. Norman Gale. HBV 1-2; OBVV

And laurel shall crown/My Blackbird with honor wherever he be. The Blackbird. *Anonymous.* NOBI; OnYI

And lay down gently now my poem is over. Windfall. F. R. Scott. CaP

And lay fools low in the light of day. Honey-Mead. *Anonymous.* AnOE

And lay in the darkness, grunting, and turning/to his rest. Mongan Laments the Change That Has Come upon Him and His Beloved. William Butler Yeats. VLP

And lay like fish/Under the net of our kisses. Drunk as drunk on turpentine. Pablo Neruda. BoLoP

And lay my heavy burden down/With Him of Galilee. Amid the Din of Earthly Strife. Henry Warburton Hawkes. TRV

And lay my vew-bow by my side,/My met-yard wi.... Robin Hood's Death. *Anonymous.* BaBo; ESPB

And lay on the floor and lay on the child and died of longing. The Poem on the Guilt. Avot Yeshurun. VWA

And lay the crucifix on this silent heart. The Young Neophyte. Alice Meynell. ACP; CAW; GoBC

And lay there prone, the soil drenched with his blood/running. The Iliad. Homer. LiTW; WaaP

And lay your leis where I lie,/And peace. Lady of Peace: Cathedral: Honolulu.. Fray Angelico Chavez. ISi

And Lazarus is still dead. Act of Faith. Arturo Trias. InW

And lead her to my secret leafy nest. Sonnets, II: "And then I sat me down, and gave the rein." Gustav Rosenhane. AWP

And lead still further on such as thy kingdom seek. The Higher Good. Theodore Parker. AA; FaBoBe; HBV 1-2

And lead the world-triumph of peace and good will. Hear, Hear, O Ye Nations. Frederick Lucian Hosmer. AH

And lead to endless day. Private Devotion. Phoebe Hinsdale Brown. AA

And lead us to the happier hunting woods. La Belle Sauvage. John Hunter Duvar. OBCV

And lead you to the source of Intellect'ual Light. To the Much Honoured R. F. Esq. Richard Chamberlain. SCAP

And leads me into conditional life. In the Fleeting Hand of Time. Gregory Corso. NAs

And leads me to the Rock of Ages, my Saviour's love is a starlit way. Bryan's Last Battle (The Scopes Trial). *Anonymous.* AmFP

And leaf shadow are lost. Evening. Hilda ("H. D.") Doolittle. CMoP

...And lean against/another autumn wind. At 85. Richard Ardinger. AMV-81

And lean flirtatiously against the door,/Tasting a green plum. After kicking on the swing. *Anonymous.* BoWoP

And leap, and dive, and see the tunnies swim. Echoes from Theocritus. Edward Cracroft Lefroy. OBVV

And leaps to life beneath a kindred spell. The Crystal. Titus Munson Coan. AA

And learn a style from a despair. This Last Pain. William Empson. CMoP; CoBMV; EBEV; FaBoMo; GTBS-P; LiTM; MoAB; MoVE; NoAm; OAEL 1-2; SeCePo

And learn each grace his pulpit taught before. Epitaph on a Worthy Clergyman. Benjamin Franklin. TRV

And learn, like many more, that life's a cable/Twisted of tedious, small, unfinished dyings. Now There Is Nothing Left. L. A. MacKay. CaP; PeCV

...And learn/That I have been an hour away. In Memoriam A.H.H., XII. Alfred, Lord Tennyson. VLP

And learn that we are better than our clay,/And equal to the peaks of our desire. The Road. James Stephens. HBMV

And learn the lip of Bethlehem's child. King Arthur's Waes-Hael. Robert Stephen Hawker. ISi; OBEV; OBVV; OxBoCh

And learn to be physically and mentally strong,/By the solemn proceeds of thy "innocent" rum. Alas! Carolina! J. Gordon Coogler. OBAL

And learn to love, in all things mortal, only/What is eternal. Ode: "My heart rebels against my generation." George Santayana. ViBoPo

And learn to sleep against this ground. Seafarer. Archibald MacLeish. NoAm; NoP

And learn with joy, the gulf, the vast, the deep. Putting to Sea. Louise Bogan. LiTM; PoA

And learned to honor first, then love him, then revere. Under the Old Elm. James Russell Lowell. PGD

And learnt her not to startle at his name. She Schools the Flighty Pupils of Her Eyes. Gerard Manley Hopkins. OBSP

And least hope wit; in Dutchmen that would be/As much improper as would honesty. Amboyna; or, The Cruelties of the Dutch.... John Dryden. OBSV

And leave a man of skin/caught in the December wind. Frozen Hands. Joseph Bruchac. CDW

And leave, a tired workman going home,/Who carved a marble image on the air. Boxer. Joseph P. Clancy. SD

And leave all the rest of the work to the string. A Receipt to Cure a Love Fit. *Anonymous.* NOEC

And leave at the foot of the cross. Consolation. *Anonymous.* STF

,And leave behind you an orange bright-/ness of fearful aptitude. Fits of Candor. Dick Gallup. ANYP

And leave both your honors' estates and your wives,/On condition that you may depart with your lives All Shams. *Anonymous.* APAS

And leave dull earth behind us! Wreathe the Bowl. Thomas Moore. HBV 1-2

And leave earth to such spirits as you, love, and me. They May Rail at This Life. Thomas Moore. NBM; PoEL 1-5

...And/leave/evil too great to resist, and mortals who grieve. Works and Days. Hesiod. LiTW

And leave for the long river drive to town. The Odd Woman. Madeline De Frees. GP

And leave for thy sweet mercy's sake/Another Hour to me Some wretched creature, savior take. Emily Dickinson. MoVE

And leave her weeping for her stupid dead. House-Mates. Leon Gellert. CBAP; NOAV

And leave him ever after dumb. Song: "Love took my life and thrill'd it." Sir Lewis Morris. OBVV

And leave his foe to sigh and cry/Alas poor thing The Mourning Conquest. *Anonymous.* CoMu

And leave, if naught so bright may live,/All earth can take or Heaven can give. The World's Great Age Begins Anew. Percy Bysshe Shelley. GoTF; TEP

And leave it with a bald head. The Little Dandelion. Lula Lowe Weeden. CDC

And leave me here alone/To tread this mist where earth and sky are one. Mist. Andrew Young. PoSH

And leave me to my loneliness again! The Dove's Loneliness. George Darley. OBNC

And leave memorial forest-kings o'erthrown. Winter. Dante Gabriel Rossetti. CBEP

And leave no grain for tomorrow. Daily Wages. Amrita Pritam. PBWP

And leave not in a single crevice/A single leaf. Priapus and the Pool. Conrad Aiken. AmLP

And leave of his volume only the mould of his girth. The Glutton. Karl Shapiro. DFF

And leave only the rise and the fall of the seas'/far Atlantic roll. In Solitary Confinement, Sea Point Police Cells. C. J. Driver. PeSA

And leave our desert to its peace! Stanzas from the Grande Chartreuse. Matthew Arnold. CoBE; MaVP; OAEL 1-2; OAEP; PoEL 1-5; TEP; VLP

And leave our old ones for a pledge. The Wooing Rogue. *Anonymous.* CoMu

And leave serenity/Which knows no pain. Solace. Clarissa Scott Delany. AmNP; CDC; PoBA; PoNe

And leave th' earth to their food. The H. Communion. George Herbert. AnAnS 1

...And leave/the bitter bullshit rotten white parts/alone. Leroy. LeRoi (Imamu Amiri Baraka) Jones. BPo; PoBA

...And leave/the bones, my stewed black skull,/an empty cage of failure. I Substitute for the Dead Lecturer. LeRoi (Imamu Amiri Baraka) Jones. NOBA

And leave the seas with their annoy,/At home at ease to live in joy. Another of Seafarers, Describing Evil Fortune. *Anonymous.* OBSS

And leave the sowers of the ground,/To eat the harvest of the fruit,/Blackbird. The Bird and the Tree. Ridgely Torrence. HBMV; PoNe

And leave their space suits/buried in the sand. The Covenant. James (Olumo) Cunningham. JB

And leave this out? I am Effie, you were my dream. Mourning Picture. Adrienne Rich. CoAP

And leave to come rest on my breast when you tire. The Cooleen. Douglas Hyde. OBVV

And leave to God and Heaven the rest. Acceptation. Margaret Junkin Preston. MC; PAH

And leave to tattered crape the drudgery of pray'r. The Dispensary. Sir Samuel Garth. OBSV

And leave to the glutton his pudding and pie. The Glutton. John Oakman. OxBChV

And leave us in peace. In Memoriam. Franco Fortini. VWA

And leave us to endure/Its immortality. Epitaphs of the War, 1914-18. Rudyard Kipling. BrPo; FaBoEE; OBWP

And leave with ancient night alone/The stedfast and enduring bone. The Immortal Part. Alfred Edward Housman. MasP; MoBrPo; UnPo; VLP

And leaves a lonesome place against the sky. Lincoln, the Man of the People. Edwin Markham. HBV 1-2; MC; MCCG; MoAmPo; OFD; OHFP; OHIP; PAH; PAL; PGD; TreFS; TrGrPo

And leaves his children to sleep on/In the one quiet bed. The Gardener. Arthur Symons. BoNaP

...And leaves his/grave Mandarins to look at each other in silence. The Emperor. Tu Fu. AWP

And leaves me at the spinning-wheel, with dark, unseeing/eyes. Spinning in April. Josephine Preston Peabody. HBV 1-2

And leaves return to willing trees for spring. Yom Kippur. Linda Pastan. VWA

And leaves the blinking world to Sleep. For the Record. Jr, Blount Roy. OBAL

And leaves them naked to the day. Myth on Mediterranean Beach: Aphrodite as Logos. Robert Penn Warren. HAP

And leaves thrust violently upon the pane. Autumn Chapter in a Novel. Thom Gunn. FaBoMo; OxBTC

And leaving, with meekness,/Her sins to her Saviour! The Bridge of Sighs. Thomas Hood. BeLS; EBEV; EnLi 1-2; EnRP; FaPoR; FPL; GoTF; GTBS; GTBS-P; HBV 1-2; OBEV; OBVV; PeD; PG; TreF; WBLP; WHA

And led him through the streets of Forbes to show the prize they/had. The Streets of Forbes. Jack McGuire. CBAP; NOAV

And led the flock away. I'll Tell You How the Sun Rose. Emily Dickinson. BrR; FaBV; LaNeLa; MoShBr; PoEL 1-5; SiSoSe; SUS; TAP; TreFS

And left at the end of the term. Limerick: "W was a wild worm." Carolyn Wells. TDH

And left her on the crag. America. Herman Melville. MAmP

And left him at peace in a lee that would feel no wind for ever. The Two Neighbours. George Campbell Hay. OxBS

And left him on his lawn not breathin'/A broken, bloody mess. Skyhook. Gary Allan Kizer. LFAC

And left his body lying. Riddle: "Around the rick, around the rick." *Anonymous.* OxNR

And left, in darkness, the fearful glimmer of joy, like a spoor. Dragon Country: To Jacob Boehme. Robert Penn Warren. PPP

...And left/me alone in this social blaze while you rest in your/cool tombs In the Heat of the Morning. Anne Szumigalski. FaBoWP

And left me listening to the sinking sound. Sonnets. Frederick Goddard Tuckerman. AP

And left me no recourse, far from my home. A Dog Named Ego, the Snowflakes as Kisses. Delmore Schwartz. LiTA; LiTM; MiAP

And left me old, and cold, and grey. May. Christina Georgina Rossetti. EG; GBL; NOBV

And left my Twittingpan to lie it out. The Encounter. Edgell Rickword. OxBTC

And left my votive chart behind/To him that rules both wave and wind. Odes. Horace. OBVE

And left, O little child, its reflex there. Laus Infantium. William Canton. HBV 1-2

And left the image that we keep. Channel U.S.A.–Live. Adrien Stoutenburg. AmFN

And left the little angleworm/With modesties enlarged. Our little kinsmen. Emily Dickinson. ImOP

And left the thorn wi' me. Ye Flowery Banks. Robert Burns. AWP; CEP; EnRP; InPo; OAEP; OBEC; PoEL 1-5; UnPo

And left the vivid air signed with their honour. I Think Continually of Those Who Were Truly Great. Stephen Spender. AtBAP; CMoP; DiPo; EaLo; ExPo; GoTF; HAP; LiTB; LiTM; MoAB; MoBrPo; MoRP; NAMP; NOBE; NoP; OAEL 1-2; OAEP; OxBTC; PoPl; PoRA; PP; TreFT; TrGrPo; ViBoPo; WaP

And left them gaping at his Midas touch. Thatcher. Seamus Heaney. FaBoIP; IPY

And left to Heaven the rest. The Happiest Heart. John Vance Cheney. AA; AnAmPo; APA; GoTF; HBV 1-2; HBVY; TreFS; WGRP

And left to shattered Seicheprey/Unending, sweet repose. Seicheprey. *Anonymous.* PAH

And left unfinished and in ruins still/The only temple He delights to fill. Enoch. Jones Very. HAP

And left us, modern, futile, banished? Exodus from a Renaissance Gallery. Ellen M. V. Acton. GoYe

And left us nothing real but the dead,/In the land where we were dreaming. In the Land Where We Were Dreaming. Daniel B. Lucas. PAH

And left you to your game. On a Dead Child. Richard Middleton. OBVV; SoSe

And lend a hand. Look Up! Edward Everett Hale. FaBoBe; FaFP

And lend a venerable dread/To the lone abbey's rocking head. A Decayed Monastery. Thomas Dermody. OnYI

And lend sweet look from airy balconies. Paul Veronese. Sir Samuel Ferguson. IrPN

And lend to loss itself a joy divine? The After-Glow. Mathilde Blind. OBNC

And lent his senses unto death himself. A Beautiful Night. Thomas Lovell Beddoes. ChRP

And Lesbia's sparrow-all alone? Per Iter Tenebricosum. Oliver St.John Gogarty AnIL; OBMV; OxBI

...And less. And/less. And less... December Sunset. Jonathan Holden. FAZ

And lest her maid should know of this disgrace,/To cover it, spilt water on the place. Shameful Impotence: Book III, Elegia VII. Ovid. ErPo

And lest the sea sands prove too few. Lyric. Philip Child. CaP

And let a Child turn homeless from our door. New Testament: Revised Edition. Sister Mary Catherine. ISi

And let a kingdom go. The Golden Age. John Vance Cheney. AA

And Let All Black People Speak This Poem/Silently/or LOUD. Black Art. LeRoi (Imamu Amiri Baraka) Jones. BP; BPo; CAPP; NIP

And let her newest lovers/be gentle as women/and longer lasting Asking for Ruthie. Judy Grahn. GP; NMM

And let her pick/Out/A pig. In These Dissenting Times. Alice Walker. PoBA

And let her prison be my arms! The Fair Thief. Charles Wyndham. HBV 1-2

And let her rival me. Song: "You wrong me, Strephon." Ephelia (Joan Philips). CavP; LiTL

And let him hate you through the glass. The Midnight Skaters. Edmund Charles Blunden. ExPo; FaBoTw; GoJo; GTBS-P; MoBrPo; NOBE

And let him know that thinks with faith to move,/They once had eyes, that are made blind by love. Caelica, LXIII. Fulke, Lord Brooke Greville. FCP

And let him mope, and wring his hands, and wail. Patient Griselda. Geoffrey Chaucer. PoRA

And let him take a warning by his friend. A Hue and Cry after Blood and Murder. *Anonymous.* APAS

And let His praise resound for/evermore. The Living God. Daniel Ben Judah. TrJP

And let it at last/Sail peacefully home. Sail Peacefully Home. Simeon S. Frug. TrJP

And let it never thee repent/To feed thy needy neighbours. Advice from Poor Robin's Almanack. *Anonymous.* OBCP

And let light perpetual shine upon him. Lament for Barney Flanagan. James Keir Baxter. NoP

And let martyr mound and tree/Be our pledge and guaranty/Of the freedom of the West! Burial of Barber. John Greenleaf Whittier. PAH

And let me be rather but honest with no wit,/Than a noisy nonsensical half-witted poet. The Poet's Prayer. *Anonymous.* OBSV

And let me be/the one you never hold. Language Lesson, 1976. Heather McHugh. MAYP

And let me deserve her, or still I say no. Song the Eighth. Edward Moore. CEP

And let me die before my death! Regeneration. Henry Vaughan. CABA; ExPo; JCP; LoBV; MeLP; MePo; NoP; OBS

And let me gaze on what ye soon must be. Disturb Me Not. *Anonymous.* WTO

And let me get out of the bar. The Judge with the Sore Rump. St. George Tucker. OBAL

And let me have my three daies' reign. To Francelia. Thomas Duffett. CavP

And let me know Thee right. Comfort for the Sleepless. H. C. Bradby. BoC

And let me laugh for you from my second mouth. Why Can't I Leave You? Ai. AmPA; GP

And let me make my earth a Heaven/Till next Communion Day. A Communion Hymn. Alice Freeman Palmer. TrPWD

And let me never never stray from THEE! The Seasons. James (1700-48) Thomson. CEP

And let me not blaspheme. De Amore. Ernest Christopher Dowson. OBNC; TrPWD

And let me taste the world/Like the fly that interprets the wine. Quarrel. *Anonymous.* WTO

And let me taste thee unexcis'd by kings. Blest Leaf! Whose Aromatic Gales Dispense (parody). Isaac Hawkins Browne. BXAP; Par

And let my cry come unto Thee. Ash-Wednesday. Thomas Stearns Eliot. AP; CoBMV; LiTA; MoAB; MoAmPo; MoPo; OxBA; SeCeV; VGW

And let my heart within travail and moan. La Vita Nuova. Dante Alighieri. AWP

And let my leaf be green with love/And let me live. Lamentation. Nissim Ezekiel. VWA

And let my mouth thy preising now bewrye. On May-Day, When the Lark Began to Ryse. *Anonymous.* LO

And let my soul, made chaste, pass for a Maid. To Saint Margaret. Henry Constable. ACP; GoBC

And let once more by mystic birth/The Lord of life be borne in Earth. Christ's Nativity. Henry Vaughan. SBVL

And let our ordered lives confess/The beauty of Thy peace. Drop Thy Still Dews. John Greenleaf Whittier. ILwL

And let our pains be less, or power more. The Riddle. Alexander Brome. OBS

And let's dig a place in de col', col' groun'/For Mr. and Mrs. Massa! Boogie-Woogie Ballads. St. Clair McKelway. PoNe

And let's drink tea. Polly Put the Kettle On. Mother Goose. BrR

And let's lynch Lucy! Lucy Lake. Ogden Nash. ShM

And let such days atone/For those when we are many and alone. Heart of Light. David Campbell. BoAV

And let that Wine be all for me! A Drinking-Song. Henry Carey. OBEV

And let the ape and tiger die. In Memoriam A.H.H., CXVIII. Alfred, Lord Tennyson. SeCeV; VLP

And let the cupp go rounde!' Drinking Song. *Anonymous.* OxBM

And let the deeps behind them be/For sturdier fish the fatal sea? Love Songs, At Once Tender and Informative. Samuel Hoffenstein. OBAL

And let the doctor etherize. To a Young Poet. Harry M. Meacham. GoYe

And let the face of God shine through. O God, I Cried, No Dark Disguise. Edna St. Vincent Millay. AH

And let the hasty hustle, if they will. Essay on Lunch. Walker Gibson. NYBP

And let the judging mind be still. On the Cliff. Hal Summers. ChMP

And let the murmuring waters/Wash over their blood-hot feet with a springing crown of tears. War. Joseph Langland. MP

...And let the paper/fall, just as I make (imaginary) love to you–Real in the mail. Correspondence. Laura Chester. APU

And let the peaceful be! The Lake. Matthew Arnold. CBEP

And let the rest of the world go by. Let the Rest of the World Go By. J. Keirn Brennan. UnPo

And let the tank fill up again. On a Lover of Books. Geoffrey Grigson. FaBoEE

And let the thirsty paper drink its fill. Spring. Boris Pasternak. LiTW

And let the world know, that green Yankees/can fight. Halifax Station. *Anonymous.* PAH

And let the world laugh, an' it will. Let Me Go Warm. Luis de Gongora y Argote. AWP

And let them know we always will be masters of the main. A New Song on the Total Defeat of the French Fleet. *Anonymous.* OBSS

And let thine earliest symbol by thy last! Two Sonnets: Harvard. Oliver Wendell Holmes. AP

...And let/Thy feet take hold on hell. To the Brave Soul. Wilbur Underwood. WGRP

And let Thy Spirit brighten/The hearts Thyself hast blessed! O God, the Rock of Ages. Edward Henry, Bishop of Exeter Bickersteth. BLPA; FPL

And let Thy step resound upon/Our night-palled earth. A Prayer. Yehoash. TrJP

And let time roll till I fill my soul/With the light from the Master's face. Be Still. Betsy W. Kline. STF

And let twenty Didos burn/So you get daily new. Dido. Thomas Campion. CBEP

And let us lose our way in woods of sombre Fate. After the Festival. Stefan George. LiTW

And let us mix a little earth with blood. The Gate's Open. John Blight. CBAP

And let us sit by the fire,/Patient until we die! The Tired Man. Anna Wickham. HBMV

And let us sleep easy,/deeply and long. Ars Poetica. Arturo Trias. InW

And let us walk through time with equal pride. Recitative. Hart Crane. FaBoMo

And let what happened so suddenly,/Never suddenly stop. Three Lyrics. Petronius Arbiter (Caius Petronius Arbiter). LiTW

And let you be, and let this break my heart. Two Solitudes. Evelyn Ames. GoYe

And let you die with bleeding heart. O Christ, Who Died. John Calvin Slemp. TrPWD

And let your full lips laugh at Fate! To A Dark Girl. Gwendolyn B. Bennett. BANP; BlSi; CDC; PoBA

And let your prothalamium be sweet. The Bed. Karl Shapiro. NYBP

And let your weeds lack dew, and duly sterve. Clear or Cloudy, Sweet as April Showering. *Anonymous.* ElL

And lets her arms sustain him in their sphere. Age. Marya Mannes. FAZ

And lets the sparks, all secular and good,/formlessly rain down. Second Horn. W. S. Di Piero. MAYP

And letting them out again. The Vacant Lot. Gwendolyn Brooks. NoAmP; NOBA

And, levelling an ancient rifle, he says "Stop/Making love outside Aras an Uachtarain." Making Love outside Aras an Uachtarain. Paul Durcan. FaBoIP

And Libye land likewise wyth warlick victorye conquoure. The Aeneid. Virgil (Publius Vergilius Maro). OBVE

And lie beside you all the night. Lovesick. *Anonymous.* UnTE

And lie down, asleep before my head hits/the pillow. The Macy's Poem. James Reiss. PoL

And lie in the sun adream while we/Hid up his scythe in flowers! The May Day Garland. Edmund Charles Blunden. HBMV

And lie, like Eve and Adam,/Unanswered under the moon. A Circle. Theodore Spencer. NYBP

And lie on the flat of my temples as proud as a wreath. Haircut. Karl Shapiro. MoPo; MoVE; MP; TwCP

And lie there with your leaden lover/For ever and a day.' The Deserter. Alfred Edward Housman. OBMV; SeCeV

And lies dreaming/Of sunlight on viable water. Requiem. Hamilton Warren. GoYe

And life again grow gentle. I Ponder on Life. Max Ehrmann. PoToHe

And life and death but shadows of the soul. On the Death of Robert Browning. Algernon Charles Swinburne. EnLit

And life for me ain't been no crystal stair. Mother to Son. Langston Hughes. AmNP; CDC; CTBA; GoSl; NTCP; OBCA; PoNe; SO; TTY

And life in me is what you give. Because She Would Ask Me Why I Loved Her. Christopher John Brennan. CBAP

And life is born anew. New Life. Joseph E. Kariuki. TTY

And life is fresh and death is salt to me. Life Flows to Death as Rivers to the Sea. J. V. Cunningham. PoL

And life is just the picture dancing on a screen. Picture-Show. Siegfried Sassoon. CMoP

And life itself is one more certainty. Two Married. Helen Frazee-Bower. HBMV

And Life lurks, evil, out of its epoch. The Dog beneath the Skin. W.H. Auden. OxBTC

...And life reborn annuls/Loss and decay and death, and all is love. Monna Innominata. Christina Georgina Rossetti. VLP

And life slips by like a field mouse/Not shaking the grass. And the Days Are Not Full Enough. Ezra Pound. PCP

And life, some think, is worthy of the Muse. Modern Love, XXV. George Meredith. NOBV; VLP

And life still smile, like child-hood's hour. To Thine Eternal Arms, O God. Thomas Wentworth Higginson. AH

And life, the throb of a revolving door. Habitue. Helen Frith Stickney. GoYe

And life will peel away, will fall and wither and peel away.   The Far Country.   Robert Greacen.   NeIP

And lift him into my arms and sing/Whether he hears my song or not.   Mutterings over the Crib of a Deaf Child.   James Wright.   LCAP; PoPl

And lift his arms and cry aloud like Man.   Childhood.   Ned O'Gorman.   PoPl

And lift my heart or bear my cross.   Pro Libra Mea.   Joseph Ignatius Constantin Clarke.   TrPWD

And lift my heart to God above/In praise for all His wondrous love.   Table Rules for Little Folk.   *Anonymous.*   FaBoUs; OxBChV

And lift my maimed creations to beg rebirth.   Son and Father.   C. Day Lewis.   EaLo

And lift off into the weather.   Our Ground Time Here Will be Brief.   Maxine W. Kumin.   AMV-81

And lift them to the sky.   A Nation's Strength (excerpt).   Ralph Waldo Emerson.   AmFN; PAL; PGD; TRV

And lift to heaven the voice of praise.   Other Sheep I Have, Which Are Not of This Fold.   William Cullen Bryant.   TrPWD

And lift up my eyes to consider more strictly the ap-/palling logic of joy.   Debate: Question, Quarry, Dream.   Robert Penn Warren.   VGW

...And lifted fearfully,/Her eyelids up, her lover and the light at once did spy.   Metamorphoses.   Ovid (Publius Ovidius Naso).   OAEL 1-2

And lifted upward to a saner view.   Plea For Tolerance.   Margaret E. Bruner.   PoToHe

And lifts to the changing moon/His changing eyes.   The Cat and the Moon.   William Butler Yeats.   CMoP; ExPo; FaBoCh; GoJo; InPo; LoGBV; LOW; PCat; RoGo

And light, and thunder of the tides.   The Masque of Queen Bersabe (excerpt).   Algernon Charles Swinburne.   AtBAP

And light her way   Pastoral.   Charles Simic.   NNaP

And light is on their wings/As they come to my shoulders.   Again My Fond Circle of Doves.   Baxter Hathaway.   HoAn

And light my pathway with His face/When the dead flesh is left behind.   The Priest Rediscovers His Psalm-Book.   *Anonymous.*   KiLC

And light the way to our native town.   Lady Day in Harvest.   Sheila Kaye-Smith.   ISi

And light the world with gas.   Gasbags.   *Anonymous.*   NOBL

And light you up your candles,/For His star it shineth clear.   Chrismas Carol.   *Anonymous.*   HBV 1-2

And lighted the way clear across for us.   Limerick: "A handy old guide from the Bosphorous."   *Anonymous.*   TDH

And lighting furtive kisses to their mark.   On the Telescopic Moon.   John Swanick [(or Swanwick)] Drennan.   BIrV; IrPN

And lightly, like the flowers.   And Lightly, Like the Flowers.   Pierre Ronsard.   AWP

And lights rising throne on throne   The Lake: Coda.   Tom Clark.   HoAn

And like a bloodhound swoops across the sky.   Design for Mediaeval Tapestry.   Abraham Moses Klein.   CaP

And like a child worn out with play,/When wearied with existence, sleep.   The Epicurean.   Sir Francis Hastings Doyle.   OBVV

And like a dream, in the Gulf-stream/Sinking, vanish all away.   Sir Humphrey Gilbert.   Henry Wadsworth Longfellow.   EtS; HBV 1-2; HBVY; MC; PAH

And, like a drunken giant, sobb'd in sleep!   The Quest of the Sangraal: The Coming of the Sangraal.   Robert Stephen Hawker.   VLP

And, like a flock of wild geese, sweeps its flowing tail.   The Kite.   Adelaide O'Keeffe.   OxBChV

And, like a kite without a tail,/He flops into the hollow vale.   Narcissus and Some Tadpoles.   Victor J. Daley.   PoAu 1-2

And like a thief he waits for you as your day approaches night.   Time.   Allan Taylor.   OBET

And like a thunderbolt he falls.   The Eagle.   Alfred, Lord Tennyson.   BoLiVe; DiPo; ExPo; FaBoCh; FF; FiP; FM; GN; GoJo; GTBS; GTBS-P; HBV 1-2; HeIP; InPK; LoGBV; MyFE; NOBV; NoP; NTCP; OAEL 1-2; OAEP; OBSP; PB; PBBP; PoPle; PPoe; PrIm; SeCePo; SeCeV; SoSe; SUS; SyP; TreFT; TrGrPo; UnPo; WiR

And like a tide you have flowed into me.   Psalm to My Beloved.   Eunice Tietjens.   ErPo

And like Black Beauty neighs his lonesomeness/For the child to come and ride.   Dexter.   Joan Byers Grayston.   PH

And like bricks fearsome in their everyday squareness.   Anniversary.   John Wain.   MP; NePoEA-2

And, like children paddling in summer brooks,/dabble their pretty feet in your heart's blood?   Go Throw Them Out.   Moishe Leib Halpern.   VWA

And like devils they danced round the piper.   The Cow Ate the Piper.   *Anonymous.*   GBP

And like him moulder into dust.   Epitaph.   Thomas Love Peacock.   FaBoUs

And like lovers hand in hand/March around and make a stand.   The Dance.   Thomas Campion.   ElL; FaBoCh; LoGBV

And, like men waking from a spell,/Grow stronger, nobler, than before,/When there is Peace.   When There Is Peace.   Henry Austin Dobson.   PAH

...And, like my grandfather,/must quiet a heart accused by its own fear.   At Cooloolah.   Judith Wright.   MoBrPo

And like my mother i shall fade/into my dreams/no longer caring/either Mother's Habits.   Nikki Giovanni.   BlSi

And like our living, where we're known/To very few, or else to none.   His Content in the Country.   Robert Herrick.   CaPo; EnLit; SeCV 1-2

And, like ten million others, dying for the people.   The Springboard.   Louis MacNeice.   ChMP; PoA

And like the panther's feet/The feet of Love.   Fragoletta.   Algernon Charles Swinburne.   UnTE

And like the sea,/is wide, is deep.   Sea-Games.   Aliza Shenhar.   VWA

And, like thy shadow, follow thee.   Compensation.   Ralph Waldo Emerson.   AP; ForPo; NOBA

And like water-lilies.   The Gods! The Gods!   D. H. Lawrence.   CMoP

And likely to come, begging, from the vault.   Hallowe'en.   Anthony Hecht.   LiTA

And likewise the neighbors that stood by my children,/Kept want and starvation away from me door.   The Shoofly.   *Anonymous.*   AmFP

And lily-coloured clothes provide/Your spouse not laboured-at, nor spun.   The Habit of Perfection.   Gerard Manley Hopkins.   ACP; BoLiVe; BrPo; CAW; CoBMV; EnLit; ForPo; LiTB; MoAB; MoBrPo; NoAm; NOBV; NoP; OAEP; OBEV; OBMV; PoPle; PoRA; TrGrPo; UnS; ViBoPo; VLP

And Lincoln dead shall lead you into life!   Lincoln.   Florence Kiper Frank.   PGD

And line with line, color with color strives.   Notes on a Child's Coloring Book.   Robert Patrick Dana.   PoPl

And lineaments of desire lit the old hag.   Moral Story II.   David Wright.   ChMP; PeSA

And lines like Virgil's, or like yours, shou'd praise.   A Letter from Italy.   Joseph Addison.   CEP; NOEC; OBTV

And lingered at the julep in the ever-brimming glass.   When the Mint Is in the Liquor.   Clarence Ousley.   PoLf

And lingers like sweet fragrance in my/soul.   Blessed Nearness.   Mary Bullock.   STF

And link'd thee to the Dunciad for thy pains.   William Lisle Bowles.   George Gordon, Lord Byron.   OBNC

And link't it self by carnal sensuality/To a degenerate and degraded state.   Chastity.   John Milton.   OBS

And link thy name by deathless art/With Richard of the Lion Heart!   Blondel.   Clarence Urmy.   AA; HBMV

And list'ning and silent, and silent and list'ning,/and list'ning and silent obey.   An Ode on the Death of Mr. Henry Purcell (excerpt).   John Dryden.   PBBP

And list to their loudest song?   The King on the Tower.   William Makepeace Thackeray.   OBVV

And listen/always listen/to the silent air.   Listen.   Jessica Hagedorn.   WPOW

And listen for my voice, if for no other/when you're all alone.   John's Song.   Joan Aiken.   DuDa

And listen! in the frosty pines/snowbirds twitter Valentines.   Valentine's Day.   Aileen Fisher.   YeAr

And listen/To his heart/beat.   On Death and Love.   Janet Campbell Hale.   VoR

And listen to man's great desire/Holding a Heart to burst?   All Fellows (excerpt).   Laurence Housman.   WGRP

And listen to subterranean voices.   At Night.   Margherita Guidacci.   WPOW

And listen to the distant cry/Of "Clo!–old Clo!"   The Lay of the Levite.   William Aytoun.   HBV 1-2

And listen/to what you think/she might say.   Three Poems for Women.   Susan Griffin.   NPGG

And listen while they say instead/The foolish things we might have said.   The Cat.   Oliver Herford.   FaBV

And listen while you may.   A Wood Song.   Ralph Hodgson.   GoJo; HBV 1-2

And listened–wretched little lad–/To what they said.   Leave Him Now Quiet.   Trumbull Stickney.   CrMA; LiTA; NCEP

...And listening still/to chanted hymns that sound from the heavenly hill.   Call Me Not Dead.   Richard Watson Gilder.   HBV 1-2; WGRP

And lit, as by a lamp from heaven,/The world's track of sin.   The Light from Within.   Jones Very.   WGRP

And lit the ages as they ran.   Conscripts of the Dream (excerpt).   Edwin Markham.   PGD

And little Adriadne sleep.   Birthright.   John Drinkwater.   CH

And little birds break out in rippling song.   Compensation.   Celia Thaxter.   HBV 1-2

And little birds were singing sweetly from each spray.   The Two Swans.   Thomas Hood.   CH

And Little Dick.   Tom Thumbkin.   *Anonymous.*   OxNR

And little feel boys o'er their heads can stray.   Snowstorm.   John Clare.   BoNaP; WiR

And little footpaths sweet to see/Go seeking sweeter places still. The Flitting. John Clare. OBRV

And little footsteps lightly print the ground. Stanzas Cancelled from the Elegy. Thomas Gray. ViBoPo

And little gap. Bo Peeper. *Anonymous.* OxNR

And little golden heads for when your head is gray. Oblation. A. Newberry Choyce. HBMV

And "Little Hatchet." That Little Hatchet. C. Butler-Andrews. PeD

And little hunted hares. The Bells of Heaven. Ralph Hodgson. BrPo; EaLo; GoJo; LiTM; MoAB; MoBrPo; NOBE; OBEV; OBSP; PPON; SiSoSe; TreFT

And little Jesus safe among/The holier gifts of love. Christmas, the Year One, A. D. Sara Henderson Hay. PoRA

And little Miss Montague screams in her ward. A Game of Consequences. Paul Dehn. ErPo; FiBHP; NOBL

And little motion in the air/Except the mill-wheel's sound. Song: "A widow bird sate mourning for her love." Percy Bysshe Shelley. NOBE; OBNC; OBSP; PoPle

And little Nanny Button-cap/Will come tomorrow night. The Moon Shines Bright. *Anonymous.* OxNR

And little russian dolls/conversing in wooden cabinets. Morning Poem. Jennivien-Diana Beenen. AMV-81

And little shoes of lavender,/To keep him from the cold. My Donkey. Rose Fyleman. TiPo

And live and die constant to Poll. Jack's Fidelity. Charles Dibdin. EtS

And live and die wi' Charlie. O'er the Water to Charlie. Robert Burns. FaBoCh

And live as long as its pure stream shall flow. Epitaph. Gabriello Chiabrera AWP

And live forever, like the dust. Poem in Three Parts. Robert Bly. CAPP; ConAP; NaP; NOBA

And live like Solomon/That Sheba led a dance. On Woman. William Butler Yeats. BiP; CMoP

And live no more to shame nore me nor you. Sonnets, LXXII: "O, lest your true love may seem false in this." William Shakespeare. LO

And live on corn dodgers the rest of my life. Starving to Death on a Government Claim. *Anonymous.* AmFP; BPAW; FSW; OBAL

And live the life whose love is free/And never swerve! Queen and Slave. Mortimer Collins. OBVV

And live the space of a door/that opens and shuts My Way Is in the Sand Flowing. Samuel Beckett. NOBI

And lived more base than that young wife/died true. The Fire i' the Flint. Lucy Robinson. AA

And lives alone, and in his secret shines/like phosphorus. At the bottom of the sea. Portrait of the Poet as Landscape. Abraham Moses Klein. NOBC

And lives and speaks, restor'd and whole. Picture of Seneca Dying in a Bath. Matthew Prior. CEP

And lives on honey like St John. Hymns for the Amusement of Children. Christopher Smart. NOCV

And lives to-day in Bread and Wine. Christmas. Sir John Betjeman. BoC; EBCP; OBCP; OxBTC

And lives with beaux,/In England. On a Judge from Scotland. Thomas Erskine, Lord Erskine. FaBoEE

And living presence of sweet music stirs/By Leac a' Chlarsair. Leac A'Chlarsair. Lucy Taylor. PoSH

And lo! a shining brightness was the brook. Cinderella. Cynthia Pickard. DFT; PoPl

And, lo, above loomed Majesty! Mount Rainier. Herbert Bashford. AA

And lo! Ben Adhem's name led all the rest. Abou Ben Adhem. [James Henry] Leigh Hunt. BeLS; BLPA; FaBoBe; FaBoRV; FaBV; FaFP; FaPoR; FPL; GN; GoTF; HBV 1-2; HBVY; MCCG; NOBE; OBEV; OBVV; OHFP; TreF; TRV; WBLP; WGRP

And lo, Christ walking on the water/Not of Gennesareth, but Thames! The Kingdom of God. Francis Thompson. AtBAP; BrPo; EaLo; FaPoR; GoBC; GTBS-P; ILwL; NOCV; OxBoCh; PoPle; SeCeV; TRV

And lo! Cities and gardens, shepherds and smiths. The Lost Child. James Reaney. NOBC

And, lo! her blushes crimson all the/west. A Sunset. Robert Loveman. AA

And lo! I tremble in my boots! To Julia in Shooting Togs (parody). Sir Owen Seaman. BXAP

And lo, I was the All-living–only God I saw. Illumination and Ecstasy. Baba Kuhi of Shiraz. ILwL

And lo! I worship at his feet! True Love. Phoebe Cary. PoToHe

And lo, in bitter sooth we all must spew it out again. The Draught of Life. Abu-l-Ala al-Maarri. LiTW

And lo, it was there I could best compare/My mother's love for me! Mother Love. Janie Alford. PGD

And lo! now art thou wretched. I, a Most Wretched Atlas. Heinrich Heine. TrJP

And, lo! so deep was Majesty in dough,/The Palace seemed the lodging of a baker. The Apple Dumplings and a King. John Wolcot. OBSV

And lo! the Christ they sing of is here in our midst to-day. On Easter Morning. Eben E. Rexford. BLRP

And lo! the cuckold with the strumpet lay. The Dream. Brian Bendo. NOEC

And lo–the dawn! Dawn. Frank Dempster Sherman. TRV

And lo! the Garden is a Paradise! Mary, Mary (parody). Anthony C. Deane. FaBoPa

And lo, the serpent of hatred raises its head in my heart, that serpent that I believed was dead. Prayer for Peace: II. Leopold Sedar Senghor. TTY

And loathe to say good night. On a Calm Summer's Night. John Nicholson. EnLoPo

And lock/all that we fear. City. Timothy P. Mocarski. AMV-81

And locked rivers open, run/In the full mid-day sun. Girl's Song. Marya Zaturenska. OLR

And locks drowning in the hall of death/Both ships and souls! The Whale. *Anonymous.* EBEV

And loneliness might bring a blessing upon us. The Absent. Edwin Muir. MoRP; NoAm

And loneliness more fleet. November Fugitive. Henry Morton Robinson. GoYe

And lonely was the forward way. I Saw Red Evening through the Rain. Robert Louis Stevenson. NOBV

And lonesome, very lonesome, is my strand. Autumn. Christina Georgina Rossetti. BrRo

And long before their time they die. The Sleepers. William Henry Davies. AnFE

And long good life to lede/All that for plowmen pray. God Speed the Plough! *Anonymous.* OxBM

And long 'tis like to be. To Think That Two and Two Are Four. Alfred Edward Housman. ImOP

And long to return/down home down home. Down Home. Randolph Outlaw. LFAC

And long to see the time to come/To be a soldier's wife. Fare You Well, My Darling. *Anonymous.* AmFP

And long, wild cries seemed shouts of fear and war. The Dutch Seamen and New Holland. William Pember Reeves. AnNZ

And look for snowdrops. After Christmas. Michael Richards. OBCP

And look into Time's eye, as into a strange house, for what/lies within. March Twilight. Louise Bogan. NePoAm-2

And look on thine, anointed King. O Lord, How Lovely Is the Place. Francis Hopkinson. AH

And look over at God and say/How about that! To Satch. Samuel ("Paul Vesey") Allen. AmNP; CTBA; LiSp; NIP; PoBA; PoNe; SD; SoSe; TTY

And look to you for refuge and relief. Thirteenth Station. William A. Donaghy. ISi

...And look/upon me as someone they didn't see awhile. The Poem on the Jews. Avot Yeshurun. VWA

And look upon these blossoms of so long ago. Landscape with the Giant Orion: Orion Seeks the Goddess Diana (excerpt. Sacheverell Sitwell. MoVE

And look west toward home Poem near midway truck stop. Lance Henson. STE

–And looked and looked our infant sight away. Over 2000 Illustrations and a Complete Concordance. Elizabeth Bishop. HaCAP; LCAP; NoAm

And, looking back, that look did sever/Him and Eurydice for ever. Orpheus. Robert Herrick. CaPo

And looking back to hillsides build/Imaginary houses. Rock Climbing. Jane Cooper. NMM

And, looking in her face, was strooken blind. Hero and Leander. Christopher Marlowe. HoPM

And looking, that we stand where he had stood. In Front of a Japanese Photograph. John Peck. SM

And, looking to Jesus,/Still trust to His word. Take Time to Be Holy. W. D. Longstaff. BLRP

And looks around for someone to come/to redeem him. Melons. Yungman. VWA

And looks on life with quiet eyes. Who Loves the Rain. Frances Shaw. BrR; HBMV; PoToHe

And looks to Thee to give the earth her/greeness/With dew. Prayer for Dew. Eleazar Ben Kalir. TrJP

And looks when well-friseur'd, amazing big. Epigram: "A head pure, sinless quite of brain or soul." Robert Burns. FaBoEE

And loosing, lost bottom, shaft, and/shooting. Among the Daffadillies. Giles Farnaby. OAEP

And looters braved the street. Celebrations. Austin Clarke. IPY; OxBI

And lopped his desperate days. Mementos. Charlotte Bronte. PeD

And Lord of all this Revelling. A Christmas Caroll, Sung to the King in the Presence at White-Hall. Robert Herrick. GoJo

And, Lord, one day, let me find again/my little brother of the Christmas crib. The Prayer of the Donkey. Carmen De Gasztold. PCh

And, Lord, to thee unite my heart,/That I may fear thy name. O Lord, Bow Down Thine Ear. Thomas Prince. AH

And, Lord, we have thy promise plain/That thou wilt walk in them again. Ascension Day. Sheila Kaye-Smith. CAW

And Lords whose parents were the Lord knows who. The True-Born Englishman. Daniel Defoe. CEP; OBSV

And lordy, give us our share. I Have Three Daughters. Ruth Stone. InPS; NMM

And lose the arid prairie in a lake. Big Dam. W. R. Moses. AmFN

And lose the name of authors. Shakespearean Soliloquy in Progress: "To print, or not to..." (parody). Richard Jago. BXAP

And lose the name of/Profits. Investor's Soliloquy. Kenneth Ward. FaFP; FPL

And lose the Nymph, to gain the Bays. In Imitation of Anacreon. Matthew Prior. CEP; FaBoEE

And lose the right to open. Shakespearean Soliloquy in Progress: "To draw, or not to..."(parody). *Anonymous.* BXAP

And lose the sun. Woodbird. Charles G. Bell. NePoAm

And lose their honour and their breath. On a Little Boy's Endeavouring to Catch a Snake. Thomas Foxton. OxBChV

And lost all wanton wisdom long since won. Magic. Lionel Pigot Johnson. VLP

And lost his gods in deep, Christ-given/rest. Maurice de Guerin. Maurice Francis Egan. AA

And lost, lives for the next total throw. Lover That I Hope You Are. Milton Acorn. NeAC

And lost teacups/full of our ashes/floated by In a Surrealist Year. Lawrence Ferlinghetti. PPON

And lost to mortals evermore! The Last Voyage of the Fairies. William Henry Davenport Adams. HBVY

And loud it screamed, the lifeless metal,/Far into the malicious night. The Bunyip and the Whistling Kettle. John Streeter Manifold. LiTB; PoAu 1-2; WaP

And loud they cried to all. The Cherry-Tree Carol, III. *Anonymous.* AmFP

...And louder the heart's dance/At parting than at meeting be. When First. Edward ("Edward Eastaway") Thomas. NoAm

And Love alone will stand omnipotent. Sonnets to My Mother. Arthur Stanley Bourinot. CaP

And, love, among them–thee! My Songs Are Poisoned. Heinrich Heine. AWP

And love and hate and life and death begin. The Good Man in Hell. Edwin Muir. MoBrPo; MoRP; TW

And love and kiss, and kiss and love. The Young Laird and Edinburgh Katy. Allan Ramsay. CEP

And love, and man's unconquerable mind. To Toussaint L'Ouverture. William Wordsworth. AnEnPo; EnLi 1-2; EnLit; ERoP 1-2; ExPo; FaBoPV; LoBV; MBW 1-2; NOBE; OAEP; OBNC; OBRV; PoNe; PoRA; PPP; TrGrPo; TRV

And love, and thought, and joy. The Sparrow's Nest. William Wordsworth. EnRP

And love arrived may find us somewhere else. Delay. Elizabeth Jennings. NePoEA; OxBTC

And love as you loved me then! Cleopatra. William Wetmore Story. AA

And love be all in all! Thou Long Disowned, Reviled, Oppressed. Eliza Scudder. AH

And love breaks on my cold hills like the sun. Love Poem. Chris Wallace-Crabbe. PoAu 1-2

And love can never lose its own! Life and Love. John Greenleaf Whittier. BLRP; TRV

And love continue still. The Spring of Joy Is Dry. *Anonymous.* EiL

And Love, dark head, is all the power/That breaks the green bough into flower. From an Irish-Latin Macaronic. Geoffrey Taylor. NeIP

And Love Domestic, smiling equably. To Hampstead. [James Henry] Leigh Hunt. EnRP

And love doth hold my hand, and makes me write. Astrophel and Stella, XC. Sir Philip Sidney. AAS; OBSC; SiPS

And love goes too...but goes the last. O Fond, but Fickle and Untrue. Walter Savage Landor. GBL

And love her as hard as you can. The Way. Robert Creeley. AP; BoLoP; LiTM; NeAP; PPP

And love in a coil. On Sunday, I wrote this. Diary. David Wagoner. CoAP

And love in life should strive to see/Sometimes what love in death would be. Too soon, too soon comes Death to show. Coventry Patmore. EG

And love in love shall make it fine. Love Unlike Love. *Anonymous.* MeEL

And love, in memory of the flourishing dead. Elegy while Pruning Roses. David Wagoner. AMV-80

And Love in tears too noble is/For pity, save of Love in smiles. The Angel in the House. Coventry Patmore. LO

And love is a game that two can play at. Ballade of Big Plans. Dorothy Parker. InMe

And love is a hard thing to outgrow. American Portrait: Old Style. Robert Penn Warren. FYAP

And Love is fled, to come no more. Marriage. Nathaniel Cotton. FaBoUs

And love is still miraculous! Chicago. John Greenleaf Whittier. MC; PAH

And love is strong, and love is wise. O, Love Is Not a Summer Mood. Richard Watson Gilder. HBV 1-2

And love is where yesterday is at. That Day. Anne Sexton. BoWoP; ConAP

And love itself be changed/To walk the earth alone. Fore Thought. May Sarton. MoLP

And love, kissed out by pleasure, seems not yet/Worth patience to regret. Before Parting. Algernon Charles Swinburne. NOBV

And love, love sang toward. The Shape of the Fire. Theodore Roethke. LCAP

And love me truly, just one minute. Snowdrop. William Wetmore Story. HBV 1-2

And Love no longer be a thing to weep. Her Epitaph. Thomas William Parsons AA; HBV 1-2

And love's best glasses reach/No fields but are his own. That Night When Joy Began. W. H. Auden. OxBTC; SoSe

And love's channel way unclogs/In the croaking of the frogs. The Early Frogs. Harry Edward Mills. PeD

And Love's midsummer will fade too soon. Midsummer. Ella Wheeler Wilcox. HBV 1-2

And love's/obscure and insatiable/appetite. Sparrows among Dry Leaves. William Carlos Williams. NYBP

...And love's the burning boy. Casabianca. Elizabeth Bishop. FaBoWP; OBSP

And love's the only oil that flows in both. The Cruse. Louise Townsend Nicholl. NYBP

And love stirs in a heart I know. Turn o' the Year. Katharine Tynan Hinkson. HBV 1-2

And love the brightest eyes, but love in vain!' A Hymn Written in Windsor Forest. Alexander Pope. NOEC; OBSP

And love the light between. Lovelight. Georgia Douglas Johnson. AmNP

And love the more impatient glows/As brighter its far object shows! Envying a Little Bird. Sisteria Gregoria Francisca. CAW

And love thee more and more. My Dear and Only Love. James Graham. BSV; CavP; JCP; OBS

And love–Thy love–that held Thee fast. Carpenter's Son. Annie Johnson Flint. BePJ

And love to thee is naught; from passionate mood/Secured by joy's complacent plenitude. Flowers I Would Bring. Aubrey Thomas De Vere. HBV 1-2; IrPN

And love triumphant treads among the stars. The Dancers. Babette Deutsch. HBMV

And love went by upon the wind/As though it had not been. Full Moon. Robert Graves. NOBE

(And Love will swear't) my dearest did not so. His Parting with Mrs. Dorothy Kennedy. Robert Herrick. MyFE

And love with old familiar love. The Convent Threshold. Christina Georgina Rossetti. MasP; NoP; PoEL 1-5

And love you so much. Steps. Frank O'Hara. ANYP; CAPP; ConAP

And love you, whom I ought to swat. Poems of Passion, Carefully Restrained So as to Offend Nobody. Samuel Hoffenstein. InMe

And loved and blessed them all in death. The Music of His Steps. Samuel Wakefield. AH

And loved to course with tempests through the night. Horses on the Camargue. Roy Campbell. AtBAP; GTBS-P; OBTV; PeSA; PoPle; SeCePo

And loved with us the beautiful and old. I Call the Old Time Back. John Greenleaf Whittier. ViBoPo

And loved you all night,/completely out of proportion. Los Angeles. Eloise Klein Healy. GP

And lovers float down from the cliffs like rain. Salvador Dali. David Gascoyne. EAS; OxBTC

And Lovers live by thinking on their loss. A Valediction. William Cartwright. OBS

And lovers shrivel into friends! Epigram: "How often, when life's summer day." Walter Savage Landor. FaBoEE

And loves for his pleasure, and 'tis time he was dead. Experience. John Boyle O'Reilly. ACP; OBVV

And loves it until death releases him. Dream and Image. Sir. Heinrich von Morungen. LiTW

And loves that drove the reason wild/But set the fancy free. Hymn to Proust. Gavin Ewart. NYBP

And loves us to the end. The Everlasting Love. Annie Johnson Flint. BLRP

And loving only giving. The Poet Speaks. Georgia Douglas Johnson. AmNP

And, loving, shall we fear to build on rock?   Sonnet: "Shall I be fearful thus to speak my mind."   Irene Rutherford McLeod.   HBMV

And low thou lies!   The Daisy.   Robert Burns.   BoNaP

And lower the price of rouge–at least some winters.   Don Juan.   George Gordon, Lord Byron.   PoEL 1-5

And loyal hearts in years to run/Shall turn to thee, O Washington. Washington.   Mary Wingate.   OHIP

And Lucifer left twinkling him alane.   A Starscape.   John Bellenden.   ACP

And Lucifer raises/his pale pearl.   Nox.   Salvador Diaz Miron.   HW

And luckier may you find the night/Than ever you found the day.   The Isle of Portland.   Alfred Edward Housman.   MoBrPo

And luckless lads will wear them/When I am dead and gone.   I Hoed and Trenched and Weeded.   Alfred Edward Housman.   LiTM; MoAB; MoBrPo; TrGrPo; VLP; WeW

And luf hir best attour all thing,/Baith gud and fair and womanlie.   Baith Gud and Fair and Womanlie.   Anonymous.   GoTS; OxBS

And lull asleep/Thy woes, and weep/No more.   Comfort to a Youth That Had Lost His Love.   Robert Herrick.   NOBE; OBEV

And lull thy dreamy eyelids to sweet forgetful bliss.   Country Music.   Plato. LiTW

And lurid placards, orange, red,/Drive through his waking dreads.   The Seraph and the Snob.   May Kendall.   CenHV

And Lydia's neighbors wonder why.   Lydia Sherman.   Anonymous.   ShM

And lyht on Alysoun.   Alison.   Anonymous.   AtBAP; CTC; EnLi 1-2; FaBoCh; MeBV; OAEL 1-2; OBEV; OxBB; PoEL 1-5

And lying in her soft place he became a swan.   Leda.   Rainer Maria Rilke. NU

And made a kind of checkered day and night.   The Castle of Indolence. James (1700-1748) Thomson.   ViBoPo

And made a useless moon-dial of the snubbing/post.   Cow-Ponies.   Maurice Lesemann.   BPAW

And made all eyes with wonder thee behold.   As in a Dusky and Tempestuous Night.   William, of Hawthornden Drummond.   LO

And made cider inside her inside.   Limerick: "There was a young lady of Ryde."   Anonymous.   CenHV; EvOK; ShM

And made her lady of halls and towers,/Into sweet Berwick town.   Young John.   Anonymous.   BuBa

And made him stir his stumps, sir.   Yankee Doodle's Expedition to Rhode Island.   Anonymous.   GBP; PAH

And made his eldest son one day/Slave in his father's stead.   Coronation. Helen Fiske Jackson.   AA; BeLS; GN; HBV 1-2

And made me cry aloud?   A Poem about Love.   G. S. Fraser.   NeBP

And made mermaids come from the sea.   Madness One Monday Evening. Julia Fields.   NIP; NNP

And made my self quiet, and happy again.   The Enquiry.   John Dyer. OBEC

And made our life a sacrament.   The House of Pride.   William James Dawson.   PoToHe

And made the appellation hideous.   Epitaph on the Late King of the Sandwich Isles.   Winthrop Mackworth Praed.   FiBHP

And made the birds explode for miles around.   Loves of the Puppets. Richard Wilbur.   CoPo; OxBC

And made the body's health depend/Upon the living soul.   Health of Body Dependent on Soul.   Jones Very.   WGRP

And made the flames burn crueller. Admire Cranmer!   Admire Cranmer! Stevie Smith.   NoAm

And made the kites to whet their beaks clack clack.   Captain Carpenter. John Crowe Ransom.   APA; AtBAP; CoBMV; FaBoMo; HoPM; LiTA; LiTM; MasP; MoAB; MoAmPo; MoVE; MP; NePA; NoAm; NOBA; OxBA; PPoe; SeCeV; TwCP

And made the pews go pair and pair/Along the aisle to the choir.   Synnove's Song.   Bjornstjerne Bjornson.   LiTW; PoPl

And made the simple scullion boy/the heir to all his land.   The Lady Isabella's Tragedy.   Anonymous.   GBP

And made their dove-wings tremble. On he flared.   The Fall of Hyperion. John Keats.   ERoP 1-2; OAEL 1-2

And made their huts and houses in the fir.   Tree.   Pat Wilson.   AnNZ

And made you his agent to answer their prayers.   Annie and Willie's Prayer. Sophia P. Snow.   BeLS; BLPA

And Maecenas paid the freight!   The Truth about Horace.   Eugene Field. InMe

And Maelstrom–in the Sky–   Behind me–dips eternity–.   Emily Dickinson. PBWP

And Mahomet and Mustapha prepare/To stem by force his madness and despair.   Pasquin to the Queen's Statue at St. Paul's, during the Procession...   William Shippen.   APAS

...And Mahoney/in his stripped skull is tortured by a lie.   Mahoney.   Sean Jennett.   NeIP

And make a dust of their seraphic song.   On Some Shells Found Inland. Trumbull Stickney.   AnFE; APA; LiTA; NCEP; NePA

And make a feast of shit and cum, of ass and thighs!   Ode: To My Lovers. Paul Verlaine.   PeHV

And make a song unique as his/And shirk responsibilities.   The Cuckoo. Patrick Reginald Chalmers.   BoAnP; CenHV

And make earth happy/As the dreamed of skies.   Wisdom.   Langston Hughes.   TiPo

And make forgotten the works of the CCC.   The CCC.   Thomas Whitbread. NYBP

And make God's perfect meadows doubly sweet/With rosy vagrancy of little feet.   Resurrection.   Harry Kemp.   HBV 1-2

And make her grave green with tear on tear.   Autumn.   Percy Bysshe Shelley.   CH

And make it follow at your call,/If you are always kind.   Mary's Lamb. Sarah Josepha Hale.   FaBoBe; FaFP; HBV 1-2; HBVY; OBCA; OxBChV

And make it last/a lifetime.   Leaving Home.   Shirley G. Cochrane. AMV-80

And make little entries/in a ledger.   Students.   Haniel Long.   AnAmPo

And make mankind its hideous secret torch.   Radiation Victim.   Colin Thiele.   NOAV

And make me, Lord, the instrument/To lead their hearts to thee.   My New Year Prayer.   Anonymous.   STF

And make me meet for heaven above,/To join Thy saints in praise and love. Self-Examination.   Anonymous.   FaBoUs

And make me more than conqu'ror in the strife.   The Harder Task. Anonymous.   BLRP

And make me smooth as balm and oil again.   To Music.   Robert Herrick. CaPo

And make me Thy belov'd abode,/And let me roam no more.   Self-Acquaintance.   William Cowper.   NOCV

And make me thy Beloved.   He Is Declared True of Word.   Book of the Dead.   AWP

And make no move; but armies come inside.   In the Sea of Tears.   Naomi Replansky.   BrRo; GP

And make our "pile," and start for home. Hurrah for Pike's Peak!   The Gold Seeker's Song.   Anonymous.   PoOW

And make our souls thy constant home!   Eternal Spirit, Source of Light. Samuel Davies.   AH

...And make/the giant bright stroke like that madman Van Gogh.   The Flowers of Politics.   Michael McClure.   NeAP

And make the gravediggers' work/heavier still.   Cancel My Subscription.   J. A. Hines.   LFAC

And make the proud Tories resign us the nation.   The Whigs' Lamentation for the Death of Their Dear Brother College....   Anonymous.   APAS

And make the sad earth happier for their bloom.   The Trailing Arbutus. John Greenleaf Whittier.   AnAmPo

And make the STOCK Immortal whence they grew.   A Congratulatory Poem to the Honoured Edmund Morris, Esq....   Elkanah Settle.   HW

And make the "vasty deep' a boulevard/For motors and joy-riders! All it's worth."   The Old Conservative.   Lewis Frank Tooker.   EtS

And make the word with my breath.   The Annunciation.   William Stanley Merwin.   AP

And make me now a blest Hermaphrodite.   To Mr. Tilman after He Had Taken Orders.   John Donne.   EBEV

And make them fair in soul as well as face.   The Looking Glass.   James Shirley.   LiTL

And make them rose-like in His name.   God's Garden.   Richard Burton. TRV; WGRP

And make these branches, leafless now so long,/Blossom again in song. From My Arm-Chair.   Henry Wadsworth Longfellow.   BLPA

And make thy Baker blest?   Ode to Miss Hoyland (parody).   Thomas Chatterton.   BXAP

And make thy Concern by reflexion his own.   Jinny the Just.   Matthew Prior.   CABL; CEP; NOBE; NOEC; OBEC; OBEV; PoEL 1-5

And make thy leaf a stain.   To a Lily.   James Matthew Legare.   AA; AnAmPo

And make thy sacrifice complete.   Hymn: "O Thou who camest from above." Charles Wesley.   SeCePo

And make up our defects with His sweet art.   Easter.   George Herbert. TrCP

And make us blest at last.   The Mistress: A Song.   John Wilmot, Earl of Rochester.   CavP; EBEV; MePo; NOBE; OBS

And make us brave to live the angels' song!   A Christmas Prayer.   Molly Anderson Haley.   PGD

And make us sages with transfigured faces.   Why I Voted the Socialist Ticket. Vachel Lindsay.   MoAmPo

And make us, whilst we pity him, forget our loyalty.   Advice to the Painter. Matthew Prior.   APAS

And make you glad and kind and wise.   Open Your Eyes.   Emma Boge Whisenand.   PoToHe

And make your eyes unfaithful to their tears.   Transience.   Sarojini Naidu. MCCG

...And make/Your opponent yours by a nicety of name.   Civilities.   Thomas Whitbread.   SD

And makes a constant sacrament of praise.   Peter Quince at the Clavier. Wallace Stevens.   AP; APA; CMoP; CoBMV; ExPo; ForPo; HBMV; InPK; InPo; InPS; LiTM; MAPA; MoAB; MoAmPo; MP; NAMP; NAWM 1-2; NOBA; OxBA; PAI; PPP; TAP; TrGrPo; TwCP; ViBoPo

And makes an end of Lenten tide.   Two Old Lenten Rhymes: I. *Anonymous.*   ACP

And makes business in the bedroom.   She Told Me.   James C. Kilgore. SOTS

And makes Heaven's loftiest roof rebound/The echoes of the noble sound. The Ascension.   Joseph Beaumont.   OxBoCh

And makes her barren Rocks and her bleak Mountains smile.   Italy and Britain.   Joseph Addison.   OBEC

And makes him bring back one leg.   Riddle: "Two legs sat upon three legs." *Anonymous.*   HBV 1-2; HBVY; NTCP; OxNR

And makes its burden less to bear.   The Hills of Sewanee.   George Marion McClellan.   BANP

And makes of me a very drear, ill-natured sort of lad.   The Contrary Boy. Gaston V. Drake.   BBGG

And makes the happiness she does not find.   Celestial Wisdom.   Juvenal (Decimas Junius Juvenalis).   AWP

And makes the slave grow pleas'd again.   Song: "Give me leave to rail at you."   John Wilmot, Earl of Rochester.   EG

And makes the World but her Periphrasis.   The Hecatomb to His Mistress. John Cleveland.   AnAnS 2

And makes them instant/democrats.   Americana.   Carl Rakosi.   InPS; PAI

And makes u/turn in/side out.   To All Sisters.   Sonia Sanchez.   PoBA

And making a morning path to the light/For the tropic traveler!   Morning Light.   Mary Effie Lee Newsome.   PoNe

And making Death a Victory.   Prometheus.   George Gordon, Lord Byron. EnRP; ERoP 1-2; InPS; NOBE; NoP; OAEL 1-2; PAI

And making joking fantasies/do for real   Suicid/ing Indian Women.   Paula Gunn Allen.   TWSS

And Malachi with garments rent,/Concludes the ancient Testament.   The Old Testament.   Thomas Russell.   TreFS

...And man and flower/and bird/Here are one at heart with all things seen/and heard.   Hawthorn Dyke.   Algernon Charles Swinburne.   VLP

And Man and Nature lived again for aye.   On Finding the Truth.   Jones Very.   TrCP

And man at least, if not his beast,/Shall bless me for my verses.   Mercy to Animals.   Martin Farquhar Tupper.   PeD

And man became a living soul./Amen. Amen.   The Creation.   James Weldon Johnson.   BALP; BANP; CDC; FaBV; GoSl; MoAmPo; PoBA; PoPl; TrCP; YaD

...—And man can never be alone.   The Wolves.   Allen Tate.   LiTA; LiTM; NoAm; NOBA; OxBA; PoA

And man fallen to his endless burden.   Spring Mountain Climb.   Richard Eberhart.   GoYe; LiSp

And man for safety ran and sought the open/field.   The Hailstorm in June 1831.   John Clare.   VLP

And man himself rewards our foes!   The Story of Cruel Psamtek. *Anonymous.*   NA

And man's immortal soul is turned to/clay.   God and the Soul.   John Lancaster Spalding.   AA

And man's religion be complete.   On the Religion of Nature.   Philip Freneau.   AmePo; AmPP; MAmP

And man's true aim shall yet be won!   The Past Is Dark with Sin and Shame. Thomas Wentworth Higginson.   AH

And man shall know again his richness.   In After Time.   Richard Eberhart. MoRP

And man, the self-destroyer, was not lucid in his mind:/With a hey nonny nonny/and a hi-de-ho.   Father and Son: 1939.   William Plomer.   NoAm; PeSA

And man, unsinning, finds all nature good.   To Sleep.   Maybury Fleming. AA

And manage wisely the last stake.   Age.   Abraham Cowley.   AWP; CavP

And mandarin ducks gather near the lotus-gathering/boat.   The Honeymooners.   Yu Ch'ien.   HW

And many a dirty street, on Thames's side,/Is yet by stool and brush unoccupied.   A Charge to the Poets (excerpt).   William Whitehead. OBSV

And many a gem in its jeweled setting/Gleamed in that war-host, the gift of a lord.   Helena Embarks for Palestine.   Cynewulf.   AnOE

And many a knave's seal's better than his soul.   Of Seals and Arms.   John Taylor.   CBEP

And many a lad will take his lass/And sit her on his knee.   The Jolly Waggoner.   *Anonymous.*   OBET

And many a life-blood owe thee still.   Address to My Malay Krees.   John Leyden.   OBTV

And many a new thing understood/That was rank folly to my head before. The Tree.   Ezra Pound.   AnFE; APA; CMoP; InPo

And many a pearly treasure/Burns in the depths below.   Oh Lovely Fishermaiden.   Heinrich Heine.   AWP

And many a wild prayer followed the wave/As he sunk into a sailor's grave. The Sailor's Grave.   *Anonymous.*   ShS

And many ae was the well-wight man/At the fetching o Johny away.   Johnie Cock (A vers.).   *Anonymous.*   BaBo; ViBoFo

And many besides may at last loose their own/for an Orange.   A New Song of an Orange.   *Anonymous.*   CoMu

And many cases of stuffed fish, vermin, and/kingfishers.   By the Ford. Edward ("Edward Eastaway") Thomas.   OBSP

And many children–God give them grace,/bringing tall candles to light Mary's face.   Christmas Morn.   Ruth Sawyer.   OBCP

And many else whose names may not be told.   Hyperion.   John Keats. OBNC; OBRV

And many folks are dying now/Who never died before.   Fin de Siecle. Newton Mackintosh.   NA

And many glories of immortal stamp.   Sonnet Written in Disgust of Vulgar Supersitition.   John Keats.   ERoP 1-2

And many humming-birds were fastened on/it.   Alicia's Bonnet.   Elisabeth Cavazza Pullen.   AA

And many, many troubled thoughts are quite breaking my/heart.   My Heart Moves as Heavy as the Horse That Climbs the Hill.   *Anonymous.*   ELU

And many other fowles mo,/The ouzel and the thrush also.   The Squire of Low Degree (excerpt).   *Anonymous.*   PBBP

And many poems like itself bring forth.   Of Sir Philip Sidney.   Sir John Beaumont.   GoBC

And many seeds like that one seed.   Fragment: "The wing'd seeds with decaying wings."   William Allingham.   IrPN

And many there were who may blush to recall/The polkas they danced at the Wooyeo Ball.   The Wooyeo Ball.   *Anonymous.*   NOAV

And map the course of man's regeneration/Over a pipe!   Inter Sodales. William Ernest Henley.   HBV 1-2

And map with my lips your warm unconscious form   Insomnia.   Elizabeth Zelvin.   AMV-80

And marbled by shadows/clocking around his face.   Windfall.   Joel Arsenault.   AMV-81

And March comes bringing flowers.   Song in March.   William Gilmore Simms.   AA; HBV 1-2

And march with our own battalions/to the beat of the muffled drum! Comrades.   Henry R. Door.   MC; PAH

And marched off home, nor'-west by nor'.   Grandfather Watts's Private Fourth.   Henry Cuyler Bunner.   PoSC; StPo; TiPo

And Marguerite I shall see no more.   Switzerland.   Matthew Arnold. MaVP; OAEP; VLP

And mark and mirror and contain/The gold and purple, rose and red.   The Puddle.   Eden Phillpotts.   HBMV

And mark'st when sparrows fall.   Shoreham: Twilight Time.   Samuel Palmer.   ERoP 1-2; NBM; OAEL 1-2

And marvel at such heights/Conquered, such blazing air.   Marriage on a Mountain Ridge.   Stewart Conn.   PoSH

And marvel at the simple amnesty of soil.   Return to the Valley.   Elfreida Read.   AMV-80

And marvellous to them his works have been.   And Truly It Is a Most Glorious Thing.   William Bradford.   AH

And marvin x and i got married/by jumping over a broom   Reincarnation. Mae Jackson.   PoBA

And Mary culls the bitter herbs ordained.   The Passover in the Holy Family. Dante Gabriel Rossetti.   GoBC; MaVP

And Mary hums a lullaby.   Christmas Lullaby.   Ulrich Troubetzkoy. YeAr

And mass her conquering glooms, then rise and flit/A shadow through the shades!'   A Moth.   Henry Bellyse Baildon.   NOBV

And match her knee for knee, grunting like thunder.   The Labors of Thor. David Wagoner.   GP

And matter's sanctified, dipped in a gold stain.   Sundown.   Léonie Adams. AmLP; MoAB; MoAmPo; TrGrPo

And may all Christian people say amen to 't.   A Satire upon the French King.   Thomas (Tom) Brown.   APAS

And may be blest Thy glory in beholding!   Adoro Te Devote.   Saint Thomas Aquinas.   CAW

And may Christ have mercy on Cassidy.   Fair Cassidy.   *Anonymous.*   BIrV

And may Great Britain rue the day/Her hostile bands came hither. Cornwallis's Surrender.   *Anonymous.*   PAH

And may Grim Pluto's inner jail,/For ever groan with Doneraile.   The Curse of Doneraile.   Patrick O'Kelly.   DBV; OnYI

And may he lend her shade to me!   Graceful Acacia.   Walter Savage Landor.   PoEL 1-5

And may his great posterity/Ne'er fail in old Scotland!   John Barleycorn. Robert Burns.   FaBoCh; HBV 1-2; LoGBV; SeCeV

And may I ask you how you find/Yourself, dear Lord, today?   A Child's Prayer.   John Banister Tabb.   GoTF; TreF; YaD

And may in time become a Solar Myth.   Giffen's Debt.   Rudyard Kipling. VLP

And may it never seem to him that she is also old.   For a Son's Marriage. Martial (Marcus Valerius Martialis).   HW

And may lead in whom she loveth as her love liketh.   The Palace of Truth. William Langland.   ACP

And may our borders blossom wide/Like Sharon's fruitful soil.   On Zion and on Lebanon.   Henry Ustic Onderdonk.   AH

And may our good country/Have quietude and wealth.   The Battle of King's Mountain.   *Anonymous.*   PAH

And may she ever rise in fame,/To honor thy immortal name!   Washington's Monument.   *Anonymous.*   OHIP; PAH

...And may the affliction of our/souls be our atonement.   The High Priest. *Anonymous.*   TrJP

And may the belt of your gown/Soon be too short.   Toast to a Departing Duchess.   Clément Marot.   HW

And may the branch (of Jesse)/spring up in Jerusalem!   Prayer for Redemption.   *Anonymous.*   TrJP

And may the evening's twilight find me gentle still.   A Prayer.   Max Ehrmann.   BLPA; BLPL; FaBoBe; PoToHe

...And may the Lord/give shelter to my soul when I leave this world!' Pilgrims in Mexico.   *Anonymous.*   OBCP

And may the Lord have mercy on your soul!   The Trial.   Henry Wadsworth Longfellow.   PAH

And may the music of thy name/Refresh my soul in death.   The Name of Jesus.   John Newton.   NOEC; OBEC; TrPWD

And may the secret of thy soul/Remain within its sanctuary!   The Sleeping Beauty.   Samuel Rogers.   GTBS; GTBS-P; HBV 1-2

And may the turf upon him laid,/Lie lightly on his breast!   A Backwoods Hero (excerpt).   Alexander McLachlan.   CaP

And may the world go well with thee.   There Is a Tavern in the Town.   F. J. Adams.   PSoN

And may their glory with his hours increase.   The Court.   *Anonymous.* APAS

And may these characters remain/When all is ruin once again.   To Be Carved on a Stone at Thoor Ballylee.   William Butler Yeats.   FaBoEE; NoAm; NoP

And may those who are married live happy.   Good & Bad Wives. *Anonymous.*   CoMu

And may we meet again where all/Are blest and freed from every thrall.   A Parting Hymn.   Charlotte Forten.   BlSi

And may ye better reck the rede,/Than ever did th' adviser!   Epistle to a Young Friend.   Robert Burns.   EBEV; MCCG

And may you be as true to your love/As I have been to mine.   Lady Alice (George Collins), I.   *Anonymous.*   AmFP

And may your happier wits grow lowd with fame/As you (my best of friends!) preserve my name.   Tristium.   Ovid (Publius Ovidius Naso).   OBVE

And maybe nearer God.   Bells in the Country.   Robert Nathan.   BrR; HBMV

And maybe tae the pox–/Ach,weill!   Elegy XIII.   Sydney Goodsir Smith. BSV

And maybe that's why it's extinct!   Wyvern.   Charles Connell.   AmMo

And maybe they hear, and wonder why,/And marvel, out in the cold.   Black Sheep.   Richard Burton.   AA; HBV 1-2

And maybe they'll find us one day,/when people finally exist.   Hominization. Miroslav Holub.   SUW

And me in my fur-about/On the warm hearthstone.   At Home, Alone with the Cat.   Walter De La Mare.   BoC

And me laid out and alive/For nothing at all, in his arms.   Drowning with Others.   James Dickey.   CoPo

And me/my own conductor.   Tubes.   Larry Mollin.   NeAC

And me splendid with love for all.   Euphoria, Euphoria.   Mark DeFoe. AMV-80

And mean, next winter, to be quite reclaimed.   Don Juan.   George Gordon, Lord Byron.   NoP

And means in tenderest Love, the Rod/To serve to thy eternal Good.   To Urania on the Death of Her First and Only Child.   Benjamin Colman. SCAP

And measured for death by their words'/grave rise, sentence them to know.   These Men.   Philip Booth.   GLGT

And measureless thy joy or grief/When TIME and thou shalt part for ever!' The Antiquary. Chapt. 10: Why Sit'st Thou by That Ruin'd Hall.   Sir Walter Scott.   BSV; EnRP; OAEP

And mechanical America Montezuma still.   Cypresses.   D. H. Lawrence. FaBoPP

And meet us at the gum-tree down in the swamp,/To wake Nicodemus today. Wake Nicodemus.   Henry Clay Work.   FSW

And meet with the one who has loved you so true/And remembered you, love, in her prayers.   I'll Remember You, Love, in My Prayers.   *Anonymous.* BLPA; FaBoBe

And meetin' julia.*   Discovering–.   Sharon Scott.   JB

And melt the icicles from off his chin.   A Meditation on Rhode Island Coal. William Cullen Bryant.   TAP

And melt to pity the annalist's iron tongue.   Scotland, 1941.   Edwin Muir. BSV; OxBS

And melted away in the storm of everyday life.   Leda.   Mona Van Duyn. NMM

And melted away in their cries.   The Crows.   Maria Valli.   CBAP

And melted them down into a bell/too heavy to ring.   Bell Too Heavy to Ring.   Tom Kryss.   NeAC

And melts in visions of eternal day.   The Vestal.   Alexander Pope.   ACP; CAW

And memories of gold and golden dreams.   London Voluntaries.   William Ernest Henley.   BrPo

And memory falls from the mast of thought.   In Summer.   Trumbull Stickney.   NCEP

And memory for the evening gray/And solitary dove.   Three Seasons. Christina Georgina Rossetti.   HBV 1-2

And memory's fabled daughter/Is Silence in the end.   Notes for a History of Poetry.   David Daiches.   PoA

And men are free to think and act/Life is worth living still.   Is Life Worth Living?   Alfred Austin.   FaPoR; GoTF; TreFS

And men, coming and going on the earth.   Clouds.   Rupert Brooke.   BoC; BrPo; GTBS; MoVE; OBEV; OBMV; OxBTC

And men cry back to God, "There shall be peace!"   Peace.   Edwin Markham.   WBLP

And men denied the jungle of young years/Grow taut, and clench their fists. Green Lions.   Douglas Stewart.   AnNZ

And men did rosy garlands wear?   A Garden.   Andrew Marvell.   OBEV

And men moved on and gave no heed/To life or death–and this is Creede. The Rise and Fall of Creede.   Cy Warman.   BPAW; PoOW

And men not measure from what height I fell.   The Poet's Prayer.   Stephen Philipps.   WGRP

And men shall call this hampered earth/The "Garden of the Lord."   The Press.   *Anonymous.*   PaPo

(And men to the arms of their brides.)   Evening Star.   Sappho.   HW

And men will hear, or when I sing or preach.   The Preacher's Prayer. George Macdonald.   TRV

And men will say they were true lovers sweet.   Medieval Norman Songs. *Anonymous.*   AWP

And men with boots will put an end/To making similes.   Monody on a Century.   Earle Birney.   CaP

And mention the dynasties/And pass them along.   Bronzes.   Carl Sandburg. EyDe

And merged forever in the all-solvent sea.   The Iceberg.   Sir Charles G. D. Roberts.   CaP

And, merged in vapour, the half-risen moon/Leans on the trunked forests, vague and dim.   April.   John Francis O'Donnell.   IrPN

And merriest, too, believe me, Sirs!/Are your Delinquent Travellers!   The Delinquent Travellers.   Samuel Taylor Coleridge.   OBTV

And merrily passeth her time away.   Tottenham Court: Song: "What a dainty life the milkmaid leads."   Thomas Nabbes.   EG

And merrily roar out Harvest Home.   Harvest Home.   John Dryden.   PrIm

And metal snake doth magnify my name.   Madonna: 1936.   John Louis Bonn.   ISi

And mice running through through the night.   Cinderella.   Feroz Ahmed-Ud-Din.   DFT

And mice to find wrapped around their bones.   Beware the Months of Fire They Are Twelve and Contain a Year.   Patrick Lane.   NeAC

And Midas now neglected stands,/With asses' ears, and dirty hands.   The Fable of Midas.   Jonathan Swift.   APAS

And Middlesex for sin.   English Counties.   *Anonymous.*   PoL

And 'midst the Stars inscribe Belinda's Name.   The Rape of the Lock. Alexander Pope.   AtBAP; ATP; DiPo

And might bring off the tricks he used to do.   Links.   Turner Cassity.   SM

And might, odds-bob, sir! in judicious hands,/Extend from here to Mesopotamy.   The Cock and the Bull.   Charles Stuart Calverley.   ALV; BXAP; FaBoCo; FaBoNo; FaBoPa; InMe; NA; Par; VLP

And miles around they'll say that I/Am quite myself again.   Oh, when I was in love with you.   Alfred Edward Housman.   BoLiVe; BoLoP; FaBV; LiTB; LiTL; MoBrPo; NBM

And miles to go before I sleep.   Stopping by Woods on a Snowy Evening. Robert Frost.   AnNE; APA; BiP; BoNaP; CMoP; CoBMV; DiPo; ExPo; FaBoCh; FaBV; FaFP; FF; ForPo; FPL; GoJo; GoTF; GrPl; HAP; HBMV; MoAmPo; MoShBr; MoVE; MP; NePA; NIP; NoAm; NOBA; NoP; NTCP; OBCA; OxBA; PAI; PoRA; PoSC; PrIm; SCV; SiSoSe; SoSe; SUS; TAP; TiPo; TreFS; TrGrPo; TRV; TwCP; UnPo; ViBoPo; WHA

And miles up there in the desert sky/A vulture specks the blue.   Spring in the Desert.   Arthur Truman Merrill.   BPAW

And milked a lioness with your hands, to make/A round of silver-bright cheese-cake.   On the Mountains.   Alcman.   LiTW

And millions of atoms/are its children.   The Brick.   Paul Roche.   NYBP

And mimic armies have begun to form.   Farewell to Winnipeg.   Roy Daniells.   OBCV

And mind condenses on old haws. Salmon Eggs. Ted Hughes. NAs

And mind when you're in love, don't pass/Too near to patches of high grass. Springfield Mountain (D vers.). *Anonymous.* ViBoFo

And mine a shielded heart for her/Who gathers simples of the moon. Simples. James Joyce. HBMV; PoPl

And mine exceptional measures are required. News of the World. Philip Levine. AMV-81

And mine, shall make earth more complete. The Last Camp-Fire. Sharlot M. Hall. HBV 1-2

And mine the stiff and automatic hand. Seance. Francis King. PoA

And mine with longing that he might re-/main. Sinfonia Eroica. Alice Archer (Sewall) James. AA

And mingle all the world with thee. In Memoriam A.H.H., CXXIX. Alfred, Lord Tennyson. VLP

And mingle all their sweets, and salts,/That none may say, the Triumph halts. Chorus. Ben Jonson. OBS

And mingle with the Blaze of Day. A Night-Piece on Death. Thomas Parnell. CEP; NOEC; OBEC; OnYI; SeCePo

And mingled white basting thread/in their hair. A Tailor Called Sorrow. Betti Alver. BoWoP

And minister the last sad Rite,/Where altar there is none, nor priest. A Year of Sorrow. Aubrey Thomas De Vere. ACP; IrPN

And mirrored to the lord of everything that is by one and one and one. Angel and Stone. Howard Nemerov. NYBP

And mirth was bounty with a humbler name. Prologue to Hugh Kelly's "A Word to the Wise'. Samuel Johnson. EBEV

And Misery's increase/Is Mercy, Pity, Peace. I Heard an Angel Singing. William Blake. CBEP

And Miss Hocket took off like a rocket. Limerick: "A young kangaroo, Miss Hocket." *Anonymous.* TDH

And, Misthriss! no more weddin's, aw good/sakes! no, no more weddin's for me! Peggu's Wedding. Thomas Edward Brown. EnLit

And mix it deftly with/Our dancing and mortal wine. Come Out of Crete. Sappho. OBVE

And mix with Walter Clark's carnations. To the Gardener at Nuneham. Horace Walpole. FaBoEE

And mix your woodland breath with Cowper's sighs. Cowper's Three Hares. Charles Tennyson Turner. FM

And mixed with quartz grains, rose and amethyst. Sandpiper. Elizabeth Bishop. HeIP; NYBP

And mock you with me after I am gone. No Longer Mourn for Me. William Shakespeare. BoLiVe

And mocked the dead bones that lay scattered by. Methought I Saw a Thousand Fearful Wrecks. William Shakespeare. EtS

And mocks my loss of liberty. The Prince of Love. William Blake. NOBE

And Modesty who, when she goes,/Is gone for ever. Of Clementina. Walter Savage Landor. HBV 1-2; OBEV

And molder in dust away. The Children's Hour. Henry Wadsworth Longfellow. AA; AmePo; AmP; AnNE; FaBoBe; FaBV; FaFP; FPL; GoTF; HBV 1-2; HBVY; LaNeLa; OBAL; OBCA; OHFP; PoEL 1-5; PoLf; PoPl; TreF; WBLP

And Molina calls it his place of birth. The Map. Gary Soto. MAYP

And Molina's eyes are lost/Between the blue of two stars. The Point. Gary Soto. MAYP

And momma's in the bedroom/with the door closed. Hanging Fire. Audre Lorde. NIP; NoP

And Monday morn stepped in a chaise/and ran away with Captain Clackit. The Lady's Diary. Charles Dibdin. NOEC

And mony wife he made a widow,/And mony ane want their son.' Lady Maisry (B version). *Anonymous.* ESPB

And more I'd give to hold her hand,/And look into her eyes! Making Port. James T. McKay. EtS

And—more–is Nature's Roman, never to be scourged. The House-Top. Herman Melville. AP; LiTA; MAmP; NCEP; NOBA; NYP; Prf

And more, much more can be obtain'd/Upon the same condition. Enterprise and Boxer. *Anonymous.* PAH

And, more often, thunderous falls of black stars. Here Is the Abattoir Where. Michael Smith. CIP

And more than half a lackey to a lord. On a Distinguished Politician. J. E. Thorold Rogers. FaBoEE

And, more than that, the baby's hair was inclining to be red. Joe Bowers. *Anonymous.* ATP

And more things true than are told. The Ballad of Minepit Shaw. Rudyard Kipling. PoPle

And more to-day than yesterday. The Amaranth. Coventry Patmore. LoBV

And more unsleeping than angel's care. The Two Children. Emily Bronte. PoEL 1-5

And morn upon her face! Blind Louise. George Washington Dewet AA

And morning dawn'd on Benvenue. The Lady of the Lake. Sir Walter Scott. EnRP

And morning shall be cold and twilight grey. The One Certainty. Christina Georgina Rossetti. OBNC

And morning shall find us identified forever. Night Alert. Alison Boodson. NeBP

And mortified, somehow, by the crunch/Of their feet on the dirt road. The Sleepers. Peter Kocan. CBAP

And mossy scabs of the worm fence, heap'd stones, elder,/mullein and poke-weed. Song of Myself. Walt Whitman. TrCP

And most of all wherewith I strive/Is that I see myself alive. I See My Plaint. John (fl. 1550) Harington. EIL

And Mother'd like to slit your throats! The Little Ones' A.B.C. Noel Coward. NLV

And mother held up her forefinger at Mary. Baby and Mary. *Anonymous.* NA

And, Mother, here we are at last. Compline. Patrick F. Kirby. GoBC

And Mother's calling me! The World's So Big. Aileen Fisher. SoPo

And mould it into heavenly forms! The Living Temple. Oliver Wendell Holmes. AA; AmePo; AP; WGRP

And mount herself, like Him, to' Eternitie in Fire. The Extasie. Abraham Cowley. AnAnS 2; SeCP

And mountain unto mountain call, Praise/God, for we are free! The Crisis. John Greenleaf Whittier. PAH

And mounted swiftly into time. Rapunzel Song. Gerard Previn Meyer. DFT

And mounting its back,/Flew up to the moon. Old Mother Goose and the Golden Egg. *Anonymous.* OxNR

And mourn'd, till Pity's self be dead. A Song from Shakespeare's "Cymbeline". William Collins. CEP; EiCP; ForPo; LAuP; NOEC; OAEP

And mourn my wasted, would-be, bright/Heritage. Heir to Several Yesterdays. Parham J. Kelley. AMV-80

And mourn the ill thy cruel hand has done. To a Little Boy, Who Had Destroyed a Nest of Young Birds. *Anonymous.* FaBoUs

And mouths to their middles split down/with laughter!/Hu! hu! hex! Speckle-Black Toad and Freckle-Green Frog. George Darley. FM

And move my inward parts with joy. Song of Joy. Uvavnuk. WTO

And move to space beneath our sky. M., Singing. Louise Bogan. CrMA; GoJo; LiTA; NePA

And move upward to the woodland. The Poet. Yone Noguchi. WGRP

And move with morning light as with massed liberating/wings. Five for the Grace. Winfield Townley Scott. VGW

And moved again and flashed again, time flashed again. Martial Cadenza. Wallace Stevens. NePA; NIP; OxBA; VGW

And moved his brush to write a new song. Sailing Homeward. Chan Fang-sheng. AWP; FaBoCh; LoGBV

And moved the balanced stars. The Organist in Heaven. Thomas Edward Brown. LoBV; OBVV

...And moves/an inch over, to put some token air/between her back and his. An Inch of Air. Robyn Sarah. CaPN

And moves like the shadow of a bird across the stone. Rock Carving. Douglas Stewart. SeCePo

And moves the hand which moves the/world,/To bring salvation down. Prayer Moves the Hand That Moves the World. John A. Wallace. STF

And Mr. Right will come along, some day. Interview. Sara Henderson Hay. DFT; OBCA

And Mrs. Roebeck will be there. Ballade of Hell and of Mrs. Roebeck. Hilaire Belloc. MoVE

And Mrs. Sippy rolls her tides/Responsive to Miss Souri. On the American Rivers. James Smith. FaBoUs

And Mrs. Walpurga and we may wake. Mrs. Walpurga. Muriel Rukeyser. NMM

And much afraid, much afraid,/Followed Mo through the shade. Kunai-Mai-Pa Mo. Ethel Anderson. PoAu 1-2

And much commend/To after times thy wit. To the Virginian Voyage. Michael Drayton. AtBAP; CBEP; HAP; HBV 1-2; MC; NOBE; OAEP; OBEV; OBS; PAH; PoEL 1-5; SeCePo; TEP; ViBoPo

And much good love, without a feather-bed. Juvenal's Sixth Satire. John Dryden. OBSV

And multiply in ignorance. The Unsettled Motorcyclist's Vision of His Death. Thom Gunn. ForPo; NePoEA-2; PoA

And murder its odor. Antigone VI. Herbert Martin. PoBA

And murdered–in the name of the father, the son and the mother. A Mad Male-Hearted Woman in a Prouder Age. Desmond O'Grady. NoAm

And murmuring of innumerable bees. The Princess. Alfred, Lord Tennyson. AnFE; AtBAP; DiPo; FF; GTBS-P; NOBV; OAEL 1-2; OAEP; SeCeV; TreFT; TrGrPo; ViBoPo; WHA

And music must cure you, so pipe it yourself. A Familiar Letter. Oliver Wendell Holmes. FaBoUs; InMe

And must be boiling them. On the Moor of Kasuga. Hitomaro. AWP

And must be forced, and forced again, to die. Death by Drowning. Elizabeth Brewster. NOBC

And must I lose a soul's inheritance? Helas! Oscar Wilde. AnIV; BrPo; GTBS; MoBrPo; TEP; UnTE; VLP

And must its little liver all/The wondrous stuff supply? Vowel Englyn to the Spider. *Anonymous.* LiTW

And must seek elsewhere for his own. The Mirror. Dante Gabriel Rossetti. SyP

And muttered, "I'm extinct." The Great Auk's Ghost. Ralph Hodgson. MoShBr; PoPl; PoPle; PV; ShM

And my aware awaking loves/The day–until I start to care. Awaking. Stephen Spender. NYBP

And my baby the angel's seal shall keep. Where Shall the Baby's Dimple Be? Josiah Gilbert Holland. BLPA

And my blind ways in darkness be no more. Adam's Song of the Visible World. Ridgely Torrence. TrPWD

And my bony fingers write/What daylight must not see. Wie Langsam Kriechet Sie Dahin. Heinrich Heine. AWP

And my boy does not return! The Fiftieth Birthday of Agassiz. Henry Wadsworth Longfellow. ImOP

And my broken heart is calling, calling for you,/Dear old girl. Dear Old Girl. Richard Henry Buck. FSN

And my buffalo have found me. The Ballad of William Sycamore. Stephen Vincent Benét. AnAmPo; HBMV; MoAmPo; PoRA; TreFT

And my cough annoys no one. Love Letter. David Ray. TW

And my day will soon be here. Africa Speaks. Michael Dei-Anang. ACV

...And my delighted eyes/Throb as with beams intense, and splendour of the skies. Love Has Eyes. William Forster. CBAP

And my delite is causer of this stryff. Rime CXXXIV: "I fynde no peace and all my warr is done." Petrarch (Francesco Petrarca). OBVE

And my dream was scared, and expired on a/moan,/And I whitely hastened away. The Dream-Follower. Thomas Hardy. VLP

And my enemies shall there/Burst with envy and despair. Songs of the People. Chaim Nachman Bialik. AWP

And my eyelids were wet/In Lethe. Southwest Passage. Dudley Fitts. PoA

...And my eyes,/shut, will not see/gorgeous flowers any more. Desire. Isaac De Botton. VWA

And my father saying things. My Father's Song. Simon J. Ortiz. MAYP; STE

And my fause luver staw the rose,/But left the thorn wi' me. The Banks o' Doon. Robert Burns. CEP; EG; LoBV; MCCG; NOBE; NOEC; OBEC; OBEV; TrGrPo; ViBoPo; WBLP; WHA

And my fear is great that you have taken God from me! Grief of a Girl's Heart. Augusta Gregory, Lady Gregory. GBL; OLR; PBWP

And my fond heart beats time with yours and cries,/"Cuckoo! Cuckoo!" Pot and Kettle. Robert Graves. HBMV

And my friend all/Shortbread and roots. Wanting a Mummy. Sandra McPherson. AmPA; LCAP

And my friend's face transfixed/In the tearing gasp of his last breath. One Thousand Feet of Shadow. David Craig. PoSH

And my girl I will find, the one I left behind,/And I'll make her as happy as can be. The First of the Emigrants. *Anonymous.* OBSS

...And my God, who could connect/With those impossible curves? Little-League Baseball Fan. W. R. Moses. LiSp; NCSH

And my hair my hair will have disappeared Song of the Old Woman. *Anonymous.* BoWoP

And my hand still suspended/as if above a letter/I long and dread to close. Toward the Solstice. Adrienne Rich. NoP

And my hand trembles...I am Oh, so weak.... Sacco Writes to His Son. Alun Lewis. DTC

...And my hands/Twitch nervously about. Two Postures Beside a Fire. James Wright. GP; HaCAP

And my heart be fill'd wholly with their old pitiless cry. The Wanderer. Christopher John Brennan. PoAu 1-2

And my heart goes out in a song/To the poet-cavalier. Sidney Godolphin. Clinton Scollard. AA

And my heart grieves no longer. Egyptian Hieroglyphics. *Anonymous.* BoWoP

And my heart is as light as the wind that blows/The leaves from off the trees. The Big Sunflower. Bobby Newcomb. BLSo

...And my heart is the reverse of yours/sister it is growing smaller Lament. George Roberts. GOYP

And my heart, my heart is longing/To be His for evermore. Waiting for the Dawning. *Anonymous.* BLRP

And my heart, O my soldiers, my veterans,/My heart gives you love. Two Veterans. Walt Whitman. GN

And my heart's right thine inward love of heart. Sonnets, XLVI: "Mine eye and heart are at a mortal war." William Shakespeare. EyDe

And my heart's song/is an eternal Sabbath. Song of the Sabbath. (or Molodovski) Kadya, [(or Kadia) Molodovsky. PBWP; WPOW

And my heart sings its praise to the Master of all,/Who is helping me serve in the road. Crowded Ways of Life. Walter S. Gresham. BLPA

And my heart still smolders in hiding,/in ashes and in blood. I Scattered My Sighs to the Wind. Hayim Nahman Bialik. VWA

And my hopes are anchored,/Safe within the veil. Jesus Only. A.B. Simpson. BePJ

And my images roared and rose on heaven's hill. I, in My Intricate Image. Dylan Thomas. EAS; LiTB

And my joy is already/Greater than the Spring. Two Springs. Li Ch'ing-chao. BoWoP

And my kisses like bees went plundering the softness/of black hair. Black Hair. Muhammadji. LiTW

And my kisses will live like birds on your shoulder Before the sun goes down. Astrid Hjertenaes Andersen. BoWoP

And my life, pitilessly demanding,/Rises forever in the morning light. The Morning Light. Louis Simpson. NNaP; NoAm

And my life to this moment/cannot be totally explained. Untitled Poem. "In the 2 A.M. Club, a working man's bar." Robert Peterson. NeAC

And my line hooks/on underbrush. Jessy. Nora Dauenhauer. TWSS

And my love lies cold in the burning wood. Fable. Frederic Prokosch. WaP

And my Love's heart. A Song of the Four Seasons. Henry Austin Dobson. BoC; HBV 1-2

And my love was slain with Nelson upon that very day. Victory. *Anonymous.* CoMu

...And my mother who bakes the bread. Journey in the Orient. Maria Luisa Spaziani. BoWoP

And my mother will make my portion up/When I return again. Fair Annie. *Anonymous.* OxBB; ViBoFo

And my name is Death!" quoth he. The Ship. Charles MacKay. BLPA

And my name is "Tiger of God." Of Iron Am I. *Anonymous.* WTO

And my nineteen years weigh heavily on my feet. October. Patrick Kavanagh. CIP; GTBS-P

And my own portion of this common life/Is more than taper flame or slender lyre. Many Indeed Must Perish in the Keel. Hugo von Hofmannsthal. AWP; TrJP

And my plump little sisters cry/"We want a drink!" Good-by! Dumpy Ducky. Lucy Larcom. OBCA

And my poem will have no meaning. Elegy and Kaddish. D. Rosenmann-Taub. VWA

And my poor heart hath felt it,/Heigh, heigho. Whither Shall I Go. *Anonymous.* GBL

...And my reason/crawls into the silence of your eyes. Spring Your Eyes Have Their Silence. Gerald William Barrax. CNA; PoBA

And my roasted body/my skull. A Witch Going Down to Egypt. Raquel Chalfi. VWA

And my sad sighs are borne on ev'ry passing breeze. Time's Balm. Cuthbert Shaw. OBEC

And my self you solely/Sovereign shall govern.' The Saga of Gisli (excerpt). *Anonymous.* OBVE

And my shadow half the size of two dates/broke Orange Chiffon. Jayne Cortez. BlSi

And my silly old collarbone's bust. Hunter Trials. Sir John Betjeman. FiBHP; PH

And my solace wherever I go. A Pastoral Ballad in Four Parts. William Shenstone. CEP

And my son Prometheus shall rise against me/Armored, bearing my name. Lucifer. Maxwell Anderson. MoRP

And, my soul, be swift to bring/All thy sweetest and thy dearest/For the triumph of our King! There's a Light upon the Mountains. Henry K. Burton. TRV

...And my/soul just can't bear/all that weight. Ancestral Weight. Alfonsina Storni. WPOW

And my soul trembles with the stillness. Moses on Mount Nebo. Abraham Regelson. VWA

And my spear is bent on more struggle! Corruption. Patu Simoko. WhB

And my stepfather dropped dead during a/photo-finish at Santa Anita. And the Winner Is. Greg Forker. LFAC

And my suit is made of wood. Cowboy Song. Charles Causley. NePoEA

And my tears fall bitterly over the stone/That covers your golden hair–my pet. Janette's Hair. Charles Graham Halpine. HBV 1-2

And my tears for very rapture/On that wee white hand should fa'. Madchen Mit Dem Rothen Mundchen. Heinrich Heine. AWP

And my tongue, unstrung, confessed to him. When He Spoke to Me of Love. M. A. Mokhomo. PeSA

And my too heavy care. The Coffin. Heinrich Heine. AWP

And my triumphant songs shall praise/The God that rules the skies. Judge Me, O God. Joel Barlow. AH

And my unspoken perturbations, even these. The Servant in Literature. Marjorie Welish. APU

And my very heart is broken. Aurelia. Robert Nichols. OBMV

And my voice ceased talking to me. Surview. Thomas Hardy. ChMP

And my vows break/Before his look. Let the Florid Music Praise. W. H. Auden. MoPo

And my whole heart will rise.   Canzonetta: Of His Lady in Absence.   Giacomino Pugliesi.   AWP

And my whole life/a rider   Morning Once More.   Joy Harjo.   TWSS

And my wife and I travel in love   Just a Few Scenes from an Autobiography.   John Tagliabue.   FAZ

And my wild bed turns slowly among the stars.   Darkness Music.   Muriel Rukeyser.   BoWoP

And my work is for naught?   Pygmalion.   Hilda ("H. D.") Doolittle.   WGRP

And my world's mask lies empty at thy feet.   Sonnets: A Sequence on Profane Love.   George Henry Boker.   AmePo

And myself as I stand or sit pass faster than you.   Leaves of Grass.   Walt Whitman.   HAP

And myself, too, if I could find/Where it lay hidden and it proved kind.   And You, Helen.   Edward ("Edward Eastaway") Thomas.   BoLoP

And naked they convey'd/To caves the sleeping maid.   The Little Girl Lost.   William Blake.   DiPo

And naked was my pastime in between.   Five Epigrams.   J. V. Cunningham.   UnTE

And name with my imperfect breath/The mortal paradox.   My Son, My Executioner.   Donald Hall.   NePoEA

And named, while Nature to its height/Quailed, the enormous Name.   Carmen Genesis.   Francis Thompson.   CoBE

And nary soul to help him/Watch the sheep feed on the hill.   The Sheep-Herder's Lament.   Arthur Chapman.   BPAW

And nathing can catch our modern sparks,/But well tochered lasses, or jointured widows.   Lass with a Lump of Land.   Allan Ramsay.   NOEC

And Nations shall learn war no more.   The Pacific Highway.   C. R. Ballard.   PAH

And nations, strangers to His name,/Shall thus be taught to sing His praise.   The American Soldier's Hymn.   *Anonymous*.   PAH

And native with night, that land from whence they came.   Native-Born.   Eve Langley.   BoAV; PoAu 1-2

And Natur's selfe did vanish, whither no man wist.   The Faerie Queene.   Edmund Spenser.   OAEL 1-2

And, nature failing, want no arts.'   The Mistress.   Sir William D'Avenant.   JCP

And Nature has her types to show/Throughout the varying year.   Resurrection.   George Crabbe.   OxBoCh

And Nature now, so long by him surpast,/Will sure have her revenge on him at last.   Ode upon Doctor Harvey.   Abraham Cowley.   CTC; OBVE; Par; PoEL 1-5

And nature one with God, at Nazareth!   Four Friends.   Leo Ward.   GoBC

And Nature renews it all.   Verses for a First Birthday.   George Barker.   MoAB; MoBrPo

And Nature's own great God adore.   The Winged Worshippers.   Charles Sprague.   AA; HBV 1-2

And Nature's purpose in her steps explore.   Almada Hill: An Epistle from Lisbon (excerpt).   William Julius Mickle.   OBTV

And nature, shuddering, feels the horrid roar.   High O'er the Poop the Audacious Seas Aspire.   William Falconer.   EtS

And naught is heard except the frogs'/small choir in distant meads.   The Old-Fashioned Garden.   John Russell Hayes.   AA

And naught is heard, save on the wind afar/The sultry whisper of the dry-eared corn.   Autumn.   Thomas Caulfield Irwin.   IrPN

And ne'er a smock to wear.   Blow the Fire, Blacksmith.   *Anonymous*.   OxNR

...And ne'er abide/One moment's separation from thy lightning bride.   The Cloud-Messenger.   Kalidasa.   LiTW

And ne'er from us depart,/Spirit of power.   Come, Thou Almighty King.   Charles Wesley.   WGRP

And ne'er held marble in its trust/Of two such wondrous men the dust.   Marmion.   Sir Walter Scott.   BSV; FaBoPP; OBRV

And ne'er the first assault to proffer.   Of Scolding Wives and the Third Day Ague.   Henricus Selyns.   SCAP

And ne'er this story tell,/But keep it to yourself.   Barber, Spare Those Hairs.   John, Jr. Love.   YaD

And ne'er was Anna Grace seen again.   The Fairy Thorn.   Sir Samuel Ferguson.   AnIV; OnMSP; OnYI; VLP

And ne'er was bribed by gold.   The Duke of Marlborough.   *Anonymous*.   OBET

And ne'er was such a burial/Sin Adam's days begun.   Sir Hugh; or, The Jew's Daughter (A vers.).   *Anonymous*.   BaBo; ESPB; FaBoBa; ViBoFo

And ne'er will tempt those seas again.   To Pyrrha.   Horace.   EnLi 1-2

And ne're did Heav'n so much a Voyage bless,/If thou canst Plant but there with like success.   To Sir William Davenant.   Abraham Cowley.   SeCV 1-2

And near his cabin, where the sound/No more was heard of lowing, died.   Aristeides.   Antipater of Sidon.   AWP

And nearby–/the real collison.   What Are We Playing At?   Andree Chedid.   BoWoP

And necklaces of laughter hung around our days/Days sparkling with new joys.   Your Presence.   David Diop.   PBA

And need not grieve alone for the boat-people.   An Apology for a Lost Classicism.   John Ciardi.   AMV-81

And neighbors toiling up the terraced land.   La Madonna di Lorenzetti.   John Williams Andrews.   HBMV

...And neighbouring thickets/ring/With jubilate from the choirs of spring!   A Place of Burial in the South of Scotland.   William Wordsworth.   VLP

And neither awful Voice be heard by thee!   Thought of a Briton on the Subjugation of Switzerland.   William Wordsworth.   BoLiVe; MBW 1-2; SeCeV; SpRo

And neither do nor say to men/Whate'er you would not take again.   Our Saviour's Golden Rule.   Isaac Watts.   OxBChV

And neither earth nor sea nor sky shall rob me then of him.   A Man's Woman.   Mary Carolyn Davies.   PoLf

And neither is young/And neither is old.   The Pulse.   Mark Van Doren.   MoAmPo; PoPl

And neither of them ever/said what they meant/and i guess nobody ever does   Legacies.   Nikki Giovanni.   CTBA

And neither one will stay.   Fair Annet's Song.   Elinor Wylie.   AmLP

And neither rains nor twilights blur the winds.   Epos.   Harold Rosenberg.   PoA

And neither stone nor steel can foil/That ambuscade of midnight flowers.   To Some Builders of Cities.   Stanley Snaith.   HaMV

And neither suspected a mutual love/Till they met in a Brunswick stew.   The Tryst.   John Banister Tabb.   OBAL

And neither wish nor fear to die.   True Happiness.   Morris Talpalar.   PoToHe

And neon death at the end of the Avenue.   Three Star Final.   Conrad Aiken.   OxBA

And Neptune, glad and fain,/Yields up to her his reign.   Her Rambling.   Thomas Lodge.   LoBV; OBSC

And nervous deer/in the grey sea.   Epigram: "Boy-mad no longer."   Rufinus Domesticus.   PeHV

And netherwards for partner draws her shade.   Light at Equinox.   Léonie Adams.   CrMA

And nets to catch the whispers/of the stars.   At the Jewish Museum.   Olga Cabral.   PoDr

And neutral voices, seen and never heard.   Mastrim: A Meditation (excerpt).   Hugh Maxton.   CIP

And never a corner for serpent sin.   Penetration and Trust.   George Meredith.   VLP

And never a dawning day will break as pure/As our grave adoration, immature.   The Grotto.   Francis Scarfe.   NeBP; PoA

And never a house between.   Strand on the Green.   *Anonymous*.   GBP

And never a person lived to tell/If ever Zachary died.   Zachary Zed.   James Reeves.   QQQ

And never a road can reach him/Who lies so far from home.   Threnody.   Ruth Guthrie Harding.   HBV 1-2

And never a tree but he lights there.   Riddle: "A white bird featherless floats down through the air."   *Anonymous*.   GBP

And never again can come, like a man slapped,/news like this.   His Toy, His Dream, His Rest.   John Berryman.   FaBoMo; NOBA

And never again in a pool of black water/Have I seen the blue eyes of the King o' Spain's daughter.   The King o' Spain's Daughter.   Jeanne Robert Foster.   HBMV

And never be put on again.   The Land of Beginning Again.   Louisa Fletcher.   BLPA

And never be we mute.   The Old Wife's Tale.   George Peele.   OBSC

And never begs anyone's pardon.   Limerick: "A strong-minded lady of Arden."   Morris Bishop.   TDH

And never came back 'till the Fourth of July.   I Asked My Mother for Fifteen Cents.   Mother Goose.   FaFP; MoShBr; TiPo

And never crush the darn thing flat/you skeptic.   Archys Autobiography.   Don (Donald Robert Marquis) Marquis.   CrMA

And never dreamed the river flowed away.   By the Beautiful Ohio.   Joan LaBombard.   SM

And never feel tired a bit.   The Mermaidens.   Laura E. Richards.   BrR; OBCA

And never forgotten," sang the Cumberland's crew.   The Cumberland's Crew.   *Anonymous*.   AmFP; ShS

And never give a thought to night.   Two doves upon the selfsame branch.   Christina Georgina Rossetti.   EG

And never going fast enough.   Morning Rush.   Constance Clark.   AmC

And never got out alive.   North Clark Street.   Raymond Thompson.   LFAC

And never hear each other's truth.   After the Murder of Jimmy Walsh.   Joan Murray.   LTB

And never know the Joy.   Song: Phillis be Gentler.   John Wilmot, Earl of Rochester.   CavP

And never knowing when you'll provoke an earthquake.   Volcanic Venus.   D. H. Lawrence.   InPS; PAI; PoL

And never leave till they have read men dead.   The Art of Poetry.   Horace.
EnLi 1-2

And never looked behind him.   The Man with Nought.   *Anonymous.*
OxNR

And never more say "Woe is me!"   Wit, Whither Wilt Thou?   *Anonymous.*
ElL

And never more we'll go and roam,/Way down in Mexico.   Way Down in
Mexico.   *Anonymous.*   CoSo

And never, never, any greater thing.   I Hold Him Happiest.   Menander
TreFT

And never, never play again/At truant from the school.   Clever Peter and the
Ogress.   Katharine Pyle.   OBCA

And never, never sulk at all.   The World's Music.   (Thomas Nicoll
Hepburn) "Setoun. Gabriel"   FaBoBe; HBV 1-2; HBVY

And never noticed till I got wet through.   On a Wet Day.   Franco Sacchetti.
AWP; BoNaP

And never once thinks of being Daddy to me.   Newspaper.   Aileen Fisher.
SoPo

And never remember/to fill his pen/again   Pen Hy Cane.   Mason Jordan
Mason.   PoNe

And never say I didn't warn you.   The Last Frontier.   John Thomas.   GP

And never scent the ground where they will lie.   Simple Autumnal.   Louise
Bogan.   MoAB; MoAmPo; QFR

And never see it, believing the form were there.   What Form the World Has.
William Bronk.   AMV-80

And never see the chasms at your feet.   Epithalamium.   Roy McFadden.
NeIP

And never shall I find the light/Of days forever flown!   Voice of the Western
Wind.   Edmund Clarence Stedman.   HBV 1-2

And never shall ill befall you!   The Sweetest Home.   *Anonymous.*   STF

...And never shall my harp thy praise/Forget, nor from thy Father's praise
disjoin.   Paradise Lost.   John Milton.   ILwL

And never shall the Bridegroom return to his Bride,/From that dark and cruel
Day,–cruel Day!   The Lamentable Ballad of the Bloody Brook.   Edward
Everett Hale.   HBV 1-2; PAH

And never since then has this Bishop been quiet.   Colenso Rhymes for
Orthodox Children.   Bret (Francis Bret Harte) Harte.   OBAL

And never since then, in the memory of men,/Has the Old Bay State seen such
a hunting again.   New England's Chevy Chase, April 19, 1775.   Edward
Everett Hale.   HBV 1-2; HBVY; PAH; PAL; YaD

And never slight a soldier because he's so poor.   Lady Flower.   *Anonymous.*
BFSS

And never spoke a word.   Camp.   Patrick Anderson.   OBCV

And never staine a cheeke for it.   Epigrams.   Martial (Marcus Valerius
Martialis).   OBVE

And never stop your joyful song/To everlasting days.   Dear Happy Souls.
Eunice Smith.   AH

And never suffer more!   Oh, for the Time When I Shall Sleep.   Emily
Bronte.   ATP

And never tell my age at all.   Pretending.   Myra Cohn Livingston.   BiCB

And never telling yourself/a lie.   Definitions.   Joseph Joel Keith.   PoToHe

And never the burning heart within you/Stirs in your sleep by the roving tide.
Marian Drury.   Bliss Carman.   HBV 1-2

And never think anything/But a white thought!   Le Medecin Malgre Lui.
William Carlos Williams.   PoA; SaC

And never to change you for no new.   Sometime I sigh, sometime I sing.
Sir Thomas Wyatt.   FCP; SiPS

And never wake to feel the day's disdain.   Care-Charmer, Sleep.   Samuel
Daniel.   ForPo; InPS; LiTB; LoBV; OAEL 1-2

And never was piping so gay.   The Host of the Air.   William Butler Yeats.
BrPo; CH; OnYI; SeCeV

And never went there again.   Doctor Foster.   *Anonymous.*   OxBoLi; OxNR

And never went to sleep again in case–   The Sluggard.   Lucilius [(or
Lucillius)].   SD

"And nevertheless we had the choice to take them!..."   Conquistador.
Archibald MacLeish.   AtBAP

And new bottled babies with real teeth/devour our fantastic/fictioned future
Frightened.   Lawrence Ferlinghetti.   NoAm; TAP

And new pervert a reconciled Maide.   A Lover's Complaint.   William
Shakespeare.   NCEP

And New Year blowing and roaring.   I Stood on a Tower in the Wet.
Alfred, Lord Tennyson.   OBSP

And New Zealand went mourning all the way!   The Burial of Sir John
McKenzie.   Jessie MacKay.   AnNZ

And next morn pored in Plato for more.   A Night-Piece; or, Modern
Philosophy.   Christopher Smart.   NOEC

And next my wife, and then I fall/Down on my knees and love the hoss.
The Kentucky Thoroughbred.   James Whitcomb Riley.   ELU

And next, the cow.   Ecological Lecture.   Burton Raffel.   AMV-81

And Niamh calling Away, come away.   The Hosting of the Sidhe.   William
Butler Yeats.   NoAm

And Nicodemus' mystery/Receives its annual reply.   An altered look about
the hills.   Emily Dickinson.   OxBA; PPP

And nigh insentient root, green from the rigid ground!   Thaw.   Jean Starr
Untermeyer.   AtBAP

And night and day, since Thou dost rise, are one.   Good Friday in My Heart.
Mary Elizabeth Coleridge.   PGD

And night approaches with her shades.   Composed Upon an Evening of
Extraordinary Splendour and Beauty.   William Wordsworth.   EnRP;
OAEL 1-2

And night at the gates where a soul would/go.   Iter Supremum.   Arthur
Sherburne Hardy.   AA

And night comes round the corner after you...   Bleecker Street.   Jean
Garrigue.   NYP; TAP

And night descends upon the desolate plain.   The Burial in Flanders.   R.
Nichols.   PeHV

And night doth nightly make grief's strength seem/stronger.   Sonnets,
XXVIII: "How can I then return in happy plight."   William Shakespeare.
OBSC

And night had settled on lake and plain/When we returned to our camp again.
The Legend of Grand Lake.   Joseph L. Westcott.   PoOW

And night is a dark tower.   Early Supper.   Barbara Howes.   DuDa; GoJo;
GrPl; NCSH; PoPl; SM

And night is freezing.   Lines for the Margin of an Old Gospel.   Sheila
Wingfield.   ChMP

And night's trees stood up   Pictures of a Gone World.   Lawrence
Ferlinghetti.   PoM

And Night shall fold him in soft wings.   Into Battle.   Julian Grenfell.
FaPoR; HBV 1-2; LoBV; MMM; OBEV; OBMV; OBWP; OxBTC; WaaP

And Night, the Negro, murmurs in his sleep.   Rounding the Cape.   Roy
Campbell.   PeSA

...And night was on the ridge/Of twilight, as the party crossed the bridge.
Don Juan.   George Gordon, Lord Byron.   PAI

And nights tumble/in a dryer.   The Field's Retention.   Jose Y., Jr. Teran.
LFAC

And nites that/multiply by twos.   –Answer to Yo/Question of Am I Not Yo/
Woman...   Sonia Sanchez.   BPo

And no accounting will open them up.   Forgiving My Father.   Lucille
Clifton.   GeTw

And no birds sing.   La Belle Dame Sans Merci.   John Keats.   AtBAP;
ATP; AWP; BeLS; BLPA; DTo; ELP; ERoP 1-2; ExPo; FaBoBe; FaBoCh;
FaFP; FiP; FPL; GoTF; GTBS; HAP; HBV 1-2; InPK; InPo; InPS; InvP;
LiTB; LoBV; LoGBV; MaC; MBW 1-2; MCCG; MyFE; NAWM 1-2; NIP;
NOBE; NoP; OAEL 1-2; OAEP; OBEV; OBNC; OBRV; OLR; PAI; PG;
PoEL 1-5; PoPle; PoRA; PPoe; Prf; PrIm; SCV; SeCeV; SoSe; StPo; TEP;
TreFT; TrGrPo; UnPo; ViBoPo; WeW; WHA; WSC

And no bread in his pocket.   The Brother.   Peter Everwine.   FYAP; NNaP

And no door anywhere.   A Door.   William Stanley Merwin.   LCAP

And no door at all, at all.   Riddle: "A long white barn."   *Anonymous.*
GBP

And no forbidding fence in sight!   My Little Lodge.   *Anonymous.*   OnYI

And no gentler than these.'   Confessions.   Elizabeth Barrett Browning.
OBVV

And no good thing will he from them withhold.   After Reading the Life of
Mrs Catherine Stubbs...   Isaac Hann.   NOCV

And no good thing withheld from me/As I walked in His own way.   His
Presence.   Dale Schulz.   STF

And no man/Lives, but to whom God gives bountiful measure of ill.   Elegiac.
Mimnermus.   LiTW

And no man sails to Babylon.   A Ballad of London.   Richard Le Gallienne.
HBMV

And no matter what we do, we'll never see one again.   Train Blues.   Paul
Zimmer.   PPJ

And no monarch alive has so many pages.   A Book.   Hannah More.   PoSC

And no more I'll go a-rovering beyond the harbor bar.   In Foreign Parts.
Laura E. Richards.   HBV 1-2; HBVY

And no more I toddle about the tree.   Alison Gross.   *Anonymous.*   BuBa;
WSC

And no need of teeth.   Making an Impression.   William Jackson.   AMV-80

And no new graves will be dug here.   Old Jewish Cemetery in Worms.
Alfred Kittner.   VWA

...And no one/around us to cry   Leave It to Me Blues.   Joel Oppenheimer.
CoPo; VGW

And no one but the baby cried for poor Lorraine, Loree.   Lorraine Loree.
Charles Kingsley.   BBV

And no one can foretell which side will win.   Mortal Combat.   Alice Fay Di
Castagnola.   GoYe

And no one dared ever betray me.   Hengest Cyning.   Jorge Luis Borges.
NYBP

And no one else/As far as I know to verify.   A Wall.   Charles Simic.
HaCAP

...And no one/else had ever/seen a mocking/bird before   Going through.
Bruce P. Woodford.   MAT

...And/no one I've ever loved has died,/exactly. Horse Chestnut. Gary Miranda. SM

...And no one/Knew where the soft-footed thief had vanished. Riddle #29: The Moon and the Sun. *Anonymous.* GoJo

And no one knows/how much I would like/to fall. A Circus Dancer. Celia Dropkin. VWA

And no one knows what is true/Who knows not what is false. Seth Compton. Edgar Lee Masters. LiTA

And no one/leaves the round table. The Round Table. Peggy Susberry Kenner. JB

And no one living looks quite human. Andre Chenier. Marina Tsvetayeva. FaBoPV

And no one noticed. Playing Pocahontas. Lew Blockcolski. VoR

And no one shall put salt on their bright tails. The Sea Birds. Van K. Brock. NYBP; SM

And no one think it worth his while/To take up to defend thee. Farewell to England. *Anonymous.* APAS

And no-one to answer the bell. The Dolgelley Hotel. Thomas Hughes. FaBoCo

And no one to believe/that heaven was really here. Heaven. Philip Levine. LCAP; NaP

And no one walks the piazza. Piazzas. Barbara Guest. NeAP

And no one will worry a bit. Does It Matter? Siegfried Sassoon. MoBrPo; PPON; WaP

And no one would complain about the parts of me that show. Soap, the Oppressor. Burges Johnson. PoLf

And no other sunshine than her beauty. Ophra. Judah Halevi. LiTW; TrJP

And no progeny to revenge their fallen manhood. Murder of a Community. Daniel Weissbort. VWA

And no remedy near till our lions come over the sea. Brightness Most Bright I Beheld on the Way, Forlorn. Aogan O Rathaille. NOBI

And no risen Redeemer/Had waited for her. Not There. *Anonymous.* STF

And no room at all for a Cherry Tyme box/with letters from a face he can't remember. Fish. Michael Hogan. GP

And no soul attains who fears. Attainment. Madison Cawein. WGRP

And no sweet chariot swung, to carry him home. Death on a Crossing. Evangeline Paterson. EBCP

...And no tree stands/ever, forever—moving, lifeless, alone. The Postures of Love. Alex Comfort. NeBP

And no turning sideways now. Beside the Road. Ken Belford. NeAC

And no voice calls, "Come in." The Child. Frank Ormsby. AMV-81

And no walls could hold him! Because. Paul Johnson. AMV-81

And no way that I chose to go/Could lead me from the grief of snow. The Snow. Clifford Dyment. MoVE

And nobler cares than listless summer knew. Sonnet: September, 1815. William Wordsworth. ChRP

And nobler for the fading of those eyes/The world seen once for all. Come Let Us Make Love Deathless. Herbert Trench. EG; HBMV; OBVV

And nobody ask me why. His Majesty. Theron Brown. AA

And nobody buys. No Buyers. Thomas Hardy. LiTB; NoP

And nobody has to think too much/About Desolation Row. Desolation Row. Bob Dylan. PAI

And nobody knew where Kilmeny had been. Kilmeny. Alfred Noyes. EnLit

And nobody knows what there befell her. Lines Scratched in Wet Cement. Ethel Jacobson. ShM

And Nobody Never was there–Nomore. The Space Childs' Mother Goose. Frederick Winsor. QQQ

And nobody, nobody knows. The Marrog. R. C. Scriven. AmMo

And nobody pulls up there. Nobody Comes. Thomas Hardy. BiP; MoVE

And nobody there to help him. The Priest of Felton. *Anonymous.* OxNR

And nobody understands Ein. Limerick: "There's a notable family named Stein." *Anonymous.* NOBL

And nobody will buy. I paints and paints. Shirley Brooks. CenHV

And nobody would commit suicide, only/To find beyond death/Bridgeport, Ohio. In Response to a Rumor That the Oldest Whorehouse... James Wright. CAPP; CoAP; NNaP; TW

And nods us/back in thru/those open doors. Elevator Landscapes. Stephen Vincent. NeAC

And noiselessly the golden curtains crash together! Midnight Show. Karl Shapiro. OxBA

And none among you shall undo her. The Metaphysical Amorist. J. V. Cunningham. VGW

And none but thou shalt be my paramour! Doctor Faustus. Christopher Marlowe. BLPL; TrGrPo; WHA

And none can comprehend/What dissolution means. To Giotto. Wesley Trimpi. NePoEA

And none else/At all. Shadow Dance. Ivy O. Eastwick. SoPo; TiPo

And none has fathomed their intent. Lavish Kindness. Elinor Wylie. AtBAP; CrMA

And none has quite escaped my smile. Let No Charitable Hope. Elinor Wylie. AnAmPo; HBMV; LiTA; LiTM; MoAB; MoAmPo; NePA; OBSP; OxBA; PBWP; SBG; TrGrPo; VGW

And none is false, and none is wholly true. American Muse. Stephen Vincent Benét. PAL

And none of us knows what can stop/the blood Breaking Off from Waiting. Clarisse Nicoidski. VWA

And none remain'd to give the rest. The Cornelian. George Gordon, Lord Byron. PeHV

And none shall know but the winds that blow/The graves wherein we lie. A Jacobite's Exile. Algernon Charles Swinburne. OBVV

And none shall spare to mock thee in/thy fall. The Torch-Bearers: America. Arlo Bates. AA; PGD

And none shall speak his name. Poet. Karl Shapiro. AnFE; CMoP; LiTM; MoAB; MoAmPo; NoAm

And none shall wear it evermore. On a Fair Woman. Francis Burdett Money-Coutts. OBVV

And none should other's worthy effort spoil. Love is Kind. Benjamin Keech. PoToHe

...And none that hath/gone may come again. Song of the Harper. *Anonymous.* LiTW

And none, till the judgment trump and shout,/Shall drive her out of the last redoubt. The Last Redoubt. Alfred Austin. HBV 1-2

And nor knows nor cares for Beeny, and will laugh there never-more. Beeny Cliff. Thomas Hardy. OBNC

And, nose to the ground, sink his teeth in a lagging hock. Tom Farley. Colin Thiele. NOAV; PoAu 1-2

And not a child but keeps some trace/Of Christmas secrets in his face. For Christmas. Rachel Field. ChBR

And not a one said sour things/to anybody any more. Mumps. Elizabeth Madox Roberts. SoPo

And not a single regret. Fiddler Jones. Edgar Lee Masters. AmP; CMoP; HBV 1-2; LiTA; LoGBV; NoAm; OxBA; TAP; TrGrPo; UnS

And not a single star chime out of tune. To Lovers of Earth: Fair Warning. Countee Cullen. CDC

And not a single thing my eyes behold/But speaks the word of Death's impending fate. Death Warnings. Francisco Gomez de Quevedo y Villegas. CAW

...And not a sound/came from the savage carpet. When the Five Prominent Poets. Josephine Jacobsen. TAP

And not a trace was left in me/of that splendid courage. The Wicked Neighbor. Zelda Shneurson. WPOW

And not a twig and not a thought/Remember where they used to be. As Night Comes On. Cecil Cobb Wesley. GoYe

And not a wave of trouble roll/Across my peaceful breast. Ninety-Fifth. *Anonymous.* AmFP

And not a wave shall trouble thee. The Faithful Shepherdess. John Fletcher. OBS

And not Alcmena's chesty son/Have room to put your ribands on! To a Boon Companion. Oliver St. John Gogarty. OBMV

And, not arriving, dream in no resentment. The Climbers. Elizabeth Jennings. NePoEA

And, not at my request, extorted from the sea. Such is Holland! Petrus Augustus de Genestet. PoL

And not be afraid. To Turn Back. John Haines. BoNaP; ConAP

And not be any better than his mother feared. Mothers and Children. Orrick Johns. AnAmPo; HBMV

...And not be/merely faint and sleepy/As they are now. Slow Movement. William Carlos Williams. PoA

And not bloody your body or the tiles. The Weight Room. Thomas Rabbit. MAYP

And not criticize as some have done/Hitherto herebefore. And Now, Kind Friends, What I Have Wrote. Julia A. Moore. FaBoCo; FiBHP

And not even a cop car goes by... Fist Fight. Doug Cockrell. Psk

And not fall. The Fundament Is Shifted. Abbie Huston Evans. MoRP; NYBP

And not far off was the churchyard gate. Both Less and More. Richard Watson Dixon. LoBV

And not fear death; it is the only way to be cleansed. Original Sin. Robinson Jeffers. MoAB; MoAmPo; MoVE

And not frighten my young son? Evening Meal in the Twentieth Century. John Holmes. MiAP

And not from your friends only/But first from yourselves! Prepare. Witter ("Emanuel Morgan") Bynner. PGD

And not Heaven itself were fairer than a world as glad as this. Give to the Living. Ida Goldsmith Morris. WBLP

And not hooked by Captain Hook but by/that ponce, Peter Pan! All the rest is fiction. Pantomime Diseases. Dannie Abse. DFT

And not in those roped arms. Masked Woman's Song. Louise Bogan. NMM

And not kill you. Try Tropic. Genevieve Taggard. MoAmPo

And not lie dead in Germany. The Heart to Carry On. Bertram Warr. PeCV

And not long dry. Mackerel Sky. *Anonymous.* OxNR

And not mis-treat the desperate. Dedication for a Building. Alan Dugan. CAD; NYP

And not one shadow moves. Midwinter Stars. Roberta Hill Whiteman. STE

"And not," said the room, "go out any more." Green Candles. Humbert Wolfe. HBMV; MoBrPo; SO

And not scream in the night–/(I trust. I trust.) A Fairy Tale. Kenneth Mackenzie. PoAu 1-2

And not she me, but I had murdered her. Ever Present. Philip Ayres. OBSP

And not so witty as you were? My Little Soul, My Vagrant Charmer. Emperor (Publius Aelius Hadrianus) Hadrian. OBVE

And not the calm or the strife. The Winds of Fate. Ella Wheeler Wilcox. BLPA; FPL; TRV; WBLP

And not the jungle green/Pasture unfolding before us can deny it. Song of Napalm. Bruce Weigl. MAYP

And not till after feast. For Christmas Day. Eleanor Farjeon. ChBR

And not to flete from feare to feare,/Such anker hold I have. The Lover Disceived by His Love Repenteth Him of the True Love ... *Anonymous.* EnPo

And not to me? Faith Trembling. Mary Ainge De Vere. AA

And not to think of it any more. The Amputation. Helen Sorrells. DFF

And not turn away. A Place to Live. Martin Grossman. AMV-80

And not within a living heart. Dead Love. Mary Mathews Adams. AA

And note how strangely you had to act. Long Term Suffering. Richard Eberhart. GLGT; GP

And nothing at all to carry home to my own dearest wife. The Jolly Shilling. *Anonymous.* OBET

And nothing but his vanity, sincere. On a Certain Poet. *Anonymous.* FaBoEE

And nothing but opened morning-glories. Getting Through. Robert P.T. Coffin. AnNE

And nothing but space is between us! Limerick: "The ladies inhabiting Venus." Al Graham. QQQ

And nothing but the willow/Remained there to be seen. A Song: "My head on moss reclining." *Anonymous.* NOEC

And nothing can take them from us or change them/Unless it is death. Not Wholly Lost. Raymond Souster. OBCV

And nothing comes between the sons of Adam and God. Let Us Learn. Melech, Ravitch. VWA

And nothing ever really at dead rest. The Road of Birds. Harry Humes. AMV-80

And nothing has changed except what brought us here. Last Visit. Robert Finch. NOBC

And nothing is as I would wish it to be. The Housewife's Lament. *Anonymous.* FSW

And nothing is too small/To thus accomplish all. A Song in Humility. Carleton Drewry. MoRP

And nothing matters in the end. After the Battle (1930). George Sylvester Viereck. GoYe

And nothing of our heart to earth returned. We Needs Must Be Divided. George Santayana. ViBoPo

And nothing permanent on earth. Nox Nocti Indicat Scientiam. William Habington. ACP; AnAnS 2; CAW; GoBC; GTBS; HBV 1-2; JCP; LoBV; MeLP; MePo; NOBE; OBEV; OBS

And nothing really matters, except to you. Poem for You. Robert Pack. NePoEA

...And nothing's/like it used to be, not even the future. O. Rita Dove. HaCAP; MAYP

And nothing stood firm/Until day again. The Story-Teller. Mark Van Doren. CTBA; LOW

And nothing tempers hard as grief,/worse, I think, than any famine. A Famished End to My Tale This Night. Maghnas O Domhnaill. NOBI

And nothing that need trouble you. The Silent Pool. Harold Monro. BrPo

And nothing to do but to pocket my gold! The Laureate (parody). William Aytoun. BXAP; Par

And nothing to say or do? Gloucester Moors. William Vaughn Moody. AP; HBV 1-2; NOBA; OxBA; TreFT; WGRP; WHA

And nothing touches the hand. Three Poems. Yakamochi. LiTW

And nothing will heal/Under the rain's broken fingers. The Elements of San Joaquin. Gary Soto. NPGG

And noting, ere they fade away,/The little lines of yesterday. Inscription on a Grot. Samuel Rogers. OBEC

And nought is all, as am I, but a dream of/thee. A Nympholept. Algernon Charles Swinburne. VLP

And nought when old enjoy'd, denied the power. Riches. *Anonymous.* AWP

And nourisheth his sacred flame/From whence no blazing sparks do fly. When Youth Had Fled. Henry Howard, Earl of Surrey. EnRePo; SiPS

And nourishing the long thoughts in my soul.... Autumn. Alexander Pushkin. AnEnPo; AWP

And now a barefoot truant and his dog. The Creek-Road. Madison Cawein. AA

And now again, her own black hair puts on/To mourn for thoughts by her worths overthrown. Caelica, LVIII. Fulke, Lord Brooke Greville. FCP

And now again the people/Call it but a weed. The Flower. Alfred, Lord Tennyson. HBV 1-2

And now again–though celestiality maroons you–as/a heron opens rising from a snag. Michael. Sandra McPherson. LCAP

And now, alas, what voice shall wake her! Wood Flower. Richard Le Gallienne. HBMV

And now an amethyst remembrance/Is all I own. I held a jewel in my fingers. Emily Dickinson. WHA

And now at last do wish thee well, and bid farewell again. To Parker. George Turberville. OBTV

And now at nearer view, no other certain/Than Dalila thy wife. Samson Agonistes. John Milton. OBS

And now begin to weep, when they have done. On the Death of Sir Philip Sidney. Henry Constable. GoBC; OBEV

And now dead, thou dost enjoy/In high heaven an angel's place. Three Epitaphs. Francis Davison. OBSC

And now, dear Lord, I cannot wait/Because I have a luncheon date. In Westminster Abbey. Sir John Betjeman. CMoP; DBV; FaBoCo; InPK; NIP; NLV; NOBL; OAEL 1-2; OBSV

"And now, fair maid, I will marry with thee." The Riddling Knight. *Anonymous.* PoEL 1-5

And now farewell, my heavenly friend. To the Archdeacon. George Farewell. NOEC

And now, good men, I pray you merry be. The Canterbury Tales: The Merchant's Tale. Geoffrey Chaucer. PCat; UnTE

And now, good sir, your horse is/shod. Robert Barnes, Fellow Fine. *Anonymous.* OxNR

And now hath made me to his hand so right/That in the manage myself take delight. Astrophel and Stella, XLIX. Sir Philip Sidney. AAS; SiPS

And now he can't button his pants. Limerick: "A cannibal bold of Penzance." *Anonymous.* LiBL

And now he could only/bar himself in and wait/for the great flint to come singing into his heart Bushed. Earle Birney. NOBC; NoP; OBCV; PeCV

And now he'll spot the withered link, and strike. The Son, Condemned. Larry Rubin. GP

And now he's a lazy old, sleepy old cat,/Timothy Tim! Tiger-Cat Tim. Edith Newlin Chase. SoPo; TiPo

And now he's bones himself. Jerry Jones. *Anonymous.* ShM

And now he's dead,/And we ain't none the sadder. Billy the Kid. *Anonymous.* CoSo

And now he's gotten a bonny young son,/And mickle grace be him upon. Willie's Lady. *Anonymous.* BaBo; ESPB; ViBoFo

And now he's mining in the promised land. Casey Jones. *Anonymous.* AmFP

And now he's sorely puzzled that no child has ever read it. Puzzled. Carolyn Wells. OBCA

And now her lap is full of trees. The Birthplace. Robert Frost. EyDe; LoGBV; OFD

And now her los biginneth to swage,/That selde y-seye is soone foryete. On the Death of Edward III. *Anonymous.* OxBM

And now his Blessing is, he can't be Curst. Against Marriage. *Anonymous.* DBV

And now his familia no esta. A Filipino Hombre (with music). *Anonymous.* AS

And now I am the wife of Hynde Etin,/Wha neer got christendame.' Hind Etin (B version). *Anonymous.* ESPB

And now I care for neither. The Divided Heart. George Wither. TrGrPo

And now...I dare not live. White Violet. Marian Osborne. CaP

And now I do not greatly care/To shoot more rockets in the air. Enough. Tom (Thomas Lansing Masson) Masson. OBAL

And now, I doubt not, the Eternal Dove/A black-fac'd house will have. On the Baptized Aethiopian. Richard Crashaw. FaBoEE; NoP; SeCV 1-2

And "Now I lay me down to sleep!" In the Firelight. Eugene Field. AA

And–now I laymen down ee beep. The Daughter at Evening. Robert Nathan. HBMV

And now I leave it to them that lust. Since so ye please to hear me plain. Sir Thomas Wyatt. FCP; SiPS

And now I live, and now my life is done. Retrospect. Chidiock Tichborne [(or Tichbourne)]. ACP; GoBC

And now I'm engaged to Miss Joan Hunter Dunn. A Subaltern's Love-Song. Sir John Betjeman. BoLoP; HAP; LiSp; MP; NOBL; OxBTC; TwCP

And now/I'm going/to say/goodbye. I Resigned Myself to Being Here. John Giorno. APU

And now I seek through the sere summer/Where no trees are shady. Daphne. Edith Sitwell. HBMV

And now I've got/A mother-in-law/From sipping ci-/Der through a straw. Sipping Cider through a Straw. *Anonymous.* FSW

And now instead of him watching TV/We all sit around watching him. Jimmy Jet and His TV Set. Shel Silverstein. CTBA; OBCA

And now is come to that same place, where first she weft. The Faerie Queene. Edmund Spenser. OBSC

And now is making nutmegs at/Moosehicmagunticook. The American Traveller. Robert Henry Newell. FaBoCo; OBAL

And now it hisses among the green rings/On fingers in coffins. Ohioan Pastoral. James Wright. LCAP

–And now it's gone! Taking Off. *Anonymous.* SoPo; TiPo

And now it's time to say goodbye,/For the old pierhead's a-drawing nigh. Leave Her, Johnny. *Anonymous.* FSW; OBSS

And now leave me to my despair. Hear Me Yet. *Anonymous.* EIL

And now let naught in memory live/But that we meet, and that we love. Meeting. George Crabbe. HBV 1-2; OBEV

And now lies down, who was my moon or more. Complaint. James Wright. NOBA; TAP; VGW

And now, like a posy, a pretty one plump in his hands. Catch. Robert Francis. HeIP; InPK; LiSp; NCSH; PP

And now like a rogue in the wide world I dwell. Insect Riddle: "I was round and small like a pearl." *Anonymous.* GBP

–And now make I ending. The Short Lay of Sigurd. *Anonymous.* EnLi 1-2

And now my heart in quiet lives,/Made murmurous with sedatives. I Wandered Angry as a Cloud (parody). Paul Dehn. SpRo

And now my story is done. I'll Tell You a Story. Mother Goose. HBV 1-2

And now my Vowes have at thy Altar paid. Deo Opt. Max. George Sandys. OBS

And now no more my trust in Him/I show. Elegy. Immanuel Di Roma. TrJP

And now of a Bloody Mary! Gold. Thomas Hood. WBLP

And now–once more to die.' The Mystic Magi. Robert Stephen Hawker. OBCP

And now one reads above his head/The words: "Completely covered." Epitaph: "Insured for every accident." Richard Armour. ShM

And now our orgies let's begin. The Witches' Song. Ben Jonson. CH

And now, our West, good-by. The Old Scout's Lament. *Anonymous.* CoSo

And now poor Simple Simon/Bids you all adieu. Simple Simon and the Pieman. *Anonymous.* OxNR; PoPl

And now, poor souls, they know not what to do. The Frowardness of the Elect in the Work of Conversion. Edward Taylor. SCAP

And now Propertius of Cynthia, taking his stand among/these. Homage to Sextus Propertius: XII. Ezra Pound. FaBoMo; OxBA

...And now returned/to remain in this poetry. To Remain. Constantine P. Cavafy. BoLoP; ErPo

And now secure in jail they rest,/The debt of blood, unpaid. Invasion Song. *Anonymous.* PoOW

And now she can't carry the tuna. Limerick: "A coloratura named Luna." J. F. Wilson. TDH

And now she has gone. After Snow. Walter Clark. NCSH

And now she is her rich sailor's wife. A Sweetheart in the Army (A vers.). *Anonymous.* BaBo

And now she's ever so good. Temper. Rose Fyleman. OxBChV

And now she's got her fisherman/To row her down the sea. The Royal Fisherman. *Anonymous.* GBP

And now that he's dead he lies still. Epitaph: "Beneath this smooth stone by the bone of his bone." *Anonymous.* FaBoEE

And now that one does not exist either. Dance-Song. Jaroslav Seifert. AMV-81

And now the brooks flow with meadow tea.... March 8, 1840. Henry David Thoreau. RFM

And now the falcon is hooded and comforted away. The Falcon and the Dove. Sir Herbert Read. BrPo; FaBoMo

And now "the girl we love the most!"/My brave Yankee boys. The Constellation and the Insurgente. *Anonymous.* PAH

And now the great ebb tides lift to the light of day/The sea-bed's briny chambers of decay. Love. Thomas Kinsella. FaBoIP

And now the lady has gotten hir luve,/The winsom laird of Ochiltrie. The Laird o Logie (B version). *Anonymous.* ESPB

And now the rain comes down!/A-a-aha, a-a-aha, my little one. The Cloud-Flower Lullaby. *Anonymous.* WTO

And now, the saints deliver/Us from fleas. Dover to Munich. Charles Stuart Calverley. NOBL

And now the song was quieted. The Man from Porlock. Helen Bevington. EvOK

And now the spring trip is ended/And everybody's feeling fine! The Spring Trip of the Schooner Ambition. *Anonymous.* ShS

And now the swallows pair! Unanswered. Martha Gilbert Dickinson. AA

And now the water seems remote, unreal, and perhaps it is. A Distance from the Sea. Weldon Kees. NoAm

And now their hour is come. Compensation. Ralph Waldo Emerson. AnNE; APA; FPL; LiTA; TAP

And now there is but Light for Love to be! To the Rosella in the Poinsettia Tree. James Picot. BoAV

And now there is merely silence, silence, silence saying/All we did not know. Sagacity. William Rose Benet. MoAmPo

And now there's nothing more to do/Except/To/Wait! Day before Christmas. Marchette Chute. ChBR; NTCP

And now they do as lively be,/As the first day he brought them/hame. Leesome Brand (A version). *Anonymous.* BaBo; ESPB

And now they keep an oyster-shop for mermaids down below. The Ballad of the Oysterman. Oliver Wendell Holmes. AnNE; AP; EtS; FaFP; HBV 1-2; HBVY; MCCG; MOS; MoShBr; TreFS

And now they live peaceful and happy,/Caroline and her young sailor bold. Caroline and Her Young Sailor Bold. *Anonymous.* AmFP

And now they say he's senator, but of that I shore don't know. A Man Named Hods. *Anonymous.* CoSo

And now thou seest my soul's angelic hue. A "Prize' Poem. Shirley Brooks. FaBoCo; FaBoNo

And now–though Planets pass, I stand/The witness to Thy shame! Epitaphs of the War, 1914-18. Rudyard Kipling. BrPo; OBWP

And now 'tis resolved that this frightful new-comer/Will winter in hell and be here in the summer. Old Nick in Sorel. Standish O'Grady. OBCV

And now 'tis silent all–Enchantress, fare thee well! The Lady of the Lake. Sir Walter Scott. OAEP; ViBoPo

And now to show that I am true to my lover,/I'll wed my darling at the blooming spring. The Lover Freed from the Gallows. *Anonymous.* BFSS

And now to us for evermore/The essence of your eighty years. For the Eightieth Birthday of a Great Singer. Edward Shanks. UnS

And now we call him by such names/As "Cookie," "Sugarplum," and Snooks!" Naming the Baby. May Richstone. BiCB

And now we three in Euston waiting-room. Parting in Wartime. Frances Cornford. FaBoWP; NIP

And now we will walk the woods our lone.' Erlington. *Anonymous.* BuBa

And now wild Beasts came forth the woods to roam. Paradise Regained. John Milton. CABL

...And now will be/taught in her/Turn to suck eggs. Self-Congratulatory Ode on Mr Auden's Election (parody). Ronald Mason. FaBoPa

And now with him she sleeps in Yarrow. The Braes of Yarrow. John Logan. BSV; GTBS; GTBS-P; HBV 1-2; OBEC

And now you grudge a spot to me. What Jenner Said on Hearing in Elysium That Complaints Had Been Made.. Shirley Brooks. EyDe; FaBoEE

And now you know my familee/And all that does belong to me. The Family. *Anonymous.* TiPo

And now you see he's made of me a honest working man. Portland County Jail. *Anonymous.* AS; FSW

And now you want me to climb on a jackass? Try to be serious! Why Mira Can't Go Back to Her Old House. Mira Bai [(or Mirabai)]. NU

And nowhere is there more despair/Than in the tangle of your hair. To a Woman. Denis Glover. AnNZ

And numberless such offices of love,/Daily and nightly, zealous to perform. The Seasons. James (1700-48) Thomson. EBEV; OAEL 1-2

And nurse it she will through one more acted night. Burning the Letters. Gwendolyn Grew. HoPM

And Nurse too is cross as she bears him away. A Child's Christmas Day. *Anonymous.* OBCP

And nuzzling each other in the smelly fold. Magnificat. Michele Roberts. BrRo

And nymphs and satyrs breaking from weathered stone. Small Park in East Germany: 1969. Gerda Mayer. OBTV

And o'er her tomb wild brambles creep. The Gulistan. Muslih-ud-Din Sa'di. AWP

And o'er his grave/Our colors wave. Mumford. Ina M. Porter. PAH

And o'er that chill and secret wave it throws/A sudden dawn of red. Rosa Rosarum. Agnes Mary Frances (Mme Emile Duclaux) Robinson. HBMV

And o'er the centuries still we hear/The Master's winsome call. We Bear the Strain of Earthly Care. Ozora S. Davis. TRV

And o'er the dark her Silver Mantle threw. Paradise Lost. John Milton. MOON

And o'er thy head destructive tiles impend. The Pell Mell Celebrated. John Gay. EnLi 1-2

And o'er your happy songs its plaudits rang. Paul Laurence Dunbar. James David Corrothers. BANP; PoNe

And O God Who art in Heaven,/Relieve my pain! How Happy the Little Birds. *Anonymous.* OnYI

And O, I'm sure my heart wad brak,/Gin ye'd prove fause to me! Dinna Ask Me. John Dunlop. HBV 1-2

And O may Cupid speed the clocks,/For she will marry me in prox! Inst., Ult., and Prox.: Answer. Sir Alan Patrick Herbert. FaBoUs

And O may its wakening be blither than mine! Lullaby. Carolina Oliphant, Lady Nairne. HBV 1-2

And, O, may no other maiden know such reproach as I! Cashel of Munster. *Anonymous.* AnIV; GBL; IrPN; OxBI

And O, my wreck'd hope,/That the cold earth's your dwelling! Lament. Edward Walsh. OBVV

And, O, pray too for me! The Maid's Lament. Walter Savage Landor. HBV 1-2; OBEV; OBNC; OBRV; OBVV

And O she was the Sunday/In every week. The Planter's Daughter. Austin Clarke. CIP; OxBI; OxBTC

(And O the bower and the hour!) Eden Bower. Dante Gabriel Rossetti. MaVP

And O! the lions I've turned away! I Am a Lioness. Aisha bint Ahmad. WPOW

And O! the merry laughter/Across the hayfield after! A Song. Ralph Hodgson. GoJo

And O the rose grow in the middle of the great world. In Crisis. Lawrence Durrell. LiTM

And O to cut the green field, leaving/One rich street with hunger in it. The Countryman's Return. Dylan Thomas. OxBTC

...And (O were I/To choose) I'd cheat the worms/And silence seek in stone. Were I to Choose. Gabriel Okara. PBA

And obdurate as stone. Hill People. Harriet Gray Blackwell. AmFN

And, obedient, learned to dread/Grave no more than marriage bed. Mother of Ten. Leonard Alfred George Strong. DBV

And observed all the ruins of Philae. Limerick: "There was an Old Person of Philae." Edward Lear. FaBoNo

And Ochil brooks and Ochil braes/Grow classic in her smile! Spring on the Ochils. James Logie Robertson. OBVV

And of a fear/That only the wind can cry and conjure of. Daybreak. Phillip Yellowhawk Minthorn. STE

And of a strange bird that chirps/With a foreign sound. Little Birds. Jacob Sternberg. TrJP

And of all glad words of prose or rhyme,/The gladdest are, "Act while there yet is time." Maud Muller Mutatur (parody). Franklin Pierce ("F.P.A.") Adams. HBMV

And of all things the infinite vanity! A Se Stesso. Giacomo Leopardi. AWP

And of alle ben lot that her thee were ilewe.' When Death Comes. *Anonymous.* MeEL

And of death the less said the better. Plain Song Talk. Richard Eberhart. PoA

And of God's voice, when man's is comfortless. La Madonna dell' Acqua. John Ruskin. NOBV

And of heaven's joys itself did disinherit. The Anatomy of Baseness: To The Detracted. John Andrews. EIL

...And of him self alas,/Doth dye unknowen, dazed with dreadfull face. Stond Who So List upon the Slipper Toppe. Sir Thomas Wyatt. AAS; PoEL 1-5

And of himself as God. Witch Doctor. Robert Earl Hayden. AmNP; MAT; NoAm

And of His bones are charnels made. Ode: "Why will they never sleep." John Peale Bishop. LiTA; LiTM; MoPo; MoVE; NePA

And, of its one movement, the depth. The Movement of Fish. James Dickey. NYBP; VGW

And of Jane Reece whom Thomas kept in dread/By Pax Romana of his board and bed. A History of Peace. Robert Graves. HBMV

And of moons and maidens at midnight. Apology for Apostasy? Etheridge Knight. NeAC

And of new love that they would learn. A Wife in London. Thomas Hardy. NOBV; OBWP

And of such/Is the kingdom of Heaven. Tombstone Epitaphs. *Anonymous.* PeD

And of the breeze–amen! The gentian weaves her fringes. Emily Dickinson. PoRA

And of the curveship lend a myth to God. To Brooklyn Bridge. Hart Crane. AP; BLPL; CrMA; DiPo; ExPo; EyDe; LiTM; NePA; OxBA; PoPl; PrIm; SeCeV

And of the eternal voice I am the thunder! Rapture. Stefan George. AWP

And of the ruins shall be made/Some yet more lovely masterpiece. Continuity. George William Russell. MoBrPo; NBM

And of the thousand Gods not one was jealous. Once on a Time a Thousand Different Men. James Henry. NOBV

And of their vain contest appeared no end. Paradise Lost. John Milton. EmL; MBW 1-2; NoP; OAEL 1-2; TrCP

And off round the herd I go dashing,/A reckless cowboy of the plains. The Cowboy's Meditation. *Anonymous.* CoSo

And off went Rumpelstiltskin, mumbling. Needles and Pins. Mark Van Doren. SO

And offal and filth of all manner in heaps. Ode to a Ditch. *Anonymous.* PeD

And offer him my heart. Spite of Thy Godhead, Powerful Love. Anne Wharton. CavP

And offers to your wayward soul and mine/The shelter of His fold. The Good Shepherd. Clyde Edwin Tuck. BePJ

And oft Disorder-like in government,/Leave even those that prosper, disconent. Chorus Primus: Wise Counsellors. Fulke, Lord Brooke Greville. OBS

And oft-rent cries may rend the skies all around through/Avondale. The Avondale Mine Disaster. *Anonymous.* AmFP; BaBo; ViBoFo

And oft th'approaching petticoat offend. The Art of Dancing. Soame Jenyns. FaBoUs

And often live beyond my means,/Tho' a captain in the army. Captain Jinks. William Horace Lingard. BLPA; BLSo

And often spoken but no longer heard. The Mixer. Louis MacNeice. FaBoTw

And often you see in a footstep/What you could not see in a face. Everything Passes and Vanishes. William Allingham. NOBV

And oftentimes a blissful dazzling smile/vanishes in this blind and breathless game. The Merry-Go-Round. Rainer Maria Rilke. CAD; WeW

And oh! but he is handsome. Cock-a-Bandy. *Anonymous.* OxNR

And oh, her breakfast is sweet indeed/To happy little Gustava! Little Gustava. Celia Thaxter. HBV 1-2; HBVY

And Oh, how oft with new life shalt thou lift/Out of the atom-drift! When I Have Gone Weird Ways. John G. Neihardt. HBV 1-2

And, oh! how taught shall I return? The Whistling Boy. George Crabbe. TrGrPo

And oh I said yes, trying to think/of anything else at all. The First Time. John Newlove. NeAC

And, oh, I thank my God tonight I am your wife. I Am Your Wife. *Anonymous.* PoToHe

And, oh! in Downing Street should Old Nick revel,/England's prime minister, then bless the devil! Loyal Effusion. Horatio and James Smith. OBRV

And oh, it may befall/In listening long to Heaven-song/I may not care at all! If You Should Tire of Loving Me. Margaret Widdemer. HBMV

And oh thank God for the simple elephant. A Difference of Zoos. Gregory Corso. VGW

And oh! the chime of children's voices in the dome. Parsifal. Paul Verlaine. SyP

And Oh, the luring thought of it/Is prayer! Envoi. John G. Neihardt. HBV 1-2; WGRP

And, oh, the pity of it all! The Indictment (excerpt). Frederick Fanning Ayer. PeD

And oh, the sweet scent, and purple skies! To My Mountain. Kathleen Raine. OxBS; PoPl

And oh! 'tis delicious to hate you! When I Loved You. Thomas Moore. ALV; HBV 1-2

And oh, when he saw pretty girls, he had a taking eye! Benjamin Franklin. Rosemary and Stephen Vincent Benét. TiPo

And oil burners roaring in the night. Saving the Harvest. Geoffrey Lehmann. CBAP

And old cringing Credible/Dies of rage and shame! Adventure. Grace Fallow Norton. HBMV

...And old earth gropes for, grasps at/steep/Heaven with it whom she childs/things by. Ashboughs. Gerard Manley Hopkins. VLP

And Old England's Roast Beef! The Roast Beef of Old England. Henry Fielding. CEP; OBEC

And old joy returns in holy presence. Come into Animal Presence. Denise Levertov. AP; HeIP; NaP; NU

And old men in the morning/Telling the town their dreams. High Summer on the Mountains. Idris Davies. OxBTC

And old men shall drop by the wayside. Shaka, King of the Zulus. *Anonymous.* PBA; TTY

And old sky and a long plain/Beyond, beyond, my bridle-rein. Texas. Amy Lowell. AmFN; BPAW

...And old, unreconciled/Blood-rites of pagan sanctity as well. L'Embarquement pour Cythere. John Streeter Manifold. CBAP

And older far than Rameses'. The Chart. Walter De La Mare. CoBMV

And, on a park bench, come to a last decision. The Nameless Ones. Conrad Aiken. NePA; OxBA

And on alle that mercy nede for charite./Amen, par amore, Amen. A Prayer to the Trinity. *Anonymous.* MeEL

And on an hey hil thu henge me,/All the werld on me to wonder. Jesus Reproaches His People. *Anonymous.* MeEL

(And on behalf)/Of the fatted calf. S. P. C. A. Sermon. Stuart Hemsley. FiBHP

And on each floor and in/each room no/one. Divorce. Kate Jennings. AMV-80

And on he pushed, a two-miles' tread,/To breakfast at his Bouwery. Peter Stuyvesant's New Year's Call. Edmund Clarence Stedman. PAH

And on her bosom I remembered all. Epitaphs of the War, 1914-18. Rudyard Kipling. BrPo; OBWP

And on her lap, the clasped, closed, iron book. The White Dress. Marya Zaturenska. MoAmPo

And on him endless youth attends. Descend, Fair Sun! George Chapman. ElL

And on his head a garland well beseene. The Faerie Queene. Edmund Spenser. GN

And on his left foot jumps over his right ear What the Violins Sing in Their Baconfat Bed. Jean Arp. WeW

And on his soul may God ha' mer-cy! The Stranger's Song. Thomas Hardy. BrPo

And on into the distance and the mist. At the Entrance. Douglas Stewart. CBAP

And on into the morning when he was beaten to death. Fable. Janos Pilinszky. OBVE

And on its topmost twig the Crow/Takes the glad morning's sun and air. The Crow. William Canton. HBV 1-2

And on Labor Day nobody works. Everyday Will Be Sunday. Anonymous. TreFT

And on land in a military train. Adelita. Anonymous. AS; FSW

And on my breast carve a turtle dove/To signify I died of love. There Is a Tavern in the Town. Anonymous. FaFP; TreF

And on my brow I feel a kiss/That I would rather die than miss. To Memory. Mary Elizabeth Coleridge. CBEP

And on my eyelids,/a tear swells/older than my body. Sierra. Alfonsina Storni. PBWP

And on my eyelids blaze/Acanthus and grape leaf. The Sibyl. Joan LaBombard. GoYe

And on my faith, good is the reason,/If it be so. If it be so... Sir Thomas Wyatt. FCP

And on my high bed,/The bed made for me/I flung myself down. The Golden Sea-Otter. Wakarpa. WTO

And on my lap the headlines loom/Like strangers in the living room. Finding a Yiddish Paper on the Riverside Line. Barry Spacks. SM

...And on my shoulders pallid/The dead leaves are falling. A Statue in a Garden. Agnes Lee. HBMV

And on my stone will pour fully/what alive my hungry heart asked/always in vain. Fear. Vittoria Pompili. PBWP

And on that day, and in that place, we will try again, and this time we/shall win. Pact. Kenneth Fearing. CMoP

And on that grace I dare depend. Lord, I Am Thine. Samuel Davies. AH

And on the assembly line/of Cadillac I heard you sigh. Poetry Concert. Michael S. Harper. TAP

And on the beach undid his corded bales. The Scholar-Gipsy. Matthew Arnold. ACV; AnFE; EBEV; EnL; FaBoPP; FiP; GoTL; HAP; HBV 1-2; HeIP; LoBV; MasP; MaVP; NOBE; NOBV; NoP; OAEL 1-2; OAEP; OBEV; OBNC; OBVV; PoEL 1-5; PoPle; SeCeV; TEP; ViBoPo; VLP

And on the bed of silence sleep till thou awakest me. Vala; or, The Four Zoas. William Blake. OBNC

And on the bleached bones, in clean sunlight, we shall begin to build. Working Class. Bertram Warr. NOBC; OBCV; WaP

And on the bridge, faces upturned to a roaring/Falcon. The Airman Who Flew over Shakespeare's England. Hyam Plutzik. PoPl

And on the cold hearth break the empty/glass. Disappointment. Thomas Stephen Collier. AA

And on the fifth day, he was–dead! The Story of Augustus Who Would Not Have Any Soup. Heinrich Hoffmann. BBGG; FaBoUs; GoJo; HBV 1-2; HBVY; MoShBr; NLV; OxBChV; ShM; SpRo; TiPo

And on the low dark verge of life/The twilight of eternal day. In Memoriam A.H.H., L. Alfred, Lord Tennyson. ELP; NAWM 1-2; PoEL 1-5; SCV

And on the Lunar world securely pry. Annus Mirabilis. John Donne. MOS

And on the magic mountain nothing moved. The Green Shepherd. Louis Simpson. MP; NePoEA; NIP; NoAm; NYBP

And on the mere the wailing died away. Morte D'Arthur. Alfred, Lord Tennyson. AnEnPo; DL; DTo; FaBoBe; FiP; HBV 1-2; NIP; NOBV; OAEL 1-2; OBNV; PoEL 1-5; SeCeV; WHA

And, on the other, lions. The Victories of Love. Coventry Patmore. FaBoRV; NBM

And on the other side, you know,/Are six, seven, eight, nine, ten. Foot Soldiers. John Banister Tabb. HBV 1-2; HBVY; OBAL

And on the other terror has rained/reigned/long enough. Man's World Dissolving. Derek Butler. LFAC

"And on the proof, and whosoever saddled you!" The Saddled Ass. Deems Taylor. NLV

And on the right the slogan Born To Lose. Black Jackets. Thom Gunn. HeIP; MP; TwCP

And on the salt wind died away. Strand-Thistle. Gustav Falke. AWP

And on the seventh, slept a great Negro sleep. New York. Leopold Sedar Senghor. NYP

And on the ships at sea. Rain. Robert Louis Stevenson. GoJo; NTCP; SoPo; SUS; TiPo

And on the way towards the window dies,/Half-open on the little garden-close? The Piano. Paul Verlaine. LiTW

And on the way/you said thanks/I love you. August Afternoon. Nancy Remaly. CTBA

And on the wrinkled earth a snipe has landed. Canadian Farmer. Genevieve Bartole. CaP

And on thine anvil shall I hammer out/The thought chaotic to prefulgid form. A Mock Invocation to Genius (excerpt). William Woty. NOEC

And on this compost, like a rose,/Fragrance of children's laughter blows. Back Lane. R. D. Murphy. PoAu 1-2

And on this lonely waste we find it true/Lost youth and love not lost, are hid with Christ. Lost Youth. Roger Casement. CAW

And on those little cheeks of thine. The Divan. Richard Henry Stoddard. AA

And on thy head shall quickly shine/The diadem of God. My Soul, Weigh Not Thy Life. Leonard Swain. AH

And on thy shining forehead/Be peace the crowning gem! O Beautiful My Country. Frederick Lucian Hosmer. AH; MC; PGD

And on thy wings bring delicate perfumes/To play the wanton with us through the leaves. David and Bethsabe. George Peele. ViBoPo

And on to Wakefield take your way. Robin Hood's Funeral. Anthony Munday. WiR

And once again we fall over/Overwhelmed with passion. Every morning I get up. Huang O. BoWoP

And once done, there is no remedy, no salvation for this,/nonentity is our portion. God and the Holy Ghost. D. H. Lawrence. MoRP

And once in twenty years, their scribes record,/By natural instinct they change their lord. Lord Shaftesbury. John Dryden. LoBV

And once rejoicing never know them more. The Seasons. James (1700-48) Thomson. PoEL 1-5

And once we've met on Claudy banks/We'll never part again.' The Banks of Claudy. Anonymous. AmFP; OBET

And one a' them's got a woman/who oughta be in hell. Five Lyrics from "Good for Nothing Man". Kenneth Ptichford. CoPo

And one an altar kept alight. Four Things. Anonymous. TRV

And One at Idbury. Country Thought. Sylvia Townsend Warner. MoBrPo

And one bewitched granddaughter. Spring Cellar. Gladys McKee. GoYe

And one boundless reach of sky. The Builders. Henry Wadsworth Longfellow. FaFP; OHFP; TreFS

And one by one back in the Closet lays. The Rubaiyat of Omar Khayyam. Omar Khayyam. EaLo; TRV

And one cat under/A witch elm/Tree. Diamond Cut Diamond. Ewart Milne. FaBoCh; LoGBV; NeIP; PCat

And one coffin when you die/Don't you know? Fin De Siecle. Edmund Vance Cook. BLPA

And one day you will call me, "Woman." Aristophanes' Symposium. Rita Mae Brown. IHMS

And one, even-breathed, on the cud of a/dream. The Milker. Eileen Duggan. CoBE

And one far-off divine event,/To which the whole creation moves. In Memoriam A.H.H., CXXXI. Alfred, Lord Tennyson. OAEP; VLP

And one feels the earth going round and round the globe of the blackening/mantle, a mad moth. Perseus. Louis MacNeice. CoBMV; LiTM

And one flew over the goose's nest. Intery, Mintery, Cutery Corn. Mother Goose. TiPo

And one for hoptoads! Pockets. Susan Adger Williams. BrR

And one for Sister Mandy. Hippety Hop to the Barber Shop. Mother Goose. SoPo; TiPo

And one for the little boy that lives in the lane. Baa, Baa, Black Sheep. Mother Goose. AmFP; FaBoBe; FaFP; HBV 1-2; HBVY; OxNR; SoPo; TiPo

And one friend Old is worth a hundred new. On Himself. William Oldys. FaBoEE

And one great Slaughter-house the warring world! The Temple of Nature. Erasmus Darwin. FM

And one hard look/Can close the book/That lovers love to see. Song: One Hard Look. Robert Graves. MoAB; MoBrPo

And one has nothing more to fear. From a Hint in the Minor Poets. Samuel Wesley. CBEP; OBEC

And one–has shut her eyes/For evermore. Where the Picnic Was. Thomas Hardy. OxBTC

And one in a velvet gown. Hark, Hark! The Dogs Do Bark. Mother Goose. HBVY; TiPo

And one is One, free in the tearing wind. In a Dark Time. Theodore Roethke. CAPP; EaLo; HAP; HeIP; MAT; MoAmPo; NoAm; NOBA; NoP; NYBP; PPP; TAP

And one is sad; her note is changed,/Because her brood is stol'n away. In Memoriam A.H.H., XXI. Alfred, Lord Tennyson. VLP

And one man bursting into the police station/Crying: "Let Justice be done. I did it, I." Law in the Country of the Cats. Ted Hughes. TW

And One Mills Bomb On a Monument in France... Anonymous. ShM

And one more day of War starts everywhere. A Wartime Dawn. David Gascoyne. LiTM; MoVE

And one more rhyme for "river"! A Drawing-Room Ballad. Henry Duff Traill. CenHV

And one more year's far gone. To a Salesgirl, Weary of Artificial Holiday Trees. James Wright. NYBP

And one must perish–let it not be he/Whom thou art sworn to obey. A Charge. Herbert Trench. HBV 1-2; OBEV; OBVV

And one of them is rather coarse. The Horse. Naomi Royde-Smith. FaBoCo; FiBHP

And one of them will carry me home,/And six I will give to thee. Fair Annie. Anonymous. BSV; CH; HBV 1-2; ViBoFo

And one old windmill,/its broken arms/clattering in the darkness. Men against the Sky. John Haines. LCAP

And one pale cry leaps/toward the stars. Late Game. B. H. Fairchild. AMV-81

And one pays down with pebbles from the shore. The Narrow Door. Charlotte Mew. SBG

And one red poppy in the corn. The Second Coming. Dannie Abse. NMP; NoAm

And one said soft to the other:/"Brother,/Mark your prey." As he lay dying. As He Lay Dying. Randolph Stow. BoAnP

And one sees o'er the long dead trail/A ghostly caravan. The Santa Fe Trail. Arthur Chapman. BPAW

And one shall live in two each year. And One Shall Live in Two. Jonathan Henderson Brooks. PoNe

And one soul in the whole world mine,/mine only. Home-Sickness. Hedwig Lachmann. TrJP

And one storm petrel rises like a whip. Sonnets for a Dying Man. Burns Singer. NePoEA-2

And one that I love is dead. At Twilight. Peyton Van Rensselaer. AA

And one the care without the cure. Diversity of Doctors. Anonymous. ALV

And one toward distant seas? The Railway Junction. Walter de la Mare. CBEP; OxBTC

And one who sings her child to sleep. An Old Song. Solomon Blumgarten (Yehoash) LiTW

And, one with Jesus, thirsts again. The Teresian Contemplative. Robert Hugh Benson. ACP; CAW

And one with the mended, broken arm of Art. A Century Piece for Poor Heine. John Logan. NNaP

And one with white hands/To comb her gleaming hair! Let Me Love Bright Things. A. Newberry Choyce. HBMV

And one with word–birds, knaves, fools, fish. The Wounded Hawk. Herbert Palmer. FaBoTw; HaMV

And onely my loke declareth my hert. Rime XLIX: "Bicause I have the still kept fro lyes and blame." Petrarch (Francesco Petrarca). OBVE

And only a step from their cottage doors/The rough hill-shepherds are emperors. The Kingship of the Hills. Will H. Ogilvie. PoSH

And only alien cities lie ahead. Long Roads. Mikhail Matusovsky. LiTW

And only all the women players. Cynicus to W. Shakspere. James Kenneth Stephen. CenHV

And only asked of heaven its aid/Her heavy lot to bear. The Little Shroud. Letitia Elizabeth Landon. PaPo

And only bitter land was washed away. Childhood. Margaret Walker. BOLo; IHMS; PBWP; PoBA; WPOW

And only death can stop him now–he's fighting for them all. The Things That Make a Soldier Great. Edgar A. Guest. NIP

And only Death himself can prove. The Trick. William Henry Davies. ChMP

And only flourish in your livery. I'll tell you whence the Rose did first grow red. William Strode. EG

And only his voice/Still echoes/Inside me. The Angel Michael. Anath Bental. VWA

And only in the light of lost words/Can we imagine our rewards. The Picture of Little J.A. in a Prospect of Flowers. John Ashbery. ConAP; PPP

And only know I should drown if you laid not your hand on me. Stillness. James Elroy Flecker. BrPo; CH; GoJo; MoBrPo; SyP

And only leaves one track. Riddle: "Goes through the mud." Anonymous. OxNR

And only men forget! Easter,1923. John G. Neihardt. AnAmPo; HBMV

And only music stays. Pediment: Ballet. Louise Townsend Nicholl. UnS

And only not so fast as we forget 'em. A Rhymester. Samuel Taylor Coleridge. PV

And only Pleasure's phantom dwells with thee. Florence. Walter Savage Landor. SeCePo

And only shadows dwell in Danger Court. Whim Alley. Hervey Allen. AnAmPo

And only should condemn the pride/That can arise from aught beside. Called Proud. Walter Savage Landor. GBL

...And only some of the/things that shine are mean. Memorandum. William Stafford. NYBP

And only the dead are wrong. Rain. Howard Moss. ErPo

And only the handkerchiefs/Wave good-bye. Stocking and Shirt. James Reeves. OnUR

And only the heart is withered and sere. Die Blauen Veilchen Der Augelein. Heinrich Heine. AWP

And only the holiest/hear it moan. Flower Ensnarer of Psalms. Rossana Ombres. BoWoP

...And only the thinking of clouds/Keeps the world on its untroubled course. Because They Were Very Poor That Winter. Kenneth Patchen. NaP

And only the young winds cry. Padraic O'Conaire–Gaelic Storyteller. Frederick Robert Higgins. OBMV; OnYI; OxBI

And only then suggest/his shorter kingdom,/Portugal. The Portrait of Prince Henry. Sydney Clouts. VWA

And only then the eye begins to see. The Counterpart. Elizabeth Jennings. LiTM

And only those who strive mightily/Shall possess it. The Village Atheist. Edgar Lee Masters. AmP; EaLo; LiTA

And only those will be secure./Who shelter 'neath Christ's blood. Noah's Carpenters. Anonymous. STF

And only wait/Till they bury me. If I Felt Less. Morris Wintchevsky. TrJP

And only your image waking in the dark. Rose in the Afternoon. Jenny Joseph. BrRo

And onward plough and ploughmen go/Into the field where farmers grow. Recitative. Ronald McCuaig. NOAV

And onward to the dark horizon flew/On their far-shadowing and soundless wings. Images. Richard Schaukal. AWP

And ony sma'er thocht's impossible. At My Father's Grave. Hugh" (Christopher Murray Grieve) MacDiarmid. ELU; GTBS-P

And ootshines't like a turnin' wing. To a Sea Eagle. Hugh" (Christopher Murray Grieve) MacDiarmid. MoBrPo

And open it,/And see her children there! An Evening Falls. James Stephens. SUS

And open little sensuous parasols, singing the nail-/in-the-foot song, drinking cool beatitudes. Afterwards, They Shall Dance. Bob Kaufman. PoNe; TwCP; VGW

And opened heaven for our delight. Saviour, Whose Love Is Like the Sun. Howard Chandler Robbins. TrPWD

And opes the Temple of Eternity. Epilogue to the Satires. Alexander Pope. CoBE

And opposition of the Stars. The Definition of Love. Andrew Marvell. AnAnS 1; BLPL; BoLiVe; BoLoP; CBEP; DiPo; EBEV; ForPo; GBL; HoPM; InPS; JCP; LiTB; LiTL; LoBV; MeLP; MePo; NOBE; NoP; OAEL 1-2; OAEP; OBEV; OBS; PAI; PoEL 1-5; SeCePo; SeCeV; SeCP; SeCV 1-2; TEP; TreFT; TrGrPo; UnPo; WHA

And oppressed that Young Lady in White. Limerick: "There was a young lady in White." Edward Lear. NBM

And or the mornin bells was rung/The threesome were a' gane. Child Maurice (D version). Anonymous. ESPB

And orange juice–for him! A Little Bird. Aileen Fisher. SoPo

And orb into the perfect star/We saw not, when we moved therein? In Memoriam A.H.H., XXIV. Alfred, Lord Tennyson. VLP

And order a washing-day! The First Proclamation of Miles Standish. Margaret Junkin Preston. MC; PAH; YaD

And ore the hill and far awa'. The Elfin Knight. Anonymous CH

And other cliffs impossible to climb. Kineo Mountain. Celeste Turner Wright. Psk

And other distant dogs respond/Beyond the fields, beyond, beyond. Night Song. Frances Cornford. FM; GDP

And other folk should get the ugly ones. Sonnet: Of All He Would Do. Cecco da Siena Angiolieri. AWP

And other love is pain, but this is joy eternal. Over the Great City. Edward Carpenter. WGRP

And other monuments. Cathedrals. W. S. Doxey. AMV-80

And other strains of woe, which now seem woe,/Compared with loss of thee will not seem so. Sonnets, XC: "Then hate me when thou wilt; if ever, now." William Shakespeare. ATP; AWP; EBEV; NOBE; OBEV; OBSC; PG; PoEL 1-5; WHA

And other things at school. Being Sick. Jimmy Garthwaite. BrR

And others doth offend when 'tis let loose. Love's Offence. Sir John Suckling. CaPo

And others round were singing out, "Hang him, hang him, shoot him!" Prospecting Dream. Anonymous. AmFP

And our ancient God calling from the mountain. Hebrew Lesson. Max Brod. AMV-80

And our ballast is old wine. Nightmare Abbey: Three Men of Gotham. Thomas Love Peacock. MyFE

And our children asleep in the attic above. Song of the Rain. Hugh McCrae. BoAV; CBAP; PoAu 1-2

And our efforts success will assuredly bless if we only are/faithful to Soccer! Eureka! Alfred Denis Godley. CenHV

And our enemy, he who keeps still! Again. Frantisek Halas. WaaP

And our eternal home! O God Our Help in Ages Past. Isaac Watts. BLRP; EaLo; FaPoR; HBV 1-2; OxBoCh; WGRP

And our fabled double kingdom/Of life and of death. Due Date. Seymour Cain. AMV-80

And our faces are like mirrors. Brothers Together in Winter. Harley Elliott. NeAC

And our fates will be like hers,/and our hems crooked forever? House Guest. Elizabeth Bishop. NCSH; NYBP; TAP

And our father, the old God-fearing man, has been dead many years. Isaac. A. C. Jacobs. VWA

And our fiery breasts they cover/As with hidden holy rain. Radiant Ranks of Seraphim. Valery Bryusov. AWP

And our friendship last long as love doth last/and stronger than death is strong. To America. Alfred Austin. GN; HBV 1-2

And our fruit gravitates toward the earth,/our fruit, indigent before its flowering. A December Frost. Vesna Krmpotic. WPOW

And our God be glad and our world be sweeter! At Little Virgil's Window. Edwin Markham. TRV

And our hair that the god had breathed upon turned laurel. Daphne. Selden Rodman. PoNe

And our hands deadly/and the dead, friends. Nightsong. Louis O. Coxe. FYAP

And our hands must melt like water. Our Hands in the Garden. Anne Hebert. BoWoP

And our hearts are restless until they rest in Thee. Thou Hast Made Us for Thyself. Saint Augustine. TRV

And our hearts, like thy waters, be mingled in peace. Meeting of the Waters. Thomas Moore. AnIL; NBM; NOBI; OxBoLi; PoEL 1-5

And our house breathes the peace/and piousness/of ryebread and evensong. Evening. Itzik Manger. VWA

And our house is a raft of shingles/sunk under leaves and vines. Rain. John Haines. NPAW

And our house, like the century,/is falling to pieces... Maybe You Cannot Comprehend. Salvador Villanueva. InW

And Our Lady sweetly smiled,/Picking cherries for her Child. A Legend of Cherries. Charles Dalmon. HBMV

And our lips in echoing song. Amen. Hymn for Laudes: Feast of Our Lady, Help of Christians. Anonymous. ISi

And our lives would be all sunshine/In the sweetness of our Lord. The All-Embracing. Frederick William Faber. BLRP; TRV

And our lofty doom fulfil. Self-Discipline. George William Russell. MoBrPo

And our only crime, that we are here to serve it. The Little Green Blackbird. Kenneth Patchen. PoCh

And our peace here, like a spring,/Make it ever flourishing. Grace for Children. Robert Herrick. EBCP; OxBChV; OxBoCh

And our pockets full too. Twelfth Night. Anonymous. OxNR

And our points/sharpening good as anybodys'. Still. Lucille Clifton. InPS; PAI

And our Pope's most recent encyclical on contraception. Alehouse Sonnets: The Dressing Station. Norman Dubie. AmPA

And our promise, too, we leave/With the flowers. More Than Flowers We Have Brought. Nancy Byrd Turner. SiSoSe

And our Saviour paid its cost! The Bible. Dorothy Conant Stroud. STF

And our shared relatives in blacktown/on the outskirts of your tongue, tied still. Tongue-Tied in Black and White. Michael S. Harper. HaCAP

And our side won, I think. Stafford in Kansas (parody). James Baker Hall. BXAP

And our skin shall see far off, as it does under water. Surprised by Evening. Robert Bly. CAPP; NaP; VGW

And our souls at home with God! Song: "Oh! that we two were Maying." Charles Kingsley. HBV 1-2

And our steeds, that through Sydney exultingly wheel,/Must graze in a week on the banks of the Peel .Songs of the Squatters, I. Robert Lowe. NOAV

And our thin dying souls against Eternity pressed. Winter Landscape. Stephen Spender. MoAB; MoBrPo

And our trim boat let her swift motion die,/Between the dim reflections floating by. Indolence. Robert Bridges. BrPo; VLP

And our two hearts will be together. Azouou. Mririda n'Ait Attik. WPOW

And our voices low in the kitchen of the moon/cooking fires. Moon Poems. John Wieners. VGW

And our wheels grazed his dead face. Dead Man's Dump. Isaac Rosenberg. BrPo; CABL; FaBoMo; GTBS-P; LiTM; MMM; MoPo; NoP; OBWP; TrJP; VWA; WaP

And our wrath shall not rest, till we finish the/deed. Apostrophe to the Island of Cuba. James Gates Percival. PAH

And our years grow deep/in a snow of roses and stones. To Vera Thompson. John Haines. LCAP

And ourselves up to keep the town. Song in a Siege. Robert Heath. CavP; OBS

And out doth keep/All feare. The Gnat. Joseph Beaumont. CBEP; FM; LoBV; OBS

AND/OUT/FELL/ME! Present. Miriam Clark Potter. BiCB

And out he came, hop, hop, hop. Handy Spandy. Mother Goose. SoPo

And out of darkness came the hands/That reach thro' nature, moulding men. In Memoriam A.H.H., CXXIV. Alfred, Lord Tennyson. VLP

And out of hell, beyond its iron bars,/My scorn of all its pains. The Gift. George William Russell. HBMV

And out of his eyes two great tears rolled, like stones, and/he died. Death of a Son. Jon Silkin. FF; GTBS-P; NePoEA; NoAm; OxBTC; TwCP; VWA

And out of Lydia Margaret's grave grows a rede, red rose,/Spread over Sweet William's breast. Sweet William. Anonymous. BaBo

And out of obvious ways/Ne'er wandering far. The Two Deserts. Coventry Patmore. BoNaP

And out of our loss is gain. Lessons of the Year. Anonymous. BLRP

And out of plain talk spin/Truth and Falsehood, the greatest weapons in the world. Sound from Leopardi. Bill Berkson. ANYP

And out of the cloud that smites, beneficent rivers of rain. Tropic Rain. Robert Louis Stevenson. OBTV

And out of the darkness they peer/With a goblin light in their eyes. The Bad Kittens. Elizabeth Jane Coatsworth. OBCA

And out of the swing of the sea. Heaven-Haven. Gerard Manley Hopkins. ACP; BrPo; CAW; DiPo; GoBC; HeIP; MoAB; MoBrPo; MOS; NoAm; NOCV; OAEP; OBEV; OBNC; OBSP; SoSe; SOTW; TrGrPo; ViBoPo; VLP

And out of the window a-tumble she did go. Mrs. Snipkin and Mrs. Wobblechin. Laura E. Richards. OxBChV; SoPo; TiPo

And out of this flower of Time/Twelve petals are wafted down. At Midnight. Frank Dempster Sherman. AA

And out she tumbles/From her warm bed. Softly, Drowsily. Walter De la Mare. SoPo; SUS

And out they creep and back again for ever. Two Houses. Edward ("Edward Eastaway") Thomas. ChMP; FaBoCh; LoGBV

And out they sally'd at the Gate. Presbyterian Knight and Independent Squire. Samuel (1602-80) Butler. OBS

And out to Simancas all knew/Where they buried Red Hugh. Red Hugh. Thomas MacGreevy. OnYI

And outside the door I heard him crying. Night Visitors. (or Molodovski) Kadya, [(or Kadia) Molodovsky. VWA

And over all/My pair of swallows. The Book I Held Grew Cold. Ernst Toller. TrJP

And over all the sky-the sky! far, far out of reach,/ studded, breaking out, the eternal stars. .Drum-Taps. Walt Whitman. AP

And over both is Heaven. The Old Burying-Ground. John Greenleaf Whittier. AP

And over both the white wings of a Dove. Ave Maria Gratia Plena. Oscar Wilde. CAW; ISi

And over it a space of watery blue/Which the keen evening star is shining through. Evening: Ponte al Mare, Pisa. Percy Bysshe Shelley. CBEP

And over tarred macadam and pavements parched and white/I've walked till my feet are sore! The Cockney of the North. Harry Graham. CenHV

...And over the left/shoulder is our distance. Moved Towards a Future. Laura Chester. NPGG

And over the quavering voice of Hem/Is the droning voice of Haw. Hem and Haw. Bliss Carman. AnAmPo; HBV 1-2

And over their city stands the pinnacled corn. Merlin. Geoffrey Hill. InPK; PoL

And over them I will take/ever more painstaking care. Wyncote, Pennsylvania: A Gloss. Thomas Kinsella. NOBI

And over those ethereal eyes/The bar of Michael Angelo. In Memoriam A.H.H., LXXXVII. Alfred, Lord Tennyson. VLP

And over waves of subtle, woolly flocks/Crashes the breaking day! Hymn to Sunrise. Anonymous. NA

And overcome by longing and by tears. The Odyssey. Homer. NAWM 1-2

And overflows with swelling storms of wrath. The Aeneid. Virgil (Publius Vergilius Maro). OAEL 1-2

And overhead the petrel wafted wide. Caesar's Lost Transport Ships. Robert Lee Frost. AmePo

And overhead they all could hear/the singing of the birds. The Boyhood of Christ. Anonymous. NOBI

And overhead wild ducks soar like racers/into forms as delicious as life or money. Untitled Poem. "A swim in Ohuira Bay." Robert Peterson. NeAC

And overlook the Little Fellow on his way to school. In the Days of Rin-Tin-Tin. Daniel Gerard Hoffman. CoPo; SM

And Ovid's GOLDEN AGE, is but a Dream. Nil Admirari. William Congreve. OBEC

And owes its being to the gazer's eye. The Image of God. Francisco de Aldana. CAW; WGRP

And own the betrayal of my unguarded heart. Voyeur. John Edward Hardy. ErPo

And ownes his offspring in their yellow eyes. The Legend of Good Women. Geoffrey Chaucer. LO

And owr kyn Harry long lyff and pease. Epitaph on Queen Elizabeth, Wife of Henry VII. *Anonymous.* AtBAP

And pa-ca, pa-ca, pa-ca, pa-ca!/Pam! pam! Pam! Rumba. Jose Z. Tallet. TTY

And paced by the sweet shrieking of the quick. The Lives of Gulls and Children. Howard Nemerov. NePoEA

And paddle in glee, my darling, while I drown. To My Daughter. James Michie. OBSP

And paddle their white canoe! The Lake of the Dismal Swamp. Thomas Moore. BLPA

And pads away/With her tail in the air. Cat. Mary Britton Miller. PCat; SoPo; SUS; TiPo

And paid for a ravaged festering weft. Shearing Grass. Peter Redgrove. NePoEA-2

And paid for Bloody Bill. Bloody Bill. D. M. Ross. AnNZ

And pain like a cat will come home to share your room. Early Spring. Sidney Keyes. MoBrPo

And paint with rapture, her inspiring shades. The Beauties of Santa Cruz. Philip Freneau. AmPP; MAmP

And painted himself a bright blue. Limerick: "An ostrich who lived at the zoo." *Anonymous.* TDH

And pale among the saints I stand,/A saint companionless. Rosalind's Scroll. Elizabeth Barrett Browning. HBV 1-2

And pale blue rice wine simmering/in the stomach of a big red fish? Who among You Knows the Essence of Garlic? Garrett Kaoru Hongo. HoAn

And Pallas eke, that warlike wench, their beauties pride to prove. Heroides: Oenone to Paris (excerpt). Ovid (Publius Ovidius Naso). OBVE

And palm the dreadful riddle of their skulls–/hoping the worst. Landlady. P. K. Page. CaP; SoSe

And pangs, and every care that into/power grows. Thanksgiving. Yehoash. TrJP

And pants against my door./Old tiger, hail! Euroclydon. Abbie Huston Evans. NePoAm

And papa flings his newspaper outward,/in disgust with discipline. Get the Gasworks. David Ignatow. InPK; PAI

And paper-boats with cargoes of his wishes. Paul Klee. Ruthven Todd. EAS

And Paradise a figuring of air. The Living Room. Gjertrud Schnackenberg. FYAP

And pardon this one. Hotel Paradiso e Commerciale. John Malcolm Brinnin. HoAn; MP; NoAm; NYBP; PoCh; TwCP

And Paris slept on by Scamander side. Menelaus and Helen. Rupert Brooke. SeCePo

And Parnell's life has been saved, which I consider/no sin. Richard Pigott, the Forger (excerpt). William McGonagall. PeD

And parson stood within the rails, a-marrying me and/thee, O! Apprenticed. Jean Ingelow. LiTL; OBVV

And part it, giving half to him. In Memoriam A.H.H., XXV. Alfred, Lord Tennyson. VLP

And part with him when he goes wrong. I Am Not Bound to Win. Abraham Lincoln. TRV

And partial view, at least, of the bright lake. Old Women of Toronto. Miriam Waddington. NOBC

And particular in turning out their toes. Robinson Crusoe. Charles Edward Carryl. AA; BaBo; BeLS; ESPB; FiBHP; HBV 1-2; HBVY; InMe; MCCG; OxBB; TreFT

And partly sound its Polity. Woman. Coventry Patmore. OBVV

And, partner once of Tiney's box,/Must soon partake his grave. Epitaph on a Hare. William Cowper. FiP; FM; HBV 1-2; HBVY; HeIP; NOEC; NoP; PoEL 1-5; PoPle; SeCeV

And pass'd a life of piety and peace. The Hermit. Thomas Parnell. GoTL

...And pass my declining years/saluting strange women and grandfather clocks. Peekaboo, I Almost See You. Ogden Nash. PoLf

And pass the sword from hand to hand! Immortality. Arthur Sherburne Hardy. AA

And passer-by along the level rows/Stooped down and whipt a bit beneath his nose. Field Path. John Clare. OBSP

And passes like a rhyme. Snowflakes. Clive Sansom. OBCP

And passeth to inherit/a residence afresh. Bhagavad Gita: Never the Spirit Was Born. *Anonymous.* GoTF; TreFT

...And passing still/go on to learn what's gone; and what I will. The Human Animal. Jane Mayhall. TAP

And passion made us Cowards grow,/Which made us brave before. An Evening's Love. John Dryden. CavP

And passionate as the dawn. The Fisherman. William Butler Yeats. MBW 1-2

And, past philosophy's surmisings, know! On the Heights. W. K. Holmes. PoSH

And past the sands and seas' blue level line,/Ceaseless, the faint far murmur of the brine. Sonnets, VIII: "The apples ripen under yellowing leaves." Thomas Caulfield Irwin. IrPN

And Patience wins the race. Bruce and the Spider. Bernard Barton. BeLS

And Patrick Sarsfield, Ireland's darling. Patrick Sarsfield, Lord Lucan. *Anonymous.* KiLC

And Paudeen Dhu, with meekly dismal face,/Receives the full possession of the place... Laurence Bloomfield in Ireland. William Allingham. NOBI

And Paul, out of Tarsus?/He is our Exegete. Our Two Worthies. John Crowe Ransom. OBAL

And Paul's will peter out. On the Triumph of Rationalism. Alfred Ainger. FaBoCo

And pause betimes in gnostic rimes/To woo the Over Soul. Moorlands of the Not. *Anonymous.* NA

And pause or stagger slightly/And go about his business. Parity. Kenneth Rexroth. GP

And pause to hear if someone calls your name. Walk Slowly. Adelaide Love. BLPA

And pausing, on the final stair/Collects her motions into shape. Nude Descending a Staircase. X. J. Kennedy. CoAP; HeIP; HoAn; HoPM; NePoEA-2; NIP; OBSP; PoA; PoL; SM

And, pausing, takes with forehead bare/The benediction of the air. Snow-Bound. John Greenleaf Whittier. AmePo; AnNE; AP; MAmP; MCCG; NOBA; OxBA; TAP

And pay againe theyr unconfused noises/with interest ever: list, I heare them singe. Sonnet XLIV. William Alabaster. AnAnS 1

And pay for the punch beside. The Dorchester Giant. Oliver Wendell Holmes. OnMSP

And pay less attention to these.' Limerick: "There was a young Fellow of Caius." *Anonymous.* NOBL

And pay no attention to runner or whore/When yer hat's on yer head and yer feet's on the shore. Liverpool Girls. *Anonymous.* OBSS

And pay Paddy Doyle for his boots. Paddy Doyle. *Anonymous.* AmSS

And pay their duties to the ruling mind? The Hurry of the Spirits, in a Fever and Nervous Disorders. Isaac Watts. NOEC

And paying a call at Dawley Bank on his way to his destination. A Shropshire Lad. Sir John Betjeman. MoBS

And pea-green zombie with X-ray eyes. Request Numbers. G. N. Sprod. FiBHP

And Peace, and Art, and Labour joined her train. Visit of Hope to Sydney Cove, near Botany-Bay. Erasmus Darwin. NOEC; OBTV

And peace begin. A Song. Joel Barlow. AmPP

And peace in all our hearts! Christmas. Henry Timrod. MAmP

And peace is in his kiss. Poem: "He lying spilt like water from a bowl." Alison Boodson. NeBP

And peace on earth for men. Afterthought. Elizabeth Jennings. OBCP

And peace on earth fulfill the angels' joy. Peace on Earth. Samuel Longfellow. PGD

And peace to adore, thou spirit of Guiding Fire! The Bacchai: The Home of Aphrodite. Euripides. AWP

And peace was born to abide alway,/In hearts that were long despairing. Three Wise Kings. William E. Brooks. PGD

And peace was Paradise! A Tempest. Emily Dickinson. MCCG

And peace, which ev'ry where/With so much earnestness you do pursue/Is only there. Peace. George Herbert. AnAnS 1; AWP; ELP; ExPo; InPo; NOCV; OxBoCh; SeCeV; TEP

And Peale is most appalling. A Saint...He Ain't. E. Y. Harburg. DBV

And peasant women such as she/who sells pine logs for firewood. The Little Donkey. Francis Jammes. PCh

And peering through the windows where they sleep. But That Is Another Story. Donald Justice. CoAP; NePoEA-2

And people are so shaken.) Granite and Cypress. Robinson Jeffers. AmPP; AnAmPo

And peoples of the Bronx, their conquerors. The Subway from New Britain to the Bronx. Randall Jarrell. NYP

And perdy to forget. Longer to muse. Sir Thomas Wyatt. FCP; SiPS

And perfect love and friendship reign/Throughout eternity. Blest Be the Tie That Binds. John Fawcett. HBV 1-2

And perfect me in love. Speak the Word. Charles Wesley. BePJ

And perfect peace, and every hope fulfilled. We See Jesus. Annie Johnson Flint. BLRP

And perfect stillness stares at perfect stream. The Stepping Stones. Conrad Aiken. CrMA

And perfore is his euyn/On Crystes owyn day. Seynt Steuyn and Herowdes. *Anonymous.* OxBB

...And perhaps also/to amuse children. Small children. The Red Herring. George MacBeth. SO

And poor indeed he who, half-alive,/Begs favour of a shadow.   Not Yet Dead, Not Yet Alone.   Osip Mandelstam.   OBVE

...And poor men bet on where a star/will rise next evening.   The Island of Geological Time.   Laura Fargas.   SUW

And poplars stand there still as death.   Southern Mansion.   Arna Bontemps. AmFN; AmNP; BALP; BANP; CNA; FB; FF; IDB; LiTM; PoBA; PoNe; TTY; WSC

And pore upon my verse, and court my grief,–.   Sonnets.   Frederick Goddard Tuckerman.   AP

And port was celestial glory.   Epitaph on John Dove.   Robert Burns. FaBoCo

And possess in sweet communion joys which earth cannot afford.   In Sweet Communion.   John Newton.   TRV

And possess the common heritage to which all flesh is heir?   The Virgin Martyr.   Ada Cambridge.   NOAV

And possibly i like the thrill of/under me you so quite new   Sonnets– Actualities.   Edward Estlin Cummings.   UnTE

And pour out your forgiveness like a wine.   The Composer.   W. H. Auden. UnS

And pour their Souls in Transport, which the SIRE/Of Love approving hears, and calls it good.   The Seasons.   James (1700-48) Thomson.   EnRP

And poured His blessing on us both.   Priest and Pagan.   Albert Durrant Watson.   CaP

And poured its treasure out upon the/leaves.   Woodbines in October. Charlotte Fiske Bates.   AA

And poured the syrup down his back.   Limerick: "Absent-minded, in his shack."   *Anonymous.*   TDH

And powerless, you cannot be recalled.   Glass Dialectic.   Howard Nemerov. WaP

And Practice drives me mad.   Multiplication Is Vexation.   Mother Goose. BrR

And praise and pray God a good haruest to sende.   A Hundreth Good Poyntes of Husbandry.   Thomas Tusser.   FaBoUs

And praise him who did make and mend our eies.   Love.   George Herbert. HoPM; SeCV 1-2

And praise his world for ever, as thou bidst.   The Poet.   Elizabeth Barrett Browning.   VLP; WGRP

And praise Mary's Child/That the harvest is done.   Harvest Song.   Joseph Campbell.   OFD

And praise the land of silver snow frozen on mossy bed.   The Silent Walls. Ian Strachan.   PoSH

And prate about an Elephant/Not one of them has seen!   The Blind Men and the Elephant.   John Godfrey Saxe.   AmePo; AnNE; BLPA; FaBoBe; FPL; GoTF; HBV 1-2; HBVY; MaC; OBCA; OnMSP; OnUR; PoToHe; StPo; TreF; WBLP

And pray for Kharma under the holy mountain.   Chard Whitlow.   Henry Reed.   BXAP; DTC; FaBoCo; FaBoNo; FiBHP; LiTM; NLV; NOBL; NoP; OxBTC; Par; UnPo

And pray God keep her heartily.   Medieval Norman Songs.   *Anonymous.* AWP

And pray that He who feeds the crying ravens/Will guide the baby's feet. Little Feet.   Elizabeth Akers.   HBV 1-2

And pray–that other hearts may Pray!   Pray-Give-Go.   Annie Johnson Flint. BLRP; STF

And pray the gods that shortly I might die.   Madrigal: "Penelope, that longed for the sight."   William Byrd.   EnRePo

And pray to God that he forgive us all.   The Epitaph, or Ballade of the Hanged.   Francois Villon.   ExPo

And prayer must now replace the dance/To keep the world from stopping dead.   Shekhina and the Kiddushim.   Edouard Roditi.   VWA

And prelude to the endless rites of love.   I Hate to See You Clad.   Paul Verlaine.   UnTE

And prepare darkness/among the stars   Remember Sabbath Days.   Larry Eigner.   VWA

And press for passage with extended hands.   The Aeneid.   Virgil (Publius Vergilius Maro).   OBVE

And press your lips to mine/till they are incandescent   Her Lips Are Copper Wire.   Jean Toomer.   NoAm

And pretty maids all of a row.   Mary, Mary, Quite Contrary.   Mother Goose.   TiPo

And pride, unmindful of its parent dust,/Scares with the dungeon and the whipping-post.   The Complaints of Poetry (excerpt).   Nicholas James. NOEC

And prime buck-venison I prefer to tripe.   Epigram: "Poet! I like not mealy fruit."   Walter Savage Landor.   FaBoEE

And prisons would palaces prove/If Jesus would dwell with me there. Nothing to Wish or to Fear.   John Newton.   BePJ

And Private James, by change of names,/Was Major-General John.   General John.   Sir William Schwenck Gilbert.   NA

...And probably a baby/or two; someone strange, respectable.   Another Night on the Porch Swing.   Cathleen Quirk.   NMM

And probably rather hard up out of the bargain.   Living? Our Supervisors Will Do That for Us!   David Holbrook.   NePoEA-2

And prolong this sad recital/By leaving careful footprints round/A wind-encircled burial mound.   Letter to Seamus Heaney.   Michael Longley. FaBoIP

And promise my own children/that there are other ways/better ways/to be chosen.   The Crippler.   Danny Siegel.   VWA

And promise of exceeding joy hereafter.   Sweet September.   George Arnold. GN

And property assures it to the swain,/Pleased and unwearied, in his guarded toil.   The Seasons.   James (1700-48) Thomson.   FaBoPP

And propt with rotten stakes   Some of Wordsworth.   Walter Savage Landor. ChTr

And protest only to the jackhammer.   On the Pavement.   David A. Sam. AMV-80

And proudly and carelessly ride for a fall.   Anarchist.   Anthony Cronin. CIP

And proudly tune their lyres to sing/Of Ethiopia's glory.   Ode to Ethiopia. Paul Laurence Dunbar.   BALP

And prove that death but routs life into victory.   Clarel.   Herman Melville. AP; MAmP

And prove that fact be true.   The Only Way to Have a Friend.   *Anonymous.* PoToHe

And prove that his mercy is boundless and free.   O Turn Ye, O Turn Ye. Josiah Hopkins.   AH

And prove the settler's worth, beyond the body's wants...   Brookfield (excerpt).   William E. Marshall.   CaP

And proved there is not anything at all/He cannot make, if that's a thing He can.   Sonnet: Of the Making of Master Messerin.   Rustico di Filippo. AWP; LiTW

And proves his faith by a consistent walk.   God Wants a Man.   *Anonymous.* BLRP

And proves the pleasanter, the colder.   Love.   Samuel (1612-80) Butler. CBEP

And prowls the fox at night.   The White-footed Deer.   William Cullen Bryant.   AnNE

And prynces twayne whom she so sore doth fray.   Medea.   Seneca (Lucius Annaeus Seneca).   OBVE

And publish that in which I mean to die.   Ballade to Our Lady of Czestochowa.   Hilaire Belloc.   ACP; ISi

And publish with our latest breath,/The love and guardian care.   Courage. Paul Gerhardt.   WGRP

And puffing his cheeks he replied "A great wig."   Orator Prigg.   William Blake.   OBSV

...And puffing proves that I/Do Stella love: fools, who doth it deny? Astrophel and Stella, CIV.   Sir Philip Sidney.   AAS; SiPS

And Pulcherie, the name it bears,/Is hidden by the enormous bloom.   Prose for Des Esseintes.   Stephane Mallarme.   OBVE

And pull and bend about these sweeps of light.   Three Poems on Morris Graves' Paintings.   John Logan.   PoDr

And pull the earth apart.   My Love Is a Tower.   Lewis, Cecil Day. AtBAP

And pull the unwilling thunder down.   To the Ship in Which Virgil Sailed to Athens (Odes, I, 3).   Horace.   AWP

And pull up the nostrils! his nose was snub.   Resurrection Song.   Thomas Lovell Beddoes.   ELU; ERoP 1-2; FaBoEE; NBM

And pulled at each end of the string.   Limerick: "Our Vicar is good Mr. Inge."   *Anonymous.*   TDH

And pulled out golden fishes.   Washing Up.   *Anonymous.*   OxNR

And pullest the heavens upon thee for a pall.   Sic Transit.   Joseph Mary Plunkett.   ACP

And, pulse of my heart! what gloom is thine?   Kitty Bhan.   Edward Walsh. ACP

And pulsing reel relaxes to a still/Of smiling passion frozen in our death of will.   As a Great Prince.   Edwin Honig.   LiTA; NoAm

And pump the valley with the tunnel dry.   Earth Has Shrunk in the Wash. William Empson.   CMoP

And pupils jump/because he jumps   Patrick Ewing Takes a Foul Shot. Diane Ackerman.   MAYP

And Purcell is the man whose shore it is.   Bounty.   Josephine Miles. NoAm

And pure religion breathing household laws.   England, 1802.   William Wordsworth.   OBEV; PPON

And purer worship may we pay/In heaven's unclouded light.   Hail to the Sabbath Day.   Stephen Greenleaf Bulfinch.   AH

And purpose clean as light from every selfish taint...   The New-Come Chief. James Russell Lowell.   MC

And pushes shaking itself loose from/the sigh.   Coda.   Fred Johnson. CNA

And pussy cat shall crowdy.   Come Dance a Jig.   *Anonymous.*   OxNR

And pussy will love me/Because I am good.   Kindness.   *Anonymous.* OxNR

...And put a tongue/In every wound of Caesar that should move/The stones of Rome to rise and mutiny   .Julius Caesar.   William Shakespeare.   LiTB

And put an end to her loneliness.   On Myself.   Edith Bone.   FaBoEE

And put him into bed? Why don't they come?   Disabled.   Wilfred Owen. BiP; BrPo; CMoP; FF; InPS; LiTM; MMM; NAMP; NIP; NoAm; OxBTC; PAI; WaP

And put him on the wall,/And that's all.   And That's All.   Anonymous. OxNR

And put his chisel down for marvelling on that stone.   A View of the Brooklyn Bridge.   William Meredith.   MoVE

And put on wisdom with the robe of dust.   Woo Not the World.   King of Seville Mu'tamid.   AWP; LiTW

...And put some chopped-up cedar boughs/In with them, and tore down the slaughter-house.   Reuben Bright.   Edwin Arlington Robinson.   AmP; AnNE; MoAB; MoAmPo; NePA; NOBA; NoP; TAP; TrGrPo

AND PUT THE SEAL OF HONOR ON HIM/WHEN HE DIED.   Thomas Wolfe's Tombstone (excerpt).   Thomas Wolfe.   TRV

And put within my cold, still hand/A monkey-wrench and the old oil can. The Dying Hogger (with music).   Anonymous.   AS

And Putid Clotts defil'd her Breasts obscene.   Cravings during Pregnancy. M. Saint-Marthe.   FaBoUs

And putting it there in a style to stay.   God in the Nation's Life. Anonymous.   BLRP; WBLP

And puzzle on the grief of the land.   The Amish.   William Doreski.   SOTS

And quack in their language still, Vive le Roy.   The Vows.   Andrew Marvell.   TW

And quaff from their cup, though you/should drink with them a double-/ draught of poison.   Distich.   Shuraikh.   TrJP

And Quardle oodle ardle wardle doodle/The magpies say.   The Magpies. Denis Glover.   AnNZ

And quarrelsome chaps in charnels/Must bear it as best they can.   The Jar of Nations.   Alfred Edward Housman.   LiTB

And question with the God that I embrace.   The Growth of Love: O Weary Pilgrims.   Robert Bridges.   MoAB; MoBrPo; NoAm

And questions Him–if he is able/to reassure her Why.   For Amy Lowell. Countee Cullen.   PoA

And quicken this dead heart of mine.   My Soul Before Thee Prostrate Lies. C. F. Richter.   AH

And quickly have my own great victory.   Sonnet VI: "The coming of that limpid Star is twice."   Louise Labe.   BoWoP

And quiet as its death/Upon a lady's breast.   Song on the Water.   Thomas Lovell Beddoes.   EG

And quiet did quiet remain.   The Song of Finis.   Walter De la Mare. MoBrPo

And quiet sleep and a sweet dream when the long trick's over.   Sea-Fever. John Masefield.   BoLiVe; EtS; FaBoBe; FaBV; FaPoR; FPL; GoTF; GTBS; HBV 1-2; HBVY; MCCG; MoAB; MoBrPo; MOS; OBTV; OBVV; OHFP; OxBTC; PoLf; PoPl; TiPo; TreF; TrGrPo; WHA

And quietly closed the drawer, and lied.   The Manual.   Larry Rubin.   GP

And quietly repeating:/burnt.   Burnt.   Boris Slutsky.   VWA

And quietly the trees casting their crowns/Into the pools.   September.   Ted Hughes.   BoLoP; OLR

And quit corn bread for the rest of my life.   Greer County.   Anonymous. ABF; CoSo

And, quit of earth's corruptions, shape/Itself, imperishably pure.   A Girl of Pompeii.   Edward Sandford Martin.   AA; HBV 1-2

And quite forget this feeling–O, this sad, sweet pain!   A Maori Girl's Song. Alfred Domett.   OBVV

And quite invisible but for the end of his nose.   Amphibious Crocodile. John Crowe Ransom.   AnAmPo; OBAL

And quivering with Cold.   Feathered Friends (parody).   Robert Peters. BXAP

And race unreined around the fields of heaven!   The Ponies.   Wilfrid Gibson.   PH

And race with dolphins at the prow.   Nantucket's Widows.   Richard Foerster.   AMV-81

And radiant as the morning is our fair land.   Salute to Life.   Dmitri Shostakovitch.   FSW

And ragwort blooming on when others fade away.   Joys of Childhood.   John Clare.   ERoP 1-2

And rain comes rattling down upon our forest/Like the doors of a country jail. St. Malachy.   Thomas Merton.   CoPo; VGW

And rain on the house-top,/But not upon me!   The Rain.   Anonymous. TiPo

And rain passing/through uneven light.   Rain.   Sister Mary Lucina. AMV-80

And raise her children to eternal day.   Along the Banks.   Joel Barlow.   AH

And raise their hands/As their names occurred.   Anseo.   Paul Muldoon. FaBoPV

And raise to immortality the rag.   The Rejected "National Hymns".   Robert Henry Newell.   InMe

And raise to thee still holier prayers!   Hymn for the Dedication of a Church. Andrews Norton.   AA

And raise us up with thee/To the new,/To the new Jerusalem.   We Are on Our Journey Home.   Anonymous.   AH

And raised such a hellabelioux?   The Sioux.   Eugene Field.   FiBHP; GoJo

And raised thee up to where thou art.   The Duke of York's Statue.   Walter Savage Landor.   FaBoEE

And raised them thus to the outer air.   Fireflies.   William Sharp.   FM

And raked the quarry to stoke his volcanic heart.   Pittsburgh.   Hy Sobiloff. NePA

And ran a bell cord through her hair.   Limerick: "A matron well known in Montclair."   William Jay Smith.   TDH

And rang like bells the vaults and the dark arches.   Bacchus.   William Empson.   NoAm; PoCh

And rang my ears, and eyes became/Veiled, as in night.   Sappho.   Caius Valerius Catullus.   AWP

And rank among the foremost class/Our evenings at Saint Cloud.   Saint Cloud.   Sir Walter Scott.   OBTV

And rapidly rushed about Dutton.   Limerick: "There was an old person of Dutton."   Edward Lear.   EBEV

And rarely wander'd in his speech, or drew/His thoughts so forth as to offend the view.   Lara.   George Gordon, Lord Byron.   OAEL 1-2; OBRV

And rather see a battle than/A dumb thing near a drunken man.   The Dumb World.   William Henry Davies.   OxBTC

And rather strive to gain from thence one thorn,/Than all the flour'shing wreaths by laureates worn   To My Worthy Friend Master George Sands.... Thomas Carew.   AnAnS 2; CaPo; JCP; MeLP; MePo; OBS; SeCV 1-2

...And rats running/over my floor (in solitary confinement).   Getting Back to Work.   Leon Baker.   LFAC

And rattles her crutch, which may put forth a small bloom, perhaps/white. Pursuit.   Robert Penn Warren.   CrMA; HAP; LiTA; MoPo; MP; NePA; PPP; TwCP

And raving, distracted, he died the next night.   The Gosport Tragedy. Anonymous.   AmFP

And ravished the daughters, and drove the fathers mad.   In Time of War. W.H. Auden.   CMoP

And ravished the poor soul you never wanted.   A Lodging for the Night. Elinor Wylie.   ErPo

And reached him sweetest water with their hands.   A Shepherd's Gift. Anyte [(or Anytes)].   AWP

And reaches down/And calls His children home?   What Bright Pushbutton? Samuel ("Paul Vesey") Allen.   PoNe

And read a book on sexual morality.   Monogamy (excerpt).   Gerald Gould. OxBTC

And read about themselves–/in color, with their eyelids shut.   A Martian Sends a Postcard Home.   Craig Raine.   NoP

And read in them, what no ill can remove,/The love that to the lover said, "I love'.   Sonnets to Aurelia.   Robert Nichols.   OBMV

And read that moderate man Voltaire.   The Respectable Burgher.   Thomas Hardy.   CMoP; NoAm; VLP

And read them by the red candles/Of garden brambles.   Poems.   Hilda Conkling.   ExPo

And read what is still unread/In the manuscripts of God.   The Manuscripts of God.   Henry Wadsworth Longfellow.   TRV

And read your Bible, sir, and mind your purse.'   Don Juan.   George Gordon, Lord Byron.   SCV

And reads dawn lifting from the shadowy hills.   Semantic.   Robert Conquest.   TEP

And realize that that never-to-be-touched/Vision is your mistress.   Circe. Louis MacNeice.   NOBV; OBMV

And reap Thy harvest: we have waited long.   Sonnet: "Nay, Lord, not thus!" Oscar Wilde.   TrPWD

And Reason confirms me a slave to her charms.   Fair Hebe.   John West. HBV 1-2

And Reason's self shall bow the knee to shadows and delusions here.   The Indian Burying Ground.   Philip Freneau.   AA; AnAmPo; AP; APA; ForPo; HAP; HBV 1-2; HeIP; LiTA; MAmP; NePA; NOBA; NoP; OxBA; PoEL 1-5; PoLf; PoPl; TAP

And reassure myself anew/That you're not me and I'm not you.   Confessions of a Born Spectator.   Ogden Nash.   LiSp

And recalling by their voices/Youth and travel.   To an Old Danish Song-Book.   Henry Wadsworth Longfellow.   OBVV

And receipts and dolls and clothes, tobacco crumbs, vases and fringes.   The Bean Eaters.   Gwendolyn Brooks.   BlSi; GrPl; HAP; HeIP; MAT; NoP; PoA; PoBA; PrIm; TAP; TTY

And recessive evening drowned in the ocean of stars.   The Blue-Hole. Charles G. Bell.   GrPl

And rechart the stars and the sins.   Paean to Eve's Apple.   James Liddy. CIP

And reckon bravely in a row/The things I am afraid to know.   The Mysteries.   Leonard Alfred George Strong.   HaMV

...And recognize its strong/shape under the gathered stars.   Power Failure. Josephine Jacobsen.   FAZ

And reconciles man to his lot.   Verses Supposed to be Written by Alexander Selkirk.   William Cowper.   CEP; NOEC; PoEL 1-5

And red at the core with the last sore-heartedness,/Sore-hearted-looking. Almond Blossom.   D. H. Lawrence.   FaBoPP

And red geraniums aflame upon my window sill.   Red Geraniums.   Martha Haskell Clark.   BLPA

And red-necked laughs still promise patient dawn.   Night Slivers.   Darwin T. Turner.   NBP

And refuse to meet him!   If Only, When One Heard.   *Anonymous.*   AWP

And refuses to come home.   His Toy, His Dream, His Rest.   John Berryman.   NOBA

And reign above the sky.   Great Shepherd of the Sheep.   Charles Wesley. BePJ

And reign the Prince o'th' Air in which it flies.   A Panegyric on the Author of "Absalom and Achitophel."   *Anonymous.*   APAS

And rein with Reason's curb fantastic Taste.'   The English Garden (excerpt). William Mason.   NOEC

And rejoice in the dust of their/land!   The Young Dove.   Moses Ibn Ezra. TrJP

And release them from cradles of cold.   In the Fishing Village.   Sheila Nickerson.   WOLT

And relief thaim with his baneir.   The Bruce.   John Barbour.   OxBS

And religion's pristine form/Shall give peace and calm the storm.   Saint Brendan's Prophecy.   *Anonymous.*   OnYI

And remain sealed, like letters which have no/address and no one to receive them.   Of Three or Four in a Room.   Yehuda Amichai.   VWA

And remarked: "I wonder now/Which will reach the bottom first?"   Some Ruthless Rhymes.   Harry Graham.   CenHV

And remember how it hurt/to be greedy and eat.   Wishing Africa.   Marilyn Bowering.   CaPN; NOBC

And remember, love, I died for thee.   Early in the Spring.   *Anonymous.* AmFP

And remember that the great harp-breasted eagle/Is now a grave.   The Death of Yeats.   George Barker.   LiTB

And remember there was something else I was hoping/for.   Double Feature. Theodore Roethke.   DFF

...And remembers/the walls of the garden, the first light.   A Map of the Western Part of the County of Essex in England.   Denise Levertov. CoAP; ConAP

And rend that glorious Empire of her Heart.   Leaving Me, and Then Loving Many.   Abraham Cowley.   AnAnS 2

And render right the chain that binds/Our fallen land!   A Lament for the Princes of Tyrone and Tyrconnel.   *Anonymous.*   AnIV

And render love for love,/Which is a just reward.   Pass forth, my wonted cries.   Sir Thomas Wyatt.   FCP; SiPS

And renew us over the night.   I Caught This Morning at Dawning.   Dennis Neagle.   AMV-80

And renowned be thy grave!   Cymbeline.   William Shakespeare.   AWP; CAW; CTC; DiPo; EBEV; EG; EiL; ELP; ExPo; FaBoCh; FaFP; FF; FiP; ForPo; GBL; GTBS; GTBS-P; HAP; HBV 1-2; HeIP; InPo; InPS; LiTB; LoBV; LoGBV; MCCG; NOBE; NoP; OAEL 1-2; OAEP; OBEV; OBSC; PAI; PoEL 1-5; PoPle; PoRA; PPoe; PrIm; QFR; RoGo; SCV; SeCeV; SoSe; TreF; TrGrPo; ViBoPo; WHA

And rented her out when they chose.   IBM Hired Her.   W. J. J. Gordon. QQQ

And repair them more than they require!   Two Mornings.   Lawrence McGaugh.   PoBA

And reply, lip and tongue/of pleasure.   The Word Plum.   Helen Chasin. NIP

And represents her at the polls.   Portrait.   Jeanne D'Orge.   AnAmPo

And reshaped it, as though it were soft/supple clay,/Into peace from His merciful throne.   Mourning.   Josephine Van Fossan.   STF

And rest and work are one.   Shekhinah.   Karl Wolfskehl.   TrJP; VWA

And rest assured, the day/Will be all sunlight, and the night/A dutiful spectrum of stars.   The Poets of the Nineties.   Derek Mahon.   FaBoIP

And rest for the night over the mantel-top.   The Flies.   Merrill Moore. AnEnPo

And rest from weary laughter/In the quiet arms of grief.   If All the Skies. Henry Van Dyke.   WBLP; WGRP

And rest in peace till another day.   Reynard the Fox (excerpt).   John Masefield.   NAMP; ViBoPo

And rest, itself unchanged, in time's estate.   The Prism.   Helen Pinkerton. NePoAm

And rest like this will be most sweet/To every tired comer.   Tree Planting. *Anonymous.*   OHIP

And rest them when she's here!   Absence.   Richard Jago.   OBEV

And rested in Heaven above.   Little Moses.   *Anonymous.*   FSW

And rested on a drying hill.   Sir Gawaine and the Green Knight.   Yvor Winters.   AnFE; CoAnAm; MoVE; NoAm; QFR; VGW

And resting gently where he chose.   Exaggerator.   Mark Van Doren. AnFE

And resting there behold/Across unmeasured space/The Majesty of God? What Called Me to the Heights?   Lawrence Pilkington.   PoSH

And restore lasting melodies of his desire.   Returning to Roots of First Feeling.   Robert Duncan.   PoA

And retreating, always retreating, behind it.   Brazil, January 1, 1502. Elizabeth Bishop.   FaBoWP; NoAm

And return from aye from the Land of Youth!   Oisin in the Land of Youth. Michael Comyn.   AnIL

And return like/birds to the flight/on the reflection of heaven.   Fast.   John Tagliabue.   SD

And return to living these your youngest years.   A Visit to Bridge House. Richard Weber.   BIrV

And return to Mars/As a Martian/Raccoon.   S F.   Ernest Leverett.   QQQ

And return to Mars as himself, a Martian/Raccoon.   Science Fiction.   Reed Whittemore.   GP

And return us to our own beloved homes.   Damn the Filipinos.   *Anonymous.* ABF

And return/With wings scorched.   The Phoenix.   Matti Megged.   VWA

And returned home the previous night.   Limerick: "There was a young lady named Bright."   A. H. Reginald Buller.   CenHV; FaBoCo; NOBL; QQQ

And returned to their homes by another way.   The Three Kings.   Henry Wadsworth Longfellow.   GN; HBV 1-2; HBVY; OnMSP

And revel o'er me, like a soulless sheep.   Lunar Stanzas.   Henry Coggswell Knight.   FaBoNo; NA

And rice and rabbit for the stranger./Thank you very much!   Driving Cattle to Casas Buenas.   Roy Campbell.   PeSA

And rich/with the cancellation of newspapers,/the stopping of milk.   The Frightened Flier Goes North.   Judith Kazantzis.   BrRo

And Richard Cory, one calm summer/night,/Went home and put a bullet through his/head.   Richard Cory.   Edwin Arlington Robinson.   AmP; AnNE; CMoP; DiPo; DL; DTC; ExPo; FaFP; FF; ForPo; FPL; GoTF; HAP; InPK; LiTM; LiTM; LoGBV; MasP; MoAB; MoAmPo; MoVE; NePA; NIP; NOBA; NoP; OxBA; PoLf; PoRA; PrIm; SoSe; StPo; TAP; TreF; TrGrPo

And rid it out of pain.   O goodly hand.   Sir Thomas Wyatt.   FCP; InvP; SiPS

And ride far away.   The World Was Never Real to Me.   George Randall Griffin.   AMV-81

And ride slowly out/Onto the thawing river.   To a Wall of Flame in a Steel Mill, Syracuse, New York, 1969.   Larry Levis.   AMV-81; MAYP

And rides God's battle-field in a flashing and golden car.   He Whom a Dream Hath Possessed.   Shaemas O'Sheel.   AnIV; HBV 1-2; HBVY; TRV; WGRP

And right through the flower-beds see him go!   Mick.   James Reeves. GDP

And rigs a little swinging gate/To let Bill Wombat under.   Weary Will.   A. B. Paterson.   BoAnP

And ring-fence-deer-park Lie.   The Lie.   Rudyard Kipling.   NOBL

And ring out, all ye laughter-peals of home.   Sirmio.   Caius Valerius Catullus.   AWP

And rip the edge off any ideal or dream.   Turf-Stacks.   Louis MacNeice. LiTM; OBMV

And rise above the hills of earth, and shine/In a serener sphere.   The Tides. William Cullen Bryant.   TAP

And rise,–be free!   He Made Us Free.   Maurice Francis Egan.   AA

And rise Thou with it in thy greater light.   Bussy d'Ambois.   George Chapman.   ViBoPo

And rise to wealth and honor,/In the State of El-a-noy.   El-A-Noy. *Anonymous.*   TrAS

And rise/up/to engulf/you.   Bog.   Leen Volwerk.   PoSH

And rival minstrels meet.   Music of the Night.   John Neal.   AA

And rivers, and women, and kings.   The Panchatantra: Kings.   *Anonymous.* AWP

And rivers of the dead around my neck.   Altarwise by Owl-Light.   Dylan Thomas.   CMoP; NoAm

And roamed there all the stupid afternoon.   Hibiscus on the Sleeping Shores. Wallace Stevens.   InPS; PAI

And roar in Numbers worthy Bounce.   An Heroick Epistle from a Dog at Twickenham to a Dog at Court.   Alexander Pope.   FM

And, roaring, set out with his awesome sword!   I Know on a Night Overcast. Hayim Nahman Bialik.   LiTW

And roars the many-sounding main.   To a Moth Crushed Within the Leaves of an Iliad.   Charles Edward Thomas.   AA

And robbed of his real function, like some men.   Superbull.   Harold Witt. FAZ

And robe me for that world of light.   Heaven's Magnificence.   William Augustus Muhlenberg.   AA

And Robin, by the cruel sparrow/Was shot quite dead with bow and arrow. Says Robin to Jenny, "If you will be mine.'.   *Anonymous.*   PBBP

And Robin shall restore amends. A Midsummer Night's Dream. William Shakespeare. BoW; CTC; EIL; EnRePo; LiTB; LoBV; MoShBr; NAs; OBSC; OxBoLi; SeCeV; TrGrPo; ViBoPo; WiR

And Robin took these brethren good/To be of his yeomandrie. Robin Hood and the Beggar. Anonymous. BaBo; ESPB

And rock about, my Saro Jane. Rock about My Saro Jane. Anonymous. FSW

And Rockefeller, junior, being bid,/Upon his knees and neighbors ever did. Compliance. Ambrose Bierce. DBV

And rocks in the air with languid hands grown cold,/The city from her thousand stairs of gold. Morgana. Gabriele D'Annunzio. LiTW

And rode away horseless to the King's white hall. Riddle of Snow and Sun. Anonymous. CBEP; NCEP

And rolled on its harmonious way/Into the boundless realms of space! The Hanging of the Crane. Henry Wadsworth Longfellow. GN

And rolled the psalm, and poured the/prayer,/From Nature's solemn altar-stair. Roslin and Hawthornden. Henry Van Dyke. AA

And rolls through all things. Lines Composed a Few Miles above Tintern Abbey. William Wordsworth. NU

And Roman Antony saw you bloom,/Flaming, on Cleopatra's ships. Italian Poppies. Joel Elias Spingarn. HBMV

And romance, and high bonnets, and Madame Le ROI! Miss Biddy Fudge to Miss Dorothy (excerpt). Thomas Moore. NBM

And rooks in families homeward go,/And so do I. Weathers. Thomas Hardy. ALV; BoLiVe; EvOK; FaBoCh; FaBV; GTBS; LoGBV; MoAB; MoBrPo; OBMV; PoPle; SeCePo

And rooted in Romance remain. Old Susan. Walter De la Mare. CMoP; GoTF; MoBrPo; TreFS

And rose and took the windswept mountain road. Synge's Grave. Winifred M. Letts. AnIV

And rose from table satisfied. Pesci Misti. Leonard Aaronson. FaBoTw

And rose is, and lily, and moon and dove. Die Rose, Die Lilie, Die Taube. Heinrich Heine. AWP

And rose up filling the sky blowsy with/fruit to come Spring. Ruth Whitman. IHMS

And rosebugs i do Gee I Like to Think of Dead. Edward Estlin Cummings. HoPM

And roses in the darkness; and my love. Slumber Song. Siegfried Sassoon. MCCG

And rotted, buried under the dust and leaves. Sonnet: "Looking into the windows that doom has broken." George Woodcock. NeBP

And round about were the wistful stars/With white faces like town children. Autumn. Thomas Ernest Hulme. FaBoMo; LoBV

And round again, and, again, round. A Poem about Breasts. James Wright. TAP

And round and round the world they went/And also stayed at home. Johnny Fife and Johnny's Wife. Mildred Plew Merryman. SoPo; TiPo

And round his heart one strangling golden hair. The House of Life. Dante Gabriel Rossetti. TrGrPo

And round it, silent, silent,/Wheels the invisible flock. The Tower. Mark Van Doren. MoPo

And round its mighty head, prophetic birds. Oedipus. Thomas Blackburn. FaBoTw

And round me stretch unfathomable skies. Lost Years. Eugene Lee-Hamilton. OBVV

And round their narrow lips the mold falls close. The House of Life. Dante Gabriel Rossetti. HBV 1-2

And round them mountain-castled lie/The hundred states of Oregon. Whitman's Ride for Oregon. Hezekiah Butterworth. PAH

And round us is the court of Day! The Hollyhocks. Craven Langstroth Betts. AA

And rounder, rounder, rounder, roared the/iron six-pounder,/Hurling death! Carmen Bellicosum. Guy Humphreys McMaster. AA; GN; HBV 1-2; MC; PAH; PAL

And rub dry their old kisses. The Horses. Maxine W. Kumin. DuDa

And rub/the wounds/together. Our People. Diane Burns. STE

And rub their ears and smooth their breast, and hold/Their paws, and gaze into their eyes of gold. Cats. Francis Scarfe. PCat

And rubbed it clean/and tried to make it work. The Harp. Bruce Weigl. MAYP

And rubbed it off again. Cressida. James Keir Baxter. AnNZ

And rubies in her hair. A Chanted Calendar. Sydney Thomas Dobell. HBV 1-2; HBVY; OBEV

And ruefully you testify his power. Defenceless Children, Your Great Enemy. Kendrick Smithyman. AnNZ

And ruin is the lot of all. The Hurricane. Philip Freneau. AP; MOS; TAP

And Ruin wildly sheds its gleam/Athwart thy path of shame. The Personified Sentimental. Bret (Francis Bret Harte) Harte. NA

And rules alike the cottage and the throne. What Is Charm? Louisa Carroll Thomas. BLPA

And run into our lives and hide. The Hare. Stanley Snaith. HaMV

And run over the pure hands/Of the souls who see all. Because. D. W. Vilakazi. PeSA

And rungs of ladders reared against the sky. Wood-cut. Victoria Mary (Vita) Sackville-West. ChMP

And rural mirth and manners are no more. The Deserted Village. Oliver Goldsmith. OBSV

And rushed home sparkling in/her yellow dress. The Physics of Ochun. Victor Hernandez Cruz. APU

And rushes at a call to meet the one/Who of his tiny universe is sun. Lost Dog. Frances Rodman. GDP

And rushing, rushing onward, gives us the day once/more. The Sun's Golden Bowl. Mimnermus. LiTW

And rushing with the tempest finds the night. The Albatross. William Pember Reeves. AnNZ

And Rustum and his son were left alone.... Sohrab and Rustum. Matthew Arnold. WHA

And rusty dump rake, the deserted farm house. Getting Loaded. Jim Thomas. AMV-80

And rusty iron in a dusty room. The Flowing Summer. Charles Bruce. CaP

And's a fair Step to reach the Heav'n above. Epithalamium on a Late Happy Marriage. Christopher Smart. HW

And saddening those waiting to be born. Not Lost in the Stars. Bruce Bliven. QQQ

And sadly mixed with blood and tears. The Festal Board. Anonymous. BLPA; TreFS

And sae brak out the feud/That gard my dearie die. The Laird of Wariston (A vers.). Anonymous. BaBo; ESPB

And sae hae they that ill woman,/Upon a scrogg-bush him beside. John Thomson and the Turk (B version). Anonymous. ESPB

And sae has he the turtle-dow/Wi the truth of his right hand. Fause Foodrage (A version). Anonymous. ESPB

And sae I flourish'd on the morn,/And sae was pu'd on noon. The Banks o' Doon. Robert Burns. BoLoP; GoTF; PrIm; TreFS

And sae the Lord be thankit. A Child's Grace. Robert Burns. BrR; MoShBr

And safe in heaven dead Mexico City Blues. Jack Kerouac. NeAP

And said, Earl Martial, but for my/oath,/Then hanged shouldst thou be. Queen Eleanor's Confession (A version). Anonymous. BaBo; ESPB; OBET; PrIm

And said: "He hadn't very far to fall." The Devil's Dictionary: Corporal. Ambrose Bierce. OBAL

And said he was very well served in his kind. The Foolish Miller. Anonymous. UnTE

And said: "Heaven pardon Brother Timothy,/And keep us from the sin of gluttony." Tales of a Wayside Inn. Henry Wadsworth Longfellow. AmPP

And said, "I don't see/so good myself." How Tuesday Began. Kathleen Fraser. CTBA; NYBP

And said, "It's a very mean trixir." Limerick: "He gave her some kind of elixir." Anonymous. TDH

And said it was the wind that stirred. Afterward. Mary Matheson. CaP

And said, "Nay, we are seven!" We Are Seven. William Wordsworth. BLPA; BLPL; EnRP; GN; GoTF; HBV 1-2; MBW 1-2; OxBChV; SpRo; TEP; TreF; WBLP

And said, "Not yet! in quiet lie." Daybreak. Henry Wadsworth Longfellow. AnNE; FPL; GoTF; HBV 1-2; PoLf; TreFT

And said though strange/they all were true. I Saw a Fishpond All on Fire. Anonymous. OxNR

And said, "What a good boy/am I!" Little Jack Horner. Mother Goose. FaBoBe; FaFP; HBV 1-2; HBVY; SoPo; SoSe

And said: "Ye ar welcum heir,/Be him that me bocht." Rauf Coilyear (excerpt). Anonymous. OxBS

And sail into the dark/With laughter on our lips. The Spark. Joseph Mary Plunkett. AnIV; AWP

And sail on the first favouring wind? Exile. Anonymous. KiLC

And sail the grey Funnel Line no more. The Grey Funnel Line. Cyril Tawney. OBET

And sail them out wandering safe on the waves of Cliona. At the News from Fal's High Plain I Cannot Sleep. Seathrun Ceitinn. NOBI

And sailed through her toward the morning light. Leda, the Lost. Eda Lou Walton. AnAmPo

And sailless seas beat the untrodden shore. At the Grave of Champernowne. John Albee. HBV 1-2

And Saint Billy Bungstarter/Have mercy on him. Secular Litany. Michael Kennedy Joseph. AnNZ

And salvaged less than the intolerable statue. The Statue. John Berryman. NYP

...And Sam, well we'll find out/whether he has an appetite for fish! Cleaning the Fish. Robert Pack. SM

And Samson is the thief and Samson is the sun. Aurora Borealis. Edouard Roditi. EAS

And sanctify this Altar to be Thine!   The Altar.   George Herbert.   AnAnS 1; ATP; HoPM; InPS; JCP; OAEL 1-2; PAI; SeCP; SeCV 1-2; TrCP; TrGrPo

And sang an original love song/That nobody understood.   Fable of the Talented Mockingbird.   Scott Bates.   BoAnP

And sang it for "Good-Night" beneath the moon.   Serenade.   *Anonymous.*   AWP

And sang of Hektor and Andromache like gods.   Andromache's Wedding.   Sappho.   BoWoP

And sang the chorus of every song at the concert in/Albert Hall.   The Dream.   *Anonymous.*   OxBoLi

And sank helplessly toward the old dream,/in which Felicia died.   Fidelity.   Jerry Kass.   AMV-80

And sank her in the sea.   The Demon Lover.   *Anonymous.*   EnSB

And Santa Anna ran away,/Along the plains of Mexico!   Santa Anna or The Plains of Mexico.   *Anonymous.*   AmSS

And sat down at his desk and wrote a story.   Herman Melville.   W. H. Auden.   LiTA; NePA; OAEP; OxBA

And sat here and let me rattle on this way.   The Transparent Man.   Anthony Hecht.   FYAP

And Satan hates mee, yet is loth to lose mee.   Holy Sonnets, II.   John Donne.   MasP; OBS

And Satan's kingdom soon shall fall!   McKinley Brook.   *Anonymous.*   ShS

And Satan's self had thoughts of taking orders.   Tophet.   Thomas Gray.   MyFE; NCEP; NOEC; OBSP

And saucily laughed at him.   Jack O'Lantern.   Anna Chandler Ayre.   SoPo

And saving nations roam o'er native wilds again!   The Last Bison: Song.   Charles Mair.   NOBC

And save the serpent in their midst.   In Memory of My Feelings.   Frank O'Hara.   NeAP; PoM

...And save the State/From selfish greed. For this we wait.   At the Lincoln Tomb.   John H. Bryant.   PGD

And save them in the time of need.   O Lord, That Art My God and King.   John Craig.   AH

And save us God's inscription in the bone.   Untitled: "Fivesucked the features of my girl by glory."   Nicholas Moore.   PoA

And save young Bobby some.   Christmas-Tide.   *Anonymous.*   OxNR

And saved a great cause that heroic day.   Opportunity.   Edward Rowland Sill.   AnNE; BLPA; GN; GoTF; HBV 1-2; HBVY; MCCG; OHFP; TreFS; WGRP; YaD

And, saved by His redemption,/We'll spread the news abroad.   We Would See Jesus.   *Anonymous.*   STF

And saved some part/Of a day I had rued.   Dust of Snow.   Robert Frost.   CMoP; MoShBr; OBSP; OxBA; PrIm; SoSe; TAP; TiPo; UnPo; WeW

And saved the sum of things for pay.   Epitaph on an Army of Mercenaries.   Alfred Edward Housman.   BrPo; CMoP; ForPo; MMM; MoAB; MoVE; NIP; NoAm; NOBE; OBEV; OBWP; OxBTC; PPP; PrIm; SaC; UnPo; ViBoPo; WaaP

And saved us twice, for Charlie's sake.   For Charlie's Sake.   John Williamson Palmer.   HBV 1-2

And saved you shall be.   The Maid Freed from the Gallows.   *Anonymous.*   AnFE; BaBo; ESPB; InPo; ViBoFo

And saw another lining/inside a further sky.   The Hatch.   Norma Farber.   SO

And saw at eve the broken sunset die/In crimson on the silent wilderness.   Temagami.   Archibald Lampman.   OBCV

And saw at last his God's dark purblind heart/In the lion's eyeball, like a wet coal.   A History.   John Williams.   NePoAm-2

And saw Himself, as one looks in a glass,/In those impassioned eyes.   In Sleep.   Alice Meynell.   BrRo

And saw his mother waiting at the door.   The Hudson.   George Sidney Hellman.   AA

...And saw/in the dew of the sandy road/faint print of a fox's paw.   On Addy Road.   May Swenson.   GOYP

And saw in the smithy his own fire burning.   Cranmer.   C. H. Sisson.   FaBoTw

And saw the ruin with rejoicing eyes.   Pharsalia: The Rivalry between Caesar and Pompey.   Lucan (Marcus Annaeus Lucanus).   OBVE

And sawdust trickled from his wounded side.   Arrogance.   Walter De la Mare.   OBSP

And say dat's good enough for nigger.   We Raise de Wheat.   *Anonymous.*   BPo; TAP

And say hello today.   Visit the Sick.   James J. Metcalfe.   PoToHe

And say him sooth in his presence.   Snatches: "Who so cometh to any hous."   *Anonymous.*   OxBM

And, say! how does it seem to you?   Far from the Madding Crowd.   Nixon Waterman.   BLPA; FaBoBe

And say, "I know. But then what can I do?"   The Deserter.   John Streeter Manifold.   CBAP

And say I love you?   The Diary of Izumi Shikibu (excerpt).   Izumi Shikibu.   BoWoP

And say I made you for Becchina's sake.   Sonnet: Of Love, in Honor of His Mistress Becchina.   Cecco da Siena Angiolieri.   AWP

And say it without voice. Praise universes/Numberless. Praise all of them. Praise Him.   The God of Galaxies.   Mark Van Doren.   ImOP; MoRP

And say my glory was I had such friends.   The Municipal Gallery Revisited.   William Butler Yeats.   GTBS-P; LiTB; OxBTC

And say my mite I will impart,/To aid the poor distress'd.   The Framework-Knitters Lamentation.   *Anonymous.*   CoMu

And say once more, Let there be light.   The Nativity.   Henry Vaughan.   SBVL

And say that I went like a ranger should go.   Roll a Rock Down.   Richard Burton.   AnAmPo

And say the lad that loved you/Was one that kept his word.   Because I Liked You Better.   Alfred Edward Housman.   EnLit; GBL; NOBV; OxBTC; PeHV

And say, "This is my Flesh and Blood"; Thy Word is my reply.   Dialogue.   Sister Mary Madeleva.   CAW

...And say those Eastern kings/Did not present thee with more precious things.   Royal Presents.   Nathaniel Wanley.   OxBoCh; TrPWD

And say to all the world "This/was a man!"   Julius Caesar.   William Shakespeare.   FaFP; TrGrPo

And say what they think in a handsomer stile.   Literary Importation.   Philip Freneau.   TAP

And say, "Why, it's a goldfinch."   Prophecy.   Jules Supervielle.   AMV-81

And say with joyous heart, "They are with Thee."   Faith.   *Anonymous.*   PoToHe

And saying so to some/Means nothing; others it leaves/Nothing to be said.   Nothing To Be Said.   Philip Larkin.   OxBTC

And saying this, drive through the falling night.   The Burial of Saint Brendan.   Padraic Colum.   OxBI

And says, "Easy, please! You'll have it right off."   Epigram: "There was this gym teacher."   Strato.   PeHV

And says, "Good-morning, love," to me.   Mrs. Barks.   Rose Fyleman.   BrR

And says our breakfast will be cold/If we play pirate any more.   Roughchin, the Pirate.   Arthur Boswell.   EtS

And says, "Why do you strike me brother? I am Man."   Rostov.   G. S. Fraser.   WaP

And says, "Why, you need sprinkling,/You thirsty little rose!"   Sprinkling.   Dorothy Mason Pierce.   SUS; TiPo

And scandal left her presence/For person more endowed!   Play-Acting.   Frances Barber.   GoYe

And scarce begun, concludes th' abortive song.   An Hymn to the Morning.   Phillis Wheatley.   TAP

And scarce fifteen of age.   Bird in a Cage.   *Anonymous.*   GBP

And scattered the thin blue petals/Of a steel rose.   Mozart.   John Heath-Stubbs.   EBEV

And scattered vowels of Jerusalem.   Anglo-Saxon.   E. L. Mayo.   MiAP

And scatters all the jewels.   Across clear drops of dew.   Asayasu.   LiTW

And schild us fro the fendes hand.   Of a Rose, a Lovely Rose.   *Anonymous.*   AtBAP; OBEV; OxBM; OxBoCh

And scholars, soldiers, kings unhonoured die.   The Traveller.   Oliver Goldsmith.   NOEC

And school-boys lag with satchels in their hands.   A Description of the Morning.   Jonathan Swift.   CABA; CEP; EBEV; EiCP; ExPo; FF; HAP; InPS; NIP; NOBE; NOEC; NoP; OAEL 1-2; Prf; SeCeV; TEP; ViBoPo; WeW

And scorn a rascal and a coach!   Tom Southerne's Birth-Day Dinner at Ld. Orrery's.   Alexander Pope.   NAs

And scorn the world's abuse–/As they dare not.   Tenth Reunion.   Edward Steese.   GoYe

And scorn to fix thy views on aught beside.   What Glorious Vision.   Thomas Cradock.   AH

And scorn to live in slavery bound down by iron chains.   Bold Jack Donahue.   *Anonymous.*   AmFP; FSW

And scorning say, "See what it is to love."   Astrophel and Stella, CVII.   Sir Philip Sidney.   AAS; HBV 1-2; NoP; SiPS

And scourged the crouching lands again.   The Awakened War God.   Margaret Widdemer.   WGRP

And scramble for what we can get.   The World.   Thomas Love Peacock.   PV

And scratched 'em in again.   There was a man of our town.   Mother Goose.   FaFP; HBV 1-2; HBVY

And scratching in its underwear,/fumbles for a heritage.   The Reports Come In.   J. D. Reed.   NYBP

And se a sad face to the sea.   At the Grave of Walker.   Joaquin Miller.   AA; AnAmPo; AnFE; APA

And sea-foam, and the earth.   The Plot to Assassinate the Chase Manhattan Bank.   Carl Larsen.   FF; PPON

And seal her to the stranger for his castle in the gloom.   Emily Hardcastle, Spinster.   John Crowe Ransom.   CMoP; OBSP

And seal the hushed casket of my soul. To Sleep. John Keats. ERoP 1-2; FaBoRV; LoBV; MBW 1-2; NIP; OAEP; OBEV; OBRV; PoEL 1-5; PrIm; TEP; WHA

And sear no more with second sight. In Festubert. Edmund Charles Blunden. OBMV

And search the oracles divine,/Till every heartfelt word is mine. My Companion. Charles Wesley. STF

And seasons, changeless since the day she died. The Cross of Snow. Henry Wadsworth Longfellow. AP; HeIP; MAmP; NOBA; OxBA; TAP

And seaweed over the marble stairs. Venetian Scene. Anne Ridler. NMP

And second-cousin to the worm!' A Ballad of a Bun. Sir Owen Seaman. CenHV

And secretly commend me to my sanct. Sonnet: "Go you, O winds that blow from north to south." Alexander Craig. EIL

And see and suffer myself/In another being, at last. The Waking. Theodore Roethke. CoAP

And see can you make out/any/noises. I Hope I Don't Have You Next Semester, But. Edwin Godsey. HoPM

And see darkness falling/away from the self. Tablerock. Darryl Wally. AMV-81

And see! descended from her chariot now,/In this related pompe shee visits you. An Angel Describes Truth. Ben Jonson. OBS

And see each other face to face as in a dream. The Return. Tu Fu. LiTW

And see God's face, Ancient of Days, Eternal! An Old Woman's Answer to a Letter from Her Girlhood. Susan L. Emory. CAW

And see him in the Face. Heaven. Digby Mackworth Dolben. BoC

And see Him in the truth of everlasting day. The Dream of Gerontius. John Henry, Cardinal Newman. OxBoCh

And see him with our Angel stand,/To waft, and welcome us to land. On the Death of His Son. Charles Wesley. NOCV

And see his children fed. For Johnny. John Pudney. HaMV; OBWP

And see if he will be moved. Ballad. Archie Randolph Ammons. GP

And see if they tasted/As good as they look. Clouds. Dorothy Aldis. SoPo

And see in clearness the Evening Star. The Evening Star. Amy Carmichael. TRV

And see in heav'n, our glorious home,/The Star of Christmas morning. The Golden Carol. Anonymous. OHIP

And see my bonnie Jean again. I'll Aye Ca' in By Yon Town. Robert Burns. BSV

And see Odell, the tax-collector, hung. Odell. James Stephens. MoAB; MoBrPo

...And/see that their wives have been loyal/in their absence. The Card-Players. David Ray. VGW

And see the blue steel redden at the word. Words. Ernest Rhys. HBMV

And see, the boy still sleeping at your side! Night Storm. William Gilmore Simms. EtS; MOS

And, see, the Boys their Flocks to Shelter drive. Pastoral Landscape. Ambrose Philips. OBEC

And see the cat play with the dog. The Rose Is Red, the Grass Is Green. Anonymous. OxNR

And see the figure he is not. Telephone Lineman. Ernest Kroll. AMV-81

And see the listening, longing maiden/Lit by the moon. The Ute Lover. Hamlin Garland. AA

...And see the longed-for land/Lie, known and very near. Sealed Orders. Richard Burton. HBV 1-2

And see the men at play. The Golf Links. Sarah N. Cleghorn. FaFP; HBMV; InMe; InPK; PoLf; PoPl; PPON

And see the rising Sun, and feel it dart/New rays of pleasance trembling to the heart. Pantisocracy. Samuel Taylor Coleridge. EnRP

And see the shadow children home again. Central Park. Howard Nemerov. NYP

And see the storm a shore. Odes. Horace. OBVE

And see them all uniting show/That man was made for man.' The Enthusiast: an Ode. William Whitehead. OBEC

And see them branching, turning into trees! Blessing Mrs. Larkin. Margery Mansfield. GoYe

And see this aged nature,/Go with a bending stature. Great Friend. Henry David Thoreau. MAmP; PoEL 1-5

And see, through heaven's gate,/Angels within it. At the Church Gate. William Makepeace Thackeray. HBV 1-2

And see thy face in Heaven, Isadore! The Widowed Heart. Albert Pike. AA

And see Thy glorious face above. Thy Glorious Face Above. Charles Wesley. BePJ

And see us play the Tragedy of Wit. Prologue to Aureng-Zebe. John Dryden. ATP; CBEP; OBS; OxBoLi; PP; SeCeV

And, see, we are landing on the island of magic...' Toward Lesbos. Renee Vivien. PeHV

And see you safely through diminished fields. Riding a One-Eyed Horse. Henry Taylor. HeIP; InPK; PH

And see, your Future Lives, Jehovah Praise. The Mercies of the Year, Commemorated. John Danforth. SCAP

And see your mother's heart's blood,/so freely running. Lamkin (K version). Anonymous. ESPB

And seeds of light/Fill the world, my whole being. When I Want to Speak. Rav Abraham I. Kook. VWA

And seeing my cast-off body lying like lumber,/I would laugh with joy. In Trouble and Shame. D. H. Lawrence. OBMV

And, seeing only faces turned away,/did not even go down the aisle as beggars do. Depression (excerpt). Charles Reznikoff. CTBA

And seek another country,–as he would do. Persistent Explorer. John Crowe Ransom. OxBA

And seek beautitude beyond the skies. To a Gentleman and Lady on the Death of the Lady's Brother and Sister. Phillis Wheatley. BlSi

And seek my harbor/Halfway round the world. A Horse Would Tire. Elizabeth Jane Coatsworth. TiPo

And seek you, not believing in you. Years. Anna Margolin. VWA

And seeks to bring the truth forgot/Again to that which he hath yet. This Discord in the Pact of Things. Boethius. LiTW

And seem to march along th' extensive plain. The Hop Garden (excerpt). Christopher Smart. FaBoPP

And seemed the desert of the night/Far down with mellow orchards to endow. The Orchard and the Heath. George Meredith. OBNC

And seems to shake the spheres. Ode on St. Cecilia's Day. John Dryden. GN

And sees a whole world. The Window. Conrad Aiken. CMoP

And sees beyond his little sphere/The waving fronds of heaven, clear. Who Loves a Garden. Louise Seymour Jones. BLPA

And sees man's slave the master of mankind. History of the Modern World. Stanton A. Coblentz. PGD

And sees Narcissus making up his face. Occam's Razor Starts in Massachusetts (parody). Edward Pygge. BXAP

And sees the grief within. Cloak of Laughter. Abigail Cresson. PoToHe

...And sees this only now that/he has himself become a mouse... The Mouse Dinners. Russell Edson. SoSe

And sees within my eyes the tears of two. Sonnets from the Portuguese, VI. Elizabeth Barrett Browning. BLPL; GTBS; HBV 1-2; OBEV; TreFS; TrGrPo; ViBoPo

And seething overflow...Hosanna, Lord! The Holy Rose. Vyacheslav Ivanov. AWP

And seize his fiery hand. Dust on Spring Street. Louis Grudin. NoP

And seizing with precipitation/The slight neglects of conversation.' Carmina. Caius Valerius Catullus. OBVE

And Self begin to be. Monochrome. Louise Imogen Guiney. AnAmPo

And self-infolds the large results/Of force that would have forged a name. In Memoriam A.H.H., LXXIII. Alfred, Lord Tennyson. HBV 1-2

And selfless self-approval of the hills. After Nightfall. William Renton. NOBV

And sell him at his own. Positive, A Coxcomb. William Plomer. PoL

And send his blessing on these poor people who have lost their sons in such/ distress. The Loss of the New Columbia. Anonymous. AmFP

And send it a thousand miles, thinking. Exile's Letter. Li Po. CTC; SeCeV

And send it in a worse estate/Than when it came to thee. The Crowned Heart. Anonymous. PoPle

And send its glorious beams afar/To fill the world with light. The Holy Star. William Cullen Bryant. BePJ

,...And send our sons/to walk out in open day. Lines for a Hard Time. Gena Ford. IHMS

And send these skirts/unravelling at my feet. Sagimusume: The White Heron Maiden. Jonny Kyoko Sullivan. WPOW

And send thy bitter cry into the storm! The City of Slaughter. Hayim Nahman Bialik. TrJP

And send thy sands to make dry lands,/when they shall want fresh water. The Powte's Complaint. Anonymous. GBP

And send us some hot in the morn. Blow, Wind, Blow! and Go, Mill, Go. Mother Goose. BrR; HBV 1-2; TiPo

And send you a happy new year. The Moon Shines Bright. Anonymous. GBP; OBET

And send you a joyful May. The Mayers' Song. Anonymous. GBP

And send you an invalid to your own native land. The Flash Frigate. Anonymous. AmSS

And sende me joy where I am nowe in pain. A! Mercy, Fortune. Anonymous. MeEL

And sending their feathers here away there away. Feathers of Snow. Anonymous. GBP

And sends me, reeling, home to bed! Tobacco. Philip Freneau. TAP

And sends us back to books, ambition, people. Sleeping Beauty: August. Douglas Knight. DFT

And sent for transportation with the Boys of Mullabaun. The Boys of Mullabaun. Anonymous. BIrV; GBP

And sent safe into exile over the waves of/Cliodhna! My Grief on Fal's Proud Plain. Geoffrey Keating. OnYI

And sent the miner home that night to Deadwood on the hills. Just from Dawson. *Anonymous.* ABF

And sent the mossbacks prancing. Bung Yer Eye. *Anonymous.* ABF

And sent them to the cruel wars in High Germany. High Germany. *Anonymous.* CBEP; FSW; WaaP

And sent this snowy spray to thee. With a Spray of Apple Blossoms. Walter Learned. AA

And separates out the wonder from the wet/and names its cause. Thomas in the Fields. Lois Moyles. NYBP

And seraphs shout, Amen! Arise, Ye Saints of Latter Days. *Anonymous.* AH

And serpent-like, that none may injure thee! Prudent Simplicity. William Cowper. FaBoEE

And serves me in my way and not another. Demands of the Muse. Vernon Watkins. PoA

And set an old bell tolling on the air. Idolatry. Arna Bontemps. AmNP; PoNe

And set it in a high, clean place,/To recall the granite strength of my desire. Clay Hills. Jean Starr Untermeyer. HBMV

And set it rose-like in your tawny hair. Twilight. Virginia McCormick. HBMV

And set its crown of glory upon your/head. Epitaph. *Anonymous.* TrJP

And set my soul at liberty/By Thy victorious love. The Conquering Love of Jesus. Charles Wesley. BePJ

And set off fireworks to praise a homemade day. Prison Song. Alan Dugan. PoA

And set off on his banal journey/When Magritte died. Homage to Rene Magritte. George Melly. EAS

And set the caup on Tintock-Tap. Tintock. *Anonymous.* GBP

And set to work to spoil the countryside. Bungaloid Growth. Colin Ellis. FaBoEE

And set your people free. Come Back, Lincoln. Chauncey R. Piety. PGD

And sets a mimic garden, cold and bright. Frost. Edith Matilda Thomas. AA

And sets the dead-land-lilies in her breast. A Roman Mirror. Sir James Rennell Rodd. OBVV

And setting out to visit you. Solitude. Charles Simic. GP

And settle like dew/over the crannies/and crevices of all our lives! The Riddles of Change. Felix Mnthali. WhB

And settled upon his eyes in a black soot. "More Light! More Light!" Anthony Hecht. CoAP; ConAP; HAP; NePoEA-2; NoAm; NOBA; NoP; OBWP; SM; SoSe; TwCP; UnPo; VGW; VWA

And settling on his shoulder/folds her wings,/caws. The Day Concludes Burning. Desmond O'Grady. CIP

And seven wondrous stags that I/Could not believe walked slowly by. Wood. Thomas Hornsby Ferril. PoRA

And severed from that element for ever. Lumber of Spring. Anne Ridler. NYBP

And severed my medical career. Pacific Epitaphs. Dudley Randall. NoAm

And shaded by historic woes/A mother mops her infant's nose. Jardin de la Chapelle Expiatoire. Robert Finch. PeCV

And shake his head at Doctor Swift. The Happy Life of a Country Parson (parody). Alexander Pope. BXAP

And shake the shade that hugs him close. Second Shadow. Theodore Roethke. PoA

And shake the very pillars/of the everlasting heavens... Patience. Frank Horne. BPo

And shakes a man as dawn shakes birds and flowers. Morning on the St. John's. Jane Cooper. NYBP

And shakes his fist at Red River Black. Idaho Jack. Jack H. Lee. BPAW

And shakes this fragile frame at eve/With throbbings of noontide. I Look into My Glass. Thomas Hardy. BrPo; CABA; EBEV; FaBoTw; HAP; NOBE; NOBV; NoP; OBSP; PoPle; PrIm; SCV; VLP

And shaking with silent laughter. The Pointed People. Rachel Field. WSC

And shall be sated with celestial mirth. The Bible. Thomas Traherne. LoBV

And shall by law deliver us. Foundation of Faith. John Drinkwater. MoRP

...And shall exalt his own anointed one. The Song of Hannah. Michael Drayton. TrCP

And shall forever span them and compactly hold and enclose them. On the Beach at Night Alone. Walt Whitman. NePA; TAP

And shall I only when I cease/To be at all, be all at peace? Peace. Irwin Edman. TrJP

And shall remain a status quo-/Without a vestige of jim crow. Status Quo. Binga Dismond. PoNe

And shall you protect? Chrysothemis. Henry Reed. MoVE

And shamble down time to doomsday? The Stranger. William Everson. FF

"And shaped like the top of a table." Lighting the Night Sky. Kenneth O. Hanson. FYAP

And share my bed with Capricorn and Cancer. Altarwise by Owl-Light. Dylan Thomas. CMoP; NoAm

And share the crusts of love in fairer weather. Sandwich Man. Louis Johnson. AnNZ

...And share/The same unholy itch. A pretty pair! They Make a Pretty Pair of Debauchees. Caius Valerius Catullus. DBV

And share their doom. My Company. Sir Herbert Read. BrPo; MMM

And share thy rest. The Dead Child. Ernest Christopher Dowson. BrPo

And share with me the grave respons./Of writing this amazing nons.! Poetical Economy. Harry Graham. CenHV; FaBoCo; TreFS

And sharp-broken/Dinner plates. Tinker's Wife. Patrick Kavanagh. CIP; InPS; NoAm

And, shattered on the roof like smallest snows,/The tiny petals of the mountain ash. Sonnets. Frederick Goddard Tuckerman. NoP

And shatters to their depths the abysses of the sea. The Mares of the Camargue. Frederic Mistral. AWP; PoPl

And she always commended me well for my seed. The Wanton Seed. *Anonymous.* OBET

And she, an avalanche of woe.' The Three Voices (parody). Lewis (Charles Lutwidge Dodgson) Carroll. BXAP

And she and I each listen in vain! Knocking at the Door. John Freeman. HBMV

And she and I went hand in hand/In the field where the daisies are. The Daisies. James Stephens. AnIV; AWP

And she and she/for a me and me– God Is a Masturbator. Gregory Corso. GP

And she answered, "I promised to cleave, and I've cleft." The Lovers. Phoebe Cary. HBV 1-2

And she answered, "No, sir, no." No, Sir, No. *Anonymous.* AmFP

And she been his Gem and Joy. The Moon Sings. *Anonymous.* MOON; OxBoLi

And she beside another lad. A Shropshire Lad. Alfred Edward Housman. OAEP

And she blew us a kiss as they copped her away/From that prominent bar in Secaucus, N.J. In a Prominent Bar in Secaucus One Day. X. J. Kennedy. ConAP; FYAP; HoAn; HoPM; NIP; NLV; OBAL; PoCh; PPP; UnTE

And she blushed to the roots of her hair when the postman/touched her fingers. Short Short Story. Josephine Jacobsen. NePoAm-2

And she can think of nothing else to do. La Pesadilla. Gerda Penfold. GP

And she chatters with Pete/during class/and/I'm glad. Foreign Student. Barbara B. Robinson. CTBA

And she claims me hers again. Magnetism. Emma Lazarus. SBG

And she compliant to his every wish. Note on Propertius 1.5. Fleur Adcock. BoLoP

And she continued to breathe evenly/from the depths of sleep. Physical Universe. Louis Simpson. InPS

And she could not have hit a more excellent plan/For making him fully and perfectly man. A Fable for Critics. James Russell Lowell. AmPP; AP; OxBA

And she counts them as they fall. Satin-Clad. Stevie Smith. OxBC

And she cows me with the lashing of her tongue. Horace, Book V, Ode III. Charles Larcom Graves. CenHV

And she crept under a pudding-pan. Ladybird, Ladybird. Mother Goose. CBEP; SoPo

And she cruelly told him he'd better. Limerick: "A young man on a journey had met her." *Anonymous.* LiBL; TDH

And she doesn't mind Waitin' a While. Whalan of Waitin' a While. James William Gordon. PoAu 1-2

And she–exposed out/of her tight shopper: a broiler. The Shebeen Queen. Mafika Pascal Gwala. WhB

And she fell into the column with a low, glad cry,/"Me-o-o-w!" Poor Kitty Popcorn (with music). *Anonymous.* AS

And she forgotten in the quiet grave. The Wanderer Recalls the Past. William Wordsworth. OBNC

And she galloped after it on a white horse. Robertin Tush. *Anonymous.* GBP

And she gently gently gently/Touched my cheek. The Hermaphrodite's Song. Lorna Mitchell. BrRo

And she had as yet hardly known God. Eve. Rainer Maria Rilke. MoRP

And she hangs in the church of Saint Hilaire,/Where you and all may see. My Madonna. Robert W. Service. BLPA

And she has crept under/The warming pan. To the Ladybird. *Anonymous.* OxNR

And she has her own resting-place at last. Mademoiselle Richarde. Edith Sitwell. MoVE

And she hauls me by the hair/Out of Hell! Family Portrait. Leonard Feeney. ISi

And she: "If I had wept!" Three Rimas, 3. Gustavo Adolfo Becquer. LiTW

And she is all thine own. On the Death of a Recluse. George Darley. CBEP; OBVV; OxBI

...And she/is caught in the trapped cat/of her children's dreams. The Perfect Mother. Susan Griffin. NPGG

...And she knows they/will answer: Hoy, hoy, hoy! Mom's Homecooked Trees. Michael Stephens. APU

And she laid a white egg in a willow tree root. The Goose and the Gander. Anonymous. GBP

And she laughed back–as if her name were Eve. In the Orchard. Robert Friend. GP

And she, like Sol, alone retires/To shine elsewhere of course. Doris. William Congreve. NOEC

And she'll bark and beg to go out again/To try and outsmart the pouring rain. Silly Dog. Myra Cohn Livingston. GDP

And she'll never more come to my call. Noonday Sun. Kathryn and Byron Jackson. TiPo

And she'll never put a stain on my jacket so blue. Jacket So Blue. Anonymous. BFSS

And she'll never/Walk the streets no more. Sweet Ethel. Linda Piper. BlSi

And she'll say that she's disgusted! Tardiness. Gelett Burgess. BBGG

...And she looked at me/with green eyes. Last Night. David Ignatow. VGW

And she man lye in his bed, but she'll/not lye neist the wa. Captain Wedderburn's Courtship (A version). Anonymous. AmFP; BaBo; ESPB; ViBoFo

And she may want, and very soon,/Her armies for her own defence. The Battle of Lake Champlain. Philip Freneau. PAH

And she not hearing a sound. Prothalamium. Donagh MacDonagh. BIrV; NeIP

And she rose up decrepitely,/For a last dim look at earth and sea. The Vision of Sir Launfal. James Russell Lowell. GN

And she rose with him flowering in her melting snow. A Winter's Tale. Dylan Thomas. AtBAP; CMoP; LiTB; SeCeV

And she's found the things she sought–/found a prize, a bully battle, and a breeze! Firstfruits in 1812. Wallace Rice. PAH

And she's gotten a father to her bairn,/The wanton laird of Young Logie. The Laird of Logie. Anonymous. BaBo; ESPB

And she's tied it about sweet Willie's/waist,/An drawn him out o Yarrow. Rare Willie Drowned in Yarrow, or, The Water o Gamrie (B version). Anonymous. ESPB

And she's wearing the Farmer's hat! The Mare. Herbert Asquith. PH

And she says I have slept too long. The Nut-Gathering Lass. Robert Burns. UnTE

And she says that I fall asleep. The Sleepy Song. Josephine Dodge Daskam Bacon. SUS

–And she/Shall be queen of the wind and the night,/Stars, sun, and the sea. The Soul. George Barlow. OBVV

And she shall have a young prince,/For her own fair sake. A Dis, a Dis, a Green Grass. Anonymous. PoPle

And she shall play the child with love, or sorrow. Caelica, XXV. Fulke, Lord Brooke Greville. AtBAP; FCP

And she singeth full like a papejay. A Description of His Ugly Lady. Thomas Hoccleve. MeEL

And she sits alone at the table, a white stone/useless except to a collector, a rich man. Behaviour of Fish in an Egyptian Tea Garden. Keith Douglas. FaBoMo; OBTV

And she sits with us only/Till next Pentecost. Miss Euphemia. John Crowe Ransom. CMoP

And she smashed my infundibuliform hat. My Infundibuliform Hat. Charles Follen Adams. OBAL

And she sold them/Three farthings a pint. The Dame of Dundee. Anonymous. OxNR

...And she spread her white apron/to their screams. The Return. Bruce Bennett Brown. TAT

And she/Stared back solemnly at me! Check. James Stephens AnIL; GTBS; HBMV; LOW; OnUR; SiSoSe; SUS; TiPo

And she stretches out a half-dried bread:/"Take." Encounter in Safed. Yungman. VWA

And she swooned away again. Aunt Nerissa's Muffin. Wallace Irwin. FiBHP

And she, the one who opened the color forever. When You Leave. Kimiko Hahn. BrSi

And she took herself to the woods of Gort! An Old Air. Frederick Robert Higgins. AnIL

And she took the loan of a stall. The Loan of a Stall. James L. Duff. ISi

And she tumbled down and broke her head. Little Blue Betty. Anonymous. OxNR

And she twisted about them like/an eel, dying, never to know. Samuel Hearne in Wintertime. John Newlove. NOBC

And she viewed their stiff pricks with horror. Limerick: "A well-bred young girl of Gomorrah." Anonymous. PeHV

...And she walked quietly/Into the house to help with the next meal. After the Storm. Elizabeth Bartlett. GoYe

And she wants you still. Papio. Eric Chock. BrSi

And she was here, her hand shut in his hand. Captured. Archibald MacLeish. HBMV

And she was not pining in sorrow like thee. Were You on the Mountain? Anonymous. PV

And she was not the ball-room's belle,/But only–Mrs. Something Rogers! Every-Day Characters. Winthrop Mackworth Praed. EnRP

And she was part of that stay at home army to keep/things going, owing that debt. On the Debt My Mother Owed to Sears Roebuck. Edward Dorn. ConAP

And she was saying oh honey. My Happiness. Greg Pape. MAYP

And she was smiling to her ears! On Mother's Day. Aileen Fisher. NTCP

And she wasn't even/a bad-looking girl, at that. Emma. Yvonne. CNA

...And she/What I do to the grass, does to my thoughts and me. The Mower's Song. Andrew Marvell. AnAnS 1; EnL; LiTL; LoBV; PoEL 1-5; PPP; SeCP; SeCV 1-2

And she who means no mischief does it all. Modesty. Aaron Hill. OBSP

And she who slays is she who bears, who bears. Parentage. Alice Meynell. SBG

And she will come like me at last. Died of Love. Anonymous. CBEP

And she will sail for evermore. The Cruise of the Mystery. Celia Thaxter. OBCA

And she wishes him cripple, or poet,/or even lonely, or sometimes,/better, my lover, dead. The Farmer's Wife. Anne Sexton. HoPM; LiTM; NePoEA-2

And she writes with his sword. To My Truly Valiant, Learned Friend.... Richard Lovelace. CaPo; PoEL 1-5

...And sheds/Her lovely hues upon the flowers' dejected heads. A Summer Storm. Charles Whitehead. OBRV

And shepherd, this is Love, I trow. A Description of Love. Sir Walter Ralegh. ALV; ElL; ELP; LiTL; OAEL 1-2; OBSC; UnTE

And shield thee, and save thee,–or perish there too! Song: "Come, rest in this bosom, my own stricken deer." Thomas Moore. PG

And shild thee fra the Fendis plicht–/Memor esto novissima. Remember the Last Things. Anonymous. MeEL

And shimmered with unheard-of consummations sterile. The New Vintage. Douglas Le Pan. OBCV

And shimmering suds of the sea! Sonnets. Frederick Goddard Tuckerman. AP

And shine among us, free from fear! Magnolia Tree in Summer. Sacheverell Sitwell. BoC

And shine in every place. Give Peace in These Our Days, O Lord. Edmund Grindal. AH

And ships are wreck'd, and shores are strewn. The Winds. John (William Kirkpatrick Magee) Eglinton. OnYI

And shivering I rub these words/together, hoping for a spark. Writing While My Father Dies. Linda Pastan. PCP

And shlopped my head into the billow. Night Shore. Barry O. Higgs. PeSA

And shone that smile on us and sang. Homage to the Empress of the Blues. Robert Earl Hayden. CNA; HaCAP; LCAP; PoBA; PoNe

And shook his fist in a cornstalk's face. Autumn. Elizabeth Madox Roberts. AnAmPo; YaD

And shook the hills with trumpeting. Orchard. Ruth Stone. PH

And shook their rusty brands,/As the Cumberland went down. How the Cumberland Went Down. Silas Weir Mitchell. MC; PAH

And shoot you four or five times/And stand over you until you finish dying Careless Love. Lonnie Johnson. BluL

And shot him. Now what could be ha.? Limerick: "A handsome young gent down in Fla." Anonymous. TDH

And should I have the right to smile? Portrait of a Lady. Thomas Stearns Eliot. AnAmPo; ForPo; HBMV; MAPA; MP; TwCP

And should that happen, I will think him you. Resolving Doubts. William Dickey. ErPo

And should we pause; the thought of Ells-/worth slain/Will steel our aching hearts to strike again! Colonel Ellsworth. Richard Henry Stoddard. PAH

And shout, "Delicious WYE, farewell!" Meandering Wye. Robert Bloomfield. OBNC

And shout of loud defiance pours,/And shook his gauntlet at the towers. Marmion. Sir Walter Scott. OHFP

And shouts, "Well, good-bye now! I'm going!" Snow. Elizabeth Jane Coatsworth. SiSoSe

And shouts, "You ain't nothing but a hound dog,"/As the spitballs begin to fly. Cruel Boys. Gary Soto. NPGG

And show her mind was altered by the rolling of an eye. Going to Mass Last Sunday. Donagh MacDonagh. BIrV; NeIP; OxBI

...And show/How that great work of Love enhances Nature's.   Sonnets from the Portuguese, X.   Elizabeth Barrett Browning.   HBV 1-2

And show mankind a righteous ruler reigns.   An Epistle to the Right Hon. Charles James Fox (excerpt).   Thomas Maurice.   NOEC

And show our plenty. They are poor/That can count all they have and more.   To His Love When He Had Obtained Her.   Sir Walter Ralegh.   FCP

And show that God is still/Holding the reins of life.   After the Dark.   Enola Chamberlain.   STF

And show the heavens more just.   King Lear.   William Shakespeare.   TrGrPo

And show the spiteful sland'rer by this/sign/That you will shield me with your/endless might.   My Inmost Hope.   Sarah Copia Sullam.   TrJP

And show to no man what I see.   He Resolves to Say No More.   Thomas Hardy.   TEP

And show us great surprises.   Life's Made up of Little Things.   Mary R. Hartman.   PoToHe

And show you St. Francis of Assisi.   Stormy Nights.   Robert Louis Stevenson.   BrPo

And show your good conduct by timely possessing.   Advice to the Ladies.   William Somervile.   FaBoUs

And showed a mouse a little house/To keep him through the cold.   Remember September.   May Justus.   SiSoSe; YeAr

...And showed/its claws streaking the gentle groins/and panting and panting.   Message from a Cross.   Max Harris.   NOAV

And showed my own place waiting by/their side.   Elegy.   Moses Ibn Ezra.   TrJP

And shows compassion to the living.   An Epitaph: "Here X. lies dead."   J. E. Thorold Rogers.   FaBoEE

And shows himself more warm and fond than thou.   Sleep.   Theophile de Viau.   AWP

And shows us, rotted and endowed,/Its senile pleasure.   University.   Karl Shapiro.   LiTA; OxBA

And shrapnel gave you, Oh, such a hugging.   On a Photo of a Baby Killed in the War.   Mark Defoe.   SOTS

And shriek with joy in that place beyond prayer.   Parting as Descent.   John Berryman.   MoAmPo

And shrill among the leaves, children impatiently calling.   Picking Apples.   Maurice Lindsay.   BSV

And shrill lark carols clear from her aerial tower.   The Minstrel.   James Beattie.   ViBoPo

And shrilling locust weaves/A song of Summer dead.   August.   William Dean Howells.   AmePo

And shrivels all the lines.   Art.   James (1834-82) Thomson.   EnLi 1-2; OBVV

And shrunk from battle's wild affray/At Manassas.   Manassas.   Catherine Ann Warfield.   MC; PAH

And shun the hovel where they might be warm.   Sheep in Winter.   John Clare.   BoAnP

And shut the lot out in firm precaution.   Page from a Diary.   Desmond O'Grady.   NoAm

And shy enquiries for literature/Come in by every post, and the side door.   From the Embassy.   Robert Graves.   PoA

And shyer than the frogs.   On Yes Tor.   Sir Edmund Gosse.   CH

And sideways a big man with buckets/sets hugely to milk a big cow.   Great Farm.   Philip Booth.   PoPl

And sigh'd for the wrongs of poor Mary le More.   Mary Le More.   George Nugent Reynolds.   OnYI

And sigh for lack of Heaven–but not/The Heaven God bestow–.   The Way I Read a Letter's–This.   Emily Dickinson.   AmePo; DiPo; InPS; PAI

And sigh for noon at midnight.   Asides from the Clowns, VII.   Jules Laforgue.   PoPl

And sigh no more!   The Clover.   Margaret Deland.   AA

And sighed, "All's well–all's well!"   Mag's Song (with music).   Anonymous.   AS

And sighing and kissing so close.   Sylvia the Fair.   John Dryden.   CBEP; UnTE

And, sighing, dream my useless life away.   Fruitionless.   Ina Donna Coolbrith.   AA

And sighing for thy motley coat again.   To the Mocking-Bird.   Richard Henry Wilde.   AA; AnAmPo; BoAnP

And sighs the sighs that loves eternal start.   The Presence of the Spirit.   Giulio Salvadori.   CAW

And sighs to find them in the wood and by the/stream no more.   The Death of the Flowers.   William Cullen Bryant.   GN

And sign crisscross with reverent thumb/Memento homo upon my bum.   Gas from a Burner.   James Joyce.   DBV; TW

And signed the canvas with his own great name.   The Artist.   Arthur Grissom.   AA

And silence filling like a cup.   Burdens.   Edward Dowden.   NOBV

And silence followed after.   Melancholetta.   Lewis (Charles Lutwidge Dodgson) Carroll.   FiBHP

And silence haunts heart's vacancy,/And even pining's done.   She Said.   Walter De la Mare.   ELP

And silence never moves,/Nor speaks nor sings.   Lines Written at the Grave of Alexander Dumas.   Gwendolyn B. Bennett.   CDC; PoNe

And silence sleeps about the glen.   Meet Me in the Primrose Lane.   John Clare.   AtBAP

...And silences/are dark windows?   The World Outside.   Denise Levertov.   ConAP

And silent is/Long Island Sound.   Geography: A Song.   Howard Moss.   CAD; PV

And silent now/Was the cicada's voice.   The Cicada.   Ou-yang Hsiu.   AWP

And silent slides the silver Brent, and mute is "Middlesex."   The Waif.   Walter De la Mare.   FaBoNo

And silently cut and run.   "The Day is Done (Parody on Longfellow).   Phoebe Cary.   ALV; BXAP; OBAL

And silently the ship is put about.   Not Gone Yet.   John Swanick [(or Swanwick)] Drennan.   IrPN

...And silver waters break/Into small waves and sparkle as he comes.   Summer Wind.   William Cullen Bryant.   AP; PoEL 1-5

And silvers on the loose not even frozen souls have seen.   Lying in a Yuma Saloon.   Jim Barnes.   CDW

And simplify me when I'm dead.   Remember Me.   Keith Douglas.   NeBP; NePoEA; OxBTC

And simulates love in a slow bitter shiver.   Life in the Castle.   Anne Hebert.   BoWoP

And sin he best to love is, and most meke,/What nedeth feyned loves for to seke?   The Love Unfeigned.   Geoffrey Chaucer.   NOBE; OBEV

And since he nipped his keeper,/He would just as soon nip you!   The Spangled Pandemonium.   Palmer Brown.   AmMo; TiPo

And since I never dare to write/As funny as I can.   The Height of the Ridiculous.   Oliver Wendell Holmes.   AA; AmePo; AnNE; FaFP; FiBHP; FPL; HBV 1-2; MCCG; MoShBr; OBAL; OBCA; PoPl; TreFT; YaD

And since nothing stopped/my sight, I let it go.   On the Porch at the Frost Place, Franconia, NH.   William Matthews.   MAYP

And since then, like a naked torch,/I have been steeped in pitch.   Not because of you, not because of me.   Natalya Gorbanyevskaya.   BoWoP

And since then she is thief and beggar,/And sovereign queen and buffoon.   The Spinning Girl.   Nathan Alterman.   VWA

And since thou own'st that praise, I spare/thee mine.   To Mary Unwin.   William Cowper.   CoBE; GTBS; GTBS-P; HBV 1-2; OBEV; TrGrPo

And since unweaponed care makes men forlorn,/Let me first make your dog an unicorn.   Caelica, XX.   Fulke, Lord Brooke Greville.   FCP

And since we won, we knew we were right.   The Great Lakes Suite.   James Reaney.   WHW

And since you, loiterer, did compose this wonder,/be with me still, and may God hold his thunder.   A Letter.   Anne Ridler.   LiTL

And sing and sing and sing to life/my praise of death.   Ancient Murderess Night.   Anna Margolin.   VWA

And sing, fal, la, la,/La, la, le.   Serenade.   Bret (Francis Bret Harte) Harte.   LBN

And sing my song of joy in perfect purity.   Prayer.   Doris Hedges.   GoYe

And sing no more.   The Song of the King's Minstrel.   Richard Middleton.   HBV 1-2

And sing no more of war   Poem to My Sister, Ethel Ennis....   June Jordan.   TAP

And sing of brave Grace Darling, who nobly saved the crew.   Grace Darling.   Anonymous.   OBET; OBSS

And sing of the praises of Muirland Meg.   She'll Do It.   Robert Burns.   UnTE

And sing song after song till we hail the new day.   How Happy the Man.   Anonymous.   OBET

And sing Te Deum.   To the Archbishop of Tuam.   Anonymous.   FaBoEE

And sing that Ektor and Andromakha/Are like two of the gods together.   The Marriage of Hector and Andromache.   Sappho.   OBVE

And sing that richt Balulalow!   Balulalow.   James, John, Robert Wedderburn.   LoBV; OBEV; OxBoCh

And sing the glad story again and again.   The Heavenly Stranger.   Ada Blenkhorn.   BLRP

And sing the songs he loved to hear.   In Memoriam A.H.H., CVII.   Alfred, Lord Tennyson.   SBVL; VLP

And sing the wildflowers up from root and seed.   Our Singing Strength.   Robert Frost.   AtBAP

And sing this song/he once heard in another village   Father Takes to the Road and Lets His Hair down.   Alan Chong Lau.   BrSi

And sing Thy praises, O my song,/alway!   The Pride of a Jew.   Judah Halevi.   TrJP

And sing to groaners high and low,/The dirge of "Hey, boys! down go ye!"   Hey, Boys! Up Go We!   Anonymous.   NOAV

And sing to our hearts as we watch again/Your fairy building grow.   The Building of the Nest.   Margaret Sangster.   HBV 1-2; HBVY

And sing, with all the heavenly choir,/That endless song above.   Jesus, the Soul of Our Joys.   Charles Wesley.   BePJ

And, singing, seize the cloth across again.   The Curtain Poem.   Edwin Brock.   NMP

And singing singing so pleasantly in their flight.   Contra Mortem.   Hayden Carruth.   PoA

And singing still the nightingales die.   Dying Thief.   Itzik Manger.   VWA

And singing too. He could be happy.   Any Night.   Philip Levine.   AMV-80

And sings a solitary song/That whistles in the wind.   Lucy Gray.   William Wordsworth.   BeLS; EnRP; ERoP 1-2; FiP; GTBS; HBV 1-2; MBW 1-2; OAEL 1-2; OAEP; OBRV; OxBChV; SeCeV; TEP; TreFS

And sings like the African sun.   Duns Scotus.   Thomas Merton.   CoPo

And sings when she chooses, her own melodies.   I Often Want to Let My Lines Go.   Leib Neidus.   VWA

And sink at last to the lasting dark.   Rondel: Autumn.   Matt Field.   AMV-80

And sink into the marsh near them.   The Widow's Lament in Springtime.   William Carlos Williams.   AP; CMoP; CoBMV; ForPo; HAP; LiTM; MoLP; NoAm; NOBA; TAP

And sink off the Lowlands low.   The Goulden Vanitie.   *Anonymous.*   AtBAP

And sink to the rhythms of El Chocolo.   The Watchers.   Charles Spear.   AnNZ

And sinks fore and aft with a bow.   Limerick:: "The cautious collapsible cow."   *Anonymous.*   LiBL

And, sipping of contrast, finds the day more fair.   The Wreck.   Walter De la Mare.   MOS

And sirens singing from our lady's sea-straw.   Altarwise by Owl-Light.   Dylan Thomas.   NoAm

And Sirius is a winterbluegreen star.   Blue Winter.   Robert Francis.   LCAP

And sit down, Robyn, and rest thee.   Snatches: "Far from thy kin kest thee."   *Anonymous.*   OxBM

And sit in peace with Thee.   Hymn to Science.   Mark Akenside.   CEP; PoEL 1-5

And sit on Proserpina's throne,/When she is up to Ceres gone.   Molly Moor.   George Farewell.   NOEC

And sit puffing smoke in the air and never say a word.   Irradiations.   John Gould Fletcher.   LaNeLa

And sit up late whenever I choose.   When I am Big, I Mean to Buy.   Mary Mapes Dodge.   BiCB

And sit where all the Gods are, in the sun.   Hialmar Speaks to the Raven.   Charles Leconte de Lisle.   AWP; SyP

And sit with Tamburlaine in all his majesty.   Tamburlaine.   Christopher Marlowe.   NIP

And sithen as we may not togeder speke,/By writinge we shall our hertes breke.   Letter to "M".   *Anonymous.*   OxBM

And sits all day in shame/Outside the office of the principal.   Zimmer in Grade School.   Paul Zimmer.   GP

And sits by your bed, and brings her knitting.   Good Luck and Bad.   John Milton Hay.   FaBoEE

And Sivin's the deel's aan sel.   A Magpie Rhyme, Northumberland.   *Anonymous.*   GBP

And six feet of earth makes us all of one size.   Six Feet of Earth.   *Anonymous.*   BLPA

And sixty people trying to relax/On little rented chairs with gilded backs.   Evening Musicale.   Phyllis McGinley.   OBAL

And skins the colour from her trembling lips.   The Pallid Thunderstricken Sigh for Gain.   Alfred, Lord Tennyson.   TW

And sky and sea, but two, which move/And form all others, life and love. To--.   Percy Bysshe Shelley.   EnRP

And slams his little door!   Song for a Little Cuckoo Clock.   Elizabeth Jane Coatsworth.   SiSoSe

And slanting o'er an ebon cloud/Falls night's last moon-beam like a sword!   Elizabethan Days.   Thomas Caulfield Irwin.   IrPN

And Slavery's spectres shriek and vanish from/the ray!   La Fayette.   Samuel Taylor Coleridge.   EnRP

And slay myself and let my blood flow/upon the cliffs!   Jerusalem the Dismembered.   Uri Z. Greenberg.   TrJP

And sleep, dark sleep, so near, so like to death.   A Summer Evening.   Archibald Lampman.   PeCV

And sleep faas drappan doun.   Caller Rain Frae Abune.   Sappho.   OBVE

And–sleep for him that wakens me!   The Sidewinder.   Charles F. Lummis.   BPAW

And sleep in death, to rest with God.   Hear Us, in This Thy House.   Philip Doddridge.   BePJ

And sleep, my brow inclined to the East,/Until sunrise.   Out of the Darkness.   Gertrud Kolmar.   WPOW

And sleep, the undivided sphere.   Credo.   Brewster Ghiselin.   PoA

And sleep thegither at the foot,/John Anderson my jo!   John Anderson My Jo.   Robert Burns.   AWP; BoLiVe; BoLoP; CABA; CBEP; CEP; CoMu; EiCP; EnLi 1-2; EnPE; ErPo; FaBV; FF; FSW; GTBS; GTBS-P; HBV 1-2; HeIP; InPK; InPo; LAuP; LiTB; LiTL; MCCG; NOBE; NOEC; NoP;

OAEP; OBEC; OBEV; OxBS; PG; PrIm; TreFT; TrGrPo; UnTE; ViBoPo; WBLP; WHA

And sleepe so guiltie and afraid,/As since he dares not come within my sight.   The Dreame.   Ben Jonson.   PoEL 1-5

And sleeping, all night long, they were hungry.   Eating.   Reginald Gibbons.   MAYP

...And sleeps/like a dumb beast, head on her paws, in the corner.   Origins and History of Consciousness.   Adrienne Rich.   NIP

And sleepy winter, like the sleep of death.   Wild Peaches.   Elinor Wylie.   AmP; FaBoWP; LiTA; LiTM; NAMP; OxBA; SBG

And slender landscape and austere.   The Lady Poverty.   Alice Meynell.   GTBS; NOBV; OBMV

And slept and would not till nearly dusk be woken.   Transfigured Bird.   James Merrill.   MoAB

And slept to tunes/Of "Quack! Quack! Quack!"   Ducks at Dawn.   James S. Tippett.   SiSoSe; SoPo; TiPo

And slew ten thousand foes.   Alfred the Harper.   John Sterling.   BeLS

And SLIDE/and SLIDE.   Sliding.   Myra Cohn.   SiSoSe

And slight luck or grace attends/Your boaters down the Bosphorus!   The Three Khalandeers.   James Clarence Mangan.   OBVV

And slight to nothing hence return.   The Swan–Vain Pleasures.   George Moses Horton.   BALP

And slime they gobble and peer/Saying "Quack! Quack!"...   Ducks.   Frederick William Harvey.   OnUR

And slit their throats, behind the barroom door..   Lupus in Fabula.   Malcolm Lowry.   OBCV; PeCV

And slow cascading of the paddle wheel.   A Simile for Her Smile.   Richard Wilbur.   HoPM; InPK; MiAP; MoLP; OLR

And slowly descend the hill, through dew-wet grass.   Miracles.   Conrad Aiken.   HBMV

And slowly fills up/with the white fruits of the snow.   The Six-Quart Basket.   Raymond Souster.   PeCV

And slowly lights his lamp.   The Firefly Lights His Lamp.   *Anonymous.*   SoPo

And slowly lose them.   Big Grave Creek.   Cid Corman.   HoAn

And slowly now, their strength renewed, the words/set off along the road, renewed.   After an Eclipse of the Sun.   Eugene Heimler.   VWA

And slowly the keys grow darker to the touch.   Sonatina in Yellow.   Donald Justice.   LCAP

And slowly the kind man comes closer, loses his rage,/sits down at table.   For My Son Noah, Ten Years Old.   Robert Bly.   InPS

And slowly up the tree trunk climbs the sun.   Among the Firs.   Eugene Lee-Hamilton.   NOBV

And slumber both stark naked, he and I?   Nudus Redibo.   Thomas Flatman.   OBSP

And sly, fat fishes sailing, watching all.   Circe.   John Byrne Leicester Warren.   VLP

And small John's kiss, three times.   It Really Happened.   Elizabeth Henley.   BiCB

And small stones/Under our feet.   The Black Bottom Bootlegger.   Esther M. Leiper.   TAT

And smash to pieces on the slate.   Tregardock.   Sir John Betjeman.   FaBoPP

And smile before he joins me, near/But underground.   Wonder and a Thousand Springs.   William Alexander Percy.   HBMV

And smile so proudly/to the camera.   Bunky Boy Bunky Boy Who's My Little Bunky Boy.   Larry Mollin.   NeAC

And smile upon his mother's breast.   The Birds of Bethlehem.   Richard Watson Gilder.   AA

And smile upon us when we meet/And greet so pleasantly.   God's Pity.   Louise Driscoll.   WGRP

And smiled a rainbow/Overhead!   April Fool.   Eleanor Hammond.   SoPo

And smilest, knowing all is well.   In Memoriam A.H.H., CXXVII.   Alfred, Lord Tennyson.   HBV 1-2; OAEL 1-2; OAEP

And smilingly she came about,/As fair a woman as fair could be.   Kemp Owyne (A version).   *Anonymous.*   BaBo; BoLiVe; BuBa; EnSB; ESPB; SeCeV; ViBoFo

And smite this sleeping world awake.   For the Briar Rose.   William Morris.   NOBV

And smoke rising quietly to the evening sky.   Thoughts from Abroad.   Patrick Maybin.   NeIP

And smoothed down my wild hair in the starred light of evening.   The Walk.   Leonard Clark.   AtBAP

And smote himself, a shuddering heap of pain.   Modern Love, II.   George Meredith.   EnLi 1-2; HBV 1-2; OAEP; VLP

And smothered truth to win a war for Greece.   Laocoon.   Donald Hall.   NePoAm-2

And smouldering wrong.   Expression.   Isaac Rosenberg.   MoBrPo

And snatch his broken snuff-box, and sneeze himself away.   Bandit.   Abraham Moses Klein.   WHW

And sniffling at my prostrate form unnerved/He licked my face!   The Turkish Trench Dog.   Geoffrey Dearmer.   GDP

And snore secure on Decks, till rosy Morn.   The Iliad.   Homer.   OBVE

And snow clouds begin to form.   Weeding in January.   Louis Daniel Brodsky.   AMV-80

And snow collects in the blind eyes of statues.   For Zbigniew Herbert, Summer, 1971, Los Angeles.   Larry Levis.   FYAP; LCAP

And snow lies inexprest in the deep lane.   Moments.   Ivor Gurney.   OBSP

And snow on the sand where in summer the water was...   Cook County.   Archibald MacLeish.   CrMA

And snuffed the nighttime out around the bed.   The Watcher.   Ruth Stone.   NYBP

And so   On His Writing Verses.   John Hawthorn.   NOEC

And so abets the shining fleet/Till it is out of gaze.   Love can do all but raise the dead.   Emily Dickinson.   LiTA; NePA

And so adieu, I thank thee for thy pain.   An Epitaph of Maister Win Drowned in the Sea.   George Turberville.   FaBoEE

And so all their multi-thousand-mile range/is too short for the hope of change.   Three Moves.   John Logan.   CAPP

And so am I now, so am I.   Lesbos.   Lawrence Durrell.   EBEV

And so appears more dreadful to the strong.   Sonnet IV: "From that first flash when awful Love took flame."   Louise Labe.   BoWoP

And so away he flew.   Upon Time.   Robert Herrick.   OBS

And so biddeth Johan Trewman and alle his felawes.   Snatches: "Johan athe Millere hath y-grounde smal."   Anonymous.   OxBM

And so, close to the flow,/the coots survive.   Coots.   Joseph Bruchac.   FAZ

And so, dear Christian Friends, how do you do?   Epigram: "The only Man that e'er I knew."   William Blake.   PV

And so dear Hodge, to church let's go,/And don't be foolish pray.   Don't Be Foolish Pray.   Anonymous.   CoMu

And so did I, my little lamb,/And so will you.   The Calf, the Goat, the Little Lamb.   Samuel Hoffenstein.   DBV

And so do I.   Maps for a Son Are Drawn as You Go.   Samuel Hazo.   AMV-81

And so ends the song of my beautiful drake.   Nell Flaherty's Drake.   Anonymous.   AnIV

And so ends the true story of Billy the Kid.   The Ballad of Billy the Kid.   Henry Herbert Knibbs.   BPAW

And so enjoy her, and none miss her.   Absence.   John Hoskyns.   EG; MeLP

And so fall asleep, Love,/Loved by thee.   A Woman's Last Word.   Robert Browning.   BLPA; BLPL; BoLiVe; FaBoBe; FaFP; HBV 1-2; InPo; LiTL; OAEP; TreFS; TrGrPo; UnTE; ViBoPo

And so, falling inwards,/is born.   St. Augustine's Pear Tree.   Marilyn Bowering.   CaPN

...And so foiled to the end/his ancient enemy.   Old Grey.   Fred Lape.   BoAnP

And so–for God's sake–hock and soda-water!   Don Juan.   George Gordon, Lord Byron.   CTC

And so, good-night, this Christmas, and God bless!   Christmas Letter Home.   G. S. Fraser.   OxBTC

And so great a boon, by a brave man's death,/is never dearly bought!   Crispus Attucks.   John Boyle O'Reilly.   PAH

And so had to leave the vicinity.   Limerick: "There was an old Fellow of Trinity."   Arthur Clement Hilton.   CenHV; LiBL

And so he left them thunderstruck and dumb,/Stung with their present guilt, and fate to come.   Naboth's Vineyard.   John Caryll.   APAS

And so he will! And so he will!   Wind.   James Stephens.   AnIL; BoNaP; ELU; HeIP; InPK; NoAm

...And so heal/The lost Son by the newly found.   The Jews.   Henry Vaughan.   OBS

And so I both enjoy and miss her.   Absence.   John Donne.   EiL; LiTL

And so I'd better call my song/"Lines after Ache-inside."   Only Seven (parody).   Henry Sambrooke Leigh.   BXAP; HBV 1-2; SpRo

And so I do my task and wait/The opening of the outer gate.   I Shall Not Cry Return.   Ellen M. Huntington Gates.   HBV 1-2

And so I guess I'll go and borrow/Johnny's boat until tomorrow.   But That Was Yesterday.   Aileen Fisher.   SoPo

And so I lay without her.   She lay all naked in her bed.   Anonymous.   BoLoP; ErPo; UnTE

And so I learned how my little tree/Was rooted deep in Eternity!   Roots.   Louis Ginsberg.   TrJP

And so I learned, luck was with glory wed.   Brother and Sister.   George Eliot.   NOBV

And so I leave to stir him, lest he stink.   Ask Not to Know This Man.   Ben Jonson.   CABA

And so I'll get the Gospel free,/You see!   To Pledge or Not to Pledge.   Anonymous.   STF

And so I love no more.   Farewell to Love.   Sir John Suckling.   CaPo

And so I made a Villanelle.   Villanelle of His Lady's Treasures.   Ernest Christopher Dowson.   HBV 1-2

And so I remain in a civil way, your Servant to command/Mary.   Mary the Cook-Maid's Letter to Dr. Sheridan.   Jonathan Swift.   LoBV; OnYI; OxBoLi

And so I rest your constant friend.   A Letter to Lady Margaret Cavendish Holles-Harley, when a Child.   Matthew Prior.   NOBE

And so I shall lose Molly Mog.   Molly Mog: or, The Fair Maid of the Inn.   John Gay.   CEP; CoMu

And so I sing again and again,/To lessen some of their bitter pain.   The Owl and the Nightingale (excerpt).   Anonymous.   PBBP

And so I sing of Him and onward plod.   The Greatest Person In the Universe.   Daniel L. Marsh.   BLRP

And so I sing/To matchless Maud/Squatting in a drawer in Spring.   Ode to a Fat Cat.   Annabel Farjeon.   PCat

And so I went singing along.   Two Simpleton Songs, II.   Anonymous.   OxNR

And so I woke and knew that he was dead.   The Dead Poet.   Lord Alfred Bruce Douglas.   HBMV; PeHV; ViBoPo

And so in mutuall Names/Of Love, burne both together.   Madrigal XI: "Love now no fire hath left him."   Giambattista Marino.   OBVE

And so interpret for us the graph of the universe/Plotted with stars...   Last Mathematician.   Hyman Edelstein.   CaP

And so/it brought us together.   Asphodel, That Greeny Flower.   William Carlos Williams.   FaBoMo

And so it did, no fooling.   Homage to Texas.   Robert Graves.   LiTB

And so it is hard times wherever you go.   Hard Times.   Anonymous.   AmFP

And so it was, all the way back to jail.   The Funeral Parlor.   Henry Johnson.   LFAC

...And so it was I entered the broken world/Hart Crane./Hart   Hart Crane.   Robert Creeley.   AP

...And so it was in all the days of my childhood.   In All the Days of My Childhood.   Russell Edson.   AmPA

And so keeps out of traffic jams/And other hippopotomusses.   Habits of the Hippopotamus.   Arthur Guiterman.   BoAnP; FaBV; FiBHP; OBCA; OnUR; TiPo

And so let him lie.   On John So.   Anonymous.   FaBoEE

And so let's all be jolly.   An Old Christmas Greeting.   Anonymous.   TiPo

And so lie down in peace.   'Twas at the Matin Hour.   Anonymous.   OHIP

And so live ever–or else swoon to death.   Sonnet Written on a Blank Page in Shakespeare's Poems....   John Keats.   PoEL 1-5

And so make a city here.   The Wish.   Abraham Cowley.   BoC; CavP; HBV 1-2; LiTB; NOBE; NoP; OAEP; OBEV; OBS; SeCV 1-2; TrGrPo; ViBoPo; WHA

And so may starve with me.   A Farewell to London In the Year 1715.   Alexander Pope.   CEP

And so may you deem of the great, by reading of the least.   To Spencer.   George Turberville.   OBTV

And so, Miss Mary Hann, forget/For hever Jeames of Buckley Square.   Jeames of Buckley Square.   William Makepeace Thackeray.   VLP

And so must you and I.   The Lover's Lament (A vers. with music).   Anonymous.   AS

And so my deare friend, for this time adue.   To My Most Dearely-loved Friend Henery Reynolds Esquire.   Michael Drayton.   AnAnS 2; OAEP; OBS; PP

And so my fist is clenched/Today–/To strike your face.   Militant.   Langston Hughes.   PoBA

And so my wife taught me to say.   Inscription in a Garden.   George Gascoigne.   CBEP; OBSC; TrGrPo

And so our debt to Lionhood must never be forgotten.   Sunt Leones.   Stevie Smith.   SBG

And so plausibly fantastic,/That one gets enthusiastic/For a bit.   Transcendentalism.   Anonymous.   NA

And so proceed ad infinitum.   On Fleas.   Jonathan Swift.   GoTF; TreFS

...And so refine/Our dust that at one draught mortality/May drink itself up, and forget to die.   An Apology for the Foregoing Hymn....   Richard Crashaw.   JCP

And so, remember me! Farewell.   Love-Letter Two.   Anonymous.   PeHV

And so repair these Rents, that men may see/And say, Where God is, all agree.   The Constellation.   Henry Vaughan.   SeCV 1-2

And so reprovde the Asses eares of Midas with theyr sound.   Metamorphoses.   Ovid (Publius Ovidius Naso).   CTC

And so saying, she gave tiny feet back to my boulder and/pain.   Combe Florey.   Paul Durcan.   FaBoIP

And so shall, in our songs' delight,/Thy power still be praised.   Psalm XXI.   Sir Philip Sidney.   FCP

And so she is, she is trembling with love and/power.   Lady Feeding the Cats (excerpt).   Douglas Stewart.   BoAnP

And so sing I, with a down a down.   Phoebe's Sonnet.   Thomas Lodge.   ViBoPo

...And so sit/Speechless while things forgotten call to us.   The House of Life.   Dante Gabriel Rossetti.   VLP

And so stand stricken, so remembering him. Time Does Not Bring Relief. Edna St. Vincent Millay. FaBV

And so the commotion arose at the fair. The Fair at Windgap. Austin Clarke. OnYI; OxBTC; SeCePo

And so the hogs streamed out of the theater crying, only/hogs, only hogs... A Performance at Hog Theater. Russell Edson. AmPA

...And so the kittens/have not yet/been drowned. Mehitabel and Her Kittens. Don (Donald Robert Marquis) Marquis. NLV

And so the lecture proceeds. Tutor's Dignity. Lewis (Charles Lutwidge Dodgson) Carroll. FaBoNo

And so the long morning/Wept itself away. The Lime Avenue. Sacheverell Sitwell. LOW

And so the night became. The Cricket Sang. Emily Dickinson. MAPA

And so the old men blundered,/And so the young men die. Scapegoats. Eleanor D. Breed. PGD

And so the pine boughs cover me. Roger Williams. Hezekiah Butterworth. PAH

And so the poor dog had none. Old Mother Hubbard. Mother Goose. FaBoBe; SoPo; TiPo

And so the poor stone was left all alone,/Fa, la, la, la, lal, de. Two Birds. *Anonymous.* OxNR

And so there would be no ex-cuse/For MILTON, but for you--Mon-goos! Child's Natural History. Oliver Herford. HBV 1-2

And so they all went home again. Three Young Rats. Mother Goose. FaBoNo; InvP; OxBoLi; OxNR; PoPle

And so they came to us once, in our youth. To the Memory of Yale College. Howard Phelps (Phelps Putnam) Putnam. AnAmPo

And so they grew ever closer together,/As all true lovers desire. The Douglas Tragedy. *Anonymous.* MaC

And so they had their way; or nearly so. Epitaph for the Race of Man. Edna St. Vincent Millay. CMoP

And so they kissed, and rode along their way. The Canterbury Tales: The Pardoner's Tale. Geoffrey Chaucer. BiP; CoBE; CTC; EBEV; EnL; FiP; HAP; MBW 1-2; NAWM 1-2; NoP; OAEL 1-2; OAEP; OxBM; PoEL 1-5; PPoe; SCV; TEP; WHA

And so they liv'd; and so they died. An Epitaph: "Interr'd beneath this marble stone." Matthew Prior. FaBoEE

And so they returned to the merry green wood,/Amongst the leaves so green. Robin Hood and Allen A Dale. *Anonymous.* BaBo; ESPB; FaBoBe; GBP; HBV 1-2; MCCG; MoShBr

And so they went back home again. A Robin and a Robin's Son. *Anonymous.* OxNR

And so think I, with a down, down, derry! A Nymph's Disdain of Love. *Anonymous.* EIL

And so this emblem shall forever be/A sign of immortality. Immortality. Joseph Jefferson. BLPA

And so this new commerce and sweet/Should all my life employ and busie me. The Odour. George Herbert. AnAnS 1; OBS

And so thy book itself turn Sodomite. Upon the Author of a Play Called Sodom. John Oldham. TW

And so to bed: pray wish us all good rest. Epitaph on Sir Edward Giles and His Wife. Robert Herrick. PoPle

And so, to clear herself in time, I leave her. Fanny's Removal in 1714. John Winstanley. NOEC

And so to where I wait come gently on. No Funeral Gloom. Ellen Terry. BLPA

...And so too everyone/who, when in Rome,/will do what the Romans do. A True Story. Marvin Bell. SV

And so turnes wine to Water backe againe. To Our Lord, upon the Water Made Wine. Richard Crashaw. MePo

And so warm the poet's tongue/You'ld read a snake, in his next song. The Humble Petition of Poor Ben to the Best of Monarchs... Ben Jonson. PP

And so was soothed my sorrow for the dead. Consolation. George Darley. ERoP 1-2

And so we are perfect sacrifice to nothing. Pacific Sonnets. George Barker. LiTM

And so we crept out of the pot. Baby and I. *Anonymous.* OxNR

...And so we sail/Steering irrevocably into the Felixstowe fog. Coming Home from Abroad. David Holbrook. OBTV

And so we seize the moment/to tell the sea Goodbye. On the Athenian Dead at Ecbatana. Plato. PoPl

And so we shall be rid of them all. Epigram: "Once in our lives." *Anonymous.* FaBoEE

And so we stoned him till he died. The Rider. Leah Bodine Drake. NePoAm-2

And so wildly in love. Folk Tale. P. Mustapaa. HW

And so, with his hand on his heart, with all possible meekness/departed. A Visitor. Lewis (Charles Lutwidge Dodgson) Carroll. FaBoNo

And so, with undiminished pride,/Each went on his respective road. Thomas Winterbottom Hance. Sir William Schwenck Gilbert. InMe

And so you may ring the bells. Dialogue, between Crab and Gillian. Thomas D'Urfey. NOEC

And so, you see, I know! The Squirrels' Christmas. Winifred Howard. ChBR

And soar to worlds that cease from pain. Permit Us, Lord, to Consecrate. Joseph Green. AH

And soars and shines, another and the same. Immortal Nature. Erasmus Darwin. OBEC

And, softer, and remote as if in history,/Rumours of what had touched my friends, my foes, or me. Melancholy. Edward ("Edward Eastaway") Thomas. MoVE; NoP

And softly part his curtains to allow/Thy visit, grateful to his burning brow. The Evening Wind. William Cullen Bryant. LaNeLa

And softly, softly breathe, lest you infect us, too. A Mock Charon. Richard Lovelace. CaPo

And softly to become as Zeus empowers. The Dream. Michael (Katherine Bradley and Edith Cooper) Field. SyP

And softly to undo the snood/That is the sign of maidenhood. Bid Adieu to Maidenhood. James Joyce. HBV 1-2; LiTL; OBEV; OnYI

...And sold/(Like our two Kings) their happiness for gold. The Fairy Maimoune. John Moultrie. OBRV

And solely attend to purity and/truth. To Purity and Truth. *Anonymous.* TrJP

...And solemn sound/Of drums, o'er came their groans. Blenheim (excerpt). John Philips. NOEC

And some bachelors hold they are best as they are. If Ever I Marry, I'll Marry a Maid. *Anonymous.* EIL

And some blue cheese, and crackers, and some fine/Ruddy-skinned pears. A Late Aubade. Richard Wilbur. SM; SoSe

And some bright hearth be made thy urn. The Tree. Anne Finch, Countess of Winchilsea. CoBE; OBEC

And some day He may use me/To water His flowers again. For the Master's Use. *Anonymous.* BLRP

...And some days all/I can want is sleep. He Said. Jean Valentine. TAP

And some hot brains are beginning to think/Of a messmate's opened vein. Song of the Seaweed. Eliza Cook. FiBHP

And some in smoke of battle lost,/Whom drums, not lutes, delighted. A Thought on Human Life. *Anonymous.* OBSP

And some me of--beauty--/was about to begin... Some Me of Beauty. Carolyn M. Rodgers. CNA

And some of the saga defied the draught in the open tomb/And was not blown. The Great Hunger. Patrick Kavanagh. BIrV

And some of them, a very few,/Stay pickled till they're ninety-two. Liquor and Longevity. *Anonymous.* FPL

And some of them followed the cars/For forty miles/Before they fell away in exhaustion. La Maquina a Houston. Edward Dorn. PoM

And some one in the Study play'd/The Wedding-march of Mendelssohn. The Angel in the House. Coventry Patmore. FaBoPP

And some read the letters now coming back from/"Amerika." Clausa Germanis Gallia. Millen Brand. GP

And some she gave to the truckler's/dog. My Little Maid. *Anonymous.* OxNR

And some street-pacing harlot his first love. Tirocinium; or, A Review of Schools. William Cowper. OBSV

...And some there are who have knowl/edge thereof... Anabasis. St.-John (Alexis Saint-Léger Léger) Perse. LiTW

And some, though mortal, have achieved their race. The Tomb of Michael Collins. Denis Devlin. OxBI

And--some verses of mine. The Hundred Best Books. Mostyn T. Pigott. InMe

And some with adoration crown her fame. Old Fortunatus. Thomas Dekker. ViBoPo

And some with your feet on lions? It is time that you were at rest. John Brown's Body. Stephen Vincent Benét. MoAmPo

--And some years hence he'll send the rest. To Lady, When about Five Years Old, with a Present of Shells. Horace Walpole. NOEC

...And some young, piteous, murdered face. The Cenotaph. Charlotte Mew. MMM

And "Somebody's Mother's" prayer was heard. Somebody's Mother. Mary Dow Brine. WBLP

And somehow find, in mirrors, colours, odours,/Their essences of lilies and of roses. Thoughts after Ruskin. Elma Mitchell. FaBoWP

...And someone/Has propped a yellow cartwheel/Against the door. The Road's End. John Montague. FaBoIP

And someone outside them, watching. Daffodils. Michael Heffernan. AMV-80; SM

And someone somewhere, playing a flute,/Has made the soldiers homesick all night long. On Hearing a Flute at Night from the Wall of Shou-Hsiang. Li Yi. UnS

And someone there stole forth a hand/To draw a brother to his side. Tenebris Interlucentem. James Elroy Flecker. CBEP; MoBrPo

...And someone will be at the door. The Knife. Jean Valentine. LCAP

And Somers has the turtle–turtle always makes him sick.   Etiquette.   Sir William Schwenck Gilbert.   CenHV; EnLi 1-2; FaBoCh; FaBoCo; FiBHP; MaC; VLP

And something else, but what I dare not name.   On the Happy Corydon and Phyllis.   Sir Charles Sedley.   BoLoP

And something in our flesh was wrong.   An Idyl in Idleness.   Robert Pack.   NePoEA

And something new will begin/though nothing like what you are thinking.   Entering the Room.   Roger Pfingston.   PoDr

And something of the Shorter-Catechist.   Apparition.   William Ernest Henley.   EnLi 1-2; TrGrPo

And something will always be falling.   The Snow.   Donald Hall.   NePoEA-2; NMP

And sometime water gushes from/Fountains that have long been dry.   Middle-Age.   E. B. C. Jones.   HBMV

And sometimes for a second really live/With magic's miracles.   Faust's Servant.   Roy Fuller.   OxBTC

And sometimes I bring her a bottle of Nuit d'Amour.   The Dover Bitch.   Anthony Hecht.   BXAP; MAT; NePoEA-2; NIP; NLV; NOBA; NOBL; OBAL; PP; PPP; UnPo; VGW

And, sometimes, leaves.   Susanna and the Elders.   Jack Gilbert.   NPGG

And sometimes referring to her mirror/as women do.   Snow White and the Seven Dwarfs.   Anne Sexton.   DFT; HaCAP

And sometimes, so relenting justice wills,/From palpable oppression of despair.   The Excursion.   William Wordsworth.   OBRV

And sometimes we may meet.   The Secret Land.   Robert Graves.   BoC

And sometimes whisper his name–/"Ishi."   The Concealment: Ishi, the Last Wild Indian.   William Stafford.   NaP

And somewhere, for the hand that seeks,/Perhaps a Sultan's pearl!   The Atlas.   Kenneth Slessor.   PoAu 1-2

And somewhere in the measured mass/of everything, imagine grass.   Imagine Grass.   Knute Skinner.   GP; SM

And somewhere Ray Bradbury and Arthur C. Clarke,/under first stars, dream up tomorrow's news.   Into the Future.   Harold Witt.   SOTS

And Son of God is made our Friend.   A Medieval Poem of the Nativity.   *Anonymous.*   TrCP

And songs of dead poets haunted me all day?   Death of a Friend.   Pauli Murray.   PoBA

And soon he will wonder what it was/he wanted to say.   Simple.   Naomi Long Madgett.   FB; PoBA

...And soon his line/Is holding the lake exactly.   Lake.   R. A. Simpson.   CBAP

And soon I shall know I was talking to my own soul.   Twenty-One Love Poems.   Adrienne Rich.   BoWoP

And soon i' the Gordon's foul heart's blude/He's wroken his dear ladye.   Edom o' Gordon.   Anonymous   BSV; HBV 1-2

And soon may give my dust their funeral shade.   The River.   Ralph Waldo Emerson.   MAmP

And soon the village brings the woodman's tale/Of having heard the new-come nightingale.   Early Nightingale.   John Clare.   PBBP

And soon they'll all smell alike, he thought, and felt sick,/And went to bed at noon.   The Last War.   Kingsley Amis.   OBSV; OxBC; SoSe

And soon those myths are silent,/placed with respect/in books nobody knows.   Because San Quentin Killed Two More Today.   Ed Lipman.   LFAC

...And soon to be swallowed/Suddenly from beneath.   Night.   Robert Bly.   NaP

And soon, too soon, we part with pain,/To sail o'er silent seas again.   The Meeting of the Ships.   Thomas Moore.   EtS

And soon upon a harlot's house I came–/Within I found him playing at solitaire!   In the Vices.   Donald Evans.   HBMV

And soon we come/to bury the hatchet   A Love Dirge to the Whitehouse (or It Soots You Right).   Bob Fletcher.   NBP

And soon wipe away with her elements/Our small fond human enclosures.   Pause.   Mary Ursula Bethell.   AnNZ

And soothe my senses with a little rest.   Green.   Paul Verlaine.   LiTW; SyP

And sorrow bloomed on a hill.   Interrogative.   Sister M. Therese.   MoRP

And sorrow darkens all the day.   Lines from an Elegy on the Death of His Wife.   Hitomaro.   LiTW

And Sorrow fold such pinions on the heart/As will not fly away?   Sunset Wings.   Dante Gabriel Rossetti.   FM; HBV 1-2

And sorrow whistles/O'er desert plains.   Lament.   Denis Florence Maccarthy.   OBVV

And sought himself in his remaining blood.   Abishag.   Rainer Maria Rilke.   AWP

And soul from soul the secret seems to keep.   Love Sonnets.   Zora Cross.   CBAP

And soul of all regret!   Autumn.   William Watson.   OBVV

And sound as this egg on my tray.   Hello There (parody).   Brian S. Salome.   BXAP

And sound integrity not more, than famed/For sanctity of manners undefiled.   The Stricken Deer.   William Cowper.   LoBV

And sound is a long journey.   Bard.   Gavin Bantock.   FaBoTw

And sound is,is,his/conjecture   The Moon Is the Number 18.   Charles Olson.   CMoP; NMP

And sound of dancing on the floor.   A Hollyhock.   Frank Dempster Sherman.   AA

And sound Thy praises everlastingly.   For Inspiration.   Buonarroti Michelangelo.   CAW; GoBC; WGRP

And sounds the same.   The Core.   John Holmes.   MiAP

And sovereign childhood with its unrelenting hand.   The Builder of Houses.   Jane Cooper.   AmPC

And space is but the span/of the long love of man.   Man.   Humbert Wolfe.   MoBrPo

And spare his golden bindings!   The Bookworms.   Robert Burns.   ELU; FiBHP

And spare that they han done amiss./Amen.   A Hymn to Jesus.   Richard of Caistre.   MeEL

And, sparing Criminals, attack the Crime.   The Borough.   George Crabbe.   CTC

And sparkly egg the bunnies bring/At Easter with the world inside!   Easter Snowfall.   Harry Behn.   TiPo

And sparrows fester in his memory.   The Cat, Caged and Shrunken.   Arthur Freeman.   BoAnP

And sparrows sweep the ceiling of our day?   Praise in Summer.   Richard Wilbur.   CAPP; NoP; PP

And speak for me–their most astonished host.   Words.   W. R. Rodgers.   OBSP

And speak no word, those sitters by the wall.   Envy the Old.   Mark Van Doren.   Prf

And speak to you in those provinces/she has in every nook and cranny of your countries.   Where Babylon Ends.   Nathaniel Tarn.   VWA

And speakest only when thy soul is stirred!   The Three Silences of Molinos.   Henry Wadsworth Longfellow.   AnFE; APA

And speaks in moments more than years.   Thus, When Soft Love Subdues the Heart.   Paul Scarron.   LO

...And speckled hatreds hide/Like toads among them.   Bona de Mortuis.   Thomas Lovell Beddoes.   ELU; TW

And specks of salt as bright to see/As lambkins to a shepherd.   The Fly.   Walter De la Mare.   OnUR; PoPle

And spede as welle!   O mestres, whye.   *Anonymous.*   EnPo

And speed, O speed the blessed day/Of justice, love, and peace.   God of the Nations, Near and Far.   John Haynes Holmes.   AH

And speeds the sun upon his golden course.   Ice-Skaters.   Elder Olson.   LiSp; SD

And spend the night mothering them instead.   Hand-Jive.   Sandie Castle.   APU

And spend the rest of their lives on Lennox Island.   Lennox Island.   David McFadden.   NOBC

And spends all his dream playing follow-my-leader.   Night Landscape.   Joan Aiken.   DuDa

And spicing the soup.   Haiku: "Winter rain at night..."   Richard Wright.   FAZ

And spill/white sugar dust/over us both.   A Sugar-Candy Bird.   Ian Young.   NeAC

And spin the horns of Ammon out of sight.   On Seeing a Little Child Spin a Coin of Alexander the Great.   Turner, Charles Tennyson.   NOBV

And spit it out into the hand/of the White man and then/wake up.   Sleeping Beauty.   Charles Johnson.   DFT

–And spit out stars/by the mouthful, eating the heart out.   How Stars and Hearts Grow in Apples.   Virginia Elson.   AMV-81

And spit whenever we wanted to.   Mrs. Trollope in America.   Helen Bevington.   NLV; OBAL

And spite of all your children seem a bride.   To–.   Thomas Rymer.   OBSP

And, spite of Truth, let Mercy guide your Pen.   Crusty Critics.   George Crabbe.   OBEC

And spits into the constellated skies.   The Poets of Hell.   Karl Shapiro.   NYBP

And splashed down in suburban grasses.   Portrait of a Young Girl Raped at a Suburban Party.   Brian Patten.   OxBTC

And splendour, splendour everywhere.   Seaside Golf.   Sir John Betjeman.   LiSp; PoPl; SD

And split the last atom/And come unto Me.   For the Fly-Leaf of a School-Book.   Norman Cameron.   OxBS

And split the tomb.   Advent.   Brother Antoninus.   NeAP; TrCP

And spoke the feeling for them, which was what they had lacked.   Large Red Man Reading.   Wallace Stevens.   HAP; LCAP

And spooky shadows creep.   Palace.   Dorothy Vena Johnson.   GoSl

And sport no more seen/On the darkening Green.   The Echoing Green.   William Blake.   CBEP; OBEC; UnPo; WiR

And sport with them in those delights,/And oft in other things.   Hawking for the Partridge.   Thomas Ravenscroft.   NCEP; OxBoLi

And spout your halo for a pint of bitter.   A Wartime Exchange: As One Non-Combatant to Another.   Alex Comfort.   OxBTC

And sprays its gold on every tree. Sunrise. Rowena Bastin Bennett. TiPo

And spread a radiance from ourselves that melts/in light. The Flowers of Politics. Michael McClure. NeAP

And spreads against the dark. A Halo. Ralph Salisbury. FAZ

And spreads the dragon's wing. A Dream of Governors. Louis Simpson. NYBP

And spreads their darkness like a sigh. Winter Rains: Cataluna. Philip Levine. NaP

And spring adorns the earth no more. The Pilgrim Fathers. Leonard Bacon. WGRP

And spring and summer both are past/And all things sweet. Late Leaves. Walter Savage Landor. HBV 1-2

And Spring herself, when she woke at dawn,/Would scarcely know that we were gone. There Will Come Soft Rains. Sara Teasdale. LiTA

And spring is upon the village./Unaya–unaya. My Breath. Orpingalik. WTO

And spring will come. Winter Crickets. John Heath-Stubbs. OBCP

...And springtime/grass/Tangles a snare to catch the tapering toe. Les Demoiselles de Sauve. John Gray. NOBV; VLP

And, sprinkling water in her face,/Would make the sacred sign. A Legend of Alhambra. Richard Chenevix Trench. OBTV

And spur him in the shoulder, with my silver spurs, of course. Oh, I Would Be a Cowboy and with the Cowboys Stand. *Anonymous.* CoSo

And squashed the Chocolate Dreams. Supermarket. Felice Holman. QQQ

And squint wryly into the light/Of our common life. His Sleep. Constance Urdang. AMV-81

And St. Mary's rings for mass! Early Morning Meadow Song. Charles Dalmon. ALV; HBMV

And stab our history to the heart. Considerations of Norfolk Island (excerpt). Kenrick Smithyman. AnNZ

And stain it with the dusty stir I make! Sonnets: A Sequence on Profane Love. George Henry Boker. AmePo

And stalk these trees of glass, these caves of stars. Manhattan Menagerie. Joseph Cherwinski. GoYe

And stamps his black marsh-feet on their white and marshy flesh. Swan. D. H. Lawrence. CMoP

And stamps to mark the tune. Finland. Robert Graves. BrPo

...And stand a moment in silence/For the passing of an era, at their own funeral. Let Us Now Praise Famous Men. C. Day-Lewis. BiP; CMoP

And stand behind your chair,/brushing the stars out of your hair. Poem for My Mother. Siv Cedering Fox. Str

And stand in lines in Seattle./Looking for work. The Late Snow and Lumber Strike of the Summer of Fifty-Four. Gary Snyder. NaP; NMP

And stand outside these nations and their noise. Braddan Vicarage. Thomas Edward Brown. FaBoPP

And stand where first they stood. A Birthday. Edwin Muir. BSV; NAs

And stare at me till I speak and speak/Lest my heart break. Elegy for a Countryman. Padraic Fallon. NeIP

And stared without a word of thanks,/Into the gutter. The Cliff. David Rowbotham. NOAV

And staring round him with a brace of beads! Ode to the Cameleopard. Thomas Hood. FaBoNo

And staring up at the house that/wears/Telephone wires like a shawl. Earth Tremor in Lugano. James Kirkup. NYBP

...And starlings in flocks/wheel over the meadows like curving hands. Midsummer Pause. Fred Lape. PoSC

And stars begotten on their night. What Do I Know? Christopher John Brennan. BoAV

And stars in the tangled limbs. Trees and Evening Sky. N. Scott Momaday. CDW

And stars move calmly overhead. The Ruined Chapel. William Allingham. IrPN

And stars shall watch another race toil on. At the Last. Vincent David Engels. CAW

And stars wash over his limbs in the mothering night? Aria for Flute and Oboe. Joseph Langland. NePoEA

And start all over again. Think of Eight Numbers. Shel Silverstein. BBGG

And start to westward through the heavy grass. A Missouri Traveller Writes Home: 1830. Robert Bly. NePoEA

And started at pipe of a sudden bird/Or wept when the wind went by. Moon-Madness. Victor Starbuck. HBMV

And started away in surprise. Limerick: "There was a young lady whose eyes." Edward Lear. EBEV; GoJo; NOBV

And started climbing the hillside back to the farm. The Victim. Lupenga Mphande. WhB

And started on another tree. The Mouse That Gnawed the Oak-Tree Down. Vachel Lindsay. LOW

And starts to be happy. Coming. Philip Larkin. MoBrPo; OxBTC

And starved a little, and brooded much/To the end of the farce! Catherine Ogg. Edgar Lee Masters. GLGT

And starved coyotes answered shriek on shriek. Dead on the Desert. Harrison Conrard. BPAW

And starved the snow he shines upon. Seasons. Christina Georgina Rossetti. YeAr

And, Statesmen by ten thousand odds/Are ANGELS, just as—are GODS. A Libel on D. Jonathan Swift. NCEP

And stay by my cradle/Till morning is nigh. Cradle Hymn. Martin Luther. BiCB; ChBR; OHIP; SUS

And stay by my side/Until morning is nigh. Away in a Manger. *Anonymous.* AH

And stay; till, sudden, it ends where the wood ends. The Path. Edward ("Edward Eastaway") Thomas. BrPo; MoVE; NoAm

And stay with their husbands the rest of their lives. Red River Shore. *Anonymous.* CoSo

And stayed His hand. What Thomas an Buile Said in a Pub. James Stephens. MoAB; MoBrPo; TrGrPo

And stayed, whose names hereon I've writ. The Posy Ring. Clément Marot. AWP

And stays long. A Fair Warning. E. L. Mayo. FAZ

And steal inglorious to the silent grave. An Ode in Imitation of Alcaeus. William, Sir Jones. HBV 1-2

And steal myself from life, and melt away. The State of Innocence. John Dryden. NOCV

And steal the bags to hold the crumbs. The Common Cormorant. Christopher Isherwood. FaBoCh; FaBoCo; FaBoNo; FiBHP; LoGBV; NLV

And steal your linen from your mould'ring clay. Epitaph on Floyd. *Anonymous.* PoL

And stealing will continue stealing. Stealing. James Russell Lowell. GoTF; TreF

And steel traffic flashing like swords/Along the highway. Spring Workman. Alan Creighton. CaP

And stench, contains the element of/chance a Christian needs. Delta Farmer in a Wet Summer. James Whitehead. TAT

And step by step will guide my way/Till dawns at last eternal day. Trials. Grace E. Troy. STF

And sticks at a job until it's done. Elegy for Alfred Hubbard. Tony Connor. SoSe

And still a kiss is sweet! The Passing Flower. Harry Kemp. HBMV

And still as a maid/Enjoy'd the Lady. I Asked a Thief to Steal Me a Peach. William Blake. CABA; CBEP; ExPo; NoP; OBNC; SeCeV; ViBoPo

And still, as darker grows the night,/Emits a brighter ray. Hope. Oliver Goldsmith. GoTF; OBEC; TreFT

And still as someone/first touching their blackness. Poem No. 21. Doughtry Long. CNA

And still be a-trying to get him a wife. The Bachelor's Complaint. *Anonymous.* AmFP

And still content, I'd find a bedding cheery/Where'er the heather grew! The Heather. Neil Munro. OBVV

And still divide the rapid mind/This way and that in search of ease. Over the Dark World Flies the Wind. Alfred, Lord Tennyson. FaBoRV

And still drunk/Between Fort Worth and/Home,/Somewhere west. Somewhere West. Andrew McCord Jones. LFAC

And still He leads us on. Through the Maze. *Anonymous.* BLRP

And still he sits, in miserie,/Upon that ruined Pump! A Pig-Tale. Lewis (Charles Lutwidge Dodgson) Carroll. WiR

And still I cannot bear it/That they take hibiscus and the salvia flower. Hibiscus and Salvia Flowers. D. H. Lawrence. FaBoPV

And still I labour to build a country fit/For heroes, knowing you'd want no part of it. A Reformer to His Father. James Simmons. BIrV

And still I'm lying in my bed alone. Alone (fragment). Sappho. AWP

And still I wait, for she is wondrous fair. Second Vision. Tadhg Dall O'Huiginn. AnIL

And still in Rome a pale-faced client be! Country Pleasures. Martial (Marcus Valerius Martialis). AWP

And still Love sang, and what he sang was this:– The House of Life. Dante Gabriel Rossetti. OAEL 1-2

And still more labyrinthine buds the rose. At Ecelin. Robert Browning. MyFE

And still must mount until no trace/Of it at all we see. The Dreadful Fate of Naughty Nate. John Kendrick Bangs. OBCA

...And still my feet hold fast. A View. Beverly Quint. NYBP

...–And still no pause in the fighting. The Iliad. Homer. WaaP

And still no sheep stirs from its place/Or lifts its Babylonian face. Sheep. Robert Francis. LCAP

And still our horses rustle like the rain. The Youth Dreams. Rainer Maria Rilke. AWP; TrJP

And still so far/from any neighboring star/in the spacious/dark The Light Year. John Ridland. OFD

And still the brown leaves drift in Russell Square. Drilling in Russell Square. Edward Shanks. OBMV

And still the cats cry mew, mew, mew. Midnight. Thomas Middleton. EiL; SeCePo

And still the clipped wing leans against/Her eagle of experience. Two Women. Naomi Replansky. NMM

And still the distant peaks have/The glow of twenty-two. Middle Age. Rudolph Chambers Lehmann. HBV 1-2

And still the dreamless body stands. Young Woman at a Window. Mark Van Doren. LiTA; MoPo; MoVE

And still the hungry, angry heart/Hangs on and howls, biting at air. The Vacuum. Howard Nemerov. NePoEA; NIP

And still the interrogation is going on. The Interrogation. Edwin Muir. CMoP; LiTB; SeCePo

And still the lilies bloom in Galilee. In Galilee. Mary Frances Butts. AA

And still the murmur with the daunce doth meete. Orchestra. Sir John Davies. FaBoEn

And still the punctual snow! New Feet Within My Garden Go–. Emily Dickinson. DiPo

–And still the roar in his mind is/unabated. Paterson. William Carlos Williams. AtBAP

And still the scatter'd Southron fled before. Marmion. Sir Walter Scott. OBRV

And still the sea is salt. Stars, I Have Seen Them Fall. Alfred Edward Housman. NoP; OBSP

And still the war goes on; he don't know why. In the Pink. Siegfried Sassoon. CMoP

And still their leaves are full of life/But there is none in my old body. Old Age. *Anonymous.* WTO

And still there is room to fill. Gitanjali. Rabindranath Tagore. ILwL

And still there's time to rest,/the night drifts. The Quiet Light of Flies. Natan Zach. VWA

And still they stab their souls and slink away. The City Church. E. H. K.. WGRP

...And still they/wanted to fasten onto and to follow her after we were in the car. The Woman Who Could Read the Minds of Dogs. Leslie Scalapino. NPGG

And still, thro' mercy, may enjoy the smell! The Adventures of Simon Swaugum. Philip Freneau. PoEL 1-5

And still thy richer gifts repeat/Till grace in glory is complete. Lord, Thou Hast Promised. Samuel K. Cox. AH

And still thy white-winged angels hover dimly/in our air! The Angels of Buena Vista. John Greenleaf Whittier. BeLS; PAH

And still "We're going South, man,' deadly near. Two Voices. Edmund Charles Blunden. OBWP

And still with branches green/Ride our ill weather out. Lovers in Winter. Robert Graves. FaBoEE; NYBP

And still you wander muttering on/Over the shades of shadows gone. Behind the Line. Edmund Charles Blunden. ChMP

And stillness falls on all the night. Nocturne. Richard Garnett. OBVV

And stillness from the pools of Paradise. Invocation. Siegfried Sassoon. MoBrPo

And stint your chatter, if you can. To My Hairdresser. Warham St. Leger. CenHV

And stir not–with their yellow eyes. Crocuses in the Grass. John Gray. CAW

And stir the petals at her feet, and kiss/The low mound where she lies. The Four Winds. Charles Henry Luders. AA; HBV 1-2

And stir 'twixt silence and a sound. Evening Song. John Vance Cheney. AA

And stirred his brains up so down:/optans coeli gaudia. The Murder of Saint Thomas of Kent. *Anonymous.* ACP

And stirs, remoteas south wind, through your breast. Heart. MacKnight Black. AnAmPo

And stirs with lover's fancies fond/The young man's eager heart. The Seasons. Kalidasa. AWP

And stitched with a rainbow seam. The Dress of Spring. May Justus. YeAr

And Stoic independence of mankind. The Filbert. Robert Southey. FM

And stole it all away. Poll Parrot. *Anonymous.* OxNR

And stole my little moppet/away. Little Moppet. *Anonymous.* OxNR

And stole them all away. A Million Little Diamonds. Mary Frances Butts. AA

And stone her face with Nixon's signature. To Mercury. X. J. Kennedy. SOTS

And stone will shove the softness from my face. Piano after War. Gwendolyn Brooks. AmNP

And stones will not fly. Mike 65. Lennox Raphael. PoBA

And stood around waiting/In their/Brown suits. In These Dissenting Times. Alice Walker. PoBA

And stood before the shimmering light/to make their vows. The First Wedding in the World. Joel Rosenberg. VWA

And stood calling back/across the water Found. Carol Muske. AmPA

...And stood watching/the boat disappear on the black waters of Lethe? A Supermarket in California. Allen Ginsberg. AmPP; CoAP; ConAP; HaCAP; HAP; HeIP; InPS; LiTM; NaP; NeAP; NOBA; PoM; PrIm; SOTW; TAP; TwCP; UnPo

And stood wondering what life is, and love,/and what they may be. Boy Wandering in Simms' Valley. Robert Penn Warren. DFF; SoSe

And stop my ears against the scream. A Northern Hoard. Seamus Heaney. CIP

And stopped the storm with a single word,/By just predicting–Rain! The Rhyme of the Rain Machine. F.W. Clarke. BoNaP

And stopped their grinning eyes. Blind Samson. William Plomer. PeSA

And stops, aghast, to see his own shade propped/Stiff at the board. Horror. Henry Treece. EAS

And stops of breath we build our Babels of. The Makers. Howard Nemerov. FYAP

And stores of gold lie buried in the/ground. The Poor Scholar. Abraham Ibn Chasdai. TrJP

And straight I called unto mind that it was Christmas day. The Burning Babe. Robert Southwell. ACP; AnFE; AtBAP; BoW; CAW; CBEP; EiL; FaBoCh; FaBoEn; GoBC; HAP; HBV 1-2; HeIP; InPS; LiTB; LoBV; LoGBV; MePo; NAs; NOBE; NOCV; NoP; OAEL 1-2; OBCP; OBEV; OBSC; OxBoCh; PAI; PoEL 1-5; PPoe; Prf; SBVL; SeCePo; TrCP; TreFT; TrGrPo; ViBoPo

And straight therewith, like wags new got to play,/Falls to shrewd turns! And I was in his way. Astrophel and Stella, XVII. Sir Philip Sidney. AAS; SiPS

And straightway all her polka-dots began a lively dance. Her Polka Dots. Peter Newell. NA

And straightway bent their unbending necks. Epigram: "If thou seekest the dread throne of God." *Anonymous.* ISi

And straightway went at it ag'in. Limerick: "There was a young lady of Lynn." *Anonymous.* LiBL

And strange-eyed constellations reign/His stars eternally. Drummer Hodge. Thomas Hardy. AWP; BrPo; CoBMV; EBEV; GTBS-P; HAP; InPo; InPS; NoAm; NOBV; NoP; OBWP; PAI; SeCeV; VLP

And strangely happy with myself. The Bagel. David Ignatow. CAPP; ConAP; FF; TwCP

And strangle it, and with it, rhetoric. Preludes for Memnon. Conrad Aiken. LiTM; MoPo; NoAm

And strawberry wire/And columbine. Song: "And can the physician make sick men well?" *Anonymous.* EiL; LoBV

And stray Song: "I love my lady's eyes." Robert Bridges. VLP

...And stray/For ever through the glens, placid and dumb. Empedocles on Etna. Matthew Arnold. GTBS-P

And stray no more, save paths Thou leadst them through. The Valley of the Heavens. Luis Ponce de Leon. CAW

And streaming in/flames. A Poem for Museum Goers. John Wieners. NeAP

And Streams of Sweat down their sow'r Foreheads flow. The Iliad. Homer. OBVE

And Streams shall murmur all around. Pastoral Hymn. Joseph Addison. OBEC

And streamward every traveler fares. The Bridge. Willibald Kohler. CAW

And strength for all duty and trial/That hour to her spirit were given. Christ and the Little Ones. Julia Gill. BLPA

And strength yet stronger grow,/Blessing and blest. International Hymn. George Huntington. PoLf

And stretch'd blind drunk beneath the table/Was how she spent her widding night. Moggy's Wedding. Charles R. Thatcher. NOAV

And stretch her luff, hio! Cheer'ly, Man. *Anonymous.* AmSS

And, stretching marvellously/Become the tracks of the Tokaido Railway Line. Fish. Takahashi Shinkichi. NU

And strews for all impartially their grave. The Tornado. Charles De Kay. EtS

And strike the key-note of each grateful prayer,/Breathed in their distant homes by wife or child! The Buoy-Bell. Charles Tennyson Turner. EtS

And strikes him dead for thine and thee. The Princess. Alfred, Lord Tennyson. OBNC; OBVV; TrGrPo

And strikes out flame from the adoring hills. Sunrise on Mansfield Mountain. Alice Brown. HBV 1-2

And strives to trim the short-liv'd blaze. The Lay of the Last Minstrel. Sir Walter Scott. OBRV

And striving Nature to conceal,/You only her defects reveal. The Goose and the Swans (excerpt). Edward Moore. PBBP

And stroked all night, with a black wing, my wings. The Black Swan. Randall Jarrell. CMoP; NMP

And strong eyes questing distances where crowd/Mist-shapes like unknown beasts half-hid in cloud. Lion Gate. Vera Rich. PoSH

And strong Orion and the Hyades. Hesiod, 1908. Alexander Mair. GoTS

And struck his hands together. Appomattox. Mackinlay Kantor. AnAmPo

And struck up a bit of a jig. Medley. *Anonymous.* OxNR

And struggle fitfully, like me, in vain,. Sonnet XXII: "O blazing Sun, how happy you are there." Louise Labe. BoWoP

And strut down the streets with paint on my face. A Song in the Front Yard. Gwendolyn Brooks. IDB; NoAm; NOBA; PoBA

And stubbed his fingers on a dead man's face. War Story. Jon Stallworthy. DFF; ELU; OxBC

And studded with ten-penny nails. Limerick: "There was a young lady of Wales." *Anonymous.* NA

And stumble away, trying not to adore her. Shrine in Nazareth. Sister Mary St. Virginia. ISi

And stun you with the quiet gaze of stone. Galatea Again. Genevieve Taggard. WHA

And submit to the grace/Of morning the adolescence of our sons. Women Hoping for Rain. David Tillinghast. AMV-81

And successor has the clap,/With a hey, trany nony nony no. A Raree Show. Stephen College. APAS

And such a lot of nice fresh air/All sandwiched in between. Cheerfulness. *Anonymous.* GoTF; TreFT

And such a love was never seen/On hill or dale or country green. Madrigal: "My love is neither young nor old." Robert Jones. EnRePo

And such a peculiar way they have of raising hunters' hair. The Buffalo Hunters. *Anonymous.* CoSo

And such as honour Heav'n, shall heav'nly Honour share. Metamorphoses. Ovid (Publius Ovidius Naso). AWP; OBVE

And such beginnings touch their END. Paradise. George Herbert. BoLiVe; OAEL 1-2; SeCP; TrGrPo

And such old winter-bitten sticks and stems they/figure the hell with. Ribald Romeos Less and Less Berattle. John Frederick Nims. MAT

And such, or my hopes fail, shall make you shine. Epistle to Elizabeth, Countess of Rutland. Ben Jonson. JCP

And such other grave affairs/As they thought of during prayers. Westland Row. James Stephens. HBMV

And such perfection here appears/It neither Wind nor Sun-shine fears. Verses Made Sometime Since upon the Picture.... John Josselyn. SCAP

And such refraction of events/As often rises ere thy rise. In Memoriam A.H.H., XCII. Alfred, Lord Tennyson. VLP

And such spirits raise, 'twill then/Trouble Death to lay agen. Upon a Wife that Dyed Mad with Jealousie. Robert Herrick. CavP

...And suck/The arteries and walk in triumph on the faces. The Trumpet: Grass on the Cliff. Robinson Jeffers. PoA

And sudden-passionate in ebbs and flows. Flawless His Heart. James Russell Lowell. MC

And suddenly are home. The Umbrella. Ann Stanford. NYBP

And suddenly: beauty/of your garments. You lay in wait. Sappho. BoWoP

And suddenly hears again the endless steps. Caesura. Kenneth MacKenzie. BoAV; CBAP; NOAV

And suddenly recognize/Who I am. My Strawlike Hair. Asya (Asya Gray). VWA

And suddenly saw Christina/Dead on the nursery floor. Christina. Louis MacNeice. BoLoP; OxBI

And suddenly saw them for the first time/By the same light that gave you away. Lantern. Gary Soto. Str

And suddenly the world becomes/A part of me and I of it. Amends to Nature. Arthur Symons. GTBS; HBMV

...And suffer/in joy, that our lives/are so familiar. Return of the Native. LeRoi (Imamu Amiri Baraka) Jones. BPo

And sugar horses painted red. The Gingerbread Man. *Anonymous.* OxNR

And suitably placed among these bright fields of food. In a Country Museum. Patricia Beer. FaBoWP

And sulky as a child when her play's done. The Poor Man's Pig. Edmund Charles Blunden. MoBrPo

And Summer, blowing over the Mediterranean/Like swans, like perfect swans. Summer Idyll. George Barker. FaBoMo; MoPo

And summer is not summer, nor can be. Three Friends of Mine. Henry Wadsworth Longfellow. MAmP

And summer not to come again. A Country God. Edmund Charles Blunden. MoBrPo

And summer rules the radiant year. Santa Barbara. Francis Fisher Browne. AA

And summer soon to be. The First Spring Morning. Robert Bridges. BoNaP

And summons read, the great consult began. Paradise Lost. John Milton. ATP; MBW 1-2; OAEP

And sundry decorations/not without meaning. Totem. Nissim Ezekiel. VWA

And sune thou shalt be thrown aside,/Like ony common weed and vile. I Do Confess Thou Art Sae Fair. Robert Burns. CBEP

And sunflowers grew up on both sides of it:/Blessing it. Effortlessly Democratic Santa Fe Trail. Martha Baird. PoPl

And sung/a sweet high hungry/single syllable Pictures of a Gone World. Lawrence Ferlinghetti. HoPM

And sung from dawn to dark, from dark to dawn. The Cricket Kept the House. Edith Matilda Thomas. OBCA

And sunk and sad was she! O I Won't Lead a Homely Life. Thomas Hardy. UnS

And sunk for to rise no more. James Harris (B vers.). *Anonymous.* AmFP; ViBoFo

And sunlight warmed the stones,/fire undressed my bones. The Dark Birds. Bert Meyers. VWA

And sunny clouds are floating over all. Castleconnell. Sir Aubrey De Vere. IrPN

And sunset splendour of July. July. John Greenleaf Whittier. YeAr

And sup with thee in glory by and by.' St. Peter. Christina Georgina Rossetti. NOCV

And surceased on the sky, and but left in the gloaming/Sea-mutterings and me. The Souls of the Slain. Thomas Hardy. CMoP; LiTB; PoEL 1-5

And sure I may look at an ugly thing. A Cat May Look at a King. *Anonymous.* OxBoLi

And sure it's not the going,/But that I find the way. Via Longa. Patrick MacDonogh. HBMV

And sure, methinks, I have great wrong/If that I be not loved again. Love Me Again. *Anonymous.* EIL

And, sure of Heaven, rides triumphing in. An Elegie on the Lady Jane Pawlet, Marchion: of Winton. Ben Jonson. SeCP

And sure to live with Christ eternally. A Copy of Verses. John Wilson. SCAP

And sure we've had enough of that,/At least within this town, sir. The Manchester Ship Canal. *Anonymous.* OBET

And sure you know there is but one Church/Can ever expect salvation. Bishop Butler of Kilcash. *Anonymous.* OnYI

And surely, myself, I'd the voyage have declined/If half what I suffred I e'er had opined! The India Guide. Sir George Dallas. OBTV

And surely on her threshold dying fall. The Gulistan. Muslih-ud-Din Sa'di. AWP; LiTW

And Susan Blouzelinda's loss repairs. The Shepherd's Week. John Gay. CEP; EiCP

And sustain me for my time in the desert/On what is essential to me. Lemuel's Blessing. William Stanley Merwin. CAPP; CoPo; NYBP

And swallow up that radiance in night? Buffalo. Florence Earle Coates. PAH

And swallowed me down like a crumb of bread. The Two Witches. Robert Graves. SO

...And swallows/fly in to my shed. Sixth-Month Song in the Foothills. Gary Snyder. HaCAP

And swash and sweep it/Blue again. Brooms. Dorothy Aldis. SoPo

And sway toward the bed/in a last chant before dawn. My Son and I. Philip Levine. FAZ; GP; NYP

And swear no day was ever passed so ill. Epistle to Richard Boyle, Earl of Burlington (excerpt). Alexander Pope. OBSV

And swear they'll have their wages rose before they reap or sow. Striking Times. *Anonymous.* OBET

And swear we'll carve our cherry-stones/no more. Trilby. Alice Brown. AA

And sweep thou on thy worldy way, O Moon! nor glance at mine! To the Moon. George Darley. MOON

And sweet Jesus we'll call him by name. All in the Morning. *Anonymous.* BiCB

And sweet, reluctant, amorous delay. Paradise Lost. John Milton. ErPo

And sweet's the air with curly smoke/From all my burning bridges. Sanctuary. Dorothy Parker. NLV

And sweet shall be thy taste, & sweet thy infant/joys renew!" Visions of the Daughters of Albion. William Blake. EnRP

And sweet to me is shipwreck in this sea. L'Infinito. Giacomo Leopardi. AWP

And sweet voice gone. On a Little Bird. Martin Armstrong. CH

And sweeter be the burden that hangs upon thee. Holy Cross. *Anonymous.* ACP; CAW

And sweeter hope, when hope despairs. To Imagination. Emily Bronte. VLP

And, sweeter numbers swelling,/Forever praise thy name. We Bring No Glittering Treasures. Harriett C. Phillips. AH

And sweeter than rosebuds than red or white clover/Is bonny young Susan to me. I Love the Blue Violet. John Clare. AtBAP

And sweeter than the violet! In the Spring. Meleager. AWP

And sweetly rocked him on her knee. Sweet Was the Song the Virgin Sung. *Anonymous.* NOCV

And sweetness comes to him. Concert. Helen Quigless. NBP

And swell in his sight and suck him thin. Relationships. Mona Van Duyn. GP

And swept away those six young youths with their foreman, young Monroe. The Jam on Jerry's Rock (II). *Anonymous.* AmFP; AS; FSW; ShS

And sweter be the birden that hanges upon thee.   Steadfast Cross.   *Anonymous.*   OxBM

And swift contending harmonies shall shake/Thy windows with a storm of jubilant praise.   Shall the Dead Praise Thee? George Macdonald.   TrCP

And Swift expires a Driv'ler and a Show.   Life's Last Scene.   Samuel Johnson.   OBEC; SeCePo

And swift to victory his master bore,   The First Olympionique to Hiero of Syracuse.   Pindar.   ATP

And swift winds on the peaks/where the light is clear.   (San Ysidro, Cabezon).   Paula Gunn Allen.   TWSS

And swilling Old Crow/out of a crystal flask.   Where Is the Black Community? Joyce Carol Thomas.   CNA

And swinges the scaly horror of his folded tail.   Lizards and Snakes.   Anthony Hecht.   CoPo; FaBoMo; NCSH; TwCP

And swirled, a strangled corpse, under His Ages.   Providence.   Cale Young Rice.   WGRP

And swirling up the blue weald landscape shifts/To the forest ridge's pine-wood darkened crest.   Woods and Kestrel.   Julian Bell.   ChMP

And swords of Damocles.   Damocles.   Robert Graves.   NYBP

And swore he belonged to somebody else.   Boxer Loses Face and Fortune.   Lucilius [(or Lucillius)].   LiSp

And swore no thing so sweet and sour as love.   Eurymachus's Fancy.   Robert Greene.   OBSC

And symbols of endurance, whispers,/"This is love."   Ostia Antica.   Anthony Hecht.   NePA

And syn prove good for nought.   Epigram: "Lasses, like nuts at bottom brown."   Allan Ramsay.   FaBoEE

And syne my logeyng I haue take/Wyth my brande dubbyd many a knyght.'   Oterborne (excerpt).   *Anonymous.*   OxBS

And t'ease the travailes of her beames to night,/In this small Lanthorn would contract her light.   To the Queen, Entertain'd at Night by the Countess of Anglesey.   Sir William Davenant.   MeLP; MePo; OBS

And T for my love Tom.   Heigh Ho! My Heart Is Low.   *Anonymous.*   OxNR

And t'other's shoes are paid for.   An Epigram: "A member of the modern great."   John Cunningham.   FaBoEE

And take a lesson from this tale, of the Spider and the Fly.   The Spider and the Fly.   Mary Howitt.   BeLS; FaFP; GoTF; HBV 1-2; HBVY; OHFP; OnUR; OxBChV; Par; TreFS; WBLP

And take a life immortall from my Verse.   To the Reverend Shade of His Religious Father.   Robert Herrick.   AnAnS 2; CaPo; JCP; OBS; SeCV 1-2

And take/From that which made us that which will make us again.   The Wheel.   Edwin Muir.   NoAm

And take from us again our living sons.   The Generations.   George M. Brady.   OnYI

And take her for a midnight stroll!   Dublin: The Old Squares.   Padraic Colum.   NePoAm

And take him at last/Up to heaven with Thee.   The Hard-Working Miner.   *Anonymous.*   AmFP

And take me back where I come from.   Careless Love.   *Anonymous.*   BLSo

And take me from my resting bed.   Riddle: "Black I am and much admired."   *Anonymous.*   OxNR

And take me to the golden hills of boyhood once again.   The Port o' Heart's Desire.   John S. McGroarty.   HBV 1-2

And take me with him by the ten taut reins/Of my skinned and burning hands.   Phaeton.   Eli Mandel.   PeCV

And take my flight/For heaven.   To Music, to Becalm His Fever.   Robert Herrick.   ATP; CaPo; EG; HBV 1-2; OBEV; QFR

And take no thing at all, or be content/With such reward as Fortune hath you sent.   Of Fortune.   Sir Thomas More.   CoBE

And take off Ladies Limitations./With a fal, la, la.   The Challenge.   Alexander Pope.   PoEL 1-5

And take off nearly/All their clothes.   August.   John Updike.   OBCA

And take off your hats,/you filthy things!   The Lady.   Elizabeth Jane Coatsworth.   MaC

And take our tea and melons in the shade.   Now Philippa Is Gone.   Anne Ridler.   FaBoTw

And take the bullet in your brain.   The Day of Battle.   Alfred Edward Housman.   OHIP; WaaP

And take the lovers unaware.   The Canoe Speaks (excerpt).   Robert Louis Stevenson.   SD

And take the plough again in peace, their/warrior's duty done.   The Minute-Men of North-Boro'.   Wallace Rice.   PAH

And take their Deaths as Watch-words unto me.   Vigilantius.   Cotton Mather.   SCAP

And take their walks across the ceiling.   The Folk Who Live in Backward Town.   Mary Ann Hoberman.   OBCA

And take these weather beaten breeches!   The Miner's Lament.   Mark (Samuel Langhorne Clemens) Twain.   BPAW

And take to thy cold arms, insensibly, thy prey.   To Death.   Anne Finch, Countess of Wilchilsea.   HBV 1-2

...And take/train into this wilderness of prisons & anthology.   To Guillaume Appollinaire.   Jim Brodey.   APU

And take your wounds from it gladly.   Ite.   Ezra Pound.   HAP; MoAB; MoAmPo; PP

And takes it with velvet lips.   Mare.   Judith Thurman.   PH

And takes this bitterest bite out of our time.   April, 1942.   Mark Van Doren.   WaP

And takes unto itself the strangest of strange lands.   My Soul Is Robbed.   Isaac Rosenberg.   MoPo

And taking pains, which is magical, tragical, funny.   For Hani, Aged Five, That She Be Better Able to Distinguish a Villain.   Gene Baro.   NYBP

And taking the moon and leaving the paper dark.   The Prediction.   Mark Strand.   EAS; LCAP

And tales in tales/Where no one fails.   The Silly Fool.   W. H. Auden.   OBMV

...And talk about/growing up in New England.   Toward a Theory of Instruction.   Danny Rendleman.   SUW

And talk about the weather/or the price of grass-seed?   The Other Side.   Seamus Heaney.   FaBoIP

And talk excitedly about ourselves, like guests.   The Couple Upstairs.   Hugo Williams.   PoL

And talk, here in the firelight,/Of him beneath the stars.   The Adventurer.   Odell Shepard.   HBMV

And talk of our deeds o'er a flask of old wine.   The Lion-Hunt.   Thomas Pringle.   OBTV

And tamed the Chaldean lions, is mighty/still to save!   Cassandra Southwick.   John Greenleaf Whittier.   PAH

And Tania's over forty!   Marvelous.   Allan Kaplan.   PoL

And tap them down with humming words.   Orpheus.   Elizabeth Madox Roberts.   MoAmPo

And tarry I may not when love cries away.   Deirdre's Farewell to Alba.   *Anonymous.*   OnYI

And taste a raindrop/warm.   I'd Like to Mark Myself.   Milton Acorn.   NeAC

And taste of Love and Death.'   Creation.   Alfred Noyes.   GoBC; OBVV

And tastes it as it goes.   Ode on the Pleasure Arising from Vicissitude.   Thomas Gray.   CEP; EiCP; GTBS; GTBS-P; LAuP; NOEC; OBEC

And taught his gorgon destinies to sing.   Luis de Camoes.   Roy Campbell.   FaBoTw; PeSA

And taunt them everyone just a tad more.   Therapy.   Ken Poyner.   AMV-81

And teach me all things–but repentance.   To His Wife on the Fourteenth Anniversary of Her Wedding-Day...   Samuel Bishop.   ViBoPo

And teach me how I may Thy dwelling find.   A Motet.   John Amner.   OBSP

And teach me the true language/Of silentness!   On Sunday in the Sunlight.   William Rose Benet.   HBMV

And teach new wonders of unselfishness.   The Joy of Love.   Allan Dowling.   BoC; ErPo

And teach the lords of empty birth a king may walk the/stage.   Edwin Booth.   Alice Brown.   HBV 1-2

And teach the rising race the way/That they may not depart.   To the First of August.   Ann Plato.   BlSi

And teach the Sons of men thy wayes.   A Prayer unto Christ the Judge of the World.   Michael Wigglesworth.   SCAP

And teach us, children of the Holy Place/Who love Thy Courts, to love Thee best of all.   At High Mass.   Robert Hugh Benson.   CAW

And teach us how to air/Our lives again.   The Goldfish Wife.   Sandra Hochman.   NYBP; UnPo

And teach us nothing, feeding not the heart.   Lines on Cambridge of 1830.   Alfred, Lord Tennyson.   GLGT

And teaches small children to do this in their turn.   To David, about His Education.   Howard Nemerov.   HaCAP

And tear through its shallow skin, and feast on it.   Flying Fox.   Thomas W. Shapcott.   CBAP

And tears are heard within the harp I touch.   The Eyes That Drew from Me.   Petrarch (Francesco Petrarca).   NAWM 1-2

And tears are longer ere they dry.   What News.   Walter Savage Landor.   BoLoP

And tears creep inward, drying on the heart.   Remembering Lincoln.   Frank Mundorf.   GoYe

And tears of sweet affection shed,–/My Mother.   My Mother.   Jane Taylor.   BLPA; BLPL; TreF

And tears stream down laughing Yuki faces/tens of thousands of years old   The Past.   William Oandasan.   STE

And tears will mingle with the wine.   Song of the Cape of Good Hope.   Christian Schubart.   NU

And teeth begin/To drill, drill?   Bitten.   Mark Van Doren.   AnAmPo

And tell her she is beautiful.   The Falcon.   Elinor Wylie.   LOW

And tell her, tell her, that I follow thee.   The Princess.   Alfred, Lord Tennyson.   AtBAP; GTBS

And tell her to take a hot mud bath/And not to wait up for me! Alligator on the Escalator. Eve Merriam. SO

And tell him, "It'll be alright–/it'll be alright tomorrow..." Trouble. Philip Brasfield. LFAC

And tell it as I saw it on the spot. My Dream. Christina Georgina Rossetti. BrRo; VLP

And tell me stories and tuck me up at night. Footnote to John ii.4. R. A. K. Mason. AnNZ

And tell me then if you'll not find/The whole lot's back in quantity. Borderline Ballad. Richard Weber. PPON

And tell me/what's the difference Love for Instance. Dan Gerber. FAZ

And tell me you believe in/The great white race. Ku Klux. Langston Hughes. BPo

And tell my brothers as they pass by/I've done robbing around the salt sea. Henry Martyn (A vers.). Anonymous. ViBoFo

And tell my sire his sons shall be/As charitably great as he. Pray Remember the Poor. Christopher Smart. NOEC

And tell the heart of England/The Spring is here again! When Spring Comes Back to England. Alfred Noyes. HBV 1-2

And tell the other girls and boys/Not to meddle with my toys. Looking Forward. Robert Louis Stevenson. BrPo; NLV; OxBChV

And tell thee when the skaters are about.' Elfin Skates. Eugene Lee-Hamilton. OBVV

And tell them all that I'm gone to sleep. Freight Train. Anonymous. FSW

And tell to his tribe that his murderer sleeps. Death Song. Alonzo Lewis. PAH

And tell which was which without looking. Limerick: "A prominent lady in Brooking." Anonymous. TDH

And tell why I have chosen thee! God of Visions. Emily Bronte. TrGrPo

And tell you love has led me to this place. Take Home This Heart. John Holmes. LiTL

And tells me at great length about apples. Getting a Poem in the Rain. Dick Lourie. NeAC

And tells the Cherub-folk in heaven/The wonder tale of Bethlehem. The Cherub-Folk. Enid Dinnis. CAW

And tells the jest without the smile. Youth and Age. Samuel Taylor Coleridge. BLPL; EnLi 1-2; ERoP 1-2; FiP; GTBS; GTBS-P; HBV 1-2; OBEV; OBNC; OBRV; PoLf

And tells the traveller on his way/That Earth shall be forgiven! Hesperus. John Clare. ERoP 1-2; FaBoRV; GTBS-P; NOBV; OAEL 1-2

And tells to man his glorious destinies. The Evening Cloud. John Wilson. HBV 1-2

And Tellus feels his forehead's cumbrous load. Endymion, III (excerpt). John Keats. MOON

And ten black cadillacs to haul it in. Italian Extravaganze. Gregory Corso. CoPo

And ten shoemakers to make/A pair of sandals to fit him. The Door-Keeper Has Big Feet. Sappho. HW

And tend the true,/The mortal flower. La Rose des Vents. Richard Wilbur. MiAP

And tending a baby that's none of your own. Run Little Dogies. Anonymous. BPAW

And terraced walls their black reflection throw/On the green-mantled moat that sleeps below. Captivity. Samuel Rogers. OBNC

And terror shall be past, and grief, and war. After Sunset. Grace Hazard Conkling. AnAmPo; HBMV; MoRP

And test their bruised omnipotence/Against the cat's austere defense. Pussycat Sits on a Chair. Edward Newman Horn. ELU

And th'other chases woman, whilst she goes/More ways and turns than hunted nature knows. Against Hope. Abraham Cowley. LiTB; LoBV; MeLP; OBS; SeCV 1-2

And tha revolution begins/just this softly It Begins Softly. Bernadine. LTB

And thagh ich habbe ido thee wrange,/Thou graunte me amendinge. A Song to Mary. of Shoreham William. MeEL

And thair lies guid Sir Patrick Spence/Wi the Scots lords at his feit. Sir Patrick Spens. Anonymous. AnFE; AtBAP; AWP; BaBo; BiP; BSV; BuBa; CABA; CABL; CH; DiPo; EBEV; ELP; EnSB; ESPB; ExPo; FaBoBa; FaBoCh; FaPoR; FF; ForPo; GN; GoJo; GoTS; HAP; HBV 1-2; HoPM; InPK; InPo; InPS; InvP; LiTB; LoBV; LoGBV; MCCG; MOS; NIP; NOBE; NoP; OAEL 1-2; OAEP; OBEV; OxBB; OxBS; PAI; PoEL 1-5; PoRA; PPP; PrIm; SeCeV; TreF; TrGrPo; UnPo; ViBoFo; ViBoPo; WeW; WHA

And thame puneist that did me wrang,/Thocht I be ald. Solace in Age. Sir Richard Maitland. OxBS

And than ys best: "Revertere." In a tyme of a somer's day. Anonymous. EnPo

...–And thank goodness they're/both of them over! A Nightmare. Sir William Schwenck Gilbert. NOBL; OxBoLi

And thank Him than. Pleasure It Is. William Cornish. CBEP; CH; MeEL

And thank my God and do not ask for more. Blind. Norman V. Pearce. PoToHe

...And thank/the enemy to whom I owe my life. Jeanne d'Arc. Louise Gluck. GeTw

And thank the great god Pan for all! For a Fountain. Bryan Waller Procter. OBEV; OBVV

And thank the kind, benignant God/For what I have not been. A Prayer. Harry Kemp. HBV 1-2; WGRP

And thank your GOD as I thank ye/For this delicious wine-cup! The Minstrel. Johann Wolfgang von Goethe. AWP

And thankit Lufe that had thair makis wunne. The Nightingale's Song. King of Scotland James I OxBM

And thanks unto the harvest's Lord who sends our/"daily bread." The First Thanksgiving. Alice Williams Brotherton. OHIP

And that a thousand Angels wait/To write them at thy inner gate. Idle Words. Walter Savage Landor. OBSV

...And that after all human/Glance, which makes all else forgiven. To T.A.R.H. Stephen Spender. PeHV

And that all Creatures for his Sake alone/Were made, for him to Tyrannize upon. The Hunting of the Hare. Margaret Cavendish, Duchess of Newcastle. FM

And that are fair to see. Go, ill-sped book. John Berryman. BoLoP

And that be thine. To Mr. ****, an Unlettered Poet, on Genius Unimproved. Ann Yearsley. NOEC

"And that Business is to serve!" Business Is Business. Berton Braley. WBLP

And that cleans up the matter. Experience. Dorothy Parker. InMe; PoPl

And that dark other mountain. That Dark Other Mountain. Robert Francis. LiSp; NCSH; SD

And that day I will tell you her name. The Lovely Village Fair; or, I Dont Mean to Tell You Her Age. Anonymous. CoMu

And that dead dogs are those who do not know/that dying is what, to live, each has to do. Curiosity. Alastair Reid. SoSe

And that, despite our dreams, the gods prevail. I Shall Never Go. A. J. Hovde. AMV-80

And that dreams themselves are a dream. Life Is a Dream. Pedro Calderon de la Barca. AWP; LiTW

And that drums had to be rolling, rolling, rolling. Dry Loaf. Wallace Stevens. AtBAP; CrMA; NOBA; OxBA; PoRA

And that ended the comedy. The Donkey and the Lapdog. Jean de La Fontaine. OBVE

And that ended Willy Wood. Willy Wood. Anonymous. OxNR

And that explains why my old friend Mike/Laid him out with a marlinespike. The Gemlike Flame. R. P. Lister. DBV; FiBHP

And that fair kneeling Goddess. Hyperion. John Keats. OBNC; OBRV

And that, Father Daly, explains why I lied/To tell how the milk soured on Mrs. McBride. Confession in Holy Week. Christopher Morley. HBMV

And that for paltry reasons given/His conscience may remain unriven. To His Importunate Mistress. Peter De Vries. NLV

And that garden shall supply/Thy delicious alchemy. Invitation to the Bee. Charlotte Smith. OxBChV

And that great day the Port Bill passed/Made us a nation hard and fast. How We Became a Nation. Harriet Prescott Spofford. MC; PAH

And that has made all the difference. The Road Not Taken. Robert Frost. AnFE; AnNE; APA; CMoP; CoBMV; DiPo; EvOK; FaBoCh; FaFP; FPL; GoTF; HAP; HeIP; LiTA; LiTM; LoGBV; MAPA; MoAB; MoAmPo; MP; NePA; NoAm; NoP; OxBA; PG; PoLf; PoPl; RFM; SeCeV; SoSe; TAP; TreFT; TwCP

And that he's Venus' runaway. Venus' Runaway. Ben Jonson. HBV 1-2

And that held her spellbound for two seconds/while I fled. Intimates. D. H. Lawrence. BoLoP; NLV; OBSP

And that his crudest and most terrifying dreams/will not return with such wide publicity. Mousemeal. Howard Nemerov. MP; NCSH; TwCP

And that Hope sows what Love shall never reap? Cloud and Wind. Dante Gabriel Rossetti. MaVP

And that I love (O soul, we must be meek!)/Is by thee only, whom I love alone. Sonnets from the Portuguese, XII. Elizabeth Barrett Browning. HBV 1-2

And that I may in her service/Ever to amend. Song for My Lady. A. Godwin. OxBoLi

And that I may myselfe well apply,/Thy sone and thee to laude and magnify. The Pastime of Pleasure. Stephen Hawes. PoEL 1-5

And that I shall lie by the waters of Waikiki and want? Twenty-Third Flight. Earle Birney. HeIP; OxBC; SoSe

And that I think's a reason fair/To fill my glass again. A Reason Fair to Fill My Glass. Charles Morris. HBV 1-2

And that I was worthy of the favor of Ibn Aamir. The Wing of Separation. al Andalusi Ibn Darraj AWP

And that intrepid Nymph, on Uri's steep descried! The Three Cottage Girls. William Wordsworth. HBV 1-2

And that is all I know of Jam. On Jam. Hilaire Belloc. NLV

And that is all it's ever going to be. Manners. Howard Nemerov. NLV

And that is all?/–That is all. I Tell of Another Young Death. Cesar Tiempo. TrJP

And that is flitting, doth abide and stay. Ruines of Rome. Joachim Du Bellay. FaBoPP

And that is how he served me. Man of Derby. *Anonymous.* OxNR

,.And that is how I came to know.) The Duel. Eugene Field. BeLS; CenHV; FaBoBe; FaFP; FPL; GoTF; HBV 1-2; HBVY; MoShBr; OBAL; OBCA; OHFP; OnMSP; PoLf; PoPl; PoRA; SoPo; TiPo; TreF

And that is how we had an accident. The Murderer. Stevie Smith. FaBoWP; OBSP; TEP

...And that is how you die. Protocols. Randall Jarrell. LCAP; OxBC; VGW

And that is life! Life. Paul Laurence Dunbar. AmNP; CDC

And that is me, Matilda Jane! Doll Song. Lewis (Charles Lutwidge Dodgson) Carroll. SoPo

And that is nothing short of hell. In Extremis. Margaret Fishback. FiBHP

And that is the meaning of Empire Day. Songs of Education. Gilbert Keith Chesterton. HBMV; OBSV

And that is the Paradise crowning her days. Effie. Sterling A. Brown. BANP

And that is the way it suppose to/be in this house of sweat and horizons. Life after Death. Richard W. Thomas. PoBA

And that is the wish to them I do give. The Antarctic Muse. Thomas Perry. OBTV

A. And that is what they require of us. A Woman Defending Herself Examines Her Own Character Witness. Susan Griffin. NPGG

And that is why I can never amount to anything politically or socially. Golly, How Truth Will Out! Ogden Nash. LiTA; MoAmPo

And that is why my Airedale dog/Is such a friend of mine. My Airedale Dog. W. L. Mason. SoPo

And that is why the noble beast/Has bitten off your head. O Have You Caught the Tiger. Alfred Edward Housman. BXAP; FaBoNo; SpRo

And that is why your Cousin May/Fell through the parlor floor today. The Termite. Ogden Nash. CenHV; NLV; OBCA; PoPl; ShM

And that - it broke! Calumny. Frances Sargent Osgood AA; HBV 1-2

And that it may be so I give thanks to the Almighty/and seek His aid. The Faith of Abraham Lincoln. Abraham Lincoln. TRV

And that it's the others who scar me/not you. The Girl I Call Alma. Linda Gregg. AmPA; NPGG

And that its purpose is to serve/Mankind, but not destroy. A Driver's Prayer. *Anonymous.* STF

And that'll be no way for me to get along. That's No Way to Get Along. Robert Wilkins. BluL

And that moment when the bird sings very close/To the music of what happens. Song: "A rowan like a lipsticked girl." Seamus Heaney. IPY

And that most distressful dire land/He'd rechristen, merely..."Ireland".' Anglo-Eire Vignette. Patric Stevenson. NeIP

And that much grief, for a day,/bankrupted our economy. Camouflage. Amy Clampitt. SUW

And that must be even more awful to bear/Than walking about on your tummy. The Snail. Sir Alan Patrick Herbert. BoAnP

And that my mother, who is dead, was by. Sonnet: He Craves Interpreting of a Dream of His. Dante da Maiano. AWP; LiTW

And that Nelly kissed her brother, and said "Billy, here's your rose"? Billy's Rose. George R. Sims. PaPo

And that no theory of pessimism is complete/which altogether ignores them Golfers. Irving Layton. SD

And that old lace, I think, falls down/Less softly on Priscilla's gown/Than when I wore it. Soliloquy of a Maiden Aunt. Dollie Radford. NOBV

And that pale sustenance,/Despair! I Cannot Live With You. Emily Dickinson. AnNE; CBEP; DiPo; MAT; MoAB; MoAmPo; NOBA; NoP; OxBA; PoEL 1-5; PPoe; SBG

And that pit an end tae his grouwin'. The Bonnie Laddie's Lang a-Growin'. *Anonymous.* OxBS

And that put an end to Lanigan's ball. Lanigan's Ball. *Anonymous.* OxBoLi

And that put him out of his pain! The Cynotaph. Richard Harris Barham. FM

(And that quickly) speake your Man. A Celebration of Charis. Ben Jonson. AnAnS 2; SeCP

And that rabbit doesn't trust me The Dream Songs. John Berryman. LCAP

And that's all he gets for his pains. Limerick: "A rheumatic old man in White Plains." *Anonymous.* LiBL

And that's all you can say. The Likeness. Leonard Nathan. GP

And that's everything. Everything. Philip Levine. AMV-80

And–that's how a good many married folk dwell./Ripperty! Kye! A-hoo! Ripperty! Kye! Ahoo! Henry Lawson. CBAP

And that's how people burn to death in hotel rooms. Life Story. Tennessee Williams. PeHV

And that's how small things/survive like grass/pushes up through/cracks in the asphalt. Postcard to a Foetus. Kirk Robertson. GP

...And that's how the favourite was beat. How We Beat the Favourite. Adam Lindsay Gordon. CBAP

–And that's how umbrellas/First were invented. The Elf and the Dormouse. Oliver Herford. AA; FaBoBe; HBV 1-2; HBVY; OnMSP; SoPo; TiPo

–And that's my earliest recollection. A Terrible Infant. Frederick Locker-Lampson. ALV; FiBHP; GoTF; HBV 1-2; InMe; NOBV; TreFS

And that's my ring around her neck/on the strongest chain in the world. Driving Carl's '56 Chevy. Warren Woessner. AmC

And that's my situation, Folks– This Form of Life Needs Sex. Allen Ginsberg. NNaP

And that's one thing I really like/That they say's good for me. Sassafras Tea. Mary Effie Lee Newsome. CDC; GoSl

And that's still a distressing sight Ecole St. Luc. Ray Fraser. NeAC

And that's the best cure for a little pussy cat.' That Little Black Cat. D'Arcy Wentworth Thompson. OxBChV

And that's the cause, says Packsaddle, that I have told this tale. Old Buck's Ghost. Frank Benton. PoOW

And that's the end of my little pig tale. A Pig Tale. James Reeves. SoPo

And that's the end of night. Evensong. Ridgely Torrence. HBV 1-2

And that's the end of three good tries. Cocoon. David McCord. OBCA

And that's the last of the cowboy. The Cowboy. *Anonymous.* BPAW; CoSo

And that's the reason why I'd almost like/To see them hawking matches in the gutter. The Case for Miners. Siegfried Sassoon. SaC

And that's the reason why you do–or do not. Don Juan. George Gordon, Lord Byron. OBRV

And that's the truth," said he. The Whale. *Anonymous.* EtS

And that's the way a sailor's life/to his sweetheart often goes. The Sailor Boy. *Anonymous.* ShS

And that's the way it comes to-day/The MISSING LINK is missing. The Missing Link. Oliver Herford. CenHV

"And that's the way it is." Impotence. Arthur Winfield Knight. SOTS

And that's the way o't noo, sirs. New Zealand Comforts. John Barr. AnNZ

And that's the way/The kissing goes. A Deux. William Wood. ELU

And that's the way they captured him, that wild Montana boy. The Wild Montana Boy. *Anonymous.* CoSo

And that's the way they captured him–the wild Colonial boy. The Wild Colonial Boy. *Anonymous.* AmFP; FaBoBa; FSW; OuSiCo; PoAu 1-2; ViBoFo

And that's the way, you see, my legs got bowed! A Sailor's Apology for Bow-Legs. Thomas Hood. EtS; MOS

And that's to keep thy Lent. To Keep a True Lent. Robert Herrick. AnAnS 2; HBV 1-2; TrCP; TRV

And that's well shod. Hob, Shoe, Hob; Hob, Shoe, Hob. *Anonymous.* OxNR

And that's what comes of reading/Pessimistic verse. Beth Appleyard's Verses. Peter DeVries. OBAL

And that's what I know about birds. Ornithology in Florida. Arthur Guiterman. BoAnP; InMe

And that's what old men are made of. What Folks Are Made Of. *Anonymous.* ABF; GoTF; TreF

And that's what she must do. The Sweet, Red Rose. Mary Mapes Dodge. BiCB

And that's what teaching is and was. History of Education. David McCord. NIP; OBAL

And that's why everything you do has some weird failure in it. The Radiance. Kabir. LLLT

And that's why he's now on Polaris. Limerick: "A Martian named Harrison Harris." Al Graham. QQQ

And that's why I'm going to Tilbury Town.' John Evereldown. Edwin Arlington Robinson. CMoP; NePA; OxBA

And that/(Said John)/Is/That. Happiness. A.(lan) A.(lexander) Milne. BoC; TiPo

And that same moon shall heap the desolate tide/Beneath the night's unchanging architrave. Sea-Sonnet. Victoria Mary (Vita) Sackville-West. SBG

And that saved the rear of Rossetti. On Himself. Dante Gabriel Rossetti. FaBoEE

And that she goes beyond my fathering. Rainbow. Robert Huff. NePoEA-2

And that she was not made for One. The Rival Sisters, III: Song. Robert Gould. CEP

And that significance precedes us–me–through the night So? Alvin Greenberg. FAZ

And that soft, gold hair by the sea-mist curled! Ulysses Returns. Roselle Mercier Montgomery. HBMV

And that some day, when the sands turn over, will resume sway. In Scorching Time. Alex Stevens. AMV-81

And that song, heard,/will stifle out this note. Sigil. Hilda ("H. D.") Doolittle. FaBoWP; VGW

And that stands all awry. Peter White. *Anonymous.* OxBoLi; OxNR

And that sticking unabidable tar. Pine Cones. Dave Smith. AMV-80

And that such Trash as we like drossy Lead,/Consume before it, and it strikes us dead. A Quarrel with Fortune. Benjamin Colman. SCAP

And that sweet man, John Clare. Heard in a Violent Ward. Theodore Roethke. HaCAP; NoAm

And that the bed was made/And that we could not stay. The Traveller Has Regrets. G. S. Fraser. BSV; OBTV

And that the colors in my eyes will vanish/when your face sets. Colors. Yevgeny Yevtushenko. LLLT

And that the earth will slide down farther down its swollen river. Something. Jared Smith. AMV-81

And that the first glance of these live Canadians/Impressed them favourably–(they were Acadians). The Emigration of the Fairies. John Hunter-Duvar. CaP

And that the same last eddy swallows up. The Orchard-Pit. Dante Gabriel Rossetti. EnLoPo; NBM; NCEP; OAEL 1-2; PoEL 1-5; SCV; SyP; VLP

And that the temples soothed in blackness/were the toys of a/foolish girl. To Egypt. Gloria Davis NBP

And that they will grasp him by the right hand at the shining throne/of grace. Charlie Rutledge. *Anonymous.* CoSo

And that this strangest spending/Buy survival at the end of time. Onwardness. Doris Hedges. CaP

And that thou have the peny redy to tak to. Money Is What Matters. *Anonymous.* MeEL

And that, thro' the wide universe,/Well-being's breath distills. A Litany for Latter-Day Mystics. Cale Young Rice. WGRP

And that thy bosom in my bosom lay. Depreciating Her Beauty. Wilfrid Scawen Blunt. OBMV

And that tied to man 'twill sever/Him and his affections ever. A Charm, or an Allay for Love. Robert Herrick. FaBoCh; FaBoUs; LoGBV

...And that uncertain heaven received/Into the bosom of the steady lake. There Was a Boy. William Wordsworth. FaBoCh; LoGBV

And that was all/My penny's worth. Buff. *Anonymous.* OxNR

And that was foolish, wasn't it, my dear? Challenge. Sterling A. Brown. CDC

And that was her final embrace. Limerick: "All young men should take note of the case." M. B. Thornton. LiBL

...And that was/how they built the harbor in Seattle. The Harbor at Seattle. Robert Hass. NPGG

And that was my castle in Spain. Reverie of a Mum. Nancy Keesing. CBAP; NOAV

And that was surely fair. One Good Turn Deserves Another. *Anonymous.* ShM

And that was the courtship of Larrie O'Dee. Larrie O'Dee. William Fink. HBV 1-2

And that was the end/Of Audrey. Audrey. Alan Dienstag. ErPo

And that was the end of the Christening. Miss Kilmansegg and Her Precious Leg. Thomas Hood. NOBV

And that was the end of the monk. Animal Fair. *Anonymous.* AS; BLPA; FaBoBe; FPL; MoShBr; NTCP; PoPle; SoPo; YaD

And that was the end of the singing-school. The Frogs' Singing-School. E. T. Carbell. SoPo

And that water these words what can they do what can they do/prince. Elegy of Fortinbras. Zbigniew Herbert. FaBoPV; OBVE

And that we call Being. Song of Myself. Walt Whitman. HoPM

And that we only saw, where ways were rough,/The flowers about our feet. First Pathways. Sidney Royse Lysaght. OBVV

And that we should be masters of the time. The Time. G. S. Fraser. WaP

And that we struggle/once twice or a thousand times/until there is built a better world. Against Negritude. Emanuel Corgo. WhB

And that, when beckoning, he should wag/The littlest in the air. The Keys of Morning. Walter De la Mare. AtBAP; MoVE; NoP

...And that which after fire/Remained, rested in one tomb as Thisbe did desire.' Pyramus and Thisbe. Ovid (Publius Ovidius Naso). LiTW

And that which fleeteth doth outrun swift time. Rome. Joachim Du Bellay. AWP

And that which most enraged me was, 'twas true. Lyce. William Walsh. BoLoP

And that which never is to die, for ever must be young. To Mr. Hobbes. Abraham Cowley. LoBV; SeCV 1-2

And that whoever seeks to know/all of the loved will see love die? O, Where Were We before Time Was. Max Dunn. NOAV

And that will be sufficient for my praise. To a Certain Lady, in Her Garden. Sterling A. Brown. CDC

And that will be the best. When Smoke Stood Up from Ludlow. Alfred Edward Housman. EnLit; MoBrPo

And that will never be. Edward. *Anonymous.* AmFP; FSW

And that will prove/I like to move! Moving. Eunice Tietjens. TiPo

And that you'd have no tail to shake! Perigoo's Horse. *Anonymous.* ShS

And that you got it from your mother. The Pansy. Samuel Hoffenstein. DBV

And that you live them, day by day. Epigram: "This is my curse, Pompous, I pray." J. V. Cunningham. PV

And thaw, though hellish slow, some day! Antenora. Hugh" (Christopher Murray Grieve) MacDiarmid. SeCePo

And thay will on you rew, as mine hes done one me. My Hairt Is Heich Aboif. *Anonymous.* OxBS

And the absence of despair/over yonder? Southeast Arkanasia. Maya Angelou. SaC

And the absolute marvel of a bunch of grapes. Seven. Nicanor Parra. PoL

And the ache is hard to bear. A thousand years, you said. Lady Heguri. BoLoP

And the aching pain of that long, long night/Will last till my life is o'er! Sundered. John Barford. PeHV

And the afflictions with which they afflict him when his loving/faints. The Tree of Love. Ramon Lull. CAW

...And the air's/Sweet with silence and vegetable smoke. Cerne Abbas. Hal Summers. HaMV

And the airy primulas, oblivious/Of the impending bee–they were fair enough sights. Coming Awake. D. H. Lawrence. BrPo

And the alabaster grain of your face, and stay. Letter to Frances. William Kistler. AMV-81

And the American royalties, and an inherited income,/To keep the wolf at bay. Public Journal. Phyllis McGinley. NLV

And the ancient cross on the hillside meant myself. A Hand of Snapshots (excerpt). Louis MacNeice. FaBoIP

And the Andalusian gentleman/on his best behaviour. Lament of the Virtues and Verses on Account of the Death of Don Guido. Antonio Machado. OBVE

And the ang-gulls convex'd. Plane Geometry. Emma Rounds. ImOP; QQQ; SpRo

And the Angels said "My! But that was near!" Limerick: "There was a young Fir-tree of Bosnia." Dante Gabriel Rossetti. FaBoNo

And the animals came forth and licked my hands. Parable. Robert Pack. NePoEA-2

And the Antipodes too have a Bothie of/Tober-na-vuolich. The Bothie of Tober-na-Vuolich. Arthur Hugh Clough. VLP

And the apple-blossom is allowed to wither on the bough.' Swineherd. Eilean Ni Chuilleanain. BIrV; CIP; FaBoWP; WPOW

And the "archaic smile' opens/again finally/to recite my doom. Wrath to Sadness. Robert Grenier. APU

And the ardent onrush of armies/Surges hot through my heart. The Forefather. Richard Burton. AA

And the armies that remained suffer'd. I Saw the Vision of Armies. Walt Whitman. WaaP

And the army was wild with cheers. Molly Pitcher. Kate Brownlee Sherwood. MC; PAH; PAL

And the ascendancy of the shadow/in the blossoming mass. A Part-Sequence for Change. Robert Duncan. VGW

And the Australia that is now my heart/Will that day hold my heart away from me. One Day. Ray Mathew. NOAV

And the awning was still there A Gone. Larry Eigner. NeAP

And the ax felt good, coming down/on a life like that. Man Arrested in Hacking Death Tells Police He Mistook Mother-in-Law... Susan Ludvigson. MAYP

And the band all playing/Nearer Oh My God to Thee Titanic Blues. Henry Brown. BluL

And the Banner of Heaven unfurl'd. Song: "My love is the flaming Sword." James (1834-82) Thomson. OBVV

And the barber kept on shaving. The Owl Critic. James Thomas Fields. BLPA; CenHV; EvOK; HBV 1-2; OBAL; StPo; TreFS; WBLP; YaD

And the basket I bear, its cords are broken. Song of a Sick Child. *Anonymous.* WTO

And the beach of sand is reached at last. The Culprit Fay. Joseph Rodman Drake. GN

And the beauty of a fair girl will soon fade away./Oh, will soon fade away. The Rejected Lover. *Anonymous.* AmFP

And the beauty of a fine young man will all soon fade away. Month of January. Frankie Armstrong. BrRo

And the bed of that sea was my bed. Awake, My Lute. Clive Staples Lewis. CenHV; FaBoNo

And the beetle drones his horn. The Field Mouse. William Sharp. MoShBr

...And the beggar lies/A lovely ghost. The Bristol Channel. Thomas Edward Brown. NOBV

And the beginning hath no end. Dawn. George B. Logan, Jr. HBV 1-2

And the beginning of reason,/the inauguration of hope. Jerusalem. Ruben Kanalenstein. VWA

And the beginning was real. The drawing of a child. Crayon House. Muriel Rukeyser. EyDe

And the bells dream. Poem: "A frail sound of a tunic trailing." Antonio Machado. AWP

And the bells of St. Sebald's Church. Durer's Piece of Turf. Norbert Krapf. PoDr

And the bells shall tinkle merrily. Sleighing Song. John Shaw. AA

And the belly-stabbing/Hobo-pariah box-car '20's. Kansas City West Bottoms. Edward Dahlberg. PoA

And the best flower in England will flourish no more. The Death of Queen Jane. *Anonymous.* AmFP; BaBo; ESPB; ViBoFo

And the best sailors in the ship lie there among the dead! The Ship of Earth. Sidney Lanier. MOS

And the best will come back to you. Life's Mirror. Bridges Madeline. BLPA; FaBoBe; GoTF; PoToHe; TreF; WBLP

...And the betrayal/Be quite undone and never more be done. The Transfiguration. Edwin Muir. MasP; OxBS

And the bewilder'd chimes. The Fountain. William Wordsworth. GTBS; GTBS-P; OBRV; SeCePo

And the bicycle ticked, ticked, ticked. A Constable Calls. Seamus Heaney. FaBoPV; IPY; NOBI

And the big baby calf grew fat! The New Baby Calf. Edith Newlin Chase. SoPo; TiPo

And the big, grown-up, cold-looking feet. The Little Girl. Nicholas Moore. ErPo; NeBP

And the big Simon more, who often rails/At what he calls ill luck or unkind fate. Simple Simon. Harriet S. Morgridge. AA

And the bird went (whistle). The Barnyard. *Anonymous.* AmFP

And the birds that sing? The Execution of Cornelius Vane. Sir Herbert Read. BrPo; NoAm

And the birds will still be there, singing. The Conclusive Voyage. Juan Ramon Jimenez. PoPl

And the birk and the broom blooms bonny. Ballad with an Ancient Refrain. *Anonymous.* NA

And the birth from the dust that is green we sing. Song (We Sing). Cosmo Pieterse. WhB

And the birthing stools of grannies long since fled. Jackson, Mississippi. Margaret Walker. FB

And the Bishop's aghast with surprise. Limerick: "Your verses, dear friend, I surmise." *Anonymous.* LiBL

And the bishop said: "The ways of God are strange!" They. Siegfried Sassoon. CMoP; HBMV; OBSV; OBWP

And the bitter groan of a Martyr's woe/Is an arrow from the Almighty's bow. Jerusalem. William Blake. OBRV

And the black feet of its night/Go walking through my room. The Myall in Prison. Mary Gilmore. BoAV; CBAP; PoAu 1-2

And the black flukes of agony/Beat at the air till the light blows out. I Only Am Escaped Alone to Tell Thee. Howard Nemerov. CoAP; HeIP; NePA; NoAm

And the black grass/is holding up the black stars. Black Maps. Mark Strand. PoA

And the black horse running/is me. Black Horse Running. Noel Maureen Valis. AMV-80

And the Black Prince goes whimpering to bed. Feigned Courage. Charles and Mary Lamb. GN; OxBChV

And the Black Rock Canal bleeds in my skin Lines from a Misplaced Person. Jeanne Hill. FAZ

And the blackberries a-growing. The Railroad. Henry David Thoreau. FaBV

And the blessed gospel's saving health/Repay your arduous toil. Laborers of Christ! Arise. Lydia Sigourney. AH

And the blessed shall bless the name/That is holy forever and ever. Blessed Is God. *Anonymous.* TrJP

And the blind cry of all the seas that roll. Sonnets to Miranda. William Watson. HBV 1-2

And the blind hands bearing the luck of the year. The Runner with the Lots. Léonie Adams. MoPo; NePA

And the blind man say told her that you/sure look good to me Tooten Out Blues. Ed Bell. BluL

And the blondes pray God to "teach us/To profit from her mistake." A Country Club Romance. Derek Walcott. OxBC

And the blood flows from the lands of the forest/with smells of animals and drying leaves. I Love What Is Not. Manfred Winkler. VWA

And the blood is black upon the unturned leaves. The Soldier Walks under the Trees of the University. Randall Jarrell. OxBA; PoPl; WaP

...And the blood is/Thin in the throat and the time not come for death? Unfinished History. Archibald MacLeish. NYBP; VGW

And the blood-red linings glow like sharp-toothed maple leaves/In Autumn. Streets. Amy Lowell. SBG

And the blue air darkened. The Thing. Theodore Roethke. CMoP

And the blue sea starred of God? Ships with Your Silver Nets. Wade Oliver. EtS

And the blue sea turns emerald as he goes. Change. Mary Elizabeth Coleridge. MoVE

And the blue snow melts about us as it falls. A Winter's Tale. Robert Patrick Dana. NYBP

...And the blue stone/Set in the tryst-ring has but worn more bright. Carrier Letter. Hart Crane. BoLoP

And the bluid rins aye frae the torn ruit. The Mandrake Hert. Sydney Goodsir Smith. AtBAP; OxBS

And the blush of the rose-petal,/lifted, of the flower. White World. Hilda ("H. D.") Doolittle. LLLT

And the boats go out and the boats come in,/But there's one away. The Fisher's Widow. Arthur Symons. HBV 1-2

And the body beginning to swell. Mountain Bride. Robert Morgan. GeTw; GP; MAYP

...And the body hangs from/the nail, and the nail holds. The New Ring. Karl Shapiro. MoLP

And the body underneath it says: I am. The Knight, Death, and the Devil. Randall Jarrell. CrMA; WeW

And the bog creeps nearer/With the bog cotton for the fairies' flag. Wester Ross. Naomi Mitchison. PoSH

And the bone he boned from its owner! The Stone Troll. J. R. R. Tolkien. SO

And the bones of sparrows. The Birds. David Posner. NYBP

"And the bottom for to break:'/"And ye to be drowned.' The Fause Knight upon the Road. *Anonymous.* OxBS

And the Bow was gone. The Rainbow. Walter De la Mare. SoPo

And the bowers of bay no more. We'll to the Woods No More. Alfred Edward Housman. LOW; OAEL 1-2; PoRA

And the boy who wrote this song, sir,/Was a lying son of a bitch. The Derby Ram, II. *Anonymous.* AmFP

And the braggart and the Gascon/Be extinguished from the land. Out and Fight. Charles Godfrey Leland. PAH

And the brave ship that bore him to glory! The Alabama. Maurice Bell. PAH

And the braves, they all hollared "Wioux-Wioux!" Limerick: "There was a young maiden, a Sioux." *Anonymous.* LiBL

And the breathless million that looked/upon/The matchless race of the Oregon. The Race of the Oregon. John James Meehan. PAH

And the breeze o'er the billows blowing. Breeze and Billow. Albert Durrant Watson. CaP

And the bridal and the churching both,/They shall be upon one day.' Child Waters. *Anonymous.* BaBo; ESPB; FaBoBa; OAEP; OBET; OxBB; ViBoFo

And the bride frae the bridegroom was stown awa. Hind Horn (B vers.). *Anonymous.* BaBo; ESPB

And the bridegroom all night through/Never turns him to the bride. A Shropshire Lad. Alfred Edward Housman. AnFE; NOBV; OAEP

And the bridegroom, taking her home at evening,/Will think he weds the Spring. Whiteness. Isobel Hume. HBMV

And the bright-bosomed Thames, in his/majesty, sweeps,/By the mound where his followers bore/him. The Fall of Tecumseh. *Anonymous.* PAH

And the bright hillside clean/Of any wind. The Bright Hillside. Rhoda Coghill. NeIP; OxBI

And the bright oar and the oar spray. Aegean. Louis Simpson. GrPl; NYBP

...And the bright sun shining on its tusks. Gratitude. Louise Gluck. FaBoWP; HeIP

And the bright winter sky as from a tube of indigo is squeezed away. North Philadelphia, Trenton, and New York. Richmond Lattimore. NYBP

And the brightness of one gold leaf/Held autumn in its silk design. Patterns. Ruth Setterberg. AMV-81

And the broad prairie melts in mist of tears. In Memoriam Rev. J. J. Lyons. Emma Lazarus. SBG

And the brown girl at my feet. Lord Thomas and Fair Annet (The Brown Girl). *Anonymous.* AmFP

And the bruised spirit flutters out/To find the happy valley. The Bird in the Room. Rudolph Chambers Lehmann. HBMV; HBVY

And the buffaloes are gone. Buffalo Dusk. Carl Sandburg. BPAW; OBCA; RFM; TiPo

And the bugles they do shine. A New Year Carol. *Anonymous.* AtBAP; CH; OxBoLi; PoSC

And the butterfly does not fear you. Lilac. Frank Stewart Flint. HBMV

And the Cabots talk only to God. A Boston Toast. John Collins Bossidy. BLPA; YaD

...And the camp we left/was a little spot in the trees when we looked back. When We Looked Back. William Stafford. NYBP

And the candle we lit casts its ray/From the window across the snow. Night Expedition from Ben Alder Cottage. Roger A. Redfern. PoSH

And the captain knows. And I know. We have it timed to the second. Pendant Watch. Madeline Defrees. NMM

And the captive's friend/From his ashes makes us freemen still. Parricide. Julia Ward Howe. PAH

And the careful trace turned fluid. Drowned Sailor. Neufville Shaw. CaP

And the cargo of young people, uninsured but liberated/From the hellish hold of the burned boat. Ode to a Lost Cargo in a Ship Called Save. Jose Craveirinha. WhB

And the cat takes a half-step, preparing to leap. Getting Up. Stephen Dobyns. MAYP

And the cat went fiddle-i-fee. Fiddle-I-Fee. *Anonymous.* AmFP

And the catbird's silver song, the wakeful bird/That to the lighted window sings for dawn. Sonnets, First Series. Frederick Goddard Tuckerman. MAmP

And the caught bee dry and fade inside/The emptied room. Under the Cliff. Geoffrey Grigson. WaP

...And the chairs applaud their one/Creator and mirror their mother chair. Chairs. Henry Petroski. PoDr

And the Chancellor said, I doubt. A Chancery Suit. Sir George Rose. FaBoCo

And the Chant that leads to War. The Song-Maker. Kingsley Fairbridge. ACV

And the charms of her mind are a heav'n to me. Enraptured I Gaze. Francis Hopkinson. BLSo

And the child draws another inscrutable house. Sestina. Elizabeth Bishop. LCAP; NoP; SM; WeW

And the child himself standing, irreducible grain. Brother Jonathan, Brother Kafka (excerpt). Vincent O'Sullivan. OCNZ

And the child softly treads behind. At God's Command. Joseph Rolnik. VWA

And the child that is born on the Sabbath day/Is bonny and blithe, and good and gay. Monday's child is fair of face. Mother Goose. FaBoCh

And the child, wakening, listens motionless. Leaves at My Window. John James Piatt. AA

And the children/had all become agents Poem: "the country". Fred Levinson. AmPA

And the children know/I am fooling. Theme in Yellow. Carl Sandburg. TiPo; YeAr

And the children of them and their chil-/dren/Wear the envenomed robe. Henry C. Calhoun. Edgar Lee Masters. AmP; LiTA; LiTM

And the children/Went.... The Next War. Osbert Sitwell. MMM

And the chin settles onto palms above/Numbed elbows propped on rotting sills. In the Attic. Donald Justice. SM

And the Chinese laundry closes on Saturday. The Avenue Bearing the Initial of Christ into the New World. Galway Kinnell. ConAP; NePoEA-2; NMP

And the choking gurgle of tepid water. The Windmills. John Gould Fletcher. CrMA

And the chosen people will serve/Themselves with orange jube-jubes/In a brand-new discount warehouse Manichean Geography I. Tom Paulin. FaBoIP

And the cigarette flies into the fire. "...I'd like to live with you." Marina Tsvetayeva. BoWoP

And the circles are hardly warm. Glycerin. Frank Lima. ANYP

And the city is lost in a wind of autumn leaves. The Fisherman. Douglas Stewart. ACV

And the city is still! Solitaire. Amy Lowell. LaNeLa; MAPA; MoAmPo

And the city rejoices mightily/at the keen melody of my voice. Fragments. Corinna. PBWP

And the city's life acknowledge the water of life. From Rome. For More Public Fountains in New York City. Alan Dugan. NYP; Prf

And the civilized scent of herbs. The Indolent Gardener. Mary Kennedy. BoNaP

And the Clam sucked, the Salmon swam, alone. Wedded Bliss. Charlotte Perkins Stetson Gilman. HBV 1-2

And the clean ones so seldom are comical. Limerick: "A limerick packs laughs anatomical." *Anonymous.* LiBL

And the climbing moon grows small. The Homecoming of the Sheep. Francis Ledwidge. EnLit; HBMV

And the close sky spreads out. The Symposium (excerpt). Leah Goldberg. PBWP

And the closeness of dry earth,/Is horses. Horses. Myra von Riedemann. OBCV

And the cloud that took the form/(When the rest of Heaven was blue)/Of a demon in my view. Alone. Edgar Allan Poe. LaNeLa; MAmP

And the clouds begin to move. In the Madness of Love. Gary Soto. NPGG

And the clouds drew round him, while he said his prayers. Old Man Mountain. Alfred Noyes. GoBC

And the clouds perish'd; Darkness had no need/Of aid from them–She was the Universe. Darkness. George Gordon, Lord Byron. EnRP; ERoP 1-2; LiTB; MBW 1-2; OAEL 1-2; OAEP; PoEL 1-5; TEP

And the club–with a couple of nicks and a bend,/I found again in the bag of a friend. The Ball and the Club. Forbes Lindsay. SD

And the Coach's light blue, shot-silk togs. Profiles of My Father. Rhyll McMaster. CBAP

And the cockatoo's head went under its wing. What the Lord High Chamberlain Said. Virginia Woodward Cloud. BBGG

And the cold silent killer's lips of the guns. The Falling of the Snow. Raymond Souster. CaP

And the collected tails of all your lives/Shall drive the moral home. Divination by a Cat. Anthony Hecht. LiTA

And the color of blue/everywhere Nocturne. Pinkie Gordon Lane. BlSi

And the colors have all passed away from her eyes! The Reverie of Poor Susan. William Wordsworth. CH; ERoP 1-2; GTBS; GTBS-P; HBV 1-2; MBW 1-2; MCCG; OxBoLi; WiR

...And the constellations/Sank nearer already, listing toward summer. Thorn Leaves in March. William Stanley Merwin. MP; TwCP

And the contented blether of the Mission sheep. At Carmel. Mary Austin. AmFN

And the cool night is a clear jewel. Letter from Des Moines. Thomas Swiss. AMV-81

And the cops keep the stash/for themselves. State School. Paul D. Shiplett. LFAC

And the cords that no man breaketh are/bound about my feet. Wild Eden. George Edward Woodberry. AA

And the corrupted year once more a child. Return. Theodore Spencer. PoA

And the countryside is well advised to be empty. Crying in Early Infancy: Sonnet. John Tranter. CBAP

And the Cow's dead, the old Cow's dead. Dead Cow Farm. Robert Graves. BrPo

And the coyotes howl over you. The Toll of the Desert. Arthur W. Monroe. BPAW; PoOW

And the crash of loud lyres! The Clouds. Aristophanes. AWP

And the crickets come creeping into our hair/To fiddle the short night away. Sleep in the Mojave Desert. Sylvia Plath. NoP

And the cries echoing around the hoarse arena. When I See Old Men. Raymond Souster. CaP

And the critics yonder say his work is alright. A Written Answer. Tom Paulin. FaBoIP

And the cross is exchanged for the crown. The School of Sorrow. Harold Hamilton. BLRP

And the Cross of Christ is there. Love Is Where the Glory Falls. Hafiz. ILwL

And the crows will finish/What I have begun. The Bush Speaks. Ernest G. Moll. NOAV

And the cry "Look out below." Look Out Below! Charles R. Thatcher. PoAu 1-2

And the cubs tangled like liquid buckskin/across the sofa back. A Gaggle of Geese, A Pride of Lions. John Moore. DuDa

And the Curse shall be on thee/For ever and ever. The Curse of Kehama. Robert Southey. LoBV; OBRV

And the cycles wheel. Called Back. Emily Dickinson. AA

And the daisies kept under. Sad Green. Sylvia Townsend Warner. MoBrPo

And the dancing light of the/lantern, homeward bound. Late October. Sara King Carleton. GoYe

And the Danes laughed loud and long. The Songs of Guthrum and Alfred. Gilbert Keith Chesterton. HBV 1-2

And the dark blue waves rolling over me. Lullaby. *Anonymous.* AmFP

And the dark brown of wet wood,/gleaming a little as it dries. January. Robert Hass. NPGG

And the dark brushes against our eyes. Violent Storm. Mark Strand. NYBP

And the dark piper/Is gone home with the birds. The Besom-Man. Joseph Campbell. OnYI

And the dark Somme flowing. The Farmer Remembers the Somme. Vance Palmer. NOAV; PoAu 1-2

And the Darkness, to Thee, is as clear as the Light. An Hymn on the Omnipresence. John Byrom. CEP; TrPWD

...And the dash/of lesser wings in the barren/marsh flew through my flesh. Heron. Philip Booth. BoAnP; NePoEA; PPJ; Psk; WOLT

And the daughters of darkness flame like Fawkes fires/still. In the White Giant's Thigh. Dylan Thomas. AtBAP; LiTB

And the day complete that we shall remember. Bidean Nam Bian. Henry Austin Dobson. PoSH

And the day's unheard-of cry. Barbed Wire. Eithne Wilkins. NeBP

And the day shall have a sun,/Which shall make thee wish it done. Manfred: An Incantation. George Gordon, Lord Byron. DBV; EnRP; OBRV; OBRV

And the day will be to-day. Weep Not To-Day. Robert Bridges. OBMV; OBVV

And the daylight's seldom seen. Greenland Fisheries. *Anonymous.* FSW

And the Days of 'Forty-nine. The Days of 'Forty-Nine. *Anonymous.* BPAW; CoSo; FSW; MC; PAH

And the days of Paolo and Francesca were gone. She Came out of the Frost. Alexander Blok. PoPl

...And the De'il pick/the bones/Of Green, Jemmy Twitcher, Lord North, and Paul Jones! Paul Jones–A New Song. *Anonymous.* PAH

And the dead begin from their dark to sing in my sleep. North American Sequence: Journey to the Interior. Theodore Roethke. LCAP

And the dead–how strangely bare! The Carillon. Rosalia Castro de Murguia. CAW

And the dead nations never rise again. The Jewish Cemetery at Newport. Henry Wadsworth Longfellow. AnNE; AP; ForPo; HAP; HeIP; HoPM; MAmP; NOBA; NoP; OxBA; PPON; TAP

And the dead saints be raised again. Spare Us, O Lord, Aloud We Pray. Isaac Watts. AH

And the dead to the desert we gave, and the glory to God in/our song. War Song of the Saracens. James Elroy Flecker. FaBV; MoBrPo; OBVV; WHA

And the deadly sins/May be bought in tins,/With instructions on the label. For the Time Being. W. H. Auden. TRV

And the Dealer will understand. Cash In. Sharlot M. Hall. BPAW

And the Debate was done. Said death to passion. Emily Dickinson. MoVE

And the deep-breathing heart grows faint/To be so near to Heaven. A Song of Arno. Grace Ellery Channing-Stetson. AA

And the deep night, and sleep, and the pines dripping. Atavism. Richard Lake. NCSH

And the deep river ran on. Song: "As I walked out one evening." W. H. Auden. MoAB; MoBrPo; OAEL 1-2

And the deep song warming her lips. The Subject of the Bishop's Miracle. John Philip. BoAV

And the defeat of grief. As He Is. W. H. Auden. MoPo

And the definite stroke/Of Seven of the Clock. Seven of the Clock. Roy MacNab. PeSA

And the delighted Audience is clapping. Concert-Interpretations (Le Sacre du Printemps). Siegfried Sassoon. CBEP

And the desert, seeing the issue grows no clearer,/Takes one long slow step nearer. Golden Calf. Norman MacCaig. OxBS

And the Devil go bury the Abbot of Derry,/And bury him deep, say I! The Abbot of Derry. John Bennett. HBMV

And the devil of a word said I coming down. Jack Hall. *Anonymous.* OBET

And the devil sent him Anna. Old Sam's Wife. *Anonymous.* ChTr

And the dish ran away with the spoon. Hey, Diddle, Diddle. Mother Goose. FaBoBe; FaFP; HBV 1-2; HBVY; OxBoLi; OxNR; SoPo; TiPo

And the distance of a foot/Becomes a thousand miles. A Wave of Coldness. Yosano Akiko. WPOW

And the doctor from Philadelphia/nods and speaks of a further bleeding. Greenwich Avenue. James Schuyler. NYP

And the donkey is he who can't see the . An Arab and His Donkey. *Anonymous.* NLV

And the doors of the best ivory.' The Outlandish Knight. *Anonymous.* OBET

And the doves come down for bread on the/sun-warmed stone. Pro Patria. Constance Carrier. NePoAm; NYBP

...And the doves will/suddenly fly out of her hands. Girl with Doves. Stephen Gray. PeSA

And the dread beauty of living/crushed us into reverence. For William Edward Burghardt Du Bois on His Eightieth Birthday. Bette Darcie Latimer. PoBA; PoNe

And the dread mirage are there. Yuma. Charles Henry Phelps. AA

And the dreamer hawk/high over that pool/in the streaming air/cries high and cool. Fisherman. Philip Booth. LiSp; WOLT

And the drifting clouds/Are drifting over the Wilderness, over the still farm. The Union Barge on Staten Island. Louis Simpson. NYP

And the drinks are Lilliputian. Evening in the Suburbs. Stella Barnett. PV

And the drowned and the shipwrecked have happy graves. Death's Jest-Book. Thomas Lovell Beddoes. NOBV

And the dull ennui of a woman's kiss! To a Sicilian Boy. Theodore Wratislaw. PeHV

And the dull pressure of beginning pain. Porch. Alden Nowlan. NeAC

And the dullness is awful! Whence and Whither. Hayim Nahman Bialik. TrJP

And the dumb shall speak. When the Dumb Speak. Robert Bly. CAPP; NoAm; NOBA

And the duo of Saturn and Mars! After an Interval. Walt Whitman AA

And the dusk. Dusk. Angelina Weld Grimke. CDC

And the dust of the dead/sings under the blade of the plow. Our People. Teresa Anderson. LTB

And the dust settled again/On the pavements of prayer. The Departure. Jeremy Robson. VWA

And the dusty bees are dozing/like pardoned sinners. Marigold. John Haines. PoL; PPJ

And the dwellings of men, the safety, and the ease. Black Tarn. Victoria Mary (Vita) Sackville-West. SBG

And the dying swan sings. On a Memory of Beauty. G. S. Fraser. NeBP

And the eagle dances across the sky. The Stars Are Thundering. *Anonymous.* WTO

And the earth grow young again. Lines Written among the Euganean Hills. Percy Bysshe Shelley. EnRP; PBBP; PoEL 1-5; ViBoPo

And the earth is warm deep soft and full/when the quietness bursts Return. Johari M. Kunjufu. BlSi

And the earth teem with saints. The Muted Screen of Graham Greene. Phyllis McGinley. FaBoEE

And the Earth will never find peace again. Inisgallun. Darrell Figgis. OnYI

And the East and the West at Her bidding/shall lie in a leash at Her feet. To San Francisco. S. J. Alexander. PAH

And the echoes edged back still further/As the silence gathered them in. Mother Goose Up-to-Date. Louis Untermeyer. MoAmPo

And the edict is written in African blood! The Caffer Commando (excerpt). Thomas Pringle. ACV

And the emerald crumbles into dust. Prologue for a Bestiary. Ronald Perry. NePoEA-2

And the emerging earth drones bass. Snow, Snow. Marge Piercy. AMV-81

And the emotion brought from a world already/Dying of what starts to infect the hills. The Green Hills of Africa. Roy Fuller. NoP; OBTV

And the empty, ocean-hymning shells. Letters to Live Poets. Bruce Beaver. CBAP

And the empty waitin yirth/–it talks loud enough? Stanes. Duncan Glen. PoSH

And the empty years have ended all their crying. The Return. Martha Ostenso. CaP

And the end is death! A Song of the Wave. George Cabot Lodge. AA; AmePo; EtS

And the end of it was he never again/In a Xanthic Xebec went sailing the main. The Zealless Xylographer. Mary Mapes Dodge. OBAL

And the end of toil and gloom. Pilgrim's Song. Bernard S. Ingemann. WGRP

And the endless beginning of prodigies suffers open.' If My Head Hurt a Hair's Foot. Dylan Thomas. NoAm

And the enduring soul holds out. Christine to Her Son. Christine de Pisan. BoWoP

And the enemies of England, they shall see me and be sick. The New Mistress. Alfred Edward Housman. MoBrPo

And the energy again/That made them what they were! Transformations. Thomas Hardy. NoAm; PPoe; PPP; TEP

And the envious, when they find/What their number is, be pin'd. To the Same. Ben Jonson. AnAnS 2; BiP; JCP; OAEL 1-2; SeCP; SeCV 1-2

And the equation solved. Mathematics of Encounter. Isabella Gardner. ErPo

And the eternal sentinels shine on. Washington and Lincoln. Wendell Phillips Stafford. PGD

And the ever-deepening track/of the unseen, feeding host. Dream of the Lynx. John Haines. NU

And the ever-moving will remain forever. Rome. Panormitanus. OBVE

And the eyes in his head see the world spinning round. The Fool on the Hill. The Beatles. PPoe

And the fabric of life, completed,/Some day will be wondrous fair. Life and the Weaver. A. W. Dewar. BLRP; WBLP

And the facade that we are; this year before it ends.' This Year, Before It Ends. Eve Langley. BoAV; NOAV

And the faint but perceptible scent of sweet clear water. Folding the Sheets. Rosemary Dobson. NOAV

And the fairest name of the Eastern shore/Bears the fairest isle of the Western coast. Verazzano. Hezekiah Butterworth. PAH

And, the fairy was laughing too. The Leprahaun. Robert Dwyer Joyce. OnYI

And the fall to doom a long way. Should the Wide World Roll Away. Stephen Crane. BiP

And the false nurse was burnt/To a stake standing by. Lamkin (C vers.). *Anonymous.* AmFP; BaBo; ESPB

And the false nurse will be burned, such a villain is she.' Lambkin. *Anonymous.* OBET

And the father of that silence. Linnets. Larry Levis. LCAP

And–the feet of my Beloved hurrying back through Time! Jobson's Amen. Rudyard Kipling. AnFE; OBTV

And the feet run in the wall. Tresco. Geoffrey Grigson. FaBoPP

...And the fellow is a fool/Who cannot find some pleasure down below. The Trucker. Will Dyson. NOAV

And the few who loved him know this until they die. Freedom, New Hampshire. Galway Kinnell. LCAP; NaP

And the field tilting always toward day. Winter Verse for His Sister. William Meredith. NYBP; TAP

And the fierce flames burnt round the heavens & round the abodes of men America A Prophecy. William Blake. OAEL 1-2

And the fiercer he burns, Dear, the better he keeps you/amused! She-Devil. Douglas Goldring. HBMV

And the fiery brown earth/Speaks in tongues Song: "All phantoms of the day." Robert Mezey. SUW

And the figure is completely/out of sight. Plucking out a Rhythm. Lawson Fusao Inada. AmPA

And the finest flower in all French land,/Five tons of gold now is his fee. King Henry Fifth's Conquest of France (B vers.). *Anonymous.* BaBo

And the finest flower that is in all France/To the Rose of England I will give free. King Henry Fifth's Conquest of France (A vers.). *Anonymous.* BaBo

And the fire and the rose are one. Four Quartets. Thomas Stearns Eliot. ExPo; NAWM 1-2

And the fire are really the same–/Upon different degrees. Nothing Is. Sun-Ra. PoBA

And the fire that maddens the poet's brain/With wild sweet ardor and heavenly pain. The Cup. John Townsend Trowbridge. HBV 1-2

And the fire will be quenched no more. I Shall Weep. Peretz Hirshbein. TrJP

And the first murderer lay upon the earth. Imperial Adam. A. D. Hope. CBAP; ErPo; HAP; NoAm; NoP; UnTE

And the first music heard among the trees. Panope. Edith Sitwell. MoAB; MoBrPo

And the first star of sunset greets you/As if you'd only gone a day. Homecoming. Stefan George. AMV-81

And the fish/shouting/with their fins. Summer. Diane Wakoski. VGW

And the fish swim in the lake/and do not even own clothing. Salutation. Ezra Pound. HeIP; LoGBV; MoAB; MoAmPo; NOBA; OxBA; TAP; VGW

And the Five Nations came. Two Souls. Marjorie Pickthall. NOBC

And the flame o' the gean tree burnin'/By the Sidlaws' side. The Gean Trees. Violet Jacob. PoSH

And the flames of the Battle were quenched/in the spray. Perry's Victory–A Song. *Anonymous.* PAH

And the flank of Aed Mac Ainmirech. Three Rounded Flanks I Loved. *Anonymous.* NOBI

And the flawed human world/return with his delicate bone. Northern Water Thrush. D. G. Jones. PeCV

And the fleeting is gathered into the glory. Many Birds. Anne Welsh. PeSA

And the flood destroyed them all. The Garden Party. Hilaire Belloc. DTC; MoVE

...And the florets more/Subtly crisp their bright profiles, or are lost in the flower. Shadows of Chrysanthemums. E. J. Scovell. MoVE

And the flutter of wings in our minds. Long-Billed Gannets. Frances D. Emery. GoYe

And the foam of longing/Over the waters. One Chord. Nelly Sachs. VWA

And the foe you cannot brave,/Scorn at least to be his slave. On Scaring Some Waterfowl in Loch Turit... Robert Burns. PBBP

And the fog rolled high on Cranberryhorn. Yankee Cradle. Robert P. Tristram Coffin. EvOK

And the forgotten people who since then/Were born in it, or lived and died in it. The Empty House. Harold Monro. BrPo

And the found voice of his buried hands/Rose in the sparrowy air. He Was. Richard Wilbur. NCSH; SaC

And the foundering shriek of the gale. Wild Iron. Allen Curnow. AnNZ

And the frail fabric shivers into dust.' The Protection of Plants. Erasmus Darwin. FaBoUs

And the free Fellowship continue so. Sonnets of the Months. Folgore da San Geminiano. AWP

And the freedom of soul he prophesied/Is gospel and law where the martyrs died. The King's Missive. John Greenleaf Whittier. PAH

And the fresh rose on yonder thorn/Gives back the bending heavens in dew. Song of Nature. Ralph Waldo Emerson. AnNE; HBV 1-2

And the fresh-severed head of it, my head. The Show. Wilfred Owen. LiTB; LiTM; MoAB; MoBrPo; NAMP; NoAm; OxBTC; ViBoPo; WaaP; WaP

And the fresh spring-tide foams the sloaky reef/As floats the white moon up the lonely land. Sonnets, IV: "Remote from smoky cities, aged and grey." Thomas Caulfield Irwin. IrPN

And the Frog peeps out of the fountain. Song: "The owl is abroad." *Anonymous.* PoPle

And the frogs singing against the fauns/in the half-light./And... Canto II. Ezra Pound. AtBAP; CoBMV; HAP; MoAB; MoAmPo; NePA; NoAm; NOBA; OxBA

And the full moon, and the white evening-star. Thyrsis. Matthew Arnold. PoPle

And the full of his arms/of strawberries, where they lay. Epigram: "The son of the King of the Moy." *Anonymous.* BIrV

And the furnace of living pain! Cleansing Fires. Adelaide Anne Procter. WGRP

And the futile difficult sounds of his old girl's crying. An Old Inmate. Kenneth Mackenzie. PoAu 1-2

...And the future, my man, is long/time gone. Letter to E. Franklin Frazier. LeRoi (Imamu Amiri Baraka) Jones. BPo; PoBA

And the Fuzzy-wuz took the bag. The Rhyme of the Kipperling. Sir Owen Seaman. CenHV

(And the G is silent as in "Fish.") A Boy He Had an Auger (with music). *Anonymous.* AS

And the gain to our church–what would it be. Just Like Me. P.W. Sinks. BLRP

And the games of scrupulous Euclid/Vanish in the gymnopaedia. Vitamins and Roughage. Kenneth Rexroth. NoAm

And the gardens that pock her face. For Doreen. Donald Davie. NMP

And the Gates of Hell shall not prevail. There Shall Always Be the Church. Thomas Stearns Eliot. TRV

And the gates of his Gaza are still asleep in the ore./And Delilah Samson. Amir Gilboa. VWA

And the gaunt earthquake rocks herself to sleep. Don Juan. Canto XVII. Isaac Clason. PeD

And the gears notch and the engines wheel. Clear Night. Charles Wright. GeTw

And the geese honk north again and/the heron's going. Elegy. Joseph Auslander. TrJP

And the generous aristocracy who admired him. George IV. William Makepeace Thackeray. FaBoEE

And the gentle breezes blow. Travel Song. Hugo von Hofmannsthal. TrJP

And the gentle sounding flute. My Master Hath a Garden. *Anonymous.* AtBAP

And the gentle tinkle/of falling rain. Jack-in-the-Pulpit. Ivy O. Eastwick. YeAr

And the gharri so slow in getting you there. Monsoon. Kenneth Slade Alling. NePoAm

And the ghost followed, like a naked cloud holding the sun's/hand. The New Ghost. Fredegond Shove. ChMP; HBMV; MoVE; OxBoCh

And the giant ever changing, living in change. A Primitive Like an Orb. Wallace Stevens. NOBA

And the gift of a sweet-faced cat. The Gift. Ed Ochester. DFF; GP; Psk

And the girl closed her window not to hear. Near Helikon. Trumbull Stickney. AnFE; LiTA; NCEP

And the girl shall shake with the cinnamon and the heat-wave/in her hair. Stony Town. John Shaw Neilson. BoAV

And the girl who serves you food/is slender and her red hair lights the wall. Degrees of Gray in Philipsburg. Richard Hugo. CoAP; NoP; NPAW

And the girls as sweet as candy. My Pretty Pink. *Anonymous.* AmFP

And the girls with their high baskets full of fruit. Lo-Yang. Emperor Ch'ien Wen-ti. AWP

And the glad earth about her strows/With treasure from her yielding boughs. To Chloris, upon a Favour Received. Edmund Waller. OBSP

And the glad earth, caressed by murmuring showers,/Wakes like a bride, to deck herself with flowers May. Henry Sylvester Cornwell. HBV 1-2

And the glad nations hailed the long-sought "Golden Fleece." The Silkworm. Marco Girolamo Vida. CAW

And the glass breaks/the sun into fragments. Children's Song. Arye Sivan. VWA

And the glass of water they've left for me/Shall "chick!' to tell them I'm drinking." The Frost. Hannah Flagg Gould. BLPA; HBV 1-2; HBVY

And the gleaming suitcases that are filling up this room. The Clock Works. Lewis MacAdams. ANYP

And the glimmering Spirit I kissed in the gloom beside me. Marriage. Walter James Turner. NOAV

And the glory of the Garden it shall never pass away! The Glory of the Garden. Rudyard Kipling. EBCP

And the goats leap into their faces shrieking. Words without Music. Irving Layton. CaP

And the God of imagination waking/In a Mucker fog. Kerr's Ass. Patrick Kavanagh. FaBoIP; NOBI

And the God that lived at Pentecost,/Is just the same to-day. Just the Same Today. *Anonymous.* BLRP; WBLP

And...the God that you took from a printed book be with you,/Tomlinson! Tomlinson. Rudyard Kipling. BeLS

And the god, the true Iacchus,/Hears now this song of mine. Evoe! Edith Matilda Thomas. HBV 1-2

And the gods from side to side. Hush! Ralph Waldo Emerson. AnNE

And the gods shook, they knew not why. Uriel. Ralph Waldo Emerson. AnNE; AP; APA; LiTA; MAmP; NePA; NOBA; OxBA

And the gods turn their eyes to some far distant/Bright constellation. Odes. George Santayana. AmePo

And the gold-dust coming up/From the trampled buttercup. Golden Stockings. Oliver St. John Gogarty. OxBI

And the golden April rains/Are my tears. Quest. Naomi Long Madgett. BPo

And the golden light is glowing. As I Came over the Grey, Grey Hills. Joseph Campbell. AnIL

And the good Lord said nothing, but with a nod/Summoned the angels of Sodom down to earth. The Psalter of Avram Haktani. Abraham Moses Klein. PeCV

And the good that I can do. What I Live For. George Linnaeus Banks. BLPA; FaBoBe; GoTF; TreFS

And the Goose lend her quill to transmit it to fame. The Peacock "At Home'. Catherine Ann Dorset. OxBChV

And the graceful arc in the sky/of a hawk he can hardly see. The Life Not Given. David Habercom. AMV-81

And the grass on the mountains. The Grass on the Mountain. Mary Austin. AmFN; AWP

And the grass stayed green that year/right through August. The Announcement. George Ellenbogen. AMV-80

And the grave is the first place I expect to find rest. Lovelye William. *Anonymous.* AmFP

And the grave whereon the bright snowdrops grow/Shall be the same soil as the beauty below. Death. John Clare. ERoP 1-2; GTBS-P

And the great bars that go on forever. Hotels. David Donnell. AMV-81

And the great brown owl flew away in her cowl,/With her large, round, shining eyes. The Great Brown Owl. Jane Euphemia Browne (Aunt Effie). OxBChV

And the great cage suffers nothing whatever no The Cage. John Berryman. PoA

And the great dreams pass on/to the common good. The Days of the Unicorns. Phyllis Webb. NOBC

And the great heart that loved the brave/and free. Margaret Fuller. Amos Bronson Alcott. AA

And the great heart that the first Morning made/Should wear all Time's destruction for a dress. The Poet Laments the Coming of Old Age. Edith Sitwell. NoAm

And the great heroes, famous for a day,/they die, they die. Mountains Are Steadfast but the Mountain Streams. Hwang Chin-i. PBWP

And the great maze of lifts and shrouds! Night Quarters. Henry Howard Brownell. GN

And the Great Pigs waddle off in the sky– The Pigs for Circe in May. Joanne Kyger. PoM

And the great song that seemed to die unsung/Triumphs upon the tongue. The Unknown City. Sir Charles G. D. Roberts. CaP

And the great wheels smash and pound beneath our feet. Variations on Southern Themes. Donald Justice. SV

And the Great Word is waiting to be spoken! Courage, All. Edwin Markham. HBMV

And the greater task, for thee to live! The National Ode. Bayard Taylor. PAH

And the greatest of all is John Bull. The World Is a Bundle of Hay. George Gordon, Lord Byron. EnRP; FF

And the green flags on their bayonets will flutter in the wind. The Connaught Rangers. Winifred M. Letts. HBMV

And the green grass growing all around! The Green Grass Growing All Around. *Anonymous.* FSW; HBVY; MoShBr

And the green grass growing over me! Forsaken. *Anonymous.* GTBS; HBV 1-2

And the green leaves they grow rarely. The Cruel Mother. *Anonymous.* InPK; OxBB

And the green silent pastures, yet remain. Composed at Neidpath Castle, the Property of Lord Queensberry, 1803. William Wordsworth. GTBS; GTBS-P

And the grey, chill day/Slips away with a frown. Chill of the Eve. James Stephens. OnYI

And the grief of a heart/going under/everyone now/can calmly finger. My White Book of Poems. Rachel (Rachel Blumstein). VWA

And the ground spinning beneath us/goes on talking. For Alva Benson, and for All Those Who have Learned to Speak. Joy Harjo. TWSS

And the guardsman's son. For the Student Strikers. Richard Wilbur. GLGT; OxBC

And the gulls tumble; and the homing ships/Peer for the harbor; and the sand drips. Eagle Sonnets. Clement Wood. HBMV

And the hair from thy crown/Be blown like thistle-down. Death. William Bell Scott. NOBV

And the halleluyahs of our second selves. Rediscovery. Kofi (George Williams) Awoonor. TTY

And the hand opens its ten thousand hold. The Idea of a University. David Shapiro. ANYP

And the hand that lies in thine is not my hand. Tristram's End. Laurence Binyon. EnLit; OBMV

And the hand trembles/at the next word to put down. A Series 5.8. John Wieners. CoPo

And the hands of the clock still knock without entering. Another Year Come. William Stanley Merwin. NYBP; OFD; PCP

And the hangman sings. The Hangman's Love Song. Stanley Moss. VGW

And the happiest eyes in the world that day were the eyes of Betsy/Jane. Betsy Jane's Sixth Birthday. Alfred Noyes. BiCB; SiSoSe

And the harbor's eyes. Lost. Carl Sandburg. AmPP; BrR; CMoP; PoPl; WHA

And the hare-lip was hidden below the coffin-lid!/And Ochone! Harvest of the Sea. Maire Mhac an tSaoi. PBWP

And the head sinks and he is gone. Death in the Corn. Detlev Freiherr von Liliencron. WaaP

And the heart be moulded. Jonathan Gentry, III: Tom's Sleeping Song. Mark Van Doren. LOW

...And the heart/By one slow wheel worn down, whetted to gladness. Instead of a Journey. Michael Hamburger. NYBP

And the heart/expands to admit its adversary. For Jane Myers. Louise Gluck. FaBoWP; GeTw

And the heart gives up its dead. A Process in the Weather of the Heart. Dylan Thomas. MoAB; NeBP

...And the heart is in tumult. Tumult. Charles Enoch Wheeler. PoNe

And the heart's awakening. Falling in Love. David Perkins. NCSH

And the heart's recollections/May hallow their shrine to the last! Disaster. James Clarence Mangan. IrPN

And the heat weighs a dreamy load. A Half-Way Pause. Dante Gabriel Rossetti. NOBV

And the Heavens for a sty! Muckish Mountain (The Pig's Back). Shane Leslie. AnIV

And the heaviest nuns walk in a pure floating/Of dark habits,/keeping their difficult balance. Love Calls Us to the Things of This World. Richard Wilbur. AmPP; CAPP; CMoP; HAP; HeIP; InPS; MoAmPo; NePA; NePoEA; NIP; NoAm; PAI; PoRA; PPP; TAP; TrGrPo; VGW

And the heavy clouds were settling/Over Flodden, like a pall.' Edinburgh after Flodden (excerpt). Ayton [(or Aytoun)] Sir Robert. OBWP

And the heavy rain to follow. Chimes. Dante Gabriel Rossetti. OBNC

And the heck with the man that works. The Great American Bum. *Anonymous.* FSW

And the hero of heroes was slain. Trafalgar. Francis Turner Palgrave. BeLS; FaBoBe

And the hill might even move a little, feeling the kick/of a child. Gnawing the Breast. Sandra McPherson. LCAP

And the hoarse nation croak'd, God save King Log. The Dunciad. Alexander Pope. CEP

And the horrible license plate on it The Sandwich Man. Ron Padgett. ANYP; ConAP

And the horse he rode/Was of ivory. The Horseman. Walter De la Mare. GoJo; SoPo; SUS; TiPo

And the horses drawing your carriage/Sing agreeably, agreeably, agreeably of love. Carry Her over the Water. W. H. Auden. FaBoTw

And the host after waiting/Must quench the lamps and pass/Alive into the house. From Scars Where Kestrels Hover. W. H. Auden. FaBoPV

And the host of airy quill-drivers/First dipped their pens in mist. Walden. Henry David Thoreau. MAmP

And the hours/Pass over us/In silence. Midnight and Ten Minutes. Shlomo Vinner. VWA

And the houses are built without walls. In the Dumps. *Anonymous.* FaBoCo; NA; OxNR

And the houses, Egypt, the great houses, had an end. The Icehouse in Summer. Howard Nemerov. NoAm

And the huge stones/of our Jerusalem hills? Answer. Leah Goldberg. VWA

And the hunt's up, and away! Hunting-Song. Richard Hovey. HBV 1-2

And the hunter home from the hill. Requiem. Robert Louis Stevenson. AnFE; BBV; BrPo; BSV; DL; FaBV; FaPoR; FPL; GoTF; GoTS; GTBS; HBV 1-2; HBVY; MCCG; MoBrPo; NLV; NOBE; NOBV; OBEV; OBNC; OBVV; OHFP; PoLf; PoPl; PoRA; TreF; TrGrPo; ViBoPo; WGRP; WHA

And the hurricane drives the dead straw into the living pine-tree. The Storm. Theodore Roethke. NCSH

And the hush of midnight falls upon the Hyde Street Grip! Ballad of the Hyde Street Grip. Gelett Burgess. BPAW

And the icy sprays of stars. Winter Night, Cold Spell. Howard Nelson. AMV-81

And the illimitable quietude/Comes gently upon us. Choricos. Richard Aldington. HBMV

–And the/immaculate white bed. Nantucket. William Carlos Williams. HAP; OxBA; SOTW; TAP; WeW

And the impossible be done/When the Wish and Deed grow one! To Mother Nature. Frederic Lawrence Knowles. HBV 1-2

...And the inanimate moon/loves him back with silences, and moonbeams made of chalk. Ghazals. Jim Harrison. PAI

And the incubus in the dream was the Lord/wrestling Sleepless on a Summer Night. Umberto Saba. VWA

And the infant's red-brown mouth a star/at the star of the girl's nipple... December 21st. Jean Valentine. LCAP

And the infinite stars in heaven are old to/me. The Mountain to the Pine. Clarence Hawkes. AA

And the inner image of a composition/beyond manipulation. Composition. Peter Blue Cloud. VoR

And the inside/of artists' stomachs itch. August 2. Norman Jordan. PoBA

And the invisible stars. Eclipse. Timothy Sheehan. SUW

And the iridescent wings/flutter and cling/all the way home. Poem for Myself and Mei: Abortion. Leslie Marmon Silko. VoR

And the iron gin that waits for Sin/Had caught us in its snare. The Ballad of Reading Gaol. Oscar Wilde. MoBrPo; TrGrPo

And the island became a wall. Hart Crane. Julian Symons. PoA

And the isles confuse him with their own black dead. The Dead in Melanesia. Randall Jarrell. MiAP

And the isles of the ocean shall wait for his law. Wake, Isles of the South. William B. Tappan. AH

...And the joy of packing/the present is enough. Almost, enough At the Nursing Home. John Cain. FAZ

And the joy of the love of men. The Kavanagh. Richard Hovey. HBV 1-2

And the joys of thee seventy times seven,/Our Lady of Pain. Dolores. Algernon Charles Swinburne. MaVP; UnTE; VLP

And the katharsis fades in the warm water of a yawn. Horatian Epode to the Duchess of Malfi. Allen Tate. FaBoMo

And the katydids and crickets hollers/"Haly!" all the night. On the Death of Little Mahala Ashcraft. James Whitcomb Riley. AA

And the Kennedys talk on TV. The New Order. Phyllis McGinley. AmFN

And the kids feel righteous–/righteous but cosy. To a Political Poet. Heinrich Heine. FaBoPV

And the kind tender Naked Boy is Love. Lycias. John Wilmot, Earl of Rochester. ErPo

And the kindly earth shall slumber, lapt in universal law. Locksley Hall. Alfred, Lord Tennyson. GoTF; WBLP

And the king dozes. The Day Closes. Carlton Talbot. ALV

And the King of Heaven will father your bairn/Till love Gregor come hame. Fair Annie of Lochryan. Anonymous. AS

And the King's clear countenance shine upon us/when we have leaped from our bodies old. To an Elderly Virgin. Mael Isu O Brolchain. NOBI

And the King slept beside the northern sea. Variations of an Air. Gilbert Keith Chesterton. Par

And the king was well and gay. The Enchanted Shirt. John Milton Hay. BBV; BLPA; GN; MaC; PaPo

And the kingdom come of peace. O Star of Galilee. Girolamo Savonarola. ISi

And the kings asleep in the ground. The Fort of Rathangan. Kuno Meyer. CH; FaBoCh; LoGBV; OxBI

And the kings began to sing. The Wise Men Ask the Children the Way. Heinrich Heine. OBCP

And the kiss that I take thou takest. The South Wind. Robert Bridges. OBNC

And the Kittens of To-day/Will be Old Cats To-morrow. Gather Kittens While You May (parody). Oliver Herford. ElL; SpRo

And the knot the parson ties will be a tight, tight, tight one. Tailor. Eleanor Farjeon. OxBChV

And the laborer's work is done. Fear Not. J. Bullock. STF

And the ladies go dancing at Whitsun. Dancing at Whitsun. Austin John Marshall. OBET

And the lady/Who taught kindergarten. Lucy McLockett. Phyllis McGinley. BiCB

And the lake her lone bosom expands to the sky. Rob Roy. Sir Walter Scott NBM

And the lake of my eyes is a cheat. Maze. Richard Eberhart. AnAmPo

...And the land by Tristram's grace was free. Tristram of Lyonesse. Algernon Charles Swinburne. WHA

And the land-lubbers lying down below. One Friday Morn. Anonymous CH; OnMSP

And the land/that in turn waits/for us... Napa, California. Ana Castillo. WPOW

And the land was a pretty woman/smiling at us/looking at her. A Pretty Woman. Simon J. Ortiz. CDW

And the land where he had been. Autumn Fields. Elizabeth Madox Roberts. BrR

And the landlord went a-mourning for his fair ladye. False Linfinn. Anonymous. BaBo

And the landscape remained lucid in the eye/even in the rain. Memory of Another Climate. Gabriel Preil. VWA

And the lapwings crying free above the plough. The Land. Victoria Mary (Vita) Sackville-West. PeHV

And the lark ascends, and his voice still rings, still rings. How Strangely This Sun Reminds Me of My Love. Stephen Spender. PeHV

And the lark sings. After Six Thousand Years. Victor Hugo. WaaP

And the lark take the keys/And hang them in heaven. The Poem. William Stanley Merwin. PP

And the last bird fly into the last light. The House of Life. Dante Gabriel Rossetti. NoP

And the last buds cease blowing. Bitter for Sweet. Christina Georgina Rossetti. GBL

And the last of my lovers/I'll light a candle still. The First of My Lovers. Sydney Carter. OBET

And the last rays of the sun/are touching/them. Tangere. Theodore Enslin. CoPo

And the last sturgeon of Thames. The Retired Colonel. Ted Hughes. NePoEA-2

And the last thing I rob will be a gong. Rome Once Alone. Clark Coolidge. APU

And the last wave romping in/To throw its boyhood on the marble sand. The Swimmer. Irving Layton. PeCV

And the laws of the prophets. Resurrection. Frank Horne. OFD; PoBA

And the lean Goths encroaching silently. Ancient Historian. Chris Wallace-Crabbe. PoAu 1-2

And the leaves of the Judgment Book unfold. Bedouin Love Song. Bayard Taylor. AA; AnAmPo; BBV; FaBoBe; HBV 1-2; MCCG; PaPo; TreFT

And the leaves stared in at the window/Like people at a play. The House across the Way. Ralph Hodgson. FaBoTw

And the leeks, and the onions, and the garlic. The Avenue Bearing the Initial of Christ into the New World. Galway Kinnell. NePoEA-2

And the lees in his beard for a fiend/outwitted! The Last Cup of Canary. Helen Gray Cone. AA

...And the leprous stones in/the sun have the splendid shine of naked, victorious gods. Spring over the City. Anne Hebert. PBWP

And the liberation from the lion's mouth. Dandelions. Howard Nemerov. DFF; NePA

And the lifting of arms to embrace. Health. Stewart Parker. CIP

And the light/always followed her to mass. "Vierge Ouvrante." Miriam Palmer. NMM

And the light in us went from stop to go. The Flower Vendor. Luis Cabalquinto. BrSi

And the light then/of the sun coming/for another morning/in the world. The World. Robert Creeley. NaP; NoAm; NoP

...And the lightening now/Is tangled in tremulous skeins of rain! Before the Rain. Thomas Bailey Aldrich. GN

And the lines of white surf come in. North of Santa Monica. Carter Revard. VoR

And the linnets are singing,"True lovers don't sever!" The Welcome. Thomas Osborne Davis. HBV 1-2

And the lion licks the man's hand with his tongue. Jerome. Randall Jarrell. PPP

And the lips and the hair of the bride. The Watcher. James Stephens. HBV 1-2; MoBrPo; OBEV; OBVV

And the lips that touch liquor must never touch mine. Lips That Touch Liquor. George W. Young. NLV; PaPo; TreFT

And the listening heart of the great world hears/The Paeans of Tennessee. Tennessee. Virginia Frazer Boyle. PAH

And the little boats of Britain shall go sailing by their side! The Little Boats of Britain. Sara E. Carsley. CaP

And the little boy ran away. The Scaredy. Anonymous. OxNR

And the little boys on the twopenny seats/Scream with laughter and suck their sweets. Circus. Eleanor Farjeon. SUS

And the little brown bird steadfastly wanders on/pulling what counts wherever it goes. Trouble-Shooting. William Stafford. AMV-80

And the little dog ran beside it. Momotara. Rose Fyleman. TiPo

And the little dream-child by the dreamland sea/Will wait for me in vain. Waking. Katharine Pyle. OBCA

And the little gilt leaves/Flicker in falling, like waifs and flakes of flame. Leaves. Frederic Manning. NOAV

And the little green cat is a bug in the grass. A Rabbit as King of the Ghosts. Wallace Stevens. SOTW

And the little one said,/"Good night." Roll Over. Anonymous. FSW

And the little ones chewed on the bones-o. The Fox. Anonymous. BaBo; StPo

And the little ones picked the bones O! A Fox Jumped up One Winter's Night. Anonymous. BLPA; OxNR; PBBP

And the little Revenge herself went down by the island crags/To be lost evermore in the main. The "Revenge." Alfred, Lord Tennyson. BeLS; DTo; FaBoCh; FaPo; HBV 1-2; MaC; MCCG; OAEP; OBWP; OnMSP; PoRA

And the little shifting pictures of people rushing/In tiny self-importance to and fro. The Crystal Gazer. Sara Teasdale. MoAmPo

And the little stars of Duna/Call me home. Duna. Marjorie Pickthall. HBV 1-2; MCCG

And the Little Waves of Breffny go stumbling through my/soul. The Little Waves of Breffny. Eva Gore-Booth. AnIV; HBV 1-2; HBVV; OnYI

And the living were made of cardboard. Canto CXV. Ezra Pound. FaBoMo

And the locked heart of man his only doubt. Proem to "The Kid." Conrad Aiken. MoAB

And the loin lies down with the limb. Limerick: "It's time to make love: douse the glim." Conrad Aiken. FaBoNo; NLV

And the lonely battle won. The Teams. Henry Lawson. CBAP; PoAu 1-2

And the lonely seabird crosses/With one waft of the wing. The Captain. Alfred, Lord Tennyson. MOS

And the lonely wind-swept ways of high Kithaeron. Epitaph of a Thessalian Hound. Simonides (of Ceos). LiTW

And the long curtains blow into the room. Robinson at Home. Weldon Kees. CoAP; NYBP

And the long flurrying flame that shoots to die... Sonnet XV. Frederick Goddard Tuckerman. TrCP

And the long labours of the toilet cease. The Rape of the Lock. Alexander Pope. FaBoPP; OBSV

And the long line of golden villages. A Sunset at Les Eboulements. Archibald Lampman. OBCV

And the long moon-beam on the hard wet sand/Lay like a jasper column half uprear'd. Gebir. Walter Savage Landor. EnRP

And the long night shall echo with our chorus. Antigone. Sophocles. WaaP

And the long sleep beside him will be sweet. Sonnet: "She is so young, and never never before." Edward Davison. ErPo

And the long stem of connection. Williams: An Essay. Denise Levertov. InPS

And the Lord can make them anywhere,/His "desert place apart." Now and Then. Margaret E. Sangster. TRV

And the lord he died on Sunday next/Before the prayer begun. Lady Maisry. *Anonymous.* OBET

(And the Lord is King above all gods!) King David. Stephen Vincent Benét. HBMV

And the Lord of the Flies must leer/At such outpouring. O Whose Are These Children. Richard Snyder. SOTS

And the Lord of the Harvest deign to own/The precious seed by the fathers sown! The Prophecy of Samuel Sewall. John Greenleaf Whittier. MAmP

And the Lord will doubly bless you/For the joy you brought His heart. Be Thankful. Mark Bullock. STF

,And the loud North again/Shall buffet the vexed forest in his rage. A Winter Piece. William Cullen Bryant. AmPP; AP; OxBA

And the love, whatever it was, an infection. Wanting to Die. Anne Sexton. ConAP; IHMS; NoAm; TAP

And the low moan of leaden-colour'd seas. Enoch Arden. Alfred, Lord Tennyson. FaBoPP

And the Lowells speak only to God. Boston. John Collins Bossidy. AmFN; FaBoCo; NLV; OBAL; OxBoLi

And the luck of our husbands and lovers, who keep free women. Pro Femina. Carolyn Kizer. MAT; NMM

And the luckier lot betide you! Gipsy Song. Ben Jonson. FaBoCh; LoGBV

And the lure is the same. A Fish to Feed All Hunger. Sandra Alcosser. WOLT

And the Lure of the East when Kipling spells/Pyjamas. Britannia Rules of Orthography. Firth". InMe

And the luve that ance was there, aye fresh and green. The Bush Aboon Traquair. John Campbell Shairp. OBVV

And the maidens who were promised still await the absent Smith. The Smiths. E. G. Murphy. NOAV

And the man/feel in his muscles the river's startled flowing. The Bridge. Derek Walcott. NYP

And the man I love as my life,/Sudden death be his fate! A Learned Mistress. Frank O'Connor. KiLC; OBMV

...And the man inside who sold it/long ago, forgot he made the deal and will not move. Landscapes. Richard Hugo. GP

And the man's eyes then were not so sunk that you saw the socket-/bones. An Anniversary. Thomas Hardy. OxBTC

And the man who plants cabbages imitates, too! The Ballad of Imitation. Henry Austin Dobson. HBV 1-2

And the man withered, strengthless, leprous, dead. Were Not the Gael Fallen. Peadar O'Mulcorny. AnIL

And the manshaped night remaining total Moonwalk. John Engels. MAT

And the Mantle of Age on my shoulders. Ichabod! The Glory Has Departed. Ludwig Uhland. AWP; IrPN

And the manuka hills/Know the slow smoke of burning. Dunedin Revisited. Denis Glover. AnNZ

And the many, many times that I held her in my arms,/Just to shield her from the foggy, foggy dew. The Weaver (with music). *Anonymous.* AS

And the marble seats are green/like woodland banks. A Charleston Garden. Henry Bellamann. PoLf

And the Marco Polo leading/With my carving in her teeth. The Old Figurehead Carver. H. A. Cody. EtS

And the marriage bell was tolled in hell/For the souls of him and her. The Bridge of Death. *Anonymous.* AWP

...And the marvel of a beautiful face. Dain do Eimhir (excerpt). Sorley MacLean. NeBP

And the masters come. Suburban Dream. Edwin Muir. OxBTC

And the memorial mosses hang their green/Upon it, as it flows ahead. Metaphor as Degeneration. Wallace Stevens. LCAP

And the memory of it like a wide heavy rain. Rainy Morning. Sotero Rivera-Aviles. InW

...And the men/in their frail boats/bow their heads and wait. The Great Wave off Kanagwa. Constance Egemo. PoDr

And the men that were boys when I was a boy/Shall sit and drink with me. The South Country. Hilaire Belloc. ACP; GoBC; HBV 1-2; MoBrPo; OBVV

And the 'mergency man in two days and a bit/Was found in the ebb tide stuck in a net. The 'Mergency Man. John Millington Synge. PoPle

And the message of the yew tree is blackness–blackness and/silence. The Moon and the Yew Tree. Sylvia Plath. CoAP; FaBoMo; FaBoWP; MOON; NaP; NYBP; PPP; VGW; WPOW

...And the/Mexican egg and the clock that will not make me know/how to leave you Les Luths. Frank O'Hara. NoAm; NOBA

And the mid-stump three somersaults in air. A Cricket Bowler. Edward Cracroft Lefroy. OBVV

And the midnight message of Paul Revere. Tales of a Wayside Inn. Henry Wadsworth Longfellow. AnNE

And the mill belonged to Sandy. Sandy. *Anonymous.* OxNR

And the miller gave it to Silly again. Silly. *Anonymous.* OxNR

And the miller that opens the hatch stands amazed at the whirl in the water. The Pike. Edmund Charles Blunden. AnFE; LiTM; MoVE

And the miller was burned at the stake nearby. The Two Sisters. *Anonymous.* FSW

And the mind drives/To the lovers' schism. Limb and Mind. John Waller. NeBP

And the mink crawls on its belly close to the ground. We Need the Tonic of Wildness. Henry David Thoreau. RFM

And the mirror maintains/The family tradition:/That she was very beautiful. My Mother's House (excerpt). Leah Goldberg. PBWP

And the misery, and the/Anger, and the vow are the same. The Bad Old Days. Kenneth Rexroth. NNaP; NoAm

And the mist along the river fix its purple in lines of a/woman's shawl on lazy shoulders. River Roads. Carl Sandburg. VGW

And the misty English trees. A Ship Sails up to Bideford. Herbert Asquith. BrR

And the moist reciprocation of his palms. Descartes and the Stove. Charles Tomlinson. FaBoMo

And the Molock of tyranny reels on his throne. Extermination. Richard D'Alton Williams. OnYI

And the mome raths outgrabe. Jabberwocky. Lewis (Charles Lutwidge Dodgson) Carroll. ALV; AmMo; BiP; DiPo; EBEV; FaBoBe; FaBoCo; FaBoNo; FaBV; FaFP; FF; FiBHP; FPL; GoJo; GoTF; HBV 1-2; HeIP; HoPM; InPK; InPS; LBN; LiTB; NA; NAMP; NBM; NIP; NLV; NOBE; NOBL; NOBV; NoP; NTCP; OAEL 1-2; OxBChV; PAI; PoPl; PoRA; PPoe; PPP; SeCeV; SpRo; TEP; TiPo; TreF; TrGrPo; VLP

And the moment broke with my/breath. The Glass Town. Alastair Reid. NYBP

And the moon and all the stars come crashing down. Grand Finale. Irving Layton. NOBC

And the moon and the stars to look upon. The Man Hunt. Madison Cawein. AnAmPo

And the moon casts a furious gleam on the many-knuckled sea The Ocean. Laura St. Martin. FF

And the moon dips and drowns, but no man heeds. Elegy. William Bell. FaBoTw

And the moon had not yet shone/In the space of this earth. I Am the Beginning. Isaiah Shembe. WTO

And the moon had slipped away/in the soft, bottomless mud. Moon Fishing. Lisel Mueller. CoAP

...And the moon in the breast of man is cold. The Moon and the Night and the Men. John Berryman. CoAP; √GW; WaP

And the moon is the same here as in Paris, as over the/Mississippi, as in Bombay. The End of a Day in the Provinces. Jules Laforgue. SyP

And the moon itself,/a pale horse of torment flying... Ryder. John Haines. LCAP

And the moon sank red. Middle Ages. Siegfried Sassoon. SO

And the moonbeams thousand strong/Past my grave each night shall file. When I Die. Fenton Johnson. CDC; PoNe

And the moons stacked up like shields I Have No Strength for Mine. Joanne Kyger. PoM

And the Moors, by noontide sun,/Were dust on Tolosa's plain. The Cid's Rising. Felicia Dorothea Hemans. OBRV

And the more I behold–only loves thee the more.   Remember Dear Mary.
John Clare.   WeW

And the morning received those stars from my hand.   I Traveled with Them.
King of Seville, Mu'tamid.   AWP

And the morning shadows of youth, and the night that fell/thereafter.   The
Moss-Rose.   Sir Henry Newbolt.   HBV 1-2

And the moss on the shore burning red.   In the Home of the Scholar Wu Su-
chiang from Hsin-an...   Wu Tsao.   BoWoP; WPOW

And the most powerful blast the gout could blow/Prove but an ignis lambens
to that toe.   One in the Gout Wishing for King Pyrrhus His Toe...   Sir
Thomas Browne.   FaBoEE

And the mother waiting at home for her boy/Will learn that he is dead.
Custer's Last Fierce Charge.   *Anonymous.*   BFSS

And the mountain/was gone.   Alaskan Mountain Poem #1.   Leslie
Marmon Silko.   VoR

And the mourner was heard no more.   The House Carpenter.   *Anonymous.*
BFSS

And the mouth gaping, a soft wound.   Fish.   Sandra Witt.   AMV-80

And the movement of the morning.   Epithalamion.   James Elroy Flecker.
BrPo

And the musick shall be praise.   Dooms-Day.   George Herbert.   JCP;
SeCP; SeCV 1-2

And the musing of my heart/when I look within.   Meditation.   Carl Rakosi.
VWA

And the name that she murmurs so oft as she weeps/Is Ivan Petrofsky Skovar.
Abdullah Bulbul Amir.   *Anonymous.*   AS; BLPA; FPL; FSW; StPo; TreF

And the name which you stumble on/Is, alas, your own.   Read Me, Please!
Robert Graves.   NYBP

And the name you called me then/I call you now–/O Liberty, my Love!
Republic to Republic.   Witter ("Emanuel Morgan") Bynner.   PAH

And the nation that plays it is lost!'   Dane-Geld.   Rudyard Kipling.
OxBTC

And the Nation was close to its Maker then.   Jack Creamer.   James Jeffrey
Roche.   MC; PAH

And the need of a world of men for me.   Parting at Morning.   Robert
Browning.   AWP; CBEP; DiPo; FaBV; FF; FiP; GTBS; HBV 1-2; HeIP;
MaVP; MBW 1-2; MCCG; MOS; NOBE; OAEP; OBEV; OBNC; OBSP;
SoSe; TreFT; UnPo; VLP; WiR

And the neighbors wondered that she should die.   Killed at the Ford.
Henry Wadsworth Longfellow.   AP; OHIP

And the nets of rain through which the farther mountains/Shine like a
shadow?   Sheep Country.   Margaret Pond.   BPAW

And the new crop exterminates the old.   The Hasty-Pudding.   Joel Barlow.
AP

And the new gospel verifes the old.   Adjustment.   John Greenleaf Whittier.
WGRP

And the new lists for new honors have/begun.   The Chronicler.   Alexander
Bergman.   TrJP

And the new sun rose bringing the new year.   The Passing of Arthur.
Alfred, Lord Tennyson.   EBEV; FaBoRV; GTBS; OBNC

And the next day have the worms/Slipping in and out between your fingers?
Scholfield Huxley.   Edgar Lee Masters.   LiTA; MoPo; TrPWD

And the next day I moved on.   Meeting the Reincarnation Analyst.   Gary
Gildner.   AmPA

And the next day smil'd on the great Event.   The Dispensary.   Sir Samuel
Garth.   CEP

And the next deepest sensual experience/is the sense of justice.   The Deepest
Sensuality.   D. H. Lawrence.   NoAm

And the next final flowering/Into a night-bird's last flight.   And the Silver
Turns into Night.   Nathan Yonathan.   VWA

And the next night you will come back/to fish for the Hand   Surf-Casting.
William Stanley Merwin.   NOBA

And the night-crow make/Me music; to my sorrow.   Tom O'Bedlam's Song.
Anonymous.   LO

And the night holds its breath.   The Bird of Night.   Randall Jarrell.
DuDa; NCSH; RFM

And the night is full of the past.   Lollingdon Downs.   John Masefield.
GoYe

And the night only heard the words they said.   Sentimental Conversation.
Paul Verlaine.   SyP; WSC

And the night pass, and the strange morning break/Upon our anguish for each
other's sake.   Sonnet: "Oh, my beloved, have you thought of this."   Edna
St. Vincent Millay.   HBMV

And the night passes–and never passes–   A Goodnight.   William Carlos
Williams.   MoAB; MoAmPo

And the nights are not separate/remember   Animula.   William Stanley
Merwin.   CAPP

And the norlan flowers spring bonny.   Sir Lionel.   *Anonymous.*   ESPB

And the nuns loved their Abbess well.   The Abbess.   Sir Walter Scott.
GoBC

And the nymph may be chaste that has never been tried.'   A Nymph and a
Swain.   William Congreve.   ALV; UnTE

...And the o-/dors of the swamp vodka/to his nostrils.   The Red-Wing
Blackbird.   William Carlos Williams.   DFF

And the oak-tree for many a season/Bears fruit for the vultures of fate!   The
Battle of Eutaw.   William Gilmore Simms.   PAH

And the occasional savage trance-like state/of people in the process of singing/
being heard.   Ode: "Midnight moonlight mobbed Dante's bridge."   Bill
Berkson.   APU

And the ocean groans darkly grey in the half-light.   Extract.   Paul Frederic
Bowles.   PoA

And the office records it.   Getting a Job.   Paul Blackburn.   NYP

And the oftener you come here the more I'll adore you.   A Welcome.
Thomas Osborne Davis.   GoTF; TreFT

And the old cast/to rehearse with.   Habitat (excerpt).   Judith Wright.
CBAP

And the old days never will come again.   Adieu, the Years Are a Broken
Song.   *Anonymous.*   NOAV

And the old enchantment lingers in the honey-heart of/earth.   Carrowmore.
George William Russell.   HBMV

And the old man went on there/beating his mule with an asphodel.   Canto
XXI.   Ezra Pound.   MoPo

And the old mind ghost-forsaken/sink into its havoc   Saint-Lo.   Samuel
Beckett.   NOBI

And the old, old love/So long ago.   Why.   Bliss Carman.   OBVV

And the old places are not sweet any more/for what they did.   The Broken
String.   *Anonymous.*   PeSA

And the old river rolls on, slowly to the gulf.   Foreclosure.   Sterling A.
Brown.   PoBA; PoNe

And the old salt replied to her, Yas'm.   Limerick: "On the deck of a ship
called the Masm."   Conrad Aiken.   FaBoNo

And the once said never finds its way back.   Nescit Vox Missa Reverti.   J.
V. Cunningham.   ELU

And the one horse in the heart/that runs/and runs   Horses.   Robert Patrick
Dana.   PH

And the only field for strife/Is the inch before the saw.   To-Day.   John
Boyle O'Reilly.   OnYI

And the only listeners now are...the rats...and the lizards.   Four Preludes on
Playthings of the Wind.   Carl Sandburg.   AmLP; MoAB; NePA; SeCeV

And the only motive perhaps that can finally take precedence of/Money.   A
Mightier Than Mammon.   Edward Carpenter.   PeHV

...And the original man on the/plate/stands and steps down, unassisted.
Xerox.   Ben Belitt.   NYP

And the other He clapped across the moon.   Jonah's Gourd Vine: I Vision
God.   Z. N. Hurston.   TTY

And the other heard only the summons of the/wind/And wondered where it
was calling.   An Adobe House.   Witter ("Emanuel Morgan") Bynner.
BPAW

And the other is gone.   Bivouac.   Alun Lewis.   ChMP

And the other little Magpie's tail.   Two Magpies Sat on a Garden Rail.
D'Arcy Wentworth Thompson.   MoShBr

And the other ranks might have got worried.   A Leaden Treasury of English
Verse.   Paul Dehn.   DBV

And the other, whose role never/Came clear to me till tonight; even/Now I do
not know his name.   The Yearbook.   Tom Clark.   ANYP

And the oxen's heavy bodies/draw His sad deeds,/and the road wails,
stumbling.   Slow Oxen.   Ilya Rubin.   VWA

And the pain of our questions will melt like the/wax of our flesh/into silence.
Under Stone.   Elaine Feinstein.   VWA

And the pain of the darkness before anything ever/was.   Under.   J. C.
Squire.   FaBoTw

And the pain speaks clearly.   A Morning Kiss.   Andrew McCord Jones.
LFAC

And the pain you are causing to me.   Red River Valley.   *Anonymous.*
FaFP

And the pale corpse of a maiden young stretched on a new-made grave.   A
Lay of the Famine.   *Anonymous.*   OnYI

And the pale day-crescent dips,/New to heaven, a slender horn.   A Frosty
Day.   John Byrne Leicester Warren, Lord De Tabley.   LoBV

And the pale fire/relinquishes its flame.   Moon Song.   Hildegarde Flanner.
AMV-81

And the palm trees I would see/Where the "sabia" is singing.   Song of Exile.
Antonio G. Dias.   TTY

And the Parthian cavalry/Will stampede at once beyond the last horizon.
Secret Weapon.   Ammonides.   LiTW

And the Pascha of salvation/Hail, with His triumphant band.   Risen with
Healing in His Wings.   Saint John of Damascus.   BePJ

And the past is dead and buried and as buried as a root.   Homecoming.
John Thompson.   MAT

And the past is immortal, the future is inexhaustible!   The Repetitive Heart.
Delmore Schwartz.   ViBoPo

And the past slips through your fingers, wishing you were/there.   A Man of
Words.   John Ashbery.   PoA

And the peace that is not in the world has flown to me.   The Fairy Wood.
Arthur Symons.   BoC

And the peaks looked toward God alone.   The Peaks.   Stephen Crane.
AA; HBV 1-2; WGRP

And the people found each other/And thereby hangs a tail.   The
Malfeasance.   Alan Bold.   AmMo

And the performing dogs are led up from below.   Vaudeville.   Lincoln
Kirstein.   NoAm

And the pettitoes to the little pig.   The Pettitoes Are Little Feet.
Anonymous.   OxNR

And the picture carried with singing into the temple.   Because I Paced My
Thought.   John Hewitt.   CIP

And the pieces of sky that will go on falling for days.   Landscape with Little
Figures.   Donald Justice.   LCAP

And the pig got up and slowly walked away.   Judged by the Company One
Keeps.   *Anonymous.*   BLPA; FPL; NLV; YaD

And the pigeon sitting awry on its carved curls.   The Statue.   Robert Finch.
OBCV; PeCV

And the pigeon with the blue ruff/She had from Monsieur d'Elboeuf.   Alas!
Poor Queen.   Marion Angus.   ACV; BSV; GoTS; OxBS

And the pikes and the muskets did trail on the ground.   The Death of Queen
Jane.   *Anonymous.*   BaBo; ESPB

And the pimpernel muddles his head.   Come into the Orchard, Anne.
Algernon Charles Swinburne.   FaBoNo

And the pimpernell pellets of Pangipoo.   In the Gloaming.   James C. Bayles.
NA

And the pin is mine.   A Song: "I'll sing you a song."   *Anonymous.*   OxNR

And the pinto wheeler draggin' in the chains.   The Oro Stage.   Henry
Herbert Knibbs.   BPAW

And the piper's name was–Spring!   The Magic Piper.   E. L. Marsh.   SiSoSe

And the plantation of my dreams.   A Charm against the Tooth-Ache.   John
Heath-Stubbs.   MP; NePoEA; TwCP

And the playground I'm passing stings/with the shouts of children.
Visitations.   Jennifer Crewe.   AMV-80

And the plumbing would howl from Hell, "We're watching/you!"
Censorship.   John Ciardi.   NLV; TW

And the plump blonde from Personnel/Is sick behind the water cooler.
Office Party.   Phyllis McGinley.   OBSV

And the plums stand by/To fill the paste that's a-kneading.   Ceremonies for
Christmas.   Robert Herrick.   AnAnS 2; GN; HBV 1-2; OHIP; PCh; TEP

And the poem he has just begun/is finished.   The House.   T. Walking Eagle
Marietta.   LFAC

And the poetic Swan shall die,/Only to sing thy elegy.   The Falcon.
Richard Lovelace.   CaPo; PBBP

And the poor fluttering captives rise in vain.   Field Sports (excerpt).
William Somervile.   FM

And the poor ghost under the castle pavement.   The Ghost in the Cellarage.
John Heath-Stubbs.   NeBP

And the poor have all the money.   Tony O!   Colin Francis.   CH; FaBoCo;
PV

And the poor is the grist that he grindeth, and/life devoureth life?   The
Pilgrims of Hope: Sending to the War.   William Morris.   VLP

And the poor love it/and think its crazy.   After Lorca.   Robert Creeley.
ConAP; LCAP; NaP; PAI; PoL

And the poor, when they're old, have little of peace!   To the Four Courts,
Please.   James Stephens.   BIrV; HBMV; MoAB; MoBrPo; UnPo

...And the power/Stokes the atomic ovens at Oak Ridge.   Norris Dam.
Selden Rodman.   PoNe

And the practice has led to abuses.   Limerick: "There was a young poet of
Thusis."   *Anonymous.*   OxBoLi

And the pretty girls are plenty.   Philadelphia.   *Anonymous.*   AmFP

...And the price/Is what the dove must pay.   Bear, Cat and Dove.   Eliezer
Greenberg.   BoAnP

And the priest still unrevealed.   Deserted Shrine.   Avner Treinin.   VWA

And the private detective idly deflowered a rose.   Anteroom: Geneva.   Denis
Devlin.   CIP

And the problems of the universe seemed solved.   Aids to Composition.
Robert Conquest.   PP

And the promise of May/to my frost-silvered lines.   With Poems Already
Begun.   Rachel Korn.   VWA

And the proud hunger/of eyes/I will never know   Poem for My Father.
Annette Arkeketa West.   TWSS

And the proud sweat glued to my skin.   Lonely.   Andre Spire.   AWP;
TrJP

And the puffin eats pancakes,/Like you/and/like/me.   There Once Was a
Puffin.   Florence Page Jaques.   NTCP; SoPo; TiPo

And the pump has frozen tonight.   Star-Talk.   Robert Graves.   BoNaP;
GoJo; HBMV; MoBrPo; OxBTC

And the pumpkins dead in the roadside fields   Thinking of You.   Dick
Lourie.   NeAC

And the pure sunlight is all from heaven.   Lovebirds.   William Jay Smith.
ErPo

And the purple peaks of Killarney/From ancient woods arise.   The Abbot of
Inisfalen.   William Allingham.   GN; HBV 1-2; OnMSP

And the quail jump from sound/Into air.   The Hunt.   Daniel Halpern.
LiSp

And the Quaker was hoarse with cheering!   Miss Kilmansegg and Her
Precious Leg.   Thomas Hood.   VLP

And the Queen's old Souldier.   An Old Souldier of the Queens.   *Anonymous.*
OBS

And the quiet of love in her feet.   The Cap and Bells.   William Butler Yeats.
BrPo; GTBS; MoAB; MoBrPo; NoAm; NoP; OBVV; OnMSP; WSC

And the rafters/Lost all laughter/Long, long ago.   Only Silence.   Arthur
Stanley Bourinot.   CaP

And the rain comes down.   The Green Corn Dance.   Alice Corbin.
BPAW

And the rain is me.   There's a Feeling.   Marcia Bullwinkle.   AMV-80

And the rain like a rumbling tune that sings/Through everything I do.   City
Rain.   Rachel Field.   SoPo; TiPo

And the rank autumn grapes/Rise in their winter flames.   Pruners: Conca di
Marini.   Joseph Langland.   NePoEA

And the raped girl in the forest.   The Voices Inescapable.   Ann Stanford.
IHMS

And the rapids that we run, oh they seem to us but fun,/For we're void of all
slavish fear.   A Shantyman's Life.   *Anonymous.*   TrAS

And the real presence is you.   All Too Little on Pictures.   Charles Black.
AMV-80

And the red clay drawing his body home.   Elegy.   Roy McFadden.   NeIP

And the red glare on Skiddaw rouzed the burgh-/ers of Carlisle.   The
Armada: A Fragment.   Thomas Babington, Lord Macaulay.   BeLS;
FaBoCh; FaPoR; GN; HBV 1-2; LoGBV; OBNC; OBRV; WBLP

And the red pike at once was king and law.   A Fauxbourg.   George Croly.
OBRV

And the red rose would but blow more red,/The white rose whiter blow.
The Ballad of Reading Gaol.   Oscar Wilde.   OAEL 1-2; OBMV

And the red wings of frost-fire rent the sky.   Life the Beloved.   Dante
Gabriel Rossetti.   MaVP

...And the refraction carrying fresh clews.   Gibbs (excerpt).   Muriel
Rukeyser.   ImOP

And the regular jolt of the horse as he moves.   Galloping.   Cordelia Chitty.
PH

And the rekindling flame.   To Shelley.   John Banister Tabb.   AA

And the rest of the story's improper.   Limerick: "There was a young lady
from Joppa."   *Anonymous.*   LiBL

And the rhythm of life returning.   A Red Glow in the Sky.   Alexander
Blok.   OBVE

And the rhythm of the smith.   Altars and Sacrifice.   Jay Wright.   FB

"And the rich He hath sent empty away."   Our Lady.   Mary Elizabeth
Coleridge.   CAW; OBEV; OBMV; OBVV

And the riderless mule went homeward from the fight of Paso del Mar!   The
Fight of Paso del Mar!   Bayard Taylor.   BeLS

And the righteous host of gods will call you fortunate/and covet, each for
himself, your arts.   No Harm to Lovers.   Albius Tibullus.   LiTW

And the ripeness all.   Preface.   W. H. Auden.   LiTA

And the ripples are thoughts coming out to the edge of a dream.   The Crane
Is My Neighbour.   Shaw Neilson.   CBAP; PoAu 1-2

And the ritual/of prayer: and cries:/and Christ's chrism.   All the Death-
Room Needs...   Michael Hartnett.   CIP

And the river grows ugly in their perpetual service.   The Dear Ladies of
Cincinnati.   Anne Stevenson.   HoAn

And the river's clean where the raw blood/flowed/When the Widow give the
party.   The Widow's Party.   Rudyard Kipling.   VLP

And the roads deep in snow?   First Death in Nova Scotia.   Elizabeth
Bishop.   CoAP; FaBoWP; LCAP; NCSH; NOBA; NYBP

And the robins are no longer afraid...   Midsummer Morn.   Frank Marshall
Davis.   GoSl

And the rocks shall raise their head,/Of his deeds to tell?   Warren's Address
at Bunker Hill.   John Pierpont.   AA; AnNE; FaBoBe; GN; GoTF; HBV
1-2; HBVY; MC; PAH; PAL; TreF

And the rocks supply the coney/With a fortress and an home.   Spring.
Christopher Smart.   OBEC

And the rocks they melt by the heat of the sun.'   The Grey Cock.
Anonymous.   ELP; OBET

And the rogues obey you well.   A Strong Hand.   Aaron Hill.   HBV 1-2

And the roll is called up yonder, I'll be there.   When the Roll Is Called up
Yonder.   James M. Black.   TreFT

And the rooster's faint shadow/Smells distinctly of the cold.   The Eggplants
Have Pins and Needles.   Novella Matveyeva.   WPOW

And the roots he left behind/tugging, tugging back.   Running the Trotline.
Jim Elledge.   WOLT

And the roots refer to the text.   The Interpreters.   D. J. Enright.   PP

And the rose-garden of my gracious home.   From Grenoble.   James Elroy
Flecker.   OBTV

And the rose it clung round the sweet briar. Mother, Mother, Make My Bed. *Anonymous.* ELP

And the rosebush gives roses. I Love You and the Rosebush. Armando Uribe. HoPM

And the round earth turn a shoulder/Into mustering gloom. Pastoral. David Wright. NYBP

And the row/Starts/to/GO Stop–Go. Dorothy Walter Baruch. SUS; TiPo

And the Royal Queen of England/Goes weeping away. The Banished Duke of Grantham. *Anonymous.* EnSB

And the Royal Queen of Grantham/Went weeping away. Six Dukes Went a-Fishing. *Anonymous.* FaBoBa; OBET

And the ruffling seas rolled mountains high. The Wind Sou'West. *Anonymous.* AmFP

And the rulers ride the blue hills/holding their black whips high. Thoughts of Chairman Mao. David Young. AmPA

And the sad soft light of evening guides me in. Jogging at Dusk. Andrew Grossbardt. AMV-80

And the sad truth which hovers o'er my desk/Turns what was once romantic to burlesque. Don Juan. George Gordon, Lord Byron. FiP

And the sadder time when mill and man/Will be both as if they never began. The Windmill. Geoffrey Johnson. HaMV

And the sailor kissed his bride with his trousers on. Jackie Tar. *Anonymous.* OBSS

And the sailor your fortune he will make. The Shepherdess and the Sailor. *Anonymous.* OBET

And the sails, with the miller dying,/Went flying, flying. The Unfortunate Miller. Alfred Edgar Coppard. FaBoTw

....,And the salty grasses/surged round her stranded body. First Love. Laurie Lee. ChMP

And the Salvation Army singing God loves us... Hope Is a Tattered Flag. Carl Sandburg. NAMP

And the sand quakes ever; and ill fare they/That look upon that light. The Ballad of Dead Men's Bay. Algernon Charles Swinburne. MOS

And the sands of the dunes are scattered/In the scud of the spray. A Paris Nocturne. William Sharp. SyP

And the sang ye sing as ye hap me ower/Is meant for him. Sang: "There's a reid lowe in yer cheek." Robert MacLellan. OxBS

And the scented eve of springtime/Greets my soul from silent bowers. Spring Nocturne. Abraham Liessin. TrJP

And the sea forgets and goes to sleep. The Queen of Crete. John Grimes. HBMV

And the sea is making love to Dionysos/in the bouncing of these small and happy whales. They Say the Sea Is Loveless. D. H. Lawrence. MOS

And the sea is not so deep/As the soul in you asleep. To a Pretty Girl. Israel Zangwill. TrJP

And the sea-mist coiled like silk about your bones. To a Seaman Dead on Land. Kay Boyle. PoA

And the sea perhaps some way/and the sea so very far. W o m a n. Magda Portal. WPOW

...And the sea robin's arc/now stilled on the rock. The Promontory Moment. May Swenson. NYBP

And the sea shouldered its salt in long gray combers hauling/new shapes on the beach sand. Adelaide Crapsey. Carl Sandburg. HBMV

And the sea that bangs in my throat. The Room of My Life. Anne Sexton. CAPP

And the sea turns white and the wind goes round. Hurricane. Archibald MacLeish. NCSII

And the sea whose sentence strikes like a leaden wave. Two Old Men Look at the Sea. J. R. Hervey. AnNZ

And the seas return to their imagined homes. Vaticide. Myron O'Higgins. IDB; PoBA

And the seed of the fire gets feeble and cold. The Song of the Old Mother. William Butler Yeats. AnIV; GTBS; LOW; MCCG; MoBrPo

And the sense that a rapture so royal may come/not again in the passage of life. A Channel Passage. Algernon Charles Swinburne. VLP

And the sentry moves not, searching/Night for menace with weary eyes. The Trenches. Frederic Manning. MCCG; NOAV

...And the Seraphim/Come tow'ring, arm'd in adamant and gold. The Solemn Noon of Night. Thomas Warton, Jr.. OBEC; SeCePo

And the Sereno knows that he has seen/The spectre of the Past,the ghost of Spain. The Andalusian Sereno. Francis Saltus Saltus. AA

And the seventh day he slept the great sleep of the Negro. To New York. Leopold Sedar Senghor. PBA

And the seventh one caught an old cart-wheel. Blackfriars. Eleanor Farjeon. OxBChV

And the shadow is only me! Hallowe'en. Frances Frost. TiPo

And the shadow of mountains will not fall on your heart. Water-Lilies. Sara Teasdale. MoAmPo

And the shadows around them that they/seeing now bark at. Dog Hospital. Peter Wild. AmPA; GP

And the shadowy pine-trees sighed. The Hill Pines Were Sighing. Robert Bridges. EG; ExPo; OAEP

And the Shamrock shine forever new! Clare's Dragoons. Thomas Osborne Davis. OnYI

And the sharpness of the straw. Christmas Morning. Steven Lautermilch. AMV-80

And the sheep faces/of those that love me. Those I Love. Victor Contoski. GP

And the shine of these small things sweeter than the face/of Ishtar. Last Words. Sylvia Plath. FYAP

...And the shining/Light be comprehended by the darkness. Autumn 1940. W. H. Auden. LiTA

And the ship went down with the fair young bride/Who sailed from Dublin Bay. Dublin Bay. *Anonymous.* BFSS

And the short quick quench of the sea. The Raid. William Everson. PrIm

And the side of Aed son of Ainmire. Wife of Aed mac Ainmirech, King of Ireland, Laments Her Husband. *Anonymous.* AnIL

And the silence ripeness,/And the ripeness all. The Sea and the Mirror. W. H. Auden. SeCeV

And the silences after their partings are very deep. The High School Band. Reed Whittemore. GLGT; NCSH

...And the silences suffered no/shadows. Teresa of Avila. Elizabeth Jennings. NePoEA-2

And The Sillies are the sweetest that I know. The Man Who Sang the Sillies. John Ciardi. OBCA

And the silt of the river is grey/In the golden sun. Arrowtown. Denis Glover. AnNZ

And the silver snake of the estuary curls to sleep/In Daymer Bay. In Memoriam: A.C., R.J.O., K.S. Sir John Betjeman. NYBP

And the singing voice has only songs that wound/with bitterness. The land is dead. The Island. Sean Jennett. NeIP; SeCePo

And the size of his gathered people/three times thirty hundred. The Fort of Ard Ruide. *Anonymous.* NOBI

And the skies are not cloudy all day. Home on the Range. *Anonymous.* BLSo; BPAW; CoSo; FaBoBe; FSW; GoTF

And the skull that lies by its salt-dry verge/Gleams pale to the death-pale moon. Laguna Perdida. Maynard Dixon. BPAW

And the sky have changed, and the further dales come up. After Midsummer. E. J. Scovell. OxBTC

And the sky is lit by static lightning,/violet flashes. Jack. Ross's Poems. Geoffrey Lehmann. CBAP

And the slaughterhouse/is as close/as I/ever/want to be/to the smell of war again Radcliff, Kentucky. Thomas G. Nickens. LFAC

And the slave who saved St. Michael's went out from its door, a man. How He Saved St. Michael's. Mary A. P. Stansbury. BLPA

And the slotted spoon in her hand. The Archaeology of a Marriage. Maxine W. Kumin. DFT

And the slow clouds go by... Spring. Richard Hovey. BBV

...And the slow, pathetic prayers/Of godly men that somehow it shall rain. Soliloquy. Frederick E. Laight. CaP

And the small child Jesus smile on you. Noel. Hilaire Belloc. HBMV

...And the small headless/Proprietor, silky, creeping & jewelled. Pet Shop. Robert Sward. ELU

And the small heart sparkles amidst the leaves/Of the one thousand flowers, and flares. The Unicorn and the Lady. Jean Garrigue. NYBP

And the small horned worms walk high with hope. Male Torso. Christopher Middleton. NePoEA-2

And the small imperialist in my body/gathered in the stars. Building in Nova Scotia. Stephen P. Dunn. GP

...And the small/knowledge that the river takes you over all. Autobiography, Chapter XVII. Jim Barnes. STE

And the small mainstreets abandoned all night. Love Poem. Robert Bly. BiP; PAI; PCP

And the small rolls of bread/in the young hands/of dark-haired mothers. Tashkent Breaks into Blossom. Anna Akhmatova. BoWoP

And the smell of a goat clinging tenaciously/through perfume and a bath. News Report. David Ignatow. ErPo; TwCP

And the smell of coffee cooking in the window above. 96 Vandam. Gerald Stern. NYP

And the smile on the face of the tiger. Limerick: "There was a young lady of Niger." Cosmo Monkhouse. GoTF; HBV 1-2; HBVY; InvP; LiBL; NA; NLV; ShM; SoPo; TiPo

And the smoke-tree puffs dun blossoms into/the blue air. The Trumpet-Vine Arbour. Amy Lowell. MAPA

And the snail/with the ticking luggage of God's time. White Serpent. Nelly Sachs. BoWoP

And the snatching dwarfs stop dancing and fight together. Maxixe. Osbert Sitwell. PoA

And the snow is deep/sleep... Lullaby. Gilles Vigneault. WHW

And the snow wraiths whirl to the eldritch/tune/Of the medicine dance of Gray Raccoon. The Dance of Gray Raccoon. Arthur Guiterman. BPAW

And the snow wreaths drift/To the canons deep and still. Winter in the Sierras. Mary Austin. BPAW

And the soft brightness which is your soul. A Sprig of Rosemary. Amy Lowell. PeHV

And the soldier of time lies calm beneath that stroke. Esthetique du Mal. Wallace Stevens. CMoP; NOBA

And the soldier with their guns. Carrickfergus. Louis MacNeice. AnIL; FaBoIP; FaBoPP; NoAm; NOBI; OnYI

And the soldiers go marching,/Marching away. Faust. Johann Wolfgang von Goethe. AWP

And the son of a gun was never there. World War I. *Anonymous.* FaFP

And the song/Break/Its jail. Oppression. Langston Hughes. CNA

;And the song was wordless; the singing will never be done. Everyone Sang. Siegfried Sassoon. AnFE; BrPo; FaBV; GTBS; GTBS-P; InvP; LOW; MoBrPo; NOBE; OBEV; OBSP; OBWP; OxBTC; PoPl; PoSC; TrJP; WaP

And the sons have remembered their deeds/As the fields have remembered the corn. The Land War. Seumas (James Starkey) O'Sullivan. OxBI

And the sons of her sons/will let the metate grow cold on the porch. Yaqui Women: Three Generations. Rick Casillas. GP

And the sons of the free may recall with pride/The day of Delegate Rodney's ride. Rodney's Ride. *Anonymous.* MC; PAH

And the sooner he pays it the bebtor." Limerick: "A merchant addressing a debtor." R. C. TDH

...And the sorrow/of things moving back to where they came from. A Procession at Candlemas. Amy Clampitt. FaBoWP; HaCAP

And the soul creeps out of the tree. All Hallows. Louise Gluck. AmPA; HaCAP; NU

And the soul feels it has not wept in vain. How We Learn. Horatius Bonar. HBV 1-2

And the soul have rest, and the air be still? Studies at Delhi. Sir Alfred Comyn Lyall. OBVV

And the soul of the man walked free in the/fields of the universe! A Beam of Light. John Jerome Rooney. AA

And the soul's fealty to none but God. America's Gospel. James Russell Lowell. PGD

And the soul within is safe from damnation,/Since it is dead. At Ease. Walter De La Mare. ChMP; GTBS-P

And the sound of Finland in your blood/could outlast the many suns of future days. The Corner. Rita Johnson. AMV-80

And the sound of her accents just sped 'em. Limerick: "There was a frank lady of Dedham." X.Y.Z. TDH

And the sound of its blue beat/matching the wine in my veins. The Stripper. Anita Endrezze Probst. CDW

And the sound of our tears, and the taste of my own. To the Wife of a Sick Friend. Edna St. Vincent Millay. SBG

And the sound of willows/Now and again dipping their long oval leaves in the water. Betrothed. Louise Bogan. NMM

And the sound that followed the couplings back/will ripple forward and hold the train. The Rescued Year. William Stafford. LCAP

...And the sound/The spray made as it hit the front of the boat. Two Sonnets. John Ashbery. VGW

And the space next to her,/which he left without a mark. Nude. Daniel Halpern. MAYP

...And the Sparrow, whose fall/Is never mentioned in the press at all. Deities and Beasts. John Updike. ELU

And the spell's over. Time Out. Oliver Jenkins. GoYe

And the spider of life sits, sleep. The Drunkards. Malcolm Lowry. NYBP

And the spinners backward go. The Ropewalk. Henry Wadsworth Longfellow. AP; MAmP

And the spirit is willing. View from the Gorge. Ben Belitt. NYBP

And the spirit within it/Is gone. Me. Walter de la Mare. BiCB; TiPo

And the spoondrift's white/Is smiling to-day/Through the salt sea spray/Upon American sailors. The First American Sailors. Wallace Rice. PAH

And the springin' corn, and the bright May morn,/When first you were my bride. Lament of the Irish Emigrant. Helen Selina Sheridan. HBV 1-2; OBVV

And the square cornbread is in the ashes,/Waiting our return. Little Puppy. Hilda Faunce Wetherill. TiPo

And the square I live in, measured out with lime. Prothalamion. Maxine W. Kumin. NYBP

And the Squire, and Lady Susan, murmur mildly to me now. Friends Beyond. Thomas Hardy. CoBMV; FaBoRV; GTBS-P; NOBV; OBEV; OBVV; VLP

And the stained moon and drift retook their places there. The Pedigree. Thomas Hardy. CoBMV

And the stake and the cross-road, fool, if you/will, does it matter to me? Despair. Alfred, Lord Tennyson. VLP

And the stars are the only ships of pleasure. Two Mornings and Two Evenings. Elizabeth Bishop. PoA

And the stars begin moving. Fish. Larry Levis. AmPA

And the stars going round in my head. Escape at Bedtime. Robert Louis Stevenson. BrR; HBVY; TiPo; TreFS; TrGrPo

And the stars in our banner shone brighter/When Sherman marched down to the sea. Sherman's March to the Sea. Samuel H. M. Byers. MC; PAH

And the stars shine bright.... Chinese Serenade for the Ut-Kam and Tong-Koo. Thomas Holley Chivers. PeD

And the stars/still remain/uncounted. Psalm of the Jealous God. Henry Abramovitch. VWA

And the Statesman, because he's so great,/Thinks his Trade as honest as mine. The Beggar's Opera. John Gay. CEP

And the static rock beat out of the radio. Making Music. Judith Minty. GeTw

And the stigma of my shame. A Rhapsody of Old Men, VII. Dimitris Tsaloumas. CBAP

And the sting of night and starlight in every heart. Music in the Rec Hut. Hubert Creekmore. WaP

And the stockmen tell the story of his ride. The Man from Snowy River. Andrew Barton ("Banjo") Paterson. CBAP; PH; PoAu 1-2

And the stone dancing/changes its dust to music. In the blue distance. Nelly Sachs. BoWoP

And the stone god of morning will restore/The rose to the vast processions of its ground. Clair de Lune. Anthony Hecht. NYBP

And the stone has taken the house/To its cold heart and is kind. The Sheiling. Edward ("Edward Eastaway") Thomas. PoSH

And the stone is rolled forever/From the soul's despair. The Return. Eleanor Rogers Cox. PAH

...And the stone/of your words as they pass, as I do not hear them. October. Bill Berkson. ANYP

And the stones. Summer Street. Ana Ilce. AMV-81

And the stores stay open terribly late. Music. Frank O'Hara. NoP; NYP

And the storm has ceased to blow. Ye Mariners of England. Thomas Campbell. BLPA; CBEP; EtS; FaPoR; GN; GTBS; GTBS-P; HBV 1-2; NOBE; OBEV; OBRV; OBWP; TreF

And the storm stood still and waited/For the stroke of the Lord, belated! Theodosia Burr. John Williamson Palmer. PAH

And the story's this: I made the monster me. The Approach to Thebes. Stanley Jasspon Kunitz. PoA

And the strange, sweet tears! Vision. Israel Zangwill. TrJP

And the stream is taking us back. The First Day Out. Thomas Reiter. WOLT

And the stream went leaping toward the stream of Ocean/first under oars, then with a following wind .The Odyssey. Homer. NAWM 1-2

And the streams of that river ran red down with blood. Braddock's Defeat. *Anonymous.* ABF

And the street slumbers on. Not without Beauty. John A. B. McLeish. CaP

And the streets ringing to the stir of life. An Egyptian Tomb. William Lisle Bowles. OBTV

And the strutting fern lay seeds on the black sill. After the Funeral. Dylan Thomas. CMoP; CoBMV; DiPo; FaBoMo; MoAB; MoVE; NoP; OAEL 1-2; OAEP

And the style of your prose growing limper and limper. Academic. Theodore Roethke. CrMA; ELU; FaBoEE; MiAP; OBAL

And the sugar hostess weeps/One year in four, but more and more. Song for February. Tom Paulin. FaBoIP

And the sun and the Father's will. Give Us This Day Our Daily Bread. Maltbie Davenport Babcock. TRV

And the sun catching it, as he swings. Coins and Coffins under My Bed. Diane Wakoski. CoPo

And the sun coming up on the Blue Mountains. H.M.S. Glory at Sydney. Charles Causley. OBTV

...And the sun/Falls in little sprays, to be picked by anyone! Pastoral. Marion Strobel. PoA

And the sun glows dull on the tracks. The Train Out. Sydney Lea. MAYP

And the sun has made/Her skin so brown. Mexican Market Woman. Langston Hughes. SaC

...And/the sun is rising in the sky. Aranda Song. *Anonymous.* CBAP

And the sun just appearing at her elbow. White Autumn. Robert Morgan. Str

...And the sun/lifts through a haze every morning/of the summer in the stomach. Self-Portrait, as a Bear. Donald Hall. SO

And the sun on its longer voyage/is melancholy. On the holy day of your going out to war. Mahodahi. BoWoP

And the sun rises, clothed in the dogs' blood. Dog Sacrifice at Lake Ronkonkoma. William Heyen. AmPA

And the sun shining soft/On the loch I have left. From Skye, Early Autumn. M. L. Michal. PoSH

And the sun smites. Today. James Schuyler. ANYP

And the sun was the same as yesterday.   Hebrew Letters in the Trees.   J. Rutherford Williams.   VWA

And the sun will shine through the whole glad day.   The Boomerang. Carrie May Nichols.   PoToHe

—And the supple-souled men—.   Three Poems.   Stephen Crane.   AP

And the swallow flies high.   The Bard's Song.   Sir Robert Stapylton. SeCePo

And the sweet name to my mouth.   Italia, Io Ti Saluto!   Christina Georgina Rossetti.   OBTV; OBVV

And the sweetest, warmest sunshine/Comes after the storm and gloom.   Life's Lessons.   Anonymous.   BLRP; FPL; PoLf; STF

And the sweetness of a lollypop/Is something that will last.   Choice.   John Farrar.   BrR; SiSoSe

And the swill'd sot drops senseless to the ground.   The Benefits and Abuse of Alcohol.   Richard Cumberland.   FaBoUs; NLV

And the swimmer arose in his nakedness and called from the opposite shore. Winter Pond.   Ben Belitt.   NYBP

And the tail of a green-eyed rat/Whipped and was gone at a gray rathole. Rat Riddles.   Carl Sandburg.   SO

And the tale he told in fo'c's'le song/Of the flagship Trenton's parting cheer. The Cheer of the Trenton.   Walter Mitchell.   EtS

And the tall reeds sigh as the wind doth blow.   The Maids of Elfin-Mere. William Allingham.   IrPN; OnYI

And the taut mind turns to its own requirings.   World I Have Not Made. Elizabeth Jennings.   ACV

And the tears of hell cannot heat my heart/When the white winds blow.   I Knew a Boy with Hair Like Gold.   Melvin Walker La Follette. NePoEA-2

And the tears of the women fall on the doilies.   Duchesses.   David Campbell.   NOAV

And the teeth/there the mouth/open   Dr. Potatohead Talks to Mothers. Judith Johnson Sherwin.   NoAm

And the Templar stars in their order said: "Rise and go."   Journey from New Zealand.   Robin Hyde.   AnNZ

...And the terrible strength/of each merciful, tucked wing.   Hotel in Paris. Dennis Trudell.   PoA

And the Texan star flashed out.   The Fight at San Jacinto.   John Williamson Palmer.   AA; BPAW; HBV 1-2; MC; PAH

And the theories sustaining your jobs you jokers.   Anthropology.   Anselm Hollo.   APU

;And the thieving guest/Was no whit the wiser for the words it ate.   Book-Moth.   Anonymous.   AnOE

And the thin cries of the gleaming, bent-winged birds.   Winter Ploughing. William Everson.   NU

And the thing itself not the thing itself,/But a metaphor.   Sex.   Jean Valentine.   FaBoWP

And the thing seen right,/For once, that winter bought.   Winter Trout. James Dickey.   LiSp

And the thing we ca the ranting o't,/The lady lies her lane.   The Earl of Errol.   Anonymous.   ESPB

...And the thing which only a moment ago/I'd thought to say, is already fled and gone.   Winter Report.   Ben Howard.   PoA

And the things we have seen and have known and have heard of, fail us.   On a Dead Child.   Robert Bridges.   BrPo; CMoP; EBEV; GTBS; LiTB; LiTM; NoAm; NOBE; NOBV; OAEP; OBMV; OBNC; ViBoPo

And the things you drew on the wall.   Country School.   Allen Curnow. AnNZ

And the things you once thought/you were rid of forever/have taken you back in their arms.   In the Basement of the Goodwill Store.   Ted Kooser. GOYP

And the thistle-down went on the wind.   Imogen—In Wales.   Thomas Caulfield Irwin.   IrPN

And the thought that, on your awaking, identity may be destroyed.   A Real Question Calling for Solution.   Robert Penn Warren.   PPP

And the thoughts of youth are long, long/thoughts.   My Lost Youth. Henry Wadsworth Longfellow   AA; AmPP; AnFE; AnNE; AP; APA; AWP; EtS; ExPo; FaBoBe; FaBV; FaFP; FaPoR; FPL; GoJo; HBV 1-2; InPo; LaNeLa; LiTA; MAmP; MCCG; NePA; OBEV; OxBA; PoEL 1-5; PoLf; PoRA; RoGo; SeCeV; TAP; TreF; ViBoPo

And the three false Halls of Girsonsfield,/They'll never be trusted nor trowed again.   The Death of Parcy Reed (A vers.).   Anonymous.   BaBo; ESPB

And the three sleeping heroes/Turn to sleep again.   Sleeping Heroes. Edward Shanks.   OBMV

And the throb wherein those old lips met/Is a living music in us yet.   The Secret Love.   George William Russell.   HBV 1-2

And the thrones of the gods and their halls, their chariots, purples and splendors.   The Plougher.   Padraic Colum.   AnFE; GoBC; GTBS; HBMV; MoBrPo; OnYI

And the tide rises, the tide falls.   The Tide Rises, the Tide Falls.   Henry Wadsworth Longfellow   AA; AnNE; AP; BLPL; FaFP; GoTF; MAmP; MOS; NePA; NOBA; OxBA; PoRA; TAP; TreFT

And the tites come down.   Stalagmites and Stalactites.   Anonymous. FaBoUs

And the title that I give it is "The Scow on Cowden Shore."   The Scow on Cowden Shore.   Anonymous.   ShS

And the toastmaster's having convulsions.)   Drinking Song for Present-Day Gatherings.   Morris Bishop.   ALV

...And the too deep/Pool of desiring fill with sleep.   Watching You Sleep under Monet's Water Lilies.   Gibbons Ruark.   SM

And the tootle, tootle, tooting of its toot.   The Amateur Flute (parody). Anonymous.   BXAP; Par; SpRo

And the tough young horns/Blared flippantly farewell.   Wedding Procession. James A. Emanuel.   NNP

And the toys came dancing from the Christmas tree/To celebrate the famous victory.   The New Nutcracker Suite (excerpt).   Ogden Nash.   PCh

...And the tracks/into the oblivion we've both been waiting for.   Memoir. Roger Weingarten.   AMV-80

And the trains going over us here in the dry hollows...   Burying Ground by the Ties.   Archibald MacLeish.   NAMP

And the trains have been constant in death.   The Stationmaster's Lament. Jerome Rothenberg.   CoPo

And the trains that go from Rouen at the ending of the day.   Rouen.   May Wedderburn Cannan.   OBWP; OxBTC

And the traitor flags come down.   The River Fight.   Henry Howard Brownell.   PAH

And the treading down of green corn.   Learning Destiny.   Herman Charles Bosman.   PeSA

And the triumph of a march/in which no one/is injured.   Sousa.   Edward Dorn.   CoPo

And the trout that struck in the thunderlight.   Flyfisherman in Wartime. Leonard Bacon.   FYAP

And the true delight of living, as you taste it only there!   Switzerland. Alfred Denis Godley.   OBTV

And the true meed of conquest our minstrels shall fix/On the promise to pay of our Willimondswicks.   A Border Ballad (parody).   Thomas Love Peacock.   BXAP

And the trumpet's song, till in woods/they are drowned.   A Piece of Black Bread.   Edward (Edward Dzyubin) Bagritsky.   TrJP

And the trusting days are past.   Trust Him.   Anonymous.   STF

And the truth is cold, as a giant's knee/Will seem cold.   A Last World. John Ashbery.   ANYP

And the truth of this nonsense/'Tis loving that proves.   The Archer. Douglas Ainslie.   OBVV

And the truth wailing there like a red babe.   If I Could Only Live at the Pitch That Is near Madness.   Richard Eberhart.   FF; LiTM; MAT; MiAP; MoAB; PoPl

And the truth was shown, for the world to/read,/That men may follow and boys may lead.   The Prize of the Margaretta.   Will Carleton.   PAH

And the tuft of his nightcap lay red in the west.   Homecoming.   Anonymous. AnIV

And the tune steps out light-footed upon the air.   Back from the Paved Way. Robert D. FitzGerald.   PoAu 1-2

And the turntable turns on a ghost of the ghosts of the past.   Old Gramophone Records.   James Kirkup.   NYBP

And the Twin Sportsmen were begotten!   To the Liffey with the Swans. Oliver St.John Gogarty.   AnIL; OxBI

And the two feasts, where light and darkness meet.   Music of Colours: the Blossom Scattered.   Vernon Watkins.   ACV; LiTB

And the tyrant that treads on her laws,/May the first honest man knock him down, Sir.   The Battle of Navarino.   Anonymous.   CoMu

And the ultimate change that we fear feels a little less far.   Sidera Cadentia. Ford Madox Ford.   OBSP

...And the umpire's throat fought in the dust for a/song.   Hits and Runs. Carl Sandburg.   SD

And the upland plover whistling beyond/The wild-rose edges of the pond. The Clamdigger.   Dionis Coffin Riggs.   TAT

And the valley is lifted to the hill/Leaving a vast still wing of darkness. Apocalypse.   Jean Lipkin.   VWA

And the vanguard of the summer host will camp with us again.   One Morning When the Rain-Birds Call.   Lloyd Roberts.   CaP

And the vast world beneath hides him/from me!   Unreturning.   Elizabeth Stoddard   AA

And the vaults are stuffed with silver/That the farmer sweated for.   Banks of Marble.   Les Rice.   FSW

...And the very best songs that ever are sung/Are sung while the heart is bleeding.   Daw's Dinner.   Joyce Kilmer.   CAW

And the very last words poor Georgie said/Was "Nearer my God to Thee." Engine 143.   Anonymous.   FSW

And the vessel sinks beneath the tide.   The Inchcape Rock.   Robert Southey. PoPle

And the Viaticum of her survival/Guiding me from the further side of Death. She of the Garden.   Emile Verhaeren.   CAW

And the victorious trumpet-peal/Dies fitfully away.　The Fight at the Bridge. Thomas Babington, Lord Macaulay.　MaC

And the villagers ran to the sound of the drum.　The Sound of the Drum. *Anonymous.*　OBET

And the virtue of being aroused/sweetly and slowly by my love.　Sonnet, X: "When I catch sight of your fair head."　Louise Labé.　PBWP

And the voice in my dreaming ear melted away.　The Soldier's Dream. Thomas Campbell.　BeLS; FaPoR; GTBS; GTBS-P; HBV 1-2; MCCG; RoGo; TreFS

And the voice of intellectual joy we go on living by.　A Letter to David Campbell on the Birthday of W. B. Yeats, 1965.　A. D. Hope.　NAs

And the voices of old years.　The Band in the Pines.　John Esten Cooke. AA

And the voices of our approaching generations.　The Drill.　Harry Brown. WaaP

And the voracious worm upbraiding you.　Drops of Gall.　Gabriela (Lucila Godoy Alcayaga) Mistral.　BoWoP

And the vultures circle the sky at eventide.　The King of Ai.　Hyam Plutzik. LiTM; VWA

And the wailing walls of single cells?　Antonina.　Felix Mnthali.　WhB

...And the waitresses too,/flying breasts and limbs,/For a free Ireland.　In Memory of Those Murdered in the Dublin Massacre, May 1974.　Paul Durcan.　FaBoIP

And the walk home always seems longer.　Open Range.　Thomas Mitchell. AMV-81

...And the walking Virtue/that you are!　Mad Sonnet 1.　Michael McClure. PoM

And the warm quivering/of the red swan's breast.　Leda.　Hilda ("H. D.") Doolittle.　HBMV; InPo

And the warmed world is sick with my sweet pains.　May-Day.　Aaron Hill. NOEC

And the warmth began, and the chill.　In the Beginning.　Jenny Lind Porter. GoYe

And the warmth, the pulsing warmth/Of human hands....　The Touch of Human Hands.　Thomas Curtis Clark.　PoToHe

And the wash of her hair that fell about me like rain.　In a Wood Clearing. Wilson MacDonald.　CaP

And the washing stops going round.　The Washing Machine.　Jeffrey Davies. PCP

And the watchdog with a nervous bark/Halts an imaginary thief.　Pastoral. Robert Hillyer.　LOW

And the water preparing its descent/To the first dead.　The Herds.　William Stanley Merwin.　NaP; NYBP

And the water's bright in a still moonlight,/As I look across the sea.　Song– Across the Sea.　William Allingham.　IrPN

And the waterfall, thinning,/Was bright as glass.　And Then It Rained. Mark Van Doren.　BoNaP

And the watermelon too many seeds.　The Old Men.　Charles Reznikoff. DFF

And the waves flowed above him, and he died.　The Death of Cuchulain. William Butler Yeats.　GoTL

And the waves have spread/The sandy bed/That holds my Love from me. The Northern Star.　*Anonymous.*　HBV 1-2

And the waves still are singing.　Homage to Marcel Proust.　Thomas MacGreevy.　CIP

And the waves which precede you/Ripple and stir/The sands at my feet. Venus Transiens.　Amy Lowell.　PoA

And the way Simon meant it/was for 300 or maybe 400 years.　Toe'osh: A Laguna Coyote Story.　Leslie Marmon Silko.　CDW; STE; VoR

And the way they feels.　The Eel.　Ogden Nash.　NTCP

And the way up to the light still there for you to find.　The Phi Beta Kappa Poem.　Richmond Lattimore.　GLGT

And the weak old country doctor/Is entitled to a furlough for his brain and for his heart.　The Country Doctor.　Will Carleton.　BLPA

And the weather drives me pazzo.　In a Shuttered Room I Roast.　Dylan Thomas.　OBTV

And the West pours/red wine/on the white/banner/of silence.　Wandering Chorus.　B. (Eliezer Blum) Alquit.　VWA

And the wheel moves slowly round.　The Old Mill.　Thomas Dunn English AA

And the wheezing, old calliope is/The very tail end of the show!　The Circus Parade.　Olive Beaupre Miller.　SoPo; TiPo

And the whirling-mad/Butterflies!　O My Love the Pretty Towns.　Kenneth Patchen.　VGW

And the Whiskey Boys are drunk outside Philadelphia.　After the Industrial Revolution, All Things Happen at Once.　Robert Bly.　CoAP; ConAP

And the white bird, enchanted,/is flying through the world, across the sea. The Troika.　Louis Simpson.　NoAm; NOBA

And the white horsemen who passed have ended their wars.　Apocalypse and Resurrection.　John Bayliss.　EAS

And the white horses of the winter sea,/sings Harry.　Themes.　Denis Glover.　AnNZ

And the white ptarmigan treads in the snow among the low hills.　Winter Scene.　Marguerite Young.　NU

And the white Ruin rises o'er the Plain.　The Iliad.　Homer.　OBVE

And the white skull grins in the fern.　Through the Dark Aisles of the Wood. Henry Treece.　NeBP

And the whole deck put on its leaves again.　The Old Ships.　James Elroy Flecker.　AnFE; BrPo; EtS; EvOK; FaBoRV; GTBS; MoBrPo; MOS; MoVE; OBMV; PoPle; PoRA; RoGo; WHA

And the whole earth/a violin.　Migration.　Joseph Bruchac.　AMV-81

And the whole heart of man.　The Landscape of the Heart.　Geoffrey Grigson.　LiTB; WaP

...And the whole island's flower is the sound of/your light.　The Murmurers. Josephine Jacobsen.　GrPl

And the whole world give back the song/Which now the angels sing.　It Came Upon the Midnight Clear.　Edmund Hamilton Sears.　AH; HBVY; TreFT

And the whole yeare bee as Halcyons day:/Oh were Canidia gone.　A Satyre Entituled the Witch.　*Anonymous.*　CoMu

...And the wide main/Wooes us in ev'ry port?　A Nation's Wealth.　John Dyer.　OBEC

And the wild gazelle with her silver feet,/I'll give thee for a playmate sweet. The Burman Lover.　John C. Baker.　TrAS

And the wild is calling, calling...let us go.　The Call of the Wild.　Robert W. Service.　CaP

And the wild sheets. O to your bed!　Spring.　Paul Verlaine.　ErPo; PeHV

And the wildfire lights as Dewey fights on the/broad Manila Bay.　Dewey and His Men.　Wallace Rice.　PAH

And the willow limbs will dance the mazurka with the wind.　An Old Polish Lesson.　Deanna Louise Pickard.　AMV-81

And the wind,/as before, fingers perfectly/its derisive music.　January. William Carlos Williams.　MoAB; MoAmPo

And the wind blew across the wild moor.　When Poor Mary Came Wandering Home (with music).　*Anonymous.*　AS

...And the wind blows in the chestnuts,/Gently discerning.　Alcestis in Ely. Nicholas Moore.　NeBP

And the wind came on as before.　Wrack.　Irving Feldman.　AmPC

And the wind crept up his accordion stair,/And under his iron door. Cupidon.　William Jay Smith.　NePoEA

And the wind drove a cloud to seaward, and the sun/ began to shine.　The Revenge of Hamish.　Sidney Lanier.　AP; PoEL 1-5

And the wind goin'/Blow my/Blues away　Big Road Blues.　Tommy Johnson.　BluL

And the wind gonna rise up, baby, blow my blues away.　I Know You Rider. *Anonymous.*　FSW

And the wind, in one word,/offered itself to the earth.　The Bat.　Roberta Spear.　MAYP

And the wind in the willow tree.　Brook Song.　James Herbert Morse.　AA

And the wind is the voice of my heart.　Night and Wind.　Arthur Symons. BrPo

And the wind it blew,/Holy Jiminy! how it blew!　The Wind It Blew Up the Railroad Track (with music).　*Anonymous.*　AS

And the wind mourns always/at being alone.　The Sorceress.　Eugene Marais.　PeSA

And the wind roars and the stream roars/As the tramping dead move on. The Sounding Portage.　Annie Charlotte Dalton.　CaP

And the wind scatters all with its hands　The Young Girl and the Beach. Sophia de Mello Breyner Andresen.　WPOW

And the wind steals the rattle of his cry.　The Measure.　Patrick Lane. NOBC

And the wind that we perfume/Sings a tune that's worth the knowing.　To Ellen at the South.　Ralph Waldo Emerson.　LaNeLa

..., And the wind/Was banging the doors of the shed in the yard.　Esyllt. Glyn Jones.　DTC

And the winds be all asleep.　The Seven Fiddlers.　Sebastian Evans. OnMSP

And the winds the crying winds/Were full of butterflies, many colored.　The Death of Old Joe Yazzie.　Ron Rogers.　STE

...And the wings unfold that cannot make/Any but natural journeys while they wake.　For a Homecoming.　Julia Randall.　NMM

And the winter called it a dreadful crime.　Soft Snow.　William Blake. AtBAP; FF; SoSe; WeW

And the winter is over/And I'm rustling yet.　Tramp Miner's Song. *Anonymous.*　AmFP

And the wisdom to know the one from the other.　Prayer for Serenity. Reinhold Niebuhr.　GoTF

And the wisest and best take the world as it is.　Take the World as It Is (excerpt).　Charles Swain.　PoToHe

And the wisest know he was more than wise.　Columbus.　Annette Wynne. TiPo

And the wit of his sharp eye.　Crows.　William Witherup.　PCP; PoL

And the Wolf is dead in Arcady and the Dragon in the sea!　Awake! Awake! John Ruskin.　HBV 1-2

And the wolf rings out with a glittering shout,/To-whit, to-whit, to-whoo! 'Tis Sweet to Roam. *Anonymous.* NA

And the woman calling. The Voice. Thomas Hardy. BoLoP; CMoP; EnLoPo; GBL; GTBS-P; HAP; InPS; MoVE; NoAm; NoP; OAEL 1-2; OAEP; OBNC; PoEL 1-5; PoPle

And the woman made for man. Man, Man, Man. *Anonymous.* ALV; FaFP; LiTL; Prf

And the woman of love tarried forever. Visual Memory. Harry Martinson. LiTW

And the woman removed the tight curlers/once she lay small in death. Angel. Robin Skelton. NMP

And the woman's pregnancy Men tell and talk. Nia Francisco. STE

...And the woman takes her sadness/and thaws it before the flames. Twenty Below. R. A. D. Ford. CaP; NOBC

And the woman wrapped in beads/shines in her familiar bones. From the Ice Age. Barbara Bloom. AMV-81

And the women get happy over some snuff. West Texas. *Anonymous.* CoSo

And the women, the pedestrians, and the detective/Desert the champ. Elegy to Sports. David Shapiro. ANYP

And the wood, swollen with mushrooms, the dark wood. The Circle. Jean Garrigue. MoPo

And the woods wail like echoes from the sea. Hoarded Joy. Dante Gabriel Rossetti. MaVP

And the woods with happy laughter/Echo all the day. The Child-King. Morris Wintchevsky. TrJP

And the word I chose is "chill." Winter. *Anonymous.* KiLC

And the word still is Forward! along/the whole line. Kearny at Seven Pines. Edmund Clarence Stedman. AA; HBV 1-2; HBVY; MC; PAH

And the Word/Will be spoken/Again. Gathering the Sparks. Howard Schwartz. VWA

And the words become/Slower,/And slower/Each time. Walls of Ice. Janet Campbell Hale. STE

And the world and the day are grey and that is all. Passage Steamer. Louis MacNeice. MOS

And the world does not know how we are greeting. Loch Lomond. Lady John Scott. TreFS

And the world goes round for ever. A Capstan Chantey. Edwin James Brady. HBMV

And the world goes turning. "The world goes turning". George Dillon. AmLP

And the world is a braver world to-day. Heroes. Edna Dean Proctor. HBV 1-2

And the world is all at our feet! The Gipsy Trail. Rudyard Kipling. HBV 1-2; PoRA

And the world is newly freshly devoured. Three Poems, I. Rosario Castellános. BoWoP

And the world is their domain. Gifts. Chauncey R. Piety. PGD

And the world is waved away. The Calyx of the Oboe Breaks. Conrad Aiken. NYBP

And the world nods to him. Jim at the Corner. Eleanor Farjeon. SoPo; SUS

And the world of man are the last voids...pendulous,/unborn. Sea. Don Gordon. EtS

And the world's flowing fates in his own mould recast. Culture. Ralph Waldo Emerson. AmePo

And the world's ill,/sings Harry. Once the Days. Denis Glover. AnNZ

...And the world–what a sight!–/is a girandole, a ring of things–all lights. Girandole. Dorothy Donnelly. NYBP

And the world with music rang. Praise and Love. William Brighty ("Matthew Browne") Rands. OBVV

And the world would be richer one poet/the more. Proem. Madison Cawein. AA; BoNaP

And the worms crawl out and the worms crawl in/And your limbs drop off of you limb by limb. The Hearse Song (with music). *Anonymous.* AS

And the worn body you will carry as your own birthmark of his scream. Kin. Michael S. Harper. LCAP

And the worst friend and enemy is but Death. Peace. Rupert Brooke. MMM; OBWP; PoA; TreFT; WGRP

And the wreath to crown the singer/Shall be gathered from my grave. Credo. Saul Tchernichovsky. LiTW

And the yacht swings on her mooring like a slave. Squaring the Circle. Louis O. Coxe. NYBP

And the year hath not worn to March. In February. John Addington Symonds. YeAr

And the year's cruel turning on the merciless. Northwind. Gene Baro. NePoEA-2

...And the/years slip by, unheeding. The Dagger. Jorge Luis Borges. NYBP

And the Yellow God forever gazes down. The Green Eye of the Yellow God. J. Milton Hayes. BLPA; PaPo

And the youngest says, "Oh, Daddy, go again!/For such good meat from town." The Fox Walked Out, A vers. *Anonymous.* BFSS

And the youth at morning shine/Makes the vow he will not keep. Westward on the High-Hilled Plains. Alfred Edward Housman. MCCG

And the youth it was told by was Allen-a-Dale! Allen-a-Dale. Sir Walter Scott. StPo

And thee returning on thy silver wheels. Tithonus. Alfred, Lord Tennyson. CABA; CABL; DiPo; ForPo; HAP; LiTB; LoBV; MBW 1-2; NAWM 1-2; NOBE; NOBV; NoP; OAEL 1-2; OAEP; OBNC; PoEL 1-5; PoPle; PPP; TEP; VLP; WHA

And Thee, the Spirit of them all! To a Highland Girl. William Wordsworth. CABL; GoTF; LoBV; TreFT

And their bodies' gold...their bodies' gold... What Is Left? Istvan Vas. VWA

And their brood perish everlastingly. The Pity of It. Thomas Hardy. CMoP; LiTM; WaP

...And their "champ clos,' the spheres. The Archangel. George Gordon, Lord Byron. LoBV

And their deeds by our bards shall forever be sung. Fort McHenry. *Anonymous.* MC

And their dogs rejoice in the bones of all my brethren. Ruins of the City of Hay. Randolph Stow. CBAP; PoAu 1-2

And their experience count as mine. On an Invitation to the United States. Thomas Hardy. AWP; InPo

And their eyes are burning. Ballad: "O what is that sound which so thrills the ear." W. H. Auden. MoAB; ViBoPo

And their girl-friends lonely–we have our consolations. Longshore Intellectual. Sean Lucy. CIP

And their great Confederacy dissolves like the diorama of a dream. The Dynasts. Thomas Hardy. WaaP

And their inveterate habits, all forbid. The Task. William Cowper. TEP

And their lips fashioned jests as they beat from their breasts/The dust of the Overland Trail. The Dust of the Overland Trail. James Barton Adams. PoOW

And their lips set to ignite one future after another. The Head Is a Paltry Matter. Pier Giorgio Di Cicco. NOBC

And their love be enduring. Song for a Country Wedding. William Jay Smith. GrPl

And their masters who are equally convinced of being/right/Beat them and hear nothing. Donkeys. Edward Field. BoAnP

And their mutual terrors heal/Within our married miracle. The Trance. Stephen Spender. ChMP; CoBMV

And their muzzles meet/On the very tuft for which he contends. The Shadow of Himself. William Renton. NOBV

And their names are engraven on honor's/bright crest. The Battle of Lovell's Pond. Henry Wadsworth Longfellow. PAH

And their opposable thumbs. The Hot Day and Human Nature. Gordon Johnston. AMV-81

...And their passion is equalled by/nothing. The Songs of Bilitis. Pierre Louys. UnTE

And their passionate hearts are quiet and cold/In the early, early days. The Early Days. Basil Dowling. AnNZ

And their portion–the wordless/permanence. Blessed... Soné. TrJP

And their snuff-laden breath blowing lightly over me in my/first sleep. Frau Bauman, Frau Schmidt, and Frau Schwartze. Theodore Roethke. CoAP; MoAB; NePoAm; NoAm; NOBA; NYBP; SaC; TAP

And their son/newborn/was the apple of his eye. Divorce. Siv Widerberg. CTBA

And their sons without one syllable of their secret treasure. For the Family of Cuchonnacht O Dalaigh. Daibhi O Bruadair. NOBI

And their terrible eyes are watching you. The Lions of Fire Shall Have Their Hunting. Kenneth Patchen. VGW

And their tongues are teasing oil from whales. The Lady in Kicking Horse Reservoir. Richard Hugo. CoAP; LCAP; NoP

...And their unshifting feet rooted/forever in the mountain's heart. In Praise of Ben Avon. Brenda G. Macrow. PoSH

And their vile carcases now left unburied.... The House of Richesse. Edmund Spenser. CH

And their white teeth sweeter than cucumbers. Day of These Days. Laurie Lee. AtBAP; BoNaP; MoVE

And their wings are split silver as they pass. Wings at Dawn. Joseph Auslander. HBMV

And theirs the dimple and the lightsome whim. Of Rama. Herman Melville. AnFE; LiTA

And theis conceiptes, digest by thoughts retire,/are turned into aprill showers of teares. Sonnet XV. William Alabaster. AnAnS 1

And them can ride as has no legs/On the Oxford and Hampton Railway. The Oxford and Hampton Railway. *Anonymous.* OBET

And them cold fishy females/With long green weeds for hair.' Cape Horn Gospel–I. John Masefield. StPo

...And themselves to go down in the first wave. Epigram for the Dead at Tegea. *Anonymous.* WaaP

And then a glad victory song may be sung. The Old Filthy Beer Pail.
Katie V. Hall. PeD

And then a Voice,–"Who next that enter-/eth?" The Doors. Lloyd Mifflin.
AA

And then, alack! to end the cruel game/Are broiled on love's quick flame.
The Angler. Bhartrihari. LiTW

And then alone, amid the beaming/Of love's stars, thou'lt meet her/In eastern
sky. Dirge: "If thou wilt ease thy heart." Thomas Lovell Beddoes. EG

And then, amazed with grief, laugh out thine eyes. Come from Thy Palace.
Thomas Randolph. OBSP

And then an awful leisure was,/Our faith to regulate. The Last Night that
She Lived. Emily Dickinson. AmP; AnFE; APA; BoWoP; CMoP;
CoAnAm; ExPo; ForPo; LiTA; MAmP; NePA; OxBA; PoEL 1-5; QFR;
SOTW

And then and how and all around we think and found that it is time to/cry
she and I. Before the Flowers of Friendship Faded Faded, XXI.
Gertrude Stein. NMM; PeHV

And then (and only then) did Aaron laugh. Aaron Stark. Edwin Arlington
Robinson. MoAB; MoAmPo

And then–and then–I'll bless/This twain that gives me happiness! Youth and
Age. George Arnold. HBV 1-2

And then another cried,"More beer, more beer." To the Memory of Yale
College. Howard Phelps (Phelps Putnam) Putnam. AnAmPo

And then appeal to the ground with their wings. Chickens the Weasel Killed.
William Stafford. NaP

And then, as usual, you'll betray me. This White and Slender Body.
Heinrich Heine. UnTE

And then at cards we better shall agree. A Maiden's Denial. Anonymous.
ErPo

And then, at least, my heart can ne'er be moved. Stanzas to the Po.
George Gordon, Lord Byron. ERoP 1-2; OAEL 1-2

And then, at the risk of breaking his neck,/Turned somersaults home to tea.
His Mother-in-Law. Walter Parke. FiBHP

And then bargain with the winde/To discharge what is behinde. L'Envoy.
George Herbert. AnAnS 1

And then be sure for aye you shall enjoy/Joyes everlasting, Everlasting joy.
The Porch. Philip Pain. SCAP

And then behind us the huge gate swung open. The Gate. Edwin Muir.
CMoP; LiTM

And then, belike, your dad will hear/An ash-stick tapping on his door.
Come Michaelmas. A. Newberry Choyce. HBMV

And then both skedaddled from Eden. Limerick: "There was a dear lady of
Eden." Anonymous. LiBL; NA

And then brought her back as his mistress. Familiarity Breeds Indifference.
Martial (Marcus Valerius Martialis). UnTE

...And then disappear into nowhere. Merce Cunningham and the Birds.
Lisel Mueller. GrPl

And then drifted away. Twelfth Night. Elizabeth Jane Coatsworth.
ChBR

And then exactly matched would be/Your house and hospitality. On a
Certain Lord Giving Some Thousand Pounds for a Horse. David Garrick.
PV

And then exit all/STAGE RIGHT How I'd Have It. John Stone.
AMV-81

And then?–Farewell, we shall meet again! A Mile with Me. Henry Van
Dyke. BLPA; FPL

And then fly back to swing on a bough,/Luriana, Lurilee. Luriana, Lurilee.
Charles Elton. PoPle

And then forever to be gone. The Falling Star. Sara Teasdale. BrR;
MoShBr; OBCA; SoPo; SUS; TiPo

...And then go home, alive,/to sleep the sleep of the awake. Graveyard by
the Sea. Thomas Lux. LCAP

...And then go off and spend the evening at the Club. The Evening Out.
Ogden Nash. MoAmPo

And then goes climbing back! Old Santa Is An Active Man. Lois Lenski.
ChBR

And then great Charles most happily will reign. The Tune to the Devonshire
Cant. John Ayloffe. APAS

And then hangs curtains up to shut it out. Essay on Man. Anonymous.
PoToHe

And then he bought a cradle. Jemmy Dawson. Anonymous. OxNR

And then he flies away. The Cuckoo Comes in April. Anonymous. OxNR

And then he knew he knew himself, grew cold. Antarctica. R. A. Simpson.
CBAP

And then he loved her very well. Peter. Anonymous. OxNR

And then he may laugh at the pigs. The Pigs. Jane Taylor. FM

And then he mizzled. On a Royal Demise. Thomas Hood. FiBHP; PV

And then he wanders among strangers all he wants. The Apple Trees at
Olema. Robert Hass. NPGG

And then he whipped them back again. Doctor Faustus. Anonymous.
GLGT

And then her red blood down did flow. Th Gypsy Countess. Anonymous.
OBET

And then his bier took him. On an Old Toper Buried in Durham
Churchyard, England. Anonymous. ShM

And then his letter seals. A Metrical Index to the Bible. Josiah Chorley.
FaBoUs

And then his voice came drifting back: "My name is Billy the Kid." Pizen
Pete's Mistake. Merrill Honey. BPAW

And then I arrived at the powerful green hill. Then I Saw What the Calling
Was. Muriel Rukeyser. FaBoWP

And then I call them in to eat. Setting the Table. Dorothy Aldis. TiPo

And then I come away– She sweeps with many-colored brooms. Emily
Dickinson. SaC

And then I cried/and made his collar wet. When My Dog Died. Freya
Littledale. NTCP

And then I'd do it again. If I Had a Firecracker. Shel Silverstein. PoSC

And then I'd hammer his old hide/Until his bones did break. An Old Man
He Courted Me. Anonymous. OBET

And then I'd hie me home! Being Gypsy. Barbara Young. SoPo

And then I'd open wide the cage, and set the singer free. People Buy a Lot
of Things. Annette Wynne. SoPo

And then I feel quite sure she'd answer Yes. Sonnet: Of Becchina, the
Shoemaker's Daughter. Cecco da Siena Angiolieri. AWP

And then I hung my head and cried. The Ludlow Massacre. Woody
Guthrie. FSW

And then I knew I had no hope at all. The Phallic Symbol. Nicholas
Moore. NeBP

And then I'll make ballads in Robin/Hood's bower,/And sing em in merry
Sherwood. Robin Hood's Birth, Breeding, Valor, and Marriage.
Anonymous. ESPB

And then I'll see my dearie. Cam' Ye By. Anonymous. AtBAP; GBP

And then I'll study how to die.' As You Like It. William Shakespeare.
CTC

And then I'll thank ye for the gift,/As something worth the giving.
Proposals for Building a Cottage. John Clare. OBRV

–And then I needs must sing. Inspirations. William James Dawson.
WGRP

And then I pressed on eye and cheek/The sightless hinges of eternity/That
make the whole world crea Imagining How It Would Be to Be Dead.
Richard Eberhart. LiTA

And then I saw no more the sun,/And lost were life and love. Eurydice.
Francis William Bourdillon. HBV 1-2

And then I saw through the swirling. The Gap in the Cedar. Roy Scheele.
Psk; SM

And then I shall blow on your flute.' Limerick: "Young Frederick the great
was a beaut." Anonymous. PeHV

And then I shivered and gave a shake,/Opened my eyes, and was wide awake.
The Midnight Court. Bryan Merryman. AnIL; KiLC

And then I smiled, and fell. The Underground Stream. James Dickey.
NOBA

And then I start getting this feeling of exaltation. A Blessing in Disguise.
John Ashbery. ANYP; PoM

And then I stopped: my father's eyes were gray. Fall Journey. William
Stafford. NaP; Str

...And then I will die either of laughing or of a/clean cut throat. And Three
Hundred and Sixty-Six in Leap Year. Ogden Nash. NePA

And then I woke–to find that I was well. Vita Benefica. Alice Wellington
Rollins. AA

And then is best, Revertere. Revertere. Anonymous. PBBP

...And then it all/Is blurred by the insistent tears! Armistice. Charles
Buxton Going. BPAW

And then it has no need for ringing,/For your voice takes its place. Poet to
His Love. Maxwell Bodenheim. PoPl

And then it's all up with the fly. The Gentle Anarchist. James Brunton
Stephens. NOAV

And then it shadows, and he darts,/With head hung, to the dormitory.
Haskell. Witter ("Emanuel Morgan") Bynner. GLGT

And then it too will know. South of the Great Sea. Anonymous. OLR

And then lead on again the universe? Crocus. Alfred Kreymborg.
HBMV

And then leave me to the mercy/Of the forest bees? Carrefour. Amy
Lowell. BoWoP; MoLP

And then lie down to rest. The Pine of Whiting Wood. John P. Sjolander.
BPAW

...And then/like losers in a poker game will cast/their own lines far, far out.
With Cindy at Vallecito. Walter McDonald. WOLT

And then moves on. Fog. Carl Sandburg. AP; FaBV; FaFP; FPL;
HBMV; HeIP; InPK; LaNeLa; MCCG; MoAB; MoAmPo; OBCA; PoPl;
SoPo; SoSe; SUS; TAP; TiPo

And then my eye rejoyce, in that I have/Thy scorne, to be a mourner at my
grave. To His Mistresse on Her Scorne. Thomas Beedome. CavP

And then my heart with pleasure fills,/And dances with the daffodils. I Wandered Lonely as a Cloud. William Wordsworth. AtBAP; BoNaP; DiPo; ERoP 1-2; ExPo; FaBoPP; HBV 1-2; HBVY; InPK; InPS; LoBV; MasP; MBW 1-2; NoP; OAEL 1-2; OAEP; OBRV; PoPl; PoRA; RoGo; SpRo; SUS; TEP; UnPo; ViBoPo; WHA

And then my senses, which too soon grow lame,/exiled from you, must go their homeless ways. You, Neighbor God. Rainer Maria Rilke. MoRP

And then my troubles oh they did begin. Love It Is Pleasing. *Anonymous.* OBET

And then no doubt your Mistresses will pay you for it soundly./With hey ho, hey, derry derry down;. Room for a Jovial Tinker: Old Brass to Mend. *Anonymous.* CoMu; OxBB

And then not Truth as seen–but as seen from. Country Walk. Geoffrey Taylor. OxBI

And then obscured, while the red blushes come. Spectrum. William Dickey. ELU

And then oh baby we loved After the Quarrel. Barbara Gibson. FF

And then–Oh, then I'll be one! The Superstitious Ghost. Arthur Guiterman. ShM

And then one day,/never look again. Strange. Kirby Doyle. NeAP

And then one Drop of Balsam will suffice. The Penitent. Jeremy Taylor. OBS; OxBoCh

And then, perhaps, regret the past,/When sorrow comes too late. Think before You Act. Mary Elliott. HBVY

And then prepare to kiss. Now come, my boon companions. Thomas Randolph. EG

And then return to where you wish and never want for more. The San Francisco Company. Isaac W. Baker. AmFP

And then returned, having marched thrice,/Into the inner room, from whence they first did rise. The Faerie Queene. Edmund Spenser. OBSC

And then rides back to shave again. Commuter. E. B. White. FaBoCo; NLV; PV; TreFT

And then rises. See him: he is a child again. In the Forest. Pinhas Sadeh. VWA

And then run down in rivers to the sea of dreams The Noonday April Sun. George Love. IDB; NNP

And then rush brightly through the summer air. Sailing after Lunch. Wallace Stevens. MoPo

And then's the end of all her mirth. The Gods of the Earth Beneath. Edmund Charles Blunden. BrPo

And then say brother–then say amn! The Soul of Man. Dora Read Goodale. AA

...And then shall I sound my heart-easing/hallelujah. The Messiah-Blower. Paul Goodman. FAZ

And then shall know both devil and man,/what I was and what I am. I Have Labored Sore. *Anonymous.* WeW

And then she laughed. Fossils. James Stephens. OnYI

And then she may walk out in two. Betty Blue. *Anonymous.* OxNR

And then she shall be a true lover of mine. Scarborough Fair. *Anonymous.* BLSo; FSW; OxBoLi

And then softly sank to silence–silence kept for evermore. The Legend of the Organ-Builder. Julia Caroline Ripley Dorr. BeLS; BLPA; FaBoBe

And then that last and shortest... To His Watch. Gerard Manley Hopkins. MoAB; MoBrPo

And then the awful, truthful catching up. Surprise. Harold Witt. AMV-81

And then the barnacles fastened on. The Critics. Theodore Spencer. NYBP

And then the blind beggar dropped five thousand more. The Blind Beggar. *Anonymous.* AmFP

And then the cat got up and started walking. Dog Body and Cat Mind. Jenny Joseph. BrRo

And then the child of future years/Shall hear what Katy did. To an Insect. Oliver Wendell Holmes. HBV 1-2; HBVY; TreF

And then the clock collected in the tower/Its strength, and struck. Eight O'Clock. Alfred Edward Housman. BrPo; CABA; CMoP; ExPo; InPK; InPo; LoBV; MoAB; MoBrPo; NoAm; NoP; OBSP; SoSe; TrGrPo

And then the golden lamps/the while/slowly filtering– On the Fine Arts Garden, Cleveland. Russell Atkins. PoBA

And then the Greeks, and Trojans both, gave up their horse/and darts. The Iliad. Homer. OBS

...And then the guns sound on another hill. The Contours of Fixation. Weldon Kees. NaP

And then the heart replies. When Summer's End Is Nighing. Alfred Edward Housman. MoVE

And then the hens–quite calmly–pecked him dead. Hens. Alden Nowlan. PoL

And then the hogs moved on once more/Upon their screaming way. Chicago Idyll. E. Merrill Root. AnAmPo

And then the individual/identity/clearing The Bare Tree/Alternate. Larry Eigner. PoM

And then the lighting of the lamps. Preludes. Thomas Stearns Eliot. AnAmPo; ExPo; FaBoMo; NAMP; TwCP

And then the minute after and the minute after the minute/after. River in Spate. Louis MacNeice. FaBoIP

And then the moon's white circle, faint and thin/Looked steady on the earth– there is no sin,. Evening. James Stephens. MoBrPo

And then the nightingale replies. Peacock and Nightingale. Robert Finch. OBCV

And then the noiseless skid/of beasts or angels skating down/into their nameless, cotton graves. V.D. Clinic. Adrien Stoutenburg. GP

And then the party ended/In jolly "hands around." October's Party. George Cooper. BrR; HBV 1-2; HBVY; PoLf; SiSoSe

And then the silence of the dead/Is held within the listening wood. Winter Sketch. Arthur Stanley Bourinot. CaP

And then the silent beaches. Two Poems. Robert J. Abrams. NNP

And then the small grass covers him. Long Feud. Louis Untermeyer. AnAmPo; APA; MoAmPo

And then!/The TAIL! On Rears. Mary Hedin. PH

And then the waking to an everlasting Love. The Kiss of God. G. Anketall "Woodbine Willie" Studdert-Kennedy. BLRP

And then–the Wharf is still! Where Ships of Purple–Gently Toss. Emily Dickinson. AmP

And then the will, and then the consciousness. An Old Atheist Pauses by the Sea. Thomas Kinsella. ELU

And then the windows failed, and then/I could not see to see. Dying. Emily Dickinson. MAPA

And then, then we shall reap,/singing, brothers, singing. Weeping and Singing. Cesar Tiempo. MoRP

And then there are always–your own two feet. There Are So Many Ways of Going Places. Leslie Thompson. SoPo

And then there comes the shutting of a door. Your Body Is Stars. Stephen Spender. FaBoTw; MoLP

...And then there was a bird. There Are Things to Be Said. Cid Corman. VGW

"And then/There wasn't any riot any more." An Old Woman Remembers. Sterling A. Brown. CNA; PoBA

And then they both shall grow together. Red, and White Roses. Thomas Carew. AnAnS 2

And then they got married, this young man and maid. The Silk Merchant's Daughter. *Anonymous.* OBSS

And then they have their answer home. The Quip. George Herbert. AnFE; JCP; LiTB; OAEP; OBS; OxBoCh; SeCP; SeCV 1-2

And then they heated Florence with old Savonarola. Merry Old Souls (excerpt). Morris Bishop. DBV

And then they shot me full of nothing. Comanche. Gary Gildner. PH

And then they sung a psalm. The Auld Seceder Cat. *Anonymous.* FaBoCh; FaBoCo

And then think how immortal anger is. Achilles. Philip Corwin. AMV-80

And then this day my life shall date. Easter. George Herbert. BoC; OBEV; TRV

And then this poor maid's heart did break. She's Like the Swallow. *Anonymous.* FSW

And then thou may'st possess Felicity. The Preparative. Thomas Traherne. PoEL 1-5

And then, to expiate our self-deceit,/Sent forth in honesty's ill rags. The Forgiven Past. Laura Riding. NoAm; PBWP

And then to fall like Phaeton. Spoken Extempore. John Wilmot, Earl of Rochester. SeCePo

And then–/to give way. Yielding. Shellie Keir Robbins. AMV-80

And then to go at once to bed. Mrs. Jaypher on Lemons. Edward Lear. FaBoNo

And then to hear a dead man chatter/Is enough to drive one mad. Maud. Alfred, Lord Tennyson. SyP

And then to kill, when strength and hope had fled. The Quarry. Juan Boscan. LiTW

And then turned homeward meditating much/About the single transferable vote. The Everlasting Mercy (parody). J. C. Squire. BXAP

...And/then, until now, she disappeared. We Were in the 8th Grade. John Berryman. GLGT

And then upbraids a Perfectness/That situates so far– Perception of an Object Costs. Emily Dickinson. MAmP; NOBA

...And then/very gently it began to rain. The Cows at Night. Hayden Carruth. SV

And then we all just naked again. Clothes Make the Man. Jack Conway. NLV

And then we did firk it, caper and jerk it/Under the greenwood tree. Under the Greenwood Tree. *Anonymous.* GBP

And then we die, in earnest, not in jest. What Is Our Life? Sir Walter Ralegh. EBEV; EnRePo; ForPo; MePo; NIP; OBSP; SiPS

And then we knelt like animals/To the body of this death, and ate. The Feast. David Wagoner. NePoEA-2

And then we laugh, with shadows in our eyes.   Nocturne of Remembered Spring.   Conrad Aiken.   HBMV

And then we may boast of our ships and their crews.   The Unseaworthy Ship. *Anonymous.*   OBSS

...And then we went to church.   Shaving.   Charles David Wright.   AMV-81

And then with patience bid me bear my fire.   Astrophel and Stella, LVI.   Sir Philip Sidney.   AAS; SiPS

...And then, would you recognize me?   Change of Address.   Kathleen Fraser.   NYBP

And then, y know, boys will be boys, and/hosses—well, hosses is hosses!   Chiquita.   Bret (Francis Bret Harte) Harte.   AA; BPAW

And then you do   Like Musical Instruments.   Tom Clark.   PPoe

And then you fall into my heart.   My Angel.   Philip Levine.   AMV-81

And then you keep your Christmas right.   The True Christmas.   Henry Vaughan.   SBVL

–And then you suddenly cried, and turned/away.   The Hill.   Rupert Brooke.   EnLit; GTBS; HBV 1-2; LiTL; MoBrPo; MoLP; OxBTC; ViBoPo

And then you will go.   Practicing.   Sonia Gernes.   AMV-80

And then you will rue it, as sure as you're born.   Army Bugle Calls: Stable Call.   *Anonymous.*   TreF

And ther-with-al he broghte us out of town.   The Canterbury Tales: A Miller.   Geoffrey Chaucer.   TrGrPo

And there a clump of houses with a/church.   The Onset.   Robert Frost.   AmP; AnNE; CMoP; CoBMV; MoAB; MoAmPo; OxBA; PPP

And there a new nest nearly made/Proclaims the winter by.   Crows in Spring.   John Clare.   EnRP

And there abide the Lord beside, the Father of us all.   Samuel Allen. *Anonymous.*   AmFP

And there and then twelve of their noblest died/Among their spears and chariots.   The Iliad.   Homer.   OBVE

And there are banners where I ride!   Shall I Go Bound and You Go Free?   Padraic Colum.   AnFE

...And there are/Many desperate arms about us and the things we know.   The Character of Love Seen as a Search for the Lost.   Kenneth Patchen.   NaP; VGW

And there are many gods in this green tree.   Irrigation.   Susan Tichy.   MAYP

And there are no pimples encircling her dimples/As ever, as yet, I have seen.   A Pretty Girl.   J. Gordon Coogler.   OBAL

...And there are no words.   Someone Sits at the Harp.   Jon Lang.   AMV-81

And there are none to show to you.   Four Wrens.   *Anonymous.*   OxNR

And there are so many things/a field can wait for when/predators wait at her edge.   Like a Field Waiting.   Raquel Chalfi.   VWA

And there are stars, but none of you, to spare.   Sunflower Sonnet Number Two.   June Jordan.   SM

And there, as in predestined grief's retreat,/Within Thy heart, as in its nest, did lie!   The Calling.   Luis Felipe Contardo.   CAW

And there beside the railroad bridge/I saw the Wandering Jew.   The Scissors-Grinder.   Vachel Lindsay.   MAPA

And there bid him rest!   Is My Lover on the Sea?   Barry (Bryan Waller Procter) Cornwall.   EtS

And there comes an answer: I am the one you love/and always shall love.   The Land That Is Not.   Edith Sodergran.   HW

And there'd be no more jokes in Music-halls/To mock the riddled corpses round Bapaume.   Blighters.   Siegfried Sassoon.   CMoP; FaBoTw; MMM; MoVE; NoAm; OBSP

And there found death, another death than hers.   Sir Eggnogg (parody).   Bayard Taylor.   BXAP

And there he cut his nose off/And flung it at the people.   There Was a Man and He Was Mad.   *Anonymous.*   GBP

And there he dwelleth, our Saviour.   Covetousness.   Peter Idley.   OxBChV

And there he kept her very well.   Peter, Peter, Pumpkin Eater.   Mother Goose.   FaBoBe; FaFP; HBV 1-2; HBVY; SoPo; TiPo

And there he sleeps beneath the sod by Antietam's rippling wave.   The Battle of Antietam Creek.   *Anonymous.*   AmFP

And there his papa's lantern, a light the boy can locate.   Floating Houses.   David Wojahn.   SM

And there I found myself more truly and more strange.   Sur Ma Guzzla Gracile.   Wallace Stevens.   PoA

And there I hear the flutes of peace,/Being a prophet and a fool.   Prophet and Fool.   Louis Golding.   HBMV

And there I met another man/Whose hat was in his hand.   Ballad: "I put my hat upon my head."   Samuel Johnson.   NOBL

And there I write Thy praise.   O How I Love Thy Law.   Isaac Watts.   STF

And there in front of me a life/would open.   A Door.   William Stanley Merwin.   CAPP

And there in secret sadness inly mourned.   The Goldfinches.   Richard Jago.   PBBP

And there in the tranquil solitude/I find my soul,–and God.   Refuge.   Lew Sarett.   HBMV

And there in the woods these bold fellows stood,/While this little babe was baptized.   Robin Hood and Little John.   *Anonymous.*   AmFP; BaBo; ViBoFo

And there in virtuous pleasure in Hymen's chains were bound.   The 'Prentice Boy.   *Anonymous.*   AmFP

And there is a certain amount of horror   Alive or Not.   Al Purdy.   NOBC

And there is a road to buried dreams/from a place beyond words.   Of Myself.   Leah Goldberg.   BoWoP

And there is no goal to reach.   The Comet.   Emil Makai.   VWA

And there is no God for Levin/but the quietness of his house.   Mashkin Hill.   Louis Simpson.   SaC

And there is no night in Creede.   Creede.   Cy Warman.   BPAW; PoOW

And there is no object so soft but it makes a hub for the wheeled/universe.   A Hub for the Universe.   Walt Whitman.   FaFP

And there is no sign of the wind.   Fear.   Charles Simic.   HaCAP

And there is no worry in a hurry.   Afterwards (excerpt).   Gertrude Stein.   LOW

And there is none so fit to keep a watch and keep/Unwearied eyes upon those horrible green birds.   On a Picture of a Black Centaur by Edmund Dulac.   William Butler Yeats.   SyP

And there is not a government in the world that wants to abolish/the factory.   The Chilean Elegies: 5. The Interior.   Tom Wayman.   NOBC

And there is nothing else.   The Black Angel.   Henri Coulette.   CoAP; NYBP

And there is nothing left remarkable/Beneath the visiting moon.   Antony and Cleopatra.   William Shakespeare.   FiP

And there is room only for one man in this house.   Abortion.   Florence Anthony ("Ai").   BoWoP

And there is something there that sounds so fair, it's a grand old name!   Mary's a Grand Old Name.   George M. Cohan.   BLSo; FSN; GoTF

And there is the trouble with pub-/licity!   Diogenes.   Morris Bishop.   NLV

And there lies gude Sir Patrick Spens/Wi' the Scots lords at his feet!   The Ballad of Sir Patrick Spens.   *Anonymous.*   EtS; RoGo

And there'll be forty lines not yet begun.   Limitations.   Siegfried Sassoon.   MoBrPo

And there may be many others, but they haven't been/discarvard.   The Elements.   Tom Lehrer.   FaBoUs

And there meet Mary and my Jane.   Newberry (Lonesome Dove). *Anonymous.*   AmFP

And there, my babe, we'll live for aye.   Her Eyes Are Wild.   William Wordsworth.   NAs

And there my love will live.   No Single Hour Can Stand for Naught.   John Clare.   OBNC

And there, O death, thy sting.   The Great Misgiving.   William Watson.   HBV 1-2; OBVV

And there, O my Father,/Be what thou art?   Come Down.   George Macdonald.   TrPWD

And there on the blue edge of the world/The young sun looked me in the eyes.   Tree-Sleeping.   Robert P. Tristram Coffin.   LOW

And there our thoughts are dull enough, God knows!   Not Such Your Burden.   Agathias.   AWP

And there repugnant it will shine.   Table Manners for the Hostess (excerpt).   Jean de Meung.   EnLi 1-2

And there's a cross for me.   Amazing Grace.   John Newton.   BLSo; FSW

And there's a poisonous cloud as dark as jet/Pouring from heaven.   The Seven Days of the Sun (excerpt).   Walter James Turner.   OBMV

And there's an end of bully.   The Bully.   John Wilmot, Earl of Rochester.   CBEP; InvP

And there's an end of your headache.   Hangover Cure.   Alexis.   FaBoUs

And there's as much corn in each o them/As they can grind in a year.   Willie O Winsbury.   *Anonymous.*   BaBo; ESPB

And there's desolation like a mountain.   On My Wandering Flute.   Abraham Sutzkever.   VWA

And there's how you AD-DRESS A CAT.   The Ad-dressing of Cats.   Thomas Stearns Eliot.   FM

And there's Joan, like Joan.   Girls' Names.   Eleanor Farjeon.   BiCB; SUS; TiPo

And there's John, like John.   Boys' Names.   Eleanor Farjeon.   BiCB; SUS; TiPo

And there's joy and peace for all,/In the Commonwealth of Toil that is to be.   The Commonwealth of Toil.   Ralph Chaplin.   FSW

And there's my song all.   My Little Cow.   *Anonymous.*   OxNR

And there's no doing anything about it.   The Rum Tum Tugger.   Thomas Stearns Eliot.   EvOK; FaBoNo; FaBV

And there's no getting around it, I am a bastard.   Oedipus at San Francisco.   Donald Finkel.   CoPo

And there's no one left to kiss me now/Over my heavy heart.   The Sailor's Sweetheart.   Duncan Campbell Scott.   PeCV

And there's nothing more to say.   Candida.   Patrick Kavanagh.   NAs

And there's nought but joy in my ain land at the comin' o' the Spring!   The Comin' o' the Spring.   Lady John Scott.   BSV

And there's the price of sinning–and I'll pay.' This Is the Horror That, Night after Night. Gerald Gould. OxBTC

And there's the trick simplicity has to win. So Graven. Josephine Miles. NoAm

And there's wrath in my swelling tide. The Song of the Flume. Anna M. Fitch. BPAW

And there's your sure-fire Western Thriller. Western Formula. *Anonymous.* PoOW

And there the king is but as the beggar. Running to Paradise. William Butler Yeats. BoLiVe; LOW; OxBoLi

And there, the Matter ends– I Read My Sentence–Steadily. Emily Dickinson. AmePo; NePA; NoAm; QFR

And there the palm tree grows in its mirror, high/in the sky's center. Coconut. Mario Satz. VWA

And there, the prize, in freedom rest and roam? The Finder Found. Edwin Muir. PoA

And there the traitor Helmut lives/A communist today. The Ballad of Helmut Franze. Jerome Sala. APU

And there they buried bold Robin Hood,/Within the fair Kirkleys. Robin Hood's Death. *Anonymous.* ESPB; OBET; TrGrPo

And there they got a Roundhead. The Character of a Roundhead. *Anonymous.* FaBoPV

And there they have buried false Sir John,/For fear he should be seen. Lady Isabel and the Elf-Knight (B vers.). *Anonymous.* BaBo

And there they lived–till the rain was over. The Haymow. Luella Markley Mockett. BrR

And there they locked in a true-lover's knot,/For true lovers to admire.] Barbara Allen. *Anonymous.* OBET; ViBoFo

And there they tied a true lover's knot,/And the rose ran round the briar. Earl Brand (B vers.). *Anonymous.* BaBo

And there this couple were lawfully married,/Whe'r their parents were willing or no. William Hall. *Anonymous.* AmFP; BFSS

And there was His blessing given. The Only One. Jo Gardner. BePJ

And there was no blood left/in my right hand. Isaac. Amir Gilboa. VWA

And there was no more use for him to be sayin'/"Higher!" Higher. *Anonymous.* FiBHP

...And there was nothing. The Dead. Louis Dudek. NOBC

And there was nothing left in the room/but mercy. Saxophonetyx. Cyn Zarco. APU; BrSi

And there was the old scolding of the birds. The Wakers. John Freeman. HBMV

And there we sit in blissful calm,/Quietly sweating palm to palm. Frascati's. Aldous Huxley. InPo; ViBoPo

And there we two stood, hands clasped; I and she! Once at Swanage. Thomas Hardy. FaBoPP

And there were many in the sky/Who laughed at this thing. God Fashioned the Ship of the World Carefully. Stephen Crane. MOS

And there, wholly dark, the pot/gay with rough moss. The Pot of Flowers. William Carlos Williams. QFR

And there wish one and all good-night. Interlude. Walter Savage Landor. GTBS-P

And there with her, his bride so true,/Now buried lies her lover too. Medelwold and Sidselille. *Anonymous.* BaBo

And there with humble sweets contents her industry. The Praise of Pindar in Imitation of Horace His Second Ode, Book 4. Abraham Cowley. OAEL 1-2

And there withal upon the hollow tree/With strained voice again thus crieth he: Psalm VI. Sir Thomas Wyatt. FCP

And there ye saw your picter. How Daur Ye Call Me Owlet Face. Robert Burns. PoPle

And there you'll burn both early and late.' The Cruel Mother. *Anonymous.* OBET

And therefore, bid I you,/And every one,/Adieu. Ah Me! Am I the Swaine. George Wither. OBS

And therefore I commend you back to Him/Whose love your love's capacity can fill. Monna Innominata. Christina Georgina Rossetti. VLP

And therefore I've sent her a couple of Quacks. Sent to a Patient, with the Present of a Couple of Ducks. Edward Jenner. FaBoUs

And therefore is his even/On Christe's own day. Saint Stephen and King Herod. *Anonymous.* BoLiVe; OxBM; OxBoCh; OxBoLi; TrGrPo

And therefore is my heart so sad. The Deserted Home. Kuno Meyer. OxBI

And therefore, my sweet Mary, this still nook,/With all its beeches, we have named from you! To M.H. William Wordsworth. EiCP

And, therefore, shalt thou be an honoured name! Tribute to the Memory of the Same Dog. William Wordsworth. FM

And therefore thou must learn fast/If thou wouldst be bishop when he is past. Symon's Lesson of Wisdom for All Manner of Children... *Anonymous.* OxBChV

And therefore vulgar authors name/Th'one Good, the other Evil Fame. Hudibras. Samuel (1612-80) Butler. OBSV

And therefore when her Aunt returned,/Matilda, and the House, were Burned. Matilda. Hilaire Belloc. CenHV; FaBoCh; LoGBV

And therewithal the kindly heat gan quench/And into wind the life forthwith resolve. The Aeneid. Virgil (Publius Vergilius Maro). FCP; NAWM 1-2; PoEL 1-5; ViBoPo

And therfor is his evyn/On Crystes owyn day. A Carol for Saint Stephen's Day. *Anonymous* CH

And therwith endeth Christmas. Sing We Yule. *Anonymous.* MeEL

And these, at least, though far between and few,/May catch the sense like subtle forest spells. Prefatory Sonnet. Henry Clarence Kendall. BoAV

And these bright legends we have learned to say. Acquaintance. David Morton. MCCG

And these de Cassagnacs speak to us now of you! Sonnet: "Dead men of 'ninety-two, also of 'ninety-three." Arthur Rimbaud. WaaP

And these failing,/Momus, there'll be you. Momus. Edwin Arlington Robinson. ViBoPo

And these few lines/Written from home, are real. Rolled over on Europe. Stephen Spender. CMoP

And these its living-dead arise no more? Night Boat. Audrey Alexandra Brown. CaP

And these my songs, my all, belong to her. Dusk. DuBose Heyward. HBMV

And these, O friend, are the Fortunate Isles. The Fortunate Isles. Joaquin Miller. WGRP

And these pronounced "Pooh!" Pooh! Walter De La Mare. FiBHP; HAP

And these same men before the autumn's fall/Shall bang old Vercingetorix out of Gaul. The Legion. Robert Graves. BrPo

And these the last verses that I write for her Tonight I can write the saddest lines. Pablo Neruda. BoLoP; OLR

And these their energetic combines/Are subduing. The Hyperboreans. Tom Paulin. FaBoIP

And these will still be beautiful/When all the wars are done. Beauty Eternal: To-Day I Saw a Butterfly. Teresa Hooley. TiPo

And Theseus leaves Pirithous in the chain/The love of comrades cannot take away. Odes. Horace. OBVE

And they all flapped their wings and cried/Billy Magee Magar! The Three Ravens (C vers.). *Anonymous.* BaBo

And they all grew ugly, and nobody cares. Three Bad Ones. *Anonymous.* BBGG

And they all lived together in a little crooked house. There Was a Crooked Man. Mother Goose. CBEP; FaBoBe; FaFP; HBV 1-2; HBVY; OxBoLi

And they all look just the same. Little Boxes. Malvina Reynolds. FSW

And they all went kneeling, kneeling/At the manger in Belen. Los Pastores. Edith Agnew. ChBR; PCh

And they always say they are well met. Swell People. Carl Sandburg. LOW

And they and we, who now are here./Together still remain. Lord, Many Times Thou Pleased Art. George Wither. AH

And they answered, gold or green. Poem to a Mule, Dead Twenty Years. Guy Owen. BoAnP; PoL

And they are abandoned of their fathers/and shut out of their mothers' hearts. The Garden of Olives. Rainer Maria Rilke. MoRP

And they are better for her praise. My November Guest. Robert Frost. AnFE; APA; BLPL; BoLiVe; HBMV; MoVE; OxBA; PoLf; ViBoPo

And they are fled that should us help. The Burgesses of Calais. Laurence Minot. ACP

And they are living still. A Coffee-House Lecture. Robert Mezey. CABA

And they are not cheap. I'm Beginning to Lose Patience. W. H. Auden. PV

And they are off a-field to work: as they do every day. The Pretty Maid. Frederick York Powell. OBMV

And they are silent. Desolation. Amy Lowell. PoA

And they are sweet as rosemary/And dim as lavender. A Song for My Mother–Her Stories. Anna Hempstead Branch. OHIP

And they are the terrifying ones The Hairs in My Nose. Aram Boyajian. NeAC

...And they are you. Cloister. Conrad Aiken. MoAB; MoAmPo

And they ate and they ate/And they ate that turnip up. Mr. Finney's Turnip. *Anonymous.* HBV 1-2; HBVY; NA

And they both rode to town on the brindled calf,/To carry it home to its mother. My Uncle Jehoshaphat. Laura E. Richards. OxBChV

And they bow to a must/though the earth in her splendor/says May. The Greedy the People. Edward Estlin Cummings. SoSe

And they buried Ben in four cross-roads,/With a stake in his inside! Faithless Nellie Gray. Thomas Hood. BXAP; EnRP; FaBoCo; HBV 1-2; InMe; NA; NOBL; ShM; TreF; VLP

And they buried him for four days. Canto XVI. Ezra Pound. ExPo; MoPo

And they buried his clothes out of pity. Limerick: "There was a young man from the city." *Anonymous.* GoTF; TreFT

And they buried them all in a row. Robin Hood's Progress to Nottingham. *Anonymous.* BaBo; ESPB; OBET

And they buried them seidel by seidel.   Limerick: "Yes, theirs was a love that was tidal."   Paul Kieffer.   LiBL

And they crumble into dust.   The Valley of Vain Verses.   Henry Van Dyke.   HBV 1-2

And they didn't wear stockings and they didn't wear sockses.   The Three Foxes.   A.(lan) A.(lexander) Milne.   GoJo; GrPl; MoShBr; OxBChV

And they flower like clockwork in her bitterest hour.   November Poppies.   Hilary Corke.   NYBP

And they folded into each other.   Uses of Poetry.   Winfield Townley Scott.   DFF; PoA

And they freed their own bold men.   Robin Hood and the Three Squires.   Anonymous.   EnSB

And they gave him three cheers in a bumper,/Drank to trade and to commerce in wine.   Bold Adventures of Captain Ross.   Anonymous.   OBSS

And they gave me this jolly red nose.   Nose, Nose, Jolly Red Nose.   Mother Goose.   BrR; FaBoCh

And they grasped the sense of words/molten in lead.   Like Groping Fingers.   Abraham Sutzkever.   TrJP

And they grow old and hard.   The Wanton (excerpt).   Vidya.   PBWP

And they have learned to live it down/As though they did not care.   Old Black Men.   Georgia Douglas Johnson.   CDC; PoBA; PoNe

And they hear no more the calling/Of the watches, or the falling/Of the sea rain in the night.   A Ballad of the Captains.   Edwin James Brady.   EtS

And they hie to their cottage–to eat bread and cheese.   To Make a Pastoral: A Receipt.   Anonymous.   FaBoUs

...And they/laugh, until they are rolling on the floor/of the heavenly TV lounge.   Rec Room in Paradise.   Tom Clark.   APU

And they lend me most of my ears to hear them   Habits.   William Stanley Merwin.   CAPP

...And they let me be.   To the Age's Insanities.   Marie Ponsot.   VGW

And they'll fight for the pretty girls, for rights and liberty.   The Jolly Soldier.   Anonymous.   AmFP

And they'll have to get a muchacho/To help with the flock next year.   Juan Quintana.   Alice Corbin.   BPAW; HBMV

And they'll never tell my father or mother/But that I'm across the sea.   The Four Maries.   Anonymous.   FSW

And they'll no be hame till noon, noon.   Hush-a-Ba Birdie, Croon, Croon.   Anonymous.   GBP; OxNR

And they'll take off your scalp in those dreary Black/Hills.   The Dreary Black Hills.   Anonymous.   ABF; AmFP; AS; BPAW; CoSo; FSW

And they lost all their lives for one,/The Earl of Cassillis' ladie.   The Gypsy Laddie (B vers.).   Anonymous.   BaBo; ESPB; FaBoBa; ViBoFo

And they/Made faces/With their noses/Up and down.   Rabbits.   Dorothy Walter Baruch.   SoPo; SUS; TiPo

And they meant it too, by thunder!   Romance.   William Ernest Henley.   EnLit; MC; PAH

...And they might cut off my limbs without recalling me/from my ecstasy.   The Songs of Bilitis.   Pierre Louys.   UnTE

...And they move sublime/Among the dews of dawning time.   The Flock at Evening.   Odell Shepard.   HBMV

And they must drink or die.   Montgomery.   Anonymous.   AmFP

And they named the stream that saved them–named it fitly–/"Christmas Creek'.   Christmas Creek.   Henry Clarence Kendall.   CBAP

And they never thank me.   The Radical.   Waring Cuney.   CDC

And they part to receive it, unawares.   Rowing Early.   John Peck.   SM

And they played together kindly/In the dark pine-tree.   The Turtle-Doves' Nest.   Anonymous.   HBVY

And they're all–for–ME!   Seven Today.   Ivy O. Eastwick.   BiCB

And they're down, down, and they're down.   The Arizona Boys and Girls.   Anonymous.   CoSo

And they're haling him to justice for the colour of his hair.   Half-Way, for One Commandment Broken.   Alfred Edward Housman.   OBSP; PeHV

And they're more happy than you'll ever know.   Son of a Gun.   Anonymous.   CoSo

And they return.   The Ritual.   Paul David Ashley.   LFAC

...And they return/They chant on every wind, and they return/In the long roll of any deep blue wave   .Our Dead.   Robert Nichols.   WGRP

And they said, "Aw, go jump in the lake!"   Limerick: "There was an old man by Salt Lake."   William Jay Smith.   TDH

And they shall not be judged unjust,/All that in him for safety trust.   Who Is the Man?   Anonymous.   TrAS

And they shall weep and feel their pain/for ever.   With Timrels.   Anonymous.   TrJP

And they sign the cross in saying: "God in mercy keep her soul!"   The Demon of the Mirror.   Bayard Taylor.   BeLS

And they, since they/Were not the one dead, turned to their affairs.   "Out, Out–".   Robert Frost.   CABA; DL; FF; HAP; HeIP; OxBA; SoSe; VGW

And they sit there and tell me/I haven't been here long enough.   Parole Board.   Derek Butler.   LFAC

And they sleep with Admiral Death.   Admiral Death.   Sir Henry Newbolt.   VLP

And they solicit far the most.   New Fashions.   George Moses Horton.   OBAL

And they stand there forever that way, locked in silence.   Woman and Nature.   Susan Griffin.   NPGG

And they stay on to talk it over.   De Imagine Mundi.   John Ashbery.   FaBoMo

And they still control the world, and you are not in my arms.   Twenty-One Love Poems.   Adrienne Rich.   BoWoP

And they sunk him in the Low Lands Low.   The Golden Vanity (B vers.).   Anonymous.   BaBo; CBEP; ELP; FaBoCh; FSW; OBET; PoPle; WiR

And they swallow the boy,/the girl,/for 15 days,/for a month,/for ever   All of a Sudden.   Teresa de Jesus.   WPOW

And they that wash on Saturday,/Oh, slovens are indeed!   They That Wash on Monday.   Anonymous.   FaBoBe; HBV 1-2; HBVY; NLV

And they think I'm normal.   Small Town: The Friendly.   Stephen P. Dunn.   PoL

And they through every neighboring land/Death and disaster sped.   The Upas Tree.   Alexander Pushkin.   LiTW

And they to thee lend ornament.   On a Violet in Her Breast.   Thomas Stanley.   OBS

And they told me how they were beguiled,/Driven out, and compelled to be chaste.   I Laid Me Down upon a Bank.   William Blake.   CBEP; EnLoPo; GBL; ViBoPo

And they turned into families/on the only land they knew.   The Israeli Navy.   Marvin Bell.   VWA

And they've given me mittens again!   Presents.   Marchette Chute.   BrR; ChBR; EvOK; SiSoSe

And they wake into a light/Whose day shall never die in night.   An Epitaph upon Husband and Wife Who Died and Were Buried Together.   Richard Crashaw.   GoTF; NOBE; TreFS

And they walked as they talked/Among ferns and bracken and clover.   Michael Walked in the Wood.   Robert Greacen.   NeIP

And they welcomed back Jacques Cartier from his perils o'er the/sea.   Jacques Cartier.   Thomas D'Arcy McGee.   CaP

And they went off a-field to work, as they do every day.   Ballade.   Paul Fort.   AWP

And they went to sea in a sieve.   The Jumblies.   Edward Lear.   BLPL; EBEV; EnLi 1-2; EvOK; FaBoBe; FaBoNo; FaFP; GoJo; HBV 1-2; HBVY; LBN; LiTB; MOS; NA; OnMSP; OxBChV; OxBoLi; PoRA; SeCeV; SoPo; TEP; TiPo; WiR

And they were down to earth.   History of World Languages.   D. J. Enright.   OxBC

And they were gestures of giving me water.   To Drink.   Gabriela (Lucila Godoy Alcayaga) Mistral.   NU

And they were happy, for to their young eyes/Each was an angel, and earth paradise.   Don Juan.   George Gordon, Lord Byron.   EnRP

And they were hard men to conquer on the scow on Cowen Shore.   The Scow on Cowden Shore (III).   Anonymous.   ShS

And they were left to hug what was, and ate the air.   The Lord's Chameleons.   Peter Klappert.   AmPA

And they were so surprised to find/Out it was me!   Hiding.   Dorothy Aldis.   SoPo; SUS; TiPo

And they who faithful serve below/Shall rule with Me on high.   Come unto Me.   John Stuart.   STF

And they will differ–if they do–/As Syllable from Sound–   The Brain–Is Wider than the Sky.   Emily Dickinson.   AmP; AnNE; MAmP; MoAB; MoAmPo; NAWM 1-2; NIP; NoAm; OxBA

And they will fight for evermore.'   Bold General Wolfe.   Anonymous.   OBET

And they will likewise all have places.   Oh No.   Robert Creeley.   AmPC; HeIP; InPK; NaP; SM

And they will on you rue,/As mine has done on me.   My Heart Is Heich Above.   Anonymous.   AtBAP; BSV; ErPo; GoTS; OBEV

..And they will think of things they have no words to utter.   October.   Thomas Wolfe.   AnEnPo

And thieves of happiness,/Sodden in the underbrush.   The Thieves of Love.   R.A.D. Ford.   PeCV

And thin-ribbed earth pokes out against the snow?   A Green Place.   William Jay Smith.   GrPl

And thine be the glory Forever, Amen.   Our Father in Heaven.   Sarah Josepha Hale.   AH

And thine the kingdom, thine the power/And glory, ever be.   Our Father, God.   Adoniram Judson.   AH

And things can gradually slip back to normal.   One of the Seven Has Somewhat to Say.   Sara Henderson Hay.   DFT

And things get left out in the rain.   Cat's Cradle.   Robyn Sarah.   CaPN

And things have a terrible permanence/When people die.   Things.   Aline Kilmer.   MCCG

And things that are yet to be done. Open the door!   On a Night of Snow.   Elizabeth Jane Coatsworth.   MoAmPo; MoShBr; OBCA

And THINGS/That go BUMP in the night,/Good Lord, deliver us!   Litany for Halloween.   Anonymous.   SiSoSe; SoPo

And things unseen do see, and things unheard do hear. The Celestial City. Giles the Younger Fletcher. NOBE; OBS

And things were as they were. A Breath of Air. James Wright. NOBA; PoPl

And things you never seem to find/In treatises and tracts. To a Child. David McCord. AnAmPo

And think how it will be in Paradise/When we're together. I Have a Room whereinto No One Enters. Christina Georgina Rossetti. OBNC

And think it's my heart that i/hear/in my ears. uh. now ain't that love? Now Ain't That Love? Carolyn M. Rodgers. BPo

And think more respectfully of the fox's sincerity. In the Library. Elizabeth Brewster. OBCV

And think not quite to end as we begin. Corda Condordia: Quest. Edmund Clarence Stedman. AA

And think not she doth hurt our solitariness,/For such company decks such solitariness. Dorus's Song. Sir Philip Sidney. LoBV

And think of Dante sweating through his hell. Walking Milwaukee. Harold Witt. HoAn; TAT

And think of gold/At Seboyeta. Seboyeta Chapel. Shirley Hill Witt. TWSS

And think of my happy condition/Surrounded by acres of clams. Acres of Clams. Anonymous. FSW

...And think of the kinds of breakings/there are, and the kinds of restraining forces. Breakings. Henry Taylor. GrPl

And think "These are the cast-off leavings of some star." Song of the Moderns. John Gould Fletcher. AWP; InPo

And think they die with pleasure, live with pain. Amoretti, XLVII. Edmund Spenser. AAS; TrGrPo

And think twice ere I'd leave it to be a dragoon! Bad Luck to This Marching. Charles James Lever. OnYI

And think 'twould lead to some bright/isle of rest. How Dear to Me the Hour. Thomas Moore. CoBE

And thinking, "Love survives/The grave,' she stepped inside to join the other wives. Bluebeard's Wife. Daryl Hine. ACV; NoAm

And, thinking over what he'd said,/Wished his friends were really there. The Fish Sonata. Winfield Townley Scott. MP

And thinks 'em the best he has tasted this season. A Fable for Critics. James Russell Lowell. NOBA

And thinks he hears the cuckoo's song. April. Samuel Thompson. BIrV

And thinks he sees no beauties like the morn. Summer Morning. John Clare. CBEP; PoSC

And thinks that he was present in the dark/When skin was chosen over root and bark. Autonomous. Mark Van Doren. LiTA

And thirty inches short of being a yard. Five Epigrams. J.V. Cunningham. UnTE

And thirty years back in a city crowd/I passed a girl when my heart cried loud! Fifty Years Spent. Struthers Burt. HBMV

And this alone," said practical Is. Was, Is, and Yet-To-Be. Ella Wheeler Wilcox. PoToHe

And this be it known is all that we know. Obituary in Bitcherel. Conrad Aiken. OBAL

And this book is but the urn/Of the ashes of love dead. Sag', Wo Ist Dein Schones Liebchen. Heinrich Heine. AWP

And this child stands/with a sopping sponge in his hand,/saying he never meant to do it. Spilled Milk. John Haines. GP

And this day's work made even that seem doubtful. The White-Tailed Hornet. Robert Frost. OxBA

And this dead thing, this dark thing/this frightful thing is my soul. She. Zinaida Gippius. WPOW

And this ends my song concerning the Farrows. Jim Farrow. Anonymous. CoSo

...And this first/sheer pain that drinking means to be alive. Workmen. Herbert Morris. NePoAm-2

And this: fish not fish but stars/that fell into their dreams. Magic Fox. James Welch. CDW

And this game rule and leede/And bring it to a good ende. Prologue to a Translation. John Trevisa. OxBM

And this green pastoral landscape, were to me/More dear, both for themselves and for thy sake! Lines Composed a Few Miles above Tintern Abbey. William Wordsworth. BiP; DiPo; ERoP 1-2; ExPo; FaBoPP; FF; FiP; ForPo; GoTF; GoTL; HBV 1-2; HeIP; InPS; LoBV; MasP; MBW; MCCG; 1-2; NAWM 1-2; NIP; NoP; OAEL 1-2; OAEP; OBNC; OBRV; PAI; PoEL 1-5; PPP; PrIm; SeCePo; SeCeV; TEP; TreFS; TrGrPo; WHA

And this, her priestess and her daughter. Avalon. Audrey McGaffin. NePoAm

And this here beauty belongs to me! Fandango. Stanley Vestal. BPAW

And this house I grow dead of, is all/That I see around or about me. Ringleted Youth of My Love. Anonymous. AnIL; AnIV; OnYI; OxBI; WTO

And this Indenture also witnesseth. A Separation Deed. Sir Lewis Morris. OBVV

And this is a judgment. Yours Truly. Leonard Nathan. AMV-80

And this is aa the life he kens there is. Auld Sanct-Aundrians–Brand the Builder. Tom Scott. BSV

And this is foolish. Still, we weep. Allergy. Walker Gibson. NePoAm

And this is grief to me. The Birds of Paradise. John Peale Bishop. GoJo

And this is it, this is it, this is it. See-Saw, Margery Daw. Anonymous. OxNR

–And this is John Adams who started them all. John Adams. Rosemary and Stephen Vincent Benét. PAL

And this is law... The Vicar of Bray. Anonymous. ALV

And this is marriage, this is love. Together. Ludwig Lewisohn. HBMV; PoToHe; TrJP

And this is me. I Am a Woman (excerpt). Akhtar Amiri. WPOW

And this is not the case with kings! The Pretzel Man. Rachel Field. SoPo

And this is only earth, my dear,/Where true love is not given. Dead Love. Elizabeth Siddal. NOBV

And this is that my soul pursueth. Song Set by Philip Rosseter: "And would you see my mistress' face?" Anonymous. OBSC

And this is the dreadful legend/Of the terrible Heinz von Stein. The Legend of Heinz Von Stein. Charles Godfrey Leland. HBV 1-2

And....this is the end of my lay. Commonplaces (parody). Rudyard Kipling. HBV 1-2

...And this is/the explanation. A Counterpoint. Robert Creeley. NeAP

And this is the last of the tailor we do hear./Tum a rally tolly dolly, tum a rolly tolly day. The Clever Skipper. Anonymous. AmFP

And this is the soul's haven to have felt. Winter Heavens. George Meredith. BoLiVe; NoP

And this is the way the baby woke. The Way the Baby Woke. James Whitcomb Riley. AA

And this is what breaks the heart. To Argos. Lawrence Durrell. MoPo

And this is what happened. The Little Bird. Anonymous. PBA

And this is what he told us, every one,/This precious priest, this goodly man, Sir John. The Canterbury Tales: The Knight's Interruption of the Monk's Tale. Geoffrey Chaucer. NAWM 1-2; OAEL 1-2

And this is what my soul pursueth. And Would You See My Mistress' Face? Thomas Campion. OAEP

And this is where we came in. Stance. Theodore Enslin. CoPo

And this is why in cloistered cell/I wait my latter day. The Fall of Maubila. Thomas Dunn English. PAH

...And this is you. Preludes for Memnon. Conrad Aiken. LiTM; MoPo; MoVE; OXBA

...And this joyless gem/That glittered on her taper finger fair. Relics. George Frederick Cameron. PeCV

And this last act of wretchedness forgive. Last Verses. Thomas Chatterton. TrGrPo

...And this late warm rain/babbling false promises in the pasture lane. Sonnet: "A warm rain whispers, but the earth knows best." Kenneth Leslie. PeCV

...And this letter was endited at Topcroft, with full/heavy heart, etc./By your own/Margery Brews. Unto My Valentine. Margery Brews. OFD

And this little dog said, Give me a/little bit please. Round About, Round About, Here Sits the Hare. Anonymous. OxNR

And this little pig had all the jam. This Little Pig Had a Rub-a-Dub. Anonymous. OxNR

And this mood by the name of melancholy/Shall no more blackened and obscured be. October. Edward ("Edward Eastaway") Thomas. ChMP; MoVE; NoAm

And this moon that leaves me dark within the door. Liberty. Edward ("Edward Eastaway") Thomas. MoAB; OAEL 1-2

And this Nightingale, kept by one Shear. The Willows. Bret (Francis Bret Harte) Harte. BXAP; InMe

And this old worn-out stuff, which is threadbare Today,/May become everlasting Tomorrow. Tomorrow. John Collins. GTBS-P; HBV 1-2

And this One–He has been dead so long!' Le Sacre-Coeur. Charlotte Mew. OBTV

And this one's bigger than–than a hundred others,/sparrows, I think it was. Sagesse. Hilda ("H. D.") Doolittle. NOCV

And this our stay on earth essential as our going. Not This Leaf Haunts Me. Tony Cosier. AMV-81

And this seven yere I have ben his page/And kept his commaundement... Dalyaunce. Anonymous. AtBAP; CH

And this should be his customary attitude! The British Tar. Sir William Schwenck Gilbert. ALV

And this should be the wise man's pattern. The Scholar in the Narrow Street. Tso Ssu. AWP

And this so alone/it was uncared for. I Saw as a Child. Zindzi Mandela. WhB

And this tale has a moral, I know,/If you'll try to find it out. The Singing-Lesson. Jean Ingelow. HBV 1-2

And this the spirit sees and is aggrieved. Anatomy of Monotony. Wallace Stevens. BiP

And this they found the beste game of alle.   The Summonee's Tale (parody).
Stanley J. Sharpless.   BXAP; FaBoPa

And this transfigured beauty wins thy love.   The Transfiguration of Beauty.
Buonarroti Michelangelo.   AWP

And this unread memento be/The only lasting part of me.   To Violet.   Basil
Bunting.   PoA

And this was reward and more for all.   Intimations.   Alma Johanna Koenig.
VWA

And this was scarcely odd, because/They'd eaten every one.   The Walrus and
the Carpenter.   Lewis (Charles Lutwidge Dodgson) Carroll.   BeLS; BLPA;
FaBoBe; FaBoCo; FaBoNo; FaBV; FaFP; FiBHP; FPL; GN; HBV 1-2;
HBVY; InMe; LBN; LiTB; MaC; MCCG; NA; NOBL; OxBChV; PoRA;
SoPo; TEP; TreF

And this was scarcely odd, because/They'd ploughed them every one!   The
Vulture and the Husbandman.   Arthur Clement Hilton.   CenHV; FaBoCo

And this was what I dreamt last night.   Flora.   Ray Fraser.   NeAC

And this way the Water comes down at Lodore.   The Cataract of Lodore.
Robert Southey.   GN; HBV 1-2; OxBChV; SpRo; TEP; TreFS; WBLP

And this way we came to love/the double negative.   Words.   Vern Rutsala.
GP

And this would cause a roar,/When your old joke was new.   Old Fashioned
Fun.   William Makepeace Thackeray.   InMe

And thistles inside.   Holding-paddock.   William Hart-Smith.   AnNZ

And thither will we go now!   The Knight of the Burning Pestle.   Francis
Beaumont and John Fletcher.   OBS

And Thomas Jefferson would have cursed.   After the Release of Ezra Pound.
Dannie Abse.   NMP

And "those a little' a long way is.   Lord, Thou Clepedest Me.   Anonymous.
OBSP

And those appear that are hateful to me and mock me.   As If a Phantom
Caress'd Me.   Walt Whitman.   GBL

And those are streams of tears which thence distil.   Describes the Place
Where Cynthia Is Sporting Herself.   Philip Ayres.   EnLoPo

And those black spaces in between that peer/so strangely at me through half-
opened doors.   The Phases of Darkness.   Paul Petrie.   TAP

And those fair Locks shall pour down showres of Gold.   On a Fair Beggar.
Philip Ayres.   EnLoPo; OBS

And those few strangers, dear indeed,/Are choked, are checked, by many a
weed.   My Birthday.   George Crabbe.   OBSP

And those high places, that are beauty's home.   Oxford.   Lionel Pigot
Johnson.   FaBoPP; OBNC; OBVV

And those of sorrows yet to come.   The Shrubbery.   William Cowper.
CBEP; CEP; FaBoRV; GTBS; NCEP; NOBE; OBEC

And those of youth, a seeming/length,/Proportion'd to their sweetness.   The
River of Life.   Thomas Campbell.   BSV; FaFP; GTBS; GTBS-P; HBV 1-2;
LiTB

And those orbits to cross again: this one and this one...   Sungrazer.   Alvin
Greenberg.   FAZ

And those roads in South Dakota that feel around in the darkness...   Come
with Me.   Robert Bly.   AmC; NoAm; NOBA

And those soft flashings of their silver/feet.   The Brook (excerpt).   William
Bull Wright.   AA

And those tears too expensive now that start/From radiant eyes and empty the
whole heart.   These Images Remain.   May Sarton.   MoLP

And those that follow will ride as free/As ever of old rode Marion's men.
Judith.   William Young.   AA

And those that Our Lord loved, He lifted into light.   The Harrowing of Hell.
William Langland.   BoC

And those that weary are of light, find rest in thee.   Hymn to Darkness.
John Norris.   GTBS

And those who are very well hung.   The Aesthetic Point of View.   W. H.
Auden.   NLV; OBAL

And those who had doubted remembering words/he had spoken.   His Last
Week.   Elinor Lennen.   PGD

And those who paint 'em truest praise 'em most.   The Campaign.   Joseph
Addison.   CEP

And those who see us/will think we are lovers.   Love Songs.   Anonymous.
BoWoP

And those who suffer with their suffering kind/Yet feel their faith, religion.'
A Conversation.   Percy Bysshe Shelley.   ERoP 1-2

And those who wisely wish to wive/Must look on Thrale at thirty-five.   To
Mrs. Thrale on Her Thirty-Fifth Birthday.   Samuel Johnson.   FaBoEE;
NAs

And those whom Our Lord loved He led into His light.   The Vision of Piers
Plowman.   William Langland.   MeEV

And those wild eyes that watch the wave/In roarings round the coral reef.
In Memoriam A.H.H., XXXVI.   Alfred, Lord Tennyson.   VLP

And those with appropriate clothing would get their chance to/dance with him
that night.   Cat or Stomp.   Laura Tohe.   STE

And those, without our schools, suffice/To make men moral, good and wise.
Fables: The Shepherd and the Philosopher.   John Gay.   CEP

And those you may end, when you please to be kind.   Advice to a Lady in
Autumn.   Philip Stanhope, Earl of Chesterfield.   CEP; FaBoUs; OBEC

And thou art strange to me, Love, to-/night.   Songs.   Richard Watson
Gilder.   AA

And thou art with me there.   The Unicorn.   Ruth Pitter.   MoBrPo; MoVE

"And thou canst answer 'nay' or 'no,'/"Or 'yea and yea and yea.'"   Sir
Magnus and the Elf-Maid.   Anonymous.   BaBo

And thou didst come/To take me home/Within thy heart to be.   I Asked for
Peace.   Digby Mackworth Dolben.   EBCP; OxBoCh

And thou dost give, with thy own loveliness,/My beauty back to me.   Laus
Virginitatis.   Arthur Symons.   EnLoPo

And Thou, enthroned, my soul shalt spare,/On Thy great Judgment Day!   O
Jesus! Sweet the Tears I Shed.   Ray Palmer.   BePJ

And thou for being alone.'   The Night Wind.   Emily Bronte.   ChRP;
NCEP; RoGo; TEP; VLP

And thou hast toiled and laboured long/With aching head and weary eye.   O
Come with Me, Thus Ran the Song.   Emily Bronte.   NOBV

And thou, His Mother, His weeping calm.   Kolendy for Christmas.
Anonymous.   CAW

And thou in clear-eyed faith hast seen God's/angels near the guns!   The
Battle of Charleston Harbor.   Paul Hamilton Hayne.   PAH

And thou in this shalt find thy monument/When tyrants' crests and tombs of
brass are spent.   Sonnets, CVII: "Not mine own fears, nor the prophetic
soul."   William Shakespeare.   AWP; CBEP; CTC; DiPo; EBEV; FiP;
HAP; InPo; LiTB; LoBV; MasP; MBW 1-2; NoP; OAEL 1-2; OAEP;
OBSC; PPoe; SeCeV

And thou lament forever/The ruin of thy soul.   As Flows the Rapid River.
Samuel Francis Smith.   AH

And thou like Adamant draw mine iron heart.   Holy Sonnets, I.   John
Donne.   EBEV; EG; MeLP; NOBE; NOCV; NoP; OAEP; OBS; OxBoCh;
PoEL 1-5; SeCP

And thou'lt never lie aside him.   Maw Bonnie Lad.   Anonymous.   GBP

And thou may'st whimper in thy sleep/These many days, and start and weep.
To a Spaniel.   Walter Savage Landor.   FM

And thou meanderest forever/At the bottom of my dream.   I Was Born upon
Thy Bank, River.   Henry David Thoreau.   ELU; PoEL 1-5

And thou, my soul, wilt still/On thine old earth-clod lie!   The Cherubic
Pilgrim.   (Johannes Scheffler) "Angelus Selesius".   WGRP

And thou'rt a Dream, O Yucatan!   The Hunter.   Walter James Turner.
HBMV

And thou's get all thy father's lands,/And dwell in Hasillgreen.'   John of
Hazelgreen (A version).   Anonymous.   BaBo; ESPB; ViBoFo

And thou, Saint Ben, shalt be/Writ in my psalter.   His Prayer to Ben Jonson.
Robert Herrick.   AnAnS 2; BoLiVe; CaPo; CavP; JCP; NoP; OAEP; OBS;
OBSP; OxBoLi; PP; SeCeV; SeCV 1-2; TrGrPo

And thou shalt be learned old Vicar.   The Spanish Curate.   John Fletcher.
OBS

And thou shalt be my ruling star!   Caroline, II.   Thomas Campbell.
OBNC

And thou shalt come, with flesh and fell,/On doomes-day to be with me.
The Debate of the Body and the Soul (excerpt).   Anonymous.   CoBE

And thou shalt find that I have written truly.   He Prayeth for Ink and Palette
That He May Write.   Book of the Dead.   AWP

And thou shalt find thy dream to be/A noonday light and truth to thee.
Beauty and Duty.   Ellen Hooper.   HBV 1-2

And thou shalt live for ever.   N.Y.   Ezra Pound.   NYP

...And thou shalt not despise/Even me, the priest of this poor sacrifice.   To
Nature.   Samuel Taylor Coleridge.   ERoP 1-2; OAEL 1-2

And thou shalt pipe and I'll come to thee.   The Shepherd.   Anonymous.
UnTE

And thou shalt Pipe, and I'll Dance to thee,/To thee, to thee, derry, derry, to
thee &c   The Merry Bagpipes.   Anonymous.   CoMu

And thou shalt sail back heavenwards. Woe is me!   To Manon, Comparing
Her to a Falcon.   Wilfrid Scawen Blunt.   OBVV

And thou shalt see thy thought another way.   The Truth.   Archibald
Lampman.   CaP

And thou shalt take a nobler leave.   In Memoriam A.H.H., LVIII.   Alfred,
Lord Tennyson.   VLP

And thou should'st wail thy case.   The Fly.   Barnabe Googe.   CH

And thou so fair–one fairest maid alone/Hath trod upon thy root.   The Sign.
Bhartrihari.   LiTW

And thou, Soul, worship her/Still in her purity.   Ballata: In Exile at Sarzana.
Guido Cavalcanti.   AWP

And thou thy joys with me.   We Have Lived and Loved Together.   Charles
Jefferys.   BLPA; FaBoBe; GoTF; PoToHe; TreFT

;And thou thyself, Mary,/Remain for ever Immaculate Maid.   Christ 1:
Advent Lyrics, IX.   Anonymous.   AnOE

"And thou thyself to all eternity!"   The House of Life.   Dante Gabriel
Rossetti.   OAEP

And thou under thy feet maist tread that foul seven-headed/beast.   Song to
Beta.   Michael Drayton.   OBSC

And Thou upholdest them all! Lord, Where Shall I Find Thee? Judah Halevi. TrJP

And thou were my ain thing,/How dearly wou'd I love thee. An Thou Were My Ain Thing (excerpt). Allan Ramsay. ViBoPo

And thou wert free and I were still in bond. His Wisdom. Nicholas Breton. ALV; OBSC

And thou wilt blow up hearts. Song: "Join once again, my Celia, join." Charles Cotton. ViBoPo

And Thou wilt find Thy dearly-bought in dust! D. O. M. Sir Henry Wotton. OxBoCh

And thou wonderst why I toll? Theme. Carl Spitteler. PoPl

And though a child, I knew it was the voice/Of one whose occupation was to die. Souvenir. Edwin Arlington Robinson. NoAm

And though full years be told,/Their forms grow slowly old. Masque of Hymen: Glad Time Is at His Point Arrived. Ben Jonson. HW

And though I kiss the salt no more/Other swimmers will. The Old Swimmer. Christopher Morley. LiSp; SD

And though ich habbe y-do thee wrong,/Thou graunte me amendinge! Hymn to the Virgin. of Shoreham William. OxBM

And though in years of sight and sound/unmet,/Known for my soul's birth-partner well/enough! The House of Life. Dante Gabriel Rossetti. OAEP

And though not in her bower, yet I/Shall in her Her Sacred Bower. Thomas Campion. HBV 1-2

And though the flame be not so great,/Yet is the heat as strong. The Fire of Love. Charles, Earl of Dorset Sackville. LiTL; UnTE

And though the task may break my back/I'll ask for no vacation! The Song of Songs. Heinrich Heine. UnTE

And though the town went crazy, she is his wife today. The Blacksmith's Serenade. Vachel Lindsay. StPo

And though they're cozened still, they still believe. The Dispensary. Sir Samuel Garth. OBSV

And though thou slay us, we will trust in/thee! Liberty. John Milton Hay. AA

And though thou wreck me, will I love/thee yet! The Sea's Spell. Susan Marr Spalding. AA; EtS

And though wild rocks about the shore appear/Yet virtue will find room to anchor there. Melancholy. William Habington. LoBV

And though you are bronzed with age/They know you are theirs. Hans Christian Andersen in Central Park. Hy Sobiloff. PoPl

And thought he was rich. Street Chants; Old Daddy Witch. Anonymous. ExPo

And thought how dark my house must be/Down in the lonesome wood. August. Katharine Pyle. OBCA

...And thought only of her? Letters Found near a Suicide. Frank Horne. BPo

And thought, "She's not hors do combat, 'tis part of an Officer's Pay." A War Bird's Burlesque (with music). Anonymous. AS

And thought suspended lie in Rapture's blissful/trance. Life. Samuel Taylor Coleridge. EnRP

And thought: "Thank God they had to amputate!" The One-Legged Man. Siegfried Sassoon. CMoP

And thought upon the music of the spheres. Zophiel: Palace of the Gnomes. Maria Gowen Brooks. AA

And thoughts of you through a mist of tears. From a Car-Window. Ruth Guthrie Harding. HBMV

And thousand worlds my silent world would light/Till broke the babel of the summer day. The Sedge-Warbler. Ralph Hodgson. PB

And thrash him at my gyvel. Nine Inch Will Please a Lady. Robert Burns. ErPo

And threaten to take our cage/away from us. We Live in a Cage. William J. Harris. PoBA

And three are one: a man, a thing, a dream. Poem: "We are such stuff as dreams are made of." Hugo von Hofmannsthal. LiTW

...And three/Beings' lives gel in my womb. Pregnancy. Sandra McPherson. BoWoP; NMM

And three cheers for the U.S.A. Song about Whiskers. P. G. Wodehouse. FiBHP

And three for dear Mamma. Eight O'Clock. Christina Georgina Rossetti. TiPo

And three-quarters of another. Riddle: "The fiddler and his wife." Anonymous. OxNR

And three ribs o' the auld wife's side/Gaed knip knap ower in twa. The Cunning Clerk. Anonymous. OxBB

And three to go. The Start. Anonymous. SD

And threw her rider in the drain. In Lincoln Lane. Anonymous. OxNR

And threw him down the stairs. Goosey Gander. Anonymous. OxNR

And threw it over the wall,/And that's all. A Tale: "There was an old woman sat spinning." Anonymous. OxNR

And threw them at the people. Johnny Went to Church One Day. Anonymous. BBGG

And thrice an elfin bugle blew/From the Gates of Faerie. The Spell. Henry Martyn Hoyt. HBMV

And thrice more happy are the happy days/That live divinely in the lingering rays. Twilight. Agnes Mary Frances (Mme Emile Duclaux) Robinson. HBV 1-2

And thrice shall the Shophar re-echo/your song/On mountain and altar to whom both/belong. To Him Who Is Feared. Eleazar Ben Kalir. TrJP

And thrice,–whereby the shadow of death is dead. The Morrow's Message. Dante Gabriel Rossetti. MaVP

And thro' a lattice on the soul/Looks thy fair face and makes it still. In Memoriam A.H.H., LXX. Alfred, Lord Tennyson. NOBV; VLP

And thro' the dusty tumult God arose. L'Avenir. Sydney Thomas Dobell. VLP

And through a tinsel gear of watch motors the heavy sky. Clock Symphony. John Frederick Nims. MiAP

And through all Brittany and Maine/Filhol shall sing to him alone. Quan Lo Ruis De La Fontana. Jaufre Rudel. LiTW

And through all the coming years, just be glad! Just Be Glad. James Whitcomb Riley. WBLP

And through chill air the puffs of milkweed hover. A Storm in April. Richard Wilbur. LCAP; NoP

And through Cripplegate went three crooked cripples. Three Crooked Cripples Went through Cripplegate. Anonymous. OxNR

And through eternity I'll sing on. Wondrous Love. Alex Means. AmFP; BLSo; FSW; TrAS

And through his misfortune it was poor Molly Bawn. Molly Bawn. Anonymous. ViBoFo

And through my thought crosses/a wingless "what is it to me?" Interior Landscape. Gloria Fuertes. BoWoP

...And through/That dance she moves, and dances too. An Epistle. A. D. Hope. PoAu 1-2

And through the changing scenes of life/I find a haven there. My Mother's Love. Anonymous. STF

And through the dim Elysian bounds/Leads all his cry of little hounds. My Last Terrier. John (G. Forrester Scott) Halsham. HBV 1-2

And through the earth a glad rebirth/of brotherhood is spreading! The Bells of Peace. Aileen Fisher. SiSoSe

And through the Garden hurls the voice of God. Adam–The First Kiss. Hal Porter. ACV

And, through the garden, through the glen/A wondrous music rings. The Old Garden. Baron Joseph von Eichendorff. LiTW

And through the gloom the wild deer shyly/gaze. Down the Bayou. Mary Ashley Townsend. AA; AnAmPo

And through the Queene of Englands/good grace/Now in England shee doth remaine. Earl Bothwell. Anonymous. ESPB

And through the sea of space we slip,/That flows all round the world. Before Sunrise in Winter. Edward Rowland Sill. AA

And through the walls run rats with small, red eyes. The Church of San Antonio de la Florida. Paul Petrie. NYBP

And through the wind-touched reddening woods shall rise/October with the rain of ruined leaves. September. Archibald Lampman. PeCV

And through unnumbered heavens/To the final flame. Arlo Will. Edgar Lee Masters. LiTA

And throw him in the deep water/that flows through the land. Deep Water. Anonymous. FSW

And throw his challenge out in lanes of light. Second Woman's Lament. Brenda Chamberlain. NeIP

And throwing back its head the sea began to sing. The Parrot Fish. James Merrill. NOBA

And throws off his covers/one by one. St. Francis Einstein of the Daffodils. William Carlos Williams. AtBAP; MoPo

And thrust my brother in the sea. Care Is Heavy. Conal O'Riordan. CAW

And thrust myself forth and am alone in the great storm. Presaging. Rainer Maria Rilke. AWP; TrJP

...And thrust/The baleful phantoms underground. Low Barometer. Robert Bridges. CMoP; CoBMV; ForPo; LiTB; NoAm; NOCV; QFR

And thrusts her deep in a dishonored grave. Full Cycle. John White Chadwick. PAH

And thus an end. Along Walking. Anonymous. CBEP

And thus and thus, vain world, again adieu. Madrigal: "Go, nightly Cares." John Dowland. EnRePo

And thus beginneth his song therewithal. Miserere mei, Domine. Sir Thomas Wyatt. FCP

And thus beginneth the game. Elinor Rumming (excerpt). John Skelton. ViBoPo

And thus believing, we rejoice. Bitter-Sweet: Hymn. Josiah Gilbert Holland. TrPWD

And thus by those of whom I hoped for/aid,/To cruel love my soul was first betrayed. Idea. Michael Drayton. OAEP

And thus complete for earth mankind's triumphal arch. Hymn for Pentecost. James Clarence Mangan. CAW

And thus did the hen reward Beecher.   Limerick: "The Reverend Henry War Beecher."   Oliver Wendell Holmes.   CenHV; FaBoNo; HBVY

And thus ended Wednesday Cocking.   Wednesday Cocking.   *Anonymous.* EnSB

And thus endis the preiching of the Swallow.   The Preiching of the Swallow. Robert Henryson.   OxBS

And thus ends the ballad of Bartleme Fair-o.   Bartleme Fair.   George Alexander Stevens.   ELP; NOEC

And thus her passion paints.   Philomela, the Nightingale (excerpt).   Patrick Hannay.   PBBP

And thus I die.   Four Ways of Dying.   Steve Chimombo.   WhB

And thus I end the bloody bout/Of brave Lord Willoughby.   Brave Lord Willoughby.   *Anonymous.*   FaPoR

And thus I guard my native land still.   The Air Sentry.   Patrick Barrington. CenHV

And thus I'll take my pilgrimage.   Pilgrimage.   Sir Walter Ralegh.   BBV; GoTF; TreFS

And thus I love them better still,/Even in extremity of ill.   Lay of the Last Minstrel.   Sir Walter Scott.   BSV

And thus I please both Lord and Lady Thrale.   On a Dog-Collar. *Anonymous.*   FaBoEE

And thus I pleased both Lord and Lady Frail.   Epitaph on the Lap-Dog of Lady Frail.   Wilkes.   ALV

And thus I see among these pleasant things/Each care decays, and yet my sorrow springs.   "The soote season..."   Henry Howard, Earl of Surrey. AAS; FCP; HeIP; InPS; NIP; NoP; SiPS

And thus I was greeted at Burns's log camp.   Burns's Log Camp. *Anonymous.*   ShS

And thus in rage/I loved, alas!   Poem About Waking.   David Ferry. NePoAm-2

And thus it is: as far as I can prove,/He loves to be beloved, but not to love. Sonnets, X: "Thus was my love, thus was my Ganymed."   Richard Barnfield.   PeHV

And thus know the all of each.   After All.   Donald Jeffrey Hayes.   CDC

And thus my Roundelay is past.   A Blith and Bonny Country Lass. Thomas Lodge.   ALV

And, thus pillowed, Pike expired.   The Death of General Pike.   Laughton Osborn.   PAH

And thus re-illumed have no humour for letting/My pilgrimage fail.   For Life I Had Never Cared Greatly.   Thomas Hardy.   CMoP; EnLit; HBMV; LiTM; NoAm

And thus reward, and practise my Advice.   Idylls.   Theocritus.   PeHV

And thus reward the toils which to those summits led.   The Isolation of Genius.   George Gordon, Lord Byron.   WBLP

And thus the little Jew died....   Biography.   Abraham Moses Klein.   TrJP

And thus the night they a' hae spent,/Just as they had been brither and/ brither.   Jock o the Side (B version).   *Anonymous.*   ESPB

And thus the year goes round, and round, and round.   Winter.   James Hurnard.   PoSC

And thus they grew like giggling fir trees.   Blocks.   Frank O'Hara.   ANYP; EAS; HaCAP

And thus, throughout, with Christmas plays/Frolic the full twelve holy-days. A New-Year's Gift Sent to Sir Simeon Steward.   Robert Herrick.   CaPo

And thus to despise the world I rede that thou lere.   Despise the World. *Anonymous.*   MeEL

And thus we dally and dip our spoon.   Poussin.   Louis MacNeice.   EyDe

And thus we see a proper tune/Is sometimes very opportune.   The Swan and the Goose.   Aesop.   AWP; LiTW; UnS

And thus went dainty Baby Bell/Out of this world of ours.   Baby Bell. Thomas Bailey Aldrich.   HBV 1-2

And thus were born/the vast multitudes/from the song/of a flute.   Elderberry Flute Song.   Peter Blue Cloud.   STE

And thus where'er I go/I ever worship God.   Hymn of Sivaite Puritans. *Anonymous.*   WGRP

And thus with waters am I crowned.   My Cabinets Are Oyster-Shells. Margaret Cavendish, Dutchess of Newcastre.   ELP

And thy atonement my salvation win.   Sonnets: A Sequence on Profane Love. George Henry Boker.   AmePo

And Thy blessing descends as the rain!   Song of the Wind and the Rain. Solomon Ibn Gabirol.   TrJP

And thy blest Saviour's blood discharge the mighty sum.   The Hind and the Panther.   John Dryden.   FiP

And thy chaste kiss in my conceit exceedeth/Others' embraces, and love's chiefest blisses.   Madrigal: "The sound of thy sweet name, my dearest treasure."   Francis Davison.   EIL

And thy delivered saints shall dwell in rest.   Hymn of the Waldenses. William Cullen Bryant.   AnNE

And thy despis'd disdain too late shall find/That none are fair but who are kind.   A Deposition from Beauty.   Thomas Stanley.   EG; HBV 1-2

And thy first youth in glory is renewed.   To Zion.   Judah Halevi.   AWP

And thy heart rends thee, and thy body endures.   Parted Love.   Dante Gabriel Rossetti.   MaVP

And thy knowledge fills the earth.   Word of God, Across the Ages. Ferdinand Q. Blanchard.   AH

And thy loneliness is ended.   Art Thou Lonely?   John Oxenham.   PoToHe

And thy right hand shall guard their fame.   On Laying the Corner-Stone of the Bunker Hill Monument.   John Pierpont.   AnNE; PAH

And thy trees whispered what he feared to know.   Farewell to the Glen. Dante Gabriel Rossetti.   MaVP

"And thynk hit is a fulle fayre tyme/In a mornynge of May."   May in the Green-Wood.   *Anonymous.*   OBEV

And tickle both the feet of Pan!   Epigrams.   Theocritus.   AWP

And tie a handkerchief round my face,/That the people may not see.'   The Laird of Wariston (B vers.).   *Anonymous.*   ESPB

And ties their little bonnets/On the buttercup and clover.   April and May. Anne Robinson.   SUS

And till I expire,/Or till I grow mad, I/Will sing unto my lyre/Peg of Limavaddy!   Peg of Limavaddy.   William Makepeace Thackeray.   OBTV

And, till its burden goes,/Our work is–where it bleeds.   Love and Sacrifice. Bernard O'Dowd.   BoAV

And till no sacrificial suffering,/On any shrine is left to tell life's sting. Kinchinjunga.   Cale Young Rice.   AnAmPo; HBV 1-2

And till seven years were past and gone/True Thomas on earth was never seen.   Thomas Rymer.   *Anonymous.*   FaBoBa; OAEP; ViBoFo

And till that death our bodies two shall part.   In Praise of His Lady. Matthew Grove.   EIl

And till the coming of the soul/To fetch the flesh, we keep the roll.   An Epitaph: On Elizabeth Chute.   Ben Jonson.   EnRePo

And till the day I die, my thoughts/will be of thee.   Un Canadien Errant. *Anonymous.*   FSW

And till then? Get some rest. Be patient. Wait.   Wait.   Timothy Steele. PoA

And till tomorrow comes defers her fate.   The Shepherd's Week:.   John Gay.   EiCP; OAEL 1-2

And Time, a sea's chaos, below.   Allegory of the Adolescent and the Adult. George Barker.   LiTB; MasP

And time and place go down the wind.   "Tu Non Se' In Terra, Si Come Tu Credi...".   Kathleen Raine.   NeBP

And time can cure the sorrow/That finds no ease in speech.   Time. Marguerite Wilkinson.   HBMV

And Time flows past them like a hundred yachts.   Out of Time (excerpt). Kenneth Slessor.   CBAP

And Time has reached a round number.   A Round Number.   Keith Douglas.   NeBP

And time is better used/for other rituals–/long nights ahead.   Rune.   Philip Brasfield.   LFAC

And Time is conquered, and thy crown is won.   Life.   Edward Rowland Sill. TRV

And Time is reckon'd a discarded thing.'   The Plea of the Midsummer Fairies.   Thomas Hood.   OBNC

And time is slowing where his shadow stands.   Old Man.   Elizabeth Jennings.   NePoEA-2

And Time is waxing old.   Motto for a Sundial.   *Anonymous.*   FaBoEE

And time itself must beat to the cadence of this river.   In Arden.   Charles Tomlinson.   OxBC

And Time locked in his tower?   Merlin.   Edwin Muir.   CBEP; FaBoTw; OxBS

And time move only in the stars and tide...   The Bells of Ste. Anne des Monts.   Leo Cox.   CaP

And Time moved on a little way in Space.   Village Noon: Mid-Day Bells. Merrill Moore.   MoAmPo

And time of attack.   The Airman's Alphabet.   W. H. Auden.   NAMP

And time restores a world of happier hours.   Eclogue.   Edward Lear. FaBoNo

And Time's last sunset flames along my blood.   Perspective of Co-Ordination. Arthur Davison Ficke.   PoA

And Time, that dooms man's love to die,/Preserves a maid's alive.   At Casterbridge Fair.   Thomas Hardy.   EnLi 1-2

And Time that other beauty mars/Can reach you not among the stars. Dream Tryst.   Richard Le Gallienne.   HBMV

And Time the ruined bridge has swept/Down the dark stream which seaward creeps.   Concord Hymn.   Ralph Waldo Emerson.   ViBoPo

And time to watch rain soak the trees.   A Nation Wrapped in Stone. Roberta Hill.   BoWoP; CDW

And Time, untiring, never late,/Sweeps by on great steel wings,/entirely out of rhyme.   Little People.   Isaac L. Peretz.   TrJP

And Time went over them a hundred years ago.   Five Visions of Captain Cook.   Kenneth Slessor.   BoAV

...And timeless/is the wheel that brings it round.   The Wheel.   Wendell Berry.   GeTw

And times his quarters on the dial/That measures two feet to the mile.   Notes on a Track Meet.   David McCord.   SD

And times to come shall, weeping, read/thy glory,/Lesse in these Marble stones, then in thy/story. A Dirge upon the Death of the Right Valiant Lord, Bernard Stuart. Robert Herrick. SeCV 1-2

And tinged the eyelids and the hands. Mona Lisa. Walter Pater. OBMV

And tiny waves that run at you/Running on the shore. There Are Big Waves. Eleanor Farjeon. OnUR

And tip the envelope, from which/Drift scraps of borage, woodbine, rue. A Letter from Home. Mary Oliver. Str

And tipple my ale in the shade. Ad Ministram. William Makepeace Thackeray. HBV 1-2

And tiptoeing gently over the stairs/Turned down the gas in the hall. Death in Leamington. Sir John Betjeman. ACV; NoP; PoPl

And 'tis a record from the dream of life. Phantom or Fact. Samuel Taylor Coleridge. EnRP; ERoP 1-2

And 'tis joy come to our jolly wassail! Wassail Song. *Anonymous.* OHIP

And 'tis my touch shall swing the gates/Of Heaven when you die! The Ballad of the Angel. Theodosia Garrison. HBV 1-2

And Titus thenceforth shall abide/In paradise with me. The Flight into Egypt. Henry Wadsworth Longfellow. OBVV

And to a gloomy Erebus transform/The destined rival of Tempean vales. Colebrook Dale (excerpt). Anna Seward. NOEC

And to all other young men I now bid adieu. My New Garden Field. *Anonymous.* AmFP

And to all such I give fair warning/Of nightmares ere to-morrow morning. Hob Gobbling's Song. James Russell Lowell. OBCA

And to all the others who made/life possible while you were/away in India/eating the natives. The Final Toast. Tom Veitch. ANYP

And to amuse children–so small, small, small. The Smoked Herring. Charles Cros. GrPl

And to be alive/Means having to go away. The Invitation. Tom Buchan. ACV

And to be buried's but to go to bed. Epigram. Samuel (1612-80) Butler. FaBoEE

And to be gather'd rather then to fall. The Green-Sickness Beauty. Edward, Lord Herbert of Cherbury. AnAnS 2

And to be idle once was no distress. Past. Winifred Howells. AA

And to bed we go. Shadrach. *Anonymous.* FaBoNo

And to begin a fresh, but never-ending/story/Of life which shall endure forevermore. We'll Meet Again. J. Danson Smith. STF

And to Bow Lane jogged nodding in a chair. The Midnight Ramble. Charles Woodward. NOEC

And to Christ, the Virgin's Son,/For the mighty men I slew. Caoilte. *Anonymous.* KiLC

And to conclude, I know myself a man,/Which is a proud, and yet a wretched thing. Affliction. Sir John Davies. NOBE; OBSC

And to deform and kill the things whereon we feed. Psyche. Samuel Taylor Coleridge. ERoP 1-2

And to die bleeding–consummate with Life. Fulfillment. Helene Johnson. CDC; PoNe

And to die is different from what any one supposed, and luckier. Song of Myself. Walt Whitman. AtBAP

And to do that to birds was why she came. Never Again Would Birds' Song Be the Same. Robert Frost. CrMA; ForPo; FYAP; HAP; InPK; NIP; NoAm; NoP; VGW

And to do this, time is very short/and the task is great. A Short Winter Tale. Natan Zach. VWA

And to dwell in a vague intermediary unit/forever and ever."/Amen. The Educational Administration Professor's Prayer. Gerald Bobango. AMV-80

And to every suitor lie in every thing,/Like a king's favourite, yea like a king. Satire. John Donne. OBSV

And to feel it beginning/to burn its way through from the core. Peter Rabbit Sex Poem. Marilyn Bowering. CaPN

And to fire the penny cannon in the bow. My Ship and I. Robert Louis Stevenson. SUS

And to have done with love/For ever, for your sake. Envoi. Arthur Symons. UnTE

And to hear her calling a man might arise and thunder/On the doors of the grave. Regina Angelorum. Gilbert Keith Chesterton. ISi

And to hear it I'd always be willing and mute. Addressed to Lady ****, Who Asked What the Passion of Love Was? Charles Morris. NOEC

And to hear the birds how they flicker their wings/In the pitfall! I say it passeth all things. The Play of the Weather: The English Schoolboy. John Heywood. ACP

And to hear them thank our God for the day. The Marching Song of Stark's Men. Edward Everett Hale. MC; PAH

And to her all sounds are music. To Her. Robert Mezey. NaP

...And to her tomb this tribute bore. Timas. Sappho. LiTW

And to him the Tiger's yell/Comes articulate and presseth/On his ear like mother-tongue. Where's the Poet? John Keats. DiPo

And to him–there wasn't a single thing/wrong! The Pastor's Friend. *Anonymous.* STF

And to his arms I turn and sleep again. On a Gloomy Easter. Alice Freeman Palmer. OHIP

And to his fettered soul be given/The glorious freedom of the just. O Thou! Whose Presence Went Before. John Greenleaf Whittier. AH

And to his law compels all creatures to obey. The Faerie Queene. Edmund Spenser. WHA

And to know she will stay in that field till you die? Landscape with Tractor. Henry Taylor. MAYP

And to know you'll never be mine. East Virginia. *Anonymous.* FSW

And to make things tidy/I'll add his–James   Epitaph: "Here lie my husbands One Two Three." *Anonymous.* PV

And to many Deaths renew mee. Out of the Italian. Richard Crashaw. SeCV 1-2

And to midday change the/midnight. And It Came to Pass at Midnight. Yannai. TrJP

And to mix with the common mould! The Fate of the Oak. Barry (Bryan Waller Procter) Cornwall. OHIP

And to-morrow I will have to die. Little Mathiue Grove. *Anonymous.* BaBo

And to-morrow's uprising to deeds shall be sweet. The Message of the March Wind. William Morris. OBNC; OBVV; WiR

And to-morrow thou must borrow,/As thou borrow'd'st yesterday. Mortal, Sneer Not at the Devil. Heinrich Heine. TrJP

And to-morrow–to-morrow the women will wail. The War Dance. Robert V. Carr. PoOW

And to my dead heart run them in! The Celestial Surgeon. Robert Louis Stevenson. BBV; BrPo; EBCP; GoTF; HBV 1-2; HBVY; MoBrPo; TreFS; TrGrPo; TrPWD; TRV; ViBoPo; WGRP

And to my whole is JESU. Jesu. George Herbert. EBCP; MeLP

And to no call can Echo more reply– On the Death of Echo. Hartley Coleridge. BoAnP; GDP

...And to offer somebody/uncomprehending, impudent thanks. Accidents of Birth. William Meredith. NoP

And to old England it may be more/Than nine sail of ships on shore. England's Great Loss by a Storm of Wind. *Anonymous.* OBSS

And to one old crippled bear/that neither of us will ever see. Statement on Our Higher Education. W. M. Ransom. CDW

And to our bold commander, brave General Brock by name! Come All You Bold Canadians. *Anonymous.* ShS

And to our plaint be ever near. How Goodly Is Thy House. Henry S. Jacobs. AH

And to pay every debt/As it falls due. Lollocks. Robert Graves. DTC; EvOK

And to possess it pay its tribute–Death. The Ideal. Francis Saltus Saltus. AA

And to possess them, honour'd Margaret. To the Lady Margaret Ley. John Milton. GTBS; GTBS-P; OBEV

...And to pour down/Upon thee many a benison. Crutches. Robert Herrick. CaPo

And to read the wall-script dares not turn his head. Blockhouse. Olga Kirsch. PeSA

And to restore/All things, he rose/To die no more. Let All Created Things. Artis Seagrave. AH

And to 'scape stormy days, I choose/An Everlasting night. A Hymn to Christ at the Author's Last Going into Germany. John Donne. AnEnPo; DiPo; EBEV; EnRePo; FaBoRV; JCP; LiTB; OAEP; OBS; OxBoCh; ViBoPo

And to send you what I shall begge, his staires/In length and ease are alike every where. Letter to Sir H. Wotton at His Going Ambassador to Venice. John Donne. OBS

And to serene and constant thoughts gives birth. The Catholic Faith. Kenelm H. Digby. CAW

And to shed abroad its effulgence/To bless humanity's night. Life Is So Short. Margaret S. Hall. STF

And to some unexpected lass,/Some gangling lad, she flings–the Flower. The Flower. Lee Wilson Dodd. HBMV

And to that end as swiftly as I can/Shall take this copy to the "Englishman'. The Holiday. Thomas Frank Bignold. OBTV

And to the child conceived in the unborn womb/War. Cycle. Sean Jennett. WaP

And to the cross by good skill/Is the harp likened well. The Bishop's Harp. [(or Manning)] Robert Mannyng. ACP

And to the dove that hatched the dovetailed world/Was faithful unto death, and shamed the Devil. Lying. Richard Wilbur. HaCAP; SV

And to the earth are wafted down his sighs. Night-Wind. Beatrix Demarest Lloyd. AA

And to the end illuminate my mind. Appeal for Illumination. Luigi Pulci. ISi

And to the ground be hurled/Before my eyes? Love Poem. Jiri Wolker. LiTW

And to the herte stongyn. Al the Meryere. *Anonymous.* AtBAP; BoW

And to the Ile the name of him then buried in it gave. Metamorphoses. Ovid (Publius Ovidius Naso). CTC; OBVE

And to the lintwhite's piping/The many's the tune I play.   The Ninepenny Fidil.   Joseph Campbell.   HBMV

And to the men on board each ship who courage have displayed.   The Glorious Victory of Navarino!   *Anonymous*.   CoMu

And to the rhythm of their delight,/Old sorceries are made anew!   Moment Musicale.   Bliss Carman.   HBMV

And to the rhythm of their slow caress/Wavers and pauses on the verge of tears.   The Louse-Catchers.   Arthur Rimbaud.   LiTW

And to the sea as happily dost haste.   To the Nile.   John Keats.   OBRV

And to the ship he rowit fast.   The Historie of Squyer William Meldrum: Squire Meldrum at.....   Sir David Lindsay.   OxBS

And to the toils of nature true,/Wreathe their capacious nests anew.   Ode X: The First of April (excerpt).   Thomas Warton, Jr..   PBBP

And to the world's tumultuous stage/Prefer the blameless hermitage?   Inscription in a Hermitage.   Thomas Warton, Jr..   HBV 1-2

And to thee, blest Spirit,/Whilst all ages run.   Now the Day Is over.   Sabine Baring-Gould.   OxBChV

And to their shady Dens each Pair retreats.   The Hymn to Venus: Venus Goes After Anchises.   Homer.   OBVE

And to think of myself/That's soon to be dust.   The Old Man to His Scythe.   Denis Wrafter.   NeIP

"And to think of the Grande Affaire I gave up for it! Lawdy!   Some Days.   Maureen Owen.   APU

And to this evening hath me brought.   Inspiration.   Henry David Thoreau.   AA; AnNE; APA; FaBoBe; HBV 1-2

And to this false plague are they now transferred.   Sonnets, CXXXVII: "Thou blind fool, Love, what dost thou to mine eyes.   William Shakespeare.   WeW

And to us all the curse of secrecy.   Mask-Maker.   Michael Jackson.   OCNZ

And to use all things for the good of Thy children.   The One Thousandth Psalm.   Edward Everett Hale.   TRV

And to wander to the water-hole.   Zebra.   Isak (Karen Blixen) Dinesen.   GoJo; RFM

And to you from the womb of the dawn/Is the dew of your youth.   To the Bridegroom.   Judah Halevi   HW

And today or tomorrow it will abandon you.   The Horse.   Alfred Edgar Coppard.   BoAnP

And today takes charge.   Memory Movie.   Diane Webster.   AMV-81

And today the delft hens have laid delft eggs.   Ornaments.   Frank Ormsby.   CIP

And told me, dear, that you were glad to come!   Forgiven.   Margaret E. Sangster.   PoToHe

And told the cops she never saw him sober.   No Great Matter.   David Lawson.   VGW

And told them nothing that they wished to know.   Jesus.   James Philip McAuley.   CBAP

And told them, "You are seeking God."   Feet.   Mary Carolyn Davies.   WGRP

And told us if we wanted/to get to buffalo we/better get out here.   Fort Wayne, Indiana 1964.   Steven Lewis.   TAT

And Tom, the neighborhood maniac, hops the bus to/the Ohio State Fair.   Labor Day.   Gary Pacernick.   TAT

And Tom Tittlemouse woke.   Tom Tittlemouse.   *Anonymous*.   OxNR

And Tom went howling down the/street.   Tom, the Piper's Son.   *Anonymous*.   OxNR

And Tom went roaring down the street.   Mother Goose Up-to-Date.   Louis Untermeyer.   MoAmPo

And tomb time, death, and substance in thy maw.   To Night.   Thomas Lovell Beddoes.   LoBV

And tombstones rewrite names on dead men's graves.   Culbin Sands.   Andrew Young.   GTBS-P; OxBS; OxBTC

And tomorrow I'll start filling it,/For next year's girls and boys.   Conversation between Mr. and Mrs. Santa Claus.   Rowena Bastin Bennett.   ChBR; SiSoSe; TiPo

And tomorrow's dust flares into breath.   The Coming of Light.   Mark Strand.   HaCAP; PPJ

...And tomorrow the fair will be gone.   Love.   Anne Stevenson.   NCSH

And tongue is prest to publish out Thy praise.   Psalm XXVI.   Sir Philip Sidney.   FCP

And tongue the alum of/a lonely heart.   Love.   Darwin T. Turner.   BALP

And tonight I had no need of sleep/beside you.   Alone with the Dawn.   Matthew Sweeney.   AMV-80

And tonight/we are returning together.   The Walker River Night.   Adrian C. Louis.   STE

And Tonson yield to Lintott's lofty name.   On a Miscellany of Poems to Bernard Lintott.   John Gay.   CEP

And too fond loving of thy hair.   Would I Might Go Far Over Sea.   Marie de France.   AWP; PoRA

And too, some images of hair and lips.   A Lean Day in a Convict's Suit.   Jean Wahl.   VWA

And took away in his little pipe/Mother Sarah's song.   Mother Sarah's Lullaby.   Itzik Manger.   TrJP

And took 'em both off and was sick in 'em.   Limerick: "Thre was a young lady of Twickenham."   Oliver Herford.   LiBL

And took his hat and went to see.   Infirm.   Edward Sandford Martin.   ALV

And took if off at night so you could see the stars.   For Sue.   Phil Hey.   PPJ

And took the flowers away.   The Reaper and the Flowers.   Henry Wadsworth Longfellow.   AnNE; HBV 1-2

...And took the long way home/By road, a matter of several miles.   Brown's Descent; or, The Willy-Nilly Slide.   Robert Frost.   EvOK; MoAmPo; PoRA; StPo

And torn from those who had no power to save.   The Rising Village.   Oliver Goldsmith.   OBCV

And/toss/me/down/a/coin.   Beggar.   Nicanor Parra.   CAD

And tossed it like a river into the grass.   Breaking Green.   Michael Ondaatje.   NOBC

And, touch'd with love like mine, preserve my absent friend.   An Ode on the Popular Superstitions of the Highlands of Scotland...   William Collins.   CEP; EiCP; EnPE; LAuP; NOEC; OAEL 1-2; OAEP; OBEC

And touch it and it stings.   With Seed the Sowers Scatter.   Alfred Edward Housman.   EnLi 1-2

And touch my tongue with songs!   A Song of Desire.   Frederic Lawrence Knowles.   HBV 1-2

And touch our damp/cheeks with our/crumbling black fingers.   A Folding and Unfolding.   Welton Smith.   PoNe

And touch the small/distances the poem/begins   If It All Went up in Smoke.   George Oppen.   VWA

And touch the very peace/They issue from.   To Look at Any Thing.   John Moffit.   RFM

And touches vulgar life with silver/light.   Death's Transfiguration.   Israel Zangwill.   TrJP

And touching, and within call.   As Rocks Rooted.   Howard G. Hanson.   AMV-80

And touching every tree upon the hill.   The Call.   James Dickey.   NePoEA-2

And toward everything I fear in my dark/mind lost to my suddenly brilliant throat.   Doe.   Philip Dow.   NPGG

And town changed us, too.   Seven Poems.   Lorine Niedecker.   VGW

And trade our children/for the most expensive/versions of old lies.   War.   Richard Shelton.   PPJ

And trade with his Eternity.   Ceremonial Ode Intended for a University.   Lascelles Abercrombie.   OBVV

And tradesmen think they are surly/In spite of the wrinkled eyes/Scored by their years of smiling.   Variation on a Theme by Francis Kilvert.   Rolfe Humphries.   UnS

And trails its blossoms in the dust!   Suspiria.   Henry Wadsworth Longfellow.   ViBoPo

And trails the stars along with them.   The Secret.   George William Russell.   MoBrPo

And trampled their watchfire out and went away southward, stepping across the/Ventana mountains.   The Inquisitors.   Robinson Jeffers.   MoAmPo

And tranquil, from whose floor the new-bathed stars/Emerge, and shine upon the Aral Sea.   Sohrab and Rustum.   Matthew Arnold.   CABL; DTo; GTBS-P; MaVP; OBNV; OBWP; VLP

And Tray responsive joins with long and piteous yell.   A Disappointment.   Joanna Baillie.   NOEC

And tread the palace of the sky!   To a Skeleton.   Anna Jane Vardhill.   BLPA

And treasured therein/A dried snake-skin.   The Book of Hours of Sister Clotilde.   Amy Lowell.   APA

And treat some rescued Breton as a comrade and a guest.   The Two Captains.   William Johnson Cory.   FaPoR

And tree and house, and hill and lake,/Are frosted like a wedding-cake.   Winter Time.   Robert Louis Stevenson.   MoBrPo; OxBChV

And tree and singing bird in this still room.   Roads.   Ruth Dallas.   AnNZ

And trees are brown/And they are trees.   When I Loved You.   Charles A. Wagner.   InMe

And trees yield up their wordless therapy.   Catalpa Tree.   Miriam Waddington.   OBCV

And tremble at the sea that froths below!   The Rape of the Lock.   Alexander Pope.   ViBoPo

And tremble for the limbs of Helen and the secrets of/the sacred isle.   The White Isle of Leuce.   Sir Herbert Read.   FaBoTw

...And trembling, the ship/cuts through the waves and flies in silence!   On Leaving Cuba, Her Native Land.   Gomez de Avellaneda Gertrudis.   WPOW

And trifles–life.   Think Naught a Trifle.   *Anonymous*.   PoToHe

And trilled all night beneath the moon and/stars/The happy nightingales.   The Thanksgiving for America.   Hezekiah Butterworth.   PAH

And trip it in comely sort. Song. "O harmless feast." Barten Holyday. ElL

And trip the teachers on the stairs! End of Term. *Anonymous.* PoPle

And triple Cerberus from below/Must leashed t' himself with him a hunting go. Cupid Far Gone. Richard Lovelace. CaPo

And triumphantly the laughter of a child resounds. Ecstasy. Helene Swarth. WPOW

And trodden out the Mills– The Brain, Within It's Groove. Emily Dickinson. DiPo; NoAm; NOBA

And trotted out of town. Little Nag. *Anonymous.* OxNR

And troubled his soul no more. How We Burned the Philadelphia. Barrett Eastman. PAH

And Trouthe shal delivere, it is no drede. Truth. Geoffrey Chaucer. AWP; CBEP; MyFE; NoP; OAEL 1-2; OxBM

And trudge to the mill in the early morn. The Weaver and the Factory Maid. *Anonymous.* OBET

And true men be you, men,/Like those of Ninety-Eight! The Memory of the Dead. John Kells Ingram. AnIV; HBV 1-2; OnYI; OxBI

And trumpet of your resurrection. The Black Rock of Kiltearn. Andrew Young. FaBoTw

And trust in God whose grace alone/Can set a captive free. Mrs. Saunder's Experience. *Anonymous.* AmFP

And trust me not at all or all in all. Idylls of the King. Alfred, Lord Tennyson. NOBV; TrGrPo

And trust only what I have built/with my own hands. Beneath the Shadow of the Freeway. Lorna Dee Cervantes. FIA

And trust that world we won for you to keep! Epitaphs of the War, 1914-18. Rudyard Kipling. BrPo; OBWP

And trust the unknown for the known. The Over-Heart. John Greenleaf Whittier. NOCV; TRV; WGRP

And trust to be so long as life shall last. Upon the Author's First Seven Years' Service. Thomas Tusser. ElL

And, trusting in his God, surmounts them all. A Reflection on the Foregoing Ode. William Cowper. OBVE

And, trusting not To-morrow, snatch To-/day for ease! To Leuconoe. Eugene Field. AA; LoBV

And Truth and Right throughout the earth be/known/As in their home above. Clerical Oppressors. John Greenleaf Whittier. PAH; PPON

And Truth diffuse her radiance from the stage. Prologue, Spoken by Mr. Garrick... Samuel Johnson. CEP; EBEV; LAuP; NOEC; NoP; OBEC; SeCeV

And truth discern, who knew but learning's lore. Inspiration. Henry David Thoreau. WGRP

And Truth, from this approving stage,/Shall beam through every act and age. Jack the Giant Queller. An Antique History. Henry Brooke. NOEC

And Truth reveal herself to you! An Insincere Wish Addressed to a Beggar. Mary Elizabeth Coleridge. NOBV

And truth's perpetual lamp forbid to wane. In Exile. Emma Lazarus. SBG

And Truth shall make thee free, there is no fear! Ballade of Good Counsel (modern version). Geoffrey Chaucer. TrGrPo

And truth stands naked under the flashing charge. Recovery. F. R. Scott. CaP

And try another Key– I am alive–I guess. Emily Dickinson. NOBA

And try his works to do. There Is a Green Hill. Cecil Frances Alexander. BLRP; HBV 1-2; OxBChV; WGRP

And try if we cannot feel forsaken. In Neglect. Robert Frost. OBSP; VGW

And try to find a way out. But he/is everywhere like a twilight-hour. The Last Supper. Rainer Maria Rilke. MoRP; OFD

And try to picture/the water going up and down. Going Up and Down. Jim Daniels. AMV-81

And try to stack them in a better load. The Armful. Robert Frost. CMoP; OBSP

And try to still/Each rising murmur, and to God's sweet will/Respond– AMEN. Amen. Frederick G. Browning. BLRP

And trying to come to terms/with bits of selves/shelved on the day of arrest. Resurrection: Fragments. Felix Mnthali. WhB

And trying to yield/is like trying to fall/asleep, or trying not to. Night Thought. Gerald Jonas. NYBP

And trying with almost no success/to bring the present to its mouth. Sunday at the State Hospital. David Ignatow. CAPP

And Tuesday, Wednesday, Thursday, Friday,/Saturday and Sunday.) Constitution for a League of Nations. Arthur Guiterman. InMe

And Tully's curule chair, and Milton's golden lyre. Ode on a Sermon against Glory. Mark Akenside. CEP

And tun'd the harsh disorders of his Soul. Davideis. Abraham Cowley. OBS

And tune to Attic themes the British lyre. The Pleasures of Imagination. Mark Akenside. OBTV

And turf-bound silence, in the frosty year. Winter Sleep. Edith Matilda Thomas. AA

And turkey-red the leaves come down. Autumn. William Jay Smith. NePoAm

And turn again to telling time/By earth's uncertain seeds. Vernal Paradox. Kim Kurt. NePoAm-2

And turn all light, all love, as well as I. Friendship in Perfection. Andrew Michael Ramsay. NOEC

And turn and wave goodbye/to the Alexandria you are losing. The Lost, Dancing. Edward Field. GP

And turn back the stone of his fate. A Curse on a Closed Gate. James H. Cousins. AnIV

And turn'd my voice/Into the noise/Of those that sit and weep. His Lachrimae or Mirth, Turn'd to Mourning. Robert Herrick. SeCV 1-2

And turn his wild brown gaze/to mine. Gone. Joanna Thompson. AMV-80

And turn its punctured eyeballs/Toward the morning? The Tomb of the Kings. Anne Hebert. BoWoP; PBWP

And turn, lady, turn. On a Grey-Haired Old Lady Knitting at an Orchestral Concert... Furnley Maurice. CBAP

And turn me thrice around, around, around. The Shepherd's Week. John Gay. PBBP

And turn misfortune to such melody/That my despair thy transports would resemble! Sonnet: "Bird that discoursest from yon poplar bough." James Clarence Mangan. IrPN

And turn my back upon them and alter my mind. The Green Briar Shore. *Anonymous.* AmFP

And turn once more our water into wine! Religion. Henry Vaughan. NOCV; OAEL 1-2; OBS; OxBoCh

And turn our blessing to a curse/By keeping you asunder. Three Songs. Francis Beaumont. GoBC

And turn their backs, and straight on backs appear/Their shameful flying. Psalm VI. Sir Philip Sidney. FCP

And turn to him and be of womankind? A Question. Edna Livingston. GoYe

And turn with disinterested/hard energy, like the stars. My Sad Captains. Thom Gunn. CMoP; FaBoMo; LiTM; NePoEA-2; PAI; PoCh

And turned away from women/to complete his studies. Epitaph for Cu Chuimne. *Anonymous.* NOBI

And turned away; never to beat so loud any more. The Mystic Drum. Gabriel Okara. TTY

And turned its head away without the least surprise. People on Sunday. Edwin Denby. ANYP

And turned me into some concoction of his own. Creed of Mr. Nicholas Culpeper. Patricia Beer. OxBC

And turned my eyes away. Seen from the Train. C. Day Lewis. BoC

And turned my face against the wall. In the Night. Elizabeth Madox Roberts. WSC

And turned the farmboy's temper wolfish,/The housewife's, desultory. The Death of Myth-Making. Sylvia Plath. PoA

And turned the lightning's darts aside! On the Death of Benjamin Franklin. Philip Freneau. PAH

And turned the meeting-house upside down. The Owl and the Eel and the Warming-Pan. Laura E. Richards. EvOK; HBVY

And turned to a squash! O dear me! Limerick: "There once was a peach on a tree." Abbie Farwell Brown. TDH

And Turners turnd a gallant man,/at making of a Ballet. Turners Dish of Lentten Stuffe. William Price Turner. CoMu

And turning out the way I am, turning out to greet you. The Chateau Hardware. John Ashbery. CAPP

And turns all their Lead to Gold. The Beggar's Opera. John Gay. CEP

And turns the shrieking mill-wheels of his mind. Ulysses' Library. David Daiches. PoA

And turns to the cool hills singing in procession. Manifesto. Paris Leary. CoPo

And 'twas years ago; but that honored word/Preserved the North in the South's parole. Lee's Parole. Marion Manville. PAH

And twenty-eight each un-leap year. Rhyme for Remembering How Many Nights There Are in the Month. Justin Richardson. FaBoUs

And twenty-five times in the fanny. Limerick: "Mussolini's pet Marshal, Graziani." Thomas Russell Ybarra. LiBL

And twenty hundred thousand more for loan. A Stolen Kiss. George Wither. HBV 1-2; LiTL

And twenty jangling wires are set at war. The Sage in Unison. Harold Stewart. NOAV

And twenty-nine in each leap year. Days in the Month. *Anonymous.* OxNR

And twenty times they passd/The squire at his baking. The Duke of Athole's Nurse (B version). *Anonymous.* ESPB

And twenty years gone in an afternoon. Anniversary. Richmond Lattimore. NYBP; PoCh

And twice is a dream. The Desk. Cid Corman. VGW

And twice it is not given thee to be born. No Trust in Time. William, of Hawthornden Drummond. LoBV

And twisted and twined in a true-lover's/knot, which made all the parish admire. Lady Alice (C version). *Anonymous.* ESPB

And 'twixt earnest and joke/Enjoy'd the Lady. The Angel. William Blake. LiTB

And two lame men to carry them away. One fine day in the middle of the night. *Anonymous.* CenHV

–And two skin-changes in my sack. Southward Bound. J.F.A. Burt. PoSH

...And 2 Thermometers stewed in treacle/for supper. More Scraps of Lear: "Hassall irritates me." Edward Lear. FaBoNo

And two to bear my soul away. Matthew, Mark, Luke and John. *Anonymous.* FaBoCh; LoGBV; OxNR

And two to guard my soul asleep. Bed Charm. *Anonymous.* HBVY

And two will carry me home,/And we'll have Lord Thomas burned. Fair Annie. *Anonymous.* BaBo

And Typify, when Death hath clos'd her Eyes,/What she shall, at the Resurrection, rise. Vox Oppressi to the Lady Phipps. Richard Henchman. SCAP

And tyrants held him up as an example. In Time of War. W.H. Auden. CMoP

And unappeased, God/and unGod. A Peaceful Song. Natan Zach. VWA

And Uncle White Sea-gull and all. Numerous Celts (parody). J. C. Squire. SpRo

And unconcerned my future fate I trust/To that sole Being, merciful and just. An Answer to a Lady Advising Me to Retirement. Mary Wortley, Lady Montagu. TEP

And under a clear sky, under a clear green sky. In a Province. Frank Templeton Prince. MoVE

And under its shade, like a lion,/Were resting the will and the power. The Ballad of New Orleans. George Henry Broker. PAH

And, under the palm, the string/Sings as it wished to sing. Musician. Louise Bogan. GoJo; NYBP; UnS

And under your hair the faun's eyes/Look out on me? What Dim Arcadian Pastures. Alice Corbin. HBMV

And underscribed it,"Let them slumber,/Who if they woke could only weep'... Goya. Conrad Aiken. AmLP

And understand the cruel and lucid tongue/Directing the migration of the herds. The Lowveld. Charles Eglington. PeSA

And understood. Not Understood. Thomas Bracken. BLPA

And undervoicings of this loss to man's futurity/May wake regret in me. A Commonplace Day. Thomas Hardy. NOBV; PoPle

And undid my belief in the trinity. Sighed a Dear Little Shipboard Divinity. Conrad Aiken. OBAL

And undispensed sustain its discipline! Religio Novissima. Aubrey Thomas De Vere. IrPN; IrPN; NBM sustain its discipline!; NBM

And undulations to and fro. In Memoriam A.H.H., CXIII. Alfred, Lord Tennyson. VLP

And unfamiliar angles of the under sea. Rousecastle. David Wright. MoBS

And universal darkness buries all. The Dunciad. Alexander Pope. AtBAP; CoBE; EBEV; EnLi 1-2; FaBoPV; FiP; NOEC; NoP; OAEL 1-2; OBSV; PoEL 1-5; SCV; ViBoPo

And unkindness, alas, hath slain/My poor true heart, all comfortless. If in the World There Be More Woe. Sir Thomas Wyatt. EG; ElL; FCP; SiPS

And unmolestit be our silver spring. Medoro's Inscription for a Cave. John Stewart of Baldynnis BSV

And unpetalled the rose-bud from Paestum. Anacreontic. Austin Clarke. NOBI

And unspeaking we eat of love and hatred./Evening bread. Evening Bread. Jacob Glatstein. VWA

...And unsustained/By tepid fluids poured in its crying mouth. The Day. Roy Fuller. OxBTC

And unto generations all/Continue doth his verity. Make Ye a Joyful Sounding Noise. *Anonymous.* AH

And unto me no second friend. In Memoriam A.H.H., VI. Alfred, Lord Tennyson. VLP

And unto miserly merchant hulks converted. Good Ships. John Crowe Ransom. WeW

"And unto Thee shall be its desire." The Royal Crown. Solomon ibn Gabirol. AWP

And unto them God calls: The world is thine. To Liebig-6. August von Platen. PeHV

And up and off and on its way to God. An Old Irish Blessing. *Anonymous.* TRV

And up from the loveliest garden/Must climb for a glimpse of sea. An Autumn Garden. Bliss Carman. HBV 1-2

And up her rock, bare-breasted, comes to die? A Sea-Spell. Dante Gabriel Rossetti. SyP; VLP; WSC

And up that hill and down that dale/I'll curse Clovelly! A Travelogue: Clovelly. Carolyn Wells. InMe

And up there the old stars rustling and whispering. Ruins under the Stars. Galway Kinnell. LCAP; NaP

And upsetting the table in their eagerness to find it. Where Two O'Clock Came From. Kenneth Patchen. SO

And use it as ye may. The Outlaw's Song. Joanna Baillie. OBEV

And use thyself betimes to hear and grant our prayers. The Georgics. Virgil (Publius Vergilius Maro). AWP

And use up all the standing room/At church next Sunday. At Church Next Sunday. *Anonymous.* BLRP

And used him till he'd done his job,"/Was all thereon she said. A Practical Woman. Thomas Hardy. NAs

And ushers our next high holiday–the dead of the/night's high-noon! Sir Roderic's Song. Sir William Schwenck Gilbert. ShM

And using for apparel what was meant/To be the curtain of the inmost soul. The Fear of God. Robert Frost. MoRP

And vain is their endeavor/Who strive to do us harm. Saratoga Song. *Anonymous.* PAH

And valor claimed her own! McIlrath of Malate. John Jerome Rooney. PAH

And vanish. No Moon, No Star. Babette Deutsch. NYBP

And vanish, though the heavens dissolve, her/stay/Is in the WORD, that shall not pass away. On the Power of Sound. William Wordsworth. VLP

And vanished from earth in a blaze of blue. Arizona. *Anonymous.* ABF

...And vanishes/again/into his darkling courses. The Star-Nosed Mole. Robert Wallace. BoAnP

And vanishes along the level of the roofs. Morning at the Window. Thomas Stearns Eliot. AnEnPo; AWP; CAD; InPo; NePA; PoA

And vanishes among the stars. Music in the Night. Harriet Prescott Spofford. AA

And vanquished Good, victorious Ill/Be lost in one repose. Enough of Thought, Philosopher. Emily Bronte. NCEP

And various vice deserves a various shame. The Authors of the Town (excerpt). Richard Savage. OBSV

And vast and vague beyond the Golden Gate/Heaved Moab of the mountains like a sea. Sonnet: "High on the wall that holds Jerusalem." Gilbert Keith Chesterton. OBTV

And vast compassion curving like the skies. The Old Gods. Edwin Muir. BSV; EaLo

And Venus to the Loves around/Remarked how ill we all dissembled. An Ode: "The merchant, to secure his treasure." Matthew Prior. InPo; NOEC; NoP; PoRA; ViBoPo

And Venus Victrix to my heart doth bring/Herself, the Helen of thy guerdoning. Venus Victrix. Dante Gabriel Rossetti. MaVP

And veriest touch of powers primordial/That any hour-girt life may understand. The House of Life. Dante Gabriel Rossetti. HBV 1-2

And verily he will find the roots of the good and the/bad, the fruitful and the fruitless,... The Prophet. Kahlil Gibran. PoToHe

And very few are asking, Why not scrap it? This Excellent Machine. John Lehmann. OxBTC

And very much like what we have to put up with daily. On the Margin: "An anniversary approaches of the birth of God." David Wright. NAs

And Vickery shall not know. Vickery's Mountain. Edwin Arlington Robinson. MoAmPo

And view the mighty spoils thou hast in battle won! Epithalamium for Helen: Song of the Sleepy Bridegroom. Theocritus. HW

And view the shining glory shore,/My heaven, my home forevermore. I've Reached the Land of Corn and Wine. Edgar P. Stites. AH

And vigour attends it by which life is lengthened. Athletic Employment. *Anonymous.* SD

And vindicate bold England's right/And die for Erin's glory. Rodney's Glory. Owen Roe O'Sullivan. OnYI

And vindicate the state's humanity. New Hampshire (excerpt). Robert Frost. DBV

And vindicates its cause. In Love for Long. Edwin Muir. BoLoP; BSV; LiTM; MoBrPo

And Virtue lead to endless bliss above. To Stella. Hester Chapone. OBEC

And virtue the cornerstone. The People's King. Lyman Whitney Allen. PGD

And visions of pure love in amaranthine bowers! The Landrail. Sir Aubrey De Vere. IrPN

And voices as low as/The flow of my blood. Monkeys. Padraic Colum. AnFE; OxBTC

And vow 't was sweet to wait. When Love Comes Knocking. William Henry Gardner. AA

And vowed he'd steal no more! The Queen of Hearts. Mother Goose. FaBoBe; HBVY

And waddles through the Louvre. Madame Dill. *Anonymous.* FiBHP

And waft me Mary-high again. Queen of Horizons. Joseph Dever. ISi

And waft us home again! At Sea. James Whitcomb Riley. MOS

And wagging of hir seemely toppe, as if it were hir crowne. Metamorphoses. Ovid (Publius Ovidius Naso). OBVE

And waggles his graves at me. Country Greeting. Frank Steele. Psk

And wait and know the coming/Of a little love. At a Window. Carl Sandburg. FaBoBe; HBMV; MoLP; PoToHe; TrPWD

And wait, and tend our agonizing seeds. From the Dark Tower. Countee Cullen. BALP; BANP; BPo; CDC; IDB; LiTM; PoBA; PoNe

And wait for Father! John Plans. Dorothy Mason Pierce. BiCB

And wait for him/to tell me/a second time/for emphasis Waiting for a Second Time. Frank LaPena. STE

And wait for nothing to happen,/as nothing will. Solutions. David Barton. AMV-81

...And wait/For the Gossamer of Paradise/To spider in our dirt-filled eyes. Osip Mandelstam. Seamus Deane. FaBoPV

And waiting for their turn/To ripen and be gone. To One Far Away, Dancing. C. Stephen Finley. AMV-81

And waiting there for Joe to go/Is pretty cold work in the snow. Joe. David McCord. TiPo

And waits an hour sometimes for such a will. Will. Ella Wheeler Wilcox. BLPA; FPL; PoToHe

And waits and looks around him. Eros Turannos. Edwin Arlington Robinson. AnAmPo

And waits for a child/to burden with this heritage. Sometimes I Think of Maryland... Jodi Braxton. CNA

And Wajir Fort lies far, lies far/underneath the first pale star. The Soldier. Uys Krige. PeSA

And wake and feed the children/and grandchildren that they love. Kyoto: March. Gary Snyder. PPP

And wake me with the morning light./Amen. Now I Lay Me. *Anonymous.* SoPo

And wake me with their screams. Words, Like Spiders. P. Wolny. PCP

And wake the coming generations with a roar like thunder. Yiddish. Abraham Sutzkever. VWA

And wake to Raptures in a Life to come. To Mrs. M. B. on Her Birth-day. Alexander Pope. CEP; EnLoPo; OBEC

And wake to serve his master loyally. Man of the World. Michael Hamburger. NePoEA-2

And wake up to ourselves, nourished and surprised. For the Sleepwalkers. Edward Hirsch. FYAP; MAYP

And wake when it is day. The Cottager to Her Infant. Dorothy Wordsworth. CH; HBV 1-2; OxBChV

And wake with the war going on. The War. William Stanley Merwin. LCAP

And wakened a murmuring child/and another child. Once in a Lifetime, Snow. Les A. Murray. CBAP

And wakening, you'll be expecting dreams again. The Departure. Robert Pack. NePoEA

And wakes the pain/That lies low in/The hollows of my chest. A Visit from Alphonse. Paul Zimmer. GOYP

And wakes to dream all night. Scholars. Walter De la Mare. NoAm

And waking cri'd, This is the Gate of Heav'n. Paradise Lost. John Milton. EBEV

And walk home across the empty/giant parking lot. Chippewa Lake Park. Warren Woessner. TAT

And walk in heaven's pathway and the peacefulness thereof. To Begin the Day. *Anonymous.* BLRP

...And walk on through a world/Renewed and fresh as far as the mind/Can create. Proportions. Joseph Stroud. NPGG

And walk over to the Emersons' for a/chicken dinner. Alimentary. Clifton Fadiman. PV

And walk the rest of the way. The Draft Horse. Robert Frost. CMoP; HeIP; HoPM

And walk to town for some cream. The Hermit Picks Berries. Maxine W. Kumin. RFM

And walk toward you along a path/from the house of enormous sighs. Inanna and Enlil. Enheduanna. BoWoP

And walk upon your heavenly death. The Advantage of the Outside. Richard Eberhart. NePA

And walk with fearless step among mankind. Canzone: "Clear, fresh, sweet waters." Petrarch (Francesco Petrarca). LiTW

And walk with you, and talk with you, like any other boy. Rioupéroux. James Elroy Flecker. OBTV; OBVV

And walke her Mourner, in this Black and Whight. An Elegie Made by Mr. Aurelian Townshend in Remembrance of the Ladie.. Aurelian Townshend. SeCP

And walked full wide in wet and in dry. The Palmer. William Langland. ACP

...And walked home alone, shoe full of blood. Verigin 3. John Newlove. NeAC

And walked in Paradise! A Death-Bed. James Aldrich AA

...And walked off into the sunset/towards the silent sea. Sea Food Thought. John W. Moser. FAZ

And walked out proud as any queen. Red. Countee Cullen. GoSl

And walked through the gates hearing/the flapping of many wings/rising upwards. Sabbath. Rivka Fried. VWA

And walks on earth unseen for evermore. Tales of a Wayside Inn. Henry Wadsworth Longfellow. AnNE

And walks upon those waves that we call ocean. The Instrument. Kathleen Raine. PoA

And, Wall-flower! do thou into Death's dark porch/Be its bridal torch! The Wall-Flower. Henrik and Arnold Thaulov Wergeland. AWP

And wallowing hateful in the eye of day! Manhood. Oliver Wendell Holmes. AP

And wanders on a hundred years. The Pilot's Walk. Lee Gerlach. HoAn

And want me back... Letters Found near a Suicide. Frank Horne. BPo; PoNe

And wanton OPTICS roll the melting eye! The Loves of the Triangles (excerpt). John Hookham Frere. FaBoNo

...And wanton rolls/The glancing eye, and turns the changeful neck. The Seasons. James (1700-48) Thomson. PBBP

And war and victory, be thine arms/My grave! King Christian. Johannes Evald. AWP

And war began next Monday on the Danes. Scyros. Karl Shapiro. HoPM; LiTA; LiTM; MoVE; NePA; SeCeV; WaP

And War's gaunt Vultures that were lean,/have grown/Gorged in the darkness in a single night! The Battle-Field. Lloyd Mifflin. PAH

And warbled out their love-sick vows,/Whilst they both slept in their grave. The West-Country Damosel's Complaint. *Anonymous.* ESPB

And warblers chaunt their lov'd notes round. In Ringlets Curl'd Thy Tresses Flow. Mary Balfour. IrPN

And ward off all impending ill/Which over vice prevails. The Happy Nightingale. *Anonymous.* OxBChV

And warm wind stolen, part by part,/Your soul through faithless hours. Song from "Chartivel." Marie de France. AWP; EnLoPo; LiTW

And warmed my hands at London and went home. Homage to Wren. Louis MacNeice. EyDe

And warms to a spectral fire.... Inscription. Donald Jeffrey Hayes. CDC

And warrant prudence in a man. A Blue Ribbon at Amesbury. Robert Frost. NePA

And was buried before she was born. In the Garden There Strayed. *Anonymous.* LO

And was clasped in his bosom in Gizeh. Limerick: "There was a young lady of Rheims." Walter De la Mare. TDH

And was deftly pulled out by the beadle. Limerick: "A nice old lady named Tweedle." *Anonymous.* LiBL

And was forced to retire to a nunnery. Limerick: "There was a young woman named Plunnery." Edward Gorey. OBAL

And was heard through the whole of West Dumpet. Limerick: "There was an old man of West Dumpet." Edward Lear. EBEV

And was helped to a hansom outside. The Arrest of Oscar Wilde at the Cadogan Hotel. Sir John Betjeman. CMoP; DTC; EBEV; InvP; MoBrPo; NoAm; NoP; OxBTC

And was never allowed any dinner. Melodies. Lewis (Charles Lutwidge Dodgson) Carroll. FaBoNo

And was not speaking to me. Night on Clinton. Robert Mezey. AmPA; NaP

And was obliged to call him woman. A Sonnet on a Monkey. Marjory Fleming. FaFP; FiBHP

And was served soup/In a miracle-whip bottle/I still keep/For a keepsake. African in Louisiana. Kojo Gyinaye Kyei. PBA

...And was strangled, as things went,/For money, by one such picked off the streets. In Santa Maria del Popolo. Thom Gunn. NMP

And wash for old sows. Hay Is for Horses. *Anonymous.* OxNR

And wash your grubby hands, my dear,/For dinner's on the table! Ann and the Fairy Song. Walter De La Mare. FaBV

And waste its little hour. Autumn Woods. William Cullen Bryant. AnNE

And watch'd, all anxious, every wind that blows. She Comes Majestic with Her Swelling Sails. Robert Southey. MOS

And watch the branches quivering by a thread/Beyond interpretation of the shade. Indolence. Vernon Watkins. FaBoTw

And watch the frost/Frail as your love/Gather in the dawn. It Is the Time of Rain and Snow. Izumi Shikibu. WPOW

And watch the moon through the clear autumn. The Jewel Stairs' Grievance. Li Po. NOBA; OBVE

And watch the other die. The Wife. Robert Creeley. AmPC; AP; VGW

And watch the product coming up. A Garden Song. George R. Sims. NOBV

...And watch/the replays, in black and white, over and over. The Brain Cells. Donald Hall. TAP

And watch the riffraft driftwood floating by? History. Robert Francis. LCAP

...And/watch the snowflakes fall in her eyes. Blue Springs, Georgia. Ree Young. GOYP

And watch thy friends' ways ever! Counsels of Sigrdrifa. *Anonymous.* AWP

And watch with hungry eyes/When hope starts staggering. Mortality.
Naomi Long Madgett. PoBA; PoNe

And watch you dance playful as a baby girl? Song of Farewell. Nellie
Wong. BrSi

And watched, all anxious, every wind that blows. Homeward Bound.
Robert Southey. EtS

And watched as fallen warriors, each in turn,/Became a stillness at the
whirlwind's core. Iulus. Eleanor Glenn Wallis. NePoAm-2

And watched our strange and desperate embrace. The Voice. Edmund
Wilson. NYBP

And watched the eastern waters gather/Into a great virile flooding wave. The
First Invasion of Ireland. *Anonymous.* BIrV

And watched the old grey hands wind out his blood. At My Grandmother's.
David Malouf. PoAu 1-2

And watches for the trout in the holy well. Gateposts. Mebdh McGuckian.
FaBoIP

And watches rain come down/On a southbound express. John Garfield.
Nicholas Christopher. MAYP; NYP

And watching ants go in a row. Dick and Will. Elizabeth Madox Roberts.
BiCB

And water mains, writhing underfoot. The Roof Garden. Howard Moss.
MAT; NYP

And water rising in a smoke of waters. Waders and Swimmers. Stanley
Plumly. GeTw

And water, water: the innocent planet,/shining and shining. The Planet.
Josephine Jacobsen. GP

And watered with the wasteful warmth/of tears? The House of Life. Dante
Gabriel Rossetti. OAEP

And wax all fresh and green again. Jason and Medea. John Gower. ACP

And Wayland's work/is worn away. Junk. Richard Wilbur. HAP; NoP;
SaC; SM; WeW

And we all die/On the down side. Salt. Ruth Stone. NMM

And we all emerge entirely where we are. On Christmas Eve. W. S. Di
Piero. AMV-81

And we all fall down! Ring-Around-a-Rosy. Mother Goose. SoPo; TiPo

And we all move and love/To the grace of her sweet face. The Clock Tower.
Colleen Thibaudeau. WHW

And we all sing. Summer Words for a Sister Addict. Sonia Sanchez.
BlSi; BPo; UnPo

And we all smile together. Song of Three Smiles. William Stanley Merwin.
CoAP; VGW

And we all three ran away,/Look ye there! Cape Ann. *Anonymous.*
BLSo; FSW

And we all went home/In a taxi-cab. Our Visit to the Zoo. Jessie Pope.
PoPle

And we anchored safe in harbor/When the morn was shining clear. The
Captain's Daughter. James Thomas Fields. FaFP; HBVY

And we are a family again,/young and laughing/on the front porch. All.
Leona Gom. Str

And we are a' put down for ane,/the earl of Cassilis' lady. Johny Faa.
Anonymous. OxBB

And we are absent till another birth. A Letter from Li Po (excerpt).
Conrad Aiken. VGW

And we are brothers, you and I,/I and you. Brotherhood. J.J.W. PeHV

And we are children. Grant us a little Spring! Snow-Girl. Yunna Mortiz.
VWA

And we are hammered into one another's dreams/of comfort in the pure
imagined past. Becoming Real. Barry Goldensohn. AMV-81

–And we are left to drink the less/Of Babel's direful prophecy. Therefore Is
the Name of It Called Babel. Osbert Sitwell. MMM

And we are lucky if we keep them still. The Cave. Glenn Ward Dresbach.
RFM

And we are not told whose gift was gold/Or whose was the gift of myrrh.
The Perfect Gift. Edmund Vance Cooke. PCh

And we are on edge The Horizon Is Definitely Speaking. Diana Chang.
BrSi

And we are praying that she'll stay forever in our U.S.A. The History of the
U.S. Winifred Sackville Stoner. TreF; YaD

And we are seized by the cold terror/and sudden realization of discovery.
Return to Prinsengracht. Janice Blue-Swartz. AMV-81

And we are taken if we wish to give,/Are needed if we need. Masters.
Kingsley Amis. NePoEA; PoPl

And we are too poor for her madness. The Vietnamese Girl in the
Madhouse. David Fisher. NPGG

And we, being they, are still ourselves made whole. Knowledge after Death.
Henry Charles Beeching. OBVV

And we believed our love/Would last a thousand years. Three Poems.
Yakamochi. LiTW

And we both know release from pain/comes from/letting/go. Sutra Blues or,
This Pain Is Bliss. Jody Aliesan. LTB

And we both play I'm only three. When a Fellow's Four. Mary Jane Carr.
BiCB

And we brought her a leaf from the green-h'us. The Young Woman from
Aenos. *Anonymous.* OBAL

And we but fretful shades that dreamed before/That love, and are no more.
Love's Mortality. Richard Middleton. WHA

And we call it wisdom. It is pain. 90 North. Randall Jarrell. AP; CoAP;
CoBMV; FYAP; MoAB; MoPo; MoVE; NoAm; NOBA; TAP

And we called the baby John. The Baby's Name. Tudor Jenks. BiCB

And we can blast another hole in ourselves without a/sound. The
Anniversary. Ai. GP

And we can conquer, though we may not share/In the rich quiet of the after-
glow/What is to come. What Is to Come. William Ernest Henley.
HBV 1-2; TreFT

And we can go barefoot/Whenever we like. Spring. Marchette Chute.
TiPo

And we can need no other rest. O God Whose Presence Glows in All.
Nathaniel Langdon Frothingham. AH

And we can take, but not keep. Wild Dreams of Summer What Is Your
Grief? George Barker. OxBTC

And we choke on the hot/quivering air In the Cellars. Jiri Gold. VWA

...And we clamber out of sleep, holding on/to it with our hands... Visiting
Emily Dickinson's Grave with Robert Francis. Robert Bly. LCAP

And we clap hands together. Green Grass. *Anonymous.* CH; GBP;
OxBoLi; OxNR

And we could be together false/if she would but stay on. The Accomplices.
Conrad Aiken. NOBA

And we cry, There dies an Adonis! The Beggar's Opera. John Gay.
AtBAP; NOEC; PoEL 1-5; SeCeV

And we'd love each other better./If we only understood. If Only We
Understood. *Anonymous.* STF

And we'd see the old sod shanty on our claim. The Little Old Sod Shanty.
Anonymous. AmFP; AS; BFSS; BPAW; CoSo; FSW

And we danced upon her grave. Ballad: "My lady was found mutilated."
Leonard Cohen. OBCV

And we deny that in your music–here/Is your unchanged, unchanging
innocent core. For M. S. Singing Fruhlingsglaube in 1945. Frances
Cornford. BrRo; UnS

And we die as the animals die. The Black Faced Sheep. Donald Hall.
LCAP; SV

And we do as He says Assassination Poems. John Ridland. MAT; OFD

And we down the golden treasure/Which is known as lemon pie. Lemon Pie.
Edgar A. Guest. OBAL

And we drop like the fruits of the tree,/Even we,/Even so. Dirge in the
Woods. George Meredith. BoLiVe; EG; FF; LoBV; OAEP; OBEV;
OBNC; OBVV; SeCeV; VLP; WHA; WiR

And we easily catch a divine catarrh,/And an immortal cough. Night on the
Shore. Heinrich Heine. LiTW

And we eat. Night. Peter Everwine. NNaP

And we eat/the last of the honeycake/behind the drapes. The Death of the
Bronx. Chana Bloch. MAYP

And we envy no landsman his dream and sleep/When we're off to the fishing
ground! Off to the Fishing Ground. L. M. Montgomery. CaP

And we even came to wonder/Where–in the name of thunder–/We had met
before this scene. In a Hotel Writing-Room. John Cowper Powys.
OxBTC

And we fall, face forward, fighting, on the deck. Thirty Bob a Week. John
Davidson. BSV; CABL; EBEV; ELU; FaBoPV; FaBoTw; FaFP; LiTB;
NBM; NoAm; NOBE; NOBV; OAEL 1-2; OBNC; OxBS; OxBTC; PAI;
VLP

...And we feel/each shuddering go through our depths. Throughout the Day
We Are Able to Ban the Voices. H. Roland-Holst. PBWP

And we feel that our weakness is pitied on high. They Never Quite Leave
Us. Margaret E. Sangster. WBLP

And we find, at the end of a perfect day,/The soul of a friend we've made.
A Perfect Day. Carrie Jacobs Bond. BLSo; GoTF; TreF; WBLP

And we find hearteners among men/That ride upon horses. At Galway
Races. William Butler Yeats. LiSp; SD

And we fly through the air on the merry-go-round! June. Mary Carolyn
Davies. SiSoSe; TiPo

And we follow ever more! The Rigveda: Pushan, God of Pasture.
Anonymous. AWP

And we from their conjunctions take/Rules to make love an almanac. An
Hymeneal Song on the Nuptials of the Lady Anne Wentworth and...
Thomas Carew. CaPo

And we gave her all our money but our subway fares. Recuerdo. Edna St.
Vincent Millay. AmFN; CTBA; EvOK; FaFP; FPL; LiTA; LiTL; LiTM;
NoAm; OxBA; PoA; TAP

And we gave three cheers for the I.R.A./and Johnson's Motor Car.
Johnson's Motor Car. *Anonymous.* FSW

And we get nothing for it but toil and vexation.' Jack Tar. *Anonymous.*
OBSS

And we get on the bus,/Taking the last of it down with us. You Know.
Jean Garrigue. NYBP; UnPo

And we go out praising. The Flea Circus at Tivoli. Nancy Willard. HoAn

And we go stripped at last the way we came. After a Time. Catherine Davis. NePoEA

And we greet in his cradle our Saviour and King! A Christmas Carol: "There's a song in the air!" Josiah Gilbert Holland. HBVY

And we grow older and less strong. The End of the Year. Su Tung-P'o. PoPl

And we guardsmen fed to the tigers. Lament of the Frontier Guard. Li Po. AP; CoBMV; OBVE; OBWP; VGW; WaaP

And we had focused back on the furniture of the air. Melodic Trains. John Ashbery. NoP

And we have brought Harvest/Home to town. Harvest. Nashe [(or Nash)] Thomas. OBSC

And we have come into our heritage. The Dead. Rupert Brooke. MCCG

And we have fosaken the day,/And we have forgotten. Nocturnal Thoughts. Avraham Huss. VWA

And we have no way of following the wind/to the world's end. Joy. Gavin Bantock. OxBTC

And we have seen Jerusalem. To F. C. in Memoriam Palestine. Gilbert Keith Chesterton. HBMV

And we hold on together. Aunt Laura Moves Toward the Open Grave of Her Father. Joseph De Roche. HeIP

And we hold such poses forever. Photographs. Charles Wright. HoPM

And we in domestic economy too/Are thriftier, shiftier, wiser than you. The Thesmophoriazusae: Women Speak Out in Defense of Themselves. Aristophanes. TreFT

And we in dreams behold the Hebrides. The Misty Island. *Anonymous.* PoSH

And we keep up the practice from that day to this. The Birth of St. Patrick. Samuel Lover. HBV 1-2

And we knew another week would have to pass. On the Island. Dennis Brutus. WhB

And we know these scars by heart. Periods of Adjustment. Shawn Wong. BrSi

And we know we are moving/towards the songs of others. Speech to the Court. Walter Lowenfels. PPON

And we laugh/laugh laugh. Laughter. Miriam Waddington. WHW

And we laughed/and we laughed. We Laughed. Rochelle Kraut. APU

And we lay scared with our lust, delirious. Biography for Traman (excerpt). Winfield Townley Scott. ErPo

And we leave the old Great Central/line/For Banbury and buns. Great Central Railway, Sheffield Victoria to Banbury. Sir John Betjeman. NYBP

And we left him alone in his glory. Not a Sou Had He Got (parody). Richard Harris Barham. HBV 1-2

And we left the crew of the junk to chew/The bark of the rubagub tree. The Walloping Window-Blind. Charles Edward Carryl. InMe; LBN; MoShBr; NA; NLV; OBCA

And we left them to rest in the green shady drill. The Sioux Indians. *Anonymous.* AmFP; BFSS

And we, like all oceans,/would know/and love each other./Salaam. After the Rain. Stanley Crouch. CNA

And we little fishes/Were staring at him. The Dirigible. Ralph W. Bergengren. SoPo

And we live on powder/And DYNAMITE! Dynamite Song. *Anonymous.* AmFP

And we live outside his garden in our tempestuous rights In Favor of One's Time. Frank O'Hara. NeAP; PoA

And we'll adore the Justice too/That strikes our comforts dead. Submission to Afflictive Providences. Isaac Watts. NOCV

And we'll advertise: "Wanted/A minister and his wife!" Wanted, a Minister's Wife. *Anonymous.* BLPA; TreFS

And we'll all hang on behind! We'll Roll the Golden Chariot Along. *Anonymous.* ShS

And we'll all shout together in that morning. Burges. *Anonymous.* ABF

And we'll be wed, my own sweet lover,/And let them talk when we are gone. The Drowsy Sleeper (B vers.). *Anonymous.* BaBo

And we'll bring him up/As other folks do. Jack and Gye. *Anonymous.* OxNR

And we'll come no more a-souling/Till this time next year. Souling Song. *Anonymous.* OBET

And we'll come no more pace-egging/Until the next year. Eastertide. *Anonymous.* OxNR

And we'll cry till then, my stormy whore! Lassitude. Paul Verlaine. ErPo

And we'll dance internationally. Dance! Dance! Dance! Nationalism. Harry Roskolenko. AMV-80

And we'll die to the tune of the stream. A Morning-Piece; or, An Hymn for the Hay-Makers. Christopher Smart. NOEC

And we'll die in defense of the rights of the land./Derry down, down, down derry down. What a Court Hath Old England. *Anonymous.* TrAS

And we'll drink to the health of Bold Gattigan, and his gallant/lumbering crew! How We Logged Katahdin Stream. Daniel Gerard Hoffman. MaC

And we'll gang nae mair a roving. The Jolly Beggar. *Anonymous.* OxBB

And we'll go to the devil together./Ri fol de rol tol de rol lol. Macbeth (parody). Horace and James Smith. BXAP

And we'll have a pudding in half-an-hour. Girls and Boys, Come out to Play. Mother Goose. BrR; TiPo

And we'll have another drink before the boat shoves off! We'll Have Another Drink before the Boat Shoves Off. *Anonymous.* ShS

And we'll hurl the rebel crew from the land/we love the best,/Shouting the battle-cry of freedom. The Battle-Cry of Freedom. George Frederick Root. FaBoBe; FSW; PAH; PSoN; TreFS; YaD

And we'll laugh at the storms, the sleet and snow,/When we reach the little town of San Antonio. Doney Gal. *Anonymous.* OuSiCo

And we'll live our whole young lives away/In the joys of a living love. I Love You. Ella Wheeler Wilcox. BLPA; FaBoBe; FPL

And we'll make her go through frost and snow,/Handy, me boys, so handy. So Handy, Me Boys, So Handy. *Anonymous.* AmFP

And we'll meet him at the round up/on the plains beyond the sky. Utah Carroll. *Anonymous.* FSW

And we'll puff cigars from noon till night/as if we were alive. Song of the Round Man. Michael Palmer. NPGG

And we'll ride the prairie that we love the best. Good-By, Old Paint. *Anonymous.* CoSo

And we'll row you to the bright celestial shore. The Old Miner's Refrain. *Anonymous.* AmFP

And we'll show 'em what free men can really do! A New Wind A-Blowin'. Langston Hughes. TrAS

And we'll sing all the songs that we love to sing. Welcome. Rose Waldo. SoPo

And we'll sit till day, but we'll find the way/To drench the world with wine. Crotchet Castle. Thomas Love Peacock. NLV

And we'll strive to please you every day. Twelfth Night. William Shakespeare. DiPo; EBEV; EiL; ExPo; FaBoCh; FiP; HBV 1-2; HeIP; InPo; LiTB; LoBV; LoGBV; NLV; NOBE; NoP; OAEL 1-2; OAEP; OBSC; OxBoLi; PoRA; PPoe; ViBoPo; WiR

And we'll tak a cup o' kindness yet/For auld lang syne! Auld Lang Syne. Robert Burns. AWP; BiP; BLPL; BLSo; BSV; CEP; CoBE; EiCP; EnLi 1-2; EnPE; EnRP; FaFP; FSW; GoTS; HBV 1-2; InPo; LAuP; LiTB; MCCG; NOBE; OAEP; OBEC; OBEV; OxBS; PoLf; TEP; TreF

And we'll taste summer all winter long! Apple Season. Frances Frost. BrR; SiSoSe

And we'll think of the cold nor'westers/That we had in Paddy West's! Paddy West. *Anonymous.* ShS

And we'll wear his skin for linen,/Says the Shan Van Vocht. What Will We Do for Linen? *Anonymous.* GBP

And we made merry work. A Little Girl. *Anonymous.* OxNR

And we merged refreshed into/the breaking of camp and day. Prospecting. Archie Randolph Ammons. ConAP

And we might listen; and the world/Be uncreated at one stroke. If They Spoke. Mark Van Doren. ImOP

And we missed it, lost it for ever. Youth and Art. Robert Browning. BoLiVe; CTC; HBV 1-2; MBW 1-2; NOBV; ViBoPo

And we mount to its summit/round by round. Gradatim. Josiah Gilbert Holland. FaFP; GoTF; HBV 1-2; HBVY; OHFP; TreFS; WGRP

And we must enquire the way/of strangers– The Country North of Belleville. Al Purdy. NOBC

And we must make Thanksgiving pies! Thanksgiving Time. *Anonymous.* SoPo

And we must take the current when it serves,/Or lose our ventures. Julius Caesar. William Shakespeare. PoPl; TRV

And we must wait for day to see the sun. Columbia's Agony. Robert Henry Newell. OBAL

And we must work hard to lose ourselves. The Straw Men. Charles Culhane. LFAC

And we, naked and alone,/awakening forever... Into the Glacier. John Haines. CoAP

And we never shall see you again, dears! The King of the Hobbledygoblins. Laura E. Richards. OBCA

And we own the night We Own the Night. LeRoi (Imamu Amiri Baraka) Jones. BOLo; PoBA

And we pass by without holding. New York. Edward Field. NYP

And we pick what gems and scraps/There are from magnificence. Half-Bent Man. Richard Eberhart. NYBP

And we played all night. Kelly. Robert Hershon. NeAC

And we plunge, prison and passenger,/into the thunder!/America! In a Dream, the Automobile. Adrianne Marcus. AmC

And we poor seamen do lie on the top,/Whilst the landmen lies below. The Seamen's Distress. *Anonymous.* OBSS

And we praise, for grace so free,/Thee, Jehovah-Jesus, Thee! Praise to Jesus! William Ball. BePJ

And we, promised by blossoms,/run gathering/bushels of cinders, black and still as nuns. The Reckoning. Alice R. Friman. AMV-81

And we publish whatever/You want us to utter. Note on Modern Journalism during the Last Campaign. E. L. Mayo. FAZ

And we're almost there. How Far Is It Called to the Grave? *Anonymous.* BLPA

And we're bound for South Australia. The Codfish Shanty. *Anonymous.* GBP

And we're late and lost unless we run. Camptown. John Ciardi. WaP

And we're taking the road together. Romany Gold. Amelia Josephine Burr. HBMV

And we're waiting to hear 'em/Sing out "'Ere she blows!" The Coast of Peru. *Anonymous.* EtS

And we rebuild our cities, not dream of islands. Paysage Moralise. W. H. Auden. OAEL 1-2; UnPo

And we rest, having done what men are best at. The Barn. Wendell Berry. EyDe

And we run because we like it/Through the broad bright land. The Song of the Ungirt Runners. Charles Hamilton Sorley. EnLit; GoTF; HBMV; MoBrPo; OBEV; TreFT

And we sail onward, and our wake is fire. As Ocean's Stream. Fyodor Tyutchev. AWP

And we sat there/king to king/with the single pawn. Spassky at Reykjavik. David Fisher. AMV-81

And we see their eyes,/Innocent as Christ's. Deer in Aspens. Kay DeBard Hall. GoYe

And we shall keep it with the keeper of the golden gates. Blind Date. Conrad Aiken. DL; MoVE; ViBoPo

And we shall know. London Town. Lionel Pigot Johnson. FaBoPP

And we shall know it's true/When the glass goes black. True Night. Rene Char. PoPl

And we shall name him darkness. Song: "Mother Mother shave me." *Anonymous.* BoWoP

And we shall sink in the impossible strife,/And be astray for ever. Life and Thought. Matthew Arnold. FiP

And we shall speak. We never spoke before. Epitaph for the Poet V. Arthur Davison Ficke. HBMV

And we sing. Two Dedications: The Wall. Gwendolyn Brooks. PoBA; PoNe

And we sit side by side/together in the canoe of our beaches. The Same Side of the Canoe. Alda Espirito Santo. PBWP

And we slept, at life's command. The Net-Menders. Brian Vrepont. BoAV; PoAu 1-2

And we slept–dreamlessly. The Sleepers. Louis Untermeyer. MoLP

And we stand all bloodied in the light. The Fire. William Burford. NePA

And we stand up before Him–what/then? What Then? *Anonymous.* STF

And we still cast shadows. A Farewell, a Welcome. Lisel Mueller. MOON

And we take it back. We give again... Tattoos. Charles Wright. GP

And we take the judgment seat. Ostrava. Petr Bezruc. LiTW

And we thank Him for His grace. Face to Face with Reality. John Oxenham. WBLP

And we took the starry lane/Back to Dublin town again. Is It a Month. John Millington Synge. BIrV

And we tracked wearily down that two-lane highway/back to Santa Fe Oh But It Was Good... Harold Littlebird. VoR

And we tramped from Lazy Harry's, not five miles from Gundagai. On the Road to Gundagai. *Anonymous.* PoAu 1-2

...And we/Turn again to our mother, our revels. The sea, the sea! The Sea. Francis Webb. CBAP; PoAu 1-2

And we've got to get ourselves/Back to the garden Woodstock. Joni Mitchell. NIP

And we've made a great mess of love, mind-perverted, ego-/perverted love. The Mess of Love. D. H. Lawrence. OAEL 1-2

...And we walk off arm in arm,/each other's windfalls, dodging the pigeons. Lady Luck. Ann Gottlieb. NMM

...And we want more: red giant,/white dwarf, black hole dense, invisible, all in one. July 4th. May Swenson. PoA

And we watch the clear sky bend. Birthday. William Stafford. NAs

And we watched him out of sight, and we conjured up the/devil! The Singing-Woman from the Wood's Edge. Edna St. Vincent Millay. HBMV

–And we, we get it all from them for nothing. A Living. D. H. Lawrence. RFM

...And we went keeled over/The streaming sea. The Nightfishing (excerpt). W. S. Graham. BSV

And we went on to heaven the long way round. Among the Worst of Men. Henry David Thoreau. LiTA; PoEL 1-5

And we went on with the game. My Grandpa Died Today. Joan Fassler. DL

And we went out into the night/Where all the constellations shine. She Wept, She Railed. Stanley Jasspon Kunitz. ErPo; VGW

And we were a' put down for ane,/A fair young wanton lady. The Gypsy Laddie (A vers.). *Anonymous.* BaBo; ESPB; HAP

And we were a' ta'en. Fish Riddle: "The robbers came to our house." *Anonymous.* GBP

"And we were black," three shades reply, "but kings." Black Majesty. Countee Cullen. PoBA; VGW

...And we were less lonely! Sinners. D. H. Lawrence. ViBoPo

And we were safe again. Tom's Angel. Walter De La Mare. BoC

And we were the only part of the night that we/Couldn't believe. The Terrace. Richard Wilbur. MiAP

And we were there, but we never said a word. Jeff Buckner. Frank Beddo. WTO

And we were wondrous merry. I Gave Her Cakes. *Anonymous.* AtBAP; TreFS

And we who are assigned to life,/Are theatre to this death. News Reel. David Ross. GoYe

And we who don't/can only look on, astonished. Mae West. Edward Field. FYAP

And we who screamed to know it/know it, and grow old. But You, My Darling, Should Have Married the Prince. Kathleen Spivack. AmPA; NMM

And we will all enlist again. When the War Is Over. William Stanley Merwin. OBSP

And we will fly to a very happy land. My Friend the Wind. King D. Kuka. VoR

And we will give them roses for each night's/reward.' The Meeting. Pierre Louys. PeHV

And we will muffle up the sheepfold bell/Whene'er thou listenest to Philomel.' The Plea of the Midsummer Fairies. Thomas Hood. OBRV

And we will not speak of life or believe in it or/remember it/as we go. Smile, Death. Charlotte Mew. WPOW

...And we will pass a pleasant week/Together, watching the falling of the leaves. A Parisian Idyl (excerpt). George Moore. SyP

And we will take this as an illumination and kiss one another. The Friendship Game. Pier Giorgio DiCicco. AMV-81

And we will talk of old days again. Moose Lake State Hospital. Dennis Shady. LFAC

And we will talk of simple homely things,/Of flowers, of laughter, of the flash of wings. To My Friend, Grown Famous. Eunice Tietjens. HBMV

And we will walk together, for a while. Afternoon. Donald Hall. Str

And we wish them a happy, a happy New Year! Comfort and Tidings of Joy. *Anonymous.* FSW

And we with God Himself commune. Communion. J.L. Spicer. BLRP

And we, with them one day shall stand/Before Him, face to face! Not One Is Turned away from God. Dorothy Conant Stroud. STF

And we won't drag on behind. Roll the Chariot (with music). *Anonymous.* AS

And we would know each other sometimes/with a love that touches indifference. The River Again and Again. Linda Gregg. NPGG

And we would walk together/Lovers the same old way. A la Claire Fontaine. *Anonymous.* FSW

And wealth is mine! To My Friend. Anne Campbell. PoToHe

And wealth to the poor, and healing/to the sick. Joy of Life. Moses Ibn Ezra. TrJP

And wear a wig of sauerkraut. On Halloween. Shel Silverstein. PoSC

And wearing sneakers, I sign with those/who have signed for me. SM. Stanley Moss. AMV-81; NYP

And wears the turning globe. The Night is Freezing Fast. Alfred Edward Housman. AtBAP; CMoP; LiTM; LoBV; MoPo; OBSP; PoPle; PrIm

And wears upon her quiet face/The Spirit's tender grace. Quaker Ladies. Ellen Mackay Hutchinson Cortissoz. AA

And weather them down to sand on the sea-floor. Rock (excerpt). Kathleen Raine. ImOP

And weave but nets to catch the wind. Vanitas Vanitatum. John Webster. NOBE; OBEV

And weave into his shame, which like the dead/Shrouds me, the hopes that from his glory fled.' Lines Written on Hearing the News of the Death of Napoleon. Percy Bysshe Shelley. ChRP; ERoP 1-2

And weave it for your head against you wake. Silex Scintillans. Henry Vaughan. AnAnS 1

And weave the many fragments/To depict a life that's real. My Book of Life. Frances Humphrey. STF

And weave us one and wave us under/Where is neither faith nor wonder. Song with Words. James Agee. MoAmPo

And weave your winding-sheet, till fair/England be your sepulchre. Song: "Men of England, Wherefore Plough." Percy Bysshe Shelley. SaC

And weaves delight through all the griev-/ing years. Electra. Francis Howard Williams. AA

And wed thy folk agein to stedfastnesse. Lak of Stedfastnesse. Geoffrey Chaucer. AWP

And weel may the keel row,/That my laddie's in. The Keel Row. *Anonymous.* PoPle

And weep amid those tresses, child,/Contented to be thus beguiled. No and Yes. Thomas Ashe. HBV 1-2

And weep his widow's tears. The Fortunate One. Harriet Monroe. AA

And weep new when a new year refits thee for weeping. Lament for Adonis. Elizabeth Barrett Browning. ATP

And weep the more because I weep in vain. Sonnet on the Death of Richard West. Thomas Gray. CEP; EiCP; EnPE; LAuP; NOEC; NoP; OAEP; OBEC; PeHV; PoEL 1-5; SeCePo; ViBoPo

And weep water ful bitterly/And teres of blood ever among. M and A, R and I. Anonymous. OxBM

And weep with Peter at the triple cock-crow. The Trappist Abbey: Matins. Thomas Merton. PoPl

And weeping with his priest, in penance died. The Bandit Peter Mancino's Death. Anonymous. CAW

And weird and childlike dreams/Sir/Like green water. The Skinny Girl. Anne Hebert. BoWoP

And welcome home the blossom of the Drynaun Dhun. The Drynaun Dhun. Anonymous. GBP

And welcome Pain, that is Love's counterpart! Beloved, from the Hour That You Were Born. Corinne Roosevelt Robinson. HBMV

And welcome Queen Alice with ninety-times-nine! To the Looking-Glass World It Was Alice That Said (parody). Lewis (Charles Lutwidge Dodgson) Carroll. Par

And welcome thee, and wish thee long. Song on May Morning. John Milton. BoLiVe; BoNaP; GN; HBV 1-2; HBVY; TrGrPo

And welcome welcome welcome him. Communion of Saints: The Poor Bastard under the Bridge. Marie Ponsot. VGW

And welcomes little fishes in/With gently smiling jaws. How Doth the Little Crocodile. Lewis (Charles Lutwidge Dodgson) Carroll. EnLi 1-2; FaBoCh; FaBoCo; FaBoEE; FaBoNo; FaFP; GoTF; LoGBV; MoShBr; NIP; NLV; NOBL; NOBV; Par; ShM; SoPo; SpRo; TiPo; TreFS

And well he ends for love who dies. Ode: "Now each creature joys the other." Samuel Daniel. LoBV; OBSC

And well it seemes a Day that never wasteth/should have a morning that for ever lasteth. Sonnet XXXVII. William Alabaster. AnAnS 1

And well it were to know no more/The burthen of the barren shore! The Barren Shore. Coventry Patmore. GBL

And well might bless the fever that was sent,/To rid him hence, and his worse fate prevent. A Satire on Samuel Butler (excerpt). John Oldham. OBSV

And well revenge may rest contented,/Since drums and parchment were invented. The Wild Boar and the Ram. John Gay. PPON

And wends his ways through the twilight the Foe of the/Gods to meet. The Story of Sigurd the Volsung (excerpt). William Morris. PoEL 1-5

And went away, and left no monument. The Coolin Ridge. William Bell. PoSH

And went dowdily on with whatever/pigeons do when they're knitting. Wild Oats. Norman MacCaig. OxBTC

And went home to my Christian school/To kick a football through the air. A Welcoming Party. John Montague. FaBoIP; IPY

And went into the room of burning lights. Victory. Lionel Pigot Johnson. NOBV

And went on working evermore/In his unweeting way. New Year's Eve. Thomas Hardy. MoBrPo; NoAm

And went to bed to mend his head/With vinegar and brown paper. Jack and Jill. Mother Goose. FaFP; HBV 1-2; HBVY; OxBoLi

And went to His death in their diadem. Address to the Crown. Charles L. O'Donnell. GoBC

And went toward the door,/which I opened all the way. A Lovely Young Moor. Anonymous. BoWoP

And went walloping, walloping,/walloping home. The Doggies Went to the Mill. Anonymous. OxNR

And went with half my life about my ways. He Would Not Stay for Me. Alfred Edward Housman. PeHV

And wept, and weep until she come again. Kore. Ezra Pound. HBV 1-2; LoBV

And wept and wrung her hands when she was/taken. Piers Plowman (excerpt). Anonymous. EnLit

And wept. (I heard her tears.) The Blessed Damozel. Dante Gabriel Rossetti. AnFE; AWP; BLPL; BoLiVe; DiPo; GoTL; GTBS; HBV 1-2; LiTB; LoBV; MasP; MaVP; NOBE; NOBV; NoP; OAEL 1-2; OAEP; OBEV; OBNC; OBVV; OHFP; PoEL 1-5; SeCeV; SpRo; TEP; TrGrPo; VLP; WHA

And wept some purple tears. The Poster Girl. Carolyn Wells. BXAP; HBV 1-2; InMe

And wept water full bitterly,/And teres of blod ever among. A New Song of Mary. Anonymous. MeEL

And were all put down for one light wife:/The Earl of Cassilis' honey. Johnny Faa, the Lord of Little Egypt. Anonymous. EnSB

And were for salt and instinct to a city. The Fishvendor. William Meredith. SaC

And were forever in a wakened world. The Path of the Stars. Thomas S. Jones, Jr. MoRP; WGRP

And wersh the wine o' victorie! The Mither's Lament. Sydney Goodsir Smith. ACV; OxBS

And west went Captain Quiros, east went Lane. Terra Australis. Douglas Stewart. NOAV

And wet the flowers with her tears where both her lovers sleep. Bill and Parson Sim. Anonymous. BPAW

And wet young oak leaves fingering the pane. To a Friend in the Country. Oliver St. John Gogarty. OnYI

And wex so mat, that joie nor penaunce/He feleth non, but lith forth in a traunce. Troilus and Criseyde. Geoffrey Chaucer. LoBV

And what a nice time/Had Mr. Pyme! Mr. Pyme. Harry Behn. TiPo

And what a time a reel of tape can play! I Was Fair Beat. Robert Garioch. OxBTC

And what/about us? The Universe. May Swenson. SUW

And what are they when these remain/The ruin'd shells of hollow towers? In Memoriam A.H.H.,LXXVI. Alfred, Lord Tennyson. VLP

And what befell them I never can tell,/For they never came back again. The Two Rats. Anonymous. PoPle

...And what breaks/on that black shore breaks in me. There. Robert Mezey. NaP

And what buildest thou?"/"Heaven," he said. The Builder. Willard Wattles. HBMV

...And what can be flatter than a flat poem? A Poem–Good or Bad–A Thing–With One Attribute–Flat. Melech Ravitch. VWA

And what care we how many petals fall! Villanelle of Marguerites. Ernest Christopher Dowson. EnLi 1-2; MoBrPo

And what could a remoter scene show more? Retirement. William Cowper. FaBoPP

And what cuckoos say you know. Bow-Wow, Says the Dog. Anonymous. OxNR

And what do you get for it? Halitosis! You Buy Some Flowers for Your Table. Samuel Hoffenstein. DBV; TrJP

And what does not die. Meridian. Brewster Ghiselin. AMV-80

And what flared up and joined the serious climb/inside our faces no one will ever know. Houses Burning: Quebec. Patrick Anderson. NOBC

And what goes on, my love, while you're away,/You'll never know. A Certain Lady. Dorothy Parker. NIP

And what good Arms shall take them away again? A Map of Verona. Henry Reed. ChMP

And what he does, all days, and years. To Know Whom One Shall Marry. Anonymous. GBP

And what her eyes enthralled her tongue unbound. Lesbia. William Congreve. OBSP

And what I am I will not see. Lais to Aphrodite. Edwin Arlington Robinson. FaBoEE

And what I don't know isn't knowledge. I Am the Great Professor Jowett. Anonymous. FiBHP; PV

And what I have, my God, I give to Thee. A Confession. Paul Verlaine. CAW; WGRP

And what I left undone. The Young Man Thinks of Sons. R. A. K. Mason. AnNZ

And what I love he snatches,/And what I love not, brings. The Farm-Woman's Winter. Thomas Hardy. VLP

And what I saw, I keep/Forever. Remainder. Frederika Blankner. GoYe

And what I see/I'll never tell. Chamber-Pot Rhyme. Anonymous. GBP

...And what I seem to have saved for my/old age is science fiction. Whatever It Was I Was Saving for My Old Age. Ann Darr. SUW

And what I sing now is for myself alone. I Looked for a Sounding-Board. H. Roland-Holst. WPOW

And what I was is no affair of yours. In Peterborough Churchyard. Anonymous. NOBL

And what I would not part with I have kept. I Could Give All to Time. Robert Frost. MoRP

And what if I don't, and what if I do? Philosophy. Dorothy Parker. InMe

And what is a Ceiling when the Ceiling has flown? The Floor and the Ceiling. William Jay Smith. GrPl; OBCA

And what is else not to be overcome? Paradise Lost. John Milton. WHA

...And what is left/of your traces/Is so goddamned beautiful. Afterword. Anonymous. ILwL

And what is wrong in woman's life/In man's cannot be right. A Double Standard. Frances E. W. Harper. BlSi

And what it covers...let all men forget. Without Regret. Lilith Lorraine. PGD

And what it says she never will remember. Improvising. Louise Townsend Nicholl. NePoAm-2

And what itself will say to me,/Beguiles the centuries of way! Though I get home how late, how late! Emily Dickinson. MoAmPo

And what long kisses and what delight/In such a night may be! Healing the Wound. Heinrich Heine. UnTE

And what loss is but one/Of his brides to the Lord? Flowering Currant. Patrick MacDonogh. ErPo

And what love as the elephant chimes. The Dance of the Elephants. Michael S. Harper. LCAP

And what man cares for withered fruit? The Ripe Fruit. *Anonymous.* UnTE

And what men say of her they mean/No more, than that on which they lean. Hudibras. Samuel (1612-80) Butler. OBSV

And what miraculous escapes! Houses. Donald Justice. EyDe; PPJ

And what my father used to say,/Is good enough for me. Lines for a Worthy Person Who Has Drifted by Accident... Sir Alan Patrick Herbert. NOBL

And what of John? The less that's said/Of John, I think, the better. A Dead Letter. Henry Austin Dobson. HBV 1-2

And what Oh what would the neighbors say! My Brother Bert. Ted Hughes. BBGG

And what on earth he means can no man say. Soul-Severance (parody). St. John Emile Clavering Hankin. FaBoPa

And what piece of me is it then/Buried down in North Carolina. A Poem for a Poet. Audre Lorde. NMM

And what rough beast, its hour come round at last,/Slouches towards Bethlehem to be born? The Second Coming. William Butler Yeats. AtBAP; BIrV; BLPL; CMoP; CoBMV; DiPo; EaLo; EnL; ExPo; FaBoMo; FaBoPV; FF; ForPo; GTBS-P; HAP; HeIP; HoPM; InPK; InPo; InPS; LiTB; LiTM; LoBV; MasP; MAT; MBW 1-2; MoAB; MoBrPo; MoRP; MoVE; NAWM 1-2; NIP; NoAm; NOBE; NoP; OAEL 1-2; OAEP; OxBI; OxBTC; PAI; PPoe; PPP; PrIm; SBVL; SCV; SeCePo; SeCeV; SoSe; TEP; UnPo; WaP; WeW

And what's a careless kiss or so/To one remembered song? The Kerry Lads. Theodosia Garrison. HBMV

And what's more, I hate you. The Complete Misanthropist. Morris Bishop. FiBHV; FPL; TW

And what's, oh, what's a Sabine farm to me without Maecenas! My Sabine Farm. Eugene Field. InMe

And what seems won paid for as in defeat. The Mountain Cemetery. Edgar Bowers. ConAP; NePoEA

And what shall happen I no longer know. Come to Birth. Abbie Huston Evans. NePoAm

And what shall I choose, if I am free to choose? The Choice. Hilary Corke. MP; NYBP

And what shall we do to the Blackbird/Who listens unawares? The Naughty Blackbird. Kate Greenaway. HBVY

...And what/she asks and what she gives. The Agonizing Memory. Pierre Louys. PeHV

And what she calls a week/Is forever and a day! Forever and a Day. Thomas Bailey Aldrich. HBV 1-2

"And what,' she said,/"Are the dead/But earth?' An Old Waterford Woman. Mary Devenport O'Neill. NeIP

And what single light is not drowned/In the glut of the sea's dark sound? Light. Jon Silkin. NoAm

And what so far from me, though nearer once? Poem: "To go, to leave the classics and the buildings." Gavin Ewart. NeBP

And what thanks do you get? The gate–I know it! Poems in Praise of Practically Nothing. Samuel Hoffenstein. InMe

And what thanks do you get? You're just as dirty! Poems in Praise of Practically Nothing. Samuel Hoffenstein. InMe

And what the Christ had done to him,/He knew, and not the Sanhedrim. Religion and Doctrine. John Milton Hay. WGRP

And what they could not eat that night,/The Queen next morning fried. Good King Arthur. Mother Goose. HBVY

And what they dared, they dare. To the Veterans of the Abraham Lincoln Brigade. Genevieve Taggard. OFD

And what they did bury was a seed. Epitaph for the Tomb of Adolfo Baez Bone. Ernesto Cardenal. PoL

And what this Couple did, Sir,/Alas I dare not Name. The London Prentice. *Anonymous.* CoMu; UnTE

And what this is all about. Companions, a Tale of a Grandfather... Charles Stuart Calverley. FaBoCo; HBV 1-2; NA; NOBL

And what thou art, America shall be. Prophecy. Gulian Verplanck. MC; PAH

And what thou art may never be destroyed. No Coward Soul Is Mine. Emily Bronte. BrRo; EaLo; FaFP; ForPo; GoTF; GTBS; HeIP; LiTB; NoP; OAEP; OBNC; OxBI; PoEL 1-5; TrCP; TreFS; TrPWD; ViBoPo; VLP

And what thy God's to thee? The Return of Napoleon From St. Helena. Lydia Huntley Sigourney. AA

And what Timotheus was, is Dryden now. Poetical Numbers. Alexander Pope. OBEC; SeCePo

And what was black she turned it red. Will the Weaver. *Anonymous.* AmFP

And what was godlike in this generation/Was never to be born.' Casino. W. H. Auden. MoPo

And what was left, I'm told, sir,/Was served out to the fleet. The Derby Ram. *Anonymous.* ViBoFo

And what was the toast?/schiehallion! schiehallion! schiehallion! Canedolia. Edwin Morgan. FaBoCo; PoSH

And what we thought, and silenced, none shall know. Nothing to Say, You Say? Conrad Aiken. LiTA

And what will be has been. Proverbial. John Seller Anson. AMV-80

And what will be left/of magnificence in/Connecticut then? The Connecticut Elm. Emma Swan. PoPl

"And what will you leave to your brother John's wife?"/"Grief and misfortune all her life." The Cruel Brother (B vers.). *Anonymous.* BaBo; ESPB

And what worked with these/Can with any words, I say. Poetry Defined. John Holmes. GrPl; PP

And what you dole will be my stay/Today and every day. God of Abraham, of Isaac, and of Jacob. *Anonymous.* TrJP

And what you give, God will re-pay,/Both here and in the Judgment day. The Framework-Knitters Petition. *Anonymous.* CoMu

And whatever else was theirs. At the Fillmore. Philip Levine. NNaP

And whatever we ask may the Son of God give us. A Hundred Thousand Welcomes. *Anonymous.* WTO

And whatsoever is consumed/The same amount remain– Hope Is a Subtle Glutton–. Emily Dickinson. DiPo

And wheels rumbling/through the dark city. The Great Figure. William Carlos Williams. InPK; NoAm; PAI; QFR

And whelm'd in deeper gulfs than/he. The Castaway. William Cowper. AtBAP; CABA; CEP; CoBE; EiCP; ELP; EnPE; FiP; GTBS; HeIP; InPo; MOS; NOBE; NOEC; NoP; OAEL 1-2; OAEP; OBEC; PoEL 1-5; PPoe; PPP

And whelpes playe with my skin.' The Hare. *Anonymous.* OxBM

And when a car pulls up a bell/rings and I say, "Fill 'er up?" Working at a Service Station, I Think of Shinkichi Takahashi. Dennis Finnell. FAZ

And when am I coming back to stay. Revelation. Carole C. Gregory. BlSi

And when another day shall break/Unto Thy service may we wake. Grace at Evening. Edgar A. Guest. TrPWD; TRV

And when do they leave there? Never... Where Are the Ones Who Lived Before? *Anonymous.* HAP

And when found, 'tis lost even then. Alas How Long. *Anonymous.* ErPo

And when from bondage we are liberated our former sufferings shall/fade from mind.' Moreton Bay. *Anonymous.* CBAP

And when God sends a cheerful hour, refrains. Sonnet XVIII: "Cyriack, whose Grandsire on the Royal Bench." John Milton. OBS

...And when has happiness ever/required much evidence to begin/its leaf-green breathing? The Truro Bear. Mary Oliver. SoSe

And when hé came to his father's years might have worn horns. On Sir John Calf. *Anonymous.* FaBoEE

And when he cried the little children died in the streets. Epitaph on a Tyrant. W. H. Auden. ELU; HeIP; OBSP

And when he does, I'll let you know. The Perils of Invisibility. Sir William Schwenck Gilbert. StPo

And when he falls, he falls like Lucifer,/Never to hope again. King Henry VIII. William Shakespeare. GoTF

And when he goes he carries/No more baggage than a bird. Fragments on the Poet and the Poetic Gift. Ralph Waldo Emerson. PP

And when he got unto the end,/Then he began again. Cock Robin Got up Early. *Anonymous.* OxNR; PBBP

And when he has it,/Gas, dikes him! The Scots in Berwick. *Anonymous.* OxBM

And, when he next doth ride abroad,/May I be there to see! The Diverting History of John Gilpin. William Cowper. BeLS; EiCP; FaBoBe; FiP; GN; HBV 1-2; HBVY; InMe; LAuP; OBEC; OBNV; PoPle; RoGo; TreFS

And, when he please, cold rocks inflame. Love's Victories. James Shirley. GoBC

And when he preaches he shuts mine. On Hearing a Lady Praise a Certain Reverend Doctor's Eyes. George Outram. DBV; GoTF; TreFT

And when he saw the beauty of her face/It took his breath away. Death Was a Woman. Sydney King Russell. GoYe

And when he sings Cuckoo, the summer draweth near. The Cuckoo. *Anonymous.* CBEP; GBP; OxNR

And when her father wad deceasd,/Heir of the crown was she. Hind Etin (A version). *Anonymous.* BaBo; ESPB

And, when I am not, the lock on my sleep, that keeps me/from waking and finding you are not there. Locks. Kenneth Koch. CoAP

And when I ascend the third time, I will fall forever,/Missing the earth entirely. Three Presidents: John F. Kennedy. Robert Bly. LCAP

And when I awoke I lay at the edge of a cliff. Dream. William Jay Smith. MoVE

And when I bake, I'll give you/a cake,/If I am not mistaken. To the Bat. *Anonymous.* OxNR

And when I change, let vengeance on me fall. The Constancy of a Lover. George Gascoigne. EnRePo; QFR

And when I'd tiptoe softly out/I'd meet the wise men coming in. Christmas Morning. Elizabeth Madox Roberts. ChBR; MoAmPo; PCh; PoSC; SUS

And when I die may I say the pater,/Virgin Mary. O Virgin. *Anonymous.* WTO

And when I die, may I still numbered be/With the rough soldier, to eternity. The Pluralist and Old Soldier. John Collier. NOEC

And when I died—the neighbors came/And buried brother John! The Twins. Henry Sambrooke Leigh. BiCB; CenHV; HBV 1-2; HBVY; MaC; PoPl; ShM; TiPo

And when I do she's there, held/sure, the very light we see by held steady, longer than even a/life. Family/Grove. Albert Goldbarth. HaCAP

And when I fart, nothing can be more pretty. Epigrams in Distich, II: To a Flatterer. *Anonymous.* FaBoEE

And when I found the door was shut,/I tried to turn the handle, but– Humpty Dumpty's Recitation. Lewis (Charles Lutwidge Dodgson) Carroll. FaBoCo; FaBoNo; FiBHP; GTBS-P; NBM; OnMSP; OxBChV; OxBoLi

And when I gently put it down/It licked me on the hand. I Held a Lamb. Kim Worthington. SoPo; TiPo

And when I hear her, I have wings. Gibberish. Mary Elizabeth Coleridge. MoVE

And when I lectured him some more/Went in his house and shut the door. The Snail. Grace Hazard Conkling. SUS

...And when I look in his eye, it/is not his eye that I see. A Poet at Twenty. Donald Hall. EAS

And when I'm dead and buried,/Susanna, don't you cry. Oh! Susanna. Stephen Collins Foster. OBAL

And when I'm sad, I take it out again. Rhyming a Friend's Poem. Yu Hsuan-chi. BoWoP

And when I mash down on your little starter,/then your spark plug would give me fire Terraplane Blues. Robert Johnson. BluL

And when I open the box, I know/What kind of self awaits me there. Things. Walter De la Mare. PoA

And when I rose, I found myself in prayer. To William Wordsworth. Samuel Taylor Coleridge. EnRP; ERoP 1-2; OAEL 1-2

And, when I saw the flower at my feet,/I understood it all. A Summer Santuary. John Hall Ingham. AA

And when I sleep he goes, because/I cannot see him then! The Ugstabuggle. Peter Wesley-Smith. AmMo

And when I take it I both live and die. Cherry Blossoms. Michael Lewis. UnTE

And when I think that Michael Angelo/Hath leaned on me, I glory in myself. The Old Bridge at Florence. Henry Wadsworth Longfellow. EyDe

And when I thought of his new joke in my sleep,/I shuddered. A Dream about an Aged Humorist. Aaron Zeitlin. VWA

And when I turn they see death in my face. Mirror. Peter De Vries. PoA

And when I've done,/My brother and son/May end their tricks in a string. Old Rowley the King. *Anonymous.* APAS

And when I will be old enough/to know. Turning Thirty. W. D. Ehrhart. AMV-81

And when I woke he'd seen to our repairs. Soldier's Dream. Wilfred Owen. ILwL

And when is it too old? Five Years Old. Lysbeth Boyd Borie. BiCB; SiSoSe

And when it comes it brings good cheer. Christmas. Mother Goose. SoPo

And when it does, we lie back in our watery hair and rock. Spider Crystal Ascension. Charles Wright. GeTw; HaCAP; LCAP

And when it gets dark he will remember something/strongly worded to say on the subject. Seascape. Elizabeth Bishop. FaBoWP; MoAB; MOS; OxBC; PPP

And when it's all gone, me lads,/we'll go whalin' for more. Coast of Peru. *Anonymous.* FSW

And when it's gone it's gone/so hurry/hurry Sale. Miller Williams. WeW

And when it's three, he'll call for you,/Cuckoo! Cuckoo! Cuckoo! Our Clock. Florence Eakman. SiSoSe

And when it shineth sometimes we shall know/That memory is possession. Sorrows Humanize Our Race. Jean Ingelow. WGRP

And when it slideth forth, it goes as nice/As when a man doth walk upon the ice. De Puero Balbutiente. Thomas Bastard. OBSP

And when it snows we'll sleep. Song: "Let's sing a song together once." Louis Simpson. NePoAm

And when kind we'll say, oh, bless you, oh! you naughty, dear, delightful men. You Naughty, Naughty Men. T. Kennick. BLSo

And when my cheery glass I tope,/I'll fancy then I am the Pope. The Pope He Leads a Happy Life. Charles James Lever. HBV 1-2

And when my flesh dissolves in death/My soul shall love thee more. O Could I Find from Day to Day. Benjamin Cleavland. AH

And when my Gotes shall han their bellies layd,/Cuddie shall have a Kidde to store his farme. The Shepheardes Calender. Edmund Spenser. EnPo; OAEL 1-2

And when our flesh is only dust,/Abide our souls with Thee. Hymn. Elizabeth Barrett Browning. TrPWD

And when our money is all gone we'll boldly go to sea. Adieu My Lovely Nancy. *Anonymous.* OBET

And when our money is all gone, we'll plough the bay some more. The Schooner Fred Dunbar. Amos Hanson. AmFP

And when our money is all spent we'll go to sea once more. The Holy Ground. *Anonymous.* OBSS

And when our money it is all spent, we'll hunt the woods for more. The Maids of Simcoe. *Anonymous.* ShS

And when Queene Katherine puts up her/finger]/Att her Graces commandement I'le/bee.' Robin Hood and Queen Katherine. *Anonymous.* ESPB

And when recalled they must bear arms again. Walking Wounded. Vernon Scannell. OBWP

And when she came back her husband was well. There Was an Old Woman, and What Do You Think? Mother Goose. HBV 1-2

And when she came back she found 'em all a-loffing. The Old Woman Who Lived in a Shoe. *Anonymous.* OxBoLi

And when she did die/She'd nothing to leave. There Was an Old Woman. *Anonymous.* OxNR

And when she moves, her mien and grace/Prove her the goddess of the place! The Indian Maid. Edward Thompson. NOEC; OBTV

And when she took it from me she left me naught/Save desiring and a yearning heart. The Lark. Bernard de Ventadour CTC

And when she wakes she will not think it long. Rest. Christina Georgina Rossetti. EnLi 1-2; HBV 1-2; NOBE; OAEL 1-2; OBEV; OBNC; OBVV; TrGrPo

And when she was bad, she was horrid. There Was a Little Girl. Henry Wadsworth Longfellow. BLPA; FaFP; OxBChV; YaD

And when th'hast done, a stench, or fog is all/The odour I bequeath. Unprofitablenes. Henry Vaughan. AtBAP; SeCV 1-2

And when thy my good lord comes home/I will say thou's my sister's son. Lord Thomas and Lady Margaret. *Anonymous.* BaBo; ESPB

And when the brave fall–ever hallow/their tomb. Fort McHenry. *Anonymous.* PAH

And when the earth shall claim your limbs, then shall you truly dance. The Prophet. Kahlil Gibran. DL

And when the evening shadows fall/Bestow thy blessing on us all. O God of Stars and Distant Space. John Franzen. AH

And when the life of Christ in men/Revives its faded image, then/Will all be Paradise again. On the Origin of Evil. John Byrom. NOEC

And when the morrow came I answered still/"Tomorrow." Tomorrow. Felix Lope de Vega Carpio. CAW

And when the night comes away flies she. Of All the Gay Birds That E'er I Did See. *Anonymous.* PBBP

And when the only tears we shed/Are of the dying on the dead. Epigram: "Our youth was happy: why repine." Walter Savage Landor. FaBoEE

And when the poor elephant suffers from bile,/Then tenderly lace up his stays! The Panther. *Anonymous.* NA

And when the singing and dancing it was all over/We raised our ports and sang out with good cheer. On Board the Leicester Castle. *Anonymous.* OBSS

And when the stormy winds do blow,/My body lies and sleeps.' Proud Lady Margaret. *Anonymous.* BaBo; ESPB

And when the town burnt in a flame,/With tan ra ra, tan ta ra ra, from thence we came. The Winning of Cales. *Anonymous.* CoMu; OBSS; OBTV

And when the water settled I could see/Two English kings among their drowned Britannias. Washing the Coins. Douglas Dunn. FaBoPV

And when their back's to me,/I will love whom I please. The Cuckoo. *Anonymous.* AmFP

And when they are Crack'd, away they are pack'd,/for Virgins, away to the City. The Merry Hay-Makers. *Anonymous.* CoMu; ErPo

And when they brung his body home/A barrel of tears was shed. Bill Peters, the Stage Driver. *Anonymous.* CoSo

And when they could na farther gae,/They coost the lovers' knot. Earl Brand; or, The Douglas Tragedy (A vers.). *Anonymous.* FaBoBa; ViBoFo

And when they gits to playing with your heart and they starts/blackin' your heart around. I Work All Day Long for You. *Anonymous.* WTO

And when they got home to their own parents dear,/They had no objections and married they were. The Silk Merchant's Daughter. *Anonymous.* BFSS 041

And when they meet the bishop's cloak,/to mak it shorter by the hood.– Hughie Graham. *Anonymous.* OxBB

And when they're child-making they're seldom crying. I Will Give My Love an Apple. *Anonymous.* CBEP

And when they snap at it, a puff of dust/comes out of their dry throats. Heaven and Hell. *Anonymous.* DL

And, when this dust falls to the urn,/In that state I came, return. The Retreat. Henry Vaughan. AtBAP; ATP; AWP; BLPL; BoC; BoLiVe; ExPo; FF; GTBS; GTBS-P; HAP; HBV 1-2; HeIP; InPo; InPS; InvP; JCP; LiTB; LoBV; MeLP; MePo; NIP; NOBE; NOCV; NoP; OAEL 1-2; OAEP; OBEV; OBS; PAI; PoEL 1-5; PoPle; PoRA; PPP; SBVL; SeCePo; SeCeV; SeCP; SeCV 1-2; TreFT; TrGrPo; ViBoPo; WHA

And when those masters stir that slave will jump. The Summing Up. James Simmons. PoL

And when thou comst to the border-side,/Remember the death of Sir Hugh of/the Grime.' Hughie Grame (A version). *Anonymous.* ESPB

And when thus well it fares with thee, wouldst thou/Have it to go unto poor Damma now? Epigrams. Martial (Marcus Valerius Martialis). OBVE

And when Thy kingdom unto us shall come,/Our servant be! The Master. S. D. Robbins. BePJ

And, when thy sight that radiant beauty blears/And dazzles thy weak eyes, see with thine ears. To My Soul. Phineas Fletcher. OxBoCh

And when thy soul and body part,/As innocent as now thou art. To His Son, Vincent. Richard Corbet. BoC 024; FaBoCh; LoGBV; OBS; OxBChV; TrGrPo

And when time comes, for old time's sake/Primrosing in our earliest brake. Threshold. Edmund Charles Blunden. HBMV

And when we are all dead, this dam will stand and give. Boulder Dam. May Sarton. SaC

And when we combine, it is matter/doing and doing and doing and doing. The Art of Love. Richard Grossman. AMV-81

And when we die, we die all over. Vita Brevis. *Anonymous.* UnTE

And when we find thy blessed mind,/Instruct our lips to speak. Almighty Lord, with One Accord. Melancthon W. Stryker. AH

And when we have the Child commended/To her warm bosome, then our Rites are ended. The New-Yeeres Gift, Sung to the King in the Presence at White Hall. Robert Herrick. SeCV 1-2

...And when we meet someone/we say, "Have a good day." The Day You Are Reading This. William Stafford. PoA

And when we were in love there was grace and good temper. Oh send to me an apple that hasn't any kernel. *Anonymous.* FaBoCh; LoGBV

And when wise poets shall search out to see/Good men, they find them all in thee. A Panegyric to Sir Lewis Pemberton. Robert Herrick. CaPo

And when would he ever stop? The Aga Khan. Steve Orlen. Psk

And when you hear her kind reply,/Return with pleasant warblings. The Message. Thomas Heywood. HBV 1-2

And when you of your neighbor speak/Use words of charity. Guard Thy Tongue. Alice M. Barr. STF

And when you rise with waking eye,/Remember then this lullaby. A Lover's Lullaby. George Gascoigne. HBV 1-2; OBEV

And when you sleep be your sad coverlet. Sonnet: "Now keep that long revolver at your side." George Hetherington. NeIP

And when you sleep you remind me of the dead. The Dug-Out. Siegfried Sassoon. AtBAP; MCCG; MoBrPo; MoVE; OHIP; WaaP; WaP

And when you snap a Wishbone, that/You'll win the larger half! Thanksgiving Wishes. Arthur Guiterman. PoSC

...And, when you wake, you find/your swag, the camp, the plains all white with frost. The Star-Tribes. *Anonymous.* NOAV

And when you wake you see again/The lovely things you saw in dream. Jack Frost. (Thomas Nicoll Hepburn) "Setoun. Gabriel" HBV 1-2; HBVY

And when your back in turned they will leave you to mourn. Polly Williams. *Anonymous.* ABF

And when your mouth is mine, I miss/The wistfulness of wanting you. Love-Songs, At Once Tender and Informative. Samuel Hoffenstein. OBAL

And whence the music no one made? Proper Clay. Mark Van Doren. PoRA; TrGrPo

And whene'er you meet a crocodile/He's ready for his dinner. If You Should Meet a Crocodile... *Anonymous.* OnUR; SoPo

And where are the galleons of Spain? A Ballad to Queen Elizabeth. Henry Austin Dobson. ALV; OBVV

And where are you off to, my son, my shadow,/with the bill unpaid, as the door swings shut? Spiv Song. Royston Ellis. PeHV

And where he is and where we are/Will never seem again so far. A Comrade Rides Ahead. Douglas Malloch. HBMV

And, where he lost his Arms, despairing dies. Halieutica. Oppian. OBVE

And where he must re-enter and re-enter. In the Tank. Thom Gunn. NoAm

And where he points that will really be the trail. A Snapshot of Uig in Montana. Richard Hugo. NPAW

And where hens lay, and when the duck will hatch. The Lout. John Clare. NBM

And where his hand touched flesh a quickened green. First Love. Charles Gullans. NePoEA

And where I faile, let Lydgate bere the lak. The Fall of Princes: Epilogue. John Lydgate. OxBM

And where I gave a pickle befor/It's now I'll give you three.' Lady Isabel and the Elf Knight (H version). *Anonymous.* ESPB

And where I heard the good priest say the Passion. Palm Sunday. Francis Jammes. CAW

And where I would be/I can not. Oh That I Were. *Anonymous.* OxNR

And where is sleep? Odes, V. Hafiz. AWP

...And where is the hand to 'gave/Words that tell so much for the lost on land? Week-End by the Sea. Edgar Lee Masters. MoAmPo

And where it was the ship went down/Is what the sea-birds know. An Inscription by the Sea. Edwin Arlington Robinson. AWP; ELU; FaBoEE

...And where perhaps remains still the reflection/of her moist lips. The Songs of Bilitis. Pierre Louys. UnTE

And where the dust is still, is still, is still. Spanish Blue. Herbert Morris. NYBP

And where the little God himself is warden. Fidessa, More Chaste Than Kind, XXXVII. Bartholomew Griffin. EG; LO

And where the old are young again,/I'll clasp my mother's hands. Beautiful Hands. Ellen M. Huntington Gates. TreF

And where the rain and river met/The water got completely wet. When I Went out. Karla Kuskin. NTCP

And where the shadows fell, they lay. Stanzas. Paul Goodman. PoA

And where the sun that shineth is/God's grace for human good. O Holy City Seen of John. Walter Russell Bowie. AH

And where the Virginians from Virginia have to ride/automobiles because the Virginians from... First Families Move Over! Ogden Nash. FaBoCo

And where they cast their anchor down,/Rose Freedom's realm to be. The Word of God to Leyden Came. Jeremiah Eames Rankin. AA; HBV 1-2; MC; PAH; PAL

And, where they've children, nobody/Will let me next or nigh them/For fear I'll say good-bye to the The Knowledgeable Child. Leonard Alfred George Strong. OBMV

And where Thou art is heaven. Dying That I Might Live. Charles Wesley. BePJ

And where thou mad'st an end, there I'le begin. Silex Scintillans. Henry Vaughan. AnAnS 1

And where 'tis safely kept, the fiend/Can do no mischief there. The Ceremonies for Candlemas Day. Robert Herrick. EnLit; OAEP

And where were the white flowers. Les Sylphides. Louis MacNeice. BoLoP; CoBMV

And where will his eyes find rest The Seventh Hell... Jerome Rothenberg. CoPo; NMP

And where you come, an exquisite/Image of death and lover of it,/Life sings a serenade. During a Chorale by Cesar Franck. Witter ("Emanuel Morgan") Bynner. AnAmPo; HBMV

And where you love you cannot break away. Reason for Not Writing Orthodox Nature Poetry. John Wain. HaMV; MP; PP

And wheresoe'er she stept, that spot transformed/Bears her soft smile amid his work of wrath. Ute Pass. Ernest Whitney. PoOW

And whether he lies to cover what he thinks. Canticles to Men. Marya Mannes. AMV-80

And whether it is fit to whisper or to shout. I Talk to You. John Newlove. PeCV

And, whether joined or separate, will not love. Preludes for Memnon. Conrad Aiken. FYAP; NoAm

And whether the Health Ministry/Are in it for their health. Citizenship. Gilbert Keith Chesterton. OxBoLi

And which cat is a witch cat,/I really cannot tell. Witch Cat. Rowena Bastin Bennett. SiSoSe

And which, improbable, remote, and true,/Was the one he kept sailing home to? Odysseus. William Stanley Merwin. NOBA; NoP

And–which is more–you'll be a Man, my son! If. Rudyard Kipling. BBV; BLPA; FaBoBe; FaFP; FaPoR; FPL; GoTF; HBV 1-2; HBVY; OHFP; OxBChV; OxBTC; PaPo; TreF; WBLP

And (which is worse) too modest to consent. Resolution in Four Sonnets. Charles Cotton. PoEL 1-5

And which no heart had for gathering. Ungathered Love. Philip Bourke Marston. OBNC

And which Velasquez or Van Dyck refuse? The Strong Heroic Line. Oliver Wendell Holmes AA

And whiffs of autumn fleck canary paint. In the Tail of the Scorpion. Genevieve Taggard. VGW

And while he digs out thee, falls in the ditch. Avarice. George Herbert. FaBoRV; LiTB

And, while I sneezed,/Was gone! The Lupracaun, or Fairy Shoemaker. William Allingham. OnYI

And while I thus at random rove/Despise the fools that whine for love. A Thousand Martyrs I Have Made. Aphra Behn. CavP; SBG

And while it lasts, we cannot wholly end. Palladium. Matthew Arnold. GTBS-P; MaVP; OAEL 1-2; OAEP; OBNC; PPP; VLP

And while seeking for the Khan/Met his first Red Indian. The Great Discovery. Eleanor Farjeon. PoSC

And, while she laughs at them, forgets/She is the thing that she despises. A Hue and Cry after Fair Amoret. William Congreve. CEP; NOEC; OBEC; OBEV

And while the others wept I smiled. White Roses. Cora Fabbri. AA

And while the whole world slept. Care. Virginia Woodward Cloud. AA; HBV 1-2

And while they strove in mutual Love,/The Parson sung a Psalm. The Presbyterian Wedding. *Anonymous.* CoMu; ErPo

And while we're on our knees, at that. And When the Revolution Came. Carolyn M. Rodgers. GP

And why people have so many lice./Ha-ya-ya-ya.   The Old Man's Song.
  Anonymous.   WTO

And why should I not speak to you?   To You.   Walt Whitman.   BiP

And why should they   White Summer Flower.   William Stanley Merwin.
  DFF

And why the devil should we stay,/When once that love is past?   Against
  Marriage to His Mistress.   William Walsh.   FaBoUs

And why the sea is boiling hot–/And whether pigs have wings.   "The Time
  Has Come," the Walrus Said.   Lewis (Charles Lutwidge Dodgson) Carroll.
  TiPo

And why they'd love him all his brief life through.   Long Tom.   Wilfrid
  Gibson.   OxBTC

And why we love you last and best/Whose hearts were broken on your breast!
  Piccadilly.   Thomas Burke.   HBMV

And why we were here, and by whose strange laws/That which mattered most
  could not be.   After the Visit.   Thomas Hardy.   NOBE; OBNC

And wi' a crack her heart did brake;/And sae this ends my sang.   Lord
  Livingston.   *Anonymous.*   ESPB; OxBB

And wi' her a' my simmer days/Like they had never been.   The Tryst.
  William Soutar.   BoLoP; BSV; EBEV; GoTS; NeBP; OxBS

And wi' his white teeth shinin' yet/The corpse lies smilin' underfit.   The
  Dead Liebknecht.   Hugh" (Christopher Murray Grieve) MacDiarmid.
  FaBoPV; OBVE

And wi oblivion's kiss/Ye win.   Defeat O' the Hert.   Sydney Goodsir Smith.
  AtBAP

And wide is the gulf, love, between you and I...   Lost Jimmie Whalen.
  Anonymous.   ABF

And widen, so, the broad life-wound/Which soon is large enough for death.
  Mystery.   Elizabeth Barrett Browning.   OBVV

And Widower of Arts.   On Professor Drennan's Verse.   Roy Campbell.
  GTBS-P

And wight in wode be fleme.   Spring.   *Anonymous.*   AtBAP; OAEL 1-2

And wild and epic music from their abodes,/Heard blend in the high night
  with those of love.   Sonnets, X: "When I had turned Catullus into rhyme."
  Thomas Caulfield Irwin.   IrPN

And wild for to hold, though I seem tame.   Whoso liest to hunt, I know
  where is an hind..   Petrarch (Francesco Petrarca).   BoLoP

And wilful Nature deacks the sod/In gentlest mockery.   The Quaker
  Graveyard.   Silas Weir Mitchell.   AA

And wilful waste, depend upon't,/Brings, almost always, woeful want!   The
  Pin.   Ann Taylor.   HBV 1-2; HBVY; OxBChV

And will also be dead/When its rude cover is shed.   Bracken Hills in
  Autumn.   Hugh" (Christopher Murray Grieve) MacDiarmid.   NoP

And will be and my birthday is.   Your Birthday Comes to Tell Me This.
  Edward Estlin Cummings.   NAs

And will be, even to the last of his dark departures.   Departure in the Dark.
  C. Day Lewis.   ChMP; CoBMV; MoPo; MP; TwCP

And will be taken to the landfill, and filled, and filled.   Landfill.   Michael S.
  Harper.   LCAP

And will expect me one day.   Winter Solstice–For Frank.   Asphodel.
  BrRo

And will keep our hearts aglow,/While the days are going by.   While the
  Days Are Going By.   George Cooper.   BLRP; STF; WBLP

And will let no lovers in tonight.   The Delta.   Michael Dennis Browne.
  NYBP

And will love thee, yes, forever and aye!   From the German of Uhland.
  James Weldon Johnson.   CDC

...And will make the same/life you surrrender to me impossible.   That Which
  You Call "Love Me."   Luis Rosales.   AMV-81

And will never turn from me.   Though My Thoughts.   Francis Daniel
  Pastorius.   AH

And will not bob it when I say,/"Bob it now!"?   Little Lady Wren.   Tom
  Robinson.   TiPo

And will not knock again.   Amor Triumphans.   Arthur Symons.   BrPo

And will not let us see His face.   Notes on a Girl.   Peter Kane Dufault.
  ErPo

And will not look, but hears/Cry as of a child/No one...   The Forests of
  Lithuania.   Donald Davie.   OxBTC

And will not open again.   Like the Touch of Rain.   Edward ("Edward
  Eastaway") Thomas.   BoLoP; EnLoPo; GBL

And will not scare.   Skunk Hour.   Robert Lowell.   AmPP; AP; BiP;
  CAPP; CMoP; CoAP; ConAP; FaBoMo; HaCAP; HAP; HeIP; InPK; InPS;
  LCAP; MoAmPo; NIP; NMP; NoAm; NOBA; NoP; OxBC; PPP; PrIm;
  SCV; TAP; WeW

And will not stop to listen to my screams.   The Smoker.   Robert Huff.
  GP; NePoEA-2

And will scribble a line to catch the post for space.   Post Early For Space.
  Peter J. Henniker-Heaton.   AmFN

And will somebody tell/me why people let go   O By the By.   Edward Estlin
  Cummings.   OxBA

...And will/stick you with it if they can.   A Bestiary.   Kenneth Rexroth.
  OBAL

And will survive us./Before it dies.   Planting a Magnolia.   W. D. Snodgrass.
  NoAm

And will tell of itself/all, all the world.   Prayer to Hermes.   Robert Creeley.
  PoM

"And will there be harmony in heaven?"   Ice Cream in Paradise.   Robert
  Hollander.   AMV-80

And will to highest name yield praises high.   Psalm VII.   Sir Philip Sidney.
  FCP

And will us, through the sacrifice/Of self, his peaceful life.   Lincoln.   James
  Whitcomb Riley.   OHIP

And will wed none but you,/Robin Adair!   Robin Adair.   Caroline Keppel.
  FaBoBe; HBV 1-2

And will, while such a lane remain.   Beyond the Last Lamp.   Thomas
  Hardy.   MoVE; NOBE; OBNC

And will you no come back again?   Will He No Come Back Again?
  Anonymous.   OBEC; OBEV

And will you testify?   Suppose a Man.   R. T. Smith.   WOLT

And William Stewart is Erle of Marr,/And his father-in-law dwells with/him
  indeed.   Will Stewart and John.   *Anonymous.*   ESPB

And William Wordsworth upon Tin-Tern!   Thou Strainest through the
  Mountain Fern.   Robert Louis Stevenson.   NOBV

And willing Nations knew their Lawful Lord.   Absalom and Achitophel.
  John Dryden.   EBEV

And willows could not hold more steady sound.   Repose of Rivers.   Hart
  Crane.   AP; AWP; CMoP; CoBMV; ExPo; ForPo; InPo; LiTM; MoAB;
  MoAmPo; NoAm; NOBA; OxBA; SeCeV

And Willy's loos'd her left-foot shee,/And latten his lady lighter be.   Sweet
  Willie.   *Anonymous.*   OxBB

And wilt thou leave me thus?/Say nay! say nay!   An Appeal.   Sir Thomas
  Wyatt.   NOBE; OBEV; OBSC

And wilt thou now to nourish my despair/Both head and feather all thy shafts
  with fear?   Caelica, XXVII.   Fulke, Lord Brooke Greville.   FCP

And win and wear a frail/Archaic wistfulness.   The Mould.   Gladys
  Cromwell.   AnAmPo

And win no more the port of home–/The only Heart's Content!   Heart's
  Content.   *Anonymous.*   HBV 1-2; PoLf

And win the wide sundrenched Pacific.   On Going to the Wars.   Earle
  Birney.   WaP

And win to Fame through indolence.   To Petronius Arbiter.   Oliver St. John
  Gogarty.   OBMV

And wind, and water to thy use/Both wash, and wing my soul.   Silex
  Scintillans.   Henry Vaughan.   AnAnS 1; FaBoPP

And wind us up for ever and ever.   Cradle Song.   Louis MacNeice.
  MoAB; MoBrPo

And windows have seaward eyes.   Sea Town.   Frances Frost.   EtS

And winds are whispering in every shutter.   Passover Eve.   Fania Kruger.
  GoYe

And winds the sea-clouds bear!   The Brooklyn Bridge.   Edna Dean Proctor.
  MC; PAH

And, wing-clipt and imprisoned, my heart's bird/Flutters against his barriers,
  wild for flight.   Lament: "Within my bosom stirs once more tonight."
  Princess Zeb-un-Nissa.   LiTW

And wing my words that they may reach/The hidden depths of many a heart.
  For Every Day.   Frances Ridley Havergal.   BLRP

And winged through ever-blooming fields/of heaven.   He Who Hath Loved.
  Walter Malone.   AA

And winne Hevene blisse./Amen.   The Five Joys of Mary.   *Anonymous.*
  MeEL

And winter again and the snows.   Over! The Sweet Summer Closes.   Alfred,
  Lord Tennyson.   GBL

And winter fought her battle strife and won.   Remembrances.   John Clare.
  SaC

And winter pulled a sheet over his head.   The Sleeping Giant.   Donald Hall.
  GrPl; MP; NCSH; NePoEA; NYBP; Psk; TwCP

...And winter slow/Increase his rule by gentlest summer means.   Pray to
  What Earth Does This Sweet Cold Belong.   Henry David Thoreau.   UnPo

And winter windes ayain,/as the worlde askes.   Sir Gawain and the Green
  Knight (excerpt).   *Anonymous.*   PoEL 1-5

And wipe your feet,/she adds.   Teeth.   Susan Griffin.   NPGG

And wiped out the sink, turning her back/on the rest of us, forever.   A
  Room in the Past.   Ted Kooser.   Str

And wisdom a five-minute silence at moonrise.   The Banished Gods.   Derek
  Mahon.   OxBC

And wise men, from the upper classes/Look very wise, in horn-rimmed glasses.
  Christmas Pageant.   Margaret Fishback.   PoSC

...And wise men here should find/Asylum from the thought and fear of Death.
  Asylum.   John Freeman.   OBMV

And wisely fair restoratives supply.   The Priest of Christ.   Thomas Ken.
  TRV

And wiser men than I went worse astray.   Epigram: "Truth I pursued, as
  Fancy sketch'd the way."   Samuel Taylor Coleridge.   FaBoEE

And with the arms of freedom cause the/wars they are all o'er. The Surrender of Cornwallis. *Anonymous.* PAH

And with the breath of kindness/Blow the rest away. Friendship. Dinah Maria Mulock Craik. BLPA; PoToHe

And with the care of the very drunk/Handed him the plate. Frying Trout While Drunk. Lynn Emanuel. MAYP

And with the drowning stars untimely drowned. Epigrams, IX: Cleonicos. Theocritus. AWP

And with the fur-wrought fly delude the prey. Fly-Fishing. John Gay. SD

And with the girls be handy. Yankee Doodle. Edward Bangs. ABF; AmFP; BLSo; ExPo; FaFP; FSW; HBV 1-2; OBAL; PAL; TrAS; TreF; YaD

And with the grind of timbers on the sides/Of cliffs resounding with the march of tides. The Ritual. Edwin John Pratt. NoAm

And with the Kings we march along the way. March of the Three Kings. *Anonymous.* OHIP

And with the last he still directs the Just. Mercy and Love. Robert Herrick. SeCV 1-2

And with the martyr's crown, crownest a life/With much to praise, little to be forgiven. Abraham Lincoln. Tom Taylor. HBV 1-2; MCCG; PAH

And with the morn those angel faces smile/Which I have loved long since, and lost awhile. The Pillar of Cloud. John Henry, Cardinal Newman. OBNC

And with the same fill every hill and dale. Daphnaida (excerpt). Edmund Spenser. PoPle

And with the second is the longing for/The mighty gladness by the third fulfill'd. Sonnet: He Speaks of a Third Love of His. Guido Cavalcanti. AWP

And with the self-same weapon, too!' Jack and Roger. Benjamin Franklin. ChTr

And with the shrieke, did wise Ulysses wake. The Odyssey. Homer. LiTW; OBS

And with the sun rises perpetual day. Question and Answer. Kathleen Raine. MoBrPo

And, with the urn, she bore my heart away! Reminiscence. Thomas Bailey Aldrich. AA; AnAmPo

And with the wounds of bulls The Spanish Girls. Ivan Arguelles. FIA

And with the Yorkshire blade/She danced a jig at night. The Old Marquis and His Blooming Wife. *Anonymous.* CoMu

And with Thee rich, take what Thou wilt away. The Task. William Cowper. EiCP

And with their blush of light descry/Thy locks crown'd with eternitie. The Dawning. Henry Vaughan. CAW

...And with/their honest mouths eat out my eyes. The Sea and the Tiger. Laurence Collinson. PoAu 1-2

And with their music/Along let them bring her. Sirena. Michael Drayton. CBEP; OBEV

And with their tow'rs his reedy head embrace. The Apollyonists. Phineas Fletcher. FaBoPP

And with them a part to take,/And so I end my song. Robin Hood and the Tinker. *Anonymous.* BaBo; ESPB

And with this verdict I conclude/One portion of my song. The Nyum-Nyum. *Anonymous.* NA

And with thy mystic spouses/Rest from the long, long way! Hymn to Horus. Mathilde Blind. OBVV

And with triumphant navies rule the main. Description of a Ninety Gun Ship. William Falconer. PeD

And with true scorpion rage she stings herself to death. The Modern Fine Lady. Soame Jenyns. NOEC; OBSV

–And with two blinks, our eyes. Mime. Dick Allen. AMV-81

And with us sing ding dong, ding dong,/Ding dong, dong,/Ding, dong. Ding Dong. *Anonymous.* EiL

And with what store of blood kings are undone. The Civil Wars between the Two Houses of Lancaster and York. Samuel Daniel. OBWP

And with your curved archaic smile you watched his passion come and go. The Sphinx (excerpt). Oscar Wilde. MoBrPo; UnTE

And with your place in the excise. Epilogue (parody). George Gordon, Lord Byron. Par

And with your soft vitality/My weary bosom fill. Variations on Sappho. Michael (Katherine Bradley and Edith Cooper) Field. PeHV

And within the indestructible night I am alone. Passage Over Water. Robert Duncan. NoAm; NOBA

And without a groan expired. Gentle River, Gentle River. *Anonymous.* AWP; LiTW

And without a seam! The Cumberland. Henry Wadsworth Longfellow AA; AnNE; EtS; MC; PAH

And without God's help/the divill will have all. A Postscript to Verses on the History of France. *Anonymous.* NOBI

And without moving he flies The Windows. William Stanley Merwin. DFF

And without pity heare their dying grones. Psalme CXXXVII. George Sandys. OBS

And wliteth in their wunne wele,/That all the woode ringeth. Lenten Is Come with Love to Town. *Anonymous.* PBBP

And wo worth right that may no favour have! Court of Sapience. John Lydgate. PoEL 1-5

And woe may come to-morrow. Song: "'Tis sweet to hear the merry lark." Hartley Coleridge. HBV 1-2

And woke the hidden boy. The Confirmation. Karl Shapiro. ErPo

And woke up on Meriador,/Drenched in the summer dew. The Shepherd of Meriador. Wilfred Rowland Childe. HBMV

And woman's beauty is the flame therein. Vashti. Lascelles Abercrombie. MoBrPo

And woman's glance shall watch me/as I go up to Heaven. Woman. Valente Malangatana. PBA; TTY

And women feel the same for worthy men. La Vita Nuova. Dante Alighieri. AWP

And women fight, like Swizzers, for their/pay. Epilogue to Mithridates, King of Pontus. John Dryden. OAEP

And women, must they wear each other's lies/against familiar breasts? For Chicle & Justina. Diane Bickston. LFAC

And won her faith, her love, her beauty. Pamela in Town. Ellen Mackay Hutchinson Cortissoz. AA; HBV 1-2

And won't play enny more. Bobby's First Poem. Norman Gale. FiBHP; MoShBr; PV

And wonder from which of his old friends in Sinder/Had burst out that muffled, "Old Jones!" J. J. Walter De la Mare. FaBoNo

And wonder is a twine of wands lodged/to spine of nothing I know at least to hold. Disturbing the Sallies Forth. Clark Coolidge. APU

And wonder, knowing better, if you hear/through some light-rooted organ of the air. Letter from Germany. Emily Grosholz. AMV-81

And wonder what the times will come to! The Progress of Dulness. John Trumbull. AnNE

And wondered again/why anyone bothered. And Was Not Improved. Lerone Jr. Bennett. CNA; PoBA

And wondered, Are they ever coming back? The Empty Glen. R. Crombie Saunders. OxBS

And wondered now whether to turn again. Turning. Robert Finch. OBCV

And wondered what was left for massacre to save. A Bronze Head. William Butler Yeats. LiTB; MBW 1-2

And wondered/what would come next The Second Coming. John William Carrington. HoPM

And wonders oh, whence come/all the petals. Faustina, or Rock Roses. Elizabeth Bishop. FaBoMo; NMP

And wonders, wonders, of His love. Joy to the World. Isaac Watts. FSW

And woodnuts rich, to make us go/Into the loneliest lanes we know. Rich Days. William Henry Davies. BoNaP

And woodthrush calling through the fog/My daughter. Marina. Thomas Stearns Eliot. AmP; CMoP; FaBoMo; GTBS-P; HeIP; InPo; LiTA; MBW 1-2; MOS; NOBE; NOCV

And woos the arts with such pure sighs. Before a Saint's Picture. Walter Savage Landor. OxBChV

And word spake never more! William and Margaret. David Mallet. CEP; NOEC; OBEC

And words and minutes fall like clothing to the floor. Time of Waiting. Geoffrey Dutton. CBAP

And words fertilize each other/in the cold and with bulging eyes This Year I Intended Children. Margaret Atwood. NeAC

And wore it well, and wore it long,/And did not die. Yahrzeit. Susan Fromberg Schaeffer. VWA

And wore the life of that bird in my hat. Shooting Ducks in South Louisiana. Richard Tillinghast. MAYP

And work for the time is a pleasant thing. The Meadow Lark. Hamlin Garland. AA

And work, nor care to rest, and find the last the best. Death. Maltbie Davenport Babcock. WGRP

And workmen whistling. Image. Thomas Ernest Hulme. InPK; OxBTC

And world-wide fluctuation sway'd/In vassal tides that follow'd thought. In Memoriam A.H.H., CXII. Alfred, Lord Tennyson. VLP

And worlds more in the grains that make mountains. The Spiral. John Holmes. MiAP

...And worms are the root. Joy Is the Blossom. Walter Savage Landor. DBV; HBV 1-2

And worry about being indiscreet. Limerick: "Aging old queers are no treat." *Anonymous.* PeHV

And worse, the woes we see not–which throb through/The immediate soul, with heart-aches ever new. The Fatal Spell. George Gordon, Lord Byron. OBNC

And would be neither Turk nor Pope. Commanders of the Faithful. William Makepeace Thackeray. ALV

And would not be instructed in how/deep/Was the forgetful kingdom of death. Janet Waking. John Crowe Ransom. AmLP; AmP; AnAmPo; CMoP; ExPo; ForPo; InPK; MoAB; MoAmPo; NCSH; NoAm; NoP; TAP

And would not let him have his way. Inscription. Ebenezer Elliott. FaBoEE

And would not speak. Despair. Denise Levertov. NNaP

And would not swap for pleasure/So mix'd with fear and trembling. The City Rat and the Country Rat. Jean de La Fontaine. OBVE

And would say more, but I am doomed/To break off in the middle.' Sally Simpkin's Lament. Thomas Hood. EnRP; MOS; ShM

And would sing like the thrush/ that sings in the thicket. Judas Iscariot. R. A. K. Mason. AnNZ

And would suffice. Fire and Ice. Robert Frost. AnFE; AnNE; APA; BiP; CABA; CMoP; CoBMV; DiPo; FaBoEE; FaFP; FaPo; FF; FPL; HBMV; HeIP; HoPM; InPK; LiTA; LiTM; MoAB; MoAmPo; MoVE; NePA; NoAm; NOBA; OxBA; PoPl; PrIm; SoSe; TAP; TreFS; TrGrPo; TW; ViBoPo; WHA

And would that make you wonder less,/O Stranger to our land? Stranger, Why Do You Wonder So? K. B. Jones-Quartey. PBA

And would that such a life were mine and thine! Glauce. Aubrey Thomas De Vere. IrPN

And, would watch this high bloom of himself, as something distant that/will be close again... An Old Man's Son. Russell Edson. LCAP

And wound them on his arm, and for her mourned. Hero and Leander. Christopher Marlowe. GBL

And wound them/until dew floods the earth. When the Angels Are Exhausted. Yona Wallach. VWA

And wound with flaming ropes of hair. The Licorice Fields at Pontefract. Sir John Betjeman. CMoP; NMP

...And woven hymns/Of night and day, and the deep heart of man. Alastor. Percy Bysshe Shelley. FiP; WHA

And wow, gin I were but young for thee! Werena My Heart Licht I Wad Dee. Lady Grizsel Baillie. OBEV

And wrap them cold in her pre-Cambrian folds. Towards the Last Spike. Edwin John Pratt. NOBC

And–wreck of wrecks!–there lie the Fair/Whose beauty wins no more! Song: "O, strew the way with rosy flowers." James Clarence Mangan. IrPN

And wring his bosom–is, to die. The Vicar of Wakefield. Oliver Goldsmith. EnLi 1-2

And wring your blood out on Hiroshima. The Enemy. Randolph Stow. NOAV

And write about daybreak/In Alabama. Daybreak in Alabama. Langston Hughes. AmFN; CNA

And write next winter more Essays on Man. Epilogue to the Satires. Alexander Pope. OAEL 1-2

And write of love on wall and sidewalk. Chalk from Eden. Howard Moss. NePA

And write on the whitest of God's white clouds/Chipeta's name in eternal blue. Chipeta. Eugene Field. PoOW

And write poems, or,/Maybe...make a wish? Doesn't It Seem to You. Gevorg Emin. AMV-81

...And write/the love poem of your life. Transformation. Quincy Troupe. CNA

And write these perishing words down/in the voice of summer rain. Summer Rain. Richard Tillinghast. MAYP

And write thine epitaph in blood and wounds. Lines on the Execution of King Charles I. James Graham. BSV; GoTS

And write this poem for money, rage, and love. The Thief. Stanley Jasspon Kunitz. VGW

And writhed to see its lethal sting/Destroying you. The Lethal Thought. Mary Boyd Wagner. GoYe

And writing novels with her broom. On the Same. Roy Campbell. OxBTC

And wrong yourselves to do her right. Secrecy. Samuel Daniel. OBSC; OLR

And wrote Principles of Political Economy. Clerihews. Edmund Clerihew Bentley. FiBHP

And wylde for to hold though I seme tame.' Rime CXC: "Who so list to hounte I know where is an hynde." Petrarch (Francesco Petrarca). OBVE

And X Y and Z is the name on our stern. The Bargeman's ABC. Anonymous. OBSS

And yawn with salty, cold, and sluggish eye. The Last Boats. Endre Ady. LiTW

And ye know what the jest is worth. Departmental Ditties: Prelude. Rudyard Kipling. VLP

And ye sall rowe me in your plaid,/My winsome dearie.' Ca' the Yowes to the Knowes. Anonymous. OxBS

And ye shall be with Me. Search. Margaret Widdemer. TrPWD

And ye shall take God's hand. The Lesbian Hell. Aleister Crowley. PeHV

And ye, that mowen alle mine harme amende,/Have minde upon my supplicacion. A Song to His Purse for the King. Geoffrey Chaucer. MeEL

"And ye to be drowned,'/Quo' the wee boy, and still he stude. The False Knight and the Wee Boy. Anonymous. FaBoCh

And ye unchanged, the same–the same? Art Thou the Same. Frances Dorr Tatnall. AA

And ye were Martin Elginbrodde. Here Lie I, Martin Elginbrodde. George Macdonald. HBV 1-2

And year by year our memory fades/From all the circle of the hills. In Memoriam A.H.H., CI. Alfred, Lord Tennyson. ELP; FaBoPP; GTBS-P; PoEL 1-5; PoPle; SCV

–And yearn indeed to become/those pure incalculable names. So it Happens. Irving Feldman. GP

And yellow harvest when the wild geese fly. There Will Be Peace. Margaret Miller Pettengill. PGD

And yellowing either bank the king-cups blow. God-Seeking. William Watson. WGRP

And "Yes, ma'am," to a Lady. Politeness. Elizabeth Turner. HBV 1-2; HBVY

And yesterday the place where we left off a little while ago. Years of Indiscretion. John Ashbery. NOBA

And yet a Spirit still, and bright/With something of angelic light. She Was a Phantom of Delight. William Wordsworth. AnFE; BLPL; EnLi 1-2; ERoP 1-2; FaBoBe; FaBV; GTBS; GTBS-P; HeIP; LiTB; LiTL; LoBV; MBW 1-2; MCCG; NoP; OAEL 1-2; OAEP; OBRV; OHFP; PoEL 1-5; PoPl; TrGrPo; ViBoPo

And yet abide the world! There Came A Wind Like A Bugle. Emily Dickinson. AtBAP; CMoP; LoBV; MAPA; MoAB; NAWM 1-2; NePA; NoAm; NOBA; OxBA

And yet after all I have but one. Tora's Song. Knut Hamsun. PoPl

And yet all those blokes are shearing for their lives. Shearing. David McKee Wright. AnNZ

And yet am lesser than a mouse. Riddle: "I am within as white as snow." Anonymous. GBP

And yet as old as Ireland, too. The Antiquary. Joseph Campbell. OxBTC

And yet behind the rascal's name/The scoundrel writes M.P.! How Different! Ebenezer Elliott. EBEV

And yet burn so high,/and fly so bright? The Aleph Bet. Fay Lipshitz. VWA

And yet, by heaven, I think my love as rare/As any she belied with false compare. Sonnets, CXXX: "My mistress' eyes are nothing like the sun." William Shakespeare. AWP; BiP; BoLoP; CBEP; DiPo; EBEV; ExPo; FF; HAP; HBV 1-2; HoPM; InPK; InPS; InvP; LiTB; LiTL; MBW 1-2; NIP; NoP; OAEL 1-2; OAEP; PAI; PoPle; PP; PPP; PrIm; SeCeV; SoSe; TEP; WeW

And yet–by Trades–the size of these/We men and women die! It's Such a Little Thing to Weep. Emily Dickinson. AmePo; AmP

And yet God has not said a word! Porphyria's Lover. Robert Browning. AtBAP; AWP; BeLS; GTBS; HAP; HBV 1-2; InPo; MaVP; MBW 1-2; OAEP; OBEV; TEP; TreFT; TrGrPo

And yet great rocks I break. Riddle: "I never speak a word." Mary Austin. TiPo

And yet, had Love been Love, he had not/died. Hic Jacet. Louise Chandler Moulton. AA; AnAmPo; APA

And yet he complained/that his stomach wasn't full. Robin the Bobbin. Anonymous. OxNR

And Yet, he Drove his Mother Crazy-he was so Slow, he was so/Lazy! An Alphabet of Famous Goops. Gelett Burgess. BBGG

And yet He loves me,/Tenderly and true. And Yet–. Arthur B. Rhinow. BLRP

And yet–He of the pierced palm/Will point the way. And Yet–. Errol B. Sloan. BLRP

–And yet he sailed but yesterday,/With Edmund Spenser, from this port. A Call on Sir Walter Raleigh. Sarah Piatt. AA

And yet he spoke of undying love. The Talker. Benjamin Appel. TrJP

And yet I aye gang barefit, barefit! The Cock Gaed to Rome. Anonymous. PBBP

And yet I bore the flower away. All Night by the Rose. Anonymous. CBEP; GBL; HeIP

And yet I can-/not like the Zoo/as much as other/people do. The Zoo. Humbert Wolfe. MoShBr

And yet I could and would not live without/Your faith that heartens and your doubts which spur. Retractions. James Branch Cabell. HBMV

And yet I do prefer it. What's my drift? Modern Love, XXXI. George Meredith. NOBV; VLP

And yet I know my fairy-land/Lies somewhere o'er their edges. Dreams. Cecil Frances Alexander. OnYI

And yet I know the splendor of the light/Will break anon. Look! where the gray is white!/ Elegy in Six Sonnets. Frederick Goddard Tuckerman. QFR

And yet I seem to get to sleep Death's Head. Phyllis Gotlieb. NOBC

And yet I think I had more fun,/When I was a cabin boy.   An Awful Responsibility.   Keith Preston.   PoPl

And yet I wait/For him.   Barren.   Rachel (Rachel Blumstein).   TrJP

And yet I want it out more than I want these words.   The Threat.   Andrei Codrescu.   APU

And yet I wondered: "What should he come/Up from out of in under for?"   The Naughty Preposition.   Morris Bishop.   FiBHP; NLV; NYBP; PV

And yet...I would go back.   The Voices of Nature.   Thomas Edward Brown.   PeD

And yet in washing one, she washed both.   Marie Magdalene.   George Herbert.   AnAnS 1

And yet is it feeble hold on a slipper eel.   The Epistle of Othea to Hector (excerpt).   Christine de Pisan.   PBWP

...And yet it seems/Sometimes that you surely found it,/John o' Dreams.   John o' Dreams.   Theodosia Garrison.   HBMV

And yet it was my heart that wanted to stay.   In the Park.   Helen Hoyt.   HBMV

And yet left eleven there.   Riddle: "Twelve pears hanging high."   Anonymous.   OxNR

And yet, like my title, have nothing to do!   Martin Luther at Potsdam.   Barry Pain.   ALV; NA

And yet linked to/pure primary numbers.   Primary Numbers.   Edvard Kochek.   AMV-81

And yet, no more shall I see my uncle,/To whom my mind would fain be revealed.   The Sun and the Moon and Fear of Loneliness.   Anonymous.   WTO

And yet nor die, nor draw a life-like breath.   Love's Despair.   Richard Lynch.   EiL

And yet not envying them their childhood/Since he endured his own?   Eight Aspects of Melissa.   Lawrence Durrell.   NeBP

And yet one feels the sumptuousness of this dirt.   California Winter (excerpt).   Karl Shapiro.   AmFN

And yet our skins hold the one and only life.   Skin.   Philip K. Jason.   AMV-81

And yet sad May must lose her flower of flowers.   On Queen Anne's Death.   Anonymous.   EiL

And yet she hath but care and wo.   A Woman Is a Worthy Thing.   Anonymous.   FaBoCo; GBP; OxBM

And yet sicker thou art still/For thinking, that thou art not ill.   Oh, England. Sick in Head and Sick in Heart.   Anonymous.   FaBoEE

And yet take them in.   The Landing.   Daniel Halpern.   AmPA

And yet that cloud bloomed only for a minute/And as I looked up vanished in the wind.   In Memory of Marie A.   Bertolt Brecht.   LiTW

And yet the furthest star/Is not so far as I.'   Lord Vyet.   Arthur Christopher Benson.   OBVV

And yet the huge bulk of a sinner/Said there was neither spirit or matter.   On the Author of the Treatise of Human Nature.   J. H. Beattie.   FaBoCo

And yet the truth is, fail we must/And be forgiven.   G.M.B.   Donald Davie.   OxBC

And yet the very fur within their armpits/Made me rise wondering and small.   One for the Ladies at the Troy Laundry Who Cooled Themselves...   Paul Zimmer.   GP

And yet these Dames, that shine so bright,/Are but the shadow of thy light.   In Praise of the Sun.   A. W.   CTC; OBSC

And yet they expose me more than all my other poems.   Here the Frailest Leaves of Me.   Walt Whitman.   AP

And yet this old woman/Could never keep quiet.   An Old Woman.   Anonymous.   OxNR

And yet thou say'st I do not love thee.   Canzonet: "See, see mine own sweet jewel."   Anonymous.   EiL; LO

And yet thou wilt; for I, being pent in thee,/Perforce am thine, and all that is in me.   Sonnets, CXXXIII: "Beshrew that heart that makes my heart to groan."   William Shakespeare.   CBEP; InvP

And yet 'tis flesh and blood alone/That makes her so divine.   Chloe Divine.   Thomas D'Urfey.   HBV 1-2; OBEV

And yet to times in hope, my verse shall stand/Praising thy worth, despite his cruel hand.   Sonnets, LX: "Like as the waves make towards the pebbled shore."   William Shakespeare.   ATP; CBEP; EBEV; ExPo; FaBoEn; FaFP; FPL; GTBS; GTBS-P; HBV 1-2; LiTB; LiTL; LoBV; NIP; NOBE; OBSC; PeHV; PoRA; SeCeV; TEP; UnPo; ViBoPo

And yet was never there a rose but died in/blooming.   Attainment.   Algernon Tassin.   AA

And yet we feel–what pain–in the intense/Desire for thee to end thy long seclusion!   The World's Desire.   William Rose Benet.   TrPWD

And yet what one of us would not/Do battle for his own!   King Philip's Last Stand.   Clinton Scollard.   PAH

And yet, who did not.   Did Not.   Thomas Moore.   ALV; BoLoP; ErPo; NBM

And yet will have him woo!   Love's Likeness.   George Darley.   OBVV

And yet with feet that bleed, I pant/On blindly,–stumbling back to God!   The Return.   Jessie Redmond Fauset.   CDC

And yet wouldst be weeping forever!   Keen Thyself, Poor Wight.   Geoffrey Keating.   OnYI

And yield more cause of terror than delight.   The Frailty of Beauty.   J. C.   EiL

And yielded to the swain.   As Chloris Full of Harmless Thought.   John Wilmot, Earl of Rochester.   TEP

And yielded with pleasure when taken by force.   A Riddle.   William Cowper.   HBV 1-2

And yonder she sits in my cane-bottom'd chair.   The Cane-Bottom'd Chair.   William Makepeace Thackeray.   HBV 1-2; PaPo

And you above them, wounded and dominant.   Messengers.   Louise Gluck.   HaCAP

And you all may be Rulers of the Queen's Navee!   The First Lord's Song.   Sir William Schwenck Gilbert.   GoTF; TreFS

And you, already, have been lost again.   Orpheus to Eurydice.   Frederick Morgan.   AMV-80

And you amid its fitful masquerade/A Thought–as I in yours but seem to be.   She, to Him.   Thomas Hardy.   OBEV; OBVV

And you and I in the world togethr.   Now Is the Cherry in Blossom.   Mary Eleanor Wilkins.   AA

And you and myself there.   The Three Mirrors.   Edwin Muir.   NoAm

...And you/are/Dead, and here is your gift: my life which is my home.   On the Death of Her Mother.   Muriel Rukeyser.   SM

And you are me, and we are two/Demonstrations that nothing is true.   Nothing.   Burns Singer.   OxBS

...And you are mine; my sweet!   Leves Amores.   Arthur Symons.   AnEnPo; UnTE

And you are pierced by a death.   Another Weeping Woman.   Wallace Stevens.   MoVE

...And you/are sick in the bathtub.   After the Agony in the Guest Bedroom.   Margaret Atwood.   NeAC

And you are still my daughter.   Heart's Needle.   W. D. Snodgrass.   AmPC; CoPo; SM

And you are the weaver's bonny.   The Devil's Nine Questions.   Anonymous.   AmFP; WSC

And you become/A goddess standing in a world of fire!   Feuerzauber.   Louis Untermeyer.   TrJP

And, you bet, the boss pair of branding irons.   The Branding Iron Herd.   Ralph Rigby.   PoOW

And you can own, as I, these gardens old/John Graydon bought with gold.   John Graydon.   Wilson MacDonald.   CaP

And you cannot gather a bowl full.   Riddle: "A house full, a hole full."   Anonymous.   OxNR

And you cheer inside?   What Kind of War?   Larry Rottman.   PoL

And you companioned I am not alone.   Monna Innominata.   Christina Georgina Rossetti.   VLP

And you could hear in the night the slice of a machete.   Maceo.   Luis Llorens Torres.   InW

And you'd better get someone who can.   Drinking Song.   James Kenneth Stephen.   NOBL

And you'd orto' heerd 'em yell!   A Liz-Town Humorist.   James Whitcomb Riley.   AmePo

And you don't/Give a damn.   Impasse.   Langston Hughes.   LiTM

And you don't mean nothing now you're dead.   Graves in Queens.   Richard Hugo.   NYP

And you draw the heart/against the emptiness she has created.   Portrait.   Louise Gluck.   Str

And you drift out with it through the trees/and into the evening.   Watertower.   Albert Bellg.   FAZ

And you fall/With the other husks of summer.   The Dragonfly.   Louise Bogan.   HeIP; NIP

And you/feel no more   To a Single Shadow without Pity.   Sam Cornish.   NBP; PoBA

And you fell/scattering your winning hand!   To an Avenue Sport.   Helen Johnson Collins.   PoNe

...And you find good reason then to adorn/yourself.   The Oyster.   Francis Ponge.   NU

And you forever will be/the words and kisses/spinning the bottle.   Kissing Game.   Bob Rosenthal.   APU

And you found me burst open/with memories, rotten memories.   To My Father.   Susannah Fried.   VWA

...And you gave me a hand job as I/tooled on happily.   The Night Was Clear and the Moon Was Yellow.   Jeffrey Miller.   APU

And you, glory-clad, reach down.   The Wife-Woman.   Anne Spencer.   BANP; NoAm

And you go on choosing me/Over and over again/Irrespective of merit   Penmanship.   Tom Clark.   ANYP

And you going to/hell!   Up against the Wall.   Cleve Phillips.   AMV-81

And you good Christians that do pass by/Just drop a tear for the Croppy Boy.   The Croppy Boy.   Anonymous.   AmFP; AnIL; AnIV; CBEP; FaBoBa; FSW; NOBI; OxBoLi

And you, good woman, saved your eggs. The Farmer's Wife and the Raven. John Gay. PBBP

...And you have been/sixteen since it began. To His Love in Middle-Age. Edwin Brock. AMV-80

And you have come instead as moon of the earth. Moon of the Earth. *Anonymous.* WTO

And you have gone to Bloomington. Poems of My Lambretta. Paul Goodman. NMP

...And you/Have made me thus! Cyrano de Bergerac, III: "Love, I love beyond Breath." Edmond Rostand. OLR

And you have only yourself to blame. The Double Shame. Stephen Spender. LiTB; LiTL; LiTM

And you, in that landscape,/are as small as a snowflake. At Nine O'Clock in the Spring. Elissa Bishop. AMV-80

And you–in whom youth never died–/Shall lead them, as a star! The Star. Marion Couthouy Smith. PAH

And you in your mild Journey pass the Hole/I made in One–ah, pay my Forfeit then! The Golfer's Rubaiyat (parody). H. W. Boynton. BXAP

And you increase his inviolability. Ode to the Chinese Paper Snake. Richard Eberhardt. CrMA

And you, inspiring chavender,/Stuff'd, chavender, or chub. A False Gallop of Analogies. Warham St. Leger. CenHV; FaBoCo; FiBHP

And you just know he knows he knows. The Sloth. Theodore Roethke. FiBHP; NePA; NePoAm; OBAL; OBCA

And you know, I believe him. The Creation: According to Coyote. Simon J. Ortiz. CDW

And you know very well whom I mean. A Certain Young Lady. Washington Irving. FaBoBe; HBV 1-2

And you, Lady–we're taking you along. Leaving Ithaca. W.D. Snodgrass. AmPC

And you land in the calaboose to–Root hog or die. Root Hog or Die. *Anonymous.* AmFP; FSW

And you, like an old Canadian trader, come whistling warning. You Are More Than I Need. Rebbekka Kaplan. AMV-80

And you listen to the sounds of this journey/to nowhere you know. Night Train. Mary C. Fineran. AMV-81

And you'll always have a chew,/In your old tobacco box. Says the Miner to the Mucker. *Anonymous.* AmFP

And you'll be as happy as little Clarence. Clarence. Shel Silverstein. OBCA

And you'll eat in the sweet bye and bye. Pie in the Sky. *Anonymous.* GBP

And you'll end up digesting the book! Limerick: "If you're apt to be ravenous, look." Myra Cohn Livingston. TDH

And you'll get an extra dose of the raging can-all. Raging Can-all. *Anonymous.* ABF

And you'll never feel lonely/at night when you're in bed. Keep a Poem in Your Pocket. Beatrice Schenk De Regniers. SoPo

And you'll never see your old rim-fire/Go drifting down the draw. Windy Bill. *Anonymous.* CoSo

And you'll often be asked to dign. Limerick: "When you turn down your glass it's a sign." James Montgomery Flagg. TDH

And you'll see them, one and all. Spooks. Nathalia Crane. ShM

And you look like hell when they're through with you. The Hearse Song. *Anonymous.* ABF; DTC; FSW; OxBoLi

And you make a thousand halts in it,/Giddily, Giddily, O! Waltzing It. William Thomas Moncrieff. UnS

And you may die in the perfumed sheets,/But I shall die in battle! The Retort Discourteous. Stephen Vincent Benét. HBMV

And you may gather garlands there/Would grace a summer queen. Edmund's Song. Sir Walter Scott. EnLi 1-2; PoRA

...And you may have seen a monkey/on a greyhound, "But Tom Fool. . ." Tom Fool at Jamaica. Marianne Moore. AP; NYBP

...And you may join her there/In those hours between sleeping and dawn. A Bed without a Woman. Raymond Souster. ELU; ErPo

And you may pray there, sir, for me. In Brittany. Charles Weekes. OnYI

And you mayhap will vaguely puzzle, "Who/Is she? and he? why do they what they do?" Sonnets to Aurelia. Robert Nichols. OBMV

And you must crush the love in your heart, and I the love/in mine! Come, the wind may never again. Emily Bronte. EnLoPo

And you must live drawn by your own sweet skill. Sonnets, XVI: "But wherefore do not you a mightier way." William Shakespeare. FaBoEn

And you must now be viewed all/As having been completely licked/By glorious Yankee Doodle. The Last Appendix to Yankee Doodle. *Anonymous.* PAH

And you must say it back. WOMEN OPEN CAUTIOUSLY. Deborah Lee. BrSi

And you must thank us for that. The Norfolk Rebellion: The Rebels' Rhyme. *Anonymous.* GBP

And you must want me to lay/down and die for you Nappy Head Blues. Bobby Grant. BluL

And you, my anonymous father,/be with me when I wake. After Grief. Stanley Plumly. AmPA; LCAP

And you nowhere. Little Elegy. Elinor Wylie. LOW

And you, our rose-deaf prison, are very/pleased with the world,/Your world. The Female God. Isaac Rosenberg. FaBoTw

And you're all set to start "The Sonnet Ca–" Sonneteering Made Easy. S. B. Botsford. NYBP

And you're aye welcome back to Northumberland!' The Fair Flower of Northumberland. *Anonymous.* BuBa

And you're on your way to Packin'town. Goody-by, Steer. Robert V. Carr. BPAW

And you're only a skittish/Child, after all,/Little foal. Foal. Mary Britton Miller. PH

And you're two months back in the middle of March. Early April. Robert Frost. YeAr

And you said, "So that's what love is." Lifesaving. Sandra McPherson. MAYP

And you say hello and see if you can survive. California, This Is Minnesota Speaking. Stephen P. Dunn. GP

And you seem One? Poem. Josephine Strongin. AnAmPo

And you shall be a true lover of mine. The Lover's Tasks. *Anonymous.* OxNR

And you shall drive our ancient crock down to the sea.' The House Next Door. Douglas Dunn. OxBC

"And you shan't wake up till you're clean plum/dead!" The Nine Little Goblins. James Whitcomb Riley. OBCA

And you should ask, I'd say "It's just a sonnet." What Is a Sonnet? Edward Watkins. AMV-80

And you,/Sitting in the firelight. What the Orderly Dog Saw. Ford Madox Ford. CTC

And you smashed the tape with your chest/and sank into the arms of many lovers. The Aging Athlete. Neil Weiss. LiSp

And you smile up at us–eternally. In Memory of My Mother. Patrick Kavanagh. CIP; FaBoIP; NoAm

And you stalwart loins. Children of Adam. Walt Whitman. AP

And you stare at his hand holding yours. Michael's Room. Reginald Gibbons. AMV-81

And you step quickly past them, into the night. The Ownership of the Night. Larry Levis. LCAP

And you tear me to pieces by being so kind. Song. John Streeter Manifold. DTC

And you tell me to go to hell! The Sailor to His Parrot. William Henry Davies. BoAnP; EtS; ViBoPo

And you that cross from shore to shore years hence are/more to me, and more in my meditations... Crowds of Men and Women. Walt Whitman. CTBA

And you the father of a glorious race/Endowed with Ch–l's strength and Low–r's face. Epistle from Mrs. Yonge to Her Husband. Mary Wortley, Lady Montagu. NoP

And you the Queen with me there and your throne in my/heart, machree,/Maureen! Maureen. John Todhunter. HBV 1-2; OBVV

And You there among them,/Staggering with the cross. Via Dolorosa. Phoebe Smith. PGD

And you through love my blackness shall endure! The Dark Brother. Lewis Alexander. CDC

And you, to tickle behind my ears. Contentment. Burges Johnson. GDP

And you upon the quarterdeck/To feed them, Mother Carey. Sea-Birds. Fray Angelico Chavez. ISi

And you've struck it,–on Poverty Flat. Her Letter. Bret (Francis Bret Harte) Harte. HBV 1-2; PoLf

And you were a butterfly, remember,/oh remember, all that day. Lupine Dew. Jarold Ramsey. NIP

And you were never more deaf and more dumb. Prayer of Little Hope. Jean Wahl. VWA

And you will always hold me/One day more. Never Will You Hold Me. Charles Divine. HBMV

And you will be jealous of our tombs. Unearthing. Betsy Rosenberg. VWA

And you will cry/and then...you will be mine as never before! The Strong Bond. Juana de Ibarbourou. PBWP

And you will find, through age and youth,/That many hearts will love you. The Best Memory Course. *Anonymous.* STF

And you will hear the music/Of the wee folks' dancing tune. When a Ring's Around the Moon. Mary Jane Carr. BrR; TiPo

And you will learn, my skeptic friend,/The truthfulness of what I've said. Proof Positive. Deems Taylor. UnTE

And you will love/The violence of our passions,/If not at first. The Estuarial Republic. Douglas Dunn. FaBoMo

And you will never catch consumption by sleeping on the ground. The Texas Cowboy. *Anonymous.* CoSo

And you will never get rid of me/until the world is Hitler-free. The Permanent Delegate. Yuri Suhl. PPON

And you will speed us onward with a cheer,/And wave beyond the stars that all is well.   Julian Grenfell.   Maurice Baring.   HBMV

And you will understand/My hatred.   Hatred.   Gwendolyn B. Bennett.   BANP; BlSi; CDC; PoBA

And you with me shall dwell....   Christ Inviting Sinners to His Grace (excerpt).   Henry Alline.   CaP

And you won't catch me!   Ring-A-Ring.   Kate Greenaway.   MoShBr

And you would die/Bleeding.../Millions of times like me!!!   Song of the Negro on the Ferry.   Jose Craveirinha.   WhB

And you would hand it back to me.   Gift.   Leonard Cohen.   SoSe

And you wouldn't dare insult me, Sir, if Jack were only here.   My Mother Was a Lady.   Edward B. Marks.   TreF; YaD

And you wrote on my slate "I love you, Joe,"/When we were a couple of kids.   School Days.   Will Cobb.   FSW

And you, you...you, you utter.../You wait!   Beyond Words.   Robert Frost.   TW

And Young Bearwell was the first man/In all that companie.   Young Bearwell.   Anonymous.   ESPB

And young Bobby Campbell lies dead in the field,/His gun still clutched in his hand.   Bobby Campbell.   Anonymous.   FSW

And young lives glad with a gladness that/knows nothing of its value for the world.   The Home.   Rabindranath Tagore.   GoJo

And young Lord Raymond stormed Jerusalem.   Crusade.   Hilaire Belloc.   GoBC

And young Roddy M'Corley goes to die/On the Bridge of Toome today.   Roddy M'Corley.   Anonymous.   FSW

And young Susan loved her sailor on a British man-of-war.   A British Man-of-War.   Anonymous.   OBET

And your alien eyes will tunnel down/like a mole, like a mole...   How.   Abraham Sutzkever.   VWA

And your ballast is old wine.   Seamen Three.   Thomas Love Peacock.   OBRV; WiR

And your belief/in the day after next.   Nuts and Bolts Poem for Mr. MacAdams, Sr.   Kathleen Fraser.   NPGG

And your brothers too, I shall ever love.   Farewell.   Death of a Ram.   Sedulius Scottus.   NOBI

And your cage shall be made of the finest of gold,/And doors of ivory.   The False-Hearted Knight.   Anonymous.   BaBo

And your children/Will live.   Face of Poverty.   Lucy Smith.   NNP; PoNe

And your coarse hands helpless, singing at a plow.   The Plowman.   Max Harris.   BoAV

And your cool palm smoothes down stern Pluto's cheek.   Ternissa! You Are Fled.   Walter Savage Landor.   ExPo; LoBV; NOBE; OBNC; PoEL 1-5; SeCeV

And your dear voice saying–/"This is my little friend."   Under All Change.   Josephine Winslow Johnson.   MoRP

And your death is victory.   Onward, Onward, Men of Heaven.   Lydia Huntley Sigourney.   AH

And your dreaming is no more!   Capilano.   A. M. Stephen.   CaP

And your eventual Rubbish Heap, and mine.   Every Thing.   Harold Monro.   AnEnPo; MoBrPo

And your eyes peel to red mud   Babylon Revisited.   LeRoi (Imamu Amiri Baraka) Jones.   BPo; NoAm; TW

And your face and the flowers/Faint away in the moon.   A Japanese Love-Song.   Alfred Noyes.   OBVV

...And your face/Shall shine with an immortal grace.   On His Mistress Looking in a Glass.   Thomas Carew.   CaPo

And your face too looks like a ridge of stone.   Animal Songs: Baboon 2.   Anonymous.   PeSA

And your father sleeps in his own name.   Someone Knocks.   Peter Everwine.   NNaP

And your fearful gaze embraces only the shadows of emptiness.   With a Book at Twilight.   Jakov Steinberg.   VWA

And your feet turned in, your ears/reddened with obituaries.   Cernunnos.   Hugh Maxton.   CIP

And your great hearts, those urns of love divine!   The Accursed.   Charles Baudelaire.   LiTW

And your growth into martyrdom.   For Malcolm: After Mecca.   Gerald William Barrax.   CNA; OFD; PoBA

And your hair is a panther's shadow.   Ballade of Muhammad Din Tilai.   Anonymous.   PG

And your hand even now grips mine as though there never/were a grave.   Lament for Sean MacDermott.   Seumas (James Starkey) O'Sullivan.   AnIV

And your head shall be deckd with the eastern wind,/And the cold rain on your breast.   The Gardener.   Anonymous.   BaBo; CBEP; ESPB

And your heart and house would be/From within swept clean and free.   Love That's Pure, Itself Disdaining.   Johann A. Gruber.   AH

And your heart, weary and alone/on the road, hostile and black.   Harlem.   Jean Brierre.   TTY

And your heart would not break, not ever.   Then.   Gary Gildner.   FiCP

And your hesitant hands/on my expectant eyes/cease to foresee/the future.   Expectation.   Aliza Shenhar.   VWA

And your high priesthood shall make earth/All hallowed ground.   Hallowed Ground.   Thomas Campbell.   BLPA; HBV 1-2

And your Honour's petitioners ever shall pray.   To the Right Hon. Henry Pelham...   Edward Moore.   OBSV

And your last trick?/A hempen rope.   House in Meudon.   Margarita Aliger.   VWA

And your latter ends melt into melody.   The New Cecilia.   Thomas Lovell Beddoes.   ERoP 1-2; OAEL 1-2

And your life is but a roses's.   The Missive.   Sir Edmund Gosse.   HBV 1-2

And your Lion shall growl, but hardly bite/more.–   An Ancient Prophecy.   Philip Freneau.   PAH

And your lips, by themselves, will then/Begin to sing young songs.   Poetics.   Andre Spire.   VWA

And your little job is done.   Madam Life.   William Ernest Henley.   CABA; InPK; MoBrPo; NBM; TrGrPo

And your love's presence, snowy, beautiful, and kind.   Sunday: New Guinea.   Karl Shapiro.   AmFN; PoPl

And your love shall be clay.   To a Cloud.   Manuel Altolaguirre.   LiTW

And your loveliness be slow to fade.   Wishes for a Bridal Couple and Their Unborn Child.   Statius Publius Papinius.   HW

And your memories will seem to begin/with the creation of the world.   Ordeal.   Nina Cassian.   PBWP

And your mother was/a princess/in darkness.   For Each of You.   Audre Lorde.   CNA

And your mother will be gooseflesh/and your father will die.   After Hilary, Age 5.   Faye Kicknosway.   APU

"And your nest shall be made of leaves of gold,/Instead of the green willow tree."   Lady Isabel and the Elf Knight (Pretty Polly).   Anonymous.   AmFP

And your other five brothers will end in hell/If they have not repented.   Dives and Lazarus.   Anonymous.   AmFP

And your pillow wet with tears.   In the Night Watches.   Sir Charles G. D. Roberts.   PeCV

And your right/to the right-hearted   The Fringes.   Harris Lenowitz.   VWA

And your ripe yeeres love-noone (he goes no higher),/Turnes all the spirits of Man into desire.   The Nurse-Life Wheat.   Fulke, Lord Brooke Greville.   AAS; NCEP

And your round little face looks as ruddy and meek/As a rose that's been washed in the rain.   The Tumble.   Ann Taylor.   HBVY

And your sorrows are less than your strength/Which he foresaw.   Faith.   Preston Clark.   HBMV

...And your sweet tongue/was the only wafer I could not wash down.   Woods Gets Religion.   John Woods.   GP

And your three-year life has been full/Of mild, steady pain.   Nansen.   Gary Snyder.   InPS; PAI

And your timing's/a week off   Three Sayings from Highlands, North Carolina.   Jonathan Williams.   OBAL

And your toothbrush–and everything–/That's helpless.   The Horse Named Bill (with music).   Anonymous.   AS; FSW

And your true name is Mistress Betty.   On a Romantic Lady.   Mary Monck.   NOEC

And your warm freshwater ripples, Horsey Mere.   East Anglian Bathe.   Sir John Betjeman.   NoP; SD

And yours is the silly head it hangs above.   Warning to One.   Merrill Moore.   MoAmPo; TrGrPo; YaD

And yours the loss and mine the deadly pain.   How oft have I, my dear and cruel foe.   Sir Thomas Wyatt.   AAS; FCP

And yours to love as lovingly.   If Love, For Love of Long Time Had.   John Heywood.   EIL

And yours, will know the taste of in their time.   Family Prime.   Mark Van Doren.   VGW

And Youth be dear, and Life be sweet to Love.   The House of Life.   Dante Gabriel Rossetti.   OBNC

And youth in Expectation.   Youth is wise.   Habitations.   Hilaire Belloc.   PV

And youth's warm gracious heart is harden'd quite.   The Plea of the Midsummer Fairies.   Thomas Hood.   OBNC

And yr/children will look at u differently/ than we looked at our parents.   Change-Up.   Don L. Lee.   CNA; PoBA

And Zero at the Bone–   A narrow Fellow in the Grass.   Emily Dickinson.   AmPP; AtBAP; BoWoP; CMoP; DiPo; ExPo; FaFP; FM; FPL; GoJo; HAP; HoPM; LiTA; LiTM; MAmP; MAPA; MoAB; NIP; NOBA; NoP; OBCA; OxBA; PoEL 1-5; PoLf; PPoe; PPP; SeCeV; SoSe; TAP; WeW

...And zero floats you into morning.   An Early Start in Mid-Winter.   Robyn Sarah.   CaPN

Andonis is the spring song, me-na-wah–   Andonis, My Daughter.   Thomas Love Peacock.   VoR

Andre Breton he said may pass here.   Sunflower.   Andre Breton.   LiTW

"Andres, my poet, I love you so much..."   Words to Remind Me of Grandmother.   Andres Castro Rios.   InW

Andrew Jackson–hickory wood!   Andrew Jackson.   Martha Keller.   AmFN; MaC

The ane a duke, the second a knight,/And third a laird o lands sae free.'
The Knight's Ghost. *Anonymous.* ESPB

Anear me Two from the Phantomland! Spirits Everywhere. Ludwig
Uhland. AWP

Anew his nuptial Toil resumes. Had I but Strength Enough, and Time
(parody). Charles Robinson. BXAP

Angel: eternally in despair. Kandinsky: "Improvision No. 27." Edward
Tick. PoDr

The angel kneeling with the wreath/Sees, in the moonlight, graves. A
Country Life. Randall Jarrell. MiAP; MoAmPo

An angel kneels, in woman's form,/And breathes a prayer for him.
Pocahontas. George Pope Morris. MC; PAH

The angel music from a demon's throat. The False Summer. Marya
Zaturenska. CrMA

An angel, now in heaven. The Bedlamite. Thomas Mozeen. NOEC

The angel of death comes to make the alienated and indestructible/One a part
of his famous society. Abraham:. Delmore Schwartz. VWA

...Angel of death/made of desire and mercy raise your wings. Resting Place.
Jon Silkin. VWA

The angel of death shall carry me. Over the River. Nancy Woodbury
Priest. HBV 1-2

Angel of poets,/Tell us how/To move men nobly,/To move them now.
Prayer for All Poets at This Time. Irwin Edman. TrPWD

An Angel robed in light hath said,/"The Lord is risen from the dead."
Light's Glittering Morn. John Mason Neale. EBCP; OxBoCh

De angel roll de stone away. De Angel Roll de Stone Away. *Anonymous.*
BoAN 1-2

The angel sent the stars to you. To Dick, on His Sixth Birthday. Sara
Teasdale. BiCB

An angel sits beside the tomb. The Mourners Came at Break of Day.
Sarah Flower Adams. HBV 1-2

The angel that we wrestle is ourselves. Reflections on Water. Kenneth
Pitchford. CoPo

The angel, treed, was trembling, that had promised peace. Jack-in-the-Box.
Elder Olson. NePA

Angelic hosts and all the sons of man! God of the World. Israel Najara.
TrJP

Angelic voices greet us there,/In the music in the air. There's Music in the
Air. Fanny J. Crosby. BLSo

Angels alone, that soar above,/Enjoy such liberty. To Althea from Prison.
Richard Lovelace. AnAnS 2; AnEnPo; AnFE; AWP; BiP; BLPA; CaPo;
CavP; EnLit; FaBoBe; FPL; GBL; GoTF; GTBS; GTBS-P; HAP; HBV 1-2;
HeIP; InPo; InPS; JCP; LiTB; LiTL; LoBV; MCCG; MeLP; MePo; NOBE;
NoP; OAEP; OBEV; OBS; PAI; PoPle; PoRA; SeCeV; SeCP; SeCV 1-2;
SoSe; TEP; TreF; TrGrPo; ViBoPo; WHA

Angels enjoy the heavens' inward quires/Stargazers only multiply desires.
Caelica, XVII. Fulke, Lord Brooke Greville. FCP

The angels had made room for the darlings to dwell/In Heav'n with their
mother that night. Two Little Children. *Anonymous.* BFSS

Angels in curling pins, with paper wings,/bells of spun glass, and drifts of
mineral snow. December Fragments. Richmond Lattimore. PCh

Angels in heaven know I love you. Down in the Valley. *Anonymous.* AS;
TreFT

The angels join, and all combine/To spread their anthems round. What If
the Saint Must Die. John Peck. AH

"Angels, Martyrs, Prophets, Virgins,/Answer, Yes!" Art Thou Weary?
John Mason Neale. CAW

Angels nor devils are of these–/The castaways on velvet ease. Passivity.
Mary Elizabeth ("E") Fullerton. BoAV

Angels of Bethlehem, echo the strain! Angel of Peace, Thou Hast Wandered
Too Long. Oliver Wendell Holmes. AH

Angels of Jazz–they don't die–they live/they live–in hipsters like you and I
Lester Young. Ted Joans. AmNP

Angels singing/To silly shepherds/Of a child born for death/To save us from
our fantasy. Christmas Myth, 1973. Robert McGovern. SOTS

The angels stream before me/like a torch. Confession. Lucille Clifton.
GeTw

Angels they are, and the day is dawning. Shepherd, Shepherd, Hark. Saint
Theresa of Avila. AWP; CAW; LiTW

Angels watch over thee,/Mary, be kind! Hymn: "Hush! oh ye billows."
Joseph Sheridan Lefanu. OnYI

Anger as soon as fed is dead–/'Tis starving makes it fat. Mine enemy is
growing old. Emily Dickinson. TW

Anger invests with such a lovely grace,/That anger's self I needs must kiss
again. Astrophel and Stella, LXXIII. Sir Philip Sidney. AAS; EG;
OAEP; SiPS

Anger, my ode is written. Envoi. J. V. Cunningham. VGW

The anger of the poor/owns one deep fire against two craters. The Anger
That Breaks a Man Down into Boys. Cesar Vallejo. EAS

Anger will make easy yet/The bitter footfalls of regret. Love-Songs, At Once
Tender and Informative. Samuel Hoffenstein. OBAL

Anguish, tough wood, and earth, remain. Prairie. K. N. Llewellyn. YeAr

Animals have it over man. Do You Love Me? Robert Watson. PoL

The animals ran, the Eagle soared and dropt. 1 September 1939. John
Berryman. NIP

Animals stand two by two, but there is only one/flood. Two Animals, One
Flood. Diane Glancy. STE

Animasaun and I went as far as Remo/Just to buy some lambs. Money!
Money! *Anonymous.* WTO

Anna anna anna anna Anna. Joe Johnson. CNA

Anna Pavlova rises like a phoenix/instead of a swan especially in your honor/
tonight. Season Ticket. Gloria Frym. APU

Anna's the name of names for me! Ballade of Ladies' Names. William
Ernest Henley. HBV 1-2

Annabella, such a ridiculous name for a breakfast cereal. The Empty Pain-
Killer Bottles. Tom Raworth. EAS

Anne,/have you made/peace with peace? Anne Sexton. Hans Juergensen.
AMV-81

Announce our love! Amen. Hymn to Joy. Julia Cunningham. PCh

Announcing me in other dells/Unto the different dawn! There is a morn by
men unseen. Emily Dickinson. OxBA

Anon, anon, anon, Sir, what is't you say? Come, Come Away, to the Tavern
I say. *Anonymous.* OBS

Anon, the lethal arrow–to upbear! Fortune's Treachery. Judah Halevi.
TrJP

Anonymous faces plastered with her smile. Standardization. A.D. Hope.
BoAV

Another, another, will follow his fright up the street. Poem in Karori.
Louis Johnson. AnNZ

Another bird assumes its furled disguise. Arras. P. K. Page. OBCV

Another camp-fire closer to its vision. The Town. David Rowbotham.
PoAu 1-2

Another cannot wake thy giant size. To Ailsa Rock. John Keats. EnRP;
MOS; OBNC

Another cross loomed dark against the sky. The Martyr. Natalie Flohr.
PGD

Another day, another dolor. A Man Can Complain, Can't He? Ogden
Nash. NLV

...Another day/begins. May. John Stevens Wade. AMV-80

Another day of honey has begun! A Summer Night in the Beehive. Charles
Tennyson Turner. FM

Another day's prose to get through. Dreambooks. Alfred Corn. DFT

Another day will find me brave,/And not afraid to dare. Interim. Clarissa
Scott Delany. CDC; PoNe

Another egg is boiling in the pot. Divorce. Erica Jong. GP

Another Father now, more strong than I,/Has borne you voiceless to your
dear blue sky. The Child's Wish Granted. George Parsons Lathrop.
AA; HBV 1-2

Another floating off, his big pouch full. Skin Diving in the Virgins. John
Malcolm Brinnin. NYBP; TAP

Another give me for that bite. Kisses. *Anonymous.* WTO

...Another/Hot day and they felt/Drowsy and wished to lie down. The
Mowing Crew. Baron Wormser. MAYP

Another man done gone. Another Man Done Gone. *Anonymous.* FSW

Another meaning is coming, wait and see. Bones. Frederick Morgan.
FAZ

Another old man, lost/In America, trying to get home. Bread Loaf to
Omaha, Twenty-Eight Hours. Patrick Worth Gray. TAT

Another reunion table/minus one more chair. My Family's under Contract
to Cancer. Greg Simison. AMV-80

Another's is as harsh as if she bray'd. The Art of Love. Ovid (Publius
Ovidius Naso). FaBoUs

Another scoop of ice cream/our smiles receive. The Greater Friendship
Baptist Church. Carole C. Gregory. BlSi

...Another/shadow that will pass. Blue Ridge. Elizabeth Hodges.
AMV-81

Another slave's/blood christened cement...Again! Toilet Bowl Congregation.
Carolyn Baxter. LFAC

Another snapp'd the cherry. Chop-Cherry. Robert Herrick. ALV; CBEP;
EnLoPo; MyFE; UnTE

Another time has other lives to live. Another Time. W. H. Auden.
OxBA

Another toucan in the/Zoo can. The Toucan. Pyke Johnson, Jr. NTCP

...Another treasure/For later scholars on generous grants to discover. A
Treasure. Reed Whittemore. NePoEA

Another two/Try. Central Park Tourney. Mildred Weston. AmFN

Another village explodes. It Is Dangerous to Read Newspapers. Margaret
Atwood. HeIP; OBWP

...Another war and/more piano tuners for my horse. The Day the Beatles
Lost One to the Flesh-Eating Horse. Dave Kelly. FAZ

Another war? No thanks. It Was the Last of the Parades. Louis Simpson.
NYBP

Another way–to see– The Tint I Cannot Take Is Best. Emily Dickinson.
MAmP; MoAmPo

Another, when they're ready, shows them game.   Upon My Lord Brohall's Wedding.   Sir John Suckling.   CaPo

Another while–and I shall drag no/more...   Another While.   Morris Rosenfeld.   TrJP

Another woman: a change of tears.   From the Notebooks.   Theodore Roethke.   PoL

Another world is also going.   Shop Talk.   Roy Fuller.   OxBC

Another year burns down to stub and ash,/And I am older.   Living.   D. S. Savage.   NeBP

Another year for Thee!   Another Year Is Dawning.   Frances Ridley Havergal.   WBLP

Anouncing peace in death and love in hate.   To Naples.   H. B. Mallalieu.   WaP

Ans ia "the same today."   Hitherto Hath the Lord Helped.   Anonymous.   BLRP

(The answer is, in a sense, no.)   Tripe.   J. B. Morton.   InMe

The answer may be nearer than we think.   Two Mountains Men Have Climbed.   Pauline Starkweather.   GoYe

Answer me, if this be done?/'Tis done.   Incantation to Oedipus.   John Dryden.   OFD; WSC

Answer my rays and cluster to a theme!   The Double Vision.   Lewis, Cecil Day.   AtBAP; NoAm

Answer quickly, "Lord, send me!/To the lands beyond the sea"?   The Master's Call.   Oswald J. Smith.   STF

The answer's yes/To that deep query.   Sehnsucht, or, What You Will.   "Corinna".   FiBHP

Answer the question, bastard. Don't waste my life.   His Side/Her Side.   Jeffrey Skinner.   AMV-81

Answer this riddle by to-morrow at noon.   Riddle: "Red and blue and delicate green."   Anonymous.   GBP

The answer to my father's tears   To My God in His Sickness.   Philip Levine.   NNaP

...The answer was/The only one earth ever got from sky.   A Walk on Snow.   Peter Viereck.   MiAP

The answer with a silent face.   Channel Crossing.   George Barker.   ACV; ChMP; GTBS-P

Answered some/Of his long marvellous letters but kept none.   Who's Who.   W.H. Auden.   CABA; CoBMV; MoAB; MoBrPo; NoAm

Answering a child's candor/Beyond the child's question.   The Knowledge of Light.   Henry Rago.   PoCh; VGW

Answering her "Miserere!"   Chicago.   John Boyle O'Reilly.   PAH

Answering note for note.   Holy Satyr.   Hilda ("H. D.") Doolittle.   MoAmPo

...Answers by/a being nothing there/where there was a man.   The Signboard.   Robert Creeley.   ConAP

The answers of the deep,/These to myself I keep.   Frutta Di Mare.   Geoffrey Scott.   EtS; OBMV

The answers that/I wish I knew!   For Vicki at Seven.   Sydney King Russell.   BiCB

Ant wyght in wode be fleme.   Spring Has Come to Town with Love.   Anonymous.   CABA

Ant yet ich bar the flour away.   Al Nist by the Rose.   Anonymous.   AtBAP

The antelope, whose feet shall bless/With their light sound thy loneliness.   Lalla Rookh.   Thomas Moore.   BIrV

The anthem rose from all the ships/Safe moored in Boston Bay.   The Thanksgiving in Boston Harbor.   Hezekiah Butterworth.   AA; MC; OHIP; PAH

Anthropophagy reigns in the kitchen.   Buttons.   Walter De La Mare.   DTC; FaBoNo

Antiochus/pours now for me!   Epigram: "I was thirsty."   Meleager.   PeHV

Antistrophe of desolation to the strophe multitude.   Still the Mind Smiles.   Robinson Jeffers.   CMoP

Antonio Stradivari's violins/Without Antonio.   Stradivarius: Working with God.   George Eliot.   TRV

Ants buried in their homes/are stopped   Stopped.   Allen Polite.   NNP

Ants gone. Cells bare.   The Ant Village.   Dorothy and Marion Edey Grider.   TiPo

The Anvil is unharmed, the hammers gone.   The Anvil of God's Word.   John Clifford.   BLRP

Anxious, and trembling for the Birth of Fate.   The Rape of the Lock.   Alexander Pope.   AtBAP; BiP; CEP; DiPo; EBEV; FiP; ForPo; HAP; MasP; MBW 1-2; MOON; NAWM 1-2; NOEC; NoP; OAEL 1-2; OAEP; OBNV; OxBoLi; PoEL 1-5; SeCeV; TEP; TrGrPo; WHA

...Anxious/for another night, singing.   Nothing Inside and Nothing Out.   Ray Amorosi.   FiCP

Any child, any girl, any woman, any surprise.   Ode in Honour.   Francis Scarfe.   EAS

Any day a fairy/Coming down the street.   I Keep Three Wishes Ready.   Annette Wynne.   SoPo

Any knowledge/of/illegitimacy.   Comments.   Peggy Susberry Kenner.   JB

Any light. Oh, any light.   The Swerve.   William Stafford.   GP; SM

...Any memory I/have of these New York places evaporates with her sweet tongue.   The Good Ship.   Michael Stephens.   APU

Any mirror except her own rivers and lakes.   A Fable for Critics.   James Russell Lowell.   AA

Any moral to this dins in drowned ears.   Salmon Drowns Eagle.   Malcolm Lowry.   OBCV

"Any more, any more, any more, never more!"   The New Vestments.   Edward Lear.   NOBV

Any music save by Handel/On the coast of Coromandel!   On the Coast of Coromandel.   Osbert Sitwell.   MoBrPo; SeCePo

Any number of consumptive Keatses and dying Gauls.   Museums.   Louis MacNeice.   MoBrPo; NAMP

Any of several/insects that bore in maize is a corn borer.   Corn.   Bernadette Mayer.   ANYP

Any old sort will suit me.   To the God of Love.   E. G. V. Knox.   ALV; HBMV; NOBL

Any old time/The mood was on ya?   Lasagna.   X. J. Kennedy.   PPJ

Any part of darling pig/Is perfectly fine with me.   Any Part of Piggy.   Noel Coward.   NLV

Any shape does for me!   The Plaint of the Camel.   Charles Edward Carryl.   AnAmPo; EvOK; HBV 1-2; HBVY; SoPo

Any ship that sails goes/To a brother's land!   An Endless Chain.   Abraham Reisen.   VWA

Any thy despis'd disdain too late shall find/That none are fair but who are kind.   When I Loved Thee.   Thomas Stanley.   LiTL

Any wall warm/When winter's deep.   Cover.   Frances Frost.   SUS

Any woman's death diminishes me   From an Old House in America.   Adrienne Rich.   NNaP

Anybody/can/get hi   Spacin.   Ronda Davis.   JB

Anybody might have found it but–His Whisper came to Me!   The Explorer.   Rudyard Kipling.   WHA

Anyone could hunt the old dog/if they could find him after that.   The One to Grieve.   Rudy Thomas.   GOYP

Anyone's life is greater than his care.   Northern Boulevard.   Edwin Denby.   CrMA

Anything and everything/Which I know and do not know!   Song.   Stephen Spender.   FaBoTw

Anything. Anything. Ridicule my arm.   In Your Bad Dream.   Richard Hugo.   LCAP

Anything but the robot manifestation/of prevailing system of exploitation.   Lecture.   Anselm Hollo.   APU

Anything lovelier/Than a white tree?   A White Tree in Bloom.   John Richard Moreland.   PGD

Anything might happen on a truly fairy night.   Sometimes.   Rose Fyleman.   SiSoSe

Anything to get me over the shock/Of finally meeting you face to face.   For Allen Ginsberg, Who Cut Off His Beard.   Sanford Pinsker.   AMV-80

Anything to me is sweeter/Than to see Shock-headed Peter.   Slovenly Peter.   Heinrich Hoffmann.   BBGG

Anyway, I'm a mouse.   We Interrupt This Broadcast.   Judith Hemschemeyer.   Str

Anyway, now Tim's dead.   In Memory of My Uncle Timothy.   Alastair Reid.   NePoEA-2

...Anyway, you should have been home/half an hour ago.   Pa.   Leo Dangel.   AMV-81; Str

..."Anywhere, anywhere, out of the world!"   Anywhere Out of the World.   Charles Baudelaire.   SyP

Anywhere, anywhere, out of this room!   A Scherzo.   Dora Greenwell.   NOBV

Anywhere in this world.   I'm on an Island.   Tom Clark.   ANYP

Anywhere nearly/ As old as me.   Five-in-June.   Lysbeth Boyd Borie.   BiCB

...Anywhere/Save in the tomb. Not there–he is not there.   Cenotaph of Lincoln.   James T. McKay.   OHIP

Ap-Cataract Ap-Pistyll Ap-Rhaiader Ap-Headlong!   Chorus: "Hail to the Headlong!"   Thomas Love Peacock.   OBRV

Apart-from-you takes half my strength/The rest I need for waiting.   Letter from a Wife.   S. Carolyn Reese.   PoNe

Apart, we left the strange sea/Within each other.   Plankton.   Ruth Miller.   PeSA

Apfel.   Concrete poem: Apfel.   Reinhard Dohl.   InPK

The aping shape of earth–sure/Of its weight now as in future.   Urn Burial.   Ted Hughes.   EBEV

Apollo is once more the golden theme!   Hyperion.   John Keats.   ViBoPo

Apollo's first, at last the true God's priest.   An Elegy upon the Death of the Dean of St. Paul's, Dr. John Donne.   Thomas Carew.   CABA

Apollo shriek'd;–and lo! from all his limbs/Celestial.   Hyperion.   John Keats.   EnRP; ERoP 1-2; OAEL 1-2; OBRV

The apotheosis of the young wife and mediocre dancer.   Made in Heaven.   Peter Porter.   PPON

The Apparatus of the Dark/To ignorance revealed.   The lightning is a yellow fork.   Emily Dickinson.   InPK

Apparel spread for drying–/heavenly Kaguyama.   Manyoshu: Spring Is
  Passing.   Empress Jito.   PBWP
Apparently he didn't. I'll teach Luke.   Of Suicide.   John Berryman.
  NoAm
Appear and plot new zodiacs upon the flesh.   The Thing Is Violent.
  Gwendolyn MacEwen.   NOBC; PeCV
Appear the argent, swan-assemblied reaches.   Reconciliation.   C. Day-Lewis.
  MP; NoAm; TwCP
...Appears/For a moment on the balconies of my chosen sleep.   Saturday
  Night in the Parthenon.   Kenneth Patchen.   EAS
Appears the dawn of heaven.   The Hour of Peaceful Rest.   William B.
  Tappan.   AA; HBV 1-2
Appears the exact color of earth.   Old Photo, 1942.   George Uba.   BrSi
Appears to transcend/The bounds of this court's jurisdiction.   The Devil's
  Dictionary: Nose.   Ambrose Bierce.   OBAL
Appease/The misery of the living and the remorse of the dead.   Purgatory.
  William Butler Yeats.   CMoP
Appease the waves where there was tumult late!   In the Depths of Night.
  Manuel Gutierrez Najera.   CAW
An appetite that must/Make do with such rough food as she, too, must.   The
  Moth.   Vernon Scannell.   OxBC
Applauding in between/bites of watermelon/to their execution.   Warden's
  Day.   Carolyn Baxter.   LFAC
Applauding just one member of the cast.   Act of Love.   Vernon Scannell.
  ErPo
An apple a day/Keeps the doctor away.   Health Food.   Anonymous.
  FaBoUs
An apple and a plum.   Bring Daddy Home.   Anonymous.   OxNR
The apple falls, falling in the quiet night.   Kentucky Mountain Farm.
  Robert Penn Warren.   MoVE
The apple that hangs unplucked, grown fabulous.   Blind Man.   Michael
  Hamburger.   NePoEA-2
The apple-tree, the singing,/And the gold?   Magic.   Thomas Wolfe.   PoPl
The apple unbitten in the palm.   As Bad As a Mile.   Philip Larkin.   ELU;
  OBSP; OxBC
The apples, Bill, the apples!   Sunday Morning Apples.   Hart Crane.
  NAMP
Apples in the orchard/Will be fire in a man!   Cider Song.   Mildred Weston.
  BoNaP
Apples, perfect for window cracking.   The Tree Is Father to the Man.   Lou
  Lipsitz.   NCSH
Apples, ripen for the dray!   The Victoria Markets Recollected in Tranquillity.
  Furnley Maurice.   NOAV; PoAu 1-2
Apply to Master Janus last of all.   Sonnet: To Brunetto Latini.   Dante
  Alighieri.   AWP
Appointments must be kept.   The Alarum.   Sylvia Townsend Warner.
  MoBrPo
...Approaches all/Stayers, and searchers of the fanged pool.   The Re-Birth of
  Venus.   Geoffrey Hill.   NePoEA
Approve, accept, know them daughters of men,/Now that your sons are dust.
  A Father of Women.   Alice Meynell.   BrRo; SBG
April/Comes like an idiot, babbling and strewing flowers.   Spring.   Edna St.
  Vincent Millay.   BoWoP; MoAB; MoAmPo; NePA; NoP
April Fool!   Oh Did You Hear?   Shel Silverstein.   PoSC
April hath a fickle mind.   April Fantasie.   Mackay Ellen Hutchinson
  Cortissoz.   AA
April's coming up the hill!   Now the Noisy Winds Are Still.   Mary Mapes
  Dodge.   YeAr
April slides her long cool fingers/under his shirt.   Time Out.   Donald
  Finkel.   HoPM
April, when you dance down these ways/Hush your awakening feet.   Late
  Winter.   Hazel Hall.   HBMV
The apron, bandana and knives/never did hide beauty from me.   The Sound
  of Rain.   David Allan Evans.   GOYP
An aptitude for mothering, an art/As painstaking as any crewel heart.   The
  New York Woman.   L. E. Sissman.   MAT
Aquarius died when/they buried atlantis this/is the age of pisces/check it out
  12 Gates to the City.   Nikki Giovanni.   IHMS; PoBA
AQUARIUS rain, the FISH comes last.   The Signs of the Zodiac.   Ebenezer
  Cobham Brewer.   FaBoUs
Ar easterlies polar easterlies pol/pole   The Windy Planet.   Annie Dillard.
  SUW
The Arab's wisdom everywhere.   A Vault inside the Castle at Goito.   Robert
  Browning.   MyFE
The arbitrary skylines of the cities/they join.   Metroliner.   Jack Du Vall.
  AMV-80
Arc-lamped thrown back upon the cutting flood.   Altarwise by Owl-Light.
  Dylan Thomas.   CMoP
Archangels, heroes,–rascals yet unhung!   Tricksters.   William Rose Benet.
  HBMV
Archangels' voices ring,/"Holy, Holy," ceaselessly.   The Angelic Vilancete.
  Gil Vicente.   CAW

Arching a world where nothing had occurred.   As It Looked Then.   Edwin
  Arlington Robinson.   CMoP; NePA; NoAm
Arching her back,/She hissed/And slipped out of the house.   My True
  Memory.   Asya (Asya Gray).   VWA
The architect, however, flew/to Afri-or Americoo.   The Picket Fence.
  Christian Morgenstern.   GrPl
The architect, though, ran away/To Afri- or Americay.   The Wooden Fence.
  Christian Morgenstern.   LiTW
...Architect, whose art/Could build so strong in a weak heart.   The Church-
  Floor.   George Herbert.   ATP; EBEV; ExPo; MeLP; OAEL 1-2; OBS;
  SeCePo; SeCeV
Arcturus and the Pleiads beckon him.   Per Aspera.   Florence Earle Coates.
  HBMV
An ardent hunter/swept to the ends of the sea.   The Moon Is Teaching Bible.
  Zelda.   VWA
Are a wooden leg–or a golden chain.   The Fortunes of War.   Anonymous.
  PoL
Are added unto them that have plenty of water.   Green, Green is El Aghir.
  Norman Cameron.   MoBS; OBWP; OxBTC
Are all biweved with bloody drops/For thine sake.'   Undo!   Anonymous.
  NOCV; OxBM
Are all growing green in my north country.   The North Country Maid.
  Anonymous.   OBET
"Are all the children in?"   Are All the Children In?   Anonymous.   STF
Are all with thee,–are all with thee!   The Building of the Ship.   Henry
  Wadsworth Longfellow.   AA; AnNE; EtS; MOS; OHFP; PGD; TreF; YaD
"Are any workmen out of work?/The Carpenter needs more."   The Carpenter
  of Galilee.   Hilda W. Smith.   TRV
Are as disordered/As my black hair.   Will he always love me?   Lady
  Horikawa.   BoWoP; LiTW; OLR
Are at the Princely tables better cheer,/Then Lamb and Kid, Lettice and
  Olives here.   Epodes.   Horace.   CavP
Are blooming bright as the night/She danced the minuet!   Miss Nancy's
  Gown.   Zitella Cocke.   AA
Are born of like/elements.   The Ring Of.   Charles Olson.   NOBA; VGW
Are born without a pang, and die/Without a pang, and so pass by.   By the
  Sea.   Christina Georgina Rossetti.   BoNaP; MOS; NOBV
Are broken glass./Good-bye.   Letter from the Street.   Thomas Brush.   LTB
Are buried here.   Neanderthal.   Michael Jackson.   OCNZ
Are but drawn curtains when the play is done.   Epitaph: "What is our life?"
  Anonymous.   FaBoEE
Are but outward symbols of/my inner ghetto.   Here I Sit in My Infested
  Cubicle.   Theresa Greenwood.   CTBA
Are but pale shadows of your dancing feet.   The Waters of Life.   Humbert
  Wolfe.   MoBrPo
Are but the recollected choice/Of what I felt for thee.   The Secret.   John
  Clare.   GBL
Are cat and dog, and rogue and whore.   Phyllis; or, The Progress of Love.
  Jonathan Swift.   OAEL 1-2; OBSV
Are cemented by common design/to invade the house.   The House.   Tania
  Van Zyl.   PeSA
Are cheap, alas! as we are dear.   Arithmetic on the Frontier.   Rudyard
  Kipling.   OBWP; VLP
Are children gazing in a sweetshop window.   Bear in Mind, O Ye Recording
  Angels.   Norman Cameron.   ELU
Are circling near the bottom/in the deepest water of the lake.   Angler.
  Mark Vinz.   WOLT
Are constant–as the fall of dice.   Constancies.   Anonymous.   UnTE
Are counted Ireland's earth, mistake, curse, shame.   Ireland.   Barten
  Holyday.   FaBoEE
...Are covered in ashes/by our slaughterer in the land of Gael/to wrap them
  from the cold air!   Mag Uidhir's Winter Campaign.   Eochaidh O
  Heoghusa.   NOBI
Are crystal mirrors of eternity.   La Beaute.   Charles Baudelaire.   AWP
Are Daphne's blushing cheeks, I swear.   To Daphne.   Walter Besant.   HBV
  1-2
Are dead and coffined with her foes.   In After Days.   George Frederick
  Cameron.   CaP
Are dimensions with room/for only two   If She Sang.   Gerald William
  Barrax.   CNA
Are each paved with the moon and these.   The Cloud: Orbed Maiden.
  Percy Bysshe Shelley.   MOON
Are filled with sea-birds and their cries.   The Echoing Cliff.   Andrew Young.
  PoSH
Are, for the most part, human but unbandaged.   Hospital.   Karl Shapiro.
  VGW
Are forced, for my greater grief, from me their face/to hide.   Psalm
  LXXXVIII.   Henry Howard, Earl of Surrey.   FCP
Are formed art, virtue, truth.   Shells.   Thomas Sturge Moore.   SeCePo
Are fought in these silent ways!   The Bravest Battle.   Joaquin Miller.
  WBLP

Are found in heaps and stacks and piles within the country store.　The Country Store.　*Anonymous.*　BLPA

Are God Almighty's bow and arrow.　Robin, Wren, Martin, Swallow.　*Anonymous.*　GBP

Are God's cock and hen.　The Robin and the Wren.　*Anonymous.*　PBBP

Are God's worst portion to mankind.　A Nameless Epitaph.　Matthew Arnold.　FaBoEE

Are gone as dust is washed from off the leaf/When comes the rain.　Nox Benigna.　William Pember Reeves.　AnNZ

Are graves become but Button-holes?　On Button the Grave-Maker.　*Anonymous.*　FaBoEE

"Are growing in my garden-plot, and this I call my dairy."　Her Dairy.　Peter Newell.　NA

Are held with his melodious harmonie/In willing chains and sweet captivitie.　At a Vacation Exercise.　John Milton.　JCP; OBS; PP

Are high-propped on a pillow of blue cloud.　To Tan Ch'iu.　Li Po.　AWP

Are hot as any hottentot and not the goods for me!'　Hornpipe.　Edith Sitwell.　FaBoMo; GTBS-P; MoVE; OAEL 1-2; SeCePo

Are "I thank you" and "If you please."　Hearts, Like Doors, Will Ope with Ease.　*Anonymous.*　HBVY; OxNR

Are just practical and do not sing,/like the crazy birds, to their offspring.　The Parents of Psychotic Children.　Marvin Bell.　SUW

Are known beyond death's door.　Threnody.　Waring Cuney.　BANP

Are like the sun, dazzling, yet plain to all eyes.　Truth.　John Donne.　SeCePo

Are like thee, young Desire.　Agathon: Song of Eros.　George Edward Woodberry.　AA

Are lying about the world.　When Green Buds Hang.　Alfred Edward Housman.　ACV

Are many as the things I hear and see.　In Your Absence.　Elizabeth Baxter.　PoToHe

Are melodiously mingled in my warm New England breast.　Longfellow's Visit to Venice.　Sir John Betjeman.　NOBL

Are merely metaphors for the void between/one pore & another　Tell Them I'm Struggling to Sing with Angels.　David Meltzer.　VWA

Are mirrored, and hover/Moonily.　Song on the Water.　Thomas Lovell Beddoes.　FaBoCh; LoGBV

Are mirrored in its round abode.　Hymn of the Earth.　William Ellery Channing, II.　AA; AnNE

Are more highly specialised than the tissues of destiny/itself?　Those Various Scalpels.　Marianne Moore.　LoBV

Are more lost than my heart, which died/not when it broke!　Dorothy.　Rose Hawthorne Lathrop.　AA

Are most remembered for your wounds and grief.　To a Crucifix.　Anna Wickham.　MoBrPo

Are never wrong and I am rhythm to strong/medicine.　In My Lifetime.　James Welch.　CDW; STE

Are not limits the sooth to formulate/Theories thereof, simply our ruler to feel?　Immortality.　Samuel Greenberg.　LiTA

Are not so warm, not so warm/As the body of my wife.　While the leaves of the bamboo rustle.　*Anonymous.*　BoLoP

Are not such furious boys with blood on their faces.　To the Woman in Bond Street Station.　Edward Weismiller.　NePA; WaP

Are not these drifting figures the chorus?　Carmen Saeculare.　Horace.　OBVE

Are not these with thousands moe/Than the court of kings do know?　The Passionate Shepherd.　Nicholas Breton.　ViBoPo

Are not to be won that way.　A Woman's Question.　Lena Lathrop.　BLPA; PoToHe; WBLP

Are not unlike/night's.　The End of Man Is His Beauty.　LeRoi (Imamu Amiri Baraka) Jones.　BALP

Are nothing but a roosing-place/For German turtle-doves!　The Doves of Venice.　Laurence Hutton.　AA

Are one inevitable element/In the great crucible of Destiny.　Fulfilment.　Elsa Barker.　HBMV

Are one of those functions/That poison their lives.　The Parting Injunctions.　Clarence Day.　DBV

Are one with all the dead, since she is gone.　The Glory of the Day Was in Her Face.　James Weldon Johnson.　BANP; CDC; IDB; PoBA

Are ornaments that well become/the wide, wild, houseless downs.　The Houseless Downs.　George Ferebe.　FaBoPP

Are pleased to wait serenely/for the coming of the spring.　The Organ Grinders' Garden.　Mildred Plew Merryman.　SoPo

Are remnants of a past life/I can't possibly understand.　The Marsh.　Marcia Southwick.　MAYP

Are rich beyond all counting and all dreams.　Poor for Our Sakes.　Mary Brainerd Smith.　BLRP

...Are riding/on soft shocks, under a sun roof,/toward the great plenty of the New World.　Big Cars.　Wesley McNair.　AmC

Are rotten in the box and mothy in the raiment.　Upon the Bankruptcy of a Physician.　Henricus Selyns.　SCAP

Are shaken with earth's old and weary cry.　The Sorrow of Love.　William Butler Yeats.　MoAB; MoBrPo; NoAm; NOBV; OAEL 1-2; PoEL 1-5; TEP; VLP

Are sitting/On the doorsteps.　Round about the Rosebush.　*Anonymous.*　OxNR

Are so choicely matched a pair,/Or with more consent do move.　On the Friendship betwixt Two Ladies.　Edmund Waller.　PeHV

Are sold on Barclay Street.　At the Shrine.　Richard Kendall Munkittrick.　AA

Are some divine foreshadowing and foreseeing/Of things beyond our reason or control.　The Sound of the Sea.　Henry Wadsworth Longfellow.　AnFE; AP; APA; EtS; GoTF; MOS; TreFT

Are still allowed to fiddle with the case.　The Glove.　Richard Lovelace.　ALV; EG

Are such things done on Albion's shore?　A Little Boy Lost.　William Blake.　CEP; ViBoPo

Are tame, indeed, beside your angry Dogs!'　Chesspieces.　Joseph Campbell.　OxBI

Are the hearts which they bear and the tales which they tell.　Know Ye the Land?　George Gordon, Lord Byron.　MCCG

Are the links of thy fetters so light that thou cravest an-/other man's chain?　Certain Maxims of Hafiz.　Rudyard Kipling.　HBV 1-2

Are the shadows of the ships.　Sketch.　Carl Sandburg.　AP

Are the things so strange and marvelous you see or have seen?　Drum-Taps.　Walt Whitman.　PoNe

Are the windows opened?/Has it rained?　Listening to the Music of Arsenio Rodriguez Is Moving Closer...　Victor Hernandez Cruz.　APU

...Are there eyes beneath the table? Laughter? A nest of birds?　Self-Portrait.　Robert Pack.　CoPo

...Are there/misprints in the Manhattan Telephone Directory?　Poem: "A clitoris is a kind of brain."　Alice Notley.　APU

Are there no more wild oats to sow?　Wild Oats.　William Henry Davies.　ACV

Are there peaks or vales or rills/Beautiful as She?　Hymn of the Angels and Sibyls.　Gil Vicente.　CAW

Are these ideas right or wrong?　Portrait of a Lady.　Thomas Stearns Eliot.　AnAmPo

Are these the same men/who played here last year?　Duel in the Park.　Lisa Grenelle.　GoYe

Are they men eating reflections of themselves?　Cuisine Bourgeoise.　Wallace Stevens.　LiTA

Are they so funny–or you?　Uncultivated Accent.　*Anonymous.*　DBV

Are things to brood on with more ardency/Than the death-day of empires.　Endymion.　John Keats.　ViBoPo

Are to the child an intimation of what glory is.　Virginia Britannia.　Marianne Moore.　MoVE

Are unchangeable firmament.　A Fever.　John Donne.　MyFE

Are walking and talking together.　Conversation.　(Taniguchi Buso) Buson.　NTCP

Are wandering over the hills of Heaven.　The Sheepherder.　Lew Sarett.　AmFN

Are we going to sleep? ask my sons, and we are surrounded by/emptiness and there is no way out.　I Left.　Tuvia Ruebner.　VWA

Are we knowing/Where we're going,/What we're doing here?　Pleasant Changes.　Jane Euphemia Browne (Aunt Effie).　OxBChV

Are welcome to sit on my bonnet!'　Limerick: "There was a young lady whose bonnet."　Edward Lear.　EBEV

Are whitening in the savage glare of truth.　Dead in Wars and in Revolutions.　Mary Devenport O'Neill.　NeIP

Are you?　"Forever."　Charles Stuart Calverley.　ALV; InMe

Are you a Lover or a Senator?　Remonstrance.　Philodemos of Gadara.　LiTW; OLR

Are you by any chance a registered/DEMOCRAT?　Crazy to Be Alive in Such a Strange World.　Lawrence Ferlinghetti.　CTBA

Are you glad you've sold us?　Are You Glad.　*Anonymous.*　WTO

"Are you hurt my child, are you hurt at all?"　Jean Richepin's Song.　Herbert Trench.　OBMV; OxBI

"Are you hurt, my lad, are you hurt at all?/O, my own!"　The Heart.　*Anonymous.*　MaC

Are you lost in the hollow/Root of the city?　Ula Masondo's Dream.　William Plomer.　MoBS

Are you not bored,/Expounding the Way?　You never touch.　Yosano Akiko.　BoWoP; PBWP

Are you not our father's father/you, Heitsi-Eibib?　Hunter's Prayer.　*Anonymous.*　PeSA

Are you not shuddering, O most benevolent God in the/skies?　Early Summer Night.　Wen I-to.　LiTW

Are you on, are you on, are you on?　In the Days of Old Rameses (with music).　*Anonymous.*　AS

...Are you really afraid of children?　These Horses Came.　Ray A. Young Bear.　CDW

Are you so tired? Unfasten your mind/And follow it hence.   Wind in the Grass.   Mark Van Doren.   FaBV

"Are you warm?"   Before the Big Storm.   William Stafford.   NaP

Are you washed in the blood of the Lamb?   General William Booth Enters into Heaven.   Vachel Lindsay.   AmLP; ATP; BoC; CMoP; HBV 1-2; InPo; LiTA; LiTM; MoAB; MoAmPo; MoPo; NoAm; NOBA; OxBA; PoA; SeCeV; TAP; TreFS; TrGrPo; WGRP

Are Zebras full of zeal?   An Alphabet.   Charles Edward Carryl.   LBN

Aren't you glad on Labor Day/There isn't any labor?   There You Sit.   Shel Silverstein.   PoSC

...Argestes/scattering the broken leaves.   Sitalkas.   Hilda ("H. D.") Doolittle.   ViBoPo

...Arguing about their/favorite mountain and the million reasons for them both.   John Button Birthday.   Frank O'Hara.   NAs

The argument/has something to do/with pleasure.   Two Paintings by Gustav Klimt.   Jorie Graham.   SV

Arise, and love me, Helena!   A Dream of Death.   Lucy White Jennison.   AA

Arise, arise.   A Morning Song for Imogen.   William Shakespeare.   AnEnPo

Arise, arise!   The Trumpet.   Edward ("Edward Eastaway") Thomas.   HBMV; MMM; MoBrPo; OHIP

Arise, ascend, be bold, desire!   To Ashtaroth and Bel.   Saul Tchernichovsky.   TrJP

Arise! come down! loved that thou art!   Morning Serenade.   Madison Cawein.   HBV 1-2

–Arise, my soul; and sing.   Now Does Our World Descend.   Edward Estlin Cummings.   AP; NYBP

Arise! thou has inherited the sky.   Nekros.   John Banister Tabb.   AmP

"Arise! Thrust in thy sickle'?   Corruption.   Henry Vaughan.   JCP; NOCV; OAEL 1-2; OBS; OxBoCh; Prf; SeCP; SeCV 1-2

Arise to prayer. Arise to divine service.   Muhammedan Call to Prayer.   Bilal.   TTY

Arise! we slept, nor of the peril recked.   Awake!   Walther von der Vogelweide.   AWP

...–Arise! ye Goths, and glut your ire!   The Dying Gladiator.   George Gordon, Lord Byron.   NOBE

The ark is borne unseen through the wilderness.   Variations on a Time Theme.   Edwin Muir.   NoAm

The ark shall ride the sea of fire,/Then rest on Sion's hill.   Like Noah's Weary Dove.   William Augustus Muhlenberg.   AH

Arm, arm, Americans! And remember, re-/member, the Tuscania!   A Call to Arms.   Mary Raymond Shipman Andrews.   MC; PAH

Arm! Arm! it is–it is–the cannon's opening roar!   Childe Harold's Pilgrimage: Canto III, XXII.   George Gordon, Lord Byron.   AnFE

Arm in arm under a sliver of blazing/moon–forever night blooms.   Night Teeth.   Peter Brett.   AMV-80

Arm in arm, without saying anything.   When I Was Conceived.   Michael Ryan.   MAYP

The arm must be bound/and bound again   The Journey with Hands and Arms.   Benjamin Saltman.   VWA

The arm of bronze outstretched against all evil!   Dance of the Macabre Mice.   Wallace Stevens.   CMoP; NePA; NOBA; OxBA; SeCeV

Armes to armes, and offspring of eche race/With mortal warr eche other may fordoe.'   From Certain Bokes of Virgiles Aenaeis.   Henry Howard, Earl of Surrey.   EnPo

...The armies move,/As out of rock, as floods unfrozen.   Gideon at the Well.   Geoffrey Hill.   NePoEA

An armillary sphere? An astrolabe?   Letters from the Astronomers, I: Nicholas Copernicus (1473-1543).   Siv Cedering Fox.   SUW

The armorer–that is I!   The Armorer's Song.   Harry Bache Smith.   AA; OHIP

Arms and legs can't be/spliced from old MGM movies   Nam.   Mike Lowery.   Psk; SOTS

Arms around her, I caress her wings.   Nightgown, Wife's Gown.   Robert Sward.   ELU

Arms cut off at the elbow.   Love's Stratagems.   Donald Justice.   NYBP

The arms of the outspread East/Receive/What I must give and give.   Surprised by Me.   Walter Darring.   NYBP

Arms outstretched/foam fingers/reaching.   Surf.   Lillian Morrison.   NTCP

Arms up, she dropp'd: our souls were in our names!   Love in the Valley.   George Meredith.   UnTE

An army of lovers shall not fail.   Sappho's Reply.   Rita Mae Brown.   PeHV

The army of unalterable law.   Cousin Nancy.   Thomas Stearns Eliot.   OBAL; OBSP

The army of unalterable law.   Lucifer in Starlight.   George Meredith.   AnEnPo; AWP; BoLiVe; CBEP; ExPo; FF; ForPo; GoTF; HAP; HBV 1-2; InPo; LiTB; LoBV; NOBE; NOBV; NoP; OAEL 1-2; OAEP; OBEV; OBNC; OBVV; PoEL 1-5; PPoe; SeCeV; TreFT; TrGrPo; UnPo; ViBoPo; VLP; WeW

Arno and April and the Apennines!   Santa Maria del Fiore.   George Herbert Clarke.   CaP

Arnold, Master of the Scud.   Arnold, Master of the Scud.   Bliss Carman.   EtS

Arnold's to blame for Andre's fame,/And Andre's to be pitied.   Sergeant Champe.   Anonymous.   PAH

Arnold shall stink to latest times.   Arnold.   Anonymous.   PAH

Aroon, Machree, Aboo!   Mavrone.   Arthur Guiterman.   BXAP; FiBHP; InMe; SpRo

Around/And round/And/Round.   Merry-Go-Round.   Dorothy Walter Baruch.   BrR; SoPo; SUS; TiPo

Around & around some imaginary dancefloor & I'd/Look up into their eyes, their eyes so far away.   My Sisters.   Bill Kushner.   APU

...Around/His yellow mouth hang crumbs of flowers.   Lie Closed, My Lately Loved.   John Woods.   ConAP

Around my feet, my bare feet, where they lay.   History Lesson for My Son.   Ted Kooser.   PoL

Around my grave go build a fence,/To show this world I had no sense.   Go Bring Me Back My Blue-Eyed Boy (with music).   Anonymous.   AS

...Around my neck/The hangman ties the holly.   Carol.   Anne Wilkinson.   OBCV

Around the corner, a vanished friend.   Around the Corner.   Charles Hanson Towne.   PoLf; PoToHe

Around the fire addressed its evening hours.   Say Not of Me That Weakly I Declined.   Robert Louis Stevenson.   EyDe; OBNC

Around the oaks the brown bats go.   Drifting.   John Francis O'Donnell.   IrPN

Around the pole, in the great room of the sun.   The May Day Dancing.   Howard Nemerov.   NoAm; NYBP

Around their lofty cradles, with the Spring's/Breath rocking slowly.   Spring.   William Allingham.   IrPN

Around us, dazing us with its light like snow.   After They Have Tired of the Brilliance of Cities.   Stephen Spender.   AtBAP; FaBoMo; LiTM

Arrange, at least, for it to have its lie.   Sonnet IX: "As soon as I lie down in my soft bed."   Louise Labe.   BoWoP

Arrange them Thyself, O Thou King of Grace.   A Low Prayer, a High Prayer.   Anonymous.   WTO

Arranged flowers growing indistinguishable/From the coldness of nocturnal trees.   Elsdon.   Freda Downie.   FaBoPP

Arrayed and strong, the battle wait.   Armistice.   Sophie Jewett.   AA

Arriving in competing waves/from the ruins of that place   Voice and Address.   Michael Palmer.   NPGG

Arriving on the moon we'll find/Our luggage sent to Mars!   Far Trek.   June Brady.   QQQ

Arrogantly/scrape/the/sky.   Change Is Not Always Progress.   Haki R. Madhubuti.   TAP

...An arrow-shower/Sent out of sight, somewhere becoming rain.   The Whitsun Weddings.   Philip Larkin.   FaBoMo; NePoEA-2; NoAm; NoP; OxBTC

An arrow turned inward has/no chance of peace.   See in the Midst of Fair Leaves.   Marianne Moore.   MoAB

Arrows to the heart.   Recollection.   Duane Big Eagle.   STE

...Art, admired in general,/is always actually personal.   In the Public Garden.   Marianne Moore.   NOBA

The Art Collection of the English Nation.   In the National Gallery.   Siegfried Sassoon.   NoAm

...An art, I tell you,/by no means given to just anyone.   One Thing to Take, Another to Keep.   Crescenzo Del Monte.   VWA

Art, I was thinking, is the imitation/of what we called nothing when we lived on the earth.   Euridice Saved.   Linda Gregg.   NPGG

Art in its arty way keeps saying: goodbye.   The Departure.   Reed Whittemore.   TAP

Art is the living–not the dead.   You Are Alms.   James W. Thompson.   PoBA

Art is the pavement that eats you...   London Pavement Artist.   James Schevill.   TAP

Art? Nature? Which do I most feel/As I read on?   On Receiving a Copy of Mr. Austin Dobson's "Old World Idylls".   James Russell Lowell.   AP

The art of his competitors the day he got the job.   Sad Story.   Clarence Day.   InMe

The art of lifting her/skirt over her ankles.   I Hear That Andromeda.   Sappho.   PBWP

Art stood amaz'd in Ambiguity.   And the Bitter Storm Augments; the Wild Winds Wage.   John Josselyn.   SCAP

Art thou gone?   The Sea Bird to the Wave.   Padraic Colum.   EtS; SUS

Art thou mine again?   The Flight of the Heart.   Dora Read Goodale.   AA

Art thou not ever, though slave of his daytime,/Choti Tinchaurya, queen of his night?   The Bride.   Laurence Hope.   HBV 1-2

Art willing to restore them now.   Christ, the Good Physician.   Charles Wesley.   BePJ

Articulate chess playin/trump holdin/cities & states   Good Times & No Bread.   Reginald Lockett.   CNA

Artist and office-holder to a claque of less/than fifty souls...to each his venomous in-group.   October and November.   Robert Lowell.   MAT

...The artist changes genre. Four Heads & How to Do Them. John Forbes. CBAP

...The artist lies/For the improvement of truth. Believe him. A Meditation on John Constable. Charles Tomlinson. NePoEA-2

Artist, who drew me so,/Must tell! The Murmur of a Bee. Emily Dickinson. AnFE; MoAmPo; TRV

The artists talking of freedom/in their chains The Will to Change. Adrienne Rich. NMM

...Arts against arms appeal! An Austrian Army. Alaric Alexander Watts. FaBoCo; FiBHP; NOBL

Arus-eyed & insistent. Letters to Walt Whitman. Ronald Johnson. VGW

As a band of brothers joined,/Peace and safety we shall find. Hail! Columbia. Joseph Hopkinson. AA; BLSo; FaBoBe; FaFP; HBV 1-2; MC; PAH; PAL; TreFS; YaD

As a bride goes combing/Her joy of hair. 'Tis the White Plum Tree. John Shaw Neilson. BoAV; PoAu 1-2

As a child, through him may speed. Hymns and Spiritual Songs. Christopher Smart. NOCV

As a cove where no swimmer is swimming. Exercise in a Meadow. Jean Elliot. GoYe

As a cow hastens to her calf, so let thy spirit speed to/me, hasten like water on its way. Charm to Quell a Rival. Anonymous. LiTW

As a coy star is there in the quiet/Of the wood's blue eye. O You among Women. Frederick Robert Higgins. BIrV

As a false snowstorm falls upon a stage. Poet in Winter. Edward Lucie-Smith. TwCP

As a free gift and offering she devotes/Herself, as long as she survives and floats. The Yacht. Caius Valerius Catullus. AWP

As a gentleman swishes his cane. The Devil's Walk. Robert Southey. PV

As a gift to the east wind, winter's friend. The young bloods come round less often now. Horace. BoLoP

As a girl beleaguered by rain, and her yellow hair? Ward Two. Francis Webb. CBAP

...As a harmless cloud. On Being Photographed. William H. Gass. AMV-81

...As a hushed footfall/In a long forgotten snow. Song: "Let it be forgotten, as a flower is forgotten." Sara Teasdale. PoA

As a lattice-gleam when midnight/moans. On Sturminster Foot-Bridge. Thomas Hardy. FaBoPP; OAEP; OBSP

As a lover, as a great wolf. Wolf Dream. Edward Lense. AMV-81

As a man bleeding, not/the reflection I desire. The Mirror. Louise Gluck. FaPON; GP; MAYP

As a man in spring desires to die in woman. The Death-Wish. Louis MacNeice. AnFE

As a man turns to face on-coming snow. The Decision. Theodore Roethke. VGW

As a masterpiece of Tact! Tact. Harry Graham. ALV

As a mother who hath borne children, as a father who hath/begotten (them), may it be glad! Penitential Psalm to the Goddess Anunit, IV. Anonymous. WGRP

As a poem erases and rewrites its poet. Knowing I Live in a Dark Age. Milton Acorn. NOBC

As a premature grief grays the strong head/Of a virile, red-haired man. Snow in October. Alice Dunbar-Nelson. BlSi; CDC

(As a pulse after the first September earthquake). Sunday Evening. Barbara Guest. NeAP

As a reed with the reeds in the river. A Musical Instrument. Elizabeth Barrett Browning. EnLi 1-2; FaBoBe; GTBS; HBV 1-2; HBVY; MCCG; NoP; OAEL 1-2; OAEP; OBEV; OBVV; OnMSP

As a restless needle held by the constant north/we always have in mind. The Constant North. J. F. Hendry. NeBP; OxBS

As a scattering of wild flowers. Resounding. Katherine Soniat. AMV-81

As a sea-shell of the sea/Ever shall I sing of thee. Lines. George Meredith. HBV 1-2

As a sign for the rapture of storm-spent eyes to discover,/Sark. Insularum Ocelle. Algernon Charles Swinburne. OBTV

As a sleepwalking monk would carry his girdle and habit. The Plough-Horse. Rhoda Coghill. OnYI

As a treasure of beauty I prize. My Heart Is in the East. Judah Halevi. TrJP

As a true confession, an istorical. Dropping Your Aitches. Joseph Warren Beach. NYBP

As a wind-mill turns in the wind on an empty sky. A Tune. Arthur Symons. BoLoP; OBNC

As a wind of dust blew under a freezing cloud. Elegy for Her Brother Sakhr. Al-Khansa. BoWoP

As a young Roe/Upon the mounts of spices. Silex Scintillans. Henry Vaughan. AnAnS 1

As Adam was beguiled by Eve. Fuller and Warren. Anonymous. BeLS

As after fire/Smoking char. Reb Hanina. Paul Raboff. VWA

As, after the screaming of jets,/the trump of Jericho. In My Own Twentieth Century. Natalya Gorbanyevskaya. PBWP

As air is given to the mouth of all? No One Ever Walking This Our Only Earth. Muriel Rukeyser. NNaP

As all folks do,/walking along W. C. W. David Ray. PoL

As all looks yellow to the jaundiced eye. An Essay on Criticism. Alexander Pope. PPoe

As all the rest, so now the stone/That tombs the two is justly one. His Being Was in Her Alone. Sir Philip Sidney. ELP

As also are those who heard/That song with me. The Selfsame Song. Thomas Hardy. CMoP; PBBP

As an old tree, when lopped of every bough,/Gathers the young leaves into itself, a frilled stump. War-Time. W. R. Rodgers. OBSP

As ancient as his walls or as his ships-/These labored Trees. Olive Trees. Padraic Colum. NePoAm

As another meeting/Is about to begin. Another Meeting. Lawrence A. Lucas. AMV-80

As any moth that in daylight/Will spread a rainbow wing. Lux in Tenebris. Katharine Tynan Hinkson. OxBI; TrPWD

As any other sad man here/american. Notes for a Speech. LeRoi (Imamu Amiri Baraka) Jones. CoPo

As any peeping Turk to the Bosphorus. Conversion. Thomas Ernest Hulme. FaBoMo; LoBV; OBSP; ViBoPo

As are the daies of sweet Zenocrate. Tamburlaine. Christopher Marlowe. AtBAP

As are the judgments of Astronomy. Thomas More to Them That Seek Fortune. Sir Thomas More. EnRePo

As at his birth he was,/So shall he be.) The Ages of Man. Abraham Ibn Ezra. TrJP

As at that moment, with a bough/Of wilding in his hand. The Two April Mornings. William Wordsworth. EBEV; EnRP; GTBS; GTBS-P; HBV 1-2

As autumn dancing, vermilion on rocks. Soliloquy in an Air-Raid. Roy Fuller. PoA

As bashful, yet impatient to be seen. The Task. William Cowper. CoBE

As beames of Corrall, but more cleare. Upon Julia's Recovery. Robert Herrick. AtBAP

As behind a cage of glass it slowly/pumps and stops, pumps and stops. Cafes. Robert B. Smith. LFAC

As behind him, perfectly timed, follows/The dumb shadow that mimes him all the way. Stormy Day. W. R. Rodgers. LiTB

As behoves/Shepheards loves. Menaphon. Robert Greene. AtBAP

As belongs to believers in Clough. On Arthur Hugh Clough. Algernon Charles Swinburne. FaBoEE

As Benjamin, and Storax, when they meet. To His Honoured Kinsman Sir William Soame. Robert Herrick. AtBAP; BoW

As between those hills, and flower and glow inside. Florence: Design for a City. Elizabeth Jennings. HaMV

As black as death, emitting a strange odor. The Inner Part. Louis Simpson. PAI

As blithe's yon lightsome lamb that plays/On Loudoun's flowery lea, lassie. Loudoun's Bonnie Woods and Braes. Robert Tannahill. HBV 1-2

As blood and water issued from thy wound,/So with thy blood, do Thou my tears compound. The Passion. Ralph Knevet. JCP

As blossoms blow on window panes. Pipings. J. Paget-Fredericks. BrR

As brave as you and as gay! Easter. Mary Carolyn Davies. OHIP

As bride and suite let pass a bier-/So pass the coming canto here. Clarel. Herman Melville. AmPP

As bright the sunshine as to-day,/A hundred years to come! A Hundred Years to Come. William Goldsmith Brown. HBV 1-2

As bright will shine Great Britain's rays,/As in King George's glorious days! The House of Peers. Sir William Schwenck Gilbert. InMe

As brooding on that"End it when you/will." The City of Dreadful Night. James (1834-82) Thomson. EBEV; LoBV; OAEP

As brothers all, we build a Friendly World. Challenge. Thomas Curtis Clark. PGD

As brothers of the Son of Man,/Rise up, O men of God! Festal Song. William Pierson Merrill. WGRP

As buzzards control,/imperceptibly, their flight. The Bear. N. Scott Momaday. CDW

As Cato's self had not disdain'd to hear. Prologue to Mr. Addison's Tragedy of Cato. Alexander Pope. CEP

As centuries past itself would do. The Waggoner. Edmund Charles Blunden. AnFE

As certain birds bred for color and song and beyond/Their youth's charm. Lines for Those to Whom Tragedy Is Denied. Joyce Carol Oates. IHMS

As certain of not dying/as is/the immense love of the dead. Razon de Amor (excerpt). Pedro Salinas. LLLT

As clean of all my dust and dirt/As that old white birch tree. I Saw God Wash the World. William L. Stidger. BLPA; PGD; TRV

As close as one brushes with truth/in half an hour. Bus Stop. Vincent O'Sullivan. OCNZ

As closing sounds of some delightful bell. The Relish of the Muse. Sir John Beaumont. PoL

As cold as ice, but just as set on me. Nothing to Fear. Kingsley Amis. DBV; ErPo; OxBC

As cold as my heart. Within the Dream You Said. Philip Larkin. InPS; PAI

As completely as I can bore it. Limerick: "Quoth the bookworm, "I don't care one bit." Oliver Herford. TDH

As Cynddylan passes proudly up the land. Cynddylan on a Tractor in Spring. R.S. Thomas. BoC

As dandelions/On a hill. The Park. James S. Tippett. BrR; SUS; TiPo

As dangerous as two colds from one source. Relativity of Spring. Artie Gold. CaPN

As dark as the air, as black as the rain/That the heavens weep... Beowulf. *Anonymous.* NU

As darkness fell, I took her in my arms. The Visit. Robert Mezey. AmPC

As darkness shows us worlds of light/We never saw by day! Oh, Thou! Who Dry'st the Mourner's Tear. Thomas Moore. TrPWD

As David, his kingdom sure, could not forget Saul. Dead Fly. Eilean Ni Chuilleanain. CIP

As dawn gleams eternally from your tall mountains and your/rocks throw back the pounding sea. The Island of Rhum. Roy Ferguson. PoSH

As daylight breaks the Indian turns his tumbril/of hacked, beheaded coconuts towards home. Nights in the Gardens of Port of Spain. Derek Walcott. OxBC

As dead as any dream of paradise. The Burning of the Birds. Shirley Kaufman. GP

...As dead bricks leap/to souvenirs like old women/remembering birth. Demolition. Philip Raisor. AMV-81

As decent to repent in, as to sin in. Epigram, in a Maid of Honour's Prayer-Book. Alexander Pope. FaBoEE

As deep, as nothing, as the grave. On Knowing Nothing. A.J.M. Smith. PeCV

As did Methusalem of old, and so I end my SONG. An Excellent New Song upon His Grace...Lord Archbishop of Dublin. Jonathan Swift. CoMu

As did the Indian and the buffalo. Pioneers. Hamlin Garland. AA

As different good, by art or nature given,/To different nations makes their blessings even. The Traveller. Oliver Goldsmith. GN

As dime flipped or gull on fire or fish/silently hurt–its mouth alive with metal. Element. P. K. Page. PeCV

As dip its wing in the wan water/An straik it on my ee-bree.' Johnie Cock (K version). *Anonymous.* ESPB

As dips the balance, Zeus from day to day/Gives great possessions, or takes all away. Advice to Kyrnos. Theognis. LiTW

As does that Part that lies between/Her Left Toe, and her Right Toe. Ballad: "Of all the Girls that e'er were seen." John Gay. CoMu

As doth a glasse the lillies faire and roses. Orlando Furioso. Lodovico Ariosto. OBVE

As down his hidy-hole he dashes/And disappears from sight. The Rabbit. Edith King. HBMV; SoPo

As downward to this world of night/The New Jerusalem they bring! Kelpius's Hymn. Arthur Peterson. AA

As due to love as thought and dreams and sighs,/Wishes and tears, poor fancy's followers. A Midsummer Night's Dream. William Shakespeare. TreFS; WHA

As dust that drives, as straws that blow,/Into the night go one and all. Ballade of Dead Actors. William Ernest Henley. ALV; OBMV

As each drew his sword/On the side of the Lord. How to Start a War. Phyllis McGinley. DBV; OBSV

...As each star/Speeds outward, goes out, or goes out of sight. Speculation. Howard Nemerov. TAP

As each year might assign. On His 86th Birthday. Thomas Hardy. ACV 010

As earth reeled blindly past. It Happened. Efua (Morgue) Sutherland. ACV

As easily as pebbles slipping into still water. In the Heartland. Mark Vinz. GP

As espying a lady named Pheasant. Miss Pheasant. Walter De la Mare. FaBoNo

As ever a second childhood understands. His Trees. Mark Van Doren. AnFE

As ever in my great Task-Master's eye. On His Having Arrived at the Age of Twenty-Three. John Milton. ATP; AWP; DiPo; MCCG; PPoe; PrIm; TrGrPo

As every devil thunders through. The Train. Alan Brownjohn. OxBTC

As every school child ought to know. Philological. John Updike. ELU

As every sense is vanquished by excess. Dante's Angels: The Angels of Protection. Dante Alighieri. BoC

As every urchin by my fence/Notes for future reference. In a Town Garden. Donald Mattam. ELU; FiBHP

As fair as a lily, as brown as a bun. Queen Anne. *Anonymous.* ChTr

As fairest of al,/And ever was and ever shal. The Fairest Flower. John Audelay. OxBM

As falling dews to thirsty flowers. The Shepherd's Calendar. John Clare. OBRV

As fancy never could have drawn,/And never can restore! To Mary. Charles Wolfe. GTBS; HBV 1-2; OBEV; OBRV; ViBoPo

As finished as you/and with a flower. Kind. Archie Randolph Ammons. NoP; PrIm

As fishbone-fine his steps through vaults resound. At the Tombs of the House of Savoy. William Jay Smith. NePoAm-2

As flat as any flounder. Fragment of a Song on the Beautiful Wife of Dr. John Overall... *Anonymous.* BoLoP

As flies run up the window-pane,/So fly my thoughts, dear love, to thee! A Love-Song by a Lunatic. *Anonymous.* NA

As fly the beauty of the light/Or dare not pledge our loyal bowls. Ode: "Without the evening dew and showers." Charles Cotton. ViBoPo

As for a florist fallen. On the Death of Mrs. Felicia Hemans (excerpt). Lydia Huntley Sigourney. PeD

As for love: it overwhelms my fear. A Letter Catches Up with Me. Eric Chaet. VWA

As for me, I am a watercolor./I wash off. For My Lover, Returning to His Wife. Anne Sexton. HaCAP; IHMS; NMM; UnPo

As for my tongue, while I have any days,/Thy justice witness shall and speak Thy praise. Psalm XXXV. Sir Philip Sidney. FCP

As for the highwayman, he's lost all his store, let him go a-robbing until he gets more. Down, Down Derry Down (with music). *Anonymous.* AS

As for the valet, he stood against a partition and tried to/imitate the tapestry. The End of a Dynasty. Zbigniew Herbert. FaBoPV

As for the verse, who list like trade to try,/I fear me much, shall hardly reach so high. In Commendation of George Gascoigne's Steel Glass (1576). Sir Walter Ralegh. SiPS

As for us, we enter your country/With our eyes closed. Witnesses. William Stanley Merwin. AmPC; LCAP

As forecast long ago by the prophets/in a circus farce The Comet. Michael Palmer. NPGG

As free as if all guilts were closed and done. The Graveyard. Jane Cooper. NePoEA-2

As from an Eagle's, cowered the plaintive Earth! Christ in the Hospital. Roy Campbell. BoC

As from my own he swept you far away. Dear gentle soul, who went so soon away. Luís de Camoens. BoLoP

As full as a tick–as solid as brass. Similes. *Anonymous.* HBVY

As full of turbulence as void of sense. London and Bristol Delineated. Richard Savage. FaBoPP

As ghost planes tirelessly orbit/The closed fields of the dead. The Odor of Blood. Thomas McGrath. NePoEA

As gifted, yet as good as God did ever plan. The Fledgling Bard and the Poetry Society. Part I (excerpt). George Reginald Margetson. BANP

As gives a power to faith to tread/All falsehood under feet. Truth. Ben Jonson. PG

As gold as morning light! The Apple Tree. Beatrice Curtis Brown. SiSoSe

As good a pair o' bed-flops as iver flopped bugs. The Dead Pig. *Anonymous.* FaBoNo

As good as most. Echo. Mildred Weston. BoNaP

As good stuff under Flanel lies, as under Silken clothes. Love and Debt Alike Troublesom. Sir John Suckling. AnAnS 2; CavP

As grave and serious at heart as you. Elegy: E. W. L. E. Sissman. NYBP

As great tears fell from the eyes of these immortals/For the dead. The Deathless Ones. Eleanor Glenn Wallis. NePoAm

As greeted our love's first accomplishment. Pure Death. Robert Graves. AWP; CoBMV; GTBS-P; InPo; MoAB; MoPo

As gud luve cumis as gais. Thir Lenterne Dayis ar Luvely Lang. William Stewart. OxBS

As guns pounded on the shore. Europe and America. David Ignatow. AmFN; NNaP; UnPo

As had she studied to misuse me so. The Taming of the Shrew. William Shakespeare. UnS

As, happily, we/freely may. A New World Symphony. Kit Wright. NLV

As happy as Cliff Klingenhagen is. Cliff Klingenhagen. Edwin Arlington Robinson. AmP; AP; CoBMV; HBMV; MoAB; MoAmPo; TreFS

As Harbinger of Heav'n, the Way to show,/The Way which thou so well hast learn'd below. To Mrs. Anne Killigrew. John Dryden. SeCV 1-2

As Harrington came, ye likewise came/And died at the door of our House of Fame. Lexington. Sidney Lanier. PAH; PAL

As He alone knows to be best. Washington's Prayer for the Nation. George Washington. PGD

As He arose in shining triumph/To immortalize this clay. The Last Day. Lola Derosier. STF

As he awakens, beautifully deceived. The Wooing Lady. William Jay Smith. NePoEA

As he chirps, "I am blammed and corruptibly jammed,/In this cuggerdom whango tree. The Whango Tree. *Anonymous.* NA

As he consigned to doom each meek, mewed band/At Pummery Fair.   A Sheep Fair.   Thomas Hardy.   Prf

As he dances in the aisles, for joy   In the Dome Car of the "Canadian'.   Sid Marty.   NOBC

As he died and decayed/His corruption was stayed.   Epitaph: "We mourn the loss."   Ambrose Bierce.   DBV

As he dips/his brown head/to drink.   Civilization.   Tom Schmidt.   NeAC

As he gazed:–"Be praised, great God,"/he said,/"For a glorious victory!"   Judgment.   Grace Ellery Channing-Stetson.   AA

As he glowed like a ruddy shield on the Lion's breast.   Maud.   Alfred, Lord Tennyson.   SyP

As he goes on his lone nightly rds.   Limerick: "On pianos and organs she lbs."   Anonymous.   TDH

As He heard the birds/Preach to St. Francis.   The Preachers.   Norman Nicholson.   NeBP

As he himself could, when above.   On the Astrologer and Almanac Maker, John Partridge.   Jonathan Swift.   FaBoEE

As he led, so he followed 'em all to the Devil.   An Epitaph upon That Profound and Learned Casuist...   Thomas (Tom) Brown.   OBSV

As he left them there, as he left them there.   O Where Are You Going?   W. H. Auden.   CMoP; LiTB; MoVE; NOBE; SoSe

As he mingled in his grandson's stupid head/the small-house prayer and the lowing fields.   Hertza.   Benjamin Fondane.   VWA

As he or she who has no more smiles left to give.   A Smile.   Anonymous.   PoToHe

As he rests there, while/he is still a human.   No Speech from the Scaffold.   Thom Gunn.   OxBTC

As he sets kisses on her face.   Nightfall.   Kalidasa.   LiTW

As he sits in his studious chair all night/reading the breathing book.   The Choice.   Frederick Morgan.   AMV-81

As he stands on the heights of his life with a/glimpse of a height that is higher.   By an Evolutionist.   Alfred, Lord Tennyson.   EnLi 1-2

As he steps so lightly over the abyss.   The Prisoner.   William Plomer.   ChMP; PeSA

As he stood against the fretted hedge, which was like white/lace.   To a Conscript of 1940.   Sir Herbert Read.   ChMP; ExPo; LiTB; LiTM; OBWP; WaP

...As he stood/before his butchered legions in the snow.   Russia 1812.   Victor Hugo.   OBWP

As he stopped to listen/for the prison helicopter.   The Flint Hills.   Lew Blockcolski.   VoR

As he takes from you, I engraft you new.   Sonnets, XV: "When I consider every thing that grows."   William Shakespeare.   AWP; BLPL; DiPo; MasP; OAEP; OBSC; TEP; TrGrPo

As he that burns must freeze, who trusts must fear,/Ill quartered coats, which yet all lovers bear.   Caelica, XV.   Fulke, Lord Brooke Greville.   FCP

...As he tries/hopelessly to hold his cup steady and make no face.   Japanese Girl with Red Table.   Stephen Dobyns.   MAYP

As he turned to go–yet, pausing, gazed?   A Sleeping Beauty.   James Whitcomb Riley.   DFT

As he weaves our web of doom.   The Weaver.   William Henry Burleigh.   BLPA

As he went on fishing his way.   The Lady and the Bear.   Theodore Roethke.   GoJo; NLV; SO

As he who died a thousand years ago.   The Fear of Death.   John Dryden.   LoBV

As he who with a joyous, loving art/Will teach the handsome lad to win your heart.   Sylvae, II (excerpt).   Statius Publius Papinius.   PeHV

As heart returns to home, year upon year.   The Heart's Wild Geese.   Henry Treece.   WaP

As Heaven and Earth were overturning.   Faust.   Johann Wolfgang von Goethe.   WSC

As Heaven's lightning strikes a tree.   An Imprecation Against Foes and Sorcerers.   Atharva Veda.   WSC

As Helen now to Paris is/Am I to him.   As Helen Once.   Muna Lee.   HBMV

As here and there a twinkling ray descried/Serves but to show how black is all beside.   Tirocinium; or, A Review of Schools.   William Cowper.   OBSV

As here I turn, I'll thank God, hastening,/That the same goal is still on the same track.   The Landmark.   Dante Gabriel Rossetti.   MaVP; NBM

As hinny to a hungry ghaist/Maun be a thocht like yon.   The Thocht.   William Soutar.   NeBP

As his cell by that sounding sea?   St. Govan.   A. G. Prys-Jones.   ACV

As his fender shivers like a tambourine.   Accident.   Sydney Lea.   NYP

As his horse on the ramparts we curried...   A Fragment: "Not a drum was heard."   Anonymous.   FaBoPa

As his lithe, fathoming heart absorbed and buried.   The Turtle Dove.   Geoffrey Hill.   FaBoTw

As his music is a preservative, for him not you.   Music.   Tony Towle.   ANYP

As his when Eden held his virgin heart.   November.   John Keble.   OBEV; OBVV

As horses in fields suddenly stop/Their gallop at a horizon and crop.   Praying.   P. J. Kavanagh.   OBSP

...As I/absurdly seek and trust to find you still.   Throwing the Racetrack Cats at Saratoga.   David Ray.   SM

As I advance,/and I with it,/sullen and sad.   Seismograph.   Ephraim Auerbach.   VWA

...As I am, as I will/never be, live with me.   Warrior with Shield.   Michael Dennis Browne.   PoDr

As I am mine, their sweating selves; but worse.   I Wake and Feel the Fell of Dark.   Gerard Manley Hopkins.   CMoP; CoBE; CoBMV; DiPo; ForPo; GTBS-P; HAP; LiTB; NoAm; NOBE; NOBV; NOCV; NoP; OAEL 1-2; OAEP; PoEL 1-5; PoPle; PPoe; PPP; SCV; SeCeV; TW; VLP

...As I bow and pass smiling.   The Young Housewife.   William Carlos Williams.   HeIP; NoAm; NoP; TAP

As I came down from Lebanon.   As I Came down from Lebanon.   Clinton Scollard.   AA; AnAmPo; HBV 1-2

As I came down to South Street by the myriad mov-/ing water.   South Street.   Francis E. Falkenbury.   EtS

As I can profit by a visit to/The fish-shaped island, population two.   On the Island.   L. E. Sissman.   NYBP

As I dig my spoon into the belly of a melon.   The Dancer.   Al Young.   PoBA

As I dipped my hands/in the bullrush slaughter.   On Living with Children for a Prolonged Time.   Mark Lowey.   AMV-81

As i dipped my mop/in/& started scrubbing.   The Clorox Kid.   Kirk Robertson.   GP

As I do now, before the advancing day.   Fatal Interview.   Edna St. Vincent Millay.   VGW

As I do now/that distant morning/In that long ago room.   Above Machu Picchu, 129 Baker Street, San Francisco.   Joseph Stroud.   NPGG

...As I flew/Parallel to where I am now standing.   Shimmering Pediment.   John Yau.   APU

...As I/found and as I saw, bring this message to the poet.   Message to the Bard.   William Livingston.   GoTS

As I go fighting down the years.   Conquest.   Georgia Douglas Johnson.   AmNP

As I go on eating, waiting for the news.   Raspberries.   Laurence Lerner.   EBEV

...As I go past them I can see/the tail light of the Chevy blinking on and off/in ecstacy.   A Meeting at the Crossroads.   Joseph Bruchac.   AmC

"As I guard o'er the fold."   Night.   William Blake.   AtBAP; BLPL; BoNaP; CBEP; EnRP; FaBoBe; HBV 1-2; HBVY; MyFE; OBEC; OBEV; OxBChV; OxBoCh; PoLf; TreFT; WiR

As I hang my head above the waters.   The Thousand and One Nights: The Song of the Narcissus.   Anonymous.   AWP

"As I have made thee now, I take thee."   Comfort in Extremity.   Christopher Harvey.   OxBoCh

As I held the rainbow near a patch of moonlight/that rose from beneath the water.   Hooking the Rainbow.   Tama Baldwin.   WOLT

...As I historically/belong to the enormous bliss of American death.   Rhapsody.   Frank O'Hara.   NoAm; NYP

As I, in such desire,/Have once a thought to turn.   Though I Regarded Not.   Henry Howard, Earl of Surrey.   AAS; SiPS

As I jump out of bed/To the world of my eyes.   The Sounds in the Morning.   Eleanor Farjeon.   SUS

As I kiss her womb/on a beach/by the tideless Aegean   God and Nature.   Musa Moris Farhi.   VWA

As I lay this Yolisday,/Alone in my longing.   Jesus Reassures His Mother.   Anonymous.   MeEL

As I look across the sea.   Song: "I walk'd in the lonesome evening."   William Allingham.   EnLoPo

As I make room for them, on one/after another filthy page of poetry.   To Hell with It.   Frank O'Hara.   NeAP

As I mind my father's house/At morning and at evening.   Lad of the Curly Locks.   Anonymous.   KiLC

As I now send you, for a beginning, praise.   Letter to the Front.   Muriel Rukeyser.   WaP

As I, O Pleiades! your beauty scan?   O Ye Sweet Heavens!   Thomas William Parsons   AA

As I parted her labia, and finally gently entered her female part.   Hmmmm, 22.   Leslie Scalapino.   NPGG

As I pass these things in the evening, as I walk.   The Bare Arms of Trees.   John Tagliabue.   Psk

As I played me with a bow/I said: "God, what is al this?"   My Purse.   Anonymous.   OxBM

As I pluck the buds of willow,/That are furry like the great wolf's beard.   I Am but a Little Woman.   Kivkarjuk.   WTO

As I pretend not to see or hear,/busy on a mission to nowhere.   To Nowhere.   David Ignatow.   CAD; NCSH

As I promise again I will wait here/for the rain, for you, to arrive.   Waiting.   Robert Pack.   GOYP; PPJ

As I remain'd thy single care. Father, How Wide Thy Glories Shine. Charles Wesley. TrPWD; TRV

As I rested and gathered and waited/For another time, another chance. Knowledge. Harold M. Grutzmacher. AMV-81

As I return to my newspaper. Daily News. Tom Clark. ANYP; EAS

As I ride, as I ride! Through the Metidja to Abd-el-Kadr. Robert Browning. PeD

As I sail home to Galveston/In oleander time! A Sailor's Song. Hazel Harper Harri. EtS

As I sail out to die. Poem on His Birthday. Dylan Thomas. DiPo; NAs

As I sang, "None maketh me afraid!" A Huguenot. Mary Elizabeth Coleridge. OBVV

As I see I must. On Stripping Bark from Myself. Alice Walker. LTB

As I set loose, like birds/In a landscape, the old words. The Words. David Wagoner. PoA

As I should like to try being young again. Wind and Mist. Edward ("Edward Eastaway") Thomas. BrPo

As I sit alone at present, dreaming darkly of a Dun. In the Gloaming. Charles Stuart Calverley. ALV; BXAP; InMe; NOBL

As I spin off beyond the front gardens/like a fresh galaxy in outer space. Conversation. Gyorgy Raba. VWA

As I start to rub your loose organ/with the tip of my toes. Till Death Do Us Part. Leila Miccolis. BoWoP

As I therein no other's face but yours can view. So Well I Love Thee, as Without Thee I. Michael Drayton. EnRePo; GBL

As I think of my days in the earth, memory long aglow. Rainscapes, Hydrangeas, Roses, and Singing Birds. Richard Eberhart. MoAmPo

As I think of my pleasant condition,/Surrounded by acres of clams. The Old Settler's Song. Francis Henry. BPAW

As I those other women? The Portrait. Robert Graves. CABA; CMoP

As I took pictures of Jimmy/with an imaginary camera. Double Exposure. Ian Young. NeAC; PeHV

As I trifled with his watch seal, red carbuncle fair to/see. Limerick Town (excerpt). John Francis O'Donnell. IrPN

As I, unblest. Statuette: Late Minoan. Lewis, Cecil Day. EnLit; OxBI

...As/I've done,/with a steady sound For one who says he feels. Petra von Morstein. BoWoP

As I wad do, were I Lord God,/An' ye were Martin Elginbrodde. Epitaph. George Macdonald. WGRP

As I wait for my love in the fir-tree alley alone with the sun. In Winter. Arthur Symons. BrPo

As I wait on the dock,/braiding the long line that knots and tangles. Rescue. Ellen Bryant Voigt. NoP

As I was by one brought forth I would bring/forth another. Fain Would I Wed a Fair Young Man. Thomas Campion. UnTE

As I was helplessly young. Childhood. Frances Cornford. FaBoWP; OBSP; OxBTC

...As I was merciful to/you just now, be merciful to me! The Pirates of Penzance. Sir William Schwenck Gilbert. NAs

As I wish silently/That the stairs were endless. Beatrix Is Three. Adrian Mitchell. NAs

...As if a curse did stain/Thy velvet leaf. The Violet. William Wetmore Story. HBV 1-2

As if a huge volcano, muffled under the sea,/Erupted with no sound. A Sea-Change: For Harold. Joseph Langland. LiTM

As if a man still swings/heavy and burning from that tree. The Carolinas. David Ray. TAT

As if a thousand girls with golden hair/Might rise from where they slept and go away. The Sheaves. Edwin Arlington Robinson. AP; AWP; CMoP; CoBMV; DiPo; FaBV; ForPo; HAP; InPo; MAmP; MoAB; MoAmPo; NePA; NoAm; NOBA; OxBA; TAP; WHA

As if, after all, God is and is about to speak. A Hymn of Form. Gordon Bottomley. BrPo

As if all/worlds were there. A Token. Robert Creeley. VGW

As if being nibbled inward by its own self. A Snap Judgement on the Llama. Peggy Bennett. ELU

As if Christ stood on yonder clouded peak/And turned its thousand waters into wine. Glencoe. Gilbert Keith Chesterton. PoSH

As if deaf to their rising chorus of squawks. The Osprey Suicides. Laurence Lieberman. HoAn

As if each leaf were, so better prepared/For falling sooner or later separate. Back to Life. Thom Gunn. NoP

As if each stalwart oak had roots/That reached to Calvary! The Cross and the Tree. William L. Stidger. PGD

As if earth were glad/To see us passing here. Daisies. Valerie Worth. PCP

As if for the last time, believing that you will leave me. Residue of Song. Marvin Bell. AmPA

As if, from the glazed balcony/of your cheeks, blue tears/had fallen. Poem: "Your face." David St. John. AmPA

As if grateful for his stark historic fading. Homage of War. Bruce Williamson. NeIP

—As if he could outpace/darkness drifting home like a flock of crows. Riverside Drive, November Fifth. Katha Pollitt. AMV-81

As if he'd been duly invited! Limerick: "There was a young man so benighted." Dayton Voorhees. HBV 1-2

...As if he'd stayed/a fisherman for life and never gone to war/was not to be expected. Seaman, 1941. Molly Holden. FaBoWP

As if he were a truckdriver, tree climber,/railroad mender, dealer in hard love. The Trouble with Truck Drivers. Margot Treitel. AmC

As if I had been dead, and now was not dead. The Fortune Teller. John Holmes. NePoAm-2

...As if I had brought/those tender stinking wings to earth. The Egg. George Bowering. NeAC

As if I had committed, against the whole scheme of life, a desecration. Moss-Gathering. Theodore Roethke. CoBMV; RFM; VGW

As if I had measured the country/And got the United States stated. A Record Stride. Robert Frost. NePA

...As if I loved games. Tennis. Nina Nyhart. AMV-81

As if in a movie Small Towns. Alejandro Murguia. FIA

As if in braille, your face. Look for Me on England. H. B. Mallalieu. WaP

As if it knows that only silence/could finally move the stars to pity. Tunes for Bears to Dance To. Ronald Wallace. GOYP

As if it were a natural creature. Sitting down, Looking up. Archie Randolph Ammons. PCP

As if it were all. This plain all. This journey all. Variations on a Time Theme. Edwin Muir. MoVE

As if it were this easy. The Deer. Laurie Sheeck. AMV-80

As if it would always move, to inner/music, and of its own passion. Ground Swell. G. Stanley Koehler. NePoAm-2

As if, like Chaucer's child, he thought/All but "O Alma!" nought. The Miracle. Walter De La Mare. CoBE; LiTB; UnPo

As if marauding winter would never come. On a Bougainvillaea Vine in Haiti. Barbara Howes. MoAmPo; NYBP

...As if on a journey/from which one does not return Things I Didn't Know I Loved. Nazim Hikmet. LLLT

As if radar were likely or handy/as bedside/as cough drops or slang. To Mind. Clark Coolidge. APU

As if remembering the way to Spring. Fall Lightly on Me. Roger Gaess. LTB

...,As if salt or money or even lust/would keep us calm and prove us whole at last. The Lost Ingredient. Anne Sexton. CoPo

As if she had known not only John,/But known of what he died. The Workbox. Thomas Hardy. UnPo

As if she had stayed on a train/one stop past her destination. For Sale. Robert Lowell. ConAP

...As if/She hid a stone in the grass. The Great Canzon. Kenneth Rexroth. NoAm

As if she, too, had heard. In the Dying of Daylight. Walter De La Mare. ACV

As if she were about to speak, or had just spoken. Two Women with Mangoes. Steven Cramer. AMV-80

As if so sure a nest were never shaped on spray. I Watched a Blackbird. Thomas Hardy. PB

As if some happy jester in the cards/Whispered the gayest secret that he knew. A Fortune-Teller. Witter ("Emanuel Morgan") Bynner. HBMV

As if tearing the bandage/From an incurable wound. Age? H. R. Hays. PoL

As if that fury of death itself were dying. Then. Edwin Muir. CMoP; PoA

...As if that habit of expecting nothing/will die with me, and that hopeless peace. Mother of Fishermen. H. Roland-Holst. PBWP

As if the air/might hold some further thing/for the listening. New Strain. George Starbuck. MP; TwCP

...As if/the city, finally, were singing itself to sleep. Night Piece. Mark Strand. NYP

As if the dark houses watching the trees from dark windows/Were simply biding their time. Domus Caedet Arborem. Charlotte Mew. PBWP

As if the dead hare were soon to awaken! The Fox Who Watched for the Midnight Sun. Norman Dubie. LCAP; MAYP

As if the design of all his words takes form/And frame from thinking and is realized. To an Old Philosopher in Rome. Wallace Stevens. AP; NoAm; NOBA

As if the flesh were a house/With too many empty rooms. Thinking of Love. Elizabeth Jennings. GOYP

As if the hue of the next feather were the shedding The Translation of Verver. Mei-mei Berssenbrugge. LTB

As if the joys of time to dreams had fled,/Or sailed away with Ines to the West. Thomas Hood. Edwin Arlington Robinson. HBMV

As if the miracle were working, on the wrong balcony. A Miracle for Breakfast. Elizabeth Bishop. AmP; LiTA; MiAP

As if the name meant once/All love, all beauty. Dublinesque. Philip Larkin. OxBC

As if the Power that chained the impatient wind/With the same fetter of repose had bound us!   A Summer Noon at Sea.   Epes Sargent.   EtS

As if the resurrection/Were nothing very odd!   A lady red upon the hill.   Emily Dickinson.   AA; BoNaP; HBV 1-2; OHIP

As if the vanished soul of Keats/Had found its new birth in a bird.   Moonlight Song of the Mocking-bird.   William Hamilton Hayne   AA

As if the walk/could cut bare feet.   This Golden Summer.   Robert Lowell.   NoP

As if the world compressed to one old man/Who was the sun, and he sole faithful planet.   Old Witherington.   Dudley Randall.   ConAP; NoAm; TW

As if the world had disappeared traceless like a dream/and rests within us finally secure   The Man without a Road: X.   Erik Lindegren.   LiTW

As if their gaze would never break.   The Annunciation.   Edwin Muir.   CMoP; NOCV

As if there had not been a battle/This morning up there on the hill.   With Corse at Allatoona.   Samuel H. M. Byers.   PAH

...As if/there were someone/who knew/the answer.   Man and Wife.   Mitchell Goodman.   VGW

As if they'd sinned, he knew not how.   Annie Shore and Johnnie Doon.   Patrick Orr.   HBV 1-2

As if they did rejoice o'er a young earthquake's birth.   Childe Harold's Pilgrimage: Canto III.   George Gordon, Lord Byron.   LiTB

As if they had been always known, yet could not be.   Bloody Cranesbill on the Dunes.   E. J. Scovell.   ChMP

...As if they knew love/is the only fortress/strong enough to trust to.   The Paper Nautilus.   Marianne Moore.   FaBoWP; VGW

As if they knew not that they weep the while.   Embarcation.   Thomas Hardy.   BrPo; OBWP

As if they never called you mine,/mine, mine.   The Masochist.   Maxine W. Kumin.   IHMS; PoA

As if they scorned both resting-place and rest!   Water Fowl.   William Wordsworth.   FM

As if they started at bo-peep,/Did soon draw in again.   Upon Her Feet.   Robert Herrick.   CaPo; OBSP; ViBoPo

As if they too knew exactly what they sought.   Hermit.   David Baker.   AMV-80

As if they were preparing cat's meat.   Hare.   Archestratus.   FaBoUs

As if this were the roadway/That carried you off forever...   I Recognized You Because When I Saw the Print.   Juan Ramon Jimenez.   OLR

As if to answer to its God through thee.   Niagara.   Lydia Huntley Sigourney.   AmLP

...As if to manifest/Thy nobler self, thy life at best!   The Lost Occasion.   John Greenleaf Whittier.   BLPL; NOBA

As if to poke chrysolites from their hiding place   For Natalya Correia.   Irving Layton.   NeAC

As if to say/it hurts, it hurts/either way.   An Emblem of Two Foxes.   Barry Spacks.   HoPM

As if to tell me which is itself?   Student.   Cheng Min.   PBWP

As if to understand, to accomplish ourselves, or become/happy!   The Technique of Love.   Jascha Kessler.   AmPC

As if we had died and gone to Dublin.   Working the Rain Shift at Flanagan's.   Gibbons Ruark.   MAYP

As if we were testing anything else.   Trying to Talk with a Man.   Adrienne Rich.   HaCAP; NIP

As if wild beasts and men did seek/To like, to love, to choose alike.   Affection and Desire.   Sir Walter Ralegh.   CBEP; OBSC

As if with plumes of grace to hover/A spirit took our part.   The Great Moth.   Robert Gittings.   OxBTC

As if within the heart a folded wing/Were making ready for a wider flight.   As Day Begins to Wane.   Helena Coleman.   CaP

As if words enclosed the secret/in myself that lasts after death.   Speaking.   Michael Ryan.   AmPA

As if yellow eyes in sunlight were answering prayer.   Red Wing Hawk.   James Applewhite.   AMV-81

As if you'd heard yourself performing.   Carnegie Hall: Rescued.   Marianne Moore.   NYP

As if you had always known it would turn out that way.   Blind Geronimo.   Bill Berkson.   ANYP

As if you had left a trace, a phantom in time at which the/olfactory dog continued to bark.   The Lateshow Diorama.   Christopher Dewdney.   CaPN

As if you hoped, of all mankind, you might/Escape the infallibility of time.   Exceptional.   Thelma Lewis.   AMV-80

...As if you were a very Cain flying from/His face?   Have Faith.   Edward Carpenter.   WGRP

...As if/you would never leave me/and were the inexorable/product of my own time.   Poetry.   Frank O'Hara.   HaCAP

As if your town were now re-paved with all/The more aching recollections of your stay.   Hardy's Plymouth.   Geoffrey Grigson.   FaBoPP

As in a Polish countryside, the flies drone in Jerusalem.   Jerusalem.   Antoni Slonimski.   VWA

As in art, in life the people/Can but kill, they cannot judge us.   If, Jerusalem, I Ever Should Forget Thee.   Heinrich Heine.   TrJP

As in Che. And so forth.   What Is Needed.   Marcos Rodriguez Frese.   InW

As in his burning throne he sits emparadis'd.   The Heavenly Jerusalem.   Giles the Younger Fletcher.   OxBoCh

As in King George's glorious days.   Iolanthe.   Sir William Schwenck Gilbert.   TrGrPo

As in "neighbour' or "weigh').   I before E.   *Anonymous*.   FaBoUs

...As in some piece of art,/Is toil cooperant to an end.   In Memoriam A.H.H., CXXVIII.   Alfred, Lord Tennyson.   VLP

As in the brilliant stillness of the sun.   The Weather of the World.   Howard Nemerov.   SUW

As in the choir the painted stone,/Death!   To Death, of His Lady.   Francois Villon.   AWP

As in the pulse/that forms these lines.   Measure.   Robert Hass.   GeTw

As, in the stranger's land, their native speech/Returns to dying lips!   The Triumph of Forgotten Things.   Edith Matilda Thomas.   HBV 1-2

As in their fate foreshadowing his own.   The Druid.   John Banister Tabb.   AA

As in their Maker ye them best may see.   Amoretti, LIII.   Edmund Spenser.   AAS; EnRePo

As in wild earth a Grecian vase!   A Poor Scholar of the 'Forties.   Padraic Colum   AnIL; GLGT; NOBI; OxBI

As innocent as our design,/Immortal as our soul.   To My Excellent Lucasia, on Our Friendship.   Katherine ("Orinda") Philips.   CavP; MeLP; OBS; PeHV; SBG; WPOW

As instantaneous penetrating sense,/In Spring's birth-hour, of other Springs gone by.   The House of Life.   Dante Gabriel Rossetti.   HBV 1-2

As into deep water/or beneath a covering wing.   March Light.   Ralph J. Mills, Jr.   AMV-81

As into her secret heart the goddess breathed a/thought/Of wedlock's glory.   Epithalamium for Stella and Violentilla: Why Do You Dally So?   Statius Publius Papinius.   HW

As is had on the rocks by the ocean's roar.   The Eddystone Light.   *Anonymous*.   StPo

As is the solemn duty of every man and wife.   When Adam Was Created.   *Anonymous*.   TrAS

As Israel's King learned wisdom from the bees.   Solomon and the Bees.   John Godfrey Saxe.   GN

As it claws away pieces of my flesh/to make me small enough to swallow.   Turtle.   Robert Lowell.   LCAP

As it cries with a sudden passion/For life or death.   The Half-Breed Girl.   Duncan Campbell Scott.   CaP

...As it cuts/your children's new names in the tombstone of thin air.   On an East Wind from the Wars.   Alan Dugan.   AP

As it did for her/In a garden?   A White Iris.   Pauline B. Barrington.   PoLf

As it grows dark/drinking wine.   After Work.   Gary Snyder.   HoPM; NNaP

As it grows older, it grows colder/And fades away like morning dew.   Down in the Meadows.   *Anonymous*.   CBEP

As it is too short to weep.   Song: "Shepherd, who can pass such wrong."   Bartholomew Young.   EIL

As it leaves the eyebrows,/it enters the heart.   Poem to the Tune of "Yi Chian Mei."   Li Ching-chao.   WPOW

As it ruined for life his digesterton.   Limerick: "There was a professor called Chesterton."   Sir William Schwenck Gilbert.   TDH

As it shone on distant Bingen–fair Bingen on the Rhine.   Bingen on the Rhine.   Carolina Elizabeth Sarah Norton.   BeLS; BLPA; HBV 1-2; TreF; WBLP

As it sounds the Matins there/O'er the graves conventual.   The Abbey.   Jose Maria Eguren.   CAW

As it sparks the impenetrable lives, like yours/Whose year revolves around the county fair.   Stud Groom.   John Glassco.   OBCV

As it tossed off the snow/to the side of the road.   The Old Flame.   Robert Lowell.   BoLoP; NoAm; NOBA

As it turns to the right on/Elm Street.   Talk.   John Perreault.   ANYP

As it were a vista upon/The suffered and fordone.   Words for the Raker of Leaves.   Léonie Adams.   PoCh

As it will no more than once or twice in our/Overlapping lives, on an empty chamber.   Finding the Pistol.   Gibbons Ruark.   MAT

As it writes it sings of each room in turn/praising each room's name.   Angels in the House.   Jerred Metz.   VWA

As its fruit gradually acquires/The bitter taste of liberty.   Africa.   David Diop.   PBA; TTY

As Jame's home flickers transformed into a Funeral Parlor.   Looking at Wealth in Newport.   James Schevill.   TAT

As Julia looks when she doth dress/Her either cheek with bashfulness.   So Look the Mornings.   Robert Herrick.   ELP

As kisses are to love.   Paradox.   Angelina Weld Grimke.   CDC

As kythed in that wild auld carline that day!   Old Wife in High Spirits.   Hugh" (Christopher Murray Grieve) MacDiarmid.   CMoP; NMP; OxBTC

As laces just reveal the surge–/Or Mists–the Appenine.   The thought beneath so slight a film.   Emily Dickinson.   AmP; AmPP; OxBA

As laughing cadets say, "In the evening/Everything has a schedule, if you can find out what it is."   Two Scenes.   John Ashbery.   ANYP

As laymen clasp their hands, we join our feet.   Upon Master Walter Montagu's Return from Travel.   Thomas Carew.   CaPo

As left you in that place,/Restless, unsatisfied.   The Lovemaker.   Robert Mezey.   CABA; NePoEA-2

As lesser men drink wine.   And Thus in Nineveh.   Ezra Pound.   PP; VGW

As Life–and you–have proved to/me!   Beyond Recall.   Mary Emily Bradley.   AA

As life exchanges semblances with death.   Mancheser by Night.   Mathilde Blind.   SBG

As light upon the wandering breeze you toss the name of/names.   To Felicity Who Calls Me Mary.   Frances Chesterton.   HBMV

As lightning does the will of God.   The Ballot.   John Pierpont.   AA

As little daunted as a star or tree.   Reciprocity.   John Drinkwater.   PoA

As little Jenny Wren/Was sitting by the shed.   Fidget.   *Anonymous.*   OxNR

As little of earth, earthy,/As his mankind proclaims.   Unkept Good Fridays.   Thomas Hardy.   MoRP

As'll make them toney seraphs sit back on their thrones an' stare!   My Mate Bill.   George Herbert Gibson ("Ironbark").   PoAu 1-2

As logs jammed between rocks.   The Fish Will Swim as Before.   Michael Spence.   AMV-81

As long ago, my love, how long ago.   Echo.   Christina Georgina Rossetti.   BoLoP; CH; ELP; GBL; LiTL; LoBV; NIP; NOBE; NOBV; NoP; OAEL 1-2; OBNC; PoEL 1-5; SeCeV; ViBoPo

...As long/as eternal earth rolls, spokes groaning, from cell to cell.   Hymn.   Otto Orban.   VWA

As long as ever you can.   John Wesley's Rule.   John Wesley.   GoTF; HBVY; TreFT

As long as he makes his meters mete and a fairly passable/rhyme.   The Wide Open Spaces.   Oscar H. Lear.   InMe

As long as I continue/to kiss you good-bye.   Riddles and Lies.   Christine Zawadiwsky.   AMV-80

As long as it watched me.   February Twilight.   Sara Teasdale.   OBCA; SoPo; YeAr

As long as Maud is there, you see–what matters all the/rest?   Rural Bliss.   Anthony C. Deane.   InMe

As long/as the wind/sleeps.   Four Choctaw Songs.   Jim Barnes.   STE

As long as there are art and girls, and onions in the stew.   At the Lavender Lantern.   Charles Divine.   HBMV

...As long as there/are those who imagine him in his name.   The Gourd Dancer.   N. Scott Momaday.   CDW; STE

As long as there is day/and part of the night.   Vision.   William Stanley Merwin.   GP

As long as thou art on my side,/What need I care for more?   A Prayer.   Humfrey [(or Humphrey)] Gifford.   OxBoCh

As long as two/and two are four.   Spring Song of a Super-Blake (parody).   Louis Untermeyer.   HBMV

As long as we had not/permanently died.   Our Blackness Did Not Come to Us Whole.   Linda Brown Bragg.   CNA

As loose on flowery beds all languishing lay.   The Castle of Indolence.   James (1700-48) Thomson.   EnRP

As lost ones seek what's lost for/ever,/At some world's end.   Sunset.   Hayim Nahman Bialik.   TrJP

As lotus blossoms are pulled out of the pool.   Mountain, Fire, Thornbush.   Harvey Shapiro.   VGW

As love is recalled to us, once/Having been so blinded.   To Ariake Kambara.   Norman Rosten.   NYBP

As Love shall help thee, when thou do'st/go hence/Unto thy everlasting residence.   His Charge to Julia at His Death.   Robert Herrick.   SeCV 1-2

As lovely as a summer night/And carefree as a lark.   Portrait.   George Leonard Allen.   CDC

As luminous as love, lost as this place.   To What Strangers, What Welcome.   J. V. Cunningham.   NoAm

...As lustful/themselves as my schemes are/and as cruel   Succubi.   John Newlove.   NeAC

As makes her seem, nor fair, nor rich, nor young.   Fair, Rich, and Young.   Martial (Marcus Valerius Martialis).   NIP

As makes her seem, nor fair, nor rich, nor young.   Of a Fair Shrew.   Sir John (1561-1612) Harington.   FaBoEE

As man behind his mask still wears a child.   Mask.   Stephen Spender.   MoAB; MoBrPo

As Man ere long, and this new World shall know.   Paradise Lost.   John Milton.   LiTB

As man to set in Parts, at first had learn'd of her.   Polyolbion.   Michael Drayton.   OBS

As many a man discovers, to his sorrow.   The Benefactors.   Sara Henderson Hay.   DFT

As many can tell.   One Thing at a Time.   *Anonymous.*   OxNR

As many feet as a hundred sheep.   Riddle: "Trip trap in a gap."   *Anonymous.*   GBP

As many looks, as many darts,/Might make them all to die.   Madrigal: "When in her face mine eyes I fix."   William Alexander, Earl of Stirling.   EIL

As many red herrings as grew in a wood.   The Man in the Wilderness.   *Anonymous.*   FaBoCo; FaBoNo; GBP; LoGBV; OxNR

As Margaret O'Brien getting adopted up there on the screen.   First Love.   Judith Hemschemeyer.   Psk

As martyrs gridirons, when God calls the roll.   Rolling the Lawn.   William Empson.   MoBrPo

As Mary once her Paradise,/Just four years old.   The Desire.   Katharine Tynan Hinkson.   HBV 1-2

...As meadows/so we wore this Land.   The Poem on Our Mother, Our Mother Rachel.   Avot Yeshurun.   VWA

As meaningful and as meaningless as any/other flower in the western field.   Two Dedications, I: The Chicago Picasso.   Gwendolyn Brooks.   LiTM

As melting quietly by his boots it fell.   Innocence.   Thom Gunn.   LiTM; NePoEA-2; NoAm

...As men are served by women/Who comfort them in darkenss and in sun.   Man without Sense of Direction.   John Crowe Ransom.   LiTM; OxBA

As men can have nothing more profit in their life than Me.   The Undertaking.   Gerrit Lansing.   CoPo

As men wedd ladyes by lycence and leve,/All ys possyble.   Ys Yt Possyble.   Sir Thomas Wyatt.   AAS; PoEL 1-5

As mendicants who see/Mimic the blind.   In Innocence.   J. V. Cunningham.   OBSP

As menstralis playis "The jolly day now dawis'.   An Evening and Morning in June.   Gavin Douglas.   BSV

As mine do this morning.   This Morning.   Jon Stallworthy.   NoP

As moon from earth, or star from star.   Atom from Atom.   Ralph Waldo Emerson.   ImOP; TiPo

As moon on man the gold foil of his brain.   Vacuum.   Josephine Miles.   MOON

As morning throws off stale moonlight and shabby sleep.   It Is the Celestial Ennui of Apartments.   Wallace Stevens.   NePA

As Moses supposes his toeses to be.   Moses Supposes His Toeses Are Roses.   *Anonymous.*   OxNR

As much as she has mine.   To My Love.   Sir John Suckling.   ALV

As much beauty as they say.   Appreciation.   Thomas Bailey Aldrich.   AA

As much, for that's an Ocean too,/That flows not every day, but ever.   This Ensuing Copy the Late Printer Hath been Pleased to Honour...   Owen Felltham.   OBS

As much regretted by mankind/As Patagonia's ACHILLES!   An Elegy on the Late King of Patagonia.   St. John Emile Clavering Hankin.   CenHV

As must, for this wise Prelate's part,/be supreme arbiters of Art.   The Handmaid of Religion.   Edgell Rickword.   OBSV

As my body/passed through the world.   The color of the flowers.   Ono no Komachi.   BoWoP

As my daily life/took over the room.   Sacrifice.   Nana Issaia.   BoWoP

As my eyes follow after/Their sunlit leaping.   The Siskins.   Theodore Roethke.   PB

As my father guided me/To the house of prayer.   How Can I See You, Love.   David Vogel.   VWA

As my strength and I walk out and look for you.   Real Life.   Ted Berrigan.   NoAm

As nail from out a plank is struck by nail.   Lady of Heaven.   Guittone d'Arezzo.   CAW

As natural as a leopard's/night cough   The Protective Grigri.   Ted Joans.   PoBA

As Nature had therein ordained some sylvan power.   Poly-Olbion.   Michael Drayton.   FaBoPP

As near as seed to fruit,/So close should be our love.   So Close Should Be Our Love.   *Anonymous.*   WTO

As near as two and two make five.   Faith and Works.   Muriel Spark.   OBSP

As neither party satisfying other,/Repentance still becomes desire's mother.   Caelica, XI.   Fulke, Lord Brooke Greville.   FCP

As never he did but that day, to the dark night with bliss.   The Temptation of Sir Gawain.   *Anonymous.*   ACP

As no god, saving only Death, can save.   Love's Assize.   Guido Cavalcanti.   LiTW

As no mere insurgent man could hope to break/With curse, fist, threat/Or love, either.   Spinster.   Sylvia Plath.   FaBoWP

As none in all the flock they like themselves would/have.   Poly-Olbion.   Michael Drayton.   FM

As nought but death may ever change thy/mind.   Who Taught Thee First to Sigh?   Edward, Earl of Oxford De Vere.   CoBE

As now in heaven!   Astraea.   John Greenleaf Whittier   AA

As now no poetaster dares to do!   To a Writer of the Day.   Langdon Elwyn Mitchell.   AA

As now, the day is over. O Tender under Her Right Breast. George Barker. MoAB; MoBrPo

As now, with earth outshone and earth's wide air,/Shows each to other as this morning fair. Sonnets, XX: "Now stands our love on that still verge of day." James Agee. MoAmPo

As nutskin, tobacco, cider, plum. Late Autumn Walk. J. D. McClatchy. AMV-80

As o'er our heads, a place of bliss. On Leaping over the Moon. Thomas Traherne. AtBAP; LiTB; LoBV; MOON; SeCV 1-2

As of broad-backed bishop/Or of crook. A Note on Master Crow. Jean Garrigue. BoAnP

As on my heavenly hills. Pandora's Song. William Vaughn Moody. AnFE; APA

As on my sweetheart's head, and draw it to me. O Ease My Spirit. Hugh" (Christopher Murray Grieve) MacDiarmid. BSV

As on the day McPherson died. Logan at Peach Tree Creek. Hamlin Garland. MC; PAH

As on two that have no longer much of any-/thing to tell. John Gorham. Edwin Arlington Robinson. MAPA; MoAB; MoAmPo; NoAm

As once in Egypt, Hellas, Ind, Iran! The Cow. Bernard O'Dowd. PoAu 1-2

As once in her fire-lit heart I felt the furies/Beating, beating. Lines to a Nasturtium. Anne Spencer. AmNP; CDC; PoNe

As once in the garden, walk again,/Centre and spirit of human kind. O Come Out of the Lily. Ruth Pitter. AnFE

As once it was, and still with tears is full. Odes, VI. Hafiz. AWP

As one by one we blow. Birthday Candles. Louise Binder Scott. BiCB

As one day will be that immortal fry/Of almost everybody born to die. The Vision of Judgment. George Gordon, Lord Byron. OxBoLi

As one expectant of her Lord's sweet will. Evening. Hugh McCrae. PoAu 1-2

As one old soldier's ballad borne on breath of battle-song. The Ballad of Chickamauga. Maurice Thompson. MC; PAH

As one who counts it freedom to believe. Authority. William Reed Huntington. AA

...As one who longs/to turn to dreams, and smiled, and played again,/The Song of Songs. The Reed-Player. Archibald MacLeish. HBMV

As one who's gladdened in a midnight wood/For having seen the moon. If You Should Lightly. Trumbull Stickney. NCEP

As one who shunneth honor—"I am he." Knowest Thou Isaac Jogues? Francis W. Grey. CAW

As one who trusted, one who knew/The common heart. The Lincoln Statue. W. F. Collins. OHIP; PGD

As one whose altitude at one time, was not so. Purgatorio. Hart Crane. NAMP

As one would hardly credit from a lesser/Person than a history professor. Don's Holiday. George Rostrevor Hamilton. FaBoCo

As other Fellows do of Trinity. On a Fellow of Trinity College, Cambridge. Richard Porson. FaBoEE

As our cries were swallowed up and all hands lost. Fog-Horn. William Stanley Merwin. NMP

As our fathers did before/Long ago. The Death of Admiral Benbow. Anonymous. GBP

As our love and our pity are, are. False Country of the Zoo. Jean Garrigue. LiTM; MP

As our lovers walk slowly towards us across a sun-dappled room. Here/There. Ken Norris. CaPN

As out of its own mouth the river's body flows. Living Poetry. Hugo Margenat. InW

As people try to deny their hidden joys. City Sparrow. Jane Mayhall. TAP

...As placid rivers/are always calling to the ruined columns. The Permanent Tourists. P. K. Page. LiTM; NOBC

As plain as at the first, when they were fresh and green. The Faerie Queene. Edmund Spenser. OBSC

As plainly, perhaps, and as bluntly as I might in our earlier/youth. Outgrown. Julia Caroline Ripley Dorr. HBV 1-2

As pleased as if the same had been a Maiden-/queen. Stanzas Written in My Pocket Copy of Thomson's "Castle of Indolence." William Wordsworth. EnRP

As pleased when shipwrecked as when safe on/shore. The Acquiescence of Pure Love. William Cowper. ILwL

As poems still conserve/the language/of old ecstasies. Illegitimate Things. William Carlos Williams. MoAB; MoAmPo

As poor as one who never knew/The treasure of the early dew. The Gombeen. Joseph Campbell. BIrV

As Pyramus did on Thisbes brest bewayle. Divers Thy Death. Henry Howard, Earl of Surrey. FCP; NCEP

As quiet and chaste as the author's own life. A Fable for Critics. James Russell Lowell. AnNE; AP; NOBA; OxBA; TAP

As racks for the Jooler-man's junk. Limerick: "Now the ears, so I always had thunk." Anthony Euwer. HBMV

As rain began greatly to fall,/And closed the door of the Ark. Chenille. James Dickey. NoAm

As, reduced to skimmed milk, to slander the cream. Old Age in His Ailing. Herman Melville. TAP

...As river-/grass on the woven current/indicates ripple./praise. A Psalm Praising the Hair of Man's Body. Denise Levertov. CAPP

As rock-hollows, tide after tide,/Glassily strand the sea. The Undead. Richard Wilbur. CAPP; CoAP; ConAP; OxBC

As rocks resist the billows and the sky. The Deserted Village. Oliver Goldsmith. BeLS; BIrV; EBEV; EnPE; FaFP; GoTL; HBV 1-2; LaA; LAuP; MasP; MCCG; NOBI; NOEC; NoP; OAEL 1-2; OAEP; OnYI; OxBI; PoEL 1-5; TEP

As roots on earth embrace to rise/Most lovely flowers in Paradise. On Thomas Carew. Anonymous. CBEP

As roses are by heaven designed/To bring the honey to the wind. The Tragic Mary Queen of Scots. Michael (Katherine Bradley and Edith Cooper) Field. EnLoPo; OBMV

As, round some citadel, the engineer/Directs his sharp stoccade. How to Build a Ha-Ha. William Mason. FaBoUs

As run its dark machinery/without sound. Tulip. Robert Wallace. PPJ

As sad as earth, as sweet as heaven! The Voiceless. Oliver Wendell Holmes. AA; ViBoPo

As scattered geese/suddenly weave a line of flight/from the wind's release. Snow Geese in the Wind. Philip Dow. NPGG

As shadows wait upon the sun. Survey Our Progress from Our Birth. John Webster. LO

As she beats her ordinary bread. In Salem. Lucille Clifton. AmPA

As she came to me out of the rain. Rain on the Down. Arthur Symons. NOBV; OBVV

As she gangs tae the kirk,/With the sun on her side. West Wind. Anonymous. PoPle

As she had sowed them with her odourous foot. Aeglamour's Lament. Ben Jonson. CH

As she lay asleep in my arms I'd Want Her Eyes to Fill with Wonder. Kenneth Patchen. LLLT

As she let out a tuck in her tunich. Limerick: "There was a young lady of Munich." Anonymous. TDH

As she passes over them. Wind and Silver. Amy Lowell. BoWoP; HeIP; MoAmPo

As she sailed on the low land low,/As she sailed on the lonesome sea. There Was a Little Ship. Anonymous. BFSS

As she shuffles into street sounds. Blind Old Woman. Clarence Major. PoBA

As She sinks in the mire of the Tarn,/Even now—even now—even now! By the Hoof of the Wild Goat. Rudyard Kipling. OBNC

As she tied her bonnet under her chin! The Love-Knot. Nora Perry. HBV 1-2

As shine on life's untrodden brink/A baby's feet. Etude Realiste. Algernon Charles Swinburne. WeW

As shuts the rose, they softly close, when he goes through/the town. The Sandman. Margaret Thomson Janvier. HBV 1-2; HBVY

As silver bracelets are liberally handed out. Raid on the Market. Polycarp Chimedza. WhB

As sinne is nothing, let it no where be. The Litanie. John Donne. AtBAP; PoEL 1-5

As sleep falls/In the innocent air. Anecdote of the Prince of Peacocks. Wallace Stevens. SOTW

As so it doth? that's pittie. Upon Jone and Jane. Robert Herrick. AnAnS 2

As some refulgent cloud in the upper sky. Smoke in Winter. Henry David Thoreau. AnNE

As some stray fawn that seeks its mother. To Chloe. Horace. AWP

As something set apart and is afraid he/Might comprehend her motor's feline purr. Lese-Majeste. Herbert Sherman Gorman. HBMV

As soon as I am grown up..." And she weeps. In Little Hands. Mani Leib. VWA

As soon as I saw you/My life ached for you, my enemy. Red Beauty. Anonymous. WTO

As soon as thou wast skilled in falconry. Sonnet: A Lady Laments for Her Lost Lover... Anonymous. AWP

As soon impeach my crown! Afraid? Of whom am I afraid? Emily Dickinson. OHIP

As soon they shall be happy to desert. Cat-Goddesses. Robert Graves. MoVE; NYBP; OBSP

As space is disappearing and your singularity. Sleeping on the Wing. Frank O'Hara. InPS; SOTW

As spoke the anguish of severest woes,/And smote his heart— Sir Roland; a Fragment. Robert Merry. NOEC

...As stake/for a new start only the fact/that scorched earth can still be used. Nearer. Judith Herzberg. BoWoP; VWA

As stars appear/In the dark/Skies. Response. Bob Kaufman. BOLo

As still he envied me, so fair she was. The Bishop Orders His Tomb at Saint Praxed's Church. Robert Browning. ATP; AWP; DiPo; ExPo; FiP; ForPo; HAP; HBV 1-2; HeIP; MaVP; MyFE; NAWM 1-2; NOBV; NoP; OAEL 1-2; OAEP; PPoe; PPP; PrIm; SeCeV; TEP; ViBoPo

As stout as our martyrs and as just as our laws! A New Catch in Praise of the Reverend Bishops. *Anonymous.* APAS

As sudden on earth's darkness streams a star! From Bethlehem Blown. Mary Sinton Leitch. PGD

As summer, lulling and so mild,/Goes golden-buttercup-wild. Summer Music. May Sarton. NCSH; NePoAm

...As sunlight/Streams into the window. Fishin' Blues. Valentino Ramirez. AMV-81

As sure to win/Under his Crosse. A Hymne to God the Father. Ben Jonson. AnAnS 2; MePo; OBS; SeCP; SeCV 1-2; TrPWD

As surely as it keeps the stroke and time/In having its undeviable say. In a Poem. Robert Frost. PP

As sweet companions as might be had. Ghost House. Robert Frost. WSC

As swift as a startled bird. The Golden Stallion. Paul Thompson. BPAW

As swift to me as heav'nly light. Come, O Come. Thomas Campion. AtBAP; EG; EIL; InvP

As tangled as my hair. How Can One E'er Be Sure. Lady Horikawa. AWP

As tell the seafarers, in the sea's disguises. Told by Seafareres. Galway Kinnell. NePoAm-2

As that insinuating, calculating, irritating,/titivating, sleepy little, creepy little, sticky... I Can't Think What He Sees in Her. Sir Alan Patrick Herbert. FiBHP

As that the congelation will/Me sooner starve than those can kill. The Frozen Zone; or, Julia Disdainful. Robert Herrick. CaPo

As the apple blossoms render/In the spring. An Apple Orchard in the Spring. William Martin. GN

As the army corps advances. An Army Corps on the March. Walt Whitman. InPS; PAI; PAL; PoLf; PPoe

As the beginning longs for the end. In an Alien Place. Leib Neidus. VWA

As the Birds flew off to the End of Next Week. The Serpent. Theodore Roethke. AmMo

As the boat's motion swept her from my sight. On the Grand Canal. David Gascoyne. SeCePo

As the branch swung beneath her dancing feet. Procne. Peter Quennell. ChMP; LiTB; LiTM; MoBrPo

As the Buffalo Bill Follies autodestruct by 1916. Wilderness Sacred Wilderness. Philip Lamantia. APU

As the cloud-foaming firmamental blue/Rests on the blue line of a foamless/ sea. The House of Life. Dante Gabriel Rossetti. OAEP

As the clouds of white/That swim in the summer skies. The Cowboy's Life. James Barton Adams. BPAW

As the cowboys rode their skintight stallions/Over the barbarous hills of California. Far West. A.J.M. Smith. PeCV

As the creation/touches him a last time all over his body? The Call across the Valley of Not Knowing. Galway Kinnell. GP

As the crossing stars took time to mark their flight/Over the mind's eye. House-Hunting. David Wagoner. DFF

As the dawn comes up like thunder/out of Brooklyn, the shaper of sunrise. East Hampton: The Structure of Sound. Philip Appleman. NYP

As the devil laughs when the keen folks cheat the cheaters. Perveril of the Peak (excerpt). Sir Walter Scott. NBM

As the dew vanished away. Another Sunday Morning. Carter Revard. VoR

As the divorc'd soul from her body parts. The Surrender. Henry, Bishop of Chichester King. EBEV; TrGrPo

As the doo flies owre the mulberry tree. Jennifer Gentle and Rosemary. *Anonymous.* OxBoLi

As the doors open and no one comes on. When You've Been Here Long Enough. Lawrence Joseph. HoAn

As the dow flies over the mulberry-tree. The Riddling Knight. *Anonymous.* AtBAP; FaBoCh; LoGBV

As the earth has patience with the life of man. The Traveller. W. H. Auden. SyP

As the earth rolls over, inverting billions of houses. Causes. Mona Van Duyn. SM

As the eternal monument of me. To Laurels. Robert Herrick. ExPo

As the firelight falls and leaps/From your feet to your lips! New Year's Eve. D. H. Lawrence. BoLoP; ErPo

As the first lovers in the garden were. Were the Bright Day No More to Visit Us. *Anonymous.* LO

As the frigate pelican/of the Caribbean. The Frigate Pelican. Marianne Moore. InvP

As the fruit is to the tree/May their children ever be! A Bridal Song. Percy Bysshe Shelley. HW

As the girl in pink on the milk-white horse/Cantered over the sawdust course. A Circus Garland. Rachel Field. OBCA; SoPo

As the grass stretches and rises,/That will go, too. Grass. Alfred Corn. MAYP

As the great cloud-utopias/burn out in the west. Dusk of the Revolutionaries. John Haines. NPAW

As the great Spirit erst with plastic sweep/Mov'd on the darkness of the unform'd deep. To the Reverend W.L. Bowles. Samuel Taylor Coleridge. EnRP

As the green grass glows upwards, strangers in the garden. Trees in the Garden. D. H. Lawrence. CMoP; MoAB; MoBrPo; NoP

As the green of the bracken amid the gloom of the heather. June Bracken and Heather. Alfred, Lord Tennyson. EnLoPo; PPoe

As the guinea corn is finely ground/in the way of a thousand stones/we take our own On the Naming Day. Johari M. Kunjufu. CNA

As the hand that plants an acorn/Shelters armies from the sun. Better, Wiser and Happier. Ella Wheeler Wilcox. WBLP

...As the/healer sings wildly, shouting to Jesus and his dead mother. Looking into a Tide Pool. Robert Bly. CAPP; MAT

As the Holy Spirit, travels the bubble of air. Ward Two. Francis Webb. CBAP

As the hot bodies of the sparrows increase each summer. Against Death. Peter Redgrove. NMP

As the Hudson retakes its thickets/and Indians reclaim their canoes. Wild Dreams of a New Beginning. Lawrence Ferlinghetti. GP

As the Indian rocks and stares and waves one hand at me. Indian. Jeanne Doriot. AMV-81

As the inhabitants of Thames right side/Do Londons Mayor; or Germans, the Popes pride. Jealosie. John Donne. AnAnS 1

As the iron gate clanged behind him, that's what he heard the warden say. Coon Can (Poor Boy) (with music). *Anonymous.* AS

...As the lad said: We must/love one another or die. Lower the Standard: That's My Motto. Karl Shapiro. NoAm

...As the Lady's skirt/moves small beyond it. The Door. Robert Creeley. NaP; NeAP; NoAm; PoM; VGW

As the leaf chars or is kindled; as the bough burns. Soldier (T. P.). Randall Jarrell. WaP

As the lean tree burst into grief. The Mad Scene. James Merrill. CoAP; NoAm; NOBA; PoA; TAP

As the light in America comes: without leaves.... Conquistador. Archibald MacLeish. NoAm

As the light's aire from a vault/which has a knob of sun. The Green Leaf. Louis Zukofsky. CoPo; VGW

As the live heat billows from pipes and pots. Forcing House. Theodore Roethke. AtBAP; CAPP

...As the long war/Begins again, not by our doing or desiring. Easter. Howard Nemerov. NoP

As the mind is overturned by memory, the heart by dread. The Overturned Lake. Charles Henri Ford. EAS

As the moon & the wave remain individually one Wavelength. David St. John. SUW

As the old man who lives in a hut on the shore drinks his glass of salt/water. Leonardo's Secret. Robert Bly. NNaP

As the old, old fabric falls apart. Portrait. Adele Naude. PeSA

As the park turns gently into evening. The Park at Evening. Leslie Norris. DuDa

As the pipes played Auld Lang Syne. The Relief of Lucknow. Robert Lowell. HBV 1-2; StPo

As the Quakeress bride's - "Until death I am thine!" The Quakeress Bride. Elizabeth Clementine Kinney AA

...As the race/Was run, the girl was beaten, and the winner/Led off his prize. Atalanta. Ovid (Publius Ovidius Naso). LiSp

As the radio begins knowingly/dealing in numbers. Numbers. Harley Elliott. LTB

As the rain was falling. Your Birds Build Sun-Castles with Song. Daniel Sloate. AMV-81

As the rancour of a cloud broke off and fell/into the back of town and foundered there. Miramichi Lightning. Alfred Goldsworthy Bailey. OBCV

As the red-haired bo'sun said. What the Red-haired Bo'sun Said. Charles H. Souter. PoAu 1-2

...As the republic accepts/the coup d'etat of spring. Spring in Washington. James Den Boer. TAT

As the rising sun slowly dries/his strange, unruly wings. The Mole. John Haines. NCSH

As the rooster walks away springily over the dampened hay. Old Boards. Robert Bly. NaP

As the sea broke wild beneath the cliff. Island of Giglio. Harold Norse. GP

As the shepherd-priest with Chaumonot led back/the remnant of a nation to Quebec. Brebeuf and His Brethren. Edwin John Pratt. NOBC

As the soft glamor of remembered rain/Hallows the gladness of a sunlit wood. From Life. Brian Hooker. HBV 1-2

As the Southern Cross rises.   On a Sea-Grape Leaf.   Katherine Garrison Chapin.   GrPl

As the sparks that fly up from the well-shod hoof.   The Forge.   Oliver St. John Gogarty.   AnIV

As the stars shine bright in the sky.   Early in the Springtime.   *Anonymous.*   OBET

As the sun got out of our eyes/and into our hungry bellies.   On the Bright Side.   Carter Revard.   VoR

As the sun, its globe compressed in/The mist-sprayed air, sinks lidless down.   Rannoch Moor.   Malcolm MacGregor.   PoSH

As the sun poured down its benediction.   Sunday Stroll.   Michael Pettit.   MAYP

As the symbol of love in heaven,/And its wavering image here.   The Bridge.   Henry Wadsworth Longfellow.   GoTF; HBV 1-2; TreF

As the tall slave sings why Father? why Father?   The Victim of Aulis.   Dannie Abse.   NoAm

As the three came past with the step of kings.   Night Piece.   John Streeter Manifold.   LiTM; MoBrPo; WaP

As the tide turned in its sleep.   The Tide in the River.   Eleanor Farjeon.   TiPo

...As the train/Carries a white-faced woman back to face the world again.   At Devlin's Siding.   Barcroft Henry Boake.   CBAP

...As the trees/Are, by the sunbeams, tickled by degrees.   The Coming of Good Luck.   Robert Herrick.   CBEP; ELU; FaBoEE; JCP; OBSP

As the two twilights of the day/Fold us music-drunken in.   Merlin.   Ralph Waldo Emerson.   AnNE; AP; CTC; EBEV; EnLi 1-2; EnLoPo; HAP; MAmp; NOBA; NoP; OxBM; PoEL 1-5

As the voracious beak, the claw's impact/Draw near.   The Hunter.   Eleanor Glenn Wallis.   NePoAm-2

As the water all night is crying to me.   The Crying of Water.   Arthur Symons.   AnEnPo

As the water cleared and sparkled in the shallows of the/ford.   The Shallows of the Ford.   Henry Herbert Knibbs.   BPAW

As the weak sun breaks on the land without a hill.   Pacifists.   George Woodcock.   NOBC

As the whole night now/Made visible behind this darkness seems/To beckon to me....   The Hamlet of A. MacLeish (excerpt).   Archibald MacLeish.   AnAmPo

As the whoreson knave men laid away/A thousand years ago.   Falstaff's Song.   Edmund Clarence Stedman.   AA; HBV 1-2

As the world's love before the world was.   The Sapphire.   William Stanley Merwin.   PoA

As the world turns once and we manage it,/only rarely getting dizzy.   Ode to the Day.   Ken Norris.   CaPN

As the Yankee :roops–with glory armed/and shod–/In Grand Review swing past the throne of/God.   For Decoration Day: 1898-1899.   Rupert Hughes.   AA

As theirs, I lay like them, my best gifts on thy shrine!   Proem.   John Greenleaf Whittier.   AA; AnNE; AP; HBV 1-2; NePA; NoP; OxBA; TAP

As then I had mine, in the place that was happy and poor.   Time's Fool.   Ruth Pitter.   ChMP; MoBrPo; OxBTC; PoRA

As then in Death, so now in Love.   Charitas Nimia, or the Deare Bargain.   Richard Crashaw.   AnAnS 1; JCP; MePo; NOCV; OxBoCh

As there seems to be/a plenty/more of gruel   Things of the Spirit.   Mason Jordan Mason.   PoNe

As these young lovers face to face/Renew their early vows!   The Palm-Tree and the Pine.   Richard Monckton, Lord Houghton Milnes.   HBV 1-2

As they carry anything/From any place you will.   Freight Boats.   James S. Tippett.   BrR

As they crowd each other toward the woods/where Stoutes Creek flows past the quarry.   About the Cows.   Roger Pfingston.   FAZ

As they did, you know when-a.   The Defeat of the Armada.   Thomas Dekker.   CoBE

As they direct the nervous spirit/on whose narrow back I ride.   Chasing the Paper-Shamans.   Wendy Rose.   TWSS

As they drain the vast vault of the night, drop by drop.   Here the Trace.   Boris Pasternak.   LiTW

As they enter the big corral above,/Through the heavenly Golden Gate.   The Cowboy.   *Anonymous.*   CoSo

As they, ever looking upward,/Watched it fly across the heavens.   The White Kite.   *Anonymous.*   LiTW

As they fell from the lips of my lover.   What My Lover Said.   Homer Greene.   AA; HBV 1-2; TreFS

As they flee across Aughty in the late evening.   On the Defeat of Ragnall by Murrough King of Leinster A.D. 994.   *Anonymous.*   OnYI

...As they generally do today, partially or wholly blind-/folded.   The Meat Epitaph.   Michael Benedikt.   FiCP

As they, in the same sense, call themselves artists.   Wigs and Beards.   Robert Graves.   NOBL

...As they lean/into the rocks, away/from my grasping fingers.   Mussels.   Mary Oliver.   NU

As they left the cold Bine Waters.   King William and King James.   *Anonymous.*   BFSS

As they meet my new eyes for the first time.   Forever.   Raymond Carver.   GeTw

As they nibble the mound/That marks his sleep.   The Shepherd.   Mary Gilmore.   ACV; PoAu 1-2

As they pad through the village street/With a sound like heavy rain.   Jersey Cattle.   Ralph Nixon Currey.   OxBTC

As they sailed on, as they sailed on,/Over his unmoving mound.   Old Hundred.   Mark Van Doren.   UnS

As they sit in the sunshine, crying no rest for the wicked.   Prize for Good Conduct.   Kenneth Allott.   OBWP

As they surely will, say "No."   A Bestiary.   Kenneth Rexroth.   OBAL

As they to glory ride therein.   In Heaven Soaring Up.   Edward Taylor.   AH

As they toast the archangels in Bundaberg rum.   Bundaberg Rum.   W. N. Scott.   NOAV

As they watch fall the uninvited/And beautiful snow onto their bed.   Rondel.   Philip Dacey.   SM

As they were once designed/In Eden for us all.   Bears and Waterfalls.   May Sarton.   GP

As they wobble from stair to stair.   Goosey Goosey Gander.   William Percy French.   CenHV

As they would vanish for a dream.   Early Morn.   William Henry Davies.   CH

...As thick mists gathered upon the horizon/vanish at the rising of the sun.   The Book of the People.   Robert de Lamennais.   PGD

As this foul Gypsie Quean.   The Author's Mock-Song to Mark Anthony.   John Cleveland.   AnAnS 2

As this imprisoned engine, night and day,/Piles its dull pulses in the darkness there?   The Hydraulic Ram.   Charles Tennyson Turner.   NBM

As this in Kew thirst for the Red Dawn.   Note on Local Flora.   William Empson.   AtBAP; EBEV; FaBoMo; MoVE

As this mere fool, huddled, a shivering form/In last year's ragged things, and nothing more.   Insights.   Catherine Davis.   NePoEA

As this moment, had love but the warrant, love's heart to/dispense!   Saul.   Robert Browning.   BBV

As this pharmacy/turns our desire into medicines and revokes the rain.   Les Realites.   Barbara Guest.   AmPC

As this quaint Quint Essence/Of Time and Patience.   Extract the Quint-essence.   Francis Daniel Pastorius.   SCAP

As this red rose, which on our terrace here/Glows in the blue of fifty miles away.   The Roses on the Terrace.   Alfred, Lord Tennyson.   VLP

As this world is made I might/live forever.   Do Not Die.   William Stanley Merwin.   CAPP

As this your silvered body/brings/&/shares   Love Poem.   Linda Wagner.   FAZ

As tho' they brought but merchants' bales,/And not the burthen that they bring.   In Memoriam A.H.H., XIII.   Alfred, Lord Tennyson.   VLP

As tho tonight were only the beginning/of all those/yester-/days   The Move Continuing.   Al Young.   PoBA

...As those/who imagine the silence of a guest/to be mysterious, or wrong.   The Parachutist.   Jon Anderson.   NYBP

As those who part look long in the eyes they lean to,/Lest they forget them.   September Midnight.   Sara Teasdale.   PoA

As those who see the far-off shadow of a fire/Gaze earnestly, and wonder if their roof-trees burn.   The Shadow.   Arthur Symons.   OBVV

As thou art now.   Odes, IV.   Hafiz.   AWP

As thou didst for Elisabeth/in the yeare 88.   A Famous Sea-Fight.   John Looke.   CoMu

As Thou didst keep Thy folk of old.   In Thine Arms.   Oliver Wendell Holmes.   TRV

As thou hadst seal'd my pardon, with thy blood.   At the Round Earth's Imagin'd Corners, Blow.   John Donne.   BLPL; CBEP; EaLo; FaBoRV; LiTB; PoPle

As thou in service true shalt be/Unto our crown and royalty.   The Parliament of Bees.   John Day.   ViBoPo

As thou rose up on Estre Day,/In joy and blisse to live aye./Amen.   A Devout Prayer of the Passion.   *Anonymous.*   MeEL

As thou sittest at the feet of God victorious,/"Philip, the king!"   Philip, My King.   Dinah Maria Mulock Craik.   HBV 1-2

As thou telst her, and none but her, my paine.   To Mr. I. L.   John Donne.   SeCP

As though a bolting tree trunk/had kicked some memory ajar?   Tete-a-Tete.   Edwin Honig.   AmC; NoAm

As though a breeze had quickened/the sea and set it blooming.   A flower of waves.   Lady Ise.   BoWoP

As though a seraph's voice had stirred/The pulses of the grass.   The Defence of Lawrence.   Richard Realf.   PAH

As though Earth were/A wonderful place.   I Have Cared for You, Moon.   Grace Hazard Conkling.   HBMV

As though forever, his appointed pigeon. Pigeons. Alastair Reid. MP;
NePoEA; NYBP; NYP; TwCP

...As though he had grown/That way, as is said of certain hill creatures. The
Mountain. William Stanley Merwin. VGW

As though he had never been. Vouchsafe me this vision! An Exeter Riddle.
Gavin Ewart. OxBC

As though his subject had decided to remain a prayer. The Painter. John
Ashbery. HaCAP; NOBA; NoP; SOTW

As though I walked the wood with sagamore George. Here, where the Red
Man Swept the Leaves away. Frederick Goddard Tuckerman. NOBA;
TAP

As though I were not beside you, "Yes! Oh, yes!" Seance. William
Abrahams. NYBP

As though I were the foul toad, said/To bear a precious jewel in his head.
Suilven. Andrew Young. OxBS

As though in storm were peace. A Sail. Mikhail Yuryevich Lermontov.
AWP; LiTW; PoPl

...As though it had drifted in/from, say, the sea, a purity of space.
Metonymy as an Approach to a Real World. William Bronk. VGW

As though it soared suchwise through heaven too. Royal Palm. Hart
Crane. AP; CMoP; MoAB; MoAmPo; NoAm; NoP; TrGrPo

As though it were hanging in the sky. Because river-fog. Kiyowara
Fukuyabu. AWP; LiTW

As though life had never been found/To progress past the sod to the sun.
Even in the Darkness. Helene Mullins. MoRP

As though more than night or a hill/Had walled you in, back of its back. A
Water Glass of Whisky. X. J. Kennedy. CoPo

As though the dead had Finis on their brows. The Imaginative Life.
Geoffrey Hill. NoAm

As though the heavens were seized with an earthquake. Reflections on the
River. Andrew Young. ACV

As though the train could think/reflecting no, no, no. Volleyball Teacher
Ends the Game. Jose Y., Jr. Teran. LFAC

As though the waters of a spring/had come to touch her burning feet.
Nightfall. Fyodor Tyutchev. LiTW

As though upon the face of Night/Lay the bright wreck of day. The Dancer.
Walter James Turner. NOAV; VGW

As thought-stones stir our heart's "Farewell!" There Is a Nook Among the
Alders. Robert Lee Frost. AmePo

As through gray caves of coral by the sea. In a Museum Cabinet. May
Swenson. WSC

As through the scattering mists of day/Came a far locomotive's shout.
Miserere. Gaspar Nunez de Arce. CAW

As through the trellis peers the sudden Bridegroom. At the Indian Killer's
Grave. Robert Lowell. NOBA; VGW

As thus my inmost soul to pour/In prayer to Thee. The Hour of Prayer.
Charlotte Elliott. STF

As 'thwart ravines of azure shouts the mountaineer. Contemplation.
Francis Thompson. BrPo; LoBV

As time comes to an end for me. Faust. Johann Wolfgang von Goethe.
DL

As 'tis my firm resolve and last farewell. The Retreat. Henry, Bishop of
Chichester King. AnAnS 2

As to harden the unhard and unhard/the hardened. It's Here In The.
Russell Atkins. AmNP; PoBA

As to just how far/she went. The Poem as Striptease. Philip Dacey. PPJ

As to make the swelling downland,/Far surrounding, seem their own. Upper
Lambourne. Sir John Betjeman. FaBoTw

As to say any moment/Which was which? I Had to Be Secret. Mark Van
Doren. SO

As to sip fast that nectarous shower/A thirstier minstrel drew in me! The
Phoenix. George Darley. CBEP; OAEL 1-2; OBEV; OBVV

As to thy Crosse reverence we may have. An A.B.C. of Devotion.
Anonymous. MeEL

As to which should be frightened of whom. Limerick: "A skeleton once in
Khartoum." *Anonymous.* ShM

As tracks lead inward to the waiting trains. Railway Station. John Hay.
WaP

As Trade had suddenly encroached/Upon a Sacrament. A light exists in
spring. Emily Dickinson. BoWoP; ExPo; LiTA; NOBA; OxBA

As tree-born instrument's soft discipline/Releases all the pent-up harmony.
Wood Music. Ethel King. GoYe

As true as metal, as deftly as surgeon's wrist. The Passer. George Abbe.
LiSp; SD

As 'twas foretold,/In the days of old,/By Gabriel. Christmas Carol.
Thomas Helmore. OHIP

As 'twas the first, shall be the last to press/This wild and noble shore. A fond
farewell! De Roberval. John Hunter-Duvar. CaP

As two true clocks together go. Song: "Silly Boy, there is no cause."
Thomas Pestel. EiL

(As Umber swears) did make his lion start. Upon Umber: Epigram. Robert
Herrick. CaPo

As unanimous verdicts/Of drilling missed holes. Drilling Missed Holes.
Don Cameron. PoOW

As unremembered,/As bird shadows on the grass. Cups of Illusion. Henry
Bellamann. HBMV

As upright as ever. Walking in a Swamp. David Wagoner. HAP; NPAW

As Venus in her ascendency/Draws triangulations on reality. The New
Litany. Rita Mae Brown. PeHV

As waiting for the better day/We ever stand on guard. O Canada! Adolphe
Routhier. FSW

As, walking clouds, she keeps from harm/The whickering child and weeping
lamb. The Village Coddled in the Valley. George Barker. OBSP

As, wan and white, to the heart of the fight/rode the little old Fighting Joe!
Wheeler at Santiago. James Lindsay Gordon. PAH

As wandering and as lost as they! The Torn Hat. Nathaniel Parker Willis
AA

As warm our hands by putting out the fire. Paradox: That Fruition Destroys
Love (excerpt). Henry, Bishop of Chichester King. ErPo

As was my pleasure when she was present. O Miserable Sorrow, withouten
Cure. Sir Thomas Wyatt. SiPS

As was screamed by that Lady of Russia. Limerick: "There was a young
lady of Russia." Edward Lear. MoShBr

As waves which lately paved his watery way/Hiss round a drowner's head in
their tempestu-/ous play. Ode to Liberty. Percy Bysshe Shelley. MBW
1-2

As we add defiant sparks/to an eternal fire The Second Generation.
Menachem Z. Rosensaft. AMV-81

As we approach a new plateau of love. The Triumph of Death. Barbara
Howes. MoAmPo; NePoAm-2

As we are grounded. Folklore. Cyril Dabydeen. BrSi

As we babble about the sky and the weather and the/forests of change.
Mixed Feelings. John Ashbery. GP; HAP

As we begin our life. August Was Foggy. Gary Snyder. NNaP

As we both watch the storm and skies. The Cotton Cat. Mary Effie Lee
Newsome. GoSl

As we burn with the fire of our flight; ah love, shall we win at/the last?
Hesperia. Algernon Charles Swinburne. OBNC; OBVV

As we come face to face, and wonder/if she understands at all what I am
saying. New Day. Naomi Long Madgett. BlSi

As we drive the nails/In the wood. Busy Carpenters. James S. Tippett.
SoPo

As we gallop into the flame. A Last World. John Ashbery. PoM

...As we/glory in our skin God Send Easter. Lucille Clifton. CNA

As we go marching on! John Brown's Body. Charles Sprague Hall. ABF;
BLSo; FaFP; FSW; MC; ShS; TrAS

As we grow smaller because of the melting of our bones. The Place of Backs.
William Stanley Merwin. HoPM

As we left that house. The Grandmother Came down to Visit Us. Joseph
Bruchac. CDW

As we lolloped back along the beach. Grandmother Jackson. David
Jackson. OBCP

As we march'd march'd, march'd in the Mulligan Guard. The Mulligan
Guard. Ed [(or Ned)] Harrigan. BLSo

As we move/out on the glowing sea of the tropics on an ice pace, you, You.
Tom Clark. ANYP; EAS

As we move slowly round to greet the dawn. Nocturne: Lake Huron.
Conor Kelly. AMV-80

As we pass in silence towards freedom–/the freedom of choice. Self-Portrait.
Edgar Jackson. LFAC

...As we/plunge forward, blindly,/brushing aside blossoms. Dogwood
Blossoms. Peter Blue Cloud. STE

As we salt and freeze and pickle/for the too little to come. Attack of the
Squash People. Marge Piercy. NLV

As we sang in de ebening by de moonlight. In the Evening by the
Moonlight. James A. Bland. FSW; PSoN; TreFS

As we, so they that treate us thus,/Must one day perish like to us. O
Fearfull, Frowning Nemesis. Samuel Daniel. PoEL 1-5

As we stand gazing at the rounded moon. Evening without Angels.
Wallace Stevens. MoPo; VGW

As we the world must now begin,/We will deal in every following thing. The
Way to Live. *Anonymous.* VLP

As we wait here with our papers. Lie here quiet. Dark in the Reich of the
Blond. William Heyen. MAYP

As we walked in the slow dark/toward home. The Horse. Faye
Kicknosway. GeTw

As weary-hearted as that hollow moon. Adam's Curse. William Butler
Yeats. BIrV; CMoP; CoBMV; DiPo; NoAm; NoP; OAEL 1-2; VLP

As weeping Beauty's cheek at Sorrow's/tale! The Bride of Abydos. George
Gordon, Lord Byron. OAEP; OBRV

As welcome to my crumbling bones. To--. Alfred, Lord Tennyson.
OBRV

As well as another body? Why May Not I Love Johnny? *Anonymous.*
OxNR

...As well as arrogance, beauty. On the Tercentenary of Milton's Death. Gavin Ewart. OxBC

As well as eggs to make hens lay. Epigram. Samuel (1612-80) Butler. FaBoEE

"As well as if a manor of thy friend's..." Ruins of a Great House. Derek Walcott. TwCP

As well as mother's lullabies.' Long John. Padraic Fallon. NeIP

As what he loves may never like too much. On My First Son. Ben Jonson. AnAnS 2; AWP; CABA.; DiPo; EBEV; EIL; ExPo; FaBoEE; FaBoEn; FF; ForPo; HAP; HeIP; HoPM; InPo; InPS; JCP; LiTB; LoBV; NIP; NOBE; NoP; OAEL 1-2; OAEP; OBSP; PoEL 1-5; PPoe; QFR; SeCP; SeCV 1-2; TEP

As when a man doth walk upon the ice. On a Child Beginning to Talk. Thomas Bastard. CBEP

As when a queen, long dead, was young. Paracelsus. Robert Browning. AnFE; GTBS; MyFE; OBEV; OBRV; WHA

As when I fell a-sleeping./Hey nonny, nonny, etc. Beauty Bathing. Anthony Munday. NOBE; OBEV

As when it deeply sighs/O'er autumn's latest bloom. O Sleep, My Babe, Hear Not the Rippling Wave. Sara Coleridge. OBNC; OBRV

As when light-/browed, swimming,/he leads. A Pair. May Swenson. RFM

As when thy moonlights, dim and sweet,/Touch some gray ruin on the hill. From Sorrow Sorrow Yet Is Born. Alfred, Lord Tennyson. OBSP

As when upon the treacherous shoals of/sleep. Becalmed. John Banister Tabb. AA

As when we grope amid the gloom of night. The Clouded Morning. Jones Very. AP; NOBA

As when you came and swept me to your heart. Sonnets of a Portrait Painter. Arthur Davison Ficke. AnAmPo

As white locks of tall waterfalls. The Canoe. Isabella Valancy Crawford. ACV; OBCV; OnYI

As white their bark, so white this lady's hours. A Virginal. Ezra Pound. AP; APA; CMoP; CoBMV; MoAB; MoAmPo; NePA; NIP; NoAm; NOBA; OxBA; TAP

...As who knows better, pray,/Than I that helped you in rehearsing it? Retractions. James Branch Cabell. HBMV

As who should swat a fly/On Titian's Virgin's nose On the Road to Vicenza. Ralph Gustafson. CaP

As who was not, in laughter, pain, and love. Days of 1964. James Merrill. CoAP; HaCAP

As wicks of thread which now are lighted up/For ceremonials of Candlemas. February. John Heath-Stubbs. OBCP

As winds unravel vagrant bells). O City, Cities! (excerpt),. R. Ellsworth Larsson. AnAmPo

As with a rampant lion's hungry/claw/Grips at the lapiz-lazuli of heaven. Dusk. Abraham Lopez-Penha. TrJP

As with a robe a mother hides/Her son, so shroud this man, O earth. Funeral Hymn. *Anonymous.* LiTW

As, with a sigh, I deem thou might'st have/been to me. Childe Harold's Pilgrimage: Canto III. George Gordon, Lord Byron. CoBE; OAEP

As with the sun a fleecy cloud. Love in Action. Coventry Patmore. EG

...As woman delights to see man/After having made love. Postman Cheval. Andre Breton. EAS

As women wear their beauty in the night. Fields at Evening. David Morton. AnAmPo; HBMV

As ye look to ither women,/Sall I to ither men. False Luve! and Hae Ye Played Me This? *Anonymous.* BSV; GBP; PoL

As ye of clay were cast by kind,/So shall ye waste to dust. The Image of Death. Thomas, Lord Vaux. GoTL; OBSC

As ye perceive by me doth fall,/And yours to love as lovingly. Love Continual. John Heywood. CBEP

As ye said, it shall be sae... The Earl of Mar's Daughter. *Anonymous* CH

As ye wend to pluck out the new world from the/fire. Love Is Enough. William Morris. PoEL 1-5

As yet unfelt among/Magnolia trees. Birmingham Sunday. Langston Hughes. PoNe

As you and I walked slowly to the station. Bluebells for Love. Patrick Kavanagh. FaBoIP; IPY

As you are come: go back and come agen. The Humble Springs of Stately Sandwich Beach. Samuel Sewall. SCAP

...As you bear/this world's dead weight and cycle on your back. Night Sweat. Robert Lowell. TAP; VGW

...As you came you may go,/Stumpaty, stumpaty, stump. Roger and Dolly. *Anonymous.* OxNR

As you cross yourself/and reach for your scalping knife. For Jean Vincent d'Abbadie, Baron St.-Castin. Alden Nowlan. NOBC

As you glow thanks. Stacking Up. Rita Rosenfeld. AMV-81

As you have perhaps, people at last attain/And find that they are rich and breathing gold. Train to Dublin. Louis MacNeice. FaBoIP

As you have visited me i will/cause you to/hunger. Hunger for Me. Alta. GP

As you may be sorry about a chance you lost/or a way or a coin or a limb you lost. Now Look What Happened. Molly Peacock. MAYP

As you no doubt delight the eye/Of other hippopotami. The Hippopotamus. Ogden Nash. FaBV; OnUR

As you paddle to destruction at the point of Lehua,/Ualapue, Kaluaaha, Molokai. The Ocean Is Like a Wreath. Kuapakaa. WTO

As you put out your hand, all night/held the small flowers. For Maria. Cleopatra Mathis. MAYP

As you saw the love in mine--as you do now, say you do! Maternity Gown. David Holbrook. OxBTC

As you shall see--three pyebalds and a roan. Walking to the Mail. Alfred, Lord Tennyson. VLP

As you were and as/you too will be When Your Parents Grow Old. Joanne Hart. AMV-80

As you with other maidens rove,/I'll smile on other men. False Love. Sir Walter Scott. ViBoPo

As you within the waters, my illimitable soul! Narcissus. Paul Valery. AWP

As you work, and sleep, and talk, and laugh, and die. Resurrection. Kenneth Fearing. CMoP

As your dear lad, and my dear lad, go on their way to France. Your Lad, and My Lad. Randall Parrish. MC; PAH

As your fate is to die, our fate is to be born. From Generation to Generation. William Dean Howells. AA

As your hand places the jar of blue crystals/By the waiting bath. The Ring. Harry Mathews. ANYP

As your inner, golden ray. God Be With You. *Anonymous.* PoToHe

As your petals open wet/to cradle my fingers. Lesbian. Paula Jennings. PeHV

Ascension and Assumption both in one! The Ascension and the Assumption. Ramon Lopez Velarde. HW

The ash grove, the ash grove alone is my home. The Ash Grove. *Anonymous.* FSW

Ash swirls like snowflakes on the passers-by. Isolation Ward. Robert L. Koenig. AMV-81

Ash trays and ashes, ashen Sybarite. After Mardi Gras. Sister Mary Honora. NePoAm-2

The ash tree stands in the stars. Invitation to a Sabbath. Harry Mathews. ANYP

Ashamed and angry to be undeceived! The Dream. Aphra Behn. PBWP

Ashby is dead! Dirge for Ashby. Margaret Junkin Preston. PAH

Ashen and wailing scattering veils and pins? White Queen. John Fuller. NePoEA-2

The ashes are cold and the image/is image no longer. House Is an Enigma. Laura Jensen. LCAP

Ashes, ashes, all fall down. Children's Lenten Wisdom. James A. Houck. AMV-80

...Ashes that wouldn't stay in/the grate but floated/out all over the room! A Letter to Hitler. James Laughlin. WaP

The ashes you leave behind are/your name. The Meeting. Gerald Constanzo. MAYP

The ashleaves froze without an ashleaf sound. Sonnet: "I saw magic ⌐ı a green country road." Michael Hartnett. BIrV

...Asia/on the one side, Afric on the other. This Narrow Stage. Theodore Weiss. NoAm

Ask Art Tatum,/He watches me. All That Jazz. Yasmeen Jamal. LFAC

Ask her what she means,/Dropping the curtain so soon! Nun Snow. Alfred Kreymborg. AnFE; APA; CoAnAm; MAPA

Ask me how it feels to be both/Exposed and doubly denied. To Be Black, To Be Lost. Hannah Kahn. GoYe

Ask me no more. Ask Me No More. Alfred, Lord Tennyson. HBV 1-2; LiTB; TreFT

Ask me nothing you can guess. A Young Man's Song. William Bell. FaBoTw; NePoEA

Ask the man struck dead by the life raft somewhere aft. Convoy. William Jay Smith. WaP

Ask that from the ashes of this fire/With new lives still to such new flames aspire. Caelica, CVIII. Fulke, Lord Brooke Greville. FCP

...Ask/This rich room how you dropped the mask! Appearances. Robert Browning. CBEP; OBSP

Ask who they were, and thou hast done. Certain True Woords Spoken Concerning One Benet Corbett. Elizabeth T. Corbett. AnAnS 2; SeCP

Ask yourself whether you've as much at stake. Epigram: "The arctic raven tracks the caribou." Raymond Wilson. PV

Asked how the warriors survived their wounds,/Or which of the young men... The Battle of Finnsburg. *Anonymous.* AnOE

Asked me for a kiss. Suicide's Note. Langston Hughes. CDC; DFF

Asked nothing else, if she had you. Miss Loo. Walter De la Mare. CMoP; HBV 1-2; OxBTC

Asking again: Where did that blood come from? Ossawatomie. Carl Sandburg. OxBA

Asking, as I do, to be loved?　Don't Sit under the Apple Tree with Anyone Else but Me!　Robert Pack.　CoPo; FF

Asking for lives filled with sweetness,/Gratitude, gladness and praise.　Just to Be Glad.　Merlin G. Miller.　STF

Asking me for my body to inhabit again.　Ancestry.　Louis Daniel Brodsky.　AMV-81

Asking something more of me,/Yet more of me.　End of Another Home Holiday.　D. H. Lawrence.　DTC; EBEV; FaBoMo; MoVE

...Asking us to travel/to the storm's blind, silent eye.　The New House.　Vern Rutsala.　GOYP

Asking "What does anyone have that we/don"t?" eating March 21st lentil soup.　Le Tombeau de Frank O'Hara.　Art Lange.　APU

Asking: "Where is the treasure?" till he died.　Troy.　Edwin Muir.　CMoP

Asking who she belonged to,/the other answering, "Whom?"　Patches of Sky.　Debora Greger.　MAYP

Asking why we should expect to translate/the hunger of poetry.　Letter to Tina Koyama from Elliot Bay Park.　Jim Mitsui.　BrSi

Asleep and sleeping with them, sleeping with women.　Sleeping with Women.　Kenneth Koch.　ANYP; NoAm; PoM

Asleep,/Asleeep,/Asleeeep....　Sweet Dreams.　Ogden Nash.　OnUR

Asleep, beautiful, the cobwebs round her.　The Sleeping Beauty.　E. L. Mayo.　DFT

Asleep before the sea.　The Black Horse Rider.　Pierre Loving.　EAS

...Asleep, I/Am a horizon.　The Thin Man.　Donald Justice.　SM

Asleep in bed?　Sing a Song of Moonlight.　Ivy O. Eastwick.　SiSoSe

Asleep in the arms of the slow-swinging seas.　Seal Lullaby.　Rudyard Kipling.　SoSe; TiPo

Asleep, not dead; a good man never dies.　Saon of Acanthus.　Callimachus.　AWP; TRV

Asleep or waking, you must ease my pain.　The Zambra Dance.　John Dryden.　CEP; SeCV 1-2

Asleep, this stupid boy is beautiful.　Nocturnal Visitor.　Carolyn Miller.　AMV-80

Asleep we are siblings. Our mother's name is Night.　To My Wife Asleep.　Edward Tick.　AMV-80

AsMERRYCHR/YSANTHEMUM　The Computer's First Christmas Card.　Edwin Morgan.　FaBoCo; NIP; PCh

An aspen, quivering there beside the burn,/And perfect peace.　A Picture.　D. C. Cuthbertson.　PoSH

Asphalt memory of blood and pain.　Harlem Gallery: From the Inside.　Larry Neal.　BPo

An aspiration fixed, a sigh made stone.　The Taj.　H. G. Keene.　OBTV

An ass like a valentine, etc.　Mare Nostrum.　Joel Oppenheimer.　NeAP

Assail him. constantly. what shall he do.　The Bus Trip.　Joel Oppenheimer.　NeAP

Assembling the self I must wake to,/Sleeping to grow back my legs.　A Dog Sleeping on My Feet.　James Dickey.　PP

Assents by eternally voting "I".　The Devil's Dictionary: Egotist.　Ambrose Bierce.　OBAL

Asserted our one night's identity.　Trilogy for X (excerpt).　Louis MacNeice.　CIP; ErPo; GBL

Asseverations that tame/The great negations with his name.　Verses for the 60th Birthday of T. S. Eliot.　George Barker.　ChMP

Assisi grew into the light, as flowers and children grow.　Assisi.　Alfred Noyes.　GoBC

Assisi lifts her towers to heaven again.　A Street Melody.　Belle Cooper.　GoBC

Assist me to resign.　Winter.　Robert Burns.　FiCP

Associate me to resign.　Mourning Letter, March 29 1963.　Edward Dorn.　ConAP

Associate, worthy of the illustrious dead,/Enjoys with them "the Liberty it loved."　Mute Is Thy Wild Harp, Now, O Bard Sublime!　Charlotte Smith.　SBG

Assume in nature's glass, in nature's eyes.　Seen in a Glass.　Kathleen Raine.　ChMP

Assumes their guilt, honours, repents, prays for them.　On the Pilots Who Destroyed Germany in the Spring of 1945.　Stephen Spender.　NeBP

Assure thy self of Welcome Love,/For Old-long-syne.　Old-Long-Syne.　Anonymous.　OBS

Assured, if I my trust betray,/I shall forever die.　A Charge to Keep I Have.　Charles Wesley.　HBV 1-2

Assured of sweet pardon and peace,/And wholly conformed to thee.　How Sweet Is the Language of Love.　Oliver Holden.　AH

Assured that He no load too great/Will make thee bear.　The Kneeling Camel.　Anna Temple Whitney.　BLPA

Assured that He will grant my quest/Or send some answer far more blessed.　Prayer.　Anonymous.　STF

The asterisk, printed panic, vanishes.　Cat.　Joe Rosenblatt.　NOBC

Astonished/at the implications of the stone.　Easter Flood.　Brenda S. Stockwell.　AMV-81

Astonished insects in worlds of feathers　I come to you with the vertigoes of the source.　Yvonne Caroutch.　BoWoP

The astonished Muse finds thousands at her side.　Ode Inscribed to W.H. Channing.　Ralph Waldo Emerson.　MAmP; NOBA; OxBA; TAP; ViBoPo

Astonishment, its endlessness.　During December's Death.　Delmore Schwartz.　NYBP

Astonishment of sky, and I, I think of you, I think that you know why.　Dead of Winter.　Anthony Towne.　NYBP

Astray from the perfect scene.　Muse, June, Related.　Brian Coffey.　BIrV

Astride his crippled mastiff's back was borne/Slowly away into the utmost dark.　An Elegy.　David Gascoyne.　FaBoTw; TwCP

At a dead man's door.　Scintilla.　William Stanley Braithwaite.　BANP; CDC

At a distance follows.　Skimmers.　Ted Walker.　NYBP

At a small secluded doorway/In the ordinary brain.　Galileo Galilei.　William Jay Smith.　PoCh

At a solemn farewell meeting.　Meeting.　William Saphier.　AnAmPo

At a white/beach (in Alabama)/Nude.　Once.　Alice Walker.　NMM; PoBA

At a white unbroken bed.　Wedding.　George Mackay Brown.　BSV

At all events it's very old.　Teatime Variations.　Peter Titheradge.　FaBoPa

At all that he is: the heart of heartlessness.　The Snow-Leopard.　Randall Jarrell.　LiTM; MoPo; MP; TwCP

At all the thoughts that in us spring/From this late-flowering lust.　Late-Flowering Lust.　Sir John Betjeman.　CMoP; ErPo; NMP; TW

At any rate shall never labour/More than thyself to love thy neighbour.　The Latest Decalogue.　Arthur Hugh Clough.　BiP; DBV; GTBS-P; HAP; NOBE; OAEL 1-2; OAEP; OBNC; OBSV; TRV; ViBoPo; VLP

At Beltane ilka body bown'd/To Peblis to the play.　Peblis to the Play.　Anonymous.　GoTS

At bequest of usura.　Canto XLV.　Ezra Pound.　CMoP; LiTM; MoPo; NePA; NOBA; TW

At chess-craft they excel the Gael.　The Fairy Host.　Anonymous.　AnIV

At Chrystis kirk on the grene.　Christ's Kirk on the Green.　King of Scotland James V,　OxBS

At compassion some logic stops!　Editorial Poem on an Incident of Effects Far-Reaching.　Russell Atkins.　NBP

At cry of thine, how proudly would they dare!'　Mother England.　Edith Matilda Thomas.　AA; HBV 1-2

At dawn I pluck, and dayward pipe my flock of dreams.　To Sleep.　Percy MacKaye.　HBMV

At dawn men ride away leaving the womenfolk/To fend for the bony goats and the crying children.　The Village.　Marina Gashe.　PBA

At dawn, Selina found him there/Strangled by a golden hair.　The Yellow Witch of Caribou.　Clyde Robertson.　BPAW; PoOW

At dawn the sun will bring good cheer to me.　The Dawn.　Anonymous.　PoToHe

At dawn there are no ripe mangoes/for miles.　Native African Revolutionaries.　Paul Jones.　AMV-80

At daybreak I chose a longer, dustier way home.　Indian Summer: Montana, 1956.　W. M. Ransom.　CDW

At daybreak saw him solitary;/And yet again at even.　Muse-Haunted.　Hugh McCrae.　PoAu 1-2

At dusk they'll dance with desperation/On muirs and hills.　To a Midge.　Eilidh Nisbet.　PoSH

At dusk waddles home with his brothers and sisters,/And says, Quack! Quack! Quack!　Walter De la Mare.　TiPo

At earth, not fire, and it would say, "This will not do."　If It Offend Thee...　Horace Gregory.　NMP

At ease, simple/as breathing.　Insomnia.　Marge Piercy.　DFF

At every turning beckoned veiled intruders/Into a midnight wood.　Mountain Convent.　Laura Benet.　GoYe

At Famine's Feast, ye ken, man.　Drone v. Worker.　Ebenezer Elliott.　FaBoPV; NBM; OBSV

At Ferns Castle yesterday I looked upon the sky!　At Ferns Castle.　Padraic Colum.　NePoAm

At first the bloody game begun.　Man the Enemy of Man.　Sir Walter Scott.　WBLP

...At first, too rich; at last, too pauvre.　Epitaph for Peter Stuyvesant, Late General of New Netherland.　Henricus Selyns.　SCAP

At freedom's call, teach manly breasts to glow,/And prompt the tender tear o'er guiltless woe.　Prospect of the Future Glory of America.　John Trumbull.　AmPP

At girls who wear glasses.　News Item.　Dorothy Parker.　FaBoUs; InMe; NLV; OBAL; TreF; YaD

At God's green caravanserai.　Camper's Night Song.　Robert Louis Stevenson.　BBV

At gulls wheeling above the Tyne, or the ship passing.　H.M.S. Hero.　Michael Roberts.　OxBTC

At hame it's hard to feel.　Parley of Beasts.　Hugh" (Christopher Murray Grieve) MacDiarmid.　BoAnP; MoBrPo; NoAm; NoP; OBMV

At Hastings, by the Bloody Lake.　Cloud and Flame.　John Berryman.　AP

At having loved one who dies–is shin-/ing.   La Bagarede.   Galway Kinnell.   NYBP

At her breast it grubs, twitching all its claws.   Halflives.   Daniel Gerard Hoffman.   SOTS

At her last maquero's/Adulteries.   Hugh Selwyn Mauberley, VI: Yeux Glauques.   Ezra Pound.   NOBA

At her lips, my nectar drinking.   O Dear Life, When Shall It Be?   Sir Philip Sidney.   EnRePo

At her pathetic signnal/the aristocracy of leaves/will begin to let go.   On Lake Pend Oreille.   Richard Shelton.   NYBP

At her sides there are long wings, folded.   Moon Is to Blood.   Richard Duerden.   NeAP

At her smile, the feast begins.   The Dream Feast.   Anita Endrezze-Probst.   VoR

At her sweet face/And my new clothes.   There'd Be an Orchestra.   F. Scott Fitzgerald.   ELU; GoJo

At his heels a stone.   Hamlet.   William Shakespeare.   LO

At his momentary song.   A Man Walking and Singing.   Wendell Berry.   AP

At his yearning desire and agony.   The Old Ghost.   Thomas Lovell Beddoes.   WiR

At home alone.   Home, Sweet Home.   Henry Cuyler Bunner.   CenHV; InMe

...At home/Ann sat beside the fire/unable to eat her dinner.   Claremont.   Robert Peters.   GP

At home, on land, on sea.   Sunday up the River.   James (1834-82) Thomson.   GTBS

At home where they are waiting. Come, come home.   Home.   Anonymous.   WTO

At home with Nature, and at one with God!   The Angelus.   Florence Earle Coates.   HBV 1-2

At just the wrong time to be heard,/Others, others.   The Common Grave.   James Dickey.   CoAP

At last, at last Earth listens:/Peace! Good will!   Earth Listens.   Katharine Lee Bates.   PGD

At last, at last, unite them there.   Qua Cursum Ventus.   Arthur Hugh Clough.   EnLi 1-2; EnLit; EtS; HBV 1-2; MOS; OAEP; OBEV; OBVV; TreFT; VLP

At last, cuck, cuck, cuck–six cucks to one coo.   Of Use.   John Heywood.   FaBoEE; PBBP

At last, far from Oriskany   The Ballad of Oriskany.   O. C. Auringer.   AA

At last, he goes to her without a word.   Elegy for a Nature Poet.   Howard Nemerov.   BoNaP; HoPM; PP

At last her fears are justified.   The Jealous Wife.   Vernon Scannell.   ErPo

At last I have the night flowers/to tend and the morning hills/to haul into sleep.   Minimum Security.   James Lewisohn.   LFAC

...At last into his cave/This Lion cowering crept, lay down, and died.   The Lion and the Wave.   William Allingham.   FM

At last into the flames he flew/And bad the world adieu.   Edom o' Gordon.   Anonymous.   OxBB

At last,/into the fog, I/hurled a lamp.   Fog 9/76.   Richard Morris Dey.   AMV-80

At last, it is I, it is I!   Eleonora Duse as Magda.   Laurence Binyon.   SyP

At last it ringeth to evensong.   Evensong.   George Tankervil.   TRV

At last, kooke, kooke, kooke; six kookes to one koo.   The Koocoo.   Anonymous.   GBP

At last my heart found voice,–"Take me, O Lord,/And do with me according to thy word."   Communion.   Edward Dowden.   TrPWD

At last, said brave Wolfe,/I die with pleasure.   Brave Wolfe.   Anonymous.   BaBo

At last,/she cried out,/and locked the door.   Gods.   Anne Sexton.   CAPP

At last the belles ringeth to evensong.   The Pastime of Pleasure.   Stephen Hawes.   MyFE

At last, there, when it turns out to be here.   Crude Foyer.   Wallace Stevens.   LiTM; NePA

At last to stand beside you and be dumb.   The Upper Lake.   Francis Stuart.   NeIP

At least, for the little man/Who stood against the mountains.   Ancestry.   Stephen Crane.   AA

At least I broke and stole that branch with love.   For C.   Philip Whalen.   NeAP; VGW

At least I have no doubt.   The Baker's Boy.   Mary Effie Lee Newsome.   CDC; GoSl

At least one dancer and one crimson flower.   She Plans Her Funeral.   Louise Morey Bowman.   CaP

At least to foresee that glory of Giotto/And Florence together, the first am I!   Old Pictures in Florence.   Robert Browning.   VLP

At least, treat me like them!   A Letter to Her Mother.   Eristi-Aya.   BoWoP

At least until the hostess has undressed.   Don't Say You Like Tchaikowsky.   Paul Rosner.   FiBHP

At length I feare thy perjur'd breath/Will blow out day, and waken death.   The Vow-Breaker.   Henry, Bishop of Chichester King.   OBS

At length the sucking jewels freeze.   The Octopus.   James Merrill.   CoAP; GP

...At long last,/even their slack jaws quiver.   Spiders.   Diane Ackerman.   MAYP

At lunchtime, they take it out,/the tongue-shaped wooden box;/today is beautiful.   History of France.   Kenward Elmslie.   ANYP

At me and you./Kuchi!/Kuchoo!   The Bubbul.   Sir Owen Seaman.   NA

At midnight blooms the flower of sin.   Flowers.   Anonymous.   WTO

At midnight no remedy for this but strong spirits/and in the cure the flaming penance.   The Grief of Our Genitals.   Henry Carlile.   GP

At midnight on the banks of Jumna/give me your vision.   Keep Me As Your Servant, O Girdhar.   Mira Bai [(or Mirabai)].   PBWP

At midnight the fig burst into flower.   Sleeper Rise.   Anonymous.   WTO

At Mo Ling's house, of endless angels,/by a horn point I shall die.   Though My Wanderings Are Many.   Suibne Geilt.   NOBI

At morning by the sea.   The Choristers.   Bliss Carman.   ACV

At Mullion in the silly time,/Is good enough for me.   Mullion.   Sir Alan Patrick Herbert.   SD

At my touch the wild/braid of creation trembles.   The Snakes of September.   Stanley Jasspon Kunitz.   AMV-81

...At night/clouds form in front of the pale moon.   The Legacy.   Judith Minty.   GeTw

At night he comes home and f–ks me.   My Husband.   Anonymous.   CoMu

At night I come back/in my mother's shoes/bedecked with the patient dust of years.   My Mother's Shoes.   Rayzel Zychlinska.   VWA

At night/I don't need/to put out the light.   Anthology Poem.   Petra von Morstein.   BoWoP

...At night/it wakes women up for miles.   The Divorce Dress.   Jeanne Finley.   AMV-80

At night the birds and insects will hide/in you.   A Letter from a Friend.   Carolyn Maisel.   IHMS

At night the old men sleep in houses that/Will always have geraniums in the windows.   Old Men on the Blue.   Thomas Hornsby Ferril.   PoOW

At night they begged for garbage/the soldiers cast away.   Portrait Philippines.   Alfred A. Duckett.   PoNe

At night when everyone's sleeping/she hears the silence of the world.   Dinosaur Tracks in Beit Zayit.   Shirley Kaufman.   FiCP

At night will sleep and keep by me.   First Cycle of Love Poems.   George Barker.   ErPo; MoPo

At once both stink and shine.   On the Countess of Dorchester.   Charles, Earl of Dorset Sackville.   APAS; CavP

At once we think you Milton, Death, and Sin.   Epigram on Voltaire.   Edward Hilton Young.   FaBoCo

At one with an astonished soldier.   The Adoration of the Magi.   Christopher Pilling.   OBCP

At others you'd better not laugh.   Limerick: "Said the elephant to the giraffe."   Charlotte Osgood Carter.   TDH

At othre fieres thy self to warme/And let theim warme with the.   A Robyn Joly Robyn.   Sir Thomas Wyatt.   AAS

At peace with beauty and needing no song at all.   November Afternoons.   Sister Mary Madeleva.   GoBC

At rats & swallows burrowed warm/in antique porticos.   Slides.   Jennifer Maiden.   CBAP

At rest in all the best that love could give!   Tennyson.   Florence Earle Coates.   AA

At rest in the blast.   At Rest in the Blast.   Marianne Moore.   MoAB; MoAmPo

At rest in the dark and silent lake.   The Snow-Shower.   William Cullen Bryant.   AnNE; HBV 1-2

At rest on its threads I am learning to fly.   Questions My Son Asked Me, Answers I Never Gave Him.   Nancy Willard.   LCAP

At see-saw across the gate.   Jack and Jill.   Anonymous.   OxNR

At seven o'clock from the houses, is roughly a distance/Of about one year and a half.   Lessons of the War.   Henry Reed.   GTBS-P; NIP

At 76, turned ghost?   Almanac.   May Swenson.   NYBP

At six o'clock some Christmas morning.   Oh Come, Little Children.   Phyllis McGinley.   FaBV

At so grotesque a blunder.   Clerihew.   Edmund Clerihew Bentley.   FiBHP; NOBL; PV

At stroke of midnight God shall win.   The Four Ages of Man.   William Butler Yeats.   MoRP; TrCP

...At such times/death isn't far from me.   He Is More Than a Hero.   Sappho.   PBWP

At Sumner on a Sunday.   For a Child.   Denis Glover.   AnNZ

At sunrise/we can look across the wasted sea for miles.   Presentation Piece.   Marilyn Hacker.   AmPA

At th' Calends, puts all out again.   Epodes.   Horace.   OBVE

At that bed's head there grows a thorn,/Which was never so blossomed since Christ was born.   Corpus Christi (B vers.).   Anonymous.   BaBo; GBP

At that cold moralist I hotly hurled/His perfect, pure, symmetrical, small world. Gift to a Jade. Anna Wickham. DBV; ELU; OBSP

At that same small, fierce-flickering fire. Prophecy in Flame. Frances Minturn Howard. AmFN

At that the pig got up and walked away! 'Twas an evening in November. *Anonymous.* CenHV

At that very instant, Siva was there with me. With My Breath I Cut My Way through the Six Forests. Lalleswari. WPOW

At the base of the cliff. The Wind of the Cliff Ka Hea. Phyllis Thompson. FAZ

At the blaring jazz/Of a morning sun. Four Glimpses of Night. Frank Marshall Davis. AmNP; NoP; PoBA; PoNe

At the bottom of every soul a spoonful of sleep. A Water-Colour of Venice. Lawrence Durrell. MoBrPo

At the center of the center where the shadows throng? Home Revisited: Midnight. John Ciardi. NYBP

At the crossroads paved/with bones. Lament. Yonathan Ratosh. VWA

At the edge of the pool with the guys No Empty Hands. Michael Brownstein. ANYP

At the end of our streets—the stars. The City by the Sea. George Sterling. BPAW

At the end of the field you are rushing by,/Is waiting for his Old Dutch? The Fat White Woman Speaks (parody). Gilbert Keith Chesterton. SpRo

At the end of your willful string. To the Carp, and Those Who Hunt Her. James Hazard. AMV-80

At the end, those are all saying things about making gardens. 13th Dance–Matching Parcels–21 February 1964. Jackson MacLow. CoPo

At the foot of the bed, and do nothing. The Morning After. Heinrich Heine. ErPo; UnTE

At the gate at the end of things. The Gate at the End of Things. *Anonymous.* BLPA

At the great conflagration there. Too Bright a Day. Norman MacCaig. GTBS-P

At the great supper of the Lamb. Accept Our Tribute. Isaac Watts. BePJ

At the head of a march to the last new Jerusalem. A Fable for Critics. James Russell Lowell. AA; AP; NOBA; OxBA; TAP

At the last silence cries for the unknown day. Time of Day. Selden Rodman. PoA

At the last, your hand feels steady. After Dark. Adrienne Rich. LCAP; LiTM; VGW

At the man who broke the bank at Monte Carlo. The Man Who Broke the Bank at Monte Carlo. Fred Gilbert. FSN; FSW; TreF

& At the music & the men, wishing it would never end Dear Old Stockholm. Al Young. NPGG

At the noise of the lambs at play and the dear wild cry of the birds. Tewkesbury Road. John Masefield. GoTF; MCCG; TreFT

At the north gate I watch for you/loosing your sleeves. Letter: The Japanese, to Her Husband at War. William Walsh. PoPl

At the old forsaken bough/Where I cling. The Last Leaf. Oliver Wendell Holmes. AA; AnNE; AP; APA; FaBoBe; GoTF; HBV 1-2; MCCG; OBVV; PoLf; SeCeV; TreF; WBLP

At the peak of the holiday rush. Limerick: "Annoying Miss Tillie McLush." Joseph S. Newman. TDH

At the pleasant time of morning/When the shepherd goes to fold. Break of Day. John Clare. CBEP

At the radiant close of labor/May our souls find rest in Thee. Come, O Lord, Like Morning Sunlight. Milton S. Littlefield. TrPWD

At the rim/of each bruised and heart-/shaped petal. The Wild Dog Rose. John Montague. BIrV; CIP; IPY

At the screen/welcoming each beast/in love's name, Your emissary. The Gift. Louise Gluck. FaBoWP; GP

At the setting of the sun. The Sin of Omission. Margaret E. Sangster. BLPA; GoTF; HBV 1-2; PoToHe; TreFS; TRV

At the shrine of the Poetry Contest in Kansas. Song Tournament: New Style. Louis Untermeyer. CrMA; OBAL

At the siege of Belle Isle. At Belle Isle. *Anonymous.* OxNR

At the sight of the beauty that greets them, for the charm they have broken. London Snow. Robert Bridges. AnFE; BoNaP; BrPo; CMoP; CoBMV; EBEV; FaBoPP; GTBS-P; LiTB; LiTM; LoBV; MoAB; MoBrPo; NBM; NoAm; NOBE; NOBV; OAEL 1-2; OBNC; OxBTC; PoEL 1-5; SeCePo; SeCeV; TrGrPo; VLP; WiR

At the sorrow of my sweet pipings. Hymn of Pan. Percy Bysshe Shelley. AtBAP; ERoP 1-2; ExPo; FaBoCh; HBV 1-2; LoGBV; MyFE; OAEP; OBEV; OBRV; PoEL 1-5; SeCeV

At the Spring o' the year. Gone Were but the Winter Cold. Allan Cunningham. CH

At the still point of the turning world. Four Quartets. Thomas Stearns Eliot. AtBAP

At the stranger who leans over their gate/Making uncouth noises. Wonder. Bernard Raymund. GDP

At the thought of touching your knees. Chloride of Lime and Charcoal. Louis Zukofsky. CoPo

At the time it seems/like a good idea. Ambitious. Jim Gustafson. APU

At the time the last clod falls to the earth/And shuddering, all things are fled. Then I'll Believe. B. W. Vilakazi. PeSA

At the turn of the palace stair. We Have Seen Her. Hilda ("H. D.") Doolittle. VGW

...At the two I stand amazed. Modern Love, XXXVI. George Meredith. NOBV; VLP

At the very next word out of you! Baby Toodles. Joseph S. Newman. BBGG

At the very tip her arched tongue/his name Ben. Amanda, Playing. C. W. Truesdale. PoDr

...At the window Daddy was screamin/bout some man and Mamma was cryin. The Killing of the Birds. Shirley Williams. BoWoP

At the woodsman's shanty there's nothing goes wrong. The Lumberman's Alphabet. *Anonymous.* AmFP

At their meeting-times here, just as these! After the Fair. Thomas Hardy. CMoP; HAP; VLP

At this hour I am always happy,/ready to be taken myself,/fully aware. Awakening. Lucien Stryk. SV

...At this last/Word I die in. This last. Letter II. W. S. Graham. NePoEA

At this lopsided crystal sweet moment... Breakthrough. Carolyn M. Rodgers. BPo

...At this moment/the poem will be happy forever. The Poem Becomes Canadian. Pier Giorgio Di Cicco. CaPN

At this the shadow wept, melting away. Concordance. Paul Violi. AMV-81

At this time whites came on the Eastern sea. Walam Olum; or, Red Score (excerpt). *Anonymous.* OBVE

At thoughts of what e'en mules may dare/In this great country of light air! Old Balaam. *Anonymous.* PoOW

At thy heart's door I stand and beat,/Though we are parted. When We Are Parted. Hamilton Aïdé. HBV 1-2

At thy right hand voluptuous, as beseems/Thy daughter and thy darling, without end.' Paradise Lost. John Milton. OAEL 1-2

At times it seems not common to explain. Of Commerce and Society. Geoffrey Hill. PPoe

At times they whisper, touch me. Song for Seven Parts of the Body, 5. Maxine W. Kumin. PoL

At turn of the tide, with wind blowing us salty weather. The Oyster-Eaters. John Blight. NOAV

At TV in Apt. 15b, East 187. One No. 7. John Frederick Frank. GoYe

At twelve bell answers bell,/as Mary to Gabriel. Angelus-Time near Dublin. W. B. Stanford. NeIP

At 12:00 he mounts, with measured tread,/The penitential stairs to bed. Mr. Eliot's Day. Robert Francis. NYBP

At twenty-one, I was elected Zeus. Youth's Progress. John Updike. FiBHP

At Tyburn half an hour's/hanging endeth all. Tybrun and Westminster. John Heywood. ACP

At us let angels hiss/From heaven that fell! The Kidnapping of Sims. John Pierpont. PAH

At what obscure in light/is now explained by shade? August Night. May Swenson. MoLP

At what time would the sun/melting tilt her into the stream? She Waited. Tania Van Zyl. PeSA

At which I cannot write since I am not lefthanded. Reflections. Louis MacNeice. FaBoIP

At which point everyone fled. Limerick: "A greedy small lassie once said." *Anonymous.* TDH

At which some needy sage/Taps out his needed fable/Across a trackless page. Another Easter. John Ridland. SM

At which the pig got up and slowly walked away. The Company One Keeps. Aimor R. Dickson. GoTF; TreFT

At whom Poseidon smoldered on/until the kingly man came home to his own shore. The Odyssey. Homer. NAWM 1-2

...At whose disposing will/The power, and rule of speaking resteth still. Ars Poetica. Horace. OBVE

At whose dumbe urn/Thus all the year I mourn. Silex Scintillans. Henry Vaughan. AnAnS 1

At yon gate theer'll be a hell of a row! Rake. Dorothy Una Ratcliffe. BoAnP; GDP

...At your/feet the fire you forgot you ever lit is out. Wolf Hunting near Nashoba. Jim Barnes. STE

Atahualpa,/Imperator Inca–/Slain. Imperator Victus. Hart Crane. OxBA

Ate her lovely ermine collar. Wihelmina Mergenthaler. Harry P. Taber. BBGG

Ate him all up O. The Frog and the Crow. *Anonymous.* GBP

Ate straight through Hickenthrift. Hickenthrift and Hickenloop. X. J. Kennedy. WSC

Ate the pudding/And left the bag. Charlie Wag. *Anonymous.* OxNR

Athena toward illustrious Lakedaimon/far over sea, to join Odysseus" son. The Odyssey. Homer. NAWM 1-2

Athens, and all the opening year on fire. A Spring Wind. Bernard Spencer. GTBS-P

...;Athens doth inherit/His corpse below. Spirit of Plato. *Anonymous.* AWP; EnLi 1-2; OBVE

Atishoo! Atishoo! Clerihew. Edmund Clerihew Bentley. PV

Atlas bare heaven, such burdens be of grace;/Caelica, in heaven, is the angel's place. Caelica, XLVII. Fulke, Lord Brooke Greville. FCP

The atom may/Return the compliment. Atomic Courtesy. Ethel Jacobson. FaFP; QQQ

...Atomic Energy, The Circus, Abominable Snowman, Napo-/leon and More... A Paragraph Made Up of Seven Sentences Which Have Entered My Memory... Chuck Wachtel. APU

An atomic submarine nudges past your belly. Sparrow in Winter. Takahashi Shinkichi. NU

Atoms, electrons–a kaleidoscope of worlds. This Only Do I Know. *Anonymous.* BePJ

Atonement for your blood/At the hands of the world/That shed it. Lament for the European Exile. Avner Strauss. VWA

The atrocity of tulips thrusting up/dog-penis red and raw. March Snow. Don McKay. NOBC

Atta boy! Atta boy! To Greet a Letter-Carrier. William Carlos Williams. OBAL

Attached to you by hooks,/tearing me as I come. Gray Silk Twisting. Patrick Lane. NeAC

Attack: The sound of jazz./The city falls. Battle Report. Bob Kaufman. CAD; TTY

Attaining, lastly, this. On a Row of Nuns in a Cemetery. Robert Guy Howarth. ELU

Attend all this. This and More. Glenn Siebert. HW

Attend his Kiddush on/A flowercup of dew. The Venerable Bee. Abraham Moses Klein. TrJP

Attend me out of time. Closing Cadence. John Moffitt. MoRP

Attended only by the loveless moon. Stars and Planets. Norman MacCaig. OBSP

Attendez a mon narration triste! The Little Peach. *Anonymous.* NA

Attracted every wondering glance. Mamba the Bright-Eyed (excerpt). George Gordon McRae. PoAu 1-2

Attracted to a blue May heaven? The Pine Bough. Richard Aldridge. NePoAm; PoSC

Attracting all, arms against acts appeal! The Siege of Belgrade. Alaric Alexander Watts. BLPA; HBV 1-2; TreF

Attracts a small downfall of dimes. Capital. Heather McHugh. MAYP

"Auch, to Hell,/I'll tak it to avizandum..." The Great Wheel. Hugh" (Christopher Murray Grieve) MacDiarmid. OxBS

Aud suddenly, and all at once, the rain! Memorial Rain. Archibald MacLeish. OBWP

Auguries of self-annihilation loom. Babylon. Siegfried Sassoon. MoRP

The august Father/Gave to me. My Wife. Robert Louis Stevenson. DL

"August's the golden month of the year." The Golden Month. Marion Doyle. YeAr

August wakens, smiling. August Smiles. Elizabeth Jane Coatsworth. SiSoSe

August will come another day. Song Set by Thomas Weelkes: "Now is my Chloris fresh as May." *Anonymous.* OBSC

Aunt Tabitha'll tell me she never did so! Aunt Tabitha. Oliver Wendell Holmes. CenHV

Aura of tattered hopes/Protesting as you dare not. Three Sermons to the Dead. Laura Riding. LiTA

Ausgang we were out of love/Und eingang we are in. In the Public Gardens. Sir John Betjeman. NYBP

Author of number, that hath all the world in Harmony framed. Come, Let Us Sound with Melody, the Praises. Thomas Campion. UnS

Automatically taking the things in, that had not been spoiled,/sordid. The Ticket. John Ashbery. ANYP

...The automobile/has been hauled away. As the Dead Prey upon Us. Charles Olson. NeAP

An automobile, I would not trade it/For any burro! Progress. Edith Agnew. AmFN

Autopsy: read/dead of acute peoplelessness. Chicken-Licken. Maya Angelou. FF

Autumn beech-leaves, flying in gold and crimson,/Fall, at thy feet, Faun. To Faunus. Horace. LiTW

Autumn is no less on me that a rose/Hugs the brown bough and sighs before it goes. Sonnet: "Say what you will." Edna St.Vincent Millay. HBMV

...An autumn leaf/hanging from a tree–I see a body! I Know I'm Not Sufficiently Obscure. Ray Durem. BPo; PoBA

Autumn nightfall too. Haiku: "On a withered branch." Basho (Matsuo Basho). WeW

Autumn's glow and sheen/Amid the summer's green! Peach Tree with Fruit. Padraic Colum. BoNaP

The autumn wind is blowing. Manyoshu: Waiting for the Emperor Tenji. Nukada. Princess. PBWP

Avarice & Chastity did shite it Epigram: "The Hebrew Nation did not write it." William Blake. OAEL 1-2

...Avarice/Gleams in the commercial eye? Garrison Town. Emanuel Litvinoff. WaP

Ave Mary! take my child! Latin Hymn. Winthrop Mackworth Praed. CoBE

Ave, Virgo! Gr-r-r–you swine! Soliloquy of the Spanish Cloister. Robert Browning. ATP; BoLiVe; DiPo; DTo; EnL; ExPo; FaBoCo; ForPo; InPK; LiTB; MaVP; NIP; NOBL; NOBV; NoP; OAEL 1-2; OAEP; SeCeV; TEP; TrGrPo; TW

Avenged in part for lifelong hidings/she has had to bear. The Whipping. Robert Earl Hayden. BP; GP; GrPl; IDB; NCSH; PoBA; TW

Avenging the friend whom I couldn't work in. Commonwealth. Ambrose Bierce. DBV

Avenue/el;in the top of his head:to tell/him Plato Told. Edward Estlin Cummings. AmFN; AmPP; CrMA; MoVE; NoAm; NOBA; NYP; OxBA; WaP

An avenue of demonstrators and police/Contained between tall buildings where the money is. An Alexandrine Magazine. Howard Nemerov. SOTS

Avert her face and pull him to her for a time before she squats to flush/him out. Floor. C. K. Williams. GeTw

Averted graciously by kind Delay! Delay. Charlotte Fiske Bates. AA

Averting face–sob in darkness. Yellow Dusk: Messenger Fails to Appear. *Anonymous.* OBVE

Averts her head/& stops chewing. Life in the Country. Michael Silverton. ELU

Avoiding the neighbors/In morning's first blush. The Last Farmer in Queens. Vickie Karp. NYP

Avoids his grim act of participation. Swing One, Swing All. George Bradley. AMV-80

Avon shall be my Thames, and she my Song,/No other prouder Brookes shall heare my wrong. None Other Fame Mine Unambitious Muse. Samuel Daniel. AAS

AW.../SH...IT/SE...DUC...ED!! Seduction. Jo Ann Hall-Evans. BlSi

Await, in fitting silence, the event. Artemis Prologizes. Robert Browning. AnEnPo

Await me in heaven, ah stand at the door. Ave Atque Vale. *Anonymous.* WTO

Await their transformation into life. The Anteroom. Denise Levertov. NeBP

Await us, weighing the unstripped bough. Farewell to Van Gogh. Charles Tomlinson. CMoP; GTBS-P; NMP

Awake all night who know/The pity of it all. Cradle Song. Louis MacNeice. OxBi; PoPl

Awake and see the rising sun. Celia Singing. Thomas Carew. EG; EnLit

Awake! Awake! Wishmakers' Town. William Young. AA

...Awake! before it is too late. Awake! W. R. Rodgers. LiTM; WaP

Awake, chaos: we have napped. Serene Immediate Silliest and Whose. Edward Estlin Cummings. MoVE

Awake in us dear memories of God's peace. San Juan Capistrano. Alice Cecilia Cooper. GoBC

"Awake, lazy earth;/Spring is coming once more." March Wind. Maud E. Uschold. YeAr

...Awake, O/Hosts! Vala; or, The Four Zoas. William Blake. ViBoPo

The awakened soul must sail or die. The Swan. Sir Edmund Gosse. SyP

Awakening transports of an inner view of things. Roots and Branches. Robert Duncan. VGW

Awakes my heart to heart's and eye's delight. Sonnets, XLVII: "Betwixt mine eye and heart a league is took." William Shakespeare. EyDe

Aware I have begun to die. The Tourist. Garret Keizer. AMV-81

Aware of One most pleased at what I do. His Adoration. David Morton. ISi

Aware that the mist will never lift to order. Wales. Norman Nicholson. ChMP

Awash with angels,/Reading alone in her chair. Warm Tea. Lewis MacAdams. ANYP

Away and back to her side, and dreams of long ago. Visions. Edmund Leamy. BBV

Away, away, away down south in Dixie! Dixie. Daniel Decatur Emmett. BLSo; FaFP; FSW; TrAS; TreF; YaD

Away, away with rum by gum;/The song of the Salvation Army. Away with Rum. *Anonymous.* FSW

Away, away! You are safer in the tomb. To a Shade. William Butler Yeats. AnIL; LiTB; PoEL 1-5

Away back before the emergence of fur or fether, back to the/unvocal sea and down deep... Silences. Edwin John Pratt. NOBC

Away both leaf and promise flew. Song: "I promised Sylvia to be true." John Wilmot, Earl of Rochester. SeCePo

Away from decay, and away from the storm. The Drowned Mariner. Elizabeth Oakes Smith AA

Away goes a reek and the rambling boy.　The Reek and the Rambling Blade. *Anonymous*.　OuSiCo

Away, haul away, Oh, haul away, Joe!　Haul away, Joe.　*Anonymous*. AmSS; ShS

Away in haste I slither,/Feeling I need a breather.　Publisher's Party. Phyllis McGinley.　OBAL

Away in the greyness/Of sundering years.　The Sheep.　Seumas (James Starkey) O'Sullivan.　OxBI

Away mine ashes, then Thy fire doth/glow.　The Ebb and Flow.　Edward Taylor.　AmP; AmPP; AnNE; AP; SCAP

Away right over the mountain!　Susiana.　*Anonymous*.　ShS

Away to best the morning at its gates!　Definition of My Brother.　W. S. Graham.　NeBP

Away up high, away down deep.　At the Playground.　William Stafford. LCAP

Away we go, away we go.　Away We Go.　Aileen Fisher.　TiPo

Away we go together, Dad and I.　Six and Thirty.　D. E. Stevenson.　BiCB

Away! who overtakes us now shall claim thee for his pains.　The Arab's Farewell to His Steed.　Carolina Elizabeth Sarah Norton.　PaPo

Away with it, let it go.　Away, Melancholy.　Stevie Smith.　OxBTC; PBWP

Away with the warrior's plume!　Ortiz.　Hezekiah Butterworth.　PAH

"Away with your blasphemies!" And laughed, and died.　Aunt Cora. Kenneth Pitchford.　CoPo

Away with your brutal disorder, and clear the field for/the tournament of Man.　The Tournament of Man.　Ernest Crosby.　PGD

Away you gallop on my saddled desires.　Patron of Flawless Serpent Beauty. F. Mayrocker.　WPOW

...Away,/You vulgar people there.　Architectural Masks.　Thomas Hardy. EyDe

Awful and awful. Good friend. You have embarrassed our/hearts.　For Victor Jara.　Miller Williams.　SM

Awkward and milky and beautiful only to hunger.　Potato.　Richard Wilbur. CAPP; CrMA; LiTA; MoAB

An awkward first audible/called language.　Solo Native.　Thomas Lux. LCAP

An awkward word,/like a tiny white parachute/follows me everywhere I go. After Spending All Day at the National Museum of Art.　Alan Britt. FAZ

Ax de Lord fer ter fetch you up higher!　Revival Hymn.　Joel Chandler Harris.　HBV 1-2; MCCG

Axa, Fatima, Marien.　Villancico.　*Anonymous*.　AWP

"Ay, a remembrancer, but nothing more."　The Corner Knot.　Robert Graves.　NYBP

Ay, and a world of pikes pass through!　His Cavalier.　Robert Herrick. CaPo; GoJo

Ay, and thy second slumber will be deep.　Sorrow.　George Santayana. WGRP

Ay, ay, and away she goes,/Bonnie Hieland laddie!　Highland Laddie. *Anonymous*.　ShS

Ay, ay, O ay–the winds that move the mere.　The Last Tournament. Alfred, Lord Tennyson.　FaBoRV

Ay, ay, Sir! Stiddy, Sir! Sou'wes-b'sou'!　A Sea Dialogue.　Oliver Wendell Holmes.　EtS; MOS; OBAL

Ay, ay, so that we may/Wend with Him at domesday.　Ay, Ay, This Is the Day.　*Anonymous*.　OxBM

"Ay, brother,–'tis well writ,/But where's the joke?"　Misapprehension.　Paul Laurence Dunbar.　BPo

Ay, by the heavens, it was a ball of gold.　A Man Saw a Ball of Gold.　Ron Padgett.　ANYP; EvOK; LiTA; NePA; PoPl

Ay–even they who say the worst about you/Can scarcely tell what I shall do without you.　Any Soul to Any Body.　Cosmo Monkhouse.　NOBV

Ay, look, and he'll smile thy gloom away.　The Gladness of Nature. William Cullen Bryant.　HBV 1-2; HBVY

Ay, man, but a'm dead now.　Wha Lies Here?　*Anonymous*.　FiBHP

Ay Manuela, Ay Manuela.　Viva la Quince Brigada.　Bart Van der Schelling.　FSW

Ay, many more which we may well divine.　Prometheus Unbound.　Percy Bysshe Shelley.　WSC

Ay me! and was this well,/O Death, to let me live when she is dead? Canzone: His Lament for Selvaggia.　Cino da Pistoia.　AWP

"Ay!" said Creep.　Old Shellover.　Walter De La Mare.　AtBAP; OxBChV; PoPle

Ay, Soul, thy very Self is unto thee/Immortal pledge of Immortality.　Soul, Wherefore Fret Thee?　Gertrude Bloede.　AA

Ay, thon's the wee bird for me.　Birds.　Moira O'Neill.　HBV 1-2

Ay, whaur are the snaws of langsyne?　Ballat O the Leddies O Langsyne. Francois Villon.　OBVE

Ay, would to God that day were back/When Andre rode to Pont-du-lac! Andre's Ride.　A. H. Beesly.　HBV 1-2

Ayain the which reson debateth,/And every creature it hateth.　Adrian and Bardus.　John Gower.　OxBM

Aye, all but my own ruffled mind.　The Bwoat.　William Barnes.　VLP

Aye, my dear and tender!　First or Last.　Thomas Hardy.　CMoP

Aye! the zwath-flow'r's a-killed by the zun.　The Child an' the Mowers. William Barnes.　VLP

"Ayeh," they both agree, and flap away.　Maine Sea Gulls.　Russell Hoban. BoAnP

Ayont ony dout/–in my mind!　Ane to Anither.　Duncan Glen.　PoSH

B

The b–r deserves to die./Glory, glory Allelujah.　The Monk of Great Renown.　*Anonymous*.　CoMu

A babbling whisper you shall hear/Of birds and blossoms, leaves and light. The Brook in February.　Sir Charles G. D. Roberts.　BoNaP; OBCV; WHW

Babe can never hunger there,/Nor poverty the mind appal.　Holy Thursday. William Blake.　CEP; EnLi 1-2; EnPE; FF; InPS; NoP; PAI; TEP

The babe cries, "Nay, for that abide I waking."　Sleep, Baby Mine, Desire. Sir Philip Sidney.　NOBE; OBSP

Babe I'm booked and I got to go　Stones in My Passway.　Robert Johnson. BluL

The babe looked up and sweetly smiled!　The Mother in the Snow-Storm. Seba ("Major Jack Downing") Smith.　PaPo

The babe/the Howling Babe　La Preface.　Charles Olson.　PoM

The Babe, the Son of Mary.　What Child Is This?　William Chatterton Dix. FSW

Babe was the only one/who came to visit gramma.　Little red riding hood. Nila NorthSun.　GP

Babes dropping quietly to the ground.　Mother.　Barry Dempster. AMV-80

The babes I've never dandled on my knee!　The Toast.　Charles Warren Stoddard.　CAW

The babies singing as if there were not/soldiers in the air.　Song My.　Susan Griffin.　NMM; WPOW

Baby!　Kadia the Young Mother Speaks.　Jessie Sampter.　TrJP

A baby asleep has no crying.　Six Questions (B vers.).　*Anonymous*.　BaBo

Baby, baby, will go there.　Father's Gone A-Flailing.　*Anonymous*.　OxNR

Baby Egypt damp with glee　Pounds and Ounces.　Michael Brownstein. ANYP

The baby fell a-thinking.　Wagtail and Baby.　Thomas Hardy.　HBMV

The baby grows.　Baby.　Joyce Carol Oates.　GeTw

A baby isn't twins!　The Twins.　Dorothy Aldis.　BiCB

Baby now must go to sleep.　Bed-Time Song.　Emilie Poulsson.　HBV 1-2; HBVY

Baby, please don't go.　Baby, Please Don't Go.　*Anonymous*.　FSW

Baby too shall fly away.　What Does Little Birdie Say?　Alfred, Lord Tennyson.　HBV 1-2; HBVY

A baby when it's sleepin', there's no cryin'.　The Riddle Song.　*Anonymous*. BLSo; FSW

Baby will come to love and grief.　Baby's in Jail; the Animal Day Plays Alone.　Charles Henri Ford.　MoVE

The babybirds pipe down. It is day.　The Avenue Bearing the Initial of Christ into the New World.　Galway Kinnell.　CAD; NePoEA-2

Babylon and Samarkand/Are mud walls in a waste of sand.　Mexican Quarter.　John Gould Fletcher.　BPAW

A baccy box without a lid,/And half a farthing candle.　Death of My Aunt. *Anonymous*.　OxBoLi

"Back Again,/BLACK AGAIN,/Home."　Back Again, Home.　Don L. Lee. BALP; BPo

Back at Tinarha I found the men/Bullied by six o'clock.　Six to Six. *Anonymous*.　PBA

Back behind a starving god/Within a Buddhist temple.　Manyoshu: To Love Someone.　Lady Kasa.　PBWP

Back down along the notched clift/To bid the world and him good-night. The Stationed Scout.　Lyman H. Sproull.　PoOW

Back & forth between us like/borrowed breath.　When Black People Are. A. B. Spellman.　BPo; CNA; PoBA

Back from mortality the huge sails slide.　At the Discharge of Cannon Rise the Drowned.　Hubert Witheford.　AnNZ

Back from the dead lake water/one at a time　Minnesota Camp Grounds. Gerald Vizenor.　STE

"Back, hell, nothin'! There's a bear in here!"　The Bosky Steer.　Henry Herbert Knibbs.　BPAW

Back in gay Paree.　If You Want to Know where the Privates Are. *Anonymous*.　ABF

Back in my own life, out on the highway.　Biography.　Maura Stanton. MAYP

Back into life, back to the gods.　The Novel.　Denise Levertov.　AP; NoAm

Back into summer light,/back into lucid air.　Black Water and Bright Air.　Constance Carrier.　SD

Back into the seat and push off.　Lost in a Corridor of Power.　Michael Brownstein.　ANYP

...Back like the joyous alarm/of the sun-greeting voice of the crow.　The Crows.　John Engels.　AMV-81

The back of his own head.　The Driver in Italy.　Nicholas Christopher.　MAYP

Back of the Job–the Dreamer/Who's making the dream come true!　The Thinker.　Berton Braley.　BLPA; WBLP

Back on the Pasc of this raw dawn./Llanon.　Night.　Glyn Jones.　NeBP

Back through midnight　Train Tune.　Louise Bogan.　NePoAm

Back to me once more–of all girls the one I/Yearn most to look on.　Note to Gongyla.　Sappho.　LiTW

Back to my self am gone.　A Queen Wasp.　Walter De La Mare.　AtBAP

Back to sleep in my dark bed on earth.　Poem Rocket.　Allen Ginsberg.　CoPo

Back to the air, to the light, to her.　Ants.　Katharyn Machan Aal.　AMV-80

Back to the alien dungeon, where all night/Unseen he burns.　November Sun.　Elizabeth Daryush.　PBWP

Back to the cold transparent ham again!　Sonnet to Vauxhall.　Thomas Hood.　PoEL 1-5

Back to the Cross, and lo! her lids are wet.　On a Sculptured Head of the Christ.　Mahlon Leonard Fisher.　HBV 1-2

Back to the grief and the toil/And the hopes and the homes of men.　Vespers.　Odell Shepard.　TrPWD

Back to the instruction manual which has made me dream of Guadalajara.　The Instruction Manual.　John Ashbery.　HAP; InPS; NeAP; NoAm; NOBA; PoM; SOTW

Back to the old eternity/Of placid, all-consoling sea.　Prairie.　Herbert Bates.　AA

Back to the rose. I cannot see/When sunlight is so close to me.　Inscription.　Ann Hamilton.　HBMV

Back to the wall, back to the wall,/To Liberty Hall.　General Vallancey's Waltz.　Paul Durcan.　FaBoIP

Back to the way!　Resolve.　Charlotte Perkins Stetson Gilman.　PoToHe; WGRP

Back to where we belong/With the cold stones and the clay.　The Song of the Heads.　*Anonymous.*　KiLC

Back to your perishing goodness, back to your heart again.　Messengers.　Charles Hanson Towne.　CAW

Back to your play, little brother.　The Palatine.　Willa Cather.　HBMV

Back to your rampart, Death.　Living.　Harold Monro.　LiTB; SeCePo

Back two his home at last.　A Misspelled Tail.　Elizabeth T. Corbett.　OBCA

Back where we ust to be so happy and so pore!　Back to Griggsby's Station.　James Whitcomb Riley.　BLPA; BLPL

A backhand explodes/Like a cloudburst.　Tennis Pro.　Lawrence Jay Dessner.　AMV-81

A backward love.　Before This Loved One.　W. H. Auden.　OBMV

Backwards and forwards to the Muslim hour.　Marrakech.　Ralph Nixon Currey.　PeSA

Backwards I compell Gloucester/to yield to Maximus, to/change/Polis/is this.　Letter 27.　Charles Olson.　CoPo

Backwards under the sun.　The Real People Loves One Another.　Rob Penny.　CNA; PoBA

Bad as Albert and Lil–what a pair!　Limerick: "She sat in a mighty fine chair."　Wendy Cope.　FaBoWP

Bad is the best, though excellent in neither.　The Passionate Pilgrim.　William Shakespeare.　ElL

Bad little kid.　Sulk when you're spoken to.　*Anonymous.*　CenHV

Bad luck to the one receiving love/and worse, I think, to the one that gives.　Love, I Think, Is a Disease.　Maghnas O Domhnaill.　NOBI

Bad luck to the pictur of Bachelor's Hall!　Bachelor's Hall.　John Finley.　HBV 1-2

Bad luck will surely follow!　A Rule for Birds' Nesters.　*Anonymous.*　HBV 1-2; HBVY

Bad luck you will have all day.　See a Pin and Pick It Up.　*Anonymous.*　HBV 1-2; HBVY

The bad man's death it well becomes to weep,–/Not so the just.　In Mortem Venerabilis Andreae Prout Carmen.　Francis Sylvester ("Father Prout") Mahony.　IrPN; NBM

...Bad neighbour and (despite the State)/A thoroughly bad lot.　The Last Democrat.　D. J. Enright.　NMP

A bad smell mixed with glory, and the cold/Eyes that belie the tessellated gold.　Ravenna.　Louis MacNeice.　OBTV

Bad women to a certainty are the downfall of men,/As Adam was beguiled by Eve.　Ye Sons of Columbia.　*Anonymous.*　BFSS

Bade them soar and sing for His joy.　The Making of Birds.　Katharine Tynan.　HBMV; OxBI

The baffled hive of helpless man laid bare.　Fog.　Laurence Binyon.　SyP

A baggy figure, equally pathetic/When sedentary and when peripatetic.　The Bear.　Robert Frost.　AmP; MoAB; MoAmPo; NoAm

Bah! there's not a colour in the bottom of the dish.　The Digger's Song.　Barcroft Henry Boake.　NOAV

The bairnie that I brocht him/Had lang been sleepin sound.　Auld Sang.　William Soutar.　OxBS

Bait it with whore, and it will hold a King.　The Royal Angler.　*Anonymous.*　OBSV

"Baith our miders sall be alike sory,/For we's baith slep soun in Gamry."　Rare Willie Drowned in Yarrow, or, The Water o Gamrie (D version).　*Anonymous.*　ESPB

Baked from sour mash and wholesome leaven.　First Hymn.　John Gill.　NeAC

Bakes off its covering of snow/like a rising blackening sun.　The Woman Thing.　Audre Lorde.　BlSi; NMM

The balance of the promise with what lasts.　Blue Waves.　David St. John.　MAYP

Balanced between reflection and reflection.　Looking Up at Leaves.　Barbara Howes.　BoNaP

Balanced I rode it like a circus horse.　Climbing in Glencoe.　Andrew Young.　LiSp; SD

Balancing on the horizon.　Invitation of the Mirrors.　Tom McKeown.　AMV-81

The baleful laughter of goats.　Omalos.　Rosanna Warren.　AMV-80

Ball, Columbia, Eisenhower.　In the Canadian Rockies.　Virginia Shearer Hopper.　AMV-80

The ball thrown nowhere and the bird in flight.　Consuelo at the Country Club.　Selden Rodman.　NAMP

Ballast by Your bright strength my failing might.　Last Plea.　Jean Starr Untermeyer.　TrPWD

...The ballet-dancer/sustains her still mercurial pose in air.　Introduction.　Clere Parsons.　FaBoTw

Balloo, wee mannie, balloo, balloo.　O Jesu Parvule.　Hugh" (Christopher Murray Grieve) MacDiarmid.　BSV

BalloonMan whistles/far/and/wee　In Just-.　Edward Estlin Cummings.　AmP; FaBV; HeIP; InPK; NCSH; NoP; PrIm; SoSe

Balls of thread growing/from the creative void–/woven for eternity.　Rebirth.　Catriona Stamp.　BrRo

Bamboo, bamboo, bamboo!　Bamboo.　William Plomer.　PeSA

Bananas and armadillos that a Captain/Carries his Monarch from another world.　Ralegh's Prizes.　Robert Pinsky.　MAYP

A band of drunken molecules.　The Fisherman.　Sam G. Harrison.　AMV-80

The bandaged elm,/and the jolly jolly chestnut.　The Book of Juniper.　Tom Paulin.　FaBoIP

...Bands of cloud-deer flee/In scattered groups of two and three.　Wind-Wolves.　William D. Sargent.　TiPo

Bang! dixieland.　Look away/Look away.　Stephen Todd Booker.　LFAC

Banish our worldliness, help us to ever/Live with eternity's values in view.　He Was Not Willing.　Lucy R. Meyer.　STF

Banishing the night/Of our griefs.　At Dawn the Virgin Is Born...　Felix Lope de Vega Carpio.　PCh

De banjo disappears!　The Banjo of the Past.　Howard Weeden.　AA

A bank of mud around me lay,/And sea-weed on the river's bed.　The Vanity of Existence.　Philip Freneau.　AmPP; AP

"A bank president on his lunch break,"/I said.　Tornado Soup.　A. K. Redwing.　VoR

The bank undid me to the shore.　From the Window Down.　Louis O. Coxe.　NYBP

Banked back/By the older flood of the ocean, to swallow it.　Haunted Country.　Robinson Jeffers.　OxBA

Banking on where I thought the road must be.　Broom at Twilight.　Robyn Sarah.　CaPN

The banners o' Scotland flaughter by/And the buskit buglers blaw.　On the Hill.　William Soutar.　PoSH

Bansai tree,/like me you are useless/and a little sad.　Relocation.　David Mura.　BrSi

A bantam clucks with a suspicious stare.　Christmas Carol.　D. J. Opperman.　PeSA

Baptism by immersion and the glorious hysteria.　A Place by the River.　William Keens.　TAT

–Baptized? buried?–One of those.　To Be a Pilgrim.　Robert Conquest.　OxBC

Bar, Song, Susan, Idol, Manasses, Maccabe, Maccab.　Memoria Technica for the Books of the Bible: Apocrypha.　*Anonymous.*　FaBoUs

Barbara stout and fine.　Song of Duke William.　Hilaire Belloc.　FaBoNo

Barbed relics of love's old war.　On the Sea Wall.　C. Day-Lewis.　SeCePo

...,Bard after bard/Shall sing thy glory, beatific Sea!　The Beatific Sea.　Thomas Campbell.　EtS

The Bard may draw his parting groan.　The Lay of the Last Minstrel.　Sir Walter Scott.　FaBoPP; OBRV

The Bard was pension'd and receiv'd the bays. An Epitaph on William Whitehead... *Anonymous.* FaBoEE

Bare was the rock, silent the sky. Sea Dawn. Francis Hackett. AnIV

The bare winds/Moving across the great plains. West of Chicago. John Dimoff. RFM

Bared again her butchered heart/To the sunrise axe of the day. News of the World. George Barker. DTC; FaBoTw; LiTB

Barefooted in the shining grass? A Little Boy in the Morning. Francis Ledwidge. MCCG; OnYI

Barely, barely repeating/themselves enough to hang on. January 25th. Maxine W. Kumin. SM

Barely empty ghosts of men/you who occupy our land? You Who Occupy Our Land. Manuela Margarido. WPOW

...Barely/Visible in the window's copper sheen. Parents. Vincent Buckley. CBAP

...A barge/That nobody roweth or steereth. The Village of Erith. *Anonymous.* WSC

Baring their crooked grins. The Horn Blow. Jeff Tagami. BrSi

Bark just trunk-chuckles, and occasionally/cuts off their sap. Bark. Don Welch. GP

Bark your crazy head off. Dog, Midwinter. Raymond Souster. GDP

Barking on and on/into the damp/fall wind Sundown at Darlington 1878. Lance Henson. VoR

Barn. This Year, Next Year... *Anonymous.* OxNR

...The barn/Blazing in darkness, all they wish to see. The Magi. Louise Gluck. PoA

The barn is old, not strange. The Barn. Edmund Charles Blunden. MoBrPo; SeCePo

Barney Google with his goo-goo-googly eyes. Barney Google. Billy Rose. OBAL

"Barren, never to know the load/of his child in you, what is your body/now if not a famine road?" The Famine Road. Eavan Boland. FaBoWP

Barriers that divide/And therefore also join,/Crazy things and holy. The Light. John Holloway. NePoEA

The barrin' of oor door weel. Get Up and Bar The Door. *Anonymous.* BFSS

The bars descending razed his plume. Marmion. Sir Walter Scott. WHA

The bars of the Tombs. Lullaby. Kenneth Fearing. CMoP

Bartering in the bazaars of genes and death. Before Passover. Seymour Mayne. NOBC

The base on which my miseries were built. A Psalm of the Early Buddhist Sisters. *Anonymous.* WGRP

Based on a volume of/Japanese prints. From the Grove Press. Anthony Hecht. OBAL

Basking in the huge limelight/of the Great Depression. Less Is More... Vern Rutsala. AMV-80

...Bass merely circles,/mouth larger and larger. Cleaning Fish. Richard Behm. WOLT

Bat lettel did the old man keen/It was his ain kittchen-boy. The Kitchie-Boy. *Anonymous.* BaBo; ESPB

...Bathe us and/bring us up together again, as we were, in the swing, above the/garden. Trellis. Laura Chester. NPGG

Bathed in the holy Stream by Hermon's thymy hill. Auras of Delight. Coventry Patmore. ACP; CAW; LoBV; OBVV

The bathers fought the ocean's hurl. Essentials. Samuel Greenberg. LiTA

The bathers think/islands are separate like them. Islands. Muriel Rukeyser. GP

Batman and Robin/are falling asleep. Goodbat Nightman. Roger McGough. NoAm

...Bats are shuttling/their delicate black silks to mesh/that dark doorway on her absence. A Journal from France: Seamstress at St. Leon. Gillian Clarke. OBTV

The bats have fled the tower. Now hoots the sleepless/hour. Lament for Better or Worse. Gene Baro. NePoEA-2

The bats headdown from roots that are its bough. The Bats. Robert Hillyer. GoYe

Battering it to death with sticks and stones. The Lake. Ted Hughes. FaBoTw; NYBP

The battle-birds! The bugles! The Call of the Bugles. Richard Hovey. AA

A battle-flag/And the victor's bays! Nancy Hanks. Harriet Monroe. OHIP

The battle is yet to be won. Angela Davis. Alice S. Cobb. BlSi

The battleline is drawn in every heart! Design for Peace. Janet Norris Bangs. PGD

Battling to the death for what is his. Gamecock. James Dickey. HoPM; UnPo

Bawdy belles-lettres,/Etc. Clerihew: "Spinoza." *Anonymous.* NOBL

A Bayonet's contrition/Is nothing to the Dead. My triumph lasted till the drums. Emily Dickinson. OBWP; WaaP

Be a child; then we will part,/Ere this love grow stronger. Ad Domnulam Suam. Ernest Christopher Dowson. HBV 1-2; PG

Be a kiss, be a ring with this posy:/Aultre n'auray! Valse Jeune. Louise Imogen Guiney. AA

Be a man and face the battle–/That's the only way to win. The Only Way to Win. *Anonymous.* WBLP

...Be a poem/without words,/which can neither be read, nor seen, nor heard. Why Don't I Write in the Language of Air? Mona Sa'udi. WPOW

–Be a purple patch/for schoolboys, and a theme for declamation! The Vanity of Human Wishes. Juvenal (Decimas Junius Juvenalis). OBVE

An' be a-waiten vor me now,/To come vor evermwore. The Wife A-Lost. William Barnes. BoLoP; ELP; EnLoPo; HAP; OBEV; OBVV

Be a wild boy and beau the fair. Soliloquy of the Returned Gold Adventurer. Syntax". PoOW

Be able every day to live/And be a better man. Resolved. Ottis Shirk. STF

Be against all sorts of mortmain. Commission. Ezra Pound. BoLoP; MP; NIP; TwCP

Be Albion still thy joy! with her remain,/Long as the surge shall lash her oak-crowned plain! Verses Written at Montauban in France, 1750. Joseph Warton. OBTV

Be all but poet, and there's way to live. A Satire. John Oldham. ViBoPo

Be all my pains remembered too!' The Two Streams. Thomas Moore. GoBC

Be all that's left to love him. The Charcoal-Burner. Sir Edmund Gosse. OBVV

Be always kind to animals wherever you may be. Kindness to Animals. Joseph Ashby-Sterry. InMe; NA

Be always sure when you come to choose the candle light. The Frolicksome Farmer. *Anonymous.* CoMu; UnTE

..."Be anyone at all"/but not that child. The Child. George Keithley. NPGG

Be as Christ would have him–brother unto brother. Brotherhood (excerpt). Sir Lewis Morris. PGD

Be as the meek wild-flower's–if transient, yet not vain. A Prayer. Felicia Dorothea Hemans. TrPWD

Be assured 'tis she or none/That I love, and love alone. Britannia's Pastorals. William Browne. EIL

"Be, be," Buddha said. The Stick in the Forest. William Stafford. CAPP

Be beautiful feather Poem to Ease Birth. *Anonymous.* BoWoP

...Be beloved of many,/Without the fear of loss or want of any. Shall I Love Again. William Browne. ViBoPo

Be bound up in our spring of blood. A Diary of the Sailors of the North. David Shulman. VWA

Be bowsum ay to knaw thy God and Lord. To the Queen. Henry Stewart, Lord Darnley. OxBS

Be calm as this impressive hour,/And lead to endless day. I Love to Steal Awhile Away. Phoebe Hinsdale Brown. AH

Be Christ's the fair and perfect life whereby/We shape our lives for all eternity. The Perfect Life. Charles Francis Richardson. BePJ

Be Christians once, and stain no more than name. The Church of England's Glory. *Anonymous.* APAS

Be covered up so tight? Otherwise. Aileen Fisher. SoPo; SUS

Be crowned with the dust that crowns the meek. Slaves of Thy Shining Eyes. Hafiz. LiTW

Be Daedalus; make wings,/Make even feathered wings... Be Daedalus. Nanina Alba. PoBA; PoNe

Be damned to us if I can see. The Houses. Eden Phillpotts. OxBTC

Be dark enough thy shades, and be thou there content. The Introduction. Anne Finch, Countess of Winchilsea. SBG; WPOW

Be decenter, and learn at least/One lesson from the cleanlier beast. A Quarrelsome Bishop. Walter Savage Landor. FaBoEE; OBSV

Be-decked, be-diamonded–be-damned!/The women of the better class. The Women of the Better Class. Oliver Herford. HBMV

Be drenched with blood, and marred with blows,/That I thereby may live. Sleep, Holy Babe. Edward Caswall. BePJ

Be dull, exceeding dull, and you'll be great. An Author's Epitaph. Written by Himself. Abel Evans. FaBoEE

..."Be dumb,/Or speak but of forgotten things to far-off times/to come." The Angel in the House. Coventry Patmore. VLP

Be dust myself pretty soon; not now. Note to Wang Wei. John Berryman. NYBP

Be each, pray God, a gentleman. Who Misses or Who Wins. William Makepeace Thackeray. SD

Be easy, October. No cackle hen, horse neigh, tree sough, duck quack. The Great Hunger. Patrick Kavanagh. NoAm; OxBTC

Be every heart with love repaid/That seeks your aid! The Return from Egypt. Pope Leo XIII. CAW

BE FAITHFUL grows upon the mind/as lichen glimmers on the wood. Two Chorale-Preludes. Geoffrey Hill. OxBC

Be for a while a little bit/Of landscape borrowed from the sky. A Bed of Campanula. John (Norman Gregor Guthrie) Crichton. CaP

Be free of fruit to all. Of Caution. Francesco da Barberino. AWP

Be God's delight–man's best estate.   What Makes a Nation Great. Alexander Blackburn.   WBLP

Be godlike in the will to serve!   The Parting of the Ways.   Joseph B. Gilder. AA; HBV 1-2; PAH

Be gone, have done! Down, wanton, down!   Down, Wanton, Down!   Robert Graves.   BoLoP; CMoP; FaBoTw; HeIP; InPK; LiTM; NoAm; NoP; OAEL 1-2; TEP

Be good, my Lord, since you cannot be pretty.   Lord Barrenstock.   Stevie Smith.   OBSV

Be guilty of yourself in the full looking-glass.   Father and Son.   Delmore Schwartz.   LiTA

Be heavy for me again or else I die!   The Complaint of Chaucer to His Empty Purse.   Geoffrey Chaucer.   CABA; TrGrPo; WHA

Be henceforth Repentance a stranger to Love.   Repentance.   George Alexander Stevens.   NOEC

Be her heart mine, her hand or eye/Be what it will, why, what care I?   The Choyce.   Thomas Beedome.   CavP

Be horrid Chimpanzees today.   The Chimpanzee.   Oliver Herford.   FaBV; FiBHP; LBN; NA

Be in my minde withoute recure?/What no, perdy!   No! Indeed.   Sir Thomas Wyatt.   MeEL

Be in the midst of them,/God's own Jerusalem!   The City of God.   Francis Turner Palgrave.   WGRP

Be it a wide or narrow place, 'tis well/So that the work it holds be only done. Send Me.   Christina Georgina Rossetti.   TRV

Be it joy or pain, endure it shall forever.   Eternal Reward, Eternal Pain.   Sir Thomas More.   CoBE

"Be it thus. Be it thus."   Adze-Head.   *Anonymous.*   BIrV

Be it thy care our age to new-create:/What built a world may sure repair a state.   To Mr. Henry Lawes.   Katherine ("Orinda") Philips.   SBG

Be joined to the small grains of the brotherhood.   Couplets, XX.   Robert Mezey.   FYAP

Be kind, but kind to me alone.   To His Mistress.   John, Duke of Buckingham Sheffield.   CavP

Be kind to human beings too./They're sometimes pretty dumb.   Humane Thought.   Rebecca McCann.   YaD

Be kind to Love, that he be kind to you.   Idylls.   Moschus.   AWP

Be kind to many wings,/Air, water, fire.   Many Wings.   Isabel Fiske Conant.   HBMV

Be kind to your old parents, although they're old and poor.   I'm a Decent Boy from Ireland.   *Anonymous.*   ShS

Be large enough for Me–   I had no time to hate.   Emily Dickinson.   FPL; PoLf

Be laying up love, I should say!/Nay, lady, smile!   To Helen in a Huff. Nathaniel Parker Willis.   OBAL

...Be left/with a memory/or an insinuation or two/of cracks in a pavement. The Cracks.   Robert Creeley.   ConAP

Be lightning for the land we love!   Invocation.   Wendell Phillips Stafford. TrPWD

Be, like the wind that fans it, free.   Abolitionist Hymn.   *Anonymous.*   TrAS

Be love their lullaby!   The Christening.   Walter De La Mare.   BiCB

An' be ma friend through eternity.   Ma Lord.   Langston Hughes.   GoSl

Be made aware that I had stopped their breath?   A Matter of Life and Death. Richard Aldridge.   NePoAm

"Be merciful to me, a fool!"   The Fool's Prayer.   Edward Rowland Sill. AA; AnNE; BeLS; FaBoBe; GoTF; HBV 1-2; OHFP; OnMSP; PG; PoLf; TreF; TrPWD; WBLP; WGRP

Be merry and glad this good New Year.   What Cheer?   *Anonymous.*   SBVL

Be mistress or, fear of the young, a wife.   Sonnet: "The point where beauty and intelligence meet."   Gavin Ewart.   WaP

Be more mighty, more lasting,/More chainless than thou!   The Ocean.   John Augustus Shea.   EtS

Be my comrade crowned/with a thousand blessings./Thus the prologue.   An Invocation.   Bishop Patrick.   NOBI

Be my law, and I shall be/Firmly bound, forever free.   Holy Spirit, Truth Divine.   Samuel Longfellow.   AH

Be my solas and my confort at my last endingge./Amen.   The Hours of the Passion.   *Anonymous.*   MeEL

Be not afraid of my body.   As Adam Early in the Morning.   Walt Whitman. AP; MAmP; OxBA

...Be not afraid/To thrust aside half-truths and grasp the whole.   Progress. Ella Wheeler Wilcox.   BLPA; FPL

Be not proud of your fair body.   Be Not Proud of Your Sweet Body. *Anonymous.*   WTO

Be not self-will'd, for thou art much too fair/To be death's conquest and make worms thine heir.   Sonnets, VI: "Then let not winter's ragged hand deface." William Shakespeare.   MasP

"Be nothing first; and then, be love."   The Healing of the Leper.   Vernon Watkins.   FaBoTw

Be off, or I'll kick you down-stairs!   Father William.   Lewis (Charles Lutwidge Dodgson) Carroll.   BiCB; BiP; FaBoNo; FiBHP; FPL; GoJo; HBV 1-2; HoPM; InMe; LiTB; NLV; PoLf; PoRA; TreF; TrGrPo

Be our strength and bush of shelter,/When our hands forsake the plough. Thanksgiving After Communion.   *Anonymous.*   WTO

Be overstrong for mortal clay.   Lowery Cot.   Leonard Alfred George Strong. MoBrPo

"Be patient, child of heaven, the time will come."   Thaba Bosio.   Sam Duby R. Sutu.   PeSA

Be patient–life itself will make us weep!   Sonnets.   Muna Lee.   HBMV

Be patient. Paul! home! home!   The Lordly Hudson.   Paul Goodman.   NYP

"Be patient," say they all.   The Trees.   Samuel Valentine Cole.   OHIP

Be patient, spring is coming quick, and ye/Shall rise again.   Lilies.   John Francis O'Donnell.   IrPN

Be patient with the living.   Patience With the Living.   Margaret E. Sangster. PoToHe

Be peace on earth, be peace on earth,/To men of gentle will.   Dr. Birch and His Young Friends: The End of the Play.   William Makepeace Thackeray. GN

Be pitiful, O God!   Convinced by Sorrow.   Elizabeth Barrett Browning. BLRP; WBLP

Be powerful above us all. Be sure.   Consecration of the House.   W. S. Fairbridge.   PoAu 1-2

Be prepared, O Man! to die.   Time.   John Huddlestone Wynne.   OxBChV

...Be proud/Of a thoroughbred bay gelding who ran fast.   Phar Lap in the Melbourne Museum.   Peter Porter.   PoAu 1-2

Be provident, and pray for cowardice/And the loaded pair of dice.   Hughie at the Inn.   Elinor Wylie.   NYBP

Be quiet, heart! home! home!   The Lordly Hudson.   Paul Goodman. CoAP; NMP; VGW

Be quiet. You need not tell me.   Intimations of Mortality.   Phyllis McGinley.   MoAmPo

Be ready to meet Jesus face to face.   Too Busy.   *Anonymous.*   STF

Be reasonable! Stop! For God's sake! Greg!...   A Colloquy with Gregory on the Balcony.   Howard Moss.   FAZ

Be reconciled to living things.   Thought for the Winter Season.   Mary Elizabeth Osborn.   NePoAm

Be salvation, homour, blessing,/Might and endless majesty. Amen.   Hymn: "Sing, my tongue, the Saviour's glory."   Saint Thomas Aquinas.   WGRP

Be satisfied–or I shall find a worse.'   Aesop's Fable of the Frogs.   Jean de La Fontaine.   OBVE

Be screwed up or warped or sick/but don't explain yourself away.   Mental Health.   Elliot Fried.   GP

Be seated, thou.   Mozart, 1935.   Wallace Stevens.   AmP; UnS

Be sent to the bottom of Botany Bay.   Botany Bay.   John Freeth.   NOEC

Be she such as neither will/Famish me, nor over-fill.   What Kind of Mistress He Would Have.   Robert Herrick.   CaPo; TrGrPo; UnTE

Be silent.   Redemption.   Stanley Cooperman.   AMV-80

Be silent as the rose.   Be Still As You Are Beautiful.   Patrick MacDonogh. AnIV; NeIP; OxBI

Be smithied all to kingly gold.   A Creed.   John Masefield.   HBMV; MoRP; WGRP

Be steady, or your pranks will rouse the ram.   Idylls.   Theocritus.   AWP

Be still alone with Thee.   My Prayer.   Horatius Bonar.   BLRP

Be still and know that I am God.   Silence, an Eloquent Applause.   Leona Gregory.   TrCP

Be still and listen/To your heart,/And hear it beating merrily!   Easter. Elizabeth Jane Coatsworth.   YeAr

Be still, my babe; sweet baby, sleep.   Sleep, Baby, Sleep.   George Wither. HBV 1-2

Be still, my soul: the waves and winds still know/His voice who ruled them while he dwelt below.   Be Still, My Soul.   Katharina von Schlegel.   TRV

Be still now, and think of April,/and the soft light thud.   Any April.   Cathy Beard.   AMV-81

Be still, refrain thyself, and wait.   Put Forth Thy Leaf, Thou Lofty Plane. Arthur Hugh Clough.   EBEV

Be still the herdsman's boy among these giants/And the ridges of laurel.   I Am Disquieted When I See Many Hills.   Hyam Plutzik.   VGW

Be still the speech that silence narrows/Into fresh song!   Music.   Anne Ryan.   CAW

Be still this night. The rite proceeds!   Winter.   Aubrey Thomas De Vere. IrPN

Be still./Wait.   The Lost Son.   Theodore Roethke.   AP; CAPP; CoBMV; HaCAP; HAP; LiTM; MiAP; MoPo; NePA; VGW

...Be still while the/Sea-wind salts your head white.   Watch the Lights Fade. Robinson Jeffers.   CMoP; NoAm; NOBA

Be strong/in the heart,/nothing lasts/forever.   Granma's Words.   Ted D. Palmanteer.   STE

Be strong in this: heaven shall be your tomb.   From William Tyndale to John Frith.   Edgar Bowers.   NePoEA; QFR

Be supple in the life of all.   Metaphysical.   Robert Fitzgerald.   PoA

Be sure a murd'rer's malice to forestall.   Song of the Flea.   Judah Al-Harizi. TrJP

Be sure, and ever shall!   As the Holly Groweth Green.   King of England Henry VIII.   ViBoPo

Be sure–be sure, we're going to do/some splendid things! Road-Song of the Bandar-Log. Rudyard Kipling. OAEP

Be sure I'll have your heart, my love,/when all your loving's done. Night Thoughts: Baby & Demon. Gwen Harwood. CBAP

Be sure it cares but little for/Thy wounded, bleeding breast! A Song About Singing. Anne Reeve Aldrich. AA

Be sure that the Poet will utter/Some beautiful thoughts on our Fate! Talking Bronco. Roy Campbell. ViBoPo

Be swallowed in its/darkness, like an eyelash. Three Landscapes (excerpt). Jerome Rothenberg. CoPo

Be thanked, O plumage of paradise, be praised. For the Sisters of the Hotel Dieu. Abraham Moses Klein. SoSe; WHW

Be thankful and glad and the Lord/extol,/Who gave us the Law on its parchment/scroll. Simhat Torah. Judah Leib Gordon. TrJP

Be thankful if in that hour of supreme vision/Life does not fiddle. Jonathan Swift Somers. Edgar Lee Masters. OBAL

"Be thankful, thou; for, if unholy deeds/Ravage the world, tranquillity is here!" Sonnet: Composed by the Side of Grasmere Lake. William Wordsworth. ChRP

Be thankful to this burcht of Aberdein. To Aberdein. William Dunbar. FaBoPP

Be the best of whatever you are! Be the Best of Whatever You Are. Douglas Malloch. BLPA; YaD

Be the citizens of the true survival! Brooklyn Heights. John Wain. LiTM; NYP; OBTV; OxBTC

Be the days dark or bright. Songs of Seven. Jean Ingelow. HBV 1-2

Be the proud captain still of thine own/fate! A Challenge. James Benjamin Kenyon. AA

Be there praise and dominion in this and every age. Epithalamium for the Dedication of a Church. Anonymous. HW

Be therefore kind, my love, whilst thou art fair. Roses. Pierre Ronsard. AWP

Be Thine the glory, and be mine the shame! The Church's Testimony. John Dryden. ACP; CAW

Be this our joy if we go or stay. Peace. Margaret E. Sangster. TRV

Be thou beside us, very near, O God! A Prayer. Frederic William Henry Myers. TrPWD

Be Thou her refuge and her trust,/Her everlasting Friend. Lord, while for All Mankind. John R. Wreford. TrPWD

Be thou mine! Psalms of Love. Peter Baum. AWP

Be Thou my guide, my strength,/My wisdom and my all. Thy Way, Not Mine. Horatius Bonar. OxBoCh; TrPWD; TRV

Be thou, O God, our dwelling-place/And our eternal home! Through Unknown Paths. Frederick Lucian Hosmer. TrPWD

Be thou our guard while troubles last,/And our eternal home. Man Frail, and God Eternal. Isaac Watts. CBEP; NOCV; NOEC; OBEC; PoEL 1-5

Be thou our master in the strife,/Until Thy will is done. Thy Will Be Done. Hugh Thomson Kerr. BLRP

Be thou prepared/To hedge us frae that black banditti,/The City-Guard. The Daft-Days. Robert Fergusson. BSV; CEP; NOEC

Be thou the Love, Love sees. Variation on Ronsard. Thomas Sturge Moore. OBMV

Be THOU the trembling sinner's stay,/Though heaven and earth shall pass away! The Lay of the Last Minstrel. Sir Walter Scott. OBRV

Be Thou to love and praise alike impelled,/Whatever boon is granted or withheld. So Fair, So Sweet, Withal So Sensitive. William Wordsworth. EnRP; NoP

Be thy first word thy last,–Ready, ay, ready! Ready, Ay, Ready. Herman Charles Merivale. HBV 1-2

Be Thy Love before, behind us,/Round us, everywhere. Lord, Save Us, We Perish. Christina Georgina Rossetti. TrPWD

Be to us both with her decease. Uncollected Poems and Epigrams, 2. J.V. Cunningham. OBAL

Be true and lead him up/Straight along the road to heaven! An Elegy on the Death of Furuhi. Yamanoue Okura. DL

Be true as these, if ye would be more wise. Thoreau. Amos Bronson Alcott. AA

Be true to me, my own sweetheart,/I'm bound to leave you here. Ten Thousand Miles. Anonymous. AmFP

Be used in heaven, when God shall feast the just. Epitaph for a Godly Man's Tomb. Robert Wild. FaBoEE

Be very much his friend indeed/To pardon or to bear it. On Friendship. William Cowper. GoTF; TreFT

...Be vigilant, strive/To recognise the damned among your friends. Annunciations. Geoffrey Hill. NePoEA-2

Be ware therfore–the blinde eteth many a fly. Snatches: "In soothe to say, though all the erthe so wanne." Anonymous. OxBM

Be wet leaves, wet grass, wet laundry, and so on. The Self and the Weather. Reed Whittemore. NMP

Be wet/with a decent happiness. The Rain. Robert Creeley. CAPP; CoAP; ConAP; VGW

Be what she thinks me, for her sweet thought's sake. Sonnets: A Sequence on Profane Love. George Henry Boker. AmePo

Be what you wish to be. Little Girl, Be Careful What You Say. Carl Sandburg. GoYe

Be where thou wilt, thou wilt not harbour here. Content. Barnabe Barnes. OBSC

Be whole again/little one./be whole. Ijajee's Story. Charlotte DeClue. STE; TWSS

Be wild aware of light unseen,/And unheard song along the air. Go to the Shine That's on a Tree. Richard Eberhart. UnS

Be with me in paradise. Julia Miller. Edgar Lee Masters. MoVE

Be with me in the summer days and I/Will for thine honor and his pleasure try. To Spenser. John Keats. CoBE

Be with us, Lord! Litany for Peace. Leslie Savage Clark. PGD

Be with us now and ever! The Trinity. Anonymous. ACP

Be with us still,–be with us still! On the Eve of War. Danske Dandridge. PAH

Be worthy of our deaths and your delight. By the Wood. Robert Nichols. ChMP 059; HBMV; MMM

Be ye fixed on your God. Days of My Youth. St. George Tucker. AA; HBV 1-2

Be ye my fictions–but her story. Wishes to His Supposed Mistress. Richard Crashaw. AnFE; ATP; BoLoP; EBEV; HBV 1-2; LiTL; MePo; OBEV; OBS; TreFT; ViBoPo

Be ye my Gods. Gods. Walt Whitman. AnAmPo

Be yet assured, thou shalt have one/Not subject to corruption. The Mount of the Muses. Robert Herrick. CaPo

Be you my Sun, I'll be your Marigold. The Riddle. Anonymous. UnTE

Be you our angel unawares. An Angel Unawares. Anonymous. BLRP; TRV

Be you with me and I have Caesar's fate. Madrigal: "Short is my rest." William Barley. EnRePo

Be yours all other bliss! Content. Norman Gale. HBV 1-2

Be zummer thoughts in winter-tide. Zummer Thoughts in Winter Time. William Barnes. VLP

The beach-tide summer of people desired. Conduct. Samuel Greenberg. CrMA; LiTA

The beach twitches with life. Rookery. Nora Dauenhauer. TWSS

The beach, with all its organ stops/Pealing again, prolonged the roar. In Romney Marsh. John Davidson. BSV; FaBoPP; GoTS; OBVV; OxBTC; PoPle; ViBoPo

A beacon in the night, to light my way. At the Tomb of Rachel. Yehoash. TrJP

The beacon light of Liberty. Washington. Denis O'Crowley. OHIP

The beads of dew on these most secret places. Morning Song. Leon Stokebury. AMV-80

The beads upon the forehead/By homely anguish strung. I Like a Look of Agony. Emily Dickinson. CBEP; InPS; NCEP; NoP; OBSP; PAI; TAP

The Beadsman, after a thousand aves told,/For aye unsought-for slept among his ashes cold. The Eve of St. Agnes. John Keats. AtBAP; BeLS; BoLiVe; DiPo; DTo; EnL; ERoP 1-2; ExPo; FiP; GoTL; HAP; HBV 1-2; HoPM; LiTL; MasP; MBW 1-2; MyFE; NIP; NoP; OAEL 1-2; OAEP; OBNC; OBNV; OBRV; PoEL 1-5; PoLf; SeCeV; TEP; TreF; TrGrPo; ViBoPo; WHA

Bear fruit of me. The Lancet. Denis Devlin. NOBI

Bear less Reproach than they who plac'd 'em there. A Hymn to the Pillory. Daniel Defoe. DBV; NCEP

Bear me now in thy deep/Bosom, Sleep,/O Sleep. O Sleep. Grace Fallow Norton. HBV 1-2

Bear me over angel pinions,/Longs my soul to be away. Let Me Go Where Saints Are Going. Lewis Hartsough. AH

Bear only perfumes and the scent/Of healing herbs to just men's fields! Low-Anchored Cloud. Henry David Thoreau. ImOP; NoP; ViBoPo

The bear's blood unable to heal them Bear's blood. Ileana Malancioiu. BoWoP

Bear's got a lot of friends. Forming Child Poems. Simon J. Ortiz. CDW

Bear still the weight of a real sun on their shoulders,/and endure. Off Viareggio. Kenneth Pitchford. CoPo

Bear them along the way of God's behest,/Breast on His breast. The Kingfisher. Blanche Mary Kelly. GoBC

Bear with my Muse, it is not as it was. Dan Bartholmew's Dolorous Discourses. George Gascoigne. EnRePo

Bear witness to his human will. A Song of Winter. Emily Davis. ACV

Beareth me with him. He Maketh Himself One with Osiris. Book of the Dead. AWP

...Bearing a message from/The invisible sole Source of specific things. In Due Season. W. H. Auden. Prf

Bearing back the perished form. Mysterious Landscape. Hans Carossa. LiTW

Bearing down with two steady eyes,/On the quaking butcher. Elegy. Theodore Roethke. CTBA; DFF; NCSH

Bearing me onward through the vast unknown.   Brother and Sister.   George Eliot.   NOBV

Bearing our fleshly burden willed to go.'   Dante's Angels: Gabriel.   Dante Alighieri.   BoC

Bearing so little ammunition.   The School Children.   Louise Gluck.   AmPA; HaCAP

Bearing the golden bough of Argicida.   Canto I.   Ezra Pound.   AtBAP; CMoP; CoBMV; LiTA; MoAB; MoAmPo; MoVE; NoAm; NoP; SeCeV; TrGrPo; VGW

Bearing the seed of my words.   If You Come Back.   Jack Cope.   PeSA

Bearing up the light.   Lumiere.   H. L. Van Brunt.   AMV-81; LTB

Bearing words, "Pro Patria.'/What do they mean, anyway?   Knowlt Hoheimer.   Edgar Lee Masters.   OxBA

Bears can be guardians; and on a sill/Whose dogs deploy, the hands of Time are still.   On a Picture by Pippin, Called "The Den."   Selden Rodman.   PoNe

Bears, lynx have made their/imprint on Rhoda's paths.   Leave the Word Alone.   Edward Marshall.   NeAP

Bears the traveler's curved baton/Fashioned like a laborer's grubber.   Hymn to the Wind God.   Anonymous.   LiTW

...Beast, brute, bastard. O dog my God!   Sacred Elegy V.   George Barker.   MoPo

The beast Nebuchadnezzar.   Bestiary.   Abraham Moses Klein.   OBCV

...Beast's most fatal message/that we die to learn it well.   In Orangeburg My Brothers Did.   A. B. Spellman.   BPo; PoBA

The beast was beauty and what we hide/is how it came from and where it goes.   The World As Wave and Idea.   Louis O. Coxe.   SOTS

The beasts blow through/their corncob pipes.../No new music   No New Music.   Stanley Crouch.   PoBA

Beasts may degenerate into men.   The Beasts' Confession.   Jonathan Swift.   CEP

...Beasts set free/On captured innocence in the den,/Confounding deities, not men.   Nebuchadnezzar's Kingdom-Come.   David Rowbotham.   NOAV

The beasts, the birds in the nest, the fireflies in the air.   The Begetting of Cain.   Hyam Plutzik.   VWA

Beat—beat—beat—drums—beat.   Drums of Haiti.   Marcus B. Christian.   GoSl

Beat for you, and bleed for you,/In the dark, in the dew!   In the Dark, in the Dew.   Mary Newmarch Prescott.   HBV 1-2

Beat heavily beyond the Atlantic roar.   Canadian Boat Song.   Anonymous.   BSV; GoTS; OxBS

Beat on my tomb, rain-gods.   Creed.   Walter Lowenfels.   PoNe

Beat out the rhythm of life/on the back of a kitchen chair.   Arkansas.   Jackman Young.   TAT

The beat that consoles them most, his blood.   The Sunbather.   Vernon Watkins.   MoPo; MoVE

Beat them, like sword and ploughshare, into one.   For an Ex-Far East Prisoner of War.   Charles Causley.   OxBC

The beaten men come into their own.   The Rider at the Gate.   John Masefield.   BrPo

Beating a way for the rising sun.   The Daybreakers.   Arna Bontemps.   GoSl; IDB; PoNe

Beating and beating at an intractable metal.   Blackberrying.   Sylvia Plath.   HaCAP; HAP; NoAm; NOBA; NYBP

Beating and beating its wings/against the glass.   The Man on the Bed.   Debora Greger.   MAYP

Beating and beating the gold alive.   How the Hen Sold Her Eggs to the Stingy Priest.   Nancy Willard.   LCAP

The beating lushness of the freely given.   Expecting.   Daniel J. Langton.   AMV-81

Beating the stars like kettle drums.   First Frost.   Edwin Curran.   HBMV

Beating their little Bibles till he died.   Grandfather in the Old Men's Home.   William Stanley Merwin.   ConAP; LiTM; SM

Beating, up from dead lakes, ascents of fire.   Rotten Lake Elegy.   Muriel Rukeyser.   MoPo; NePA

The beauteous Irish lady,/Who/Gives/Potatoes/Eyes.   The Potatoes' Dance.   Vachel Lindsay.   SUS

The beauties of my Father's house, which shall/No more be shut from me!   Music.   Charles Phillips.   CAW

Beautiful, also, are the souls of my people.   Poem.   Langston Hughes.   CDC

Beautiful and appalling.   Microcosmos.   "Susan Miles."   OxBTC

The beautiful and young/all poems are for.   In a Spring Still Not Written Of.   Robert Wallace.   BoNaP; PP

Beautiful, beauti–FUL SOUP!   Turtle Soup.   Lewis (Charles Lutwidge Dodgson) Carroll.   BrR; FaBoNo; InMe; NLV

...Beautiful beautiful/black men with outasight afros   Beautiful Black Men.   Nikki Giovanni.   BPo; NMM

Beautiful both in labor and repose.   Man Carrying Bale.   Harold Monro.   BrPo; MoBrPo

Beautiful bruises on the crusted/glittering snow.   Tracks.   Brad Lee Shurmantine.   AMV-81

The beautiful City of Prague!   The City of Prague.   William Jeffery Prowse.   CenHV

Beautiful dreamer, awake unto me.   Beautiful Dreamer.   Stephen Collins Foster.   BiP; BLSo; FSW

Beautiful element of unreason under it?   Black Earth.   Marianne Moore.   FaBoMo

Beautiful flocks of the mind.   Deer.   John Drinkwater.   CH

Beautiful gods stroll unconcerned/among our mortal apprehensions.   Seagulls.   John Updike.   Psk

Beautiful in the manner of his country.   Aborigine.   Hugo Williams.   OBTV

The Beautiful is born, and sea and earth/May well revere the hour of that mysterious birth.   The Birth of Venus.   Anonymous.   EtS

The Beautiful is good, the good is true.   Rydal.   Hartley Coleridge.   VLP

Beautiful is the Puerto Rican flag.   Que Bonita Bandera.   Anonymous.   FSW

...Beautiful Jerusalem,/Over which Christ wept.   I Have Been through the Gates.   Charlotte Mew.   MoAB; MoBrPo; TrGrPo

Beautiful Judas Tree,/April in bloom.   The Morning After.   Dorothy Wellesley.   OBMV

Beautiful little hands, hands that will close our eyes!   Sonnet: "And I have seen again the marvellous child."   Paul Verlaine.   LiTW

Beautiful motherly monster, watch over me still.   Because the Three Moirai Have Become the Three Maries...   Constance Urdang.   MOON

Beautiful mouth, murmurs/of pleasure. Theresa, you.   Theresa.   John Pass.   AMV-81

Beautiful Savior! I'm Thine evermore.   Beautiful Savior.   Charlotte M. Kruger.   BePJ

The beautiful scapegoats arrive by boat.   To the Islands.   Howard Moss.   SM

The beautiful slipper deposited there/By his highness, the Prince of Wales.   Baron Renfrew's Ball.   Charles Graham Halpine.   PAH

Beautiful souls who were gentle when I was a child.   Twilight.   John Masefield.   OxBTC

Beautiful Still-heart rests/With the queens of old.   Still-Heart.   Frank Pearce Sturm.   OBMV

The beautiful, the terrible Accost.   My Most. My Most. O My Lost.   Jose Garcia Villa.   BoW

Beautiful the youth who in green Spring/Broke earth with song.   Song: "Bone-aged is my white horse."   Brenda Chamberlain.   NeIP

Beautiful winners, collared with pink roses.   The Beautiful Horses.   Donald Hall.   NePoAm-2

Beautiful winter, with snowflakes again.   Beautiful.   W. A. Bixler.   WBLP

"Beauty and all sorts of good fortunes arrive."   Oracle: Iwori Wotura.   Anonymous.   WTO

Beauty and fool together laid.   Symbols.   William Butler Yeats.   OBMV

...Beauty and good/Show from the mountainside of solitude.   Compensation.   Robinson Jeffers.   MoAB; MoAmPo

The beauty as the marriage steadily failed.   All the Way from There to Here.   Jack Gilbert.   NPGG

Beauty, beauty, beauty!   Sic Vita.   William Stanley Braithwaite.   BANP

Beauty blue and beauty white/Be her own by day and night.   Shopping Day.   Orrick Johns.   InMe

Beauty decays, love dies, desire doth fly.   Beauty, a Silver Dew.   Anonymous.   CBEP

Beauty does fade, at thirty dies.   Fading Beauty.   Anonymous.   FaBoEE

Beauty, eternal fugitive,/Seeks the home that we cannot give.   The Last Days.   George Sterling.   AnAmPo; HBMV

Beauty, ever let thy magic presence/Shed its glory round my clouded lot.   Enthusiasm.   James Clarence Mangan.   IrPN

The beauty fades, and man's life ends.   Hos Ego Versiculos.   Francis Quarles.   OBS

Beauty, grave, and virtue wait/On lovely Kate of Garnyvillo!   Garnyvillo.   Edward Lysaght.   IrPN

Beauty is everlasting/and dust is for a time.   In Distrust of Merits.   Marianne Moore.   AP; CoBMV; EaLo; LiTA; LiTM; MoAB; MoAmPo; NePA; OBWP; OxBA; SeCeV; TreFT; TrGrPo; ViBoPo; WaaP; WaP

Beauty is everywhere kin.   Music Stirs Me.   Ricarda Huch.   PBWP

Beauty is hers, and she is beauty instead.   I Know a Lovely Lady Who Is Dead.   Struthers Burt.   HBMV

The beauty is, how wholly/they attend their huntings here.   On the College Archery Range.   Robert Wallace.   LiSp

Beauty is like remembrance, cast/From Time long past.   Time Long Past.   Percy Bysshe Shelley.   HBV 1-2

"Beauty is truth, truth beauty,"–that is all/Ye know on earth, and all ye need to know.   Ode on a Grecian Urn.   John Keats.   AnEnPo; AtBAP; ATP; AWP; BiP; CBEP; ChRP; DiPo; EBEV; EnLi 1-2; EnRP; ERoP 1-2; ExPo; FaBoBe; FaFP; FF; FiP; ForPo; FPL; GoTF; GTBS; HAP; HBV 1-2; HBVY; HeIP; HoPM; InPK; InPo; InPS; LiTB; LoBV; MasP; MBW 1-2; MCCG; NAWM 1-2; NIP; NOBE; NoP; OAEL 1-2; OAEP; OBEV; OBNC; OBRV; OHFP; PAI; PoEL 1-5; PPoe; PPP; PrIm; SeCeV; SoSe; TEP; TreF; TrGrPo; UnPo; WHA

Beauty like thine makes usurpation fair.   On a Miniature.   Henry Augustin Beers.   AA

The beauty of its present flesh.   Our Vegetable Love Shall Grow.   Elaine Feinstein.   PoL

The beauty of man never disappears/But drives a blue car through the parking lot.   Two Years Later.   John Wieners.   CoPo; PoM

A beauty of sorts is nearly always within reach.   Point Grey.   Daryl Hine.   NOBC

Beauty's home, Killarney, ever fair Killarney.   Killarney.   Edward Falconer.   TreFS

Beauty shall shed a tear.   I Have Loved Flowers.   Robert Bridges.   EG; GoJo; MoAB; MoBrPo

Beauty so sudden for that time of year.   November Cotton Flower.   Jean Toomer.   CDC; NoAm; UnPo

A beauty, that can charm like you.   An Ode on Miss Harriet Hanbury.   Sir Charles Hanbury Williams.   OBEC

Beauty that in this dim world, I adore.   Sonnet.   Joachim Du Bellay.   CAW

Beauty, that's colour, and proportion.   The First Anniversary: The New Philosophy.   John Donne.   ExPo

The beauty that was Walsingham, that patience/that is Rome.   The Holy Land of Walsingham.   Benjamin Francis Musser.   ISi

Beauty took from those who loved them/In other days.   Fare Well.   Walter De La Mare.   CoBMV; GTBS-P; MoVE; NOBE; OBEV

Beauty walks forth to light the world for-/ever!   The White City.   Richard Watson Gilder.   PAH

...–A beauty/we have less than not/deserved.   May Song.   Wendell Berry.   AP

Beauty when we wake will be/a solitude on land and sea.'   The Seven Sleepers.   Sir Herbert Read.   SeCePo

Beauty with the flame shawl, do not repulse me.   Ghazal of Isa Akhun Zada.   Anonymous.   PG

Beauty-worshipping I of mine!   Circe.   Alfred Kreymborg.   MAPA

Became as white as snow.   The Child.   John Banister Tabb.   AA

Became at once of pure pearl made.   Variations: The Air Is Sweetest That a Thistle Guards.   James Merrill.   NePoEA

...Became/much more than there was time for him to be.   El-Hajj Malik El-Shabazz (Malcolm X).   Robert Earl Hayden.   CNA; PoBA

Becasue I praise.   Praise.   Rainer Maria Rilke.   ChTr

Becasue that he, sufficiently,/Hath tried the female kind.   Take Heed of Gazing Overmuch.   Thomas Richardson.   ElL

Because a cricket, who/had minstrelled every night outside/her window, died.   Heart's Needle.   W.D. Snodgrass.   NePoEA

...Because a sage/Here dwelling taught the wisdom of the coming age.   Kinfauns Castle (excerpt).   William Montgomerie.   OxBS

...Because/always this great box flowers over us/with all the coloured faces of mankind...   Grain Elevator.   Abraham Moses Klein.   CaP

Because among them all thou art the best.   Sonnet: To His Lady Joan, of Florence.   Guido Cavalcanti.   AWP

Because an owl goes home.   Dawn.   Gordon Bottomley.   MoBrPo

Because because because because because.   Sonnets for Roseblush, XVIII.   John Hollander.   SM

...Because charm/will save itself before it remembers us.   Charming.   William Matthews.   MAYP

Because for all the things he left undone/There is no possible excuse.   Anonymous Gravestone.   Erich Kastner.   ELU

Because, for just a little while,/The way seemed dark and dreary.   Recompense.   Nixon Waterman.   HBV 1-2

Because, forsooth, "I'm married!"   To Be or Not to Be (parody).   William H. Edmunds.   FaBoPa

Because from friends we're never/parted.   Just Folks.   Edgar A. Guest.   FaFP; TreFS

Because God made thee mine.   Because.   Edward Teschemacher.   BLSo; FSN; TreFT

Because God's gifts put man's best dreams to shame.   Sonnets from the Portuguese, XXVI.   Elizabeth Barrett Browning.   EnLi 1-2

Because he believed in fairy tales.   The Four-Leaf Clover.   Monica Shannon.   BrR

Because he cried, "Democracy" was lynched.   The Black Draftee from Dixie.   Carrie Williams Clifford.   BlSi

Because he forgot how to walk and learned how to fly/before he thinked.   Consider the Auk.   Ogden Nash.   QQQ

Because he gave himself.   Christmas Brownie.   Rowena Bastin Bennett.   ChBR

Because he is he and I am I.   Friends.   Edward Verrall Lucas.   HBV 1-2

Because He is my true love/He wore them instead.   Wardrobe.   Sister Mary Madeleva.   GoBC

Because he loved the peanuts so.   Peanuts.   Anonymous.   FaFP

Because he meant to picke the locke.   On a Puritanicall Lock-Smith.   William Camden.   ShM

Because he played with Beauty for a toy!'   October XXIX, 1795.   William Stanley Braithwaite.   CDC

Because he's busy being wrong.   How to Forget.   Rebecca Foresman.   PoToHe

Because he walks at peace with life/And death.   He Walks at Peace.   Tao Te Ching.   TRV

Because he was a bad man.   Juan Rulfo Moved Away.   Alberto Rios.   APU

Because he was of that royal blood,/And was loved by a virtuous lady.   Geordie (C vers.).   Anonymous.   BaBo

Because he wouldn't teach/and he couldn't porter.   Giles Johnson, Ph.D.   Frank Marshall Davis.   BPo; PoBA

Because her Cheekes are neere.   To Lucasta: The Rose.   Richard Lovelace.   SeCV 1-2

Because her glory in my death will die.   Sweet Pity, Wake.   Anonymous.   ElL

Because her griefs were worthy to be known,/And telling hers, might hap forget mine own.   Rosamond's Appeal.   Samuel Daniel.   OBSC

"Because her own Leg had killed her!"   Miss Kilmansegg and Her Precious Leg.   Thomas Hood.   NOBV

Because his heart went with you in your hand.   Sonnets of the Months.   Folgore da San Geminiano.   AWP

Because his hope is dead.   The Pessimist.   Anonymous.   PoToHe

Because I am with them no more?   Do They Miss Me at Home?   S. M. Grannis.   TreFS

Because I couldn't sit down.   I stood on the bridge at midnight.   Anonymous.   FaFP

Because I do not give a damn.   Observation.   Dorothy Parker.   FiBHP; InMe

"Because I don't want you to shear my fleece."   An Answer to the Parson.   William Blake.   FaBoEE; NLV

Because I dreamed the thicket and the thorn?   Sleeping Beauty.   Howard Nemerov.   DFT

Because I fell in the soft and pale sands/of Ashdod/in the War of Liberation.   Since Then.   Yehuda Amichai.   VWA

Because I gave you a false face/and a light of my own making.   Saint Pumpkin.   Nancy Willard.   LCAP

Because I guess really we were the only ones there   Fortune.   Lawrence Ferlinghetti.   CAD

Because I have copied everything I have seen.   Penicillin.   Frank Lima.   ANYP

Because I have loved life, I shall have no sorrow to die.   A Song of Living.   Amelia Josephine Burr.   HBV 1-2

Because I have no heart to give you.   Violet.   Arthur Symons.   BrPo

Because I know for me my work is best.   Work.   Henry Van Dyke.   TRV

"Because I KNOW this man, let him be clear.'"   The Meaning of the Look.   Elizabeth Barrett Browning.   TrCP; TRV

Because I know Thou lovest me.   An Evening Prayer.   Anonymous.   STF

Because I love you, and I know you're right.   What's Hard.   Laurence Lerner.   NePoEA-2

Because I'm breathing an absurd music/that will not stop.   Man on Move Despite Failures.   Jeffery Alan Triggs.   AMV-80

Because I'm 'quainted with John Law/and they won't let me down   Brownsville Blues.   Sleepy John Estes.   BluL

Because I'm sure it considers every knock a boost.   Traveler's Rest.   Ogden Nash.   DBV

Because I murdered that Knoxville girl,/The girl I loved so well.   Knoxville Girl.   Anonymous.   FSW

Because I never liked to work-a nohow.   Ain't Workin' Song.   Anonymous.   OuSiCo

Because I never was married before!   Wedding of the Clans.   Aubrey Thomas De Vere.   AnIL; IrPN

...Because I shall let the poem out of my house/and it will beam.   To Build a Poem.   Christine E. Hemp.   GOYP

Because I silenced, long ago,/The only voice that they obey.   The Gray Folk.   Edith Nesbit.   NOBV

Because I was flesh/I was my worst fear   Effectively coming through slaughter.   Judith Fitzgerald.   CaPN

Because I wear a yellow wig.   The Wasp's Song.   Lewis (Charles Lutwidge Dodgson) Carroll.   FaBoNo

Because if you don't I shall starve or freeze.   Up from the Wheelbarrow.   Ogden Nash.   FaBoBe

Because in such a plight I lie/Dying because I do not die.   Coplas about the Soul Which Suffers with Impatience...(excerpt).   San Juan de la Cruz.   OBVE

Because, in the road, I met her foster-nurse.   Remembering Golden Bells.   Po Chu-i.   AtBAP; AWP

Because Incertainties we cannot know/Be sure, not to believe.   Sure, There's a Tie of Bodies!   Henry Vaughan.   NCEP

Because it erst was nought, it turns to nought.   This Life, Which Seems So Fair.   William, of Hawthornden Drummond.   GTBS; GTBS-P

Because it has a very important moral, which is, Don't be a discoverer, be a/promoter.   Columbus.   Ogden Nash.   NoP; OFD

Because it is bitter,/And because it is my heart. In the Desert. Stephen Crane. AmePo; LiTM; NOBA; OBSP; TAP

Because it is primitive. Grid Erectile. Christopher Dewdney. CaPN

Because it is their doom, so maun I. Admiral Byng. *Anonymous.* OBSS

Because it is winter and the new year. Elegy for My Father. Mark Strand. GeTw; HaCAP; LCAP; UnPo

Because it only lives, doubly alive. By the Waterfall. Friedrich Adler. TrJP

Because it's soon or late/we have to go down in that old lonesome ground. Everybody Ought to Make a Change. Sleepy John Estes. BluL

Because it shaws we're gey near Judgment-day. Campidoglio. Giuseppe Belli. OBVE

Because it takes less time than the other kind? Anti-Love Poems. Elizabeth Brewster. NOBC

Because me mother come back the very next day. Hullabaloo Belay. *Anonymous.* FSW

Because men say there's better things/In the modern cattle show. The Last Longhorn. R. W. Hall. BPAW; CoSo

Because men suffer it, their toy the world. Playthings. William Cowper. WaaP

Because—my dear, you see; I'm blind. Sight. Cora Ball Moton. GoSl

"Because my fathers and I/are owned by the living/warmth of the earth/ through our naked feet." You Laughed and Laughed and Laughed. Gabriel Okara. PBA

Because my heel is as long as my toe! Up in the Lift Go We. *Anonymous.* PBBP

Because my name is Lazarus and I live. The Convent. Gilbert Keith Chesterton. GoBC

Because my silkworms were hungry. Tzu Yeh Songs. *Anonymous.* BoWoP

Because no wreath we owe. Stonewall Jackson. Herman Melville. AmePo

Because none e'er lay in her bed,/Unless they first were knocked o' th' head. On Honour. Bernard Mandeville. NOEC

Because of a child of man. With a rocking. Prince Yuke. LiTW

Because of all things known/That is most difficult. To a Friend Whose Work Has Come to Nothing. William Butler Yeats. AnFE; AWP; BiP; BoC; DiPo; ForPo; InPo; LiTM; MBW 1-2; MoAB; MoBrPo; OAEL 1-2; OBMV; PoA

Because of nobler work and sweeter rest. Backward–Forward. *Anonymous.* BLRP

Because of the love that I bore them, Dona Eis Requiem. Heretics All. Hilaire Belloc. ACP

Because of you, Madame Moon/It rains. You Made It Rain. Fareedah Allah. BlSi

Because of you the Ark must sail without the Unicorn.' The Late Passenger. Clive Staples Lewis. EBCP; TrCP

Because on Him their trust is laid. Psalm XXXVII. Sir Philip Sidney. FCP

Because one March afternoon/you gave me/a between/a beat. Pre-positions. Jose Isaacson. VWA

...Because our love is whole/Whether I live or fail. V-Letter. Karl Shapiro. AP; CoBMV; MiAP; MOLP; NoAm; TrJP; WaP

Because our trip's always/Put off till to-morrow. In Go-Cart So Tiny. Kate Greenway. TiPo

Because people could not pay/was no reason why they should not eat. The Last Families in the Cabins. Millen Brand. GP

Because she had been one of them/And greatly loved in Bethlehem. Mary of Bethlehem. Mary King. ISi

Because she loved, because she had always loved. Centerfold Reflected in a Jet Window. Sandra McPherson. GeTw; MAYP

Because she never lets up,/even in bed–and she beats him there, too. The Retired Boxer. Lucilius [[or Lucillius]]. LiSp

Because she's touched her perfect body/with her mind. Suzanne Takes You Down. Leonard Cohen. BiP; NIP; NoP

Because she's unable to Postulate How. The Space Child's Mother Goose. Frederick Winsor. QQQ

Because she thinks I ate that worm! The Worm. Ralph W. Bergengren. SiSoSe

Because she was cozen'd (in being too kind)/By three or four men before so. The Shepheard and the Milkmaid. *Anonymous.* CoMu

Because she will not heed him. Fountains. Sacheverell Sitwell. MoBrPo

Because somebody/called him/black. Black Sketches, 7. Don L. Lee. NeAC

Because that he could hew/And hammer, he was glad. The Ridiculous Optimist. *Anonymous.* STF

Because—that's Hallowe'en! If You've Never. Elsie Melchert Fowler. SoPo

Because the beginning shall remind us of the end/And the first coming of the second coming. The Cultivation of Christmas Trees. Thomas Stearns Eliot. OFD

Because the birthday of my life/Is come, my love is come to me. A Birthday. Christina Georgina Rossetti. AWP; BLPL; BoLiVe; FaFP;

GoTF; GTBS; InvP; LiTB; LiTL; LoBV; NAs; NOBE; NOBV; OAEL 1-2; OAEP; OBEV; OBVV; OLR; TreFS; TrGrPo; ViBoPo; VLP; WHA; WiR

Because the brutes within, I do not doubt,/Are archetypal of the brutes without. Eden's Courtesy. Clive Staples Lewis. EBCP

Because the chain is broke, though no link lost. Elegy on Mistress Boulstred. John Donne. JCP

Because the Chaplain's here as well, damn his eyes. Captain Hall. *Anonymous.* GBP

Because the envelope–is empty. A Letter. Rachel Korn. VWA

Because the fairies/still are there/beneath the red and green. Holly Fairies. Aileen Fisher. ChBR

Because the fullness of the time was come. Mary's Girlhood. Dante Gabriel Rossetti. CAW; GoBC; ISi; MaVP; WGRP

–Because the heaven, moved moth-like by thy beauty, goes/Still turning round the earth. The Naked Seed. Clive Staples Lewis. TrCP

Because the highest manifestation of/Hagia Sophia/is old and a woman. In Praise of Old Women. Marya Fiamengo. WPOW

Because the King of Life is entered in. Supersensual. Evelyn Underhill. WGRP

Because the longed-for Christ looked up/In Mary's happy eyes! While Shepherds Watched. Margaret Deland. GN; HBVY

Because the Lord to thee, himself/Hath bounteously expressed. I Love the Lord. *Anonymous.* AH

Because the mind's eye lit the sun. The Blue Swallows. Howard Nemerov. BiP; NoP

Because the moon is coming down/Beyond the branches and will drown. Watching the Moon. David McCord. YeAr

Because the Morne, with Roses strew's the way. The Vision of Delight. Ben Jonson. SeCV 1-2

Because the mother of my wife/Has come–and means to stay with me. An Unexpected Pleasure. *Anonymous.* FaBoCo

Because the night is here. Light the Lamps Up, Lamplighter. Eleanor Farjeon. CH; SiSoSe; TiPo

Because the night was fair? I Gazed upon the Cloudless Moon. Emily Bronte. MOON

Because the prick is laid beneath the stones. On Mr. Pricke. *Anonymous.* FaBoEE

Because the road's last turn will be the best. The Zest of Life. Henry Van Dyke. WBLP

Because the sun has whispered/That Summer's on the way. Secret. Esther Hull Doolittle. YeAr

Because the sun is there. Rain. Vladimir Nabokov. GrPl

Because the time was wrong. Mockingbird in Winter. Ernest Kroll. AMV-80

Because the truth can know no ownership. A Letter from When. Bernadine. LTB

Because the world had failed us both. The Tragedy of the Leaves. Charles Bukowski. HoPM

Because their mother's dead. Old Gray Goose. *Anonymous.* ABF

Because there are no proportions in death. The Fox. Kenneth Patchen. AnAmPo

Because there is no time for love. Time. Avraham Huss. VWA

Because there is nothing to be said. Lover's Meeting. Ray Mathew. CBAP

...Because there's a difference between being hurt and being afraid. By-Products. Baron Wormser. MAYP

Because these men of strength are with us. For Edwin R. Embree. Owen Dodson. CNA

Because they are mine/According to their deserving. The Right to Life. John N. Morris. AMV-80

Because they are not strong. Orator. Ralph Waldo Emerson. AnNE; OxBA

Because they could not help believing right. Absalom and Achitophel. John Dryden. OBS

Because they died before that I was born. Why Do We Love. Sir Benjamin Rudyerd. EIL

Because they know by doing so they'd be breaking of the ac'. The Merchant Shipping Act. *Anonymous.* OBSS

Because they're going to be cremated. Some Folks I Know. Samuel Hoffenstein. ALV

Because they're living; so I leave 'em. Free Thoughts on Several Eminent Composers. Charles Lamb. DBV; FaBoCo; OBRV; OxBoLi

Because they see me gazing where thou art. I Do Not Love Thee! Carolina Elizabeth Sarah Norton. GTBS; HBV 1-2; OBEV

Because they were even faster/than any cloud. A Story from the Bushmen. Joseph Ceravolo. ANYP

Because thou must not dream, thou need'st not then despair. The Hymn of Empedocles (excerpt). Matthew Arnold. OBEV

Because thy name moves right in what they say. Sonnets from the Portuguese, VII. Elizabeth Barrett Browning. CTC; HBV 1-2; OAEP; VLP

Because touching ourselves/we touched everything. Walking on the Prayerstick. Wendy Rose. TWSS

Because we are strangers. Gaeltacht. Pearse Hutchinson. BIrV

Because we have promised tomorrow to ourselves. Blackmen: Who Make Morning. Angela Jackson. CNA

Because we love, he is. Then trust awhile. Afterward. Elizabeth Stuart Phelps Ward. HBV 1-2

Because we take no interest in poltix of the day.) The Children of the Owl and the Pussy-Cat. Edward Lear. FaBoNo

Because–well, because he's my friend. Loyalty. Berton Braley. BLPA

Because what keeps me/From my honey/Is money. Basic. Ray Durem. PoNe

Because when I gets mad I/acts just like I sound Peach Orchard Mama. Blind Lemon Jefferson. BluL

Because when they come to full flower/I will be off away. Heart's Needle. W.D. Snodgrass. NePoEA

Because with five Frigats we did them destroy. The Famous Fight at Malago. Anonymous. CoMu; OBSS

Because with Isaac I am wed today. A Letter to His Friend Isaac. Judah Halevi. TrJP

Because you are so like your daddy. I'll Buy You a Tartan Bonnet. Anonymous. OxNR

Because you are wedded to the flux of life, because we are/words and our meanings change. Two Words: A Wedding. John Nichol. NOBC

Because you find me dangerously/Independently/Passive? Pavlov. Naomi Long Madgett. BPo

Because you have made them so out of your hearts. I Am What You Make Me. Franklin K. Lane. PGD

Because you will not gain will not buy a thing/beyond what she herself can offer you Listening to a Confucious. Henryk Grynberg. VWA

Because you wont be/out/of/it/when i need you Signals. Johari (Jewel C. Latimore) Amini. PoBA

Because you wouldn't/let it just be Young Woman's Neo-Aramaic Jewish Persian Blues. Jerome Rothenberg. BoWoP

Because your blazing eyes my bale have bred. For That He Looked Not Upon Her. George Gascoigne. EIL; NoP

Because your eyes have ruled this a mismatch already. All Thumbs. David Giber. AMV-81

Because your husband is captive,/your rage increases, your heart is never calm. Final Prayer. Enheduanna. BoWoP

Beck'ning the tardy ships, the ships that never come! The Cocoa-Tree. Charles Warren Stoddard. AA; AmePo; CAW

Beckoned, and so did the/Harriman firm. Albany Schmalbany. George Starbuck. PV

Become a single being, sure and true. World without Peculiarity. Wallace Stevens. HaCAP

Become both food, and Shepheard to thy sheep! Silex Scintillans. Henry Vaughan. AnAnS 1

Become more fragile and more fine/Breathing the atmosphere divine. The Hawkbit. Sir Charles G. D. Roberts. HBV 1-2

Become my universe that feels and knows. Dramatis Personae: Epilogue. Robert Browning. VLP

Become so shining that we cease to be. Out. Nathaniel Burt. MoLP

Become the night's blown wave. Off Saguenay. Alfred Goldsworthy Bailey. ACV

Become the slave of what his slaves create. Portrait of a Machine. Louis Untermeyer. MoAmPo

Becomes at last no meaning and no place. The Stoic: for Laura von Courten. Edgar Bowers. CoAP; NePoEA; QFR

...Becomes/only a way I remember people looking. Face-Paintings of the Caduveo Indians. William Dickey. FAZ

Becomes the night of snow! The Lover. Richard Henry Stoddard. AA

Becoming an osprey frozen skyhigh/to challenge me. Peyote Poem. Michael McClure. NeAP; PoM

Becoming furious bitter rising up sounds The Sound of Afroamerican History Chapt II. S. E. Anderson. PoBA

Becoming her mother and my own. The Late Mother. Cynthia Macdonald. Psk

Becoming high and dry on the sand as we talked. Farewell. Pat Wilson. AnNZ

Becoming transparent. Everlasting. Ice. Ai. FYAP

A bed, and sleep/To wake in thee. Come, Come, What Doe I Here? Henry Vaughan. MePo; SeCV 1-2

The bed creaks/as I make it. Senryu. Pat Nolan. APU

Bed me and beget my son. The Female Principle. A. D. Hope. OxBC

Bed me strike a match and blow. In Memory of Eva Gore-Booth and Con Markiewicz. William Butler Yeats. CABA; FaBoPV; MBW 1-2; MoAB; NoAm; OAEL 1-2; OBMV; OxBTC

A bed of blighted corn. The Four Winds. Shane Leslie. OnYI

The bed we give him, though of softest down. Liberty (excerpt). William Wordsworth. FaBoCo; FiBHP; Par

Bedlam! this is pretty sport. Pretty Sport. William Habington. NOBE

Bedraggled from their dunking when the ducks took to the water. The Parliament of the Three Ages (excerpt). Anonymous. PBBP

The beds are narrow,/but I'm coming in with you. Moon Tiger. Denise Levertov. MOON

The beds of fleur-de-lys. The Beds of Fleur-De-Lys. Charlotte Perkins Stetson Gilman. AA

The bedsteads and the tables, kitchen pokers, and the floors. A New Song on the Birth of the Prince of Wales. Anonymous. CoMu; FaBoBa; NOBV; VLP

The Bee committed Paricide. Fuscara or the Bee Errant. John Cleveland. AnAnS 2

Bee given to such as honor him with feare and reverence trew. Metamorphoses. Ovid (Publius Ovidius Naso). CTC; EnPo

The bee of hearts, which mortals name/Cupid, Love, and Fie for shame. Song of the Stygian Naiades. Thomas Lovell Beddoes. EnRP; ERoP 1-2; OAEL 1-2

The Beech amid the forest lives. Trees. Sara Coleridge. OHIP; OxBChV

Beeches in May, beeches in February. Beech Trees. Sister Mary Madeleva. BBV

Beelzebub, will butt at blue! Because of Her Who Flowered So Fair. Leonard Feeney. ISi

Been brought to life again. At Kenneth Burke's Place. William Carlos Williams. NOBA

Been doing something: I can tell by the way they smell I Can Tell by the Way You Smell. Walter Davis. BluL

Been in the pen so long,/O honey, I'll be long gone. Been in the Pen So Long (with music). Anonymous. AS

Been operating on nubs since it first called us niggahs. Parasitosis. Ronda Davis. JB

Been tempered to a man's defiant hate. Hagar. Elisabeth Eybers. PeSA

BEEP...bEEP/joy.../BEEP! Christmas 1959 et Cetera. Gerald William Barrax. OFD; PCh

Beer upon wine, let that be. Proverbial Advice on Eating and Drinking. Anonymous. FaBoUs

The bees are flying. They taste the spring. Wintering. Sylvia Plath. NMM

Bees! bees! was it your hydromel/Under the lindens? Under the Lindens. William Landor. HBV 1-2

Bees bring you honey from their hoard,/When you awake. Mary Was Watching. Anonymous. ISi

Bees, humming in the storm, carry their cold/Wild honey to cold cells. The Rainy Summer. Alice Meynell. GoJo; MoVE; OBSP; OxBTC; SBG

Bees in the stomach, sweat across the brow. Now. Appendix to the Anniad. Gwendolyn Brooks. BlSi

...Bees with their noise invade/His rest, and on his lips their honey made. Love Sleeping. Plato. AWP; FaBoEE

...Beethoven's Tenth is what it breathes. An die Musik. David Malouf. CBAP

Beetle and locust and flies and lice and moth and rust/and mold. Today. Margaret Walker. FB

Beetles were blind in the ages of yore. A Song from the Coptic. James Clarence Mangan. NOBI

Befitting emblems of adversity. Meditations in Time of Civil War. William Butler Yeats. CABL

Before dawn/I would take up the breathing of ocean. Night Dive. Don Johnson. MAYP

Before dawn kindles a new day. A Gateway to the Sea–St. Andrews. George Bruce. MAYP

Before God's last Put out the Light was spoken. Once by the Pacific. Robert Frost. AmLP; AnFE; BPAW; CMoP; CoBMV; HAP; HeIP; InPo; LiTA; LiTM; MoAB; MoAmPo; MOS; NePA; NOBA; PrIm; VGW; WeW

Before goodbye/of all we know. Seven Poems. Lorine Niedecker. VGW

Before he crow to cause others wake or rise. The Ship of Fools. Alexander Barclay. ACP

Before he died. Pheasant. Zulfikar Ghose. ACV

...Before he fills and sails down. Sled Burial, Dream Ceremony. James Dickey. CAPP

Before her old grandmother/Grows a young man. Nancy Cock. Anonymous. OxNR

Before his ample Chest the frothy Waters fly. The Aeneid. Virgil (Publius Vergilius Maro). OBVE

Before his arms encompass/The sweet comptometress. Calculating Female. Jill Hellyer. PoL

Before his soul was stolen by the sea. The Parrot. Wilfrid Gibson. OBMV

"Before I'd marry that kind, I'd rather die!" De Mexico Ha Venido. Anonymous. TrAS

Before I'd part with you, my dear. 'Tis You That Makes My Friends My Foes. Anonymous. YaD

Before I die, a book-eared dog. Nature in Couplets. Charlton Ogburn. GrPl

Before I die/I'll bake a cathedral. Hope. Edith Sodergran. PBWP

Before I dive, God's mercy in my claws.   Falconry.   Anne Wilkinson. OBCV

Before I hear your cries as they come to drag you captive.   The Iliad. Homer.   WaaP

Before I pull my colors down you can sink me and be hanged!   Maggie Mac. *Anonymous.*   AmFP

Before I seen your smilin' face/An' heard your lyin' tongue.   Lonesome Road (with music).   *Anonymous.*   AS

Before I sing 'em all again/I'd see you all in hell.   Raccoon's Got a Bushy Tail.   *Anonymous.*   FSW

Before I were ca'd traitor Mains!/That eats and drinks of meal and maut. Hobie Noble.   *Anonymous.*   BaBo; ESPB; OxBB; ViBoFo

Before I will pillage or part/buy a ship, I'll be a shepherd.   A Poem to Show the Trouble That Befell Him When He Was at Sea.   Thomas Prys.   OBTV

Before in infancy/The world you first did see.   Now Sleep My Little Child So Dear.   Casper Kriebel.   AH

Before it bowed politely/and softly went away.   The Visitor.   Jack Prelutsky. AmMo

Before it grows too late.   The Sisters Kastemaloff.   Carlton Talbot.   ALV

Before it has picked up the heart of/a continent and shoved it into the Gulf of Mexico.   The River.   Pare Lorentz.   AmFN; NAMP

Before it is too late.   Before It Is Too Late.   Frank Herbert Sweet. PoToHe

Before it left, barking down the road.   Coming Back Home.   Ray A. Young Bear.   CDW

...Before it swoops me up, feather/The hawk of the world's forgetting with the down of/Your memory.   Faintly and from Far away.   Vassar Miller. CoPo

Before it turns up-/side down with the lark.   Morning, Noon, and...   Hawley Truax.   NYBP

Before it was quite unsheathed from/reality.   Hurt Hawks.   Robinson Jeffers.   AmP; AtBAP; CMoP; CoBMV; DiPo; FYAP; LiTA; LiTM; MoAB; MoAmPo; MoVE; NoAm; NOBA; NoP; OxBA; PrIm; TAP; UnPo

Before jealous destiny burns you to ashes to nourish the roots of life.   Black Woman.   Leopold Sedar Senghor.   TTY

Before landing on another expedition.   Flies Love Me.   Nuala Archer. AMV-81

Before light withdraws we would like to say/unforgettable words.   Late Afternoon.   Elizabeth Sullam.   AmC

Before man's laughter hunts our fear!   Journal to Stella.   Morton Dauwen Zabel.   PoA

Before me on each path there stood/The witty and the tender Hood.   On Thomas Hood.   Walter Savage Landor.   PV

Before my altar's dark rose tree.   Where Do I Love You, Lovely Maid? Raymond F. Roseliep.   ISi

Before my life, my love shall end.   The Queen of Paphos, Erycine. *Anonymous.*   EIL; GBL

Before my pen by help of fame/Cease to recite thy sacred name.   A Fancy. Thomas Lodge.   EIL; LoBV; OBSC

Before our eyes there stand/somewhere, in freer lands, the/children Jacob's goodly tents!...   My Song to the Jewish People.   Leib Olitski.   TrJP

Before our hearts were broken/Like sticks in a fire.   Portmanteau Parodies: After W.B. Yeats.   Gilbert Keith Chesterton.   FaBoPa

...Before our own parents touched that way.   Persimmon Trees, She Remembers, Not Far Away.   David Baker.   AMV-81

Before pursuing its scratchy path again.   Partial Draft.   Robert B. Shaw. AMV-81

Before she got half-way there.   Mother Niddity Nod.   *Anonymous.*   OxNR

Before she went out for a walk.   Limerick: "There once was a girl of New York."   Cosmo Monkhouse.   LiBL; NA

Before striking out in their sea.   On Galveston Beach.   Barbara Howes. MoAmPo

Before the apple-red and hungry mornings rise.   The Third Continent. Mary Erulkar.   ACV

Before the boss comes 'round.   Rain.   Frank Marshall Davis.   GoSl

Before the children's bones, on the holy mountain.   On the Mountain. Michael Kennedy Joseph.   AnNZ

Before the chilly dawn can blight/The delicate frail buds of light.   The Lamplighter.   Seumas (James Starkey) O'Sullivan.   BIrV; OxBI

Before the circle they inscribe/Becomes a full moon/At rest.   Blessing of the Firstborn.   Howard Schwartz.   VWA

Before the colors deepened and grew small.   Anglais Mort a Florence. Wallace Stevens.   AP

Before the cross was the body laid,/With hands clasped fast, as if still he prayed.   Sir William of Deloraine at the Wizard's Tomb.   Sir Walter Scott. OBNC

Before the dark.   This Evening, without Blinking.   Pattiann Rogers. AMV-80

Before the dawning of the day/She fades away.   Sing-Song: Is the Moon Tired?   Christina Georgina Rossetti.   MOON

Before the day she sinks in death, my Ros geal dubh!   Roisin Dubh.   Owen Roe MacWard.   OnYI

Before the fairest of all girls is by parsons led astray.   The Frolicsome Parson Outwitted.   *Anonymous.*   CoMu

Before the game is up.   A Coney Island Life.   James L. Weil.   AmFN

Before the heavy drop/of the apples.   Tropics.   Ellen Bryant Voigt.   SM

Before the indifferent beak could let her drop?   Leda And The Swan. William Butler Yeats.   AnIL; AtBAP; CABA; CMoP; CoBMV; DiPo; EBEV; ExPo; FF; FPL; GTBS-P; HAP; HeIP; InPK; InPo; LiTM; MoAB; MoBrPo; MoVE; NAWM 1-2; NIP; NoAm; NOBE; NoP; OAEL 1-2; OAEP; PBBP; PPoe; PPP; PrIm; SCV; SeCeV; SoSe; TEP; TrGrPo; WeW

Before the Judge, who thenceforth bid thee rest/And drink thy fill of pure immortal streams.   Sonnet XIV: "When Faith and Love which parted from thee never."   John Milton.   OBS

Before the man with the blown balloons goes home.   Public Holiday: Paris. Joyce Horner.   GoYe

Before the memories we bear,/The flames leap backward everywhere.   The Ordeal by Fire (excerpt).   Edmund Clarence Stedman.   WGRP

Before the name of Attila.   Dirge of Alaric the Visigoth.   Edward Everett. BeLS

Before the old gentleman miss'd her.   Limerick: "There was an old soldier of Bicester."   *Anonymous.*   FaBoNo; OxBChV

Before the old Inn-sign.   The Old Inn-Sign.   Wilfrid Thorley.   BrR

Before the sandbags dragged his compressed body/into the dark hole, into total oblivion.   A Hanging.   Frank Mkalawile Chipasula.   WhB

...Before the screen doors/of their suddenly forbidden houses.   Going Away. Howard Nemerov.   DFF

Before the Second Word.   A Poet's Proverbs.   Arthur Guiterman.   TiPo

Before the spray is white with May,/Or blooms the eglantine.   The Milkmaid. Henry Austin Dobson.   HBV 1-2

Before the startling ring/and the long unwinding of curses/and cloth.   My Father Kept His Cats Well Fed.   Kenneth Sherman.   HeIP

Before the thirst for red/has found a track to follow!   Toulouse Lautrec. Astrid Tollefsen.   PBWP

Before the Voice of Man was heard;/In the beginning was the Word.'   The Missal.   Rosemary Dobson.   BoAV

Before the white body of the poor dog slain by chance bullets,/the divine Francis wept.   Brother Dog.   Luis Anibal Sanchez.   CAW

Before the wind's feet/In the wheat!   A Dakota Wheat-Field.   Hamlin Garland.   OBCA

Before the Wonder of your form and face.   Sonnets to Miranda.   William Watson.   HBV 1-2

...Before then, Holy Player,/do not break off!   The Fiddler.   Martin Buber. VWA

Before there was any water there were tides of fire, both our tones/flow from the older fountain.   Continent's End.   Robinson Jeffers.   AnFE; AWP; FaBV; ImOP; InPo

Before these nuptial days some sign to me for promise show.   An Epithalamion upon the Marquis of Huntilies Marriage.   King of England, James I   HW

Before they are off with the old?   Dictum Sapienti.   Charles Henry ("John Paul") Webb.   ALV

Before they die and turn to mud/And I have gone.   Oblivion.   Ellis Ayitey Komey.   PBA

Before they disappear beyond/These white-hooded mountains and appetites. Requiem for My Mother.   Keorapetse Kgositsile.   WhB

Before they saw through it and found me.   The Diggers.   William Stanley Merwin.   EAS

Before they started, he and she, to play.   The Guitarist Tunes Up.   Frances Cornford.   ELU; SoSe

Before Thine altar, Lord Most High,/Thy Name we bless and magnify.   Thy Name We Bless and Magnify.   John Power.   BLRP

Before thy ark Earth keeps her sacred dance.   Ode to the Setting Sun: The Sun.   Francis Thompson.   GoBC; InMe; MoAB; MoBrPo; OBNC; WHA

Before thy sovereign scratch nor rub thee nought.   The Boy Serving at Table. John Lydgate.   OxBChV

Before too late, too late, too late, too late,/Becomes a deafening clamor in the ear?   Personal.   Samuel Yellen.   NYBP

Before us lies the valley/Of the Walker of the Snow!   The Walker of the Snow.   Charles Dawson Shanly.   OnYI

Before us, too, they found the hope/of islands, and the hope of dawns,/was of another day.   Shetland, Hill Dawn.   Robin Munro.   PoSH

Before we fall to kissing and to bed.   Preludes for Memnon.   Conrad Aiken. LiTM

Before we go to Paradise by way of Kensal Green.   The Rolling English Road.   Gilbert Keith Chesterton.   EvOK; FaBoCh; HBMV; LoGBV; NOBE; NOBL; OBEV; OBMV; OxBTC; SeCeV

Before we met the man who ate glass/& asked about our dreams.   Public School 168.   Stewart Brisby.   LFAC

Before we soiled our lips with crime,/That you and I went our two ways.   If I Have Wronged You.   Trumbull Stickney.   NCEP

Before you disappeared/Into the mountain.   Poem to Han-Shan.   Joseph Stroud.   NPGG

Before you gave to Texas/The rugged strength of oak. The Road to Texas. Berta Hart Nance. BPAW

Before you halt at the lines again! Lofty Lane. Edwin Gerard. PoAu 1-2

Before you have finished, again evening will have come. It Is Not Likely Now. Frances Bellerby. ChMP

Before you leave. Cities #8. Victor Hernandez Cruz. BOLo

Before you'll be through dancing o'er Sally our Queen. The Rich Lady from Dublin. *Anonymous.* BFSS

Before your pity I would choose your hate. Ephelia to Bajazet. Sir George Etherege. APAS

Befriend us, Time, Love's gaunt executor! In Time. Robert Graves. FaBoEE

Befringe the rails of Bedlam and Soho. The First Epistle of the Second Book of Horace. Alexander Pope. CEP

Beg for mercy. Follow, Follow. Thomas Campion. EnLoPo

Beg him to take off the spell again. Fable. Joan Aiken. WSC

Beg pardon, I'm soiling the doileys/With afternoon tea-cakes and scones. How to Get On in Society. Sir John Betjeman. NOBL; OBSV; OxBTC

Begeled, parde,/Withouten grace. Men Only Pretend. *Anonymous.* MeEL

A begetter/who abandons his offspring. The Empty Apartment. Aaron Zeitlin. VWA

Beggar am I that wait and pray/To feast my soul on His beauteous Face. The Poor. Speer Strahan. CAW

The beggar is happy to lie on his back in the dirt. The Beggar. H. L. Doak. HBMV

A beggar with a flaming sore. The Grey Ones. Louis MacNeice. CMoP

The beggars have changed places, but the lash goes on. The Great Day. William Butler Yeats. BIrV; CMoP; FF; OBSP

Begge thou wouldst take thy Tenants Rent. Silex Scintillans. Henry Vaughan. AnAnS 1

Begging all the world/to enter in it. Queer Things. Emanuel Carnevali. EAS

Begging not to be stolen still again from/this grave, which is in a field of clover. A Piece of Shrapnel. David Ray. NIP

Begging one rosebud-but my rose was/dead. My Rose. Hildegarde Hawthorne. AA

Begin a gentle hymn of praise. The Silent Town. Richard Dehmel. AWP

Begin, and then the work will be completed. Faust. Johann Wolfgang von Goethe. PoLf; TRV

...Begin/as male and female, thrust and ache. Palais des Arts. Louise Gluck. MAYP

Begin, New Year-and bring that/joyous day! Hymn for the Eve of the New Year. Abraham Gerondi. TrJP

Begin the talk/of HYenaaaAAS. Hospital/Poem. Sonia Sanchez. BPo; PoBA

Begin to gleam across the mournful plain? The Raven Days. Sidney Lanier. AmePo; CBEP; NePA; OxBA

Begin to perish now. I Should Not Dare to Be So Sad. Emily Dickinson. InPo

Beginning a new row. The Natural Order of Things. Harley Elliott. NeAC

The beginning of every end, and the end of every place. Riddle: "The beginning of eternity." *Anonymous.* GoTF; TreFT

...Beginning to fall/into my arms like a solar panel/melting with friction. How the Sky Begins to Fall. Joan Colby. AMV-81

Beginning to remember/as its leaves fell. The Horse. William Stanley Merwin. GP

Beginning with my ending. The Golden Heart. Witter ("Emanuel Morgan") Bynner. HBMV

Beginning with the woman/in the early morning. Early Morning Woman. Joy Harjo. TWSS

Begins the vast biography. But now the dentist cannot die. Andrew Lang. CenHV

Begins to take shape. The Overgrown Back Yard. John Holmes. CrMA; NePoAm

Begins to wonder if it is possible he has been forsaken. Cocteau's Opium: 1. Donald Finkel. CoPo

Begone! no tramper gets a farthing here. Epigram on the Refusal of the University of Oxford to Subscribe... William Cowper. TW

"Begone! we'll have no fools in paradise!" Paradise: A Hindoo Legend. George Birdseye. HBV 1-2

Begotten without thought, born without pains,/The ropy drivel of rheumatic brains. The Della Cruscans. William Gifford. OBEC

...Beguiled/By which of this is fiction which is real. Discourse on the Real. Samuel Yellen. NePoAm

Beheld thy glorious childhood, and rejoiced. The Antiquity of Freedom. William Cullen Bryant. AA; AnNE; AP

Beheld thy lovely form; and now, he glowed; The First Olympionique to Hiero. Pindar. ATP

Behind a cloud, the Robber laughed/In a mad white carouse. The Robber. Walter James Turner. MoBrPo

Behind bruised eyelids, start the years again. Prisoner of War. Gertrude May Lutz. GoYe

Behind drawn curtains; play a harpsichord/And circumvent the storm. Mid-Century. Mary Elizabeth Osborn. NePoAm

...Behind dry lips/a loaded gun. Face to Face. Adrienne Rich. LiTM; NoP

Behind everything there is always/The unknown unwanted life. The Orient Express. Randall Jarrell. AmP; AP; CMoP; CoAP; CoBMV; NOBA

Behind him the plate glass of the store only cracked. The Hongo Store 29 Miles Volcano Hilo, Hawaii. Garrett Kaoru Hongo. MAYP

Behind his Delphian rock he sinks to sleep. Sunset over the Aegean. George Gordon, Lord Byron. OBNC

Behind in the fields. Haiku: "The crow flew so fast..." Richard Wright. FAZ

Behind me, the folly of my flight. A Translation of the Cywdd to Morvydd.... *Anonymous.* NOEC

Behind the box of frozen peas/and ice cubes. Now It Is Broccoli. Jeff Tagami. BrSi

Behind the cloud-topped hill, an humbler heaven. An Essay on Man. Alexander Pope. TrGrPo

Behind the coffin lid/closing like an office door. Daredevil. Kirby Congdon. PeHV

Behind the future's screen a great dawn watches,/Keeping guard on Massada. Massada. Yitzhak Lamdan. VWA

...Behind the shapes/my breath ghosts in sharp air. Taking to the Woods. Henry Taylor. MAYP

Behind the veil, behind the veil. In Memoriam A.H.H., LVI. Alfred, Lord Tennyson. HBV 1-2; LoBV; NAWM 1-2; OAEL 1-2; OAEP; OBNC

Behind their mortgaged houses. Men at Forty. Donald Justice. GP; LCAP; PPP; Prf

...Behind them/the sun went down and all the roads grew dark. The Odyssey. Homer. NAWM 1-2

Behind us one death comes/and goes as it pleases/it is the one/we are. Sounds. Paul David Ashley. LFAC

Behold-a man! Serenade for Strings. Dorothy Livesay. NAs

Behold, behold the Lamb! Jesus, the Name Most High. Charles Wesley. BePJ

Behold! He, too, hears but the voice of the Laws, the flutes of/the God! The Reply of Socrates. Edith Matilda Thomas. WGRP

Behold him! from the region of the blest/He speaks: he bids thee rest. To the Sister of Elia. Walter Savage Landor. HBV 1-2

Behold him, full and perfect quite,/A false saint, and true hypocrite. The Duellist. Charles Churchill. OBSV

Behold, how God each April gives/The miracle of Spring. Easter. Edwin L. Sabin. OHIP; PoSC

Behold I am Ra of the Eastern and Western Skies! He Overcometh the Serpent of Evil in the Name of Ra. Book of the Dead. AWP

Behold, I breathe and touch Thee too. God. John Banister Tabb. GoTF; TreFT

Behold, I slept with them! In Egypt. Paul Celan. VWA

Behold it, our Land of Beyond! Rhymes of a Rolling Stone. Robert W. Service. TRV

Behold, it was Death I had met. Death Seed. Ricarda Huch. PBWP

"Behold me! I am May!" Spring. Henry Timrod. HBV 1-2

Behold: my cross was gone! Behold, My Cross Was Gone! Alice Mortenson. BePJ

Behold, my Samsons are returning in the thick of the night/Lit up by the flaming foxes. My Samsons. Haim Guri. VWA

Behold our darkness only there! The Mediator. Elizabeth Barrett Browning. TrPWD

Behold our life unto our old life true. Morn. Helen Fiske Jackson. AA

Behold our Vegetable Athens rise/Where all the acres in the Land are wise! The Wayzgoose. Roy Campbell. OBSV

Behold the atom I preferred/To all the lists of clay! Choice. Emily Dickinson. AA

Behold the blaze of thy immortal name. A New-Year's Sacrifice. Thomas Carew. CaPo

Behold the city street! Manhattan. Morris Abel Beer. AmFN

Behold the deeds that are done of Mrs. Jones! Behold the Deeds! Henry Cuyler Bunner. ALV; HBV 1-2; InMe; NLV

Behold the Helen of the heart! On the Bust of Helen by Canova. George Gordon, Lord Byron. EyDe

Behold the Imperial Mount! 'tis thus the mighty falls. Childe Harold's Pilgrimage: Canto IV. George Gordon, Lord Byron. EBEV; FaBoPP; FaBV; GN; MBW 1-2; MOS; OAEL 1-2; OAEP; OBRV; TrGrPo; WaaP; WHA

Behold!-the Rondeau, tasteful, light,/You bid me try! The Rondeau. Henry Austin Dobson. HBV 1-2

Behold the shield; He shall not take thee all. For E. McC. Ezra Pound. LiSp; SD

Behold the smiling happy land,/That freedom calls her own. No More Beneath the Oppressive Hand. *Anonymous.* AH

Behold the Very Beauty/Thou worshipest the shadow upon earth.   A Sonnet to Heavenly Beauty.   Joachim Du Bellay.   AWP; CTC

Behold, the weary West!   Villanelle of Sunset.   Ernest Christopher Dowson.   BrPo

Behold the works of William Morris!   Rondel (parody).   *Anonymous.*   BXAP; Par

Behold the world! and curse your victories!   Don Juan.   George Gordon, Lord Byron.   FiP; OBRV

Behold this lovely world.   Behold.   Mary Kawena Pukui.   WTO

"Behold this walrus-tooth!"   The Discoverer of the North Cape.   Henry Wadsworth Longfellow.   AnNE; AtBAP

Behold this wreched body/That your unkindness haith slaine.'   Unkindness Has Killed Me.   *Anonymous.*   MeEL

Behold thy glorious face/And count all other things but loss.   Blest Be the Wondrous Grace.   George Barrell Cheever.   AH

"Behold thy slave, all day that walks these woods unknown!"   Actaeon.   Bewe.   OBSC

Behold where monumental States/Immortalize their lives sublime!   The Founders of Ohio.   William Henry Venable.   MC; PAH

Beholden still in blinking reveries,/With sombre sea-green gaze inscrutable.   To My Cat.   Graham R. Tomson.   PCat

Beholds the hairy/pappus of a dandelion.   The Medium IV Sights.   Carl Rakosi.   PAI

Being a Christian is seeking/The many lost souls to win.   Being a Christian.   *Anonymous.*   STF

Being always/poor.   Ennui.   Langston Hughes.   OBAL; OBCA

Being american we were/born without this knowledge.   The Cities Are Washed into Time.   John Oliver Simon.   NeAC

Being at once the fuel and the fire.   Song.   *Anonymous.*   CBEP

Being bark-bound, flagged, snapped, fell out-/right,/And in his fall felled me!   The Ivy-Wife.   Thomas Hardy.   VLP

Being born in good days, but deceased in bad.   An Epitaph on His Grandfather.   Thomas Shipman.   CBEP

Being double dead, going and bidding go.   The Expiration.   John Donne.   AtBAP; CBEP; EIL; MeLP; MePo; OBSP; SeCP

Being earth, at last I knew/the vibrance under the hill.   Things Known: Under the Hill.   Richard Eberhart.   PoA

Being glad of you, O pine-trees and the sky!   Pine Trees and the Sky: Evening.   Rupert Brooke.   MCCG

Being in thine owne heart, from all malice free.   Witchcraft by a Picture.   John Donne.   EyDe

Being intelligent, I measure him/by his mere look.   A Rapier of Treason.   *Anonymous.*   BoWoP

Being mighty a master, being a father and fond.   In the Valley of the Elwy.   Gerard Manley Hopkins.   EG; InPo; NOBV; NOCV; ViBoPo

Being neither white nor black?   Cross.   Langston Hughes.   BANP; IDB; LiTM; PoBA; PoLf; SoSe; TAP

Being on whiskey, ragtime, chicken, and the scriptures fed.   The Wisdom of Old Jelly Roll.   A.J.M. Smith.   PeCV

Being pecked upon/by the wind's wont   Metagnomy.   N. H. Pritchard.   NBP

Being primed for the big game, hungering for the cup.   Fall Practice.   Dabney Stuart.   SM

Being Proteus, he never dreamed at all.   The Shape-Changer.   Chris Wallace-Crabbe.   NOAV

Being threshed at hip and thigh, against that trash/Of pale wild flowers and their drifting legs.   Sunday at the End of Summer.   Howard Nemerov.   BoNaP

Being thus declin'd, in what a case was she.   Aenigma on the Six Cases.   *Anonymous.*   FaBoUs

...& Being tired of the mystic rose you wear in your/hair.   In Pursuit of Love.   Ken Norris.   CaPN

Being told on KWYK radio/in Navajo   Story Tellers Summer, 1980.   Nia Francisco.   STE

Being unsure, there is the fate/of doing nothing right.   For the New Year.   Robert Creeley.   NaP

Being useful, small   The School Bus.   Larry Eigner.   FAZ

...Beleaguered/Up to its sills by the gnawing fact.   Not to Forget Miss Dickinson.   Marshall Schacht.   LiTM

Beleeve and leave to wonder.   Wit Wonders.   *Anonymous.*   MeEL

The Belfry swarm'd with Monks; it seem'd alive.   King Arthur and His Round Table: Bees and Monks.   John Hookham Frere.   OBRV

Belie the most learned:/Autant en emporte le vent.   Autant en Emporte le Vent.   Marguerite de Navarre.   PBWP

The belief, and the love, and the truth.   Mein Kind, Wir Waren Kinder.   Heinrich Heine.   AWP; TrJP

Believe, and Dare, and Do!   To Labor.   Charlotte Perkins Stetson Gilman.   PoLf

Believe, and leave to wonder.   The Divine Paradox.   *Anonymous.*   MeEV

"Believe. Believe this is what I see."   The Wish to Be Believed.   Mona Van Duyn.   PoA

...Believe/me all else is rationalization.   Guns.   Ronald Crowe.   AMV-81

Believe me, i know, i know the moon/is a diamond.   The Moon Is a Diamond.   Arthur Sze.   AMV-81

Believe that all my griefs were true/And all my joys were dreamt.   How to Read Me.   Walter Savage Landor.   NOBV

Believing as I always have believed/That God is just.   The Condemned.   Edward Howland.   AA

Believing his daddy's all right.   The Little Child's Faith.   Louis Edwin Thayer.   PoToHe

...Believing I could give him/the sun and the moon.   On Certain Days of the Year.   Nancy Simpson.   AMV-81

Believing in fire/for not knowing/my place.   Territory.   Susan Wood-Thompson.   AMV-81

Believing nothing or believing all.   The Popish Plot.   John Dryden.   ACP

Believing what he believed/and did what doing.   Difference.   Clere Parsons.   FaBoTw

Belinda smiled, and all the world was gay...   The Rape of the Lock.   Alexander Pope.   ExPo

The bell of Christ's, tolling its hundred times.   Oxford Bells.   Sister Maris Stella.   GoBC

The bell of the blood in a deep sea/Drowns, the hood of the face is eyeless.   Leave Train.   Alan Ross.   ChMP

The bell rings, and it is enough.   You want the summer lightning, throw the knives.   Ingeborg Bachmann.   BoWoP

The bell rope broke,/And down she fell.   A Scottish Shoe.   *Anonymous.*   OxNR

Bell–that swings slowly and slowly over.   Still and All.   Burns Singer.   NePoEA-2; OxBS

Bell them at dawn, tell them at evening/In what fold they must sleep.   The Shepherds.   Beren Van Slyke.   GoYe

Bella has gone back to her cape of nettles.   Bella and the Golem.   Rossana Ombres.   VWA

The belle of the Mohawk Vale.   Bonny Eloise.   J.R. and Elliot. C. W. Thomas.   FSW

Bellows of joy into the sodden air.   Dementia Praecox.   Morris Bishop.   PoA

The bells cannot ring it, but long years, oh, bring it!/Such as I wish it to be.   Songs of Seven.   Jean Ingelow.   HBV 1-2

Bells, far off, very faint.   Waking Up.   Edward Lense.   AMV-80

"Bells, guard our Baby Cobina from all devils and all/harm."   Baby Cobina.   Gladys May Casely Hayford.   CDC

The bells of the world are ringing/For anguish and war again?   Bitter Question.   Arthur R., Jr. Macdougall.   PGD

...Bells/waiting with their tongues cut out/for this particular silence.   The Memory of Elena.   Carolyn Forche.   MAYP

Belly fringed and curving like an horizon.   New Forms.   Peter Redgrove.   NMP

Belong to you, a woman.   Dance Instructions for a Young Girl.   Kimiko Hahn.   BrSi

Belonged to wind and world the toil/And venture, and to Guy the oil.   Guy.   Ralph Waldo Emerson.   NOBA

Belongs, though he never knew it, to the Kingdom.   The Kingdom.   Louis MacNeice.   LiTM

Beloved, beautiful, come!   Will You Come?   Edward ("Edward Eastaway") Thomas.   CH; GoJo; GrPl; LoBV

Beloved, can you hear?   Serenade.   Richard Middleton.   HBV 1-2

Beloved, I only love thee! let it pass.   Sonnets from the Portuguese, IX.   Elizabeth Barrett Browning.   CTC; HBV 1-2

Beloved, in memory.   Farewell to Anactoria.   Sappho.   AWP; LiTW

Beloved, let us love: for only thus/Shall we behold that God who loveth us.   Love Is of God.   Horatius Bonar.   TRV

The beloved of damsels and dames–/Och, ochone!   A Farewell to Patrick Sarsfield, Earl of Lucan.   *Anonymous.*   AnIV

Beloved, world-without-end lamented face;/And not a blindfold mask on a pillar of dust.   The Cloud.   Edwin Muir.   OBTV

Below, a sea of stars!/Above, of stars a sea!   From Russian Hill.   Ina Donna Coolbrith.   BPAW

Below, alone, lying on pieces of unbleached/Canvas, with a violent premonition of sails!...   Poets Seven Years Old.   Arthur Rimbaud.   SOTW

Below the ragged/Line he signed/His chummy name.   Walt Whitman.   Edwin Honig.   NePA; TAP

Belt by the folk descend frome Agenoir.   The Aeneid.   Virgil (Publius Vergilius Maro).   OBVE

Bemoaning distresses of maidens/In the clump of eucalyptus trees.   Sancho.   William Edwin Collin.   CaP

Ben-an heaved high his forehead bare.   The Lady of the Lake.   Sir Walter Scott.   PoEL 1-5

Ben-Anna split/Burma-Shave.   Burma-Shave.   *Anonymous.*   NLV

Ben in the way no more!   The Lyttel Boy.   Eugene Field.   AA

Benchers only live by rules.   The Humours of the King's Bench Prison, a Ballad.   Leonard Howard.   NOEC

Bend down and touch lightly with my lips the white face in the coffin. Reconciliation. Walt Whitman. AnEnPo; HAP; MoAmPo; NoP; OBSP; OBWP; OxBA; TrGrPo; WaaP

Bend down and weep. I have not tears. Willow Bend and Weep. Herbert Clark Johnson. PoNe

Bend down the branches yonder/To shield my Darling's rest. The Lullaby. Felix Lope de Vega Carpio. CAW

Bend, great God, before thy shrine,/The bournless macrocosm's thine. Ode to Solitude (excerpt). James Grainger. ViBoPo

Bend to your need Orion's hounds/Or the small fagot of a rose. Ownership. Lizette Woodworth Reese. MoAmPo

Bending forward/hornlike at the top. Young Sycamore. William Carlos Williams. TAP

Bending in the green rain. 100 Year Old Woman at Christmas Dinner. Colin Style. AMV-80

Bending like a finger-tip, and beckoning to you. Parliament Hill. Sir Henry Howarth Bashford. BrR

Bending on cold knees. Burning Love Letters. Howard Moss. DFF; HoPM

Beneath a blinding sky, one blaze of sun. The Gorse. Wilfred Wilson Gibson. AtBAP

Beneath a tree that had no name,/Silence turned and slept. Daphne. Hildegarde Flanner. HBMV

Beneath heaven's cloudless dome. Death of Gaudentis. Harriet Annie". WBLP

Beneath it all, desire of oblivion runs,. Wants. Philip Larkin. GTBS-P; NoP

Beneath it paused the Duke of Shaou. The Pear-Tree. Anonymous. AWP

Beneath its breast my mother lies asleep. My Mother. Claude McKay. AnEnPo

(Beneath my feet the golden pavement burned.) A Dream. Helen Hunt Jackson. AnFE; APA

Beneath my home town that was/slaughtered, was slain. The Secret Town (excerpt). Abraham Sutzkever. TrJP

Beneath my Lord the Lamb. God's Dominion and Decrees. Isaac Watts. CEP; OBEC

Beneath our elms, along our grass. A Circus Garland. Rachel Field. OBCA; SoPo

Beneath quivering of molten flesh,/of veins, purple as violets?) Hippolytus Temporizes. Hilda ("H. D.") Doolittle. SBG

Beneath, Sir Olaf was lyind dead. Sir Olaf. Johann Gottfried von Herder. AWP

...Beneath the blankets/They have spread, until they are fast asleep. Indian Summer. A. S. Draper. YeAr

Beneath the burden of the years, and praise the earth/once more. To M. E. W. Gilbert Keith Chesterton. HBV 1-2

Beneath the cumbering dust of years,/In silence seemed to smile! First Communion. Jose Asuncion Silva. CAW

Beneath the dancing feet of crowds/Of other still-living suns and stars. The Red Heart. James Reaney. CaP

Beneath the dark, like a star. Ties. Dabney Stuart. GrPl; LiSp

Beneath, the earth is six feet deep;/the grass is optional and spare. Assembly Line. Adrien Stoutenburg. AmC

Beneath the folds of drapery suggested the languor of a convales-/cent. Autumn Melancholy. Janet Hamill. APU

Beneath the good how far–but far above the great. The Progress of Poesy. Thomas Gray. ATP; AWP; CEP; EiCP; EnPE; GTBS; GTBS-P; HBV 1-2; LAuP; NOEC; OAEP; OBEC; OBEV; PP; ViBoPo

Beneath the gray November cloud. Snow-Bound. John Greenleaf Whittier. AA; WiR

Beneath the lucid ripples/to have found so monstrous/an obscurity. To a Dead Journalist. William Carlos Williams. QFR

Beneath the moon I know her equals. Love-Songs, At Once Tender and Informative. Samuel Hoffenstein. OBAL

Beneath the poinsettia's red in warm December. Flame-Heart. Claude McKay. AmNP; BANP; CDC

Beneath the shadow of Thy throne a hundred years from now. A Hundred Years from Now. Mary A. Ford. BLPA

Beneath the shadows/stetching across/this day of love. Funeral of Rufino Contreras. Ruth Wildes Schuler. SOTS

Beneath the white ring of ice. Toward the Splendid City. Ed Ochester. LTB

Beneath the yew the glad day through/There romps a little gnuey new. The Gnu Wooing. Burges Johnson. HBVY

Beneath their feet, the knife-sharp gibber-stone. The Tank. Roland Robinson. PoAu 1-2

Beneath worse ailments of the mind. The Matron of Jedborough and Her Husband (excerpt). William Wordsworth. PeD

Beneficent, believe me,/His Eccentricities– The bat is dun, with wrinkled wings. Emily Dickinson. FM

...Benjamin: six months old. Seeing and Doing. John Dean. AMV-81

Benny's an/empty bag. The Memory of Boxer Benny (Kid) Paret. Frank Lima. PoNe

Bent by the wind/their edges shine. Grasses. Ralph J. Mills, Jr. FAZ

Bent, following the cherub at the top/That points to God with his paired half-moon wings. Transcendentalism: A Poem in Twelve Books. Robert Browning. DiPo; PP; VLP

Bent in a wind which bore to me a sound/Of far-off piteous bleat of lambs and sheep. On the Wing. Christina Georgina Rossetti. SBG

Bent in the squares of moonlight, dreaming of the north. The Cabin North of It All. James McMichael. AmPA

Bent low, deafened, I plunge/On, blind in the face of the storm. Mistral. Barbara Howes. NYBP

Bequeathed us lovelier to recall/Than this dead boy! A Volunteer's Grave. William Alexander Percy. HBMV

Ber low, therffor, geve god the sterne,/For sure, circa Regna tonat. V. Innocentia Veritas Viat Fides Circumdederunt Me Inimici Mei. Sir Thomas Wyatt. AAS

Bereaved, we started home, leaving that animal there. Part of the Darkness. Isabella Gardner. BoAnP

Bereft of these and thee! Song of the Palm. Tracy Robinson. AA

Bermudian damsels are not fair! Amanda's Complaint. Philip Freneau. AP

Berness/ionalis/deliber. Ghost. Clark Coolidge. ANYP

Beseech the glorious one/To keep me near you/At the Judgement. Tenson. Iselda Carenza. WPOW

Beside an eternal river of scented honey. The Thousand and One Nights: Psalm of the Bottle. Anonymous. AWP

Beside God's ancient everlasting rune. Nodes. Alice Corbin Henderson. WGRP

Beside her grandfather's elderly puppet walk. Gardeners. David Ignatow. PCP

Beside me still. Then. John Morgan. AMV-81

Beside the boisterous brook of Green-head Ghyll. Michael. William Wordsworth. DiPo; EnL; ERoP 1-2; GoTL; OAEL 1-2; OAEP; WHA

Beside the idle summer sea. Rondel: Beside the Idle Summer Sea. William Ernest Henley. OBNC

Beside the rose, the sangria and the happy earth. Today I Am Envying the Glorious Mexicans. Michael C. Blumenthal. MAYP

Beside the sun of Schemmelfennig! Schemmelfennig. Bret (Francis Bret Harte) Harte. OBAL

Beside the sweet and delicate face/that by thy hearth-stone smiles. The Pilgrim from the East. Gustave Kahn. TrJP

Beside the white/chickens. The Red Wheelbarrow. William Carlos Williams. AmLP; BLPL; CMoP; ForPo; GrPl; HeIP; HoPM; InPS; LiTA; LiTM; MoAB; MoAmPo; NIP; NoAm; NOBA; NoP; PrIm; SoSe; SOTW; TAP; UnPo

Beside those eyes all other beauty's/vain. My Sweet Gazelle! Immanuel Di Roma. TrJP

Besides a little feather bed/To rest my little back. The Squirrel. Anonymous. OxNR

Besides, a penknife sticks in my heart,/So out I cannot creep.' Little Sir Hugh. Anonymous. OBET

Besides, everybody admits it's a Man's World./And just look what they've done to it! Why, Some of My Best Friends Are Women. Phyllis McGinley. NMM

Besides, it's grand for bailing. Sartorial Solecism. R. E. C. Stringer. FiBHP

Besides, it's not my tree at all,/But overhanging from next door. Best of Two Worlds. John Basil Boothroyd. BoAnP

Besides, the number of my years/Is over forty. Ad Xanthiam Phoceum. Horace. AWP

Besides the slow oxidation of carbohydrates and amino-acids. Animals. Robinson Jeffers. NU

...Besides the taxes are due on the/Thirty-first and the mirrors forget everything they see. Doctor Bill Williams. Ernest Walsh. InvP

...Besides/These there are many/Thousands of other truths, more/Than can ever be numbered. The City of the Moon (excerpt). Kenneth Rexroth. GP

Besides, when not a creature's by/'Tis inward satisfaction. Song: "Think of dress in every light." John Gay. OBEC; OBSP

Besieging the blossoming/Towers of the roses. Frost. Stella Benson. OxBTC

Bessy always had to wait,/While Mary lived in plenty. Bessy and Mary. Anonymous. OxNR

The best-beloved Night! Hymn to the Night. Henry Wadsworth Longfellow. AA; AnFE; AnNE; AP; APA; BLPL; ExPo; GoTF; HBV 1-2; HBVY; LaNeLa; LoBV; NePA; NOBA; OxBA; TAP; TreFS; TrGrPo; ViBoPo; WHA

The best damn glass of water I ever had. Sparkling Water. Richard Schaaf. TAT

The best days are the first/To flee. Mantova. James Wright. LCAP; NNaP

Best for you and best for me.　In the Gloaming.　Meta Orred.　BLSo;
FaFP; FSW; TreF

The best friends of the world.　Us Tasting the Air.　David Shapiro.　ANYP

The best little donkey that ever was born.　Kindness.　Anonymous.　OxNR

Best lover, secretary, and perfect staff.　The Secretary.　Peter Redgrove.
OxBTC

Best now I luif that graceles gane.'　The Man of Valour to His Fair Lady.
William Dunbar.　MeEL

The Best of All to find–is Jesus!　What Christ Is to Us.　Anonymous.
BLRP

Best of show!　Best of Show.　Barbara Howes.　GDP

The best of Tuscan cheer to feed your youth.　Sonnets of the Months.
Folgore da San Geminiano.　AWP

The best old man a-living in the land,/The best old man for life.　My Good
Old Man.　Anonymous.　BFSS

(Best Prince) then use best; which is Poesies worth.　The Epistle Dedicatory
to Chapman's Translation of the Iliad.　George Chapman.　OBS

Best recollection's/opposite number/on a ordinary day.　It's A.　Kit
Robinson.　APU

Best suited for the match/upcoming with the Masked Executioner.　Ripper
Collins' Legacy.　Don Johnson.　LiSp

...Best that you and I/Should live together, or together die.　United.　Paulus
Silentiarius.　AWP

The best time/Of the year for me.　I Like Christmas.　James S. Tippett.
ChBR

The best way is to come up hill with me/And have our fire and laugh and be
afraid.'　The Bonfire.　Robert Frost.　InvP

The best we shall find is a friend.　The Best Treasure.　John J. Moment.
TRV

The best work hasn't been done.　Opportunity.　Berton Braley.　WBLP

The best you get is an even break.　Ballade of Schopenhauer's Philosophy.
Franklin Pierce ("F.P.A.") Adams.　HBMV

The beste may be amended:–/But I will nott say so.　These Women All.
Heath.　FaBoCo

Bestial and natural of/any beast, you dig?　Small Comment.　Sonia Sanchez.
NBP

Bestowing on my grave/Perpetual care.　Country Cemetery.　Freda Newton
Bunner.　AMV-80

Bet–this is/the house where the table stands with/the light and the light.
Hut Window.　Paul Celan.　VWA

Bet were him that knewe/The false fro the trewe.　Snatches: "Wel were him
that wiste."　Anonymous.　OxBM

Bet yo' life dey got/Each and de udder's man.　Dey Got Each and de
Udder's Man.　Anonymous.　WTO

Bethink the lineage of a Pine.　Family Trees.　Douglas Malloch.　OHIP

Bethink ye, now ye hold your heavenly place.　To the Moon.　Pierre
Ronsard.　AWP

Betray the elf that loves to dwell/In Robin's bosom, as a chosen cell.　The
Redbreast (excerpt).　William Wordsworth.　PBBP

Betray what has been and what might have been.　A View of the Present
State of Ireland.　Edmund Charles Blunden.　BrPo

Betrothed in life, in death to be allied.　The Suttee.　Thomas Skinner.
OBTV

Better a cross, and nails through either hand,/Than Pilate's palace and a
frozen soul!　If Love Were Jester at the Court of Death.　Frederic
Lawrence Knowles.　HBV 1-2

Better all life forget her than this thing,/That Willowwood should hold her
wandering!'　The House of Life.　Dante Gabriel Rossetti.　OAEL 1-2

Better an ignis fatuus/Than no illume at all–.　Those–Dying Then.　Emily
Dickinson.　AmePo; CABA; NAWM 1-2; NoP

Better be blind than see what we must see.　Merry Christmas!　Elder Olson.
FAZ

Better be cheated to the last/Than lose the blessed hope of truth.　Faith.
Frances Anne Kemble.　FaBoBe; HBV 1-2; OBVV

Better by far you should forget and smile/Than that you should remember and
be sad.　Remember.　Christina Georgina Rossetti.　AnEnPo; AWP;
BoLiVe; BoLoP; EnLoPo; FaBV; FPL; GoTF; GTBS; MCCG;
NOBE; NOBV; NoP; OAEL 1-2; OAEP; OBEV; OBNC; OBVV; PoLf;
PoPle; PoRA; SBG; TreFS; TrGrPo; ViBoPo; WHA

Better–Could I bring?　I could bring you jewels–had I a mind to.　Emily
Dickinson.　TAP

...Better far/Pursue a frivolous trade by serious means,/Than a sublime art
frivolously.'　Aurora Leigh.　Elizabeth Barrett Browning.　BrRo

Better for birders, but for birds not so good.　Of Birds and Birders.　John
Heywood.　PBBP

Better get a home in-a dat Rock,/Don't you see?　I Got a Home in-a Dat
Rock.　Anonymous.　BoAN 1-2; BPo

A better grave than this.　Epitaph.　Elinor Wylie.　MoAmPo; SBG

Better, I think, than an embittered whine.　The Fox and the Grapes.
Marianne Moore.　FM

Better if it were a cockroach, simply to squash it.　Birds in the Night.　Luis
Cernuda.　PeHV

Better keep quiet and act like the/others/Or they'll begin to make fun of your/
nose.　Now You're Content.　Andre Spire.　TrJP

...Better/Not hear that "which' for "who'/And risk eternal doom.　Burial of
an Irish President.　Austin Clarke.　BIrV; IPY

Better not lock it/up again.　What Happened?　John Wieners.　PoM

Better or worse, we're in for life.　Reuben and Rachel.　Harry Birch.
PSoN

Better put a strong fence round the top of the cliff/Than an ambulance down
in the valley.　A Fence or an Ambulance.　Joseph Malins.　BLPA

Better quit fooling, fooling me.　All Night Long Fooling Me.　Anonymous.
AmFP

Better safe port, then be in seas distrest.　Now Strike Your Sailes Ye Jolly
Mariners!　Edmund Spenser.　EtS

...Better still to burn/Upon that gloom where all have felt a chill.　A Winter
Talent.　Donald Davie.　NePoEA-2; OAEL 1-2

Better than a pre-fab–/No rent!　Down in the Jungle.　Anonymous.　WTO

Better than anyone, he knows/what must be done/to save us.　Charlton
Heston.　Elliot Fried.　AMV-80

Better than day they know the day.　From Soil Somehow the Poet's Word.
Kenneth Leslie.　OBCV

Better than death in life is life in death:–/Good night!　Icarus.　Harry
Lyman Koopman.　AA

Better than lust for boys, with Pope and Turk,/Or others' spouses, like my
Lord of York.'　The Second Satire of the First Book of Horace (excerpt).
Alexander Pope.　OBSV

Better than the summit raptures/And the deep-sea sorrows?　No.　Middle-
Aged Conversation.　Arthur Seymour John Tessimond.　PoL

Better than us; less wide.　Dream Songs.　John Berryman.　HaCAP

Better than waking is to sleep! Albuera!　Albuera.　Thomas Hardy.　WaaP

Better the choking sigh, the sobbing breath/Than passion's death!　Dead
Fires.　Jessie Redmond Fauset.　BANP; PoNe

Better the swan's brief note than thousand cries/Of rooks in springtime blown
about the skies.　Erinna.　Antipater of Sidon.　AWP

The better thou thryuest, the gladder am I.　A Hundreth Good Poyntes of
Husbandry.　Thomas Tusser.　FaBoUs

Better 'tis that one should fall,/Than by one to hazard all.　The Scare-Fire.
Robert Herrick.　HAP; NoP

Better to abdicate/From a material and spiritual terrain/Fit only for
barbarians.　Translation.　Roy Fuller.　ChMP; NOBE; OxBTC

Better to die, you think./But nothing happens.　Execution.　James A.
Randall, Jr.　BPo

Better to leave it so–and to escape/Whatever in the landscape may be strange.
The Dam, Glen Garry.　Robert Symmons.　PoSH

Better to leave it standing wide.　Gates.　Ted Kooser.　GP

Better to pray for the Restoration/Than the overseer of a patch-work nation.
The Misses Poar Drive to Church.　Josephine Pinckney.　AnAmPo

Better 'twere my book were dead/Than to live not perfected.　His Request to
Julia.　Robert Herrick.　CaPo; OBS

...A better way of killing a louse/than by destroying the body it feeds on.
With the Most Susceptible Element, the Mind, Already Turned...　Walter
Benton.　WaP

Better when I had nothing but happiness.　Then and Now.　Kath Walker.
IHMS

...Between, a rock/inside, you hold the wild bird still/like this, in here, in here.
A Bird inside a Box.　William Stafford.　NPAW

Between bare branches, the cold steel-blue of the sea.　The House in the
Green Well.　John Hall Wheelock.　MoAmPo

Between. Between. Between. Between. Between.　Dead Center.　Chester
Kallman.　PoA

Between death's republic and his kingdom　For Now.　William Stanley
Merwin.　CoPo; NaP

Between halves of a moon/That rides all night at the full.　Full Moon.
Galway Kinnell.　NePoAm-2

Between her bestowal and her desire.　Oh the Inconstant.　N. P. Van Wyk
Louw.　PeSA

Between her Bosom and His hayre!　Tryste Noel.　Louise Imogen Guiney.
HBV 1-2; OBVV

Between leaps to its burrow.　The Jerboa.　Marianne Moore.　AtBAP;
FaBoWP; FYAP; MoPo

Between my comely bachelors/And blushing bridal maids.　The Ballad of the
Dark Ladie.　Samuel Taylor Coleridge.　EnRP

Between my thighs like a valentine before you have time to/wipe them.　You.
Tom Clark.　ANYP; EAS

Between my trembling hands.　The Morning of the Red-Tailed Hawk.
Bettie M. Sellers.　AMV-80

Between myself and the place I inhabit.　Everything Has Its History.　Phillis
Levin.　AMV-81

Between Orion and the Pleiades.　Ceremony.　Howard Nemerov.　AMV-80

Between our banks of steep embraces.　Juniper.　Laurie Lee.　NeBP

Between promise and pleading stance,/you are devil, flesh, and earth.　She
Proves the Inconsistency of the Desires and Criticism of Men...　Sister
Juana Ines de la Cruz.　BoWoP

Between Selma, Peking,/Westchester/And me. Undertow. Langston Hughes. LiTM

Between sun-wilted hedgerows into town. Pegasus Lost. Elinor Wylie. MoAmPo

Between the cold waves of his hair, as he tip-/toes off. Death. Maxwell Bodenheim. AnAmPo; MAPA; TrJP

Between the cradle and the grave/Lies a haircut and a shave. Babies Haven't Any Hair. Samuel Hoffenstein. NLV

Between the end of the Chatterley ban/And the Beatles' first L.P. Annus Mirabilis. Philip Larkin. NIP; NLV; NOBL

Between the faggot and the flame/I see his face return. Evidence at the Witch Trials. James Keir Baxter. OxBC

Between the Karim Shahir/M'lefaat-Zawi/record says/in the/kurdish hills. Between the Karim Shahir. Rochelle Owens. CoPo

Between the music and the soundless scream. The City. Ben Maddow. WaP

Between the North Star and the Southern Cross. On a Monument to Marti. Walter Adolphe Roberts. TTY

Between the sailing cloud and the seasick sea. Put Off Thy Bark from Shore, Though Near the Night. Frederick Goddard Tuckerman. MOS

Between the solid earth and welkin flit. Pluto's Council. Edward Fairfax. OBSC

Between the South and the North Countrie. The Man of the North Countrie. Thomas D'Arcy McGee. OnYI

Between the streamlets she does not sleep./Sleep a little. The Sleep Song of Diarmaid and Grainne. Anonymous. OnYI

Between those two great beams on plumes outspread/Hovers and gleams the everlasting Dove! Hymn for the Feast of the Annunciation. Sir Aubrey De Vere. ISi

Between two drinking-bouts a masterpiece. The Old Masters. Emile Verhaeren. AnEnPo

Between two fires. The Conflict. C. Day Lewis. AnEnPo; LiTB; LiTM; MoAB; MoBrPo; NoP

Between two gusts, cold waves, the golden tide. Homage to the Weather. Michael Hamburger. NMP

Between two vigils fallen asleep. This Quiet Dust. John Hall Wheelock. AnEnPo; MoAmPo; WHA

Between two wretched dying men, of whom/One doubts, and one for pity's sake believes. A Thorn Forever in the Breast. Countee Cullen. BiP

Between us and the scene before us, fading/Softly to darkness. By the Sea. John Hollander. AmPC

Between us are many fish. Canadice Lake. Bob Mondy. WOLT

Between us still we breed a mystery. The Chalk-Pit. Edward ("Edward Eastaway") Thomas. BrPo

Between us, though we rot to feed the crow. Poem: "You, who in April laughed, a green god in the sun." Brenda Chamberlain. NeBP

Between yourself and me. Evidence Read at the Trial of the Knave of Hearts. Lewis (Charles Lutwidge Dodgson) Carroll. FaBoNo; FaFP; GTBS-P; NBM; OxBoLi

Betweenpie mountains–lights a lovely mile. My Own Heart Let Me More Have Pity On. Gerard Manley Hopkins. CoBMV; FaBoMo; InPS; LiTM; NOBV; NoP; PAI; VLP

Betwene hire kurtle and hire smok/I wolde ben hid. The White Beauty. Anonymous. MeEL; OxBM

Betwixt Atrides Great, and Thetis God-like Son. The Iliad. Homer. OBVE

Betwixt the two of them, all opposites meet. Sonnet XIII. Winfield Townley Scott. ErPo

Bewail one hour the more, when sea/And wind are one with memory. Penumbra. Dante Gabriel Rossetti. VLP

Beware!...I shall not always wait/Before thy doors! Extremum Tanain. Horace. AWP

Beware, lest this little brook of life/Some burning noon go dry! Have You Got a Brook. Emily Dickinson. FaBV

Beware, O Man–for knowledge must to thee,/Like the great flood to Egypt, ever be. To the Nile. Percy Bysshe Shelley. OBRV

Beware of it,–/for long ago you strangled two great snakes. Drunken Heracles. Wallace Gould. AnAmPo

Beware of the man who praises liberated women;/he is planning to quit his job. Seventeen Warnings in Search of a Feminist Poem. Erica Jong. AmPA

"Beware of the semblance/of lard at thy flanks." One Modern Poet. Carl Sandburg. OBAL

Beware, oh, take care. Beware, Oh, Take Care. Anonymous. FSW

Beware such silly vanity and fraud. Night Comes Apace. Evan V. Shute. CaP

Beware the ale foam in your way/Or you will end like Zimmer. A Zimmershire Lad. Paul Zimmer. SM

Beware the hour/It uproots trees! Warning. Langston Hughes. BPo

Beware the Warden of Light has married/an old piece of string! The Wheelchair Butterfly. James Tate. NoAm

Beware! therfore: the blind eteth many a fly. Against Women. Anonymous. MeEL

Beware to whom thou tellest thy tale,/But bere a horn and blow it naught. Bear a Horn and Blow It Not. Anonymous. OxBM

"Beware, you are dead sheaves,/I am a flaming fire." The Prophet. Yehoash. TrJP

Bewigged Descartes looks more outre than the painted wizard. Unpredictable but Providential. W. H. Auden. SUW

The bewilderment from their eyes? A Nisei Picnic. David Mura. BrSi

Bewitched gods tracking time toward our release in/light. Stones: Avesbury. Daisy Aldan. PoA

Beyond, a green continent. Locations. Jim Harrison. AmPA

Beyond all measure/of time. Between the Tides. Emily Sargent Councilman. AMV-80

Beyond blue walls/black death is waiting. Pshytik. Nahum Bomze. VWA

Beyond fixed sight, beyond nothing? Sestina. Judith Kroll. AmPA; SM

Beyond her worried hands. Flight. Ruth Whitman. SO

Beyond his hopes, with joy and plenty crowned. The Rising Village. Oliver Goldsmith. OBCV

Beyond its own sweet will! Amy Wentworth. John Greenleaf Whittier. BeLS

Beyond my sight the cloudless sky/Is troubled with artillery. Macrocosm. Philip Child. CaP

Beyond our fate/And distant from our eyes. Cartography. Louise Bogan. PoPl

Beyond our hearing is the hearing of the community. Requiem. William Stafford. NaP

Beyond potential beauty, beautiful. Design for a Stream-Lined Sunrise. Sister Mary Madeleva. GoBC

Beyond self's vanquishment/We feed upon our kill. The Meaning of Violence. John Williams. NePoAm-2

Beyond sly bramble, misted kiln/And the dried voluptuary veins. Mould of Castile. Jack R. Clemo. NOCV

Beyond some swinging open door/Into eternity. These Men. Leon Gellert. BoAV; PoAu 1-2

Beyond the confines of the tomb/Appears the dawn of heaven! There Is an Hour of Peaceful Rest. William B. Tappan. AH

Beyond the crackle/of death's stinking certainty. The Yellow Season. William Carlos Williams. MoAB; MoAmPo

Beyond the dark, into the dream/Over the hills and far away. Stanzas. William Ernest Henley. HBV 1-2

Beyond the Day of Jubilo. Jubilo. Allen Tate. WaP

Beyond the end of our understanding. Omphalos: The Well. Sean Jennett. NeIP

Beyond the flicker of/a puffed-out candle A Poem for Integration. Alvin Saxon. PoBA

Beyond the gray spaces around tree branches/where the silences of birds are the answer. A Colloquy of Silences. Michael Heffernan. SM

Beyond the hope of touch. The Overtakelessness of Those. Emily Dickinson. MoRP

Beyond the mountains of the west,/Their children go to die. Indians. Charles Sprague. GN

Beyond the prism/still. Leaving Smoke's. Gordon Henry. STE

Beyond the rim of his plate/Trudged the disinherited./Ipse dixit, 1938. Portrait of a Senator. Charles Norman. DBV

Beyond the shadows of Aegina's rocks,/Amidst the dark Aegean's distant surge. Greece. William Haygarth. OBTV

Beyond the stomach walls/of the shark. The Sea-Turtle and the Shark. Melvin B. Tolson. BP; PoBA

Beyond the wall of tears/the phoenix period/in flames Phoenix. Rose Auslander. VWA

Beyond the woodpile, the air I could almost hold. In the Dream of the Body. David Keller. AMV-80

Beyond tomorrow's mystic gates. The New Year. Horatio Nelson Powers. PoToHe

Beyond what glittering stars and in what ultimate re-/gions! The Sound of the Sea. John Hall Wheelock. EtS

Beyond what I have asked or thought. After the Rain. Edward A. Collier. BLRP

Biafra. O mother, hear the growl, the night/is cold, cold, cold. Biafra. L. V. Mack. PoBA

Bible school would have helped/But Daddy wouldn't go. Does Daddy Go? Anonymous. STF

The bicycles barely moving, the sun posted Snapshot of Hue. Daniel Halpern. MAYP

Bid adieu to the kind friends and boarders/That hang 'round at Duffy's Hotel! Duffy's Hotel. Anonymous. ShS

Bid Cleobulus not refuse/The gift of love I give. To Dionysus. Anacreon. LiTW

Bid earth and its delusions pass away/But leave the mind as its creator free. Written in a Thunder Storm July 15th 1841. John Clare. ERoP 1-2; VLP

Bid him judge me gently for the sake of long ago. To Her–Unspoken. Amelia Josephine Burr. HBV 1-2

Bid him renounce his wish and kneel/In thanks for this same kindly clay. Clay. Edward Verrall Lucas. HBV 1-2

Bid joy back, have at the harvest, keep Hope pale. Fragment. Gerard Manley Hopkins. NAMP

Bid Love be still, nor ever speak,/Lest he his own rejection seek. If She Be Made of White and Red. Herbert P. Horne. HBV 1-2

Bid me farewell when the last stars awake,/Or else my wounded heart will break, will break! In Summer. Charles Hanson Towne. HBMV

Bid me Good Morning! Life! I Know Not What Thou Art. Anna Laetitia Barbauld. GTBS; GTBS-P

"Bid me not live," I sigh, "till all be gone." Love's Rosary. George Edward Woodberry. AA

Bid me, O Lord, in that most dreadful hour,/Not fall, but fly away! Death. Mary Elizabeth Coleridge. TrPWD

Bid the day be born. Christmas Antiphones (excerpt). Algernon Charles Swinburne. PGD; TrPWD; TRV

Bid the setting sun adieu. Day: A Pastoral. John Cunningham. OBEC

Bid the stars shine forever. Centaur Song. Hilda ("H. D.") Doolittle. VGW

Bid the world's hounds come to horn! The White Stag. Ezra Pound. LOW

Bid Time and Nature gently spare/The shaft we raise to them and thee. Hymn Sung at the Completion of the Concord Monument April 19, 1836. Ralph Waldo Emerson. PoPl

Bid us sing thy Harvest Home! Harvest Home. Henry Alford. WGRP

Bid you be merry and remember death. De Coenatione Micae. Martial (Marcus Valerius Martialis). FaBoCh; LoGBV

Bidde we God and oure Ledy/To thilke blisse Jesus us sende./Amen. The Death of King Edward I. Anonymous. MeEL

The bidding of a monarch, and his countenance/Enforces homage. King Henry V. William Shakespeare. PH

–"Bide a wee, and dinna weary!"/Is a heartsome song. Bide a Wee! John Oxenham. TRV

...Bids/Silence, and drinks our soul through closed eye-lids. Partings. Charles Guerin. AWP

Bids spheres and atoms in just order move. The Hand and Foot. Jones Very. AP; NePA

Bids the young eyes of spring witness eternal pain. Soon with the Lilac Fades Another Spring. Patrick MacDonogh. OxBI

Bids us save the great To-day. The Present. Adelaide Anne Procter. WGRP

Bids you alleviate the fever. Epithalamium. Vassar Miller. NePoEA

BIG BIRD SENSATION, MISSING LOCAL BOY. Ganymede. William Plomer. PeHV

...The big black dog/comes running, wet and smelling of/the fields, the mud, the edge. The Edge of Town. William Clamurro. AMV-81

A big center slice/of fried ham. Butcher's Wife. Herbert Scott. GP

A big, fat, lazy slug that, even then,/Killed women, children, and defenceless men. The White Monster. William Henry Davies. AmMo; LiTB

Big fish alone escape from thee! The Net of Law. James Jeffrey Roche. HBV 1-2; PV

Big love or angler's luck. And Only Our Shadow Walks with Us. Eithne Wilkins. NeBP

A big one! A big one! An Incorrigible Music. Allen Curnow. OCNZ

The big rain that rattles and roars. Rain Sizes. John Ciardi. SoPo

Big sound on the ground It's Over a(See Just. Edward Estlin Cummings. OxBA; VGW

Big-toothed one. Animal Songs: Hyena. Anonymous. PeSA

Big with a death to nourish him/during a long sleep. The Snake. Wendell Berry. GeTw

Big with tenderness Tell Our Daughters. Besmilr Brigham. IHMS

Bigger bogies, bigger Jennies,/Frichten muckle men. Jenny wi' the Airn Teeth. Alexander ("Surface man") Anderson. HBV 1-2

The bigger fuss, the smaller the result. The Mountain in Labor. Aesop. AWP

...Bigger than/this poem, smaller than the whole world. Natural History. Laura Fargas. SUW

The biggest fish are still outside the nets. Psychoanalysis. Gavin Ewart. NYBP

Bill and mittens, lie ye there! The Wood-Cutter's Night Song. John Clare. EnRP; OBRV

Bill Bailey won't you please come home. Bill Bailey. Hughie Cannon. BLSo; FSN; FSW; OBAL

Bill's in the Legislatur', but he doesn't say what fur. Billy, He's in Trouble. James Barton Adams. YaD

The billboards of the sky. Skywriting. Mary Maxtone. BrR

Billy the Kid wakes up in the morning and She is not in love. The Return of Philista. Dick Gallup. ANYP

Billy Whistle,/Tripping-go. Toe Tipe. Anonymous. OxNR

BIM BAM BOO!–an' the dope gave out. Willy the Weeper. Anonymous. AS; GBP

Bind me forever in your ritual, your/Worship and prayer, me, and all mankind! Bread. Abraham Moses Klein. PeCV

Bind us the Morning, and restore our own! Thefts of the Morning. Edith Matilda Thomas. AA

Binding black beetles round its eyes/Placed in walnut shells. Mary Arnold the Female Monster. Anonymous. GBP; OBET

Binding, blood-brotherly/Beyond-speech answer. The Flash. James Dickey. LCAP

...Binding up in an unlimited way what/otherwise goes unexpressed. Live Acts. Charles Bernstein. APU

Bing on the ring! Bing, bang! (Hey) The Raftsmen. Anonymous. FSW

Bingo was his name, sir. Bingo. Anonymous. FSW

Binnae the mowdie-man's. Molecatcher. Albert D. Mackie. GoTS

Binoculars/raised/like pistols. Waiting for E. gularis. Linda Pastan. SUW

Birches falling down the hillside. For My Grandmother, Bridget Halpin. Michael Hartnett. BIrV; CIP

The bird as it beats its blunt head/again and again into the earth. At the Edge of the Jungle. Patrick Lane. NOBC

A bird dipped wing, and, swift and white,/Peace brooded there. On the Height. Eunice Tietjens. HBMV

The bird drops home. L'Oiseau Bleu. Gordon Bottomley. BrPo

The bird flies yonder o'er the field. Of the Child with the Bird at the Bush. John Bunyan. CBEP; OxBChV

A bird had erected her nest to stay/And sing to the soul of the sleeper below. The Emigrant's Child. Lyman H. Sproull. PoOW

A bird I cannot name crows. A New Poem (for Jack Spicer). Robert Duncan. NNaP; PoM

The bird is to die I'm Sad. Forugh Farrokzad. BoWoP

The bird moves apart from his cry. The Black Plateau. William Stanley Merwin. NNaP

A bird my body,/My bird-blood ready. The Young Girl. Theodore Roethke. NoAm

The bird my trap gave me,/My faithful, useful trap. O Lamb Give Me My Salt. Anonymous. PBA

Bird, O my bird, listen to me, do not close your wings. The Bird. Rabindranath Tagore. LiTW; PoPl

The bird of god descends between two moments/Like silence into music, opening a way through time. Air. Kathleen Raine. MoAB; MoBrPo

The Bird of Time has but a little way/To fluter–and the Bird is on the Wing. The Rubaiyat of Omar Khayyam. Omar Khayyam. SeCeV

...A bird rising over the ashes, a dream. Wishful Thinking. Michael C. Blumenthal. HaCAP

The bird's-eye glory to full sight/Bring, and outcasts into delight. A Mile from Eden. Anne Ridler. MoPo

The bird's fire-fangled feathers dangle down. Of Mere Being. Wallace Stevens. HaCAP

A bird's song after rain./Melissa. Melissa. Carolyn D. Redl-Hlus. AMV-80

The Bird's transfigured in the Flower. The Blue-Bird. Herman Melville. BLPL; NOBA

A bird sits in its cage alone. Captive. Peretz Hirshbein. TrJP

The bird so fair, for its putrid sake,/is flung to the dogs in the junk's white wake. The Flying Fish. John Gray. LoBV; OBNC

A bird that shuts his wings for better speed. Sonnets. Frederick Goddard Tuckerman. NoP

A bird that wakes a fellow up,/Should have been a buttercup. The Bird. Samuel Hoffenstein. FiBHP; PV

Bird that was shot ne'er dropped so quick as he. On Zacchaeus. Francis Quarles. HAP; LoBV; MePo; OBS; OBSP

Bird, the long throat bent back, and the eyes in hiding. Winter Swan. Louise Bogan. AnAmPo

"The bird upon its lonely bough/Sings sweetest at the close of day." Dull Is My Verse. Walter Savage Landor. PoEL 1-5

The bird was on the brier! Topsyturvey-World. William Brighty ("Matthew Browne") Rands. OxBChV

The bird who watched/what would be called/a dream Aswelay. Norman Henry Pritchard II. PoBA

The bird will call at longer intervals. Heigh-Ho on a Winter Afternoon. Donald Davie. NePoEA-2; OxBTC

Bird wings clipped, birds feet chained Okinawa Kanashii Monogatari. Geraldine Kudaka. BrSi

The bird with the wisp of straw. Spring. Caroline Giltinan. HBMV

The bird would sing as it sang in the Palace of old. Hearing the Early Oriole. Po Chu-i. UnS

"Birdie!" Sylvia cried, "come back!" Dove's Nest. Joseph Russell Taylor. HBV 1-2

Birdlike from a cage in a freedom of flight. Imagery. Harindranath Chattopadhyaya. ACV

The birds are in the bushes and the wolf is at the door. Everything in Its Place. Arthur Guiterman. NLV; OBAL

The birds are still in flight. Believe the birds. Imaginary Elegies, I-IV. Jack Spicer. NeAP

The birds, but notes of thine imperial own! The Mocking-bird. Henry Jerome Stockard. AA

Birds flittered over the new grass, the moles hummed. Cinderella. Roger Mitchell. DFT

Birds fly by like falling stars. Landscape. Abraham Sutzkever. VWA

Birds go flying by. At the Doors. Der Nistor. TrJP

The birds go to sleep by the sweet wild twist of her song. The Outlaw of Loch Lene. Jeremiah Joseph Callanan. AnIV; BIrV; CH; GBL; IrPN; OBEV; OBRV; OnYI; OxBI

Birds I never met before/act like this is their home. Silica Carbonate Rock. Fred Berry. NU

...Birds/in it don't remember/it wasn't there. In One Place. Robert Wallace. Psk

The birds in the air, that fly together pair and pair,/Bear witness, Ann, that I love thee. Geordie (B vers.). Anonymous. BaBo

Birds make all about those sippers and smilers ceremonies of/very sweet sound. Tea Poems: Chinaman. George Mackay Brown. OxBC

Birds (O unreal whitewashed station!)/Compose no more that invisible architecture. Daphne Stillorgan. Denis Devlin. CIP

The birds that are singing. Winter Song. Juan Ramon Jimenez. WSC

The birds that call to you, and all the shoals/That swim in the natal waters of her ocean. Message from Home. Kathleen Raine. ImOP

The birds that day/More cheerfully will sing. Song Set by Thomas Weelkes: "In pride of May." Anonymous. OBSC

The birds, the birds, sob for the time of man. The Conspirators. Frederic Prokosch. LiTM; NAMP; NePA; PrIm; WaP

The birds, they never cease/and their souls are only air. Praise of God. Anonymous. NOBI

Birds, trampling the lily foliage, eating the soft round roots! The Moon-Bone Cycle: The Birds. Anonymous. WTO

The birds which are flying/And gliding about above/Will some day tire/And descend to earth. Colonialism. Cabdullaahi Qarshe. WTO

Birds, wild swans, glide palely o'er a charming stream. Peace. Samuel Greenberg. CrMA

Birds will not approach. Song from the Unfinished Man. Paul David Ashley. LFAC

Birth and the grave, that are not as they were. Alastor. Percy Bysshe Shelley. CABL; OAEL 1-2; OAEP

Birth announcement/of Your/Day Star Stars in Apple Cores. Luci Shaw. TrCP

The Birth-day shines, when logs not burne, but/men. Ode: To Sir William Sydney, on His Birth-Day. Ben Jonson. NAs

Birth is its dying. Solstice. Emery George. HoAn

The birth of JESUS in the human soul. The Salutation of the Blessed Virgin. John Byrom. ISi

A birth of joy—not like the first of tears and woe. Hymn to the Supreme Being on Recovery (excerpt). Christopher Smart. NOEC

The birthdays of the old require such candles. Strokes. William Stafford. ConAP; PCP

Birthing aboriginal psychosis. Custer Must Have Learned to Dance. Elizabeth Woody. STE

Birthmarked that dawn! What Birds Were There. Brother Antoninus. NoAm

The birthplace of the Messiah, had I known! The Inn That Missed Its Chance. Amos R. Wells. TrCP

A Bishop or at least a Dean. A Wykehamist's Address to Learning. P. N. Shuttleworth. FaBoCo

A bit of the Book in the evening,/To hallow the end of the day. A Bit of the Book. Margaret E. Sangster. TRV

A bit on the grand side. What about you? The Evans Country. Kingsley Amis. NOBL

Bit shee's Juno, when she walkes,/And Minerva, when she talks. A Celebration of Charis. Ben Jonson. AnAnS 2; SeCP

A bit too much/because the car was hot. Early June. R. P. Dickey. TAT

The bitch eternity is going to be eternal. Death with a Coda. Giuseppe Gioachino Belli. AMV-81

Bite me and be born. In the Root Cellar. Maxine W. Kumin. FaBoWP

Bite me./Hard. New York, Summer. Jack Gilbert. NPGG

The bits of a photograph lie on the/dresser... Lamentations. Alter Brody. TrJP; VWA

The bits of chalk and the precious/stones. The End of Man Is Death. Moses Ibn Ezra. TrJP

Bits of me splintered in to a mirror/falling falling rolling,/in... Look at My Face. Carolyn M. Rodgers. JB

Bitter for remembrance of the healing which has passed. Lincoln. John Gould Fletcher. HBMV; LaNeLa; MoAmPo

Bitter grief tastes me best, pain is my ease,/Sick to the death, still loving my disease. Like Those Sick Folks. Sir Philip Sidney. OBSP

Bitter had been thy punishment. The Culprit Fay. Joseph Rodman Drake. GN

Bitter is your trouble–and I am far from you. The Kine of My Father. Dora Sigerson Shorter. OnYI; OxBI

Bitter landscapes,/unlovely. The Distances to the Friend. Jonathan Williams. NeAP

Bitter sadness,/That's the road I go. Lonely Road. Peter Abrahams. PBA

Bitter the wail of a spirit;/Lost after all. Lost after All. Charlie D. Tillman. PeD

Bitterer, too, are ye? The Tuft of Kelp. Herman Melville. FaBoEE; FaBoRV; MAmP; MOS

The bitterness, the folly and the pain. Abraham Lincoln Walks at Midnight. Vachel Lindsay. OHIP

Bittersweet, sumac,/snow, and frozen seed. The Round. Philip Booth. BoNaP; GrPl; NCSH

Black against the same moon in an unsame sky. At the Edge of the Bay. Thomas Caldecot Chubb. EtS

Black, among the English newspapers. Three Women. Lauris Edmond. OCNZ

...Black/and enormous, wobbling to his feet, the dumb bull, Copernicus. The First Birth. Rodney Jones. MAYP

...A black and/impudent Voltairean crow has spoiled/the sacrament. And I can rise and go. Sunday in the Country. May Swenson. NePoAm-2

Black/Angry/Proud Washiri (Poet). Kattie M. Cumbo. BOLo

Black Angus, wagging his tail by the white laburnums,/Greet their Laird's shade! The Lairdless Place. Kate Rennie Archer. GoYe

Black as auld widdie-fruit, Mahoun/Bestrides a redeless mapamound. The Deevil's Waltz. Sydney Goodsir Smith. FaBoTw

Black as tar and tar it isn't. Riddle: "White as snow and snow it isn't." Anonymous. GBP

The black bass rises to the fly. A Rise. Ernest McGaffey. AA

Black Bear sang, drumming on a log. Moon of Huckleberries. Phil George. VoR

The black belt scarcely buckles, maw. Chicago Allegory. Stewart Parker. CIP

The black berries again on their red twigs. Difficult Times. Bertolt Brecht. ELU

Black Betty, where'd you come from?/ Bambalamb. Black Betty. Anonymous. ABF

The black bird of your death flaps,/calling our names. Phil. Ted Kooser. AMV-81

The black bird sang as if it had a song. Sail away. Robert Adamson. CBAP

Black birds, the wind, cover their heart. Man of My Time. Salvatore Quasimodo. PoPl

Black, black, black is the color of my true love's hair. Black Is the Color. Anonymous. FF

Black buckles dangling/from dusty black vests The Old Men. Cid Corman. PCP

A black cat comes, wide-eyed and thin;/And we take him in. Snow in the Suburbs. Thomas Hardy. BoNaP; CMoP; GoJo; MoAB; MoBrPo; OAEL 1-2; OBMV; OxBTC; PPP

Black coffee in a big tin can. Trail Crew Camp at Bear Valley, 9000 Feet.... Gary Snyder. HaCAP

The black cow is two native carriers/Bringing its belly home, slung from a pole. Fetching Cows. Norman MacCaig. BoAnP; OxBC

Black cows and white cows and red. Cow Time. Monica Shannon. SiSoSe

The black creek and/the small leaf slips in. Treaties. Archie Randolph Ammons. HaCAP

Black-crested,/Soft, and neat. Quail Walk. Heather Ross Miller. BoAnP

Black dada nihilismus. Black Dada Nihilismus. LeRoi (Imamu Amiri Baraka) Jones. PoM

...Black horned pout/doze on the bottom. The Farm. Donald Hall. LiTM

The black hound running in fierce despair,/With his grief of a thousand year. Gluskap's Hound. Theodore Goodridge Roberts. WHW

Black is my cry, black to the roots of sight. The Murder Trial. Perseus Adams. PeSA

Black/magic is your/touch/making/me breathe. Black Magic. Sonia Sanchez. BPo

A Black man/again. Two Jazz Poems. Carl Wendell Hines, Jr. AmNP

The Black Man's son held a terror, you see. The Black Man's Son. Oswald Durand. TTY

Black mother, I still am/One of the soil. A Lament to My Mother. Guy C. Z. Mhone. WhB

Black neighborhoods which surround the small airfield. A Dimpled Cloud. Frederick Seidel. FYAP

The black, numb fingernails. On a Field at Fredericksburg. Dave Smith. GeTw; HaCAP

Black out. Black. Nicholas Rinaldi. AMV-80

Black plush, a dark flame. Paterson. William Carlos Williams. CMoP

BLACK POWER. Stereo. Don L. Lee. PoL

A black rock avalanche repaints/the persiflage of the victim's "Greece". Another Island Groupage.   Kenward Elmslie   ANYP

...Black rocks and billows looming/In the dim chill dawn of day!   The Dawning of the Day.   James Clarence Mangan.   GoBC

Black rocks for thy thorns.   The Gardens of Cymodoce.   Algernon Charles Swinburne.   FaBoPP

Black roots shaped like fingernails and shoes.   Lone Gentleman.   Pablo Neruda.   ErPo

The black seed in its brain/parachuting toward earth.   Silence.   Gregory Orr.   GeTw

Black skins, babel–and the sun/That burns all colours into one.   Jamaica Market.   Agnes Maxwell-Hall.   TTY

The black snow falls, and the wind blows.   The Wind Carol.   Lewis Turco.   SM

A black snowman/and place him upon/Malcolm's grave.   I remember... Mae Jackson.   BOLo; CNA; PoBA

Black, something very bright, from inside him.   In the Dead of the Night.   Norman Dubie.   AmPA

The black soul cracks the universe./free.   Beyond the Nigger.   Sterling D. Plumpp.   PoBA

...The black spot on your head is your own mourn-/ing cap.   Looking at a Dead Wren in My Hand.   Robert Bly.   GP; NNaP

Black taxes,/on everything I do.   Taxes.   Don L. Lee.   BOLo

Black the way a hero dies.   Negritude.   James A. Emanuel.   BPo; CNA

Black trout,/Ye're oot.   Dips or Counting Out Rhymes: "I saw a doo flee our the dam."   Anonymous.   GBP

Black unison/our heartbeats   Uhuru.   Mari E. Evans.   CNA

Black water breaking into reality.   Extracts from Addresses to the Academy of Fine Ideas (excerpt).   Wallace Stevens.   LiTM

Black, white, and red, O red like the soil of Africa.   We Delighted, My Friend.   Leopold Sedar Senghor.   PBA; TTY

Black & white/over & over/again.   The Kiss.   Claude Clayton Smith.   PoDr

Black with birds of carrion prey.   Villanelle.   John Nist.   AMV-81

The blackberries sweating in their bucket.   Among Blackberries.   Michael Waters.   GeTw

–A blackbird, a branch/a mass of yellow.   Four Glosses.   Anonymous.   NOBI

Blackbird builds his fire. Outside, a quick thirty below.   Christmas Comes to Moccasin Flat.   James Welch.   CDW; GP; MAT

A blackbird on/His leafy throne/Tossed it alone/Across the bay.   The Blackbird by Belfast Lough.   Anonymous.   KiLC

...A blackbird resting/on a telephone wire that moves/quietly with the wind./a southwind.   Man Thinking about Woman.   Don L. Lee.   CNA; NoAm

The blackbird saith.   Vesper.   Thomas Edward Brown.   BoC

The blackbird sat in the cedar-limbs.   Thirteen Ways of Looking at a Blackbird.   Wallace Stevens.   AP; BLPL; CABA; CMoP; CoBMV; DiPo; HaCAP; HeIP; InPK; LiTM; MAPA; NoAm; NOBA; NoP; SOTW; TAP

The blackbirds have their wills,/The poets too.   Early Spring.   Alfred, Lord Tennyson.   HBV 1-2; HBVY

...Blackened/because born that way.   Propriety.   Marianne Moore.   UnS

The blacker are their crimes, he louder sings.   The Parliament of Bees.   John Day.   ViBoPo

Blackness, and scalding stench, for love and flowers.   Sonnets.   Frederick Goddard Tuckerman.   HAP

The blackout like scarves in our new hair.   Negatives.   Charles Wright.   PoA

The blacks should cultivate the Cane-land isles.   The Sugar Cane.   James Grainger.   NOEC

...The blade,/Blood-stained, continue cutting weeds and shade.   Reapers.   Jean Toomer.   BPo; CDC; HAP; InPK; NoAm; PoBA; PPP

The blade gestures in my hand/for my parents to run.   Taking Care of It.   Deborah Lee.   BrSi

A blade of gold flashed on the ocean's rim.   The New Day: Prelude.   Richard Watson Gilder.   HBV 1-2; PoLf

...A/blade of grass was then born, an immortal springtime!   The Stone and the Blade of Grass in the Warsaw Ghetto.   David Scheinert.   VWA

...Bladed/Like a shell, and as it opens, cuts.   Earliness at the Cape.   Babette Deutsch.   FYAP; NePoAm-2; NYBP

Blades of a feather.   Henley, July 4: 1914–1964.   L. E. Sissman.   PrIm

Blades of limpid seashell.   Daisy.   William Carlos Williams.   MoAB; MoAmPo

The blades will crack his big black eyes.   Thaw.   Walker Gibson.   ELU; NePoAm

Blah, blah, blah, blah, blah, darling, with you!   Blah, Blah, Blah.   Ira Gershwin.   OBAL

Blake snake, mama, done/run my darling home   That Black Snake Mama.   Blind Lemon Jefferson.   BluL

Blame me not if at last I meanst/More to be pleased than innocent.   I Pressed Her Rebel Lips.   Anonymous.   ErPo

Blame not my lute!   The Lute Obeys.   Sir Thomas Wyatt.   OBSC; QFR

Blame the Spring wind.   I Had Not Fastened My Sash over My Gown.   Tzu Yeh.   WPOW

Blamed your death on (IT! Martyrdom.   Richard W. Thomas.   PoBA

Blank through the dalehead and the bony face.   William Wordsworth.   Sidney Keyes.   ChMP; OxBTC; SeCePo

The blankets crackle with bright blue sparks.   Static.   Barton Sutter.   AMV-81

The blast of triumph o'er thy grave.   The Battle-Field.   William Cullen Bryant.   AA; FPL; PoLf; TRV

The blast with her too late warning/And testimony of love.   Earthquake.   R.A.D. Ford.   NOBC

...Blasting/Such beauty into nothing.   Snowy Egret.   Bruce Weigl.   MAYP

An' blaw my father heame to my moother.   Rhyme of the Fishermen's Children.   Anonymous.   GBP

The blaze grows greater, but 'tis sooner out.   Love and Jealousy.   William Walsh.   BoLoP

A blaze of grandeur, permanence of the impersonal.   Sea-Hawk.   Richard Eberhart.   BoAnP

Blaze two red eyes as hot as cooking-coals.   Dog.   John Crowe Ransom.   InPS; LiTA; OBAL; PAI

Blazed with his cross and set on living rock.   The Mountain.   Robert Finch.   CaP

Blazes from the paper without lifting your hands.   The Luminous.   Barbara Guest.   PoM

Blazing creatures of my kind/Will cry–Glory to God and peace to men.   Stone Angel.   Anne Ridler.   EaLo

Blazing fire and Christmas treat.   January Brings the Snow.   Mother Goose.   TiPo

...Blazing forms ascending the centuries/in their muted sheens, matter to me.   The Convert.   Margaret Danner.   BPo

Blazing in the light of all-year eternal/holy August.   Insomniac Poem.   Ron Loewinsohn.   NeAP

A blazing red harsh head tear up/And the dear floods of his hair.   The Tombstone Told When She Died.   Dylan Thomas.   OxBTC

...Blazing/with kisses that smoulder toward heaven.   Love Poem.   Ron Padgett.   APU

Blazing with noon and dripping with its pomp.   Drought.   Geoffrey Johnson.   HaMV

Bleak Envy these dull frauds with pleasure sees,/And wonders at the senseless mysteries.   The Dispensary.   Sir Samuel Garth.   OBSV

A bleak Siberia of the soul.   Exiles.   William Hamilton Hayne.   AA

Bleed up the fact of one anemone?   Tammuz.   Rayner Heppenstall.   WaP

Bleeding to death. The counter-attack had failed.   Counter-Attack.   Siegfried Sassoon.   BrPo; EnLit; MoBrPo; WaP

The bleeding wedge had not once split true/before I bashed the sledge askew/and smashed its shaft.   At the Woodpile.   Raymond Henri.   SaC

Bleeds drop by drop, and pants his life away.   To Mr. Gay...On Finishing His House.   Alexander Pope.   NOEC

Bleeds with its death-wound, but deeper yet for thee.   Serenade of a Loyal Martyr.   George Darley.   NOBE; OBNC; OBRV; OnYI

Bleeds with its death-wound, its wound of love for thee!   Song: "Sweet in her green dell the flower of beauty slumbers."   George Darley.   OBEV; OBVV

Blending into pigments/and arching back again.   To Morris Louis of the Blue Veil 1958-9.   Anne Cherner.   PoDr

Blending the arrested figures upon the arched/sarcophagus of pain.   Minna.   Maxwell Bodenheim.   MAPA

Bless God for Christ, that kept them all.   The Ten Commandments.   Anonymous.   FaBoUs

Bless her in earth and heaven.   A Mother's Birthday.   Henry Van Dyke.   OHIP

Bless him with many children to tumble and romp at his/feet.   Dicamus Bona Verba.   Albius Tibullus.   NAs

Bless it. Soon. Can she talk?   Natalya Nikolayevna Goncharov.   Don Coles.   NOBC

Bless me, and by repentance make/A holy day in heaven.   Song: "Whenever, Chloe, I begin."   Philip Stanhope, Earl of Chesterfield.   NOEC

Bless me! this is pleasant,/Riding on the Rail!   Rhyme of the Rails.   John Godfrey Saxe.   InMe; MoShBr; PoLf

Bless my tripudiation, stellify/my verses, Ferd., be ever at my scrutoire.   Homage to Ferd. Holthausen.   Gwen Harwood.   NOAV

Bless our mountain greenery home.   Mountain Greenery.   Lorenz Hart.   OBAL

Bless the labor of my hand.   Lord, Dear God! To Thy Attending.   Heinrich Otto.   AH

...Bless the Lord both now/And ever henceforth. Praise the Lord!   Not to Us, Not unto Us, Lord.   Anonymous.   AH

Bless the orchards/And the grain!   Grace for Gardens.   Louise Driscoll.   TrPWD

Bless the pine outside my window bless/the stranger in my midst.   Time to Myself.   Paulette Jiles.   NOBC

"Bless the toil of doing well!   To the Right Honourable Robert Walpole, Esq.   Ambrose Philips.   CEP

A blinded mole, or else a burned fly. Absence. Sir Philip Sidney. SiPS

The blinded poet who balks at stammering love/Stamps on through slapdash rhythms of fate or pride. The Motives of Rhythm. Robert Conquest. PP

Blinder than you. Tiresias. George Garrett. NePoAm-2; SM

Blindingly behind each lover's eye! Incidents in Playfair House. Nicholas Moore. ErPo; NeBP

Blindly from wave to wave toward Ararat. The Great Wave: Hokusai. Donald Finkel. PoPl

Blood all over the tiles, clutching at nothing. Stepfathers. David Donnell. NOBC

Blood already running there. A Poem for Painters. John Wieners. NeAP; PoM

Blood, bone, breath. It's in the Name. Kitty Tsui. BrSi

The blood divine invites us near. The Work That Saves! Horatius Bonar. BePJ

Blood dripping through crusted thighs. Praise for Sick Women. Gary Snyder. NeAP

Blood faultlessly broached redeemed the sullied air, the earth's/grossness. The Goring. Sylvia Plath. OBTV

Blood flows: a film on our eyes. Politics (excerpt). Tom Marshall. NOBC

The blood flows one imposed way, and no other. Parting: 1940. John Frederick Nims. PoA

Blood in my body drags me/Down with my brother. To a Blossoming Pear Tree. James Wright. HAP

Blood is thicker, sir, than water, now as then. Blood Is Thicker Than Water. Wallace Rice. PAH

Blood lines catching at my breath. For Leningrad, and My Jewish Ancestors. L. M. Rosenberg. AMV-81

Blood mixed with mud was drying on my ear. Picture Postcards. Miklos Radnoti. VWA

The blood of us a lighted dew. Wind on the Lyre. George Meredith. EG; NBM

Blood on your finger-tips for Lazarus who was poor. In Memory of Arthur Winslow. Robert Lowell. AP; MiAP

The blood-red flower of revolution. Roses and Revolutions. Dudley Randall. BPo; CNA; ConAP; NIP; NoAm; PoBA; TAP

The blood searching in his head without metaphor Letters & Other Worlds. Michael Ondaatje. NOBC; NoP

Blood shot and scattered to the winds of light/The ribbed original of love. In the Beginning. Dylan Thomas. MoRP

Blood & spit... Birthright. Geraldine Kudaka. BrSi

Blood streaks his shimmering beauty; in his eyes/Lingers incredulous and shocked surprise. For the Opening of the Hunting Season. Morris Bishop. BoAnP

The blood that we see shed, the tears that we/Shed, the wall, and the anonymous cross. Untitled. Daryl Hine. NoAm; TwCP

...Blood, veins,/machinery and love: our names. Love Medley: Patrice Cuchulain. Michael S. Harper. GeTw

Blood will not serve. A Poem for Heroes. Julia Fields. CNA

The blood with each revolving of the breath/Cries: "Who will come to kiss me from this sleep?" False Enchantment. Jean Starr Untermeyer. MoAmPo

The blood wrung from the cursing sailors' shirts. Sea Turtle. Liston Pope. AMV-80

...The bloody and/shabby/Pathos of the result. Eagle Valor, Chicken Mind. Robinson Jeffers. ELU; LiTA; OBSP; OxBA; WaP

The bloody fields of Flanders He so loves. God, How I Hate You. Arthur Graeme West. MMM

The bloody lot all rolled in one. Jim's mad. The Chances. Wilfred Owen. MMM; OxBTC

Bloody race of flowers, do you know? In the land of dwarfs. Forugh Farrokhzad. BoWoP

Bloom in th beauty of your giving, each/By each, in mankind's heart, brave Finnish dead. Ode to the Finnish Dead. Chad Walsh. HoAn

The bloom of young desire, and purple light of love. The Progress of Poesy. Thomas Gray. ATP

The bloom of youth from all, and fair curls turn to grey. Epigram: "Most inexplicable the wiles of boys I deem." Rhianus. PeHV

Bloomed forth the fragrant rose that all delight to view. The Slave. Jones Very. AP; TAP

Blooming, blooming, blooming/into the sweet blood of woman. The Fury of Cocks. Anne Sexton. CAPP

Blooms in a world made innocent again. A Lot of Night Music. Anthony Hecht. NIP; OxBC

Blooms the unchanging Rose of all the World. A Portrait. Brian Hooker. HBV 1-2

Blossom, beyond all reason, in the park. Fugue for One Voice. Anthony Hecht. LiTA

Blossom on the plum. March. Nora Hopper. HBV 1-2

...The blossoms are/white, and I am almost there. White Blossoms. Robert Mezey. NaP; VWA

The Blossoms of Eternal Life!' To the Queen. William Blake. EnRP

Blossoms of mercy/in the midst of the holocaust. In This Life. Robert Mezey. SUW

Blossoms/swaying in the wind. Voices. Nora Dauenhauer. TWSS

Blossy boys, bubble oh!/Over the brow. The Ploughboy in Luck. Anonymous. OxNR

Blots for a moment/My sleepy star. Mopoke. Louis Lavater. PoAu 1-2

Blou! blou! blou! Blou Northerne Wynd (excerpt). Anonymous. AtBAP

The bloudie crosse of my deare Lord/Is both my physick and my sword. Conscience. George Herbert. AnAnS 1

Blow away the morning dew,/how sweet the winds do blow. Blow away the Morning Dew. Anonymous. FSW

Blow, boys, blow!/Blow, my bully boys, blow! Blow, Boys, Blow. Anonymous. ShS; TrAS

"Blow bright, blow bright/The coal of this unquickened world." Night-Music. Philip Larkin. InPS; PAI

Blow high, blow low! let tempest tear.... Blow High! Blow Low! Charles Dibdin. HBV 1-2

A blow is delighted. Sacred Emily. Gertrude Stein. OBAL

Blow, my bully boys, blow! Blow, Bullies, Blow. Anonymous. AmSS

Blow, northerne wind,/Blow, blow, blow! Blow, Northern Wind. Anonymous. GBL; OBEV; OxBM

Blow on our flesh your crystal cure. Song of January. Gerta Kennedy. PoPl

A blow on the weam,/Or a kick on the arse. The Description of an Irish Feast, or O'Rourk's Frolic. Hugh MacGowran. OBVE; OnYI

Blow out the candles of your cake. For K.R. on Her Sixtieth Birthday. Richard Wilbur. NoP

Blow, salt wind from the north upstarting,/Scatter such dreams away! A Tropical Morning at Sea. Edward Rowland Sill. EtS

Blow the bellows old man. As I Went up the Brandy Hill. Anonymous. OxNR

Blow, thou wind of God! Ode to the North-East Wind. Charles Kingsley. FaPoR; GN

Blow, ye winds of morning,/Blow. Peter Gray. Anonymous. BLSo; FSW; OuSiCo

Blow your shrill pipes, and I will follow after. Ship near Shoals. Anna Wickham. HBMV

Blowing in mists, their spectral sails like light. Old Ships. David Morton. BBV; EtS

Blowing kisses from an/increasing distance. For Steph. Wendy Rose. CDW

Blowing spittle and sound/From insulting lips. Keep a Hand on Your Dream. X. J. Kennedy. Psk

Blowing strong against our faces. Viewing Russian Peasants from a Leningrad-Bound Train. Roger Gaess. LTB

Blowing the lights out, one by one. Peppergrass. Stanley Plumly. LCAP

Blowing the oak leaves pale side out.... Weather. Archibald MacLeish. MoAmPo

Blowing the right way/at just that moment in history The Song Turning Back into Itself 3. Al Young. CNA; NPGG

Blowing up balloons the size of the/Hall of Justice. The Day They Busted the Grateful Dead. Richard Brautigan. MAT

Blown away in the street. See-Saw, Down in My Lap. Anonymous. OxNR

Blown by the night wind/with the moon for an icy sail. Wolves. John Haines. BoAnP; LCAP

...Blown by the/Wind, like the dodo's. Bedtime Story. George MacBeth. NePoEA-2; NoAm; SoSe

Blown by the wind slowly scatters away. Clearing at Dawn. Li Po. AWP

Blown from night and the North. Old Age. Sophocles. LiTW

Blown maggots in by flatterers. Epigram. Samuel (1612-80) Butler. FaBoEE

Blown through the stifling streets of slums. At Piccadilly Circus. Vivian de Sola Pinto. OBMV

Blown worlds beyond by the destroying storms. Desolate. Claude McKay. CDC

Blows as the dust blows the ghost of the/ Hunt! The Hunt. Harriet Prescott Spofford. AA

The blud outbullerand on the nakit swerd,/Hir handis furthsprent. The Aeneid. Virgil (Publius Vergilius Maro). OBVE

Blue across the country and away across/the sea. Dirge. Kenneth Fearing. AmP

Blue as an eyelid, godless, and I write. Alone. Anna Akhmatova. BoWoP

Blue at the prow of my desire. Postlude. William Carlos Williams. AnAmPo

A blue bird in a nest. Sailor. Langston Hughes. GoSl; PoA

A blue-black negro with gleaming teeth waits for his/chance to leap. Down the Mississippi. John Gould Fletcher. LiTA

Blue butterflies/Are chasing at play. Corn-Blossom Maidens. Masahongva. WTO

The blue expanse, with foam besprent,/is his too glorious monument. Song of Gwythno. Thomas Love Peacock. OBRV

The blue-eyed flower, that blooms to-day,/To honey turns to-morrow. The Rosemary Spray. Luis de Gongora y Argote. AWP; LiTW

Blue-eyed Mary is a flower. Blue-Eyed Mary. Mary E. Wilkins Freeman. OBCA

Blue eyes he had and such waving gold hair! Touche. Jessie Redmond Fauset. BlSi; CDC

Blue forget-me-nots/glaze cracked Monogram 4. Martina Werner. BoWoP

Blue halo. Me. No hand, no wife, no song. Note in a Sanitorium. Ray Amorosi. FAZ

Blue idiom, blue embrace. The Fever Toy. Charles Wright. AmPA

Blue / indigo /bodies............. Poem for Etheridge. Sonia Sanchez. BPo

The blue kingfisher dives on you in fire. Colloquy in Black Rock. Robert Lowell. AnNE; CAPP; CoBMV; MiAP; MoAB; MoAmPo; NoAm

...Blue/like midnight sometimes/or a robin's egg/sometimes Spectrum. Mari E. Evans. BPo

Blue night was exposed. Blue Bottle. Patricia Hampl. AMV-81

Blue nights and casual canzonets,/Creole Girl? Creole Girl. Leslie Morgan Collins. PoNe

Blue rivers running their course,/a gesture of calm. The Diary of Amanda McFadden. Linda Hogan. TWSS

A blue sea-poem, joy, moon-ripple on wave. The Morality of Poetry. James Wright. PP

The blue settled, finally,/in the sky. In Its Place. Carol Stager. AMV-80

The blue shimmering/of lake-water. The Walk. W. W. Eustace Ross. PeCV; SD

Blue Shoes may go quite alone. Little Blue Shoes. Kate Greenaway. TiPo

A blue sky, a soft breeze,–/That's June. That's June. Mary Frances Butts. YeAr

Blue sky came! A Shower. Izembo. SUS; TiPo

The blue sky is accessible merriment to any, or we can try. Summer Mansions. Ruth Herschberger. HoAn

Blue treed a possum in Noah's ark Old Dog Blue. Jim Jackson. BluL

The blue vein, bright on her temple, pitifully beating. Boy with His Hair Cut Short. Muriel Rukeyser. ExPo; LiTM; MoAB; MP; NAMP; PoPl; RoGo; TwCP; VGW

Blue with sweat, the violinist/Crashes into the orchestra, which explodes. Cadenza. Ted Hughes. CMoP; NYBP

Bluebloods blue books as in dogs and sex-freaks The American Dream. Johnie Scott. NBP

Bluejay screeches from a pine. What Happened Here before. Gary Snyder. NNaP; PoM

Blues is that/little black gal/of mine. Blues. Horace Mungin. BOLo

The bluid ye drave til ilka airt/Sall feed its ain reid sleepan hert. Ye Mongers Aye Need Masks for Cheatrie. Sydney Goodsir Smith. OxBS

Bluish snakes slid/Into the dissolution of a smile. Gioconda. Thomas MacGreevy. OnYI

The blundering German cannon wuld provide/Their shame forever and our Parthenon. The Cathedral of Rheims. Edmond Rostand. CAW

The blunt blade dives through the flesh/long dead, soon stacked, used up, mute. Chopping Wood. Dave Smith. SM

Blush, Christians, if you can, and copy Tray. Tray's Epitaph. Peter Pindar. GoTF; TreFS

The Blush/Of shame? Query. Mildred Weston. PoL

Blushing as the young blond Polish priest/bites into his chicken next to her. Around the Kitchen Table. Gary Gildner. Str

Blushing from the field of battle. The Challenge. Anonymous. UnTE

Blushing quietly beneath the skin/of a face lit up in the black light/of paranoia. City Jail. J. J. Maloney. LFAC

Blythe and merry may she be,/The lass that made the bed for me. The Lass That Made the Bed for Me. Robert Burns. InvP; UnTE

The Board votes:/Turn control reset dials to Blob Culture. Soft-Man 3. Ed Sanders. ANYP

Boarded the train there's no getting off. Metaphors. Sylvia Plath. HeIP; InPK; SoSe

The boat has gone. On the Balcony. D. H. Lawrence. BrPo; GBL

A boat, to which the world itself is sea,/Wherein the mind sails on her fatal way. Caelica, XCVI. Fulke, Lord Brooke Greville. FCP; NOCV

The boatmen rest their oars and say,/'Miserere Domine! Hear, Sweet Spirit. Samuel Taylor Coleridge. ViBoPo

Boats bound south for Georges/Sway in a slow farewell. Out from Gloucester. Harlan Trott. EtS

The boats moved silently and the low whistles blew. Relating to Robinson. Weldon Kees. NaP; NYP

Bob was Dob's dog,/Chitterabob Mob's cat. Dob and Mob. Anonymous. OxNR

Bob White! Bob White! Bob White! Bob White. George Cooper. HBVY

Bob white! Peas ripe! For E.C.J. Emmett Jarrett. NeAC

Bobbed on the river like children's little boats. The Swans. Clifford Dyment. BoAnP; MoVE

Bobbing by Ahab's whaleboats in the East. The Quaker Graveyard in Nantucket. Robert Lowell. NMP

Bobolincon, Wadolincon, Winterseeble, follow, follow, fol-/low me! The O'Lincon Family. William Flagg. HBV 1-2; HBVY

...The bobwhite's/whistle opens in the air, broad and pointed like a leaf. Independence Day. Wendell Berry. OFD

(The bodies/all buried/in shallow graves? The Songs of Maximus, 2. Charles Olson. NoAm

Bodies approach; they wish to fulfill you. Little Lullaby. Irving Feldman. NYBP

Bodies of little foxes may hide and sleep. Night of Wind. Frances Frost. TiPo

The bodies of men on his wings he bears,/The serpent bright: but now must I sink. The Elder Edda: The Beginning and the End (abridged). Anonymous. LiTW

Bodies thick with food and lovers/After twenty years. Looking at Pictures to Be Put away. Gary Snyder. FF; InPS; NNaP; PAI

An bodily sicht o nocht. The Man in the Moon. Hugh" (Christopher Murray Grieve) MacDiarmid. NeBP

A boding of unknown, foreshadowed things. The Flight of the Geese. Sir Charles G. D. Roberts. PeCV

The body a roving, singing automation. Black Students. Julia Fields. NBP

The body and the soul know how to play/In that dark world where gods have lost their way. Four for Sir John Davies. Theodore Roethke. NOBA

Body awaits the tolerance of crows. The Tolerance of Crows. Charles Donnelly. CIP

The body but a wisp of smoke, that lightly wove/Through the shadows of the waiting City. Encounter in Jerusalem. Fay Lipshitz. VWA

The body flies/within the bone. Body's Freedom. Helen Neville. NePA

A body melting On the 25th Anniversary of the Liberation of Auschwitz... Eli Mandel. NOBC

A body of being/from the ashes in the ground. Soweto. Sipho Sepamla. WhB

The body of your life goes under. Corps d'Esprit. Heather McHugh. AmPA

The body outside the shadow moving/down once more. Views. Harriet Susskind. AMV-80

The Body Shop would not receive his body. The Maladjusted: A Tragedy (excerpt). Morris Bishop. NLV

The body/the blood/both unknown. There's an Unknown River in Soweto. Zindzi Mandela. WhB

Bogart is staring at Lauren Bacall's breasts/as if they might start speaking. Breasts. Maxine Chernoff. APU

The boisterous joys of Odin's hall. Heap on More Wood. Sir Walter Scott. OBCP; TiPo

Bold, brave and undaunted/Was young Brennan on the Moor. Brennan on the Moor. Anonymous. AmFP; FSW; GBP; OnYI; OuSiCo

Bold, cautious, true, and my loving comrade. As Toilsome I Wander'd Virginia's Woods. Walt Whitman. AmePo; HBV 1-2; SeCeV; ViBoPo

Bold, gay, and daring stood old Charlie Quantrell-o. Quantrell (II). Anonymous. CoSo

The bold, reprehensible, brave, indispensable/Sensible lads of the press. The Reporters. Newman Levy. InMe

The bold, significant, successful man. Success. Emma Lazarus. SBG

The bold trail, the old trail./The trail to Laramie. Laramie Trail. Joseph Mills Hanson. BPAW; PoOW

Bold with the thought, in reverence I sate down,/And, for a moment, filled that empty Throne. At Florence. William Wordsworth. VLP

Boldly bring I up the rear. Song of Allegiance. R. A. K. Mason. AnNZ

Boldly I scrawl the descriptive phrase–"Self-Portrait." Artist and Ape. Gordden Link. GoYe

The bomb domanial in the dome of blue. Snow. W. R. Rodgers. LiTM

Bomb-pitted with Contentment and the/Pain of Breathing. Friends. Mary Goose. STE

The bomber roared over their dream. The Bomber. Brian Vrepont. BoAV; NOAV

The bombing-planes of Jove. Battle Hymn of the Spanish Rebellion. L. A. Mackey. OBCV

The bombs are falling darkly for our fate. Full Moon: New Guinea. Karl Shapiro. MiAP

The bombs showered us in the air. A Fete. Larry Eigner. NeAP

The bond of kinship, the heritage of Empire. One Race, One Flag. A. R. D. Fairburn. AnNZ

Bone dry, old, in a dry land, Jim, my Jim. Dream Barker. Jean Valentine. PrIm; VGW

The bone-filled suit of armor/That lies rusting at his door. In That Dark Cave. Shel Silverstein. ELU

The bone symmetry/of my lovely skull. I'm Lucky. Charlotte Mandel. AMV-81

A bone wave-whitened and dried in the wind. Words for Music Perhaps. William Butler Yeats. AtBAP

Bones and vermillion gills. Lutra, the Fisher. James McMichael. AmPA

...Bones of Black strength/have always been/poems for our people. A Poem about Beauty, Blackness, Poetry. Linda Brown Bragg. CNA

The bones of your face are pinned with autographs. Femina. Daphne Marlatt. NOBC

The bones that underneath thee lie/Shall live for Hell or Heaven! The Holy Field. Henry Hart Milman. OxBoCh

Boney broke his heart and died./John Franswah! Boney Was a Warrior. *Anonymous.* FSW

Bonfires of roses in the snow. How can you look at the Neva. Anna Akhmatova. BoWoP

Bong, Mr., bong, Mr., bong, Mr., bong. Dirge. Kenneth Fearing. AmP; FF; HeIP; HoPM; NAMP; NIP; PoRA; TrJP

Bonie lassie, will ye go/To the birks of Aberfeldy! The Birks of Aberfeldy. Robert Burns. CTC; ViBoPo

...Bonnet crowned with flowers/that casually tries itself on her. At the Millinery Shop. Daniel Mark Epstein. MAYP

Bonnie Jean of Bethelny was scarce fif-/teen year auld. Glenlogie, or, Jean o Bethelnie (A version). *Anonymous.* ESPB; GN

Bonnie. What are you eating? Dear Bonnie, consider! Giving Rabbit to My Cat Bonnie. Anne Stevenson. FaBoWP

Bonniest bairn in a' the warl'. The Bonniest Bairn in a' the Warl'. Robert Ford. GN

The bonny holms of Yarrow! Yarrow Unvisited. William Wordsworth. EnLi 1-2; EnRP; GTBS; GTBS-P; HBV 1-2; PoRA

A bonny lass with a black e'e? A Cow and a Calf. *Anonymous.* OxNR

Bonny lassie O! Bonny Lassie O! John Clare. CH

Bonny St. Johnstone stands on Tay. The Twa Sisters of Binnorie. *Anonymous.* EnSB

The bony structure of the universe. Failure. E. L. Mayo. FAZ

Boo boo/poop poo/pup/gh. The Black Hat. Clayton Eshleman. VGW

Boogie-woogie, ragtime! A Cappella. Michael Pettit. GrPl

Book-lore ne'er served, when trial came,/Nor gifts, when faith was dead. Zeal and Love. John Henry, Cardinal Newman. TW

A book/May be a staff, a crook. A Book. Lizette Woodworth Reese. YeAr

The book of life still closed in her dead hand. On a Dead Lady. Alfred de Musset. EnLi 1-2

A book of myths/in which/our names do not appear. Diving into the Wreck. Adrienne Rich. CAPP; HaCAP; HeIP; InPK; InPS; MOS; NIP; NoAm; NOBA; NoP

A book that is never done, never done. The Walk in the Garden. Conrad Aiken. PoCh

Books are a load of crap. A Study of Reading Habits. Philip Larkin. NOBL; SoSe; TW

Books are friends. Come let us read. Books Are Keys. Emilie Poulsson. SiSoSe

Books; china; a life/Reprehensibly perfect. Poetry of Departures. Philip Larkin. CMoP; FF; HeIP; MP; NMP; OxBC; PrIm; TwCP

Books hold all things for their lovers. Books. Eleanor Farjeon. YeAr

The books tumble on our heads and we are buried. On Meeting a Stranger in a Bookshop. Oscar Williams. NePA

Boola boola Pensacoola hullabaloo! Boston Charlie. Walt Kelly. FiBHP; GoJo

Boom, boom, ain't it great to be crazy? The Elephant and the Flea. *Anonymous.* TrAS

...Boom/Of the far waterfall like doom. Tarantella. Hilaire Belloc. GoBC

Booming and mourning of the new-come bee. Notes Toward a Supreme Fiction: The President Ordains the Bee to Be. Wallace Stevens. AtBAP; LiTA; LiTM; MoPo; NOBA

Boot, saddle, to horse, and away! Cavalier Tunes. Robert Browning. HBV 1-2; MCCG

Booted and spurred/To ride! An Oration, Entitled "Old, Old, Old, Old Andrew Jackson." Vachel Lindsay. YaD

Boots and saddles, mount and ride. Boots and Saddles. Nicolas Saboly. OHIP

Booze and the blowens cop the lot. Villon's Straight Tip to All Cross Coves. William Ernest Henley. AWP; CenHV; FaBoCo; HBV 1-2; InMe; InvP; NA; SeCePo

Booze in the morning–for my sake. From the Epigrams of Martial. James Michie. FaBoEE

The border-land of Nature's harmony. New Zealand. Hubert Church. AnNZ

The borderlines of sense in the morning light/are naked as a line of poetry in a war. The Song of the Borderguard. Robert Duncan. NeAP; PoM

Bore him the greetings of the deathless/dead! The Cranes of Ibycus. Emma Lazarus. AA

Boreal armature. Styro. Clark Coolidge. ANYP

Bored and impatient in the monster's mouth. Dying. Robert Pinsky. AMV-81; HaCAP; MAYP

Bored with immortality. Dean Inge. Humbert Wolfe. FaBoEE

Bores! through his castle wall, and farewell king! Richard II. William Shakespeare. DiPo; DL

Born again/thinking of you Bean Spasms. Ted Berrigan. ANYP

Born and reborn/I,embrace,the whole. The Turnaround for Higherground. Pancho Aguila. LFAC

Born, born, we know how it goes. Holy Family. Muriel Rukeyser. MoAmPo

...The born child cries. Multipara: Gravida 5. Marie Ponsot. VGW

Born from a dark void/where Thunder sleeps. A Time of Turquoise. Judith Mountain Leaf Volborth. TWSS

Born is the King of Israel. The First Nowell. *Anonymous.* LiTB; PCh; ViBoPo

Born of rejection, of the boundless snow. From the Highest Camp. Thom Gunn. MP; TwCP

Borne from the fight and the full endeavour/On an ebb tide. Ebb Tide. Marjorie Pickthall. CaP

Borscht and wurst around the samovar. Shootin' with Rasputin. *Anonymous.* FSW

Bosom nor barn is filled with these. A Dead Harvest. Alice Meynell. MoVE

A bosom/not his own? Hard Questions. Margaret Tsuda. RFM

The bosom of his Father and his God. Elegy Written in a Country Churchyard. Thomas Gray. BiP; BoLiVe; DL; EiCP; EnPE; ExPo; FaBoBe; FaBoPP; FaBoPV; FaBoRV; FaFP; FaPoR; FPL; GN; GoTF; GoTL; GTBS; GTBS-P; HAP; HBV 1-2; HBVY; HeIP; HoPM; InPK; InPo; InPS; LaA; LiTB; LoBV; MasP; MCCG; MyFE; NOBE; NOEC; NoP; OAEL 1-2; OBEC; OBEV; OHFP; PAI; PoEL 1-5; PoLf; PPoe; PPP; PrIm; SCV; SeCeV; TEP; TreF; TrGrPo; UnPo; ViBoPo; WBLP; WHA

The boss will sing a different tune. Great Day (Union Version). *Anonymous.* FSW

Bot I am he/That shall los thee/From Satan the Phinnes bonde. Christ Calls Man Home. *Anonymous.* MeEL

Bot I beseik God for to send the grace/To rewle thy realme in unitie and peace. The Dreme: The Compleynt of the Comoun Weill of Scotland. Sir David Lindsay. OxBS

Bot now I luif that graceles gane.' In Secreit Place This Hyndir Nycht. William Dunbar. OxBoLi

Bot othir wayis all yheid the gle. The Bruce. John Barbour. OxBS

Bot weit your lippis & labor hully. Of May. Alexander Scott. OxBS

Botanical calm slips from stills. Specimen of an Induction to a Poem. Alan Bernheimer. APU

Bote ley thou thi fet to my pappe,/And wite the from the colde. Our Lady's Song. *Anonymous.* OBEV

Both)Self adventures deathlessness Noone and a Star Stand, Am to Am. Edward Estlin Cummings. NePoAm-2

Both are enjoyable only when hot. Recipe. *Anonymous.* UnTE

Both at home and o'er the sea. Missions. *Anonymous.* STF

Both bud and fade, both blow and wither. To A. L. Thomas Carew. AnAnS 2; CaPo; SeCP

Both comic/and full of unspeakable grief. Animals That Stand in Dreams: The Panda. Harley Elliott. NeAC

Both counterpoint and chord. Fugue. Constance Carrier. GoYe

"Both!" cried Jane,/Quite bold and plain. Greedy Jane. *Anonymous.* HBVY; OxBChV

Both empty are within. The Church and Clergy Here. Jonathan Swift. DBV

Both eternally lost to news or rumours of spring. Myths. Guy Butler. PeSA

Both fool is called and knave. A Jewish Poet Counsels a King. Santob De Carrion. TrJP

...Both/Have found their sleeping armies massacred. Two Wise Generals. Ted Hughes. MoBS

Both heart in heart and hand in hand. Jerusalem. William Blake. OBRV

Both her first born and all her bleating Gods. Paradise Lost. John Milton. EBEV

Both her mourner and her tomb. On the Countess Dowager of Pembroke. William Browne. AWP; CABA; EnLi 1-2; GoTF; HAP; InvP; JCP; NoP; OBEV; PoEL 1-5; SeCeV; TreFS; ViBoPo; WeW

Both, of course, being perfectly correct. Two Roads, Etc. Dorothy Walters. IHMS

Both of us hearing/The roar of our dreams. The Boxer Turned Bartender. Gary Allan Kizer. LFAC

Both of us kept on going. Catechism, 1958. W. M. Ransom. CDW

Both of us, of the love which makes us one. Monna Innominata. Christina Georgina Rossetti. VLP

Both of us trying to stay well/who move and crave. Trying to Stay. Diana Chang. PoDr

Both officers and privates,/Who liberty pursue. Trenton and Princeton. *Anonymous.* PAH

Both old and young commended the/maid/That such a witty prank had plaid. The Friar in the Well (A version). *Anonymous.* ESPB

Both our professions/are being ruined/by amateurs.   The Old Trouper.   Don (Donald Robert Marquis) Marquis.   FaBoCo

Both pain the heart when exquisitely keen.   As in Smooth Oil the Razor Best Is Whet.   *Anonymous.*   HBV 1-2

Both Paynim, and the Peers of Charlemane.   Paradise Regained.   John Milton.   OBS

Both quiet on the old brown dresser.   Duck.   John Lyle Donaghy.   BIrV; OxBI

Both relieved to stop play-acting/When the part gets too exacting.   Cote d'Azure.   Katherine Hoskins.   NYBP

Both serve, and still/our need mocks our gear.   Double Monologue.   Adrienne Rich.   NePoEA-2

Both shade and substance, beef and bone.   The Dog in the River.   Phaedrus.   AWP

Both the year's, and the day's deep midnight is.   A Nocturnal upon St Lucy's Day, Being the Shortest Day.   John Donne.   AnAnS 1; AtBAP; BoW; CBEP; EBEV; EnRePo; GBL; JCP; LiTB; MeLP; MePo; NOBE; NoP; OAEL 1-2; OBS; PoEL 1-5; PoPle; PPP; SeCP; SeCV 1-2; TEP

Both them I serve and of their train am I.   Sonnet I: "O Nightingale, that on yon bloomy Spray."   John Milton.   OBS

Both think thee poor and cruel.   The Relapse.   Thomas Stanley.   AnAnS 2; OBEV

Both Up and Down wish you were here.   Ode to a Vanished Operator in an Automatized Elevator.   Loyd Rosenfield.   QQQ

Both when first ev'ning was, and when first morn.   The First Day of Creation.   John Milton.   OxBoCh

Both with her Husband's, and her own tough fleame.   Upon Suddes a Laundresse.   Robert Herrick.   AnAnS 2; DBV

Both wood and iron, to seal/The dream-world with the real.   The Water-Wheel.   Jack R. Clemo.   ChMP

Both word and prayer, when it is true love's token.   Love.   Torquato Tasso.   AWP

Both wrathful Bible and the fuming shotgun/Saw the serpent glisten in their buckshot.   Quatrina.   Joseph Bennett.   LiTA

Bothe by dayes and by nightes! et in nomine Patris et/Filii, etc.   Rats Away!   *Anonymous.*   OxBM

A bottle and a kind landlady/Cure all again.   How Stands the Glass Around?   James Wolfe.   PAH

A bottle of good brandy and on each arm a girl.   Jackson.   *Anonymous.*   FSW

Bottles, rags, gelignite.   The Wheel.   James Cole.   FAZ

The bottom.   Getting Under.   Alan P. Lightman.   AMV-81

The bottom of the sea is cruel.   The Sea.   Hart Crane.   CrMA

The bottom with your ballast full was laded.'   Of an Heroical Answer of a Great Roman Lady to Her Husband.   Sir John (1561-1612) Harington.   BoLoP; ErPo

The boughs are bare, the stem is twisted now.   Epigram: "The scentless laurel a broad leaf displays."   Walter Savage Landor.   FaBoEE

The bouncing ball you turned from for solace.   All of Us Always Turning away for Solace.   Delmore Schwartz.   OxBA

Bound and weary I thought best/To sulk upon my mother's breast.   Infant Sorrow.   William Blake.   BoLiVe; InPS; NAs; OBNC; OBSP; PAI; PoPle

Bound away in the Dreadnought to the westward we'll go.   The Dreadnought.   *Anonymous.*   AmSS; ShS

Bound away in the Waterwitch to the west'ard we go.   The Waterwitch.   *Anonymous.*   PoAu 1-2

Bound blindfold to the groaning wheel of Time.   The Sakiyeh.   Mathilde Blind.   SBG

Bound by gold chains about the feet of God....   Morte d'Arthur.   Alfred, Lord Tennyson.   GoBC

Bound by the heart-beat pulse of a drum!   The Inheritors.   Dorothy Livesay.   CaP

Bound down to Newfoundland.   Bound down to Newfoundland.   *Anonymous.*   ShS

Bound each to each, like flower to wedded flower.   A Vow to Heavenly Venus.   Joachim Du Bellay.   AWP

Bound for the Dam of Rotter.   The Wedding.   Tom (Thomas Hood, Jr.) Hood.   InMe

Bound him in darkness, till the glorious morrow/Unsealed his eyes to that he had not known.   Paul.   John Oxenham.   TRV

Bound in those Ivy Chains by thee.   Song: "Take, oh take those Lips away."   Francis Beaumont and John Fletcher.   PoEL 1-5

Bound to a petty tyrant's nod,/Because he wears a paler face.   America (excerpt).   James M. Whitfield.   BPo

Bound up in the unquenchable flames of double suns.   Letters to Walt Whitman.   Ronald Johnson.   VGW

Bound with rubber that smolders into morning.   Street Fire.   Daniel Halpern.   AmPA; NYP

Bounded on the near side/By uncertain ground/And on the far side by frenzy.   A Garden of Situations.   Jack Anderson.   PoA

Bountiful and Bare.   Wave.   Barbara Guest.   AmPC

The bouquet of your flesh turn sad by mine.   Winter and Red Berries.   Nicholas Moore.   NeBP

Bourbon and orange juice is a rotten way to get drunk   Orange Juice Song.   David Phillips.   NeAC

Bow down your head and cry.   Poor Boy.   *Anonymous.*   FSW

Bow each in turn,–why tears for birth or death?   Time.   Bhartrihari.   AWP

Bow hither out of heaven and see and save.   Easter Hymn.   Alfred Edward Housman.   CABA; EaLo; EBEV; MoAB; OAEP; OFD; SeCeV

Bow low down in de valley for to pray,/An' I ain't done prayin' yet.   Religion Is a Fortune I Really Do Believe.   *Anonymous.*   BoAN 1-2

Bow lowly down before the sacred sight/Of man's Divinity alive in stone.   St. Isaac's Chruch, Petrograd.   Claude McKay.   AmNP; PoBA

Bow-wow! bow-wow! bow-wow-wow! bow-wow!   Jippy and Jimmy.   Laura E. Richards.   SoPo; TiPo

The bow-wows came and chased/him/right up there!   Round About There Sat a Little Hare.   *Anonymous.*   OxNR

Bow your forehead/like a headstone sinking/towards the sun and rising winds.   In the First Cave.   Seymour Mayne.   VWA

Bowe thu down to the brinke,/And mekely taste of the welle.   The Wells of Jesus Wounds.   *Anonymous.*   MeEL

Bowed heads look up, and lo, the day is done...   The Belfry.   Laurence Binyon.   CH

The Bowery! The Bowery! I'll never go there anymore!   The Bowery.   Charles Hale Hoyt.   FSN; GoTF; TreF

Bowling or collecting coins,/writing about it.   The Song.   David Ignatow.   CAPP

The box is a box is a box.   Late Late.   George Starbuck.   PPON

The box is only temporary.   The Arrival of the Bee Box.   Sylvia Plath.   FaBoMo; FaBoWP; HaCAP; NaP

Box it/back in?   Blue Alert.   Eve Merriam.   PCP

Boxes of fallen stars/shunt along the track/that shines before us.   Boxcars.   Diane Keating.   CaPN

A boy asleep in the high heavenly forest/Of innumerable & open arms   Two Sorrows.   David St. John.   SUW

Boy, at the lovely tip of your external urethral orifice, all my poetries/terminate   Gay Epiphany.   James Mitchell.   PeHV

...The boy attained thereat/Dhyana, first step of "the path."   The Light of Asia.   Sir Edwin Arnold.   VLP

The boy believed the sound had made a curse,/Jarring on the piles of broken shells.   Shelly Beach.   C. J. Koch.   NOAV

A boy feels when the poet he pores upon/Grows less and less sweet to him, and knows/no cause.   The Beginning of the End.   Gerard Manley Hopkins.   VLP

The boy hath stol'n your thoughts some other way,/Where wantonlike they do with many play.   Caelica, LXX.   Fulke, Lord Brooke Greville.   FCP

A boy he is–/for him a kiss.   Epigram: "He is my love."   *Anonymous.*   BIrV

A boy is told to eat his meal in silence.   The Tomboy.   William Burford.   NePA

The boy lay dead in the father's arms.   The Invisible King.   Johann Wolfgang von Goethe.   NU

The boy lifts the pail.   Ram Time.   William Heyen.   GeTw

The boy liked coming home better than going.   Going to Town.   Fred Lape.   PH

Boy sails north or approaches coral islands.   Up There.   W. H. Auden.   OxBTC

A boy that sings on Duncton Hill.   Duncton Hill.   Hilaire Belloc.   GoBC

The boy, the myrtle boughs, the triple spell/Of moth and snake and white witch terrible.   Le Jeune Homme Caressant Sa Chimere.   John Addington Symonds.   OBVV

Boy, what a racquet!   Advice from an Expert.   John Kieran.   InMe

A boy with a window to the east/is a boy with an extra eye!   Window to the East.   Virginia Moran Evans.   AMV-80

Boy! Won't you show them how to write!   Advice to a Young Man (of Letters)...   Irwin Edman.   InMe

Boys and girls run round and round.   Fishes Swim.   *Anonymous.*   OxNR

The boys can't beat our time.   Roll, Johnny Booger.   *Anonymous.*   BFSS

"Boys, I got the limit."   The Mighty Hunter.   Mrs. J. B. Worley.   PoLf

Boys, it's a very tough titty/but the milk is so doggone good   Jersey Belle Blues.   Lonnie Johnson.   BluL

Boys, that was the show that paid.   The Clown's Baby.   Vanier, Margaret Thomson.   PaPo

...Br'er Sterling's rocker glows.   Br'er Sterling and the Rocker.   Michael S. Harper.   LCAP

...Braces for throat-/cutting ice, bandaging snow.   November through a Giant Copper Beech.   Edwin Honig.   NoAm; NYBP

The bracts and bright white flowerets/of horse-parsnips.   Weed.   Robert Hass.   MAYP

Brady, where you at?/Struttin' in hell with his Stetson hat!   Brady (with music).   *Anonymous.*   AS

Braggart voust is naught t' his fancy.   Canzo of Bird-Songs and Love.   Daniel Arnaut.   LiTW

The brain which takes that in its stride/is yours & mine & it is late.   T.V. (1).   Anselm Hollo.   APU

Bran, come your purpose be not swirled until to us you/come away!   The Sea-God's Song to Bran.   *Anonymous.*   LiTW

Branch, green, the sudden burden of the leaves.   American Ash.   Stanley Plumly.   GeTw

Branches above my head/extend their dark blessing.   A Last Address to My Ghosts.   Gregory Orr.   GeTw

Branching from the brilliant/Radiating cold.   Snow Queen's Portrait.   Ruth Berman.   PoDr

The Brand is on the Seed!   Emily's Haunted Housman (parody).   David Cummings.   BXAP

The brand new world of Nature holds/So much for him to see!   Nature at Three.   Bettye Breeser.   BiCB

Brandy in my bottle and money in my purse.   I've Rambled This Country Both Earlye and Late.   *Anonymous.*   OuSiCo

The brave man with a sword!   The Ballad of Reading Gaol.   Oscar Wilde.   AnFE; BeLS; BrPo; DTo; GoTF; HBV 1-2; LiTB; OnYI; PoPl; TreF

The brave old fisher from whom I came!   Thrustararorum.   Henry Nehemiah Dodge.   EtS

The brave Queen Bess.   Yes: I Write Verses.   Walter Savage Landor.   EnLi 1-2; EnRP

Brave Songs, with sleepless eyes.   Sentinel Songs.   Abram Joseph Ryan.   HBV 1-2

Brave though her sons, how shall they meet/The spirit of the Maine!   The Spirit of the Maine.   Tudor Jenks.   AA; MC; PAH

The brave who, having fought, can never die.   Two Heroes.   Harriet Monroe.   OHIP

Brave, wise, and Venus' son.   In a Bye-Canal.   Herman Melville.   MAmP

Bravery runs in my family.   Coward.   Archie Randolph Ammons.   OBAL

The bravest of all shanty-boys, the foreman, Young Monroe.   Young Monroe at Gerry's Rock.   *Anonymous.*   AmSS

Bread, Beauty and Brotherhood.   The New Trinity.   Edwin Markham.   PGD

The bread-crumbs and the tea.   The boy stood in the supper-room.   *Anonymous.*   CenHV

The bread of life sent down from Heaven.   Table Graces, or Prayers for Adults: Evening Meal.   *Anonymous.*   BLRP

Bread taste sour.   Church and State.   William Butler Yeats.   CMoP

Break, break, because thou needs must part/From thine own Love, from thine own Sweet!   Song: "Fair is the night, and fair the day."   William Morris.   HBV 1-2

...Break, brother,/sister, and die.   When the Wine Was Gone.   Alvin Aubert.   CNA

Break down the four-square walls of standing time.   The House of Splendour.   Ezra Pound.   InPo

Break from electric trees/their tops, fall completely and forever/into star dust.   The Indian Women Are Listening: To the Nuke Devils.   Wendy Rose.   TWSS

Break in by making any reply!   Passing Visit to Helen.   D. H. Lawrence.   CMoP

...Break-/ing into a little run, passed from my sight.   The Ox.   Mary Morison Webster.   PeSA

Break it, and hold at last my soul's clear pearl.   He the Beloved (excerpt).   Qorratu'l-Ayn.   WPOW

...Break me: thus am I dead,/Am resurrected now in wine and bread.   At Communion.   Madeleine L'Engle.   TrCP

Break not his sweet repose.   A Soldier's Grave.   John Albee.   AA

—A Break of camera calm.   Body Fished from the Seine.   Gregory Corso.   GP; SM

Break off the yoke and set me free.   The Battle Within.   Christina Georgina Rossetti.   TRV

Break roof and let my death come in.   Prayer Against Indifference.   Joy Davidman.   AnEnPo; TrPWD

Break sullen on the last inviolate shore.   Tunnel Beach.   James Keir Baxter.   AnNZ

Break them, wear them,/With the blossoms on your breast?   For a Girl in Love.   Florence Hynes Willette.   GoBC

The break with the past, the major operation.   Consider These, For We Have Condemned Them.   C. Day Lewis.   LiTB; LiTM; NAMP; SeCePo

The breaker breaking on the beach.   In Memoriam A.H.H., LXXI.   Alfred, Lord Tennyson.   VLP

Breakfast in Elko.   Hitch Haiku.   Gary Snyder.   LCAP

Breaking a flower/from its green stem.   Piano Pieces (excerpt).   Thomas W. Shapcott.   CBAP

Breaking the night's maidenhead.   The Dog.   Valentin Iremonger.   BIrV; NeIP

Breaking with honey buds, shall ever equal.   The Express.   Stephen Spender.   BBV; CMoP; EnLi 1-2; ExPo; GoJo; LiTM; MoAB; MoBrPo; MoVE; MP; NAMP; NIP; NoAm; PoPl; RoGo; SeCeV; TwCP

Breaking/Your laws.   Inviolable.   Daniel Gerard Hoffman.   GrPl

Breaks, and in accents mellifluous, follows the thoughts of the author.   The Metre Columbian (parody).   *Anonymous.*   BXAP; Par; SpRo

Breaks from her tuneful lips, "Rome! Italy!"   Petrarch.   Giosue Carducci.   AWP

Breaks his leg/while she lies/sleeping.   The Child Who Walks Backwards.   Lorna Crozier.   CaPN

Breaks like the Atlantic Ocean on my head.   Man and Wife.   Robert Lowell.   AmPP; BoLoP; ConAP

Breaks, O my heart's blood, like a heart and hill.   We Lying by Seasand.   Dylan Thomas.   BiP; PoA; SyP

Breaks the first Christmas morn.   Calm, on the Listening Ear of Night.   Edmund Hamilton Sears.   AH

A breast for men to love.   He Praises Her Hair.   *Anonymous.*   AnIL

Breast/Is best.   Note on Feeding.   *Anonymous.*   FaBoUs

The breast, which beat to former joy,/Will ne'er desert its pledge, my Boy!   To My Son.   George Gordon, Lord Byron.   NAs

The breastes round, and long small armes twain.   The Smiling Mouth and Laughing Eyen Grey.   Charles, duc d' Orleans.   HAP; NoP

...The/breasts hung innocent/in the morning light.   The Innocent Breasts.   Joel Oppenheimer.   PoM

A breath, a wind, a sound, a voice, a tinkling of the camel-bell.   Do What Thy Manhood Bids Thee Do.   Richard Burton.   GoTF; TreFS

Breath for breath yr. breath my breath gone   I Don't Hear Any Melody Breathing I Hear.   John Gill.   NeAC

The breath of Heaven must swell the sail,/Or all the toil is lost.   Human Frailty.   William Cowper.   HBV 1-2

The breath of kindred plumes against/its feet?   The House of Life.   Dante Gabriel Rossetti.   OAEP

The Breath of Nature, and her endless Bloom.   Spring Flowers.   James (1700-48) Thomson.   AtBAP; NOBE; OBEC

A breath/of what the dark/wood took.   Dark Wood.   Ian Wedde.   OCNZ

The breath that gave it life was thine.   Posthumous.   Henry Augustin Beers.   AA

The breath that should go howling to the moon/Blows out the lamp and wheezes off to bed.   The Wolf.   Donald Davidson.   AnAmPo

Breath 2 u 2 u velvet sumthin blkman   Positives.   Johari (Jewel C. Latimore) Amini.   PoBA

Breathe a gay goodnight.   When.   George William ("A.E.") Russell.   ATP; OnYI

Breathe a prayer and a tear for the Croppy boy.   The Croppy Boy.   William B. McBurney.   OnYI

Breathe, and I vanish/Instantly.   The Snowflake.   Walter De la Mare.   NCSH

Breathe; burn; and change.   The Break.   E. N. Sargent.   NYBP

Breathe deeply and begin/to whistle/as I walked back home.   The Jump Shooter.   Dennis Trudell.   LiSp

Breathe deeply:/how good and sweet the air is.   I Will Go into the Ghetto.   Charles Reznikoff.   VGW

Breathe in—/a large thrush eats the mistletoe.   Four Stories.   David Shapiro.   ANYP

Breathe in,/Breathe out.   January.   H. R. Hays.   EAS

Breathe into it and let my secrets go   Lock the Place in Your Heart.   Zindzi Mandela.   LLLT

Breathe it;/taste it; how it/Feeds the brain.   It.   Gary Snyder.   LCAP

Breathe it, veery thrush!   Blow Softly, Thrush.   Joseph Russell Taylor.   HBV 1-2

Breathe low her name, my soul; for that/means more.   The House of Life.   Dante Gabriel Rossetti.   VLP

Breathe./Make./Be.   My Son, My Son...   Seymour Cain.   AMV-81

Breathe my breath also through these songs.   Chanting the Square Deific.   Walt Whitman.   AmePo

Breathe only roses,/Fallen at their feet.   Seville.   L. D'O. Walters.   HBMV

...Breathe thou, and there's the rich perfume.   The Perfume.   Robert Herrick.   CaPo

Breathed darkness forth (dark night is Cupid's day).   Hero and Leander.   Christopher Marlowe.   SeCePo

Breathes a new myth into the elegy.   Elegy.   Louis Johnson.   AnNZ

Breathes a pure and holy feeling,/All through the night.   All through the Night.   Harold Boulton.   FSW

Breathes like a flute/As he flits high and low.   The Summer Is Coming.   Bryan Guinness.   OxBI

...Breathes/upon these vessels by the sea,/to be wrought in the frothing waves.   Aubade.   Frank O'Hara.   SM

Breathing but the breath of ages.   Kol Nidra.   Joseph Leiser.   AA; TrJP

Breathing delight to-day, but none to-morrow.   Fair Is the Rose.   *Anonymous.*   EG; EiL

Breathing his bronzen breath at the azury centre of time.   This Solitude of Cataracts.   Wallace Stevens.   LCAP

Breathing in the glow of herself.   The Chandelier as Protagonist.   William Virgil Davis.   AMV-80

Breathing in this stone room,/without evidence.   The Small Lizard.   Linda Gregg.   MAYP

Breathing knowledge into them   Ellas and the Statues.   Guften Akin. PBWP

Breathing poppies. Thinking.   Spots of Blood.   Phyllis Webb.   NOBC

Breathing, robbing the air.   The Breathers.   James Reiss.   AmPA

...Breathless above/your overpowering grasp of reality.   The Basement Watch. Thomas Tolnay.   AMV-80

Breathless, I pretend to enter her with knives.   Barren Poem.   Michael Ryan.   AmPA

A breathless swimmer in that cold green element.   The Cold Green Element. Irving Layton.   NOBC; NoP; OBCV

The breeze that stirs the little loch/On silent Lochnagar.   Ante Mortem. Syd Scroggie.   PoSH

Breezy, Sneezy, Freezy.   The Twelve Months.   Gregory Gander.   GoTF; TreFT

Breton poets rhymed the tale,/Calling it The Nightingale.   The Nightingale. Marie de France.   BoWoP

The Brewer's dog too poured a note of thunder,/Rattled his chain, and wagged his tail for wonder.   Instructions to a Celebrated Laureat (excerpt). John Wolcot.   NOEC

Bribing the Marys of the world to sell,/For tinseled star, their flesh and blood to hell!   The Starred Mother.   Robert Whitaker.   PGD

A brick not used in building/Can smash a window pane.   A Brick Not Used in Building.   Naomi Replansky.   PoL

The bridal bed already made,/The crypt also richly arrayed.   An Old Picture. Howard Nemerov.   OBSP

The bridal gown used as a shroud, an old custom.   The Child-Bride.   Joyce Carol Oates.   GeTw

The bridal is over!   The Bride's Toilette.   Ellen Mackay Hutchinson Cortissoz.   AA

The bride hides herself.   Haiku: "Did I see her."   *Anonymous.*   HW

The bride lay clasped in her living tomb!   The Mistletoe Bough.   Thomas Haynes Bayly.   BLPA; GoTF; HBV 1-2; PaPo; TreFS; VLP

The Bridegroom started from his Trance at last,/And pipeing homeward jocoundly he past.   Idylls.   Theocritus.   OBVE

The bridegroom went in,/And the door was shut.   Five Were Foolish. Arthur J. Hodge.   AH

The bridegroom wished he knew.   Love and a Question.   Robert Frost. MoBS

The Bridegroom with his bride!   St. Agnes' Eve.   Alfred, Lord Tennyson. CAW; CoBE; EnLit; GoBC; GTBS; HBV 1-2; LiTB; MaVP; OAEP; OBEV; OBVV; OxBoCh

The bridge is everlasting monument.   The Bridge from Brooklyn (excerpt). Raymond Henri.   EyDe

A bridge to stop asses at, once for all.   Sincere Flattery of R. B.   James Kenneth Stephen.   FaBoPa; NOBL; Par

...The brief and everlasting/human story written on the lapsing sands.   The Entertainer.   Bruce Beaver.   NOAV

Brief be the twilight as I pass/From light to dark, from dark to light. Vespers.   Silas Weir Mitchell.   WGRP

Bright and fleeting as the path of a snail.   In the Madison Zoo.   Roberta Hill.   CDW

Bright-arm'd, high-crested, and athirst for war.   The Iliad.   Homer.   OBVE

Bright as the listening stars.   Sea Lyric.   William Stanley Braithwaite. GoSl

...The bright bead/of your woman's laughter.   Tight Rope.   LeRoi (Imamu Amiri Baraka) Jones.   CNA

The bright blood that swells through the currants.   The fruits you give me are more savory than others.   Marguerite Burnat-Provins.   BoWoP

A bright burst of light and holiness/were/ever   Funeral Poem.   LeRoi (Imamu Amiri Baraka) Jones.   CNA

A bright butterfly for our slow perusal?   Coin in the Fist.   Florence Kerr Brownell.   GoYe

The bright, clean, strong words still remain.   Seizure.   James E. Warren, Jr. AMV-81

Bright cobwebs on a Christmas tree.   Golden Cobwebs.   Rowena Bastin Bennett.   ChBR

A bright fire and a casement closed at night/To keep the warm air in.   The Contented Bachelor.   John Kendall.   InMe

A bright fountain of red eyes/tinkling sightless to the road.   A Trucker. Thom Gunn.   PCP

Bright-harnest Angels sit in order serviceable.   Hymn on the Morning of Christ's Nativity.   John Milton.   NOBE; OBEV

Bright healthful waves flow forth, to each glad wanderer/free!   To the Poet Wordsworth.   Felicia Dorothea Hemans.   BrRo

Bright leaps a living brook!   From the Flats.   Sidney Lanier.   NOBA; OxBA

...Bright let be the air/About my lonely cloud of care.   The Victories of Love. Coventry Patmore.   FaBoRV

A bright new world of peace.   Bells of New Year.   Arthur Gordon Field. PGD

The bright obvious stands motionless in cold.   Man Carrying Thing. Wallace Stevens.   SyP

Bright over Europe fell her golden hair.   Letty's Globe.   Charles Tennyson Turner.   CBEP; HBV 1-2; NOBV; OBEV; OBVV; OnUR

The bright procession/Of eddying forms,/Sweep through my soul!   The Strayed Reveller.   Matthew Arnold.   LoBV; OAEL 1-2; OBEV; VLP

Bright she is, no daisy whiter.   Madrigal: "My mistress is as fair as fine." Thomas Ravenscroft.   OxBoLi

Bright shines the sun upon the shipless sea.   The Ship and the Sea.   Blanche Edith Baughan.   AnNZ

A bright silver penny.   The Silver Penny.   Walter de la Mare.   CMoP; ExPo; OBMV

Bright sky, bright sky, carbon scarred with ciphers.   End of a Year.   Robert Lowell.   HaCAP

The bright sun sharpens it.   Sharpeville Inquiry.   Anne Welsh.   PeSA

...Bright teeth/that surely time will cut through/like a rough knife kerneling corn.   After Reading Nelly Sachs.   Linda Pastan.   VWA

A bright torch, and a casement ope at night,/To let the warm Love in!   Ode to Psyche.   John Keats.   CABA; CBEP; DiPo; ERoP 1-2; HBV 1-2; InPS; LiTB; LoBV; MBW 1-2; NOBE; NoP; OAEL 1-2; OAEP; OBEV; OBNC; OBRV; PAI; PoEL 1-5; PP; PPP; WHA

The bright wallpaper, imperishably old,/Uncurls and flutters; it will never fall. Mother and Son.   Allen Tate.   LiTA; MoAB; MoAmPo; MoVE

The bright watchers are still there.   Country Stars.   William Meredith. GrPl

Bright wavelets unbroken/to the rim spread round him.   The Solitary. Mary Barnard.   FAZ

A bright yellow flower and a new red pot.   Five Little Sisters Walking in a Row.   Kate Greenaway.   MoShBr

A bright yellow nut, so they say!   Yearning.   Alfred Kreymborg.   MAPA

Brightening, enlarging the rock-pools.   Sisters.   Robin Hyde.   AnNZ

Brightening the littered leaves upon the ground?   Love Fallen to Earth. Paul Verlaine.   SyP

Brightening with every shade that on its surge doth/ride.   Approach of Evening.   George Croly.   IrPN

A brighter Phoebus of their own.   Eutaw Springs.   Philip Freneau.   AA; BeLS; PAH

Brighter than the brightness they destroy.   Beauty and Terror.   Lesbia Harford.   CBAP; PoAu 1-2

The brightest Angels bowing round/Jehovah and his golden crown. Springfield Mountain (A vers.).   *Anonymous.*   ViBoFo

The brightest gift, the gladdest gift/The world has ever known.   Christmas. Mary Mapes Dodge.   BiCB

The brightest jewel in my Crown/Wad be my Queen, wad be my Queen.   O Wert Thou in the Cauld Blast.   Robert Burns.   BoLiVe; EBEV; EnL; EnPE; HeIP; NOBE; NoP; OAEP; OBEC; OxBS; TrGrPo; WHA

The brightest light the sun e'er threw/Is lifeless to one gleam of thine!   Sweet Innisfallen.   Thomas Moore.   HBV 1-2; OBNC

The Brightest of the Bright, whom I met upon my way.   The Brightest of the Bright.   Egan O'Rahilly.   BIrV

Brightest truth, purest trust in the universe–all/were for me/In the kiss of one girl.   Summum Bonum.   Robert Browning.   ELU; EnLi 1-2; GTBS; HBV 1-2; LiTL; OHFP

Brightly shine our neighbours, Venus, Mars.   The Survivors.   Daryl Hine. TwCP

Brightness falls from the air.   A Litany in Time of Plague.   Nashe [(or Nash)] Thomas.   CABA

The brightness from on high/will cover the earth with beauty, and/inhabit the human sky.   Our Love Shall Be the Brightness.   James Wreford Watson. CaP

Brilliant as day and rocks are so ready/for the stamping of little feet. Rumplestiltskin Poems.   William Hathaway.   DFT

Brimmed with reflected day.   The Bindweed.   Walter De la Mare.   BrPo

...Bring at last/That perfect pardon which is perfect peace.   With Snow White Veil.   Henry Wadsworth Longfellow.   TreFT

Bring back, bring back, Oh, bring back my Bonnie to me.   My Bonnie Lies over the Ocean.   *Anonymous.*   FSW

Bring back the same, then dye and dying last.   Can Doleful Notes to Mesur'd Accents Set.   John Danyel.   UnS

Bring dreams of Christ to dusky cane-lipped throngs.   Georgia Dusk.   Jean Toomer.   AnAmPo; BP; BPo; CDC; NoAm; NoP; PoBA

Bring 'em home, bring 'em home.   Bring 'Em Home.   Barbara Dane.   FSW

Bring faith in God, a beacon in the night/To guide mankind aright.   The Old Year's Prayer.   Minna Irving.   PGD

Bring forth May flowers.   March Winds.   Mother Goose.   SoPo

Bring forth the self-same men?   The Death of Leonidas.   George Croly. BeLS

Bring her home on the crupper,/A scalp on either side.   After the Comanches.   *Anonymous.*   PAH

Bring me to my arms on the first May night.   Love in the Valley.   George Meredith.   VLP

Bring him his supper nights, and clean the cave.   Lot Later.   Howard Nemerov.   NMP

Bring home the goat, bring the child home to its mother. Hesperos, you bring home all the bright dawn disperses. Sappho. BoWoP

Bring home the poet, let him rest/In the old land he loved the best. Bring Home the Poet. Patrick MacDonogh. OnYI

Bring in her bill, once more, the Branch of Peace. Farewell Frost, or Welcome the Spring. Robert Herrick. CaPo

Bring it; and bring enough for two. Hearts-Ease. Walter Savage Landor. EnRP

Bring Love back, Love! Love in Dreams. John Addington Symonds. HBV 1-2

Bring me a little water, Sylvie,/Ev'ry little once in a while. Bring Me a Little Water, Sylvie. Anonymous. FSW

Bring me Men. The Coming American. Sam Walter Foss. AmFN; BBV; BLPA; FaBoBe

Bring me to winne with the self God. A Cry to Mary. Saint Godric. MeEL

Bring me your tears! Your Tears. Edwin Markham. HBMV

Bring near the Brotherhood of Man. Resurgence. Laura Bell Everett. PGD

Bring summer and ripe fruits/in their purple hearts. Pear Tree. Hilda ("H. D.") Doolittle. AP; BoWoP; CMoP; HBMV; MoAmPo; NOBA; UnPo

BRING THE MUSIC Bring the Soul Blocks. Victor Hernandez Cruz. CAD

Bring the North. Bring the North. William Stafford. LCAP

Bring the rain upon his head. Evening Red and Morning Gray. Anonymous. FaBoBe; HBV 1-2; OxNR

Bring the wounded, Martha! Bring the wounded, men. Washington in Love. John Berryman. LCAP

...Bring their play to ruin. About a Year after He Got Married He Would Sit Alone... James Whitehead. GP

Bring them back to their homes. Praise of a Train. Anonymous. WTO

Bring thy Baby back to me! Communion. Caroline Giltinan. CAW

Bring up the flowers. There Is but One May in the Year. Christina Georgina Rossetti. TiPo

Bring us the sacred sword! To Africa. Raymond Mazisi Kunene. WhB

Bring us to that palace that is built/For penitents that be to mercy able./Amen. La Priere de Nostre Dame. Geoffrey Chaucer. ISi

Bring yellow-sun pollen/with song to the comb. The Poems Come Easier. Ray Mathew. BoAV

Bring you down/to me. Daring. Carol Konek. IHMS

Bringing back to me/Simple joys I once knew. Thoughts after Work. David Rubadiri. WhB

Bringing bullet holes/and death/and apple pie! The Prophet's Warning; or, Shoot to Kill. Ebon. PoBA

Bringing frankincense and praise/For her gift of the Infinite One. The Springfield of the Far Future. Vachel Lindsay. MoRP

Bringing in our arms, like game wardens,/a warm shot for her Doe-Face. Erin Moure. CaPN

Bringing long peace to Cornland, Alp, and Sea. Abraham Lincoln Walks at Midnight. Vachel Lindsay. AmFN

Bringing peace to many. Summary of the Distance between the Bomber and the Objective. Walter Benton. WaP

Bringing peace to their humid limbs. Dionysus. Irving Layton. ErPo

Bringing sal volatile/And a glass of brandy neat. Sweeney Erect. Thomas Stearns Eliot. OxBTC; VGW

Bringing shark to door of cabin. Storm at Sea. Anonymous. WTO

Bringing the child his body and his mind. For the Time Being. W. H. Auden. PCh

Bringing the summer and bringing the sun. Fly away, Fly away over the Sea. Christina Georgina Rossetti. SUS

Bringing with them nothing/but that sound. Why Do You Write about Russia? Louis Simpson. AMV-81; InPS; LCAP

Brings a fresh fragrance of heaven to our senses. New Moon. D.H. Lawrence. BoNaP

Brings a six-foot teddy bear/From the Birmingham Toy Fair. Another Prince Is Born. Adrian Mitchell. NAs

Brings health/To the place of feasting. Ayii, Ayii. I Walked on the Ice of the Sea. Anonymous. RFM

Brings Heaven near. Faith, Hope and Love. Anonymous. BLRP

Brings him the end he could not find. The Traveller. Allen Tate. LiTM

Brings him to you, for he gets there just the same. The Cowboy at Work. Anonymous. CoSo

Brings him with gold to the shrine, brings him in arms to the/gate? Amours de Voyage. Arthur Hugh Clough. OBNC

...Brings mosaic/to dusty windshields, to the waking, music. Aspects of Spring in Greater Boston. George Starbuck. NYBP

Brings those we love before us, as they were,/with faults and all, not nobler, just there. Sea Canes. Derek Walcott. HeIP

Brings to me thoughts of care and sorrow/out of the airt where dwells my lass. Song: "Day will rise and the sun from eastward." George Campbell Hay. OxBS

Bristled with cities, us the sea received. A Dream. Matthew Arnold. GBL; OBTV; SeCePo

Britain had nothing else to fear, as far as you could/think... The Death of Prince Leopold. William McGonagall. EvOK

The British tar forever is the dandy-o. The Shannon and the Chesapeake. Anonymous. AmSS; OBSS

Britons, if undone, can go,/Where tobacco loves to grow. Boy! Bring an Ounce of Freeman's Best (parody). Isaac Hawkins Browne. BXAP; Par

"Britons never will be slaves." Rule Britannia. James (1700-48) Thomson. CEP; EiCP; EnLi 1-2; FaPoR; GTBS; GTBS-P; HBV 1-2; NOEC; OAEP; OBEC; OBWP; TreF; WBLP

Brittle as jelly jars. The Lizards of La Brea. Marc De Baca. AMV-80

Brittle as the green bones/beneath. Circa 1814. David Staudt. AMV-80

...Brittle great fig-trees/Snap off, figs and all.... The Englishman in Italy. Robert Browning. SeCePo

The brittle rock of bone,/My people,/Cries out to God. My People. Else Lasker-Schüler. WPOW

"Bro, they been callin that sister by the wrong name." Gwendolyn Brooks. Don L. Lee. NoAm

The broad magnolia bud and wants the branch. Spring's on the Curb. Hildegarde Flanner. AnAmPo

Broadcast it all over the world./Amen. The Banks of a River. Abraham Sutzkever. VWA

Broke earth with song. Song–Talysarn. Brenda Chamberlain. NeBP

The broken and their children born and unborn/of the endless war. Endless. Muriel Rukeyser. NYBP

The broken bread Thy body be,/To cheer each languid heart. The Cup of Blessing. Charles Wesley. BePJ

A broken bundle of mirrors....! Near Perigord. Ezra Pound. CABL; FaBoMo; LiTA; LiTM

Broken by strength/and still strong. The Lonely Land. A.J.M. Smith. CaP; NOBC

The broken glass was chinking as she sank among the wrecks. An Old Song Re-sung. John Masefield. EvOK; ExPo; LiTB

...Broken/ground, uninhabited, pure space. La Banditaccia, 1979. Rika Lesser. MAYP

...A broken heart lies here. A Jacobite's Epitaph. Thomas Babington, Lord Macaulay. FaPoR; NOBE; OBEV; OBNC; OBVV

Broken light bulb/for her contact lens. A Horror Story Written for the Cover of a Matchbook. Chuck Wachtel. APU

Broken me with love for a slender boy. Mother darling, I cannot work the loom. Sappho. BoWoP

Broken or sold. Or given away. Or used and forgotten. Or/lost. Green Light. Kenneth Fearing. VGW

The broken-throated cry of the woman smashing the/near horizon. This Particular Christian. Louis Johnson. OCNZ

A broken weathercock seeking/Its own north, its own lost/Bearings. Squall. John Moore. NCSH

The broken wing. Geological Faults. Barbara Unger. AMV-81

The broken word, the broken arch. Colosseum. Harold Norse. TrJP

A bronze bodhisattva's ancient smile. The Peacock Room. Robert Earl Hayden. FB

Bronze of a sea,/under the flame. Dorothy. Alfred Kreymborg. AnAmPo

Bronzed peacock feathers, red combs of her cocks. Nineteen Hundred and Nineteen. William Butler Yeats. BIrV; LiTB; MasP; MoAB; MoPo

Brood her high lonely mysteries. He Remembers Forgotten Beauty. William Butler Yeats. CTC; LLLT

A brood of goslings, cackling in debate. To the Marquis of Graham on His Marriage. Anonymous. OBSV

The brooding and blissful halcyon days! Halcyon Days. Walt Whitman. NePA; OxBA

...The brook/Reminding the stones where, under a breath, it falls. Waterfalls. Vernon Watkins. NoAm

A broom, a flame, a foot, a stronger mate. Spider. Thomas Cole. PoA

The broth flows over the rust/And mingles with Kedron. Hunger. Arthur Rimbaud. AWP

A broth of passion and boredom for the world. A Summing Up. Gabriel Preil. VWA

The brothas, the beautiful brothas/sho will! Yuh Lookin GOOD. Carolyn M. Rodgers. BPo

...Brothels and Sex Shops everywhere./Wish you were here. The School Hockey Team in Amsterdam. Frank Ormsby. OBTV

Brother beloved, we are thy funeral trees! The Tears of the Poplars. Edith Matilda Thomas. AA; AnAmPo

Brother by worthier brother I may come/To all unknowing that is loving God. St. Francis and the Cloud. Marie De L. Welch. MoRP

Brother-gods, they wait for me! Residential Rhymes (excerpt). Osman Edwards. OBTV

Brother: Good-bye. At the Grave of My Brother. William Stafford. Str

Brother, he's our father! A Rouse for Stevens. Theodore Roethke. OBAL

Brother, hear my last farewell. The Dying Californian. Anonymous. AmFP; BFSS; BPAW; TrAS

Brother, I pardon thee.   Marsh Song–At Sunset.   Sidney Lanier.   AmePo; NOBA

...Brother, my heart/races for sea-room–we are out of breath.   Her Dead Brother.   Robert Lowell.   NePoEA

Brother owl has told me/respect your elders   In Respect of the Elderly. Thomas Love Peacock.   VoR

A brother's right to freedom. That is "Why."   Why I Am a Liberal.   Robert Browning.   EnLi 1-2

Brother."...This is the way we are.   The Way My Ideas Think Me.   Jose Garcia Villa.   AnFE; EaLo

Brother to brother pressed,/Tara, tantara, teino!   A Song of the Open Road. Anonymous.   AWP

Brother to brother should be kind,/Yet bear the Littletons in mind.   Satire on Old Rowley.   Anonymous.   APAS

A brother who has walked his thousand miles.   Poem for My Father's Ghost. Mary Oliver.   InPS; Str

Brothers in blood, a beastly, bitter brood.   The Rout of San Romano.   Jon Manchip White.   NePoEA

Brothers in bond of the water's ring.   The Gift of Water.   Hamlin Garland. AnAmPo; BPAW

"Brothers in spirit, brothers in deed are we"?   Brothers.   James Weldon Johnson.   BANP

Brought on by my English.   For My Father: Two Poems.   David Kherdian. GP

Brought safely home.   Rise, Glorious Conqueror! Rise.   Matthew Bridges. BePJ

Brought thither from the blossom'd limes.   The Storm.   Coventry Patmore. EnLoPo

Brought to blaze on the head of one creature–King Saul!   Saul.   Robert Browning.   BoLiVe; FiP

Brown and perfect below the descending of tides.   The Distances.   Jim Carroll.   PoA

Brown and purple kingdoms/Offered to me.   A New Hampshire Boy. Morris Bishop.   HBMV

The brown, clear stream/that cuts its lifetime into/the dimming strata.   In the Redwood Forest.   Ralph Pomeroy.   CoPo

The brown earth crimsons as he dies,/The strong and dusky stag.   The Dark Stag.   Isabella Valancy Crawford.   NOBC; PeCV

The brown feathers of such a bird as fathered this phoenix?   The Father. Richmond Lattimore.   EyDe; NePoAm-2

Brown gingham, pink, and skirts of Alice blue.   In an Iridescent Time. Ruth Stone.   MoAmPo; PoPl

Brown hawthorne berry, red dog rose.   Stranger to Europe.   Guy Butler. ACV

Brown junks with brown sails/Windward and lee.   The Fishing Fleet. Lincoln Colcord.   HBMV

The brown of her–her eyes, her hair, her hair!   The Farmer's Bride. Charlotte Mew.   BoLoP; ErPo; FaBoWP; HBMV; MoAB; MoBrPo; OxBTC; PoRA; SBG; TrGrPo

Brownish white, whitish brown–and sings.   A Negro Judge.   Frederick Seidel.   CoPo

The browns built up to show/the monotony of waiting.   In the Sitting Room of the Opera.   Criss E. Cannady.   PoDr

...The browns/of these men and their music.   Here Where Coltrane Is. Michael S. Harper.   CNA; PoBA

Brucie keeps on asking, "When/Is Percy comin' back?"   The Murder. Gwendolyn Brooks.   DBV

The bruise of life burns outward.   Summer.   Tom Marshall.   NOBC

...The bruise/you might have kissed and might not yet refuse.   Under the Scub Oak, a Red Shoe.   Dave Smith.   GeTw

The Bruiser in his ritzy suit.   Three Cheers for the Black, White and Blue. Ruth Pitter.   BoAnP

Brush against our one innocent/life.   Little Sis.   David Kherdian.   AMV-80

Brush up your Shakespeare/And they'll all kowtow.   Brush Up Your Shakespeare.   Cole Porter.   NLV; OBAL

Brushes a grain of quartz from the unmoved hill.   Beinn Naomh, IV: The Summit.   Kathleen Raine.   OxBS

Brushing my blond hair.   A Letter from the Hotel.   Aliki Barnstone.   FAZ

...Brusquely we separate.   The Songs of Bilitis.   Pierre Louys.   UnTE

The brute approach of ecstasy.   Boys, By Girls Held in Their Thighs.   John Peale Bishop.   ErPo

Bt those who chose/To survive survival.   Masada.   Isaac Eichanan Mozeson. AMV-81

Bu gosh! how I'm stuck on my honor!   Limerick: "Lucasta," said Terence O'Connor."   Edwin Meade Robinson.   HBMV

Bu joy drops from me like ripe apples.   Immoral.   James Oppenheim. HBV 1-2

Bubble from depths of the Icarian sea.   On the Death of a Metaphysician. George Santayana.   AA; AmLP; APA; ViBoPo

...The bubbling cry/Of some strong swimmer in his agony.   Don Juan. George Gordon, Lord Byron.   LiTB; MCCG; OBRV; ViBoPo; WHA

Bubbling molten, wobbling top heavy/Into one and many.   A Dove.   Ted Hughes.   OxBC

Bubbling up through the earth all the way from the/other side.   Sunlight. Joseph Bruchac.   AMV-80

A bucket of clear water from the well/Be in its homely brightness beautiful. A Coast View (excerpt).   Charles Harpur.   CBAP

A bucket of steaming water/slop slop.   Pretty Vomit.   Bob Rosenthal. APU

A bud in the shadows/kissing its way/into this world.   Boundaries.   Roberta Spear.   MAYP

Buddha accepts/The money/And the flowers.   Oraga Haru.   Issa.   OFD

...The budding leaves/stab mercilessly in my heart.   Two Poems.   Robert J. Abrams.   NNP

Buddy, can you spare a dime?   Brother, Can You Spare a Dime?   E. Y. Harburg.   SaC

...Buddy, you know the drill.   The Author to His Body on Their Fifteenth Birthday 29.ii.80.   Howard Nemerov.   NAs

Buffalo gals won't you come out tonight,/And dance by the light of the moon? Buffalo Gals.   Anonymous.   BLSo; FSW

Buffalo woman/this is all/this is all.   Buffalo marrow on black.   Lance Henson.   STE

A buffered aspirin for a splitting leg.   Party Knee.   John Updike.   FiBHP

The bugle's dying notes that say,/"Another night; another day."   In Barracks. Siegfried Sassoon.   FaBoTw

Build a nest of bone feather and leaf/on treebranch/just below the sun. Conquistador.   Georgia Lee McElhaney.   CoPo

Build a world where life rejoices,/Generous Youth.   Youth.   Katharine Lee Bates.   PGD

Build strongly, for her name must be/With Carthage of the sail-white sea. San Francisco Arising.   Edwin Markham.   BPAW

...Build the log pyramid/in my cold chambers at the Meson Brujo.   Meson Brujo.   E. A. Lacey.   PeHV

Build you an ark! I tell you, it's going to rain.   Noah.   Hermann Hagedorn. MoRP

The builders of the pyramid everywhere!   Pyramis or The House of Ascent. A. D. Hope.   PoAu 1-2

...The building glaring,/as it rumbles, at itself.   The Sow's Ear.   Theodore Weiss.   NoAm

The building of the honeycomb.   No New Thing.   Vincent Buckley.   CBAP

Building, perching, pecking, fluttering,/Everywhere!   Wrens and Robins in the Hedge.   Christina Georgina Rossetti.   SUS; TiPo

Building the cart again.   Ox Cart Man.   Donald Hall.   InPS

The/building/will/fall.   For H. W. Fuller.   Carolyn M. Rodgers.   BPo

Builds his battlements of music up/Amid a falling world.   Boy Playing an Organ.   Francis Sweeney.   GoBC

Built in Jerusalem's wall.   Jerusalem.   William Blake.   OBRV

Built/with that in mind.   The House.   Robert Creeley.   CoPo

Bulgari–/Dulgari–/Sagharimainz.   Soldier, Rest!   Robert Jones Burdette. OBAL

The bulge was Algy.   Algy.   Anonymous.   MoShBr; PoPle; ShM

...A bulk/that writhes and fat-/tens as it speeds.   River Rhyme.   William Carlos Williams.   PoA

...The bull and the great mute swan/Strain into life with their notorious cries. Of Commerce and Society.   Geoffrey Hill.   PPoe

The Bull of Heaven charging down/To graze the pastures, tame and lourd. Buffalo.   Charles Eglington.   PeSA

Bull's Eye: the water cries out.   Stone and the Obliging Pond.   Duane Ackerson.   PoL

The bullets of my quick sixshooter glittering song.   Request for a Song. Julian Tuwim.   LiTW

Bullets, whose armature soul can hold no fear.   No Credit.   Kenneth Fearing.   CMoP

"A bumpity ride in a wagon of hay/For me," says Jane.   Bunches of Grapes. Walter De la mare.   GoJo; GrPl; HBV 1-2; HBVY; MoShBr; OxBChV; SUS; TiPo

Bundle in the bush of radiance: birth-cry of poem!   I Sing an Old Song. Oscar Williams.   LiTM; NePA

Bunkers, barracks, crematoria....   Dachau.   John Malcolm Brinnin.   GP

The Bunny and the Baby and the Prophylactic Pup.   Strictly Germ-Proof. Arthur Guiterman.   BLPA; HBV 1-2; TreF; TrJP; YaD

Bunuel, Bunuel,/is the world? Did you?   Flowers for Luis Bunuel.   Stuart Z. Perkoff.   NeAP

The bunyip paddling in the dark.   The Sundowner.   Shaw Neilson.   CBAP; PoAu 1-2

Bur'ing thy grave in thy sepulchre's reach.   The Angels Sung a Carol. Edward Taylor.   AH

Bur s/(t into a stale shriek/like an alarm-clock)   Impressions, Number III. Edward Estlin Cummings.   UnPo

The burden of the sea.   Answers to the Snails.   Arthur Solway.   AMV-81

Burdened with love she cannot give away.   Daguerreotype of a Grandmother. Celeste Turner Wright.   Str

Burdened, yet to the nascent future bound!   Ode to the Sea.   Howard Baker.
OxBA

Buried alive in this, their language.   Swedish Lesson.   Barton Sutter.   SM

Buried in dust, once dead by fate.   On the Tombs in Westminster Abbey.
Francis Beaumont.   ACP; CH; GTBS; GTBS-P; HBV 1-2; OBEV; PoPle;
TrGrPo; ViBoPo

Buried,/Is a silver skull.   In Memory of Garcia Lorca.   Eldon Grier.
PeCV

Buried under the grade of the new/highway.   Elephants.   Patrick Lane.
NeAC

Buried within the blue vault of the air?   A Dead Mole.   Andrew Young.
FM; GTBS-P; OBSP

Buries the talent to manure the vice.   Sir Francis Bacon.   Ambrose Bierce.
DBV

Burn'd Him to th'Pot, and sour'd his curdled Blood.   The Divine Blacksmith.
Matthew Prior.   FaBoNo

Burn in my heart, burn evermore,/Till I burn out for Thee.   The Soul
Winner's Prayer.   Eugene M. Harrison.   STF

Burn this.   An Oregon Message.   William Stafford.   CoAP; MOON

Burned for the glory of Heaven continually.   Life After Death.   Pindar.
EaLo

Burned in a sea of ice, and drowned amidst a fire.   Idea.   Michael Drayton.
TrGrPo

...Burned not to lie/in the ashes of our dust, it will be to grow.   Violet.
John Hollander.   FYAP

The burner is both burned and blessed.   Twelfth Night.   Philip Booth.
NePoEA

Burning.   The Waste Land.   Thomas Stearns Eliot.   FaBoMo

Burning a house burning in the wilderness.   Burning.   Galway Kinnell.
CoAP

Burning blacker softly, softer.   African Poems: We're an Africanpeople.
Don L. Lee.   CNA

Burning burning   The Hungry Black Child.   Adam David Miller.   PoBA

Burning dinner is not incompetence but war.   What's That Smell in the
Kitchen?   Marge Piercy.   NLV

Burning down Fear Village/And last week's jokes.   Cowboy Song.   Tom
Veitch.   ANYP

Burning forever in consuming fire.   The Wild Knight.   Gilbert Keith
Chesterton.   WGRP

Burning from streetlight/to streetlight.   The Fire Breather, Mexico City.
Jaime Jacinto.   BrSi

The burning grin of space, knelled hell, is sprung.   To George Barker.   Gene
Derwood.   NePA

Burning intensely in the centre of a cold sky.   Hoelderlin's Old Age.
Stephen Spender.   NoAm

Burning its sullen depths with one red blaze.   The Tower of the Dream
(excerpt).   Charles Harpur.   PoAu 1-2

The burning left for another season.   Spring Sequence.   Judith Minty.
AMV-80

Burning righteous,/but burning blind.   Black Mail.   Alice Walker.   AmPA

The burning secret of this mountain, that coal.   An Unseen Fire.   Michael
G. Cooke.   AMV-81

...The burning shiver/Of August strikes like a hawk the crouching hare.
Emblems.   Allen Tate.   InPo; VGW

Burning straight upward.   Sleep.   Del Marie Rogers.   LTB

Burning the/bleeding/sun   The New Manong.   Luis Syquia.   BrSi

A burning void/Upheld by stillness.   The World.   Kathleen Raine.   OxBTC

Burns again for the steelman/who burned like hell for their women.   Driving
at Dawn.   William Heyen.   SaC

Burns in their bones. The world is in their eyes.   Variations on a Theme.
John Hay.   NePoAm

Burns up the building: Lord forbid the same.   When Let By Rain.   Edward
Taylor.   MAmP

Burns with terrible flames and smells.   Air.   Tomaz Salamun.   VWA

Burnt by the boys to get a swarm of bees   The Badger Grunting on His
Woodland Track.   John Clare.   FM; InPS; PAI

A burnt space through ripe fields/A fair mouth's broken tooth.   August 1914.
Isaac Rosenberg.   EBEV; OxBTC

Burpee.   Max Schling, Max Schling, Lend Me Your Green Thumb.   Ogden
Nash.   PV

Burr-like he closes over us.   August 18.   Joanne Kyger.   PoM

Burst like a poppy in this solitude,/In this cool silence.   The Thousand and
One Nights: The Sleeper.   Anonymous.   AWP; LiTW

A burst of fragrance/from black branches.   Love Song.   William Carlos
Williams.   MoAB; MoAmPo

Burst the bonds that we abhor.   Lord, Deliver, Thou Canst Save.   Eliza Lee
Follen.   AH

Burst through the gloomy shades of death,/And shine above the skies.   Deep
Spring.   Anonymous.   AmFP

Burst to illumine our tempestuous day.   Sonnet: England in 1819.   Percy
Bysshe Shelley.   CBEP; EnL; ERoP 1-2; FiP; OAEP; PPP; SeCePo; SeCeV

Burst your bowels!   Phantasus.   Arno Holz.   LiTW

Bursting from the rip in the sun.   On Leaving Baltimore.   Duane Niatum.
CDW

The bursting Randolph ruin spread,/And lost what honor won.   On the
Death of Captain Nicholas Biddle.   Philip Freneau.   PAH

Bursting the air with perennial desperations.   In Memory of My First
Chapatis.   Diane Di Prima.   PoM

Bursts in unexpected laughs?   He Tries out the Concords Gently.   Edward
(Edward Dzyubin) Bagritsky.   TrJP

Bursts upon the enfranchised Bride/The triumphant "Come and see."   Rabbi,
Where Dwellest Thou? Come and See.   Anonymous.   BePJ

...Bury a man/When the last of his dreams is dead.   Dreamer of Dreams.
William Herbert Carruth.   PoLf

Bury her at even,/And then leave her!   Bury Her at Even.   Michael
(Katherine Bradley and Edith Cooper) Field.   CAW; OBMV

Bury it, bury it, bury it where it was born.   Should Thy Love Die.   George
Meredith.   ELP

Bury me not Bunko damned Catholic I pray in Egypt.   The Avenue Bearing
the Initial of Christ into the New World.   Galway Kinnell.   LiTM; NMP

Bury me on old Smoky, old Smoky so high,/Where the wild birds in heaven
can hear my sad cry.   Way Up on Old Smoky.   Anonymous.   TrAS

& Bury my face in my hands.   A Swell Idea.   Steve Kowit.   APU

Bury my heart at Wounded Knee.   American Names.   Stephen Vincent
Benét.   AmFN; LaNeLa; LoGBV; OBAL; OxBA; PG; TreFT; YaD

Bury nothing.   The Eternal Return.   Alan Loney.   OCNZ

Bury that agony, bury this hate, take our black hands in yours.   Open Letter.
Owen Dodson.   BALP

The bush is still a bush, and fire is fire.'   The Burning Bush.   Norman
Nicholson.   EaLo; EBCP; NeBP; SeCePo

The Bush, the hills, the range,/And the dark flats under.   Emus.   Mary
Elizabeth ("E") Fullerton.   BoAnP; PoAu 1-2

Bushels they take/And spread over the streets.   Ishmael.   Gabriel Levin.
VWA

The bushmen of the western side/Rode in to Talbragar.   Talbragar.   Henry
Lawson.   PoAu 1-2

Business is back to normal.   Policy of the House.   Charles Stetler.   GP

Bust in, and hold the ground!   Stand Up!-.   D. H. Lawrence.   OxBTC

Bustling monks/tilling their green precincts.   Starlings.   Norman MacCaig.
BoAnP

The busy day and social night.   Marmion.   Sir Walter Scott.   OBRV

Busy in the unhurt stillness, breeding and dying.   Storm.   Judith Wright.
PoAu 1-2

But a bare hedge and bleak December.   The Stallion.   Alan Porter.   PH

But a bird sings on in the almond tree.   A Fiddler.   Walter De La Mare.
LOW; UnS

But a blush of grief tears my   The Distaff.   Erinna.   WPOW

But a bold peasantry, their country's pride,/When once destroyed, can never
be supplied.   Sweet Auburn.   Oliver Goldsmith.   NOBE

But a boy's best friend is his mother.   Go Get the Axe.   Anonymous.   AS;
TrAS

But a brightly colored fan/Folding and unfolding there?   A Circus Garland.
Rachel Field.   SoPo

But a calm of ordinary bliss/Bears me to sleep unmarred.   Charlotte Nicholls.
Jack R. Clemo.   NAs

But a canner can't can a can, can he?   Limerick: "A canner, exceedingly
canny."   Carolyn Wells.   HBV 1-2; HBVY; LiBL; YaD

But a cat too is an extension of God.   Thoughts on Capital Punishment.
Rod McKuen.   InPK

But a chance lens flare/surrounds her face/with a rim of fire.   The
Photographer's Wife.   Janet Beeler.   AMV-81

But a charmer has to know.   Ballad of Old Women & of How They Are
Constrained to Stimulate...   Norman Talbot.   NOAV

But a collie, a pony and a gun.   Sheep Ranching.   Owen Wister.   BPAW

But a daughter shouldn't be a picture/on a prison bunk/on her birthday.
Birthday: Tara Regina.   George, Jr Mosby.   AMV-81

But a dog ate him up in the hall.   Limerick: "There once was a man of
Bengal."   Anonymous.   CenHV; OnUR; OxBoLi

But a dream within a dream?   A Dream Within a Dream.   Edgar Allan Poe.
AP

But a false hearted lover will lead you to the grave.   My Horses Ain't
Hungry.   Anonymous.   FSW

But a flame in my heart and my eyes, the Maid with her/banner of snow!
The Maid.   Theodore Goodridge Roberts.   HBV 1-2; MoShBr

But a flint holds fire.   An Emerald Is as Green as Grass.   Christina
Georgina Rossetti.   TiPo

But a flint holds fire.   Flint.   Christina Georgina Rossetti.   OxBChV

...But a force/that water welcomes and displays.   Whiplash.   William
Matthews.   AmC; MAYP

But a garland of fresh flowers.   My mother always said.   Sappho.   BoWoP

But a god, a god indeed/Is the man whose bed receives you as his bride!   To
Melite.   Rufinus Domesticus.   LiTW

But a good grip/Will break the heart/Of the best hound in the land.   The
Grip.   Brendan Kennelly.   CIP

But a handful of dirt to the rat. Blake Leads a Walk on the Milky Way. Nancy Willard. OBCA

But a horse will stand always/Backed up to a gale. Straws. Elizabeth Jane Coatsworth. AmFN

But a hundred yearly/Would be very nice. Love. Charles Stuart Calverley. ALV; FiBHP

But a' is for my own son dear,/The heir o Rothiemay.' The Fire of Frendraught (C version). Anonymous. ESPB

But a' is for your fair confession/You've made upon the sea.' Brown Robyn's Confession. Anonymous. ACP; CH; ESPB; GBP

But a jerky bum, humming/with a gentleness less than human. The Fights. Milton Acorn. NOBC

But a knot in the tangled skein of things where chance and/chance combine? Heir and Serf. Don (Donald Robert Marquis) Marquis. HBMV

But a last poor man set sail commander, on a ship that never returned. The Ship That Never Returned (with music). Anonymous. AS

But a last wildrose tells a beautiful lie/to the frost-bitten earth and funereal sky. Bohernabreena. Leslie Daiken. OnYI

But a llama is numero uno.' Limerick: "An Argentine gaucho named Bruno." Anonymous. NOBL

–But a locked door. Midnight Lamentation. Harold Monro. BrPo; ChMP; OBMV; OxBTC; ViBoPo

But a longing dead as its kindred sped/A thousand years ago! I Took a Hansom on To-Day. William Ernest Henley. HBV 1-2

But a mouth kisses and a hand soothes the moment away. You Have the Lovers. Leonard Cohen. NOBC

But a new earth healed, and a new sun rising. We Shall Say. Miriam Allen DeFord. GoYe

But a new-fashioned three-cornered cambric country-cut handkerchief. My Grandmother Sent Me a New-Fashioned Three-Cornered Cambric... Anonymous. OxNR

But a piece of hell will batter her. Le Christianisme. Wilfred Owen. BrPo

But a piece/of/it/all. Who Am I? Felice Holman. RFM

But a sadder, to come to die/Before having loved at all. Folk Songs, 1. Anonymous. LiTW

But a score of my friends soon will/make mock of thee. The Grey Hair. Judah Halevi. TrJP

But a second-hand-dealer in light. Limerick: "Q is a quoter who'll cite." Oliver Herford. TDH

But a second look at Felicity,/Who resembled her mother,/Was less reassuring. Mrs. Crudeman. Osbert Sitwell. HaMV

But a shadow hovering in our midst/Prevented a possible communion. A Sunday in Cambridge. Eddie Linden. PeHV

But a small wind sighed, colder than the rose/Blooming in desolation, "No one knows." The Innocent Spring. Edith Sitwell. NOBE

But a song is lifting its wings. Morning Song. Afanasy Afanasyevich Foeth. AWP

...;But a thought/of that late death took all my heart for speech. In Memory of Major Robert Gregory. William Butler Yeats. AnIL; DiPo; EBEV; OAEL 1-2; OAEP

But a very great Sin they said it had been,/If it had been done by another. The Quaker's Song. Anonymous. CoMu

But a warm wall in winter, an old coat thrown around you. The Center of the Garden. Ann Stanford. AMV-80

But a' was for him, Glenkindie,/In bower he must go mad. Glasgerion (B version). Anonymous. BaBo; ESPB

But a' was for that ill woman,/In the fields mad she gaed. Lady Isabel. Anonymous. BaBo; ESPB

But a' was for the bonnie babe/That lay blabbering in her bleed. Lord Ingram and Chiel Wyet (B version). Anonymous. ESPB

But a woman's love is long/And grows when it is waiting. Two Loves. Laurence Housman. HBMV

But Adam nevuh had no dear old Ma-am-my. Why Adam Sinned. Alex Rogers. BANP

But add an "a' or an "e'/and it gives your Christian name away... Lay Your Weapons Down, Young Lady. Piaras Feiritear. NOBI

But after all, my comfort rests in this,/That for thy sake my youth decayed is. Youth. Bartholomew Griffin. OBSC

But, after all, they didn't do it! To a Friend. Grace Stricker Dawson. BLPA

But, after all, what may be Heaven indeed? The Human Plan. Charles Henry Crandall. AA

But after dark all cats are gray./Love, it is night! The Passionate Professor. Bert Leston Taylor. NLV

But after her I'll whoop and hollo. Birds' Lament. John Clare. PoEL 1-5

But after one such love, can love no more. The Broken Heart. John Donne. AtBAP; DiPo; EBEV; LiTL

But after their names, not on sweaters. Limerick: "The British in branding their betters." David McCord. InMe

But after thirty days a ghostly sun/Gave sickly promise that the storms were done. Dauber. John Masefield. CMoP

But again, he did not know the answer. Lousy Peter. Osbert Sitwell. HaMV

But age hath brought me right to bed. His Own Epitaph. Robert Herrick. CaPo

But age-soured infancy, a darkened dawn. Not in Narrow Seas. Allen Curnow. AnNZ

But Age will keep for pleasure/What Youth thought misery. Since Youth Is All for Gladness. Glenn Ward Dresbach. FiBHP; HBMV; InMe

But Ah, and Ah, again, my imbecility! Contemplations. Anne Bradstreet. PBWP

But ah, Desire still cries, give me some food. Astrophel and Stella, LXXI. Sir Philip Sidney. AAS; CABA; InPS; NoP; OAEL 1-2; SiPS

But ah, how few the God that loves! Heaven and Hell. Francis Thompson. OBSP

But ah! how wondrously they slew/With what they had to go on. The Conquerors. Phyllis McGinley. DBV

But ah! I co'd not: sho'd it move/To Life Eternal, I co'd love. Julia's Petticoat. Robert Herrick. AnAnS 2; CaPo

But ah! more wondrous still the charming fair. A Compliment to the Ladies (parody). William Blake. BXAP

But, ah, my little readers, will you mark and understand? Here Is the Tale. Anthony C. Deane. InMe; NA

But ah! poor parson! when he died,/His breath he could not draw! Parson Gray. Oliver Goldsmith. NA

But ah the worst and last is yet behind,/For of a Gryphon she doth beare the mind. My Ladies Haire Is Threeds of Beaten Gold. Bartholomew Griffin. AAS

But ah! the Wretch the speechless lyes,/Attends but Death to close his Eyes. Sylvce: A Song. John Dryden. CavP

But, ah, thy little Baby sweet/Who was indeed thy God! Regina Coeli. Coventry Patmore. ISi

But ah! to know that bliss shall fail not, and/Our hearts be dust! Sextains. William Baylebridge. BoAV

But ah! what served it to be happy so?/Sith passed pleasures double but new woe? Spring Bereaved. William, of Hawthornden Drummond. OBEV

(But, alas, we never do.) The Flaw in Paganism. Dorothy Parker. DBV; NLV

But, alas, who less could do, that found so good occasion? Think'st Thou to Seduce Me Then. Thomas Campion. BiP; EiL; OBSP; SoSe

But all appeared either the native ground,/Or twisted, wrought, and interwoven with the piece. Upon the Works of Ben Jonson (excerpt). John Oldham. PP

But all delights rejoice his days/Who takes with thanks and never seeks. Sensuality. Coventry Patmore. OBVV

But all do not afford such food to thee/As this poor one, the worser part of me. The Cypress Curtain of the Night. Thomas Campion. LoBV

But all I'll own of the old man's pride/Are rows of rivets along her side. Rivets. N. S. Olds. EtS

But all I want to talk about/Would be unspeakable things. Guilt. Lorenzo Thomas. APU

But all is found in Christ my Lord. My Need. Anonymous. STF

But all is new unhallow'd ground. In Memoriam A.H.H., CIV. Alfred, Lord Tennyson. SBVL; VLP

But all life here is carried on/Against the crash and cry of the moving tides. Zennor. Anne Ridler. MoVE

But all my sighs and griefs are fully paid,/When I but see the shadow of her shade. On My Late Dear Wife. Jonathan Richardson. NOEC

But all of these my unwearying ardor mocks/when sunfire ignites the miles of rippling corn. The Beauty of My Land Peers Warily. Dennis Brutus. WhB

But all's one for that, since I must and will away. On Leaving Mrs. Brown's Lodgings. Sir Walter Scott. NBM

But all's one level plain he hunts for flowers. The Thousand and One Nights: Death. Anonymous. AWP

But all that night the sound of wheels/Kept rumbling through my head. The Circus Parade. Katharine Pyle. OBCA

But all the time you keep going away, away. Grandmother Watching at Her Window. William Stanley Merwin. PrIm; VGW

But all the year my suit must be/That I may please, and she love me. Song Set by Thomas Weelkes: "Three times a day my prayer is." Anonymous. OBSC

But all through your life, remember child/All that glitters is not gold. All That Glitters Is Not Gold. Anonymous. TreFT

But all time roars outside this room. Baby Song. Thom Gunn. NAs

But all was silent save for parrots occasionally,/in the haunted blue bush. Delicate Mother Kangaroo. D. H. Lawrence. GrPl

...But almost certain that they can/never really come to be together. The Way Sun Keeps Falling Away from Every Window. Lyn Lifshin. NeAC

But also cucumbers that are ripe, and pears, and apples. Loveliest of What I Leave behind Is the Sunlight. Praxilla. WPOW

But alwaies oon, your owne boeth ferme and stable. Eche Man Me Telleth I Chaunge Moost My Devise. Sir Thomas Wyatt. AAS

But always and for ever he/At night will sleep and keep by me.   My Joy, My Jockey, My Gabriel.   George Barker.   MoAB; MoBrPo

...But always deft/with wry smiles and excuses.   The First Goodbye Letter.   James Simmons.   AMV-81

But always his skill is superior.   The Evangelist.   Bennie Lee Sinclair.   TAT

But always of the island as a dream.   Southward Sidonian Hanno.   Hervey Allen.   EtS

But always, when a lover speaks,/Look kindly and reply.   Riddles Wisely Expounded.   *Anonymous.*   BaBo; ViBoFo

But always, without fail THE NECK.   Traveler's Curse after Misdirection.   Robert Graves.   DBV; FiBHP; HoPM; MoAB; MoBrPo; NLV; TW

But an emperor of Tartary has died for love of me.   The Memory.   Edward John, Lord Dunsany.   OxBI

But an honest joy/Does itself destroy/For a harlot coy.   Silent, Silent Night.   William Blake.   CBEP

But an old age serene and bright,/And lovely as a Lapland night,/Shall lead thee to thy grave.   To a Young Lady.   William Wordsworth.   EG; EnRP

But an unconstant lover/Will tote ye to yer grave!   The Unconstant Lover.   *Anonymous.*   TrAS

"But," answered Turner, "don't you wish you could?"   Turner's Sunrise.   Helen Bevington.   EyDe

But appears to know/only vertical words.   Sunday Rain.   John Updike.   DFF

But are not of?   Midnight on the Great Western.   Thomas Hardy.   CH; CoBMV; NOBE

But–are you sure you shut the door?   The Cautious Struggle.   *Anonymous.*   UnTE

But aren't they–/in wax/paper for the/moment–beautiful!   To Flossie.   William Carlos Williams.   NePoAm-2

But armed with the invincible sword and shield/of our own names and faces.   Exits and Entrances.   Naomi Long Madgett.   BlSi

But as for little Bill he made him/The Captain of a Seventy-three.   Little Billee.   William Makepeace Thackeray.   CenHV; EtS; FaBoCh; FaBoCo; HBV 1-2; HBVY; LBN; LoGBV; MOS; NA; NOBL; PoPle; ShM; TreFS

But as for me, I never could.   Walter Savage Landor.   Dorothy Parker.   DBV

But as for me I think that He/Is like an abalone.   The Abalone Song.   George Sterling.   BPAW

But as for the bucket, Pawtucket.   Limerick: "But he followed the pair to Pawtucket."   *Anonymous.*   GoTF

But as green/As anything:/As spring.   Dying: An Introduction.   L. E. Sissman.   NYBP

But, as I lift mine eyes above,–His banner over me is love.   His Banner over Me.   Gerald Massey.   HBV 1-2; WGRP

But as I wave I see, appalled,/The new fast bowler's wicked grin.   Spot-Check at Fifty.   Vernon Scannell.   NAs

But as long-lived as present love.   Of English Verse.   Edmund Waller.   AnAnS 2; CavP; OAEL 1-2; OBS; PP; SeCP

But as love is long-winded,/the moving wind/describes its moving colors of sound and flight.   The Wind.   Robert Creeley.   AmPC

But as pretty a thing as may be.   Fain Would I Have a Prettie Thing to Give unto My Ladie.   *Anonymous.*   CoMu; ElL; EnPo; InvP; OAEP; ViBoPo

But as the Devil not half so true.   The Apostasy of One and But One Lady.   Richard Lovelace.   CaPo

But as the mute had thought.   Mute Opinion.   Thomas Hardy.   CMoP

But as the winds the waters stir/The mirrors change & flye.   I Wish I Was Where I Would Be.   John Clare.   NOBV

But as though the birds were in on the secret.   If the Birds Knew.   John Ashbery.   PoA

But as yet there's nae chickens appear'd at Cockpen.   The Laird O' Cockpen.   Carolina Oliphant, Lady Nairne.   BeLS; BSV; HBV 1-2; OBRV

But, as you will! we'll sit contentedly,/And eat our pot of honey on the grave.   Am I Failing?   George Meredith.   CABA; GBL

But ask whatever else, and we will dare!   Ode Recited at the Harvard Commemoration.   James Russell Lowell.   AA; AP; HBV 1-2; MAmP; NOBA; OBWP; OHIP; PAH

But asks our leave to spread himself in prose.   The Sweeniad (parody).   Myra Buttle.   FaBoPa

But at a distance, in another tree.   No Possum, No Sop, No Taters.   Wallace Stevens.   AmP; HaCAP; MoVE; OxBA; TAP; VGW

But at dusk when I lifted her, laughing, laughing,/Over the brook–I knew.   And of Laughter That Was a Changeling.   Elizabeth Rendall.   HBMV

But, at her feet, how blest were I/For any need of hers to die!   The Henchman.   John Greenleaf Whittier.   HBV 1-2; OBEV; OBVV

But at last he cried, "I am lost."   A Learned Man.   Stephen Crane.   LiTA; MoAmPo; NePA

But at last to the one same house.   Songs of T'ang.   Confucius.   CTC

But at least, my sinner, we will spend tonight together.   Tonight at Least, My Sinner.   *Anonymous.*   WTO

But at noon I pulled away.   Two Poems.   Edward Marshall.   CoPo

...But at Rossroe hordes/Of village cats have massacred his birds.   The Philosopher and the Birds.   Richard Murphy.   CIP

But at the immolation of a race who cries?   Death of a Whale.   John Blight.   CBAP; PoAu 1-2

But at the stable-door he'll say good-night.   Together.   Siegfried Sassoon.   BrPo

But, at the touch of wrong, without a strife,/Slips in a moment out of life.   To Hartley Coleridge.   William Wordsworth.   HBV 1-2

...But at times I am ravenous.   Misanthropos (excerpt).   Thom Gunn.   OxBC

But baby's cries can't waken her,/In the baggage coach ahead.   In the Baggage Coach Ahead.   Gussie L. Davis.   FSN; TreFS

But, baby, where are you?   Ballad of Birmingham.   Dudley Randall.   BPo; HeIP; InPK; NIP; NoAm

But Baldy saved the gold.   Baldy Green.   *Anonymous.*   PoOW

But bang my head against the wall/and write this poem   Poem to Help My Father.   Norma Hope Richman.   Str

But bargains: those he will not strike.   Age.   Walter Savage Landor.   ELU; FaBoEE; NBM; NOBV

But be a fine fellow at bottom.   Limerick: "There once was a warden of Wadham."   *Anonymous.*   PeHV

But be a loving father to thee,/And brag the name o't.   A Poet's Welcome to His Love-Begotten Daughter.   Robert Burns.   LiTB; NAs; NOEC; OxBoLi; PoEL 1-5; ViBoPo

But be damned if you can damn us/Frisco-by-the-Bay!   Frisco's Defi.   H. S. Hooper.   BPAW

But be he once to Hymen's close yoke sworn,/Thou straight brav'st this good fellow with the horn.   Caelica, XXXI.   Fulke, Lord Brooke Greville.   FCP

But be In a defiant land/of its own a real right thing.   To the Poem.   Frank O'Hara.   SM

...But be/Its shadow upon life enough for thee.   Aspecta Medusa.   Dante Gabriel Rossetti.   OBSP; VLP

But be this so or not, who can take water down him/Another had to drown in?   Reasons For and Against Marrying Widows.   Henricus Selyns.   SCAP

But bear a horn and blow it not.   Discretion.   *Anonymous.*   CBEP

But beat the bullion–husbands, wives–/And spread it over all your lives.   Advice to Julia.   Henry Luttrell.   OBRV

But beauty and the starlight of her eyes.   Ravished by all that to the eyes is fair.   Buonarroti Michelangelo.   AWP

–But beauty is more now than dying's when.   Life Is More True.   Edward Estlin Cummings.   WaP

But Beauty's self she is,/When all her robes are gone.   My Love in Her Attire.   *Anonymous.*   BLPL; EG; FF; GTBS; HeIP; LiTB; NIP; OBSP; ViBoPo

But beauty's soul abideth still.   Ballad of the Faded Field.   Robert Burns Wilson.   AA

But because it comes first,/and is pledge of the rest.   The Queen of Seasons.   John Henry, Cardinal Newman.   GoBC

But before 't was ten o'clock at night/He gaed it oer as shamefully.   The Bonny Lass of Anglesey.   *Anonymous.*   ESPB

But, before tears can fall, they are asleep.   If Man, That Angel of Bright Consciousness.   Conrad Aiken.   NePA

But begin with the sun to have done before noon,/That the carts may come down for the blubber.   The Greenland Voyage.   *Anonymous.*   OBSS

But behind the yellow piss-pine/crouched the trickster, waiting/to put a mountain there.   Detective Work.   Wendy Rose.   TWSS

But being afraid that I will be afraid.   Moving In.   Paul Engle.   PoA

...But being all/Are gone, the Many-headed Beast must fall.   On the Queens Return from the Low Countries.   William Cartwright.   MePo

But, being shy enough, may yet survive our love.   The Distances They Keep.   Howard Nemerov.   BoAnP

But, being so much too good for earth,/Heaven vowes to keepe him.   Epitaph on S.P. a Child of Q. El. Chappel.   Ben Jonson.   SeCP; SeCV 1-2

But being the secret hidden from yourself.   Runes.   Howard Nemerov.   PoCh

But, belly, God send thee good ale enough,/Whether it be new or old.   Of Jolly Good Ale and Old.   William Frederic Stevenson.   EIL

But, best of all, I love a road that leads to God knows where.   The Best Road of All.   Charles Hanson Towne.   HBMV

But best of all I love my pig.   St. Anthony and His Pig. A Cantata.   Frederick Forrest.   NOEC

But best of all when evening's sigh/Was murmuring at its close.   I Love My Love in the Morning.   Gerald Griffin.   ACP; GoBC; IrPN; OnYI

But better had they ne'er been born/That read to doubt or read to scorn.   The Book of Books.   Sir Walter Scott.   GoTF; TreFT

But better than all of them is the absolutely last chord/of the apparently inexhaustible...   Sincere Flattery of W. W.   James Kenneth Stephen.   HBV 1-2; NOBL; Par; SpRo

But bid good-night, and close their lids for ever.   The Sadness of Things for Sappho's Sickness.   Robert Herrick.   PoPle

But bid them go, bid them bring night, and you. Capriccio. Babette Deutsch. HBMV

But Binker's always Binker, and is certain to be there. Binker. A.(lan) A.(lexander) Milne. PoPl

But Biography is about Chaps. Clerihews. Edmund Clerihew Bentley. FiBHP

But bitterer is the cup than can be told. Fairy Godmothers. Eugene Lee-Hamilton. OBVV

But bless our hands that ebb away. The Players Ask for a Blessing on the Psalteries and Themselves. William Butler Yeats. UnS; VLP

But blessings be about you, dear, wherever you may go. Lovely Mary Donnelly. William Allingham. AnIV; HBV 1-2; IrPN

But blest to fold but thee. L'Envoi: The Return of the Sire de Nesle A.D. 16–. Herman Melville. APA

But blood is manifest, and words are vain. The Gods Are Mighty. N. P. Van Wyk Louw. PeSA

But blood seeps where/I sign before tearing/down the perforated line. Special Delivery. John Montague. CIP; IPY

But boldly march up sword in hand/And that's the way to win her. Would You in Venus' Wars Succeed. Anonymous. ErPo

But born of the rock and the air, not of a woman. Signpost. Robinson Jeffers. GoYe; ViBoPo

But bowed his comely head/Down, as upon a bed. The Execution of King Charles. Andrew Marvell. AnEnPo; PoRA

But Boys! O Boys! O Boys! O Boys! O Boys! Oliver St. John Gogarty. OBMV

But bravely stood where still she stands at bay. Sonnet on the Crimean War. William Forster. CBAP

But break them when she's kind. I Lately Vowed. John Oldmixon. ErPo; HBV 1-2

But breathless all, Fitz-James arose. The Lady of the Lake. Sir Walter Scott. OxBS

But bring my love-ship home to me. My Ships. Ella Wheeler Wilcox. PoLf

But bring us in good ale! Bring Us in Good Ale. Anonymous. CH; EBEV; EG; FaBoCo; MeEL; OAEL 1-2; OxBM; ViBoPo

But brush this dust off me, lest horror it brings/Ere I know it–next moment I dance at the King's! The Laboratory. Robert Browning. ATP; BoLiVe; OBEV; OBVV

But bryng us in good ale. Bring Good Ale. Anonymous. SeCePo

...But Buchenwald flows right/From German lips into my English ear. Dreams in German. David Martin. NOAV

But burrow seed, you're root and rind. The Corrs. Tom MacIntyre. CIP

But by his death which some perhaps will mone,/Ye shall condemned be of many a one. Amoretti, XXXVI. Edmund Spenser. AAS

But, by jingo, next election/I shall put up as MP. Old Brown's Daughter. Anonymous. OBET

But by the way be sure he did not miss/To give her many a sweet and friendly kiss. Angelica and the Ork. Sir John (1561-1612) Harington. OBSC

...But by then/it will have returned to its place. The Statue. Robert Creeley. LCAP

But carved cross-pipes, and, underneath,/A pint-pot neatly graven. Will Waterproof's Lyrical Monologue. Alfred, Lord Tennyson. VLP

But catch, like Peter, men of sin,/For catching is to take them in. The Methodist. Evan Lloyd. NOEC; OBSV

But caught submerged in current of the years/See, wavering, each a shape that never clears. Sisters. Dorothy Roberts. CaP

But celery, stewed,/Is more quickly chewed. Celery. Ogden Nash. FaBoUs; NePoAm

But chiefly, in their hearts with Grace divine preside. The Cotter's Saturday Night. Robert Burns. OBEC

...But childhood, small as a thimble,/looses its genie to the ends of night. Eros out of the Sea. Dilys Bennett Laing. PoA

But children, remember Sarah Stout/And always take the garbage out! Sarah Cynthia Sylvia Stout Would Not Take the Garbage Out. Shel Silverstein. BBGG; OBCA

But "Children will be children," Mamma said. Our Polite Parents. Carolyn Wells. BBGG

But choose amazed to ride you down with hunger. In My First Hard Springtime. James Welch. AmPA; CDW

But clasped to his bosom, the infant lies dead. The Erl-King. Johann Wolfgang von Goethe. MaC

But close behind,–the pipes, the pipes,–the hoofs! Faun-Taken. Rose O'Neill. AnAmPo; HBMV

But close by, unchanging, incomplete. Bachelor Farmer. Roger McDonald. CBAP

But cold Buck's merciless, locked to the Eagles. The Ancestor. Dave Smith. SM

But cold security, the one and only/Right of a workless man without a home. Death and the Plowman. Sidney Keyes. OxBTC

But colourless. Colourless. Poppies in July. Sylvia Plath. FaBoWP; LCAP; NaP

But come, come in till then! Come in till then! Cinderella. Randall Jarrell. DFT; LCAP

But coming home it's miles and miles. Adventure. Harry Behn. TiPo

But complaint cannot redress/Of my great grief the great excess. Farewell all my welfare. Sir Thomas Wyatt. EnPo; FCP; GBL; SiPS

But confident of praise, if praise be due,/Trusts without fear, to merit, and to you. The Good-Natur'd Man: Prologue. Samuel Johnson. LoBV

But copy the things that I wear! Limerick: "Said a lady who wore a swell cape." Oliver Herford. TDH

But copying is, what, in her, Nature writes. Astrophel and Stella, III. Sir Philip Sidney. AAS; OAEL 1-2; OBSC; SiPS

But could not hear its peak. My Sense of Sight. Oliver Herford. HBMV; HBVY

But could not make the sickle yield. The Sword and the Sickle. William Blake. BoLiVe

But could they not have holden me/When I was in all that wrath? Childe Maurice. Anonymous. TrGrPo

But Crist ich hire biteche/That was my lemman. His Sweetheart Slain. Anonymous. OxBM

But Cristes lore, and his apostles twelve,/He taughte, and first he folwed it him-selve. The Canterbury Tales: The Poure Persoun. Geoffrey Chaucer. GoBC

But cruel She I lov'd in vain. A Song from the Italian. John Dryden. CEP; SeCV 1-2

But, Cupid, now farewell, I will go play me/With thoughts that please me less, and less betray me. Caelica, LXXXIV. Fulke, Lord Brooke Greville. FCP

But Custard keeps crying for a nice safe cage. The Tale of Custard the Dragon. Ogden Nash. OBCA; PoPl; PoRA; TiPo

But customer to nothing,/even air. Catalogue Army. Naomi Shihab Nye. MAYP

But d'aint no smokin' possum while de cook am lyin'/sick. Black Sailor's Chanty. Charles Augustus Keeler. EtS

But dark has not yet come. Threshold. Charles David Webb. NePoAm-2

But darker days and hungrier I must spend/Till hunger and darkness make an end. The Little Boy Lost. Stevie Smith. FaBoTw

But daurna come ashore for Bover and his gang. Captain Bover. Anonymous. GBP

But David's harp was gold. Negro Spirituals. Rosemary and Stephen Vincent Benét. AmFN

But day already smells of autumn. Camel. Laila Akhyaliyya. BoWoP

But day by day I spin my shroud. Arachne. Rose T. Cooke. AA; AnAmPo

But day shall bring back delight. Song: "Love laid his sleepless head." Algernon Charles Swinburne. TrGrPo

But dead as a door nail; God be thanked. Epitaph: "Here lies my poor wife, without bed or blanket." Anonymous. FaBoEE

But dead on the level was my gal Sal. My Gal Sal. Paul Dresser. BLSo; FSN; TreFT

But Deadbelly get Ahead/Ha ha ha   Mexico City Blues. Jack Kerouac. NeAP

But dearer far than all surmise/Are sudden tear-drops in your eyes. Sonnet: "Some things are very dear to me." Gwendolyn B. Bennett. PoBA; PoNe

But Death himself to your pride defers,/Adventurers–O Adventurers! The Adventurers. Mary C. G. Byron. HBV 1-2

But Death's what even Politicians fail/To bribe or swindle, bully or blackmail. Another on the Same. Hilaire Belloc. OBSV

But declared she would never leave Portugal. Limerick: "There was a young lady of Portugal." Edward Lear. OxBoLi

But defines for the fortunate, that joy in which all joys should/rejoice. To a Little Girl, One Year Old, in a Ruined Fortress (excerpt). Robert Penn Warren. MoVE

But deplorable absence of ecticut. Limerick: "There was a brave girl of Connecticut." Ogden Nash. NePA

But descend and enter into your embodiment. Invitation to a Spirit. Anonymous. WTO

But Desire Gratified/Plants fruits of life and beauty there. Abstinence Sows Sand All Over. William Blake. EBEV; FF; GBL; ViBoPo

But did Helen of Troy/Run away with the boy/On such very triangular legs? Triangular Legs. Sir Alan Patrick Herbert. NLV

But did not make a single sound! Snow. Alice Wilkins. TiPo

But did not understand. The Seekers. Victor Starbuck. WGRP

But did she know how ill these two accord,/Such cruelty she would have soone abhord. Amoretti, XXXI. Edmund Spenser. AAS

But did wrap the thing in its rejection slip/that saw to it I am here. A Test of Competence. Greg Forker. LFAC

But did you cut off enough? Insufficient Vengeance. Martial (Marcus Valerius Martialis). UnTE

But die a sad and scornful death down in this foreign land. The Flying Cloud. Anonymous. AmFP

But die, by whom each joy doth pass? Song: "How can that tree but withered be." Anonymous. EIL

,But/die in you and am/never born again in/the same place; never/stop! Ho Ho Ho Caribou.   Joseph Ceravolo.   ANYP

But die you must, fair maid, ere long,/As he, the maker of this song.   A Meditation for His Mistress.   Robert Herrick.   CaPo; JCP; NOBE; OBEV; OBS; SeCP

But Dionysus led them home/In a chariot of pain.   Rye Bread.   William Stanley Braithwaite.   CDC

But disguised thus at the Atlantic balls/It is very difficult to single them out I Am Partly Moon...   Vincente Huidobro.   LiTW

But dissolves them to itself in weariness.   Letter of a Mother.   Robert Penn Warren.   MoAmPo

But do not be vexed, I will postdate a cheque for you.   Tree Party.   Louis MacNeice.   FaBoIP; OxBTC

But do not breathe at home one word of this!   Love's Caution.   William Henry Davies.   ChMP

But do not fall in love with thine owne selfe;/Narcissus earst was lost on such a shelfe.   Aurora: Sonnet XXVI.   William Alexander, Earl of Stirling.   OxBS

But do not give advice at all.   A Garland of Precepts.   Phyllis McGinley.   NLV

But do not leave your questioning mind, brother,/to be nibbled in this dance of mice.   The Redeemer.   Kizito Z. Muchemwa.   WhB

But do not so; I love thee in such sort/As thou being mine, mine is thy good/ report.   Sonnets, XXXVI: "Let me confess that we two must be twain."   William Shakespeare.   CBEP; OAEP; PeHV

But do not travel down dumb wind like prodigals.   The Spire Cranes.   Dylan Thomas.   PoA

But does a Human Form display/To those who dwell in realms of Day.   Auguries of Innocence.   William Blake.   AtBAP; BiP; BLPL; BoLiVe; DiPo; EBEV; FaBV; FaFP; FaPoR; FM; LAuP; LiTB; LoBV; MasP; OAEL 1-2; OAEP; OBNC; OBRV; PoEL 1-5; SeCeV; TrGrPo; TRV; WGRP

But does not need to know/Why spirit was flesh-bound.   Winter Night.   Cecil Day-Lewis.   PoA

(But Don John of Austria rides home from the Crusade.)   Lepanto.   Gilbert Keith Chesterton.   AnFE; CAW; FaBV; FaPo; FaPoR; GoBC; HBMV; HBVY; MoBrPo; MOS; OBMV; OBNV; PoRA; TreFS; WHA

But don't be so rude as all that!   Limerick: "There once was a sensitive cat."   Alice Brown.   TDH

But don't forget our chaplain/With his head out of the port.   Manila Bay.   Arthur Hale.   PAH

But don't pass me dried-apple pies.   Dried Apple Pies.   *Anonymous.*   BLPA

But don't say to Dr. Freud/Jenny kiss'd me.   Such Stuff as Dreams.   Franklin Pierce ("F.P.A.") Adams.   FiBHP; SpRo

But don't think to stop it, it is of no use,/For people will talk.   People Will Talk.   Samuel Dodge.   WBLP

But don't weep the minutes away/Along with the dust/That cloaks the light.   To You Building the New House.   Nelly Sachs.   VWA

But don't you be the one to choose me: poor.   Sunflower Sonnet Number One.   June Jordan.   SM

But don't you fence it in.   Way Out West.   Charles A. Siringo.   CoSo

But–don't you take no sail off 'er," said the Ol' Man,/said 'e.   What the Old Man Said.   C. Fox Smith.   EtS

But dont run/I wont just think pigeon   Pigeon.   Elouise Loftin.   CNA

But doth waste with greediness.   Confined Love.   John Donne.   AnEnPo

But double L and Double T,/The de'il may ken wha they may be.   The Spelling of Elliot.   *Anonymous.*   FaBoUs

But, down on down, the uninhabitable sorrow.   The Kingfisher.   Amy Clampitt.   HaCAP

But drappit o Childe Owlet's blude/and pieces o his flesh.   Child Owlet.   *Anonymous.*   ESPB

But drawing the water down to the deepest wonder.   Fountain.   Elizabeth Jennings.   BoC; PoCh

But dried among the bric-a-brac/On mantlepieces of Peru and Mexico.   The Republic 1939.   James Liddy.   CIP

But drift to sleep where canvas hides the stars/Of the long, planetary wagon train.   Wagon Train.   E. L. Mayo.   MiAP

But droop into mine arms, and understand!   Terre Promise.   Ernest Christopher Dowson.   NOBV

But drop a parting tear/For town, whose greatest gift to us/Was to be lovers here.   A Song of Parting.   Compton Mackenzie.   HBV 1-2; OBVV

But drops caught up in the bough/Fall murderously on me now.   The Letter.   Patricia Beer.   OxBC

But Duty First is the rule and plan/Of a Prince who is also a family man.   The Warrior's Lament.   Sir Owen Seaman.   FiBHP

But dwell in darkness; for your god is blind.   A Coronet for His Mistress Philosophy.   George Chapman.   CoBE

But dying is a pleasure,/When living is a pain.   Farewell ungrateful traitor.   John Dryden.   BoLoP; CBEP; ELP; HAP; InPo; LiTB; NOBE; ViBoPo

...But each ear/Is listening to its hearing, so none hear.   At the Party.   W. H. Auden.   OBSP

But each one to his taste, I always say.   The Legend of Success, the Salesman's Story.   Louis Simpson.   NYBP

But each unto each, as in Thy sight, one.   Plighted.   Dinah Maria Mulock Craik.   HBV 1-2

But earth and will are stronger/And nearer–and we stay.   Nostalgia.   Louis MacNeice.   OnYI

But Earth has specialized in little men.   Go Fly a Saucer.   David McCord.   ImOP

But easy writing's vile hard reading.   Clio's Protest.   Richard Brinsley Sheridan.   FaBoEE

But Edison made light of it.   Fable.   James Facos.   NLV

But "Emigrated to another star!"   Emigravit.   Helen Hunt Jackson.   AnFE; APA

But empresses came back as cats!   Bast.   William Rose Benet.   HBMV

"But empty sends the rich away."   Joseph Mary Plunkett.   Wilfrid Meynell.   ISi

But envy strikes to the marrow/and sticks there for ever.   Epigram: "Heat goes deep as cold."   *Anonymous.*   NOBI

But equally a want of books and men!   England, 1802.   William Wordsworth.   OBEV

But ere I could flie thence, it pierc'd my heart.   Astrophel and Stella, XX.   Sir Philip Sidney.   AAS; OAEL 1-2; SiPS; TEP

But ere they wan to the tap o the hill/The wedding was a' bye.   Young Peggy.   *Anonymous.*   BaBo; ESPB

But, ere you get another, 'ti'n't amiss/To try a year or two how you'll keep this.'   The Beggar Woman.   William King.   NOEC

But Error, wounded, writhes with pain,/And dies among his worshippers.   Truth, the Invincible.   William Cullen Bryant.   GoTF; TreF

But especially Englishmen.   A Bestiary.   Kenneth Rexroth.   OBAL

But especially those that can't tell/murder from phenomenology.   Gunfighter.   Gerald Locklin.   AMV-80

But etched on our minds/Forever.   Eagle.   Tom Bowker.   PoSH

But evade the sesquipedalian school inspector/With his muzzle and his bag!   Birth of a Great Man.   Robert Graves.   NYBP

But, even then, an honest eye should wink.   At Lucky Moments We Seem on the Brink.   W. H. Auden.   PV

But even there he failed, they say,/To get a likeness once.   The Imperfect Artist.   George Rostrevor Hamilton.   DBV

But ever alive, struggling and rising again, seeking/the light, freeing the world.   The Hotel.   Harriet Monroe.   AnAmPo

But ever in my lavender/I hear the brawling bees.   That Day You Came.   Lizette Woodworth Reese.   HBV 1-2

But ever rises on the cheeks again.   Wine.   Daqiqi.   LiTW

But ever sleep in your mystery,/And in your silence rejoice.   The Cliff Dwelling.   Arthur W. Monroe.   PoOW

But ever-smiling Spring, and Pleasure reign.   The Swallows: An Elegy.   Richard Jago.   CEP

But evermore a life behind.   In Memoriam A.H.H., XLI.   Alfred, Lord Tennyson.   VLP

But every Jack/He must study the knack/If he wants to make sure of his Jill.   The Yeoman of the Guard (excerpt).   Sir William Schwenck Gilbert.   FaBoUs

But every moment adds to the cry/Of that dead army driving by.   Trees on the Calais Road.   Edmund Charles Blunden.   BrPo

But every morning he still is/Too little to look.   Little.   Dorothy Aldis.   NTCP; SUS; TiPo

But every pane of glass is still whole.   Allegro.   Tomas Transtromer.   EAS

But every time she winks or smiles,/She thinks of the foggy dew.   The Foggy Dew.   *Anonymous.*   CoMu; ELP; UnTE

–But every woman there will look at me.   The Gown.   Mary Carolyn Davies.   HBMV

But every wrong way I take,/Can become the right way towards your wisdom.   Alajire.   *Anonymous.*   WTO

But everything passes...   Water-Front.   Cecil Ffrench Salkeld.   OnYI

But expect nothing. Live frugally/On surprise.   Expect Nothing.   Alice Walker.   AmPA; FF

But expects to return with gold and silver store.   The Greenland Men.   *Anonymous.*   OBSS

But ez fur myself, I thank ye,/I'll not take any in mine.   The Pledge at Spunky Point.   John Milton Hay.   OBAL

But failte and hospitality, inducing fresh acquaintance.   Galway Races.   *Anonymous.*   OxBoLi; SD

But fair and faithful few there be.   That He Findeth Others as Fair, But Not So Faithful as His Friend.   George Turberville.   EIL

But fairies have broke their wands,/And wishing has lost its power!   Song: "A lake and a fairy boat."   Thomas Hood.   HBV 1-2

But, faith, he fears the Irish knack/Of handling the shillay.   Irish Astronomy.   Charles Graham Halpine.   HBV 1-2

But faith like thine will never pass away.   Erin.   Kenelm H. Digby.   CAW

But falls into a whore-house by the way.   In Fuscum.   Sir John Davies.   FaBoEE

But falsely called Euxine–its meaning is "hospitable"–/holds me.   Tristium.   Ovid (Publius Ovidius Naso).   NAs

But fancy builds a prison still for thee! Stay, Shade of My Shy Treasure! Sister Juana Ines de la Cruz. WPOW

But Fancy still will sometimes deem/Her fond creation true. A Day Dream. Emily Bronte. VLP

But, far and near: "Cuckoo! Cuckoo! Cuckoo!" The Fresh Air. Harold Monro. CH

But far down the road a tall stone stood... The Wounded. Louise Louis. GoYe

But fast it runneth on and passen shall/As doth a dream, or shadow on the wall. The Twelve Weapons of Spiritual Battle. Sir Thomas More. EnRePo

But Fate and gloomy Night encompass thee around. To the Memory of Mr. Oldham. John Dryden. ATP; AWP; CABA; DiPo; EBEV; ExPo; FiP; ForPo; HAP; HeIP; InPK; InPo; InPS; LoBV; NIP; NOBE; NoP; OAEL 1-2; OBS; PAI; PoEL 1-5; PP; PPoe; PPP; Prf; SeCeV; SeCV 1-2; ViBoPo

But, Father, pity poverty,–/I have no other coat to wear. A Proud Song. Marguerite Wilkinson. HBMV

But father, son and clerk join up/To talk about the Football Cup. The City. Sir John Betjeman. TEP

But fear perhaps my little son/Should break his hands, as I have done. The Rebel. Hilaire Belloc. CoBE

But fear, thirst, hunger, and this huddled chill. Montana Pastoral. J. V. Cunningham. MAT; MoAmPo; PrIm; VGW

But feels the death that all must die/As fuller life is won. O Thou Eternal Source of Life. Rolland W. Schloerb. TrPWD

But fell in the pond and croaked in it. Nursery Rhyme. Kenneth Burke. OBAL

But Feridoun was not content/Though Ajum's kingdom was his own! Contentment. Muslih-ud-Din Sa'di. LiTW

But few, I fear, will tell their wives/The doleful tale of wo. The Battle of Queenstown. William, Jr Banker. PAH

But fight back, gambol/while you can, then go with grace in your prime. The Old Whore Speaks to a Young Poet. Dave Smith. SM

But fight on to the last/With a stiff upper lip. Keep a Stiff Upper Lip. Phoebe Cary. FaFP

But, fighting or flying,–I'm your very very/humble. General Howe's Letter. *Anonymous.* PAH

But finding nothing, sullenly withdrew. Range-Finding. Robert Frost. AmLP; CABA; NIP; NoAm; NoP; OBWP

But first/he unbuttoned my gown,/inflamed me. Freely, from a Song Sung by Jewish Women of Yemen. Stephen Levy. VWA

But first I'll drink at the spring below, and/whet again my scythe. The Mower in Ohio. John James Piatt. AA

But first I'll take my watering-pot/And wash the pansies' faces. Rain in the Night. Amelia Josephine Burr. TiPo

"But first let's do as Jane has done." The Penitent Nun. John Lockman. UnTE

But first let's learn to do what Jane has done. Repentance. Louis Untermeyer. NLV

"But first, my dear, I'd have you learn to swim." Epigram: "When Pontius wished an edict might be passed." Matthew Prior. DBV

But first set my poor heart free,/Bound in those icy chains by thee. Hide, O Hide Those Hills of Snow. John Fletcher. HBV 1-2; ViBoPo

But first, to make a marriage, shot his wife. Five Epigrams. Donald Hall. NePoAm-2

...But fishermen know/there are days when you don't catch anything. Angling, a Day. Galway Kinnell. WOLT

...But fled/Murmuring, and with him fled the shades of night. Paradise Lost. John Milton. OAEL 1-2; WHA

But floats the flag of forty stars/By Chickamauga River. Garfield's Ride at Chickamauga. Hezekiah Butterworth. PAH

But follow sorry phantoms to and fro,/And let a kingdom go. The Man with the Hoe: A Reply. John Vance Cheney. HBV 1-2

But following her such hope remaineth none. She That Holds Me Under the Laws of Love. Sir Arthur Gorges. GBL

But, fool, seekst not to get into her heart. Astrophel and Stella, XI. Sir Philip Sidney. AAS; SiPS

But for a day the nickle bet/Made your hopes ten feet tall. A Nickle Bet. Etheridge Knight. CAD

But, for a parting present, leave her/A rooted pox to last for ever! The Progress of Marriage. Jonathan Swift. EiCP

But for a' that they ca'd, and for a' that they socht,/They left the young squire busy bakin'. The Duke o' Athole's Nurse. *Anonymous.* OxBB

But for a truth, or for the common's sake. The True Knight. Stephen Hawes. AnEnPo; OBEV; TrGrPo

...But/For all his clothes, his face, his face is black! Shadows. *Anonymous.* WTO

But for nine-till-fiver Linda, a thrifty working girl. Belle de Jour (parody). George Melly. FaBoPa

But for one hour/Come back to me. Susannah Prout. Walter De la Mare. FaBoEE

But for perfect worship leave/Dora to her poet. Margaret and Dora. Thomas Campbell. HBV 1-2

But for strong new growth/Under midnight moons Remembering Fannie Lou Hamer. Thadious M. Davis. BlSi

But, for such as our earth is now, it lasted long. The Season of Phantasmal Peace. Derek Walcott. NoP

But for The Thing. The Runes on Weland's Sword. Rudyard Kipling. AtBAP; PoEL 1-5

But for the way the waif befits my life. The Road. Herbert Morris. NePoAm-2

But for their falling/I might see her still. Two Poems. Hitomaro. LiTW

But for their powers, accept my piety. To William Camden. Ben Jonson. AnAnS 2; AWP; InPo; JCP; OBS; SeCV 1-2

But for them the bombers answer everything. 2nd Air Force. Randall Jarrell. CMoP; WaP

But for those who Love/Time is/Eternity. Time. *Anonymous.* GoTF; TreFT

But for whose brave-hearted Son we had never/Known the sweet hurt of the sorrowful love. The Hurt of Love. George Macdonald. TrCP

But forthwith bade my Julia shew/A bud in either cheek. The Rosarie. Robert Herrick. InMe

But fortune favors fools, as old men say,/And lets them live, and takes the wise away. An Epitaph of the Death of Nicholas Grimald. Barnabe Googe. EnRePo

But foul fare the filthy bird that singeth cuckoo. Madrigal: "Well fare the nightingale." *Anonymous.* PBBP

But found no winter anywhere to see. Mid-Winter Walking. Robert Graves. MoAB

But found themselves beguiled, beguiled/By her indifferent breast. Nature. Walter Stone. NYBP

But Francis, kneeling/Prays for their souls. Saint Francis Borgia or a Refutation for Heredity. Phyllis McGinley. NePoAm-2

But frankly gaily shall be got the gods. Meditation at Kew. Anna Wickham. AnEnPo; FaBoTw; MoBrPo

But fresh always with new tears. A Blackbird Singing. R. S. Thomas. BoANP; BoC

But fresh and honey-like; and Need/No household skeleton at all. In the Study. Thomas Hardy. BrPo

But, friend of Mine, who wounded, knowest thou,/My hands? Roundel of Passion-Tide. *Anonymous.* CAW

But from a sober perspective. The Horatians. W. H. Auden. NYBP

But from its own divine vitality. A Poet!–He Hath Put His Heart to School. William Wordsworth. EnRP; VLP

But from that eve he was alone on earth. Rhoecus. James Russell Lowell. AA; MCCG

But from that mark how far they rove we see/for all this waste of wealth, and loss of blood. On the Detraction which Followed upon My Writing Certain Treatises. John Milton. ATP; ExPo; FaBoPV; SeCeV

...But from the deep/recesses of the heart before the darkness falls. Ballykinlar: May 1940. Patrick Maybin. NeIP

...But from/the next it is fixed in shadow and light. The Field. David Huddle. Str

But from those gifts which Heav'n has heap'd on her. At Penshurst. Edmund Waller. AnAnS 2; OAEP; OEAL 1-2; SeCV 1-2

But, gaining back my will, may find it thine. Laid on Thine Altar. *Anonymous.* TrPWD

But get married, my boys, and have all night in, and go to sea no more! Jack Wrack. *Anonymous.* ABF

But get some color and music out of life? The Investment. Robert Frost. CMoP; OxBA

But get thee to a nunnery-go! Shakespearean Soliloquy in Progress: "To be, or not to be..."(parody). Twain Mark. BXAP

But gi'e her my breast-knot, white an' blue? White an' Blue. William Barnes. GBL; GTBS-P

But give me leisure every time. The Dignity of Labor. Robert Bersohn. NLV; PoPl

But give the wild will never. Egrets. Max Eastman. AnEnPo

But give to the haughtiest question,/Smiling, a sweet reply. The Sunshine of the Gods (excerpt). Bayard Taylor. AA

But gives me love and weeping. In a Wood. E. J. Scovell. GBL

But go, behold Arpasia's face,/And read it perfect there. Song: "The shape alone let others prize." Mark Akenside. HBV 1-2

But go on shedding blood/to sign our doors. Agent Orange. Rita Brady Kiefer. SOTS

But God has heard, and the storm is gone, so hush and/lullaby! The Mother's Lullaby. John Clare. NAs

But God himself can't kill them when they're said! Words. *Anonymous.* PoLf

But God his owne will guard, and their sharp paines and griefe/in time asswage. Author of Light, Revive My Dying Spright. Thomas Campion. AAS; AtBAP

But God, if one of them could farm! Ballad of the Bushman. Eileen Duggan. CoBE

But God is ever dear. Jonah. *Anonymous.* ACP

But God knows you are stronger than I am. Limerick: "There was once a maiden of Siam." *Anonymous.* GoTF; TreFT

But God on his repealless list/Can summon every face. They dropped like flakes. Emily Dickinson. AA; OHIP

...But God the performer/Is walking about with the bird in His hand. Spring. Oscar Williams. LiTA

But God was seen no longer any more. He Said: "If in His Image I Was Made." Trumbull Stickney. AnFE; APA; LiTA

But God will bring him where the Blessed are. The Way. Henry Van Dyke. TRV

But Godes mercy is us alle beheeve,/For this world fareth as a fantasye. This World Fares as a Fantasy. *Anonymous.* OxBM

But going on to search her cruel mind/for better excuses to leave my narrow bed. Why Do We Lie. B. S. Johnson. ELU

But going, took the stars and moon/And sun away with her. Pierrette in Memory. William Griffith. HBV 1-2

...But golfers play it as it lies. Golf Ball. John Delaney. AMV-81

But good enough for them, the suckers. Wm. Brazier. Robert Graves. NOBL

But good night to the Session, good night! A Grouchy Good Night to the Academic Year. Ted Pauker. NOBL

But good ones love the dark, and find/The night as pleasant as the day. Queen Mab. Thomas Hood. HBV 1-2; HBVY

But grant my brother's need shall find/I thought of him instead. Prayer. May Carleton Lord. PGD

But grant, O God, that when he dies/One prayer should rise! Shame. Arthur Rimbaud. SyP

But grave and piano,/When pension's withdrawn-O! A Courtier's a Riddle. Ralph Schomberg. TrJP

But Grey is slyer than Black: "Why, I am practically/White." The "Black' Country. D. J. Enright. HaMV

But grief's redress is happiness,/Alternate through the years. Song: "We only ask for sunshine." Helen Hay Whitney. HBV 1-2

But grief shone here, while joy was one with/shame,/Beloved and blest. In Guernsey. Algernon Charles Swinburne. VLP

But ha! ha! ha! full well is me,/For I am now at liberty. Love's Snare. Sir Thomas Wyatt. LiTL

...But had begun/serious work on staring at a face/his hammer had laid bare by luck alone. The Crack. Michael Goldman. NYBP

But had no throat like yours, my bird,/Nor such a listener. Joy of the Morning. Edwin Markham. HBV 1-2

But hadst thou seen her plaster'd up before,/'Twas so unlike a face, it seem'd a sore.... Against Women. Juvenal (Decimas Junius Juvenalis). LiTW

But hallowed thoughts around thee twine o' hame and in-/fancy,/O rowan tree! The Rowan Tree. Carolina Oliphant, Lady Nairne. HBV 1-2

But handy for the crucified. Poem. R. A. K. Mason. ACV

But Happy be, though in a Dying Hour,/O're whom the Second Death obtains no power. Matthew X. 28. Roger Wolcott. SCAP

But hardly anyone feels/he has to be equal to his own fate Time Was. Pati Hill. FAZ

But hark! a sheep's bell calls me up,/Like Oxford college bells, to sup. On Westwell Downs. William Strode. CBEP; FaBoPP; JCP; PoEL 1-5

But has an eye, at once, to all the Nine. On a Squinting Poetess. Thomas Moore. FaBoCo

But has bad dreams; I fear he has bad dreams. King Borborigmi. Conrad Aiken. MAPA

But has for Him some treasure chaste. Sons of Promise. Thomas Curtis Clark. PoToHe

But hast thou bliss in youth? O sweet estate! Content. Thomas Campion. OBSC

But hasten home, and I'll bespeak/Your services another day! A Valentine. Matilda Betham-Edwards. OBVV; PeHV

But have, at present, other fish to fry. Sir Launfal. John Moultrie. OBRV

But have you/Caught, among small/Stars, his flute? Delicate the Toad. Robert Francis. DuDa

But having perfected what He had to do,/stood off shrouded in his loneliness. Watchmaker God. Robert Lowell. HaCAP

But he always came home to tea, tea, tea, tea, tea,/Tea to the n-th. Poe at Tea. Barry Pain. HBV 1-2

But he belly laughs. He's not wise. Three Fitts. Stewart Parker. CIP

But he by many deaths will bless her days. A Young Highland Girl Studying Poetry. Iain Crichton Smith. NePoEA-2; PP

But he by this Diviner Art/makes conquest of the Heavenly part. Reply. Sidney Godolphin. OBS

But he came home again, with "Damaged Goods." Song for Mother's Day. T. S. Matthews. ELU

But he can't/So he don't. He Loves Me. *Anonymous.* OxNR

But he cares not a penny for that. A Baker's Dozen of Wild Beasts. Carolyn Wells. OBCA

...But he couldn't move, the track was so deep. Variations on a Theme. Oscar Williams. LiTA

But he'd a good time doin' it, did'ney? Limerick: "There was a young fellow named Sydney." Don (Donald Robert Marquis) Marquis. LiBL

But he dared not stay/Over-long! The Unicorn. Ella Young. SoPo; TiPo

But he did for them both with his plan of attack. The General. Siegfried Sassoon. ELU; FiBHP; TW

But he did give Elizabeth a Dodo/And he never even offered one to me. Of a Certain Green-Eyed Monster. Esther Lilian Duff. HBMV

But He did love His servant. Abraham and Isaac. Else Lasker-Schüler. BoWoP; VWA

But he didn't catch me. The Little Turtle. Vachel Lindsay. GoJo; NTCP; OBAL; OBCA; SoPo; SUS; TiPo

But he didn't-he died in the fall. Limerick: "There once was a young man named Hall." *Anonymous.* ShM

But he doesn't know it may be the last time. Shake Hands with Your Bets, Friend. Lorenzo Thomas. APU

But he goes unappeased/Who is on kindness bent. Love. Henry David Thoreau. CBEP; OBVV

But he got in behind-and oh,/the difference to us! The Man from Inversnaid. Robert Fuller Murray. SD

But he had squatted at the end of steel. End of Steel. Thomas Saunders. CaP

But he had to git out o' dere. A Garland of Recital Programs. Franklin Pierce ("F.P.A.") Adams. InMe

But he has got a wife-and O!/The difference to me! Jacob. Phoebe Cary. InMe; OBAL

But he has his apple trees still in bloom./Johnny Appleseed! Johnny Appleseed! Johnny Appleseed. Rosemary Benet. TrAS

But he her smell jes' de same. Black Gal. *Anonymous.* ABF

But he holds to his North or South/Blows-and again is quiet. My Mouth Is Very Quiet. Jose Garcia Villa. AnFE; CoAnAm

But he is come in cold-as-workhouse weather,/Poor as a Salford child. Carol. John Short. DTC; FaBoTw

But he knowed too much to go dat way. Old Man Know-All. *Anonymous.* BPo

But he'll lug the whole dark/across your door sill. The Bear Who Came to Dinner. Adrien Stoutenburg. SO

But he'll miss him once the old dog's dead. Hector the Dog. Kate Barnes. GDP

But he'll swallow with never a spasm/What ostriches couldn't digest. The Singular Sangfroid of Baby Bunting. Guy Wetmore Carryl. NA

But he mighty lak' a rose! Sweetes' Li'l' Feller. Frank Lebby Stanton. FaFP; TreFS

But he must shovel coal to make the engine smoke. Ol' John Brown. *Anonymous.* ABF

But he never ate abalone. Abalone (with music). *Anonymous.* AS

But he never came back any more. A Leave-Taking. Arno Holz. AWP

...But he/Never can tell where shall his landing be. Man's Dying-Place Uncertain. Robert Herrick. CaPo

But he never could tell which he liked the best. Gregory Griggs. Laura E. Richards. OxNR; SoPo

But He never gives in, so we two shall win-/Jesus and I. Jesus and I. Dan Crawford. BLRP; TRV

But he never had a son. Family 8. Lyn Lifshin. NeAC

But he never shall send our ancient friend/To be tossed on the stormy sea. The Brave Old Oak. Henry Fothergill Chorley. FaBoBe; HBV 1-2

But he never would indicate how. Limerick: "An eccentric old person of Slough." George Robey. CenHV

But he only wanted to have a time in the woods of Michigan. Harry Dunne (I). *Anonymous.* ShS

But he proved a gander. Epitaph: "Here lies Landor." Walter Savage Landor. FaBoEE

But he pulled it out by the tail. A Scot, a Welsh and an Irish Man. *Anonymous.* GBP

But, He Restor'd, 'tis now become a Throne. To My Friend, Dr. Charleton, on His Learned and Useful Works. John Dryden. SeCV 1-2

But he rose up and knew himself a Greek. Keats. Lizette Woodworth Reese. AA

But he's as good as anybody going. Waspish. Robert Frost. BoAnP

But he's comin' back if he goes ten thousand miles. He's Gone Away (with music). *Anonymous.* AS

But he's just a little pig still. The Space Child's Mother Goose. Frederick Winsor. QQQ

But he's just as dead as if he'd been wrong. Mike O'Day. *Anonymous.* GoTF; TreFT

But he's known all the same/As the dark ne plus ultra of Reason. De Sade. John Fuller. NLV

But he's not the only pebble on the beach! You're Not the Only Pebble on the Beach. Harry Braisted. FSN

But he's such a very great musician/Grimacing and fingering his fiddle-strings. A Tragedy. Theophile Marzials. HBV 1-2

But he scarce reads his Bible, and never loves thinking. The Sluggard. Isaac Watts. OxBoLi; Par; TreFS

But he sets my blood a-going/Where his song will never be. The Tree-Toad. Orrick Johns. HBMV

But he shall come at twilight's close,/And bring his golden sheaves. The Harvest Dawn Is Near. George Burgess. AH

But he shall put to flight the host of/my sorrows. Bring Me the Cup. Moses Ibn Ezra. TrJP

But he shall walk with Me, his God. The Old Road. Jones Very AA

But he shook his little tail/And away he flew. Little Bird. Anonymous. OxNR

But he smacked me upon my bare bottom, Anne!' Limerick: "Charlotte Bronte said, "Wow, sister! What a man!" Victor Gray. NOBL

But he stare afterward, wonder me thinketh. Snatches: "What! why didest thou wink." Anonymous. OxBM

But he started at once to bow-wow hard. Limerick: "There was a young puppy called Howard." A.(lan) A.(lexander) Milne. GDP; TDH

But he still was a Master of Arts. Limerick: "There once was a Master of Arts." Cosmo Monkhouse. TDH

But he takes it wherever he goes. The Elephant. Anonymous. OnUR

But he that fights and runs away/Will live to fight another day. Fight. Anonymous. FaFP

But he that is cast down/From enjoy'd beauty, feels a woe,/Only deposed Kings can know. A Deposition from Love. Thomas Carew. AnAnS 2; CaPo; CavP; MeLP; OAEP; OBS

But he that learns these letters fair/Shall have a coach to take the air. He That Ne'er Learns His ABC. Anonymous. GBP; GLGT

But he that of repetition is most master. Whistle Aloud, Too Weedy Wren. Wallace Stevens. LiTA

But he thinks upon the dear old folks he left in Gaspereaux. The Banks of the Gaspereaux. Anonymous. AmFP; ShS

But he 'twas made for did not know/Whether 'twas a thing or no. Riddle: "There was a man made a thing." Anonymous. GBP

But he wanted you to be/proud of him, so he invented/the telephone before he called. The Invention of the Telephone. Peter Klappert. AmPA; PPJ

But he wants the other half It's the Same at Four A.M. Joy Harjo. TWSS

But he was apprehended, bare,/By one who rose up from the dead. Three Epigrams. Theodore Roethke. NLV

But he was backed through thick and thin/By all his kin. Adam Smith. Edmund Clerihew Bentley. FaBoCo

But he was bespoken for. That's Life? Alan Bold. FF

But he was not, was not, so he is nought. Fear Death by Water. Richard Eberhart. AMV-81

But he went down;/That's where I'm going. Spike Driver Blues. Mississippi John Hurt. BluL

But he went the house cat in. Lancaster County Tragedy. W. Lowrie Kay. ShM

But he who is well married is near to Paradise. Prayers of a Christian Bridegroom. Pierre Poupo. HW

But he who kisses the joy as it flies/Lives in eternity's sun rise. He Who Binds to Himself a Joy. William Blake. EBEV

But he, who loved them, is at rest. Laleham: Matthew Arnold's Grave. Lionel Pigot Johnson. FaBoPP

But He who paid our hopeless debt,/Our constancy shall prove. Shall We Forget. William Mitchell. BePJ

But he who speaks, or him who's spoken to,/Must both remain as strangers still to you. Yourself. Jones Very. AA; AmLP; MAmP; NePA; NOBA; OxBA; PoEL 1-5

But he whose name in grav'd in the white stone,/Shall last and shine when all of these are gone. Contemplations. Anne Bradstreet. AmPP; AnFE; AnNE; AP; APA; MAmP; PBWP; PoEL 1-5; SCAP; WPOW;

But hears the proud dead/Whimpering. Now in the Bloom. Florence Kiper Frank. GoYe

But heaven breathes softly/by her side. Though She Slumbers. Joseph Joel Keith. ISi

But heaven is very far away. At the Fountain. Marcabrun. AWP

But heaven stooped under the roof on the morn/That it brought them only a baby. Only. Harriet Prescott Spofford. HBV 1-2

But Heaven will protect the working girl. Heaven Will Protect the Working Girl. Edgar Smith. FaFP; FiBHP; TreF

But heavy like a bough in spring. Song from a Country Fair. Léonie Adams. GoJo; GrPl

But heed Thou that I need not thank Thee long. Gratitude. Mikhail Yuryevich Lermontov. LiTW

But held the first his whole life long/Deep hidden in his heart. The First Song. Richard Burton. AA

...But Helen stayed/In Troy...I know...Cease, child—you trouble me! Helen–Old. Isabel Eccleston MacKay. CaP

But hell, we'll take the pike/If this don't stop. New National Anthem. Anonymous. CoSo

But help not, though she call. Song: "Hold back thy hours, dark night, till we have done." Francis Beaumont and John Fletcher. OBSP

But henceforth I maun mind the plow,/And ye maun bide at hame. John Grumlie. Anonymous. GBP

But her heart is some place far away upon the Wexford/shore. In Service. Winifred M. Letts. HBMV

But her lip was gray and writhen. In Hospital. William Ernest Henley. VLP

But her own words are night's and mine. In Shadow. Hart Crane. NOBA

But her sisester usest to boosest her. Limerick: "There was a young lady of Woosester." Anonymous. LiBL

But here are no fat fish to bolt and bring/My treasure back from limbo, therefore–splash! On a Spring-Board. Edward Cracroft Lefroy. OBVV

But here I find Him, in your quickening dust. O Earth, Sufficing All Our Needs. Sir Charles G. D. Roberts. CaP

But here I lie as warm as they. Outside the Chancel Door. Anonymous. ShM

But here, in Bloemfontein,/Keep closed the door. In Bloemfontein. Alan Ross. BoLoP

But here, Kind Reader, here is our bruised goose. One Man's Goose; or, Poetry Redefined. George Starbuck. PP

But here lies Henry, Duke of Grafton. Epitaph on the Duke of Grafton. Sir Fleetwood Shepherd. FaBoEE

But here on earth to have such heaven's bliss. Amoretti, LXXII. Edmund Spenser. AAS; EG; EnLi 1-2; OAEP; OBSC

But here's a more difficult matter remains,/To tell if he showed us less manners or brains. The Vision. Daniel Defoe. APAS

But here's the cure; Thy presence, Lord, alone/Will make a stall a court, a cratch a throne. But Art Thou Come, Dear Saviour? Anonymous. OxBoCh

But here's the joy; my friend and I are one;/Sweet flattery! then she loves but me alone. Sonnets, XLII: "Thou that last her, it is not all my grief." William Shakespeare. CBEP; InvP

But here's twenty thousand Cornish bold/Will know the reason why!' The Song of the Western Men. Robert Stephen Hawker. CBEP; EnRP; FaPoR; GoBC; HBV 1-2; OBNC; OBRV; OBVV; PaPo; RoGo

But here the huge hotels still sway in space/with the exactness of a foreign place. Early Arrival: Sydney. Vivian Smith. NOAV

But here the stitches are–and I will take a quid. To My Cousin Mary, for Mending My Tobacco Pouch. Francis Scott Key. OBAL

But here they hold their breath, as if/for shame. The Solitary. Rainer Maria Rilke. TrJP

But here 'tis time to rest myself and you. The Art of Love. Ovid (Publius Ovidius Naso). FaBoUs; UnTE

But here we are, we are. All Intents. Larry Eigner. VGW

...But here you are. Sayer. George P. Elliott. FAZ

But him her host that unkind guest had slain. Astrophel and Stella, XXXVIII. Sir Philip Sidney. AAS; SiPS

But his actual candle blazed with artifice. A Quiet Normal Life. Wallace Stevens. LCAP

But his is act to fill an alien town/With friends, who make his tomb their loving care. Epigrams. Theocritus. AWP

But his bones lie stark hereunder. Body of John. R. A. K. Mason. AnNZ

But his heart runs. The Runner. Alexandra Grilikhes. SD

But his mangled corpse lies buried on Lake Erie's distant shore. James Bird. Anonymous. AmFP; BFSS

But his parents said look it is fall. The Fall. Russell Edson. LCAP

But his poor forgetful body swallows spirits by mistake. Sanctimony. Anonymous. WTO

But his shadow hurries from his feet to his face. The Death of Vitellozzo Vitelli. Irving Feldman. MP; TwCP

(But his shoes were far too tight). Incidents in the Life of My Uncle Arly. Edward Lear. FaBoNo; FPL; MoShBr; NA; NBM; OAEL 1-2; OxBoLi; TrGrPo

But his sorrow runs deeper, the woman/has long since died in his dreams... The Old Man. David Fisher. NPGG

But his Trull, but his Trull, but his Trull/holds up the Kettle. A Ballad of All the Trades. Anonymous. CoMu; ErPo; UnTE

But his voice in a softened accent broke: The Culprit Fay. Joseph Rodman Drake. GN

But his word cauterizes our infection/unifying blackness Saint Malcolm. Johari (Jewel C. Latimore) Amini. BPo

But hit's mighty ha'd to giggle w'en dey's nuffin in de/pot. Philosophy. Paul Laurence Dunbar. BPo

But hit to your toil in the mornin' or you'll soon be driftin' away. The Dry-Landers. Anonymous. CoSo

But hoary heads crowneth the farmer and wife. Thank God for the Country! Mrs. Major Arnold. WBLP

But holds them all beneath his hands at last. Craftsmen. Victoria Mary (Vita) Sackville-West. OxBTC

But holy death is kinder? Early Death. Hartley Coleridge. GoTF; HBV 1-2; OBEV; TreFS

But, Holy Saltmartin, why can't you beat time? The Ondt and the Gracehoper. *Anonymous.* BIrV

But honestly/Don't come/If they have improved you. In This Shanty Shebeen without You. Richard Augustine Chima. WhB

But hope, for all the shifts I try,/Will be my sovereign till I die. Hope. Gamaliel Bradford. HBMV

But how bone-masonry/Outweighs the skeleton. Song for a Marriage. Vassar Miller. HW

But how can I a weed become/If I am shadowed with the Son? The Flower. Samuel Speed. OxBoCh

But how can I describe it by a hair? The Hair's-Breadth. Nicholas Moore. NeBP

But how can I give silence/My whole life long? Night Song at Amalfi. Sara Teasdale. MoAmPo

But how can 2 and 3 make four,/If 3 and 2 make faces? Crazy Arithmetic. D'Arcy Wentworth Thompson. FaBoCo

But how I hate the wabbly gink,/Like me, who knows not what to think! Thoughts on the Cosmos. Franklin Pierce ("F.P.A.") Adams. HBMV

But how I wish I were abroad again,/My dear, my dear! I Shall Not Be Afraid. Aline Kilmer. HBMV

But–"How many were sorry when he/passed away?" The Measure of a Man. *Anonymous.* BLPL; PoLf; STF

But–how they fastened me. Warblers. Marsden Hartley. AnFE

But how thoroughly departmental. Departmental. Robert Frost. AnNE; DiPo; GoYe; HeIP; HoPM; MoAB; MoAmPo; NIP; NOBA; NOBL; OBAL; SoSe

But how to tell without dying/Is not told by the dying trees. Witness. Josephine Miles. GP

...But (how unlike All else/We seek on Earth?) 'tis never sought in vain. The Art of Happiness. Edward Hilton Young. PoL

But how will Nan prefer my boon,/In tatter'd hose and clouted shoon! The Country Inn: Song: "Though richer swains thy love pursue." Joanna Baillie. OBRV

But human lives vanish/In dark night. Stars Fade. Peretz Hirshbein. TrJP

...But hurry, for/The terror is, all promises are kept./Even happiness. Treasure Hunt. Robert Penn Warren. NoP

But hush! hark! a deep sound strikes like a rising knell! Childe Harold's Pilgrimage: Canto III, XXI. George Gordon,Lord Byron. AnFE

But hush! Remind not Eros of his wings. Love. William Watson. TrGrPo

But I ain't got nobody/For to call me sweet. Dressed Up. Langston Hughes. GoSl

But I ain't worth a darn, at spinnin' a yarn/What wanders away from the truth. A Nautical Extravaganza. Wallace Irwin. StPo

But I also dreamt, which charmed me most,/That you loved me still the same. I Dreamt I Dwelt in Marble Halls. Alfred Bunn. TreFS

But I always try to get as many words into the/last line as ever I possibly can.' Limerick: "There was a young man of Japan." *Anonymous.* FaBoCo

But I am come to autumn,/When all the leaves are gold. Gold Leaves. Gilbert Keith Chesterton. OxBTC

But I am completely nourished. A Decade. Amy Lowell. MoAmPo; PoPl

But I am far away, searching the rooms/Of my house, looking for my children. Missing the Children. Paul Zimmer. Str

But I am greater than he.../I escaped him. Man and Bat. D. H. Lawrence. BoAnP

"But I am here.' "You are not,' your mother said. A Queer Thing. Nancy Keesing. NOAV

But I am no longer thirsty. Wallflower to a Moonbeam (parody). Louis Untermeyer. BXAP

But I am not an angel nor have I come in a dream. And on My Return. Haim Guri. VWA

But I am not ordained to preach. The Calf-Path. Sam Walter Foss. HBV 1-2; HBVY; PoLf

But I am ready against the dark/to listen for more than love. Quick Now, Here, Now, Always–. William J. Rewak. AMV-81

But I am sure the spellbound king/drawing out his reign/a little longer Autumn Music. Gabriel Preil. VWA

But I am writing little songs,/As little ladies will. Song of Perfect Propriety. Dorothy Parker. DBV; InMe

But I behold in all the range of Night/Only the splendor of your loveliness. Sonnets to Miranda. William Watson. HBV 1-2

But I, beholding thy bright shining eyes,/Shall heaven enjoy amidst hell's miseries. If When I Die. William Fowler. EiL

But I believe it was no more/Than thou and I have done before/With Bridget, and with Nell. A Ballad upon a Wedding. Sir John Suckling. AtBAP; CABA; CABL; CaPo; EBEV; InvP; JCP; LoBV; NoP; OBS; Par; SeCeV; UnTE; ViBoPo

But I cam' here to bonny Scotland/To the man that I lo'e best! The Gay Gos-hawk. *Anonymous.* BuBa; GN; HBV 1-2

But I came down the stair. A Child Asleep. Elizabeth Madox Roberts. AnAmPo

But I can give love-talk to you, you little blue flower of the/Spring! To a Blue Flower. John Shaw Neilson. BoAV; PoAu 1-2

But I can outwit him. The Outwit Song. Daniel Gerard Hoffman. SaC

But i can see in my eyes/a nice, gentle, generous young man. Poem: "you can look into my face." Mike Todachine. CTBA

But I can squeeze through the/space beneath/The little back-yard gate. The Difference. Eleanor Alletta Chaffee. BiCB

But I can't change it Trash. Earl Gene Box. LFAC

But I can't drop it if I tried! For to Admire. Rudyard Kipling. MoBrPo

But I can't live without/that sound that sound that sound that sOWnd. Umbilical. Eve Merriam. CTBA

But I can't: she is me. Punto Final. Shirley Hill Witt. TWSS

But I can't stay here by myself. I Wish I Was a Little Bird (with music). *Anonymous.* AS

But I can't, you know; I have to keep on walking. Spring Night. Richard Aldridge. NePoAm

But I cannot care/That is my madness. They Have Taken It from Me. Timothy Corsellis. WaP

But I cannot hide them away from Him! By the Conemaugh. Florence Earle Coates. PAH

But I close my door on none/Lest Christ close his door on me. The Open Door. *Anonymous.* KiLC

...But I come/back, far down these evenings, faithful, to glean. Priest Lake. William Stafford. PoA

But I could not both live and utter it. "My Life Has Been the Poem..." Henry David Thoreau. AmePo

But I cried, "Stuff–/I've had enough." She Found Me Roots (parody). R. W. Ransford. BXAP

But I'd give my pony and saddle to be at home, sweet home. Home, Sweet Home. *Anonymous.* CoSo

But I'd like to get at least a million more! Telegram. William Wise. TiPo

But I'd like to see my mammy, oh,/Who lives in Alabamy, ah. Gwine to Alabamy. *Anonymous.* TrAS

But I did not find even the echo of your steps. In My Dreams I Searched for You. *Anonymous.* WTO

But I did not know how/with difficult eyes. Reunion. Judith Herzberg. BoWoP

But I didn't get none from you! Valentine. Shel Silverstein. PoSC

But I didn't see him eat. The Circus. Elizabeth Madox Roberts. SoPo

But I do compare/Now that she's gone. For Anne. Leonard Cohen. ELU; FF; PoCh

"But I do know how to paint." Clerihew. Edmund Clerihew Bentley. NLV

But I do not know yet/How to go and forget! How to Go and Forget. Edwin Markham. HBMV

But I do not look, move, or make a noise. The Centaur Overheard. Edgar Bowers. ConAP

But I do not mourn, nor do I weep; I only stare/Steadfastly at pain and I am silent. Epilogue. Joseph Eliyia. VWA

But I do say it's hard to lose either/ When you have both. Toads. Philip Larkin. CMoP; ForPo; NePoEA; NMP; NoAm; NOBL; OxBTC; SoSe

But I do/The best I can/For a middle-aged child. Middle-Aged Child. Inez Hogan. BiCB

But I does ma wark, if ma consonants/Be properly mixed with ma vowels! A Rustic Song. Anthony C. Deane. FiBHP; InMe

But I don't bring her flowers/and I don't bring her pills. Disguised. John Perreault. ANYP

But I don't care!/I'm still here! Still Here. Langston Hughes. BPo

But I don't care where the water goes if it doesn't get into/the wine. Wine and Water. Gilbert Keith Chesterton. ACP; CenHV; FaBoCo; FiBHP; GoBC; HBMV; InMe; MoBrPo; ViBoPo

But I don't give a damn,/I don't give a river,/I don't give a duck. Poem in Time of Winter. Ray Mathew. NOAV

But I don't like the sound of the moddle. A Woman's Reason. Gelett Burgess. FaBoNo

But I doubt he'd suit the office, Clancy, of The Overflow. Clancy of the Overflow. Andrew Barton ("Banjo") Paterson. PoAu 1-2

But I fear that is almost too few. Limerick: "There was an old man who said, "Do." *Anonymous.* LiBL; NA

But I fear we may have to inter'm.' Limerick: "There was a good Canon of Durham." William Ralph Inge. CenHV

But I feel I am coming unsexed. Limerick: "A lady who signs herself "Vexed.".". Edward Gorey. OBAL

But I feel I am in very good company. Good Company. *Anonymous.* OBET

...But I felt my spine/Squirm suddenly. I admit it. It was mine. The Rural Carrier Stops to Kill a Nine-Foot Cottonmouth. T. R. Hummer. SM

But I forget which ones they are. The Flag. Shel Silverstein. PoSC

But I give buns to the elephant when I go down to the Zoo! At the Zoo. A.(lan) A.(lexander) Milne. TiPo

But I go for ever and come again no more. Home No More Home to Me. Robert Louis Stevenson. CH

But I had to stop her snoring! Necessity. Harry Graham. FaBoCo

But I hardly think I will. Hardly Think I Will. *Anonymous.* ABF

But I have a birthday, so.../I feel finer. Richer. Aileen Fisher. BiCB

But I have certainty enough/For I am sure of you. Certainty Enough. Amelia Josephine Burr. HBMV

"But I have entered in." The Land of Heart's Desire. Emily Huntington Miller. HBV 1-2

But I have heard the word she spoke/In her man's arms as the dawn broke. The Free Woman. Theodosia Garrison. HBMV

But I have never known/the eternal word for "open'. I Have Heard Them Knock. Michael Hartnett. NOBI

But I have to smile Naphtha. Frank O'Hara. ANYP

But I haven't a penny to spare. Limerick: "B was a beggarly bear." Carolyn Wells. TDH

But I haven't come to that–and I hope I never shall–/and that's the Village Poor House! Our Village. Thomas Hood. CBEP; InMe; OBSV; PoEL 1-5; PoPle

But I hear the beating of dead boughs. Blight. Arna Bontemps. BANP; CDC

But I hear the living rush/far away from my heart Nobody Riding the Roads Today. June Jordan. BPo

But I hope some day/I will/overcome Parchman Farm Blues. Booker White. BluL

But I inclined to every kind,/All seven on one hill. The Mystic. Witter ("Emanuel Morgan") Bynner. HBV 1-2

But I keep, against the ice and the fire,/the memory of your profile on the pillow. The Profile on the Pillow. Dudley Randall. BP; BPo; PoBA; TAP

But I keep each olden, golden while/All to myself. All to Myself. Wilbur D. Nesbit. BLPA

But I keep saying:/Black is best. Black is Best. Larry Thompson. BOLo; PoBA

But I know I flew when I heard them. I, Icarus. Alden Nowlan. NCSH; WHW

But I know I would like you much better,/If you'd be a good girl, and shut up. Me and Samantha. Pyke Johnson, Jr. GDP

But I know the lovely Etan/will not be sleeping alone. The Lovely Etan. *Anonymous.* NOBI

But I know you will learn it too late, my dear. The Way of It. John Vance Cheney. HBV 1-2

But I lay awake; and my heart was heavy with pain. Before Dawn. Elinor Chipp. HBMV

But I learned how the wind would sound/After these things should be. The New House. Edward ("Edward Eastaway") Thomas. EBEV; MoAB; MoBrPo; NOBE; OBEV

But I like magic made by cooks! Thanksgiving Magic. Rowena Barrett. BrR; SiSoSe; TiPo

But I like mine best of course. My Policeman. Rose Fyleman. SoPo; TiPo

But I like not the coat that you come in–the colour of death. I Spoke to the Violet. John Shaw Neilson. BoAV

But I like to get as many words in the last line as I can. Limerick: "There was a young man from Japan." *Anonymous.* LiBL

But I'll bet you that B is for Bella. Limerick: "B is for beautiful Bella." *Anonymous.* TDH

But I'll butter my ears on the Fourth of July,/And then I'll be able to skate. Father William. *Anonymous.* NA

But I'll give your nose a bit of a warming. The Devil and the Governor (excerpt). William Forster. CBAP; PoAu 1-2

But I'll hear de trumpet sound/In-a dat mornin'. Song: "Sometimes I feel like an eagle in de air." *Anonymous.* NAMP

But I'll keep up the struggle for as long I dare. On Dressing to Go Hunting. *Anonymous.* PH

But I'll leave you where I found you, at the foot of the Sweet/Brown Knowe. The Maid of the Sweet Brown Knowe. *Anonymous.* AnIV; OnYI

But I'll let a rainbow ravel/Through the wings of my silver plane. Silver Ships. Mildred Plew Meigs. TiPo

But I'll like Spring because it is simply Spring/As the thrushes do. I So Liked Spring. Charlotte Mew. OxBTC

But I'll live in peace in my own country,/And so I end my tragedy. Captain Glen's Unhappy Voyage to New Barbary. *Anonymous.* OBSS

But I'll never forget Johnny Murphy, on the banks of the Little Eau Pleine. On the Banks of the Little Eau Pleine. *Anonymous.* AmFP

But I'll quit the herd of longhorns for the sake of my little wife. The Jolly Cowboy. *Anonymous.* CoSo

But I'll take a lot/From the candy pot. I'd like a little. *Anonymous.* FaFP

...But I loitered, while the dews/Fell fast I loitered still. An Apple Gathering. Christina Georgina Rossetti. OBNC; OLR

But I long to clutch my lover's body/& he sink into me. After Li Ch'ing-Chao. Anne Waldman. APU

But I love a man that dares to act, Bob Ander-/son, my beau. Bob Anderson, My Beau. *Anonymous.* PAH

But I'm damned if I see how the helican! Limerick: "A wonderful bird is the pelican." Dixon Lanier Merritt. CenHV; FaBoCo; LiBL

But I'm fine, unmarked, floating/in the bath of their self-love. The Sickness of Friends. Henri Coulette. NYBP

But I'm going back to Friar's Point if I be rocking/to my head Traveling Riverside Blues. Robert Johnson. BluL

"But I'm not scared now/because of you." A Riddle. Charlotte Zolotow. NTCP

But I'm not so think as you drunk I am. Ballade of Soporific Absorption. J. C. Squire. InMe

But I'm off to join the others, for the rumor might be true. The Ballad of Tonopah Bill. *Anonymous.* BPAW

But I'm still in Fairport. Pippa Passes, but I Can't Get around This Truck. Margaret Blaker. NLV

But I'm sure that these garments St. Mhomas. Limerick: "A bright little maid in St. Thomas." Ferdinand G. Christgau. HBV 1-2; TDH

But I'm talking about/Harlem to you! Lenox Avenue Mural. Langston Hughes. AmNP

But I'm wild in love/With the planet we've got! Valentine for Earth. Frances Frost. QQQ

But I'm with you up at Wyndcroft,/Over Tintern on the Wye. The Iron Music. Ford Madox Ford. HBMV

But I make a rule of always trying to get just/as many words into the last line as I/possibly can. Limerick: "There was a young bard of Japan." *Anonymous.* CenHV

But I molest thy quiet; sleep, whilst we/That live, would leave our lives to die like thee. Funeral Elegy on the Death of His Very Good Friend Mr. Michael Drayton. Sir Aston Cokayne. OBS

But I mourn for Cean-Salla! Cean-Salla. James Clarence Mangan. OnYI

But I must build and build and build/Until a temple stands. The Builder. Caroline Giltinan. HBMV

But I must love her (Tigresse) too too much,/Forc'd must I love, because I finde none such. But Thou My Deere Sweet-Sounding Lute Be Still. Richard Lynche. AAS

But I must stop this play and go–/Or choke you with your pillow-lace! Morning. Hugh McCrae. BoAV

But I must wash the baby's panties! Babysitter's Song. *Anonymous.* FSW

But I my burning and my death foresee. Like to the seely fly. Francis Davison. EG

But I never can recollect whom.' Limerick: "There was an old man of Khartoum." William Ralph Inge. LiBL; NOBL; OxBoLi

...But I never dar'd/To drive the pauper from the yard. To Our House-Dog Captain. Walter Savage Landor. NBM; PoEL 1-5

But I never heard/He caught the Blue Bird. Old Cat Care. Richard Hughes. OBMV

But I never heard/That the frogs stopped croaking. Poetry Today. John Heath-Stubbs. PoL

But I never saw a mustache/On a baby's face before. The Drunken Fool. *Anonymous.* BFSS

But I never will be married till my soldier comes again. The Soldier's Farewell to Manchester. *Anonymous.* BFSS; CoMu

But I on it securely play,/And gall its horsemen all the day. Upon Appleton House, to My Lord Fairfax. Andrew Marvell. JCP

But I only desire she mayn't have a beard. Song: "Give Isaac the nymph who no beauty can boast." Richard Brinsley Sheridan. NOBI

But I own that I love a good fire,/And occasional herring and mouse. An Old Cat's Confession. Christopher Pearse Cranch. OBCA

But I proclaim from the dust/That he slew me to gratify his hatred. Amanda Barker. Edgar Lee Masters. NoAm

But I rather think he went the other way./Singing fol diggy di-do, fol diggy day. The Miller. *Anonymous.* FSW

But I reflect–which women never do. Written on a Looking-Glass. *Anonymous.* FaBoEE; HBV 1-2

But I remember one pale woman's face/In San Pedro. Spain, 1809. F. L. Lucas. HaMV

But I sacked the presumptuous hag the next week,/I was that lonely. The Geranium. Theodore Roethke. CoAP; UnPo; WeW

But I see a wise man/When I look into a pool. A Thought. William Henry Davies. GTBS; MoShBr

But I sees their point of view.' Clerihew. Edmund Clerihew Bentley. NOBL

But I shall be hearing the harsh cries of wild fowl. She Walked Unaware. Patrick MacDonogh. BoLoP; ErPo; FaBoTw; NeIP; OnYI; OxBI

...But I shall depart to sleep forever in the/hall of the dead bards. Another Song. William Ross. GoTS

But I shall find the farthest dream/That kisses me, asleep. Rubric. Josephine Preston Peabody. AA

...But I shall hear her laugh/Soon, when she shows the crimson blade to God. A Last Confession. Dante Gabriel Rossetti. NCEP

But I shall not be awake at that time. Life Is a Platform. Peter Levi. FaBoTw

But I shall not, doing it, look backward. The Plowman. Raymond Knister. OBCV; PeCV

But I shall smile with less than joy,/And laugh with more than pain. Courage. Helen Frazee-Bower. HBMV

But I shall weep...I shall weep. But I Shall Weep. Beatrice Redpath. CaP

But I shan't get lost/For Themison is a torch. Epigram: "Since I am completely drunk." Anonymous. PeHV

But I should have had my Annabel Lee. Annabel Lee (parody). Stanley Huntley. SpRo

But I sing of the quality of bamboo. Bamboo. Eric Rolls. NOAV

But I slacken my pace to watch them. Three Colts Exercising in a Six-Acre. Joseph Campbell. BoAnP; OnYI

But I somehow fancy we'll all be pen-mates on the day when/they call the Roll of the Sky. While the Billy Boils. David McKee Wright. AnNZ

But I TALK! I Speak, I Say, I Talk. Arnold L. Shapiro. GrPl

But i tell you, i came out of those marriages/one smart bitch. Daily Courage Doesnt Count. Alta. GP

But I thank Thee, God, for my life! Requiem. F. Norreys Connell. HBV 1-2

But I think/careful copies might/be made, which will be/just as good. An Angler's Vade Mecum. John Engels. WOLT

But I think I'd rather see one/Than to be one, anyhow. Diversions of the Re-Echo Club. Carolyn Wells. OBAL

But I think I was somewhat to blame. Papa Love Baby. Stevie Smith. DBV; SBG

But I think it soon will, it's so like you. On a Lady Who Beat Her Husband. Anonymous. FiBHP

But I think it will be hard to be with me. The Color of Many Deer Running. Linda Gregg. NPGG

But I think mice/Are nice. Mice. Rose Fyleman. EvOK; NTCP; SoPo; SUS; TiPo

But I think our conscience is too bad/For any remedy Sleeplessness of Our Time. R. A. D. Ford. AMV-81

But I think they are simply repegnant. Limerick: "The styles that at present are regnant." Anonymous. LiBL

But I, though fair he still mid glow,/Do miss a zight he cannot show. Air an' Light. William Barnes. VLP

But I thought all the time 'twas a hornet. Limerick: "There was a young man of St. Bees." Sir William Schwenck Gilbert. LiBL

But I thought I'd say distinctly/What I feel about it, James. Retrospection. Sir Arthur Thomas ("Q") Quiller-Couch. CenHV

But I thought it was Tangiers I wanted. I Thought It Was Tangiers I Wanted. Langston Hughes. PoNe

But I thought that I would choose thee/For encomium, as a change. Lines on Hearing the Organ. Charles Stuart Calverley. CenHV; FaBoCo; FiBHP; InMe; NBM; NOBL

But I tug childish at my bars/Only to fail again. I never hear the word "escape'. Emily Dickinson. CMoP; NCEP; NOBA

But I've got the giggles today! I've Got the Giggles. Sir Alan Patrick Herbert. FiBHP

But I've had my say, and now, Amen. The Cowman's Prayer. Anonymous. CoSo

But I've not come to see you hang/Nor hung you shall not be. The Sycamore Tree. Anonymous. AmFP

But I waked, and all was done. A Report Song in a Dream, between a Shepherd and His Nymph. Nicholas Breton. GBL; OBSC; SeCePo

But I walked ahead on the open road/Into the day that was breaking. In the Open Fields. Hugo Sonnenschein. VWA

But I want instead to see/if you yourself will pass this way. A Small Dragon. Brian Patten. AmMo

But I want to look like me. I Have Got to Stop Loving You. Florence Anthony ("Ai"). GeTw

But I was always ready to bark–/And so was she. Of an Ancient Spaniel in Her Fifteenth Year. Christopher Morley. GDP

But I was born to other things. In Memoriam A.H.H., CXX. Alfred, Lord Tennyson. ImOP; OAEL 1-2; SeCePo

But I was young and foolish, and now am full of tears. Down by the Salley Gardens. William Butler Yeats. CMoP; CTC; EnLoPo; FSW; HBV 1-2; NoAm; OBEV; OBVV; OnYI; OxBI; PG; PoEL 1-5; PrIm; SoSe

But I went to Beckley/And they spoke directly. I Went to Noke. Anonymous. GBP; OxNR

But I, what do I here? The City of Dreadful Night. James (1834-82) Thomson. WiR

But I, who have but thinly thrived,/Should much prefer to be revived. Madrigal Macabre. Samuel Hoffenstein. ShM

–But I will escape, with my dog, on the far side of the Fair. The Individualist Speaks. Louis MacNeice. MoVE; OBMV

But I will never marry you/Nor to you will I be tied! The Wexford Girl (I). Anonymous. ShS

But I will never wend from thee! Song: "The streams that wind among the hills." George Darley. NBM

But I will not say so. Women. Heath. CTC; OBSC

But I will plight with the dainty rose,/For fairest of all is she. Flowers. Thomas Hood. HBV 1-2

But I will remember to sing for him also. After the Pow-Wow (excerpt). Harold Littlebird. STE

But I wish that every honest man might/enjoy his own.' Lord Delamere. Anonymous. ESPB

But I, with Aaron, faint yet unafraid,/Held up the hands of Moses while he prayed. Three Helpers in Battle. Mary Elizabeth Coleridge. EaLo

...But I won't... The Skunk. Dorothy Walter Baruch. SoPo

(But I won't be back no more, mama) Drive Away Blues. Blind Willie McTell. BluL

But I wot he did God's will wha made/Siccar o' Calvary. I Heard Christ Sing. Hugh" (Christopher Murray Grieve) MacDiarmid. ACV; NoAm

But I would begin too–I would begin again. To Spring. Virginia Moore. AnEnPo

But I would eat and drink of the best, and no work would I do. The Knight of the Burning Pestle. Francis Beaumont and John Fletcher. OBS

But I would gladly forfeit both/For tales my father told. Garland for a Storyteller. Jessie Farnham. GoYe

But I would not engage the wombat/In any form of mortal combat. The Wombat. Ogden Nash. CenHV

But I would rather, could I choose,/Feed him than buy his boots and shoes. The Centipede. Samuel Hopkins Adams. InMe

But I would that I knew where my Lord is gone! Ballade of Faith. Tom MacInnes. CaP

But I would wish, to both our hearts' delight,/For his will to be joined with my desire. Non Que Je Veuille Oter La Liberte. Pernette de Guillet. WPOW

But icy light icy dark and green wet leaves/above. For Artaud. Michael McClure. NeAP

But if an ass thou meetest, simply/bray! Adapt Thyself. Shem-Tob Palquera. TrJP

But if, Baby, I'm the bottom,/You're the top! You're the Top. Cole Porter. FSN; NLV; OBAL; UnPo

But if God of his goodnesse graunt us a trewe. Snatches: "When ye see the sunne amis." Anonymous. OxBM

But if he bring us drink, the rather/With "How, butler, how!" How, Butler, How! Anonymous. ViBoPo

But if he comes not what becomes of London?/Undone. London Sad London. Anonymous. OBS

But if he were alive/He would turn in his grave. Final Curtain (parody). Roger Woddis. FaBoPa

But if heaven take thee, envying us thy Lyre,/'Tis to pen Anthems for an Angels quire. A Gratulatory to Mr. Ben. Johnson for His Adopting of Him... Thomas Randolph. AnAnS 2; JCP; OBS

But if I arrive safe home, no more will I sail/With a drunken captain in a heavy gale! Canso Strait. Anonymous. ShS

"But if I can't be sorry, why,/I might as well be glad!" The Penitent. Edna St. Vincent Millay. YaD

But if I'm right in my surmise he's gone the other way. Sam Bass. Anonymous. AS; BeLS; BeLS 004; CoSo; FSW

But, if it's got so they like the flavor...well... Nightmare Number Three. Stephen Vincent Benét. MaC; MoAmPo; SaC

But if Robin walke easte, or he walke/west,/He shall neuer be sought for me.' Robin Hood and the Butcher. Anonymous. ESPB

But if she doth of sorrow speak,/E'en from my heart the strings do break. When to Her Lute Corinna Sings. Thomas Campion. AAS; AtBAP; CABA; EnLi 1-2; ExPo; NoP; OAEL 1-2; SeCeV

But if she ever proves true to me/I'll marry and settle down. As I Went out for a Ramble. Anonymous. OuSiCo

But if she gave to his satiety/To no avail, what then? It had to be. The Happening. Mary Aldis. HBMV

But if she loves as I have loved, she never can forget. Oh, No! We Never Mention Her. Thomas Haynes Bayly. PaPo

But if she soften not her eye/I know that life and I must part. My Love, Oh, She Is My Love. Anonymous. AnIV

But if that effort be too great,/To go away at any rate. On Queen Caroline. Anonymous. FaBoEE

But if the blood hounds ever catch me/in the 'lectric chair I'll die. Blood Hound Blues. Victoria Spivey. BluL

But if the dead could write, would we bother to? Rocks and Deals. Geoffrey Young. APU

But if thou do not, Love, I'll truly serve her/In spite of thee, and by firm faith deserve her. Love Guards the Roses of Thy Lips. Thomas Lodge. EIL

But if thou live, remembered not to be,/Die single, and thine image dies with thee. Sonnets, III: "Look in thy glass, and tell the face thou viewest." William Shakespeare. LiTB; MasP; OBSC

But if thou love me not, I languish/and I die. Solomon. Heinrich Heine. TrJP

But if thou wilt amendes make. A Warning. *Anonymous.* EnLit

But if thy lips' loud cry leap to his smart,/The inspir'd recoil pierce thy brother's heart. The Song-Throe. Dante Gabriel Rossetti. MaVP

But if we could see and hear, this Vision–were it/not He? The Higher Pantheism. Alfred, Lord Tennyson. EnLi 1-2; HBV 1-2; MaVP; SpRo; TRV; VLP

But if we still in virtue delight, our souls are in heaven placed. Song Set by Philip Rosseter: "What is a day.." *Anonymous.* OBSC

But, if ye wish her gratefu' prayer,/Gie her a haggis! Address to a Haggis. Robert Burns. ViBoPo

But if you break the bloody glass you won't hold up the weather. Bagpipe Music. Louis MacNeice. CMoP; ExPo; GTBS-P; LiTB; LiTM; NLV; NoAm; NOBE; NOBL; NoP; OAEL 1-2; OAEP; OBSV; OnYI; OxBTC; SeCePo; SeCeV; ViBoPo

But if you can see it, though no one else can, it will yours. Where? Arthur Seymour John Tessimond. OBTV

But if you cast your greedy eyes on Myiscus,/I'll scratch them out. Epigram: "Diodorus is nice..." Meleager. PeHV

But if you come with dreams for baggage/Sit with us by the cedar fire! Desert Song. Glenn Ward Dresbach. BPAW

But if you don't, I'll lay it on, by G–d! Don Juan. George Gordon, Lord Byron. OBRV

But if you don't know/shut up, we'll understand What Is Poetry. James Scully. FYAP

But–if you find a fish on land,/oh throw it in the sea. On the Dangers Attending Altruism on the High Seas. Gilbert Keith Chesterton. FaBoNo

But if you look long enough,/eventually/you will be able to see me.) This Is a Photograph of Me. Margaret Atwood. NoP

But if you're dead and gone to hell you must remain. Sweet William's Ghost (B vers.). *Anonymous.* ViBoFo

But, if you succeed, you must/Paddle your own canoe. Paddle Your Own Canoe. Sarah Knowles Bolton. FaFP

But if your selfe in me ye playne will see,/Remove the cause by which your fayre beames darkned be. Amoretti, XLV. Edmund Spenser. AAS

But Ile spend my comming houres,/Drinking wine, and crown'd with flowres. On Himselfe. Robert Herrick. FaBoEE; SeCV 1-2

But ilka blade o' grass/Keps its ain drap o' dew. Its Ain Drap o' Dew. James Ballantine. HBV 1-2

But imagine the/Ride, when you start. Remarkable Art. Gelett Burgess. FaBoNo

But in at my dure thou go. Who Is at My Window. *Anonymous.* EG; TrGrPo

But in beween times life has been such fun!' A Shot in the Park. William Plomer. MP

But in by the dark hearth-fire/My hopes lay ashen and dead. Lament. Gudmundur Gudmundsson. LiTW

But in drunkeship I dide/The werste that mighten been thought. Snatches: "Whil that I was sobre." *Anonymous.* OxBM

...But in each rose there grows/A greater power and mastery than blows. Dogrose. Patric Stevenson. NeIP

But in England's song for ever/She's the Fighting Temeraire. The Fighting Temeraire. Sir Henry Newbolt. HBV 1-2

But in faith I bless you again a thousand times,/For lending me now some leisure to make rhymes. To Fortune. Sir Thomas More. ACP

But in fresh deluge, Heav'n it selfe came downe. Eugenia: Presage of Storme. George Chapman. FaBoEn

But in gladness of God evermore make thou thy glee. Ghostly Gladness. Richard Rolle. HAP

But in her heart a cold December. April Is in My Mistress' Face. *Anonymous.* GBL; HeIP

But in her room...an empty room.../She had no pride. Loss. Julia Johnson Davis. HBMV

But in His still and shadowed face I saw/The agony of Man. A Vision. Geoffrey Dearmer. HBMV

But in less than half an hour/Kneeled and whined at Celia's feet. The Declaimer. Sir Henry William Baker. NOEC

But in little June-buggies and automobeetles/And dragonflying machines! Contrary Mary. Nancy Byrd Turner. HBMV; HBVY

But in memory and oblivion only at the/last in the nothingness that is everything. Memory as Memorial in the Last. Edward Marshall. CoPo

But in my room alone I sighed. Popular Songs of Tuscany. *Anonymous.* AWP

But in Return did make the work more Rare. On an Indian Tomineois, the Least of Birds. Thomas Heyrick. FM

But in stone the Virgin listened,–never smiled nor spoke again. La Preciosa. Thomas Walsh. ISi

But in such matters Russia's mighty empress/Behaved no better than a common sempstess. Don Juan. George Gordon, Lord Byron. OAEL 1-2

But in th' obverse/'Tis worse. Upon Julia (parody). Ernest Radford. BXAP

But in that far-off cattle land/He sometimes acted like a man. The Texas Song. *Anonymous.* CoSo

But in that safe and secret dust/Which shall not rise again. A Dead Warrior. Laurence Housman. HBMV

But in the cliff-grass Love builds deep/A place where wandering wings may sleep. Swallow Song. Marjorie Pickthall. CaP

But in the crowded darkness not a word did they say. The Old-Marrieds. Gwendolyn Brooks. AmNP; PoBA

But in the journeyman's labour. Epigram: "Give pensions to the Learned Pig." William Blake. FaBoEE

But in the shade I will believe what in the sun I loved. On the Sun Coming out in the Afternoon. Henry David Thoreau. OBSP; PoEL 1-5

But in the Spirit's secret cell/May hymn and prayer forever dwell. Again as Evening's Shadow Falls. Samuel Longfellow. AH

But in the twinkling of an eye,/My wee, wee man was clean awa. The Wee Wee Man. *Anonymous.* BaBo; CH; EBEV; ELP; ESPB; FaBoCh; GBP; OAEL 1-2; OxBB

But in the wilderness of my brain/the cock of the future crows. The Cock. Ewa Lipska. VWA

But in the winter the children like the calm and the/radiant made me remember these words. The Riding Stable in Winter. John Tagliabue. PH

But in the world of thought and mental might! Written upon the Top of Ben Nevis. John Keats. ERoP 1-2; PoSH

But in the wrinkled old crones with/silver-white hair. Virtue. Immanuel Di Roma. TrJP

But in their company the night is/luminous. Without My Friends the Day Is Dark. Moses Ibn Ezra. TrJP

But in this country/there is war. Poem for the Young White Man Who Asked Me How I, an Intelligent... Lorna Dee Cervantes. WPOW

But in thy love I live and die. Rosader's Sonnet. Thomas Lodge. OBSC

But in thy presence ever blest,/O God of my salvation. Hymn. Paul Laurence Dunbar. TrPWD; TRV

But in thy tender jealosy dost doubt/Least the World, Fleshe, yea Devill putt thee out. Holy Sonnets, XVII. John Donne. MasP; OAEP

But in whose dust all brighter dust must lie. The Wraith-Friend. George Barker. OBMV

But in your breast his leaf and love embrace. Amoretti, XXVIII. Edmund Spenser. AAS; CABA

But in yourself your own. Dear Child Whom I Begot. J. V. Cunningham. NAs

But, inches from it, felt, and turned aside. At a Low Mass for Two Hot-Rodders. X. J. Kennedy. Psk

...But inside everything/was moving, shivering with wind. We knew that much. Children among the Hills. Linda Gregg. NPGG

But inside–/Gee, that poor shine! Bottled. Helene Johnson. BlSi; CDC; GoSl; PoBA

But iron tore him, and his flame died. The Dragon's Hoard. J. R. R. Tolkien. AmMo

But is a singing in a dark place. A Music. Wendell Berry. VGW

But is certainly rough on Abraham. Epitaph: "Mary Ann has gone to rest." *Anonymous.* FaBoCo

But is for others undiminished somewhere. Sad Steps. Philip Larkin. NoP

But is forced to fly before it,/Or else worship and adore it. Love. Sir Henry William Baker. NOEC

But is healed, but is glad,/'Tis so sweet. Aucassin and Nicolette: Who Would List. *Anonymous.* CTC

But is lord of the earldom as much as he. The Vision of Sir Launfal. James Russell Lowell. AnNE

But is love itself/realised. Highland Loves. Rennie McOwan. PoSH

But is sewn on with needle and thread. The Bison. Hilaire Belloc. NA

But is there nothing you can leave alone? Stop, Science–Stop! Sir Alan Patrick Herbert. FiBHP

But island by island we must go across. Do Not Embrace Your Mind's New Negro Friend. William Meredith. WaP

But isn't it lovely/Kicking up leaves! October. Rose Fyleman. SiSoSe; TiPo

But it can stab. Prelude. R. A. K. Mason. AnNZ

But it didn't make me feel better Pearl Harbor Day 1970. Dick Lourie. NeAC

But it does tell me my soul has a shadow. Writ on the Eve of My 32nd Birthday. Gregory Corso. NAs

...But it doesn't bear dwelling on. Wholesome. William Meredith. TAP

But it grows old and waxeth cold,/And fades away like evening dew. Waillie, Waillie! (with music). *Anonymous.* AS

But it is All Friends' Night, a traveler's good-night. Good-Night. Edward ("Edward Eastaway") Thomas. NoP

...But it is already too late. The/children have vanished. Grand Abacus. John Ashbery. EAS

But it is different light. Farolita. Mei-Mei Berssenbrugge. BrSi

(But it is far away.) Cockayne Country. Agnes Mary Frances (Mme Emile Duclaux) Robinson. OBVV

But...It is my shadow that I kiss, my shadow I embrace. Dream. Joseph Eliyia. VWA

...But it is not so with me. It Is Not So with Me. William Blake. SeCePo

But it is/to the heart universal, for the soul of/the world is abroad to-night. The Soul of the World. Ernest Crosby. AA

But it keeps them on my knife. I Eat My Peas with Honey. *Anonymous.* OnUR

But it leads at last to a golden Town where/golden Houses are. Roofs. Joyce Kilmer. BLPL; PoLf

But it made my property mine once more. Trespass. Robert Frost. FaBV

...But it makes you/feel so good in your bones and it's all free! Poems. Gary Gildner. Psk

But it may clip thee in thy prime. Like to the Grass That's Green Today. Peter, the Younger Bulkeley. AH

But it never comes again. The Flight of Youth. Richard Henry Stoddard. AA; HBV 1-2

But it prowls forever powerless, cut off from its jungle. The Wooden Tiger. Samuel Yellen. NePoAm

But it's better on down the road. Mule Skinner Blues. *Anonymous.* FSW

But it's dabbling in the dew makes the milkmaids fair! Dabbling in the Dew. *Anonymous.* CH; UnTE

"But it's far in advance of the age." Limerick: "A canary, its woe to assuage." Oliver Herford. TDH

But it's got to come out liverwurst. Leaning on a Limerick. Eve Merriam. TDH

But it's hard tu tell: snaix is snaix. Some Verses to Snaix. *Anonymous.* NA

But it's helpful when reading in bed! Limerick: "There was an old person who said." William Jay Smith. TDH

But it's just a headache to any teacher. The Merry Month. *Anonymous.* InMe

But it's more fun to be more to be fun to be little joe gould) Little Joe Gould Has Lost His Teeth and Doesn't Know Where. Edward Estlin Cummings. NoAm

But it's nearly over now, and now I'm easy. Now I'm Easy. Eric Bogle. OBET

But it's not any fun for her. Blues. John Fuller. NOBL

But it's oh! in my heart that/I do wish he may not die. The Blue Bells of Scotland. Dorothy and Annie McVicar Jordan. FSW; HBV 1-2; TreFS

But it's thinking that leads to the grave. Existentialism. Lloyd Frankenberg. FiBHP

But it's true about the bird, believe me. Bird Song. Betsy Rosenberg. VWA

But it's v-i-c-t-o-r-y to know I've Christ within. It's G-L-O-R-Y to Know I'm S-A-V-E-D. *Anonymous.* FSW

But it's War! And–Orderly, clean this knife! War. Edgar Wallace. OBWP

But it's with strength alone that I prevail. The Spartan Wrestler. Damagetus. LiSp

But it's woe be unto you. Woe Be Unto You. *Anonymous.* ABF

But it shall never bring to you/The hapless fate of Anne Boleyn! My Dearling. Elizabeth Akers Allen. AA

But it shone long enough for one/To know that hands held up the sun. The Secret Heart. Robert P. Tristram Coffin. PoSC

But it stirred in me as the seed in sod,/Or a broken rhyme. Song of a Factory Girl. Marya Zaturenska. HBMV

But it stopped short–never to go again–/When the old man died. Grandfather's Clock. Henry Clay Work. BLPA; BLSo; FaFP; FSW; PSoN; TreF

...But it takes/a while. It takes a while. Hurting. Vi Gale. GP

...But it took him a long time/finally to make his mind up to go home. The Prodigal. Elizabeth Bishop. CoAP; InvP; LCAP; LiTM; MoAB; MP; NYBP; PPP; TwCP

But it was all through dread and/fears. The Soldier's Wooing. *Anonymous.* AmFP

But it was in the good green-wood,/Among the lily-flower. The Birth of Robin Hood. *Anonymous.* BuBa; OAEL 1-2; OxBB; ViBoPo

But it was life to hear you speak,/And heaven to see your face. Voyager's Song. Clement Wood. HBMV

But it was my love's splashing oar. A Loon I Thought It Was. *Anonymous.* OBVE

But it was really to see you! By Way of Pretext. Yakamochi. AWP

But it wasn't the stars that thrilled me. Word of Art. Alan Bernheimer. APU

But it works every time. Songs of the Transformed: Siren Song. Margaret Atwood. PoA

But it would have made your heart/right sair,/To see the bridegroom rive his haire. The Cruel Brother (A version). *Anonymous.* BaBo; EnLit; ESPB; OxBB; ViBoFo

But it would seem some major operation/(On head and heart) may be the only way. "No Quarrel." Sir Alan Patrick Herbert. DBV

But its pause has legs. Call It a Louse. Cid Corman. VGW

But jackson/thanks two gods for that/every sunday Dirty Joke. Daniel L. Klauck. LTB

But James was only a snail. The Four Friends. A.(lan) A.(lexander) Milne. TiPo

But Jesus, 'tis thy light alone,/Can shine upon the heart. Olney Hymns. William Cowper. CEP

But Jesus went weeping away, and left him there wondering why. Children of Love. Harold Monro. MoBrPo

But join with heart and soul and voice/for Jefferson and Liberty. Jefferson and Liberty. *Anonymous.* FSW; TrAS

But joyous hours do fly away too fast. Amoretti, LXXXVI. Edmund Spenser. AAS; EG

But just a drop of dew instead/Swinging on a spider's thread. For a Dewdrop. Eleanor Farjeon. HBVY

But just give me an army cot/At home when I need rest. Thanks Just the Same. *Anonymous.* PoLf

But just how close was core to corse/Could only William tell. Archery. Walter De la Mare. FaBoNo

But just like poor Billy he wanders astray/And loses his life in the very same way. Billy the Kid. *Anonymous.* CoSo

But just to all the ladies,/I'm sure I wish you well. The Texas Rangers. *Anonymous.* BFSS

But keep me, guide me, love me, Lord,/Just for to-day. Just for To-day. Sybil F. Partridge. HBV 1-2; TreF; TRV

But keep that earlier, wilder image bright. To Cole, the Painter, Departing for Europe. William Cullen Bryant. AmePo; AP; MAmP; TAP

But keep ye white forever–keep ye whole/The battlements of dream within the soul! A Prayer for the Old Courage. Charles Hanson Towne. TrPWD

But keeps you grinding through/a granite air. The Carousel. Gloria C. Oden. AmNP; PoBA

But killed the mice in his father's barn. Ding, Dong, Bell. Mother Goose. SoPo; TiPo

But kin of the trembling ocean, not of the dust. The Sorcerer. A.J.M. Smith. PeCV

But kiss and unkiss till we die. Courtship. Alexander Brome. CavP

But kiss him, & give him both drink and apparel. The Little Vagabond. William Blake. CBEP; CEP; NLV; OBSV; SeCeV

But - kiss me, darling! dear old Smiler's dead. Obituary. Thomas William Parsons AA; HBV 1-2; HBVY

"But kiss me first," she says. And so I stay. Infatuated. *Anonymous.* UnTE

But kneel no more upon the sands/To mount the kings of Eastern lands. Camel. Mary Britton Miller. TiPo

But kneel to him she hates to crave/The absolution of the grave. Rest. Mathilde Blind. SBG

But knocked them all down with his poker. Limerick: "There was an Old Man with a poker." Edward Lear. HBV 1-2

But know the dismal day draws neer wherein/The fire shall earth it self dissolve and sin. The Town Called Providence Its Fate. Benjamin Tompson. SCAP

But know, what stupid asses prize,/Lions and noble beasts despise. The Lion and the Cub. John Gay. GN; HBV 1-2

But knows the taste of his meat. The Teacher. Virginia Brady Young. GoYe

But Labor vaster than myself/I find it to infer. The Frost Was Never Seen. Emily Dickinson. MAmP

But, laddie, seek to ken nae mair! The Women Folk. James Hogg. HBV 1-2

"But, lady, if you see that I must liue," Sir Lionel. *Anonymous.* BaBo; ESPB

But lang-bearded maidens/I saw never nane.' Our Goodman (A version). *Anonymous.* BaBo; EnLi 1-2; ESPB; ViBoFo

But lang ere he came down again/Was convoyed by lords fifteen. The Heir of Linne. *Anonymous.* BaBo; ESPB

But lang we'll mind and sair we'll rue/The bloody battle of Bothwell Hill. The Battle of Bothwell Bridge. *Anonymous.* OxBB

But lang we'll mind, and sair we'll rue,/The bloody battle of Bothwell Hill. Bothwell Bridge. *Anonymous.* BaBo; ESPB

...But last night the Italians/cheered the violence in one of our westerns. A Map of Montana in Italy. Richard Hugo. LCAP

But laughing gaily, her delighted breasts/Sent ripples down her body to her knees. Her Merriment. William Henry Davies. EnLoPo

But lay my lady on the upper hand,/For she came of the better kin. Little Musgrave and Lady Barnard. *Anonymous.* BaBo; CABL; ESPB; FaBoBa; InvP; OBET

But lay Thy feet to my breast/And keep Thee from the cold. Cradle Song of the Virgin. *Anonymous.* ISi

But learn that death is not, if such a fate be thine. Epitaph for Elizabeth Ranquet. Pierre Corneille. CAW

But leave, because I cannot as I should! To John Donne. Ben Jonson. AnAnS 2; OAEP; OBS; SeCV 1-2

But leave me one spoonful of Bonnie Dundee. Ode to the Last Pot of Marmalade. "John." OBTV

But leave my thoughts to me. Chiaroscuro: Rose. Conrad Aiken. MAPA

But– leave/the/dead/noisemakers/alone. Come on Home. Sharon Scott. JB

But leave the thread with God. Leave the Thread with God. *Anonymous.* BLRP

But leaves lots of room/For me and the bears. The Pear Tree. E. Elizabeth Longwell. BrR

But leaves what you desire! The Ways of Trains. Elizabeth Jane Coatsworth. SoPo; TiPo

But left Church and State to Charles Townshend and Squire. Sketch of his Own Character. Thomas Gray. CEP; EiCP; LAuP

But left her lace to whiten on/Each weed-entangled way! Queen Anne's Lace. Mary Leslie Newton. BrR; MoShBr

But left the Sun her Curate-light. Upon Phillis Walking in a Morning before Sun-rising. John Cleveland. AnAnS 2; MeLP

But Leonard tarries long! Datur Hora Quieti. Sir Walter Scott. GTBS; GTBS-P

But let her go, man, let her go. Catullus Talks to Himself. Caius Valerius Catullus. UnTE

But let her prayses yet be low and meane,/Fit for the handmayd of the Faery Queene. Amoretti, LXXX. Edmund Spenser. AAS

But let it passe and think it is of kinde/That often chaunge doth plese a womans minde. Dyvers Dothe Use as I Have Hard and Kno. Sir Thomas Wyatt. AAS

But let me have bold Zimri's fate/Within the arms of Cozbi. I Murder Hate by Field or Flood. Robert Burns. CBEP; NCEP

But let me sing and return/to the root of my song, the deepest to me. A Return to the Tree of Time. Vesna Parun. WPOW

But let my chief endeavours be,/To know my self, thy will, and Thee. For Scholars and Pupils. George Wither. OxBChV

But let my loves fayre Planet short her wayes/This year ensuing, or else short my dayes. Amoretti, LX. Edmund Spenser. AAS

But let's, like Origen, since other hopes are past,/Hope the poor devil may be saved at last. The Great Despair of the London Whigs. *Anonymous.* APAS

But let's walk along together. Your Church and Mine. Phillips H. Lord. BLPA

But let us hence depart, whilest wether serves and wind. The Faerie Queene. Edmund Spenser. OAEL 1-2

But let us to the story as before. Don Juan. George Gordon, Lord Byron. OAEL 1-2

But let us wipe out a few hundred million. Come! David Ignatow. CAPP

But let your enemy present his case/In the least favourable time and place. Fable. Maurice James Craig. NeIP

But lets the poet see how heav'n can shine. Coleridge. Theodore Watts-Dunton. HBV 1-2; OBVV

...But Liddy/outdid me: she'd pretend/to be grateful. Dancing School. Jonathan Holden. Psk

But lif' up yo' haid w'en de King go by! A Spiritual. Paul Laurence Dunbar. BPo

But life has told on you. To Hasekawa. William Arensberg. HBV 1-2

But light were night didst thou no love/me so. Starlight. John White Chadwick. AA

But light your candles/to bless what is at hand. Ode on a Decision to Settle for Less. [(or Pillin)] William Pillen. VWA

But, like a child, with words thou cheatest me. Immortality Conferred in Vain. Theognis. LiTW

But like a flowered cloth you show,/That when 'tis washed will sweeter smell. A Battle of Similes. *Anonymous.* WTO

But like a man with nothing to do/Except walk straight upright like me and you. The Man Upright. Thomas Macdonagh. BIrV

But, like a noble Phidian marble, stands/The memory of him. The Dead Player. Robert Burns Wilson. AA

But like an Oriental Tale/To others, fabulous– Reportless subjects, to the quick. Emily Dickinson. NOBA

But like flask of rose-water in fashion/Is the cure my dear flame can bestow. Red Ants. *Anonymous.* WTO

But like fox and smoke I gleam among the thrushes/And light your streets. I Light Your Streets. Meridel Le Sueur. GP

But like it, enjoy it, and thankfully eat. Loving and Liking. Dorothy Wordsworth. OxBChV

But, like the eyes that mark great Guido's/fame,/It follows every one, as if by name. The Living Book. Charlotte Fiske Bates. AA

But, like the rainbow, seems,though born/Of earth,a part of heaven. Leila. George Hill. AmLP

But like the shriek of misery/That wild, wild music wailed to me. Redbreast, Early in the Morning. Emily Bronte. NCEP

But linger, linger long,/Singers of song. To John Greenleaf Whittier. William Hayes Ward. AA

But liquor/Is quicker. Reflections on Ice-Breaking. Ogden Nash. BLPL; FaBoCo; FaFP; LiTM; NePA; NLV; NoP; OBAL

But listen, it was thursday, there was this boy,/Manzini– Manzini: Escape Artist. Gwendolyn MacEwen. NOBC

"But listen, Warsaw is there!" so he doesn't understand. Conversation with a Countryman. Antoni Slonimski. VWA

But Litle Iohn, with an arrow broade/Did cleaue his heart in twinn. Robin Hood and Guy of Gisborne. *Anonymous.* BaBo; BuBa; CoBE; ESPB; OAEP

But Little John his grave hath digged–/It was hard by Kirkeslie. The Death of Robin Hood. *Anonymous.* EnSB

But little John Nobody, that dare not once speak. Little John Nobody. *Anonymous.* OxBoLi

But little recks the world in its distress/The sorrow that is silent on the hill. Nature in War-Time. Herbert Palmer. HaMV

But little she knew I was Gorman,/The man who made the songs! Beware of Larry Gorman. *Anonymous.* ShS

But little things are seen by God/From His watchtower in heaven. Little Things. *Anonymous.* STF

But little things/On little wings/Bear little souls to heaven. Written in a Little Lady's Little Album. Frederick William Faber. HBV 1-2; HBVY

But Liverpool doth all bewail/Their Fate; likewise his Garden Quail. Dingle Bank. Edward Lear. FaBoNo

But lonely bells across gray wastes of sea. Fog. John Reed. AnEnPo

But long June evenings when I came this way. Nightfall on Sedgemoor. Andrew Young. FaBoPP

But longer time doth ask resolution.' Mine Old Dear Enemy, My Froward Master. Petrarch (Francesco Petrarca). SiPS

But look at the footprint. There's hair between the toes!' The Progress of Poetry. Christopher (Christopher St. John Sprigg) Caudwell. OxBTC

But look inwards, and begin to live! Advice against Travel. James Clarence Mangan. OBVV

But look on me with an eye of pity, for it is now my only claim. President Parker. *Anonymous.* OBSS

But look out, girls, he's telling you a lie. The Dodger. *Anonymous.* GBP

But looked, and changed their mind! A North Pole Story. Menella Bute Smedley. OxBChV

But–Lord ha'e mercy!–the ring was gone! The Two Wives. Daniel Henderson. ShM

But–Lord, how usual! The Innovator. Stephen Vincent Benét. EyDe

But–Losh keep me,/What did I speir?' The Wishin' Well. Helen B. Cruickshank. BSV

But lost somewhere in space the whooping crane's/final cry is speeding toward a star. Okeechobee. John Allison. GrPl

But louder sang that ghost, "What then?" What Then? William Butler Yeats. CMoP

But Love and Grace took Glorie by the hand,/And built a braver Palace than before. The World. George Herbert. OBS; SeCV 1-2

But Love, and Joy, and smiling Spring/Inspire their little souls to sing! An Epitaph on a Robin-Redbreast. Samuel Rogers. FaBoEE; FM; PBBP

...But Love assaileth/Me and sets my words t' his dancing. Autet e Bas. Arnaut Daniel. CTC

But Love being blind, how should he know of this? Hermaphroditus. Algernon Charles Swinburne. SyP; TEP; VLP

But love it is, is strong as death,/And I love Thee. A Song for the Least of All Saints. Christina Georgina Rossetti. BePJ

But love me for love's sake, that evermore/Thou mayst love on, through love's eternity. If Thou Must Love Me. Elizabeth Barrett Browning. FaFP

But love, more potent than your haughtiest/anger,/Subdues the souls which hate could only/wound! The Stricken South to the North. Paul Hamilton Hayne. PAH

But love/my own/feeling Nineteen Pieces for Love: # 15. Susan Griffin. LLLT

But love not one continuous/downpour. Advice to Bores. Abraham Ibn Chasdai. TrJP

But love now whilst thou may'st be loved again. Sonnet: "Look, Delia, how we esteem the half-blown rose." Samuel Daniel. EiL

But Love, once gone, goes for ever, and/all that endures is the grief. Love in Exile. Mathilde Blind. TrJP

...But love/Perceives without a mirror in the hands. Mirrors. Elizabeth Jennings. NePoEA

But love's way never changes of promising never to/change. Four Folk-Songs in Hokku Form, 3. *Anonymous.* LiTW

But love survives the venom of the snake. In Hospital: Poona. Alun Lewis. DTC; NeBP; SeCePo

But love was in her eye betray'd. The Eye of Love. George Moses Horton. BALP

But love whom ye list; for I care not. Hate Whom Ye List. Sir Thomas Wyatt. EnRePo; FCP; SiPS

But love will lean to a smaller flame/Forever and forever. String Stars for Pearls. J. U. Nicolson. HBMV

But Lucifer saw himself, too, fair. Revelation. Blanche Taylor Dickinson. CDC

But mad dogs and Englishmen/Go out in the midday sun. Mad Dogs and Englishmen. Noel Coward. CenHV; FiBHP; NLV; NOBL; OBTV

"But, madam, is there nothing else/That we can show to-day?" I asked no other thing. Emily Dickinson. NOBA; OxBA

But make him kick the dead. On Supporters of the Baconian Theory. Alfred, Lord Tennyson. FaBoEE

But make my constant meales at home. Chloris Farewell. *Anonymous.* OBS

But make my strengths, such as they are,/Here in my bosom, and at home. To the World: a Farewell for a Gentlewoman, Virtuous and Noble. Ben Jonson. EnRePo; JCP

–But make no bones. The Woods No More. Jay Macpherson. PeCV

But make no efforts to propound/Any solution of the question. Gemini and Virgo. Charles Stuart Calverley. FiBHP

But make not a mute of me. The Burden. Francesca Yetunde Pereira. PBA

But makes a curtsey to the heart. Kissing. Fred Emerson Brooks. PeD

But making it/the shiny seed's/your prize and/genesis. Back into the Garden. Sarah Webster Fabio. BlSi

But Man grows old, lies down, remains where once he's/laid. Contemplations. Anne Bradstreet. PBWP

But Man is great and strong and wise–/And so he dies. Irony. Louis Untermeyer. TrJP

But Man may better, if he will/Apply his wit to make it right. That All Things Are as They Are Used. George Turberville. EnRePo

But man never severs the stalk/Which bears this palatable fruit. The Moon Now Rises to Her Absolute Rule. Henry David Thoreau. PoEL 1-5

But man, oh Lord, how thin you've grown. Easter Poem. Kathleen Raine. LiTB

But man/permitted to be man. In the Mourning Time. Robert Earl Hayden. BPo

But man was made for endless immortality. Contemplations. Anne Bradstreet. AmLP; PBWP

But many a man, yif I shal not tarye,/Ofte daunceth, but no thinge of herte. The Dance of Death. John Lydgate. PoEL 1-5

But many a rude player hallowed the wave/That closed above the sailor's grave. The Sailor's Grave. Eliza Cook. BLPA

But many more refuse to die/Wonder! Quatrains. Salah Jahin. TTY

(But marriage is a yet more awful doom.) Rooming-House Melancholy. Erich Kastner. LiTW

But Mary, beside the cross-tree, could not understand,/Looking upon the tired, human face. It Is Finished. John Hall Wheelock. MoRP

But MAUDSLEY'S FEATHERING SCREW of/double blade/Threw these, and all the rest, into the shade. Means of Propulsion for Steam-Ships. Thomas Baker. FaBoUs

But may be ravenously unripped in hell? Sonnet for a Picture (parody). Algernon Charles Swinburne. BXAP

But may great kindness come of it in the end. September, the First Day of School. Howard Nemerov. GLGT; OxBC

But me an' mine, by rain an' shine/We do be thinkin' long. A Song of Glenann. Moira O'Neill. HBV 1-2

...But meaning motion fans fresh our wits with wonder. Henry Purcell. Gerard Manley Hopkins. TEP; UnS; VLP

But–meet no we angels, Pansie? Meet We No Angels, Pansie? Thomas Ashe. HBV 1-2; OBVV

But meets the angel in the proper hour. Tobias and the Angel. John Gray. NOBV

But Meggie reave her yellow hair. Willie's Fatal Visit. *Anonymous.* BaBo; ESPB

But men, my horse, with men! Alexander to His Horse. Eleanor Farjeon. PH

But men prefer to take the cash/And let such fragile credit go. Wiser Than the Children of Light. Monk Gibbon. NeIP

But men shall know nothing thereof. Penumbra. Pierre Louys. PeHV

But men will love you, flower, fairy, non-mortal/spirit burdened with flesh,/Forever, life-long. To O.E.A. Claude McKay. BANP; BPo

But Mercy first and last shall brightest shine. Paradise Lost. John Milton. ExPo

But Merlin's Isle of Gramarye/Where you and I will fare! Puck's Song. Rudyard Kipling. FaBoCh; FaBV; LoGBV; OxBChV; PoPle

But merrier were they in Dunfermline gray,/When all the bells were ringing. The Lady of the Lake. Sir Walter Scott. HBVY

But mind from its fire, a phoenix, fly. In This Strange House. Carleton Drewry. MoRP

But mine should be a fiercer howl than/yours! African Moonrise. Roy Campbell. CoBE

But Money gives me pleasure all the time. Fatigue. Hilaire Belloc. FaBoCo; GoTF; MoVE; NLV; NOBL; OxBTC; PV; TreFT

But more for pledge of what remains/Past the horizon's utmost rim! We Praise Thee, God, for Harvests Earned. John Coleman Adams. AH

But more swarm into his place, or dart/Up the rigging to drop on deck. The Legend of Ghost Lagoon: The Pirates' Fight. Joseph Schull. CaP

But most–for that he crassly snares his mate/In no such spangled net of love and hate. The Man in the Dress Suit. Robert L. Wolfe. HBMV

But most of all I want my poems sung/unthinkingly between your lips like air. New Numbers: Foreword. Christopher Logue. OxBTC

But most of all, I wish, my dearest darling,/To be the Blessed Morning when you wake! Wild Wishes. Ethel M. Hewitt. HBV 1-2

But, most of all, my heart, beware thyself. Be Sad, My Heart. Francis Quarles. NIP

But most say that she stricken was, with the March Hare as her mate. The Wizard of Alderley Edge. Peter Coe. OBET

But most those Friends, whose much-lov'd converse gave/Thy gentle charms a tenfold power to please. Sonnet to Oxford. Thomas Russell. OBEC

But most with murmur sigh "God save the King'. Bosworth Field: Richard III's Speech. Sir John Beaumont. JCP

But mostly/we just danced. The Dance. Jim Gustafson. APU

But Mother...she must never know/That I have sunk to depths so low. Thoughts of Loved Ones. Margaret Fishback. FiBHP

But mothers never change at all./Jesus! His Mother in Her Hood of Blue. Lizette Woodworth Reese. ISi; OHIP

But Mrs. Aherne sold taste rainbows at/Two for one cent, and from her shelves rained sugar. Dakota: Five Times Six. Joseph Hansen. NYBP

But muddy for hours and days/When it melts. Jerusalem in the Snow. Anath Bental. VWA

But Mudville hearts are happy now–for Casey hit the ball! Casey's Revenge. James Wilson. BLPA; GoTF; OnMSP; TreFS

But must, before she goes to bed,/Rub off the daubs of white and red. A Beautiful Young Nymph Going to Bed. Jonathan Swift. PPON

[But must suffer all, being poor.] To me he seems like a god. Sappho. BoWoP

But my ambitious ranging mind approves? Amores. Ovid (Publius Ovidius Naso). UnTE

But my blessings on Susan, the Pride of Kildare. The Pride of Kildare. *Anonymous.* OBET

But my comrade sprang to save me,/And receiv'd it in his heart! Comrades. Felix McGlennon. FSN

But my darling, it's when I think of thee. The Leaving of Liverpool. *Anonymous.* FSW; ShS

But my ear still kept the sound of the sea like a shell. Mid-Country Blow. Theodore Roethke. BoNaP

...But my eyes/are no longer strong, and I am tired now of looking. Deuteronomy. Robert Bringhurst. NOBC

But my father brings fresh glazed donuts in a white bag. Love from My Father. Carole Gregory Clemmons. CNA; PoBA

But my fause luver staw my rose,/And left the thorn wi' me. False Love. Robert Burns. LiTL

But my fetters of iron are stronger–/sevenfold! His Wife. Rachel Blaustein. WPOW

But my fiddle knows–and I talk to her. The Dark Man. Nora Hopper. HBV 1-2

But my hands, clinging,/Remain/Clinging. My Mother Once Told Me. Yehuda Amichai. NYBP

But my head's a cracking seed which will not grow. The Forbidden. Phyllis Haring. PeSA

But my heart is cold in the cold night-tide,/Where the elfins ride. The Fairy Thrall. Mary C. G. Byron. HBV 1-2; HBVY

...But, my/heart is with the deep thing that/ticks in secret, and surfaces to speak. Mine. Frank Polite. NYBP

But my horse always takes table d'oat. Limerick: "Said a sporty young person named Groat." *Anonymous.* TDH

But my jealous heart would break/Should we live one day asunder. A Song: "My dear mistress has a heart." John Wilmot, Earl of Rochester. HBV 1-2; LiTL; LoBV; SeCV 1-2

But my lady Mary fell asleep and the cowards ran away. Lisnagade. *Anonymous.* WTO

But my laugh has gone for good,/And gone the charm of tears. Shall I Do This. Purohit Swami. OBMV

But my name in the heart of a child. To Death. Padraic Pearse. AnIV

But my poor Heart alone is harm'd,/Whilst thine the Victor is, and free. Song. Love Arm'd. Aphra Behn. CavP; OBS

But my songs must tickle and bite/And burn with the ardor of living. Ardor. Gamaliel Bradford. HBMV

But my true love is false! She Is Overheard Singing. Edna St. Vincent Millay. InMe

But my way is to be patient, and I have survived/even to this year not worse than the last. Good Riddance to Bad Rubbish O at Last! Paul Goodman. TW

But my will runs to waste/In incontinent tears. My Son and I. Rosemary Norman. BrRo

...But my words none draws/Within the vast reach of the huge statute laws. Satire.   John Donne.   ViBoPo

But nae bonnie laddie will tak' me awa'.   A Song: "My name is sweet Jenny, my age is sixteen."   *Anonymous.*   PoL

But, naked on your couch, wear them for me.   With a Gift of Rings. Robert Graves.   GBL

But name upon the canvas, none.   *Anonymous.*   John Banister Tabb.   AA

But nane but thee for me, bonie lovie,/But nane but thee for me.   The False Lover.   *Anonymous.*   OxBB

But Nature lost the date of this/And left it in the sky.   It struck me every day.   Emily Dickinson.   PPP

But naught is found and all is given o'er/Till the young brood come chirping to the door.   Hen's Nest.   John Clare.   PBBP

But ne'er were hearts so light and gay/As then shall meet in thee!   If Thou Wert by My Side, My Love.   Reginald Heber.   HBV 1-2

But near the eternal Peace I lay, nor stirred,/Knowing the happy dead hear not at all.   In Extremis.   George Sterling.   HBV 1-2

But near the Sacred Feet she sits and waits.   The Flying Lesson.   Petrarch. CAW

But 'neath its wrath the proudest/cedars fall.   The Meek and the Proud. Abraham Ibn Chasdai.   TrJP

But 'neath thy much loved stars, a fitter tomb.   Washington's Tomb.   Ruth Lawrence.   OHIP

But needn't expect me to drink it at their house.   Tirade on Tea.   Phyllis McGinley.   InMe

But needs must call a spade a spade.   Song: "A woman's face is full of wiles." Humfrey [(or Humphrey[) Gifford.   ElL

But neither has it/much to carry.   Snow Fence.   Ted Kooser.   PPJ

But neither side a winner,/For things are as they were.   The Secular Masque. John Dryden.   OBSP

But neither sun nor moon, my dear,/Has yet caught me.   Variations on an Old Nursery Rhyme.   Edith Sitwell.   HBMV

But never a lad that ever I found,/Was able to Curl my Hair'o./Finis   A New Song Called The Curling of the Hair.   *Anonymous.*   CoMu

But never a mortal understands/Their strange immortal speech.   Sleep and His Brother Death.   William Hamilton Hayne.   AA

But never a word says he.   The Scarecrow.   Michael Franklin.   SUS

But never, as you dreame, in bed, or grave.   So Quicke, So Hot, So Mad Is Thy Fond Sute.   Thomas Campion.   NCEP; PoEL 1-5

But never ask me why.   Never Ask Me Why.   Silvia Margolis.   GoYe

But never before wi a courteous knight/That ga me a' my will.   King Henry. *Anonymous.*   BaBo; ESPB; OxBB

But never can be quite so any more.   The First Step.   Andrew Bice Saxton. AA

But never changed the coin and gift/Of Bonaparte.   Napoleon and the British Sailor.   Thomas Campbell.   BeLS

But never doubt your gift. You are right! You are right!   To a Reviewer Who Admired My Book.   John Ciardi.   OBAL

But never go back on the poor.   Jim Fisk.   *Anonymous.*   AS; ViBoFo

But never got a likeness–no, not once.   The Artist as Cuckold.   *Anonymous.* UnTE

But never, I ween, could any hand/Write half of its toil and glory.   The Maul.   Mary E. Nealy.   MC

But never knew substantial joys,/Until I heard my Savior's voice.   Mission. *Anonymous.*   AmFP

But never let me lose my song/Before the hardest day is through.   A Mother's Prayer.   Margaret E. Sangster.   TrPWD

(But never my love, my love for you).   Candle Song.   Anna Elizabeth Bennett.   GoYe

But never, never match our wee/White Rose of all the world.   Our Wee White Rose.   Gerald Massey.   HBV 1-2

But never, never with the slain.   Just behind the Battle, Mother. *Anonymous.*   FiBHP

But never one likeness.   Fortunatus the R. A.   Nicarchos [(or Nicarchus)]. LiTW

But never put back together a broken heart.   Complaint of a Young Girl. Wang Chung-ju.   PCP

But never speak a word.   The Message.   Heinrich Heine.   AWP

But never the Son who cannot change.   San Lorenzo Giustiniani's Mother. Alice Meynell.   HBV 1-2

But never to catch the vision which glorified his clay.   Joses, the Brother of Jesus.   Harry Kemp.   HBMV

But never–to our sorrow–/The little, pagan Faun.   The Visitor.   Patrick Reginald Chalmers.   HBV 1-2; HBVY

But nevermore the people spied/The tall men or the bull.   The Three Tall Men.   *Anonymous.*   OBET

But night being come they hasted home,/and kindly kist and parted.   The Coy Shepherdess; or, Phillis and Amintas.   *Anonymous.*   CoMu

But night determines here, away!   The Apparition of His Mistress Calling Him to Elysium.   Robert Herrick.   AnAnS 2; CaPo; ExPo; SeCP; SeCV 1-2

But night, the reserved, the reticent, gives more than it takes.   As One Put Drunk into the Packet-Boat.   John Ashbery.   HaCAP; HAP

But no, ah no, they're only butterflies.   The fallen flowers seemed.   Arakida Moritake.   LiTW

But no answer comes from stoat or bird or hill/Whether it is man's cross to kill, or die.   The Temple.   Clifford Dyment.   ChMP

But no City, great or small,/Have I ever seen at all!   The Pilgrim and the Herdboy.   Robert Williams Buchanan.   OBVV

But no friend to the breed that threw them out.   Escape to Love.   Patrick MacDonogh.   BIrV

...But no frown of mine/Will betray the company I keep.   The Disquieting Muses.   Sylvia Plath.   NMM; SBG

But no good girl's lip out of Paris.   Ballad of the Women of Paris.   Francois Villon.   AWP

But no knowledge in the grave/Where the nameless followers sleep.   Sheridan at Cedar Creek.   Herman Melville.   LiTA; PAH

But no little feast/Is spread any more.   The Mouse.   Elizabeth Jane Coatsworth.   MoShBr; OBCA; SoPo; SUS; TiPo

But no man can change/His earthen body.   This Earthen Body. *Anonymous.*   WTO

But no man has entered/The conversation.   I Suppose Her Mother Told Her. Francine Corcos.   AMV-80

...But no matter, the sequel/Is easily guessed.   Dora versus Rose.   Henry Austin Dobson.   ALV; NOBL

But no more Jack, and we were more/Dull and baffled than before.   Ballad of a Strange Thing.   Howard Phelps (Phelps Putnam) Putnam.   MoVE; OxBA

But no one/believes her; no one.   In Mysterious Ways.   Faye Kicknosway. GeTw

But no one blames Wisga/anymore.   Wisga.   Lew Blockcolski.   VoR

But no one else's mother/Is quite so dear as mine.   My Mother. *Anonymous.*   STF

–But no one gave me/a diploma when I was born.   Hard Way to Learn. James Hearst.   AMV-80

But no one knows.   To a Hurt Child.   Grace Denio Litchfield.   AA

But no one, no one, can ever bring me down.   The Fat Boy's Dream. Richard McCann.   GrPl

But no one said how slow, how willing.   How Morning Glories Could Bloom at Dusk.   Jorie Graham.   NPGG

But no one took him home to dinner either.   This One Is about the Others. Dan Jaffe.   FAZ

But no onle knows my agony and grief.   Eighteen Verses Sing to a Tatar Reed Whistle.   Ts'ai Yen.   BoWoP; PBWP; WPOW

But no queen comes/In slipper green.   Depression before Spring.   Wallace Stevens.   OBAL; SOTW

...But no vain terror thrills/His perfect harvesting; he sleeps at ease.   Late Autumn.   William Allingham.   IrPN

But nobody dares/Because of the bears!   Night Watchmen.   Wymond Garthwaite.   BrR

But nobody may give a tree/Excepting Santa Claus.   For Allan.   Robert Frost.   PCh

But nobody seems to know whose.   Limerick: "From Number Nine, Penwiper Mews."   Edward Gorey.   TDH

But nobody sees, nobody hears.   The White Peacock.   Mary Mills. NePoAm

But none, alas! shall mourn for me!   My Life Is Like the Summer Rose. Richard Henry Wilde.   HBV 1-2; TreFT

But none, alas! shall mourn for me!   Stanzas.   Richard Henry Wilde.   AA

But none, by saber or by shot,/Fell half so flat as Walter Scott.   On Scott's Poem "The Field of Waterloo."   *Anonymous.*   DBV; FiBHP

But none except the pure of heart/may hear.   Legends of Christmas.   Aileen Fisher.   ChBR

But none of them have got such spouses,/No such baccy, no such beer.   My Old Wife's a Good Old Cratur.   *Anonymous.*   OBET

But none of them wept for their FREDDY, except/HUM PICKITY WIMPLE TIP.   The King of Canoodle-Dum.   Sir William Schwenck Gilbert.   CenHV

But none of us desired to have them again.   The Locust Hunt.   Philip Murray.   NePoAm-2

But none of us hold it aginst her.   Limerick: "When our dean took a pious young spinster."   Victor Gray.   NOBL

But none-the-less a mirror for a life/that is less substantial than reflection. Snow White.   Robert M. Chute.   DFT

But nonetheless important. Mistresses.   *Anonymous.*   KiLC

But not a knight asleep.   The Virginians of the Valley.   Francis Orrery [(or Orray)] Ticknor.   AA; AnAmPo; HBV 1-2; PAH

But not all that many. Cheers!   Ode to Me.   Kingsley Amis.   NAs

But not always a hero like this–and that's all.   Caldwell of Springfield.   Bret (Francis Bret Harte) Harte.   MC; PAH

...But not being great in mind/Have left undone the greatest–and mankind. Don Juan.   George Gordon, Lord Byron.   OBSV

But not by thee my steps shall be,/For ever and for ever. A Farewell.
Alfred, Lord Tennyson. FaBoRV; HBV 1-2

But not for me. After Death. R. A. K. Mason. AnNZ

But not in our alley! Sally in Our Alley. Henry Carey. AWP; BLPL;
BLSo; BoLoP; CBEP; CoMu; FaBoBe; FaFP; FSW; GTBS; GTBS-P; HBV
1-2; InMe; LiTL; NOBE; OBEV; PG; PoPle; PoSC; TreF; ViBoPo

But not/in the same way. Apology. William Carlos Williams. OxBA

But not like what the child has seen. The Happy Child. William Henry
Davies. AtBAP

But not, my beloved, will fading wither you. Requiem. John Frederick
Matheus. CDC

But not on my back,/Because of my wings! Duet. Leonora Speyer.
HBMV

But not on Sunday night. Not on Sunday Night. *Anonymous.* STF

But not one hair of the head of the/seven-year-old boy/in a village that went
up in napalm. Another Late Edition (excerpt). Olga Cabral. PPON

But not so easy. A Letter for Marian. Thomas McGrath. VGW

But not so friendly and not quite so near. Reunion. Edwin Arlington
Robinson. NoAm; NOBA

But not so loud as on Eurystheus of old. Antaeus: A Fragment. Wilfred
Owen. PeHV

But not to make a constant stay. The Familie. George Herbert. AnAnS 1

But not to make it right, or take it down. Robert Frost's Left-Leaning
TRESPASSERS WILL BE SHOT Sign (parody). William Zaranka.
BXAP

But not to read the law, to reap greens, greens/Forever in her small, pathetic
pail. Greens. David Ray. SM; VGW

But not to sleep. He finds it hard to sleep. Journey toward Evening. Phyllis
McGinley. GoYe; NYBP

But not touch with my hands? What Am I to Do With My Sister? Prince
Yuhara. AWP

But not very far at all. Origins. Joy Harjo. TWSS

But not with water, ice, nor snow,/But with an equal fire. The Snow-Ball.
Petronius Arbiter (Caius Petronius Arbiter). LiTW; OBVE

But note I will this text,/To draw better the next. Patience of all my smart.
Sir Thomas Wyatt. FCP; SiPS

"But nothin' else than wut he sells/Wears long, an' thet J.B./May larn, like
you an' me!" Jonathan to John. James Russell Lowell. PAH

But nothing answered anything. The Hens. Elizabeth Madox Roberts.
GoJo; HBMV; OBCA; SoPo; SUS; TiPo

But nothing happens. Exposure. Wilfred Owen. FaBoMo; InPS; MMM;
MoVE; NoAm; OBWP; PAI; WaP

But nothing much unusual occurred;/don't get the wrong idea. Eyewitness.
Rodney Hall. PoAu 1-2

But nothing promised that is not performed. To Juan at the Winter Solstice.
Robert Graves. CMoP; CoBMV; EBEV; FaBoMo; LiTB; LiTM; MoBrPo;
MoPo; MP; NoAm; OAEL 1-2; SeCeV; TwCP

But nothing that he can fix. The Misery of Mechanics. Philip Booth.
MAT

But nothing will happen until we pause/to flame what we know, before any
signal's given. Near. William Stafford. ConAP

But nought is found, by sea or land,/That can a wayward wife withstand.
Wedlock. Jenny Grahame. LiTL

But now all I eat is the whip! Disillusion. *Anonymous.* WTO

...But now and then our lies/betray us into truth. A True Confession. Jon
Stallworthy. NoAm

But now, even more widely scattered lie our dead. The Land. Struthers
Burt. HBMV

But now he is sleeping on the old staked plains. Only a Cowboy.
Anonymous. CoSo

But now he laughs their threats to scorn with the Union at his back. The
English Labourer. *Anonymous.* OBET

But now I always say it fast. The Twins. Elizabeth Madox Roberts.
BiCB; TiPo

But now I am content to sleep. The Old King. John Heath-Stubbs.
NePoEA

But now I call him dirty louse. The Immortals. Isaac Rosenberg.
FaBoTw; MMM; TrJP

But now I fear her trip will be a/Damn'd business for my Miss Medea, &c.
&c. The Nurse's Dole in the Medea. Euripides. OBVE

But now I finde the glasse abused me. Lovers Conceits Are Like a Flattring
Glasse. *Anonymous.* OBS

But now I have a deity. Poverty. Thomas Traherne. OxBoCh; Prf; TEP;
TrCP

But now I have to go and feed the pig. Ambition. Edith Agnew. TiPo

But now I know why: they knew better. The Radical in the Alligator Shirt.
Lou Lipsitz. AMV-80

But now I must depart from thee,/And never more return. The Time Is
Swiftly Rolling On. Berryman Hicks. AH

But now I only know I am,–that's all. I Feel I Am. John Clare. ERoP
1-2; OAEL 1-2; SeCePo

But now I've come to an old straw pad/With the gipsies dancing round me.
The Gipsy Laddie. *Anonymous.* FaBoCh; LoGBV; OxBoLi

...But now impart/That sterner grace–to offer Thee my head. Consecration.
Anonymous. TRV

But now it's down the road, and we're in it. Ride. Josephine Miles.
FaBoWP

...But now it would hold even more/people who never in their lives have to
know the score. Telling the Cousins. Les A. Murray. AMV-81

But now, my little boy, you preach to me. The Atheist Buries His Son.
Abu'l-Atahija. LiTW

But now my pony's grazin' at the rancho I call home. The Wandering
Cowboy. *Anonymous.* CoSo

But now my wits are crazy and leaden is my tongue. The Green Autumn
Stubble. Patrick Browne. OxBI; WTO

But now...oh now the moon comes shining through! Winterscape. Jess
Perlman. AMV-80

But now (old man) flye on, as swift as thought,/Sith eyes from love and hope
from heart is wrought. When We in Kind Embracements Had Agre'd.
Anonymous. AAS

But now she's Leddy Gowrie. The Lass o' Gowrie. Carolina Oliphant,
Lady Nairne. HBV 1-2

But now stop dancing in my eyes/Or I will tie you round my neck. Pearly
Beads. *Anonymous.* WTO

But now that I have seen my lord/My heart is at rest. Thick Grows the
Tarragon. *Anonymous.* HW

But now the curtain lifts:–my soul's swift powers/Rise robed and crowned–for
lo! the play is ours Summons. Arthur Davison Ficke. HBMV

But now the solitudes are here. At the "Ye that do truly." Charles
Williams. NOCV; OxBoCh

...But now the winter's come. The Private Meeting Place. James Wright.
NYBP

But now they stand in every bodies way. Epitaph: "Here lies John Trot, the
friend of all mankind." William Blake. FaBoEE

But now thou seemest far away. The Judgment of the May. Richard
Watson Dixon. OBNC

But now thy tree is left so bare and poor/That they can hardly gather one
plum more. Of the Theme of Love. Margaret Cavendish, Duchess of
Newcastle. OBSP

But now you come at noon. A Dillar, a Dollar, a Ten O'Clock Scholar.
Mother Goose. FaBoBe; FaFP; HBV 1-2; HBVY; TiPo

But nowhere could I find Him who walks/Master's cornfield in the morning.
Who Is That A-Walking in the Corn? Fenton Johnson. GoSl; PoNe

But, O! delighting me. Reason Has Moons. Ralph Hodgson. FaBoCh;
LoGBV; OBSP

But O! far sweeter, if they please/Thy nymph for whom these notes are sung.
A Persian Song of Hafiz. Sir William Jones. OBEC

But O! if Fortune fill thy sail/With more than a propitious gale,/Take half thy
canvas in. The Golden Mean. William Cowper. HBV 1-2

But, O my heart, hear thou, hear thou, the sailors' song! Sea-Wind.
Stephane Mallarme. AWP; SyP

But O my prince of Friends, do you? A Parting. Wang Wei. LiTW

But O the lure of chancing winds/Outriding rain! What Price. Lulu
Minerva Schultz. GoYe

But o the starhushed silence which our third's. 72: wild(at our first)beasts
uttered human words. Edward Estlin Cummings. FaBoMo; NYBP

But O, the very reason why/I clasp them, is because they die. Mimnermus in
Church. William Johnson Cory. HBV 1-2; NOBE; OBEV; TreFT; VLP

But O the wind, the sun, the light! Beyond. Hannah Parker Kimball. AA

But O, Thy grief! For Thou canst see and hear. Spring, and the Blind
Children. Alfred Noyes. OxBTC

But O Thy grief, Thy grief, doth kill! The Eclipse. Henry Vaughan. HBV
1-2; OBSP

But O!–what ray ere shone from Heaven/Like God's first smile on a soul
forgiven. Pure is the Dewy Gem. Jeremiah Joseph Callanan. IrPN

But O, you tarry still! I Say I'll Seek Her. Thomas Hardy. QFR

But oblivion, not thy forgiveness, FRANCE. The Pisan Cantos (excerpt).
Ezra Pound. FaBoTw

...But of a spirit that demands/to be compensated for its skill. The
Professional. David Ignatow. NNaP

But of almighty love a brighter sign,/Shines forth thy law, pure, perfect and
divine. Athalie: Chorus (excerpt). Jean Baptiste Racine. WGRP

But of broad, peaceful oak-leaves for citizens saved! A Fable for Critics.
James Russell Lowell. AnNE; NOBA

But of course they can sit still at home,/And get dismally drunk upon whisky.
Let Us All Be Unhappy on Sunday. Lord Charles Neaves. FaBoCo

But, of course, they couldn't hear me. No one could. Homecoming. Peter
Viereck. CoAP

But of course you already know about that/from your own random suffering/
& sudden inexplicable bliss. Birthday Poem. Al Young. NPGG

But of course you can never be quite sure of these things. Fearful Symmetry.
Basil Bunting. PoA

But of Love I an't foretoken:/Ask some older sage than I! Toujours Amour. Edmund Clarence Stedman. HBV 1-2

But of new Monsters, Earth created more. Metamorphoses. Ovid (Publius Ovidius Naso). OBVE

But of one, if short he came,/I can rest me where I am. A Celebration of Charis. Ben Jonson. SeCP

But of the beautiful disrelation of the spiritual. Dam Neck, Virginia. Richard Eberhart. LiTA; MoAB; WaP

But of the towns which I have seen/Worst luck to Clonakilty. Clonakilty. *Anonymous.* FaBoEE

But of what, they could hardly say. The Fox. C. Day-Lewis. BoAnP

But oftentimes it pleaseth her to stay/In simple cotes closed in with walls of clay. Content. Geffrey Whitney. EIL

But oh! a brighter home than ours/In heaven, is now thine own. Dirge. Felicia Dorothea Hemans. HBV 1-2

But, oh, dear friends, you should have seen/The one that got away! Tombstones in the Starlight. Dorothy Parker. NIP

But, oh dear, how it tires one's legs! Limerick: "An elephant sat on some kegs." J. G. Francis. TDH

But oh, far sweeter, if they please/The Nymph for whom these notes are sung. A Persian Song of Hafiz. Hafiz. AWP

But oh, her heart was like to break/To count another year. The Gentlest Lady. Dorothy Parker. ISi

But oh, her lower half remains/Impenetrably pure. Tormenting Virgin. *Anonymous.* UnTE

But, oh, how far we see! A Hillside Farmer. John Farrar. HBMV

But, oh, I longed to ask the Fish/Whence came their silver scales! The Silver Question. Oliver Herford. NA

But oh! I miss the little moon/Who played there in the afternoon. The Lost Playmate. Abbie Farwell Brown. HBVY

But, oh, I wish my bones would wait/Till I grow up inside me! Growing Up. Edna Kingsley Wallace. BiCB

But Oh, if you love me, forgive me,/And none of this is true. Song. Theodore Spencer. AnFE

But Oh it's the small bit of furze between two towns/Is what makes the Kilfenora teaboy really run. The Kilfenora Teaboy. Paul Durcan. FaBoIP

But, oh! met with scorn.' The Wild Flower's Song. William Blake. CBEP

But oh, no man could hold it, for twas thine. The Legacie. John Donne. AtBAP; SeCP; TrGrPo

But Oh! she's but a young thing just come frae her Mammy. My Boy Tammy. Hector Macneill. CH

But oh, that we could sleep up there... Sleeping on the Ceiling. Elizabeth Bishop. MiAP

But oh the ache of the heart that longs/Night and day for the other one! The Other One. Harry Thurston Peck. AA

But oh, the debt is terrible/That must be paid in song. Song Making. Sara Teasdale. WGRP

–But oh, the den of wild things in/The darkness of her eyes! The Gipsy Girl. Ralph Hodgson. EnLit; MCCG; MoBrPo

But, oh, the loaves of bread I've made. Compensation. Virginia Maughan Kammeyer. AMV-80

But, oh! the smile that gave the charm/No longer beams for me! The Dew Each Trembling Leaf Inwreath'd. Mary Balfour. IrPN

But oh, the things I learned from her/When Sorrow walked with me! Along the Road. Robert Browning Hamilton. BLPA; BLPL; GoTF; TreFS

But oh, to-day! To-Day. Sister Mary Philip. GoBC

But, oh, what a sight/Is the fuzzy brown dog next door! Bingo Has an Enemy. Rose Fyleman. TiPo

But, oh, what anguish to discover/Her lover has become–her friend! Friend and Lover. Bridges Madeline. AA; HBV 1-2

But, oh, you'll not forget me, mother,/If I'm numbered with the slain. Just before the Battle, Mother. George Frederick Root. FSW; PSoN; TreFS

But, oh! you've wholly lost the youth/The instant that he tells you truth! Lying. Thomas Moore. FiBHP

But ol' man river, he jus' keeps rollin' along. Ol' Man River. Oscar, II Hammerstein. BLSo

But old Cornwall's bounding daughters/For gray Dundagel's tide. Queen Guennivar's Round. Robert Stephen Hawker. CoBE

But Old Dog happily lay in the sun/Much too lazy to rise and run. Sunning. James S. Tippett. GDP; SiSoSe; SUS; TiPo

But ole Mosser hain't cotch me, an' he never will! Wild Negro Bill. *Anonymous.* BPo

But on heaven's bright and flowery plain/I hope to meet you all again. McAfee's Confession. *Anonymous.* AmFP

But on her or my raincoat go roughly to it. Nausicaa. Irving Layton. ErPo

But on poisons thrive, and in death survive/Through ghostly night. Roisin Dubh. Aubrey Thomas De Vere. AnIV

But on the turn, you're virile, true and straight! To Grosphus. Godfrey the Satirist. PeHV

But on this Bank contented ever rest. Twas Night. *Anonymous.* OBS

But on Venus it must be venereal. For Travelers Going Sidereal. Robert Frost. OBAL

But on well-run farms pests have to be kept down. The Early Purges. Seamus Heaney. NCSH

But once more, as before, accepted and refused. The Winter Twilight, Glowing Black and Gold. Delmore Schwartz. NoAm

But once to have the liberty/That I have lack'd so long. Now Must I Learn to Live at Rest. Sir Thomas Wyatt. AAS; FCP; SiPS

But–once you have slept on an island/You'll never be quite the same! If Once You Have Slept on an Island. Rachel Field. BrR

But one command is thine: be pure! Star Morals. Friedrich Wilhelm Nietzsche. AWP

But one day that's fun day/Is Sunday afternoon. On a Sunday Afternoon. Andrew B. Sterling. FSN

But one dead albatross they found/At Karehana Bay. Threnody. Denis Glover. AnNZ

...But ONE ETERNAL/in the love of Beauty and in the selfhood of Love. The Testament of Beauty. Robert Bridges. OxBoCh

But one green Branch and a white robe. Palm-Sunday. Henry Vaughan. AtBAP

But one is currency. One is mine. One. The Letter. John Holmes. NePoAm

But one kiss from her honey mouth/Would make me whole again! Molly Asthore. Sir Samuel Ferguson. IrPN

But one of the nicer gods. A Bestiary. Kenneth Rexroth. OBAL

But one poor life, that my own land may live! Nathan Hale. William Ordway Partridge. PAL

But one remembers yet. One Sea-Side Grave. Christina Georgina Rossetti. NOBV

But one ruined candle/And your tears. Letter in Winter. Raymond Richard Patterson. PoBA

But one–shall be like blood. The White Ships and the Red. Joyce Kilmer. MC; PAH

But one that takes no food save blood. Family Poem. John Holloway. NMP

But one thing is left us now; that is–/Begin it again. Da Capo. Henry Cuyler Bunner. HBV 1-2

But one unending NOW, to be/A boundless circle around us cast! The True Heaven. Paul Hamilton Hayes. WGRP

...But one, with nothing left/beside/His dog to love, crept down among the ferns and/died. Exodus for Oregon. Joaquin Miller. BPAW

...;But one would not be he/who has nothing but plenty. The Jerboa. Marianne Moore. CMoP

But only a huge bobbin of black wire unwinding. Hello up There. Marge Piercy. NLV

But only at Wit's-End Corner/Is the "God who is able" proved. Wit's-End Corner. *Anonymous.* BLRP; STF

But only fools like me, you see,/Can make a God, who makes a tree. Atheist. E. Y. Harburg. PV

But only for a day as we/Shall not be here tomorrow. Some Are Born. Stevie Smith. FaBoCo

But only for this worthy knight durst prove/To loose his Crowne, rather then faile his Love. Astrophel and Stella, LXXV. Sir Philip Sidney. AAS; SiPS

But only gaze upon the glass/Of water that he could not drink. Mark Anderson. Wilfred Wilson Gibson. MMM

But only God. There. Mary Elizabeth Coleridge. EBCP

But only God can make a tree. Trees. Joyce Kilmer. BLPA; FaBoBc; FaFP; FPL; GoTF; HBV 1-2; HBVY; MCCG; OHFP; WBLP; WGRP

But only great as I am good. Tall Oaks from Little Acorns Grow. David Everett. FaFP; GoTF; TreF

But only in meditation/The Mystery speaks to us. The Infinite. John Boyle O'Reilly. OnYI

But only lark and nightingale forlorn/Fill up the silences of night and morn. False Poets and True. Thomas Hood. HBV 1-2; PP

But only multiply in the green grass. Necropolis. Karl Shapiro. MoAB; PoA

But/only one man–like a city. Paterson. William Carlos Williams. TAP

But only one mother the wide world over. Only One Mother. George Cooper. SiSoSe

But only scornful Echo made reply. Doris and Philemon (parody) (excerpt). J. C. Squire. BXAP

But only spell and point and punctuate. On Editing Scott Fitzgerald's Papers. Edmund Wilson. CrMA; NYBP

But only spirit wandering wide/Through infinite immensity. I'm Happiest When Most Away. Emily Bronte. SeCePo

But only Stella's eyes and Stella's heart. Astrophel and Stella, XXIII. Sir Philip Sidney. AAS; SiPS

But only that sweet laugh wherewith she slays me. Madame D'Albert's Laugh. Clément Marot. ALV; AWP

But only to build memories of spiritual gates. Emblems of Conduct. Hart Crane. LiTM; NAMP; NePA

But only to build memories of spiritual gates. Emblems of Conduct. Samuel Greenberg. LiTA

But only two hairs on his chest. The Lavender Cowboy. Harold Hersey. BPAW; CoSo; FSW

But only under the condition/that you swear to do my bidding. Handsome Friend, Charming and Kind. Beatrice de Dia. WPOW

But only what's sung,/when love's over, endures. Iliad. Humbert Wolfe. MoBrPo

But our hired man he sets close by/An' squirts an'squirts an' squirts. The Moo-Cow-Moo. Edmund Vance Cooke. FaFP; MoShBr

But Our Lady stands above the world/With the white Moon at Her feet. Our Lord and Our Lady. Hilaire Belloc. GoBC; HBMV; ISi

But our lips shall be silent, uncommitted. Without Name. Pauli Murray. AmNP; PoBA; PoNe

But our lot crawls between dry ribs/To keep our metaphysics warm. Whispers of Immortality. Thomas Stearns Eliot. ATP; CMoP; CTC; LiTA; MAPA; NePA; NoAm; NOBA; NoP; OBMV

But out of fear/of the unknown. On the Death of Neruda. H. L. Van Brunt. LTB

But out of hope his wife might die to bear 'em. Upon Batt. Robert Herrick. AnAnS 2; FaBoEE

But over my gray head/The plover's unageing cry. By the River Eden. Kathleen Raine. NYBP

But over their shoulders, God and/our mother, signaling: "Ridiculous." Our Kind. William Stafford. AMV-81

But over there is Fryer hill/Quietly producing millions still. The Ballad of Chicken Bill. F. E. Vaughn. PoOW

But overlooked my father's house/Just quartering a tree. A Thunder-Storm. Emily Dickinson. BoNaP

But parents ne'er should let you go unpunished for a pun. Cautionary Verses to Youth of Both Sexes. Theodore Hook. HBV 1-2; OxBChV

But pass for theirs who had the luck to light/Upon them by mistake or oversight. Inventions. Samuel (1612-80) Butler. PV

But, passing forth for knowledge sake, to cut the foaming/seas. Going Towards Spain. Barnabe Googe. EnRePo

But Patience clips her wings. I'm on My Way to Canaan. Anonymous. AH

But peace and plenty gar them sing/Frae year to year! Glasgow (excerpt). John Mayne. BSV

But peer outside of his prison room/With the eye of an anarchist? To Carry the Child. Stevie Smith. NoAm; NYBP

But Peesy-weesy paid for a'. Thumbikin, Thumbikin, Broke the Barn. Anonymous. OxNR

But people you can pierce forever,/What will you create from them? The Bayonet and the Needle. Eliezer Steinbarg. VWA

But perhaps I shall meet thee and know thee again/When the sea gives up her dead. Song of the Old Love. Jean Ingelow. HBV 1-2

–But /perhaps (though how was one to believe it?)/only because it was one's own? P.S. Jascha Kessler. AmPC

But perish they and their effigies. Painture. Richard Lovelace. CaPo

But pinned to the heart of darkness a tattered fire-flag flies. The Stand-To. C. Day-Lewis. OBWP

But pity for the grief they cannot feel. The Prisoners. Stephen Spender. FaBoMo; MoAB; MoBrPo

(But plain black hats rode the thoughts that made our/code.) One Home. William Stafford. AmFN

"But planet-and-space-ship,/Rocket or race-ship/Never shall part me from that." The Witch's Cat. Ian Serraillier. SO; WSC

But play'd so lightly on your Mind,/It left no lasting Print behind. To a Lady Sitting before Her Glass. Elijah Fenton. OBEC

But play the pretentious ass again, and/some other young captain will do. Songs of Cheng. Confucius. CTC

But please don't sing while I work. To a Young Woman on the World Staff. Franklin Pierce ("F.P.A.") Adams. ALV

But please remember that I am not dead,/Nor even dying. Dartmoor: Sunset at Chagford. Thomas Edward Brown. NOBV

But please, sir, to mention your pay. Epistle to Mr. Murray. George Gordon, Lord Byron. FaBoUs

But Pleasure then is cold and dumb,/And sings and laughs with strangers near. Joy and Pleasure. William Henry Davies. OBMV

But poems are far, far better/For putting boys to sleep! The Critic. John Farrar. SoPo

...But poets still,/And duly seated on the Immortal Hill. Don Juan. George Gordon, Lord Byron. PPoe

But–Pony Club, here I come! Learner. J. A. Lindon. PH

But poor old uncle's groaning. My Singing Aunt. James Reeves. ShM

But poor Queen Jane beloved lay cold as a stone. The Death of Queen Jane. Anonymous. OBET

But pray don't touch my sweet little lips. Precious Things. Anonymous. GoSl; TTY

But pray God's mercy upon all of us. Ballade of the Hanged Men. Francois Villon. LiTW

But pray the Lord shaws mercy til us aa. Ballat O the Hingit. Francois Villon. OBVE

But pray to God that he forgive us all. The Epitaph in Form of a Ballad. Francois Villon. CTC; EnLi 1-2

But Psyche–where, oh where, is she? Two Kitchen Songs. Edith Sitwell. CMoP

But purer than a tall candle before the Holy Rood/Is Cathleen, the daughter of Houlihan. Red Hanrahan's Song about Ireland. William Butler Yeats. ACV; CMoP; FaBoCh; LoGBV; NOBI; OnYI; OxBI

But Pussy and I/very gently will play. I Love Little Pussy. Jane Taylor. SoPo; TiPo

But questions were/asked. The Three Dead and the Three Living. George Barker. LiTB

But quite forgets her frowns and antics rude,/So kindly hath she grown to her new use. The Whole World Now Is but the Minister. Robert Bridges. VLP

But rarest of all is the pearls that fall/From a truthful mariner's lips. The Powerful Eyes O' Jeremy Tait. Wallace Irwin. FiBHP; StPo

But rather more expensive, now, of course. Beside the Seaside. Sir John Betjeman. OxBTC

But rather save my little store/To give poor folks, who want it more.' Greedy Richard. Jane Taylor. OxBChV

But rather will in that sweet bondage die/Than break one hair to gain its liberty. Her Hair. Anonymous. LiTL

But read not those which in our hearts are writ. Knowledge and Reason. Sir John Davies. OBSC

But readily resort/To Bellenden's or Lepell's. Damon and Cupid. John Gay. SeCeV

But really it's a funnier joke/To meet a head that's lost its folk! The Untutored Giraffe. Oliver Herford. ShM

But really, it takes a lot of grace/To be a preacher's wife. The Preacher's Wife. Anonymous. STF

But reduce no Human Spirit/To Disgrace of Price–. Publication Is the Auction. Emily Dickinson. AmePo; NoP

But rejected still to rave/Alive in his uncovered grave. Hurry Me Nymphs. George Darley. NBM

But remember Gengulphus's wife!–and reflect/On the moral enforced by her terrible tale! A Lay of St. Gengulphus (excerpt). Richard Harris Barham. VLP

But remember the Red River Valley,/And the girl that has loved you so true. Red River Valley. Anonymous. AS; FaBoBe; TrAS

(But remember to pay the bill). And. Ricardo Gonsalves. FIA

But returned in the evening to Anerley. Limerick: "There was an Old Person of Anerley." Edward Lear. FaBoCo; LiBL

But reverence for the archetype. Greek Architecture. Herman Melville. NoP

But right now the other side's winning. Limerick: "God's plan had a hopeful beginning." Anonymous. LiBL; NIP

But ring the fuller minstrel in. Ring Out, Wild Bells. Alfred, Lord Tennyson. WiR

But Roaring Bill (who killed him) thought it right. The Pacifist. Hilaire Belloc. MoVE

But rode to find a Child. The Riding of the Kings. Eleanor Farjeon. ChBR; YeAr

But rooks all talk together. The Rooks. Jane Euphemia Browne (Aunt Effie). OxBChV

But roses snow-silver from the dead!) To the Sun. Roy Campbell. EaLo

But Sa'di cried against the unloving heart of the Belov'd. Ode. Muslih-ud-Din Sa'di. AWP

But sairer grat the nourice,/when she was tied to the stake. Lamkin (A version). Anonymous. BaBo; CBEP; ESPB; FaBoBa; OxBB; ViBoFo

But sang, "O sea-starved, hungry sea." A Crazed Girl. William Butler Yeats. PAI

But Sartre is smartre. Graffiti. Anonymous. NLV

But say, is yours without compare? The Question. James Beattie. FaBoCo

...But say love died/Out of a cold and calculating pride. Somewhere I Chanced to Read. Gustav Davidson. HBMV

But say my verses do not scan,/And I get me another man! Fighting Words. Dorothy Parker. InMe; NAMP

But saying, "Fathers! Fathers!" Hunting Civil War Relics at Nimblewill Creek. James Dickey. ConAP

But sceptres, scutcheons, mitres gold/Flew up and kicked the beam. The Vision. William Taylor. NOEC

But secrete a skilful shell and stone and perfect be? A Tall Tale; or, A Moral Song. Phyllis Webb. OBCV

But see all wind-stirred. Now Close the Windows. Robert Frost. LOW

But see not twice unveiled the veiled God's face. Sonnet: "This is the golden book of spirit and sense." Algernon Charles Swinburne. SyP

But see, the sun speeds on his western path/To glad the nations with expected light. Prophecy. Luigi Pulci. PAH

But, seeing what/The man will do/Unbribed, there's no/Occasion to.   The British Journalist.   Humbert Wolfe.   DBV; FiBHP; PV

...But seen from the angle of her/death.   Burial.   Alice Walker.   AmPA; PrIm

But send some kind centurion,/An expert with the lance.   Security.   Charles L. O'Donnell.   TrPWD

But sequence ravelled out of reach/Like balls upon a floor.   I felt a cleavage in my mind.   Emily Dickinson.   DiPo; NOBA; OxBA

But shake your head, and scatter day!   To Amarantha.   Richard Lovelace.   CaPo; HoPM; LiTL; MePo; NIP; NoP; OBEV; SeCP; SeCV 1-2; TrGrPo; UnTE; ViBoPo

But Shakespeare knows it will be met.)   W.S. In spirit (Through S.S.).   Found.   Sarah Taylor Shatford.   PeD

But Shakespeare's extra, as you ought to know.   Xmas for the Boys.   Gavin Ewart.   OBSV

But shame has kept them late in bed.   A Welshman to Any Tourist.   R. S. Thomas.   OxBC

But shared with me the strangest happiness.   Lonely Love.   Edmund Charles Blunden.   OxBTC

...But she,/And night, shall be/Drowned in one endless day.   Eternity.   Robert Herrick.   WHA

But she came never back again,/Her auld father to see.   Brown Robin (A version).   Anonymous.   ESPB; OxBB

But she can tell and so can he.   The Flea.   Roland Young.   PoPl

But she cried, "What the heck will my fel.?"   Limerick: "There was a young lady from Del."   Anonymous.   TDH

But she didn't care much about that.   Limerick: "The girl with the theater hat."   Carolyn Wells.   TDH

But she didn't do it. And now it's too late.   Too Many Daves.   Dr. Seuss.   OBCA

But she does look and look for me.   This is a real story!   Poem to Be Read and Sung.   Cesar Vallejo.   EAS

But she got away from kitty,/Long time ago.   Kitty.   Elizabeth Payson Prentiss.   MoShBr

But she has listen'd to the voice/On city breezes   A London Plane-Tree.   Amy Levy.   OBVV

But she hath built an altar to Repose.   Nubia.   Bayard Taylor.   HBV 1-2

But she hath kiss'd her Flower/Where the wounds are to be.   Carol.   Louise Imogen Guiney.   CAW; OBVV

But she is changeless/And seems more beautiful as time/passes.   The Constant Lover.   Louis Simpson.   NYBP

...But she/is gripped in spastic fists of fear,/trembling at noises made by me.   Midnight.   Arthur Nortje.   WhB

But she is in her grave, and O,/The difference to me!   Lucy.   William Wordsworth.   BLPA; FaBV; FPL; GoTF; LoBV; MaC; OBEV; TreF; TrGrPo

But she is not kind.   In Mind.   Denise Levertov.   NMM; PAI

But she is worse: in time she will forestall/The Devil, and be the damning of us all.   A Rodomontade on His Cruel Mistress.   John Wilmot, Earl of Rochester.   OBSP

But she it is who names the wedding-day.   Love and Marriage.   Ray Mathew.   PoAu 1-2

But she/never showed up/at the shack last night/And—   M & O Blues.   Willie Brown.   BluL

But she plays soberly with the sea's/small change and hums back to it its slow vowels.   A Mongoloid Child Handling Shells on the Beach.   Richard Snyder.   InPK

But she rests, at the end of the path, in the city/Whose "builder and maker is God."   My Daughter Louise.   Homer Greene.   HBV 1-2

But she's been gone some ten years since, and I know not what to do.   Peggy Said Good Morning.   John Clare.   ELP

But she's divine!   The Water Lady.   Thomas Hood.   CH; HBV 1-2

But she's got such a start that I doubt if you'll find her.   The Careful Husband.   Anonymous.   OnYI; OxBI

But she shouldn't be so fat.   The Perils of Obesity.   Harry Graham.   FiBHP

But she slipped on the stairs and came down.   Limerick: "A housewife called out with a frown."   Anonymous.   TDH

But she softly whispered him,/"I darena this avow."   The Holy Nunnery.   Anonymous.   BaBo; ESPB

But she turned her eyes away.   To Adhiambo.   Gabriel Okara.   PBA

But she was my daughter, only three,/who had to pee.   Award.   Ray Durem.   BP; BPo; NNP; SoSe; TTY

But she who carries the sun/has no fear of night.   Song for the Divine Bride and Mother.   Felix Lope de Vega Carpio.   HW

But she will come like me again.   I Wish, I Wish.   Anonymous.   OBET

But shee'le gett one to starch her Ruffe/That never troubles mee Boy.   The Maids of Honour.   Anonymous.   CoMu

But sheltered only from the ruffling wind.   The Little Lough.   John Hewitt.   NeIP

But shew'd mixt tongs from many a land of men cald to their/aid.   The Iliad.   Homer.   OBVE

But shift you, for money, from friend to friend.   The Modes of the Court.   John Gay.   HeIP

But show me the more tricky if you can.   Pigmies and Cranes.   Walter Savage Landor.   NOBV

But silence steals the song.   Wild Eden.   George Edward Woodberry.   AA

But simple people would like to know/Who carries his business on?   The Devil.   Anonymous.   STF

But simply as the natural and sweet/Continuance of days spent here with thee.   Many Things Thou Hast Given Me, Dear Heart.   Alice Wellington Rollins.   AA

But since he cannot, Reader, look/Not on his picture, but his book.   To the Reader.   Ben Jonson.   EnRePo

But since he did it you restore,/See that you play the fool no more.   The Fair Maid of the West.   Anonymous.   CoMu

But since he died, and poets better prove,/Theirs for their style I'll read, his for his love.   Sonnets, XXXII: "If thou survive my well-contented day."   William Shakespeare.   CBEP; GTBS; GTBS-P; HBV 1-2; LiTL; OBSC; PP

But since I thus have sought her,/Will run me out of breath till I have caught her.   I Follow, Lo, the Footing.   Ben Jonson.   LiTL

But since, thank God, we have got free,/Revenged the Terrible's cause shall be.   A Sea Song.   Anonymous.   OBSS

But since that everie one cannot be wittie,/Pardon I crave of them, and of thee, pitty.   Sonnets, XX: "But now my Muse toyled with continuall care."   Richard Barnfield.   PeHV

But since ye are my scourge, I will entreat/That for my faults ye will me gently beat.   Amoretti, XXIV.   Edmund Spenser.   AAS; HBV 1-2

But, since your eyes are blind, you'd say,/"Where? What?' and turn away.   A Sketch.   Christina Georgina Rossetti.   GTBS-P

But sing-a-ling-a-ling for me.   The Bells.   Anonymous.   FiBHP

But singe this song, "By, by, loullay,"/To drive away all heivynis.'   Jesus Comforts His Mother.   Anonymous.   MeEL

But, sir, I may not, till you abdicate.   To a Captious Critic.   Paul Laurence Dunbar.   BPo

But sit upon the Pyrenees/And use the...   Midsummer Melancholy.   Margaret Fishback.   PV

But sleeps upon it, and for action–snores.   An Attorney General.   Ambrose Bierce.   DBV

But so as still the mother's power/Lives in the pretty lady-flower.   A Lady Dying in Childbed.   Robert Herrick.   EG

But so much patience as a blade of grass/Grows by, contented through the heat and cold.   Patience Taught by Nature.   Elizabeth Barrett Browning.   EBCP; OxBoCh

But soar in air, a wandering spirit.   Wild Swan.   Anonymous.   AnOE

...But society,/totally narrow-minded, had all its values wrong.   Days of 1896.   Constantine P. Cavafy.   PeHV

But softer than the breath of summer/Was the kiss she gave to me.   Song: "O, it was out by Donncarney."   James Joyce.   MoBrPo; OBVV

But softly the snow falls.   Wednesday at North Hatley.   Ralph Gustafson.   NOBC

But some day I will grow up and see/faces.   Feet.   Harry".   TiPo

But some day you will come back to me,/And love me tenderly,/So good bye, my lady love, good bye.   Good Bye, My Lady Love.   Joseph E. Howard.   FSN

But some had opportunity to squeal.   Many Workmen.   Stephen Crane.   LiTA; NePA; TAP

But some little mite is learning how to write/To write a little book about you!   There's Money in Mother and Father.   Morris Bishop.   FiBHP

But some man may hime greeve.   Snatches: "There is none so wise a man."   Anonymous.   OxBM

But some of us were more afraid/To keep on living like we been.   Riot Rhymes U.S.A. (excerpt).   Raymond Richard Patterson.   GP

But some people will bet on anything.   First Precinct Fourth Ward.   Daniel Mark Epstein.   TAT

But some pure lustre from their light/All future worlds shall have.   Tragic Love.   Walter James Turner.   OBMV

But some wille I save, and some wille I not.'   Snatches: "The formest of these bestes three."   Anonymous.   OxBM

But somebody hasta black hisself/For somebody else to stay white.   Sootie Joe.   Melvin B. Tolson.   FAZ

But somehow tenderness survives.   Somehow We Survive.   Dennis Brutus.   WhB

But something has to be left to God.   Good-by and Keep Cold.   Robert Frost.   CMoP

But something. One finds out as one goes aughan.   The Spell Against Spelling.   George Starbuck.   FYAP

But something that is just my size:I'm eight.   Something Very Elegant.   Aileen Fisher.   BiCB

But something went wrong with the plan: I am still on the train.   Observation Car.   A. D. Hope.   NoAm

But sometimes he just sits and watches me work.   I've Gone and Stained with the Color of Love.   Milton Acorn.   NeAC

But sometimes/I wish/That they wouldn't. Politeness. A.(lan) A.(lexander) Milne. PoPl

But sometimes look into thy grave, alive. Quatrain. Joshua Sylvester. FaBoEE

But somewhere in your head the old soldiers/are dying, dying into the fullness of spring. Old Soldiers Home at Marshalltown, Iowa. Jim Barnes. AMV-80; FAZ

But, son,/always serve wine. Advice to My Son. Peter Meinke. Psk

But soon it grows quite big and furious. Adolphus Elfinstone. Gelett Burgess. BBGG

But soon or late the man who wins/Is the one who thinks he can. Thinking. Walter D. Wintle. SoSe; WBLP

But souls ye have none fit for Paradise. Mourning Women. Mathilde Blind. SBG

But spare me thy disdain! Arab Song. Richard Henry Stoddard. AA

But spirits, penumbral, of the colour blue. Australia. Michael Jackson. OCNZ

But spite of thy hap, hap hath well happed. In faith I wot not well what to say. Sir Thomas Wyatt. FCP; SiPS

But Spring hums everywhere: the nesting birds/Are stammering out their sympathy for me. Weaving Love-Knots 2. Hsueh T'ao. BoWoP

But spring was gone from his step. Hep-Cat. John L. Sellers. LFAC

But St. Swithin smiled and slept. St. Swithin. Daniel Henderson. HBMV; ShM

But stand for ever by his own/Firm and well-fixed foundation. The Pillar of Fame. Robert Herrick. CaPo; NIP

But standing here, remembering, I hurt. Humiliation Revisited. Nova Trimble Ashley. AMV-80

But steeple-sliding's best! The Best Game the Fairies Play. Rose Fyleman. SoPo

But still flows on the eternal river. The Sun-Dial. Thomas Love Peacock. ERoP 1-2; OBNC; OBRV

But still he answered with a sigh:/"Unhappily I'm married." The Shades of Night Were Falling Fast (parody). Alfred Edward Housman. BXAP; FaBoNo; FiBHP; NLV; SpRo

But still he stands/Addressing his ball. A Public Nuisance. Reginald Arkell. LiSp; SD

But still he waits the risen Sun,/For still 'tis only dawning Day. The Burial of King Cormac. Sir Samuel Ferguson. IrPN; NOBI; OnYI

But still I am glad I'm alive. A Vagrant. Erik Axel Karlfeldt. PoPl

But still I am not drunk enough/to dream us into Spring Song of the Hesitations. Paul Blackburn. NMP

But still I can hear the birds sing on over my head. Exit Molloy. Derek Mahon. PoL

But still I find no bottom. Sounding. David Jauss. Str

But still I hope the time will come/When you and I will be as one. Black Is the Color. Anonymous. FSW

But still, I see your point of view. Simon Gerty. Elinor Wylie. OBAL

But still in Israel's path they shine. Mockery. William Blake. TrGrPo

But still in vain; pen, hand, and intellect/In the first effort conquer'd are and check'd. Sonnets to Laura. Petrarch. EnLi 1-2

But still, it makes you wonder, sort of. The Immoral Arctic. Morris Bishop. FiBHP

But still it's pretty good for me/Every time I climb a tree Every Time I Climb a Tree. David McCord. NTCP; SoPo; TiPo

But still, like the heat lightning you've/only skirted, within striking distance. Manitou. Ron Ikan. PPJ

But still my fancy wanders free/Through that which might have been. Castles in the Air. Thomas Love Peacock. HBV 1-2

...But still no sound/Breathes 'mid the green fern-spaces round. Australian Transcripts, V: Mid-Noon in January. William Sharp. FM

But still our Country's nobler planet glows/While the eternal stars of Heaven are fast. The Rejected "National Hymns". Robert Henry Newell. InMe

But still regard the destitute. Lord, Hear My Prayer. John Clare. NoP

But still singing,/"Baby, baby, o baby." Heaven. Gary Soto. NPGG

But still the child squealed on. As With My Hat. Samuel Johnson. LBN

But still the hands of mem'ry weave/The blissful dreams of long ago. Sweet Genevieve. George Cooper. BLSo; FSW; PSoN; TreFS

But still their nigritude offends the sight,/We mean to gild 'em! A Black Job. Thomas Hood. VLP

But still we cling, and still regret, regret.... Lament in Autumn. Harold Stewart. PoAu 1-2

But still within my bosom's core/Shall live my Highland Mary. Highland Mary. Robert Burns. AnFE; AWP; BoLiVe; GoTF; GTBS; GTBS-P; HBV 1-2; InPo; OAEP; OBEC; OBEV; TreFS; TrGrPo; ViBoPo; WBLP

But still within the elder tree/The strong sap rose, though none could see. At Candlemas. Charles Causley. OBCP

But stony, death-like sleep, too deep for dreams. Sonnets: A Sequence on Profane Love. George Henry Boker. AmePo

But stood as at the great white throne,/Unmindful of things dead. The Return. Annie Fields. AA

But stop and loiter all the time to sing it in ecstatic songs. Beginning My Studies. Walt Whitman. CBEP; OxBA

But stoutly at the outer brink/Defends the fort he overthrows. The Defender. Arthuir M. Sampley. GoYe

But strange how blood brings curiosity. My Father Died This Spring. Joanne Kyger. PoM

But stream nor fire shall part/This and this joined heart. Madrigal: "Wake, sleepy Thyrsis." Francis Pilkington. EnRePo

But struck one target. Pacific Epitaphs. Dudley Randall. NoAm

But such a heart whose Pulse may be/Thy Praise. A Heart to Praise Thee. George Herbert. TRV

But such a mind, mak'st God thy guest. The Picture of Her Mind. Ben Jonson. GoBC

But such as thou art printed in the heart,/In changeless baby loveliness still there. Mimma Bella. Eugene Lee-Hamilton. HBV 1-2

But such as will loiter, and lazy will be,/Shall for their labour be brought on their knee. A Schoolmaster's Admonition. Anonymous. OxBChV

But such creatures; much of this wild-shaped chance! Crab. John Blight. BoAV

But such is love--- Line Like. Nelly Sachs. BoWoP

But such it is I not how to begin. Such vain thought as wonted to mislead me. Sir Thomas Wyatt. FCP

But Summer, silence and sleep. War Poem. Ilya Ehrenburg. AMV-81

"But–supper, darling, still is in the pot." Hors d'Oeuvre. Deems Taylor. UnTE

But supper is na ready./Fal, lal, etc. Supper Is Na Ready. Anonymous. GBP

But sure as oft as Women weep,/It is to be suppos'd they grieve. Mourning. Andrew Marvell. CABA; SeCP

But sure I shall find some friends where I go. Sir Thomas Armstrong's Last Farewell to the World. Anonymous. APAS

But sure they were out, for he forfeits his crown/When he lends any poet about the Town. The Wits. Sir John Suckling. CaPo

But swaying, linking, blessing all/A family of boys. Bind-Weed. Susan (Sarah Chauncey Woolsey) Coolidge. GN

But swear to defend her,/And scorn to survive, if unable to save. Massachusetts Song of Liberty. Mrs. Mercy Warren. PAH

But sweeter still two lovers when one mantle covers both. Sweetest of All. Anonymous. UnTE

But sweeter yet, the sun-beauteous wife of Isaac. Rebecca. Joseph Eliyia. VWA

But sweetly chiselled and curled/Your inscrutable lips? A Proud Lady. Elinor Wylie. SBG

But swiftness is the Vice I only fear. The Fable of Acis, Polyphemus, and Galatea. John Dryden. AtBAP

But 't will be talk'd in Carlisle town/That these two Bewick and Graham. Anonymous. BaBo; ESPB

But take it from me...he gets my vote! My Candidate. Norman H. Crowell. YaD

But, "Take me home again," she cried,/"And I will sing and sing!" Burning Bush. Karle Wilson Baker. HBMV

But take our greatness with our bitterness? Meditations in Time of Civil War. William Butler Yeats. CABL; MoVE

But tarries yet the Cause for which He died. A Christmas Ghost-Story. Thomas Hardy. EnLi 1-2; OBWP

But tasks, in hours of insight will'd,/May be through hours of gloom fulfilled. We Cannot Kindle. Matthew Arnold. TRV

But tears of sorrow shed by me. By Coelia's Arbor. Richard Brinsley Sheridan. OnYI

But tell her that I love her, and say I drank/her health/To-day at Deadman's Bar. A Health at the Ford. Robert Cameron Rogers. AA; FaBoBe

But tell me, Nymphs, what power divine/Shall henceforth wash the river Rhine? Cologne. Samuel Taylor Coleridge. DBV; FaBoEE; HBV 1-2; InMe; NLV; OBTV; PV; TW

But terrible things were done/Long, long ago. Glencoe. Douglas Stewart. CBAP

But than a river vast his haste will seem. Epigram: "Oh! Trouble not Menedemos by guile." Strato. PeHV

But thank the Lord you're not forbidden/To covet your neighbour's daughter. Addendum to the Ten Commandments. Anonymous. DBV

But thanks to a' the powers in heaven/That I gae maiden hame!' Fair Annie. Anonymous. AnFE; BaBo; ESPB; FaBoBa; ViBoFo

"But thanks to my friend here, I've hum-/bled your pride." The World Turned Upside Down. Anonymous. PAH

But that dirty little coward that shot Mr. Howard/And laid poor Jesse in the grave! Jesse James (A vers.). Anonymous. ABF; AmFN; AS; BaBo; BFSS; CoSo; FaBoBe; FSW; MaC; TrAS; TreFS; ViBoFo; WiR; YaD

But that doesn't really matter. Clerihew: "Albert Durer." W. Leslie Nicholls. PV

But that fool just off and left me/just moved to the piney wood Piney Woods Money Mama. Blind Lemon Jefferson. BluL

But that heart was worthy thee!   Warning and Reply.   Emily Bronte. OBVV; OxBI

But that hour/he bequeathed to his descendants/still to be born/a knife/in the heart.   Isaac.   Haim Guri.   VWA

But that I'd pluck and wear in my wreath,/If thou wert but a flower!   Anklet Song.   *Anonymous.*   WTO

But that is not/For him to think about, far less to say.   Reformed Drunkard. Vernon Scannell.   AMV-80

But that is not today...   Glimpses # xii (excerpt).   Lawrence McGaugh. BOLo

But that it's Wealth is Infinite, to Set us up Anew.   Pindarick Elegy upon the Renowned Mr. Samuel Willard.   John Danforth.   PeD

But that its wings were weak-so it became/A dusky speck again, that was a winged flame.   Sonnet: "I stood beside a pool, from whence ascended." Richard Chenevix Trench.   IrPN

But that large grief which these enfold/Is given in outline and no more.   In Memoriam A.H.H., V.   Alfred, Lord Tennyson.   NAWM 1-2; OAEL 1-2; OAEP

...But that/my darling should be crooked and a liar.   Knightsbridge of Libya. Sorley MacLean.   NeBP

But that my pain is unenjoyed.   Neaera When I'm There Is Adamant. George Buchanan.   OBVE

But that, O me! I both must write and love.   I Know That All beneath the Moon Decays.   William, of Hawthornden Drummond.   BSV

But that one scar grew greater/and does not cease to grow.   Forgive and Forget.   Totius" [(J. D. Du Toit)].   PeSA

But that's Fred all over. Need I say more?   Fred.   David McCord.   TiPo

But that's probably because they are sensibler.   An Intoduction to Dogs. Ogden Nash.   MoShBr

But that she had smothered him.   Britannia's Pastorals.   William Browne. EIL

But that sun shines on and on-/Bright as a fresh dropped egg.   Rollo's Miracle.   Paul Zimmer.   GOYP

But that they stopt his furie from the same,/Because their forefront bare sweet Stellas name.   Astrophel and Stella, L.   Sir Philip Sidney.   AAS; SiPS

But that two-handed engine at the door/Stands ready to smite once, and smite no more.   Last Came, and Last Did Go.   John Milton.   TW

But that was long ago!   The Parrot.   James Elroy Flecker.   FaBoTw

But that was long before this jump and jive.   Tales of the Islands, VI. Derek Walcott.   OxBTC

...But that was yesterday.   Don Larsen's Perfect Game.   Paul Goodman. LiSp

But that we done for God's love have we no mair.   Phantasy.   *Anonymous.* ACP

But that we may bring to Jesus, and leave at the foot of the/cross.   There Is Never a Day So Dreary.   Lilla M. Alexander.   BLRP

But that which Crowneth all the Rest/In his own language better is Exprest. A Lamentation on My Dear Son Simon Who Dyed of the Small Pox... John Saffin.   SCAP

But that which fairest is, but few behold,/Her mind adornd with vertues manifold.   Amoretti, XV.   Edmund Spenser.   AAS; HeIP; OAEL 1-2; TrGrPo

But that which has no birth/Or breath within the ken/Of transitory men. Blue Hills Beneath the Haze.   Charles Goodrich Whiting.   AA

But that which looks from maiden eyes/Should last of all be broken.   Maiden Eyes.   Gerald Griffin.   HBV 1-2

But that world can only be better/That knows they have died in vain.   In Postures That Call.   Oscar Williams.   WaP

But that your trespass now becomes a fee;/Mine ransoms yours, and yours must ransom me.   Sonnets, CXX: "That you were once unkind befriends me now."   William Shakespeare.   InvP

But the acceptance, that must be,/My Christ, by thee.   A Thanksgiving to God for His House.   Robert Herrick.   BLPL; BoC; EnLit; FaBoBe; HAP; HBV 1-2; InPo; OBS; OFD; OHIP; PoRA; SeCeV; SeCP; SeCV 1-2; TrCP; TrPWD; ViBoPo; WGRP

But the ae best dance e'er cam to our lan',/Was-the De'il's awa wi' the Excise-/man.   The De'il's awa' wi' the Exciseman.   Robert Burns.   OAEP

(But the air can not stand my singing long.)   The Violent Space.   Etheridge Knight.   BPo

But the appearance of choice/In their sad and fatal voice.   January 1940. Roy Fuller.   LiTM; SeCePo; WaP

But the appearance of choice/In their sad and fatal voice.   War Poet.   Roy Fuller.   HoPM; PP

But the ashes dance. Each ashfleck leaps at the sun.   Noon of the Sunbather. Marge Piercy.   NMM

But the axles of their wheels were hot/With the same frenzies as our own. Empires.   Francis Burdett Money-Coutts.   OBVV

But the baby wasn't right.   The Night Was Smooth.   James Bertolino.   PoL

But the beating of our singing hearts.   A Circle Begins.   Harold Littlebird. STE

But the beginners well deserve the praise.   On a Fortification at Boston Begun By Women.   Benjamin Tompson.   PAH; SCAP

But the berries of the rowan-tree/are burning like beacon fires.   Winter Is Here.   Katri Vala.   PBWP

But the best is probably "Grinn & Barrett."   The Best Firm.   Walter G. Doty.   HBV 1-2; HBVY

But the best thing for us, we believe, is to go on for as long as we can, living/upstream...   The Hours of a Bridge.   William Stanley Merwin.   LCAP

But the bird with a broken pinion/Never soars as high again.   The Bird with a Broken Wing.   Hezekiah Butterworth.   WBLP

But the blest volume thou has writ/Reveals thy justice and thy grace.   The Heavens Declare Thy Glory, Lord!   Isaac Watts.   TreFT

But the boot prints remain. He will never come/back.   Turn (a poem in 4 parts).   Ken Belford.   NOBC

But the boss said never mind old scout/time wears disgraces out.   Confession of a Glutton.   Don (Donald Robert Marquis) Marquis.   GDP

But the breeze has dropped, and silence is the last word.   Fear of Death. John Ashbery.   FaBoMo; TAP

...But the bridge from the/abstract to the specific/was too much.   Fruit and Government.   Mira Teru Kurka.   APU

But the bridge wasn't built yet. Oh! it's good-by Liza Jane.   Good-By Liza Jane (with music).   *Anonymous.*   AS

But the cat came back for it wouldn't stay away.   The Cat Came Back. Otto Bonnell.   FSN

But the chaste Muse, with blushes covered o'er,/Retires confused, and will reveal no more.   On the Masquerades.   Christopher Pitt.   NOEC

But the cherry tree's in flourish!   A Catch for Singing.   Wilfred Wilson Gibson.   AnFE

But the chief point of all is the cookery.   How to Catch a Trout.   Thomas Barker.   FaBoUs

But the child keeps on playing, so I play.   The Lost Children.   Randall Jarrell.   CoAP; PrIm; TAP

But the child's sob in the silence curses deeper/Than the strong man in his wrath.   The Cry of the Children.   Elizabeth Barrett Browning.   EnLi 1-2; HBV 1-2; OAEP; ViBoPo; VLP

But the child that stands amid the blossoms gay/Is sweeter, quainter, brighter e'en than they.   Nikolina.   Celia Thaxter.   GN; HBV 1-2

But the choir-boy is happy and gay.   Low Church.   Stanley J. Sharpless. NLV

But the city, dusk and mute,/Slept, and there was no pursuit.   Hell Gate. Alfred Edward Housman.   NoAm; UnPo

But the city's towers grow straight and high!   Song of the Builders.   Jessie Wilmore Murton.   AmFN

But the clover is honey and sun and the smell of sleep.   Nebuchadnezzar. Elinor Wylie.   MoAmPo; SBG

But the colt was too heavy.   A Row of Stalls: Nell.   Raymond Knister. OBCV

But the cord isn't long enough.   My Invention.   Shel Silverstein.   PV; QQQ

But the corpse of my name/Lies there till this very day.   Mother.   Julian Tuwim.   VWA

But the dark wind is earless, and the day/is endless, and the grasses hiss and hiss.   Civil War.   Mark Van Doren.   MoVE

But the darndest lake among them is the lake of the Caogama.   The Lake of the Caogama.   *Anonymous.*   WTO

But the dead say only the earth endures.   The Passion Drinker.   Anita Endrezze-Probst.   VoR

But the dead women in my soul/Knew all that summer knows.   Heritage. Dorothea Mackellar.   NOAV

But the dear knows who I'll marry.   I Know Where I'm Going. *Anonymous.*   AnIV; ELP; GBP; IrPN; MoShBr; OBET; OLR; OnYI; ViBoPo; WTO

But the dearest, truest Christmas/Is the Christmas in the heart.   Christmas in the Heart.   *Anonymous.*   ChBR; OHIP; SiSoSe

But the devil a penny was there in it/Except the binding round it.   Lucy Locket and Kitty Fisher.   *Anonymous.*   OxBoLi

...But the dog of the house/Fled howling through the open door.   Scapegoat. W. R. Rodgers.   CIP

But the Dreadnought's the clipper to beat one and all.   The Dreadnought. *Anonymous.*   AmFP; OBSS

...But the dreams of Homer neither/grow nor wilt...   I Sing No New Songs. Frank Marshall Davis.   PoBA; PoNe

But the dull need to make some kind of house/Out of the life lived, out of the love spent.   An Urban Convalescence.   James Merrill.   CoAP; NOBA; NYP

But the dunce would produce if he could.   Riddle: "Take of letters the first." *Anonymous.*   CoBE

But the dust sinks/like loosened pearl/in a tide softly.   Ebb.   John Lyle Donaghy.   NeIP

But the eagle will never fly.   America.   Henry Dumas.   BOLo; PoBA

...But the empress/(How like an empress) was implacably shocked.   Beyond Biology.   Robert Francis.   NePoAm

But the energy it draws on/might lead to racing a cold engine, cracking the frozen spiderweb...   Re-Forming the Crystal.   Adrienne Rich.   CAPP; TAP

But the English live at home. Home. J. H. Goring. MoShBr

But the everlasting teamwork/Of every bloomin' soul. Co-operation. J. Mason Knox. BLPA; YaD

...But the experienced walker knows/That the other explanation is more often true. Pilgrim's Problem. Clive Staples Lewis. TrCP

But the face at the rail is farther and farther away. Song: "Lovers in ladies' magazines." Thomas McGrath. VGW

But the flash cut him, and he lies in the stubble. At Great Torrington, Devon. *Anonymous.* ShM

But the folk maun funder the auld house/and bigg up anither. The Auld House. William Soutar. OxBS

But the force of her farts/Is like stones from a sling. No Names. *Anonymous.* KiLC

But the Forest Department are rubbing their hands. Afforestation. E. A. Wodehouse. FiBHP; SD

But the forest–I sometimes wonder about the forest! The World Is Really a Sugarplum House in the Forest. Aram Boyajian. NeAC

But the ghosts of our old madness/Will rise and walk again. Alienation. Harry Kemp. HBMV

But the Glory of Heaven/Shines forth in God's Son. Christmas. Betty Scott Stam. BePJ

But the glory of the Lord is all in all. Dominus Illuminatio Mea. Richard Doddridge Blackmore. GoTF; OBEV; OBVV; TreFS

But the god the pilot pitied,/Saved, and made him rich and great. Rhododaphne. Thomas Love Peacock. OBRV

But the god who climbs, is I. Ecce Homo. Witter ("Emanuel Morgan") Bynner. WGRP

But the golden ring he gave me/From my finger never part. Rosewood Casket. *Anonymous.* FSW

But the great and flashing magpie/He flies as poets might.) Magpies in Picardy. T. P. Cameron Wilson. HBV 1-2; MMM

But the great fall is/When you fall in love. Love. *Anonymous.* TTY

But the great heart of the mountain glows/With deathless fire below. Christine. John Milton Hay. AA

But the green nuts are falling on my heart. I Sat among the Green Leaves. Marjorie Pickthall. HBMV

But the gulls fly over. Compensation. Gerald Gould. HBMV

...But the hand/did not loosen, in the darkness, its grip. The Breakdown. Sherod Santos. MAYP; SM

But–the hand that ope'd the gate/Shall forever hold the key! Panama. James Jeffrey Roche. MC; PAH

But the handle was good and strong. Arawata Bill. Denis Glover. ACV

But the harvest time of Love is there. Love Indestructible. Robert Southey. OBNC

But the head and the hoof of the Law and the haunch/and the hump is–Obey! The Law of the Jungle. Rudyard Kipling. LiTB; PoEL 1-5

But the hearts of the young are brittle as glass. Homework for Annabelle. Phyllis McGinley. GLGT

But the heat! I can feel it yet,/And that conniving cold. Piccola Commedia. Richard Wilbur. GP

But the heavens/Were hard above us/Like the earth of the summer beneath. We Did It. Yehuda Amichai. BoLoP

But the hedgerows renew their green breath/When taken each winter by death. Easter Thought. Leo Cox. CaP

But the hogs find it simply appalling. Limerick: "A bull-voiced young fellow of Pauling." Morris Bishop. TDH

But the hope of the City of God at the other end of the road. The Seekers. John Masefield. HBV 1-2; WGRP

But the horrible double entendre. Limerick: "There was an old man of Boulogne." *Anonymous.* CenHV; FaBoCo; OxBoLi

But the horrible double ontong. Limerick: "There was a young man of Hong Kong." *Anonymous.* LiBL

But the Host went by with averted eye/And barred the outer door. The Inn of Earth. Sara Teasdale. LiTA

But the hot sun of the South is to fully ripen my songs. Drum-Taps. Walt Whitman. AP

But the hour that brought the scent of rose, she lived it in Paradise. The Rose of Eden. Susan K. Phillips. BeLS

But the hulls mak feels o's a'! Feels. J. C. Milne. PoSH

But the human mind existed before/there was worship or righteousness. The Human Mind. Ai Shih-te. TrJP

But the image of her graces/Fills my heart and leaves no spaces. Written in My Lady Speke's Singing-Book. Edmund Waller. CavP

...But the Indians,/whoever they were, did not arrive. During the Pageant at Medicine Lodge. Charles G. Ballard. VoR

But the inward flavor of the infinite. Ode to Salt. Pablo Neruda. NU

But the jewels were never found. The Ballad of Sir Brian and the Three Wishes. Newman Levy. FiBHP

But the lady gets in. Stuff. H. B. Johnson. AMV-80

But the lady had floated into the leaves/With the blue mist of the fire. Birthday Gifts. Herbert Asquith. BiCB; OFD; SiSoSe

But the landscape of New England holds a rapture hard/to win. A Painter in New England. Charles Wharton Stork. HBMV

But the lass I adore, the lass for me,/Is the lass in the Female Factory. The Lass in the Female Factory. *Anonymous.* NOAV

But the last day before Christmas/Is–slow–slow–slow. Counting the Days. James S. Tippett. ChBR

But the leaves of the willow are bright as wine. Farewell, Sweet Dust. Elinor Wylie. AnAmPo; LiTA

But the little clown puppet, he parachuted! Little Clown Puppet. Carolyn Haywood. BrR

But the Lord has need of all. Three Trees. Charles Henry Crandall. OHIP

But the Lord in whom we trust/Will yet give us crumb for crust/Over here, over here. Famine Song. *Anonymous.* WTO

But the love of the warm heart lingers/here. Browning at Asolo. Robert Underwood Johnson. AA

But the lover will be well. A Shropshire Lad. Alfred Edward Housman. OLR

But the man closing up/Does not say the word. The Man Closing Up. Donald Justice. CoAP

But the man fears depths,/and could not save them if they tipped. Inside and Out. Robert Phillips. GeTw

But the man I'm loving lives/down in Jacksonville Jacksonville Blues. Nellie Florence. BluL

But the man went out to die. The King. Mary Elizabeth Coleridge. OBVV

But the man who told this story, sir,/Was a lyin' son of a —-. The Darby Ram. *Anonymous.* FSW

–But the marble is not lost! The Temple. Josephine Winslow Johnson. MoRP

But the memory of the lime-white mansions his right hand/has laid/In ashes warms the hero's heart! O'Hussey's Ode to the Maguire. James Clarence Mangan. AnIV; IrPN; NOBI; SeCePo; TW

But the miller makes the money. God Made the Bees. Mother Goose. SaC

But the mind as Ixion, unstill, ever turning. Canto CXIII. Ezra Pound. NYBP

But the most remarkable thing about England,/Was that the bread was white. For England, in Grateful Appreciation (excerpt). Anton Vogt. AnNZ

But the mouse stays his nibbling, to explore/My eye with his bright eye. The Recovery. Edmund Charles Blunden. CBEP; MoBrPo

But the multitude saw why she wore the/bandage. Carl Hamblin. Edgar Lee Masters. AmP; CMoP; LiTA; LiTM; OBSV

But the names still remain. Names. Jorge Guillen. LiTW

But the nearest friends are the auldest friends/And the grave's the place to seek them. It's an Owercome Sooth for Age an' Youth. Robert Louis Stevenson. NOBV

But the neighbours slept behind sealed doors, with feather/dusters beside their beds. Dust. Randolph Stow. CBAP; PoAu 1-2

But the nettle's over all. Nettles. Neil Munro. PoSH

But the newly budding blossoms/Are equally gay. Cycle. Langston Hughes. GoSl

But the next dearest blessing that Heaven can give/Is the pride of thus dying for thee. When He Who Adores Thee. Thomas Moore. HoPM; OBRV

But the night is the day of my cock. The Torn Nightgown. Joel Oppenheimer. CoPo

But the noblest thing that perished there/Was that young, faithful heart. Casabianca. Felicia Dorothea Hemans. BeLS; BLPA; EtS; FaBoBe; FaFP; FPL; GoTF; HBV 1-2; HBVY; PaPo; TreF; WBLP

But the old cowboy will soon be gone,/Just like the buffalo. The Old Cowboy. *Anonymous.* CoSo

But the old man would not so, but slew his son,/And half the seed of Europe, one by one. The Parable of the Old Man and the Young. Wilfred Owen. FaBoRV

But the old men know when an old man dies. Old Men. Ogden Nash. DFF; EvOK; InPS

But the older woman only/Knows the ebb tide leaves her lonely/With the shining fields of mud. Youth and Age on Beaulieu River, Hants. Sir John Betjeman. ChMP; FaBoTw; MP; TwCP

But the one I liked best/Was, "I do not always tell the truth." A Catch-22 Test. John L. Sellers. LFAC

But the one that is hindmost/Will meet with a great mistake.' How Many Miles to Barley-Bridge? *Anonymous.* OxBoLi

–But the One who framed us of clay on earth/not so has ordered. My Sorrow, Donncha. Padraig O Heigeartaigh. NOBI

But the one you are hiding/will fly Song of Man Chipping an Arrowhead. William Stanley Merwin. InPK

But the only man/I met/threw knives–/moonlight/through my eyes. Mooncalf I. Diane Keating. CaPN

But the order of summits,/the order of ruins,/is wedding gladness. The Book Rises Out of the Fire. Edmond Jabes. VWA

But the oriole, the oriole,/Sings "Joy! joy! joy!" Bird Song. Laura E. Richards. HBV 1-2

But the other won several prizes. Limerick: "There was a young man of Devizes." Archibald Marshall. CenHV

But the owl's brown eye's the sky's new blue./Heigho! Foolscap! Mandrake's Song. Thomas Lovell Beddoes. NBM

But the oyster loves the dredging sang,/For they come of a gentle kind. The Herring Loves the Merry Moonlight. Sir Walter Scott. FaBoCh; LoGBV; PoPle

But the pack moves away. Newborn Baby. Miroslav Holub. SUW

But the pastor–for not knowing,/Simply "gets it in the neck." Let Your Pastor Know. *Anonymous.* STF

But the patience and poise of flowers from the earth. Prayer for This Day. Hildegarde Flanner. TrPWD

But the people in the sky really love/to have dinner & to take a walk with you. Frank O'Hara. Ted Berrigan. APU

But the pettiest sight in those chaming ooms/Was he white sik fock and he bida booms. Sime Ines. Jane Stubbs. FiBHP

But the plumber lays his pipes. The Difference. Stoddard King. OBAL

...But the police were too late./It had already happened. At That Moment. Raymond Richard Patterson. PoBA

But the rest of the way through is clear. Limerick: "There was a young fellow named Shear." John Ciardi. TDH

But the Restitution/Of Idolatry. Now I knew I lost her. Emily Dickinson. PeHV

But the rich Food on which we live/Demands more Praise than Tongues can give. The Church the Garden of Christ. Isaac Watts. NOCV

But the rich odor some fine day/Shall (what I can not do) repay/That little care. Widcombe Churchyard. Walter Savage Landor. FaBoPP

But the river shall flow like the song of birds. During Thoughts after Ofay-Watching. Mongane Wally Serote. WhB

But the Road that runs by Atholl will be doing yet for me. The Road. Christine Orr. PoSH

But the robin's song is the best! The Song of the Robin. Beatrice Bergquist. SUS

But the rose with all its thorns excels them both. Comparisons. Christina Georgina Rossetti. OxBCV

But the rowan's deid. The Rowan. Violet Jacob. PoSH

But the sage was a sage. The Black Riders. Stephen Crane. YaD

But the scent of the roses will hang round/it still. Farewell!–but Whenever You Welcome the Hour. Thomas Moore. HBV 1-2; OAEP

But the sea-caves rung, and the wild winds sung,/The dirge of lovely Rosabelle. Rosabelle. Sir Walter Scott. BeLS; EnLi 1-2; GTBS; GTBS-P; HBV 1-2

But the secret sits in the middle and knows. The Secret Sits. Robert Frost. InPK; LOW; SoPo

But the set came suddenly right about,/and so they never did find out. Teevee. Eve Merriam. QQQ

But the sheet was Belfast linen. The Ballad of William Bloat. *Anonymous.* DBV; NOBL

But the show was over. The Artist. William Carlos Williams. InPS; LCAP; NYBP; PAI

But the sin forgiven by Christ in Heaven/By man is cursed alway! Two Women. Nathaniel Parker Willis. BeLS; OBVV

But the skin of the thing that made her go. In Memory of Anna Hopewell. *Anonymous.* ShM

But the sky/was blue. Once. Alice Walker. PoBA

But the smell of the hay/to be baled today. Morning. M. A. George. AMV-80

But the snow keeps whispering of you over and over. Letters to a Stranger. Thomas James. AmPA

But the soul knows no time/Nor any sleep. Sops of Light. Fredegond Shove. ChMP

But the soul that courts it, it must die, a low unlovely thing. The Merry Jovial Beggar. Peter Casey. WTO

But the source of light is hidden in the leaves. Summer Garden. Anna Akhmatova. BoWoP

But the speed, the swiftness, walking into clarity,/Like last year's briony, are gone. The High Hills. Ivor Gurney. FaBoPP

But the spicery of their savor entrances his scent. Amid the Myrtles. Judah Halevi HW

But the spirit curls and sleeps/Huddled up/Within me. Seaweed, Seaweed. Hannah Tatana. WTO

But the Spirit of Adventure.../Chuck it, Heath! A Trifle for Trafalgar Day. Ted Pauker. NOBL

But the spirit of this place just the same,/Felt here as joy. In the Marble Quarry. James Dickey. AmFN; NoP

But the stars! all night long the stars are clover,/Over, and over, and over! In the Field Forever. Robert Wallace. PPJ

But the stars and the stillness/Are always at home. A Baby-Sermon. George Macdonald. OxBChV

But the still grass, the leaves, the trembling flower/Keep, through dead time, that everlasting hour Wherever Beauty Has Been Quick in Clay. John Masefield. MoRP

But the strong are saying nothing until they see. The Strong Are Saying Nothing. Robert Frost. CMoP

But the summerdusk darkens; leaves turn red overnight. July in the Jardin des Plantes. Claire McAllister. NePA

But the sure light of sweet eyes bright/Shines on forever and forever. Under the Blue. Francis Fisher Browne. AA

But the surf drowns out what might have been/their battle song, a song beginning "O love..." Green Frogs. David Rigsbee. AMV-81

But the surgeon cut off his escape. Limerick: "A surgeon once owned a big ape." *Anonymous.* TDH

But the sweet little Bees large Monument. A Black Patch on Lucasta's Face. Richard Lovelace. AnAnS 2; CaPo; SeCP

But the sweet taste of wine/Aging in the landlady's glass. The Laborer. Samuel Chimsoro. WhB

But the sweetest of all music/The pipes at Lucknow played! The Pipes at Lucknow. John Greenleaf Whittier. GN; HBVY

But the sweetest smile she ever wore/Was the smile she wore in death. The Maiden of the Smile. Alfred Austin. TEP

But the sword-shaped moon/Has cut my heart in two. A Year Passes. Amy Lowell. MOON

But the tail end was friendly and waggy. Maggie. *Anonymous.* OnUR

But the tender grace of a day that is dead/Will never come back to me. Break, Break, Break. Alfred, Lord Tennyson. ATP; AWP; BiP; BoLiVe; DiPo; DL; EtS; FaBoBe; FaBV; FaPoR; FF; FiP; GoJo; GoTF; GTBS; GTBS-P; HAP; HBV 1-2; HeIP; InPo; LiTB; MaVP; MBW 1-2; MCCG; MOS; NIP; NOBE; NOBV; NoP; OAEP; OBNC; PoEL 1-5; PoPl; PoRA; PPoe; PrIm; TEP; TreF; TrGrPo; WBLP; WeW; WHA

But the things that are honour'd of Zion/Are most of them made from wood. Woodworker's Ballad. Herbert Palmer. HaMV; OBEV

But the thunder/was all over her mind. The Sound. Robert Kelly. PoM

But the tide is sure to win! The Tide Will Win. Priscilla Leonard. TRV

But the tiny grains of sand down beneath. The Stars. Ping Hsin (Hsieh Wang-ying). WPOW

But the trayv'lin's near its endin',/An' the end's aye the best. The Last o' the Tinkler. Violet Jacob. OxBS

But the trip around the garment's hem/Is not the path I tread. Needle Travel. Margaret French Patton. HBMV

But the very song of(as mountains/feel and lovers)singing is silence. All Which Isn't Singing Is Mere Talking. Edward Estlin Cummings. VGW

But the weary ne'er return/To their ain countrie! The Exile's Song. Robert Gilfillan. HBV 1-2

But the wheel that does the squeaking,/Is the one that gets the grease. Explanation. Josh Billings. GoTF; TreFT

...;But the white fomy creame/Did shine with silver, and shoot forth his beame. Next unto Him Was Neptune Pictured. Edmund Spenser. EtS

But the white man he works but a day,/My dollar and a half a day. A Dollar and a Half a Day. *Anonymous.* TrAS

...But the whole affair is only a hare-/brained episode in the life of the planet. Fourth Act. Robinson Jeffers. LiTA; WaP

But the wickedest born from the Pole to the Horn/Was the Hermit of Shark-Tooth Shoal! The Ballad of Yukon Jake. Edward E., Jr. Paramore. BeLS; BLPA

But the wide Republic's emblem/Is the bounteous, golden Corn! Columbia's Emblem. Edna Dean Proctor. GN

But the wild goat bounding on the barren hill/Droops in the grassy pen. The Wild Goat. Claude McKay. CDC

But the wild swans they know me,/And the horse that draws the plough. The Fairy Fiddler. Nora Hopper. HBMV; ViBoPo

...But the wind/In the wake of her skirts is cold. Indian Summer Here, You in Honolulu. Donald Johnson. AMV-80

But the wind knows! Wind's Work. Thomas Sturge Moore. BrPo; HBMV; HBVY

But the women are my favorite vessels of wrath. It's No Good! D. H. Lawrence. InPS; PAI; PV

But the words may be true ones: "Obedience is ice to the wine." The Young Bride's Dream. Rhoda Coghill. OxBI

But the words will fail to come out. Symmetrical Poem. Michael Palmer. NPGG

But the world shall end when I forget. Itylus. Algernon Charles Swinburne. GTBS; HBV 1-2; WHA

But the worst of it all was, nobody knew/What the Mayor of Scuttleton next would do. The Mayor of Scuttleton. Mary Mapes Dodge. NA

But the wreck of the line that have held it in sway. Newstead Abbey. George Gordon, Lord Byron. ChRP

But the wretch that can number his kisses/With few will be ever content. An Epigram of Martial, Imitated. Sir Charles Hanbury Williams. OBEC

But the years–years–/Like leaves falling. Thorn Piece. Amy Lowell. PeHV

But the Yellow Rose of Texas/beat the belles of Tennessee. The Yellow Rose of Texas. *Anonymous.* BLSo; FSW; PSoN; TreFT

But the young must eat pomegranate seeds in the darkness under the/earth. Pity. Babette Deutsch. WHA

But their Creator, whom sin nor nature tied,/For us, His creatures, and His foes, hath died. Holy Sonnets, XII. John Donne. JCP; NOCV; TrCP

But their dreams are all inscrutable by eight or nine. Some Dreams They Forgot. Elizabeth Bishop. NoAm

But their hearts, they do not so/In their love and duty. Of Cynthia. *Anonymous.* OBSC

But their love is not equal to mine. A Pastoral Ballad in Four Parts. William Shenstone. CEP; OBEC

But their thirst would remain/unquenched forever. Men Are Children of This World. Moses Ibn Ezra. TrJP

But their tongue gets caught in his "Hms' and "Haws'. The New Style. David O'Bruadair. BIrV

But theirs is all the youth we might have had. The Garden Party. Donald Davie. NePoEA

But then again I've never been/near Orion, or the Tannhauser/gates,/I've only been here. Final Farewell. Tom Clark. APU

But then, how it was sweet! Confessions. Robert Browning. ELP; GTBS-P; MBW 1-2; NOBE; NOBV; PoPle; ViBoPo

But then, I still have each other. Limerick: "A staid schizophrenic named Struther." *Anonymous.* NIP

But then in spots she was so rich,–/I wonder which? On the Death of the Giraffe. Thomas Hood. FaBoEE

But then the nation will be truly blessed. The Medal Reversed. Elkanah Settle. APAS

But then the world is tired, very tired of reality. Sunday Night Walk. Raymond Souster. CaP

...But then you notice/how far away you have moved. Far Be It. Laura Chester. APU

But then you step out/in the end Monkshood XXI. Kristjana Gunnars. CaPN

But thence I learn, and find the lesson true,/Drugs poison him that so fell sick of you. Sonnets, CXVIII: "Like as to make our appetites more keep". William Shakespeare. CBEP

But there ain't no bugs on me. There Ain't No Bugs on Me. *Anonymous.* FSW

But there ain't none what can compare with my own sweetheart's/curls. I Am Fur from My Sweetheart. *Anonymous.* CoSo

But there are little rooms in your life like/this pause at the door, Someone Here. For a Plaque on the Door of an Isolated House. William Stafford. FAZ

But there are millions I'd forget/Will have their laugh at passing me. I've Thirty Months. John Millington Synge. OBMV

But there are no young angels/like the one I was in my golden days. The Love of Older Men. James Kirkup. PeHV

But there are skies that look so pure. And beautiful things. Women at the Market. Angela Aymrich. PBWP

But there are souls that in this lovely hour/Know all I mean, and feel whate'er I feel. Nature. John Clare. CBEP

But there are the trees,/darling, over there. In the Forest. George Bowering. NOBC

But there I have been living ever since. Sea Island Miscellany. Richard P. Blackmur. MoVE

But there is a great deal about it you don't understand. Poem about Morning. William Meredith. NYBP

But there is always at least one germ around/O mortals. Bonner's Ferry. Peter Schjeldahl. ANYP

But there is no joy in Mudville: Mighty Casey has struck out. Casey at the Bat. Ernest Lawrence Thayer. AmePo; BBV; BeLS; BLPA; FaBoBe; FaFP; FPL; GoTF; HBV 1-2; InMe; LiSp; MaC; OBAL; OBCA; PaPo; PoPl; PoRA; SD; StPo; TreF; YaD

But there is no road through the woods! The Way Through the Woods. Rudyard Kipling. CH; FaBoCh; LoGBV; MCCG; MoVE; NOBE; OBEV; OBNC; OBVV; OxBChV; OxBTC; PoPle; RFM; SeCeV; VLP

But there is no sting in death,/no sting for you. For Tony, Dougal, Mick, Bugs, Nick et al. Dave Bathgate. PoSH

But there is silence/In the houses of Nagoya/And the hills of Ise. The Snow Party. Derek Mahon. CIP; FaBoIP; FaBoPV; OxBC

But there it lies, for ever and a day. On a Hand. Hilaire Belloc. ELU

But there it stings for evermore/The soul that must endure it. All Is Vanity, Saith the Preacher. George Gordon, Lord Byron. TrCP

But there's a penance: I'll repay your crime/embalmed in verses, you shall stink through time. Two Poems against His Rival, II. Caius Valerius Catullus. LiTW

But there's none so sweet a flower/As the lad that I adore. Arise and Pick a Posy. *Anonymous.* OBET

But there's still no joy in Mudville–Casey's daughter/has struck out. Casey's Daughter at the Bat. Al Graham. InMe

But there's you, and me, and Bindlestiff–/And remember Mary's Bindlestiff. Edwin Ford Piper. HBMV

But there, up there, 'tis heart to heart. Lorena. H. D. L. Webster. BLPA; FSW; PSoN

But there wasn't a man of them that day/Who was fitter to die than he! Ready. Phoebe Cary. PAH

But there were days, O tender elf,/When you were Poetry itself! To A Child. Christopher Morley. BiCB; HBMV

...But there will be/Fifty-six new sonnets by tomorrow night. Notes for a Sonnet (parody). Edward Pygge. BXAP

But there will be less to say. Length of Moon. Arna Bontemps. CDC; LiTM; PoNe

But these are they who have conquer'd and kept, the People/of Eighty-Nine. Wind Song. Zoe A. Tilghman. BPAW

But these human creatures cease not from their reaping/While the corn stands high, waiting to be cut Reapers. Mathilde Blind. SBG

But these I wear as a signet set,/As a seal upon my heart. Four Years Were Mine at Princeton. John Peale Bishop. GLGT

But these travellers have received a pardon,/and pass freely among the ruins. The Journey of the Suicides. Marilyn Bowering. CaPN

But these tunneled through pit blackness:/Scarlet; yellow; blue. Primary. Abbie Huston Evans. GP

But these were luxuries not for him who went for the/Simple Life. The Good Rich Man. Gilbert Keith Chesterton. DTC

But they are not like Shu,/So beautiful, so brave. In Our Lane. *Anonymous.* LiTW

But they are not the Life for which they stand. Art. James (1834-82) Thomson. NOBV

But they bound him up in straps–/phylacteries. Before the Statue of Apollo. Saul Tchernichovsky. TrJP

But they can't find me. Forty Years Ago. John Perreault. ANYP

But they did not speak; it was not worth while. The Toys Talk of the World. Katharine Pyle. OBCA

But they die hard. Stepney Green. John Singer. WaP

But they do not sing. The Plum Gatherer. Edna St. Vincent Millay. NoAm

...But they fail to see/The great Idealist who looms behind. The Great Idealist. Jami. LiTW

But they failed to reach/the glistening silk that nestles/the twin doves/in my breast. Mother's Inheritance. Abu Khalid. Fawziyya. WPOW

But they feel quite chummy with God. To New Haven and Boston. Walter Foster Angell. GoTF; TreFS

But they have raised no cry./I wonder why. Scottsboro, Too, Is Worth Its Song. Countee Cullen. PoBA

But they I think/resent being owned or/written into roses. Imperialist. Archie Randolph Ammons. GP

(But) they intoxicated him, and made/him a worshiper of idols. Quatrain. Sarmed the Yahud. TrJP

But they keep such a beautiful shape. Limerick: "There was an old man of the Cape." *Anonymous.* LiBL

But they knew the way. Contrast. Eileen Duggan. ACV; AnNZ

But they know me round the backblocks as Flash Jack from Gundagai. Flash Jack from Gundagai. *Anonymous.* PoAu 1-2

But they made Spurgeon do. To Live and Die in Dixie (excerpt). John Beecher. GP

But they never stand still long enough/as they serve serve serve. Daily I Fall in Love with Waitresses. Elliot Fried. GP

But they're claiming, right now, you were eight. Limerick: "A salmon remarked to his mate." Norman R. Jaffray. TDH

But they're one thing that should be done by halves. A Semi-Revolution. Robert Frost. LiTM

But they saw a flock o' pretty birds/That took their bride away. Earl Mar's Daughter. *Anonymous.* BuBa; GN; HBV 1-2

But they seemed to have frozen there ere they ran,/The Company's man. Labor and Capital: Impression. William Dean Howells. AmePo

But they shall neither know nor care/Who hold Valhalla's height. The First Division Marches. Grantland Rice. PAL; YaD

But they stand round with griefless eye,/Whilst my regret consumes like fire! She. Thomas Hardy. VLP

But they still got an itch for heavenly grass. Heavenly Grass. Tennessee Williams. PoPl

But they/Still walk/About heavily/In everybody's/Head. Dinosaurs. Valerie Worth. NTCP

But they told me I had ruined my dress. Strawberries. Judith Hemschemeyer. DFF

But they wake not where you are sleeping. The Moon behind High Tranquil Leaves. Robert Nichols. OBMV

But they want nothing that are drunk. Let Minions Marshal Every Hair. *Anonymous.* ALV

But they were died with crimson/Before the day was done. Ballad. Maurice Baring. HBV 1-2

But they were multitudes. When God First Said. Natan Zach. VWA

But they, while their companions slept/Wcrc toiling upward in the night. The Ladder of St. Augustine: The Heights. Henry Wadsworth Longfellow. GoTF; TreF

But they who love the greater love/Lay down their life; they do not hate. At a Calvary Near the Ancre. Wilfred Owen. MoRP

But they will not dream of us poor lads/Lost in the ground. Miners. Wilfred Owen. BrPo; MoAB; MoBrPo; NOBE

But they would pierce our heart/if they could only fly the distance. Man and Wife. Anne Sexton. CAPP

But thine arithmetic is quite correct. Fragment of a Greek Tragedy. Alfred Edward Housman. CenHV; FaBoNo; NOBL; Par; SpRo

But things for him will not be what they seem/To average men since he has dreamt his dream! My House. Claude McKay. CDC

But think it as sweet as her own. Market Women's Cries. Jonathan Swift. AnIV

But think not I dream of thee, Tybalt, my love. Anna-Marie, Love, Up Is the Sun. Sir Walter Scott. ViBoPo

But think, those Worlds, which deck the Skies,/Were only form'd to please their Eyes. On Mites, To a Lady. Stephen Duck. FM

But this beats dancin' at the Cowboys' Ball. The Cowboy's Ball. Henry Herbert Knibbs. PoOW

But this here air was too hot for him. John Coil. Anonymous. ShM

But this I know–He'll be with me/Until those years shall end. I Know. Verda Group. STF

But this I may: a man might howl a space/Of many years who once had seen his face. They Say, in Other Days. John Gray. NOBV

But this involves the grave. There is a shame of nobleness. Emily Dickinson. NePA

But this is heaven's way,/and possibly, nature's. As Sand. Natan Zach. VWA

But this is the sport in Country and Court,/Then let not these pastimes betray thee. To Friend and Foe. Anonymous. CoMu

"But this is where he lives!" To Some Millions Who Survive Joseph E. Mander, Senior. Sarah E. Wright. PoBA

But this little amputation/will shift the balance of the universe. Cutting the Jewish Bride's Hair. Ruth Whitman. HW

But this New World is forever new to hands that keep it/new. The New World (excerpt). Edgar Lee Masters. AmFN

But this pursues us to the urn,/And marries either's dust. La Belle Confidente. Thomas Stanley. JCP; MeLP; MePo; OBS

But this stranger no one knew. The Emigrant. Alexander McLachlan. NOBC

But this the worke of harts astonishment. Amoretti, LXXXI. Edmund Spenser. AAS; NoP

But this time is the last. New Love, New Life. Amy Levy. OBVV

But this tomb here be alone,/The only melancholy stone. Epitaph on Erotion. [James Henry] Leigh Hunt. OBRV

...But those dark men/looked at his load and laughed, and turned away. Merchandise. Sean Jennett. NeIP

But those in gray come close to me/And take my hand in theirs. The Days. Theodosia Garrison. HBMV

But thou alone to Him wert dear. God's Plans. Anonymous. BLRP

But, Thou art good; and Goodness still/Delighteth to forgive. A Prayer in the Prospect of Death. Robert Burns. HBV 1-2; TrPWD; WGRP

But thou art playing with it absently/And dreaming, like a girl. Animula Vagula. A. Y. Campbell. HBMV

But thou canst add to that, coward and slave. The Medal of John Bayes. Thomas Shadwell. APAS

But thou Desire, because thou wouldst have all,/Now banisht art, but yet alas how shall? Astrophel and Stella, LXXII. Sir Philip Sidney. AAS; SiPS

But thou, O God, for ever shine the same. A Contemplation on Night. John Gay. CEP

But thou read'st black where I read white. The Everlasting Gospel. William Blake. OBRV

But thou's as weil at thy ain ingle side/Now sitting, I think, 'twixt thee and me! Jock o' the Side. Anonymous. OxBB

But thou wilt abide and see them all/to fade, for thou livest and/endurest to all eternity. Hymn of Unity. Anonymous. TrJP

But (thou wilt see): He brings joy. Birth of Christ. Rainer Maria Rilke. MoRP

But though I had an hundred mair,/;I'd gie them a' to King Charlie. The Bonnie House of Airlie. Anonymous. BaBo; ESPB; OBEV; OxBB; OxBS

But though it scared, it did not bite. The Silken Snake. Robert Herrick. OBSP

But though the noise of falling blows was heard/The anvil is unchanged; the hammers gone. God's Word. John Clifford. TRV

But though the whole world turn to coal,/Then chiefly lives. Virtue. George Herbert. AWP; CH; ELP; EnLit; ExPo; ForPo; HAP; HBV 1-2; HeIP; InPo; InPS; InvP; JCP; LoBV; NOBE; NOCV; NoP; OAEL 1-2; OBEV; PoRA; PPP; SeCeV; SoSe; TEP; TreFT; TrGrPo; ViBoPo; WGRP; WHA

But thought is free, and dreams are dreams, and so/I dream, and dream, and dream; but let that go. Sonnet: "It is as true as strange, else trial feigns." John, of Hereford Davies. ElL

But thought she should go back to Sweden. Limerick: "There was a young lady of Sweden." Edward Lear. EBEV

But thought the deepening blue thought of the fly. Truth. Howard Nemerov. HoPM; LiTM; MoVE

But thought will glow when the sun grows cold,/And mix with Deity. Thought. Ralph Waldo Emerson. AmePo

But three brother again we never were to be. Archie O Cawfield (A vers.). Anonymous. BaBo; ESPB

But throned in Self, the changeless Light of Lights. Pythagoras. Thomas S. Jones, Jr. AnAmPo

But through a little hole in the boring report/God watches us faking it. Against Meaning. Andrei Codrescu. APU

But through how many years sinks down/My sullen heel. Walking in Beech Leaves. Andrew Young. MoVE

But through long nights she stared into the dark,/And knew she lied. The Dead Faith. Fanny Heaslip Lea. HBV 1-2; WGRP

But through the gate sleeps his lost paradise. Flower of Exile. Max Dunn. BoAV

But Thy palms toil-worn by nails are torn,/O Christ, on Calvary. The Way of the World. James Jeffrey Roche. CAW

But thyme and parsley underneath the moon. Walking at Night. Henry Treece. WaP

But, till she fetches open sea/Let no man deem that he is free! The Storm Cone. Rudyard Kipling. ChMP; OxBTC

But till that day, plaise God, I'll stick to the Wearin' o' the/Green. The Wearin' o' the Green. Anonymous. AnIL; AnIV; HBV 1-2; NOBI; OnYI; PoSC; TreF

But till then he could never believe it/That Strumbolo lay in the straits. A Hot Engagement between a French Privateer and an English Fireship. Anonymous. OBSS

But time or tide won't wait for you, if you are tied for/time. Address to Children. Anonymous. FaBoUs

...But time shall come/When France shall reign, and laws be all repealed! Inscription (parody). J. H. Frere and George Canning. Par

But 'tis enough that Christ knows all,/And I shall be with him. Lord, It Belongs Not to My Care. Richard Baxter. EBCP; OxBoCh

But 'tis in vermin that about thee throng. Upon the Anonymous Author of Legion's Humble Address to the Lords. Thomas (Tom) Brown. APAS

But 'tis the tenderest reed of all/That trembles first when Earth is shaken. "Picciola". Robert Henry Newell. AA

But 'tis the wet that makes it die, no doubt. What Is Liquid. Margaret Cavendish, Duchess of Newcastle. FaBoUs

But 'tis your Suffrage makes Authentique Wit. Prologue to the University of Oxford, 1673... John Dryden. OBS; PP

But to abolish the working classes for ever/and have a world of men. O! Start a Revolution. D. H. Lawrence. FaBoEE

But to be lonesome, you have to love. Leaving Here. Stephen Philbrick. AMV-81

...But to comprehend/Him, as He is, is labour without end. 'Tis Hard to Find God. Robert Herrick. LiTB

"But to divide your heart again." The Weed. Elizabeth Bishop. MoPo

But to forget is slow, Babe. Belle. Anonymous. OuSiCo

But to frolic and sing and then go off to sleep! Lullaby Town. John Irving Diller. BLPA

But to fugues and sonatas that possibly hide/Uncomposed in her–well–in her tuneful inside.' The Music of the Future. Oliver Herford. CenHV

But to get quick relief, just confide in a friend. Confide in a Friend. Anonymous. PoToHe

But to her it was full great comfort. A Maid of Brenten Arse. Anonymous. GBP

But to her sisteris feast na mair she gaed. The Tale of the Upland Mouse and the Burgess Mouse. Robert Henryson. OBNV

But to know that He is coming/Fills the soul with pure delight. He Is Coming. Gladys M. Gearhart. STF

But to live a little, invoking/the old powers. Pure Products. Denise Levertov. NMP

But to live in the tragic world forever. A Story about Chicken Soup. Louis Simpson. LCAP; NMP; NNaP; NoAm; TAP

But to me it is an honour/To be born an Irishman. No Irish Need Apply. Anonymous. WTO

But to me they bring a promise/which should be in you–not them–high, in your room. The Belongings. Theodore Enslin. CoPo

But to me you're as fair as you were, Maggie,/When you and I were young. When You and I Were Young, Maggie. James, and George W. Johnson Butterfield. BLSo; FSW; PSoN; TreF

But to morphology, the shape that cannot die. The Cicada (excerpt). Conrad Aiken. PoCh

But to perish as these things perish'd. The Rhyme of Joyous Garde (excerpt). Adam Lindsay Gordon. PoAu 1-2

But to prop the earth and the stone.   The Lament for Art O'Leary. *Anonymous.*   AnIL; KiLC

But to refuse before you're asked displays/Inventive genius worthy of the bays! Sextus the Usurer.   Martial (Marcus Valerius Martialis).   AWP

But to take this softness and this plenitude/As aesthetic, and control it as it falls.   A Snowfall.   Richard Eberhart.   FiCP

But to the East–the East! Go, say this, Pilgrim dear!   Rudel to the Lady of Tripoli.   Robert Browning.   LoBV

But to the heavens, lo, it fled, for to receive his doom.   "In winter's just return..."   Henry Howard, Earl of Surrey.   AAS; FCP; SiPS

But to the wide, clear-windowed room/It is rebirth.   Light.   Hermann Hagedorn.   MoRP

But to this later light they saw in him,/Their day was dark, and dim.   Silex Scintillans.   Henry Vaughan.   AnAnS 1

But to throw out the bishops who threw out the bill.   A Ballad, November 1680.   *Anonymous.*   APAS

But today someone gave me/A little carved bowl.   The Little Carved Bowl. Margaret Widdemer.   BrR

But too content at heart/To care.   Three Girls on a Buttress.   Eilidh Nisbet. PoSH

But too much reason on each side?   Epigram: "What makes all subjects discontent."   Samuel (1612-80) Butler.   FaBoEE

But took what e'er he proffer'd her,/"I, marry, and thank you too!"   The Thankful Country Lass.   *Anonymous.*   CoMu

But touch'd with virtue's magnet force,/It trembles doing wrong.   To a Lady, with a Compass.   George Napier.   FaBoUs

But touch me with thy wand, or hovering/Above mine eyelids sweep me with thy train.   Sleep.   Statius Publius Papinius.   AWP

But trailing clouds of glory do we come.   Intimations of Immortality from Recollections of Early Childhood.   William Wordsworth.   ATP

But trees of life light up/with their own power.   The Tree of Life is Also a Tree of Fire.   Gerda Norvig.   VWA

But trembled if one passed him with a frown.   In Time of War.   W.H. Auden.   CMoP

But Trinity sets thee free again.   Close Season for Marriage.   *Anonymous.* FaBoUs

But triumph rather in this faithful pledge/Of innocence, and fair virginity/ Inviolate.   The Oeconomy of Love (excerpt).   John Armstrong.   NOEC

But trust the guidance of the One Who Knows.   On Australian Hills.   Ada Cambridge.   PoAu 1-2

But trust the Master Weaver/And His steady, guiding Hand.   The Master Weaver.   *Anonymous.*   STF

But trusting it, a mystery that would keep.   Night Blooming Flowers. Katha Pollitt.   MAYP

But try to live each day He sends/To serve my gracious Master's ends.   If But One Year.   *Anonymous.*   STF

...But turning the permanent also/into the transient takes up all the time that's left.   The Put-Down Come On.   Archie Randolph Ammons.   NoP

"But 'twas a famous victory."   The Battle of Blenheim.   Robert Southey. BeLS; EnRP; FaBoPV; FaBV; FaPoR; FPL; GN; HBV 1-2; HBVY; InMe; MCCG; OBNC; OBRV; OBWP; PaPo; PoLf; TreF; TrGrPo; WBLP

But 'twas Cerinthus that is lost.   A Death in the Desert.   Robert Browning. GoTL; OxBoCh

But 'twas–the fact that He was dead–.   A Dying Tiger–Moaned for Drink. Emily Dickinson.   PeD

But unconcern'd, can lett thy glories passe.   Clarinda's Indifference at Parting with Her Beauty.   Anne Finch, Countess of Winchilsea.   SBG

But "Union forever,"/Shall be our last toast.   The Times.   *Anonymous.* PAH

But unknown to the slim hands' betrayal.   Timers.   Flora J. Arnstein. GoYe

But unlike God in heaven, come and go.   Secular Games.   Richard Howard. PoA

But unmanned spirit or unfleshed man/I cannot cradle. Child, no one can. The Pieta, Rhenish, 14th C., the Cloisters.   Mona Van Duyn.   Prf

But unto any pious motion/There's little coin and less devotion.   The Bounty of Our Age.   Henry Farley.   FaBoCh

But unto love/Resign your simple natures/To tender love.   I Heard a Linnet Courting.   Robert Bridges.   BrPo; LiTB; LiTM; OBMV

But unto us the light/Dies once for all; and sleep brings on eternal night. Aminta: Chorus I.   Torquato Tasso.   AWP; OBVE

But unto you pertains the loss.   For Pity, Pretty Eyes, Surcease.   Thomas Lodge.   ElL

But up what corridors thrums the flood's growl?   Her Mood around Me. Brewster Ghiselin.   LiTL

But upright as the staff of one who watcheth o'er his sheep.   The Three Poplars.   Philip Francis Little.   OxBI

But Vanderdecken himself could tell you more!   The Flying Dutchman.   A. M. Sullivan.   EtS

But vindicate the ways of God to Man.   The Wild Garden.   Alexander Pope.   PrIm

But vines bear grapes–and Bacchus loves a song.   A Blackbird.   Marcus Argentarius.   LiTW

But wander, an imperishable name,/Kurnos, about the isles and shores of Greece!   To Kurnos.   Theognis.   PeHV

But wanting still the glory of the spire.   Giotto's Tower.   Henry Wadsworth Longfellow.   EyDe

But was there ever dog that praised his fleas?   To a Poet, Who Would Have Me Praise Certain Bad Poets...   William Butler Yeats.   CTC; DBV; FaBoEE; PV

But was told they were kept for the Dons.   Limerick: "There was a young gourmand of John's".   Arthur Clement Hilton.   CenHV

But Wastmuir king he made it oot,/An an ill deid mat he dee!   Fause Foodrage (C version).   *Anonymous.*   ESPB

But Water's wider, thank the Lord, than Blood.   Ninth Philosopher's Song. Aldous Huxley.   ViBoPo

But waur than a', the mickle craw/Has ta'en and killed our poussie, O!   The Craw's Killed the Poussie, O!   *Anonymous.*   BoAnP

But we all like Fourth/Of July a lot.   Fourth of July.   Marchette Chute. SiSoSe

But we are exiles from our fathers' land.   Canadian Boat Song.   John Galt. BLPA; CaP; CBEP; FaBoCh; FaPoR; LoGBV; OBEV; OBNC; OBRV

But we bear.   Woman and Nature.   Susan Griffin.   NPGG

But we believe it was for us He hung and suffered there.   We May Not Know.   Cecil Frances Alexander.   TRV

But we can go, if by God's power/We only bear the burden of the hour.   As Thy Days So Shall Thy Strength Be.   Georgiana Holmes.   TRV

But we can have some conversation before it is too late.'   He Told His Life Story to Mrs. Courtly.   Stevie Smith.   NLV

But we can offer you a home, a haven,/That might prove even worse.   Pet Shop.   Louis MacNeice.   BoAnP

But we cannot/Buy with gold the old associations!   The Golden Mile-Stone. Henry Wadsworth Longfellow.   PoEL 1-5

But we care not a whit, as we jovial sit/Before our blazing fire.   Old Winter. Thomas Noel.   PoSC

But we'd hasten to the rescue/Of those souls near death's abode.   Could We. *Anonymous.*   STF

But we do. That's the wonder.   J.B. (excerpt).   Archibald MacLeish.   EaLo

But we don't call this cold in Quebec.'   Limerick: "There was a young boy of Quebec."   Rudyard Kipling.   FaBoNo

But we hae meat and we can eat,/For which the Lord be thankit!   Grace. *Anonymous.*   LoGBV

But we have come in tattered penury/Begging at the door of a Master.   A Plea for Mercy.   Kwesi Brew.   PBA

But we have none! but we have none!   Siren Chorus.   George Darley. BIrV; FaBoRV; OxBI; ViBoPo; WSC

But we have only one bed!/Cried the fair young maiden.   Rollicking Bill the Sailor.   *Anonymous.*   AmSS

But we have taken out papers and will become citizens.   Exile.   Chana Bloch.   GP

But we hope in a short time to see you again.   Spanish Ladies.   *Anonymous.* AmSS

But we, Jehovah, His people, are dual/and so undone.   Israel.   Israel Zangwill.   TrJP

But we left him alone with his glory.   The Burial of Sir John Moore after Corunna.   Charles Wolfe.   AnIV; BBV; FaBoRV; FaFP; FaPoR; GN; GoTF; GTBS; GTBS-P; HBV 1-2; HBVY; MaC; MCCG; NOBE; OBEV; OBRV; OBWP; OnYI; OxBI; PaPo; PoRA; RoGo; TreF; WaaP; WBLP; WHA

But we left him alone with the Devil.   The Lay of the Vigilantes. *Anonymous.*   PoOW

But we'll find some action that fits your style./Can you drive?   Unsolicited Letters to Five Artists (parody).   Clive James.   FaBoPa

But we'll leave it to be hackneyed by the fellows in the rear.   The Men Who Come Behind.   Henry Lawson.   NOAV

But we'll ne'ver forget sweet Manchester and the girls we leave/behind. Lancashire Lads.   *Anonymous.*   CoMu

But we'll not sport together on the banks of Salee.   On the Banks of Salee. *Anonymous.*   AmFP

But we'll pull 'em into Bend/If we are both drunk.   Pete Orman. *Anonymous.*   BPAW

But we'll shut the door on him!   Jittery Jim.   William Jay Smith.   BBGG

But we must give our gnu to some zu.   Limerick: "It was a refractory gnu." *Anonymous.*   TDH

But we must hear God's trumpet clear/Sound peace upon His Hill.   The Promised Land.   Jessie E. Sampter.   TrJP

But we must not stare.   Sitting.   Susan Griffin.   NPGG

But we never will be beat by any mortal foe,/boys!/Tullalo, tullalo, tullalo-o-o-o, boys!   The Progress of Sir Jack Brag.   *Anonymous.*   PAH

But we, once dead, no more do see the sun.   Spring Bereaved.   William, of Hawthornden Drummond.   OBEV

But we're all in the old school List.   The Old School List.   James Kenneth Stephen.   CenHV

But we're extensible; we don't leave room. After the Spanish Chroniclers. William Bronk. GP

But we're full inside!' Mr. Ody met a body. Edith Nesbit. CenHV; FaBoNo

But we're going West tomorrow, with our fortune in our hands. Western Wagons. Rosemary and Stephen Vincent Benét. BPAW

But we're slaves, and we're orphans, Eoghan!–why did you/die? Lament for the Death of Eoghan Ruadh O'Neill. Thomas Osborne Davis. AnIv; IrPN; NOBI; OnYI; OxBI

But we remember how they shot/Rory O'Connor. Civil War. Austin Clarke. NOBI

But we/ruminate with our heads. Late Again. Gabriel Zaid. AMV-81

...But we shall prosper yet. Transport. William Meredith. WaP

But we shall sleep in Clyde's water/Like sister an like brither. Clyde's Water. Anonymous. BaBo; OxBB

But we should all be ready/Before our time has come. The Santa Barbara Earthquake. Anonymous. AmFP

But we slide past forlornly/Upon the great sea-flow. Mein Liebchen, Wir Sassen Zusammen. Heinrich Heine. AWP

But we soon again shall meet them in that better land above. The Boys of Sanpete County. Anonymous. AmFP

...But we stay behind, among them,/The injured, the adored. Many Wagons Ago. John Ashbery. HaCAP

But we were not born to survive/Only to live The River of Bees. William Stanley Merwin. HeIP; LCAP

But we/Will read it together The Way to the River. William Stanley Merwin. CoAP; NYBP

But we will spend them on shore with our sweethearts and wives. New Sea Song. Anonymous. OBSS

But we, with rifles poised, kept on our search. The Asylum, II. Hayden Carruth. SM

But wear it and it will not fade. Shot? So Quick, So Clean an Ending? Alfred Edward Housman. PeHV

But wears a floury head, and talks in flow'ry speech! The Irish Schoolmaster (parody). Thomas Hood. BXAP

But wel I wot they lake none othes. On the Times. Anonymous. OxBM

But went on being awfully nice/And took a lot of prizes. Miss Snooks, Poetess. Stevie Smith. PV

But went on into marble that does not weep. Island Quarry. Hart Crane. CrMA; PPP

But were some child of yours alive that time,/You should live twice–in it and in my rhyme. Sonnets, XVII: "Who will believe my verse in time to come." William Shakespeare. DiPo; OBSC

But westward, look, the land is bright. Say Not the Struggle Nought Availeth. Arthur Hugh Clough. ATP; AWP; EaLo; FaBoRV; FaFP; FaPoR; GoTF; GTBS; GTBS-P; HBV 1-2; HBVY; LiTB; LoBV; NOBE; NOBV; OAEL 1-2; OAEP; OBEV; OBNC; OBVV; SoSe; TEP; TreF; TrGrPo; TRV; ViBoPo; VLP; WaaP; WGRP

But, what a waste of rocks/For that "chapel," they called it. Spokane Falls. Phil George. VoR

...But what altho she had sworn,/Sure quondam was I. Quondam Was I in My Lady's Grace. Sir Thomas Wyatt. EnPo; GBL

But what are you going to do in spring? Men Are the Devil. Mary Carolyn Davies. HBMV; YaD

But what befell them I never can tell,/For they never came back again. What Became of Them? Anonymous. OBCA; OxBChV

But what do you do, Polycharmus, I pray,/When a lover's stiff prick stops your bum? To Polycharmus. Martial (Marcus Valerius Martialis). PeHV

But what do you expect me to do? We Didn't Know. Tom Paxton. PPON

But what does it mean? What are we going to do? It's No Use Raising a Shout. W. H. Auden. OBMV

But what does that have to do/with the 78 dead miners/of Mannington, West Virginia? 78 Miners in Mannington, West Virginia. Louis Phillips. TAT

But what gives greater heat than coal on fire? Didyma. Anonymous. UnTE

But what has been, has been, and I have had my hour. Happy the Man. John Dryden. FaPoR

But what he taught me I learnt all by heart. A Dream of Venus. Bion. AWP

But what he will/strain the ocean for and/what he needs. Salt. Lucille Clifton. GP

But what I have, my God, I give to you. My God, You Have Wounded Me with Love. Paul Verlaine. ILwL

But what if he was/completely somebody else? Being Somebody. Edwin Honig. TAP

But what if I heard my first love calling me once more? The Flight. Sara Teasdale. HBMV

But what is better still–we shall be friends. Any Wife or Husband. Carol Haynes. BLPA

But what is your opinion, Mrs. Grundy? An Open Question. Thomas Hood. NBM

But what it means, we cannot call to mind. Apparition. John Erskine. HBMV

But what it ought to be/Has quite escaped my mind! A Chronicle. Anonymous. BLPL; NA

But what makes the city what it is. The Bed. Dennis Saleh. NeAC

But what no force, his reason is no better. Manhood. Sir Thomas More. EnRePo

But what of all the lovers now/Parted by Death,/Grey Death? Spring in War-Time. Sara Teasdale. OHIP

But what of me? And What of Me? Liz Sohappy Bahe. CDW

But–what of me?/And–what of you? Lines Written on November 15, 1933 by a Man Born November 14, 1881... Clayton Hamilton. InMe

But what's the use of telling what everybody knows? Mabel, in New Hampshire. James Thomas Fields. HBV 1-2

But what still deepening clouds of Care survive! Life. George Crabbe. OBEC

But what that I shalle say, nowe herken me. Too Much Sex. Anonymous. MeEL

But what the Devil can be done/With Wit and Beauty too? Song: Wit and Beauty. Robert Gould. CavP

But what the waur am I? Rigid Body Sings. James Clerk Maxwell. FaBoCo; FaBoPa; Par; SpRo

But what torments of grief you endured/From evils which never arrived! Needless Worry. Ralph Waldo Emerson. GoTF; TreFT

But what we have to remember, ma'am,/Is to keep our eye on the moral. It Might Be a Lump of Amber. Walter De la Mare. FaBoNo

But what were you searching for/in such dark places/where I was searching for love. Brother. Richard Shelton. Str

...But what women say to kind/Lovers, we write in rapid streams and wind. Carmina. Caius Valerius Catullus. OBVE

But what you are I do not know. Carnal Knowledge. Gwen Harwood. CBAP

But whate'er smack'd of Noyance, or Unrest,/Was far far off expell'd from this delicous Nest. The Land of Indolence. James (1700-48) Thomson. OBEC

But whaur his hame, or what his/name,/I dinna care to tell. Comin' Thro' the Rye. Robert Burns. ExPo; FaFP; FSW; HBV 1-2; LiTB; LiTL; OxBS; SpRo; TreF; UnTE; WBLP

But whaur's the Minister? Last Lauch. Douglas Young. BSV; FaBoCo; NLV; OxBS; SeCePo

But when a glance is sparkling black/It drives me wild. Epigram: "I like them pale." Strato. PeHV

But when a man's in trouble, it's a long freight-train and ride. The Railroad Blues. Anonymous. AmFP

But when as our short light/Comes once to set, it makes eternal night. A Pastoral of Tasso. Samuel Daniel. OBSC

But when Coleridge began to inquire furthur,/Off they ran! We Saw Three Boys. Dorothy Wordsworth. GLGT

But when could their steeds, so mule-footed and slow,/Compare with the birds of the free Navajo? Song of the Navajo. Albert Pike. PoOW

–But when he laughed, then you could see/He was as young as young could be! Danny Murphy. James Stephens. OnUR; RoGo

But when he's a hundred and a day/He gets a little pipe to play! The Seven Ages of Elf-Hood. Rachel Field. BiCB

But when he sang his song for me, 'twas Darling that I heard. At Bedtime. Mariana Griswold Van Rensselaear. HBMV

But when he saw me stung and cry,/He tooke his wings and away did fly. Four Anacreontic Poems, 1. Edmund Spenser. AAS

But when he stood up, that face/Was lost in a maze of water. The Premonition. Theodore Roethke. CAPP

But, when he thought of publishing,/His face grew stern and sad. Poeta Fit, non Nascitur. Lewis (Charles Lutwidge Dodgson) Carroll. FaBoNo; NBM; OBSV

But when I come that red Rose leaps/To battle for my sake. The Battle. William Henry Davies. BrPo

But when I die, they will find me in the dark/By this jewel's light. Author Unknown. William Montgomerie. OxBS

But when I sleep, Thou sleepest not,/But watchest patiently. The Nearest Friend. Frederic W. Faber. TreFS

But when I tell of city things,/He sniffs and shuts one eye! The Fisherman. Abbie Farwell Brown. EtS

But when I thought myself of herself free,/All's changed, she understands all men but me. Caelica, XXXIX. Fulke, Lord Brooke Greville. FCP

But when I turn'd to make my peace/That one short hour was told. The Apparition. Stephen Phillips. OBEV; OBVV

But when it's gone it's never near. Bounce Buckram. Anonymous. OxNR

But when it's old, it groweth cold/And fades away like morning dew. Waly, Waly. Anonymous. AmFP

But when Myrtilla sleeps till ten,/Aurora steals them back agen. Sweet Slug-a-Bed. Anonymous. FaBoCo

But when our day of judgment comes,/They'll have to share their pretty things.   I Lived in a Town.   *Anonymous.*   TrAS

But when she asks for money, how she stings!   Melissa.   *Anonymous.*   UnTE

But when she died, the Fairy Queen it brought/To Fairy Land, where yet it may be seen, if sought.   The Faerie Queene.   Edmund Spenser.   OBSC

But when she goes I still can hear/The water say, "And do you think?"   Water Noises.   Elizabeth Madox Roberts.   BoNaP

But when she lifted to the moon in heaven/Her face, two moons together I surveyed.   Shame Hitherto.   Al Mutanabbi.   LiTW

But when the crowing syrens blare/I with another ghost am lain.   Shadwell Stair.   Wilfred Owen.   FaBoTw

But when the flesh was gone,/the light was gone too.   The Project.   Gregory Orr.   GeTw

But when the heart's attorney once is mute,/The client breaks, as desperate in his suit.   The Courser and the Jennet.   William Shakespeare.   LoBV

But when the hour came–to his surprise/She sent him from her with remorseful eyes.   The Other One Comes to Her.   Mary Aldis.   HBMV

...But when the state/Plays with death, it really dies.   A Bestiary.   Kenneth Rexroth.   OBAL

But when the trees bow down their heads,/The wind is passing by.   The Wind.   Christina Georgina Rossetti.   BLPL; FaBoBe; OxBChV

But when these eyes encountered Tim's/Mine was the emptier stare.   Why?   Walter De La Mare.   FiBHP

But when they came away/They had all bought age.   Bargain.   Louise Driscoll.   HBMV

But when they fear no brother's face/Truth walks about the market-place.   In the Mood of Blake.   William Soutar.   HaMV

But when they lit the candle, then I/smiled!   Riddle: What Am I?   Dorothy Aldis.   SoPo

But when was that ever a bar,/To any watch they keep?   Neither Out Far Nor In Deep.   Robert Frost.   AmP; AP; CoBMV; CrMA; DiPo; HAP; LiTA; MoAB; MOS; NoAm; NOBA; NoP; TAP; WeW

But when we come where comfort is,/She never will say no.   I Care Not for These Ladies.   Thomas Campion.   AAS; CABA; ErPo; HAP; LiTL; NIP; NoP; OAEP; ViBoPo

But when we do not understand it–/We say it is of no account.   Ifa.   *Anonymous.*   WTO

But when will we love ourselves?   Love Your Enemy.   Yusef Iman.   BPo; TTY

But when you're only halfway up,/You're neither up nor down.   The Noble Duke of York.   *Anonymous.*   FSW

But when your countenance filled up his line,/Then lacked I matter; that enfeebled mine.   Sonnets, LXXXVI: "Was it the proud full sail of his great verse."   William Shakespeare.   InvP; MBW 1-2; OAEL 1-2; OAEP; TEP

But whence no messenger comes back.   A Summer Christmas in Australia.   Douglas Brook Wheelton Sladen.   OBCP

But whenever she goes to the play,/She never sits near to the trumpeter.   The Trumpeter.   *Anonymous.*   CoMu

But where are all the beautiful ships/I knew so long ago?   The Ships of Saint John.   Bliss Carman.   EtS

But where are the Crooks of Yesteryear?   Another Villon-ous Variation.   Don (Donald Robert Marquis) Marquis.   HBMV

But where are the snows of yester-year?   The Ballad of Dead Ladies.   Francois Villon.   AWP; CTC; ExPo; GoBC; HBV 1-2; OBVE

But where art thou?   Still Barred Thy Doors.   Aru Dutt.   ACV

But where God's gone, there's no man knows.   The Hunchback.   John Peale Bishop.   PoA

But where has this Praxiteles been prying?   Spoken by Venus on Seeing Her Statue Done by Praxiteles.   *Anonymous.*   EyDe; FaBoEE

But where in the world did the children vanish?   Ballade of Lost Objects.   Phyllis McGinley.   NLV; PoCh

But where in the world is the path for me/Except the river that runs to the sea!   Norah.   Zoë Akins.   HBV 1-2

But where is County Guy?   County Guy.   Sir Walter Scott.   OBRV

But where is the man that can live without dining?   What We May Live Without.   Owen Meredith.   GoTF; TreF

(But where is what I started for so long ago?/And why is it yet unfound?)   Facing West from California's Shores.   Walt Whitman.   MoAmPo; TAP

But where, oh where, do the failed fathers go?   Failed Fathers.   Lewis Turco.   AMV-81

But where's the bloody horse?   On Some South African Novelists.   Roy Campbell.   AnFE; FaBoCo; FaBoEE; GTBS-P; InPK; MoBrPo; MoVE; NOBL; OxBTC; PoPl

But where's the Queen of Sheba?/Where King Solomon?   Gone.   Walter De la Mare.   GoJo

But where the crime's committed/The crime can be forgot.   Consolation.   William Butler Yeats.   OBSP

But where the Mole all silent glides/Dwells Peace–and Peace is wealth to me.   Shooter's Hill.   Robert Bloomfield.   OBNC

But where to go late at night?/All alone!   Alone.   Itzik Manger.   VWA

But where you passed there is a trail/Of blossoms in my heart.   Where You Passed.   Amelia Josephine Burr.   HBMV

But which are worse, kings ill or easily led,/Schools of this truth are yet not brought a-bed.   Caelica, XXXVI.   Fulke, Lord Brooke Greville.   FCP

But which, bound hand and foot, he, close on night,/Can only see.   Eyes.   Walter De la Mare.   BrPo

But which could any face call good, for calling/Infinity a number does not make it one.   Numbers and Faces (excerpt).   W. H. Auden.   ImOP

But which it only needs that we fulfil.   A Prayer in Spring.   Robert Frost.   MoRP; TrCP; TrPWD; YeAr

But which sense cannot note by note define.   The Face.   Thomas Wade.   ERoP 1-2

But while I live, be true.   Until Death.   Elizabeth Akers.   HBV 1-2

But whiskers on a baby's face,/I never saw before.   Our Goodman (B vers.).   *Anonymous.*   AmFP; ESPB; UnTE; ViBoFo

But who, among the rest,/will deny me/my place.   The Pink Locust.   William Carlos Williams.   PP

"But/who are you!"   Following the Sun.   Jascha Kessler.   AmPC

But who, bar me, hawks in this town/A dead branch and an evil eye?'   The Beggar.   Adrian Mitchell.   FaBoTw

–But who, being human, wishes to be a gull,/Knows nothing much, though birds are beautiful.   The Self Unsatisfied Runs Everywhere.   Delmore Schwartz.   PoA

But who belonging to me will they know/When I am gone.   The Garden by Moonlight.   Amy Lowell.   NMM

But who can ever tell what peairs/O' veet trod vu'st the steairs?   The Stwonen Steps.   William Barnes.   NOBV

But who can guess, or even surmise/The countless things she served with her eyes?   The Serving Girl.   Gladys May Casely Hayford.   CDC; GoSl

But who can tell the sorrow of her heart?   Who Can Tell?   *Anonymous.*   WTO

But who can think without a fear/Of horrors that happen so?   The Apparition.   Herman Melville.   MAmP

But who could have woke them/While you were not near?   Spring.   Isaac Rosenberg.   TrJP

But who for fellow men endured the shame/Shall have eternal glory for his own.   The Glory of Lincoln.   Thomas Curtis Clark.   PGD

But who for the brief moment he has chosen to believe.   The Triangular Field.   Stephen Dobyns.   MAYP

But who, his art in worlds of woe, would prove,/Let him within his heart but cipher love.   Caelica, XXIV.   Fulke, Lord Brooke Greville.   FCP

But who his name and word abuse/Shall feel his wrath and melt away.   Thrice Blest the Man.   John Barnard.   AH

But who is seldom mentioned in the fable.   Fabulary Satire, IV.   Daryl Hine.   NOBC

But who killed the Jews?   Riddle.   William Heyen.   GP; SM

But who knows the name/of the new-born son/Of the beautiful swan?   A Son Just Born.   Mary Britton Miller.   TiPo

But who knows what gay roisterer/before this dawn will pay their fare.   Viaticum.   Ethna MacCarthy.   NeIP

But who shall find a pen fit for thy glory,/Or make posterity believe thy story?/Vive St. George!   Iter Boreale.   Robert Wild.   APAS

But who sits still and holdeth fast the nets.   Pains and Gains.   Edward, Earl of Oxford De Vere.   EIL

But who th' Almightie feare, deride/Pale death, and meete with triumph in the tombe.   What Am I Who Dare.   William Habington.   OxBoCh; TrPWD

But who then is a louse?   Contrast.   Mvula Ya Nangolo.   WhB

But who there weeping sits,/Hath got the Prize.   Silex Scintillans.   Henry Vaughan.   AnAnS 1

But who will help me.   My Mother's Death.   Judith Hemschemeyer.   Str

But who will reap them when our scythes are falling?   Before Olympus.   John Gould Fletcher.   MoAmPo

But whoso reaps the ripened corn/Shall shout in his delight,/While silences vanish away.   Golden Silences.   Christina Georgina Rossetti.   NBM

But why chasterize you an' me?   It Ain't Necessarily So.   Ira Gershwin.   OBAL

But–why did you kick me down stairs?   An Expostulation.   Isaac Bickerstaffe.   FaBoCo; FiBHP; NIP; PV

But why they called that thing a horse,/That's what is Greek to me.   The Hippopotamus.   Oliver Herford.   NA

"But why were all the poets dumb?"   Glasgow Street.   William Montgomerie.   OxBS

But wickedly he dyed.   Giles Corey.   *Anonymous.*   PAH

But wild Ambition loves to slide, not stand,/And Fortune's ice prefers to Virtue's land.   Achitophel: the Earl of Shaftesbury.   John Dryden.   NOBE

...But will death let/Our eyes the longed-for vision see?/We know not yet.   Mors et Vita.   Samuel Waddington.   HBV 1-2

But will start childbearing again/through potash and bromide.   The Dead Sea.   Henryk Grynberg.   VWA

But will they, can they, bear thy darling back?   Epigrams.   Theocritus.   AWP

But win, as once their fathers won,/The laurel wreath of fame. The True Aristocrat. W. Stewart. WBLP

But wind, quixotic in its dance,/Has tried for conquest more than once. Windmill on the Cape. William Vincent Sieller. GoYe

But wine of the best/Shall have no rest,/Good gossipes mine-a... Good Gossips Mine. *Anonymous.* OxBM

But winter lasts forever. The Reach of Silence. Charles Black. AMV-81

But wishing us well,/wishing us a life/in another story. An Overture. Michael Knoll. LFAC

But with a face as towards a friend, and with thin sparkling tears. To the Spirit Great and Good. [(James Henry[) Leigh Hunt. TrPWD

But, with a smile as happy as a child's,/blew out the golden light. Shall Then Another. Kenneth Mackenzie. NOAV

But with blood, pus, horror, death, stepmothers, and lies. The School Globe. James Reaney. NOBC

But with fair spring water/With which we were christened. As Joseph Was A-Walking. *Anonymous.* OHIP; ViBoPo

But with fruit in its hair. The Death of Carmen Miranda. Stephen E. Smith. AMV-81

But with its sorrow on that day/My heart itself was cast away. Lassitude. Mathilde Blind. SBG

But with long use her tears are dry. In Memoriam A.H.H., LXXVIII. Alfred, Lord Tennyson. NAWM 1-2; OAEL 1-2; OAEP

But with my soul had from above/This endless holy fire. A Song to Amoret. Henry Vaughan. HBV 1-2; LiTL; ViBoPo

But with no one to blame. Now I Am a Man. Russell Marano. AMV-80

But, with remembered blessings then/Made every day Thanksgiving Day. Every Day Thanksgiving Day. Harriet Prescott Spofford. OHIP

But with such brightnesse whylest I fill my mind,/I starve my body and mine eyes doe blynd. Amoretti, LXXXVIII. Edmund Spenser. AAS

But with the blue sea and sky there was always benevolent sun. On First Looking into Michael Grant's Cities of Vesuvius. Gavin Ewart. OBTV

But with the next returning spring,/Retire to shades–you'll hear her sing. Lines Occasioned by the Burning of Some Letters. Sarah Dixon. NOEC

But with their false Plots I hope they will end,/At Tyburn where th' Rabble will surely attend. A Ballad upon the Popish Plot. John Gadbury. CoMu

But with this I haven't said much. Conjuration. Agnes Gergely. VWA

But with work, and hope, and the right to call/Upon Him who sees it and knows us all! I Saw a New World. William Brighty ("Matthew Browne") Rands. NBM

But within a stall. The Cherry-Tree Carol, IV. *Anonymous.* AmFP

But without the crow/–of the cock. Cock. Aharon Amir. AMV-81

But, woe is me, I have never a pocket! The Highwayman's Ghost. Richard Garnett. StPo

But, woe is me! though thou now brought the day,/Day shall but serve more sorrow to display. Poems. William, of Hawthornden Drummond. JCP

But woman's work is never done. Man May Work from Sun to Sun. *Anonymous.* SaC

But wood, with a gift for burning Song: "You're wondering if I'm lonely." Adrienne Rich. PBWP

But Wood would not rhyme with gun, but Bun would. John Bun. *Anonymous.* NLV; PoPle; ShM

But words are weak.' A Valediction. Ernest Christopher Dowson. BoLoP

But words like:/Supreme Court/graceful/wise. A Grandfather Poem. William J. Harris. CNA; PoBA

But worse to trust to my own mind/And find the same corruption there. I Am the Only Being Whose Doom. Emily Bronte. MAT; NCEP; TW; VLP

But worst was the silence whose words/stung like whips and remained unspoken. Poem for the Atomic Age. Emanuel Litvinoff. NeBP

But would the sound of your sticks on the floor/Thundered in her skull for evermore! In the Children's Hospital. Hugh" (Christopher Murray Grieve) MacDiarmid. NoP

But would you to the marriage of true minds/Admit impediment? Beauty in Trouble. Robert Graves. NYBP

But wouldst thou know (deere sweet) for all. The Complement. Thomas Carew. CavP

But write reams of the clothes she has on her. Limerick: "'Tis strange how the newspapers honor." Eugene Field. TDH

But wusser yet, the blue-tail fly. The Blue-Tail Fly. *Anonymous.* GBP

But Wyatt said true, the scar doth aye endure. Exhortation to Learn by Others' Trouble. Henry Howard, Earl of Surrey. FaBoEE

But ye shall gae hame a wedded wife with child. Willie's Lyke-Wake. *Anonymous.* BaBo; ESPB

But ye to blame, thus to refuse/My service, and to let me die. Cruel You Be. George Puttenham. EIL

But years shall see the cypress spread,/Immutable as my regret. Beneath the Cypress Shade. Thomas Love Peacock. EnRP; OBRV; OBSP

But yet, alas, the scar shall still remain. Epigram: "Sighs are my food, drink are my tears." Sir Thomas Wyatt. SiPS

But yet amongst those cares which cross my rest,/This comfort grows, I think I love thee best. A Poem Put into My Lady Laiton's Pocket. Sir Walter Ralegh. FCP; SiPS

But yet beware lest burning with desires,/That all thy waters cannot quench thy fires. Sonet XXV. William Alexander, Earl of Stirling. OxBS

But yet more stately were the power and ease/That with a whisper deepen'd all the seas. The Quiet Tide near Ardrossan. Charles Tennyson Turner. FaBoPP

But yet of him I ask no more/Than Pity for my Pain. Song: "Know, Celadon, in vain you use." Ephelia (Joan Philips). CavP

But yet with me still/Shall ever rest my own beloved. Dirge Sung at Death. *Anonymous.* WTO

But yet ye wot not whome I mene. The Lytyll Pretty Nyghtyngale. *Anonymous.* OAEP

But yield to me my darling, Stamford's finest Susan Kitchell. The Best Line Yet. Edward Allen. PoL

But, yielding to the common lot,/Lie unrecorded and forgot. San Francisco from the Sea. Bret (Francis Bret Harte) Harte. BPAW

But "yiet' and "yiet' was endless,/and "thole a little' a long way is. Prayer for Forbearance. *Anonymous.* LoBV

But you and I aren't going to let it rain. Getting Drunk with Daughter. Robert Huff. NePoEA-2

But you and I knew–Oh, too well!–/Life went another way!) At the Comedy. Arthur Stringer. HBV 1-2

But you and I know better...'Tis good-bye to Horn and Hound. Blue Peter. Stanislaus Lynch. OnYI

But you and I remember/Through every starlit night. Song: "I saw the day's white rapture." Charles Hanson Towne. HBV 1-2

But you are dead and gone. Wise. Lizette Woodworth Reese. HBV 1-2

But you are left like memory,/Or hope, in the heart of man. The Pearly Everlasting. Ernest Fewster. CaP

But you/Are the earth I hover over. Release. D. H. Lawrence. CMoP

But you are the quietest fish in the sea. Lament for a Sailor. Paul Dehn. WaP

But you are tir'd, and so am I./Farewel. A Letter from Artemisa... John Wilmot, Earl of Rochester. SeCV 1-2

But you believe nothing, with the evidence lost. Notes on a Life to Be Lived. Robert Penn Warren. NoAm

But you better stay at home with your kind and loving little wife. The Cowboy's Life Is a Very Dreary Life. *Anonymous.* AmFP

But you, broad woak, wi' ribby rind,/Wer here so long as I can mind. The Vield Path. William Barnes. NOBV

But you can often call their blough. One, Two, Three–Gough! Eve Merriam. NTCP

But you can't expect them to wait forever. The Midnight Court. Brian Merriman. BIrV

...But you can't get away from the guns! Screw-Guns. Rudyard Kipling. ViBoPo

But you, Catullus, your destiny's obdurate. Carmina. Caius Valerius Catullus. OBVE

But you'd be a bigger tract of land/If you were thin out-spread. Pike's Peak. *Anonymous.* BPAW

But you'd oughter git a liddle mo' pull in de head. The Turtle's Song. *Anonymous.* BPo

But you do not know/A single one of the mourners. Letter with a Black Border. Sandra McPherson. GeTw

But you–do you hear it, Yankee boys? Treason's Last Device. Edmund Clarence Stedman. PAH

But you feel all warm.../with Christmas coming! December. Aileen Fisher. SiSoSe

But you forget everything. It Was You, Attis. Sappho. PeHV

But you frolic in the meadow, still in clover,/never having had a master ride astride you. The Thracian Filly. Anacreon. LiSp

But you gonna want me some of these mornings/and poor James won't have you T-Bone Steak Blues. Yank (James) Rachel. BluL

But you have gone, old one, into the night–alas. Lament for Apirana Ngata. Arnold Reedy. WTO

But you have to feel for it My Life, the Quality of Which. Etheridge Knight. NNaP

But you haven't made it across and never will. Traffic Lights. Lina Kasdaglis. BoWoP

But you know it never fit me right/at all. Cousin Ella Goes to Town. George Ella Lyon. Str

But you'll come back again/For that good old mountain dew. Mountain Dew. *Anonymous.* FSW

But you'll look sweet/On the seat of a bicycle built for two! Daisy Bell (A Bicycle Built for Two). Harry Dacre. BLSo; FSN; GoTF; TreF

But you'll ne'er stop a lover–/He will find out his way. The Great Adventurer. *Anonymous.* FaFP; GTBS; GTBS-P

...But you'll never want/to eat with it again. Poem: "In the stump of the old tree." Hugh Sykes Davies. EAS

But you'll wait years maybe/for the next doomed expedition. Climbing You. Erica Jong. PoA

But you'll walk like a man! Do You Fear the Wind? Hamlin Garland. AA; GoTF; HBV 1-2; HBVY; MCCG; PoPl; TreFT; YaD

But you man, man,/the way you spoze to be. Compozishun–To James Herndon and Others. Ronald J. Goba. NCSH

But you must die, and you know why,/By Honeyman's N.P.C.' James Honeyman. W. H. Auden. MoBS

But you must die/As well as I. The Changes to Corinna. Robert Herrick. JCP

But you must pay the gage of promist weal. Arcadia. Sir Philip Sidney. SiPS

But you must smell them. On Apples. David Ross. NYBP

But you're my cup of tea. The Soldier Loves His Rifle. W. H. Auden. TEP

But you're rude when you get in the whey! The Embarrassing Episode of Little Miss Muffet. Guy Wetmore Carryl. OBCA; OnMSP; StPo

But you're the one for me Phoebe in a Rosebush. Clyde Watson. NTCP

...But you remain/with your Jewishness. Crossing. Anthony Barnett. VWA

But you shall not tell the gray from the gold/Or the stone from the shining hair. Not Three–But One. Esther Lilian Duff. HBMV

But you shall see gray beards in a long row,/Upon the rustic roads where I now go. His Statement of the Case. James Herbert Morse. AA

But you still have to wait Waitress. Michael Brownstein. ANYP

But you the cash must instant pay,/Or else Dorinda will not play. To an Artful Theatre Manager. Lorenzo Da Ponte. TrJP

But you've something behind, neatly shaven and shorn,/That's scarcely a mistress's toy. To Labienus. Martial (Marcus Valerius Martialis). PeHV

But you want to watch out where it goes. Limerick: "Now.the sneeze is a joy-vent, I s'pose." Anthony Euwer. HBMV

But you were always ambitious. They Eat Out. Margaret Atwood. NoP

But you were blind, and slept, and did not know. Rachel. Ruth Gilbert. AnNZ

But You–were crowned in June– Ourselves were wed one summer–dear. Emily Dickinson. PeHV

But you will die to-day. Her Strong Enchantments Failing. Alfred Edward Housman. CBEP; FaBoTw; MAT; NOBE; NOBV; OAEL 1-2

But you will have to go and knock at the House of the Dead. Elephants May Parade Before Your House. Anonymous. WTO

But you will last very long. Calamus. Walt Whitman. AP

But you will not ask me to go. Faith. Lorenzo Thomas. APU

But you ye untold latencies will thrill to every page. Shut Not Your Doors. Walt Whitman. NOBA; OxBA

But you yourself would be to blame. The Boy and the Wolf. John Hookham Frere. HBV 1-2; HBVY

But young Hind Horn he took her to bed. Hind Horn (A vers.). Anonymous. ATP; BaBo; ESPB; ViBoFo

But, young man, shove me down as a milliner.' Taking the Census. Charles R. Thatcher. NOAV

But young men think it is, and we were young. Epitaph: "Here dead lie we because we did not choose." Alfred Edward Housman. FaBoEE

But your daddie's a-rockin'/Upon the saut sea. Can Ye Sew Cushions? Anonymous. FaBoCh; LoGBV

But your damn'd poet lives and writes agen. On Poets. Alexander Pope. FaBoEE

But your gown to wrap about our heads,/And my coat around our feet. The Coolun. Maurice O'Dugan. AnIV; OnYI; OxBI

...But your many busts will/always have a place in my Hall of Fame. Jeep. Charles Stetler. GP

But your thoughts are all guileful and gloomy! Andrew Magrath's Reply to John O'Tuomy. Andrew Magrath. OnYI

But youth's brief agony can glaze/Into a posthumous joy. The Chrysanthemum Show. C. Day-Lewis. MoVE

...But zoo tricks are cut/And make everybody laugh. A Bestiary. Kenneth Rexroth. OBAL

The butcher-bird sings, sings, sings. Recruiting Drive. Charles Causley. NePoEA; OxBTC; PPON; PrIm

...A butcher with hands frightfully red/with the blood of their civilization. Put Down. Leon Damas. TTY

...Butchered out of their/own bodies good to eat a thousand years. Howl, I. Allen Ginsberg. NeAP

(The Butler gone) the keys are left behind. In Obitum Promi. Henry Parrot. FaBoCo

Butterflies, away! Corn-Grinding Song. Anonymous. AWP; SUS

The butterfly clicks its heels/in time to a much higher music. The Hoofer. A. K. Redwing. VoR

A butterfly goes. Up the Barley Rows. Sora. SoPo

A butterfly whose bite can kill a man. The Devil-Dancers. William Plomer. PeSA

Button your lip. Monarch of the Sea. George Starbuck. OBAL

Buttons, a farthing a pair. Buy Any Buttons? Anonymous. OxNR

Buttons his coat against the wind When the spent day begins to frail. Edward Estlin Cummings. ErPo

Buy hyacinths to feed thy soul. Hyacinths to Feed Thy Soul. Muslih-ud-Din Sa'di. BLPA; BLPL; FaBoBe; TRV

Buy Lads, or else your Lasses cry: Come buy. The Pedlar's Song. William Shakespeare. CH

–Buy my cherries, whiteheart, blackheart, golden girls, O/buy! For Exmoor. Jean Ingelow. OBEV; OBVV

–Buy oranges! The Marketwoman. Agostinho Neto. WhB

"Buy some sandwiches. You guys saved my life." Mission Tire Factory, 1969. Gary Soto. NPAW; NPGG

Buy what you need–and never pay. Covet. Ambrose Bierce. DBV

...Buy whatever hunger/looks good on the stand. Museum of Cruel Days. Richard Hugo. NPAW

Buy your ticket at the station on the Rock Island Line. The Rock Island Line. Anonymous. AmFP; FSW

Buzz with prayer/in the forsaken silences Locusts of Silence. Seymour Mayne. VWA

The buzzard circles like a clock. Holding the Mirror up to Nature. Howard Nemerov. PoA

Buzzards ride their back. Jackson State Prison. Leon Baker. LFAC

Buzzing about, now to, now from,/All the constellations in God's kingDOM. Gemini Jones. Willard R. Espy. FaBoUs

Bwagamoyo–lay down your heart here on the coast of your/homeland. Bwagamoyo. Lebert Bethune. PoBA

By a churl of a squirl named Earl. The Squirrel. Ogden Nash. CenHV

By a more desperate adaptation. Rain in the Southwest. Reeve Spencer Kelley. AmFN

By a shrill/piping of plenty. To Waken an Old Lady. William Carlos Williams. HAP; InPK; InPo; NoP; QFR

By a soundless crystal/of cocaine Lacrimas; or, There Is a Need to Scream. K. Curtis Lyle. PoBA

By a thousand, thousand things! The Heart's Proof. James Buckham. BLRP; WBLP

By a way Love knows. Love's Resurrection Day. Louisa May Alcott. AA; HBV 1-2

By all means let us appease the terse gods. Of Commerce and Society. Geoffrey Hill. PPoe

By all means play Lucretia by day. But I need a Lais at night. From the Epigrams of Martial. James Michie. FaBoEE

By all our roots connected/with the deepest wells/of the world. In Vistas of Stone. Abo Stoltzenberg. VWA

By all that he has been and yet must be. O Thou Immortal Deity. Percy Bysshe Shelley. TrPWD

By all those migrations/of thousands and thousands of birds. The Crossing. Paul Blackburn. NYBP

By all Thy woes, by all Thy joys, Lord Jesus grant them peace. Oh, Give Us Back the Days of Old. John Mason Neale. NOCV

By an inner love, as if it had no part/In what I say: it is his praise I sing. As when Some Hungry Fledgling Hears and Sees. Vittoria da Colonna. BoWoP

By and by we shall meet on that beautiful shore. Sweet By and By. S. Fillmore Bennett. PSoN

By any pledge of any God or man. Memorial Sonnet. Marjorie Meeker. AnAmPo

By applying the book/As well as applying the text. Double Duty. W. E. Farbstein. PoPl

By at the gallop he goes, and then/By he comes back at the gallop again. Windy Nights. Robert Louis Stevenson. GoJo; OxBChV; PH; PoRA; SiSoSe; TiPo

By bed and board stands Duty/To snatch my dreams from me! The Forbidden Lure. Fannie Stearns Davis. HBV 1-2

By being planted too close to our parents. Dilemma. David Ignatow. VGW

By being so frank of her/hye nonny nonny noe. Hye Nonny Nonny Noe. Anonymous. FaBoCo; NOBL

...By bestowing it on the/most UNWORTHY of ALL MORTALS. Colonel Chartres. John Arbuthnot. OBSV

By bridge or log, he'll always feel its beat/Against his body, even in his dreams. Crossing a Creek. Herbert Clark Johnson. PoNe

By bringing a prettier one here. Hog Drovers. Anonymous. AmFP

By broken fence is proved a common field. Caelica, XXXVIII. Fulke, Lord Brooke Greville. EnRePo; FCP

By bums venereal, ruefully discharged/By Ward's mysterious drop or magic pill. To the Revd. Mr.— on His Drinking Sea Water. John Winstanley. NOEC

By chance, he on his road and I on mine? The Killing. Edwin Muir. ACV; ChMP; MoRP; PoPl

By Chreist and St. Patrick, the nation's our own! Lilliburlero (A New Song). Thomas, Marquess of Wharton. APAS

By sea and sky! she shall be mine,/The bonnie lass amang the heather.   Owre the Muir amang the Heather.   Jean Glover.   HBV 1-2

"By Shakespeare.' And walked away.   Sasha and the Poet.   Jean Valentine.   VGW

By silver reeds in a silver stream.   Silver.   Walter De La Mare.   AnEnPo; BoNaP; BrR; GoTF; GTBS; MoAB; MoBrPo; PoPl; SiSoSe; SUS; TiPo; TreF

By simply looking at a heron crossing a stream.   The China Policy.   Carl Rakosi.   FAZ

By simply looking toward the light.   Transformed.   D. Weston Gates.   STF

By slant and twist, which way the wind hath blown?   On Seeing Weather-Beaten Trees.   Adelaide Crapsey.   MCCG

By some farm-yard gate, perhaps,/That led back from nature into history. MacDuff.   Charles Tomlinson.   NAs; OxBC

By starlight and by candle-light and dreamlight/She comes to me.   She Comes Not When Noon Is on the Roses.   Herbert Trench.   HBMV; OBEV; OBVV

By stirring suddenly, by bringing/Back the broad echoes of those beating wings.   The Visitation.   Elizabeth Jennings.   MoBS

By strict necessity, along the path/Of order and of good.'   The Excursion. William Wordsworth.   EnRP

By strict observance of this rule, keep good accounts/you may.   How to Keep Accounts.   Anonymous.   FaBoUs

...By/Summerhill, I have a lust/for words in my mouth.   Beast Enough. Robert Billings.   AMV-81

By sweet fount or murmuring shore,/Never more!   Fairy Song.   Felicia Dorothea Hemans.   HBVY

By tapping it gently/with a stick.   Braille.   Gerald Costanzo.   AMV-81

By terms of grief which her example holds, and pardons.   Elegy Against a Latter Day.   Kendrick Smithyman.   AnNZ

By that bed's side there stands a stone,/"Corpus Christi" writ thereon.   He Bare Him Up, He Bare Him Down.   Anonymous.   MeEV

By that which is and never could be me.   Reflections.   Merle Molofsky. AMV-81

By the all-immanent Will.   The Unborn.   Thomas Hardy.   CMoP

By the Assention of thy Lawn, see All.   To Dianeme.   Robert Herrick. AnAnS 2; CaPo; PoL

By the awful breath of God.   The Children of Stare.   Walter De la Mare. BrPo

By the beautiful hands of Sleep.   Hushed by the Hands of Sleep.   Angelina Weld Grimke.   CDC

By the benignant touch of love and beauty.   The Dungeon.   Samuel Taylor Coleridge.   MCCG

By the bivouac's fitful flame.   Drum-Taps.   Walt Whitman.   AP

By the bonnie green woods of Killeevy.   Sir Turlough; or, The Churchyard Bride.   William Carleton.   IrPN

By the bonny milldams of Binnorie.   The Cruel Sister.   Anonymous.   OxBB

By the bright strange light of a star!   The Barn.   Elizabeth Jane Coatsworth. AnNE; ChBR; OBCP; SoPo

By the brook where we two were not side by side...   The Parting.   Sappho. LiTW

By the celebrant above, they are raised, Valor's breath.   On the Lacedaemonian Dead at Plataea.   Simonides (of Ceos).   WaaP

By the curve of the nude mouth or the laugh up the sleeve.   O Make Me a Mask.   Dylan Thomas.   PoA

By the dark music/Blown from Sleep's trumpet.   Louse Hunting.   Isaac Rosenberg.   EBEV; NoP; OxBTC

By the dear dust it roofs, I too shall rest.   Sonnets, XI: "Ye two fair trees that I so long have known."   Thomas Caulfield Irwin.   IrPN

By the favor of God we might know as much–as our/father Adam knew. The Conundrum of the Workshops.   Rudyard Kipling.   HBV 1-2; MoBrPo

By the feat he performed on the banks of Champlain.   The Banks of Champlain.   Anonymous.   AmFP

By the hearth a holier Lar!   Celia's Home-Coming.   Agnes Mary Frances (Mme Emile Duclaux) Robinson.   OBEV; OBVV

By the injustice of the skies for punish-/ment?   The Cold Heaven.   William Butler Yeats.   AWP; CTC; GTBS-P; HAP; InPo; MoVE; NAMP; NoAm; OAEL 1-2; OAEP; OBSP; TEP; WeW

By the lemonade springs where the bluebird sings,/In the Big Rock Candy Mountain.   The Big Rock Candy Mountain.   Anonymous.   AmFP; FSW; GBP; MaC; NOBA; OBAL; TreFT

By the living God, we'll try the game again!   Tomorrow.   John Masefield. MoBrPo; TrGrPo

By the loud surf of Los Muertos which is beating in my ears.   Spanish Waters.   John Masefield.   BeLS; FaBoBe; MCCG; OnMSP

By the lovely, sweet banks of the roses.   Banks of the Roses.   Anonymous. FSW

By the manly love of classics   A Classic Waits for Me.   E. B. White. BXAP; InPK; NYBP; Par; SpRo

By the mystery and the function of his denying.   The Scientist.   Janet Burroway.   SoSe

By the noise of the wind!   Although It Is Not Plainly Visible to the Eye. Fujiwara-No- Toshiyuki.   AWP

By the pale marge of Acheron,/Beyond the scope of any sun.   Villanelle of Acheron.   Ernest Christopher Dowson.   VLP

By the poor Courtier of the King's, and the King's poor Courtier.   The Old and the New Courtier.   Anonymous.   CoMu

By the rifle, the good rifle!/In our hands it is no trifle!   The Rifleman's Song at Bennington.   Anonymous.   PAH

By the river running down/Sings Harry.   I Remember.   Denis Glover. AnNZ

By the same token,/Sustenance is.   Song from the Gulf.   Rolfe Humphries. MoLP

By the same wonder wounded be.   Prayer of the Maidens to Mary.   Rainer Maria Rilke.   AWP

By the sea's side hear the dark-vowelled birds.   Especially When the October Wind.   Dylan Thomas.   CABA; DiPo; LiTB; MoAB; MoBrPo; NeBP; OAEP; OxBTC

By the sea-shore, whereon she loved to dwell.   Don Juan.   George Gordon, Lord Byron.   EnLit

By the side of the Black Jack boy.   Black Jack Davy.   Anonymous. OuSiCo

By the silver of the stars.   Elements of Grammar.   Calvin C. Hernton. NBP

By the sins of their fathers scarred.   The Price He Paid.   Ella Wheeler Wilcox.   WBLP

By the so deviate sensual delight he has enjoyed.   On the Street. Constantine P. Cavafy.   BoLoP

By the song of the crickets there./(...)   Urn I: Silent for Twenty-Five Years, The Father of My Mother Advises..   Walter Lew.   BrSi

By the Strife that moves the stars.   The Breath of Night.   Randall Jarrell. CrMA

By the strong pulling of her bladed mind/Through that ever-reluctant element. On Portents.   Robert Graves.   FaBoMo

By the taste of honey I knew it was he.   Song: "The bee-keeper kissed me." Anonymous.   BoWoP

By the throned gods, tall, golden-coloured, joyful, young.   The City.   George William Russell.   WGRP

By the time we reach the shore, it seems as though the/Fifth Month were Autumn.   The Excursion.   Tu Fu.   AWP; SD

By the torn waters.   Doctor Faustus.   Geoffrey Hill.   NMP

By the touch of the Master's hand.   The Touch of the Master's Hand. Myra Brooks Welch.   BLPA; PoToHe; STF; TRV

By the way Baby, what day do you shop?   Canteen Pimpin'.   Yasmeen Jamal.   LFAC

By the wayside, on a mossy stone.   Old.   Ralph Hoyt   AA

By the Wind that walks the Night/I am baptized into sight.   Dithyramb in Retrospect.   Peter Hopegood.   BoAV; PoAu 1-2

By thee I please, by thee I live.   The Gift of Song.   Horace.   LiTW

By their decree he soon transformed was/Into a patient burden-bearing Ass. A Gulling Sonnet.   Sir John Davies.   ElL

By their rebellion, from the Books of Life.   Paradise Lost.   John Milton. FiP

By then, everyone would be looking.   Overcoats.   Larry Kramer.   AMV-80

By these aboding mountains, this lovely glen.   Invocation.   Valentin Iremonger.   BIrV

By this example you may see/That when I sleep I may not wake.   Lord, How Shall I Me Complain.   Anonymous.   CBEP

By this good wicked spirit, sweet angel devil.   An Evil Spirit, Your Beauty Haunts Me Still.   Michael Drayton.   GBL

By this hand, the third day of August . '55/from the ARSIA/in a timeless sea . The Letter.   Paul Blackburn.   CoPo

By this one Scotchman, pacing in the Square.   Caledonia.   Anthony Powell. NOBL

By this small dark spot/Without which it were not.   The Clouds That Are So Light.   Edward ("Edward Eastaway") Thomas.   FaBoTw

By this time he has tested his first plough,/And studied his last chapter of St. John.   Bishop Blougram's Apology.   Robert Browning.   FaBV; OBNC; PoEL 1-5; TRV; VLP

By this white, awful Mystery,/Haggard and dead.   The Dead Moon. Danske Dandridge.   AA

By this you see/I have children three/Depend on me.   Tax Return. Anonymous.   FaBoUs

By those true tears y'are weeping.   To a Gentleman Objecting to Him His Grey Hairs.   Robert Herrick.   CaPo; JCP; MyFE

By three days' loss eternally to save.   Qui Perdiderit Animam Suam. Richard Crashaw.   ACP

By three or four men before so.   The Shepherd and the Milkmaid. Anonymous.   UnTE

By thunders of white silence, overthrown.   Hiram Powers' "Greek Slave." Elizabeth Barrett Browning.   SBG; VLP

By thy damned snake, which does about thee crawl/In reach of my bliss, to beget my fall.   To a Fine Young Woman.   William Wycherley.   TW

By thy dear Son are we all saved–/Gramercy, lady free. The Annunciation. Margaret Devereaux Conway. ISi

"By Thy Grace, we will." Hold the Fort. Philip Bliss. FSW

By thy wild and stormy steep,/Elsinore! The Battle of the Baltic. Thomas Campbell. FaPoR; OBEV

By traytrous gyft that poysoned shyrt receaved of his wyfe. Medea. Seneca (Lucius Annaeus Seneca). OBVE

By turf embers she gives tongue/When the choirs are silenced in wood and stone. Wolfhound. Richard Murphy. NOBI

By unnumbered ways of dream to death. Immortality. George William Russell. AnIV; AWP; OBMV

By violent mouldings through the tunnelled ways/Of all he would regain. Christ in the Clay-Pit. Jack R. Clemo. EBCP; GTBS-P

By virtue of divine intelligence! Love. Ben Jonson. UnTE

By virtue of the invocation "There is no God but/Allah and Muhammad is His Prophet." Love Charm. *Anonymous.* WTO

By vows you're mine, by love is yours/A heart that cannot wander. Song: "At setting day and rising morn." Allan Ramsay. HBV 1-2

By way of souvenir? They Part. Dorothy Parker. ALV

By what grand eye were these images summoned there? Mise en Scene. Robert Fitzgerald. NYBP; VGW

...By what means he shall achieve/Mankind's deliverance. Paradise Lost. John Milton. FaBoPV

By what remains each cycle's year is seen. To Find the Golden Number, Cycle of the Sun, and Roman Indiction. *Anonymous.* FaBoUs

By which alone the mortal heart is led/Unto the thinking of the thought divine. Faith. George Santayana. WGRP

By which each of us moves/toward the other/in a series of subtractions. Bar Harbor. Marita Garin. AMV-81

By which he meant my grandmama,/find out about it. Shooting Crows. David Huddle. GOYP

"By which she yet must raise herselfe againe,/Ere she can judge all other knowledge vaine." Of Human Learning. Fulke, Lord Brooke Greville. OBS

By which the spirit gains. An Art of Poetry. James Philip McAuley. ACV; NOCV

By which thou shalt be judged, are written down. Earth. William Cullen Bryant. AmePo; AP

By which, when all consumes, your fame shall live. To the Lady Lucy, Countess of Bedford. Samuel Daniel. OBSC

By whistling the only tune he knows:–/"Yankee Doodle!" Barnyard Melodies. Fred Emerson Brooks. OBAL

By whom hell may be felt or death assail! My love is like unto th' eternal fire. Sir Thomas Wyatt. FCP

By whome I hope to ryse againe from death and earthly dust./Haud ictus sapio Gascoygnes Good Night. George Gascoigne. AAS

By whose descent among us/The worlds are reconciled. A Christmas Hymn. Richard Wilbur. CoPo; MoRP; OBCP; OFD; PCh; TrCP

By whose indifferent consent they rule. On the Eve of the Plebiscite. Kenneth Rexroth. NNaP

By whose light my soul will gladly/Wing her passage to the skies. Only Waiting. Frances Laughton Mace. BLPA

By wisdom learned since we were dead. Helen. Susan (Sarah Chauncey Woolsey) Coolidge. AA

By your ever-dying poet/Who remains/Your humble servant. To My Children Unknown, Produced by Artificial Insemination. James Kirkup. NAs

By your own jewels set on fire. To His Mistresses. Robert Herrick. CaPo

–By your roomy skull where most men might well spend/Longer than you did in Arabia, friend! Stony Limits. Hugh" (Christopher Murray Grieve) MacDiarmid. CABL

By your silence and acceptance of sorrow/as the bread itself. Threnody. David Ignatow. FAZ

By your will bind the laurel./My hair, Delphic laurel. Odes. Horace. CTC

Bygone canon, bygone spleen. Orange March. Richard Murphy. NOBI

C

C'est li mo'oule, c'est li ma pren. Aurore Pradere. *Anonymous.* ABF

The C Major of this life: so, now I will/try to sleep. Abt Vogler. Robert Browning. CoBE; DiPo; GoTL; HBV 1-2; MBW 1-2; OAEL 1-2; OAEP; VLP; WGRP

C'mon down from yo / wite / highs/and live. A Chant for Young / Brothas & Sistuhs. Sonia Sanchez. BPo

The C# moon strikes/a chord across/the sunset clef, and all/is music, music. Riding with the Fireworks. Ann Darr. AmC

Ca, c'est l'acacia. Part of a Letter. Richard Wilbur. CMoP

...Ca/n/is/ell drunk if i/be pencils A He as O. Edward Estlin Cummings. InPS; PAI

Ca' them where the burnie rows/My bonnie dearie. Hark! the Mavis. Robert Burns. OBEV

Cabbage and bones, said she. Cabbage/and bones. The Ballad of Ballymote. Tess Gallagher. GP

The cabin is a bed and desk–a shroud/Of moth wings on the screen, starving for light. Arriving. Daniel Halpern. HoPM

A cabin rich in all that's fair–/It's quare. Quantity and Quality. Winifred M. Letts. HBMV

Cable her care of casino TIME TERROR GONE/STOP SEAWARD DREAM GREAT STOP (actually, a lie) Circus Nerves and Worries. Kenward Elmslie. ANYP

CABOOSE! Crossing. Philip Booth. AmFN

Cadets must envy every elder brother,/The little poet must the great. To Poets. Walter Savage Landor. ViBoPo

Caelica, you say you love me, but you fear,/Then hide me in your heart, and keep me there. Caelica, LXV. Fulke, Lord Brooke Greville. FCP

Caesar, shivering,/Heard repeat/Spades on the hillside,/Sentries' feet. Caesar Remembers. William Kean Seymour. HBMV

Caged in his stone-ribbed side. Sunk Lyonesse. Walter De La Mare. CoBMV; FaBoCh; LiTM

Cain son of man/tell him that i Scrawled in Pencil in a Sealed Railway Car. Dan Pagis. VWA

Cain't yoh pahson stand it foh you,/You got to stand it foh yohself. You Got to Cross It Foh Yohself (with music). *Anonymous.* AS

A Cain without a country, a Judas at the board! The League of Nations. Mary Siegrist. MC; PAH

...A calabash/intact, for drawing water;/in pieces, bridges for my guitar. Song of a Common Lover. Flavien Ranaivo. TTY

Calendars tear, and their clothes blow. O yes! Nuns in the Wind. Muriel Rukeyser. NNaP

Calenus, you'll die of starvation. Sealed Bags of Ducats. Martial (Marcus Valerius Martialis). LiTW

The calf has gone to a stranger's land. The Bride's Farewell: Two Songs. *Anonymous.* WTO

California. I have never been there. This Song Shows Me Pictures: Morningside Drive, New York City... Richard Oyama. BrSi

Call all the elves of June together. Harebells in June. Annette Wynne. SUS

Call and I follow, I follow! Let me die. The Song of Love and Death. Alfred, Lord Tennyson. OBNC

The call boy rudely raps. Mask. Elizabeth Cox. GoYe

Call each and all! Call us! And then call her! The Night Court. Ruth Comfort Mitchell. HBV 1-2

Call for more pens, more paper, and more ink. Cacoethes Scribendi. Oliver Wendell Holmes. AA; NLV

...The call for/water. Sestina with Refrain. Thomas W. Shapcott. CBAP

Call her the/laughing one. Sarah. Edna Aphek. VWA

Call him brother,/semblance, prey. Tracking Rabbits: Night. Jim Barnes. CDW

Call him high Shelley now and praise his wake. A Man Whom Men Deplore. Alfred Kreymborg. HBMV

Call it autumn. This Fall. Jody Aliesan. AMV-81

Call it Peace? Peace. D. H. Lawrence. FaBoPP

Call me: Child, come here,/come this way. Like an Elephant. Mahadevi (Mahadeviyakka). PRWP

Call me when you get up. Another Coast. David Wojahn. MAYP

Call my spirit to the fields above. Song of Fionnuala. Thomas Moore. AnIL; BIrV; OnYI

Call not that mirror me, for I have slipped/Your grasp, I have eluded. The Flame. Ezra Pound. AnFE

Call on my name and it shall never fail. Akhnaton. Thomas S. Jones, Jr. AnAmPo

The call that I heard and made words to/early this morning. No One Cares Less Than I. Edward ("Edward Eastaway") Thomas. MoVE

Call that I love on the deep yellow/Between me and the Spring? To a School-Girl. Shaw Neilson. PoAu 1-2

Call the cows home! Thunder. Walter De la Mare. BoNaP

Call the most wretched of us: my brother,/My brother-abcess! St. Francis of Assisi and the Miserable Jews. Jozef Wittlin. VWA

...Call the soldiers back. Kent State, May 4, 1970. Paul Goodman. MAT

Call the tired Love back! O sweet is love, and sweet is lack! Francis Thompson. EG

Call upon him; He is near. Brother, Hast Thou Wandered Far. James Freeman Clarke. AH

Call us to shelter, hearth, and fireside chair. Winter Nights. Lora Dunetz. AMV-80

Call your hounds up, lady. Moon Rock. E. Louise Mally. PoL

Called Earth Over Luna Lagoon. Limerick: "By rocket, to visit the moon." Al Graham. QQQ

Called him Loon-Heart, Mahn-go-taysee! The Song of Hiawatha. Henry Wadsworth Longfellow. AnNE

Called out by the clap of the thunder. The Hag. Robert Herrick. CaPo; EnL; FaBoCh; LoGBV; PoSC; WiR; WSC

Called them "Hiawatha's Brothers." The Song of Hiawatha. Henry Wadsworth Longfellow. TiPo; WBLP

Calling all black people, come in, black people, come/on in. SOS. LeRoi (Imamu Amiri Baraka) Jones. BPo; CNA; PoBA

Calling all life/to Come! Come!/Come! Drum. Langston Hughes. MoAmPo

Calling down the many birds/to brutalize the air. Graveside. Don Domanski. CaPN

Calling down to their helpless trees The Stone Garden. Richard Shelton. NPAW

...Calling for a thesaurus/to explain sex in all its musical failure. Letter to Kafka. Maura Stanton. AmPA

Calling from the open door,/With her soft voice, o'er and o'er,/Robin's come! Robin's Come! William Warner Caldwell. HBVY

Calling home the museums. Calling Home the Scientists. Wendy Rose. AMV-81

Calling me from sleep after decades. My Young Mother. Jane Cooper. FaBoWP

Calling me home! The Last Fairy. Rosamund Marriott Watson. OBVV

Calling on all. A Robin. Walter De la Mare. CMoP; FaBoRV; PB

Calling the Chippewa in The Ice-Fishing House: Long Lake, Minnesota. Michael S. Harper. TAT

Calling to you, ye swinging spears of the larkspur. The New God. James Oppenheim. WGRP

Calling with voices of young birds/to its wheat. The Chaff. William Stanley Merwin. PPP

Calling you home Calumet Early Evening. Annette Arkeketa West. TWSS

The callow and the sallow and the fallow wiped off/the page! Memoirs of a Turcoman Diplomat. Denis Devlin. IPY; NOBI

Calls himself poor, that we may call him rich. Epigrams in Distich, III: The Purse-Proud. Anonymous. FaBoEE

Calls home its own/and the children enter. Spirit-Like before Light. Arthur Gregor. VWA

Calls, mocking, up the stair. Mima. Walter De la Mare. BiCB; BrPo

Call▸ through the valleys of Hall. Song of the Chattahoochee. Sidney Lanier. AA; AmFN; AP; BoNaP; DiPo; FaBoBe; FaBV; HBV 1-2; LaNeLa; LiTA; MCCG; NePA; OHFP; TreF; YaD

The calm and serious face. The speaking eyes. In Memory. Katha Pollitt. MAYP

Calm and unmoved as in battle he sat,/The gray-bearded man in the black slouched/hat. Lee to the Rear. John Randolph Thompson. MC; PAH

A calm breath, a silent breath, a slow breath breathes outward from/the nostrils. Thus Crosslegged on Round Pillow Sat in Space. Allen Ginsberg. NNaP

Calm, calm me more! nor let me die/Before I have begun to live. Lines Written in Kensington Gardens. Matthew Arnold. EnLi 1-2; FaBoPP; NIP; TrPWD

Calm hair, meandering in pellucid gold. On Seeing a Hair of Lucretia Borgia. Walter Savage Landor. AnFE; CABA; HAP; InPK; OAEP

The calm petals around the stem:/God! Sodom's Sister City. Yehuda Amichai. VWA

Calm thou may'st smile, whilst all around thee weep. Epigram: "On parent knees, a naked new-born child." Sir William Jones. OBEV; PoPl

Calmed, as that gray church tower/Checks the wild pigeons taking them to breast. Letter Across Doubt and Distance. M. Carl Holman. AmNP; PoNe

The calmer sea, that bring/all other dreams to me. Nightmares. Siv Cedering Fox. WSC

The calmest degree that you know is superlative? A Fable for Critics. James Russell Lowell. AmePo

Calmness within the wind, the warmth in cold. Winter Encounters. Charles Tomlinson. LiTM

Calvary, Calvary, Calvary,/Sho'ly He died on Calvary. Calvary. Anonymous. AH; BoAN 1-2

Calvary's cross a suffering Christ adorns. Motherhood. William L. Stidger. PGD

Came Christ, the Swordless, on an ass! The Conquerors. Harry Kemp. AnAmPo; HBV 1-2

Came clitter-clatter down the stairs/And galloped away. The Huntsmen. Walter De la Mare. CenHV; DuDa; HBMV; PH; SiSoSe; TiPo

Came fresh transfigurings of freshest blue. Sea Surface Full of Clouds. Wallace Stevens. AP; CMoP; CoBMV; MoAB; MoAmPo; MOS; VGW

Came love, and parting, birth and death,/And all that women know. Farm Wife. John Hanlon Mitchell. CaP

Came on at Winter's sober pace/(O careless lover!) Affaire d'Amour. Margaret Deland. HBV 1-2

Came proudly down the steps to greet/The happy Crocodile! Crocodile. William Jay Smith. OBCA

Came riding on a nanny goat, selling of pigstails. Shon a Morgan. Anonymous. GBP

...Came the classical murmurous movement of a hundred herds. On the Appeal From the Race of Sheba: II. Leopold Sedar Senghor. TTY

Came the climax, "How's your parents?" Conversational. Anonymous. ALV; FiBHP

Came to bless the earth that day,/Long ago on Christmas. The First Christmas. Emilie Poulsson. OHIP

Came to my side, and put down his head in love. The Dream. Louise Bogan. MoAB

Came to us easily,/Came to us then. For M–. Bruce Williamson. NeIP

Camel-slaughterer/rebel's refuge/healer of broken bones. Elegy for Her Brother, Sakhr. Khansa. WPOW

The camera may/do justice to laughter, but must/degrade sorrow. I Am Not a Camera. W. H. Auden. EyDe

The camera photographs the cameraman. On a Photo of Sgt. Ciardi a Year Later. John Ciardi. MiAP

The Campbells are comin',/O-ho, O-ho! The Campbells Are Comin'. Anonymous. FSW

The campfire, flaring to a star,/Fans the wind where hunters are. Indian Song. Willard Johnson. BPAW

Camping with quick hands. What It Means, Living in the City. William Dickey. PoL

Can all the world's bliss/Save thee from this? When the Turf Is Thy Tower. Anonymous. MeEV; SeCePo

"Can any good thing come to God out of poor Nazareth?" The Divine Office of the Kitchen. Cecily Hallack. BLRP; GoTF; PoLf; TreFT

Can bid us, in turn, o gentle Saviour:/"take, eat–/live'. For Dr. and Mrs. Dresser. Margaret Avison. PeCV

Can blaze be done in cochineal,/Or noon in mazarin? I Found the Phrase. Emily Dickinson. AA; AmPP; AnFE; APA

Can bless them as the bell's/Transfixing tongue can bless. Crusoe's Island. Derek Walcott. NoAm

Can Bourbon or Nassau claim higher? Prior's Epitaph. Matthew Prior. TrGrPo

Can bring thee no stillier peace than is found in the/Sultan's dominions. A Triplet on the Reign of the Great Sultan. James Clarence Mangan. IrPN

Can center both the worlds of Heaven and/Hell. Often Rebuked, Yet Always Back Returning. Emily Bronte. EnLit

Can change it to the fount which maketh/green my own. A Dream. Elizabeth Clementine Kinney AA

Can charm, if you please,/The fish from the seas. Terence McDiddler. Anonymous. OxNR

Can deary be cheated/When nothing is miss'd. Sally Sweetbread. Henry Carey. CoMu

Can do a thing about the snow/But let it fall! Snow in the City. Rachel Field. TiPo

Can erase the worst heartaches. Erasers. Anonymous. PoToHe

Can fan into a fire. Youth Sings a Song of Rosebuds. Countee Cullen. BANP; PoLf

Can feed the fire as in its youth–/Can hold the runners lest they fall! After the Centennial. Christopher Pearse Cranch. PAH

Can God be God till we ourselves are whole! The New World: The New God. Witter ("Emanuel Morgan") Bynner. WGRP

Can God bring back the day when we two stood/Beneath the clinging trees in that dark wood? A Silent Wood. Elizabeth Siddal. NOBV

Can hold a sigh? March Evening. Leonard Alfred George Strong. MoBrPo

Can I cease to love thee? No! Maid of Athens, Ere We Part. George Gordon, Lord Byron. EBEV; EnLi 1-2; EnRP; FaBV; FaFP; HBV 1-2; MBW 1-2; MCCG; OAEP; PrIm; TreF

Can I disrust Eternity? Prayer in April. Sara Henderson Hay. TrPWD

Can I ever know you/Or you know me? The Mystery. Sara Teasdale. HBMV

Can I get you now, or must I hesitate? Hesitation Blues. Anonymous. FSW

Can I go home wid yuh, sweetie?"/"Sure." Jazz Band in a Parisian Cabaret. Langston Hughes. BANP; MoAmPo

Can I hope, though I am burnt,/That spring will come again? If I Consider. Lady Ise. WPOW

Can I keep it from eroding? Educational Music or Erosion. William H. Schubert. AMV-81

Can I lean/on it, lean more than on all/his accomplishments, those greeny/asphodel triumphs. Yes, But... Theodore Weiss. TAP

Can I make out of moonlight/a heavy, tangible object? Sleepwalkers. Bella Akhmadulina. BoWoP

Can I not sing but "hoy"/When the jolly shepherd made so much joy? The Jolly Shepherd Wat. Anonymous. NOBE; OxBM; SBVL

Can I say people, sitting in parks, are kinder? But I Do Not Need Kindness. Gregory Corso. CoPo; NeAP

Can I wish your lives unmade/though the pain of them is on me. To My Children, Fearing for Them. Wendell Berry. Str

Can it be he is one of those queers? Limerick: "The treatment by old Mr. Mears." *Anonymous.* PeHV

Can keep mine own away from me. Waiting. John Burroughs. AA

Can let out an Anagram/even as he list. Mr. Ward of Anagrams Thus. Nathaniel Ward. SCAP

Can make me, as it made you, Master of the Comic Spirit. To Harold Jacoby. Irwin Edman. InMe

Can make me see each time anew/The beauty of the rose? The Reversible Metaphor. Troubadour". InMe

Can make the stall a Court, the cratch a Throne. Carol. *Anonymous.* BoC

Can man forget this Storie? A Hymne on the Nativitie of My Saviour. Ben Jonson. SeCV 1-2

Can more on love than al this town. Snatches: "Joly sheperde of Ascell Down." *Anonymous.* OxBM

Can my love fade too? Longing for the Emperor. Empress Iwa no Hime. BoWoP

CAN NEVER BE DISTURB'D BY SUCH AS THOU!' Whisperings in Wattle-Boughs. Adam Lindsay Gordon. OBVU

Can never fail cuckolding two or three spouses Two or Three: A Recipe to Make a Cuckold. Alexander Pope. BoLoP; FaBoEE

Can never have "a solitary way." There Is a Mystery in Human Hearts. *Anonymous.* PoToHe

Can no longer hold my weight. Foreign Soil. Dianne Hai-Jew. BrSi

Can now take root in life, inherit love? Poem: "Some are too much at home in the role of wanderer." Denise Levertov. NeBP

Can only find/the/alley For Sammy Younge. Charlie Cobb. PoBA

Can place, or stamp make current aught but worth? Caelica, LXXX. Fulke, Lord Brooke Greville. FCP

Can read without its glasses/On revelation's wall. Belshazzar. Emily Dickinson. AmePo; CBEP; MoRP

Can reek and retch and rot in perfect safety. Civil Defense. Kenneth Burke. OBAL

Can sing without his robe or glass. Loyalty. William Henry Davies. BrPo

Can sneer at him who drew "Achitophel!" Don Juan. George Gordon, Lord Byron. OAEL 1-2; SeCeV

Can split the infinite of light/That shutters nothing out. The Nature of Love. James Kirkup. EaLo

Can Stuart, or Nassau go higher. On Himself. Matthew Prior. FaBoEE

Can sweethearts all their thirst allay/With strawberries? With Strawberries. William Ernest Henley. HBV 1-2

Can't be traffic. There's no one here but you. County Roads. Thomas Rabbit. MAYP

Can't find what you can't see/can you? American History. Michael S. Harper. BPo; HaCAP

Can't get away to marry you today/My wife won't let me! Waiting at the Church; or, My Wife Won't Let Me. Fred W. Leigh. FSN

Can't get loose/can't/be yourself/can't.... Real Deal Revelation. Raymond Ringo Fernandez. LFAC

Can't hold her pure little han'! I Went to the City. Kenneth Patchen. PoPl

Can't I soften the heart of a/stone! The Piper's Progress. Francis Sylvester ("Fathus Prout") Mahony. FiBHP

Can't I stay one minute more? Bedtime. Eleanor Farjeon. SoPo; TiPo

Can't make a buck! Poor Kid. William Cole. OBAL; PV

Can't someone have the rumba banned?/(Shicker-shick) And Now... John Basil Boothroyd. FiBHP

Can't we just quietly/Swallow The Pill?' Misericordia! James Lipton. NLV

Can't you live humble/To de dyin' Lam'? Can't You Live Humble? *Anonymous.* BoAN 1-2

"Can't you play a quiet game/Of some kind or other?" "Sh." James S. Tippett. SUS; TiPo

Can't you see our shadows/when the light licks hard? The Torch. Greg Forker. LFAC

Can't you spare me over for another year? O Death. *Anonymous.* TrAS

Can tell, mayhap, what greatness is. The Chronicle of the Drum (excerpt). William Makepeace Thackeray. ViBoPo

Can the long waiting on a wonder/Obliterate the long bleak pain? Austere the Music of My Songs. Fyodor Sologub. AWP

Can the spice-rose/drip such acrid fragrance/hardened in a leaf? Sea Rose. Hilda ("H. D.") Doolittle. FaBoMo; NoAm; NoP

Can there anything/good come out of/prison. Cell Song. Etheridge Knight. NNaP; PoBA

Can there be any trusting to our words? The Art of Politics. James Bramston. NOEC

Can these bring cordial peace? False world, thou liest. False World, Thou Liest. Francis Quarles. SeCePo

Can this be, Master, what thine eyes have done? Poem: "I know not if from uncreated spheres." Niccolo Machiavelli. AWP

Can warm my heart to gladness and to love. Ode. In Imitation of Pastor Fido Written Abroad, in 1729. George, Lord Lyttelton. CEP

Can we accept the unexplained, the loss,/The crushing agony, and hold us still. Yet Listen Now. Amy Carmichael. TRV

Can we be sure that such a deathless kiss/Holds nothing from beyond the dark abyss! Eternal Moment. Katherine"(Amelia Beers Warnock Garvin) "Hale. CaP

Can with a single Look inflame/The coldest Breast, the rudest Tame. Of Loving at First Sight. Edmund Waller. SeCP

Can work the unknown number harm. To Lesbia. Caius Valerius Catullus. UnTE

...Can you believe/that? I give you my word. The Book of Lies. James Tate. SM

Can you endure such grief/At any hand but hers? Symptoms of Love. Robert Graves. BoLoP

Can you ever be less than kind? A Bronze Statuette of Kwan-Yin. Charles Wharton Stork. GoYe

Can you forgive our foolish condescension,/Now you are gone? The Masquerader. Aline Kilmer. HBMV

Can you forgive us, now?-/Your fallen gods? To a Dog. Josephine Preston Peabody. BLPA; WGRP

Can you hear the song that tells you/All my heart's true love? Gipsy Love Song. Harry Bache Smith. FSN

Can you question the folly of man in the creation of God?/Who are you? Mother, among the Dustbins. Stevie Smith. PBWP

Can you sleep, sleep, Peter? Four Sides to a House. Amy Lowell. PoRA

Can you stand on your hind legs like an angel and sing/the perfectly circular song? Round Trip. Stan Rice. NPGG

Can you tell me aught of England or of Spring in England now? In Springtime. Rudyard Kipling. BrPo

Canaan/where the fight is The Approaches. William Stanley Merwin. NOBA; Prf

The Canadian border/He holds in his hand The Furniture Man. Dick Gallup. ANYP

The cancer ate her like horse piss eats deep snow. The Funeral. Norman Dubie. MAYP

CANDIDATE; So, Echo, you will vote for me I know./ECHO; No. By-Election Idyll. Peter Dickinson. FiBHP

A candle flamed upon a table;/A candle flamed. Winter Night. Boris Pasternak. PoPl

The candle-flames beside the surplices. Giorno dei Morti. D. H. Lawrence. BrPo; FaBoRV; NOBE; SeCePo

The candle flares. A Star is in the east. The Protagonist. Peter Hopegood. PoAu 1-2

Candle, I dream. Come, come away! To a Candle. Walter De La Mare. ChMP; ELP

The candle in its sconce. The Resolution. Vassar Miller. CoPo

A candle in my darkest need,/Twin to a star. Dwell with Me, Lovely Images. Theodore Maynard. GoBC

...A/Candlelight and spotlight/Kind of a place. Tonight in Chicago... *Anonymous.* AmFN

Candles are extinguished. Small bones/ache. Small Bones Ache. Moshe Dor. VWA

Candles in the windows of a safe earth. North Sea Off Carnoustie. Anne Stevenson. HoAn

The candles of new Camelot shone through the fought/field. Mount Badon. Charles Williams. FaBoTw

Candour still thy substance is. Age of Gold. Pietro Metastasio. CTC

Canna turn Arthur O'Bower. Riddle: "Arthur O'Bower had broken his bands." *Anonymous.* GBP; OxNR

Cannot allay the anger of God/towards a soul sin-freighted. The Seafarer. *Anonymous.* OBVE

Cannot be lived again, yet has not died. The Window. Francis Scarfe. NeBP

Cannot express my thoughts on birds. On Another. Hilaire Belloc. FaBoEE

Cannot get off so light. Prelude to Commencement. Marie De L. Welch. NYBP

Cannot meet his eye. Sparrow in an Airport. Richard Snyder. PPJ

Cannot put Humpty Dumpty together again. Riddle: "Humpty Dumpty sat on a wall." *Anonymous.* HBV 1-2; HBVY

...Cannot stop the sweat/that runs from his eyes and opened palms. Midewiwan. Phyllis Wolf. STE

Cannot, the tempest tells me, disappoint. Rain. Edward ("Edward Eastaway") Thomas. OBWP; OxBTC

The cans shall be filled with wine, ale and beer. Lustily, Lustily. *Anonymous.* OBSS

The canticle a million maids have cried,/Finding in you themselves: and justified. A Nun to Mary, Virgin. Sister Mary St. Virginia. ISi

Cap-a-pie with nakedness. Woman's Arms. Anacreon. UnTE

A cap by night-a stocking all the day! A Description of an Author's Bedchamber. Oliver Goldsmith. BIrV

Cap'n, I believe, believe, believe I'll die.   Cap'n, I Believe (with music).
Anonymous.   AS
Caparison elephants, teach bears to juggle.   The Lion Roars at the Enraging
Desert.   Wallace Stevens.   NePA
Capework of the wind.   Sleepless at Crown Point.   Richard Wilbur.   InPK
...Capricorn is drawing the threads   Across Space and Time.   Charles Olson.
PoM
Captain, can't you see this four o'clock trouble 'bout to kill poor me?   Lights
in the Quarters Burnin' Mighty Dim.   *Anonymous.*   OuSiCo
"Captain, Captain, there's no one watching us."   The Distant Winter.   Philip
Levine.   VGW
Captain James for cruel murder/Now must on a gibbet die.   Captain James.
Anonymous.   OBSS
Captain O'Flan dismissed each man/To breakfast on cold porridge.   The
Battle of Muskingum.   William Harrison Safford.   PAH
The captain said "Quack! Quack!"   I Saw a Ship A-Sailing.   Mother Goose.
MoShBr; NTCP; SoPo; TiPo
...A captain to command us,/And the word we must obey.   Waiting.   John
Davidson.   ViBoPo
Captains among the ghosts, heroes among the dead.   The Battle.   Chu Yuan.
WaaP
Captives of the camera.   Family Portrait.   Rebecca Hood-Adams.   AMV-80
Captivity is Consciousness–/So's Liberty.   No Rack Can Torture Me.   Emily
Dickinson.   MAmP; MoAB; MoPo
Capture my heart, and teach my memory to forget!   Dreams.   Arthur
Symons.   PoA
Captured another brave and then there were ten.   Ten Little Indian Boys.
M. M. Hutchinson.   SoPo
The captured stars exert their dim,/funereal, phosphorescent light.   Insects.
Isidor Schneider.   AnAmPo; TrJP
The car conveys us where we've been.   Moving between Beloit and Monroe.
Bink. Noll.   AmC; GrPl
...A car ran/over Charlotte. This is her book.   Charlotte, Her Book.
Elizabeth Bartlett.   FaBoWP
The car was gone and shifting sand/had drifted in so soon/and covered up its
track.   The Shack.   Nellie Burget Miller.   PoOW
Caramel, brown sugar,/A chocolate treat.   Harlem Sweeties.   Langston
Hughes.   TTY
The caravans go down to Death/The king of Zidon and of Tyre.   The March
of Humanity.   J. Corson Miller.   HBMV
The carcase comes to me, and he will get the skin.   The Peasant and the
Sheep.   Ivan Andreevich Kriloff.   AWP
The cardinal bird.   The Cardinal Bird.   William Davis Gallagher   AA
The cardinal's red cursive/Line, written on winter, writing to spring...
Cardinal.   Barbara Howes.   DFF
Cardinal Spellman/Lies in state.   Dirge.   Austin Clarke.   CIP
...The Cardinals would win the pennant, there would be no change in the/
weather.   Hopper's "Nighthawks. (1942).   Ira Sadoff.   PoDr
Care for every living thing,/In summer, Winter, Fall, and Spring.   The
Bobolink.   Thomas Hill.   HBV 1-2
Care less, eyes, lips, and hands to miss.   But We by a Love, So Much
Refined.   John Donne.   LO
...Care, like a drowsy child,/Is laid asleep in flowers.   Music.   Percy Bysshe
Shelley.   TrGrPo
Careful not to curtail our lives/Or change the names he has given us.   The
Lodger.   Michael Longley.   FaBoIP
A careful queen/She bows to no one   I Know a Lady.   Joyce Carol Thomas.
CNA
Careful to replace them/until they are truly quartets.   River Road Studio.
Barbara Guest.   PoM
The careless carpentry of snow!   Nature: The Artist.   Frederic Lawrence
Knowles.   AA
The careless hand he sickly stings.   The Impulse of October.   W. R. Moses.
NCSH
A careless mumble/Of/one/night/Stands.   The Good Old Days.   Barbara
Fried.   NLV
Careless of agate,/Careless of jade.   I Change.   Witter ("Emanuel Morgan")
Bynner.   HBMV
A careless touch should pour unbidden/Its bitterness upon my breast.   The
Amphora.   Fyodor Sologub.   AWP
Cares nothing/for the flicker of my warmth.   Lake Harriet: Wind.   Laurie
Taylor.   AMV-81
Caressed a trigger absently/And wandered out of life.   He scanned it,
staggered, dropped the loop.   Emily Dickinson.   PoEL 1-5
Caressed by light, I lay/small, in the human day.   Arrival.   John Wain.
EBEV
Caressing a penis with ears.   Limerick: "In a high-fashion journal for queers."
Anonymous.   PeHV
Caring no more to dwell within/The house where faith is dead.   The
Deserter.   Joseph Seamon, Jr Cotter.   CDC
Caring not to stir at all,/'Till the dew begins to fall.   Noon.   John Clare.
OBRV; SeCePo

Carlotta./I gotta!   Mia Carlotta.   Thomas Augustin Daly.   GoTF; InMe;
NLV; TreFS
Carmen Sylva is warbling/An Ode to Humanity.   Lines on Carmen Sylva.
Emma Lazarus.   TrJP
Carnation: my Lord and my God.   Easter Monday.   Michael McFee.
AMV-80
Carol, Carol, we have come/Back to heaven, back to home.   Epilogue: The
Flower of Old Japan.   Alfred Noyes.   MoBrPo
Caroline Pink from China Town.   Caroline Pink.   *Anonymous.*   PoPle
Caroling softly souls of slavery.   Song of the Son.   Jean Toomer.   AmNP;
BP; CDC; NIP; PoBA
Carouse on the affluent kisses of the tide.   Tide Turning.   John Frederick
Nims.   FYAP
Carpenter Christ!   Carpenter Christ.   Mildred Fowler Field.   PGD
Carpenter's son, carpenter's son,/was it a job well done?   Craftsman.   Luci
Shaw.   TrCP
The carpenter tendin to his own/movin north   Frank Albert & Viola Benzena
Owens.   Ntozake Shange.   BlSi
The carpet underneath their feet.   The Happy Sheep.   Wilfrid Thorley.
SoPo
Carrara, instructed, immaculate,/Is permanent; study this marble man.
Carrara.   Philip Murray.   NePoAm
Carried away on the stream of your might,/Dionysos.   Hail, Dionysos.
Dudley Randall.   BPo
Carried into the sky/on the backs of bees/pollinating with poems.   Entering
the Desert: Big Circles Running.   Wendy Rose.   TWSS
Carried po' man to cemetery but failed to bring him back,/Ev'ybody been
dodgin' Stagolee.   Stagolee (B vers.).   *Anonymous.*   ViBoFo
Carried with her the shining armour, the gift of Hephaistos.   The Iliad.
Homer.   NAWM 1-2
The carrion-birds a-wheeling round your head.   I Went Down into the Desert
to Meet Elijah.   Vachel Lindsay.   WGRP
Carrots bell pepper onions   What the Rooster Does before Mounting.   Cyn.
Zarco.   APU; BrSi
Carry a palm for me.   Palm Sunday: Naples.   Arthur Symons.   BrPo
Carry its political news/to Castile and to Aragon.   El Gusano.   Irving
Layton.   PeCV
Carry my holla, holla, ce,la,ho,ho,hu.   Love Pursued.   *Anonymous.*   GBL
Carry on man's work/the great design of life.   Here We Were Born.
Marcelin Dos Santos.   WhB
Carry on, my soul! Carry on!   Carry On!   Robert W. Service.   HBV 1-2
Carry the grapes up into the solemn house,/Where I was born.   Picking
Grapes in an Abandoned Vineyard.   Larry Levis.   MAYP
Carry the lad who was born for a king/Over the sea to Skye!   Flora
MacDonald and the King.   *Anonymous.*   BFSS
Carry this forthwith to the Governor!   The Ring and the Book.   Robert
Browning.   OAEP
Carrying ahead of us/our twin bouquets of light.   Country Singer.   Jean
Nordhaus.   AmC
Carrying anything I want downstairs to take it for/a ride on the bicycle .   17.
IV. 71.   Paul Blackburn.   PoM
Carrying crossbows, seeing it lead/and finesse the climactic horse.   Picture
Collection.   Marjorie Welish.   APU
Carrying groceries/on Saturday mornings.   Poems about Playmates.   Ronda
Davis.   JB
Carrying her full cargo of roses.   Big Wind.   Theodore Roethke.   AmPP;
CMoP; GoJo; InvP; NCSH; NoP; PPoe; VGW; ViBoPo
Carrying messages/across the cloudless night...   Snakes.   Peter Wild.
AmPA; GP
Carrying the larks upward.   Pennines in April.   Ted Hughes.   PPP
Carrying the robber down with him.   Three Presidents: Theodore Roosevelt.
Robert Bly.   LCAP
Carrying us giddily away and over/The bright, green terraces of summer.
Merry-Go-Round.   Oliver Jenkins.   GoYe
Cartridges on a deserted rifle range.   Poem Beginning with a Line by Cavafy.
Derek Mahon.   FaBoIP
Carve, inflict upon this brow/The majesty of its doomed Now.   Now, If You
Will Look in My Brain.   Jose Garcia Villa.   AnFE; CoAnAm
Carve love deep on my death.   Prayer for Living and Dying.   Christopher
La Farge.   TrPWD
Carved on a tree, her name is in the park.   Poem: "We used to float the
paper boats in spring."   Donald D. Olsen.   PoPl
A carven face forever weeping.   La Rue de la Montagne Sainte-Genevieve.
Dorothy Dudley.   HBMV
The carver Holm; the Maple seldom inward sound.   The Faerie Queene.
Edmund Spenser.   OHIP
Carving out my heart with yesterday's pain.   The Mask.   Irma McClaurin.
BlSi
The case continues.   Come Live with Me (parody).   Naomi Marks.   BXAP
'Case he been on the Charlie so long.   On the Charlie So Long.   *Anonymous.*
AS

...The case presents/No adjunct to the Muses' diadem.   Hugh Selwyn Mauberley.   Ezra Pound.   NOBA

...A casement ope at night,/To let the warm Love in!   To Psyche.   John Keats.   ViBoPo

"Cash er charge?"   Trout Fishing in Virginia.   Michael Beirne McMahon.   AMV-80

Cassock, bands, and hymn-book too.   If I were a Cassowary.   Samuel Wilberforce.   CenHV

Cast down from light into this loathsome home.   Christ and Satan: Lamentations of the Fallen Angels.   *Anonymous*.   AnOE

Cast down in the dirt,/Of death's filthy sport.   Epitaph for My Cat.   Jean Garrigue.   TAP

Cast forth redounding smoke and ruddy/flame....   Paradise Lost.   John Milton.   EnL

Cast not a clout/Till May be out.   Button to Chin.   *Anonymous*.   OxNR

Cast off, and nab him; when you have him, call.   The Plot against Proteus.   A. J. M. Smith.   OBCV; PeCV

Cast on the name of genuine whiteness, which/Doth thee alone, for chastity, enrich.   Whiteness, or Chastity.   Joseph Beaumont.   LiTL; LoBV

Cast them now on the new tidal line,/All that was left of gull and mine.   The Glaucous-Gull's Death.   D. J. O'Sullivan.   NeIP

Cast us back/into isolation   For the New Union Dead in Alabama.   Edward Dorn.   PoM

Castaways of wind and weather/Drifting aimlessly together.   Drift.   Denis Glover.   AnNZ

Casting his bowler glumly on the sideboard:/"Gimme my dinner."   Sapphics.   Dominic Bevin Wyndham Lewis.   NOBL

Casting shadows without a sound.   Sunday.   Lawrence R. Rungren.   AMV-80

Casting your baited hook/Into the world of men.   To a Little Boy Learning to Fish.   Robert D. Hoeft.   AMV-81

The castle at its toils, the lapwings love/To glean among at grape-time.   Sordello's Birth-Place.   Robert Browning.   MyFE

Castles crane forward, puff themselves up, and watch/For the foolhardy twinkle of my match.   Laid Off.   Francis Webb.   BoAV

Casts round the world an equal eye,/And feels for all that lives.   The Mouse's Petition.   Anna Laetitia Barbauld.   OxBChV

...A casual glance/would tell you there could be no silver here.   Graves at Elkhorn.   Richard Hugo.   UnPo

Casual interrogations, short/walks with attendant...   At the Corner of Muck and Myer.   Paul Violi.   APU

The cat ate him.   The Flattered Lightning Bug.   Don (Donald Robert Marquis) Marquis.   StPo

Cat-call the cat-gut "fiddles"? Fiddlesticks!   Old King Cole (parody).   Gilbert Keith Chesterton.   BXAP

...Cat, contrary to being put out,/is brought in/and fed for sleep   Inner-City Lullaby.   Russell Atkins.   CNA

A cat, five minutes created, sits with a pigeon./Happy birthday.   Birthday Poem from Venice.   Patricia Beer.   OxBC

The Cat looked long and softly at the King.   Maerchen.   Walter De La Mare.   CoBMV

The cat's in the cupboard/And can't see me.   Great A, Little a.   *Anonymous*.   OxNR

The cat's run away/With the pudding too!   Sing, Sing.   *Anonymous*.   OxNR

The cat!...SKAT!!!   The Cat!   Joseph Payne Brennan.   ShM

The cat sleeps like an old campaigner/During this season of the long rains.   Wet Thursday.   Weldon Kees.   NaP; NYBP

The cat spotted black and white/you will have to divide/for that you'll need God's guidance.   The Will.   Sipho Sepamla.   WhB

The Cat that follows his nose.   The Cat That Followed His Nose.   John Kaye Kendall.   CenHV

Cat, under myriad stars, do you forget years?   Cat of Many Years.   Gertrude May Lutz.   AMV-80

The cat went fiddle-i-fee, fiddle-i-fee.   The Farmyard.   *Anonymous*.   BFSS; OxNR

...The cat/who shuttles easily between two worlds.   The Bat.   Ellen Bryant Voigt.   MAYP

...The cataclysmic moment,/verse or song, does not last long.   Meeting Mick Jagger (parody).   Robert Peters.   BXAP

The cataract of Death far thundering from the heights.   Mezzo Cammin.   Henry Wadsworth Longfellow.   AmePo; CBEP; FPL; NoP; TAP

Catch a flea, catch a flea.   Brow, Brow, Brenty.   *Anonymous*.   OxNR

Catch/catch/catch/(if you can)   Grunion.   Myra Cohn Livingston.   RFM

Catch him who you can!   When I Was a Young Maid.   *Anonymous*.   AmFP

Catch it if you can.   Mix a Pancake.   Christina Georgina Rossetti.   NTCP; SoPo; SUS

Catch of night, as slowly he began to name/The far off, alien stars.   Naming.   Joseph Stroud.   NPGG

Catch the distant klingle-klang/Of the cow-bells tinkling home!   Sassafras.   Samuel Minturn Peck.   AA

Catch the glad sounds, and shout, "Jerusalem, all hail!"   The Crusaders Behold Jerusalem.   Torquato Tasso.   CAW

Catch up with you at last.   Speed.   William Henry Davies.   MoRP

Catch yuh later on Jesus, i mean motha!/it must be/deeeeeep...   Jesus Was Crucified or: It Must Be Deep.   Carolyn M. Rodgers.   BlSi; PoBA

Catches celestial wind in its sails/propelling the world through space.   Speak Like Rain.   Jerred Metz.   VWA

Catches the light/and sends it back.   The River.   D.G. Jones.   NOBC

Catches tigers/In red weather.   Disillusionment of Ten O'Clock.   Wallace Stevens.   AmP; CMoP; CrMA; FF; ForPo; InPK; InPS; LOW; NIP; OxBA; PAI; PPoe; SOTW; WeW

Catching of happiness is called.   Born Yesterday.   Philip Larkin.   HaMV; NAs

Catching roach and gudgeon in the orchard pond.   Vigils: Down the Glimmering Staircase.   Siegfried Sassoon.   PoLf

Catching the merest fraction/Of sleep, you will know what I mean.   You and It.   Mark Strand.   NYBP

Catching their difficult breath.   The Stadium.   William Heyen.   LiSp

Catfish didn't register/to swim this brook.   Sensational Relatives.   Alexis Krasilovsky.   AMV-80

Cathedral Mary,/shine!–   The Bridge: Three Songs.   Hart Crane.   LiTA

A Catholic, Madonna fair, to worship thee.   Aspiration.   Charles Lamb.   CAW

Catholic/pleasure/treasure.   Men Walked To and Fro.   Blanaid Salkeld.   NeIP

Catnip from the other side.   The King of Cats Sends a Postcard to His Wife.   Nancy Willard.   OBCA

Cato, in pity, hear our just demur,/Man to be critic, must be connoisseur.   Friend Cato.   Anna Wickham.   MoBrPo

The cats are keeping store!   Sunday.   Elizabeth Jane Coatsworth.   AmFN

The cats claws/lie sleepun.   Cats Is Wheels.   Faye Kicknosway.   APU

Cats/in/the form of/images/come feeding.   Cannibalism.   Diana Chang.   WPOW

Cats, no less liquid than their shadows,/Offer no angles to the wind.   Cats.   Arthur Seymour John Tessimond.   BoAnP; HaMV; PCat

Cats sleep/Anywhere.   Cats.   Eleanor Farjeon.   PCat

Cats walk neatly.   Cats.   Robert Francis.   DFF

...The cattle come,/reeling to left and right, and always, down.   Metaphysic of Snow.   Donald Finkel.   PoA

The cattle then are sick.   'Tis Summer Time on Bredon (parody).   Hugh Kingsmill.   FaBoCo

Catullus, still remember to be strong.   To Himself.   Caius Valerius Catullus.   AWP; LiTW

& Caught a plane/to/petit bourgeois/negro/heaven.   At the National Black Assembly.   LeRoi (Imamu Amiri Baraka) Jones.   GP

Caught and held in the light that spills/off the floor and stains the bed/like wine.   Beautiful Woman.   Dale Zieroth.   NOBC

Caught by pains of menacing death, I falter,/Lost in the love-trance.   Ode: "Peer of gods he seemeth to me."   Sappho.   LiTW

Caught him in metamorphosis, were/Left him as epilogues.   Mauberley.   Ezra Pound.   NoP

...Caught in a strange country/for which no man would die.   The Negatives.   Philip Levine.   NePoEA-2

Caught in an anger exact as a machine!   Tired and Unhappy, You Think of Houses.   Delmore Schwartz.   LiTM; MoAB; MoAmPo; NePA

Caught in her eyes the late years wept, seeing/th' impossibility of her being.   Princess Elizabeth of Bohemia, as Perdita.   Frank O'Hara.   PoA

Caught in Love's restless sway.   Epigram: "Perchance some coming after."   Strato.   PeHV

Caught in that alien axis, grown immense/In that green will.   Winter Juniper.   Joseph Langland.   NePoEA

Caught in the frozen palms of Spring.   The Blackbird.   Alfred, Lord Tennyson.   FM; HBV 1-2; PB; PBBP

...Caught/In the rear-view mirrors of the passing cars.   The War against the Trees.   Stanley Jasspon Kunitz.   HAP; NoAm; PPON

Caught in the wide, implacable,/Clear gaze of the basilisk.   Dark Earth and Summer.   Edgar Bowers.   QFR

Caught on each glistening/Valley and hill.   Sleet Storm.   James S. Tippett.   BrR; SiSoSe

...Caught with his britches down/By death, whom he'd imagined out of town?   At Shagger's Funeral.   Bruce Dawe.   NOAV

Cauliflower, Cauliflower.   Life Is Butter, Life Is Butter.   *Anonymous*.   FaBoNo

Caulk the draughty shingles/With threads of rock.   Noah in New England.   Tom Lowenstein.   VWA

'Cause a gold tooth makes a woman look old!   Gold Tooth Blues.   Tennessee Williams.   OBAL

'Cause a secret is inside.   Secrets.   E. Kathryn Fowler.   BiCB; ChBR

The cause acquits you not, but I that wink.   Amores.   Ovid (Publius Ovidius Naso).   UnTE

'Cause all my sins are taken away.   Hand Me Down My Walking Cane.   *Anonymous*.   FSW

...Cause areas of torment in the unreal like stones in an open/field. Correspondences. Robert Duncan. PoM

'Cause Franklin knows/Anything goes. Anything Goes. Cole Porter. OBAL

'Cause he's got the best thing out. Get Into the Boosting Business. *Anonymous.* WBLP

'Cause her head is curly/Baby, and bushy too Hunkie Tunkie. Charlie Jordan. BluL

'Cause I ain't gonna stay here any longer. You Can Dig My Grave. *Anonymous.* FSW

Cause I do/where I am Poem for a "Divorced" Daughter. Horace Coleman. LTB

'Cause I don't play the dozen, I declare, man, and neither the ten Kentucky Blues. Little Hat Jones. BluL

'Cause I just wanna stay home. I Just Wanna Stay Home. Irwin Silber. FSW

'Cause I'm a traveling man/boys, I can't stay here The Gone Dead Train. King Solomon Hill. BluL

'Cause I'm goin' round the world, baby mine. Baby Mine. *Anonymous.* FSW

'Cause I'm going in the world/to sing long distance blues You Can't Keep No Brown. Bo Weavil Jackson. BluL

"'Cause I never have tried raisin' any." Limerick: "Here is the reply made by Benny." Lee Blair. TDH

'Cause I've been warned and I've decided/To sleep alone all of my life. Don't Sing Love Songs. *Anonymous.* FSW

The cause is nowhere found in rhyme. Song: "Who can say." Alfred, Lord Tennyson. LoGBV

'Cause it pleases the eye,/And I like the effect. Hence These Rimes. Bert Leston Taylor. FiBHP

'Cause it's snitch on your neighbor time. Lawn Order. William Franklin. LFAC

'Cause it was the last vacation/Grandpa ever had. Poor Grandpa. R. C. O'Brien. ShM

Cause its the only/for real thing/i/know Woman Poem. Nikki Giovanni. BlSi; NMM; NoAm

A cause ruined before, a world betrayed. The War Horse. Eavan Boland. BlrV; CIP

'Cause that way we get two desserts/Instead of only one! Neighborly. Violet Alleyn Storey. TiPo

'Cause the next gal I get will have to do what poppa say. Number Twelve Train. *Anonymous.* FSW

'Cause the stuff'll be here/Baby when the boat get back Stew Meat Blues. Bessie Jackson. BluL

Cause there ain't a good man/Like me left around. Request for Requiems. Langston Hughes. ShM

Cause there ain't no sense/In my bein' dead. Wake. Langston Hughes. OBAL; ShM

'Cause there's still a lot of cottages/down at Carmel-by-the-sea. Aimee McPherson. *Anonymous.* FSW

'Cause they never did find willie's thumb. How One-Thumb Willie Got His Name. John L. Sellers. LFAC

'Cause to be of one possest/Barr'd the hope of all the rest. Amaryllis I did woo. George Wither. EG

'Cause when I'm drunk, nothing don't worry my mind Dead Drunk Blues. Lillian Miller. BluL

'Cause wormy apples are organic. Eco Right. Walt Gavenda. QQQ

'Cause you know when I carry that gun/lord I can't keep it hid 45 Pistol Blues. Walter Roland. BluL

'Cause your body's gonna swivel when you come to die, sugar babe. Sugar Babe. *Anonymous.* ABF

Caution, shyness, and pretense–/O foolish wind! The Maiden. Peter Hille. AWP

...Cautiously, a frayed/black monocle cord starts to make its way back across my/cheek... Clement Attlee. Michael Benedikt. PAI

Cavafy, it was your song/from which I borrowed/both the manner & the courage. It Was Your Song. Steve Kowit. APU

The cave by the Mississippi/Where Tom and Becky strayed. When the Mississippi Flowed in Indiana. Vachel Lindsay. CMoP

Cave of night blooms/with fresh explosions. The Cave of Night. John Montague. CIP

The cave re-echoed to her sighs. Fingal: an Ancient Epic Poem (excerpt). James MacPherson. EnLi 1-2

The caves of generation and the terraces of the stars Walking Westward (excerpt). C. K. Stead. OCNZ

Caw. Caw. Caw. Caw. Sheaf-Tosser. Eric Rolls. PoAu 1-2

Caws of unnumbered Springs. There Blooms No Bud in May. Walter De la Mare. MoAB; MoBrPo

Ce! la! ho! ho! hu! The Chase. William Rowley. CH

Cease, gentle muse! the solemn gloom of night/Now seals the fair creation from my sight. To S. M. a Young African Painter, on Seeing His Work. Phillis Wheatley. BlSi

Cease, my doubts, my fears to move,/Spare the honour of my Love. Song: "Thyrsis, when we parted, swore." Thomas Gray. OAEP

Cease now my song, my woe now wasted is./O joyfull verse. The Shepheardes Calender:. Edmund Spenser. AtBAP; PoEL 1-5

Cease then, my song, cease the unequal lay. On Imagination. Phillis Wheatley. BlSi; PoNe

Cease thy vain dreams of beauty's warmth–forget/The face thou longest for! Lost Desire. Meleager. AWP

Cease to recite thy sacred name. Love's Protestation. Thomas Lodge. ACP

Cease we to praise, now pray we for a kisse. Astrophel and Stella, LXXIX. Sir Philip Sidney. AAS; SiPS

Ceaseless, changeless, malign, searching into the very soul/The rushing desolation reigns. Winter Westerlies. James Devaney. BoAV

Ceaseless her joyful deathwail she/Sang to departing Araby! Nepenthe. George Darley. OBNC; OBRV

A ceaseless song of praise begin,/And shout redeeming grace. In God's Eternity. Hosea Ballou I. AH

Ceaselessly heave and swoon a wish to cry. The Lice-Finders. Arthur Rimbaud. SOTW; SyP

Ceasse then myne eyes, to seeke her selfe to see,/And let my thoughts behold her selfe in mee. Amoretti, LXXVIII. Edmund Spenser. AAS

Ceasse then, till she vouchsafe to grawnt me rest,/Or lend you me another living brest. Amoretti, XXXIII. Edmund Spenser. AAS

Ceiling unlimited. Visibility unlimited. Ceiling Unlimited. Muriel Rukeyser. MoAmPo

Celebrate the end of anything. Landscape, New Mexico. Kell Robertson. TAT

Celebrating the marriage/Of flesh and air. Life Is Motion. Wallace Stevens. AmLP; SD; WeW

...A celebrity who tells/what it is like in the altitude. Kite. Laura Jensen. LCAP

Celui mo lais, celui mo prends. U, Deux, Trois. *Anonymous.* ABF

...Cemeteries and all that is/dead breed pestilence. Things Dead. Marcel Schwob. TrJP

Cenotaph'd and paragraph'd,/And reckon'd quite a bore. Love, You've Been a Villain. James Robinson Planché. NOBL

The Censor attending a risque Revue/And combining Stern Duty with pleasure. The Smile of the Goat. Oliver Herford. FiBHP

The cent'ries complete, or odd years beside. To Know If It Be Leap Year. *Anonymous.* FaBoUs

Center of lake of light Mexico City Blues. Jack Kerouac. NeAP

Center of/their workaday world Pictures from Brueghel. William Carlos Williams. PPP

Center on center unfold, lotus petals,/the boundless wave of bliss. Not Yet. Joanne Kyger. APU

...The center,/where there are no clues except pleasure. Whole and Without Blessing. Linda Gregg. MAYP; NPGG

...The centerfielder drifts under/the last fly ball of the summer, and puts it away. A Difference. Tom Clark. HoAn

Centimeters deep yawns the abyss. In Nine Sleep Valley (excerpt). James Merrill. HaCAP

Central High School, yes, yes, yes! Strawberry Shortcake, Blueberry Pie. *Anonymous.* LoGBV

The central stream of what we feel indeed. Below the Surface-Stream, Shallow and Light. Matthew Arnold. InPK; NOBV; OBSP

Centrally lo-/cated under 21/white males/& i'll be yr slave. Poem: "It's a dull poem." Steve Jonas. PeHV

The centuries are stars, and stud the way. The Seven Sleepers. Mark Van Doren. FYAP

Centuries hence, this scavenged place/May spring again in grass! Highway Construction. Carol Earle Chapin. QQQ

...Centuries of crushed shells,/plus the new. Italian Woman. Diane Wakoski. GrPl

The centuries surround me with fire. Lines Concerning the Unknown Soldier: "Arteries juicy with blood." Osip Mandelstam. NAs

Centuries will have to pass/before it will extinguish itself. To a Victim of Radiation. Arturo Vivante. FAZ

A century after, Sarsfield's laughter/Was echoed from Dungannon. A Ballad of Sarsfield. Aubrey Thomas De Vere. GoBC

The Century's blind man! Melting Pot. Michael Echeruo. TTY

'Cept, he admire him/for his sin/cerity. Abu. Dudley Randall. BPo

Ceres, Queen of Plenty, hallows/Growing fields as well as fallows. Praise of Ceres. Thomas Heywood. ElL

A certain awe of profound marveling. La Vita Nuova. Dante Alighieri. AWP

The certain faith of a March daffodil. The Lilies of the Field. Compton Mackenzie. OBVV

Certain flights require total risk. The Acrobat from Xanadu Disdained All Nets. Dan Georgakas. FF

Certain is nothing but Death! Mors et Vita. Richard Henry Stoddard. AA

Certain of one thing, now the worst is passed/The last must be the best because the last. Fisbo (excerpt). Robert Nichols. OBSV

A certain spirit/I hope/you've passed on to me. Placing a $2 Bet for a Man Who Will Never Go to the Horse Races ... Diane Wakoski. UnPo

The certain taste and surer smell/of a dim-lit past when we slept well. Spring Poem. Bin Ramke. AMV-81

Certain they are blue, without ever looking up at the sky. The Party. Jerome Sala. APU

Certainly as apples, around me. When It Rains. H. A. Maxson. AMV-80

Certainly not. Just what shall we tell the children? Plus Ca Change... Philip Whalen. WeW

Certainly the means must not defeat the end. Values in Use. Marianne Moore. NePoAm-2

Cette dent, d'importance et d'orgueil. Limerick: "Il etait un gendarme a Nanteuil." George Du Maurier. LiBL

The chaff of life, the most of it,/its miscellaneous debris. The Dump. Greg Kuzma. PoA

Chain me to thee with that hair. Madrigal: "Have I found her." Francis Pilkington. EnRePo

A chain of souls connected by/Names. Crow, Straight Flier, but Dark. Laya Firestone. VWA

...Chained hang the/stars of thee fast to the rocks with hempen ropes/set unmoveable. The Night Long. Imr el Kais. LiTW

Challenge Fate to throw the main. Holiday. John Davidson. OBVV

A challenge full of deathless hate. The Rattlesnake. Robert V. Carr. PoOW

The challenge of the line, not even the title/of a single poem. Modern Poetry. Anita Skeen. IHMS

Challenge yourself for a fool, call me no more knave! Against Garnesche (excerpt). John Skelton. ViBoPo

A chamber for His splendor, without bound. Sea-Voyage. John Hall Wheelock. EtS

The chamber is there! Bluebeards's Closet. Rose T. Cooke. AA

Chance flicks his tail & swims, through. Steveston: Imagine: A Town. Daphne Marlatt. NOBC

A chance light shines and suddenly it is spring. September. Aldous Huxley. EBEV

A chance to put on my own brand. My Own Brand. Art Cuelho. TAT

The chance to/scares you off To Poem. Lyn Lifshin. NeAC

Change and contempt, you know, ill speakers be,/Caelica, and such are all your thoughts of me. Caelica, XVIII. Fulke, Lord Brooke Greville. FCP

Change cannot harm him now, nor fortune/touch him more. The Burial of Latane. John Reuben Thompson. PAH

Change change your change change change./your/mind nigger. A Poem to Complement Other Poems. Don L. Lee. BPo; NoAm

Change hands ma'am/Celere—run away, just in sham. A Holiday Task. Gilbert Abbott A Becket. NA

Change, in the Arts, is nearly always good. A New Poet Arrives. Gavin Ewart. OxBTC

Change is illusion—yet I hate/The silence and the changeless dark. Against Seasons. Robert Mezey. AmPC; NYBP

...Change is the nursery/Of music, joy, life and eternity. Change. John Donne. ViBoPo

Change my sorrow/Into song. Like Barley Bending. Sara Teasdale. HBMV

A change of name requires no change of vow. Lycoris darling, once I burned for you. Martial (Marcus Valerius Martialis). BoLoP

The change onward from ours to that of beings who walk/other spheres. "The world below the brine". Walt Whitman. AmLP; BiP; BoNaP; FM; MAT; NePA; NoP; PAI

Change, to include a new horse. Birth. James Dickey. NOBA

...Change/to the plural/where you will/never be/lonely again. Grammar Lesson. Linda Paston. Psk

The changeable Whirlpool of Life. The Whirlpool. Anonymous. PoToHe

...Changed places with statues of wax/Banyans banyans. The Spectral Attitudes. Andre Breton. EAS

...Changed/Snow into grass and gave to all such powers. A Suit of Nettles. James Reaney. OBCV

Changeless, eternal,/For ever and ever. Bhagavad-Gita: Debate Between Arjuna and Sri Krishna. Prabhavananda,Isherwood,tr Anonymous. WaaP

The changeless God's eternal fane. Morwennae Statio. Robert Stephen Hawker. GoBC

The changeless Polynesia of my poem. Nude. Harold Witt. ErPo

Changes a slave into a child,/And duty into choice. Love Constraining to Obedience. William Cowper. NOCV

Changes with the ebbing tide. Old Woman of Beare. Anonymous. AnIL; KiLC; OnYI

Changing itself by slow degrees/Into thick flowing molten gold. African Easter. Abioseh Nicol. PBA

Changing until we find that which/cannot be changed. Human Dilemma. Jim Rosemergy. AMV-80

Chant: "Come in peace, O blissful/Seventh Day!" Sabbath, My Love. Judah Halevi. TrJP

Chanted in love that casts out fear/By Seraphim. At the Grave of Burns. William Wordsworth. EnLi 1-2; EnRP

The chanter, the drones. Fleadh. Michael Longley. CIP

The chanting cuckoo's double note! "I Am the Resurrection and the Life," Saith the Lord! Robert Stephen Hawker. GoBC

Chanting of sorrow, joy, and love. Medieval Norman Songs. Anonymous. AWP

Chanting solemn music for the souls that/passed below. The Battle in the Clouds. William Dean Howells. PAH

Chaos in windy grays/through a red prairie. The Last Quatrain of the Ballad of Emmet Till. Gwendolyn Brooks. CNA; PoBA

Chapeau bas!/Gloire au Marquis de Carabas! The Marquis of Carabas. Robert Barnabas Brough. FiBHP; HBV 1-2

Chaplet of perfumes on the Rosary of Love. The Child's Prayer. Robert de Montesquiou-Fezensac CAW

Chaps in whose light we are/Now being Conned. Progress. Sally Belfrage. PV

The character is gone. Being Natural. Carl Rakosi. GP

Characteristic of his neighbors. Neighbors. Charles Malam. AMV-80

Characteristic of only the spirits/attributed only to gods. The Beacon. Arthur Gregor. GP

Characteristically,/Saul only admires/their thick souls. King Saul. Allan Kolski Horvitz. VWA

Characters only a priest can read. A Card Game: Kinjiro Sawada. Patricia Y. Ikeda. BrSi

Charge–charge, O'Donnell and conq'ring O'Neill! O'Neill's War Song. Michael Hogan. OnYI

Charge, charge! 'tis too late to retreat. The Ode on St. Cecilia's Day. John Dryden. GN

Chargeable matters shall of love oppress/The childish game and idle business. Age. Sir Thomas More. EnRePo

A chariot softly glanced down, and stayed hard thereby. The Metamorphoses. Ovid (Publius Ovidius Naso). MOON

Charity, come home,/Begin. We Continue. William Stanley Merwin. CAPP

Charley Warlie's old cow. Charley Warlie. Anonymous. OxNR

Charley with the motor running and that girl goosed. Death-Lace. David Ray. MAT

Charlie he's my darling, the young Chevalier. Charlie He's My Darling. Robert Burns. ALV; FaBoPV; FSW; HBV 1-2; ViBoPo

Charlie hugs and kisses the girls,/For he knows they taste like candy. Weevily Wheat. Anonymous. ABF; AmFP; AS; FSW; TrAS

Charm'd with the Saphir-winged Mist. The Kingfisher. Andrew Marvell. AtBAP; PB

Charm of the Magic Ring! Midsummer Courtship. James (1834-82) Thomson. OBVV

The charmed boat approached, and there its haven found. Ever as We Sailed. Percy Bysshe Shelley. SeCePo

Charmed magic casements, opening on the foam/Of perilous seas, in faery lands forlorn. Ode to a Nightingale: The Nightingale. John Keats. FaBV

Charmed with the splendour of this northern star,/Shall here unlade him and depart no more. London after the Great Fire, 1666. John Dryden. NOBE

Charming as a yacht. Christmas Eve. Patricia Beer. OBCP

The charnel of yon desecrated fane! Kilmallock. Sir Aubrey De Vere. IrPN

A charred and blackened bough. Revenge! Horace. AWP

...Charring darker/bodies with your/caucasian flames Custer (1). Alison Baker. FAZ

Chart the tides of millennium! Let Dreamers Wake. Lilith Lorraine. PGD

Charts the course of every Christian,/Leads us on to paradise. Light and Love, Hope and Faith. Eva Gray. STF

Chase the little the etc. it's 10 a.m. White Country. Peter Schjeldahl. ANYP

Chasing into nothing. Death Songs. L.V. Mack. PoBA

Chasing skeeters out of sunny Tennessee. I Was Born about Ten Thousand Years Ago. Anonymous. AS; FSW

Chasing that shade/Which my sins made,/While I so spring, as if I could not fade! Looking Back (excerpt). Henry Vaughan. FaBoPP

Chaste be her conduct, and sublime her views. The Instalment (excerpt). Edward Hilton Young. FaBoCo

Chaste, biddable, out of all likelihood. Cover Her Face. Thomas Kinsella. CIP; IPY

...The chatter of cultured apes/Which is called civilization over there. Australia. A. D. Hope. ACV; BoAV; NoP

Chawing chewing gum, chewing chawing gum. Chewing Chawing Gum. Anonymous. AmFP; FSW

Cheap as sunlight,/And morning air. Repetitions. Carl Sandburg. HBMV

The cheap hotels stood in shadows of/each/with/a practiced/solemnity Image of City.   Lance Henson.   VoR

Cheated of all the summer should have brought.   After the Show.   Sam Harrison.   NeIP

A checkered taxi runs him down.   Songs about Life and Brighter Things Yet. Samuel Hoffenstein.   NLV

Chee, chee, chee.   Robert of Lincoln.   William Cullen Bryant.   AnNE; FaBoBe; HBV 1-2; HBVY; OBCA; WBLP

Cheek by jowl, my dog and I.   George Ridler's Oven.   *Anonymous.*   OBET

...Cheek/grow warm next to your own in hushed dark familial December. December.   James Schuyler.   NoAm

Cheerer of age, youth's kind unrest,/And half the heaven of the blest.   The Lucky Chance: Song.   Aphra Behn.   WPOW

Cheerily they may arrive, three months behind.   A Campus in Summer. Reed Whittemore.   GLGT

Cheers the repast, and celebrates the chase.   Epigram.   Richard Garnett. OBVV

Chefs and saints still appear to blithe it.   Moon Landing.   W. H. Auden. MOON; SUW; WeW

A chemist's shop, a street, a lamp.   Dances of Death.   Alexander Blok. OBVE

The chequered landscape varying as it goes,/Still adds to hope and promises repose.   The Emigrant.   Standish O'Grady.   CaP

Cherish the cure, as if it were good to keep.   Misery.   John Holmes. NYBP

Cherished ones without number and never enough!   Thousands and Three. Paul Verlaine.   PeHV

The cherl n'il nought adown er the day dawe.   The Man in the Moon. *Anonymous.*   MeEL; OxBM

Cherrish the cheek, but make none blush/at all.   The Meddow Verse or Aniversary to Mistris Bridget Lowman.   Robert Herrick.   SeCV 1-2

The cherry and hoary pear/Scatter their snow around.   Spring Goeth All in White.   Robert Bridges.   BoNaP; HBMV

Cherry and pear, and me, myself,/Pasting a name on each.   Harvesting. Selma Robinson.   InMe

The cherry boy, once the sweetest prize,/was growing gnarled before my eyes. The Cherry Boy (excerpt).   Royston Ellis.   PeHV

The cherub with the fiery sword/Was waiting there as well.   New Moses. Michael Kennedy Joseph.   AnNZ

The Cheshire smile–which sets me fearfully free.   Objects.   Richard Wilbur. FF; NoP

A-chewing,/A-mooing,/To pass the hours away.   Cows.   James Reeves. NTCP; PoSC

Cheyenne-a, Cheyenne, I'm a-leaving Cheyenne.   Cheyenne.   *Anonymous.* CoSo

The Cheyenne climbed that winter, fleeing.   Fort Robinson.   Ted Kooser. GP

Chicago, in half an hour.   Flight 382.   Doris Longman.   AMV-81

Chick-a-chick, and left me here behind.   Uncle Reuben.   *Anonymous.*   FSW

A chicken too might do me good.   The Fox at the Point of Death.   John Gay.   OBEC

...chicken/yard, ma's apron an' my head cool in its bonnet.   Gracie.   Faye Kicknosway.   GeTw; NMM

The chickens they are crowing, for it is almost daylight.   The Chickens Are A-Crowing.   *Anonymous.*   TrAS

Chief Bald Eagle was/The tomahawk of hell.   Brady's Bend.   Martha Keller. StPo

A chief is no bigger than his blanket,/I said, waving her away.   Chicken. Dave Etter.   MAT

The chiefest of ten thousand, Thou;/The chief of sinners, we.   Jesus, How Much Thy Name Unfolds!   Mary Peters.   BePJ

...Chiefly, if thy name/Wise Pallas and the immortal Muses own.   Inscription for a Grotto.   Mark Akenside.   CEP; NOEC; OBEC; PoEL 1-5

The chiefs of the two great armies met/Beneath the old apple-tree.   Mr. Johnson's Policy of Reconstruction.   Charles Graham Halpine.   PAH

The Chiefs of Tyrone and Tyrconnell,/Live on through the years!   In Memoriam: Francis Ledwidge.   Norreys Jephson O'Conor.   HBMV

The Chieftain's pride, his heir, is dead.   An Irish Lamentation.   Johann Wolfgang von Goethe.   AWP

The child and the ocean still smile on each other,/Whilst–   A Vision of the Sea.   Percy Bysshe Shelley.   MOS

"Child, as it was with others, so with you."   The Girl Takes Her Place among the Mothers.   Marya Zaturenska.   HBMV

Child beloved, child adored.   Dawning Fair, Morning Wonderful. *Anonymous.*   AH

A child can wave as the boats go by.   July 4th.   Anne Waldman.   APU

"Child, child, be not afraid. Your Cross/Is occupied by Me."   There Was No Room on the Cross.   *Anonymous.*   GoBC

–A child enduring a dream/That grows, at the first touch of day,/ Unendurable.   First Light.   Thomas Kinsella.   BIrV; CMoP; NoAm

The child grown into a giant journeys over the whole world/Without a pass. The Child Who Was Shot Dead by Soldiers at Nyanga.   Ingrid Jonker. PeSA

A child had been taken from bed/and broken in our hands.   Garcia Lorca. Louis Dudek.   NOBC

The child himself stayed fast asleep.   Three Kings Came.   Thomas W. Shapcott.   PoAu 1-2

Child, how did you come so softly?   At Daybreak.   Helen Hoyt.   BiCB

Child, if you have a rummy kind of name,/Remember to be thankful for the same.   Various Beasts.   Hilaire Belloc.   FaBoNo

The Child in their stable/Whose name lives forever.   The Quiet-Eyed Cattle. Leslie Norris.   PCh

The Child is born in blood, O child of blood.   New Year's Day.   Robert Lowell.   AmPP; ConAP; LiTM; NePoEA; PPoe

...Child, it lies/Within your power of choosing to/Conceive the Child who chooses you.   Dialogue between Mary and Gabriel.   W. H. Auden.   ISi

Child, it's a tender string to touch,/That sounds, "Thou'rt mine."   To an Infant Daughter.   John Clare.   NAs

A child lay weeping.   The Lonely.   George William Russell.   AWP; OnYI

Child, love's flesh and bone.   Stabilities.   Anne Stevenson.   NCSH

The child of a diviner will.   Heinrich Heine.   Ludwig Lewisohn.   TrJP

Child of a starveling sod.   The Road to Castaly: Revelation.   Alice Brown. WGRP

Child of green lovebird and the raven death.   Dollar Bill.   John Frederick Nims.   MiAP

A child of human hopes and human fears.   Renunciation.   Wathen Mark Wilks Call.   OBVV; WGRP

The Child of Light who findeth his Father in the/Evening.   He Maketh Himself One with the God Ra.   Book of the Dead.   AWP

The Child of Misery, baptiz'd in Tears!   Apology for Vagrants.   John Langhorne.   OBEC

...The child's cry comes from the house.   Notes on a Life to Be Lived. Robert Penn Warren.   NoAm

A child's first finger exercise/Before her on the music stand.   In Passing. Roy Helton.   HBMV

The child's first vision of the insatiate sea.   Enigma.   Hugh McCrae. BoAV; PoAu 1-2

A child's unfinished body,/waxy & insistent.   Kindergarten.   Dennis Schmitz.   NPGG

The child's walk in the darkening afternoon.   An Elegy.   E. J. Scovell. ChMP

A child's wish to do something simply superb.   Windshield.   Robert Fitzgerald.   AmC; CrMA

A child should never feel a fear,/Wherever he may be.   Friends.   Abbie Farwell Brown.   HBV 1-2; HBVY

A Child so blessed, and full of love,/Sent for your joy from Heaven above. From Heaven High I Come to You.   Martin Luther.   PCh

A Child stretched out His arms that we might pray!   A Christmas Dawn at Sea.   Eva Morgan.   EtS

The child swelling the womb.   Bread.   Nancy Keesing.   PoAu 1-2

The child that will lead you.   The Child.   William Stanley Merwin.   NoAm

Child, they will come.   To Insure Survival.   Simon J. Ortiz.   CDW

Child, though magician, elf, you're not/My imagination but my daughter. Separate Parties.   Dabney Stuart.   NYBP

Child too soon buried.   Ophelia.   Vernon Watkins.   MoVE

The Child was not with her.   Tribute to the Angels.   Hilda ("H. D.") Doolittle.   InPS; NMM; NOBA

The child was still/alive. Admit you're glad.   The Search Party.   William Matthews.   GeTw

A child will go on being tortured.   Something about It.   John Hollander. GP

Childe Rolandine bowed her head and in the evening/Drew the picture of the spirit from heaven.   Childe Rolandine.   Stevie Smith.   BrRo

Childhood is health.   Holy Baptism.   George Herbert.   HBV 1-2; PoEL 1-5

The childhood, the gestures, the rigid travellers.   Poem out of Childhood. Muriel Rukeyser.   NMM

A childless woman hears.   No Child.   Padraic Colum.   AnFE; OBMV

Childlike, with childish things not put away.   Epitaphs of the War, 1914-18. Rudyard Kipling.   BrPo; OBWP

Children almost never tap on the glass.   Sharks at the New York Aquarium. Charles Martin.   SM

Children are all happy/On Christmas Day.   It's Almost Day.   *Anonymous.* FSW

Children be children.   School Days/Rule Days.   Derek Butler.   LFAC

Children building this rainman out of snow   Sonnet Entitled How to Run the World.   Edward Estlin Cummings.   NePA

The children came to tell me when she died.   Care.   Richard Murphy. IPY

...(Children, children,/oh see that waterfall.)   Any Time.   William Stafford. LCAP

The children cried so when his eyes were shut.   Into the World and Out. Sarah Piatt.   HBV 1-2

The children don't know it, and Santa won't tell.   For the Children or the Grown-Ups? *Anonymous.* OBCP

The children gathered, the candles alight–That music to hear, to see that sight.   The Christmas Tree.   Peter Cornelius.   PCh

...The children/growing up drunk.   Poem for viet nam.   Ray A. Young Bear.   STE

The children had put small Siennese banners in its prickly/sides and the colors drooped...   Country Villa.   Jean Garrigue.   TAP

The children have scrawled it: BIG NORM IS DEAD.   Twenty-One Sonnets.   C. K. Stead.   OCNZ

(Children in boxes at a play/Stand up to watch it well.)   Epitaphs of the War, 1914-18.   Rudyard Kipling.   BrPo; OBWP

Children in ordinary Dress/May always play with Sand.   Franklin Hyde.   Hilaire Belloc.   FaBoUs; NLV

The children knew what it was all about.   Ghosts' Stories.   Alastair Reid.   NePoEA-2

...The children/laughed in the tree.   I Sought All over the World.   John Tagliabue.   Psk

...Children leave the greatest/show on earth/and see the circus?   What Happens.   June Jordan.   BPo

The children live, the children/rise from My Lai ditch.   Patience, Hard Virtue.   Daniel Berrigan.   LFAC

The children need Prang paints, tablets,/spelling books.   Bordello, Revisited.   Eve Triem.   GP

The children never forget them. They can never forget.   Bay Violets.   Sister Maris Stella.   GoBC

Children of God and heirs of heaven!   Great God, the Followers of Thy Son.   Henry, Jr. Ware.   AH

Children of the Lord.   Rise and Shine.   *Anonymous.*   FSW

The children of the Pilgrim sires/This hallowed day like us shall keep.   The Twenty-Second of December.   William Cullen Bryant.   GN

The children of the sod, and this/Rose in the sun, and flew for hours.   The Angel in the House.   Coventry Patmore.   VLP

The Children of the State/forever countable/forever indispensable.   The Children of the State.   James Lewisohn.   LFAC

Children out for holiday,–/That's July.   That's July.   Mary Frances Butts.   YeAr

The children sang. Who Mary love/The long year through have Christmas nigh them!   Festum Nativitatis.   Aubrey Thomas De Vere.   IrPN

"Children should be seen, not heard!"   Some Ruthless Rhymes.   Harry Graham.   CenHV

...The children swing in blue/And green, and the wet clouds extend.   The Professionals.   Geoffrey Grigson.   PoA

Children/They teach to walk,/Soldiers/To fall.   Training on the Shore.   Shlomo Vinner.   VWA

...Children wait with dreaming faces/the Eve when The Child is born.   The Long Night Moon: December.   Frances Frost.   YeAr

Children watering their charges, the black lulled elephants.   The Ganges.   Norman Dubie.   LCAP

...Children who believe/like he does, in today, and today, and today.   A Veteran of the Great War.   John Bensko.   MAYP

The children who never cry.   Other Women's Children.   Marilyn Waniek.   AMV-80

Chill December brings the sleet,/Blazing fire, and Christmas treat.   The Garden Year.   Sara Coleridge.   FaBoBe; GoTF; HBV 1-2; HBVY; TreFT

Chill my heart with fear to-night!   Phantoms of the Steppe.   Alexander Pushkin.   WSC

The chill settles in around the place where I have moved/with everything.   Evaporation Poems.   Kathleen Norris.   IHMS

Chill Silence, like a surging sea,/Slowly enveloped me.   Clowns' Houses.   Edith Sitwell.   SyP

Chilled to crystal tears.   Nocturne.   Gwendolyn B. Bennett.   BANP

Chilled with a miserly comparison/Of the toy's purchase with the length of life.   Blight.   Ralph Waldo Emerson.   AmePo; AP; NOBA; NoP

Chillun, an achin' heart Lord!   Up on de Mountain.   *Anonymous.*   BoAN 1-2

Chillun, I know you go'n to miss me/When I'm gone.   Zek'l Weep (with music).   *Anonymous.*   AS

Chilly water, Chilly water,/Hallelujah to dat Lam'.   Chilly Water.   *Anonymous.*   BoAN 1-2

The Chim-pan-zee can-not forget.   Having a Wonderful Time.   Dominic Bevin Wyndham Lewis.   FiBHP

Chimborazo, Cotopaxi,/They had stolen my soul away!   Romance.   Walter James Turner.   BiCB; CH; GoJo; HBMV; HBVY; MoBrPo; NOAV; NOBE; OBMV; PoRA; TrGrPo; WHA

The chime of the silver bells.   Ticonderoga.   V. B. Wilson.   PAL

Chime, sing! rhyme, ring! over fields and fells!   The Green Gnome.   Robert Williams Buchanan.   StPo

Chime up like silver-winged dreams in flight.   Love Sonnets, VIII.   Charles Harpur.   PoAu 1-2

...Chimes reach,/like lianas, from life to death, room to room.   Nightpiece.   Lewis Turco.   SOTS

The chimney smoke we saw was bramble fire.   Neighbors.   Marilyn Francis.   GoYe

Chin chopper, chin chopper, chin chopper, chin.   Here Sits the Lord Mayor.   Mother Goose.   ExPo; HBV 1-2; HBVY; OxNR

The chin is where you fall off/When I look at my shoes.   Cosmogony (parody).   D. C. Berry.   BXAP

China must be broken in pieces.   Ching a Ring.   James Robinson Planché.   NOBL

A Chinese baby fell/And cried as any other.   Five Vignettes.   Jean Toomer.   BALP; PoBA

Chinese boxes, each containing/the World, and its shadow.   The Vigil.   Denise Levertov.   NePoEA-2

The Chinese know all about/Sweet 'n sour   Sweet 'n Sour.   Genny Lim.   BrSi

A Chinese moment in the Mearns.   Aberdeen Train.   Edwin Morgan.   BSV

...The chipmunk/Dives to his rest.   The Chipmunk's Day.   Randall Jarrell.   NCSH; OBCA

Chipmunk, do you like the sun,/The blowing snow and me?   Winter Noon.   Sara Teasdale.   YeAr

Chirping in the sleeves/Of a scarecrow.   Haiku: "Grasshoppers."   Kawai Chigetsu-Ni.   WPOW

...Chirping (not a/great songster) in the bay cherry bushes wild of leaf.   Mechanism.   Archie Randolph Ammons.   HAP

The chisel fell.   The Death of Azron.   Alice Wellington Rollins.   AA

Chisels men's hands to magnify.   To Iron-Founders and Others.   Gordon Bottomley.   GTBS; OBEV; OBMV; OBVV

Chitter and quarrel/in the piercing dark/above the killed.   A Plague of Starlings.   Robert Earl Hayden.   HoAn

Chloris, at worst, you'll in the end/But change your Lover for a Friend.   Chloris, 'Tis Not in Your Power.   Sir George Etherege.   OBS

Cho-chop comee blackie bird,/Nipee off her nose!   Nursery Song in Pidgin English (parody).   *Anonymous.*   SpRo

The choicest is the gift of melody.   To Melody.   George Leonard Allen.   CDC

...The choir/of assembled carrion crows.   Sunstrike.   Douglas Livingstone.   PeSA

Chokes me as it hugs me in its fire.   Metamorphosis.   Peter Porter.   OxBTC

Choking through the whole attack.   Wanderings: Champs d'Honneur.   Ernest Hemingway.   PoA

Choose from out that company/Whom to serve, and whom to love.   Valentine to a Little Girl.   John Henry, Cardinal Newman.   GoBC

Choose the squirming sea.   Eating Fish.   George Johnston.   WHW

"Choose then".   Choosing a Death.   Alberta Turner.   LCAP

Chop some wood, 'twill do you good, And you'll eat in the sweet bye and bye.   The Preacher and the Slave (with music).   *Anonymous.*   AS; FSW; TrAS

A chord, a dream, a longing, love of Thee!   Reality.   Martha Gilbert Dickinson.   AA

Chose rather to be praysed for dooing good,/Then to be blam'd for spilling guiltlesse blood.   Amoretti, XXXVIII.   Edmund Spenser.   AAS

Chose to belaurel Robinson instead/Of famous men like Richard Watson Gilder.   T. R.   Donald Hall.   PoA

Chose to have it out at last/on your own premises.   I Am in Danger–Sir–.   Adrienne Rich.   HaCAP; NOBA

The chosen ruby and the reprobate.   In the Dark None Dainty.   Robert Herrick.   CaPo; CBEP; ELU; PoPle

Christ abiding to the end.   Christ for Everything.   R. A. Belsham.   STF

Christ, at this Highbury altar, I offer myself to Thee.   St. Saviour's, Aberdeen Park, Highbury, London, N.   Sir John Betjeman.   MoVE

"Christ be with us!" he said, as the ship sped west.   Christopher Columbus (excerpt).   William Hart-Smith.   PoAu 1-2

Christ bring us all to the Homeland/Of His eternal love.   The Homeland.   Hugh Reginald Haweis.   BLRP

Christ, charging well his chosen ones, forbade/Offence: "for lo! of such my kingdom is."   On the "Vita Nuova" of Dante.   Dante Gabriel Rossetti.   MaVP; VLP

"The Christ Child hath been here."   When the Christ Child Came.   Frederic Edward Weatherly.   OHIP

The Christ-child knocks.   Through the Ages.   Margaret Hope.   PGD

Christ died between two felons. Mozart lay/With twenty poor, anonymous as they.   Mozart's Grave.   Paul Scott Mowrer.   GoYe

Christ! for a horse between my legs/And the sagebrush once again.   Sagebrush.   Charles Erskine Scott Wood.   BPAW

Christ found my heart full of sorrow,/Cleansed it and filled it with love.   Secret of Song.   Christine White.   STF

"Christ! get that dirty player, Death!"   Down the Field.   Rolfe Humphries.   AnAmPo

Christ-gladness with no equal, and His everlasting snows.   Hail, Maiden Root.   Caelius Sedulius.   ISi

"Christ has risen from the dead!"   Not in Vain.   *Anonymous.*   BLRP

Christ His Cross shall be my speed!   A Christ-Cross Rhyme.   Robert Stephen Hawker.   CAW; GoBC

The city boils/black men/jump out of trees.   Death of Dr. King.   Sam Cornish.   CNA; OFD; PoBA

...The City Hall all clean/gleams like silver like the magnolias in the moonlight.   Hudson Ferry.   James Schuyler.   NYP

A/city/is a bumpy/thing.   City.   Jane Stembridge.   NMM

City lights mark the horizon.   The Party at the Contessa's House.   Brian Robertson.   AMV-80

The city looks flimsy as a movie set.   Shoe Shop.   Barton Sutter.   SM; SoSe

City nested in bays! My city!   Mannahatta.   Walt Whitman   AA; EyDe; HBV 1-2; MoAmPo; NYP

The city/never did get/all the names   The Louisiana Weekly #4.   David Henderson.   PoBA

City of our rendezvous.   The Rendezvous.   Bernard Spencer.   GTBS-P

The City of Quivira whose streets are paved/with gold.   Quivira.   Arthur Guiterman.   BPAW; PAH

The city running to weed patch right on time.   Where or When.   Philip Whalen.   PoM

City that constantly squirms/but never screams.   The Idea of San Francisco. Jim Gustafson.   APU

The city that will not die.   The Doomed City.   E. L. Mayo.   FAZ

The City/was taken exactly forty-eight hours later/when we were washing away the blood.   The Bridal Bed.   Jenny Mastoraki.   PBWP

A city without joy or weariness,/Itself beholding, from itself aloof.   Venice. Arthur Symons.   OBSP

The Civet sented Musquash smelling ever.   The Kingly Lyon, and the Strong Arm'd Beare.   William Wood.   SCAP

The civil man to his lust/And the lookout to his mast.   The Veteran.   Louis O. Coxe.   MoVE

The civil war of that household.   A Small Farm.   Michael Hartnett.   CIP

The civil words I have to say. And yet...   Enemy, Enemy.   Cecil J. Mullins. AMV-80

Civilian, is the child he then begot/To be allow'd legitimate, or not?   A Case to the Civilians.   *Anonymous.*   FaBoEE

Civilization continually shifts/Upon the places of the earth.   Dust.   Waring Cuney.   CDC

Ck-thrash-ub! Ck-ck-tish-u!)   To Bary Jade.   Charles Follen Adams. OBAL

Clad in silver tissue, I/March magnificently by!   Washed in Silver.   James Stephens.   ELU; MOON

Claim her impetuously!   The Swimmer.   Roden and Wriothesley Berkeley Noel.   OBVV

Claim this my country, though today/Timor mortis conturbat me.   A Letter to Three Irish Poets.   Michael Longley.   BIrV

Claiming me, Charon, for life.   At the Ferry.   U. A. Fanthorpe.   FaBoWP

Claims its huge dominions not by kinship, nor bond/Of common ending. Breadth. Circle. Desert. Monarch. Month. Wisdom.   John Hollander. PoA

...The clamour of history/Will never deafen or decrease their glory.   Were I to Mount beyond the Field.   Sidney Keyes.   MoPo

Clanging its bars until I was deaf/with the knuckles of my fists.   Leaving Raiford.   Mario Petaccia.   LFAC

Clap your hands, and I can do it.   Acrobat.   Edward Watkins.   AMV-80

& A clarity/that pierced through to the other world.   Kicking from Centre Field.   David McFadden.   NeAC

Clarity The logic is not The Boats and O, I am not/alone   LXXII A Sonnet for Dick Gallup.   Ted Berrigan.   ANYP

Clasp hands–/Companions of long ago.   Meditation.   Schaechter-Gottesman VWA

Clasp her and hold and love.   At Sunset.   Louis V. Ledoux.   HBV 1-2

Clasped in final union/On one cross of dread.   Christ and His Mother at the Cross.   Jacopone da Todi.   CAW

Clasping tenderly a crumpled/Cheese-cake to his lonely breast.   Burglar Bill. Thomas Anstey Guthrie.   FiBHP

Clasps thee with arms that cling like/Death's embrace:/Les morts vont vite! Les Morts Vont Vite.   Henry Cuyler Bunner.   AA

Clatt'ring within the flabby lean, their pith/Exhaust, and tide of every art'ry frore.   Freedom: A Poem, Written in Time of Recess...   Andrew Brice. NOEC

Claude, I'm not writing anymore poems about you.   Barbara's Land Revisited–August 1978.   Geary Hobson.   STE

The claws of the beast were wide, long his thrashing tail.   The Fisher Cat. Richard Eberhart.   GrPl

The claws of the tropics will gather your pile and the dealer gets it all. Down and Out.   Clarence Leonard Hay.   BeLS; BLPA

The claws remain, but worms, wind, rain, and heat/Have sifted out the substance of thy feet.   The Lion's Skeleton.   Charles Tennyson Turner. FM; NBM; NOBV; VLP

The clay grows less, and, leaving it, the mind/Dwells with the stars. Standing on Tiptoe.   George Frederick Cameron.   CaP; OBCV; PeCV

Clay in his thoughts,/And lightning in his tread!   The Dancer.   Joseph Campbell.   OBMV; OxBI

Clay of his mould and to his image prest!   Smoking Flax.   Mary Josephine Benson.   CaP

The clay of their departed lover.   The Heart of All the Scene (From "Woodnotes").   Ralph Waldo Emerson   AA

A clean and clever lad/who is doing/his best/to get on....   The Omelet of A. MacLeish.   Edmund Wilson.   NYBP; Par

The clean bones crying in the flesh.   Full Moon.   Elinor Wylie.   CrMA; MoAB; MoAmPo; SBG; VGW

Clean/brick walls.   Come Visit My Garden.   Tom Dent.   NNP

Clean new bombers from America muffle their engines/and glide down now. Eisenhower's Visit to Franco, 1959.   James Wright.   NMP

Clean sheets, again,/just in case   Strung out with Elgar on a Hill (excerpt). Jonathan Williams.   GP

A clean slate, with your own face on.   You're.   Sylvia Plath.   FaBoTw; FaBoWP; NAs; NCSH

Clean, soft and shining/on her chest.   Motherhood.   May Swenson.   CoAP

Clean with rejoicing, complete in/outgiving, come, day without end.   Glad Day.   Louis Untermeyer.   TrJP

Clean wounds, but terrible,/Are those made with the Cross.   Pieta.   James Philip McAuley.   CBAP; PoAu 1-2

Clean yir feeties,/An' walk in.   Knock at the Doorie.   *Anonymous.*   OxNR

Cleaner than Sunday, warmer than leaves.   Spring Is a Looping-Free Time. Martin Robbins.   SD

Cleaning and caressing,/Creeping and healing.   The Minimal.   Theodore Roethke.   BiP; HaCAP; NoAm; NOBA

Cleanliness is godliness/Said the sphinx.   The Blessing.   Ruth Berman. AMV-81

Cleanse from thy skirts the slaughter shed,/Or make thyself an ashen bed,/O Baltimore!   Through Baltimore.   Bayard Taylor.   PAH

Clear across/loud acres of sun.   Cicada.   John Haines.   NPAW

Clear as a milk-white feather in a crow/Or a black stallion on a field of snow. A Good Resolution.   Roy Campbell.   OBSV

...Clear as tracks,/are callings and cold signals on the wind.   Depot in Rapid City.   Roberta Hill.   BoWoP

Clear away your running gear, and blow, ye winds, high-o!   Blow, Ye Winds. *Anonymous.*   AmFP; AmSS; FSW

The clear blue California sun surrounds us.   Terminal Version.   Diana O Hehir.   NPGG

...A/clear broth–just water/that tastes of these roots.   Recipe.   Albert Goldbarth.   VWA

The clear church-bells ring in the Christmas-/morn.   Morte d'Arthur. Alfred, Lord Tennyson.   VLP

...Clear mental image, against/the lingering headache of sky.   White Zombie. Harrison Fisher.   APU

Clear of the myriad images that still–/do what I will–encumber its pure line. After Rain.   P.K. Page.   NOBC

The clear Promethean spirit/Through a broken tragic age.   Adriatic.   Robert Conquest.   PP

Clear rang their voices through the ocean's roar,/"Hooray, hooray, hooray!" The Three Badgers.   Lewis (Charles Lutwidge Dodgson) Carroll.   FaBoNo

The clear sweet taste/Of a summer tree!   Apple Song.   Frances Frost. TiPo

Clear things may not be seen.   Miracles.   Conrad Aiken.   MoAmPo

Clear, trembling, tart as fresh pineapple.   The Judgment.   Kathleen Spivack. BoWoP

The clear vowels rise like balloons.   Morning Song.   Sylvia Plath.   BoWoP; HaCAP; HeIP; IHMS; InPK; InPS; LCAP; NAs; NOBA; PAI; PrIm; SBG

Clear whom he meant.   Dream Songs.   John Berryman.   HaCAP

The clearest well your eyes behold/Has sand to foul it at the base.   Omnia Vanitas.   Dugald Buchanan.   GoTS

Clearing of tenantry, exile, exploitation.   Sgurr Nan Gillean.   Sorley MacLean.   PoSH

Clearness between: our nod is barely civil.   Meeting Myself.   Edward Lucie-Smith.   NePoEA-2

Clearness for me, frailty for her.   In a Glass-Window for Inconstancy. Edward, Lord Herbert of Cherbury.   AnAnS 2; OBSP; SeCP

Cleave the wood, and I am there.   The Oxyrhyncus Sayings of Jesus. *Anonymous.*   TRV

Cleave thou thy destined way!   A Voice from the Invisible World.   Johann Wolfgang von Goethe.   AWP

Cleaves to mischance and unrepaired loss./For tender stalks–   A Poem Entreating of Sorrow.   Sir Walter Ralegh.   SiPS

Cleaving the clouds, and quivering to the sky–/"Orate pro nobis!"   All Souls' Eve.   Mary E. Mannix.   GoBC

Cleaving the green/Twilight like a rhythmic sword.   Woodlands.   Sir Herbert Read.   BrPo

Cleaving the ocean waves,/Parting the wild rushing seas!   Canoe-Hauling Chant.   Apirana Ngata.   WTO

An' cleek my duds for auld lang syne.   Justice to Scotland.   *Anonymous.* InMe; NLV

Cleft and dimpled/the apples she brings to bed.   Evesong.   Maureen Duffy. PeHV

Clench your heart into your fists and/your mouth–seal it firmly.   Deportation. A. Glanz-Leyeles.   TrJP

Clenching and opening one small hand.   Making a Fist.   Naomi Shihab Nye. MAYP

Cleopatra, Rome, farewell! Antony to Cleopatra.   William Haines Lytle. AA; BeLS; BLPA; FaPo; HBV 1-2; TreF

Clerks, bishops, kings go by–/To-morrow so shall I!   The Dust.   Lizette Woodworth Reese.   HBMV

Cleveland Hailed Cleveland Made Ruler Twice.   Presidents of the United States.   *Anonymous.*   FaBoUs

Cleveland Indians was the confirmation.   The Maestro's Barber Shop. Ricardo Vasquez.   FIA

Clever lady (with a/strength which seemed incredible).   Introducing a Madman.   Keith Waldrop.   TW

CLICK CLICK, knowing we owe it our lives, more hazy and/blurred with each day.   Utopia TV Store.   Maxine Chernoff.   APU

Clickety-clack/Horseman, pass by.   Clickety-Clack.   Paul Blackburn. NoAm

Clickety, clickety,/Clackety/Clack.   Song of the Train.   David McCord. NTCP; SoPo

The cliffed escarpment ends in stormclad strength.   The Testament of a Man Forbid.   John Davidson.   BSV

Climate and the affections. Jews quote that.   Land of Nations (excerpt). Gertrude Stein.   AtBAP

"The climate's very healthy once you're used to being dead."   On Learning to Adjust to Things.   John Ciardi.   OBCA

...Climate where how swiftly/the dark grows, and the time comes.   A Woman.   Denis Johnson.   MAYP

...Climb/the arc of the world.   Ship Bottom.   Richmond Lattimore. NePoAm-2

Climb toward the turnip-colour sun.   Rapunzel.   Eli Mandel.   DFT

Climbed a tree at night to get a chicken for a lady.   Some Modern Good Turns.   Dennis Dibben.   FAZ

...Climbed my growing/body's staircase to the very tip of sleep.   Twins. William Matthews.   MAYP

The climbers will change, the hills remain.   Mountaineering Bus.   Rennie McOwan.   PoSH

Climbing, he withers into light.   The Dragonfly.   Howard Nemerov.   PoA

...Climbing the slopes/Of uneatable soft green!   Bare Almond-Trees.   D. H. Lawrence.   FaBoPP; OBTV

Climbing up to heaven above/Night and wind and storm.   My Delight. Gamaliel Bradford.   HBMV

Climbs back up to claim herself again.   The Woman Hanging from the 13th Floor Window.   Joy Harjo.   TWSS

Cling closer, love, and close thine eyes.   Laura's Song.   Oliver Madox Brown.   HBV 1-2

Cling to His arms and sleep, and sleeping, dream,/And dreaming, look for me. The Lamp of Poor Souls.   Marjorie Pickthall.   HBV 1-2

Cling to what's divine in him.   Your Friend.   *Anonymous.*   GoTF; TreFT

Clinging/to lost/horizons/i   Upon Leaving the Parole Board Hearing. Conyus.   PoBA

Clip thy wild tongue, and tie thee to the table.   Ode to a Country Hoyden. John Wolcot.   NOEC

Clipped it and left it.   Farewell to Lesbia.   Caius Valerius Catullus.   LiTW

...Clipped them like ends of/split hair.   Hypocrite Women.   Denise Levertov. CAPP; MAT; NMM; PoM

Clipping the same sad alnage of the years.   The Clerks.   Edwin Arlington Robinson.   AA; AnNE; MAmP; MoAB; MoAmPo; MoVE; PoEL 1-5

The cloak he wears around his shoulders is the woods.   Jacob and Esau. Else Lasker-Schüler.   BoWoP

The clock dropping its shoes and/No floor   Resolution.   William Stanley Merwin.   NYBP

The clock just now has nothing more to say.   The Campus on the Hill. W.D. Snodgrass.   AP; LiTM; MP; NIP; NoAm; TAP; TwCP

...The clocks/Chime muted underneath domestic calm.   At Delft.   Charles Tomlinson.   NYBP

Clockwise and counter-clockwise turning.   A Poem beginning with a Line by Pindar.   Robert Duncan.   ConAP; NeAP; NMP; NNaP; PoM

A clood aince mair cam' owre me/Wi' Jock the byreman's braith. Cloudburst and Soaring Moon.   Hugh" (Christopher Murray Grieve) MacDiarmid.   NoAm

An' close, an' close into your ear/I'll tell ye how I lo'e ye, dear.   My Laddie. Amelie Rives.   HBV 1-2

The close call packed away and sniffing at the edge   The Elms Dispatch. Ron Padgett.   ANYP

Close interweaved, I quaff the rosy wine.   Fie on Eastern Luxury!   Hartley Coleridge.   NLV

Close it and lay it in God's hand.   The Old Year.   Clarence Urmy.   PGD; PoToHe

...Close now your golden wings!   Fountains.   Osbert Sitwell.   MoBrPo

Close or far away, it doesn't matter, I am sure of it.   I Am Sure of It. Jimmy Santiago Baca.   LFAC

The close, sequestered, colorless retreat/Where she was born, where she will always stay.   The Travel Bureau.   Ruth Comfort Mitchell.   HBMV

Close/stars crowd   Frost.   George Johnson.   WHW

Close the door on love and hang/The key upon the nail.   Suburban Song. Elizabeth Riddell.   CBAP; NOAV

Close the front door. This is/The front porch. Goodnight, house.   A Room I Once Knew.   Henry Birnbaum.   GoYe

...Close thy burning eyes with a kiss, as if they/were thy lips.   The Songs of Bilitis.   Pierre Louys.   UnTE

...Close to his private/parts. blood to blood.   Blood to Blood.   Alvin Aubert. GP

Close to the crosses, my own name dances about.   Funeral Notices. Alfonsina Storni.   AMV-81

Close to the end of my tether.   Down on My Luck.   A. R. D. Fairburn. AnNZ

Close to the last red embers draw/Your welcome soul.   The Last Guest. Frances Shaw.   HBMV

Close to the only motor/in the world.   Coming Home.   John Stone.   NIP

Close up your fingers tight and hold him fast.   A Pinch of Salt.   Robert Graves.   HBMV; MoBrPo

Close yo' eyes in sleep.   Kentucky Babe.   Richard Henry Buck.   AA; FSN; HBV 1-2

Close your eyes; walk bravely through.   Close Your Eyes!   Arna Bontemps. AmNP; CDC; FB; PoBA; PoNe

Closed down the hatch of his vault/and slept.   The Knell.   Muhammad Al-Fituri.   TTY

Closed in beating heart we could not be/To the sunk sun, the far, surrendered sea.   Ebbtide at Sundown.   Michael (Katherine Bradley and Edith Cooper) Field.   CAW

The closer Good, the less my chance to see.   Epigram.   Pernette Du Guillet. PBWP

Closer your arms shall twine.   Your Snow-White Shoulder.   Heinrich Heine. UnTE

Closing in an azure sky.   A Landscape.   John Cunningham.   CEP

Closing my ears I hear her footstep as she does not walk away.   The Four Cardinal Times of Day.   Rene Daumal.   AMV-81

Closing the compass of its legs/In a prayer to the Absolute   Lilith.   Yvan Goll.   VWA

Closing the door upon/Those half-remembered things–   Wood-Thrush.   John Hall Wheelock.   NePoAm

Closing the doors of the house and the head also!   Asmodai.   Geoffrey Hill. NePoEA

Closing the doors of the sun.   For Alan Blanchard.   John Oliver Simon. NeAC

Closing the eyes. As/simple an act. You float   Way out West.   LeRoi (Imamu Amiri Baraka) Jones.   NeAP; NMP; PoBA

Closing their lids, bestow a dirge-like death!   The Poet.   Cornelius Mathews AA

Closing upon her spikes.   City Afternoon.   Barbara Howes.   AmFN

...Cloth of gold/where lightly pass/the delicate feet of Spring.   Casual Gold. Maud E. Uschold.   SoPo; YeAr

Clothe Thou the fiels, as in the prophet's/vision,/With peace Elysian.   God Save the Nation.   Theodore Tilton.   AA

...Clothed like the curved/camellia, whiter than winter's moons.   A Prospect of Swans.   Dorothy Donnelly.   HoAn

Clothes, drying in the breeze.   To the Old Masters.   Wing Tek Lum.   BrSi

The clothes like blossoms, all sweet and fresh and fluffy.   Old Ellen Sullivan. Winifred Welles.   TiPo

Clothes sodden, the out-of-work stay on.   Rainy Midnight.   Ivor Gurney. FaBoPP

Clothing us in a robe of more than glory.   The Coliseum.   Edgar Allan Poe. AP; NOBA

A cloud is even now passing across the clear face of the/moon.   The River of Heaven.   *Anonymous.*   AWP; LiTW

A cloud of birds that to and fro/Dart joyous midst the sunrise-glow. Australian Transcripts, X: The Wood-Swallows.   William Sharp.   FM

...Cloud-reflecting lakes/In the old mountains of time.   Guide to the Ruins. Howard Nemerov.   EyDe

The cloud's deep voice, the wind's low/sigh.   The Exile at Rest.   John Pierpont.   AA

The cloud, the sky, can see. We are the blind.   Above Ben Loyal.   Arthur Ball.   PoSH

...Cloud wagons move/outward still, dreaming of a Pacific.   In California. Louis Simpson.   NoAm

Cloud your eyes/with pain   Old Story.   Lance Henson.   VoR

Clouded in flesh;–yet, Shepherds! sit we here.   A Carol.   Edmund Bolton. OxBoCh

The cloudless azure whence they came!   After the Fire.   Oliver Wendell Holmes.   MC; PAH

The clouds are fitted to the wind,/The wind is to the snow.   As birds are fitted to the boughs.   Louis Simpson.   BoLoP; NePoEA; OLR

The clouds are torn asunder/one by one.   Fishermen.   Gabriel Preil.   VWA

Colossal hoax of clocks and calendars If(Touched by Love's Own Secret)We,Like Homing.   Edward Estlin Cummings.   PoA

Colossal the star of death/Standing like the clock of the times.   What Secret Desires of the Blood.   Nelly Sachs.   VWA

The colour of the sky.   The Iris.   Gasetsu.   TiPo

The colours of a million dusks and dawns/Lay low where she was laid. From Burton the Anatomist.   Maurice James Craig.   NeIP

Colours that change whene'er they wave their wings.   The Rape of the Lock,. Alexander Pope.   NOBE

Columbia, bless the God who built the skies.   Columbia, Trust the Lord. *Anonymous.*   AH

Columbo and Adonis died.   The Turtle and the Sparrow (excerpt).   Matthew Prior.   PBBP

Columbus' doom-burdened caravels/Slant to the shore, and all their seamen land.   The Discovery.   Sir John Collings Squire.   OFD; PoSC

Columbus found/that far beyond the flat on flat/the world was round?   12 October.   Myra Cohn Livingston.   NTCP

Columbus's doom-burdened caravels/Slant to the shore, and all their seamen land.   There Was an Indian.   J.C. Squire.   AmFN

"Column! Forward!"   Bethel.   A. J. H. Duganne.   PAH

Column on column comes the drenching rain.   A Thunderstorm.   Archibald Lampman.   CaP; NOBC

Com-a-ti-yi yippi, yippi yea.   The Old Chisholm Trail.   *Anonymous.* AmFP; BeLS; BFSS; BPAW; CoSo; FaBoBe; FSW; TreFT

Com'mere, boy!   Brass Spittoons.   Langston Hughes.   BANP; MoAmPo; NoAm

"Com out' hath felld it al with fight.   Come Out, Lazarus!   *Anonymous.* OxBM

Coma-cow-cow, coma-cow-cow, yicky-yicky-yee.   When I Was a Cowboy. *Anonymous.*   ABF

Comatas sang this as dusk came.   Comatas.   Harry Mathews.   ANYP

The/comb/Fathoming her flowing selves.   A Fantasy of Little Waters. James Scully.   NYBP

Comb, Garters, Stockins, Gloves.   Verses to Be Repeated by an Attorney... John Willis.   FaBoUs

Combed their stone hair, laughed, and made no reply.   A Visit to Van Gogh. Charles Causley.   PoCh

Combs her electrical head.   At Morning an Iris.   Patrick Evans.   NeBP

Combustion joins all elements in fire.   Dies Irae.   Inger Hagerup.   LiTW

Come a dairy, come a dairy.   Devilish Mary.   *Anonymous.*   FSW

Come a fa la ling, come a derry.   Devilish Mary.   *Anonymous.*   OuSiCo

Come a little closer./Where you from?   Okay "Negroes."   June Jordan. BPo

Come a' to me, come a' to me.   Witch's Milking Charm.   *Anonymous.* GBP

Come again and again,/And still welcome, Gentlemen.   The Man in the Moon Drinks Clarret.   *Anonymous.*   CoMu

Come again, Jack! Come again, Jill!   There Were Two Blackbirds Sitting on a Hill.   Mother Goose.   HBV 1-2; HBVY

"Come again, little girl!" they called, and I/Called back, "You come see me!" A Visit to the Asylum.   Edna St. Vincent Millay.   SO

Come again to the earth/for all men to remember.   Christmas Songs.   Gerta Kennedy.   PoPl

Come all you heavy laden/I'll ease you of your pain.'   New Year's Carol. *Anonymous.*   OBET

Come all young men a warning take/Bid a curse to the pirate sea.   The Flying Cloud.   *Anonymous.*   BaBo; ViBoFo

Come along ten million strong.   Harriet Tubman.   Margaret Walker.   PoNe

Come: among the sons of men is one/Welcomer than art Alfred Tennyson?   To Alfred Tennyson.   Walter Savage Landor.   FaBoUs; PoL

Come an' meet me, wi' the childern, on the/road.   Come an' Meet Me wi' the Childern on the Road.   William Barnes.   VLP

Come, and abide in me, and I in thee.   Abide in Me, O Lord, and I in Thee. Harriet Beecher Stowe.   AH

Come and ask him/what he dreamed?   Song: "When the birds sang." *Anonymous.*   BoWoP

Come and celebrate with me.   Rondel.   Muriel Rukeyser.   FF

Come, and claim thy part thereof,–/I have fashioned it for thee!   The Builder. Francis Sherman.   CaP

Come and dance with me/In Ireland.   Irish Dancer.   *Anonymous.*   AnIL; EnL; FaBoCh; LoGBV; NOBE; OBEV; OxBM; SeCePo

Come and fight me, Man to Man!   Apache Kid.   Ned White.   BPAW

...Come and/get it.   It's Food.   Cid Corman.   GP

Come, and I will gaze on thee!   Song of Egla.   Maria Gowen Brooks.   AA; AnAmPo

Come, and in coming to Me you find/A sweet and perfect rest.   Come unto Me.   Flora L. Osgood.   STF

Come, and in this glowing nest,/Phoenix, learn to die.   Appeal to the Phoenix.   Louis Untermeyer.   UnTE

Come and listen while we pray/Whack fol the diddle lol the dido day. Whack Fol the Diddle.   Peadar Kearney.   FiBHP; OnYI

Come and picket on the picket line.   The Picket Line Song.   *Anonymous.* FSW

Come and play a little/In the middle of the square.   Ten Brothers. *Anonymous.*   MaC

Come and play oh yes   The Story of Good.   Phyllis Janik.   IHMS

Come and sacrifice, that you may have rest in your body,/Inside and outside. Wisdom Is the Finest Beauty of a Person.   *Anonymous.*   WTO

Come and see my shining palace built/upon the sand!   Second Fig.   Edna St-Vincent Millay.   AmP; FaBV; NoP

Come and talk the Man-Talk, that's the cure for you!   Willy and the Lady. Gelett Burgess.   HBMV

Come and welcome, sinner, come.   Come and Welcome.   Thomas Haweis. BePJ

Come and worship with me now.   I Want to Write a Jewish Poem.   Gary Pacernick.   VWA

Come ant daunce wyt me/In Irlaunde.   I Am of Ireland.   *Anonymous.* GBP; OnYI

Come as thou wilt, and what thou wilt bequeath,/I long to kisse the Image of my Death.   Sonnet IX.   William, of Hawthornden Drummond.   OBS

Come, as we could not hold it fast/We'll play it o'er again.   A Copy of Verses Sent by Cleone to Aspasia.   Walter Savage Landor.   LoBV

Come at light of dawn,/and bring no good friend.   Song: "Come at dawn, good friend."   *Anonymous.*   BoWoP

Come away, come away, my darling.   What Then Is Love But Mourning. Thomas Campion.   EnRePo

Come back again from blood; and they are strong.'   Elder Tree.   Conrad Aiken.   AP

Come back along to me.   In a Low Rocking-Chair.   Helen Coale Crew. HBMV

...Come back, bitch. Eat me alive.   Please.   Ronald Koertge.   GP

Come back! come back! and help me pay for/The bread and cheese and Lager Bier.   The Ballad of Lager Bier.   Edmund Clarence Stedman.   OBAL

Come back, come back, my own true lover,/And I will go away with you. Wake Up, You Drowsy Sleepers.   *Anonymous.*   BFSS

Come back early or never come.   Autobiography.   Louis MacNeice. FaBoIP; NOBI

Come back in a year/for the second.   Shakuhachi.   Jim Mitsui.   BrSi

Come back, my Beloved, I am waiting/To rise up and be caressed!   To the Sun.   Guido Gezelle.   LiTW

–Come back, O Day! said he.   Night and Day.   Sidney Lanier.   AA; AnAmPo

Come back, old graying guides,/That I, in tribute, may atone.   In Tribute. Vernal House.   CaP

Come back, Paul!   Two Little Dicky Birds.   *Anonymous.*   OxNR

...Come back to Elfin Town/For it's here that you were born!   Elfin Town. Rachel Field.   WSC

Come back to me! Come back to me!   Coeur de Lion to Berengaria. Theodore Tilton.   AA

Come back to seek the girl she was in these familiar/stones.   To a Young Girl Leaving the Hill Country.   Arna Bontemps.   CDC

Come back to us, child, if you love us,/And bring us your love.   Child and Poet.   Algernon Charles Swinburne.   EnLit

Come, be instructed of my Lamb.   Spiel of the Three Mountebanks.   John Crowe Ransom.   MoAB; MoAmPo

Come, be my valentine!   Shepherdess' Valentine.   Francis Andrewes.   OFD

Come, beauteous in thine after form,/And like a finer light in light.   In Memoriam A.H.H., XCI.   Alfred, Lord Tennyson.   OBNC

Come behind and kiss me milking the cow!   Song of the Milkmaid.   Alfred, Lord Tennyson.   HBV 1-2

Come bill, and kiss, and I'll show you.   Invitation to Dalliance.   *Anonymous.* FaBoEE

Come Boys a good health to our selves.   The Roaring Lad and the Ranting Lass.   *Anonymous.*   CoMu

Come, brother, roll, roll!   Cotton Song.   Jean Toomer.   BPo; CDC

Come build in the empty house of the stare.   Meditations in Time of Civil War.   William Butler Yeats.   CABL

Come, butter, come.   Churning.   *Anonymous.*   OxNR

Come buy o' me a broom.   The Broom Squire's Song.   *Anonymous.*   OxNR

Come choose the one/You love the best.   Here's a Poor Widow. *Anonymous.*   OxNR

Come, choose your road and away.   The Call of the Spring (excerpt). Alfred Noyes.   SUS

Come close, warm me, even/If I die in the flame.   Ode to a Beautiful Woman.   Carl Clark.   JB

Come, come home.   Come Home.   *Anonymous.*   PeSA

Come, cruel ease.   Come, Break with Time.   Louise Bogan.   ATP; MoAmPo

Come dear Lord/Upon the Clouds again to judge this world!   Silex Scintillans.   Henry Vaughan.   AnAnS 1

Come, Dora, my darling, my angel, and help me to ask him to dine.   Lord Walter's Wife.   Elizabeth Barrett Browning.   BeLS; HAP

Come down. Come down. Why dost/thou hide thy face? Speak. James Wright. HAP; SM; TAP; WeW

Come down, O Icarus, come down, down, O. Bird, Bird. Gene Derwood. LiTA

Come down this ev'ning, I'll introduce you. Under the Anheuser Bush. Andrew B. Sterling. OBAL

Come down to Kew in lilac-time (it isn't far/from London!) The Barrel-Organ. Alfred Noyes. BLPL; EnLit; FaBV; HBV 1-2; MCCG; MoBrPo; PoRA; TreF

Come drink, my boys, you're welcome, for I am young and the world is/wide. Sally's Garden. Anonymous. AmFP

Come, drink, you won't get licker/In the sweet bye and bye. Cow-Boy Fun. Wallace D. Coburn. PoOW

Come dyry, come dyry, come dawn, hey ho! Dawn. Anonymous. OBSC

Come equally handy to Whistler. Limerick: "There is a young artist named Whistler." Dante Gabriel Rossetti. LiBL

Come, every one who thirsts, to me. The Broken Bowl. Jones Very. AP

Come for the cool waters and thirsty men. The Fountain. Pavlos Liasides. AMV-80

Come for to show you/My diamond ring. Cotton Eye Joe. Anonymous. FSW; OuSiCo

Come forth, and bring with you a heart/That watches and receives. The Tables Turned. William Wordsworth. CBEP; DiPo; ERoP 1-2; HBV 1-2; MBW 1-2; OAEL 1-2; OAEP; OBRV

Come forth, O Quiet Heart,–I have avenged thee. He Biddeth Osiris to Arise from the Dead. Book of the Dead. AWP

Come fresh-from-the-oven flakes direct from the heart of the corn. Breakfast with Gerard Manley Hopkins. Anthony Brode. BXAP; FaBoPa; FiBHP; NOBL; Par

Come from the dead, and from the sky. Two Loves. Richard Eberhart. CMoP

Come from thy forest, and with me/Learn what it is to go to sea. Captain Jones' Invitation. Philip Freneau. MOS

Come Gaul or Briton; if array'd/For fight–he'll feel a freeman's blade. The Battle of Tippecanoe. Anonymous. PAH

Come get him–they knew where to search. A Lone Striker. Robert Frost. SaC

Come, gi'e me your hand,–we are brethren a'. We Are Brethren A'. Robert Nicoll. HBV 1-2

Come haste! the hour sets its face/Unto great Happenings. The Maine Trail. Gertrude Huntington McGiffert. HBV 1-2

Come hear me pray nine times a day,/And fill your heads with crotchets. The Distracted Puritan. Richard Corbet. OxBoLi

Come here, Lord!/Sinner cryin' come here, Lord. Come Here Lord! Anonymous. BoAN 1-2

Come here, my peek-a-boo ball! The Lost Ball. Lucy Sprague Mitchell. TiPo

Come, hide thee in mine arms,/If not for love, yet to shun greater harms. To Chloris. William, of Hawthornden Drummond. OBSP

Come/Home. The Shortest and Sweetest of Songs. George Macdonald. NOBV

Come home again, come home again! The Call. Anonymous. OBEV

Come home, dead man, who made your mind my home. Father. John Wheelwright. UnPo

"Come in and leave the play." The End of Day. William Butler Yeats. LiTB

Come in by the fire. Carol: "Fire is what's precious now..." Alison Boodson. NeBP

Come in, come in, they call. Alpha November Golf Sierra Tango. Tom Clark. APU

"Come in, I care not who you are,/I'm Belle Starr." Belle Starr. Anonymous. BPAW

Come in, John Wesley/For it rains. John Wesley Gaines. Anonymous. ELU; FiBHP

Come in, my dears, and tarry awhile! A Nursery Song. Laura E. Richards. HBV 1-2; HBVY

Come in, O Spring, come prettily in/All human hearts, I pray! O Spring, Come Prettily In. Adolf Strodtmann. CAW

...Come, in stream we'll cool/The wine ere quaffing.–Muleteer! Clarel. Herman Melville. OxBA

Come into me, and I will make you full. Ode to Food. Darrell Gray. APU

Come, knit hands, and beat the ground,/In a light fantastic sound. A Masque Presented at Ludlow Castle (Comus). John Milton. BoLiVe; NOBE; OBEV; PPoe; SeCeV; TrGrPo; ViBoPo

–Come, let me wash it in this big tin basin,/battered and shiny like the moon. The Shampoo. Elizabeth Bishop. FaBoWP; OxBC

Come, let's be drunk together! Song of the Vivandiere. Heinrich Heine. UnTE

"Come, let us all now mery be,/Since she has made such a happy/choice." Willie o Winsbury (D version). Anonymous. ESPB

Come let us be bold with our songs. The Pontoon Bridge Miracle. Vachel Lindsay. LoBV; NePA

"Come let us clasp your hands, we're/brothers all,/Over their graves!" Over Their Graves. Henry Jerome Stockard. AA; OHIP

...Come, let us feast our eyes. L'Art, 1910. Ezra Pound. HeIP; OxBA

Come, let us give some man his glory, or make it our own. The Iliad. Homer. WaaP

Come, let us go and listen to his flute. Love and Music. Anonymous. WTO

Come, let us in Him rest. Amen. Roll Out, O Song. Frank Sewall. AA

"Come, let us talk of former days." Sweet Was the Song. Walter Savage Landor. ViBoPo

Come life and light. Heavenward. Carolina Oliphant, Lady Nairne. HBV 1-2

Come life or come death I couldn't do less/than follow his guide. A Christopher of the Shenandoah. Edith Matilda Thomas. PAH

Come, light, now. Suilven and the Eagle (excerpt). Gordon Bottomley. MoBrPo

Come like this flower between thy God and thee.' The Pansy and the Prayer-Book. Mathilda Betham Edwards. OBVV

Come, love, come close, and murder me with a kiss. A Bedtime Story. Robert Mezey. NePoEA

Come, love; come, love, for sweet love's sake. Song for Autumn. Andrew Young. GBL

Come, Love, let us away from here. Away. Max Ehrmann. PoToHe

Come, maidens, come quickly, let me take a penny. New Brooms. Robert Wilson. EIL

"Come, Mary Winslow, come;I bell thee home." Mary Winslow. Robert Lowell. AnNE; MiAP; MoVE; PPP

Come, memory, let us seek them there in the shadows. On the Death of Friends in Childhood. Donald Justice. ConAP; LCAP; NCSH

Come, my Corinna, come, let's go a-Maying. Corinna's Going A-Maying. Robert Herrick. AtBAP; ATP; BiP; BoNaP; CaPo; CBEP; CoBE; DiPo; EnL; ExPo; GTBS; HAP; HBV 1-2; InPS; JCP; NIP; NOBE; NoP; OAEL 1-2; OAEP; OBEV; OBS; PoEL 1-5; PoPle; PPP; PrIm; SeCeV; SeCP; SeCV 1-2; TEP; TreFT; TrGrPo; WHA

Come my friends come/I am waiting for you. Call from the Afterworld. Jozef Habib Gerez. VWA

"Come, my lad, and drink some beer." Hermit Hoar... Samuel Johnson. EnLi 1-2; NLV; PV; ViBoPo

Come near, that even so/They may have peace. For All in Pain. Amy Carmichael. TRV

Come not along my way. I seek my rest. Troubles of the Day. William Barnes. GTBS-P

"Come not! Come not again!" The Flown Soul. George Parsons Lathrop. AA

Come now–appease me just a little/With the why-and-wherefore of your sex! Without the Moon. Jules Laforgue. LiTW

Come, O Bride. Come, O Friend, to Greet the Bride. Solomon H Alkabez. TrJP

Come, O Hymenaeus. Song for the Third Marriage of Lucrezia Borgia (excerpt). Lodovico Ariosto. HW

Come of'en wi' your work vrom hwome,/Up here a while. Do come. Lwonesomeness. William Barnes. NOBV

Come, of your Buttercup buy! Little Buttercup. Sir William Schwenck Gilbert. GoTF; TreFS

Come, old friend, come thro' the darkness and let us be/playmates again. Pirates. Alfred Noyes. MCCG

Come, old Goliath, come and play! Goliath and David. Louis Untermeyer. TrJP

Come on Catullus, you can/take it. Catullus viii. Louis Zukofsky. NoAm

Come on, Chaplin, we mean business. Patriotic Ode on the...Persecution of Charlie Chaplin. Bob Kaufman. PoBA

Come on down. It's time. Black Boy. Norman Rosten. TrJP

Come on. Let's go. I want an answer. Coming Up & Falling Down. Stephen Vincent. NeAC

Come on, men,/Give it a trial! Ballyhoo for a Mendicant. Carlton Talbott. AnAmPo

Come on, open that window/or I'll go home. Serenade. Emanuel Carnevali. AnAmPo

"Come on out, we are burning a fairy!" Limerick: "Some Harvard men, stalwart and hairy." Edward Gorey. OBAL

Come on Phidon, add deeds to words! Epigram: "Stolen kisses, wary eyes." Strato. PeHV

...Come on, play ball! Polo Grounds. Rolfe Humphries. HoPM; LiSp; SD

Come on up, come on up. At the Party. Patricia Goedicke. FAZ

"Come on, you...Do you want to live forever?" Losers. Carl Sandburg. CMoP; HBMV; MoAB; MoAmPo; MoVE; NoAm; TrGrPo

Come one, come all, the oven's full of bread Nineteen Sections from a Twenty Acre Poem (excerpt). David Martinson. TAT

Come out from the bath. The Bath. Gary Snyder. CAPP; GP; NNaP; TAP

Come out into the sun!   Though Bodies Are Apart.   C. Day-Lewis.   NAs

Come peace. Come violence. Come violent peace.   The House.   Winfield Townley Scott.   MiAP

Come people; Aaron's drest.   Aaron.   George Herbert.   MeLP; MePo; OAEP; OBS

"Come, play with me, my treasure!"   A Pastoral.   *Anonymous.*   AWP; UnTE

Come, pledge me on this ground, aground, aground!   We Be Three Poor Mariners.   *Anonymous.*   AmSS

Come Poet shut up eat my word, and taste my mouth in your/ear.   The End.   Allen Ginsberg.   ConAP

Come, precious–I'm not good at waiting.   Invitation to a Mistress.   *Anonymous.*   UnTE

Come quick, come quick, come quick, come quick.   The Watch.   Frances Cornford.   DTC; HBMV; HeIP; InPK; MoBrPo; OxBTC

"Come quickly, dear!/The keeper has turned on the tap!"   Otters.   William Hart-Smith.   BoAnP

Come, rains,/come,/come again/and again.   Winter Journey.   Stanislaw Wygodski.   VWA

Come safe to land and Love be left behind.   Adrift.   Elizabeth Dickinson Dowden.   WGRP

Come safely back. There was nothing in her arms.   Leaving Something Behind.   David Wagoner.   CoAP

Come see the monster.   If.   Anselm Hollo.   APU

Come sing, come sing, come sing sing/And sing.   Yardbird's Skull.   Owen Dodson.   AmNP; CNA; IDB; PoBA; VGW

Come, sing my jealous fears to rest,/And let your songs be those I've written.   To Phyllis.   Eugene Field.   InMe

Come! sip it freshly as it flows.   The Enchanted Spring.   George Darley.   BoNaP; NBM

Come sleep, come lightning, comes the dove at last.   The Usk.   C. H. Sisson.   NOCV

Come/smile at me/with your breasts   Smile at Me.   Musa Moris Farhi.   VWA

Come soon, my love, my bride, and share this meal.   The Lion's Bride.   Gwen Harwood.   BoWoP

Come soon, soon!   To Night.   Percy Bysshe Shelley.   AWP; HBVY; MCCG; NoP; TEP; TrGrPo

Come, sorrow, come, her eyes that sings/By thee are turned into springs.   Song Set by John Dowland: "Come, ye heavy states of night."   *Anonymous.*   OBSC

Come steering safely home.   Ships.   Nancy Byrd Turner.   SoPo; SUS

Come strong veiled women, bearing their perfect jars.   Archaeology.   Katha Pollitt.   MAYP

Come stump away to Stamford.   The Bullard's Song.   *Anonymous.*   OBET

Come, take the footpath way with me!   The Footpath Way.   Katharine Tynan Hinkson.   HBV 1-2

Come, talk with me. My body is alone.   Come Laugh with Me.   *Anonymous.*   WTO

Come, tell me then how great's the smart/Of those thou woundest with thy dart!   The Wounded Cupid.   Robert Herrick.   AWP; OFD

Come the dusky plumes of red "Singing Leaves'.   The Camp of Souls.   Isabella Valancy Crawford.   NOBC

Come the king and Pompadour.   The Pompadour.   George Walter Thornbury.   BeLS

Come the little clouds out of the Ice-Caves,/To bring us rain for our harvests!   Rain Chant.   Louis Mertins.   BPAW

Come then and help us, or we die.   Help, Good Shepherd.   Ruth Pitter.   OxBoCh

Come, then, and make thy flight/As swift to me, as heavenly light.   My Life's Delight.   Thomas Campion.   TrGrPo

Come, then, at least we may enjoy/Some pleasure for our punishment!   An Argument: To Any Phillis or Chloe.   Thomas Moore.   NIP; OBSP

Come then, expressive Silence, muse HIS Praise.   A Hymn on the Seasons.   James (1700-48) Thomson.   LAuP; OxBoCh

Come then thou faithful witness! come dear Lord/Upon the clouds again to judge this world!   Ascension-Day.   Henry Vaughan.   OxBoCh

Come there as to a Paradise.   In Provence.   Jean Aicard.   CAW

Come those last, late, lingering hours before/Christmas Day.   Those Last, Late Hours of Christmas Eve.   Lou Ann Welte.   PCh

Come, thou silver-breasted moonbeam of desire!   The Snake-Charmer.   Sarojini Naidu.   PBWP

Come to behold the death of the poor heart.   Sonnet: To a Friend Who Does Not Pity His Love.   Guido Cavalcanti.   AWP

Come to me, love, the twilight star/Shall guide thee to my bower.   Song: "Where is the nymph, whose azure eye."   Thomas Moore.   EnLoPo

Come to me, loving Mary.   A Poem to Mary.   Blathmac Mac Con Brettan.   NOBI

Come to me quickly–Shadow of Darkness.   Shadow of Darkness.   Gladys May Casely Hayford.   PBA

Come to my arms, naked in the dark.   From the Persian.   Kenneth Rexroth.   FaBoEE

Come to my haggard gate, my very doorstep.   Ad Limina.   Joseph Campbell.   BIrV

Come to our ignorant hearts and be forgiven.   Veni Creator.   Alice Meynell.   ILwL

Come to papa, come to papa, do!/My sweet embraceable you!   Embraceable You.   Ira Gershwin.   BLSo

Come to share the festal show.   Song of the Mermaids and Mermen.   Sir Walter Scott.   WSC

Come to the burialie/Between four and five.   Ding Dang, Bell Rang.   *Anonymous.*   OxNR

Come to the heart which is throbbing to press thee!   Come to Me, Dearest.   Joseph Brenan.   HBV 1-2

Come to the stone and tell me why I died.   Come to the Stone.   Randall Jarrell.   VGW

Come to the top, O wicked swimmer!   The Swimmer.   John Crowe Ransom.   SD

Come to the valley where my ashes are blown by the wind/And laid to rest.   Memento Vivendi.   Eva Brudne.   VWA

Come to their terms, your plans unmade,–/And be belied, and be betrayed.   Exhortation.   Louise Bogan.   QFR

Come to thy God at last!'   The Silent Tower of Bottreaux.   Robert Stephen Hawker.   GoBC; OBRV

Come to your Wedding Song.   A Black Wedding Song.   Gwendolyn Brooks.   CNA

Come try! come try! come try!   A Hoggie Dead!   *Anonymous.*   PBBP

Come unto me, and I will give you rest.   Come unto Me, When Shadows Darkly Gather.   Catharine H. Watterman.   AH

"Come unto me and rest.'"   The Call to the Strong.   William Pierson Merrill.   BLRP

"Come up higher!" cry the angels: "come up to the/Royal Arch."   Farewell to Earth.   Elizabeth Doten.   PeD

Come uppe Jetty, follow, follow,/Jetty5 to the milking shed.'   The High Tide on the Coast of Lincolnshire.   Jean Ingelow.   BeLS; FaBoPP; GN; GTBS; HBV 1-2; NBM; OBVV; OnMSP; PaPo

Come visit. I shall welcome you.   Elegy for Former Students.   Virginia Scott Miner.   AMV-81

Come walk with me! Come walk with me!   Man of Galilee.   Mary Louise Deissler.   BePJ

Come, we'll associate this jolly pilgrimage!   What Fair Pomp Have I Spied of Glittering Ladies.   Thomas Campion.   AtBAP; GBL; PoEL 1-5; Prf

Come welcome, sweet Jesus, and lodge in our hearts.   No Room at the Inn.   *Anonymous.*   FSW

Come west and see; touch these leaves.   West of Your City.   William Stafford.   LiTM

Come, what do you make of it, Watson?/By me!   Wasted Ammunition.   Stoddard King.   InMe

Come where my love lies dreaming,/Dreaming the happy hours away.   Come Where My Love Lies Dreaming.   Stephen Collins Foster.   GoTF; TreFS

Come with a rattle, a jingle, a tone and a word.   Whispering Clouds.   Mariquita Platov.   AMV-80

Come with your medicine making,/O caller of Buffalo!   Caller of the Buffalo.   Mary Austin.   BPAW

Come yee my servants of my father Blessed   Upon the First Sight of New-England June 29, 1638.   Thomas Tillam.   SCAP

Come yield me the sweets of thy heart.'   Far Sweeter Than Honey.   Abraham Ibn Ezra.   TrJP

Comely, comely, love trembles/and the sweet-shrub   A Vulnerary.   Jonathan Williams.   PoM

The comely Girdhar, Mira's Lord,/saves those who for salvation come.   Wake Up, Dear Boy That Holds the Flute!   Mira Bai [(or Mirabai)].   WPOW

Comes a flash from my world,/A cutting cold light.   Like the Eyes of Wolves.   Nachum Yud.   TrJP

Comes alive when I remember.   Loveliness.   Hilda Conkling.   TiPo

Comes articulate and presseth/On his ear like mother-tongue.   The Poet.   John Keats.   PP

Comes beautifully back to me/In blossoms, everywhere.   Symbol.   David Morton.   HBMV

Comes (best of all) himself–our welcome James.   Henry James.   Robert Louis Stevenson.   OBNC

Comes Death, and takes the table clean away.   A Comparison of the Life of Man.   Richard Barnfield.   OBSC; OBSP

Comes down,/As soon it must, from the mountain.   Here in Katmandu.   Donald Justice.   CoAP; ConAP; HeIP; LiSp; NIP; RFM

...Comes haply on the verge/Of happiness, haply hysterics. Is.   The Rites for Cousin Vit.   Gwendolyn Brooks.   BPo; HAP; SM

Comes like a tiger crunching through the stones.   The Hermit.   William Henry Davies.   BrPo; MoBrPo

Comes pouring like sunlight the lark's noisiest music.   Spring Doggerel.   Rhoda Coghill.   NeIP

Comes/Revolution.   Huey.   Etheridge Knight.   NNaP

Comes stealing; comes creeping.   The Rock-A-By Lady.   Eugene Field.
HBVY; TiPo

Comes the deer to my singing.   Hunting-Song.   *Anonymous.*   AWP

Comes the one scar that your heart shall hide/Till the day you die!
Certainties.   Margaret Widdemer.   HBMV

Comes the rain with me.   Song of the Rain Chant.   *Anonymous.*   AWP

The comet's pulsing rose.   Exposure.   Seamus Heaney.   CIP; IPY

Cometh al this newe science that men lere.   Proem to the Parlement of
Foules.   Geoffrey Chaucer.   FiP

Comets! come every day–and stay a year.   Comets and Princes.   Samuel
Johnson.   FaBoEE

...Comfort/As lying with a man./To come down, down.....   Tottingham
Frolic.   *Anonymous.*   UnTE

Comfort in the steady sun, time beating down.   The Book of Persephone.
Robert Kelly.   PoM

The comfort of the poor man's sleep.   Sleep That Like the Couched Dove.
Gerald Griffin.   OnYI

Comfort that does not comprehend.   The Return.   Edna St. Vincent Millay.
LiTA; MoAB; MoAmPo; MoPo; NoAm; OxBA; PoPl

Comfort Thy care-stricken, Christ in Thy Kingdom.   Prayer for Rich and
Poor.   William Langland.   BoC

Comforted, warmed, remembering the womb.   Momist.   Amy Groesbeck.
GoYe

...Coming all the way/from a grave in Haiti.   Haitian Suite.   Gregory Orr.
MAYP

Coming and coming and coming. She screamed.   Woman's Liberation.
Sister Maura.   AMV-81

Coming back, coming back, going over.   On the Hill below the Lighthouse.
James Dickey.   NePoEA-2; SM

...Coming back home to an invisible/town and a wife made of clear air and
smoke.   I Point Out a Bird.   Quinton Duval.   FAZ

Coming for to carry me home.   Swing Low, Sweet Chariot.   *Anonymous.*
AA; ABF; AmFN; BLSo; BoAN 1-2; FSW; GBP; GoSl; LoGBV; UnPo

Coming home to roost.   The Happy Poem.   Thomas Brush.   LTB

Coming like madness in the snow.   Passing into Storm.   Patrick Lane.
NOBC

Coming like the ruby in the invisible dark,/glowing/with his own
annunciation, towards us.   Lucifer.   D. H. Lawrence.   OAEP

The coming of that age/When man shall find his wings!   Let Us Declare!
(excerpt).   Angela Morgan.   PGD

Coming out again and again.   Coming out of.   Robert Duncan.   EAS

Coming over by Ben Buy they have word of May,/O Donacha Ban!   There Is
Snowdrift on the Mountain.   W. P. Ker.   PoSH

Coming to no sure conclusion, nor anxious to come.   The Wasps' Nest.
George Macbeth.   OxBTC

Coming to that level and spoiled.   Areas.   Leslie Scalapino.   NPGG

Coming together   Feasts of Death, Feasts of Love.   Stuart Perkoff.   NeAP

Coming toward wholeness towards singleness   From the Rain Forest.
Desiree Flynn.   BrRo

Coming up from Richmond,/On the way to Kew.   Life and Death.   William
Ernest Henley.   OBNC

Coming up the canon from the smoke-blue plains!   The Smoke-Blue Plains.
Badger Clark.   YaD

Command, and we obey!   The Voice of God Is Calling.   John Haynes
Holmes.   AH

Command me to her hertely!   She Saw Me in Church.   *Anonymous.*   MeEL

Command their son to take the post that fits the/Geraldine.   The Geraldines.
Thomas Osborne Davis.   IrPN

Command your sleepy poet to descend.   Laudanum.   *Anonymous.*   NOEC

Commander, sweet good night.   When Death Came April Twelve 1945.   Carl
Sandburg.   AP

Commanding all consciousness forever to rejoice!   I Wakened to a Calling.
Delmore Schwartz.   PoPl

Commenced a more than Newton in abstruse philosophy.   Death's Vision
(excerpt).   John Reynolds.   NOEC

Commend me all to my good-mother,/At night when ye gang home.'   Lord
William, or, Lord Lundy.   *Anonymous.*   ESPB

Commend thou me to each, as doth behove.   Ladies That Have Intelligence
in Love.   Dante Alighieri.   LiTW

The Commies are using it now.   Surveyor.   Guy Butler.   PeSA

Commin' owre the Hill o' Hoos.   Insect Riddle: "As I went owre the.Hill o'
Hoos."   *Anonymous.*   GBP

Commission'd to steal, and commission'd to/lie.   On Sir Henry Clinton's
Recall.   *Anonymous.*   PAH

The committee shivers/With delight in/Its manure.   Un-American
Investigators.   Langston Hughes.   BPo

Commodious to conquer heaven and Thee/Planted in me.   Fraility.   George
Herbert.   NOCC; OxBoCh

The common man, perhaps, is Not Allowed?   The Crucifix.   Alexander
Pushkin.   LiTW

The common rituals of life.   Folding a Shirt.   Denise Levertov.   NeBP

The common things of life are all so dear.   Life's Common Things.   Alice E.
Allen.   WBLP

A common triumph or a single grave.   Call All.   *Anonymous.*   PAH

The common-wealth still safe, must studie thee.   To William Earle of
Pembroke.   Ben Jonson.   SeCP

The common woman is as common/as a rattlesnake.   Ella, in a Square
Apron, along Highway 80.   Judy Grahn.   NMM

The common woman is as common/as a thunderstorm.   Carol, in the Park,
Chewing on Straws.   Judy Grahn.   PeHV

The common woman is as solemn as a monkey/or a new moon.   The
Common Woman.   Judy Grahn.   GP

The commonplace, average man.   The Average Man.   Margaret E. Sangster.
WBLP

The commonwealth of man,/The City of our God!   The Prophecy Sublime.
Frederick Lucian Hosmer.   TrPWD

The Commonwealth of Man without the man.   Great Powers Conference.
Edith Lovejoy Pierce.   PGD

Commotion for/every syllable.   The Empress.   Diane Wakoski.   CoPo

Companion in repose with those who once were men.   Everyman.   Siegfried
Sassoon.   BoLiVe; MoBrPo

Companion, mourner, thief.   Harmless Streets.   Tess Gallagher.   LTB

Companioned by those powers who keep me unafraid.   The Wisdom of the
World.   Siegfried Sassoon.   MoBrPo

Companions of the spring.   Ode: To the Cuckoo.   Michael Bruce.   NOEC;
OBEC; PBBP

The company is the best you'll ever have.   How to Eat Alone.   Daniel
Halpern.   MAYP

Compared to the creatures in the seas entrall.   The Faerie Queene.   Edmund
Spenser.   AtBAP

Compass lost and rudder broken,/Drifting, drifting, thoughtlessly.   A Home
without a Bible (excerpt).   Charles D. Meigs.   WBLP

Compelling a recognition.   Paring the Apple.   Charles Tomlinson.   CMoP;
NePoEA-2; NMP; OxBTC

The competitive product you said you'd send.   A Consumer's Report.   Peter
Porter.   FaBoCo; NOBL

Complain, and are not fain/To say what they saw in her heart.   Proem.
Heinrich Heine.   AWP

"Complaine, my lute, complaine with me,/Untill that he doth come againe."
A Pleasant New Ballad of Two Lovers.   *Anonymous.*   CoMu

Complaine not whatsoever Need invades,/But heaviest fortunes beare as
lightest shades.   A Hymne to Our Saviour on the Cross.   George
Chapman.   PoEL 1-5

Complete days reach/harmonic proportions, narrowly/entering the flood.
Archangel.   Kit Robinson.   APU

Complete in a completed scene, speaking/Their parts as in a youthful
happiness.   Credences of Summer.   Wallace Stevens.   AP; CoBMV

Complete neither/beard nor/breast/neither.   The Numbers.   Joel
Oppenheimer.   CoPo

Complete Thy purpose, that we may become/Thy perfect image, O our God
and Lord!   The Master's Touch.   Horatius Bonar.   BePJ; HBV 1-2;
TrPWD

Completed Faust when eighty years were past.   It Is Too late!   Henry
Wadsworth Longfellow.   BLPL; PoLf

Completely new, yet linked to paradise.   Mendel's Law.   Peter Meinke.
SUW

...Completing this/poem, would be like entering my own house.   My Own
House.   David Ignatow.   AMV-80

A completion like the exhaling/of a single breath   Growing Together.   Joyce
Carol Oates.   IHMS

...Complex/As the needs of your new and childfree girl.   On Not Being Your
Lover.   Mebdh McGuckian.   FaBoIP

A complex, or assistant foreman!   Poems in Praise of Practically Nothing.
Samuel Hoffenstein.   InMe

The complex reason of your simple doubt.   The Doppelganger.   Daryl Hine.
OBCV

Completions marked with still unmalignant moles/Of the actual, scabs on
unfolding leaves?   Those of Pure Origin.   Roy Fuller.   FaBoMo

...A compliment/To all accomplishment.   The Drowning Poet.   James
Merrill.   PP

Complique, mais eurythmique.   After a Passage in Baudelaire.   Robert
Duncan.   CMoP; PoA

Composed around the echo of a pistol-shot.   Sarajevo.   Lawrence Durrell.
GTBS-P; OBTV

Composed, they suffer your coming.   Elk Ghosts: A Birth Memory.   Dave
Smith.   GeTw

A composing of senses of the guitar.   The Man with the Blue Guitar.
Wallace Stevens.   CMoP

Composing stillness round their careless will.   The Idler.   Elizabeth Jennings.
NePoEA

Composite span–an actuality.   Granite and Steel.   Marianne Moore.   NYBP

Composted in their fertile hecatombs.   Proserpine at Enna.   Ronald Bottrall.
SeCePo

Comprehending all,/All eligible to all. Song of the Universal. Walt Whitman. PGD

–Comrade, it serves to feel/The sackcloth next the skin. Renunciants. Edward Dowden. OBVV

Comrade Jesus hath his red card. Comrade Jesus. Sarah N. Cleghorn. AnAmPo; HBMV; WGRP

Comrade of ocean, playmate of the hills. Love in the Wind. Richard Hovey. AA; HBV 1-2

A comrade peered–"Yes, he'd 'a' got 'em!" It's Three No Trumps. Guy Innes. FiBHP

Concatenation of the poppet heads. The Brides. A. D. Hope. HAP

Conceal'd and dormant under ground. The Eagle and the Beetle. Jean de La Fontaine. OBVE

Conceded to the jaw,/Of toothed, blue steel. Heart's Needle. W.D. Snodgrass. AP

Conceiv'd with grief are, and with teares brought forth. To Primroses Fill'd with Morning-Dew. Robert Herrick. AnAnS 2; OBS; PoPl; SeCV 1-2; ViBoPo

...Conceive it how you please/But paint me these. Epiphany: For the Artist. Elizabeth Sewell. EyDe

Conceive the bard the hero of the story. That Idiot, Wordsworth. George Gordon, Lord Byron. DBV

Concentrates what Time forgave! Postscript, on a Name. Stephen Ratcliffe. AMV-80

Concentric rings, those many marriages/That life on each live thing bestows. For a Second Marriage. James Merrill. NePoEA

Concerning life in an attempted passage/From ancient history. I Am Not the Constant Reader. Michael Brownstein. ANYP

Concerning the slithery, slimy eel? Song of Hate for Eels. Arthur Guiterman. OBAL

...The concertmaster rubs a little resin on his bow. Guide to the Symphony. Weldon Kees. VGW

...Conclude/Our kneeling as cattle by all-generous waters? Wedding Wind. Philip Larkin. HW; MAT

Concord and Charity in circles move. The Pilgrim Fathers. William Wordsworth. PAH

Concourse of light and cloud that would never come back. The Yorkshire Moors. Hal Summers. HaMV

[Concrete poem] Forsythia. Mary Ellen Solt. BoWoP

[Concrete poem] Marriage. Mary Ellen Solt. BoWoP

[Concrete poem] Moonshot Sonnet. Mary Ellen Solt. BoWoP

[Concrete poem] Rain Down. Mary Ellen Solt. BoWoP

[Concrete poem] Wild Crab. Mary Ellen Solt. BoWoP

Condemned, like all his family, to Clear the Way! Clear the Way. John Montague. FaBoIP

Condemned to live, I speak now Looting. Jascha Kessler. HoAn

A condition which I could face with equanimity. The Anatomy of Happiness. Ogden Nash. LiTA; TAP

Conduct you soonest to the Stygian shores. The Dispensary. Sir Samuel Garth. DBV

Conduct your blooming in the noise and whip of the/whirlwind. The Second Sermon on the Warpland. Gwendolyn Brooks. BPo; NOBA; PoBA

...The conductress/Was dark and lost, refused to change. Hold-Up. Louis MacNeice. FaBoIP

Confess, laconically:/"Hard." Anabasis. Eithne Wilkins. NeBP

Confess, Marpessa, who is your new lover? Confess, Marpessa. Robert Graves. TEP

Confess no trouble like unto a Wife. The Wife-Hater. Anonymous. CoMu

Confesses to the other's ghost. The Ghost. William Henry Davies. BrPo

Confessionals and agonies of prayer. A Butterfly in Church. George Marion McClellan. BANP

The confetti's tourbillons again will bluster/And lay our happiness waste-wide with the rest. Calm Winter Sleep. Hilary Corke. MP; NYBP

Confided to her trust,/The key to lands of gold! Cuba. Harvey Rice. PAH

Confident that life will not begin tomorrow.... The Jewish Cemetery. Cesar Tiempo. VWA

Confiding always on His excellent greatness. Johannes Milton, Senex. Robert Bridges. CMoP; LiTB; NAMP; PoEL 1-5; PoPl

Confirm, as once it clawed, a mind made free. Appalachian Convalescence. Robert Conquest. OxBC

Confirm the tales her sons relate! The Passions. William Collins. EiCP; GoTL; GTBS; GTBS-P; HBV 1-2

Confirmed in her instinctive guess/That letters always bring distress. Sarah Byng. Hilaire Belloc. CenHV; GoJo

Conflagrant world against world The Making of Color. Hugh Seidman. AmPA

Confound his ffoes, Lord, wee beseeche,/And loue His Grace both night and/day! The Rose of England. Anonymous. ESPB

Confused the drama with the true Amphimachos the Dandy. Vincent McHugh. NePoAm-2

Confused with my life, that is commonplace and solitary. Next Day. Randall Jarrell. HAP; NoAm; NoP; NYBP

Confusedly among the rout that in thine Orgies trots. Metamorphoses. Ovid (Publius Ovidius Naso). OBVE

Confusing the star-dazed tourists/with our incomparable sense of loss Queen Victoria and Me. Leonard Cohen. NoAm

...Confusing/The tongues and tasks of her children's children. My Grandmother. Karl Shapiro. VGW

(The confusion is called harem scarem.) Limerick: "The sultan got sore on his harem." Anonymous. GoTF; TDH; TreFT

The congressed candles fuming in the nave. On the Nativity of Christ Our Lord. Joseph Bennett. NePA

The congruence of the complement is vain, if it exists. To a Steam Roller. Marianne Moore. BoWoP; CMoP; FaBoMo; MoAB; MoAmPo; OxBA; PP; VGW

Connecting youtometoyoutometo/you to me/to you. Noises. Fred Johnson. CNA

Conqu'ring and to conquer go. Jesus, Thou Art the King. Charles Wesley. BePJ

The conqu'ring Force of unresisted Steel? The Rape of the Lock. Alexander Pope. AtBAP; CABL; CEP; CoBE; DiPo; EnL

Conscience perfect. Skylarks. Ted Hughes. HAP

...Conscience within/Is guidance enough for the conduct of men. Credo. Georgia Douglas Johnson. BALP; PoBA

Conscious of her reed neck/that the smallest stone can break. In the Library. Ed Ochester. Psk

Conscious of our pleasing God. Jesus, Master, O Discover. Anonymous. AH

Consciousness aches in the void for the physical thud of your/heart. Separation. D. S. Savage. NeBP

The consecrated spot shall hold/The name of "Gelert's Grave." Beth Gelert. William Robert Spencer. BeLS; BLPA; GDP; OBNV; TreFS

The consecration wondrous (being their own)/As when the water reddened at the feast. Cana Revisited. Seamus Heaney. FaBoMo

–Consent, consent, consent to be/My many-branched, small and dearest tree. Mentreche il Vento, Come Fa, Si Tace. Delmore Schwartz. AnFE; CoAnAm

Consents to his inexorable will. Playboy. Richard Wilbur. FF; NoAm; NOBA; NoP; WeW

Consequently the tongue is a chair. The Domestic Stones. Hans Arp. EAS

Consider all this wonder, O my soul! A Meditation for Christmas. Selwyn Image. OBEV

Consider how briefly its beauty is going to last. The Apple. Plato. WeW

Consider how the other half lives. Saints Lose Back. Nancy Willard. HoAn

Consider it, then,/A finished performance. Over. R. S. Thomas. FF

Consider Phlebas, who was once handsome and tall as you. Death by Water. Thomas Stearns Eliot. OBVE

Considering how to run. A Centipede Was Happy Quite. Anonymous. ALV; OnUR; SoPo; TiPo

Considering she came from such/A pleasant familee. Such a Pleasant Familee. Wallace Irwin. ShM

Considering what wild infancy/Drove horror from His Mother's/breast. Wisdom. William Butler Yeats. TrCP

Considering whom to please. The Redwoods. Louis Simpson. AmFN; CoAP; PP

Consigning dry leaves to the winter sea. The Young Men Come Less Often– Isn't It So? Horace. ErPo

Consistent in his preference for every kind of corruption. George I,–Star of Brunswick. William Makepeace Thackeray. FaBoEE

A consort of blue trombones. How the Laws of Physics Love Chocolate! Reg Saner. GP

Conspicuous on our fields the shadow of man. Midwest. John Frederick Nims. MoVE; PoPl

The constable told him brusquely/To put it away. Six Reasons for Drinking. Vernon Scannell. OxBC

A constant interchange of growth and blight! Laodamia. William Wordsworth. EnRP; ERoP 1-2; OAEP

Constrained by the will/to believe. Machine Out of the God. Thomas E. Sanders. AMV-81

The constriction killing me also. The Rabbit Catcher. Sylvia Plath. SBG

Constructing puzzled strictures for his God. Job. Eli Mandel. PeCV

Consubstantial, co-eternal/While unending ages run,/Evermore and evermore! Of the Father's Love Begotten. Prudentius (Aurelius Clemens Prudentius). BePJ

Consul, or King, can sound himself to know/The destiny of Man, and live in hope. Calais, August 15, 1802. William Wordsworth. NAs

Consumed by either fire or fire. The Dove. Thomas Stearns Eliot. BoC

The consummate symmetry of the dead. On the Dates of Poets. Michael L. Johnson. AMV-80

...The consummation of rain/on the tin roof, the tides of drowning sound. Domestic Quarrel.   Sally McInerney.   GrPl

The contact lens/you are looking for!   Lost Contact.   William Cole.   PoL

Contain my heart's/merry-making.   When You Reach the Hilltop the Sky Is on Top of You.   Etta Blum.   GoYe

Contained my hate in embryo.   Written on a Paper Napkin.   Len Gasparini. NeAC

Containing passion still,/Who cared enough to sing.   To a Western Bard Still a Whoop and a Holler away from English Poetry.   William Meredith.   PP

Content in His love, you will never grow/old.   In His Service.   Clarence E. Clar.   STF

Content should Time confess/How sweet you were.   The Queen's Song. James Elroy Flecker.   BrPo; HBV 1-2

Content though blind, had I no better guide.   To Mr. Cyriack Skinner Upon His Blindness.   John Milton.   DiPo; MBW 1-2; OBS

...Content to be/my own incredible imagery.   Adman into Toad.   Frank Polite.   APU

Content to dream, and sing no more.   Poet and Lark.   Mary Ainge De Vere. AA; HBV 1-2

Content to know He doeth all things/well.   God Doeth All Things Well. *Anonymous.*   STF

Content to know, where'er He leads/That we can trust Him still.   Thy Will Be Done.   Albert Simpson Reitz.   STF

Content to pray in life and love/And toil, till all are thine.   O Gracious Father of Mankind.   Henry Hallam Tweedy.   AH

Content to remain content.   Oxen: Ploughing at Fiesole.   Charles Tomlinson. OxBTC

Content to serve and suffer still I must.   Suffering in sorrow in hope to attain. Sir Thomas Wyatt.   FCP

Content to suffer while we know,/Living and dying, Thou art near!   Hymn of Trust.   Oliver Wendell Holmes.   AA; TrPWD

Content wi' you to mak a pair,/Whare'er I gang.   Epistle to James Smith. Robert Burns.   BSV; CABL; MCCG; OBEC

Content, with De Monts and Champlain,/With this, for Cathay.   The Saint John.   George Frederick Clarke.   CaP

...Content with one warm kiss/had there been anyone to offer this. Incendiary.   Vernon Scannell.   OxBC

Content you with Nay, for you get no more.   Of Few Words, Sir, You Seem to Be.   *Anonymous.*   SiPS

"Content yourselves with laughing at the/antics of the fools who do."   The House of a Hundred Lights.   Ridgely Torrence.   AA

Content yow. This ye get no moir.   The Bankis of Helicon: Remeidis of Luve. *Anonymous.*   OxBS

Contented and calm as the mountains,/And deep as the woods and the sea. The Great Voices.   Charles Timothy Brooks.   HBV 1-2

Contented, half to please.   A Prayer for Indifference.   Fanny Macartney Greville.   LoBV; NOEC; OBEV

Contented like the road that dozes/In panniered gown of briar roses.   The Road to the Pool.   Grace Hazard Conkling.   HBMV

Contented live, and then contented die.   To Mr. Izaak Walton.   Charles Cotton.   ViBoPo

Contented with the bed of one.   An Epitaph upon a Sober Matron.   Robert Herrick.   CaPo

Contented with thine own estate,/Neither wish death nor fear his might. "Martial, the things for to attain."   Henry Howard, Earl of Surrey.   FCP

Contentedly he glides away, serene.   The Year's End.   Timothy Cole.   HBV 1-2

...A continent they had/To ravage, and raving romped from sea to sea.   O Pioneers!   John Peale Bishop.   VGW

The continent, whole,/We will take, by my soul,/If the cowardly Yankees will let us.   A New War Song by Sir Peter Parker.   *Anonymous.*   PAH

Continue still/With their good will.   L'Envoy: To His Book.   John Skelton. EnRePo

Continue to think that I really intend to forget you.   This Way Out. Margaret Fishback.   ALV

Continuing yet/Not to cut with your own?   The Preacher.   Al-Mahdi. TTY

Contra hos Motores Bos!   Motor Bus.   Alfred Denis Godley.   FaBoCo; NOBL

Contra regis consilia.   The Martyrdom of Becket.   *Anonymous.*   EnPo

...The/contraction/of that is.   Three Tiny Songs.   Cid Corman.   HoAn

A contrite heart, a humble thought,/Are mine accepted sacrifice.   Ivanhoe. Chapt. 39: Rebecca's Hymn.   Sir Walter Scott.   EnRP

Contrive that the poor may have something to eat.   A Song: "While a thousand fine projects are planned ev'ry day."   *Anonymous.*   NOEC

Contrives that none go out again—   No passenger was known to flee.   Emily Dickinson.   MoVE

Control me for/i am and need   A Sun Heals.   Johari (Jewel C. Latimore) Amini.   JB

Control the rhythms of my soul.   Variations on a Late October Day. George, Jr Mosby.   LFAC

Control thy more voracious bill,/Nor for a breakfast nations kill.   The Turkey and the Ant.   John Gay.   PBBP

Control your environment.   A Bestiary.   Kenneth Rexroth.   OBAL

Controlled woolgathering is my work too.   Sheepdog Trials in Hyde Park. C. Day-Lewis.   NoAm; NoP; OxBTC

A conversation of stone.   The Cutting Edge.   Philip Levine.   NYBP

Converting all your notes of woe/Into hey money, money.   Much Ado about Nothing in the City (parody).   *Anonymous.*   FaBoPa

Converting all your sounds of woe/Into Hey nonny, nonny.   Much Ado about Nothing.   William Shakespeare.   ALV; AWP; BoLiVe; CTC; DiPo; EIL; ELP; ExPo; FF; FiP; GoTF; HBV 1-2; InMe; InPo; LiTB; LiTL; MCCG; OAEP; OBSC; PoEL 1-5; SeCeV; TreFS; TrGrPo; ViBoPo

Convicted of the great eternities/Before two worlds.   Aurora Leigh. Elizabeth Barrett Browning.   WPOW

Convinc'd that, of all the earth's nations,/Not one would be faultless to/Q. A Hot Day in Sydney.   *Anonymous.*   NOAV

Convulsed, foaming immortal blood: farewell.   A Professor's Song.   John Berryman.   HeIP; NoAm; NOBA; OxBC

Coo ahh, choo eee, coo coo!   The Birds of America.   James Richard Broughton.   AmFN; BoAnP

..."Coo, Coo" is Metaphysics.   Literary Landscape with Dove and Poet. Phyllis McGinley.   NePoAm-2

Cook mapped the coast, with one eye cocked for game.   Five Visions of Captain Cook.   Kenneth Slessor.   BoAV

A cook may get credit for what's really science's.   Deus Ex Machina. Richard Armour.   QQQ

Cool as from underground springs and pure enough to/drink.   The Man-Moth.   Elizabeth Bishop.   LiTA; LiTM; MAT; MiAP; MoAB; MoAmPo; NoAm; NOBA; NYP; PoCh; PPP

Cool as sundown/I lived there too.   Pachuta, Mississippi / A Memoir.   Al Young.   TAT

Cool madness.   The Assault.   Robert Nichols.   MCCG

Cool reek of the field. Reek of companions.   Cobb Would Have Caught It. Robert Fitzgerald.   GrPl; HAP; InvP; MP; SD; TwCP; WeW

Cool shadows and with native grace bestow/Even on unbelievers vast shelters... The House-Builders.   Kamala Das.   PBWP

Cool, sober murderers of their neighbours' fame.   Modern Critics.   Samuel Taylor Coleridge.   FaBoEE

The cooling brooks that from thy nooks/Singing and dancing go.   Echoes from the Sabine Farm.   Eugene Field.   AA

Cools its small grey feet in the grasses.   The Ruin.   Richard Hughes. OBMV

"Coors," I said, that being/what I seemed to be/drinking.   And Then What? Dave Kelly.   PoL

The cop at the door unwraps a stick of gum.   Father of the Victim.   Rae Ballard.   AMV-80

"Cop's bitch."   Quotations.   George Oppen.   NNaP

Copious and new into the morning,/celebrated.   Unspeakable.   Margaret Avison.   NOBC

Copping a doorknob and wondering where/in hell you tell people to go.   The Destruction of Bulfinch's House.   Stephen Sandy.   CoPo

Copulating with sixteen year old/Nymphomaniacs of my imagination.   The Advantages of Learning.   Martial (Marcus Valerius Martialis).   ErPo

Copy this ten times and pass it on.   Chain Letters.   Alice Fulton.   LTB

The copywriter is flushed by the client's sun.   Nine O'Clock Thoughts on the 73 Bus.   Peter Porter.   PoL

A coral paisley cobra.   The Paisley Ceiling.   Lila Arnold.   IHMS

Cordelia's/In stony/Lonesome/Ground!   Stony Lonesome.   Langston Hughes.   NOBA

The cordiality of Death/Who drills his welcome in.   That after horror that was His.   Emily Dickinson.   MoPo

...Corduroy/Gayla that makes you stand out/Even in a festive crowd.   At Long Last.   Lindsay Patterson.   CNA

The corn is eaten, the animal howls, the sun flowers.   Sun of the Center. Robert Kelly.   CoPo

The Corn King beckoning to his Spring Queen.   A Girl in a Library. Randall Jarrell.   NoAm; NOBA; NoP

"Corn rigs are bonny'.   The Piper.   *Anonymous.*   OxNR

The corn under my shirt awkward a little rough light brown dry/and making me itch at times   The Canadian Prairies View of Literature.   David Donnell.   NOBC

The corners been far flung.   Elysee.   Larry Eigner.   VGW

Cornwall, Monmouth–that's enough.   Rhymed Mnemonic of the Forty Counties of England.   Donald Monat.   FaBoUs

Coronation Day was over in the little town of Melrose.   Coronation Day at Melrose.   Peter Bladen.   PoAu 1-2

The Coroner upon them/SAT.   One Week.   Carolyn Wells.   LBN

A coronet for Mabel!   A Portrait.   Joseph Ashby-Sterry.   HBV 1-2

A corpse once young and sweet.   Brendan Gone.   Padraic Fiacc.   CIP

"A corpse should be transported by express,' said the Consul/mysteriously, waking up suddenly.   For Under the Volcano.   Malcolm Lowry.   NOBC

The corpse that here in fourteen lines is wrapped/Had otherwise been covered with a hundred. On a Magazine Sonnet. Russell Hillard Loines. AA; OBAL

The corpse/was wrapped like panetone in Italian tinfoil. Sailing Home from Rapallo. Robert Lowell. HaCAP; NoAm; TAP

...A correct compassion, that performs its love, and makes it live. A Correct Compassion. James Kirkup. ChMP; FaBoTw; ImOP; OxBTC; SeCePo

Correct my faults, protect my life, direct me when I die! A Child My Choice. Robert Southwell. CAW; GoBC; HBV 1-2; OxBoCh

Correctly labeled, Homo sap. Brief Essay on Man. Arthur Guiterman. OBAL

Corrects the tongues of bungling, churlish men. Lynched Negro. Maxwell Bodenheim. PoNe

Corroborate and order/Mean average temperature/For the last million years. Glacier. Norman Nicholson. OBTV

The corroboree is gone./And we are going.' We Are Going. Kath Walker. CBAP; NOAV

The Corsican, prophetic and renowned,/To whom I spake, one awful night alone! The Sphinx Speaks. Francis Saltus Saltus. AA

Corydon made his choice and took—Well, which do you/suppose? Phillis and Corydon. Arthur Colton. HBV 1-2

'Cos I am so fond of him. The Christening. A.(lan) A.(lexander) Milne. BiCB

'Cos my friend here didn't see. Some Ruthless Rhymes. Harry Graham. CenHV

'Cos Pope does a lot but Chapman more/(If you can't read Homer in Greek). On First Looking into Chapman's Homer I (parody). T. Griffiths. BXAP

'Cos they haven't got a rabbit, not anywhere there! Market Square. A.(lan) A.(lexander) Milne. TiPo

The Cosbosecontic and Millenkikuk! The Lovely Rivers and Lakes of Maine. George B. Wallis. BLPA

Cost us lives, as true as our blood is red,/And probably always will. The Miner. Alfred Castner King. PoOW

...The costly price/I paid for laurel wreath and marble shaft! A Mother before a Soldier's Monument. Winnie Lynch Rockett. PGD

Costumeless Consciousness–/That is he– Those Not Live Yet. Emily Dickinson. MAmP

'Cotia was a colliery./Her men were true and bold. Robens' Promised Land. George Purdom. WTO

...Cottage in the woods/with milk and strawberries on a wooden table. Housing Starts. Peter Davison. EyDe

A Cottage is Wood-Park with you. Stella at Wood-Park. Jonathan Swift. BIrV

The cotton clouds/should merely fall. The Graceful Bastion. William Carlos Williams. NYBP

Cotton threads and clear clean water and jesting and a/friend. Needs. Elizabeth Rendall. HBMV

Cottonwoods, and the gray-green/leaves of the buffalo/grass. Funeral at Ansley. Don Welch. GP; TAT

The cottonwoods stood somnolent and still/Beneath the sun. First Winter Storm. William Everson. NU

Couch a hogshead with me then,/In the darkmans clip and kiss... The Maunder's Praise of His Strowling Mort. Anonymous. OxBoLi

Couched triumphant, calm and brave,/In the ever-holy grave. A Requiem. James (1834-82) Thomson. EnLit; HBV 1-2

A cough, a creaking stair. Still Life. Reed Whittemore. CoAP; ConAP

Coughed up the shirts,/And flagged the train. Bill Groggin's Goat. Anonymous. FSW

Coughed up those shirts and flagged the train. The Goat. Anonymous. BLPL; OnUR; PoLf

Could anyone alive survive it? Conversation. Florence Anthony ("Ai"). LTB

Could barely tell what name were thine. In Memoriam, A.H.H., LIX. Alfred, Lord Tennyson. VLP

Could be any day every day now and forever! Christmas Comes... Earle Birney. ACV

Could be found where the cold waves had toucester. Limerick: "An old couple living in Gloucester." Anonymous. TDH

Could be happy to just go on missing out/on all the fun/"out there" Hardon ("get one today"). Ian Wedde. OCNZ

Could do a little/of/mebby Mrs. Sadie Grindstaff, Weaver and Factotum, Explains... Jonathan Williams. OBAL

Could he plead guilty in a lovelier way?/His judges acquitted him. Youth. Laurence Hope. WeW

Could he see us, would reject us. On Evolution. John Ciardi. OBAL

...Could I be moved/to believe in new beginnings? Could I be moved? In a U-Haul North of Damascus. David Bottoms. FYAP; MAYP

Could I but find the words. Song to a Negro Wash-Woman. Langston Hughes. GoSl

Could I but know she was not this,–not this! The Lament of Edward Blastock. Edith Sitwell. OBMV

Could I but teach the hundredth part/Of what from thee I learn. Anecdote for Fathers. William Wordsworth. EnRP

Could I go/on one wing,/the white one? The Wings. Denise Levertov. CAPP

Could I not stay at least until dewfall? King Duffus. Sylvia Townsend Warner. FaBoWP

Could I so entertain him, hee'd love Me. Martial. Thomas Heyrick. CavP

Could it be known what they discreetly blot. Poets Lose Half the Praise. Edmund Waller. PP

Could it be that he's the falling snow? Snail. Takahashi Shinkichi. NU

Could it be that/it never/was? A Little Girl's Dream World. Della Burt. BlSi

Could it be that we neither celebrate nor mourn? Wreathmakertraining. Karl Patten. FAZ

Could it be, when I was young,/Some one dropped me on my head? Theory. Dorothy Parker. SBG

Could learn to shape my action to it. My Creed. S. E. Kiser. PoToHe

...Could lie down and fit/Our desolate arms and bodies into it. Cruciform. Winifred Welles. NYBP

Could love like thee, and turn as brave to rest.... The Golden Elegy. Leopold Staff. LiTW

Could love you for yourself alone/And not your yellow hair. For Anne Gregory. William Butler Yeats. BiP; CMoP; DiPo; DTC; ExPo; FaFP; ForPo; InPo; LiTL; LiTM; LoBV; SeCeV; SOTW

Could man outlook that mark! Dear, Beazuteous Death! Henry Vaughan. LO

...Could not/bear my eyes to break you apart. Nystagmus. Joseph Matuzak. SUW

Could not cosset their deformity/Save in a Granada lacking/Federico Garcia Lorca. Garcia Lorca Murdered in Granada. John Streeter Manifold. CBAP

Could not Professor Charles Darwin/Graft annual upon perennial trees? Invitation to Juno. William Empson. AtBAP; CMoP; FaBoMo

Could not snap the spectrum up for food/as you have done. To a Chameleon. Marianne Moore. GoYe; PoPl

Could paint the scent as well. Plum Blossoms. Anonymous. SoPo

Could peace not bloom, too, in the world once more? Midwinter. Margaret E. Bruner. PoToHe

...Could put on lookes, of no more overthrow/Than now fraid life. The Iliad. Homer. OBS

Could reflect on the improvement of Man/who's really not built too well. Brief Reflection on the Insect. Miroslav Holub. SUW

Could remember/No more? Elegy for Mr. Goodbeare. Osbert Sitwell. MoBrPo

Could scarcely catch the feeble moan/Which told her heart was broken. The Maid of Neidpath. Sir Walter Scott. BeLS; GTBS; GTBS-P

Could see my love's gold eye/And feel his fire. Weathercock. Elizabeth Jennings. NePoEA

Could set their crushed hopes at the summit again. Humpty Dumpty. Adeline D. T. Whitney. HBV 1-2

Could they have seen that she had overheard. The Tree in Pamela's Garden. Edwin Arlington Robinson. MoLP

Could to my sight that heavenly face restore. Sonnet: "Surprised by joy– impatient as the Wind." William Wordsworth. ViBoPo

Could Venus yield more love-delight/than here she grants in Love's requite? Phyllis Corydon clutched to him. Caius Valerius Catullus. BoLoP

Could we be so now! Even So. Dante Gabriel Rossetti. NOBE; NOBV; OBNC; VLP

Could you explain it to your she-gull? The Sea-Gull. Ogden Nash. FaFP; FPL; MOS; NePA

Could you, without you could,/could ye? I Would If I Could. Anonymous. OxNR

Couldn't be no action like what/i dun already seen. U Name This One. Carolyn M. Rodgers. BlSi; NMM; PoBA

Couldn't put Humpty Dumpty together again. Humpty Dumpty Sat on a Wall. Mother Goose. FaBoBe; OxBoLi; OxNR

(Couldn't you wait until I took you out?) Verse for a Certain Dog. Dorothy Parker. GDP

Count and put in place like hand-sewn jewels/On your sweater from Hong Kong. Sisters. Sandra McPherson. AmPA

Count it the lists that God hath built/For haughty hearts to ride a-tilt. The Splendid Spur. Sir Arthur Thomas ("Q") Quiller-Couch. HBV 1-2; HBVY

Count me among all Faithful Souls. The Nameless Saints. Edward Everett Hale. WGRP

Count not the years, but take of each its boon. To His Wife. Decimus Magnus Ausonius. AWP

Count on a friend, in faith an' practice,/In ROBERT BURNS. To William Simpson, Ochiltree. Robert Burns. MCCG; OxBS

Counter dark clouds like the seven-tiered arch of the rainbow! Consider the Lilies. Dorothy Donnelly. HoAn

Counting its money/and throwing it away? Wind Song. Carl Sandburg.
MoAB; MoAmPo; MoShBr

Counting out in her counting-house/My pennies of time. Gold Watch.
Patrick Kavanagh. InPS

...Counting/sheep before I know it. Somewhere Near Phu Bai. Yusef
Komunyakaa. MAYP

Counting the common strokes of the empty swings Tropisms on John
Berryman. Gerald Vizenor. VoR

Counting the frequent drop from reeded eaves. On a Wet Summer. John
Codrington Bampfylde. NOEC

Counting the singles carefully. After Midnight. Louis Simpson. CAPP;
NoAm

Counting with kingly eye the subjects of his power/Who sleep with beauty and
are unappeased. Among the Coffee Cups and Soup Toureens Walked
Beauty. Jack Spicer. PeHV

The countless countless dead. Edmonton, Thy Cemetery... Stevie Smith.
OxBTC

Countless little nails/squirming and dropping out of it. His Father's Hands.
Thomas Kinsella. FaBoIP

Countries, Towns, Courts: Beg from above/A pattern of your love! The
Canonization. John Donne. AnAnS 1; ATP; BiP; BLPL; BoLiVe;
CABA; CBEP; CoBE; DiPo; ElL; EnLoPo; ForPo; HAP; InPS; JCP; LiTB;
LiTL; LoBV; MasP; MBW 1-2; MePo; NAWM 1-2; NIP; NOBE; NoP;
OAEL 1-2; OBS; PoEL 1-5; PPoe; PPP; SeCePo; SeCeV; SeCP; SeCV 1-2;
TEP; TrGrPo; UnPo; UnTE; ViBoPo

The country blooms–a garden and a grave. The Deserted Village. Oliver
Goldsmith. OBSV

...A country climb is the best disgrace, a/couple of practices any of them in
order is so left. A Waist. Gertrude Stein. NMM

The country grand they wrought for,/Is their monument to-day, and for aye.
The Battle of Monmouth. Thomas Dunn English. PAH

...The country house/stares forward, hallucinated, at the road to the
metropolis. September. Boris Pasternak. NaP

A country rising from its knees/To upset all the histories. The Young
Fenians. Padraic Fallon. BIrV

The Country's best, is accent hit,/And partly sound its polity. Preludes.
Coventry Patmore. HBV 1-2

A country-wedding shall thy hopes deprive. Elegy. John, Lord Dreghorn
Maclaurin. NOEC

...The county cleared the field. Bystanders. William Matthews. NPAW

...The county/womenfolk are in Iowa City Iowa/asking for you and for the St.
Patrick's Hospital. Double Semi-Sestina. George Starbuck. SM

A couple of miles from the tram terminus. A Jewish Cemetery Near
Leningrad. Joseph Brodsky. VWA

Courage in our own. Question Not. Adam Lindsay Gordon. PoToHe

...Courage/is grey-green growing wild. Flowers of the Foothills & Mountain
Valleys. Alice Notley. APU

Courage is in that bottle,/the driest thing there is. The Hole in the Sea.
Marvin Bell. NYBP

...A course which homes/outward, and misses nothing at all. The Ghost of a
Ghost. Brad Leithauser. MAYP

Coursed, coted, mouthed by an unfeeling bore. The Fortunes of Nigel
(excerpt). Sir Walter Scott. NBM

The court says white is black or that black crimes are white. The Animals
Sick of the Plague. Marianne Moore. InPS

Cousins and friends/laugh and say–"aye" A Teacher Taught Me. Anna
Walters. VoR

Cover her face: mine eyes dazzle: she died young. The Duchess of Malfi.
John Webster. AnFE

Cover the face. After. Robert Browning. BoLiVe; EG; TrGrPo

Cover the words we form with flesh. Madonna of the Dons. Arthur
MacGillvray. ISi

Cover thy countenance, and watch, and fear. The House of Life. Dante
Gabriel Rossetti. HBV 1-2

Cover us with your pools of fir. Oread. Hilda ("H. D.") Doolittle. AP;
AWP; CMoP; ExPo; GoJo; InPS; MoAmPo; MoVE; NoAm; NOBA; OxBA;
SBG; TAP; WeW

Covered now by that handkerchief, kissed by the children. Belita. Alberto
Rios. LTB

..Covered/up like younger siblings, so no one may see, in sacred/taboo-ness...
The Djanggawul Cycle, 172. Anonymous. WTO

Covering my probings, as you do,/With quiet conversation. Carious
Exposure. Gladys Cardiff. CDW

...The covering of our feet/Offends, for the ground where we find we stand is
holy White Goat, White Ram. William Stanley Merwin. NePoEA

Covers his eyes with memory like a sheet. Idiot. Allen Tate. AnAmPo;
FaBoMo; LiTA; NAMP

Covers your father's tracks. The Red Flag. Michael Jackson. OCNZ

A cow! Miserly Paron. Anonymous. AnIL

The cow brake loose, the rope ran home,/Sir, God give you good-morrow! A
Nonsense Carol. Anonymous. OxBoLi

The cow is a black globe. Going. Peter Everwine. NNaP

A cow might enjoy in a tree. Limerick: "There is little in afternoon tea."
Gelett Burgess. FaBoNo

...Cow's blood/we'll mix with mash for pigs. Haitian Suite. Gregory Orr.
MAYP

Coward! regard it with unhurried breath,/And know this outrage for the last.
Reflections. A. Deshoulieres. PBWP

Coward, take my coward's hand. The Coward. Eve Merriam. TrJP

A cowboy drunk his heart did plunk./As you do you'll git according. Jesse
James (B vers.). Anonymous. BaBo; ViBoFo

The cowboy's eyes of bitter blue/Or the brave black fellow. Country Tune.
Elizabeth Riddell. BoAV

A cowboy's life for me. The Gay Jolly Cowboy Is up with the Sun.
Anonymous. CoSo

Cowhide, rabbit fur, the five fingers of my hand. The Glove. Harold Bond.
NYBP

The cows are coming home in Maine. Cows Are Coming Home in Maine.
Robert P. Tristram Coffin. DuDa

Cowslips for her covering. An Epitaph upon a Virgin. Robert Herrick.
FaBoEE

Coyning thee a Philip and Mary. Upon an Hermaphrodite. John Cleveland.
AnAnS 1

Coyote,/he belongs to none. Coyote, Coyote, Please Tell Me. Peter Blue
Cloud. STE

The coyote, lonely on the wind swept summit. Voyageur. R. E. Rashley.
CaP

The coyotes and the bells. The Sound of Morning in New Mexico. Reeve
Spencer Kelley. AmFN

Coyotes are circling around our truth. Outside. William Stafford.
NePoAm-2

"Crab-apple red!"/Said they, and I woke up in bed. Crab-Apple. Ethel
Talbot. BiCB; TiPo

A crab puts its face into the pit. Afternoon 3. Saburoh Kuroda. EAS

...Crablike,/over the slippery, seaweed-covered shore. The Visitor. Gregory
Orr. MAYP

Crack nature's molds, all germins spill at once/That make ingrateful man!
King Lear. William Shakespeare. TW

Cracked corn, cracked wheat, peanuts and split peas, hail! The Seed-Eaters.
Robert Francis. NePoAm-2

The cracked disc goes round/With a creaking sound. Song of Occident.
Claude Vigee. VWA

The cracked teacup screams. Haiku: "In the August grass." Etheridge
Knight. NeAC; SM; TAP

Cracking his cruel whip/To the gathering shades? Winter the Huntsman.
Osbert Sitwell. AtBAP; BoW

Crackles like paper money. O Catch Miss Daisy Pinks. Alistair Campbell.
AnNZ

The crackling terrible furnace of the sun. Going In. Marge Piercy. DFF

Cracks, and rejoices in the flame. A Description of Maidenhead.
Anonymous. NOBL

Cracks its light on the fissile planes of the mirror. Always, from My First
Boyhood. John Peale Bishop. VGW

The cradle of God. The Reed. Caryll Houselander. ISi

Cradle your tremble/to the end. Songs of the Priestess. Malka Tussman.
VWA

Cradles you in the trees, as the arm/of the mountain holds the light of the
farm. The Cradle. Roland Robinson. NOAV

...Cradling space/and then/filling it with verdure? Ode to Arnold
Schoenberg. Charles Tomlinson. NePoEA-2

Cradling your spark through blizzard, drift and tomb. In the Shelter. C.
Day Lewis. BoC

Craft with which I don't know how to deal. The Mind, Intractable Thing.
Marianne Moore. LiTM; NYBP

The crags weigh/No more than our shadows. Landscape. Octavio Paz.
OBVE

Cramming all those almonds into a bag. Edward Lear in February.
Christopher Middleton. TwCP

Cranes hover over shale. Slow rivers shine. Sonnet to Seabrook. David
Ray. AMV-80

The crash of battle that are never won. Sonnet: "The master and the slave go
hand in hand." Edwin Arlington Robinson. PP

Crash of machineguns, ring of locusts, airplane roar,/calliope yell, bzzzs.
Bayonne Turnpike to Tuscarora. Allen Ginsberg. NNaP

Crashing, as I lie here, stretched out, running running. On the Couch.
Oscar Williams. WaP

Crashing foams and ravels once/Was muted marble Athens owned. At the
Ocean's Verge. Ralph Gustafson. OBCV

A craven spirit and a heart/That never will be whole. My Father's Cot
(parody) (excerpt). J. C. Squire. BXAP

The craving Carkesses of those Souls that need. Could'st Thou (O Earth)
Live Thus Obscure. George Alsop. SCAP

Crawl, all/exits/from/hibernaculum! In England's Green &. Jonathan
Williams. CoPo

Crawl, and wait. This Is an African Worm. Margaret Danner. BPo

Crawl through muddy marshes/Wallow in foul waters. My Little Love Lies on the Ground. Larin Paraske. PBWP

Crawling out of the water/and onto the tracks. The Sixties. Thomas Listmann. AMV-80

The crazed and hooded creatures of the heart. The Heart. Harvey Shapiro. HoPM

"Crazy dogholkoda, hah?" he growled,/looking over his shoulder. Crazy Dogholkoda. Mary Tallmountain. TWSS

A crazy old blind man in Windsor Tower? George III. William Makepeace Thackeray. FaBoEE

Crazy swallows/turn somersaults in the air. Speaking for Them. Hayden Carruth. GP

Creaking, creaking,/High in the hangman's tree. The Gallows Tree. Frederick Robert Higgins. OnYI

Creaks the small rocking chair. Sometimes a Little House Will Please. Elizabeth Jane Coatsworth. BrR

The cream of/genes! Ovid, Meet a Metamorphodite. Jonathan Williams. PoM

Creased and bundled with a rubber band,/In which she is the first one. Brown Like Us. Gary Soto. NPGG

Create a self of your own. One/that will love me. The Dance. LeRoi (Imamu Amiri Baraka) Jones. CoPo

Create her out of sorrow/That, never perishing,/Is a stately thing. The Stranger. Jean Garrigue. LiTM; MP; NOBA; TwCP

Create me well, or I shall be self-born. At 21. Eugene L. Belisle. AMV-81

Creates within that barren water-way/New life, new loveliness, and passes on. The Canal. Aldous Huxley. HBMV

Creating the hardship, the infinite variety. Day and Night Handball. Stephen P. Dunn. AmPA

CREATION Some Days/Out Walking above. De Leon Harrison. PoBA

Creation moveth, and the farmboy sleeps,/A still strong sleep till but the east is red. Sonnets. Frederick Goddard Tuckerman. MAmP

Creation seemed a mighty crack/To make me visible. To My Quick Ear. Emily Dickinson. AnFE; APA; CoAnAm; MAPA

Creative Commerce, these are thine! A Descriptive Poem, Addressed to Two Ladies.... John Dalton. NOEC

The creator of every creature. Two Invocations of the Virgin. Geoffrey Chaucer. ACP

The Creator of night and of birth/was the Maker of the stars. Special Starlight. Carl Sandburg. MoRP

"Creator! shall I bloom?" God Made a Little Gentian. Emily Dickinson. AA; FaBV

Creature and creature,/we stared down centuries. On the Coast near Sausalito. Robert Hass. WOLT

The creature is protected you see/From silly people like you and me. Hipporhinostricow. Spike Milligan. AmMo

The creature madly climbing back/Into his chrysalis. A Conservative. Charlotte Perkins Stetson Gilman. AA; HBV 1-2

The creature nodded, and he went away. Homage. George O'Neil. AnAmPo

...A creature progressively/Thirsty for life will be for death too. Age in Prospect. Robinson Jeffers. MoAB; MoAmPo

The creatured Image became the Likeness. Negative Passage. Michael Newman. PoA

Creatures passed through the wet sieve/Without enrichment or decay. The White Ship. Geoffrey Hill. OxBC

Creels and all, creels and all. Riding. William Allingham. OxBChV

Creep awa', my bairnie, creep afore ye gang. Creep Afore Ye Gang. James Ballantine. HBV 1-2

Creep into the season's river/and the ruin. Mortally. James Kirkup. NeBP

Creep-mouse, creep-mouse,/In the twilight! Chanson Naive. John McClure. HBMV

A creeping mystic what-is-it. The Sins of Kalamazoo. Carl Sandburg. VGW

Creeping, silently creeping everywhere. The Voice of the Grass. Sarah Roberts Boyle. AA; HBV 1-2; HBVY

Crept into the dead bird, ceased to exist. The Sea Bird. Keith Douglas. ChMP

Crept near the windowpane, to feast. Mill Valley. Myra Cohn Livingston. RFM

A crescent ship without a sail! A Ship, an Isle, a Sickle Moon. James Elroy Flecker. BrPo; FaBoRV; SyP

...Crevice where/azure striation swirls beyond the stones. La Fontaine de Vaucluse. Marilyn Hacker. FYAP

The crew plans its escape. Father. Lois Reiner. AMV-80

The crew to row, the boat to go,/The eight to win the race. A Racing Eight. James L. Cuthbertson. PoAu 1-2

The Cricket cheers the dusk with mirth. Nature's Key-Notes. Thomas Caulfield Irwin. IrPN

"A cricket chirps and then dies." Tall Trees by Still Waters. James Tate. MAYP

A cricket like a dwindled hearse/Crawls from the dry grass. Exeunt. Richard Wilbur. BoNaP; ELU; HeIP; NCSH; PoLf; Psk

Crickets Crickets. Aram Saroyan. ANYP; MAT

Cried, ah! And can Death enter Paradise? Madrigal: The Beautie, and the Life. William, of Hawthornden Drummond. AtBAP; EIL; PoEL 1-5

Cried as the wind now cries/through this flute of stone. The Old Prison. Judith Wright. PoAu 1-2

Cried "Damn it, how hot we shall be!" A Stanza Completed. William Lort Mansel. FaBoEE

Cried Dick, as he surveyed them o'er,/"You wouldn't do for Australia." Dick Briggs from Australia. Charles R. Thatcher. NOAV

Cried enough tears/died enough times/died enough times. 8:00 a.m. Monday Morning. William Welsh. SOTS

...Cried/Mortally, like a bird the cat has caught. The Appointment. Leonard Alfred George Strong. OxBTC

Cries–"Go to it, Tom Agnew, Bill Agnew!" Tom Agnew, Bill Agnew. Dante Gabriel Rossetti. ChTr

Cries of snow-crimson children leaving school. Getting Through. James Merrill. NYBP

Cries out, cries out/For its true mate. I Take Thee Life. Margot Ruddock. OBMV

Cries out/for something like that... A Welcome for Etheridge. James (Olumo) Cunningham. JB

Cries the still passionate, the walking woman. Against a Second Coming: The Walking Woman. Sidney Keyes. AtBAP

CriesWhichAreWings. What Is. Edward Estlin Cummings. MOS

The crime he had committed/Will send his soul to hell. Ellen Flannery. *Anonymous.* AmFP

Criminal, he wants to be my toy, my crazy plaything. Cops and Robbers. Bill Middleton. AMV-80

Cripes! but I'm agin it! Dry (parody). Samuel Hoffenstein. BXAP

A criss-crossed pile of/sun-bleached bones. Evil Is No Black Thing. Sarah Webster Fabio. PoBA

Croak–croak–/SPLASH! Grandfather Frog. Louise Seaman Bechtel. TiPo

Croak his two words: More weight. Going to Press. Judith Moffett. AMV-80

Crocus in the shade. When the World is Burning. Ebenezer Jones. ACV; OBEV; OBVV; PoPle; VLP

The cross in thine own heart/Alone can make thee whole. In Thine Own Heart. (Johanne Scheffler) "Angelus Silesius" TRV

'Cross the country/with my long clothes on Roberta. Leadbelly. BluL

The Cross, the Crown, the Scales, may all/As well have been the Sword. A Sky Pair. Robert Frost. MoAB; MoAmPo

'Cross the ford o' Kabul river in the dark! Ford O' Kabul River. Rudyard Kipling. FaBoTw

'Cross the wide Missouri. Shenandoah. *Anonymous.* ABF; AmFN

The Cross was His own. The Cross Was His Own. *Anonymous.* BePJ; BLPA

Crossed by the bridge/of frequent sighs On the Way to Language. Michael Palmer. NPGG

Crossed out delete and wrote his patient stet. The Proof. Richard Wilbur. EaLo; OBSP

Crossed over a storm, and rained down murder. Andromache. Euripides. WaaP

Crosses do still bring forth the best events. Crosses. Robert Herrick. CaPo

The crosses we make for ourselves,alas!/are the heaviest ones of all. The Heaviest Cross of All. Katherine Eleanor Conway. AA

Crossing a Ford, the Torrent sweeps away,/An unregarded Carcase to the Sea. The Iliad. Homer. OBVE

Crossing back and forth/the men... Men in the City. Alfonsina Storni. PBWP

Crossing cream-beams yellowly/Held aloft the roof. The Vision of Mac Conglinne. *Anonymous.* CAW

Crouch low thy neck to eleemosynary gifts. To the Pending Year. Walt Whitman. OBSP

A crow digs endlessly/but no longer bleeds. Lighthouse in the Night. Alfonsina Storni. BoWoP

Crow flew guiltily off. Crow's First Lesson. Ted Hughes. NoAm; PAI

Crow had to start searching for something to eat. That Moment. Ted Hughes. FF

The Crow Indian had said about Coyote/hitting the nail at last The Structural Study of Myth. Jerome Rothenberg. PoM

Crow lost in a world of wrack. The Ark. Irving Feldman. AmPC

...A crow/on either shoulder. The Boxcar Poem. David Young. AmPA

Crow's eye-pupil, in the tower of its scorched fort. Crow's Last Stand. Ted Hughes. PAI

The crow shall find new mud to walk upon. Where We Must Look for Help. Robert Bly. ConAP; NePoEA

Crow went on laughing. A Childish Prank. Ted Hughes. OAEL 1-2; OxBC

Crowd murmuring popeyes/for the last look King Lives. Jill Witherspoon Boyer. CNA

Crowd not your table: let your number be/Not more than seven, and never less than three. The Art of Cookery. William King. FaBoUs

The crowd sucks her last tear and turns away. Aftermath. Sylvia Plath. SBG

Crowded in a gesture/Of homesickness. The Hill of Intrusion. W. S. Graham. NePoEA

Crowded into the forest of tables to eat. New York. Tony Towle. ANYP

Crowding east where the sun waits. A Jerusalem Notebook. Harvey Shapiro. AMV-81

Crowds round her lap/hearing itself spoken of. Portrait of My Mother on Her Wedding Day. Celia Gilbert. AMV-81; DFF

A crown, a mansion, and a throne that shine,/With gold unfading, Washington! be thine. To His Excellency, General Washington. Phillis Wheatley. OFD; SBG

The crown awaits the conquest; Lead on, O God of might. Lead On, O King Eternal. Ernest W. Shurtleff. AH

Crown'd once with joy, and light: crown'd now with fire and/paines. Sin, Despair, and Lucifer. Phineas Fletcher. OBS

Crown her seven hills with flowers. Sing, Woods and Rivers All. Claudian. HW

A crown of splendour/On beauty's brow! The Islands of the Ever Living. Anonymous. AnIV

The crown that burns on thine immortal head/Of indivisible supremacy! Homeric Unity. Andrew Lang. HBV 1-2

A crown upon thy head, and scepter in thy hand. An Epithalamium upon the Marriage of Captain William Bedloe. Richard Duke. APAS

Crows await your eyes. Iron-Door-Woman. Judith Mountain Leaf Volborth. TWSS

Crows for a dawn he shall not see again/And cannot but desire. In the Web. E. L. Mayo. MiAP

The crows in possession. Crows. Philip Booth. DFF

The crows, that brought him bread and meat.' On Barclay's Apology for the Quakers. Matthew Green. NOEC

Crrreeet, crrreeet, crrreeet. Ice. Dorothy Aldis. SUS; TiPo

..."Crucial figures" in/the "pageantry" of "Western thought." Humanities Course. John Updike. GLGT

The crucifix that came of Nazareth. The Garden of Epicurus. George Meredith. ATP

Cruel, cruel to describe/what there is no reason to describe. The Operation. Robert Creeley. NaP

Cruel fingers setting the ocean's curls. The Dyke-Builder. Henry Treece. LiTB; WaP

The cruel frost encrusts the cornland! Winter in Durnover Field. Thomas Hardy. MoBrPo

The cruel little naughty boy,/Was never heard of more. The Cruel Naughty Boy. Anonymous. BBGG

A cruel mistress thus conspires/With a delusive dream. The Dream. Sir Edward Sherburne. OBSP

Cruel to be kind to all his kind is he. Holy Poems. George Barker. MoPo

Cruel, unkind! I say farewell, farewell! Heaven and earth and all that hear me plain. Sir Thomas Wyatt. FCP; SiPS

Cruell death vanquishing so noble beautie/Oft makes me wayle so hard a destenie. Visions. Petrarch. EnLi 1-2

The cruelties of ages past affect us now. MMDCCXIII 1/2. Lorenzo Thomas. APU

The cruelty that the Universe feeds/while displaying its glories. To the Moon, 1969. Babette Deutsch. MOON

Cruising down along the coast of the High Barbaree! The High Barbaree. Anonymous. AmSS; FSW; OuSiCo; ViBoFo

Crushed by the silence, bolt it down. Herman Moon's Hourbook. Christopher Middleton. NePoEA-2

Crushed, drowned, or with harsh saws/asunder sawn. Thy Faithful Sons. Eleazar. TrJP

Crushed eggs whence snakes could crawl! When I Vexed You. Robert Browning. OBSP

Crushed the longings of my sentimental heart. The Sentimentalist. Edward Field. PPJ

Crushed will be the carriages, engine and all. Rock away, passenger. Anonymous. CenHV

Crushing a dandelion/skull. Beer Drops. Melba Joyce Boyd. BlSi

Crushing the humble underfoot, indulging the cruel. The Stars Have Given Me a Hard Fate. Gaspara Stampa. PBWP

The crust snaps/with the sound/of breaking bones. The Home Place. Robert Currie. PPJ

Crux in a savage tongue none of us know. Trainwrecked Soldiers. John Frederick Nims. MiAP

A cry; a living sleep. Eclogue. Frederic Prokosch. ViBoPo

Cry Cock-a-diddle-dow! The Tempest. William Shakespeare. AnFE; CH

Cry, Damn it, how hot we shall be! Beginning of an Undergraduate Poem. Anonymous. FaBoCo

Cry, every bird is in some sort/that leader clamouring at dawngate.' Copernicus. Robert D. FitzGerald. BoAV; NOAV

Cry "God for Harry, England, and Saint George!" King Henry V. William Shakespeare. TreF; WaaP

A cry is at the lips, and then is gone. The Horsemen. Gene Baro. NePoEA-2

The cry is my own, the force of breath/the last blossoms to grow. In Impressions of Hawk Feathers Willow Leaves Shadow. Elizabeth Woody. STE

Cry "non sum dignus" o'er and o'er/For her dear sake. The Sanctum. Thomas Augustin Daly. TrPWD

The cry of Lilith's child. Lilith's Child. Edward Francisco. DL

The cry of my dogs was the only choir/In which my spirit did take delight. The Friar. Thomas Love Peacock. SD

The cry of the first wild-goose. In My Boat That Goes. Saigyo Hoshi. AWP

The cry of the heart/Till it ceases to beat. The Dreams of the Dreamer. Georgia Douglas Johnson. CDC

The cry of the heron, suddenly stilled/as it flies from the landing/over this cold lake at evening. For Daphne at Lone Lake. John Haines. NPAW

A cry of which/nothing remains. The Mute City. Lazer Eichenrand. VWA

Cry out as they fly off,/indifferent to us. Elegy: Ise Lamenting the Death of Empress Onshi. Lady Ise. BoWoP

Cry out in pride and blessedness: O children! The Cow Wandering in the Bare Field. Randall Jarrell. MoVE

Cry, song, cry,/And hear your crying lost. Chanson un Peu Naive. Louise Bogan. HBMV

Cry stinking fish? To Calliope. Robert Graves. CMoP

The cry–"uhuru" The West Ridge Is Menthol-Cool. D. L. Graham. PoBA

Cry wellaway, but well befall the right. A Year's Burden. Algernon Charles Swinburne. VLP

Crye (thee/Hy A Pair of Wings. Stephen Hawes. MeEL

Cryin', "Cockles and mussels, alive, alive, oh!" Molly Malone. Anonymous. FSW; MaC

Cryin' I was standin' right there/po-lice had me barred Dark Road Blues. Willie Lofton. BluL

Crying aloud, "How beautiful they are,/But not our English hills!" Where a Roman Villa Stood, above Freiburg. Mary Elizabeth Coleridge. OBNC; OBTV

Crying, as the rays disappear from the inner peak of the mat,/from its transverse fibre. The Djanggawul Cycle, 84. Anonymous. WTO

Crying, "Cockles and mussels: alive, alive O!" Cockles and Mussels. Anonymous. ELP; OnYI

Crying: Fools! Where is our bread? Landscape near a Steel Mill. Herschel Horn. PPON

Crying for the pleasures/of the poor. Eternities. Norman Mailer. NYBP

Crying, "Sweetly may they sleep/'Neath the wave." The Battle of Valparaiso. Anonymous. PAH

Crying, world without end? Peewits on the Hills. Alice V. Stuart. ACV

The crystal cast into the light. A Sitch Cut in April. Clifford Dyment. MoVE

A crystal tree lets fall a crystal leaf. Decoration. Louise Bogan. MoAB; MoAmPo

...The crystal world/Is inverted, slow and gay. The Operation. W. D. Snodgrass. InPK; TAP

Crystals both dark and bright of the rain/That begins again. After Rain. Edward ("Edward Eastaway") Thomas. NCSH

Cryste may send sich a yere. Who Wot Nowe That Ys Here. Anonymous. InPS; PAI

Cuba, the widow, passes. Two Countries. Jose Marti. TTY

The cuckoo-flowers grow mauver and mauver. Winter Is Gone, and Spring Is Over. Alfred Austin. FaBoCo

The cuckoo is the bird that bears the bell. Madrigal: "The nightingale, the organ of delight." Anonymous. PBBP

The cuckoo's note would be drowned by the voice of my dead. The Cuckoo. Edward ("Edward Eastaway") Thomas. BrPo

Cuckoo to welcome in the spring! Trico's Song. John Lyly. EG; OBSC; TrGrPo

(The cuckoo who singeth it all day long). Which Is the Bow? Anonymous. GBP

Cuddle-down hide-away/house in the grass. The House of the Mouse. Lucy Sprague Mitchell. NTCP; SoPo; TiPo

Cuddy shall have a kid to store his farm. The Contempt of Poetry. Edmund Spenser. OBSC

A cudgel for his enemies,/And money for his friends. The Youth and the Northwind. John Godfrey Saxe. StPo

A culture is no better than its woods. Woods. W. H. Auden. NePA; NePoAm

The culture of Athens was a nation's awaking. Winter Homily on the Calton Hill. Douglas Young. OxBS

Cumberlands/Smokies/Unakas– My South. Don West. PoNe

A cunning language of/their own. January. Deborah Godin. AMV-80

The cunning rod of Moses. At Last. Rosemarie Newcombe. PoL

...The cup of his glory/Needed but that death to render it full. Custer's Last Charge. Frederick Whittaker. BPAW; HBV 1-2; MC; OnMSP; PAH; PoLf

The cup of life's for him that drinks/And not for him that sips. Away with Funeral Music. Robert Louis Stevenson. GoTF; TreFT

The cup that runneth over still remains. A Pagan Reinvokes the Twenty-Third Psalm. Robert Leopold Wolf. HBMV; TrPWD

Cupid plague thee for thy treason. Ode: "Now I find thy looks were feigned." Thomas Lodge. EnRePo; OBSC

A cure for habit, some beneficent/Simplicity or steadiness of heart. Canberra in April. J. R. Rowland. NOAV; PoAu 1-2

Cured, I am frizzled, stale and small. Home after Three Months Away. Robert Lowell. HaCAP; NoP

The curfew tells me - cover up the fire. The Iron Gate (excerpt). Oliver Wendell Holmes AA

Curfew will not ring to-night! Curfew Must Not Ring To-Night. Rose Hartwick Thorpe. BeLS; BLPA; BLPL; FaBoBe; HBV 1-2; PaPo; TreF; WBLP

Curious anticlimax to thy dreams/Twenty golden years ago! Twenty Golden Years Ago. James Clarence Mangan. IrPN; NOBV; OnYI

A curious carpenter. The Carpenter. Michael Perkins. PoL

...The curious look/Of conquerors on their silly, silly faces. On a Very Young, Very Dead Soldier. Richard Gillman. NePoAm

Curled in the dark of a winged pod/knows flourishing. In Weather. Robert Hass. AmPA; GeTw

Curled like a question mark asleep. Christ Walking on the Water. W.R. Rodgers. AnIL; MoAB; NoAm; OxBI

Curled neatly round his neat and evil head. Spate in Winter Midnight. Norman Maccaig. BoC; GTBS-P; PoSH

Curled, rolled, woven, lover. It Is That Bane of Self in Love. Richard Eberhart. LiTL

The curled-up figure of the woman lies/And lost within that passive sea my words. The Lost Continent. Jenny Joseph. BrRo

Curling downwards at the corners,/Like a bent twig/For a kayak rib. Men's Impotence. Anonymous. WTO

A curling wall back when I'm thistle-burning. House in Denver. Thomas Hornsby Ferril. AmFN

Curls down for a nap/And purrs and purrs. Wind Is a Cat. Ethel Romig Fuller. SoPo

...The curriculum/Vitae of sailors and the sick at heart. Leaving Inishmore. Michael Longley. FaBoIP

"A curse light on me if ever again,/My lands be in jeopardy!" The Heir of Linne. Anonymous. BuBa; ESPB

Curse lightly and pronounce Your serious name. Christmas Eve. Karl Shapiro. NYBP

The curse of a mother light on them. A Leitrim Woman. John Lyle Donaghy. OnYI; OxBI

Curse the corm'rants! stone 'em, shoot 'em,/Any thing–to save our cherries. The Cherries. A Parable. Thomas Moore. OBSV

The curse, the hope, the beauty/That never must be told. John Darrow. Donald Davidson. HBMV

Curse their children who became junk. To My Daughter the Junkie on a Train. Audre Lorde. CNA

...Cursing, stumble out like ghosts into the frozen dark. Mess Deck Casualty. Alan Ross. WaP

Cursing the hunger as we feed. The Last Fish. Barry Spacks. AMV-80

...The cursive adder writes/Quick V's and Q's in the dust and rubs them out. Movements. Norman MacCaig. OxBC

Curst be the coachman that did drive so fast,/With no less curse than absence makes me taste. Astrophel and Stella, CV. Sir Philip Sidney. AAS; SiPS; SiPS 10]

The curtains are stiff and prim and still. Gallant Chateau. Wallace Stevens. MoAB; MoAmPo

The curtains billow and the doors move on their hinges. Piyyut for Rosh Hashana. Haim Guri. OFD

...Curtains/blowing at the window/speaking to me. The Departure. Frank Steele. GOYP; PPJ

Curv'd like a flower o'er the waters of Nemi. The Swimmer of Nemi. William Sharp. SyP

The curve and plunge of everlasting flight? Dolphin Seen Alone. Richmond Lattimore. BoAnP

Curved in a smile. The mystery remains. Hands. Louis Untermeyer. AnAmPo 013; MoLP

The custom of the world is wearing clothes. The Custom of the World. Louis Simpson. BoLoP

Cut down, and up again as blithe as ever. Ianthe. Walter Savage Landor. BoLiVe; GBL; OBEV; TrGrPo; ViBoPo

Cut down by my best friend. Epitaphs of the War, 1914-18. Rudyard Kipling. BrPo; OBWP

Cut down our Lettuce/To make a salad. Tombstone Epitaphs. Anonymous. PeD

Cut me a switch to whip old ghosts/through sunsets to the morning. Witch Hazel. Theodore Enslin. CoPo

The cut of the moon/in my mind. Trying to Sleep. Ralph Pomeroy. ELU

The cut of your pattern/like the design in a bolt of memory Relics. Suzanne Gegna. AMV-81

Cut off his nose,/And popped it in a basin. Close Shave. Anonymous. OxNR

Cut off, hurtling forward in the cold sky. War Requiem. Del Marie Rogers. LTB

Cut square and thin in a bowl of ice water. Eastward to Eden. Edgar Bogardus. PoL

Cut the currents of strife. Rhythm. Jean Percival Waddell. CaP

...Cut the fields, and suck/The treasure from all cities.... Six Epigrams (excerpt). Gerard Manley Hopkins. SeCePo

Cut them in July,/Then they will die. Cut Thistles in May. Anonymous. OxNR

Cut–with no music–on her smile. Notes for a Movie Script. M. Carl Holman. AmNP; PoBA; PoNe; WeW

A cutout, a fancy French silhouette. Widow's Walk. Elizabeth Spires. MAYP

Cutting brush every day/And folding his clothes carefully. Dusk. Ken Belford. NeAC

Cutting each other's hair. The Tales the Barbers Tell. Morris Bishop. ALV

Cutting off the edge of time, falling, endlessly. Falling. Bob Kaufman. PoBA

The cycles of Heaven in twenty centuries/Bring us farther from God and nearer to the Dust. The Rock. Thomas Stearns Eliot. OBMV; TRV

The cymbals now have whitened. The Crucifixion of Noel. Marsden Hartley. AnAmPo

D

Da bird 'e just spread-a 'ees wing an' make flight. The Educated Love Bird. Peter Newell. FiBHP

Da colour an scent o a million flooers. Tuslag. T. A. ("Vagaland") Robertson. OxBS

Da nita'ga, "They are standing/together as one." Where Fire Burns. Gladys Cardiff. TWSS

Da's all righ'. baby. Da's All Right, Baby. Anonymous. ABF

Dabbling among those cold stones. Baiamai's Never-failing Stream. William Hart-Smith. BoAV

Dabbling much in rhyme. Tell Me Not in Joyous Numbers. Stephen Crane. OBAL

Dacca is lost from the roll of the kings! The Dove of Dacca. Rudyard Kipling. GN

The dachs-hound, Geist, their little friend. Geist's Grave. Matthew Arnold. FM; HBV 1-2; NOBV; TEP

DACTYLICS, call'st thou 'em?–"God help thee, silly one!" The Soldier's Wife (parody). J. H. and George Canning Frere. Par

,Dad with all his bottons on/back in the watch fob days. Ilford Rose Book. James Schuyler. ANYP

Daddy, ain't you heard? Lenox Avenue Mural. Langston Hughes. AmNP

Daddy, daddy, you bastard, I'm through. Daddy. Sylvia Plath. BiP; BoWoP; CAPP; CMoP; CoAP; HaCAP; InPK; InPS; LiTM; NaP; NIP; NMM; NMP; NoAm; NOBA; NoP; PAI; PrIm; TW; TwCP; UnPo

"Daddy, you haven't got it right!" Teasing. Anonymous. OxNR

The daffodils beside the lake in spring. In the Lake Country. Kay Wissinger. AMV-80

Daffodils like drifting flaws/of sunlight on these winter hills. Spring in These Hills. Archibald MacLeish. NCSH

A dagger, a rope, a fan,/carved in the tufa. Etruscan Notebook. Elena Clementelli. PBWP

DAILY AT FIVE WEEKENDS AT NIGHTFALL. Signs. Charles Martin. SM

Daily calling me to heaven,/Even from my trundle bed. My Mother's Prayer. T. C. O'Kane. BLPA; FaBoBe

Daily cup, the Holy Grail. Mentis Trist. Robert Hillyer. HBMV

The daily dirge, and rites divine. The Grave of King ARthur. Thomas Warton, Jr.. CEP; GoTL

The daily flight/at my senses of these couplets. Saint Patrick's Day, 1973. Wendy Rose. CDW

Daily stoops to harbour there. Astraea. Ralph Waldo Emerson. AnNE

Daily strength for daily needs. Day by Day. Stephen F. Winward. TRV

Daily the ocean between us/Grows deeper but not wider. Daily the Ocean between Us. Patricia Goedicke. TAP

Daily to turn in Paul's, and help the trade. On English Monsieur. Ben Jonson. NLV; NoP

Dainty white lilies and sad flowers well prized. Brown Is My Love. Anonymous. AtBAP; CBEP; EG; EiL; GBL

Dairy Queen and Buttercup! Steeds. Paul Hiebert. WHW

Daisies and kingcups and honeysuckle-flowers.' The City Child. Alfred, Lord Tennyson. OxBChV

Daisies, daisies, in a field of daisies? Hogwash. Robert Francis. LCAP

Daisies grasped in Phoebe's fist/Would be charming, I insist. Anniversary in September. Beatrice Curtis Brown. BiCB

Daisies round the dish and a pearl on every/scale. The Zodiac Song. John Ruskin. NOBV

The Daisy, by the shadow that it casts,/Protects the lingering dew-drop from the sun. In a Child's Album. William Wordsworth. GN

A daisy dead and dry. For the Candle Light. Angelina Weld Grimke. BlSi; CDC; PoNe

The daisy is the flower that opens. Star Song of the Bushman Women. Anonymous. PeSA

The Daisy never dies! A Field Flower. James Montgomery. HBV 1-2

Daith an rebellion blinn ma ee! Largo. Sidney Goodsir Smith. NeBP

Dallied more wantonly/With the fair Egyptian Queen. Whenas the Nightingale. John Cleveland. LiTL; UnTE

Damascus! Damascus! Saul, afterward, Riding East. John Malcolm Brinnin. HoAn; Prf

Dame Favor is my mistress' name, Dame Fortune is her/maid. Gascoigne's Praise of His Mistress. George Gascoigne. EnRePo

Dame Fortune advanced him to eminence, d– her. Epitaph: "Here lies the remains of great Senator Vrooman." Ambrose Bierce. DBV

Dame Jolt's brown horse, old Dobbin, is no more. An Elegy on the Death of Dobbin, the Butterwoman's Horse. Francis Fawkes. NOEC

Dame Luna, with her twinkling spies, from azure tow'rs. Theophila: Cynthia. Edward Benlowes. MOON

Damn'd for thy false apostacy. To My Inconstant Mistress. Thomas Carew. EnLit; EnLoPo; GBL

Damn./Damn./Damn. 22 Miles. Jose Angel Gutierrez. FIA

Damn my neighbors. Damn Brewster Diffenbach. In the Hole. John Ciardi. HoAn

Damn the dull critics,/And die of obscurity. Ultra-Germano-Criticasterism. [James Henry] Leigh Hunt. PP

Damn the young poets! Let them rather learn/cooking or prosody and study the dull Masters. Onan. Paris Leary. CoPo

Damn your hides! Samuel Hall. Anonymous. ChTr

Damned his soul to water springs. Epitaph after Reading Ronsard's Lines from Rabelais. John Millington Synge. FaBoEE

Damned if Willie didn't drown. Silly Willy. R. L. B. ShM

Damned road/and get hit. Song of the Breed. Carroll Arnett. STE

The damp, despised, and aimless Doze. The Doze. James Reeves. AmMo

The damp terror of space. A July Storm: Johnson, Nemaha Country, Nebraska. Steve Hahn. AMV-81

...The dampness/of sheets and the panic of self, alone and peculiar, entire and full. I am the sorrow in the wheat fields. Ellen Bass. NMM

The damsel she laught, and was pleas'd in her mind,/And said he was very well serv'd in his kind. The Unfortunate Miller; or, The Country Lasses Witty Invention. Anonymous. CoMu; OxBB

Dan we bofe can haul. Go Way F'om Mah Window. Anonymous. ABF; AS

Dana/and me/in wet fear/walking to the parking lot/gray lines of/soaked cars. Kora for March 5th. Lewis MacAdams. ANYP

Dance all the colors of Life/For a lover of pleasure/Now dead. Song for the Dead, III. Anonymous. TTY

Dance alone in the same place at the same time Stumbling. Dick Lourie. NeAC

Dance, and make the village hum! Patapan. Bernard De La Monnoye. ChBR; PCh

Dance before dead England's hearse. Auguries of Innocence. William Blake. OxBoLi

Dance, gal, gimme de banjo! Gimme de Banjo. Anonymous. ShS

"Dance light, for my heart it lies under your feet, love!" Kitty Neil. John Francis Waller. HBV 1-2

...The dance of the/Dream-led masses down the dark mountain. Rearmament. Robinson Jeffers. OxBA

...The dance/of the multiple suns is done. By the Bridge. Ted Walker. NYBP

The dance of two words that are all/autumn and silk and nothingness. Turn Blind. Paul Celan. VWA

Dance on in this museum case. Love Song to Eohippus. Peter Viereck. MoAmPo

Dance & tell me black african things/i know you know African Things. Victor Hernandez Cruz. InW

Dance the gay daffodils in smocks of gold. Holiday. Henry Dawson Lowry. OBVV

Dance the ghost-dance, O Dakotah!/For to-morrow thy people come home. Remember the Promise, Dakotah. Robert V. Carr. PoOW

An dance the Hielan Laddie. Some Say the Deil's Deid. Anonymous. FaBoCh; LoGBV

Dance thy dainty foot and straying/Come, come away! Silly Sweetheart. Anonymous. CH

Dance to show how very little a/thing happiness can be really. Elephant. Alan Brownjohn. OnUR

Dance to the tinkling tambourine. The Cocooning. Frederic Mistral. AWP; PoPl

Dance to your daddy, my little lamb. Dance to Your Daddy. Anonymous. FSW

...Dance with them/this silent, simple dance. Return to Lake Emily Chequamegon National Forest. Richard Behm. WOLT

Dance with you, my sweet brown Harlem girl. Juke Box Love Song. Langston Hughes. GrPl; IDB; OLR; PoBA

Danced by the streams. Upon Julia's Hair Filled with Dew. Robert Herrick. AtBAP; EG

Danced round the dreadful thing in fiendish glee. The Lynching. Claude McKay. BALP; BANP; IDB; PoBA

...The dancer falls/Then rises like an oriole over walls. Dancer: Four Poems. Paul Engle. AMV-80

The dancers come forward to represent unclaimed things. The Interlude. Robert Duncan. CMoP

The dancers dance while the dawn is grey. Aux Carmelites. Katharine Tynan Hinkson. OnYI

Dances like Italy, imagining red. Walt Whitman at Bear Mountain. Louis Simpson. CAPP; ConAP; LiTM; NePoEA-2; PoCh; PP

Dancing before last night's dishes/Like a thief. Aubade after the Party. Tom O'Grady. FAZ

The dancing city is filled with storm,/driving young men to you, captive. Inanna and Ebih. Enheduanna. BoWoP

Dancing hailstones spin,/The wine's own kin. Bubbling Wine. Abu Zakariya. TTY

Dancing in the meadows where the hayfields were. Where the Hayfields Were. Archibald MacLeish. DuDa; LOW

Dancing in the somber light/Of history, shiny pencils/At the edge of things. Relaxation. Dick Gallup. ANYP; APU

The dancing Pleiads and eternal men. Bacchus. Ralph Waldo Emerson. AmePo; AnNE; AP; APA; AWP; HBV 1-2; LiTA; MAmP; NOBA; OBEV; OxBA; PoEL 1-5; ViBoPo

A dancing sword of tempered steel. A Sword. Karin Boye. WPOW

Dancing with a woman as gold/as the river bottom. New Orleans. Joy Harjo. STE; TWSS

Danger face, maintain your ground/And see your country righted. Come, Ye Lads, Who Wish to Shine. Anonymous. PAH

...Dangerous/to yourself, more dangerous to others? Harriet. Robert Lowell. HaCAP

Dangling from a horn. Haiku: "Coming from the woods..." Richard Wright. FAZ

Daniel saw de stone,/Cut out de mountain widout hands. Daniel Saw de Stone. Anonymous. BoAN 1-2

Daniel, the mount whence the great stone was taken! The Assumption. Saint Nerses. CAW

Dansa au clair de la lune. Le Hibou et la Poussiquette. Francis Steegmuller. NYBP

Danse calinda, bou-doum, bou-doum,/Danse calinda, bou-doum,bou-doum. Michie Preval. Anonymous. ABF

Dapper Irishman. Uptown. Allen Ginsberg. FF

Dapple in France the fertile plains. Who Has Not Walked Upon the Shore. Robert Bridges. CMoP; MOS

Dare I well give, I say, my heart to year. To seek each where, where man doth live. Sir Thomas Wyatt. FCP; SiPS

Dare not defile bread you baked/but never blessed. For Jeanette Piccard Ordained at 79. Renny Golden. AMV-80

Dare to have pity and forgive. Armistice Day. Lucia Trent. PGD

Dare to hold or dare let go,/What abysses gape below! Suburban Lullaby. John Streeter Manifold. BoAV

...Dare we land upon a dream? Landing on the Moon. May Swenson. MOON; TAP

Dared to stand out/and say/Madaza was a "Wanted." From the Outside. Mafika Pascal Gwala. WhB

The dareemo grass is the best hay,/Of this I have always been sure. The Best Dance. Anonymous. WTO

Dares trust such Power with so much Piety. To the King on His Navy. Edmund Waller. CEP

Daring Dave Farragut/Thunderbolt stroke! Farragut. William Tuckey Meredith. AA; EtS; FaBoBe; HBV 1-2; HBVY; PAH

Daring to live for the impossible. To Be a Jew in the Twentieth Century. Muriel Rukeyser. TrJP

"The Dark and Bloody Ground." The Mothers of the West. William Davis Gallagher. MC; PAH

Dark, and rain in the air. O Lyric Love. Winfield Townley Scott. VGW

Dark as it is, all change would aggravate. To —. Percy Bysshe Shelley. ERoP 1-2

Dark Bedouin of the waves. A Cyclone at Sea. William Hamilton Hayne. AA

The dark blood of the folk. Night of Battle. Yvor Winters. PoA

Dark blood strands of wool Marrakesh Women. Lyn Lifshin. LTB

The dark bloom of the world. The Ritual. Joy Gwillim. AMV-80

Dark blue rings/Around our necks. Song of the Hanged. Eleni Vakalo. PBWP

Dark bronze, bright leaves, pure silken threads, in triple/flower. A Dream of November. Sir Edmund Gosse. SyP

...A dark cricket begins/In the castles of maple. Depressed by a Book of Bad Poetry, I Walk toward an Unused Pasture... James Wright. ConAP

Dark Danny knows all/These lovely things. Dark Danny. Ivy O. Eastwick. BrR; TiPo

The dark days o' winter were simmer to me! The Braes o' Gleniffer. Robert Tannahill. OBRV

The dark deep emerald that Rossetti wrought/For his own soul, to wear for ever more. What the Sonnet Is. Eugene Lee Hamilton. HoPM; OBVV

Dark down, the stone, in its fall,/Found the sea: I could do that much, after all. Two Pieces after Suetonius. Robert Penn Warren. NOBA

The Dark Dragon from Darkfell,/bears on his pinions the bodies of men,/ Soars overhead. I sink now. The Song of the Seeress. Anonymous. NAWM 1-2

The dark, dreary winter, an' wild-driving snaw,/Alane can delight me–now Nannie's awa'. My Nannie's Awa'. Robert Burns. GN; HBV 1-2

Dark drum the vanishing horses' hooves. The Closing of the Rodeo. William Jay Smith. MP; NePoEA; SaC; SD; TwCP

The dark dust already fallen for tomorrow/from long since gentle stars. Woman Seed Player. Roberta Hill Whiteman. STE

The dark earth, furry as a bear,/Grumbled too! Dark Song. Edith Sitwell. CMoP; FaBoTw; PBWP

Dark earth would ope and hide us in our graves. The Conspiracy of Charles, Duke of Byron. George Chapman. MOON; ViBoPo

Dark-eyed lad of long ago! Dark-Eyed Lad Columbus. Nancy Byrd Turner. SiSoSe

...–Dark eyes are dearer far/Than orbs that mock the hyacinthine-bell. Sonnet: "Sweet poets of the gentle antique line." John Hamilton Reynolds. OBRV

The dark figure awaited/and pacing below. To Emily. Arthur Gregor. AMV-80

Dark hair, dark eyes, slim shoulder.../God-speed, K.M.! To K.M. Walter De La Mare. BoC

The dark has many doors. The Dark. William Heyen. EyDe

Dark head, dark eyes, slim shoulder.../God speed, K. M. Horse in a Field. Walter De La Mare. HBMV

Dark hidden beauty/In the faces of black women,/Which only black men/See. Jungle Taste. Edward S. Silvera. CDC

Dark hours of grief and pain reveal/The undreamed constancy of love. By Night. Philip Jerome Cleveland. TRV

The dark is melting. We touch like cripples. Event. Sylvia Plath. NOBA

The dark Lieutenant from the sea. The Summer Story. John Lehmann. MP

Dark look, and overhanging thorn. Poem: "I cannot tell, not I, why she." Walter Savage Landor. OAEL 1-2

Dark of heart, dark of mind. Like Odysseus under the Ram. Archilochus. OBVE

Dark of night, and light of sun. In a Grave-Yard. William Stanley Braithwaite. PoBA

The dark passed through her into the dark. Eve in Old Age. Rob Holland. NIP

Dark people do. Dark People. Kattie M. Cumbo. BOLo

The dark Religions are departed & sweet Science reigns/END OF THE DREAM Night the Ninth Being the Last Judgment. William Blake. OAEL 1-2

The dark stiff little compact spots you see on these white fields/are not shadows. Rag Doll and Summer Birds. Owen Dodson. PoNe

The dark, the horrible pain, the anguish, the bloody sweat.... The Words of Jesus. William Rose Benet. MoRP

...Dark/the sharp lift of the fins. The Sharks. Denise Levertov. NeAP

Dark threads, brushed wetly over my hands/like nerves, quickening. Gemini Elegy. Margaret Gibson. MAYP

...Dark voices tell you/how after many nightmares we are friends. The Dream. Paul Petrie. TAP

...The dark watermark of your absence, a hush. Hush. David St. John. LCAP; MAYP

Dark with no dream is hateful: let me live! The Town without a Market. James Elroy Flecker. MoBrPo

Darkened to slate by melting frost. October. Fredric Koeppel. AMV-80

Darkening the sky/With driven rain. Retrospect. An Pilibin. OnYl

Darkens and deepens and takes/Tints of purple-maroon, rose-madder and straw. In the Fall. Hugh" (Christopher Murray Grieve) MacDiarmid. FaBoMo

Darker by far than any Coalpit Stone. Gods Determinations. Edward Taylor. AP; MamP; SCAP

Darker nights for Leonora than to-night shall ever be. Leonora. Edwin Arlington Robinson. NePA

Darkey,take your hat off when the train goes past. Charley Snyder. Anonymous. ABF

Darkly he rose, and then I slept. A True Account of Talking to the Sun at Fire Island. Frank O'Hara. ANYP; HaCAP; NNaP; SOTW

...Darkly your grace proffers/The grave accusation of innocence. Small Colored Boy in the Subway. Babette Deutsch. PoNe

Darkness and silence, the two eyes that see God. Great/staring eyes. Black-Out. Robinson Jeffers. LiTA; LiTM; NePA; WaP

The darkness and the thunder and the rain. To Germany. Charles Hamilton Sorley. MoBrPo

...The darkness around us is deep. A Ritual to Read to Each Other. William Stafford. NePA

Darkness, black moth the light burns up in. Death. Charles Wright. FiCP

...Darkness broods/O'er ghastly shapes, and sounds not to be borne. Sacred Poetry. John Wilson. WBLP

The darkness I desire is full of you. Unborn. John Le Gay Brereton. NOAV

Darkness in and out of rooms, mouths, words. Dome Poem. Dave Smith. PoA

Darkness in the purple rushes–/Weet, a-weet, a-weet, weet weet! Sandpipers. Helen Merrill Egerton. CaP

The darkness is cold/because the stars do not believe in each other Sunset after Rain. William Stanley Merwin. PoA

The darkness of that battle in the West/Where all of high and holy dies away. Idylls of the King. Alfred, Lord Tennyson. VLP

Darkness only gives us leisure/Our stol'n joys to number. Wherefore Peep'st Thou, Envious Day? Anonymous. GBL

The darkness pushing down upon the land. By the Pacific. Herbert Bashford. AA

Darkness that man must dread at last. Tenebrae. Austin Clarke. AnIL; BIrV; CIP; IPY; NeIP; NOBI

Darkness that was before the worlds were made,/And will be after they are dead. A Hymn to the Sea. Richard Henry Stoddard. EtS

The darkness they command/Is utter, and their kiss a final calm. In Memory of Robin Hyde, 1906-39. Charles Brasch. AnNZ

Darlin', what have,/Have I done? Look down That Lonesome Road. Anonymous. OuSiCo

Darling girl, do you love me? Up Street and Down Street. Anonymous. OxNR

Darling, I've been waiting/long/for you to come. Chippewa Love Song. Anonymous. BoWoP

The Darling of the Nile. The Sphinx. Henry Howard Brownell AA

Darling! take my answer so. Do I Love Thee? John Godfrey Saxe. HBV 1-2

...Darling,/we have escaped our death-struggle with our lives. Marriage. Robert Lowell. NAs

Darnel, Ragweed, Wortle Preface. Theodore Weiss. NMP; VGW

Das Ding an sich is all of life,/a task to be dispatched. The Lacemaker (Vermeer). Anne Marx. GoYe

Das iss doch kein Climate fur a mittelaged Mann. Vor a Gauguin Picture zu Singen. Kurt M. Stein. FiBHP

Dash, dash, upon the ground,/To gentle slumbers call. Ah Fading Joy. John Dryden. GoTF; LoBV; OAEP; TreFT; ViBoPo

Dash down yon cup of Samian wine! Don Juan. George Gordon,Lord Byron. AnFE; OBTV; SeCeV

Dash him to dust, and let the world repose. Advice to a Raven in Russia December 1812. Joel Barlow. AmLP; NePA; NOBA; OBWP; OxBA

Dash me, partner, if I don't! The Blanket Injun. Arthur Chapman. BPAW

Dashing airman, Curate pale. Soldier Brave, Sailor True. Anonymous. OxNR

Dashing, toward the sea. Snacks. Ronald P. Tanaka. BrSi

Dat dare ain't a-gwine to be no rain today. The Rain Song. Alex Rogers. BANP

An' dat lil' brack sheep–wuz–me! The Little Black Sheep. Paul Laurence Dunbar. WBLP

Dat man got a heart lak a rock cast in de sea/Or else he wouldn't gone so far from me. St. Louis Blues. W. C. Handy. FF

Dat Nigger tore up de whole co'n field. Run, Nigger, Run! Anonymous. BPo

Dat's de deed to it. A Little Cabin. Charles Bertram Johnson. BANP

Dat's de reason I's a-sighin' an' a-singin' now fu' you,/Li'l' gal. Li'l' Gal. Paul Laurence Dunbar. GoSl

An' dat's de way dat hyporite 'ten'. That Hypocrite. *Anonymous.* BPo

Dat's de way you proves yo'se'f/An' shows yo'se'f a man. Settin' on de Fence. *Anonymous.* WBLP

"Dat's my only son, Lawd, Lawd, dat's my only son." Po' Laz'us (Poor Lazarus). *Anonymous.* ABF

Dat's why de king an' queen an' princess so rich now. The Maid Freed from the Gallows (C vers.). *Anonymous.* ViBoFo

Dat side de river, again I'll be/Wid my boy Kree. Kree. Armistead Churchill Gordon. AA

Dat you cain't git yo' lodgin' here. Song to the Runaway Slave. *Anonymous.* BPo

The dates on their way from Basra cut off by the seas. Lament for a Dead Lover. Siraad Haad. WTO

Dats'/What D blues/Is. D Blues. Calvin C. Hernton. PoBA

...Daubed/With war-paint, teeters some lust-red manitou? A Country without a Mythology. Douglas LePan. NOBC

Daughter/daughters/I love you. Going to Town. Linda Hogan. TWSS

The daughters died because they'd rather/Go to their mother than stay with their father. Epitaph from a Yorkshire Churchyard. *Anonymous.* DBV

Daughters, I love you. The Women Speaking. Linda Hogan. TWSS

The Daughters of Albion hear her woes, & eccho back/her sighs. Visions of the Daughters of Albion. William Blake. ERoP 1-2; OAEL 1-2

Daughters will throw up their hands/and cry, "Not me! Not me!" A Voice from our of the Night. Lisel Mueller. GP

Daughterwife, look upon me. Westland Row. Thomas Kinsella. NoAm

David alone, with sling and stone, ten thousand kill'd or/more. A Metrical Version of the Bible....(excerpt). *Anonymous.* FaBoUs

David killed Goliath—dead! Who Did Swallow Jonah? *Anonymous.* FSW

"David, King of Israel, yet liveth and/endureth!" The Death of David. Hayim Nahman Bialik. TrJP

David's brethren/in the Land of Goliath. The Cave of Night. John Montague. CIP

David's city after dark./Honor tibi, Domine. Christmas Carols. Patricia Beer. OxBC

Davus, I detest/Persian decoration. Persicos Odi: Pocket Version. Henry Austin Dobson. NLV

A daw is a daw, and a daw shall be ever.' Of a Daw. John Heywood. PBBP

Dawn after mortal dawn, with vulgar joy/Acclaim the sun. A Black November Turkey. Richard Wilbur. AmLP; BoAnP; LCAP; MoAB; NCSH

Dawn enters; my Love wakens; here is day. Nuptial Song. John Byrne Leicester Warren, Lord De Tabley. GTBS-P; NOBV; OBVV

Dawn has broken, Dwarf,/Stiffen now to stone. The Words of the All-Wise (excerpt). *Anonymous.* OBVE

Dawn is not one of them. Alba. Derek Walcott. GoJo; PCP

Dawn lightly laid her rosy hand. A Ballad of a Nun. John Davidson. BeLS; HBMV; MoBrPo; OnMSP

Dawn like a thief/fell upon me. In gold sandals. Sappho. BoWoP

The dawn of every day is as the close is,/You would lay roses! If You Had Known. Thomas Hardy. FaBoRV; GBL

...Dawn/Of sallow and grey bricks, and newsboys crying war. Aubade. Louis MacNeice. ViBoPo

The dawn on earth of Freedom's perfect day. On the Completion of the Pacific Telegraph. Jones Very. AP; TAP

The dawn, with silver-sandaled feet,/Crept like a frightened girl. The Harlot's House. Oscar Wilde. MoBrPo; SyP

The dawning's crimson flush. The North Wind Came Up Yesternight. Robert Bridges. SeCeV

Dawns into the Jubilee of the Ages. On the Jubilee of Queen Victoria (excerpt). Alfred, Lord Tennyson. UnPo

Day after happy day,/Night after night. Marriage. Wilfred Wilson Gibson. HBV 1-2

Day and night. Day and night. The Muse. Barry Spacks. MAT; PoL

Day and night/Eat fish Pepsi Generation. Walasse Ting. MAT

Day and night she dances,/between the suns/she dreams Shulamit in Her Dreams. Marcia Falk. VWA

The day begins its dark/journey, across nine bridges/wrecked one by one. Foreboding. John Haines. ConAP

The day comes soon when I must let You in. Unwelcome. Irma Dovey. AMV-80

Day has begun. Sunrise in the Hills of Satsuma. Mary McNeil Fenollosa. AA

The day has come for all. Aubade Triste. Agnes Mary Frances (Mme Emile Duclaux) Robinson. NOBV

The day has dawned at last. Bugle Song of Peace. Thomas Curtis Clarke. WBLP; WGRP

The day has dawned, my beloved. Nihon Shoki: Dawn Song. *Anonymous.* HW

The day held no insurmountable fears/for me. Black Power. Alvin Saxon. PoBA

Day holding one and moving solemnly—/Night holding two. Chariots. Witter ("Emanuel Morgan") Bynner. HBMV

Day in, Day out, you just kept belching. To a Publisher...cut-out. LeRoi (Imamu Amiri Baraka) Jones. NeAP

The day is always now and is vacant. Inertia. Kirti Chaudhari. WPOW

The Day is dawning, the Day is dawning, which shall be our own. The Garibaldi Hymn. Luigi Mercantini. WBLP

The day is fading, and the dusk is cold. Dreams. Victor J. Daley. PoAu 1-2

The day is gone, and all the restless night/Is bound about with ribbons of pale stars. Evening on the Harbor. Virginia Lyne Tunstall. HBMV

The day is never darken'd/That had thee here obscure. Phoebus and Admetus. George Meredith. EnLi 1-2; NOBE; OBEV; OBVV

...Day/is so deep already with involvement. Pas de Deux for Lovers. Michael Dransfield. CBAP

The day is tired. Solstice. Charles Weekes. OnYI

The day lay in the glass and the blood was gone. The Last Supper. Oscar Williams. FaFP; LiTA; LiTM; MoRP; NePA

The/day most clearly begins. A Meditation: What is a Stocking in Eternity? Lewis MacAdams. ANYP

The day my love came home to me. In Misty Blue. Laurence Binyon. HBMV

The Day of Days is here. The Day of Days. William Morris. VLP

THE DAY OF HUMANITY. Black Mother. Viriato Da Cruz. WhB

The day of perfect righteousnessThe promised day of God. Thy Kingdom Come. Frederick Lucian Hosmer. WGRP

Day of rest, God hath blest Israel's/Sabbath day. Keep Ye Holy Sabbath Rest. *Anonymous.* TrJP

A day of Stevenson's will prove to be/Not part of Time, but Immortality. Stevenson's Birthday. Katherine Miller. AA

Day of the vernal winds/1967. Do Nothing Till You Hear from Me. David Henderson. PoBA

The day on which the nuptials/Of Stella and Violentilla/Are to the world proclaimed. Ah, Now I Know What Day This Is. Statius Publius Papinius. HW

The day revolving, and the sun stood still. How Copernicus Stopped the Sun. R. H. W. Dillard. SUW

...Day rises in words like huge poppies/exploding on their stems. The Alchemy of Day. Anne Hebert. BoWoP

Day's lord erases. Envoy. Robert Duncan. VGW

Day that I loved, day that I loved, the Night is here! Day That I Have Loved. Rupert Brooke. FPL; GTBS; PoLf

The day though came no later, in spite of all I said. Lente, Lente. Ovid. AWP; LiTW

The day we went to Rothesay, O. Rothesay, O. *Anonymous.* FSW

The day whose end shall give this hour as sheer/As chaos to the irrevocable Past. Dawn on the Night-Journey. Dante Gabriel Rossetti. NCEP

Day without rice. Rice. Carol Muske. AmPA

The day you answered yes! Darling, Tell Me Yes. John Godfrey Saxe. HBV 1-2

Daybreak and a candle-end. Wild Old Wicked Man. William Butler Yeats. AnIL; AtBAP; CMoP; MBW 1-2

Daybreak their very faces proved divine! Theologians. Walter De La Mare. EaLo

Daylight and moonlight, all the fun in the world. The Statue. Kenneth Allott. EAS

Days and nights whirl by to that first kiss/so full of promise and surprise. Rumplestiltskin Poems. William Hathaway. DFT

The days are beginning to fall. Pub. Julian Symons. LiTB; WaP

The days draw in, the winter has begun. Farm Wife. Matt Field. AMV-81

The days go I remain The Mirabeau Bridge. Guillaume Apollinaire. OBVE

The days have fled,/My well-beloved. It Was Not You. Andre Spire. TrJP

The days that make us happy make us wise. Biography (excerpt). John Masefield. OxBTC

Days when I got the front seat to myself/to chew with my father/singing with the radio. Dentyne. Annie Lurie. AmC

The Daystar that was risen in your heart. To J. S. Bach. Michael Thwaites. MoRP

Dazed as the couple I'd saved from the cake,/jacked in their tracks by the onrushing beams. There Should Have Been. Sydney Lea. SM

A dazzling city, suburbia or Jerusalem,/a mirage in the bleak light. Evening Walk. Sonja Akesson. WPOW

Dazzling petals from dark fate. Almond Blossom in Wartime. Stephen Spender. ACV

The dazzling violence of atomic death. Improvisation on an Old Theme. Dorothy Livesay. ACV; CaP

The dead against the dead and on the silent ground/The silent slain— The Silent Slain. Archibald MacLeish. CMoP; CoBMV; ExPo; LiTM; MoVE; NePA; PoL f10]; TiPo

Dead, and clos'd up in Yvorie. Upon a Flie. Robert Herrick. FM

Dead and divine and brother of all, and here again he lies. Drum-Taps. Walt Whitman. AP

The dead and I/we swim/through the new doors/of our old houses. Cologne. Hilde Domin. VWA

The dead and the serious old/Do not expect the main thing from us. A Letter from a Friend. John N. Morris. CABA

The dead are a cadmium blue, and they understand. Homage to Paul Cezanne (excerpt). Charles Wright. HaCAP

...The dead are not dead but alive. Vastness. Alfred, Lord Tennyson. VLP

Dead as stone! Ramon. Bret (Francis Bret Harte) Harte. BeLS

...Dead beside you,/his shared cigarette still alive in your lips. No Man Knows War. Edwin Rolfe. TrJP; WaP

The dead bird be reborn. That Bright Chimeric Beast. Countee Cullen. AmNP

The dead/but who hears them Who Says. Musa Moris Farhi. VWA

The dead by the side of the road. The Dead by the Side of the Road. Gary Snyder. HAP; InPS

Dead Cats and Turnip-Tops come tumbling down the Flood. A Description of a City Shower. Jonathan Swift. CABL; CBEP; CEP; EiCP; EnLi 1-2; ExPo; HeIP; LoBV; MAT; NOEC; NoP; OAEL 1-2; OBSV; OnYI; PPP; SeCePo; SeCeV; TEP; ViBoPo

Dead cones upon the alder shook. In Memory of Jane Fraser. Geoffrey Hill. NoAm; OxBTC

The dead dance/flower stalks of the wind– Oblivion! Nelly Sachs. PBWP

A dead, drowned face stares up immutably. Morning on the Shore. Wilfred (William Wilfred Campbell) Campbell. NOBC

The dead-end quarry held us there till dawn. Snake Hill. Jay Parini. AMV-81; MAYP

Dead, even great Darius is not his peer. Alive, this man was Manes, a common slave. Anyte. BoWoP

The dead fields, women rooted to the river. The Apple Trees. Louise Gluck. HaCAP

...A dead fly swept/under the carpet, wrinkling to fulfillment. Harriet. Robert Lowell. NoP

Dead for each other's sake. Heaven. Martha Gilbert Dickinson. AA; HBV 1-2

...The dead have said/What these can only memorize and mumble. Grandeur of Ghosts. Siegfried Sassoon. AnFE; HaMV; MoBrPo; OBMV

Dead in his meagreness. In the Prison Pen. Herman Melville. PoEL 1-5; TAP

Dead in loves firmament, no starre shall shine/So nobly faire, so purely chaste as thine. His Muse Speakes to Him. William Habington. AnAnS 2

The dead in that death-haunted dream. The Dream. John Peale Bishop. LiTA; LiTM

Dead in the rice paddies, dead on the nameless hills. Ode for the American Dead in Korea. Thomas McGrath. NePoEA; PoPl; VGW

Dead is the holy Alciphron! Modo and Alciphron. Sylvia Townsend Warner. MoBrPo

Dead is the root whence all these fancies grew. A Farewell to False Love. Sir Walter Ralegh. BoLoP; EiL; FCP

...Dead is the year! The Last Day of the Year (New Year's Eve). Annette Von Droste-Hulshoff. BoWoP

Dead joys unburied breed us death and pain. Joy's Treachery. Wilfrid Scawen Blunt. VLP

The dead know nought of sorrow. Selfishness. Margaret E. Bruner. PoToHe

Dead leaves pile round her feet. Anne and the Peacock. Noel Welch. FF

The dead lie deep in me. Summer Pogrom. Fay Zwicky. CBAP

Dead loves that were born for me. Stony Grey Soil. Patrick Kavanagh. CIP

The dead must rest, the dead shall rest. Oh, Earlier Shall the Rosebuds Blow. William Johnson Cory. HBV 1-2

Dead, oh, Kincora! Kincora. James Clarence Mangan. AnIV; OnYI; OxBI

Dead pilot adrift in raft. Time Zones for Forty-Four. Donald A. Stauffer. WaP

The dead pride of our own/Mother country, weeping/To be let down. Nightmare Inspection Tour for American Generals. Gibbons Ruark. TW

...The dead/Remain, and the once inestimable caskets. The Middle of a War. Roy Fuller. OBWP

The dead rises from his grave/in the clothes of a magician,/shedding his miracles. A Death in the Streets. Mario Petaccia. LFAC

Dead sculs and bones of men, whose life had gone astray. The Faerie Queene. Edmund Spenser. PPP

Dead sea of the dead god of the dead stars. Sonnets of the Triple-Headed Manichee: II. George Barker. PoA

...The dead/Sleep light this wind being overhead. Winter Night. Robert Fitzgerald. PoPl

Dead space opposing,/to and fro. Poplar. Gottfried Benn. PoPl

Dead, strayed, to love-strange lover. Wedded. Isaac Rosenberg. PoPle

Dead the fire, though we blow. Another to the Maids. Robert Herrick. OHIP

Dead to myself, I live in Thee. A Song: "Lord, when the sense of thy sweet grace." Richard Crashaw. SeCeV; ViBoPo

"Dead," was all he answered. The Death of the Hired Man. Robert Frost. AnNE; CMoP; HoPM; MaC; MoAB; MoAmPo; NoP; OxBA; SeCeV; SoSe; TrGrPo

The dead were the fortunate ones. The Wreck of the Deutschland (parody). David Annett. BXAP

Dead whales are rendered down,/Give oil. Killing a Whale. David Gill. BoAnP

The dead will not rehabilitate us. Posthumous Rehabilitation. Tadeusz Rozewicz. FaBoPV

Dead women tell no tales. Elegy on Any Lady by George Moore. Max Beerbohm. FaBoEE

Deadlocked with them, taking root as/cradles rock. All the Dead Dears. Sylvia Plath. IHMS

Deadly as the icy sleet of skag that froze your blood. Burying Blues for Janis. Marge Piercy. GeTw; NeAC

A deadly life in woe? What death is worse than this." Sir Thomas Wyatt. FCP; SiPS

The deaf and mute may feel where I have failed. What Five Books Would You Pick To Be Marooned with... Paris Leary. CoPo

Deaf dumb and blind can only stare at the sky. On First Hearing Beethoven. George Barker. UnS

A deaf policeman heard the noise/And came and killed those two dead boys. One Bright Morning... Anonymous. EvOK

Deaf to the pathos circling in the air. A Pauper. Allen Tate. LiTM

Deaf to your call, though shades of his eyes/Break through and stare. Madrigal: "Your love is dead, lady, your love is dead." R. S. Thomas. BoLoP; ELU

Deaf, unable to feed herself, demented... The Henyard Round. Donald Hall. Psk

Dear ancestors, all this is still one in my mind. The Poet Imagines His Grandfather's Thoughts on the Day He Died. Wing Tek Lum. BrSi

Dear as the mother to the son,/More than my brothers are to me. In Memoriam A.H.H., IX. Alfred, Lord Tennyson. PeHV; VLP

Dear C, you are a ca-ca pee-pee head. Hate Mail. Steve Kowit. APU

Dear Christ, to be born for this! In the Snack-Bar. Edwin Morgan. FF

Dear city of my pilgrimage. Leap in the Smoke. John Buchan. PoSH

Dear death, kind death! oh, read this idly, friend. Inscription in a Book. Gilean Douglas. AMV-81

Dear Dionysus, give me back again/Ten fingertips that leave the world alone. King Midas. Howard Moss. CoAP; TAP

Dear, doting Dick, for O! she saved my life. Privy-Love for my Landlady. George Farewell. NOEC

Dear dreams of our first Love–lost Heliodore! Heliodore. J. D. Logan. CaP

Dear Emily Sparks! Reuben Pantier. Edgar Lee Masters. GLGT

Dear endless argument! yet sometimes we/Even as we argue kiss. There! Let it be. The Pleasures of Love. Wilfrid Scawen Blunt. HBV 1-2

Dear Father, take care of thy children, THE BOYS! The Boys. Oliver Wendell Holmes. HBV 1-2; WBLP

Dear, foiled enthusiast, teach our hearts to/feel! Don Quixote. Craven Langstroth Betts. AA

Dear for her reputation through the world... Richard II. William Shakespeare. FaBV; FaPoR

Dear, for thy love I would not wear the willow.' Buen Matina. Sir John Salusbury. EiL

Dear friend, of Easter when it means all this. What Does Easter Mean to You? May Ricker Conrad. PGD

Dear friend! our fresh delight in simplest nature's hues! Foliage. Felicia Dorothea Hemans. OBRV

Dear God, be kind with the heart-sick child/Who steps on the Lonely Road. In Dark Hour. Seumas MacManus. WGRP

Dear God, wilt thou not set a lamp/Low in the West for me? The Lamp in the West. Ella Higginson. AA; HBV 1-2

Dear guests, you now have seen Love's corpse-light shine. Modern Love, XVII. George Meredith. BoLoP; HeIP; NOBV; NoP; OAEP; VLP

Dear Heart, no more–no more. Rhymes and Rhythms: Prologue. William Ernest Henley. VLP

Dear heart, pale and long. Dusk Song. William H. A. Moore. BANP

Dear heart, the wise forget.–/I am not wise! A Valentine. Jeannette Bliss Gillespy. AA

Dear heart, you lay above the ground. The Yew-Tree. Anonymous. GBL

Dear Home Home. Nellie Womack Hines. PoToHe

Dear home in England, won at last. Green Fields of England. Arthur Hugh Clough. OAEP

Dear, how long ago we knew! Love Triumphant. Frederic Lawrence Knowles. GoTF; HBV 1-2; TreFT

Dear, I still believe in love,/But no more–in you! Love-Faith. Harry Kemp. HBMV

Dear Lord, be kind to those who wait. The Cod-Fisher. Joseph C. Lincoln. EtS

"Dear Lord, dear Lord, that I may be like/thee! Thomas a Kempis. Richard Rogers. Bowker. AA

Dear Lord, kind Lord, remember me. A Father's Prayer. *Anonymous.* STF

Dear Lord, to thee. Master, No Offering. Edwin Pond Parker. AH

Dear love, how can I care? Song: "How can I care?" Robert Graves. GBL

Dear! love me not, that ye may love me more! Astrophel and Stella, LXII. Sir Philip Sidney. AAS; HBV 1-2; SiPS

Dear Messrs. T., I'm yours without a farthing./For executors and self, GEORGE HARDING Reply to a Creditor. George Harding. FaBoUs

...Dear mother, bends,/With love's true instinct, back to thee! To My Mother. Thomas Moore. OHIP

"Dear mother, had I minded you,/I need not now have died." The Little Fish That Would Not Do as It Was Bid. Jane and Ann Taylor. OHIP

Dear mother of fresh thoughts and joyous health! To Sleep. William Wordsworth. BoLiVe; EnRP; GTBS; GTBS-P; HBV 1-2; InPo; MyFE; OBRV; TrGrPo; ViBoPo

Dear old Ions was asleep. Music. William Bell Scott. NOBV

"Dear Pound, I am leaving England." Villanelle: The Psychological Hour. Ezra Pound. CTC

Dear priceless nothings, which outweigh/All riches that the sun shines on. Love Hath a Language. Helen Selina Sheridan. HBV 1-2

Dear reader, take heed &/by the way, will you marry me? Usage. Sharon Thesen. CaPN

Dear, red-faced father God who lit your mind. To His Dead Body. Siegfried Sassoon. NoAm

Dear sir, and make me yours for ever. Chaste Florimel. Matthew Prior. BoLoP; ErPo

Dear steed! our ride hath been in vain/To the halls where my love lay dying. The King of Denmark's Ride. Carolina Elizabeth Sarah Norton. GN; HBV 1-2

Dear to me here in my Alpine exile. Alcaics: to H. F. B. Robert Louis Stevenson. EG; NBM; OBEV; OBVV

Dear under-song in Clamor's hour. Recollections of Love. Samuel Taylor Coleridge. ChRP

Dear, we must go again/To where the town ends.... A Song of Two Wanderers. Marguerite Wilkinson. HBMV

"Dear wife'...'devoted mother'.../"Beloved child'... The Mistress. Joan Barton. OxBTC

The dearer for the tears. May Margaret. Theophile Marzials. HBV 1-2

Dearer to God are the prayers of the poor. Hymn: "Brightest and best of the sons of the morning." Reginald Heber. NBM

Dearer to me than every other/Are you, my Russia, even so. Russia. Alexander Blok. AWP

Dearer twenty-thousand-fold/Than gold, is Amy Margaret. Amy Margaret. William Allingham. BiCB

...Dearest Atthis,/can you now forget all those days? Sappho, if you do not come out. Sappho. BoWoP

The dearest look nor the longest kiss assuages? The Door and the Window. Henry Reed. NeBP

Dearest Mabel!-dearest.... At Her Window. Frederick Locker-Lampson. HBV 1-2; OBVV

Dearest of all God's creations,/Great and wondrous motherhood. Wondrous Motherhood. *Anonymous.* PGD

The dearest though I keep myself,/I keep for sake o' somebody. I've Had Many an Aching Pain. John Clare. NOBV

Death shall take you in his arms/And shatter your virginity. Corinna in Vendome. Pierre de Ronsard. BoLoP; ErPo

Death. He. Lawrence Ferlinghetti. NeAP; PoM

Death. So Be My Passing. William Ernest Henley. HBVY

Death a settlement, or a long, long strike. Binding Arbitration. Robert Wrigley. SOTS

Death ain't/No jive. Death in Yorkville. Langston Hughes. PoBA

"Death, also, has its further shore!" The Sea Is His. Edward Sandford Martin. EtS

Death and all winter absolutes at bay. Apostasy. Mary Mills. NePoAm

Death and hate on the rocks, as sandward and landward it/roars. The Winter Lakes. Wilfred (William Wilfred Campbell) Campbell. BoNaP; NOBC; OBCV

Death and Sleep, who came unsought. Sleep. Lewis Frank Tooker. AA

Death, and the gloom which round me even now/Thickens, and to its inner gulph recalls. The Second Asgard. Matthew Arnold. FiP

Death and the Rain and Tomorrow. A Fence. Carl Sandburg. WeW

Death, are you come/To lay hands upon your prey? Soliloquy on Death. F. K. Fiawoo. PBA

Death attends each rank and station,/Whether he is call'd or not. Odes. Horace. OBVE

Death, be a chum and make it soon. Death, Don't Be Boring (parody). Roy Kelly. BXAP

Death bears the blame, 'tis his envenom'd dart/That strikes the suff'ring mortal to the heart. The Rising Village. Oliver Goldsmith. PeCV

Death being kittens/who once chased their tails. Geometry. Alfred Kreymborg. AnAmPo

Death brought him blisse that ever shall endure. Upon the Death of Sir Antony Denny. *Anonymous.* EnPo

...Death can never get true lovers' goats! Tristram and Isolt. Don (Donald Robert Marquis) Marquis. HBMV

Death cometh at last. An Old Man's Song. Richard Le Gallienne. HBV 1-2

The death-cry drowning in the battle's roar. Don Juan. George Gordon, Lord Byron. OBWP

Death-defying/Eatna! For an Eskimo. Annie Charlotte Dalton. CaP

Death, do you hear me singing in your key. Finale: Presto. Peter Davidson. CoPo

Death doth draw nigh;/There is no remedy. O Death, Rock Me Asleep. Anne Boleyn. EIL; FF

Death draws his cordons in. The Company of Lovers. Judith Wright. BoAV

Death drones the answer, far away, Chiffons! William Johnson. HBV 1-2

Death fang'd the remnant of his lugs. On William Prynne. Samuel (1602-80) Butler. FaBoEE

Death follows with uplifted dart. On the Dead. Walter Savage Landor. NBM

Death for this is ne'er the nigher,/Welcome mirth, and fear farewell. The Battle of Monmouth. *Anonymous.* PAH

Death goes indoors/exhausted The Peachtree. Denise Levertov. CAPP

Death has it in her hand, cut like a cross.' Sonnet: Of His Pain from a New Love. Guido Cavalcanti. AWP

Death has not changed my opinion. Genealogy. Eleni Vakalo. PBWP

Death, honour, and fierce battle wait. Battery Moving Up to a New Position from Rest Camp: Dawn. Robert Nichols. MMM

Death, however reckoned, is hard to dispose of. Burning the Cat. William Stanley Merwin. NIP

Death, in a dark, in a deep, in a dream, for ever. Sonnet of Fishes. George Barker. FaBoMo

Death in her heart! When London Calls. Victor J. Daley. CBAP

Death is a useful comma/which punctuates, and labors to convince/of more to follow. Thesis. William Walter De Bolt. AMV-80

Death is abroad...oh, the black season!/The deep–the dim! Song Be Delicate. John Shaw Neilson. BoAV; PoAu 1-2

Death is better for every earl/Than life besmirched with the brand of shame!"... Beowulf. *Anonymous.* AnOE; HeIP; ViBoPo; WTO

Death is dancing me ragged. The Women Are Grieving. Linda Hogan. TWSS

Death is gwineter lay his cold icy hands on me, Lord! Death's Gwineter Lay His Cold Icy Hands on Me. *Anonymous.* BoAN 1-2

Death is on your side: you can't lose. The Advice of an Efficiency Expert. Augustus Young. CIP

Death is only a quiet door/In an old wall. Death Is a Door. Nancy Byrd Turner. BLPA

Death, is that you calling? Your wind-harp/sighing with the element of form? Black Bagatelles. Rodney Hall. CBAP

Death is the gentlest of the world's replies. Give Me Not Tears. Rose Hawthorne Lathrop. AA

Death is the lighter evil of the two. Poverty. Theognis. AWP

Death is your lover and our body bends/To meet his dark, possessive head. A Game of Chance. Howard Moss. PoA

DEATH JUST MAKES IT SEEM REAL/ Death May Leap on a Sunny Day. Raymond Thompson. LFAC

Death keeps open house house. Farmer and Sailor. Plato. LiTW

Death killed Kildare–who dare kill whom he will. Who Killed Kildare? Jonathan Swift. GoTF; HBV 1-2

Death lies dead. A Forsaken Garden. Algernon Charles Swinburne. BoLiVe; CBEP; EBEV; FaBoPP; GTBS; GTBS-P; HBV 1-2; LiTB; LoBV; MaVP; NOBE; NOBV; NoP; OAEL 1-2; OBNC; OBVV; TEP; VLP; WHA

Death/like homesickness/like homecoming after captivity. Dying. Alfred Alvarez. VWA

Death like pomatum, tea, and crabs must fall. The Ocean Wanderer. *Anonymous.* NA

Death made wide a million gates/So to close her tragic story. A Memory of Earth. George William Russell. OBVV

Death may not on its unmasked slope/Take you without all soul, all hope. Teach Us to Mark This, God. Franz Werfel. TrJP

...Death met I too,/And saw the dawn glow through. Hymn to Colour. George Meredith. OBNC

Death neither wish, nor feare to see. Epigrams. Martial (Marcus Valerius Martialis). OBVE

...The death of a year,/And watch it go down in thunder. Year's End. Brother Antoninus. NoAm

Death of kinsmen/death death!' The Tain: The Armies Enter Cuailnge. *Anonymous.* NOBI

THE DEATH OF NOTHING, FUNERAL OF GAIUS!　Lean Gaius, Who Was Thinner Than a Straw.　Lucilius [(or Lucillius)].　OBVE

The death of pancakes in America.　The Metamorphosis of Aunt Jemima.　William Childress.　MAT

The death of the afternoon to them/Is but the lengthening of blue-black shadows on brick walls.　Rear Porches of an Apartment Building.　Maxwell Bodenheim.　AnAmPo

The death of those we love as/The hint of your death, love.　A Space in the Air.　Jon Silkin.　NePoEA; TrJP

Death on the pillow be thine,/Thy Saviour's presence.　Good Wish.　*Anonymous*.　FaBoCh; LoGBV

Death only was so amorous/I let him have his way.　Three Epitaphs: For a Virgin Lady.　Countee Cullen.　MoAmPo

Death opens unknown doors. It is most grand to die.　The Tragedy of Pompey the Great (excerpt).　John Masefield.　WGRP

Death passeth by.　Omens.　James H. Cousins.　OnYI

Death's child and mine: My name will be poet.　Poem to My Death.　Julia de Burgos.　BoWoP

Death's/little victory flags.　Overheard in a Barbershop.　Irving Layton.　NMP

Death's narrow but oppressive sea/Looks not unnavigable to me.　The Narrow Sea.　Robert Graves.　FaBoEE; FaBoMo; MOS

...Death's own pale horses,/That raced in the tracks behind.　A Gallop of Fire.　Marie E. J. Pitt.　PoAu 1-2

Death's towering ruin from the past/Makes black the land that round me/lies.　Death.　Madison Cawein.　AA

Death said to the Lady.　Death and the Lady.　Léonie Adams.　MoAB; MoAmPo

...Death seemed but the shade/That those heavenly branches made.　An Old Woman Laments in Spring-Time.　Edith Sitwell.　ViBoPo

...Death seems a comely thing/In Autumn at the fall of the leaf?　Autumn Song.　Dante Gabriel Rossetti.　ViBoPo

Death shall change as the light 'twixt moonset and dawn.　Among the Ferns.　Edward Carpenter.　WGRP

Death shall come in with thee.　A Ballad of Death.　Algernon Charles Swinburne.　MaVP

A death-shocked nation lived, a world was bettered.　Lincoln.　Clyde Walton Hill.　PGD

...–Death, stay thy phantoms!　Kaddish.　Allen Ginsberg.　NeAP; NOBA; PoM; VWA

Death-still–and sudden as death.　The Blue Heron.　Theodore Goodridge Roberts.　CaP; NOBC; OBCV; PeCV

Death succeeds Atimetus.　Epigram: "The golden one is gone from the banquets."　Hilda ("H. D.") Doolittle.　PoA

Death surely ends at once the dreamer and the dream?　Sonnet on Life.　Sir Brooke Boothby.　ViBoPo

Death, that great/Underliner, has made me notice this today.　Che Guevara Is Dead.　Peter Schjeldahl.　ANYP

Death, the great poet, adds the lacking rhyme.　The Great Poet.　King of Seville Mu'tamid.　LiTW

Death times death is–being.　Two Times Two Is Four.　Halper Leivick.　VWA

Death to all cats! The Rule/of Dogs shall last a thousand years!　Mort aux Chats.　Peter Porter.　OxBC

Death to him's a strange surprise.　The Quiet Life.　Seneca (Lucius Annaeus Seneca).　LiTW

Death, to mark them in the Spring.　Spring and Death.　Gerard Manley Hopkins.　BrPo; SyP

Death to the killers, bringing light to life.　Not Palaces.　Stephen Spender.　CMoP; FaBoMo; LiTB; LiTM; MoAB; MoBrPo; NoAm; NoP; WaP

Death–unsubdued–the last one of my race.　The Last Longhorn's Farewell.　John P. Sjolander.　BPAW

Death unto us must be freedom and rest.　Parted Souls.　Edward, Lord Herbert of Cherbury.　AnAnS 2; SeCP

Death waits and watches where he lies!　The Massasauga.　Hamlin Garland.　AA; BPAW

Death was but the good King's jest,/It was hid so carefully.　The Skeleton.　Gilbert Keith Chesterton.　FaBoTw

Death was the end of every such desire.　Love's Ending.　*Anonymous*.　OBSC

Death will be lurking near the base lines.　Near the Base Line.　Samuel L. Albert.　NePoAm-2

Death will come, if it comes,/through my love for the men of Ireland.　If I Owned All of Alba.　Colum Cille.　NOBI

Death will end our crying/For friends that come and go.　Ballade of Dead Friends.　Edwin Arlington Robinson.　AA

Death will have gathered me.　A Tragedy.　Edith Nesbit.　HBV 1-2

Death will not have it so.　Before Sedan.　Henry Austin Dobson.　GoTF; TreFS

Death winks at me.　You Hide.　Edith Bruck.　BoWoP

Death would be then between us two/The passing of a summer's night.　If I Could Touch.　William Stanley Braithwaite.　BALP

Death would have been only/an abstraction,/evil only a rhyme.　Supreme Fiction.　Howard Winn.　SOTS

Debas'd, debas'd the nation lyes/In gloom fanatic, cant, and lies!　Arthur's Seat (excerpt).　Thomas Mercer.　OxBS

Debate of my thoughts, or an unlikely presence.　On My Stand.　Sharon Scott.　JB

Decades of arrogance between/The dial life and him.　A Clock Stopped.　Emily Dickinson.　AnFE; APA; CoAnAm; MAmP; MAPA; NCEP; NoP; PoEL 1-5

Deceit. Deceit. Deceit.　To the Tune "The Phoenix Hairpin."　T'ang Wan.　WPOW

Deceive and captivate the mind:　The First Olympionique to Hiero of Syracuse.　Pindar.　ATP

Deceive, deceive me once again!　You smiled, you spoke, and I believed.　Walter Savage Landor.　BoLoP; GBL; OAEP

December: And a Cristesmasse I drinke red wine.　The Months.　*Anonymous*.　OxBM

December bones in a sweet whore of May.　Apocalypse.　John Frederick Nims.　MiAP

Decent behavior/From a popular savior.　Question and Answer.　Samuel Hoffenstein.　DBV; FiBHP; PV

A decent, quiet end, if you please, Master Death.　Disquisition on Death (excerpt).　A. R. D. Fairburn.　AnNZ

Decide. Oh, coincide!　Somewhere the Equation Breaks Down.　Daniel Berrigan.　NYBP

Decisive action in the hour of need/Denotes the Hero, but does not succeed.　B Stands for Bear.　Hilaire Belloc.　ShM

Deck'd in Oriental pride,/By homely British fire-side.　Address to Certain Gold Fishes.　Hartley Coleridge.　VLP

Deck thee with flowers which fear not rage of days!　Change Should Breed Change.　William, of Hawthornden Drummond.　OBEV; OxBoCh

Decked all with flowers, and wings of gold fit to employ.　The Faerie Queene.　Edmund Spenser.　OBSC

...Declared that man had given/A sentence, unapproved, and overruled by Heaven.　The Prisoner.　Emily Bronte.　BFSS; BoC; EG; ELP; EnLi 1-2; NOBE; NOBV; NoP; OBEV; OBVV

Declares, O clams, thy case is shocking hard!　Sonnet to a Clam.　John Godfrey Saxe.　AnNE; BoAnP

Decline, Fall, to futility and larks,/to the bright crustaceans of the oversky.　To Friends Who Have Also Considered Suicide.　Phyllis Webb.　NOBC

Decorating a highway/on the very edge of Manhattan.　To Desi as Joe as Smoky the Lover of 115th Street.　Audre Lorde.　CNA

Decoy/for sharks in the night　Cornwallis.　Tony Beyer.　OCNZ

The decrepit persistent folly within this place/Will sow with itself the last paddock of space.　Ward Two.　Francis Webb.　CBAP

...Decry/The backward glance, I think we can guess why.　On a Vulgar Error.　Clive Staples Lewis.　OxBTC

Dedicated to the canning works!　Willis Beggs.　Edgar Lee Masters.　SaC

Deedle, deedle, dumpling, my son John.　Deedle, Deedle, Dumpling, My Son John.　Mother Goose.　BrR

Deeds shall be done for her none ever did.　The Love Secret.　*Anonymous*.　AWP

...Deeds were their last words.　Elegy for Our Dead.　Edwin Rolfe.　WaP

The deeds you wrought are not in vain!　A Ballad of Heroes.　Henry Austin Dobson.　HBV 1-2; HBVY; OHIP

Deem me all these, but love me as your/love.　A Sonnet.　Alice Duer Miller.　AA

Deems as a bubble all your waves!　Lake Superior.　Samuel Griswold Goodrich.　AA

...Deep/and comfortable/as a growl.　An Example of How a Daily Temporary Madness Can Help a Man...　John Stone.　TAT

Deep and inscrutable singular Name.　The Naming of Cats.　Thomas Stearns Eliot.　NLV

Deep anger unto me was lent/To write this strain.　The Whisperer.　James Stephens.　WGRP

DEEP APPLE PIE/TARTE AUX POMMES PROFONDES.　Bonne Entente.　F. R. Scott.　FiBHP; OBCV; PeCV

Deep as this hour, ready again to sleep.　Night Feeding.　Muriel Rukeyser.　MiAP; NMM

Deep at our deepest, strong and free.　Enrica, 1865.　Christina Georgina Rossetti.　TEP

Deep beneath and bright above.　Reflection from Sea and Sky.　Walter Savage Landor.　FaBoEE

...The deep, dark, full and flowing River!　River-Mates.　Padraic Colum.　AnIV; AWP

Deep down green/they are told to let go　The Swimming Lesson.　Robert Hershon.　NeAC

Deep down under ground.　A Catch.　Richard Henry Stoddard.　AA

Deep draught drink down my soul!　The Wine Cup.　Meleager.　OLR

The deep forest, the bright heavens,/These comprehend my woe.　Two Folk Songs, 1.　*Anonymous*.　LiTW

The deep gold of the flames/of death.　Elegy.　Pinhas Sadeh.　VWA

A deep groan was answered from hell. St. Irvyne (excerpt). Percy Bysshe Shelley. PeD

A deep-heard river in the heart's deep earth. Love Is Not Solace. Sister Maris Stella. GoBC

Deep in his soul, to win the preferred bride. The First Olympionique to Hiero of Syracuse. Pindar. ATP

Deep in his sweet flesh, the pond ebbs/and flows its sure, slow heart. The Snapper. William Heyen. AmPA; MAYP; PCP

Deep in the brain, far back. Night Crow. Theodore Roethke. AmP; DFF; ELU; HoPM; InPK; MoVE; NCSH; OBSP; VGW

Deep in the centre of her brain. Art's Variety. David McFadden. NeAC

Deep in the earth's dark breast. God's Will. Mildred Howells. HBV 1-2

Deep in the heart whereto it came/Of old as some wind-wearied bird/Drops to its nest. Splendid and Terrible. Seumas (James Starkey) O'Sullivan. HBMV

Deep in the night dark shapes of cows are feeding. Song for Past Midnight. Geoffrey Lehmann. CBAP

Deep in the roaring tide he plunged to endless night. The Bard. A Pindaric Ode. Thomas Gray. CEP; EiCP; EnL; EnPE; GTBS; GTBS-P; LAuP; NOBE; NOEC; OAEL 1-2; OAEP; OBEC; SeCePo; TW

Deep in the shadow of Rome! On the Campagna. Elizabeth Stoddard AA

Deep in their roots, all flowers keep the light. From the Notebooks. Theodore Roethke. PoL

Deep in thy tangled wood he sinks entwin'd. Polonged Sonnet. Simone dall' Antella. AWP

Deep in your heart to sleep, to sleep,/In the darlingest tomb of lovers. Song: "There is many a love in the land, my love." Joaquin Miller. HBV 1-2

The deep intelligence living at peace would have. Life at War. Denise Levertov. NMM; VGW

Deep-lowing for his deep content. The Old Ox. George Rostrevor Hamilton. FaBoEE

The deep midnight's/Perpetual day. A Sky of Late Summer (excerpt). Henry Rago. NMP

Deep river, Lord; I want to cross over into camp ground. Deep River. Anonymous. ABF; BoAN 1-2; BPo; FSW; TAP; TrAS

The deep sound-not-heard-by-ears of silence. Of Snow. Norman Brick. WaP

A deep, still pool. Falling from the ridge. Emperor Yozei. LiTW

The deep-voiced neighboring ocean/Speaks, and in accents disconsolate answers the wail of the forest. Evangeline. Henry Wadsworth Longfellow. BeLS

Deepen our spirits for a love like Thine. For Deeper Life. Katharine Lee Bates. TrPWD

Deepen to purple, and are one with night. The Last Romantic. Alexander Laing. AnAmPo

Deeper and deeper down, before the dark. Conservative. Harold Witt. AMV-80

Deeper and deeper now, and more and more. The Divine Insect. John Hall Wheelock. GoYe; NYBP

Deeper than thought, earthed in the feeling heart. Zimbabwe. F. D. Sinclair. PeSA

The deepest, bitterest curse thine ancient house hath/borne! Ajax. Sophocles. AWP

The deepest bow of all-/and the most painful. The Deepest Bow. Marie Takvan. AMV-81

"The deepest need of men-/"More prayer!" More Prayer. Anonymous. STF

The deeps them covered; they sank down/Into the bottoms as a stone. Unto Jehovah Sing Will I. Henry Ainsworth. AH

The deer have formed their snow circle/two hills beyond. The Cherokee Dean. Norman H. Russell. STE

...A deer/standing alone in a meadow. Late Starting Dawn. Richard Brautigan. PCP

Defamed by every charlatan,/And soil'd with all ignoble use. In Memoriam A.H.H., CXI. Alfred, Lord Tennyson. VLP

Defeats me, calling me through strange earths/to this place suddenly yours. The Onion. John Thompson. NOBC

Defend the bad against the worse. Where Are the War Poets? C. Day-Lewis. OBWP

Defiant to the last! Albatross. Charles Warren Stoddard. AA; EtS

Definitionless in this strict atmosphere. A Lovely Love. Gwendolyn Brooks. BPo

Deformed remnants of the fairy-days. The Ants. John Clare. BoAnP

—Deftly you've caught it-that carton/of-ice cream! Willy. Richard Moore. MAT

Defying him/through this poem of pain. Old Dog. Raymond Souster. GDP

Deid for a ducat deid/By the crueltie o his ain maistress. Under the Eildon Tree. Sydney Goodsir Smith. OxBS

Deign to forget not Peter and his pence. Wishmakers' Town. William Young. AA

Deigne at my hands this crowne of prayer and praise. Ascension. John Donne. AnAnS 1; OBS

Deity will see to it/That You never do it— Beauty–be not caused–it is. Emily Dickinson. TAP

Del tempo felice nella miseria. If I Ever Grow Old. Elinor Nauen. APU

Delia's gone, one more round. Delia's Gone. Anonymous. FSW

Deliberately plant them all where throbs/Thy bleeding heart, and stifling with its sobs. To a Madonna. Charles Baudelaire. SyP

–Delicate/as a flintflake–the knifed nous... A Technical Supplement. Thomas Kinsella. CIP

Delicate beauty/Trembles and goes. Lichen. Mary Elizabeth ("E") Fullerton. PoAu 1-2

A delicate crop/of criminal mystic immortelles/stands to the censor's scythe. Apology of Genius. Mina Loy. QFR

...The delicate cross-bow mark/Of bird, left in the ebbing sand. The Other Journey. Katherine Garrison Chapin. MoVE

Delicate, delicate, delicate, delicate–now! The Base Stealer. Robert Francis. GoJo; LiSp; NCSH; NTCP; SD

The delicate, firm, whole flesh of the still unburned. Advent 1966. Denise Levertov. NNaP; PAI; Prf

Delicate-hued, delightful May. In Praise of May. Anonymous. AnIV

A delicate pink veil. Plum Blossoms. Basho (Matsuo Basho). SUS

Delicately bordered by poplars. In the Dordogne. John Peale Bishop. AnAmPo; OBWP; VGW

Delicious, fine Sugar Hill. Harlem Sweeties. Langston Hughes. LiTM; NoP

Delight like the sun's mouth and the water's weight.... Conquistador. Archibald MacLeish. AtBAP

Delight thy self in that which worthless is. A Song of Emptiness to Fill up the Empty Pages Following. Michael Wigglesworth. SCAP

Delightful at all times is Arran! Arran. Anonymous. FaBoCh; FaBoPP; LoGBV

Delightful Muse, and be my love. Invocation (parody). Samuel Hoffenstein. BXAP

The delights of hirsute sex/let us leave to Welsh shepherds. Epigram: "It is true that I held Thero fair." Meleager. PeHV

Delights us yet, as Lady A–. Epitaph on a Warthog. J. B. Morton. PV

Deliver me, O Lord, from all/Activity centripetal. Prayer before Study. Theodore Roethke. TrPWD

Deliver me once more from my daily bread. Deliver Me, O Lord, from My Daily Bread. Jeanne Murray Walker. AMV-80

Deliver us from ourselves. Litany of the Lost. Siegfried Sassoon. MoRP

Deliver us, O Lord,/With bread of health from life's abundant board. De Profundis. Amos N. Wilder. TrPWD

Delivered/palpable/ours. Snapshots of a Daughter-in-Law. Adrienne Rich. FaBoWP; HaCAP; NIP; NMM; NoP

Delivering o'er to executors pale/The lazy, yawning drone. King Henry V. William Shakespeare. GN

The dell an excuse for one more delay/on our homeward way. The Dell. Gavin Ewart. OxBC

Delmore, Delmore! His Toy, His Dream, His Rest. John Berryman. FaBoMo; NOBA

...The demand/will arouse/some of these men and women The Maximus Poems. Charles Olson. NoAm

...Demanded he/was like any one of us. He Held Radical Light. Archie Randolph Ammons. NoAm

Democracy's divine protagonist. Walt Whitman. Francis Howard Williams. AA

The democratic wisdom underneath, like solid ground for all. The Commonplace. Walt Whitman. MoAmPo; TrGrPo

Demophilus strikes up; the screech-owl dies. Demophilus. Henry Wellesley. ALV

Demosthenes has vanished/In Waters Green– His mansion in the pool. Emily Dickinson. OBAL

Demur–you're straightway dangerous–/And handled with a Chain– Much madness is divinest sense. Emily Dickinson. AmPP; BoWoP; CBEP; CMoP; DiPo; ELU; HeIP; LiTA; LiTM; MAT; NAWM 1-2; NoAm; NOBA; NoP; OxBA

Den he hung down his head, an' he died. Never Said a Mumbalin' Word. Anonymous. ABF; GBP; TrAS

Den I axed her w'en she'd have me,/An' she jes say "Go long!" She Hugged Me and Kissed Me. Anonymous. BPo

Den lubly Fan will you cum out tonight,/An' dance by de lite ob de moon. Lubly Fan. Cool White. TrAS

Den sometimes I think she ought to be buried alive. Cornfield Holler. Anonymous. ABF

Denied to ages, but betroth'd to me. The Inspiration. James Montgomery. PAH

Denies you the beer/to cry into. Prohibition. Don (Donald Robert Marquis) Marquis. PoPl

Denise of the delicate crossed paws. Denise. Robert Beverly Hale. GDP; GrPl

Dennis Jerry Josh Efficiency Apartment. Gerald William Barrax. PoBA

...Deny/The dog is us, the everyman. The Dog in Us. John Barnie. AMV-81

Deo gracias therto–alas, I go with chylde!/"Kyrieleyson." "Kyrie, so Kyrie.'. *Anonymous.* EnPo

Depart,–be off,–excede,–evade,–crump! Intramural Aestivation; or, Summer in Town, by a Teacher of Latin. Oliver Wendell Holmes. FaBoNo

Depart not till on earth thou shower! May Carols. Aubrey Thomas De Vere.

Depart to Hell, there may you yell,/and roar eternally. The Day of Doom. Michael Wigglesworth. OBCA

Depart you in peace, you angels of/peace! Queen Sabbath. Hayim Nahman Bialik. TrJP

Departed with a muffled cry of pain. The Lord of the Isle. Stefan George. AWP

Depend on us. Things. William Stanley Merwin. HAP

Depending on where you stand/or whom you try to please. A Mountain Heritage. Joan Wyrick Ellison. AMV-80

Deplorable abortion/more and/more In Memoriam: Martin Luther King, Jr. June Jordan. PoBA

Deplore what is to be deplored,/and then find out the rest. King Billy. Edwin Morgan. BSV

Deployed, they search, shouting "Sey-sahm, Sey-sahm." Stray Dog, near Ecully. Margaret Avison. OBCV; PoA

The depressed who are also the defeated. For the Depressed. Julian Symons. WaP

Deprive you of honour to yourselves. Perry Zoll. Edgar Lee Masters. CrMA

Deprived of human graces, not divine,/Thus hath his death raised up this soul of mine. Caelica, XCIX. Fulke, Lord Brooke Greville. EnRePo; FCP; OxBoCh; PPoe

...Depth/Measured within its level gaze. Icos. Charles Tomlinson. GTBS-P

The depth of ocean in mid-stream. For Jan. John Wieners. CoPo

Dere's no hidin' place down dere. Dere's No Hidin' Place down Dere. *Anonymous.* BoAN 1-2; BPo

Dere's one mo' river to cross. O, Wasn't Dat a Wide River! *Anonymous.* BoAN 1-2

Deride the hackneyed misery–/Earth's only yield. The Deserted Homestead. Loren C. Eiseley. PoA

The derivation of that word and/what rocks Sirens. Elliott Coleman. FAZ

Dern frae aa men/the ferlies ye ha seen. For a Wife in Jizzen. Douglas Young. OxBS

Derrum, kimmy quo qua. Old Bangham. *Anonymous.* FSW; OuSiCo

Derry down, down, down, derry down. Red Iron Ore. *Anonymous.* ABF; AS; FSW

Descend, while three birds watch and the fourth flies. Winter Landscape. John Berryman. AP; LiTA; LiTM; MoAmPo; MP; PoPl; TwCP

Descendants of Dingana/And of Senzangakhona. Come In. Isaiah Shembe. WTO

Descended/into the abyss of secret self. Thou Shalt Not. Malka Tussman. VWA

Descends in silver to his proper bride. Malediction upon Myself. Elinor Wylie. AnAmPo

Descent's a nasty dinner. Satisfaction. Archie Randolph Ammons. GP

Describing its own voice/its/reason Evil Nigger Waits for Lightnin'. LeRoi (Imamu Amiri Baraka) Jones. NoAm; NOBA

Describing the familiar bow-wow/as I make my plans. Joan Brown, about Her Painting. Kathleen Fraser. NPGG

Dese bones gwine to rise again. Dese Bones Gwine to Rise Again. *Anonymous.* ABF; AS; OxBoLi

The desert is their grave, the sand their shroud. The African Desert (excerpt). Martin Farquhar Tupper. OBTV

Deserts hold court on earth's last judgment day. On Some Trees Needlessly Slain. Stanton A. Coblentz. TRV

Deserve a better heritage than this. Cigarette for the Bambino. Gavin Ewart. WaP

Desire and love/Must in the height of all their rapture move,/Where there is true felicity. Christian Ethics. Thomas Traherne. OxBoCh

Desire continu/ING. A 4 Part Geometry Lesson. Robin Blaser. NeAP

...Desire/Grown violent does either die or tire. Love Me Little, Love Me Long. Robert Herrick. CaPo

Desire is guide to me, and Love no lodestar needs. O Night, O Jealous Night. *Anonymous.* EG

Desire it is that flies; then wings are freight/That only bear the feathered heart no weight. A Gull Goes Up. Léonie Adams. WHA

Desire of all the orient host/Is here upon my breast. Songs of the Sea-Children. Bliss Carman. OBCV

Desiring him in all your works/For to direct your ways. The Exhortation of a Father to His Children. Robert Smith. OxBChV

Desiring nought but how to kill desire. Thou Blind Man's Mark. Sir Philip Sidney. CABA; EnRePo; HeIP; PPP; ViBoPo

The desolate nest is broken/And torn with storms and rain! Lost Beliefs. William Dean Howells. AmePo

Desolation will not vanish out of the/Negev/Ere it vanishes out of the hearts. Zealots of Yearning. David Rokeah. TrJP

Desophisticate identizoid–African sculptines. Disinterment. James Sherry. APU

Despair before us, vanity behind. As in the Midst of Battle There Is Room. George Santayana. AnFE; APA; AWP; NePA

Despair, distress,/and all self-sickness. Against Dark's Harm. Anne Halley. NMM

Despair of violin. Songs. Edward Estlin Cummings. APA

Despairing of the State, Euripides/Became a quietist. Thus creators end. Consolations of Art. Roy Fuller. OxBC

Desperate, righteous, clawing to be free. Eczema. David R. Slavitt. TW

Despise all moderns, thinking more/Of Shakespeare and Praxiteles. Statistics. Stephen Spender. MoBrPo

Despite all my efforts/the world continues the same. Disillusionment. Claribel Alegría. AMV-80

Despite green woods,/blossoms and seed,/my spirit rots. The Cambridge Songs (excerpt). *Anonymous.* BoWoP

Despite mistake after mistake after mistake. In Winter. Michael Ryan. MAYP

Despite of all your generals, ye prevail. The Crimean Heroes. Walter Savage Landor. ALV

Despite the falling snow. She Tells Her Love while Half Asleep. Robert Graves. BoLoP; EBEV; FaBoTw; GBL; NOBE; OxBTC

Despite the rhapsodies of Robert Browning. That English Weather: After Browning (parody). *Anonymous.* Par

Despite the washers arguing. Imagine that. Saturday Morning at the Laundry. Christopher Gilbert. MAYP

Despite their bad character, their art is mild. Ciampino. Edwin Denby. ANYP

A despot thou, and yet thy people free,/And by the heart, not hand, enslaving us. Sonnet to the Prince Regent. George Gordon, Lord Byron. MBW 1-2

The destiny of the stone house brooding over this place. The Mountain. Musaemura Bonus Zimunya. WhB

Destroy the evidence to keep them secret still. Ego. Norman MacCaig. GTBS-P

Destroy the Universe/With a solution. Human Cylinders. Mina Loy. AnAmPo

Destroy this spirit, and we have planted the seeds of despotism/at our own doors. The Bulwark of Liberty. Abraham Lincoln. PGD

Destroy thy children:/Thy valuable children,/Thy valuable children. The Earthquake. *Anonymous.* WTO

Destroying life alone, not peace! Lines Written in the Bay of Lerici. Percy Bysshe Shelley. ERoP 1-2; OAEL 1-2

The destruction that brings an eagle from heaven is better than mercy. Fire on the Hills. Robinson Jeffers. CMoP

Detached in love where pygmies cannot pin you/To the ground like Gulliver. So good luck and cheers. Dear Folks. Patrick Kavanagh. FaBoTw

Details guarding the line! Bridge-Guard in the Karroo. Rudyard Kipling. OBWP

DETERMINED, DARED, and DONE A Song to David. Christopher Smart. AnFE; AtBAP; CEP; EaLo; EBEV; EiCP; EnPE; FaBoCh; GoTL; HAP; HBV 1-2; LaA; LAuP; LoBV; MasP; MyFE; NOBE; NOEC; OAEL 1-2; OBEC; OBEV; OxBoCh; PoEL 1-5; TrGrPo; TRV; UnS; ViBoPo; WGRP

Detestable, stupid, degraded/Pig of a public! Cynical Ode to an Ultra-Cynical Public. Charles Mackay. DBV

Deus meus adjuva me. Deus Meus. Mael-Isu. CAW

The devel is shent,/Crist, through the might of thee. Lovely Tear of Lovely Eye. *Anonymous.* OxBM

Developing someone else's negative. Small Moon. Howard Nemerov. PCP

The devil a pitcher was whole in Coleraine. Kitty of Coleraine. Charles Dawson Shanly. HBV 1-2; MCCG; OnYI; StPo

The devil and he had both one nurse. On Tom-O-Combe. *Anonymous.* FaBoEE

The Devil and not God must be their Sire. An Account of the Cruelty of the Papists... Benjamin Harris. SCAP

The Devil below was ringing his knell. The Inchcape Rock. Robert Southey. BeLS; FaBoBe; GN; HBV 1-2; HBVY; OBNV; OBRV; PaPo; TreFS

Devil/devil/wheeEEE Hist Whist. Edward Estlin Cummings. OFD; SO

The devil is a-working in a Texian's head-/In a Texian's head. The Texian Boys. *Anonymous.* CoSo

The Devil, long since, had had this dish. Epitaph on Sir Walter Pye, Attorney of the Wards... John Hoskyns. FaBoEE

The devil mob had here no more to say,/But charmed at William's name marched all away. On the Late Metamorphosis of an Old Picture.... *Anonymous.* APAS

The devil's an ass, for Jesuits on this spot/Broke both the neck of Godfrey and their Plot. On the Murder of Sir Edmund Berry Godfrey. *Anonymous.* APAS

The devil's had the final say. Elegy for Two Banjos. Karl Shapiro. AtBAP; LiTA; TrJP; WaP

Devil's in the women if they take a notion. Sourwood Mountain. *Anonymous.* FSW

The devil take her! Why So Pale and Wan? Sir John Suckling. ALV; AWP; DiPo; ELP; EvOK; FaBV; FPL; GoTF; HAP; HoPM; InPo; LiTL; MCCG; NLV; NOBE; OBEV; OBS; PoRA; SeCePo; TEP; TreFS; TrGrPo; WHA

The devil take the pynot,/And God save me. I Crossed the Pynot. *Anonymous.* PBBP

The devil tempts not least. Temptation. Robert Herrick. LiTB

Devils! if in hell such devils do abide, to the hell I do go. Go. Arcadia. Sir Philip Sidney. FCP; SiPS

Devils, there many be, and Gods but one. Caelica, CV. Fulke, Lord Brooke Greville. FCP; NOCV; PoEL 1-5

Devoted, Lord, to thee. In Mercy, Lord, Incline Thine Ear. Isaac M. Wise. AH

The devotion to something afar/From the sphere of our sorrow? One Word Is Too Often Profaned. Percy Bysshe Shelley. BLPL; CBEP; GoTF; GTBS-P; LiTB; LiTL; MCCG; OBRV; TreFT; WHA

Devoured by wind and sea in sight of land. Grasmere Sonnets. David Wright. NoAm

Devouring a poor pregnant rabbit. Agamemnon. Aeschylus. CTC

The dew-damp daisies in the grass/Laugh up to greet me as I pass/To meet the upland sun. The Serf's Secret. William Vaughn Moody. HBV 1-2

Dew falls from frosty reed, and flowers bend in the wind. A Mirage. Ruth Setterberg. AMV-80

The dew flashes from its brown feathers! Pleasant Sounds. John Clare. CBEP

Dew has turned to rime. The Road to School. Joy M. Lane. AMV-81

The dew it falls na sooner down/Then ay it is full weet. Clark Sanders. *Anonymous.* OxBB

The dew shines bright; I bide forlorn,/and shudder with the chill of morn. Stanzas. Solomon Ibn Gabirol. TrJP

Dews of thyself to fetch/And holy balms. The world feels dusty. Emily Dickinson. MoAmPo

The dewy bells of evening ring,/And all is melody. Fairy Music. Francis Ledwidge. YeAr

The dewy rest they dream of and call heaven. Dew on a Dusty Heart. Jean Starr Untermeyer. MoAmPo

Dextra paw Elevant a Jugg of beare. The Poem: "What ailes Pigmalion? Is it Lunacy." Thomas Morton. SCAP

An' dey ain't no use in talkin', we jes' had one scrumptious/time! The Party. Paul Laurence Dunbar. AmNP

Dey all comes gadderin' in. De Sheepfol'. Sarah Pratt McLean Greene. AA; HBV 1-2

Dey brought Bill home wid his toes a-dragging',/Dis mornin' dis evenin', so soon. Dis Mornin', Dis Evenin', So Soon (with music). *Anonymous.* AS

Dey eats mos' all our victuals from us. Blessing without Company. *Anonymous.* BPo; PoL

Dey git all de farmer make. Po' Farmer. *Anonymous.* OuSiCo

Dey'll git home bime-by. Song: "I wrastled wid Satan, I wrastled wid sin." *Anonymous.* NAMP

Dey makes um mit dog und dey makes em mit horse,/I guess de makes em mit he.... Der Deitcher's Dog. Septimus Winner. PSoN

Dey tell me Joe Turner he done come/Come with fohty links of chain. Joe Turner Blues. *Anonymous.* AS; TrAS

Dey want me to help score d ambush Badman of the Guest Professor. Ishmael Reed. BPo

The diabolic clock/of moderation. On Riots. Cy Leslie. NBP

The Diadem that beares. To The New Yeere. Michael Drayton. AtBAP; PoEL 1-5

A diadem woven with rue. Crowned. Amy Lowell. HBV 1-2

The diamond body of his being. The Lost Dancer. Jean Toomer. BALP; PoBA

Diamond opal do you hear Life in the City. In Memoriam Edward Gibbon. Philip Whalen. PoM

Diamonds are forever so I give you softer things. The Hardness Scale. Joyce Peseroff. LLLT

Diamonds one way,/rubies the other. Beltway. Laura McLaughlin. AmC

Diane does not remember. To Diane. Helen Hay Whitney. AA; HBV 1-2

The diapason thunders shake the shore/And chant the song of freedom evermore. Spirit of Freedom, Thou Dost Love the Sea. Henry Nehemiah Dodge. EtS

The Diars Shumach, with more trees there be,/That are both good to use, and rare to see. Trees Both in Hills and Plaines, in Plenty Be. William Wood. SCAP

The dice were cast. I lost. One-Two-Three. Hannah Senesh. WPOW

Dick drinks from your eyes and he finds no lack! Bridegroom Dick (excerpt). Herman Melville. PoEL 1-5

Dick said to old Pike, innocent of Shakespeare. From Plane to Plane. Robert Frost. MoAmPo

Dick the jewels,/There they lie. A Marriage Betwixt Scrape, Monarch of the Maunders...(excerpt). Alexander Pennecuik. NOEC

Dickery, dickery, dare. The Flying Pig. *Anonymous.* OxNR

Did a few tears fall? Light Casualties. Robert Francis. PPJ

Did both conduct and teach me, how by it/To climb to thee. The Pearl. George Herbert. HAP; MePo; NOCV; OAEL 1-2; OxBoCh; PoEL 1-5; SeCP; SeCV 1-2

Did certain persons die before they sing. On a Bad Singer. Samuel Taylor Coleridge. FaBoEE; GoTF; TreF

Did dreadful death forbear his fume/For beauty, pride, or lust? On the Vanity of Man's Life. *Anonymous.* OBSC

Did ever libel yet so sharply bite? On Mr. Edward Howard, upon His British Princes. Charles, Earl of Dorset Sackville. OBSV

Did ever you see such a sight in your life,/As three blind mice? Three Blind Mice. *Anonymous.* FSW; OxNR

...Did he, didn't he,/Bellow: "Forgive me!"? Volcanoes. Bella Akhmadulina. PBWP

Did he get on? Nancy Hanks. Rosemary and Stephen Vincent Benét. FaBV; LaNeLa; NTCP; PoPl; SiSoSe; TiPo

Did he not bear the greatest pain of all,/Silent, upon the cross on Calvary? A Virile Christ. Rex Boundy. TRV; WGRP

Did her raw wristbone scrape against my hair? My Grandmother Had Bones. Judith Hemschemeyer. DFF

Did hold my wand'ring thoughts, when thy sweet eye/Bade me leave all, and only think on thee. Sonnet: "How that vast heaven intitled First is rolled." William, of Hawthornden Drummond. EIL

Did I but ken your heart still dreamed/O' bygane days and me! Jeanie Morrison. William Motherwell. HBV 1-2

Did I learn a lesson in translation? A Lesson in Translation. Gabriel Preil. VWA

(Did I not venerate/Sung's line and state.) Wide, Ho? *Anonymous.* OBVE

Did it cover Jerome? Only half! Limerick: "Jerome was a dizzy giraffe." *Anonymous.* TDH

Did it not know that she was sleeping on my arm? You Know Not How Deep Was the Love Your Eyes Did Kindle. Ibn al-Abbar. PeHV

Did meake the hag bewitch em woo'se. A Witch. William Barnes. VLP

Did moonlight sift into her mouth. Rapunzel. Anne Sexton. DFT

...Did not confuse/The Gates of Ivory with the Gates of Horn. Homage to Malcolm Lowry. Derek Mahon. FaBoIP

Did not ourselves the Cubits warp/For fear to be a King— We Never Know How High We Are. Emily Dickinson. AmP; AnFE; APA; TRV

Did not the rowling Earth snatch her away. Song: "Stay Phoebus, stay." Edmund Waller. SeCP

Did Percy Bysshe have any balls? Percy Shelley. John Peale Bishop. ErPo

Did Robin-a-bobbin/Who bent his bow. Robin-a-Bobbin. *Anonymous.* OxNR

Did Shakespeare? If so, the less Shakespeare he! House. Robert Browning. DiPo; OAEP; PP

Did Shriner die or make it to New York? A Disappearance in West Cedar Street. L. E. Sissman. TwCP

Did/Somebody/Die? World War II. Langston Hughes. HaCAP

Did soon draw in again. Upon Mistress Susanna Southwell Her Feet. Robert Herrick. EnLi 1-2

Did take a priest at last for pure devotion. Of a Zealous Lady. Sir John (1561-1612) Harington. FaBoEE

Did take Ianthee to his wife, and so her love enjoy. Metamorphoses. Ovid (Publius Ovidius Naso). PeHV

Did the city swarm out to the rails of the jetty, as one. Landscape of the Vomiting Multitudes. Federico Garcia Lorca. NYP

Did the medals go home to my cat? Gunner. Randall Jarrell. OFD

Did their Catullus walk that way? The Scholars. William Butler Yeats. CMoP; NoP; OAEL 1-2; PoA

Did they hear Heaven's great "Well done"? A Ballad of the Conemaugh Flood. Hardwick Drummond Rawnsley. PAH

Did we not underwrite them when we were born? Elegy for Minor Poets. Louis MacNeice. FaBoIP; HaMV; PP

Did wonder pour down/on the whole goddamn town. The Memory. Robert Creeley. CAPP; VGW

Did you ever feel the pain, my dear, Mary Ann. Mary Ann. *Anonymous.* FSW

Did you ever see/Cattle, vale, or mountain range/As beautiful as she? Song: "Grace and beauty has the maid." Gil Vicente. LiTW

Did you ever see/Such a funny thing before? Cosher Bailey's Engine. *Anonymous.* FSW

Did you ever see such a neat little growth/On two blind mice? Rhymes for a Modern Nursery: Two Blind Mice. Paul Dehn. FiBHP

...Did you imagine/A Woodbine passing to and fro, a face/That stabilizes like a smoke ring? The Third Light. Michael Longley. FaBoIP

...Did you know/you still had green tears? Quarry/Rock. Paul Mariah. PeHV

Did you not then sigh/my voices my voices of course? To Joan. Lucille Clifton. GeTw

Did you ride your madman? Hag-Ridden. Robert Graves. BIrV

Did you run your fingers through your kids' hair? For My Torturer, Lieutenant D–. Leila Djabali. WPOW

...Did you see that? A square! Squares. Michael Hamburger. FF

Did you see the wicked sun that winked? Ballad of Another Ophelia. D. H. Lawrence. CoBMV; MoVE

Did you think you'd caught me?/Blind, blind man! Blind Man's Buff. Anonymous. OxNR

...Diddain not my ill-uttered plea,/Which would not have been made, except to thee. Phaedra: The Conquest of Love. Jean Baptiste Racine. LiTW

Diddle, diddle, dumpling, my son John. Diddle, Diddle, Dumpling, My Son John. Anonymous. OxNR

Diddlety, diddlety, dumpty. Puss up the Plum Tree. Anonymous. OxNR

Didn' ol' John wade the water, water on his knees? Didn' Ol' John Cross the Water on His Knees? Anonymous. OuSiCo

Didn't and ain't got/no color. Mama's God. Carolyn M. Rodgers. GP

Didn't come to see you hangin'/By the gallows pole. The Gallows Pole. Anonymous. FSW

Didn't get the rise that he expected. Aunt Eliza. Anonymous. ShM

& Didn't have a/dime. Black Sketches, 2. Don L. Lee. NeAC

Didn't have no blues, I couldn't be satisfied Motherless Child Blues. Elvie Thomas. BluL

Didn't my Lord deliver Daniel/An' why not-a every man. Didn't My Lord Deliver Daniel? Anonymous. BoAN 1-2; FSW

Didn't old Pharaoh get los'./In de Red Sea True believer, O. Didn't Old Pharaoh Get Los'? Anonymous. BoAN 1-2

Didn't we all block big as trees. Revisiting the Field. Walter Pavlich. AMV-81

Didn't you feel them there at the hem?/APRIL FOOL! April Fool. Elizabeth Jane Coatsworth. YeAr

Didsdain'st we see thee stained with other's light. Madrigal: "Why dost thou haste away." Sir Philip Sidney. EG; OBSC; SiPS

Didst bear a happy burden, oh maiden undefiled! Maria Bright. Walther von der Vogelweide. ISi

Didst fettle for the great grey drayhorse his bright and battering sandal! Felix Randal. Gerard Manley Hopkins. BrPo; DiPo; EBEV; EnL; FaBoMo; GTBS-P; HAP; InPo; InPS; LiTB; LiTM; MoAB; MoBrPo; MoPo; NAMP; NoAm; NOBE; NoP; OAEP; OBEV; OBNC; PAI; PoPle; PoRA; PrIm; RoGo; SOTW; VLP

Die, and be turn'd into a Lute. Againe. Robert Herrick. SeCP

Die as you are, or living speak like them. But choose. But Choose. John Holmes. MiAP

Die, driven against the wall.' The Kings. Louise Imogen Guiney. GoBC; HBV 1-2

Die, dying clasp'd in his embrace. Fatima. Alfred, Lord Tennyson. GBL; SeCePo; UnPo; UnTE

Die late, beloved of earth, and change for heaven. To the Excellent Pattern of Beauty and Virtue, Lady Elizabeth... James Shirley. GoBC

...Die like a man/which, as things were, wasn't so easy. Marshall. George Macbeth. NoAm

Die, pussy, die. Stopping the Swing. Anonymous. OxNR

"Die," she screams, riding. Artemis. Peter Davidson. ErPo

Die the starch-neck Philistine!/Scoffers and defamers! Gaudeamus Igitur. John Addington Symonds. HBV 1-2

Died away in the night as frost will blacken a dahlia. The Heart of Thomas Hardy. Sir John Betjeman. TW

Died dancing/on treasure island Lolo Died Yesterday. Cyn. Zarco. BrSi

Died for and sung for and fought for,/And worked for,/Is living yet. Plain-Chant for America. Katherine Garrison Chapin. PAL

(Died from a weakness of the lungs/On an Ohio coal train)/For comradeship. Coal for Mike. Bertolt Brecht. PoPl

Died in half an hour. Butterfly. Anonymous. OxNR

Died upon those wind-blown gallows/At twenty-one or so! Pirates. Elizabeth Jane Coatsworth. EtS

Died without star or cross or ribbon. Distribution of Honours for Literature. Walter Savage Landor. FaBoEE

...Dies,/If he must or lives on the bread of faithful speech. Soldier, There Is a War between the Mind. Wallace Stevens. LiTM; NePA

...Dies/unspoken and unspeaking/lily-white. My Friends, This Storm. Kizito Z. Muchemwa. WhB

A Difference–A Daisy-/Is all the rest I knew! Went up a year this evening! Emily Dickinson. HAP

Difference between the living and the dead. Strange Meetings. Harold Monro. PoA

The difference/is obvious: the people/disappeared. Translations. Wing Tek Lum. BrSi

The differences between shadows. Around the Block. Keith Waldrop. AMV-80

...Different/From the hands around me, raising schooners at closing time. A Finished Gentleman. Geoffrey Dutton. NOAV

Different yet the same as before. Ah (You Say), This Is Holy Wisdom. Hilda ("H. D.") Doolittle. CrMA

Difficult stems: she sings it, she sings! Sonnets to Orpheus. Rainer Maria Rilke. SOTW

Difficult though its meter was to tackle,/I'm glad i wrote it. Lady Jane. Sir Arthur Thomas ("Q") Quiller-Couch. FiBHP; InMe

Dig and be dug/In return. Motto. Langston Hughes. PoBA; PoNe

Dig deep, dig deep,/You will find my bones. I Am a Jew. David Martin. VWA

Dig, dig; and if I come to ledges, blast. Intention to Escape from Him. Edna St. Vincent Millay. SBG

Dig for the withered herb through heaps of snow. The Seasons. James (1700-48) Thomson. FM

Dig in your heels against the slippery grave! Twenty Years After. Evan V. Shute. CaP

DIG WE MUST/They dig . The Slogan. Paul Blackburn. PoM

DIGDOG. Digdog. Ruth Pitter. AnFE

Digging my fingers into my cheek! A Letter to Her Father. Inib-sarri. BoWoP

Digitoxin, Filaxis, Alka-/Butazoliden, Tal-/Win Simples. Gladys Cardiff. TWSS

The dignity of room, the value of rareness. November Surf. Robinson Jeffers. CrMA; MoPo; OxBA

Dim apparition thou!–and bitter is my tear. Eyam (excerpt). Anna Seward. NOEC

–Dim as a ghost he flies/Through the night mysteries. Moth-Song. Ellen Mackay Hutchinson Cortissoz. AA

Dim bodings wherefore? Now indeed I know. Sonnets. Frederick Goddard Tuckerman. MAmP

The dim boy claps because the others clap. The Freaks at Spurgin Road Field. Richard Hugo. LCAP; SM

Dim fields of fading stars! Interlude: The Casement. Christopher John Brennan. PoAu 1-2

...Dim men with old robes/walk gravely through the Danube mists/their arms outstretched for me. The Celt in Me. Keith Wilson. GP

Un Dimanche, au milieu d'Edimbourg. Limerick: "Il etait un Hebreu de Hambourg." George Du Maurier. CenHV

A DIME WIL OPEN THE DOOR. Another Day. Isabella Maria Brown. PoNe

Dimes and to carry the inscrutable bruise like a bride. The Horse in the Drugstore. Tess Gallagher. AmPA

A dimple in the smile of nature. Jeannie Marsh. George Pope Morris. AA

"Dinah, blow your horn." I've Been Workin' on the Railroad. Anonymous. BLSo; FaFP; FSW; SaC; TreF

Dined and danced upon their heads/Till they toddled to their beds. The Table and the Chair. Edward Lear. GoTF; HBVY; SoPo; TreFT

Ding ding dong, ding ding dong. Frere Jacques. Anonymous. FSW

Ding, dong, bell. The Merchant of Venice. William Shakespeare. BoLiVe; CTC; DiPo; EG; ElL; ELP; EnLi 1-2; EnRePo; GoTF; GTBS; GTBS-P; InPo; LiTB; OAEL 1-2; OAEP; OBEV; OBSC; PoEL 1-5; SeCeV; TreFS; TrGrPo; ViBoPo; WHA

Ding, Dong, Ding! The Big Bell in Zion. Theodore Henry Shackleford. BANP

Ding-dong, ding-dong, ding-dong. Dirge for a Righteous Kitten. Vachel Lindsay. SUS

Ding-dong....Ding-dong....Unwillingly I drink/the wine/Of consolation of a God that is not mine. Angelus. Solomon Blumgarten (Yehoash) LiTW

Dining at the white house He's Doing Natural Life. Conyus. PoBA

Dinna cheat, but drink fair,/Huzza, huzza, and huzza lads yet,/Up wi't, &c. Up in the Air. Allan Ramsay. NOEC

Dinna ye hear th' bagpipes play? The Pipes o' Gordon's Men. J. Scott Glasgow. HBV 1-2

Diogenes sold sucker lists/To Hellenistic slickers. The Complete Cynic. Keith Preston. NLV

A dip-a-de-do. Do! The Morning Duke Ellington Praised the Lord... Owen Dodson. FB

Dip into this river with your ebony cups. Black Star Line. Henry Dumas. CNA; PoBA

Dip the song in the stream. Lethe. Edna St. Vincent Millay. PG

Diplomats and clever girls/Know when to be seduced. The Right Time. Anonymous. UnTE

Dipped long in wisdom's fount to heal the soul. The Marathon Runner. Fenton Johnson. CDC

–Dipping into Death like a soup. A Dreamed Realization. Gregory Corso. NeAP; PoM; VGW

Dipping their fingers in a stream. Spring Pastoral. Elinor Wylie. AnEnPo

Dips to the icy pool. A Spring Serpent. Yvor Winters. ExPo

The dire and sweet alarm/Of beauty that outruns the eager eye.   Poem: "As rock to sun or storm."   Niall Sheridan.   OnYI

...Dire figures of the past/That veil a young girl in her tomb.   The Pill. Austin Clarke.   TW

Dire rocks! near which whoever came,/Was sure to split, and sink and damn.   An Epistle to My Friend J. B.   Robert Dodsley.   NOEC

Directing another vein the world's heart–Rome!   A Road in the Weald. Richard Church.   HaMV

Directing it to the house of no known address.   Ward Two.   Francis Webb. CBAP

Direction and velocity, to accommodate you, dear.   Hello.   John Berryman. NAs

Directly away from/unsupported world.   From Vice, 1966.   Jim Brodey. ANYP

The dirge of lovely Rosabelle.   The Lay of the Last Minstrel.   Sir Walter Scott.   BSV

Dirges from the pine and cypress/Mingle with the tears we shed.   The Vacant Chair.   Henry Stevenson Washburn.   TreFS

Dirt of my flesh, defeated, underground.   At the Executed Murderer's Grave. James Wright.   AmPC; HaCAP

Dirty girl,/Thumb stump.   Cut.   Sylvia Plath.   CAPP; TAP

Dis mornin', dis evenin', so soon.   Old Bill.   *Anonymous.*   ABF

Dis yere hammer, nin-pound hammer,/Kill mah partner, kill Joh Henry,/Kill him dead.   Ever Since Uncle John Henry Been Dead (with music).   *Anonymous.*   AS

...Disappeared in the abyss/(Vanitas vanitatum!)/of white Charybdis.   PSI. Melvin B. Tolson.   PoBA

Disappearing mysteriously all too soon behind a low-flying flight of clouds.   Flight of the Roller Coaster.   Raymond Souster.   ACV; NOBC; PeCV; SO; WHW

Disarm the hearts, for that is peace.   Disarm the Hearts.   Ethel Blair Jordan.   PGD

Disarmed before the archers of the King.   Archers of the King.   Sister Mary Genoveva.   GoBC

A discard, your dense self your last/Enormity.   Malediction.   Barry Spacks. TW

Discarded ermine to reveal a pig.   On the Relinquishment of a Title. Geoffrey Grigson.   FaBoEE

Discarding peace over all the sea and land.   I Hear and See Not Strips of Cloth Alone.   Walt Whitman.   WaaP

Discern the patient whole in every part.   Theophany.   Evelyn Underhill. WGRP

"Discharge me? No! He knew I did just right."   The Code.   Robert Frost. MaC; OBNV; PAI; PoA; UnPo

Discharge the debt, and walk away.   Human Frailty.   Philip Freneau. AnAmPo

The discipline of thy rebuke/Shall be refining fire!   With Self Dissatisfied. Frederick Lucian Hosmer.   TrPWD

Disclosed the gentle hand grown horned and cruel.   Six Winters.   Ruthven Todd.   NeBP

Disconnect the telephone;/cut the wires.   Tombstone with Cherubim. Horace Gregory.   NAMP

Discovering subtleties and profundities in/Any slightest gesture, or delicate glance.   Hardy Perennial.   Richard Eberhart.   GOYP

Discovering truths I do not care to know.   It Rolls On.   Morris Bishop. ImOP

Discovers in/it, after all, a place for the genuine.   Poetry.   Marianne Moore. OBSP

Discumbered of their Persian luxury.   The Fall of the Leaf.   Henry David Thoreau.   AP

Disdain me not.   Disdain Me Not without Desert.   Sir Thomas Wyatt. FCP; SiPS

"Disdaining to strike while a stick is left standing."   Change the Can Cheerily.   *Anonymous.*   AmSS

Disdains to crop a weed, and will not come.   Inexorable.   William, of Hawthornden Drummond.   NOBE; OBEV

...Disengaged stairways wake/me to the sky. And I fly,/I fly.   The News & the Weather.   Rika Lesser.   MAYP

The disfigured legs that with a stolid/magnificence used to hold up the world. The Sums.   Lauris Edmond.   FaBoWP

...Dislodging a single cone/Which drops away without a sound.   Confrontions of March.   H. C. Dillow.   AMV-80

Dismissing me to my imprisonment/Of thinking free.   An Interview.   Philip Brasfield.   LFAC

Disorderly, drunk, and obscene.   Sonnet and Limerick.   Morris Bishop. FiBHP

Dispatch this note to our hero at once   After the Broken Arm.   Ron Padgett.   ANYP; ConAP; EAS

Dispenser of dreams,/collector of pain.   Folk Tune.   Esther Raab.   VWA

Dispers'd and broken thro' the ruffled Skies.   The Iliad.   Homer.   OBVE

Disperse it, as now light dispels the dark.   Morning Hymn of Adam and Eve. John Milton.   OxBoCh

Displaced, condensed, as by my dreamed regard.   Dream.   Josephine Miles. PoA

Displaying to us her white robes?   Near a Waterfall at Ryumon.   Lady Ise. BoWoP

A disposition lower than Australia.   Madrid, Iowa.   Ron Ikan.   PPJ

Dispulit of the tresur that he yemit:/Surrexit Dominus de sepulchro.   On the Resurrection of Christ.   William Dunbar.   NOCV; OxBS; PoEL 1-5

The disrespectful giggles of the street.   The Perturbations of Uranus.   Roy Fuller.   ErPo

Dissemble well, and win the field!   To Flavia.   Edmund Waller.   HBV 1-2

Disseminating their/Circumference.   The Poets Light but Lamps.   Emily Dickinson.   AmePo; HeIP; PP

Dissolve inversion,/positive appears.   Winter Developing.   Nora Dauenhauer. TWSS

Dissolve us in pleasure, and soft repose.   If the Heart of a Man.   John Gay. CBEP; ELP; EnLoPo; HeIP

Dissolved in blossom dew, and washed away/In delicate spring rains.   In April.   Ethelwyn Wetherald.   CaP

Dissolves at her touch and is weaved anew.   Promontory Moon.   Galway Kinnell.   MOON

...Dissolves/in dark cement.   The Countershadow.   Philip Booth.   NYBP

Dissolves my dream, his task, and the name/Of the wretched place from whence he came...   Lines Written near Linton, on Exmoor (parody). Daniel Gerard Hoffman.   BXAP

...Dissolving everything: Time,/Space and Fortune in its ferocious fashion. The Sun.   Andrew Oerke.   PoA

...Dissonance/Is far below, where man is.   Winter Climb.   Beinn Eunaich. PoSH

Distance is dead and light can only die.   Terminal.   Karl Shapiro.   AmLP

Distance re-inflates the hills.   In the Cheviots.   Maurice Lindsay.   PoSH

The distances to every side of us/as in a poem   The Alphabet Came to Me. Jerome Rothenberg.   VWA

...Distant/as the cloud I came in on.   Arizona Highways.   James Welch. CDW

Distant City made wholly of light.   The Milky Way.   Jon Anderson. MAYP

...Distant/cousin to the floating traffic of uncrowded stars.   Wheels. Dorothy Donnelly.   HoAn

The distant dripping of water wasting through clay.   Roots Go Down. Lloyd Frankenberg.   AnEnPo

The distant strains of triumph/Burst agonized and clear!   Success is counted sweetest.   Emily Dickinson.   AWP; CBEP; CMoP; DiPo; FPL; GoJo; InPo; InPS; LiTA; LiTM; MAmP; MCCG; MoAB; MoAmPo; NOBA; OxBA; PAI; PG; PoRA; SBG; TAP; TreFT; WaaP

The distant swans' far floated cry.   Swans at Night.   Mary Gilmore.   PoAu 1-2

Distaste which takes no credit to itself is best.   Snakes, Mongooses, Snake-Charmers and the Like.   Marianne Moore.   ExPo

Distilled in wholesome dew named rosmarine.   Pebbles.   Herman Melville. AP; MAmP

Distinct, but distant–clear–but, oh how cold!   Sun of the Sleepless.   George Gordon, Lord Byron.   AtBAP; MOON

Distinguished, and familiar, and aloof.   And What Is Love? Misunderstanding, Pain.   J. V. Cunningham.   HoPM

Distinguished only from the ruck/By their impressive long run back.   The Unfinished Race.   Norman Cameron.   OxBS

Distinguished the belt feed lever from/the belt holding pawl.   The Fury of Aerial Bombardment.   Richard Eberhart.   AmP; BiP; CMoP; ExPo; FaBoMo; FF; FYAP; HeIP; HoPM; InPK; LiTA; LiTM; MiAP; MP; NIP; NMP; NoAm; NoP; OBWP; PrIm; TAP; TwCP; UnPo; VGW; WaP

...Distorted features/That wept, and grew enormous, and cried Woe.   Poem: "He watched with all his organs of concern."   W. H. Auden.   PoA

Distractions and the human crowd.   Distractions and the Human Crowd. Stevie Smith.   OxBC

Distress would somehow know the thing to do.   If Lincoln Should Return. Margaret E. Bruner.   PoToHe

Distressed the New Forest unduly.   Limerick: "There was a professor of Beaulieu."   C.E.M. Joad.   FaBoCo

Disturb the privacy of those/About to wash or change their clothes.   Lord High-Bo.   Hilaire Belloc.   FiBHP

Disturbed by swords, like Damocles's feast.   A Very Heroical Epistle in Answer to Ephelia.   John Wilmot, Earl of Rochester.   APAS

Disturbs the Sabbath of that deeper sea.   Hymn.   Harriet Beecher Stowe. PoToHe

Ditto, ditto my song–and thank good-/ness they're both of them over! Iolanthe.   Sir William Schwenck Gilbert.   CoBE

Divels there many be, and Gods but one.   Sonnet CV.   Fulke, Lord Brooke Greville.   OBS

Divers,/do not lose consciousness before/you reach the bell.   The Nets on the Andrea Doria.   Karen G. Tepfer.   AMV-81

Diversity that never tires!   Preludes.   Coventry Patmore.   HBV 1-2

Diverted from swimming a moment when he dropped. The Preacher Sought to Find Out Acceptable Words. Richard Eberhart. WaP

Divide my love and me. Song II. The Landskip. William Shenstone. CEP

Divided, with but half a heart,/Til we shall meet and never part. The Exequy. To His Matchlesse Never to Be Forgotten Freind. Henry, Bishop of Chichester King. AtBAP; BoLoP; ForPo; GBL; HAP; HBV 1-2; InPS; InvP; JCP; LiTL; LoBV; MeLP; MePo; NOBE; NoP; OBEV; OBS; PoEL 1-5; PPoe; PrIm; QFR; SeCePo; SeCP; TEP; ViBoPo

The divil a man would eat fish of a Friday. Blackbirds and Thrushes. *Anonymous.* GBP

Divine Abodes shall own his Pow'r,/When Time and Death shall be no more. Song: "Sweet are the Charms of her I love." Barton Booth. OBEC

Divine approval is thy sweetest praise. To My Father. Henrietta Cordelia Ray. BlSi

...Divine/Child, this importunate guest. Ecstasy. Arthur Symons. UnTE

The divine intoxication,/Of the first league out from land? Exultation is the going. Emily Dickinson. NCEP

The divine presence there too is,/But to torment men, not to give them bliss. The Thief. Abraham Cowley. EnLi 1-2; EnLit; JCP; OAEP; WHA

Divine, to the Divinity. The Dark Angel. Lionel Pigot Johnson. ACP; CAW; GTBS-P; LiTB; MoBrPo; NOBE; NOBV; OAEL 1-2; OBMV; VLP; WHA

Divinely inaccessible, the scorn. Marsyas. Sir Charles G. D. Roberts. PeCV

Divinely superfluous beauty. Divinely Superfluous Beauty. Robinson Jeffers. HeIP; LiTL; MoLP; PoPl

A dizziness of the things I have not said. The Soul of Time. Trumbull Stickney. LiTA; NePA

Dizzy, lost, yet unbewailing! Prometheus Unbound. Percy Bysshe Shelley. FiP; PoEL 1-5

Do again what lordly Joshua did. Afternoon in the Garden. Ethel Anderson. NOAV

Do angels pick the cherry-blood of folk like me, Lord? Plaint. Charles Henri Ford. AtBAP; EAS; MoVE; PPON

Do be my enemy for friendship's sake. To Hayley. William Blake. FaBoEE; TrGrPo

"Do better, now, my child." A New Leaf. Kathleen Wheeler. PGD; WBLP

Do bring to mind what we did do/Among the dock-leaves years agoo. Dock-Leaves. William Barnes. VLP

Do change your mind, and answer, "Yes,'/And save me from starvation. The Gourmet's Love-Song. P. G. Wodehouse. NOBL

Do flowers and butterflies belong/To a blind December? The Haunted House. Robert Graves. OxBI

Do I astonish more than they? Song of Myself. Walt Whitman. AtBAP

Do I carry the moon in my pocket? Master Hugues of Saxe-Gotha. Robert Browning. OAEL 1-2

...Do I flicker there like coal? Cold Fire. George Starbuck. NYBP

Do I get anything so easily? Animal Songs: Hyena's Song to Her Children. *Anonymous.* PeSA

Do I?/It might be so. A Slice of Wedding Cake. Robert Graves. BoLoP; NOBE; OxBTC

..."Do I know/Whether my motion makes the wind that moves me?" The Wind in the Tree. Frank Templeton Prince. OBSP

Do I love you? A Love Song. Raymond Richard Patterson. BOLo

Do I make faces like that at you./Pinkie. Sacred Family (excerpt). Gertrude Stein. AtBAP

Do I move toward form, do I use all my fears? Double Ode. Muriel Rukeyser. LCAP

Do I not know her lips are cold. A Moment. Stopford Augustus Brooke. IrPN

Do I really want to go in drag on such a hot day? Aka. Frederick Eckman. FAZ

Do it now! Do It Now! *Anonymous.* BLPA; FaFP

Do it well or not at all. Always Finish. *Anonymous.* BLPA; FaBoBe; WBLP

Do, Lawd, delibbah po' me! All Night Long (with music). *Anonymous.* AS

Do li th' dil len dol,/Do lia a. Do Li A. *Anonymous.* GBP

Do make me a pallet, I'll lie on the floor. Jack O' Diamonds; or, The Rabble Soldier. *Anonymous.* CoSo

Do more bewitch me than when art/Is too precise in every part. Delight in Disorder. Robert Herrick. ALV; AnAnS 2; AnFE; BiP; BoLiVe; CaPo; EnLoPo; FaBV; FF; GTBS; HAP; HBV 1-2; HeIP; InMe; InPK; InPS; JCP; LiTB; LiTL; LoBV; NIP; NOBE; NoP; OAEL 1-2; OAEP; OBEV; OBS; PAI; PoPle; PoRA; PP; PPoe; PPP; PrIm; SeCePo; SeCeV; SeCP; SeCV; TreFS; TrGrPo; ViBoPo; WHA 1-2

Do, my Johnny Boker, do! Johnny Boker. *Anonymous.* AmSS; FSW

Do not ask his nation; that/Was History's confederate. Epitaph on a Bombing Victim. Roy Fuller. NeBP

"Do not awaken," written in haste. March Wind. Lewis Warsh. APU

"Do not be such a glutton again." The Plum-Cake. Ann Taylor. HBVY

Do not bring flowers here as homage/Of love, nor twigs of green! Bring stone! At the Jewish Cemetery in Prague. Oscar Levertin. VWA

Do not call her—let the strangers pass! Love's Guerdons. Edith Nesbit. NOBV

...Do not cry/Because its light fails to be obvious. Beach Talk. Norman MacCaig. PoA

Do not cry out again in clumsiness and shame. Straus Park. Gerald Stern. NYP

Do not dare to breathe aloud. Hush, Hush. Mani Leib. TrJP

Do not deny it. Two Decisions. Vernon Watkins. OxBTC

...Do not expect applause. Johann Joachim Quantz's Five Lessons. W. S. Graham. FaBoMo

Do not expect to feel so free on land. Letter to Pearse Hutchinson. Eilean Ni Chuilleanain. FaBoWP

Do not fail to tell men so! Tell Him So. *Anonymous.* BLPA; BLPL; WBLP

Do not forget me quite,/O Severn meadows. Song: "Only the wanderer." Ivor. Gurney. FaBoPP

Do not forget the poor old man. The Old Age of Michelangelo. Frank Templeton Prince. PeSA

Do not get the unsifted thistles stuck in thy tongue. Theophilus Thistledown, the Successful Thistle Sifter. *Anonymous.* OxNR

Do not go/Away, Christmas. Stay, Christmas! Ivy O. Eastwick. SiSoSe

Do not go in. The door is closed. The Ilex Tree. Agnes Lee. PoA

"Do not go, linger a while/among us here in this place." If it is you, there. Lady Ise. BoWoP

Do not keep but give away. Keeping Christmas. Eleanor Farjeon. OBCP

Do not laugh at her shame and downfall. She Is More to Be Pitied Than Censured. William B. Gray. FSW

Do not leave me, God. Prayer for the Useless Days. Edith Lovejoy Pierce. TrPWD

Do not leave your love like Johnny,/Marry her before you go. Johnny Todd. *Anonymous.* FSW

Do not let him weep. The Last Words. Maurice Maeterlinck. AWP; PoPl

Do not let me wait in vain. The Lover's Prayer. *Anonymous.* WTO

...Do not look/back. The bridge is a clock. How to Find Your Way Home. Mario Petaccia. LFAC

Do not look for the permanent for it/exists neither upon the earth nor in/the heavens. Actions. Marcel Schwob. TrJP

Do not mock me in thy bed,/While these cold nights freeze me dead. A Lover's Plea. Thomas Campion. NOBE

Do not my love detain. Sweet Trees Who Shade This Mould. James Mabbe. GBL

Do not overlook me, your slave,/in your measureless mercy. Mary Magdalene. Kassia. BoWoP

Do not repent. It is too late. Faces from a Bestiary. X. J. Kennedy. NePoEA-2

Do not slip from my arms:/sleep close to me! Close to Me. Gabriela (Lucila Godoy Alcayaga) Mistral. PoPl

Do not spare. Subject. Marie Ponsot. VGW

Do not stir/Do not stir. Feather or Fur. John Becker. TiPo

Do not think they lack/Precisely the same intentions. Barbarians. John Fowles. PoL

Do not withhold from me Thine Eternal Beauty. Two Prayers. Rabi'a al-Adawiyya. BoWoP; WPOW

Do nothing by halves/Which can be done by quarters. W.L.M.K. F. R. Scott. NOBC

Do others feel like this? Where do they go? Housewife. Susan Fromberg Schaeffer. IHMS

Do please tell me all about it, what you do and who you are. Arrogance Repressed. Sir John Betjeman. FiBHP

Do something for somebody, quick! How To Be Happy. *Anonymous.* BLPA

Do speak that speech of wondrous beauty/That our fathers wrought. I'r hen Iaith A'i Chanedon (To the Old Tongue and its Songs). Walter Dowding. ACV

Do suckle thee/Upon my breast. The Child Compassion. Margot Ruddock. OBMV

Do the bones repeat: It's a good act—/we got a good hand....? Hazardous Occupations. Carl Sandburg. SaC

Do they call virtue there ungratefulness? Astrophel and Stella, XXXI. Sir Philip Sidney. AAS; AWP; CoBE; GBL; HAP; HBV 1-2; InPS; NoP; OAEP; OBSC; PAI; PoEL 1-5; PPoe; SiPS; TEP; TrGrPo; ViBoPo; WeW

Do they come back to you? The Little Ghosts. Thomas S. Jones, Jr. HBV 1-2

Do they go lost and aimless to the deep? The Night Moths. Edwin Markham. HBMV

Do they know he will die? Rock Painting. Jack Cope. PeSA

Do they look like small clotting hearts? Irapuato. Earle Birney. NIP; PeCV

"Do they think of me at home?" Do They Think of Me at Home. Joseph Edward Carpenter. FaBoBe; TreFS

Do thou, as thou art wont, repair/My heart with gladness, and a share/Of thy meek nature! To the Same Flower. William Wordsworth. EnRP

Do Thou my Strength, my Saviour be,/And make me to Thy glory live! A Prayer. Anne Bronte. TrPWD

Do to His mother Mary reverence! The Canterbury Tales: The Prioress's Tale. Geoffrey Chaucer. GoBC; ISi; LoBV; OAEP; OxBoCh

Do watch her to madness when woonce she do move. Her Skin Is So White as a Lily. Padraic Colum. LO

Do we need such shadows/Here in life? Tis a Little Journey. Anonymous. PoToHe

Do we not touch/across the censorious years? Invocation to Sappho. Elsa Gidlow. IHMS

...Do we seek forgiveness/From ourselves, for ourselves? As Difference Blends into Identity. Josephine Miles. NoAm

Do what you list, I will your thrall be founde,/Thogh ye to me ne do no daliance. Ballade to Rosamund. Geoffrey Chaucer. MeEL

Do what you will, his every want supply,/Keep him–but out of Newgate, Mrs. Fry! A Friendly Address. Thomas Hood. PoEL 1-5

...Do you believe/love, and how much. The Mechanic. Robert Creeley. NaP

Do you float up to the surface of this my tank,/Or you shall be a rebel to God. Tin-Ore. Anonymous. WTO

Do you have time for only these? Stop a Minute! Anonymous. STF

Do you hear me bawling to you across the hearthrug?' Ireland 1977. Paul Durcan. FaBoIP

Do you hear me, whispering/your name voicelessly,/tenderly?/Or must I shout? To a God Unknown. David Eller. VWA

Do you hear this praise of you,/Little park that I pass through? Ellis Park. Helen Hoyt. HBMV

Do you know more? Challenge. Kenton Foster Murray. HBV 1-2

Do you love barberries? Barberries. Mary Aldis. HBMV

Do you love it? quoth she,/So do I, Sir. I'd Have You, Quoth He. Anonymous. FF

Do you love me Judas, Peter. Luci Shaw. AMV-80

Do you make me notice you! The Reminder. Thomas Hardy. CMoP; OBCP

Do you mourn the lost fingers/or offer them in sacrifice. Old Man Hall. P. L. Jacobs. LFAC

...Do you need to sit/beside the buried rotting peel of a banana/to recall its fruit? The Argument. Jane P. Moreland. AMV-80

Do you not see the Christmas star/That we are guided by? Song of the Wise Men. Edith Lovejoy Pierce. PGD

Do you open the pane and pop out the flame/Just to see how the wind do blow. The Candlelight Fisherman. Anonymous. OBSS

Do you play as before, little jester? To His Soul. Emperor (Publius Aelius Hadrianus) Hadrian. PoPl

Do you see? It must be the aprons of silence. Aprons of Silence. Carl Sandburg. NoAm; NOBA

Do you see what I mean about the rain? Biography of Southern Rain. Kenneth Patchen. VGW

Do you suppose, Max, of which she is made. Sara in Her Father's Arms. George Oppen. GP; NNaP

"Do you teach these boys at night as well?" Epigram: "I dined with Demetrius." Automedon. PeHV

Do you? The night is falling.... The Captive. William Franklin. LFAC

"Do you think?...I hear...in the frozen north..." The Refrigerator. Howard Moss. GP

Do you think I know not God's law? Unity. Jakov De Haan. VWA

Do you think, Mr. Green, it was cricket?' Limerick: "An angry young husband called Bicket." John Galsworthy. CenHV

Do you think one has nothing to do but forgive? Delia Very Angry. Anonymous. NOEC

Do you think, perhaps, that some one/Would say that I was fair? Snowfall. "I. V. S. W." InMe

Do you think that I'd tell you a lie? The Bongaloo. Spike Milligan. AmMo

Do you think that Spoon River/Had been any the worse? Mrs. Williams. Edgar Lee Masters. NAMP

...Do you think/Wax could have stopped us, or chains? The Sirens. Donald Finkel. NePoEA

Do you think your mother/Will ask me in to tea? The New Neighbor. Rose Fyleman. SoPo; TiPo

Do you understand? you/Horses ass In the Bar. Robert Vander Molen. TAT

Do you wish to go home from the ball? At the Ball! Charles Henry ("John Paul") Webb. OBAL

Do your good will to cure a wight that liveth in distress. The Lady Again Complains. Henry Howard, Earl of Surrey. SiPS

Doch doch I assure thee Enueg. Samuel Beckett. NoAm

Dochter of God, I cry, sich breasts/Are nae for human een. Skye. John Gawsworth. PoSH

The docile bus-queue moons. The Fragments. Peter Dale. NOCV

(Le Docteur), sont les plus awful bores! Limerick: "Chaque epoque a ses grands noms sonores." George Du Maurier. CenHV

Doctor/Lawyer/Indian Chief. Rich Man. Anonymous. SaC

Doctor, mind the sick/And leave the well alone. A Doctor Fell in a Deep Well. Anonymous. ShM

Doctor's orders. Pass the bran. Breakfast Song in Time of Diet. Stoddard King. OBAL

The Doctor slid a little down the pillow. A Hundred Collars. Robert Frost. YaD

Doctors' medicines; sweet swallow down. Moors, Angels, Civil Wars. Keith Sinclair. AnNZ

Doctors were called, and he agreed to sail. The Poet on the Island. Richard Murphy. CIP; NMP

Dodona's oaks were still. Dodona's Oaks Were Still. Patrick MacDonogh. NeIP

Dodsley's your man–the poem's ended. To a Gentleman, Who Desired Proper Materials for a Monody. Anonymous. NOEC

Doe eyes. Africa. James Russell Grant. OBTV

Doe, shall, and must obey. The Broken Heart. John Ford. AtBAP

Doe throw you downe from your high estate,/And make you low and desolate. Of Boston in New England. William Bradford. SCAP

Does a very foolish thing, and seldom gets another. Landlord Fill the Flowing Bowl. Anonymous. FSW

Does half my heart lie buried there/In Texas, down by the Rio Grande? Lasca. Frank Desprez. BeLS; BLPA; BPAW; FaBoBe; HBV 1-2; TreF

Does he his duty well as I do mine? The Night Express. Cosmo Monkhouse. OBVV

Does he hunch up, as I do,/Against the dark of the night? Pete at the Zoo. Gwendolyn Brooks. LOW

Does he regard on what we dine? Epigram on Fasting. Anonymous. OBVE

Does himself all the good he can by stealing. A Misconception. James Russell Lowell. OBAL

Does in the World but more successful grow,/Than the True, which does True Wits most undo. Upon the Most Useful Knowledge, Craft or Cunning... William Wycherley. SeCV 1-2

Does it matter about the turnin's? The Ways O' Men. Angelina Weld Grimke. CDC

Does it not seem/That love can all control? Idyl: Sunset. Henrietta Cordelia Ray. BlSi

Does it pay, do you think, just to care? Life's Little Things. Anonymous. STF

"Does my old friend remember me?" In Memoriam A.H.H., LXIV. Alfred, Lord Tennyson. VLP

Does not my fear cover her fear? A Doe at Evening. D. H. Lawrence. BrPo

...Does spare/This child of hers, that most deserves her care. The Happy Night. John, of Buckingham Sheffield. UnTE

Does the free wind care? A Summer Wooing. Louise Chandler Moulton. HBV 1-2

Does the heart know? Does the Pearl Know? Helen Hay. AA

Does the maiden still swing in thy giant clasp? The Grape-Vine Swing. William Gilmore Simms. AnAmPo; HBV 1-2

Does the man hear the small feet of the frightened ideal. The Man Coming Toward You. Oscar Williams. LiTA

Does the one tempo of the movement flow. Incense. Louise Townsend Nicholl. NePoAm-2

Does the Spearmint lose its flavor on the bedpost overnight? Does the Spearmint Lose Its Flavor on the Bedpost Overnight? Billy Rose. OBAL

"Doesn't it seem to you she's fumbling/About up there?" Lois in Concert. Charles Moorman. AMV-81

Doesn't live here/Any more. The Dinosaur. Carl S. Junge. SoPo

Doesn't take flight anymore/on wings of innocence. Let's Talk, Mother. Edith Bruck. VWA

Doesn't the wild wind/whistle. Deaf. Barry O. Higgs. PeSA

Doff sorry pride for pardon,/Or ever love go by. Amantium Irae. Ernest Christopher Dowson. HBV 1-2; OBEV

Dog around the block, sniff. Dog around the Block. E. B. White. GDP

Dog, goes bow-wow, bow-wow. A Farmyard Song. Maria Hastings. SoPo

Dog-gone!/He ain't gone. Gone Boy. Langston Hughes. NePoAm-2

The dog howled and howled and listened and howled and/howled and howled. One-Line Poems from a New Statesman Competition. Alison Prince. PoL

The dog it was that died! Elegy on the Death of a Mad Dog. Oliver Goldsmith. BeLS; BLPA; CBEP; FaBoBe; FPL; GDP; GoTF; HBV 1-2; HBVY; LBN; MCCG; NA; NLV; NOBI; OAEP; PoPle; RoGo; ShM; TEP; TreF

...The Dog/of Art turns to the world/the quietness of his eyes. The Dog of Art. Denise Levertov. NoAm

The dog of my heart will not bark.   Love without Love.   Luis Llorens Torres.   InW

...Dog on a leash/gone crazy with the aroma of flagpoles.   Shoe.   John Perreault.   EAS

The dog said "Bow-wow'.   The Comic Adventures of Old Mother Hubbard and Her Dog.   Sarah Catherine Martin.   OxBChV

Dog-skins squashed and beaten flat.   How Old's the Moon?   *Anonymous.*   MOON

The dog swallows the doll.   Snapshot.   John Fuller.   NePoEA-2

...The dog/Turns and turns about, stops and sleeps.   Nooksack Valley.   Gary Snyder.   NaP

The dog, who was starving, is dead.   Children's Crusade, 1939.   Bertolt Brecht.   MoBS

Dogchains hanging out of the mouths & sides.   The Dogchain Gang.   Stan Rice.   NPGG

Doggie scampers when I call,/And has a heart to love us all.   Pussy Has a Whiskered Face.   Christina Georgina Rossetti.   TiPo

Dogging with rage and joy over the broken backs/of words words words   To an Athlete Turned Poet.   Peter Meinke.   LiSp

Doggone! I'm late!   The Cow Has a Cud.   David McCord.   TiPo

Dogs are random   Probability and Birds.   Russell Atkins.   CNA; FB

The dogs closed in, and finally, the men.   Hunt.   Melvin Walker La Follette.   NePoEA

Dogs get in the way.   Back Country.   Joyce Carol Oates.   Psk

The dogs have had a good long wait.   Going to the Dogs.   *Anonymous.*   GoTF; TreFS

The dogs' track and the deer's.   Epigram: The Hunt Goes By.   Howard Nemerov.   OBAL

"Dogs, trucks and guns belong to them/but the soil, the spirit in the earth/is ours."   To a Detainee.   Musaemura Bonus Zimunya.   WhB

Dogtrots out of that valley/forever   Nevada.   Stanley Noyes.   PH

Doin' the twist with my mind stayed on freedom,/Hallelu, hallelu, hallelu, hallelu, hallelujah!   Woke Up This Morning with My Mind on Freedom.   *Anonymous.*   FSW

Doing the duties of her grave delight?   The Elfin Wife.   Jake Falstaff.   BoC

Doing the Hucklebuck   Poem for Otis Redding.   Joyce Carol Thomas.   CNA

Doing the thing that you cannot do!   Talents Differ.   Laura E. Richards.   TiPo

...Doing your best/to remember that, so far, you have returned.   Off to Patagonia.   Theodore Weiss.   TAP

The doldrums/have dealt this deuce/of a dull day...   Inertia.   Audrey McGaffin.   NePoAm

A doll found in the river.   My Sister, My Self.   Raymond Filip.   CaPN

A dollar a day is all they pay/For work on the boulevard.   Sh-Ta-Ra-Dah-Dey (Irish Lullaby). (with music).   *Anonymous.*   AS

Dollhouse of Mama War.   Paris.   Gregory Corso.   VGW

A dome compact of all but visible stars.   Description of a View.   William Empson.   ACV

The domes with songs, the theaters with plays.   The Aeneid.   Virgil (Publius Vergilius Maro).   WaaP

Domestic character you and i/had hoped she might become/archy   Mehitabel Sings a Song.   Don (Donald Robert Marquis) Marquis.   InMe

Domine, defende nos/Contra hos Motores Bos!   On the Motor Bus.   Alfred Denis Godley.   NLV

Dominion and ancestral sway.   Twilight of the Earth.   George William Russell.   AnIL

Don sheets, wear stars in your hair, fix tinsel wings?   Evolution.   John Blight.   CBAP

Don't–Ah'll die!   Calling the Doctor.   John Wesley Holloway.   BANP

Don't anther.   The Panther.   Ogden Nash.   MoShBr; OBAL; OBCA; SoPo; TiPo

Don't be afraid, Here I am, Here I am!   The Furniture of the Poem.   Dennis Saleh.   NeAC

Don't be angry, I was only, only teasing you.   Teasing.   Cecil Mack.   FSN

...Don't be envied or/armed with a measuring-rod.   His Shield.   Marianne Moore.   DTC; LiTM; NePA

Don't be lazy, do-si-do, and a little more dough...   The Girl I Left Behind Me.   *Anonymous.*   AmFP

Don't bite the hand that's feeding you.   America, I Love You.   Harry and Bert Kalmar Ruby.   FiBHP; InMe

Don't blame us if we meditate a mild attempt at parricide.   "Everybody Works but Father" as W. S. Gilbert Would Have Written It.   Arthur G. Burgoyne.   FiBHP

Don't brathe upon my neck so much.   At the Theater.   Sir Alan Patrick Herbert.   FiBHP

Don't care if I do,/So long as I'm near you.   Where Have You Been, My Good Old Man?   *Anonymous.*   OuSiCo

Don't Care was put in a pot/And boiled till he was done.   Don't Care.   *Anonymous.*   GBP

Don't crowd aroun' me, (hanh!)/'Roun me, if you do I'll die. (hanh!)   Don't Talk about It.   *Anonymous.*   OuSiCo

Don't cry. Your wounds are/beautiful if you'll love mine.   Oh Yes.   William Matthews.   AmPA

Don't drink too much WINE, BRANDY, GIN, or anything/strong.   Epitaph in a Churchyard at Thetford, in Norfolk.   *Anonymous.*   FaBoUs

Don't ever fear sweet Mary, beware of sweet Marie!   Mary's a Grand Old Name.   George M. Cohan.   TreFT

Don't ever let the devil get/The upper hand on you.   The Lexington Murder.   *Anonymous.*   OuSiCo

Don't fear me! There's the grey beginning. Zooks!   Fra Lippo Lippi.   Robert Browning.   BiP; BoLiVe; CABL; CTC; MaVP; MBW 1-2; NoP; OAEL 1-2; OAEP; Prf; TEP; ViBoPo; VLP

...Don't feel/badly it could happen/to anyone   A Midwife's Story: Two.   Anne Szumigalski.   NOBC

Don't forget!/Do not forgive!   Babi Yar.   Lev Ozerov.   VWA

Don't forget henna for the palms of your hands....   Poem to Her Daughter (excerpt).   Mwana Kupona Msham.   WPOW

Don't forget my love.   Huesca.   John Cornford.   BoLoP; ChMP

Don't forget to bloom each spring!   When I have gone away.   Sugawara Michizane.   LiTW

Don't give up the ship!   Defeat and Victory.   Wallace Rice.   MC; PAH

"Don't give yo/right name no/No NO"   Blackie Thinks of His Brothers.   Stanley Crouch.   PoBA

Don't go past me, my friend!– shout! and I'll rise again.   Forced March.   Miklos Radnoti.   VWA

Don't go to the wilds of Australia.   The Settler's Lament.   *Anonymous.*   PoAu 1-2

Don't grow weary, boys,/For we're going to the ball.   Don't Grow Weary, Boys.   *Anonymous.*   CoSo

Don't hide the madness.   On Burroughs' Work.   Allen Ginsberg.   NoAm; NOBA

Don't hurt de liddle babies; dey/is too sweet to kill-o.   Chuck Will's Widow Song.   *Anonymous.*   BPo

Don't it make you feel all right?   The Bishop of Atlanta: Ray Charles.   Julian Bond.   AmNP; CNA; NIP

Don't it make you want to cry?   Those Boys That Ran Together.   Lucille Clifton.   CNA; PoBA

–Don't know the place I'm for. Don't know the day.   Winter Wakens All My Care.   *Anonymous.*   HAP; OxBM

Don't let anyone in to wake us   As We Are So Wonderfully Done with Each Other.   Kenneth Patchen.   ErPo

...Don't let them have a chance with you.   Sonnets of the Months.   Folgore da San Geminiano.   AWP

Don't let this last piece of cake go begging, begged the upstairs apartment.   Moving In.   Josephine Miles.   NoP

Don't let your left hand/Know what your right hand do   Never Let Your Left Hand Know.   Lil Johnson.   BluL

Don't listen to the story some villain's tongue will tell/Or you are sure to meet Naomi's fate.   Naomi Wise.   *Anonymous.*   AmFP

Don't long for someone who will never come back.   Advice to a Neighbour Girl.   Yu Hsuan-chi.   PBWP

Don't look for this to happen any time soon.   Jeane Dixon's America.   Gerald Costanzo.   MAYP

"Don't make it harder for use,' the hangman whispered.   The Execution.   Alden Nowlan.   PeCV

Don't mean nothing./Never has.   Old Man.   Faye Kicknosway.   APU

Don't mind the weather so the wind don't blow.   Hop Up, My Ladies.   *Anonymous.*   OuSiCo

Don't mind you sailin', but you'll be gone so dog-gone long.   Dupree.   *Anonymous.*   OuSiCo

Don't Poke more than Twice/At an Intimate Place like his Gizzard.   The Lizard.   Theodore Roethke.   GrPl

Don't pretend, and I won't,/I ever looked at you before.   Take My Song of Love to Heart.   *Anonymous.*   NOBI

Don't put your trust in young men/Or they astray they may lead.   Fair Florella (B vers.).   *Anonymous.*   BaBo

Don't read the fine/print, there isn't any.   The Market Economy.   Marge Piercy.   GeTw

Don't say I can heal/or bring back/the dead.   Bumi.   LeRoi (Imamu Amiri Baraka) Jones.   PoBA

Don't say nay,/Charming Judy Callaghan.   The Sabine Farmer's Serenade.   Francis Sylvester ("Father Prout") Mahony.   HBV 1-2

Don't say what you hope to be,/But tell me what you are.   Don't Tell Me.   *Anonymous.*   STF

...Don't shake/your shinkolobwe at me   What Maisie Know She Don't Want No/Anger Game at Shinkolobwe.   Judith Johnson Sherwin.   NoAm

Don't shout.   Underwear.   Lawrence Ferlinghetti.   CoPo; OBAL

"Don't shrug away," he said, "There's nowhere to go."   Birthday.   John Ciardi.   NAs

Don't speak of others' faults until/We have none of our own.   Be Careful What You Say.   Joseph Kronthal.   STF

Don't stab ourselves in the left pulmonary,/I'm Romeo, Juliet!   Romeo and Juliet.   Fred Newton Scott.   InMe

Don't stop him saying what we knew before/we came.   Town Meeting.
  John Hay.   NePoAm

Don't tell me anymore./Don't.   Don't Show Me.   Ruth Beker.   VWA

Don't tell me what you dreamt last night, for I've been reading/Freud.   Song:
  "Don't Tell Me What You Dreamt Last Night."   Franklin Pierce
  ("F.P.A.") Adams.   FiBHP

Don't touch that bird of paradise,/Perched on the bedpost there!'   The Bird
  of Paradise.   William Henry Davies.   AtBAP; BrPo; MoVE

"Don't touch this or you'll die!"/It's too late.   Living with Children.   Jim
  Wayne Miller.   GOYP

Don't try for things too far beyond your reach!   The Greedy Fox and the
  Elusive Grapes.   Aesop.   MaC

DON'T WAIT, MOTHER/THEY ARE COMING, SWIFTLY...   When My
  Brothers Come Home.   Aires de A. Santos.   WhB

Don't wait till Judgment Day.   Shady Grove.   Anonymous.   FSW

Don't wake me up.   Don't Say.   Moshe Yungman.   VWA

"Don't worry, kid, the wages of sin is birth."   Tales of the Islands, IV.
  Derek Walcott.   OxBTC

"Don't yall forget to water/my purple petunias."   Revolutionary Petunias.
  Alice Walker.   BlSi

Don't you drive me around   Sic 'Em Dogs On.   Booker White.   BluL

Don't you hear His foot on the treetop,/Soft like the south wind blow?   The
  Little Cradle Rocks Tonight in Glory.   Anonymous.   AmFP

Don't you hear it?   Desnos Reading the Palms of Men on Their Way to the
  Gas Chambers.   Stephen Berg.   VWA

Don't you hear them sinners cryin'?   Judgement Day.   Anonymous.   WTO

Don't you know it's Halloween?   Halloween.   Marie A. Lawson.   SiSoSe;
  TiPo

Don't you let me die an old maid, but take me out of pity.   Old Maid's Song.
  Anonymous.   FSW

Don't you? like when you ask to leave the room/& go to the moon.   Bean
  Spasms.   Ted Berrigan.   EAS

Don't you rock 'im die-dy-o.   Sail away Ladies.   Anonymous.   FSW

Don't you see/Your sons are/Almost men?   The Return of the Dead
  (excerpt).   Samar Attar.   PBWP

Don't you take no wooden nickels, hear?/Tin dimes neither.   So long, pal.
  Aunt Jemima of the Ocean Waves.   Robert Earl Hayden.   LCAP; PoBA

Don't you think I did well with my red herring?   The Red Herring.
  Anonymous.   FaBoNo

Don't you think that Christmas/Is pleasantest of all?   Santa Claus.
  Anonymous.   SoPo

& Don't You Tread On Me.   Resolution.   Ted Berrigan.   ANYP; OFD

Donald Caird's come again.   Donald Caird.   Sir Walter Scott.   BSV

Donder and Blitzen licked off his paint.   The Boy Who Laughed at Santa
  Claus.   Ogden Nash.   BBGG; CenHV; MaC; StPo

Done foun' my los' sheep,/Done foun' my los' sheep.   Done Foun' My Los'
  Sheep.   Anonymous.   BoAN 1-2

Done groun' it all in molazzis, O–O–O.   Ain' No Mo' Cane on de Brazis.
  Anonymous.   ABF

...Done with all disasters but the one.   The Brief Journey West.   Howard
  Nemerov.   NoAm

Done with casting, reeling in slowly, casting...   San Pedro Road.   Robert
  Hass.   GeTw; WOLT

"The Dong with a luminous Nose!"   The Dong with a Luminous Nose.
  Edward Lear.   AmMo; CBEP; CenHV; FaBoCo; FaBoNo; FaBV; LBN;
  NBM; NOBV; PoEL 1-5; VLP; WiR

The donkey's got the whooping-cough.   Up in the North.   Anonymous.
  OxBoLi

Donnor's or Donnee's to their practise shall/Find you to reckon nothing, me
  owe all.   An Epistle to Sir Edward Sackville, Now Earl of Dorset.   Ben
  Jonson.   NCEP

Dont breathe heavy less u really mean it.   Dialogue 4 1 Voice Only.   Doug
  Fetherling.   NeAC

Dont forget to fly   For Poets.   Al Young.   CNA; DFF; PoBA; RFM

Doodleldy, doodledly, doodledy, dan.   Doodledy, Doodledy, Doodledy, Dan.
  Anonymous.   OxNR

The doom of lone Alulvan!   Alulvan.   Walter De la Mare.   MoVE

Doomed at the age of one and twenty,/To die a dreadful death of scorn.
  Farewell to the World of Richard Bishop.   Anonymous.   CoMu

The doomed only trade that he knows.   Coronary Thrombosis.   William
  Price Turner.   OxBS

Doomed to dismay, disgrace, despair.   Frenzy.   George Crabbe.   NOBE

The door-butler lets the strangers in.   Power-Cut.   Mebdh McGuckian.
  FaBoIP

The door has a creaking latch.   Hugh Selwyn Mauberley, X.   Ezra Pound.
  CoBMV; NOBA

The door in the chest standing open.   Simple Song.   Marge Piercy.   CTBA;
  LLLT

The door is not used to be opened/With a cigarette for a key.'   The Tale of
  Lord Lovell.   Anonymous.   NOBL

...The door is opened/to sleep which brings me to my sun.   When the Orient
  Is Lit by the Great Light.   Vittoria da Colonna.   WPOW

Door shuts/under dream water.   The Town of Hill.   Donald Hall.   FiCP;
  InPK; TAP

A door stands open in the heart/And all good things are true.   Song Under
  Shadow.   William Rose Benet.   MoRP

Doors forget but only doors know what it is/doors forget.   Doors.   Carl
  Sandburg.   LOW

The Doors that let the dark leap in/Across my sunny life!   The Narrow
  Doors.   Fannie Stearns Gifford.   HBMV

The doors, the little doors, swing wide.   Jim Desterland.   Hyam Plutzik.
  VGW

Dooth cast like shadowe, making it seeme ruddye therwithall.
  Metamorphoses.   Ovid (Publius Ovidius Naso).   OBVE

Doris lay down, all out of pity.   When Doris Danced.   Richard Eberhart.
  CMoP

The dormant bear.   D-Y Bar.   James Welch.   CDW; STE

Dorset cock and cockatoo; and raven ends.   To Eliza, Duchess of Dorset.
  Joseph Bennett.   LiTA; NePA

"Dost think with such unwieldy bundle/The mart of Paradise to gain?"   The
  Caravan.   Hovhannes Blouz.   CAW

Dost thou not see my baby at my breast,/That sucks the nurse asleep?
  Antony and Cleopatra.   William Shakespeare.   TreFS

"Dost thou prefer a widow to a maid?"   Four Love Poems.   Moses Ibn
  Ezra.   TrJP

Dost thou remember Jeames?   When Moonlike Ore the Hazure Seas.
  William Makepeace Thackeray.   InMe; NA

Dost thou remember Sicily?   Theocritus.   Oscar Wilde.   HBV 1-2; NOBE;
  OxBI

A dot on Long Island Sound.   Black Jess.   Peter Kane Dufault.   NYBP

Dot's pest as anydings I know;/Yaw, dot is so!   Yaw, Dot Is So!   Charles
  Follen Adams.   HBV 1-2

Doth but borrow/Sorrow.   Judgment Day.   John Oxenham.   TRV

Doth in eternal glory shine.   He That Never Read a Line.   Anonymous.
  AnIL

Doth keep us daily schooled and exercised/Lest that the fright thereof should
  overbear us.   Grieve Not, Dear Love.   John Digby, Earl of Bristol.
  OBSP

Doth make my heart give to my tongue the lie.   Astrophel and Stella, XLVII.
  Sir Philip Sidney.   AAS; GBL; NoP; PoEL 1-5; SiPS

Doth move the spirits with brave delights,/Who Beauty's darlings be.   Song:
  "The primrose in the green forest."   Thomas Deloney.   TiPo; ViBoPo

Doth neither wish, nor fear, his dying day.   In Praise of Country Life.
  Robert Chamberlain.   CavP

Doth Order order so/Disorder's overthrow?   Cleopatra: Chorus.   Samuel
  Daniel.   OBSC

Doth practice dying by a little sleep.   The Obsequies of the Lord Harrington.
  John Donne.   MyFE

Doth seem to be herself, though darkened be her light.   The Faerie Queene.
  Edmund Spenser.   OBSC

Doth yield to Immortality.   Ode to England.   William Wilberforce Lord
  AA

Dotting the points to a constellation/you had yet to name.   Losing Track.
  Cathy Song.   BrSi

The double axe will fall like boulders of thunder.   The Double Axe.   Anne
  Hazlewood-Brady.   IHMS

Double-lived in regions new!   Ode: "Bards of Passion and of Mirth."   John
  Keats.   OAEP; OBRV

Double/the empty spaces.   Parting: A Game.   Lynn Sukenick.   NMM

Double your glory is who perished thus,/For you have died for France and
  vindicated us.   Ode in Memory of the American Volunteers Fallen for
  France.   Alan Seeger.   PAH

Doublenesse, and tresoun, and envye,/Poisoun, manslaughtre, and mordre in
  sondry wise.   The Former Age.   Geoffrey Chaucer.   OxBM

Doubling back now/Through a knotted sleeve   Shirt.   Charles Simic.
  HaCAP

Doubling each look of Care, each token of Distress.   A Slum Dwelling.
  George Crabbe.   OBNC

"Doubloons!" they said. The words crashed gold./"Doubloons!"   Portrait of a
  Boy.   Stephen Vincent Benét.   HBMV; MCCG

Doubt is disease.   Believe and Take Heart.   John Lancaster Spalding.   AA

...Doubt/Is the house dick and time whistles taxis.   Nocturne, Central Park
  South.   L. E. Sissman.   NYP

Doubt will have a dwelling there.   The Companion.   Edwin Arlington
  Robinson.   NoAm

Doubtful if it be crowned!   Delayed till she had ceased to know.   Emily
  Dickinson.   AA

"Doubtless there are other roads."   The Wayfarer.   Stephen Crane.   AA;
  AmePo; LiTA; MoAmPo; NePA

Doubtless there'll be many/Surprised to see you there.   Surprises.
  Anonymous.   STF

Doug is the tall one.   Dining out with Doug and Frank.   James Schuyler.
  NYP

Dough lone de way, my dearie.   On the Road.   Paul Laurence Dunbar. AA

Douglas, Douglas, tender and true!   Too Late.   Dinah Maria Mulock Craik. HBV 1-2

Doun i' the meadow, where we twa met.   The Padda Song.   *Anonymous.* GBP

Dour as the diamant, cauld as the starns.   Calvinist Sang.   Alexander Scott. OxBS

Dour, malignant to the core,/they will try to outlive him.   Breakwaters. Ted Walker.   NYBP

'Dout a lovah's lane.   Lover's Lane.   Paul Laurence Dunbar.   BANP

–The dove/An ancient turtle egging love.   Aboriginal Sin.   John Hay. NePoAm-2

The dove has brought an olive branch to eat.   Where the Rainbow Ends. Robert Lowell.   AnNE; CoBMV; HaCAP; MoAB; MoAmPo; NePoEA; TrGrPo

The dove in the heavens/Is the one I choose.   The Dove.   *Anonymous.* GBP

Dover Andover Depew!   Sing a Song of the Cities.   Morris Bishop.   CAD

Doves did not know where to fly, and.   The Epitaph Ending in And. William Stafford.   LCAP; NaP; NIP

The doves, the hawthorn merge in the wrack and foam.   Venus of the Salty Shell.   Denis Devlin.   BIrV; NOBI

Down and down her slanting country, her hair straight out behind her/Like a sail.   Private Rooms.   Diana O Hehir.   NPGG

Down and down; the compass needle dead on terror.   Lady Ralegh's Lament. Robert Lowell.   OBSP

Down, at once, we sunk to heaven.   The Enjoyment.   *Anonymous.*   ErPo

Down below the keel of her the lost ships lying/In the weed and the coral, far below...   In the Trades.   C. Fox Smith.   EtS

Down, boys, down for the morning swim!   Song for a Camper.   John Farrar. YeAr

Down by de ribber-side, down by de ribber-side, I'm go'n' to ride with my King Jesus.   Ain' Go'n' to Study War No Mo'(with music).   *Anonymous.* AS

Down came wheelbarrow,/Little wife and all.   When I Was a Bachelor. *Anonymous.*   HBV 1-2

Down, down, be finished at/last.   America Bleeds.   Angelo Lewis.   PoBA

Down down into the earth!   The Old Men.   Irving Feldman.   MP

Down, down,/Now jentil belly down.   Now Jentil Belly Down.   *Anonymous.* GBP

Down, down the mountain/They hunt on, and on.   Three Jovial Gentlemen. Daniel Gerard Hoffman.   MoBS

Down, down together even as I wake.   The Course.   Robert Huff.   CoAP

Down, down with the Devil.   Simon Legree–A Negro Sermon.   Vachel Lindsay.   HBMV; InMe; LiTA; LoGBV; MoVE; NAMP; NePA; NLV; TAP

Down drough the orch'd, where my ears/Do miss the vaices gone.   The Vaices That Be Gone.   William Barnes.   NOBV

Down for ever with Wat o' the Cleuch!   Walsinghame's Song (parody). James Hogg.   BXAP

Down from her towers a ray shall hover,/Touch you–a passer-by!   Alma Mater.   Sir Arthur Thomas ("Q") Quiller-Couch.   OBVV

Down he stumbled! down she tumbled!/Right at the Parson's feet! Wheelbarrow.   Eleanor Farjeon.   FiBHP

"Down here among my people."   The Preacher's Mistake.   William Croswell Doane.   BLPA; PoToHe

Down here it is raucous and gritty and crude. I love it.   Saturday in the County Seat.   Elijah L. Jacobs.   AmFN

...Down highway and river/to the deaf and hungry cities.   White Pines. Barry Silesky.   AMV-80

Down hill screaming/our heads off!   This Is Pioneer Weather.   William Carlos Williams.   NePoAm-2

Down hills floating by heart on the bulldozed land.   For Robert Frost. Galway Kinnell.   NOBA; PP; VGW

Down in the barley gold.   The Walking of the Moon-Women.   Shaw Neilson.   ACV

Down in the ditch you go!   Army Bugle Calls: Fatigue Call.   *Anonymous.* TreF

Down in the flood of remembrance, I weep/like a child for the past.   Piano. D. H. Lawrence.   BLPL; CBEP; CMoP; GrPl; GTBS-P; HAP; HeIP; InPK; InvP; LiTB; MoAB; MoBrPo; NIP; NoAm; NOBE; NoP; OAEL 1-2; OAEP; OBSP; PoPle; UnPo; WeW

Down in the green wood shady.   Three little children sitting in the sand. *Anonymous.*   ExPo

Down in the meadow where th cowslips grow!   Oh, Susan Blue.   Kate Greenaway.   TiPo

Down in the ragged canyon where "Martha's younket" sleeps.   Old Red Hoss Mountain.   Cy Warman.   PoOW

Down on the cushions, a-tremble with dread/while the others hide their eyes. In the Seraglio.   David R. Slavitt.   ErPo; PeHV

Down on your knees for mercy cry, lest you in sin like Polly die.   Wicked Polly.   *Anonymous.*   ABF

...Down rush the showers,/And float the deluged paths and miry fields.   On the Dark, Still, Dry, Warm Weather ...   Gilbert White.   NOEC

Down scrip and sheep-hook goes,/When foxes Shepherds be.   The Pastoral on the King's Death. Written in 1648.   Alexander Brome.   OBS

Down Sheet Lane/to Blanket Fair.   Up the Wooden Hill.   *Anonymous.* OxNR

Down the cattle come again!   Highland Cattle.   Dinah Maria Mulock.   GN

Down the dense sweetness of oblivion.   The Final Hunger.   Vassar Miller. LiTM

...Down the dusk hillside/Lumbers the wain; and day fades out like smoke. The Potato Harvest.   Sir Charles G. D. Roberts.   CaP; NOBC

Down the gray disastrous morn,/Laughter and rallying!   Of Wounds and Sore Defeats.   William Moody.   HBV 1-2

Down the long combers of his pride.   In Memoriam Roy Campbell.   Ralph Nixon Currey.   ACV; PeSA

Down the long lanes of the vanished years,/Echoing frailly and far away.   To a Scarlatti Passepied.   Robert Hillyer.   HBMV

Down the North Channel Paul Jones did/steer just at the break of day.   The Yankee Man-of-War.   *Anonymous.*   AA; EtS; FaBoBe; LaNeLa; OBSS; PAH; PaPo

Down the old high roads of inexhaustible light.   A Coal Fire in Winter. Thomas McGrath.   NU

Down the page and on out like this over the edge.   The Escape.   William Stafford.   NNaP

Down the polished floors of space.   Butterflies.   Clive Sansom.   BoAnP

Down the rocky road and all the way to Dublin./Whack-fol-lol-de-ra.   The Rocky Road to Dublin.   *Anonymous.*   FaBoBa

Down the Santa Clara Valley through the world from far/away–/Far and far away–far away.   On the Great Plateau.   Edith Wyatt.   HBMV

Down the stairs.   Confession.   Ralph Pomeroy.   CoPo

Down their carved names the rain-drop ploughs.   During Wind and Rain. Thomas Hardy.   CMoP; ELP; ExPo; ForPo; GTBS-P; HAP; NIP; OAEL 1-2; OxBTC; PoPle; PPoe; PPP; QFR; SeCeV; TEP

Down there, looking up, crying and reaching/As they go under.   Dragon. Joseph Stroud.   NPGG

Down there, we're just another noise.   Cockpit in the Clouds.   Dick Dorrance.   TiPo

Down through the streams of my palms,/The deep lifelines.   Lifelines.   T. R. Hummer.   AMV-80

Down through the years to us shall be/Ever and ever the victory!   The Ballad of Paco Town.   Clinton Scollard.   PAH

Down thru cloud-floor to Chicago, sunset fire obliterate in black gas.   Friday the Thirteenth.   Allen Ginsberg.   NNaP

Down to firm, century-anchored earth, to pace/In safety amid the treacheries of space.   Parachute.   Stanley Snaith.   HaMV

Down to Kill Roy   Mexico City Blues.   Jack Kerouac.   NeAP

Down to soft welcoming feathers, warm eggs.   Mating Answer.   Ronald Bottrall.   PoA

Down to the drowned lands of Lincolnshire;/To make ewes cast their lambs. The Sad Shepherd.   Ben Jonson.   FaBoPP

Down to the edge, down to the hard, final edge.   Deer Hunt, Salt Lake Valley.   Helen Handley.   GrPl

Down to the grave–ARE ITS HOPES IN VAIN?   Life.   Ella Wheeler Wilcox.   PoToHe

Down to the ground at once, as butcher felleth ox.   The Castle of Indolence. James (1700-48) Thomson.   CEP; EiCP; LAuP

Down to the last little lizard, even as other men.   Lines to Dr. Ditmars. Kenneth Allan Robinson.   ImOP

Down to the old mill stream/where lies of love are fair.   Stutterer.   Alan Dugan.   CAPP; NYBP

...Down to the/river! into the street!   Howl, II.   Allen Ginsberg.   NeAP; PoCh

"Down to the river to water my geese,/And over the river to Charlie."   My Pretty Little Miss.   *Anonymous.*   BFSS

Down to the shining, pebbly sea/And kick the frothing waves aside.   Beech Leaves.   James Reeves.   OnUR

Down to the silence I come, in the shadow I will rest.   Snowfall.   Giosue Carducci.   AWP

Down twenty, thirty feet below.   Anchorage.   Pat Wilson.   AnNZ

Down we come again.   Sliding.   Marchette Chute.   TiPo

Down where he lies to-night, silent, and under the storms.   Pasa Thalassa Thalassa.   Edwin Arlington Robinson.   EtS; LaNeLa; MOS

Down where the Dream Woman dwells.   The Paradox.   Paul Laurence Dunbar.   PoBA

Down will come baby, cradle, and/all.   Hush-a-Bye, Baby, on the Tree Top. *Anonymous.*   OxNR

Down you go alone, so late, into the surge-black/fissure.   You Will Know When You Get There.   Allen Curnow.   OCNZ

Downstream where the yolk of the sun breaks,/bleeding in the water.   The Woman.   George Keithley.   NPGG

Downward and downward/into the murmurous/waters of sleep.   Shooting Whales.   Mark Strand.   LCAP

Downward thousands of enormous dreams   I go to this window.   Edward Estlin Cummings.   NAMP

Downward to darkness, on extended/wings.   Sunday Morning.   Wallace Stevens.   AmP; AP; BiP; BLPL; CMoP; CoBMV; CrMA; ForPo; HaCAP; HAP; HeIP; InPo; InPS; LiTA; LiTM; MasP; MoAB; MoAmPo; MoVE; NAWM 1-2; NePA; NIP; NOBA; NoP; OxBA; PPoe; QFR; SeCeV; TAP; WeW

...Downy/hair fragrant with leafsmoke.   Downy Hair.   Lucien Stryk.   FAZ

A dozen dozen in her place.   The Constant Lover.   Sir John Suckling.   AWP; CaPo; FaBV; FaFP; FPL; HBV 1-2; HeIP; InPo; JCP; LiTB; LiTL; MCCG; NOBE; OBEV; OLR; SeCePo; TreFS; TrGrPo

Dozens of languages we heard/And walked amid them dumb.   Newcomers.   Abraham Reisen.   VWA

Dozle tivy-too.   Marezle Toats.   *Anonymous.*   FaBoNo

A drab and dingy bird.   Self-Protection.   D. H. Lawrence.   NoP

Drag heavy bundles of dreams to their Moriahs.   The Messiah.   Yungman.   VWA

Dragged to oblivion by the foundering weight.   On the Edition of Mr. Pope's Works with a Commentary and Notes.   Thomas Edwards.   TW

Draggin' his claws/down a mirror glass.   Jis' Knowin'.   Thomas G. Nickens.   LFAC

Dragging a moth to inspect/in the long afternoon.   The Woman Who Loved Women.   Colette Inez.   NMM

...Dragging/a shadow-plane, an anchor/that will not grab.   An Airline Breakfast.   William Matthews.   AMV-80; MAYP

Dragging from behind only/A skull on a rope/Tied to his belt.   Considering the Bleakness.   Moishe Leib Halpern.   VWA

Dragging him up the stairs to one who lies dead.   The Conversation of Prayer.   Dylan Thomas.   EBEV; GTBS-P; NoP

Dragging the corn by her golden hair,/Into a dark and lonely wood.   The Villain.   William Henry Davies.   MoBrPo; OBSP; OxBTC; SoSe; WHA

Dragging the night behind/us on a web of steel.   South Shore Line.   John Schlesinger.   AMV-80

Draggle tail, dreary dun.   Master and Man.   *Anonymous.*   NA; OxNR

A dragon a-draggin' a drag?   Limerick: "A dragon, who was a great wag."   Carolyn Wells.   TDH

The dragon banner floating in the sun.   How Goes the Night?   *Anonymous.*   AWP

The dragonfly.   Seven Poems.   Lorine Niedecker.   VGW

Dragons blazing like Northern Lights/would leap out and frighten the stars.   Prison Break.   Michael Hogan.   GP

Drags the dead horse away to hollow swelling growls.   Ghazals.   Jim Harrison.   NoAm

Drained spittle from his pipe, then scrammed.   For William Carlos Williams.   Galway Kinnell.   SM

The drama of the world's annihilation!   Ode to the Hayden Planetarium.   Arthur Guiterman.   ImOP

Drank three quick beers/& left in a hurry.   Between a Good Hat & Good Boots.   Kell Robertson.   TAT

"Drank up their drink and gone to bed."   Horace Paraphrased.   Isaac Watts.   LoBV

The draught from the leaves sifts down and shakes your hands   The Italian Air.   Lewis MacAdams.   ANYP

Draughts of tomorrow/drawn slow/into empty lungs.   Herman Moon's Hourbook.   Christopher Middleton.   NePoEA-2

Draughts of vanilla extract.   The Gerbil Who Got Away.   Judith C. Root.   AMV-81

Draw back the bolts, and give up to Love/Your easiest chair.   Carol for Advent.   John Heath-Stubbs.   OxBC

Draw fear in white threads back and forth through my body.   Port Bou.   Stephen Spender.   MoPo; MP; OBTV; TwCP

Draw, from every beast they snare,/Comfort for a wedded pair!   The Ballad of Hiram Hover.   Bayard Taylor.   BXAP; FaBoCo; OBAL

Draw me a pot of beer, mother, and, mother, draw it mild!   The Biter Bit.   Ayton [(or Aytoun) Sir Robert.   InMe

Draw me another pint of old and mild.   At the Ship.   R. P. Lister.   FiBHP

Draw me by charity, mother of mine.   Rosa Mystica.   Gerard Manley Hopkins.   ACP; GoBC

Draw them from my heart and from my eyes wipe/My constant flood of tears.   Swift Floods.   Kata S. Petroczi.   WPOW

Draw those dark braids lower, Lady!/But to Krishna go.   A Song from the Gita Govinda.   Jayadeva.   LiTW

Draw up my love to shower on him sleeping!   Sonnet: "In heaven there is a star I call my own."   Irene Rutherford McLeod.   HBMV

Draw up my prisoned spirit to thy soul!   Love's Testament.   Dante Gabriel Rossetti.   MaVP

Drawing the soul to its anchorage.   Greyport Legend.   Bret (Francis Bret Harte) Harte.   EtS; GN; MOS

Drawing to inside straights.   Poker Poem.   Michael Pettit.   AMV-80

Drawn back again.   Mid-Plains Tornado.   Linda Bierds.   AMV-80

Drawn of fair peacocks, that excel in pride,/And full of Argus eyes*their tayles dispredden wide.   The Faerie Queene.   Edmund Spenser.   WHA

Drawn simply by the seasons, by their lives.   Hotel Sierra.   David St. John.   MAYP

Draws in, and at his Trunk spouts out a Sea.   Paradise Lost.   John Milton.   MOS

...Draws out of the infinite spaces/all things down to its own/niggardly miserable earth.   Friends.   Richard Moore.   SM

Draws rein and sings to the swing of the tide.   The Phantom Horsewoman.   Thomas Hardy.   CMoP; FaBoPP; NOBE; PoEL 1-5; WSC

Draws round his head, knowing what/change is near.   On a Great Man Whose Mind is Clouding.   Edmund Clarence. Stedman.   AA

The dread inquiry meets my soul,/What shall it answer there?   Advertisement of a Lost Day.   Lydia Sigourney.   WBLP

The Dread of Tyrants, and the sole Resource/Of those that under grim Oppression groan.   Happy Britannia.   James (1700-48) Thomson.   OBEC

Dread poetry, and damn the poet.   Satire.   Alexander Geddes.   ACP

The dread that my old love may be alive/Has seized my nursling new love by the throat.   Modern Love, XL.   George Meredith.   VLP

Dreadful murderer/B U D D H A   Mexico City Blues.   Jack Kerouac.   NeAP

Dreadful sorry Clementine.   Oh, My Darling Clementine.   Percy Montross.   FaBoBe

Dreadful sorry, Clementine.   Rhymes for a Modern Nursery.   Paul Dehn.   FiBHP; ShM

A dreadful tremor, a panic in all the frame of things.   The Clock.   Jovan Ducic.   LiTW

The dreadfull spectacle of that sad house/of Pride.   The Faerie Queene.   Edmund Spenser.   OAEP

A dream,–a dream, Autonoe!   To a Greek Girl.   Henry Austin Dobson.   HBV 1-2

Dream! and be one with these.   Ceylon.   A. Hugh Fisher.   HBV 1-2

Dream: and the great anthropomorphic rose.   Nijinsky.   Parker Tyler.   PoA

...A dream/bends when the night in it dissolves   End Song.   Ruth Krauss.   LLLT

A dream can bring me to your arms once more.   Compensation.   Lizette Woodworth Reese.   HBMV

...The dream/Comes of God's good pleasure.   The Dream.   Francis Burdett Money-Coutts.   OBVV

Dream, dream, for this is also sooth.   The Song of the Happy Shepherd.   William Butler Yeats.   NoAm; VLP

A dream drips softly.   Impression of a Fountain.   Hakushu Kitahara.   LiTW

The dream grain whirls like freakish Easter snows.   Glanmore Sonnets.   Seamus Heaney.   NoP

The dream had not been broken,/And love were with us yet.   A Song of Autumn.   Rennell Rodd.   HBV 1-2

The dream is lovelier than the song.   Dream and the Song.   James David Corrothers.   BANP

Dream music fills the air/like the scent of dried herbs.   Herbs in the Attic.   Marilyn Waniek.   AMV-81; MAYP

...Dream of contempt/Which clothes in his useless exile the Swan.   Sonnet: "This virgin, beautiful and lively day."   Stephane Mallarme.   PoPl

A dream of misty elms to plague the mind.   To the Memory of Yale College.   Howard Phelps (Phelps Putnam) Putnam.   AnAmPo

The dream of passion soon or late/Is broken–don't anticipate.   Advice to Julia.   Henry Luttrell.   IrPN

Dream of the golden splendors of your smile,/Dream you remember yet.   Ave Atque Vale.   Rosamund Marriott Watson.   HBV 1-2

The dream peace/that would satisfy/as immortality.   To This Hill Again.   James Macmillan.   PoSH

The dream that baffles me, may you fulfill.   Muse in Late November.   Jonathan Henderson Brooks.   PoNe

The dream that comes, the wish that goes,/The memories that follow!   Collige Rosas.   William Ernest Henley.   OBVV; PG

Dream thou–and from thy sleep/Then wake to weep.   Mutability.   Percy Bysshe Shelley.   EnLi 1-2; HBV 1-2; NoP; OBNC; ViBoPo

Dream thru the mind/like the beautiful words.   Twelfth Raga/for John Wieners.   David Meltzer.   NeAP

Dream, while the innumerable choir of day/Welcome the dawn.   Nightingales.   Robert Bridges.   AtBAP; BrPo; CMoP; CoBMV; ExPo; ForPo; HBMV; LiTB; LiTM; MoAB; MoBrPo; OAEL 1-2; OBEV; OBMV; OBNC; OBVV; PBBP; PoPl; SeCeV; TrGrPo; UnPo; VLP

Dream while you may.   At the Manger.   W. H. Auden.   EBCP; ILwL

...Dreamed of Angels' Spelling Bee and thought of/Truthful James.   The Spelling Bee at Angels.   Bret (Francis Bret Harte) Harte.   StPo

Dreamed up in fantasies/of bygone glory.   Ancestors.   Dudley Randall.   BPo; CNA

A dreamer and a prodigal.   Phantasus.   Arno Holz.   AWP

The dreamer of brave deeds that might have been,/Shall cureless ache with wounds forever green. In Vinculis: The Deeds That Might Have Been. Wilfrid Scawen Blunt. TrGrPo

Dreamin', dreamin' that you love me. The Trail Herd. *Anonymous.* BPAW

Dreaming, dreaming pleasantly. Pagan Epitaph. Richard Middleton. OBVV

(Dreaming,/et/cetera, of/Your smile/eyes knees and of your Etcetera) Is 5. Edward Estlin Cummings. AnAmPo

Dreaming/her children were coming home Raising the Flag. Gerald Vizenor. VoR

Dreaming is still on the house. The Katskills Kiss Romance Goodbye. Ishmael Reed. APU

Dreaming only on the yellow/and green magnificence/that is hardening within them. The Cauliflower. John Haines. GP

Dreaming the flower I have never seen. Moly. Thom Gunn. HAP; NoAm; PrIm

Dreaming toward natural grace in a green town. Willows. Joseph Langland. NePoEA

Dreams aloud that it is God. The Church. Jules Romain. WGRP

The dreams–and faith–and love! The Dreams Ahead. Edwin Carlile Litsey. PoToHe

Dreams of girls, about yr girl friend, writing letters, wanting children,/Making plans. Things to Do around a Ship at Sea. Gary Snyder. CAPP

Dreams shake my loosened hair–the wind/Lone listener to my spirit wild. On the Tower. Annette von Droste-Hulshoff. PBWP; WPOW

Dreams, trees, and water's bright babblings. Talking with Soldiers. Walter James Turner. ChMP; MoBrPo

Dreams, Whimseys, and no more. Troas, II: Chorus (latter end). Seneca (Lucius Annaeus Seneca). OBVE

Dreamt as a prelude to realities.) What Sanguine Beast? LeRoy Smith, Jr. NePoAm

Dreamt of a sword at my side and a battle-horse underneath/me. Amours de Voyage. Arthur Hugh Clough. FaBoPV

Dreamwater/bears me away. Dreamwater. Hilde Domin. VWA

A dreamy watchfulness of tranquil things,/And not unblest. From My Window. Mary Elizabeth Coleridge. OBNC

A dreary glory smiled. Upon Her Soothing Breast. Emily Bronte. BoWoP

...The dreary snowflakes do not cease/drifting past my window in the demi-dark. Long Lines. Paul Goodman. NMP; VGW

Drenching all the trees between the two sandhills. Thunderstorm. Sam Mitchell. NOAV

Dress'd in his best suit of clothes. Down Went McGinty. Joseph Flynn. FSN; TreF; YaD

A dressed man and a naked man/Stood by the kip-house fire. A Dressed Man and a Naked Man. George Orwell. EBEV

Drew down upon his heels to help him die. The Thief's Niece. George Keithley. NPGG

Drew one angel–borne, see, on my bosom! One Word More. Robert Browning. FiP; HBV 1-2; PoEL 1-5; ViBoPo; VLP

Dribbles a bit, dries up, and is done for? March 1st. Kathleen Spivak. NYBP

Dribbling salt water into flowers' eyes. Sheep Dipping. Norman MacCaig. OxBC

Drift on through slumber to a dream, and through a/dream to death. Music (after Sully Prudhomme). George Du Maurier. CBEP

Drift slowly away. El Dorado. Richard Ryan. BIrV

The drift-wood fire without that burned,/The thoughts that burned and glowed within. The Fire of Drift-Wood. Henry Wadsworth Longfellow. AP; BLPL; HBV 1-2; MAmP; NOBA; NoP; OxBA; TAP

Drifting in casually, one by one. Icarus. Valentin Iremonger. BIrV; CIP; NeIP; OnYI; OxBI

Drifting in his watery nursery/of brazen pomps, old nightmares stink romantic. The Malefic Surgeon. Gerrit Lansing. CoPo

...The drifting shroud/of everything men once had thought they owned. Highland Shooting Lodge. Maurice Lindsay. PoSH

Drifting the summer/labyrinths of love. On the Range. Raymond Souster. NOBC

Drifting, the Ten Tribes there, lost forever. Scene of a Summer Morning. Irving Feldman. NYBP

Drifting to the desert gleaming/Underneath a jewelled sky. Drifting. D. Maitland Bushby. BPAW

Drifting up and down Woodward Avenue. In Detroit. R. R. Cuscaden. PoL

The drifting wilderness of snow. The Rehearsal. Horace Gregory. VGW

Drifts evermore to the west the scanty smokes of thy/wigwams! To the Driving Cloud. Henry Wadsworth Longfellow. FaBoRV; PoEL 1-5

...Drifts free of Him/whose breath gave it shape. Haiku: "That silver balloon." Robert Phillips. GrPl

Drifts in the song, complete/as an archangel. The Drowned. Norman MacCaig. OxBC

The driftwood of the town who have no roof-tops, and no home! City Roofs. Charles Hanson Towne. BLPA

Drink, and be filled, and ye shall understand! Comfort of the Fields. Archibald Lampman. CaP

Drink and be whole again beyond confusion. Directive. Robert Frost. AP; BLPL; CMoP; CoBMV; CrMA; DiPo; ForPo; HAP; InPS; LiTA; LiTM; MasP; MAT; MoAB; NePA; NoAm; NOBA; NoP; PPP; PrIm; SeCeV

Drink and drain the brimming cup/Till wine drives out the anguish. Epigram: "Drink, unhappy lover." Meleager. PeHV

...Drink, children, sing. Charming the Moon. James DenBoer. MAT

Drink deep and don't dribble for you are drinking my/dreams. Teatime Variations. Peter Titheradge. FaBoPa

Drink deep the image solid of the bone. High Dive. William Empson. AtBAP

Drink! for you know not why you go, nor where. The Rubaiyat of Omar Khayyam. Omar Khayyam. FaBoRV

Drink, gossips mine! we drink no wine. Medieval Norman Songs. *Anonymous.* AWP

Drink it straight and swig it mighty,/Till the world goes round and round! Drinking Song: "Drink that rotgut, drink that rotgut". *Anonymous.* CoSo

Drink success to the tars of the Blanche. The Tars of the Blanche. *Anonymous.* OBSS

Drink the rivers of thy grace. Saviour, Who Thy Flock Art Feeding. William Augustus Muhlenberg. AH

Drink to his resurrection later on. The Elegy. A. D. Hope. ErPo; NoP

Drink to Our Native Land! God Bless the State! A Toast to Our Native Land. Robert Bridges. MC; PAH; PAL

Drink to the pioneer! The Pioneer. Eugene Field. BPAW; PoOW

Drink to the troop that never shall die! The Grey Horse Troop. Robert William Chambers. HBV 1-2; PAH

Drink water/and you drink sky Food. Victor M. Valle. FIA

Drink wine from quite extraordinary grapes. Two Gardens. Arlene De Bevoise. AMV-80

Drink with my Guddame, as ye ga by,/Anys for my saik. The Ballad of Kynd Kittok. William Dunbar. BSV; GoTS

The drink would taste sweeter from dad's dinner pail. My Dad's Dinner Pail. Edward Harrigan. BLPA

Drinking beer and lemon-squashes, taking baths and cooling down. Up the Country. Henry Lawson. CBAP

Drinking beneath the wine. Frippery. Horace. LiTW

Drinking great ardours; and the rapturous birth/Of winged things. An Autumn Song. Edward Dowden. ACV; OnYI

Drinking in its golden showers,/but sadder still. Rains on the Island. Gabriel Preil. VWA

Drinking muscatel and swapping stories/Until the buttons drive us home. Literary Life in the Golden West. Philip Whalen. NAs

Drinking the dewdrop's/Mystery. The Snail. Langston Hughes. GoSl; TiPo

Drinking the moon. Plowing at Full Moon. Leo Dangel. AMV-80

Drinking the waters/of death with/the new dead. The Old Man Who Is Gone Now. Margarita Baldenegro Reyes. FIA

Drinks and drinks up the heart. Black Angel. Lewis Thompson. AtBAP

Drinks wine i' th' very height o' th' fever. To Master Davenant for Absence. Sir John Suckling. CaPo

Dripping red with blood. North Country. Kenneth Slessor. CBAP

Dripping slantwise into my side. I Am Almost Asleep. Eldon Grier. PV

A dripping stringer of night-caught crappies. Sunday Crappies. Jim Thomas. WOLT

Drips, drips, drips from the leaves. A Soft Day. Winifred M. Letts. AnIV; OnYI

Drips into my present and their present/Like seasoned wisdom from the land of Lethe. Proust on Noah. Eisig Silberschlag. VWA

Driv'n else to graunt by Angels sophistrie,/That I love not, without I leave to love. Astrophel and Stella, LXI. Sir Philip Sidney. AAS; SiPS

Drive a tractor. Drive a Tractor. *Anonymous.* NLV

Drive all hurtfull Feinds us fro,/By the Time the Cocks first crow. The Old Wives Prayer. Robert Herrick. SeCV 1-2

...Drive/as fast as they could,/Away from their beds. Pornography, Nebraska. Sandra McPherson. MAYP

Drive, he sd, for/christ's sake, look/out where yr going. I Know a Man. Robert Creeley. AmC; AmPC; CAPP; ConAP; CoPo; InPS; MAT; NOBA; OBSP; PAI; PoM; PPP

Drive me back to the lime-juice tub. The Limejuice Tub. *Anonymous.* NOAV

Drive on and on,/On and on! Solitary Song. *Anonymous.* WTO

Drive Pretender to the D–l, keep K. George in his place,/Derry Down. A New Song Entitled the Warming Pan. *Anonymous.* CoMu

Drive the colour from her cheek? Twilight. Henry Wadsworth Longfellow. CH

Drive to Chicago,/and get drunk/on Welfare checks. Corn-Planter. Maurice Kenny. STE

Driven crazy on a locust/post. The Poem. Galway Kinnell. NaP

Driven here and there–/with only itself to love. Elvin's Blues. Michael S. Harper. BPo

Driven out, thrown away, married too soon! The Plaint of the Wife. W. R. S. Ralston. AWP

Driven to smash the blank unsilvered mirror. The White Horse. Mary Mills. NePoAm

Driver held Car swerves,/injures 11; driver held. Aram Saroyan. ANYP

Driver, there's an awful glitter in the air. What is the weather/forecast? Internal Injuries. Robert Penn Warren. NYP

The drivers, therefore, didn't do. Limerick: "A man hired by John Smith and Co." Mark (Samuel Langhorne Clemens) Twain. FaBoNo; TDH

...Drives through cold/towards his roped stone quay, his dead fish fold. End of the Season on a Stormy Day–Oban. Iain Crichton Smith. NePoEA-2

Driving around, I will waste more time. Driving to Town Late to Mail a Letter. Robert Bly. BoNaP; CAPP; ELU; HeIP; InPK; NaP; VGW

Driving my car hard north/Against their fragile yearnings. Driving North from Savannah on My Birthday. Paul Zimmer. AmC; AMV-81

Driving the first of its withered leaves/Over the stones where the fountain broke. Fragment. Edwin Arlington Robinson. MAPA

A drizzling rain set in. The Rosy Bosom'd Hours. Coventry Patmore. EnLoPo; NOBV

Drooping his swift wings on either side. The Power of Music (excerpt). Pindar. UnS

Droops, dies, and falls without the cleaver's stroke. All Things Decay and Die. Robert Herrick. CaPo

Drop a little/On the table/Top a little. Baby's Drinking Song. James Kirkup. NTCP

Drop anything except a tear. Another. J. E. Thorold Rogers. FaBoEE

Drop by drop Time fades, and rose by rose! Autumn Twilight. Henri de Regnier. LiTW

Drop by drop/without restraint/forever– My Soul Hovers Over Me. Joshua Tan Pai. VWA

Drop/Dead./Flip, flop./Plop. A Tragedy. Theophile Marzials. PeD

Drop from Thy lips Thy syllables of quiet! Agnus Dei. Victor Kinon. CAW

Drop Gabriel–and Me– I envy seas, whereon he rides–. Emily Dickinson. OLR

Drop heavy on my heart. Always in the Parting Year. Else Lasker-Schüler. TrJP

Drop him in the sepulchre/With his Uncle Jerry. Mr. Slimmer's Funeral Verses for the Morning Argus. Charles Heber Clark. OBAL

Drop him in the sepulchre/With his Uncle Jerry. Obituary. Max (Charles Heber Clark) Adeler. DTC

Drop into living with my blind, punished hero. Mythics. Helen Chasin. DFT

Drop into water.../Chick-a-dee-dee-dee... Chickadee. Hilda Conkling. TiPo

Drop me a kiss–I'm the bird dead-struck! Juggling Jerry. George Meredith. BeLS; HBV 1-2; OAEP; SeCePo; VLP

& Drop my chalky crap, my gnats & flies,/in the gutter with such distinction. After an All-Night Cackle with Sloth & Co. I Enter the Mansion... Gary Gildner. GP

...Drop my harp/Through a green wave, off Yesnaby,/Next time you row to the lobsters. The Five Voyages of Arnor. George Mackay Brown. NePoEA-2

Dropped a handful of flakes in the oriole's empty nest. Kriss Kringle. Thomas Bailey Aldrich. HBVY

Dropped a tin can over the smoke stack. Field Work. Doug Cockrell. Psk

Dropped by the Black Prince. Clerihew. Edmund Clerihew Bentley. PV

Dropped–mockery of life's a quick-wasted lot–Dropped on a virgin sheet 't is but a blot! A Drop of Ink. Joseph Ernest Whitney. AA

Dropped science, and took up divinity. There Was a Young Man from Trinity. *Anonymous.* ImOP

"Dropped something?" The Wren. Issa. NTCP

Dropping at eve in coral bays/A vapoury footfall on the ocean's sleepy/blaze. An Indian Song. William Butler Yeats. VLP

...Dropping down/Weary some dawn by a lake where wild rice/Whispers to water. Night Flight. George Whalley. CaP

Dropping gold foil/on field and wall. Leaflight. Dorothy Donnelly. NCSH

Dropping to the ground and rolling down the bowling alley of/the sky. After Dinner We Take a Drive into the Night. Tony Towle. ANYP

Droppings on the rocks, and rain/glides slowly down. A Footnote to a Gray Bird's Pause. James (Olumo) Cunningham. JB

Drops be on our cheeks–O world, they are not tears but dew. Lessons from the Gorse. Elizabeth Barrett Browning. HBV 1-2

Drops her among stones/and cracked shells. Pregnant Teenager on the Beach. Mary Balazs. AMV-80

Drops on four feet. Yet he has bleeding paws. The Allegory of the Wolf Boy. Thom Gunn. OxBC

...Drops/sparkle and fall to the power of a thousand from her body. The One Girl at the Boys Party. Sharon Olds. MAYP

Dropt it, as loth to drop it, on the rest. Faesulan Idyl. Walter Savage Landor. OBRV; SeCePo

Drown all the dogs,' said the fierce young woman. The Renowned Generations. William Butler Yeats. OxBoLi

Drown in despair when his days darken. The Answer. Robinson Jeffers. MoRP

Drown me on my return–but spare me as I go. On Leander's Swimming over the Hellespont to Hero. Thomas Warton, Jr.. FaBoEE

A drowned face waits at the mirror. Now, before Shaving. Aaron Kramer. AMV-81

A drowned fish and a sea-bird's feather. Loss of an Oil Tanker. Charles Causley. OxBC

Drowned in the blood of rubies there, not die. A Nuptial Verse to Mistress Elizabeth Lee Now Lady Tracy. Robert Herrick. HW

Drowned in the royal court of my ghetto. The Golem. Shlomo Reich. VWA

Drowned out by the winds and a promise. Graduation Day, 1965. Julio Marzan. InW

...The drowning sea/Is all he has between himself and drowning. Swimmer. Robert Francis. LiSp

Drowning thy music with their cry for gold! The Poet. Angela Morgan. WGRP

Drowns us in drouth, nor no man ever loved. Lovers' Debouchment (parody). William Zaranka. BXAP

Drowsily come the sheep. Slumber Song. Louis V. Ledoux. HBMV

The drum and fife is her delight,/And a merry man in the morning. I'm Seventeen Come Sunday. *Anonymous.* UnTE

...Drums, drums should have beaten/for the arrival of my mother. The Arrival of My Mother. Keith Wilson. DFF; GP

"Drunk/"blest/"gebentsht A Letter to Paul Celan in Memory. Jerome Rothenberg. VWA

Drunk on its own scents,/Asks nothing of life. Paralytic. Sylvia Plath. FaBoWP

Drunk water cold and clear from an inexhaustible hidden fountain. The Wilderness. Kathleen Raine. BoWoP; PoSH

The drunken butterflies sit/With opening and shutting wings. Song of the Fallen Deer. *Anonymous.* OBVE

A drunken parson and wicked people. Legsby, Lincolnshire. *Anonymous.* GBP

The drunken sea bards come/to lounge on all its Capes. Still Pond, No More Moving. Howard Moss. NYBP

Drunken/Stricken with fists. The Drunk Man. *Anonymous.* NOAV

Drunkenly in the billows/Of your nude jubilation. Our Canoe Idles in the Idling Current. Kenneth Rexroth. ErPo

Dry bones make good flutes. The Hollow Flute. Avner Strauss. VWA

The dry bones shall awake, and shout–"Our God is nigh!" The Desolate Valley. Thomas Pringle. OBTV

The dry indifferent glare in my mind's eye/wavered but burned on. The Closed World. Denise Levertov. NoP

The dry land Earth, and the great receptacle/Of congregated waters He call'd Seas. Over All the Face of Earth Main Ocean Flowed. John Milton. EtS

Dry-mouthed and still/Beneath the charmed hill? The Firstling. Peter Davison. WeW

A dry old clerk in sleeves gathers it all. Missouri Town. John Palen. AMV-80

Dry-rot at ease till the Judgment-day! Garden Fancies. Robert Browning. CTC; EnLi 1-2; VLP

...The dry stalks of daylilies/marking a stillness we can't keep. Over and Over Stitch. Jorie Graham. HaCAP

A dry tuft of grass. Haiku: "Once upon a time". Issa. WSC

Dry up/like/unwatered/weed Incantation to Get Rid of a Sometime Friend. Emanuel DiPasquale. TW

Dry up my tears, and dwell within her heart. Violets and Roses. *Anonymous.* OBSC

The dry/wet buds/and the cut. Purple Dry Buds. Michelle Roberts. LFAC

Dry wind only is still talking among the oldest stones. Conserving the Magnitude of Uselessness. Archie Randolph Ammons. NoAm

Dubois returning condemned lives/to pure glories... The Living Truth. Sterling D. Plumpp. PoBA

Duck and cover! It takes a man/to be a mouse this night," he said. Mouse Night: One of Our Games. William Stafford. NCSH

The duck/'s web-/foot, like a candle, in a quart of gin we'd killed. To Delmore Schwartz. Robert Lowell. NoAm

Duck shee shantamar. Dips or Counting Out Rhymes: "Dip, dip, allebadar." *Anonymous.* GBP

Duckle, duckle, daisy. Duckle, Duckle, Daisy. Leroy F. Jackson. ChBR

Ducks, crying out! We look at them, and leave them to go their/way. The Djanggawul Cycle, 57. *Anonymous.* WTO

E

'E'd 'a' split 'is fice in 'arf.   Epitaph on a Marf. *Anonymous.*   PV

E'een the olf stone pit, deep as house is high,/Was brimming o'er and floated o'er the top.   Deluge.   John Clare.   BoNaP

E'en for itself to love thy soul-ennobling art.   To Benjamin West. Washington Allston.   AnAmPo

E'en from my heart the strings do break.   Of Corinna's Singing.   Thomas Campion.   EnLit; HBV 1-2

E'en like the passage of an angel's tear/That falls through the clear ether silently.   Sonnet: "To one who has been long in city pent."   John Keats. FaBoBe; FPL; LoBV

E'en on death's journey remember thou me.   Remember Thou Me. *Anonymous.*   WTO

E'en should'st thou wed a woman,/From thee we'll not depart.   Epigram: "Now art thou fair, Diodorus."   Strato.   PeHV

–'E'en so, it is so!'   Saul.   Robert Browning.   OAEP; VLP

E'en such is he who died and yet did laugh/To see these lines writ for his epitaph.   Like to the Thundering Tone.   Richard Corbet.   NA

E'en then let Fate my Matty spare,/And when thou dy'st then turn a Star.   On My Pretty Marten.   Charles Cotton.   FM

E'er once again we shall drift/On the turbulent, open sea.   Quiet Waters. Blanche Shoemaker Wagstaff.   BLPA

E.g. your rage when I switched off the light!   Do Not Go Gentle (parody). Tim Hopkins.   BXAP

E-I, E-I, Oh!   Old MacDonald Had a Farm.   *Anonymous.*   FSW

E're I prove false to faith, or strange to you.   Deare, If You Change. *Anonymous.*   AtBAP; PoEL 1-5

'E's crowdin' us out!–'er majesty's poet–soldier an' sailor too!   A Ballad (parody).   Guy Wetmore Carryl.   BXAP; Par

An' 'e winked back–the same as us!   When 'omer Smote 'is Bloomin' Lyre. Rudyard Kipling.   Par

Each a glimpse and gone for ever!   From a Railway Carriage.   Robert Louis Stevenson.   OxBChV; TiPo

Each a mirror/for man's eyes.   During the Eichmann Trial (excerpt). Denise Levertov.   NMP

...Each a potential source of precision/and invention, given a hand to hold it. La Reproduction Interdite / Not to Be Reproduced.   Kathleen Fraser. NPGG

Each and all these,–and more, and more than these!   In a Spring Grove. William Allingham.   IrPN

Each answering other, praises pouring forth.   Benedicite.   Anna Callender Brackett.   AA

Each beaten leaf contains/Ten thousand pains.   Stormy Night in Autumn. Chu Shu-chen.   BoWoP

Each beating hour/Rings false.   Low Tide.   Lynette Roberts.   NeBP

Each bird is husd'd, that stretch'd its pinions to the/day.   Sleep upon the World.   Alcman.   AWP

Each breast does feel, no braver fuel choose/Than that, which one day worms may chance refuse?   Sonnet: "My God, where is that ancient heat towards thee."   George Herbert.   OAEL 1-2

...Each bubble/Contains a complete eye of water.   The Glass Bubbles. Samuel Greenberg.   LiTA; NePA

Each by contraction multiply'de.   An Hymeneall Dialogue.   Thomas Carew. AnAnS 2; SeCP

Each calling on the other's name!   So Beautiful You Are, Indeed.   Irene Rutherford McLeod.   HBMV

Each care decays, and yet my sorrow springs.   Description of Spring.   Henry Howard.   AnEnPo; AtBAP; ElL; LiTB; LoBV; OAEP; OBEV; SeCePo; SeCeV

Each carefully telling you/what it knows about light.   Psalm.   Patricia Hooper.   HoAn

Each cruel deed unto his brow/Adds one thorn more.   Quatrain.   Charles G. Blanden.   PGD

Each day rises barren and bare.   Brow of Nephin.   *Anonymous.*   AnIL

Each day's light has more significance these days   Getting Up Ahead of Someone (Sun).   Frank O'Hara.   ANYP

Each day/transforms/into another day.   Circles.   Elizabeth Knies. AMV-80

Each does us credit, and we know it too.   The Evangelist.   Donald Davie. NePoEA

Each doing what it should be doing,/and ignoring you completely.   Time Piece.   William Cole.   ELU; GrPl; PPJ

Each drug that numbs alerts another nerve to pain.   Soft Wood.   Robert Lowell.   LiTM

Each dune looked up from dreamy memories.   The Sea.   Herman Gorter. LiTW

Each dusty road leads to Appomattox now.   John Brown's Body.   Stephen Vincent Benét.   BeLS

Each feels the amazing, murderous legends move.   The Figures on the Frieze. Alastair Reid.   ErPo; NYBP

Each finds his hurt heart strangely comforted.   I Think That God Is Proud. Grace Noll Crowell.   PoToHe

Each fled away to heaven, winged like a bird.   The Apple-Tree.   Nancy Campbell.   AnIV

...Each flowering shrub,/hides a policeman with a club.   Central Park. Robert Lowell.   LiTM; NYP

Each found the likeness in his thought.   The Painter Who Pleased Nobody and Everybody.   John Gay.   BeLS

Each from a blue-veined pot.   Crockery.   Julia Budenz.   AMV-80

Each furious thought that's driving through my brain/Screams in its fresh young wonder and delight.   Lamorna Cove.   William Henry Davies. BrPo

Each gift is gold and frankincense and myrrh.   Alchemy.   Adelaide Love. PGD

"Each heart holds the secret;/Kindness is the word."   What Is Good.   John Boyle O'Reilly.   GoTF; HBV 1-2; HBVY; PoToHe; TreF; WBLP

Each holds that bruise to her heart like a stone/And aches for rain. Kingfisher Flat.   William Empson.   PoM

Each hour,/That hath bewitched me.   Love's Witchery.   Thomas Lodge. EIL

Each hour we are new souls: o love, each hour/Meet me the first time, say me last good-bye.   A Valentine.   Hal Summers.   ChMP

Each hunger-striking for its daily bread.   Virgin Country.   Roy McFadden. NeIP

...Each/In a soft hat, fill/With dust-dolls their long boxes).   Nightdream. Charles Wright.   LCAP

Each in an empty frame!   Luck.   Evan V. Shute.   CaP

Each in his paradoxical way/Does a lot for the famous critic K.   A St. Cecilia's Day Epigram.   Peter Porter.   ELU

Each in his turn.   The Man Who Named Children.   Alberto Rios.   LTB

Each in the end when each is overthrown.   Beyond Religion.   Lucretius (Titus Lucretius Carus).   AWP

...Each indiscretion/a caress of faithlessness/a feather to touch/you by.   On Why I Would Betray You.   Jorie Graham.   AMV-81

Each leading its oafishonging/To be a shooting star.   Fireflies.   Carolyn Hall.   FaPON; HBVY

...Each leaf/imprinted, syllables in our lives.   Writing to Aaron.   Denise Levertov.   FAZ

Each life its task to do.   Summer Sabbath.   Jessie E. Sampter.   TrJP

Each little lyrical/Grave or satirical/Musical miracle!   On a Fly-Leaf of Burn's Songs.   Frederic Lawrence Knowles.   HBV 1-2

Each lonely and earthly, wanting to be celestial.   His Body.   Sandra McPherson.   AmPA; GeTw; GP

Each making answer, Here am I, send me.   O God, Send Men.   Elizabeth Burrowes.   AH

Each man take his share!   Fair Thou Art.   Mordecai Ben Isaac.   TrJP

Each man where he can, wearing out the day in his manner.   Sextus Propertius: Turning Aside from Battles.   Ezra Pound.   WaaP

Each minute the last minute.   Living.   Denise Levertov.   VGW

Each morning I will know it.   Search.   Claribel Alegría.   BoWoP

Each muscle sink to itself, and separately enjoy.   High Summer.   Ebenezer Jones.   NOBV

Each night a star to guide thy feet to Heaven.   Opportunity.   Walter Malone.   BLPA; BLPL; FaBoBe; WBLP; YaD

Each night/I prepare our departures.   The Elephant.   Sandra Hochman. BoAnP

Each night, in that cement silence,/we were the only witnesses.   The Slaughterhouse Boys.   William Meissner.   AMV-81

Each night/Is trifoliate, strange to the touch.   The Wrong Kind of Insurance. John Ashbery.   NYP

...Each night, the city becomes a butterfly,/trembling in its oil.   Suburban Dusk.   Bert Meyers.   EAS

Each of her tones and of her looks/Would have its four, not lines, but books.   To Helen.   Winthrop Mackworth Praed.   LoBV

Each of them a sight more lovely/Than the screens around your bed.   Shitty. Kingsley Amis.   OxBC; TW

Each of these a promise you could never keep.   The Wrecker Driver Foresees Your Death.   David Baker.   MAYP

Each of us here as divinely as any is here.   You, Whoever You Are.   Walt Whitman.   AmFN

Each of us like you/stands apart, like you/fit to be worshiped.   Adonis. Hilda ("H. D.") Doolittle.   AP; AWP; BoC; InPo; LiTA; PoPl

Each on her shining glockenspiel.   Two Hundred Girls in Tights & Halters. Daniel Gerard Hoffman.   ELU

Each one a word resisting/everything that conspires to silence.   In the City of Bogota.   Greg Pape.   MAYP

Each one, by nature, loves to be a king.   Ambition.   Robert Herrick.   CaPo

Each one has ermine or satin robes, and bears above/A wand and crown. The Queens.   Robert Fitzgerald.   NYBP

Each one, in form grotesque, playing its part/In the fantastic Mardi Gras of Night. Night's Mardi Gras. Edward J. Wheeler. HBV 1-2

Each one kept shroud, nor to his neighbour gave/Or word, or look, or action of despair. Hyperion. John Keats. FaBoPP

Each one left a little token,/For above they live again. Ashtabula Disaster. Julia A. Moore. OBAL

Each one making possible the next From a Survivor. Adrienne Rich. CAPP; GP

Each one/With earth foundation/Reaches up. Against Gravity. Edith E. Cutting. AMV-80

Each ordinance appointed/To save us, will reveal. Arise, O Glorious Zion. William G. Mills. AH

...Each pause/brings us to bells or flames. Earliest Spring. Denise Levertov. LCAP

...Each pointed, star-tipped breast/Invites complete approval east and west. Epitaph of a Stripper. William Jay Smith. AMV-80

Each raindrop shares the ocean's fate. Rain. Einar Benediktsson. LiTW

...Each rung/on the drainrack trumpets swansong, swansong. The Psychonaut Sonnets: Jones. Albert Goldbarth. SM

Each second I'm new-born from some new grave. Struggle. Sidney Lanier. CBEP; LiTA; OxBA

Each silently, but not alone. You Are the Brave. Raymond Richard Patterson. NBP; NIP; PoBA

Each Song a Sacrifice. The Masque of the Inner-Temple and Gray's Inne. Francis Beaumont. OBS

Each song I write leaves in its wake. My Flying Machine. Louis Daniel Brodsky. AMV-80

Each Soul doth tend its own immortal flame,/Fans it to Heaven, or smothers it in shame. Life's Chequer-Board. John Oxenham. TRV

Each springtime when my friends, not I,/sit in some bar or outdoor cafe,/drinking beer. Sestina to the Common Glass of Beer: I Do Not Drink Beer. Diane Wakoski. SM

Each squelch of leather on mud complaining, "But where are you going?" Remembering Lunch. Douglas Dunn. OxBC

Each stares at his own self-love. The Triumph of Chastity. Barbara Howes. NePoAm-2

Each step tuned to the flap of your wings. Raven at Lemon Creek Jail. Thomas Waltner. LFAC

Each stone on your roads speaks to us of the beating of/your heart Open Earth. Clarisse Nicoidski. VWA

...Each subnormal boot-/black heart is pulsing to its ant-egg dole. A Mad Negro Soldier Confined at Munich. Robert Lowell. FaBoMo; NMP; OxBC

Each thought the other/A bit of a twitch. Geeandess. William Cole. PV

Each time men touch you and you freeze in hell The Comedian. Irving Layton. AMV-81

Each time with gently disapproving hands. Baptism. Alden Nowlan. PoL

Each to their cloister did they gone/Sine temptationibus. The Friar and the Nun. Anonymous. GBP

An' each took aff his several way,/Resolv'd to meet some ither day. The Twa Dogs. Robert Burns. CABL; CEP

Each vainly rubbing the 'cursed spot/Which brands him Cain. For Mack C. Parker. Pauli Murray. PoBA

Each virgin flowerest faint and wan/With the bliss of her own sweet breath so pure. The White Anemone. "Owen Meredith." GN

Each waiting for a comet in the sky. Death & Empedocles 444 B.C. Horace Gregory. PoA

Each was an angel, and earth paradise. Don Juan. George Gordon, Lord Byron. CoBE; HAP

Each wave with a counterfeit shimmer. Sexy Food Stamps. Jeffrey Miller. APU

Each week he lives one brief and glorious day. Pedro. Phoebe W. Hoffman. GoYe

Each will eat of the provision he acquired. Humorous Verse: "The caliph shot a gazelle." Abu Dolama. TTY

Each wishing for the sword that severs all. Modern Love, I. George Meredith. EnLoPo; HBV 1-2; HeIP; NBM; NOBV; NoP; OAEL 1-2; OAEP; PoEL 1-5; VLP

Each with a little lighter heart. Christmas at Melrose. Leslie Pinckney Hill. BANP

Each word by itself, and all if it need be. Piers the Plowman's Creed. Anonymous. MeEV

Each year a daughter or a son. The River Don. Anonymous. GBP

Each year I hoped they'd keep, knew they would not. Blackberry-Picking. Seamus Heaney. BoNaP

Each year they are the first to rise. Crocus. Joan Murray. AMV-80

Eachie, peachie, pearie, plum. Dips or Counting Out Rhymes: "Eachie, peachie, pearie, plum." Anonymous. GBP

Eager saints and angels ask in Heaven's zone,/Who is this? Bride Song. Christina Georgina Rossetti. OBVV

Eager to reach the land of Prester John. On the Edge of the Pacific. Theodore Maynard. CAW

Eagle beagle, bug grub, boar bear. Florida. Dannie Abse. OxBC

The Eagle of the Blue. The Eagle of the Blue. Herman Melville AA

Eagle of the north-west, thou hast heard/the voice of the Reim-kennar. The Pirate (excerpt). Sir Walter Scott. OAEP

...Eagle Runner/Abandons the city of red rain, and dives/Into the sea at the end of the pier. The Novelty Shop. Duane Niatum. CDW

The eagle scans his vast domain. The Eagle. William Sharp. FM

The eagle waves away/turning the earth/as an edge in the sky. Eagles. Elizabeth Woody. STE

An eagle, weary of his mighty wings,/With anxious inquest fills his mortal span! On Startling Some Pigeons. Charles Tennyson Turner. PB

...The ear/hear's time's cadence, her ontoward flight. Ear Is Not Deaf. Irene Dayton. GoYe

Earl Douglas was buried at the braken-bush/And the Percy led captive away. The Battle of Otterburn (B vers.). Anonymous. BaBo; BSV; ESPB; FaBoCh; GoTS; HBV 1-2; OnMSP; OxBB

The Earl of Stamford's ae dochter/And the kind o' England's brither. The Shepherd's Dochter. Anonymous. OxBB

Early and late the backdrop is for joy. This World. Abbie Huston Evans. NePoAm

...Early/and late, this hour has closed/around us. The Meeting. Tess Gallagher. GeTw

The early and the latter rain! For an Autumn Festival (excerpt). John Greenleaf Whittier. PGD

Early Early Early/Huuuuuuuuuuuuuuuuuuuu–beeeeeeeeeeeeeeee Prelude to Akwasidae. Anonymous. TTY

Early, early Easter Day. Early, Early Easter Day. Aileen Fisher. SiSoSe

Early in the morning! Early in the Morning. Anonymous. AmSS

Early may fly the Babylonian woe. On the Late Massacre in Piedmont. John Milton. ATP; AWP; BiP; DiPo; EnL; EnLit; ExPo; FaPo; GTBS; GTBS-P; HAP; HBV 1-2; HeIP; InPo; JCP; LiTB; LoBV; MBW 1-2; NIP; NOBE; NOCV; NoP; OAEP; OBWP; PoEL 1-5; PPoe; PPP; SeCeV; UnPo; ViBoPo; WaaP; WeW

Early to Bed and Early to Rise. Four Epitaphs. Sylvia Townsend Warner. MoBrPo

Early, with my own name in mind. The Well-Travelled Roadway. John Newlove. NeAC

Earnest of mind and of motion lithe. The Confirmers. Archie Randolph Ammons. TAP

Earnestly they are inflated, diminished...and away... School Cadets. Anne Elder. CBAP

An earring for the goddess of the east. The Sun (excerpt). Vidya. PBWP

Ears poise before decision, scenting danger. The Watershed. W. H. Auden. OAEL 1-2

The earth again with honey sweet and salty. True Vine. Elinor Wylie. AnFE; APA; LiTA

Earth and heaven's latest born. See the Crocus' Golden Cup. Joseph Mary Plunkett. OnYI

Earth and her vines may shroud our murderings,/But what shall kill immortal memory? To God. Furnley Maurice. BoAV 030

–Earth, and the world to come. Chorus of the Elements. John Henry, Cardinal Newman. OBVV

Earth around will resound/Joyful hymns to heaven. God of Might, God of Right. Anonymous. TrJP

Earth breeds and beckons to the stubborn plough. Farm Child. R. S. Thomas. BoNaP; ChMP

Earth crumbles Some San Francisco Poems. George Oppen. NNaP

Earth, earth, earth, thy cold is keen,/Earth grown old. Advent. Christina Georgina Rossetti. TrCP; VLP

The earth exhales. Slough. Sir John Betjeman. DBV; MoBrPo

Earth fell on the box and the biscuit tin. Heart Burial. Geoffrey Grigson. PoL

Earth has become a smiling Paradise. A Christmas Carol. Anonymous. OHIP

"Earth has no sorrow that God cannot heal." Come, Ye Disconsolate. Thomas Moore. CAW; WGRP

The earth his bones, the heavens possess his goost. Wyat Resteth Here, that Quicke Coulde Never Rest. Henry Howard, Earl of Surrey. AAS; EnPo; FCP; NCEP; NoP

The earth his sober inn/And quiet pilgrimage. The Man of Life Upright. Thomas Campion. AAS; ElL; OAEP; PoRA; ViBoPo

...Earth holds firm under my heel. Asphodel. David Malouf. CBAP

Earth holds her breath to hear/White silence on white silence, whirl. Snowflakes. Alice Behrend. GoYe

Earth into the space that is earth. Day Twenty-Three. Victor Coleman. NOBC

The earth is created, and moves us/on our journey/towards remembering. Tonight Everyone in the World Is Dreaming the Same Dream. Susan Litwack. VWA

Earth is enlarged to inherit/The soul of your Lincoln and mine. The Soul of Lincoln. Chauncey R. Piety. PGD

The earth is friendly as a mother's breast.   Rules for the Road.   Edwin Markham.   GoTF; TreFT

The earth is hell when thou leav'st to appear.   Fair Summer Droops.   Nashe [(or Nash)] Thomas.   EIL; LoBV; OBSP

...The earth is hot,/Alive beneath me with an ageless rot.   The Dead.   John Williams.   NePoAm-2

Earth is our dancing place now.   All the Spirit Powers Went to Their Dancing Place.   Gary Snyder.   UnPo

The earth is taken: this is not your home.   Travelogue for Exiles.   Karl Shapiro.   AnFE; MoAmPo; TrJP

Earth is too harsh for Heaven to be/One little hour in jeopardy.   To a Calvinist in Bali.   Edna St. Vincent Millay.   NoAm

The earth is white/far inland.   Far inland go my sad thoughts.   Anonymous.   BoWoP

Earth its home and earth its tomb.   First Philosopher's Song.   Aldous Huxley.   AWP; HBMV; InPo

...Earth itself/Appeared the place of pilgrimage it is.   Recollections of a Day's Journey in Spain.   Robert Southey.   OBTV

The earth lost in/A shudder of heat.   On Mt. Iron.   Charles Brasch.   AnNZ

The earth made windows. Who watched our homecoming.   Crabbing.   Norman Levine.   CaP; OBCV

The earth must burn, ere we for Christ can look.   Caelica, LXXXIX.   Fulke, Lord Brooke Greville.   FCP; NOCV

The earth no gain.   The Blank Book Letter.   Samuel Greenberg.   LiTA

The Earth poised on his broad hands.   Ploughman at the Plough.   Louis Golding.   HBMV; OHIP

The earth renders the farmer in due season/Corn.   Seed.   Herman Charles Bosman.   PeSA

Earth reserves no blessing/For the unblessed of Heaven!   A. E.   Emily Bronte.   NBM

Earth's axis varies; your dark central cone/Wavers, a candle's shadow, at the end.   Legal Fiction.   William Empson.   CMoP; ExPo; FaBoMo; LiTB; LiTM; MoVE; NoAm; NoP

Earth's blackest day and whitest day,/Were just three days apart.   Calvary and Easter.   Susan (Sarah Chauncey Woolsey) Coolidge.   WBLP

Earth's bluish animals are few.   Variation on a Sentence.   Louise Bogan.   FM; ImOP

Earth's dearest treasure is the few/True friends who love and prize you.   Don't.   Anonymous.   STF

Earth's ignorant nullity made strange with flowers.   Prehistoric Burials.   Siegfried Sassoon.   MoBrPo

Earth's last diaper hung in the sun to dry.   Letter to Karl Shapiro.   E. L. Mayo.   MiAP

Earth's loftiest head, found upright to the end.   To Victor Hugo.   Algernon Charles Swinburne.   OBVV

The earth's moving nearer to truth and to dread.   I Was Washing outside in the Darkness.   Osip Mandelstam.   FaBoPV

The earth's refreshed by frequent showers.   Weather Wisdom.   Anonymous.   GoTF; HBVY; TreF

Earth's saddest day and gladdest day,/Were just three days apart!   An Easter Song.   Susan (Sarah Chauncey Woolsey) Coolidge.   TRV

Earth's sea white with waves.   Adore We the Lord.   Anonymous.   NOBI

Earth's wish, and the sun's prayer, in granite kept.   Who Shapes a Balustrade?   Conrad Aiken.   EyDe

Earth's wrongs are ended.   Of Those Who Walk Alone.   Richard Burton.   HBV 1-2

The earth says to the earth, All this is ours.   Inscribed in Melrose Abbey.   Anonymous.   FaBoEE; FaBoRV

The earth sees his works, and heaven knows his/name!   God.   Alphonse Marie Louis de Lamartine.   ILwL

Earth shall be fair, and all her folk be one.   Turn Back, O Man.   Clifford Bax.   NOCV; TRV

The earth-soul Freedom, that only/Lives, and that only is God.   To Walt Whitman in America.   Algernon Charles Swinburne.   EnLi 1-2; VLP

The earth, that first time/seen from the air.   Lamentations.   Louise Gluck.   MAYP

The earth that wakes one human heart to feeling/Can centre both the worlds of Heaven and Hell.   Stanzas.   Emily Bronte.   ChRP; HBV 1-2; LiTB; LoBV; OAEL 1-2; OAEP; OBNC; PBWP

Earth, the chatterer, father of all/speech . . . . .   Paterson.   William Carlos Williams.   NoAm

The earth, the living church of ancient joy.   I Never See the Red Rose Crown the Year.   John Masefield.   EnLi 1-2

The earth, the sea, and the air!   The Song of a Heathen.   Richard Watson Gilder.   AA; WGRP

Earth, thou hast not such another.   On Margaret Ratcliffe.   Ben Jonson.   SeCP

Earth-thrown singer, who burnt his bridges.   The Moment of Vision.   Richard Eberhart.   MoRP

"Earth to earth, and dust to dust!"   Death and Resurrection.   George Croly.   WGRP

Earth to my mother earth,/Spirit to thee.   Overlord.   Bliss Carman.   CaP

The earth too, as my cradle swung,/Drifted into slumber deep.   Night.   Gabriela (Lucila Godoy Alcayaga) Mistral.   LiTW

Earth trembles waiting/For the sun again...   Earth Trembles Waiting.   Blanche Shoemaker Wagstaff.   PoLf

The earth turns over, though the street is still.   Waiting for the Post.   Dorothy Auchterlonie.   CBAP

The earth turns white,/far inland./Ija-je-ja.   Song of the Rejected Woman.   Kibkarjuk.   WPOW

The earth was covered/with the bones of winter/for as far as the eye could see   The Year of Winter.   Frank LaPena.   STE

Earth were exchanged for heaven,/Could Time his passing cease!   Beside the Blackwater.   Norreys Jephson O'Conor.   HBMV

Earth, whom the vast stars crown.   To a Traveler.   Lionel Pigot Johnson.   AnEnPo; MoBrPo; NBM

The earth will silently open,/silently close.   Sinkholes.   Janet Reed McFatter.   GrPl

Earth, with her thousand voices, praises GOD.   Hymn before Sunrise, in the Vale of Chamouni.   Samuel Taylor Coleridge.   EnRP; ERoP 1-2; MCCG; OAEP; OxBoCh; WGRP

Earth your face fern coal   After Elegies.   Jean Valentine.   LCAP

Earthlings! If you are my equals,/prove it and fly! Fly!   Crippled Child at the Window.   Melissa Cannon.   AMV-80

An earthly mansion is only grief,/prisoners all the living.   A Child in Prison.   Gofraidh Fionn O Dalaigh.   NOBI

Earthward to lift to the dazzle/Any answering form.   Dazzle.   Dorothy Roberts.   NOBC

Ease after war, death after life does greatly please.   The Faerie Queene.   Edmund Spenser.   MOS; PoPle; SeCePo

Ease came with song, he could not buy with gold.   Idylls.   Theocritus.   AWP; OBVE

The ease with which beauty is beauty   By Fiat of Adoration.   Oscar Williams.   LiTL; LiTM; NePA

Easier to love, we so should find,/It is than to be just and kind.   The Victories of Love.   Coventry Patmore.   GBL

Easily onward, through flowers and weed.   Endymion.   John Keats.   ATP

Easily stopped what/had hardly started,/our song together.   Wulf and Eadwacer.   Richard Ryan.   BoWoP; CIP; TrGrPo

The East put out a single flag,/And signed the fete away.   A drop fell on the apple tree.   Emily Dickinson.   BoNaP

The east sky glints with light,/And it is Christmas Day!   Hagar.   Francis Lauderdale Adams.   OxBS

The East wind blows it back again.   The South Wind Brings Wet Weather.   Anonymous.   HBV 1-2

Easter is back in the beautiful world--/Sing, everyone, sing!   Easter Joy.   Nancy Byrd Turner.   YeAr

Easter's coming!"/And they hurried.   Down a Sunny Easter Meadow.   Nancy Byrd Turner.   SiSoSe; SoPo

Eastward, into sunrise.   Ya Se Van Los Pastores.   Dudley Fitts.   FYAP

...Easy are the great governments and the great steamboats.   Trinity Place.   Carl Sandburg.   NYP

Easy in the presence of her lover.   Laboratory Poem.   James Merrill.   InPK; MAT; MP; NePoEA-2; TwCP

Easy lies the head that wears/A crown among both bulls and bears.   For Little Boys Destined for Big Business.   Samuel Hoffenstein.   DBV

Easy live and quiet die.   The Bride of Lammermoor (excerpt).   Sir Walter Scott.   BSV

An easy morning's ride.   A route of evanescence.   Emily Dickinson.   AmePo; AmLP; ForPo; NoP; PoEL 1-5; SoSe

Easy to grow.   Easy to Grow.   John Giorno.   ANYP

Easy to see how starlight/becomes deadly/when you walk with him.   The Access.   Henry Kanabus.   APU

& Eat & drink & wave their hands, clear at the top.   Technique.   Philip Pierson.   AMV-80

"Eat, eat me, soul, and thou shalt never die."   I Kenning Through Astronomy.   Edward Taylor.   AmPP

Eat it/and find a pearl in my mouth.   Art.   Hjalmar Flax.   InW

Eat oats, eating hay, munch! munch! munch!   Work Horses.   Edith Newlin Chase.   SoPo

Eat soda crackers,/Roll on the ground.   Roll on the Ground.   Anonymous.   AmFP; FSW

Eat! Stuff! and turn your back on pork.   Mutton (parody).   Anonymous.   BXAP

Eat the/quarterpound reality.   Diner.   Archie Randolph Ammons.   PoL

...Eat, then watch/the core brown in your hand.   Adam and Eve at the Garden Gate.   Marsha Pomerantz.   VWA

EAT/300 FEET.   The Anthropophagites See a Sign on NC Highway 177...   Jonathan Williams.   OBAL

Eat up the honey.   What Does the Bee Do?   Christina Georgina Rossetti.   OxBChV; SUS; TiPo

Eate, Eate me, Soul, and thou shalt never dy.   Meditations.   Edward Taylor.   AmP; AP; LiTA; NoP; TAP

Eaten by a woman/Who saw nothing   Seated on her bed legs spread open. Joyce Mansour.   BoWoP

Eating cherries off a plate.   One, Two, Three, Four.   *Anonymous.*   OxNR

Eating only enough so as not to say good-bye.   The Street.   Gary Soto. NPGG

Eating our way down.   Millions of Strawberries.   Genevieve Taggard. MoShBr; TiPo

Eating peanuts and throwing the shells.   Peanuts.   Ken Belford.   NeAC

Eating the green heart of the tree/Of man!   The Thousand and One Nights: Love.   *Anonymous.*   AWP; LiTW

Eating what I like, sound as a bell.   The Uninfected.   E. L. Mayo.   MiAP

Eats joyously with her own/real teeth.   Big Momma.   Don L. Lee.   BPo; CNA

Eats not, frequents no plays, no balls:–she's dead.   Epigrams in Distich, I: The Fine Lady Reform'd.   *Anonymous.*   FaBoEE

Eats the whole land at home.   The Sea Eats the Land at Home.   Kofi (George Williams) Awoonor.   CAD

Eavesdropping/on the talk/and laughter/of others   Tune: Endless Union.   Li Ching-chao.   PBWP

Ebony-tree with the big spreading leaves.   Animal Songs.   *Anonymous.* PeSA

Ebry time I wheel about,/I jump Jim Crow.   Jump Jim Crow.   Thomas D. Rice.   BLSo

The eccentric circle of your years.   Poet Wondering What He Is Up To.   D. J. Enright.   OxBC

Eche carde decayes, and yet my sorow springes.   Imitated from Sonetto in Morte 42.   Petrarch (Francesco Petrarca).   OBVE

Eche lovings harte would see his frynde,/And soe woulde I doe mine.   Where One Would Be.   Sir Edward Dyer.   PoEL 1-5

...Eche partie did applie/Good reasons to defende their case.... Metamorphoses.   Ovid (Publius Ovidius Naso).   CTC

Echo. Ever. Heaven.   George Herbert.   AnAnS 1; BoLiVe; SeCP; TrCP; TrGrPo

The echo groping for the sound.   Deja Vu.   J. B. Mulligan.   AMV-80

Echo I am.   Echo in a Church.   Edward, Lord Herbert of Cherbury. AnAnS 2

The echo of an echo.   To My Son, Not Yet Born.   William Virgil Davis. AMV-81

Echo of echoes, shadower of shades!   A Man of Culture.   Arthur Seymour John Tessimond.   HaMV

Echo of mine, I am amenable.   Mirror.   James Merrill.   CoAP; NePoEA-2; SM

The echo of the crippled Negro, king of the city, makes a/turn around the night in the sky...   Deep Night.   Juan Ramon Jimenez.   NYP

The echo of the grave perfects desire.   Sestina on Her Portrait.   Howard Nemerov.   WaP

The echo of thy flout of Noah's ark!   The Loon.   Theodore Harding Rand. CaP

The echo of Thy voice still feebler grows!   The Age Is Great and Strong. Victor Hugo.   WGRP

Echo through ruins like yours, Mykenai.   Remembering Mykenai.   Alfred Corn.   SM

The echo waits, the years close in.   Echo.   Elizabeth Stanton Hardy.   GoYe

Echo your thought in ours? "Destroy! Destroy!"   Brother Fire.   Louis MacNeice.   AtBAP; MoAB; NoAm; NOBE; OAEP; WaaP

Echoes!–Oh, wintery cricket, welcome thou!   Written in July, 1824.   Mary Russell Mitford.   OBRV

The echoing shore resounds Castalio's name.   The Goff. An Heroi-Comical Poem (excerpt).   Thomas Mathison.   NOEC

Echoing the light/After you were gone/Of our white-on-white.   The Snow Light.   May Sarton.   NLV

An eclipse of the sun for days and weeks/Forebodes disaster in Constantinople! Dark Aspect and Prospect.   *Anonymous.*   PeD

Eclipse while he lived, and decease at his dying.   Cardinal Bembo's Epitaph on Raphael.   Thomas Hardy.   EyDe; FaBoEE

–The Economist has gone out & heavily invested in hat-stocks.   Of How Scientists Are Often Ahead of Others in Thinking...   Michael Benedikt. SUW

Economy, economy! Who'll till this land?   American Farm, 1934.   Genevieve Taggard.   VGW

...Eden is enchanted/only till night awakes the shadow in the brush.   Eve. Jakov Fichman.   VWA

An Eden of that dim lake.   The Lake.   Edgar Allan Poe.   OBRV

Eden smells of cedar.   Raven holds his wings and sucks his stone.   Imperfect Sestina.   Phyllis Webb.   NOBC

An Eden, with my hoe and rake:/the Serpent only God could make.   In a Garden.   Donald Campbell Babcock.   NePoAm

The edge of the orchard country.   Lightning Bug.   Robert Morgan.   GeTw

The edges white/and sleek as a swan...   Swan.   Donald Hall.   LCAP

Edible necklaces/and caged red birds.   Sentences (excerpt).   Tony Harrison. OBTV

Edith Sitwell fell in love with Pope.)   A Thought in Time.   Robert Hillyer. NYBP

The edition is limited/and will soon be out of print.   Snow Anthology. Arthur Stanley Bourinot.   GoYe

Edward, thou dudest ase a shreward,/Forsoke thine eme's lore.   Against the Barons' Enemies.   *Anonymous.*   MeEL

Een de mighty fine house on de mighty high hill!   Ol' Doc' Hyar.   James Edwin Campbell.   BANP

Eena, meena, mina, mo.   Eena, Meena, Mina, Mo.   *Anonymous.*   OxNR

Eer she see the Earl of Murray/Come sounding thro the town!   The Bonny Earl of Murray (A vers.).   *Anonymous.*   BaBo

Eerie, oorie, you're oot.   Dips or Counting Out Rhymes: "Zeenty, peenty, heathery, mithery."   *Anonymous.*   GBP

Ef de train don' run, I got a mule to ride.   Alabama-Bound.   *Anonymous.* ABF

Ef He's willin', we'll pull through–/Say good-by er howdy-do!   Good-By er Howdy-Do.   James Whitcomb Riley.   CTC

Ef I leave here walkin', it's chances I might ride.   Dink's Blues. *Anonymous.*   ABF

Ef I's layin' 'mong de t'ings I's allus/knowed.   A Death Song.   Paul Laurence Dunbar.   AA; BANP; CDC; PoLf; PoNe

Ef there's thousands o' my mind.   The Biglow Papers.   James Russell Lowell.   AnNE

Ef trouble don't kill me, I'll live a long time.   I'm Sad and I'm Lonely. *Anonymous.*   AS; FSW; TrAS

Ef you don't want a lickin' all over, be sho dat dey allers/go "punk!" Kentucky Philosophy.   Harrison Robertson.   HBV 1-2

The effect is nature's/Who ignores it, and in whose impoverishment we domi-/cile.   The Ruin.   Charles Tomlinson.   NePoEA-2

Effect their beauty without robbery.   New Year.   Stephen Spender.   AWP

Eftir our deid that live may we:/Timor mortis conturbat me.   Timor Mortis Conturbat Me.   William Dunbar.   FaBoRV; NOBE

Ego needs must spoil/Such a beautiful friendship!   Paysage Moralise.   John Hollander.   ErPo; NePoEA

Egypt, Antony, farewell.   Cleopatra Dying.   Thomas Stephen Collier. BLPA; BLPL; FaBoBe; TreFT

Eh, Kathleen, the cat is gone.   The Celtic Fringe.   Stevie Smith.   FaBoNo

Eh's melten tut, arise!   Morning Song.   Kurt M. Stein.   FiBHP

...Eia, Domine Deus.   A, a, a, Domine Deus.   David Jones.   FaBoTw; NOCV

Eidolons, adrift on the night air.   The Lost Children.   Gregory Orr.   GeTw

Eight bells have struck, and my watch is/below.   Tacking Ship Off Shore. Walter Mitchell.   AA; EtS; FaBoBe; GN; HBV 1-2

Eight bells in a cracked steeple.   Preston.   *Anonymous.*   GBP

Eight men! Who speaks?   Eight Volunteers.   Lansing C. Bailey.   PAH

82. MY WHISKERS–THE WOLF'S BEARD.   Moire.   Michael McClure. EAS

Eileen! Eileen!...   The Clock's Song.   Rose Hawthorne Lathrop.   AA

Either impound it for a stray,/Or send it back to me!   The Crier.   Michael Drayton.   ElL; InvP; OAEP

Either in this world or the next.   Preludes.   Coventry Patmore.   GoBC

Either now or tomorrow or the day after that.   Girl in a Nightgown. Wallace Stevens.   OxBA

Either of them know the human thing/is not to be snow-white but to be ugly. The Dwarf.   Gerald Locklin.   DFT; GP

...Either region affords him, now his/day is done, the means of sport.   A Fisher's Apology.   Arthur Johnstone.   GoTS

Either the lunches or the dead soldiers.   Dead Soldiers.   James Fenton. OBTV; OBWP

Either thou'dst die, or thou must run away.   Sonnet: Of an Ill-Favored Lady. Guido Cavalcanti.   AWP

Either way I'll be in.   Spring.   Carole Gregory Clemmons.   PoBA

Either way, now he is dead and done with that lot.   On the Suicide of a Friend.   Reed Whittemore.   ConAP; NMP

An' eke the Council-chawmir,/Wi' shame that day.   Hallow-Fair.   Robert Fergusson.   OxBS

Elain, Tireis, Allodetta/Quiet this metal.   The Alchemist.   Ezra Pound. LiTA; NePA; WSC

"Elbow room!" laughs Daniel Boone.   Daniel Boone.   Arthur Guiterman. MaC; MoShBr

Elbows, knees, dreams, goodnight.   Young.   Anne Sexton.   NCSH

An elder was he in the Church of Christ,/Immortal at thirty; his faith sufficed. A Ballad of Redhead's Day.   Richard Butler Glaenzer.   MC; PAH

The elders find them chill, I think.   At Eighty-Seven.   Dachine Rainer. NePoAm

Eleanor, he said, or Janet Janet Janet do you dream me?   Herself.   John Holmes.   HoPM; MiAP

Eleazar was the faculty and the whole curriculum/Was five hundred gallons of New England rum.   Eleazar Wheelock.   Richard Hovey.   OBAL

Elective Monarchs cannot stand,/Nor Loves, without an equal dart.   I Am No Subject unto Fate.   *Anonymous.*   OBS

Electricity's a riot!/The End.   Electricity Is Funny!   John Currier.   GrPl

Elegant past blown out like a torchere. Cypress Grove. Austin Clarke. IPY

Element to element. The Foundered Tram. Harold Monro. BrPo

An elemental alphabet/Of splintered atom, stalking germs. Signatures. Candace Thurber Stevenson. AmFN

The elements have heard, and rock and cave replied. The Leaves That Rustled on This Oak-Crowned Hill. William Wordsworth. FM; VLP

Elephant hunter, take your bow! The Elephant II. *Anonymous.* TTY

An elephant is not a load for an old man–/Nor for a young man either. Erin (Elephant). *Anonymous.* PBA

Eleu loro!/Never, O never! Song: "Where shall the lover rest." Sir Walter Scott. NBM

Eleven for England, twelve for France. One for Sorrow, Two for Mirth. *Anonymous.* PBBP

Eleven, nine, seven, five, three and one. Wheel of Fortune. *Anonymous.* FSW

The Elfin from the green grass, and from me/The summer dream beneath the tamarind tree? Sonnet–To Silence. Edgar Allan Poe. PPON

Elibank hunt again, Wat's snug at hame. Muckle-Mou'd Meg. James Ballantine. HBV 1-2

Elijah's Chariot born on Seraph's wings,/Mounts with this Treasure to the port of Bliss. An Elegiack Verse On the Death of the Pious and Profound... Nehemiah Walter. SCAP

Elle continua de rire comme une hyene. Everything Is Swimming. Stevie Smith. FaBoNo

"Elliot of Lariston, Elliot for aye!" Lock the Door, Lariston. James Hogg. BSV; GoTS; OxBS

& The elm branch is the dryad's breast. Elm Fuck Poem. Ed Sanders. ANYP

Elongations of the coils of light itself/(engine of color) and motion (motor of form). At the Museum of Modern Art. May Swenson. NYP

The elopers/Stay at the beautiful place. Haiku: "The first night." *Anonymous.* HW

Else Crossfield, Dietzsch,/nee Schubert–British bitch! Schwiegermutterlieder. Tony Harrison. PAI

Else, how sir, did you come to be American? For My Father. Paul Potts. FaBoTw

Else I'd been riding in the clouds with angels long ago. The Stampede. Wallace D. Coburn. PoOW

Else I'm a servant to the glass/That's with Canary lined. The Resolve. Alexander Brome. CavP; EG; LiTL; OBEV

Else is he a man unkind. A Minion Wife. Nicholas Udall. EIL

Else it was he. Oberon, the Fairy Prince: A Catch. Ben Jonson. EIL; FM

Else Muse, awake her not. To His Valentine. Michael Drayton. AtBAP; PoEL 1-5

Else never rejoice, till I hear the voice,/That The King Enjoys His Own Again. Martin Parker. OBS

Else none at all in aught proves excellent. Love's Labour's Lost. William Shakespeare. PP

Else tears heap all within one clay-cold hill. To Emily Dickinson. Hart Crane. CMoP; ForPo; NoAm; NoP; TAP

Else the next cloud that vails my skies,/Drives all these thoughts away. O Lord, My Best Desire Fulfil. William Cowper. OxBoCh

–Else what is born lies nameless in her lap. The Rape of Europa. Richard P. Blackmur. CrMA

Else why these low graves laid so near,/In this forgotten place? Sometime It May Be. Arthur Colton. HBV 1-2

Else you'll be singing Too-ral-loo, etc. Vilikins and His Dinah. Edward Laman Blanchard. VLP

Elsewhere and far He died, but here, oh at heart, He rises! London Night. Kathleen Raine. NeBP

Elsewhere you must write this poem/because there is nothing more to do. Notes towards a Poem That Can Never Be Written. Margaret Atwood. NOBC

Elude me and go drifting out of sight/like the receding fields. Journey. Sam Harrison. NeIP

Eluding every word I would fit it to. The Effect of Snow. Robert Finch. ACV

Elusively life's mystery. Simplicity Aims Circularly. Anna Walters. VoR

The Elysian ghosts shall never know the same. To Delia. Samuel Daniel. OBSC

Le 'em put their trust in the hands of God. Jay Gould's Daughter (with music). *Anonymous.* AS

Embedded in this crystalline/precipitate of time. Quod Tegit Omnia. Yvor Winters. MoVE; QFR

Embers of a dying winter fire. Pilgrimage to Hennessey's. Steven Sher. AMV-81

Emblem, earnest, of the rest/That remaineth for the blest. Day of God! Thou Blessed Day. Hannah Flagg Gould. AH

Emblem of hope and love through future years. The Lady of the Lake. Sir Walter Scott. ViBoPo

Emblems, assurance/of a world that was always his own. My Father & the Figtree. Naomi Shihab. GP

Emblems of the bright and better land. Flowers. Henry Wadsworth Longfellow. HBV 1-2

Emblems of the inexplicable will. Reconciliation. John Hall Wheelock. CrMA

Embrace and kiss and love me in despite. Thou Art Not Fair. Thomas Campion. AAS; AtBAP; EG; EIL; EnLoPo; EnRePo; InvP; ViBoPo

Embroidered on my sleeve/is wet with tears. Correspondence:. Lady Ise. BoWoP

Embroidered the mantle is/Of your maidenhead. To Mistress Margery Wentworth. John Skelton. CBEP; EBEV; EG; EnLoPo; LoBV; NOBE; OAEL 1-2; OBEV; OBSC; TrGrPo; ViBoPo

The emerald dragon breaks his teeth. A Seamark. Bliss Carman. PeCV

Emeralds big as half the county. Epigram: "Ireland never was contented." Walter Savage Landor. FaBoEE

Emerson's the last famous poet/I thought I'd ever meet. In the Garden. Tom Schmidt. NeAC

Emit small propitious birds. Conditions. Jose Luis Vega. InW

Emitting crumby titters. The Haunted Oven. X. J. Kennedy. WSC

Empire is no more! and now the lion & wolf shall cease. The Marriage of Heaven and Hell. William Blake. LAuP

Employ me discreetly,/That peace may possess me. Prayer. Eduard Moricke. TrPWD

Employ me, mighty Love, to dig the Mine. The Thraldome. Abraham Cowley. SeCV 1-2

Emporcelained, became/A term for excellence. The Byfield Rabbit. Katherine Hoskins. SaC

Emptied of all its sorrow and its dread! Head of Medusa. Marya Zaturenska. MoAmPo

Empty as a new boat,/Home. Sleeping Pill. Diana O Hehir. AMV-81

An empty boat, floating, adrift. Written on the Wall at Chang's Hermitage. Tu Fu. HoPM; NaP

Empty chrysalids of that bright ephemerid the soul. Natura Naturans. Kathleen Raine. NYBP

The empty conclusion that is rooted/In the convulsion of our lives. Our lives in captivity. A Green Refrain. Avraham Huss. VWA

Empty empty empty/As death Embrace the Bride. Joyce Mansour. PBWP

An empty lap, an hour to tea, a knit, a nod, a nap, ennui. Anno Domini. E. M. Walker. PoL

Empty me of myself, that when I work,/All that I work for, never concerns me. Invocation (excerpt). Theodore Spencer. TrPWD

Empty/receives most. Blessings Are. Cid Corman. GP

...The empty road/soared east and west. No static. Air. Ohio. John Updike. AMV-80

Empty saddles in the old corral. Empty Saddles. *Anonymous.* BPAW

The empty salads of English advent and the formulae of/seajoy. Lusty Juventus. Charles Madge. FaBoMo

The empty shacks/home A Dream of Women. Carolyn Maisel. IHMS

An empty sky, shadowy with consummations Sleep. Mei-mei Berssenbrugge. LTB

Empty temples–a decade of dark-blue/sins, son, worse than you. Dream Songs. John Berryman. TAP

Empty the rummer while you are able,/Two Sundays before Lent. Gracey Nugent. Austin Clarke. CIP

The empyrean is a void abyss. The City of Dreadful Night. James (1834-82) Thomson. GTBS

En mi poema/sorpresa. Poem in Nueva York. Cyn Zarco. APU

The enamelled bank, bruising nor herb nor flower,/That place illumined. An Interview near Florence. Samuel Rogers. OBNC

Enamored–of the Conjuror–/That spurned us–Yesterday! Heaven–Is What I Cannot Reach! Emily Dickinson. MAmP; NOCV

The enamoured rustic worships its fair hues,/Nor knows he makes the shadow, he pursues! Constancy to an Ideal Object. Samuel Taylor Coleridge. ERoP 1-2

Encapsulated everything we sought to find/And never felt to end. Lochan. Roger Smith. PoSH

Encased in his fear or facing your own Fear. Roger Stump. AMV-80

The enchanting tale, the tale of pleasing woe. Sonnet to Byron. John Keats. ERoP 1-2

Enchantress, wake again! The Lady of the Lake. Sir Walter Scott. ViBoPo

Encircles itself to a star/and dies in our place. This House. Ray A. Young Bear. CDW

Enclasped and grasped/Within thy cold embrace! To Ruin. Robert Burns. CoBE

Enclosed in my/fruit/with breath inside Swimming Pool. Maria Teresa Horta. PBWP

Enclosing us, cutting us from them personally. Glen Pean. Denis Rixson. PoSH

Encourage peace, and take to heart/A goose.   A Panegyric on Geese. Francis Sylvester ("Father Prout") Mahony.   OnYI

The end comes back. It always comes too soon.   Traction: November 22,1963. Howard Moss.   AmFN

...End fair enough.   On Spies.   Ben Jonson.   NoP; OBSP

The end is now!   The End Is Now.   Madelaine Marie.   PeHV

An end locked fast,/Bent we cannot re-bend.   Summer Is Ended. Christina Georgina Rossetti.   NOBV

End nymphs, your songs, that in the clouds are/ringing.   Diana Enamorada: Ring Forth, Fair Nymphs, Your Joyful Songs.   Gaspar Gil Polo.   HW

End o' dat mornin' when de Lord said to hurry.   O, Gambler, Git Up Off o' Yo' Knees.   *Anonymous.*   BoAN 1-2

The end of love is that the heart is still.   The Moment of the Rose. Dunstan Thompson.   LiTA

End of the factory-window song.   Factory Windows Are Always Broken. Vachel Lindsay.   CrMA; FaFP; LiTA; NAMP; NePA; OBCA; OBSP

The end of the mantic Muskrat and the Seal/Is the end of you, my inarticulate friends.   Is There a Voice (parody).   Philip Appleman.   BXAP

The end of the matter! The Justice of/God I acknowledge.   Elegy (For Himself).   Moses Rimos.   TrJP

End of the pony's tail, and mine!   The Tale of a Pony.   Bret (Francis Bret Harte) Harte.   OBNV

...The end which ends with no way out.   Voice of a Dissipated Woman inside a Tomb...   Sor Violante do Ceu.   BoWoP

The end won't come in darkness but a/blinding flash of light.   Out of the Darkness.   Frankie Armstrong.   BrRo

End your groan, and come away.   The Duchess of Malfi.   John Webster. FaBoEn; HAP; HW; NoP; OBEV; OBS; PAI; QFR; SeCePo; ViBoPo

Ending howls in sounds/of peace.   To a Captain in Sinai.   Ada Aharoni. AMV-81

Ending I praise her for putting the basket down.   The Goods She Can Carry: Canticle of Her Basket Made of Reeds.   Gibbons Ruark.   MAYP

Ending my long blind years, a fistful of blood-red weed in my/hand.   Coming Suddenly to the Sea.   Louis Dudek.   NOBC

Ending up tending shop up in Fiesole.   Tourists.   Howard Moss.   FiBHP; NYBP

Endless and no/Whisper of death.   Atropos.   John Myers O'Hara. AnAmPo

The endless drummers of subtracting night.   He Came to Visit Me.   Martin Seymour-Smith.   FaBoTw

Endless hymns of praise I sing.   Precious Child, So Sweetly Sleeping.   Anna Hoppe.   AH

The endless miracle that embodies thee.   Stone Too Can Pray.   Conrad Aiken.   EaLo; MoRP

The endless repetitions of his own murmurous blood.   A Letter.   Anthony Hecht.   NYBP; OxBC

Endow the fallow plain.   At My Whisper.   John Lyle Donaghy.   AnIV

Ends the epic/makes the night lyric   The Scribe.   Endre Farkas.   CaPN

Endungeoned it in dust.   Lines to a Blind Girl.   Thomas Buchanan Read. AA

Endurance asks no recompense.   Desert Claypan.   Frederick T. Macartney. PoAu 1-2

...Endure/In silence and disdain/Love's utmost treacheries.   Fourteenth Birthday.   Phyllis McGinley.   NePoAm-2

Endure it, doubtful whether God be Lord,/Or Dagon.   Samson Agonistes. John Milton.   TRV

Endure till day and night shall cease/to be!   Immortal Israel.   Judah Halevi. TrJP

The enemy roamed the desert, and everyone itched.   A Day with the Foreign Legion.   Reed Whittemore.   CoAP; ConAP; LiTM; NePoEA

Energy is needed, people remember yours.   The Sanctimonious Poets. Friedrich Holderlin.   NU

Enfold me in your arms!   Tonight.   Louise Chandler Moulton.   AA

Enfolds the spheric wonder of the sky.   Greenwich Observatory.   Sidney Keyes.   MoAB; MoBrPo

Engadu forgot where he was born.   Gilgamesh: The Seduction of Engadu. William Ellery Leonard.   ErPo

Engage not a Coolie Chinee.   The Coolie Chinee.   Septimus Winner. OBAL

Engirt with azure and with Saphire veines./(Cetera desunt).   She Dwelt aong the Untrodden Ways (parody).   J. C. Squire.   BXAP

England hath need of thee, and not/Of Leavis and Eliot.   Thou should'st be living at this hour.   Heathcote William Garrod.   CenHV

England, in one small subject, such contains.   Parthenope.   Barnabe Barnes. CBEP

England's shores, adieu! adieu!   Song of the Pilgrims.   Thomas Cogswell Upham.   MC; PAH

English cot by English water/That shall see the German sea.   The German Legion.   Sydney Thomas Dobell.   PeD

The English knowing prize it not,/But fling't like drosse away.   The Indians Prize Not English Gold.   Roger Williams.   SCAP

The English lady, and little wee boy,/Went a' to Benachie.   Lang Johnny More.   *Anonymous.*   ESPB

An English Pilot too, (O Shame, O Sin!)/Cheated of Pay, was he that show'd them in.   The Last Instructions to a Painter.   Andrew Marvell.   OBS

Englishmen in ennui.   Handling Synne.   Robert De Brunne.   DBV

Engulf the planets. I have seen the best.   After Grey Vigils.   George Santayana.   WHA

Enhungered, thirsting as they daily sink/Beneath the trampling multitude. Priest Or Poet.   Shane Leslie.   CAW; WGRP

Enigma rules, and the heart has no certainty.   Flux.   Richard Eberhart. Psk; VGW

Enjoy it a', ye've nae mair for't.   Odes.   Horace.   OBVE

Enjoy them both in bloom before they wither.   Double Gift.   *Anonymous.* UnTE

Enjoy thy great possessions as thou may'st.'   I Dreamed a Dream.   Arthur Hugh Clough.   NOBV

Enjoy yourself in this world,/Never mind what they say.   Let's Get Going. Leyla Hanim.   PBWP

Enjoyed them precisely with a sharp pencil.   The Cancer Cells.   Richard Eberhart.   HAP; LiTM; MiAP

Enjoying of myself I lie.   Love Made in the First Age.   Richard Lovelace. AnAnS 2; CaPo; JCP; OAEL 1-2; SeCP

Enjoying perfect boredom up in Hull.   Mr. Strugnell (parody).   Wendy Cope.   FaBoPa

Enjoys his Wish, and well imploys his time.   The Advice.   Charles, Earl of Dorset Sackville.   FaBoUs

Enlightened by the luster they inflict.   Touchstone.   James Worley. AMV-80

Enlisted on the other front.   Beach Burial.   Kenneth Slessor.   BoAV; CBAP; PoAu 1-2

The enormous power of their peacefulness.   The Hills.   Frances Cornford. MoBrPo

Enormous thin sheep/Intent as wolves/Surround Him.   A Child's Nativity. John N. Morris.   GP

Enough. As yet disquiet clings/About us. Rest shall we.   The Impercipient. Thomas Hardy.   OAEP; PrIm; TrGrPo; ViBoPo; WGRP

Enough confusion of my own, I've got.   Japanese Beetles.   X.J. Kennedy. HoAn; OBAL

Enough! Enough! it is enough for me/To dream of thee!   Lines to Fanny (excerpt).   John Keats.   ChRP

Enough for him Fall's golden glows,/And colors in the sunset wrought.   The Dead Prospector.   Arthur Chapman.   BPAW

Enough, he died with conquering Graeme.   The Lay of the Last Minstrel. Sir Walter Scott.   OBRV

Enough in any man's own conscience.   From One of Case's Pill-Boxes. John Case.   FaBoUs

Enough it is for one man to sustaine,/The stormes, which she alone on me doth raine.   Amoretti, XLVI.   Edmund Spenser.   AAS

Enough! Let us two be one.   The Glimpse of a Plain Cap.   *Anonymous.* LiTW

Enough, more than enough, for everyone.   Cataract.   Margoret Smith. NYBP

Enough of fear and shadowy despair,/To frame her cloudy prison for the soul! Autumn.   Thomas Hood.   LiTB

Enough! or Too much.   Proverbs of Hell.   William Blake.   AtBAP

Enough that the touch of the shell/Be warm to my hand.   For This, the Tide. Val Vallis.   BoAV

Enough that we have justified our birth,/Ere entering the inscrutable abode. Love's Immortality.   Elsa Barker.   HBMV

Enough to hush the screams within   Just Making It.   Richard Thomas. PoNe

Enough to make him homesick, what home was really like.   I've Got a Home in That Rock.   Raymond Richard Patterson.   FF; PoBA; PoNe

Enough. You have returned. And all is well.   In the Evening.   Thomas Hardy.   ImOP

Enraptured by the sunset's charm divine.   Twilight.   Joaquin A. Pagaza. CAW

Enraptured child still fond enough to sing.   Independence.   Roy McFadden. OxBI

Enrich our souls in secret/With abundant life.   O God, in Restless Living. Harry Emerson Fosdick.   TrPWD

Enshrine her and she dies, who had/The hard heart of a child.   Beauty. Elinor Wylie.   OxBA

Enshrined with snakes within his tomb, did yield her part-/ing breath.   In Praise of a Gentlewoman.   George Gascoigne.   CBEP

Enter Shakespear, with a loud clap.   On the Erection of Shakespeare's Statue in Westminster Abbey.   Alexander Pope.   FaBoEE

Entered I into the subway station/Known as Cathedral Parkway.   Life. Franklin Pierce ("F.P.A.") Adams.   InMe

The Entering–takes away–.   I Had Been Hungry, All the Years.   Emily Dickinson.   AmePo; LiTA; LiTM; MoAmPo; SBG

The enterprise is sick.   Troilus and Cressida.   William Shakespeare.   ImOP

Enters–and is lost in Balms.   Come Slowly–Eden.   Emily Dickinson. CMoP; UnTE

Enthrone thy Rosy-self within mine Eyes.   The Reflection.   Edward Taylor. AmPP; AtBAP; NePA; OxBA

Enticed to the release of the sky.   Seals, Terns, Time.   Richard Eberhart. LiTM; MoAB; MoAmPo

Enticing the gingerbread goodies that grew/At the top of the cooky-nut tree.   The Cooky-Nut Trees (A Tale of the Pilliwinks).   Albert Bigelow Paine. OBCA

Entirely a flower at the end.   Counting on Flowers.   John Ciardi.   PP

An entity in name only/and that taken in vain.   Dodo.   Henry Carlile. GP; Psk

Entrust the flag of liberty/At last, to Russian hands.   A Hymn.   Nikolai Nekrasov.   LiTW

Entwine like harp notes on time's weltering curve.   Die Pelzaffen.   Charles Spear.   AnNZ

...Entwined in one anguished knot/around his blood-stained neck!   To See Him Again.   Gabriela (Lucila Godoy Alcayaga) Mistral.   OLR

Envy, ye monarchs with our proud excess,/At our low sail, and our high happiness.   Virgidemiarum.   Joseph Hall.   OBSV

Envying none, and envied not.   Written on the Walls of His Dungeon.   Luis Ponce de Leon.   TrJP

The Epilogue no mortal yet can know.   New-Englands Crisis: The Prologue. Benjamin Tompson.   AnAmPo; SCAP

Equal, equipped at last, (O joy! O fruit of all!) them to fulfil, O soul!   Darest Thou Now O Soul.   Walt Whitman   AA

An equal wisdom, I'd surmise.   Wisdom.   Linda Peavy.   PH

...An equation for X,/as it, too, now grows by subtraction.   Little Ode for X. Maura Stanton.   MAYP

The equation is the interdependence of parts.'   Resolution of Dependence. George Barker.   FaBoTw; LiTB; LiTM

Equypollent with Marcus Tulius.   Epithalamium for Gloucester.   John Lydgate.   HW

Er an sei Back muss floateh.   An Unserer Beach.   Kurt M. Stein.   InMe

Er cloudy trophies hung.   Ode on Melanch   Oly.   W. H. Auden.   NOBE

"Er–I mean "Quite!"/Or, simply, "Right!"'   Preface ShrinkLit: Elements of Style William Strunk, Jr. & E. B. White.   Maurice Sagoff.   NLV

Er sith his lif, Quoth Hending.   Snatches: "Tel thou never thy fomon." Anonymous.   OxBM

Er the gobble-uns'll git you/Ef you/Don't/Watch/Out!   The Elf Child. James Whitcomb Riley.   AmePo

Er the Gobble-uns'll git you/Ef you don't watch out!   Little Orphant Annie. James Whitcomb Riley.   AA; BBGG; FaFP; HBV 1-2; HBVY; MoShBr; NLV; OBAL; OBCA; OxBChV; PaPo; TiPo; TreF

Er Troilus out of Criseides herte.   But Whan the Cok: Troilus and Criseide. Geoffrey Chaucer.   AtBAP

Er we cain't git no courtin' done!   Our Hired Girl.   James Whitcomb Riley. HBV 1-2; HBVY

An era's gesture entombed in their crackling dismay.   A House All Pictures. Emery George.   AMV-81

The era with a testament.   Chanson de Chateaulaire.   Herbert Sherman Gorman.   AnAmPo

Erasing the night evidence   Morning Has No House.   Rosemarie Waldrop. MAT

Ere, dear Alabama! They turn cold on thee!   A Missouri Maiden's Farewell to Alabama.   Mark (Samuel Langhorne Clemens) Twain.   InMe

Ere death, once let us stand/As we stood then!   At an Inn.   Thomas Hardy. NOBV

Ere freedom out of man.   Ode Sung in the Town Hall.   Ralph Waldo Emerson.   AnNE

–Ere he enter that school/not for study or for music/but to bear clay and stones.   The Lament for Art O Laoghaire (excerpt).   Eibhlin Dubh O'Connell.   NOBI

Ere her chaste will lay vanquished in my chains.   Sonnets: A Sequence on Profane Love.   George Henry Boker.   AmePo

Ere Hopkins and Sternhold knew how to scan.   The Office of Poetry. Nathaniel Whiting.   OBS

Ere I be brought to ground.   A Rhyme-beginning Fragment.   Anonymous. AnIL

Ere I cease to love her, my queen, my queen!   My Queen.   Anonymous. HBV 1-2

Ere I do thrum thee such a thwacking thump/As all the bawds of tizzy never twanged.   To a Loudmouth Pontificator.   Ray Mizer.   TW

Ere I'll die for love, I'll fairly forego it.   The Careless Lover.   Sir John Suckling.   CavP

Ere I pass life's sunset stile.   To A Skull.   Joshua Henry Jones.   BANP

Ere I prove false to faith, or strange to you.   Madrigal: "Dear, if you change."   John Dowland.   EnRePo

Ere Ishmael's spirit drives them forth/again.   The Bedouins of the Skies. James Benjamin Kenyon.   AA

Ere it be long within the earth to rest.   Visions.   Petrarch.   EnLi 1-2

Ere lang the waves war foamin'.   The Mermaid.   Anonymous.   CH

Ere long, alive, alas, thou shalt not see me.   Madrigal: "In nets of golden wire."   Thomas Morley.   EnRePo

Ere nescience shall be reaffirmed/How long, how long?   Before Life and After.   Thomas Hardy.   FaBoRV

Ere pestilence or famine sweep the land.   On Seeing an Officer's Widow Distracted.   Mary Barber.   NOEC

Ere rivers run dry and rocks melt with the sun.   Bring Back.   Anne Ridler. ACV

Ere she see the Earl of Moray/Come sounding thro' the toun.   The Bonnie Earl of Moray.   Anonymous.   AnFE; ESPB; FaBoCh; FSW; LoGBV; OBS

Ere Sigurd came to the Niblungs and faced their gathered foes.   The Brooding of Sigurd.   William Morris.   SeCePo

Ere smoky towns shall vie with rural plains,/And city cockneys rival country swains.   The Comparison (excerpt).   Anonymous.   NOEC

Ere the night cometh and she may not work.   Saint Luke the Painter. Dante Gabriel Rossetti.   GoBC

Ere the Sunset and the Drooping Leaf!   Song of Basket-Weaving.   Constance Lindsay Skinner.   AnAmPo; BPAW

Ere they see Sir Patrick and his men/Come sailing to the land.   Sir Patrick Spens.   Anonymous.   ESPB

Ere thy whole soul be slain by cankerous sin.   Heart of Oak.   Charles Henry Luders.   AA

Ere time has brushed cold fingers through my hair!   Welt.   Georgia Douglas Johnson.   BANP

Ere to the wind's twelve quarters/I take my endless way.   From Far, from Eve and Morning.   Alfred Edward Housman.   CMoP; HAP; HeIP; MoBrPo; NBM; NoP; PoEL 1-5; PrIm

Ere we exhaust the theme of love.   Welcome, Ye Hopeful Heirs of Heaven. Phoebe Hinsdale Brown.   AH

Ere we have left to feed it, feeds on us.   On the Cuckoo.   Francis Quarles. PBBP

Ere Work, alack, came in with Wail.   My Jacket Old.   Herman Melville. SaC

Ere yet the misty herds/Leave warm 'mid the gray grass their dusky bed. Song: "Softly, O midnight Hours!"   Aubrey Thomas De Vere.   IrPN

Ere you can fade, ere you can die,/My Dark Rosaleen!   Dark Rosaleen. Hugh O'Donnell.   AWP; LiTW

Ere you in Dinnybristle town/Will daurna to be seen.   The Bonny Earl of Murray (B vers.).   Anonymous.   BaBo

Ere you were born was beauty's summer dead.   Sonnets, CIV: "To me, fair friend, you never can be old."   William Shakespeare.   FaBoEn; FPL; GBL; GTBS; GTBS-P; HBV 1-2; HeIP; LiTL; OAEP; OBEV; OBSC; PeHV; Prf; ViBoPo

Erebus of earth's ancestral mind.   Presences Perfected.   Siegfried Sassoon. MoBrPo

Erect no Mausoloeums: for his best/Monument is his Spouses Marble brest. Upon the Death of the Lord Hastings.   John Dryden.   CEP; PeD; SeCV 1-2

Ergo, Good wine carrieth a man to heaven.   Logic.   Anonymous.   FaBoUs

Erin mavournin, Erin go bragh!   Exile of Erin.   Thomas Campbell.   HBV 1-2

Erinna, handmaid of the Muses, penned.   Baucis.   Erinna.   AWP

Eros wings down to a fir to sit/and hoot like a Long-eared Owl.   The Ballad of Blossom.   Mona Van Duyn.   SM

...Erosion/is its very face.   Wanting a Child.   Jorie Graham.   MAYP

Error's brought in to blind men damningly.   Good News from New-England. Edward Johnson.   SCAP

Erstwhile eagle-scout/bed-mate   The Honey Lamb.   Jonathan Williams. PoM

Escape from prison.   The Choice.   John Masefield.   MoAB; MoBrPo

Escape from the weekday time. Which deadens and/endures.   Sunday Morning.   Louis MacNeice.   CoBMV; FaBoIP; FaBoMo; HeIP; LiTB; MoAB; MoBrPo; MoVE; NIP

Escaped bubbles of gas crawl/Like maggots everywhere.   The Death Balloon. Patricia Goedicke.   FAZ

Eschew the golden hall, thy thatched house is best.   On Edward Seymour, Duke of Somerset.   Anonymous.   OBSC

Esemplastic was always a ridiculous word.   At Lake Geneva.   Richard Eberhart.   LiTA

Esmeralda, immer, immer.   Lines Written in Oregon.   Vladimir Nabokov. NYBP

Especially a dark girl dressed in blue.   The Dark Girl Dressed in Blue. Anonymous.   BeLS

Especially as I had tied her girdle/With the wrong bow.   The Great Offence. Abu Nuwas.   LiTW

Especially Ellen M'Jones Aberdeen.   Ellen M'Jones Aberdeen.   Sir William Schwenck Gilbert.   InMe

Especially when those con-/cerned/Possess neither (sang the nightin-/gale). Fable.   Norman Harris.   NYBP

Essay me no villany/In the lands where we go.   Carol in Praise of the Holly and Ivy.   Anonymous.   OHIP

The essence of great bosoms now no more. A Fragment. George Gordon, Lord Byron. ERoP 1-2

Essential but secret like a rose. Be Beautiful. Jose Garcia Villa. AnFE; CrMA

Est bene for him/Relinqui id alone. Puer Ex Jersey. *Anonymous.* NA

Est summum nefas fallere:/Deceit is gross impiety. Memorial Lines on the Gender of Latin Substantives. Benjamin Hall Kennedy. FaBoUs

Establish him firmly there. Inscription on the Pyramid of Pepi I. *Anonymous.* LiTW

Establish them, that values may go on. Boy-Man. Karl Shapiro. NYBP; SoSe

Establish thy serenity o'er the fields. Haze. Henry David Thoreau. HeIP; InPo; NoP; PoPl

Establish thy serenity o'er the fields. Woof of the Sun, Ethereal Gauze. Henry David Thoreau. AnNE; AP; TAP; ViBoPo

Et c'est la fin pour quoy sommes ensemble. Aubade. Karl Shapiro. GP; VGW

Et des p'tits pantalons au velours. Limerick: "Il y avait une jeune fille de Tours." *Anonymous.* LiBL

Et le Grec l'enrhumait. Ce fut moi. Limerick: "Il naquit pres de Choisy-le-Roi." *Anonymous.* LiBL

Et les soldats faisaient la haie? ILS LA FAISAIENT. Triumphal March. Thomas Stearns Eliot. MBW 1-2; OBWP

Et profugi gemitus exgrabuere rathae. Mors Iabrochii. *Anonymous.* NA

"Et ton the,t'a-t-il ote la toux?" Limerick: "Un vieux duc (le meilleur des epoux)." *Anonymous.* LiBL

L'Etat C'est Moi and Ich Dien. Clerihew. Edmund Clerihew Bentley. PV

Etched a ripple, eloquent/Of a freshening wind and a fair day. The Cachalot. Edwin John Pratt. CaP

Etched by a foreign stylus never used/On the outmoded page of the Apocalypse. Come away, Death. Edwin John Pratt. PeCV

Etched/by love. Now in my heart. Sappho. BoWoP

The Eternal alone dwells within you for aye. The Eternal. Esaias Tegner. LiTW

Eternal be the sleep/Unless to waken so! Lines: "When youthful faith hath fled." John Gibson Lockhart. OBVV

Eternal beauty is for ever new. To Rotenham–3. August von Platen. PeHV

Eternal/bright The End of a War. Sir Herbert Read. OBMV

The eternal city shall be free! her sons shall walk with princes. Rienzi to the Romans. Mary Russell Mitford. GoTF; TreFS

The Eternal City stands. The City of God. Samuel Johnson AA; FaPoR; TRV; WGRP

Eternal Comforter. Lord, Thou Hast Suffered. Amy Carmichael. TRV

An eternal deathday light/forever flickering? Memorial Poem. Jacob Glatstein. VWA

Eternal dreams, blood samples/pouring from one glass to the next. Batyushkov. Osip Mandelstam. OBVE

Eternal Good that rules the summer flower/And all the worlds that people starry space! Credo (excerpt). Richard Watson Gilder. TrPWD

Eternal in the heav'ns this dwelling stands. In Him. Annie Johnson Flint. BLRP; TRV

Eternal is the Prince who grants such bliss. The Phoenix (excerpt). *Anonymous.* PBBP

The eternal jewels of the short-lived night. The Stars. Mary Mapes Dodge. AA

Eternal joy which nothing can molest. Love Which Is Here a Care. William, of Hawthornden Drummond. OxBoCh

Eternal Lord, afterwards made–/for men earth, Master almighty. Hymn: "Now we must praise heaven-kingdom's Guardian." Caedmon. TrCP

Eternal Love, maintain thy life in me. Astrophel and Stella, CX. Sir Philip Sidney. NIP; TEP

Eternal pain! Philomela. Matthew Arnold. AtBAP; BoLiVe; EnLi 1-2; GTBS; HBV 1-2; MaVP; MCCG; OAEL 1-2; OAEP; OBEV; PBBP; PPP; SeCeV; UnPo; VLP; WHA

...Eternal peace/Be to us both with her decease. Here Lies My Wife. J. V. Cunningham. NIP

The eternal reciprocity of tears. Insensibility. Wilfred Owen. CMoP; ExPo; FaBoTw; LiTB; LiTM; MMM; MoAB; OAEP; OBWP; OxBTC; PAI; SeCeV; WaP

Eternal solitude water solitude. The Great Fountains. Anne Hebert. BoWoP

Eternal sunshine settles on its head. The Deserted Village. Oliver Goldsmith. TrGrPo; TRV; WGRP

The eternal thing in man,/That heeds no call to die. Heredity. Thomas Hardy. CBEP; CTC; EBEV; ImOP

The eternal things of life can never die. Eternal Values. Grace Noll Crowell. PoToHe

Eternally distant and luminous in the air. The Book of How. Merrill Moore. MoAmPo

Eternally eternally bud and blossom/Evolve the particulars of doom. Sequence. George Barker. PoA

Eternally, in nineteen hundred thirty-six. Portrait de Femme. Irving Feldman. NoAm

Eternally/To behold and see/The Trinity!/Amen. Upon a Dead Man's Head. John Skelton. CoBE; HAP; SeCePo

The eternally wilting daisy and sandals are extra. Free Enterprise. Charles Stetler. GP

"Eternity alone our wrong can right,/That makes all young again in Time's despite." Love's Remorse. Edwin Muir. LiTL; OxBTC

Eternity in heaven. The Power of Littles. *Anonymous.* TreFT

...Eternity is where we forget we are as we call out: Hello! Hello! Goodby "Hello." Philip Dow. NPGG

Eternity!–Will this same sense recur,/That once this life was really mine? A Song of Life. Franz Werfel. TrJP

...Ether-shod,/Ran straight for comfort up to God. Do What You Will. Dorothy Hobson. GoBC

An ether/that muds its nose/and feet? Three Songs from the Temple. Don Domanski. NOBC

Ethiopes' lips are soft as thine. A Paradox. William Herbert, Earl of Pembroke. EiL

Euboea's neighbor. Athens! Farewell, Sea! Farewell. Plato. AWP

Euerye such a louely ladye,/God send her well to speede! The Boy and the Mantle. *Anonymous.* BaBo; ESPB; OxBB; UnTE

Eunuchs in court-dress preparing a bed. A Palace Poem. Hsueh Feng. LiTW

Ev'n eternitie is too short/To extoll thee. Praise. George Herbert. AnAnS 1

Ev'n God himself, being pressed for my sake. The Bunch of Grapes. George Herbert. AnAnS 1

Ev'n thou may'st come too late,/And not restore my life, but close my eyes. Orinda to Lucasia. Katherine ("Orinda") Philips. PeHV

Ev'ning and morn solemnized the fifth day. Paradise Lost. John Milton. PBBP

Ev'ry roun' goes higher higher,/Soldiers of de cross. We Am Clim'in' Jacob's Ladder. *Anonymous.* BoAN 1-2

Ev'rybody loves Saturday night. Everybody Loves Saturday Night. *Anonymous.* FSW

"Eva!" again. Eve. Ralph Hodgson. ALV; AnFE; BoLiVe; BrPo; EvOK; HBV 1-2; LiTB; LiTM; MoAB; MoBrPo; OnMSP; SeCeV; TrCP; TrGrPo; UnPo

...Evade/Whatever hand might reach and touch our hand. Exile. Donald Hall. NePA

Evading believers, he hurries off down Pitt Street. An Absolutely Ordinary Rainbow. Les A. Murray. CBAP

Evahmo'... Southern Road. Sterling A. Brown. BALP

Evangelize! Evangelize! Evangelize! Henry Crocker. BLRP

Evanished in a cloud of mist,/And left her all alone. Sweet William's Ghost. *Anonymous.* BuBa

Evanishes at crowing of the cock. The Grave. Robert Blair. CoBE; NOEC

Evaporates a naked corpse inside the pharmacy. Chaplin's Sad Speech. Rafael Alberti. LiTW

Evaporation in ascent. Expansion to Aveline's. Jim Brodey. ANYP

The eve of New Year's Day/Left the Old Year lost to all. The Old Year. John Clare. NOBV; OBCP; PG

Eve stretched her hand and plucked the fruit. The Tree. Dorothy Auchterlonie. NOAV

Even a deaf mute can hear. Abraham and Sarah. Itzik Manger. VWA

Even a dog is better than you. Money Is King. *Anonymous.* FSW

Even a good wind blows some ill. Notes on the Post-Industrial Revolution. Edward Morin. FAZ

Even a little joy/Is too heavy for us to bear. In Fine, Transparent Words. David Vogel. VWA

Even a queen must not defy a king. Diptych. Velma West Sykes. IHMS

Even a rain. Even If. Rachel Fishman. VWA

Even an endless sleep would be/Stirred by the dreams of you! The Last Word. Frederic Lawrence Knowles. HBV 1-2

Even as a holy martyr sheds her blood. Stanzas on Mutability. Hugo von Hofmannsthal. AWP; TrJP

Even as a mother her sweet infant heir/That wan and sickly droops upon her breast. On a Discovery Made Too Late. Samuel Taylor Coleridge. EnRP

...Even as charcoal dusk/Effaced his lazy semaphore. L'Ile du Levant: The Nudist Colony. Barbara Howes. NePoAm-2; PoCh

"Even as he led his life, so did he die." To Graecinus, on Loving Two Women at Once. Ovid (Publius Ovidius Naso). EBEV

–Even as he spoke, the sun's one spark/Withdrew, and left the dusk more dark.– The Incentive. Sarah N. Cleghorn. HBMV

Even as herself, O friend!/I will of you! Constant. Emily Dickinson. AA; FaBoBe

Even as I die and am born. He Is Like the Serpent Saka. Book of the Dead. AWP

Even as I stand or sit passing faster than you. Stallion. Walt Whitman. PH

Even as it happens. The Death of the First Man. Nancy Sullivan. NIP

Even as my youth sings through my years. Sweet Clover. William Rice. HBV 1-2

Even as our common doom/Saddens their bloom. Immortal Flowers. Wallace Rice. AA

Even as the day into this room. The Room. William Soutar. EBEV

...Even as the/evening slowly took the forest into night... In the Forest. Russell Edson. LCAP

Even as the pool cleanses the defiled! God to Man. Talmud. TrJP

...Even as the Power divine/Which then lulled all things, brooded upon mine. Ode to Naples (excerpt). Percy Bysshe Shelley. FaBoPP

Even as you prime your feathers and set sail. The Raven. Adrienne Rich. NePoEA-2

Even ashes of lovers find no rest. The Hour Glass. Ben Jonson. BLPL; CBEP; EnLoPo; LiTB; NIP; OAEL 1-2; SeCP

Even at intervals during the day I would/suffer an occasional eclair/for the sake of appearance. Beauty I Would Suffer for. Marge Piercy. NIP

Even at the moment when they should array/Themselves in pensive order. The Coliseum. George Gordon, Lord Byron. MCCG

Even becoming precious, concentrates to burn us where we've/chosen to make our stands. R. W. Artie Gold. CaPN

Even before I speak, she serves. Nani. Alberto Rios. GP; SM

Even Belphoebe's, whom they gave their lives for! The Queen's Men. Rudyard Kipling. AtBAP

Even Christ's palms, unhealed,/Smart and cannot fish there. Limbo. Seamus Heaney. CIP; OxBC

Even crawling inside O/it yowls at U and I. Genesis of Vowels. James Richard Broughton. CrMA

Even for a cab. Knight, with Umbrella. Elder Olson. FiBHP

Even for a while, hear an exalted speech/And know Death by his smile. Cesar Franck. Joseph Auslander. HBMV

Even for kings, the rag-poor past, the purple that may set.' Quebec Liquor Commission Store. Abraham Moses Klein. ACV; OBCV

Even from far off smell the true water. Camel. William Stanley Merwin. NePA

Even from my heart the strings do break. Corinna. Thomas Campion. ElL; TrGrPo; UnS

Even grass has a song,/'though only wind hears it. Song-Maker. Anita Endrezze-Danielson. STE

...Even grim lids in/grass jaws ponder over them. The Tall Toms. Edwin Honig. NePA

Even happiness. Fairy Story. Robert Penn Warren. NYBP

Even he/Could not live long enough. With a Sliver of Marble from Carrara. James Wright. EyDe

...Even he/is gibberish to their ears Ohms. Irving Layton. NeAC

Even her hand disturbed her as she lay. Five Epigrams. J.V. Cunningham. UnTE

–Even I/Regain'd my freedom with a sigh. The Prisoner of Chillon. George Gordon, Lord Byron. BeLS; DTo; EnLi 1-2; EnRP; HBV 1-2; MaC; MCCG; NOBE; OBRV; PoLf

...Even I/will be a believer. The Quilt. Larry Levis. MAYP

Even if a foolish girl, not yet full grown,/Confronts you with a scarcely decent passion. Advice to Colonel Valentine. Robert Graves. NYBP

Even/if I only/pass them Justice. Petra von Morstein. BoWoP

...Even if it is the book of nightmares. The Book of Nightmares. Galway Kinnell. NNaP

Even if it's only in the whiteness of a washed pocket-handkerchief. We Are Transmitters–. D. H. Lawrence. OxBTC

Even if that blind groping but achieves/A darker head, a few more aspen leaves. The Aspen and the Stream. Richard Wilbur. NYBP

Even if the darkness precedes and follows/us, we have a chance, briefly, to shine. The Chance. Arthur Sze. BrSi

Even if we cease life is a miracle. It May Be So with Us. John Masefield. ATP

.......Even if you forgot. Your Hands. Angelina Weld Grimke. CDC; PoBA

Even in colocynth and calomel?/I cannot tell. Oh, Hollow! Hollow! Hollow! Sir William Schwenck Gilbert. FaBoNo

Even in death we have no luck. Exile Song. Morris Rosenfeld. LiTW

Even in Hades/I am with you. Andromeda forgot. Sappho. BoWoP

Even in my place he weeps. Even I, not he. He and I. Dante Gabriel Rossetti. MaVP; NBM

Even in that loneliest wave we are not alone. Answering a Letter from a Younger Poet. Brewster Ghiselin. PoCh

Even in this being alone I meet with you. Alone. E. J. Scovell. GBL

Even in thyn armes, thair doutles had I deit. To His Maistres. Alexander Montgomerie. OxBS

Even like these to rail and sweat/Staring upon his sinewy thigh. On Those That Hated "The Playboy of the Western World", 1907. William Butler Yeats. NOBI

Even love does now no longer find/A place in female souls. A Song on the South Sea. Anne Finch, Countess of Winchilsea. NOEC

Even love will drop around to smile goodbye. Elegy. Aleksandr Pushkin. AMV-81

Even lowlier bowed my head, and bowed my heart. Homage. Helen Hoyt. AnAmPo

Even lust and envy sleep, yet loves denies/Rest to my soul and slumber to my eyes. Midnight. John Dryden. ACP

Even me. Black Sketches, 10. Don L. Lee. NeAC

Even now. Recollection Long Ago: Sad Music. Robert Penn Warren. SV

Even now by hate again I doubt the same. Desire, alas, my master and my foe. Sir Thomas Wyatt. FCP

Even now–even now–even now! Predestination. Rudyard Kipling. LoBV

Even now, from scratching ravens of the mind. The Grave. John Lyle Donaghy. NeIP

...Even now, I dream/of choosing. Learning to Live without You. Susan Wood. AMV-81

Even now the horses of the stars/canter, early on Sunday mornings. Watching the Out-Door Movie Show. Ann Struthers. FAZ

Even on board the Lisbon Packet? The Lisbon Packet. George Gordon, Lord Byron. NLV

Even on Calvary's slope,/I sing! Out of the Depths. Frederic Lawrence Knowles. TrPWD

Even on lonely winter evenings refusing/not to point to the stars. My Penis. Ed Ochester. GP

Even on that secret world from this/Her twilight enters in. Moonlight. Walter De la Mare. EnLoPo

Even our souls may leak away/then, and only return to us/with Hell and horned beasts! In Memory of Francois Rabelais. Yunna Moritz. VWA

Even sea gulls love the shape of roses/ere day closes. Confidence. Marsden. Hartley. AnFE

Even small talents live at ease. To the Minister Liu. Yu Hsuan-chi. BoWoP

Even so likewise by death was freedom wrought. Elegy Wrote in the Tower, 1554. John (fl. 1550) Harington. ElL

Even so of all the vowels, I and U,/Are dearest unto me, as doth ensue. Sonnets, XIX: "Ah no; nor I my selfe: though my pure love." Richard Barnfield. PeHV

Even so, perhaps we no longer/belong here. For the Minority. Robert Peterson. NeAC

Even so, poor bird, like thee/None alive will pity me. The Nightingale. Richard Barnfield. AWP; EG; GTBS-P

"Even so!" said the Queen. Jealousy. Mary Elizabeth Coleridge. EnLoPo; NBM; OBNC

...Even so the kingdoms falter/and go down of themselves! Lafayette to Washington. Maxwell Anderson. PAL

Even so, through eyes and voice, your soul doth move/My soul with changeful light of infinite love. Soul-Light. Dante Gabriel Rossetti. MaVP

Even Solomon in all his glory was not arrayed like one of these. God Provides. St. Matthew Bible, N.T.. BLRP

Even such is man, who died and then did laugh/To see such strange lines writ on's epitaph. Nonsense. Elizabeth T. Corbett. FaBoNo

The even tenour of her ways. Poems, X. Philip O'Connor. EAS

Even the acrobatic swift/has not his flying-crooked gift. Flying Crooked. Robert Graves. FaBoMo; LiTM; MP; OBSP; PCP; TwCP

Even the alarm clock/Had its hands all over me. On Certain Mornings Everything Is Sensual. David Jauss. GOYP

Even the angels were standing in line. Rip the Apple Seller Awakes; or, after 50 Years, the Great Depression. Duane Ackerson. SOTS

Even the best rum tasted better, shared. The Drove-Road. Wilfred Wilson Gibson. EnLit; OxBTC

& Even the birds are made joyful/by our shouts Sukkot. Sol Lachman. VWA

Even the blessed Virgin/She's now brought forth a son. The Carnal and the Crane. *Anonymous.* ESPB

Even the blind will sense that something's wrong. In Perspective. Robert Graves. OBSP

...Even/the body must finally end. Instead of Features. Jim Moore. PoDr

Even the dead shall rise. The Raising of Lazarus. Lucille Clifton. CNA

Even the dead sing them an unending hymn. Divinities. William Stanley Merwin. PoA

Even the dirt kept breathing a small breath. Root Cellar. Theodore Roethke. AmPP; BoNaP; HeIP; InPK; NoP; PPP

Even the great and loving heart of God,/Whereby all love doth live. Living Waters. Caroline Spencer. HBV 1-2

Even the low belch of the brunette behind the flippers. Writing on Napkins at the Sunshine Club Macon, Georgia 1971. David Bottoms. TAT

...Even the moss grows old/Upon the shallowest rocks. At the Western Shore. Sarah Youngblood. IHMS

Even the moth is my disciple. Though I am Laila of the Persian romance. Princess Zeb-un-Nissa. BoWoP

Even the mountains vast and tall/The sea dissolves away.   Perspectives.
Dudley Randall.   AmNP

Even the night will blossom as the rose.   On Growing Old.   John Masefield.
CMoP; CoBE; FaFP; FPL; GoTF; HBMV; LiTB; LiTM; MoAB; MoBrPo;
MoRP; PG; PoLf; PoRA; TreFS; ViBoPo; WHA

Even the roses spilt on youth's red mouth/Will soon blow down the road all
roses go.   June.   Francis Ledwidge.   BBV; BIrV; HBMV; HBV 1-2;
NOBI

Even the stones speak.   Meditations of an Old Woman.   Theodore Roethke.
NaP

Even the street-cars/song   The Songs of Maximus, 1.   Charles Olson.
NoAm

...Even the sun/Seems washed, and with adored heat burns my back.   Wet
Through.   Hal Summers.   HaMV

"Even the sunbeams falter, flicker and bend–/I am the end."   The End.
Marguerite Wilkinson.   HBMV

Even the Viet Cong were called Charlie.   Who Needs Charlie Manson?
Raymond Thompson.   LFAC

Even the voices calling them to bed.   Village before Sunset.   Frances
Cornford.   BoNaP; LoGBV

Even the waves rise in the image of flowers.   The Diary of the Waning Moon
(excerpt).   Abutsu.   PBWP

Even the wildest beast afar/Knows the light of the Saviour's star.   Christmas
Legends.   Denis Aloysius McCarthy.   ChBR

Even the women could detect/Their awful fall from intellect.   Recapitulations.
Karl Shapiro.   PoNe

Even then, damn me if I'd work a day/For the Company underground./Nor
over ground.   For the Company Underground.   Francis MacNamara.
NOAV

Even then not in fear of error.   On a Recent Protest against Social
Conditions.   David Posner.   NYBP

Even then, yes–they will behold another sunrise.   Winter Count of Sean
Spotted Wolf.   Earle Thompson.   STE

Even these feathers freed from their wings forever/are afraid.   The Book of
Nightmares.   Galway Kinnell.   NNaP

Even this love's heat must be its curb and rein.   Cantica: Our Lord Christ.
Saint Francis of Assisi.   AWP; OBVE

...Even this melting/lifts the sleepless ship toward grass.   To You on the
Broken Iceberg.   Tess Gallagher.   GP

Even this, oh Love, for thee to Death!   Of His Death.   Meleager.   AWP

"Even this shall pass away.'"   The King's Ring.   Theodore Tilton.   GoTF;
TreFS

Even tho, I must remember this, I have forgotten you.   Words.   Helen
Morgan Brooks.   NNP; PoNe

Even those sad words, even in sad me did breed.   Astrophel and Stella,
LVIII.   Sir Philip Sidney.   AAS; SiPS

Even though birds/Are creatures with wings.   Footpaths Cross in the Rice
Field.   Lin Ling.   PBWP

Even though I am quiescent as in death/I soar amongst the stars.
Ruaumoko–The Earthquake God.   Mohi Turei.   WTO

...Even though/it was a woman to blame as usual, died.   Helen.   James
Harrison.   NLV

Even though the oldest kings had their singers and/clowns calling, "Oh king,
you shall live forever   Good Morning America (excerpt).   Carl Sandburg.
OFD

Even though they cannot be heard.   Variations on a Theme.   Mark Vinz.
LiTA; Psk

Even though you cover it/with careful wrappings.   Love, that dwarfs our life.
Akahito (Yamabe no Akahito).   LiTW

Even thus do the favors flow of disgustful Fortune.   Aweary Am I.   Abu-l-
Ala al-Maarri.   AWP; LiTW

Even to Envy, sharpening a knife,/His interest.   Music in Venice.   Louis
Simpson.   NYBP

...Even/to one on this night train.   On the Night Train from Oxford.   E. L.
Mayo.   FAZ

Even to the bourne of all, to the unbeholden land.   The Seven against Thebes.
Aeschylus.   AWP

Even to the icy winter, and the siege.   Leningrad Cemetery, Winter of 1941.
Sharon Olds.   NIP

Even to the rich she can forgive/Their regal selfishness,–and let them live!
Charity.   George Parsons Lathrop.   CAW

Even today I get proud/when I remember/this all took place in Chinese.
Chronicle.   Mei-Mei Berssenbrugge.   GP

Even two like Don Alonzo Estaban San/Salvador.   El Capitan-General.
Charles Godfrey Leland.   AA; HBV 1-2; YaD

...Even we/Who are still blind a while, facing the sun.   The Day.   Witter
("Emanuel Morgan") Bynner.   PGD

Even when he looks away/he sees his uncle's body fall   What He Saw.
Robert Currie.   Str

Even when sun is not.   Banalbufar, A Brazier, Relativity, Cloud Formations...
Paul Blackburn.   CoPo

Even when the liar speaks the truth.   The Shepherd-Boy and the Wolf.
Aesop.   AWP

Even when we went the two of us together?   How Will You Manage.
Princess Daihaku.   AWP

Even when we went/together.   How will you cross.   Princess Oku.   BoWoP

Even where the gravestone's single/flower blows.   First Joy.   Vernon
Watkins.   ChMP

Even whose recktie/are covered by lloyd's.   Flotsam and Jetsam.   Edward
Estlin Cummings.   NOBA; OBAL

Even with the good knight Charlemain.   Ballad of the Lords of Old Time.
Francois Villon.   AWP

Even yet, perhaps, a trifle piqued–who knows?   The Troll's Nosegay.   Robert
Graves.   PoCh

...Even you/Might close hands with this/crew?   Son.   James A. Emanuel.
PoNe

Even your summer in another clime.   Sonnet: "I know I am but summer to
your heart."   Edna St. Vincent Millay.   HBMV

Evening beyond the point/where the lighthouse breaks.   Six Ten Sixty-Nine.
Conyus.   PoBA

Evening bring us to our beds with/Grateful thoughts, forgiving, and/Forgiven,
for Jesus' sake. Amen   A Christmas Prayer.   Robert Louis Stevenson.
TrCP

The evening can be awfully jolly.   When Lovely Woman Stoops to Folly
(parody).   Mary Demetriadis.   FaBoPa

Evening/cannot conceal the stark/nudity of trees.   For Spring.   D. G. Jones.
NOBC

Evening clouds are glowing/And dusk is full of song.   Spring.   Harry Behn.
TiPo

The evening comes, the fields are still.   Bacchanalia (excerpt).   Matthew
Arnold.   FaBoRV; OAEL 1-2

–The evening darkness gathers round/By virtue's holiest powers attended.
Lines Written near Richmond, upon the Thames, at Evening.   William
Wordsworth.   OBEC

Evening is comforting flame.   Friend.   Gwendolyn Brooks.   CNA

The evening kicks him on his homing tangent.   The Daily Round.   Ronald
McCuaig.   BoAV

Evening mist-tides hissing past my brogues.   I Stroll.   Peter Redgrove.
NePoEA-2

The evening mists are rising now.   The Mists Are Rising Now.   Hasye
Cooperman.   GoYe

The evening paper, in an Irving Place cafe.   Problems of a Journalist.
Weldon Kees.   NaP; NYP

Evening's first star and golden as a bee/In the sun's hair–for happiness is here!
Don Juan's Address to the Sunset.   Robert Nichols.   OBMV

Evening, star of the sea.   Sea Pieces.   Robert Fitzgerald.   PoPl

...The evening star, the pale/cool-throated star, that rises with the Danish
nightingale.   Denmark.   Humbert Wolfe.   OBTV

The evening–/zippe, zappe!–/it goes.   Puerto Rico Song.   William Carlos
Williams.   NYBP

The evenings Sunne beheld there sweltred in their gore.   Polyolbion.
Michael Drayton.   OBS

Evenly of an assize.   The Round Table.   [(or Manning)] Robert
Mannyng.   ACP

Event he foresees for each of us–a reckoning, our own.   Last Things.
William Meredith.   NoAm

...Events/can bring back, they think, something that got away.   Berkeley,
Madison, Ann Arbor, Kent...   William Stafford.   SOTS

Eventually,/Friday comes.   Robinson Crusoe Daniel Defoe.   Maurice Sagoff.
NLV; PoRA

Eventually it becomes a/CAT.   The Kitten.   Ogden Nash.   DFF; MoShBr

Ever after live in strife, and wish again for Mallow.   The Rakes of Mallow.
Anonymous.   IrPN; OnYI

Ever after thy calm, look I for a storm.   Fortune.   Sir Thomas More.
GoBC

Ever again my handkerchief/Is scented with White Heliotrope.   White
Heliotrope.   Arthur Symons.   BoLoP; EBEV; PAI

Ever calling, "Blanca! Blanca!" through the desert halls/of Heaven.   Durand
of Blonden.   Ludwig Uhland.   AWP

Ever distant and dark, ever returning.   For a College Yearbook.   J. V.
Cunningham.   NoAm

Ever elegant in woe.   To the Memory of Lord Halifax (excerpt).   Ambrose
Philips.   FaBoCo

Ever faithful, ever sure.   Praise the Lord.   John Milton.   FaBoCh; LoGBV

Ever for your presence sighs.   Hymn to Artemis, the Destroyer.   Marya
Zaturenska.   MOON

Ever gratefully, Your little friend...   Matinees.   James Merrill.   HaCAP;
NOBA; Prf

Ever heard Bird/flap his wings   Mellowness & Flight.   George Barlow.
CNA

The ever-imminent gleamed a space/Through the dull wear of commonplace.
Vision.   James Devaney.   NOAV

Ever perfect, ever in them-/Selves eternal.　Rose-Cheeked Laura.　Thomas
　Campion.　AAS; AtBAP; EnL; EnLoPo; ExPo; InPK; InPo; InPS; InvP;
　LoBV; NoP; OAEL 1-2; OAEP; PAI; PoEL 1-5; SeCeV; TrGrPo; ViBoPo;

Ever Queen and Mother of God.　Our Lady on Calvary.　Sister Michael
　Marie.　ISi

Ever/Removed!　Life in a Love.　Robert Browning.　HBV 1-2; MaVP;
　OAEP; OBNC; OBVV; TrGrPo

Ever shall the circling sun/Find the Many still are One!　Additional Verses to
　Hail Columbia.　Oliver Wendell Holmes.　PAH

Ever since, o'er all our loss/Shines the glory of the cross.　A Thought.
　Margaret E. Sangster.　TRV

Ever singing "die, oh! die."　The Phantom-Wooer.　Thomas Lovell Beddoes.
　EnRP; ERoP 1-2; OBRV; TrGrPo; ViBoPo; WiR

Ever so quietly/when we weren't looking.　Why Did You Go.　Edward
　Estlin Cummings.　VGW

Ever stop me/loving/even you!　There's Somethin'.　Adam Small.　PeSA

Ever to make all men in soul and body/free.　Oh, Let Thy Teachings.
　Immanuel Di Roma.　TrJP

Evere beeth his geres to the grove grene.　Snatches: "Thei thou the wulf hore
　hode to preste."　Anonymous.　OxBM

The evergreen pricking its cool needles.　To Mark Rothko of Untitled (Blue,
　Green), 1969.　Anne Cherner.　PoDr

Evergreens that ne'er decay.　To a Child Five Years Old.　Nathaniel Cotton.
　OxBChV

Everlasting as a thought.　Night at an Airport.　David Ignatow.　NNaP

The everlasting cat!　The Cat of Cats.　William Brighty ("Matthew
　Browne") Rands.　OxBChV

...The everlasting/gaudeamus igitur of the elder students.　The Academic
　Overture.　Richmond Lattimore.　GLGT

Everlasting omen of what is.　Often I Am Permitted to Return to a Meadow.
　Robert Duncan.　CAPP; CMoP; HeIP; NOBA; NU

The everlasting surges of the tide.　George Washington.　John Hall Ingham.
　AA; OHIP; PAH; PAL

Evermore Thy child to be.　A Child's Prayer.　Anonymous.　BLRP

Evermore was the flight/Of the fire-bird of Rangi.　The Noosing of the Sun-
　God.　Jessie MacKay.　ACV

Every afternoon,/Boom! Boom!　Sally Go Round the Sunshine.　Anonymous.
　OuSiCo

Every beauty takes my minde,/Tied to all, to none confin'd.　Loves Heretick.
　Thomas Stanley.　CavP

...Every Bird of song/Attending his loud harmony with admiration and love.
　Milton.　William Blake.　OBRV; PB; PBBP

Every bird, sky's prey and bereft of origins.　Every Land Is Exile.　Claude
　Vigee.　VWA

...Every bug that can fly/is down at the spotlight.　Ballet under the Stars.
　Robert Stewart.　FAZ

Every compass is looking at you.　Traveling North.　John Woods.　PoL

Every critic–don't you know it?/Is himself a minor poet.　Every Critic in the
　Town.　Robert Fuller Murray.　PoL

Every day a new landscape/and the heart, peeled like an onion.　Bouzouki.
　Kenneth O. Hanson.　GP

Every day/a new map of the same terrain.　Six Years.　Alice Bloch.　PeHV

Every day at sundown for your dear sake my love.　Out of the Rolling Ocean
　the Crowd.　Walt Whitman.　ViBoPo

Every day he comes to weep.　On a Wife.　Francis Coutts.　OBSP; OBVV

Every day I did not spend in solitude was wasted.　After Long Busyness.
　Robert Bly.　CAPP; PoA

...Every day/Speaks a new scene; the last act crown the play.　Epigram: "My
　soul, sit thou a patient looker-on."　Francis Quarles.　PoPle

Every day, walking the city jungles.　The Nature of Jungles.　W. R. Moses.
　NCSH

...Every day we separate.　Villanelle.　Marilyn Hacker.　AmPA; SM

Every drawer I will paint a different color.　Eclipse.　Tomaz Salamun.
　VWA

Every drop we sprinkle/O'er the brow of Care/Smooths away a wrinkle.　Fill
　the Bumper Fair.　Thomas Moore.　HBV 1-2

Every evening now throughout the summer.　A Cold Spring.　Elizabeth
　Bishop.　MP; TwCP

Every finger a bird.　Bird Watcher.　Ronald Wallace.　PPJ

Every footprint/is a rose.　Cat in the Snow.　Aileen Fisher.　NTCP

Every gem/Is perfect; and with care I polished/them!　To a Plagiarist.
　Moses Ibn Ezra.　TrJP

Every greasy nuisance has been banisht–/Hurraw for Gass!　An Ode on Gas.
　Anonymous.　OBAL

Every hour there is less of that touch in the world.　For a Masseuse and
　Prostitute.　Kenneth Rexroth.　NNaP

Every imaginable pattern of constraint.　Ration Party.　John Streeter
　Manifold.　WaP

Every inch of you, a terrible vision, not bear, but virgin!　Elizabeth's War
　with the Christmas Bear: 1601.　Norman Dubie.　LCAP; MAYP

Every inch of your life is like theirs, you move out.　So Long Solon.　Jack
　Myers.　AmPA

Every kind of life immortal in its Maker!　Proverbial Philosophy.　Martin
　Farquhar Tupper.　VLP

Every lake in Canada under the stars.　Night Wind in Fall.　W. R. Moses.
　NCSH

Every land my imagination knew.　Pegasus.　Patrick Kavanagh.　FaBoIP;
　MoAB; OxBI

Every living creature is/Woman, Man, and Child.　The Riddle.　W. H.
　Auden.　EnLi 1-2

Every man is a King of Dreams!　The King of Dreams.　Clinton Scollard.
　HBV 1-2

(Every man's woman and every/woman's man, said Suetonius　The Switch
　Blade (or, John's Other Wife.).　Jonathan Williams.　NeAP

Every man who has no hair/Generally wears a wig.　Hickety, Pickety, I-
　Silicity.　Anonymous.　OxNR

Every man wished Andre clear, and Arnold in his stead.　Major Andre
　(Arnold's Treason).　Anonymous.　AmFP

Every mither had her son,/But sweet Sir Hew was dead.　Sir Hugh, or, The
　Jew's Daughter (C version).　Anonymous.　BaBo; CH; ESPB

Every morning, rising, rising, rising, ask yourself.　Cocteau's Opium: 2.
　Donald Finkel.　CoPo

Every morning the sun comes, the sun.　The Arc Inside and Out.　Archie
　Randolph Ammons.　NoAm; NoP

Every morsel snap, snap, snap.　Giant Bonaparte.　Anonymous.　OxNR

Every mountain valley and bog in Ireland will shake/one day, before she shall
　perish, my Roisin Dub　Little Black Rose.　Anonymous.　NOBI

Every nail slides down/its passageway as if/that destination/had been chosen.
　Hammer.　Erica Funkhouser.　AMV-81

Every natural action obeys by/the straightest possible process.　The Praises.
　Charles Olson.　VGW

Every night, by my lamp, hair turning white.　Regretful Thoughts, II.　Yu
　Hsuan-chi.　BoWoP

Every night it's not like life.　Keno.　Dara Wier.　MAYP

Every night the same stew.　The Young Wife.　C. K. Stead.　OCNZ

Every Night with our Beauties lie.　The Happy Husbandman; or, Country
　Innocence.　Anonymous.　CoMu

Every Nymph may read thee–Here.　A Sigh.　Anne Finch, Countess of
　Wilchilsea.　CEP

Every one with a bell and a blue hat,/And what is that?　Riddle: "Down by
　the waterside stand a house and a plat."　Anonymous.　GBP

Every place, everywhere, every day.　The Lord Has a Child.　Langston
　Hughes.　AH

Every prayer is heard in heaven/That is breathed from a truthful mind.　Who
　Has Our Redeemer Heard.　Stephen Collins Foster.　AH

Every round goes higher higher,/Some o' these days.　God's Goin' to Set
　This World On Fire (B vers.) (with music).　Anonymous.　AS

Every scrap of disaster's your/Privilege./Anything.　Payments.　Diana O
　Hehir.　NPGG

...Every sidewalk on the block/was scribbled with obscenities and hearts.
　Tar.　C. K. Williams.　GeTw

Every single Australian/every single one of them,/every single one.　They'll
　Tell You About Me.　Ian Mudie.　PoAu 1-2

–"Every step an arrival."　Overland to the Islands.　Denise Levertov.
　ConAP; UnPo

Every step of the way shining out of them.　My Mother's Feet.　Stanley
　Plumly.　GeTw

Every tendon move of the years, sitting, staring, in the/hallway...　Houston
　Street, N.Y.　Carolyn Baxter.　LFAC

Every time he farts, he shits.　Family Life.　Anonymous.　DBV

Every time is the first anew.　Finding a Poem.　Eve Merriam.　RFM

Every time it shakes/it's a sign my baby's home　Deceitful Brownskin Blues.
　Blind Lemon Jefferson.　BluL

Every two hours I wipe off my glasses.　Eyeglasses.　Tom Clark.　ConAP

Every window has been abused with the rocks of departing children.　Los
　Mineros.　Edward Dorn.　PoM

An' every work her love ha' wrought/To eyezight's woone, but two to thought.
　Tokens.　William Barnes.　NBM; PoEL 1-5; VLP

Every work of noble mind/is a noble work of God.　Remember the Source.
　Richard Eberhart.　MoRP

Every year thou claimest a heart.　The Dart.　Anonymous.　GBP

Every year we're surprised/how this old chestnut still grabs/a couple squirrels.
　The Graduate.　Charles Stetler.　GP

Everybody is dangerous.　Triolet.　Sandra McPherson.　SM

Everybody looks his best/At this annual ball.　Autumn's Fete.　Alice Sutton
　McGeorge.　YeAr

Everybody loose and at a distance.　Zimmer Envying Elephants.　Paul
　Zimmer.　GP

Everybody's naked.　Chugachimute I Love the Name.　Rochelle Owens.
　CoPo

Everybody try/to do the hop, skip, and jump.　Hop, Skip, and Jump.　Gary
　Snyder.　LCAP

Everybody works in our house, but my old man.　Everybody Works but
　Father.　Charles W. McClintock.　TreFS

Everyday is august second.   The August Second Syndrome Poem.   J. A. Hines.   LFAC

Everyday now are as unreliable/As their eyes.   The Lie.   Al Lee.   AmPA

...Everyone and I stopped breathing.   The Day Lady Died.   Frank O'Hara.   ANYP; CAPP; HaCAP; HoAn; NeAP; NoAm; NOBA; NoP; NYP; PoM; SOTW

Everyone believes in his own luck.   In the Middle of August.   Edward Hirsch.   MAYP

...Everyone gaping/and elaborate Louis Quatorze wondering at his envy.   My Marriage with Mrs. Johnson.   Jack Gilbert.   NPGG

Everyone is dead who would know/the little there is to know/about Abraham. Abraham.   George Bogin.   GOYP

Everyone silent, moving....Take my hand. Speak to me.   Effort at Speech between Two People.   Muriel Rukeyser.   FYAP; MoAB; MoAmPo; MP; TrGrPo; TrJP; TwCP; WeW

& Everyone simply dances away.   Slow Dance.   David St. John.   AmPA; LCAP

Everyone wants to get at her.   The Incentive.   Martial (Marcus Valerius Martialis).   UnTE

(Everyone wants to meet him).   Lines to Ralph Hodgson, Esqre.   Thomas Stearns Eliot.   NLV; OBAL

Everyone wished to walk.   Klaxon.   James Reaney.   AmC

...Everything/As on my heavenly hills.   The Fire-bringer.   William Vaughn Moody.   WGRP

Everything else, drunken/dumbshow.   Memory Gardens.   Allen Ginsberg. NNaP

Everything good is from the Indian.   Comanche.   Tom Clark.   ANYP

Everything has happened.   The Babysitters.   Sylvia Plath.   NoP

Everything I do is stitched with its color.   Separation.   William Stanley Merwin.   AmPC; HAP; NoP; PCP

Everything I say/is a garment.   Sous-Entendu.   Anne Stevenson.   OBSP

Everything is air-conditioned except the air.   I Hear America Griping. Morris Bishop.   AmFN; QQQ

Everything is blissfully quiet now. I am ready for sleep.   The Conversation in the Drawingroom.   Weldon Kees.   EAS

...Everything is/done against Time.   A Cold Night.   Bernard Spencer. WaP

Everything is known to a god. The gods are desperate.   Poem: "Like a deaf man meshed in his endless silence."   John Wain.   PoCh

Everything is water/if you look long enough.   Just Friends.   Robert Creeley. NeAP

Everything just grows/More beautiful.   Haiku: "Spring rain."   Kaga no Chiyo.   PBWP

Everything knows its way.   The Sky.   Anonymous.   TTY

Everything/makes/its music   Lowriders #2.   Reyes Cardenas.   FIA

"EVERYthing's robins/when you're still just three."   Little Brother.   Aileen Fisher.   BiCB; DTC

Everything that is not God consumed with intel-/lectual fire.   Blood and the Moon.   William Butler Yeats.   MBW 1-2

Everything that never held a single thing at all.   Elegy in a Theatrical Warehouse.   Kenneth Fearing.   NYBP

Everything they say/And everything they do.   Faults, Male and Female. Anonymous.   DBV

Everything/was/all right.   Black Sketches, 5.   Don L. Lee.   NeAC

Everything we cannot see is here.   The Glass Door.   Robert Watson.   GP

Everything we look upon is blest.   A Dialogue of Self and Soul.   William Butler Yeats.   CABA; CMoP; DTC; ExPo; FaBoMo; LiTB; LiTM; MasP; MoBrPo; NoAm; OAEP

Everything you are gone slightly mad./America.   Lady.   Ted Berrigan. APU

Everywhere bacteria swim.   World of Bacteria.   Sakutaro Hagiwara. AMV-80

Everywhere, everywhere, Christmas to-night!   A Christmas Carol.   Phillips Brooks.   OHIP; SoPo

Everywhere, far and near,/It will shine–water-shine.   Flute Song.   Kavangho Masaveimah.   WTO

Everywhere he wrote in sand/But in the language of Heaven.   The Wandering Jew.   Benjamin Fondane.   VWA

Everywhere, teethmarks on this and that.   Kindertotenlieder.   Michael Longley.   CIP

Everywhere the solemn/malignancy of life/is the burden/to be carried into the mountains.   Longjaunes His Periplus (excerpt).   Howard McCord.   GP

Everywhere the wind blows,/From Cruz to Quoddy Head.   The Coasters. Thomas Fleming Day.   AA

Everywhere was full of the pulsing of the loud and fallen dusk.   The Dark and Falling Summer.   Delmore Schwartz.   NYBP

Everywhere you turn is luck.   The Undertaking.   Louise Gluck.   FaBoWP

The evidence inviting me to trace/it where it was before it left its place. Playmates.   Lillian Everts.   GoYe

Evidence of/chaotic times.   Dark Shadows.   John Hall.   NBP

Evidently-veiled griefs; impervious tombs.   A Pastoral.   Geoffrey Hill. NePoEA-2

Evil example will never come of me.   The Song of Roland, LXXIX. Anonymous.   WaaP

Evil king is known by his imposts.   The Chinese Book of Rites (excerpt). Anonymous.   OBVE

Evil they sow, and sorrow will they reap for their/harvest.   A Vision of Judgement.   Robert Southey.   EnRP

An evil word it is,/This love.   In Memory of Radio.   LeRoi (Imamu Amiri Baraka) Jones.   NeAP; NIP; NoP; PoM

Evolved calmness,/my heart enfold.   The Sorrow of Unicume.   Sir Herbert Read.   BrPo; ChMP

Exact more interest than my casual pity.   The Spring Vacation.   Derek Mahon.   FaBoIP

Exalted in/the streaming rain.   And When the Green Man Comes.   John Haines.   ConAP; NCSH

Exalted there they ought to Shine.   My Spirit.   Thomas Traherne.   SeCV 1-2

Examples be of mine estate, though there appear no wound.   No Pains Comparable to His Attempt.   Anonymous.   PBBP

Exceeds a thousand days of mirth.   Ballstown.   Anonymous.   AmFP

Excellency of stars, precious stone of the night.   Welcome to the Moon. Anonymous.   BoNaP; MOON

Except a certain awful look/of terrible depression   In Golden Gate Park That Day.   Lawrence Ferlinghetti.   NoAm

Except a space where the wind whistles,/but you cannot see that.   Drawings by Children.   Lisel Mueller.   PoDr

Except as he find it/In the security of all.   A Free Nation.   Edwin Markham.   TRV

Except at Harvest Festival.   Diary of a Church Mouse.   Sir John Betjeman. BoC; OxBTC

Except at sunset when it mingles milk with blood and urine.   Serengeti Sunset.   Andrew Oerke.   PoL

Except by ancient crabs like me, who served/their time in sail.   The Old Quartermaster.   Gordon Grant.   EtS

... Except dread Jove/Think it enough for me to have had thy love.   To His Mistress Desiring to Travel with Him as His Page.   John Donne.   NOBE

Except for its marauding hand/It had been Heaven below.   Immortal is an ample word.   Emily Dickinson.   NOCV

Except for one squeamish old spinster.   There Once Was a Wicked Young Minister.   Conrad Aiken.   OBAL

Except for that stifling thought.   War.   Michael Brownstein.   ANYP

(Except for the French/who still want to be Mensch)   Can. Hist.   Earle Birney.   OxBC

Except for the green and Tipperary, boys.   Tipperary Recruiting Song. Anonymous.   OnYI

...Except I'd have your tongue cut out.   A Lesson in Oblivion.   Dabney Stuart.   GP

Except in Fenchurch Street alone,/And there by Peter Cockburn.   From a Tobacco Wrapper.   Anonymous.   FaBoUs

Except in you who keep no single spark.   Sonnet II: "O handsome chestnut eyes, evasive gaze."   Louise Labe.   BoWoP

Except Love's fires the virtue have/To fright the frost out of the grave. Death and Love.   Ben Jonson.   NOBE

Except of seeing the world's self submerged.   Sonnet: He Is Out of Heart with His Time.   di Montecanti Guerzo.   AWP

Except summer and a dog scratching at his side.   Accident at Three Mile Island.   Jim Barnes.   AMV-81; FAZ

Except that each looks at it with his mortal face.   City without Smoke. Edwin Denby.   NYP

Except that I am a fool.   Punchinello.   Hugh de Burgh.   CAW

Except that I'm stuck for better or worse/In Tolman's elastic universe. Richard Tolman's Universe.   Leonard Bacon.   ImOP

Except that lonely woman with white hair.   The Hero.   Siegfried Sassoon. OBWP

Except that old vacation boredom, and/A deep desire to be returned to land. Vacationer.   Walker Gibson.   SD

Except the body is moved,/still, to some other use.   Moment.   Robert Creeley.   CAPP

Except the gallows claim his due,/For hey! then up go we!   Song: "Know then, my brethren, heaven is clear."   Anonymous.   FaBoCo

Except the love of God, which shall live and last for aye!   The Love of God. Bernard Rascas.   CAW; WGRP

Except the wind that far away/Comes sighing o'er the heathy sea.   The Sun Has Set.   Emily Bronte.   UnPo; ViBoPo; VLP

Except their shaggy little child,/Who cried and cried.   The Satyrs and the Moon.   Herbert Sherman Gorman.   HBV 1-2

Except through death, a refuge and a crown.   To Vittoria Colonna. Buonarroti Michelangelo.   AWP

Except thy beauty, virtues, and thy friend.   Licia (excerpt).   Giles the Elder Fletcher.   EBEV

Except to prove the sweetness of a shower.   Tall Nettles.   Edward ("Edward Eastaway") Thomas.   BrPo; CBEP; ELU; FaBoTw; HBMV; MoAB; MoBrPo; OBSP

Except to raise some earth to shelter those/Whom the Madonna gathers for respose? Madonna di Campagna. Alfred Kreymborg. HBMV

Except trying/to see you with me. Apron Strings. Marge Piercy. TAP

Except you picked up small stones from the bridge/and seeded the water with them, making rings. The Ring Poem: A Husband Loses His Wedding Band... Philip Dacey. FAZ

Excepting he was up on yonder gallows tree/And my faith could bring him down. The Lover Proved False. *Anonymous.* AmFP

Excepting Paul and Peter. The Twins. Kathryn Jackson. BiCB

Excepting such who all this time/Had reason good against my rime. Almanac Verse. Samuel Danforth. SCAP

Excess of pride can bring the greatest misery. I Sing a Song Reluctantly. Countess Beatriz de Die. PBWP

Exchange a glance that marshals all death's field. A March with All Drums Muffled. Reuel Denney. NYP

Exchanging shells, which placed against the ear,/Occasionally echo the throbbing of a heart. Martin Buber in the Pub. Max Harris. BoAV; NOAV; PoAu 1-2

An excited Alexander you've mistaken for a match. Forgiven. A.(lan) A.(lexander) Milne. SoPo

Exclaimed, "This, too, I owe to thee, Jaffar!" Jaffar. [James Henry] Leigh Hunt. BeLS; HBV 1-2

Exclamation line of dots close quote. What Hath Man Wrought Exclamation Point. Morris Bishop. NYBP

...Exclusive ORLANDO/the new seamless nylon. The Orlando Commercial. George Macbeth. NOBL

Excuse me while I go and have a drink. Ballade of Liquid Refreshment. Edmund Clerihew Bentley. FaBoCo

Excuse us, Animals in the Zoo,/I'm sure we're very rude to you. Excuse Us, Animals in the Zoo. Annette Wynne. TiPo

Executor,/estranged, prayerless,/by a followed memory. Celan. Anthony Barnett. VWA

Exempt from mortal sin. The Double Vision of Manannan. *Anonymous.* BIrV

Exert our malice, gratify our pride,/And settle Satan's kingdom ev'rywhere. The Extravagant Drunkard's Wish. Edward Ward. NOEC

Exerts a healing power and a calm control. The Moon in September. Kashiprosad Ghose. ACV

Exhaled from open flanks, the sea. The Lido. Edmund Wilson. ErPo

Exhaling, weeping, trembling/With ever-yearning love. Die Lotosblume Angstigt. Heinrich Heine. AWP

Exhorts for God, for freedom, and the ballot box. Security. Denis Glover. AnNZ

(Exil'd for ay from those high treasures, which/He knowes not) grow in only follie rich. Astrophel and Stella, XXIV. Sir Philip Sidney. AAS; OAEP; SiPS

Exiles, sons of Eve, the accursed seed of Cain. On the Jewish Day of Judgment in the Year 1942. Jozef Wittlin. VWA

Existence is/before it gets wiped off. Existence. Sheila Moon. AMV-80

Existence, no doubt, precedes essence, but things/Became worse when the roof caved in. Synthesizing Several Abstruse Concepts with an Experience (parody). Carol Poster. BXAP

"Exit, pursued by a bear." The Shakespearean Bear. Arthur Guiterman. CenHV; EvOK

(Exit the hors d'oeuvres) ITEM. Edward Estlin Cummings. MoAB; MoAmPo

Exotic bird, haunter of autumn hedgerows. Pheasant. Sidney Keyes. HaMV

Expanding with the starr'd nocturnal flowers. From My Diary, July 1914. Wilfred Owen. CoBMV; FaBoMo; LiTM; MoAB; MoBrPo

Expect/nothing Notes on a Long Evening. David Phillips. NeAC

Expect nothing but advice on metrics. From the Provinces. Norman Rosten. HoAn

Expectant of the certain end. He Hears with Gladdened Heart the Thunder. Robert Louis Stevenson. GoTF; TreFT

Expectant of the silence of the skies. The Heavens Are Our Riddle. Herbert Bates. AA

Expecting the main things from you. Poets to Come. Walt Whitman. AnAmPo; FF; LiTA; TrGrPo; YaD

Expecting till thy Saviour comes/To dress them, and unswadle death. The Burial of an Infant. Henry Vaughan. OAEP

Expelled from the golden bars! Ass-Face. Edith Sitwell. OBMV

Experience is defendant, and the jury/Peers of tradition, and the judge is fury. The Judge is Fury: Epigraph. J. V. Cunningham. QFR

...The/Experience of the disaster fell the/Seventies. Hookerlumps in the Love Canal. William Sylvester. SOTS

Experience runs through me like a tape. Plexus and Nexus. Judson Jerome. AMV-81

...Experiment frittered. The Cross Spider. May Swenson. SUW

Experimenters, Enablers, Encouragers,/And Associates in Accomplishment. The Middle-Time. Lona M. Fowler. TRV

Experts, passionate and deft,/wait while Berra flies to left. Tao in the Yankee Stadium Bleachers. John Updike. LiSp

Expir'd To-day, entomb'd To-morrow,/When known, will save a double Sorrow. In Sickness. Jonathan Swift. CEP; NOEC; OBEC

Expiring notes–they and these lines are done. Balsham Bells. Kenrick Prescot. NOEC

Explains why I'm Eveready, why/you're a strange new story every time. Rechargeable Dry Cell Poem. Jim Wayne Miller. GOYP

Explicit prologus in decimumtertium librum Eneados. The Aeneid. Virgil (Publius Vergilius Maro). OxBS

Exploding color in the light. Powwow 79, Durango. Paula Gunn Allen. STE

Expose himself to light, and be/Developed just in time for bed. Some Frenchmen. John Updike. FaBoCo; NLV

Exposed to lose his life as well as breeches. Don Juan. George Gordon, Lord Byron. OBSV

Exposed to the polished strangeness,/asleep or awake. The 20th Century. Darrell Gray. APU

Exposing most, when most it gilds distress. Rural Life. George Crabbe. NOBE

An exquisite beast, the giraffe. The Giraffe. Nikolai Gumilev. LiTW

An Exquisite Reply! Within my Garden, rides a Bird. Emily Dickinson. AmPP

Extending your bleak shadow/into the bright web of song. That Is Not Indifference. Howard G. Hanson. AMV-81

Extends across the seventeenth parallel where head-/sized jungle flowers bloom. Dandelions for Chains. Sarah Kirsch. WPOW

Extends me holy fruit. Timid Lover. Countee Cullen. BANP

Extinct in the dry morning air. Bombing Casualties: Spain. Sir Herbert Read. PPON

Extols the silence of how soon a loss. Objects. W. H. Auden. NePoAm-2

An extraordinary thing for Aberdeen. On an Aberdeen Favourite. *Anonymous.* FaBoEE; FaBoPP

The Extreame Scabbe take thee, and thine, for me. To the Soure Reader. Robert Herrick. AnAnS 2; NLV; NoP; OAEP; SeCP

The exuberant light and burning bloom of/love. Apologia. Algernon Charles Swinburne. VLP

Exudes from the dried fish and the brown jug and the bowl. Nature Morte. Louis MacNeice. NoAm

Exultant shriek the demons of the gale! The Snowstorm. Pearl Riggs Crouch. BPAW; PoOW

...Eye-deep it led/to the naked and cold. In Memoriam Paul Celan. Gad Hollander. VWA

The eye in the leaf/Wombs Parody. Martha Paley Francescato. BoWoP

...The eye/luminous, price of solitude. The Offender. Denise Levertov. NePoEA-2

...The eye of flesh/that saw love couldn't last. Definition. Lauren Shakely. FYAP

Eye of the earth, and what it watches is not our wars. The Eye. Robinson Jeffers. AmLP; AP; CrMA; LiTA; LiTM; NOBA; OxBA; WaP

The eye of the realist is inflatable. The Eye. Michael Benedikt. ConAP

The eye-pits darted a dark ray/That searched me to my shadowy skeleton. The Dead Sheep. Andrew Young. FM

Eye, the cauldron of morning. Ariel. Sylvia Plath. CMoP; HaCAP; HeIP; LCAP; NMP; NoAm; NOBA; NoP; PBWP

The eye walking/around you/me. Eyes. Clarisse Nicoidski. VWA

The eyelids fall, the star-charts. The Invention of Astronomy. William Matthews. PoL

Eyes advance, waver as they feed/upon the rich succulence/of words. Public Library. Candace Thurber Stevenson. GoYe

Eyes and nose on a cabbage head I never did see before. Three Nights Drunk. *Anonymous.* OuSiCo

Eyes, from whose beauty God has/banished weeping/And wiped away the tear. Comforting Lines. *Anonymous.* STF

Eyes livid invitations,/as you challenged me one-on-one. The Challenge. Calvin Murry. LFAC

Eyes made for glory soon discover thee. That Thou Art Nowhere to Be Found. George Macdonald. TrCP

The eyes of lovers everywhere. A Stone. Richard Eberhart. NePoAm-2

—The eyes of my Regret. The Eyes of My Regret. Angelina Weld Grimke. CDC

The eyes of Texas are upon you/Till Gabriel blows his horn. The Eyes of Texas. *Anonymous.* FSW

The eyes of the dying and those of the dead. Eyes of Men Running, Falling, Screaming. *Anonymous.* OBWP

Eyes open aching from the cold and faced a trout. Water. Gary Snyder. LCAP

The eyes stay empty. The sky grows full. Comcomly's Skull. Jim Barnes. STE

...Eyes that see,/Beyond the dark, the dawn and thee. Spirit of Life, in This New Dawn. Earl Bowman Marlatt. AH

The eyes turn topaz. Mauberley. Ezra Pound. MoPo

...The eyes turning as the/fingers tighten on the scrawny neck.　The Lesson.
Paul Mariani.　MAYP

F

The fabled queen of love.　Sonnet: "When Phoebe form'd a wanton smile."
William Collins.　EnLoPo; OBSP

The fabric that death was weaving around you.　The Small Square.　Sophia
de Mello Breyner Andresen.　WPOW

Face Antichrist in each disguise.　Upon the Weathercock.　John Bunyan.
OxBChV

Face full of tears.　Fantasy Street.　Andrew Glaze.　NYP

The face he saw in heaven, looked down on me.　Lux in Tenebris.
Anonymous.　GoBC

A face I am ashamed to show.　Even in my dreams.　Lady Ise.　BoWoP

The face in a hoop of grim ecstasy　Her careful distinct sex whose sharp lips
comb.　Edward Estlin Cummings.　ErPo

Face in the mirror,/my tiny nightmare.　Landcrab.　Margaret Atwood.
SoSe

Face it. You must. You can.　Autumnal.　Rolfe Humphries.　MoRP

A face more like/A soup-tureen.　Queen Elizabeth.　*Anonymous.*　DBV

...The face of dusk/wanders between the never and the never.　Sabbath.　D.
Rosenmann-Taub.　VWA

The face of Him who walked on Galilee.　If I Could Grasp a Wave from the
Great Sea.　John Richard Moreland.　EtS

Face of my beloved/the face of love.　The Face of Love.　Ingrid Jonker.
PeSA

A face, once young, in age loved all the more.　Slow Summer Twilight.
John Hall Wheelock.　LiTM

Face stuffed and sneering, "Gratt has what it takes."　Professor Gratt.
Donald Hall.　OBAL

A face that was simply the front skin of the self concealed and separate.
Deaf School.　Ted Hughes.　NoP

Faces still reflecting Light from communion with/the Unknown God.　Black
Church on Sunday.　Joseph M., Jr. Mosley.　NBP

Facing the empty house and its laden barns.　On the Hall at Stowey.
Charles Tomlinson.　CMoP; NoAm

Facing the sun, untalkative, out of reach.　Here.　Philip Larkin.　CMoP

Facing west from home.　To Some Few Hopi Ancestors.　Wendy Rose.
TWSS

FACIT cry I!!!　The Typewriter Revolution.　D. J. Enright.　NoP

The Fact could not be sadder than the Thought!　Realization.　Mahlon
Leonard Fisher.　AnAmPo

"The fact has not created in me/A sense of obligation."　A Man Said.
Stephen Crane.　FF; GoTF; ImOP; LiTM; NCEP; OBAL; OBSP; OBSV;
PrIm; TAP; TreFT; WeW; YaD

The fact:–I've heard it,–once perhaps too much.　Don Juan.　George
Gordon, Lord Byron.　OBRV

A fact of which men spend their lives/Attempting to convince their wives.
The Bat.　Ogden Nash.　PV

"A fact so dread," he faintly said,/"Extinguishes all hope!"　The Mad
Gardener's Song.　Lewis (Charles Lutwidge Dodgson) Carroll.　BLPL;
FaBoCo; FaBoNo; NBM; OxBChV; WiR

Fade at forethought's touch of life's unknown/surprises/Far beyond.　Plus
Ultra.　Algernon Charles Swinburne.　VLP

Fade in a fragrant mist of tears away/When weeping noon leads on the altered
day.　Maquillage.　Arthur Symons.　OBSP; VLP

Fade then and fall–thou hast had all/That Life can give: ask somewhat now of
Death.'　Fading-Leaf and Fallen-Leaf.　Richard Garnett.　OBVV

Faded Face,/Sorrow-wrung!　The Faded Face.　Thomas Hardy.　QFR

A faded flower, a broken ring,/A tress of golden hair.　'Tis but a Little Faded
Flower.　Ellen Clementine Howarth.　AA; HBV 1-2

Faded in mist/O'er the river's banks.　I Saw a Ghost.　Joan Boilleau.　TiPo

Fader of Grace,/Whether thou has/Forgeten thy litel sone?'...　Lullay, My
Child.　*Anonymous.*　OxBM

Fades and shrinks, a red leaf/drenched and torn in the cold rain.　Phaedra.
Hilda ("H. D.") Doolittle.　SBG

A fading dust covering the hammer's tracks　Ember Grease.　Dick Gallup.
ANYP

...The fading sound/Is blent of falling embers, weeping kings.　Helen Grown
Old.　Janet Lewis.　QFR

A fag-end dropped on the silent road.　Corporal Stare.　Robert Graves.
BrPo

A faggot in steel boots.　2 Poems for Black Relocation Centers.　Etheridge
Knight.　NNaP; NoAm

Fail, Sun and Breath!–yet, for thy peace, She shall endure.　Trust Thou Thy
Love.　John Ruskin.　OBEV; OBVV

Failing the stature that such sires forecast!　Our First Century.　George
Edward Woodberry.　AmePo; PAH

Fails from sight,/Fails in the west.　Three Trees at Solstice.　Mary Finnin.
BoAV

A failure, and complete,/Was your Old Stone Fleet.　The Stone Fleet.
Herman Melville.　EtS

...A failure at expression/by this mass of death; unable to follow its vast
progression.　The Coral Reef.　John Blight.　NOAV

...Failure/the first day of the rest of our lives.　Little Yellow Leaf.　James
Tate.　NoAm

Failure, the longed-for valley, takes him in.　In the Smoking Car.　Richard
Wilbur.　ConAP; LiTM; MoAmPo

Fain, fain am I, O CHRIST, to pass the grave!　Resurrection.　Sidney
Lanier.　PoEL 1-5

Fain would fling the net, and fain have her free.　Love in the Valley.
George Meredith.　TrGrPo

Fain would I die to end this stress,/Remediless.　Of Misery.　Thomas
Howell.　EIL; FF

Fain would my Tongue adore my King/And pay the Worship due.　Sincere
Praise.　Isaac Watts.　TrPWD

Faint as shed flowers, the attenuated dream.　The House of Life.　Dante
Gabriel Rossetti.　BoLoP; SyP

Faint but distinct, uttered by drinking ground.　Dialogue of the Way.
Harold Stewart.　BoAV

The faint leaf vanishes to light.　Grapes Making.　Léonie Adams.　FYAP;
MoVE; NePA; UnPo

...The faint/light of snow, the blood stopped cold in my feet.　Ice River.
David Baker.　SM

Faint not–fight on! To-morrow/comes the song.　Be Strong.　Maltbie
Davenport Babcock.　AH; BLPA; FaBoBe; FaFP; OHFP; WBLP

The faint odor of fish I couldn't quite/wash from my fingers.　The Smell of
Fish.　William Meissner.　WOLT

A faint odour of bone/Withers quickly, my brain is stone.　Kohoutek.
Richard Ryan.　CIP

A faint star caravan.　Happy Christmases (excerpt).　John Francis
O'Donnell.　IrPN

Faint yet pursuing, faint yet still pursuing/Ever.　A Life's Parallels.
Christina Georgina Rossetti.　NBM; PoEL 1-5

Faintly answering still the notes that once were so dear.　At the Mid Hour of
Night.　Thomas Moore.　AnIV; GoBC; GTBS; GTBS-P; HBV 1-2; NBM;
NOBE; OAEP; OBEV; OBNC; OBRV; OxBI; PoEL 1-5; TreFS; ViBoPo

A faintly bilious look/perpetually on her face.　The Invention of New Jersey.
Jack Anderson.　InPS; PAI; TAT; TW

Faintly, like falling dew,/His fast notes shower.　The Skylark.　Frederick
Tennyson.　GN

Fair as she was, she never was so fair!　The One White Hair.　Walter Savage
Landor.　HBV 1-2

Fair beauty mixed with chastity.　Come, Love, Let's Walk.　*Anonymous.*
EIl

Fair but faded Summer,/Sweet, farewell!　Farewell to Summer.　George
Arnold.　AA

Fair by eleven.　Rain before Seven.　*Anonymous.*　FaBoBe; OxNR

Fair Conway sends this sweet wild rose to/thee!　With a Rose from Conway
Castle.　Julia Caroline Ripley Dorr.　AA

Fair fall the shadow-seekers!" quoth the king.　The First Voyage of John
Cabot.　*Anonymous.*　MC; PAH

Fair flowers thrive round the little grave, I pray.　To Two Bereaved.
Thomas Ashe.　NOBV

Fair head, her chainmail cap of golden curls./Penbyn Gwyr.　Gold.　Glyn
Jones.　NeBP

Fair Idea his mistress,/Child of Eternity.　A Wealthy Man.　William
Allingham.　IrPN

...A fair if privileged/Mind veined with gold.　Respectabilities.　Jon Silkin.
NePoEA-2; NoAm

A fair mouth's broken tooth.　August 1914.　Isaac Rosenberg.　EBEV;
NOBE; OBWP; OxBTC

Fair or weather or a two-reef gale.　The Ballad of Halfmoon Bay (excerpt).
Keith Sinclair.　AnNZ

Fair Play–/Both went to se–　The Show is not the Show.　Emily Dickinson.
AmePo; AmPP; DiPo

The fair report of seven good children's deeds.　The Mother.　*Anonymous.*
OHIP

Fair & strengthless as seafoam/under a deserted sky.　The Black Book.
John Berryman.　VGW

Fair virgins, learn by me/To count Love a toy.　Fie, Fie on Blind Fancy!
Robert Greene.　EIL

The fair, young Angel of my infancy.　A Mother's Picture.　Edmund
Clarence Stedman.　OHIP

A fair young wanton lady.　The Gipsy Laddie.　*Anonymous.*　BSV

Faire be no lenger proud of that shall perish,/But that which shal you make
immortall, cherish.　Amoretti, XXVII.　Edmund Spenser.　AAS

A fairer rose did never bloom/Than now lies cropp'd on Yarrow.　The Dowie
Houms o' Yarrow.　*Anonymous.*　OBS

The fairest blossom of the garden dies.　Visions.　William Browne.　ViBoPo

"The fairest flower o woman-kind/Is my sweet, bonie lady!" Geordie (A version). *Anonymous.* BaBo; ESPB; FaBoBa; OxBB

The fairest form, the sweetest breath,/Away he bore. Death of the Day. Walter Savage Landor. NoP

Fairest land while land of slaves/Yields their free souls no fit graves. E. B. B. James (1834-82) Thomson. HBV 1-2

The fairest of earthkin/My leman she shall be. The Hawthorn. *Anonymous.* GBP; OxBM

Fairest of them all/Is my handsome, winsome Johnny. I Know Where I'm Going. *Anonymous.* FSW

The fairest one that I can see, sir,/Innamen, senaman, see. Here Come Three Merchants A-Riding. *Anonymous.* TrAS

The fairest rose in shortest time decays. If Crossed with All Mishaps. William, of Hawthornden Drummond. CBEP

The fairest shepherd on our green,/A love for any lady. Fair and Fair. George Peele. EiL; OBEV; ViBoPo

The Fairies' Kangaroo. An Explanation of the GrassWalking the Fields. Robert Siegel. GeTw

The Fairies' sleep is warm and sweet! The Fairies' Shopping. Margaret Deland. HBVY

Fairweill. I say no moir. Gife Langour–. Henry Stewart, Lord Darnley. OxBS

The fairy isle is seen no more. The Enchanted Island. Luke Aylmer Conolly. OBRV

A fairy may be near you–but you may/never know. Once When You Were Walking. Annette Wynne. SUS

The Fairy mimbling mambling in the garden. The Mocking Fairy. Walter De la Mare. MoBrPo; MoShBr

The fairy month, the merry month, the laughter/of the year! June. Douglas Malloch. YeAr

A fairy-tale! Only–I feel it! Natural Magic. Robert Browning. VLP

...The faith and morals/hold/Which Milton held. Faith and Freedom. William Wordsworth. GN

Faith bleats to understand. I should have been too glad. Emily Dickinson. NOCV

Faith failing her, Love dyed in mee. Shall I Then Hope When Faith Is Fled? Thomas Campion. AAS

Faith, Hope, and Love–abide. The Old Year and the New. Annie Johnson Flint. BLRP

Faith, I could spare thee all, my dear. Epigram: "Thy eyes and eyebrows I could spare." *Anonymous.* FaBoEE

Faith in a dying Lord. Thy Conquering Name. Charles Wesley. BePJ

A faith in man, a trust in God. Recipe for Living. Alfred Grant Walton. PoToHe

Faith, let her go, or come, or tarry! Farewell, Dear Love! Since Thou Wilt Needs Be Gone. *Anonymous.* EiL; OAEP

A Faith more fix'd, a Rapture more divine/Shall gild their passage to eternal Rest. Sonnet: "Could then the Babes from yon unshelter'd cot." Thomas Russell. OBEC

Faith revives when faith was/failing. Hymn: "Framer of the earth and sky." Saint Ambrose of Milan. TrCP

Faith's mountain spreads its roots beyond this ground. After Laughter. Grace Buchanan Sherwood. GoYe

Faith, truth, worth, law, all popular protections. Caelica, LXXVII. Fulke, Lord Brooke Greville. FCP

Faith will be,/Never till they both believe. Tell Me, Dearest. John Fletcher. EiL; ViBoPo

Faithful as enemy, or friend. Roosters. Elizabeth Bishop. AmLP; CrMA; LiTM; NePA

The faithful fire of vision still awaiting our return. The Sacred Hearth. David Gascoyne. FaBoTw

A faithful former slave set free. Slave Story. Hodding Carter. PoNe

Faithful, fugitive, abolished Fili-Mele. Doorway to Time in Three Voices. Luis Palés Matos. InW

Faithful guardian, would you destroy me? Watch-Dog. Charles Brasch. OCNZ

A faithful love, a faithful love. The Fool by the Roadside. William Butler Yeats. MoVE

The faithful swain here lastly made an end,/Whom all good shepherds ever shall defend. Pastoral: The Tenth Eclogue. Michael Drayton. JCP

Faithful to God and thee. Beloved, It Is Morn. Emily Henrietta Hickey. CAW; GoBC; OnYI

The faithfulest–hardiest–last. You Lingering Sparse Leaves of Me. Walt Whitman. CBEP

Faithfully kept through hunger and through/cold,/By the good Christian knight, ELISHA KANE! Kane. Fitz-James O'Brien. PAH

Faithless Reader, you'll still feel like a leaf/lost in a pile of gloves. Outside Baby Moon's. Paul Violi. APU

Faithless to thee, false, unforgiven,/And lose my everlasting rest. Song: "Absent from thee, I languish still." John Wilmot, Earl of Rochester. BoLoP; ELP; EnLoPo; GBL; LoBV; MePo; OBS; SeCePo; SeCV 1-2; ViBoPo

"Faix, we're jisht the most peaceable race on the earth,/If ye l'ave us alone." The Peaceable Race. Thomas Augustin Daly. HBV 1-2

The falcon hath borne my Mate away. The Falcon. *Anonymous.* ACP; EG; InPo; LiTB; NU; SeCeV; ViBoPo

Fall asleep, or, hearing, die. Music. John Fletcher. FaBoCh; LoGBV

...A/Fall bonfire in summer that only/Lets one eye sleep Patience of a People. F. J. Bryant, Jr., CNA

Fall downe, fall downe, and worship it, for that is shee. Tell Me You Wandering Spirits. *Anonymous.* OBS

Fall, gall themselves, and gash gold-vermilion. The Windhover. Gerard Manley Hopkins. AtBAP; BiP; BrPo; CAW; CMoP; CoBMV; DiPo; EaLo; EBCP; ExPo; FaBoMo; ForPo; GTBS-P; HAP; InPK; InPS; InvP; LiTB; LiTM; LoBV; MoAB; MoBrPo; MoPo; MoVE; NIP; NoAm; NOBE; NOBV; NoP; OAEL 1-2; OAEP; OBNC; PAI; PBBP; PoEL 1-5; PoPl; PoPle; PoRA; PPoe; PPP; PrIm; SCV; SeCeV; SyP; TEP; TreFT; UnPo; VLP; WeW

Fall in! Fall in! Reveille. Michael O'Connor. AA; HBV 1-2

"Fall in!" I shouted; "Fall in for your pay!" I Stood with the Dead. Siegfried Sassoon. ChMP

Fall in Long Island. Lake Success. Robert Conquest. OxBC

Fall like rain to the hungry sea. On the Edge at Santorini. Michael C. Blumenthal. AMV-80

Fall/loosely/(waiting)/at her sides. Philomena Andronico. William Carlos Williams. FaBoMo

A fall, no flight. The Egg of Nothing. John Taylor. AMV-81

The fall of a fairy tear/On a fairy lute? Chopin Prelude. Eleanor Norton. HBMV

A fall of purest snow. The Fall of the Plum Blossoms. Ranko. TiPo

...Fall/of seeds and sleet, petal and limb. In the Surgery. J. M. Ditta. AMV-80

Fall on the seeming void, and find/The rock beneath. Faith. John Greenleaf Whittier. TRV

The fall-out of our clinking/Brattling chains... View from the Window. Jane McCoy. AMV-80

Fall, tyrants, fall! The Trumpet of Liberty. John Taylor. NOEC

...Fall upon corroded monuments and the/graves of the forgotten dead. Yes, the Agency Can Handle That. Kenneth Fearing. WeW

Fall wavering down to cover/The poet and his song. Auspex. James Russell Lowell. AnFE; AnNE; AP; APA; HBV 1-2; NePA; OBVV; PoEL 1-5; TAP

Fall yet triumphant in thy woe,/Bound with the entrails of thy foe. A Fly Caught in a Cobweb. Richard Lovelace. CaPo; SeCP

Fallen around the vase, saying they were sorry. Poppies. Sandra McPherson. GeTw

Fallen cold and dead. Oh Captain! My Captain! Walt Whitman. LoGBV

The fallen girl her grave effaces. Lyrics. James Agee. MoAmPo; PoPl

Fallen in the sword-swing of his stormy hand. Tall Stately Plants with Spikes and Forks of Gold. Frederick Goddard Tuckerman. AnNE

Fallen out of it/and vanished. My Father after Work. Gary Gildner. AMV-80; Psk

The fallen rain glitters like stars/In the dark river of her hair. Queen. Dom Moraes. NePoEA-2

The fallen, struggling monarch that has thrust/His tongue in rage and roll'd his red eyes in/disgust Vaquero. Joaquin Miller. AA; BPAW

...The fallen tree/weeps silently from dead, fringed eyes. The Felled Plane Tree. Anna Hajnal. BoWoP

The fallen trees/keep ringing. Occupational Hazards. David Young. FiCP

Falling afraid lest any keel come near! The Derelict. Rudyard Kipling. BrPo

Falling as rain. Autumn Rain. D. H. Lawrence. BrPo

Falling asleep I listen/To the falling London rain. London Rain. Louis MacNeice. HeIP; NoP

Falling blossoms. Haiku: "These branches..." Joso. FAZ

Falling, delicate, merging. Light Morning Snow, We Wait for a Warmer Season. John Garmon. AMV-80

The falling falling Snow? For Snow. Eleanor Farjeon. CH

Falling fast oh fast. Haiku: "Neither earth nor sky." Hashin. WeW

The falling fruits' uneven spastic/extrasystolic beats. Words to a Song. Agnes Nemes Nagy. BoWoP

The falling/gun/shells on our blk/ tomorrows. Right On: White America. Sonia Sanchez. BOLo; PoBA

Falling into the deep grass/they want to live with green forever. Girl with the Green Skirt. Dana Naone. CDW

Falling, no less, yet surely no more, than I. Caves. David Baker. MAYP

The falling out of faithful friends, renewing is of love. Amantium Irae. Richard Edwards. EiL; HBV 1-2; LoBV; OBSC

...Falling/petal by petal on the muzzles of the transfigured/horses. Letter from a Black Soldier. Bill Anderson. VGW

Falling six miles. Hitch Haiku. Gary Snyder. LCAP

Falling snow. Snowfall. Artis Bernard. NTCP

The far-off splendid semblance of my maid.   Shadows of His Lady.   Jacques Tahureau.   AWP

Far off, the sound/of "Walkin' the Dog"/fading.   West Lake.   Kenneth O. Hanson.   CoAP

Far off, with head as high, old Babylon.   The Impious Feast.   Robert Eyres Landor.   OBRV

Far-out voice calls, "Look, no moon!"   Winter: The Abandoned Nest.   Ron Baxter.   WeW

Far over sands marbled with moon and cloud,/From less and less to nothing.   The Last Tournament.   Alfred, Lord Tennyson.   FaBoPP

Far southward where a single chimney stands out aloof/in the sky.   Down the Mississippi.   John Gould Fletcher.   LiTA

Far toward the hills of heaven unveiled/and bright.   The Flight of the War-Eagle.   O. C. Auringer.   AA

Far-wel, and lok thou never eft Love defye!   L'Envoy de Chaucer a Scogan.   Geoffrey Chaucer.   EnLi 1-2

Far worse than any death to me.'   The Sailor Boy.   Alfred, Lord Tennyson.   MOS

Fara diddle dyno,/This is idle fyno.   Madrigal: "Ha ha! ha ha! This world doth pass."   Thomas Weelkes.   OxBoLi

The farcical, tragic impotence of our world.   Speakers, Columbus Circle.   Raymond Souster.   CaP

Fare thee well, Jamie Douglas!/Be kind to the three babes I've born to thee.   Jamie Douglas (A vers.).   Anonymous.   BaBo; ESPB; ViBoFo

Fare thee well, my charming girl,/With golden slippers on.   Cuckoo Waltz (with music).   Anonymous.   AS

Fare-thee-well now forever, my bonnie black Bess.   Dick Turpin and Black Bess.   Anonymous.   AmFP

Fare thee well, O Honey, fare thee well.   Dink's Song.   Anonymous.   ABF; FSW; OxBoLi

Fare weel and have gude nicht:/I say no more.   Lament of the Master of Erskine.   Alexander Scott.   BSV; GBL

"Fare wel my joy and welcom pain/Til I see my lady again!"   Go Heart, Hurt with Adversity.   Anonymous.   MeEL; OxBM

Fare well, From your dream/I only shall not rise.   Ark Parting.   Jay Macpherson.   NOBC

Fare ye well, Old Joe Clark,/I'm a-goin' away.   Old Joe Clark.   Anonymous.   ABF; FSW; TrAS

Fare you well, fare you well.   Great Getting Up Morning.   Anonymous.   FSW

Fare you well, my darling.   Little Brass Wagon.   Anonymous.   FSW

Fare you well, my own true love, for growing.   The Trees They Do Grow High.   Anonymous.   OBET

Fare you well; your suit is cold.'   The Merchant of Venice.   William Shakespeare.   CTC

Fareweill, with patience perforce till day.   The Solsequium.   Alexander Montgomerie.   GoTS; NoP; OxBS

Farewel, and you attending Stars that wheel/Round Nights black Axle-tree, bright Stars, farewel.   Idylls.   Theocritus.   OBVE

Farewel my book and my devocioun!   The Legend of Good Women.   Geoffrey Chaucer.   OxBM

Farewel you Puritannick Prig,/I scorn to take your Shilling.   The Penurious Quaker; or, The High Priz'd Harlot.   Anonymous.   CoMu

Farewell! adieu! good-by! so long!   To a Thesaurus.   Franklin Pierce ("F.P.A.") Adams.   BLPL; NLV; PoPl

Farewell all pleasure, welcome pain and smart!   Absence absenting causeth me to complain.   Sir Thomas Wyatt.   FCP; SiPS

Farewell and adieu./Echo: Adieu!   Lover and Echo.   Carroll O'Daly.   OnYI

Farewell, and overlook/these white ashes among the black.   Now in This Long-Deferred Spring.   Sylvia Townsend Warner.   FaBoWP

Farewell, bright jasmine flower, sweet maiden rose!   Popular Songs of Tuscany.   Anonymous.   AWP

Farewell direction, farewell all affection.   Arcadia.   Sir Philip Sidney.   FCP

Farewell, Erin! farewell all,/Who live to weep our fall!   Oh! Where's the Slave So Lowly.   Thomas Moore.   NOBI

Farewell, fare you well, my own true love.   The Anchor's Aweigh.   Anonymous.   ShS

"Farewell, farewell, my darling,/I'll never see thee more!"   O Strassburg.   Anonymous.   WaaP

Farewell, farewell, sweet hour of prayer!   Sweet Hour of Prayer.   William W. Walford.   BLRP; TreFT; WBLP

Farewell, farewell, temptation.   Brother Green.   Anonymous.   BFSS

Farewell, farewell, Your Royal Highness.   A Luncheon.   Max Beerbohm.   FaBoCo; NOBL; OBSV; OxBTC

Farewell, forever and a day!   Resurge San Francisco.   Joaquin Miller.   PAH

"Farewell from one whose love still burns for thee!"   Cordova.   Ibn Zaydun.   AWP; LiTW

Farewell. I waste no vainer words. I hope for better day.   A Refusal.   Barnabe Googe.   EnRePo; NoP

Farewell, lightbringer, fly to thy heaven again!   Terence MacSwiney.   George William Russell.   AnIV

Farewell, Miss Melerlee!   Miss Melerlee.   John Wesley Holloway.   BANP; PoNe

Farewell; my blessing season this in thee!   Hamlet.   William Shakespeare.   MasP

Farewell, my bonie banks of Ayr.   The Gloomy Night Is Gath'ring Fast.   Robert Burns.   MCCG

Farewell, my brother/Comrade, son.   For You, My Son.   Horace Gregory.   MoAmPo

Farewell, my dearest dear, till our next meeting.   The Seamen and Soldiers' Last Farewell to Their Dearest Jewels.   Anonymous.   OBSS

Farewell, my sweetest foe, mine Emily!   Arcite's Farewell.   Geoffrey Chaucer.   LiTL

Farewell, old bachelor.   Madrigal: "O I do love, then kiss me."   Robert Jones.   OxBoLi

Farewell! Othello's occupation's gone!   Othello.   William Shakespeare.   TreFT; TrGrPo

Farewell poor Turkeys I must say.   A Melancholy Lay.   Marjory Fleming.   FaBoCh; FiBHP; LoGBV; NLV

Farewell! Some day you'll merely be/"Among the patronesses"!   Debutantrum.   William Rose Benet.   InMe

Farewell, sweet heart of mine, farewell.   Medieval Norman Songs.   Anonymous.   AWP

Farewell! the birds of Eden/Ye shall hear nevermore!   Farewells from Paradise.   Elizabeth Barrett Browning.   OBEV; OBVV

Farewell the rest, the soil will be disdain'd.   The Advice.   Sir Walter Ralegh.   AAS; FCP; NCEP; SiPS

Farewell, then, my dear one-/My Mary, farewell.   Serenade.   Jeremiah Joseph Callanan.   IrPN; OnYI

Farewell, thou humid main.   O Billows Bounding Far.   Alfred Edward Housman.   BoNaP

Farewell, till spring days come again-/My Old Straw Hat!   My Old Straw Hat.   Eliza Cook.   BrRo

Farewell to charming Mollie; I died for the love of you.   The Sheffield Apprentice.   Anonymous.   AmFP; BFSS

Farewell to Ierne! Ierne, farewell.   Lay of the Forlorn.   George Darley.   OnYI

Farewell to splint, choke damp/and blast!/Hurrah, for Californy!   California.   J. P. Robson.   VLP

Farewell to the flowers in the valley.   Flowers in the Valley.   Anonymous.   AtBAP; OLR; OnMSP; OxBoLi

Farewell to the old Kentucky shore.   Darling Nellie Gray.   Benjamin Russel Hanby.   BLSo; FSW; PSoN; TrAS; TreFS

Farewell to your lover, honey, my love,/I love her to my heart.   This Lady She Wears a Dark Green Shawl.   Anonymous.   AmFP

Farewell, unkissed!   What Should I Say.   Sir Thomas Wyatt.   EnRePo; FCP; GBL; NoP; SiPS

"Farewell! We lose ourselves in light."   In Memoriam A.H.H., XLVII.   Alfred, Lord Tennyson.   VLP

Farewell wheelbarrow,/Little wife and all.   The Bachelor's Lament.   Anonymous.   OxNR

Farewell, whilst I live below,/my merry darling, my Sion.   On the Death of His Son.   Lewis Glyn Cothi.   PoPl

Farewell! who living didst support the State,/And coud'st not fall but with thy Counry's Fate.   Upon the Death of the Viscount of Dundee.   John Dryden.   OBS

Farm within farm and in the centre, me.   Summer Farm.   Norman MacCaig.   ACV; BSV; OxBTC

...A farmer cursed/the mess his body made.   Taught to Be Polite.   Virginia Brady Young.   AMV-81

A farmer ought to do his best for/every single seed!   The Anxious Farmer.   Burges Johnson.   BoNaP

The farmer take offense.   Little Boy Blue.   Guy Wetmore Carryl.   ALV

The farmer watching by the hedge/Shot both with his lang gun.   The Corbie and the Crow.   Anonymous.   PoPle

The farmers clean their boots, and whittle, and drowse.   Oregon Winter.   Jeanne McGahey   AmFN

Farther and farther, all the birds/Of Oxfordshire and Gloucestershire.   Adlestrop.   Edward ("Edward Eastaway") Thomas.   BrPo; CH; FaBoPP; GoJo; HAP; LiTB; NOBE; OBEV; OxBTC

Farther and farther from them yet/The road that lies before us.   Farewell to Town.   Laurence Housman.   HBMV

The Fascists sing the ancient hymn,/"The Peeler and the Goat."   O'Duffy's Ironsides.   Anonymous.

Fashioned bellcords to summon butlers/from my cousins' hair that grew no more.   Hair.   Maxine Silverman.   VWA

Fashioned of pearl and rose/This lonely shell.   The Lonely Shell.   Martha Eugenie Perry.   CaP

Fashioning, for the world and me,/A wholeness from our opposites.   Presence.   John Moffit.   MoRP

Fast fell the driving snow.　How One Winter Came in the Lake Region.　Wilfred (William Wilfred Campbell) Campbell.　CaP; NOBC; OBCV; PeCV

Fast-fixed as they in Time like glass.　In Time Like Glass.　Walter James Turner.　MoBrPo; NAMP; OBMV

Fast in the little General's fragile hand.　The Little General.　Edwin Muir.　BSV

Fasten'd her down for ever!　Ginevra.　Samuel Rogers.　BeLS; PoLf

The faster I run.　Riddle: "Two bodies have I."　*Anonymous.*　OxNR

Faster than a novel　A Poem.　Richard Meltzer.　PoL

Faster than the applauding coins of the world can ever fall.　Under the Umbrella of Blood.　William Pitt Root.　GeTw

The faster we go, the louder we get.　Progress.　Suzanne Douglass.　QQQ

Fat as she can waller.　Little Gal at Our House.　*Anonymous.*　ABF

Fat capons, quails and fish,/Each upon a lordly dish.　How Sweet Thy Precious Gift of Rest.　Ben Makhir.　TrJP

Fat, cold-eyed crows lighten our day.　Reading Indian Poetry.　Ramona Wilson.　VoR

The fat sky gurgles like a swollen bladder/With the foul rain that rains on poverty.　Lean Street.　G. S. Fraser.　NeBP; OxBS

A fat swan loved he best of eny roost.　The Canterbury Tales: A Monk.　Geoffrey Chaucer.　TrGrPo

Fat/with the baby happy land　A Heifer Clambers Up.　Gary Snyder.　NoAm; NOBA

Fate cannot harm me, I have dined today.　Recipe for Salad.　Sydney Goodsir Smith.　FaBoUs

"Fate cannot touch me: I have dined to-day."　Beer.　Charles Stuart Calverley.　BXAP; CenHV; FaBoCo; FiBHP

Fate, Fate has ordained us to plague one another.　The Poet and the Dun.　William Shenstone.　PP

Fate gave, what chance shall not control,/His sad lucidity of soul.　Resignation.　Matthew Arnold.　FaBoRV

A fate he shared–it bears much thinking on–/With certain persons at the Pentagon.　Here Lies Fierce Strephon.　Anthony Hecht.　TW

Fate is quick to revenge.　Epigram: "Just as he is growing a beard."　Aulus Persius Flaccus.　PeHV

Fate's King and not its Executioner.　To a Good Physician.　William Wycherley.　ACP

Fate's left instead of luck: what's candle lit in sun for?　Queen Anne's Musicians.　Thomas Hennell.　FaBoTw

Fate should snatch from me the jewel/Which I bought for one and sixpence on the beach.　On the Beach.　Charles Stuart Calverley.　ALV; FiBHP

Fated of grief to die,/Impart it to a solitary lyre?　Wherefore, Unlaurelled Boy.　George Darley.　ERoP 1-2; FaBoRV; NOBE; OBRV

Fates, be kind.　Moguls and Monks.　Lewis MacAdams.　APU

Father and Holy Spirit, Three–/Through ages without end!　Death-Bed Hymn of Saint Anthony of Padua.　Saint Anthony of Padua.　CAW

Father and mother rejoice,/And I in comfort live.　To My Youngest Kinsman, R. L.　Abraham Chear.　OxBChV

Father and mother watch an automobile with a just married sign on it grow-/ing smaller in a road.　The Automobile.　Russell Edson.　LCAP

Father, away! Our road is over there!　Mignon.　Johann Wolfgang von Goethe.　AWP

Father, be thou at our side!　Father, Hear the Prayer We Offer.　Love Maria Willis.　AH

Father begat me,/A simpleton./Whirr, whirr!　Foolish Child.　*Anonymous.*　PBA

A father betrayed by his son, all of us/sometime abandoned, lonely, denied.　The New Calf.　James Hearst.　TAT

...Father/carrion for the wild beasts and all the great vultures.　The Mu'Allaqa of Antar.　Antar [(or Antana)].　TTY

"Father, do Thou bless my child."　My Trundle Bed.　J. G. Baker.　BLPA; FaBoBe

"Father forgive," He said.　The Death of Goody Nurse.　Rose Terry Clarke.　PAH

Father, forgive me./I did not know what I was doing.　Confession to J. Edgar Hoover.　James Wright.　CAPP; ConAP

The father have dominion over hers.　Leaving Seoul: 1953.　Walter Lew.　BrSi

Father,/have you really come home?　The Father of My Country.　Diane Wakoski.　NoAm; TAP

Father hid his face and sigh'd,/Mother turn'd and wept.　Mother Wept.　Joseph Skipsey.　HBV 1-2; OBVV; VLP

"Father," I observed to Heaven,/"You are punctual!"　Lightly stepped a yellow star.　Emily Dickinson.　MoAmPo; MoShBr; OxBA

"Father, I thank thee!"　Evangeline.　Henry Wadsworth Longfellow.　AA

Father in heaven, we thank Thee.　Thanksgiving.　Ralph Waldo Emerson.　SoPo

Father, in Thy gracious keeping/Leave we now Thy servant sleeping.　Now the Laborer's Task Is O'er.　John Lodge Ellerton.　BLPA; GoTF; HBV 1-2; TreFS; WGRP

...Father/Mispronounced the French. But he had grace.　Ballet.　Brenda Hillman.　AMV-81

Father-/Nature, the Great Flame.　Faustus Triumphant.　Thom Gunn.　FaBoMo

Father, "Not my Will, but Thine."　Disappointment.　Edith Lillian Young.　TRV

The father of a friend just sickened and sickened.　Obsessive.　Marvin Bell.　LCAP

Father of Nile and Creator of Egypt.　Kilimandjaro.　Bayard Taylor.　AmP

Father's house is a better place/When the stormy rain is pouring.　A Story for a Child.　Bayard Taylor.　HBV 1-2; HBVY

A father's warmth in his son's house:/his own two knees to his chest.　Epigram: "Broad and ample he warms himself."　*Anonymous.*　NOBI

Father, Son and the Holy Ghost,/Through all eternity.　The Seven Blessings of Mary.　*Anonymous.*　FSW

Father, that I do not understand.　On the Subject of Poetry.　William Stanley Merwin.　PP

Fathered centuries ago by the noble Remus.　Whom Lesbia Loved.　Caius Valerius Catullus.　LiTW

The fathers/are coming　The New Mothers.　Carol Shields.　Str

Fathers are Time/And sons are thyme.　Concertmaster.　Richard Burgin.　AMV-81

"Fathers, forgive me. I cannot follow."　The Law.　Grace Schulman.　GP

The fathers of daughters/cannot say this.　Father Poem.　Joel Oppenheimer.　PoM

The fathers will hear you.　The Children's Bells.　Eleanor Farjeon.　CH

Fathomless, deep is my love/To thee, my passion, my mate.　Fathomless Is My Love.　Kalola.　WTO

The Fathoms they abide–　She Rose to His Requirement–Dropt.　Emily Dickinson.　CABA

Fatigu'd with dirt, drink, and embrace.　A Pastoral.　George Alexander Stevens.　CoMu; ErPo

The fattest ox the first must bleed.　Supreme Fortune Falls Soonest.　Robert Herrick.　CaPo

The faucon hath borne my make away.　Lully, Lulley.　*Anonymous.*　AtBAP; DiPo

Faultless, immortal, till he change or die./Love not!　Love Not.　Carolina Elizabeth Sarah Norton.　HBV 1-2; IrPN; OBVV

...The faun for whom/no curtain falls upon the mystery that he has always known.　Homage to Vaslav Nijinsky.　James Kirkup.　UnS

The fav'rite grand march that is played in Black Beard.　The Undertakers' Club.　*Anonymous.*　GBP

Favorite Grandson Braid touches my heart.　Favorite Grandson Braid.　Phil George.　VoR

The fawn dreams/With wide brown eyes.　The Fawn in the Snow.　William Rose Benet.　AnAmPo; MoAmPo

Fawning, and licked the ground whereon she trod.　Paradise Lost.　John Milton.　FM

Fayrer then fayrest, let none ever say,/That ye were blooded in a yeelded pray.　Amoretti, XX.　Edmund Spenser.　AAS

FE–Fi–FO–FUM!　I Do Like Ogres–.　Dorothy Brown Thompson.　ShM

Feace after feace, an' smile by smile.　The Fall.　William Barnes.　NBM; PoEL 1-5

A fear–a future state;–'tis positive Negation!　Limbo.　Samuel Taylor Coleridge.　ERoP 1-2; OAEL 1-2

Fear Bute, fear Mansfield, North and me,/And be as blest as slaves can be.　A Proclamation.　*Anonymous.*　PAH

Fear fills the chamber. Darkness decks the bride.　Hero and Leander.　George Chapman.　OAEL 1-2

Fear kills./Watch out.　Observation of a Bee.　Leah Goldberg.　WPOW

Fear not at all; for a slave, if he fears not, is free.　A Child's Future.　Algernon Charles Swinburne.　EnLi 1-2

"Fear not, I will pilot thee."　Jesus, Saviour, Pilot Me.　Edward Hopper.　AH; BLRP

Fear not, with my Zenophile/remain thou here to dwell.　The Little Love-God.　Meleager.　AWP

Fear now no thing but immortality.　The Book of Day-Dreams.　Charles Leonard Moore.　AA

The fear of death, I mean.　Exchange.　Dabney Stuart.　HoPM

...A fear/That runs by analogy/On your page, in your house, for your dear.　The Chinese Banyan.　William Meredith.　NePoEA

...Fear,/The yellow chirper, beaks its cage.　In the Cage.　Robert Lowell.　FF; NOBA; SM; SyP

Fear turns to sleep as one who dreamt of falling, an abyss!　Tall and Singularly Dark You Pass among the Breakers.　Louis Zukofsky.　NoAm

Feare Women that Sweare, Nay; and know they lye.　Satan, No Woman.　Fulke, Lord Brooke Greville.　NCEP

Feared to advance, feared to return–That's all.　The Knight in the Wood.　John Byrne Leicester Warren, Lord De Tabley.　NCEP; NOBV; VLP

Fearful for my children.　First Surf.　Emanuel DiPasquale.　Str

A fearful heart' betrays the knave–/Success to the Hyder Ali.　Barney's Invitation.　Philip Freneau.　PAH

Fearful though they be, fearful though they be.　We Will Not Fear.　David Diamond.　AH

Fearing the firmament to be the Khan/Of grotesque Caliph or blotched Caliban.　The New Moon.　Edmund Charles Blunden.　BrPo

Fearing to die if I but sleep alone.　Anguish.　Stephane Mallarme.　AWP; SyP

The fearless leave/Their names.　The Fearless.　Mortimer J. Adler.　PoA

The fears of years, like a biting whip,/Had cut grooves too deeply across our backs.　Hard Rock Returns to Prison from the Hospital for the Criminal Insane.　Etheridge Knight.　BP; ConAP; InPS; LFAC; NIP; NNaP; NoAm; TAP; UnPo

...The feast is ended.　Oberon's Feast.　Robert Herrick.　BoLiVe; CaPo; OAEP; SeCV 1-2; TrGrPo

A feast of heavenly mortar/an orgy of stones.　How Things Fall.　Donald Finkel.　VWA

A Feast unknown/to stone/or tree or beast.　Evolution.　May Swenson.　TrGrPo

Feather calligraphy avenue feathers　Some Feathers.　Dick Gallup.　ANYP

A feather from their breasts　Year of the Bird.　Brian Swann.　AmPA

A feather often turns the scale.　A Feather's Weight.　George Parsons Lathrop.　FaBoUs

...Feathers, glistening warm/with his own heartstain, fell through infinite space.　Panther and Peacock.　Gwen Harwood.　CBAP; PoAu 1-2

The feathers land selectively in living rooms/from Maine to Seattle...　Chrome Babies Eating Chocolate Snowmen in the Moonlight.　A. K. Redwing.　VoR

Feathers lopped off, spurs everywhere did lie.　Ad Johannuelem Leporem, Lepidissimum, Carmen Heroicum.　Anonymous.　FaBoNo

Feathers of a flee wad feather up his bonnet.　Wee Willie Gray.　Robert Burns.　OxBChV

Feathers of seed/have touched the Earth.　Open.　Joseph Bruchac.　FAZ

Featureless and alone.　Valediction.　Lawrence Raab.　AMV-81

The features are fixed with the dull metallic glow/of an ancient face, cast in bronze or brass.　My Father Dreams of Baseball.　Laurence Lieberman.　LiSp

Features so horrid, were it light,/Would put the Devil himself to flight.　The Ghost.　Charles Churchill.　OBSV

February's days are twenty-nine.　Days of the Month.　Anonymous.　HBV 1-2; HBVY; TreFT

The feckless, simple scent/of feathers, of fleece, of wet fur/in winter rain.　Nursing the Hide.　Carol Dunne.　AMV-81

Fed on the salt and blood of me.　Maritimes.　Penelope Shuttle.　BrRo

The Federal Constitution, boys, and Wash-/ington forever.　The Federal Constitution.　William Milns.　PAH

Feeble insects made it/In the stormy sea.　O Sailor, Come Ashore.　Christina Georgina Rossetti.　BrR; FM

Feed and come home again.　My Dame Hath a Lame Tame Crane.　Anonymous.　OxNR

Feed and lift them up for aye.　Psalm XXVIII.　Sir Philip Sidney.　FCP

Feed me till I want no more.　The Divine Hand.　William Williams.　BLRP

Feed on the bait, but yet beware the hooks.　To Alexander Neville.　Barnabe Googe.　EnRePo; NoP

Feed Thou my feeble shoots.　Long Barren.　Christina Georgina Rossetti.　PBWP; TrCP; VLP

Feeding our minds...the mind which is also flesh.　Mexico.　Robert Lowell.　BiP

...Feel/a soft, inward squeeze like a rubber ball.　Chicago, Summer Past.　Richard Snyder.　Psk

Feel each and all the inhumanities.　Ah Me! The Mighty Love.　George Frederick Cameron.　CaP

Feel her own soul through all the brooding air.　May, 1840.　Hartley Coleridge.　OBVV

Feel I but His hand.　It's Just the Same to Me.　Hermann Hesse.　ILwL

...Feel me, to do right.　Feel Me.　May Swenson.　GP

Feel not the world's despite.　Lachrimae.　Anonymous.　AtBAP

Feel o' the red earth!/Devon to me!　Devon to Me.　John Galsworthy.　HBMV

–The feel of my own body/New to me, as I struck, as he struck.　Experience.　James Simmons.　BIrV; CIP

"Feel'st not, Sir Dick," say saucy Moll,/"A Pious Melancholy?"　Praise-God Barebones.　Ellen Mackay Hutchinson Cortissoz.　AA

Feel–that it all is cold and gone.　Stanzas.　John Gardiner Calkins Brainard.　AnAmPo

Feel the Arabian/Winds floating from the fan.　The Fan.　Edith Sitwell.　HBMV

...Feel the quiet/and stability they make,/and lasting custom.　Park.　David Ignatow.　Psk

Feel the small shape of light/going out of my arms.　Her Going.　Shirley Kaufman.　PCP

Feel the whiskey burn.　Sunflower Rock.　Paul Blackburn.　NoAm

Feel their glass canopies flutter in the heav'nward prayer.　The Testament of Beauty.　Robert Bridges.　MoVE

Feeling everything that/we are it's not enough.　What We Can.　Ray A. Young Bear.　VoR

The feeling is a jewel like a pearl.　Friends.　John Ashbery.　LCAP

The feeling/is a little like when the Tarot cards by chance/turn up the Hanged Man.　Dream of the Forgotten Lover.　Lucia Fox.　BoWoP

The feeling is of/terrible slowness/overtaking haste.　The Tortoise.　Cid Corman.　InPK; SM; VGW

Feeling more in two worlds than one in all worlds the growing encounters.　The Shark's Parlor.　James Dickey.　NYBP

Feeling neither too ill nor too old.　At Home in Dakar.　Margaret Danner.　BlSi; FB

Feeling's magnification and the work in our words.　The Collector.　Robert F. Whisler.　AMV-81

Feeling their bodies/for bruises.　The Tough Ones.　Errol Miller.　AMV-80

Feels the dampness of the garden like a caress.　Poems.　Antonio Machado.　AWP; LiTW

Feet for glue or cloven feet or hooves/that split the world from knowing too much　Panegyric.　Harris Lenowitz.　VWA

Feet incorrigible/ragging the world,　Spring Omnipotent Goddess.　Edward Estlin Cummings.　OxBA

The feet it has/where eer they go/archy.　Fat Is Unfair.　Don (Donald Robert Marquis) Marquis.　EvOK

The feet of fierce or humble priests/trample out the green.　Credo.　Leonard Cohen.　PeCV

The feet & the pedals a single blur.　The Cyclists.　Lawrence Kearney.　AMV-80

–Fegs, God's no blate gin he stirs up/The men o' Crowdieknowe!　Crowdieknowe.　Hugh" (Christopher Murray Grieve) MacDiarmid.　InPS; NoM; NoP; OxBS; PAI

Felicitous phenomenon!　O to Be a Dragon.　Marianne Moore.　CTC; GoYe; NMM; PoPl

Fell as one dead at Desiderio's feet.　Charlemagne.　Henry Wadsworth Longfellow.　AnAmPo; FaFP

Fell down on you,/And made ye white.　How Lillies Came White.　Robert Herrick.　AnAnS 2; CaPo

Fell from the patriot's heaven down to the/loyalist's hell!　Arnold at Stillwater.　Thomas Dunn English.　PAH

Fell in love with it/and clung there.　Father.　Rose Auslander.　VWA

"Fell through a crack in the Floor of the/Sea"?　Of the Lost Ship.　Eugene Richard White.　AA

Fell to her death/from a great height/in Arizona.　Modern Romance.　William J. Harris.　GP

Fell with the falling night.　Snow Toward Evening.　Melville Cane.　SUS; TiPo

Felled, through which low laughters expire.　The Execrators.　David Galler.　NMP

A feller's always mostly man,/Out fishin'.　Out Fishin'.　Edgar A. Guest.　BLPL; PoLf

A fellow-angel to that godly bone!　Savage Portraits.　Don (Donald Robert Marquis) Marquis.　HBMV

The fellow sitting here thinking,/minutes ago.　Call It Goofus.　Bill Berkson.　ANYP

Fellow to the falling leaves.　The Solitary Woodsman.　Sir Charles G. D. Roberts.　CaP; OBCV

Fellowship for all the world!　The Message of Peace.　Julia Ward Howe.　PGD

...Felt as deeply/As any of these, with as much or as little reason.　Barnsley and District.　Donald Davie.　OxBC

Felt for thee as a lover or a child!　England, 1802.　William Wordsworth.　OBEV

Felt its intense reality with love and wonder, this lonely rock.　Oh, Lovely Rock.　Robinson Jeffers.　NoAm; NU

Felt my own littleness, and want of strength,/And thought no more to aim at works of length.　On Descending the River Po.　William Parsons.　OBTV

Felt the bewilderment of one/Who has recalled his murdering.　Jew.　James A. Randall, Jr.　BPo

Felt the first sunshine of the early spring!　France.　Langdon Elwyn Mitchell.　AA

Felt the pain/greater than pain/knew exactly/what it meant　The Musician at His Work.　Robert Currie.　Str

Felt the pang of transcience.　At Sea.　Jean Toomer.　BALP

The female hyena, it is/Very large.　Fact.　Kenneth Rexroth.　OBAL

The female moon/Beckons to darkness/And disappears.　Sand Paintings.　Alice Corbin.　AnAmPo; BPAW

A female Oedipus with half his sight.　Captain's Table.　Witter ("Emanuel Morgan") Bynner.　AnFE

Feminine marvelous and tough.　XXXVI.　Ted Berrigan.　ANYP

...The Fenians sped/Three mighty shouts to heaven; and left/Ben Edar to the dead.　Aideen's Grave.　Sir Samuel Ferguson.　NOBI

Fer over dat road Ise bound to go.　Ida Red.　Anonymous.　ABF; FSW

Fer she knows a thing or two.　Comin' to Town.　Robert V. Carr.　BPAW

Fer there warn't no use in stayin'/When one bird could sing fer all! The Mocking-bird. Frank Lebby Stanton. AA

A ferociousness of light/in the cold dark of the seas. The Medusa. Guy Davenport. GP

The fertile midnight, straining/in the lavish bed of morning. A Constant Labor. James W. Thompson. BPo

The fertile tears of women/That water the dreams of men. Lake-Song. Jean Starr Untermeyer. AnAmPo; HBMV; TrJP

Festive, clear, crowded with delight. The Handball Players at Brighton Beach. Irving Feldman. NYP

Fetch me far and far away. Invocation. Louis MacNeice. SO

Fetterless, lawless, a maiden free! A Mood. Amelie Troubetzkoy. AA

Fever port,/Port of Holy Peter. Port of Holy Peter. John Masefield. AtBAP; OBMV

Feverish people require more sleep than most,/And need to learn all they can about repose. Fever. Thom Gunn. PeHV

Few be my days of loneliness and pain/Until I meet in love with thee again. Sonnet: "In every dream thy lovely features rise." William Barnes. BoLoP

Few be they/Who, reaching Friendship's port, have there found rest. Ajax. Sophocles. LiTW

A few lean chimneys streaming/violently southward The Storm. William Carlos Williams. PCP; PPJ

A few minutes/only/for the sake of living We Fooled Ourselves. Jozef Habib Gerez. VWA

A few people are talking low in a boat. Driving toward the Lac Qui Parle River. Robert Bly. ConAP; LCAP; NaP; NCSH; NoP

Few people knew she died, but oh,/The difference to her! Lucy Lake (parody). Newton Mackintosh. BXAP; HBV 1-2; SpRo

...The few poems/that are the holy spaces of my life. Ghosts, Places, Stories, Questions. Vincent Buckley. NOAV

A few sad vacant hours,/And then, the Curtain. He Abjures Love. Thomas Hardy. OBNC

A few survive in deeps, very/Wily, large, and solitary. Poets Observed. Francis Coleman Rosenberger. AMV-80

A few yet lived, to languish and to mourn/For good old manners never to return. The Frank Courtship. George Crabbe. OBRV

Fewer leaves and more fruit ever/We find on the little tree. Spanish Folk Songs. Anonymous. AWP

Ffrom Thomas a Pott I'le turne his/name,/And the Lord of Arrundale hee shall/bee.' Tom Potts. Anonymous. ESPB

A Fiction superseding Faith-/By so much-as 'twas real- Her sweet weight on my heart a night. Emily Dickinson. PeHV

...Fiction/that there is work to be done,/and almost inconsolably. Loyal. William Matthews. MAYP

-A fiction, while I/breath and/change pace. The Third Dimension. Denise Levertov. NeAP; NoAm

Fictions of will and need. After Sex. Greg Kuzma. GP

Fiddle and aw' together. Greensleeves and Pudding Pies. Anonymous. LO

Fiddle, we know, is diddle: and diddle, we take it,/is dee. The Higher Pantheism in a Nutshell. Algernon Charles Swinburne. ALV; BXAP; FaBoNo; HBV 1-2; NA; Par; SpRo

Fie, fie, fie on you! And the word has power! The Buzz Plane. Robert Francis. TW

Fie, pleasure, fie! I dare not trust to this. Fie, Pleasure, Fie! George Gascoigne. EIL; InvP

Fie upon Love and all his Laws. Such bitter fruit thy love doth yield. Anonymous. EG

Fie upon you,/Bold-faced jig! Jenny Wren. Anonymous. EvOK

The field his arms. Hero and Leander. George Chapman. EG

Field, Lawn and Cape Onion, Juniper Stump, Turk's Gut, and/Spanish Room. Gazeteer of Newfoundland. Michael Harrington. CaP

The fields and dresses grey with dust Frederick Douglass. Sam Cornish. PoBA

Fields, hills, and cots, and every forest brake/Slumber in dew. Three Fragments. William Allingham. IrPN

The Fields of Peace have been given to me as my City. He Knoweth the Souls of the East. Book of the Dead. AWP

The fields once blossomy we scour/Where the old poets plucked the flower. Dandelion. Annie Rankin Annan. HBV 1-2

Fields without walls that all the people/own!' Ireland. John James Piatt. AA

...The fierce flower from its steep/flamed upon the sounding deep. Waratah. Roland Robinson. PoAu 1-2

The fierce old Irish dead! The Call. Daniel Corkery. OnYI

Fierce party in the streets. The evening falls. June 10. Marcos Rodriguez Frese. WPOW

The fierce wasp settle on a golden pear. Transition. May Sarton. NePoAm

Fierce without strength; o'erflowing, though not full. The Modern Fine Gentleman (excerpt). Soame Jenyns. OBSV

A fiercer glitter in their eyes. Ship from Thames. Rex Ingamells. PoAu 1-2

The fiery and the snuffy are raring to go. I Ride an Old Paint. Anonymous. AmFP; AS; FSW; TrAS

A fiery furnace where the cattle trod. Prairie Fires. Hamlin Garland. OBCA

A fiery-hearted thing to do? The Feckenham Men. John Drinkwater. GTBS

15 cents is plenty to keep you in the sky. How to Get to Canada. Ted Berrigan. APU

Fifty men own the lemon grove/and no man is a slave. A Song for the Spanish Anarchists. Sir Herbert Read. ChMP

Fifty million dumb cops in the world/and this one has to be a genius. Driving While under the Influence. Michael Casey. AmC

Fifty years syne come Christmas Day. Under the Snow. Robert Collyer. AA

-A Fig, an Olive, and a Bay. Detail. Mary Ursula Bethell. AnNZ

The fig leaf lays a shadow on the dust. Greek Archipelagoes. Patrick Leigh-Fermor. OBTV

The fight is lost-and he knows it is lost-and yet he is/fighting still! The Fighting Failure. Everard Jack Appleton. HBV 1-2; YaD

Fight on and take another. Locks and Bolts. Anonymous. FSW; OBET

Fightin' like divils for concilialtion,/And hatin' each other, for the love of God. No Place So Grand. Anonymous. WTO

Fighting and pleading/to be let out. The Palomino Stallion. Alden Nowlan. BoAnP; PH; PoL

Fighting skeeters down in sunny Tennessee. Highly Educated Man. Anonymous. ABF

Fights on and on in the endless wars,/Then silent, unseen-goes down. The Mothers of Men. Joaquin Miller. PGD

...Figured and pre-figured in the nothing-transfiguring wheel. The Figured Wheel. Robert Pinsky. MAYP; NPGG

The figures of women at repose to/signify the strength of the waves' lash. Lear. William Carlos Williams. NOBA; PoA

"Fill 'er up. Fill 'er up, Charlie." Looking for the Buckhead Boys. James Dickey. LiSp

...Fill my faltering human/Heart's hunger with a more celestial love. Animal. Max Eastman. FYAP

Fill my heart with light divine. Morning Star, O Cheering Sight! Anonymous. AH

Fill our gold cups with love/stirred into clear nectar You Know the Place. Sappho. PBWP

Fill the bowl, butler, and let the cup rought. Fill the Bowl, Butler! Anonymous. MeEL; OxBM

Filled for tomorrow and the days ahead/With everything that's thought or done or said. The Time Is Today. John Farrar. GoYe

Filled full of the foam of the river. Atalanta in Calydon. Algernon Charles Swinburne. EnLi 1-2; MaVP

Filled in the fine detail complete/To the least flower, to the last leaf. Pennsylvania Academy of Fine Arts. Ernest Kroll. AMV-80

Filled with a remote sense of eternity. The Well. Luis Palés Matos. InW

...Filled/with deaf cries, like an invisible river. Grand Street & the Bowery. David Ghitelman. FAZ

Filled with dreams. A Comparison. John Farrar. BrR

Filled with itself and yet transparent. A Drop of Dew. Shimon Halkin. TrJP

Filled with skilfully stuffed memories It Is So Long Since My Heart Has Been with Yours. Edward Estlin Cummings. NoAm

Filled with the presence of God, whose voice was the sound of the/ocean. The Courtship of Miles Standish. Henry Wadsworth Longfellow. TreFS

Filling all wind/fall/day Scattered Leaves. Lance Henson. VoR

Filling the hollow of my throat. To My Father. Tony Curtis. AMV-81

Filling the road up with colors, faces,/Tender speeches, until they feed us to the truth. Never Seek to Tell Thy Love. John Ashbery. HaCAP; InPS

...Filling the room/like a flood and flushing me out. Tenant at Number 9. John Blight. CBAP

Filling the songs of poets everywhere. A Wish. Vidal de Nicolas. BoC

Filling up the night like a well. Village in Snowstorm. Norbert Krapf. FAZ

Filling with water the dark space/that goes between us/when we are not even looking. Death on the Farm. Cary Waterman. GP

Fills my walled garden with your honey breath/wherein I move, a mote. The Dream Songs. John Berryman. NoAm

Fills the next grave - the beautiful and young. The Past. William Cullen Bryant. AA

Fills the road with sea-shadows that drift in figure/eights, knot and snarl and draw me forward. Night Fishing for Blues. Dave Smith. GeTw; LiSp; WOLT

Fills the silence of God that has lasted forty-two years. Twenty-One Sonnets. C. K. Stead. OCNZ

Fills the universe around. Evening Hymn. William Henry Furness. AA

Fills them with having arrived.   Palm of the Hand.   Rainer Maria Rilke. NU

A film of hope and a memoried day.   Dream Girl.   Carl Sandburg.   MoLP

...A film/over water that's deep and abiding.   A Film.   Albert Goldbarth. MAYP

Filming that one wheel still spinning/in the motionless air.   Cut.   David J. Feela.   AMV-81

The filter here, not innocence but guilt.   Photos of a Salt Mine.   P.K. Page. NOBC

A filth on the floor of that room.   How the Joy of It Was Used Up Long Ago.   Linda Gregg.   NPGG

The finale is always the same.   ...The Dancer from the Dance.   Suzanne Juhasz.   IHMS

Finally/a clear sign.   Not the Arms Race.   Sam Abrams.   APU

& Finally button her blood around my hands   My Wife Is My Shirt. Stephen Tropp.   InPK; PeD

& Finally either rewards someone for something or goes up/under something. 1st Dance–Making Things New–6 February 1964.   Jackson MacLow. CoPo

Finally enfold the season's cloves,/Cover a somnolent face on Sundays. Newsboy.   Irving Layton.   CaP

Finally gets into a fight–rip, goes the engine.   A Ripping Trip.   Anonymous. CoSo

Finally, he became a perfect gentleman/just in time for rigor mortis.   My Uncle Joe.   Robert B. Smith.   LFAC

Finally I tried to define why divine silence...   Vowel Movements.   Daryl Hine.   PoA

...Finally in grains, a dry/precipitate, the irony of salt.   Calypso.   Richard Kell.   CIP

Finally, let us say, I have been asked to write simply.   There Is No Reason Why Not to Look at Death.   Robert Sward.   CoPo

Find all the witchcraft that we need/Around us, every day–   Witchcraft was hung, in history.   Emily Dickinson.   WSC

Find but those faults, which they want wit to make.   Tyrannic Love.   John Dryden.   ViBoPo

Find in the shade of such a tree/The innocence of childhood's eye.   The Apple.   Ray Smith.   TrCP

...Find/interdependence in the flux of things.   All the Farewells.   Byron Vazakas.   MoPo

...Find/Known channels with a red nun on my right.   Red Right Returning. Louis O. Coxe.   MoVE;.; WaP

Find me, and turn thy back on heaven.   Brahma.   Ralph Waldo Emerson
AA; AnNE; AP; APA; AWP; BiP; DiPo; EaLo; GoTF; HAP; HBV; 1-2; ILwL; InPo; LiTA; MAmP; NePA; NOBA; NoP; OBEV; OBVV; OxBA; PoRA; SeCeV; TAP; TreF; TrGrPo; UnPo; ViBoPo; WGRP; WHA

Find my tomb in the palm of her hand.   Sick unto Death of Love. Anonymous.   WTO

...Find one's/misery made clear, borne, as if also, by a hedge of ice.   Grace Abounding.   Archie Randolph Ammons.   HaCAP

Find out a hundred you in London may/Of Presbyterian asses in one day. Upon Saul Seeking His Father's Asses.   Rowland Watkyns.   FaBoEE

Find the central human urge/To make a thousand roads converge?   Conflict. F. R. Scott.   CaP; PeCV

Find the fair Pierides!   A Garden Song.   Henry Austin Dobson.   BoNaP; HBV 1-2; LoBV; OBEV; OBNC; OBVV

Find the penknife there and plunge it/Into your false heart.   Lady, Weeping at the Crossroads.   W. H. Auden.   MoVE

Find their sole speech in that victorious brow.   Shakespeare.   Matthew Arnold.   ATP; BiP; BoLiVe; CBEP; FiP; GTBS; HBV 1-2; InvP; NoP; OBEV; OBVV; ViBoPo; WHA

Finding any motherhood/Most sweet.   The Old Mare.   Elizabeth Jane Coatsworth.   MoAmPo

Finding fish before the birds.   12 Oct.   Allen Planz.   WOLT

Finding, if not the place, the way there.   A View of Jersey.   Edward Field. NeAP

Finding love was lust.   Love and Lust.   Isaac Rosenberg.   ChMP; TrJP

Finding our way to Beauty–and to God!   My Garden.   Janice Appleby Succorsa.   HoPM

Finding shadows to lie down in/and the quiet that finally touches my palms Quiet By Hillsides in the Afternoon.   Martha Lifson.   AMV-80

Finds a neat and compact space/In the hollow of his hand.   The Egoist Dead.   Elizabeth Brewster.   CaP

Finds blood spotting her legs/from the long ride.   Uneasy Rider.   Diane Wakoski.   NIP

Finds the frost in the day's air, and the nights which appear too/long. Address Not Known.   John Heath-Stubbs.   ChMP

Finds this fair fruit too well suffice/To pay the peace, and honest praise,/Of EDEN lost.   Rondeau: "Of Eden lost."   George Ellis.   OBEC

Finds, to conclude in music, only death.   Perfect Rhyme.   John Frederick Nims.   InPK

Finds ways enough to ease thine heaviness.   Of Money.   Barnabe Googe. ElL; EnRePo; FF; ForPo; NLV; NoP

The fine blue dust that a god leaves/when it is flying toward new worlds/to be born.   Hammerstoke.   Don Domanski.   CaPN

The fine bones of my hand/have nothing to say about God.   In the Van Gogh Room.   Traise Yamamoto.   BrSi

A fine flash Yankee barman, and once more cut a shine.   The Flash Colonial Barman.   William W. Coxon.   NOAV

A fine, fresh HYLAS, a delicious boy,/To serve our purposes of beastly joy. The Times.   Charles Churchill.   OBSV; PeHV

Fine Lapis tandem coelo descendis ab alto/et fundum rursus, cum gravitate petid.   Resplendent Studs of Heaven's Frame.   Anonymous.   SCAP

A fine rain falls,/greened is their garden.   The Visitor.   Michael Dennis Browne.   OBTV

Fine sounds are floating wild/About the earth: happy are ye and glad.   Sleep and Poetry.   John Keats.   ATP

...A fine thunder peals/will with its friends and soon, from agony/put the fire out.   Dream Songs.   John Berryman.   NaP

Fine, vulgar man, you got your fill.   Poem to the Memory of H. L. Mencken. Baron Wormser.   MAYP

Fine will be the day.   If Bees Stay at Home.   Anonymous.   OxNR

A fine yellow film follows where they go/The ancient rugged Eskimoes. Eskimoes Again.   Dick Gallup.   ANYP

...Finely, slenderly made.   Classical Autumn.   Robert Clayton Casto. AMV-81

The finest entertainment known,/And given rag-cheap?   What Did I Dream? Robert Graves.   DuDa

The finest Hampshire rabbits/That e'er crept from a hole.   The Rabbit Man. Anonymous.   OxNR

...The finger of ice/in a glove that does not care/how we are wakened.   Ice. Jack Driscoll.   AMV-80

Fingered the frolic bones beneath the clock.   Carnival.   J. R. Hervey. AnNZ

Fingering the ring with its silver bat, the foreign/And credible Chinese symbol of happiness.   From Government Buildings.   Denis Devlin.   IPY

Fingers all together!   The Mitten Song.   Marie Louise Allen.   BrR; NTCP; SoPo; SUS; TiPo

The fingers hidden, home/to a name written in water.   After.   Philip Levine. VWA

The finished ships disturb it, and depart.   The Way to the Sea.   Laurence Lerner.   NePoEA-2

Finisher off! Black Finisher off!   Shaka.   Anonymous.   WTO

A Finn And German Vault And Hop.   The Cranial Nerves.   Anonymous. FaBoUs

Fire above, and fire below,/With a whip i' your hand, to make him goe.   The Masque of Queenes.   Ben Jonson.   FM; OFD; WSC

Fire and fleet and candle light,/And Christ receive thy soul.   A Lyke-Wake Dirge.   Anonymous.   AnFE; AtBAP; BuBa; CH; EaLo; FaBoCh; FaBoRV; GBP; GoBC; HAP; HBV 1-2; HoPM; LoBV; OBEV; PoEL 1-5; SeCeV

Fire and sword with ease subdues.   Beauty.   Thomas Stanley.   AWP

The fire burns and Penelope sews.../He never tells–but Penelope knows! Ulysses Returns.   Roselle Mercier Montgomery.   HBMV

...Fire cracks/from common stone, a sunrise in evening.   October Elegy. Margaret Gibson.   FYAP

The fire-doomed Empire of a myriad Ants.   Immanent.   Walter De la Mare. PoA

Fire gonna burn ma soul!   Fire.   Langston Hughes.   NoAm; NOBA

...Fire/his white messengers/& come find out/for himself...   I Told Jesus. Sterling D. Plumpp.   PoBA

Fire in the main well,/The captain didn't know.   Fire Down Below. Anonymous.   FSW

Fire is living,/Fire death.   The Firing Squad.   Harry Mathews.   ANYP

The fire is out, the house dark.   The Nurse's Lament.   Mary Elizabeth Coleridge.   NOBV; OBSP

A fire is passing up through the soles of my feet!   Evolution from the Fish. Robert Bly.   NoAm; NOBA

Fire mounts aloft, and they my heart have fired.   Madrigal: "You black bright stars."   Thomas Morley.   EnRePo

"A fire o coals to burn her, wi hearty/cheer,/And she'll never get mair o me." Edward (A version).   Anonymous.   BaBo; ESPB

& Fire of new iris.   May All Earth Be Clothed in Light.   George Hitchcock. VGW

The fire of whose furnaces may/sleep, but never dies!   Prejudice.   Georgia Douglas Johnson.   AmNP; PoBA

The fire rubs/itself for warmth & the windows/go white with frost.   Eclogues. Dennis Schmitz.   NPGG

Fire, spoke to fire, and mixed in heaven, Maid.   The Saint.   Humbert Wolfe. CAW

Fire-spreading, foe-spurning,/Steeds of the Ocean!–   Ethelstan: O'er the Wild Gannet's Bath.   George Darley.   PoEL 1-5

The fire that cried in pure crystal/Out of its cloud!   To Rosemary.   Stephen Vincent Benét.   LaNeLa

Fire that freed the slave.   Would I Might Rouse the Lincoln in You All. Vachel Lindsay.   PoSC

Fire where it burns more truly dwells/Than where it scatters light.   Claim to Love.   Giovanni Battista Guarini.   AWP

The fire will come out of the sun/and I shall look in the heart of it.   Non Piangere, Liu.   Peter Porter.   OxBC

The fire will freeze and be like ice,/And the raging sea will burn.   No Change in Me.   *Anonymous.*   AmFP

Fire within fire, desire in deity.   The House of Life.   Dante Gabriel Rossetti.   VLP

The fireflies are naked and cold/in the rags of their light   Alone.   Richard Shelton.   NYBP

Fires in the fall!   Autumn Fires.   Robert Louis Stevenson.   BrR; SUS; TiPo; YeAr

Fires lit, laughter now,/And a new day calling.   Dawn Wail for the Dead.   Kath Walker.   CBAP

Firewood, iron-ware, and cheap tin trays.   Cargoes.   John Masefield.   AnEnPo; BLPL; CMoP; DiPo; ExPo; FaBV; FaPo; FaPoR; GoTF; GTBS; InPK; LiTM; MCCG; MoAB; MoBrPo; MOS; NOBE; OBEV; OBMV; OBVV; PoRA; RoGo; SeCeV; TEP; TreF

Firm hand and high heart for the further task.   Prayer of a Teacher.   Dorothy Littlewort.   TrPWD

The first and foremost in the fight/Are sure to win the day!   To Arms.   Park Benjamin.   PAH

First and/freedom.   Warriors Prancing, Women Dancing...   Niema Rashidd.   NBP

First and second and third voice/yeah, yeah.   Requiem for "Bird" Parker.   Gregory Corso.   PoNe

The first-born of Neptune are Lords of the/Main!   The Lords of the Main.   Joseph Stansbury.   PAH

The first cat that was ever killed by Care.   New England.   Edwin Arlington Robinson.   AmP; HeIP; MoAB; NoP; TAP

First–Chill–then Stupor–then the letting go–   After great pain, a formal feeling comes.   Emily Dickinson.   BoWoP; CABA; ForPo; HAP; InPo; InPS; LiTA; MAmP; MoAB; MoAmPo; MoPo; MoVE; NAWM 1-2; NePA; NIP; NoEu; NoP; PAI; PPoe; PrIm; SBG; TAP; UnPo; WeW

First Christmas night of all!   First Christmas Night of All.   Nancy Byrd Turner.   BiCB

The first cock crows: the morrow is begun.   Fetching the Wounded.   Laurence Binyon.   MMM

First cousin to Ragged-and-Tough.   Not Ragged-and-Tough.   *Anonymous.*   FaBoNo

...The first deep whisper of the rising sun.   Aubade.   Mekeel McBride.   MAYP

The first dry rattle of new-drawn steel/Changes the world to-day!   Edgehill Fight.   Rudyard Kipling.   PoPle

The first dull thunder stills the lake.   Walleye.   Allen Hoey.   WOLT

The first eschue is remedy alone.   Comparison of Love to a Streame Falling from the Alpes.   Sir Thomas Wyatt.   FaBoEn

The first estew is remedy alone.   From these high hills...   Sir Thomas Wyatt.   FCP

...The first fact is the social body,/one from another, nor needs no other.   The Kiwi Bird in the Kiwi Tree.   Charles Bernstein.   APU

First for food and then also for flowers.   Lilith.   Linda Gregg.   WPOW

A first foundation of shells to be/fired at the winter's muddy back.   Canning Time.   Robert Morgan.   Str

First go get a reputation.   Lines to Be Embroidered on a Bib....   Ogden Nash.   FaBoUs

The first great movies made flesh.   Sunday Afternoon.   Philip Levine.   NaP

The first hibiscus flower/falls.   Twilight.   Ch'en Yun.   LiTW

The first in Danger as the first in Fame.   Hector and Andromache.   Alexander Pope.   OBEC

First in my heart of all her sweet warm body/are those two human breasts.   The Miracle.   Allan Dowling.   ErPo

"First in the hearts of his countrymen."   Washington.   B. Y. Williams.   PGD

First in these fields I sung the sylvan strains.   Windsor-Forest To the Right Honourable George Lord Lansdown.   Alexander Pope.   CEP

First into this five, women may take us all.   The Primrose, Being at Montgomery Castle, upon the Hill...   John Donne.   FaBoPP; GBL

The first Jew was God; the second/Denied him; I am alive.   The Turning.   Philip Levine.   VGW

First let me see that you are growing old.   To a Lady.   John James Piatt.   AA

...The first line/of this poem; itself, especially, suddenly,/from nothing.   Metaphysical Shock while Watching a TV Cartoon.   Stan Rice.   NPGG

The first link in the mighty plan/Is still–and all upbraideth man.   Nature's Hymn to the Deity.   John Clare.   EBCP; VLP

The first morning of May.   There Gowans Are Gay.   *Anonymous.*   GBP

The first morning of winter   Loft.   Michael Dransfield.   CBAP

The first New England slave-ship with the/Negroes in the hold.   Hearing Men Shout at Night on MacDougal Street.   Robert Bly.   CAD; InPS

The first to the second o the third o   An Autobiography.   Bairam at Tunisie.   LiTW

"First of summer, lovely sight!"   First of Summer, Lovely Sight.   *Anonymous.*   NOBI

The first pressure on the trigger.   The Verdict.   Norman Cameron.   SeCePo

The first snow.   A Dead Leaf.   Howard Moss.   NYBP; NYP

...The first snow falls too late.   Sudden Frost.   David Wagoner.   PoPl

The first snow of the year danced on the lawn.   The First Snow of the Year.   Mark Van Doren.   NCSH

The first sorrow comes from the first hope.   Family Cups.   Steve Orlen.   Str

The first Thanksgiving of all.   First Thanksgiving of All.   Nancy Byrd Turner.   PAL; SiSoSe

First, though,/let me consume all/with a craving like this,/a craving like this.   A Childless Witch.   Raquel Chalfi.   VWA

The first, thus matcht, were scantly Gentlemen.   Astrophel and Stella, XIII.   Sir Philip Sidney.   AAS; SiPS

The first time I have/Ever seen them close.   Four Poems for Robin.   Gary Snyder.   NOBA; SOTW

The first time they saw Paris they resolved to make the last?   Unromantic Song.   Anthony Brode.   DBV; FiBHP

First to God and then to you.   Roundel: "My ghostly fadir, Y me confesse."   Charles, duc d' Orleans.   EnPo

The first tool I step on/Turned into a weapon.   The Objection to Being Stepped On.   Robert Frost.   NLV

First touch of hand in hand–Did one but/know!   Monna Innominata.   Christina Georgina Rossetti.   VLP

First whale, then pig, then man, some day/The worm will make it square.   The Whaler's Pig.   Edwin James Brady.   NOAV

The first white wall of the village.../The fruit-trees...   Metaphors of a Magnifico.   Wallace Stevens.   SOTW

First William, or the Conqueror, who did this realm/enthrall.   Lines on the Succession of the Kings of England (reversed).   *Anonymous.*   FaBoUs

The Firstborn He, and we shall heaven fill!   The Son of Man.   Dorothy J. Langford.   BePJ

The fish bending to touch her.   Fish.   Daniel Halpern.   AmPA

Fish-bones choke us.   Eat with Care.   *Anonymous.*   FaBoUs

The fish dripping/sparkling water.   Fish.   W. W. Eustace Ross.   PeCV

A fish hook/an open eye.   You Fit into Me.   Margaret Atwood.   NoP; PoL; TW

The fish in deep water, swim over my head.   I Never Will Marry.   *Anonymous.*   FSW

The fish swim in the dark, and cannot see.   The Fisherman Casts His Line into the Sea.   Robert Holland.   AMV-80

The Fish with glittering tails.   The Zodiac Rhyme.   *Anonymous.*   GBP

The fisherman's wife knits/his death into the sweater.   The Sweater.   Gregory Orr.   PPJ

The fishers mumble, waiting till the night/Urge on the clouds, and cover up the moon.   Wings in the Dark.   John Gray.   NOBV

Fishing for people/And hooking the sun.   Aged Fisherman.   Witter ("Emanuel Morgan") Bynner.   GoYe

Fishing in the ponds/of Hell.   A Bodhisattva Undoes Hell.   Jerome Rothenberg.   CoPo

Fishing words dangle/untouched/as the hack fumbles through/our pocket-contents and his job.   State Prison 4:00 p.m.   Thomas G. Nickens.   LFAC

A fission! A fission!/We all fall down.   A Leaden Treasury of English Verse.   Paul Dehn.   QQQ

...The/fist is pounding and pounding, and the mouth answering.   Gargoyle.   Carl Sandburg.   NoAm; NOBA

The fists of the wind are clenched.   Three Songs: Thessalian.   Winifred Bryher.   PoA

Fit for the soul to wear those clothes again.   The Soul's Garment.   Margaret Cavendish, Dutchess of Newcastre.   OxBoCh; SeCePo

Fit for their only listener, Heaven.   'Twas When the Spousal Time of May.   Coventry Patmore.   GBL

Fit him to breed aught but a servile race.   Deep Down the Blackman's Mind.   R. E. G. Armattoe.   ACV

Fitly where beasts and flowers wed shall meet/Our lips, our limbs, beneath the look of God.   Golden Bough.   Helen Hoyt.   HBMV

The fitter and turner, his wife who sings, and their child.   The Handloom.   Judith Rodriguez.   FaBoWP

Fitter, where it died to tell,/Than that it lived at all.   Farewell.   Epitaph on Elizabeth, L. H.   Ben Jonson.   AnAnS 2; BiP; CABA; EIL; ELP; EnL; FaBoEE ForPo; HAP; HBV 1-2; HeIP; InPo; NIP; NoP; OBEV; OBS; SeCP; SeCV 1-2 ViBoPo; WHA

Fitting your hawks their jesses!")   Song: "Give her but a least excuse to love me!"   Robert Browning.   ViBoPo

Five balls! Five bright brass balls!/To juggle with, my love, when the sky falls.   By Candlelight.   Sylvia Plath.   SBG

Five belated addresses/to the Lord.   Winter's Edge.   P. R. Roberts.   SOTS

...Five bells coldly ringing out./Five bells.   Five Bells.   Kenneth Slessor.   BoAV; CBAP; NOAV; PoAu 1-2; PoRA; SeCePo

Flesh is merely a lesson./We learn it/& pass on.   The Buddha in the Womb.
Erica Jong.   MAYP

The flesh of dark.   Night Out, Tom Cat.   Charles deGravelles.   AMV-81

Flesh of the cherry, dark and sweet.   Cherry.   Gene Baro.   ErPo

The flesh, the blood, the sheaf, the grape,/That feed His man–the bread, the
wine.   The Fugitive.   Alice Meynell.   NOCV

"Flesh to feed hell's worm upon."   After Death.   Algernon Charles
Swinburne.   NOBV

Fleshing his dream of the beautiful, needful thing.   Frederick Douglass.
Robert Earl Hayden.   AmNP; BiP; CNA; GP; HaCAP; HoAn; IDB;
PoBA; PoNe; TTY

Flew to their nests from the birdies' ball.   The Birds' Ball.   C. W. Bardeen.
BLPA

Flicker as snow flickers, blown from those inland hills.   The Mudtower.
Anne Stevenson.   HoAn

Flicker in the embers on the hill.   What Trinkets?   Thomas Hornsby Ferril.
NePoAm-2

A flicker of a light or two/Far above and beyond the large cage.   The Cold.
Charles Simic.   HaCAP

Flickers of dust in a lighted window.   Akriel's Consolation.   [(or Pillin)]
William Pillen.   AMV-80

Flickers of unlikely heat/at the edge of our belief bud forth.   Food for Fire,
Food for Thought.   Robert Duncan.   NeAP

Flies contented across the great plain/home to his welcome in the honeycomb.
A Busy Yellow Bee.   Anonymous.   NOBI

Flies/even in the winter/live here   Your Mother.   Sam Cornish.   CNA

Flies, flies are on the plane tree, on the streets.   As a Plane Tree by the
Water.   Robert Lowell.   AP; CMoP; CoAP; CoBMV; CrMA; DTC;
ForPo; LiTM; MoAB; MoAmPo; NePA; NePoEA; NoAm; NOBA; OxBA;
TrGrPo

Flies o'er the unbending corn, and skims along the main.   An Essay on
Criticism.   Alexander Pope.   BoLiVe

Flies off, blue and white and host/to a freedom/it knows nothing of.   In
What Manner the Body Is United with the Soule.   Jorie Graham.   NPGG

Flies the Phoenix bird,/Singing.   Roses Red.   Arno Holz.   AWP

Flies to its haven of securest rest!   The Wife to Her Husband.   Anonymous.
HBV 1-2

The flight is deeper than your father, boy.   A Presentation of Two Birds to
My Son.   James Wright.   PPP

The Flight is past: and Man forgot.   Sic Vita.   Henry, Bishop of Chichester
King.   AnAnS 2; DiPo; EG; ELP; HBV 1-2; MePo; NOBE; OBS; OBSP;
SeCP

The Flight of the Earls.   Lament for the O'Neills.   John Montague.   CIP

A flightless timorous landrail/whose cry is rusted, hard, like chains.   A Rum
Cove, a Stout Cove.   Tom Paulin.   FaBoIP

Fling out his blazoned banner!   The Shoemakers.   John Greenleaf Whittier.
AnNE

Fling their towering crests to the stars on high/To shield me from the sea.
Aunt Zillah Speaks.   Herbert Palmer.   FaBoTw

Fling us a handful of stars!   Caliban in the Coal Mines.   Louis Untermeyer.
HBV 1-2; MoAmPo; PoPl; TreFS; TrJP; TRV

Flings out its arms, day breaks on Inishtrahull!   Dawn in Inishtrahull.   D. J.
O'Sullivan.   OnYI

Flinkywisty pomm,/Slushypipp.   A Letter to Evelyn Baring.   Edward Lear.
FaBoNo

Flint and steel I'll ever name ye.   The Tinder.   Thomas Carew.   CaPo

Flirts from his Cart the Mud in Walpole's Face.   On Dreams.   Jonathan
Swift.   BIrV

Flit down the hedgerows in the frozen plain/And hang on little twigs and start
again.   Emmonsail's Heath in Winter.   John Clare.   PoEL 1-5

Flit to the silent world and other summers,/With wings that dip beyond the
silver seas.   My Heart Shall Be Thy Garden.   Alice Meynell.   HBV 1-2

Flitted and sipped, and sipped again!   On Time.   Richard Hughes.
MoBrPo

Flitters of hair wave at the sun.   Site of Ambush: Narration.   Eilean Ni
Chuilleanain.   CIP

Float less than April fog below our hermit-/age.   Sanctuary.   Louise Imogen
Guiney.   AA

Float on the waves like ravelled lace.   Impressions.   Oscar Wilde.   SyP

Float with me there, Pauline, but not like air.   Water and Air.   Robert
Browning.   OBRV; VLP

The floating ashore into sleep and to morning.   Gimboling.   Isabella
Gardner.   ErPo; WeW

Floating/down/stream.   And the Old Folks Said.   Diane Mei Lin Mark.
BrSi

Floating, floating, one forever, in the light of God's great/smile.   Hereafter.
Harriet Prescott Spofford.   HBV 1-2

Floating frog.   Haiku: "No need to cling."   Joso.   FAZ

Floating, like a vapor, on the soft summer air.   Jeanie with the Light Brown
Hair.   Stephen Collins Foster.   BLSo

Floating slowly down the escalator,/Slowly, lonely, to another train.   The
Escalator.   Alex Glasgow.   OBET

Floating with/their broken plums   In War.   Mason Jordan Mason.   PoNe

Floats down, - "Auf Wiedersehen!"   Palinode.   James Russell Lowell   AA

Floats through the azure air–an island of the blest!   Childe Harold's
Pilgrimage: Canto IV, XXVII.   George Gordon, Lord Byron.   AnFE

Flock ev'ry Sunday to the seat,/To stare about them, and to eat.   The Cit's
Country Box.   Robert Lloyd.   NOEC

Flock o'er their carrion, just like men below.   Don Juan.   George Gordon,
Lord Byron.   EBEV

A flock of bright red lanterns/has settled.   About an Excavation.   Charles
Reznikoff.   NTCP; PCP; PrIm; VGW; WeW

(A flock of swans)/drives forward   A New Siege: An Historical Meditation
(excerpt).   John Montague.   CIP

Flocks, herds, and waterfalls, along the hoar profound!   Nature's Charms.
James Beattie.   OBEC

"A flood of fish/fish-teeming sea!"'   Amergin's Songs.   Anonymous.   NOBI

"A flood of painful memories," says Dr. Doctor.   Dr. Dimity Is Forced to
Complain.   Cynthia Macdonald.   SUW

Flood the sea marsh, salt down another spring.   The Farm Near Norman's
Lane.   Mary Finnin.   PoAu 1-2

Flooded by dawn's pale courage, rapt in/eve's/Rich acquiescence.   Word over
All.   Cecil Day Lewis.   OAEP

Flooding level and bright along the verandah.   Verandahs.   R. F.
Brissenden.   CBAP; NOAV

The floodlights/in the guard towers.   Begotten of the Spleen.   Charles Simic.
LCAP

Floods all the soul with its melodious seas.   Milton.   Henry Wadsworth
Longfellow   AA; AmPP; AP; AWP; InPo; MAmP; NePA; NoP; TAP;
TrGrPo

Floods the womb until I drown.   Malcolm.   Sonia Sanchez.   BP

The floor so far away I can't determine/Which room I'm in, which year,
which life.   Childhood.   Maura Stanton.   MAYP; SM

...The floor ticked/And she turned to listen.   The Widow Perez.   Gary Soto.
MAYP

"Flop! Flop! Flop!"   Did You Feed My Cow?   Anonymous.   GoSl

A floud that drowns both tears, and grones,/My Saviours bloud.   Silex
Scintillans.   Henry Vaughan.   AnAnS 1

Flounders in mud. O Jesu, make it stop!   Attack.   Siegfried Sassoon.
MCCG; MoBrPo; NOBE; OxBTC

Flour the board for kneading.   Still Birth.   Catherine Rutan.   AMV-81

Flow gently, sweet Afton, disturb not her dream.   Afton Water.   Robert
Burns.   BiP; BoNaP; FaBoPP; HeIP; LAuP; OAEP; PG

Flow,/Ice,/Snow.   Sound of Water.   Mary Devenport O'Neill.   NTCP

Flow on, flow unconfin'd, my Tale!   Marmion.   Sir Walter Scott.   OBRV

Flow still in the Prophet's word/And the People's liberty!   Inspiration.
Samuel Johnson.   AA; HBV 1-2; TrPWD; WGRP

Flow swiftly into thee, and in thee ever end.   Upon Nothing.   John Wilmot,
Earl of Rochester.   AtBAP; MePo; OBS; OBSV; PoEL 1-5; TrGrPo;
ViBoPo

Flowed into each other's arms, like dreams.   Daybreak.   Stephen Spender.
MoLP

Flower and youth with an arrow offshot   Image-Nation 3.   Robin Blaser.
PoM

The flower imperishable of this valiant age,–/A true American!   A Man!
Clinton Scollard.   OHIP

Flower into a cold wind that smells/of the moon   North.   Lance Henson.
STE

The flower of England/Shall never be no more.   The Death of Queen Jane.
Anonymous.   BaBo

Flower/of Love and of Persuasion.   Desire Knows.   Asclepiades.   LiTW

Flower of the moon!   The Night-Blooming Cereus.   Harriet Monroe.   AA

The flower upon its inmost side!   The Pressed Gentian.   John Greenleaf
Whittier.   AnAmPo

The flower will then reveal its blossom-heart.   Like an April Day.   Johan
Sebastian C. Welhaven.   LiTW

The flower you loved, in times that were.   Ashore.   Laurence Hope.   HBV
1-2

The flowere she touch'd on, dipt and rose,/And turned to look at her.   The
Talking Oak: Olivia.   Alfred, Lord Tennyson.   GN

The flowered paper peeling from the walls.   Midnight.   Weldon Kees.
NoAm

The flowering love.   The Intruder.   Marya Zaturenska.   OLR

The flowers are driving me wild.   Song to My Love.   Laurence McKinney.
InMe

The flowers are hidden lately   Keep Me Still, for I Do Not Want to Dream.
Larry Eigner.   NeAP

Flowers cast no/fragrance backward over the weary way.   Alabaster Boxes.
Anonymous.   PoToHe

The flowers from his helmet toward the deserving of France.   St. Aubin
d'Aubigne.   Paul Dehn.   OBWP

Flowers, I said, will come of it.   April 5, 1974.   Richard Wilbur.   GP;
HaCAP

Flowers in her hair, castanets in her hands.   Spain.   Arthur Symons. OBTV

"The Flowers of the Forest are a' wede away."   The Flowers of the Forest. Jane Elliot.   BSV; CH; FaBoCh; FaBoRV; GoTS; OBEC; CxBS

The flowers of the town are all turned away.   Two Songs.   Cecil Day Lewis. HAP

The flowers seem to nod   Open.   Larry Eigner.   NeAP

The flowers wince,/But drink.   Vernal Showers.   David O'Neil.   AnAmPo

A flowery, green, bird-singing land.   In May.   William Henry Davies. OBVV

The flowing of all men's tears beneath the sky.   Before the Mirror. Algernon Charles Swinburne.   OBEV; OBVV

The flowing of water, the Way of Love.   Four Folk-Songs in Hokku Form, 1. *Anonymous.*   LiTW

The flowing waters collected grateful about/her.   Actaeon.   Arthur Hugh Clough.   VLP

Flows an immense river with doves of steel and hope.   The International Brigade Arrives at Madrid.   Pablo Neruda.   WaaP

Flows from the heart of Love, the Lord.   May-Day: April and May.   Ralph Waldo Emerson.   GN

Flows to the ray and warbles as it flows.   Religious Musings.   Samuel Taylor Coleridge.   EnRP

Flows where the green tree perfectly/Curves to its perfect shadow.   The Snow-Gum.   Douglas Stewart.   PoAu 1-2

A fluid substance.   Pretty Beads.   Dick Gallup.   ANYP

Flukes flashing/silver/before the dive.   Before the Dive.   Elizabeth Kempf. AMV-81

Flung on the sands of a sunless eternity.   Dead Embryos.   Judit Toth. WPOW

Fluorescent-lighted/wastes of geology   A Night in the Royal Ontario Museum.   Margaret Atwood.   PBWP

...A flush/Ruddy and vague, the grace/(A rose!) of her lyric face.   Pastel: Masks and Faces.   Arthur Symons.   NOBV; SyP

Flutter, and float, and change to butterflies.   The Genesis of Butterflies. Victor Hugo.   AWP

Flutter/and shatter/against the Great Divide.   Hearing of the End of the War.   Richard Tillinghast.   MAYP

Flutter'd and flam'd the original Star Spangled Banner.   The Rejected "National Hymns".   Robert Henry Newell.   InMe

Fluttering about a white azalea bush.   Proportion.   Amy Lowell.   BoWoP

Fluttering they move their weedy Beds among,/Or instant diving, hide their plumeless Young.   Sailing upon the River.   George Crabbe.   OBNC

Flux, efflorescence–whatever you care to call it!   Pro Femina.   Carolyn Kizer.   NMM

Fly around my blue-eyed gal,/You almost drove me crazy.   Fly around My Blue-Eyed Gal.   *Anonymous.*   FSW

Fly down, Death.   Madboy's Song.   Muriel Rukeyser.   MoAmPo; TrJP

Fly, fly, from the old city/Into the field!   The Old City.   Ruth Manning-Sanders.   CH

Fly hence, shadows, that do keep/Watchful sorrows charm'd in sleep!   Dawn. John Ford.   OBEV

The fly I envy settling in the sun/On the green leaf, and wish my goal was won.   Written in Prison.   John Clare.   OAEL 1-2

A fly on the ceiling–the click-/snicking cannons on so peacefully.   Peace Delegate.   Douglas Livingstone.   PeSA

Fly through the air, perhaps it is–that elevator car!   A Modern Ballad. Caroline D. Emerson.   BrR

Fly to him I love the best.   Bless You, Bless You, Burnie-Bee.   *Anonymous.* OxNR

Fly to Jesus, sinner, fly!   Sinner, Is Thy Heart at Rest?   Jared B. Waterbury. AH

Fly to the city and stand there and wait/For the beggar at the gate Mandelstam.   Richard Burns.   VWA

Fly to the one that you love best.   Little Sally Waters.   Mother Goose. AmFP; FSW; TiPo

Fly to Wild Eden!   Wild Eden.   George Edward Woodberry.   HBV 1-2

Fly, witch, to the wood; healed be this hurt!/So help thee the Lord!   Charm for a Sudden Stitch.   *Anonymous.*   AnOE

The flying bird turned back to hear.   Music.   *Anonymous.*   WTO

The flying fish sing to light.   The Flying Fish.   Jack Cope.   PeSA

...Flying (flying, that's the word/I was looking for) right out of sight.   Love Is.   Ann Darr.   GrPl

Flying full tilt already.   Running.   Richard Wilbur.   CoAP

Flying, he lands–and holds on.   Monkey Difference.   Barbara Howes.   GP

Flying the black flag of himself.   Crow Blacker Than Ever.   Ted Hughes. TEP

Flying with green in her beak; the dove also had come.   The Animals. Josephine Jacobsen.   GoYe

An' fo' de little feller/Runnin' space...   After Winter.   Sterling A. Brown. GoSl; PoBA; PoNe

Foam brightens like the dogwood now/at home, in my own country.   The Long Voyaage.   Malcolm Cowley.   AnFE; NePA

Focus and rose are one.   On Waking.   Alida Carey Gulick.   GoYe

The focus of attendant spheres/And keystone of the arching years.   Eppur Si Muove?   Robert Hillyer.   GoYe

The foe had better ne'er been born,/That gets in Stonewall's Way.   Stonewall Jackson's Way.   John Williamson Palmer.   AA; HBV 1-2; MC; PAH

Foeman and friend were flying when he flew.   The High Jump.   *Anonymous.* LiSp

The foetus stifling in the mind's gloom.   A Person from Porlock.   R.S. Thomas.   BoC

The fog-blurred grave.   Hiroshige.   Mark M. Perlberg.   NYBP

The fog unfolds its bitter scent.   November Night, Edinburgh.   Norman MacCaig.   BSV; NMP

Fogo, Twillingate, Morton's Harbor,/All around the circle!   I's the B'y. *Anonymous.*   FSW

Fol de riddle, lol de riddle, hi ding do.   The Carrion Crow.   *Anonymous.* OxNR; PBBP

Fol de rol, fol de rol.   Words for Music Perhaps.   William Butler Yeats. AtBAP

Fol he is the on hire is bold.   Where Is Paris and Helene?   Thomas of Hales.   OxBM

Fold ancient pity/over new-turned earth.   Wisdom.   Phyllis Hanson.   GoYe

Fold close my little one!   Missing.   John Banister Tabb.   TrPWD

Fold dun garments of night,/Trembling, shudder away.   Half-Light.   Jean Percival Waddell.   CaP

Fold her hands across her breast–/Let her sleep on.   The Sleeper.   Isobel Hume.   HBMV

An' fold his arms an' shet his eyes,/An' set, an' set, an' flosserfize.   A Philosopher.   Sam Walter Foss.   OBAL

Fold home, fast fold thy child.   The Blessed Virgin compared to the Air we Breathe.   Gerard Manley Hopkins.   BrPo; ISi; MoPo; NOBV; OxBoCh; VLP

Fold up the deck-chairs, dear. There will be some/Not needed next year, no matter how warm the sun.   Afternoon in Anglo-Ireland.   Bruce Williamson.   NeIP

Folded close under deepening snow.   The First Snow-Fall.   James Russell Lowell.   AA; AnNE; HBV 1-2; MCCG; TreF

Folded her silver wings and slept/Upon the slopes of Tamalpais.   As I Came Down Mount Tamalpais.   Clarence Urmy.   AA; HBMV

Foldeth the sheep in pastures of eternal life.   The Testament of Beauty. Robert Bridges.   OxBTC

Folds her fingers around it.   In the Small Boats of Their Hands.   Pamela Kircher.   AMV-80

...Folds in your palm/That fall aside like breasts,/Creating the letter M.   The Hard Summer.   Medbh McGuckian.   FaBoIP

Folds/neatly/away.   Barbie-Doll Goes to College.   Ronald Gross.   WeW

Folk need not on frets to be standing/That's wooed and married and a'. Woo'd and Married and A'.   Alexander Ross.   OxBS

Folks either must avoid temptation/Or face my nasal accusation.   The Bloodhound.   Edward Anthony.   GDP

Folks need a lot of loving all the while.   Need of Loving.   Strickland Gillilan.   BLPA; PoToHe; WBLP

The folks will say, "Here's one by/woman slain."   The Unhappy Lover. Judah Al-Harizi.   TrJP

"Foller de drinkin' gou'd."   Foller de Drinkin' Gou'd.   *Anonymous.*   ABF

Follies of love are love's true ministers.   Love's Baubles.   Dante Gabriel Rossetti.   MaVP

Follow Barker's advice to cook the fish.   Baits for Various Fish.   Thomas Barker.   FaBoUs

Follow him till he sleeps, and kill him with a stone.   John Standish, Artist. Kenneth Fearing.   AnAmPo

Follow its old footprints/In the winter night.   Eskimo Chant.   *Anonymous.* RFM; WHW

Follow me–follow me 'ome!   Follow Me 'Ome.   Rudyard Kipling.   OAEP

Follow me, I'll guide thee home!   Holy Spirit, Faithful Guide.   Marcus Morris Wells.   AH

Follow the desultory feet of Death?   The House of Life.   Dante Gabriel Rossetti.   EnLi 1-2

Follow The Gleam.   Merlin and the Gleam.   Alfred, Lord Tennyson. MaVP; OAEL 1-2; OAEP; VLP

Follow the terrible drone of a cockchafer, or the bleak/Oracle of a barking dog.   The Ear.   Louis MacNeice.   OBSP

Follow through/The country dance.   Lachlan Gorach's Rhyme.   *Anonymous.* PoPle

Follow thy life, and she will sue/To pour for thee the cup of honour!   Hebe. James Russell Lowell.   AA; AnFE; AnNE; APA; HBV 1-2

Follow up! Follow up!   Forty Years On.   Edward Ernest Bowen.   HBV 1-2

Follow your nose, follow the sun or/follow the dreaming sea, but follow! Intimacy.   Al Young.   NPGG

Follow your own nose.   Many Happy Returns.   W. H. Auden.   NAs

Followed by a long beam of/light skyward, slowly sweeping in a circle/the breath.   Europe.   John Ashbery.   CoPo

Followed by darker shame. Thus I was made. Beginning. Alden Nowlan. NeAC; NOBC

Followed by the sight of you when you are gone. Lightning. Witter ("Emanuel Morgan") Bynner. MoLP

Followed her bright vivacity. A Small Elegy. Richard Snyder. PCP

Following/and falling endlessly/from/her thoughts. Rain. William Carlos Williams. AP; CoBMV

Following in Thy perfect way. Heartsearch. Evelyn K. Gibson. STF

The following morning, urged by my affairs,/I left bright Venice.... Julian and Maddalo (excerpt). Percy Bysshe Shelley. OAEL 1-2; OBTV

Following my doggy ends to doggy end. Timon Speaks to a Dog. Philip Hobsbaum. TW

Following so fair a prize/I could nevermore go wrong. Bel M'es Quan Lo Vens M'Alena. Arnaut Daniel. AWP; LiTW

Following the bird with no name. The Long Joke. R. T. Smith. STE

Following the easy fucking stupid plot to town. Walking to Bellrock. Michael Ondaatje. NOBC

...Following/The hundred-footed sea-wind and the gull. Oedipus at Colonus. Sophocles. LiTW

Following the stars/her mind a star Stars. Robert Earl Hayden. CNA; LCAP

Following the stately and rapid ship, in the wake/following. After the Sea-Ship. Walt Whitman. CBEP; MOS; NePA

Following the white swan through the hedge. A Little Girl on Her Way to School. James Wright. GLGT

...Following us/into the north. Crossing the Border into Canada. Joy Harjo. STE

Follows a meal and the simple urge to sing. Envying the Pelican. Richard Weber. CIP

Follows the mouse, and all is open field. Aylmer's Field. Alfred, Lord Tennyson. VLP

Follows the naked work, profoundly moved by it. Story of a Hotel Room. Rosemary Tonks. OxBTC

Folly, flee, sing going down Don Giovanni on His Way to Hell. Jack Gilbert. NPGG

The folly of Love's sacrifices. Cythera. Paul Verlaine. AWP; SyP

Fomenters as forefathers we? Southern Cross. Herman Melville. AnFE; LiTA

Fond and severe, as looks the groom on bride. The Rival. Sylvia Townsend Warner. MoAB; MoBrPo

Fond dream! which now the east and south winds bear/Away to far Armenia's spicy lands. The Recantation. Albius Tibullus. LiTW

A fond goodnight/Wherever you are. Last Song. James Guthrie. TiPo

Fondly shall my last look wander/To thee, beloved, far away. The Canadian Exile. Antoine Gerin-Lajoie. CaP

Fondness it were for any being free,/To covet fetters, though they golden be. What Guile Is This. Edmund Spenser. ForPo; LiTL

The food and raiment of the Child. Advent Meditation. Alice Meynell. MoRP

Food of the spirit, the soul's hive,/Home and haven of Holy Ghost? The Earth. Leonard Mann. BoAV

Food only for vultures and high-flying crows. Epigram: "Those snooty boys in all their purple drag." Strato. PeHV

Food rife with chlorophyl/Is orophyl! No Mixed Green Salad for Me, Thanks. Georgie Starbuck Galbraith. QQQ

A foodless journey home, as pilgrimage. Marston. Stephen Spender. FaBoTw

A fool among the ruins findeth gold. The Gulistan. Muslih-ud-Din Sa'di. AWP; LiTW

A fool I bring thee to be made a child. A Prayer. George Macdonald. TrPWD

Fool, if thou canst not pass her, rest her/slave! In Harmony with Nature. Matthew Arnold. OAEP

A fool of HAFIZ!–yea, a fool of fools. Odes, I. Hafiz. AWP

"Fool," said my Muse to me, "look in thy heart, and/write." Astrophel and Stella, I. Sir Philip Sidney. AAS; AWP; CABA; EBEV; EG; EnLi 1-2; GBL; HAP; HBV 1-2; InPS; NoP; OAEL 1-2; OAEP; OBSC; SiPS; TEP; TreFT; TrGrPo; ViBoPo

"Fool!" the poems said,/Scornfully. But he is dead. Talk with a Poet. Helen Bevington. SaC

"Fool," they sang in voices more like angels watching/"Fool." The Book of Percival. Jack Spicer. CoPo

Fool, to stand here cursing/When I might be running! The Faun Sees Snow for the First Time. Richard Aldington. MoBrPo

Foolish, delicate, in the lower right-hand corner. Two Views of a Cadaver Room. Sylvia Plath. CMoP; GoYe; NMP

A foolish Toy, yet once more I/Would with Thee live, and for thee die. A Dialogue betwixt GOD and the Soul. Sir Henry Wotton. MeLP; OBS; OxBoCh

The foolishness is on me, and the wild tears/fall! In Leinster. Louise Imogen Guiney. AA; GOBC; HBV 1-2; OBVV

Fools as we met, so fools again we parted. As Love and I, Late Harbour'd in One Inn. Michael Drayton. GBL

Fools banter heav'n itself, O Young!–and thee! New Night Thoughts on Death. A Parody. William Whitehead. NOEC

...Fools like me/Should never try to shave a tree. Winter Trees. Conrad Diekmann. LiSp; SD

A foot in mouth gives safisfaction rare/As two left feet belied with false compare. Conceit upon the Feet (parody). William Zaranka. BXAP

A foot like a cat, a tail like a rat. How a Good Greyhound Is Shaped. *Anonymous.* BoAnP

The foot of Adam leaves the mark/Of some child scrabbling in the dark. Adam's Footprint. Vassar Miller. NePoEA; NIP

The foot of my verse is the knell of their hearse. Dismissing Progress and its Progenitors. George Reavey. EAS

Footnotes in treatises on orchestration. On a Portrait of Mme. Rimsky-Korsakov. Kingsley Amis. NePoEA-2

Footprints of birds record a brief alighting/In flight begun and ended in the air. All That Was Mortal. Sara Teasdale. MoRP

Footprints of fiery moments/Flash out memorials in silent ice. Chinese Winter. Frederick Robert Higgins. BIrV

The footstep of a foreign lord/Profaned the soil no more. Seventy-Six. William Cullen Bryant. HBV 1-2; MC; PAH

For a bad master, and a/worse dame. Father Short. *Anonymous.* OxNR

For a benison to fall/On our meat and on us all. Amen. Grace for a Child. Robert Herrick. AWP; InPo; InPS; LoBV; MoShBr; OAEP; PAI; PoRA; TrGrPo; ViBoPo

For a bloody death. The Wife Speaks. Mary Stanley. AnNZ

For a broad-wheel'd waggon went over my head. Epitaph: "Here lies I, no wonder I'm dead." *Anonymous.* FaBoEE

For a chance to drown in that blue water of his./Sigismundo. Sigismundo. Linda Gregg. AmPA

For a cloudy morning, a cloudy morning/Oft brings a pleasant day. The Dark-Eyed Sailor. *Anonymous.* FSW; ShS

For a couple of hours, but I am not that person. How to Get There. Frank O'Hara. NoP

For a creed that will not let you dance? Magalu. Helene Johnson. BlSi; CDC; PoBA; PoNe

For a dill doul, dil doul, dil doul doul,/take all my money, give me a dill doul. The Maid's Complaint for Want of a Dil Doul. *Anonymous.* CoMu

For a dimness worse than under floors. Not Blindly in the Dark. Robert M. Stanley. AMV-81

For a doe never ran through the street so fast/As the maid ran through the town. The Broomfield Hill. *Anonymous.* AmFP

For a dozen naked hours of coming and coming. Homosexual Sonnets. Kenneth Pitchford. GP

For a few thousand battered books. Hugh Selwyn Mauberley, V. Ezra Pound. CoBMV; NOBA; OxBA

For a fift sort I know thou canst not find. In Librum. Sir John Davies. FaBoEE

For a figleaf fallen from the withered tree. The Statues in the Public Garden. Howard Nemerov. ConAP; EyDe

For a god goes with it and makes it store/To the soul that is starving in darkness be-fore. The Vision of Sir Launfal. James Russell Lowell. GN

...For a house/is where/deep/purposes are/broken/off. The Eyes of Flesh. Sandra Hochman. NMM

For a jollie goode Booke whereon to looke,/is better to me than Golde. "O For a Booke." *Anonymous.* CH; PoSC; SiSoSe

For a large conscience is all one,/And signifies the same with none. Hudibras. Samuel (1612-80) Butler. OBSV

For a lazy man I won't maintain. Georgia Boy. *Anonymous.* OuSiCo

For a like amount you could just as well buy a face. A Valentine for a Lady. Lucilius [(or Lucillius)]. LiTW; OFD

For a little of that which Harry gave Doll. As I Walked in the Woods. *Anonymous.* UnTE

For a little while! The Spanish War. Hugh" (Christopher Murray Grieve) MacDiarmid. CMoP; NMP

For a little while. Tenantry. George Scarbrough. TAT

For a maid again I'll never be. O Waly, Waly Up the Bank. *Anonymous.* EnLoPo; FaBoBa; GBP; OBS

...For a minute, she shuts her eyes. For the Field. Eric Chock. BrSi

For a moment all that it touches back to wonder. The Beautiful Changes. Richard Wilbur. CMoP; CoAP; HaCAP; InPS; NIP; PAI

For a moment I saw the aunt of a potter's wife. Impermanence. Lal Ded. BoWoP

For a plate of steaming sausage like the kind my mother fried. Sausage. Edgar A. Guest. OBAL

For a poor sinner in his bed. Dirge for a Bad Boy. Emile Victor Rieu. BBGG

For a proud idleness like this/Crowns all thy mean affairs. Waldeinsamkeit. Ralph Waldo Emerson. AP; HBV 1-2; NOBA; WGRP

For a ragged man/With a pound or two. Asses. Padraic Colum. LOW

For a rainbow footing it nor he for his bones risen.   The Caged Skylark.
Gerard Manley Hopkins.   CMoP; FM; LiTM; MoAB; MoBrPo; MoPo;
OBMV; PBBP; SoSe

For a row of wind-blown poplars against an English sky.   The Poplars.
Bernard Freeman Trotter.   CaP

For a second, with slightly more patience, more time/for reflection?   One
Almost Might.   Arthur Seymour John Tessimond.   ChMP

For a single general's reputation/Is made out of ten thousand corpses.   A
Protest in the Sixth Year of Ch'ien Fu.   Ts'ao Sung.   FaBV; LiTW

For a small admission price/the public can visit/Monday thru Friday.   Louie.
Paul D. Shiplett.   LFAC

For a smile of God thou art.   Maidenhood.   Henry Wadsworth Longfellow.
HBV 1-2

For a soldier always makes a perfect lover!   Stragglers.   Pietro Aretino.
ErPo

For a soul that thou slightest-/Thine own.   The Zeal of Jehu.   John Henry,
Cardinal Newman.   OBRV

For a time never to be lived in.   The Fourth Dimension.   Leonard Nathan.
AMV-81

For a week or two I'll miss her.   Hen Dying.   Alasdair MacLean.   BoAnP

For a while, I'll let it make you strong,/make your heart lion,/then I'll take it
back.   Woman to Man.   Ai.   GP

For a whole minute against all the dark, as if I were a child.   Swedish Angel.
Winfield Townley Scott.   LiTM

For a wind's in the heart of me, a fire's in my heels.   A Wanderer's Song.
John Masefield.   MCCG; MoAB; MoBrPo

For a world without greed, without guns.   It Is Not Too Late.   Lucia Trent.
PGD

For ae man that ye droon/I droon twa.   Tweed and Till.   Anonymous.
BoNaP; FaBoCh; FaBoPP; GBP; PV

For after death there's a judgement due.'   The Lady's Complaint.   John
Heath-Stubbs.   MP; TwCP

For after dying all reprieve's too late.   A Song: "Fair, sweet and young,
receive a prize."   John Dryden.   LiTL; OBS

For after the blaze, as is no wonder,/Of deadly "nay" hear I the fearful
thunder.   The lively sparks that issue from those eyes.   Sir Thomas Wyatt.
FCP

For age itself would leave me there and I'd be young again.   County Mayo.
Anthony Raftery.   AnIL

For al was vanished me fro through the freshe sightes.   Mum and the
Sothsegger: A Dream.   Anonymous.   OxBM

For all a full atonement made.   I Believe Thy Precious Blood.   John Wesley.
BePJ

For all a green willow is your garland.   All a Green Willow Is My Garland.
John Heywood.   EIL

For all (a second choice) you/present for my passionate caresses.   Sappho, Be
Comforted.   William Carlos Williams.   NePoAm-2

For all do know, unto their woe/all things be dear but poor mens labour.   All
Things Be Dear but Poor Mens Labour.   Anonymous.   CoMu

For all doctors are not mice,/Some are dogs, you see!   Mother Tabbyskins.
Elizabeth Anna Hart.   CenHV; OxBChV

For all had put on Christ's righteousness.   No Sect in Heaven.   Elizabeth H.
Jocelyn Cleaveland.   BLPA; TreFS

For all I know, he is crying yet.   The Man in the Onion Bed.   John Ciardi.
SO

For all I see/Are naught to me,/Save her that's but a lassie yet.   My Love
She's But a Lassie Yet.   James Hogg.   HBV 1-2

For all is thine, be it good or bad that grows.   A Proper Sonnet, How Time
Consumeth All Earthly Things.   Thomas Proctor.   FaBoRV; OBSC

For all its giddy laughter/holds a smarting edge.   Song of the Intruder.
Maria Jacobs.   AMV-81

For all lover true to admire.   Lord Lovel.   Anonymous.   BLPA

For all my passions centered, dear, in you.   Aja's Lament over His Dead
Wife.   Kalidasa.   LiTW

For all my steeds and the rest of my property/We'll retain to her lady's side.
Lord Derwentwater (The King's Love-Letter).   Anonymous.   AmFP

For all of these, the early dead,/Who've gone where no ovations are.   The
Ballad of Dead Yankees.   Donald Petersen.   HeIP; LiSp

For all old Homer's life e'er since he died till now.   Life and Fame.
Abraham Cowley.   AnEnPo

For all our pains, no prospect can we see/Attend us, but old age and poverty.
The Woman's Labour.   Mary Collier.   NOEC

For all our songs are to the night.   Letter to the Night.   Lloyd Frankenberg.
AnAmPo

For all salvation wholly comes/From the almighty Lord.   I to the Lord from
My Distress.   Anonymous.   AH

For all that childhood teaches us of Thee:/We thank Thee, Lord!   A Little Te
Deum of the Commonplace (excerpt).   John Oxenham.   TRV

For all that ever has been ours....   For All That Ever Has Been Ours.   Ziche
Landau.   LiTW

For all/that is lovely in women.   All That Is Lovely in Men.   Robert
Creeley.   NaP

...For all that the cannibals/Ate her one day they had nothing else to do.   As
in Their Time.   Louis MacNeice.   PoL

For all the boundless universe/Is Life–there are no dead!   There Is No Death.
John Luckey McCreery.   BLPA; FaBoBe; HBV 1-2; TreF; WBLP

For all the brave lives of the mariners lost,/That are sunk in the watery main.
Henry Martyn.   Anonymous.   BaBo

(For all the danger thou wert in)/Of the infectious dart.   Confess We All,
Before the Lord.   John Wilson.   AH

For all the Fairies' evidence/Were lost if that were addle.   The Fairies'
Farewell.   Richard Corbet.   NOBE

For all the glories which the Fight did yield.   Annus Mirabilis.   John
Dryden.   OBS

For all the happiness mankind can gain/Is not in pleasure, but in rest from
pain.   The Indian Emperor.   John Dryden.   FiP

For all the love encompassing/Thy children constantly.   So Touch Our
Hearts with Loveliness.   Gail Brook Burket.   AH

For all the next week you'll be ruled by the devil.   Finger Nails.
Anonymous.   OxNR

For all the Sin wherewith the Face of Man/Is blacken'd, Man's Forgiveness
give–and take!   The Rubaiyat of Omar Khayyam.   Omar Khayyam.
EaLo; LoBV

For all the summer islands where the gulf tides flow.   Hemlock Mountain.
Sarah N. Cleghorn.   HBV 1-2

For all the words of God are pure.   I Come to Supplicate.   Simeon Ben
Abun.   TrJP

For all the world belonged to me/When I was six years old.   When I Was
Six.   Zora Cross.   BiCB; HBVY

For all the World is our Pan's Quire.   Clorinda and Damon.   Andrew
Marvell.   AnAnS 1; SeCP

For all things trite shall leap alight/And bloom again for you!   With a First
Reader.   Rupert Hughes.   HBMV

For all this waste of wealth and loss of blood.   On the Same.   John Milton.
SeCeV

For all those powers were ready to embrace/The present means to give our
shepherds grace.   Britannia's Pastorals.   William Browne.   JCP

...For all those things that we have done/At your Command?   Fire and
Brimstone; or, The Destruction of Sodom (excerpt).   George Lestey.
PeHV

For all thoughts and all acts/Trouble the limpid eyes of the world.   Homer.
Albert Ehrenstein.   TrJP

For all thy pride and boasting, into nought.   Eternity.   Sir Thomas More.
EnRePo

For all thy wealth, one penny is his fare.   To a Covetous Churl.   Edward
May.   FaBoEE

For all time, the Lord eternal./Amen.   The Seafarer.   Anonymous.   EBEV

For all true loves to admire.   Lord Thomas and Fair Ellinor.   Anonymous.
OBET

For all we are worth.   My Way Is Not Thy Way.   D. H. Lawrence.
CMoP

For all your Greek and your glory,/To be sent back to A B C.   An A B C
for Grown Gentlemen.   Marquise de Bouflers.   GLGT

For ambition too humble, for meanness too high.   Epitaphium Vivi Auctoris
1792.   Horace Walpole.   FaBoEE

For an approving God.   Apparently with No Surprise.   Emily Dickinson.
AmePo; AnFE; AnNE; APA; NoP; PPP; SoSe; TrGrPo

For an audience of gods, and superwords.   Doctors' Row.   Conrad Aiken.
AP; HAP; NYP; PoPl

For an hour/we are incorruptible.   Amanda Dreams She Has Died and Gone
to the Elysian Fields.   Maxine W. Kumin.   GP

For answer from their icy Elysee.   Sur Ma Guzzla Gracile.   Wallace
Stevens.   PoA

For any eye is an evil eye/That looks in on to a mood apart.   A Mood
Apart.   Robert Frost.   OBSP

For anything they'll buy.   A Song with a Discord.   Arthur Colton.   AA

For are we not God's children both,/Thou, little sandpiper, and I?   The
Sandpiper.   Celia Thaxter.   AA; FaBoBe; GN; HBV 1-2; HBVY; OBCA;
OxBChV

For around Cape Horn and home again, oh, that is the sailor's way!   The
Sailor's Way.   Anonymous.   ShS

For arrows, for pens,/for prophecy.   Elsewhere.   Linda Pastan.   VWA

For as a child I knew I was no child/as now I know I am not old   Elijah
Speaking.   Doug Fetherling.   NOBC

For as He ascended to heaven/So will your King reappear!   Let Not Your
Heart Be Troubled.   Alice Mortenson.   BePJ

For as many days as they had taken to die.   The Stranded Whales.   Geoffrey
Dutton.   CBAP

For as my heart is love, love not in me,/So beauty thou, beauty is not in thee.
Needs Must I Leave, and Yet Needs Must I Love.   Henry Constable.
InvP

For as on you our Muse begun, in you all music endeth!'   Phyllis.   Nicholas
Breton.   OBSC; TrGrPo

For, as our God was never of wood or bone,/our land is not of stones or earth. Luzzato. Charles Reznikoff. VWA

For as sure as you go rambling,/She'll marry another man. The Girl I Left behind Me (My Parents Raised Me Tenderly). *Anonymous.* AmFP

For as the Head is made more weak,/Man is more busie, bold, and free. A Drinking-Song... William Wycherley. SeCV 1-2

For as there is a certeyne tyme to rage,/So ys there tyme suche madnes to asswage. Mye Love Toke Skorne My Servise to Retaine. Sir Thomas Wyatt. AAS

For as they have not found me Gay,/They have not left me Sterne. Book-Lender's Lament. *Anonymous.* FaBoUs

For as Thy days, Thy strength shall be. As Thy Days. Grant Colfax Tullar. BLRP

For at dawn is the reckoning and the last night is long. Cain Shall Not Slay Abel Today on Our Good Ground. Malcolm Lowry. OBCV; PeCV

For at dawning to assail ye/Here no bugles sound reveille. The Lady of the Lake. Sir Walter Scott. OBRV; TrGrPo

For at then ende it binimeth hevenriche winne. "A Lutel Soth Sermun': Going to Hell. *Anonymous.* OxBM

For audience in the good green Bus! Good Green Bus. Rachel Field. BrR

For auld Robin Gray he is kind unto me. Auld Robin Gray. Lady Anne Barnard. BeLS; HBV 1-2

For aye, thy leal and silent lover. Love's Despair. Diarmad O'Curnain. OnYI; OxBI

For base earth was far unfit/For thy beauty, grace, and wit. Three Epitaphs. Francis Davison. OBSC

For be the old love ne'er so true,/She is ever for the new. Let Her Give Her Hand. *Anonymous.* ELP

For beast and man must be fed. The Sower's Song. Thomas Carlyle. OBVV

For beautie, wit, and matchlesse dignitie/yeeld to Samela. Doron's Description of Samela. Robert Greene. LoBV; PoEL 1-5

For beauty born of beauty–that remains. To a Wind-Flower. Madison Cawein. AA; HBV 1-2

For beauty hath created been/T'undo, or be undone. Ulysses and the Siren. Samuel Daniel. CABA; EiL; EnRePo; HAP; LoBV; NOBE; NoP; OBEV; OBSC; PoEL 1-5; TEP; ViBoPo

For beauty, wit, and matchless dignity,/Yield to Samela. Samela. Robert Greene. EiL; GBL; HBV 1-2; NOBE; OBEV; OBSC; ViBoPo

For, behold, there's a little grey nun peeping out/From a bunch of green leaves at his side. The Grey Linnet. James McCarroll. CaP

For being a part of me, somewhere in time Could I Say I Touched You. Harold Littlebird. VoR

For benefits that still survive, by faith/In progress, under laws divine, maintained. Poems Chiefly of Early and Late Years: Prelude. William Wordsworth. VLP

For beste of bon and blod. I Live in Great Sorrow. *Anonymous.* MeEL

For Betsy's battle-flag! Betsy's Battle-Flag. Minna Irving. MC; PAH

For bewtie,/Of dewtie/Sould yeild and give hir place. The Bankis of Helicon: "Declair, ye banks of Helicon." *Anonymous.* OxBS

For birds, and fields, and for bread. Bread. Stanley Burnshaw. TrJP

For birds of a feather will all flock together,/Let their parents say little or much. Three Maids a-Milking Would Go. *Anonymous.* CoMu

...For birds that will/swoop down and pluck them off. Leave the Top Plums. Janet Carncross Chandler. AMV-80

For bloody lies and tyranny/Have made a murderer of McCaffery. McCaffery. *Anonymous.* OBET

For Blueskin's sharp penknife hath set thee at ease,/And every man round me may rob if he please. Newgate's Garland. *Anonymous.* FaBoBa

For bodies/eating/at drink/thank her Womanwork. Paula Gunn Allen. TWSS

For body, soul, wit, cunning, mind and thought,/Part will He none, but either all or naught. The Twelve Properties or Conditions of a Lover. Sir Thomas More. EnRePo

For bombers; and bears the earth upon his head. Native Working on the Aerodrome. Roy Fuller. NeBP

For both have reared the minster that shrines the sacred fire. The Glory of Toil. Edna Dean Proctor. PGD

For bounteously hath he/Rewarded unto me. How Long, Jehovah? Henry Ainsworth. AH

For bratticed wrackers are singing aloud,/And the throngers croon in May! Sing for the Garish Eye. Sir William Schwenck Gilbert. NA

For bread this brave/bard also gave/a clean-cut shave. Lyric Barber. Liboria E. Romano. GoYe

For breaking of the Lord's birthday. In Dessexshire as It Befel. *Anonymous.* GBP

For but a single palmful/Of water now for thee. An Aboriginal Mother's Lament. Charles Harpur. ACV

...For by itself onion/Is bitter and unpleasant to the taste. Onions. Philemon. FaBoUs

For by such plans you'll never gain/The height of one who should be tall. The Down-Pullers. Walter E. Isenhour. STF

For by the death-blow of my Hope/My Memory immortal grew. Lines Written beneath a Picture. George Gordon, Lord Byron. OBSP

For by the evening I shall be a star. Climb. Winifred Welles. BiCB

For by the wind which from my sighs doth come,/Your praises round about the world are blown. Diana. Henry Constable. OBSC

For by tomorrow I may think so too. Woman's Constancy. John Donne. EnLit; LiTL; MBW 1-2; NLV; NoP

For calmness to remember,/Or courage to forget. Remember or Forget. Hamilton Aïdé. HBV 1-2

For carrots are unable to engage in conversation. The Parrot and the Carrot We May Easily Confound. Robert Williams Wood. PV

For certain years, for certain months and days. Retro me, Sathana! Dante Gabriel Rossetti. MaVP

For Chaos stirs when you have sounded. Night Wind. Fyodor Tyutchev. LiTW

For chil-dren to de-ride and scorn? Child's Natural History. Oliver Herford. HBV 1-2

For Christ is risen, the angels say/At blessed Easter time! At Easter Time. Laura E. Richards. OHIP

For Christ is risen today! Go Tell Them That Jesus Is Living. *Anonymous.* BePJ

For Christ, who lived for all the world,/Was part of all the year. Not Only in the Christmas-Tide. Mary Mapes Dodge. ChBR

For Church's good; she rises high,/When such as you fall down. A Prognostication on Will Laud, Late Archbishop of Canterbury. *Anonymous.* OxBoLi

For clever deils he'll mak them! Epitaph on a Schoolmaster. Robert Burns. FaBoCo

...For cocks do sleep/when clocks do wake for thee. Of the Clock and the Cock. George Turberville. EnRePo

For Colly will give me/no more milk now! Colly, My Cow. *Anonymous.* EvOK

For Communism and for liberty. Full Moon at Tierz: Before the Storming of Huesca. John Cornford. OBWP

For comrades and lovers. No Labor-Saving Machine. Walt Whitman. PCP

For constant faith is made a drudge/But when requiting love is judge. Caelica, LXI. Fulke, Lord Brooke Greville. FCP

For Curio dresses nothing–but himself. On a Stingy Beau. John Winstanley. FaBoEE

For custom conquers fear and shame. Fable XIII: The Tame Stag. John Gay. EiCP

For cutting loose from habit. An Original Cuss. Keith Preston. ALV

For Daffodil comes home today. Daffodil's Return. Bliss Carman. CaP

For dancing is love's proper exercise.' Orchestra. Sir John Davies. UnS

For Danger halt your mercy in his chaine. Three Roundels of Love Unreturned. Geoffrey Chaucer. MeEL

For, Dante, I'm the goad and you're the bull. Sonnet: To Dante Alighieri (He Writes to Dante...). Cecco da Siena Angiolieri. AWP

For David his anoint, and his seed, evermore. Psalm XVIII. Sir Philip Sidney. FCP

For David lived, but Juan nearly died. Don Juan. George Gordon, Lord Byron. UnTE

For days when it rains too hard/to be trowelling in the garden. Return to Astolat. Gail White. AMV-81

For dead he lay. The Road to Zoagli. Max Beerbohm. FaBoNo

For dearly do I love his sweet bonnet so blue. Bonnets So Blue. *Anonymous.* OBET

For death has slaine my sweeting,/Which hath my heart in keeping. Tan Ta Ra Ran Tan Tant: Cries Mars on Bloody Rapier. *Anonymous.* NCEP

For Death, he taketh all away, but them he cannot take. Heraclitus. William Johnson Cory. AWP; CBEP; ELU; FaBoEE; FaPoR; GoTF; GTBS; HBV 1-2; NOBE; OBEV; OBNC; OBSP; OBVV; PeHV; PoRA; SeCePo; TreF; ViBoPo; VLP

For Death thou art a Mower too. Damon the Mower. Andrew Marvell. AnAnS 1; JCP; OAEL 1-2

"For death to flap in on. But I carry the knife." Casa de Pollos. Kathleen Fraser. AmPA

For death to you was one more victory. Joyce Kilmer. Amelia Josephine Burr. HBMV

For delaying our walk this fine morning. Arthur McBride. *Anonymous.* GBP; OBET

For Dick Turpin she lived and she died. Dick Turpin's Ride. *Anonymous.* OBET

...For distant islands/so remote we can never know their names. At Pont-Aven, Gauguin's Last Home in France. Andrew Grossbardt. AMV-81

...For doing so Crow Breast, the/Gros Ventre chief, called me a fool. Poor Wolf Speaks. Poor Wolf. NU

For dread to fall I stand not fast. It May Be Good. Sir Thomas Wyatt. AAS; EnRePo; FaBoPV; FCP; SiPS

For dreams are licensed as they never were. I Dreamed That in a City Dark as Paris. Louis Simpson. CoAP; NePoEA

For dreams are your life/In the night/And my hope in the day. Love Song. Flavien Ranaivo. PBA

For drowning of my sister Kate. The Two Sisters. *Anonymous.* PrIm

For dust and clay is the Serpent's meat,/Which never was made for Man to eat. The Everlasting Gospel. William Blake. OBRV

For Dust is insatiate and invincible. Mrs. Southern's Enemy. Osbert Sitwell. AtBAP; ViBoPo

For each age is a dream that is dying,/Or one that is coming to birth. Ode: "We are the music-makers." Arthur William Edgar O'Shaughnessy. FaPoR; GoTF; GTBS; HBV 1-2; OBEV; OBVV; OnYI; OxBI; TreF; TrGrPo; ViBoPo; VLP; WHA

For each breath of the south-wind makes a new bamboo! Eating Bamboo-Shoots. Po Chu-i. OBVE

For each light there is another light/wanting to stifle it. Kinneret. Judith Herzberg. VWA

For each pearl my eyes have wept. The Portrait. Edward Robert Bulwer, Earl of Lytton. HBV 1-2

For each, the whole of the devoted sun. A General Communion. Alice Meynell. NOCV

For early I in love was crossed,/Before my flower of love was lost. An Old Maid Early. William Blake. OBSP

For earth for fire and water for table chair and blood. Ode for Soft Voice. Michael McClure. NeAP

For either the rain is destroying his grain/Or the drought is destroying his roots. The Farmer. Sir Alan Patrick Herbert. CenHV

For else all other suit/Is clean in vain. All heavy minds. Sir Thomas Wyatt. EG; FCP; SiPS

For else will magistrates and lawyers/Divide thy wealth, thy purse retain. Advice to Hotheads. Samuel Isaac. TrJP

For endless rest–though risen is he. A Drizzling Easter Morning. Thomas Hardy. CMoP

For England and America/Will keep and hold the sea! The Battle of Manila. Richard Hovey. PAH

For England's sinking unless they/Do take the helm, and better sway. The Sea Martyrs. *Anonymous.* OBSS

For entertaining Plated Wares/Upon my Silver Shelf– It Dropped So Low–in My Regard. Emily Dickinson. CABA; CMoP; HAP; InPK; OBSP; OxBA; PoPl

For envy of her precious neighborhood. Sonnetto XXXV: "My Lady's face it is they worship there." Guido Cavalcanti. CTC

For 'er Majesty's bold troubleshooters is flyin' to sort out the mess. Bold Troubleshooters. Peter Veale. NOBL

For ere this-day-month come and gang/My wedded wife ye'se be.' Blancheflour and Jellyflorice. *Anonymous.* ESPB

For Essex's sake they would fight all. The Young Earl of Essex's Victory over the Emperor of Germany. *Anonymous.* ESPB; OBET

For euery roome is either there, or here. To My Lady Rogers, the Authors Wiues Mother... Sir John (1561-1612) Harington. EyDe

For even as water could you touch and behold/my heart, as through our hands it flowed. This Evening, My Love, Even as I Spoke Vainly. Sister Juana Ines de la Cruz. PBWP

For even if at dusk she choose to fly/Afterwards she must rest. The Final Word. Dom Moraes. NePoEA-2

For even if I beat, their hate/Will grow to more than this mere grin. The Judgement of God. William Morris. OBVV

For even now our brackish waters can/be sweetened by a strange tree. The Magic Apple Tree. Elaine Feinstein. BrRo

For even this earth bears its fruits in due season and blesses/Thee,/O Lord! The Lament of Saint Ann. *Anonymous.* CAW

For ever alone, the palm. August. Laurence Binyon. SyP

FOR EVER AND FOR EVER/ARE CLAD IN ROBES OF WHITE! For Thee, O Dear Dear Country! John Mason Neale. VLP

For ever at peace with the sea! The Song of the Derelict. John McCrae. EtS

For ever be folded, protecting and warm. The Horn. James Reeves. SO

For ever be my ghost. Nocturne. Edward Davison. CH

For ever cursed–because mine eyes/Are fashioned so! Vagabonds. Madelaine Marie. PeHV

For ever from that fatal tree debarred,/Which flaming swords and angry cherubs guard. Solomon on the Vanity of the World. Matthew Prior. EiCP

For ever its fire breaks out at last,/And shrivels all the lines. Art. James (1834-82) Thomson. OBVV

For ever let Britannia wield/The tea-pot of her sires! The Poets at Tea. Barry Pain. Par

For ever shepherd you across/The shining field of heaven. Among the Millet. Archibald Lampman. CaP; WHW

For ever/The wind of the south. South Wind. Nathan Yonathan. VWA

For ever, though they lived so short a time. On Two Brothers. Simonides (of Ceos). AWP

For ever through the glens, placid and dumb. Cadmus and Harmonia. Matthew Arnold. OBVV

For ever where the bravest fall/The best beloved die. The Battle of Bennington. Thomas P. Rodman. MC; PAH

For ever with the baby at her breast. Flemish Primitive. G. S. Fraser. BSV

For ever with thee to remain/within thy town Jerusalem. A Prisoner's Song of Jerusalem. *Anonymous.* ACP

For evermore I'll gladly stay/With the girl I left behind me. The Girl I Left behind Me. Samuel Lover. FSW

For evermore with me to last/The power wherein I am possess'd. Since Love Is Such That as Ye Wot. Sir Thomas Wyatt. FCP; SiPS

For every danger, every fear,/Our shield and our defender. The Name of Jesus. Annie Johnson Flint. BePJ

For every Gael that shows so brave/Is nothing better than a slave! To an Anti-poetical Priest. Giolla Brighde MacNamee. AnIV

For every girl at all,/They all love Jack! They All Love Jack. *Anonymous.* ShS

For every infant severed from the breast. Living in Sin. Austin Clarke. ELU

For every joy the seedling of a dream. In the Grass. Annette Von Droste-Hulshoff. PBWP

For every little boy like me/The temperance pledge should sign. Temperance Song. *Anonymous.* FaBoUs

For every man an idiot was,/And every house a folly. For Though the Caves Were Rabbited. Henry David Thoreau. OBSP; PoEL 1-5

For every man who hears this song will know we're not to blame. The Durham Lock-Out. *Anonymous.* CoMu

For every mile the feet go/the heart goes nine Doll's Boy's Asleep. Edward Estlin Cummings. DuDa

...For/every neighborhood child to find/under the Christmas tree next year. Pipe Dreams. Diane Bickston. LFAC

...For every pest you slay/Ten more rank flies pollute the breath of day. Savage Portraits. Don (Donald Robert Marquis) Marquis. HBMV

For every thing that lives is Holy The Marriage of Heaven and Hell. William Blake. CEP; LAuP

For every time I lose a friend/A little lamp goes out. My Friends Are Little Lamps to Me. Elizabeth Whittemore. PoToHe

For every time the sun goes up/Over the heavens,/ayi, yai, ya. Dead Man's Song, Dreamed by One Who Is Alive. *Anonymous.* WTO

For every word has its marrow in the English tongue for order and for delight. The Instruments. Christopher Smart. WiR

For everyone knew them in the Lord, and they lived by the/water of life forever./Hallelujah. Solomon: Inspiration. *Anonymous.* WGRP

For everything give thanks! Thanks for Everything. Helen Isabella Tupper. WBLP

For everything that lives is Holy. A Song of Liberty. William Blake. EnLi 1-2

For everywhere the Irish are,/Much gayety's aborning. Dawn Song–St. Patrick's Day. Violet Alleyn Storey. YeAr

For Falseness and Lamkin/Deserved well to die. Lamkin (B vers.). *Anonymous.* BaBo

For fame of families is all a cheat,/'Tis personal virtue only makes us great. The True-Born Englishman. Daniel Defoe. OBSV

For father's got money,/But mother's got none. Clap Hands, Clap Hands. *Anonymous.* OxNR

For father's ship is coming home/With wondrous things from foreign lands. The Wind's Song. (Thomas Nicoll Hepburn) "Setoun. Gabriel" HBV 1-2; HBVY

For fear he is the flea. Lines for an Eminent Poet and Critic. Patric Dickinson. PV

For fear, I would seem to limit/The love of the illimitable God. My Church. E., O. G. BLPA; SoSe

For fear lest Mans Array/Should Him to Manly Deeds betray? Odes. Horace. OBVE

For fear like us you spend your days upon Van Diemen's shore. The Female Transport. *Anonymous.* NOAV

For fear my Cradle prove my Urn. Youth and Beauty. Aurelian Townsend. AnAnS 2; GBL; MePo; SeCP

For fear of human eyes swerved from his plan. And When I Am Entombed. Ralph Waldo Emerson. ViBoPo

For fear that she wile your fancy frae me. Whistle an' I'll Come to Ye, My Lad. Robert Burns. BoLiVe; LiTL; OxBoLi; UnTE; ViBoPo

For fear the children might hear me. In the Season of Wolves and Names. Marieve Rugo. AMV-80

For fear the king should rule again,/I'd pull down Tiburn too. The Downfall of Charing Cross. *Anonymous.* FaBoCo

For fear they burn a hole through two-foot steel. Spoils. Robert Graves. HAP; MoLP; NYBP; WeW

For fear You may not strike again/I will not draw the steel. Resolution. Charles L. O'Donnell. GoBC; TrPWD

For fear you should return the compliment. To a Poetic Lover. W. Hay. ALV

For fegs, it's aye high time/The claith was owre the parrot! The Parrot Cry. Hugh" (Christopher Murray Grieve) MacDiarmid. OxBS

For feind a crumb of thee sho faws. Return Thee, Hairt. Alexander Scott. BSV

For fellowship at night. The mountains grow unnoticed. Emily Dickinson. MoAB; MoAmPo; TrGrPo

For fere of nyght, so hateth she derknesse!..... And As For Me. Geoffrey Chaucer. CH

For few can be good, like the clever,/Or clever, so well as the good. Good and Clever. Elizabeth Wordsworth. OxBTC

...For few or none/Hears thy voice right, now he is gone. Memorial Verses. Matthew Arnold. CABA; FiP; HBV 1-2; OAEL 1-2; OAEP; PP; VLP

For fient a bit o't's rotten. Epitaph for William Nicol. Robert Burns. FaBoEE

For fighting's part of what a Yankee knows! Dewey in Manila Bay. R. V. Risley. MC; PAH

For flesh/that becomes garbage on the roads/at night and in the wind and the rain. Refugees. Chaim Grade. VWA

For food, for fun, for poison/They are a help to man. The Wild Mushroom. Gary Snyder. NoP

For footsteps/stopping short of my door/then leaving forever. The Well-intentioned question. Wendy Rose. STE; TWSS

For fortune often mocks the careless lover's eyes. Hylas. Sextus Propertius. AWP

...For free he says/so that I can't refuse. My Garden, My Daylight. Jorie Graham. HaCAP; MAYP

For freedom's right;/In flushing fight/To conquer if then to fall. Oh! for a Steed. Thomas Osborne Davis. IrPN

For friends in all the ag'd you'll meet,/And brothers in the young. Song: "Had I a heart for falsehood fram'd." Richard Brinsley Sheridan. HBV 1-2; OBEC

For from all seasons shall we new jewels borrow/To deck the Mother born Immaculate. Vigil of the Immaculate Conception. Maurice Francis Egan. CAW

For from the Body can they fly? The Duel. Abraham Cowley. AnAnS 2

For from the King of Kings/Eternal mercy springs. The Bounty of Jehovah Praise. George Sandys. AH

For from thence there is no stealing away,/As there was on the road from Moscow. The March to Moscow. Robert Southey. FaBoCo

For gambling on the Sabbath day. Macaffie's Confession. Anonymous. BeLS; CoSo

For gazing at girls while I uncurl like greed. Variation on the Gothic Spiral. William Stanley Merwin. PoA

For generations to choke on. Day of the Parade. Alan Chong Lau. BrSi

For giving out with the wrong combination/of notes. The Perfectionist. Bernice Fleisher. PoDr

For gladness, shedding piteous tears between. The Dawn in Britain. Charles M. Doughty. PoEL 1-5

For Glorie's of eternitie a frame,/That by all bodies else obscures her name. Love Is the Peace, whereto All Thoughts Doe Strive. Fulke, Lord Brooke Greville. AAS

For glory or for shame. A Name in the Sand. Hannah Flagg Gould. AA

For glory's of eternity a frame,/That by all bodies else obscures her name. Caelica, LXXXV. Fulke, Lord Brooke Greville. FCP; JCP

For God alone doth know how blest/My early years have been in thee! It Is Too late to Call Thee Now. Emily Bronte. NOBV

For God, by grace, shall dwell in Thee,/And God himself is Light! Walking in the Light. Bernard Barton. VLP

"For God, for Country and for Yale!" Yale Boola March. Charles H. Loomis. FSN

For God had set His likeness on all the things that were. I Saw the Winter Weaving. Jalal ed-Din or al-Din Rumi. LiTW

For God has something still to teach/In that diviner vale. A Little Sequence (excerpt). Francis Burdett Money-Coutts. OBVV

For God hath given to Love to keep/Its own eternally. My Dead. Frederick Lucian Hosmer. WGRP

For God is good, and, lo, my ships/Are coming home from sea! Jubilate. George Arnold. EtS

...For God is life, and death perhaps/Exile from God. Exile from God. John Hall Wheelock. GoBC; WGRP

For God is love, and His bright law/Should find our hearts without one flaw. Unless. Ella Dietz Glynes. AA

(For god likes girls/and tomorrow and the earth). Dive for Dreams. Edward Estlin Cummings. OLR

For God may suffer for a time/But will disclose it in the end. The Lord of Lorn and the Fals Steward. Anonymous. OxBB

For God never ranks His sailors by the Regis-/ter of earth! Reuben James. James Jeffrey Roche. NA

For–God of Waves!–none could repress/One choking thought–the loneliness! The Death of Colman. Thomas Frost. PAH

For God requires no more than thou hast done,/And takes thy work to bless it for his own. Laus Deo. Robert Bridges. VLP

For God's forsaken the buffalo range and the damned old buffalo. Buffalo Skinners. Anonymous. ABF; AmFP; AS; BaBo; BFSS; BPAW; CoSo; FSW; GBP; ViBoFo

For God's own angel of the resurrection/Shall rend the grave, and roll the stone away. I Know That My Redeemer Liveth. Virginia Frazer Boyle. BePJ

"For God's sake be careful or someone will hear you!" Sacred and Profane Love, or, There's Nothing New under the Moon Either. Peter De Vries. NLV

For God's sake, call the hangman. Gulliver. Kenneth Slessor. ACV

For god's sake, is there anyone out there listening?/If so, Peace. Living with Chris. Ted Berrigan. NoAm

For God's sake/Let me be me. Africa's Plea. Roland Tombekai Dempster. PBA; TTY

For God's sake, reader! take them not for mine! Don Juan. George Gordon, Lord Byron. EnL; MBW 1-2; OAEL 1-2; OAEP

For God's Word abides for all eternity. My Bible and I. Anonymous. STF

For God sent out a warning through the land. The Tupelo Destruction. Anonymous. AmFP

For God, the great Headmaster. Schoolmaster. George Rostrevor Hamilton. FaBoEE

For God who sendeth/He only lendeth. In Trust. Mary Mapes Dodge. SiSoSe

For, God wot, ther hartes wold be wo/To spende ther husbondes money so. What Women Are Not. Anonymous. MeEL

For good and forever–heavy as turf and heartscalded. The Father. Desmond O'Grady. NoAm

For good is dede, the land is sinful. Four Wise Men on Edward II's Reign. Anonymous. OxBM

For good to sound the coral at the hearts of men. Dead Marine. Louis O. Coxe. WaP

For goode is the liff, ending faithfully. Rime CXL: "The longe love, that in my thought doeth harbar." Petrarch (Francesco Petrarca). OBVE

For goodness only doth God comprehend,/Knows what was first, and what shall be the end. Caelica, LXXXVIII. Fulke, Lord Brooke Greville. FCP; JCP; OxBoCh

For Greiv-Ill, pain, forlorn estate do best decipher me. Caelica, LXXXIII. Fulke, Lord Brooke Greville. FCP; PoEL 1-5

For grey morn breaks from thine eyes. Rise, Lady Mistress, Rise! Nathaniel Field. EiL

For grocery shops were grocery shops,/Not hemispheres to me! Counters. Elizabeth Jane Coatsworth. SoPo; SUS

For guilt must all be compensated. Who Never Ate with Tears His Bread. Johann Wolfgang von Goethe. WGRP

For Guinever is but a child. Little Guinever. Annie Fields. AA

For "had I wist" cometh to late for to louse it. Snatches: "Know or thou knitte." Anonymous. OxBM

For, had we here said lesse, we had sung nothing then. New Yeares, Expect New Gifts. Ben Jonson. SeCP

For hadde ye ratones youre reed, ye couthe not reule/youselven. The Vision of Piers Plowman. William Langland. OxBM

For half an hour in the street to-day. A Piper. Seumas (James Starkey) O'Sullivan. CH; MoShBr; OxBI; TiPo

For happiness is your dower,/Your morning-gift is rest. Imagined Happiness. Erik Axe Karlfeldt. LiTW; PoPl

For hark! still, still the bell doth toll/For some but now departed soul. The Passing Bell. Thomas Heywood. FaBoRV

For Harry our King is gone hunting,/To bring his deer to bay. The Hunt Is Up. Anonymous. CH

For having lost but once your prime,/You may for ever tarry. To the Virgins, To Make Much of Time. Robert Herrick. ALV; AnAnS 2; AWP; BLPA; BoLiVe 026; BoLoP; CaPo; DiPo; ELP; EnLoPo; ExPo; FaBV; FaFP; FF; ForPo; FPL; GBL; GoTF; HAP; HBV 1-2; HeIP; InMe; InPo; InPS; JCP; LiTB; LiTL; LoBV; MasP; NIP; NLV; NOBE; NoP; OAEL 1-2; OAEP; OBEV; OBS; OLR; PAI; PG; PoEL 1-5; PoPl; PPoe; PrIm; QFR; SCV; SeCeV; SeCV 1-2; SoSe; SpRo; TreFS; TrGrPo; ViBoPo; WHA

For he ain't like some of the swabs I've seen,/As would go and lie to a poor marine. A Sailor's Yarn. James Jeffrey Roche. MOS; NA

For he can creep. Jubilate Agno. Christopher Smart. CTC

For he can thoroughly enjoy/The pepper when he pleases!/Wow! wow! wow! The Duchess's Lullaby. Lewis (Charles Lutwidge Dodgson) Carroll. FaBoNo; SpRo

For he cannot read his tombstone when he's dead. Do It Now. Berton Braley. BLPA; FaFP; WBLP

...For he/Combines domestication,/Venery, and independence. A Bestiary. Kenneth Rexroth. OBAL

For he could think without congestion,/Upon both sides of every question. The Dinosaur. Bert Leston Taylor. ImOP

For He dearly loves His children/And will lead them safely through.   Jesus Never Fails.   Walter E. Isenhour.   STF

For he, doing only things fit for his nature,/Did seem to me by much the wiser creature.   Tunbridge Wells.   John Wilmot, Earl of Rochester.   FaBoPP; OBSV

For he doth more good unto the poor/Than many a crowned king!   Old Christmas.   Mary Howitt.   GN

For he doth suck our eggs, and sing cuckoo.   Of the Cuckoo.   John Bunyan.   PBBP

For he gave all his heart and lost.   Never Give All the Heart.   William Butler Yeats.   BoLoP; CMoP; GTBS; HBV 1-2; MoLP

For he has gotten his little triangle,/Quod erat faciendum!   The New Ballad of Sir Patrick Spens (parody).   Sir Arthur Thomas ("Q") Quiller-Couch.   BXAP

For He has planned the best for us/And will lead us all the way!   The Best for Us.   Olive H. Burnett.   STF

For He hath triumphed gloriously!   Tell Forth His Fame.   *Anonymous.*   BePJ

For He is God and Ghost and Everyman.   Second Seeing.   Louis Golding.   WGRP

For He is God Omnipotent.   To-Day a Shepherd.   Saint Theresa of Avila.   AWP

For He is King above, no Power is like to Love./Glory here, Diggers all!'   The Diggers' Song.   Gerrard Winstanley.   FaBoPV

For he is lechoure.   Snatches: "Wake wel, Annot."   *Anonymous.*   OxBM

For He is made man for thy sake.   Three Christmas Carols: II.   *Anonymous.*   ACP

For he is sadder than God knows.   Judaeus Errans.   Louis Golding.   TrJP

...For he knows as well as I do/That the branch will not break.   Two Hangovers.   James Wright.   AmPC; LCAP

For he liv'd by the rope, and died by the halter.   On a Rope Maker Hanged.   William Browne.   CavP

For he mightn't like it, Mama, Mama.   I Love Little Willie.   *Anonymous.*   ABF

For he murdered my girl when I paid for a Duke.   Rigoletto.   Newman Levy.   OBAL

For he ne fond nones kinnes blisse,/Ne of dintes foryevenesse.   The Fox and the Wolf.   *Anonymous.*   OxBM

For he never played cricket at all.   Limerick: "There was an old man of Bengal."   Thomas Anstey Guthrie.   CenHV

For he never rode the hell-bound train.   The Hell-Bound Train.   *Anonymous.*   BeLS; BLPA; BPAW; CoSo

For he offered his life for the people's/sake!   The Ride of Collins Graves.   John Boyle O'Reilly.   PAH

For he on honey-dew hath fed,/And drunk the milk of Paradise.   Kubla Khan.   Samuel Taylor Coleridge.   AtBAP; AWP; BiP; BoLiVe; CH; DiPo; ELP; ERoP 1-2; ExPo; EyDe; FaBoBe; FaBoCh; FaBV; FaFP; FF; FiP; ForPo; FPL; GN; GoJo; GoTF; GTBS; HAP; HBV 1-2; HeIP; HoPM; InPK; InPo; InPS; InvP; LiTB; LoBV; LoGBV; MaC; MasP; MAT; MBW 1-2; MCCG; MyFE; NAWM 1-2; NIP; NOBE; NoP; OAEL 1-2; OAEP; OBEV; OBNC; OBRV; PAI; PoEL 1-5; PoPl; PoRA; PP; PPoe; PrIm; RoGo; SCV; SeCeV; SoSe; SyP; TEP; TreFS; TrGrPo; UnPo; ViBoPo; WeW; WHA; WSC

For he pronounced them good.   Almighty God in Being Was.   Silas Ballou.   AH

For he pu'ed up the bonny brier,/And flang't in St. Mary's Lough.   The Douglas Tragedy.   *Anonymous* BoLiVe; HBV 1-2; NoP

For he's a raving Nimrod will not start/To bathe his hands in such a royal heart.   An Ironical Encomium.   *Anonymous.*   APAS

For he's low doun, he's in the broom,/That's waitin' on me.   Low Doun in the Broom.   *Anonymous.*   BSV; GoTS

For he's made her his lady instead of his whore.   Blackberry Fold.   *Anonymous.*   OBET

For he's madly mistaken/If he thinks that I mourn.   The Cuckoo (B vers.).   *Anonymous.*   OBET

For he saith, "Tjou passest through."   Passing Through.   Annie Johnson Flint.   BLRP

For he seemed like a man leaving his mind behind him/Somewhere there on the ground   The X of the Unknown.   Tom Clark.   LiSp

For he sees thee yet, he sees thee yet!   The Witch o' Fife.   James Hogg.   BSV

For he shall eat your sweetbreads, like a dog.   Didactic Sonnet.   Melvin Walker La Follette.   NePoEA; PoA

For He shall speak peace.   He Shall Speak Peace.   Thomas Curtis Clark.   WBLP

For he sings of what the world will be/When the years have died away.'   The Poet's Song.   Alfred, Lord Tennyson.   ELP; FiP; VLP

For he that believeth bearing in hand,/Ploweth in water and soweth in the sand.   My heart I gave thee...   Sir Thomas Wyatt.   FCP

For he was a blade of the April sod/That bowed and blew with the whisper of God.   Threnody for a Poet.   Bliss Carman.   CaP

For he was a good outlawe,/And dyde pore men moch god.   A Gest of Robyn Hode.   *Anonymous.*   ESPB; OxBB

For he was a jovial hunter.   Sir Lionel.   *Anonymous.*   AmFP; ESPB

For he was drown'd and I've the ague.   Written After Swimming From Sestos to Abydos.   George Gordon, Lord Byron.   ALV; ERoP 1-2; InMe; LiSp; MBW 1-2; MOS; NLV; NoP; OBRV; OBTV

For he was just a farmer's boy/And she a Jersey cow...   A Farmer's Boy.   *Anonymous.*   OBET; PoPle

For he was the one who changed/her name.   I like coffee, I like tea.   *Anonymous.*   FaFP

For he was tired, like me.   Clouds.   Norman Ault.   HBVY

For he who bus'nesse would from storms procure,/Soon his affairs above his mannage findes.   Gondibert.   Sir William Davenant.   SeCV 1-2

For he who dies believing/Dies safely in Thy love!   O Spacred Head! Now Wounded.   Paul Gerhardt.   BePJ

For he who his pleasures puts off for/a day,/Deserves to be reckon'd an Ass.   The Ass.   Moses Mendes.   TrJP

For he who is honest is noble,/Whatever his fortunes or birth.   Nobility.   Alice Cary.   OHFP; WBLP

For he who lives more lives than one/More deaths than one must die.   The Ballad of Reading Gaol.   Oscar Wilde.   NOBV; ViBoPo

For he wiped his feet clean on the scraper.   Limerick: "T was a tidy young tapir."   Carolyn Wells.   TDH

For hearts to apprehend Thee everywhere;–/We thank Thee, Lord.   Thanksgiving.   John Oxenham.   BLRP; WBLP

For hearts will break, and bands will/bow;/So dear will I love my lady now!'   Prince Heathen (A version).   *Anonymous.*   ESPB

For heaven and hell are childhood playmates still.   For Two Girls Setting out in Life.   Peter Viereck.   MiAP

For Heaven is a different thing,/Conjectured and waked sudden in,/And might extinguish me.   'Tis so much joy!   Emily Dickinson.   NOCV

For heaven's sufficed with a single sun.   The Golden Sestina.   Giovanni Pico della Mirandola   LiTW

For heaven shouldn't purchase/That little sister hand.   The Hand.   Ebenezer Jones.   OBVV

For her and me, I'll drive her there afore she skids awa.   The Deean Tractorman, Deleerit.   Edith Anne Robertson.   OxBS

For her children are grown and her work is done.   The Old Mother.   *Anonymous.*   PoToHe

For her children now/Oppress her children.   Mother Dark.   Francesca Yetunde Pereira.   PBA

For her I made this song and for her I sing it.   The Bear's Song.   *Anonymous.*   AWP

For her lost shoe.   The Lost Shoe.   Walter De la Mare.   BrR

For her love I mourning make,/More than any man.   For Her Love I Cark and Care.   *Anonymous.*   CBEP

For her–oh, God!–who brought this torment to me.   My Thirty Years.   Juan F. Manzano.   TTY

For her peace no less.   Fatherland Song.   Bjornstjerne Bjornson.   AWP

For her sweet eyes own that she/Also loves her neighbor.   Thoughts on the Commandments.   George Augustus Baker.   AA; HBV 1-2

For her the time passes slowly.   Tonight the Famous Psychiatrist.   Louis Simpson.   OxBC

For here day and night toileth the summer/lest deedless his time pass away.   Gunnar's Howe above the House at Lithend.   William Morris.   OBTV

For here my eye has seen but few,/Who in each act that act have done.   The Strangers.   Jones Very.   CBEP; OxBA

For here the sun was followed by a star.   On the Nativity of Our Saviour.   Thomas Philipott.   JCP

For here with joy and dutiful regard/In all my rural comforts he had shared.   Lines Descriptive of Thomson's Island.   Benjamin Lynde.   SCAP

For hete of cold, for cold of hete I dye.   The Song of Troylus.   Petrarch.   AWP

For Highland Harry back again.   Highland Harry Back Again.   Robert Burns.   EBEV

For him it is impossible, for he is God.   The Great Sad One.   Uri Z. Greenberg.   VWA

For him, sweet blossomings and death.   A Russian Spring Song with Minaiev.   Thomas Walsh.   GoBC

For him that can breake vowes but not returne.   Oft have I sigh'd for him that heares me not.   Thomas Campion.   FaBoEn

For him that was of men most true.   The knight of the Burning Pestle.   Francis Beaumont and John Fletcher.   AtBAP

For him who hears, in soundless strains/The music of intangible things.   Tree-Building.   Franklin Cable.   PGD

For hire love mourning I make,/More then eny mon.   Love for a Beautiful Lady.   *Anonymous.*   MeEL

For his bronco fell on him/And mashed in his head.   Blood on the Saddle.   *Anonymous.*   FSW

For his clean hands and love-submissive heart.   Intercession in Late October.   Robert Graves.   MoAB

For his father had protected his good estate.   The Pitt-Rivers Museum, Oxford.   James Fenton.   FaBoMo

For his favorite hobby is trimming goatees.   I Know a Barber.   Edward Anthony.   TiPo

For His grace and power are such/None can ever ask too much.   Thou Art Coming to a King.   John Newton.   TRV

For his Heart belies his Haires.   Anacreontea: Young Men Dancing. *Anonymous.*   OBVE

For his heart belies his hairs.   Youthful Age.   Thomas Stanley.   AWP

For his home in the sea, which was moister.   Limerick: "O was an ossified oyster."   Carolyn Wells.   TDH

For his ignorance I could strike him dead.   Goodbye to Regal.   Daniel Huws.   NYBP

For His is a kingdom in the hearts of men.   I Have Lighted the Candles, Mary.   Kenneth Patchen.   TrCP

For his long absence, some againe are glad/To waste his goods unwreak't, all talking still.   The Odyssey.   Homer.   CTC

For His love is always shining.   God's Sunshine.   John Oxenham.   WBLP

For his loyal brothers, who were shot on Dunlavin Green.   Dunlavin Green. *Anonymous.*   FaBoBa

For his mercies aye endure,/Ever faithful, ever sure.   Let Us with a Gladsome Mind.   John Milton.   TRV; WGRP

For his name it is young Edward, who ploughed the lowlands low.   Edwin in the Lowlands Low.   *Anonymous.*   AmFP

For his soul's peace this life to song has given.   The Succession.   Frances Laughton Mace.   AA

For his sow has eaten her pigs and turned into stone.   The Boar of Badenoch and the Sow of Atholl.   Naomi Mitchison.   PoSH

For His star it shineth clear.   Christmas Carol.   *Anonymous.*   GN

For history is a record of good men gone wrong on licker.   Chantey of Notorious Bibbers.   Henry Morton Robinson.   InMe

For Hob is Cupid in disguise.   Hob upon a Holiday.   *Anonymous.*   NOEC

...For holy Children, Maids, and Men/Make up the King of Glory's Diadem.   Christendom.   Thomas Traherne.   PoEL 1-5

For holy wimman am I on.   A Student Courting.   *Anonymous.*   OxBM

For home's the best place for/All people like me!   Jonathan Bing.   Beatrice Curtis Brown.   OnMSP; SiSoSe; SoPo; TiPo

For home-staying/Vagabonds!   Maps.   Dorothy Brown Thompson.   BrR

For Horror starts, like Charity, at home.   Homage to William Cowper.   Donald Davie.   NePoEA

For how can no-thing be annihilated?/Ex nihilo nihil fit.   Epitaph on James Moore Smythe.   Alexander Pope.   FaBoEE

For how could such a wretch succeed,/But that, alas, it was decreed?   Written over a Gate.   John, Duke of Buckingham Sheffield.   NIP

For how to manage my damned soul/Will puzzle many a flaming devil.   I Am the Poet Davies, William.   William Henry Davies.   CBEP; OBSP

For huge ferocious stars.   Slow Riff for Billy.   James (Olumo) Cunningham.   JB

"For hunger or for love they bite and tear."   Reflection from Rochester.   William Empson.   PoA

For Hymen will their coupled joys maintain.   Epithalamium.   Sir Philip Sidney.   SiPS

For I always was washing my hair.   Limerick: "I have heard," said a maid of Montclair."   Morris Bishop.   TDH

For I am a rusty cowboy/And Pumpkin Creek's my home.   The Drifter. *Anonymous.*   CoSo

For I am bald and old and green.   The Olympic Girl.   Sir John Betjeman.   SD

For I am come to see you saved,/And saved you shall be.   The Man Freed from the Gallows.   *Anonymous.*   AWP

For I am Death!   The Voice of the Void.   George Parsons Lathrop.   AA

For I am friend and comrade of the hills.   Bright Abandon.   Tessa Sweazy Webb.   GoYe

For I am going/Into everlasting joys/Where fountains are flowing.   Our Captain Cried All Hands.   *Anonymous.*   OBET

For I am gone for evermore.   Where shall I have at mine own will.   Sir Thomas Wyatt.   FCP; SiPS

For I am he, and he is I.   Egotism.   Edward Sandford Martin.   AA

For I am he that shall fill your young veins with the seeds of all/futurity.   Song of My Soul.   Ralph Chubb.   PeHV

For I am lonely/And a stranger in this land.   A Stranger in This Land.   Cliff Ashby.   NOCV

For I am now at liberty.   Liberty.   Sir Thomas Wyatt.   OBSC

For I am old, and very very cold, and never wear a Jerkin.   Have You Any Work for a Tinker, Mistris.   *Anonymous.*   OBS

...For I am one touched by the hand of God.   Club 82: Lisa.   Cynthia Kraman Genser.   NYP

For I am ready to admit/That you are wrong and I am right.   The Ideal Husband to His Wife.   Sam Walter Foss.   InMe

For I am the only daughter.   The Only Daughter.   *Anonymous.*   OBET

For I am the soul of man.   The Poet Confides.   Herbert T. J. Coleman.   CaP

For I am the spirit of light, and life, and/mirth.   Ode.   Richard Watson Gilder.   AA

For I and this house will never do weil.'   The Wife of Auchtermuchty. *Anonymous.*   BSV; GoTS

For I bestow upon any man or woman the entrance to all the/gifts of the universe.   To Rich Givers.   Walt Whitman.   AnAmPo

For I bless God for every feather from the wren in the sedge to the/ CHERUBS and their MATES.   Jubilate Agno.   Christopher Smart.   AtBAP

For I, by this, do at their meaning guess/That beat a whelp afore a lioness.   To His Wife, for Striking Her Dog.   Sir John (1561-1612) Harington.   OBSP

"For I came in wid the Donkey—on Your Honour's invi-/tation."   The Legends of Evil.   Rudyard Kipling.   MoShBr

For I can leave at once and hunt/me somewhere to go   Broke and Hungry.   Blind Lemon Jefferson.   BluL

For I can never collect my self-respect/When I use a revolving door.   When West Comes East.   Corey Ford.   InMe

"For I can see it blazing!"   Joshua Hight.   *Anonymous.*   ShM

For I can see that he loves me,/And that's as good as gold.   The Shepherd and the Shepherdess.   *Anonymous.*   OBET

For I can't help thinking the poor old house is a house with a broken/heart.   The House with Nobody in It.   Joyce Kilmer.   BLPA; BLPL

For—"I can't stay quiet,"/Little Lucy said.   Lucy Lavender.   Ivy O. Eastwick.   BiCB; SiSoSe

For I choose that very girl/As my Valentine.   The Lovable Child.   Emilie Poulsson.   HBV 1-2; HBVY

For I'd rather be on the raging sea/As to be in a false love's company.   Earlye, Earlye, in the Spring.   *Anonymous.*   AmFP

For I'd sooner have them here this night than you, deceiving Molly.   Mulberry Mountain.   *Anonymous.*   AmFP

For I don't care, you know, my Ma.   I Love Somebody (I Love Little Willie). *Anonymous.*   AmFP

For I fished a lifetime boy and man,/And the final trawl scarcely makes a cran.   The Final Trawl.   *Anonymous.*   OBSS

For I found a bachelor's button/In black-eyed Susan's bed.   I Used to Love My Garden.   C. P. Sawyer.   FaBoCo

For I go walking night and noon/To spare my sack of coals.   Winter.   John Millington Synge.   NOBI; OBMV; OxBTC

For I had always loved it so!   Remembrance.   Aline Kilmer.   CAW

For I had rather owner be/Of thee one hour, than all else ever.   A Fever.   John Donne.   DiPo; OAEL 1-2

For I have a hidden fairy tune/In the bottom of my heart.   The Green Fiddler.   Rachel Field.   StPo

For I have a home up yonder,/Glory Glory.   I Have Some Friends Before Me Gone.   *Anonymous.*   AH

For I have been a cow-puncher on the U-S-U range.   The U-S-U Range.   G. W. Barr.   CoSo

For I have but the power to kill,/Without—the power to die—   My Life had stood—a Loaded Gun.   Emily Dickinson.   AmPP; HAP; NAWM 1-2; NoP; SBG; WeW; WPOW

For I have gravyd her wythin the secret wall/Of my trew hart, to love her best of all!   Knowledge, Acquaintance.   John Skelton.   NCEP

For I have jined this low-down gang,/And no one cares for me.   My Father Gave Me a Lump of Gold.   *Anonymous.*   OuSiCo

For I have learned by the unlikely way/of deficiency and excess temperance.   Lines.   Paul Goodman.   PeHV

For I have made captive Hodeirah's Son.'   Thalaba and the Magic Thread.   Robert Southey.   SeCePo

For I have murdered my own true love,/Whose name was Rose Connelly.   Down in the Willow Garden.   *Anonymous.*   FSW

For I have reached that stage of life when youth/can be contracted solely by contagion.   Amen.   Jaime Sabines.   AMV-81

For I have sworne thee faire, and thought thee bright,/Who art as black as hell, as darke as night.   Sonnets, CXLVII: "My love is as a feaver longing still."   William Shakespeare.   CBEP; DiPo; EBEV; HoPM; PoEL 1-5; TEP

For I have taken Krazy (phew!) five hundred miles to/Maine!   Apex.   Nate Salsbury.   InMe; NLV

For I have the gift/Of the Murrain Stone!   Herb-Leech.   Joseph Campbell.   AnIL; OnYI

For I have towchyd his owyn dere tre.   Eva's Lament (excerpt). *Anonymous.*   AtBAP

For I have vowed in strangest fashion,/To love and never seek compassion.   Caelica, IV.   Fulke, Lord Brooke Greville.   FCP

For I hold forever, forever my own,/The passionate rose.   Fulfilment.   Louis V. Ledoux.   HBMV

For I knew o'er the grave o' the Harbor Belle the sea-gulls fly.   From the Harbor Hill.   Gustav Kobbe.   HBV 1-2

For I know, in the tombs/There's no carousing.   Anacreontic.   Robert Herrick.   CaPo; OAEP; OxBoLi

For I know the hand of Nature/Will not make a fairer creature.   The Choice. George Wither.   OBEV

For I know where she bought it.   Bought Locks.   Martial (Marcus Valerius Martialis).   AWP; LiTW

For I know you will be true/Till we meet at the golden gate.   The Wreck of Number Nine.   *Anonymous.*   BFSS

For I'll believe I have her heart/As much as she hath mine.   Song: "I prithee send me back my heart."   Henry Hughes.   CavP; HBV 1-2; JCP; LiTL; ViBoPo

For I'll catch the moon by her silver hair and dance her around/the sky. The Bunyip.   Douglas Stewart.   AmMo

For I'll know I've been successful as a/little fellow's dad.   Dad's Greatest Job.   *Anonymous.*   STF

For I'll neither eat nor drink,/Nor set a fit on ground.'   The Clerk's Twa Sons o Owensford.   *Anonymous.*   BaBo; ESPB

For I love my wife.   Thespian in Jerusalem.   Myra Glazer Schotz.   VWA

For I love/thee/more than Durer/loved a seaweed.   The Vow.   Carl Rakosi. FAZ

For I'm a poor cowboy and I know I've done wrong.   The Cowboy's Lament. *Anonymous.*   BFSS

For I'm a wild lumberjack, and I know I've done wrong.   The Cowboy's Lament; or, The Streets of Laredo (B vers.).   *Anonymous.*   ViBoFo

For I'm a young cowboy and dying alone.   The Cowboy's Lament; or, The Streets of Laredo (A vers.).   *Anonymous.*   ViBoFo

For I'm afraid you will sarve me like you sarved/Your little Scotch-ee,/Your little Scotch-ee.   Little Scotch-ee (with music).   *Anonymous.*   AS

For I'm as tired as I can be.   The Fairies of the Caldon Low.   Mary Howitt. BeLS; HBV 1-2; HBVY

For I'm fond of tobacco and ladies.   Mickey Free's Song.   Charles James Lever.   ALV

For I'm gettin' old an' wrinkled in de face.   Cotton-eyed Joe.   *Anonymous.* ABF

For I'm going to end my troubles/By drowning in the deep blue sea.   Sailor on the Deep Blue Sea.   *Anonymous.*   FSW

For I'm my mother's bouncing girl.   What Care I?   *Anonymous.*   OxNR

For I'm never "all there' at a time!"   Limerick: "There was an old looney of Rhyme."   *Anonymous.*   TDH

For I'm on the road to my own true love, ten thousand miles away!   Ten Thousand Miles Away (with music).   *Anonymous.*   AS

For I'm riding away on my Brown Girl,/Where the sun is sinking low.   The Dying Cowboy of Rim Rock Ranch.   *Anonymous.*   CoSo

For I'm sick at the heart, and I fain wald lie down.   Lord Randal. *Anonymous.*   AtBAP; ATP; AWP; BaBo; BSV; DiPo; EBEV; ESPB; FaBoBa; FF; ForPo; FPL; HAP; HBV 1-2; HeIP; HoPM; InPo; LiTB; LiTL; LoBV; MaC; NIP; NoP; OAEL 1-2; OxBB; OxBS; SeCeV; TreF; TrGrPo; ViBoFo; WeW

For I'm so fond of liberty/That I cannot be a slave.   Oh! Isn't It a Pity. Harriet H. Robinson.   SaC

For I'm sure it is nothing but Love!   A Song of Love.   Lewis (Charles Lutwidge Dodgson) Carroll.   GN

For I'm sure they know the story of the so-called "rabbit pie".   My Other Chinee Cook.   Brunton Stephens.   PoAu 1-2

For I'm wearied with hunting and fain would lie down.'   Lord Rendal. *Anonymous.*   EnSB

For I may misunderstand how you act but/never how you live.   How Do You Live?   *Anonymous.*   STF

For I may need it in the sweet by-and-by.   The Pecos Puncher.   *Anonymous.* CoSo

For I may never touch, smell, taste, or see/Again, because I could not hear. The Fifth Sense.   Patricia Beer.   MoBS

For I meddle me to know/Love, and naught can cure it.   I Am Dark and Fair to See.   *Anonymous.*   UnTE

For I must go and live with she!   Grieve Not for Me.   *Anonymous.*   ShM

For I must hurry after/To overtake my near.   We Met on Roads of Laughter.   Charles Divine.   FaBoBe; HBMV

For I must worship and adore/What'er is brave and best.   To England. Charles Leonard Moore.   AA

For I own no more castles in Spain!   Aladdin.   James Russell Lowell. AnNE; HBV 1-2; RoGo; TreFT

For I paid for my seat in St. Paul's, when I was six years old, and took possession against the evil   Jubilate Agno.   Christopher Smart.   AtBAP

For I reck not a bean:/I wot what I do mean.   Me List No More to Sing. Sir Thomas Wyatt.   AAS; FCP; SiPS

For I sat myself like a cormorant once/Hard by the tree of knowledge.   The Devil's Thoughts (excerpt).   Richard Porson.   DBV

For I saw it more than once/and a city of light many times.   The Ancient One.   Charles Culhane.   LFAC

For I sell the future in a mere flower!   The Fable Merchant.   Charles Dobzynski.   VWA

For I shall be no deader then/Than they have been for years.   The Bishop's Last Directions.   *Anonymous.*   DBV

For I shall know Olivia by her Voice.   Endimion Porter and Olivia.   Sir William Davenant.   MePo; NOBE

For I shall look upon thee, if thou seest not me.   He Poet in His Poverty. Nizami.   LiTW

For I shall love the very scorne/which for my sake you do put on.   Song: "Or love mee lesse, or love mee more."   Sidney Godolphin.   CavP; JCP; MePo; OBS

For I shall mind not, slumbering peacefully.   Regret Not Me.   Thomas Hardy.   MoVE; PoPle; SeCeV

For I spy the woolly, woolly wolf.   Last Words before Winter.   Louis. Untermeyer.   MoAmPo

For I think there must be/Inside of me/A bird!   The Little Shepherd's Song. William Alexander Percy.   YeAr

For I thought of my doll and–sakes/alive!–I answered, "Mary Ann!"   A Mortifying Mistake.   Anna Maria Pratt.   AA; HBV 1-2; HBVY

For I, thy Saviour, died for thee.   He Died for Me.   George Washington Bethune.   BePJ

For I tried it and changed ranges to a far and better land.   Curly Joe. *Anonymous.*   BPAW

For I've a carol which some shepherds heard/Once in a wintry field. December.   Christina Georgina Rossetti.   YeAr

"For I've gotten my lot and my heart's/desire,/And what Providence has ordered for/me."   Richie Story (A version).   *Anonymous.*   BaBo; ESPB

For I've made a vow, I'll keep it true,/I'll never marry a man but thee. James Hatley.   *Anonymous.*   BaBo; ESPB

For I've pull'd out the sting/Of the marriage ring.   The Marriage Ring. William Blake.   HW

For I want to have supper ready/As soon as Dad comes home.   Domestic Science.   *Anonymous.*   WBLP

For I was all of her, and she was all of me.   All of Her.   Samuel L. Albert. NePoAm-2

For I was born under a kind star.   I was born under a kind star.   Katharine Tynan.   EG

For I will be her champion new,/Her fame I will repair.   The Great Adventure.   Henry David Thoreau.   HBV 1-2; OBVV

For I will dare none, Good Lord, walke dead still.   On Some-Thing, That Walkes Some-Where.   Ben Jonson.   CoBE; OBSP; SeCP; SeCV 1-2

For I will go to the wedding, and be wedding-guest/At the marriage of the living dark.   Bavarian Gentians.   D. H. Lawrence.   CMoP; OAEL 1-2; PPoe

For I will just be gathered to/My incubator.   Orphan Born.   Robert Jones Burdette.   OBAL

For I will never come again/With you, with love, to such a time.   Picnic. Ray Mathew.   BoAV

For I will rest/in an easy bed tonight.   In Rain.   Wendell Berry.   GeTw

For I wore the bitterness/From it long ago.   Transformation.   Lewis Alexander.   CDC; PoNe

For I would have thine Image be/White as I can, though not as Thee.   The Nymph Complaining for the Death of Her Faun.   Andrew Marvell. AnAnS 1; AtBAP; CBEP; CH; FM; GoTL; HBV 1-2; HeIP; LoBV; MePo; OAEL 1-2; OBS; PoEL 1-5; SeCP; SeCV 1-2

For if again that shirt is wet/'Twill vanish from our sight.   Song of the All-Wool Shirt.   Eugene Field.   StPo

For if ever I have a Man, Square-Cap for me.   Square-Cap.   John Cleveland. AnAnS 2

For if he gapes, by Josh, you're dead.   Epitaph: "Here lies the body of Andrew Gear."   *Anonymous.*   FaBoCo

For if He thunder by law the thunder is yet His voice.   The Higher Pantheism.   Alfred, Lord Tennyson.   WGRP

For if I breake, you may mistrust/The vow I made to love you too.   The Selfe-Banished.   Edmund Waller.   MePo; OBS

For if I do, he'll be sure to cry.   Little Boy Blue.   Mother Goose.   FaFP

For if I do,/He's sure to cry.   Boy Blue.   *Anonymous.*   OxNR

For if I were single again, I'd be cussed if I ever got married.   Come All You Young Ladies and Gentlemen.   *Anonymous.*   OBET

For if it prosper, none dare call it treason.   Epigram: Of Treason.   Sir John (1561-1612) Harington.   NIP

For if she be not for me,/What care I for whom she be?   The Lover's Resolution.   George Wither.   AWP; BoLoP; GoTF; HBV 1-2; InMe; LiTL; NOBE; OBEV; PG; TreFS

For if she do, O cruel thou,/Would wrong them: O who can tell how?/Balow, balow, &c   The New Balow.   *Anonymous.*   CoMu

For if she spie my Love, (alas) aie me,/My mirth is turn'd to extreame miserie. Sonnets, VII: "Sweet Thames I honour thee."   Richard Barnfield.   PeHV

For, if shee be not for me,/What care I, for whome she be.   Faire Virtue, the Mistresse of Phil'arete: Shall I, Wasting in Dispair.   George Wither.   SeCV 1-2

For if someone returned it/It made him impossibly nervous.   At the Tennis Clinic.   I. L. Martin.   SD

For if the prayer dies from my heart I will be quite alone.   A Prayer for Faith.   Margaret E. Sangster.   PoToHe

For if the Quakers be not Gelt/Your Troopes will have the Staggers.   The Four-Legg'd Quaker. *Anonymous.* CoMu

For, if the world hath loved thee not,/Its absence may be borne.   Lines on Leaving a Scene in Bavaria.   Thomas Campbell. OBNC

For if they beat us in the fight, we beat them/in the race.   The King's Own Regulars. *Anonymous.* PAH

For if we carried them away/They'd die of homesickness that day.   Fringed Gentians.   Amy Lowell. BrR

For if we get our orders mixed/It'll surely be too late.   The Wreck of the Royal Palm. *Anonymous.* AmFP

For if ye were laid in your weel made/bed,/Your days will nae be lang.'   Sweet William's Ghost (F version). *Anonymous.* ESPB

For if you bawl, you bawl alone.   Mamma Sings.   Samuel Hoffenstein. DBV

For if you don't, they'll order you off with an old Colt's forty-/four.   The Melancholy Cowboy. *Anonymous.* CoSo

For if you ever cross those plains,/She'll marry another man.   The Rambling Cowboy. *Anonymous.* BFSS; CoSo

For if you had told me he was your son,/He should neer have been slain by me.'   Child Maurice (B version). *Anonymous.* ESPB

For if you hit me, slave, I'll call thee, beggar.   Cupid. *Anonymous.* ElL

For if you knew our hardships you'd never poach again.   Van Dieman's Land (B vers.). *Anonymous.* CoMu; FaBoBa; NOAV; OBET

For if you sport with pretty maids you are sure to have your/change.   Leicester Chambermaid. *Anonymous.* CoMu; OBET

For if you start to rustling you will surely come to see/The State of Sonora–be an outcast like me .Juan Murray. *Anonymous.* CoSo

For ilka ane that ye droon,/I droon twa.   Quo' the Tweed. *Anonymous.* CH

For in a wife it is no worse to find/A common body, than a common mind.   Miriam: Chorus.   Lady Elizabeth Carew. LiTL

For in all of these appeareth clear/The handiwork of God.   Nature's Creed. *Anonymous.* OHIP

For in death is resurrection.   The Song of Chess.   Abraham Ibn Ezra. TrJP

For in good faith   Now World. *Anonymous.* CH

For in her eyes I saw his torchlight blazing.   Thus Saith My Chloris Bright.   Giovanni Battista Guarini. GBL

For in his heart and in his hand there lingered/Some remnant of the ancient melodies.   Plato, a Musician.   Leontius. UnS

For in His keeping I shall still abide.   Safe in His Keeping.   Edgar Cooper Mason. BLRP

For in his Logic, he used even the least of birds.   Piers the Ploughman.   William Langland. PBBP

For in his pipe he made so much joy.   The Shepherd upon a Hill. *Anonymous.* GoBC; OxBoCh

For in 'is cabin he can sit/And sail and sail–and let 'er knit.   A Grain of Salt.   William Irwin. HBV 1-2

For in Salem also is His tabernacle.   Tabernacle of Peace.   Hayim Be'er. VWA

For in the body's health the soul's forgot.   The Grave-Yard.   Jones Very. NOBA

For in the morning you went out to battle/And at night you did not return.   Fighting South of the Ramparts. *Anonymous.* LiTW

For in these ordered days a woman only/Is free to be very hungry, very lonely.   The Affinity.   Anna Wickham. HBMV

...For in vain she cares/For wand'ring planets that has fixed stars./Praelucendo pereo.   A Pulpit to Be Let. *Anonymous.* APAS

For in you are gaiety and happiness,/and all good things one could ask of a woman.   Lady Maria, in You Merit and Distinction.   Bieiris de Romans. PeHV

For indeed and forever would he be/to them/just dad.   Poems, IX.   Philip O'Connor. EAS

"For indeed–the clocks have struck."   Striking.   Charles Stuart Calverley. CenHV

For Ireland, time-foundered, that Ireland has lost.   Pattern of Saint Brendan.   Francis MacManus. AnIV; OxBI

For it belongs to/A world of fire before the rocks and waters.   The View of Rangitoto.   Charles Brasch. AnNZ

For it brings the time nearer when Santa Claus comes.   When Santa Claus Comes. *Anonymous.* ChBR

For it chanced that that door was the Dean's.   Limerick: "There was a young genius of Queens."   Arthur Clement Hilton. CenHV

For it inspired a bard to win/Ecstatic heights in thought and rhyme.   Shelley's Skylark.   Thomas Hardy. CoBMV; FaBV; PBBP; VLP

For it is Irish, too.   Irish.   Edward J. O'Brien. SiSoSe

For it is neither just nor fit/That poets should each other eat.   To a Swallow.   Bishop Euenos. OBVE

For it is sweet to be a little mad/When a friend comes home.   Odes.   Horace. WaaP

For "it is worthy," for it is all worthy.   Christmas at a Decade's End.   Richard Snyder. SOTS

For it is written, That thou shalt not murther.   To the Reverend Joseph Trapp, on the First Volume...   Abel Evans. FaBoEE

For it makes us tell the story of our whole lives.   Rejoicing at the Arrival of Ch'en Hsiung.   Po Chu-i. AWP

For it must be kept going.   A Soldier's Plea for the Y.M.C.A.   Joseph Samuel Reed. PeD

For it ne'er shall see the like of Captain Paton no mo!   Lament for Captain Paton.   John Gibson Lockhart. OBRV

For it never will be clear,/Never mirror heaven again.'   Trouble Not the Maiden's Soul.   Johan Ludvig Runeberg. LiTW

For it raises my flowers and covers my wife.   From a Churchyard in Wales. *Anonymous.* FiBHP

For it's a darn good layout/For the shape it's in.   For Sale. *Anonymous.* BPAW

For it's great to fight for Freedom/With a Rebel Girl.   The Rebel Girl.   Joe Hill. FSW

For it's now ten o'clock.   Wee Willie Winkie.   Mother Goose. SiSoSe; SoPo; TiPo

For it's one two three strikes, you're out/At the old ball game.   Take Me Out to the Ball Game.   Jack Norworth. OBAL

For it's up with the bonnets of Bonny Dundee!   The Doom of Devorgoil, II, ii: Bonny Dundee.   Sir Walter Scott. EnRP

For it's virtue and baths and good cooking go hand in/glove!   Streets.   Douglas Goldring. HBMV

For it seems a fact still of some importance, that I am dying.   Because in This Sorrowing Statue of Flesh.   Kenneth Patchen. NaP

For it seems compassion sticks longer than the other colors, in this/bleaching cloth.   Crumbs or the Loaf.   Robinson Jeffers. CMoP

For it seems to me and him/that America/happened most there.   The Poem I Am Writing.   Artie Gold. CaPN

For it takes the Texas Aggies/To produce real fighting men!   College Song.   Edward Anthony. InMe

For it to be beyond our human powers/Even to orchestrate another's fugue.   Reading in the Night.   Roy Fuller. OxBC

For it was neither lord nor loune/That was in bower last night wi mee.'   Clerk Saunders. *Anonymous.* BaBo; CPEP; ESPB; OAEP

For it will all the power of art outdo/To join the new reformer and the beau.   More Reformation.   Daniel Defoe. OBSV

For it would please her to forgive.   To His Verse.   Walter Savage Landor. OBVV

For its last name is called Gates of Paradise.   Fleshflower.   William Pitt Root. GeTw

For its light is the light eternal/That burns at both its ends.   If Mr. H.W. Longfellow Had Written Miss Millay's.   Franklin Pierce ("F.P.A.") Adams. OBAL

For its people's hopes are fled!   The Conquered Banner.   Abram Joseph Ryan. AA; GoTF; HBV 1-2; PAH; TreF

For its thump thump scold scold/Thump thump away/The deil a bit of comfort is therre.   Washing Day. *Anonymous.* CoMu

For Jackson swears he'll never send/The Druid to sea again!   The Loss of the Druid. *Anonymous.* ShS

For Jesus Christ arose again/To everlasting life.   Victory. *Anonymous.* STF

For Jesus Christ, our Saviour,/Was born on Christmas Day.   God Rest You Merry, Gentlemen.   Dinah Maria Mulock Craik. FaFP; FSW; GN; HBV 1-2; HBVY; LiTB; OHIP; TreFS; ViBoPo

For Jesus hath risen, and man shall not die.   Lift Your Glad Voices in Triumph on High.   Henry, Jr. Ware. AH

For Jesus pleads, and must prevail.   The Great Redeemer Lives.   Anne Steele. BePJ

For Joan of Arc goes riding by.   The Good Joan.   Lizette Woodworth Reese. MoShBr

For Jock's to be married to Maggie,/The lass wi the gowden hair.   Blythsome Bridal. *Anonymous.* GBP

For Jove dwells here: And 'tis no pity,/If Troynovant be now no more a City.   Troynovant.   Thomas Dekker. LoBV; OBSC

For joy our Saviour Christ was born/On Christmas Day in the morning.   As I Sat on a Sunny Bank. *Anonymous.* OxBoLi

For just one plaudit banishing/The might of human love.   There is No Trumpet Like the Tomb.   Emily Dickinson. BoLiVe

For killin' pretty Polly will send my soul to Hell.   Pretty Polly. *Anonymous.* AmFP

For killing of my mother dear,/And her not hurting thee.   Jellon Grame (B version). *Anonymous.* ESPB

For killing pretty Polly and running away.   Pretty Polly. *Anonymous.* FSW; OuSiCo

For kingdom, power, and glory thine./Both now and ever be.   Our Father Which in Heaven Art. *Anonymous.* AH

For/know/he lived   A Marriage.   Anthony Barnett. VWA

For know that you are clay, and they are brass.   The Story of the Pot and the Kettle.   Charles Montagu. APAS

For know, the last word is the word that lasts longest.   On Colley Cibber's Declaration That He Will Have the Last Word...   Alexander Pope.   FaBoEE

For L is found in Lubberkin and Love!   Traditional Charms for Finding the Identity of One's True Love.   John Gay.   FaBoUs

For labor has her rugged peers/Who glorify the gown she wears!   Tomorrow's Men.   Georgia Douglas Johnson.   GoSl

For lake and village-pump and sea,/For You–but also room for Me!   A Sermon.   Lady Margaret Sackville.   HBMV

For lending me now some leisure to make rhymes.   Davy, the Dicer.   Sir Thomas More.   DiPo

For less than they quote/For the table d'hote.   La Carte.   Justin Richardson.   ELU; FiBHP

For lest man should think flesh a seat of bliss,/God works that his joy mixed with sorrow is.   Caelica, XCIV.   Fulke, Lord Brooke Greville.   FCP

For life goes backward nor tarries with yesterday...   The Prophet.   Kahlil Gibran.   PoPl; PoToHe

For life goes on, I say   Greeting from a Distance.   Hans Sahl.   VWA

For life, I give you love, that fears no death.   Truth.   Cecil Francis Lloyd.   CaP

For life was filling us/Like jugs of wine.   Days Were Great as Lakes.   David Vogel.   VWA

For lifting intangible weights/Into real walls.   The Crane.   Charles Tomlinson.   MoBrPo

For light doth seize my brain/With frantic pain.   Mad Song.   William Blake.   CEP; ERoP 1-2; NOEC; OAEL 1-2; PoEL 1-5; PoRA; PrIm; TEP; TrGrPo

For light enough to get back down to you.   Talking Myself to Sleep in the Mountains.   Gibbons Ruark.   MAYP

For Lincoln leads them all.   Lincoln Leads.   Minna Irving.   OHIP

For lipstick/I wear my lips.   My Makeup.   Rochelle Kraut.   APU

For little dreams to go.   Hold Fast Your Dreams.   Louise Driscoll.   SoPo

For Little Peetookle is spared the strain/Of the Rollicking Mastodon over in Spain.   The Rollicking Mastodon.   Arthur Macy.   NA

For living is lying with Howell.   Limerick: "There's a Portuguese person named Howell."   Dante Gabriel Rossetti.   CenHV; DBV

For living lives as gentle as we can.   Stopping near Highway 80.   David Ray.   TAT

For lo! his breast was stricken very sore.   Christ and the Soul.   John of the Cross.   BoC

For lo! I too would follow/Hathor, who is Love.   He Entereth the House of the Goddess Hathor.   Book of the Dead.   AWP

For lo! mine heart, resolved to moistening air,/Feedeth mine eyes which double tear for tear.   Diana.   Henry Constable.   OBSC

For Lochnagar? Wi' clook and claw!   The Patriot.   J. C. Milne.   PoSH

For lone survivors like him/who remember its virtues.   Marginalia (excerpt).   W. H. Auden.   FaBoEE; OAEL 1-2

For long and in loneliness.   I Explain.   Stephen Crane.   AA

...For, look, the night is near!   The Mahabharata (excerpt).   Anonymous.   DL

For losing of her maidenhood.   From Citron-Bower.   Hilda Doolithe.   AP

For lost honour among thieves.   The Thieves.   Robert Graves.   BoLoP; CMoP; GTBS-P; LiTM; OAEL 1-2; OxBI; WeW

For lost like these, 'twill be/As Time had never known ye.   To a Bed of Tulips.   Robert Herrick.   CaPo

For love: each petal of each rose a kiss!   With Roses.   Beatrix Demarest Lloyd.   AA

For love has grown up like a hair.'   Soluble Noughts and Crosses; or, California, Here I Come.   Roger Roughton.   EAS

For Love hath made but one of twain.   Love's Calendar.   William Bell Scott.   HBV 1-2

For Love hath many loves in store.   Tomorrow Is the Marriage Day.   Anonymous.   NCEP

For love–if love's accompanied with gold.   Aphrodite Pandemos.   Anonymous.   UnTE

For Love is full of showers.   Love's Servile Lot.   Robert Southwell.   ACP

For love is heaven, and heaven is love.   The Lay of the Last Minstrel.   Sir Walter Scott.   BSV; ViBoPo

For love is of the Soul.   She who hath felt a real pain.   John Gay.   EnLoPo

...For Love/Is only stronger far than death.   The Incarnation and Passion.   Henry Vaughan.   TrCP

For love is the kind of a tree whose fruit/Grows not on the branches, but at the root.   This Is What the Watchbird Sings, Who Perches in the Lovetree.   Bruce Boyd.   NeAP

For love me hath in bales brought,/Me think it do me good, y-wis.   I Have Set My Heart So High.   Anonymous.   OAEL 1-2; OxBM

For love of her, each mother-sheep/And baby-lamb He blessed.   The Lamb-Child.   John Banister Tabb.   ChBR

For love of maide and moder thyn benigne!   Troilus and Criseyde.   Geoffrey Chaucer.   ExPo; OxBM

For love of you, old slit, for love of you.   Romeo and Juliet.   Howard Phelps (Phelps Putnam) Putnam.   ErPo

For Love shall never, never return to me again!   Vixi.   Charles Mackay.   HBV 1-2

For Love shall still be lord of all!   Lay of the Last Minstrel.   Sir Walter Scott.   ATP; OBRV

For Love, that conquers Death and Fear,/Is risen–That was dead.   Resurrexit.   Henry Longan Stuart.   CAW

For love, that had made his friend's peace/ with Death,/ Alone could make his with life.   The Two Wives.   William Dean Howells.   AA

For love to get well started, really needs propinquity/(Hence my title).   Propinquity Needed.   Charles Battell Loomis.   InMe

For love uninterrupted night.   Briggflatts.   Basil Bunting.   OAEL 1-2

For love will creep where well it cannot go.   Upon Sir John Lawrence's Bringing Water over the Hills...   Sir John Suckling.   CaPo

For lovers should be loved again.   March.   Alfred Edward Housman.   FaBoCh; LoGBV; NoP

For lower I can find no place to stand.   O Thou Who Art Our Author and Our End.   Sir John Beaumont.   GoTF; TreFT

For Lydia will be seventeen.   L'Eau Dormante.   Thomas Bailey Aldrich.   HBV 1-2

For making her Nigras mean.   H. Rap Brown.   Henry Blakely.   CNA

For making their work one hell of a lot lighter.   Monument to a Boxer.   Lucilius [(or Lucillius)].   LiSp

For man is a brute and a fool.   Callypso Speaks.   Hilda ("H. D.") Doolittle.   SBG

For Man's dominion–beauty swept away!   The Passing of the Forest.   William Pember Reeves.   AnNZ

For man's no bigger than the way he/treats his fellow man.   Measuring a Man.   Anonymous.   STF

For man shall be at one with God/In bonds of firm necessity.   These Things Shall Be.   John Addington Symonds.   TRV

For many a dark and cloudy morning/Turns to a bright and sunshiny day.   False Nancy.   Anonymous.   AmFP

For many a man such fire oft kindleth,/That with the blaze his beard singeth.   Right true it is...   Sir Thomas Wyatt.   FCP

For many a stormy wind shall blow/ere Jack comes home again.   Sailing Sailing.   Godfrey Marks.   FSW

For me but sighs.   The Moon-Child.   Fiona Macleod.   CH; EtS

For me, doth wear the veil of Night.   Days Too Short.   William Henry Davies.   MoBrPo

For me, I ken na ane o' them,/But what the waur am I?   In Memory of Edward Wilson (parody).   James Clerk Maxwell.   BXAP

For me is death.   April–And Dying.   Anne Reeve Aldrich.   AA

For me it never sings in vain.   The Cuckoo.   Frederick Locker-Lampson.   HBV 1-2

For me, my vision of the long ago!   Two Sonnets.   David P. Berenberg.   HBMV

For me, supine beneath this vine,/Doing my best to get a jag on!   The Preference Declared.   Eugene Field.   NLV

For me that place hath chiefest charms,/That brings me, dearest, to thine arms.   Happiness Amidst Troubles.   Immanuel Di Roma.   TrJP

For me, the autumn hills!   Manyoshu: When, Loosened from the Winter's Bonds.   Nukada. Princess   PBWP

For me the birth,/The sorrows of the crucified?   Faith's Difficulty.   Theodore Maynard.   TrPWD

For me, the death in darkness; to you, now, a hard dawn.   Poem for Jacqueline Hill.   Anonymous.   BrRo

For me, the death of all desires/In deep, eternal calm.   Night.   Thomas William Rolleston.   HBV 1-2

For me, the world crumbles beneath my feet.   Sonnets of a Portrait Painter.   Arthur Davison Ficke.   AnAmPo

...For me/There is no peace but one.   The Poet to the Birds.   Alice Meynell.   FM

For me they all to wear them seemed/When I was born.   Wonder.   Thomas Traherne.   AnAnS 1; AtBAP; CBEP; HAP; LiTB; LoBV; NoP; PPoe; SeCePo; SeCeV; SeCP; SeCV 1-2; TrGrPo; WHA

For me to naturalize/and acclimate/and choose it for my own.   The Yellow Flower.   William Carlos Williams.   HAP

For me you are a light on the mantelpiece,/A half shadow on the wall.   Poem for My Grandfather.   A. C. Jacobs.   VWA

For me, you may hang 'em, or drown 'em.   Verses Written upon Windows.   Jonathan Swift.   DBV

For memories are preserved in my feet/ever since, ever since.   Rachel.   Rachel (Rachel Blumstein).   VWA

For Memory locks her chaff in bins/And throws away the grain.   Recollection.   Anne Reeve Aldrich.   AA

For men and dreams like these, we make/Thanksgiving every year!   The First Thanksgiving.   Nancy Byrd Turner.   YeAr

For men may come and men may go/But I go on for ever.   The Brook.   Alfred, Lord Tennyson.   BoNaP; FaBV; GN; GoJo; MCCG; PoPle

For men of better palate will by it/Take the just elevation of your wit.   To the Reader of Master William Davenant's Play, The Wits.   Thomas Carew.   CaPo

For men to use their fortune reverently,/Even in youth. The Noble Balm. Ben Jonson. OBEV

For men will only laugh at woe. Medieval Norman Songs. *Anonymous.* AWP

For methinks thou stay'st too long. The Passionate Pilgrim. William Shakespeare. EiL; FaBoEn; GBL; LiTB; TreFS; UnTE

For might hath maistry and skill goth under. Snatches: "Wit hat wonder and kind ne can." *Anonymous.* OxBM

For might is right unti a mightier/come. Might Is Right. Israel Zangwill. TrJP

For mine, alas! hath left me,/Falero, lero, loo! I Loved a Lass. George Wither. CH; EnLi 1-2; HBV 1-2; NOBE; OBEV; PG; PoPle; UnTE

For mirthful, gentle, delicate, and warm. Wild Rose. William Allingham. GN

For misery is trodden on by many,/And being low never relieved by any. Poor Wat. William Shakespeare. OBSC

For Mistress Andrew Jackson. Madam Hickory. Wilbur Larremore. AA

For mock begger hall stands empty. The Map of Mock-Begger Hall. *Anonymous.* CoMu

For monuments and all must die. To Thee, Dear Henry Morison. Fynes Moryson. OBTV

For mony a heart thou has made sair,/That ne'er did wrang to thine or thee! The Lovely Lass o' Inverness. Robert Burns. GoTS

For more empty and hopeful boats and their sails. A Coconut for Katerina. Sandra McPherson. FiCP; LCAP

For morn nor eve can change that fiery gloom/That glares within the spirit's living tomb. What Is Young Passion. Hartley Coleridge. NCEP

For mortal love, that might not die of it. Endymion. Edna St. Vincent Millay. AnEnPo

For Mother's kiss,–sweeter this/Than any other thing! Wishing. William Allingham. HBV 1-2; HBVY; OHIP; OxBChV

For mourning to enter a home of poetry. It would be wrong for us. Sappho. BoWoP

For Munday hath hang'd himselfe. Epitaph in St. Olave's Church, Southwark, on Mr. Munday. Francis, Lord Jeffrey Jeffery. OxBoLi

For murdering Maria Marten, I was hang'd upon the tree. The Murder of Maria Marten. W. Corder. CoMu

For my answer is a rose. The Rose. George Herbert. AtBAP; LiTB; PoEL 1-5

For my beautiful, dutiful Lily Adair. Lily Adair. Thomas Holley Chivers. OBAL

For my dream is to conquer the heavens and battle for king-/ship on high. A Farewell. George William Russell. AnIV

For my dreams of your image that blossoms a rose in the deeps of my/heart. The Lover Tells of the Rose in His Heart. William Butler Yeats. CMoP; ViBoPo

For my heart being yours released no blood to make ready for love. This Is My Beloved (excerpt). Walter Benton. UnTE

For my heart heeds nothing, only loving you. Motets: "My love, how could your heart consider." *Anonymous.* PBWP

For my heart is more than often back/By the hills of Donegal. It's a Far, Far, Cry. Patrick Macgill. HBMV

For my heart's in his holdin',/My mind in his mind. The Green Hunters. Florence M. Wilson. AnIV

For my innocent days will come back no more. The Girl's Lamentation. William Allingham. SeCePo

For my just hand may sometime move/The wheel of Fortune, not the sphere of Love. A Lover, upon an Accident Necessitating His Departure.... Thomas Carew. CaPo

For my last old dollar's gone. Don't Let Your Deal Go Down. *Anonymous.* FSW

For my Other is not a woman but a man/the King upon whose bosom let me lie. The Torso: Passages 18. Robert Duncan. CAPP; GP

For my part I/Am sitting in a bus. The Underground. Guy Boas. CenHV

For my Rose of October there promised/She'd bloom for me aye, as–my wife. A Rose in October. James Whitcomb Riley. OBAL

For my soul yearns and fears. Saul. Isaac Rosenberg. VWA

For my soule to say a Pater Noster and an Ave. A Second Epitaph. *Anonymous.* MeEL

For my will goes the other way,/And it were perjury! I Have a King. Emily Dickinson. MAPA

For my young lord is coming,/I hear his bugle blow. Lady Maisry. *Anonymous.* BaBo

For mystery–the dream of things/Beyond our power of seeing! Thanksgiving. Florence Earle Coates. TrPWD

For nations all shall worship thee,/For judgments thine are known. O Lord, Almighty God. *Anonymous.* AH

For Nature has a bitter season/When she informs upon her own. Late Autumn. A. M. Sullivan. GoBC

For never a beggar need now despair, And every rogue has a/chance.' The Speculators. William Makepeace Thackeray. OBSV

For new things to play! I Like House Cleaning. Dorothy Brown Thompson. BrR

For night is day, and darkness light,/O Father of all lights, to thee. Psalm CXXXIX. Mary Herbert, Countess of Pembroke. OBSC

For night is yours. It is never/against you. You are not its enemy. Talking to the Mule. Laura Jensen. AmPA

For no man knows, on the morrow, whether/We two pass by, or but one alone. Interlude. Ella Wheeler Wilcox. HBV 1-2

For no one fool is hunted from the herd. Sir Fopling Flutter. John Dryden. DiPo

For no one must suppose I've anything/To hide–and show myself in Grafton Street. At the Polo-Ground. Sir Samuel Ferguson. NOBI

For no one stock can ever serve/To love so much as shee'l deserve. My Dearest Rival. Sir John Suckling. MeLP

For no one there could compare with the field artilleree. Old King Cole. *Anonymous.* OuSiCo

...For no reason, and for no reason/taken away. Evensong. Peter Kane Dufault. AMV-80

For no reason that I can tell. Little Elegy. Denis Devlin. NOBI

For no such shadow shalbe had againe. Visions. Petrarch. EnLi 1-2

For no watchman is waiting for you and for me. The Butterfly's Ball. William Caldwell Roscoe. OnUR; OxBChV

...For Non-existence/Proclaims in organ tones, "To Him we shall return." Happy the Moment When We Are Seated in the Palace, Thou and I. Jalal ed-Din or al-Din Rumi. ILwL

For none are rich without content. The Consolation of Philosophy. Boethius. OBVE

For none can call again the passed time. Amoretti, LXX. Edmund Spenser. AAS; AWP; CABA; FaBoEn; HAP; HBV 1-2; InPS; NoP; OBSC; SeCeV

For none I find My Sweet Sweeting. *Anonymous.* CH

For None see God and live– To Pile Like Thunder to Its Close. Emily Dickinson. MAmP

For none would use with disrespect,/Whom Heaven thinks proper to protect. The Wren. *Anonymous.* OxBChV

For noo, alas, 'tis winter/That gangs a twalmonth roun'. Langsyne, When Life Was Bonnie. Alexander ("Surface man") Anderson. HBV 1-2

For not the faintest motion could be seen/Of all the shades that slanted o'er the green. The Sigh of Silence. John Keats. GN

For nothing can untwine/Thy life from mine. A Prayer. *Anonymous.* STF

For nothing now can ever come to any good. Song: Stop All the Clocks. W. H. Auden. MoBrPo

For nothing's left in either of the Scales. The Balance of Europe. Alexander Pope. SeCeV

For nothing shalt thou find but bones and dust. Eumares. Asclepiades. AWP

For nothing this wide universe I call,/Save thou, my rose: in it thou art my all. Sonnets, CIX: "O, never say that I was false of heart." William Shakespeare. GTBS; GTBS-P; HBV 1-2; LiTL; NOBE; OBEV; OBSC

For now he ne're will be my love agen. Sawney Was Tall. Thomas D'Urfey. OAEP

For now, I am the first to know. Degas. Paul Monette. AmPA

For now I dye,/I die, I die. O Death, Rock Me Asleep. George Boleyn. EnPo; FaBoRV

For now I have found mine own true-love,/Whom I thought I should never see more. The Bailiff's Daughter of Islington. *Anonymous* AmFP; BaBo; ESPB; FaBoBa; FSW; GN; HBV 1-2; OAEP; OBET; OxBB; OxBoLi; ViBoFo

For now I know you never shall deceive/Till my belief your truth shall misbelieve. Sonnets to Aurelia. Robert Nichols. OBMV

For now I try that awful road. Frankie Silvers. Frances (Frankie) Silvers. AmFP

For now is the time of Christmas. Now Is the Time of Christmas. *Anonymous.* MeEL; OxBM

For now my song is ended. The Passionate Pilgrim. William Shakespeare. EiL

For now the people have the light Now the People Have the Light. Charles G. Ballard. VoR

For now they solace swift desire. At a Hasty Wedding. Thomas Hardy. InPK; VLP

...For now we know/Both how to make men sick and keep them so. On Hygiene. Hilaire Belloc. DBV

...For now you see my heart which met/your touch–and so is shattered in your hands. In Which She Satisfies a Fear with the Rhetoric of Tears. Sister Juana Ines de la Cruz. BoWoP

"For of a' the lads that I do ken,/The lads o Wamphr The Lads of Wamphray. *Anonymous.* BaBo; ESPB

For of all heaven's gifts the sweetest/Sure is peace,–the sweetest, best. While to Bethlehem We Are Going. Sister Violante Do Ceo. CAW

For of God,–of God they are. Yes, It Was the Mountain Echo. William Wordsworth. EnRP

For oft beneath fair friendship's specious show/Lurks the false, trait'rous, undermining foe.   Sarah Hazard's Love Letter.   John Ellis.   NOEC

For oh, she talks of wisdom/With challenge in her eyes.   Look Not to Me for Wisdom.   Charles Divine.   HBMV

For Oh, the British Public is a lucky little man!   Britannia's Baby.   D. H. Lawrence.   NAs

For oh! Thou'rt all kind, and all soft at the bottom.   Young Strephon and Phillis.   *Anonymous.*   UnTE

For oh tonight/it's Halloween!   It's Halloween.   Jack Prelutsky.   NTCP

For oh what running river/Can stand against the sea?   The Tides Run Up the Wairau.   Eileen Duggan.   AnNZ

For old gray death upon his crutch/To rake into his Bag of Nought.   Of Change of Opinions.   Victor Plarr.   NOBV

For on his heart it stamps disgrace/Who formed the base design.   The Cottager's Complaint.   *Anonymous.*   OBET

For on the turbid current of his passion/Thy face is shining still!   The Mountain Heart's-Ease.   Bret (Francis Bret Harte) Harte.   HBV 1-2

For once a little looking down face/Seemed to be saying: "How do you do?"   The Story of the Baby Squirrel.   Dorothy Aldis.   TiPo

For once he was a true love of mine.   Whittingham Fair.   *Anonymous.*   GBP

For once I stood/In the white windy presence of eternity.   The Most-Sacred Mountain.   Eunice Tietjens.   HBMV; MoRP

For once out of the woods, all the fears are forgot.   Wprroes/.   *Anonymous.*   PoToHe

For once we acted as we ought.   Epigram: "Above all gifts we most should prize."   Walter Savage Landor.   FaBoEE

For once wuz enough for us.   Si Hubbard (with music).   *Anonymous.*   AS

For once you git the habit, why, you can't keep still.   Once You Git the Habit.   *Anonymous.*   CoSo

For one brief moment dazzlingly.   Dawn Amid Scotch Firs.   William Sharp.   SyP

For one day/You'll die!   What Was Your Dream, Doctor Murricombe?   Osbert Sitwell.   AtBAP

For one far summit, blue against the sky.   Barter.   Marie Blake.   PoPl; PoToHe

For one I never know before/The day he came to die.   Simon the Cyrenean.   Lucy Lyttleton.   HBV 1-2

For one is gone–who shall not go–/From Sagamore!   Sagamore.   Corinne Roosevelt Robinson.   HBMV

For one is one and stands alone/And ever more shall be-O.   Carol of the Numbers.   *Anonymous.*   AmFP

For one moment,/I chased the lines away.   I Followed a Path.   Patricia Parker.   BlSi

...For one moment,/stopped in time and doubt,/we are each other.   Audiences.   Robert Hollander.   GLGT

For one must return/To fulfill one's nature.   Once More Fields and Gardens.   T'ao Ch'ien.   AWP

For one of us could drink it all alone.   Drunk Last Night.   *Anonymous.*   FSW

For one that you remember/And ten that you forget.   Rococo.   Algernon Charles Swinburne.   HBV 1-2; ViBoPo

For one the mire, the hurry and the throng.   Life.   Amory Hare.   HBMV

For one was wise and one was fair,/But one was mine.   The Three Sisters.   Arthur Davison Ficke.   HBV 1-2

For one who could not understand.   A Woman's Answer to the Vampire.   Felicia Blake.   BLPA

For one who forsook for my garden/His Paradise!   The Beloved.   Katharine Tynan Hinkson.   IIBV 1-2

For one whose egg swells awkwardly of late.   Cousin Emily and the Night Visitor.   Kendrick Smithyman.   ACV

For only a while longer./I am afraid.   Aaron Nicholas, Almost Ten.   Janet Campbell Hale.   VoR

For only in darkness/Grow hatred and strife.   Kind Hearts.   *Anonymous.*   HBV 1-2

For only in Unmeaning Might is met/The intolerable thought none can ignore.   Submarine Mountains.   Cale Young Rice.   EtS

For only men who are brave and good/Can come out changeless from a wood.   Out of the Earth.   Mary Carolyn Davies.   HBMV

For only peace and pardon pass/The watchful guard of prayer.   The Sentinel.   Annie Johnson Flint.   BLRP

For or the morn at ten o clock/Ye's deal'd as fast as mine.'   Lord Thomas and Fair Annet (I version).   *Anonymous.*   ESPB

For others to live in/before moving somewhere else.   Lives.   Gerald Dawe.   AMV-81

For otherwise, how could I shrink/At entering these walls?   He Visits a Hospital.   Rolfe Humphries.   AnAmPo

For our brave Queen-a.   The Elves' Dance.   *Anonymous.*   CH

For our Dragon hath vanquished the St. George.   A Mock Song.   Richard Lovelace.   CaPo

For our glorious meeting there.   Walking with Him in White.   Charles Wesley.   BePJ

For our little lost horse herder, wrangler Joe.   Little Joe the Wrangler.   N. Howard Thorp.   BPAW; CoSo; FSW

For our own lady's dying, brother dear.'   Sonnet: On the 9th of June 1290.   Dante Alighieri.   AWP

"For our sake, brother, eat it all."   The Last Rite.   Richard Frost.   AMV-80

For our Tita is this day/Married to a noble fay.   The Muses Elizium.   Michael Drayton.   HW

For our world was death without grief and all holds broken.   The Spoilers and the Spoils.   Judith Johnson Sherwin.   SM

For out of backward love all hate doth grow.   Hate and Debate Rome through the World Hath Spread.   Sir John (1561-1612) Harington.   TW

For out of backward love, all hate doth grow.   In Roman.   Sir John (1561-1612) Harington.   PV

For out of the infinite past it came/With the love in the eyes of you!   Song: "Flame at the core of the world."   Arthur Upson.   HBV 1-2

For over thee I'll build a bridge,/That ye never more true love may sever.   Annan Water.   *Anonymous.*   BaBo

For P. has wrote upon their tomb.   Epitaph on the Stanton Harcourt Lovers.   Mary Wortley, Lady Montagu.   FaBoEE

For pants he makes his skindoo.   Limerick: "The poor benighted Hindoo."   Cosmo Monkhouse.   HBV 1-2

For parting me and you.   In Exile.   Blanche Edith Baughan.   ACV; AnNZ

For past is now thy wrath, and thou/dost comfort me.   My God.   Solomon Ibn Gabirol.   TrJP

For pastime in a field with blossoms strewn.   Three Ballate.   Angelo Poliziano.   AWP

For peace and blessing may she stand,/America our land!   Prayer on Fourth of July.   Nancy Byrd Turner.   YeAr

For peace on earth–a lasting peace, and just!   The New Mars.   Florence Earle Coates.   PGD

For Peace will light the country on that Thanksgiving Day.   The Volunteer's Thanksgiving.   Lucy Larcom.   OBCA

For period exhaled.   Great Streets of Silence Led Away.   Emily Dickinson.   AtBAP; NOCV

For place a coronet on him you will,/You straight see all great in him, but his ill.   Caelica, XCII.   Fulke, Lord Brooke Greville.   FCP

For pleasure or gain, to the hunting of men?   The Hunters of Men.   John Greenleaf Whittier.   AnAmPo

For plotting Adam's fall.   Swan.   Edward Lowbury.   GTBS-P

For ploughing on Our Lord's birthday.   On Christmas Day.   *Anonymous.*   OBET

For Plymouth Town it flowed with tears/When they heard of the sad and dread affair.   The Wreck of the Rambler.   *Anonymous.*   OBSS

For poems diluted with plenty of water.   On the Lake Poets.   Charles Townsend.   FaBoEE

For poor Mark Lee at last had come upon/One thing that M.L. couldn't do for him.   Black Boy.   Carl Carmer.   AnAmPo

For present pleasure soon is o'er,/And all the past is vain.   Solitude.   James Beattie.   OBEC

For Progress comes early, and Freedom too soon.'   Songs of Education.   Gilbert Keith Chesterton.   FaBoCo

For Pussy can't bear to be worried or teased.   I Like Little Pussy.   Jane Taylor.   FaBoBe; HBV 1-2; HBVY

For pussy don't like to be worried and teased.   Pussy.   *Anonymous.*   OxBChV

For rain and wind together/Here through the summer make a chill wet weather.   The Falls of Glomach.   Andrew Young.   OxBS; PoSH

For rainsmell on pale blue winds/from China   When Sun Came to Riverwoman.   Leslie Marmon Silko.   VoR

...For reasons having nothing at all/to do with ego, guilt, ambition, or even money.   The Cormorant in Its Element.   Amy Clampitt.   SUW

For reverie, for freedom, and for love.   From Mistra: A Prospect.   Ted Higgs.   AMV-80

For rushing to the rescue/as if you'd heard yourself performing.   Glory.   Marianne Moore.   NYBP

"For," said they, "we're Colonial Dames."   Limerick: "Two ladies with high social aims."   Sam S. Stinson.   TDH

For scarcely all its snows can cool that color.   Farm Boy after Summer.   Robert Francis.   NCSH

For secondly he kicks up behind to clear away there.   Jubilate Agno.   Christopher Smart.   NCEP

For see the God takes vengeance on my scorn.   Idylls.   Theocritus.   PeHV

For see, the hounds are just in view.   The Hare with Many Friends.   John Gay.   HBV 1-2

For seeming to presume?   On Seeming to Presume.   Lawrence Durrell.   LiTM

For seldom they land that go swimming with me.   Song of the White Lady of Avenel.   Sir Walter Scott.   NBM

For seven long years, this precious syllogism/Hath baffled justice and humanity!   The Dancing Bear.   Robert Southey.   FM

For she can earn no other way/The bread which she doth eat.   The Watercress Seller.   Thomas Miller.   OxBChV

For she can take away the dread of things.   My Comrade.   Edwin Markham.   AA

For she conquers shame and Death.   Love Is Strong.   Richard Burton.   AA; HBV 1-2

For she dreamt she had married the Devil!   Miss Kilmansegg's Honeymoon.   Thomas Hood.   NBM

For she grows Poison Ivy!   Poison Ivy!   Katharine Gallagher.   SiSoSe

For she has seen the mothers' children/And knows that it is well.   The Little Ghost.   Katharine Tynan Hinkson.   HBV 1-2

For she herself, my Queen of Love,/Is Rose, and Lily, and Sun, and Dove!   Love's Resume.   Heinrich Heine.   TrJP

For she is dead, and human flesh is frail.   The Spirit of Night.   Thomas Rogers.   EIL

For she is Queen of Courtesy.   The Queen of Courtesy.   Anonymous.   ISi

For she'll go no more to Conland, this winter-time to lye.   Walter Lesly.   Anonymous.   BaBo; ESPB

For she my mind hath so displaced/That I shall never find my home.   The Mower to the Glow-worms.   Andrew Marvell.   AnAnS 1; AtBAP; AWP; EG; ELP; EnLoPo; InPo; InvP; MePo; NOBE; NoP; OAEL 1-2; OBS; OxBoLi; PoEL 1-5; PoPle; PPP; SeCP; TrGrPo

For she's gone to Manchester the summer months to stay.   Ellen Taylor.   Anonymous.   OBET

For she took a bottle to church.   The Well of St. Keyne.   Robert Southey.   BeLS; FaBoBe; HBV 1-2

...For she turns to thee,/And trembles.   To Sultan Murad II.   James Clarence Mangan.   NOBI

For she was a young and a sweet noble lady,/The fairest young bride that I ever have seen.   The Nobleman's Wedding.   William Allingham.   IrPN

For she was not unwed.   The Faithless Wife.   Federico Garcia Lorca.   LiTW

For she was the cause of my lying down.   Lord Randal.   Anonymous.   AmFP

For she was the nearest linesman/And he didn't like the call.   Dark Eyes at Forest Hills.   I. L. Martin.   SD

For she, who made of home a Heaven,/Wakes–to find Heaven her home!   Mother.   Anonymous.   PGD

For she yelled, "How shall I fix the 'taters,/Fried, lionized, baked, biled, or mashed?"   The Cultured Girl Again.   Ben King.   FiBHP; OBAL

For Sherman and Grant, hurrah!   The Song of Sherman's Army.   Charles Graham Halpine.   MC; PAH

For should I not supply/The cause, th' effect would die.   To Critics.   Robert Herrick.   CaPo; PV

For should the bow unbended be,/Yet that can never help the cure.   The Expostulation.   Thomas Shadwell.   OAEP

For silence doth forgive and cancel all.   A Fugue.   Hubert Church.   AnNZ

For silence is a sounding thing/To one who listens hungrily.   Your Songs.   Gwendolyn B. Bennett.   CDC

For since I have found thee, lovely youth,/We never more will part.   The Friar of Orders Gray.   Thomas Percy.   CEP; HBV 1-2; NOEC; OBEC

For since that stormy night not a mortal hath had sight/Of the flag of the last Buccaneer.   The Last Buccaneer.   Thomas Babington, Lord Macaulay.   EtS; HBV 1-2

...For, since thou thoughtst it best/Not to dream all my dream, let's act the rest.   The Dream.   John Donne.   EG

For singing/Whatever beauty there is.   Alabama.   Julia Fields.   PoBA; PoNe

For sleep is fair and warm–   A Beautiful Night.   Thomas Lovell Beddoes.   LoBV

For sluttish spoils of opportunity/And daughters of the game.   Troilus and Cressida.   William Shakespeare.   TrGrPo

...For so/Based, his poems are his own land.   Ovid on the Dacian Coast.   Dunstan Thompson.   NYBP

For so God gives us twice our daily bread.   Twice Fed.   A. A. Bassett.   HBV 1-2

For so it is: we love no shallower land.   Why, Lord?   Mark Van Doren.   AH; TrPWD

For so should it be.   A Maid of Kent.   Anonymous.   OxBoLi

For so the whole round earth is every way/Bound by gold chains about the feet of God.   Idylls of the King.   Alfred, Lord Tennyson.   TreF; WGRP

For so to seek and find you prove/One selfsame motion.   How Far?   Vassar Miller.   CoPo

For some are lucky, leaving their curved faces/Propped in the moonlight while their bodies drown.   Moonlight Night on the Port.   Sidney Keyes.   DTC

For some day the goose girl will marry a king!   The Goose Girl.   Dorothy Roberts.   CaP

For some long time all wondered if they'd seen/A womanly king or a male queen.   A Portrait of Henri III.   Theodore Agrippa d' Aubigne.   PeHV

For some seeds/meal is the end of the journey.   Seed Journey.   Gregory Corso.   VGW

For some slight cause of wrath, whence life's warm stream must flow.   Childe Harold's Pilgrimage: Canto I.   George Gordon, Lord Byron.   LiSp

For some time she sat stiffly in the chair,/Then slowly raised her hand and stroked his hair.   Jack Rose.   Maxwell Bodenheim.   HBMV

For Somebody's sake, wherever we are.   Somebody's Birthday.   Abbie Farwell Brown.   BiCB

For someone had drawn (ah, who could it be?)/A knife across her throat.   Going Back Again.   Edward Robert Bulwer, Earl of Lytton.   EvOK; FiBHP

For something, ere in vain you die.   Time To Die.   Ray Garfield Dandridge.   BANP; PoBA

For something fulfilled this hour, loved or endured.   Taller To-Day.   W. H. Auden.   CMoP

For something is amiss or out of place/When mice with wings can wear a human face.   The Bat.   Theodore Roethke.   GoJo

For Sons of Drake are lords of Colon's/world.   The Sailing of the Fleet.   Anonymous.   PAH

For soon by what it tells the clock is stilled.   A Timepiece.   James Merrill.   HoPM; NePoEA-2; NoAm

For soon or late Love is his own avenger.   Don Juan.   George Gordon, Lord Byron.   EnRP; OAEP; WHA

...For soon they seek/The neighbouring spring; and drink, and swell, and die.   The Sugar Cane.   James Grainger.   FaBoUs

For sorrow, and a new view past where the tree fell.   The New View.   John Holmes.   MiAP

For sorrow that poor John Thompson's gone.   Epitaph: "Come knock your heads against this stone."   William Blake.   TEP

For soul is form, and doth the body make.   Beauty.   Edmund Spenser.   OBSC

For, south of the Border, I left her my heart!   Song of the Border.   Gordon W. Norris.   BPAW

For spent is his last groat.   And Now a Fig for the Lower House.   Patrick Cary.   JCP

For spoiling her nice new clothes.   Little Polly Flinders.   Mother Goose.   HBV 1-2; HBVY

For Spring is here!   Glad Earth.   Ella C. Forbes.   YeAr

For spring is in the making!   Spring Is in the Making.   Nona Keen Duffy.   YeAr

For spying to be done to death with sticks.   Three Dreams.   James Michie.   NePoEA-2

For sticks or stones or softest coaxing words.   Beaver Pond.   Anne Marriott.   ACV; NOBC

For still dear to my soul, as 'twas then to my eyes,/Is that barrel of porter at Tammany Hall.   Song: "There's a barrel of porter at Tammany Hall."   Fitz-Greene Halleck.   OBAL

For still her cheeks possess the same/Which native she doth owe.   Love's Labour's Lost.   William Shakespeare.   CTC

For still I hold it that to give/Is sweeter than to take.   Dare Quam Accipere.   Mathilde Blind.   OBVV

For still my children play,/And shall tomorrow, if the weather holds.   Security.   Michael Hamburger.   NMP; PoCh

For still the craft of genius is/To mask a king in weeds.   Quatrain: Poet.   Ralph Waldo Emerson.   OBSP

For still 'tis found too true a case,/That poor men pay for all.   The Poor Man Pays for All.   Anonymous.   OBET

For still 'tis only dawning Day.   Abdication of Fergus Mac Roy.   Sir Samuel Ferguson.   AnIL

For strife comes with manhood, and waking with day.   Lullaby of an Infant Chief.   Sir Walter Scott.   HBV 1-2; OxBChV

For subjects are the surest guard of kings.   A Dialogue between King William and the Late King James...   Charles Blount.   APAS

For such a bold rider's soul.   The Knight's Leap.   Charles Kingsley.   StPo

For such a faithful tender Heart/Can never break, can never break in vain.   Constancy: A Song.   John Wilmot, Earl of Rochester.   CavP; OBS

For such a pair of wings as thine,/And such a head between 'em.   The Jackdaw.   William Cowper.   HBV 1-2; HBVY; PB; PBBP

For such a pleasant chance,/To sing some pleasant song.   Marvel No More Although.   Sir Thomas Wyatt.   AAS; SiPS

For such company decks such solitariness   Arcadia.   Sir Philip Sidney.   AtBAP; FaBoRV; FCP; SiPS

For such loss in such young years.   Three Epitaphs.   Francis Davison.   OBSC

For suffering humankind, a wiser pity/For those who lift a heavier cross with Thee!   Prayer in Affliction.   Violet Alleyn Storey.   TrPWD

For sufferinges beforehand wee must tender.   Sonnet II.   William Alabaster.   AnAnS 1

For sure, circa Regna tonat.   Who lyst his welthe and eas retayne.   Sir Thomas Wyatt.   EnPo

For sure I will assay/If I can give thee mate.   Although I Had a Check.   Henry Howard, Earl of Surrey.   SiPS

For sure that is the narrow way.   Childhood.   Henry Vaughan.   OxBoCh

For surely God and all his saints above,/High in their other heaven, pardon love. To a Nun. John Ormond. FaBoTw

For surfeits sooner kill than fasts. Against Absence. Sir John Suckling. CaPo

For, take my tip, you'll miss the bus, old boy. If Not (parody). H. A. C. Evans. FaBoPa

For, take which you please, it must needs be a bastard. A Wicked Treasonable Libel. Jonathan Swift. UnTE

For Talbot's de dog, and James is de ass. Lilliburlero. Anonymous. ViBoFo

For Tammuz, the beautiful Tammuz is/dead. The Death of Tammuz. Saul Tchernichovsky. TrJP; VWA

For Teeney and Weeney to have for drinking. Green Grass and White Milk. Winifred Welles. TiPo

For tell me how they differ, tell me pray,/A cloudy tempest, and a too fair day. Advice to My Best Brother, Colonel Francis Lovelace. Richard Lovelace. CaPo

For telling such lies o' the kirk. Little Billy. Anonymous. GBP

For ten-and-sixpence sterling. Alnwick Castle. Fitz-Greene Halleck. AA

For ten miles, till day at last breaks. Starting Early from the Ch'U-Ch'eng Inn. Po Chu-i. OBVE

For than fine madness still he did retain/Which rightly should possess a poet's brain... Christopher Marlowe. Michael Drayton. ChTr

For that, as mine your Beauties now,/Imploy'd his utmost sight. An Apologie for Having Loved Before. Edmund Waller. MePo

For that at length yet doth invite some rest,/Thou though still tired, yet still doost it detest. Astrophel and Stella, XCVI. Sir Philip Sidney. AAS; SiPS

For that at once all languor will dispel,/As sure as cabbage. Hangover Cure. Amphis. FaBoUs

For that beautiful unseen temple/Was a child's immortal soul. Two Temples. Hattie Vose Hall. BLPA

For that bud is only mine/on the back of my own stone/and reserved for my next night. Do Not Ask. Christine Lavant. WPOW

For that flame-winged Creator who fulfils. The Immortal Spirit. Stephen Spender. MoRP

For that I could never forgive you. The Heart Has Its Reasons. Felice Picano. PeHV

...For that insight may the Wife/To her indulgent Lord become more dear. Composed on the Eve of the Marriage of a Friend ... William Wordsworth. HW

For that is more than I can do. Prayer. Thomas Ellwood. WGRP

For that is our sweet Aunt Mary's tree. Aunt Mary. Robert Stephen Hawker. OHIP

For that may be the reason/Her lips with dew are wet. The Rose's Cup. Frank Dempster Sherman. AA

For that may not be far away,/Ye dorty blackleg miners! The Blackleg Miners. Anonymous. GBP; OBET; VLP

For that/most of all. The Secret. Denise Levertov. NaP

For that old faded midnight/That frightened but an hour. When night is almost done. Emily Dickinson. TRV

For that one, two/Thousand score. To Dianeme. Robert Herrick. CaPo; FaBoBe; LiTL

For that other young guy who died too late. Grandfather Gabriel. Robert Penn Warren. AnAmPo

For that reason, we stand up and kill. Lying Down with Men and Women. John Woods. GP

For that road leads directly to the heart. On a Lady Who P-ssed at the Tragedy of Cato. Alexander Pope. OBSP

For that's the best cure for a little pussy cat. Who's That Ringing At My Door Bell? Anonymous. FaBoCh; LoGBV

For that's the best way to forget her. The Lambs on the Green Hills Stood Gazing on Me. Anonymous. AnIV

For that's the penance he maun drie,/To scug his deadly sin. Young Benjie. Anonymous. BaBo; OxBB

For that's the style in the Army. Captain Jinks. Anonymous. FSW

"For that/She is beautiful, delicate;/Therefore." Susanna and the Elders. Adelaide Crapsey. AnAmPo

For that they housed Him from the cold! A Christmas Fold-Song. Lizette Woodworth Reese. ChBR; HBMV; HBVY; OBCA; OHIP; OnMSP; SUS; TrCP

For that Thou bearest all that Thou hast made;/We thank Thee, Lord! For Beauty, We Thank Thee. John Oxenham. PGD

For that thy face is in my eyes/impressed. The Elusive Maid. Abraham Ibn Chasdai. TrJP

For that unwanted babe, for comfort too long ago, too/far away. My Mother's Birthday: "I used to watch you sleeping." Kathleen Raine. NAs

For that vast love, that hangs upon the Cross. Death-Bed Reflections of Michel-Angelo. Hartley Coleridge. EyDe

For that was the Riff in the Lieut. Limerick: "A lieutenant who went out to shoot." Morgan Taylor. LiBL

For that which God doth touch and own/Cannot for less be told. The Elixir. George Herbert. FaBoCh; GN; LoGBV; NoP; OHIP; TrGrPo; WGRP

For that will still be free/In spite of jealousy. Turn All Thy Thoughts. Thomas Campion. LiTL

For the beating of our own hearts/Was all the sound we heard. The Brookside. Richard Monckton, Lord Houghton Milnes. GoTF; HBV 1-2; TreFS

For the best of bone and blood. Fowls in the Frith. Anonymous. CBEP; NCEP; OBSP

For the big dog/at the end of the drive. Stone Age. Pat Nolan. APU

For the blessings that remain. The Blessings That Remain. Annie Johnson Flint. BLRP

For the blue sky bends over all! Christabel. Samuel Taylor Coleridge. OBRV

For the blue waves to roll over her pretty blue eyes. The Lover's Lament for Her Sailor. Anonymous. AmFP

For the bold Princess Royal from the pirate sailed away! The Bold Princess Royal. Anonymous. ShS

For the bonnie ship the Diamond,/Goes a-fishing for the whale. The Bonnie Ship the Diamond. Anonymous. FSW

For the book that I got from my Grandfather Hyde. I've Got a New Book from My Grandfather Hyde. Leroy F. Jackson. BrR; SiSoSe

For the bounties of song are no jealous god's mercies,/Far-fetched and dear bought. A Singing Lesson. Algernon Charles Swinburne. HBV 1-2

For the breath of the face of the Lord that is/felt in the bones of the dead. A Song in Time of Revolution 1860. Algernon Charles Swinburne. VLP

For the builders are not gone. Song: "Why do the houses stand." George Macdonald. OBVV

For the butterfly-soul that is in it/Longs for the winds again! A Yellow Pansy. Helen Gray Cone. HBMV

For the change of the face of thy colour I know thee not who/thou art. Johnny, I Hardly Knew Ye: Swinburnese (parody). Robert Yelverton Tyrrell. OnYI

For the child of her love is no longer a slave. She's Free! Frances E. W. Harper. BlSi

For the chosen have no choice. Moses. Sydney Tremayne. OxBS

For the clear cut sky. New England Greenhouse. Rennie McQuilkin. AMV-80

For the Colonel's Lady an' Judy O'Grady/Are sisters under their skins! The Ladies. Rudyard Kipling. ALV; EnLit; GoTF; MoBrPo; TreFT

For the contemplation of the Sages. Thanksgiving for the Body. Thomas Traherne. ImOP

For the corn is gone (so is her teaux). Limerick: "A lady who lived at Bordeaux." Anonymous. TDH

For the correct/yes. In Celebration of My Uterus. Anne Sexton. CAPP

For the country will bring us/no peace. Raleigh Was Right. William Carlos Williams. AmPP; NoAm; PP

"For the crime these boys committed/They surely must be hung." Pearl Bryan. Anonymous. ViBoFo

For the customary ram/Familiar to our darkness. Isaac and Esau. Rose Drachler. VWA

For the cut of all cuts is a Birmingham cut. The New Navigation. Anonymous. OBET

For the darling of the ladies is Hildebrand/Montrose. I'll Strike You with a Feather. Arthur Lloyd. VLP

For the dawn that only rises/in the heart of unity. Vanguardia. Sandra Maria Esteves. LTB

For the day when I make merry,. But Give Me Holly, Bold and Jolly. Christina Georgina Rossetti. BrR; ChBR; TiPo

For the dead live, and I am of their kind. Gravestones. Vernon Watkins. ChMP; TEP

For the dearest girl in all the world has gone square back on me. Lackey Bill. Anonymous. CoSo

For the deeds of tomorrow night. The Green Mountain Boys. William Cullen Bryant. AnNE; MC; PAH; PoPl

For the deep limits of sorrow's tears are not yet found. The Depths of Sorrow. Anonymous. WTO

For the depth of the font was abysmal. Limerick: "The babe, with a cry brief and dismal." Edward Gorey. OBAL

For the desert keeps her secrets,/When she has claimed her own. Bones in the Desert. Ned White. BPAW

For the devil, after prospectin' round, called it a damn poor place for/hell. The Peeler's Lament. Anonymous. CoSo; WTO

For the Duke of Parma's ear. Duke of Parma's Ear. Eli Siegel. ELU

For the England they had fought for on that wild October day. Balaclava. Anonymous. OBET

For the evening air is chilly in Cremona. Cremona. Arthur Conan Doyle. HBV 1-2

For the evil crew who murdered Kevin Barry/That day in November? Kevin Barry. Terence Ward. OnYI

For the Fatherless Children and widows are never deserted of the Lord. Jubilate Agno. Christopher Smart. NCEP

For the fighting Captain and the men/Of the Yankee Privateer.   The Armstrong at Fayal.   Wallace Rice.   PAH

For the fire of Sirius/Withers heads and knees.   Two Drinking Songs.   Alcaeus.   LiTW

For the first step along the Calvary road?   The Misfit-1939-1945.   C. Day Lewis.   BoC

For the first time my heart/Is filled with many thoughts.   Never Could I Think.   Izumi Shikibu.   PBWP

For the first time, now for the first time seen.   Green.   D. H. Lawrence.   ELU; GBL; MoBrPo; PoA

For the first time/she can breathe.   That First Gulp of Air We All Took When First Born.   Nancy Paddock.   PoDr

& For the first time/wanting each other/only.   For a Marriage.   Erica Jong.   CTBA

For the fisher-wife an' the weary lady,/Maisrie, Maisrie!""   Maisrie.   Jessie MacKay.   AnNZ

For the flare, polestar, pulley toward the edge.   On the Mountain.   Ruth Stone.   BoWoP

For the flowers of the forest are withered away.   The Flowers of the Forest.   Alison Cockburn.   BSV; OBEC

For the forced-fire/of roses.   The Porcupine.   Galway Kinnell.   NaP; NOBA

For the Fourth so glorious/And our flag so free!   Fourth of July Song.   Lois Lenski.   SiSoSe

For the future...for your century.   Only in This Way.   Margaret Goss Burroughs.   BlSi

For the future in the distance, and the good that I can do.   My Aim.   George Linnaeus Banks.   WBLP

For the Giant feels he's got a call to plug him if he comes.   A Friendly Game of Football.   Edward Dyson.   CBAP

For the girl I loved so well with dark brown eyes and hair.   Brown-Eyed Lee.   Anonymous.   CoSo

For the girls have got the tow-rope, an' they're hauling in the slack.   Homeward Bound.   D.H. Rogers.   AnNZ; EtS

For the glory of the garden glorifieth every one.   The Job That's Crying to Be Done.   Rudyard Kipling.   TRV

For the God of earth and heaven/Always meets His children there.   God Is There.   Walter E. Isenhour.   STF

For the God whose love we sing/Lends a little of his heaven/To every living thing.   Out of the Vast.   Augustus Wright Bamberger.   TRV

For the good chance that hapened was to Sir Gawaine and his/lady gay.   The Marriage of Sir Gawain.   Anonymous.   BaBo; ESPB

For the good Lord knows I can buy more clothes, but never a friend/like that!   Bum.   W. Dayton Wedgefarth.   BLPA

For the grapes' sake along the wall.   October.   Robert Frost.   GoJo; MAmP

For the gray morn breaks from thine eyes.   Matin Song.   Nathaniel Field.   HBV 1-2

For the great heart of the nation, throbbing, answered,/"Lord, we come!"   The Reveille.   Bret (Francis Bret Harte) Harte.   GN; HBV 1-2; MC; OHIP; PAH; PAL

For the great visions are past but do/not fade/and fortify and mollify.   Inscription on the Flyleaf of a Bible.   Dannie Abse.   TrJP

For the green leaves all turn yellow.'   The Green Leaves All Turn Yellow.   James Kenney.   IrPN

For the grim Idiot at the gate/Is deathless and eternal there.   The City of the End of Things.   Archibald Lampman.   NOBC; OBCV

For the hand that rocks the cradle/Is the hand that rules the world.   The Hand That Rocks the Cradle Is the Hand That Rules the World.   William Ross Wallace.   BLPL; FaFP; PoLf; TreF; WBLP

For the hazardous cliff-face and the promised land.   Darkened Windows.   Ronald Bottrall.   PoA

For the Head of the Serpent we know should/be bruis'd.   On the Snake.   Anonymous.   PAH

For the heart of a girl is a wonderful thing!   The Heart of a Girl is a Wonderful Things.   Anonymous.   BLPA

For the Heart of all hearts, through the fire of love, and the/wine of love, and the wings.   The Wings of Love.   James H. Cousins.   AnIV

For the hearts of these others are double.   Love-Song of the Water Carriers.   Anonymous.   PeSA

For "The Heavenly' made the earth/common to all.   There Is a City.   Anonymous.   TrJP

For the heavy hearts of soldiers.   Hush'd Be the Camps To-Day.   Walt Whitman.   MC; OHIP

For the Highland hills are ill to climb,/And the bluidy swords woud fear ye.   The Trooper and Maid.   Anonymous.   BaBo

For the human voice and the good news of friends   The Telephone.   Edward Field.   PPJ

For the hunter, death, disaster.   Early Morning Feed.   Peter Redgrove.   BoC

For the I offered my blood in sacryfice.   Vox Ultima Crucis.   John Lydgate.   OBEV; OxBoCh

For the journey back to a separate life/And to a very different Hebrew.   Buying a Shop on Dizengoff.   Erez Biton.   VWA

For the joy of feeling the thing inside.   Swallowing.   Harold Bond.   AMV-81

For the joyful days are coming./Fal la la.   Durham Old Women.   Anonymous.   GBP

For the joys we now may prove,/Take advice of present love.   To Phillis.   Edmund Waller.   CavP; OAEP; SeCP; TrGrPo

For the just shall rise to meet their Lord/In the flicker of an eye.   Rapture.   Randolph Carlson.   AMV-80

For the killing of James A. Garfield, for that I'm doomed to die.   Charles Guiteau, II.   Anonymous.   AmFP; ViBoFo

For the last sad sight of her face and the little grace of an hour.   Impenitentia Ultima.   Ernest Christopher Dowson.   BrPo; HBV 1-2

For the last time?   The Daughter of Jairus.   Marina Tsvetayeva   BoWoP

For the last time, we seem to be hearing the music.   Concert at the Station.   Osip Mandelstam.   AMV-81; VWA

For the life of us/we cannot stand to stay.   Form.   Heather McHugh.   GeTw

For the/life that we,/in our killing,/failed/to give them.   On the Birth of My Son, Malcolm Coltrane.   Julius Lester.   PoBA

For the like of the wan little fellow there?   Thoughts at the Museum.   Eileen Brennan.   OnYI

For the lily of the mountain foot/That withered far away.   The Irish Peasant Girl.   Charles Joseph Kickham.   AnIV

For the little boy who's waiting to grow/up to be like you.   To Any Daddy.   Anonymous.   STF

For the lone patrol, with his life in his hand,/Is hunting for blood in No-Man's Land.   No-Man's Land.   J. H. Knight-Adkin.   MCCG

For the long wait till our meeting.   Wings and Seeds.   Sandra McPherson.   GeTw

For the longer I live/The more fool am I.   Lack Wit.   Anonymous.   OxNR

For the Lord is risen; He dies no/more.   The Cross and the Tomb.   Annie Johnson Flint.   STF

For the Lord said, "Let Whale Be!'/And there was Whale!"   Whale.   William Rose Benet.   EtS; MoAmPo

For the loss, as for the life,/there will be no excuse, there/is no justification.   Confessions of the Life Artist.   Thom Gunn.   CMoP

For the lost fury of the fight.   Achilles and the King.   John Logan.   AmPC

For the love o thee now I maun die;/I come, my bonny Annie!'   Andrew Lammie.   Anonymous.   ESPB

For the love that is purest and sweetest/Has a kiss of desire on the lips.   A White Rose.   John Boyle O'Reilly.   AA; AnAmPo; HBV 1-2; OBEV; OBVV; OnYI; PoPl; SoSe

...For the lungs/Are dusted with the particles of death.   Poems from the Coalfields, 1: Air Shaft.   Ian Healy.   PoAu 1-2

For the maister brunt the whistle that the wee herd/made!   The Whistle.   Charles Murray.   GoTS; OxBS

For the man/of whom you reminded me once   This Journey.   Ingrid Jonker.   BoWoP

For the mighty wind arises, roaring seaward,/and I go.   Locksley Hall.   Alfred, Lord Tennyson.   BLPL; CABA; DiPo; EBEV; FaBoBe; FaFP; HBV 1-2; MaVP; MBW 1-2; OAEL 1-2; OAEP; VLP; WHA

For the moon/is an old family treasure.   Proposition.   Nicolas Guillen.   TTY

For the more we are envied, the higher we rise.   Harry Carey's General Reply...   Henry Carey.   HBV 1-2

For the mortgage man's the one who gets it all.   The Farmer Comes to Town.   Anonymous.   TrAS

For the mother and ransomed maiden,/That morning in Carlisle.   The Captive's Hymn.   Edna Dean Proctor.   PAH

For the murderous gallows, black and grim, is cheated of its dead!   Death-Doomed.   Will Carleton.   PaPo

For the name of the kitten was Love.   The Little Cat Angel.   Leontine Stanfield.   BLPA

For the Night Bird's/Inscrutable cry.   Seneca.   Thomas Merton.   CoPo

For the nimble trick on the friar she played.   The Friar and the Fair Maid.   Anonymous.   UnTE

For the no man's land/of my existence/breaks out anew.   Listening.   Hanny Michaelis.   VWA

For the occupant and house alike grow old.   The Ruined Cabin.   Alfred Castner King.   PoOW

For the old Kentucky home, far/away.   My Old Kentucky Home.   Stephen Collins Foster.   AA; AnAmPo; APA; BLSo; FaBoBe; FaBV; FaFP; GoTF; PoLf; PSoN; TreF; TrGrPo

For the old road to Paradise,/That's a crowded way!   The Old Road to Paradise.   Margaret Widdemer.   HBMV

For the one more cast-off shell.   Sand Dunes.   Robert Frost.   MoAB; MoAmPo; RFM

For the packet they watched, "homeward bound"/At the breakin' of day.   The Homeward Bound.   Bill Adams.   EtS

For the paper-boy, their go-between, to bring them/Lonely but hopeful, to a bed somewhere? Personal Column. Tom Paulin. FaBoIP

For the pattern which He planned. The Loom of Time. *Anonymous.* BLPA

For the people that dwell in the North can tell/Of Marian and bold Robin Hood. Robin Hood and Maid Marian. *Anonymous.* BaBo; ESPB

For the pikes must be together/By the rising of the moon. The Rising of the Moon. *Anonymous.* FSW

For the plural of spouse, it is spice. Limerick: "There was a young fellow named Dice." *Anonymous.* LiBL

For the Poorman's nosegay is an introduction to a Prince... Jubilate Agno. Christopher Smart. AtBAP

For the purposes of what intrinsic studies? The White Rat. Marguerite Young. MoPo

FOR THE RAISING OF THE SEED/TRIES WAITING EXALTATION. Fall To. Howard Jones. NBP

For the razor blade was German made,/But the sheet was Belfast linen. Belfast Linen. *Anonymous.* WTO

For the real powers to make fishers of men. Fishing Lines. Donald M. Hassler. WOLT

For the receipt is learned Dr Harmer's. The Art of Making Puddings. William King. FaBoUs

...For the relief of the body/and the reconstruction of the mind. Planetarium. Adrienne Rich. CAPP; FaBoWP; HaCAP; NIP; NoAm; NOBA

For the river's new earth. Going to the Water. Geary Hobson. STE

For the roaring wind and the blessed time/That brings him home again. A Wife's Song. William C. Bennett. HBV 1-2

For the robbing of the house carpenter,/And the taking away of his wife. The House Carpenter (with music). *Anonymous.* AS

For the Rose is Beauty; the Gardener, Time. A Fancy from Fontenelle. Henry Austin Dobson. HBV 1-2; OBVV

For the sad, pale melon, the squash, and the grain! A Hopi Prayer. Harrison Conrard. BPAW

For the sake o' Somebody! For the Sake O' Somebody. Robert Burns. AtBAP

For the sake of the bent bow and the silent archer,/Ganga, river of God, come down from the sky.' Ganga. Thomas Blackburn. MoBS

For the sake of the pleasure one cannot hear,/And the pleasure that only one can see? Langley Lane. Robert Williams Buchanan. HBV 1-2

For the sake of the rider who would /not heed! On the Road to Chorrera. Arlo Bates. AA

For the sake of the sun. In the Badlands. David Wagoner. UnPo

For the sake of the tree. Song: "Those rivers run from that land." Robert Creeley. VGW

For the sake of your Burns, you loved, oh, so dear. Burns and His Highland Mary. *Anonymous.* ShS

For the same little cherub that sits up aloft/Will look out a good berth for poor Jack! Poor Jack. Charles Dibdin. BeLS; HBV 1-2

For the same reason you probly stopped shufflin. W. H. Auden & Mantan Moreland. Al Young. NPGG

For the sands are in his heart,/And the killing snows. Siberia. James Clarence Mangan. NBM

For the sap has commenced to run. Sugar Weather. Peter McArthur. CaP

For the sea is his truest home! The Seagull. Mary Howitt. OxBChV

For the second the process was reversed/And that one was without pride. Adam and Eve. C. H. Sisson. FaBoTw

For the seventh time/explained the origin of death. Why I Didn't Go to Delphi. James Welch. CDW

For the ship that never returned. The Ship That Never Returned. Henry Clay Work. BLPA; FSW

For the sicht o'ts eneuch/To turn my soul nesh! In the Pantry. Hugh" (Christopher Murray Grieve) MacDiarmid. NoAm

For the 'skeeter was fleeter than Peter. Limerick: "There was a bright fellow named Peter." Marie Bruckman MacDonald. TDH

For the sky to put on/When the weather's bad. Garment. Langston Hughes. GoSl

For the sleep which now is thine! To Allegra Florence in Heaven. Thomas Holley Chivers. BXAP; PeD

For the small time/we have/by our own/light. Wonders. Shirley Kaufman. VWA

For the Snark was a Boojum, you see. The Hunting of the Snark. Lewis (Charles Lutwidge Dodgson) Carroll. FaBoNo; FiBHP; MasP; NOBV; OBNC; OBNV; OnMSP; PoEL 1-5

For the song/of the meadowlark/is always/new. The Seed of Reality. Max Von Hartmann. AMV-80

For the soul and the mind that repose not,/O, give us a rest! Home, Sweet Home. Henry Cuyler Bunner. InMe

For the spirit, born to bless,/Lives but in its own excess. A Song. Laurence Binyon. HBMV; MoBrPo

For the sportsman inborn shall the memory bless/Of the horse of the highwaymen, Bonny Black Bess. My Bonny Black Bess. *Anonymous.* CoMu; ViBoFo

For the still proud people of Banba! Lament for Banba. Egan O'Rahilly. AnIV; AWP

For the story ends this way. The Owl and the Nightingale. *Anonymous.* MeEV

...For the strength/That is not of the Heavens is of Hell. A Battle. Isabella Valancy Crawford. NOBC

For the subject I've touched, will make us root hog, or die. A Hit at the Times. A. O. McGrew. PoOW

For the sucking mouths/of light. But Perhaps. Nelly Sachs. BoWoP

;For the sufferings of this life,...are not worthy to be compared with the glory which shall The Royal Way of the Holy Cross. Thomas à Kempis. BoC

For the sweet surety of the common air. A Flower of Mullein. Lizette Woodworth Reese. MoAmPo

For the Swift passing of our visiting guests. Building a House. Dick Gallup. ANYP

For the taste o' a mornin's mornin' in Shanahan's ould shebeen! The Mornin's Mornin'. Gerald Brennan. BLPA

For the things that are pleasing to/God are made known unto us. The Path of Wisdom. *Anonymous.* TrJP

For the third time my body rises/and finds the good, the lasting shore! And in That Drowning Instant. Abraham Moses Klein. VWA

For the thorns that it must wear. The Little Child. Albert Bigelow Paine. AA

For the tie is unbroken on the Plains of Emu. The Exile of Erin. *Anonymous.* NOAV

For the time being, for the time being,/Peace. Conversation with Rain. Louise D. Gunn. GoYe

For the toothless old tykes of tomorrow/Were the Tigers of Yesterday. The Last of the Grand Old Masters. Tom Patey. PoSH

For the trail he cut so long ago/Runs straight through the heart of the West. The Texas Ranger. Margie B. Boswell. BPAW

For the unjustest act/Is still the pleasant'st jest. Lucasta Laughing. Richard Lovelace. PoEL 1-5

For the victims of this great and dreadful fire. The Milwaukee Fire. *Anonymous.* AmFP

For the virgin roadsteads of our hearts an unwavering keel. Perhaps. W. H. Auden. MoPo; NePA; OAEP

For the voice that speaks to the heart/Pleases the Master best. To a Boy. *Anonymous.* KiLC

For the voyage of oblivion awaits you. The Ship of Death. D. H. Lawrence. CMoP; FaBoRV; FaBoTw; GTBS-P; LiTB; LoBV; MasP; MOS; NoP; OAEL 1-2; OAEP; PrIm

For the want of a life-boat they all went/down,/And she sank to the bottom of the sea. The Mermaid (B version). *Anonymous.* AmFP; BaBo; ESPB; FSW; TreF; ViBoFo

For the War-King thunder-stricken from his fiery battle-car! Funeral of Napoleon I. Sir John H. Hagarty. CaP

For the warst sin, neebours, is pride, ay, pride! Pride. Violet Jacob. OxBS

For the way to fight is to fight. Just One Signal. *Anonymous.* PAH

For the West Wind told me so. The West Wind's Secret. Mary Jane Carr. BrR

For the wife of the Red-haired man. The Red Man's Wife. Douglas Hyde. OnYI; OxBI; SeCePo

For the winds of the dawn say, "Follow, follow/Jesus Bar-Joseph, the carpenter's son." The Bridegroom of Cana. Marjorie Pickthall. CaP; TrCP

For the yellow-hair'd laddie my gudeman shall be. The Yellow-haired Laddie. *Anonymous.* GBP

For the Yonghy-Bonghy-Bo. The Courtship of the Yonghy-Bonghy-Bo. Edward Lear. EnLoPo; EvOK; FaBoNo; HBV 1-2; OAEL 1-2; OnMSP; WiR

For the young child, Christ, straight and wise. Child. Carl Sandburg. TRV

For thee, against myself I'll vow debate,/For I must ne'er love him whom thou/dost hate. Sonnets, LXXXIX: "Say that thou didst forsake me for some fault." William Shakespeare. OAEP

For thee, and for myself, no quiet find. Sonnets, XXVII: "Weary with toil, I haste me to my bed." William Shakespeare. DiPo; OBSC

For thee, fair Virtue, welcome even the last! Apologia pro Vita Sua. Alexander Pope. NOBE

For Thee, O Lord, the light. The Shadows. George Macdonald. TRV

For thee watch I, whilst thou dost wake elsewhere,/From me farre off, with others all too neere. Sonnets, LXI: "Is it thy wil, thy Image should keepe open." William Shakespeare. PoEL 1-5

For their loves naked/and damned–/for all Mary Magdalenes. For All Mary Magdalenes. Desanka Maksimovic. WPOW

For their perilous march was o'er. The Migration of the Grey Squirrels. William Howitt. OxBChV

For their song ceased, and they were dead. The Blue Closet. William Morris. NBM; VLP

For their unjust extortion/And vile offences, swing. The File-Hewer's Lamentation. Joseph Mather. FaBoPV; NOEC

For them in life, or death provides. On the Universality and Other Attributes of the God of Nature. Philip Freneau. AP; ForPo

For them prepare/The road! The Road. Zalman Schneour. TrJP

...For them she is alive,/and warm, and wet. For Great Grandmother and Her Settlement House. Ann Darr. GP

For them/there is no/embarrassment. The Lovers. Joan Murray. LTB

For them to read when they're in trouble/And I am not. They Say My Verse Is Sad: No Wonder. Alfred Edward Housman. NoAm

For then I greet you from the stars. Last Words. Annette von Droste-Hulshoff. CAW

...For then I knew/It must break with as little warning. That Summer. Henry Treece. NYBP

For then, I know, thou wilt the rest impart. For Her Heart Only. *Anonymous.* ElL

For then, I swear, the world today/No rarer picture could display. The Likeness. Martial (Marcus Valerius Martialis). PeHV

For then the night will more than pay/The hopeless longing of the day. Longing. Matthew Arnold. CBEP; FPL; HBV 1-2; LO; OAEP; PoLf

...For then they plaine may see,/How hony-combs from his lips dropping bee. Sonnets, VIII: "Sometimes I wish that I his pillow were." Richard Barnfield. PeHV

For then you are/listening in heaven. To Mark Anthony in Heaven. William Carlos Williams. NOBA

For ther as the wolfe devoured him,/There lyes all this great erles gold. Young Andrew. *Anonymous.* ESPB

For there are many of those infants' souls/Crying out for the help of Me. The Holy Well. *Anonymous.* BaBo; FaBoCh; GBP; LoGBV

For there be more devouring beasts of prey/Than haunt the woods, among the human race. Volto Sciolto e Pensieri Stretti. James Clarence Mangan. IrPN

For there is a point to be learned in that. A Hundreth Good Poyntes of Husbandry. Thomas Tusser. FaBoUs

For there is joy in long dried tears,/For whetted passions of a throng! To Usward. Gwendolyn B. Bennett. BlSi

For there is no god found stronger than death;/and death is a sleep. Hymn to Proserpine. Algernon Charles Swinburne. EnL; EnLi 1-2; MaVP; OAEL 1-2; OAEP; OBNC; OBVV; PoEL 1-5; SeCeV; TEP; VLP; WHA

For there is no place so homelike/As a cow camp on the range. A Cow Camp on the Range. *Anonymous.* CoSo

For there is not another man alive,/In the world, to pull my legs! The Last Man. Thomas Hood. OBRV; VLP

For there is nothing to talk about. Peace. George Jonas. NeAC

For there is one more fair than thou, beloved of Alexis'. Hexametra Alexis in Laudem Rosamundi. Robert Greene. ElL; GBL; PoEL 1-5

For there is prepared thy nuptial bed. Epithalamium for Charlotte Corday and Francis Ravaillac. Percy Bysshe Shelley. HW

For there is that which never should be known. Sonnets: A Sequence on Profane Love. George Henry Boker. AmePo

For there never was man of woman born/Sae fair as him that is slain. Lady Diamond. *Anonymous.* BaBo; ESPB

For there's a town that's a trunk by the railroad corral. The Railroad Corral. *Anonymous.* CoSo

For there's Christmas, merry Christmas in the air. Christmas Shoppers. Aileen Fisher. ChBR

For there's life in the Old Land yet. England. Gerald Massey. HBV 1-2

For there's luck in odd numbers," says Rory O'More. Rory O'More; or, Good Omens. Samuel Lover. HBV 1-2

For there's more enterprise/In walking naked. A Coat. William Butler Yeats. CMoP; LiTM; NoAm; OBSP; PoEL 1-5

For there's neer a lord shall enter my bower,/Since my first love has so slighted me. Jamie Douglas (B vers.). *Anonymous.* BaBo

For there's neither a limb nor a tree. Once I Was a Shepherd Boy. *Anonymous.* OBET

For there's no place for Mormons but the lowest pits of hell. The Mormon Bishop's Lament. *Anonymous.* CoSo

For there's no true spell in Connacht or hell/(Bis) That's able to raise a Cain. The Ballad of Persse O'Reilly. James Joyce. FaBoBa; LiTB

For there's not a colleen sweeter,/Where the River Shannon flows. Where the River Shannon Flows. James I. Russell. FSN

For there's not a stunt that's in it with the Maple Leaf Rag. Maple Leaf Rag. Sydney Brown. BLSo

For there's plenty of gold,/So I've been told,/On the banks of the Sacramento. The Banks of the Sacramento. *Anonymous.* AmSS

For there shall we nothing lack./Veni, coronaberis. In Praise of Ivy. *Anonymous.* MeEL

For there, the air, everywhere full of planes. A Leg in a Plaster Cast. Muriel Rukeyser. MoAmPo

For these dead birds sigh a prayer. The Phoenix and the Turtle. William Shakespeare. CABA; CBEP; FaBoEn; LiTB; LiTL; LoBV; MasP; MePo; MyFE; NOBE; NoP; OAEL 1-2; OBEV; OBSC; PoEL 1-5; SeCePo; SeCeV; TEP

For these girls of the city were the ruin of me. The Sailor Cut down in His Prime. *Anonymous.* OBET

For these, O Lord, our thanks! Thanksgiving Day. Robert Bridges. OHIP

For these things occur...in the Flowery Land. Story of the Flowery Kingdom. James Branch Cabell. HBMV; OnMSP

For these vast hearts it was a narrow room. Cloister. Charles L. O'Donnell. CAW

For they already know to where we are going. The Dead Men. Sophia de Mello Breyner Andresen. PBWP

For they appeal from tyranny to God. Sonnet on Chillon. George Gordon, Lord Byron. AnEnPo; ExPo; FiP; GoTF; LiTB; LoBV; MBW 1-2; OAEP; SeCeV; TreFS; TrGrPo

For they are coming, and they are three! Isabelle (parody). James Hogg. BXAP; Par

For they are Nature's dreams. Night Mists. William Hamilton Hayne. AA

For they are needed against ogres. In Black Chasms. Leslie Norris. WSC

For they, at least, remembered Him/While other songs forgot. Lament for a Poor Poet. Myles Connolly. CAW

For they come of the same undaunted strain/As Wayne, Anthony Wayne! Anthony Wayne. Arthur Guiterman. TiPo

For they cut the pine in the wintertime and drive it in the spring. The Farmer and the Shanty Boy (Trenton Town). *Anonymous.* AmFP

For they'd none of 'em be missed–they'd none/of 'em be missed! The Mikado. Sir William Schwenck Gilbert. EnLi 1-2

...For they flamed and it was me they burned. Some Eyes Condemn. Edward ("Edward Eastaway") Thomas. NoAm

For they hae vanquishd great Montrose,/Our cruel enemy. The Battle of Philiphaugh. *Anonymous.* ESPB

For they have been the Christmas tree. Ashes of the Christmas Tree. Yetza Gillespie. ChBR

For they have passed away. New England's Dead. Isaac McLellan AA

For they have the dogs, and are riding tantivy. The Old Pack. *Anonymous.* APAS

For they know when their shepherd is nigh. The Shepherd. William Blake. CBEP; EnRP; ExPo; HBV 1-2; LoBV; OBEC; TiPo

For they lie at ease and know that life is done. The City of the Dead. Richard Burton. HBV 1-2

For they love so to play, that by Night or by Day,/They will turn up their Silver Hair. The Hunt. *Anonymous.* CoMu

For they must have motion/Through the vague snow of many clay pipes. Pantoum. John Ashbery. SM

For they're looking for lads like the cock of the game. The Cock of the Game. *Anonymous.* OBET

For they say you are taking the sunshine,/Which has brightened our pathway a while. Red River Valley. *Anonymous.* BLSo

For they see, hear, smell, feel not/what Heaven reveals all about. Revealed. Harry Lyman Koopman. AA

For they sped, first swallows,/and passed me by/to star the sky. What Are You Thinking About? James Macmillan. PoSH

For they, the after-life, shall live/With him, in New Jerusalem. O Christmas Night. Henricus Selyns. AH

For they, too, have been on the heights,/and have come down. Among Friends. Greg Kuzma. AMV-80

For they've done their hitch in hell. We've Done Our Hitch in Hell. *Anonymous.* ABF

For they were first to look with love/Upon the Christmas Child! Christmas Song. Elizabeth-Ellen Long. ChBR; SiSoSe

For they were only your fathers/But I was your officer. In Memoriam, Private D. Sutherland. Ewart Alan Mackintosh. BSV

For they were sent to do judgment on him! God's Judgment on a Wicked Bishop. Robert Southey. HBV 1-2; HBVY; OBRV; OnMSP

For Thine am I, Thy servant aye most bound. Domine Exaudi. Sir Thomas Wyatt. FCP

For Thine is the Kingdom and the Power and the Glory. Amen. Footnote to the Lord's Prayer (excerpt). Kay Smith. TrCP

For things are as they were. The Song of Momus to Mars. John Dryden. CBEP

For things unknown, only in mind. The Flesh and the Spirit. Anne Bradstreet. AnAmPo

For things we are too blind to see. The Shut-In. Nellie De Hearn. PoToHe

For thinking that thou art not ill. England. *Anonymous.* CBEP; ELU

For thirty pieces Judas sold/Himself, not Christ. Betrayal. Hester H. Cholmondeley. TRV

For this, and all, my soul doth worship Thee. A Thankful Acknowledgment of God's Providence. John Cotton. SCAP

For this bit of green costume jewellery/A nescient, obscure love.   At Roblin Lake.   Alfred W. Purdy.   PeCV

For this, dear wife, I've lost my life, to put down this rebellion.   Brother Green.   *Anonymous.*   AmFP

For this great Union Railroad it will fetch the Devil through.   The Utah Iron Horse.   *Anonymous.*   AmFP

...For this I have abandoned/all my other lives.   Waxwings.   Robert Francis.   LCAP; NU

For this I pray. For this alone I pray.   Supplication.   Edith Lovejoy Pierce.   TrPWD

For this is Christ.'   On the Swag.   R. A. K. Mason.   AnNZ

For this is Love's prerogative–/To give–and give–and give.   Love's Prerogative.   John Oxenham.   BLRP

For this is our Remembering Day.   Remembering Day.   Mary Wight Saunders.   YeAr

For this is the way the gentlemen are   Cantata for Two Lovers.   Helga Sandburg.   UnTE

For this is the way the old bachelor done.   The Bachelor's Lay.   *Anonymous.*   OuSiCo

For this is true:–they need your eyes/To light the ways of Paradise.   To–.   Katharine Morse.   HBMV

For this is Tuesday,–Wednesday is tomorrow.   Spouse.   Witter ("Emanuel Morgan") Bynner.   AnFE

For this little while in the sun's season.   The Double Tree.   Winfield Townley Scott.   PoPl

For this, O human beings, mourn we may.   Darkness.   Arthur Hugh Clough.   OBSP

For this poor wreath, give thee a crown of praise.   A Wreath.   George Herbert.   OBSP

For this the monk is to blame.   The Weak Monk.   Stevie Smith.   BoWoP; FaBoTw

For this the poets lived–and died.   Ballade of the Poetic Life.   Sir John Collings Squire.   OBMV

For this, this, 'twas worth my while/To flit across the sea.   The Bride's Song.   William Johnson Cory.   OBTV

For this time it was Henry who/Hopped the twig, and a good job too.   Henry VIII.   Eleanor and Herbert Farjeon.   StPo

For this were to give up your kingdom, and bow down your/neck to death.   The Wandering Lunatic Mind.   Edward Carpenter.   WGRP

For this, which shall be lost/Before what is, is done.   Tiresias' Lament.   Ellen de Young Kay.   NePoEA

For this world is but fantasy.   The World an Illusion.   *Anonymous.*   MeEL

For those ideals for which, since Homer sang,/The hosts of thirty centuries have died.   Sonnets Written in the Fall of 1914.   George Edward Woodberry.   HBV 1-2; MC; PAH

For those of us who drop our eyes/And no one picks them up.   Disillusionment.   Virginia Graham.   NLV

For those prepared who merit just applause/By bravely dying in their country's cause.   The Death of Wolfe.   *Anonymous.*   PAH

For those who live in cities/they have no need to see.   Indigo.   Lorna Crozier.   CaPN

"For those you never see."   "I Would," Says Fox, "A Tax Devise."   Richard Brinsley Sheridan.   HBV 1-2

For Thou alone canst save.   Thou Alone Canst Save.   Amelia Wakeford.   BePJ

For thou art a girl as much brighter than her,/As he was a poet sublimer than me.   A Better Answer (to Cloe Jealous).   Matthew Prior.   AWP; ELP; ExPo; InPo; NOEC; PoEL 1-5; SeCeV

For thou art heavenly, she an empty dream.   Paradise Lost.   John Milton.   ChTr; EBEV; FaBoPV; FiP; MBW 1-2; OAEL 1-2

For thou art of her clay.   The Lacking Sense.   Thomas Hardy.   CMoP; PoEL 1-5

For thou art the man that alone art/The cause of my misery.   My Lodging It Is on the Cold Ground.   Sir William D'Avenant.   JCP

For thou art the whole wide world to me.   Songs.   Richard Watson Gilder.   AA

For thou art with me, for thou art with me wheresoe'er I go.   All in the Downs (Susan and William).   *Anonymous.*   AmFP

For thou, Destroyer, art man's only Hope!   Charleston.   Richard Watson Gilder.   PAH

For thou didst see how deeply I/repent.   Thanksgiving.   David Abenatar Melo.   TrJP

For thou hast lost thy glory.   Songs Set by Thomas Morley, II.   *Anonymous.*   OBSC

For Thou hast stooped to ask of me/The love of my poor heart.   Our Heavenly Father (excerpt).   Frederick William Faber.   TrPWD

For Thou must one day wake for me/To suffer and to weep!   Jesus, Child and Lord.   Frederick William Faber.   BePJ

For thou shall get a better mare, and weel paid shall thy cowte foal be.   The Lochmaben Harper.   *Anonymous.*   ESPB; OxBB

...For thou shalt be/Damn'd for thy false apostasy.   To His Inconstant Mistress.   Thomas Carew.   OBEV

For thou shalt reign unrivalled there.   By Babel's Streams.   Philip Freneau.   AH

For Thou upon the Cross hast saved our souls!   Everyman.   *Anonymous.*   CAW

For though in France awhile my body be,/My heart remains (dear Paradise) in thee.   King Henry to Rosamond.   Michael Drayton.   OBSC

For, though killin' 's repperhensible, it's/somethin' ye can stan'.   The Salvation of Texas Peters.   James W. Foley.   ShM

For though some virtues he might lack,/He had his pleasant side.   Exit God.   Gamaliel Bradford.   HBMV; InMe

For though the world be burned, this never will be Brent.   Brent: A Poem to Thomas Palmer Esq.   William Diaper.   OBSV

For though we throw the dog his bone/He wants it back with interest.   The Lady's-Maid's Song.   John Hollander.   LiTM; MP; NePoEA; TW; TwCP

For thoughts, like angels, wage eternal war.   To a Writer of the Day.   Langdon Elwyn Mitchell.   AA

For thousands of miles on the water.   The Driver.   James Dickey.   VGW

For three dayes space they wine did/chase,/And drank themselves good friends.   Robin Hood's Delight.   *Anonymous.*   ESPB

For thu art he that hath all wrought,/and I thi moder alone.'   Here I Sit Alone.   *Anonymous.*   OxBoCh

For thunder, a break in the weather.   New York in August.   Donald Davie.   NMP

For thus I leave the world, the flesh, the devil.   Holy Sonnets, VI.   John Donne.   EBEV; JCP; LoBV

For thy allegiance to the poet's art.   Wapentake.   Henry Wadsworth Longfellow   AA

For thy dear sake, nae care I'll take,/Tho' ne'er another trow me.   O Tell Me How to Woo Thee.   Robert Graham.   OBEC

For-thy I chase to cheve as chaunce is me demed.'   Alexander and the Gymnosophists.   *Anonymous.*   OxBM

For-thy is love leader of our Lord's folk of heaven.   Et Incarnatus Est.   William Langland.   NOBE

For thy love, like a mark, is stamped on all.   All-Over Love.   Abraham Cowley.   LiTL

For thy name's sake, O hear us.   Jehovah, Lord and Majesty.   Conrad Weiser.   AH

For Thy new Heaven, Lord, give me new earth!   She Asks for New Earth.   Katharine Tynan Hinkson.   HBMV

For thy own Pox will they Revenge contrive.   To Scilla.   Sir Charles Sedley.   FaBoEE; PV

For thy parting/Neither say nor sing/By by, lully lullay!   The Coventry Carol.   *Anonymous.*   EBCP; ELP; MeEL; OFD; PCh

For thy sweet love remembered such wealth brings,/That then I scorn to change my state with Kings.   Sonnets, XXIX: "When in disgrace with fortune and men's eyes."   William Shakespeare.   ATP; AWP; CBEP; CTC; DiPo; EBEV; ExPo; FaBoEn; FaBoRV; FaBoWP; FaBV; GBL; GoTF; GTBS; GTBS-P; HAP; HBV 1-2; HeIP; InPK; InPo; InPS; InvP; LiTB; LiTL; LoBV; MasP; NOBE; NoP; OAEL 1-2; OAEP; OBEV; OBSC; PeHV; PG; PoEL 1-5; PoPl; PoRA; PPoe; PPP; Prf; PrIm; SCV; SeCeV; TEP; TreF; TrGrPo; TRV; ViBoPo; WHA

For thy Ways cannot be shown/By any Light, but by thine own.   A Morning Hymn.   Joseph Beaumont.   OxBoCh; TrPWD

For time and strength, O Lord! on Thee,/My spirit calls.   The Man's Prayer.   Thomas Augustin Daly.   TrPWD

For time is brief from cradle to the grave.   I Sing America Now!   Jesse Stuart.   AmFN

For time sic causis has repairit.   The Reeds in the Loch Sayis.   *Anonymous.*   BSV; GoTS

For tincture, wonder at.   The Weeping Cherry.   Robert Herrick.   AtBAP

For Tips/that will bring home/Toys of death.   Begging A.I.D.   David Rubadiri.   WhB

For 'tis in Jesus' name I pray. Amen.   My Daily Prayer.   Eva Gray.   STF

For 'tis NOT the same in a hundred years!   In a Hundred Years.   Elizabeth Doten.   BLPA

For 'tis their glory to be short, and sweet.   Epigram: "If true that notion, which but few contest."   *Anonymous.*   FaBoEE

For 'tis true as the gospel, believe it or not,/Who are born to be hang'd, will never be shot.   Sir Henry Clinton's Invitation to the Refugees.   Philip Freneau.   PAH

For to be alone with Silence/Is to be alone with God.   Silence.   Samuel Miller Hageman.   TRV

For to be paid to her unjust disdains.   Caelia: Sonnet.   Sir David Murray.   EIL

For to-day we have naming of parts.   Naming of Parts.   Henry Reed.   DTC; FF; GoJo; HeIP; HoPM; InPK; InPS; LiTB; LiTM; MP; NOBE; NoP; PAI; PrIm; SeCePo; SoSe; UnPo; WaP

For to let these jolly wassailers in.   Gloucestershire Wassail.   *Anonymous.*   OBET

For to live is to act in terms of death.   Ritual Three.   David Ignatow.   ConAP

For to make a scolding woman hold her/Tongue, tongue, tongue.   The Dumb Wife Cured.   *Anonymous.*   MaC

For to no earthly dwelling-place seems God so strangely/near!   The House of Pain.   Florence Earle Coates.   HBV 1-2

For to number sorrow by/Their departures hence, and die.   Upon the Losse of His Mistresses.   Robert Herrick.   AnAnS 2; CaPo; OAEP; SeCV 1-2

For to pray to our heavenly Queen.   The Leaves of Life.   *Anonymous.*   OBET

For to repent your cruelness.   Since Ye Delight to Know.   Sir Thomas Wyatt.   FCP; SiPS

For to sit upon a serpent's knee.   Diverus and Lazarus.   *Anonymous.*   ATP; OBET

For to wed with a poor country girl/That's no fortune to be had?   Jack Tar.   *Anonymous.*   ShS

For today are poor fold raised up/and cast a-down the proud.   Masters in This Hall.   William Morris.   FSW

For today my heart was brought to tears.   My spouse, Chunaychunay.   *Anonymous.*   BoWoP

For tonight together billet,/And tomorrow wend our ways.   And Tomorrow Wend Our Ways.   *Anonymous.*   WTO

For tonight we'll drink the health/Of every overlander.   The Overlander.   *Anonymous.*   PoAu 1-2

For Tony was a Turtle/Delicately bred.   Tony the Turtle.   Emile Victor Rieu.   SO

For traveller there could do me no good/Were I in trouble with night tonight.   Were I in Trouble.   Robert Frost.   OBSP

For truly they are soothed with drifting.   Report from California.   Lois Moyles.   NYBP

For truth and justice, and God's valiant right!   Armistice Day Vow.   Dorothy Gould.   PGD

For truth is precious and Divine,/Too rich a Pearl for Carnal Swine.   Godly Casuistry.   Samuel (1612-80) Butler.   OBS

For Truth shines brightest through the plainest dress.   An Essay on Translated Verse (excerpt).   Wentworth Dillon, Earl of Roscommon.   FaBoUs

For Turk and Brahmin, monk and Jew/Had reached Him through the gods they knew.   Ad Coelum.   Harry Romaine.   BLPA; FaBoBe

For 'twas he made the noggin to rowl.   Larry O'Toole (Parody on Lever).   William Makepeace Thackeray.   ALV

For twenty-one years, boys, is a mighty long time.   Twenty-One Years.   *Anonymous.*   AmFP

For two to sleep with sorrow on a hazardous Bed.   Mists and Rain.   Charles Baudelaire.   SyP

For tyme sic caussis hes reparit.   The Gude and Godlie Ballatis: The Reid in the Loch Sayis.   *Anonymous.*   OxBS

For unto Thee our eyes turn evermore.   Hymn of Weeping.   A. Ben Shefatiah.   TrJP

For unto us this day is born,/A Saviour and a King.   Hark! Hark! With Harps of Gold.   Edwin Hubbell Chapin.   AH

For upon the field I will make a bran-mash of his brains, mixed/with the maille of his armor.   A Perigord pres del Muralh.   Bertrand.   CTC

For us, and friends, and laughter!   Our House.   Dorothy Brown Thompson.   BrR

For us fellers, what was dyin'/And a-soakin' in the water of Manilly.   Off Manilly.   Edmund Vance Cooke.   PAH

For us, more human and less holy,/In time like air is essence stated.   In Time Like Air.   May Sarton.   MoLP; NYBP

For us the passage brief;–the happy dead/Are ever by great beauty visited.   The Dead.   David Morton.   PAH

For us tired children, now our games are played.   Sonnet: "We will not whisper, we have found the place."   Hilaire Belloc.   MoBrPo

For uses therefore I must count worth while.   Aurora Leigh.   Elizabeth Barrett Browning.   NOBV

For venturing her sweet life for the sake of her dear.   The Silk Merchant's Daughter (II).   *Anonymous.*   ShS

For wale o aa the manly sports/Climbin bears the gree.   O Aa the Manly Sports.   J. K. Annand.   PoSH

For want of vultures, we have crows.   Prometheus.   Jonathan Swift.   FaBoPV

For war is eating now.   The Times.   Charles Madge.   OBMV

For was it not thy happy lot/To live and die a rose?   To a Withered Rose.   John Kendrick Bangs.   AA

For we always go to church/When we've nothing else to do.   Attending Church.   *Anonymous.*   STF

For we are bound in common dread/Of what we do not know.   The News.   "Sec."   TRV

For we are Love, and God Himself is made/Only of thee and me.   Only of Thee and Me.   Louis Untermeyer.   HBV 1-2

For we are quite alone,/Here 'mid the ash trees.   La Fraisne.   Ezra Pound.   PG

For we are right, but these gluttons are wrong.   The Song of Roland, XCIII.   *Anonymous.*   WaaP

For we are the Ancient People,/Born with the wind and rain.   The Song of the Ancient People.   John Hay.   AA

For we are the poets/writing poems by/paying the rent/with our lives.   A Poem of Broken Pieces.   Andrew McCord Jones.   LFAC

For we are their children in the light of humanness, and under the/shadow of God's closing hand.   Promises, VIII. Founding Fathers....   Robert Penn Warren.   NoAm

For we, being ghosts, cannot catch hold of things.   August.   Louis MacNeice.   LiTM; PoPle

For we both have been blessed.   Ending.   Norman Jordan.   PoNe

For we carry the Heavens with us, Dear,/While the Earth slips from our feet!   Sunday at Hampstead, X.   James (1834-82) Thomson.   ViBoPo

For we find them but once in a while.   Worth While.   Ella Wheeler Wilcox.   BLPA; FPL; GoTF; PoToHe; TreF

For we have all in thee.   The Hazard of Loving the Creatures.   Isaac Watts.   CEP

"For we have heard/"That the Lord, our God, is with you."   Zechariah.   Earl Bowman Marlatt.   MoRP

For we have one Anacreon Moore.   On Tom Moore's Translation of Anacreon.   Thomas Erskine, Lord Erskine.   FaBoEE

(For we have to look trim in the port) and in/The high-piled ambiguous cargo.   Sailors' Harbour.   Henry Reed.   MOS

For we increase the sea with our tears/And the wandering wind with our sighs.   A Poem Written in Time of Trouble by an Irish Priest...   Augusta Gregory, Lady Gregory.   OBMV

For we know that in Heaven above at this moment he's saving/God.   Addition to Kipling's "The Dead King (Edward VII), 1910."   Max Beerbohm.   FaBoEE

For we left father and mother at hame/Breaking their heart for thee.'   The Gay Goshawk (E version).   *Anonymous.*   ESPB

For we'll be back in a few short years./Hinky, dinky, parley voo.   Mademoiselle from Armentieres.   *Anonymous.*   BLSo; FSW; OBAL

For we'll sleep in Lake Michigan where the stormy winds blow.   The Beaver Island Boys.   *Anonymous.*   OuSiCo

For we played Molongo cricket–and McDougal topped the score!   How McDougal Topped the Score.   Thomas E. Spencer.   PoAu 1-2

For we're bound for the Rio Grande.   Rio Grande.   *Anonymous.*   ABF; FSW; TrAS

For we're bound for the Rio Grandy.   Down in the Land of the Center-Fire Saddle.   CoSo

For we're due to be dawned on, I guess.   Aus Einer Kindheit.   Kenneth Koch.   AmPC

For we're well on the road to the railroad corral.   The Railroad Corral.   *Anonymous.*   FSW

For we scorn to live in slavery, bound down with iron/chains.   Jack Donahoe.   *Anonymous.*   CoSo

For we shall know, too late to know/Or care.   Beforehand.   Witter ("Emanuel Morgan") Bynner.   HBMV

For we took our shoes off/As we fell.   Martyrdom of Two Pagans.   Philip Whalen.   NeAP

For we, which now behold these present/days,/Have eyes to wonder, but lack tongues to/praise.   Sonnets, CVI: "When in the chronicle of wasted time."   William Shakespeare.   AWP; BLPL; CBEP; CTC; DiPo; EnRePo; ExPo; FaBV; FiP; GTBS; GTBS-P; HBV 1-2; InPo; LiTB; LiTL; LoBV; LoGBV; MasP; MBW 1-2; MCCG; NOBE; NoP; OAEL 1-2; OAEP; OBEV; OBSC; PoRA; PPoe; SeCeV; TEP; TreFT; TrGrPo; ViBoPo

For we, who all the Wonder might have told,/Kept silence, for our mouths were stopped with gold.   A Guard of the Sepulcher.   Edwin Markham.   WGRP

For we will not live here forever   The Whole Universe Is Full of God.   Yunus Emre.   LLLT

For weariness of life, not love of Thee.   Good and Great God!   Ben Jonson.   OxBoCh

For weeks she went untidy, she went sullen.   Miriam Tazewell.   John Crowe Ransom.   TW

For weel I wot this typical Scot/Was a michty loss to the nation!   The Pawky Duke.   David Rorie.   BSV; GoTS

For, weeping, they are Father, Mother.   At Last.   Richard Henry Stoddard.   HBV 1-2

For, were I not, you'd leave me too.   Get You Gone.   Sir Charles Sedley.   ELP

For were the worthiest woman curst/To love one man, he'd leave her first.   Another. In Defence of Their Inconstancie.   Ben Jonson.   SeCP

For what before was filled by me alone,/I now discern hath room for everyone.   Caelica, LXIV.   Fulke, Lord Brooke Greville.   FCP

For what can neither ask nor heed his death.   There Was a Time.   Edward ("Edward Eastaway") Thomas.   MMM

...For what can words tell/Of things that have no yesterday, tomorrow or to-/day?   On Trust in the Heart.   Seng-Ts'an.   ILwL

For what concerns my knowledge God reveals.   Paradise Regained.   John Milton.   OBS

For what could fathom God were more than He. Finite Reason. John Dryden. LoBV

For what could she complain of but his love? The Metamorphoses. Ovid (Publius Ovidius Naso). JCP

For what flower, plucked,/Lingers long? Flowers of Darkness. Frank Marshall Davis. AmNP; IDB; NoP; PoBA; PoNe

For what I have done/you can do/and what I am/you/can/be. A Message from Reverend Fat Back Made Possible by... Melvin Douglass Brown. LFAC

For what is gold bute ston/But if it haveth wis man? The Proverbs of Alfred: Wealth and Wisdom. Anonymous. OxBM

For what it came to find and will die for. Under the Sign of the Moth. David Wagoner. AMV-81

For what my senses can themselves perceive/I need no revelation to believe. The Hind and the Panther. John Dryden. OBS

For what old crime of theirs I do not gather. Tall Ambrosia. Henry David Thoreau. PoEL 1-5

For what one is, one sees not; 'tis the lot/Of him at peace to contemplate it not. The Grave. Yvor Winters. MoVE; NoAm

For what thou hast done thou hast done. Irrevocable. Mary Wright Plummer. WGRP

(For what was done there/I ask no man pardon.) For the Goddess Too Well Known. Elsa Gidlow. PeHV

For what would America be without the lads that look for coals? Down in a Coal Mine. Anonymous. AmFP

For whatever new comes from it/something old died. The Pitch Piles Up in Part. Desmond O'Grady. CIP

For when flesh fell/In my arms, soul did as well. Poem. Keith Sinclair. ACV

For when He frowns, 'tis then ye shine! My Springs. Sidney Lanier. UnPo

For when he kicked Miss Roe, she kicked him again. Captain Wattle and Miss Roe. Charles Dibdin. OxBoLi

For when he shoots he shoots for keeps and piles his victims up in/heaps. The Dying Desperado. Anonymous. CoSo

For, when his hand's upon it, you may know/That there's go in it, and he'll make it go. Whittling. John Pierpont. GN

For, when I awoke, ther was but I alone. Waking Alone. Anonymous. MeEL

For when I wrote I did thy beauty lack. Sonnet: "Like Memnon's rock, touched with the rising sun." Giles the Elder Fletcher. EIL

For when my tongue is loosed most, then most I lose my/speech. The Maltworm's Madrigal. Henry Austin Dobson. HBV 1-2

For when she calls lavender summer must die! Lavender's for Ladies. Patrick Reginald Chalmers. HBMV

For when the corn's to shear the bairn's to bear. A Scottish Proverb. Anonymous. FaBoUs

For when their work begins to wither/Their worth decays. When Youth and Beauty Meet Together. Anonymous. EIL

For when they see this town they fly,/And anxiously increase their speed. Anno 1829. Heinrich Heine. AWP; LiTW

For when we have no money, we shall find chalk. The Wench in the Street. Anonymous. CBEP

For when you flow into me/You're not at all through. The Great Lakes Suite. James Reaney. WHW

For when you go you're coming back,/In Topsy-Turvy Land. Topsy-Turvy Land. H. E. Wilkinson. SoPo

For where I am would I not be,/And where I would be I can not. Suspira. Anonymous. OBEV

For "Where there's a will there's a way." Where There's a Will There's a Way. Eliza Cook. BLPA; FaFP; GoTF; TreF

For where they bloom God is, and I am free. Poets Love Nature. John Clare. CBEP; ERoP 1-2; OAEL 1-2

...For which act/I think to say this/wrongly. The Whip. Robert Creeley. NaP; NeAP; NoAm; PoM

For which he cannot find/a means or time. The Pool. Robert Creeley. CoAP

For which I wanted the night to retreat! Quite Forsaken. D. H. Lawrence. BrPo

For which Ile repent all the dayes of/my life,/And god be with them all three!' Little Musgrave and Lady Barnard (B version). Anonymous. ESPB

For which or pay me quickly or I'll pay you. To Fine Grand. Ben Jonson. JCP

For which the intricate Alps are a single nest. Connoisseur of Chaos. Wallace Stevens. CABA; LiTM; MoPo; SUW

For which the Lord be thankit! Two Graces. Anonymous. FaBoCh

For which your petitioners ever will pray,/&c. &c. &c. &c. &c. The Petition of the Orangemen of Ireland. Thomas Moore. NOBI

For Whigs admit no force but argument. Oxford & Cambridge. Sir William Browne. FaBoCo

For while in him confiding,/I cannot but rejoice.' Joy and Peace in Believing. William Cowper. NOCV; TRV

For while they are robbing the House-Carpenter,/And coaxing away their wives. The Demon Lover. Anonymous. BaBo

For while thy beza is in hand/Man's salvation's at a stand. To Dr. Kipling. Richard Porson. FaBoCo

For while we've got sea room, bold lads, never fear.' Bold Princess Royal. Anonymous. OBSS

For who can bear to feel himself/At Christmas?/Yours documentarily,/W. H. AUDEN (master). Dear Father Christmas (parody). Russell Davies. FaBoPa

For who can bear to feel himself forgotten? Night Mail. W. H. Auden. OxBTC

For who can say "Misfortunes know not me'? The Art of Wenching (excerpt). Anonymous. NOEC

For who could have foretold/That the heart grows old? A Song: I Thought No More Was Needed. William Butler Yeats. AtBAP

For who could see the passage of a goddess/unless she wished his mortal eyes aware? The Odyssey. Homer. NAWM 1-2

...For who dares move/Reward for his delight? Sonnet: "Madam, 'tis true, your beauties move." Sidney Godolphin. JCP

For who else could I get in my place/to do the job in dark, airless conditions? Self-Employed. David Ignatow. NNaP

(For who except myself has yet conceiv'd what your children en-masse/really are?) Long, Too Long America. Walt Whitman. NoAm

For who pretends to ticking clocks,/Or wooden chair and stool? The Busy Body. Rachel Field. InMe

For who would want a lollypop/To chase one, don't you know? The Lollypops. Cordia Thomas. SoPo

...For whoever joins me/in the ceremony of dreams. Night Song for an Old Lover. Susan Glickman. AMV-81

For whoever pays the taxes, old Mus' Hobden owns the land. The Land. Rudyard Kipling. MoBrPo; OnMSP

For whom He hath prepared it, they shall/stand/On the Right Hand and Left! Peace. Adeline D. T. Whitney. PAH

For whom, it seems, the sacraments have failed. The Envy of Poor Lovers. Austin Clarke. CIP; CMoP; NMP

For whom, more rude than a beggar's rhyme in the gutter,/These songs are sung. The Return of Eve. Gilbert Keith Chesterton. ISi

For whom my life, however it may teem/With petty faults, will not have been in vain. O, Let Me Kiss—. Karl Gjellerup. PoPl

...For whom/This glorious sight, when sleep hath shut all eyes? Paradise Lost. John Milton. TrGrPo

For whose eyes, for whose lips, but mine! Thisbe. Helen Gray Cone. AA

For whoso wants Money with them shall not speed. London Lickpenny. John Lydgate. GoTL; MeEV; OxBM

For why should we mourn for the blest? Bright Be the Place of Thy Soul! George Gordon, Lord Byron. HoPM

For, William McBride, it all happened again/And again and again and again and again. No Man's Land. Eric Bogle. OBET

For Wind's been everywhere today, and has an alibi. Small Dark Song. Philip Dacey. PPJ

For winter drought rewards the peasant's pain,/And broods indulgent on the buried grain. Georgics. Virgil (Publius Vergilius Maro). EiCP

For wisdom, courage and strength/A man the like of Fionn? The Praise of Fionn. Anonymous. KiLC

For wisest conquerors do towns desire,/On honourable terms and not with fire. To His Lady, Who Had Vowed Virginity. Walter Davison. OBSC

For with a full hand that does bring/All that was promis'd by the spring. To My Young Lady Lucy Sidney. Edmund Waller. MePo; OAEP

For with his nails he'll dig them up again. The White Devil, V, iv: "Call for the Robin Redbreast." John Webster. AnFE; EBEV; FaBoCh; FaBoEn; GTBS; GTBS-P; HAP; HBV 1-2; HeIP; LiTB; LoBV; LoGBV; NoP; OBEV; OBS; PAI; PoEL 1-5; PoRA; PrIm; SeCePo; TrGrPo; ViBoPo

For with his own realm it compares so well/He feels assured it surpasses hell. The History of Arizona: How It Was Made and Who Made It. Charles O. Brown. BPAW

For with my hand I have indost/To pay quhatevir his trappouris cost. The Petition of the Gray Horse, Auld Dunbar. William Dunbar. OxBS

...For woman 'tis to/ply/The spinning wheel–then to herself/she's true. Sonnet: "My soul surcharged with grief now loud complains." Rachel Morpurgo. TrJP

For women grieve to think they must be old. To Delia. Samuel Daniel. EnRePo

For women's looks are such enchanting charms,/As can subdue the greatest god in arms. Mars and Venus. Robert Greene. OBSC

For words, and birds, not apples/On the tongue, nor roast in the gut. Yaddo. Ruth Herschberger. FAZ

For work to do, and strength to do the work,/We thank Thee, Lord! Gratitude for Work. John Oxenham. PGD

For y not whider y shal, ne hou longe her duelle. Wynter Wakeneth. Anonymous. OxBoCh; SeCePo

For ye have been famed/The worst in this contray! A Call for a Song. Anonymous. OxBM

For ye'll be a' i' the tod's hole/In less than a hunner year.   The Tod's Hole. *Anonymous.* GBP

For ye're great Macdonald's braw lady,/And will be to the day that ye dee.' Lizie Lindsay (B version). *Anonymous.* ESPB

For ye shall be married ere this day week/Tho' the same death you should die. The Bonny Earl of Livingston. *Anonymous.* OxBB

For ye turned my true love fae my door,/When she came sae far to me.   The Lass of Roch Royal (A vers.). *Anonymous.* ViBoFo

For yellow, fresh and full-blown once it bloomed.   Lost Love. *Anonymous.* WTO

For yesterday I was your prisoner,/But now the night I am set free.'   Archie of Cafield. *Anonymous.* BuBa; OxBS

For yesterday is always sad, its nature/Darker than love would wish in every feature.   Loss.   Charles Madge.   FaBoMo

For, yet unskaith'd by Death's gleg gullie,/Tam Samson's leevin!   Tam Samson's Elegy.   Robert Burns.   PoEL 1-5

For you and bibacious young Quintus Horatius–/Stewed.   Persicos Odi. Franklin Pierce ("F.P.A.") Adams.   HBMV

For you, and for the rest who cannot share/Your gold of unrevealed awakenings.   For Arvia.   Edwin Arlington Robinson.   BiCB

For you and me/There's/Woe.   Angola Question Mark.   Langston Hughes. BPo; TTY

For you and that big dark blue.   Down at the Docks.   Kenneth Koch. PrIm; VGW

For you are a cross/Of the old sea-hoss/And a regular terror-pin.   The Turtle. *Anonymous.* PAH

For you are driving your horses through/The mist where Genesis begins.   To the Man after the Harrow.   Patrick Kavanagh.   CIP; FaBoIP; GTBS-P

For you are made one/With the Christ on the cross.   For His Sake.   Annie Denman.   BePJ

For you are two years old/This morning.   Crawl, Laugh.   Issa.   OFD

...For you bring,/to what you define now, all/there is, ever, of future.   Vox Humana.   Thom Gunn.   NePoEA-2

For you cain't get yo' money when it's due.   Hard To Be A Nigger. *Anonymous.* ABF

For you can take your lives away/By giving up your purses.   The Gallant Highwayman.   James De Mille.   WHW

For you can watch it grow.   Poem of Circumstance.   Jean Cocteau.   CAW

For you cannot deny but my shepherd's to blame.   The Lamentation of Chloris. *Anonymous.* CoMu

For you, "Dudley"/and your beardless, baubled clan,/these loathings/to suck on.   For "Mr. Dudley," a Black Spy.   James A. Emanuel.   BPo

For you, fairy music through all your days!   To a Little Sister, Aged Ten. Alison Elizabeth Cummings.   BiCB

For you, for you I am trilling these songs.   For You, O Democracy.   Walt Whitman.   TrGrPo

For you have learned, not what to say,/But how the saying must be said.   To a Friend, on Her Examination for the Doctorate in English.   J. V. Cunningham.   EiCP; VGW

For you have tied my hands.   Johnny Sands. *Anonymous.* AmFP; CoMu; OBET; ViBoFo

For you know when I have money the devil's in me./Derry, down, down, down derry down.   The Rackets around the Blue Mountain Lake. *Anonymous.* FSW

For you know Wyoming will be your new home.   Git Along, Little Dogies. *Anonymous.* ABF; FSW; MoShBr

For you like a child's drawing on a piece of paper.   We Have Been Happy. Max Eastman.   AnEnPo

For you love me truly, truly, dear.   I Love You Truly.   Carrie Jacobs Bond. BLSo; FSN; TreFS

For you may save the life of/A pretty Muffin Bird!   The High Barbaree. Laura E. Richards.   SoPo

For you must be stuffed and my customers filled!   Dilly Dilly. *Anonymous.* OxNR

For you must shut the baby there.   John of Tours. *Anonymous.* AWP

For you only can say "Wee! wee!"   The Three Little Pigs.   Alfred Scott Gatty.   OxBChV

For you're not at all well!   Out of Sorts.   Sir William Schwenck Gilbert. ALV

For you that not remember it.   Juana.   Alfred de Musset.   AWP

For you've killed all the devils and rent over Hell."/Scrath-a-fillee, fillee, filiddle, filum.   The Farmer's Curst Wife (B vers.). *Anonymous.* BaBo; ESPB

—For you were a lover in the world.   The Word of God.   Einar Skjaeraasen. HW

For you, wi aa the pikes ye claim,/Wi him to battle.   To a Hedgehog. Samuel Thompson.   BIrV

For you will have trouble the whole of the week.   Sneeze on a Monday, You Sneeze for Danger. *Anonymous.* EvOK; HBV 1-2; HBVY; NLV

For you will shortly come to me,/Where we shall never part.   The Dying Father's Farewell. *Anonymous.* AmFP

For your good luck to master even twelve.   Fortitude.   Sir Eeinmar von Zweter.   LiTW

...For your incurable sins some salve.   College of Flunkeys, and a Few Gentlemen.   John Berryman.   GLGT

For your marriage an your kirkin too/Sal baith be in ae day.'   Child Waters. *Anonymous.* ESPB

For your monument–a people/Laughing, laughing all the year.   Sholom Aleichem.   Elias Lieberman.   TrJP

...For your mouth has wrapped my life in a/thin gauze of hope.   Your Mouth.   Jenab Shehabuddin.   LiTW

For your possible/discovery.   Towards a City That Sings.   June Jordan. NYP

For your quite unoriginal sin.   A Hawthorne Garland.   Richard Harter Fogle.   OBAL

For your sake, oh my secret,/My life.   In Terror of Hospital Bills.   James Wright.   GP

For your sake storm we any height.   The Lost Colors.   Elizabeth Stuart Phelps Ward.   AA; HBV 1-2; HBVY

For youthful friendship is a thing/More precious than succeeding.   Hersilia. William Cory Johnson.   NOBV

Forbear incessant to adore that Power/Who fills, sustains and actuates the whole?   To the Memory of Sir Isaac Newton (excerpt).   James (1700-48) Thomson.   ImOP; NOEC

Forbid that we should vainly rove/Beyond the freedom of thy love.   O God, in Whom the Flow of Days.   Donald Campbell Babcock.   AH

A Force drunk with its own infinitude.   Tree of Time.   K. D. Sethna. ACV

The force of habit is so strong.   The Elephant, or The Force of Habit. Alfred Edward Housman.   NOBL; PV

The force of nature can no further go.   Three Blessings (Parody on Dryden). *Anonymous.* ALV

Forced by their lord, who is asham'd to find/Such light in sense with such a darkened mind.   Astrophel and Stella, XCIX.   Sir Philip Sidney.   SiPS

Forcing boy & girl to lie/down together untaught/in the adjacent dark. Adolescence.   Dennis Schmitz.   FAZ

Forcing me to drink/from the trough of reality.   Tim.   John Montague. FaBoIP

Forebear, survivor, have I lost my way?   The Pack Rat.   Robert Pack. PPP; WeW

A forecast 'tis of heav'nly bliss!   Three Love Poems.   Judah Halevi.   TrJP

"Forego me now; come to me soon."   Come to Me Soon.   Sir Walter Ralegh.   UnTE

Foregoe me now, come to me soon.   On Dulcina.   Sir Walter Ralegh. CoMu

...Forehead/against his forearm, leaning up against the barn.   Land of Little Sticks, 1945.   James Tate.   MAYP

A foreign thing desertless in origin.   Apologia pro Vita Sua.   Archie Randolph Ammons.   HaCAP; NOBA

...Foreign tongues/Commune above her in a drift of wings.   Assumption. Padraic Fallon.   BIrV; NOBI

The foreknowledge veiled in our face.   Autochthon.   Sir Charles G. D. Roberts.   CaP

Foremost he marched with swift and/haughty step.   The Exodus from Egypt. Ezekielos.   TrJP

Forerunners of a sterner power,/Heralds of me?   I'll Come When Thou Art Sadder.   Emily Bronte.   VLP

...Foreseeing/its purpose is to haunt the shell like singing.   Not in the Poet. George Barker.   OBSP

The forest is mute.   Song.   Sophie Jewett.   AA

...The forest knows/Where you are. You must let it find you.   Lost.   David Wagoner.   GP; PoA

A forest of loose ends/Where sewing never mends.   The Tapestry.   Howard Nemerov.   Prf

...The forester,/slept under arms on duty for his masters.   The Odyssey. Homer.   NAWM 1-2

Forever after the water tastes fiery.   A Fire a Simple Fire.   Frederic Will. FAZ

Forever awkward,/each partner dreaming of grace.   American Bandstand. Michael Waters.   MAYP

Forever certain if forever slow.   Girod Street Cemetery: New Orleans. Harry Morris.   GoYe

Forever changeless, against a changing sky?   Gestures to the Dead (excerpt). John Wheelwright.   MoVE

Forever for the people's good should spin.   An Oriental Apologue.   James Russell Lowell.   PoEL 1-5

Forever, from our shore.   Song of Marion's Men.   William Cullen Bryant. AnNE; HBV 1-2; HBVY; MC; PAH; TreF

Forever in beauty/Always   Wishes.   Patty L. Harjo.   VoR

Forever in the sweat of fire   Hermetic Bird.   Philip Lamantia.   VGW

Forever intervene!   Our lives are Swiss.   Emily Dickinson.   NOBA; PoL; TAP

Forever is deciduous/Except to those who die.   Summer Has Two Beginnings.
  Emily Dickinson.   InPo
The forever itself a circling of the hooves of horses.   A Dream of Horses.
  Ted Hughes.   NePoEA-2
Forever let Britannia wield/The teapot and her sires!   Macaulay at Tea.
  Barry Pain.   HBV 1-2
Forever looking back/over his stooped shoulder   Poem for Jan.   Joseph
  Bruchac.   CDW
Forever. Motion is all.   King Wind.   Mark Van Doren.   NCSH
Forever mourning themselves/into dust.   The Beads.   Jaime Jacinto.   BrSi
Forever, my thou-/sand blessings be with them!   Last Leave of the Hills.
  Duncan Ban MacIntyre.   GoTS
"Forever–never!/Never–forever!"   The Old Clock on the Stairs.   Henry
  Wadsworth Longfellow.   HBV 1-2; WBLP
Forever of my company!   The Pilgrim.   Sarah Hammond Palfrey.   AA
Forever, on a   My Poker Girl.   Tom (Thomas Lansing Masson) Masson.
  OBAL
Forever on their own!   To Walt Whitman.   Tom MacInnes.   CaP
Forever playing where a boy I played,/By hill and grove, by field and stream
  delayed.   The Song.   Jones Very.   MAmP
Forever runs on the song of the clock!   The Time-Clock.   Charles Hanson
  Towne.   HBMV
Forever shall the Lord be King!   The Lord Is King.   Anonymous.   TrJP
Forever the lover/of every small town.   Lady of Lidice.   Fray Angelico
  Chavez.   ISi
Forever to cry aloud/In anguish: I love the black swan.   The Black Swan.
  James Merrill.   MoPo
Forever, to the skies!   To Mary Magdalen.   Bartolome Leonardo de
  Argensola.   CAW
Forevermore at home with Thee!   This Easter Day.   Martha Snell
  Nicholson.   BePJ
Forfeit their Paradise by their pride.   The Flower.   George Herbert.
  AtBAP; AWP; ELP; FaBoRV; InPo; JCP; MePo; NIP; NOBE; NOCV;
  NoP; OBS; OxBoCh; PoEL 1-5; PPP; SeCP; SeCV 1-2
Forfeit through endless self-evasion/The estate of simple being.   The Tourists.
  Cecil Day-Lewis.   OBTV
Forgane thir stannyris schane the beryall strandis.   Proloug of the Twelft
  Buik of the Aenead.   Gavin Douglas.   AtBAP
Forge molten gold into the image of keys/one must surely fit this gate.   The
  Spell.   Michelle Roberts.   LFAC
The forge of bitter hate.   Birmingham.   Margaret Walker.   PoBA
The forgeries of death.   Ode to the Muse on Behalf of a Young Poet.   David
  Wagoner.   AMV-80
Forget.   All Our Joy Is Enough.   Geoffrey Scott.   OBMV
Forget him and forget her.   To the Tune of the Coventry Carol.   Stevie
  Smith.   FaBoTw
Forget long hates in one consummate faith.   The Road to Dieppe.   John
  Finley.   MCCG
Forget me not.   Up the Hill.   Anonymous.   PH
Forget me not, en vogant la galere.   Though this the port and I thy servant
  true.   Sir Thomas Wyatt.   FCP; SiPS
Forget me then; but ne'er believe that thou canst be forgot!   Forget Thee?
  John Moultrie.   BLPA; FaBoBe; PoToHe
Forget not it is yours and ours.   Our Mother Tongue; or, An Envoy to an
  American Lady.   Richard Monckton, Lord Houghton Milnes.   GN
Forget not the one potter and...the...lathe.   So, Man?   Gene Derwood.
  NePA
Forget not this!   Forget Not Yet.   Sir Thomas Wyatt.   AAS; AnFE;
  AtBAP; BiP; CBEP; ElL; EnLi 1-2; FCP; GoBC; HAP; HBV 1-2; NoP;
  OAEP; OBEV; SiPS
Forget sad thoughts forlorn.   The Seasons.   Kalidasa.   AWP
Forget that we bore the burden/And carry away the song.   Our Burden
  Bearer.   Phillips Brooks.   TRV
...Forget/The nonsense and the farce of what the fools call great?   Upon the
  Downs.   Sir George Etherege.   ViBoPo
Forget the vows made in that cloistered/nook.   Ghost-Flowers.   Mary
  Thacher Higginson.   AA
Forget/we ever met.   Should We Legalize Abortion?   Frank O'Hara.
  NoAm
Forget what I've been proving,/Sweet Phyllis, and love me!   Don't.   James
  Jeffrey Roche.   HBV 1-2
Forget when traveling or at home.   Just Forget.   Myrtle May Dryden.
  WBLP
Forget Yourself and think of Those Around.   A Poet's Proverbs.   Arthur
  Guiterman.   TiPo
The forgetful surf creaming on those ledges.   Suicide off Egg Rock.   Sylvia
  Plath.   NMP; PPP
Forgetful, you too may grasp it time and again/in an open field, among
  flowers.   Stinging Nettle.   Gwen Head.   GP
...Forgets/All the truth and returns to his dream.   Habakkuk.   Edouard
  Roditi.   VWA

Forgets the rush and rapture of his wings.   The Soul's Travelling (excerpt).
  Elizabeth Barrett Browning.   ILwL
Forgetting his own flesh and blood!   On the Death of Doctor Swift.
  Jonathan Swift.   ViBoPo
Forgetting the black seasons of a race.   The Crimson Cherry Tree.   Henry
  Treece.   WaP
Forgive and bless all men like the holy light.   An Old Woman.   Edith
  Sitwell.   CoBMV; MoPo
Forgive, and make me whole.   A Little Song.   Robert Grosseteste.   ISi
"Forgive, but ah, never forget."   The Song of the Flags.   Silas Weir
  Mitchell.   PAH
...Forgive, forgive/My cigarettes, I swallowed smoke alive.   He Records a
  Little Song for a Smoking Girl.   James Whitehead.   GP
Forgive, forgive, we pray!   They've Crucified Our Lord.   Alice Mortenson.
  BePJ
Forgive him for his Neolithic sins.   Prayer for the Age.   Myron H.
  Broomell.   TrPWD
Forgive, if I have tarried long.   Troubadour Song.   Bernard of Ventadour
  EnLi 1-2
Forgive it, Kitty,/'Tis man's way.   Man's Way.   Leonard Alfred George
  Strong.   HBMV
"Forgive me, Caesar, I want to come home."   Ovid.   Richard Pevear.
  AMV-81
Forgive me, father,/as I have forgiven you/my sins.   Epitaph.   David
  Ignatow.   CAPP
Forgive me, Lord, tomorrow as today.   Finale.   James Picot.   BoAV
Forgive me, Mother, for the guilt of song.   The Slacker Apologizes.   Peter
  Viereck.   MiAP
Forgive me my tresspasses.   Letter to My Mother.   Dom Moraes.   NoAm
Forgive me that I am so young.   To One Older.   Marion M. Boyd.
  HBMV
Forgive me this or that, or Hell or Heaven.   A Prospect of Death.   Andrew
  Young.   DTC
Forgive me those whom I mistook/For you–alas, they were too many.   Broad
  Gold.   Anna Akhmatova.   LiTW
Forgive my vain repentances,/And bid me sin no more.   Times without
  Number Have I Pray'd.   Charles Wesley.   OxBoCh
Forgive, O Lord, forgive our Trespasses.   And Forgive Us Our Trespasses.
  Aphra Behn.   EBEV
Forgive our memory stain! e'er this might of love/Hath meekly found its room,
  so called immortality   Spirituality.   Samuel Greenberg.   LiTA
Forgive the anguish of the turning wheel!   Faith.   Ada Cambridge.   PoAu
  1-2
Forgive the bells their jingle.   The Jester's Plea.   Frederick Locker-Lampson.
  CenHV
Forgive the guilt, that grew in youth's vain ways.   The Sins of Youth.
  Thomas, Lord Vaux.   ACP
Forgive the past, and strive to mend.   Darby and Joan.   St. John
  Honeywood.   AA
Forgive the world's fond idolatries.   If I Have Lifted up Mine Eyes to
  Admire.   Amos N. Wilder.   TrPWD
Forgive Them–Even as Myself–/Or else–forgive not me–   'Tis true–they shut
  me in the cold.   Emily Dickinson.   SBG
"Forgive them, for they know not what they do!"   Easter Eve.   James
  Branch Cabell.   HBMV
Forgive these nigguhs that know not what they do.   Riot.   Gwendolyn
  Brooks.   BP; BPo; CAPP; PoBA; TAP
Forgive us all that we have done.   Forgive.   Lalia Mitchell Thornton.
  BePJ
Forgive, when I remember.   Roses in December.   G. Anketall "Woodbine
  Willie" Studdert-Kennedy.   BLPA
Forgive your son!   Ecce Puer.   James Joyce.   BIrV; EBEV; NAs; NoAm;
  PoPl; TrCP
Forgo me now, come to me soon.   Dulcina.   Sir Walter Ralegh.   ALV
Forgot it, I forgot it, the name "man."   Space-Wanderer's Homecoming.
  Peter Viereck.   AMV-80
Forgot to close my hungry eyes/After giving them this wasted passion.
  Someone Could Certainly Be Found.   F. R. Scott.   CaP
Forgotten.   Epitaph for John Camden Hotten.   G. A. Sala.   DBV
Forgotten, dead, disconsolate.   A Memento for Mortality.   William Basse.
  FaBoCh; LoGBV
Forgotten flowers on the empty grate.   Intempestiva.   Henry Longan Stuart.
  CAW
Forgotten they live, and forgotten die.   Oxford Canal.   James Elroy Flecker.
  OxBTC
Forgotten tides.   Haiku: "Seaweed..."   Kito.   FAZ
Forlorn suburbs, but with golden names!   Childhood.   Donald Justice.
  LCAP
Forlorn the sea's forsaken bride/Awaits the end that shall betide.   A Cinque
  Port.   John Davidson.   BrPo; PoPle; VLP
The form of one he hates no longer now,/Alas! even in dreams, shall he espy.
  Sonnets to Karl Theodor German.   August von Platen.   PeHV

Form that is energy from these seas risen,/Identified. Resumed in God. The Place at Alert Bay. Muriel Rukeyser. PoA

Formed in each believing heart. For Christmas-Day. Charles Wesley. CEP

The former and the latter rain,/On this, my seed. The Husbandman. Frances Beatrice Taylor. CaP

The former, it were not so great a curse/To read on the steel-mirror of her smile. Modern Love, VII. George Meredith. NOBV; VLP

Formerly cruel, but now immensely sweet. Sonnet VII: "We see each living thing finally die." Louise Labe. BoWoP

...Formic acid to bite with as its unregarded jaws grow. Reclaimed Area. Jon Silkin. NoAm

The formic wine within the purple grail. The Lesson. Larry Rubin. GoYe

Forming out of all that darkness, that huge disorder. At the Sign-Painter's. Jared Carter. FYAP

Formless ice on a formless plain/that was and is and comes again. Summer. Conrad Aiken. NoAm

Forms, flames, and the flakes of flames. Nomad Exquisite. Wallace Stevens. AtBAP

The forms that swim and the shapes that creep/Under the waters of sleep? The Marshes of Glynn. Sidney Lanier. AnFE; LiTA

Formulae/the one for place He accepts the circle, speech and so. Anne-Marie Albiach. BoWoP

Forsake it not, it is Thine own,/Though weak, yet longing to believe. The Doubter's Prayer. Anne Bronte. WGRP

Forsaken He went down, and was afraid. The Crucifixion. Alice Meynell. OxBoCh

Forsooth, though I men's master be,/Theirs is the teaching mind! God's Education. Thomas Hardy. MoRP

Forth, and make firm a highway for the King! Battle-Song of Failure. Amelia Josephine Burr. HBMV

Forth came the red bull/And licked them all. Riddle: "Four and twenty white bulls." *Anonymous.* GBP

...Forth they wandered,/John-a-dreams and Low-lie-down. Ballad of Low-Lie-Down. Madison Cawein. HBV 1-2

Fortoun is fikkill, quhen scho beginnis and steiris. Cresseid's Complaint against Fortune. Robert Henryson. MeEL

The fortresses and bastions of our fears. I Have Approached. Alan Paton. PeSA

Fortune, adieu! Love and Fortune. Fulke, Lord Brooke Greville. OBSC

Fortune can here claim nothing truly great,/But that this princely creature is her seat. Caelica, LXXXI. Fulke, Lord Brooke Greville. FCP

Fortune have cast on thee so her chaunce/That alwaies thow must stand in variaunce... A Letter Sent by the Mayor.....(excerpt). *Anonymous.* NOBI

Fortune in battle, glory and fame/And an earthly kingdom, through the Holy Cross. Elene. Cynewulf. AnOE

Fortune is God—all you endure and do/Depends on circumstance as much as you. Circumstance. Percy Bysshe Shelley. CBEP

Fortuned have his lady for to win. Balade Simple: "Fairest of stars." John Lydgate. GBL

Forty cents a pound in a paper sack. Seven Cent Cotton and Forty Cent Meat. *Anonymous.* FSW

Forty days of pardon God grant him. Ave Maris Stella. *Anonymous.* CTC

44 years to do. So That Even a Lover. Louis Zukofsky. CoPo

Forty miles from farms. Hitch Haiku. Gary Snyder. LCAP

Forty years younger/and/twenty years freer. State Prison 5:00 p.m. Thomas G. Nickens. LFAC

Forward! and not back;/And lend a hand. Lend a Hand. Edward Everett Hale. TreFS

Forward, clutching the twitching/shape, humming...humming... Knockmany. Richard Ryan. CIP

Forward-like, but however, and like favourable heaven heard these. The Bugler's First Communion. Gerard Manley Hopkins. NoAm; OAEP; PeHV

An' forward tho' I canna see,/I guess an' fear! To a Mouse. Robert Burns. AnEnPo; AnFE; ATP; BiP; BSV; DiPo; EiCP; EnL; FaFP; FF; FM; GoTS; GTBS; HAP; HBV 1-2; HBVY; HeIP; InPS; LAuP; LoBV; MCCG; NOEC; NoP; OAEL 1-2; OAEP; OBEC; OxBS; PAI; PoLf; PPP; PrIm; SeCeV; TEP; TreFS; TrGrPo; WHA

Forward Thy church throughout the coming years/Wide as the world and broad as humankind. Eternal God Whose Searching Eye Doth Scan. Edwin McNeill Poteat. TrPWD

Forwards in reverse, always holding their caps. Glasgow Schoolboys, Running Backwards. Douglas Dunn. OxBC

The fossil virgin of the skies/waxes and wanes. Lunar Baedeker. Mina Loy. VGW

The foul hyena's prey. The African Chief. William Cullen Bryant. AnNE; BLPA; PaPo; TreFS

...Found/A word for, while I gathered sight and sound. The Brook. Edward ("Edward Eastaway") Thomas. MoVE; SeCeV

Found comfort in the moving green of trees. The Comfort of the Trees. Richard Watson Gilder. PAH

Found her forgetting/which was her or which was him. All One. Millen Brand. GP

Found him with crabs upon his face. The Newcomer's Wife. Thomas Hardy. BoLoP; OxBTC

Found justice, truth, and human liberty! Columbus. Florence Earle Coates. MC

Found that it contained that very new/Verse form, the clerihew. Clerihew: "Edmund Clerihew Bentley." William Jay Smith. PV

Found truest, best, immaculate. Mulier Amicta Sole. Fray Angelico Chavez. ISi

Found us at tears and wept for company. Sonnets. Frederick Goddard Tuckerman. AP

The Foundation Stone/did not make its own back tremble/nor did it falter. The Drunkeness of Pain. Aliza Shenhar. VWA

Founded in righteousness and peace and love/to bring forth fruits joy and eternal bliss. Paradise Lost. John Milton. FaBoPV

The founder thou; these are thy race! Experience. Ralph Waldo Emerson. AnNE; FPL; LiTA; PoEL 1-5; TAP

A fount of strength to brim earth's loving-cup. The Vintage. Belle Cooper. GoBC

The fountain is slowed down, as if controlled/by your calm hands. About This Course. David Shapiro. PoA

Fountain of light, the glory of a star. The Sun Men Call It. John Hall Wheelock. NePoAm-2

The fountain tosses pallid spray/Far in the sorrowful, silent sky. Irradiations. John Gould Fletcher. AnFE; APA; CoAnAm

The fountain unbroken. Truth. George William Russell. AnIL; GTBS; MoBrPo

The fountains of the boiling stars, the/flowers on the foreland, the ever-/returning roses of dawn. Apology for Bad Dreams. Robinson Jeffers. AmP; AP; CoBMV; LiTA; MoAB; MoAmPo; NOBA; OxBA; SeCeV

Four corners round about. Riddle: "Black within and red without." *Anonymous.* GBP; OxNR

A four foot box, a foot for every year. Mid-Term Break. Seamus Heaney. NCSH; NoP

A four-footed friar in orders of gray! Coyote. Bret (Francis Bret Harte) Harte. BPAW

Four hundred and fifty years ago/He wrote that Testament. In Paris. Thomas Macdonagh. OnYI

Four kisses on his cheek! Victorian Song. John Farrar. GoYe

Four sparks of phosphor shone like flame. Femme et Chatte. Paul Verlaine. AWP; OBVE

4 walls/& 3 settees. On a School-Teacher. *Anonymous.* GLGT

The Four Winds dry their wooden shoes. Fishing Boats in Martigues. Roy Campbell. FaBoEE; FaBoPP; OBSP; PeSA

Fourfooted, tiptoe. The Fallow Deer at the Lonely House. Thomas Hardy. AWP; BoAnP; CH; CMoP; InPo; MoVE; OBSP

Fourteen miles to the Cumberland Gap. Cumberland Gap. *Anonymous.* AmFN; FSW

Fourth, I am eaten. Riddle: "First I am frosted." Mary Austin. TiPo

Fourth of July—Hurrah! Hooray! Fourth of July. Rachel Field. SiSoSe

The fox drags its wounded belly. January. R. S. Thomas. ELU

The fox is after dinner, too. The Sycophantic Fox and the Gullible Raven. Guy Wetmore Carryl. AA; AnAmPo; BLPA; CenHV; FaFP; FiBHP; HBV 1-2; InMe; NLV; OBCA; TreFT

Foxes round churchyards bare/Gnawing the guts of men. The End of Clonmacnois. Frank O'Connor. CIP

The Foxglove by the garden gate/Looked down and smiled on Four and Eight. Four and Eight. ffrida Wolfe. BiCB; SiSoSe

...Foxheads,/sharp-nosed,/amber-eyed,/dreaming her dreams. A Life. Chana Bloch. MAYP

Foxy's at the back door,/Picking a marrow bone. Put Your Finger in Foxy's Hole. *Anonymous.* OxNR

Fractures well cur'd make us more/strong. Repentance. George Herbert. OAEP

Frae earth mak you immortal images. The Real Muse. Tom Scott. PoA

Frae the burst craters o the hert. Ye Spier Me. Sydney Goodsir Smith. AtBAP; BSV

Fragile, insolent, absolute. The Altars in the Street. Denise Levertov. CAPP

Fragments of bliss & roses/decorating your fists. Praxis. Sharon Thesen. CaPN

Fragments of cloudlets break/into light rain. Sunset. Mafika Pascal Gwala. WhB

Fragments of idea/lost forever/in the empty/empties./Amen. Principally. Tom Veitch. ANYP

Fragments of suns and chains sank/in the Gaza sea. Samson Rends His Clothes. Anadad Eldan. VWA

The fragrance of the autumn warmest,/Closest and strongest.   On the Road Home.   Wallace Stevens.   NU

Fragrant as the rose at dawn in spring etc.   My Regrets.   Michael André.   APU

The fragrant Work with Diligence proceeds.   The Aeneid.   Virgil (Publius Vergilius Maro).   OBVE

Frail as the Cord, and brittle as the Urn.   Power.   Matthew Prior.   LoBV

The frail/boat/is to/reach/the three/holy/mountains.   Sky links cloud waves.   Li Ch'ing-chao.   BoWoP

The frail body must wait till dusk/To be lowered/In the hot and sandy earth.   At the Funeral of Great-Aunt Mary.   Robert Bly.   Str

The frail duration of a flower.   The Wild Honey Suckle.   Philip Freneau.   AmLP; AP; BLPL; OxBA; TAP

Frail, on frail rafts, across wide-wallowing waves,/Shapes here and there of child and mother pass.   John Webster.   Algernon Charles Swinburne.   InvP

Frail stairs the careless wind blows through.   The Spider.   Loren C. Eiseley.   SUW

Frail violets, freshly born.   Lament.   Laurence Binyon.   MoVE

Frailest and bravest! the Bay State still/Counts with her worthies John Underhill.   John Underhill.   John Greenleaf Whittier.   PAH

The frailest of the unsubstantial forms/That leave the shores that are for those that seem!   Mimma Bella.   Eugene Lee-Hamilton.   HBV 1-2

Fram the schoure of pinis sure/Thou sild him her and thare! Amen.   Swet Jesus.   Michael of Kildare.   NOBI

The frame defines oblivion: against night/a septet of reflections holds the scene.   Pure Nails Brightly Flashing.   Stephane Mallarme.   LiTW

Framed in the midnight thicket of your hair.   Vieux Carre.   Walter Adolphe Roberts.   PoNe

Framing her like the borders of a valentine!   A New Orleans Balcony–1880.   Dorothy Haight.   CAW

Frangible, a honeycomb of pores.   Earthly Love.   Joseph Bennett.   NePA

Frankincense, flowers, upon touching her.   In Panelled Rooms.   Ruth Herschberger.   LiTA

Frantic with their reasons to live?   Arsenic.   Howard Moss.   CoAP; NYBP

Frayed reconciliation between truth and lie.   Eden Revisited.   Vassar Miller.   FAZ; GP

The frayed rope and the boot tht slips on the rocks.   Buachaille Etive Mor and Buachaille Etive Beag.   Naomi Mitchison.   PoSH

...A freak tide raised/The feathered stick she took to lure me home.   Trouvaille.   Richard Murphy.   CIP; IPY

The freaks of the cosmic circus are men.   Carrousel Tune.   Tennessee Williams.   NLV; OBAL

...Fredome mar to pryss/Than all the gold in warld that is.   The Bruce.   John Barbour.   ViBoPo

A free and frank young Yankee maiden.   An American Girl.   Brander Matthews.   AA

A free and gallant Congo–black blossom from black seed!   Dawn in the Heart of Africa.   Patrice Emery Lumumba.   PBA; TTY

Free, black & forty-one.   Dream Song.   John Berryman.   CoAP

Free, equal, and fraternally,/A seat for three.   A Seat for Three: Written on a Settle.   Walter Crane.   OBVV

Free grace an' dyin' love,/To ring dem charmin' bells.   Mary an' Martha Jes' Gone 'Long.   Anonymous.   BoAN 1-2

Free hearth for thee, and honest fame.'   The Sea-Watcher.   Aubrey Thomas De Vere.   IrPN

The free man's chosen land.   Song of Liberty (excerpt).   Louise Ayres Garnett.   PGD

Free men set themselves free.   The Slave.   James Oppenheim.   TrJP

Free through whom?/Free through Kane.   Prayer of the Fishing Net.   Anonymous.   WTO

Free trade, or sable brothers free?/Oh, will we choose the latter!   Shop and Freedom.   Anonymous.   PAH

Freed by your thrall.   The One Lost.   Isaac Rosenberg.   MoBrPo

Freed some, but Martin Luther freed them all.   The Pope from Penance Purgatorial.   George Buchanan.   OBVE

Freedom and Honor and sweet Loving-kind-/ness.   To the United States of America.   Robert Bridges.   HBV 1-2; PAH

Freedom in mah soul.   Freedom in Mah Soul.   David Wadsworth Cannon, Jr..   PoNe

Freedom's crusaders/Who war against war.   The New Crusade.   Katharine Lee Bates.   MC

Freedom's song, freedom's song.   World Youth Song.   Anonymous.   FSW

Freedom that flows in form and still is free.   Seagulls.   Robert Francis.   RFM

Freedom through Kane, the life-giving one!   O Kane, O Lono of the Blue Sea.   Anonymous.   WTO

Freedom to find to find to find/That nakedness.   Song: "The world is full of loss."   Muriel Rukeyser.   MiAP

Freedom to worship God.   The Landing of the Pilgrim Fathers.   Felicia Dorothea Hemans.   BeLS; BLPA; FaBoBe; FaBV; FaFP; FaPo; GN;

GoTF; HBV 1-2; HBVY; MC; OHIP; PAH; PAL; PaPo; PGD; SBG; TreF; WBLP

Freedom,/wings!   Bilogy Lesson.   John D. Engle, Jr.   AMV-80

Freeze into an attitude/Recalling the dead.   Picture of a Nativity.   Geoffrey Hill.   NoAm; OxBC

Freezing wet or hot humid black/in a dragon's belly.   Modern Architecture.   Norman Nathan.   AMV-81

The French probably have/an expression for it.   The Lift.   Raymond Souster.   PoL

A Frenchman, a Spaniard, a Yankee!/Derry down, down, hey derry down.   A New Ballad.   Anonymous.   PAH

The Frenchmen strolling and taking it easy/and the sun/burning.   Guadalupe, W.I.   Nicolas Guillen.   TTY

The frenzied kisses that you gave and got.   Ad Lesbiam.   Niall Sheridan.   OxBI

The frenzy of hands the frenzy/of feet of statues.   They Came This Evening.   Leon Damas.   TTY

La Frere Lubin is not the man!   Ballade of a Friar.   Andrew Lang.   HBV 1-2

Fresh and fragrant little nightful.   Darling, If You Only Knew.   Edward Newman Horn.   ErPo

Fresh as God's latest word!   As Rivers of Water in a Dry Place.   Anna Bunston de Bary.   HBMV

Fresh as the lips love's earliest sighs enthrall.   Toledo.   Antonio Gomez Restrepo.   CAW

Fresh as the new flowers in the graveyard.   Family Reunion.   Jim Wayne Miller.   Str

...Fresh as this particular/flood of burn breaking across us now/from the sun.   Easter Morning.   Archie Randolph Ammons.   HaCAP; NoP

Fresh beads upon the rosary of a saint!   Post-Meridian.   Wendell Phillips Garrison.   AA

Fresh branches of the trees surviving winter.   Above the Rocking Heads of the Mothers.   Nelly Sachs.   PBWP

Fresh, changeful, constant,/Upward, like thee!   The Fountain.   James Russell Lowell.   OBCA

Fresh Codfish, Fine Codfish!'   Mrs. Busk.   Osbert Sitwell.   OxBTC

Fresh from the beauty and the bliss/Of English liberty?   Incident at Bruges.   William Wordsworth.   OBTV

A fresh roost for the Holy Ghost.   First Confession.   X. J. Kennedy.   ConAP; NCSH; NePoEA-2; NIP; PPP

Fresh, spicie mornings; and eternal beams/These are his due.   Silex Scintillans.   Henry Vaughan.   AnAnS 1

Freshly bourgeons every bough.   Spring.   Thomas Stanley.   AWP

Freshly escaped from the drygoods factory/across the bay   On the Beach.   Pati Hill.   FAZ

The freshly fallen snow.   Willows in the Snow.   Tsuru.   SUS

The friar he walked on the street,/And shaking his lugs like a well-washen/ sheep.   The Friar in the Well (B version).   Anonymous.   ESPB

Friar Lubin cannot do it.   Friar Lubin.   Clément Marot.   AWP; DBV

Friend and brother to every other man.   Dark Testament.   Pauli Murray.   AmNP; BlSi

Friend, listen: the God whom I love is inside.   The Clay Jug.   Anonymous.   NU

Friend, newly found, accept my full heart's thanks.   Accept My Full Heart's Thanks.   Ella Wheeler Wilcox.   PoToHe

Friend of the golden-haired Dawn, friend of the gods/of the hearth?   Work.   Alexander Pushkin.   AWP

Friend, partake not of the flesh of the/kid, drink not the wine which is/white.   Five Arabic Verses in Praise of Wine.   Anonymous.   TrJP

Friend to no one, continual crossing/back and forth of the sea.   Halfbreed Chronicles: Isamu.   Wendy Rose.   TWSS

The friend we trust, the fair we love,/And we desire no more.   A Poet's Grace.   Robert Burns.   TrPWD

A friend who is not firm as a great rock/Is of no profit and idly bears the name.   A bright moon illumines the night-prospect.   Anonymous.   BoWoP

Friend, why don't you come?   Song: "Since the night is dark."   Anonymous.   BoWoP

Friend, yourself now say a last Amen.   To a Friend Going on a Journey.   Mahammed A. Hassan.   WTO

Friended thus, I have let nothing pass.   Monody to the Sound of Zithers.   Kay Boyle.   PoA

The Friendly Cow, all red and white,/Will fill her up again.   The Milk Jug.   Oliver Herford.   HBMV; HBVY

The friendly thief sea wealthy with the drowned.   Night's Fall.   W. S. Graham.   NeBP

A friendly, wistful name and airy–/Mary.   Gentle Name.   Selma Robinson.   BiCB; MoShBr

Friends fail and Love grow cold.   Song Set by John Farmer: "Take Time while Time doth last."   Anonymous.   OBSC

Friendship in Him gain'd an Ubiquity.   To the Memory of the Learned and Reverend, Mr. Jonathan Mitchell...   Francis Drake.   SCAP

"Friendship is Love without his wings!" Friendship Is Love without His Wings. George Gordon, Lord Byron. GoTF; TreFT

Friendship takes time to overcome. If Along the Highroad. *Anonymous.* LiTW

Frighted the reign of Chaos and old Night. Paradise Lost. John Milton. TrGrPo

(Frightened? No. Happy? Yes.)/Out into sunlight. The Trial. W. H. Auden. NePA

The fringes of the sunsets and the hills. The Word. Richard Realf. AA; AmLP

Frisbee and I performed the flying change. Flying Changes. Mary Wood. PH

Frisco hilly tincan evening sitdown vision. Sunflower Sutra. Allen Ginsberg. CoAP; HaCAP; InPS; MAT; NeAP; NOBA

The frolic architecture of the snow. The Snow-Storm. Ralph Waldo Emerson AA; AnNE; AP; BLPL; DiPo; FaBoBe; GN; GoTF; LaNeLa; LiTA; MAmP; NePA; NOBA; OxBA; PoEL 1-5; PoLf; Prf; TreFT; UnPo; WiR

From a branch nothing cried from ever in my life. How Many Nights. Galway Kinnell. CAPP; MAT; NaP

From a castaway ox-bone they carve her more splendid than/stone. Ox-Bone Madonna. James J. Galvin. ISi

From a cheap and chippy chopper on a big black block! To Sit in Solemn Silence. Sir William Schwenck Gilbert. FiBHP

From a grave or a bed, from a grave or a bed. Fourth Song the Night Nurse Sang. Robert Duncan. VGW

...From a million pinholes/the giant steel ant machine/pours forth galaxies. View from the Planetarium. David Barker. GP

From a place that will not mend for you? Winter Evening Poem. Laura Jensen. LCAP

From a shining night if 'tis our delight in the season of the year. A Shining Night; or, Dick Daring, the Poacher. *Anonymous.* CoMu

From a tray marked IN to another marked OUT. Endurance Test. Dacre Balsdon. DBV; FiBHP

From a world more full of weeping than he can understand. The Stolen Child. William Butler Yeats. CMoP; EnLi 1-2; NoP; OnYI; OxBI; WSC

From a world not his. That Man in Manhattan. Shannon Keith Kelley. AMV-80

From above and below/As if before/Being. A Grain of Moonlight. Asya (Asya Gray). VWA

From age to age, the only Lord. Come, All Ye People. George R. Seltzer. AH

From all his ill-got honors flung,/Turned to that dirt from whence he sprung. A Satirical Elegy on the Death of a Late Famous General. Jonathan Swift. CABA; ExPo; FF; HoPM; NIP; NLV; NoP; OBSV; PoEL 1-5; SeCeV

From all I was–what may The God not do? Epitaphs of the War, 1914-18. Rudyard Kipling. BrPo

From all mishap now hardily/This end to make. "To make an end of all this strife." Sir Thomas Wyatt. FCP

From all that fondles life and feed the/heart. On a Ferry Boat. Richard Burton. AA

From all the Just on earth, and all the Blest above. Sonnet to William Wilberforce, Esq. William Cowper. CEP; OAEP

From alle wymmen mi love is lent/Ant lyht on Alysoun. Bytuene Mersh and Averil. *Anonymous.* ViBoPo

From amongst the fifty/Camels on the slopes? The White, Orphaned Camel Kid... *Anonymous.* WTO

From andrew hill's steel fingers/guaran/teed to set us back on our souls again Energy for a New Thang. Ernie Mkalimoto. NBP

From beatings of hearts, and reachings of hands. The Sea-Maiden. J. W. De Forest. EtS

From beauty to the other beauty, peace, the night splendor. Gale in April. Robinson Jeffers. MoAB; MoAmPo

From being trampled to death by stampeding beasts. Buffalo. Louis Daniel Brodsky. AMV-80

From blood-drenched shore to shore! The Hymn of Hate. Joseph Dana Miller. PGD

From both I learn. Just an Old Man. Mary Goose. STE

From brawling, from desimeling/And from dicing. Snatches: "If that a yong man wold atain." *Anonymous.* OxBM

From Brooklyn, over the Brooklyn Bridge, on this fine/morning,/please come flying. Invitation to Miss Marianne Moore. Elizabeth Bishop. MoVE

From burning my city again. Limerick: "Said Nero to one of his train." *Anonymous.* LiBL

From can–to can–to can. Repast. Gertrude Tiemer-Wille. GoYe

...From Chatterton/to the bitter & present scene. Dream Songs. John Berryman. TAP

From chin to toe smooth as a pebble. Boy at a Certain Age. Robert Francis. DFF

From cluttered void God plucks my mind sweat-sodden/Into His hush all of a gracious sudden. Fulfillment. Vassar Miller. NePoEA-2

From curfew time to the next prime. Saint Francis and Saint Benedight. *Anonymous.* EaLo

From dawn to night unquenched their light–/As are my thoughts of you. Star Song. Robert Underwood Johnson. HBV 1-2

From day to night, from night to day. Rooks. Charles Hamilton Sorley. MoBrPo

From dead/on the side/of the road. Waking on a Greyhound. Gordon Henry. STE

From Death to Life, thou might'st him yet recover. Idea. Michael Drayton. FaBoEn; GTBS; HAP; HBV 1-2; PoEL 1-5; PPoe; TrGrPo

From drama of pleasures inconstant/To saintly sins of delight. She Was All That You Loved. Halldor Laxness. LiTW; PoPl

...From each impassive dream,/Repentantly the sleepers come. Chanticleer. Margaret Irvin. PoAu 1-2

From early Homer to the precious here. Sickle Pears (For Glidden Parker). Owen Dodson. AmNP

From Earth all came, to Earth must all return;/Frail as the Cord, and brittle as the Urn. Solomon on the Vanity of the World. Matthew Prior. NOEC; PoEL 1-5

From earth arose the flaming Name/From floral whorls from spectral horns/ On the high hour of death Raziel. Yvan Goll. VWA

From East to West ran one white shiver,/And waxen strong their song was Day. Dawn-Angels. Agnes Mary Frances (Mme Emile Duclaux) Robinson. HBV 1-2

From everlasting night to everlasting noon. Epitaphs on Two Piping-Bullfinches of Lady Ossory's. Horace Walpole. FaBoEE

From every cloud, in mighty streams, to refresh it! A Reply to Zaidun's Complaint... Wallada. PBWP

From every note devotion springs,/Rapture and harmony and love/O'er spread the list'ning choir. The Adventurous Muse. Isaac Watts. NOEC

From farther than the market wagon– I Saw a Delicate Flower Had Grown up 2 Feet High. Henry David Thoreau. MAmP

From flying straight to Your Heart Whose Rays conduct me to/the SONG! Morning Light Song. Philip Lamantia. NeAP

From Fools and Knaves, in our Parliament free,/Libera nos, Domine! A Free Parliament Litany. *Anonymous.* OxBoLi

From fury into weary/Surrendering of feeling. Fox. Clifford Dyment. HaMV; OBSP

From generation to generation/Grant us, O Lord, thy grace and salvation! St. Patrick's Hymn before Tara. James Clarence Mangan. EnRP; GoBC

From God's side even on such a simple thing? To a Daisy. Alice Meynell. MoBrPo; WGRP

From grave to grave. How I came to be a graduate student. Wendy Rose. STE

From green and blue things and arguments that cannot be/proven. Canal Bank Walk. Patrick Kavanagh. CIP; CMoP; FaBoTw; IPY; MoBrPo; NoAm; NOBI

"From grief and groan, to a golden throne, beside the King/of Heaven." Lenore. Edgar Allan Poe. AA; AnFE; AP; APA; CoAnAm; LiTA; TreFS; WHA

From hard hearts huge tears are wrung. The Survivor. R. S. Thomas. FaBoTw

From Heav'n on Earth, to Heav'n in Heav'n ascend,/Where our felicities can know no/End. Earth Felicities, Heavens Allowances. A Blank Poem. Richard Steere. SCAP

From heaven, O spirit, come! complete/My heart, with Christ's perfection sweet! The New Heart. *Anonymous.* WGRP

From her fountain divine, 'tis sufficient for me. This Life Is All Chequer'd with Pleasures and Woes. Thomas Moore. ELP

From her own lov'd island of sorrow. She Is Far from the Land. Thomas Moore. AnIL; EnRP; HBV 1-2; NOBI; OBNC

From here, the summit of Suilven,/my net returns glittering. Ascent. Donald G. Saunders. PoSH

From here to yonder, to become silent emptiness at last. Cubist Portrait. Marjorie Allen Seiffert. PoA

From highest heavens along he's come/To dy for mans Redemption. For Innocents Day. Luke Wadding. NOBI

From him tho Aged, is not whimsey Pated,/Or prone to Dote, nor Superanuated. To His Excellency Joseph Dudley Eqr Gover: &c. John Saffin. SCAP

From His beard, O joy, O wonders!/Falls a shower of little mice. The House of God. A. D. Hope. OxBC

From his/hands, it/is in/the stone. Rock Painting. Carroll Arnett. VoR

From His Highness, and the Devil,/Libera nos, etc. The Litany. Charles Cotton. OBSV

From his own gates? Hippolytus. Euripides. AWP

From his perfect darkness a voice says, I have not. Why Hast Thou Forsaken Me? Chad Walsh. TrCP

From Hull and Halifax and Hell,/Good Lord, deliver me. The Dalesman's Litany. *Anonymous.* OBET

From it ne'er let me remove/Nor let it remove from me. Batte's Song. Michael Drayton. LoBV

From its fair face, shall bid our spirits fly. To My Brothers. John Keats. EnLi 1-2; NAs; TEP

From joy I part, still living in annoy. A Farewell. Sir Philip Sidney. EIL; EnLi 1-2; NOBE; OBSC; SiPS

From lamp of lonely toll-gate streamed athwart the night. Guilt and Sorrow. William Wordsworth. FaBoPP

From Life, the gem/He died for. So Death–I live! Divine Poems. Jose Garcia Villa. MoRP

From light, so with their substance he awaits the night. Nightflight and Sunrise. Geoffrey Dutton. BoAV

From little knowledge where great sorrows brood. A Twilight in Middle March. Francis Ledwidge. BIrV; OnYI; OxBI; WHA

From loneliest regions at all hours,/Unsought-for, come. Epitaph. Aubrey Thomas De Vere. OBVV

From long ago it has been thus. Farming. Anonymous. LiTW

From Lord to Lackey, and at last to all. Beware Fair Maide. Anonymous. OBS

From loving with a single will. Letter I. Randall Swingler. WaP

From manuscripts like winding-sheets/Her risen praises steal! Our Lady of the Libraries. Sister Mary Ignatius. ISi

From maple sweetness, maple wonder! Maple Feast. Frances Frost. SiSoSe

From mathematics further off/Than from Eternity. If I Could Tell How Glad I Was. Emily Dickinson. MAmP

From matrimony free. Old Bachelor. Anonymous. ABF

From men and from the angel-host/Be praise and glory evermore. The Old Hundredth. William Kethe. FaPoR

From millions whose hands can turn this rock into children. Laurentian Shield. F. R. Scott. NOBC; OBCV

From Moaning Hill towards the mead–/The Mead of Memories. The Dead Quire. Thomas Hardy. OAEP

From mourning, there is no relief. Elegy for the Wife of a Friend. Yu Hsuan-chi. BoWoP

From my family I have learned the secrets/of never having a home. Heritage. Linda Hogan. TWSS

From my feet The Maximus Poems. Charles Olson. CAPP; CMoP; NeAP; NMP; PoM; VGW

From my kennel white moon, white master/in the night. Dog. Ingrid Jonker. PBWP

From my mind a space is taken away. Death of a Bird. Jon Silkin. BoAnP; NePoEA

From New South Wales to Paddington the shortest way's the/High. Lines on a Mysterious Occurrence. Alfred Denis Godley. CenHV

From noisy anger to the sullen spleen. The Fan. John Gay. ViBoPo

From north alabama ridges/over bridges sherman didnt burn. First Monday Scottsboro Alabama. Tom Weatherly. PoBA

From nothing human let us hold apart! Nihil Humani Alienum. Titus Munson Coan. AA

From now on, mama, I said I'm gonna let you go From Now On. Barefoot Bill. BluL

From nowhere to nowhere across/our faces that lonely stunned look. Bushed. Charles Lillard. NOBC

From one of the white throats which it hid among? Vision by Sweetwater. John Crowe Ransom. AP; CMoP; CoBMV; FaBoMo; MoAB; NOBA; OxBA

From our contemporary Dr.—, of —. An Ecclesiastical Chronicle (excerpt). John Heath-Stubbs. NOBL

From our old Vilna streets/They drive us to Berlin. A Cartload of Shoes. Abraham Sutzkever. VWA

From our snug fire-side this Christmas-tide/We'll keep old Winter out. Old Winter. Thomas Noel. GN; HBV 1-2

...From our tree/dropped, that she not wither,/autumn in our terrible breath. An Abortion. Frank O'Hara. TAP

From out his secret altar touched with hal-/lowed fire. On the Morning of Christ's Nativity. John Milton. AnFE; CoBE

From out its chaliced pearl the Angel came/To strengthen Him. Gethsemane. Annette von Droste-Hulshoff. CAW

From out my reins,/those small, cold hands. She Contrasts with Herself Hippolyta. Hilda ("H. D.") Doolittle. SBG

From out my weary prison, my life of woes so mean! Prayer to Santa Maria Del Vade. Juan, Archpriest of Hita, Ruiz. CAW

From out the dreadful stones it dies away. The Melancholy Year. Trumbull Stickney. NCEP

From out the Southland in the old year's noon. The Vision of Lazarus (excerpt). Fenton Johnson. BANP

From out your bloom of light the Maker's beauty shines. Spring-Joy Praising God. Praise of the Sun. C Greiffenberg. WPOW

From Oxford comes the throng and hum of bells/Breakin the. . . . air of spring. Oxford Bells. Gerard Manley Hopkins. FaBoPP

From perfect day to perfect night/And wonder what they mean. Tom Pringle. Louis Simpson. NePoAm-2

From present griefs, and future unknown harms,/And baby sleeps. Baby Sleeps. Samuel Hinds. HBV 1-2

From purple rhetoric of evening skies. Nearing Again the Legendary Isle. C. Day-Lewis. CoBMV; FaBoTw; LiTB; MoAB; MoBrPo

From Pyrrha's pebbles or old Adam's seed. A Real Woman. John Keats. LiTL

From real griefs, from factious elves,/Will speedily relieve ye. Maryland Resolves. Anonymous. PAH

From Saskatoon, Saskatchewan, to Walla Walla, Wash. Etude Geographique. Stoddard King. AmFN; BPAW

From scabby eyes,scales from/the mind and husbands from wives. The Winds. William Carlos Williams. AnAmPo

From sea to sea drifting,/drops of bright ruby. From My Lai the Thunder Went West. Richard Ryan. CIP

From silent life I'd steal into my grave. The Choice. Nahum Tate. OBSP

From simplest nest may soar the sweetest song. The Skylark's Nest. R. H. Long. PoAu 1-2

From sky to sky they rake/our lives with pins of light Another Night with Telescope. Leonard Cohen. PeCV

From snow that melted only yesterday Spring Pools. Robert Frost. AmPP; DiPo; MoAB

From so many different and interesting/points of view Books. William Baer. AMV-81

From so much sorrow–of whom I am one. Deem Not. George Santayana. AnEnPo; TrGrPo

From sopranino to contrabass. Vow. John Updike. NYBP

From south to north/For this fresh air and fragrant wine. Garden at Heidelberg. Walter Savage Landor. OBTV

From star to star, until I see his face. The Last Good-By. Louise Chandler Moulton. AA

From stoker's flame to gunner's aim/The race that rules the wave! Battle-Song of the Oregon. Wallace Rice. PAH

From storm-lashed Erie's wintry shore,/Shall spring the Volunteers once more. The Volunteers. William Haines Lytle. MC; PAH

From sucking cider/Through a straw. Sucking Cider Through a Straw. Anonymous. AS; GBP

From that/corked catch-up bottle. No Bargains Today. Peggy Susberry Kenner. JB

From that deep chord which Hampden smote/Will vibrate to the doom. England and America in 1782. Alfred, Lord Tennyson. MC; PAH

From that fierce marriage falling, gently going. Compelled to Love. Walter Stone. ErPo

From that place the morn is broke/To that place day doth unyoke! Hymn to Pan. John Fletcher. NOBE; OBEV

From the beginning to the end/And with absolutely nothing left untold. Ballad of the Hidden Dragon. Anonymous. WTO

From the Beyond of this earth. War. Guillaume Apollinaire. WaaP

From the blood-stained lips of a youth who lay/On the battlefield of Chickamauga. Bury Me Not on the Chickamauga. Anonymous. BFSS

From the book that journeys in somebody's jacket. Madrigal to a Streetcar Token. Rafael Alberti. LiTW

From the bottom of the pool, fixed stars/Govern a life. Words. Sylvia Plath. ConAP; HaCAP

From the centuries that are gone/To the centuries that shall be. Follow Me. Henry Wadsworth Longfellow. PGD

From the cradle to the grave,–/Save, O Save! Desire. Matthew Arnold. WGRP

From the crucible of life when you've poured off the/scum. The Crucible of Life (excerpt). Edgar A. Guest. PeD

From the cupped palms of a stranger's hands. Your lynx-eyes, Asia. Anna Akhmatova. BoWoP

From the dark bay hissing/like crabs, red tropic suns. This Day, under My Hand. David Malouf. CBAP

From the darkened hands of the universal Cain. Invocation. Edith Sitwell. AtBAP

From the darkling caves. The Mermaids. Walter De la Mare. BrPo

...From the day/On which it should be touch'd, would melt away! Admonition to a Traveller. William Wordsworth. GTBS; GTBS-P

From the death in the teeth of the tornado. The Tornado. Norman H. Russell. STE

From the dim north bringing snow? O Wind, Why Do You Never Rest. Christina Georgina Rossetti. TiPo

From the doorsill of heaven came the word:/"Welcome!" The Restoration of Enheduanna to Her Former Station. Enheduanna. BoWoP

...From the dust gets up a buster named Tucson. Bronco Busting, Event #1. May Swenson. LiSp; PH

From the dust my mother was. The Housecleaner. Gail White. AMV-80

From the dust of my bosom! Anne Rutledge. Edgar Lee Masters. AmFN; AmLP; CMoP; FaFP; FaPo; HAP; InPo; LiTA; LiTM; MCCG; MoAmPo; MoVE; NePA; NoAm; NOBA; OFD; OxBA; PoPl; PoSC

From the emptying/bottle of bourbon. Lilies for Neal. James Minor. WOLT

From where the sun now stands I will fight no more forever! War. Chief Joseph. PGD

From which but fools like me would roam! Love-Songs, At Once Tender and Informative. Samuel Hoffenstein. OBAL

From which constellation shall you sail/to the mandala/that only a knife can find? Original Strawberry. Nancy Willard. LCAP

From which he climbed. After the Swimmer. Robert Wallace. LiSp

From which our lives are made. Good Thoughts. Katherine Maurine Haaff. PoToHe

From which there will be no more flying. The Poor Relation. Edwin Arlington Robinson. AnAmPo

:From which to be/Exempted, is in death to follow thee. Elegie. William Habington. AnAnS 2

From which war I do not know/and I'm terrified. From Which War. Phillip Yellowhawk Minthorn. STE

From which we fall toward a window The Theory of the Flower. Michael Palmer. NPGG

From whom, in happier hours, we wept to part. To the River Itchin, near Winton. William Lisle Bowles. OAEL 1-2

From whom she picks and chews,/absorbed, the viral nits. Clinic: Examination. Audrey Conard. AMV-80

...From whose floor the new-bathed stars/Emerge, and shine upon the Aral Sea. The Death of Sohrab. Matthew Arnold. FiP

From whose happy spark here let/Spring the purple violet. Upon Prue, His Maid. Robert Herrick. ForPo; JCP; NoP; OAEP

From whose solicitous and shining grace/a name descends on the anonymous. Cape Ann: A View. John Malcolm Brinnin. NYBP

From Wibbleton to Wobbleton is/fifteen miles. From Wibbleton to Wobbleton Is Fifteen Miles. Anonymous. OxNR

From Wicking to Weep. Berries. Walter De La Mare. AtBAP; MoBrPo; TiPo

From Winchester, twenty miles away! Sheridan's Ride. Thomas Buchanan Read. BBV; BeLS; FaBoBe; FaBV; FaFP; GN; HBV 1-2; HBVY; MC; OHFP; OHIP; PAH; TreF; WBLP; YaD

From winter, plague and pestilence, good Lord, deliver us! Autumn. Nashe [(or Nash)] Thomas. EiL; LoBV; OAEL 1-2; OBSC; TrGrPo

From Woolfe and Foxe I will defend ye. To His Flocks. Henry Constable. FM

From worlds before and after. Poetry. Edwin Markham. AA

From year to year, the promised nuptials wait The First Olympionique to Hiero of Syracuse. Pindar. ATP

From zealous Churchmen's pick and plane/Deliver us O Lord! Amen!' The Levelled Churchyard. Thomas Hardy. NOBL

Front page, sporting section, and all. Limerick: "A trendy young girl from St. Paul." Anonymous. NIP

Front Street will be waiting at our/backs. Front Street. Howard Moss. NYBP

Frost, a star edges with its fire. Sea Violet. Hilda ("H. D.") Doolittle. NoP

Frost-bitten cheek blooming again/in the kitchen heat. March Sound. Harry Thurston. AMV-81

A frost-mailed warrior striding/A shadowy steed of snow. January Is Here. Edgar Fawcett. YeAr

Frosted alders:/shapes of coral/clawing outward. Skiing on Russian Christmas. Nora Dauenhauer. TWSS

Froth beneath the Peacock's tongue. Vihio Images. Judith Mountain Leaf Volborth. TWSS

FROUDE, WHATELY, GROTE, and HAMILTON, a brilliant list/might fill. Principal British Writers. Edward B. Goodwin. FaBoUs

Frozen for bravery, beautiful. Four Poems for April. Louis Adeane. NeBP

Frozen for new eyes/At break of another dawn... Remnant Ghosts at Dawn. Oliver La Grone. FB

Frozen, his beard tucked in–He stands and counts the stars. Vilna. Moishe Kulbak. VWA

Frozen, holds on, and sings. Mad Day in March. Philip Levine. NYBP

Frozen like a star/All winter long you are. Harlem in January. Julia Fields. CAD; CNA

Fruit, flower, or stone, or given or taken. The Gift. Ann Stanford. GP

Fruit will be falling,/September is here. September Is Here. Edward Bliss Reed. YeAr

Fruits begin to sprout there,/Some sweet and some bitter. The Pillar-Box. Jiri Wolker. LiTW

The fruits I look for; everything/As on my heavenly hills. I Stood Within the Heart of God. William Vaughn Moody. AH

Fruits of dull Heat, and Sooterkins of Wit. The Dunciad. Alexander Pope. AtBAP

The fruits of Necessity ripen in all weathers. The Night There Was Dancing in the Streets. Elder Olson. NePA

Fuck with the moon, the sun don't like it. The View from a Cab. Henry Taylor. NLV

"Fuck you"/I said/"I quit" The Water-Truck. Patrick Lane. NeAC

Fucking is so very lovely/Who can say no to it later? LIII. Ted Berrigan. ANYP

The fuel small, how be the fires so great? Arcadia. Sir Philip Sidney. SiPS

...The fuel/streaming down the sides, like fun in the sun, air in the air. "Blue Is the Hero... Bill Berkson. ANYP

The fugue erupting, shaking/its captive soul, the dance. Tambour. Istvan Vas. VWA

Fuit in manibus cupidorum. Snatches: "Tax has teened us alle." Anonymous. OxBM

Ful cler was than the morowtyde,/And ful attempre, out of drede. The Dream of the Romaunt of the Rose. Geoffrey Chaucer. LoBV

Fulfil your doom, disordered minds, and fly/The infinite you carry in your soul. Damned Women. Charles Baudelaire. BoLoP

Fulfilling absolute Decree/In casual simplicity– How Happy Is the Little Stone. Emily Dickinson. AmP; NePA

Full acceptance in His favor,/And among His sons a place. The God in Whom We Trust. Anonymous. STF

The full caught pause of their embrace. The Discovery of the Pacific. Thom Gunn. HeIP

Full dearly Tom would rue it! Tommy Was a Silly Boy. Kate Greenaway. TiPo

Full forty at a meal. Riddle: "A wide mouth, no ears nor eyes." Anonymous. CoBE

Full hardly earneth Mat. his dinner. Earning a Dinner. Matthew Prior. NLV

Full harvest tilted high/In the ruts of tomorrow's ice. Returning from Harvest. Vernon Watkins. NYBP

Full many a bard shall chant his lays,/Their requiem. The Ocean-Fight. Anonymous. PAH

Full many a Girl will lead her Brindled Pup. An Omar for Ladies. Josephine Dodge Daskam Bacon. HBV 1-2

The full measure/Of cool pleasure,/The secret shared. Mountain Vigil. Douglas Fraser. PoSH

The full moon dominates the dark. Full Moon. Robert Earl Hayden. BPo

The full/moon/in the center of the sky. Once Only. Gary Snyder. SUW

Full moon not come into view/stars not journey by night. Wait Till the Darkness Is Deep. Wallada. WPOW

The full moon sank beneath the sea. The Play. Charles Otis Judkins. PeD

Full of beauty waiting till we enter. Kindly Vision. Otto Julius Bierbaum. AWP

Full of deep blue/Mysterious stars. Christmas Lights. Valerie Worth. PCh

Full of Indians street-people/and other workers of the world. Lonnie Kramer. Geary Hobson. STE

Full of letters lying in the dark,/from the world to the world. Just before Dawn. Roo Borson. CaPN

...Full/of life, death, insanity, and grace! American against Solitude. Alan Dugan. CAPP

Full of meaning and shining, the kingdom to which I awoke. The Hills of Pomeroy. Ewart Milne. NeIP

Full of people sitting together. Animal Songs: Giraffe. Anonymous. PeSA

Full of real death and enormous explosions that actually go bang. A Nice Part of Town. Alfred Hayes. NYBP

Full of still longing for a scarlet mouth. Candles. Helene Swarth. WPOW

Full of sweet breath. The End of the Parade. William Carlos Williams. NYBP

Full of the God, having drunk fire. Noon. Robinson Jeffers. MoAmPo

Full of the importance/of carrying briefcases. The Citizen. Vilma Howard. NNP

...Full of/the night in their faces. Pickers. Peter Brett. AMV-81

Full of wonder and of fate–/Prosit Neujahr! Prosit Neujahr. George Santayana. InMe

The full-throated kingdom of the truly dead. Virgin Pictured in Profile. Rosanna Warren. AMV-81; MAYP

Fulness of joy, and faith, and love/To every waiting heart. Prayer. Anonymous. STF

Fumble the ropes of her long swinging beads. Nuns at Eve. John Malcolm Brinnin. MoAB; MP; TwCP

Fumbled and forced–yet willing, ready to learn the knack. Mill Girl. James Keir Baxter. AnNZ

...Fumbled/for her coat and bag, and lurched out. An Egyptian Passage. Theodore Weiss. CoPo; TAP

The funeral North–the black dark sky/Alike mourned I Now Had Only to Retrace. Charlotte Bronte. NOBV

The funny old bagpipe man! The Bagpipe Man. Nancy Byrd Turner. TiPo

Funny old Saint Nicholas. Stocking Song on Christmas Eve. Mary Mapes Dodge. ChBR; OHIP

Fur I weant shed a drop on 'is blood, noa, not fur Sally's oan kin.   The Northern Cobbler.   Alfred, Lord Tennyson.   EBEV

Fur whar you finds de nigger–dar's de/banjo an' de 'possum!   De Fust Banjo. Irwin Russell.   AA; BLPA; HBV 1-2

The furious spirit you are letting go.   The Genie.   Ann Stanford.   WSC

The furious words and minerals which destroy.   Two Armies.   Stephen Spender.   ChMP; CoBMV; OBWP; OxBTC; SeCeV; WaP

Furling his wings at last to rock and rest/In the green hollow of the the stormy wave.   Winged Mariner.   Grace Clementine Howes.   EtS

The furniture will not move/unless you are there to move it yourself   Silent Movies.   Pedro Juan Pietri.   InW

Further and further south of Hadrian's Wall.   Feliks Skrzynecki.   Peter Skrzynecki.   CBAP

...Further harmonies/are implied in the harmonies we state   Against the Silences to Come.   Ron Loewinsohn.   PoM

The further he doth goe, the further he doth stray.   The Faerie Queene. Edmund Spenser.   FaBoEn

Further, old Baba rather briskly enter'd.   Don Juan.   George Gordon, Lord Byron.   PoEL 1-5

Further out, Time and Chance are waiting to happen.   Coastline.   Elaine Feinstein.   BrRo

Further than New Zealand or a nebula.   Triumphal Ode MCMXXXIX. George Barker.   LiTB; WaP

Further than target ever showed or stone.   A Soldier.   Robert Frost. MoPo; NePA; OFD; SeCeV; WaaP; WaP; WeW

Furthermore, he stutters.   Neighbors.   Lennox.   DBV

Fusty Christopher.   To Christopher North.   Alfred, Lord Tennyson. EvOk; FaBoEE; FiBHP

The futile folly of the Infinite.   Prayer to the Virgin of Chartres.   Henry Adams.   CAW; GoBC; ISi

The future creeps like a shadow across the meadow/And while I lose I love unspeakably.   The Deaths.   Solveig von Schoultz.   LiTW

The future is for tomorrow.   The Future Is for Tomorrow.   Anna Greki. WPOW

The FUTURE only holds thee and can hold thee.   Thou Mother with Thy Equal Brood.   Walt Whitman.   AmePo

The future slave may lisp the patriot's name/And his breast kindle with a kindred flame!   Colonial Nomenclature.   John Dunmore Lang.   NOAV

A future summer gleams,/Passing the fairest glories of the present! September.   George Arnold.   HBV 1-2

Fuzzy Wuzzy wasn't fuzzy,/Was he?   Fuzzy Wuzzy Was a Bear. Anonymous.   NTCP

G

"G–d– your books!" the testy father said,/"I'd not give–for all you've read." The Discontented Student.   St. George Tucker.   OBAL

G—lle, whose eyes have power to make/A Pope of every swain.   Written at Mr. Pope's House at Twickenham.   George, Lord Lyttelton.   CEP

Gaa-a-muna, a mountain flower/With tender blue petals   Gaa-A-Muna, a Mountain Flower.   Harold Littlebird.   OxBS; VoR

Gabbling wild lies of ruffians, skids or snow.   Not Late Enough.   Hazel Townson.   PV

Gables and red tiled roofs and twisted chimneys.   Fragment: "–you see." William Allingham.   IrPN

Gaed hame and married that lady,/And heird her father's land.   Young Ronald.   Anonymous.   ESPB

The Gael will lose respect/and freemen turn to clowns.   A Defence of Poetry. Giollabrighde Macconmidhe.   NOBI

Gaily it sets out into the depths of my profoundest/closet, to do battle with the dusts of summer.   The European Shoe.   Michael Benedikt.   AmPA; ConAP; TwCP

Gaily they drank their wedding feast,/Nor has their friendship ever ceas'd. Sir Helmer Blaa and His Bride's Brothers.   Anonymous.   BaBo

The gain is gloss.   To the Reader.   J. V. Cunningham.   NoAm; QFR

The gain is hers, the loss is mine,/Of evil sown seed such is the fruit.   Of Love.   Sir Thomas Wyatt.   FCP

'Gainst a woman that was a brute.   A Hate-Song.   Percy Bysshe Shelley. EnLoPo

'Gainst fearful odds, till set of sun,/We battle–and the field is won!   The Guns in the Grass.   Thomas Frost.   MC; PAH

'Gainst the Saxon stranger on the day of danger/Out of Aileach Neid.   The Dark Palace.   Alice Milligan.   AnIV

The gal I left behind me.   Gal I Left Behind Me.   Anonymous.   ABF; BPAW; CoSo

Galaxies were thick, weather was clear.   A Poem to Explain Everything about a Certain Day in Vermont.   Genevieve Taggard.   NYBP

Gallant band of Fifty-one!   The Gallant Fifty-One.   Henry Lynden Flash. PAH

Gallant young Lieutenant Miles/And his valiant volunteers!   Ballad of Lieutenant Miles.   Clinton Scollard.   MC

Gallop the miles, the straight-backed miles without number.   Cycling to Dublin.   Robert Greacen.   OnYI

Galloping deception, giving us visions/hysteric   Air (parody).   Philip Dow. BXAP

"Galumph, galumph!' go my galoshes.   Thaw.   Eunice Tietjens.   BrR

Gamble hath wisely laid of ut re mi.   To My Noble Kinsman, Thomas Stanley, Esquire, on His Lyric Poems...   Richard Lovelace.   CaPo

The game is worth the candle if there's flame.   Catch What You Can.   Jean Garrigue.   VGW

Game of chess, which he will always win.   Old Montague.   Michael Kennedy Joseph.   AnNZ

The game you play at is not to my mind.   Modern Love, XIV.   George Meredith.   HBV 1-2; VLP

Games that call for patience, foresight, maneuver,/like war, like marriage. Fairground.   W. H. Auden.   NYBP

Gamey snorting of hot breath/on the back of my neck.   Zoo Dream.   David Barker.   GP

Gang doun wi' a sang, gang doun.   Song: "Whaur yon broken brig hings owre."   William Soutar.   GoTS; OxBS

Gangrene was corn, and monuments went mad.   Armistice.   Paul Dehn. OxBTC

Gangway, girls: I'll show you trouble.   Prologue to a Saga.   Dorothy Parker. InMe

Gannin alang the Scotswood Road te see the Blaydon Races.   Blaydon Races. Anonymous.   ELP

Ganymede feels the talons in his spine/Lift him Olympian to lustier wine. Ganymede.   Witter ("Emanuel Morgan") Bynner.   AnFE; CoAnAm

The Gap is real & there is no such thing as/female intelligence. We're dumber than hell.   Mean Drunk Poem.   Sharon Thesen.   CaPN; NOBC

Gape at your porridge, munch it like a god!   Ward Two.   Francis Webb. CBAP

Gape on, as they do to be paid, gape on!   A Parley with His Empty Purse. Thomas Randolph.   JCP; OBS

Gaps in the low-hung gloom, and, bright in air,/Orion or the Bear. Remembered Grace.   Coventry Patmore.   OxBoCh

...A/garbage can lid smashed into a likeness of the mad English/king, George the Third.   You Were Wearing.   Kenneth Koch.   ANYP; CoAP; EAS; NIP; NNaP; NoAm; NoP

...The garden/A little overgrown now/Despite the freshly raked sand.   A Nobleman's House (excerpt).   May Sarton.   EyDe

The garden-boy is leading the cranes home.   The Cranes.   Po Chu-i. OBVE

...Garden, falsified by snow/Waiting to melt, and become real again.   Winter and Summer.   Stephen Spender.   MoAB; MoBrPo; MoPo

A garden full of weeds.   What Do They Say.   Gary Snyder.   NNaP

The garden is not ours.   Casa d'Amunt.   Alastair Reid.   NePoEA

The Garden Master's gone.   Dream Songs.   John Berryman.   NOBA

The garden reverberate with the voice/I hid from once, now run to find.   The Crack.   J. C. Hall.   HaMV

...The garden/where jets flash like swords above your head?   Miami.   Daniel Mark Epstein.   MAYP

Gardener of Eden–and Gethsemane!   Unearth.   Alfred Joseph Barrett. GoBC

The gardener of the World, he goes.   Summer Sun.   Robert Louis Stevenson. MoBrPo

The garibaldian cape shot full of bullet holes.   The City of Beggars.   Alfred Hayes.   WaP

The garland briefer than a girl's.   To an Athlete Dying Young.   Alfred Edward Housman.   ATP; BiP; BLPL; BrPo; CMoP; DL; ExPo; GoTF; HAP; HeIP; InPK; LiSp; LiTB; LiTM; MaC; MasP; MoAB; MoBrPo; NBM; NIP; NoAm; NoP; PoEL 1-5; PoPl; PoRA; PPoe; PrIm; SD; SeCeV; SoSe; TEP; TreF; TrGrPo; UnPo; VLP; WHA

A garland for his forehead made/For roses drops of blood instead.   A Legend.   Tschaikovsky.   OHIP

A garland, where comes neither rain, nor wind.   The Garland.   Henry Vaughan.   AnEnPo

Garlanded with blood-red lilies, for ever/And ever and ever, in love.   Virgin Martyrs.   John Heath-Stubbs.   OxBC

...Garnishing/the aviary, burnishing this zoo.   Garnishing the Aviary. Margaret Danner.   BP; BPo

...Garrulous kings/Who at last can agree.   Armagh.   W. R. Rodgers. NoAm

Garrulous to the very last.   After the Supper and Talk.   Walt Whitman. MoAmPo

...The garrulous/Water has dried up at last.   The Last Utterance of the Delphic Oracle.   Anonymous.   OBVE

The garter snake leaves behind/One of his silver glittering crystal annual sleeves.   June.   James Reaney.   WHW

Gas, powder and a/little rubble.   Primitives.   Dudley Randall.   BALP; BPo

Gasp thy gasp, and groan thy groan,/Day is near the breaking. Guy Mannering. Chapt. 27: Wasted, Weary, Wherefore Stay. Sir Walter Scott. EnRP

Gassed underground the quiet Nazi way. Woodchucks. Maxine W. Kumin. HoPM; InPK; NIP

The gate must be closed, logic tells me. At night/the dark is darkest. When the Last Riders. Natan Zach. VWA

The gate of polished reed closes behind them/And the West is let in. Stanley Meets Mutesa. James D. Rubadiri. PBA

The gate that leads out of life, good wife,/Is the gate that leads to Him. Don't Be Sorrowful, Darling. Rembrandt Peale. HBV 1-2

...Gates-/Closing behind the hill of the road/That narrows behind me–beckon me back. Descending. Robert Pack. NePoEA-2

The gates of Heaven are nearer/Than the body of my beloved. Year after year I have watched. Li Ch'ing-chao. BoWoP

Gather, gather, gather, etc. MacGregor's Gathering. Sir Walter Scott. AnFE; OxBS

Gather–gather–gather them in. The Old Sexton. Park Benjamin. AA; HBV 1-2

Gather it up from the dust,/That its sparkle may amuse you. A Lady. Amy Lowell. MAPA; MoAmPo

Gather my pine-brush and light fires unmolested underneath/my trees. Funeral in Hungary. Kay Boyle. AnEnPo

Gather the dead as the first dead scrape home. The Guardians. Geoffrey Hill. NePoEA-2; NoP

Gather the fragrant petals of my life/And crush them, Lord, then help me sing the song. The Poet Prays. Grace Noll Crowell. TrPWD

Gather the Rose of love, whilest yet is time,/Whilest loving thou mayst loved be with equall crime. The Faerie Queene. Edmund Spenser. FaBoEn; NOBE

Gather Thy dispersed children in/Jerusalem! We Sit Solitary. Anonymous. TrJP

Gather under the prayer shawls/of the fathers these benedictions/as under so many tents. Benediction. Myra Sklarew. VWA

Gather us sweets from the blossoming clover. Honey Bee. Lucy Fitch Perkins. SUS

Gather with the saints at the river/That flows from the throne of God. Shall We Gather at the River? Robert Lowry. AH

Gather ye roses while ye may. Gather Ye Roses. Robert Louis Stevenson. GoTF; TreFT

Gather ye soup-suds while ye may. Counsel to Girls. Archibald Stodart-Walker. CenHV

The gathered brasses want to go/boom—boom. View of the Capitol from the Library of Congress. Elizabeth Bishop. AmFN

Gathered exulting to insult your/Great eagle in his fall? The Eagle's Fall. Charles Goodrich Whiting. AA

Gathered the grey trunks as I stumbled homeward. This Morning I Wakened among Loud Cries of Seagulls. Patrick MacDonogh. NeIP

Gathering at the river's edge A River in Asia. Andrew Grossbardt. FAZ

...Gathering grasses/in the middle morning. Telephone. Robin Shectman. AMV-81

Gathering strength for flight. Survivors. Michael Hogan. FAZ

Gathering strength, gaining breath,–/naught can sever/Me from the Spirit of Life! Dryad Song. Margaret Fuller. AA; WGRP

Gathering the still-warm eggs with held breath. The Sergeant. Don Johnson. MAYP

Gathering to its shell my startled soul. Champ de Manoeuvres. Sir Herbert Read. BrPo

Gathering to itself sound and silence /Mine and the sea wind's. The Rose. Theodore Roethke. BiP; CH; HBV 1-2; NaP; NOBA; NYBP; PAI; PPoe

...Gathers/all colour to itself/and gives it to the sky Walking through the Door. Brian Henderson. CaPN

Gathers me nearer to be born. When a Girl Looks Down. Kay Smith. OBCV

...The gaudy moths and millers,/Are only dressed-up caterpillars. The Butterfly and the Caterpillar. Joseph Lauren. OnMSP

Gauze flutterings of vegetation. For My Mother. Louise Gluck. GeTw; UnPo

Gave from their hollow throats the name of "Saturn!" Hyperion. John Keats. SeCePo

Gave out all its sweets to love's exquisite flame! I Saw from the Beach. Thomas Moore. OBNC; OxBI

Gave them likewise hardy strength/And patient hearts to bear. Buttercups and Daisies. Mary Howitt. HBV 1-2; HBVY; OHIP; OxBChV

Gave them their marching orders and was moving. The Mountain. Robert Frost. FaBV

Gave to love's feast its choicest gust,/A vague, faint augury of despair. The Angel in the House. Coventry Patmore. VLP

Gavst immortality, free will,/And language not involved in dark! Adam's Hymn in Paradise. Joost van den Vondel. WGRP

GAWD SAVE THE/QUEEN! Shillin' a Day. Rudyard Kipling. OAEP; ViBoPo

Gay cotes graceles,/maketh Englande thriftles. The English. Anonymous. GBP

Gay go up and gay go down/To ring the bells of London town. The Bells of London. Anonymous. BrR; EvOK

The gay time is begun. First Spring Morning. Robert Bridges. YeAr

Gay with fond glances/Good with long talks. Death in the Home. Thomas Sturge Moore. BrPo

Gayle Marie, you're beautiful. Untitled. King D. Kuka. VoR

Gayly swinging/nectarine penticles like apricots. Some Stories of the Beauty Wapiti. Ebbe Borregaard. NeAP

A gaze in the eyes, a kiss–/Why will it not go by! Winter Song. George Macdonald. NOBV

Gaze no more in the bitter glass. The Two Trees. William Butler Yeats. BrPo; OAEL 1-2; VLP

Gazed at each other. Turned their backs. The Brothers. John Holloway. NMP

Gazed back, and would not offer one look round. Don Juan in Hell. Charles Baudelaire. AWP; SyP

Gazing and blazing, blessing and possessing all vividness/and all darkness. A Little Morning Music. Delmore Schwartz. BoNaP; NYBP

Gazing at last from the martial heights whereunder/Deathless memories roll to an ageless sea. Edinburgh. Alfred Noyes. HBV 1-2

Gazing in safety at/a star solid as flesh. Christmas Night. Lawrence Sail. OBCP

...Gazing/straight ahead into the uncertain future. Grandfather Yoneh. Emily Borenstein. AMV-81

Gazing upon the ground, with thoughts which dare not/glow? Childe Harold's Pilgrimage: Canto III. George Gordon, Lord Byron. PoEL 1-5

The gazing world afar/Shall greet with shouts the Bonnie Blue/Flag/That bears the cross and star! The Bonnie Blue Flag. Annie Chambers Ketchum. PAH

The gears grind; somewhere a suffering creature calls. Shore Leave Lorry. Roy Fuller. NoAm

Gee, but I want to go, Gee, but I want to go home. Gee, but I Want to Go Home. Anonymous. FSW

"Gee, I never knew you/played," says your astonished high school/principal. Hey Fella Would You Mind Holding This Piano a Moment. William J. Harris. GP

Gee, Officer Krupke, krup you! Gee, Officer Krupke. Steven Sondheim. OBAL

Gee up, Neddy, to the fair. Gee up, Neddy, to the Fair. Anonymous. OxNR

The geese follow after. Titty Cum Tawtay. Anonymous. OxNR

Gehazi, Judge in Israel,/A leper white as snow! Gehazi. Rudyard Kipling. FaBoPV

The general of the patronymic march. Towards the Last Spike. Edwin John Pratt. OBCV

Generalissimo:/Able to cope. Chip. George Starbuck. OBAL

A generation laughs...and lights again. Anatole France at Eighty. Gladys Oaks. AnAmPo

Genital/faces/from the dark/mouth. The Voice of the Power of This World. Gregory Hall. NU

...The genitals mark his centre exactly. Four Heads & How to Do Them. John Forbes. CBAP

Genius, left to shiver/On the bank, 'tis said,/Died of that cold river. Common Sense and Genius. Thomas Moore. NBM

Genteelly damn'd beside a Duke,/Than sav'd in vulgar company. Epitaph on a Tuft-Hunter. Thomas Moore. FaBoEE

The gentiles/will tell you had some special deal Portrait of a Jew Old Country Style. Jerome Rothenberg. NNaP

"Gentle dreams, steal over Thee." Latin Lullaby. Anonymous. CAW

Gentle Jane felt shooting pains. The Swift Bullets. Carolyn Wells. ShM

"Gentle Jesus, meek and mild,/Look upon a little child." A Foxhole for the Night. John Robert Quinn. BoAV

...The gentle Lake/Lies like a sleeping child too blest to wake! Written on the Banks of Wastwater during a Calm. John Wilson. OBRV

Gentle lords and ladies gay. The Lay of the Last Minstrel. Sir Walter Scott. TrGrPo

"A gentle man on Earth/And gentle 'mid the Shades. Palinode. Oliver St. John Gogarty. OBMV

Gentle people are dull/At the end of the day. Day's End. Lesbia Harford. PoAu 1-2

Gentle springs, freshly your salt tears/Must still fall dropping from their spheres. Madrigal: "Flow not so fast." John Dowland. EnRePo

Gentle swain at thy request/I am here. A Masic Presented at Ludlow Castle (Comus). John Milton. EBEV; EG; GN; NOBE; OBEV; OBS; SeCeV

The gentle warbling wind low answered to all. The Bower of Bliss. Edmund Spenser. CH; LoBV; UnS

...The gentle word Son that she gave/to each of the seed of Ethiopia? Aunt Jane Allen. Fenton Johnson. GoSl; IDB; PoBA; PoNe

Gentlefolk fall away in crumble sadness/past the shifting potholes of our day. Driving through Belgium. Michael Brownstein. ANYP

A gentleman, no matter what he did. A Portrait. Caroline Duer. AA

The gentleness of rain was in the wind. Fragment: Rain. Percy Bysshe Shelley. ChRP

The gentlest current yet to take/The first bewildered flake. Presence of Snow. Melville Cane. GoYe

Gentlest fair, mourn, mourn no moe. Weep No More. John Fletcher. EIL; OBEV; ViBoPo

Gentlest of women, lay your arms aside. Lay Your Arms Aside. Pierce Ferriter. BIrV

Gently, dreamily, quietly over desolate sands! Sorrow of Mydath. John Masefield. MoBrPo

"Gently, Johnny, my Jingalo." Gently, Johnny, My Jingalo. Anonymous. FSW; OBET

Gently, now, lay your flowers down. Burial of the Young Love. Waring Cuney. BANP

Gently shakes our ladder. Stonehouse. Jeff Tagami. BrSi

Gently to hear, kindly to judge, our play. King Henry V. William Shakespeare. SCV

The genuine passions of the nether pit! Ranolf and Amohia. Alfred Domett. ACV; AnNZ; OBTV

...Genuine, you are interested in poetry. Poetry. Marianne Moore. BiP; CMoP

Geometry indeed is God. Letters from the Astronomers, II: Johannes Kepler (1571-1630). Siv Cedering Fox. SUW

George is gonna build a new barn,/So we'll tear the old one down. The Harrington Barn Dance. Anonymous. CoSo

George the Third said with a smile:/"Seventeen-sixty yards in a mile." Useful Dates. Anonymous. FaBoUs

Georgie Porgie ran away. Georgie Porgie. Anonymous. OxNR

Gesture Coquette--/And shake your Head! Going to her. Emily Dickinson. PeHV

...A gesture of the hands/Can hardly hold so vast an emptiness. John Nobody. Dom Moraes. NoAm

Get a-long, get a-long,/Youpi-ya,/Yo-o-u-u-p! Texas Trains and Trails. Mary Austin. SoPo; TiPo

Get a sponge. Get a shovel. Call God. Soup's on. The Last Supper. Stan Rice. NPGG

Get a stick and make them mind. Children When They're Very Sweet. John Ciardi. BBGG

..."Get about your business, Paraclete!" Nausea. E. L. Mayo. MiAP

Get along home, Cindy, Cindy, I'll marry you some day. Cindy. Anonymous. BLSo; FSW; GoTF; TrAS; TreFS

Get beat like the devil and flogged with the broom--/And it's hard times. Johnny McCardner. Anonymous. OuSiCo

Get Black Bitterness/NOW Poem (No Name No. 2). Nikki Giovanni. BOLo

Get down into the water, fish!/(Or you'll be dead.) The Sea Gull Curves His Wings. Elizabeth Jane Coatsworth. TiPo

...Get down to/playing war, celebrating my son's life. Rite of Passage. Sharon Olds. MAYP

Get down you dirty rascal. King of the Castle. Anonymous. OxNR

Get him up and be gone as one shaped awry; he disturbs the order here. In Tenebris. Thomas Hardy. BrPo; CMoP; LiTB; LiTM; NoAm; NOBE; NoP; OAEP; OxBTC; PrIm; SeCePo; TreFS; VLP

Get his half-dollah back,/zzZ. Parody on Thomas Hood's "The Bridge of Sighs." Anonymous. FiBHP

Get hold of yourself, and say: "I can." Equipment. Edgar A. Guest. PoToHe

Get home unto thy plow. Braddock's Fate, with an Incitement to Revenge. Stephen Tilden. PAH

Get more than the lovers...in the dust...in the cool/tombs. Cool Tombs. Carl Sandburg. AmP; AmPP; AnFE; AP; AtBAP; BLPL; BoLiVe; CMoP; CoAnAm; HAP; HBMV; HeIP; MoAB; MoAmPo; MoVE; NoAm; NOBA; OBSP; PAL; PoLf; TAP; TrGrPo; ViBoPo; WHA

Get off the stage ere we begin our booing! Lament. Gelett Burgess. InMe

Get on board, little chillun,/There's room for many a more. The Gospel Train. Anonymous. BLSo; GoSl; TrAS

"Get our self another bit once the pants/are off them what's the difference?" Visitors' Parking. Anne Szumigalski. NOBC

Get out--get out! He knows not shame nor fear. Epitaphs of the War, 1914-18. Rudyard Kipling. BrPo

Get out of the way--one, two, three, fire! A Shooting Song. William Brightly ("Matthew Browne") Rands. OxBChV

Get out the way, Big Bill Snyder/We'll tar your coat and feather your hide, sir. Old Dan Tucker (Down Rent Verses). Anonymous. TrAS

Get ready for the snow, get ready/To go down. Things to Do around a Lookout. Gary Snyder. CAPP; NaP; TAP

Get real nigger/And stop making gestures. You're Nothing but a Spanish Colored Kid. Felipe Luciano. PoBA

Get the wish I wish tonight. Star-Light, Star-Bright. Mother Goose. OxNR; SoPo; TiPo

Get thee away/with a rose/in your heart. Birthing: 2000. Pancho Aguila. LFAC

Get up and bar the door. Get Up and Bar the Door. Anonymous. ATP; BaBo; BiP; BoLiVe; BSV; EnSB; FaBoBa; GoTS; HeIP; MaC; NoP; OnMSP; OxBS; StPo; TrGrPo; ViBoPo

Get up and clean the grate. Baldy Bane. W. S. Graham. NePoEA

Get up and get my breakfast, you good-for-nothing thing! Hello, Girls (with music). Anonymous. AS

Get up got here bow/It's Nation/Time! It's Nation Time. LeRoi (Imamu Amiri Baraka) Jones. NoP

Get up, Jack! John sit down! Get Up, Jack! John,Sit Down! Anonymous. ABF

"Get up, my dear, it is to-day." A Summer Morning. Rachel Field. SoPo; SUS; TiPo

Get up/only men erect bind heavens to the earth Your cheeks flat on the sand. Venus Khoury-Gata. BoWoP

Get you gone,/You silly blockhead. A Grenadier. Anonymous. OxNR

Get you half a gallon of whiskey and get on you a big drunk Packin' Trunk Blues. Leadbelly. BluL

Get you the sons your fathers got,/And God will save the Queen. A Shropshire Lad. Alfred Edward Housman. NOBV

Get yourself up--and go find a book! Limerick: "If you don't know the meaning of snook." Myra Cohn Livingston. TDH

Gets no pity, but just her lover's spurn. Women, whoever wishes to know my lord. Gaspara Stampa. BoWoP

Gets warmed when coal is fired. The Opportune Overthrow of Humpty Dumpty. Guy Wetmore Carryl. BBGG

Gettin to the next town/Baby. Pickin Em Up and Layin Em Down. Maya Angelou. NLV

Getting back together! Getting Back. Dorothy Brown Thompson. SiSoSe

Getting fat on the outside/while inside we grow thin. Oil. Linda Hogan. TWSS

Getting off/the ground Cleavage. Archie Randolph Ammons. OBAL

Getting so clean/all clean inside That Old Sauna High. Anselm Hollo. PoM

Getting used to themselves having been numb too long. Cranes. J. R. S. Davies. PoL

The ghost of a woman, her body overboard/Laid, in the waters around/GREENLAND. Gudveig. Francis Berry. OBTV

The ghost of Agamemnon, like a bee,/Hums in the groining of his vaulted tomb. Invasion Weather. Douglas Newton. NeBP

Ghost of my self The Poet Haunted. Wendy Rose. TWSS

Ghost on my desk, speak, speak. Ghosts. Alastair Reid. NYBP

Ghost or God, evermore moves on the face of the deep. Evening on the Broads. Algernon Charles Swinburne. TEP

...A ghost/orbiting forever lost/in our monotonous sublime. Waking Early Sunday Morning. Robert Lowell. FaBoMo; HaCAP; NOBA; OxBC

A ghost picked up a skull; from underneath/we watched the cancer, spewing through the teeth. Cinco de Mayo, 1862. Albert Rios. GP

A ghost upon this common earth. The Twilight of Disquietude: The Years That Go to Make Me Man. Christopher John Brennan. PoAu 1-2

Ghosting glory from the water! The Ballad of O'Bruadir. Frederick Robert Higgins. EtS; OBMV

The ghostly glimmering/of the gum. Pine Gum. W. W. Eustace Ross. OBCV

...Ghosts dance/a new dance, pushing from their hearts/a new song. I Expected My Skin and My Blood to Ripen. Wendy Rose. TWSS; WPOW

Ghosts of black hands through the ruins Monte Alban. Joseph Stroud. NPGG

The ghosts of grief and loss/walking beyond the Sea of Serenity Nine Bean-Rows on the Moon. Al Purdy. MOON

The ghosts of lovers, who had lived and died/Within its walls, were sleeping in our bed. Tenants. Wilfred Wilson Gibson. HBV 1-2

The ghosts of mid-channel, the banging doors/of the state sirocco. On This Day I Complete My Fortieth Year. Peter Porter. NAs

Ghosts of miners--wanting air. Miners. John C. Frohlicher. BPAW

The ghosts of the Kellys still ride from the range. The Bushrangers. Edward Harrington. PoAu 1-2

...Ghosts shall shake/The dead, until they wake/In the grave. Death's Jest-Book. Thomas Lovell Beddoes. OBRV

The ghosts stood gossiping. Monument. Milton Acorn. NeAC

The giant presence of a terrible God. In an Empty Window. Ray Fraser. NeAC

Giant thing inhabits none,/But vast Desolation! Hundred-Gated Thebes. George Darley. NOBE

The giantess shuffles nearer, cries "Deceiver'. Prologue. W. H. Auden. NoAm

Giddy with grandeur where you stood. Ezry. Archibald MacLeish. MoVE; NOBA

Gif that the tryackill cum nocht tyt/To swage the swalme of my dispyt! Remonstrance to the King. William Dunbar. OxBS

Gif ye will advise me to marry/The lad I lo'e dearly, Tam Glen. Tam Glen. Robert Burns. ALV; AWP; BSV; InPo; OAEP; OBEC; OxBS

The gift he gave Immanuel. The Friendly Beasts. *Anonymous.* BiCB; ChBR; OnMSP; PCh; SiSoSe

The gift of Faith, the crown of Song! Our Country. Julia Ward Howe. MC; PAH; PAL

The gift of friends, to share the way I go. Friends. Thomas Curtis Clark. PoToHe

The gift of gladness will not die!/Sing nonny non, hey nonny no. Hey Nonny No. Marguerite Merington. AA

The gift of work; its fellowship/And rugged fruitfulness. A Little Song of Work. Sarah Elizabeth Sprouse. BLRP

The gift to be a miracle/Shall never pass away. The Higher Calling. W. M. Czamanske. STF

...The gift which gives/A vision of the beautiful. Poetry. William Soutar. HaMV

The gifts her kinship and our loves reveal. Chicago. Bret (Francis Bret Harte) Harte. PAH

The gifts, the firstlings, weathered/on that forging stone. The Reapings. Theodore Weiss. NMP

Gifts will get ye, or the man. To Virgins. Robert Herrick. CaPo; UnTE; ViBoPo

Giggling all the way/about some fat unmarried neighbor/or some poor man's cock. In an Arab Town. Susan Tichy. MAYP

Giggling maids push/a trolley of fresh/linen down the corridor. Tracks. John Montague. FaBoIP

"Gil Brenton is my father's name." Gil Brenton. *Anonymous.* BaBo; ESPB; OxBB

Gilboa, my man. Mount Gilboa. Malka Tussman. PBWP

Gilded and sticky, with a little sting. Pretty Words. Elinor Wylie. HBMV; YaD

...The gills/have an almost human grin. Planting Trout in the Chicago River. Dennis Schmitz. NPGG

Gills/to survive/immersion/in that deep/wet world. The Home. Susan Axelrod. NMM

Gimme them, and the feelin' of solid domestic comfort. Home, Sweet Home. Henry Cuyler Bunner. CenHV

Gimmie dat ol time/religion/it's good enough/for me! Sermonette. Ishmael Reed. NIP; PoBA

Gin I had kend he'd bin your son,/He'd neir bin slain for mee. Gil Morrice. *Anonymous.* OxBB

Gin I had na sworn by the croun an the/septer roun,/Eearl Marchell sud ben gared dee.' Queen Eleanor's Confession (B version). *Anonymous.* ESPB

Gin is better than all the water in Lethe. The Scarlet Woman. Fenton Johnson. BANP; PoBA; PoNe

Gin nouthe and answere thou me. My Folk, What Have I Done Thee? William Herebert. OxBM

Gin on the bun-shops and copy-book stalls. G. K. Chesterton on His Birth. Alfred Edward Housman. FaBoNo; NLV

"Gin us peace an' joy. Amen!" In the Morning. Paul Laurence Dunbar. BPo; GoSl

Ginkgo leaves/the color of teeth. Skull of a Neandertal. Michael Cadnum. SUW

Girl from strange boy, that strange boy from his girl. Why the British Girls Give in So Easily. Nicholas Moore. WaP

"The girl I love in England,'/I drink at Rotterdam! To–. Thomas Hood. OBTV

The girl in a grey frock.... A Grey Frock. Zenaida Hippius. PBWP

A girl in pyjamas and bangles/Slept with her hands in my hair. Zalinka. Tom MacInnes. PeCV

Girl of three cows don't crow! Showing Off. *Anonymous.* KiLC

The girl parachutes onto the plain. Behind the Wheel. Michael Brownstein. ANYP

The girl, the singing, and the Christmas child. Jesu, Joy of Man's Desiring. Robert Fitzgerald. NYBP

A girl waiting/shy, brown, soft-eyed–/to guide you/Upstairs, sir. The Jungle. William Carlos Williams. CABA

A girl walking by along the platform/explodes the whole Glen area. When I'm Going Well. Ronald G. Everson. PeCV

The girl who screamed had fallen in a faint. In the Snake Park. William Plomer. NoAm; NYBP; OxBTC

A girl/whose hair is yellower than/torchlight should wear no/headdress but fresh flowers. Don't Ask Me What to Wear. Sappho. PBWP

Girls believe and men deceive the whole world over. Birds and Bees. *Anonymous.* UnTE

The girls had not merely touched for future luck. Wax. Winfield Townley Scott. ErPo

The girls with braided hair whom I/loved most shyly/Are women with children. Home-Coming. Albert Ehrenstein. TrJP

A girly, womanly, female, feminine dame! There Is Nothin' Like a Dame. Oscar, II Hammerstein. OBAL

Git on board, little chillen,/Dere's room for many a mo'. Git on Board, Little Chillen. *Anonymous.* BoAN 1-2; BPo

Git ready and let us go home. He Raise a Poor Lazarus. *Anonymous.* AH

Git up and smile white at'em with your hands/crossed thataway. A Man by the Name of Bolus. James Whitcomb Riley. AA

Git up now and get it while it's hot. Cowboy's Gettin'-Up Holler. *Anonymous.* CoSo; TrAS

Give a rouse: here's, in hell's de-/spite now,/King Charles! Cavalier Tunes. Robert Browning. BoLiVe; EnLit; HBV 1-2

Give a rousing fuck for Pearl! Janis Joplin and the Folding Company. Bayla Winters. AMV-80

Give a single penny that we may not sing in vain. The Children's Carol. Eleanor Farjeon. PCh

Give as you would of your substance/If his hand the offering took. How to Give. *Anonymous.* BLRP

Give away our possessions and live for him. O people who live in the world. Andal. BoWoP

"Give back the Singing Man!" The Singing Man. Josephine Preston Peabody. HBV 1-2

Give back this universe/Its pristine bloom. On Receiving News of the War. Isaac Rosenberg. MMM; MoBrPo; OBWP

Give birth/bleak as a goddess Calliope in the Labour Ward. Elaine Feinstein. BrRo

Give consolation for the "might have been"? Too Late. Nora Perry. PoToHe

Give day to other worlds; for me/It must suffice to dream of thee. Farewell. John Addington Symonds. HBV 1-2

Give dogs the guts, and leave the wolves the rest. Cominus, You Reprobate Old Goat. Caius Valerius Catullus. DBV

Give earth yourself, go up for gain above! The Ancient Doctrine. Robert Browning. OBVV

Give her a nickname: Slippery. Slippery. Carl Sandburg. BiCB; TiPo

Give her an Empire, she pines for a name! Unsatisfied. Oliver Wendell Holmes. AnNE

Give her as sweet and pure a kiss. The Kiss. Walter Savage Landor. OBVV

Give her strewings, but not stir/The earth that lightly covers her. Epitaph upon a Child That Died. Robert Herrick. OBEV

Give her strewings, but not stir/The earth that lightly covers her. Upon a Child That Died. Robert Herrick. CaPo; CavP; CH; ForPo; InPK; LoBV; NoP; OBS; SeCV 1-2; TrGrPo

Give her, swallows,/my tenderness. Swallows over the Camp. Uys Krige. PeSA

Give her the unfading crown!' The Birthday Crown. William Alexander. OBVV

Give her the wages of going on, and not/to die. Wages. Alfred, Lord Tennyson. OAEP

Give her then the glass rings/And the blue bracelets. After Twenty Years. Fadwa Tuquan. PBWP

Give him a drink of milk and watch him go. Birthday. Yevgeny Yevtushenko. NAs

Give him amongst thy works a place,/Who in them lov'd and sought thy face! The Book. Henry Vaughan. JCP; SeCV 1-2

Give him his sword, and set him free! The Viking. Whitley Stokes. OnYI

Give him the victor's glistening robe,/The palm-wreath and the crown. O Thou, Who Didst Ordain the Word. Edwin Hubbell Chapin. AH

...Give him your love. The Beast in the Space. W.S. Graham. FaBoTw; PoA

Give it a free trial in the privacy/of your own home. Highway Patrol Stops Me, Going Too Slow. Robert Peterson. NeAC

Give it a home. The World Narrowed to a Point. William Carlos Williams. MoLP

Give it my brother. Cuckoo, Cherry Tree. *Anonymous.* PBBP

Give it strict form. Prayer before Work. May Sarton. SaC

Give it time, it will rise up again. The Seeds of Love. *Anonymous.* FaBoCh; LoGBV; OBET; WiR

Give/life to me as thou didst to my fathers and pardon the sins of/all my people! Salutation. Emperor of Abyssinia Zerea Jacob. ISi

Give, Lord! Their weakned Hearts strong Consolations./Amen. Two Vast Enjoyments Commemorated. John Danforth. SCAP

Give me a drink. Last Will of the Drunk. Myra von Riedemann. OBCV

Give me a faint glimpse of Heaven. Petition of Youth before Battle. John Bunker. CAW

Give me a little time,/Eternity,/& I will mend. Lives of the Saints. Jon Anderson. FiCP

Give me an equal kiss, as I kiss you. Pygmalion to Galatea. Robert Graves. PG

Give me an extra set of wings. Where Is My Butterfly Net? David McCord. FiBHP

Give me back my job again. I Don't Want Your Millions, Mister. Jim Garland. FSW

Give me back my stones! The Testing-Tree. Stanley Jasspon Kunitz. FYAP; MAT; UnPo

Give me but a Barrack, a Fig for the Clergy. A Soldier and a Scholar. Jonathan Swift. OBEC

Give me, I say, our own American. The True Knight. Ella Wheeler Wilcox. PeD

Give me, Lord God, to look upon that dung,/My body and my heart, without disgust. Voyage to Cythera. Charles Baudelaire. LiTW; NAWM 1-2; SyP

Give me more love, or more disdain. Mediocrity in Love Rejected. Thomas Carew. ALV; AnAnS 2; ATP; CaPo; GBL; HBV 1-2; MeLP; MePo; NoP; SeCV 1-2; TEP

Give me my own child. Shango. *Anonymous.* PBA

Give me my robes of earth/and my black milk. New Year's Eve in Solitude. Robert Mezey. NaP; VWA

Give me myself but for an hour. Go back, dark blood. The Dream and the Blood. Louis Untermeyer. UnTE

Give me new phoenix-wings to fly at my desire. On Sitting Down to Read "King Lear" Once Again. John Keats. ATP; DiPo; EBEV; EnRP; ERoP 1-2; MBW 1-2; NoP

Give me new sight; O grant me strength to find/From lamp and flower simplicity of mind. A Midnight Interior. Siegfried Sassoon. MoRP

Give me one perfect thing. Envoi. Anna Wickham. MoBrPo

Give me Peace; that is all, that is all I seek.../Say, starting on Saturday week. From a Full Heart. A.(lan) A.(lexander) Milne. InMe

An' give me sech a startle thet I woke. Sunthin' in the Pastoral Line. James Russell Lowell. AP

Give me solitude, give me Nature, give me again, O Nature,/Your primal sanities!... Give Me the Splendid Silent Sun. Walt Whitman. BoLiVe; BoNaP

Give me some little lyric of my own. I Like to Quote. Mitchell D. Follansbee. PoPl

Give me some time to blow the man down. Blow the Man Down. *Anonymous.* ABF; AmFP; BLSo; FSW; TrAS

Give me the bad new days. Soaps. Harold Witt. SOTS

Give me the broom. The left-overs sweep the leavings away. The Floor Is Dirty. Edward Field. NeAP

Give me the confused self that you can do nothing with;/I can do something. The Just Vengeance (excerpt). Dorothy L. Sayers. BoC

Give me the days when I was twenty-one! The Garrett. William Makepeace Thackeray. HBV 1-2

Give me the inspiration/of war mongers/and throw their causes/to the orphans. For Myself. J. A. Hines. LFAC

"Give me the knife. They move." The Sunflowers. Douglas Stewart. BoAV; PoL

Give me the pure, or none. To a Painted Lady. Alexander Brome. CavP

Give me the straight and ordered flame! Self-Analysis. Anna Wickham. MoBrPo

Give me the sunlight and the sea/And who shall take my heaven from me? Sunlight and Sea. Alfred Noyes. MOS

Give me the vision,/And they may live. Prayer. Frank Stewart Flint. TrPWD

Give me the whole fire of your heart. Astrology. Tom Marshall. PeCV

Give me the withered leaves I chose/Before in the old time. Song: "Oh roses for the flush of youth." Christina Georgina Rossetti. GTBS-P; LoBV; ViBoPo

Give me the Woman here. Sonnet: "Oh! for some honest Lovers ghost." Sir John Suckling. MeLP; MePo; PoEL 1-5

Give me three grains of corn. Give Me Three Grains of Corn, Mother. Amelia Blandford Edwards. AS; BLPA

Give me thy flannel petticoat/To wrap around my head! Comfort in Affliction. Ayton [(or Aytoun)] Sir Robert. InMe

Give me treatment, but don't put me in hospital! Modern Love Songs. Faarah Nuur. TTY

Give me wide walls to build my house of Life. Wide Walls. *Anonymous.* PoToHe

Give me your light and hide the world from me! Blindness. Delmira Agustini. PBWP

Give mind to what I pray, and have it done! Envoy (To King Henry IV). Geoffrey Chaucer. WHA

Give my heart. In the Bleak Mid-Winter. Christina Georgina Rossetti. BoC; OxBoCh; TRV

Give my Love fame faster than Time wastes life;/So thou prevent'st his scythe and crooked knife. Sonnets, C: "Where art thou, Muse, that thou forget'st so long." William Shakespeare. OBSC

Give my regards to old Broadway and say that I'll be there, e'er long. Give My Regards to Broadway. George M. Cohan. BLSo; FSN

Give my respects to Mrs. Jones, and say I'm pretty well! Misadventures at Margate. Richard Harris Barham. HBV 1-2

...Give/Or take a day or two, my days are numbered. An Unborn Child. Derek Mahon. FaBoIP

Give or withhold, let pain or pleasure be,/Enough to know that we are serving Thee. Hymn. John Chadwick. TrPWD

Give our love to the Beatles, good-bye. Below Hekla. Selima Hill. FaBoWP

Give peace, O God, give peace again! Christ the Consoler. Sir Henry William Baker. BePJ

Give peace to write and read and think. Darling of Gods and Men, beneath the Gliding Stars. Basil Bunting. NoAm

Give shelter from storms and from dyioux. Limerick: "When they go out walking the Sioux." *Anonymous.* TDH

Give thanks for this turn for the better. A Change in Style. Eochaidh O Heoghusa. NOBI

Give thanks never to have/seen them/real and alive/among/us. The Litanies of Julia Pastrana. Thomas W. Shapcott. CBAP; NOAV

Give the barber a pinch of snuff. Barber, Barber, Shave a Pig. Mother Goose. HBV 1-2; HBVY

Give the shantyboys doughnuts and nothing goes wrong! The Shantyboys' Song. *Anonymous.* ShS

Give their earthen floors/The ease of trampolines. Dancers at the Moy. Paul Muldoon. BIrV

Give them me. Give them./No. Overheard on a Saltmarsh. Harold Monro. CH; GoJo; MoShBr; SO; TiPo; WSC

Give them the roll of the drum! The Charge by the Ford. Thomas Dunn English. PAH

Give them to your sons. Hot-Cross Buns. Mother Goose. OxNR; SoPo

Give thou my sacred relics burial. His Return to London. Robert Herrick. AnAnS 2; CaPo; EnLit; FaBoPP; FF

"Give thy name!'–"Sir! Genius.'" God Said, "I Made a Man". Jose Garcia Villa. AnFE

Give to our children all the happy days you gave/To Ralph, Vasey, Alastair, Biddy, John and me. Trebetherick. Sir John Betjeman. CMoP; EvOK; ExPo

Give unto us thy breadth of love,/In loving all mankind. O Mind of God, Broad as the Sky. Oliver Huckel. TrPWD

Give us again the solace of belief. The Poets. Scudder Middleton. HBMV

Give us laughter, Puck! To Puck. Beatrice Llewellyn Thomas. HBMV

Give us love, and give us peace! One Morning, Oh! So Early. Jean Ingelow. HBV 1-2; OxBChV

Give us one drink ere we go henne. Omnes Gentes Plaudite! *Anonymous.* OBSP

Give us our daily bread! The People's Petition. Wathen Mark Wilks Call. OBVV

Give us our swords again, and hold thy hand. The Prayer of Beaten Men. Margaret Louisa Woods. HBV 1-2

Give us the courage of our leisure/To make the unimagined world more real. A Peony for Apollo. Charles Edward Eaton. GoYe

Give us this court and rule without a guard. The Last Instructions to a Painter. Andrew Marvell. APAS

Give us this day our daily news. Bar-Room Matins. Louis MacNeice. EaLo

Give us thy light, forgive us what we are. Sonnet: "O little self, within whose smallness lies." John Masefield. WGRP

Give us to build above the deep intent/The deed, the deed. A Prayer. John Drinkwater. HBV 1-2; OBVV; TrPWD; WGRP

Give you such birthday presents, if I could. For a Birthday. Elaine V. Emans. BiCB

Give you welcome to the Glories with the Song of/the Gulf Stream. Song of the Gulf Stream. Francis Alan Ford. EtS

Give your attendance to my mistress' call. You Blessed Bowers. *Anonymous.* ElL

Give your thanks that to a woman/Tears are given, and be at ease. A Wasted Sympathy. Winifred Howells. AA

Given to lewdness and/Rodomontade. Paradise Lost: V. Anthony Hecht. NLV

Given under our hand with a quillet/This day of our era. On a Cock Which Was Stolen from a Good Priest. Egan O'Rahilly. OnYI

The giver given from gift shall never part. Arcadia. Sir Philip Sidney. SiPS

Giver of good, so answer each request/With Thine own giving, better than my/best. The Answered Prayer. Annie Johnson Flint. STF

Gives earth and heaven, for song's sake and the soul's,/Their glory. The Interpreters. Algernon Charles Swinburne. PoEL 1-5

Gives everybody on his plate of malathion/A rich spoonful of air. Conservancies. Josephine Miles. GP

Gives her a dampy touch, that doth benumb/Her soul, and strikes her contemplation dumb. The Lark. *Anonymous.* PBBP

Gives irresponsive absence flesh and vesture. Epigram: "Dear, my familiar hand in love's own gesture." J. V. Cunningham. PV

Gives it a wipe–and all is gone. The Poet's Fate. Thomas Hood. ELU; FiBHP; PV

Gives it a wipe,–and all is gone. To the Reviewers. Thomas Hood. TW

Gives its worn body back to earth again. Let Me Go down to Dust. Lew Sarett. TrPWD

Gives me just what I want, and asks back nothing. My Stearine Candles. James Henry. NOBV

Gives our loved ones naught to fear. Muster Out the Rangers. *Anonymous.* CoSo

Giving a curious feeling to the mind/Of peopled solitude. The Quantocks. William Wordsworth. FaBoPP

Giving a sense of someone, or something/being born/Hyeeeeee-a. The Two Coyotes. T. Walking Eagle Marietta. LFAC

Giving everyone I know a dirty look. I Cannot Wash My Eye without an Eyecup. *Anonymous.* PV

Giving light, dying. Moon's Ending. Sara Teasdale. MOON

Giving me back to life. Thirty Childbirths. Millen Brand. AMV-80

Giving off the odor that partridges love. Solitude Late at Night in the Woods. Robert Bly. BiP; VGW

Giving psalm/and ease. Miniatures IV. Mute the Hand Moves from the Heart. Lynn Strongin. IHMS

Giving the soul of man, though the last trump/blare throught the curtains, the right to his own The Uncelestial City (excerpt). Humbert Wolfe. BoC

Giving us gifts at hand, the glitter of all their eyes. Eyes of Night-Time. Muriel Rukeyser. BoWoP; MiAP; NePA

...Giving us the poles/That are His own, not merely balanced strife. Pain. Thomas Edward Brown. PeD

,Giving you a sense of satisfaction/Understandable in any language Citizen. Peter Schjeldahl. ANYP

Giving you back her deathless love of you! Ave Atque Vale. Thomas S. Jones, Jr. HBV 1-2

A glacial age demands a glacial heart. Spring. Frederick Feirstein. AMV-81

A glacier suffocating a siren. The Welder. Frank Lima. ANYP

Glad am I that I came to Him./And found His truth and grace. I Came to Jesus. George White. STF

Glad captives of Thy matchless grace,/Thy righteous rule obey. Compassion So Divine. Anne Steele. BePJ

The glad indomitable sea,/The strong white sun. A Sea Child. Bliss Carman. HBV 1-2

(Glad is the wind and tall is the fire). The World in Making. Sir Gilbert Parker. CaP

Glad shall ring, "A Christ is born!" The Christmas Candle. Kate Louise Brown. SoPo

Glad that, in loving you, the whole world lives afresh. Watching You Walk. Ruthven Todd. LiTL; NeBP

Glad tidings shout to all abroad,/So be it, Lord, Amen. Th' Almighty Spake, and Gabriel Sped. George Richards. AH

Glad to be flying. The Pelican. Greg Kuzma. AmPA

Glad to be hid, and proud to be forgot. The Young Author. Samuel Johnson. EiCP; LAuP

Glad to be Nothing, to be All. To Henry Vaughan. A. J. M. Smith. OBCV

Glad to conceal her tears, her blushes there. Fond Youth. Samuel Rogers. OBRV

Glad to find a spark among the ashes/and make the time seem warm. Behind the Stove. James Hearst. TAT

Glad to find release in heaven's care. For You. Ted Berrigan. ANYP

Glad, when is opened unto my need/Some sea-like glimpse of thee. A Strip of Blue. Lucy Larcom. AA; HBV 1-2; WGRP

Gladden the poor and sad/For love's dear sake. While Stars of Christmas Shine. Emilie Poulsson. OHIP

Gladly I follow Heaven's command,/With Jesus near! Jesus Is Near. Robert Cassie Waterston. BePJ

Gladly I turn me from the sight,/Unto my tale again. Marmion. Sir Walter Scott. BSV

Gladly to run, or to inherit/In Thine eternal dwelling peace. The Return (excerpt). Margaret Louisa Woods. TrPWD

Gladly would I be free,/this landscape I would be,/that rushes past! Express Train. Karl Kraus. TrJP

...A glance of your eyes/Beneath their brown lashes. Verse Written in the Album of Mademoiselle—. Pierre Dalcour. PoNe; TTY

Glanced out and down and said "Oh no, only about ten/feet more." Mr. Artesian's Conscientiousness. Ogden Nash. NLV

...Glancing at the dark, waiting/for another scrap of it/to seek him out. Nightswim. William Pitt Root. MAYP

Glancing, I go by–dry-eyed–/(I've swung.) Conversation Piece. Arthur Freeman. ErPo

Glancing off you like the light/That hovers but will not stay. After the Second Operation. Patricia Goedicke. TAP

The glaring sunshine never knew! All's Well. John Greenleaf Whittier. CBEP; OBSP

The glass falls from the window, part by part,/And ringeth faintly in the grassy stones. Elegy in Six Sonnets. Frederick Goddard Tuckerman. QFR

The glass man, without external reference. Asides on the Oboe. Wallace Stevens. AP; FaBoMo; MoAB; MoAmPo

The glass of fat, the blue flame. Uncle. Philip Levine. NNaP

A glass of Schaeffer'll/Make your kid a general. Booze Turns Men into Women. Bernadette Mayer. APU

...A glass vase which reflects/The world's grief weeping in its daughter. The Vase of Tears. Stephen Spender. AtBAP

Glazed now with ice the cloistral vine/That hid the shyest grape. Monody. Herman Melville. AP; LiTA; MAmP; NCEP; OBSP; PoEL 1-5

Glazing the pale hair, the duplicate gray standard faces. Dolor. Theodore Roethke. AP; BiP; CMoP; CoBMV; HaCAP; HeIP; HoPM; LiTM; MoVE; NMP; NoAm; OBSP; PAI; PoA; PPON

The gleam of irrecoverable gold. Sunken Gold. Eugene Lee-Hamilton. EtS; NCEP; NOBV

The gleam of one more broken dream, O Ottawa! Deep Dark River. Lloyd Roberts. CaP

Gleaming like a new promise, that silently carried you away. Trading Chicago. Charles O. Hartman. AMV-80

Gleaming silver threads, making one garment/for high priest and swineherd. Summer Night. Hayim Nahman Bialik. VWA

The gleaming wineglass and the golden wine. The Dandelion Gatherer. Robert Francis. PPJ

Gleams like a glorious emerald Gueneyere's. Love That Is First and Last. Algernon Charles Swinburne. LiTL

Glide on, and holy Peace assumes her woodland sway. Sunset. William Julius Mickle. OBEC

Gliding/north & south, speeding with/a slurred sound– Merritt Parkway. Denise Levertov. AmC; AmPP; NeAP; PoM

A glimpse of joy that we have met/Shall shine, and dry the tear. To the Rev. Mr. Newton. William Cowper. LoBV

Glimpse of that fierce green land of mink and henna. To the Lady Portrayed by Margaret Dumont. John Hollander. OBAL

The glint of golden sunlight on His wings. The Great Man. Eunice Tietjens. WGRP

A glint of snows above Baluchistan. Camel. Jon Stallworthy. BoAnP

The glinting birthday of a fractious star. The Wit. Elizabeth Bishop. NePoAm-2

Glistening like drops of copper, agonised, in our path. Chrysalides. Thomas Kinsella. BIrV; NoAm

...Glistening snout/ready to shove up the privates of the world. Ego. Robert Siegel. PoA

Glistens on the crushed cups/and papers floating by. Lost Moments. Glover Davis. SM

Glitter green with sunny showers. Ode on the Departing Year. Samuel Taylor Coleridge. FaBoPP

Glittering and still shall come the awful night. Winter Evening. Archibald Lampman. OBCV; PeCV

The glittering, angelic meadow. The Dove of New Snow. Vachel Lindsay. MoAmPo

Glittering/gold/trembling/on darkness. The List. Michael McClure. NU

...Glittering virgin/Who is dying and glass on her marvelous bier. The Ways and the Peoples. Randall Jarrell. PoA

Gloor! Gloor! Gloor! Crow's Ditty. *Anonymous.* GBP

Gloria in excelsis Deo. Angels We Have Heard on High. *Anonymous.* FSW

Gloria Patri. Celebrated Return. Clarence Major. AmNP

Glorified all else beside–the Red and White and Blue! Your Flag and My Flag. Wilbur D. Nesbit. FaFP; WBLP

"Glorified and sanctified be His great name!" Invocation. of Berditshev, Levi Isaac. EaLo

Glorified in full release upward–/songs cease. Dawn. William Carlos Williams. MoAB; MoAmPo; PoPl

Glorious it is/When wandering time is come./Yayai-ya-yiya. Song of Caribou, Musk Oxen, Women, and Men Who Would Be Manly. *Anonymous.* WTO

Glorious Lord, and coming King! Abiding. A. B. Simpson. STF

A glorious nothing it would be,/To say, his tomb were rich, not he. Epitaph Inscribed on a Small Piece of Marble. James Shirley. CavP

A glorious picture by the wind unrolled. Gibraltar. Richard Chenevix Trench. OBRV; OBTV; OBVV

The Glorious Soul that was the King/Made to possess them, did appear/A Small and little thing! The Third Century. Thomas Traherne. AnAnS 1

Glorious: to walk across the field/towards my beloved. The Bird Catcher. *Anonymous.* TTY

The glorious wonders of the Deity. Eden. Thomas Traherne. AnAnS 1; PoEL 1-5; SeCV 1-2; TrGrPo

Glory be! I'm sixty! Emancipation. *Anonymous.* BLPA; FPL

Glory be to God on high/And on earth peace/Good will towards men. Love. George Herbert. TrCP

Glory be to God on high, who grants us our/salvation! The Wanderer. *Anonymous.* EnLi 1-2

Glory be to the new-born King. Virgin Mary Had One Son. *Anonymous.* FSW

A glory for one is another's Lost Cause. The Surrender of New Orleans. Marion Manville. PAH

The glory from his gray hairs gone/Forevermore! Ichabod. John Greenleaf Whittier. AmP

Glory Hallelujah, Hi ro je-rum. The Rich Man and the Poor Man. *Anonymous.* FSW

The glory, jest, and riddle of the world! An Essay on Man. Alexander Pope. DiPo; GoBC; GoTF; NOEC; PrIm; TreFS; TrGrPo; TRV; ViBoPo

The glory, Lord, we give to thee alone. God Set Us Here. Nicasius de Sille. AH

Glory O! Glory O! to the Bold Fenian Men. Down by the Glenside. Peadar Kearney. AnIV

A glory of olive and amber and wine,/Runs the color in the wheat. Color in the Wheat. Hamlin Garland. BPAW

The glory of the sum of things/Will flash along the chords and go. In Memoriam A.H.H, LXXXVIII. Alfred, Lord Tennyson. NoP; PBBP; VLP

The glory of this perfect day/Grow dim or cease to be! I Want to Die while You Love Me. Georgia Douglas Johnson. AmNP; BANP; BlSi; CDC

Glory's burning, generous swell,/Fancy, and the poet's shell. Go, Forget Me. Charles Wolfe. HBV 1-2

Glory sing to the Lord. Glory. Joseph Wise. AH

The glory that men in good kingdoms see/Is when both young and old in traffic be. Caelica, XIX. Fulke, Lord Brooke Greville. FCP

The glory/The power, the glory. Brasilia. Sylvia Plath. CAPP

Glory to Man in the highest! for Man is the/master of things. Hymn of Man. Algernon Charles Swinburne. VLP; WGRP

Glory to the new-born King. Hark! The Herald Angels Sing. Charles Wesley. FSW; GoTF; SBVL; TreFS

Glory to You forever and ever. Amen. O Glory of Virgins. Saint Venantius Fortunatus. ISi

The glottals of a Sweeney prayer/Are drowned in great expectorations. Sweeney, Old and Phthisic, among the Hippopotami (parody). David Cummings. BXAP

Gloves waiting for hands. The Daughters of Blum. Charles Wright. CoAP; SM

Glow at a smile and sicken at a frown! To a Friend in Love during the Riots. William Parsons. NOEC

Glow, little glow-worm, glow. The Glow-Worm. Johnny Mercer. OBAL

The glow of what has gone. Separate Peace. Harrison Smith Morris. MC

The glow-worm lights us home to bed. The Queen of Fairies. *Anonymous.* ViBoPo

The glowing coales: so leysurly his spirit from him drew. Metamorphoses. Ovid (Publius Ovidius Naso). CTC

Glowing yet with gratitude! Daily Bread. *Anonymous.* BePJ

GLUMP. Bye Bye. Sean O'Huigin. WHW

The Glurpy Slurpy Skakagrall–/Who's standing right behind you. The Worst. Shel Silverstein. WSC

Glytterand on every spar and ruf on hycht. The Aeneid. Virgil (Publius Vergilius Maro). OBVE

"Gnawing the guts of men." The End of Clonmacnois. *Anonymous.* KiLC

Go and find work. What the Chairman Told Tom. Basil Bunting. OxBTC

Go and get your candle lit! The Stranger in the Pumpkin. John Ciardi. NTCP

Go and love and suffer! Wedding Song. Conrad Ferninand Meyer. HW

Go and make somebody else/Unsatisfied. To the Tune "Red Embroiderd Shoes'. Huang O. PBWP; WPOW

Go as gently as you came. Primroses. Alfred Austin. OBVV

"Go ask Papa." Proposal. *Anonymous.* GoTF; TreFS

"Go away,' I said, "Go away.' By the Road. Geoffrey Grigson. OxBTC

Go back so that Flight-of-the-Chiefs will be inhabited.'/Nabosulu/Nabusele Tip-of-the-Single-Feather. Velema. WTO

Go back to the city/so sudden-like The Proposition. Paul Blackburn. ErPo

Go back when you're rich, behung with lice! A Terrestrial Cuckoo. Frank O'Hara. SOTW

Go, bar the door, you fool, she cries. An Epigram on Florio. John Winstanley. FaBoEE

Go bare, bare, bare. Shoe a Little Horse. *Anonymous.* OxNR

Go boldly on with no land-looking doubt/Through the increasing seas to yet more sea. The Deeper Seas. Henry Bellamann. EtS

Go bomb a canoe. Dear America. Robert Peterson. PPON

Go by, go by. Come Not When I Am Dead. Alfred, Lord Tennyson. FaBoRV; GBL

Go by, linked fin by fin, most odiously. Three Sonnets. [James Henry] Leigh Hunt. NOBL

Go child, who is my sin and nothing more. Unknown Girl in the Maternity Ward. Anne Sexton. CoPo; NAs; NoAm

Go chipping off and dancing/through the flat blue keening/air. On a Morning Full of Sun. Philip Appleman. SOTS

...Go/contrary, go/sing The Songs of Maximus: 3. Charles Olson. PPP

Go dancing to school. May Mornings. Ivy O. Eastwick. BrR; SiSoSe

Go do the dishes. Go to bed. The Ballad of Mary Baldwin. Stephen Sandy. MAT

Go down the street. A Catch of Shy Fish. Gwendolyn Brooks. CAPP

Go down you blood red roses, go down. Blood Red Roses. *Anonymous.* FSW

Go! dull complaint, my lady this report. Go, Sad Complaint. Charles, duc d' Orleans. MeEL

Go dwell thou with them as a mourner dwells. La Vita Nuova. Dante Alighieri. AWP

Go early, go quick, and get a good view. The Camels Have Come. *Anonymous.* PoOW

Go farther! let it serve to trample on. Sonnets from the Portuguese, II. Elizabeth Barrett Browning. OBVV

...Go/Find a park. Poems from the Coalfields, 2: Advice from a Nightwatchman. Ian Healy. PoAu 1-2

Go find the answers, right away, and tell me in September!' I Wish. Nancy Byrd Turner. SiSoSe

(Go flower child, in peace bloom free.) Patty, 1949-1961. Sharon Mayer Libera. IHMS

Go forth from life in guise of mendicants. For, Lord, the Crowded Cities Be... Rainer Maria Rilke. AWP; TrJP

Go forth I say–attain–attain. With Every Rising of the Sun. Ella Wheeler Wilcox. GoTF; TreFT

Go forth no longer as my body-slave,/But as the heir of all the Universe. Soul-Drift. Mathilde Blind. SBG

Go, go from the martial plain which you have forgotten! Satires. Juvenal (Decimas Junius Juvenalis). PeHV

"Go, go, go, seek some otherwhere,/Importune me no more!" Youth and Cupid. Queen of England Elizabeth I. OBSC

Go hang my self, and thy desire. Song: "Fire, fire." Henry Bold. GBL

Go hang thyself, and burn thy Marianne. Poet, Whoe'er Thou Art. John Wilmot, Earl of Rochester. DBV

Go headlong down among the deep/Whales. A Mother's Song. Francis Ledwidge. EtS

Go, heart, unto thy Saviour. Go, Heart, unto the Lamp of Licht. *Anonymous.* BSV; GoTS

Go hence, for it is useless to pretend. Innocent Landscape. Elinor Wylie. OxBA

Go hippity hop to bed. Hippity Hop to Bed. Leroy F. Jackson. TiPo

Go home and look after your wives. An Encomium upon a Parliament. Daniel Defoe. APAS

Go home. Go home to my noisy wife. The Drunken Man. Steve Orlen. MAYP

Go home, you see, well I wouldn't run a risk like that. My Hat. Stevie Smith. BrRo

Go hunt the hurtful fly, and bear/My blessing to your kind in air. The Bat. Ruth Pitter. FM

...Go hunting/lightly as pampooties/over the skull-capped ground. Viking Dublin: Trial Pieces. Seamus Heaney. IPY

Go! I forgive thee all/In weeping over this! Disarmed. Laura Redden Searing. AA

Go in one ear/and out the other A Deposition by John Wilmot. Vincent McHugh. ErPo

Go kill the dying swan! Ode: "Once more the country calls." Allen Tate. WaP

Go kiss their hands and make your own/With every touch more white. Song to the Masquers. James Shirley. OBSP

Go, little verse, and lay in vesture meet/Of poesy, my homage at her feet. In February. Henry Simpson. HBV 1-2

Go 'long, Blue Dog. On the Trail to Idaho. *Anonymous.* CoSo

Go, love without the help of anything on earth.' Gnomic Verses. William Blake. OBRV; TrGrPo

Go not the way lamenting goes. A Weightless Element. Gottfried Benn. PoPl

Go now/I think you are ready. Tract. William Carlos Williams. AmP; AP; BiP; BLPL; CoBMV; DL; FF; LiTA; LiTM; MoAB; MoAmPo; MP; NePA; NoAm; NOBA; TAP; TrGrPo; TwCP; VGW

Go on brave doctor, a third volume write,/And find us paper while you make us sh–. Upon the Author of the "Satire against Wit." Sir Charles Sedley. APAS

Go on riding while you got the chance. For Jack Chatham. Jared Carter. AMV-81

Go on to build cathedrals, like the Gauls. Peter at Fourteen. Constance Carrier. NePoAm

Go on with less ambition than I came. Fight with a Water-Spirit. Norman Cameron. HaMV

Go out/make fruitful the earth Journey Round the World. Ingrid Jonker. PBWP

Go, peny, go! Snatches: "Spende, and God shal sende." *Anonymous.* OxBM

Go, ring out all the bells! A Testament. *Anonymous.* OBSC

Go sail with your soldier, he'll find you a home. The Lame Soldier. *Anonymous.* OuSiCo

Go sailing off with Peter Pan/Along the Tree-top Way! The Tree-Top Road. May Riley Smith. HBV 1-2

...Go screw, taste–/itself a tasteless suggestion. Taste. John Updike. AMV-81

Go see 'em in the room! Johnnie Bought a Ham. *Anonymous.* OuSiCo

Go sen'-a dem angels down, O, bretheren. My Way's Cloudy. *Anonymous.* BoAN 1-2

Go, shut the leaves, and clasp the book. In My Own Album. Charles Lamb. CBEP; OBRV

Go sleep, ma honey, m–m. Go Sleep, Ma Honey. Edward D. Barker. AA

Go, stepping soft in your star-buttoned moccasins, A-zlay. Navajo Song. Maynard Dixon. BPAW

Go Stranger, sojourn in the woodland cot/Of INNOCENCE, and thou shalt find her there. Inscription for a Tablet on the Banks of a Stream. Robert Southey. OBEC

"Go take up her body and get it out of my way,"/Was the words the rich man said. The Coal Miner's Child. *Anonymous.* OuSiCo

Go, talk to him, and tell him who you are,/Face to face, at last, Scott; and kiss his scar. Green Breeks. Douglas Dunn. FaBoPV

Go talking and have easy hours. The Sun Used to Shine. Edward ("Edward Eastaway") Thomas. FaBoTw

Go tell it on the mountain,/Our Jesus Christ is born. Go Tell It on the Mountain. *Anonymous.* FSW

Go the route, old scout, and be merry,/For tomorrow you may die. Is It Really Worth the While? *Anonymous.* BLPA

Go then, my dust, to dust, but thou my soul/Return unto thy rest above the pole. The Circulation. Thomas Washbourne. NOCV

Go then, Sweet Sara, take thy Sabbath Rest,/With thy Great Lord, and all in Heaven Blest. In Saram. John Cotton. SCAP

Go then thy way with thine accustomed cheer,/Nor heed my churlish greeting, O New Year. Thysia. Morton Luce. HBV 1-2

Go through my window, my little bird,/And buy molasses candy. Little Bird, Go through My Window. *Anonymous.* OuSiCo

Go to bed and undress you. Good Night, God Bless You. *Anonymous.* OxNR

Go to bed third/A golden bird. Go to Bed First. *Anonymous.* GBP; OxNR

Go to hell,/and I walk off. In a Dream. David Ignatow. GP

Go/to it, O jazzmen. Jazz Fantasia. Carl Sandburg. AnFE; CoAnAm; MoAB; MoAmPo; PoNe

Go to making/Dust? Must. Must. Alun Lewis. ELU

Go to my son, by whom my medicine's sold. Epitaph on a Quack. *Anonymous.* FaBoUs

Go to sleepy, little baby. All the Pretty Little Horses. *Anonymous.* ABF; AmFP; FSW; OxBoLi

Go to the moon/where they belong. So This Is Our Revolution. Sonia Sanchez. GP

Go to thy little senseless play–/Thou dost not heed my lay. A Mother to Her Waking Infant. Joanna Baillie. NOEC

Go to thy nest and lay. The Hen Keeper. *Anonymous.* OxNR

Go, True Child, heart of song, sing out, sing out! True Child. Marion Hodge. AMV-81

Go up from fold and rick,/The cattle then are sick. Two Poems after A. E. Housman. Hugh Kingsmill. NOBL

Go way down cellar/and eat apples. Ring the Bell. *Anonymous.* OxNR

Go weave and spin, you can't go,/Buckeye Jim. Buckeye Jim. *Anonymous.* FSW

Go, Wedlock, to the men of leaden brains,/Who hate variety, and sigh for chains. Ode: "That I have often been in love, deep love." John Wolcot. NOEC

Go where I will, thou lucky Lar stay here,/Warm by a glittering chimney all the year. To Lar. Robert Herrick. BoW; CaPo; SeCV 1-2

Go with me to that land where I'm bound. Come and Go with Me to That Land. *Anonymous.* FSW

Go. You are not allowed to forget. Instructions for Crossing the Border. Dan Pagis. VWA

...Goat. Skunk. Some snakes. A History of the Pets. David Huddle. PPJ

...The goatherd blows his flute/and calls the cattle up the slope. Campi Flegrei. Barend Toerien. PeSA

Goats lolled at the doorways,/innocently spreading a smell of peace. End of Summer. Berl Pomerantz. VWA

Goats of cast bronze danced into/sunlight on the window sill. Into & At. Edmund Pennant. SOTS

A goblin lives in our house all the year round. The Goblin. Rose Fyleman. NTCP; TiPo

God, a motion of thy lip! A Hymn to God in Time of Stress. Max Eastman. TrPWD

God abide the coming day! Adios. Donald Campbell Babcock. NePoAm-2

God accept him, Christ receive him. Ode on the Death of the Duke of Wellington. Alfred, Lord Tennyson. ACV; OBVV; VLP

God Almighty sees we keep/Religiously to one another? The True Confession of George Barker. George Barker. ErPo

God alone suffices. Nothing Move Thee. Saint Theresa of Avila. PBWP

God am I for the time. Homage to Sextus Propertius, VII. Ezra Pound. VGW

God and flesh were one. Incarnation Poem. John Leax. TrCP

God and His ark are onward rolled,/High above earth in heaven. The Eagle Swift. Adam of St. Victor. BePJ

God and His heaven are globed in you. The Locomotive to the Little Boy. Benjamin R. C. Low. HBMV

God and man, and so He is for aye,/Ascendit super sidera. The Five Joys of the Virgin. *Anonymous.* ISi

God, angels' gifts on bodies, may bestow. Of the Blessed Sacrament of the Altar. Robert Southwell. GoBC; OBEV

God answered: where I was the day/My Son was crucified. Calvary. Libby Stopple. GoYe

God be at my end and at my departing. God Be in My Head. *Anonymous.* BoC; OxBoCh; TRV

"God be kind to the noble boy,/Who is somebody's son, and pride and joy!" Somebody's Mother. Mary Dow Brine. BeLS; BLPA; FaFP; TreF

(God be praised!) the Georges ended. The Georges. Walter Savage Landor. ChTr; DBV; FaBoEE; FiBHP; NIP; OBSV

God be thanked, I carry a knife. Arms and the Woman. Dorothea Mackellar. NOAV

God be thanked! Whate'er comes after, I have lived and toiled with men! The Galley-Slave. Rudyard Kipling. BrPo

God be with the night that's gone! The Vanished Night. Niall MacMurray. KiLC

God be with us, together with the prayer of Patrick, chief/apostle. Prayer to St. Patrick. Ninine. OnYI

God be with you in the Winter,/Just to guide you into rest. Through the Year. Julian S. Cutler. BLPA

God be with you till we meet again! God Be with You Till We Meet Again. Jeremiah Eames Rankin. AH; TreFS

God become human and man grown divine. The Line of Beauty. Arthur William Edgar O'Shaughnessy. OnYI

A God beheld in dreams that were/Beheld of her! The Laud of Saint Catherine. Algernon Charles Swinburne. CAW

God being with thee when we know it not. Sonnet: "It is a beauteous evening, calm and free." William Wordsworth. LoBV; ViBoPo

God bless all in this house till we do come again. Somerset Wassail. *Anonymous.* OBET

God bless America, My home sweet home. God Bless America. Irving Berlin. BLSo; TreFT

God bless America, the home of the brave! Kearsarge and Alabama. *Anonymous.* PAH

"God Bless America,"/With an Irish accent. Poem to a Nigger Cop. Bobb Hamilton. TTY

God bless and keep you far, John-John!/And that's my prayer. John-John. Thomas Macdonagh. AnIV; AWP; HBMV; OnYI; OxBI

"God bless and keep you," mother dear, today. My Mother. Bertha Nolan. PGD

God bless him then forever. A Trick for Tyburn; or, A Prison Rant. *Anonymous.* APAS

God bless me, what a deal you've seen! Nonsense. Thomas Moore. FaBoEE; InMe; NA

God bless my babe, and lullaby/From this thy father's quality. A Cradle Song. Nicholas Breton. HBV 1-2; NOBE; OBEV

"God bless our little ghost!" Our Little Ghost. Louisa May Alcott. OBCA

God bless pawnbrokers!/They are quiet men. Pawnbrokers. Marguerite Wilkinson. HBMV

God bless the Bastard king of England. The Bastard King of England. *Anonymous.* FSW

God bless the child! The Wood, the Weed, the Wag. Sir Walter Ralegh. CBEP; SiPS; TrGrPo

God bless the Dean and make his deanship plenary. Lucretius Versus the Lake Poets. Robert Frost. GLGT

God bless the fish-hawk and the/fisher! The Fisherman's Hymn. Alexander Wilson. AA; EtS

"God bless the friend who just "stands by'!" The Friend Who Just Stands By. B. Y. Williams. PoLf; PoToHe

God bless the little villages and guard them night and day! Song of the Little Villages. James B. Dollard. CAW

God bless/The mortician's wife/Who lives forever The Fishermen's Wives. Elaine Namanworth. AMV-80

God bless the U.S.A., so large,/So friendly, and so rich. On the Circuit. W. H. Auden. NOBL; OxBTC

God bless thee, when winds blow,/Our home, and all we know. A Prayer for a Little Home. Florence Bone. BLPA; FaBoBe; FaFP; GoTF; TreFT

God bless them, that each Christmas they/May furnish so their board. A Carol for Twelfth Day. Anonymous. OHIP

God bless these wives and their strong/Men's endeavour. The Well of Life. Sir Herbert Read. NoAm

"God bless those pretty Spanish girls we left around Cape Horn." Rounding the Horn. Anonymous. OBSS

God bless us all! That's quite another thing. A Jacobite Toast. John Byrom. FaBoCo

God bless you, and God bless me! The Robin's Song. C. Lovat Fraser. MoShBr

God bless you, brother. This Holy Night. Eleanor Farjeon. ChBR

God bless you, dear, and all who sail in you. A Note on Wyatt. Kingsley Amis. WeW

God bless you, dear, good night! The Sun Was Slumbering in the West. Thomas Hood. FiBHP

God bless you, dear Maggie, you've given new life to a poor volunteer. The Cripple for Life. Anonymous. AmFP

God bless you, dear, to-day! God Bless You, Dear, To-Day! John Bennett. AA

God bless you. Guilt is magical. Adultery. James Dickey. TAP; WeW

God bless you old girl!–So unafraid! The Statue of Liberty. Sheila Jane Crooke. YaD

"God bless you, sir!' and lay their rammers by. Tadlow. Abel Evans. FaBoCo

God bring us all to his in,/"Amen, amen,' dicentes. Tutivillus, the Devil. Anonymous. EBEV; MeEL

God bring you to a fairer place/Than even Oxford town. The Spires of Oxford. Winifred M. Letts. EnLit; FaFP; HBV 1-2; MCCG; OHFP; OnYI; PoLf; PoRA; TreF; WGRP

God! but the interest! The Debt. Paul Laurence Dunbar. BANP; CDC; SoSe; TRV

God! but the night is cold! Monsieur Qui Passe. Charlotte Mew. SBG

God cannot be expressed. Silence. John Lancaster Spalding. AA

God cannot let it come to naught. Fifty Years. James Weldon Johnson. BANP

God cares, He always cares! God Cares. Helen Annis Casterline. BLRP

God carry her to Paradise/and dance there with her immortal soul. Winter in Another Country. Florence Anthony ("Ai"). AMV-81

God caught his eye. Epitaph on a Waiter. David McCord. NIP; NLV; OBAL; PPJ

God cloth'd himselfe in vile mans flesh, that so/Hee might be weake enough to suffer woe. Holy Sonnets, XI. John Donne. MasP; OBS

God curse the man who saddled me/as Jesus' wife. I am a young girl, gay. Anonymous. BoWoP

God damn their eyes! Ballad of Sam Hall. Anonymous. FSW; VLP

God does do such wonderful things! God Does Do Such Wonderful Things! Angela Morgan. TRV

God does not live to explain. New Hampshire, February. Richard Eberhart. LiTM; MP; TwCP

God don't like it, no, no,/It's a scandalous and a shame. God Don't Like It. Anonymous. OuSiCo

God don't never change/Ohhhh-ahh/Always will be God God Don't Never Change. Blind Willie Johnson. BluL

God doth despise,/Abhor, and spew out all neutralities. Neutrality Loathsome. Robert Herrick. LiTB; NoP

God finds united being in the beingless death he dies,/And lifts it up to secret majesty of skies. Why the Resurrection Was Revealed to Women. C Greiffenberg. PBWP

God, for a man that solicits insurance! Bohemia. Dorothy Parker. CrMA; NAMP; NLV

God forbid, you might become a donkey with epaulets. In Life's Stable. (or Molodovski) Kadya, (or Kadia) Molodovsky. VWA

God, forgive! Phantoms. Harry McGuire. CAW

God found I wasn't there–/At least not over half. Not All There. Robert Frost. FaBoCo

God gave Noah the rainbow sign. Sowing on the Mountain. Anonymous. FSW

God gave you/all that strength/for you to kill/my people./Love–Delilah Love Letter. Carole C. Gregory. BlSi

God gif him dolour and disease/That breaks their hairt, and nocht the better. To Luve Unluvit. Alexander Scott. GoTS; OxBS

God, give me hills to climb,/And strength for climbing! Hills. Arthur Guiterman. HBVY

God give thee strength, O gentel trout,/To pull the raskall in!! Ballade: To a Fish of the Brooke. John Wolcot. CBEP

God, give thy wayward children peace! Let There Be Light. William M. Vories. AH

"God, give us another chance!" The Song of the Unsuccessful. Richard Burton. WGRP

God give us grace to live as Bradley died! Conductor Bradley. John Greenleaf Whittier. PaPo

God, God am I. The Seven Days, III: On First Knowing God. Reed Whittemore. GP

God, God have pity on man apart. American Twilights, 1957. James Wright. CoAP

God goeth with you, Greatheart! Where Are You Going, Greatheart? John Oxenham. BLPA; PAL; PGD

God grant her now hevyn to encrese/and owr kyng Harry long lyff and pease On the Death of Elizabeth, Queen of Henry VII... Anonymous. FaBoRV

God grant that I may be/(My sweet) sweet company. Benediction. Stanley Jasspon Kunitz. MoRP; VGW

God grant, that in the mills, a day/May be blest, "Ten hours" long. Ah! Leave My Harp and Me Alone. Anonymous. SaC

God grant thee thine own wish, and grant thee mine. Vota Amico Facta, Fol. 160. Gazaeus. OBVE

God grant them all his blessing/That now maken cheer. Lullay My Liking. Anonymous. EG; ELP

God grant thy daughter a Cordelia be! To England. George Henry Boker. AA

God grant 'twill bring us Andy. Andy's Gone with Cattle. Henry Lawson. PoAu 1-2

God grant us all (a) good ending,/Regnat Dei gracia. Nunc Gaudet Maria. Anonymous. ISi

God grant us all as well to fare. Sir Orfeo. Anonymous. AtBAP; MeEV; OxBM

God grant you find one face there/You loved when all was young! The Old Song. Charles Kingsley. CBEP; OBVV; PG

God granting these, before I die, I'd ask no more of life. Wishes. A. C. Child. PoToHe

God ha' mercy on his soul! Hamlet. William Shakespeare. InPo; TrGrPo; ViBoPo

God ha' mercy on such as we,/Baa! Yah! Bah! Gentlemen-Rankers. Rudyard Kipling. NOBV

God had released her. The Widow. Robert Southey. NOEC; OBEC

...God had/thrown a lamp-post at the Captain, temporarily disabling/him. Poems, VIII. Philip O'Connor. EAS

God haffe mersey on Roben Hodys solle,/And saffe all god yemanrey! Robin Hood and the Potter. Anonymous. BaBo; ESPB

God hangs tapestries in a worked-out mine, way back in the woods. The Puritan Hacking away at Oak. Todd Gitlin. AMV-80

God has blest you. The Daily Grind. Fenton Johnson. AmNP

God has done well to me. After Two Years. Richard Aldington. GTBS; HBV 1-2; MoBrPo; PG; PoPl; WHA

God has fogotten the world! A Song of Doubt. Josiah Gilbert Holland. WGRP

God has forgotten, or he never knew–/This want of you. The Want of You. Ivan Leonard Wright. BLPA; FaBoBe

God hath the soul. Linen Bands. Vance Thompson. AA

God have her soul, I can no better say. Oft in My Thoughts. Charles, duc d' Orleans. NoP

God help all poor souls lost in the dark! The Heretic's Tragedy. Robert Browning. OAEL 1-2

God help him, he was cryin',/An', maybe, so was I. Wee Hughie. Elizabeth Shane. HBMV

...God help the many/who will die of soap foam. How Come? David Ignatow. CAD; NYP

God help us all to kindly view/The world that we are passing through! The World I Am Passing Through. Lydia Maria Child. AA; HBV 1-2

God help us to be brave. Litany of the Heroes. Vachel Lindsay. MoRP

God help who follow in my footsteps. Men's Loving Is a False Affection. Anonymous. NOBI

God help who looks upon its like. A Visit to Enniskillen. Tadhg Dall O Huiginn. NOBI

God help you on that fatal day. Be Frugal. Richard Church. OBSP; OxBTC

God hid the whole world in thy heart. The Mighty Heart. Ralph Waldo Emerson AA

God Himself will humble you. A Conceited Man. Anonymous. WTO

God, how have we led ourselves astray and gone wrong? Windows. Mordechai Husid. VWA

God, how I long for stars/to mark where/I've taken you in. Fecundity. Diane Keating. CaPN

A god humbled Shadow. Guillaume Apollinaire. WaaP

God, I'm tired, I said. The Couch. Fred W. Wright, Jr. AMV-80

God, I shall not forget the four last things. Ballade on Eschatology. Sister Mary Madeleva. GoYe

God, if they prayed to Him,/Would give fine weather. When I Was a Little Girl. Alice Milligan. OnYI; OxBI

God in all the concord of their mirth/Heard the adoration-song of Earth. An April Adoration. Sir Charles G. D. Roberts. HBV 1-2

God in himself is bliss enough,/For we have all in Thee. Where-e'er My Flatt'ring Passions Rove. Isaac Watts. NOCV; OxBoCh

God in his heaven bidding light arise. The Master Singers. Rhys Carpenter. WGRP

God in his mercy lend her/grace,/The Lady of Shalott. The Lady of Shalott. Alfred, Lord Tennyson. ATP; BeLS; BLPL; DiPo; EnLit; FaFP; FiP; GN; GTBS; HBV 1-2; InPS; MaC; MaVP; MBW 1-2; MCCG; NOBE; OAEL 1-2; OAEP; OBEV; OBNV; OBRV; OBVV; SeCeV; TEP; TreF; VLP; WHA; WiR

...God in his time/Or out of time will correct him. The Country Clergy. R.S. Thomas. GTBS-P; OxBTC

God in His wisdom created them all. The Chemistry of Character. Elizabeth Dorney. BLPA

The god in the forest of the heart. A Way of Keeping. Nancy Willard. IHMS

God in Three Persons, Blessed Trinity! Holy, Holy, Holy. Reginald Heber. HBV 1-2; OHIP; TreFT; VLP

God is a junkie and he has sold salvation/for a week's supply. Blues for Sister Sally. Lenore Kandel. NMM

God is all-sufficient/For the coming year. God Is Faithful. Frances Ridley Havergal. BLRP

God is–and in the morning fire. Monserrat. William Edwin Collin. CaP

God is cold. A Man Adrift on a Slim Spar. Stephen Crane. MOS

God is death. The Ant Trap. Joe Rosenblatt. NOBC

God is God forevermore. Foundations. Henry Van Dyke. TRV

God is his own interpreter,/And he will make it plain. Light Shining out of Darkness. William Cowper. CBEP; EaLo; EBEV; EiCP; ELP; EnPE; FaBoCh; FaFP; FiP; FPL; GoTF; HBV 1-2; HeIP; LiTB; LoGBV; NOBE; NOCV; NOEC; OBEC; PoEL 1-5; SeCeV; STF; TreF; TrGrPo; TRV; WGRP

God is in league with their forgetfulness. At Toledo. Arthur Symons. BrPo

God is it who transcends. Asolando. Robert Browning. OAEL 1-2; VLP

God is my God, by me praised. Psalm XLII. Sir Philip Sidney. FCP

God is neglected–/The old soldier slighted. God and the Soldier. Anonymous. GoTF; TreFS

...God is/On High. He can see you. You will die. Small Woman on Swallow Street. William Stanley Merwin. CoAP; ConAP

God is wisdom, God is love. God Is Love. John Bowring. FaBoBe

God keep him from all fear. Medieval Norman Songs. Anonymous. AWP

God, keep me still unsatisfied. Prayer. Louis Untermeyer. MoAmPo; TrJP; WGRP

God keep our land forever free! This Is America. Thomas Curtis Clark. PGD

God keep us struggling shapes. Unit. Mary Elizabeth ("E") Fullerton. BoAV; NOAV

God keep us whole and true, my distant love. Love Letter from an Impossible Land. William Meredith. WaP

God keep you every time and every-/where. God Keep You. Mary Ainge De Vere. AA

"God keep you safely, brother,/Who go to die for me." Hail and Farewell. Anne Higginson Spicer. HBMV

God kepe hem, bothe in feeld and towne,/And thenne shal I be kept ful wel. The Dark Lady. Anonymous. OxBM

God, King, who sittest on a gracious/Throne. These Things I Do Remember. Salaman Solomon ben Aaron. TrJP

God! knit Thou sure the cord/Of my thralldom to my Lord. I Bind My Heart. Lauchlan MacLean Watt. TRV

God knoweth why. There Is No Unbelief. Lizzie York Case. HBV 1-2; TreFS

God knows how many/lonely men the loaves/have eaten. Two Windows by Magritte. Ruth Roston. PoDr

God knows I hope he's right. Poem for Nana. June Jordan. BlSi

God knows, I sing! Arrivals and Departures. Melvin Walker La Follette. CoPo

God knows I've been all around this world–/And started around again. The Horse Trader's Song. Anonymous. AmFP

God knows my soul's been anchored in de Lord. My Soul's Been Anchored in de Lord. Anonymous. BoAN 1-2

God knows, no rime nor reason except his. The One Thing Needful. Vassar Miller. PoCh

God knows, some curse themselves, in cursing him. On Judas Iscariot. Francis Quarles. FaBoEE

God knows what God is coming next. The Seven Spiritual Ages of Mrs. Marmaduke Moore. Ogden Nash. MoAmPo

God knows which God is the God God recognizes. The Day after Sunday. Phyllis McGinley. MoAmPo; OBSV; UnPo

God knows why/Anyone would bother/To forward such a thing. Love Poem: The Dispossessed. T. R. Hummer. MAYP

God lay upon this tongue. The Jewels. Austin Clarke. MoAB

God, let me flower as I will! Let Me Flower as I Will. Lew Sarett. TrPWD

God lets alone. Inspiration. Henry David Thoreau. EBCP

God-like you have grasped the Whole! Artemis. Dulcie Deamer. PoAu 1-2

God lives and loves and cares for me. The Father Knows. F.L. H.. BLRP

God lost, hell fownd: ever, never begune:/now bidd mee into flame from smoake to runne. Sonnet XLVI. William Alabaster. AnAnS 1

God loves all prettiness, and on this/Surely his angels lay their kiss. To a New York Shop-Girl Dressed for Sunday. Anna Hempstead Branch. HBV 1-2

God loves an idle rainbow,/No less than labouring seas. Reason Has Moons. Ralph Hodgson. MoVE

God made Himself an awful rose of dawn. The Vision of Sin. Alfred, Lord Tennyson. OAEL 1-2; VLP

God made little lads/To kiss pretty wenches. God Made Trees. Anonymous. LO

God made my soul for Hungary! Music of Hungary. Anne Reeve Aldrich. AA

"God made to cater unto me!" The Umbrella, the Cane, and the Broom. Eliezer Steinbarg. VWA

God make me worthy of my friends. A Prayer. Frank Dempster Sherman. GoTF; TreFS

God, make thy people live. The City, Lord, Where Thy Dear Life. William E. Dudley. AH

God make us saints, and brave. Franciscan Aspiration. Vachel Lindsay. CAW

God! may I never, never lose that too! Childhood. Jens Baggesen. AWP

God means just what He says. Why Doubt God's Word? A.B. Simpson. BLRP

God might suffocate/between these fingers. Labour of the Brain, Ballad of the Body. Nicole Forman. NMM

God moves on the water,/And the people had to run and pray. God Moves on the Water. Anonymous. OuSiCo

God must be with her in her solitude! To a Deaf and Dumb Little Girl. Hartley Coleridge. PoEL 1-5; VLP

God must have made thee in His anger, and/forgot. To the Colorado Desert. Madge Morris. BPAW

...God, must I sit and sew? I Sit and Sew. Alice Dunbar Nelson. BlSi; CDC; WPOW

God must remake the world, or me, or you! Sonnets. Muna Lee. HBMV

God needs body and burns in unjust anger until the man is/faithful and his work be satisfied. Tabernacles. Gerrit Lansing. CoPo

The God of Bethel heard. The God of Bethel Heard Her Cries. Richard Allen. AH

God of justice, when wilt thou teach them to save themselves? When Wilt Thou Teach the People—? D. H. Lawrence. OBSV

God of Life! Creator! It was I! It was I! The Factories. Margaret Widdemer. HBV 1-2

The god of light, poetry, and movies/still laughs at that one, Buster. Buster Keaton. Michael McFee. AMV-81

The God of Music dwelleth out of doors. Music. Edith Matilda Thomas. HBV 1-2

The GOD of nature in the feilds of grace. M. Crashaws Answer for Hope. Richard Crashaw. OBS; SeCV 1-2

(The God of order is called Love.) Entropy. Theodore Spencer. ImOP

"God of our Fathers! Thou art blessed!" Nativity Ode. Saint Cosmas. CAW

God of our Fathers, we Thy children lie. Midnight. Margaret E. Sangster. TRV

God of silent noon,/Hear my salutation! A Chant out of Doors. Marguerite Wilkinson. TrPWD

God of the Christlike, grant that we/Do follow, follow worthily! Braving the Wilds All Unexplored. Robert Freeman. AH

God of the rich there never was. Overseer of the Poor. James Hayford. NePoAm-2

God of the worlds which Death reveals/To all our race.... God (excerpt). Alexander McLachlan. CaP

God of this ceiling, let us worship you! Homage to the Carracci. Tom Disch. PoA

God of thy people, hear us cry to thee. God of the Nations. Walter Russell Bowie. AH; TrPWD

The god of war himself, and all mankind. Venus Accoutered as Mars. Anonymous. UnTE

God of wisdom and of love. Thou Remainest. Annie Johnson Flint. BLRP

God of youth, let this day here/Enter neither care nor fear. God Lyaeus. John Fletcher. OBEV; ViBoPo

God one morning, glad of heaven,/Laughed–and that was you! A Little Person. Brian Hooker. HBMV

God only knows, said the stare. A Starling and a Willow-Wren. W. H. Auden. FaBoMo

God only waited for me till/I prayed the larger prayer. Prayer–Answer. Ednah D. Cheney. STF

God only, who made us rich, can make us poor. Sonnets from the Portuguese, XXIV. Elizabeth Barrett Browning. NOBV; VLP

God order'd motion, but ordain'd no rest. Man. Henry Vaughan. AnEnPo; CBEP; ForPo; HBV 1-2; MeLP; MePo; NOBE; NOCV; OBEV; OBS; PoEL 1-5; SeCV 1-2

God ought surely to shut up soon,/As I go. To the Moon. Thomas Hardy. BoNaP

God ought to bow profoundly for the favour. Epigram: "Exhausted now her sighs, and dry her tears." Walter Savage Landor. FaBoEE

The God our things all tost and turned quight/Rolles with a whyrle wynde. Thyestes, III: Chorus. Seneca (Lucius Annaeus Seneca). OBVE

God pardon priest and people and so I bid farewell. The Romish Lady. Anonymous. BFSS; OuSiCo

God pardon them, O insect king,/Who fancy so unjust a thing! Lines to a Dragon-Fly. Walter Savage Landor. FM; OBNC; OBRV

God pity and pardon/The poor prisoner for life. A Prisoner for Life. Anonymous. CoSo

God pity any Mormon that attempts to follow me! A Mormon Immigrant Song. Anonymous. CoSo

God planted a scarlet maple tree. Trees. Bliss Carman. OHIP

God proffers all, 'twere grievous sin/To live content in less! Tamerton Church-Tower; or, First Love. Coventry Patmore. FaBoPP

God promptly bring them down with/pestilence! The Canterbury Tales: The Wife of Bath's Tale. Geoffrey Chaucer. EnL; EnLit; OAEL 1-2; TW; ViBoPo

God provideth for the morrow. Providence. Reginald Heber. GN; HBV 1-2; OHIP

God punishes in the person of his mother/One who endured before he chose his fate. Baudelaire in Brussels. Anthony Cronin. BIrV

"God reigns and the Republic lives!" Faithful unto Death. Richard Handfield Titherington. PAH

"God reigns: at His feet earth's Destiny sleeps like a/child." Parvuli Ejus. Aubrey Thomas De Vere. IrPN

God reigns, let the earth be glad! This Is My Father's World. Maltbie Davenport Babcock. AH; TRV

God rest him! I'm the victor, to-day in/Cherokee! The Ride to Cherokee. Amelia Walstein Carpenter. AA

God rest him! Never hero had/A nobler funeral pyre! John Maynard. Horatio, Jr Alger. BeLS; BLPA; FaBoBe

God's a-gonna trouble the water. Wade in the Water. Anonymous. FSW

God's all of this, God's everything, God's fact. Sonnet XI. Adele Greeff. GoYe

God's ancient cry Neila. Yvan Goll. VWA

God's blessing on the monarch who rules on Lombard/Street in Philadelphia. Rulers: Philadelphia. Fenton Johnson. AmFN; GoSI; PoNe

God's bright and intricate device/Of days and seasons doth suffice. The House Beautiful. Robert Louis Stevenson. NOBE

"God's crypt is sealed! 'Twill stand revealed in His own/good time," quoth he. Henry Hudson's Quest. Burton Egbert Stevenson. HBV 1-2; MC; PAH; PAL

God's curse on him who made me a nun. Motets, II. Anonymous. PBWP

God's, East–mine, West: good friends,/behold my Land! The Triumph. Sidney Lanier. PAH

God's Embryo within thy womb. Epigram: "Hail, blissfulest maiden." Anonymous. ISi

God's gwinter build up Zion's walls. Great Day. Anonymous. BoAN 1-2

God's Heaven,/for Heaven's where's God. Mary. Robert Farren. ISi

God's in his heaven–/All's right with the world! The Year's at the Spring. Robert Browning. BLPA; FaBoBe; FaBV; YeAr

God's interrupted wish-fulfillment, told/Some of the story. The Wave. Daryl Hine. Prf

God's love, God's wisdom, Child of loneliness. Child of Loneliness. Norman Gale. WGRP

God's own fox will have his way/This night or some other night. Now the Holy Lamp of Love. Patrick MacDonogh. BIrV

God's perfect wisdom, power, and love. A World Beyond. Nathaniel Ingersoll Bowditch. AA

God's pity then, say I,/On some poor king. Poor Kings. William Henry Davies. HBV 1-2

...God's puppets, best and worst,/Are we; there is no last or first. All Service Ranks the Same with God. Robert Browning. TreFT

God's servant, born of Bethlehem! Invitation. Solomon Ibn Gabirol. TrJP

God's touch will keep the one chord quivering. L'Envoi. Edwin Arlington Robinson. TrCP

God's way adore. The Fall of Richmond. Herman Melville. MC; PAH

"God's ways are dark and very seldom pleasant." Death and the Bridge. Robert Lowell. HaCAP

God's ways are strange. God's Ways Are Strange. Margaret E. Bruner. PoToHe

God's will to love. God's Will. Charles E. Guthrie. BLRP

God's wrath must on the miscreant lie/Who dares offend her! The School Girl. William Henry Venable. AA

God said, Let Newton be! and all was light. Epitaph Intended for Sir Isaac Newton, in Westminster Abbey. Alexander Pope. FaBoEE; InPK

God save our president! God Save Our President. Francis DeHaes Janvier. PAH; PAL

God save the King! God, somehow, free the free. The English Rider. Robin Hyde. AnNZ

God save the lives of them and their wives,/Whether they be young or old! A Song of Ale. Anonymous. AnFE; OBSC

God save the people! God Save The People. Ebenezer Elliott. WBLP

God save the plough! God Save the Plough. Lydia Huntley Sigourney. OBAL

God save the Sundays where he rode. Hudson Hornet. William W. Cook. AMV-80

God save us all from death when we are fed. Sehnsucht. Anna Wickham. MoBrPo

God sees sweet flowers growing. Under the Leaves. Albert Laighton. HBV 1-2; OHIP

God send every gentleman/Such hawks, such hounds, and such a leman. The Three Ravens. Anonymous. ExPo; FSW; InPK; NoP; OBET

God send fine weather to carry home the sheaves!' A Memory. Katharine Tynan. OxBI

God send me an ending as fair as his/Who died in his stirrups there! Hippodromania; or Whiffs from the Pipe (excerpt). Adam Lindsay Gordon. CBAP

God send my sparrow's soul good rest. The Funeral of Philip Sparrow. John Skelton. ACP

God send/No end/To line/Divine/Of George and Caroline! A Lilliputian Ode on Their Majesties' Accession. Henry Carey. NOEC

God send that I may die out there! The Pilgrimage. Albrecht von Johannsdorf. LiTW

God send the West a many such/To make our country thrive! Kit Carson's Last Smoke. Stanley Vestal. PoOW

"God send this Crum-well-down!" The Three Troopers. George Walter Thornbury. BeLS; HBV 1-2

God send us all good ending! Chevy Chase. Anonymous. BuBa; EnRP; EnSB; OxBB; ViBoPo; WHA

God sende him hap that wolde wel do! Snatches: "Hope is hard ther hap is fo." Anonymous. OxBM

"God sends a Voice, a Voice!" The Poet's Call. Thomas Curtis Clarke. WGRP

God! Set me glowing! Let me shine! A Very Minor Poet Speaks. Isabel Valle. BLPA

God shall speak to thee out of the sky. Solitude. Edward Rowland Sill. AnNE

God shield the stock! If heaven send no supplies,/The fairest blossom of the garden dies. The Rose. William Browne. HBV 1-2; OBEV

God show, God blind these children! Sunday: Outskirts of Knoxville, Tennessee. James Agee. ErPo; InPK

...God, since if it were that you/Were to exist, then I would really too. The Atheist's Prayer. Miguel de Unamuno. ILwL

"God smite their souls to the depths of hell." Studies at Delhi. Sir Alfred Comyn Lyall. OBTV; OBVV

God stand its sentinel/For evermore. A National Hymn. John William DeForest. PAL

The god stays alive. Apollo. James Wright. LCAP

God suffer little men/the taste of soul's desire. God Give to Men. Arna Bontemps. BANP; BPo; CDC; PoNe

God takes a text, and preacheth patience. The Church Porch. George Herbert. TRV

...A god that can do villainy/With a good grace and glib facility. Satire. John Marston. ViBoPo

God, that is euer a crowned kyng,/Bryng us all to his blisse! Robin Hood and the Monk. Anonymous. BaBo; ESPB; FaBoBa; MeEV; OBNV; ViBoFo; ViBoPo

God that is over us all! Songs of Seven. Jean Ingelow. HBV 1-2

God, that mad'st her well regard her. Dieu Qu'il la Fait. Charles d'Orleans. AWP

God the Father, God the Son, and God the/Holy Ghost adore. All Saints' Day, Nov. 1. Christopher Wordsworth. VLP

God the Great Musician/Calling life anew. Rain Music. Joseph Seamon, Jr Cotter. BANP; BrR; CDC

God, the slow withering! Suddenly. Leonora Speyer. PG

God the Son/Brought my release. Lost, But Won. Henry J. Von Schlichten. BePJ

The God their gifts confess aright! The Magi Visit Herod. Caelius Sedulius. CAW

God, there were Men like Spiro Agnew. The Banquet of the Century in Persepolis. Alamgir Hashmi. SOTS

God–they ate Catholics and their Catholic God! Poem against Catholics. James and Fenton Fuller. John OBSV

A god thou art or made of stone. Epigram: "When 'mongst the youths." *Anonymous.* PeHV

God thought about you, and so I am here. Baby. George Macdonald. BiCB; GoTF; HBV 1-2; HBVY; TreF; TRV

God to bestow a second benefit. Thanksgiving. Robert Herrick. LiTB; OFD

God to guard me, God to love me. Bega. Marjorie Pickthall. CaP

God to His people strength shall give,/That they in peace shall blessed live. Psalm XXIX. Sir Philip Sidney. FCP

God took the spinning-jenny/Out of his side. Fragments. William Butler Yeats. PrIm

God touched the man, and Lincoln stood revealed! Lincoln. Jane L. Hardy. OHIP

...God/Unworshipped withers to the Futile One. Auditors In. Patrick Kavanagh. OxBI

God waited for me till/I prayed the larger prayer. The Larger Prayer. Ednah D. Cheney. BLRP; WGRP

God was just your little Boy,/And you know the way. To Our Lady. Mary Dixon Thayer. TreFS

God was made man once more. Night and Morning. Austin Clarke. AnIL; CIP; IPY; MoAB; NeIP; NoAm

...God was right/about him–he wasn't ready to be imperfect. Eve's Version. James Harrison. AMV-81

God were not God, whom knowledge cannot know. Sonnets, First Series. Frederick Goddard Tuckerman. MAmP

God, what a dancing spectre seems the moon! Modern Love, XXXIX. George Meredith. VLP

God! what a little accident of gold/Fences our weakness from the wolves of old! Honour Dishonoured. Wilfrid Scawen Blunt. OBMV

"God, what a place! What is it? Life or Death?" Life or Death. Glenn Ward Dresbach. HBMV

God, when he walked on earth. Shine, Perishing Republic. Robinson Jeffers. AmLP; AnAmPo; CMoP; FF; LiTA; LiTM; MoAB; MoAmPo; NAMP; NePA; NOBA; NoP; OxBA; PrIm; TAP; TRV; UnPo; VGW; ViBoPo

God who also watched over me/was my old granny's friend. To the Anxious Mother. Valente Malangatana. PBA

God, who bade me walk,/sets in my path an angel for my devil. On the Path. Avner Strauss. VWA

The God who gave all worlds that are,/And all that are to be. Awake, Awake to Love and Work. G. Anketall "Woodbine Willie" Studdert-Kennedy. TRV

God, who made thee mighty, make thee mightier yet. Land of Hope and Glory. Arthur Christopher Benson. FaPoR

...God who such a mother gave/This poor bird-hearted singer of a day. My Mother. Francis Ledwidge. HBMV; OHIP

God, why have you ruined us? Job's Ancient Lament. Owen Dodson. FB

God will advance a mile in blazing light to him. Whoso Draws Nigh to God. *Anonymous.* TRV

God will cheat no one, not even the world of its triumph. For the Time Being. W. H. Auden. MoAB; OAEL 1-2

God will give me medicine from his stocks/and I'll recover/straight after death. If God Exists. Ewa Lipska. VWA

God will help thee bear what comes/Of joy or sorrow. Today. Mary Frances Butts. GoTF; TreFT; TRV

God will remember the world! A Song of Faith. Josiah Gilbert Holland. WGRP

God will sentence me to repeating it endlessly and forever. When I Hear Your Name. Gloria Fuertes. AMV-81

God will take care of you. God's Goodness. C. D. Martin. WBLP

God wills it–for the enchanted Soul's fair/sake. The Garden Where There is No Winter. Louis James Block. AA

God! wilt Thou grant aid to me/Who came o'er th' upheaving main? The Heavenly Pilot. Cormac Mac Cuilenan. CAW; OnYI

The God with meate hath not Thy hunger fed,/Nor goddesse laid thee in a little bed. Eclogues. Virgil (Publius Vergilius Maro). OBVE

God workes that his joy mixt with sorrow is. Sonnet XCIV. Fulke, Lord Brooke Greville. OBS

God would never understand. On a Catholic Childhood. Janet Campbell Hale. VoR

God wrought as like a botcher, as God might do. On Botching. John Heywood. FaBoCo

God yielding to descend cut off our thrall. Our Lady's Salutation. Robert Southwell. ISi

God yive that so mighte it be! Snatches: "Have good day now, Mergerete." *Anonymous.* OxBM

God, you are vast. We Are All Workmen. Rainer Maria Rilke. EaLo

Goddamn everything! The Retirement of the Elephant. Russell Edson. AmPA

Goddess, allow this aged man his right/To be your beadsman now that was your knight. A Farewell to Arms. George Peele. BoC; HBV 1-2; NIP; NOBE; OBEV; OBWP; PoPle; PoRA

Goddess by god, with Antony. Cleopatra. Algernon Charles Swinburne. BeLS

Goddess, excellently bright. Cynthia's Revels. Ben Jonson. AtBAP; GN; MOON; TrGrPo

Goddesse, allow this aged man his right,/To be your Beads-man now, that was your Knight. Polyhymnia: His Golden Lock. George Peele. AtBAP; FaBoEn; PPoe

Goddesse, allow this aged man his right,/To be your Beads-man now, that was your Knight. A Sonet: "His Golden lockes, Time hath to Silver turn'd." George Peele. PoEL 1-5

GodFrey Gordon Gustavus Gore! Godfrey Gordon Gustavus Gore. William Brighty ("Matthew Browne") Rands. BBGG; HBVY; TiPo

Godhead in the mortal element. Man Is God's Nature. Richard Eberhart. EaLo; MoRP

Godlike, he makes provision for mankind. The Sower. Sir Charles G. D. Roberts. CaP; OBCV

...Godly milky/nascency succulent miracle Love Child–a Black Aesthetic. Everett Hoagland. BPo

The Gods are jealous–now, as then,/Giving no quarter. Epitaphs of the War, 1914-18. Rudyard Kipling. BrPo

The Gods are just, and compensation comes. Philoctetes. John Byrne Leicester Warren, Lord De Tabley. NOBV

The Gods are pleas'd alone with Purcells' Layes,/Nor know to mend their Choice. On the Death of Mr. Purcell. John Dryden. NOBE; UnS

Gods are powerless to save/Their own children from death? Never Again, Orpheus. Antipater of Sidon. OBVE

Gods are we, Thou hast said; and we pay dearly. Scazons. Clive Staples Lewis. EBEV

...The gods can blow/Life into marble, but not into wood. Pygmalion. Hans Brockerhoff. AMV-80

The gods defrocked, and Troy a rubbish heap. In a Bed-Sitter. Hal Porter. NOAV

The gods have set a sign for us, the tomb. The Setting of the Moon. Giacomo Leopardi. MOON

...The gods know best. The Song of the Arrow. Isabella Valancy Crawford. PeCV

The gods lie cold where the leaves are gold,/And a Child comes forth alone. The Feast of the Snow. Gilbert Keith Chesterton. HBV 1-2

...Gods make their own importance. Epic. Patrick Kavanagh. BIrV; FaBoIP; IPY; NOBI; OxBI

The gods must not know us well or they would/not dance so openly, so happily before us. The Gods Must Not Know Us. Linda Gregg. NPGG

The Gods of the Copybook Headings with terror and slaughter return! The Gods of the Copybook Headings. Rudyard Kipling. FaPoR; OBSV; OHFP; OxBTC; TW

Gods speak from the torn waves' droning eloquence. Land's End. Stanton A. Coblentz. BPAW; EtS

The gods their god-like fun. Letter to My Sister. Anne Spencer. AmNP; BlSi; PoBA; PoNe

The Gods themselves with us do dwell. The Mower against Gardens. Andrew Marvell. AnAnS 1; EBEV; FaBoPV; LiTB; NoP; OAEL 1-2; OAEP; PoEL 1-5; PP; PPP; SeCV 1-2

The Gods, though beasts they do not Love,/Yet like them when they'r burnt in Sacrifice. Written in Juice of Lemmon. Abraham Cowley. AnAnS 2; SeCP; SeCV 1-2

Gods what a terrible tragedy/not to make good with the tragic/archy The Wail of Archy (excerpt). Don (Donald Robert Marquis) Marquis. FiBHP

Gods wonders I have seene. They See Gods Wonders That Are Call'd. Roger Williams. SCAP

Goe and prosper for a space,/Till I rob thee of thy place. The Letter. John Tatham. CavP

Goe see the angry kynges. Hercules Furens, IV: Chorus. Seneca (Lucius Annaeus Seneca). OBVE

Goes back like a lord, alone. Little Black Man with a Rose in His Hat. Audrey Wurdemann. YaD

Goes dispiritedly, glad to finish. Phases of the Moon. Robert Browning. MOON

Goes flaunting out, and, in her trim of pride,/Think all she says or does, is justified. Juvenal's Sixth Satire. John Dryden. OBSV

Goes on stating his abhorrence/of the prudery of Lawrence. D. H. Lawrence and James Joyce. Humbert Wolfe. FaBoEE

Goes reluctantly on to the race with the hurrying wheels. Autumn Love. Ibycus. LiTW

Goes running on,/From nowhere to nowhere,/Without me. Now I Have Forgotten All. David Vogel. VWA

Goes safely–where an open eye–/Would drop Him–Bone by Bone. There is a pain–so utter. Emily Dickinson. BoWoP; NOBA

Goes straight up to heaven and nothing more is heard of it. Her Husband. Ted Hughes. OxBC

Goes the great fathingale. A Royal Pickle. Carlton Talbot. ALV

Goes to bed beneath this stone/Early, sober, and alone. Epitaph on a Party Girl. Richard Usborne. FaBoEE

Goes to the piano/and begins to play. The Light Passages. Debora Greger. MAYP

Goes to the window and lets them flow/into the ochres of the afternoon. In the Fall. Alina Rivero. AMV-81

Goes up in steam, comes down in less! Cloud. Samuel Hoffenstein. AnAmPo

Goin' 'cross the mountain/You can hear my banjo tell. Goin' 'Cross the Mountain. Anonymous. AmFP

Goin' down Cripple Creek/To 'ave some fun. Cripple Creek. Anonymous. AmFP; FSW

Goin' down the Platte River for death or for life. In the Summer of Sixty. Anonymous. CoSo; PoOW

Goin' to have the best old farm/That you have ever seen. Times Are Getting Hard. Anonymous. FSW

Goin' to make you run, sir. You Kicked and Stomped and Beat Me. Anonymous. OuSiCo

Goin' to shiver when the cold winds blow. To the Pines. Anonymous. WTO

Going back to spend the rest of my life beneath that Rising Sun. The Rising Sun Blues. Anonymous. OuSiCo

Going back we looked at the few/plastic clouds into the dark moony/trees. Don't Break It. Joseph Ceravolo. ANYP

Going back, you heap the creel with phlox and marigolds. Fishing with My Daughter in Miller's Meadow. Lucien Stryk. GP

Going, buddy, to my country,/Somebody dying every day. John Henry (F vers.). Anonymous. ViBoFo

The going-elsewhere of ripples incessantly shaping. Swimming Chenango Lake. Charles Tomlinson. FaBoMo; NoAm

Going hammer and tongs like a couple of dogs. The Midnight Court. Brian Merriman. BIrV

Going home. Things to Do around Kyoto. Gary Snyder. NaP

Going nowhere, with nowhere to be from. Friday Evening. Julio Marzan. InW

Going on inside. Out There. Bill Berkson. ANYP

Going outside with all the others. Party Going. Bill Manhire. OCNZ

Going to bed was a journey. The Journey. David Ignatow. Psk

Going to work. Early Meadow-Rue. Stanley Plumly. LCAP

...Going with/the wind as they always did. Milkweed. Philip Levine. LCAP

Gold and brown. College Formal: Renaissance Casino. Langston Hughes. BALP

Gold are all heaven's rivers,/And silver her streams. The Heavenly City. Stevie Smith. FaBoTw

Gold atoms dancing underground. Calling Myself Home. Linda Hogan. TWSS

The gold earth turned to good–forever. Long Summer. Laurie Lee. BoNaP

Gold give us, God forgive us. Inscription above the Entrance to the Abbey of Theleme. Sir Thomas Urquhart. FaBoRV

Gold, gold, gold. The Golden Whales of California. Vachel Lindsay. AtBAP

Gold gold the water rises. The Right True End. Anonymous. WTO

The gold I miss for dreaming is all yours. Dear Friends. Edwin Arlington Robinson. AmePo

The gold of dreams we fashioned long ago. When This Tide Ebbs. Verna Loveday Harden. CaP

The gold of Thy gate is melting/in my yearning. Zebaoth. Else Lasker-Schüler. TrJP

...Gold stars stuck to its fin. Skins. Elizabeth Spires. MAYP

The gold that clustered there/about the Host? Saint Apollinare in Classe. R. N. D. Wilson. CAW

Gold wings across the sea. Song: "Gold wings across the sea!" William Morris. LoBV

A Golden Age, must be as free,/For Acorns, as for Honesty. The Moral. Bernard Mandeville. CEP

A golden cataract that comes/Out of the cornucopia of dream. Indian Summer. Barbara Howes. IHMS

Golden chalices, wooden priests,/as the wretched world stands now. Epigram: "Gold priests, wooden chalices." Anonymous. NOBI

The golden cloud above the pond. In Hellbrunn. Georg Trakl. LiTW

The golden daffodillies/Are blowing in the sun. An April Morning. Bliss Carman. HBMV; HBVY

The golden dogs I'm going to/Are handsome dogs and gay. Says Something Too (parody). Samuel Hoffenstein. BXAP

The Golden Gate is going down/To beat the Yankee Blade. Humbug Steamship Companies. Anonymous. BPAW

Golden gleamed the woman's hair. Along the Strand. Alfred Mombert. TrJP

The golden heresy of truth. On Behalf of Some Irishmen Not Followers of Tradition. George William Russell. AnIL; PoLf

The golden orange every prince will fight/to own. Smudging. Diane Wakoski. AmPA; PrIm

A golden prince of pictorial war Uccello. Gregory Corso. NeAP; PoM

Golden slippers I,m gwinter wear,/To walk de golden streets. Oh, Dem Golden Slippers. James A. Bland. GoSl; PSoN

Golden spurs/For you to find! Golden Spurs. Virginia Scott Miner. SiSoSe

Golden-tinted and fair, as thy own Pumpkin pie! The Pumpkin. John Greenleaf Whittier. OHIP

Golden wolves are/guarding the lambs. In Chagall's Village. Rose Auslander. VWA

Goliathus was better and he/not a native. The Zoo. Gilbert Sorrentino. NeAP

Gomorrah was lost to them. Of the Beloved Caravan. Conny Hannes Meyer. VWA

Gone agin.–Finnigin. Finnigin to Flannigan. Strickland Gillilan. FaBoBe; GoTF; HBV 1-2; StPo; TreF; YaD

...Gone, alas! like our youth too soon. The Kerry Dance. James Lyman Molloy. OnYI

Gone as his mouth's last sighs. The Burning of the Temple. Isaac Rosenberg. FaBoMo; TrJP

Gone his soul into all nations, gone to live and/not to die. The Death of Jefferson. Hezekiah Butterworth. PAH

...Gone/in the silver glinting on the river. Sharks, Caloosahatchee River. Greg Pape. MAYP

Gone into the cherry tree. Pit, Pat. Anonymous. OxNR

Gone is another summer's day. Summer Evening. Walter De la Mare. FM; MoAB; MoBrPo; MoShBr; TiPo

Gone is she, scorning my bough! The Tree and the Lady. Thomas Hardy. MoAB; MoBrPo

Gone is the heart of Man. Three Poems of the Atomic Age: Dirge for the New Sunrise. Edith Sitwell. AtBAP

Gone is the sweet swallow–/Gone, Philomell' Waltz. Edith Sitwell. OAEP

Gone like a never perfectly recalled air. Celandine. Edward ("Edward Eastaway") Thomas. OxBTC

Gone like a snatch of song upon the stair. Daffodils. Lizette Woodworth Reese. AA

Gone like the summer in their yellow bus. 1930's. Robert Lowell. NoP

Gone off in company with Music! Fifine at the Fair, XCIII (excerpt). Robert Browning. Par

Gone suddenly straight beyond this blood/of our deaths. Blood. Ray Bremser. NeAP

Gone to a television/test pattern/in the city. Pine Point, you are:. Gordon Henry. STE

Gone to his death-bed/All under the willow tree. My Love Is Dead. Thomas Chatterton. WiR

...Gone/under the final two strokes of Trinity's bell. The Assassination of President McKinley. Paul Blackburn. NYP

Gone was the radiant world of gossamer. His Dream of the Sky-Land: A Farewell Poem (excerpt). Li Po. WSC

Gone-With-The-Grin Lip Remover. Brainwashing Dramatized. Don Johnson. PoNe

Gong/steam end/end. The Hammer. Clark Coolidge. ANYP

Gongula? August (parody). Robert Frost. BXAP

Gonna beat the record of the Robert E. Lee. Steamboat Bill. Anonymous. FSW

Gonna fix it/so I won't have to drift no more/Mmmmmmmm. Rolling Log Blues. Lottie Kimbrough. BluL

Gonna fly all over God's heaven. All God's Children Got Shoes. Anonymous. FSW

Gonna lay that poor boy down,/He won't get up no more. Round and Round Hitler's Grave. Anonymous. FSW

Gonna let my little light shine. This Little Light of Mine. Anonymous. FSW

Gonna make white/a twentyfourhour/lifetime/J.O.B. Vive Noir! Mari E. Evans. BOLo; PoBA

Gonna meet my father Blow Gabriel. Blind Gary Davis. BluL

Gonna set my banjo down. Git Along Down to Town. Anonymous. AmFP

Gonna take my baby/And leave me lonesome here That Lonesome Train Took My Baby Away. Charlie McCoy. BluL

Gonna take my master charge/and get everything in town Master Charge Blues. Nikki Giovanni. OBAL

Good and drunk and goozy all the time. Keep My Skillet Good and Greasy. Anonymous. FSW

Good books that say, at some length, "yea,"/And thereby spite the Noes. An Ode. John Updike. FiBHP

Good-by, Liza, poor gal,/She died on the plain. Bronc Peeler's Song. *Anonymous.* CoSo

Good-by, Miss Liza Jane! Bedbug. *Anonymous.* GoSl

Good-by, my wayside posy! The Milking-Maid. Christina Georgina Rossetti. BeLS

Good-by, old Paint, I'm a-leavin' Cheyenne. Good-by, Old Paint. *Anonymous.* ABF; FSW

Good-by, the last of my good-bys. Rondel: "Good-by, the tears are in my eyes." Francois Villon. AWP

Good-by to dull old Hesiod. Class-Dismissed. *Anonymous.* UnTE

"Good-by, you big lummox, I'm glad you've backed out!" Sweet Betsey from Pike. *Anonymous.* ABF; AmFP; AS; BFSS; BLSo; BPAW; CoSo; FaBoBa; FSW; GoTF; OBAL; OxBoLi; TrAS; TreFT; ViBoFo

"Good-by, young man, good-by." Oh, See How Thick the Goldcup Flowers. Alfred Edward Housman. EnLi 1-2; FaBV; MoBrPo

Good-bye–and hail! my Fancy. Drum-Taps. Walt Whitman. AP

Good bye. Good bye. The Secret. Lonny Kaneko. BrSi

Good-bye, good-bye, to everything! Farewell to the Farm. Robert Louis Stevenson. TiPo

Good-bye, mother, friends and all;/All I had done gone. Delia Holmes. *Anonymous.* AmFP

...Good-bye,/Mrs. Pappadopoulos, and thanks. So-and-So Reclining on Her Couch. Wallace Stevens. AmPP; LiTM; NOBA

"Good-bye," said the river, "I'm going downstream." Exit Line. Howard Nemerov. WeW

Good-bye to playwrights, and good-bye to you! Deeper into the Forest. Roy Daniells. PeCV

Good-bye, with a handshake,/Vincent. The Potato Eaters. Frank Graziano. PoDr

Good Christopher Finch, and David Frier. By the Dominical Letter, to Find on What Day of the Week... *Anonymous.* FaBoUs

Good claret is my mistress now. Once, Twice, Thrice. *Anonymous.* DBV; PV

Good day to you, Pablo Picasso! A "Twiner." J. A. Lindon. DBV

Good drunkards, pledge him with your laughs/Before the city's taverns close. Epitaph. Lawrence Durrell. FaBoCo

Good engineer but he's dead and gone./Dead and gone./On the road again... Casey Jones (E vers.). *Anonymous.* ViBoFo

Good English hospitality, O then it did not fail! The Mayors. William Blake. CH

Good faith, Mr. Parson, excuse me from that! On Marriage. Thomas Flatman. ELU; FaBoUs; FiBHP; NOBL

A good fat goose shall thank you well. When Molly Smiles. *Anonymous.* HBV 1-2

Good for the spirit, good/For body, thou! to both art wine and bread! The Appeasement of Demeter. George Meredith. EnLi 1-2; VLP

Good fortune for us, our living here/At a station/Along the way. A Bird's Nest. Erez Biton. VWA

Good friend, I am building the bridge for him. The Bridge Builder. Will Allen Dromgoole. BLPA; GoTF; PoToHe; TreFS; TRV

Good friends/who console her/by growing old/simultaneously No More Than Five. Fred Levinson. AmPA

Good God, and what is all this beauty for? Landscapes. Louis Untermeyer. HBV 1-2

Good God–I must marry him I suppose! In the Room of the Bride-Elect. Thomas Hardy. BrPo

Good God, we ha' bought it fair. Labor. *Anonymous.* PGD

Good grease. Good Grease. Mary Tallmountain. STE; TWSS

A good guy coming home, the long day done. Back through the Looking Glass to This Side. John Ciardi. NLV

"Good heavens! is this the Borue?" The Dream. *Anonymous.* WTO

Good husewiues know best all the rest how to guide. A Hundreth Good Poyntes of Husbandry. Thomas Tusser. FaBoUs

Good is Heaven. Evil is Hell. The Marriage of Heaven and Hell. William Blake. EnRP; LAuP

Good its yews among all yew-trees,/and its sweet birches better! My Fixed Abode Is Glen Bolcain. Suibne Geilt. NOBI

Good Langston sat too long to lift me. Reading Walt Whitman. Calvin Forbes. PoBA

Good Lawd, by'm by. By'm By (with music). *Anonymous.* AS

The good life returns to us in perfect weather or/perfect pleasure/nipples showing. Archilochos:. John Tagliabue. FAZ

Good little kid. Speak when you're spoken to. *Anonymous.* CenHV

Good Lord, by and by. By and By. *Anonymous.* FSW

"The good Lord Clifford' was the name he bore. Song at the Feast of Brougham Castle. William Wordsworth. EnRP

Good Lord, deliver us! Ring Out Your Bells. Sir Philip Sidney. CABA; ElL; GBL; NoP; SiPS; TEP; ViBoPo

Good Lord, Good Lord, I'm gwine home. Do Don't Touch-A My Garment, Good Lord, I'm Gwine Home. *Anonymous.* BoAN 1-2

"Good Lord! only think,–black and curly already!" Paddy's Metamorphosis. Thomas Moore. OnYI

"Good Lord! what fools ye be." The Man Who Frets at Worldly Strife. Joseph R., and Halleck, Fitz-Greene Drake. AA

Good love-sport to the lady of Ch'i! To the Lady of Ch'i. *Anonymous.* HW

Good luck! Four Heads & How to Do Them. John Forbes. CBAP

Good luck comes with mistletoe! Mistletoe Sprites. Solveig Paulson Russell. ChBR

Good luck has he that deals with none! A Double Ballad of Good Counsel. Francois Villon. AWP

The good man pouring from his pitcher clear/But brims the poisoned well. Fragments of a Lost Gnostic Poem of the Twelfth Century. Herman Melville. NOBA; NoP; OBSP; PoEL 1-5; ViBoPo

A good man's Word exceeds a bad ones Bond. If Any Be Pleased to Walk into My Poor Garden... Francis Daniel Pastorius. SCAP

Good men and women gone too soon to bed. Dear Uncle Stranger. Conrad Aiken. NoAm; NOBA

Good men/Go to your home again. The Shepherd Boys. Nicolas Saboly. OHIP

"Good-morning, Bobby Blue." Bobby Blue. John Drinkwater. SoPo

Good morning brother, let me/fight by your side Revolutionary Letters. Diane Di Prima. GP

Good morning, daddy!/Ain't you heard? Island. Langston Hughes. HaCAP

"Good morning! good morning! our work is begun!" Good Night and Good Morning. Richard Monckton, Lord Houghton Milnes. OxBChV

Good-morning, goodmorning, goodmorning–sir. Out of Soundings. Padraic Fallon. NeIP

Good morning, Life–and all/Things glad and beautiful. A Greeting. William Henry Davies. MoBrPo; MoRP

Good morning, Mrs. Roebeck. Christ have mercy! On Mundane Acquaintances. Hilaire Belloc. ELU; FaBoEE; FiBHP; MoVE; OxBTC

Good morning, young lady, my hosses won't stand. Good-Bye Old Paint. *Anonymous.* TrAS

Good morrow fair maidens, on Tuesday morning. I Shall Be Married on Monday Morning. *Anonymous.* ErPo

Good morrow to you, Valentine. St. Valentine's Day. *Anonymous.* OxNR

Good news, good news. Letter Written on a Ferry Crossing Long Island Sound. Anne Sexton. CoAP; MP; NYBP; TwCP

Good night, dear heart,/Good night, good night. Epitaph Placed on His Daughter's Tomb. Mark (Samuel Langhorne Clemens) Twain. TreF

Good night, good night. Epitaph Placed on His Daughter's Tomb. Mark (Samuel Langhorne Clemens) Twain. GoTF

Good night! Good night! Good Night. Victor Hugo. SiSoSe; SoPo; SUS; TiPo

Good-night, good-night,...good-night. The Ghosts of the Buffaloes. Vachel Lindsay. MoAmPo; NePA

Good night, ladies, good night, sweet ladies, good night, good night. The Waste Land. Thomas Stearns Eliot. CMoP; CoBMV; HAP; LiTA; LiTM; MasP; MoAmPo; MoPo; MoVE; NAWM 1-2; NoAm; NOBE; NoP; OxBA; OxBTC; PPoe; TAP

Good night my children For the Girls 'Cause They Know. Harold Littlebird. VoR

Good night, my love! good night! Good Night. John Nichol. OBVV

Good night, Old Dear, "Good Egg." Mac. Mark Vinz. Str

"Good night! Sweet dreams! God keep you everywhere!" My Little Love. Charles B. Hawley. HBV 1-2

Good night t' ye, Mounseer Nongtongpaw! Nongtongpaw. Charles Dibdin. HBV 1-2

Good-night to the Season!–Good-night! Good-Night to the Season. Winthrop Mackworth Praed. ALV; NOBE; NOBL; OBNC; OxBoLi; PoEL 1-5

Good: now it is time. An Introduction to Some Poems. William Stafford. CAPP

Good nut-brown ale and toast. O Thou That Sleep'st. Sir William Davenant. CBEP; InvP

Good old money, which is nothing short of providential. Bankers Are Just Like Anybody Else, Except Richer. Ogden Nash. ATP; LiTA

Good, our first fire is lighted! October Morning. John James Piatt. YeAr

Good sense and skill/Of madness cured me. For My Contemporaries. J. V. Cunningham. CoAP; PP; SM

The good shepherd feeds his sheep. Let Thy Kingdom. *Anonymous.* AH

Good Shepherd, may I sing Thy praise/Within Thy house forever. The King of Love. Sir Henry William Baker. BePJ

The good smell of the dust/that is the same/everywhere around the earth. Blood River Day. Dennis Brutus. WhB

Good St. Joseph, come this night. Carol of the Russian Children. *Anonymous.* OHIP

Good! the air of the/uplands is stimulating. The Aftermath. William Carlos Williams. FAZ

The good, the joy, that it may bring/Eternity shall tell.　Speak Gently. David Bates.　PaPo; SpRo

Good things with glad....Yes, Caroline!　To C.F.H. on Her Christening-Day. Thomas Hardy.　NAs

Good tidings of great joy.　The Light in the Temple.　William Rose Benet. MoRP

Good vinegar of sorry wine.　Damis, an Author Cold and Weak. Anonymous.　HBV 1-2

Good weather for work.　Work Room.　Kenward Elmslie.　ANYP

Good will henceforth from Heaven to men/Begin and never cease.　While Shepherds Watched Their Flocks by Night.　Nahum Tate.　GN; HBV 1-2; HBVY; NOCV; OnYI; OxBI; TreFS

...The good will/of the good white folks downtown,/who hired him.　The Idiot.　Dudley Randall.　BPo

Good will towards men.　Finis.　George Herbert.　JCP

Good wives make amulets/Against her, to protect themselves./Lilith is jealous. Lilith.　Ruth Fainlight.　VWA

Good woman, take my arm.　I Am a Hunchback.　Robert Louis Stevenson. OBSP

...Good work done/comes back into the mind,/a free breath drawn. Reverdure.　Wendell Berry.　SaC

Good year and good luck,/With chuck, chuck, chuck, chuck!　To Mistress Isabel Pennell.　John Skelton.　CBEP; LiTL; NOBE; OAEP; OBEV; OBSC; PoEL 1-5; SeCeV; TrGrPo

"Goodby, you big lummix, I'm glad you backed out."　Betsy from Pike. Anonymous.　BaBo

Goodbye, Cynthie Jane.　Goin' Up the River.　Anonymous.　TrAS

Goodbye Elvis/Goodbye Groucho.　A Sort of Elegy.　Blanche Farley. SOTS

Goodbye, goodbye. It/seemed so real.　Moving.　Darrell Gray.　APU

Goodbye, little Bonnie, goodbye.　Goodbye, Little Bonnie, Goodbye. Anonymous.　FSW

(Goodbye my dear goodbye)　Six O'Clock.　Owen Dodson.　PoNe

Goodbye, my lover, goodbye.　Goodbye, My Lover, Goodbye.　Anonymous. FSW

Goodbye–perhaps your flight has just begun/Under the sun.　Vernon Castle. Harriet Monroe.　HBMV

Goodbye the day. Good luck to me.　A Ballad of a Mine.　Robin Skelton. MoBS

Goodbye you ugly Detroit.　Abandoning Your Car in a Snowstorm: Rosslyn, Virginia.　Michael C. Blumenthal.　AmC

Goodbyes creaking in the pines.　Visit.　James Welch.　AmPA

A goodly company, the Devil go with all!/Tweedle tweedle twino.　The Marriage of the Frog and the Mouse.　Anonymous.　EBEV

A goodly inheritance!　Bequest.　S. Gale Gilburt.　AMV-81

"Goodman, you've spoken the foremost/word,/Get up and bar the door." Get Up and Bar the Door (A version).　Anonymous.　ESPB

Goodness how delicious, eating goober peas!　Goober Peas.　Pindar.　FSW; PSoN

Goodness, how we'd like to know/If things will always alter so.　Children's Song.　Ford Madox Ford.　HBV 1-2

Goodnight.　Bedtime Story.　Lou Lipsitz.　VGW

Goodnight, goodnight./signed Joseph.　Mary Passed This Morning.　Owen Dodson.　PoBA

..."Goodnight,/love. It was good."　Rondeau after a Transatlantic Telephone Call.　Marilyn Hacker.　SM

Goodnight, pretty maidens, till Wednesday morning.'　The Sign of the Bonny Blue Bell.　Anonymous.　OBET

The goodwife was a Scots woman,/And she came to his hand.　Gude Wallace (G version).　Anonymous.　ESPB

GOOOOOOOOOOOJOOOOOB.　I Am the Walrus.　The Beatles.　PPoe

Goops like that annoy me much!　Felicia Ropps.　Gelett Burgess.　BBGG; TiPo

Goose-giblets, too, are good.　The Best Religion.　Heinrich Heine.　TrJP

...Goose/who waddles, slopping/noisily in the mud of/his pool.　To Daphne and Virginia.　William Carlos Williams.　CrMA

The Gordian knot need not be cut.　Charity Overcoming Envy.　Marianne Moore.　NYBP

Gorged with yew trees that were good for bows.　In the Oregon Country. William Stafford.　AmFN

The gorgeous cabbages of Ghent!　The End of My Sister's Guggenheim. John Malcolm Brinnin.　GLGT

The gorgeous tiger-lilies,/That in our garden grow!　Tiger-Lilies.　Thomas Bailey Aldrich.　GN

Gorgons and Hydra's, and Chimera's dire.　Paradise Lost.　John Milton. AtBAP; OBS

The Goshawk feeds on your timid heart.　The Goshawk.　John Haines. GP

...The gossip/Of the wind in her hair will be stopped much too soon.　Going down the Mountain.　Valentin Iremonger.　NeIP

Got a message from heaven of peace and good will.　The Cowboy. Anonymous.　CoSo

Got a sound sleep, indeed, indeed I did,/Though all this stuff laid somewhere in my head.　Verses to Miss –-.　J. Wilde.　NOEC

Got anothr papa on the Salt Lake Line!　Casey Jones.　Anonymous. OxBoLi

Got my hooks on the ladder an I'm climbin up the wall　Crawl Blues. Vincent McHugh.　ErPo

Got rattled, and shouted, "Who's next?"　Limerick: "A clergyman told from his text."　Anonymous.　TDH

Got shot though the bowels, and you see where I lay.　The Cowboy's Lament (III).　Anonymous.　CoSo

Got to drive these dogies down the trail.　Doney Gal.　Anonymous.　FSW

Got to get out here, got to get out/of the music.　A Short History of the Better Life.　Tess Gallagher.　LTB

Got to get your can filled Monday.　No More Booze.　Anonymous.　OBAL

Gott pulls mit me und I mit Him–/Meinself–und Gott.　Kaiser & Co. Alexander Macgregor Rose.　HBV 1-2

Gotten at last with labour and long toil　Amoretti, LXIX.　Edmund Spenser.　AAS; CoBE

Gra machree a coolin bawn.　The Cruiskeen Lawn.　Anonymous.　HBV 1-2; OnYI

Grab a handful of heart/and run like hell.　Strip Mining Pit.　Dan Gillespie. TAT

Grace and Persuasion dwell in young Theoxenos.　Ode on Theoxenos. Pindar.　PeHV

Grace can make our foes our friends.　Come, Follow Me.　Thomas Campion.　EnRePo

Grace informing with silent soul.　Gulf-Weed.　Cornelius George Fenner. EtS

Grace more than thine, but Gods, the world hath none.　At Home in Heaven. Robert Southwell.　AnAnS 1

Grace ran/a dripping wet/nude/to the car.　Married Three Months.　Sheryl L. Nelms.　AmC

The grace that shines from her body/Giveth to lover all great joy.　Medieval Norman Songs.　Anonymous.　AWP

...Grace, the largest space we know,/may be just across the threshold.　A Wish for Waving Goodbye.　Roberta Hill.　AMV-80

Grace the soft Warbles of her honied Voice.　The Enthusiast: or, The Lover of Nature.　Joseph Warton.　CEP; EnPE; LAuP

Grace to reach the home on high!　Father, Into Thy Hands.　Thomas B. Pollack.　BePJ

A graceful error may correct the cave.　Mind.　Richard Wilbur.　CMoP; ForPo; HaCAP; HoPM; NCSH; NePA; NePoEA; OBSP

The Graces daunced, and Apollo play'd.　Gratiana Dauncing and Singing. Richard Lovelace.　AnAnS 2; CaPo; CBEP; JCP; LiTL; LoBV; MeLP; MePo; OAEP; OBEV; OBS; SeCV 1-2

Gracious and eternal death/who permits departure.　Things That Are Worse Than Death.　Sharon Olds.　MAYP

Gracious and helpful, wise and good,/The Fairy Princess Moe stood.　To an Island Princess.　Robert Louis Stevenson.　OBTV

The gracious gift of this New Year.　Ane Sang of the Birth of Christ, with the Tune of Baw Lula Low.　Anonymous.　BSV

Gradual as flowers, gradual as rust.　Emily Dickinson.　Michael Longley. CIP

The gradual self-effacement of the dead.　Song: "The first month of his absence."　Alun Lewis.　LiTM; OBWP; WaaP

The gradual shade is drawn.　Sun and Cloud.　Melville Cane.　PoPl

The Grafin's greed, her son's need, mine, nor how to supply them.　Das Schloss.　Lincoln Kirstein.　NoAm

...Grains of dirt/strewn thru my body　Elegy.　Alan Loney.　OCNZ

Grains through the hourglass glint and spring.　Tattoos.　Charles Wright. GP

"Gramercy, father, so mote I thee,/For all these thinges liketh not me." Diversions for an Unhappy Princess.　Anonymous.　OxBM

Granada and Leon and haughty Navarre/Shall lower their banner to Cuba's lone star!　Battle Cry.　William Henry Venable.　PAH

Grand manchons, et terribles duffeurs.　Limerick: "A Potsdam, les totaux absteneurs."　George Du Maurier.　CenHV; LiBL

The grand Napoleon of the realms of rhyme.　Don Juan.　George Gordon, Lord Byron.　OAEP

Granddady, they tore/his/neck.　Biography.　LeRoi (Imamu Amiri Baraka) Jones.　TAP

Granddaughter of King P'ing.　Of Silk Is Her Fishing-Line.　Anonymous. HW

...Grander, build the edifice/Begun so long ago by Washington.　Washington's Birthday.　Arthur J. Burdick.　OHIP

Grandeur has nothing so sublime,/Nor Beauty half so fair.　The Unknown God.　Henry Francis Lyte.　TRV

Grandeur of the perfect sphere/Thanks the atoms that cohere.　Prudence. Ralph Waldo Emerson.　OBAL

The grandeurs of his Babylonian heart.　All's Vast.　Francis Thompson. MoAB; MoBrPo

The grandfather of all/dream.　The last dream.　Ray A. Young Bear.　STE

Grandfather of the days is he,/Of dawn the ancestor. The Mountain Sat upon the Plain. Emily Dickinson. FaBV

"Grandfather's dying. He's going to die,' I sang. Ulinda. David Campbell. CBAP

Grandfather smooths out/footprints. Akawense. Phyllis Wolf. STE

...A grandiose/talking headstone for my tooth. The Root Canal. Marge Piercy. DFF; HoAn

Grandly the thought rides the words, as a good/horseman his steed. The English Language. William Wetmore Story. GN

Grandma is a widow. Pennsylvania Deutsch. Christopher Morley. NLV

Grandma picked up her scissors and struck him through the/heart Une Vie. Pentti Saarikoski. ELU

...Grandma's hair, secret, let down only here.' The Boy Who Dreamed the Country Night. C. J. Koch. NOAV

Grandmaw always expected the worst, and waits/for desperately sensual bathers to drown. The Nude on the Bathroom Wall. Gena Ford. IHMS

Grandmother Granger's wedding gift/To every girl on her marriage day. The Wedding Gift. Minna Irving. BLPA

Grandmother/used to chain herself/to the postoffice/for woman rights The River. Sam Cornish. PoBA

Grandmothers, & spinster aunts/& all those babies. Family Chronicle. Anselm Parlatore. SUW

Grandpapa was quite annoyed. Our Polite Parents. Carolyn Wells. BBGG

Grandson, he said, if that is true/then these flowers are like the whiteman. Someone Gave Him Some Plastic Flowers Once. Dennis Shady. LFAC

The granite blocks/that line the causeway/flash by like fish. The Fisherman's Wife. Nora Mitchell. AMV-80

Grant from Thy faith we all/May never, never fall!/Kyrie Eleison. Media Vita. Notker Balbulus. CAW

Grant me now my soul's desire,/"None of self and all of Thee." None of Self and All of Thee. Theodore Monod. BLRP

Grant me, O Gods, to prize aright/Sorrow, since sorrow gives me sight. Pain. St. John Lucas. HBV 1-2

Grant me, O Lord, a sunny mind,/Thy windy will to bear! Besides the autumn poets sing. Emily Dickinson. OxBA

Grant me the grace, I beg upon my knees,/Not to forget that I was one of these. Prayer. Arthur Guiterman. TrPWD

Grant me thy presence, Lord, I pray,/And keep me from all sin. Awake My Soul, Betimes Awake. Isaac Chanler. AH

Grant me to be beautiful in the inner man. The Inner Man. Plato. PoPl

Grant me to see the light! In the Dark. George Arnold. HBV 1-2

Grant me wisdom Mary had/When she taught her little Lad. The Housewife. Catherine Cate Coblentz BLRP; TrPWD; TRV

Grant my son's ashes lie where these men are! Virtue. Walter De la Mare. MMM

Grant that our willing, though unworthy quest/May, through thy grace, admit us 'mongst the blest. Hierarchie of the Blessed Angels (excerpt). Thomas Heywood. WGRP

Grant that the woman who bore me/Suffered to suckle a Man! Battle Cry. John G. Neihardt. HBMV

Grant them, good Lord, as thou mayst of thy might,/To fret inward for losing such a loss. Satires. Sir Thomas Wyatt. FCP; SiPS

Grant then, dear Lord, that all who love may be/Heirs of Thy glorious Immortality. Thysia. Morton Luce. HBV 1-2

Grant Thy pardon excellent/for all my crimes, since I repent! The Time Is Ripe and I Repent. Oengus Ceile De. NOBI

Grant to my poor soul amorous the dark gift of this/illusion. Povre Ame Amoureuse. Louise Labe. AWP

Grant us, Great God,/Thou Joy of men, that we find Thy face/Mild with mercy on that Great Day! Amen Juliana. Cynewulf. AnOE

Grant us, O mother, therefore, unto who pray,/Some little of thy light and majesty. A Prayer. Archibald Lampman. TrPWD

Grant us thy Spirit's help, thy will/In every deed to do. Salutation to Jesus Christ. John Calvin. WGRP

Grante me in Paradise to have a mansion/That shede His blode for my redempcion! Farewell This World! Anonymous. EnPo; OxBM

Grante us, Crist,/With thyn uprist/To gone. An Easter Song. Anonymous. OxBM

The grape will redden on your fingers/Through the lit crystal of the cup. Autumn. Roy Campbell. GTBS-P; MoBrPo; OBMV; OxBTC

Grapple with pride/the thin and perilous wheel. Model T. Adrien Stoutenburg. CTBA

The grass below–above the vaulted sky. I Am. John Clare. CBEP; EBCP; EBEV; ERoP 1-2; GTBS-P; HAP; LiTB; NBM; NOBE; NOBV; NoP; OAEL 1-2; OBNC; PG; PoEL 1-5; PoPl; Prf; PrIm; TrGrPo; VLP; WHA

Grass by the sea/in quiet smells/a little way Flake Diamond of/the Sea. Larry Eigner. PoM

Grass in the splendor/of thighs/without words–/worth My Spring Thing. Everett Hoagland. BPo

The grass is green here too; I call/My draw a fair one. Mezzo Cammin. Judith Moffett. SM

Grass nibbling inward/Like green fire. Former Barn Lot. Mark Van Doren. FaBV; LOW; MoAmPo; PoPl

The grass so little has to do/I wish I were the hay! The grass so little has to do. Emily Dickinson. GN; HBVY

Grass sprang out of my skull,/My head was of black earth. Suffering. Albert Ehrenstein. TrJP

The grass that fades. Sob, Heavy World. W. H. Auden. DTC

Grass, trees, and flower-/ing season, for no clear reason. For No Clear Reason. Robert Creeley. VGW

Grasses and leaves, come from the meadows green. Sonnets, XII: "A roadside inn this summer Saturday." Thomas Caulfield Irwin. IrPN

The grasses vanish. Poem for Dorothy Holt. Susan Irene Rea. AMV-81

The grasshopper's among some grassy hills. On the Grasshopper and the Cricket. John Keats. BiP; BoC; BoLiVe; DiPo; ERoP 1-2; ExPo; FaBoBe; GN; HBV 1-2; InPo; LiTB; MBW 1-2; NIP; OAEL 1-2; SeCeV; TrGrPo

The grasshopper will look good to us./So it goes... Accomplished Facts. Carl Sandburg. WHA

Grassroots down under put fingers into dark dirt. Grassroots. Carl Sandburg. RFM

The Grateful Dead & Amelia Earhart hello to you from me 25 Spontaneous Lines Greeting the World. Jim Tyack. AMV-80

Grateful for you/all the same. A Tardy Epithalamium for E. and N. Ralph Pomeroy. PeHV

...Grateful that you/never hit one of them, erect this statue. The World's Worst Boxer. Lucilius [(or Lucillius)]. SD

Gratefully through it and it parts a little while. Green Pastures. Dick Allen. AMV-80

Graunt hem his blissing,/That now maken chere. A Lullaby of the Nativity. Anonymous. MeEL

Graunt theim, goode lorde, as thou maist of thy myght,/To frete inward for losing suche a losse. My Mothers Maydes when They Did Sowe and Spynne. Sir Thomas Wyatt. AAS

Grave as the birds in last solemnities/Assembling to depart. Beauty Imposes. Shaw Neilson. PoAu 1-2

Grave his name, and pour the fragrant/Balm upon the icy stone. The Burial of the Dead. Prudentius (Aurelius Clemens Prudentius). LiTW

The grave is cold enough for me/Without you and your poetry. Alas! 'Tis Very Sad to Hear. Walter Savage Landor. GTBS-P; TW; WeW

Grave is conquered! Christ is King! Triumph. L. D. Stearns. BLRP

The grave is neatly kept by you and me. Decent Burial. Lois Seyster Montross. HBMV

...Grave mama, I caught/the silliest and it was me. Please Forward. James Welch. CDW

The grave marked only by the green/Memorial of grass! Memorial. Mae Winkler Goodman. PGD

The grave of my firstlove murdered by my brother. Ireland 1972. Paul Durcan. FaBoIP

A grave, on which to rest from singing?/Choose. Sonnets from the Portuguese, XVII. Elizabeth Barrett Browning. BrRo; HBV 1-2; VLP; WHA

The grave's narrow too/But you lie there alone. The Family of Eight. Abraham Reisen. VWA

The Grave said to the Rose. The Grave and the Rose. Victor Hugo. AWP

The grave was finished, but the spade/Remained in memory. Bereaved of All, I Went Abroad. Emily Dickinson. MAPA

Gravedigger turning/daisy-filled clods/on a fresh made/bed. To Turn from Love. Sarah Webster Fabio. BlSi

Gravely accepts and eats my offering. Tortoise. Joanne De Longchamps. BoAnP

Graver follies must thou follow,/But as senseless, false, and hollow. Youth! Thou Wear'st to Manhood Now. Sir Walter Scott. OBSP

...Gravid/with bodies, trembling/to give birth. The Disconnections. John Engels. WOLT

The gray bull will browse, his back to me, when I go by. Evening before Rain. Leonard Alfred George Strong. OxBTC

A gray gull/into a room. Halcyon. Hilda ("H. D.") Doolittle. MoAmPo

The gray rags fluttered on the dead. Festubert: The Old German Line. Edmund Charles Blunden. MMM

The gray shape with the palaeolithic face/Was still the master of the longitudes. The Titanic (excerpt). Edwin John Pratt. NOBC; PeCV

The gray street and a crumbling wall. In Old Tucson. Sharlot M. Hall. BPAW

Graze the great machines. Grazing Locomotives. Archibald MacLeish. PPJ

The great Ahkoond of Swat/Is not! A Threnody. George Thomas Lanigan. AA; CBEP; CenHV; FiBHP; HBV 1-2; InMe; NA; NLV; PeCV; WHW

The great and holy Baal Shem Tov awaits. The Strange Guest. Itzik Manger. VWA

Green corn, don't-cha tell Polly./Green corn.   Green Corn.   *Anonymous.* FSW

The green cove below the light.   What Must (iii).   Archibald MacLeish. MoLP

Green diamond, or gem of girosol!   Sonnets.   Frederick Goddard Tuckerman.   AP

Green-eyed, bedizened, at the dappled center.   Errantry.   Robert Fitzgerald. NYBP

Green fields call us on.   Sunday Morning.   Isidor Schneider.   AnAmPo

The green Forum's sparrows are the sparrows of home.   The Augsburg Adoration.   Randall Jarrell.   NYBP

The green fruit ripen, or the rotten drop?   An Old Folks Home.   Paul Lake. AMV-81

Green grapes may be touched, but his ripe/chastity will be guarded.   Epigram: "I am provoked."   Strato.   PeHV

Green, green grows the grass/Behind our tired feet.   Descent for the Lost. Philip Child.   CaP

Green groweth the holly.   Green Groweth the Holly.   King of England Henry VIII.   EBEV; SBVL; TrGrPo

Green grows the grass in North Amerikee!   Home, Boys, Home. *Anonymous.*   FSW

...The green has begun to emerge from the rind of/the cantaloupe, and everything seems possible.   Museum.   Robert Hass.   NPGG

The green hills break as our graves embrace.   Summer Rain.   Laurie Lee. MoVE

Green in summer, and in winter/Musical with wind.   Monaghan.   Shane Leslie.   OnYI

Green jacket, red cap,/And white owl's feather.   Up the Airy Mountain. William Allingham.   FaFP

Green mould on its hand-made leather casing   TV.   John Forbes.   CBAP

Green-plover cry: "Pee-weet, pee-weet!"   January.   D. J. O'Sullivan.   NeIP

The green-robed Spring has come to town tonight.   Villanelle of Washington Square.   Walter Adolphe Roberts.   PoNe

Green scapulars to wear over your shroud.   The Strand at Lough Beg. Seamus Heaney.   NoP; OBWP

Green Spring trips forth to set the world aflower.   May-day on Magdalen Tower.   Thomas Herbert Warren.   OBVV

Green trees that in the forest grew.   A Dialogue between the Soul and Body. Andrew Marvell.   AnAnS 1; HAP; InPS; JCP; MeLP; MePo; NoP; OAEL 1-2; OBS; OxBoCh; PoEL 1-5; PPP; SeCP; TEP

The green were one wide grave.   The Bay Fight.   Henry Howard Brownell. PAH

The greener wood has private ways/That posted death may not remark. Defeated Farmer.   Mark Van Doren.   AnAmPo

The greenest/singing leaves/grew/tendresses/of trust   One, the Other, And. Wendy Wieber.   NMM

Greenish, pulsing, a clutch/of snake eggs.   Shaman: For Malcolm.   Erika Mumford.   PoDr

The greenleaf is flowing/In flame out of sight!   October's Song.   Eleanor Farjeon.   PoSC

...Greet with an eye to love/The hard or simple chore.   Praise to Light. Thomas Cole.   NePoAm-2

Greeting you joyfully.   Roaches.   Edward Field.   NYP

Grenada of mine!   Grenada.   Mikhail A. Svetlov.   WaaP

Grew so broad-minded he was scatter-brained.   This Humanist Whom No Beliefs Constrained.   J. V. Cunningham.   ELU; InPK

Grey, and dear heart, how grey!   Vain Finding.   Walter De la Mare.   BrPo

Grey evil, which has no path, and shows neither light nor dark/and has no home, no home anywhere.   Evil Is Homeless.   D. H. Lawrence.   MoRP

Grey stone, grey water,/And brick upon grey brick.   The Closing Album. Louis MacNeice.   OBTV

The grey towns where the wishes and the fears are done.   Fugue.   Howard Nemerov.   AmC; TAP

Grey were the geese and green was the grazing.   Three Grey Geese in a Green Field Grazing.   *Anonymous.*   OxNR; PBBP

The griddle-cake's thar, anyway.   Home, Sweet Home.   Henry Cuyler Bunner.   InMe

Grief, an untimely doom, fame that/eternal abides.   Song, Youth, and Sorrow.   William Cranston Lawton.   AA

Grief builds no barns; its plough/Rusts at the door.   Nurse No Long Grief. Mary Gilmore.   PoAu 1-2

...Grief for them/who wait longing for love.   The Wife's Lament. *Anonymous.*   BoWoP

The grief is fixed too deeply/That mourns a man like thee.   Joseph Rodman Drake.   Fitz-Greene Halleck.   BLPA

The grief my heart is bearing/Will waste away my life.   The Crusade. Rinaldo d'Aquino.   CAW

The grief of all weary steps/That softly come to me.   I Am the Autumn. Itzik Manger.   TrJP

The grief that must have way.   Resignation.   Henry Wadsworth Longfellow. HBV 1-2

...The grief/Which for His sake/Came upon His mother.   The Crucifixion. *Anonymous.*   OnYI

Grief will not turn again.   Hymn to Dispel Hatred at Midnight.   Yvor Winters.   TW

The grief-wrung minds are shuttled/Between the agony of the factory/And the misery at home.   The Factory Hands.   Polycarp Chimedza.   WhB

Griefe, interrupted speach with teares supplyes.   A Pastorall Dialogue. Thomas Carew.   AnAnS 2; SeCP

The griefs and hates, and all the meaner parts/That balance thy one grim misgotten pile.   To a Millionaire.   Archibald Lampman.   NOBC

The griefs and pains that we know well!   Medieval Norman Songs. *Anonymous.*   AWP

Grieved that they bound it, grieves that they are broken.   Pericles and Aspasia.   Walter Savage Landor.   ViBoPo

Grill me some bones!'   At the Keyhole.   Walter De La Mare.   DTC; MoAB; MoBrPo

Grim suicides in bottom-rock and stone.   Suicide Pond.   Kathy McLaughlin. PoA

Grimacing to break the seal   Smiles.   Peter Schjeldahl.   ANYP

Grind, O mill, keep grinding!   Harvest Song.   Richard Dehmel.   AWP; LiTW

Grinding the wounds/Of poverty.   May Bright Mushrooms Grow.   Innocent Banda.   WhB

Grinds up/flaming graves/and gives birth/to ashes.   When the Day. Thomas Sessler.   VWA

Grinly I tell you this. And this is all.   Mother Goose Up-to-Date.   Louis Untermeyer.   MoAmPo

Grinned an evil grin and thrust/His tongue out with its fork.   Eve. Christina Georgina Rossetti.   CH; FM; GTBS-P; NBM; NIP; OxBoCh; PoEL 1-5; SeCeV

Grinning/& stoned/& desolate   A Small Faculty Stag for the Visiting Poet. Earle Birney.   OxBC

Grins at the fellow–grunts–and lounges on!   Steam (excerpt).   Ebenezer Elliott.   VLP

Grip earth and let burn.   Like This Together.   Adrienne Rich.   CoPo; VGW

Grip on the seed and lets our future breathe.   A Hard Frost.   C. Day Lewis. HaMV

Grip the ground astride, press teeth to lip.   How Can Man Die Better. Tyrtaeus.   WaaP

Gripped on the shoulder of the man in front.   War Blinded.   Douglas Dunn. OBWP

Gripping the shoulders/before or after our deaths   Noise Grimaced.   Larry Eigner.   NeAP

Grips his arm, draws him down to his own dark home.   The White Skirt. Stephen Dobyns.   MAYP

Groaning when the/Wind moves it.   Backyard Swing.   Janet Campbell Hale. STE

The Grocer trembles; for his time,/Just like his weight, is short.   The Song against Grocers.   Gilbert Keith Chesterton.   CenHV; DBV; FaBoCo

Groom into singing clans.   In Hotels Public and Private.   Ralph Pomeroy. CoPo

The groom retails the favours of his lord.   London: A Poem in Imitation of the Third Satire of Juvenal (excerpt).   Samuel Johnson.   OBSV

...Grope/In the alien light, toward a goal/He could be sure of never reaching. Abraham.   Stephen Mitchell.   VWA

Groping, you may like Omar grasp a pearl.   In a Copy of Omar Khayyam. James Russell Lowell   AA

Grotesque experience, embittered form.   Catacombs.   Istvan Vas.   VWA

Grotesquely garbed/In his master's clothes.   Who Translates a Poet Badly. Gonzalez Prada.   ELU

Ground and mobile air, combined/reactively, could have in mind.   Actual Vision of Morning's Extrusion.   Alan Dugan.   PPP

Grounded,/I return home.   Desert March.   Gerda Norvig.   VWA

The grounding of arms/toys, and the blinding gulls   Passages.   Larry Eigner. NeAP

...The grounds are a formal ruin/whereon the lucky who lived/come to resemble so much that does not   Two Pictures of a Leaf.   Marvin Bell. LCAP

Groundsel in flower.   Through Storm and Wind.   *Anonymous.*   OxNR

Grow fragrant for the Judgment day.   Mutans Nomen Evae.   Eric Gill. CAW

Grow high above my head.   Invocation.   Helene Johnson.   BANP; PoNe

Grow more distant from the others on/the beach.   Bathing with Father. Doug Fetherling.   NeAC

Grow now. Sing. Fly. Do what you're here for.   The Magician Suspends the Children.   Carole Oles.   SoSe

Grow out in lines like cabbages while men/In gold braid blow among the hollyhocks.   Band Music.   John Fuller.   NePoEA-2

Grow up, Juniper, like Maine!   Christening-Day Wishes for My God-Child Grace Lane Berkley II.   Robert P. Tristam Coffin.   BiCB; OFD

Grow very tall.   Go to Bed Late.   *Anonymous.*   OxNR

Grow well, good tree! Planting a Tree. Nancy Byrd Turner. YeAr

Growing, day by day, more closely into oneness with each/other. A Prayer for Broken Little Families. Violet Alleyn Storey. PoToHe

Growing green down on the Gila; there's a home for you and/me. Freighting from Wilcox to Globe. *Anonymous.* AmFP; CoSo

Growing one with its silent stream. By the Margin of the Great Deep. George William Russell. HBMV; OBEV; OBVV

Growing smug, feeling like/a balloon in a world with no pins. Ten Week Wife. Rhoda Donovan. Str

Growing the lives we give away/when we wake. Taking the Train Home. William Matthews. GeTw

Grown fat/With eating many a miching/Mouse. A Cat. Robert Herrick. PCat

Grown men, so sad, in coats too big too fit. Cleaning Up, Clearing Out. Daniel Ross Bronson. AMV-80

Grown up again to love. This Blonde Girl. Kendrick Smithyman. AnNZ

The grown-up white man and the grown-up black. The Castle. Sidney Alexander. PoNe

Grows a fair plant, bears flowers and fruit. Nonpareil. Matthew Prior. EnLoPo

Grows stoutly toward our future... The Long Night Home. Charles F. Gordon. NBP

...Grows to an envious fever/Of pale and bloodless emulation. Troilus and Cressida. William Shakespeare. NIP

...The growth will be less for the/libation a while, and then more. Cow Pissing. Robert Morgan. GeTw

The grunion are building/a star tunnel Grunion. Wendy Rose. CDW

The grunting pigs, that wait for all,/Scramble and hurry where they fall. Autumn. John Clare. EG

Gryll/Will/Be borne out by history yet. Gryll's State. Jr, Blount Roy. OBAL

Gryll will not therefore say a Grace for it. Upon Gryll. Robert Herrick. AnAnS 2

Guantanamera guajira Guantanamera. Guantanamera. Jose Marti. FSW

A guard celestial from Omnipotence. Stand by the Flag. John Nichols Wilder. GN; PGD

Guard him well whose child I bear! Channel Water. Virginia Scott Miner. AMV-80

Guard me mine and my own rooftree./"Man of the House!" The Man of the House. Katharine Tynan Hinkson. CAW

Guard the poor from treachery. Hawks. James Stephens. HBMV

Guard thy emblematic flower. The Evening Primrose. John Langhorne. CEP; OBEC

The guard turns, grinning,/and shoots the bird. Reaching. William Carson Fagg. LFAC

Guard well the rest of him, their rare sweet worshipper. Bereavement of the Fields. Wilfred (William Wilfred Campbell) Campbell. CaP

...Guarding a costly orchid tuft,/plebeian in our land. Land of the Free. Sister Mary Honora. NePoAm-2

Guarding my family with guns. War on the Periphery. George Johnston. NOBC; PeCV

Guarding the invisible sheaves/The risen watchers stand. The Myth. Edwin Muir. CMoP

A' gude things may attend you! To Miss Ferrier. Robert Burns. CBEP

Guess her name, three times I've telled it. Riddle: "There was a girl in our town." *Anonymous.* HBV 1-2; HBVY; OxNR

Guess I got nothing left to say Cokboy, Part Two. Jerome Rothenberg. NNaP

Guess I'll have to/Count to ten. Come on In. *Anonymous.* SD

Guess that's sifficient, "Good-night." What You Goin' to Do When the Rent Comes 'Round? Andrew B. Sterling. OBAL

Guess we'll give it one mo' try. Strange Legacies. Sterling A. Brown. CNA; PoBA; TTY

Guess who knew he'd got them wrong. The Riddle. Ralph Hodgson. PoPl

Guessing what color and raiment. When the Fairies. Edward Dorn. NeAP; TAT

The guest-eructed nesselrode. Drafts for a Quatrain. Edmund Wilson. OBAL

...Guest/only casually invited, and that several months ago. Poem: "The eager note on my door said 'Call me.'. Frank O'Hara. EAS; NoAm; NOBA

The guests' departure leaves us soon alone. After the Hunt. Detlev Freiherr von Liliencron. AWP

The Guests that Come hereto shall swim in bliss. Meditations. Edward Taylor. TAP

Guide, and support, and cheer me to the end! The Recluse. William Wordsworth. OBRV

The guide, the guardian of my heart, and soul/Of all my moral being. Lines Composed a Few Miles above Tintern Abbey. William Wordsworth. WGRP

Guide the steps that go astray. The Golden Sequence. Pope Innocent III. CAW

Guide them in faith beneath familiar stars–/Our Lady of the Refuges. Our Lady of the Refuges. Sister Maura. ISi

Guide them with their sacrifice of frankincense and myrrh. A Christmas Carol. Gilbert Thomas. MoRP

Guide thou my efforts and inspire my song. Celestial Queen. Jacopo Sannazaro. ISi

Guide Thou the pen within my wavering hand! The Scribe's Prayer. Arthur Guiterman. TrPWD

Guide us safe through the torments/And shoutings of pain. I Place Myself. *Anonymous.* WTO

Guide where our country's redeemer is laid. Government Official. Paul Dehn. WaP

Guided by wide eyes that never seem to see. Soil Searcher. James Joyce. CTBA

Guides the shuddering nose to Buchanan. On Robert Buchanan, Who Attacked Him under the Pseudonym... Dante Gabriel Rossetti. FaBoEE

Guiding with strength and tenderness. I See God. *Anonymous.* STF

The guidon flags flutter gayly in the wind. Drum-Taps. Walt Whitman. AP

Guild lay under his engine dead. Guild's Signal. Bret (Francis Bret Harte) Harte. PaPo

Guiltless they'll gaze, and innocent adore. Isabella: or, the Morning (excerpt). Sir Charles Hanbury Williams. NOEC

The gulf of Fear, 'twixt Heaven and Hell. Death the Great. Elis Wyn o Lasynys. LiTW

A gull above the ploughshare hears/The ironic song of our defeat. Two Generations. Leonard Alfred George Strong. OBMV

Gulls circle Veradero/with cries. Cuban Refugees on Key Biscayne. Barbara Winder. TAT

The gulls moved seaward very quietly. Gulls. William Carlos Williams. NoP; OxBA

Gulls to the landless drop of the wind-gray cloud. Heraclitus in the West. Charles G. Bell. NePoAm

Gully, gully, gully. Head Bumper. *Anonymous.* OxNR

Gumming the keys/of her baby grand How About. Sheryl L. Nelms. Str

The gun-towers eager/for a fight.../to kill... St. Valentine. Pancho Aguila. LFAC

The gunner twitches, and unreprimanded/Eases two tensions, running home the bolt. Defensive Position. John Streeter Manifold. MoBrPo

The guns and enemies that face/Into this delicate and dangerous place. Conversation. John Berryman. LiTA; LiTM; NePA; WaP

...Guns learn everything/From your thin body pinned against the light. An Officers' Prison Camp Seen from a Troop-Train. Randall Jarrell. WaP

The gunshot he fires/up into the silent air/is to awaken Loneliness. Al Young. PoBA

Gur-gur-gur and gur-gur-gur,/That is all I heard. That Is All I Heard. Yehoash. TrJP

Gurgled in the fog/and freely outgassed. First Rainfall. Alan P. Lightman. SUW

Gus Cannon gulping, "I called myself Banjo Joe!" LI. Ted Berrigan. ANYP

The gush of water from a thousand precious wells. The Water-Witch. Martha Eugenie Perry. CaP

A gust in the big tree/splatters raindrops/on the roof Heavy, Heavy–What Hangs Over? Kenneth Burke. PoL

A gute Noodlesupp' tut Wunders workeh. Mama's Advice. Kurt M. Stein. InMe

The gutteral sorrow of the refugees. The British Museum Reading Room. Louis MacNeice. LiTM; MoAB; MoBrPo; NOBE; SeCePo; WaP

Guzzlewopper. Eyewinker. *Anonymous.* OxNR

Gwan-n, mules! Gee-up dar, mules! Gee-Up Dar, Mules. Edwin Ford Piper. YaD

Gwine up gwine up to see de heabenly lan'. Gwine Up. *Anonymous.* BoAN 1-2

Gwineter harness in de morning soon. Gwineter Harness in de Morning Soon. *Anonymous.* ABF

Gwineter hug my Julie,/Oho! Julie Ann Johnson. *Anonymous.* ABF

Gyf Rowley, Iscamm, or Tyb Gorges be ne/seene. The Accounte of W. Canynge's Feast. Thomas Chatterton. EnLi 1-2

The gypsy cages lions in a song. The Sleeping Gypsy–a Painting by Rousseau. Nick Johnson. PoDr

Gyres run on, and we poor souls/Hurry after. Crazy Bill to the Bishop (parody). Robert Peters. BXAP

H

H'as metamorphosed me into an ass! The Metamorphosis.   Sir John Suckling. CaPo; FaBoEE

H' as turnd his Mistresse, not she him, away. Il Pastor Fido.   Giovanni Battista Guarini. OBVE

H'had Shows of Reason, and few Men have more. On the Death of a Monkey. Thomas Heyrick. FM; MePo

H O L D M E T I G H T L Y. Balloon. Colleen Thibaudeau. WHW

H-O-M-E-S is the 5-letter key. The Great Lakes of Canada. Gordon Perry. FaBoUs

Ha' done, ha' done, ha' done, for I ha' done my ditty. A Ditty. John Day. EIL

Ha! France will hear of him yet one/day! The Hero of the Commune. Margaret Junkin Preston. AA

Ha! give me ale! Give Me Ale. Anonymous. HBV 1-2

Ha, ha, ha, ha, ha! For a Mocking Voice. Eleanor Farjeon. CH; TiPo

Ha, ha, ha! Hangtown gals. Hangtown Girls. Anonymous. FSW

Ha! ha! ha! what fantastic lovers! The Indolent. Paul Verlaine. SyP

Ha! ha! ha! you and me, little brown jug don't I love thee! Little Brown Jug. Joseph E. Winner. ABF; BLSo; FaFP; FSW; OBAL; PSoN; TrAS; TreF

Ha ha ha, you pretty young girls,/that feeling's off of me. Lolly-Too-Dum. Anonymous. FSW

Ha, ha! methinks I make a lie. Of Women. Richard Edwards. EIL

Ha! ha! the soul regains her place,/And sweetens all the skies. Hymns for the Amusement of Children. Christopher Smart. EiCP; LAuP; NOCV

Ha, ha, the wooing o't. Duncan Gray. Robert Burns. ALV; BSV; CoMu; EnLit; ErPo; GoTS; GTBS; GTBS-P; LiTL; MCCG; OBEC

Ha! I go barefoot all the day! Her Favorites. Mattie Lee Hausgen. PoPl

"Ha!" I say. "It's you." My Brother. Dorothy Aldis. SoPo; TiPo

Ha! no music like that crushing through/the skull-bone to the brain. The Battle of the Cowpens. Thomas Dunn English. PAH

Ha! they finished them off! Lalela Zulu. Anonymous. PeSA

Ha! this scent is hot! Piere Vidal Old. Ezra Pound. MoAB

Habille dans sa meilleure costume. Monsieur McGinte. Anonymous. NA

Habit of conversation/(thickly turned thing) may make none. Je Suis une Table. Donald Hall. NePoEA

A habit unpleasant, but curious. Limerick: "There was a young girl of Asturias." Anonymous. TDH

An habitation I will build,/Where they shall live in peace and/rest.' The Noble Fisherman, or Robin Hood's Preferment. Anonymous. ESPB

Had a definite flavour of gin. Limerick: "From the bathing machine came a din." Edward Gorey. OBAL

Had a nip from the flea, had a bite from the louse. My Father Kept a Horse. Anonymous. GBP

Had anything been wrong, we should certainly have heard. The Unknown Citizen. W. H. Auden. BiP; CABA; FF; GoTF; HeIP; InPK; LiTA; LiTM; MoAB; MoRP; NePA; NIP; NLV; NOBL; NYBP; OBSV; PoRA; PPON; SoSe; TreFT; UnPo

Had been mimicked in fairy masonry/By the elfin builders of the frost. The Vision of Sir Launfal. James Russell Lowell. GN

Had broken and thrown away! The Slave's Dream. Henry Wadsworth Longfellow. AnNE; FaPoR; OBVV; PoNe

Had built this stack of thigh-bones, jaws and shins. In Kerry. John Millington Synge. AWP; FaBoPP; GBL; MoBrPo

Had damn'd him to the depths of impoctence. The Disappointment. John Wilmot, Earl of Rochester. UnTE

Had Deborah fear? or was that vision vain/That Actia, Arlotte, and Mandane dreamed? Sonnets, First Series. Frederick Goddard Tuckerman. MAmP

Had fallen asleep on his chest. Limerick: "There was a young fellow named West." Anonymous. TDH

...Had filled/Them up, would keep them filled until the end/Of Time. Towards the Last Spike. Edwin John Pratt. NOBC

Had followed the hunchback/To his kennel in the dark. The Hunchback in the Park. Dylan Thomas. DiPo; EBEV; FaBoTw; MoAB; MoBrPo; MP; NoP; PrIm; TwCP

Had frightened off the eye of day/And kept the Moon reflected there. The Witches' Wood. Mary Elizabeth Coleridge. PBWP

Had he lived a day longer/He'd have been a day older. The Wonderful Old Man. Anonymous. NA

Had He not met me on the road/And helped me on the way! My Cross. Zitella Cocke. HBV 1-2

Had I a golden pound to spend. Had I a Golden Pound. Francis Ledwidge. AnIV

Had I a thousand hearts to give,/Lord! they should all be Thine. Majestic Sweetness. Stennett Samuel. BePJ

Had I not come with my beloved. Deirdre's Farewell to Scotland. Anonymous. OnYI

Had I on earth but wishes three,/The first should be my Anna. The Gowden Locks of Anna. Robert Burns. CBEP

Had I the Art to stun myself/With Bolts of Melody! I Would Not Paint a Picture. Emily Dickinson. MAmP; NOBA

Had it lived long, it would have been/Lilies without-roses within. The Girl Describes Her Fawn. Andrew Marvell. GTBS

Had learned that Heaven is pleased thy simple joys to share. The Robin. Jones Very. AnNE

Had lived like the wives in the patriarchs' days. Over the Coffin. Thomas Hardy. BrPo

Had made brutes men, and men divine. Preludes. Coventry Patmore. GoBC; HBV 1-2

Had made them certain earth returned their love. Two Look at Two. Robert Frost. AP; CoBMV; CrMA; LiTL; MoAB; MoAmPo; NU

Had man to learn himself anew/Beyond the second birth of Death. In Memoriam A.H.H., XLV. Alfred, Lord Tennyson. VLP

Had not David, the perfect warrior, taught/That of my fault thus pardon should be sought. "When reckless youth in an unquiet breast." Henry Howard, Earl of Surrey. FCP

Had not her blush rebuked me. The Shoe-Tying. Robert Herrick. CaPo

Had not these me against myself defended. Grace. Ralph Waldo Emerson. AmPP; NoP; TrPWD

Had not thy waves forbade the rest. Upon Julia Washing Herself in the River. Robert Herrick. CaPo

Had not we women radicals/Just got right in the way.... Deliverance. Frances E. W. Harper. WPOW

Had pity on the least of things/Asleep upon a chair. The Ballad of Father Gilligan. William Butler Yeats. AnIV; EaLo; HBV 1-2; InPo; MoBrPo; OnYI; PoRA

Had plashed the water up the farther strand. Pericles and Aspasia. Walter Savage Landor. ViBoPo

Had seen a lonely dog pass by that night. A Dog's Vigil. Margaret E. Bruner. PoToHe

Had seldom seen a costlier funeral. Enoch Arden. Alfred, Lord Tennyson. BeLS

Had she not so doon, sure I had bene slayne,/Yet as it was, I hardly scap't with paine. Amoretti, XVI. Edmund Spenser. AAS; OAEL 1-2

Had shown under the shattered sky a people that were/free. The Old Song. Gilbert Keith Chesterton. FaBoTw

Had sold the ship and cargo, sent the money to the States. Coming Around the Horn. Anonymous. ABF; AmFP

Had somewhere to get to and sailed calmly on. Musee des Beaux Arts. W. H. Auden. BiP; CABA; CMoP; CoBMV; DiPo; ExPo; FaFP; FF; ForPo; GTBS-P; HAP; HeIP; InPK; InPS; LiTB; LiTM; MoAB; MoPo; MP; NePa; NIP; NoAm; NOBE; NoP; OAEP; PAI; PoRA; PPP; PrIm; SCV; SeCePo; SeCeV; SoSe; TEP; TrCP; TreFT; TrGrPo; TwCP; WeW

Had starlings chattering without stop. Jenny Wren. William Henry Davies. MoBrPo

Had stayed at home behind me and was fast asleep in bed. My Shadow. Robert Louis Stevenson. FaBoBe; FaBV; GoTF; HBV 1-2; HBVY; OnUR; OxBChV; SoPo; TEP; TiPo; TreF

Had stood the one behind the other/If it had been. On One Condition. Charles Madge. EAS

Had swamped the sacred poets with themselves. Poets and Their Bibliographies. Alfred, Lord Tennyson. PP

Had swept in drifts across the ground. Monkey. William Jay Smith. TiPo

Had the Devil a bed, he would pray him to take him. Epitaph on a Great Sleeper. Sir Aston Cokayne. FaBoEE

Had the Elders bcen sprightly and able. Susannah and the Elders. Anonymous. ALV; OLR

Had the love of a bird for a child. The Watch of a Swan. Sarah Piatt. AA

Had theirs/nailed down/too. In-Group. Lionel Kearns. PeCV

Had they only not come too late-too late! Too Late. Fitz Hugh Ludlow. PoLf

Had thou or I or both been wise. Sonnet: "Chloris, whilst thou and I were free." Charles Cotton. ViBoPo

Had to go out and dig another "rear." Rookie's Lament. Anonymous. ABF

Had tried deeply but could not/so that that was why The Modes of Vallejo Street San Diego, Los Angeles (excerpt). Hugh Seidman. UnPo

Had we remained together/We could have become a silence. Quick and Bitter. Yehuda Amichai. BoLoP

Had wearied of the Summer and the Sun. In Memorabilia Mortis. Francis Sherman. CaP

Hadn't a-been for Cotton-eyed Joe,/I'd a-been married a long time ago. The Bank of the Arkansaw. Anonymous. OuSiCo

The haggard daylight steer. The Death of a Toad. Richard Wilbur. AmP; AP; BiP; CMoP; ForPo; LiTM; MiAP; MoVE; NMP; NoAm; NoP; PoA

Hags away, while Children sleep. Charm: "Bring the holy crust of Bread." Robert Herrick. WSC

Hah! Hah! la belle jaune giroflee.   The Gilliflower of Gold.   William Morris. AnFE; WHA

Hai hai!/Young moon   Prayer to the Young Moon.   *Anonymous.*   PeSA

...Hail and beware them, when they/come.   A Newly Discovered "Homeric' Hymn.   Charles Olson.   NeAP; NoAm; PoM

Hail and farewell. Hello, goodbye. O keeper/Of the profane grail, the dreaming skull.   The Ghost's Leavetaking.   Sylvia Plath.   NePoEA-2

Hail, as aforesaid, coming Spring!   The Lawyer's Invocation to Spring. Henry Howard Brownell.   PoLf

..."Hail, daughter! robed in the loveliest robe of the/year."   Song: Under the Bronze Leaves.   Saint-John Perse.   AtBAP; PoPl

Hail Earth, the Rose of Stars.   Wild Eden.   George Edward Woodberry. AA

Hail him, and both joys prolong.   Songs: "Now in golden glory goes." Lionel Pigot Johnson.   VLP

"Hail, Hyacinths and Roses!"   A Pretty Ambition.   Mary E. Wilkins Freeman.   OBCA

Hail, Jew Antonio, methinks you sit/With mien ironic in the prompter's pit. Da Silva Gives the Cue.   Walter Hart Blumenthal.   TrJP

Hail, lady, be gracious to usward; that alway her honor/abide.   Alcestis. Euripides.   AWP

Hail, noble bridegroom, hail!   If They Honoured Me, Giving Me Their Gifts. Michael (Katherine Bradley and Edith Cooper) Field.   OBMV

Hail, O Sun of Righteousness!   Chanticleer.   William Austin.   EBCP; OxBoCh

Hail oracle, shine/in that dark night!   Dylan, Who Is Dead.   Samuel ("Paul Vesey") Allen.   PoBA

Hail this eet cross at last.   The Crossed Swords.   Nathaniel Langdon Frothingham.   AA

Hail to the black!   The Song of the Smoke.   William Edward Burghardt Du Bois.   OBVV; PoBA; UnPo

Hail to the coming time!   The Fine Old English Gentleman New Version. Charles Dickens.   CoMu; FaBoBa; NOBV; OBSV

Hail! to the courage of the Boys in Blue,/Who fought so grandly, to their Country true.   The Battle of Murfreesboro.   Kinahan Cornwallis.   PAH

"Hail to the victor who passes by!"   The Victor.   William Young.   HBMV

Hail to thee our Alma Mater/Hail! all hail! Cornell!   Far above Cayuga's Waters.   *Anonymous.*   FSW

Hail to you, goddess, Lady of stately Cypros...   Homeric Hymns: Hymn to Aphrodite (abridged).   *Anonymous.*   LiTW

Hail, with His triumphant band.   Easter Hymn.   Saint John of Damascus. CAW

Hailing the dream for which they died–/Alleluia!   Pax Nobiscum.   Earl Bowman Marlatt.   MoRP

The haill clanjamfrie!   The Bonnie Broukit Bairn.   Hugh" (Christopher Murray Grieve) MacDiarmid.   FaBoCh; GoTS; HAP; InPS; PAI

Hair become a ring first of rays around you/And then a crown.   To a Young Leader of the First World War.   Stefan George.   WaaP

The hair on our shoulders dangles and shines.   The Natives.   David Mura. BrSi

"Hair on the back of the hand/denotes extreme cruelty in a woman."   Look to the Back of the Hand.   Judith Minty.   PoA

Hairs less in sight, or any Hairs but these!   The Rape of the Lock. Alexander Pope.   AtBAP; CABL; CEP; CoBE; DiPo

... Half a hundred sons and daughters/Mourned and lamented his departing spirit.   The Devil and the Angel.   Rosemary Dobson.   BoAV; PoAu 1-2

Half a kiss, half a tear,/Saying good-night.   Sowing.   Edward ("Edward Eastaway") Thomas.   HBMV

Half a length of red lace, a slip of damask/Dropped on the ox–is payment in full!   An Old Charcoal Seller.   Po Chu-i.   SaC

Half an hour after his head was cut off.   Riddle: "King Charles the First walked and talked."   *Anonymous.*   OxNR

...The half-back/raised his fractured head, and cried: "I/call this fun!" Football.   Walt Mason.   SD

Half-born tendrils, grasping, gasp.   The Vines.   John Gray.   NOBV

Half clouded with a crimson fall/Of roses thrown on marble stairs.   The Gift of God.   Edwin Arlington Robinson.   AnAmPo; AP; CoBMV; MAPA; MoAB; MoAmPo; OxBA

Half-drunk, I get up and comb my hair.   Letting My Feelings Out.   Yu Hsuan-chi.   BoWoP

Half dumb Vandal,/half wild Dane.   Qua Song.   Colette Inez.   FAZ

Half expecting/To find the garden/Cratered like a moon.   Pumpkins.   John Cotton.   BoNaP

Half fish,/Half girl/To marry.   Catch.   Langston Hughes.   NoAm

Half-folded like an April bud/On winter-haunted trees.   Sleeping Beauty. Walter De La Mare.   DFT

Half-forgotten lust runs through me–/Senex becomes seventeen.   Betjeman at the Post Office (parody).   Stanley J. Sharpless.   FaBoPa

Half-glad, half-tearful, as the vision pales!   Cader Idris at Sunset.   Charles Tennyson Turner.   FaBoPP

Half hating you,/half eaten by the moon.   Dear Reader.   James Tate.   EAS

Half-heard and half-created.   The Voice of the Derwent.   William Wordsworth.   FaBoPP

Half-high, or tapering off at summer's end.   Sonnets.   Frederick Goddard Tuckerman.   MAmP

Half his delighted offspring mount his knees.   The Parish Register.   George Crabbe.   OBRV

The half-hushed sobbing of the hearts that weep.   The Harvest of the Sea. John McCrae.   EtS

Half is the hearing.   Seeds.   Augusta Webster.   OBVV

Half lion, half child, is at peace.   Against Unworthy Praise.   William Butler Yeats.   AnFE

Half loth, for sorrow, to awaken/The lesser music of the grass.   Clearing for the Plough.   Ernest G. Moll.   NOAV

A half-loved creature, motionless and bloated.   The Image.   Roy Fuller. ChMP; GTBS-P; OxBTC

...Half maid/Half tree?   Daphne.   Thomas S. Jones, Jr.   OHIP

Half metal she stayed.   Tulip.   Humbert Wolfe.   MoBrPo

The half-moon frowns on the city,/on the faces of tenement children, thin as relief checks.   Canal Street, Chicago.   Clyde Fixmer.   TAT

The half o' winter's gone at Yule.   If Candlemas Day Be Dry and Fair. *Anonymous.*   PoSC

Half of a clasp.   Half.   Hawley Truax.   NYBP

Half of primroses.   Minnie and Mattie.   Christina Georgina Rossetti. GoJo; InvP; SUS; TiPo

Half soul and half body.   Written Forty Miles South of a Spreading City. Robert Bly.   NNaP

Half-starved and lonely/crawling into a bleeding spring   Songs for the Cisco Kid or Singing for the Face.   K. Curtis Lyle.   PoBA

The half-starved children/In the desert slums.   Sakhara.   R.A.D. Ford. NOBC

Half-stirred memories and regrets/Drowning in that iron din.   Murphy in Manchester.   John Montague.   NMP

Half strange seems Earth, and sweeter than/her flowers.   Meditation under Stars.   George Meredith.   OAEP

Half the answer hangs upon a thread.   Riddle: "There is one that has a head without an eye."   Christina Georgina Rossetti.   OxBChV

Half the bed and all the clothes.   Good Night, Sweet Repose.   *Anonymous.* OxNR

..Half-tipsy with the wonder/of being alive, and wholly enveloped in love. Great Things Have Happened.   Alden Nowlan.   GOYP

Half-way with rosy fingers meet,/To kiss and play together.   A Bunch of Roses.   John Banister Tabb.   HBVY

Half white/half immigrant/taking up the city and losing at cards.   Family Photograph.   Gerald Vizenor.   VoR

Halfway up, already full dark.   The Second Night.   M. L. Hester, Jr. AMV-80

Halleloo, halleloo, halleloo, hallelujah!   Brother Noah.   *Anonymous.*   AmSS

The hallelujah chorus forever shifting its star soloists.   The People, Yes. Carl Sandburg.   BBV; NAMP

Hallelujah, give us a handout/to revive us again.   Hallelujah, I'm a Bum. *Anonymous.*   AS; FSW; TrAS

Hallelujah!/Glory to the bleeding Lamb!   It Is Finished.   Jonathan Evans. BePJ

Hallelujah!/Hallelujee!   Epitaph at Leeds.   *Anonymous.*   FaBoCo

Hallelujah, I'm a travelin'/Down Freedom's main line.   Hallelujah, I'm A-Travelin'.   Harry Raymond.   FSW

Hallelujah! Jesus lives.   Christ Is Risen!   Christoph Christian Sturm.   BePJ

Hallelujah, Lord I've been down into the sea.   Hallelujah!   *Anonymous.* BoAN 1-2

Hallelujah! Thine the glory,/Revive us again!   Revive Us Again.   John J. and William Porter Mackay Husband.   FSW

"Hallo!" said the barn-yard cock,/"Cock-a-doodle-doo."   The Clocking Hen. *Anonymous.*   HBVY

Hallowed be Thy name–Halleluiah!   The Human Cry.   Alfred, Lord Tennyson.   ILwL

Hallowed by neglect and an air so tame/that people celebrate it by forgetting its name.   At the Un-National Monument along the Canadian Border. William Stafford.   HAP; HeIP

Halloween, Halloween,/scritch,/scratch,/squeak.   Halloween Concert. Aileen Fisher.   SiSoSe

HALT glitters, but I choose/Your way.   May Trees in a Storm.   Geoffrey Grigson.   GBL

Halt, hang hump-backed, and look into his crater.   The Raider.   W.R. Rodgers.   AnIL; MoBrPo

An hame again!/Emly-amly,/Emly-amly,/Fill, fill, fill!   The Miller's Wife's Lullaby.   *Anonymous.*   GBP

Hame, hame, hame, to my ain countrie!   Loyalty.   Allan Cunningham. GN

Hamlet vacillated–so does this stuff.   Virtual Particles.   Frank Wilczek. NLV

Hammer at it brightly.   Smith's Song.   George Sigerson.   OnYI

Hammer ring.   Hammer Song.   *Anonymous.*   ABF

...Hammered/By Roman nails and hung on a Jewish hill.   Invisible Trumpets Blowing.   Edwin John Pratt.   CaP

"Hamor, (donkey) he cried,/and proved the language living.   The Test. Robert Friend.   GP

The hand from which it fell/Was thy lost angel's, too.   Messages.   Alfred Noyes.   GoBC

The hand gropes on the breast, rewinds the clock.   Fracture of Light: Song in the Cold Season.   Samuel French Morse.   PoA

Hand in hand now you now I going on and off.   Greenwich Village Saturday Night.   Irving Feldman.   AmPC

Hand in hand we begin the walk across Wonder Lake/walking on water. Lake Walk at New Year's.   Leigh Perez-Diotima.   AMV-81

Hand-in-hand with beauty.   Rendezvous.   Mary Scott Fitzgerald.   PoToHe

The hand in the breast pocket.   Marriage.   Marianne Moore.   NMM; NOBA

A hand in winter, resisting the glove.   The Misogynist.   Jean Morgan.   FF

...A hand moves across/a pencil drawing of the world/and smudges everything. The Weather.   Lorna Crozier.   CaPN

The hand of creation/weeps.   The Light of the World.   B. (Eliezer Blum) Alquit.   VWA

The hand of friendship down Life's sunless hill?   She, to Him.   Thomas Hardy.   OxBTC

The hand that held it scarce was seen.   The Hand That Held It.   W. G. Elmslie.   TRV

The Hand that made us is Divine.   The Spacious Firmament on High. Joseph Addison.   EaLo; ELP; FaBoBe; FaPoR; GN; HBV 1-2; HBVY; MCCG; NIP; PoEL 1-5; TreFT

The hand that marks the face of time is still,/And all the ages sleep. Pyramus and Thisbe.   Laurence Dakin.   CaP

Hand upraised and face into the wind/That no longer brings tears to my eyes. The Statute of Liberty.   Edward Field.   TAT

Hand us a Sonnet cool and dry as/Your very best, and we shall freeze.   To the Poet T. J. Mathias.   Walter Savage Landor.   PV

The hand which after the appointed days/And hours shall give a Future to their Past?   Old and New Art.   Dante Gabriel Rossetti.   MaVP

A hand will find us in the dark/And guide us on our way.   The Blind Man. Margaret E. Sangster.   PoToHe

...A handful of men./No two from one country.   Report from a Planet. Richmond Lattimore.   FYAP

A handful of paper ashes,/My mother would drift away.   The Great Blue Heron.   Carolyn Kizer.   CoAP; NePoEA-2

Handfuls again.   Handfuls.   Carl Sandburg.   AP

...Handling/his word we feel his flesh, his bones, and hear/his voice saying our early-morning name   ....For They Shall See God.   Luci Shaw.   TrCP

Handmaid and Hangman to your need,/Is audience.   Gaiety: Queer's Song. Richard Howard.   ErPo

The hands and voice of Allah   Theme One: The Variations.   August Wilson. PoBA

Hands, bind my eyes, infallibly restore my/Share in perdition.   A Lost Soul. Jay Macpherson.   NOBC

The hands gripped hard on the desert.   At the Bomb Testing Site.   William Stafford.   CAPP; CoAP; LiTM; NoP; OBWP

Hands have no tears to flow.   The Hand That Signed the Paper.   Dylan Thomas.   HaMV; InPo; MoAB; MoBrPo; MoPo; MoRP; NoAm; NOBE; NoP; OBWP; SeCePo; TrGrPo; WaP; WeW

Hands have opened doors/to let the dead wind in.   Written.   Mary Ruelfe. AMV-81

The hands of a girl, and most, your hands.   Your Hands.   Ernest Christopher Dowson.   UnTE

Hands of earth, of this clay/I'm also made from.   Turtle Mountain Reservation.   Louise Erdrich.   TWSS

The hands of the shepherd were like glass/Polished with glimmering fever. The Island.   Giuseppe Ungaretti.   LiTW

...Hands/on skin; how good it feels.   Adolescence.   Gregory Orr.   Psk

Hands over face/invisible men   They Are Killing All the Young Men. David Henderson.   PoBA

Hands plucking and twisting the stems,/Came the sauntering sorrowful stranger.   Pastoral.   Clifford Dyment.   MoVE

Hands to waist clinging on/for dear life.   Chinatown Games.   Wing Tek Lum.   BrSi

...Hands which lay curled and still/near the soft gray felt hat on the table.   In January, 1962.   Ted Kooser.   Psk

Hands, wings, are found....   Discovered in Mid-Ocean.   Stephen Spender. MoBrPo

The hands you/love to touch.   A Work of Artifice.   Marge Piercy.   IHMS; Psk

Handsome Girdhar, Mira's lord,/saves those who come to be saved.   Wake, child.   Mira Bai [(or Mirabai[).   BoWoP

Handsome Molly! Little Molly darling!)   Handsome Molly.   Anonymous. FSW

Hang down your head and cry.   Long Lonesome Road.   Anonymous. OuSiCo

Hang him, and so let him go.   Love Is a Babel.   Anonymous.   CBEP

Hang it up till the rings fall.   Dead Hand.   William Stanley Merwin. CAPP

Hang new heavens with new birds, all is renewed.   Shiva.   Robinson Jeffers. NoAm; NOBA

...The/hang of its waxen cloud exalts this house.   Jubilate Herbis.   Norma Farber.   PCh

Hang on/for dear life.   Dinosaur.   Bonnie Hearn.   AMV-80

Hang the miller by his neck.   To the Puss Moth.   Anonymous.   OxNR

Hang them, oh Christ, all three!   Prayer for the Speedy End of Three Great Misfortunes.   Frank O'Connor.   DTC; OBMV

Hang them, sweet Christ, all three.   Inheritance.   Frank O'Connor.   DBV; TW

Hang thou there upon the tomb,/Praising her when I am dumb.   Much Ado about Nothing.   William Shakespeare.   CTC; OBSC; ViBoPo

Hang up the broken spear, and blow/A dirge upon the horn.   The Last Hunt. William Roscoe Thayer.   AA; FaBoBe; HBV 1-2

Hang up thy wife, and she'll make four.   To the Landlord.   Jonathan Swift. DBV

Hang your head over, hear the wind blow.   Down in the Valley. Anonymous.   BLSo

A-hanging for the mother's sake/On Chester's fatal tree.   Execution of Alice Holt.   Anonymous.   OxBoLi

Hanging from the/old/sky   Moth.   Lance Henson.   VoR

Hanging isn't good enough for me.   Song: "When the echo of the last footstep dies."   E. W. Mandel.   OBCV

Hanging lights/About its head.   City: San Francisco.   Langston Hughes. AmFN; GoSl

Hanging like an oasis in his air/of lost connections.   Memories of West Street and Lepke.   Robert Lowell.   AmPP; CAPP; CMoP; ConAP; InPS; NaP; NOBA; PAI

...Hanging on until the end.   Mismatch.   Carl Lindner.   AMV-80

Hanging over the edge/like a root.   Brooklyn Summer.   Lou Lipsitz.   LTB

The hangman mutters: "Plenty/even for Housman's verse."   When Lads Have Done (parody).   Humbert Wolfe.   BXAP; Par; SpRo

Hangs deep in the dark body/A divining heart.   Ark Anatomical.   Jay Macpherson.   NOBC

Hangs like a foot-note from my shoulders.   On Solomon Lazarus Lee, Exhibitioner of Balliol.   Henry Charles Beeching.   FaBoEE

Hannah's at the window, binding shoes.   Hannah Binding Shoes.   Lucy Larcom.   GN; HBV 1-2

Haply I may remember,/And haply may forget.   Song: "When I am dead, my dearest."   Christina Georgina Rossetti.   BiP; BoLoP; DL; EBEV; FF; FPL; GBL; GoTF; GTBS; HBV 1-2; InPS; LiTL; NOBE; NoP; OAEL 1-2; OAEP; OBEV; OBVV; PoLf; PoRA; SCV; SoSe; TreFS; ViBoPo; VLP; WHA

Haply to mind them that your love endures.   Invocation.   Arthur J. Little. ISi

Haply you live a day longer in verse.   Young Reynard.   George Meredith. HoPM

Happens to like is one/Of the ways things happen to fall.   Table Talk. Wallace Stevens.   NoP

A happier, brighter, purer Heaven than theirs.   Where Lies the Truth? Has Man, in Wisdom's Creed.   William Wordsworth.   TrCP

...Happier lives,/settled in ruts, and great for wanting less.   The Chelsea. Derek Walcott.   NYP

A happier man today I'd be/Had a visiting adult done it to me.   To a Small Boy Standing on My Shoes While I Am Wearing Them.   Ogden Nash. ALV; DBV; FiBHP

...Happiest if ye seek/No happier state, and know to know no more.   Paradise Lost.   John Milton.   EBEV

...Happiness/dreamed for, brain spinner,/garbage maker.   Don't Hope to Gain by What Has Preceded.   Joanne Kyger.   PoM

Happiness! Happiness! Happiness!   Alleluya.   Ruben Dario.   TTY

Happiness/the least and best of human attainments   Poem Read at Joan Mitchell's.   Frank O'Hara.   ANYP

Happiness, (which whoever hears me let him or her set out in search of this day.)   Song of Myself.   Walt Whitman.   AtBAP

Happy, and all your poems still to be found.   You Hated Spain.   Ted Hughes.   OBTV

Happy as one walks by a woman's side.   Sensation.   Arthur Rimbaud. AWP

Happy Cadaver's hunger as you take/The kissproof world.   When, Like a Running Grave.   Dylan Thomas.   OAEL 1-2

Happy Christmas to all, and to all a good/night.   A Visit from St. Nicholas. Clement Clarke Moore.   AA; BeLS; BLPA; ChBR; FaBoBe; FaBV; FaFP; FaPo; FPL; GoTF; HBV 1-2; HBVY; NTCP; OBAL; OBCA; OBCP; OnMSP; OxBChV; PaPo; PCh; PoPl; SiSoSe; TiPo; TreF; YaD

The happy earth looks at the sky/And sings.   Easter.   Joyce Kilmer.   SoPo; TiPo

Happy field or mossy cavern,/Choicer than the Mermaid Tavern?   Lines on the Mermaid Tavern.   John Keats.   AWP; DiPo; EnRP; HBV 1-2; InMe; InPo; LoBV; NLV; OAEP; OBRV; PoRA; PP; SeCeV; TreFS; ViBoPo

Happy for man could he say so.   On a Dog of Lord Eglinton's.   Robert Burns.   OBSP

Happy for the snow clean hands of you, my friends.   Plea to Those Who Matter.   James Welch.   AmPA

Happy he can compass it!   True Beauty.   Francis Beaumont.   EiL; HBV 1-2

Happy heart so light!   Oh! To Have A Birthday.   Lois Lenski.   BiCB

The happy highways where I went/And cannot come again.   A Shropshire Lad.   Alfred Edward Housman.   EvOK; NOBV; OAEP

Happy if it be thy call/In the holy cause to fall.   The Young American.   Alexander H. Everett.   PaPo

Happy is he that can obtain her love.   Description and Praise of His Love Geraldine.   Henry Howard, Earl of Surrey.   AAS; OAEP

Happy is the girl/That marries the miner boy.   The Miner Boy, I. *Anonymous.*   AmFP

Happy man, that soon doth knock/Babble babes against the rock!   Loss in Delay.   Robert Southwell.   OBSC

Happy mayst thou be if thou canst be only/Happy without love.   Sapphic Stanzas.   Alexander Radishchev.   LiTW

Happy our hill then/feed her children.   Men of the Rocks.   Joseph Gordon ("Adam Drinan") MacLeod.   OxBS

The happy streets in Babylon, when once the dream was/truth.   Babylon.   Viola Taylor.   HBV 1-2

Happy the heart that sighed for such a one!   To Delia.   Samuel Daniel.   OBEV; PoPle

Happy the heart that thinks of no removes!   Fine Knacks for Ladies.   John Dowland.   CBEP; CH; EBEV; EiL; ForPo; HAP; LiTB; LoBV; NoP; QFR; ViBoPo

Happy the man.   Beatus Vir.   Richard Le Gallienne.   HBMV; OHIP

Happy the ripe stalks and the harvested grain.   Happy Are Those Who Have Died.   Charles Peguy.   WaaP

Happy, they gave themselves to love.   Two Young Men, 23 to 24 Years Old.   Constantine P. Cavafy.   PeHV

Happy though my choice may be/Empty tree for empty tree.   Flight.   George Johnson.   WHW

Happy to the point of hopelessness.   This Beach Can Be Dangerous.   Allen Curnow.   OCNZ

Happy was Cologne/To be worthy of such a bishop!   The Good Bishop. *Anonymous.*   CAW; WGRP

Happy with friends to watch the turning of the stars.   Herman Moon's Hourbook.   Christopher Middleton.   NePoEA-2

Happy yourself, you feel another's woe.   Stanzas to Edward Williams.   Percy Bysshe Shelley.   OBNC

The harbingers of summer heats/Which from afar he bears.   The Inward Morning.   Henry David Thoreau.   AP; MAmP

...Harbor/Hard in a cold pale storm that falls all over.   Faeryland.   Robert Pinsky.   MAYP

A harbor of bone.   Winter Morning.   William Jay Smith.   BoNaP; NCSH

The harbor whither those were bound/Lieth, nor yet is found.   Unfulfilment.   Frances Louisa Bushnell.   AA

The harbour darkens above me.   Three Poems for Your Eyes.   Rachel McAlpine.   OCNZ

...The hard ancestral stone/where your head will rest at last.   Guinea.   Jacques Roumain.   TTY

Hard and it's hard ain't it hard, great God,/to love one that never will be true.   Hard, Ain't It Hard. *Anonymous.*   FSW

The hard bodies–are they/their guts or their brains?   Southbound on the Freeway.   May Swenson.   AmC; AmFN; NTCP; NYBP

Hard, but O the glory of the winning were she won!   Love in the Valley.   George Meredith.   TreFT

The hard core of the purpose and will of man.   Hydro Works.   J. R. Hervey.   AnNZ

Hard diamond, infinite sun.   Tears.   Edith Sitwell.   CMoP; MoPo

...Hard is the lot/of one that longs for love in vain.   Wife's Lament. *Anonymous.*   PBWP

Hard it must be, beyond this day,/For even the grass to rest.   A True Picture Restored.   Vernon Watkins.   NoAm

Hard love, it's hard love.   Copacetic Mingus.   Yusef Komunyakaa.   MAYP

Hard old oaks drip honey.   Eclogue.   Virgil (Publius Vergilius Maro).   PoPl

Hard on the land wears the strong sea/and empty grows every bed.   Dream Songs.   John Berryman.   CAPP; HaCAP; NoP

Hard times will drive you, from door to door   Hard Time Killin' Floor Blues.   Skip James.   BluL

Hard to be pleased at all, and never long.   The True-Born Englishman.   Daniel Defoe.   OBSV

Hard wood is worn by the stone,/So is stone by the softness of feet.   Newness.   Tom Paulin.   FaBoIP

Harden and echo at a statue's voice.   Capital Square.   Patrick Anderson.   OBCV

Hardening tender green/to insensate lumber.   Hampstead: The Horse Chestnut Trees.   Thom Gunn.   NoP

Hardening through the mind and night of the first freeze.   Hardweed Path Going.   Archie Randolph Ammons.   HaCAP; UnPo; VGW

Harder day comes (Purity. Purity!)/With sweetly reeking coins.   Herman Moon's Hourbook.   Christopher Middleton.   NePoEA-2

A harder time is coming.   The Respite.   Ingeborg Bachmann.   WPOW

...Harder yet/are the chances, for a man/to be reborn a man/in this Karma earth   Mexico City Blues.   Jack Kerouac.   PoM

The hardest knife ill-used doth lose his edge.   Sonnets, XCV: "How sweet and lovely dost thou make the shame."   William Shakespeare.   CBEP 047; MasP; TrGrPo

The hardest stone on which to found/Altar and shelter for Eternity.   Ex Nihilo.   David Gascoyne.   GTBS-P

Hardly in the underwood/Russet pinions softly whir.   Summer.   John Davidson.   BoNaP

Hardlye ye may kisse mee, where no such gnomon apeereth.   Of Tyndarus.   Richard Stanihurst.   BIrV

Hardy har./Friendlies!   Poison Meat.   Tom Veitch.   ANYP

The hardy whaleman has no envied fare.   A Perilous Life. *Anonymous.*   EtS

Hark, happy lovers, hark!   A Kiss.   William, of Hawthornden Drummond.   EiL

Hark, hear in the distance/The beat of my heart!   Absent Yet Present.   Edward Robert Bulwer, Earl of Lytton.   OBVV

Hark! her love too discloses.   Madrigal: "Sweet nymph, come to thy lover." *Anonymous.*   PBBP

Hark hither; and thy selfe be HE.   Temperance or the Cheap Physitian upon the Translation of Lessius.   Richard Crashaw.   SeCV 1-2

Hark! now I hear them–Ding-dong, bell.   The Tempest.   William Shakespeare.   BiP; EBEV; ELP; EnLi 1-2; ForPo; GTBS; HAP; HBV 1-2; HeIP; InPS; NoP; OAEP; OBEV; OBSC; OBSP; PAI; PoPle; PoRA; PPoe; SeCePo; SeCeV; TEP; ViBoPo; WHA

Hark, now! that Owl, a-snoring in his tree,/Till it grow dark enough for him to see.   The Owl.   Walter De la Mare.   OBSP

Hark, the bell tolls! up, sexton and delve!   A Rhyme of the Sun-Dial.   William Bell Scott.   NOBV

Hark!–the black squadrons wheeling down/to Death!   Fredericksburg.   Thomas Bailey Aldrich.   PAH

Hark! the redemption hour's/resounding stroke,/For him who bore with patient heart/the yoke!   Spring Song.   Nahum.   TrJP

...Hark, thy evening gun/Startles the desert over Africa!   At Gibraltar.   George Edward Woodberry.   GN; HBV 1-2

(Hark to the thrush's trilling).   The King's Ballad.   Joyce Kilmer.   HBV 1-2

Hark to the tolling bell!   In Respectful Memory of Mr. Yarker.   John Close.   FaBoCo

Hark, what a tone of love passed through the night.   God's Harp.   Gustav Falke.   AWP

The harmless thistle that his hand had pluck'd/From the wild common, melancholy crop.   James Rigg (parody).   James Hogg.   BXAP; Par

Harnessed angels, hand on sword.   Epithalamium.   Alfred Edward Housman.   HW

Harnessed scorpions/before her.   We have seen how the most amiable.   Hilda ("H. D.") Doolittle.   BoWoP

Harps without pause, building with song the world.   Vita Nuova.   William Watson.   OBVV

The harrow for his team/is a fistful of pens.   The Scholar's Life. *Anonymous.*   NOBI

The harsh and bitter seeding/Of the dragon-rooted flower.   Three Barrows Down.   Jocelyn Brooke.   ChMP

Harsh as the loose sheet of iron that bangs in the wind.   The Birdsville Track.   Douglas Stewart.   CBAP

A harsh, dry rattle assembling within my craw.   On Scafell Pike.   Ted Walker.   NYBP

Harsh Gods and hostile Fates/Are dreams! this only is–   Empedocles on Etna.   Matthew Arnold.   TW

The harsh russet of dried blood.   Buried at Springs.   James Schuyler.   ANYP; CoAP; PoM

A harvest–come and reap.   I Bore with Thee, Long, Weary Days.   Christina Georgina Rossetti.   BePJ

Harvest lost, and all our store-houses empty.   In This River.   Valentin Iremonger.   NeIP

A harvest of barren regrets.   One Thing.   Owen Meredith.   WBLP

Harvester, harbinger, harrow my heaven.   A Blason.   A. D. Hope.   NOAV

Has a grain of common sense in it, except my own.   Crochet Castle.   Thomas Love Peacock.   ALV

Has anything worth writing down to say.   Ghetto Summer School.   Douglas Worth.   FF

Has asked me to say that at this moment he is especially grateful/to you/For wearing a blue gown. A Blue Valentine. Joyce Kilmer. ISi

...Has become, since their earliest days, a familiar/practice for trees. Trees Lose Parts of Themselves inside a Circle of Fog. Francis Ponge. NU

Has brought them life at last./Because you prayed. Because You Prayed. C. B. B. STF

Has clothed my nakedness in ceremony. Ceremony. Vassar Miller. NePoEA

Has cocked a leg against your Family Tree. On a Female Snob, Surprised. Patric Dickinson. DBV

Has come, has come! The Dawn's Awake! Otto Leland Bohanan. BANP

Has Death its wisest victims called/When idiots are born? Abstrosophy. Gelett Burgess. CenHV; NA

...Has deceived/The unwary into an immoderate love of death. The Night-Walker. Horace Gregory. MOON

Has drained the cup of beauty drop by drop. Who Pilots Ships. Daniel Whitehead Hicky. BrR

Has ever reached half high enough/To write a mother's name. A Mother's Name. Anonymous. PGD

Has fallen onto the shoulders of my parents/Whom it is eating to the bone. Childlessness. James Merrill. ConAP

Has forgotten those men and that beautiful bride. A Lady Comes to an Inn. Elizabeth Jane Coatsworth. MoAmPo; SO; StPo

Has gone to the city Ispahan. When the Sultan Goes to Ispahan. Thomas Bailey Aldrich. AA; BeLS; FaBoBe; HBV 1-2

Has had no luck at all. Now Dreary Dawns the Eastern Light. William Butler Yeats. CMoP

Has he no friend, no loving mother near? The Fruit Plucker. Samuel Taylor Coleridge. CH; SeCeV

Has light as Air each Limb, each Thought as clear as Day. The Praise of Industry. James (1700-48) Thomson. OBEC

Has made me receptive to greens. I Take 'Em and Like 'Em. Margaret Fishback. PoPl

Has made this poet my dumb slave. On Hearing Mrs. Woodhouse Play the Harpsichord. William Henry Davies. BrPo

Has my sobbing ever/Waked you from your sleep? In the Silent Night. Isaac L. Peretz. TrJP

Has nailed us suffering Jews/Onto the cross once more. A Jewish Child Prays to Jesus. I. Blumenthal-Weiss. VWA

Has never drowned the silent sound/Within my happy heart. Buffalo Creek. John Le Gay Brereton. PoAu 1-2

Has no actual characteristics. Bureaucratic Limerick. William Harmon. OBAL

Has no one heard the sound of his horn? When the Days Grow Long. Hayim Nahman Bialik. TrJP; VWA

Has nobody got a fire to light? The Hounds. Patric Dickinson. ChMP

Has passed from the dream, passed from the trees' long/shadows. Farmyard. Ruth Dallas. AnNZ

Has proved that the arse of the hedgehog/Can hardly be buggered at all. Exhaustive Experimentation. Anonymous. DBV

Has pulled up at a roadblock/a shade far from Garrison? Descendancy. Tom Paulin. FaBoIP

Has reared his monument and crowned him saint. Lincoln. John Townsend Trowbridge. PGD

Has saved the country more than one billion. The Death of King Edward VII. Anonymous. OxBoLi

Has seen something strange... Haiku: "That duck, bobbing up". Joso. WSC

Has smiled and said "Good Night", and gone to rest. On a Dead Hostess. Hilaire Belloc. MoVE

Has something special to enjoy. Gifts. Hazel Harper Harris. BiCB

Has spring, too, felt the doom of years? Primo Vere. Giosue Carducci. AWP

Has sung to such as me this undersong. Undersong. Mark Van Doren. PoCh

Has telegraphed thrice already for money. The Last of the Princes. A. K. Ramanujan. OxBC

Has to carry evenings up the hill/to make it dark. Seventh Son. Ed Roberson. PoBA

Has, to her boundless beauty, join'd/A boundless will to ease us. Epigram: "Cloe's the wonder of her sex." Charles, Earl of Dorset Sackville. FaBoEE

Has trouble hearing. Three Poems for Women. Susan Griffin. NPGG

Hasn't anybody seen my mouse? Missing. A.(lan) A.(lexander) Milne. MoShBr

Hasn't found the baby yet. Our Polite Parents. Carolyn Wells. BBGG

Hast then sweet Love our wished flight. Come away, Come Sweet Love. Anonymous. OAEP; PoEL 1-5

Hast thou an easy stool? The Inner Significance of the Statues Seated Outside the Boston... Walter Conrad Arensberg. AnAmPo

Hast thou returned to pay the debt of kisses/Thou owest to me? Clarimonde. Theophile Gautier. AWP

Hast thou still some secret nest/On the tree or billow? The World's Wanderers. Percy Bysshe Shelley. EnLit; ViBoPo

Haste then, sweet love, our wished flight! Come away, Sweet Love. John Dowland. LoBV

The hat with the rattlesnake band/is gathering dust. The Rattlesnake Band. Robert J. Conley. STE

Hate is its ignorant paradigm. The Paradigm. Allen Tate. NOBA

Hate laugh shimmy. One X. Edward Estlin Cummings. FaBoMo

Hated, as their age increases,/By their nephews and their nieces. Good and Bad Children. Robert Louis Stevenson. BBGG; FaBoCh; FaFP; GoTF; HBV 1-2; HBVY; LoGBV; NBM; NLV; OxBChV; TreF

The hated dog killed the Moon. In Memory of the Moon. (A Killing.). Charlotte DeClue. STE; TWSS

Hates, instead, him self/him black self. Black Bourgeoisie. LeRoi (Imamu Amiri Baraka) Jones. BPo

Hatful, capful, pocketful, lapful,/Holla, boys, holla, hip hip hurrah! Apple Wassail. Anonymous. OBET

Hath cared to look upon thy face. Eros. Robert Bridges. CMoP

Hath found the art/To turn his double pains to double praise. Man's Medley. George Herbert. ViBoPo

Hath guest fire-fledged as thine, whose lord is Love? The House of Life. Dante Gabriel Rossetti. SyP

Hath his grave not been hollowed, and woven/his pall,/Since they passed o'er the river? Beyond the Potomac. Paul Hamilton Hayne. PAH

Hath in't more value, though less seen. The Apostasy. Thomas Traherne. CoBE

Hath left it ever rosy round the rim! To an Old Venetian Wine-Glass. Lloyd Mifflin. AA

Hath less the characters of dark and cold/Than warmth and light asleep. The Unknown Eros. Coventry Patmore. LO

Hath loved your tangled locks enwound. Mystical Poets. Amado Nervo. CAW

Hath me defended hitherto, and will do still I trust. "Girt in my guiltless gown..." Henry Howard, Earl of Surrey. FCP

Hath melted like snow in the glance of the Lord! The Destruction of Sennacherib. George Gordon, Lord Byron. BeLS; BLPA; BLPL; BoLiVe; DiPo; ERoP 1-2; EvOK; FaBoBe; FaBoCh; FaFP; FaPo; FaPoR; FF; GN; HAP; HBV 1-2; InPK; InPS; LoGBV; MBW 1-2; MCCG; NIP; NoP; OAEP; OBWP; OnMSP; PoLf; TrCP; TreF; WBLP; WeW; WGRP

Hath no warrant to aqquire/The dainties of his chaste desire. He That Loves. Sir Philip Sidney. ErPo

Hath not enough of sadness, and my heart/Is stifled for a cry. Awake. Mary Elizabeth Coleridge. OBNC

Hath planted his most true and holy word. Hail, Holy Land. Thomas Tillam. AH

Hath reaped a joy, which never shall have end. The Martyrdom of Father Campion. Henry Walpole. GoBC

Hath shut these doores of heaven that/durst/Thus set them ope. I Am the Door. Richard Crashaw. OAEP

Hath steel somewhat advantage over water. The Fountain. King of Seville, Mu'tamid. AWP

Hath taught still peace to grow. Limerick: "The daughter of debate." Queen of England Elizabeth I. LiBL

Hath this world aught so fair as Stella is? Astrophel and Stella, XXI. Sir Philip Sidney. AAS; CABA; SiPS; TEP

Hatred and guilt have left us without language/who might have held discourse. Effort at Speech. William Meredith. NYP; Prf; SM; WeW

Hatred of/my light/brown/outer. The Self-Hatred of Don L. Lee. Don L. Lee. BPo; TW

The hatreds of a hundred thousand years. The Festival. Frederic Prokosch. LiTA; WaP

The hats of small barbarians/who lie drunken in the leaves. October. Steve Hahn. PPJ

"Haue done and tell it me;'/"If that thou will goe to merry green-/wood,... Robin Hood and the Curtal Friar. Anonymous. ESPB

Haue done sowing wheate before halowmas eve. A Hundreth Good Poyntes of Husbandry. Thomas Tusser. FaBoUs

Haul away, my Johnsy-o. Haul away, My Rosy. Anonymous. AmFP; FSW; OuSiCo

Haul on the bowline,/So early in the morning. Haul on the Bowline. Anonymous. AmSS; FSW; ShS

Haul on the rope. Smite the metals. Make huge, long sound. To the Bell-Ringer. Robert Farren. OnYI

Haul taut your bowlines—well all—belay! Reefing Topsails. Walter Mitchell. EtS

Haul the wind! Put out again to sea! Seaway. Grace Wilson. AMV-81

Haunt him in his massive hour-/child, I call. The Brother-in-Law. Larry Rubin. GP; TW

A haunt of ancient Peace. The Palace of Art. Alfred, Lord Tennyson. UnPo

The haunt of seals and orcs, and sea-mews' clang. Paradise Lost. John Milton. FaBoPV

(Haunted by that gentle fire). A Mother Is a Sun. Peggy Bennett. PoSC

The haunted tow'rs of Cumnor Halle. Cumnor Hall. William Julius Mickle. BeLS; CEP; OBEC; OxBB; ViBoPo

The haunting fragrance that still lingers here/As in a rose-jar, so within my heart. As in a Rose-Jar. Thomas S. Jones, Jr. PoLf

The haunting stories of a thousand years/Waken to fragrance in the English Spring! Spring in England. Charles Buxton Going. HBMV

Haunts me night and day. The Look. Sara Teasdale. ALV; HBV 1-2; LiTL

Hava na Shira Shire Hallelujah. Hava Na Shira. *Anonymous.* FSW

Have a being less durable even than he. The Poplar Field. William Cowper. CH; ELP; FaBoPP; FaBoRV; FiP; ForPo; HAP; HBV 1-2; InPo; LAuP; NOBE; NOEC; OBEC; PoEL 1-5; RoGo; SeCeV; TrGrPo; WiR

Have a heart, Chung,/it's awful. Songs of Cheng. Confucius. CTC

Have a still shorter date, and die sooner than we. The Poplar Field. William Cowper. GTBS; GTBS-P

Have a turnip than his father. The Turnip Vender. *Anonymous.* OxNR

Have all built their nests in my beard!' Limerick: "There was an Old Man with a beard." Edward Lear. FaBoCo; FaBoNo; HBV 1-2; LiBL; NOBL; NoP; NTCP; OnUR; OxBChV; TEP; TiPo

Have all their might conserved/In treasure, finally. Lines with a Gift of Herbs. Janet Lewis. QFR

Have and play the with-alle/And go to the tenys. The Second Shepherd's Play: Haylle, Comely and Clene. *Anonymous.* BoW; NAs; OBEV

Have another cheese straw! Rhinoceros. William Hart-Smith. BoAnP

Have another man an' play sick on you. Dirty Mistreatin' Women. *Anonymous.* ABF

"Have at the Faith!' each cries: "good bye till our/Next merry meeting!' Lambeth Lyric. Lionel Pigot Johnson. NOBV

Have been hurled/triumphantly out of sight. First Day at School. Michael Ivens. OxBTC

Have broods to succeed us a hundred years hence.... The Epicure Sung by One in the Habit of a Town Gallant. Thomas Jordan. NOBE

Have but hopeless, hard/rebellion for bard. Throw away the Flowers. Elizabeth Daryush. PBWP

Have cenotaphed his fame. Poe's Cottage at Fordham. John Henry Boner. AA

Have certain periods set, and hidden fates. Sonnet. I. Sir John Suckling. AnAnS 2; CaPo

Have courage, my boy, to say no. Have Courage, My Boy, to Say No! L. M. Hilton. WTO

Have cried on love so bitterly, with so true a tongue? There's Wisdom in Women. Rupert Brooke. HBV 1-2

Have developed from a flea! Darwinism in the Kitchen. *Anonymous.* FiBHP; NLV

Have died upon the tree. Rinaldo. Henry Peterson AA

Have entered, and I am/Alone, and it is late. The Old Pastor. John Banister Tabb. AmP

Have eyes to wonder, but lack tongues to praise. When in the Chronicle. William Shakespeare. BoLiVe

Have faded from our ken, we from their knowledge fallen. Old Paintings on Italian Walls. Kathleen Raine. NYBP

Have fallen on another's sight/And been broken! Love-Songs, At Once Tender and Informative. Samuel Hoffenstein. OBAL

Have found a quiet needed for so long. Return. Sterling A. Brown. BALP; CDC

Have gathered them and will do never again. In Memoriam (Easter, 1915). Edward ("Edward Eastaway") Thomas. GTBS-P; NOBE; OBWP; OxBTC

Have good care of all the three. With a Rod No Man Alive. Walther von der Vogelweide. AWP

Have grandchildren half/behind half/with them. Voice in the Blood. Barney Bush. STE

Have hamburgers! Have hamburgers! Louisiana Perch. Ron Padgett. APU

Have heard a kitten in the wilderness. Chaplinesque. Hart Crane. AP; CMoP; CrMA; LiTM; NoAm; NOBA; OxBA; VGW

Have heard her massive sandal set on stone. Euclid Alone Has Looked on Beauty Bare. Edna St. Vincent Millay. ATP; CMoP; FaBV; FaFP; HBMV; ImOP; InPo; MoAB; MoAmPo; MoVE; NoP; TAP; WHA

Have I anything to declare/to the marshalled dead? The Road to Bologna. Roy MacNab. PeSA

Have I broken my shin, a bone which cannot be mended? Poet's Lament on the Death of His Wife. Raage Ugaas. WTO

Have I learned to understand you? You Say, "I Will Come." Lady Otomo of Sakanoe. LiTW; OLR

Have I not any charity to give? Modern Love, XX. George Meredith. VLP

Have I not proved his wisdom is no fable? Eyes. William Henry Davies. BrPo; FM

Have I not reason to lament/What man has made of man? Lines Written in Early Spring. William Wordsworth. ACV; CBEP; EnLi 1-2; ERoP 1-2; FPL; HBV 1-2; MBW 1-2; MCCG; OAEL 1-2; OAEP; OBRV; PG; PoLf

"Have I penciled my eyebrows/sharply enough?" The Toilette. Chu Ching-Yu. HW

Have I (think!) wanted to be the tree, or/one, two or three stanzas about a tree? 3 Stanzas about a Tree. Marvin Bell. Prf

Have I undone her by my vehemence? The Straw. Robert Graves. MoVE; OxBTC

Have left it younger than a boy. The Earth and Man. Stopford Augustus Brooke. HBV 1-2; OnYI

Have love enough will I have love/enough when it's not just a game? Step on His Head. James Laughlin. VGW

Have made the silence deeper by degrees. After Commencement. Howard Nemerov. GLGT

Have mercy, and give light, and stablish me! The Darkness. Lionel Pigot Johnson. BrPo

Have mercy on a humble bard, O Lord! The World Is a Mighty Ogre. Fenton Johnson. AmNP

Have mercy on my poor old prurient interest. The Poor Old Prurient Interest Blues. John Hartford. MAT

Have mercy on us, Future Girl! A Dresscessional. Carolyn Wells. WBLP

(Have mercy on us) we must use the/knife. The Knife. Milton Kaplan. TrJP

Have mercy on your miseries and your sins. Go Far, Come Near. Walter De La Mare. CoBMV

Have mercy, Tuka says. The Restless Heart. *Anonymous.* WGRP

Have mercy upon us, O Lord! Stigmata. Charles Warren Stoddard. TrPWD

Have mickly holp thereto. Anglo-Irishman's Complaint. *Anonymous.* AnIL

Have mind upon my supplication! The Complaint of Chaucer to His Empty Purse. Geoffrey Chaucer. CoBE; EnL; EnLi 1-2; GoBC; NoP; OAEL 1-2; OxBM; ViBoPo

Have moved through years, changed/And disappeared. Mimosa. Cleopatra Mathis. MAYP

Have my hand under/Her blue dress when she is there. The Dress. Christopher Middleton. NMP

Have never, will never/face death having known. Wynyard Sailor. Ray Mathew. CBAP

Have no forked tongues like mortals–/here on Iona. There Are Gods. C. L. Riley. PoSH

Have not the slightest need of sorcery. To a Lady. J. B. Morton. PoL

Have nothing much to say and more to learn. Relativities (parody). Louis Untermeyer. BXAP

Have nowhere we can hide/From those who refuse to change. Disguises. Elizabeth Jennings. NePoEA-2

Have paid my birth-dues; am quits with the people. Birth-Dues. Robinson Jeffers. MoAB; MoAmPo

Have pictured in our mind. Worry. *Anonymous.* PoToHe

Have pity–and remember/How soon thy roses die! O Youth with Blossoms Laden. Arthur Wallace Peach. HBMV

Have pity at least on the spuds. Prayer for Fine Weather. Shane Leslie. PoL

Have pity, master. This is a wicked land. Holstenwall. Sidney Keyes. FaBoTw

Have pity on me/lying here by myself/in the feather bed. Yourself and Myself. *Anonymous.* NOBI

Have place in the flashing throng/That spangle your banner bright. Song of Texas. William Henry Cuyler Hosmer. PAH

Have plucked no thorns from thy dear/brow, but planted thousands there! Why the Robin's Breast Was Red. James Ryder Randall. AA; CAW

Have power for aye in wonted gult to glide. The Lover to the Thames of London. George Turberville. EIL; NoP; OBSC

Have proved by every line you write. A Critic. Walter Savage Landor. ChTr; DBV; FaBoEE

Have pulled down with fangs of poison A Sense of Coolness. Quincy Troupe. PoBA

Have reached had our shyness and/each other's namelessness been breached. A Nameless Recognition. Arthur Gregor. GP

Have realized a little what they meant, and for the first time/been afraid. The Entertainment of War. Roy Fisher. FaBoMo

Have rowed away from one another! Two Poems. Saigyo Hoshi. LiTW

Have seared his own with flame. For John Keats, Apostle of Beauty. Countee Cullen. CDC

Have stood aside and watched yourself go by. Watch Yourself Go By. Strickland Gillilan. BLPA; PoToHe

Have the life-surging heavens no/business but this? As to Being Alone. James Oppenheim. TrJP

Have their reflected light/Danc'd by the streams. Dew Sat on Julia's Hair. Robert Herrick. ELP

Have them and hold them over-long,/Out of Thy wondrous treasuries. A Hymn of Thanksgiving. Wilbur D. Nesbit. OHIP

Have they learned to live/in a flowerless country? Seeing the Returning Geese. Lady Ise. BoWoP

Have thou care for my last ending.   Dies Irae.   Thomas of Celano.   LiTW

Have thought the thing Napoleon thought was to their/interest.   Napoleon Hoped That All the World Would Fall beneath His Sway.   *Anonymous.* FaBoCo

Have thoughts yet colder than the thing he is.   The Generous Years. Stephen Spender.   PoCh

Have to express our need of forgiveness.   Crisis.   W.H. Auden.   AtBAP

Have waked marooned upon the coast of morning.   Bout with Burning. Vassar Miller.   LiTM; MoAmPo; NePoEA

Have waved at last in union o'er the world.   The Columbiad: One Centred System.   Joel Barlow.   AP

Have we not learnt our histories?   October.   John Bayliss.   NeBP

Have worshipped, not the incarnate Christ,/But tinsel on the Christmas tree. African Christmas.   John Press.   OBCP

Have woven round you, in the burning Now,/A lure unknown to Helen's Phidian brow.   Her Pedigree.   Arthur Davison Ficke.   HBMV

Have y-gete Scotlande?/With rombylogh.   Snatches: "Maidenes of Engelande, sare may ye morne."   *Anonymous.*   OxBM

Have ye e'er heard of gallant like young Lochinvar?   Young Lochinvar.   Sir Walter Scott.   FiBHP; HBVY; InMe; OBNV

Have yet a long while to go before nightfall/Brings you to sure effulgence! To the Afternoon Moon, at Sea.   Cale Young Rice.   EtS

Have you armed your children?   How Will You Call Me, Brother?   Mari E. Evans.   BlSi

Have you been a good girl, Jane?   The Good Little Girl.   A.(lan) A.(lexander) Milne.   BBGG

Have you charmed them all again?   For Kuo Hsiang.   Yu Hsuan-chi. BoWoP

Have you cut off your hands yet?   The Friend.   Marge Piercy.   NMM

Have you ever tried to buy them without money?   The Terrible People. Ogden Nash.   NePA; TAP

Have you eyes to find the five/Which five hundred did survive?   The Test. Ralph Waldo Emerson.   AA; OBAL; PP

"Have you heard sheep? is right!"   How Low Is the Lowing Herd.   Walt Kelly.   FiBHP

Have you left us nothing but your blindness?   In the Gorge.   William Stanley Merwin.   AmPC

Have you looked in the glass/that mirrors you?   From the Ballad of Evil. N. P. Van Wyk Louw.   PeSA

Have you no thought O dreamer that it may be all maya, illusion?   Are You the New Person Drawn toward Me?   Walt Whitman.   NePA; NoAm; OBSP; PPP

"Have you nothing better for Nancy?"   Neglectful Edward.   Robert Graves. BrPo; MoBrPo

Have you nothing for me?   The Tax-Gatherer.   John Banister Tabb.   GN

Have you prayed, lately, for that?   A Negro Soldier's Viet Nam Diary. Herbert Martin.   PoBA

Have you seen yourself retreating?   What's the Use.   Ogden Nash.   PoPl

Have you slain the sweet birds/In your brother's face?   Abel.   Else Lasker-Schüler.   VWA

Have your name in his big Tally Book!   The Cowboy's Dream.   *Anonymous.* MaC

The haven reached to which I first was bound.   To Crown It.   Robert Herrick.   CaPo

Haven't got wet!   Haiku: "Spring rain! And as yet."   Buson (Taniguchi Buso).   LiTW

...Haven't I/Danced the bigger dance?/Haven't I?   The New Platform Dances.   Jack A. Mapanje.   WhB

...Haven't seen an Elm/in thirteen American Years.   Guess Who.   Fred Chappell.   NLV

Having another glass of booze like a necktie like a/velvet noose like a nurse/ like sleep.   I Scream You Scream.   Don McKay.   NOBC

Having been nursed beyond the sopping rain,/Back down the stair.   At Thomas Hardy's Birthplace, 1953.   James Wright.   ConAP

Having been whipped across the eyes/Like penitents, to make us see. December Storm.   John Hay.   NePoAm

Having cocoa and animals once more for tea!   Animal Crackers. Christopher Morley.   SoPo; SUS; TiPo

Having contemplated without template to/flower so.   This Is after All Vacation.   Louis Zukofsky.   CoPo

Having destroyed the House of Atreus which has ruined/us utterly.   The Trojan Women: Cassandra's Epithalamium.   Euripides.   HW

....–Having discovered/that the innkeeper was the inn.   Orgy.   Norman MacCaig.   OxBC

...Having eaten it/all these years.   Red Dust.   Philip Levine.   NNaP

Having found none worthier of his confidence!   The Old Peasant in the Billiard Saloon.   Huw Menai.   ACV

Having her arms about me. And I shall trust her then.   The Sea-Captain. Gerald Gould.   EtS

Having her picture taken–by–is it Rembrandt?   A Floridian Museum of Art. Reed Whittemore.   EyDe

Having located himself/through my place.   My Place.   David Ignatow. CAPP

...Having no thought/Of the river, and the irony underneath.   The Age of Sheen.   Dorothy Hughes.   NYBP

Having nowhere to go:/I am one of them.   Carrier Indians.   Ken Belford. NOBC

Having outfaced three English kings/And kept a people's faith.   Robert the Bruce.   Edwin Muir.   OxBS

Having overwalked/the Eye of God/without a consequence.   Peripatetic. Robert Lima.   AMV-81

Having seen every sight/But never anyone struck by lightning.   The Postilion Has Been Struck by Lightning.   Patricia Beer.   OxBC

Having so much to choose/out of the teeming air.   Lyric.   John Hewitt. NeIP

Having that once drunk sweetness to the dregs.   And What Sordello Would See There.   Robert Browning.   MyFE

Having to accuse/and accuse.   The Line-Up.   Joan Swift.   FiCP; SM

Having to do at times with love or in one time/the understanding of final pain, I go with that.   Time's Times Again.   Archie Randolph Ammons.   SUW

Having to hear the wenches wail/And the dying Negro moan.   Southern Cop. Sterling A. Brown.   SoSe

Hawaii appeared an island.   Born Was the Island.   *Anonymous.*   WTO

A hawk flew into heading home,/Killed instantly.   The Forgotten Rock. Richard Eberhart.   NePA

A hawk for every dove!   A Child Screening a Dove from a Hawk.   Letitia Elizabeth Landon.   VLP

The hawk replied, "I will not lose my diet/To let a thousand such enjoy their quiet."   A Sparrow-Hawk Proud.   *Anonymous.*   CH; EBEV; OBSP

Hawklike, as the rod you leave/Instantly, and down–you're over!   The Pole-Vaulter.   *Anonymous.*   LiSp

The hawthorn hedge took root, grew wild and high/to hide behind.   The Hawthorn Hedge.   Judith Wright.   PoAu 1-2

Hay, ma laddie, they won't come down!   Post-Rail Song (with music). *Anonymous.*   AS

The hayricks of Its fields/and artless find time.   Ask of the Sun.   Louis Zukofsky.   NoAm

(The haystack's the one at the back.)   Limerick: "There was once a fastidious yak."   Oliver Herford.   TDH

Hazel nuts thud in the forest/From the wearied boughs.   Autumn. *Anonymous.*   KiLC

Hazel nuts thud in the forest/From the wearied boughs.   Autumn.   Frank O'Connor.   PoSC

He ahold of my hand has completely satisfied me.   Of the Terrible Doubt of Appearances.   Walt Whitman.   NePA

He aims. At her. Then drops his aim. Idly.   The Guard at the Binh Thuy Bridge.   John Balaban.   FYAP

He allus felt "tollable well."   "Tollable Well."   Frank Lebby Stanton. FaFP

He alone is great/Who by a life heroic conquers fate.   The Inevitable.   Sarah Knowles Bolton.   AA; WGRP

He also died in vain.   The Jewish Conscript.   Florence Kiper Frank.   TrJP

He altered the expression of my face/And gave me back my beauty.   The Fired Pot.   Anna Wickham.   FaBoTw; FaBoWP; OxBTC

He always ends up green and sad/And sitting on a lily pad.   What Is the Opposite of a Prince?   Richard Wilbur.   WSC

He always had a shrewd head for business.   And Dust to Dust.   Charles David Webb.   NePoAm-2

He always picks her up/when he's through.   Harelip Mary.   Ronald Koertge.   GP

He always said my eyes were blue,/And often swore my lips were sweet. Poems, XCIII: "Mother, I cannot mind my wheel."   Walter Savage Landor. PG

–He always set his goals beyond the seen.   Three Cezannes.   George Whipple.   AMV-80

He, and about him his, are turned to stone.   Elegy on the L.C.   John Donne.   ATP

He and his golden bearded curls....   Saga of Leif the Lucky (excerpt). Hervey Allen.   EtS

He and she/Treading with naked foot/A running burning sea.   Song at the Skirts of Heaven.   Uri Z. Greenberg.   VWA

He answered, "I am here."   Adsum.   Richard Henry Stoddard.   AA

He ask'd, and hoped, through Christ. Do thou the same!   Epitaph on Himself.   Samuel Taylor Coleridge.   OxBoCh

He asked for bread, and he received a stone.   On the Setting Up of Mr. Butler's Monument in Westminster Abbey.   Samuel Wesley.   PPON

He asked me once–and squeaked at me/Because I hadn't any!   The Organ-Grinder.   Jimmy Garthwaite.   BrR

He ate, drank, slept, talk'd politics, and died.   On a Certain Alderman. John Cunningham.   FaBoEE

He ate the buttons off his shirt.   Dilly Dilly Piccalilli.   Clyde Watson. NTCP

He ate the dormouse,/Else it was he. "Buzz," Quoth the Blue Fly. Ben Jonson. TEP

He aught never gentilman called to be. Snatches: "In whom is trauth, petee, fredome, and hardinesse." *Anonymous.* OxBM

He balled was, and highte Lord Longenforde. Portrait of the Pornographer (parody). G. W. Jones. BXAP

He bears the insult–Love his only crime. Crucifixion. Hugh O. Isbell. PGD

He bears the load, He paid the price,/That bought me liberty. No Greater Love. *Anonymous.* STF

He beats them easily. Quoits. Mary Effie Lee Newsome. CDC; GoSl

He became/A millionaire. The Story of Ug. Edwin Meade Robinson. HBMV; YaD

He becomes frightened,/unable to finish his sentence. The Emergency Room. David Fisher. NPGG

He began to speak. The Bad Apple. Bruce Bennett. LTB

He believes there's stowaways down there–but, good/lord, what kind? Down Below. Joan Aiken. WSC

He bends his strength against the flood. Midstream. D. J. Enright. OxBC

...He bent and drank/in bondage to the ground. The Springs. Wendell Berry. GP

He best can paint 'em who shall feel 'em most. Eloisa to Abelard. Alexander Pope. CEP; LoBV; PoEL 1-5; TEP

He bet it was out today,/And would I see if he was right? Not of School Age. Robert Frost. GLGT

He betides himself to wake his own body/Before he crow to cause others wake or rise. Preachment for Preachers. Alexander Barclay. CAW

He bid her adieu. Then I withdrew from Erin's flowery vale. The Irish Girl's Lament. *Anonymous.* ShS

He biddeth a prayer to bless his youth/With Truth, and Purity, mother of Truth. Founder's Day. Robert Bridges. OBVV

He bids His world Good Night. Good Night. Dorothy Mason Pierce. BrR; SiSoSe

He bites their legs off and he beats them/Into a pulp, and then he eats them. The Swank. V. C. Vickers. AmMo

He blesseth thee, He blesseth me,/And we are near. Mizpah. Julia Aldrich Baker. BLPA; FaBoBe

He blusters still and walks with seaman's legs. The Old Sailor. Glenn Ward Dresbach. EtS

He bore/her smile out in the heat to her, as a gift. Developing a Wife. Andrew Taylor. CBAP

He bought her a ring/And a damascene gown. Down by the River. *Anonymous.* OxNR

He bow'd his head an' died, head an' died, head an' died, head an' died, head an' died. Look-a How Dey Done My Lord. *Anonymous.* BoAN 1-2

He bowed His head and, shuddering died,/Who was the Life. Signum Cui Contradicetur. Sister Mary Angelita. GoBC

He bows his head/To the sacred offerings/Of the New Year. Oraga Haru. Issa. OFD

He bows, turns round, and whip - the man's a black! The Sister: Epilogue. Oliver Goldsmith. OBSV

He brays like a man. Her Dwarf. George P. Elliott. MAT

He brays, the laureate of the long-eared kind. English Bards, and Scotch Reviewers. George Gordon, Lord Byron. AtBAP; ERoP 1-2; OAEL 1-2; PP

He breathed deep pleasure and trotted on. Reynard the Fox (excerpt). John Masefield. OBNV

He breathes out the last of the wind/as if it were a word. Definitions of the Word Gout. Tina Koyama. BrSi

He bring us to winne,/That hath us dere boght! The Crucifixion. *Anonymous.* MeEL

He brings a change of mood. The Grammar of Love. Pott and Wright. ALV

He brings my need before the Father/Every day. Interceding. Opal Leonore Gibbs. BePJ

He brought terror to my heart. There Came a Gray Owl at Sunset. *Anonymous.* WSC

He brushed by as he flew. You on the Tower. Thomas Hardy. SaC

He builds him a crimson nest. An Indian Summer Day on the Prairie. Vachel Lindsay. BPAW; RFM; SoPo

He builds in faith and doubt his shaking house. The Mythical Journey. Edwin Muir. NoAm; OxBS

He burnt unwares his wings, and cannot fly away. Astrophel and Stella, VIII. Sir Philip Sidney. AAS; SiPS

He calmly return'd/To his cottage again. The Despairing Lover. William Walsh. ALV; CEP; ELP; FaBoCh; LoGBV; NLV; NOBL; OBEC; OxBoLi

He came into the world with Absolute Continuity. Assuming the Name of Any Next Child. John Tagliabue. AMV-80

He came up again and said there was/none there. Blue Bell. *Anonymous.* OxNR

He can be content with two thousand a year. The Insatiable Priest. Matthew Prior. OBSP

He can be the body that casts/That white shadow across the waters/Just offshore. Rip. James Wright. NaP

He can curse the God that made him for the colour of his hair. Oh Who Is That Young Sinner with the Handcuffs on His Wrists? Alfred Edward Housman. AtBAP; FaBoTw; NOBV; PeHV; SoSe

He can exult and die in the same breath. The Good Hour. Louise Driscoll. HBMV

He can go among strangers/To save lives. Conception. Josephine Miles. FaBoWP; GP

He can move a big ship–or p'raps win me. Taunt. *Anonymous.* WTO

He can never name ocean. German Shepherd. Myra Cohn Livingston. RFM

He can only hurt me a piece at a time. Everything: Eloy, Arizona, 1956. Florence Anthony ("AI"). AmPA; FF

He can read my mind/through my knees and heels. Hossolalia. Mildred Luton. PH

He can snatch a man bald-headed while he waits. The Desperado. *Anonymous.* CoSo; TreFS

He can snuggle back in the telephone pole. The Woodpecker. Elizabeth Madox Roberts. OBCA; TiPo

...He can stand the sweetness. The Shirts. Tess Gallagher. MAYP

He can stay with me while I do not lift them. The End of the World. Gordon Bottomley. BrPo; CH; MoBrPo; MoVE

He can't find a penis that fits. Limerick: "A smooth-bottomed fellow named Fritz." *Anonymous.* PeHV

He can take at a wonderful pace. Limerick: "His figure's not noted for grace." Kenyon Cox. TDH

He cannot cut a pair of green/galligaskins,/If he were to die. Tailor of Bicester. *Anonymous.* OxNR

He cannot fly. Jailbird. Vernon Scannell. OxBC

He cannot know, he cannot tell/Where Spring performs her miracle. Springtime in Cookham Dean. Cecil Roberts. HBMV

He cannot sit alone. The Warm of Heart Shall Never Lack a Fire. Elizabeth Jane Coatsworth. TiPo

...He cannot stop from staring/all the way to the back of his brain. The Photographer Whose Shutter Died. William Meissner. PoDr

He cannot walk, borne down by his giant wings. The Albatross. Charles Baudelaire. EnLi 1-2; SyP

He cannot warm up his shot corpse, whose food/is syrup-green Lethean ooze, not blood. Spleen. Charles Baudelaire. NAWM 1-2

He carelessly stuck a verbena. Limerick: "There once was a happy hyena." Carolyn Wells. TDH

He cares not–yet prithee be kind to his fame. For My Own Monument. Matthew Prior. CEP; EiCP; HBV 1-2; LoBV; OBEC; OBEV

He carried kids until his back was broke on the/Oregon Trail. The Oregon Trail. *Anonymous.* BPAW

He catched at love, and filled his arm with bays. The Story of Phoebus and Daphne Applied... Edmund Waller. InvP; OBS

He catches a brief glimpse of bloodied hair/And hears an unintelligible prayer. The Feast of Stephen. Anthony Hecht. HAP; NoP

He catches them/And makes them pay Pursuit. Vern Rutsala. FAZ

He caught fishes/In other men's ditches. Tommy Tittlemouse. *Anonymous.* OxNR

He caught the whale all by the tail and turned him inside out. Jack Was Every Inch a Sailor. *Anonymous.* WHW

He chirped for joy to see himself deceived. Upon Mistress Elizabeth Wheeler under the Name of Amarillis. Robert Herrick. CaPo

...He chooses to dictate his poems/through me rather than write them down himself. Boogie with O. O. Gabugah. Al Young. NPGG

He chose a book called Storyland and lost himself in that. Seven Times One Are Seven. Robert Hillyer. BiCB

...He climbed our vines/and hid, on hands and knees, along our veins. Variations on a Theme. Oscar Williams. LiTA

He closed his eyes, no more to rise on the sweet Dundee. Pretty Mary. *Anonymous.* BFSS

He comes, a lyric at his lip,/Unstudied Poesy. Comradery. Madison Cawein. AA

He comes and I, in ancient grief, descend. Sonnet VIII: "I live, I die, I burn myself and drown." Louise Labe. BoWoP

He comes back through the dark singing/so quietly that you can hear nothing. Translation into the Original. Jack Gilbert. NPGG

He comes, he runs, he leaps to my desiring arms. Eclogues. Virgil (Publius Vergilius Maro). EiCP

He comes to brood and sit. Peace. Gerard Manley Hopkins. AtBAP; EBCP; ELP; GTBS-P; OAEP; OBSP; TrCP

He comes to remind us of sunshine and/pleasure. The Blue-Bird. Alexander Wilson. AA

"He cometh, so I wait." Idyl: Sunrise. Henrietta Cordelia Ray. BlSi

He conjures tangled forests in a furnished flat. London Tom-Cat. Michael Hamburger. BoAnP

He consented, himself, to/the finality of/an event.   For Tinkers Who Travel on Foot.   Margaret Avison.   NoAm

He could have sent khomeini/the fish.   Wasp.   William Welsh.   SOTS

He could hit an ant with his spear.   A Skilful Spearman!   *Anonymous.*   WTO

He could na preach for thinkin o't.   My Love, She's but a Lassie Yet.   Robert Burns.   ViBoPo

...He could no longer tarry,/But was returned again unto the quarry.   In Obitum Ben. Jons.   Mildmay Fane, Earl of Westmoreland.   OBSP

He could not carry off, so now he's carri-on.   On John Adams, of Southwell.   George Gordon, Lord Byron.   PV

He could not determine his journey's direction/But for your bright scintillating protection.   The Little Star.   *Anonymous.*   InMe; SpRo

He could not keep his head above water!   The Briefless Barrister.   John Godfrey Saxe.   ShM

He could no say it.   Gnat on My Paper.   Richard Eberhart.   DFF

He could not see which way to go/If you did not twinkle so.   The Star.   Jane Taylor.   Par

He could only say, "I'll/talk about them when I understand them."   W. S. Landor.   Marianne Moore.   OBAL

He could range like Paracelsus/Through his field and someone else's.   Specialist.   Theodore Roethke.   PV

He couldn't carve a duck.   When Father Carves the Duck.   Ernest Vincent Wright.   FaBV

He couldn't find the stick.   The Stick.   Bruce Bennett.   LTB

...He couldn't move, the track was so deep.   Variations on a Theme.   Oscar Whitman.   NePA

He couldn't shut up, the way the lonely can't. I can. Dick.   Letter to Garber from Skye.   Richard Hugo.   AMV-81

"He couldn't stay awake for you, he had to go to bed!"   A Song of Twilight.   *Anonymous.*   HBV 1-2

He crows more loudly in defeat.   The French, 1870-1871.   *Anonymous.*   FaBoEE

He cuddles up and laps my hand/And tells me he can understand.   My Dog.   Tom Robinson.   SoPo

He curses, curses all the way.   The Donkey.   P. R. Kaikini.   ACV

He cut it through the middle.   My Father Was a Frenchman.   *Anonymous.*   OxNR

He cuts the line, conceding defeat.   Charlie Johnson in Kettletown.   Claude Clayton Smith.   WOLT

He'd be four time as tall as me,/And live three times as long.   Fragment in Imitation of Wordsworth.   Catherine Fanshawe.   FaBoNo; FaBoPa; HBV 1-2

He'd bring him to a proper sense/Of what was due to gentlemen!'   Peter Bell the Third.   Percy Bysshe Shelley.   ChRP

He'd find less changed than his own daughter.   For My Father.   Rachel Field.   InMe

He'd given our dream to you.   A Rhyme of the Dream-Maker Man.   William Allen White.   PoLf

He'd heard/such a thing   Rice and Rose Bowl Blues.   Diane Mei Lin Mark.   BrSi

He'd like to cut/The tithes that bind.   Alma Mater, Forget Me.   William Cole.   FiBHP

He'd love me sure–/And maybe praise!   A Little Page's Song.   William Alexander Percy.   HBV 1-2

He'd have every beast in the Ark ill!   Limerick: "A chap has a shark up in Sparkill."   Morris Bishop.   TDH

He'd many a mile to go that night,/Before he reached the town-o.   The Fox.   *Anonymous.*   FSW

...He'd nailed her fast/Between two thieves, him and herself.   Solitary Confinement.   X. J. Kennedy.   NePoEA-2

He'd ne'er leave the girl with the strawberry curls,/And the Band played on.   The Band Played On.   John E. Palmer.   FSN; OBAL; TreF

He'd never been Man in the Moon so high.   The Man in the Moon.   *Anonymous.*   MOON; OxNR

He'd pay his reck'ning in the realms below.   On a Poet.   Henry Luttrell.   FaBoEE

...He'd say, "Wanna play kick the can?"   We Used to Play.   Don Welch.   Psk

He'd shrivel up at once or turn to stone.   The Playboy of the Demi-World: 1938.   William Plomer.   OxBTC; PeHV; TW

He'd stood up straight–it broke his back!   Johnny.   Emma Rounds.   ShM

He'd worked as a pony on a merry-go-round.   The Wooden Horse then said.   Jenny Mastoraki.   BoWoP

He danc'd full fast, but tired at last,/And gae it up as shamefullie.   The Bonny Lass of Anglesey.   *Anonymous.*   ESPB

He dared their margins with silver   New Storefront.   Russell Atkins.   FB

He dares to weep/in the midst of us.   Closing Piece.   Rainer Maria Rilke.   PCP

He deals in dreams, and calls it–work!   The Ticket Agent.   Edmund Leamy.   HBMV

He definitely listened to the usual AM broadcasts/You know: shake the hand, the hand falls off.   Anti-Memoirs.   Simon Schuchat.   APU

He did not answer: I started out.   The Future.   James Oppenheim.   TrJP

He did not know us then; he might/Upon another day!   A Ballad of the Gold Country.   Helen Hunt Jackson.   BPAW

He did not think me strange or older,/Nor I, him.   All Souls' Night.   Frances Cornford.   EnLoPo; OBSP; OxBTC

He did not try.   The Urban Experience.   Lew Blockcolski.   VoR

He did nothing but basking until he was saved!   The Old Sailor.   A.(lan) A.(lexander) Milne.   CenHV

He did ramble till those butchers cut 'im down.   The Ram of Darby.   *Anonymous.*   OuSiCo

He did, the scaffold, "Je sais ou je vais."   Saint-Just 1767-93.   Robert Lowell.   FaBoMo

He didn't love back.   Two-Volume Novel.   Dorothy Parker.   InMe

He didn't use to/talk.../but/he does now.   The Emancipation of George-Hector (a colored turtle).   Mari E. Evans.   AmNP

He died amidst their whole.   Phineas within and without.   Paul Zimmer.   VGW

He died close to the dirt.   The Dirt Doctor.   Melvin Douglass Brown.   LFAC

"He died for us. For what in hell do we?"   The Sit-In.   Darwin T. Turner.   BALP

He died in 1895./He is not dead.   Frederick Douglass: 1817-1895.   Langston Hughes.   BPo

He died in public. He claimed the secret right/To be ashamed.   Two Poems About President Harding.   James Wright.   CoAP

He died in war, and yet he died in peace.   The Atheist's Tragedy.   Cyril Tourneur.   EIL

He died like one who dared not hope to live.   W. H. Eheu!   Samuel Taylor Coleridge.   FaBoEE

...He died looking towards my face.   Dream.   Richard Watson Dixon.   EBEV; LoBV; NOBV; VLP

He died, regretted by a mourning world.   Epitaph on Washington.   *Anonymous.*   OHIP

He died so quietly.   The Dying Child.   John Clare.   CBEP; EnRP; NCEP; TrGrPo

He died. Was twenty-four years young.   Epitaph.   Jiri Wolker.   WaaP

He died when he could live no longer.   Epigram: "Tom's sickness did his morals mend."   Matthew Prior.   FaBoEE

He died years ago.   Cynical Portraits.   Louis Paul.   InMe; NLV

He dies who loves it,–if the worm be there.   Pelleas and Ettarre (excerpt).   Alfred, Lord Tennyson.   PoEL 1-5

He dives, I suppose,/For divers reasons.   Cold Logic.   Barney Hutchinson.   SD

He does enjoy his little bit of fun.   Quiet Fun.   Harry Graham.   DBV; ShM

He does it from this time, and will/Do it forever more.   I Lift My Eyes Up to the Hills.   Cotton Mather.   AH

He does not choose to cause her life to stop.   An Evasion.   Douglas Livingstone.   PeSA

...He does not know/How it was he lost his bright blue fly.   Blue Fly.   Joaquim M. De Assis.   TTY

He does not rightly love himself/Who does not love another more.   Love Serviceable.   Coventry Patmore.   EnLoPo

He does not want even these few lines written.   Angel.   James Merrill.   ConAP; PoA

He does the only thing he knows,/And does it very thorough.   Old Man Platypus.   A. B. Paterson.   BoAnP

He doesn't stretch/At all!   Walking.   Grace Ellen Glaubitz.   SoPo; TiPo

He done what he didn't intend.   Limerick: "There was a young man of Ostend."   *Anonymous.*   LiBL

He doth lie and she doth kneel.   An Epitaph for Sir Henry Lee...   *Anonymous.*   FaBoEE

He doth not crave less time, but more.   Time.   George Herbert.   TEP

He doth sit by us and moan.   On Another's Sorrow.   William Blake.   AWP; CBEP; CEP; EBCP; EnRP; FaBV; ViBoPo

He drank his kumis and wine,/Ate his pure food,/And lived happily ever after.   Zong Belegt Baatar.   *Anonymous.*   WTO

He draws his heavy brows and will not rest.   The Onondaga Madonna.   Duncan Campbell Scott.   PeCV

He dreamed the midnight dancers/buried him head down.   The Urban Experience.   Lew Blockcolski.   VoR

He dreams of being tried and pronounced–"Dead."   After Some Day of Decision.   Reed Whittemore.   NePoEA

...He dreams/of hunting with hounds in the snow.   Rural Lines after Breughel.   Norbert Krapf.   PoDr

He dreams of marbles and of tops, and nods.   The Schoolboy Reads His Iliad.   David Morton.   MCCG

He dredged forth the break-away tunes/Green from winter's bayous.   Troubador.   J. Edgar Simmons.   TAT

He drew them on the glass. The Frosted Pane. Sir Charles G. D. Roberts. HBV 1-2

He drives her four-in-hand. The Coachman. *Anonymous.* OxNR

He drives them through the town. Thistledown. Lizette Woodworth Reese. YeAr

–He drove a white horse and went splash in the sea. Play-Song. *Anonymous.* LiTW

He dwells, transformed into a tongue. Vert-Vert, the Parrot. Louis Gresset. CAW

He earned his outlaw fame. Jesse James. Rosemary and Stephen Vincent Benét. BPAW

...He eats/Fish from his Saviour's hands, and it tastes black. Penguin on the Beach. Ruth Miller. PeSA

He enjoys and grows by love. From Solitude to Solitude towards Life. Paul Eluard. LiTW

He enjoys as full content, without his cares. The Suet Dumpling (parody). *Anonymous.* BXAP

...He entered into the last dream/of Offa the King. Mercian Hymns (excerpt). Geoffrey Hill. FaBoMo; HAP

He enters without knocking. Notes for the Chart in 306. Ogden Nash. NYBP

He escaped/Into a telephone pole/On the long straight west of Swinton. A Motorbike. Ted Hughes. InPS

He faced the arrows and died in front of his church. Brebeuf and His Brethren. Edwin John Pratt. ACV; OBCV; PeCV

(He failed in business, took to drink and died). An Epitaph. Colin Ellis. OxBTC

He falls–and yet old Arlington will never rise again! Arlington. David McKee Wright. AnNZ

He far in the dungeon-tower! In a Lovely Garden Walking. Ludwig Uhland. AWP

He fathers-forth whose beauty is past change:/Praise Him. Pied Beauty. Gerard Manley Hopkins. AnEnPo; ATP; AWP; BiP; BoLiVe; BrPo; CMoP; CoBMV; DiPo; EaLo; EBCP; FaBoMo; FaFP; GoJo; GTBS-P; HAP; HeIP; HoPM; InPK; InPo; InPS; InvP; LiTB; LiTM; MoAB; MoBrPo; MoRP; MoVE; NAMP; NIP; NoAm; NOBE; NOBV; NoP; OAEL 1-2; OAEP; OBEV; OBMV; OBNC; OBSP; PAI; PoPl; PoRA; PPP; PrIm; SCV; SoSe; SOTW; TEP; TreFS; TrGrPo; TRV; ViBoPo; VLP; WeW

He feared but two things–to turn thief, and lie.' Stoklewath; or, The Cymbrian Village. Susanna Blamire. NOEC

He fears, and flies from Marion's men. The Swamp Fox. William Gilmore Simms AA; AmePo; BeLS; FaBoBe; MC; PAH

He feels the vaguely sweet content/Of perfect sloth in limb and brain. Day-Dreams. William Canton. NOBV

He fell asleep upon the swell... The Cachalot. Edwin John Pratt. OBCV

He fell down and broke his bones. The Man Who Jumped. *Anonymous.* OxNR

He fell that day amongst the slain, a valiant/man was he. Sainclaire's Defeat. *Anonymous.* PAH

He fell the day that Richmond fell,/And took the first despatch. My Correspondent's Last Ride. George Alfred Townsend. AA

He felt a chair in Scotland. And sat down. Five Visions of Captain Cook. Kenneth Slessor. BoAV

He felt like burying his head/and sobbing in the grass. Jealous Adam. Itzik Manger. TrJP

He felt puzzled licking the rain/from the trees. The Way the Bird Sat. Ray A. Young Bear. CDW; VoR

...He felt that spell begin/To work, not needing words. He Could Have Found His Way. Kathleen Dalziel. PoAu 1-2

He figured he was in motion. Retired Farmer. David Allan Evans. Psk

He findes the God there, farre unlike his Bookes. Chorus: Sacerdotum. Fulke, Lord Brooke Greville. EG; FaBoEn; InvP; JCP; MePo; NOBE; OAEL 1-2; PPP; SeCePo

He finds night day. The Two Spirits. Percy Bysshe Shelley. CH; LO; WiR

He finds no worship alien or odd. When Mahalia Sings. Quandra Prettyman. IDB; PoBA

He finds that private business asserts a prior claim. A Bully. *Anonymous.* WTO

He finished him, beginning with his shoes. An Accommodating Lion. Tudor Jenks. OBCA

He flew awa in a blazing flame. Riddles Wisely Expounded. *Anonymous.* ESPB; FaBoBa; GBP; ViBoFo

He flew away. He left with me/Despair and my disgrace. My Angel. Jonathan Henderson Brooks. PoNe

He flies so easy, when he sings. Driving in Oklahoma. Carter Revard. VoR

He floated upwards, and regain'd the steep. The White Horse of Westbury. Charles Tennyson Turner. EBEV; VLP

He floats through high dark branches, a corpse tangled in a tree on a river. A Journey through the Moonlight. Russell Edson. LCAP

He follows after shadows-the King of Ireland's Son. King of Ireland's Son. Nora Hopper. AnIL

He follows on his horny toes,/The little dog under the wagon. The Little Dog under the Wagon. *Anonymous.* PoLf

He fondled with steeled heart Milady's cat. The Cat-o-Nine-Tails. John Blight. BoAV

...He forgot how to walk and learned how to fly before/he thinked. A Caution to Everybody. Ogden Nash. NePA

He forgot why his lips moved, his body swayed. Tales of Shatz. Dannie Abse. OxBC; VWA

He found his prize–the Land of Liberty. The Dreamer. Dorothy Gould. PGD

He found one shelter–in a caravan/Bound for the hills. The Mountaineer. Robert Nathan. TrJP

He from her presence sneaked, completely humbled! Animal Magnetism. Laurence Hynes Halloran. NOEC

...He from his welling throat untied/A kerchief, crying "Give Sal that!'–and died. Don Juan. George Gordon, Lord Byron. FiP

He gaed tae the byre/And swallowed the coo. Sandy Kildandy. *Anonymous.* OxNR

He gallops; and the dark wind brings;/His lonely human cry. The King's Son. Thomas Boyd. AnIV; OBMV; OxBI

He gave and I, who sing/His praise, bring all I have to bring. A Friend. Lionel Pigot Johnson. HBV 1-2

He gave His all and knew no loss. My Master Was So Very Poor. Harry Lee. TRV

He gave it up, and scuttled to his hole. World's End. G. K. Chettur. ACV

He gave not protection to Temair. Tara. *Anonymous.* OnYI

...He gave that world/Its grandest lesson: "On! sail on!" Columbus. Joaquin Miller. AA; AmePo; BeLS; EtS; FaBoBe; FaFP; GN; GoTF; HBV 1-2; HBVY; MC; MCCG; MOS; OHFP; PAH; PAL; PaPo; PGD; TreF; YaD; YeAr

He gave them the spirit his own to defy. America. Arthur Cleveland Coxe. MC; PAH

He gave with a zest and he gave his best–/Give him the best to come. Peter Cooper. Joaquin Miller. AA

He gets behind, driving off–into the city's secret heart. Amsterdam Street Scene, 1972. Raphael Rudnik. AMV-81

He gets his uniform out. Baseball Note. Franklin Pierce ("F.P.A.") Adams. SD

He gets pains in his arms and legs/And a rheumatic cramp. Sleep My Child. *Anonymous.* FSW

He gives the very best to those/Who leave the choice with Him. The Best Choice. *Anonymous.* STF

He gives what his style allows:/cows. An Insult. *Anonymous.* NOBI

He giveth and giveth and giveth again. He Giveth More. Annie Johnson Flint. BLRP; TRV; WBLP

He giveth His beloved rest,/To the weary one. With Him. Julia E. Martin. STF

He giveth his beloved sleep. The Sleep. Elizabeth Barrett Browning. HBV 1-2; TRV; WGRP

He glided silent through the wide/vistas of the Tyger's slumber. The Clown: He Dances in the Clearing by Night. Ramon Guthrie. NMP

He glides/sleek in the spirit/of fish. Into Fish. Sheryl L. Nelms. GOYP

He goes again-goes his own gait. The Game. Winfield Townley Scott. AnAmPo

He goes before them and commands them all,/That to himself is a law rational. The Master Spirit. George Chapman. EtS

He goes on talking soundlessly, moving his raised hands furiously, a final spark of blood... In the Subway. Juan Ramon Jimenez. NYP

He goes out every night/With a new one by his side. Tom Cat Blues. *Anonymous.* FSW

He goes to swallow it down./He steals away. The Song of Nu-Numma-Kwiten. *Anonymous.* PeSA

He got married, and then there were none. Ten Little Nigger Boys. *Anonymous.* OxNR

He got struck severe at the fair ground/For which he took a rest. Grand Rapids Cricket Club (excerpt). Julia A. Moore. PeD

He grew, or else his comrades lied,/Confounded dull before he died. The Life and Character of Dean Swift (excerpt). Jonathan Swift. NOBI; NOBL

...He grew smaller and sputtered into sleep. Traverse City Zoo. Jim Harrison. BoAnP

He grows drunk with them,/he who is at our side. Battle Song. Macuilxochitl. WPOW

He guides the conq'ring sword, he governs in/the fight. On the Late Successful Expedition against Louisbourg. Francis Hopkinson. PAH

He had a bien plaisaunt jag on. Limerick: "When that Seint George hadde sleyne ye draggon." *Anonymous.* NA

He had a heart to praise, an eye to see,/And beauty was his king. Petition. John Drinkwater. TrPWD

He had an eunuch cat hight Ganymed.   Lost Lines from Chaucer's Prologue to The Canterbury Tales.   *Anonymous.*   PeHV

He had an excellence which you miss.   The Deceased.   Keith Douglas.   FaBoTw

He had been shaped like a drunken pyramid, ir-/regularly triangular.   The Stone.   Paul Blackburn.   NYP

He had better be without her.   He That Marries a Merry Lass.   *Anonymous.*   ALV

He had both purse and person too,/And all at his command.   The Knight and Shepherd's Daughter (A version).   *Anonymous.*   ESPB

He had come a long way since he named the animals.   Since Then.   D. J. Enright.   OBSV

He had discovered something called "le jazz hot'/& found it of some interest.   Le Jazz Hot.   Anselm Hollo.   PoM

He had got manhood at the testing-place.   Dauber.   John Masefield.   BBV

He had his fill, Oh,/Of what he pleased.   Happy Myrtillo.   Henry Carey.   SeCePo

He had in fact been drowned the night before.   Subjectivity at Sestos.   P. M. Hubbard.   NYBP

He had many true-loves–but never one.   The Lucifer.   Guy Glover.   CaP

He had no fear of death;/Nor Death of him.   Corporal Pym.   Walter De la Mare.   FaBoEE

He had no trousers of his own/And so he wore his sister's...   A Fragment: "The boy stood on the burning deck. (parody).   *Anonymous.*   FaBoPa

He had not sung of Wales, nor I of him.   English Bards and Scotch Reviewers.   George Gordon, Lord Byron.   EiCP

–He had nothing to say.   To Hell with Your Fertility Cult.   Gary Snyder.   NAs; TW

He had one more poem/And that poem is lost,/For ever.   After My Death.   Hayim Nahman Bialik.   VWA

He had only one mania–/Pennsylvania.   Clerihew: "William Penn."   William Jay Smith.   PV

He had saved the world.   The Passion of Our Lady.   Charles Peguy.   ISi

He had sent this Ship of Air.   The Phantom Ship.   Henry Wadsworth Longfellow.   EtS

He had shellac on all his feet/And rubber on his nose.   A Little Pig Asleep.   Leroy F. Jackson.   BrR

He had such a chance, with a new mor-/rice-dance,/He never went home againe.   Flodden Field.   *Anonymous.*   ESPB

He had the Hunter led away.   Lord Epsom.   Hilaire Belloc.   PH

He had the wyte o his ain death,/And bonny lady"s overthrow."   The Laird of Wariston (B vers.).   *Anonymous.*   BaBo

He had to be four times cuckold.   The Temperaments.   Ezra Pound.   BoLoP; ErPo; NoAm; NOBA

He had to put Descartes before the horse.)   Theological.   Clifton Fadiman.   FiBHP; PV

He handles us severely,/That despicable White man!   Work Song.   Raymond Mazisi Kunene.   WTO

He hands it to me through the fence.   Milking Time.   Elizabeth Madox Roberts.   GoJo; OBCA; SUS

He hands them back when he sees they are done.   The Toaster.   William Jay Smith.   GrPl; SoPo

He hands these words/songs once lived/to a young boy/a part of the earth.   Stories Relate Life.   Dennis Shady.   LFAC

He hangs on tight/As if I might.   Generations.   Joseph Awad.   AMV-81

...He hardly knew the man/But it felt funny to leave him just lying there.   John Brown's Body.   Stephen Vincent Benét.   PoLf

He has a hcart, and gets his speeches by it.   On J. W. Ward.   Samuel Rogers.   ALV; DBV

He has a prince's eyes.   Schoolroom: 158–.   James E. Warren, Jr.   GoYe

He has been eaten by the bear.   The Grizzly Bear is huge and wild.   Alfred Edward Housman.   CenHV

...He has been gone/twenty years and not heard from.   Dream 2: Brian the Still-Hunter.   Margaret Atwood.   BoWoP

...He has been hiding here for/Many generations.   Out of the Dark Wood.   Peter".   AmMo

He has been pierced by Spring,/That sharp knife.   That Sharp Knife.   Thomas Wolfe.   NCSH

He has come in his dotage to live a life free from care/In a fool's pastoral setting getting tanned   Shakespeare, Possibly, in California.   Reed Whittemore.   • MoVE

He has discovered it first, and perhaps I/shall find it to-morrow.   The Lily of Torrow.   Henry Van Dyke.   AA

He has escaped the private wars of peace.   The Young Recruit.   Arthur Davison Fiche.   ELU

He has forestalled death.   The Man Without Faith.   Richard Church.   MoRP

He has forgot to make me mad/to love your body and your mind.'   To a Lady on Her Marriage.   William Bell.   NePoEA

He has found the snake's egg.   Merlin and the Snake's Egg.   Leslie Norris.   WSC

He has given himself a deadly wound/And word spake never mair].   Fair Isabell of Rochroyall.   *Anonymous.*   OxBB

He has "God" on his lips in his rise/and his fall.   The Eternal Jew.   Jacob Cohen.   TrJP

...He has/gone out of you.   Room.   Shirley Kaufman.   NMM

He has himself begun to crow,/To himself "Good morning" said.   Gingilee.   Moishe-Leib Halpern.   TrJP

"He has his head well screwed on," Flann agreed.   Frankenstein Gets His Man.   Frank Carr.   AmMo

...He/Has made at the most something wooden and empty.   A Fable for Critics.   James Fenimore Cooper.   DBV

He has more horns/Than all the king's sheep.   Riddle: "Little Billy Breek."   *Anonymous.*   OxNR

He has never a story to tell!   A Toad.   Elizabeth Akers Allen.   OBCA

& He has never fought/a thief.   Zapata & the Landlord.   A. B. Spellman.   NNP; PoBA

He has no bite/And very little bark.   The Bogus-Boo.   James Reeves.   AmMo

He has no hair on his behind.   The Ape.   Roland Young.   PoPl

He has no principles at all.   A Levantine.   William Plomer.   OBMV

He has no teeth/But is kind.   Love (excerpt).   Alice Walker.   NMM

He has not been seen since/not once   Time of fish dying.   Gabriela Melinescu.   BoWoP

He has not known his God.   Who Does Not Love True Poetry.   Henry Clay Hall.   PoToHe

He has sung.   My Song.   King D. Kuka.   VoR

An he has tane that gay lady,/An ther he did her burne.   The Laily Worm and the Machrel of the Sea.   *Anonymous.*   ESPB; InvP; LoBV; OxBB; PoEL 1-5

He has the beauty of them all/Hidden beneath his hair.   The Hairy Dog.   Herbert Asquith.   SoPo; SUS; TiPo

He has won that storm-tight roof of hers/Which Earth grants all her kind.   She Hears the Storm.   Thomas Hardy.   ATP

He hasn't dogs or polliwogs/Like any other child.   Radiator Lions.   Dorothy Aldis.   SoPo

He hasn't got far yet, but he's a damn good starter.   A Toast.   *Anonymous.*   PV

...He hates him/That would upon the rack of this tough world/Stretch him out longer.   King Lear.   William Shakespeare.   FiP

He hath his love; but I–I have my song.   A Song's Worth.   Susan Marr Spalding.   AA

He hath it still complete.   My Father's Close.   *Anonymous.*   AWP

He hath the watchword and the key,/In peace, or wars.   The Way to Heaven.   Charles Goodrich Whiting.   AA

He haveth brought us to blis/Superni,/That haves y-dit the foule pit/Inferni.   Of One That Is So Fair and Bright.   *Anonymous.*   CoBE; HAP; ISi; OxBM

He heard and he knew this life's secret/I hear and I know.   The Englishman in Italy.   Robert Browning.   FaBoPP

He heard the good pastor/Cry, All flesh is grass.   On a Clergyman's Horse Biting Him.   *Anonymous.*   FaBoEE; GoTF; NLV; TreFT

"He hears it not now, but used to notice such things"?   Afterwards.   Thomas Hardy.   AnFE; BoNaP; CBEP; CH; CMoP; EBEV; FaBoRV; ForPo; GTBS-P; InPS; LiTB; LiTM; MoAB; MoBrPo; MoVE; NOBE; NoP; OAEL 1-2; OAEP; OBNC; PAI; PoEL 1-5; PoPle; QFR; SeCeV; TreFT; TrGrPo; ViBoPo

He hears the rustling leaf and running/stream.   The Evening Wind.   William Cullen Bryant.   AA; AnNE

He hears the silence shattered by the laughter of the loon.   The Fruit Rancher.   Lloyd Roberts.   CaP

He held before a shouting throng,/A crowning of his own.   The Crowning of Dreaming John.   John Drinkwater.   HBMV

He held me by His hand.   Upheld by His Hand.   Grace B. Renfrow.   BePJ

He helped to bury whom he helped to starve.   An Epistle from Mr. Pope to Dr. Arbuthnot.   Alexander Pope.   OBSV

He helps himself to applejack,/And she to Paris Green.   The Farmer and the Farmer's Wife.   P. G. Herbert.   FiBHP; NLV

He, hi, he can tell time...   Track-Lining Song.   *Anonymous.*   AmFP

He hides them deep, like the secret sleep/Of him he loved so well.   The Burial of Moses.   Cecil Frances Alexander.   BeLS; BLPA; BLRP; GN; HBV 1-2; WBLP

...He hides them/To be published in his seventies.   Confidential.   Winfield Townley Scott.   ELU

He hies him once more to the runlet,/To fetch her the Drake!   The Manlet (parody).   Lewis (Charles Lutwidge Dodgson) Carroll.   BXAP; Par

He hoped to write one good line; died believing in God.   A Funeral Oration.   David Wright.   MP

He/hopes/the scent/won't destroy/the universe   They Live in Parallel Worlds.   William J. Harris.   CNA

He huffed "Of Course she flew!"   African Sunday.   Maureen Owen.   APU

He hugs the soul he calls his own.   Family Life.   Allan M. Laing.   FiBHP

He humbled and hewed down until at last he fell himself.... The Battle of Maldon. *Anonymous.* OBWP

He hurries to another school/and waits...perhaps for you. The Ghoul. Jack Prelutsky. OBCA

He imagines a speckled trout/coming up shining and raging with life. Spring. Michael Hogan. LFAC; TAT

He is a bastard if he dare to mock/Old Jamestown's shrine or Plymouth's/ famous rock. Ode to Jamestown. James Kirke Paulding. PAH

He is a better poet than us all. The Thrush. Alfred Austin. TEP

He is a businessman,/and his business is bad Suite from Catullus. Vincent McHugh. ErPo

He is a conscious black and white/Little symphony of night. The Skunk. Robert P. Tristram Coffin. TiPo

He is a friendly TOAD. A Friend in the Garden. Juliana Horatia Ewing. OxBChV

He is a leopard–he bought himself in a shop. Leopard Skin. Douglas Stewart. NOAV

He is a most unpleasant brute/To find in bed, at night. The Scorpion. Hilaire Belloc. BoAnP

...He is a sensation,/for newspapers and headaches. He is exploded! The Raspberry in the Pudding. Philip O'Connor. EAS

He is a stranger to me now/Who was my friend. Chamber Music. James Joyce. OLR

He is an artist, not an artisan. Eclogue. John Davidson. BrPo

He is. As you imagined Him. Neo-Classical Poem. William Jay Smith. WaP

He is brought home to her, as she brings a child. A Legend of Viable Women. Richard Eberhart. MiAP; MoVE

He is buried somewhere else. The Underground Gardens. Robert Mezey. NaP

He is caught in the spell. I Find My Love Fishing. *Anonymous.* PBWP

He is coming back to thee! Baby mine! Baby Mine. Charles Mackey. BLSo

He is dangerous even though asleep and unarmed. He. John Ashbery. SOTW

He is drifting sideways toward the dusty places. The Teeth Mother Naked at Last. Robert Bly. GP

...He is engaged/To marry/The Electric Holding Company. Always We Watch Them. Paul Mariah. LFAC

He is ever fair and great. The Thought Eternal. Johann Wolfgang von Goethe. AWP

He is fashioning a frame/For the shimmering silver beauty of the evening stars. God Is at the Anvil. Lew Sarett. HBMV; TRV; WGRP

He is feeling/excellent too, I guess, and/weightless and/"smiling'. In a Season of Unemployment. Margaret Avison. NOBC

He is gone out from Burgos... The Lay of the Cid: Pawning the Coffers of Sand. *Anonymous.* LiTW

He is, he was, or is to be. Inscription for a Statue of Love. Voltaire (Francois Marie Arouet). LiTW

He is heard to speak through a mother's love. Mother. Emily Taylor. PGD

He is impatient now. To Celia. Charles Cotton. OBEV

...He is in my company,/with the first smashed bottle. Thoughts. David Ignatow. FAZ

He is king of the donjon deeps. The Song of the Turnkey. Harry Bache Smith. AA

He is knit with his doom. Germinal. George William Russell. BIrV; MoBrPo; OBEV; OBMV

He is led forward by their announcing wings. Signs Everywhere of Birds Nesting, While. William Carlos Williams. MoVE

He is lettuce planted by the water. Inanna's Song. *Anonymous.* LLLT

He is like a rippling wave/That passes by. Like Ripples on the Water. *Anonymous.* WTO

He is loving us now, he is loving all. Ward Two. Francis Webb. CBAP

He is my brother-man. He is humanity. He Is My Countryman. Antoni Slonimski. TrJP

He is my flesh and I/am what he was. Poems for My Daughter. Horace Gregory. MoAmPo

He is my Shepherd indeed! Mercies and Blessings. *Anonymous.* STF

He is my son. Sons. Don Polson. AMV-81

He is not at home. The Kingdom. Jon Swan. NYBP

He is not dead. The Lizard. Rona Murray. NOBC

He is not dead–he is just away. Away. James Whitcomb Riley. BLRP; TreFT; TRV; WGRP

...He is not in third/Grade,/Will he ever be in fourth? At Their Place. Paul Mariah. LFAC

He is not of the Island race! England. Grace Ellery Channing-Stetson. AA

He is not to leave. The Inland Lighthouse. James McMichael. AmPA

He is not wise that will be dum/In ortu Regis omnium. Farewell Advent! James Ryman. MeEL; OxBM

He is only a good alien, nominally happy. Washington Cathedral. Karl Shapiro. MiAP

He is only thistledown planted on the wind. Thistledown. Denis Glover. AnNZ

He is really perfectly serious/About the universe being mysterious. Clerihew. Edmund Clerihew Bentley. NLV

He is repuls'd indeed, but You'r undone. A Letter to the Countess of Denbigh. Richard Crashaw. MePo; SeCP

He is snug and out of all the weather. Covered Bridge. Robert P. Tristram Coffin. AmFN

He is so beguiling,/That dearest of dears. Apprehension. Douglas Ainslie. OBVV

He is still inside. Dream. Nana Issaia. BoWoP

He is taken, stripped, and bound. Leichhardt in Theatre: The Room. Francis Webb. PoAu 1-2

He is the Brownies' racehorse,/The Fairies' Kangaroo. An Explanaton of the Grasshopper. Vachel Lindsay. SoPo

He is the core of the heart of love, and He, beyond laboring seas, our/ultimate shore. How Many Heavens... Edith Sitwell. MoRP; TrCP

He is the Lie: one true thought, and he's gone. Antichrist. Edwin Muir. EaLo

He is the most exciting thing/In town on Sabbath day. The Organist. George W. Stevens. BLPA

...He is/the observer. He watches, He does not interfere. The Observer. David C. Yates. AMV-81

He is the one who looks after my child. Oriki Erinle. *Anonymous.* PBA; TTY

He is the one who waited for the things we are running away from Shango II. *Anonymous.* TTY

He is the one who waves. Salt Water Story. Richard Hugo. NoP

...He is the one with us/Beginning and end.' I Am the One. Thomas Hardy. OxBTC

He is the primal rock. Nation. Mendel Naigreshel. VWA

He is the wonderful glad New Year. The New Year. Dinah M. Mulock Craik. BrR; YeAr

He is too skilled in bleeding hearts/To turn this way and pity mine. Song from the Bride of Smithfield. Sylvia Townsend Warner. MoBrPo

He is trying to forget, his briefcase/With everybody's initials on it. Man Lying on a Wall. Michael Longley. CIP; FaBoIP

...He is visibly moved by the/open-hearted and believable way I say this. Dream with Fred Astaire. Bill Berkson. APU

He is weary of nothing; he watches air-planes; he watches/pelicans. Pelicans. Robinson Jeffers. FM; MoAmPo

...He is what is left of my life. The Dreadful Has Already Happened. Mark Strand. NoAm

...He is willing/To fork out his penny and pocket your shilling. On Communists. Ebenezer Elliott. NLV; NOBL

He is wise; follow him. Arabian Proverb. *Anonymous.* TreF

He is "with me always" there! Let Me Go Back. Mary E. Albright. BLRP

...He it is/That I shall sleep with–happier fate."... Dinnshenchas: The Enchanted Fawn. *Anonymous.* OnYI

He jigs me five times every nicht/Young man, could you do that? Could You Do That? Robert Burns. UnTE

He joy'd in Hope, that now were laid Foundations/Of Piety for many Generations./Maestus Composuit. An Elegy in Memory of the Worshipful Major Thomas Leonard Esq.... Samuel Danforth II. SCAP

He jumped into another bush/And scratched them in again. A Man of Thessaly. *Anonymous.* CBEP; FaBoCo; OxNR

He jumped on the poop crying, Maintops'l haul. The Fishes. *Anonymous.* GBP

He just goes "ffffffff-ut!" Primer of Consequences. Virginia Brasier. ShM

He just laughed/At my tears. Nightmare. James A. Emanuel. BPo

...He just lays there. Rhode Island. William Meredith. NoP

He just nodded. Adam's Apple. Coleman Barks. PPJ

He just stood there behind the display case. Cash Only, No Refund, No Return. Daniel Mark Epstein. MAYP

...He just wins or loses. My Father: October 1942. William Stafford. CAPP; NaP

He kept thinking of/his own 8 grandchildren. Future generation. Nila NorthSun. STE

He kicked up his heels and belched till he died,/Sing, "raw riddle," sing, "ray." The Miller That Made His Will. *Anonymous.* BFSS

He kindly trains us to endure. The Angel of Patience. John Greenleaf Whittier. WGRP

He kissed the Dawn-Star pale. Betrayal. John Banister Tabb. ACP

He knew as much about Divinity/As other fellows do of Trinity. On a Doctor of Divinity. Richard Porson. FaBoCo

He knew me intimately too...! Poet. Donald Jeffrey Hayes. AmNP

He knew the whole–and could not choose/but turn! In Hades. Anna Callender Brackett. AA

He knew the whole prison/Yard/By the feel of his tongue/Against each grey rock. Gravel. Paul Mariah. LFAC

He knew there was reason, but couldn't find it/and marched to battle half an inch behind it. Cullen. P. K. Page. CaP

He knew they were his Children ruind in his ruind world The Four Zoas. William Blake. TW

He knows as well, it seems, as we/The time is come to fly away. The Robin. William Bell Scott. FM

He knows me by the little song I start to sing,/shifting from foot to foot. The Burden of Decision. Peter Everwine. NNaP

He knows not when nor how. Forever in My Dream and in My Morning Thought. Henry David Thoreau. PoEL 1-5

He knows the Steward–he is known afar/To magistrates and bums–great man, John Marr! The Splendid Village. Ebenezer Elliott. NBM

He knows where he needs to be/and puts himself there/eight hours a day. The Prison Guard. J. J. Maloney. LFAC

He knows why the scientist/in secret delight/strokes the fern's/voluptuous braille. The Fish in the Stone. Rita Dove. HaCAP

He labors good on good to fix, and owes/To virtue every triumph that he knows. Character of the Happy Warrior. William Wordsworth. BoLiVe

He labors greatly/He cannot breathe. Annales: "Like a shower of rain." Ennius. WaaP

He late that night/Followed the leaping tide. Song: "Where in blind files." Eavan Boland. CIP

He laughed out with A ha ha ha ha. An Evening's Love. John Dryden. CavP; FF

He laughingly kisses them/with his gashed tongue/of poems. The Death of the Epileptic Poet Yesenin. Aram Boyajian. NeAC

He lay in jewelled feathers, dead. The Pheasant. Robert P. Tristram Coffin. TiPo

He lays his head in a lady's lap/As gently as a child. Unicorn. William Jay Smith. SO

He leans to life, conspires to give and get/Other serving yet. Old Tennis Player. Gwendolyn Brooks. LiSp; SD

He learned his place among the weeds. The Birth of a Shark. David Wevill. TwCP

He learned it from Penelope.../Penelope, who really cried. An Ancient Gesture. Edna St. Vincent Millay. NMM

He leaves to room with some old Reverend. Development. D. J. Enright. OBSP

He left behind coins, for his lodging, and traces of/red mud. Mercian Hymns (excerpt). Geoffrey Hill. NoP

He left her on her sick sick bed,/Sheding the saut saut tear. Proud Lady Margaret. Anonymous. ESPB; OxBB

He left me and went in search/of wealth. What She Said. Okkur Macatti. PBWP

...He left no money and no clothes. The Boarder. Frederick Feirstein. NYP

He left not Faction, but of that was left. Zimri. John Dryden. AnFE

He left off living single/And lived with his wife. Jacky Jingle. Anonymous. OxNR

He left the name, at which the world grew pale,/To point a moral, or adorn a tale. Charles XII of Sweden. Samuel Johnson. NOBE; OBEC

He left, to seek the light! She Wandered after Strange Gods... Laura Benet. HBMV

He left us so partisan. The Gentle Snorer. Mona Van Duyn. NePA

He lies down and curls himself around the cottage, listening to the insect/that rubs its wings... A Cottage in the Wood. Russell Edson. LCAP

He lies down in his boots and overcoat,/And shuts his eyes. Darwin in 1881. Gjertrud Schnackenberg. SM

He lifted the tablets up before them saying/The word that gave them all words: Listen. The Eleventh Commandment (excerpt). John Holmes. MoRP

He lifted up the pity of His face. Judgment Day. William Dean Howells. AA

He listens to the shell and says:/"The freeway?" For Richard Chase. Jim Wayne Miller. GOYP

He lived in the odium/Of having discovered sodium. Clerihew. Edmund Clerihew Bentley. NLV

He lived in woods and bowers. The Fairy King. William Allingham. IrPN

He lived outside of books. The Manner of a Poet's Germination. Jose Garcia Villa. PP

He lived to chase the hounds another day. The Fox. John Clare. BoAnP

He lived while waiting but to die. Epitaph. Tristan Corbiere. AWP

He lives, and peace is in His heavenly realm! The Sages. Adam Mickiewicz. CAW

He lives century after century, and the test I set for him he/has passed. The Clouds. Mira Bai [(or Mirabai(]. NU

He lives forever, while his children perish. The Ailing Parent. Lora Dunetz. NePoAm-2

He lives in the heart/Of everyone. A Reply to Nancy Hanks. Julius Silberger. TiPo

He lives the Crusoe of his lonely fields/Which dark green oaks his noontide leisure shields. There Is a Charm in Solitude That Cheers. John Clare. NOBV

He'll aid your reading of Horatius. For Sale, a Horse. Charles Edward Taylor. AA

He'll be a month older when comes next moon. Ringely, Ringely. Eliza Lee Follen. BiCB

"He'll be your man, but he'll not come home." Josie (with music). Anonymous. AS

He'll bid us live forever where pleasure never dies. The Little Family. Anonymous. BaBo; BFSS

He'll come back again/If we are good. Robin Hood. Anonymous. OxNR

He'll come home to rest in England where the golden willows/blow! Saint George of England. Cecily Fox-Smith. BBV

He'll court you and pet you and leave you and go/In the spring up the trail on his bucking bronco. Bucking Bronco. Anonymove. BPAW

He'll face my door and won't come in. Every Night When the Sun Goes In. Anonymous. TrAS

He'll fight, they say, another day,/Who saves himself by running! The Battle of Plattsburg. Anonymous. PAH

...He'll find me still a reed,/Though sighing at his breath, indeed. Variation on a Theme by John Lyly. Sacheverell Sitwell. ViBoPo

He'll forgive this night's tryst with the Widow/Prevost! Aaron Burr's Wooing. Edmund Clarence Stedman. PAH

He'll give His Spirit's grace and power/To fill, to comfort, and direct. Our Times Are in His Hands. Mary D. Freeze. STF

He'll give you what his kind allows,/Cows. Epigram: "I know him." Anonymous. BIrV

He'll go to sleep until/it puts itself right. Cat & the Weather. May Swenson. HAP; WeW

He'll hang himself upon a party line. Frigate Jones, the Pussyfooter. Kenneth Burke. OBAL

He'll hear a sample of my mind, the chief of the Black Tail/Range. The Black Tail Range. Anonymous. CoSo

He'll hide his head under his wing. Little Cock Robin. Anonymous. PBBP

He'll labour night and day/To be a Pilgrim. The Pilgrim's Progress. John Bunyan. EBCP; EBEV; WiR

He'll let me sleep, seeing I fast and pray. The Day Is Gone. John Keats. EnRP

He'll live–to go hunting–/Another fine day. The Hunt. Walter De La Mare. BoAnP

He'll make his gold repeater chime. Mr. Coggs. Edward Verrall Lucas. HBV 1-2; HBVY

He'll never be on the prowl for other women/he has so many at home Wasp Sex Myth (One). Anselm Hollo. PoM

He'll never start. The Kaleidoscope. David Gill. OBTV

He'll not be back any more. Griesly Wife. John Streeter Manifold. ATP; MoBrPo; MoBS

He'll not say a word because he need not, he said so many. Letter for Melville 1951. Charles Olson. CoPo

He'll only be deported. On the Park Bench. Kenneth Slade Alling. NePoAm

He'll plead for me. The All-Sufficient Christ. Bernice W. Lubke. BLRP

"He'll raise up his head and come knock at the door." The Trooper's Horse. Anonymous. OBET

He'll roll me in his Highland plaiddie. My Bonnie Highland Laddie. Robert Burns. UnTE

...He'll run/toward the flamingos in the sun. Boy in the Roman Zoo. Archibald MacLeish. NCSH

He'll see only the back from which he broke,/Bleeding, chilling,/Of the other. The Couple. Ana Blandiana. WPOW

He'll shoot both my young son and me.' The Great Silkie of Sule Skerrie. Anonymous. BuBa; MOS

He'll smile at last/On a golden bed. The Frowning Cliff. Herbert Asquith. BrR

He'll so supply, you'll think you've got your own. Ye Beauties, Beaux, Ye Pleaders at the Bar. Anonymous. FaBoUs

He'll stay right with it/Till it's fixed beyond repair. Handyman. Homer Phillips. QQQ

He'll stop up the chink of the wide Universe. This World and This Life Are So Scattered, They Try Me. Heinrich Heine. ELU

He'll take my two hands in his own, and stoop to kiss my/mouth. My Blessing Be on Waterford. Winifred M. Letts. HBMV

He'll take what he can find. Rue. Anonymous. FSW

He'll tell us/Why/we are. Yesterday. Carol Lee Sanchez. TWSS

He'll think that I'm cute/and a little moon-trap. Honey Moon. Kathleen Leland Baker. NLV

He'll turn a papist, ranker than before. Upon Glass: Epigram. Robert Herrick. JCP

He loans me eyes that look on heaven? Vision. Frank Sidgwick. MMM

He loathed the fraud, yet would not bed alone. Ulysses. Robert Graves. ChMP; CMoP; FaBoTw; NoAm; OxBI; PrIm

He longs to feel his kind of love once more. In Despair. Constantine P. Cavafy. PeHV

He looked at my face but he was looking at my skull. Portrait: The Freedom Fighter. George Jonas. NeAC; NOBC

He looked in the glass/at the bare boughs of his face. At Eighty. Rosamund Stanhope. AMV-80

He looked into himself, and was deceived. King James II. John Dryden. ACP

He looked up and answered, "Why, no'm." Limerick: "There was once a dear little gnome." Carolyn Wells. TDH

He looked upon the twain, like Joseph standing by. O Child of Beauty Rare. Johann Wolfgang von Goethe. ISi

He looks, and she looks forth: there are no other eyes. The Lady with the Unicorn. Vernon Watkins. LiTB; MP; TwCP

He looks as though from his own wings/He hung down crucified. The Eagle. Andrew Young. ELU; PoSH

He looks from his grave for life,and/judgment/Rides over his city like a star. The Angels at Hamburg. Randall Jarrell. AmP

He looks to Heaven, and lulls his cares to rest. The Rising Village. Oliver Goldsmith. NOBC

He, Lord everlasting, Omnipotent God! The Hymn of the World's Creator (excerpt). Caedmon. CAW

He lost, at one fell swoop (or plunge)/His aunt, his honour, and his sponge! The Bath. Harry Graham. CenHV; ShM

He "lost his life"? He found his death. For Any Beachhead. Michael Kennedy Joseph. AnNZ

He lost in errors his vain heart prefers,/She safe in the simplicity of her's. Simple Faith. William Cowper. OBEC

He lost that hope which, having gained,/We too would lose in Thee attained. Plea for Hope. Francis Carlin. TrPWD

He lost/there too. Black Sketches, 8. Don L. Lee. NeAC

He loved America all his life! Washington. Nancy Byrd Turner. SoPo; TiPo; YeAr

He loved, he died. No one knows which came first. A Romance. Chester Kallman. PoA

...He loves/salt, itself. Stony Brook Tavern. J. D. Reed. NeAC

He loves the gain that vanity brings in. Upon Rook: Epigram. Robert Herrick. CaPo

He made a hole in a giant cactus/and put them away, inside. I'd run about. Anonymous. BoWoP

He made ablaze with light my soul of shade! The Dream of Dakiki. Firdausi. WGRP

...He made good sport that night. The General Public. Stephen Vincent Benét. GLGT

He made his love a coffin of the gowd/sae yellow,/And buried his bonnie love doun in a/sea valley. Bonnie Annie (A version). Anonymous. ESPB

He made it in his senses by imagination free. A Man of Sense. Richard Eberhart. MiAP

He made me blest–and broke my heart. No Cold Approach. Robert Burns. EBEV

He made my home till Death should call me thence. The Master of Time. Jan van Nijlen. LiTW

He made not one mistake. He Maketh No Mistake. A. M. Overton. STF

He made our bodies each for each,/Then put your hand into my hand. Magnificat. Arthur Symons. UnTE

He made our Souls to make his Creatures/Higher. Amendment. Thomas Traherne. SeCV 1-2

...He made that craft this art. The Makers. David Galler. NYBP

He made the pencilled map alive with war. Timoshenko. Sidney Keyes. OBWP

He made the world to be a grassy road/Before her wandering feet. The Rose of the World. William Butler Yeats. BoLiVe; BrPo; CMoP; HBV 1-2; MoAB; MoBrPo; OBVV

He made us hear the ranks of shining feet/Treading to glory's throne up Tremont Street. A Revivalist in Boston. Adrienne Rich. EaLo

He makes a mess of me to nourish you,/Then makes a mess of you to nourish me. The Cryptic Streets. Abu-l-Ala al-Maarri. LiTW

He makes a nice dish in this region/To eat in the spring! Mary and the Lamb. Frank Dempster Sherman. InMe

He makes me seem bright by comparison! Limerick: "I'm bored to extinction with Harrison." Anonymous. TDH

He makes the grass the mountains crown/And corn in valleys grow. Edom. Anonymous. AmFP

He makes two not alike, but one. To Chloe, Who Wished Herself Young Enough For Me. William Cartwright. LiTB; LiTL

He mastered men and trees and birds and winds. The Kabbalist. Deborah Eibel. VWA

He may as well deny a world to me. The Author to His Booke. Thomas Heywood. OBS

He may call cousin with the bell of France. Great Tom. Richard Corbet. OxBoLi

He may find a place in God's Paradise. From the Garden of Heaven. Hafiz. LiTW

He may leave you and never return. The Wreck of the Old 97. Anonymous. FSW; ViBoFo

He may, say we, but not well, be a lover. Tell Me No More. William, of Hawthornden Drummond. TrGrPo

He may tell you quite succinctly it is Hell. A Ballad of Abbreviations. Gilbert Keith Chesterton. NOBL

He meade the maidens squeal an' run,/Because 'twer Easter Zunday. Easter Zunday. William Barnes. VLP

He means all to the hearts of men. Star of the Morning. D. V. Johnstone. BePJ

He MEANT them, HOW he meant them–at the time. Epitaph: Lloyd George. Anonymous. FaBoCo

He merely barked: "A lady doll/I found out in the garden!" The Buccaneer. Nancy Byrd Turner. TiPo

He merely mows and leaves no unsightly scars. Old Man with a Mowing Machine. May Carleton Lord. GoYe

He merges awhile into the lie/Of his own silhouette. The Poet in Old Age Fishing at Evening. Desmond O'Grady. CIP

He might happen to take thee for one, my dear. The Young May Moon. Thomas Moore. ELP; EnRP; HBV 1-2; MOON; OAEP; OBEV

He might have passed in July,/And not so cheated!' The Pink Frock. Thomas Hardy. OBSP

...He might/well be a cocker spaniel. P.C. Plod Versus the Dale St. Dog Strangler. Roger McGough. NoAm

He moved the gates of heaven apart/And gave to earth–a Mother! The Gift. Anonymous. PGD

He moves no more   The New Pieta: For the Mothers and Children of Detroit. June Jordan. PoBA

He murmured, "After many days." The Teacher's Dream. William Henry Venable. BeLS

He must be dead first, let' it alone for mee. An Epitaph on Doctor Donne, Deane of Pauls. Elizabeth T. Corbett. AnAnS 2

He must have raised/rare orchids/years ago. Senile. Pat Folk. PCP

He must him seeken esilye/In the bosom of Marye,/For ther he is, forsoothe, pardee! Truth. Anonymous. OxBM

He must stride/Ere he can feed. The Foal. William Renton. NOBV

He must wear a crown of sorrow/Who would be a Son of Man. Young and Radiant, He Is Standing. Allen Eastman Cross. AH

He muttered, "The good Great Spirit loves His white children/best!" The First Thanksgiving Day. Margaret Junkin Preston. MC; PAH

He muttering squats, aloof, forlorn,/Dangling a baitless hook. The Old Angler. Walter De La Mare. OAEP

He names that kidlet after me! The Cowboy and the Stork. Robert V. Carr. BPAW

He ne'er will get translated to the skies. Epitaph on an Engraver. Henry David Thoreau. EyDe

He nearly/touches his shadow. Afternoon, with Just Enough of a Breeze. Robert Sund. BoAnP

He needs me, calls me, loves me: let me go!' Mary Magdalene. Dante Gabriel Rossetti. GoBC; MaVP

He needs no foil, but shines by his own proper light. The Character of a Good Person. John Dryden. NOCV

He needs the earthly city not/Who hath the heavenly found. Norembega. John Greenleaf Whittier. PAH

He never brings them once to th' push of pikes. Good Men Afflicted Most. Robert Herrick. LiTB

He never did that to me. He Never Did That to Me. Noel Coward. NLV

He never gazed on Carcassonne. Carcassonne. Gustave Nadaud. BLPA; FaBoBe; HBV 1-2

He never has been living since. A Guinea-Pig Song. Anonymous. OxBChV

He never responds,/But says "SHIT!".../Without being heard. The Garden Boy. Bonisile Joshua Motaung. WhB

He never saw her from that day. There Lived a Lady in Milan. William Rose Benet. HBMV

He never sent up his address. The Headless Gardener. Ian Serraillier. BoC

He never smiled again! He Never Smiled Again. Felicia Dorothea Hemans. HBV 1-2

He never took toll/Of a mouse in his life. An Old Woman. Anonymous. OxNR

He never was married,/divided or touched. Sum. James Nolan. Str

He never would have waxed in my care   A Poem against Rats. Fred Levinson. AmPA

He now must lead the morris daunce before us. Our Bonny-Boots Could Toot It, Yea and Foot It. Anonymous. NCEP

He now presents as marrons glacees. Ingenious Raconteur. Renee Haynes. PV

He offers us nothing but the vision of the illumination that/he is. Buddha. Theodore Holmes. CoPo

(He once met Morgan Forster)/My contact and my pal. Naturally the Foundation Will Bear Your Expenses. Philip Larkin. FaBoPV

He only craved an understanding friend. The Lonely Dog. Margaret E. Bruner. PoToHe

He only knows his mother–give him back. Motherhood. Josephine Dodge Daskam Bacon. HBV 1-2

He only knows, or haply he may know not. The Rigveda: Hymn of Creation. Anonymous. LiTW

He only let them grow! Old Quin Queeribus. Nancy Byrd Turner. EvOK; SoPo; TiPo

He only once indulged the whim/Of asking Meyer to lunch with him. Lord Lucky. Hilaire Belloc. NLV

He only that no death doth dread/Doth live at rest. Of Fortune. Thomas Kyd. EIL

...He only wishes they would hear him sing. The Airy Christ. Stevie Smith. NOCV

He open'd it: and taking of the cover,/He straight perceav'd himselfe to be my Lover. Sonnets, XI: "Sighing, and sadly sitting by my Love." Richard Barnfield. PeHV

He opened the door and met the young/woman who waited for him. In the Old House. Donald Hall. NePoEA-2

He opens it up with a flick of his tail. From Oddity Land. Edward Anthony. TiPo

He opens suddenly and lets you in. Bert Schultz. Colin Thiele. PoAu 1-2

He or she that loves too long/Sell their freedom for a song. The Indifferent. Francis Beaumont. EIL; EnLit; HBV 1-2

He orders that we keep immaculate. The Easter Song. Caelius Sedulius. OnYI

He owned he was the man that killed poor Oma Wise. Naomi Wise. Anonymous. BaBo

He paddles the canoe-ark with deer and prairie hens/over the rabbiteye and red haw. There Won't Be Another. Diane Glancy. STE

He paints a portrait for a candid future. Portrait in Winter. Katherine Garrison Chapin. GoYe

He paints it once; and paints no more. This Morning Tom Child, the Painter, Died. Samuel Sewall. SCAP

He passes by and I turn round. Epigram: "Even if I try not to ogle a boy in the street." Strato. PeHV

He passeth, and all again for awhile is bright. North Wind in October. Robert Bridges. VLP

He paw his dirt in the heifer's faces,/Long time ago. Hoosen Johnny. Anonymous. AS; FSW He pays the half who does confess the debt. To the Most Virtuous Mistress Pot, Who Many Times Entertained Him. Robert Herrick. CaPo

He pays the whole, and yet am I not free. Sonnets, CXXXIV: "So, now I have confessed that he is thine." William Shakespeare. CBEP; InvP

He peopled it with living beings, that was the/grand, divine, eternal drama. God's Work. Charlotte Cushman. TreFT

He perishes toward Hercules. This Dim and Ptolemaic Man. John Peale Bishop. AmC; CrMA; ImOP; LiTA; LiTM; NePA

He pistis sou sesoke se. Jericho's Blind Beggar. Henry Wadsworth Longfellow. WBLP

He pitied "them that only asked for peace." A Post-Mortem. Siegfried Sassoon. DFF

He placed the jewel in the casket and lay down to sleep. In the Henry James Country. William Abrahams. WaP

He played a tune and he danced it roon'/About the gallows tree. MacPherson's Farewell. Anonymous. FSW

...He played/('Fore Midas,) in the Phrygian shade,/With Pan, and to the Sylvan host. A Vision (excerpt). Bryan Waller Procter. OBRV

He plops at your side/With a mouthful of fish! Seal. William Jay Smith. GrPl; RFM

He ploughed, all glowing, and planted/The apples of her breast. Eve. Robert Leopold Wolf. HBMV

He plunged in,/But never raise again. The Mother's Malison, or, Clyde's Water. Anonymous. ESPB

He points to Marc laughing/At the mud hens, surfacing from underneath the pier. On Visiting My Son, Port Angeles, Washington. Duane Niatum. CDW

He pokes at it obsessively/With the instrument of his chastened line A Younger Poet. Peter Schjeldahl. PoA

...He ponder'd for a while,/Then met his Fanny with a borrow'd smile. Delay Has Danger. George Crabbe. FaBoPP

He pondered; his tears are creeping/Down to the desert still. The Mountain. Mikhail Yuryevich Lermontov. AWP

He popped his head under her wing, and lay/As still as a stone, till King Sun was away. Sir Lark and King Sun: A Parable. George Macdonald. GN; HBV 1-2; HBVY

He pours wine that you'd hate to give Fido. The Antiquary. Martial (Marcus Valerius Martialis). LiTW

He preserved but a burgher at most,/But Lansdown delivered a king. The Shash. Anonymous. APAS

He preses down on my face/Ringing again and again. The Obscene Caller. Cheri Fein. TW

He pricked his fingers very much,/Which made poor Simon whistle. Simple Simon. Anonymous. HBV 1-2

He pried from the insect jaws the bright crumb of steel. Metropolitan Nightmare. Stephen Vincent Benét. ImOP; NYBP

He promised Noah not to flood again. Dissatisfaction with Metaphysics. William Empson. CMoP

He prospered greatly long ago! Beowulf: The Tale of Sigemund. Anonymous. AnOE

He proves, less happy than his favour'd brute,/A life of ease a difficult pursuit. Absence of Occupation. William Cowper. OBEC

He pulls mankind in after him, to die. Jeremiah. Witter ("Emanuel Morgan") Bynner. CrMA

He put on dark glasses. Eclipse. F.R. Scott. WHW

He put our lives so far apart/We cannot hear each other speak. In Memoriam A.H.H., LXXXII. Alfred, Lord Tennyson. LiTB

He put the head upon a swords point,... King Arthur and King Cornwall. Anonymous. ESPB

He puts me to rest. He Puts Me to Rest. David Ignatow. VGW

He puts the mug to his head,/grunts, and drains it clean. A Drink of Milk. John Montague. FaBoIP

He puts them under a microscope and falls asleep counting/them... Counting Sheep. Russell Edson. FiCP; LCAP

He quotes the Scripture and eats hares.' A Case at Sessions. Walter Savage Landor. OBSV

He raised a mortal to the skies;/She drew an angel down. Alexander's Feast. John Dryden. ATP; CEP; CoBE; FiP; GoBC; GTBS; GTBS-P; HBV 1-2; LoBV; NOBE; OAEP; OBS; SeCeV; SeCV 1-2; TrGrPo; WHA

He raised his eyes to follow my progress. We All Have a Bench in the Park to Reach. George Jonas. NeAC

...He reaches for me in his sleep. Bridal Piece. Louise Gluck. SM

He reaches the haven through tears. The Rosary of My Tears. Abram Joseph Ryan. HBV 1-2

He read the other half. Epigram: "Cu Chuimne in youth." Anonymous. BIrV

He really presented a comical sight. Limerick: "Sir Bedivere Bors was a chivalrous knight." Frederick B. Opper. TDH

He reeleth with his own heart,/That great rich Vine. Sunday up the River. James (1834-82) Thomson. ViBoPo

He rehearses steps, soloist in compulsions of a dream. Stanley Matthews. Alan Ross. LiSp; OxBTC

He reigned, is reigning yet; they call His realm/The kingdom of the Truth. The Man Christ. Therese Lindsey. BePJ; TRV

He reigns not but by her preserving voice. On Leaving Holland (excerpt). Mark Akenside. OBTV

He relinquished his hold/At the faraway call/Of a downstairs voice. True to a Dream. Donald Petersen. NePoEA-2

He relives again the day he died... The Fire Burns Low. John Leax. TrCP

He replied, "But the day was so rainy." Limerick: "There was a young man of Fort Blainy." Anonymous. LiBL

He replied, "But, you see, it's my hobby." Limerick: "A certain young fellow, named Bobbie." Anonymous. LiBL

He rests, he is quiet, he sleeps in a strange land. Memorial Rain. Archibald MacLeish. BoLiVe; CMoP; LiTA; MoAB; MoAmPo; NoAm

He rewarded me with a box of yodel spume/& a ride on his sunset machine. A Chasm. Michael Silverton. PV

He rises with the Crown! Stonewall Jackson. Henry Lynden Flash. AA; PAH

He rode contented through a summer idyll. Pastoral. Gavin Ewart. OxBC

& He rolls/up his/sleeves Ray Charles. Sam Cornish. CNA

He rose again behind the stone. Easter Night. Alice Meynell. BrRo; OHIP

He rose, and crawled away into the night. Between the Lines. Wilfred Wilson Gibson. MCCG

He rose. There are things men can never slay. Madonna of the Exiles. James Edward Tobin. ISi

...He rose upward like a stone. Two Birds. Kathleen Linnell. AMV-81

He rubbed his eyes again and went to sleep. Little Boy Blue. John Crowe Ransom. LiTM

He rules today with great renown/The Kingdom of the Spirit! The Lord of Heaven to Earth Came Down. Kathryn Blackburn Peck. BePJ

He runs Fur-bear-ance in the ground. Child's Natural History. Oliver Herford. HBV 1-2

He runs like the rough satyr Sun./Come away! Country Dance. Edith Sitwell. NoAm

He runs up the bank–and away he goes! Antelope. William Jay Smith. TiPo

He runs with all his mane.   The lion is a beast to fight.   Sir Arthur Thomas ("Q") Quiller-Couch.   CenHV

He rush'd into the field, and, foremost fighting, fell.   Childe Harold's Pilgrimage: Canto III, XXIII.   George Gordon, Lord Byron.   AnFE

He's a bit thick–not a high-flyer–/but he'll do the trick.   And Where Do You Stand on the National Question?   Tom Paulin.   FaBoIP

He's a-choppin in de new groun',/Great Godamighty.   Great Godamighty.   *Anonymous.*   ABF

"He's a clever versifier."   The Curse of Faint Praise.   Irwin Edman.   InMe

He's a dancer too.   Nowhere, Not among the Warriors at Their Festival.   Atimantiyar.   WPOW

He's a fool for not joining the union.   He's a Fool.   *Anonymous.*   FSW

He's a Gold Pencil tipt with Lead.   Verses Wrote in a Lady's Ivory Table-Book.   Jonathan Swift.   NCEP

He's a high-faluting, scooting,/shooting son-of-a-gun from Arizona,/Ragtime Cowboy Joe.   Rag Time Cowboy Joe.   Lewis F. and Grant Clarke Muir.   FSW

He's a loyal Ribbon man,/Says the Shan Van Vocht.   The Shan Van Vocht.   *Anonymous.*   AnIL; AnIV; FaBoPV; FSW; GBP; NOBI; OnYI; OxBoLi

He's a man who won't fit in.   The Men That Don't Fit In.   Robert W. Service.   BLPA; BLPL

He's a Moppsikon Floppsikon Bear!'   Limerick: "There was an Old Person of Ware."   Edward Lear.   CenHV; LiBL; NA; PoPl

He's a no good weed/swear he done me wrong   Stepfather Blues.   Big Joe Williams.   BluL

He's a rider but he'll leave that rail some time.   Pay Day at Coal Creek.   *Anonymous.*   FSW; OuSiCo

He's a Whigg that will not follow.   A Carrouse to the Emperor, the Royal Pole...   *Anonymous.*   CoMu

He's a young sailor cut down in his prime.   The Young Sailor Cut down in His Prime.   Anonymous.   OBSS

He's allus the first aboard her when the lifeboat wants a crew.   The Lifeboat.   George R. Sims.   PaPo

He's always glad to stop his work/And come and talk to me.   The Hired Man's Way.   John Kendrick Bangs.   OBCA

He's been there many times before.   My Friend.   Marjorie Lorene Buster.   STF

He's bound for the Frankfort Jail.   Frank James, the Roving Gambler.   *Anonymous.*   AmFP

He's broken his leg in trying to spell/Tommy without a T.   Poor Dear Grandpapa.   D'Arcy Wentworth Thompson.   NA

He's Christian enough that repents, and that stitches.   The Candidate.   Thomas Gray.   PPP

"He 's come! The Saviour has come!"   He's Come! The Saviour Has Come!   Alice Mortenson.   BePJ

He's danc'd awa' wi' the Exciseman.   The Exciseman.   Robert Burns.   GoTS

He's eat till his pants won't button at all./Ground hog.   Ground Hog.   *Anonymous.*   TrAS

He's fair to look on as the rose/And gentle as a kitzen.   The Ovibos.   Robert Beverly Hale.   FiBHP

He's forgot that he's the man who feeds them all.   The Farmer Is the Man.   *Anonymous.*   FSW

He's gard him leave a better pledge,/Four fingers o his right han.   Brown Adam (A version).   *Anonymous.*   ESPB

He's going to marry Mary Ann!   Mary Ann.   Joseph Tabrar.   PV

He's gone a long, old time.   White House Blues.   *Anonymous.*   FSW; OuSiCo

He's gone John,/He's long gone.   Long Gone.   *Anonymous.*   ABF

He's gone to Heaven–because he lived so well/That many a wretch through him has gone to hell.   An Epitaph.   William Henry Davies.   ChMP

He's gone: up bubbles all his amorous breath!   On an Engraved Gem of Leander.   John Keats.   CBEP

He's got roots and herbs/steals a woman, man, every where he land   Snake Doctor Blues.   J. D. (Jelly Jaw) Short.   BluL

He's got the whole world in His hands.   He's Got the Whole World in His Hands.   *Anonymous.*   BLSo; FSW

He's got to go there by himself.   Lonesome Valley.   *Anonymous.*   FSW

He's greedy of his life who will not fall,/Whenas a public ruin bears down all.   To His Book.   Robert Herrick.   CaPo; FaBoUs

He's gwyne to git his.   Doan't You Be What You Ain't.   Edwin Milton Royle.   BLPA

He's haild her lady of Douglassdale,/Himsel the lord within.   Willie O Douglas Dale.   *Anonymous.*   BaBo; ESPB

He's just as good as free.   Initials.   Michael S. Glaser.   AMV-81

...He's just like his father   Dear Mother.   Emmett Jarrett.   NeAC

He's just like rock of Gibraltar.   Limerick: "A canny old codger at Yalta."   Anonymous.   LiBL

He's laying her dust, for fear of it rising.   Peter's Tears.   Thomas Hood.   GoTF; TreFT

He's left his home to return no more.   Lady Franklin's Lament (I).   Anonymous.   OBSS; ShS

He's lighted down at Ararat,/And there he's made his hame.   Ballad of the Flood.   Edwin Muir.   MoBS

...He's like the stupid swain/Who seeks the lamb his bosom hides.   Ritual Not Religion.   Telugu E. Indian.   WGRP

He's long gone, He's long gone John.   Long John.   *Anonymous.*   FSW

He's more contented in the zoo.   The Miscegenous Zebra.   Roland Young.   BoAnP

...He's/most definitely/(my father's died)/against parting.   Against Parting.   Natan Zach.   VWA

He's mourning for his own true love/Just like I mourn for mine.   George Collins.   *Anonymous.*   FSW

He's my Christ forever more!   The Ageless Christ.   B. L. Byer.   BePJ

He's my love fro evermair/Bonny Bobby Shaftoe.   Bobby Shaftoe's Gone to Sea.   Mother Goose.   BrR; HBV 1-2

He's never spry–/Don't ask me why.   The Newt.   David McCord.   TiPo

He's not one jot better than monsieur Pantin.   The Lady's Receipt for a Beau's Dress.   *Anonymous.*   CoMu

He's not the only one to feel that way.   Courthouse Square.   Herbert Merrill.   AmFN

"He's not there, He's not there."/Goodbye, Johnny.   Benign Neglect/Mississippi, 1970.   Primus St. John.   PoBA

He's out in the meadows/And milking his cows.   The Milkman.   Seumas (James Starkey) O'Sullivan.   SUS

He's proud of being short and stout.   Teddy Bear.   A.(lan) A.(lexander) Milne.   OnUR

He's publishing a book next May/On "How to Make Bee-keeping Pay'.   Opportunity.   Harry Graham.   DTC; FaBoCo

He's quaffing in a world of spirits.   Original Epitaph on a Drunkard.   Royall Tyler.   OBAL

"He's really nicer than he seems."   Little Willie.   *Anonymous.*   ShM

He's resigned, and when you hit him/he lets you hit him twice.   Willy Wet-Leg.   D. H. Lawrence.   CMoP; TW

He's set about building something in his barn/and it's big.   The Neighbor.   Miller Williams.   GP

He's so scared his buttocks quake.   Hitler, Frothy-Mouth.   *Anonymous.*   WTO

He's standin' there out in the air,/A promissory chicken.   Gettin' Born.   Anthony Euwer.   PoPl

He's taen his lady, and he's gaen hame,/An noo he's king ower a' his ain.   King Orfeo.   *Anonymous.*   BuBa; ESPB; OxBB; OxBoLi

He's taken out his wee pen-knife,/And he's twyned himsel o his ain sweet life.   The Bonnie Banks O Fordie (A vers.).   *Anonymous.*   BaBo; BuBa

He's the Earl of Fitzdotterel's eldest son.   My Lord Tomnoddy.   Robert Barnabas Brough.   FiBHP; VLP

He's the figure in the carpet.   The Figure in the Carpet.   James Camp.   TW

...He's the guest/of my knowing, though not asked.   The Guest.   Wendell Berry.   AP

He's the man-eating shark/Who will eat neither woman nor child.   The Chivalrous Shark.   *Anonymous.*   FSW

He's the spit of his da in every feature...   The Midnight Court.   Bryan Merryman.   OBVE

He's the very Lord of glory/Who has risen up today!   Alleluia! Alleluia! Let the Holy Anthem Rise.   *Anonymous.*   PoSC

He's thinking more of shortening sail than striking the bell.   Strike the Bell.   Anonymous.   OBSS

He's weary o' the thrusting of it.   The Thrusting of It.   Robert Burns.   UnTE

He's won the heart and got the hand o' Kate Dalrymple.   Kate Dalrymple.   *Anonymous.*   GBP

He said, "Darling, I pay through the nose."   Limerick: "There was a young man of Montrose."   Arnold Bennett.   CenHV; FaBoNo; OxBoLi

He said, "Don't call me sir, call me modom."   Limerick: "There was a young Fellow of Wadham."   Anonymous.   NOBL

He said, "Don't stand in the chill."   Hands Clenched under My Shawl...   Anna Akhmatova.   PBWP

He said for me to run along/And not to bother him any more.   Horse.   Elizabeth Madox Roberts.   PH; TiPo

He said he didn't want to go alone   The Shooting.   Laura Tohe.   STE

He said he supposed 'twas the cat.   Limerick: "N is for naughty young Nat."   Isabel Frances Bellows.   TDH

He said he was drinking too much.   The Corrupt Man in the French Pub.   Brian Higgins.   OxBTC

He said it like goodbye.   Angle of Vision.   Martha Bosworth.   AMV-80

He said looking back/back/at beauty.   The Women in Vietnam.   Grace Paley.   NMM

He said: "My dear friend, I beg pawarden!"   Limerick: "A very polite man named Hawarden."   *Anonymous.*   TDH

...He said, Now.   First Practice.   Gary Gildner.   AmPA; InPK; LiSp; Psk; TW

He said: "O God, my world in Thee!"   World's Worth.   Dante Gabriel Rossetti.   GoBC; VLP

He said: Oh;/I thought I'd like to know;/but I can't wait.   Odiham.   John Gray.   FaBoCo

He said, "Put it together; the world's like that too."   Jigsaw Puzzle.   Russell Hoban.   NTCP

He said, "son you look like me,/please be a man like me."   Midwife.   Earl Gene Box.   LFAC

He said there is no man with the law in his hand/Can take Jesse James when alive.   Jesse James.   *Anonymous.*   AmFP

He said you brute, I'll never go out mending any more.   The Cunning Cobbler Done Over.   *Anonymous.*   CoMu

He said, "You're too late, ma, I am!"   Limerick: "There was a young hopeful named Sam."   Elizabeth Ripley.   TDH

He sall at my agane cumyng/Mak homage and oblissing,/I mak myne avow!'   Golagros and Gawane (excerpt).   Anonymous.   OxBS

He sang a Freedom Song, hanging from a limb.   The Flood Viewed by the Tourist from Iowa.   James Whitehead.   SM

He sang the Song of the Sheet.   Song of the Sheet (parody).   *Anonymous.*   BXAP

He sang to himself and I still remember the tune.   Greystone Cottage.   Richard Hugo.   NPAW

He sank in those white arms of guile/To seek the false moon in the sea.   True and False.   Isabella Valancy Crawford.   PeCV

He sank into his sister's arms,/And they died as white as snaw.   The King's Dochter Lady Jean.   Anonymous.   ESPB

He sat in a chair,/And gave all the people a nod.   Docteur Foster.   *Anonymous.*   OxNR

He sat quiet as a mouse.   Henry Adams.   W. H. Auden.   OBAL

He saw a place green as welcome/on whose still water the sky lay white.   Inland Passages, I: The Long Hunter.   Wendell Berry.   GP

He saw Flame/he saw flame.   Paradise.   Willis Barnstone.   VWA

He saw heaven fall and the world end,/O God, how long ago!   The Ballad of the White Horse.   Gilbert Keith Chesterton.   ACP

He saw the giant sea above his head.   Endymion, II.   John Keats.   EnRP

He saw the lord of all His creatures/stand.   The Created.   Jones Very.   AmP; MAmP; NOCV; QFR

He saw the peak which he had trod/with the Angelus was grown/innocent, and stood alone   On a Ledge.   William Bell.   PoSH

He say if I just stay out of the grave/Old John I see you won't go to the pen   Lawyer Clark Blues.   Sleepy John Estes.   BluL

He says again, "Good fences make good neighbors."   Mending Wall.   Robert Frost.   AmFN; AnNE; AP; CMoP; CoBMV; DiPo; ExPo; FaBoPV; FaBV; FaFP; FPL; HAP; HBV 1-2; HeIP; HoPM; InPK; InPo; InPS; LaNeLa; LiTA; LiTM; MCCG; MoAB; MoAmPo; MoVE; NePA; NoAm; NOBA; NoP; OHFP; OxBA; PAI; PrIm; SCV; SeCeV; SoSe; TAP; VGW; ViBoPo; WHA

He says, "An' now I got-n my way,/I'll tear the buildin' down."   Samson.   *Anonymous.*   OuSiCo

He says confusing tender words/to the beasts,/The mutilated Soldier.   The Mutilated Soldier.   David Fisher.   NPGG

He says, How do you do?   Manners.   Mariana Griswold Van Rensselaer.   HBMV; HBVY

He scarce could stand on any ground,/He was so full of mettle.   Pigwiggin Arms Himself.   Michael Drayton.   MoShBr

He scarcely saw the play at all/For watching his reaction to it.   Critic.   E. B. White.   NLV

He scattered the enemy/he struck the nations.   Battle Songs of the King Tshaka.   *Anonymous.*   PeSA

He scornes them now, but o they'l sute full well/With th'Purple hee must weare in Hell.   Upon Lazarus His Teres.   Richard Crashaw.   SeCV 1-2

He scorneth once to shrink or start for any stormy wind.   The Jovial Marriner; or, The Sea-Man's Renown.   John Playford.   CoMu

He screams the silent screams.   But, Still, He.   Henry N. Lucas.   AMV-81

He searched, but never searched his heart.   His Quest.   Lewis Frank Tooker.   AA

He seeks a hill where living day shall stand.   With Hands Like Leaves.   James Still.   GrPl

He seeks them headlong, and is seen no/more.   The Task.   William Cowper.   CoBE

He seeks with holy love to lure/The wanderer 'neath His wing.   The Unerring Guide.   Anna Shipton.   BLRP

He seemed bored by our/questions, interested/more in our women.   Great Man.   B. S. Johnson.   ELU

He seems alone up there, but he is warm.   Beside the Sea.   George Johnston.   ACV

...He seems content/to warm himself on my cold thighs.   Cats and Egypt.   Andrew Hughes.   AMV-81

He seems odd in the forest.   The King of Sunshine.   Michael Silverton.   PV

He sees, He hears, and from on high/Will make our cause His care.   All Our Griefs to Tell.   John Newton.   BePJ

He sees through stone.   He Sees Through Stone.   Etheridge Knight.   BALP; ConAP; LFAC; NBP; NNaP

He sees what Children dwell in Love,/And marks them for his own.   Against Quarrelling and Fighting.   Isaac Watts.   OBEC; OxBChV; SeCcPo

He seldom hears/my voice at all.   Listening.   Aileen Fisher.   NTCP

He sends us clothed about with wings,/And finds them ragged babes that weep!   The Children of the Poor.   Victor Hugo.   LiTW

He sends us, stripped and naked, to the grave.   Ambition.   Nathaniel Parker Willis.   OBCA

He sent him home again!   Exile.   Virna Sheard.   PeCV

He served his kind by Word and Deed,/In God's grand greenwood chapel.   Johnny Appleseed.   William Henry Venable.   PAH

He serves all who dares be true.   Love's Nobility.   Ralph Waldo Emerson.   GoTF; TreF

He set her on her steede, and forward forth/did beare.   The Faerie Queene.   Edmund Spenser.   OAEP

He set them all a-laughing,/Ha, ha, ha!   Willy, Willy Wilkin.   *Anonymous.*   OxNR

He sets the wave afire and still is cold.   The Goldfish.   Audrey Alexandra Brown.   CaP

He settled down/Again to sleep.   The Wonder Clock.   Katharine Pyle.   OBCA

He shall dig Gravel next Horn-Fair/and that he is like to do.   The Scolding Wives Vindication.   Anonymous.   CoMu

He shall have nothing but mustard.   When Jacky's a Very Good Boy.   Mother Goose.   BrR; EvOK

He shall most utterly abase,/And set a desert in their place.   A Ballad of London.   Richard Le Gallienne.   FaBoPP

He shall not blind his soul with clay.   The Princess.   Alfred, Lord Tennyson.   PGD

He shaped a kiss: all day she smiled.   Apocrypha.   Babette Deutsch.   HBMV

He sheds the roughness, lays it by,/And boldly plows his day there.   The Plowman.   Robert Burns.   UnTE

He shelled out his soul/Which flew to God.   On Samuel Pease.   *Anonymous.*   ShM

He shifted his trumpet, and only took snuff.   Retaliation.   Oliver Goldsmith.   CEP; DBV; FaBoPV; LaA; NOBI; NOEC; OxBoLi

He shone wi' gold aboon them a',/And the bride frae the bridegroom's stown awa'.   Hynd Horn.   *Anonymous.*   BuBa; GN; OxBB

He shook himself. Must breed, drink, rot with motion.   Tales of the Islands, VII.   Derek Walcott.   OxBTC

He shook his head/And shook his fist.   Building Bridges.   Solomon Mahaka.   WhB

He shot an otter because he had a gun.   The Shooting.   Robert Pack.   CoPo

He shot and killed me and now I am gone.   Molly Bawn.   *Anonymous.*   BaBo

He shot me and killed me. My name's Molly Ban.   Shooting of His Dear.   *Anonymous.*   OxBoLi

He should be glad they did not wring his neck.   Who Killed Lawless Lean?   Stevie Smith.   TEP

He should from her full lips derive/Honey enough to fill his hive.   The Captived Bee; or, The Little Filcher.   Robert Herrick.   CaPo

He should, he could, he would, he did the best.   Look Home.   Robert Southwell.   NOCV

He should just face the facts/and get his ass home.   Saturday Afternoon at the Movies.   John Logan.   NNaP

He should learn to drink cider and/brandy.   The Man in the Moon.   *Anonymous.*   OxNR

He should not continue in this stay,/But sink away.   Old Furniture.   Thomas Hardy.   MoVE; OxBTC

...He shows no interest in flying.   Letter to a Friend in an Unknown Place.   Anita Barrows.   NMM

He shrugs, and turns away from me.   An Israeli Soldier's Nightmare.   Alison B. Carb.   AMV-80

He shyly turns and shields his eyes/And, smiling, gives his blessing.   Wedding Song.   Johann Wolfgang von Goethe.   HW

He sigh'd and expired at the oar.   The Galley Slave (excerpt).   *Anonymous.*   PeD

He signd a bond o unity,/And visits now they pay.   The Earl of Mar's Daughter.   *Anonymous.*   BaBo; ESPB

He sings in his cracked voice and we/are all laughter.   Oblique Birth Poem.   Ann Darr.   GP

He sits upon the throne of hearts!   The King of Kings.   Lon Woodrum.   BePJ

He sleeps. In his right side are two red holes.   Eighteen-Seventy.   Arthur Rimbaud.   OBWP

He sleeps in the place of the name/As it was doomed to be.   Ticonderoga: A Legend of the West Highlands.   Robert Louis Stevenson.   OBNV

He sleeps late, days before Christmas.   Tenant Farmer.   Robert Ward.   AMV-81

...He sleeps less tremulous, less cold/Than we who must awake, and waking, say Alas!   Asleep.   Wilfred Owen.   MMM

He sleeps like fair Endymion. The Poet. Joel Benton. WGRP

He sleeps the faster that he wept before. Comfort. Elizabeth Barrett Browning. HBV 1-2; TRV

He slept like a rock or a man that's dead. The Weary Blues. Langston Hughes. BALP; FaBV; NoAm; NOBA; NoP; PoNe; UnS

He slept without a shirt on. Old Boniface. *Anonymous.* OxNR

He slipped away like one who went/To a lovers' rendezvous. The Last Trail. Stanton A. Coblentz. BPAW

He slips the mooring of his consciousness. Over Bright Summer Seas. Robert Hillyer. NYBP

He slouches down the centuries. The Australian. Arthur H. Adams. PoAu 1-2

He slowly went off for to cool. Collusion between a Alegaiter and a Water-Snaik. J. W. Morris. NA

He smarteth most that hides his smart,/And sues for no compassion. The Silent Lover. Sir Walter Ralegh. EIL; PG; ViBoPo

He smashed all the glass in the room. (Bill: $50.) Delirium in Vera Cruz. Malcolm Lowry. FaBoTw; OxBTC

He smil'd to see his merry young men/Had gotten a taste of the tree. Robin Hood and the Beggar. *Anonymous.* BaBo; ESPB

He smiled: "Abide in me." Concerning Them That Are Asleep. Rossiter Worthington Raymond. STF

He smiled as one who vanquisheth. The Two Lovers. Richard Hovey. HBV 1-2

He smiled, expecting wings of liberty. The Man Who Wanted to be a Seagull. J. R. Hervey. AnNZ

He smiles and looks gay. The Description of a Good Boy. Henry Dixon. OxBChV

He smiles at the prize: it sparkles: junk. Junk. William Zaranka. AMV-80

He smiles, of course–but oh, the rude/Remarks that cross his mind! The Lesser Lynx. Emile Victor Rieu. CenHV; FiBHP

He smiles with his father's hesitant smile/And speaks with his voice. For a Father. Anthony Cronin. FaBoTw

He snarls, and mews, and flies. My Catbird. William Henry Venable. AA; HBV 1-2

He snatched a remnant flying into light/And strewed it with the stars, and called it Night. He Made the Night. Lloyd Mifflin. HBV 1-2

He sneak'd to Hell without 'em. Epigram on Lord Chesterfield and His Son. *Anonymous.* FaBoCo

He snores in his sleep and rubs his nose. The Jolly Woodchuck. Dorothy and Marion Edey Grider. TiPo

He sometimes dreamed of losing. The Fisherman. Will Wells. AMV-80

...He sought a shorter path/To distant Ind, and here he found–a world. The Discoverer. Arthur Gordon Field. PGD

He spits his apple out and shoots himself in the mouth with his/finger. Blossom. Stanley Plumly. GeTw

...He split/the lying Hare's lip to this day. How Death Came. *Anonymous.* PeSA; TTY

He spoke. And drank rapidly a glass of water. Next to of Course God America I. Edward Estlin Cummings. AmFN; AmP; AnNE; BiP; ExPo; FaBoPV; InPo; LiTM; NCSH; NePA; NLV; NoP; OBWP; OFD; OxBA; TAP; VGW; WaaP; YaD

He spoke, and shouting held on in the foremost his single-foot/horses. The Iliad. Homer. NAWM 1-2

He squalls patrician goddamits from the magnolia. Starlings. Ted Olson. PV

He squoffled once, he squirled, and then/He wrote what's writ above. The Cruise of the P.C. *Anonymous.* NA

He stalls above me like an elephant. To Speak of Woe That Is in Marriage. Robert Lowell. CAPP; NoAm

He standeth ever at thy side,/And ever brings relief. Fear Not, Poor Weary One. Thomas Cogswell Upham. AH

He stands/gleaming on the world/with his drums A Portrait of Rudy. Jim Cunningham. CNA

He stands, who was my future, claiming me. The Mirror. Edgar Bowers. QFR

...He stared/beyond the serpent in the apple tree/to the round sweet dangerous apple. Family. Norman MacCaig. FF

He still called me Annie Mexico. My Mother Shoots the Breeze (excerpt). Fred Chappell. NLV

He still has two more serves– The Midnight Tennis Match. Thomas Lux. AmPA

He still may leave thy garland green. Love and Friendship. Emily Bronte. VLP

He still must love that pensive melody. Sonnet: "If I might choose where my tired limbs shall lie." John Anster. IrPN

He still sees the green-richness of Ben More/rooted in the seas. Island of Mull. *Anonymous.* PoSH

He still shall live, shall live as long/–As ever dead man did. A Great Man. Oliver Goldsmith. NA

He still wore the Holland handkerchief/Around his head. The Suffolk Miracle (B vers.). *Anonymous.* BaBo

He still would be a distant stranger/And not the Baby in the manger. Advent 1955. Sir John Betjeman. OBCP

He stirs the dust where the feet of my dreams had passed. The Rat. Arthur Symons. SyP

He stole my locket,/my heart as well! The Robber. Ivy O. Eastwick. SiSoSe

He stood and they bound him foot and hand/To the cross of a rifle sight. Down in Dallas. X. J. Kennedy. CoPo; FF; OFD

He stood entranced, enchained by her/Full-breasted loveliness. The Fisher. Roderic Quinn. BoAV; CBAP; PoAu 1-2

He stood in his/Shoes and he wonder'd. A Song About Myself, st. 4. John Keats. CoBE; DiPo; FaBoCh; InvP; PoEL 1-5; PP

He stood there, without a railing, owner of pain. Silent. Christ's Descent into Hell. Rainer Maria Rilke. Prf

He stops suddenly/to hear the black water. The Child. Donald Hall. NCSH; NePoEA-2

He strains his cripped knees, and struts along. The Old General. Sir Charles Hanbury Williams. OBEC

He strong as Jove, she like Alcmena fair! To a Friend on His Nuptials. Matthew Prior. HW

He suddenly seems young, the water old. Old Triton Time. Vernon Watkins. OBSP

He suffered–God alone knows it–/In secret–revealed it no none. Epitaph. Sholom Aleichem. TrJP

He summons back the light! Chanticleer. Katharine Tynan. HBV 1-2; HBVY; TiPo

He supped it all. Greedy Tom. *Anonymous.* OxNR

He suppose to die. War. William Alfred, Jr. McLean. BOLo

He surely knows–or maybe He does not! The Vedic Hymns: The Song of Creation. Anonymous. ILwL

He surpasses all, as the poets of Lesbos/Surpass the poets of other lands. The Bridegroom Is So Tall. Sappho. HW

He swallows his own face in half a second! My Garden. William Henry Davies. BoNaP

He swole to be a Lord: and then he burst. In Gaetam. Thomas Bastard. FaBoEE

He swore by the rood that he had not lied. A Conquest. Walter Herries Pollock. OBVV

He swore she could do more work in a day/Than he could do in seven. The Old Man Who Lived in the Woods. *Anonymous.* OnUR

...He takes/A secret wound out of the world. The Mud Turtle. Howard Nemerov. NYBP

He takes it with brandy, and thinks it no sin./Oh, Punkydoodle and Jollapin! Punkydoodle and Jollapin. Laura E. Richards. OBCA

...He takes/the old man's detonation device. He has a big plan. TV Blooper Spotter. Jack Skelley. APU

He taketh his leve and goth away,/Exibit tunc de patria. The Boar's Head. *Anonymous.* MeEL; MeEV; OxBM

He taught no more, I held him fast,/And killed him wiz a rough. O-U-G-H. Charles Battell Loomis. NLV

He taxed him ten dollars and costs, just the same. At Cheyenne. Eugene Field. BPAW

He tears the stocking from his head/& is the girl of your dreams. The Man. Michael Dennis Browne. GP

He that departs with his owne honesty/For vulgar praise, doth it too dearely buy. To My Booke. Ben Jonson. AnAnS 2; OAEP; SeCV 1-2

He that died at Azan gave/This to those who made his grave. After Death in Arabia. Sir Edwin Arnold. HBV 1-2; WGRP

He that doth not, his error is as great/As who by clyster gave the stomach eat. Love's Progress. John Donne. LiTB; ViBoPo

He that had hid the gold and found it not,/Of that he found he shaped his neck a knot. For shamefast harm of great and hateful need. Sir Thomas Wyatt. FCP

He that is crownit abone the sky/Pro nobis Puer natus est! On the Nativity of Christ. William Dunbar. OBEV; OxBoCh

He that is far from me is far from the Kingdom. He That Is Near Me Is Near the Fire. Origen. TRV

He that lies in the middle/Shall have a gold fiddle. Rock, Ball, Fiddle. *Anonymous.* CBEP; OxBoLi

He that made bellows, could not make breath. The Bellows Maker of Oxford. John Hoskyns. FaBoEE

He that parteth from you never/Shall enjoy a spring for ever. A Welcome. William Browne. HBV 1-2; LiTL; OBEV

He that so much for you did do,/Will do yet more, and care for you. Casting All Your Care upon God, for He Careth for You. Thomas Washbourne. OxBoCh

...He/That wants himself, is poor indeed. The Grasshopper. Richard Lovelace. MeLP; SeCePo; SeCV 1-2

He that wealth and power craves,/Shall become a slave of slaves. Freedom. Abraham Ibn Ezra. TrJP

He that will fetch it, let him take it!'   The Melancholy Knight: Sir Eglamour. Samuel Rowlands.   ElL

He that will never thrive/May lie till eleven.   He That Would Thrive. *Anonymous.*   HBV 1-2; HBVY; OxNR

He the Eternal appeared.   Love's Vision.   Edward Carpenter.   WGRP

He then asks money for the time/It took to perpetrate the crime.   The Artist. Sir Walter Ralegh.   DBV

...He then flew into his friend's apartment/through the willingly open window. Poems, VII.   Philip O'Connor.   EAS

He then set her behind her love,/And they went singing hame.   The Bent Sae Brown.   *Anonymous.*   ESPB

–He then unties the string.   Warning to Children.   Robert Graves. FaBoCh; FaFP; LoGBV; NoP; OAEL 1-2; SO

He, there, me, here.   God, Is, Like, Scissors.   Jose Garcia Villa.   EaLo

He thinks, poor cuckold, that he bears the rule,/When heaven knows I do but gull the fool.   Dialogue between a Squeamish Cotting Mechanic and his Sluttish Wife...   Edward Ward.   NOEC

He thinks the rain begun,/And hastes to sheltering bowers.   Summer Images. John Clare.   CBEP; EG; OBNC; OBRV

He thinks too much: such men are dangerous.   Julius Caesar.   William Shakespeare.   TreFS

He thinks with mild surprise that it is true.   Five Domestic Interiors. Vernon Scannell.   OxBC

He thought a thimble/Was the phallic symbol.   Diodorus Siculus. *Anonymous.*   ErPo

He thought I thought he thought I slept.'   The Kiss.   Coventry Patmore. ALV; BoLoP; EnLoPo; FiBHP; LiTL; NOBV; OBVV; PoPle

He thought, ringing the bell for more of both.   The Evans Country. Kingsley Amis.   NOBL

He threw some dirt o'er her and turned to go home,/The birds to weep, nobody to mourn.   Pretty Molly.   *Anonymous.*   BFSS

He threw the baboon heels over head,/And there he stuck tight in the mire, -ire, -ire...   Lord Lovel (parody).   *Anonymous.*   ViBoFo

He through simple faith will show you/Bright and clear, the harbor light. The Pilot.   Anonymous.   STF

He thrust it through and through his heart,/And word spak never more.   The Lass of Lochroyan.   *Anonymous.*   HBV 1-2

...He/told it like it/was...   Langston.   Mari E. Evans.   BOLo; CNA

He told that story well.   Stratagem.   Allen Curnow.   AnNZ

He told where all the running water goes,/And dressed me gently in my little clothes.   The Boat.   Robert Pack.   CoAP; NePoEA-2; SM

He too, at last, became no more than goat.   Castaway.   John Nerber.   PoA

He too had tears for all souls in trouble/Here and in Hell.   The Nameless One.   James Clarence Mangan.   ACP; BIrV; EnRP; GoBC; HBV 1-2; IrPN; NBM; NOBI; OBEV; OBVV; OnYI; OxBI

He, too, is a king/To whom God giveth song.   A Crowned Poet.   Anne Reeve Aldrich.   AA

He too lowered the shutter and locked the door,/and with all those who prayed, I went home.   On the Day of Atonement.   Yehuda Amichai. VWA

He, too, must close his youthful life, and slumber with the dead."]   Mary Wyatt and Henry Green.   *Anonymous.*   AmFP

He, too, will find he is undone,/And that she was not made for one.   Fair, and Soft, and Gay, and Young.   Robert Gould.   UnTE

He took a ruler in his hand,/And struck the white dove dead.   The Dove. Victor J. Daley.   NOAV

He took his father's silver spoons,/And after that he took his leave.   What He Took.   *Anonymous.*   CoMu

He took her with a sigh.   Never Seek to Tell Thy Love.   William Blake. ChRP; ELP; EnLoPo; FaBV; InPS; LiTL; NOBE; OAEP; OBEC; OBNC; PAI; PoEL 1-5; PoPle; TreFT; ViBoPo

He took in thought the course Athena gave him.   The Odyssey.   Homer. NAWM 1-2

He took no apples off, yet left no apples on it.   Riddle: "There was a man who had no eyes."   *Anonymous.*   OxNR

He took two steps, he took two steps,/past the sociologist.   At the Klamath Berry Festival.   William Stafford.   InPK

He tosses high the spray and leaves/The other boats behind.   Boats. Rowena Bastin Bennett.   SoPo; TiPo

He travels the fastest who travels alone!   The Winners.   Rudyard Kipling. BLPA; FaPoR; FPL

He treads the kindly furrow, nor turns his head.   The Sower.   Laurence Binyon.   MMM

He tries in vain his oath to keep by ent'ring Table Bay!   The Flying Dutchman.   *Anonymous.*   OBSS; ShS

He tucked a shrewd hand in his miser's vest.   Vignette: 1922.   Lawrence P. Spingarn.   AMV-81

He tumbled down into the dark/A hundred towns or more.   The Portrait of a Florentine Lady.   Lizette Woodworth Reese.   HBMV

He turned, and vanished in the bright'ning dell.   Ode: "To orisons, the midnight bell."   William Beckford.   OBTV

He turned him homeward sick and slow.   Tragedy.   George William Russell. MoBrPo

He turned over and closed his eyes like a little bird.   The Stranger.   Juan Gelman.   VWA

...He turned to me/The white ignorant hollow of his face.   Father and Son. Stanley Jasspon Kunitz.   MP; NoAm; TwCP

He turns around, and waves his hand,/And blows his horn again.   The Balloon Man.   Dorothy Aldis.   TiPo

He turns the morning's earnest gaze away.   Sunrise in Summer.   John Clare. FaBoPP

He up and shot himself–well out of season.   The Sportsman.   David McCord.   LiSp

He us all to Heven bring,/Qui mortem Cruce voluit.   The Nativity. *Anonymous.*   MeEL

He used to be swoopinaroundhere all–/–of the time.   Ski Trail.   Samuel ("Paul Vesey") Allen.   FB

He used to wear a long brown coat/That buttoned down before.   Abram Brown.   *Anonymous.*   OxNR

He vanishes in the ripples/among the green slim reeds.   The Snake Trying. W. W. Eustace Ross.   NOBC; OBCV

He vowed, he prayed, he found the maid/Forgiving all and good.   Blooming Nelly.   Robert Burns.   UnTE

He waddles through the ditch to look for spring.   Ground Hog Day. Marnie Pomeroy.   PoSC

He wades into the pool of her/stagnant desire.   Cafe Tableau.   May Swenson.   ErPo

He waits for the new commitments to be made.   Traveling Boy.   William Meredith.   NoAm

He waits to greet the gallant tars/Who fought in Mobile Bay.   Through Fire in Mobile Bay.   *Anonymous.*   PAH

He wakes from deepest sleep/upon a distant signal and waits/as if crouching, springs/to life.   Dante.   Robert Duncan.   PoM

He walks again on the Seas of Blood, He comes in the terrible Rain.   The Shadow of Cain.   Edith Sitwell.   CoBMV; OxBTC

"He walks on the earth no longer, your grey-eyed king..."   The Grey-Eyed King.   Anna Akhmatova.   PBWP

He walks out briskly to infect a city,/Whose terrible future may have just arrived.   Gare du Midi.   W. H. Auden.   OBSP

He wandered through a valley steep./Lovely in a lonely place.   I Met at Eve. Walter De La Mare.   HBMV

He wanders with his Country too.   Another.   Richard Lovelace.   AtBAP; CaPo; PoEL 1-5

He wanted no blood on his head!   Motive for Mercy.   Ken Milburn.   PoSH

He wants noan o' th' bonnet, thae foo'!   The Dule's i' This Bonnet o' Mine. Edwin Waugh.   HBV 1-2

...He wants/To vanish into its hard, cold light.   Dino Campana and the Bear. Edward Hirsch.   MAYP

He warranted no better, I don't know.   Mr. Bleaney.   Philip Larkin. HoPM; InPS; NePoEA-2; OxBC; PAI; PPoe

He wars on Death–for Life; not men–for flags.   The Next War.   Wilfred Owen.   AnEnPo; WaP

He was a blacksmith/and was/a brave/man.   Ned Christie.   Robert J. Conley.   STE

He was a friend of mine.   He Was a Friend of Mine.   *Anonymous.*   FSW

"He was a man, let him go'.   Penny Is a Hardy Knight.   *Anonymous.* OxBM

He was a real nice man. He liked me, too.   Seumas Beg.   James Stephens. EvOK; GrPl; OxBTC; RoGo

He was a truly perfect, noble knight.   The Canterbury Tales: Prologue. A Knight.   Geoffrey Chaucer.   MaC; TrGrPo

...He/was alive/his spit in the glue.   War Bride.   Douglas Worth.   FF

He was always here.   Wide Empty Landscape with a Death in the Foreground.   N. Scott Momaday.   CDW

He was as full of tears and trust as a child.   Virgin and Unicorn.   John Heath-Stubbs.   NeBP

He was blasted to nothing.   Truth Kills Everybody.   Ted Hughes.   PAI

He was born, bred, and hanged, all in the same parish.   Epitaph on Will Smith.   *Anonymous.*   FaBoCo

He was born upon the deep blue sea.   Jack Was Every Inch a Sailor. *Anonymous.*   FSW

He was drowned the next day/In the waters of Okeefinokee. the next day/In the waters of Okeefinokee.   A Legend of Lake Okeefinokee.   Laura E. Richards.   StPo

He was eating a nut/And wouldn't look at me.   I Saw a Little Squirrel. *Anonymous.*   TiPo

...He was for men the artist/Of woes unnumbered, and their deadly foe.   The Worst Horror.   Euripides.   DBV

He was free as air when the girl's father found him,/returning from an evening out with friends.   Suicide.   Anne Stevenson.   FaBoWP

He was gone. He pushed his heavy/cap slowly off. Then he sang praise. Joseph's Suspicion.   Rainer Maria Rilke.   MoRP; TrCP

He was her man but he done her wrong, so wrong. Frankie and Johnny, I (with music). *Anonymous.* ABF; AmFP; AS; ATP; BaBo; BeLS; BiP; BLSo; BluL; FaFP; FF; FSW; LiTL; NIP; NOBA; OxBoLi; TrAS; TreF; TrGrPo; UnPo; ViBoFo; YaD

...He was his own/delight and solar system. Shadow. Anthony Delius. PeSA

He was I and I am he. Forebears. Elizabeth Riddell. BoAV

He was my servant–and the better man. Epitaphs of the War, 1914-18. Rudyard Kipling. BrPo; OBWP

He was my sovereign, my heart's delight, my charming young/Gilderoy. Gilderoy. *Anonymous.* OBET

He was neither up nor down. The Grand Old Duke of York. Mother Goose. GBP; SoPo; TiPo

He was no dope. Clippety Cloppity. George Starbuck. PV

He was not the Godric who fled from the fight. The Battle of Maldon. *Anonymous.* AnOE; OAEL 1-2

He was nothing he had ever been and existed not/knowing how to do so. The Turtle's Belly. Ellen Pearce. IHMS

...He was offspring of the generation in between. After Five Years. Augustus Young. BIrV

He was our peacemaker, who mid the storm/Of the great conflict, served the Prince/of Peace. Andrew. Thomas William Parsons. AA

He was paid for the foal he had never lost,/And three times o'er for the good grey mare. The Lochmabyn Harper. *Anonymous.* BuBa

"He was pure straight; God rest him; not like us." November 1967. Paul Durcan. FaBoIP

He was rapidly shouting this as he ran from/the barn. The Farmer's Head. Ron Padgett. ANYP

...He was reading a story so hopeless,/so starless, we all belonged. In Sepia. Jon Anderson. PoA

He was Revere and I was Dawes. What's in a Name? Helen F. More. PAH

He was Sadie's man, that had done her wrong, he wouldn't come home. Sadie (with music). *Anonymous.* AS

He was scandalizin' my name. Scandalize My Name. *Anonymous.* FSW

He was seen way over yander/in Oklahomie. Hill Hunger. John Foster West. TAT

He was so clever he could take the sun. Crow Voices. Gail Tremblay. AMV-81

He was so cold, me leetla boy,/He no could wait. Da Leetla Boy. Thomas Augustin Daly. HBV 1-2

He was so great a loss to good society. Don Juan. George Gordon, Lord Byron. OBRV

He was so happy, I gave him also/My vivid coloured crayons and my big glass marble. The Toy Horse. Valentin Iremonger. NOBI

He was so tired, poor thing. The Funeral. Walter De la Mare. CMoP; MoVE

He was strong and of God! The Serpent of God. Cerise Farallon. UnTE

He was the first and strongest in the barn/when he was stabled. February. Barbara Winder. PH

He was the first to see the snow. First Snow in Alsace. Richard Wilbur. AP; NoP; OBWP

He was the Flame eternal,/He was the Light. Venite Adoremus. Margery Cannon. GoBC

He was "the old man" of a gunboat on the Yangtze. Commander Lowell. Robert Lowell. VGW

He was there, he was there, he was there! Kilroy. Peter Viereck. FF

He was thinking, "A cluster of deep-red flowers/Would pay the taxes of ten poor houses." The Flower Market. Po Chu-i. PPON

He was third engineer, a Scotsman, a good neighbor/lost. Twenty-One Sonnets. C. K. Stead. OCNZ

He was up and away at dawn of day/With the rose-bush under his arm. The Wars of the Roses. Anonymous. GBP

He was wise. Hunting Song. Donald Finkel. CoAP; MoBS; NePoEA

He was, you might say, killed by implication. Epitaph for a Scientist. Lex Banning. NOAV

He wasn't the wiz that he woz. Limerick: "The fabulous wizard of Oz." Anonymous. QQQ; TDH

He watched the lark's flight–/I, the dollar's. For a Little Lady. Fred Saidy. InMe

He watches in the lonely street. Serenade. Henry Timrod. HBV 1-2

He watches me for Mother, and will turn/The bier and baby-carriage where I burn. Between the Porch and the Altar. Robert Lowell. MiAP; NePoEA; PAI

He watches the angelic mouth stain/with the sweet wine. The Angel. Alfred Hayes. FYAP; MAYP; TrJP]

He watches the mills prosper and grow derelict,/As he starts his journey to the Finland Station. Anastasia McLaughlin. Tom Paulin. FaBoIP

He waves th frayed emblems of his wings/And warns us off. The Road the Crows Own. Susan Astor. AMV-81

He wears Earth's livery still. Earth's Bondman. Betty Page Dabney. GoYe

He weeps for a single neck. Outside the Supermarket. Roy Fuller. OxBC

He well might find it in this fret/Of lilies rusted, rotting, wet/With rain. A Room on a Garden. Wallace Stevens. NoP

He went inside just as the convoy passed. After the War. Douglas Dunn. OxBC

He went to bed with what he thought the girls were symbols of. Philander. Donald Hall. ELU; ErPo

He went to look for bigger rocks. A Handful of Small Secret Stones. Chris Bursk. AMV-81

He wept his Friend in verse: then let us try,/Now Shepard's faln, to write his Elegy. To the Reader. Urian Oakes. SCAP

He which hath business and makes love doth do/Such wrong as when a married man doth woo. Break of Day. John Donne. CABA; EG; EiL; EnRePo; LiTB; LiTL; TrGrPo

He whistled that he might not weep. The Blithe Mask. Dollett Fuguet. TRV

He who broke bread with her/tipped his hat. Short Eulogy. Zali Gurevitch. VWA

He who can make the most of transient skies,/It seems to me deserves the only prize. Credo. Alfred Kreymborg. AnAmPo

He who climbs a thorny tree,/Gathers juicy berries she. Count Filippo. Charles Heavysege. PeCV

He who contracts his swelling sail/Eludes the fury of the gale. Contentment. Nathaniel Cotton. OxBChV

"He who creates true beauty ever lives." The Craftsman. Marcus B. Christian. PoNe

He who desires but acts not, breeds pestilence. The Marriage of Heaven and Hell. William Blake. FF

"He who doubts all things" Philonous' Paradox. Christopher Gilbert. FAZ

He who earns praise/Has under heaven the greatest glory. Widsith, the Minstrel. *Anonymous.* AnOE

He who hath braved Youth's dizzy heat/Dreads not the frost of Age. To Age. Walter Savage Landor. EnRP; HBV 1-2; TreFS

He who knows all, fears not. Great Death shall die. Deep Sea Soundings. Sarah Williams. EtS; WGRP

He who knows, and knows that he knows, is wise, follow him. He Who Knows. *Anonymous.* BLPA

He who might have wrought in flame/Only traced upon the foam. Epilogue. George William Russell. MoBrPo

He who misled them all–the butler, Toomes. The Feckless Dinner Party. Walter De la Mare. FaBoTw

He who of those delights can judge, and spare/To interpose them oft, is not unwise. Sonnet XX: To Mr. Lawrence. John Milton. MyFE

He who shall hurt the little wren/Shall never be beloved by men. Three Things to Remember. William Blake. MoShBr

He who the morn may awake from her kisses/Drinks from the cup of the blessed in heaven! The Damsel. Omar B. Abi Rabi'a. AWP; LiTW

He who the ox to wrath had moved/Shall never be by woman loved. Auguries of Innocence. William Blake. PPoe

He, who to heaven aspired,/Needs only earth. Portrait of a Very Old Man. Sara E. Carsley. CaP

He who was like the maned lion. Praises of the King Tshaka. Anonymous. PeSA

He who watches over it in the highest heaven/Knows indeed–or haply knows not. Brahma, the World Idea. *Anonymous.* WGRP

"He whom I loved for what he might have been/Freezes with traitors in the ultimate pit." Upon the Death of George Santayana. Anthony Hecht. AmLP; CoPo; NePA

He whom you dubbed unclubbable/Don't say the same of you!' Johnsonian Poem in Progress: "I put my hat upon my head" (parody). F.A.V. Madden BXAP

He will be an uncle,/if we are lucky. Game after Supper. Margaret Atwood. FaBoWP

He will become a monkey with one leg/And he will hop hop hop away. Song of Abuse. *Anonymous.* WTO

He will bless his mother too. The Beadle's Testimony. Jerome Rothenberg. NNaP

He will cancel the machines we have got. Work. D. H. Lawrence. OBMV

He will constrain thee to depart unheard. The Gulistan. Muslih-ud-Din Sa'di. AWP; LiTW

...He will eat little/And speak less before he hangs. Chief Leschi of the Nisqually. Duane Niatum. CDW; STE

He will forget, he will forget. Warning. Robert Lee Frost. AmePo

He will gather us together some day. The Song of Cove Creek Dam. *Anonymous.* AmFP

He will itch. The Hermit Has a Visitor. Maxine W. Kumin. BoWoP

He will keep me by His pow'r. God Is with Me. Oswald J. Smith. STF

...He will lead me and no man/Can violate or circumvent His plan. The Pagan Isms. Claude McKay. BPo

He will let go   The Earth Cycle Dream.   Phillip Yellowhawk Minthorn.
STE

He will not heal her withered, widowed heart.   Fourth Station.   William A.
Donaghy.   ISi

He will not let my field lie fallow.   The Ploughman.   Karle Wilson Baker.
WGRP

...He will/order many, this time, to be killed/for a single, beautiful word.
Parsley.   Rita Dove.   HaCAP

He will reach before the sun is set.   The Sea-God's Address to Bran.
Anonymous.   OnYI

He will refund us finally/Our confiscated Gods.   Because that you are going.
Emily Dickinson.   MoAmPo

He will remember the blade's/white silence,/the waiting/under his father's
eyes.   The Sacrifice.   Chana Bloch.   VWA

He will save you now.   Come, Every Soul.   John H. Stockton.   AH

He will see, in its stead, with his/spiritual eye.   Epitaph.   *Anonymous.*
TrJP

He will stay sweeter longer.   Lying in State.   Adrian Mitchell.   ELU

He will thee guard and keep.   Rules for Daily Life.   *Anonymous.*   STF

He will trip it trip it trip it on the toe/Diddle diddle diddle doe.   Since Robin
Hood.   *Anonymous.*   NCEP

He wishes he could hug them like big friends from home.   The Stalin
Epigram.   Osip Mandelstam.   FaBoPV

He with his head swung backward.   Courtship.   Diana O Hehir.   NPGG

He with his one lord/And I with my many.   Monasteries.   Charles David
Webb.   NePoAm-2

He with the King of glory/Shall reign eternally.   Stand Up for Jesus.
George Duffield, Jr..   AH; TreFS

He, with the martyr's amaranthine wreath,/Twining the victor's crown!   John
Pelham.   James Ryder Randall.   AA; PAH

He without hair, and thou without a crown.   A Fable.   Matthew Prior.
NoP

He woke, and wondered more: for there she lay.   Nuptial Sleep.   Dante
Gabriel Rossetti.   LoBV; MaVP; NOBV; VLP

He woke–His smile alone illumined/space.   Creation.   Ambrose Bierce.
AA

He wolde nothing wete his clawes.   Snatches: "For ye be like thw sweinte
cat."   *Anonymous.*   OxBM

...He/wolfed down dark red catsup with his french fries.   Beef.   Leon
Stokesbury.   GP

He won't be coming back–   Buying the Dog.   Michael Ondaatje.   Str

...He won't come back.   Down, Down, Down.   Heather McHugh.   SUW

He won't come hazing us no more,/O poor old Joe.   Old Joe.   *Anonymous.*
OxBoLi

He won't get his hundred here today.   Poor Little Johnny.   *Anonymous.*
AmFP

He won't take the advantage no more.   Jim Haggerty's Story.   *Anonymous.*
ABF

...He wonders when/He'll grow into his sleep so sound again.   Ten Days
Leave.   W.D. Snodgrass.   MoAmPo; Psk; UnPo

He wooed, he wooed that fair Janet/An' ca'd her Dear-Coft till her name.
Sir Colin.   *Anonymous.*   OxBB

He works hard, he drinks hard, and goes to hell at last!   Click Go the Shears.
Anonymous.   NOAV

He would berth us/to schedule.   The Anathemata.   David Jones.   FaBoTw

He would bestow upon me a good blessing.   The Feast of Saint Brigid of
Kildare.   Saint Brigid.   CAW; OnYI

He would have been eleventh.   Variations of Greek Themes.   Edwin
Arlington Robinson.   OBAL

He would have no heart who denied you love.   My Own Dark Head (My
Own, My Own).   *Anonymous.*   NOBI

He would have spared thee, and tak'n a bribe.   On the Death of the Lord
Treasurer.   Anonymous.   FaBoEE

He would have the visage/of a prophet/or a priest.   Chambers of Jerusalem.
Yehuda Karni.   VWA

He would like birds be far more near to heaven.   Britannia's Pastorals.
William Browne.   PBBP

He would not be so violent in his repetition/if it were not a questionable
proposition.   On Lavater's Song of a Christian to Christ.   Johann
Wolfgang von Goethe.   ELU

...He would not in mine age/Have left me naked to mine enemies.   King
Henry VIII.   William Shakespeare.   TrGrPo

He would not reave them of their happy breath.   As Life What Is So Sweet?
Anonymous.   OBSP

He would rather be stinking dead.   Dog and Tiger.   Eliezer Greenberg.
BoAnP

He would surely ordain a Fourth Amendment for the sky.   Peek-A-Boo.
Robert Lowenstein.   AMV-81

He wouldn't be any the happier if he did, so what's the/good?   Charlie
Piecan.   *Anonymous.*   OxBoLi

He wrapped in wisdom, and they whirled by whim.   An Elegy, to an Old
Beauty.   Thomas Parnell.   NOEC

He writes himself; he has no time.   The Writer.   Hildebrand Jacob.
FaBoCo

He writes–not that you won or lost–but/how you played the Game.
Alumnus Football.   Grantland Rice.   FPL; GoTF; PoLf; TreFS

He writhes his motionless metallic reins.   The Brass Horse.   Drummond
Allison.   FaBoTw

He wrote the Inferno/On a bottle of Pernod.   Clerihew.   Edmund Clerihew
Bentley.   NLV

Head arched, eyes glancing/toward the passing school bus.   The Corral.
Earle Thompson.   STE

Head bent, hair loosed now mingles with your mane.   Unbridled Now.
Laura Lourene LeGear.   GoYe

...Head, dis-/Membered, floats out over the singing stones.   Paros.   Robin
Macgowan.   EAS

The head falls and/hangs and cannot wake itself.   Laser.   Archie Randolph
Ammons.   NOBA

Head for, and nest with her adored!   A Daughter of Admetus.   Thomas
Sturge Moore.   FaBoTw

...Head in wings,/Or upside-down, they doze behind the walls.   To My
Friend, behind Walls.   Carolyn Kizer.   NePoAm-2

The head that I shall dream of,/And 'twill not dream of me.   The Rainy
Pleiads Wester.   Alfred Edward Housman.   BoLoP; NoAm

...Head up, and watch for talking: we're not/Expected to pray!'   What
Schoolmasters Say.   Martin Seymour-Smith.   OxBTC

The head with its vocabulary useless/Among the flogged plantains.   Stations.
Ted Hughes.   NoAm

Heading for Eugene   Heading for Eugene.   Lorenza Schmidt.   FIA

Heading for where the banks of silver thresh.   The Virgins.   Derek Walcott.
OxBC; SoSe

Heading straight/into the alcove of bubbling flesh.   The Women of Rubens.
Wislawa Szymborska.   WPOW

Headless torsos, faceless lovers, friends of mine.   The Onion, Memory.
Craig Raine.   NoP

Heads.   The Art of Holding On.   Dwight Okita.   BrSi

Heads swiftliest for the state of grace.   The Happy Hen.   James Agee.
ErPo 064

Heah, Rattler, heah.   Ol' Rattler.   *Anonymous.*   ABF

Heal me, and keep me in thy dwelling-place.   I Sought On Earth.   George
Santayana.   AnEnPo

Heal me like her, or else wound her like me.   To Cupid.   Francis Davison.
OBSC

The Healer by Gennesaret/Shall walk the rounds with thee.   The Healer
(excerpt).   John Greenleaf Whittier.   PGD

The health of other absent Lords.   A Toast.   *Anonymous.*   ALV

Health, peace, and joy to Washington!   Evacuation of New York by the
British.   Anonymous.   PAH

Health to all that love hunting the hare.   The Hunting of the Gods.
Anonymous.   OxBoLi

A health to the dashing Spanish girls I met around Cape Horn.   The Girls
around Cape Horn.   *Anonymous.*   AmFP

Heap earth upon it.   Requiescat.   Oscar Wilde.   BrPo; EnLit; GoTF;
GTBS; HBV 1-2; InvP; MoBrPo; OBNC; OBVV; OnYI; OxBI; TreF;
TrGrPo; WHA

Hear a suppliant! Let me be/partner in thy destiny!   To an Infant Expiring
the Second Day of its Birth.   Hetty Wright.   NOEC

Hear again the spirit sound of silence.   The Collector.   Desiree Flynn.
BrRo

Hear all about it! News! they cried.   How They Brought the Good News by
Sea.   Norma Farber.   PCh

Hear all men speak, but credit few or none.   Distrust.   Robert Herrick.
CaPo

Hear all the wheels/hiss in the street, turning/anxiously into themselves.
Parts Man.   Michael West.   AmC

Hear/another voice/singing under ice   The Uninvited.   Dorothy Livesay.
NOBC

Hear from his Father's lips that all is good.   Nature.   Jones Very.   AP;
HBV 1-2

Hear her singing Handy Dandy up and down the stair.   Down in Yonder
Meadow.   *Anonymous.*   PoPle

Hear how it booms out, Time and Tide,/Solemnly, Time and Tide.   Ticking
Clocks.   Rachel Field.   TiPo

Hear in the wind/The bush sob:/It is the ancestors' breath.   Breaths.   Birago
Diop.   TTY

Hear in thy heart the Master's words, "Well done."   This Day Is Thine.
Verna Whinery.   BLRP

Hear it not, Duncan, for it is a knell/That summons thee to heaven, or to hell.
Macbeth.   William Shakespeare.   TreFS

Hear Lydiat's life, and Galileo's end.   The Scholar's Life.   Samuel Johnson.
NOBE; OBEC; SeCePo

Hear'st thou the groans that rend his breast?   Thou Lingering Star.   Robert
Burns.   OBEC

(Hear that Missouri roll!). Jesse James. William Rose Benet. BBV; BPAW; FYAP; MoAmPo; NAMP; StPo; TrGrPo

Hear the crack of thunder! Over and Under. William Jay Smith. TiPo

Hear the lost sisters innocently tease. The Little Brother. James Reeves. OxBTC

Hear the music, the thunder of the wings. Love the wild swan. Love the Wild Swan. Robinson Jeffers. AnFE; HeIP; MoAB; MoAmPo; PAI; TW

Hear the prayers our hearts are urging. Victimae Paschali Laudes. Wipo. CAW

Hear the unison of their voices.... A Unison. William Carlos Williams. NOBA; SeCeV

Hear the yarn of a sailor,/An old yarn learned at sea. The Yarn of the Loch Achray. John Masefield. SeCeV; StPo

Hear them and come: they call you home. For My Brother. Thomas Merton. GoTF; InPo; TreFS

Hear unconcern'd the oar/That dips itself in wine! Champagne Rosee. John Kenyon. OBEV; OBRV; OBVV

Hear us, hear us, O Good Sun! Three Songs from the Haida, III: Queen Charlotte's Island, B.C. Constance Lindsay Skinner. BPAW

...Hear what he says,/The dauntless master, as he starts the human tale. Puella Parvula. Wallace Stevens. HaCAP; LCAP

"Hear what the Lord has done for me!" Exhortation to Prayer. William Cowper. NOCV

Hear what the newsboys shout,/Or see the raincoats pass. Lobsters in the Window. W. D. Snodgrass. BiP; BoAnP; NCSH; NYBP; TAP

Heard all the crickets singing, and was glad. A Prayer in Darkness. Gilbert Keith Chesterton. BoC; FPL; MoBrPo; PoLf; TrGrPo

Heard on this coast, the music of the spheres/Would sound like something from The Gondoliers. Afternoons with Baedeker. Osbert Lancaster. FaBoCo; NOBL

Heard someone talking about. Distinctions. Charles Tomlinson. CMoP

Heard the pulse of you when all was still ringing little/bells last night under my ear. I Heard You Solemn-Sweet Pipes of the Organ. Walt Whitman. CBEP; NePA; OxBA

...Heard this heavy curse,/Servant of servants, on his vicious race. Paradise Lost. John Milton. FaBoPV

Heard unheeded, leaves me a lonely began. To Seem the Stranger Lies My Lot. Gerard Manley Hopkins. NOBV

Hearing church organs grind out canticles/for all souls dynamited into heaven. Letters from Birmingham. Harold Bond. TAT

Hearing her sister come, waiting the hiss/To turn her to a Mrs. from a Miss...? To the Ladies. Arnold Kenseth. PPON

Hearing the horizons endure. The Horses. Ted Hughes. NoAm; PH

Hearing the Infinite whisper there. Lest Thou Forget. William L. Stidger. PoToHe

Hearing the stones cry out under the horizons. Wind. Ted Hughes. SoSe

Hearing the worms gnaw in the satin and grinding my teeth. They Have Turned the Church Where I Ate God. Gary Gildner. GP

Hearing them, year to year, I talk to myself alone. Sea Bells. Richard Eberhart. AMV-80

Hearing, to hear them. Sapphics. Algernon Charles Swinburne. AnEnPo; PoEL 1-5

Hearing under the breath the stone/that is ours alone. The Rock. William Stanley Merwin. NYP

Hearing you/beating off under covers. First Pregnancy. Alta. NMM

Heark'ning in the aspect/of th'eternal silence. Noel: Christmas Eve, 1913. Robert Bridges. CAW; LiTB; MoVE; NOCV; OBCP; OxBoCh; PoEL 1-5

Hears the dry thunder roll, and knows no rain. And So the Day Drops By. Frederick Goddard Tuckerman. AnNE

Hears the thrush, while all is still,/Within the groves of Grongar Hill. Grongar Hill. John Dyer. CEP; FaBoPP; GoTL; LAuP; LoBV; NOEC; NoP; OBEC; PoEL 1-5; SeCePo; TrGrPo; ViBoPo

Heart aches,/lungs pant/dry air/sorry, scant. Breathless. Wilfred Noyce. OBTV

Heart and soul do sing in me. Song: "O fair! O sweet! when I do look on thee." Sir Philip Sidney. SiPS

The heart ay's the part ay,/That makes us right or wrang. Epistle to Davie, a Brother Poet. Robert Burns. OBEC

...The heart beats away wishes/before they fester on the drum. Avoidances. Ron Welburn. PoBA

The heart burns–but has to keep out of face how heart burns. Strange Hells. Ivor Gurney. OxBTC

The heart cries out like a conductor/On a morning train, "Change! All/change!" We Settled by the Lake. F. D. Reeve. NYBP

The heart distrusting asks, if this be joy? The Deserted Village. Oliver Goldsmith. EBEV; LoBV

Heart, Ear, and Eye, and everything/Awake! A Christmas Carol. Robert Herrick. PCh

Heart emptied, and scarce hoping to amend. Here Have I Been These One and Twenty Years. Arthur Hugh Clough. NAs

...The heart expands/to claim this world, blue vapor without end. Monet Refused the Operation. Lisel Mueller. FYAP

The heart gives out/Silence. The Last Fire. Moishe Steingart. VWA

Heart has found rest on heart. Meeting After Long Absence. Lilla Cabot Perry. AA

The heart has not stopped. Mystic. Sylvia Plath. NYBP

Heart heavily wounded/by five sharp swords. Guitar. Federico Garcia Lorca. InPK

A heart in love/Becomes a deep ravine? Recklessly I Cast Myself away. Izumi Shikibu. PBWP

The heart is sensual, though five eyes break. When All My Five and Country Senses See. Dylan Thomas. MoAB; MoBrPo; NoAm; PoA; SeCePo

...Heart is slow to learn/What the swift mind beholds at every turn. Pity Me Not. Edna St. Vincent Millay. AnNE; CMoP; MoAB; MoAmPo; NePA; OxBA; TrGrPo

A heart less perfect, needing cure/By Love's own music, softly played. With Lilacs. Charles Henry Crandall. AA

The heart lives by the faith the lips deny,/God knoweth why. There Is No Unbelief. Elizabeth York Case. WBLP; WGRP

A Heart may bee your sacrifice/Too weake to bee your shrine. Song: "Noe more unto my thoughts appeare." Sidney Godolphin. MeLP; MePo

The heart must beat as the times require. Lines. Herbert Martin. PoBA

The heart of all the perfumes of the wood. After the Shower. Archibald Lampman. CaP

The heart of it is Love, the end of it/Is Peace and Consummation sweet. Obey! The Light of Asia. Sir Edwin Arnold. VLP

The heart of London beating warm. London. John Davidson. NOBE; OBNC

The heart of man has long been sore/And long 'tis like to be. Last Poems. Alfred Edward Housman. OAEP

Heart of my heart. Colloquial. Rupert Brooke. BrPo

Heart of my heart, Hilaire! The Summons. Elizabeth Roberts MacDonald. CaP

The heart of our green season. Natural History. Richard Howard. TAP

The heart of standing is we cannot fly. Aubade. William Empson. FaBoMo; FaBoTw; LiTB; OxBTC

The heart of the shepherd is sore. The Shepherd's Lament. Johann Wolfgang von Goethe. AWP

The heart's a chess game where the queen's lost/or the closest thing to death in life. Romance of the Cigarette. Mary di Michele. CaPN

The heart's calm voice that stills the baying hounds. In Hospital: Poona. Alun Lewis. DTC

The heart's each pulse shall keep the sense/it had/With all, though the mind's labour run to/nought For An Allegorical Dance of Women by Andrea Mantegna. Dante Gabriel Rossetti. VLP

The heart says heart will never cease. The Time Has Come, the Clock Says Time Has Come. Conrad Aiken. NePA

The heart set beating in the side/Has but the wisdom of a hare? The Horn. Léonie Adams. AnAmPo; MoAB; MoAmPo

The heart shall still remember/Christ in its very sleep. Before Sleep. Prudentius (Aurelius Clemens Prudentius). LiTW

...A heart-shaped/wing. A beating stillness. A/motionless weight. The Argument Begins with A. Sharon Thesen. CaPN

The heart should rise on wings of love to Heaven. The Right Use of Prayer. Sir Aubrey De Vere. OBVV; WGRP

A heart-sick yearning for the time/When it should never more be spoken. Partings. Maria Jane Jewsbury. OxBChV

Heart speaks to heart, and still is under-/stood. On a Cast from an Antique. George Pellew. AA

Heart, star, rood, rose, swan, gyre, and Ballylee. Parachuting Thoor Ballylee (parody). William Zaranka. BXAP

The heart still hankers for the rounded shape. First Corncrake. John Hewitt. NeIP

A heart still prisoned in the frost of war. St Mary's Loch. Geoffrey Faber. PoSH

Heart straining, to utter that cry?–But/Cannot, breath short. Sila. Robert Penn Warren. NoP

The heart struck silly by Love's shaft/Forgets its arithmetic! Dialogue. Agathias. OLR

A heart that still can feel, and eyes that still can weep. Divine Compassion. John Greenleaf Whittier. MAmP

The heart the great/thrower/of every ball. Catalogue. Hilde Domin. VWA

A heart-throb in the sky–/Then not at all! The Lark. Lizette Woodworth Reese. HBMV

Heart to heart as we lay/In the dawning of the day. My Delight and Thy Delight. Robert Bridges. AnFE; CMoP; GTBS; HBV 1-2; LiTL; NBM; NOBE; OAEP; OBEV; PoEL 1-5

A heart whose love is innocent. She Walks in Beauty. George Gordon, Lord Byron. AtBAP; ATP; AWP; BLPA; BoLoP; ELP; ExPo; FaBoBe; FaFP; FF; FiP; FPL; GoTF; GTBS; GTBS-P; HBV 1-2; HBVY; HeIP; InPo; InPS; LiTB; LiTL; LoBV; MBW 1-2; MCCG; NIP; NOBE; NoP; OAEP; OBEV; OBNC; OBRV; PAI; PG; PoEL 1-5; PrIm; RoGo; SeCeV; TreF; TrGrPo; WHA

Hearts are broken, heads are turned, wi' castles in the air.   Castles in the Air. James Ballantine.   HBV 1-2

Hearts beating against my hands/burst inside   February Park.   Gerald Vizenor.   VoR

Hearts like lead in our breasts.   Clare Coast.   Emily Lawless.   OxBI

Hearts may breake, that be in love.   The Broken Heart.   Thomas Beedome. OBS

The hearts of men are merciless.   Two Poems About President Harding. James Wright.   CoAP

The hearts of the maids, and the gentlemen's heads, were/bothered I'm sure by this Irishman.   The Irishman and the Lady.   William Maginn.   HBV 1-2

Hearts of true British mould.   A Song About Charleston.   *Anonymous.* PAH

Hearts sure of brass they had, who tempted first/Rude Seas that spare not what themselves have nurs   The Battel of the Summer-Islands.   Edmund Waller.   SeCV 1-2

The hearts that made the Nation were the Women of the West.   The Women of the West.   George Essex Evans.   PoAu 1-2

Hearts were made to give away/On Valentine's dear day.   Hearts Were Made to Give Away.   Annette Wynne.   TiPo

Heartscalds and torments–but sorra a mother/Has got one to spare.   Boys. Winifred M. Letts.   HBMV

The heartwood thrown open against the blade.   Progress.   Connie Martin. PPJ

...Heat comes/out of the center, radiates faintly and no paper will burn. Ghazals.   Jim Harrison.   NoAm

The heat compels me to go,/I must go.   Cold and Heat.   *Anonymous.* WTO

Heat creates both light and motion.   Science for the Young.   Wallace Irwin. ShM

The heat of steel/aging as it passes through/throbbing cells.   Hand Saw. Erica Funkhouser.   AMV-81

Heat wove the air/and we smoked dime cigars.   Thirteen, Full of Life. Graham Everett.   WOLT

The heathen Chinee is peculiar–/Which the same I am free to maintain.   The Heathen Chinee.   Bret (Francis Bret Harte) Harte.   BPAW; CTC; FaBoCo; InMe

Heating coffee for the Prince, her master.   The Morning After.   Walter Clark.   NCSH

Heav'n, Heav'n will make amends for all!   A Consolatory Poem.   Nicholas Noyes.   SCAP

A heav'nly count'nance, and a heart infernal.   An Epigram on Woman. Philip Ayres.   FaBoEE

Heave away! and don't you make a noise,/For we're bound for Australia. Cape Cod Girls.   *Anonymous.*   TrAS

Heave away! yellow gal I want to go.   Heave Away.   *Anonymous.*   ABF; TrAS

Heave her up and away we'll go,/All on the plains of Mexico.   Santy Anno. *Anonymous.*   FSW; OuSiCo; ShS

Heave-ho! Away with her/Into the stalls.   Song of the Ballet.   J. B. Morton. DBV; FiBHP

Heave us a wrack to beguile our grief. Amen.   The Wrecker's Prayer. Theodore Goodridge Roberts.   OBCV; PeCV

Heave, ye rollers, heave!   The Landlubber's Chantey.   James Stuart Montgomery.   HBMV

Heaven aint the only H in the dictionary   Ho.   Al Young.   GP; NPGG

Heaven and earth are full of thee!   Day Is Dying in the West.   Mary Artemisia ("Aunt Mary") Lathbury.   AH; TRV

Heaven and earth to peace beguiles.   A Cradle Song.   William Blake. EnRP; OBCP; OBEC; SBVL; ViBoPo

Heaven, crowded with stars, trembled from rim to rim.   The Fish-Hawk. John Hall Wheelock.   AnAmPo; EtS; HBMV

Heaven had not won, nor earth so timely lost.   Epitaph on Thomas Clere. Henry Howard, Earl of Surrey.   SiPS

Heaven have her in its tender care!/O medeto gozarimas!   The Musmee. Mrs. Major Arnold.   OBTV

"Heaven," he said.   The Builder.   Willard Wattles.   AnAmPo; HBMV

Heaven, his friend, the earth his follower.   For John Berryman I.   Robert Lowell.   NOBA

Heaven I hope will seat him on his Throne.   Heavens Bright Lamp, Shine Forth Some of Thy Light.   George Alsop.   SCAP

Heaven is blessed with perfect rest,/but the blessing of earth is toil.   The Gospel of Labor.   Henry Van Dyke.   TRV; WBLP; WGRP

Heaven is not built of country seats/But little queer suburban streets!   To the Little House.   Christopher Morley.   HBMV

Heaven is older than you!   Song.   Florence Smith.   BLPA

The Heaven itself, is blinded throughout night.   Hyperion.   John Keats. WHA

Heaven keep our loves away.   Phyllida's Love-Call to Her Corydon, and His Replying.   *Anonymous.*   AnFE; ElL; OBEV; OBSC

Heaven keep us Protestants from harm: the/rest...no ill betide!   The Cardinal and the Dog.   Robert Browning.   VLP

Heaven may be stol'n again!   The Thief.   *Anonymous.*   OxBoCh

A heaven of unborn evanescent stars.   From the Sea.   Sara Teasdale. MoLP

Heaven ope to Indians wild, but shut to thee.   Boast Not Proud English, of Thy Birth and Blood.   Roger Williams.   SCAP

Heaven-pointing spires shall beautify thy plain   The Avon.   Henry Jacobs. AnNZ

Heaven put his hand forth, and did glean.   To His Sister, Mrs. S. the Rose. William Hammond.   OBS

Heaven reechoes the auto-da-fe.   El Emplazado.   William Henry Venable. PAH

Heaven's gate to me while I live–/Forbidden though it is.   I Have a Blue Piano.   Else Lasker-Schüler.   TrJP

Heaven's lights and you to me will shine.   Madrigal: "Dear, when I did from you remove."   Edward, Lord Herbert of Cherbury.   ElL

...The heaven's river has/drowned its banks and the flood of joy is abroad.   A Song-Offering.   Rabindranath Tagore.   LiTW

Heaven sent us Soda Water/As a torment for our crimes.   Feast on Wine or Fast on Water.   Gilbert Keith Chesterton.   ALV

Heaven stoops to give it life.   The Soul.   *Anonymous.*   STF

A heaven taken by storm where none are left but the slain!   The Desolate City.   Wilfrid Scawen Blunt.   OBEV; OBVV

Heaven vowes to keepe him.   Epitaph on S.P. a Child of Q. El. Chappel. Ben Jonson.   AnAnS 2; SeCP

A Heaven will banish all corruption thence.   Upon Thought Castara May Die.   William Habington.   ACP

Heaven, with a host of eyes to gaze on thee.   My Star.   Plato.   EnLi 1-2

Heavenly Archer, loose thy string.   Dust to Dust.   Walter De La Mare. TrPWD

Heavenly Buddhas smiling in their sleep.'   A Short History of British India. Geoffrey Hill.   OxBC

Heavenly Father be it so.   God Supreme! To Thee We Pray.   Penina and Edward N. Calishch Moise.   AH

The heavenly harbor at last!   In Harbor.   Paul Hamilton Hayne.   AA; HBV 1-2

An heavenly plant it was, and sweetly grew.   Peace.   Samuel Speed. OxBoCh

The heavens are red.   War Comes.   Zalman Schneour.   TrJP

...Heavens are shallow as the sea/is now deep, and you love me.   Insomnia. Elizabeth Bishop.   LLLT

The heavens at last will end, as all things must–/To let new heavens ripple out of dust.   Eagle Sonnets.   Clement Wood.   HBMV

The heavens sagged; there was nothing to say.   Contemporary Song. Theodore Spencer.   LiTA

The heavens' sun perfected in your eyes.   Woman.   Randall Jarrell. NoAm; NOBA

The heavens themselves look brighter, Love,/Since thy sweet soul is there. The Warrior to His Dead Bride.   Adelaide Anne Procter.   OBVV

Heavily borne away on the exhausted blast.   The Revolt of Islam.   Percy Bysshe Shelley.   ChRP

Heavily hangs the tiger-lily.   Song: A Spirit Haunts the Year's Last Hours. Alfred, Lord Tennyson.   AtBAP; GTBS; GTBS-P; HeIP; OAEP; OBNC; PoEL 1-5; PoPle

Heavily on this little heart/Presses this immortality.   A Song of Derivations. Alice Meynell.   WGRP

Heavily weighted, they struggled well,/kicking up the water, then went down. The Hands.   Tony Harrison.   FaBpTw

Heavy and cold as a stone.   Leaving Mexico One More Time.   Constance Urdang.   AMV-80

Heavy and frisky in your freshened pelt,/Printing the stones.   The Otter. Seamus Heaney.   FaBoIP; IPY

...Heavy deeds/make heavy hearts and to them/life is suffering. stand clear. Revolutionary Letters.   Diane Di Prima.   GP

The heavy-hooft below.   On the Heights.   Walter Savage Landor.   FaBoEE

The heavy hyacinth remembering death.   Admonition for Spring.   L. A. Mackay.   CaP; OBCV; PeCV

The heavy iron gates/are closing in my breasts.   Nothing More Will Happen. Marge Piercy.   NeAC

The heavy knife. As to a gala day.   Black Marigolds.   Bilhana.   AWP; ErPo; LiTW

Heavy, oh Heavy, is mine to keep.   The Sad Child's Song.   Mark Van Doren.   SO

The heavy-shouldered ox, and eagle, lion, man.   Carolers.   Nancy G. Westerfield.   AMV-81

Heavy, the wind a low portent of rain.   Dictum: For a Masque of Deluge. William Stanley Merwin.   AP; NoAm

The heavy tundra slowly/rolls over and sinks/in the darkness.   The Tundra. John Haines.   ConAP

Heb'n gate opened, and he rolled right in.   Two White Horses (with music). *Anonymous.*   AS

An' Hebben is up,/I'm upward boun'.   Northboun'.   Lucy Ariel Williams Holloway.   BANP; BlSi; CDC; GoSl; PoNe

Hebrews, James, Peter, and John,/Jude and Revelation.　The New Testament. *Anonymous.*　FaBoUs

Hector withdrew his spear and said/"Perhaps."　The Iliad.　Homer.　OBVE

Hedges freaked with snow.　Hedges Freaked with Snow.　Robert Graves. OxBTC

The hedonism and the arts of/Alexandria/kept him a devoted disciple.　One of the Jews.　Constantine P. Cavafy.　TrJP

Hee! Hee! Hee! Hee! Ha! Ha! Ha! Ha! Ha!　Laughing Time.　William Jay Smith.　SoPo

Hee is a bisconted Hypocrite.　The Lancashire Puritane.　*Anonymous.* CoMu

Hee is the author of our peace.　A New-Yeares-Gift Sung to King Charles, 1635.　Ben Jonson.　SeCP

Hee smarteth most that hides his smart,/And sues for no Compassion.　Sir Walter Ralegh to the Queen.　Sir Walter Ralegh.　AAS; OAEP

Heed Mercy's call.　Come, Friends and Neighbors, Come.　Lewis Hartsough. AH

Heed that low music, and be mute.　Silentium.　Fyodor Tyutchev.　LiTW; PoPl

Heedless and wilful, took their knights to bed.　Sonnet: "Women have loved before as I love now."　Edna St. Vincent Millay.　PoA

–Heedless of Sabbath/and immune to echoes.　With Due Deference to Thomas Wolfe.　Joanne Townsend.　AMV-81

Heedless of the reins or the charioteer.　Georgics.　Virgil (Publius Vergilius Maro).　LiTW

Heedless of the wind and weather./Fa la la la la, la la la la.　Deck the Halls. *Anonymous.*　FSW

Heedless of where the next bright bold may fall.　The White Goddess. Robert Graves.　MoBrPo; OAEL 1-2

The heedless virgin, unaware,/Plays with the dart that wounds her. Strephon.　John Smyth.　UnTE

The heedless world upon a heaving/shoulder.　The Coat of Fire.　Edith Sitwell.　OAEP

"Heel and toe from dawn to dusk,/Round the world and home again".　The Testament of John Davidson: The Last Journey.　John Davidson.　BSV; GoTS

Heel cannot bruise, nor weight break/The shadow shape of gold. Recollection.　Dorothy Donnelly.　NCSH

Heels to the shoes and lipstick on the mouth.　A Certain Age.　Phyllis McGinley.　NePoAm-2

Heigh-ho! and yet he eyes me not.　Beauty, Alas, Where Wast Thou Born. Lodge, Thomas Greene, Robert.　EIL

Heigh-ho, back again.　A Big Ship Sailing.　*Anonymous.*　FSW

Heigh ho, heigh ho, 'chill love no more.　Though Amaryllis Dance in Green. *Anonymous.*　NIP; OAEP

Heigh ho, my heart! would God that she were mine!　Rosalynde.　Thomas Lodge.　EIL; GoBC; GTBS; GTBS-P; LiTB; OBEV; OBSC; TrGrPo; UnTE

Heigh ho! says Anthony Rowley.　The Love-Sick Frog.　*Anonymous.* OxNR

Heigho, dot and go one,/Fal lal de ral de ra, &c.　The Lover's Arithmetic. *Anonymous.*　OxBoLi

Heigho! yea thee and nay thee.　The Quaker's Meeting.　Samuel Lover. CenHV; OnYI

Heightening the horror of its gloomy shades.　The Rising Village.　Oliver Goldsmith.　OBCV

The heirdom all converged in thee!　To-Day and Thee.　Walt Whitman. NePA

Held captive in this painted tin/For us, who now can sing no more.　Alle Vogel Sind Schon Da.　Frances Chesterton.　UnS

Held high the gleaming colors/Of the flag they loved so well.　Our Country's Emblem.　*Anonymous.*　WBLP

Held in eternal bondage there.　A Diamond.　Robert Loveman.　AA

Held in memory.　Hunter's Morning.　Harold Littlebird.　STE

Held in that eye of his, which is every bit as real/as he is invisible.　A Natural History of Dragons and Unicorns My Daughter and I Have Known. William Pitt Root.　AMV-81; SM

Held Ministers in my palm and, laughing, blew/Confusion on the fleets of Blefuscu!　A Tryst in Brobdingnag.　Adrienne Rich.　NYBP

Held the pebbles in our hands/and ate the freckled pears.　September 7. Ellen Bass.　NMM

...Held to the knowledge that a bird's beak,/born of cells of bone, discourages the worm.　I Move to Random Consolations.　William Heyen.　AmPA

Held together by/something sweet in the dark.　For We Are All Madwomen. Barbara Sweeney.　AMV-81

Held up by slow friendly winds.　The People, Yes.　Carl Sandburg.　CMoP

Helen, foiler of beauty.　New Legends.　Robert Graves.　AtBAP

Helen, grown old, no longer cold,/Said, "you to all men I prefer."　Helen. Mary Ann Lamb.　OBRV

Helen, it seems, is more/herself the more she's reproduced.　The Ultimate Antientropy.　Theodore Weiss.　NoAm

Helicopters colliding with tenements/in orange surprise　Walk with De Mayor of Harlem.　David Henderson.　PoBA

Hell and pain and terror, I.　Eve.　*Anonymous.*　BIrV

Hell blot black for alway the thought "Peace!"　Sestina: Altaforte.　Ezra Pound.　AmP; CMoP; CoBMV; FaBoTw; LiTA; MoAB; NOBA; SoSe; SOTW

–Hell came when I saw/MYSELF.../and couldn't stand/what I see...　Herbert White.　Frank Bidart.　AmPA

Hell must open like a red rose/for the dead to pass.　Eurydice.　Hilda ("H. D.") Doolittle.　VGW

...Hell needs its/teeth kicked out, here and now!　Testimony.　Carolyn M. Rodgers.　BPo

Hell, no, Baby!/They can't win!　Funky Football.　Fareedah Allah.　BlSi

A hell of a fat chance my orange bears had!　The Orange Bears.　Kenneth Patchen.　NaP

Hell raised a hoarse, half-human cheer.　A Ballad of Hell.　John Davidson. AnEnPo; HBMV; HoPM; MoBrPo; WHA

Hell, rising from a thousand thrones,/Shall do it reverence.　The City in the Sea.　Edgar Allan Poe.　AA; AnAmPo; APA; ForPo; HBV 1-2; LiTA; MAmP; MAT; MOS; NePA; NOBA; NoP; OxBA; PoEL 1-5; TAP; ViBoPo; WHA

Hell shall rise in grim derision and make/room!　Twilight on Sumter. Richard Henry Stoddard.　PAH

Hell there are no more islands.　Hershey Kiss.　Patti Renner-Tana.　SOTS

Hell we may as well/be doing this/as anything else/as silly.　July 1st, French Creek.　Kevin Roberts.　WOLT

Hell, well, Heavens!　Hell, Well, Heaven.　Mongane Wally Serote.　WhB

The hell where youth and laughter go.　Suicide in Trenches.　Siegfried Sassoon.　BrPo; MMM

Hellas re-born from death.　Egypt.　Hilda ("H. D.") Doolittle.　HBMV

Hellelujah!/Throne and Cross forever.　Cross and Throne.　Horatius Bonar. BePJ

Hello death　Ayohu Kanogisdi Death Song.　Carroll Arnett.　STE

...Hello,/Good-bye is the only story. We know, we know.　The Story We Know.　Martha Collins.　SM

...Hello'ing/them & howling them & hallowing them.　Earthly.　Ian Wedde. OCNZ

Hello? Is there anyone there?　Central.　Ted Kooser.　Psk

("Hello!" says my own.)　Who Wants a Birthday?　David McCord.　BiCB

Hello, Somebody, hello.　Hello, Somebody.　*Anonymous.*　ShS

A help, a love, a you, a wife.　Love Song: I and Thou.　Alan Dugan.　AP; CAPP; FF; HoPM; InPK; NoAm; SoSe

Help!/Fire!/Thief!　Trials of a Tourist.　Anne Tibble.　FaBoCo; NLV

Help help madness help.　Madness.　James Dickey.　NYBP

Help him play a manly part.　Keep the Glad Flag Flying.　*Anonymous.* FaFP

Help, Lord! Lest I should crucify,/By thought or deed, Thy Love again.　The Prince of Life.　John Oxenham.　TrPWD

Help me.　Care.　Josephine Miles.　NYBP

Help me accept its fate with Christmas feeling.　To a Young Wretch. Robert Frost.　OFD

Help me down Cemetery Road.　Toads Revisited.　Philip Larkin.　CMoP; NOBL; SaC

Help me endure the Pit, until/Thou wilt not have forgotten me.　An Outdoor Litany.　Louise Imogen Guiney.　TrPWD

Help me lean against this wind?　Burning against the Wind.　Judith Minty. GeTw

Help me, Lord, in stress and struggle/Just to keep my eyes on Thee.　Credit. *Anonymous.*　STF

Help me now!　Song: "Help me now."　Emmett Jarrett.　NeAC

Help me, Sir, and so I will.　Bad I am, but yet they child.　Gerard Manley Hopkins.　BoC

Help me to die, O Lord!　Before Action.　William Noel Hodgson.　WGRP

Help me to live.　My Evening Prayer.　Charles H. Gabriel.　BLPA; FaBoBe

Help me to live for others,/That I may live like Thee.　Others.　Charles D. Meigs.　WBLP

Help me to my lives ende,/And make me with thyn Sone y-saught...　Queen of Heaven.　*Anonymous.*　OxBM

Help me to need no aid from men,/That I may help such men as need!　A Dedication.　Rudyard Kipling.　GTBS; HBV 1-2; OBVV

Help me to tell it in my reverence.　The Canterbury Tales: Invocation. Geoffrey Chaucer.　CAW

Help me today.　Help Me Today.　Elsie Robinson.　PoToHe

Help me/turn the face of history/to your face.　Getting down to Get over. June Jordan.　TAP

Help on reform in every way you can.'/Then the old man died.　An Old Man's Advice.　*Anonymous.*　OBET

Help out of thee, since nature hath revealed,/That with thy tongue thy bitings may be healed.　Caelica, II.　Fulke, Lord Brooke Greville.　FCP

Help pull out my horse. He's down below.　The Old Sussex Road.　Ian Serraillier.　NTCP

Help to chant Immanuel's praise.　Hail, Thou Once Despised Jesus!　John Bakewell.　BePJ

Help to make the earth happy/Like the heaven above.   Little Things.   Julia A. Fletcher Carney.   HBV 1-2

Help us, oh God, we're rich.   Harlem, Montana: Just Off the Reservation.   James Welch.   CDW; GP; STE

...Help us see/That without dust the rainbow would not be.   Two Somewhat Different Epigrams.   Langston Hughes.   NePoAm-2

Help us sin to flee,/That we may thy son see/In joy without end.   Ubi Sunt Qui Ante Nos Fuerunt?   *Anonymous.*   CoBE; NoP; OAEP; OxBM; PrIm; SeCeV; WeW

Help us to break like oaks in the soughing bacterial wind.   Tennyson.   Alan Ansen.   CoAP

Help us to save free conscience from the paw/Of hireling wolves, whose Gospel is their maw.   To the Lord General Cromwell.   John Milton.   AnEnPo; EnLit; FaBoPV; NoP; OBS; TrGrPo; ViBoPo

Help whom thou may'st–for surely unto thee/Sharp need of help will e'er the end be borne.   The Gulistan.   Muslih-ud-Din Sa'di.   AWP

Help yourself to the jellyfish, the goose down,/the chocolate-covered cotton balls.   I Have Lived This Way for Years and Do Not Wish to Change.   Michael C. Blumenthal.   HaCAP

Helped him make the whole world neighbor.   Alexander Graham Bell Did Not Invent the Telephone.   Robert P. Tristram Coffin.   TiPo

Helped, with drinking, to keep them alive.   Two Comical Folk.   *Anonymous.*   OxNR

Helping us keep time   Player.   Stephen Dunning.   FAZ

The helpless, hungry, nervous shrew/lives for a year of hurly-burly/and dies intolerably early.   The Masked Shrew.   Isabella Gardner.   ImOP

Helpless the charioteer is carried at the will of his horses.   Georgics.   Virgil (Publius Vergilius Maro).   WaaP

Hemingway play the fool and Faulkner forget his art.   Let Them Alone.   Robinson Jeffers.   AP

The hemlock shakes in the rafter, the oak in the driving keel.   Misgivings.   Herman Melville.   AP; MAmP; NePA; NOBA; OxBA

The hemlocks, muffled,/deepen to the grim/taking of a further beauty on.   Bonus.   Archie Randolph Ammons.   HaCAP

The hempen Haschish of the East/Is powerless to our Western Cotton!   The Haschish.   John Greenleaf Whittier.   OBAL

Hence alive the Past must be.   A Dead Past.   C. C. Munson.   BLRP; WBLP

Hence away, therefore, and leave me!   Song: "Fond affection, hence, and leave me!"   Robert Parry.   EIl

Hence come thy misery. Answer, if you can.   Errors of Ecstasie.   George Darley.   OnYI

Hence-forth be this your posture; AS YOU WERE.   The Sigh.   Nathaniel Wanley.   OBS; OxBoCh

Hence his contentment.   Ancient Wisdom, Rather Cosmic.   Ezra Pound.   NOBA

Hence my claw is tired of scribing.   My Claw Is Tired of Scribing!   Colum Cille.   NOBI

Hence pass till Hallow-mass!–my spell is spoken.   Claud Halcro's Invocation.   Sir Walter Scott.   NBM

Hence rules the circling deep, and awes the/world.   Summer.   James (1700-48) Thomson.   CoBE

Hence the grief that is in my heart.   The Blackbird Calls in Grief.   *Anonymous.*   NOBI

Hence! to the water-side, away!   The Culprit Fay.   Joseph Rodman Drake.   GN

Henceforth he talks in Hades with the dead.   Ajax.   Sophocles.   LiTW

Henceforth, henceforth/Will echo sea and earth.   Henceforth, from the Mind.   Louise Bogan.   LiTA; MoPo; MoVE; NePA; QFR

Henceforth its sweetest song shall be the/song of sin forgiven!   The Two Angels.   John Greenleaf Whittier.   AA

Henceforth take warning by the fall/Of cruel Barbara Allen.   Barbara Allen's Cruelty.   Anonymous   HBV 1-2; OBEV; ViBoPo

Henceforth thy going out and in God keep for ever will.   I to the Hills Will Lift Mine Eyes.   Francis Rous.   AH

Henry nodded, un-.   Dream Songs.   John Berryman.   CAPP; HaCAP

...Henry springs youthfully/in his six-by-two like a dancer.   Dream Songs.   John Berryman.   HaCAP

Henry was not his favourite.   Dream Songs.   John Berryman.   NaP

...Her and the/bed: one quiet ache of white.   Three Women.   Barry Dempster.   CaPN

Her angel looks upon God's face.   The Eternal Image.   Ruth Pitter.   MoBrPo; OxBTC

Her anthem, "Salve, Redemptoris Mater."   Mater Amabilis.   Sir Aubrey De Vere.   ISi

Her arm, her flesh, warm in the sun, and bleeding.   Transformation Scene.   Constance Carrier.   FYAP; GoYe

Her bandage hides two festering sores/That once perhaps were eyes.   Justice.   Langston Hughes.   BPo

Her battered hulk is heaving to and fro.   The Derelict.   Lucius Harwood Foote.   AA

Her beads and her beauty/Were raiment rare!   The Ballad of Adam's First.   Leland Davis.   HBMV

Her beauty conquers all.   Love's Emblem.   John Clare.   NIP

Her beauty is her own and she is not proud.   Mabel Kelly.   Turlough O'Carolan.   BIrV

Her beauty, not his sin, had struck him blind.   Peeping Tom.   Francis Hope.   ErPo

Her beauty's clear prerogative/To profit so by Eden's blame.   Preludes.   Coventry Patmore.   HBV 1-2

Her beauty's wonder lives again in me.   Diana.   Henry Constable.   OBSC

Her bed a rosy nest/By a bed of roses prest.   The Rose.   Richard Lovelace.   EG

Her bed is India; there she lies, a pearl.   Troilus and Cressida.   William Shakespeare.   GBL

Her beneath the woman/I seem to be!   The Woman I Am.   Glen Allen.   BLPA

Her bird-delighting citron-trees/In every purple vale!   Tartary.   Walter De La Mare.   HBMV; OxBChV

Her black gazelle eyes I have seen.   Krishnakali.   Rabindranath Tagore.   ACV

Her blacks crackle and drag.   Edge.   Sylvia Plath.   FaBoWP; HaCAP; TAP

Her blows did make ye blue.   How Violets Came Blue.   Robert Herrick.   CaPo; EnL

Her body, lithe and brown.   The Cat.   Charles Baudelaire.   PoPl

Her bones leak radium.   Artificial Death, II.   Elizabeth Ann James.   SOTS

Her bracelets will glitter,/becoming the lights/of a village you turned from years ago.   For Her.   Mark Strand.   GOYP

Her bread upon the water.   Gastric.   C. T.   PeD

Her break shook me and a brown arm closed down/A show I would have stayed a season with.   Visionary Oklahoma Sunday Beer.   James Whitehead.   SM

Her breasts are still filling with milk.   On the Death of a New Born Child.   Mei Yao Ch'en.   NaP

Her breath always only half an inch from the corner of my eye.   Collapsible.   Tom Raworth.   EAS

...Her breath as it/flows in and out like light through opals.   Chinese Baby Asleep.   Dorothy Donnelly.   NCSH

Her breath grow slow and light/As it joined with his own.   The Harvest.   William Aberg.   LFAC

Her brest that table was so richly spredd,/My thoughts the guests, which would thereon have fedd.   Amoretti, LXXVII.   Edmund Spenser.   AAS

Her burning eyes on her forgetful hands.   The Power of Interval.   John Byrne Leicester Warren, Lord De Tabley.   NOBV; OBSP; VLP

...Her/changeableness. My unchangingness.   Questions ⅛.   Donald Hall.   FF

...Her chase/The God of Nature in the fields of grace.   For Hope.   Richard Crashaw.   LiTB; ViBoPo

Her chaste desires, and angel's face.   Nuptial Hymn.   Henry Peacham.   EIl

...Her chewed fingers/are tatooed SUE on one hand DAVE on the other.   Driving into Enid.   Michael Van Walleghen.   FYAP

Her child, her sex, her tyrant, and herself.   An Indian Mother about to Destroy Her Child.   James Montgomery.   PaPo

Her child it must have been.   After the Death of Her Daughter in Childbirth...   Izumi Shikibu.   PBWP

Her child stops and mumbles...   A Child of Hers.   T. Walking Eagle Marietta.   LFAC

Her children suffer: without her   Must Be the Season of the Witch.   Alurista.   FIA

Her clowns, with cobbled shoon stuck full of iron tackets.   On the Road to Anster Fair.   William Tennant.   OBRV

Her cold divinities of death and change.   The Cold Divinities.   James Wright.   AmPC

...Her constitutional majesty/in the red world of love.   Poem: "The person who can do."   Alan Dugan.   NoAm

Her coral lips, her snow-white dimpled chin.   Midnight.   William Shakespeare.   OBSC

Her crowned self submits to her own laws.   Love Enthroned.   Richard Lovelace.   CaPo

Her Cupid is a black-guard boy,/That runs his link full in your face.   Song: "Dorinda's sparkling wit, and eyes."   Charles, Earl of Dorset Sackville.   CavP; OBS; SeCV 1-2

Her dead face, my fallen city,/are more real to me than love./My fate, my sorrow.)   Under the Ruins of Poland.   Itzik Manger.   VWA

Her deathless syllable.   Step lightly on this narrow spot!   Emily Dickinson.   NePA

Her doom (unknown),/her unmown green.   The Picture of J. T. in a Prospect of Stone.   Charles Tomlinson.   PoCh; PPP

...Her dress unwrinkled/Like the Rhone passing through Geneva.   The Standing.   Medbh McGuckian.   FaBoIP

Her dusky face is lit with sober light,/Sibylline, yet benign.   Formerly a Slave.   Herman Melville.   PoNe; TAP

Her ear, she never/Would have bounced.   Zimmer's Last Gig.   Paul Zimmer.   AMV-80

Her entrance was wet, and she came.   Rite of Spring.   Seamus Heaney.   OxBC

Her escort is like a river.   In the Wicker Fish-Trap.   *Anonymous.*   HW

Her exquisite yellow youth...   Jessie Mitchell's Mother.   Gwendolyn Brooks.   BoWoP; NAs; NMM

Her eyebrows wove with a golden thread.   Ibby Damsel.   *Anonymous.*   AmFP

Her eyes blink, tirelessly winking.   A Pair of Fireflies.   Stephen Shu Ning Liu.   BrSi

Her eyes have not shut all night.   The Jealous Lovers.   Donald Hall.   NYBP

Her eyes kept watch on her people.   Seeing Oloalok.   Marilyn Bowering.   NOBC

Her eyes shall give me brighter days,/Her arms much softer nights.   May the Ambitious Ever Find.   Charles, Earl of Dorset Sackville.   UnTE

Her eyes staring clear, through white flakes of sea-salt.   Five Lyrics from "Good for Nothing Man".   Kenneth Pitchford.   CoPo

Her eyes unfocused, mouth half-open.   Beets.   Alden Nowlan.   PeCV

Her eyes were fixed and mad, like mine and the panthers.'   Here and There: Nocturnal Landscape.   Malcolm Cowley.   PoA

Her eyes were kind.   Song: "Singer within the little streets."   Monk Gibbon.   NeIP

Her face and will athirst against the light.   A Soul.   Christina Georgina Rossetti.   WPOW

Her face lily-white, kissed and dry and cold.   Wildflower.   Stanley Plumly.   LCAP

...Her face/Still in the rictus of victory?   Resuscitation Team.   U. A. Fanthorpe.   FaBoWP

Her fair eternal form/spreadeagled in the empty air/of existence.   A Coney Island of the Mind.   Lawrence Ferlinghetti.   LiTM; NeAP; PoM

Her faulty snowfall brilliantly denied.   The Phenomenon.   Karl Shapiro.   CMoP; NMP; NYBP

Her feathers full of water and her neck/Under the water like a bar of light.   Swans Mating.   Michael Longley.   FaBoIP

Her filthie parbreake all the place defiled has.   The Faerie Queene.   Edmund Spenser.   EBEV

Her fire has already started.   A Sale of Smoke.   Roberta Spear.   AmPA

Her five American children and their mates/never did grow quite prosperous enough to send).   Kennedy Airport.   Aaron Kramer.   AMV-80

Her food was more divine.   Sarah Threeneedles.   Katharine Lee Bates.   HBMV

Her four sons, my father/and me   Requiem.   Stephen Vincent.   NeAC

Her fugitive pieces will find themselves safe.   A Fable for Critics.   James Russell Lowell.   OBSV

Her future is an apple tree, his past a dark old yew/Growing together in this orchard now.   Enigma.   Richard Murphy.   CIP

Her God upon her lap: the Virgin-Bride,/Her awful Child: her Son!   Aishah-Schechinah.   Robert Stephen Hawker.   GoBC; ISi; OBNC; OxBoCh

Her golden hair hanging down to her knees.   The Hog-Eye Man (with music).   *Anonymous.*   AS

Her goofs her goons her big galoots/under the red-face moon?   Yes, What?   Robert Francis.   LCAP

Her great sou knotted in a handkerchief.   Eighteen-Seventy.   Arthur Rimbaud.   OBWP

...Her grief/left no after-taste.   How I Was Her Kitchen-Boy.   Gunter Grass.   AMV-81

Her hair, like rain, closed on the thorny rose.   The Fortunate Fall.   Alfred Alvarez.   VWA

Her hair pulled/back her face/wide open   Martha Graham.   Lyn Lifshin.   LTB

...Her hair/Reverberates with light.   The Minotaur.   Robert Gibb.   FAZ

Her hair that touched the ground, and, shown/Between her Swan's legs, feathers and white down.   The Swan.   Stephen Spender.   UnS

Her hand moved into the dense plumes/on his breast to touch/the utter stranger.   Leda Reconsidered.   Mona Van Duyn.   NMM

Her hand on your sleeve.   There Is Something.   Deborah Pope.   AMV-81

...Her hand opened/again, and the streets opened, and she wished all well.   Bess.   William Stafford.   GP; NNaP; NoP

Her hand seemed milk in milk, it was so white.   Of Phyllis.   William, of Hawthornden Drummond.   EIL; HBV 1-2; LiTL

Her head covered with black feathers...   Descending Figure.   Louise Gluck.   FaBoWP; GeTw

Her heart did break, it was so sore,/But she shed not any tear.   Prince Robert.   *Anonymous.*   AmFP

Her heart had had a sonnet.   Auf Meiner Herzliebsten Augelein.   Heinrich Heine.   AWP

Her heart is empire, and her love is heaven.   Verses Copied From the Window of an Obscure Lodging-House.   *Anonymous.*   LiTL; ViBoPo

Her hearts of oak!   Ode.   Philip Freneau.   AP

Her honest fame shall ever live/Within the mouth of man.   On the Princess Mary.   John Heywood.   OBSC

Her hose of Honesty, I guess,/I should for her provide.   The Garment of Good Ladies.   Robert Henryson.   ACP

Her I should recognize/years later, anywhere.   Sisters.   Adrienne Rich.   IHMS

Her jag, her jag, her jagged tail.   Jonah and the Whale.   *Anonymous.*   BLPA

Her joyes, her smiles, her loves, as readers take/For Venus Ceston, every line you make.   A Sonnet, to the Noble Lady, the Lady Mary Worth.   Ben Jonson.   AnAnS 2

...Her King, who smiled upon/Her tears and said: "Behold, thy son."   Esther.   Fray Angelico Chavez.   GoBC

Her kisses/Dissolve us in pleasure, and soft repose.   The Beggar's Opera.   John Gay.   CEP; EnLoPo; TEP

Her Knees and elbows are only/glued together.   When a Man Has Married a Wife.   William Blake.   ErPo; FF

...Her knees/which looked up at opposite ends/of the sky.   Lost on September Trail, 1967.   Alberto Rios.   FYAP

Her last breath, disappointed.   Martha Blake at Fifty-One.   Austin Clarke.   CIP; IPY; NOBI

Her leg was drowned first, and/her head followed after.   Peg.   *Anonymous.*   OxNR

Her life is his.   Hari, look at me a while.   Mira Bai [(or Mirabai)].   BoWoP

Her life–she feels it closing about her now/Like a small theater, empty, without lights.   A Dancer's Life.   Donald Justice.   LCAP

Her lily breast doth stain/All flowers and lilies far.   Daphnis Came on a Summer's Day.   *Anonymous.*   ViBoPo

Her lips as red as a cherry.   How to Choose a Wife.   *Anonymous.*   FaBoUs

Her lips my kisses alway.   On a Rainy Night (excerpt).   Harry Edward Mills.   PeD

Her little boy weeping sought.   The Little Boy Found.   William Blake.   CBEP; NoP

Her livan bouk back i the licht. Juist byde a wee.   Ice-Flumes Owregie Their Lades.   Douglas Young.   SeCePo

Her lonely voice still calls him–but her panther won't/come in!   The Cat.   Richard Church.   BoAnP; PCat

Her lost moist hand clings mortally to mine.   Modern Love, XXI.   George Meredith.   NOBV; VLP

Her lot to bear, to nurse, to rear,/To love,–and then to lose.   Songs of Seven.   Jean Ingelow.   HVB 1-2

Her love hath end; my woe must ever last.   The Eleventh and Last Book of the Ocean to Cynthia.   Sir Walter Ralegh.   NCEP

Her love is true I know.   True Love.   Waring Cuney.   CDC

...Her love our own showing/Her love in all her honor.'   A (excerpt).   Louis Zukofsky.   VGW

Her love prevented my one dream,/To soar across the skies.   On the Road There Stands a Tree.   Itzik Manger.   VWA

Her love was pure and willing,/And so was mine forever.   Rainbow Willow.   *Anonymous.*   BFSS

Her lover vanish'd in the air/And she gaed weeping away.   Clerk Saunders.   *Anonymous.*   OxBS

...Her makeup left/upon the second face, she smiles.   Chamber Music.   John Ditsky.   AMV-81

Her meanings lost in manners, she will walk/Alone in brilliant circles to the end.   Pathedy of Manners.   Ellen de Young Kay.   SoSe

Her mind, adorned with virtues manifold.   All This World's Riches.   Edmund Spenser.   LiTL

...Her mind/drinks up/the full meaning/of it/all!   The Mental Hospital Garden.   William Carlos Williams.   FYAP

Her mother feels relieved.   Haiku: "When the daughter."   *Anonymous.*   HW

Her motto is "Glory! we conquer or we die."   The United States and Macedonian.   *Anonymous.*   PAH

Her mouth blooms with a beloved name, her own.   Sappho.   Jack Cope.   PeSA

Her much-adored delightful Fairy Prince!   Modern Love, X.   George Meredith.   NBM; PoEL 1-5; VLP

Her naked love, my great good news.   O Night O Trembling Night.   Stephen Spender.   ErPo; NeBP

Her name, her nature, wither'd from the world!   The Pleasures of Hope.   Thomas Campbell.   EnRP

Her name is Dragon Fly.   Lalai (Dreamtime).   Sam Woolagoodjah.   NOAV

Her name of Sinless Child.   From "The Sinless Child."   Elizabeth Oakes Smith   AA

Her neck and breast was like the snow,/Then from the bore I was forced to go.   The Whummil Bore.   *Anonymous.*   ESPB

Her neck is so long and strangly/I'm afraid she will never die.   Old Maid's Song.   *Anonymous.*   AmFP

Her nose in the tail of the hound. The Angry Poet. Frank O'Connor. CIP

...Her/old cunt chews/like it still had teeth. Mr. Muscle-On. Faye Kicknosway. GeTw

Her only answer from the reed he blew. Pan and Syrinx. W. R. Rodgers. NMP

Her only treasure,/and never spent. Early Losses: A Requiem. Alice Walker. BlSi

Her own self-will made void her own self's will. The End of It. Francis Thompson. NOBV; OBSP

Her own smile becoming tighter and tighter. Rivalry. Alden Nowlan. PoL

Her pale head heavy as metal. Snowdrop. Ted Hughes. FaBoMo

Her pale lavender outline/startled into eternity. Four Mountain Wolves. Leslie Marmon Silko. VoR

Her pelvis may be ruined/For a thousand years. We Are a Young Nation, Uncle. Marilyn Chin. BrSi

Her placket no longer open to the Saxon. Eire. David O'Bruadair. BIrV

Her planetary eyes, and touch her voice/With such a sorrow... The Fall of Hyperion. John Keats. MBW 1-2

Her playmate, and her wooer in the shade. Endymion. John Keats. OAEP; OBEV; OBRV

Her position by now is much higher! Limerick: "A new servant maid named Maria." Anonymous. TDH

Her powdering, with her eyes on me. Body and Spirit. William Henry Davies. AtBAP

Her praise and worth I'll sing alway. The Virtuous Wife. Von Trimberg Susskind. TrJP

Her pride in her denial lies/And mine is in my victories. O What Pleasure 'Tis to Find. Aphra Behn. UnTE

Her pulses flutter'd like a dove/To hear him speak. She listen'd like a cushat dove. Christina Georgina Rossetti. EG

Her pupils glow with pleasure all night long. Song: "The engine screams and Murphy, isolate." Thomas Kinsella. FaBoIP

Her quiet eyelids closed–she had/Another morn than ours! We Watch'd Her Breathing. Thomas Hood. ELP

Her red, rosy cheeks is moulderin' away. The Fair Damsel from London (The Brown Girl–Pretty Sarah). Anonymous. AmFP

Her rust-red autumn-beech-leaf hair. Song: "Rousing to rein his pad's head back." Geoffrey Taylor. NeIP; OxBI

Her's ever and her's still, come life, come death!/God save Elizabeth! God Save Elizabeth! Francis Turner Palgrave. HBV 1-2

Her scaly heart flaking until dawn. Mythics. Helen Chasin. DFT

Her setting star, like Bethlehem's,/To Thee shall point the way! Vesta. John Greenleaf Whittier. TrPWD; WHA

Her sheaves too heavy for the talkers there. On Bertrand Russell's "Portraits from Memory'. Donald Davie. FaBoTw

Her shrieks were for Young Edwin that ploughed the Lowlands low. Young Edwin in the Lowlands Low. Anonymous. BaBo; OBET

Her silent fury of bones hammering the boards. The Old Peasant Woman at the Monastery of Zagorsk. James Schevill. NMP

Her skin was satin and gold. Escapist's Song. Theodore Spencer. PoL

Her small body impressed/in needles on the dark green floor Step father. Judith Fitzgerald. CaPN

Her songs died on the air. Song: "She sat and sang alway." Christina Georgina Rossetti. GBL

Her sons from the waters return once again. The Grimsby Lads. Anonymous. OBSS

Her soul is from her body reft;/Her spirit be forgiven!' William and Helen. Sir Walter Scott. EnRP; OAEP

Her soul spoke thus (I know it did). Servant Girl and Grocer's Boy. Joyce Kilmer. YaD

Her soules into sin/For any worldes win,/That was so dere y-boght! I Sigh when I Sing. Anonymous. OxBM

Her spirit stands unhoused before my door. Grey Woman. Gladys Cardiff. CDW; TWSS

Her stockings are torn but she is beautiful. Women. Adrienne Rich. NMM

Her stockings of finely-knitted silk. Sonnet: "Idly she yawned, and threw her heavy hair." George Moore. ErPo

Her tall boyfriend/with the fast car/and paul newman smile/is no competition For Your Inferiority Complex. David O'Rourke. AMV-81

...Her teeth whiten/the bloodsea of her mouth. Nina Simone. Lance Jeffers. CNA

Her temples chafe–but all too late–/The wound's A BROKEN HEART! The Forced Bridal. Anonymous. PaPo

An' her tender heart did brak in three. The Great Silkie of Sule Skerry (B vers.). Anonymous. ViBoFo

Her that in life was not content with two. On a Whore. John Hoskyns. FaBoEE

Her thieves are never hung. Epigram on a Lawyer's Desiring One of the Tribe to Look.... Robert Fergusson. OxBS

Her thoughts a moment since of one who shines/Apart, and would be hers if he had known. Firelight. Edwin Arlington Robinson. NoAm

...Her three/Children follow like figures in effigy. Home Leave. Barbara Howes. MP; TwCP

Her titled language crowned in high/entail. Two Argosies. Wallace Bruce. AA

Her tongue has been replaced by/a single mute camellia. The United States Prepare for the Permanent Revolution. George Hitchcock. EAS

Her touch is a perfume, a melody. Mishka. John Gray. NOBV; SyP

Her towers, and lone sands heap her/crowned merchants' graves. United States. John Keble. CoBE

Her trail is this twisting stream/that she sends, milky, to the sea. Message from Ohanapecosh Glacier. W. M. Ransom. CDW

Her udder shrivels and the milk goes dry. The Cow in Apple Time. Robert Frost. CABA; MoAB; MoAmPo; OBSP; PoLf

Her uncontrollable, aching cry of love. Circe. A. D. Hope. PPP

Her value is above the pearl,/That takes delight in sporting. Song: "If she be not as kind as fair." Sir George Etherege. CavP; CEP

Her vertu meriteth more prayse, than parlye can utter. Nature in Her Working. Richard Stanyhurst. NCEP

Her very frowns are fairer far/Than smiles of other maidens are. She Is Not Fair to Outward View. Hartley Coleridge. FaBV; GTBS; GTBS-P; LiTL

Her very individual,/Unpliable/Own. Offspring. Naomi Long Madgett. FB

Her Voice and Smiles my Song shall grace. Odes. Horace. OBVE

Her voice comes to you through the lips of a crone. Change of Life. Constance Urdang. VWA

Her voice could not be softer/When she told it in confession. Her Voice Could Not Be Softer. Austin Clarke. NOBI

Her voice lifting us into trees. A Dangerous Music. Michael Knoll. LFAC

Her weary lips beat on without a sound. A Look into the Gulf. Edwin Markham. AA

Her wedding gown it was she wrought,/Sewing the long white seam. The Long White Seam. Jean Ingelow. GN; HBV 1-2; NOBV

Her whose graceful beauty/Lost is now to me! Tripping down the Field-Path. Charles Swain. HBV 1-2

Her woman's heart for me! Song: "O, like a queen's her happy tread." William Watson. HBV 1-2

Her wounds came from the same source as her power Power. Adrienne Rich. TAP

Her young disciples leaves behind. The River Swelleth More and More. Henry David Thoreau. NOBA

Hera of the gold throne beside/him. The Iliad. Homer. NAWM 1-2

An herald strange, the like was never born,/Whose very beard is flesh, and mouth is horn. On the Cards and Dice. Sir Walter Ralegh. EnRePo; FCP

Herald the Spring with a battle of melody/and music of clarinet droning. The Clouds. Aristophanes. LiTW

Heralds all of day's approaching. Dawn. Anonymous. WTO

The herb that beat back fever and sore/went home to its family: the lilies. Garlic. Marvin Bell. GP

The herb, the flower, is eaten by the snail. Upon a Snail. John Bunyan. OxBChV

An' herds o' common men! The Blind Boy's Pranks. William Thom. OBEV

Here, a dark sea speaks with white hands. Bone Thoughts on a Dry Day. George Starbuck. GoYe; MP; TwCP

Here a false face won't help you. A Bestiary. Kenneth Rexroth. OBAL

...Here a fountain/bubbles forth a cold and stainless water. I am Hermes. Anyte. BoWoP

Here a nail and there a nail,/tick, tack, too. Is John Smith Within? Anonymous. OxNR

"Here am I, send me, send me." Something You Can Do. Anonymous. STF

"Here and here, man, m-a-a-n." Sheep. Hal Porter. PoAu 1-2

Here and hereafter, touch a Paradise. To Ned. Herman Melville. MOS; NOBA; PoEL 1-5; ViBoPo

Here and there, defiant,/A shout of gold. Judean Summer. Fay Lipshitz. VWA

Here and there, in cold pockets/Of remembrance, whispers out of time. Self-Portrait in a Convex Mirror. John Ashbery. HaCAP

Here behold it open laid. Of His Mistress. Peter Hausted. EG

Here by the eastern sea. A Tribute of Grasses. Hamlin Garland. AA; AnAmPo

Here come the jets. Seven Sharp Propeller Blades. John Ciardi. QQQ

Here come the trains. Trains. James S. Tippett. SoPo; SUS; TiPo

Here comes a chopper to chop off your head. Oranges and Lemons. Anonymous. OxNR

Here comes a cropper'. That's what I said. American Lights, Seen from Off Abroad. John Berryman. LCAP; OBAL

Here comes another, flopping among the sage.   Tumbleweed.   David Wagoner.   BoNaP

Here comes baby, apples and all.   Catch Him, Crow! Carry Him, Kite!   *Anonymous.*   OxNR

Here comes Keery galloping by!   Husky Hi.   Rose Fyleman.   TiPo

Here comes my husband from his whist.   Dis Alitr Visum; or, le Byron de nos Jours.   Robert Browning.   VLP

Here comes old Jack with a broken pack,/A gallop, a gallop, a gallop.   Here Comes My Lady with Her Little Baby.   *Anonymous.*   OxNR

Here comes the lady; let her witness it.   Othello.   William Shakespeare.   BoC; EBEV; SCV; TreF

Here comes the man in the green flannel suit.   Speaking of Television: Robin Hood.   Phyllis McGinley.   OBSV

–Here comes the smoking Bouillabaisse!   The Ballad of Bouillabaisse.   William Makepeace Thackeray.   FaBoUs; HBV 1-2; InMe; OBEV; OBTV; OBVV; ViBoPo

Here comes trotting, snorting death/let loose again.   Death Invited.   May Swenson.   BoAnP; LiSp

Here Damon lies, whose Songes did some-time grace/The murmuring Esk; may Roses shade the place.   To Sir William, of Hawthornden Alexander.   William, of Hawthornden Drummond.   OBS

Here dead men speake their last, and so/do I;/Love-slaine, loe, here I lye.   The Paradox.   John Donne.   OAEP

Here drifted/An hedonist.   The Age Demanded.   Ezra Pound.   InPo; NoP

Here Dulness reigns, with mighty wings outspread,/And brings the true Saturnian age of lead.   Inscriptio.   Alexander Pope.   OBSP

Here ends the days of a faithful youth.   Young Forbest.   *Anonymous.*   ShS

Here ends the story of my Aunt/And her ungrateful weed.   My Aunt.   Ted Hughes.   WSC

Here ends the Will of Cathaeir Mor, who was King of Ireland.   The Testament of Cathaeir Mor.   *Anonymous.*   OnYI

Here error is all in the not done,/all in the diffidence that faltered.   The Pisan Cantos (excerpt).   Ezra Pound.   FaBoTw; NOBE

Here, every thought and mood and fancy rise/From common earth, and soar to mystic skies.   Laurence Bloomfield in Ireland.   William Allingham.   IrPN

Here follow untranslatable French puns.   Sonnet Ending with a Film Subtitle.   Marilyn Hacker.   MAYP; SM

Here, for a moment, I am Thou.   Uriel.   William Force Stead.   TrPWD

Here, for just a season,/Among these clever citizens.   Winter in Etienburgh.   Stephen Parker.   NYBP

Here gives a prison, there a throne.   To Aaron Burr, under Trial for High Treason.   Sarah Wentworth Morton.   PAH

Here, Hannah, take these breakfast things away.   Morning.   *Anonymous.*   NOEC

Here he is near!   Satan Is Following Me.   *Anonymous.*   WTO

Here he paused and did stay,/Sighed, and rose, and went away.   Philomela's Second Ode.   Robert Greene.   OBSC

Here–here–here is my finishing line.   There Is No Place.   Aleksander Wat.   VWA

Here: here is his trail.   The Trail.   Edward Weismiller.   WaP

Here, here the Tomb of Robin Herrick is.   To Robin Red-Breast.   Robert Herrick.   OBS; PBBP; TrGrPo

Here I am–HAUF-ROADS UP PIGGIN SCHIEHALLION/Aa for the guid o my health!   Hauf-Roads Up Schiehallion.   Donald Campbell.   PoSH

Here i come, dear shoes.   Aubade.   Anselm Hollo.   APU

Here I feel/my wide forehead/a shore of eternity   Song for a Day (excerpt).   Francisco Arrivi.   InW

Here I fix my habitation,/In thy sheltering love at home.   Laboring and Heavy Laden.   Jeremiah Eames Rankin.   AH

Here. I insist. I want/to pay them all back.   Flesh Coupon.   Jeff Wright.   APU

Here I live, lone clock-a-clay,/Watching for the time of day.   Clock-a-clay.   John Clare.   CBEP; ERoP 1-2; LiTB; LoBV; NBM; OAEL 1-2; OBNC; PoEL 1-5; SeCeV; TrGrPo; VLP; WHA

...Here I've related/Just what the lay commemorated.   Honeysuckle (Chevrefoil).   Marie de France.   BoWoP

Here I will drift through time like a lazy swimmer/and cities may pass me by.   Early Dutch.   Jennie M. Palen.   GoYe

Here, if you care, and lie full-length,/Is water deep enough to drown.   A Muse of Water.   Carolyn Kizer.   NMM

Here in His own abode,/Thy jealous God.   The Staff and Scrip.   Dante Gabriel Rossetti.   OAEP

Here in my breast!   The Water-Nymph and the Boy.   Roden and Wriothesley Berkeley Noel.   OBVV

Here in my crystalline,/Here in my breast!   I Flung Me Round Him.   Roden Noel.   HBV 1-2

...Here in one common sty/Men and their fellow-brutes with equal honor lie.   Brent: A Poem to Thomas Palmer, Esq.   William Diaper.   FaBoPP; NOEC; OBSV

Here in the book it cannot stay forever and there on the/sea the text is lost.   Seascape with Bookends.   Charles Edward Eaton.   AMV-80

Here in the car and in Queens and in Brooklyn.   Riding Westward.   Harvey Shapiro.   GP; NYP; VWA

Here, in the dark, it is being.   By Canoe through the Fir Forest.   James Dickey.   NYBP

Here in the forest-heart, hung blackening/The wolfbait on the bush beside the spring.   Elegy in Six Sonnets.   Frederick Goddard Tuckerman.   QFR

Here, in the mingling of our bloods.   Prothalamion.   Terence Tiller.   NeBP

Here in the suburb of the cruel city/and the swift tide out to sea.   A Jew Walks in Westminster Abbey.   Aubrey Hodes.   TrJP

Here in the sun I put apart from me/Cassandra, Helen, and Persephone.   Troubadours.   Arthur Davison Ficke.   HBMV

Here in the whelming abyss/As it were in the crook of an arm.   In Space-Time Aware–.   Abbie Huston Evans.   GP

Here in these beating valves, you will/For all my mortal time reside!   Montreal.   Abraham Moses Klein.   CaP; OBCV

Here in this other life.   South Inlet.   Greg Kuzma.   WOLT

Here in this simmering marsh.   River Roses.   D. H. Lawrence.   BrPo; CMoP; GBL; OAEL 1-2; ViBoPo

Here into pure green depth drop down from lofty ledges.   The Bothie of Tober-na-Vuolich.   Arthur Hugh Clough.   BoNaP

...Here is a bed.   Sailing to an Island.   Richard Murphy.   IPY; NMP

Here is a tale of right nought.   Snatches: "There was a man that hadde nought."   *Anonymous.*   OxBM

Here is a task for all that a man has of fortitude and delicacy.   A Christmas Sermon: To Be Honest, To Be Kind.   Robert Louis Stevenson.   PoLf

Here is Africa the great/Glittering/In the light of dawn.   I Am a Negro.   Muhammad Al-Fituri.   TTY

"Here is beauty, here is hope, here is peace."   The Wall.   Arthur L. Phelps.   CaP

Here is himself, marred, as you see, with traitors.   Julius Caesar.   William Shakespeare.   FaPoR

Here is life's holy amplitude/Thee who perhaps art not at all!   Doubt.   Fernand Gregh.   WGRP

Here is love, naked, lying in great state/On the bare ground, as in all human faces.   Nativity.   May Sarton.   NePoAm-2

Here is my heart for your valentine.   A Valentine.   Laura E. Richards.   YeAr

Here is my hope,/And my pyramides.   His Poetry His Pillar.   Robert Herrick.   AnAnS 2; CaPo; EG; EnL; JCP; LoBV; MyFE; OBS; QFR; SeCP

Here is no room for thee; go down to hell.   A Dead King.   Algernon Charles Swinburne.   VLP

"Here is one who senses the fitness of things."   Abandonment of Autos.   Bruce Dawe.   CBAP

"HERE IS REST!"   Last Lines.   Richard Harris Barham.   OBVV

"Here is that very selfsame smile/Come back with us to bed."   Keep Smiling.   *Anonymous.*   WBLP

Here is the alchemy of art that brings to this room/The face and the spirit of Israel.   Pictures at an Exhibition.   Nathan Rosenbaum.   GoYe

Here is the bleak radiance that levels the world.   Snow Train.   Louise Erdrich.   TWSS

"Here is the first pretty snowdrop"–and it was the dung of a/crow!   Epigram: "I ran upon life unknowing, without or science or art."   Alfred, Lord Tennyson.   FaBoEE

Here is the Land of Song!   To Arcady.   Charles Buxton Going.   HBV 1-2

Here is the peace of the fathers.   The Urn.   Hart Crane.   PoA

Here is the pillow./Rest.   Lullaby.   Léonie Adams.   AmLP; MoAB; MoAmPo

Here is the place to wake.   The Swallows.   Patric Dickinson.   ChMP

Here is three times three/For the Yankee Privateer!   The Yankee Privateer.   Arthur Hale.   PAH

"Here is your freedom. Taste–and come again!"   Freedom of the Hills.   Douglas Fraser.   PoSH

Here is your vicious, central shape/That has no need of cheer or tape.   This Runner.   Francis Webb.   CBAP

Here it is found.   Napkin and Stone.   Vernon Watkins.   NYBP

Here Klito spent eighty years.   Poems from the Greek Anthology.   of Tarentum Leonidas.   NNaP

"Here lay Julio/He were crazy for Truck."   Julio.   Kell Robertson.   TAT

Here lie I as warm as they.   On Elizabeth Ireland.   *Anonymous.*   FaBoEE

Here lie two poor lovers, who had the mishap/Though very chaste people, to die of a clap.   Three Epitaphs on John Hewet and Sarah Drew.   Alexander Pope.   NIP

Here lie Walker's particles.   On William Walker, Author of "A Treatise of English Particles."   *Anonymous.*   FaBoEE

"Here lies a bearer of the pall/At the funeral of Shakespeare."   In the Old Churchyard at Fredericksburg.   Frederick Wadsworth Loring.   AA

Here lies Ben Jonson, every age will look/With sorrow here, with wonder on his book.   On Ben Jonson.   Sidney Godolphin.   CBEP

Here lies blood, and let it lie/Speechless still, and never cry.   Epitaph on the Earl of Strafford.   John Cleveland.   CavP; FaBoEE; FaBoPV; NOBE; SeCePo

Here we go looby loo,/All on a Saturday night.   Here We Go Looby Loo. *Anonymous.*   FSW

Here we go,/The Umbrella Brigade!   The Umbrella Brigade.   Laura E. Richards.   SoPo; SUS; TiPo

Here we who loved so, were so cold and bitter,/Hardly can disagree.   You would have understood me, had you waited.   Paul Verlaine.   BoLoP

...Here, where he begins.   To Landrum Guy, Beginning to Write at Sixty. James Dickey.   PP

Here, where she used to love me,/Here, where she loves me not.   Song: "Has summer come without the rose."   Arthur William Edgar O'Shaughnessy. HBV 1-2

Here where the wind skins Drumochter/Only the storm moves fast. Drumochter.   Anne B. Murray.   PoSH

Here, where Time brings pasture to the sea.   By the North Sea.   Algernon Charles Swinburne.   FaBoPP

Here where you lay the sheep will browse.   The Fallen Zulu Commander. C. M. Van Den Heever.   PeSA

Hereafter comes not yet.   Patience, for I have wrong.   Sir Thomas Wyatt. FCP; SiPS

Hereafter fame, here martyrdom.   The Prophet.   Abraham Cowley.   JCP; TrGrPo

Hereafter, he that lacks this hour,/May be as great as I.   Hymns for the Amusement of Children.   Christopher Smart.   NOCV

Herein the gospel mystery lies,/Through Christ revealed by sacrifice.   Living Bread.   Eva Weaver Sefton.   BePJ

Herewith, therefore, to take effect at once, I resign.   Operative No. 174 Resigns.   Kenneth Fearing.   NYBP

A heritage, it seems to me,/Well worth a life to hold in fee.   The Heritage. James Russell Lowell.   HBV 1-2; HBVY

Herkne to my roun!   Alison.   *Anonymous.*   MeEL; NoP

Hermes' moly, growing solely/To undo enchanter's wile!   Moly.   Edith Matilda Thomas.   HBV 1-2

The hermit's chapel, the pilgrim's prayer.   Landscapes.   Thomas Stearns Eliot.   BiP; LoGBV

A hermit-soul gone raving mad,/And beating at his bars.   The Loon.   Lew Sarett.   HBMV

The hern, the curlew are silent,/Silent a' thing.   Benighted to the Foothills of the Cairngorms.   Olive Fraser.   PoSH

The hero's garland his, the martyr's crown.   J. A. G.   Julia Ward Howe. PAH

Hero waits with she-goat's face.   On a Landscape of Sestos.   Carlos Baker. EyDe

Hero, who was a girl/track star from Gyara   I Taught the Talented. Sappho.   GLGT

Herod and Pilate riding by,/And Judas, one of three.   A Ballad of Christmas. Walter De la Mare.   OBCP

Herod is his name.   Innocent's Song.   Charles Causley.   GTBS-P; OBCP

Heroes to mate them.   Portait with Background.   Oliver St. John Gogarty. OBMV

Heroic hearts, upon our lonely way.   The Two Old Kings.   John Byrne Leicester Warren, Lord De Tabley.   OBEV; OBVV

The heroic Hektor who raised/that reflection of the heroic/in his shield...   At the Loom.   Robert Duncan.   VGW

Herr Love, Herr Lucifer,/Your flash/In the pan.   Godiva (parody).   D. C. Berry.   BXAP

Herrick shall make the meddow-verse for/you.   The Parting Verse, the Feast There Ended.   Robert Herrick.   SeCV 1-2

Herrick, thou art too coarse to love.'   The Vision.   Robert Herrick. AnAnS 2; CaPo; EAS; ErPo; JCP; SeCP

Hers, by thy beauty tempting her to thee,/Thine, by thy beauty being false to me.   Sonnets, XLI: "Those pretty wrongs that liberty commits."   William Shakespeare.   CBEP; InvP

Hers could not stay, for sympathy.   The Loveliness of Love.   George Darley. EG; GTBS-P

...Hers is the/Linear kingdom.   The Lady of the Castle.   John Hollander. GP

Hers is the shame if such forgotten be!   On the Proposal to Erect a Monument in England to Lord Byron.   Emma Lazarus.   AA

Hers never was the heart for you.   The Test.   Walter Savage Landor.   HBV 1-2

Hers. Not yours, my love. Hers.   Lost.   Alfred Alvarez.   NMP

Herself grow Eden once again, possest of Love and/thee.   A World for Love. John Clare.   PG

Herself the star, eclipsing those above her,/That shines, and to her chamber lights her Lover.   Moonlight.   Edward Moxon.   OBRV

Heven I tolde al his/That o night were hir gest.   A Maid Mars Me. *Anonymous.*   OxBM

Hevene blisse I shall yeve thee,/That lasteth ay and oo.'   Jesus Contrasts Man and Himself.   *Anonymous.*   MeEL

Hevene to ben our heritage.   A Warning to Those Who Serve Lords. *Anonymous.*   MeEL

Hey, are you just back for a visit or are you going to/stay?   Are You Just Back for a Visit or Are You Going to Stay?   Francis Coleman Rosenberger. AMV-81

Hey Betty Martin, Tip-toe fine!   Hey, Betty Martin!   *Anonymous.*   AS; ExPo

Hey boy, if you think we gon' help you/swear you better change your mind. Don't Want No Hungry Woman.   Floyd Council.   BluL

Hey boys, can't you line, ho boys, just a hair.   Lining Track.   *Anonymous.* AmFP

Hey, Buddy. Look!/I'm makin' a road!   Florida Road Workers.   Langston Hughes.   CTBA; GoSl; MoAmPo

Hey cat lady, you eat it.   Finger of Necessity.   Coleman Barks.   TW

Hey, cowboy! Bring 'em HOT!/HOT IR'N!   Hot Ir'n!   Squire Omar Barker. PoOW

Hey derry down, down adown.   Would God That It Were Holiday!   Thomas Deloney.   EIL

Hey! down-a-down, a-down.   The Death of Robin Hood.   *Anonymous.* BuBa

Hey down a down hey down derry.   Why Should Not We All Be Merry. *Anonymous.*   OBS

Hey down (Ho down)! Derry, derry down./Among the leaves so green, O. The Keeper.   *Anonymous.*   FSW

Hey, drag away, drag away!   Hey Dorolot.   *Anonymous.*   OxNR

Hey, Duke, why do you go ride/On a terrible old nag like that?   Considering the Death of John Wayne.   Louis Phillips.   SOTS

Hey, for cattle cook'd and cut!   Donought Would Have Everything. Ebenezer Elliott.   NOBV

Hey for home! Lo, for our guiding,/Hesper in the dusk abiding!   A Woodland Revel.   Clarence Urmy.   HBMV

An' hey for houghmagandie.   Gie the Lass Her Fairin'.   Robert Burns. CoMu; ErPo

Hey for the heart's delight!   In Kensington Gardens.   Arthur Symons. EnLoPo

Hey, good old Bowling Green.   Bowling Green.   *Anonymous.*   FSW

Hey, ho, away we go,/My Bonnie Hieland Laddie.   Hieland Laddie. *Anonymous.*   FSW

Hey, ho! Away we go!/Riding on a donkey.   Donkey Riding.   *Anonymous.* WHW

Hey ho! chill love no more.   Through Amaryllis Dance in Green. *Anonymous.*   EIL

Hey-how for Hallowe'en!   Hey-How For Hallowe'en!   *Anonymous.* FaBoCh; LoGBV

Hey, I wish it was Sunday then.   Courtship.   *Anonymous.*   OxNR

"Hey! Jolly Roger, O."   Pirate Treasure.   Abbie Farwell Brown.   EtS

Hey lee lee, and lye li lo.   Leatherwing Bat.   *Anonymous.*   FSW

Hey, little black-eyed Susie, hey!   Black-Eyed Susie.   *Anonymous.*   ABF; AmFP; FSW

Hey nonny no!   Hey Nonny No!   *Anonymous.*   EIL

Hey nonny ronny!   Colin.   Anthony Munday.   GTBS; GTBS-P

Hey? Of what doth the noble poet brood/In a tragic mood?   "These are the live."   Kenneth Fearing.   NAMP

Hey pretty mama/Tell me what have you done   No More Good Water. Jaybird Coleman.   BluL

Hey that's my cat!/Coming home.   Nature Green Shit.   Gary Snyder. LCAP

Hey, the sun gonna shine in/my back door some day   Bullfrog Blues. William J. Harris.   BluL

Hey, Willie Winkie!--See, there he comes!   Willie Winkie.   William Miller. FaFP; HBV 1-2; HBVY; OxBChV; OxNR

Hi cockalorum, jig, jig, jig.   Hush, My Baby, Do Not Cry.   *Anonymous.* OxNR

Hi, Hi, Curlywig, you've got it in/your pocket.   Hi, Hi, Curlywig. *Anonymous.*   PoPle

Hi Monkey/I'm home   Primavera.   Frank Lima.   ANYP

"Hi ya, gang!"   School Begins.   Nell Goodale Price.   BrR

Hi, yai! The world, how fair!   The Rainbow.   *Anonymous.*   WTO

Hi-yip! We've still got the ol' rodeo!   Rodeo Days.   Squire Omar Barker. PoOW

Hic habitat Felicitas!   The Library.   Frank Dempster Sherman.   AA

Hic hoc horum genitivo.   Amo, Amas.   John O'Keefe.   GBL

Hic jacet Joe. Hic jacet Bill.   Bill and Joe.   Oliver Wendell Holmes.   AA; HBV 1-2

Hickory, dickory, dock.   Hickory, Dickory, Dock.   Mother Goose. FaBoBe; FaFP; HBV 1-2; HBVY; OxNR; PoPl; SoPo; TiPo

Hid in the husks which on that day/My instinct would not throw away! Doubt.   Helen Hunt Jackson.   WGRP

Hidden behind the flower/of the moon   Three Moments.   Susan Sherman. DFF

Hidden behind the hills of sky.   Weather.   Hilda Conkling.   TiPo

The hidden boundary between/God's patience and His wrath.   The Doomed Man.   Joseph Addison Alexander.   TRV

Hidden by a minstrel-smile.   Heritage.   Gwendolyn B. Bennett.   BANP; BlSi

...A hidden ground/Of thought and of austerity within.   Austerity of Poetry. Matthew Arnold.   EnLi 1-2; OAEP; OBVV

Hidden in cellars when the boughs are bare.   The Ungathered Apples. James Wright.   ErPo

Hidden in darkness, I make my way to the east.   The Lord of the East. Chu Yuan.   LiTW

Hidden mischiefe to conceale in State and Love is treason.   Were My Hart as Some Mens Are.   Thomas Campion.   AAS; HBV 1-2

Hidden springs wine/and shoulder blades.   Divination.   Jerred Metz. VWA

Hidden under/wild hyacinths   People Do Gossip.   Sappho.   PBWP

Hide from me my dead pages/Against the black wall oblivion.   You Who Dog My Footsteps.   Leib Kwitko.   TrJP

Hide in deep herbage....   Endymion.   John Keats.   CTC

& Hide my fists/in my hands.   The Piano.   Frank Davey.   NOBC; WHW

Hide not Thyself, let first love prove not wrong.   A Psalm.   Edmund Charles Blunden.   TrPWD

Hide private parts which I disclose/To those who know what a poem knows. What Curious Dresses All Men Wear.   Delmore Schwartz.   ELU

Hide Thou me, Rock of Ages, safe in Thee.   Hide Thou Me.   Anonymous. AmFP

...Hide/your blonde strawed skull from the/white/multitude of drips.   Fag-End.   Philip O'Connor.   EAS

The Hidebehind's behind you.   The Hidebehind.   Michael Rosen.   AmMo

Hides in her heart an alien Paradise?   The Nun.   Arthur Symons.   BrPo

Hiding her lovely eyes until day break.   Secretary.   Ted Hughes.   ErPo

Hiding her thoughts away.   Waiting.   John Freeman.   CH

The hiding place of my rejected/prayers.   Beneath Thy Wing.   Hayim Nahman Bialik.   TrJP

Hiding, water-polished, under our sleep's blue shelf.   Anima.   Diana O Hehir.   NPGG

Higgledy piggledy, "fiddledum diddledum."   The Soldiers' Friend (parody). J. H. Frere and George Canning.   Par

Higgledy, piggledy, my black hen.   Higgledy, Piggledy, My Black Hen. Mother Goose.   FaBoBe; HBV 1-2; PBBP; TiPo

Higgledy, piggledy, niggledy, niggledy,/Gallop a dreary dun.   Master I Have, and I Am His Man.   Mother Goose.   TiPo

High above the world of talk/he slips honestly, falls/into the wind.   Wires. Lee Bassett.   SOTS

High above them/Blinding crystal is the sunlit steep.   Vermont.   Sarah N. Cleghorn.   HBMV

High bliss is only for a higher state.   To the Reverend Mr. Murdoch.   James (1700-48) Thomson.   OBEC

High brave glee!   Moon Mission.   Ron Baxter.   WeW

A high complexion without fleck/Or flaw, and curls about her neck.   At a Reading.   Thomas Bailey Aldrich.   OBAL

High diddledydee.   Says I to Myself.   Edward Lear.   FiBHP

High her call to us rings: Come to me...   Arignota Remembers.   Sappho. LiTW

...High, high/are the mountains, etc.   Southern Liebeslieder.   Joan Retallack. AmC

High, high up in the air.   What's in There?   Anonymous.   CH; OxNR

High in the Valais-depth profound,/I saw the morning break.   Obermann Once More.   Matthew Arnold.   PoEL 1-5

High in their other heaven, pardon love.   To a Nun.   Anonymous.   EBEV

The High King of Glory permit her to get the mange.   A Glass of Beer. James Stephens.   AnFE; CMoP; DBV; DTC; ExPo; FaBoCo; FiBHP; GoTF; InPK; NCSH; NLV; NoAm; OBMV; OBSP; OxBTC; SeCePo; TreFT; TW

...The high lean country/full of old stories that still go walking in my sleep. South of My Days.   Judith Wright.   FaBoWP; PoAu 1-2

High noon hummed,/all parts in place--/or nearly so.   Cicada.   Adrien Stoutenburg.   RFM

...High on a wall/spitting on Ira Rosenblatt   Spitting on Ira Rosenblatt. Robert Hershon.   NeAC

High on the hill/Here...   Song of the Hill.   Edith Lodge.   GoYe

High on the peak of Fuji.   I passed by the beach.   Akahito (Yamabe no Akahito).   HoPM

"High over all the lonely bugle grieves."   The Singer of One Song.   Henry Augustin Beers.   AA

High over many lives/may he be raised and glorified.   Joshua's Face.   Amir Gilboa.   VWA

High overhead the crow of night/Patrols eternity.   Pocomania.   Derek Walcott.   NoAm

High priestess of your home.   Autumn.   Jean Starr Untermeyer.   MCCG; MoAmPo

A high rushing tide of dark hair   Am Driven Mad.   Allen Polite.   NNP

High stepped the horses for us, proud riders in autumn.   Proud Riders. H.L. Davis.   AnAmPo

High the sun stood in the heavens,/But no shadow followed him.   The Parklands.   Stevie Smith.   MoBS

High up in the clear butter of her mother floated).   The Eggs.   Peter Redgrove.   NAs

The higher up the altitude,/The swifter down the plummet.   Alpine View. Melville Cane.   PoPl

The highest earthly bloom of matter's brief commotion.   Tides.   Will H. Blackwell.   AMV-80

The highest spires were ablaze with the movement of feet.   Victoria Market. Francis Brabazon.   BoAV; NOAV

The highest symbol is in the reality.   The Tree of Death.   Claude Vigee. VWA

A highly inflammable/balloon eclipsed by seminal/and nubile/loving.   For My Mother.   June Jordan.   BoWoP; NMM

A highly susceptible Chancellor!   The Susceptible Chancellor.   Sir William Schwenck Gilbert.   ALV

Highly th' imperial sign/shone in his glory!   Christophe.   Russell Atkins. PoNe

Highly transcendental.   80-Proof.   Archie Randolph Ammons.   SUW

Highway still must lead to thee!   The Highway.   William Channing Gannett. WGRP

The hill all summer hid from me.   Autumn Daybreak.   Edna St. Vincent Millay.   LaNeLa

The hill of Astonishment,/And the hill of Babylon.   The Burglar of Babylon. Elizabeth Bishop.   NYBP

Hill over that far-off hill.   Animal Songs: Baboon.   Anonymous.   PeSA

The hill steep and slick, and what/One other reason do I fumble over?   In a Mirror.   Marcia Stubbs.   MAT

The hills are mute: yet how they speak of God!   Silence.   Charles Hanson Towne.   TRV; WGRP

The hills breathing like a horse's flank/with grasses combed and clean of the last snow.   Tasmania.   Vivian Smith.   NOAV

Hills of the middle distance: storm and calm,/each with its friendliness.   Hills of the Middle Distance.   Archie Mitchell.   PoSH

Hills peep o'er hills, and Alps on Alps arise!...   An Essay on Criticism. Alexander Pope.   ChTr

The hills sleep on in their eternity.   To a Friend.   Hartley Coleridge. CBEP; HBV 1-2; OBRV; PoLf

The hills where his life rose,/And the sea where it goes.   The Buried Life. Matthew Arnold.   BoLiVe; EnL; ForPo; MaVP; OAEL 1-2; OAEP; SeCeV; VLP

Hills, where light poplars, the firm oak,/Loosen into a little smoke.   Last Hill in a Vista.   Louise Bogan.   FaBoWP

Him bare a maide-moder, Marye.   A Hymn of the Incarnation.   Anonymous. MeEL

Him born of maid-mother, Mary.   Glad and Blithe Might Ye Be. Anonymous.   SBVL

Him here retain, blest he whom Christ hath call'd.   The Reverend Mr. Higginson...   Edward Johnson.   SCAP

Him in the empty hall.   Seasons of the Soul.   Allen Tate.   MoVE; NePA; OxBA

Him lodging in your bosom to have lent.   Amoretti, LXXIII.   Edmund Spenser.   AAS; CoBE

An' him no more to me nor me to him/Than the wind goin' over my hand. Sea Love.   Charlotte Mew.   ELU; MoAB; MoBrPo; OxBTC; TrGrPo; ViBoPo

Him, said the Lord, him you shall hate.   Amalek.   Friedrich Torberg. VWA

Him, she brings in.   Still Life: Lady with Birds.   Quandra Prettyman. CAD; PoBA

Him so her for to serven/That he us to him take.   The Annunciation. Anonymous.   MeEL; OxBM

Him tellee no lie, gottee pigtail on.   Foreigners at the Fair.   Fred Emerson Brooks.   OBAL

Him that I am fashioning of fine white clay.   Fine Clay.   Winifred Shaw. PoAu 1-2

"Him through handmaiden me."   A Faith on Trial (excerpt).   George Meredith.   WGRP

Him, upon Him, prithee, call,/For to save us one and all.   Horologium: The Mother of God.   Anonymous.   ISi

Himself his father, son and bride/And his own Word   The Phoenix. Howard Nemerov.   LiTM; NePA

Himself, his Maker, and the Angel Death.   The Good Great Man.   Samuel Taylor Coleridge.   HBV 1-2

Himself into the air, straight up,/hand over hand.   Shepherd and the Hawk. William Hart-Smith.   AnNZ

Himself our bravest crown.   On Board the '76.   James Russell Lowell. MOS

Himself our Father, and the World our Home.   Lines Written in the Album at Elbingerode, in the Hartz Forest.   Samuel Taylor Coleridge.   OBTV

Himself,/The Bread and Wine.   Exchange.   Sister Mary Dorothy Ann. GoBC

Himself, the "guilty" child!   "Guilty or Not Guilty?"   *Anonymous.*   BeLS; BLPA

Himself the middle of a roaring world.   From the Notebooks.   Theodore Roethke.   PoL

Himself–to Him–a Fortune–/Exterior–to Time–   This Was a Poet.   Emily Dickinson.   AmePo; MAmP; NOBA; PP

The Hind did first her country Cates provide;/Then couch'd her self securely by her side.   The Hind and the Panther.   John Dryden.   PoEL 1-5

Hing on a tree till they be deid.   Against the Thieves of Liddesdale.   Sir Richard Maitland.   BSV

Hinky dinky parlay-voo.   Hinky Dinky.   *Anonymous.*   ABF; AS; TrAS

Hio, hark away!   Master Skylark.   John Bennett.   AA

"Hip, hip. Eyes front. Chin up," to the tick/Of the marvellous stomach clock.   Recall.   Reed Whittemore.   NYBP

Hip, hip, hip! Hop, hop!   Harlot's Catch.   Robert Nichols.   ErPo

Hippety-hoppity!   The Wapiti.   Ogden Nash.   MoShBr

Hir briddes yet, as it is seene,/Of Alceoun the name bere.   Ceix and Alceone.   John Gower.   OxBM

Hir countenance was full light.   Besse Bunting.   *Anonymous.*   EnPo; MeEL

His action won such reverence sweet/As hid all measure of the feat.   Character.   Ralph Waldo Emerson.   AA; AnFE; AnNE; APA; LiTA; OBSP

His All-Mind bids us keep this sacred place!   Substitution.   Anne Spencer.   BlSi; CDC

His all the mercy and the power.   Father Mapple's Hymn.

His Am'rous Tusks sing'd in the Flame.   The Death of Adonis.   Theocritus.   OBVE

His aqualung was the wrong size.   Full Fathom Five Thy Father Lies (parody).   June Mercer Langfield.   FaBoPa

His Ark drown in the deluge of the King.   Charles the Fifth and the Peasant.   Robert Lowell.   MiAP

...His arms full of school drawings he hoped/not to drop in the mud.   Churchyard.   Robert Hass.   NPGG

His arrow has become the pillar of my house.   The Arrow of Desire.   *Anonymous.*   WTO

...His artists are guaranteed peace,/good food and total isolation from infernal life.   Pan Cogito's Thoughts on Hell.   Zbigniew Herbert.   FaBoPV

His axe cut off my cares from cumberd breast.   The Martyrdom of Mary, Queen of Scots.   Robert Southwell.   ACP

His barge ycleped was the Maudeline.   The Canterbury Tales: General Prologue.   Geoffrey Chaucer.   MOS; PPP

...His bas-relief/name chisels to dust.   Elegy for a School-Friend.   Augustus Young.   BIrV

His beard and dewy hair shed trickling drops of brine.   The Court of Neptune.   John Hughes.   EtS

His beauty shall in these black lines be seen,/And they shall live, and he in them still green.   Sonnets, LXIII: "Against my Love shall be, as I am now."   William Shakespeare.   OBSC

His Bed, Male children shall beget.   Observation.   Robert Herrick.   FaBoUs

His beggarman bones with the charity of their wings.   Birds.   Ruth Miller.   PeSA

His bellman cockerel crying the first round.   The Veteran.   Edmund Charles Blunden.   BrPo

...His benigne-mercie/continueth forever.   Confess Jehovah.   *Anonymous.*   TrAS

His bicycle has/A motor fastened on.   Different Bicycles.   Dorothy Walter Baruch.   SUS; TiPo

His birthright name Pacelli will be sung/In glad Te Deums by celestial choirs.   Eugenio Pacelli.   Francis Neilson.   GoYe

His bite is at the growly end.   The Ambiguous Dog.   Arthur Guiterman.   GDP

His blaze in my blood/flowing forever.   Interval with Fire.   Dorothy Livesay.   CaP

His blessing He extendeth.   Psalm III.   Sir Philip Sidney.   FCP

His blood availed for me.   Triumph of His Grace.   Charles Wesley.   BePJ

His blood had been poured down the River Moskva.   The Murder of the Tsarevich Dimitri by Boris Godunov.   *Anonymous.*   LiTW

His Blood, thy Bane; my Balsam, Bliss, Joy, Wine;/Shall Thee Destroy; Heal, Feed, make me Divine.   The Third Century.   Thomas Traherne.   AnAnS 1

His body couched in a curious bed,/When care, mistrust, and treason waits on him.   King Henry VI.   William Shakespeare.   TreFS

His body is in motion,/I hope his soul's at rest.   Young Edwin in the Lowlands Low (B vers.).   *Anonymous.*   BaBo

His body lies at Shiloh.   The Battle of Shiloh.   *Anonymous.*   AmFP

His body lithe and strong and free as a whip in the wind!   Genius.   Louis Saunders Perkins.   PeHV

His body renewed by the birth of fire,/Taint of evil all taken away.   The Phoenix (excerpt).   *Anonymous.*   LiTW

His body's white, the sun is red./The Moonsheep.   The Moonsheep.   Christian Morgenstern.   FaBoNo; MOON

His bones now rot on the lone prairie.   Oh, Bury Me Not on The Lone Prairie (with music).   *Anonymous.*   AS

His book in them finds judgement, with you/love.   To His Noble Friend, Mr. Richard Lovelace, upon His Poems.   Andrew Marvell.   PP

His born brothers, their buried bodies/Be an unlikely treasure hoard.   The Seafarer.   Ezra Pound.   AmP; AnAmPo; AP; CTC; ExPo; FaBoTw; HeIP; InPK; LiTA; LiTW; NoP; OxBA

His bow and arrow across his breast/That he might sleep so sweet.   The Two Brothers.   *Anonymous.*   AmFP

His breast to my bosom./His mouth to my mouth.   My Grief on the Sea.   *Anonymous.*   AnIL; LiTW; NOBI; OnYI; WTO

His breath, long spent, now finds a vent,/Like steam from boiler gushing.   Brand Fire New Whaling Song Right from the Pacific Ocean.   *Anonymous.*   EtS

...His breath/was as sour as an orchard/after the first frost.   My Grandfather Dying.   Ted Kooser.   Str

His bride and his darling to be.   Leezie Lindsay.   *Anonymous.*   BFSS; FaBoCh; LoGBV

His bright black face above me/saying, Say hello to John.   Say Hello to John.   Sherley Anne Williams.   BlSi

His brither he has unbent his bow,/'T was never bent by him again.   Clerk Colvill (A version).   *Anonymous.*   BuBa; EnSB; ESPB

His career on earth, was marred/By his own misdeeds.   Sketch of Lord Byron's Life.   Julia A. Moore.   FiBHP

His cigar on fire for the sensual life.   A Lesson in Hammocks.   James Schevill.   FAZ

His clay to nourish yet the longing root/Of the wild daffodil, the ivy leaf.   Old Michael.   George M. Brady.   NeIP

His coat is of scarlet in a thousand patches.   I Gathered Mosses in Easedale.   Dorothy Wordsworth.   SaC

His comrade stole his coat and hat and kept on headin' West.   The Dying Hobo.   *Anonymous.*   AmFP

His countenance, his hands' motion,/Serene even to a fault.   Orpheus and Eurydice.   Geoffrey Hill.   NePoEA-2

His courage is as little as his wit.   The Exercise of Affection.   Ayton [(or Aytoun)] Sir Robert.   BSV

..His course/the music they drank as from a golden cup.   The Greater Music.   Theodore Weiss.   NePoAm-2

His creatures mosten thee obeye.   O Maister Deere and Fader Reverent!   Thomas Hoccleve.   EBEV

His creeping soul in Sternhold's creeping lays!   The Country Justice.   John Langhorne.   NOEC

His cringing courtiers played the shameful farce,/But I still seemed to bid him kiss my a—.   Journal of a Tour through the Courts of Germany (excerpt).   James Boswell.   OBTV

His Cross is every tree.   I See His Blood upon the Rose.   Joseph Mary Plunkett.   CAW; GoBC; HBMV; MoRP; OnYI; OxBI; PoLf; TRV; WGRP

His daily and all-nourishing bread.   La Condition Botanique.   Anthony Hecht.   MP; NePoEA; NoAm

His days he wasted, an imbecile mind.   Residence in France: The Prelude.   William Wordsworth.   ChRP

His deeds are more to God, yea more than/finest gold.   Ahab Mohammed.   James Matthew Legare.   AA

His dreams led nowhere–yet alive he sang.   Yiddish Poet.   A. C. Jacobs.   VWA

...His dry music/still singing in our ears.   The Rattlesnake.   Robert Wrigley.   AMV-80

His eager gun at rest, a hunter stalking game.   Autumn Dawn.   Antonio Machado.   PoPl

His ear can hear/My Song of Sleep.)   The Virgin's Slumber Song.   Francis Carlin.   ISi; YeAr

His ears erect with certainty   If I Could Meet God.   Dennis Schmitz.   NPGG

His equal or his better ne'er was born.   The Soul of Dante.   Buonarroti Michelangelo.   GoBC

His evening lectionary, and reciting the Book at dawn.   The lips of the one I love are my perpetual pleasure.   Hafiz.   BoLoP

...His eye/alert to the providing water.   The Predicter of Famine.   William Carlos Williams.   VGW

His eye is dry as the splitting sky/And his face is yellow.   On the Thirteenth Day of Christmas.   Charles Causley.   OBCP

...His eye/Would find in hers a startled twin of wonder.   Droving Man.   Thea Astley.   PoAu 1-2

His eyes burned shrewdly as emerging stars.   The Star Watcher.   Peter Davison.   TwCP

His eyes now charged with fire/ready to strangle her.   In Days of New.   Elizabeth Bartlett.   AMV-81

His eyes went slimy with the look of snails.   Sonnets for a Dying Man.   Burns Singer.   NePoEA-2

His face is deadly pale.   Poem: "High on a ridge of tiles."   Maurice James Craig.   BoAnP; NeIP

His face is that of a man terribly glad to be selling fish,/terribly glad that God made fish,... Fish Crier. Carl Sandburg. AmFN; OxBA

His face is trodden deeper in the mud. Glory of Women. Siegfried Sassoon. MMM; OBWP

His face is very nearly/only eye! The Dragonfly. Chisoku. SoPo

His face, wounded by us, for us and over us watches. In Time. Kathleen Raine. NeBP

His faithful dog shall bear him company. An Essay on Man. Alexander Pope. GoTF; NU; OBEC; TreFS

His far weigheth down: Jesus is born. Sonnet LXXIV. William Alabaster. SBVL

His farces are physic; his physic a farce is. On Sir John Hill, M.D., Playwright. David Garrick. FaBoCo; NLV

His Father, and his God. Faith. Louise Morgan Sill. CAW

His finger pressed the trigger and he shot him through the heart. Annie Breen. Anonymous. CoSo

His five pure notes succeeding pensively. Solitude. Archibald Lampman. BoNaP; CBEP; ExPo; OBCV; PeCV

...His flesh is warmed/By blood that never need be drained. On a Fifteenth-Century Flemish Angel. David Ray. NePoEA-2

His flowing mane protecting me always/ta wa nee ta wa nee ta wa nee Ta Wa Nee. Ronald James Dessus. LFAC

His foot is upon my threshold. Sun in the East. Anonymous. LiTW

His footprint is his image fallen from heaven. Afternoon: Amagansett Beach. John Hall Wheelock. BoNaP; MoVE; NePA

His form unseen, his voice unheard– Threnody. Thomas Lovell Beddoes. EnRP

His foster brother thar was dede. Bruce Meets Three Men with a Wethe. John Barbour. OxBM

His friends, who stayed and wept. A Death in Hospital. John Lehmann. AtBAP

His furniture is love. God's Residence. Emily Dickinson. TRV

His gateway is wide and the folk of the moor/Come singing so gaily right up to the door. From the Day-Book of a Forgotten Prince. Jean Starr Untermeyer. HBMV

His ghost and only song. Breath. Heather McHugh. GeTw

His Ghost shall glide over the Green. Colin's Complaint. Nicholas Rowe. OBEC

His gifted ken can see/Phantoms of sublimity. Apologia Pro Vita Sua. Samuel Taylor Coleridge. EnRP; ERoP 1-2; OBSP; PP

HIS gifts never mystified. Neither Shadow of Turning. Jack R. Clemo. NOCV

His glorious Face! which glistereth else so bright/That the angels' selves cannot endure His sight. Cease, Then, My Tongue! Edmund Spenser. ILwL

His glory and his monuments are gone. Meru. William Butler Yeats. NoAm; OAEL 1-2; PAI; PoA

His goal half-won, but Dulcinea still his talisman. The Bridge of Heraclitus. George Reavey. BIrV

His god-like image, till it sinks where blends/Time's dim horizon with Eternity. On the Defeat of Henry Clay. William Wilberforce Lord. PAH

His godhead shines through clay. Wherein Consists the High Estate. Ebenezer Dayton. AH

His golden prophecy/Lighting the doorway of the pioneer. Farther. John James Piatt. AmePo

His grace accepts and now sustains/our load. Casting All Your Care Upon Him. Anonymous. STF

"His grace was sufficient for me." My Grace Is Sufficient for Thee. Anonymous. BLRP

His grandson George now Britain's sceptre sways,/Whom God preserve, and bless with length of/days. Lines on Succession of the Kings of England. Anonymous. FaBoUs

His grave broke open, did affright the boors. The Portents. Christopher Marlowe. OBSC

His grave was deckt with flowers by strangers' hands/to-day. Memorial Day. Richard Watson Gilder. OHIP

His great confessional unread. Final Autumn. Josephine Winslow Johnson. NAMP; NePA

His grin must drag his breeches out of Hell. Comedian. Louis Johnson. AnNZ

His hair had all turned white. Tom Starr. Robert J. Conley. STE

His hair shines like that of a young boy–/It is crinkled and crisp as lettuce. Ben. Thomas Wolfe. NCSH

His halter and his traces all/Of fresh butter. Wheatlet Son of Milklet. MacConglinne. OnYI

His hand his tune, his mind sought his lay,/Which to the Lord with sober voice did say: Psalm XXXII. Sir Thomas Wyatt. FCP

His hand is the black basalt, and his veins/Are rocky veins, ablaze with gold and fire. Nunc Scio, Quid Sit Amor. L. A. Mackay. OBCV

His hands behind his back, a tiny smile/Flickering from the distance like a glowworm. Adam in Love. Stephen Mitchell. VWA

His hands for whom thou claim'st the freedom of the mind! To Ronge. John Greenleaf Whittier. AnEnPo

His happier fortune in this mound you see. On the Grave of a Young Cavalry Officer Killed in the Valley... Herman Melville. AP

His happiness was not completed/Until that a helpmate was found. When Adam Was First Created. Anonymous. OBET

His harvest-sweepings on a winter sea/To feed the primal hungers of a reef. The Ground-Swell. Edwin John Pratt. CaP

His hated foes to hell shall fare,/His lovers to his realm. The Nature of the Turtle Dove. Anonymous. PBBP

His head alone remained to tell/The cruel death he died. On the Death of Mrs. Throckmorton's Bullfinch. William Cowper. HBV 1-2; NOEC; PBBP; PPP

His head fell off like a leaf. Revenge Fable. Ted Hughes. TW

...His head full/& his heart full, he's making ready to move on. Dream Songs. John Berryman. HaCAP; NaP

His head sank, and a radiance flowed. Socrates Prays a Day and a Night. George O'Neil. AnAmPo

His head shone honey-gold. The Dream. Helen Spalding. ChMP

His head upon his lover's breast/Of the terrors of the flight. Grania. Anonymous. KiLC

His head was in his hat. A Second Stanza for Dr. Johnson. Donald Hall. FiBHP; ShM

His heart divine/Will enter thine, and lead the way/To blissful day. Keep on Praying. Roger H. Lyon. BLRP

His heart had learned, through weariness and care,/The patience, that he deemed he'd sought in vain His Answer. Clara Ann Thompson. BlSi

His heart held breathless with beatitude. The Old Adam. William Rose Benet. YaD

His heart lay down, took ether, and gave birth. An Unfinished Work (Excerpt). X. J. Kennedy. PeD

His heart makes music of the tears of/my Spring. Abishag. Jacob Fichman. TrJP; VWA

His heart to the darkness and into the sadness/of joy. First Song. Galway Kinnell. CAPP; LiTM; NCSH; NePoAm; NoP

His heart unbiassed, and his mind his own. The Bastard. Richard Savage. NOEC; OBSV

His Heaven commences ere the world be past! Blest Retirement. Oliver Goldsmith. OBEC

His heaven would be a place where all day long/he'd lay his head upon somebody's knees. Puppy. Fred Lape. BoAnP; GDP

His heels upright. Baby Taffy. Anonymous. OxNR

His heir, the Adam that he wrought! Brand Speaks. Henrik Ibsen. WGRP

His heir you were not, had he seen you twice. Epigram. Leonard Welsted. ALV

His helpers wash and bow, laughing. A Glimpse of the Body Shop. Stephen Berg. NaP

His hide is sure to flatten 'em. The Hippopotamus. Hilaire Belloc. FiBHP; InPK; PoPl

His Holy Spirit is here! Apocalypse. Edith Lovejoy Pierce. MoRP

His hooves have rest. The Mount. Léonie Adams. MoAB; MoAmPo; MoVE

...His hope/that heat would be arrested on its shore. Heat. Kenneth Mackenzie. AP; PoAu 1-2

His horns dip into the sun. The Deer. Asya (Asya Gray). VWA

His horse and him, unconscious of them all. The Task. William Cowper. CoBE

His horse's trampling echoes now. Swift. Thomas Caulfield Irwin. BIrV

...His horses's shoes/Were heavy, and he headed for the barn. Parable. Richard Wilbur. OBSP

His imagination is a gnat's and he crawls through muck. The Confession. Wen Yi-tuo. ChTr; LiTW

HIS INVENTORY thus is ended. An Inventory of the Furniture of a Collegian's Chamber. John Winstanley. OBSV

His invitation to stay a while longer/in this place. Happening In. Mark Sanders. WOLT

His iron-armed hoofs gleam in the morning ray. Sunday Morning. James Grahame. OBRV

His is a world-wide fatherland! The Fatherland. James Russell Lowell. GN; HBV 1-2; HBVY; PGD; PoPl

His jealousy makes bastards of us all. You, Whose Mother's Lover Was Grass. Gregory Corso. NoAm

His jest eternal, and our lives so short. As One Who Bears beneath His Neighbor's Roof. Robert Hillyer. MoAmPo

His Joys I wish may ne'r have end,/but gain his subjects' love and praise. England's Triumph. Anonymous. CoMu

His kingdom in thy heart shall never pass away. A Happy Christmas. Frances Ridley Havergal. BLRP

His kingdom is forever. A Mighty Fortress Is Our God. Martin Luther. AWP; EaLo; HBV 1-2; TreFS

His Kingdom is forever. Paraphrase of Luther's Hymn. Frederic Henry Hedge AA

His Kingdom shall yet rule though stars be dust. The Centuries Are His. Georgia Moore Ebeling. TRV

His kiss on my mouth! Across the Door. Padraic Colum. HBV 1-2

His knees and thighs like silver, & his breast and/head like gold.' America: A Prophecy. William Blake. EnRP

His languid tail above us, lit with myriad spots of light. The Indian upon God. William Butler Yeats. MoBrPo; WGRP

His last white earms, an' they stood still. The Turnstile. William Barnes. CH; NOBV; OBVV

His last words were for Mary in the rolling silvery tide. Mary in the Silvery Tide. Anonymous. OBET; ShS

His Laws require His Creatures all to prais/His Name, and when they do 't be most my Joys. Hosanna. Thomas Traherne. PoEL 1-5; SeCV 1-2

His leprosy was cleansed, and he fell down/Prostrate at Jesus' feet and worshipped him. The Leper. Nathaniel Parker Willis. WGRP

His life he gave! Requiem. George Lunt AA

His life is a watch or a vision/Between a sleep and a sleep. Atalanta in Calydon. Algernon Charles Swinburne. ACV; BoLiVe; FaFP; HeIP; MasP; NoP; OBEV; OBVV; TrGrPo; ViBoPo; WHA

His life links Shakespeare's with the probable. Lincoln. Rembrandt William B. Ditmars. HBMV

His life runs through/them Panther. Sam Cornish. PoBA

His life sings me! Shaman. Will Inman. GP

His Life still kept alive in Thee. An Epitaph upon Mr. Ashton a Conformable Citizen. Richard Crashaw. OBS

His life time is eternity,/His limit is infinity. The Cannibal Hymn. Anonymous. TTY

His light shall in my darkness shine,/And guide me to His throne. Ah! Give Me, LORD, the Single Eye. Augustus Montague Toplady. OxBoCh

His light was there. I miss the light. A Celebration. May Sarton. NePoAm-2

His light will illumine the way. Try the Uplook. Anonymous. BLRP

His limbs wer a-fringed wi' the vrost or the snow. The May Tree. William Barnes. LiTB; LoBV

His little sparks of song/Like promises of Spring. January. Douglas Gibson. OBCP

His livelie face thy brest how did it freate,/Whose cynders yet with envye doo the eate. In the Rude Age. Henry Howard, Earl of Surrey. AAS; FCP; NCEP

His look will flow like oil over us. Ank'hor Vat. Denis Devlin. BIrV; CIP; IPY; NOBI

His love has given me so great a worth,/That I care no more for things of this earth. A Ditty. Bertha Jacobs. WPOW

His love is sweetest breath,/beyond all things on earth. When I went into my garden. Sister Bertken. BoWoP

An' his luik was like the luik o' man/Wha's heart in twa is riven. Willie and Helen. Hew Ainslie. HBV 1-2; LO

His magnetic and mastering song. The Spirit of Wine. William Ernest Henley. HBV 1-2

"His Majesty's turned parsimonious/And keeps no whore now but his Consort." Queen Mother to New Queen. Robert Graves. OBSV

His manly face turned to the sky,/And beaten by the rain. The General's Death. Joseph O'Connor. AA

His Master cries—"he has no gratitude!" The Hottentot. Thomas Pringle. OBRV; OBTV

His meal the whole world. Darkness. Peggy Bacon. BrR

His medal somewhere in the pages/of a book. Dory Miller. Sam Cornish. CNA

His men shall haue halfe a crowne a day/To bring them to my brother, King Iamye. Sir Andrew Barton. Anonymous. BaBo; EnSB; ESPB; OxBB; ViBoFo

His message will be short and voluble. Samson Agonistes. John Milton. OBS

His metamorphosed shade,/Leaving the flesh it had,/Breathes on the words they made. Lector Aere Perennior. J. V. Cunningham. QFR

His mighty frame was refuge, while his/mien/Did make dispute of stature with the/gods. The Voice of Webster (excerpt). Robert Underwood Johnson. AA

His milking-maid the ploughman sung/Till all the fields around him rung. The Crow Sat on the Willow. John Clare. VLP

His mind is rapt above the starry sky. The Secrets of Angling. John Dennys. MyFE

His mind was a thanksgiving to the power/That made him; it was blessedness and love. The Excursion. William Wordsworth. OBRV

His mining's all over, poor miner farewell. Hard-Working Miner. Anonymous. ABF; AmFP

His miraculous lantern will shine,/effulgent forever. The Boy and the Lantern (excerpt). Evaristo Ribera Chevremont. InW

His momma too. Black Sketches, 6. Don L. Lee. NeAC

...His moneys he gets in with paine,/At th'Calends, puts all out againe. The Praises of a Countrie Life. (Horace, Epode 2). Ben Jonson. SeCP

His monogram on the silver. Teahouse. Nicholas Rinaldi. AMV-81

His monument a people free! President Lincoln's Grave. Caroline Atherton Briggs Mason. OHIP

His mother's kindness is a debt,/He never, never will forget. The Baby. Ann Taylor. OHIP

...His mother's/last hope: that he'll give up vice for art. The Young Conquistador. Robert Peterson. GP

His mother's poor body lay mouldering away. Queen Jane. Anonymous. FSW

His mother was too/busy praying for salvation/to answer that question The Night Has Twenty-Four Hours. Pedro Juan Pietri. InW

His mouth on mine,/kissing my mama. Stepfather: A Girl's Song. Yusef Komunyakaa. Str

His mouth to my mouth. My Grief on the Sea. Douglas Hyde. OBEV; OBVV; OxBI

His mouth upon my mouth has said/Pater and Ave for my peace. Posthumous Coquetry. Theophile Gautier. AWP

His movements are graceful, all girls he does please, and my move he has stolen away. The Man on the Flying Trapeze. George Leybourne. BLSo; FaBoBe

His name from blank oblivion,/Who never had a grave. John Filson. William Henry Venable. PAH

His name hath saved us from these wicked men. Now Israel May Say, and That Truly. William Whittingham. AH

His name is whispered in the God's abode. The Father's Business. Edwin Markham. TRV

His name will follow me on the interstate/all the way into the center of oklahoma. He Told Me His Name Was Sitting Bull. Joy Harjo. TAT

His name/Would mean nothing to me, his questions are not/His own, but let my answers/Be mine. Walk-Up. William Stanley Merwin. CoPo

His narrow forehead ruffled by the Jutland wind. Chief Petty Officer. Charles Causley. OxBTC

His neck-nerves sunder'd, and his spirits shrunke. The Odyssey. Homer. OBS

His net is broke, the fowl go free, the fowler ta'en. The Overthrow of Lucifer. Phineas Fletcher. OBS

His new-fangled rifle, his green new steel helmet. The March 1. Robert Lowell. HaCAP

His next may be a rod in piss. The Virtues of Sid Hamet, the Magician's Rod. Jonathan Swift. APAS

His nobler task is–to forget. The Crowing of the Red Cock. Emma Lazarus. AA; HBV 1-2

His numbers rais'd a shade from hell,/Hers lift the soul to heav'n. Ode for Music on St. Cecilia's Day. Alexander Pope. CEP

His obscene victory vain. There's A Regret. William Ernest Henley. AnEnPo

His old decaying mortal eye,/desiring it, despising it. The Spectacle of Truth. John Hewitt. CIP

His old Ford door WIDE OPEN on that/Promised Land. Rock and Roll. Sibyl James. AmC

His only beauty to be/all moose. Poetry, a Natural Thing. Robert Duncan. CAPP; NoAm; NOBA

His own bombs burst on his own tomb. The Killer Too. Walker Gibson. FF

...His own breathing a shamble-sound. Scarabs for the Living. Richard P. Blackmur. AnFE; CrMA

His own Oneiza, his Arabian Maid. Thalaba and the Banquet. Robert Southey. SeCePo

His own tongue only, and of it not much. Japanese Beetles. X.J. Kennedy. HoAn; OBAL

His oxen face invents the smile. Jacob. Else Lasker-Schüler. BoWoP; VWA

His page concluded with the dawn. Diary of a Raccoon. Gertrude Ryder Bennett. GoYe

His penis erect with/fantasy Along History. Muriel Rukeyser. NNaP

His people dead, his gay pots broken. Joan Miro. Ruthven Todd. EAS

His Persian lovers all shall leave him/And swear faith to Thy sweeter powers. New Year's Day. Richard Crashaw. JCP

His pillow haunted–. On the Victory of Poland and Her Allies over the Sultan Osman, 1621. Casimir Sarbiewski. CAW

His plaintive music gone–/While they rave on. Mozart Perhaps. John Hall Wheelock. UnS

His pleasure lies, but in the piety/Of consecrated hearts and lives devout. The End of Being. (Lucius Annaeus Seneca) Seneca. WGRP

His praise to celebrate in songs/Is lovely in his sight. How Glorious Are the Morning Stars. Benjamin Keach. AH

His presence all that place with sanctity did fill. The Life of San Millan (excerpt). Gonzalo de Berceo. CAW

His presence and His power/Are everywhere. Tree-Planting. Samuel Francis Smith. OHIP

His presence brings forth fragrance without fail. Lilies of the Valley. Jo Gardner. BePJ

His presence makes my heaven/And I am satisfied. God's Presence Makes My Heaven. Oswald J. Smith. STF

His presence will my soul sustain/In days of deepest grief and pain. The Sun Now Risen. Johann Conrad Beissel. AH

His price is everything. The Bear. Ted Hughes. FaBoMo

His prince, his country and his friends. Against Love. Sir John Denham. CBEP

His pristine peace of mind's his final prayer. Home, Sweet Home. Henry Cuyler Bunner. CenHV; InMe

His prow is always there! Purpose. John James Piatt. AA

His quick veins shying in the wind's war. The Silver Leaf. John Hay. NePoAm

His quiet hand will lead the sunshine in. Wild Weather. Katharine Lee Bates. PGD

His reeds bequeath'd, his bird-lime, and his snares. On a Fowler. Isidorus. AWP

His reign forever shall endure. Nations That Long in Darkness Walked. John Barnard. AH

His reply was the same as before. The True Facts of the Case. Anthony Euwer. OBAL

His rod and His staff will uphold me. The Lord Is My Shepherd. John Knox. BePJ

His rubber boots are full of feet/and his tippet full of ears. The Boy. Eugene Field. NA

His saddle his kingly throne. The Cowboy's Life. *Anonymous.* AmFN; SoPo; TiPo

His scream still rising a block away. Sirens in Bad Weather. Sherod Santos. MAYP

His secret architecture knows. The Snake. Roy Campbell. AtBAP

His servants may we be, or shine,/Pure pearls, according to his will./Amen. Amen. The Pearl. *Anonymous.* MeEV

His service is the golden cord/Close binding all mankind. In Christ. John Oxenham. STF

His shadow gone into the sun. Perspectives Are Precipices. John Peale Bishop. LiTA; MoVE; NePA

His shadow has missed you by a mile. Too high. Camping Out on Rainy Mountain. Jim Barnes. CDW

His shotgun pulls him into the sky. Usually an Old Female Is the Leader. Tom Hennen. FAZ

His silent laugh still shakes the hills at dawn. Jerusalem Sonnets. James Keir Baxter. NoP; OCNZ

His silver balls, that, softly dropt,/Ring into golden bowls. An Opium Fantasy. Maria White Lowell. AnFE; APA

His singular way, a gentle lunatic at large/In the societies of cross and reasonable men. The Poet. James Kirkup. PP

"His sins were scarlet, but his books were read." On His Books. Hilaire Belloc. ACP; FaBoCo; FaBoEE; GoTF; NLV; OxBoLi; PoPl; TreFT; WeW

His sister's bedroom lights/Blink off, on, then off again. Dividing the Field. William Aberg. LFAC

His skin/will keep/me warm. Four Choctaw Songs. Jim Barnes. STE

His small soft foghorn quavering through the air. By Achmelvich Bridge. Norman MacCaig. OxBS

His smile at parting bright through April haze. A Letter to Charles Townsend Copeland (excerpt). Robert Hillyer. GLGT

...His smile/Is the official seal on my marriage. The Butcher. Hugo Williams. OxBTC

His son keeps on the business still,/Resigned unto the heavenly will. Epitaph at Upton-on-Severn. *Anonymous.* FaBoCo

His songs drop like plum. Haiku: "The piano man." Etheridge Knight. NeAC; SM; TAP

His soul had gone forth to discover/The beautiful Fountain of Youth. The Fountain of Youth. Hezekiah Butterworth. PAH

His soul has gone aloft. Tom Bowling. Charles Dibdin. EtS; HBV 1-2

His soul is back again among the sabres/Yelling, "The Deed!ç The Deed!" Makhno's Philosophers. John Streeter Manifold. CBAP; NOAV

His soul is with the saints, I trust. The Knight's Tomb. Samuel Taylor Coleridge. CBEP; EROP 1-2; FaBoCh; GN; LoGBV

His soul sings like a sahophone. A Hex on the Mexican X. David McCord. FiBHP

His soul well-knit, and all his battles won,/Mounts, and that hardly, to eternal life. Immortality. Matthew Arnold. FiP

His soul will leap to Ocean's arms! Richard Somers. Barrett Eastman. AA

His spectacles perched handsome on his nose. Love. Nicholas Moore. ErPo

His spent soul to that river where none grow old. Hermit. James Keir Baxter. AnNZ

His spirit fled into the gloom below. The Aeneid. Virgil (Publius Vergilius Maro). NAWM 1-2

His spirit, from its earthly bondage freed,/Had to some better region fled for ever. Beachy Head (excerpt). Charlotte Smith. SBG

His spirit heed, still winged with golden prophecies. Chavez. Mildred McNeal Sweeney. HBV 1-2

His spirit is awake. Tom Thomson. Arthur Stanley Bourinot. CaP

His spirit that has fled/Blind as a worm. The Chambermaid's Second Song. William Butler Yeats. ErPo

His spirit was gone for to sport aloft/In the realms of the good and great. Emmeline Grangerford's "Ode to Stephen Dowling Bots, Dec'd." Mark (Samuel Langhorne Clemens) Twain. NLV; OBAL

His stature, since he died. In Manchester Square. Alice Meynell. SBG

His steed he spurred, in haste to lead such noble men. Bunker Hill. George Henry Calvert. BeLS; FaBoBe; MC; PAH

His studies too little regd. Limerick: "When an All-American gd." *Anonymous.* TDH

His style/has other outstanding/virtues/which delight me. Poem: "on getting a card." William Carlos Williams. VGW

His sweeter voice a just accordance kept. Homeric Hymns: Hymn to Mercury. *Anonymous.* LiTW

His swiftest and his sweetest thought/Can never poet say. Evanescence. Frederic William Henry Myers. OBVV

His tear-wet feet still drying with her hair. For the Magdalene. William, of Hawthornden Drummond. AtBAP; LoBV; PoEL 1-5

His teeth they chatter, chatter still. Goody Blake and Harry Gill (excerpt). William Wordsworth. Par

...His temples/Are found beside his mother's in many cities. Metamorphoses. Ovid (Publius Ovidius Naso). NAWM 1-2

His tender, loving, joyous will–be done"? His Will Be Done. Annie Johnson Flint. BLRP

His the divinest face I ever looked into! His Face. Florence Earle Coates. OHIP

His thirty coins held fast,/Goes dark Iscariot. This Very Hour. Lizette Woodworth Reese. AnAmPo; HBMV

His thoughts flew back to where she said, "I'm growing warmer now." The Frozen Girl (with music). *Anonymous.* AS

His throne is with the outcast and the weak. His Throne Is with the Outcast. James Russell Lowell. TrCP

...His tobacco pouch,/I observed, was already missing from beside his bed. The Wolves. Galway Kinnell. NePoEA-2

His toiles had rack't, t'a labouring womans paines. The Odyssey. Homer. OBS

His tomb bears the date that he said it on. Limerick: "A certain young gourmet of Crediton." Charles Cuthbert Inge. CenHV; LiBL; TDH

His tongue lay there by way of mat,/And he would wipe his feet on that! An Unsuspected Fact. Edward Cannon. NA

His trail let him lay! The Brother Eagles. *Anonymous.* NOAV

His tree is not my tree, His word, my word;/His Yale, my Yale. Monkey. Josephine Miles. LiTM

His trowel catches the light and becomes precious. On Roofs of Terry Street. Douglas Dunn. OxBTC

His truth acceptable to lying men. Rimbaud. W. H. Auden. SyP

His truth at all times firmly stood/And shall from age to age endure. Scotch Te Deum. William Kethe. WGRP

His two-story house he turned/into a forest,/where both he and I are the hunters. My Father's Wedding 1924. Robert Bly. InPS

...His unfinished glass of water/Appears to beg me for a flower. Alleys. Sandra McPherson. MAYP

His voice he strains, and from his heart out brings/This song that I not whether he cries or sings. Domine ne in Furore. Sir Thomas Wyatt. FCP

His voice rose in the noisy streets of Detroit. Andrew Jackson's Speech. Robert Bly. ConAP

His voice was so worn and sonorous. Limerick: "An extinct old ichthyosaurus." *Anonymous.* TDH

His voice/went on/and on/through the leaves.... Pound at Spoleto. Lawrence Ferlinghetti. CAPP; PoM

His war was not hers. A Jealous Man. Robert Graves. CMoP

His was a sacred way/That only the strong dare follow. Peter. Earl Bowman Marlatt. MoRP

His was the nation's sacrifice,/And ours the priceless gain. The Emancipation Group (excerpt). John Greenleaf Whittier. PGD

His weary soul may sweetly slumber/Within the vale, heaven sublime. The Ashtabula Disaster. Julia A. Moore. EvOK

His wheels click in the single road. The Monument and the Shrine. John Logan. LCAP

His whole territory/shut against trespassers. The Specialist. Anne S. Perlman. SUW

His wife could do more work in a day/Than he could do in seven. Father Grumble. *Anonymous.* AmFP; ViBoFo

His wife had never noticed that he died/His songs unsung. Toll the Bell for Damon. Maxwell Anderson. InMe

His wife looked it up in her dream book/and played it.   Hope.   Langston Hughes.   OBAL

His wife, that he may live.   A Reasonable Affliction.   Matthew Prior. ALV; GoTF; HBV 1-2; NOEC; NoP; ShM; TreFT; TrGrPo

His will shall yet be done.   Thy Will Be Done.   Annie Johnson Flint.   STF

His wit & passion, gift, the whole young man/alive with surplus love.   Dream Songs.   John Berryman.   NoP

His words hang in the air, unanswered,/then drift away, slow feathers.   The Fog Dream.   Sandra M. Gilbert.   PoA

His words jump down/to stand/in their/places.   Corner Meeting.   Langston Hughes.   CAD

His words of beauty floom/Forevermore!   On a Dead Poet.   Frances Sargent Osgood   AA

His work goes on increasing through all time.   Abraham Lincoln.   A. S. Ames.   OHIP

His work, his dream, bridging the span of death.   Blueprint.   D. B. Steinman.   GoYe

His work shall bide, silver tride, but thine by death is staid.   Mr. Roger Harlackenden.   Edward Johnson.   SCAP

His works are the apocalypse of verse.   On the Death of Mr. Pope.   *Anonymous.*   NOEC

His would survive, though never to him cleave.   The Enigma.   Richard Eberhart.   NYBP

His wrath which one day will destroy ye both.   Paradise Lost.   John Milton.   EBEV

His year's all spring, and hath no fall.   Occasioned by Seeing a Walk of Bay Trees.   Mildmay Fane, Earl of Westmoreland.   OBSP

His years with others must the sweeter be/For those brief days he spent in loving me.   Brother and Sister.   George Eliot.   GN

His yoke to bear, his work to do,/Study his life to learn his will.   Jesus a Child His Course Begun.   Margaret Fuller.   AH

His zeal may freeze, whilst we, kept warm/With love and wine, can know no harm.   The Winter Glass.   Charles Cotton.   HBV 1-2

Hissed like a snake, and swallowed him at one mouthful.   Grotesque.   Robert Graves.   DTC

History, has ordained us a grave/from which there is no resurrection.   Out of the corpse-warm vestibule of heaven steps the sun.   Ingeborg Bachmann.   BoWoP

History is them; it is also theirs to make.   Driving Wheel.   Sherley Anne Williams.   BlSi

History moves like an old woman/crossing the street.   Who Makes the Journey.   Cathy Song.   BrSi

...History, not wanted yet,/Lean'd on her elbow, watching Time...   Yardley-Oak.   William Cowper.   LaA; NCEP; NOEC

History of their deeds can tell–/But ourselves must set us free.   Our Fathers Fought for Liberty.   James Russell Lowell.   PAL

The history theirs whose language is the sun.   An Elementary School Class Room in a Slum.   Stephen Spender.   MoPo; MP; OAEP; PPON; TwCP

History will say of you: "That pack of G...d... fools."   Christians at War.   John F. Kendrick.   TW

Hitch up and promenade to your seats.   Salute Your Partner.   *Anonymous.*   AmFP

Hitching, forever hitching/Ships–shallops to a star.   I, Who Fade with the Lilacs.   William Griffith.   HBMV

Hither and thither crying.   Montgomery.   J. C. Hall.   ChMP

Hither, by singer's magic,/The pilgrim world must come.   Yattendon.   Sir Henry Newbolt.   HBMV

Hits me cleanly in the heart,/never winging honour:/this I do know!   Chanson: "If they say my furred cloak."   Pernette Du Guillet.   PBWP

Hitty Pitty will bite you.   Riddle: "Hitty Pitty within the wall."   *Anonymous.*   OxNR

Hm Lord, I'm mos' done toilin' here.   Mos' Done Toilin' Here.   *Anonymous.*   BoAN 1-2

Hnag down yo' heads an' cry.   Don' Let Yo' Watch Run Down (with music).   *Anonymous.*   AS

Ho! Bullee in the Al-lee.   Lost and Given Over.   Edwin James Brady.   PoAu 1-2

Ho, Father Bull, I hear you roar,/and the zodiac-beasts neigh a star-reply.   Epos.   Julian Tuwim.   LiTW

Ho, ho, honey, take a whiff on me.   Honey, Take a Whiff On Me.   *Anonymous.*   ABF; OxBoLi

Ho hum./Good-by,/scum.   Epilogue.   Dallas E. Wiebe.   TW

Ho, landlord, fill the bowl!   The Swashbuckler's Song.   James Stuart Montgomery.   HBMV

"Ho!" thought the page, "she loves his hound,/So this is Lady Clare!"   Love Me, Love My Dog.   Isabella Valancy Crawford.   WHW

Hoar with salt-sleet and chalkings of the birds.   Sometimes I Walk where the Deep Water Dips.   Frederick Goddard Tuckerman.   NOBA

Hoarded like happy summers in my/heart.   One Who Watches.   Siegfried Sassoon.   TrJP

Hoarse with fulfilment, I never made promises.   Noah's Raven.   William Stanley Merwin.   AmPC; HaCAP

Hobson and his men.   Hobson and His Men.   Robert Loveman.   PAH

Hobson has supt, and's newly gone to bed.   On the University Carrier Who Sickn'd in the Time of His Vacancy...   John Milton.   MePo

Hoecakes, hominy, sassafrass tea.   Kansas Boys.   *Anonymous.*   FSW

Hogging it down like a pig I call the feeding of corpses.   Mystic.   D. H. Lawrence.   WeW

Hoist your burdens, get on down the road.   Gravelly Run.   Archie Randolph Ammons.   CoAP; PoA; Prf

Hol' de win'! Hol' de win' don't let it blow.   Hol' de Win' Don't Let It Blow.   *Anonymous.*   BoAN 1-2

Hold ajar the wicket gate.   The Quiet Enemy.   Walter De la Mare.   BrPo

Hold and fold us all beneath the shadow of Thy wing.   Love is Life.   Richard Rolle.   GoBC

Hold: and I grind your manhood bone on bone.   The Ghost.   Robert Lowell.   AtBAP; MoVE; PoA

Hold back the world from you and me.   Urban Roses.   Ted Isaac.   PoPl

Hold fast–hold fast your dreams!   Hold Fast Your Dreams.   Louise Driscoll.   BLPA; FaBoBe; FPL; HBMV

Hold hard then, heart. This way at least you live.   The Fist.   Derek Walcott.   LLLT

Hold Him gently by the hand/And know His will is best.   God's Will Is Best.   Thelma Curtis.   STF

Hold His Own Nod Your Head.   The Cooper & Bailey Great London Circus.   Robert Hershon.   MAT

Hold in the faces of inheritors/a tight precarious old man's embrace.   Poems from a First Year in Boston.   George Starbuck.   NePoEA-2

Hold infinity in the palm of your hand/And eternity in an hour.   To See a World in a Grain of Sand.   William Blake.   InPK

Hold, men, hold!   Hold, Men, Hold!   *Anonymous.*   ChBR

Hold on hard, hold on, my stevedore heart.   First Things.   Lucienne Desnoues.   WPOW

Hold on:/off the coast,/glass falling.   Hydrographic Report.   Frances Frost.   EtS

Hold onto the heart & the hearts of others./I love you   Dance of the Infidels.   Al Young.   PoBA

Hold out–that's all.   Swans in Flight.   Miroslav Holub.   FaBoPV

Hold out yo' light,/You heav'n boun' soldier,/Let yo' light shine a-roun' de world.   Heav'n Boun' Soldier.   *Anonymous.*   BoAN 1-2

Hold the answer if only he could find it.   The Ring.   Paul Mariani.   GeTw

...Hold them gently/in the softness of my jaws.   Suppositions.   Margherita Faulkner.   AMV-80

Hold these branches at rest,–/My babe is asleep.   A Christmas Cradlesong.   Felix Lope de Vega Carpio.   PoPl

"Hold thine tunge stille/And have al thine wille."   Wight in the Broom.   *Anonymous.*   OxBM

Hold tight, squeeze.   If It Would All Please Hurry.   James Tate.   MAYP

Hold us and pick us to pieces.   Operation.   Alfred Alvarez.   NMP

Hold you poison or grapes?   Ears in the Turrets Hear.   Dylan Thomas.   FaBoTw

Holding a box of shoe-laces in unendingly shaking hands.   Reality.   Raymond Souster.   CaP

Holding a calm face against the opening world.   In Time of Need.   William Stafford.   UnPo

Holding a lady's wornout shoe.   Water.   Anne Sexton.   CoPo

...Holding/an enormous rope of silence.   Distance.   Peter Everwine.   NNaP

...Holding an old red pinwheel,/ran ran ran ran.   Goose.   Richard Emil Braun.   NoAm

Holding close to his ear the shell of the world.   Portrait of the Boy as Artist.   Barbara Howes.   DFF; MoAmPo

Holding due course to Harfleur.   King Henry V.   William Shakespeare.   MOS

Holding his destiny within his hands.   The New Negro.   James Edward McCall.   CDC

Holding,/holding/to keep.   Near Drowning.   Ralph Pomeroy.   DFF

Holding in his heart a secret/Which in vain he seeks to break.   The Dragonfly.   Theodore Harding Rand.   CaP

Holding it/gingerly/with/the very/tips/of her/fingers.   Once.   Alice Walker.   BlSi

Holding it, not for enjoyment, but simply because we are in/it.   The Bothie of Tober-Na-Vuolich.   Arthur Hugh Clough.   FaBoPV

Holding me earthbound/by all that is at once/most vulnerable/most destructive.   Slug.   Gwen Head.   GP

Holding myself hostage and there's no way out   Dear Patty Dear Tania.   Richard Mathews.   GP

Holding our day more firm in unbelief.   Odes.   Horace.   CTC

...Holding out/straw after others have got your harvest.   Epigram: "You were a pretty boy once."   Philip of Thessaloni.   PeHV

Holding second position/till six when the mothers came.   Swansong.   Carol Muske.   AmPA

Holding the bandage ready for your eyes.   The Children of the Poor.   Gwendolyn Brooks.   PoA; PoCh

Holding the histories of the night/In yet unmelted tracks. Like Snow. Robert Graves. AtBAP

Holding the lily and the Child. Childhood. Donagh MacDonagh. NeIP

Holding the planet/in place. The Man Who Dreamt He Was Turquoise. Wendy Rose. TWSS

Holding the restless finches and a single star. Deep Well. Roland Robinson. CBAP; NOAV

Holding them/close to the earth. Daybreak on a Pennsylvania Highway. John Daunt. AMV-80

Holding them not in vain! Supplication. Josephine Johnson. TrPWD

Holding to her thin breast his bald weeping head. Three Seasons. Francis Sparshott. NOBC

...Holds a season/Constant, green and perfect. The Tray. Thomas Cole. NePoAm

Holds all my moments in His hand/And gives them, one by one. Step by Step. Barbara C. Ryberg. STF

Holds half the secret of success. To know thy bent and then pursue. Ella Wheeler Wilcox. CenHV

Holds its peace and holds its own. Athene's Song. Eavan Boland. CIP

Holds me as I drift to dreamland, safe inside my slumberwear. Indoor Games near Newbury. Sir John Betjeman. MoVE

Holds up his little crumb of crust/And cries, "Behold the loaf!" Miniature. Eden Phillpotts. OBSP

Holds you,/holds you/close and tenderly before he vanishes. The Poem Rising by Its Own Weight. Denise Levertov. GP

Hole in the ice;/Golden gates. Golden Gates. Anonymous. ShM

The hole in which my body lies/Would not contain one-half my speeches. The Orator's Epitaph. Lord Brougham. NLV

& The hole is closed & the boat has left & the day is closed. Memorial Day: A Collaboration. Ted and Anne Waldman Berrigan. EAS

Holes in maps look through to nowhere. The Map of Places. Laura Riding. LiTA; NoAm

Holiday (boys), cry Holiday! The Song in Making of the Arrows. John Lily. LoBV; OBSC

Hollerin' TIMBER! Lord, this timber's gotta roll. Timber. Jerry the Mule. FSW

The hollow and the whole. Autumn Apples. Laurie Lee. BoC

The hollow Eccho will reply, 'Twas I. The Farwell. Henry, Bishop of Chichester King. CavP

The hollow, famished cup of Love, replete! Prayer. Hazel J. Fowler. TrPWD

A hollow life is beautiful with shame. Epigram: A Spiral Shell. Howard Nemerov. OBAL

A hollow note. The Leaping Fire. John Montague. IPY

The hollow-roaring Forties echo, "Where?" Clipper Ships. John Anderson. EtS

Hollows the hedge-bound track, a sealed/Furrow on dark, closing behind him. Civilities of Lamplight. Charles Tomlinson. OxBC

The holly bears the crown. The Holly and the Ivy. Anonymous. ELP; GBP

The holy bread, the food unpriced,/Thy everlasting mercy, Christ. The Everlasting Mercy. John Masefield. BoC; GoTF; ILwL; TreFS; TRV; WGRP

The Holy Ghost, the truth that stands/When turned to dust are lips and hands. Life's Testament. William Baylebridge. BoAV; PoAu 1-2

Holy God makes no reply/Yet. De Civitate Hominum. Thomas MacGreevy. CIP

The holy Halo shoots it's arrowy beams.' The Action of Electricity. Erasmus Darwin. FaBoUs

Holy, holy, holy Lord. Holy God, We Praise Thy Name. Clarence A. Walworth. AH; TreFT

Holy is the deed you do! Hymn to Evil. Louis Ginsberg. PoA

The holy melodies of love arise. The Arsenal at Springfield. Henry Wadsworth Longfellow. AmPP; AnNE; AP; HBV 1-2; MCCG; PGD; WaaP

The holy One, blessed be He. Shalom Aleichem. Anonymous. TrJP

The holy peace that fills the air/Of those calm solitudes is there. The Forest Maid. William Cullen Bryant. OBVV

Holy the silence of your calm retreat. Sonnet: Leaves. William Barnes. FaBoRV; OBNC

Holy the supernatural extra brilliant intelligent kindness of the soul! Footnote to "Howl." Allen Ginsberg. AmPP; CAPP

A holy trimmer in this Protestant city:/you cannot hide the evidence of grace. Lais. Elaine Feinstein. FaBoWP

Holy Virgin, Mother, Queen! The Benedictine Ultima. Anonymous. CAW

Holy with self-forgotten charities. Golden Wedding (excerpt). Alan Mulgan. ACV

The holy word/Grew white and still. The First Autumn. Marshall Schacht. MoRP

Homage I pay, my Lord, that now am free. Homage. R. J. Schoeck. GoYe

Home, a sound of bells,/In the huge, quiet night. Memory. Joseph Stroud. NPGG

Home again, home again, market is/done. To market, to market. Mother Goose. FaBoBe; FaFP; HBV 1-2; HBVY; OxNR; SoPo; TiPo

Home again, home again,master/and dame. Come up, My Horse, to Budleigh Fair. Anonymous. OxNR

A home all holy for each Host/That comes in love to me. A Child's Wish. Abram Joseph Ryan. AA; CAW

Home, away home, ere the lightning floated forth again. Lightning. D. H. Lawrence. CMoP; LiTL; MoAB; MoBrPo; UnTE

Home, dear heart,/To you. My Life Is a Bowl. May Riley Smith. BLPA

Home for herself./I said. Wait for Me. Robert Creeley. NOBA; PPP

Home, he still dreams of going home. Finding Them Lost. Howard Moss. CoAP; NYBP; SM

Home, home, here's my baby's home! Anne Hutchinson's Exile. Edward Everett Hale. PAH

Home in the hands/of strangers A Poem for the Old Man. John Wieners. NeAP

The home in the heavens above. I Buried the Year. W. Luff. STF

A home is built of loving deeds/That stand a thousand years. House and Home. Victor Hugo. TRV

Home is sweet, and only sweet,/Where there's one we love to meet us! Home Is Where There Is One to Love Us. Charles Swain. BLPA; BLPL; FaBoBe

Home is where we have to gather grace. Enterprise. Nissim Ezekiel. ACV

A home not mine, dear outcast. Choosing a Name. Anne Ridler. NOBE

The home of beautiful boys. Epigram: "Listen, you who know the pains of love." Meleager. PeHV

Home of fair poesy, realm of pure harmony,/Santa Lucia, Santa Lucia! Santa Lucia. Anonymous. FSW

The home of Silence and of Heat! The Arid Lands. Herbert Bashford. AA

Home once more. The Song of the Shadows. Walter De la Mare. CMoP

Home, poor heart, you cannot rediscover/If the dream alone does not suffice. To Nature. Friedrich Hoelderlin. LiTW

Home they go, yo ho! Harvest Song. Ludwig Heinrich Christoph Holty. AWP

Home through the gloomy wood in wonderment. Endymion, IV. John Keats. EnRP

Home through the greenwood–home. The Wife from Fairyland. Richard Le Gallienne. HBV 1-2

Home to Corca Bascinn, in the morning light. Fontenoy. 1745. Emily Lawless. AnIV

Home to his Mothers house privat returnd. Paradise Regained. John Milton. CABL

Home to me...is love! Home. June Brown Harris. PoToHe

Home to my provincial town/having spoken to no one. Arrival: The Capital. Desmond O'Grady. NMP

Home to the coral fathoms of my day. Leviathan. Kenneth Pitchford. CoPo

Home to the heart of God! The Way. Leslie Savage Clark. PGD

Home to the heart of his sinning land where she stumbled/and sinned in the dark. On a Soldier Fallen in the Philippines. William Vaughn Moody. AP; HBV 1-2; MC; NOBA; PAH

Home to their mother, hop. Frog Hunting. Peter Cooley. MAYP

Home to thy father thou shalt bear/Another child made like to thee. The Carpenter. George Macdonald. TrPWD; TRV

The home undisturbed, the green Isle of/the Lover! The Green Isle of Lovers. Robert Charles Sands. AA

Home–what a perfect place! Home Thoughts in Laventie. Edward Wyndham Tennant. HBMV

Home with him he brought it. Riddle: "He went to the wood and caught it." Anonymous. GBP; OxNR

Home with the tide into the mighty river. The Estuary. Ruth Pitter. MoVE

The homefelt joys, beyond expression dear,/Deserve an elegy, a parting tear. Corydon's Farewell, on Sailing in the Late Expedition Fleet. Anonymous. NOEC

A homeless land and friendless, but a land/I did not know and that I wished to know. Two Sonnets. Charles Hamilton Sorley. MMM

Homely old hags always snoring? Paradise. Immanuel Di Roma. TrJP

Homer himself, in a long work, may sleep. To the Generous Reader. Robert Herrick. CaPo

Homer his sight, David his little lad. Tears. Lizette Woodworth Reese. AA; GoTF; HBV 1-2; HBVY; MCCG; MoAmPo; TreFS; WGRP; WHA

Homer was blind, and Bennet could not read.' On the Death of Old Bennet the News-Crier. Anonymous. NOEC

Homesick for harpings of eternity. The Dead Musician. Charles L. O'Donnell. CAW

Homesick for the Black Land. Return of the Prodigal Son. Leopold Sedar Senghor. GrPl

The homestead of the free!   The Kansas Emigrants.   John Greenleaf Whittier.   MC; PAH

Homeward/To a dreamless slumber.   Stevedore.   Leslie Morgan Collins. AmNP

Homeward to the deep.   Legend.   Ridgely Torrence.   EtS

The homicidal hurry in his soul/embarrassed into an uncertain smile.   A Classical Quatrain.   Paul Goodman.   VGW

Homing the bride, and harvest, and men dead.   The Waggon-Maker.   John Masefield.   EBEV

Homo called sapiens.   Apostrophe to Man.   Edna St. Vincent Millay.   DBV; SBG

Honest labour bears a lovely face,/Then hey noney, noney, hey noney, noney. Art Thou Poor, Yet Hast Thou Golden Slumbers?   Thomas Dekker.   CBEP; HAP; InPS; OAEP; PAI; UnPo; ViBoPo

The honest Layman's Faith is still the same.   To Mr. Bays.   Charles, Earl of Dorset Sackville.   APAS

An honest man's the noblest work of God.   An Essay on Man.   Alexander Pope.   AnFE; GoTF

The honest ox, rejoiced, into the shade.   My Ox Duke.   John Dyer.   NOEC

Honestly I don't know why/everybody's looking at me like this.   Who Can Tell When He Is Awake.   James Tate.   MAYP

Honesty coupled to beauty is to have honey a sauce to sugar.   As You Like It.   William Shakespeare.   PP

Honey and Sherry and little Bashaw.   Golden Grain.   Helen M. Wright.   PH

The honey crystallized,/and the honey-lover smoke.   Lost Silvertip.   J. D. Reed.   NYBP

Honey for tea, and nothing/Will ever really happen again.   Send for Lord Timothy.   John Heath-Stubbs.   OxBC

Honey in a beehive,/And me in bed.   Where.   Walter De La Mare.   NYBP

Honey, let me be your salty dog.   Salty Dog Blues.   Anonymous.   CoSo; FSW

The honey of peace in old poems.   To the Stone-Cutters.   Robinson Jeffers.   AmP; MoAB; MoAmPo; MoVE; NIP; NOBA; NoP; OxBA; PoCh; PoPl; PP; PrIm; TrGrPo

Honey, sugar baby mine.   Crawdad.   Anonymous.   FSW

Honey, take yo' bressed time.   Sister Lou.   Sterling A. Brown.   AmNP; GoSl; PoBA; PoNe

Honey, they're struttin' that thing/night and day/(Let's get back)   I Don't Know.   Cripple Clarence Lofton.   BluL

Honey, trus' de Lawd a bit, an' doan' fohgit to smile!   Trus' an' Smile.   B.Y. Williams.   BLRP

The honeycomb, the holy land/Broken and bleeding in my hand.   Text.   Audrey Wurdemann.   FYAP

The honeyed lips I have known.   The Day Death Comes.   Faiz Ahmen Faiz.   AMV-81

Honeyed notes that never fail/Upon my lips they laid.   Song for a Dancer.   Kenneth Rexroth.   TAP

The honeysuckle scent,/raspberries–black & red,/greenleaf, rose, & thorn.   Reading Sign.   Jack Anderson.   LFAC

The honky-tonk out of the somnolent grasses/Is a memorizing, a trying out, to keep.   These Locusts by Day.   Wallace Stevens.   PoA

Honor and joy were lost in the shadow of the/question.   Trees Once Walked and Stood.   Joshua Tan Pai.   VWA

Honor and point of dust.   Marianne Moore (1887-1972).   Raymond F. Roseliep.   SOTS

Honor be to old Ishmael Day!   The Ballad of Ishmael Day.   Anonymous.   PAH

Honor, for death shy valentine.   Letter from a Coward to a Hero.   Robert Penn Warren.   MoAmPo

Honor him for their memory whose bones he goes among!   The Forging of the Anchor.   Sir Samuel Ferguson.   HBV 1-2; IrPN

Honor partners, balance all.   Mississippi Sawyer.   Anonymous.   AmFP

Honor the brave/Who died to save/Your all upon "Our Left."   Our Left.   Francis Orrery Tichnor.   MC; PAH

Honor, then, for all time be/To the brave Montgomery!   Montgomery at Quebec.   Clinton Scollard.   PAH

Honor to Lexington,/Our first immortal name!   A Song for Lexington.   Robert Kelley Weeks.   AA

Honor with aige till every vertew drawis.'   Honour with Age.   Walter Kennedy.   OxBS

Honorable distinguished Christofo Colombo.   Mysterious Biography.   Carl Sandburg.   OFD; SiSoSe

Honour, a friend, anguish, untimely death.   Achilles.   Ernest Myers.   OBVV

Honour, high honour, and renown/To Hymen, god of every town!   As You Like It.   William Shakespeare.   HW; ViBoPo

Honour, in spite of love, pronounced thy death.   Epitaph on a Child Killed by Procured Abortion.   Anonymous.   NOEC

Honour meant most. She listened by the door/For who'd betray it; but too spent to care   The People (excerpt).   Robin Hyde.   AnNZ

Honour paid to Mudjekeewis,/But no honour to the muse.   What I Think of Hiawatha (parody).   J. W. Morris.   Par; SpRo

Honour the Kremlin, boys, but now and then/Admit some signs of grace at Number Ten.   Less Nonsense.   Sir Alan Herbert.   OxBTC

Honour the shrine where you alone are placed.   More Than Most Fair.   Fulke, Lord Brooke Greville.   EIL

Hony Soyt Qui Mal Pence.   Sir Gawain and the Green Knight.   Anonymous.   EnLi 1-2; OAEL 1-2

Hoo, hoo, Lord, baby June, what a day, what a day!   Four O'Clock Flower Blues.   Anonymous.   AmFP

An' hoo says hoo can tell when hoo's hurt.   Jone o' Grinfield.   Anonymous.   VLP

Hoogh, quoth he.   The Lady in Love.   Anonymous.   OxNR

Hooked fishes of the factory world.   City Life.   D. H. Lawrence.   CAD; OAEP

Hoopoe, if of that tribe which sing/Articulate in the desert ring!   Nepenthe.   George Darley.   OBNC; OBRV; PBBP

Hooray!/The cat/is/dead!   Death of the Cat.   Ian Serraillier.   SO

The hooves and horn-points anagrammed in stars.   Europa.   Derek Walcott.   NoP

Hop light, ladies,/Oh, Miss Loo!   Plantation Play-Song.   Joel Chandler Harris.   MCCG

Hope, and press forward, your face to the light.   Press Onward.   Anonymous.   FaFP

Hope, blossoming within my heart,/May look to heaven as I depart.   To the Fringed Gentian.   William Cullen Bryant.   AA; AnFE; AnNE; AP; APA; AWP; FaBoBe; FPL; GN; GoTF; HBV 1-2; NePA; NoP; OBRV; PoLf; TAP; TreFT

Hope cannot give/That hap denies.   Love Cannot Live.   Anonymous.   EIL

Hope for you yet, then.   St. Asaph's.   Kingsley Amis.   OxBTC

Hope is a sad-faced clown/in sneakers.   Hope.   Kenneth L. Anderson.   AMV-80

Hope is reality and time is life.   On Ascending a Hill Leading to a Convent.   Francisco Manuel de Mello.   CAW

Hope not for mind in women; at their best/Sweetness and wit, they are but mummy, possessed.   Love's Alchemy.   John Donne.   CABA; LiTL; NoP; OAEL 1-2; OAEP; SUW; ViBoPo

"Hope not thou much, and fear thou not at all."   Hope and Fear.   Algernon Charles Swinburne.   FaBoBe; HBV 1-2

The Hope of all/The world was born.   Bethlehem of Judea.   Anonymous.   BiCB; ChBR

Hope of burning off at least the top crust of the time's un-/cleanness, from the acid bottles.   Prescription of Painful Ends.   Robinson Jeffers.   LiTA; MoAB; MoAmPo; OxBA

The Hope of the Worlds hidden under her heart!   Annunciation Night.   Katherine Eleanor Conway.   CAW

Hope revolving him/past sense.   Hope.   William Dickey.   GDP; PoL

Hope's the strangest game we play.   Saving the Fish.   R. T. Smith.   WOLT

Hope! Saith the holly.   Green Grow'th the Holly.   Anonymous.   PCh

Hope she dies of shame.   Sally Free and Easy.   Cyril Tawney.   OBET

Hope spreads on heavenward wing.   Light of the World.   Slyvester Judd.   BePJ

Hope still lives on time depending,/By thy plagues my torments ending.   Song Set by Robert Jones: "She whose matchless beauty staineth."   Anonymous.   OBSC

The hope that floods thy throat!   An Early Bluebird.   Maurice Thompson.   AA

Hope thrives in straits, in weakness love,/And faith in this world's shame.   A Thanksgiving.   John Henry, Cardinal Newman.   TrPWD

Hope to have more time to tell you about/The latter in the foreseeable future.   Tenth Symphony.   John Ashbery.   NOBA

...Hope/was the hollowness in their cold clean skulls.   The Ruined Motel.   Reginald Gibbons.   MAYP

Hope, we do live yet.   Arcadia.   Sir Philip Sidney.   FCP; SiPS

...Hopeful as a/rainwashed hill of moonlit pines.   Who Shall Speak for the People?   Carl Sandburg.   OxBA

Hopelessness somewhere, and bring me a friend.   Minutes of Gold.   Anonymous.   PoToHe

Hoping he's dead.   Caesar.   William Stanley Merwin.   LCAP; NaP

Hoping/is a form/of forgetting   The Hopes.   Dieter Fringell.   AMV-80

Hoping that she would understand/and take me quickly into hand.   Organ Solo.   Knute Skinner.   GP

...Hoping that the Resurrection/Will not catch him unawares whenever it takes place.   Epitaph.   John Heath-Stubbs.   OxBTC

Hoping that when the tide is full I may seek my/unhaunted bed.   Caedmon.   Norman Nicholson.   FaBoTw

Hoping to ask my mother and father/for forgiveness for the years/they have taken from their lives?   Visit.   Vic Coccimiglio.   Str

Hoping to find a mislaid dream somewhere!   To the New Owner.   Lucile Hargrove Reynolds.   PoToHe

...Hoping to see/how we wear the things that happen in the world.   Newspaper Hats.   Jim Howard.   AMV-81; FAZ

Hoping you/are the same/archy   Archy Confesses.   Don (Donald Robert Marquis) Marquis.   EvOK; FiBHP

Hoping you'll turn and snap at me/To pick my feet up, and not to slouch. Desires.   Connie Bensley.   FaBoWP

Hoppity,/Hoppity,/Hop.   Hoppity.   A.(lan) A.(lexander) Milne.   FaBV; NTCP; TiPo

The horizon comes down,/Beating hard on his shoulders.   Pole Vault.   Shiro Murano.   SD

"Horn Head' would be better.   I Am Suibne the Wanderer.   Suibne Geilt. NOBI

The horn's sweet note and the tooth of the hound.   Two Songs of a Fool. William Butler Yeats.   CMoP

(The horn sounds hoarsely)   Ballad of Faith.   William Carlos Williams. OBAL

The horn, the horn, the lusty horn,/Is not a thing to laugh to scorn.   As You Like It.   William Shakespeare.   CTC; OBSC; ViBoPo

The horns of morning sound above the/storm.   To a Town Poet.   Lizette Woodworth Reese.   AA

...The horrid/blast,/From Hell with furious tempest!   Song of the Sea. Rumann MacColmain.   OnYI

A horrid winter overtakes my soul.   Often I Compare My Lord to Heaven. Gaspara Stampa.   PBWP

Horror, horror!   Ulf of Ireland.   Charles De Kay.   AA

...The horror of their years/stoned me to death.   Waiting in Front of the Columnar High School.   Karl Shapiro.   HAP

The Horror welcomes her, again,/These, are not brayed of Tongue—   The Soul Has Bandaged Moments.   Emily Dickinson.   MAmP

—The horrors of O'Hare.   747 (London–Chicago).   Robert Conquest. OxBC

The horse above on the mountain.   Sleepwalkers' Ballad.   Federico Garcia Lorca.   WeW

Horse and pelatis, Ho, ho!   Witch's Broomstick Spell.   Anonymous.   GBP

A horse-cab driver, looking straight ahead,/Smiles quietly, just because it is morning.   The Sickness.   Frederick Seidel.   CoPo

A horse can trot, for all he's old.   How the Old Horse Won the Bet.   Oliver Wendell Holmes.   AnNE

The horse doth with the horseman run away.   To Fuscus Aristus.   Horace. AWP

A horse gazes steadily at me.   A Late Spring Day in My Life.   Robert Bly. NCSH

...Horse hooves mixed/with the howling of a piano.   Links.   Barry Dempster.   CaPN

The horse/Is more so ( )   Horse & Rider.   Wey Robinson.   BXAP; SD

The horse, of course.   The Horse.   Shel Silverstein.   PH

A horse, plunging into darkness,/kicks a stone out of its path.   Lantern. Frank Polite.   GP

A horse's head where his tail should be.   Riddle: "See, see, what shall I see?" Anonymous.   OxNR

Horse, sky, cow, tree, thank you, I mean,/Beauty, and love.   Amsterdam Letter.   Jean Garrigue.   NYBP

...The horse/Stood saddled, browsing in grass,/Waiting for me.   A Dream of Burial.   James Wright.   NaP

A horse that no one rides!   I Saw the Wind To-Day.   Padraic Colum. GoJo; SUS

A horse that runs over wooden bridges, and sleeps/In abandoned barns... Three Presidents: Andrew Jackson.   Robert Bly.   LCAP

The horse that wore the shoe his name was Mike.   I Found a Horseshoe (with music).   Anonymous.   AS

The horse wades in the city of grammar.   Perspective He Would Mutter Going to Bed.   Jack Gilbert.   NPGG

Horseman, pass by!   Under Ben Bulben.   William Butler Yeats.   AnIV; CMoP; CoBMV; FaBoRV; HAP; LiTM; LoBV; NoAm; NoP; OxBI; OxBTC; WeW

The horses like hours standing hours in a row.   The Stable.   Jill Hoffman. PH

The horses on the hill that browse.   Somnambulistic Ballad.   Federico Garcia Lorca.   LiTW

The horses run back into the barn.   Barn Fire.   Thomas Lux.   LCAP

...The horses/slowly turned and moved toward the barn.   Miss Creighton. Henry Taylor.   GrPl

...The horses waited for the dawn to mount to her high/place.   The Iliad. Homer.   NAWM 1-2

Hosanna! and Thy glorious footsteps greet./Amen.   Christ's Coming in Triumph.   Jeremy Taylor.   BePJ

Hosanna for evermore!   The Holy City.   Frederic Edward Weatherly. BLRP; WBLP

Hosannah the home run!   Dream of a Baseball Star.   Gregory Corso. NoAm; SD; VGW

...Hoses,/lax in their dreams of spring,/sleep deep.   Snow.   Ralph Pomeroy. Psk

Hoses/were coming to whip back to water, wash to the sewers the/nuisance-freight.   Snow in New York.   May Swenson.   NYP

...Hospitable to all/who can endure the cold intensity of art.   A Poet's Progress.   Michael Hamburger.   NePoEA; PP

The hospital where someone's dead.   The Message.   Jacques Prevert.   WeW

De hoss I fancy am de bobtail nag;/He'll walk away from de bay.   De Camptown Races.   Stephen Collins Foster.   TrAS

The hostess reads, with gentle zest,/The poetry of Edg-r Gu-st.   Mrs. Brown and the Famous Author.   Stoddard King.   ATP

The hostess writes/B. Y. O. B.   Thoughts on Being Invited to Dinner. Christopher Morley.   HBMV

Hot and intent with a strange love/for what they can light upon and keep. Brobdingnag.   Adrien Stoutenburg.   NYBP

Hot are my pease, hot.   The Hot Pease Man.   Anonymous.   OxNR

Hot as hell outside.   Same Tits.   James Tate.   FAZ

Hot diggity!   Your Birthday in Wisconsin You Are 140.   John Berryman. NAs

Hot, naked, unashamed beauty!   Summer Afternoon.   Raymond Souster. BoNaP

Hot suns of Africa are burning still!   To a Brown Girl.   Ossie Davis. PoNe

Hot the tears Del Cascar wept.   Del Cascar.   William Stanley Braithwaite. BANP; CDC

A hound stands o'er the carcass of a man.   Between the Traveller and the Setting Sun.   Henry David Thoreau.   PoEL 1-5

The hounds of doorways think this is no great matter.   Dirge for Two Clavichords and Bowler Hat.   Kendrick Smithyman.   AnNZ

The hounds wail for the dead.   The Ballad of the Foxhunter.   William Butler Yeats.   EnLit

The hour has struck, though I heard not the bell!   Modern Love, III. George Meredith.   HBV 1-2; VLP

The hour I first believed.   Amazing Grace.   Anonymous.   ABF

The hour is late, and far that shining town.   Sonnet: "Since I keep only what I give away."   George Hetherington.   NeIP

The hour of waking together.   The Garret.   Ezra Pound.   PoPl; SOTW

The hour that brings us back to back/But harbingers the larger light. Greeting from England.   Anonymous.   PAH

The hour when Liberty is born.   Valley Forge.   Thomas Buchanan Read. MC; PAH

Hourly growing more haggard from the weight of the/grave.   Variations on a Theme.   Oscar Williams.   LiTA

...The hours advance/Like flecks of foam borne landward and destroyed. Before an Old Painting of the Crucifixion.   N. Scott Momaday.   QFR

Hours eating from this planet's tasty/Dwindling peace of mind.   Declaration of Independence.   Michael Brownstein.   APU

The house above, when all is love/There'll be no parting there.   Our School Now Closes Out.   Edmund Dumas.   AH

The house in which his mother was born.   Mnemosyne Lay in Dust.   Austin Clarke.   CIP; CMoP; IPY

The house is a maelstrom of loves and hates where you–/Having got down– belong.   Under the Mountain.   Louis MacNeice.   FaBoIP

The house is a witness that must be effaced.   Moving Out.   Joyce Carol Oates.   AMV-81

The house is going/And will soon be gone.   The Abandoned House. Patricia Hubbell.   WSC

The house is in order in heaven–/I hope I shall see you up there.   A Coal Miner's Goodbye.   Anonymous.   AmFP

The house is poor but open is the gate.   The Marriage of Geraint: Enid's Song.   Alfred, Lord Tennyson.   FaBoRV

...A house of strife/Built far back in the fundaments of life.   The Rooftree. Allen Tate.   PoA

House of the Future, built upon the sand.   Danger.   Theodora L. Paine. PGD

...A house-/shaped mound of ivy/grows on dust.   Epithalamium.   John Ditsky.   DFT

The house that cannot pass away be ours.   The Most Alluring Clouds That Mount the Sky.   William Wordsworth.   NOBV

The house trembled with my coughs/and the breaths of my phantoms of the night.   Explorations Bronchitis: The Rosario Beach House.   Aleida Rodriguez.   FIA

The house where all is still.   A Farewell.   Alice Brown.   HBV 1-2

Household words, no more depart.   Seaweed.   Henry Wadsworth Longfellow.   AP; HBV 1-2; MOS; OxBA; TAP

& The houseplants continue to shine.   House Plants.   David McFadden. NOBC

Houses and sky, a dream, a dream!   November.   Laurence Binyon.   SyP

Houses should have homes to live in.   Houses Should Have Homes to Live in.   David Ross.   PG

Houses sway at the slightest/tremor.   The California Phrasebook.   Dennis Schmitz.   AmPA; NPGG

Housman the draught that's black.   Thomas Hardy and A. E. Housman. Max Beerbohm.   NLV

Hover, phoenix-free, above the deep Edens of the valley.   Westering. Douglas V. Kane.   GoYe

...Hovering/journeys over the fathomless waters.   The Dragonfly-Mother. Denise Levertov.   InPS

Hovering over ten thousand acres/Of young fir.   Logging (excerpt).   Gary Snyder.   NOBA

Hovering over the sound is a mother buried/inside me, her bare arms cover the sea.   The Voices.   Janine Pommy-Vega.   APU

...Hovering/So still, in the windless sky.   Nothing.   Charles Simic.   NNaP

Hoves thy black flag!...Therefore I hate thee, Death!   Mors, Morituri Te Salutamus.   Francis Burdett Money-Coutts.   OBVV

How a daughter of their sires/Saved a captive Englishman.   Pocahontas. William Makepeace Thackeray.   AmFN; GN; MC; OnMSP; PAH; PAL

How a shepherd-swain did conquer them;/The like did never none.   Robin Hood and the Shepherd.   Anonymous.   ESPB

How about that!   American Gothic.   Samuel ("Paul Vesey") Allen.   IDB

How alien the lovers of your ghost.   Rome Remember.   Sidney Keyes. MoAB

How all bright things decay.   Ballad of the Drinker in His Pub.   N. P. Van Wyk Louw.   PeSA

How all things/cried out to share them   Those Who Come What Will They Say of Us.   John Knoepfle.   FAZ

How am I to be cured against my will?   Mad Song.   Denise Levertov. TAP

How amazed the children/there/will be.   On This Day.   M. B. Goffstein. NTCP

How ancient, and how full of grace.   Slowly, Slowly Wisdom Gathers. Mark Van Doren.   PoA

How animal is soul, and not its opposite.   Animal Song.   Heather McHugh. MAYP

How are the mighty fallen/and the weapons of war, are they perished! Nearly Everybody Loves Harvey Martin.   William D. Barney.   LiSp

How are they then conjoined? As God would.   Sonnet LXVI.   William Alabaster.   SBVL

How are things on the Great Divide,/O Whiskey Bill?   Whiskey Bill,–A Fragment.   Anonymous.   BPAW

"How are you!" is a greeting, not a question.   Of Tact.   Arthur Guiterman. MoShBr

How art thou Nothing when th' art most of all!   On an Houre-Glasse.   John Hall.   MeLP; MePo

How at my sheet goes the same crooked worm.   The Force That through the Green Fuse Drives the Flower.   Dylan Thomas.   ATP; BiP; BLPL; CABA; CMoP; CoBMV; DiPo; EBEV; ExPo; FaBoMo; ImOP; InPo; InPS; LiTB; LiTM; MoAB; MoBrPo; MoPo; MoVE; NeBP; NIP; NoAm; NOBE; NoP; OAEP; OxBTC; PAI; PoPle; PPP; PrIm; SCV; TEP; UnPo; ViBoPo

How bad I do feel!   Jack of Diamonds.   Anonymous.   AmFP

How beautiful are both these nothings.   Shane O'Neill's Cairn.   Robinson Jeffers.   NoAm; NOBA

How beautiful are your breasts with their two russet/berries.   Song: "If you love God, take your mirror between your hands and look.   Mahmud Djellaladin Pasha.   LiTW

How beautiful is night!   Night.   Robert Southey.   GN

How beautiful it might have been to live.   The Massacre of the Innocents. William Jay Smith.   EaLo

How beautiful their feet, who follow in that train.   The Train of Religion (excerpt).   Martin Farquhar Tupper.   FaBoCo

How beautiful thy feet are on the hills!   No Single Thing Abides.   Lucretius (Titus Lucretius Carus).   AWP; ImOP; PG

How beggared wilt thou leave us, how obscure!–   At the Ascension.   Luis Ponce de Leon.   CAW

How best these precious gifts to use/Thou hast bestowed on me. Understanding.   Anonymous.   PoToHe

How better than in shock to learn of/terms?   You Are a Jew!   Delmore Schwartz.   TrJP

How bitter black that trail to town!   Frozen Fire.   Floris Clark McLaren. CaP

...How black it is/Beneath these thick-boughed trees!   The Empty House. Walter De la Mare.   BrPo

How black it is, how fast it is, below?   Neurasthenia.   Agnes Mary Frances (Mme Emile Duclaux) Robinson.   NOBV

How blessed it is,/Lion.   Lucky Lion!   Anonymous.   WTO

How blossomed so ye leafless bough.   Why Ye Blossome Cometh before Ye Leafe.   Oliver Herford.   AA

How both Revenge, and Sympathy consent/To make two Rocks each others Monument.   Sonnet: The Double Rock.   Henry, Bishop of Chichester King.   SeCP

How brain secretes dog's soul, we'll see!'   Tray.   Robert Browning.   FM

How break and enter what will only bend?   Reply to Mr. Wordsworth (excerpt).   Archibald MacLeish.   ImOP

How calm you are. And the burning wheel/passes gently over us.   Happiness. Louise Gluck.   MAYP

How came it that the peasants died.   Louis XV.   John Sterling.   BeLS

How can darkness look to our house for light?   To His Father on Praising the Honest Life of the Peasant.   Parvin E'tesami.   WPOW

How can he be? The words are wild.   The Child Is Father to the Man. Gerard Manley Hopkins.   FaBoCo; NOBV

How can I any more be sad?   Wind and Rain.   Anonymous.   HW

How can I be content/when there is still/that odor in the world?   Mock Orange.   Louise Gluck.   MAYP

How can I be happy/While you are not here?   Song: "I could make you songs."   Dorothy Dow.   HBMV

How can I believe/you ran under a low maple limb/to knock me off?   Horse. Jim Harrison.   BoAnP; PH

How can I breathe? You can't, you fool!   Sanctuary.   Elinor Wylie. BoWoP; MoAB; MoAmPo

How can I die while Jesus lives?   The Man of Calvary (Easter Day Service). Anonymous.   AmFP

How can I drive off this word–/Hopelessness?   A Weary Song to a Slow Sad Tune.   Li Ch'ing-chao.   BoWoP

How can I fit her mammoth grief/into the dark below my matchstick ribs? Country Drive-In.   Josephine Jacobsen.   AmC

How can I keep from singing?   How Can I Keep from Singing? (excerpt). Robert Lowry.   FSW; TRV

How can I keep my maidenhead/Among so many men?   How Can I Keep My Maidenhead.   Robert Burns.   ErPo; UnTE

"How can I live now my William is gone?"   A Sailor's Life.   Anonymous. OBSS

How can I roll, when the wheels won't go?   Nine Pound Hammer. Anonymous.   FSW

How can I stop to unload this burden/when the cry of generations drives me on.   The Cry of Generations.   Mordechai Husid.   VWA

How can I tell   The Market.   Gary Snyder.   NaP

How can I tell her/I am thinking that transformations are not forever?   From the Journals of the Frog Prince.   Susan Mitchell.   DFT; NIP

How can I tell them I have no reply?   Cante Hondo.   Ellen de Young Kay. NePoEA

How can I turn from Africa and live?   A Far Cry from Africa.   Derek Walcott.   HeIP; NoAm; TTY; UnPo

How can I wash my outside?   Hunger.   Anonymous.   WTO

How can she live till in her blood He live!   Ribh Considers Christian Love Insufficient.   William Butler Yeats.   TW

How can the young do such a/thing?   Along the River.   D. J. Enright. DFF

How can they bury in a grave/Someone who died from love?   Death Songs. Anonymous.   BoWoP

How can they know that I long to leave?   Analogy.   Brian Higgins. FaBoTw

How can they stand so patiently!   The Old Wharves.   Rachel Field.   SoPo

How can this be justified, how can it/Be justified?   My Mother's Sister.   C. Day-Lewis.   OxBTC

How can we hope to help Him/And hasten His return?   The World's Bible. Annie Johnson Flint.   STF; TRV

How can we know the dancer from the dance.   Among School Children. William Butler Yeats.   AnIL; BLPL; CMoP; CoBMV; DiPo; ForPo; GTBS-P; HAP; InPS; LiTB; LiTM; MBW 1-2; MoAB; MoBrPo; MoVE; NAWM 1-2; NIP; NoAm; NOBE; NoP; OAEL 1-2; OAEP; OxBTC; PPoe; PPP; PrIm; SeCeV; TrGrPo; WeW

How can we learn upon our knees,/That ironside unropes the bell?   Three Poems about Children.   Austin Clarke.   CIP

How can ye love God,/Whom ye have not seen?   More Love.   Anonymous. AH

How can you be a man this morning?   A Riddle.   Martial (Marcus Valerius Martialis).   PeHV

How can you go on saying you're happy?   The Beckett Kit.   Linda Gregg. AmPA

How canst thou dream Pan dead when/still/Thou seem'st to hear him sing! The Dancing Faun.   Robert Cameron Rogers.   AA

How changeful are the ways of humankind.   Tossed on a Sea of Trouble. Archilochus.   PoPl

How charming now, and cool it is!   Lines Written in the Dog-Days. William Woty.   NOEC

How close the Christ Child comes! how near the Star!   Noel! Noel!   Laura Simmons.   PGD

How Cob gave his life for the kiddy an' went straight up to glory.   Panhandle Cob.   Anonymous.   CoSo

How cold are thy baths, Apollo!   Jugurtha.   Henry Wadsworth Longfellow AA; AP

How cold my/TOES-tiddely-pom/Are/Growing.   The More It Snows. A.(lan) A.(lexander) Milne.   NTCP

How cold the stars are, how clear!   At the Telephone Club.   Henri Coulette. CoAP

How comes it that he wrote a book/Of five thousand words?   Lao-Tzu.   Po Chu-i.   LiTW

How could a blind rock satisfy/The hungers of the sea?   The Feather. Vernon Watkins.   FaBoTw; MoVE

How could I bear to see you die/Upon this hangman's line?   The Maid Freed from the Gallows ("Hangman, Slack on the Line").   *Anonymous.*   AmFP

How could I love thee, Dear, the most,/Loved I not others, some?   Alibi (parody).   Arthur Guiterman.   BXAP

How could I seek the empty world again?   Remembrance.   Emily Bronte.   BLPL; BoLoP; BoWoP; CH; EBEV; EnLoPo; FaFP; ForPo; GTBS; HAP; HBV 1-2; LiTB; LiTL; MasP; NOBE; NoP; OAEP; OBNC; OxBI; PoEL 1-5; TEP; TreFT; TrGrPo; VLP

How could such sweet and wholesome hours/Be reckoned but with herbs and flowers?   The Garden.   Andrew Marvell.   AnAnS 1; AnEnPo; AtBAP; AWP; BiP; BLPL; CEP; DiPo; ExPo; ForPo; HAP; HBV 1-2; InPo; InPS; InvP; JCP; LiTB; LoBV; MasP; MeLP; MePo; NIP; NOBE; NoP; OAEL 1-2; OAEP; OBS; PAI; PoEL 1-5; PoLf; PoPle; PoRA; PPoe; PPP; QFR; SeCePo; SeCeV; SeCP; SeCV 1-2; TEP; TrGrPo; WHA

How could that comfort you?   For the Rain It Raineth Every Day.   Robert Graves.   NYBP

How could the spirit flee?   In the Still, Star-Lit Night.   Elizabeth Stoddard   AA

How could they recover from the sword?   Lament after Her Husband Bishr's Murder.   Al-Khirniq.   BoWoP

How could you ever doubt that God/Sees you and hears your prayer?   No Doubt.   Helen Baker Adams.   STF

How craven so to strike me stricken so,/Yet from you fully armed conceal his bow!   It Was the Morning.   Petrarch (Francesco Petrarca).   NAWM 1-2

How crowded is the heavenly House of Light/With those who marched–for us–into the night.!   For Those Who Died.   Thomas Curtis Clark.   PGD

How Cyrus laid the cable!   How Cyrus Laid the Cable.   John Godfrey Saxe.   MC

How dare disbelieve/the Indians' orenda, or the Greeks'/Athene, the owl?   Owl.   Peter Kane Dufault.   NYBP

How dare they deserve?/Love, even.   Fragment.   Bruce Berlind.   FAZ

How dare you place any thing before a man?   By Blue Ontario's Shore (excerpt).   Walt Whitman.   FaBoPV

..."How dare you write/Such stuff on me, as dead outright;....   John Baynham's Epitaph.   Thomas Dermody.   OnYI

How dark his darkness, who till latest eve/Still slumbers on, nor then his couch will leave!   The Day of Denial.   Jones Very.   NOBA

How dead we are.   Not Any Sunny Tone.   Emily Dickinson.   AnFE; APA; MAPA

How dear comes beauty when a skin is black.   McDonogh Day in New Orleans.   Marcus B. Christian.   AmNP; PoNe

How dear it is, they mutter.   On the High Cost of Dairy Products.   James McIntyre.   FiBHP

How death takes/gifts of hair/and makes/itself a shawl   Wrapped Hair Bundles.   Frank LaPena.   STE

How deep the earth can be.   Sky Diver.   Adrien Stoutenburg.   LiSp

How deep the woods are.   Jacklight.   Louise Erdrich.   TWSS

...How deep this pool is/Only the dark cranes know that never come.   The Ancient Couple on Lu Mountain.   Mark Van Doren.   VGW

How delicate the dream/that even ice/attempts to hold.   The Ice Castle.   Michael Harris.   AMV-80

How delicately thou teachest love to me!   O Flame of Living Love.   Saint John of Damascus.   AWP; CAW

How did he fall/into my power?   The Experiment with a Rat.   Carl Rakosi.   GP; PoL

How did thou ever begin?   Hail to Thee, Blithe Owl.   Ring Lardner.   OBAL

How did you think of a star?   God, the Artist.   Angela Morgan.   BLPA; PoToHe

How different from the way it ever stood?   The Star-Splitter.   Robert Frost.   ImOP

How different from us,/Miss Beale and Miss Buss.   Of the Principal and Vice-Principal of the Ladies' College, Cheltenham.   *Anonymous.*   FaBoEE

How divine my Flora's flower!   Flora's Flower.   *Anonymous.*   UnTE

How do angels learn to sing?   Obligatory Love Poem.   P. L. Jacobs.   LFAC

How do I learn to love her/as you have loved me?   Chain.   Audre Lorde.   BlSi

How do I wear you/on this imperfect arm?   Six Divine Circles.   Gail Ghai.   AMV-81

How do you carry your spores,/the stars, and will you/let them go?   How to Reach the Moon.   Marsha Pomerantz.   VWA

How do you explain this?   Life Studies.   Peter Schjeldahl.   ANYP

How do you know?   The Year's Awakening.   Thomas Hardy.   CMoP; OxBTC

How do you like my silence from mouths stopped/With the dust of my triumphant care?   Elliott Hawkins.   Edgar Lee Masters.   OxBA

How do you like your blueeyed boy/Mister Death.   Buffalo Bill's.   Edward Estlin Cummings.   AmFN; CMoP; HeIP; InPK; LiTA; NePA; NOBA; OBSP; TAP; VGW

How do you spell Success?/With an S-S-S!   Cheers.   Eve Merriam.   LiSp

"How do you spell your last name?"   Young Girl.   Thomas Waltner.   LFAC

How does it feel/well–you know.   Abbreviated Rumination.   P. L. Jacobs.   LFAC

...How dry/the ghosts of dryness are.   Two Views of Two Ghost Towns.   Charles Tomlinson.   NoAm

How e'er it hits, there is no dough.   On Maids and Cats.   Henricus Selyns.   SCAP

How each hour moves toward their awakening?   Message.   Dorothy M. Richardson.   PoA

How each Summer day is won/from soil, the old clay soil/and that long, cold kingdom.   June.   Elaine Feinstein.   BrRo

How easily we forget   Sitting Alone in Tulsa Three A.M.   Lance Henson.   VoR

How easy is a bush suppos'd a bear!   Midsummer Night's Dream.   William Shakespeare.   BoLiVe; CTC; DiPo; FiP; GN; GoTF; HW; LBN; LiTB; MasP; PP; TreFS; WSC

How eill it be when we shall sleep indeed?   Sleep.   Thomas Bailey Aldrich.   AA

How else could He have saved a world/Filled with such diverse souls?   Diversity.   Evarard V. Thompson.   BePJ

How else to be fecund if not/to put up with a man.   The Couple.   Joel Oppenheimer.   CoPo

..How else will you take bonds of/the future, against the wolf in men's hearts?   Ascent to the Sierras.   Robinson Jeffers.   LoGBV; OxBA

How even he did not get to keep that lovely body.   The Racer's Widow.   Louise Gluck.   AmPA; GeTw; LiSp; NYBP; SM

How every watcher in whole spellbound crowds/Would light the wrong end of a cigarette.   The Death of Professor Backwards.   X. J. Kennedy.   SOTS

...How everything in God's earth or heaven/Can be known.   City.   Joseph Stroud.   NPGG

..."How everything shines."   An Allegory.   David Ignatow.   VGW

How faint, how loud the bravest hearts have cried.   Prayer.   James Elroy Flecker.   TrPWD

How fair a day was near–oh punished eyes,/That I had been more foolish, or more wise!   Astrophel and Stella, XXXIII.   Sir Philip Sidney.   AAS; OAEL 1-2; OBSC; SiPS

How fair a lot to fill/Is left to each man still.   A Summer Night.   Matthew Arnold.   CBEP; ExPo; GTBS; MCCG; OAEP; SeCePo; SeCeV

...How fair is youth that flies so fast!   Triumph of Bacchus and Ariadne.   Lorenzo de Medici.   CTC

How far can the noun expand, lacking the lust of the verb.   For the Noun C.   BL.   Parker Tyler.   PoA

How far how deep I don't know.   Rain.   Peter Sears.   AMV-80

...How far/mere honesty or justice is from all they need.   Behind the Falls.   William Stafford.   RFM

How far the unknown transcends the what/we know.   Nature.   Henry Wadsworth Longfellow   AA; AmePo; AmLP; AnNE; AP; AWP; FaBoBe; FPL; GoTF; InPo; PoLf; TAP; TrGrPo; TRV; WHA

How fast the time goes!   When I Saw You Last, Rose.   Henry Austin Dobson.   HBV 1-2

"How fatal are blind Cupid's ways."   Love and Honour.   Fulke, Lord Brooke Greville.   OBSC

How few its joys, how little they endure!   The Nightingale.   Petrarch (Francesco Petrarca).   LiTW; PoPl

How finish better than that?   Haste to the Wedding.   Alex Comfort.   ErPo

How five and twenty shillings were/Expended in one week.   How Five and Twenty Shillings Were Expended in a Week.   *Anonymous.*   OBET

How fleeting and how frail is human life!   Epitaph.   Gabriello Chiabrera.   AWP

How foolish he who fool calls me,/If frequently to mass I go.   If Frequently to Mass.   Christianne Pisan.   PoPl

How, for your sake,/to confront his pride and fear.   Going the Rounds: A Sort of Love Poem.   Anthony Hecht.   BoLoP

How frugal is the chariot/That bears a human soul!   There is no frigate like a book.   Emily Dickinson.   FPL; GoJo; GoTF; MoAmPo; NIP; OBCA; PoLf; PoPl; SiSoSe; SoSe; TAP; TreFS; TrGrPo; YeAr

"How funny, Hope."   The Assassination.   Robert Hillyer.   AnNE; MoAmPo; OFD

How gaily would I put my work away/And go with you.   Bed-Time.   Ralph M. Jones.   HBMV

"How glad I am that I crossed the sea!"   The Ambitious Ant.   Amos R. Wells.   OBCA

How glorious is the hour of secret prayer!   The Hour of Prayer.   Albert L. Hoy.   AMV-80

How God will be glad of thee,/Little Sister Rose-Marie!   Rose-Marie of the Angels.   Adelaide Crapsey.   HBV 1-2

How goes a life?   Something like the ocean/Building dead coral.   Squall.   Stanley Moss.   CoAP

How good Castara is, how deare my friend.   To a Friend, Inviting Him to a Meeting upon Promise.   William Habington.   AnAnS 2

"How good! how kind! and he is gone." In Memoriam A.H.H., XX. Alfred, Lord Tennyson. VLP

How good it was to see him again! The Visitor. George Bogin. FAZ

How good to see you again/shining, gleaming. Car Wash. Myra Cohn Livingston. NTCP

How goot dere Athol Boetry must be!' Athol Brose. Thomas Hood. FaBoCo

How grandly glow the bays! On the Death of Francis Thompson. Alfred Noyes. OBVV

How great is God Almighty,/Who has made all things well. All Things Bright and Beautiful. Cecil Frances Alexander. FaPoR; OHIP; OxBChV

How greater care of me can you demand? Death's Apology. Francisco Manuel de Mello. CAW

How green your Tree grows there. Earth and Sky. Eleanor Farjeon. PoSC; SUS

How had it blessed mankind, and rescued me! The Complaint, or Night Thoughts on Life, Death and Immortality. Edward Hilton Young. EnPE

How happy for us, that it is not at home! The Place of the Damned. Jonathan Swift. FaBoEE; OBSV

How happy this young man keeps bachelor hall./Larey-wo, wo, larey wo. When Boys Go A-Courting. Anonymous. TrAS

How happy we were in all those days! Blue Bottle. Anonymous. OuSiCo

How have your trousers fared? The Jam-Pot. Rudyard Kipling. HBV 1-2

How he came to be christened Maginnis! A Bush Christening. Andrew Barton ("Banjo") Paterson. PoAu 1-2

How he crossed the seas, a sailor bold,/In fourteen-ninety-two. Columbus. Leroy F. Jackson. SiSoSe

How he left my heart sore/And my eyes wet! Song: "Going down the old way." Margaret Widdemer. HBMV

How he met the Moorish maiden beside the lonely well. The Broken Pitcher. Ayton [(or Aytoun)] Sir Robert. InMe

How He rose, the Lord of glory. Easter Song. Mary Artemisia ("Aunt Mary") Lathbury. OHIP

How he turned without a word/followed him back to the highway. Incident. Karl Kopp. GOYP

How Heathen shrubs kisse Jesus for their King. Awake Yee Westerne Nymphs, Arise and Sing. Samuel Danforth. SCAP

How her hands are safe/As the eyelids of birds. Hats. R. H. W. Dillard. GP

How her heart hums! Love! Love! Rhoda McMahon. WeW

How high his honor holds his haughty head! Cacophonous Couplet on Cardinal Wolsey. Anonymous. DBV

...How his sealed lips sang/The Ite, Missa Est! A Martyr's Mass. Alfred Joseph Barrett. GoBC

How–how in God's name–I could pay! Bankrupt. Cortlandt W. Sayres. PoLf; PoToHe

How huge a body she was, how she corrected/The very tilt of the earth on its new course? Mater Dei. Padraic Fallon. NOCV

How I could be at twenty-two/as old as all mankind. Empty Holds a Question. Pat Folk. GOYP

How I'd like to have wings/and fly back to him. The Road to Pengya. Tu Fu. Prf

How I died waiting in my dream. The Gardener at Thirty. Jascha Kessler. AmPC

How I fell in the spring in the fall. Limerick: "There was a young fellow named Hall." J. F. Wilson. TDH

How I hate my destiny. The Photos. Diane Wakoski. NIP

How I hate to live this way! Eighteen Verse Sung to a Tatar Reed Whistle. Ts'ai Yen. BoWoP; WPOW

How I hold my daddy/like an old stone tree. The Moss of His Skin. Anne Sexton. CoAP; IHMS; SM

How I lived with you is the wonder. Epigram: "My heart still hovering round about you." Robert Nugent, Earl Nugent. NOEC

How I long to go,/For to hear de trumpet soun',/In dat mornin'. You May Bury Me in de Eas'. Anonymous. BoAN 1-2

How I long to see dat day./Gwine to see dat day,/To see dat day. De Band o' Gideon. Anonymous. BoAN 1-2

How I long to take you/All to myself/As a mother takes her child. The New Wife. Anonymous. WTO

How I look for your melodies! The Quest. Gladys Cromwell. HBMV

How I love Thy precious name! O My Saviour and Redeemer. Alice Mortenson. BePJ

How I love you for making things in the/morning. Sunday Morning. Wayne Moreland. PoBA

...How I shook the water/from my eyes at each return of the beautiful stranger. To My Mother. L. M. Rosenberg. AMV-81

How I wept and I wept and I wept and I wept! The Jokesmith's Vacation. Don (Donald Robert Marquis) Marquis. ALV; FiBHP

How I wish I/Could calculate pie. The Value of Pi. Anonymous. FaBoUs

How I wish I had that crust/That once I threw away. Wilful Waste Brings Woeful Want. Anonymous. OxNR

How I wonder which you are. Back Yard, July Night. William Cole. BoNaP

How I would dig it up! Kojiki: Metal Hoe Hill. Anonymous. HW

...How I would take you from,/Now, if I could, its whirling vacuum. Elegy for My Father. Howard Moss. NePoEA; VWA

How ill it becomes it Sonnes of God/To want Humanity? The Courteous Pagan Shall Condemne. Roger Williams. SCAP

How in that Eden could Adam/Be really, wholly lost? An American Takes a Walk. Reed Whittemore. MoVE

How, in the dark of time, he lost his way. Legend. John Hall Wheelock. LiTL; MoLP

...How/in this world we were going/to be necessary. An American Boyhood. Jonathan Holden. Psk

How infinite the compromise/That indicates I will! There are two mays. Emily Dickinson. NOBA

How insufficient is/The endearment and the look. May with Its Light Behaving. W. H. Auden. EBEV

How is it, my love? Worse than for me/With another man? An Attempt at Jealousy. Marina Tsvetayeva. WPOW

How is it that we know the world is changed? Camels of the Kings. Leslie Norris. OBCP; PCh

How is it you cannot hear/Your loved yoke-fellow? Longing. Anonymous. WTO

How it befell, when we our foes did choke/Like bees, and put them pell-mell to the Smoke. On Tobacco. Thomas Pestel. EIL

How it can/hang you up/for good Insight. Lionel Kearns. PeCV

How it hangs upon the trees,/A mystery of mysteries! Spirits of the Dead. Edgar Allan Poe. MAmP

How it heartens us to strip you off!/& this is no matter of fashion. In Praise of Clothes. Erica Jong. MAYP

...How it is these selves,/recently, are coming more quickly. Before the Statue of a Laughing Man. William C. Bowie. AMV-81

How joyous his neigh! Song of the Horse. Anonymous. AWP

How keen the cold! The New Moon. Kobayashi Issa. MOON

How knowest whether this night the tempest will not/come? Four Folk-Songs in Hokku Form, 2. Anonymous. LiTW

How life was but a name for loneliness. The Fog. Robert P. Tristram Coffin. CrMA

How lightly I have fled beneath thy hand. Opportunity. Niccolo Machiavelli. AWP

How like Eve's apple doth thy beauty grow,/If thy sweet virtue answer not thy show! Sonnets, XCIII: "So shall I live, supposing thou art true." William Shakespeare. InvP; MasP

How like the dream is life, like life the dream. Thus Spoke My Love. Pieter Corneliszoon Hooft. LiTW

How like this Big Baboon would be/to Mister So-and-so! The Big Baboon. Hilaire Belloc. MoShBr

How like you this, what hath she now deserved? The Lover Sheweth How He Is Forsaken of Such as He Sometime Enjoyed. Sir Thomas Wyatt. AAS; AtBAP; EIL; ELP; EnPo; FaBoEn; GBL; HoPM; InPS; OAEP; PAI; PoEL 1-5; PoRA; TrGrPo; ViBoPo

How little good my health did anyone near me. Robert Frost. Robert Lowell. NoAm

How little reaped where they had sown-/The generous Ascendancy. Lines Written in a Country Parson's Orchard. Leslie Daiken. OnYI

How little thought them two Chinese,/They'd both be smash'd to shivers. Domestic Didactics by an Old Servant: The Broken Dish. Thomas Hood. OBRV

How lonely all men are. Jodrell Bank. Patric Dickinson. SUW

How lonely all the years will run/Until I rest by thee. The Churchyard on the Sands. John Byrne Leicester Warren, Lord De Tabley. CH; FaBoPP; GBL; HBV 1-2; LoBV; NOBV; OBNC

How long has this got to go on? We Have Been Here Before. Morris Bishop. EvOK; FiBHP; InMe; NYBP

...How long have I not known/where waking ends and the dream begins... Infidelity. Olga Berggolts. BoWoP

How long, how long, till spade and hearse/Put to sleep my mother's curse? The Welsh Marches. Alfred Edward Housman. FaBoTw

How long it waits to soak beneath the bait. Jersey Bait Shack. Peter Balakian. MAYP

How long or brief/it seems to be. Twice Times Then Is Now. Ibn Hazm Al-Andalusi. OBVE

How long thy temples worshipless, Oh God? On Jordan's Bank. George Gordon, Lord Byron. ChRP

How long was he standing there/like that, before I came? Bearhug. Michael Ondaatje. PPJ

...How loose/ourselves from the disinterested/blaze of his wide pure eye? The Stranger. Adrienne Rich. CoPo; NNaP

How love so young could be so sweet. So Sweet Love Seemed. Robert Bridges. EnLit; FaBV; GTBS; HBV 1-2; LiTL

How lovely is the self this day discloses. Roses on the Breakfast Table. D. H. Lawrence. BrPo

How lovely the head/Made gourd. For Stephen Dixon. Zack Gilbert. PoBA

How lovely their scared, gentle eyes. Small Poem about the Hounds and the Hares. Lisel Mueller. GP

How low are the ceilings. Love, Love! What Nonsense It Is. Natalya Gorbanyevskaya. WPOW

How low, how mean, and full as poor as I./Cetera desunt. The Dedication to the Sermons. Charles Churchill. QFR

How man in his wretchedness waits for mercy. Christ 1: Advent Lyrics, III. *Anonymous*. AnOE

How mannerly and how polite/Their little John can be. The Visitor. Katharine Pyle. BBGG; OnUR

How many adieus? The Sense of Smell. Louis MacNeice. NYBP

How many brooms will sweep the sky? Halloween Witches. Felice Holman. WSC

How many chickens, for your sweetness, paid in blood! Shatnes or Uncleanliness. Eliezer Steinbarg. VWA

How many children make a family. Accents in Alsace: Alsace or Alsatians. Gertrude Stein. AtBAP

How many heavens at once it is/To have her God become her lover. On a Prayer Book Sent to Mrs. M. R. (excerpt). Richard Crashaw. ErPo

How many inert molecules are ready to break into life? Cells Breathe in the Emptiness. Galway Kinnell. NaP; VGW

How many kisses did he give you?/One, two, three, &c. I Had a Black Man. *Anonymous*. OxBoLi

How many leaves/open their green shutters now/to let April through. April. Linda Pastan. Psk

...How many, like/this dog, could I not wish/had been here in my/place, only a little closer! The Savage Beast. William Carlos Williams. TW

How many loved the drummer boy/Who prayed before he died! The Drummer Boy of Shiloh. *Anonymous*. AmFP

How many lovers does it take/to weave a sweater from a snake? Two Lovers Sitting on a Tomb. Pati Hill. FAZ

How many men of England died/To prove they were not dead. For a War Memorial. Gilbert Keith Chesterton. MMM

How many monkeys are you? The Tree. Alfred Kreymborg. HBMV; PoPl

How many pounds did it weigh?/One, two three, &c. Nursery Rhyme: "Judge, judge, tell the judge." *Anonymous*. OxBoLi

How many prompters! what a chorus! Plays. Walter Savage Landor. HBV 1-2; NLV; OBSP; OxBoLi; PV

..How many/shall be emancipated in company with them! Nanak and the Sikhs (excerpt). *Anonymous*. WGRP

How many shoelaces will they make of that! The Mad Yak. Gregory Corso. CoPo; NoAm

How many T's in that? Timothy Titus Took Two Ties. *Anonymous*. OxNR

How many the fictitious Shores–/Or any Harbor be– I Many Times Thought Peace Had Come. Emily Dickinson. AmP

How many things a child may do/For others by its love. Deeds of Kindness. Epes Sargent. HBV 1-2; HBVY

How many were going to St. Ives? Riddle: "As I was going to St. Ives." Mother Goose. SoPo

How many will her coldness kill! Song: "See, see, she wakes! Sabina wakes!" William Congreve. HBV 1-2; NOEC; OBSP

How many years they have been teaching birds/In little schools, by little skills,/How to be shadows Cypresses. Robert Francis. LCAP

How marvelous to be a thought entirely surrounded by brains! Shack Poem. Robert Bly. CAPP

How matchless would it be if she were well! Sonnets to Philomel. Sir John Davies. SiPS

How may the death of that dull insect be/The life of yon trim Shakespeare on the/tree? The Mocking Bird. Sidney Lanier. AA

...How meek/Were those mute signs of dire soul-shattering pain. Midnight at Baiae. A Dream Fragment of Imperial Rome. John Addington Symonds. PeHV

How men were ever cheerful. Epigram: "O death, thy certainty is such." Henry Luttrell. FaBoEE

How might this goodness draw our soules above/Which drew downe God with such attractive Love. Incarnatio Est Maximum Donum Dei. William Alabaster. MePo

How most it hurts that most delights the sense. Lonely Beauty. Samuel Daniel. CTC; OBSC

How much a dunce that has been sent to roam/Excels a dunce that has been kept at home. The Progress of Error. William Cowper. OBTV

How much a freeborn woman's favour costs. Epitaphs of the War, 1914-18. Rudyard Kipling. BrPo; OBWP

How much an animal death. The Zoo. John Logan. LCAP

–How much?–and–do you love me, kid? Threes. Carl Sandburg. CMoP; OxBA; PoLf

How much better the poets! Gormley's Laments (excerpt). Gormley. PBWP

How much by labour can/The feeble race of man! Express. William Allingham. NOBV

How much fewer volumes of verse there'd be! Lovers, and a Reflection. Charles Stuart Calverley. FaBoCo; FaBoPa; NA; SpRo; VLP

How much, Jesus Christ only knows. I'm Only a Broken-Down Miner. *Anonymous*. AmFP

How much that loyal body wanted learning. Epigram. Joseph Trapp. FaBoCo

How music's made is not a thing of luck. How Music's Made. Dilys Bennett Laing. ELU

How must the heart, ah, Cupid! be,/The hapless heart that's stung by thee! Cupid Stung. Thomas Moore. HBV 1-2

How my heart would never yield/To me the joy I long to feel. The Eighteenth Song. Hadewijch. LiTW

How naked go the sometime nude! The Naked and the Nude. Robert Graves. NYBP; SoSe

How near they are at last to finding me. Alien. Helen Frazee-Bower. HBMV

How nearer by a universe/to their divinity. My Sun-Killed Tree. Marguerite Harris. GoYe

How nice mud feels/Between the toes. Mud. Polly Chase Boyden. NTCP; SoPo; TiPo

How now? fie fie fie! you dance false. Strike It up, Tabor. *Anonymous*. NCEP

How numb, the Bellows feels! I breathed enough to take the trick. Emily Dickinson. NoAm

How oft, and by what means we did agree. To Cypassis, Corinna's Maid. Ovid (Publius Ovidius Naso). EBEV

How oft your pellets pass them/Is singular–like grouse. A Plea for a Plural. Rudolph Chambers Lehmann. CenHV

How often, oh! how oft. How Often (parody). Ben King. HBV 1-2

How old is Spring, Miranda? A Lady Thinks She Is Thirty. Ogden Nash. PoPl

How old is the ghetto? Ask the question, nobody knows. Promised Land. Mary Engel. AMV-80

How on the Cross this day a Saviour died. Sonnet. Petrarch. CAW

How on the moor above it stand/Stone row and mound and pagan ring. Sheepstor. Leonard Alfred George Strong. HBMV

How on thy breast, and o'er thy brow,/Bursts the uprising sun! Canada. Sir Charles G. D. Roberts. PeCV

How once a woman's breast was white. History. Paul Tanaquil. HBMV

How our lifespan has become/an American crayon drawing The dots of de dondi. Kristjana Gunnars. CaPN

...How paltry is the Devil's power/to destroy compared to what can momentarily be. Prospero without His Magic. Jack Gilbert. NPGG

How patient he has been with God! The Toiler (excerpt). Edwin Markham. PGD

How patiently is waited for/The lighthouse-keeper's leave on shore! Epitaph for a Lighthouse-Keeper's Horse. J. B. Morton. PV

,...How perfectly/mirrors God's face, the workings of his mind. The Sea. Lloyd Frankenberg. AnFE; CoAnAm; MOS

How pleasant it is to have money. Spectator Ab Extra. Arthur Hugh Clough. ALV; FaBoCo; FiBHP; GTBS-P; NBM; NLV; OBSV; OxBoLi

How pleasant life was in the eighties! Reflections outside of a Gymnasium. Phyllis McGinley. SD

How pleasant to know Mr. Lear! How Pleasant to Know Mr. Lear. Edward Lear. CBEP; ChTr; EBEV; FaBoCo; FiBHP; HAP; NOBE; NOBL; NOBV; NoP; SpRo; VLP

How pleased she is looking! A Greek Gift. Henry Austin Dobson. CenHV

How poor and stingy–/compared with Mozart's legacy–/is the Sermon on the Mount. Mozart. Jacob Glatstein. VWA

How poor if you should turn him from the door. Decision. *Anonymous*. PoToHe

How punctual death is, or else how slow. The True Weather for Women. Louis Simpson. NePoAm

How pure brave my wet thrasher, my enemy. The Pike. John Bruce. LiSp

How quickly the strangeness would pass from things/if it were not for them. For Guillaume Apollinaire. William Meredith. CoAP

How quickly you must die. Three Poems. Basho (Matsuo Basho). LiTW

How rapidly the iron age/Succeeds the age of brass! This House, Where Once a Lawyer Dwelt. William Erskine. GoTF; HBV 1-2; TreF

How rewarding to know Mr. Smith! Mr. Smith. William Jay Smith. FiBHP; SpRo

How rich, how full is their reward,/Reserved until the final day! Thus Spake the Saviour. Jeremy Belknap. AH

How right I was! How right I was! Regarding (1) the U. S. and (2) New York. Franklin Pierce ("F.P.A.") Adams. HBMV

How rough with thorns! O nights, how harsh to me! To Sleep. Giovanni della Casa. AWP

How to bear the blackened night/And the dreadful dawn. The Masters. Margaret Widdemer. HBMV

How to realize his question/Let alone his answer? The History of the World as Pictures. Nancy Sullivan. CoPo

"How toothless than a serpent's child/It is to have a sharper's thanks!" A Bad Break. W. T. Goodge. NOAV

How trembles if I chance to hear/Elizabeth! Elizabeth! The Voice. Norman Gale. HBV 1-2; OHIP

How unhappy. How his mind moves dreaming. The Man in the Recreation Room. Edward Harkness. SM

How unpleasant to meet Mr. Eliot!/(Whether his mouth be open or shut). Lines for Cuscuscaraway and Mirza Murad Ali Beg. Thomas Stearns Eliot. FiBHP; NLV; OBAL; PoPl; SpRo

How vastly we improve our style! A Word of Encouragement. J. R. Pope. ELU; FiBHP; FPL; NLV; NOBL; PV

How very far away, easily/that much further away. Going. Robert Kelly. CoPo

How very like to all the world, except/Menodotis. Menodotis. Leonidas of Alexandria. AWP; LiTW

How very wise I am. How very/very wise. The Insidious Dr. Fu Man Chu. LeRoi (Imamu Amiri Baraka) Jones. CoPo

How wan her cheeks are, and what heavy/tears! Masks. Thomas Bailey Aldrich. AA

How wan they are, and shrunken, when they come back! How It Is. Uri Z. Greenberg. VWA

How was I shock'd to think the hero's trade/Of such materials, fame and triumph made! One to Destroy, Is Murder by the Law. Edward Hilton Young. FF

How was it?/Sweet. Came to me—/Who? Rudaki. BoLoP; OBVE

How water must do just that for stone. Observation. Derk Wynard. AMV-80

How we love the starry banner,/The emblem of the free! When This Cruel War Is Over. Anonymous. AmFP

How we metabolize loss/as fast as we have to. In Memory of the Utah Stars. William Matthews. GeTw; MAYP; NPAW; Psk

How we noble Un-Employeds/Had rare hard work to do the Midnight/March. The Midnight March. Fred Gilbert. VLP

How we played by the water's edge/Till the April sun set. Allie. Robert Graves. GoJo; LOW

How we thrill with the joy of their fame! The Fleet at Santiago. Charles E. Russell. MC; PAH

How we Worcesters lie where we redeem'd the battle. Gheluvelt. Robert Bridges. BrPo

How welcome will the last blast be that lays me low. When Each Bright Star Is Clouded. Jeremiah Joseph Callanan. IrPN

How well God works for you and me. To Men. Anna Wickham. MoBrPo

How well Horatius kept the bridge/In the brave days of old. Horatius. Thomas Babington, Lord Macaulay. BBV; BeLS; FaFP; FaPoR; HBV 1-2; HBVY; MCCG; OBNV; OBWP; OHFP; PoLf; TreF; VLP

How well to live, and not how long. A Skeltoniad. Michael Drayton. PoEL 1-5; PP

How wetly your father came down at Lodore! The Cataract at Lodore (parody). Helen Bevington. SpRo

How what goes up so frequently/So seldom cometh down. Enigma for Christmas Shoppers. Phyllis McGinley. PoPl

How will he be married/Without e'er a wife? Tommy Tucker. Anonymous. OxNR

How will my pup, if I'm so tall,/Reach up to kiss me on the nose? Growing. Frances Frost. BiCB

How will she through our little maze/ever in future thread her ways? Sleep-Walking Child. Elisabeth Eybers. PeSA

How will you lift that bankrupt head/When all the butterfly beauty's dead? The Question. Norman Gale. ELU; FiBHP

How wisely wanton is this epicene! Four Winds. Hal Porter. NOAV

How wonderful in the new eye the world will appear! Eyesight II. Robert Duncan. EAS

...How worthy every man/To hold high tournament in Camelot. Sonnets of the Months. Folgore da San Geminiano. AWP

How would grass/be as a substitute? cement? The Artist. Kenneth Koch. AmPC

–How you and i are blossoming The First of All My Dreams. Edward Estlin Cummings. NYBP; VGW

How you boomed,/Vibrated, shouted/In utter self-restraint. Thoughts for My Grandmother. Laya Firestone. VWA

How you puncture bloods/and fingernails. Moral Ode. D. Rosenmann-Taub. VWA

How you shine. For My Wife. Steven Lautermilch. AMV-80

Howcome you pulled the trigger on me,/John...Wilkes...Booth? Honest Abe Lincoln. Max Shulman. OBAL

Howdy, honey, howdy, won't you step right in? Howdy, Honey, Howdy! Paul Laurence Dunbar. PoLf

Howe'er strong talents exercise their skill. An Essay on the Genius of Pope (excerpt). Charles Lloyd. OBRV

However brightly leap the brass-hinged bone,/Beam and rafter, joist and cellar-stone? The Homer Mitchell Place. John Engels. SM

However I wander/Or walk in my sleep. Peregrine's Sunday Song. Elinor Wylie. NYBP

However miniatured/i will speak/me Voting Machine. Norman Nathan. AMV-80

However we may scream we are/suffering quietly. Burning Oneself In. Adrienne Rich. NYP

"However you frown, no matter how,/I will sing as I am singing now." First Miracle. Genevieve Taggard. HBMV

However you will not read in books/the exploits of these family/men. The Disgrace. Mary di Michele. CaPN

Howl along the hostile trail–hideous slaughter of the host. Genesis: The Approach of Pharaoh. Caedmon. WaaP

The howlet read the order,/They held a bonnie work. The Kirk of the Birds, Beasts and Fishes. Anonymous. GBP

Howlin/Like a guitar player Make Music with Your Life. Bob O'Meally. CNA

Howling much worse, and oh the door is open. Who Is This Who Howls and Mutters? Stevie Smith. OxBC

Howling of dogs at the empty homes... 1867: Last Sounds. Gerry O'Egan. PoL

...The howling of the/women of Argyle! The Day of Inverlochy. Iain Lom. GoTS

Howls to her sundered cubs with piteous rage/And savage agony. The Destiny of Nations. Samuel Taylor Coleridge. ChRP

Huddled in dark, and hold,/Waiting for when they fill. The Rooftop. Thom Gunn. NoP

Huddled in Dirt this reasoning Engine lies/Who was so Proud, so Witty, and so Wise. A Satire against Reason and Mankind. John Wilmot, Earl of Rochester. SCV

Huddled together for a little while by the fire/in the Ice Age, two hundred thousand years ago. He Sits down on the Floor of a School for the Retarded. Alden Nowlan. GOYP

Hug her neat and kiss her sweet,/Then you may rise upon your feet. King William Was King George's Son. Anonymous. OuSiCo

Hug her nice and kiss her twice/For the prettiest girl I know. London's Bridge Is A-Burning Down. Anonymous. AmFP

Hug me round/In your solitude/Profound. Escape. Georgia Douglas Johnson. PoBA

Huge and beautifully black as he ever was.../But dead. Best Loved of Africa. Margaret Danner. PoBA; PoNe

The huge and desolate ranges of the Coast. Canterbury. Basil Dowling. AnNZ

The huge concept of Ben Dorain. One of the Many Days. Norman MacCaig. PoSH

A huge, hammer-headed spirit/Shall pass, as if led by the nose into Heaven. Walking on Water. James Dickey. NePoEA-2

...The huge mountain/Of rectifying darkness, now all but level with her sight. My Grandmother. Perseus Adams. PeSA

...Huge/, on the pillow's dark side. The Night Mirror. John Hollander. NYBP; Prf

The huge, sorrowful human face. Goldfish on the Writing Desk. Max Brod. TrJP

The huge tide hurries them away. The Logs. Sir Charles G. D. Roberts. ACV

–A huge tractor wheels by/the edge of the sky. Wagon Wheels. S. E. LaMoure. AMV-81

Huge, unblushing. Dreams of Water. Donald Justice. LCAP; NYBP

The hugest hearts that break. Love's Stricken "Why." Emily Dickinson. BoLiVe

Hugging some ancient sorrow to his breast. The House of Colour. Francis Sherman. CaP

Hugh/a mhuirnin! The Beset Wife. Robert Farren. OxBI

Huh! Are you the great grandchildren of the West! The Legend of Boastful Bill. Charles Badger Clark, Jr. BPAW

Huh uh! Chillun, let us pray! An Ante-Bellum Sermon. Paul Laurence Dunbar. BALP; BPo

Hull-down the bilge-sprung tankers limp/To pale Atlantic afternoons. Tangier: Hotel Rif. Donald Thomas. OBTV

The human being is a lonely creature. The Human Being Is a Lonely Creature. Richard Eberhart. NePoAm

Human eyes must fall asleep. Shadow-Love. Heinrich Heine. TrJP

The human face a furnace sealed,/The human heart its hungry gorge. A Divine Image. William Blake. AtBAP; ChTr; NoP; OBNC; TEP

...The human/Face has its own beauty. Skiers. Robert Penn Warren. LiSp

The human face shines like a dark sky/As it speaks of those things that oppress the living. Late at Night during a Visit of Friends. Robert Bly. InPS

A human soul knows and adores its God! Worship. William Wilberforce Lord AA

Humanity can understand, and would flow likewise/If power and desire were perch-mates. The Excesses of God. Robinson Jeffers. MoRP

Humble, yes, but not unsung,/Strictly modern 5-rm. bung.! Hearth and Home. Stoddard King. OBAL

Humble yo'self, de bell done ring. Humble Yo'self de Bell Done Ring. *Anonymous.* BoAN 1-2

Humiliatus sum vermis. Farewell, This World. *Anonymous.* MeEL

"Humility and greatness grace the task/Which he who does it deems impossible!" Th Child's Purchase. Coventry Patmore. CoBE

Humming his elegy out o'er a flowing glass. To the Memory of Gavin Wilson (Boot, Leg and Arm Maker). George Galloway. NOEC

Humming in the dark the songs he'd have sung. In Memory of W. H. Auden. David R. Slavitt. SM

Humming softly, something ancient. Zeyde. Roberta Metz. AMV-81

Humor and boredom from the everlasting dross! T. S. Eliot. Robert Lowell. NoAm; NOBA

Humouring age with filial flowers,/Childhood with pebbles? Time. Robert Graves. AtBAP; LiTM

Hump and heavy-tongue combined. Self-Portrait. Moses Mendelssohn. TrJP

"Humph!" said he. The Lady Who Loved a Swine. *Anonymous.* OuSiCo

Hunc, hunc, hunc, he said./And away went he. There Was a Lady Loved a Swine. *Anonymous.* GBP

Hunched above us, waiting what earth means. En Route. E. L. Mayo. MiAP

A hundred and some odd years old. Untitled: "fisk is/a/negroid/ institution..." Sharon Scott. JB

The hundred evils enterd him,/And he fell oure the brim. Burd Isabel and Earl Patrick. *Anonymous.* BaBo; ESPB

A hundred eyes and never a nose! Riddle: "A riddle, a riddle, as I suppose." Mother Goose. TiPo

The hundred last leaves stream upon the willow. The Long Small Room. Edward ("Edward Eastaway") Thomas. BrPo

Hundred per cent, red-blood American. Immigrants. Nancy Byrd Turner. AmFN

A hundred praises, Christ, 'tis meet,/For all we drink, for all we eat. Four Prayers, II. *Anonymous.* OnYI

A hundred spirits whisper "Peace." In Memoriam A.H.H., LXXXVI. Alfred, Lord Tennyson. VLP

A hundred voices answer'd, "I!" The Rising. Thomas Buchanan Read. PAH; TreFS

A hundred white stones/turn to raging phlox. Scribe. Paul Auster. VWA

"A hundred years are but a moment of sleep." Sleeping on Horseback. Po Chu-i. LiTW

A hundred years past due./Now! Alabama Centennial. Naomi Long Madgett. BALP; BPo

A hundred years will come once more,/A hundred years ago. A Hundred Years Ago (with music). *Anonymous.* AS

Hundreds of able-bodied men are wanted on the drive. The Lumber Camp Song ("The Shanty Boy's Song"). *Anonymous.* ShS

Hundreds of yeares you Stellas feet may kisse. Astrophel and Stella, LXXXIV. Sir Philip Sidney. AAS; OAEP; OBSC; SiPS

Hung down my head and cried, po' boy! Po' Boy (with music). *Anonymous.* AS

Hung on the kitchen door. Riddle: "Hick-a-more, Hack-a-more." *Anonymous.* OxNR

Hung owre his hurdies wi' a swirl. Luath. Robert Burns. GDP

Hung poised, forgetting how to fall. Green Rain. Mary Webb. BoNaP; CH

Hung up to be dried by God/in the cosmos– Landscape of Screams. Nelly Sachs. NYBP

Hung with the bloody calves' heads in the butcher shop. Testimonies. Weldon Kees. NYP

Hunger for bread and peace. Lessons. Helen Weber. PGD

The hunger for lost arms.../Death. Things. Dorothy Dow. HBMV

...Hunger/for what is naked and approachable,/tangible and delicious. Squid. Michael C. Blumenthal. MAYP

The hunger in each of us making her smile. The Last Job I Held in Bridgeport. D. W. Donzella. TAT

Hunger of glory gat/Hold of the land. The Battle of Brunanburh. *Anonymous.* CoBE; EnLit; OBVE; OBWP; TrGrPo; WaaP

Hungered for what my heart shall never say. Before Day. Siegfried Sassoon. WGRP

hungry, and plucking/the fruit. O Taste and See. Denise Levertov. NoP; PBWP; PPP; TAP

Hungry and thirsty we break these stones in the cold of winter. The Roadmenders' Song. *Anonymous.* WTO

Hungry clouds swag on the deep. The Marriage of Heaven and Hell. William Blake. LoBV

The hungry fiend/Screams the apocalypse of clay/In every corner of this land. The Great Hunger. Patrick Kavanagh. CIP; FaBoIP

Hungry, to the hands of the holy man. Far and Wide She Went. Caedmon. EtS

The Huns gelded and feeding in a ring. More Sonnets at Christmas. Allen Tate. LiTA; NePA

The hunt for food/Brings glory to the/Warrior of knowledge Sunrise. Jim Tollerud. VoR

Hunted creatures in their flight/Find a refuge for the night. The Granite Mountain. Lew Sarett. HBMV

Hunted, lonely, and spent,/Broken and dying. The Waradgery Tribe. Mary Gilmore. BoAV; PoAu 1-2

The hunter and his game. Love Equals Swift and Slow. Henry David Thoreau. NoP

Hunters watch so narrowly.' The Lady of the Lake. Sir Walter Scott. EnRP

...Hunting you in the dark/Mountains to eat your tender heart. For Mary. Kenneth Rexroth. PoPl

Hunts for a mate, and the tired footman reels/'Twixt chairmen, torches, and the hackney wheels. A Rhapsody (excerpt). Henry Vaughan. FaBoPP

A huntsman not to be outdone in politeness. Toujours la Politesse. *Anonymous.* OBVE

Hurl a courageous splendid light/Into the eye,–and then,–the FIGHT! Gallantly within the Ring. John Hamilton Reynolds. SD

Hurling defiance toward the vault of Heav'n. Paradise Lost. John Milton. PoEL 1-5

Hurly, hurly, AMEN. Two Graces. *Anonymous.* FaBoCh

Hurrah! for bright Water! hurrah, hurrah! The Water-Drinker. Edward Johnson. BXAP; PeD

Hurrah for the Black Ball Line! Black Ball Line. *Anonymous.* ABF

Hurrah! for the Bonnie Blue Flag that bears a Single Star! The Bonnie Blue Flag. Harry Macarthy. BLSo; PSoN

Hurrah, for the cowboy's cattle are sold/Whenever he thinks they will bring the most gold! A Kansas Cowboy. *Anonymous.* CoSo

Hurrah for the Monitor's famous cruise! The Cruise of the Monitor. George Henry Boker. MC; PAH

Hurrah for the next that dies! The Revel. Bartholomew Dowling. BLPA; HBV 1-2; OnYI

Hurrah for the pumpkin-pie! Thanksgiving Day. Lydia Maria Child. NTCP; OHIP; SiSoSe; TreFS

Hurrah!/For the true-born Englishman! The Englishman. Sir William Schwenck Gilbert. NOBL

Hurrah! Hurrah! Our country forever, Hurrah! Paul Jones's Victory. *Anonymous.* AmFP; TrAS

Hurrah, my boys, we're homeward bound! Good-Bye, Fare You Well. *Anonymous.* AmSS

Hurried back to the digs where Banquo/Sat up late with a hole in his head. Fleance. Michael Longley. FaBoIP

Hurry, and come right back again. Themes for Country-Western Singers (excerpt). Ted Kooser. PoL

Hurry, hurry down to the shores of your island. War Song of O'Driscol. Gerald Griffin. OnYI

Hurry, hurry to the field! The Fatal Sisters. Thomas Gray. CEP; CoBE; EiCP; EnPE; LAuP; OAEP

Hurry! Let her in! The Confessional. *Anonymous.* UnTE

Hurry me, burry me, hickey ho,/To wag dum mingo. Dandoo. *Anonymous.* BFSS

Hurry, my heart, be swift, my heart,–/How did we wait so long! Click o' the Latch. Nancy Byrd Turner. HBMV

Hurry, Tomorrow!/ hurry, do! Hurry Tomorrow. Ivy O. Eastwick. BiCB

Hurry up!/Make haste! Cultural Exchange. Langston Hughes. BPo; PoBA; PoNe

...The hurrying eyes/pause, waiting for an outdistanced/gladness to overtake them. Self-Portrait. R. S. Thomas. NAs

Hurrying through the underworld, soundless. Second Glance at a Jaguar. Ted Hughes. NoAm; NYBP; PrIm

Hurt beyond hurting, never to forget. Good-Bye for a Long Time. Roy Fuller. NeBP

Hurt, can I laugh? and honest, need I cry? Democritus and Heraclitus. Matthew Prior. OBSP

The hurt healed, and the mind was filled with light. The Fishers. Ruth Pitter. BoC

Hurt my knee and scraped my hand and built my pectoral muscles/big as vagina. In the Baggage Room at Greyhound. Allen Ginsberg. NaP; NoP

Hurt not the face which nothing can amend. When Two Suns Do Appear. Sir Philip Sidney. EnRePo; MOON; SiPS

"Hurt not the trees." The Trees Are Down. Charlotte Mew. BoNaP; BrRo; MoAB; MoBrPo; TrCP; WPOW

...The hurt we feel is delicate–/all for ourselves and all for nothing. Champagne. Rita Dove. MAYP

Hurtling/through the tape/to victory... Letters Found near a Suicide. Frank Horne. BPo; PoNe

Husband and wife/Man and wife. Decoy. John Ashbery. PoM

Husband, show me the way. Show Me the Way. *Anonymous.* PBWP

An' hush-a-by, wee babbie O. The Rantin Laddie (B vers.). *Anonymous.* BaBo

Hush, ah hush! and the Scythes are swinging/Over the clover, over the grass! Scythe Song. Andrew Lang. GN; HBV 1-2

Hush anarchy's sway, and give peace to the world. Columbia. *Anonymous.* AmFP

Hush, child, listen, and believe. Halloween. Myra Cohn Livingston. OFD

"Hush!' cried a voice at his shoulder. The Court Historian. Walter Thornbury. HBV 1-2; OBVV

Hush! he's at the window-sill. Tiptoe Night. John Drinkwater. SiSoSe

"Hush, hush, he is come!" Tom, Tom, the Piper's Son. John Crowe Ransom. ViBoPo

Hush! Hush! see how He smiles in dreams. Bring a Torch, Jeanette, Isabella. Nicolas Saboly. OHIP

Hush! hush! wild heart. Beauty Rohtraut. Eduard Moricke. AWP; OBVE

Hush–hushing... The Main-Deep. James Stephens. MoBrPo; MOS; OBMV; UnPo

Hush me, O slumbering mountains–/Send me dreams. The Blue Ridge. Harriet Monroe. HBMV

Hush–Only to me! Many a Phrase Has the English Language–. Emily Dickinson. DiPo

Hush! said the sea, and hush. Gray Shore. James Rorty. EtS

Hush thee, hush thee, dear little soul. A Ballade of the Nurserie. John Twig. NA

Hush thee, princeling,/God's own blessed Son. Hush Thee, Princeling. Anna Elizabeth Bennett. AH

Hush! they rest in Bethlehem. St. Bridget's Lullaby. Dorothy Una Ratcliffe. CAW

Hush, woman, do not speak to me! The Tryst after Death. *Anonymous.* LiTW

"Hush your mouth, don't draw a breath;/We'll draw a pension from Casey's death!" Casey Jones (B vers.). *Anonymous.* ViBoFo

Hushed lie the sedges, and the vapours creep,/Thick, grey and humid, while the marshes sleep. Marshlands. [(Emily[) Pauline Johnson. NOBC

Hushing the heart that beats and beats and beats? Greeness. Angelina Weld Grimke. CDC

Hut two, hut two, hut said the corp'rals/Merry men are we. Old King Cole. *Anonymous.* FSW

Huzza! Father Malebranche and shorthand for ever. To Henry Wright of Mobberley, Esq. on Buying the Picture... John Byrom. NOEC

Huzza for the King and Prevost, sir. About Savannah. *Anonymous.* PAH

Huzza for the right and the white cockade! The White Cockade. *Anonymous.* OnYI

Huzza! 'twill last for ages long,/With a gay lady. London Bridge. *Anonymous.* CH; EyDe; GBP; OxBoLi; OxNR

A hyacinth I wish'd me in her hand. Like the Idalian Queen. William, of Hawthornden Drummond. BSV; GoTS; ScCcPo

The hyacinth my garden gave/Shall lie upon that Roman grave! After a Lecture on Keats. Oliver Wendell Holmes. AA; ViBoPo

Hyah, bound away,/To the wild Missouri! Shenandoah. *Anonymous.* ShS

The hyaline of drifting glooms... The Fish. Rupert Brooke. BoC

Hyde Park at best–though counted ultra-grand–/The "Boston Common" of Victoria's land. The Rejected "National Hymns". Robert Henry Newell. InMe

Hyeh come de chahcoal man-n-n-n./Chahcoal! Chahcoal Man (with music). *Anonymous.* AS

Hymen oh Hymenaeus, come, Hymen oh Hymenaeus. A Debate on Marriage versus Virginity. Caius Valerius Catullus. HW

A hymn, a snare, and an exceeding sun. Boy Breaking Glass. Gwendolyn Brooks. NoAm; NoP

The hymn to beauty written on her face. Being Her Friend. John Masefield. GTBS

Hymns of high praise, and I among them chief. Paradise Lost. John Milton. ILwL

Hyperion's march they spy and glittering shafts of war. The Progress of Poesy. Thomas Gray. ATP

Hypocrite Swift sent Stella a green apron/And dead desire. Hypocrite Swift. Louise Bogan. PoA; SBG

–Hypocritical Reader–my co-equal–no, my Brother! To the Reader. Charles Baudelaire. SyP

The hypothetic frog alone/Is the one frog we dwell upon. A Frog's Fate. Christina Georgina Rossetti. NOBV

Hysteric in the elemental act. The Pick-Up. J. V. Cunningham. UnTE

I

I!/A man among many/citizens of a Nation which has yet to exist. Poem of the Future Citizen. Jose Craveirinha. TTY

I, above all, promote brave soldiers. As I Pondered in Silence. Walt Whitman. WHA

I add, "Corinna, don't do this again!" Amores. Ovid (Publius Ovidius Naso). NAs

I admire her spirit. Cheerio My Deario. Don (Donald Robert Marquis) Marquis. FaBoCo

I admit it, at the last. Farewell to Kurdistan. Rosemary Tonks. OxBTC

I advance for as long as forever is. Twenty-Four Years. Dylan Thomas. CMoP; DiPo; InPK; MAT; MoAB; NAs; NoAm; OBSP

I agree with you cheerfully, ladies. Life. Alfred Kreymborg. ELU

I ain't gonna study war no more. Study War No More. *Anonymous.* FSW

I ain't got long to stay here. Steal away. *Anonymous.* BoAN 1-2; BPo; FSW; TrGrPo

I ain't got no sweetheart,/To sit and talk with me. Poor Lonesome Cowboy (with music). *Anonymous.* AS

I ain't got nobody to/Really comfort me Going Away Blues. Lottie Kimbrough. BluL

I ain't got the man that I thought I had! Great Gawd, I'm Feelin' Bad (with music). *Anonymous.* AS

I ain't got time to kiss you now,/I'm busy with this mule. The Kicking Mule. *Anonymous.* AmFP

I ain't nothin' but a yearlin'. Youth of the Mountain. Walter Hand. AnNE

I all my days/Could gladly spend. Love Unknown. Samuel Crossman. BoC

I almost could have slapped the child. Indifference. Harry Graham. DBV; NLV

I almost never dream of anyone,/except my sons,/who is still alive. Living among the Dead. William Matthews. GeTw

I almost scratch Persephone. Leo to His Mistress. Henry Dwight Sedgwick. BLPA

I almost wish I were a Tory. A Primrose Dame. Gleason White. HBV 1-2

I/alone/in a room. Testament. Lucille Clifton. GeTw

I already knew the answer. Mythology. Michael Waters. MAYP

I also bless the eldertree/Where you surrendered, dear, to me. Knight Olaf. Heinrich Heine. HW

I also might take my share. Only a Smile. *Anonymous.* STF

I always come in prostrate; Yeats & Frost. Dream Songs. John Berryman. CAPP

I always eat bananas now! My First Love. Harry Graham. FiBHP

I always take a road that brings/Me halt upon a hill. I Love a Hill. Ralph Hodgson. BrPo

I am a bird. The Elements. William Henry Davies. MoBrPo; OBVV

I am a blind fiddler and far from my home. The Blind Fiddler. *Anonymous.* FSW

I am a boy. A Young David: Birmingham. Helen Morgan Brooks. PoNe

I am a brittle bone projecting from the sand. Cycle. Sean Jennett. OnYI

I am a drowsy grass-blade/In the greenest shadow. Irradiations. John Gould Fletcher. MAPA

I am a Fool. The Kingdom of Poetry: Swift. Delmore Schwartz. PoA

I am a girl in pain./No! Song: "I don't want to be a nun." *Anonymous.* BoWoP

I am a gray frog/Out there in the chorus. Ceremonies. Ann Stanford. HW

I am a lady young in beauty waiting. Piazza Piece. John Crowe Ransom. AP; BoLoP; CoBMV; GoTF; HeIP; InPo; MoAB; MoAmPo; MoVE; NoAm; NOBA; NoP; OxBA; SoSe; TAP; TreFT; TrGrPo

I am a loosed boat floating a thousand miles. At the End of Spring. Yu Hsuan-chi. BoWoP

I am a Merry Jest! Ballade of the Primitive Jest. Andrew Lang. HBV 1-2

I am a miser/Counting my gold. Miser. Harold Vinal. MCCG

I am a naked candle burning on your grave. All Souls. D. H. Lawrence. FaBoRV

I am a phantom, and all mortals seem/But phantoms, and my life fades as a dream. The Coup de Grace. Edward Rowland Sill. AA

I am a rebel soldier and far from my home. The Rebel Soldier. *Anonymous.* LoGBV; OxBoLi

I am a roving gambler; rambling, gambling man. Roving Gambler Blues. *Anonymous.* FSW

I am a shadow in the light. Shadow. Richard Bruce. CDC

I am a Sheep, and not an Ass. The Blind Sheep. Randall Jarrell. NYBP; OBAL

I am a son of the sea/and the sea's wife, the wind. North Atlantic. Carl Sandburg. MOS

I am a star that is dead.   She Warns Him.   Frances Cornford.   EnLoPo

I am a stranger in an alien port.   At the Battery Sea-Wall.   Clifford James Laube.   GoYe

I am a troubled soldier, no friend and no home.   The Troubled Soldier. *Anonymous.*   AS

I am a Union man,/Gonna leave you behind.   Get Thee Behind Me, Satan. Millard and Lee Hays Lampell.   FSW

I am a very small violet/Thinking of May.   I Am.   Hilda Conkling.   TiPo

I am a whit impatient, and 'tis ill/To cross a hungry dog, Messieurs, en garde. En Garde, Messieurs.   William Lindsey.   AA

I am a widow, robed in black, alone.   I am a widow, robed in black, alone. Christine de Pisan.   BoWoP

I am a woman.   Bitter Herbs.   Alta.   NMM

I am a woman and must be told/Lies to warm me when I am old.   Talk to Me Tenderly.   Vivian Yeiser Laramore.   HBMV

I am afraid.   I Am Afraid.   *Anonymous.*   WSC

I am afraid of.   Song of the Trees.   *Anonymous.*   OBVE

"I am afraid of silence. I am afraid."   This One Heart-Shaken.   Sister Maris Stella.   GoBC

I am afraid of the name that you will name me.   The Succubus.   Harriet Rose.   BrRo

I am alive–and that is beautiful.   Thank God for Life.   *Anonymous.*   PGD

"I am all that is and was and shall be,/My garment may no man put by." The Swan.   Jay Macpherson.   PeCV

I am all yours.   Surrender.   Amelia Josephine Burr.   HBV 1-2

I am alone, yet someone else is with me,/drinking coffee, looking out at the snow.   Six Winter Privacy Poems.   Robert Bly.   LCAP

I am always behind.   A Grammar.   Andrei Codrescu.   EAS

I am amazed anew/At the inexhaustible fertility of the natural world.   The Invention of Zero.   Constance Urdang.   VWA

I am among all men, most richly blessed.   Prayer of an Unknown Confederate Soldier.   *Anonymous.*   GoTF; TreFT

I am an American.   I Am an American.   Elias Lieberman.   PAL; PoLf; TreFT

I am an ancient reluctant conscript.   Old Timers.   Carl Sandburg. AnAmPo; NoAm; YaD

...I/Am an old mountain warming his tired bones.   Internal.   Joseph Auslander.   FYAP

...I am another.   Telemachus and the Bow.   Randall Colaizzi.   AMV-81

I am as disturbed as before.   Autumn.   Princess Shikishi.   PBWP

I am as one disembodied, triumphant, dead.   So Long!   Walt Whitman. AmP

I am as vulnerable/to your least touch as a wandering clove of dust.   House Poem.   Jane Cooper.   AMV-81

I am ashamed/for soon I will be as you....   My Brothers...   Anna Walters. VoR

I am ashamed of my fortune in the presence of God.   When I Think of the Hungry People.   O-Shi-O.   TRV

I am at ease.   A free woman. At last free!   *Anonymous.*   BoWoP

I am becoming a vegetable/of stiff gold.   The King in May.   Michael Dennis Browne.   NYBP

I am becoming them.   The Marsh, New Year's Day.   Peter Everwine. NNaP

I am being/eaten away by light   Daguerreotype Taken in Old Age. Margaret Atwood.   BoWoP

I am beside you, now.   The Shadow's Song.   Yvor Winters.   PoL

I am beyond blame.   The Suburb.   Anne Stevenson.   NMM

I am blind, and do not play-/Dallan De! Dallan De!   Butterfly in the Fields. Joseph Campbell.   BoAnP

I am born to love them.   Song of the Last Jewish Child.   Edmond Jabes. VWA

I am bound for the promised land.   The Promised Land.   *Anonymous.* AmFP; TrAS

I am bound on a journey without end,/And can not bear the song of the cuckoo.   The Trail Up Wu Gorge.   Sun Yun-feng.   BoWoP; PBWP

I am bound to follow the F A steers until I am too old./Ho-loo-loo-loo-loo. The Texas Cowboy.   *Anonymous.*   AmFP

I am bringing up my children to be you   Peasant.   William Stanley Merwin. NYBP

I am busy writing a critical piece.   Notes on a Certain Terribly Critical Piece. Reed Whittemore.   PP

I am but an alien and a Genovese.   Columbus (excerpt).   Alfred, Lord Tennyson.   OFD

I am but finite, yet thine infinitely.   Artillerie.   George Herbert.   InPS; NoP; PAI; PoEL 1-5; SeCV 1-2

I am caught and Love goes free!   The Golden Fish.   George Arnold.   HBV 1-2

...I am closer to you/Than land and I am in a stranger ocean/Than I wished. Parachutes, My Love, Could Carry Us Higher.   Barbara Guest.   NeAP

"I am coming–Sciar–and for you and to you!/Sciar–and to you!"   The Venetian Serenade.   Richard Moncton, Lord Houghton Milnes.   OBRV

I am Content, I do not care.   Careless Content.   John Byrom.   CEP; HBV 1-2; NOEC; OBEC

I am content to know the air.   They Say the Butterfly Is the Hardest Stroke. Paul Durcan.   FaBoIP

I am content to wait and watch the night.   I Never Asked for More Than Thou Hast Given.   G. Lowes Dickinson.   PeHV

I am cursed still to live:–even/Death loved him the best.   Envy.   Adelaide Anne Procter.   NOBV

I am damned to Hell what/alarmclock is ringing   My Alba.   Allen Ginsberg.   NoAm; NOBA

I am dazzled.   Dazzled.   Arthur Sze.   BrSi

I am dead weed cast upon the shore.   A Song of Sickness.   Hine Tangikuku. WTO

I am deaf to your notes and dead/by a soldier's body in Burma.   In Memory of Basil, Marquess of Dufferin and Ava.   Sir John Betjeman.   OBWP

I am dressed in a whirlpool of leech skins.   Tlanusi'yi, the Leech Place. Gladys Cardiff.   CDW; STE; TWSS

I am drowning.   Camp Notes.   Mitsuye Yamada.   WPOW

..."I am drying myself, my red/breast feathers, my rangga feathers–my children!"   The Djanggawul Cycle, 33.   *Anonymous.*   WTO

I am dying of wisecracks   Hose and Iron.   Greg Kuzma.   MAT

I am eighteen.   Eighteen.   Maria Banus.   BoWoP; VWA

I am elemental fire. I burn.   Saint Stephen in San Francisco.   Melvin Walker La Follette.   CoPo

I am ever in His care.   How Can I Smile?   Florence B. Hodgdon.   BLRP

I am falling/inside the walls of Arles/full of sun...   Midnight.   Gabriela (Lucila Godoy Alcayaga) Mistral.   BoWoP

I am fat and honored/before you.   Protecting the Burial Grounds.   Wendy Rose.   TWSS

,I am filled/With queer affection for the human race.   The Tomb of Lt. John Learmonth, A.I.F.   John Streeter Manifold.   BoAV; CBAP; PoAu 1-2; WaP

I am, finally, an incompetent, after all   From the Sustaining Air.   Larry Eigner.   PoM

...I am fine thank/you.   Summer.   Bill Manhire.   OCNZ

I am fire,/I'll be dumb.   Six Movements on a Theme.   David Ignatow. NNaP

...I am/flooded to that realm the lightnings/coil, I inmost far out in the world. To Forget Me.   Theodore Weiss.   CoAP

I am flying flying flying/in the trees of your eyes.   We Become New.   Marge Piercy.   TAP

I am foolish enough always to find it in wind   Poem: "Khrushchev is coming on the right day!"   Frank O'Hara.   NeAP; PoM

I am. For you.   You.   Carroll Arnett.   VoR

...I am free to go/From darkness into darkness to my peace.   Oedipus to the Oracle.   Wesley Trimpi.   NePoEA

I am fulfilled of Love.   Completion.   Eunice Tietjens.   HBMV

I am Gabriel.   Kingdom of Heaven.   Léonie Adams.   MoAB; MoAmPo

I am glad, I am glad, that my friends don't know what I think.   In My Dreams.   Stevie Smith.   FaBoWP

I am glad–I am glad–the stone is of your choosing...   Now I Have Nothing. Stella Benson.   OxBTC

...I am glad of a drop of cold water/That runs from town to town.   Adieu to Old England.   *Anonymous.*   OBET

I/I'm glad/she/chose/to/run   Romp.   Dave Etter.   WeW

I am glad that the Prince of Peace is hovering over No/Man's Land.   The New Day.   Fenton Johnson.   BANP

I am glad that they whom I have loved are as far off as the/stars. Communion.   Wallace Gould.   AnAmPo

I am God's soul, fused in the soul of man.   Poetry.   Ella Heath.   HBV 1-2; WGRP

I am going. He calls.   Rizpah.   Alfred, Lord Tennyson.   CABL; PoEL 1-5; VLP

I am going home.   Few Days.   *Anonymous.*   ABF

I am going into the night to find a world of my own.   Love, My Machine. Louis Simpson.   CAPP

I am going to do nothing for ever and ever.'   On a Tired Housewife. *Anonymous.*   EvOK

I am going to help them/Turn the new hay.   Willy Boy.   *Anonymous.* OxNR

I am going to keep things like this.   Hawk Roosting.   Ted Hughes.   CMoP; GTBS-P; HAP; HeIP; LiTM; MP; NePoEA-2; NMP; OxBTC; PB; PPP; TwCP; UnPo

I am going to sell your shop,/you to be remembered in my lines.   The Inheritance.   David Ignatow.   CAPP

I am grateful to him.   Little White Fox.   David Rowbotham.   BoAV

I am happy as I hold this sky/in my hands, in my eyes, and in myself.   The Serenity in Stones.   Simon J. Ortiz.   CDW

I am happy only/with the door open between us.   With the Door Open. David Ignatow.   CTBA

I am happy to-night: I have laughed to-night at death.   The Happy Night. J. C. Squire.   HBMV

I am so close to good. I have no need to see God.   Like a Mourningless Child.   Kenneth Patchen.   MoAmPo

I am so doggone evil, evil as a man can be.   Evil-Hearted Man.   *Anonymous.* FSW

I am so happy.   Northern Pike.   James Wright.   CAPP

"I am so old!"..."Good-night, Babette!"   Good-Night, Babette.   Henry Austin Dobson.   HBV 1-2; OBVV

I am so pleased with myself.   The Way It Is.   Gloria C. Oden.   CNA

"I am so tired," she has written to me, "of appreciating/the gift of life."   The 90th Year.   Denise Levertov.   FiCP

I am sorry, but I quite forgot/It was your resting-place.   Ah, Are You Digging on My Grave?   Thomas Hardy.   BoAnP; BrPo; DL; MoAB; MoBrPo; PAI; TEP

I am sorry for my horse.   Epigram.   *Anonymous.*   ALV

I am still a child.   Moses.   Amir Gilboa.   VWA

I am still a fool,/since I am the one who keeps the fire.   January.   Ellen Bryant Voigt.   NoP

I am still happy.   Meditations of an Old Woman.   Theodore Roethke.   AP; LCAP; NaP; NOBA

..I am still/The black swan of trespass on alien waters.   Durer: Innsbruck, 1495.   Ern Malley.   CBAP

I am still too awake/to do what I do.   To Sleep.   Barbara Fialkowski. AMV-81

I am strange Lee altered; you are still L'e-Strange.   Nathaniel Lee to Sir Roger L'Estrange, Who Visited Him in His Madhouse.   Nathaniel Lee. FaBoEE

I am stuffed with myself/and ready to digest.   As I Grow Older and Fatten on Myself.   Joseph Carson.   AMV-80

I am sure I don't know,/Says the great bell at Bow.   The Bells of London. *Anonymous.*   HBV 1-2; HBVY

I am sure I shall then be somebody's child.   Nobody's Child.   Phila H. Case. TreF

I am sure this Jesus will not do,/Either for Englishman or Jew.   The Everlasting Gospel.   William Blake.   OBRV

I am talking about how we have been able/to survive insignificance.   The Significance of a Veteran's Day.   Simon J. Ortiz.   GP

I am telling you this:/history is your own heartbeat.   Blue Ruth: America. Michael S. Harper.   PoBA

I am the ark and He that dwells/therein.   To My People.   Edwin Seaver. TrJP

...I am the background/upon which you will build your empire.   Russia. William Carlos Williams.   VGW

I am the blank between the colors/the interspace between tongues/the one who foresees the end.   When the Storms Come.   Lupenga Mphande.   WhB

I am the bugle for the mouth of love.   Carmina Amico.   Edward James. PeHV

I am the burden of an old despair!/Footfall...   Footsteps.   Hazel Hall. HBMV

I am the captain of my soul.   Invictus.   William Ernest Henley.   AnEnPo; BLPA; FaBoBe; FaBV; FaFP; FaPo; FaPoR; FPL; GoTF; GTBS; HBV 1-2; HBVY; HoPM; LiTB; MCCG; MoBrPo; NOBE; OBEV; OBMV; OBVV; OHFP; PoPl; TEP; TreF; TrGrPo; ViBoPo; VLP; WGRP; WHA

I am THE CAT.   I Am the Cat.   Leila Usher.   BLPA

I am the cinnamon/peeler's wife. Smell me.   The Cinnamon Peeler.   Michael Ondaatje.   NOBC

I AM THE COLD WATER/THAT RESTORES YOUR SOUL   Inscription for a Wayside Spring.   Frances Cornford.   BrRo

I am the darling of your god.   Granny Crack.   James Reaney.   NOBC

I am the dead, the only happy one.'   Elegy on the Eve.   George Barker. WaaP

I am the dust of men.   Prairie.   Carl Sandburg.   LaNeLa

An I am the earl o the Isle o Sky,/And surely my Peggie will be calle Glasgow Peggie.   *Anonymous.*   BaBo; ESPB

...I am the/egg, the sperm.   A Woman's Song.   Colleen J. McElroy.   BlSi

I am the figure writhing on the backcloth.   Landscape with Figures.   Keith Douglas.   NePoEA

I am the final judgement and the rock.   Eagle.   Robin Skelton.   NOBC

I AM THE FLAG.   I Am the Flag.   Lawrence M. Jones.   PAL; PGD

I am the Flower-Bush that blooms for ever.   He Defendeth His Heart against the Destroyer.   Book of the Dead.   AWP

I am the grass./Let me work.   Grass.   Carl Sandburg.   AWP; BBV; BLPL; BoLiVe; FaBV; MCCG; MoAB; MoAmPo; MoVE; NoAm; NOBA; NoP; OBWP; OHFP; OxBA; PoLf; PoPl; TrGrPo; WaaP; WHA

I am the grave: of every hope.   Song of Amergin.   *Anonymous.*   MOON

I am the guest, the one to be indulged.   Guest.   D. J. Enright.   OxBC

I am the human heart!   I Thirst...   Katherine Bregy.   CAW

I am the Hunter of grasses and flowers.'   The Great South Land (excerpt). Rex Ingamells.   CBAP; NOAV

I am the inheritor. Kneel at my feet.   Senior Members.   Sean Lucy.   CIP

I am the keeper of the goal.   Inflictis.   Archibald Stodart-Walker.   CenHV

I am the killer who kills today for five million killers who wish/a killing. Killers.   Carl Sandburg.   MoVE

"I am the King of Terrors,' Want replied.   Epigram: "Prepare to meet the King of Terrors."   Ebenezer Elliott.   NOBV

...I am the king of the dead.   The Song of the Demented Priest.   John Berryman.   MoPo

I am the lean gray deer/running on the edge of the rainbow.   Indian Song: Survival.   Leslie Marmon Silko.   CDW; VoR

I am the little child you used to be.   The Child in the Garden.   Henry Van Dyke.   HBV 1-2

I am the lord of everything!   I Blow My Pipes.   Hugh McCrae.   PoAu 1-2

I am the Lord/Of the Dance, said he.   Lord of the Dance.   Sydney Carter. OBET

I am the loser for my tenderness.   The Elephant to the Girl in Bertram Mills' Circus.   Anthony Cronin.   CIP

I am the Love that dare not speak its name.'   Two Loves.   Lord Alfred Bruce Douglas.   PeHV

I am the man to shun Hamlet's soliloquy.   If So the Man You Are.   Percy Wyndham Lewis.   OBSV

I am the measure of Felicitie.   Mustapha.   Fulke, Lord Brooke Greville. OBS

"I am the mother of Iscariot."   Motherhood.   Agnes Lee.   BLPA; HBMV

I am the one who bathes the dust from your feet.   There Are Flowers of Zait in the Garden.   *Anonymous.*   PBWP

I am the only Messenger today on Miramichi.   The Messenger Song. *Anonymous.*   ShS

I am the only one who loves.   Letter Out of the Gray.   Gabriel Preil. VWA

I am the open sesame,/And the unwitting tool of fate.   The Tool of Fate. Yehoash.   TrJP

I am the place and not the places me?   To London the Train Gallops, Its Shrill Steel Hooves'.   Clifford Dyment.   HaMV

I am the pulse of the cosmos whose life is to God/as a wave.   The.Wave. John Curtis Underwood.   EtS

I am the pure lotus,/that blossomed in the field.   Death as a Lotus Flower. *Anonymous.*   TTY

I am the resurrection and the life.   Message Clear.   Edwin Morgan.   NIP

I am the rider, it is I.   Who.   Moishe-Leib Halpern.   TrJP

I am the root of life;/I am the chord.   The Song of the Woman-Drawer. Mary Gilmore.   PoAu 1-2

I am the sign who names you.   I'll act out a weird dream.   Marie-Francoise Prager.   BoWoP

"I am the Spring, the Spring, the Spring with laughter on my lips."   Who Calls.   Frances Clarke Sayers.   SiSoSe

I am the stem that fed the fruit/the link that joins you to the night.   Woman to Child.   Judith Wright.   PBWP

I am the stray one.   One.   Carolyn M. Rodgers.   BPo

I am the string, the bow and the arrow   They Tell Me I Am Lost.   Maurice Kenny.   STE

I am the Tiger of Desire!   The Tiger of Desire.   Tom MacInnes.   OBCV

I am the vey model of a modern Major-/General.   The Pirates of Penzance. Sir William Schwenck Gilbert.   CoBE

I am the vine,/the branches, you/and you.   The Mysteries Remain.   Hilda ("H. D.") Doolittle.   NOBA; TAP; VGW; WPOW

I am the voice of music and the ended dance.   The Blind Man (excerpt). Judith Wright.   CBAP

I am the Whom It May Concern.   Notation in Haste.   Elias Lieberman. GoYe

I am the womb and the grave,/The Now and the Ever.   Life and Death. William Ernest Henley.   OBNC

I am the Yankee Doodle Boy.   The Yankee Doodle Boy.   George M. Cohan.   BLSo; FSN

I am thinking about the cannisters of nerve gas/honeycombed outside Salt Lake City.   At Night.   Alan Proctor.   FAZ

...I am thinking how we can use what we have/to invent what we need. Leaflets.   Adrienne Rich.   NoAm

I am thrilled by my own loneliness.   Buildings.   Daniela Gioseffi.   FAZ

I am through you so i   I Am So Glad and Very.   Edward Estlin Cummings. CMoP

I am thy rose, my dear, and thou my tree.   To Her Love.   Edward May. FaBoEE

I am tired. Everyone's tired of my turmoil.   Eye and Tooth.   Robert Lowell. CAPP

I am tired of civilization.   Tired.   Fenton Johnson.   BANP; IDB; PoBA; PoLf; PoNe; TTY

I am to see to it that I do not lose you.   To a Stranger.   Walt Whitman. NoAm; NOBA

I am too glad to be alone,/come forth with me to-day!   Come Forth, Come Forth!   John Wilson.   OBRV

I am topsy-turvy once more.   Lives.   Cyril Dabydeen.   BrSi

I am tragedian in this scene alone.   On His Own Agamemnon and Iphigeneia. Walter Savage Landor.   OBRV

I am troubled, I'm dissatisfied, I'm Irish. Spenser's Ireland. Marianne Moore. FaBoWP; LiTA; LiTM; MasP; NePA; NoAm; NOBA; OxBA; TAP

I am trying to operate/from the fire that is the bush. Yom Kippur. Eric Chaet. VWA

I am trying to tell you something. Endurance. Carolyn Forche. SV

...I am/under their lids, growing black. Goodbye. Bill Knott. EAS

I am...waiting Minotaur. Robert Fisher. AmMo

I am waiting for/a BLACK POETRY DAY. A Black Poetry Day. Alicia Loy Johnson. BOLo

I am waiting for my turn. Foetal Song. Joyce Carol Oates. IHMS; NAs

I am waiting for someone to swallow me up,/but with all my thorns. Orgy. Gina Labriola. WPOW

I am wandering down/thankful/as I ask. Home Alone These Last Hours of the Afternoon... Stephen Levy. VWA

I am where I go Winter. Samuel Menashe. GrPl

I am who you turn to when the world stops. Wake. Elizabeth Spires. AMV-80

I am Wind and Sky and Sea! Outward. John G. Neihardt. HBV 1-2

I am with/the old men/watching one/spring go out. The Process. Robert Kelly. CoPo

I am with thee, and most take all. The Quidditie. George Herbert. PoEL 1-5

I am Woman as Heaven made Me. Song: "With my frailty don't upbraid me." William Congreve. PoL

I am wrong, but give me someone/to talk to. Hegel. LeRoi (Imamu Amiri Baraka) Jones. CoPo

I am, you have heard it, the Beginning and the End. Time. Allen Curnow. AnNZ

I am young and young are you:/'Tis the time for playing. Phyllis. *Anonymous.* UnTE

I am your Bread? The Anathemata. David Jones. AtBAP

I am your child. Child of the World. Edna L. S. Baker. GoYe

"I am your child: O parents, ye have come!" The House of Life. Dante Gabriel Rossetti. EnLi 1-2

I am your divine name. Plain Song. Jean Cocteau. PoPl

I am your elements, Lord,/In their nothingness. The Way up Is the Way down. Charles Brasch. OCNZ

I am your servant and your thrall. Beauty Clear and Fair. John Fletcher. CBEP; OAEP; OBEV; ViBoPo

I am your singer,singing my last note. Moritura. Margaret Gilman (George) Davidson. AA

"I am your slave," said the Jinn. Aladdin and the Jinn. Vachel Lindsay. AnAmPo; AnFE; APA; CoAnAm; MAPA

I an my rose/Are one. The Rose. G. A. Studdert Kennedy. EBCP

I anchored,/in the darkness of harbors/laid-by. Reclining Figure. Donald Hall. ConAP; LCAP

I and a marsh bird only make a wail. Evening in England. Francis Ledwidge. MCCG

I and all the others that will love you/if they love you/3/unless they love you. Cascando. Samuel Beckett. NOBI

I and my wordy lust/Long since away. All Day and All October. Laurence Lerner. PeSA

I and my works were caught in the gale of the world. Mihailovich. Roy McFadden. NeIP

I and my worn symbols see up the sun. A Valley where I Don't Belong. Marge Piercy. IHMS

I and this Love are one, and I am Death. The House of Life. Dante Gabriel Rossetti. SyP; VLP

I announce your resurrection/and your death. The Beirut–Hell Express. Etel Adnan. WPOW

I answer not, and I return no more!' Opportunity. John James Ingalls. AA; FaFP; GoTF; HBV 1-2; HBVY; OHFP; PoLf; TreF; WBLP; YaD

I answer you/amen. Christmas Mass for a Little Atheist Jesus. Claude Maillard. BoWoP

I anticipate, drinking, the concentric circles/of the other consciousness. Fishing Drunk. Bob Mondy. WOLT

I, Antiphanes,/The son of Antiphanes,/Dedicate to Hermes. This Torch, Still Burning in My Hand. Crinagoras. SD

I appeal to thee, Laka! The Rainbow Stands Red...A Tiring Song. *Anonymous.* WTO

I apprehend will get some blame/On her good name. Her Eyes. John Crowe Ransom. LiTM; NePA; OBAL; PoPl

I, as the night invites me, fall asleep. To a Lady Who Sent Me a Copy of Verses at My Going to Bed. Henry, Bishop of Chichester King. PP

I, as wooer, perhaps might come/To so sweet an Artium/Magistra. Ad Chloen, M.A. Mortimer Collins. HBV 1-2

I ask a man in the smoker where he is going and he answers: "Omaha." Limited. Carl Sandburg. AmP; HAP; LoGBV; MoAB; MoAmPo; OxBA

I ask but right for my redress. When that I call unto my mind. Sir Thomas Wyatt. FCP

I ask but Silence whilst I dye. To the Nightingale. Philip Ayres. CEP

I ask each river where is Ebbw's voice–/In memory of the sweet days that have been. Days That Have Been. William Henry Davies. FaBoPP

I ask for pillows/the nurse brings pudding. Stroke. Mike Lowery. Psk

I ask God to help you and bid you farewell. The Lovesick Cowboy. *Anonymous.* CoSo

I ask no more, for that affords/What is not in the force of words. Tree-Topped Hill. *Anonymous.* NOEC

I ask no more–I stayed. The Shepherd Who Stayed. Theodosia Garrison. OHIP; PCh

I ask no other till then. Taisigh Agat Fein Do Phog. *Anonymous.* BIrV

I ask that I may perish/By a soldier's death! Andre's Request to Washington. Nathaniel Parker Willis. MC; PAH

I ask thee not my joys to multiply,–/Only to make me worthier of the least. Adequacy. Elizabeth Barrett Browning. SBG

I ask to be taken in. Spring Again. Ronald Wallace. PPJ

..I ask you can that behaviour have a good/end come to it? A Translation from Walter von der Vogelweide. John Millington Synge. MoBrPo

I ask you, cranes,/to warm my child in your wings. Mother's Song. *Anonymous.* BoWoP

I ask you, mountain, be my final resting place. From Mount Nebo. Karl Wolfskehl. VWA

I ask you often, but you never say? Furnished Lives. Jon Silkin. NePoEA-2; NMP; NoAm

I ask you, Sirs, what thought you then/On Christmas long ago? It Seems That God Bestowed Somehow. Amanda Benjamin Hall. AH

I asked a little power,/Thou gavest me a begging-bowl. A Miracle Indeed. Purohit Swami. OBMV

I asked him to lend me eighteenpence,/But he borrowed a shilling of me. My Dream. *Anonymous.* NA

I asked his work; he dealt in coal,/And shipped it up the Tyne, he said. The Counselor. Dorothy Parker. InMe

I asked the Lord could it be mine. Every Time I Feel the Spirit. *Anonymous.* FSW

I at least can learn/to live with obesity/and a little fame. Since. W. H. Auden. PAI

I ate the food I ne'er had eat. Bread. James Dickey. LCAP

I await your dark claw. Glory Be to God for Dappled Things. Diane Keating. CaPN

...I awake/at the unforgettable instant/he dies. Creation of the Child. Susan Litwack. VWA

I awake to find/my heart pumps/like a wing without air. The Burial. Glover Davis. SM

I awaken/on all fours. The Skunk (parody). Philip Dow. BXAP

I awoke all broken-hearted, lying in Van Dieman's Land. Van Dieman's Land. *Anonymous.* BaBo

I awoke before you got in. Dream of a Father. Shirley G. Cochrane. AmC

I awoke in my cradle/In the dark sun's light. This Night. Osip Mandelstam. VWA

"I baked the tart for my little sweetheart." The Tale of a Tart. Frederic Edward Weatherly. SUS

I bang on the empty drums/alone Rhapsodies. Cyril Dabydeen. BrSi

I bared my soul to all the woods, and God. May. Stephen Moylan Bird. HBMV

...I barely can right myself/fountain of tears, river of grief. Fountain of Tears, River of Grief. Christine de Pisan. WPOW

I bear a little more than I can bear. Sonnet from "One Person". Elinor Wylie. MoAB; MoAmPo

I bear the rainbow bubble Earth/Square on my scornful back. The Tortoise in Eternity. Elinor Wylie. ImOP

I became suspicious even of those who had real eyes. My Father's Eye. Eleni Vakalo. BoWoP

I become them, sometimes. Pure flight. Pure fantasy. Lean. The Turncoat. LeRoi (Imamu Amiri Baraka) Jones. NeAP

I been doin' all I can, honey,/Just tryin' to get along with you. Lowdown Dirty Blues. *Anonymous.* AmFP

I been talked 'bout sure as you're born. Hell and Heaven. *Anonymous.* ABF

I beg death's pardon now. And mourn the dead. The Pardon. Richard Wilbur. NePoEA; NIP; NoAm; NOBA; NoP

I beg of Love that ever I/May in like chains of darkness lie! Upon a Black Twist, Rounding the Arm of the Countess of Carlisle. Robert Herrick. CaPo

"I beg you pardon but we believe we have made some degree/of progress on the residual qualities.... Mr. Attila. Carl Sandburg. ImOP

I beg you very gently break the news. A Petition. Thomas Bailey Aldrich. AA

I believe, even our deaths are forgiven. Nor Mars His Sword. Dunstan Thompson. NePA

I believe everything, I am here. The Owl King. James Dickey. CoPo

I believe I'll lay down/take mor-phine and die The Jailhouse Blues. Sam Collins. BluL

I believe I will leave here mama/a long way from my home   Leaving Town Blues. Ishman Bracey. BluL

I believe in the singing, and sleep.   The Horse Show at Midnight. Henry Taylor. PH

I believe it all, and for no man's death I grieve.   A Letter from Brooklyn. Derek Walcott. OxBTC

I believe that I'm not given to croaking,/But you'll admit that it's provoking! Hard to Bear. Tudor. Jenks. OBCA

I believe the dose will do.   Receipt for the Vapours. Mary Wortley, Lady Montagu. PBWP

I believe the heart/overflows its beats....   Beginning. Marcos Rodriguez Frese. InW

I believe the world will rip apart/From the inside/Of our next moment alive. Homage to Elvis, Homage to the Fathers. Bruce Weigl. MAYP

I believe you's gone asleep.   Dolly's Lesson. *Anonymous.* FaBoUs

I believed him, and lit another cigar.   Waiting for Nighthawks in Illinois. Roger Pfingston. FAZ

I bend and enter   Lying Here, Everything In Me. Margaret Atwood. NeAC

I bend close to the floorboards hoping/for at least one flower to appear.   Ode on Celestial Music. Brian Patten. OxBTC

I bet a birthday CHEESE cake/would please them most of all.   Birthday Cake. Aileen Fisher. BiCB

I bet God can dance too.   I Bet God Understands about Givin up Five. Yasmeen Jamal. LFAC

"I bet I can eat a lot monia."   Limerick: "A hearty old cook of Lithonia." Jr, Blount Roy. TDH

I bet my life on Christ, Christ crucified,/Aye risen, and alive forevermore. The Great Wager. G. Anketall "Woodbine Willie" Studdert-Kennedy. TrCP

I bet she scratched/When she was itchy.   Taboo to Boot. Ogden Nash. FiBHP

I bet you somethin to eat.   Translations from the English. George Starbuck. VGW

I bid him farewell and I wished him in hell/With his old gray beard a-shaking. Old.Gray Beard A-Shaking. *Anonymous.* AmFP

I bid, Lord, Thy passion/To mine mend look.   Hours of the Passion. William of Shoreham. ACP; CAW

I bid my days turn back, I broke my windows, I unsealed my locks.   The Magnet. Ruth Stone. MoAmPo; NePA

I bid thee carve them, knowing what I know.'   Opifex. Thomas Edward Brown. OBVV

I bid thee hail, bright lady-bird!   Lines to a Lady-Bird. Lord De Tabley. FM

...I bid thee know/That answering God's own love thy womb shall throe.' Mary and the Bramble. Lascelles Abercrombie. OBMV

I bid them bring to you/Dreams, and strange imaginings, and sleep. Greeting. Ella Young. AnIV

I bleed my bones, their marrow to bestow/Upon that God who knows what I would know. The Marrow. Theodore Roethke. NYBP

...I bless/all knowledge of love, all ways of publishing it.   Open Letter from a Constant Reader. Mona Van Duyn. GP; PoA

I bless'd with learning, takes a pen and writes.   Evening: an Elegy (parody). Horace (or Horatio) Smith. BXAP

I bless Thy goad of discontent.   The Aim. Sir Charles G. D. Roberts. PeCV

I blew as he said!   Written at the End of a Book. Langdon Elwyn Mitchell. AA

I blossom in the Field.   He Is Like the Lotus. Book of the Dead. AWP

I bobbed with a hook through the palm of my hand.   Under the Boathouse. David Bottoms. MAYP

I bought a pack of smokes for the journey.   Precious Mettle. Lewis Warsh. APU

...I bought the car/with dollars I earned from the sale of love poems.   Last of the Poet's Car. Tony Connor. OxBTC

I bought zome aggs, but now ha' nwone to zell.   Shop O' Meat-Weare. William Barnes. NOBV

I bow—if not, your mighty wills be done.   An Humble Wish (excerpt). Edward Thompson. NOEC; OBTV

I bow not to the monkey bands.   The Deserted Kingdom. Edward John, Lord Dunsany. AnIV

I bow to him, exalt his name!   On the Capture and Imprisonment of Crazy Snake, January, 1900. Alexander L. Posey. BPAW

I bow to Master Takayama/who smiles all the way from Japan.   Away. Lucien Stryk. GP

I bow with great thanksgiving!   Thanksgiving. Gene H. Osborne. PGD

I bowed before the altar,/I laid my banjo by.   Rufus Mitchell's Confession. *Anonymous.* AmFP

...I boxed him in my plain pine/arms and let him take his ease just for a minute.   Letter to an Absent Son. Madeline De Frees. GP; NMM

I break the toils around thy head/And from their gibbets take thy dead.   The Study of a Spider. John Byrne, Leicester Warren, Lord De Tabley. NOBV; VLP

I break water, a fish left high and dry/under the new moon./Goodbye.   The Magnolia's Shadow. Eugenio Montale. NaP

I breathe and let my eyes/close, there is probably trouble.   A Day in My Union Suit. Michael Pettit. MAYP

I breathe dust spreading down in/a great wing.   From the Dust. Elaine Dallman. VWA

I breathe into his mouth/& make him real   The Man under the Bed. Erica Jong. AmPA

I breathe/the pungent scent/of her terror.   Trembling. Aliza Shenhar. VWA

I breathed, and this truth burned up my breath.   The Hand. Irving Feldman. AmPC

...I breed the shape of your grave in the dirt.   The Supper after the Last. Galway Kinnell. NOBA; PoCh

I bring back the petticoat and the bottle of scent.   Lent. W. R. Rodgers. NeBP; OxBI

"I bring freedom for all."   The Guerrilla. Frelimo. WhB

I bring from the shadow-world only/Pale blossoms that perish in air.   Song: "If once I could gather in song." Wilfred Wilson Gibson. OBVV

I bring her to drink the dregs of cisterns all mire and/if she mislikes it...   The Mufaddaliyat: His Camel. Alqamah. AWP

I bring my stocking feet close to the faint incense.   Thinking of "The Autumn Fields." Robert Bly. NNaP

I bring you as offering.   Orchard. Hilda ("H. D.") Doolittle. APA; AtBAP; CMoP; ExPo; LiTA; LiTM; MoAmPo; OxBA

I bring you my moon song/To sing at moonlit sands at night/In joy or sorrow alike. Moon Song. Chuba Nweke. PBA

I bring you my passionate rhyme.   A Poet to His Beloved. William Butler Yeats. BrPo

I bring you my songs/To sing on the Georgia roads.   Sun Song. Langston Hughes. CNA

I broke from sleep, forgot my pain,/And woke to light and life again.   The Midnight Court. Brian Merriman. OnYI

I brood on the uselessness of letters.   Snow Storm. Tu Fu. NaP

I brood upon uncompleted tasks.   Tom on the Beach. George Bruce. BSV

I brought him to grief, woman!   Goll Mac Morna Parts from his Wife. *Anonymous.* NOBI

I brush my watery eyes, and breathe.   Grandpa's .45. W. M. Ransom. CDW

I build the place of my leaving/that the dark may come clean.   For the Rebuilding of a House. Wendell Berry. EyDe

I buried you deeper last night.   To a Persistent Phantom. Frank Horne. BANP; CDC

I burn as a lonely taper/In blackest night.   Canto Cantare Cantavi Cantatum. Rita Mae Brown. PeHV

I burn like St Catherine's wheel/Spun on fires I cannot feel.   Memorial Couplets for the Dying Ego. George Barker. EBEV

I burn these words in praise,/of our meeting, our friendship.   It Started. Jimmy Santiago Baca. LFAC

I burned my hand—to save this bit.   A Fragment. John Bancks. NOEC

I burst for thee, and thy dear love.   Mir Traumte Von Einem Konigskind. Heinrich Heine. AWP

I burst out laughing.   The Lesson. Charles Simic. HaCAP

I bury my dead. I mourn/for four full days.   Coyote's Daylight Trip. Paula Gunn Allen. TWSS

I button and unbutton/what I feel   On the New Road. Lyn Lifshin. NeAC

...I buy a small necklace for/my wife. Promise to write him a poem.   Scrimshaw. Michael Hogan. LFAC

I cain't stay, no—I cain't stay.   John Henry (D vers.). *Anonymous.* ViBoFo

I call it stupid of the pig.   The Pig. Ogden Nash. DBV; FPL

I call no-one to witness/But the clanging birds of the air.   Ibycus. John Heath-Stubbs. PoCh

I called that milk"—she blushed with pride–/"You bade me speak the truth." Wordsworth at Tea. Barry Pain. HBV 1-2

I called upon your pretty Caroline/For to drive the old cat   Lady Isabel and the Elf-Knight (B vers.). *Anonymous.* ViBoFo

I calm down,/undress, and slip/in between them and think/of household gods. New York. Thom Gunn. NYP

I came as a black feather/that had moved/against wind.   For Michael. Karen L. Mitchell. AMV-80

I came as a shadow,/to dazzle your night!   Nocturne Varial. Lewis Alexander. PoBA; PoNe

I came back to myself,/To the real work, to/"What is to be done."   I Went into the Maverick Bar. Gary Snyder. HaCAP; MAT

"I came from martyrdom unto this peace!"   President Garfield. Henry Wadsworth Longfellow. PAH

I came from the wilderness.   Wilderness. Carl Sandburg. AP

"I came like Water, and like wind I go." The Rubaiyat of Omar Khayyam. Edward Fitzgerald.   EBEV; TRV

I came not for this.   Man of Crete.   J. R. Hervey.   AnNZ

I came out living. Of me there are many.   Brief Thunder at Sharpeville. Arthur Nortje.   WhB

I came to buy/a few bananas by the ganges/while waiting for my wife.   The Market.   Gary Snyder.   CoPo

I came to love, I came into my own.   The Dream.   Theodore Roethke. AmP; LLLT; MoVE; NIP; NoP; NYBP; UnPo

"I came up and pulled the string, and you came down and let/me in."   Jack the Jolly Tar.   Anonymous.   BaBo

I came upon a man with the face of a bull.   Minotaur Poems.   E.W. Mandel.   OBCV

I came with nothing, found nothing there.   Tangier.   Stephen P. Dunn. SM

I can almost feel the tushes in your throat.   Epigrams.   Martial (Marcus Valerius Martialis).   OBVE

I can almost hear them/yammering in strange tongues.   Neural Folds. Lucille Day.   SUW

I can almost name.   The Vestal in the Forum.   James Wright.   AMV-81

I can be touched/and not feel like a passing shadow.   Dusk.   Marcia Southwick.   MAYP

I can break my chrysalis too!   The Butterfly.   Alice Freeman Palmer.   HBV 1-2

...I can but fortell/The worm where once the kiss clung, and that last less chasm-/deep farewell.   The Hambone and the Heart.   Edith Sitwell. OBMV

I can but know thee as my star,/My angel and my dream!   Night and Love. Edward Robert Bulwer, Earl of Lytton.   HBV 1-2

I can die now I just begun to live   Moonset, Gloucester, December 1, 1957, 1:58 AM.   Charles Olson.   CAPP

...I can/eat as I go.   Stepping Westward.   Denise Levertov.   NMM; VGW

I can endure my own despair,/But not another's hope.   Rivals.   William Walsh.   HBV 1-2; OBEV

I can feel my cheek/still burning.   The Portrait.   Stanley Jasspon Kunitz. CTBA; GP; Psk

...I can/feel my eye breaking.   The Window.   Robert Creeley.   CAPP; NoAm; NOBA; TAP; VGW

I can feel that I have been changed, I feel that/death has come near to me. Life the Very Gods in My Sight Is He Who.   Sappho.   WPOW

I can find a job with a crawling mob/On the banks of the Maranoa.   The Overlander.   Anonymous.   NOAV

I can go and heed Thy call/By traveling on my knees.   Traveling on My Knees.   Sandra Goodwin.   STF

I can hardly think you will not turn over and creep/Along the furrows trenchward as if to die.   Youth in Arms: IV. Carrion.   Harold Monro. MMM

I can hear cars, moving on steel rails, colliding/Underground.   Miners. James Wright.   ConAP; CTBA

I can hear God, leaning over Safed.   Safed.   Dovid Knut.   VWA

I can hear it crying/When I sit like this away from life.   The Animal I Wanted.   Kenneth Patchen.   VGW

I can hear it swallow.   The Garden Hose.   Beatrice Janosco.   NTCP; PoL

I can hear my father saying/you had to let it go   Drop the Wires.   Hugh Seidman.   AmPA

I can hear them/making soft liquid sounds/of contentment.   Speech.   Henry Taylor.   MAT; NLV

I can hear today's key sounds fading softly/& almost see opening sleep's epic novel.   Things to Do in Providence.   Ted Berrigan.   APU

I can ignore the way they grow.   Dilemma of the Elm.   Genevieve Taggard. MoAmPo

I can leave you now.   How to Get to New Mexico.   John Brandi.   TAT

I can lick the mick that threw the overalls in Mistress Murphy's chowder. Who Threw the Overalls in Mistress Murphy's Chowder.   George L. Geifer. FSN

I can light cheroots and gaspers with my tail.   I Wish I Were.   Anonymous. FaBoNo; OxBoLi

I can love any, so she be not true....   The Indifferent.   John Donne.   EG

I can namore, my tale is at an ende.   The Canterbury Tales: The Franklin's Tale.   Geoffrey Chaucer.   OAEL 1-2

I can never more return with my poor dog Tray.   The Harper.   Thomas Campbell.   CBEP; NCEP

I can no longer sense/the wings' dry flutter.   The Therapeutist.   Beth Bentley.   AMV-80

I can no more cross this room/Than Zeno's arrow.   Depression.   Wendy Cope.   FaBoWP

...I can no more/Foresee or more control than robin and wren.   Fifty Faggots.   Edward ("Edward Eastaway") Thomas.   BrPo; MoAB; MoBrPo

...I can-/not touch you and this is the oppressor's language.   The Burning of Paper Instead of Children.   Adrienne Rich.   LCAP

I can now wipe em away.   Heedless o' My Love.   William Barnes.   GBL

I can only be whatever you are.   Brotherhood.   Jose Luis Vega.   InW

I can only bougaloo & bop   Missing Beat.   Carolyn M. Rodgers.   JB

I can only roll you under/the carpet now   Naming the Rain.   Annette Arkeketa West.   TWSS

I can play the fiddle with my left/hind-leg.   I Wish I Were.   Anonymous. FaFP

I can promise you we shall not get first in a rage.   My Master and I. Anonymous.   CoMu; OBET

I can remember/nothing about it now/but the geese.   Wild Geese.   William Hart-Smith.   BoAnP

I can remember when he was a pup.   The Span of Life.   Robert Frost. DiPo; GDP; HoPM; LiTM; SoSe

I can rest me where I am.   A Celebration of Charis.   Ben Jonson.   AtBAP

"I can see," he begins,/"that you two have problems..."   Wayman in Love. Tom Wayman.   NIP; NOBC

I can see over to Brooklyn and Jersey,/and beyond there are meadows,/and mountains and plains.   The Hour of Feeling.   Louis Simpson.   FiCP

I can see thy flaming heart/Burn already through thy vest.   Dearest Friend, Thou Art in Love.   Heinrich Heine.   TrJP

I can sing about it still.   The Song of the Reed Sparrow.   Anonymous. OxBChV

I can sleep in the sea and be none the wetter.   Quatrain: "Good-looking, I'll never stoop for you."   Mahsati.   WPOW

I can still see her, patially./through the lace curtains streaming through the window.   The Lace Curtains.   Lewis MacAdams.   ANYP

I can still smell him/in my dreams.   Poems about Playmates.   Ronda Davis. JB

I can't. Confusion on the man!   Aaron Burr.   Stephen Vincent Benét. InMe

I can't congratulate the Devil.   On the Reverend Jonathan Doe. Anonymous.   ChTr; FaBoEE

I can't do it myself, but my sister, she can.'   Nine Times a Night. Anonymous.   OBET

I can't find my way home.   This Little Pig Went to Market.   Anonymous. OxNR; SoPo; TiPo

I can't forbear to flog the wicked witch.   An Adieu to My Landlady. George Farewell.   NOEC

I can't get no sassin', baby, on the tele–telephone.   Depot Blues. Anonymous.   AmFP

I can't get over the barn door sill.   This Pig Got in the Barn.   Anonymous. OxNR

I can't hardly wait, he said.   Standing on the Corner.   Philip Levine. NNaP

I can't learn how to know men, or conceal/How strange they are to me. Strange Meetings.   Harold Monro.   MoBrPo

I can't remember, he said, but I'm all right.   The Patient.   Nicholas Moore. EAS

I can't remember what he done.   Mystery Story.   Howard Nemerov.   NLV

I can't say it!/Manikin!   Manikin and Minikin.   Alfred Kreymborg. MAPA

"I can't talk," I cried offended,/"To a man I've never met."   Interrupted Romance.   Anonymous.   UnTE

...I can't/think of anything like us before. No wonder it scares me. Homosexual Sonnets.   Kenneth Pitchford.   GP

I can't think of one, can you?   A Bestiary.   Kenneth Rexroth.   OBAL

"I can't tie mine up, Mom,/I might get a call."   Hot Line.   Louella Dunann.   QQQ

...I can't/Understand, Vacerra, why,/You don't have more money.   Poems from a Greek Anthology (excerpt).   Martial (Marcus Valerius Martialis). NNaP

I can't whistle/you can't kiss/eating salty fish.   A Song for New Orleans. George Keithley.   NPGG

I can tell you no more if I preach for a year.   A Brief Sermon.   Anonymous. GoTF; TreFS

I can walk across.   The Return.   Stanley Moss.   PoL

I/can walk/thru calendar years/without ever/losing my stride....   For Mulatto.   Raymond Ringo Fernandez.   LFAC

I can well say this of me:/Heavy hangs my sorrow.   Though I've a Clever Head.   Anonymous.   HAP

I canna sing, and maunna say/How sair I grieve for somebody.   Somebody. Anonymous.   OxBS

I cannot, and I won't.   Blind but Happy.   Fanny J. Crosby.   TRV

I cannot be destroyed.   Us.   Julius Lester.   PoBA

...I cannot/be more than the man/who watches.   The Name.   Robert Creeley.   CoPo

(I cannot be positive which).   The Yak.   Hilaire Belloc.   ALV; FaBV; HBVY; InMe; NA; NLV; NOBL; OxBChV; TreFS

I cannot bear the still grief of the sky.   When Nature Hath Betrayed the Heart That Loved Her.   Sophie Jewett.   AA

I cannot believe the find.   I Cannot Believe That I Am of Wind.   Samuel Greenberg.   LiTA

I cannot believe them old.   Lost Companions.   Helen Bryant.   AMV-80

...I cannot bite the day to the core. The Glory. Edward ("Edward Eastaway") Thomas. OxBTC

...I cannot budge. Encirclement. Mieczyslaw Jastrun. AMV-81

I cannot cut the cane today. A Creole Slave-Song. Maurice Thompson. AA

I cannot deny what I know would undo me! To Little or No Purpose. Sir George Etherege. UnTE

I cannot die/Unless I walk outside these whitethorn hedges. Innocence. Patrick Kavanagh. FaBoIP

I cannot drive it from mine ear,/That crying in the dark. Midnight. Archibald Lampman. OBCV; PeCV

I cannot explain it. I do not/want to explain it. Dreamscape. Philip Booth. FiCP

I cannot find your peer in any pasture. A Mare. Kate Barnes. NYBP; PH

I cannot grasp the rapture now of you,/Who were so close to dawn, and trees, and dew. Resurgam. Struthers Burt. HBMV

I cannot grind; love wastes me so. Popular Songs of Tuscany. Anonymous. AWP

I cannot halt that mindless stream,/whose will is my necessity,/overthrow or victory. The Riders. Robert Friend. GP

I cannot help but deem the grackle/An ornithological debacle. The Grackle. Ogden Nash. DBV; NLV; PV

I cannot help this. It is noblesse oblige. One-Way Song. Percy Wyndham Lewis. PP

I cannot leave the unburied bones,/And I fain would go my way. Death Song. Robert Stephen Hawker. OBNC; OBRV; OBVV

I cannot live without thee. To His Coy Love. Michael Drayton. EiL; ErPo; HBV 1-2; LiTL; OBEV; OBS; ViBoPo

I cannot love Him if I love not you. Monna Innaminata. Christina Georgina Rossetti. VLP

I cannot love thee.–Come, come thou!– Rimas. Gustavo Adolfo Becquer. CAW

I cannot love thee less nor more. Song: "Why, lovely charmer, tell me why." Sir Richard Steele. LiTL; ViBoPo

I cannot recall. Haiku: "A balmy spring wind..." Richard Wright. FAZ

I cannot remember our love. Memory. Helen Hoyt. PoLf

I cannot return. Pirouette. Audre Lorde. NNP

I cannot say if their catch is shrimp,/Or fireflies buring clear. Nocturne: Georgia Coast. Daniel Whitehead Hicky. AmFN

I cannot see you till I doubt my eyes. Some Refrains at the Charles River. Peter Viereck. PoCh

I cannot sleep as long as there is wire/running from his eye to his ear. The Middleaged Man. Louis Simpson. NNaP

I cannot stand the man who wears/a ring/on his little finger;/not even if it is you. Ringless. Diane Wakoski. Prf

I cannot take/any man in my arms but my lord/white as jasmine. Other men are thorn. Mahadevi (Mahadeviyakka). BoWoP

I cannot tell for I do not know. I Had Two Pigeons Bright and Gay. Anonymous. OxNR; PBBP

I cannot tell, I cannot see. The Watchman. Abraham Reisen. TrJP

I cannot tell your voice from my own voice. The Anniversary. William Dickey. GOYP

I cannot think that they have done/A great amount of riding. The Racing-Man. Sir Alan Patrick Herbert. BoAnP; FiBHP; PH

I cannot think the thing farewell. In Memoriam A.H.H., CXXIII. Alfred, Lord Tennyson. HAP; NOBE; OAEL 1-2; OAEP; SeCePo

I cannot, till I reconcile my time/With your eternal charity of light. Rest O Sun I Cannot. Joseph Tusiani. GoYe

"I cannot understand: I love." In Memoriam A.H.H., XCVII. Alfred, Lord Tennyson. VLP

I cannot walk without it. I Have to Have It. Dorothy Aldis. SoPo

I cannot wish it Less. Song. Thomas Parnell. CEP

I cannot write unless he's sent above. A Parental Ode to My Son. Thomas Hood. FiBHP; HBV 1-2; PoLf

I cant stand bein sorry & colored at the same time/it's so redundant in the modern world No More Love Poems #1. Ntozake Shange. BlSi

...I captive raz'd a town. The Trojan Horse. William, of Hawthornden Drummond. EyDe

"I care for nobody, not I,/If no one cares for me." Love in a Village (excerpt). Isaac Bickerstaffe. ViBoPo

"I care not now how soon 'tis done/Or cut, if cut by you." The Parcae, or Three Dainty Destinies: The Armillet. Robert Herrick. CaPo

I care with my breasts. I care with my belly's blood./Come down. Summoned. Diana O Hehir. NPGG

I carry the offense of my flat belly,/the silent red loss of monthly bleeding. The Wife Takes a Child. Ellen Bryant Voigt. SM

I catch myself. Harbor. Nancy Price. IHMS

I caught her terror then. I have it still. NW5 & N6. Sir John Betjeman. SCV

I caught the cold flash of the blue/unappeasable sky. Robin Redbreast. Stanley Jasspon Kunitz. Prf

I change bot seas, bot cannot change my love. In Orknay. William Fowler. GoTS; OxBS

I cheer a dead man's sweetheart,/Never ask me whose. A Shropshire Lad. Alfred Edward Housman. OAEP

I chew and I spit/All over my sweetheart's behind. Driving the Mule. Anonymous. GBP

I choose a place that is unfrequented by men. Madly Singing in the Mountains. Po Chu-i. CBEP

I choose (and I thank you) to die of old age. The King and the Clown. Anonymous. MaC

I choose the opposite direction. 5 Poems. Robert Gray. CBAP

I choose to be twozi not threezi. Limerick: "A bigamist born in Zambezi." David McCord. InMe

I choose to sleep. The Birds Do Thus. Robert Lee Frost. AmePo

I chose a modern subject as more meet. Don Juan. George Gordon, Lord Byron. OAEL 1-2

I chose death to save my honor. White as Snow. Anonymous. OuSiCo

I chose the sun and every chance of blood.... Nilotic Elegy. G. S. Fraser. WaP

I clack, clack/into the veins of all Creation. O, Beautiful They Move. [(or Pillin)] William Pillen. VWA

I claim his soul and body,/And I will share his doom.' The Woman at the Washtub. Victor J. Daley. NOAV

"I clasp you all; my own Child waits,' she said. Madonna of the Empty Arms. Maurice Francis Egan. ISi

...I climb aboard/my tractor and sail. Yachting in Arkansas. Craig Weeden. AMV-80; PPP

...I climb the cliff and go home the other way. The Dead Seal near McClure's Beach. Robert Bly. NNaP; NU

I climb to crown my chaste desire. Mistress, Since You So Much Desire. Thomas Campion. OAEL 1-2

I close her eyes, and keep them tight/Whene'er we come to kiss. I Close Her Eyes. Heinrich Heine. UnTE

I close my eyes and listen,/as she goes out to sing this city home. The Homecoming Singer. Jay Wright. PoBA

I close up like a frightened flower. Frightened Flower. William J. Harris. BOLo

...I/clutch here at words,/having no force to fly. Pine Boat a-Shift. Anonymous. OBVE

I clutch the world's mutations. In flight in escape. Nelly Sachs. BoWoP

I coincide with my skin. One Morning. Ellen Levine. AMV-81

I come and go/In the calm and the storm and the rain. Farmer. Liberty Hyde Bailey. YeAr

I come from Alabama with a banjo on my knee. Oh, Susanna. Anonymous. FSW

I come from an uncouth land as a sely pilgrim/That far hath sought. The Coming of Christ. Anonymous. ACP

I come here to add my own/to the growing silence Poplars. Henryk Grynberg. VWA

I come, my bonnie Annie! The Trumpeter of Fyvie. Anonymous. OxBB

I come quietly to find/A flower to place upon my heart. Puna's Fragrant Glades. Queen Lydia Lili, u-o-ka-lani. WTO

I come to myself/a beast in a shoe box/sport/of the king of the cats. We Were Permitted to Meet Together in Prison to Prepare for Trial. Daniel Berrigan. LFAC

I come to thee, thou stream of life,/My Saviour and my God! Lines to the Blessed Sacrament. Jeremiah Joseph Callanan. OnYI

I come with my word alive. The Question. Muriel Rukeyser. IHMS; WPOW

I come with the dust and I'm gone with the wind. Pastures of Plenty. Woody Guthrie. WTO

I come with the wind and the water upon me,/And never a care! The Faun. Haniel Long. HBMV

I come you go/like the waves/of loving. Erotic Suite (excerpt). Jose Luis Vega. InW

I comfort my son with the hope/the life in the confident man. Daddy. Lucille Clifton. NIP

I confess, my friend, I am puzzled. Meditatio. Ezra Pound. FaBoCh; LoGBV; LOW; OBAL

I confess that this beautiful Nigguh is ready. For Real. Jayne Cortez. PoBA

I confirm, sign, and seal,/This, the true act and deed of/WILL JACKETT. Extraordinary Will. Will Jackett. FaBoUs

I cost my foolish mistress fifty pound. On the Same. Hilaire Belloc. PoL

I could break so easily. Surcease. Patrick Lane. NeAC

I could bring great silence on armies/–though tonight I am freezing cold.' Cold Is the Winter. Anonymous. NOBI

I could eat it now. Rumpty-Iddity, Row, Row, Row. Anonymous. OxNR

I could endure this all/If autumn ended and the cold light came. Winter is Another Country. Archibald MacLeish. NCSH

I could find it only by chance. The white chrysanthemum. Mitsune (Oshikochi no Mitsune). LiTW

I could go on writing like this forever... Squeal (parody). Louis Simpson. BXAP; FiBHP; Par; UnPo

I could have had some/good times in high school... Elegy for the Forgotten Oldsmobile. Adrian C. Louis. STE

I could have went the beaten track/But I will lay quite here. A Spring Lay. Oliver Opdyke. InMe

I could never understand–/JESUS SAVES Elephant Rock. Primus St. John. PoBA

I could no more through all eternity! Men Told Me, Lord! David Starr Jordan. WGRP

I could not add. Wardance Soup. Phil George. VoR

I could not/be saved. The Mood. Quandra Prettyman. PoBA

I could not be so sure of Spring/Save that it sings in me. April. Sara Teasdale. PoSC; SoPo; TiPo; YeAr

I could not deny it love if I tried. Giant Decorative Dahlia. Molly Holden. OxBTC

I could not disappoint you and so prevailed. Encouraged. Paul laurence Dunbar. TRV

I could not get a rhyme for roman/And was oblidged to call it weoman. A Sonnet: "O lovely O most charming pug." Marjory Fleming. FaBoCo; NLV

I could not give you any goodlier thing/If I were king. If I Were King. Justin Huntly McCarthy. FaFP; GoTF; PoLf; TreF

I could not hate you more if hatred were my bones. I Don't Have No Bunny Tail on My Behind. Alta. GP; TW

I could not have endured it had he called my name Seravezza. Hoyt W. Fuller. PoBA

I could not live alone. The Wife. Anna Peyre Dinnies AA

I could not love thee, dear, so much,/Loved I not Honour more. To Lucasta, Going to the Wars. Richard Lovelace. ALV; AnFE; AtBAP; CABA; CaPo; CoBE; ELP; EnLi 1-2; EnLoPo; ExPo; FaBV; FPL; GBL; GoTF; HAP; HBV 1-2; HeIP; InPS; LiTL; LoBV; MeLP; MePo; NIP; NOBE; NoP; OAEL 1-2; OAEP; OBEV; OBSP; OBWP; PAI; PoEL 1-5; PoRA; SCV; SeCeV; SeCP; SeCV 1-2; TreF; ViBoPo; WHA

I could not love you half so well/without my practice shots. Cavalier Lyric. James Simmons. PoL

I could not/mainline it/away.../was your/love To Mother and Steve. Mari E. Evans. BPo; PoBA

I could not see to see– I Heard a Fly Buzz–When I Died. Emily Dickinson. AmePo; AmLP; APA; BoWoP; CABA; CMoP; DiPo; DL; ExPo; FF; ForPo; HAP; HoPM; InPK; InPo; LiTA; LiTM; MAmP; MasP; MoAB; MoAmPo; MoVE; NAWM 1-2; NePA; NoAm; NOBA; NoP; OxBA; PoRA; PPP; SCV; SeCeV; SOTW; TAP

...I could not show myself/Worthy of you unless I sought your death. The Cid: Two Lovers in the Toils of Honor. Pierre Corneille. LiTW

I could not swallow the lake Swallow the Lake. Clarence Major. PoBA

I could not take three steps. I picked up my mother. Ishikawa Takuboku. LiTW

I could only sleep through the night,/my mouth slightly open. Clams. Ishigaki Rin. PBWP

...I could please/With these poor offerings, a man like thee. Dedication, to Leigh Hunt, Esq. John Keats. ViBoPo

I could read what page eight had said to try. Japanese Beetles. X.J. Kennedy. HoAn; OBAL

I could run on till Doomsday in this shrill,/Pindaric fashion, and, dear Clive, no doubt I will. Letter to Myself (parody). Christopher Reid. FaBoPa

I could see/her devotion/to literature/was not/perfect. Misunderstanding. Irving Layton. PV

I could see/her white thighs/glistening with rain. Therese. Alden Nowlan. NeAC

I could see the baby and I/Would be going places together. What the Donkey Saw. U. A. Fanthorpe. OBCP

I could tell it to the world right now. Last Statement. Vladimir Mayakovsky. FaBoPV

I could tell you more about him, but there ain't no use. Everyday Dirt. Anonymous. FSW

I could turn to gold for thee. The Sunshine of Thine Eyes. George Parsons Lathrop. AA

I could use it. Money. Richard Armour. FaFP; GoTF; NLV; PoPl; TreFS

...I could weep/For joy. But I fall asleep. Falling Asleep. Ian Serraillier. DuDa

I couldn't. She Went to Stay. Robert Creeley. OBAL

I couldn't have liked it more. I've Been to a Marvellous Party. Noel Coward. NLV

I couldn't help it! I just laughed and laughed. Montana Wives. Gwendolen Haste. AmFN

I couldn't help myself. I had to smile. The Rapist's Villanelle. Thomas M. Disch. SM

...I couldn't help wishing/you'd rolled it down into the city,/sun setting, caving in the crowds. Mary Speaks to Jesus. Barry Dempster. CaPN

...I couldn't/quite say: I do not want you to go. Since You Seem Intent... Gerald Locklin. GOYP

I couldn't see no body home and/Wasn't no one to be found High Water Everywhere. Charlie Patton. BluL

I count each moment for a day,/Each minute for a year. Alas, My God. Thomas Shepherd. OxBoCh

I count the bars of his cage while we wait. To a Foreign Friend. Leonard Nathan. GP

I court them all and marry none,/And still be a rambling sailor. The Rambling Sailor. Anonymous. OBSS

...I covet/what they think we've got. The Converts. Chana Bloch. AMV-81

I cower in silence/And in anguish/Lick the boots of my burning conscience. Conscience. Melech Ravitch. VWA

I crave the moments that pass me by. Love's Will. Lewis Warsh. APU

I cremated Sam McGee. The Cremation of Sam McGee. Robert W. Service. BLPL; FaFP; GoTF; MaC; NOBC; OBNV; PoLf; ShM; StPo; TreF

I cried to dream again. The Tempest. William Shakespeare. TrGrPo

...I cros myself/with her confessionals. A Poem for My Father. Sonia Sanchez. BPo; IHMS

I cross my arms on my breast,/And all is peace within. The Windmill. Henry Wadsworth Longfellow. MoShBr

I cross the deliberate gulf of man. Prince Henry the Navigator. Sydney Clouts. PeSA

I cross the mountains into the light of the sea. Songs for the Four Parts of the Night. Owl Woman. PBWP

I cry, bursting free... After Reading Sylvia Plath:. Alta. IHMS

I cry/for myself. Carmina Burana (excerpt). Anonymous. BoWoP

I cry out to You/that You should bind them for me,/my Lord. Foul Water. Mordecai Temkin. VWA

I cry thy sighs, my dear, thy tears I bleed. Astrophel and Stella, XCIII. Sir Philip Sidney. AAS; SiPS

I cry to you beyond upon this bitter air. Immortal Autumn. Archibald MacLeish. AP; BiP; BoLiVe; CMoP; CoBMV; LiTA; MoAB; MoAmPo; TrGrPo

I, cumbered with good manners, answer do,/But know not how. For still I think of you. Astrophel and Stella, XXX. Sir Philip Sidney. AAS; SiPS

I curse–and quit the land. The Royal Adventurer. Philip Freneau. PAH

I curse it present, I regret it past. Have I, This Moment, Led Thee from the Beach. Walter Savage Landor. GBL

I cut a watermelon. To be a mistress. Kiyoko Tsuda. BoWoP

I'd-a been at home sleeping/in a doggone feather bed Three Women Blues. Blind Willie McTell. BluL

I'd accept it at once without making a fuss. The Birthday Bus. Mary Ann Hoberman. BiCB

I'd be a butterfly; living, a rover,/Dying when fair things are fading away! I'd Be a Butterfly. Thomas Haynes Bayly. HBV 1-2

I'd be home in mama's bed, darlin', darlin'. Darlin'. Anonymous. FSW

"I'd be the greatest trumpeter in the Universe,/if old Satchmo had never been born!" Satchmo. Melvin B. Tolson. BPo

I'd been taking a nap in my bed and had not been asleep at the switch. Asleep at the.Switch. Anonymous. PaPo

...I'd/been through enough of a/war to know courage/when I saw it. In White Tie. David Huddle. Str

"I'd better pick the white bits up,/And put them on the heap, for tidiness." On Catching a Dog-Daisy in the Mower. Peter Redgrove. NePoEA-2

I'd buy me a johnny to fill up my trunk,/I'd go for a soldier the bounty to jump. The Alphabet. Anonymous. BFSS

I'd change my ways. That's what I'd do. Lazy Lou. Mary Mapes Dodge. BBGG

I'd choose his bark, however bad. The Dog. Oliver Herford. FaBV

I'd color every tree and bush/And spill paint on the ground. Autumn Color. Tom Robinson. YeAr

I'd come a long way for someone scared to trust. Possession. Lynne Lawner. ErPo

I'd dance a measure on his grave. Tom O'Roughley. William Butler Yeats. CMoP

I'd die from these things. Vertigos or Contemplation of Something That Is Over. Alejandra Pizarnik. VWA

I'd do it all over again. The Unknown Soldier. Billy Rose. BLPA; FPL; PAL

I'd double your pleasure, I'd double my/pain,/This moment forever to bury, The Ferry. George Henry Boker. AA

I'd drink in science at each look,/Nor fear the lapse of time. Verses on a Cat. Charles Daubeny. HBV 1-2

I'd drive the rainbow-wickets in/And ask someone to play. The Rainbow. David McCord. SoPo

I'd ever want another man/Like you? He and She. Eugene Fitch Ware. PoLf; YaD

I'd fly away to some tall tree/And there I'd sit and sing. Young Hunting (Loving Henry). Anonymous. AmFP

I'd fly to the side of my mother/And there let me lay down and die. Seven Long Years in State Prison (with music). *Anonymous.* AS

I'd give the whole world if my Lulu was hyer. A Way Up on Clinch Mountain (B vers. with music). *Anonymous.* AS

I'd gnaw on it a thousand years. If Justice Moved. Bettie M. Sellers. TW

I'd go absolutely right straight crazy to heaven. This Darknight Speed. Eloise Klein Healy. AmC

I'd go in freedom to my grave,/Than rule yon isle and be a slave. Holyhead. Sept. 25, 1727. Jonathan Swift. BIrV; NOBI

I'd hate to be me, were I you. Limerick: "Said a saucy young skunk to a gnu." Gerard Neyroud. TDH

I'd have a home, I'd have a home. De Ballet of De Boll Weevil (with music). *Anonymous.* AS

I'd have a new string to tie to my bow."/Towdy owdy, dil-do dum/tol-lol-li-do dil-do day. The Birds' Courting Song. *Anonymous.* TrAS

I'd have him love the thing that was/Before the world was made. Before the World Was Made. William Butler Yeats. GTBS-P

I'd have paid my tithe seven times to hell,/Ere you'd been won away.' Tamlane. *Anonymous.* BuBa; WSC

I'd have you say–"No! no! I will not let you!" A Love-Lesson. Clément Marot. AWP

I'd heard/a night hawk calling 4th of July. William Carlos Williams. PoA

I'd hop all the way down the next long block. Boy Trash Picker. Jim Howard. FAZ

I'd just as soon be pushed by events to where I belong. Parentage. William Stafford. BiP

I'd leave my home, honey, I'd leave my home. Swannanoa Tunnel. *Anonymous.* FSW

I'd leave them both for lovin' you. Careless Love. *Anonymous.* UnTE

...I'd left the poem/seated motionless upon a wooden bench/with tears in its eyes. The Poem in the Park. Peter Davison. GOYP

I'd like a rondeau Getting by on Honesty. Stephen E. Smith. AMV-80

"I'd like a swig of ink." Said the monkey to the donkey. *Anonymous.* FaFP

I'd like to be/A grownup soon. Grownups. William Wise. TiPo

I'd like to be a lighthouse/With the ships all watching me. I'd Like to Be a Lighthouse. Rachel Field. SoPo

I'd like to be in Texas when they round-up in the spring. I'd Like to Be in Texas when They Round-Up in the Spring. *Anonymous.* CoSo

I'd like to be the sort of friend that you have been to me. A Friend's Greeting. Edgar A. Guest. BLPA; BLPL

I'd like to have served in the can. The Grandiloquent Goat. Carolyn Wells. MoShBr

I'd like to see the signs. Marx, the Sign Painter. Edgar Lee Masters. NoAm; TAP

I'd like you to meet/my daughter, Nebraska. Under Which Heading Does All This Information Go? Mira Teru Kurka. APU

I'd love to be a Fairy's child. I'd Love to Be a Fairy's Child. Robert Graves. BiCB; HBVY; SoPo

I'd love to meet that bloke who rode/The big white bull through Wagga. The Search. Charles Shaw. NOAV

I'd love to turn you on. A Day in the Life. The Beatles. PPoe

I'd love you just the same! To My Valentine. *Anonymous.* SoPo

...I'd make a quarry/With thousands of these quarter'd slaves, as high/As I could pick my lance. Coriolanus. William Shakespeare. FaBoPV

I'd make you Queen,/For I'd marry you. If I Were a Queen. Christina Georgina Rossetti. SiSoSe

I'd mastered it when I was five! Hints on Pronunciation for Foreigners. *Anonymous.* FaBoUs

I'd much rather sit here in the sun. Song: "I'd much rather sit there in the sun." Ruth Krauss. SO

I'd never get through that at all! In the Library. Michael Patrick Hearn. NTCP

I'd never have let Sir Hoker Poker/Carry away campeenio. As I Went up the Humber Jumber. *Anonymous.* FaBoNo

I'd never seen one like it. A Form of Passion. David McFadden. NOBC

I'd not move/Till you tired/Of my love. To a Butterfly. William Henry Davies. FM

"I'd rather be a swineheard in the hut, understood/by swine, than be a poet misunderstood by men." To a Young Poet Who Fled. John Logan. SM

I'd rather be with Rosie Nell, a-swinging in the lane. Rosie Nell (with music). *Anonymous.* AS

I'd rather choose to dye in Wine. The Fly. Francisco Gomez de Quevedo y Villegas. OBVE

I'd rather have a kiss from Johnny Faa's lips/Than all his gold and his money.' The Gypsy Countess. *Anonymous.* PoPle

I'd rather have Jesus, there's nothing beside. My Choice. Grace B. Renfrow. BePJ

I'd rather have one blossom now/Than a truck load when I'm dead. Kindness during Life. *Anonymous.* STF

I'd rather SEE than BE one! The Purple Cow. Gelett Burgess. AmePo; FaBoCo; FaBoNo; FaFP; FiBHP; FPL; GoTF; GrPl; HBV 1-2; HBVY; LBN; NA; NePA; NLV; NTCP; OBAL; OBCA; PoLf; PoPl; SoPo; TiPo; TreFS; YaD

I'd rather wade in wiggly mud/Than smell a yellow rose. Mud. Polly Chase Boyden. FaBV

I'd rather whistle for a man than for a sheep or cow. Whistle, Daughter, Whistle. *Anonymous.* FSW

I'd rather you'd not go unless you must. A Servant to Servants. Robert Frost. CMoP

I'd rather you'd remember and be sad. Remember (parody). *Anonymous.* ALV; BXAP

I'd really like/a few things with/qualities of their own. Thing Poem. Petra von Morstein. BoWoP

I'd remind them please, look at those knees/you got a Miss Ann's scrubbing. Sepia Fashion Show. Maya Angelou. BlSi

I'd sail all around this whole wide world/To the girl I love the best. Foggy Mountain Top. *Anonymous.* FSW

I'd sail with you,/Though I never sailed back again. A Sea-Song from the Shore. James Whitcomb Riley. TiPo

I'd say I love you but I don't know how. White-Haired Lover (excerpt). Karl Shapiro. PoA

I'd scratch out both his eyes. Hard Daddy. Langston Hughes. BANP

I'd see you all in hell. Cotton Field Song. *Anonymous.* ABF

I'd seen the tide,/it, too, and gone. Time and Tide. Hazel Washington Lamarre. PoNe

I'd set my foot on some fine ship/And sail the ocean around. When You and I Must Part. *Anonymous.* AmFP

I'd show you a good way to get in it. Heaven. *Anonymous.* UnTE

I'd silence all those cries/That desolate the land. The White Bird. Roy McFadden. ACV; NeIP

I'd sit astride the stem and guide/It straight to Fairyland and stay. A Fairy Voyage. *Anonymous.* SoPo

I'd slaughter/melons with my cock/for you. Melon-Slaughterer; or, A Sick Man's Praise for a Well Woman (parody). Robert Peters. BXAP

I'd sleep all the winter in a big fur bed. Furry Bear. A.(lan) A.(lexander) Milne. SoPo; TiPo

I'd sooner be here with my friends/Than at the diggins-oh. The Diggins-Oh. *Anonymous.* NOAV

I'd sooner walk the bottom of the ocean/Than I'd give up my collier sweetheart. I'll Have a Collier for My Sweetheart. Widnes Oliver. WTO

I'd spend it all upon you. As I Was Going up Pippen Hill. *Anonymous.* OxNR

I'd strangle in your raucous throat that song you sing. Sleepless Night. Egan O'Rahilly. AnIL; KiLC

I'd take the mountain-side e'en now,/And walk to Luggelaw again! The Pretty Girl of Loch Dan. Sir Samuel Ferguson. HBV 1-2

I'd tell my ardent love to you,/If I but knew–if I but knew. If I But Knew. Amy E. Leigh. AA

I'd tell the soldiers, "I'm the King!" If I Were King. A.(lan) A.(lexander) Milne. OnUR

I'd then sound the noise. Dorothy. Alfred Kreymborg. AnAmPo

I'd thwack you well to cure your pride, my Woman of/Three Cows! The Woman of Three Cows. James Clarence Mangan. AnIL; IrPN; NOBI; OnYI; OxBI

I'd toddle safely home and die–in bed. Base Details. Siegfried Sassoon. DBV; FF; HeIP; MMM; MoBrPo; NIP; OBSP; SoSe

I'd trade you the world just to share her pillow/On a Monday morning. On a Monday Morning. Cyril Tawney. OBET

I'd turn your snow to flame. The Amorist. *Anonymous.* UnTE

I'd want you away. Arthur. Tom Paulin. FaBoIP

I'd wear one by my side. If Wishes Were Horses. *Anonymous.* FaBoBe; HBV 1-2; OxNR

I'd wedge your ugly howling down your throat! The Drenching Night Drags On. Aogan O Rathaille. NOBI

I daily weep/And keep my sheep/That feed upon the down. The Maiden's Complaint. *Anonymous.* OLR

I damn such Fools! Go, go, you're bit.' The Day of Judgement. Jonathan Swift. BIrV; CEP; FaBoRV; NOBE; NOEC; OAEL 1-2; OBSV; PPP; TW

I damn such fools!–Go, go, you're bit. On the World. Jonathan Swift. AnIV

I damn your gods,/And thank you too. No More. Carl Clark. JB

I dance, for the joy of surviving,/on the edge of the road. An Old Cracked Tune. Stanley Jasspon Kunitz. GP; SM

I dangle, drowned in fire. Hera, Hung from the Sky. Carolyn Kizer. NMM

I dar not seyn quan che seyght "Pes!" How! Hey! It is non les. *Anonymous.* EnPo

I dare not hear my own footfall. Trees. Ted Hughes. NYBP

I dare not let my thought walk through? Of Love and Time. John Henderson. BoAV

I do not proclaim them to the sober.　Drinking Alone in the Moonlight.　Li T'ai-po.　AWP

I do not speak of mercy/Which is your name too　As I Am My Father's.　Rose Drachler.　VWA

I do not sprawl. I saw to the level of need.　The Beaver's Story.　Vernon Watkins.　NYBP

I do not think you want to hear/About this unimportant Peer.　Lord Heygate.　Hilaire Belloc.　OxBoLi

...I do not torture myself/with my shortcomings.　The Signal.　David Ignatow.　NNaP

I do not utter now/the word "love."　Letter to P.　Robert Friend.　NYBP

I do not want no patent thing/A-squealin' over me!　The New Church Organ.　Will Carleton.　PoLf

I do not want to walk that way again.　For Eager Lovers.　Genevieve Taggard.　AnAmPo

I do not waste my breath.　What the Bones Know.　Carolyn Kizer.　NePoAm-2

I do not wish to wake/to the cruel day of love.　Leave me my rest.　Fire at Murdering Hut.　Judith Wright.　ACV

I do this out of a certain humility.　Release.　Peter Schjeldahl.　ANYP

I do without all and face the winter regretting./The child in me who can play no longer.　Ago.　Elizabeth Jennings.　GOYP

I do your work so why ask.　Small Game.　Philip Levine.　AmPC

(I doe beleeve) they'd live no other where.　The Pleasant Life in Newfoundland.　Robert Hayman.　NOBC

"I don't agree,"/Said W. E. B.　Booker T. and W. E. B.　Dudley Randall.　BP; NoAm

I don't always understand his business.　The Orange Tree.　Ellen Pearce.　IHMS

"I don't believe that all of it is true!"　Always Battling.　Thomas O'Brien.　NeIP

I don't care!　Ou Phrontis.　Charles Causley.　AtBAP; NePoEA

I don't care a fig for her, so now let her go.　So I Let Her Go.　Anonymous.　AmFP

...I don't care a single straw, my love,/What the world says of me.'　The Saucy Sailor.　Anonymous.　OBET

"I don't care if I see another xerox as long as I live."　The Ty Cobb Story.　Tom Clark.　LiSp

I don't come/every fifteen seconds.　Blank Verse for a Fat Demanding Wife.　Jim Lindsey.　TW

I don't fancy he.　Disillusion.　Maureen Burge.　BrRo

I don't get nothing but the/mean old high sheriff.　Big Rock Jail.　Barefoot Bill.　BluL

I don't have to look for what will be/there, dark, pure, calling incomprehensibly.　Running Back.　Dave Smith.　LiSp

...I don't hear the calling/And dancing of cockatoo-crested morning.　'Morning, Morning.　Ray Mathew.　PoAu 1-2

I don't know any state I'd rather be in.　Affidavit in Platitudes.　E. B. White.　InMe

...I don't know/how much he's grasped/of our delicate situation.　Some Kind of Giant.　Sheila Pritchard.　BoAnP

I don't know. I don't know.　Recovery.　Patricia Y. Ikeda.　BrSi

"I don't know–I just came for/the ride."　Just for the Ride.　Anonymous.　FaFP

I don't know, I've always wanted to be Vera Lynn.　Flood.　Roger McGough.　FF

I don't know what will happen to me.　A Friend Advises Me to Stop Drinking.　Mei Yao Ch'en.　HoPM

I don't know whether it's pain.　Crickets and Locusts, Cicadas.　Rosalia de Castro.　PBWP

I don't know which loss hurt the worse–/My God or Santa Claus.　The Skeptic.　Robert W. Service.　PV

I don't know why I'm here.　Rilke.　Phyllis Webb.　PeCV

I don't like no railroad fool.　I Don't Like No Railroad Man (with music).　Anonymous.　AS

I/don't love.　A Poem Looking for a Reader.　Don L. Lee.　BP

I don't mind eels/Except as meals.　The Eel.　Ogden Nash.　FaBV

I don't see any cat-bird here.　The Cat Heard a Cat-Bird.　John Ciardi.　SO

I don't see it that way, O my Kamikaze heart.　The Japanese Consulate.　Frank Polite.　APU

"I don't see very many tears," he says.　Brest Left behind.　John Chipman Farrar.　PAH

I don't see why grown people stay/At home when they could be away.　When I Grow Up.　Rupert Sargent Holland.　BiCB

I don't see why you don't stay a little longer.　Stay All Night, Stay a Little Longer.　Anonymous.　AmFP

I don't sell for nothing less.　The Lady in the Pink Mustang.　Louise Erdrich.　TWSS

I don't think he'll ever come back.　On a Bookseller.　Oliver Goldsmith.　PV

...I don't think/I shall ever close my windows again.　This Morning.　Jay Wright.　NNP

"I don't think it's gonna make it."　Plato Instructs a Midwest Farmer.　David Palmer.　SUW

I don't understand.　A Boy Thirteen.　Jerry Irish.　DL

I don't want/more responsibility.　Tryst.　Eve Merriam.　NMM

I don't want that fistful/of glazed tulips you will bring.　Cold Snap.　Kathy Mangan.　AMV-80

...I don't want them/to learn anything, & no thunder crash/in their eyes.　Giving the Moon a New Chance.　Terry Stokes.　MOON

I don't want to get adjusted to this world.　I Don't Want to Get Adjusted.　Anonymous.　FSW

I don't want to live forever.　Portraits.　William Carson Fagg.　LFAC

I don't want to play in your yard/If you won't be good to me.　I Don't Want to Play in Your Yard.　Philip Wingate.　FSN; TreFT

I don't want your whiskey and I don't want your wine,/'Cause I don't let the girls worry my mind.　I Don't Let the Girls Worry My Mind.　Anonymous.　AmFP

I done done a-what ya' tol' me to do.　I Done Done What Ya' Tol' Me to Do.　Anonymous.　BoAN 1-2

I done give you my money/I done give you most anything　Poor Man Blues.　Henry Townsend.　BluL

I done sting my baby/and she won't stay away from me.　Mojo Hiding Woman.　Blind Boy Fuller.　BluL

I doodle handlebar/mustaches on the last Russian Czar.　Grandparents.　Robert Lowell.　LiTM

I doubt I could do it again.　June Song.　Abby Rosenthal.　AMV-81

I drag the cross of sacrifice/To the top of the cruel hill!　The Way of the Cross.　Joseph Ignatius Constantin Clarke.　CAW

I drained the madness/from your womb.　Reflections.　Anita Barrows.　NMM

I drank it when we met the gas/Beyond Gethsemane.　Gethsemane.　Rudyard Kipling.　FaBoTw

I dread it still at sixty-two.　The Dark.　Roy Fuller.　DuDa

I dreaded even a heaven with doors so chained.　The Unreturning.　Wilfred Owen.　MoBrPo

I dreaded you two thundering behind!　The Service.　Burges Johnson.　HBMV

I dream, I dream, I dream.　Old War-Dreams.　Walt Whitman.　OBSP

...I dream I/only dream I am awake.　The Great Bear Lake Meditations (excerpt).　J. Michael Yates.　NOBC

I dream no ill of Death.　Confession of Faith.　Elinor Wylie.　AnAmPo; APA; MoAmPo; SBG

I dream of axes.　Tables.　Naomi Clark.　AMV-80

I dream of/The New Now,/nebulous, nomadic.　Revving Up La Reve.　Joel Dailey.　APU

I dream that I'm a tree!　Moschatel.　D. J. O'Sullivan.　NeIP

I dreamt I saw a ghost last night/Under the apple tree!　Miss Jennian Jones.　Anonymous.　AmFP

I dred the Grekes; yea! when they offer gyftes!'　The Aeneid.　Virgil (Publius Vergilius Maro).　OBVE

I dremt that madness passes like a dream　That Which We Call a Rose.　Michael Dransfield.　CBAP

I drift across and dream the time/when ever-after time was mine.　Remembering Apple Times.　John T. Hitchner.　AMV-80

I drift in sweet enchantment back to rest.　Such Stuff as Dreams Are Made Of.　Thomas Wentworth Higginson.　AA

I/drink Alka Selzer/in my sleeping tin pot　Vision of Turtle (One).　Jim Brodey.　ANYP

I drink–and live–what has destroyed some men.　Thou Art Not Lovelier Than Lilacs.　Edna St.Vincent Millay.　BoLiVe

I drink from the well of cattle.　Wells.　Donald Hall.　NMP

I drink (from this full glass) to your return.　Letter to a Friend.　John Thompson.　BoAV; PoAu 1-2

I drink that water, and find it cool and clear.　The River.　Dabney Stuart.　NYBP

I drink to you/in smoke-mirled, blue-black,/polished sloes, bitter/and dependable.　Sloe Gin.　Seamus Heaney.　FaBoIP

I drive home/the proud cattle of my hands.　Picture Framing.　Bert Meyers.　ELU

I drive the spike.　Mike.　Anonymous.　ABF

I drop hook and worm, settle back,/wait for the pull.　Summit Lake.　Mark Thalman.　AMV-81

I drown in silence and endure/The thought of never getting better.　Convalescence.　James Philip McAuley.　CBAP

...I/drown in that/green sea.　Green Grass and Sea.　George Woodcock.　AMV-81

I durst hae ridden the world around/Had Christie Graeme been at my back.　The Bewick and the Graeme.　Anonymous.　OxBB

I dust the frame and set the picture straight.　Intaglio.　Henri Coulette.　NePoEA; PoCh

I dwell among the people.   The Voice of God.   Louis I. Newman.   GoTF; PoToHe; TreF

I dwell, laid up in safest nest.   Psalm IV.   Sir Philip Sidney.   FCP

I dwell, who fain would be where she is gone.   Fiammetta.   Giovanni Boccaccio.   GoBC

...I,e. we make it crazy or/no, and sometimes in the afternoon.   The Love Bit.   Joel Oppenheimer.   CoPo; PoM

I eat the world.   The Fat Man.   Vern Rutsala.   DFF

I eat two/and am full from the five.   Houses, Past and Present.   Eli Bachar.   VWA

I embrace the purpose of God, and the/doom assign'd.   Maud.   Alfred, Lord Tennyson.   MBW 1-2; OAEL; OAEP; OBWP; VLP

I embrace the world.   The Long Waters.   Theodore Roethke.   NaP; NYBP

I embraced in my heart that they hate/The diamond of justice   Jew.   Pierre Morhange.   VWA

I empty myself of my life and my life remains.   The Remains.   Mark Strand.   NYBP; PPP

& I end up having to leave the radio on all nite/for fear of missing something   She Employed the Familiar "Tu" Form.   Doug Fetherling.   NeAC

I ended my dream, I opened my eyes/and sprang from my pangs in a leap–awake!   The Midnight Court.   Brian Merriman.   NOBI

I enjoy a small enclave of the sun.   Guide to Jerusalem.   Dennis Silk.   VWA

I enter the lit house.   Parliament Hill Fields.   Sylvia Plath.   HaCAP

I envy the man with the hoe.   Lament while Descending a Shaft.   *Anonymous.*   AmFP

I erased her!   Magical Eraser.   Shel Silverstein.   WSC

I even feel sure you will assist me again, Master of insight & beauty.   Eleven Addresses to the Lord.   John Berryman.   CAPP; OxBC

I even forget english.   Song for My Father.   Jessica Hagedorn.   BrSi

I ever liked thy wine, though salt with/tears.   Departure.   May Riley Smith.   AA

I ever will with my weak able pen/Subscribe myself your Servant/Francis Ben.   A Messe of Nonsense.   *Anonymous.*   OBS

...I expect at any time/to see a man-bat flap/away from a stony turret.   Sarentino–South Tyrol.   Philip Brantingham.   AMV-80

I expect the stars will be bright/The woods full of bears.   My Cheap Lifestyle.   Eileen Myles.   APU

I expect to join the army by and by.   Shout for Joy.   *Anonymous.*   AmFP

...I explained/the blood each month and blood the first time.   Before Breakup on the Chena outside Fairbanks.   David McElroy.   Psk

I explore the pantry shelf.   Nursery Rhymes for the Tender-Hearted.   Christopher Morley.   FaFP

I fail for breath and cannot keep that pace.   The Wind Blows.   Donagh MacDonagh.   NeIP

I fain would bring my soul back safe to thee.   A Prayer.   Richard Le Gallienne.   TrPWD

I fain would hear, before I go, the wood-/notes of the veery.   The Veery.   Henry Van Dyke.   AA

I fain would know what she hath deserved.   Vixi Puellis Nuper Idoneus...   Sir Thomas Wyatt.   LiTL; OBEV

I fain would rest,/After a little while.   After a Little While.   James Ryder Randall.   CAW

I faint and fail when (thou, the perfect/whole)/I think of thee.   Infinity.   Philip Henry Savage.   AA

I faint in this obscurity,/Thou dewy dawn of memory.   Ode to Memory.   Alfred, Lord Tennyson.   VLP

I fainted, sunk, and dy'd away.   Fragment of Sappho.   Ambrose Philips.   OBEC

I' faith, in love am I!   Be Ye in Love with April-Tide?   Clinton Scollard.   AA; HBV 1-2

...I fall a/sleep in sweaty hay and dream my hair is made of feathers.   Childs Memory.   Terri Meyette Wilkins.   LFAC

I fall asleep/and dream of/almost touching you.   The Porch.   Gary Gildner.   AMV-80

I fashion a wedding for death/and I am the bride.   How Do I Enter the Silence of Stones.   Mona Sa'udi.   WPOW

I fear at night he will not come again.   Care-Charmer Sleep.   Bartholomew Griffin.   AAS; NIP

I fear I am a problem for whom/some new sorcery may be in store.   Learning to Speak.   Melvin Wilk.   AMV-81

(I fear I'd better drop the song/Of elephop and telephong!)   Eletelephony.   Laura E. Richards.   GoJo; NLV; NTCP; OBCA; OnUR; OxBChV; SoPo; TiPo; YaD

I fear Iambus would have grabbed his clothes/And written the ode at Weimar.   Not Lotte.   Katherine Hoskins.   ErPo

I fear no more.   For Forgiveness.   John Donne.   WGRP

I fear that I Should Be!   The Invisible Bridge.   Gelett Burgess.   NA; TreFT

I fear that, otherwise they will not know!   Tell All the World.   Harry Kemp.   HBMV

I fear that you will never know or guess.   At the beginning of winter a cold spirit comes.   *Anonymous.*   BoWoP

I fear the stab, the graunch, the touch of metal.   A Dentist's Window.   James Keir Baxter.   OxBC

I fear thee more than hadst thou stood/Full-panoplied in womanhood.   To Olivia.   Francis Thompson.   MoBrPo

I fear what I shall find.   On a Return from Egypt.   Keith Douglas.   NeBP; NePoEA

I feasted on your vintage.   In Celebration.   Ellen Bass.   NMM

I fed this child/through the night/whom now/I run from.   Chance Meeting.   Susan Griffin.   NPGG

I, fed with judgment, in a fleshly tomb, am/Buried above ground.   Lines Written during a Period of Insanity.   William Cowper.   EBEV; FiP; HAP; InPo; NoP; OAEL 1-2; PPP; Prf; TW

I feed on your Name like a cockroach on a crumb–this cock-/roach is holy.   Psalm III.   Allen Ginsberg.   CAPP

I feed the porch with fragrant smoke,/Strew roses on the stair.   Prelude.   Arthur Christopher Benson.   OBVV

I feel as hollow as a fiddle,/Working so many hours,' said Liddell.   Liddell and Scott.   Thomas Hardy.   OxBoLi

I feel at peace: tonight at least, content.   Eating Lechon, with my Brothers and Sisters.   Luis Cabalquinto.   BrSi

...I feel chilly/and grown old.   A Toccata of Galuppi's.   Robert Browning.   AnFE; EnLi 1-2; GTBS-P; HAP; HBV 1-2; LiTB; LoBV; MaVP; NCEP; NOBE; NOBV; NoP; OAEL 1-2; OAEP; TEP; WHA

I feel de spirit, move-in' in my heart,/I will pray Jordan pray.   Ev'ry Time I Feel de Spirit.   *Anonymous.*   BoAN 1-2

–I feel faint kisses creeping on my lips.   Charleville.   Arthur Rimbaud.   SyP

I feel footsteps moving under mine.   High Field–First Day of Winter.   Gary Eddy.   AMV-80

"I feel good."   Image in the Mirror.   Peggy Susberry Kenner.   JB

I feel him tickling my heart-strings.   Cupid Drowned.   [James Henry] Leigh Hunt.   HBV 1-2

"I feel I'd like to go:/"Around the corner..."   Around the Corner.   *Anonymous.*   FSW

I feel, I feel, I feel, I feel like a morning star.   Shew! Fly, Don't Bother Me.   Billy Reeves.   PSoN

I feel its energy, its calm.   Snowdrops.   George MacBeth.   OBCP

I feel its tears upon my hand.   The Shamrock.   Maurice Francis Egan.   AA; HBV 1-2

I feel its texture, though the gate is fast.   Those Hours When Happy Hours Were My Estate.   Edna St. Vincent Millay.   PrIm

I feel like, I feel like, Lord,/I feel like my time ain't long.   I Feel Like My Time Ain't Long.   *Anonymous.*   BoAN 1-2; OuSiCo

I feel like I'm on my journey home.   The Saint's Delight.   *Anonymous.*   TrAS

I feel like the road.   Unemployment.   William Mills.   HoPM

...I feel/Most at home with what is Real.   Doggerel by a Senior Citizen.   W. H. Auden.   NLV; NOBL

I feel my sun's heat, though his light I miss.   Diana.   Henry Constable.   OBSC

...I feel no single/treachery but what you are having been these few seconds/something like my self   The People's Choice: The Dream Poems II.   LeRoi (Imamu Amiri Baraka) Jones.   BiP

I feel nostalgic.   Old Movies.   John Cotton.   FF

I feel safe from my own or even Milton's hell?   A Willing Suspension.   John Holmes.   PoCh

I feel so break-up, I want to go home.   John B. Sails.   *Anonymous.*   AS; FSW

I feel so disgusted/I've got them lowdown rounder blues   Lowdown Rounder's Blues.   Peg Leg Howell.   BluL

I feel so shy, I'll really die, A walking for that cake.   Walking for That Cake.   Ed [(or Ned)] Harrigan.   BLSo

I feel that Bunny's at my bedside/In a white cotton nightcap,/Tickling me with his whiskers.   Mr. McGregor's Garden.   Mebdh McGuckian.   FaBoIP

I feel the autumn fail–all that slow fire/Denied in me, who has denied desire.   The Sequel.   Theodore Roethke.   NYBP

I feel the coming glory of the Light!   Credo.   Edwin Arlington Robinson.   AnNE; CMoP; MoAmPo; NePA; OxBA; TAP; TrCP; TreFT; WGRP

...I feel the ease/of whiskey and the gallows and I rest.   Depression.   Rex Burwell.   AMV-80

I feel the flames of hottest summer day.   Astrophel and Stella, LXXXIX.   Sir Philip Sidney.   AAS; SiPS

I feel the moon's hub unhinge from center/And roll berserk.   Hitchhiker.   Jack Marshall.   NYBP

I feel the promptings of Satanic power,/While you do homage unto me alone.   Modern Love, XXVIII.   George Meredith.   VLP

I feel the same when you are near.   When You're Away.   Samuel Hoffenstein.   FiBHP; PoL

I feel the summer in the spring.   Spring Song.   *Anonymous.*   OBVE

I feel the truth; so let the world surmise.   Modern Love, XLVIII.   George Meredith.   EnLi 1-2; NoP; OAEL 1-2; OAEP; VLP

I had been vext, if vext I had not been.   Astrophel and Stella, LXXXVII. Sir Philip Sidney.   AAS; SiPS

I had bent and broke, I should not dare/To linger in the shadows there. Tolerance.   Thomas Hardy.   MoRP

I had borne thee savage daughters/And beautiful fierce sons.   The Warrior Maid.   Anna Hempstead Branch.   HBV 1-2

I had buried it so low/In my mind!   The Secret.   James Stephens.   WSC

I had eaten the apple ere you were weaned.'   At the Altar-Rail.   Thomas Hardy.   BrPo

I had him sit next me at table....   Song of Myself.   Walt Whitman.   PoNe

I had his answer, wise as yours.   Colloquy.   Weldon Kees.   NaP; NYBP

I had holes in my feet/from the nails.   Invitation.   Victor Contoski.   PV

I had liefer go to a tryst with thee/Than to a tryst with a foolish woman. The Bell of the Hermitage.   Anonymous.   CAW

I had more pleasure in the other dream.   Another Way.   Ambrose Bierce. AA

I had no hope of getting home.   In the Snowfall.   Gwerfyl Mechain. BoWoP

I had not expected this. The kids/Are screaming and tearing at my eyes.   The Election.   Robert Pack.   CoPo

I had not expected to be/an ordinary woman.   The thirty eighth year. Lucille Clifton.   AmPA

I had not learned I could dispense with love/Like a blind man unhindered by the gloom.   Dedication.   Drummond Allison.   FaBoTw

I had rather love Phillis both false and unkind,/Than ever be freed from her power.   The Conquest of Granada.   John Dryden.   DiPo

I had slept too deeply/to enjoy that beautiful scene.   All Night Long.   Nina Cassian.   VWA

I had stones in my hands.   Heron.   Stanley Plumly.   AmPA

...I had to climb up/18 years to hear their names.   August 12, 1952. Charles Fishman.   AMV-81

I had to let those storm-lit valleys heal.   The Wound.   Thom Gunn. NePoEA

I had to scrape my canvas clean/to begin again with a voluptuous death/ posing naked on a bed.   A Fiction of Edvard Munch.   Mary di Michele. CaPN

I had walked out the back door/onto scorched ground–safe again.   Staying Ahead.   Malcolm Glass.   AMV-81; FAZ

I hadn't oughter passed her up the time I had the chance.   Thais.   Newman Levy.   FiBHP; InMe

I hae but only ae daughter,/And wedded to her ye'se be.   Young Allan. Anonymous.   BaBo

I hail'd the place where months before,/The Tories took me from the shore. The Descent on Middlesex.   Peter St. John.   PAH

I hail my fathers, sing their blood to the leaf.   Summer Acres.   Anne Wilkinson.   CaP

I hand her the saw.   Making a Door.   Dennis Schmitz.   LCAP

I hand it back to gather dust on the shelf.   The Miner's Helmet.   George Macbeth.   OxBTC

I hang, behead, electrocute.   The Hanging.   J. E. H. MacDonald.   OBCV

I happy am, if well with you.   In Reference to Her Children, 23. June, 1656. Anne Bradstreet.   BoWoP; SBG; TAP

I harden like a scab.   Dido: Swarming.   Kathleen Spivack.   PoA

I hardly dare come close to you.   The Little Boy to the Locomotive. Benjamin R. C. Low.   HBMV

I hardly ever repent.   Reminiscent Reflection.   Ogden Nash.   FaBoCo

I hardly hear a Woman's Clack.   On His Own Deafness.   Jonathan Swift. BIrV; FaBoEE

"I hardly know–I've only written ten."   What hundred books are best.   John Kendrick Bangs.   CenHV

I hardly know/Why Wattle should not do.'   Under the Wattle.   Douglas Brook Wheelton Sladen.   OBVV

–I hastily walk away fill'd with the/bitterest envy.   When I Peruse the Conquer'd Fame.   Walt Whitman.   ELU; MCCG; PoEL 1-5

I hate a fool that starves her love/Onely to feed her pride.   'Tis Now Since I Sate Down.   Sir John Suckling.   AnAnS 2; CavP; PoEL 1-5; SeCV 1-2

I hate poetry with a passion/& write poems.   The External Element.   David McFadden.   NeAC

I hate such noodles, I do.   Fragment of a Song.   Lewis (Charles Lutwidge Dodgson) Carroll.   FaBoNo

I hate the sin, and yet I sin alway.   Sonnet.   Pedro Malon de Chaide. CAW

I hate to go above you.   The Fear of Flying.   Mona Van Duyn.   NMM

...I hated him. He weeps,/Solemnizing his loss.   The Dead Bride.   Geoffrey Hill.   TW

I have a great desire to move elsewhere.   Work.   Andrei Codrescu.   EAS

I have a kind of halloween mask/Which I am afraid to put on.   Empire of Dreams.   Charles Simic.   LCAP

I have a need of water near.   Exiled.   Edna St. Vincent Millay.   EtS; MOS; PoRA

I have a place where my spirit sings,/In the hollow of God's Palm.   The Place of Peace.   Edwin Markham.   GoTF; TreFT; TRV

I have a sorrow not wholly mine, but another's.   On a Certain Engagement South of Seoul.   Hayden Carruth.   AmFN; NMP

I have all sensuous hell to love you in.   Epithalamium for Cavorting Ghosts. Dachine Rainer.   NePoAm-2

I have always found it so.   I Have Always Found It So.   Birdie Bell. BLRP

I have always loved the word guitar.   Guitar.   David St. John.   MAYP

I have asked to be left a few tears/And some laughter.   Bundles.   Carl Sandburg.   MoAmPo

I have awakened at Missoula, Montana, utterly happy.   In a Train.   Robert Bly.   CAPP; NaP; PoL

I have beaten out my exile.   The Rest.   Ezra Pound.   AmP; MoAB; MoAmPo; NoAm; NOBA; OxBA; PP

I have been a good provider, but I/B'lieve I been misled   Revenue Man Blues.   Charlie Patton.   BluL

"I have been a man," the clod said.   The Clod.   Edwin Curran.   HBMV

"I have been a tormentor the whole of/my life,/But I neer was tormented so as with/your wife."   The Farmer's Curst Wife (A version).   Anonymous. BaBo; ESPB; ViBoFo

I have been faithful to thee, Cynara! in my fashion.   Non Sum Qualis Eram Bonae Sub Regno Cynarae.   Ernest Christopher Dowson.   AWP; BLPA; BoLoP; BrPo; EnLoPo; FaBoBe; FaFP; FPL; GBL; GoTF; GTBS-P; HAP; HBV 1-2; HeIP; InPo; LitL; MoBrPo; NOBE; NoP; OAEL 1-2; OBEV; OBMV; OBNC; OBVV; PG; PoPl; PrIm; TEP; TreF; TrGrPo; ViBoPo; VLP

I have been happy, so long.   Night Song from Backbone Mountain.   Daniel Mark Epstein.   TAT

I have been her kind.   Her Kind.   Anne Sexton.   CAPP; CoAP; FF; HaCAP; HeIP; LiTM; MP; PPP; TAP; TwCP; WPOW

I have been one acquainted with the Night.   Acquainted with the Night. Robert Frost.   AmP; AP; CMoP; CoBMV; DiPo; ForPo; FPL; HAP; LiTM; MoAmPo; MP; NePA; NoAm; NOBA; PoLf; PPP; SoSe; TAP; TwCP; VGW; WeW

I have been proud, and said, "My love, my own!"   Sonnets from the Portuguese, XXXVIII.   Elizabeth Barrett Browning.   BLPA; BLPL; CTC; FaBoBe; HBV 1-2; PoPl; ViBoPo

I have been so instinctively thorough/About my crevice and burrow.   A Drumlin Woodchuck.   Robert Frost.   GoYe; NoAm; NOBA

"I have been too prolific."   I Knew a Cappadocian.   Alfred Edward Housman.   FiBHP

I have been waiting/for you to come by.   Waiting for You to Come By. Simon J. Ortiz.   CDW

I have begun to think.   Forthfaring.   Winifred Howells.   AA

I have bitten myself underneath!'   Limerick: "There was an old man of Blackheath."   Anonymous.   CenHV

I have but this to say.   Lydia.   Lizette Woodworth Reese.   AA

I have carried it with me too long. I give it back.   Elegy for My Father. Mark Strand.   Prf

I have caught the shining falcon.   Mariushka's Wedding Song.   Anonymous. HW

I have chatter'd like a pye.   Anacreon's Dove.   Samuel Johnson.   AWP

I have come a long way/after Death.   Elegy and Flame.   Horace Gregory. FYAP

I have come back/As empty-handed as I went.   Back.   Weldon Kees. NaP; PrIm

I have come to rest beneath its sheer net.   The Poem.   David Schloss.   PoA

I have done my duty, as a public spirited citizen, in any/case.   Confession Overheard in a Subway.   Kenneth Fearing.   LiTA; LiTM; WaP

I have dreamed: let me wake!   The Dream.   Arthur Symons.   SyP

I have driven, I have driven, the maiden into the damp/earth!   Sorrow. Anonymous.   AWP

I have endured as best I could,/Threescore and ten!   Threescore and Ten. Richard Henry Stoddard.   HBV 1-2

I have felt to soar in freedom and in the fullness of/power, joy, volition.   I Have Not So Much Emulated the Birds that Musically Sing.   Walt Whitman.   RFM

I have forgotten what.   Shadow Life.   Robert F. Reid, III.   AMV-81

I have forgotten you.   Death Songs.   L.V. Mack.   PoBA

I have found that Amon is given to me thereby/For ever and ever.   The Lovely Delightful Song of Thy Sister.   Anonymous.   LiTW

I have found Thee–/My Hiding Place!   My Hiding Place.   Kathryn T. Bowsher.   STF

I have given my answer.   Personal.   Langston Hughes.   AmNP; NOBA

I have gone forever,/Forever.   Bride's Lament.   Sappho.   HW

I have got ten,/And keep them all like gentlemen.   The Dove Says, Coo, Coo. Anonymous.   PBBP

I have got wet/With the dew of the lower boughs!   Two Poems.   Hitomaro. LiTW

I have grown more frail than a thin yellow/chrysanthemum   Poem to the Tune of "Tsui Hua Yin."   Li Ching-chao.   WPOW

I have heard Thy voice, I have met Thy/call.   God's Call.   Anonymous. STF

I have watched them and I know.   How the Flowers Grow.   (Thomas Nicoll Hepburn) "Setoun. Gabriel"   SoPo

I have work to dream.   (End) of Summer (1966).   Bill Knott.   EAS

I have wrapped my dreams in a silken cloth,/And laid them away in a box of gold.   For a Poet.   Countee Cullen.   GoSl; PoNe; TTY

I haven't got a key!   Lock the Dairy Door.   *Anonymous.*   OxNR; PBBP

I haven't seen the moon in two years.   He Says He Wrote by Moonlight. Katharyn Machan Aal.   AMV-81

I haven't the heart to poke poor Billy   Some Ruthless Rhymes.   Harry Graham.   CenHV

I haven't the slightest thing to fear.   The Bird.   John Hollander.   PPP

I haven't thought for thirty years/Of Lalage and Barbara.   The Private Dining Room.   Ogden Nash.   ExPo; NYBP; PoCh

I having no power over my shadow.   Song of a Jewish Boy.   J.M.   TrJP

I heap the stones to make his cairn/Where many sleep as sound as he.   A Girl's Song.   Katharine Tynan Hinkson.   OnYI

I hear and is my heart not badly shaken?   Shancoduff.   Patrick Kavanagh. CIP; FaBoIP; FaBoTw; IPY; NoP; OxBI

I hear grass breaking in rabbits' teeth.   Lenox Christmas Eve 68.   Sam Cornish.   CNA

I hear her passing sigh/Her final whisperings.   Bird and the Muse.   Marya Zaturenska.   PoA

I hear His voice among the trees,/And I am not afraid.   Eventide.   Caroline Atherton Briggs Mason.   GoTF; TreFS

I hear it in the deep heart's core.   The Lake Isle of Innisfree.   William Butler Yeats.   BoC; BrPo; CMoP; CoBMV; DiPo; FaBoPa; FaBoPP; FaBV; FaFP; FaPoR; FPL; GoTF; GTBS; InPK; InPS; LiTM; MBW 1-2; MCCG; MoAB; MoBrPo; NoAm; NOBE; NoP; OAEP; OBEV; OBVV; OnYI; OxBTC; PAI; PoPl; PoRA; PrIm; RoGo; TEP; TreF; TrGrPo; VLP; WeW; WHA

I hear it with longing/as they cry out the hours.   Sweet Voice of the Garb. Suibne Geilt.   NOBI

I hear my neighbour's bees.   By the Road to the Air-Base.   Yvor Winters. CrMA

I hear my sweet bird sing.   The White Bird.   Anna Akhmatova.   LiTW

I hear myself hearing/my breathing. Loud.   Next Year, in Jerusalem. Shirley Kaufman.   VWA

I hear names leaving the bark/in growing numbers and flying north Footprints on the Glacier.   William Stanley Merwin.   NoAm

I hear strange voices calling through the night.   The Haunted House. George Sylvester Viereck.   AnAmPo

I hear that fathomless ocean breaking about us/In sleep, and all things borne to dissolution.   The Estate: "Waking by Night'.   Charles Brasch.   AnNZ

I hear the autumn winds; and it is cold.   The Widow.   Mariana B. Davenport.   AMV-80

I hear the beat/Of the Talking Drums!   The Talking Drums.   Kojo Gyinaye Kyei.   PBA

I hear the call of the singing firs/In the hush of the golden moon.   The Lost Lagoon.   [(Emily() Pauline Johnson.   BPAW

I hear the faery spirits shriek in hell.   The Salesman.   Robert Mezey. NePoEA

I hear the frosty clatter of goat hooves.   The Teacher.   David Fisher. NPGG

I hear the knelling horn.   Cries Out of Blindness.   Tristan Corbiere.   LiTW

I hear the world's weeping/and my unborn song.   My Body.   Rachel Korn. VWA

I hear their broken consonants...   Remains of an Indian Village.   Al Purdy. NOBC

I hear their gentle voices calling "Old Black Joe."   Old Black Joe.   Stephen Collins Foster.   FaFP; GoTF; PSoN; TreFS

I hear their wae/Greetan greetan dark and daw,/Their dregy ere I dae. Coronach.   Alexander Scott.   OxBS

I hear what she is saying!   Mad Song.   Hester Sigerson.   AnIV

I hear you, I will come.   A Shropshire Lad.   Alfred Edward Housman. BrPo

I hear your clock tick out the hour of grace.   Moriturus.   Madelaine Marie. PeHV

I heard a hearty laugh performed.   Protect Me.   Hans Adler.   AMV-80

I heard a horseman riding/And the sound of running feet.   The Song of Samuel Sweet.   Charles Causley.   OBNV

I heard a mourner say,/Give me Jesus.   Give Me Jesus.   *Anonymous.* BoAN 1-2; BPo

...I heard him squeal/Before he died beneath my wheel.   Love for a Hare. Melvin Walker La Follette.   NePoEA-2

I heard his vow,–God heard it too,/Before he pass'd!   Solemn Rondeau. Charles Dent Bell.   OBVV

I heard my companion say/I won't see your smiling face again   Memphis Minnie-Jitis Blues.   Memphis Minnie.   BluL

I heard new feet sound in the statued porch/And salutations I had heard before.   The Lady of Life.   Thomas Michael Kettle.   ACP

I heard only the sigh of the wind.   While I walked in the moonlight.   Lady Murasaki Shibiku.   LiTW

I heard that cry as though/It were of a heart-moving voice long dead/The deathless echo.   An Inconclusive Evening.   Frances Bellerby.   FaBoTw

I heard the dead men singing in the sun.   Supremacy.   Edwin Arlington Robinson.   NoAm

I heard the dust falling between the walls.   Redeployment.   Howard Nemerov.   LiTM; NePA; OBWP; TrJP

I heard the lament of all other pain,/all other life.   The Goat.   Umberto Saba.   VWA

I heard the mighty bars/Of thunder-gusts that shook heaven's dome,/And moved the balanced stars.   Wesley in Heaven.   Thomas Edward Brown. OBNC

I heard the soothing summer-rain.   At Sea.   John Townsend Trowbridge. AmePo; EtS

I heard the tapping of a blind man's stick.   Sight.   W. W. Gibson. MoBrPo

...I heard the throng/Of inner voices praise her golden head.   Beauty and the Bird.   Dante Gabriel Rossetti.   FM

I heard the wild geese flying/In the dead of the night.   Wild Geese.   Elinor Chipp.   HBMV; TiPo

I heard them their speech was foreign already/and blazed like the extinguishing of a mountain   Emigration.   Anita Barrows.   NMM

I heard your laughter rumble from my belly.   My Dim-Wit Cousin. Theodore Roethke.   DFF

I held Harriet until my lips burned   True Love.   Joe Johnson.   CNA

I held the man for nothing in my arms.   Saint Judas.   James Wright. ConAP; LCAP; NMP; NOBA; SM

I here, thou there, yet both but one.   A Letter to Her Husband, Absent upon Public Employment.   Anne Bradstreet.   AmP; APA; CBEP; HAP; HeIP; LiTA; MAmP; NoP; OxBA; SCAP

I hide & watch/he will never find my wooden legs   I Have Cut an Eagle. James Koller.   PoM

I hoe in one furrow/And heap all my fill.   Monogamania.   Eve Merriam. UnTE

I hold in both hands such weight/it is my only description.   I Keep to Myself Such Measures.   Robert Creeley.   NoAm

I hold in fief/Four square feet of the orient.   The Prayer Rug.   Sara Beaumont Kennedy.   HBMV

I hold it towards you.   This Living Hand.   John Keats.   BoLoP; CABA; HAP; InPK; InPS; MBW 1-2; NoP; OAEL 1-2; OBSP; PAI; SyP

I hold my daughter's hand/For comfort.   Scene from a Dream.   Janet Campbell Hale.   STE

I hold/My father's ghost in my arms in his dark doorway.   My Father's Ghost.   David Wagoner.   Str

I hold my head as proudly high/As any man.   The Road to the Bow. James David Corrothers.   BANP

I hold my head in my hands/and bring away hair.   Radiation Leak.   Jody Aliesan.   LTB

I hold my word tight to my breast.   Therefore I Must Tell the Truth. Torlino.   ExPo

I hold thee and my thoughts arise/To Christ, His Cross!   The Stick.   May O'Rourke.   HBMV

...I hold/whatever offers refuge.   Cold is cold.   Rooftop Winter.   Dwayne Thorpe.   AMV-80

...I hold–whatever tugs/the other end–I hold that string.   Father and Son. William Stafford.   GP

I hold you in my hands.   Heart's Needle.   W.D. Snodgrass.   NCSH; NMP; NoPoEA

I hold you in those arms.   I Hid You.   Miklos Radnoti.   LLLT; VWA

I holler "CHOW!" and then I RUN!   Have I Got Dogs!   William Cole. GDP

I home on the lock/and my life explodes about me.   Walking Home at Night. Daniel Weissbort.   VWA

I honor shit for saying: We go on.   The Excrement Poem.   Maxine W. Kumin.   FaBoWP

I hope he dies before/they teach him a new tongue.   Alien.   William Price Turner.   OxBS

I hope/Her mother washed her mouth with soap.   Story.   Dorothy Parker. InMe; MaC

I hope his soul's in Heaven for now and eternity.   Jimmy Judge. *Anonymous.*   AmFP

I hope I haven't offended you/If I've said anything wrong.   Teamster's Song. *Anonymous.*   TrAS

I hope I shall lie down some day,/Lie down and sleep.   A blue-eyed phantom far before.   Christina Georgina Rossetti.   EG

I hope I shall with Jesus reign,/And therefore I will serve him.   O, That I Had Some Secret Place.   *Anonymous.*   AmFP

I hope I still may play the lyre.   Epitaph on an Irish Priest.   *Anonymous.* FaBoEE

An I hope ilk ane sal sae be servd/That treats ane honest man sae.   The Bonny Birdy.   *Anonymous.*   ESPB

I hope it's Michael Dan.   An Ulsterman.   Lynn Doyle.   OnYI

I hope nobody gets the worst.   I Married in My Youth a Wife.   J. V. Cunningham.   TW

I hope she will not come again!   Aunt Selina.   Carol Haynes.   HBVY

I hope she will not now complain/to high, to low, to high, to low, to low. The Jovial Tinker; or, The Willing Couple.   *Anonymous.*   CoMu; UnTE

(I hope someone looked after the pigs.)   Hernando de Soto.   Rosemary and Stephen Vincent Benét.   NLV

I hope that none of our enemies will know for the want of places.   The Owslebury Lads.   *Anonymous.*   OBET

I hope the whole unimportant affair is/soon forgotten. The analogies are too trite.   A Sparrow's Feather.   George Barker.   NYBP

I hope they had time, and light/Enough to read it.   An Image from Beckett. Derek Mahon.   CIP

I hope they'll lay us where we play'd, just twenty years ago.   Twenty Years Ago.   Dill Armor Smith.   BFSS; BLPA

I hope to be an emperor under my own mausoleum.   Marcus Aurelius.   C. H. Sisson.   OxBC

...I hope to be proud/Of the little rascal when I come back.   Old Father Annum.   Leroy F. Jackson.   SiSoSe

I hope to please you better, love, for now is the time.   Polly Oliver's Rambles. *Anonymous.*   ViBoFo

I hope to see my Pilot face to face/When I have crost the bar.   Crossing the Bar.   Alfred, Lord Tennyson.   BiP; BLRP; BoLiVe; DiPo; DL; EnL; EtS; FaBoRV; FaBV; FaFP; FaPoR; FF; FiP; FPL; GoTF; GTBS; HBV 1-2; HBVY; HeIP; LiTB; MaVP; MBW 1-2; MCCG; MOS; NOBE; NOBV; NoP; OAEL 1-2; OAEP; OBEV; OBNC; OBVV; OHFP; PoLf; SoSe; TEP; TrCP; TreF; TrGrPo; TRV; ViBoPo; VLP; WBLP; WGRP; WHA

I hope to see the day when you'll/Be working for a dollar.   Song of the Leadville Mine Boss.   Don Cameron.   PoOW

I hope to win her in the end–/My daughter.   An Old Song Resung.   Charles Larcom Graves.   CenHV

I hope we can be together in the next.   There is a soldier on a battlefield. *Anonymous.*   BoWoP

I hope we'll meet on Canaan's shore.   Parting Friends.   *Anonymous.*   ABF

I hope we'll meet with those we loved some forty years ago.   Forty Years Ago.   *Anonymous.*   HBV 1-2

...I hope/you always remember our pact. I will.   With Schoolchildren. Willis Barnstone.   GLGT

I hope you are smothered/in the fall of a huge yellow moon.   The Nigga Section.   Welton Smith.   BPo

"I hope you/don't mind."   A Remembrance of a Color inside a Forest.   Ray A. Young Bear.   CDW

I hope you have better luck in your poem/Than you had in mine.   The Newly Pressed Suit.   Roger McGough.   NoAm

I hope you'll make sense of the notes.   Limerick: "No water. dry rocks and dry throats."   Wendy Cope.   FaBoWP

I hope you'll relieve me and let me carry on./Derry down, down, down derry down.   The Coal-Owner and the Pitman's Wife.   *Anonymous.*   CoMu

I hoped you'd see the sandgrains on my coat.   The Beaches (excerpt). Robin Hyde.   AnNZ; FaBoWP

I huddle, hoard, hold out, hold on, hold on.   Cold.   Robert Francis. LCAP; NePoAm-2; PoA

An' I hug her, an' hug my Pa/An' love him purt'nigh much as Ma.   A Boy's Mother.   James Whitcomb Riley.   HBVY; OHIP

I hum a mortal tune/and/am all and none of those.   At Veronica's.   Robert Peterson.   NeAC

I hump the jug and fill her up with fiction.   The Minstrel's Last Lay.   John Barth.   OBAL

I hung his coat and trousers to roast before a fire.   Taffy.   *Anonymous.* BBGG

I hung his coat and trousers to roast before a fire.   Taffy Was a Welshman. *Anonymous.*   GBP; OxNR

I, hungry, kissed the brogue upon her mouth.   Nora.   Dora Sigerson Shorter.   HBMV

I hunt among stones   The Kingfishers.   Charles Olson.   CMoP; InPS; NeAP; NOBA; PoM

I hurl a brick through/a store front window/and disappear.   Black Warrior. Norman Jordan.   PoBA

I, I, The future that mends everything.   The Elementary Scene.   Randall Jarrell.   CMoP; LCAP

I identify with everybody, even the heresiarchs.   Eleven Addresses to the Lord.   John Berryman.   CAPP; OxBC

I, if I perish, perish; in the name of God I go.   A Royal Princess.   Christina Georgina Rossetti.   BrRo

I implore Neptune to claim his child to-day!   At the Carnival.   Anne Spencer.   BANP; BlSi; CDC; NoAm; PoNe

I, in a dimness, still, silent,/in the twilight before morning,/expired.   Raya Brenner.   Pinhas Sadeh.   VWA

I in a new understanding of my confusion.   In Broken Images.   Robert Graves.   PPoe

...I, in mine, celebrate the love-choir.   Ovid in the Third Reich.   Geoffrey Hill.   FaBoMo; NoAm; PoL

I in my deanery, she in her booth.   Wildtrack: "Lie easy in your secret cradle."   John Wain.   NAs

I inch along the labyrinth,/scarcely in motion.   Bridges and Tunnels.   Beth Bentley.   EyDe

I intended an Ode;/And it turn'd to a Sonnet.   Urceus Exit: Triolet.   Henry Austin Dobson.   CenHV; GTBS; HBV 1-2; OBEV

I invited them home   An Easy Decision.   Kenneth Patchen.   CTBA; LOW

I invoke the land of Ireland!   Invocation to Ireland.   Amergin.   AnIV; OnYI

I, Jesus, saw thee,–doubt it not,–/And read the secrets of thy heart!   I Saw Thee.   Ray Palmer.   HBV 1-2

I joy, may I sweet flowers for glory breed,/Whether thou getst them green, or let them seed.   Upon Wedlock, and Death of Children.   Edward Taylor. AmPP; AP; NoP

I just can't bring myself to go and get some meat.   Personal Song. Arnatkoak.   WTO

I just deswear we won't be here long   Big Apple Blues.   Sonny Boy Williamson.   BluL

I just love to hear my/baby call my name   Take a Walk around the Corner. Leroy Carr.   BluL

I just need a few moments to recover   Poem after Apollinaire.   Ira Sadoff. AmPA

I just saw a lady-bug/And heard a robin sing.   Wise Johnny.   Edwina Fallis. SiSoSe; SUS; TiPo

I just sit here all a-lone and cry an' moan, cry an' moan.   Friendless Blues. Mercedes Gilbert.   TrAS

I just was telling Adela/How many birds it struck since May.   Count Gismond.   Robert Browning.   VLP

I just whispered back that the Seminole must/also feel Kachina.   Poem to a Redskin.   Wendy Rose.   CDW

I keep asking.   Looking for a Rest Area.   Stephen P. Dunn.   AmPA

I keep for life/how light/shapes how/lives deepen.   Photographer.   Philip Booth.   EyDe

I keep for you a running account.   The History of Communications and a Running Account.   Pien Chih-lin.   LiTW

I keep me to myself.   Three.   John N. Morris.   GP

I keep my money in an old tow bag/Oh! doo dah day!   Gwine to Run All Night; or, De Camptown Races.   Stephen Collins Foster.   OBAL

"I keep my nerve, I keep my nerve!"   Winter Song.   David Daiches. NYBP

I keep the old track of mortality.   Inspiration.   Wilfred Wilson Gibson. WGRP

I keep them wide apart.   The Songs I Sing.   Charles G. Blanden.   HBV 1-2

I keep what you gave.   On Devenish Island.   Frank Ormsby.   CIP

I kept it till it ran alone.   Riddle: "As I was walking in a field of wheat." *Anonymous.*   OxNR

I kept losing my way.   How I Escaped from the Labyrinth.   Philip Dacey. PoL; PPJ

I kept my king, gold, child, and secret.   Mythics.   Helen Chasin.   DFT

I kept my mouth/shut.   Vegas.   Charles Bukowski.   NoP

I kept the door wide,/Closed it after him and pushed the bolt.   The Bull Moses.   Ted Hughes.   NoP

I kept the little fortress fast./–Be good to me.   The Door.   Mary Carolyn Davies.   HBMV

I killed even the Thembu king.'   Boast of Masopha.   Z. D. Mangoaela. PeSA

I killed him there and threw him out,   Another Sin I Had Forgot. *Anonymous.*   PeD

I kiss each bead, and strive at last to learn/To kiss the Cross.   The Rosary. Robert Cameron Rogers.   AA; BLSo; FaBoBe; FSN; HBV 1-2; TreF; WBLP

I kiss her feet and deem it sweet/To perish for my queen.   The Little Knight in Green.   Katharine Lee Bates.   AA

I KISS YOUR HANDS.   Film Vermouth: Six O'Clock Show.   Magda Portal.   PBWP

I kissed the foot that bruised me as it passed.   The Ladder.   Leonora Speyer. HBMV; PG

I kneel and bow.   Gnostology.   Sam Hamill.   AMV-81

I knelt and cried and almost prayed.   The Coweta County Courthouse. James Miller Robinson.   AMV-80

...I knelt in a corner and tried to/imagine what I would say to her, the girl in the field.   Deaf Girl Playing.   James Tate.   AmPA

I knew before it was spoken.   Quatrain: "I knew like a song your vows weren't strong."   Mahsati.   WPOW

I knew God dwelt within my heart.   Vestigia.   Bliss Carman.   CaP; WGRP

I knew her self was not in that strange place.   The Harlem Dancer.   Claude McKay.   BALP; BANP; BPo; FF; NoAm; TAP

I knew how a growing tree is true.   I Did Not Know the Truth of Growing Trees.   Delmore Schwartz.   LiTM

I knew how dark it was.   Girl with Long Dark Hair.   Stephen Gray. PeSA

I knew, I knew that he would come no more! Ulysses Returns. Roselle Mercier Montgomery. HBMV

I knew I walked that weary way/In a great company. Heartbreak Road. Helen Gray Cone. HBMV

I knew it was love, and I felt it was glory. Stanzas Written on the Road between Florence and Pisa. George Gordon, Lord Byron. EnLi 1-2; HBV 1-2; MCCG; OBRV

I knew my dog had got/To Heaven as well as I. A Heterodoxy. Edward John, Lord Dunsany. OnYI

I knew my face would not be young again. The Road. Conrad Aiken. AP; MoAmPo

I knew that I had known enduring love. The Buried Lake. Allen Tate. CrMA

I knew that once: but now–I think it. Senex to Matt. Prior. James Kenneth Stephen. CenHV; FiBHP

I knew the brain of Hercules! The Threshing Machine. Alice Meynell. SeCePo

I knew the chipped fire of pond ice/Was in her eyes like a widow's soul. Coleridge Crossing the Plain of Jars: 1833. Norman Dubie. LCAP

I knew the train was going down to Hell. A Dream. Evan Jones. NOAV

...I/knew we'd all live as long as Hokusai. Spring Street in '58. Derek Walcott. NYP

I knew you when you/still had hair! For Emily (Dickinson). Maureen Owen. APU

I knew your brow was cooled, you well again. With Long Black Wings. Trumbull Stickney. NCEP

I know. Haywood. Harold LaMont Otey. LFAC

"I know a person who has died." A Recollection. Frances Cornford. ELU; FaBoWP

I know a Rose in overhead. Rose and Root. John James Piatt. AA

I know a thing too strange for knowing,/I, the clay. The Poet. Haniel Long. HBMV

I know a thousand others just like you. No Madam Butterfly. Louise Hajek. AMV-80

I know! Ah, Friend, I know! In the Matter of Two Men. James David Carrothers. BANP

I know an old lady who swallowed a horse./She died, of course. The Old Lady Who Swallowed a Fly. Anonymous. ShM

I know at last 'tis God who prays. God Prays. Angela Morgan. WGRP

I know by proof that love is long annoy. My Love Is Past. Thomas Watson. PBBP

I know de Lord's laid his hands on me. I Know de Lord's Laid His Hands on Me. Anonymous. BoAN 1-2

I know de udder worl' is not like dis,/Oh, not like dis. Run, Mary, Run (I Know de Udder Worl' Is Not Like Dis). Anonymous. BoAN 1-2

I know, dear James–but then/It's I or none at all! To a Portrait of Whistler in the Brooklyn Art Museum. Eleanor Rogers Cox. HBMV

...I know everything, but she's/like heaven and knows nothing. Which is her fate. My Sister. Alfonsina Storni. BoWoP

I know exactly what I look like. Remembering My Father. Jonathan Holden. Str

I know half my life belongs to the wild darkness. Middle of the Way. Galway Kinnell. NU

I know He will abide with me today. Faith and Sight. Anna M. King. BLRP

I know her name is Love. My April Lady. Henry Van Dyke. HBV 1-2

...I know her tomb/Is yonder in the shapeless gloom. Glasgow. Alexander Smith. BSV

I know how the fingers of late October/Loosen the hazel nuts". Localities. Carl Sandburg. AmFN

I know how to behave. Complaint. Ian Hamilton. NoAm

I know how you be tonight! Ivory Masks in Orbit. Keorapetse Kgositsile. PoBA

I know. I also left a skin there. Cottonmouth Country. Louise Gluck. CoAP; GeTw

I know I am in your honest presence. Americana. Carl Rakosi. PAI

I know. I know. On the Last Page of the Last Yellow Pad in Rome before Taking Off... Miller Williams. AMV-80

I know I'll have another mess of beans. Beans, Bacon and Gravy. Anonymous. FSW

I know I look/square, but do/you see/a humpbacked/Camel/printed on/me? Gotta' Smoke? William Franklin. LFAC

I know/I'm black/AND/beautiful. On Getting a Natural. Dudley Randall. FB; PoBA

I know I'm just as close to You/As all those children were! Finding You. Mary Dixon Thayer. CAW

I know I should be happy with them. This Moment Yearning and Thoughtful. Walt Whitman. MCCG

I know it happened, just because/I was not there at all. A Tragedy. Tom (Thomas Lansing Masson) Masson. OBAL

I know it would've/come right up/and gave me/five! The Roach. John Raven. BPo; HoPM

I know it–Yes I know it! Superstition. Minji Karibo. WPOW

I know my love can never die. The Reason Why. Thomas Lovell Beddoes. OBRV

...I know myself a man,/Which is a proud and yet a wretched thing. The Immortality of the Soul. Sir John Davies. ViBoPo

I know no couple better can agree! On Giles and Joan. Ben Jonson. NOBL

"I know no Heaven but fair Wentworth's eyes." Upon My Lord Chief Justice's Election of My Lady Anne Wentworth... Thomas Carew. CaPo

I know no more than this. At Brill on the Hill. Anonymous. GBP; OxNR

I know not, but He knows. Not I, But God. Annie Johnson Flint. STF

I know not, but I burn and feel it so. Carmina. Caius Valerius Catullus. OBVE

I know not, but I know that both are ill. To Stand Up Straight. Alfred Edward Housman. EnLi 1-2; OAEL 1-2

I know not, but it is a spotless spot. De Naevo in Facie Faustinae. Thomas Bastard. FaBoEE

I know not–He is fond of flowers. Between Our Folding Lips. Thomas Edward Brown. PeD

I know not if earth is merely earth,/Only that heaven is heaven. Heaven Is Heaven. Christina Georgina Rossetti. YeAr

I know not what I think; I know/Only that thou art what I need. The Doubter. Richard Watson Gilder. TrPWD

I know not what to fear or hope,/Nor aught but that Thy will is best. A Heathen Hymn (excerpt). Sir Lewis Morris. TrPWD

I know not where is that Promethean heat/That can thy light relume. Othello. William Shakespeare. FiP

I know not whether I shall live or die. A Woman's Sorrow (excerpt). Ho Nansorhon. PBWP

I know not whither I must fare. Three Sorrowful Things. Anonymous. MeEV

I know nothing/learn of me February. William Stanley Merwin. NNaP

I know now that they are beautiful as God. Of Wounds. Sister Mary Madeleva. ISi

I know she hath both wives and widows loved,/Though she would neither wife nor widow be. A Contention betwixt a Wife, a Widow, and a Maid. Sir John Davies. OBSC; SiPS

...I know she wipes her hands. A Lady. W. D. Snodgrass. TW

I know something good about you? I Know Something Good About You. Louis C. Shimon. BLPA; PoToHe

I know that God is good! The Eternal Goodness. John Greenleaf Whittier. TRV

I know that his hand has reached hers/Just as she was about to turn on the lights. Old Couple. Charles Simic. HaCAP

I know that I would smile to see you dead. Sonnet to a Tyrant. Mary Anne Ellis. AMV-80

I know that now at last/it is beginning to grow light. The Total Influence or Outcome of the Matter: THE SUN. Marge Piercy. WPOW

I know that soon I will stand before you/And spit at your face with my blood. A Dark Hand. Itzik Manger. VWA

I know that summer, scarcely here,/Is gone until another year. The End of Summer. Edna St. Vincent Millay. BoNaP

I know that this is the way in ours. In Hardwood Groves. Robert Frost. AmLP; HAP

"I know that Utah Carl won't be lost on that great day." Utah Carl. Anonymous. BFSS

I know that when they walk in grass/She wears balmorals. Mrs. Smith. Frederick Locker-Lampson. HBV 1-2

I know the blood about his heart/Is dry as dust. My Creed. Alice Cary. WGRP

...I know the dove/Outsang me down the afternoon. Woodpigeons at Raheny. Donald Davie. PP

I know the hunched and running grass/Will feel the lashes of the rain/Ere of the sun it comfort has. Meditation in Winter. Leonard Mann. BoAV

I know the Inskips very well indeed. Bristol and Clifton. Sir John Betjeman. CMoP

I know the night/undaunted, relates location/to the sun. Night Crackles. Elizabeth Woody. STE

I know/the waving sun/the/constant ephemerals B. Larry Eigner. NeAP

I know the weed and moss too well,/To be afraid to sing. Song: "I know that any weed can tell." Louis Ginsberg. TrJP

I know the woman well. Mary Magdalene. Leonora Speyer. HBMV

I know Thee not. Abide with me! Depart from Me. Mary Elizabeth Coleridge. TrPWD

...I know/There is God. In the Hospital. Arthur Guiterman. WGRP

I know to greet the day/by listening carefully first. A Good Start. Larry Moffi. AMV-81

I know to what brown country/My homing thoughts will fly. My Country. Dorothea Mackellar. PoAu 1-2

I know very well I could not. I Saw in Louisiana a Live-Oak Growing.
Walt Whitman. AP; AWP; InPK; InPo; InPS; LiTA; MAT; MCCG;
NePA; NoAm; NOBA; NoP; OxBA; PrIm

I know we can make it/With just a little bit of soul. Keep on Pushing.
David Henderson. PoBA

I know we grow more lovely/Growing wise. Two Voices. Alice Corbin.
HBMV

I know what it is not but I don't know what it is Ars Poetica. Adam
Wazyk. VWA

I know what Nature will soon be, I feel/Within my heart the blend of God
and man. Anticipation. Joseph Tusiani. GoYe

I know what sound is there. City Trees. Edna St. Vincent Millay.
LaNeLa

I know what they have done. The Last Wolf. Mary Tallmountain. TWSS

I know when I'me well, I was never so mad,/To forsake a good thing when 'tis
to be had. An Amorous Dialogue between John and His Mistress.
Anonymous. CoMu; UnTE

I know why; I'll see you tomorrow; I'll tell/you everything tomorrow.
Potomac Town in February. Carl Sandburg. EvOK

I know why the caged bird sings! Sympathy. Paul Laurence Dunbar.
AmNP; CDC; IDB; PoBA; PoNe

I know You are there. The sweat is, I am here. Certainty before Lunch.
John Berryman. LCAP; OxBC

I know you'll see/the love that wings/to you from me. Small Song. Luci
Shaw. EBCP

I know you well enough, my son,/To know that's what you would have done.
Advice. Ambrose Bierce. DBV

I knows it, dem bones gona rise agin. In Come de Animuls Two by Two.
Anonymous. GBP

I'l never be 'stead of a Lover,/An aged Chronicle's new Cover. A Young
Man to an Old Woman Courting Him. John Cleveland. AnAnS 2

I laden will return to thee,/Ev'n sated with variety. The Scrutiny. Richard
Lovelace. AnAnS 2; BoLoP; CaPo; CavP; EnLit; EnLoPo; GBL; MeLP;
MePo; NoP; OBS; SeCP; TrGrPo

I laugh at fortune, as in jest to die. Idea. Michael Drayton. OAEP;
TrGrPo

I laugh at you through strings and snakes/of blood, my furious lovers with
your tiny bows. Like Gulliver. Nina Cassian. BoWoP; VWA

I laugh, close my eyes, and relax. One Man Down. Florence Anthony
("Ai"). GeTw

...I laughed and you were gone. Ballade of the Session after Camarillo.
David Galler. NMP

I launched a boat frail as a butterfly LXXIV. Ted Berrigan. ANYP

I lay a lonely heart/Before Thy feet. Mea Culpa. Ethna (Anna Johnston
MacManus) Carbery. CAW; TrPWD

I lay it all to thinkin' of Casey's tabble dote. Casey's Table d'Hote. Eugene
Field. PoOW

I lay my lute beside thy door! I Lay My Lute beside Thy Door. Clarence
Urmy. HBMV

I lay silently, waiting, waiting... Night Poem in an Abandoned Music Room.
[(or Pillin)] William Pillen. VWA

I lay until I slept; and when the day/Found us, my soul knelt at our feet to
pray. Mother of Men. Stephen Southwold. HBMV

I'le bring a fever; since thou keep'st no fire. The Invitation. Robert
Herrick. CaPo; OAEP

I'le disapparell, and to buy/But one half glaunce, most gladly dye. Silex
Scintillans. Henry Vaughan. AnAnS 1

I'le not be won with all thy store. To Plautia. Sir Aston Cokayne. CavP

I'le rather keepe this frost, and snow,/Then to be thaw'd, or heated so. The
Frozen Heart. Robert Herrick. CavP

I'le take my benbowe in my hande,/And come into the grenwoode to/thee.'
The Jolly Pinder of Wakefield (B version). *Anonymous.* ESPB

I'le yield to destiny. Corydon's Complaint. Samuel Pordage. CavP

I lean my wondering, wayward heart on Thine. To Jesus of Nazareth.
Frederic Lawrence Knowles. TrPWD

I leaned against a rock, out of the wind. The Galloway Shore. Sydney
Tremayne. BSV

I leaned upon my staff and fell asleep.' The New River Head, a Fragment.
E. Dower. NOEC

I leap, for love's ultimate ploy,/crying, "Darling, take me, I'm a changed boy!"
Ontogeny. Jarold Ramsey. NIP

I leap onto our neighbor's/Roof and devour their dreams. The Man in the
Ocelot Suit. Christopher Brookhouse. CAD

...I learn about/policemen who shoot real bullets into real people. James
Powell on Imagination. Larry Neal. BPo

I learn by going where I have to go. The Waking. Theodore Roethke.
AP; BiP; CAPP; CoAP; CoBMV; CrMA; HaCAP; HAP; HeIP; InPK; InPS;
LiTM; MoAmPo; MP; NIP; NoAm; NOBA; NoP; PAI; PoPl; PPP; PrIm;
SM; SoSe; TAP; TwCP

I learn to seek the fruitful thing or act. By Rail through Istria. Robert
Conquest. NoAm

I/learned. 18,000 FEET. Ed Roberson. PoNe

I learned the little that I know by this. Don Juan". George Gordon, Lord
Byron. ViBoPo

I leave her in wise Hands. Eleven Addresses to the Lord. John Berryman.
OxBC

I leave him to his lot, and like my own. Samson Agonistes. John Milton.
EBEV

I leave him, while the daylight gleam de-/clines/Upon the capes and chines.
A Singer Asleep. Thomas Hardy. OAEP

I leave in him revolt, (latent right of insurrection! O quenchless, indispensable
fire!). Still Though the One I Sing. Walt Whitman AA

I leave it to the sunlight, like the one/Landor the master left his voice upon.
Your Name in Arezzo. James Wright. SM

I leave on the canvas such weight/it is only my knuckles popping. Listens,
Too (parody). D. C. Berry. BXAP

I leave them as a father does his son. Sleep and Poetry. John Keats.
EnRP; ERoP 1-2; PP

I leave with a prayer in my heart:/black water won't rise no more Rising
High Water Blues. Blind Lemon Jefferson. BluL

I leave ye as I got ye–/A maist unceevil crew. Drumdelgie. *Anonymous.*
GBP

I left him practising the hundredth psalm. The Vision of Judgment. George
Gordon, Lord Byron. MasP; OBSV

I left the commonwealth mine air. Epitaph on the Fart in the Parliament
House. John Hoskyns. FaBoEE

"I left them in the Stapler,/Sleeping in their sheen." Willie Macintosh.
Anonymous. CBEP; ESPB; OxBoLi; ViBoFo

I left you to your adorning. At the Drapers. Thomas Hardy. BrPo

I lent a sigh to them. My Days Have Been So Wondrous Free.
Anonymous. TrAS

I let it be. Read and let read. Serious Readers. Peter Redgrove. OxBC

I let the whole sea/wash in. Incident at Mossel Bay. Mary Balazs.
AMV-81

I let them know/that I was christened. Perambulator Poem. David
McCord. OFD

I let them sprinkle water on my child. Cross Ties. X. J. Kennedy. CoPo;
HoPM

I let you–I repine. Girl to Soldier on Leave. Isaac Rosenberg. MMM

I lick the cream off property! that's what it seems to say! Lord Tennyson and
Lord Melchett. D. H. Lawrence. FaBoEE

I lie alone. The Silver Moon. Sappho. EnLi 1-2

I lie and listen, and rejoice. Midsummer. John Townsend Trowbridge.
AA; HBV 1-2; HBVY

...I lie down, my hands/supporting my head. The Feral Pioneers. Ishmael
Reed. UnPo

...I lie here and plot/the agony of resurrection. Antrim. Robinson Jeffers.
BIrV; NOBA; VGW

I lie in restlessness/all the night/comfortless. Songs of Ch'en. Confucius.
CTC

I lie in stolid hopelessness/and they lay my soul in strips. Remembering.
Maya Angelou. PPJ

I lie near a shade of willow, willow. Song: "Roses and pinks will be strewn
where you go." Sir William Davenant. ViBoPo

I lie secure in Jesus' arms. What Happiness Can Equal Mine. John David.
AH

...I lie still/In a green sack on a green hill. Here and There. Jon
Stallworthy. NoAm

I lift my head and read their names/In powerless envy. On a Visit to Ch'ung
Chen Taoist Temple... Yu Hsuan-chi. PBWP

I lift my head and smile. The Day's March. Robert Nichols. MMM

I lift my lamp beside the golden door! The New Colossus. Emma Lazarus.
AmFN; FaBV; FaFP; FaPo; FPL; GoTF; PAL; PGD; PoLf; PoPl; PrIm;
SBG; TreFS; TRV

I lift the catch...and in my heart/open a gate. Farm Gate. Uys Krige.
PeSA

I lifted up my foot, and squashed/The God damn little fool. How to Treat
Elves. Morris Bishop. DBV; FiBHP; OBAL; OBCA; PoPl

I light the second yahrzeit candle. Esther. Erev Shabbos. Marc Kaminsky.
VWA

...I/Lightly with dry lips brush your placid neck. A Bought Embrace. G.
S. Fraser. WaP

...I, like a/Fish out of water, am dangling in the sun. Love Dirge.
Anonymous. WTO

I like him very, very much. Mr. Minnitt. Rose Fyleman. HBVY

I like it fine in Jail/And I don't want no Bail. Girl Held without Bail.
Margaret Walker. BPo; CNA; PoBA

I like not any fashion that turns glum/The heart, and makes the visage sick
and ill. Sonnet: He Will Not Be Too Deeply in Love. Cecco da Siena
Angiolieri. AWP

I LIKE/SURPRISES! Surprises. Jean Conder Soule. BiCB

...I like that you/cover your teeth. Kalaloch. Carolyn Forche. AmPA

I, like the child, whom nurse hath overthrown,/Not crying, yet am whipped, if
you be known. Caelica, XLIII. Fulke, Lord Brooke Greville. FCP

I like the clouds up in the sky.   Summer Sky.   Ruth McKee Gordon.   TiPo

I like the fall–/The mist and all.–   The Mist and All.   Dixie Willson.   BrR; SoPo; YeAr

I, like the field burnt-over,/awaited the return of Spring!   On Seeing the Field Being Singed.   Lady Ise.   BoWoP

I, like the fish bequeathed to Neptune's bed,/No sooner taste of air but I am dead.   Caelica, LVII.   Fulke, Lord Brooke Greville.   FCP

I like the Game of Tennis best.   A Ballade of Lawn Tennis.   Franklin Pierce ("F.P.A.") Adams.   SD

I like the sight/Of crows for my good night.   Crows.   David McCord.   RFM; TiPo

I like those goddamn green bananas   The History of the Human Body....   Elinor Nauen.   APU

I like to be as my fathers were,/In the days e'er I was born.   The Old Squire.   Wilfrid Scawen Blunt.   FaPoR; HBV 1-2; OBEV; OBVV; SD

I like to be only/Squat and bunchy–/Do You-oo-oo-oo, too?   The Little Fox.   Dorothy and Marion Edey Grider.   TiPo

I like to fight/Sometimes on my way back to the block.   Sometimes on My Way Back Down to the Block.   Victor Hernandez Cruz.   BOLo

I like to pick and choose/and who knows someone/like you might arrive...   Whore.   Linda King.   GP

I like to see you living in the world.   Young Heroes.   Frank Horne.   BPo

I like to sit around with mammals.   Penguins in the Home.   Helen Bevington.   OBAL

I like to watch and wonder/Who's hiding halfway under...   Umbrellas.   Rowena Bastin Bennett.   TiPo

...I like your voice./Look where it's come from.   Codex.   Stephen Rodefer.   APU

I liked him.   The Stone.   Paul Blackburn.   NYBP

I liked their footman, John, the best.   Bored.   Horatio Brown.   PeHV

I lingered, thinking of heads held higher/When shawls were many–on Easter Day.   The Shawls.   Monk Gibbon.   NeIP; OxBI

I listen, and it cheers me long.   Woods in Winter.   Henry Wadsworth Longfellow.   CBEP; MAmP

I listen for its singing all the day!   The Harp of Sorrow.   Ethel Clifford.   HBV 1-2; WGRP

I listen/for my name.   Listening.   Nancy Passy.   AMV-81

I listen for the coming of His feet.   The Coming of His Feet.   Lyman Whitney Allen.   BLPA

I listen like a farmer in the rows.   A House of Readers.   Jim Wayne Miller.   GP; PPJ

I listen to its happy squeak.   New Shoes.   Marjorie Seymour Watts.   SoPo

I listen to the summer expand.   Thieves.   Perseus Adams.   ACV

I listened, beyond mourning, for her wings.   In Her Song She Is Alone.   Jon Swan.   NYBP

...I live a spine tingling life/of delirious sex & intense happiness.   Success Story.   Terence Winch.   APU

I live and breath the joy of it.'   The Vesture of the Soul.   George William ("A.E.") Russell.   ACV

"I live because he has passed my way."   Growing Old.   Rollin J. Wells.   BLPA; GoTF; TreFT; WBLP

I live for such moments.   Living with Others.   Al Zolynas.   LTB

I live in pleasure, when I live to Thee.   Live while You Live.   Philip Doddridge.   OxBoCh

I lived in pleasant times.   The Deserted Mountain.   Anonymous.   BIrV

I lived in the first century of these wars.   Poem (I Lived in the First Century).   Muriel Rukeyser.   UnPo

I lived past eighty,/I liked it all, sir.   Thomas Jefferson.   Rosemary and Stephen Vincent Benét.   TiPo

I'll always be faithful to you.   Sinful to Flirt (Willie down by the Pond).   Anonymous.   AmFP

I'll always dress in black and rave.   I'll always dress in black and rave.   Christine de Pisan.   BoWoP

I'll always love the dog days best.   A Dog Day.   Rachel Field.   SiSoSe

I'll always remember my town by the sea.   Block City.   Robert Louis Stevenson.   EyDe; NTCP; SoPo; TiPo

I'll ask no thing,/Of God or king,/But to clear away his shadow.   Diogenes.   Max Eastman.   HBV 1-2

I'll be a Party hack, Sir!   Garland for a Propagandist.   Ted Pauker.   NOBL

I'll be an Indian./Ogalala?/Iroquois.   The Longing.   Theodore Roethke.   NaP

I'll be Awfully Sad, when it Goes!   On Digital Extremities.   Gelett Burgess.   HBVY

I'll be blamed ef I can see/How all my money got away from me./For sometime.   What Kin' O Pants Does the Gambler Wear (with music).   Anonymous.   AS

I'll be content to take them both.   Les Amours.   Charles Cotton.   HBV 1-2

...I'll/be cruel, I'll be cruel   My Gang.   Jack Kerouac.   PoM

I'll be in a position/to offer ten centavos to a beggar/and to feel compassion.   Small Country.   Claribel Alegria.   BoWoP

I'll be reborn upon this earth/Forever in the sun.   Toroi Bandi.   Anonymous.   WTO

I'll be remembering what I see tonight.   Edward Weston in Mexico City.   Philip Dacey.   LTB; PoDr

I'll be Santa Claus to him!   A Real Santa Claus.   Frank Dempster Sherman.   ChBR

I'll be so false as to be true, and such a/fool as to be wise.   The House of a Hundred Lights.   Ridgely Torrence.   AA

I'll be true to the end all the same.   Dreaming in the Trenches.   William Gordon McCabe.   AA

I'll be up the country/Drinking that cool canned beer   She's Gone Blues.   Barbecue Bob Hicks.   BluL

I'll be waiting for you,/In the shade of the old apple tree.   In the Shade of the Old Apple Tree.   Harry H. Williams.   FSN; TreFT

An' I'll be wi' thee–noo.   The Hobthrush.   Anonymous.   GBP

I'll be your tootsie, wootsie,/If you'll coax me."/"But you must Coax me."   Coax Me.   Andrew B. Sterling.   FSN

I'll beat my poem in a trap/for the stingy fox, to prove/that you were here.   Dead Center.   Ruth Whitman.   NYBP

I'll beguile ye if I can.   Nievie Nievie Nick Nack.   Anonymous.   OxNR

I'll blow a kiss to you.   The Baby's Debut (Parody on Wordsworth).   Horace and James Smith.   ALV; OBRV; Par

I'll bring her to a parley yet.   She's But a Lassie Yet.   James Hogg.   LiTL

I'll build my nest in the ruffle of her dress/Where the bad boys can never bother me.   Free Little Bird.   Anonymous.   FSW

I'll burn away such sickness from the Earth.   The Employee.   Rudi Holzapfel.   DBV

I'll burn my books!–Ah, Mephistophilis!   Doctor Faustus.   Christopher Marlowe.   AtBAP; HeIP

I'll burn you on yon high hill-head,/Blaw your ashes in the sea.   The Auld Matrons.   Anonymous.   BaBo; ESPB

I'll bury me in Sule Skerry.   The Great Silkie.   Anonymous.   FSW

I'll buy you a farewell dinner/And take you home to meet the wife.   The Conservative Shepherd to His Love.   Jack D'Arcy.   InMe

I'll change a mistress till I'me dead–/And fate change me to worms.   Against Constancy.   John Wilmot, Earl of Rochester.   GBL

I'll change your singing Q.'   Miss Ellen Gee of Kew.   Anonymous.   FaBoNo

I'll climb the roots like a grey staircase, and watch you/from the purple lilies.   Life-Hook.   Juana de Ibarbourou.   WPOW

"I'll come with you, Puppy," said I.   Puppy and I.   A.(lan) A.(lexander) Milne.   OnUR; SoPo; TiPo

I'll crown and deck thee all with bays,/And love thee more and more.   I'll Never Love Thee More.   James Graham.   CBEP; GBL; HBV 1-2; NOBE; OBEV; PoPle

I'll cry thou canst be kind.   Brothers.   Gerard Manley Hopkins.   OAEP

I'll dance above your green, green grave/Where you do lie beneath.'   The Brown Girl (B version).   Anonymous.   ESPB

I'll dance and sing on my love's grave/A whole twelvemonth and a day.'   The Brown Girl (A version).   Anonymous.   ESPB

I'll die in harness with my scheme.   Is.   Patrick Kavanagh.   FaBoTw

I'll die thy valour's sacrifice.   For a Picture Where a Queen Laments over the Tomb of a Slain Knight.   Thomas Carew.   CaPo

I'll die with the one that loves me best."   W   Who's That at My Bedroom Window?   Anonymous.   ShS

I'll dig with it.   Digging.   Seamus Heaney.   BIrV; CIP; IPY; TwCP

I'll do better with English than a poem.   The Change.   David O'Bruadair.   BIrV

I'll do,–I'll plough or dig as DELIA's slave.   Elegy: On Delia's Being in the Country.   James Hammond.   CEP

I'll do my best to keep in touch with You./Faithfully yours,/Theodore.   A Letter from the Pygmies.   Theodore Weiss.   VGW

I'll do what I said, now, and close you in neatly.   Stocking Fairy.   Winifred Welles.   SoPo; TiPo

I'll draw the coleus again, its leaves/a curvilinear trap for light.   Alba: March.   Marilyn Hacker.   GP

I'll dream of it tonight.   Birth of a Country.   Agnes Gergely.   VWA

"I'll dress you up in satin so fine,"/Al down by the greenwood si-de.   The Cruel Mother (C vers.).   Anonymous.   BaBo; ESPB

I'll drink it down right smilingly.   The Stirrup-Cup.   Sidney Lanier.   AA; WHA

I'll drink my arrowroot, and go/To bed.   Changed.   Charles Stuart Calverley.   ALV; FiBHP; NOBV

I'll drink the aged Cecubum,/Until the roof turn round.   A Frolic.   Robert Herrick.   FaBoEE

I'll drink thy Muse's health, thou shalt quaff mine.   A Letter to Ben Jonson.   Francis Beaumont.   LoBV

I'll drink thy Muses health, thou shalt quaff mine.   Mr. Francis Beaumont's Letter to Ben Johnson...   Francis Beaumont.   OBS; ViBoPo

I'll drink to the health of the Creole girl on the lakes of Ponchartrain.   On the Lakes of Ponchartrain.   Anonymous.   AmFP

I'll drop my burden at his feet,/And bear a song away.   How Gentle God's Commands.   Philip Doddridge.   TRV

I'll drop through the sea-air/Till everything stops.   Girl at the Seaside. Richard Murphy.   BIrV; NMP

I'll enjoy him forever, I vow and declare.   The Golden Glove.   *Anonymous.* AmFP; MaC

I'll fairly and squairly/Quite a' and seek nae mair.   The Poet's Wish: An Ode.   Allan Ramsay.   OBEC

I'll ferry you.   Ferry Me across the Water.   Christina Georgina Rossetti. BiP; GoJo; OxBChV; SoPo; SUS

I'll fight 'gainst every odds–and I'll gain the victory.   The Captain Stood on the Carronade.   Frederick Marryat.   EtS; HBV 1-2; MOS

I'll fin' me a woman, babe, an' roam no' mo'.   "Cholly" Blues.   *Anonymous.* ABF

I'll find my cap a feather,/And kiss a Highland bride!   The Rose Is a Royal Lady.   Charles G. Blanden.   HBMV

I'll find the stable and pull out the bolt.   The Fascination of What's Difficult. William Butler Yeats.   BIrV; BrPo; PoEL 1-5

...I'll find you/in a rocking raft or lying close/against the ground like its lover. Dream.   David Ignatow.   VWA

I'll fix on my canvas if so I may dare/The boys who bathe in Saint Andrew's Bay.   Ballade of Boys Bathing.   Frederick William Rolfe.   PeHV

I'll follow and bring you back by force. I will!–".   Home Burial.   Robert Frost.   AnNE; APA; CoBMV; MAPA; PrIm; TAP

I'll follow Him at home, abroad/'Til time becomes eternity.   On Time with God.   C. D. Nutter.   STF

"I'll follow my true love wherever he may go,/If I have to beg my food from door to door."   Hind Horn (In Scotland Town).   *Anonymous.*   AmFP

I'll forsake them all and follow thee.   The Queen of Hearts.   *Anonymous.* FSW; OBET

I'll gaze upon it while I run/And watch the rising day.   My Former Hopes Are Fled.   William Cowper.   OxBoCh

I'll get no notions in my head/Beginning with: "When I am dead."   When I Am Dead.   Albert Stillman.   InMe

I'll get up and/be a man again.   Big Dog.   Anselm Hollo.   APU

I'll git down and waller there, And obleeged to you at that!   Knee-Deep in June.   James Whitcomb Riley.   AmePo; OHFP

I'll give any man a pint o' wine/That'll read my riddle right.   Riddle: "I sat wi' my love, and I drank wi' my love."   *Anonymous.*   GBP

I'll give her medicine made by men.   The Doctor's Story.   Will Carleton. BLPA

I'll give the devil two for pay,/If he will fetch the third away.   De Se.   John Weever.   FaBoEE

I'll give thee for a playmate sweet.   Ossian's Serenade.   Calder Campbell. BLPA

I'll give to you a butter-cake.   Charm for Hiccups.   *Anonymous.*   FaBoUs

I'll give you a groat.   Riddle: "Riddle me, riddle me ree."   *Anonymous.* OxNR

I'll give you a ring.   Riddle: "Flour of England, fruit of Spain."   *Anonymous.* HBV 1-2; HBVY; OxNR

I'll give you my thumb.   Father Greybeard.   *Anonymous.*   OxNR

I'll go and close the mountains' door/On the city's strife and din.   Behind the Closed Eye.   Francis Ledwidge.   MCCG

I'll go and make love to Nature/In some more quiet spot.   Three Sweethearts. Heinrich Heine.   UnTE

I'll go forward and do and dare.   Young Africa's Resolve.   Dennis C. Osadebay.   ACV

I'll go in and build a fire.   Beginning to Live.   Ruth Stone.   GP

I'll go no more a-roving/With you fair maid.   A-Roving.   *Anonymous.* FSW; ShS; UnTE

...I'll go scrve,/With willing mind, his majesty King George.'   The Linen Weaver.   *Anonymous.*   NOEC

I'll go spend my days with/My little Mohee.   Little Mohee.   *Anonymous.* ABF; AmFP; AmSS; BaBo; FSW

I'll go to Santiago.   Song of Black Cubans.   Federico Garcia Lorca. SOTW

I'll go where the mariner's going;/And be the mariner's bride.   The Mariner's Bride.   James Clarence Mangan.   IrPN

I'll go with him wherever he goes.   When I Was Single.   *Anonymous.*   FSW

I'll grab my darling Siilenboor/As she goes to her wedding.   Siilenboor. *Anonymous.*   WTO

–I'll greet them all once more   Once More.   Forugh Farrokhzad.   BoWoP

I'll grind his bones to make my bread.   Fe, Fi, Fo, Fum.   Mother Goose. EvOK; ExPo; ShM

I'll hae ma piece at hame, mun.   Aye, There's Hills.   Hamish Brown. PoSH

I'll hang my harp on a weeping willow tree,/And may the world go well with thee.   There Is a Tavern in the Town.   *Anonymous.*   BLSo

An' I'll har a' your ribbons reel/In the morn ere I leave ye.   The Trooper and the Maid.   *Anonymous.*   FSW

I'll have a home, I'll have a home.   The Ballet of the Boll Weevil (B vers.). *Anonymous.*   ViBoFo

I'll have my girl I love the best, in spite of her darned old mammy.   As I Walked Out One Morning.   *Anonymous.*   AmFP

I'll have the blues, Corinna, long as you stay gone.   Corinna.   *Anonymous.* FSW

I'll have to learn to leave myself alone.   Peregrine Prykke's Pilgrimage (parody).   Clive James.   FaBoPa

I'll have to say Good-night again!   Palabras Carinosas.   Thomas Bailey Aldrich.   AA; HBV 1-2

I'll have to wear my own.   Shoes.   Tom Robinson.   SoPo; TiPo

I'll help You some other day.   Think It Over.   *Anonymous.*   STF

I'll hide beneath my waistcoat. Mum's the word.   Leavings (parody). Gerard Benson.   BXAP

I'll hold no more, false Caelica, live free,/Seem fair to all the world, and foul to me.   Caelica, XLII.   Fulke, Lord Brooke Greville.   FCP

I'll hold the string said I.   Play.   Frank Asch.   NTCP

...I'll/hole it back until I dies.   Bim Bam.   Dorothy Rosenberg.   PoNe

I'll hug thee more than ever I have done.   The Ghost of Lucrece: To Vesta. Thomas Middleton.   MOON

...I'll join those kings/my people served before the death of Christ.   No Help I'll Call Till I'm Put in the Narrow Coffin.   Aogan O Rathaille.   NOBI

I'll joy in my salvation's God.   The Sun and Moon So High and Bright. *Anonymous.*   AH

I'll keep you as my guest.   Death Songs.   *Anonymous.*   BoWoP

I'll kill you.   Ohio Valley Swains.   James Wright.   NNaP

I'll kill you if you quote it!   Ah, Yes, I Wrote "The Purple Cow."   Gelett Burgess.   DBV; FiBHP; PoPl

"I'll know that it hasn't been sat on."   Limerick: "There was, in the village of Patton."   *Anonymous.*   TDH

I'll know that moment divine,/When all the things you are, are mine.   All the Things You Are.   Oscar, II Hammerstein.   BLSo

I'll know you even less.   Eight Lines for a Script Girl.   George Jonas. NeAC

I'll lay a man a pint o'rum,/There are no more than thirty-two.   Go-d'ling. *Anonymous.*   BFSS

I'll lay down my life for the Emerald Isle.   Bold Robert Emmet.   Tom Maguire.   OnYI

I'll lead ye right, you needen doubt.   Walken Hwome at Night.   William Barnes.   NOBV

I'll learn from you,/old witch,/who bewitches men/and women, too.   Safed and I.   Molly Myerowitz Levine.   VWA

I'll learn the art of prayer/And be properly pardoned/ In time/   Journey. Raymond Thompson.   LFAC

I'll leave behind/perhaps an echo/for man, who forgets/and remembers/and starts again....   Why Would I Have Survived?   Edith Bruck.   VWA

I'll leave her more to nag about/Than she's got breath.   Testament. Langston Hughes.   NePoAm-2

I'll leave the turnkeys all behind,/The wheel to tread and the corn to grind. The Gaol Song.   *Anonymous.*   GBP

I'll leave thy heart a-dying.   The Cheat of Cupid: or, The Ungentle Guest. Robert Herrick.   AWP; PG; SeCeV

I'll let you know which shortly–farewell, a long farewell.   On the Threshold. *Anonymous.*   BLPA

I'll lie and feed my sheep/On a green Lawn.   In the Trench.   Leon Gellert. BoAV; PoAu 1-2

I'll live, and as he pulls me down, mount higher...   Elegies.   Ovid (Publius Ovidius Naso).   ChTr

I'll love my Country, Prince, and Laws; and those, that love/the King.   Plain Dealing.   Alexander Brome.   OBS

I'll love no woman young or old/because her kiss is–what it is!   Keep Your Kiss to Yourself.   *Anonymous.*   NOBI

I'll love you till the day I die,/And then you know I'm done.   The True Lover's Farewell.   *Anonymous.*   AS

I'll make a smile of teeth. I'll make my mark.   Getting On.   Stephen Sandy. CAD

I'll make her my little wife–/Root hog or die.   The Bullwhacker. *Anonymous.*   CoSo

I'll make you a small/silk purse.   Hog at the Manger.   Norma Farber. PCh

I'll make you shine in a light and friendly way.   I'll Give My Love a Light and Friendly Kiss.   *Anonymous.*   OuSiCo

"I'll make you what you want to be."   The Promise.   Mary B. Fowler. STF

I'll marry the widow, and keep the Cock Inn.   The Widow That Keeps the Cock Inn.   *Anonymous.*   CoMu

I'll meet a trooper with a soft, wide hat/who will take away my Earth-rocks and debrief me.   Earth Walk.   William Meredith.   MAT

I'll meet the saints and chosen up in the heavenly skies.   The West Palm Beach Storm.   *Anonymous.*   AmFP

I'll meet them both in heaven/At the spring of the year.   The Spring of the Year.   Allan Cunningham.   HBV 1-2

I'll meet them in the country when I can.   Anxiety about Dying.   Alicia Ostriker.   AMV-80

I'll meet you in the world above/Where parting is no more.   The Vance Song. *Anonymous.*   OuSiCo

I'll tell thee, when the end is come,/How we may best forget. A Little While. Dante Gabriel Rossetti. ViBoPo; VLP

I'll tell you nothing/but you will know why I fight. If You Ask Me Who I Am. Armando Guebuza. WhB

I'll thank the Gods for my Reward,/And smile at ilka Fop. The Twa Books. Allan Ramsay. OxBS

I'll think it's noon at half-past four! Country Towns. Kenneth Slessor. CBAP; PoAu 1-2

I'll think of the leech-gatherer on the lonely moor! Resolution and Independence. William Wordsworth. BoNaP; CABA; CBEP; DiPo; EBEV; ERoP 1-2; FaBoRV; HAP; InPS; LiTB; MasP; MAT; MBW 1-2; NOBE; NOCV; NoP; OAEL 1-2; OAEP; OBNC; OBRV; PAI; Par; PoEL 1-5; PPP; SpRo; TEP

I'll think of what must soon approach,/And fit myself to fit a coach. Modern Midnight Conversation: Between a Contractor and His Wife. Anonymous. NOEC

I'll think upon my own true love in the Isle of Germany. High Germany. Anonymous. OBET

I'll toast you in Congaree mud. To Amy. J. Gordon Coogler. OBAL

I'll toll the bell. Leaves. Ted Hughes. OxBC

I'll travel the world over wherever he may roam. The Gamboling Man (C vers.). Anonymous. AS

I'll trust alone in thee. Jesus, I Come to Thee. Nathan S. S. Beman. AH

I'll try/the whole/cause,/and/condemn/you/to/death. Fury Said to a Mouse. Lewis (Charles Lutwidge Dodgson) Carroll. NoP

I'll tune Thy Elegies to Trumpet-sounds,/And write Thy Epitaph in Blood and Wounds! His Metrical Vow. James Graham. OxBS; ViBoPo

I'll turn my course backward across the salt sea,/And there I will dwell with the little Mohee. The Indian Mohee. Anonymous. BFSS

I'll turn my eyes away from him,/And look instead at me. Let Me Look At Me. Bessie June Martin. STF

I'll wagon-loads of love and glory bring. Meditations. Edward Taylor. AnNE

I'll wait until eleven strikes–/Perhaps a little after. Pendulum Rhyme. Selma Robinson. InMe

I'll wake up by and by/And play squash for an hour. And Again (parody). Humphrey Evans. BXAP

I'll warrant I'll make him quickly give out. The Buxom Young Dairy Maid. Anonymous. OBET

I'll warrant she'll prove an excuse for the glass. School for Scandal. Richard Brinsley Sheridan. NOEC; TreF

I'll wash thee, Lord, till I be clean. The Leper Cleansed. John Collop. TrGrPo

I'll weep all the day by my red fuchsia tree! O What if the Fowler. Charles Dalmon. CH

I'll weep with thee, tear for tear. Has Sorrow Thy Young Days Shaded? Thomas Moore. OxBI

I'll write chaste sonnets of imagined Loves. The Fresh Start. Anna Wickham. ViBoPo

I loathe her. Self Portrait 4. Tove Ditlevsen. WPOW

...I long/for something permanent. The Them Decade. Terence Winch. APU

I long for thy narrow breasts,/Thou restless, ungathered. O Atthis. Ezra Pound. PoA

I long for time to pass, so I/Can think of all this with nostalgia. Christmas Family Reunion. Peter De Vries. NLV; NOBL

I long to fade back/into this door of sun forever Myself When I Am Real. Al Young. CNA; PoBA

I long to hear some good gal call my good gal call my name No No Blues. Willie Baker. BluL

I long to kiss the image of my death. Sleep, Silence' Child, Sweet Father of Soft Rest. William, of Hawthornden Drummond. BSV; HBV 1-2

I long, when we shall meet again,/To be as tall as you. A Child's Song to Her Mother. Winifred Welles. HBMV

...I longed for/Mortal or centaur to surprise me. Tiresias (excerpt). Austin Clarke. CIP

I longed to forgive them, but they never/smiled. My Parents Kept Me from Children Who Were Rough. Stephen Spender. OAEP

I look across the waves, alone/In the misty filigree. The Ships of Arcady. Francis Ledwidge. EtS

I look, and do not doubt that He is there. The Church. Edwin Muir. MoRP

I look at it, and pass on. Darkness. Joseph Campbell. BIrV

I look at my face in the glass and see/a halfborn woman. Upper Broadway. Adrienne Rich. HaCAP; InPS

I look at you, and I sigh. A Drinking Song. William Butler Yeats. BoLoP; OAEL 1-2; PoL

I look at your beautiful wings/and sense your flight. Hawk Nailed to a Barn Door. Peter Blue Cloud. VoR

I look back. Nowhere. Meanwhile, one or more wives/Go on stilts for the mail. Movies, Left to Right. Robert Sward. NYBP

I look, but it is never there. 999 Call. Elizabeth Bartlett. FaBoWP

I look for you with smiles, with tears,/But look for you in vain! The Quest. Ellen Mackay Hutchinson Cortissoz. HBV 1-2

I look into the crater of the ant. The Vantage Point. Robert Frost. CoBMV; MAmP; OxBA

I look just like/That dark/Bunch of woods/Over there. Working near Lake Traverse. Tom Hennen. FAZ

I look up angrily at the light. Getting Up Early. Robert Bly. NaP

...I/Looked after him thro' happy tears. An Athenian Garden. Trumbull Stickney. NCEP

I looked again–the Kid was dead! The Kid's Last Fight. Anonymous. GoTF; TreF

I looked, and I was healed! Sin and Its Cure. Anonymous. STF

I looked, and it was He! Disguises. Thomas Edward Brown. VLP; WGRP

I looked, and saw the room was filled/With Dawn. I watched it grow. I Dreamed I Saw the Crescent Moon. Anonymous. PoL

I looked and three whin bushes rode across/The horizon–the Three Wise Kings. A Christmas Childhood. Patrick Kavanagh. PCh

I looked at you once, and the half of my soul was lost. At Mass. Robin Flower. OxBI

I looked in the mirror before I was born but I didn't see nothin Song: "She was lyin face down in her face." Bill Knott. MAT

I looked over in the corner: grandma and grandpa had 'em too. Statesboro Blues. Blind Willie McTell. BluL

I lose. Goodbye Broadway,/Hello Rilke. In the Gazebo (parody). Philip Appleman. BXAP

I lose the power of eating.– Shakespearean Soliloquy in Progress: "To starve, or not to..."(parody). W. H. Ireland. BXAP

I lose to keep, and choose/Tamer as prey. Tamer and Hawk. Thom Gunn. FaBoTw; NePoEA

I lost my color/tending the flock. Song: "Though I am dark." Anonymous. BoWoP

I lost my true lover/For courtin' too slow. On Top of Old Smoky. Anonymous. BLSo; FSW

I lost not thee, nor any shape of thine. The Image of Delight. William Ellery Leonard. AnFE; APA; HBMV

I lost the best feather i my wing/For my crowse crawing. Willie Macintosh (B version). Anonymous. ESPB

I lost the prejudice of paradise/And wound up caring for the babies of these guys. Eve of Easter. Bernadette Mayer. APU

I lov'd him so well, and so very, very well,/That I built him a bow'r in my breast. I Once Lov'd a Boy. Anonymous. WTO

I love a Bedouin cavalier! She Scorns Her Husband the Caliph. Lady Maisun. LiTW

I love, and the world is mine! The World Is Mine. Florence Earle Coates. AA

I love at eyes' length! The Peeper. Peter Davison. ErPo

I love best thee–/Thou pretty pretty lady! Lady April. Richard Le Gallienne. YeAr

I love 'em when they get that way! The Lady with Technique. Hughes Mearns. FiBHP

"I love her," he said as he pulled on his pajamas. The Accountant in His Bath. Adrian Mitchell. NYBP

I love him best of all! Child's Song in Spring. Edith Nesbit. HBV 1-2; OHIP; OxBChV

I love him, love him, love him past belief! A Chaplet of Southernwood (excerpt). John Gambril Nicholson. PeHV

I love him more than daddie/And I'm only thirty two. The Fat Budgie. John Lennon. NLV

I love His love for evermore. The Love of God. John Audelay. OxBM

I love His precept more. Sensitiveness. John Henry, Cardinal Newman. TrCP

I love, I love his home. Lost But Found. Horatius Bonar. HBV 1-2

I love my country best. The Rejected National Hymns. Robert Henry Newell. InMe

I love my darlin'-o. The Rich Old Lady. Anonymous. OuSiCo

I love my life, but not too well. I Love My Life, but Not Too Well. Harriet Monroe. HBV 1-2

"I love my Love, and my Love loves me!" Answer to a Child's Question. Samuel Taylor Coleridge. EnRP; FaBoBe; HBV 1-2; HBVY; OxBChV; PoPle

I love my mother,/And she's my sweetheart. Her Eyes Don't Shine Like Diamonds. David Marion. FSN

I love my wee miner lad an' wha can me blame? Six Jolly Wee Miners. Anonymous. CoMu

I love no love but thee. My True Love Hath My Heart and I Have His. Mary Elizabeth Coleridge. BoLiVe; BoLoP; CH; DiPo; FaBoBe; GBL; HBV 1-2; LiTL; OAEP; PoEL 1-5; PoPle; SeCeV; TrGrPo; ViBoPo; WHA

I love nothing better than my wife. The Jolly Tester. Anonymous. OxNR

I love school. Indian Education. Adrian C. Louis. STE

I love sweet Rosie O'Grady,/And Rosie O'Grady, loves me. Sweet Rosie O'Grady. Maude Nugent. FSN

"I love the clouds, the clouds that pass, eternally, the/marvellous clouds." The Stranger. Charles Baudelaire. SyP

I love the fond,/The faithful, and the true. Song. John Clare. NoP; OBVV

I love the ground whereon she stands. Black Is the Colour. Anonymous. GBP

I love the silent majority/That will rise earlier than the sun. I Love. Samuel Chimsoro. WhB

I love them,/wanting them gone The Children. Susan MacDonald. IHMS

I love thy loveliness that hears no cry. In an Autumn Wood. William Alexander Percy. HBMV

I love to skip alone and play/Along the sand when mist is falling. Skipping along Alone. Winifred Welles. SoPo; TiPo

I love waves, and winds, and storms... I Love Snow and All the Forms. Percy Bysshe Shelley. TiPo

I love with pity, pity me with love. Pity and Love. Anonymous. ALV

"I love you." Husband and Wife. Arthur Guiterman. PoToHe

I love you Phone Call. Tom Crawford. AMV-81

"I love you, alta" his voice/in my whole body like a blessing. He Said, Lying There. Alta. GP

I love you and you love me... The Purse–Seine. Paul Blackburn. CoPo

I love you and your great way of forgetting. Graves. Carl Sandburg. AnEnPo

I love you daddy/what you done it for Eagles on a Half. Geechie Wiley. BluL

I love you Emerald/Tell the world I do/Em Travelin' Blues. Blind Willie McTell. BluL

I love you forever, always and in all ways Mother/Deer/Lady. Harold Littlebird. VoR

I love you. Goodbye. Goodbye. In the Yellow Light of Brooklyn. Al Lee. NYP

I love you, I'd like to go. You. Tom Clark. ANYP; EAS

I love you, I love you. At Dawning. Nelle Richmond Eberhart. BLSo

"I love you I love you" again (never often enough)/"I love you" Thinking of Bookshops. James Liddy. CIP

I love you, Ida, 'deed I do. Ida, Sweet as Apple Cider. Eddie Leonard. BLSo; FSN; TreFT

I love you most because you please to love me. Song: "Lady, you are with beauties so enriched." Francis Davison. ElL

"I love you? My Lord!"/Was all that she said. Triolet. Paul T. Gilbert. PV

I love you, Pocahontas/where his feet are You at the Pump (History of North and South). Frank O'Hara. ANYP

I love you so much, my heart is singing. Infelice. Stevie Smith. FaBoWP

I loved a false young man. Green Willow, Green Willow. Anonymous. AmFP

I loved him so Remembering Him. Joe Reccardi. AMV-80

I loved my friend. Poem: "I loved my friend." Langston Hughes. DFF; NTCP

I loved myself, because myself loved you. The Excuse. Sir Walter Ralegh. AAS; FCP; SiPS

I loved thee ere I loved a woman, Love. To Art. Dante Gabriel Rossetti. PoL

I loved you all. The Mother. Gwendolyn Brooks. BPo; GP

I loved you then, I love you yet. Say "Au Revoir," but Not "Good-Bye." Harry Kennedy. FSN

I loved you Wednesday,–yes–but what/Is that to me? Thursday. Edna St. Vincent Millay. InMe

"I lust for nothing." Sexual Soup. Erica Jong. GP

I'm a bit of a bisexual, you know.' Limerick: "Said a gabby old queer in Saint-Lo." Anonymous. PeHV

I'm a broken-down digger on Kiandra plain. The Broken-Down Digger. Anonymous. PoAu 1-2

I'm a fighter, I am fly, and I am flip. The Bad Man from the Brazos. Anonymous. CoSo

I'm a-goin' down to Lynchburg town,/To carry my tobacco down. Goin' Down to Town (with music). Anonymous. AS

I'm a-going to leave this town. Goodbye, Little Bonny Blue Eyes. Anonymous. AmFP

I'm a good hater,/But a bad lover. Peregrine. Elinor Wylie. BLPL; HBMV

I'm a high-lopin' cowboy, an' a wild buckeroo. The High-Loping Cowboy. Curley W. Fletcher. BPAW

I'm a-hunting a home to go to. Bear the News, Mary. Anonymous. ABF

I'm a killer diller from the South Killer Diller. Memphis Minnie. BluL

An' I'm a-layin' neah huh! Song of Summer. Paul Laurence Dunbar. MCCG

I'm a lookin' for that bully and he must be found. The Bully Song. Charles E. Trevathan. BLSo

I'm a lousy miner, I'm a lousy miner in search of shining gold. Lousy Miner. Anonymous. AmFP

I'm a man for ev'ry Sceane. Love Dislikes Nothing. Robert Herrick. AnAnS 2; CBEP

I'm a natural born eas'man, don't have to work. Kassie Jones. Furry Lewis. BluL

I'm a nigger from de state of Alabam! Walky-Talky Jenny (with music). Anonymous. AS

I'm a peach, and that's all there is tutte. Limerick: "Miss Minnie McFinney of Butte." Carolyn Wells. LiBL; TDH

I'm a rambler I'm a gambler/And I gamble when I can. Rambling, Gambling Man. Anonymous. FSW

I'm a-rollin', through an unfriendly worl'. I'm A-Rollin'. Anonymous. BoAN 1-2

I'm a round-town gent, and I don't choose/To work in the mud and do without shoes. I'm a Round-Town Gent. Anonymous. GoSl

I'm a roving rake of poverty and son of a gun for beer. The Ramble-eer. Anonymous. PoAu 1-2

I'm a sheep without a fold. A Rich Tuft of Ivy. Suibne Geilt. NOBI

I'm a soul–again confide me/To a lover, ere I perish. The Violin's Complaint. William Roscoe Thayer. AA

I'm a woman with a husband!/Good luck to you. St. Kilda. Barrie Reid. BoAV

I'm a young maiden. I know I've done wrong. The Bad Girl's Lament; or, St. James Hospital. Anonymous. ViBoFo

I'm about to show you a mighty river. Map Reading. David Citino. AMV-81

I'm absolutely starving. The Diet. Maureen Burge. BrRo

I'm afraid 'twill be past twelve o'clock. Sheep Shearing. Anonymous. OBET

I'm again a fair maid on the shore. The Fair Maid by the Shore. Anonymous. AmFP; BaBo

I'm Alabama bound. Alabama Bound. Anonymous. FSW

I'm alive and from afar I hear its swansong. Days in White. Ingeborg Bachmann. BoWoP

"I'm all alone/By the telephone!" The Gramophone. James Reaney. CaP

...I'm all there is/Forever, chum, just see it my way, & I do. American Landscape with Clouds & a Zoo. Jon Anderson. MAYP

I'm always glad to see you such/An idiot, they won't hurt you much. A Father's Heart Is Touched. Samuel Hoffenstein. FiBHP

I'm always alone. Here Am I, Little Jumping Joan. Mother Goose. TiPo

I'm always glad when the chickens come home to roost The Gangster's Death. Ishmael Reed. PoBA

I'm always sorry/When the ride ends. Ferry-Boats. James S. Tippett. SoPo; SUS; TiPo

I'm as happy as I've ever been. Important Statement. Patrick Kavanagh. PoCh

I'm back in those forgotten days,/And watch her at her binding. On the Fly-Leaf of a Book of Old Plays. Walter Learned. HBV 1-2

"I'm better because he passed my way." As We Grow Older. Rollin J. Wells. PoToHe

I'm black. I'm black/& I'm from Look Back. Black Is a Soul. Joseph Blanco White. IDB; PoBA

I'm bound away for ever,/Away somewhere, away for ever. Early One Morning. Edward ("Edward Eastaway") Thomas. MoVE

I'm bound away for the fishing ground. Round the Bay of Mexico. Anonymous. FSW

I'm bound away for ther wild Miz-zou-rye. Wild Miz-zou-rye. Anonymous. ABF

I'm bound for San Francisco/ With my washbowl on my knee! I Come from Salem City. Anonymous. AmSS

I'm bound to gamble all my life, Du-da, du-da, day. The Gambler. Anonymous. AmFP

I'm bound to go to heaven when I die. Dig My Grave. Anonymous. AmFP; FSW; OuSiCo

I'm bound to march in endless bliss,/And die a shouting Methodist. The World, the Devil, and Tom Paine. Anonymous. AH

I'm bound to the hills. Lonesome Water. Roy Helton. AmFN; MoAmPo

I'm building for years to be–/That little chap who follows me. Service Supreme. Anonymous. STF

I'm called "The Collision" Rosewood Vision. Jim Brodey. ANYP

I'm certain that he thought the place/Belonged by rights to him. The Spring. Rose Fyleman. BrR; FaPON

I'm charged for her annuity! The Annuity. George Outram. HBV 1-2

I'm cold already and I'm fainting. On the Rising Generation. Howard Dietz. ALV

...I'm comforted/By this narcotic thought: I know my soul. I Know My Soul. Claude McKay. BPo

"I'm damned if I don't–or I do." Limerick: "A half-baked potato, named Sue." George Libaire. LiBL

I'm darned if I know how the helican. The Pelican. Anonymous. GoTF; TreFS

I'm driving on The U.S. Coast and Geodetic Survey Ship Pioneer. Robert Hershon. NeAC

...I may not as I would, yet must I as I may.   I Could Not Though I Would.
George Gascoigne.   PoEL 1-5

I may not be a nice person.   If I Leave Here Alive.   Solomon Mahaka.
WhB

I may not go on the gypsies' road–/The road that has no ending.   The
Gypsies' Road.   Dora Sigerson Shorter.   OBVV

I may not shake my bagge for you.'   The Cricket and the Greshope Wenten
Hem to Fight.   *Anonymous.*   EBEV

I may not wish to seek your door again.   Understanding.   Pauline E. Soroka.
PoLf

I may remember him!   Heart, We Will Forget Him.   Emily Dickinson.
AA; LiTL; OLR; ViBoPo

...I/may sell it to you, and/I may not.   Buying a Record (parody).   Robert
Peters.   BXAP

I may show him visible.   Person, or A Hymn on and to the Holy Ghost.
Margaret Avison.   PeCV

I may stretch out a loving hand/To wrestlers with the troubled sea.   For
Every Day.   Frances Ridley Havergal.   BLRP

I mean...I...can fly/like a bird in the sky...   Ego Tripping.   Nikki Giovanni.
NoAm; Psk

I mean. Like that.   W. W.   LeRoi (Imamu Amiri Baraka) Jones.   HeIP;
NBP; NOBA; PoBA

I mean my weary/sooooooul.   Oh Ambulance Man.   Memphis Jug Band.
BluL

I mean Santy–singing about Fee–/be on my my way to what you call/loving
Tennessee   Bad Luck Blues.   Blind Lemon Jefferson.   BluL

I mean so I will know if I should/feel resentful or honored.   Zeppelin.
Andrew Glaze.   WeW

I mean the church, the king, and me.   A Maypole.   Jonathan Swift.
CBEP; NCEP

I mean the moment when it seems most plain/is the moment when you must
begin again.   The Discovery.   Gwendolyn MacEwen.   NOBC

I mean the thread that breaks./The dust between/typewriter keys.
Maintenance.   Robyn Sarah.   CaPN

"I mean to mark the Guinea pigs/From other common Swine."   On Mr.
Pitt's Hair-Powder Tax.   Robert Burns.   FaBoEE

I mean to ride the swells and tides till I gain young Billy Crane.   Young Billy
Crane.   *Anonymous.*   ShS

I mean to take to writing it myself!   The Ballad of the Billycock.   Anthony
C. Deane.   ALV

I mean–well, really, that's just what I mean.   La Donna Perpetuum Mobile.
Irwin Edman.   FiBHP; NYBP

...I mean, with/those four red wheels.   The Keys of the Jail.   *Anonymous.*
OuSiCo

I meant to tell you...   I Meant to Tell You.   Sean Haldane.   PoL

(I measure time by how a body sways.)   Poem: "I knew a woman, lovely in
her bones."   Theodore Roethke.   TrGrPo

I meet my true love at the rising of the sun.   At the Setting of the Sun.
Anonymous.   CBEP

I meet myself on stairs & pass without nodding.   The Apartment-Hunter.
Philip Schultz.   NYP

I meet the evening face to face.   This Is My Rock.   David McCord.
GeTw; NTCP; SiSoSe; SoPo; TiPo

I meet the sunlight flashing like a blade.   Walking in Bush.   Basil Dowling.
AnNZ

I meet you as a lover.   Night Harvest.   Susan Pence.   AMV-80

I meet you as a lover.   Night Sowing.   David Campbell.   BoAV; CBAP;
PoAu 1-2

...I melt into the air with a voluptuousness so delicate/that I am content to be
alone.   From a Letter.   John Keats.   NU

I merely thee ejaculate!   Thou Mother with Thy Equal Brood (excerpt).
Walt Whitman.   PeD

I met a friend.   Cincinnati.   Cid Corman.   GP

I met her at the fountain in the park.   While Strolling through the Park.   Ed
Haley.   BLSo; FSW

I met his eyes...And then I knew...   Who Are My People?   Rosa Zagnoni
Marinoni.   BLPA; PoToHe

I met the Master face to face.   I Met the Master.   *Anonymous.*   BePJ;
BLRP; PoLf; STF

I met the wolf alone/And was devoured in peace.   The True Encounter.
Edna St. Vincent Millay.   OBSP

I might, and yet thou goest safe, supreme.   Modern Love, IX.   George
Meredith.   NOBV; VLP

I might arise the while,/But I'd drop dead again.   If I Should Die To-Night.
Ben King.   BLPL; FiBHP; GoTF; HBV 1-2; InMe; PoLf; TreFS; YaD

I might be likened to a bird,'/Quoth he, "that did defile it nest."   King James
and Brown.   *Anonymous.*   ESPB

I might have grown up at last/And learnt what is meant by home.
Afterlives.   Derek Mahon.   CIP

I might have kissed him as I would a maid.   Hate.   James Stephens.
MoAB; MoBrPo; OBVV

I might have known I would not be the last.   Rapunzel.   Sara Henderson
Hay.   DFT

I might have plucked the rose, and I did not.   The Proffered Rose.   King of
Bohemia Wenceslas.   LiTW

I might have set the honey-maker free.   Julius Caesar and the Honey-Bee.
Charles Tennyson Turner.   FM; NBM

I might in fact be seeing my first sheep.   Philosophy Is Born.   Christian
Morgenstern.   FaBoNo

I might not bring myself at last/To–do without you altogether.   To Cloe.
Thomas Moore.   NLV

I might thy scorn as justly move,/As now thou sufferest mine.   Song: "I
prithee let my heart alone."   Thomas Stanley.   ViBoPo

I might tumble into bed with a nobody.   It's nice that though you are casual
about me.   Sulpicia.   BoWoP

I miss the crazy bastard,/and wish him back to abuse me/into song.   At the
St. Louis Institute of Music.   Ronald Wallace.   GOYP

I miss the old four pounds. Let's start again!   A Roman Thank-You Letter.
Martial (Marcus Valerius Martialis).   OBCP

I mourn for house, and tribe, and home.   Oh, How My Love with a Whirling
Power.   Tu-kehu and Wetea.   WTO

I move and remain.   River God's Song.   Anne Ridler.   NYBP

I move at the heart of the world.   In the Tree House at Night.   James
Dickey.   NoP

I move in darkness till he finds his light.   Nightfall.   Elder Olson.   DFF

I move the meeting be adjourned.   I Move the Meeting Be Adjourned.
Nicanor Parra.   HoPM

I move/to keep things whole.   Keeping Things Whole.   Mark Strand.
CoAP; HaCAP; HeIP; LCAP; NoAm; PPP; TAP

I moved with the morning.   A Field of Light.   Theodore Roethke.   LiTM;
MP; TwCP

I mun be married a Sunday.   I Mun Be Married a Sunday.   Nicholas Udall.
EIL

I murdered my own true lover; I'll never reach the sky.   Poor Omie.
Anonymous.   PrIm

I murmur with a sour grimace,/""Where's me?"   Who'd Be a Hero
(Fictional)?   Morris Bishop.   FiBHP; OBAL

I muse how she had such a grace/To seem a hawk, and be a kite.   A
Farewell to a Fondling.   Thomas Churchyard.   EIL

I must a little taste its opposite.   Sonnet: To Love, in Great Bitterness.   Cino
da Pistoia.   AWP

I must admire aloof, and for my part/Be well contented, since you do't with
art.   An Answer to Some Verses Made in His Praise.   Sir John Suckling.
PP

I must air out the regalia.   Spring Cleaning.   Phil George.   VoR

I must and I will get married, I'm in the notion now.   I Must and I Will Get
Married.   *Anonymous.*   TrAS

I must, and so I dare!   The Gray Hills Taught Me Patience.   Allen Eastman
Cross.   AH

"I must be here," she said,/"somewhere/between John and Joseph."   The
Wall.   Ludvik Askenazy.   VWA

I must be sometime taking.   Night Train.   Robert Francis.   DuDa; LOW

I must be still.   Reflections.   Edna Becker.   TRV

I must becom a Child again.   Innocence.   Thomas Traherne.   AnAnS 1

...I must confess/I love thee more, but I esteem thee less.   Carmina.   Caius
Valerius Catullus.   OBVE

I must confess, mine eye and heart/Dotes less on Nature, then on Art.   Art
above Nature, to Julia.   Robert Herrick.   AnAnS 2

I must earnestly warn you that you will eventually lose the habit.   Gather Ye
Rosebuds (parody).   Laurence Fowler.   BXAP

I must endure the timid sun.   Lines Written in Dejection.   William Butler
Yeats.   MBW 1-2; NAs

I must endure you, for you'll never sin/By robbing coaches, until dead men
travel.   Black Bart, P08.   Ambrose Bierce.   BPAW

I must get those jeans taken up   My House.   Robert Adamson.   CBAP

I must go back. It aches still where his head/Long pressed against my bosom
heavily.   Aut Caesar Aut Nullus.   Lilian White Spencer.   CAW

I must go, but my soul lies helpless/Beside your bed.   The Virgin Mother
(excerpt).   D. H. Lawrence.   ViBoPo

I must have dropped it when transfering.   Journey.   Diane Wakoski.
IHMS

I must have love enough to run a factory on,/Or give a city power, or drive a
train.   Acts Passed beyond the Boundary of Mere Wishing.   Stephen
Spender.   OxBTC

I must have lunch alone forever. Terrible.   The Things I Say Are True.
Blanca Varela.   BoWoP

I must have new dreams!/New for old!   New Dreams for Old.   Cale Young
Rice.   HBV 1-2

I must/Have passed it in my sleep.   To Critics.   Walter Learned.   AA;
AnAmPo; HBV 1-2

I must lay him on the shelf,/And make up the tale myself.   The Dumb
Soldier.   Robert Louis Stevenson.   OxBChV

I must/Look like someone else   In My New Clothing.   Basho (Matsuo Basho).   SoPo

I must myself therewith content/And bear it as I can.   If ever man might him avant.   Sir Thomas Wyatt.   FCP; SiPS

I must not falter on my wall.   Father Father Son and Son.   Jon Swan.   NYBP

I must not give you birth!   Black Woman.   Georgia Douglas Johnson.   BALP

I must own, Sir, but I blush indeed with Shame,/Your Pennance is prevailing.   A Lovely Lass to a Friar Came.   John Wilmot, Earl of Rochester.   CoMu

I must perforce ga seik my fathers sword.   To Henry Constable and Henry Keir.   Alexander Montgomerie.   OxBS

...I must pity/even the destruction of such small life.   A Dead Weasel.   David Helwig.   NOBC

I must pray, for it is the hour of the Sovereign of the world.   Shadows.   Paul Claudel.   CAW

I must read more carefully.   Volcano.   Derek Walcott.   OxBC

I must return to/like my own boke.   Off the Back of a Lorry.   Tom Paulin.   FaBoIP

...I must start/to sit with a blind brow/above an empty heart.   He Resigns.   John Berryman.   OBSP; SM; WeW

I must stay here with my hurt.   Here.   R. S. Thomas.   GTBS-P

I must suffer everything, being poor.   Seizure.   Sappho.   LLLT

I must tell you, these discover/What doubts and fears are in a lover.   The Primrose.   Thomas Carew.   FaBoUs

I must turn on the air conditioner and/drive back toward the house.   The Dazzling Day.   Lewis MacAdams.   ANYP

I must visit the cactus once more/and then, we'll have that drink.   Gunslinger.   Edward Dorn.   NoAm; NOBA

I must wait that I may be/Great enough to mother thee.   Unborn.   Irene Rutherford McLeod.   HBMV

"I my-/self/Am Reason. and the Other was a Dream."   The Bride.   Ambrose Bierce.   AA

I myself am a complete orchestra./So long.   Variations on an Air Composed on Having to Appear in a Pageant...   Gilbert Keith Chesterton.   NLV

I myself am but little known in China.   Translations from the Chinese.   Christopher Morley.   EvOK

An I nae mair maun writhle about the tree.   Allison Gross.   *Anonymous*   BaBo; CH; ESPB

I name them over and over.   Thistle, Yarrow, Clover.   Kenneth Porter.   NePoAm

I ne'er feared to give defiance to my/oppressor.   Oh, Ye Censurers.   Al-Samua'al Ibn Adiya.   TrJP

"I ne'er had been in this condition/But for my mother's prohibition."   Fable XX: The Old Hen and the Cock.   John Gay.   EiCP

I ne wot whider I shal fare.   Snatches: "Whenne I thenke thinges three."   *Anonymous.*   OxBM

I near me to your sleeping city.   Beyond.   Lionel Pigot Johnson.   BrPo

I near you, you near him, all of us must die.   Poem: "Old man in the crystal morning after snow."   Delmore Schwartz.   PoA

I need no more, I have no less.   Upon a Rich Country Gentleman.   *Anonymous.*   FaBoEE

I need no revelation to believe.   Confessio Fidei.   John Dryden.   NOBE

I need not fear the hordes of Hell/Coursing the Irish Channel.   The Viking Terror.   *Anonymous.*   KiLC

I need so much more than you do.   Your Need Is Greater Than Mine.   Theodore Enslin.   CoPo

I need Thee greatly–now.   A Mother's Prayer.   Jeanette Saxton Coon.   STF

I need your poisoned arrow tomorrow.   Hunter's Song.   Mvula Ya Nangolo.   WhB

I negotiate the steps of paradise/Leaping to measures that I cannot hear.   The Trout.   Daryl Hine.   CoAP

...I neither love nor see/And cannot be a man.   To Miss B.   John Clare.   NOBV

I neuer knew shepeard that goot such a liuinge/But David, the shepeard, that was a king.   King John and the Bishop.   *Anonymous.*   BaBo

I nevah inten' to give de journey ovah,/until I reach ma home.   Until I Reach-a Ma Home.   *Anonymous.*   BoAN 1-2

I never can forgive her, the Lily of the West.   The Lily of the West.   *Anonymous.*   AmFP; BFSS; FSW

I never can have a new dress.   Limerick: "Said the spider, in tones of distress."   Oliver Herford.   TDH

I never could list the ills I got–/Too big a shipment.   Count William's Escapade.   Guillaume de Poitiers.   ErPo

"I never died," says he.   Joe Hill.   Alfred Hayes.   UnPo

I never do a worthy thing, a decent deed or wise.   Temper.   *Anonymous.*   PoToHe

"I never expected the big nasturtiums/To come in my lifetime!" Grandpa said.   The Big Nasturtiums.   Robert Beverly Hale.   BoNaP; NYBP

I never follow an inferior way.   The Marigold.   George Wither.   CBEP; OBS

I never heard of tulips amidst musk-shedding hya-/cinths.   To a Young Lover.   Amur Mu'izzi.   LiTW

I never heard that sound by day.   By Night.   Robert Francis.   PoL; VGW

I never her it ring without/That funny little thrill.   The Door-Bell.   Charlotte Becker.   PoToHe

I never knew a friend could be/Like Him, my Friend divine.   I Never Knew.   Glenn E. Wagoner.   STF

I never knew but one–and here he lies.   Epitaph to a Dog.   George Gordon, Lord Byron.   BLPA; GDP

I never knew how many/many/stars there really are!   Until We Built a Cabin.   Aileen Fisher.   TiPo

I never knew I would ever get lost.   How a Girl Got Her Chinese Name.   Nellie Wong.   WPOW

I never knew so sure, so right a fit.   The Melmac Year.   David Hilton.   APU

I never knew that. A Divinity School at Harvard.   Experiential Religion.   Travis Du Priest.   AMV-80

I never knew the worth of him/Until he died.   An Old Story.   Edwin Arlington Robinson.   AnNE; GoTF; HBMV; MoAmPo; OBSP; TreFS

I never know from day to day/Which ones I'll have to eat.   Be Careful.   *Anonymous.*   NLV

I never learned to bat or bowl/But I heard the curtain going up.   The Boy Actor.   Noel Coward.   OxBTC

I never lived at all until the thrill of that moment when my heart stood still.   My Heart Stood Still.   Lorenz Hart.   BLSo

"I never loved you so."   Priapus and the Pool.   Conrad Aiken.   AmLP; NoAm

I never meant to live and die a maid.   O Stay, Sweet Love.   *Anonymous.*   EG; TrGrPo

I never more may steer!   The Sailor.   William Allingham.   HBV 1-2

I never resent a communication.   1,000 Illustrations & a Complete Concordance.   Michael André.   APU

I never saw a woman die/from living.   The Truth about My Sister and Me.   Anita Endrezze Probst.   CDW

I never saw her again.   Ritratto.   Ezra Pound.   PP

I never saw Mary more provoked.   Mary Ames.   *Anonymous.*   NA

I never shall forget that lovely afternoon,/When I met her at the fountain in the park.   The Fountain in the Park.   Ed Haley.   FSN

I never want to see you in your new straw hat.   To William Allen White.   Edna Ferber.   InMe

I never wanted to be a Dianne Arbus.   Captivity Narrative: September 1981.   Adrian C. Louis.   STE

I never was so happy since the hour I was born.   Turkey in the Straw.   *Anonymous.*   GBP

I never would cry my songs to sell.   Vendor's Song.   Adelaide Crapsey.   AnFE; APA; HBV 1-2

I never would cry, Old chairs to mend.   Chairs to Mend.   *Anonymous.*   OxNR

I never would cry old clothes to sell.   If I had as much money as I could/spend.   Mother Goose.   FaFP; HBV 1-2

I never would cry, Young lambs to sell!   The Toy Lamb Seller.   *Anonymous.*   OxNR

I never would feel lonesome with the two of us alone.   Little Mary Cassidy.   Francis A. Fahy.   HBV 1-2

I never writ, nor no man ever loved.   The Marriage of True Minds.   William Shakespeare.   AnEnPo

I no great Adam and you no bright Eve.   At the Firth of Lorne.   Iain Crichton Smith.   BSV

I no longer want to meet/people who have swallowed no living light from black soil.   For a Young South Dakota Man.   Freya Manfred.   TAT

I nod as I write good evening, lonely/And sick for home.   Outside Fargo, North Dakota.   James Wright.   LCAP; NNaP

I nod, Sure, the kids went to sleep easily.   The Confession.   Peter Cooley.   AmPA

...I not doubt/He came alive to land.   The Tempest.   William Shakespeare.   MOS

I not the bride can be!   Who? Who?   *Anonymous.*   CH

I note it has outlasted all the bombings.   The Ivory Tower.   Robert Hillyer.   NYBP

I note with what calm grace the French relax.   La Grande Jatte: Sunday Afternoon.   Thomas Cole.   NePoAm

I nothing buy or sell or lack.   Fish Riddle: "Although it's cold no clothes I wear."   *Anonymous.*   GBP

I notice she did not rebuchre.   Limerick: "Said a maid, "I will marry for lucre."   *Anonymous.*   TDH

I notice the surprise/of people who look at me as I pass.   The Sound of Rain.   Bella Akhmadulina.   BoWoP

I now have learn'd love right, and learn'd even so/As they that being poison'd poison know.   Astrophel and Stella, XVI.   Sir Philip Sidney.   AAS; SiPS

...I nurture the hole i was, fill it up.   From 2nd Chance Man: The Cigarette Poem.   Faye Kicknosway.   IHMS

I pictured it with cock/& balls that weighed on me for days.   How the Death of a City Is Never More Than the Sum of the Deaths...   Victor Coleman.   NOBC

I piss in the sink/with a feeling of/eternity.   The Garden of Earthly Delights.   Charles Simic.   NoP

I pitched my wishes back into the black water.   Fish.   Joe Rosenblatt.   NOBC

I pitied him for his small strategy.   The Compassionate Fool.   Norman Cameron.   CBEP; GTBS-P; OBSP; OxBTC

"I pity the thief."   The Bishop and His Portmanteau.   *Anonymous.*   ALV; DBV

...I place my feet/with care in such a world.   The Well Rising.   William Stafford.   NaP

I plan to freeze my neighbors to the marrow/By being the inventor of the bow and arrow.   Brave Old World.   Elisabeth Lambert.   FaFP

I plant money in the asphalt;/I lunch on bitter apples   Under Your Voice, among Legends.   Phyllis Beauvais.   NMM

I planted him in this country/like a flag.   Death of a Young Son by Drowning.   Margaret Atwood.   BoWoP; NOBC

I play in the moonlight/Any old how.   On My Old Ramkiekie.   C. Louis Leipoldt.   PeSA

I play with syllables, and sport in song.   Table Talk.   William Cowper.   PP

I plead instead for us/Against the sons we hoped we would not hurt.   Lines to His Son on Reaching Adolescence.   John Logan.   CAPP; NePoEA-2

I pleas'd my master, and I pleas'd my dame.   Epigram on a Dog.   Samuel Johnson.   FaBoEE

I pluck a rose–to let it fall/And perish in the gloom.   Old Gardens.   Arthur Upson.   HBV 1-2

I plucked a rose, and, lo! it had no thorn.   Simple Nature.   George John Romanes.   HBV 1-2

I ponder the exchange/Itself/And salvage mostly/The leaning.   In These Dissenting Times.   Alice Walker.   PoBA

I ponder too long the X-ray child in his mother's womb.   Third and Fourth.   Keidrych Rhys.   NeBP

I pondered long that cold majestic face/Whose vision seemed of infinite void space.   The City of Dreadful Night.   James (1834-82) Thomson.   OAEP

I pour the cream.   Vacation.   William Stafford.   AmFN; PoL; Psk

I pr'ythee help me over on thy back.   Epigram.   *Anonymous.*   ALV

I praise God's one name.   All Is God's.   Jakov De Haan.   VWA

I praise my days for all they bring,/Yet are they only not enough.   Dejection.   Robert Bridges.   QFR

I praise the lava holes/whence issued my first passport.   En Passant.   Andrei Codrescu.   APU

I praise the mortal wound that made me His!   Variations on a Theme by George Herbert.   Marya Zaturenska.   TrPWD

...I praise the star that slings my body free.   Sent Ahead.   John Hay.   NePoAm

I praise thee, God.   Hymn.   Wathen Mark Wilks Call.   OBVV

I praise Thee, Lord, and better praise Thee/would,/If what I had, my heart might ever hold.   The Experience.   Edward Taylor.   AmPP

...I pray for the fantastic/Messages one can learn to receive when the heartbeat skips.   Orange County Plague: Scenes.   Laurence Lieberman.   CoPo

I pray, God bless the good old town!   Haverhill, 1640-1890.   John Greenleaf Whittier.   MAmP

I pray God grant another love you so.   I loved you; even now I may confess.   Alexander Pushkin.   BoLoP

I pray God let me never see ryng/Into this realm so young ane King.   So Young Ane King.   Sir David Lindsay.   SeCePo

I pray I may be ready with my witness.   Eleven Addresses to the Lord.   John Berryman.   CAPP

I pray that e'er this world be done,/Christ may relieve his piteous pain.   Himself (excerpt).   Edwin John Ellis.   OBMV

I pray that my will may be attuned to/Your will for & with me.   Alcoholic.   John Berryman.   NOCV

I pray that Thou wilt find me, Lord,/Waiting patiently.   A Morning Prayer.   Betty Perpetuo.   STF

I pray that you will/come soon.   Be Kind to Me.   Sappho.   PeHV

I pray the Lord my soul to take.   Children's Prayers.   Eugene Henry Pullen.   BLRP

I pray thee Lord my body take.   Aunt Jane.   Alden Nowlan.   SoSe

I pray Thee O Lord from the depths of/my heart.   A Prayer.   Julian Tuwim.   TrJP

I pray to God another love you so.   I Loved You Once (From the Russian of Alexander Pushkin).   Dudley Randall.   AmNP

I pray to God that evil fire him brenne!'   The Cuckoo and the Nightingale.   Thomas Clanvowe.   PBBP

I pray to Jesus that Mary bare/Send us him again.   Two Old Lenten Rhymes: II.   *Anonymous.*   ACP

I pray you every day.   Friends.   Lionel Pigot Johnson.   GoBC

I pray you, for my own pain's sake,/Break the rules that I shall make!   The Dead Make Rules.   Mary Carolyn Davies.   HBMV

"I pray you, sir, let me go milk my cow."   Pastourelle.   *Anonymous.*   OBSC

I prayed for grace, that I might love/The rain only.   A Valediction.   Melvin Walker La Follette.   CoPo

I prayed I had not become human.   The Judas Goat.   Susan Musgrave.   NOBC

I prayed that you would love me/and that you would not love me   You Do Not Have to Love Me.   Leonard Cohen.   NoAm

I prayed the world/Might be good to him.   The Donkey.   *Anonymous.*   BiCB

I prays der Lord, "Dake anyding,/But leaf dot Yawcob Strauss."   Yawcob Strauss.   Charles Follen Adams.   PaPo

I preach for ever; but I preach in vain!   The Parish Register.   George Crabbe.   OBRV

I prefer another diet.   Parisian Nectar.   Gelett Burgess.   FaBoNo

I prefer the nether-treasure of the one who runs away.   The One Who Runs Away.   Callimachus.   LiSp

I prefer violins in repose/to some undefined yearning.   Violins in Repose.   Jorge Plescoff.   VWA

I presume there are equal facilities yet.   I Kissed You.   *Anonymous.*   BLPA

I promise this machine will not be lost/For want of this one nail.   The Bulldozer.   Donald A. Stauffer.   WaP

I promise you. Time will not take away that.   The Fortress.   Anne Sexton.   LiTM

I propped my rifle toward heaven/and fired a shot in the air/for the others to hear.   The Donner Party (excerpt).   George Keithley.   NPGG

I pull my pillow over my ear/but I hear.   Survivor.   Archibald MacLeish.   NCSH; PrIm

I pump him full of lost watches.   Birthplace Revisited.   Gregory Corso.   CAD; NeAP; PoM; VGW

I pushed him in the well, and he wished me in hell,/With his old gray beard a-shakin'.   Old Beard A-Shakin'.   *Anonymous.*   BFSS

I put it in my meal-poke,/to eat it to my bread.   A Scottish Cat.   *Anonymous.*   OxNR

I quail, lean to beginnings, sheath-wet.   Cuttings, later.   Theodore Roethke.   AP; HaCAP; LCAP; NoAm; NOBA; PPoe; TAP

I quake not till earth quakes,/Firm set as earth's axis.   Om.   *Anonymous.*   WTO

I quit th' enterprise of that that I have lost,/To whomsoever lust for to proffer most.   Alas the grief and deadly woeful smart!   Sir Thomas Wyatt.   FCP; SiPS

I race the shadows of the trees.   Routes.   Peter Everwine.   FiCP; NNaP

I raise the human race within my loins/And fire it off to home!   Zimmer's Hard Dream.   Paul Zimmer.   GP

...I rake the mess/the vines I rake/the vines.   The Creeper.   Tom Schmidt.   NeAC

I ran between them,/drumming the uprights of the fence.   The Fence.   Heather McHugh.   GeTw

I ran down the stairs/out the door/into his arms.   Alone in the House.   George Bogin.   AMV-80

...I ran into the night/Wondering why I smiled.   Before Action.   Leon Gellert.   BoAV; CBAP

I ran off with it, as happy as a faggot/in boy's town.   The Woman.   Frank Lima.   ANYP

I ran until gallows tripped over/remembering the skill of love.   Escape.   Ilya Rubin.   VWA

I, rapt in your dear heav'n, my loss describe.   Whitehall Stairs.   Aaron Hill.   NOEC

I rasp like a sick dog; I can't find my life.   From the Notebooks.   Theodore Roethke.   PoL

I rather lost my taste for butter.   A Present of Butter.   Tadhg Dall O'Huiginn.   BIrV

I reach, I touch, I begin to know you.   St. Roach.   Muriel Rukeyser.   GP

...I reach over, feel-/ing the gutteral vibration ebbing off the red brick crevices;/I fall a sleep   Prison Walls–Red Brick Crevices.   Terri Meyette Wilkins.   LFAC

I read, and, bending, kiss her reverently.   The Corpse.   George Moore.   SyP

I read my murder in their eyes.   Abraham's Knife.   George Garrett.   PoPl

I read you everywhere.   Hallowed Places.   Alice Freeman Palmer.   HBV 1-2

I realize my life isn't going to turn out/the way I had planned.   Summer Visitors.   Stephen Clark.   AMV-81

I realize that it, for those,/Has been a common day.   First Sight of Her and After.   Thomas Hardy.   PoEL 1-5

I really believed/it might all/be possible.   Ballet.   Milton Kaplan.   SOTS

I really can't remember.   Simple Sam.   Leroy F. Jackson.   ChBR; PoSC

I really do not like that cat!   What Could It Be?   William Cole.   BoAnP

I really hate to say it but I need a lady's room.   The Motorcyclists.   James Tate.   MAYP

I really hold a million million rocks here in my hand.   Rocks.   Florence Parry Heide.   NTCP

I reap and I don't think of next/year's harvest.   Calm.   Aldo Camerino.
VWA

I recall these Mephistopheles lines.   Reading Faust.   Judah Goldin.
AMV-81

I recke never, for he ne rought.   Snatches: "Here lieth under this marbel
ston."   *Anonymous*.   OxBM

I recreated, even by thy creature, live.   To Mr. R.W.   John Donne.
AnAnS 1

I reek with sorrow.   Diary. Moon of the Hiding Doe.   Charlotte De Clue.
TWSS

I refer to the United States of America,/Goes marching on.   Christopher
Columbus.   Franklin Pierce ("F.P.A.") Adams.   InMe

...I regret nothing.   Portrait of the Artist as an Old Man.   Michael
Dransfield.   CBAP

...I regret/This enterprise no more than I regret/My life; and I am glad that I
was born.   Captain Craig (excerpt).   Edwin Arlington Robinson.   PoEL
1-5

I rejoice in the spring, as though no spring ever had been.   Vernal Sentiment.
Theodore Roethke.   ELU; MiAP

I rejoice in their family fealty now.   Responsibilities.   J. C. Hall.   HaMV

I rejoice that my soul and I/Are mortal and will not last.   Poem for the Year
Twenty Twenty.   Al Lee.   AmPA

I remember a slice of lemon, and a bitten macaroon.   Mr. Apollinax.
Thomas Stearns Eliot.   PoA

I remember him!   Heart! We will forget him!   Emily Dickinson.   LLLT

I remember how the grass was trampled/and how finally they loved each
other.   Envoy.   Alasdair MacLean.   PoSH

I remember how we called it down, how down/we desired it to fall: the rain.
Farmers.   Thomas Lux.   LCAP

I remember Mama's voice humming mezzo/as I walked out into the light.
Light under the Door.   Marilyn Waniek.   MAYP

I remember my mother.   Mending the Adobe.   Hayden Carruth.   EyDe;
Psk

I remember now, and your mouth left the slightest aftertaste of/earth.
Kissing Natalia.   Eldon Grier.   NOBC

I remember the past.   Three Poems.   Hitomaro.   LiTW

I remember the rain as the feathery fringe of her shawl.   Green Rain.
Dorothy Livesay.   NIP; NOBC

I remember you,/Love,/In my prayers.   When the Curtains of Night Are
Pinned Back (with music).   *Anonymous*.   AS

I remember/your black mustache.   Love Songs.   *Anonymous*.   BoWoP

I repeat asking to myself/the question whose answer I know.   An Early
Illinois Winter.   Alex Kuo.   BrSi

I replied, "Quite a few, I believe."   Limerick: "Quoth a cat to me once: Pray
relieve."   Oliver Herford.   TDH

I rescue them again and again.   Beyond the Firehouse.   Patrick Worth Gray.
AMV-80

I rest as soft and true/As bird that clings to snow.   Different Winter.
Louise Townsend Nicholl.   NePoAm-2

I rest in the grace of the world, and am free.   The Peace of Wild Things.
Wendell Berry.   GeTw; HeIP; NU; PCP; VGW

I rest upon Thy word alone.   The Word of God.   Annie Johnson Flint.
BLRP

I return lowly, blind, at work too.   Landscape with Minute Wildflowers.
Hugh Maxton.   CIP

I return, return, return.   When the Dews Are Earliest Falling.   Arthur Hugh
Clough.   OAEP

I return to the first number one, which is the prime candle/Muting a gracious
hollow upward flame.   The Million.   Peter Redgrove.   OxBC

I return your Almes agen.   The Beggar to Mab, the Fairie Queen.   Robert
Herrick.   CaPo; WSC

I returned the handshake you taught me as a boy.   The Summer Rentals.
Daniel Halpern.   MAYP

...I rhyme/To see myself, to set the darkness echoing.   Personal Helicon.
Seamus Heaney.   FaBoIP; IPY

I ride like Joan to conquer my whole man.   Will to Win.   F. R. Scott.
OBCV

I ride protected.   Slave.   Langston Hughes.   LiTM

I ride you unseene wave/wee rise together/under daddye's roof & hand.
Song: Time Drawes Neere.   Anne Waldman.   APU

I rise/I rise/I rise   Still I Rise.   Maya Angelou.   BlSi

I rise to God to make death sweet by thee.   From Thy Fair Face I Learn.
Buonarroti Michelangelo.   PeHV

I roamed/a thousand miles/before you came.   In the Silence.   Stephany.
BPo

I roar like a sick lion/between her breasts.   Woman.   Irving Layton.   ErPo

I roll upon my side and break my glasses;/Time passes.   Beetle Bemused.
R. P. Lister.   PV

I romp with joy in the bookish dark.   Eating Poetry.   Mark Strand.   GrPl;
MAT; NoAm; PPP; TAP

I run, I run, I am gathered to thy heart.   Renouncement.   Alice Meynell.
AnFE; BoLoP; CAW; GoTF; GTBS; HBV 1-2; LiTL; MoBrPo; NOBE;
OBEV; OBMV; OBNC; OBVV; TreFT; ViBoPo

I run my hand along those old grooves in the rock.   Touches.   William
Stafford.   CAPP

...I run/Till the fawn smoke settles on the earth.   Smoke.   Mebdh
McGuckian.   FaBoIP

I's frustrated!   Bad Morning.   Langston Hughes.   OBAL

I s'pose no man before or since/Dreamt such a funny thing?   What the
Prince of I Dreamt.   Henry Cholmondeley-Pennell.   NA

I sad and pensive wholly.   The Earth, Late Choked with Showers.   Thomas
Lodge.   ElL; ViBoPo

I safely sheltered in thy heart at last.   Sonnets: A Sequence on Profane Love.
George Henry Boker.   AmePo

I said aloud: "Look out that you don't fall!"   Rispetti: On the Death of a
Child.   Paul Heyse.   PoPl

I said: "God, what is al this?"   Singe We Alle and Say We Thus.
Anonymous.   EBEV

I said how many years do you get/if they give you life.   How to Swing Those
Obbligatos Around.   Alice Fulton.   LTB

...I said I'd be converted and do good/If he would let me off–he said he would.
Midnight.   James Stephens.   DTC

I said: "I know. I am looking for it."   The Snake.   Hilary Corke.   PV

...I said/"I'm happy" to the Sun.   The Sun.   John Drinkwater.   NTCP;
SoPo; TiPo

I said, "I will, then, be a toad."   Think as I Think.   Stephen Crane.   WeW

I said, lest we should die alone.   Shadow and Shade.   Allen Tate.   InPo;
LiTA; VGW; ViBoPo

I said petals from an appletree.   Portrait of a Lady.   William Carlos
Williams.   AmPP; CMoP; NoAm; NOBA; OxBA

I said so once, and now I know it.   Life Is a Jest, and All Things Show It.
John Gay.   HBV 1-2

I said, "SO"/when I was 8.   The Photos from Summer Camp.   Izora
Corpman.   FAZ

I said "That's all right sweet mama/our   Dough Roller Blues.   Garfield
Akers.   BluL

I said, "That's good, that's enough."   Each Bird Walking.   Tess Gallagher.
FaBoWP; MAYP; SV

I," said the dove from the rafters high.   The Friendly Beast.   *Anonymous*.
PoSC; SoPo

I, said the gray fox,/All alone.   The Secret Song.   Margaret Wise Brown.
OBCA

I said "Vernon Lee?"   Inapprehensiveness.   Robert Browning.   NOBV;
VLP

I said your name but silence answered me.   Gethsemane.   Arna Bontemps.
CDC

I sail in a boat of factories and sparrows/out of sight.   Thaw in the City.
Lou Lipsitz.   MAT; NCSH

...I sailed from New York/For Bonnie Dundee, my heart it felt as light as a
cork.   Jottings of New York.   William McGonagall.   OBTV

...I salute/that various field.   Salute.   James Schuyler.   ANYP; FYAP;
NeAP

I sang of these things,/Because they are so nice to think about.   Song of
Sukkaartik, the Assistant Spirit.   *Anonymous*.   WTO

I sang praise to the Father,/The Son and Holy Ghost.   Christmas Day.
Andrew Young.   OBCP

I sank in arms that folded me from fears,/And like an infant, slept.   Chimney
Swallows.   Horatio Nelson Powers.   HBV 1-2

...I sat and ate/Some frozen dinner while I watched/The Late Show, and the
Late Late.   No Country You Remember.   Robert Mezey.   AmPC; FF

I sat down in my house and ate a carrot.   Denunciation; or, Unfrock'd Again.
Philip Whalen.   NeAP

I saw a Bishop with puce gloves go by.   In Freiburg Station.   Rupert
Brooke.   OBTV

I saw a girl with one leg/over the rail of a balcony   The Right of Way.
William Carlos Williams.   MoVE

I saw a million flowers for the bee.   The Bee.   John Fandel.   GoYe

I saw again the common face/And heard the ordinary speech.   The
Epiphany.   George Strong.   GoYe

I saw all colours through her, and through her for a moment/I saw the Castle.
The Princess Who Fled to the Castle.   Francis Landy.   VWA

I saw as I lay dying that unbroken sea.   The Islands.   Randall Jarrell.
EAS

I saw her eat my heart.   The Spider and the Ghost of the Fly.   Vachel
Lindsay.   VGW

I saw him–in his golden prime,/THE GOOD HAROUN ALRASCHID.
Recollections of the Arabian Nights.   Alfred, Lord Tennyson.   VLP

...I saw/him looking up, say to us "All clear. All clear."   Air Raid.   Peter
Wild.   Psk

I saw it where your mother hung it/hopelessly/above her kitchen stove.
Bunny.   Christopher Fahy.   TAT

...I saw my father's eyes were warm.   The Addict.   Larry Rubin.   GoYe

I saw my Father's face frown through the glass.   My Father's Watch.   John Ciardi.   ImOP

I saw my Lord,/The one I love,/Last night..in sleep.   On the Death of Emperor Tenji.   *Anonymous.*   BoWoP

–I saw nobody coming, so I went instead.   Dream Songs.   John Berryman.   LCAP; NaP; NoAm

I saw that it was his umbrella!   Little Snail.   Hilda Conkling.   TiPo

I saw the Ghost of Youth!   The Lost Genius.   John James Piatt.   AA

I saw the gilded vapours fly/And leave me as I was before.   Why Do I Hate That Lone Green Dell?   Emily Bronte.   VLP

I saw the heart of summer start.   Winter's End.   Howard Moss.   NePoEA

I saw the Man that saw this wondrous sight.   I Saw a Peacock.   *Anonymous.*   CH; FaBoCh; GBP; ImOP; LoGBV; OBSP; OxBoLi; PoPle

I saw the mark/Of tears upon her, as she stept/Into the dark.   In the Street.   Shaw Neilson.   CBAP

I saw the morning break.   Victory.   *Anonymous.*   WGRP

I saw the picnic vanish down the hill,/And waved the moon awake, with empty hands.   The Assignation.   James Wright.   NePoEA

I saw the rendezvous.   Beaver Sign.   Kenneth Porter.   NePoAm

I saw the sheep with their lambs,/And thought on the Lamb of God.   Sheep and Lambs.   Katharine Tynan Hinkson.   AnIV; HBV 1-2; OBEV; OBVV; OnYI; OxBI

I saw the stony, rocky road where the tinker's children bide.   Tinker's Moon.   Ewart Milne.   OnYI

I saw the thing that should have pierced his heart/Turn to a golden staff.   Gifts.   Mary Elizabeth Coleridge.   PBWP

I saw their emu feather tails sticking out behind them.   War Dance.   Miidhu.   NOAV

I saw them mirrored from her bosom fly/Back to the moon on high.   Love in Moonlight.   Bhartrihari.   LiTW

I saw there was no harm/at all, though you were gone.   The Blue Animals.   John Anderson.   AmPA; SM

"I saw through the joke!" the man replied/They re-seated themselves beside.   Adam, Lilith, and Eve.   Robert Browning.   HBV 1-2

I saw you'd fallen back, you were wrapped/in some huge fold of darkness!   Vision.   Delmira Augustini.   WPOW

I saw you/on my walk last/night./Running.   Glimpse.   Pearl Cleage Lomax.   PoBA

...I saw you vanish into air.   Butterfly.   D. H. Lawrence.   SOTW

I saw your hand ascending/to bid a last adieu.   Fourth Station.   Ruth Schaumann.   ISi

I say, dear friend, good morning and good night.   Elegy.   William Jay Smith.   NePoEA

I say, God send me better speed; and, Fancy, now/farewell!   The Green Knight's Farewell to Fancy.   George Gascoigne.   EnRePo

I say he only WAS–he did not LIVE.   He Lives Long Who Lives Well.   Thomas Randolph.   WBLP

I say it don't make no difference/'cause they both life time   Ol' Hannah.   Doc Reese.   BluL

...I say it's funny/That life is dearest when it costs us money.   Epistle to the Reader.   Walker Gibson.   PP

I say moon, I see white,/a foam of sea of sky/over fire, consumed.   Tongues of Fire.   Jorge Plescoff.   VWA

I say no moir.   A Lament: 1547.   Alexander Scott.   CH

I say no more, because I loved her.   Song Set by Robert Jones: "Once did I love and yet I live."   *Anonymous.*   OBSC

I say no more for Clavering.   Clavering.   Edwin Arlington Robinson.   CrMA; HBMV; OxBA

I say no more.–I care not though thou cease.   The Dispute of the Heart and Body of Francois Villon.   Francois Villon.   AWP; OBVE

I say not this of Chartres' dame,/Mother of Louis!   Prison Song.   Richard Coeur de Lion (Richard Lion-Heart).   LiTW

I say: son, wed you half as well.   The Aged Wino's Counsel to a Young Man on the Brink of Marriage.   X. J. Kennedy.   FF

I say that Pollard is none mery gollard.   Snatches: "Walterius Pollard non est but a dullard."   *Anonymous.*   OxBM

I say them in ceremony again:/Oak, fern, ivy and pine.   Little Epithalamium.   Chester Kallman.   CrMA

I say there will be no fruit in Britain for seven years unless/something happens.   The Book of Merlin.   Jack Spicer.   CoPo

I say "Thy breadth and thy depth for ever/Are bridged by his thoughts that cross to/me."   Divided.   Jean Ingelow.   HBV 1-2; OBNC; SpRo; VLP

I say to myself he is coming.   Funeral Song.   *Anonymous.*   PeSA

I say, when I marry gonna marry a Indian squaw/So the Big Chief can be my daddy-in-law.   Big Chief Blues.   Furry Lewis.   BluL

...I say with all my/heart and soul, "AMERICA FIRST!"   America First!   G. Ashton Oldham.   PGD

I say yes but it will take a long time.   For My Daughter.   Ronald Koertge.   GP; Str

I says let's bring her down.   First Flight.   Daniel Gerard Hoffman.   GrPl

I sayt an sayt again.   Women's Wather.   T. S. Law.   OxBS

I scampered/and fell.../–Mamma!...Mamma!...   Mamma!   Frank Horne.   BPo

I scarce should be unclasp'd at night.   The Miller's Daughter.   Alfred, Lord Tennyson.   CBEP; GTBS; LiTL; OBEV; OBVV; TrGrPo; UnTE; VLP

I scorn all earthly dung-bred scarabies.   Sonnet–To the Critic.   Michael Drayton.   LoBV

I scorn the multitude, alive and dead.   Be Gone Ye Blockheads.   Diogenes Laertius.   GLGT

I scrabble my toes.../Glunk!   Oiseaurie (parody).   Margaret Widdemer.   BXAP

I'se got a gal in the Sourwood Mountain,/Hey-tank-toodle all the day.   Sourwood Mountain.   *Anonymous.*   AmFP

I search for them, you are/hidden You.   Tom Clark.   ANYP

I search for words for her–and there are none.   Definition.   Grace Noll Crowell.   PoToHe

I search my mind for possible wounds and feel/The victim's body heavy on the victor's heart.   The Praying Mantis Visits a Penthouse.   Oscar Williams.   FaFP; LiTM; NePA

I see a chance for peace! What about water?   Sonnet: "Cry, crow."   Hayden Carruth.   NNaP

I see a culture of twigs and bird-shit/Waving a gaudy flag it loves and curses.   Desertmartin.   Tom Paulin.   FaBoIP

I see a long lean god/Standing in painted splendor.   Dancing Gal.   Frank Marshall Davis.   FB

I see all number, time, and space/Looking from my neighbor's face.   Life's Testament.   William Baylebridge.   PoAu 1-2

I see alps, ice, stars and white starlight/In a dry, high silence.   Nocturne of the Self-Evident Presence.   Thomas MacGreevy.   BIrV; CIP

I see an angel stand, guarding the way,/Somebody's mother and mine.   Old Ladies.   Will Allen Dromgoole.   WeW

I see and yet no greater sorow take,/Then that I loose no more for Stellas sake.   Astrophel and Stella, XVIII.   Sir Philip Sidney.   AAS; SiPS

I see forms of old time talking,/Who smile on me.   The House of Hospitalities.   Thomas Hardy.   NoAm

I see hell as a collection of warm fires.   Quite Shy Actually but Obsessed.   Jeffrey Miller.   APU

I see her close beside me with silent lips sad and tremulous.   Once I Pass'd Through a Populous City.   Walt Whitman.   AmPP; NePA; OxBA

I see his dreams.   The Skylark.   Frederick Tennyson.   HBV 1-2

I see it etched in fire.   Checking the Firing.   R. T. Smith.   AMV-80

I see it not, nor hear Adieu.   Years.   Walter Savage Landor.   CBEP; HBV 1-2; OBEV

I see it prophesy the path winds take.   In the Beginning Was the Bird.   Henry Treece.   LiTB; WaP

I see me I see me again.   Dawn.   Eileen Myles.   APU

I see Mike's painting, called SARDINES.   Why I Am Not a Painter.   Frank O'Hara.   ANYP; ConAP; HaCAP; HoAn; NeAP; NoAm; NOBA; PoM

I see mine own face over me,/With tears upon its cheek.   Little Gray Songs from St. Joseph's, XXX.   Grace Fallow Norton.   HBV 1-2

I see my self/Alive/A life   Poem for My Family: Hazel Griffin and Victor Hernandez Cruz.   June Jordan.   BPo

...I see my slaughtered joy/Bursting its cerement.   To Daisies.   Francis Thompson.   HBV 1-2

I see no ending to such plight/Except my usual; more insight.   Families.   Thomas Blackburn.   OBSP

I see/no more.   Landscape with Figures.   Theodore Enslin.   CoPo

I see no reason/Why gunpowder treason/Should ever be forgot.   Gunpowder Plot Day.   *Anonymous.*   FaBoPV; OxNR

I see that I am to wait for what will be exhibited by death.   Night on the Prairies.   Walt Whitman.   MoRP; RFM

I see that the new will not compare with the old.   Old and New.   *Anonymous.*   AWP; LiTW

I see that their arrows/are really boomerangs.   Image.   Henry Dumas.   BOLo

I see the constellations,/But by their gaps.   Can the Mole Take.   Cecil Day-Lewis.   OBMV

I see the future, and I will not see.   Spring-Gazing Song.   Hsueh T'ao.   BoWoP

...I see the/gods themselves rolled crashing down the great steps of the/temple in the darkness.   Investiture.   Brian Henderson.   BIrV

I see the head well-waves break out.   Portrait.   John Lyle Donaghy.   BIrV

I see/the image of my gun/on every eye.   The Famous Outlaw Stops in for a Drink.   David James.   AMV-81

I see the risen Lord again!   Faith.   John Richard Moreland.   OHIP

I see the solid hill/Flow backward for a moment and stand still.   At Arley.   Andrew Young.   FaBoPP

I see the world half otherwise/And tremble at its mysteries.   The Edge.   Rosemary Dobson.   NOAV

I see them now/but they aren't there.   Eastside Incidents.   Gregory Corso.   GP; NYP

"I see they've put a new streetlight out there."   The Planetary Arc-Light.   August Derleth.   GoYe

I see things from/the under side Ballade of the under Side. Don (Donald Robert Marquis) Marquis. InvP

I see those mice skittering back/night after night in the dusty plate. The American Poet–"But Since It Came to Good..." William Hathaway. APU

I see 'tis folly, but I feel 'tis woe. Carmina. Caius Valerius Catullus. OBVE

I see who e'ers freed, you for Slaves are decreed/Until you burn again, burn again. On the Lord Mayor and Court of Aldermen... Andrew Marvell. CoMu; FaBoBa

I see you, after all my pains,/So much resemble man! On a Spaniel Called Beau Killing a Young Bird. William Cowper. FaBoCh

...I see/you are afraid of yourself. Woman, You Are Afraid of the Forest. Maria Wine. PBWP

I see you diving, diving into the/darkest waters of your birthplace. For Mariella, in Antrona. Tobey A. Simpson. AMV-80

I see you every day. On Sir Henry Ferrett, M.P. J. B. Morton. PV

I see you sitting. Matmiya. Mary Tallmountain. TWSS

"I see your lights!" But ours had long died out. The Sentry. Wilfred Owen. AnEnPo; MMM

I seek a care-less home/home to my heart's content/home. Home. Sipho Sepamla. WhB

I seek her again; and I love you not now. The Shiver. Thomas Hardy. InPo

I seek not mine but his/Who sent me, and thereby witness what I am. Paradise Regained. John Milton. LiTB; OBS

I seem again to meet/the blue eyes of the images in the church. Enfidaville. Keith Douglas. HaMV

I seem to fail from out my blood/And grow incorporate into thee. In Memoriam A.H.H., II. Alfred, Lord Tennyson. ELP; GTBS-P; NAWM 1-2; NOBE; OAEL 1-2; OBNC; PoEL 1-5; UnPo

I seem to hear the rushing wave/I heard far out at sea. Wind and Wave. Charles Warren Stoddard. AA

I seem to know them, though this body of mine/Passed into spirit at the touch of hers! The First Kiss. Theodore Watts-Dunton. HBV 1-2

I seem to look through on the glories that lie in that great Home/Corral. The Range Rider's Soliloquy. Earl Alonzo Brininstool. PoOW

I seem to love the little ghost I made. On Shooting a Swallow in Early Youth. Turner, Charles Tennyson. FM; NOBV

I seen uncle willie cry some. When My Uncle Willie Saw. Carol [(or Carole)] Freeman. NMM

I sells mah chah-coal two bits a sack/Chah-coal, chah-coal. Charcoal Man. *Anonymous.* TrAS

I send a thought–of marigolds. A Thought of Marigolds. Janice Farrar. GoYe

I send defiance, since if overthrown,/Thou vanquishing, the conquest is mine own. Idea. Michael Drayton. NoP

I send my soul through time and space/To greet you. You will understand. To a Poet a Thousand Years Hence. James Elroy Flecker. ChTr; FaBoRV; HBV 1-2; MoBrPo; PoRA

I send the tears caught in my bandana. Traditional Funeral Songs. *Anonymous.* BoWoP

I send this/Kiss for him. A Kiss. *Anonymous.* KiLC

I send this verse along to make you see. By Return Mail. Richard Aldridge. NePoAm-2

I send you my constancy./Take it,/please. Love-Letter One. *Anonymous.* PeHV

I sent a letter to my love/On a sheet of stone. The True Confession of George Barker. George Barker. FaBoTw

I serve thee with my heart,/And fall before thee. Devotion. *Anonymous.* LiTB; OBEV

I set my love a seal upon your arm. A Marriage Charm. Nora Hopper. HBV 1-2

I sh'd think 'e'll get right again. The Collier's Wife. D. H. Lawrence. HaMV; OxBTC

I shake my own hand and pretend/we are making up for good. Absent Star. Quinton Duval. FAZ

I shake my wings/and fly into its boughs. The Knot. Stanley Jasspon Kunitz. HAP

I shall arise,/And with these eyes/My Saviour see. I Said Sometimes with Tears. Samuel Crossman. OxBoCh

I shall be an old bum loved but unrespected. The Good Boy (with music). *Anonymous.* AS

I shall be beside the noble ones. Deirdre's Lament. *Anonymous.* LiTW; OnYI

I shall be forever killing; and be killed. Nice Day for a Lynching. Kenneth Patchen. PoNe

I shall be gone, and you may whistle for me. Oh, oh, you will be sorry for that word! Edna St. Vincent Millay. BoWoP

I shall be good as new. The Stones. Sylvia Plath. CAPP; SBG; SM

I shall be more (alas!) than one be sold. Christus Matthaeum et Discipulos Alloquitur. Sir Edward Sherburne. ACP

I shall be rich and splendid/With the spoils of the Indies of Age. Come, Captain Age. Sarah N. Cleghorn. HBMV

I shall be satisfied/If only the dreams abide. If Only the Dreams Abide. Clinton Scollard. HBV 1-2

I shall be sorry for its wife! The Perfect Child. Adrian Porter. NLV

I shall be still. The child may keep his toy. Sonnets from a Sequence. Shirley Barker. AnAmPo

I shall be sure to find old Daniel Gray. Daniel Gray. Josiah Gilbert Holland. AA; HBV 1-2

I shall become a part of them. My Hereafter. Juanita De Long. WGRP

I shall bigge me a bowr at the wodes ende,/There to lede my life. The Forester. *Anonymous.* OxBM

I shall build me a bower at the woodes end/There to lead my life. I Have Been a Forester. *Anonymous.* CBEP; EBEV; FaBoRV; GBP; OBSP

I shall but love thee better after death. Sonnets from the Portuguese, XLIII. Elizabeth Barrett Browning. BoLoP; CTC; FaBoBe; FaBV; FF; FPL; GoTF; GTBS; HBV 1-2; HeIP; HoPM; LiTB; LiTL; NIP; NoP; OAEP; OLR; PAI; PG; PoLf; PoPl; PoRA; TEP; TreF; TrGrPo; TRV; UnPo; WHA

I shall buy a little orphan-girl/And bring her up as mine. If No One Ever Marries Me. Laurence Alma-Tadema. BiCB; OxBChV

I shall come back at last/In this dark house to die. In This Dark House. Edward Davison. OBMV

I shall creep out into darkness. Blue Symphony. John Gould Fletcher. AnAmPo; MAPA

I shall crown your innocent heads/with twelve stars of Israel. If I Forget Thee. Emanuel Litvinoff. TrJP; VWA

I shall cry out to heaven, "The sun! the/sun!" Helios. Joel Elias Spingarn. AA

I shall do nothing but look at the sky. Over the Heather the Wet Wind Blows. W. H. Auden. EnLi 1-2; PoRA

I shall dream of a crown til I do. The Scratch. James Dickey. AP

...I/Shall drink it to the full, and go content! Morning in the North-West. Arthur Stringer. CaP

I shall ebb out with them, who homeward go. The Autumnal. John Donne. TEP; ViBoPo

...I shall emerge some day. O Never Star Was Lost. Robert Browning. TreFT

I shall, even before the Resurrection, attain my full stature. Magdalene. Boris Pasternak. MoRP

I shall explain, with love and luck,/Three Chinese sailors and a duck. Gets Hung up on a Dirty, of All Things, Joke (parody). Henry Taylor. BXAP

I shall fare alone–/Nor track nor trace. Beauty Is Most at Twilight's Close. Par Lagerkvist. LiTW; PoPl

I shall find ten as fair, and yet more true. To His Unconstant Friend. Henry, Bishop of Chichester King. AnAnS 2

I shall forever be with Thee/Because Thou art with me. Companionship. Maltbie Davenport Babcock. STF

I shall forget, in Nineteen-twenty,/You ever hurt a bit! The One before the Last. Rupert Brooke. OBVV

I shall forget the drop of Anguish/That scalds me now–that scalds me now! I shall know why. Emily Dickinson. NoAm; NOCV

I shall give birth to my daughter here,/holding up the sky. Lineage. Reba Terry. AMV-81

I shall give them all to my elder daughter. If I Should Ever By Chance. Edward ("Edward Eastaway") Thomas. FaBoCh; GoJo; GTBS; HBMV; LoGBV; MoAB; MoBrPo; MoShBr; OBMV; OxBChV

I shall go haunting in search of a friend, a friend. The Ghost at Anlaby. Randolph Stow. NOAV

I shall go hence that I may weep alone. Sonnets. Robert Hillyer. HBMV

I shall go homewards in the Western Star. Country Press. Rosemary Dobson. FaBoWP; NOAV

...I shall go/Thoughtfully toward the distant fields that show/Emptiness, white and endless. A Vision. Maria Konopnicka. WPOW

I shall hate sweet music my whole life long. The Triumph of Time. Algernon Charles Swinburne. ViBoPo

I shall have had my day. Maud. Alfred, Lord Tennyson. NOBV

...I shall have/heard/Death; I shall know that I have lived/too long. Strangeness of Heart. Siegfried Sassoon. MoRP; TrJP

I shall have less to say,/But I shall be gone. The Sound of the Trees. Robert Frost. AnFE; APA; AtBAP; MAPA; OxBA; PG

I shall have lost/Half my delight. The Stream's Song. Lascelles Abercrombie. OBMV

I shall have need of them, when you are gone. Lover to Lover. David Morton. HBMV

I shall have sung! I shall have sung! Rebel. Irene Rutherford McLeod. HBMV

I shall have the best and fairest May/That ever I saw. That Ever I Saw. *Anonymous.* CBEP; TrGrPo

I shall hear distinct the sweet echo of my prayers from/Thy Abode of Songs. Divine Songs to Ahura Mazda. Zoroaster. LiTW

I shall hear, I doubt not, thy pangs in Limbo related. Dido to Aeneas. Richard Stanihurst. AnIV

I shall hear the click-click of the gun I'd/Omitted to load! My Woodcock. Patrick Reginald Chalmers. CenHV

I shall lament the inevitable loss of my sight. To the Sun. Ingeborg Bachmann. BoNaP

I shall lese my right arm! For Sore Eyes. *Anonymous.* OxBM

I shall look for loving crops from the birth, life, death, im-/mortality, I plant so lovingly now. A Woman Waits for Me. Walt Whitman. ErPo; NOBA

I shall lose God et vitam eternam. Up I Arose in Verno Tempore. *Anonymous.* GBP

I shall never come back. My Mother Said. *Anonymous.* LoGBV; OBSP; OxNR; PoPle

I shall never come back again! The Changeling. Charlotte Mew. CH

I shall never find any/greater than you. The Great Hunt. Carl Sandburg. MoLP

...I shall never fly. That "Craning of the Neck". Isabella Gardner. NePA

I shall never leave you, darling,/Do not fear. Ballad: "Father, through the dark that parts us." Roy Fuller. ELU

I shall not come to harm. Ophelia's Song. Marya Zaturenska. OLR

I shall not die! I Shall Not Die for Thee. Padraic Colum. CTC

I shall not die because of you. I Shall Not Die. *Anonymous.* KiLC

I shall not fail that rendezvous. I Have a Rendezvous with Death. Alan Seeger. BBV; BLPA; DL; FaBV; FaFP; GoTF; HBV 1-2; MCCG; OHFP; PoPl; ViBoPo; WaP

I shall not find his equal anywhere. I Saw My Father. E. L. Mayo. MiAP

I shall not know the sun is there/When next I see the sun. The Supreme Sacrifice. Furnley Maurice. CBAP

I shall not lie to you ever again–/Will you love me still? The Modern Woman to Her Lover. Margaret Widdemer. HBMV

I shall not listen to you,/Shall not come. Dead "Wessex" the Dog to the Household. Thomas Hardy. FM

I shall not live in vain. If I Can Stop One Heart from Breaking. Emily Dickinson. AH; FPL; GoTF; OHFP; PoLf; PoToHe; TreF; TRV

I shall not lose thee though I die. In Memoriam A.H.H., CXXX. Alfred, Lord Tennyson. HBV 1-2; OAEL 1-2

I shall not pass this way again. I Shall Not Pass This Way Again. *Anonymous.* BLPA; BLRP; FPL; GoTF; TreF; TreFS; WBLP

I shall not quit her feet in Paradise! The Shed. Charles L. O'Donnell. ISi

I shall not repeat others' comments about me. Wet Casements. John Ashbery. PoM

I shall not return to Ur. Abraham. Eisig Silberschlag. VWA

I shall not sing again. The Last Song. Eileen Duggan. CAW

I shall not sleep tonight when I hear the plane. Nightmare at Noon. Stephen Vincent Benét. OxBA

I shall not tell how much I loved him then. Sonnet: On the Detection of a False Friend. Guido Cavalcanti. AWP

I shall not think of taking/even my comb of boxwood. If you go away. *Anonymous.* BoWoP

I shall not walk the clover snows.) Spring Song. LeRoy Smith, Jr. NePoAm

...I shall not/want him for long. Neo-Thomist Poem. Ernest Hemingway. OBAL

I shall not wonder more, then,/But I shall know. Change. Raymond Knister. CaP; OBCV; PeCV

I shall nurse my love and keep it/Faithfully, for you, till then. Fidelis. Adelaide Anne Procter. BLPA; FaBoBe

I shall pay no rust as rent/For the house that is mine. The Tenancy. Mary Gilmore. BoAV; CBAP; PoAu 1-2

I shall pluck my love from my chest/And bury its memory under the ground. Prostration. David Semah. VWA

I shall possess the field. Two Voices in a Meadow. Richard Wilbur. NePoAm-2; UnPo

I shall quite simply never speak to the fellow again. The Deserter. Stevie Smith. FaBoWP

I shall rejoice Thy yoke to share! The Carpenter's Son. Kathryn Blackburn Peck. BePJ

I shall release my hold, and be blown away. The Flagpole Sitter. Donald Finkel. CoAP

I shall remember them with tears. Farewell. Katharine Tynan. CH

"I shall return dearies/and don't you motherfuck forget it!!!" Toe Queen Poems (excerpt). Ed Sanders. ANYP

"I shall rise from the dead," I am saying. In the Mountain Tent. James Dickey. CAPP

...I shall rise/from the dead to say the sun is shining. Mounds of Human Heads Are Wandering into the Distance. Osip Mandelstam. FaBoPV

I shall rouse her in the morn,/My fiddle and I thegither. Green Sleeves. *Anonymous.* GBP

I shall see him eat my words/When he grovels hither. Academic Curse: An Epitaph. Wesli Court. TW

I shall see justice done. Witch. Patricia Beer. OxBC

I shall see Messiah ride. Besieged. Zalman Schneour. TrJP

I shall see Thee in likeness Thine. Psalm XVII. Sir Philip Sidney. FCP

I shall see them walk hand in hand,/Her head on his hated breast. The Desolate Lover. Eileen Shanahan. NeIP

I shall shout for help! The Crow. Rita Boumi-Pappas. PBWP

I shall spring up, a sparkle from the coal. The Cloud of Unknowing. Philip Murray. NePoAm-2

I shall stay here long. Strangeness, at last, brings peace. Traveling America. Jan Struther. AmFN

I shall suffice that they were breathed and died for her delight. Follow Your Saint. Thomas Campion. AAS; AtBAP; EBEV; EiL; EnLoPo; ExPo; ForPo; HAP; InPo; OAEL 1-2; SeCePo; TrGrPo; ViBoPo

I shall tell those who pass that Midas here lies buried. Cleobulus' Epitaph. Simonides (of Ceos). PoPl

I shall use the shivered glass for my own collage. Ella of the Cinders. Mary Blake French. DFT

I shall wait. But I shall not weep. I shall not care. After Tschaikowsky. Wallace Gould. AnAmPo

I shall walk out bravely into the daily accident. Morning Song. Alan Dugan. CAD; ELU

I shall want just one kiss more. To Anne. William Stirling-Maxwell. HBV 1-2

I shall weep, oh, I shall weep, I know/For joy or for misery. Wedding Morn. D. H. Lawrence. MoAB; MoBrPo

I shall whistle him, time's fool,/Back to the present. Soliloquy by the Shore. Martin Scholten. GoYe

I shall work better all my other days. The Book. Winfred Ernest Garrison. TRV

I shall yet be footloose. Broken-Face Gargoyles. Carl Sandburg. AmPP; MoAmPo; OxBA

I shan't be gone long.–You come too. The Pasture. Robert Frost. AnNE; BiP; BLPL; BoC; CMoP; DiPo; GoJo; LaNeLa; MoAB; MoAmPo; MoShBr; NOBA; OxBA; PoPl; SoPo; SoSe; TiPo; ViBoPo

I shan't look up to see it drop. Sonic Boom. John Updike. QQQ

I shan't steal kisses from you any more. Juventius, My Honey. Caius Valerius Catullus. PeHV

I shape with bare/and desperate hands/its likeness in myself. The Likeness. Arthur Gregor. VGW

I share Thy dream tonight! Christmas Eve. Catherine Parmenter. PGD

I shelter a song for you/Secretly.... Secret. Gwendolyn B. Bennett. BlSi; CDC

I shold haue purcchased three of the/best churches/That stands by any highway.' Little John a Begging (A version). *Anonymous.* ESPB

I shoot wild ducks down deep snake-holes,/And drink gin-sling from two-quart bowls. My Home. *Anonymous.* NA

I should be glad of another death. Journey of the Magi. Thomas Stearns Eliot. BoC; DiPo; DTC; EaLo; EBCP; FaBoCh; FaBoMo; FaFP; HAP; HeIP; InPK; InPo; LiTA; LiTM; LoGBV; MoAB; MoAmPo; MoRP; MP; NePA; NIP; NOCV; OAEP; OBCP; OBMV; OxBTC; PCh; PPoe; SBVL; SoSe; TAP; TrGrPo; TwCP

I should be more than a page of print she knows by heart. Old Fellow. Ernest Walsh. ErPo

I should be pleased to lie in one grave with'em. My Burial Place. Robinson Jeffers. AP

I should be told that there is, after all,/An essence and an irony in fall. Autumn Orchard. Catherine Haydon Jacobs. AMV-80

"I should be very ill!" The Mad Gardener's Song. Lewis (Charles Lutwidge Dodgson) Carroll. FiBHP

I should die of the love that I bear the Gael! On His Exile to Iona. Saint Columcille. CAW; LiTW

I should dumbfounder every jail-bird there. Fresco-Sonnets to Christian Sethe. Heinrich Heine. AWP

I should go riding up and down upon the velvet chair. The Dentist. Rose Fyleman. SoPo; TiPo

I should go with him in the gloom,/Hoping it might be so. The Oxen. Thomas Hardy. BiP; BoLiVe; CMoP; CoBMV; EBEV; GTBS; HAP; HBMV; InPK; LiTM; MoAB; MoBrPo; MoRP; NoAm; NOBE; OAEL 1-2; OAEP; OBCP; OxBTC; PCh; PPoe; PPP; SoSe

I should have been cruel enough to bring/You through the flame. Last Words to Miriam. D. H. Lawrence. CoBMV

I should have kissed her if the rain/Had lasted a minute more. A Thunderstorm in Town. Thomas Hardy. BoLoP; EnLoPo; GBL; OBSP

I should have made a lighter cross/To bear up Calvary! A Little Parable. Anne Reeve Aldrich. AA; HBV 1-2

I should have written/"doubt"/when I had it. Doubt. Pat Nolan. APU

I should know what God and man is. Flower in the Crannied Wall. Alfred, Lord Tennyson. BBV; BoNaP; DiPo; FaBV; FaFP; GoTF; InPK; LiTB; MaVP; MCCG; NIP; PoPl; TEP; TreFS; TrGrPo; TRV; WGRP

...I should leap from heaven or hell with a/whole spirit and heart. I Walked with My Reason. Sorley MacLean. LiTW

I stayed many weeks in England/Instead of just one.   The White Cliffs.
Alice Duer Miller.   PoLf

I stayed. On my peacetime feet. There was little alternative.   Autumn Sequel,
IV.   Louis MacNeice.   FaBoIP

I steadier step when I recall/That, if I slip, Thou dost not fall.   With Whom
Is No Variableness, Neither Shadow of Turning.   Arthur Hugh Clough.
EnLi 1-2; GoTF; TreFS; TRV; WGRP

I steer my course with every wind/To all the ports she has designed.   A
Letter to Lord Middleton.   Sir George Etherege.   CavP

...I stifle my/sobs in the grass.   The Songs of Bilitis.   Pierre Louys.   UnTE

–I still/Am Belisarius!   Belisarius.   Henry Wadsworth Longfellow.   PoEL
1-5; WiR

I still can see the light I dreamed you were.   Two Sonnets for a Lost Love.
Samuel A. DeWitt.   GoYe

I still can't.   Blades.   C. K. Williams.   GeTw

I still could tell you less of it/Than blind Homer may.   Tourist.   Mark Van
Doren.   NePoAm-2

I still dont know.   The Art of Enforced Deprivation.   Alta.   GP

I still go there, looking for him/among the empty tables.   Remembering
Lutsky.   Rayzel Zychlinska.   VWA

...I still long/To sail forgotten ships to Arcady.   Arcady Revisited.   Robert
Funge.   AMV-80

I still take tigers/safely home.   Paper Words.   William Franklin.   LFAC

I still wish with passion/that you were here.   To J.F.K. 14 Years after.
Roger Weaver.   AMV-80

...I stood and watched her little lamp uselessly lost/among lights.   On the
Slope of the Desolate River.   Rabindranath Tagore.   OBMV

I stood before it for hours in wintertime.   A Hill.   Anthony Hecht.   CoAP;
NYBP

I stood so near upon the height/That my flesh felt the carillon.   Antwerp and
Bruges.   Dante Gabriel Rossetti.   OBTV; VLP

I stood there, fifteen.   Fifteen.   William Stafford.   CAD

I stood there like a child, scared, new,/bird-eyed, not knowing why I came.
Desks.   Dave Smith.   HaCAP

I stop somewhere waiting for you.   Song of Myself.   Walt Whitman.   AmP;
AP; APA; LiTA; MAmP; MoAmPo; NOBA; OxBA; TAP

I stop to wonder at our/stubborn appetite for joy.   As in the Land of
Darkness.   Robert Miklitsch.   AMV-80

I strain my heart, I stretch my hands,/And catch at hope.   De Profundis.
Christina Georgina Rossetti.   CoBE

I strew lilies on the grave/Of the bravest of the brave.   Decoration.   Thomas
Wentworth Higginson.   AA; OHIP

I strike a match and watch it burn, finding/in its one act of mercy what we
are.   Elegy for My Mother.   Richard Katrovas.   SM

I strike for life.   Ojibwa War Songs.   Anonymous.   AWP

I strive to recall it if I may.   The Dream.   William Allingham.   BIrV;
NOBV; OxBI

I stroke him/but cannot find the dial.   The Secret in the Cat.   May
Swenson.   DFF; GP

I stuck it on with cellotape. Not quite straight.   Trees, Effigies, Moving
Objects.   Allen Curnow.   OCNZ

I stumbled like a drunkard.   The Potter.   Anonymous.   TTY

I suck smoke/out of my eyes.   Fighting Her.   David Phillips.   NeAC

I suckle coyotes/and grieve.   Long Division: A Tribal History.   Wendy
Rose.   TWSS

I suffered facts,/And have the bloody photographs to prove it.   History:
Madness.   Stan Rice.   NPGG

I suppose, by one of those tall, dark, handsome/Gentlemen the Victorians were
so crazy about.   Mourningsong for Anne.   David Posner.   FAZ

I suppose if I must starve, I must!   The Crocodile.   Oliver Herford.   OBCA

...I suppose/it is the nearest I will get to home.   Postcards from Kodai.
Kevin Crossley-Holland.   OBTV

I suppose we should leave him there,/alone, nodding off to sleep, dreaming.
Old Ego Song.   John Minczeski.   AMV-80

I suppose where all the rest of us must go.   The Mantis Friend.   Vincent
McHugh.   NePoAm-2

I sure hopes I get invited,/When they let her out of jail next year.   Mae's
Rent Party.   Ernest J. Wilson, Jr.   PoNe

I surely will die.   Rye Whisky.   Anonymous.   ABF; CoSo

...I surely will return/To my native Ballyshannon, and the winding banks of/
Erne.   The Winding Banks of Erne.   William Allingham.   AnIV; IrPN;
NBM

I surfet with excess of joy, and dye.   Murdering Beauty.   Thomas Carew.
OAEP; SeCP

I surrender myself   What to Say to the Pasha.   George Hitchcock.   OBAL

I survive/survive/survive   This Morning.   Lucille Clifton.   GLGT

I survived His innocence/without my own.   All the World Moved.   June
Jordan.   NBP; PoBA

...I suspect I'll find you/on the scaffold of the Knowable,/furiously soaping the
noose.   St. Augustine Contemplating the Bust of Einstein.   Diane
Ackerman.   SUW

I swallowed sighs that seeped into my bones.   My Song.   Hayim Nahman
Bialik.   VWA

I swear I don't want no body ooo, lord, baby always hanging 'round   I'm
Gonna Move to the Outskirts of Town.   Big Bill Broonzy.   BluL

I swear I hear those sisters still humming.   I, Woman.   Irma McClaurin.
BlSi

I swear I remember nothing.   Friends, you are lucky you can talk.   Vidya.
BoWoP

I swear it to you on my common/woman's/head.   The Common Woman.
Judy Grahn.   GP

I/swear/nothing   Incidental Pieces to a Walk: for Conrad.   James (Olumo)
Cunningham.   JB

I swear to you I knew it once.   Empty Dwelling Places.   Kenneth Patchen.
PoA

I sweep away blossoms and dust,/Small claims to my care,/Which lend the
sunset its colors.   Roof Garden.   Raymond Filip.   CaPN

I sweetly fell asleep.   For Lo! My Jonah How He Slumped.   John Wilson.
AH

I swer by Heven-King/Thos beeth five lither thing!   Snatches: "Bishop
lorless."   Anonymous.   OxBM

I swore I would, yet still she said I should not/Do what I would, and yet for
all I could not.   A Little Pretty Bonny Lass.   Anonymous.   EiL; NCEP

...I swore,/nothing, but nothing, would be beneath me.   I Knew I'd Sing.
Heather McHugh.   GeTw

I tak my leif aganis my will.   The Bankis of Helicon: Fairweill.   Anonymous.
OxBS

I take his head upon my breast,/And hold my dearest till he wakes.   When
My Beloved Sleeping Lies.   Irene Rutherford McLeod.   HBV 1-2

I take it you are he?   Incident in a Rose Garden.   Donald Justice.   NCSH

I take my leve a-gaynst my wyll.   A Farewell to His Mistress.   Anonymous.
ABF; AtBAP

I take my whole body off,/and throw it/in the river.   Summer.   Frank Asch.
NTCP

I take on shapes like water.   When the Loneliness of the Tomb Went down
into the Marketplace.   Mona Sa'udi.   WPOW

I take smiles/and draw bright nooses around you.   Metaphors.   Miklos
Radnoti.   VWA

I take the gift, Lord, look on me/As one who has Thy gift received.   He
Took My Place.   Horatius Bonar.   BePJ

I take the globe and roll it away: where/On it now is someone like you?   For
Elizabeth Bishop.   Sandra McPherson.   GeTw; MAYP

...I take/the risk of you in the hay's rot.   Having Read Books.   Heather
McHugh.   GeTw

I take the wound, and die at Venus' foot.   O Gentle Love.   George Peele.
EiL

I take these things,/not much more, from/my shelter from/the hurricane.
Jeronimo's House.   Elizabeth Bishop.   MiAP; NoP

I take your life into my living head.   Readings of History.   Adrienne Rich.
ConAP

I Taliessin came.   Taliessin's Return to Logres.   Charles Williams.   ACV

...I tame/The world around me till it names my name.   Pot Shot.   Padraic
Fallon.   CIP

I taped the book back together/for my sleeping children.   Langston Hughes.
Lew Blockcolski.   VoR

I taste honey and wine.   The Harvester.   Terry Lawrence.   AMV-80

I taste tomorrow's/tears.   At the Well.   Malka Tussman.   VWA

I taste unutterable bliss,/And everlasting rest.   I Know That My Redeemer
Lives.   Charles Wesley.   TreFS

I teach this forsaken town to howl.   Small Town.   William Joyce.   FAZ

I tear myself down from my double meaning.   Apart from Oneself.
Alejandra Pizarnik.   VWA

...I tell them I will share/my string of beads/if they give me Manhattan.   The
Indian.   Thomas Reed.   AMV-81

I tell this tale, as she told it to me,/In the year of eighteen ninety three.
Chipeta's Ride.   John W. Taylor.   PoOW

I tell you   Letter.   William Stanley Merwin.   HAP

I tell you love is possible./We have to try.   To a Child.   S. S. Gardons.
NePoEA-2

I tell you the kingliest victories fought/Are fought in these silent ways.   The
Greatest Battle That Ever Was Fought.   Joaquin Miller.   GoTF; TreF

I tell you this across the blackened vine.   Even in the Moment of Our
Earliest Kiss.   Edna St. Vincent Millay.   ATP

I tell you this across the blackened vine.   Fatal Interview.   Edna St. Vincent
Millay.   VGW

I tell you this, young man, so that your expectations of life/Will not be too
great.   Improvisations: Light and Snow (excerpt).   Conrad Aiken.
BoNaP

...I tell you. you're singing.   Song of the Strange Young Duckling.   Deborah
Munro.   IHMS

I, tempest-tossed, and wrecked at last,/Come home to port no more.   To Mr.
Newton on His Return from Ramsgate.   William Cowper.   NOEC

I thank God I'm free at las'.   I Thank God I'm Free at Las'.   *Anonymous.* BoAN 1-2; BPo; TAP

–I thank heaven somebody's crazy/enough to give me a daisy   One Winter Afternoon.   Edward Estlin Cummings.   NCSH

I thank her hands when the maple leaves turn,/hear her chants in the thrush's song.   Yonosa House.   R. T. Smith.   STE; Str

I thank thee for the slice of bread and the prayerful mood.   Kibbutz Sabbath.   Levi ben Amittai.   EaLo

I thank Thee, O my God!   A Thanksgiving.   Lucy Larcom.   OHIP

I thank Thee while my days go on.   De Produndis (excerpt).   Elizabeth Barrett Browning.   TrPWD

"I thank ye for nothing," Bold Dickie says he,/"And you're a damn fool for following me."   Archie O Cawfield (B vers.).   *Anonymous.*   AmFP; BaBo; ESPB

I thank you for the sunrise   Voices That Have Filled My Day.   Fay Chiang.   BrSi

I thank you, Old Man, the Sweat Lodge.   Old Man, the Sweat Lodge.   Phil George.   GrPl

"I thank you very kindly, Sir, I hear you quite clearly."   The Deaf Woman's Courtship.   *Anonymous.*   BFSS

I thanked her but I wouldn't dream/Of eating cake without ice cream.   Catherine.   Karla Kuskin.   NTCP

...I' the fifth diseases clog/And trouble him; then death's his epilogue.   De Morte.   *Anonymous.*   OBSP

I' the licht nichts o' the year.   The Licht Nichts.   Violet Jacob.   ACV

I, the swinging needle in the compass of the world;/Thou, the perpetual North.   Prayer.   Edith Lovejoy Pierce.   TrPWD

I then should have need/Of your needles indeed.   I Need Not Your Needles.   *Anonymous.*   OxNR

I thenche on hir that I ne see nought ofte.   An Unfortunate Lover.   *Anonymous.*   OxBM

I therefore must recommend,/Though not without some regret,/The extinction of poems.   Memo from the Desk of X.   Donald Justice.   TwCP

I therefore strive to follow those/Whom he to follow him hath chose.   The Anglers Song.   William Basse.   OBS

I think a heart must moan somewhere.   Voice in Darkness.   Richard Dehmel.   AWP

I think about them when I think of you.   Codicil.   Ruth Stone.   BoWoP

I think back when I had you.   Four Poems for Robin.   Gary Snyder.   NOBA; SOTW

...I think better/lost back there in our old brown car.   Strangers.   William Stafford.   NNaP

I think God in His ecstasy/Was startled...and was still.   The Star.   Beatrice Redpath.   CaP

I think God took these precious things, and made of them–/the Mothers.   Mothers.   *Anonymous.*   PGD

I/think/he/had.   Once.   Alice Walker.   PoBA

I think he only loves himself out loud.   The Talker.   Mona Van Duyn.   PoL

I think I am/alone and I will/still shiver.   Whose Voice.   Barney Bush.   STE

I think I can be even with mankind.   On the Phrase, "To Kill Time."   Voltaire (Francois Marie Arouet).   ALV; PV

I think I know no finer things than dogs.   I Think I Know No Finer Things Than Dogs.   Hally Carrington Brent.   BBV; BLPA

I think I know what the shape of the field was/That made the old man weep.   Field Day.   W. R. Rodgers.   BIrV

I think I'll be all of them/By taking turns.   When I Grow Up.   William Wise.   BiCB

I think I'll go and try it out on mine!   Run, Kitty, Run!   Jimmy Garthwaite.   BBGG

I think I'm the hot tuna.   Custer (2).   Alison Baker.   FAZ

I think I maun wed him to-morrow!   Last May a Braw Wooer.   Robert Burns.   EnLi 1-2

I think I never saw fairies skinnier.   Trapping Fairies in West Virginia.   Gelett Burgess.   FaBoNo

I think I robbed your ancestors/When I was young as you.   In Glencullen.   John Millington Synge.   ELU; FM; OBMV; OxBI

I think I should be a better boy.   A Little Boy's Vain Regret.   Edith Matilda Thomas.   AA

I think I should be covered up with snow!   Says Something, Too (parody).   Henry Taylor.   BXAP

I think I will not hang myself to-day.   A Ballade of Suicide.   Gilbert Keith Chesterton.   ALV; FiBHP; HBV 1-2; InMe; NLV

I think I will not quarrel with the Bond.   Portia.   Oscar Wilde.   BrPo

I think, if I went back, that she/Would take me to her breast.   San Francisco.   Walter Adolphe Roberts.   PoNe

I think it clever of the turtle/In such a fix to be so fertile.   The Turtle.   Ogden Nash.   FaFP; FiBHP; FPL; NePA; NIP; NoP; OBAL; SoSe; TAP

...I think it has an orange/bed in it, more than the ear can hold.   Radio.   Frank O'Hara.   PoA

I think it mercy if thou wilt forget.   Holy Sonnets, IX.   John Donne.   ATP; BiP; EBEV; JCP; NoP; OBS; PPP

I think it only came.   Little Phillis.   Kate Greenaway.   BiCB

I think it's pretty there, don't you?   Hair Ribbons.   *Anonymous.*   BiCB

I think it's worth it/that a good poet's life/is well spent.   Souster.   Ray Fraser.   NeAC

I think it was a very good/relationship.   Aaron.   Edwin Denby.   ANYP

I think it will be Golgotha.   Golgotha Is a Mountain.   Arna Bontemps.   AmNP; CDC; PoNe

I think it would like you to awaken.   Falling in Love.   Jon Anderson.   MAYP

...I think its mother wakens it.   Breakfast Time.   James Stephens.   SUS

I think of her, each night/dreaming intruders, their bloody forearms raised.   Rumors of War in Wyoming.   Tom Rea.   SOTS

I think of how the dead, my dead, once lay.   Reserve.   Richard Aldington.   BrPo

(I think of the flame carved like an asparagus tip.)   To the Statue.   May Swenson.   NYP

I think of the masts at Cette and the sweet rain.   American Letter.   Archibald MacLeish.   AmFN; AmPP; OxBA

I think of what will yet be seen/In Johnsonville and Geraldine.   Home Thoughts.   Denis Glover.   AnNZ

I think of you always.   Two Poems.   Akahito (Yamabe no Akahito).   LiTW

I think of you, and mercy! my/Tunic's got a tent-pole in it.   An Invitation to an Invitation.   Caius Valerius Catullus.   ErPo

I think of you,/and wonder if either of us/will ever come home.   To Maynard on the Long Road Home.   W. D. Ehrhart.   LTB

I think of you/restless,/journeying.   When I strip.   Anne-Marie Kegels.   BoWoP

I think of you with bitter longing always   Goddess.   Judith Johnson Sherwin.   BoWoP

I think of you with nothing on.   Celia Celia.   Adrian Mitchell.   FaBoEE

I think once more he seems to die.   In Memoriam A.H.H., C.   Alfred, Lord Tennyson.   VLP

I think, perhaps, hell sent the invitation,/long ago, to watch my bark go down.   Sonnet, XX: "A seer foretold that I would love one day."   Louise Labé.   PBWP

I think she gives the right answer, before/the light dims, bluing, then purpling the retina.   My Mother's Life.   William Meredith.   AMV-81

I think "Sorry Missus' was what he said.   Wounds.   Michael Longley.   FaBoIP; FaBoPV

An' I think that mebbe at last I ken/What your look meant then.   The Watergaw.   Hugh" (Christopher Murray Grieve) MacDiarmid.   BSV; GoTS; NeBP; NoP

I think that's all you ever really wanted/Not jails pain or death.   To an Old San Francisco Poet.   Keith Abbott.   APU

I think that the girl is gone mad.   The Comedy of Billy and Betty.   *Anonymous.*   OxNR

I think that we deserve to freeze.   The Arctic Ox.   Marianne Moore.   NYBP

I think that we will say, "God knew the best!"   Sometime.   May Riley Smith.   BLPA; HBV 1-2

I think the distance/Is nowhere.   Border Line.   Langston Hughes.   PoCh

I think the mountains ought to be/Taught a little modesty.   The Paps of Dana.   James Stephens.   NoAm

I think the result was a dead heat.   A Farewell to English (excerpt).   Michael Hartnett.   CIP

I think there are most tigers in the wood.   Ceremony.   Richard Wilbur.   CoAP; MiAP; NoAm; PP

I think there possibly might be/E'en greater geese than thou.   Precious Stones.   Charles Stuart Calverley.   InMe

I think there's no man speaks better Welch.   King Henry IV.   William Shakespeare.   NAs

(I think they are meant to be trippy.)   Limerick: "You have to be brainy, not drippy."   *Anonymous.*   TDH

I think they'd both be happier, for the nonce.   Savage Portraits.   Don (Donald Robert Marquis) Marquis.   HBMV

I think they need some tranquillizers.   A Bestiary of the Garden for Children Who Should Know Better.   Phyllis Gotlieb.   WHW

I think they're strolling still.   Road Fellows.   Barbara Young.   BrR

I think this is the Sea of Disappointment.   Nightwalker.   Thomas Kinsella.   BIrV; IPY

I think thou'rt Jester at the Court of/Heaven!   The Harlequin of Dreams.   Sidney Lanier.   AA; AP

I think was probably me.   Tracks in the Snow.   Marchette Chute.   SiSoSe

I think we all ought to do that   For Muh' Dear.   Carolyn M. Rodgers.   CNA

I think we're drifting apart.   Rift Tide.   Ruth M. Walsh.   QQQ

I think we should all go to sleep now,/And not care anymore.   Gautama in the Deer Park at Benares.   Kenneth Patchen.   NaP

I think, we've fared, my heart and I.   My Heart and I.   Elizabeth Barrett Browning.   HBV 1-2

I think we've played this one before.   Conversation.   K. Malley.   AMV-80

I think, whose lips have prest me, I am proud.   Epigrams.   Theocritus.   AWP

I think with doubtful view/Whether you be the rose, or the rose is you.   The Rose.   Thomas Lodge.   OBSC

I think you're great.   So Long as Time & Space Are the Stars.   Michael Silverton.   PV

I thinks I mus' 'a' been called to preach.   This Sun Is Hot.   Anonymous.   BPo

...I-Thou, cat, I-Thou.   The Cat as Cat.   Denise Levertov.   NOBA

I thought all earthly creatures knelt/From rapture of the joy I felt.   The Everlasting Mercy.   John Masefield.   TRV

"I thought all people understood/The difference 'twixt "might" and "could"!"   The Cumberbunce.   Paul West.   NA

I thought an Abyssinian child/Had cried out in the whitethroat's scream.   The Prize Cat.   Edwin John Pratt.   NoAm; PeCV

I thought, and took a street-car back to Harvard Square.   I Walked over the Grave of Henry James.   Richard Eberhart.   VGW

I thought I had beheld it from the flood.   Lines on Seeing a Lock of Milton's Hair.   John Keats.   PeD

I thought I loved the song; but no!/It was her singing of it!   The Song.   John Erskine.   AA

I thought I should never/see you again.   Paterson.   William Carlos Williams.   MoLP

I thought I was wounded to the core/but I was only bruised.   Epilogue.   Denise Levertov.   LLLT

I thought it was heavy–/& I liked the idea/before I came down/from my high.   Slow Death.   Lorri Martinez.   LFAC

I thought of the snake,/of his quick motion.   Castoff Skin.   Ruth Whitman.   InPK

I thought of Troy, what we had built her for.   Aeneas at Washington.   Allen Tate.   AP; FYAP; LiTA; MoPo; MoVE; NePA; NoAm; NOBA; OxBA

I thought of you, dear Dorothy!   The Mouse.   Hugh McCrae.   PoAu 1-2

I thought probably I would hate you, but I have not.   Lindeman.   Mary Jane White.   AMV-81

I thought she had a pre-dynastic look.   Early Chronology.   Siegfried Sassoon.   GLGT

I thought she kind o' wished me to!   The Smack in School.   William Palmer.   HBV 1-2

I thought so once; but now I know it.   My Own Epitaph.   John Gay.   FaBoEE; FF; GoTF; NIP; NOEC; SeCePo; SeCeV; TreFT

I thought that was/rather good.   Another Academy.   Charles Bukowski.   TAT

I thought the river stood still and did not flow.   Tzu Yeh Songs.   Anonymous.   BoWoP

"I thought they were the bitterest enemies?"   The Enemy's Portrait.   Thomas Hardy.   EyDe; TW

I thought, "What lovely poems this will make!"   Literary Love.   Harry Kemp.   HBMV

I thought: why me, why her, & knew it wouldn't last.   Family Romance.   Larry Levis.   MAYP

I thought why not ride the rest of the way together?   Jump Cabling.   Linda Pastan.   AmC

...I thought, with that/other mind, and stood still.   Black Silk.   Tess Gallagher.   FaBoWP; MAYP

I thought you'd be good after this.   Washing and Dressing.   Ann Taylor.   FaBoUs

I thought you was alone.   The Food Drops Off a Fork.   Michael Silverton.   PoL

I throw away my life/and my life comes back.   Boomerang.   John Perreault.   ANYP; EAS

"I thynk hit is a fulle fayre tyme/In a mornynge of May."   In Summer.   Anonymous.   CH

I titty-atty-ing I-o.   Kitty Morey.   Anonymous.   AmFP

I toast with this bitter cup/and offer up as prayer,/on our road, let us repair.   Of Pardons, Presidents, and Whiskey Labels.   Richard Snyder.   SOTS

"I told my wife/that besides marriage/and the mystery of children,/I have one friend."   108 Tales of a Po'Buckra, No. 106.   Will Inman.   GP

I, too, a shade!   Her Shadow.   Elisabeth Cavazza Pullen.   AA

I, too, am America.   I, Too.   Langston Hughes.   CDC; FF; HaCAP; HeIP

I too am of that royal race/Who do what we are born to do.   Tiger.   A. D. Hope.   OxBC

"I, too, but seem."   In Utrumque Paratus.   Matthew Arnold.   MaVP; OAEP; OBNC; PoEL 1-5; VLP

I too came to know the right side/of the world.   The Armless.   Don Welch.   AMV-81

I too find it delicious.   Gislebertus' Eve.   John Berryman.   LCAP

I, too, have plucked a stalk of grass/from your ample prairie, Walt.   Letters to Walt Whitman.   Ronald Johnson.   VGW

I too heard, like Lord Jim,/A voice which tempted: "Jump!"   Conrad.   Antoni Slonimski.   VWA

"I, too, joyfully trod my hills and came away,/"And bore a Burden up a stony road.'   Levavi Oculos.   Marion Campbell.   PoSH

I, too, know "Christ is risen, as he said."   Assurance.   Ida Norton Munson.   PGD

I too lie safe beneath his wing.   Parting.   William Caldwell Roscoe.   OBVV

I too make my excursions/into the land of the living/no different than anyone else.   Vampirella.   Elaine Equi.   APU

I too, making dark things clear,/Am of my trade a master.   The Scholar and the Cat.   Anonymous.   KiLC

I too must worship blindly, Jonathan.   Whaddaya Do for Action in This Place?   George Starbuck.   NePoEA-2

I, too, once dwelt in Arcady.   On a Picture by Poussin Representing Shepherds in Arcadia.   John Addington Symonds.   FaBoBe; HBV 1-2

I, too, once trusted air/that plunged me down./Yes, I!   "...As When Emotion Too Far Exceeds its Cause"–Elizabeth Bishop.   Gloria C. Oden.   AmNP

I too wanted love pure and simple.   Each Day.   David Ignatow.   NNaP

I too when my time comes/Shall do mightily.   A Song of Greatness.   Mary Austin.   AmFN; TiPo

I took a glance around before I wiped my mouth. Feeling weary.   Hmmm, 15.   Leslie Scalapino.   NPGG

I took a rung and I claw'd her,/An' a braw guid bairn was she.   My Wife's a Wanton Wee Thing.   Anonymous.   CoMu

I took by the throat the circumcised dog/And smote him, thus.   Othello.   William Shakespeare.   FiP; GoTF; TreFS

I took him by his left leg/And threw him down the stairs.   Goosey, Goosey, Gander.   Mother Goose.   HBV 1-2; PBBP

I took his face in my hands.   Earth Changes.   Kent Shire.   AMV-80

...I took it for an omen.   Ghost Pet.   Horatio Colony.   GoYe

I took my love in my icy arms/In the Spring on Ringwood Hill.   In the Ringwood.   Thomas Kinsella.   CMoP; FaBoIP; NMP; OxBI

I took the way that pleas'd mysel,/And sae did Death.   Death and Doctor Hornbook.   Robert Burns.   OxBS

I took thee for an angel, but have wooed/A cacodaemon in mine ignorant mood.   Night.   Charles Heavysege.   OBCV

I took up my little black stick,/And kocked out all their teeth.   As I Went over the Water.   Anonymous.   PBBP

I took up my position by the keyhole in the door.   The Keyhole in the Door.   Anonymous.   CoMu

I took you for your likeness, Cloe.   Cupid Mistaken.   Matthew Prior.   EiCP; InMe

I tore the bat's wing: what would you have more?   I Went to the Toad That Lies under the Wall.   Anonymous.   OxNR

I toss to-day; for you and I/Over the world are met!   To-Day.   Benjamin R. C. Low.   HBV 1-2

I touch my groin.   The Hemingway Syndrome.   Adrian C. Louis.   STE

I touch the hand there on the pillow.   Fall Comes in Back-Country Vermont.   Robert Penn Warren.   NYBP; VGW

I touch you/as a blind man touches the dice/and finds he has won.   My Love.   Richard Shelton.   GOYP

I touched center/and forgave myself   When I Cut My Hair.   Rayna Green.   TWSS

I touched her hand and she/disintegrated.   Eclipse.   Amir Rashidd.   NBP

I trace the dancing of their secular swarm.   The Sense of Responsibility.   Harry Mathews.   ANYP

I track him in vain!   In the Forest.   Oscar Wilde.   SyP

I travel the risk of the end. O perilous love.   The Little Girl with Bands on Her Teeth.   Genevieve Taggard.   VGW

I travel the road, alone.   Walking at Night.   Amory Hare.   PoLf

I tremble at the sorrow of the time.   October 1803.   William Wordsworth.   EnRP

I tremble, cold with dread,/Lest I wake up dead.   The Fear.   Wilfred Wilson Gibson.   GTBS

I tremble for the rosy boys.   Design for a Bowl.   Anacreon.   UnTE

I tried not to think/Of Caesar Chavez.   Salad La Raza.   Janet Campbell Hale.   VoR

I tried to be/oh tried to be/tried to be/a man to you/a man to you.   Evil Devil Woman.   (Kansas) Joe McCoy.   BluL

I tried to throw away the bud,/But the blossom would remain.   Love's Pains.   John Clare.   NOBV

I tried to turn the handle, but–   In Winter, When the Fields Are White.   Lewis (Charles Lutwidge Dodgson) Carroll.   EBEV; NOBV

I tripped up his heels and he fell on/his nose.   Old Bandy Legs.   Anonymous.   OxNR

I trow ye be nocht wyse.   The Pardoner's Sermon.   Sir David Lyndsay.   BSV

I trust the God–but oh! I fear the child!   The Blessed Virgin's Expostulation.   Nahum Tate.   ISi

I trust them more than the foot rule. Bach may yet have been right.   All Those Hymnings Up to God.   Abbie Huston Evans.   MoRP

I trust to recouer my harte agayne,/And Crystes curse goo wythe yow!'
Crow and Pie. *Anonymous.* ESPB

I trust you, James, to do your best/To save the soup at Grosvenor Gardens.
Vers de Societe (parody). Henry Duff Traill. Par

I trusted it. A Form of Adaptation. Robert Creeley. AmPC

I try it first upon her/youngest girl. The Newlyweds' Cuisine. Wang Chien.
HW

I try to find/the proper retrospective. The Edward Hopper Retrospective.
Tony Quagliano. PoDr

I try to strangle my sobs/But my tears stream down my face. Eighteen
Verses Sung to a Tatar Reed Whistle. Ts'ai Yen. WPOW

I'ts when things seem worst that you mustn't quit. Don't Quit. *Anonymous.*
FPL

I turn and the world turns on the other side. In the Night. Elizabeth
Jennings. MP; NePoEA; NYBP

...I turn,/and touch my glass to his. Out of the Deepness. William Jackson.
AMV-81

I turn away in shame. Not Even in Dreams. Lady Ise. WPOW

I turn'd from all she brought to those she could not bring. Childe Harold's
Pilgrimage: Canto III. George Gordon, Lord Byron. FiP; MCCG; OBRV

I turn over to my third side. Hotel. Adam Wazyk. VWA

I turn to last/Perhaps. It's Hard to See but Think of a Sea. Louis
Zukofsky. VGW

I turn you out of doors/stubborn desire I turn you out of doors. Alain
Chartier. BoLoP

I turned,–a tawdry simpering little dowd/Passed by, and left me trembling on
the curb. Jerked Heartstrings in Town. E.B.C. Jones. HBMV

I turned about, and gave a look,/Just at the foot of Benachie. The Little
Wee Man. *Anonymous.* BuBa

I turned, and saw them whispering about it. I Bended unto Me. Thomas
Edward Brown. NOBV; NTCP; PeD; PoSC

I turned–and so she kissed me. The Garden. Digby Mackworth Dolben.
GoBC

I turned around and broke them locks,/I broke 'em all asinder (asunder). I
Dreamed Last Night of My True Love (with music). *Anonymous.* AS

I turned aside and bowed my head and wept. The Tropics in New York.
Claude McKay. AmNP; GoSl; NoAm; PoBA; PoNe; TTY

I turned aside until the mask/Was slipped once more in place. The Mask.
Clarissa Scott Delany. CDC; PoNe

I turned away and wept. The Bull Calf. Irving Layton. InPK; OBCV;
PeCV

I turned into the house of God. The Lesser Evil. George Orwell. OBTV

...I turned the fragrant earth/And laid him in. Raccoon on the Road.
Joseph Payne Brennan. GoYe

I twist them in a crown today,/And tonight they die.' A Crown of
Wildflowers. Christina Georgina Rossetti. OxBChV

...I understand/and won't give assertion up. Working with Tools. Archie
Randolph Ammons. NoAm

I understand my childhood. Mythology. Earle Thompson. STE

I understand my clinging/to the thought of you. Who Is Not a Stranger
Still. Stephany. BPo

I understand the shore when I hear its sound. I Hear the Wave.
Anonymous. OnYI

I understand these people better, now I know. Loneliness. Brooks Jenkins.
CTBA

I understood Christ was a carpenter/And not a brewer's servant, my good Sir.
Epigram: To English Connoisseurs. William Blake. OxBoLi

I understood it as you did: indifference. Elegy for N. N. Czeslaw Milosz.
SV

I understood that I was to stay and eat with him Finding a Teacher.
William Stanley Merwin. GLGT; NNaP

I use three fingers/to strike a match. March 23, 1982 Tuesday Night.
Thomas Waltner. LFAC

I used to get all revved up. Ego. Philip Booth. MP; TwCP

I used to get there on my bike. Phone Number. Jack Collom. APU

I used to laugh and smile/once upon a time when I was like you. Once
Upon a Time. Gabriel Okara. PBA

I value not half a score,/Nor their noise, nor their noise. The Death of
Admiral Benbow. *Anonymous.* CoMu

"I vas a bride,/But now I is a vidor." Mr. and Mrs. Vite's Journey.
Anonymous. NOBL

"I've a hell on the inside as well as without." Hell in Texas. *Anonymous.*;
ABF; BPAW; CoSo

I've a mind to raise your rent! Lord Gorbals. Harry Graham. FaBoCo

I've a short while to be here,/And a long time to be gone. Little Birdie.
Anonymous. FSW

I've been around a long time, um, I really paid some dues. Why I Sing the
Blues. B. B. King. MAT

I've been sitting here a long time/And always it feels like I'm falling. The
Weight. William Aberg. LFAC

I've been wondering about. Stove. Ken Belford. NeAC

I've brought you a white cheese/From my island, and the sea's/Voice in a
shell. Manos Karastefanis. James Merrill. TAP

I've come from Alabama/Wid my banjo on my knee. O! Susanna.
Anonymous. GoTF

I've died at my post like an Irish lad, or a wild colonial boy. I Am a Wild
Young Irish Boy. *Anonymous.* ShS

I've done; unto my elders I give way,/for 'tis but little that a child can say.
Childhood. Anne Bradstreet. SBG

I've dreaded all the guilty dread,/And done what they would fear to do. Sir
Eustace Grey. George Crabbe. ELP; MyFE; PoEL 1-5

I've dreamed of my first love, the subtle serpent. In Nature There Is Neither
Right nor Left nor Wrong. Randall Jarrell. OxBC

I've enjoyed this visit,/your wife's sheets/are Irish linen. The Sonnet.
Daniel Gerard Hoffman. GP

I've fixed it somehow/so the clock is/resting. The Clock. Felice Holman.
GrPl

I've gambled in the wildwoods/And I never lost a game. Yonder Comes My
Pretty Girl (B vers.). *Anonymous.* AS

I've got a frog/Inside my hat. Notice. David McCord. SoPo

I've got Death really thinking/because she couldn't make me mad. Climbing.
Gloria Fuertes. PBWP

I've got to know friend, I've got to know. I've Got to Know. Woody
Guthrie. FSW

I've got.../WHAT? Suburbia. Maurice Martinez. PoNe

I've gotten now the bonniest lass/That is in the hale country.' The Broom of
Cowdenknows (A version). *Anonymous.* ESPB

I've had to make do with you. Bobbie's Cat. Gerald Locklin. GP

I've heard of "gift of tears" but did not know,/Until this moment, what the
words could mean. A Birthday in Hospital. Elizabeth Jennings. NAs

"I've hell on the inside as well as the out!" The Devil in Texas.
Anonymous. NLV

I've know it from a boy, and love it well. The Milking Shed. John Clare.
VLP

I've known/ all fading past me into peace. Falling Asleep. Siegfried
Sassoon. MCCG; MoBrPo; MoVE; OxBTC

I've left it rent-paid to the villainous Scot! The Sally from Coventry.
William Thornbury. HBV 1-2

I've lost all my claim on fortune and fame,/A-sleepin' at the foot o' the bed.
Sleepin' at the Foot O' the Bed. Luther Patrick. BLPA

"I've lost all taste for joy," he said. The Ascetic. Victor J. Daley. PoAu
1-2

I've lost my way. Mexico City Blues. Jack Kerouac. NeAP

I've made this reference to halitosis! Bishop Orders His Tomb in St.
Praxed's. Morris Bishop. OBAL

I've made up my mind to steal ye, steal ye, steal ye, Bedelia dear. Bedelia.
William Jerome. FSN

I've met Love a-smiling–for Love's in my heart! Song: "Love's on the
highroad." Dana Burnet. HBV 1-2

...I've my own faults to face. The Wind at Your Door. Robert D.
FitzGerald. NOAV; PoAu 1-2

I've never been more serious./Love, J. Letter from an Island. John
Malcolm Brinnin. TAP

I've never been nine till now, you know! Christmas Birthday. Grace Ellen
Glaubitz. BiCB; SiSoSe

I've never seen a black cat before/Wearing a hat and trousers. Coplas.
Anonymous. FSW

I've no more time. When I Get Time. Tom (Thomas Lansing Masson)
Masson. BLPA; FPL

I've no time to throw away. Ay or Nay? Ralph Schomberg. TrJP

I've noticed nearly all the dead/Were hardly more than boys. Two Sides of
War. Grantland Rice. GoTF; TreFT

I've promised mamma to remember/He's only a talented man! The Talented
Man. Winthrop Mackworth Praed. ALV; CoBE; FiBHP; HBV 1-2;
NOBL

I've rode many horses all over the range,/But none like Pattonio, the pride of
the plains. Pattonio, the Pride of the Plain. *Anonymous.* CoSo

I've said enough of linsey-woolsey Hyde–/His sacrilege, ambition, lust, and
pride. The Downfall of the Chancellor. *Anonymous.* APAS

I've seen him but three times today! Of All the Men. Thomas Moore.
FiBHP

I've seen them,/Hanging on the old barbed wire. The Old Battalion.
Anonymous. OBET

I've somebody sleeping/In every bed! The Old Woman. Marjorie Allen
Seiffert. AnAmPo

"I've stabled mysel,' quo' Tam o' the linn. Tam o' the linn cam up the gait.
Anonymous. FaBoCh

I've taken to hiding a piece of flint in my shoe. Dark. Eloise Klein Healy.
AMV-80

I've tasted my blood too much/to abide what I was born to. I've Tasted My
Blood. Milton Acorn. NOBC

I've the prettiest birthday-garden/and I'm six years old today. Birthday
Garden. Ivy O. Eastwick. BiCB

I will sing unto the Lord/In a voice that is cheerfully dry.   New Lines for Cuscuscaraway and Mirza Murad Ali Beg.   Louis Simpson.   OBAL

I will take them up/And gently gent-/Ly love them, tell them/What they have probably meant.   Bibliographer.   Josephine Miles.   FaBoWP

I will teach the blind to find Him/Who can turn their night to day.   Lord, I Know Thy Grace Is Nigh Me.   Hervey Doddridge Ganse.   AH

"I will tell you nothing! Nothing, do you hear?" he/shrieked. "Go away! Go away!"   Variations, Calypso and Fugue on a Theme of Ella Wheeler Wilcox.   John Ashbery.   ANYP; LCAP

I will Thee thanks forever sing.   Psalm XXX.   Sir Philip Sidney.   FCP

I will to know you, even serve you.   To the Unknown God.   Friedrich Wilhelm Nietzsche.   ILwL

I will try counting the notes/instead of sheep.   Love Letter Postmarked Van Beethoven.   Diane Wakoski.   BiP

I will turn to sleep again.   Whirring Wheels.   John Oxenham.   TRV

I will wait for her to wake.   Grandmother Sleeps.   Liz Sohappy Bahe.   CDW

I will waltz to the tune of your slow sadness.   The Scorner.   Tchicaya U. Tam'si.   TTY

I will wash the ploughman's clothes,/And dry them on the dyke, O.   The Ploughman.   Anonymous.   GBP

...I will write some more forever though only poetry and therefore always/failure. Dick.   Letter to Reed from Lolo.   Richard Hugo.   NNaP

I will yield to fate and be a golfer too!   The City of Golf.   Robert Fuller Murray.   SD

I wind you to my weather.   To Helen Frankenthaler of Circe, 1974.   Anne Cherner.   PoDr

"I winna gang wi you,' she said,/"Nor ony Highland loon.'   The Lady of Arngosk.   Anonymous.   ESPB

I wis my mother then shall us see.   Pastourelle.   Anonymous.   LO

I wish all his tomorrows fair.   Per Diem et per Noctem.   Mary Stanley AnNZ

I wish as I was there.'   Port of Many Ships.   John Masefield.   MOS; OBMV

I wish eastern standard/time, etc. rang the/changes in our hearts.   Blue Funk.   Joel Oppenheimer.   NeAP

I wish her with her wedded mate.   To Clarissa.   Robert Nugent, Earl Nugent.   NOEC

I wish I could call my mother/or eat death like candy.   Homecoming Blues.   Vassar Miller.   GP

I wish I could tell you.   The Birthday.   Philip Dacey.   AmPA

I wish I could tell you how it is in that dark,/standing in the huge singing and the alien world.   Don Giovanni on His Way to Hell.   Jack Gilbert.   NMP; NPGG

I wish I'd never been born.   Po' Boy Blues.   Langston Hughes.   BANP

I wish I didn't talk so much,/When I am at a party.   Reflections at Dawn.   Phyllis McGinley.   FiBHP; NLV; NOBL

"I wish I had a yellow crown/As glistering...as...the moon."   The Haughty Snail-King.   Vachel Lindsay.   LOW; SO

I wish I had something to eat.   Fifteen Years Past.   Tom Veitch.   ANYP

...I wish I had the guts/to tell you this is a place I hope/I never have to go through again.   Cumberland Station.   Dave Smith.   HaCAP; MAYP

"I wish I hadn't come."   Vacation Trip.   William Stafford.   AmC; CTBA; PV

I wish i knew/your secret.   Sister Bernardo.   Heather Wilde.   FAZ

I wish I may, I wish I might/Get the wish I wish tonight.   Star Wish.   Anonymous.   HBVY

I wish I thought What Jolly Fun!   Wishes of an Elderly Man.   Sir Walter Ralegh.   DBV; FaBoCh; FaBoCo; FaBoEE; FiBHP; FPL; LoGBV; NLV; NOBL; PV

I wish I was a maid again,/And in my own country.   Song: "How happy were my days, till now."   Isaac Bickerstaffe.   OBEC

I wish I was single again.   I Wish I Was Single Again.   Anonymous.   AS; BFSS; FSW

"I wish I were a jelly fish/That cannot fall downstairs."   Triolet.   Gilbert Keith Chesterton.   NOBL

I wish I were a leprechaun/Beneath a hawthorn tree!   Faith, I Wish I Were a Leprechaun.   Margaret Tod Ritter.   TiPo

...I wish/I were like zinnias.   Zinnias.   Valerie Worth.   NTCP

I wish I were over a bottle,/Which goes gluggity, gluggity–glug–glug–glug!   Gluggity Glug.   George Coleman the Younger.   HBV 1-2

I wish, I wish, he'd go away.   The Little Man Who Wasn't There.   Hughes Mearns.   FaFP; SoPo

I wish–I wish/It came again in June.   School after Christmas.   Wymond Garthwaite.   ChBR

I wish it was like Annika's place/at our place.   At Annika's Place.   Siv Widerberg.   NTCP

I wish myself in old Ireland/And you in the middle of the sea.   Earl Brand; or, The Douglas Tragedy (B vers.) (excerpt).   Anonymous.   ViBoFo

I wish she could rule her tong!   Keep a Good Tongue in Your Head...   Martin Parker.   CoMu

I wish some weird looking animal/would come along.   Epistrophe.   LeRoi (Imamu Amiri Baraka) Jones.   CAD; NNP; PoNe

I wish somebody would tell me what diddie wa diddie means.   Diddie Wa Diddie.   Blind Blake.   BluL

I wish that I could make you yelp just once.   Hmmmm, 19.   Leslie Scalapino.   NPGG

I wish that I were dead.   A Trysting.   Richard Dehmel.   AWP

I wish that I were dead.   La Vie C'est La Vie.   Jessie Redmond Fauset.   BANP; CDC; PoNe

I wish that I were very tall,/High up above the trees.   Playgrounds.   Laurence Alma-Tadema.   HBV 1-2; HBVY

I wish that man would go away!   As I was coming down the stair.   Anonymous.   CenHV

"I wish that my wagon had one!"   The Gold-Tinted Dragon.   Karla Kuskin.   SoPo

I wish that the needle-point may break,/And the craws pyke out yer een.'   The Maid Freed from the Gallows (I version).   Anonymous.   ESPB

I wish that you may constant prove/unto the man that you do love.   Riddles Wisely Expounded.   Anonymous.   BaBo

I wish the church-yard was his doom,/Who murders my content.   The Cottager's Complaint.   John Freeth.   NOEC

I wish the pompous Pekinese/Could know the Jolly Pup!   The Ordinary Dog.   Nancy Byrd Turner.   TiPo

I wish them choked, all three!   There Are Three Who Await My Death.   Anonymous.   NOBI

I wish then, dear George, it were better or worse.   On Gaulstown House.   Jonathan Swift.   CBEP

I wish they made pantyhose.   The Great Pretender.   Pat Nolan.   APU

I wish they were/Grass.   Late November in a Field.   James Wright.   CAPP; NNaP

I wish they would make provisions for this,/Those rocket gentlemen.   A Projection.   Reed Whittemore.   NePoEA

I wish to God he'd go away!   A Case.   Anonymous.   FaBoCo

I wish to God I'd been cremated.   The Author's Epitaph.   Anonymous.   FiBHP

...I/wish to remain a phony the rest of my life.   Voice.   Ron Padgett.   APU

I wish we could do it all again,/with clown hats on.   Loving.   Jane Stembridge.   NMM

...I wish/What I wished you before, but harder.   The Writer.   Richard Wilbur.   CAPP; HaCAP; OxBC; Str

I wish with my breast I could crush it, perish it all.   Nostalgia.   D. H. Lawrence.   PoA

I wish you a Merry Christmas/And a Happy New Year.   Christmas Carol.   Anonymous.   BrR; ChBR; OHIP; SiSoSe; TiPo

I wish you'd go away.   The Postman.   Laura E. Richards.   SoPo; TiPo

...I wish you had been/there, I was so interested to hear about it.   The Horse Show.   William Carlos Williams.   CMoP; NOBA; TAP; VGW

I wish you well, wish/Tall angels whose rib-freezing/Beauty attend you.   Wishes for Her.   Denis Devlin.   CIP; NOBI

I wish your burly fist on the front door/Had banged yet oftener in literature   The Person from Porlock.   Robert Graves.   BoC

...I wished the second feature/Dark and dreadful.   Midweek.   Josephine Miles.   NoP

I wished you well again.   Mementos.   W.D. Snodgrass.   AmPC; NePoEA-2

I wiss that they had a' gane mad,/Whan they cam' first to Yarrow.'   The Dowie Houms o' Yarrow.   Anonymous.   BSV; GoTS; OBEV; OxBS

I with a whistle shut the door,/I may not ope again.   Get Up!   Joseph Skipsey.   NOBV; VLP

I with the deer, and with the nightingale!   When in the Woods I Wander All Alone.   Edward Hovell-Thurlow.   HBV 1-2; HBVY

I witness patterns but I don't care/what they mean.   The Owner of My Face.   Rodney Hall.   CBAP

I woke–and found the coach had missed/the train!   The Journey.   Mary Berri (Chapman) Hansbrough.   AA

I woke and found 'twas but a dream.   A Convict's Tour to Hell.   Francis MacNamara.   NOAV

I woke and saw the dark small trees that burn/suddenly into flowers more lovely than the white moon   Train Journey.   Judith Wright.   PBWP

I woke up.   My Dream.   Lew Blockcolski.   VoR

I woke up broken-hearted with a yearling by the tail.   The Lone Star Trail.   Anonymous.   CoSo

I wol yow telle a litel thing in prose...   The Canterbury Tales: Sir Thopas.   Geoffrey Chaucer.   Par

I wole mone my song/On wham that it is on ilong.   Fairest between Lincoln and Lindsey.   Anonymous.   MeEL

I, Woman, must be/the child of myself.   From the Cavities of Bones.   Patricia Parker.   BlSi

I won'be back, oh, babe, I won'be back.   Heavy-Hipted Woman.   Anonymous.   ABF

I won't be reconstructed and I don't give a damn.   The Rebel.   Innes Randolph.   NLV; OBAL; OxBoLi

I would like to be watching Heaven's family/drinking it through all eternity. The Heavenly Banquet. Saint Brigid. OnYI

I would listen even again to that labouring breath. Remorse. Sir John Betjeman. MoBrPo; OBSP

I would look up–and laugh–and love–and lift. My Creed. Howard Arnold Walter. FaFP; PoLf; WBLP

I would look/with authority down/the tops of white dresses. The Purpose of Altar Boys. Alberto Rios. MAYP

I would love Thee as Thou lov'st me,/O Jesus most desired! I Give My Heart to Thee. Ray Palmer. BePJ

I would my guests should praise it, not the cooks. Critics. Martial (Marcus Valerius Martialis). AWP

I would my heart had been as thine,/Or else thy heart had been as mine. When First Mine Eyes Did View and Mark. Sir Thomas Wyatt. FCP; SiPS

I would not alter thy cold eyes. Flos Lunae. Ernest Christopher Dowson. OBMV

I would not bar a single door/Where love might enter in. Christmas Eve. *Anonymous.* TRV

I would not be–not quite–so pure as you. A Prayer. Samuel Butler the Second. FaBoEE

I would not be singing her song. House in St. Petersburg. Stanley Burnshaw. VWA

I would not do by thee as thou hast done! Lines on Hearing That Lady Byron Was Ill. George Gordon, Lord Byron. EBEV

I would not give my loss for all his gain. Sonnets: A Sequence on Profane Love. George Henry Boker. AmePo

I would not have it so/But for the stars. The Part of Fortune. Ann Sanfedele. AMV-81

I would not know it; I would know but thee. To One Who Would Make a Confession. Wilfrid Scawen Blunt. HBV 1-2; ViBoPo

I would not lend my pony now/For all the lady's hire. I Had a Little Pony. Mother Goose. SoPo

I would not part with my sweetheart/For tuppence ha'penny farden. The Rose Is Red, the Rose Is White. *Anonymous.* OxNR

I would not sail again with sheep. Sheep. William Henry Davies. LiTM; MoBrPo; StPo

I would not see myself as I am now. To Aphrodite: With a Mirror. Aline Kilmer. HBMV

I would not see the light of morning fall/On any world but this. For He Had Great Possessions. Richard Middleton. HBV 1-2

I would not take a day of drink/for these tears upon my cheek. My Sins in Their Completeness. Mael Isu O Brolchain. NOBI

I would not the good bishop be. The Problem. Ralph Waldo Emerson AA; AnNE; AP; AWP; HBV 1-2; LiTA; MAmP; NePA; NOBA; NoP; OxBA; TAP; WGRP

I would only soar from sight/If I could return each night. Little Satellite. Jane W. Krows. SoPo

I would put on my coat and galoshes White Apples. Donald Hall. TAP

I would rather answer that/than meet with a wicked woman! A Sweet Little Bell. *Anonymous.* NOBI

I would rather have geese for their mystery. The Boy and the Geese. Padraic Fiacc. NeIP

...I would rather see before my/eyes than Lydia's chariots in all their glory/armored for battle. Some There Are Who Say That the Fairest Thing Seen. Sappho. WPOW

I would rather the bellowings/of a stag with forty prongs! The Starry Frost Descends. Suibne Geilt. NOBI

I would regret nothing. Incident on a Journey. Thom Gunn. NePoEA

I would say good morrow,/Then, aunts, all three. Riddle: "There were three sisters in a hall." *Anonymous.* OxNR

I would seek the house of Quiet,/That the Master Workman made! The Song of the Forest Ranger. Herbert Bashford. HBV 1-2; OHIP

I would serve like Jesus. Father, Teach Me. Walter M. Lee. STF

I would sleep, my leaves all dissolved in flight. September 2. Wendell Berry. PoA

I would study your dark tongue... Verses Written During a Sleepless Night. Alexander Pushkin. CBEP; OBEC; PoPl

I would tear thy tendrils from my heart and die for/love of thee! Uncourtly Love. Walther von der Vogelweide. LiTW

I would that all remembrances/As gently pierced my breast! Lucy. Walter De la Mare. CMoP; EnRP; NOBE; OBEV; TrGrPo

I would to God that he were hang'd/That does not love a coney. Of All the Seas That's Coming. *Anonymous.* EBEV

I would touch them in a dream The Carnation. Paul Hannigan. PoL

I would wish to catch in my arms,/Endlessly,/One such as you. Phallus. Shiraishi Kazuko. BoWoP

I wouldn't be a private car/In sober black, would you? Taxis. Rachel Field. SoPo; TiPo

"I wouldn't dare name that tree." Uncle Mells and the Witches' Tree. Elizabeth Madox Roberts. WSC

"I wouldn't do that dear," Mamma said. Our Polite Parents. Carolyn Wells. BBGG

I wouldn't even make mincemeat to give to a poodle of/you. Lines in Dispraise of Dispraise. Ogden Nash. NAMP

I wouldn't trade a circus/For some crocuses, Would you? C Is for the Circus. Phyllis McGinley. SoPo; TiPo

I wouldn't want to undertake her! The Jilted Funeral. Gelett Burgess. ShM

"I wrap it up neatly and send it by post/To my friends and relations who need it the most." A New Song to Sing about Jonathan Bing. Beatrice Curtis Brown. SoPo

I write in a shady seat. A Hedge before Me. Saint Columcille. BIrV

I write/in exactly/this way. Bio-Poetic Statement: Instruction to Warriors on Security. Carroll Arnett. STE

I write of Hell; I sing (and ever shall)/Of Heaven, and hope to have it after all. The Argument of His Book. Robert Herrick. AnAnS 2; AtBAP; AWP; CaPo; CoBE; EBEV; EnL; EnLi 1-2; EnLit; ForPo; HAP; HBV 1-2; InPo; InvP; JCP; NoP; OAEL 1-2; OAEP; OBS; PoEL 1-5; PoPle; PoRA; SeCeV; SeCP; SeCV 1-2; TrGrPo; ViBoPo; WHA

I write the sun's Love, and the stars' No. Night in Martindale. Kathleen Raine. NeBP

I write these verses in acknowledgment. A Crucifix. Paul Verlaine. SyP

I write this poem on a fallen leaf and send it out to a wandering man. Written on a Leaf. *Anonymous.* BoWoP

I write this sad, left-handed poem. The T.E. Lawrence Poems: The Void. Gwendolyn MacEwen. NOBC

I write well under the greenwood. The Scribe. *Anonymous.* AnIL; OnYI

I wronged the sire: some Satyr he, or an uncouth-limbed/Pan. Idylls. Theocritus. AWP

I wrote these verses down/And left them and was gone. Epilogue. James Burns Singer. FaBoTw

I wrote Who wrote Icon Basilike? On Christopher Wordsworth, Master of Trinity. Benjamin Hall Kennedy. FaBoCo

I wud sooner sleep. Old Shepherd's Prayer. Charlotte Mew. EaLo; MoAB; MoBrPo; OxBTC

I wys, powle hachet, she bleryd thyne I. With Lullay, Lullay. John Skelton. AAS; InvP; NCEP

I yield before the silence and I know/Your servants who are waiting at my side. Alone. Hubert Witheford. AnNZ

I yield, I'll love you, lest it be/I die of you ere you of me! Escalade. Arthur Symons. UnTE

I yield Thee to the cruel cross! Dialogue at the Cross. Frederick Spee. CAW

I yielded myself to the perfect whole. Each and All. Ralph Waldo Emerson AA; AnNE; AP; AWP; BLPL; HBV 1-2; MAmP; MCCG; NePA; NOBA; OHFP; OxBA; TAP; WGRP

I/you, whatever that conundrum may yet/prove to be, amounts to nothing. The Woodlot. Amy Clampitt. HaCAP

Ice-clear fire of your name Epistle for Spring. R. Ellsworth Larsson. CAW

An ice-cream cone. Puppy. Aileen Fisher. SoPo

The ice eagle can do nothing/but melt. The Ice Eagle. Diane Wakoski. PAI

An ice horse/galloping into/the fire. Ice Horses. Joy Harjo. TWSS

Ice tolled fey moon-scenes! Loss! Loss! Rhoda McMahon. WeW

An iceberg is a large, drifting/Piece of ice, broken off a glacier. Winter Night. Charles Simic. HaCAP

Ich am a maide–that me ofthunche!/Leef me were gome boute gile.' The Lady in the Wood. *Anonymous.* OxBM

"Ich kann nicht Englisch!" civilly said/The lady from over the Rhine. The Puzzled Census Taker. John Godfrey Saxe. HBV 1-2

"Ich shal be king, that men shulle see,/When thou, wreche, ded shalt be." King I Sit. *Anonymous.* OxBM

Ich thither Hie, for this place I/Do take it in great dudgeon. A Devonshire Song. *Anonymous.* OBS

Ichthyos, the sign of Jesus. Fish Shop Windows. Geoffrey Dutton. NOAV

...An icicle/Is something about which to be illogical. Out of My Study Window. Reed Whittemore. PoPl

Icicle roots/I know, by now, must melt. By Now. Ralph Salisbury. STE

The icicles on the eaves/Drone in the wind like the swords/Of murderers. The Terrace in the Snow. Su Tung-P'o. NaP

...The icicles/stroked by an amorous sun. Party at Bannon Brook. Alden Nowlan. NeAC

Ickerman, chickerman, chinee-choo. Ah, Ra, Chickera. *Anonymous.* OxNR

Iconographically,/Just what she meant. Firmness. Anthony Hecht. OBAL; PV

Icy cerecloth, exiled and useless Swan. The Swan. Stephane Mallarme. SyP

An icy season./That's my news. I Bring You News. *Anonymous.* NOBI

Icy time–/that's my rime. Scel Lem Duib. *Anonymous.* BIrV; OxBI

The icy wind through the darkness whines. The Rats. Georg Trakl. LiTW

"The ideal age for a man is two,"/That's what I say, when I look at you. The Ideal Age for a Man. Monica Shannon. BiCB

The ideal pet, however,/is unrecognizable when it arrives/in the river awash in the land afar. Riven Doggeries. James Tate. MAYP

An ideal the wisest man/has not yet formulated/into truth,/as the earth has. The Locus. Cid Corman. VGW

...Identity/Lost, he stood in swollen ecstasy. Saint Francis and the Birds. Roy McFadden. OxBI

The idiot radiance of Thy dawn. Father. Arthur Davison Ficke. TrPWD

The idle singer of an empty day. L'Envoi. William Morris. EnLi 1-2

An idle wind blew round an empty throne/And stirred the heavy curtains on the walls. Failure. Rupert Brooke. ILwL

Idol of the ox herd/the prime demon Finnbennach. How the Bulls Were Begotten: The Two Bulls. Anonymous. NOBI

If a blinder soul there be,/Let me guide him nearer Thee. Thou, Our Elder Brother. John Greenleaf Whittier. ILwL

If a cloud floated over it/I would hate the sky Surfaces. Peter Meinke. Str

If a flow in Age appear,/'Tis but rain, and runs not clear. Tyrannic Love. John Dryden. CavP

If a God decrees my downfall, I shall stand it like a man. The Agnostic's Creed. William Malone. HBV 1-2

If a Joyce is found cleaning/The boots of a Rumbold. The Right Heart in the Wrong Place. James Joyce. FaBoPV

If a king's brother can such mischief bring,/Then how much greater mischief as a king? An Historical Poem. Anonymous. APAS

If a loved one is lost. See true grief. Sandpaper, Sandpiper, Sandpit. Warren Slesinger. AMV-80

If a man could measure up/even to his clothes. In the Cafe. Roo Borson. PPJ

If a man were married to/Anyone but his wife. Pleasure. Anonymous. UnTE

If a roof on stormy evenings/Isn't nicer to be under. U is for Umbrellas. Phyllis McGinley. TiPo

If a swallow cannot make a summer,/It can bring on a summary fall! Little Red Riding Hood. Guy Wetmore Carryl. FiBHP

If a tree don't fall on me/I'll live until I die. Mountain Top. Anonymous. AS

If a wood-chuck could chuck wood. How Much Wood Would a Wood-Chuck Chuck. Mother Goose. TiPo

If age bereave us of this bliss,/Then will no more such sport be found. Madrigal: "Sweet Cupid, ripen her desire." William Corkine. EnRePo

If all ice and fire she be. Ice and Fire. Sir Edward Sherburne. CavP

If all your servants prove not true,/May steale a heart or two from you. To the Countesse of Salisbury. Aurelian Townsend. AnAnS 2; MePo; OBS; SeCP

If any do, it is not I. There Was a Frog. Anonymous. NA

If any one knows it,/Let him disclose it! Dirge of the Moolla of Kotal. George Thomas Lanigan. NA

If any seek her favor, deeming it/A garden of delights–such are its/fruits. The World's Illusion. Moses Ibn Ezra. TrJP

If anybody happens to ask you,/Then I've got those gambler's blues. The Gambler's Blues (St. James Infirmary Blues). Anonymous. TrAS

–If anyone were to listen/they'd know/about humans Night Song for a Woman. Al Purdy. NOBC

If at first you don't succeed,/Why, cry, cry again. A Maxim Revised. Anonymous. BLPA; FPL; NLV; WBLP

An' if aw gan back tiv Elsdon,/"The de'il may carry me." At Elsdon. George Chatt. FaBoPP

If Bugger Burns was a brother of mine,/I'd kill that bastard and serve my time. Bugger Burns. Anonymous. OuSiCo

If but a few shall know my worth/And proudly call me friend. Success. Edgar A. Guest. TreF

If but God weærieth. Antique Harvesters. John Crowe Ransom. AnFE; AP; APA; CoBMV; CrMA; InPo; MoAB; MoAmPo; NoP; OxBA

If but the rights of subjects they receive,/'Tis all they ask–or all a crown can give. A Prophecy. Arthur Lee. PAH

If but the window/Love illuminate. Eyes That Queenly Sit. Elizabeth Daryush. QFR

If chestnut men forgot to come/To cities in the fall. Chestnut Stands. Rachel Field. SiSoSe

If children you have ten, Sir John/Won't for his tenth part ask you one. The Tithe: To the Bride. Robert Herrick. CaPo

If constant to your pets, I hold/You'll faithful be in friendships after. To a Young Brother. Maria Jane Jewsbury. OxBChV

If Damons, all my Hopes are crost;/Or that of my Alexis, I am lost. On Her Loving Two Equally. Aphra Behn. SBG

If daylight and night-shine/Were not in your kiss. Dark Rosaleen, IX. David McKee Wright. PoAu 1-2

If Death should stroke thee, Thompson, scratch Him for me. Elegy. Howard Nemerov. PPJ

If death so glorious be our doom at all! The Philosophic Flight. Giordano Bruno. AWP

If design govern in a thing so small. Design. Robert Frost. AP; BLPL; CMoP; CoBMV; CrMA; ForPo; HeIP; InPS; NIP; NoAm; NOBA; NoP; PAI; PPP; PrIm; SeCeV; SoSe; TAP

If England drive us forth/We shall not fall alone! Ulster. Rudyard Kipling. FaBoPV

If ere I leave bright Celias love. The Protestation, A Sonnet. Thomas Carew. CavP

If euer your Grace doe stand in neede,/Champion to your Highnesse again/I'le bee.' The Earl of Westmoreland. Anonymous. ESPB

If ever I could dare despise/My Mother? My Mother. Ann Taylor. OHIP; OxBChV; PaPo

If ever I false prove to you,/The sea would rage and burn. The Lass of Roch Royal (C vers.). Anonymous. ViBoFo

If ever I get married,/A soldier's wife I'll be. Soldier Boy for Me. Anonymous. AmFP

If ever I go out from home a cuckold I come in. The Old Farmer and His Young Wife. Anonymous. GBP

If ever I'll gaze on thy glorious behind. Poetic Thought. Anonymous. FiBHP

If ever I marry in this wide world,/A railroader's bride I'll be. A Railroader for Me. Anonymous. AmFP

If ever I prove false/To my Love that loves me. Valentine Promise. Anonymous. PoSC

If ever sonnet held so true a speech! Sonnet: He Is Past All Help. Cecco da Siena Angiolieri. AWP

If ever thou comest to merry Tamworth,/thou shalt have clouting-leather for thy shone. King Edward the Fourth and a Tanner. Anonymous. BaBo; ESPB

If ever world were blessed, now it is. April Rise. Laurie Lee. BoC

If everybody says he is valuable/It will be comforting for him. Valuable. Stevie Smith. OxBTC

If felt by me, will be smilingly deflected/by your mysterious concern Poem: "Hate is only one of many responses." Frank O'Hara. NeAP; SOTW

If few those faults, you must not flout him. Early Thoughts of Marriage. Nathaniel Cotton. OxBChV

If, finding it, he fails to find/Its master. The Snail. Vincent Bourne. HBV 1-2; HBVY; OBVE

If flowers can wake,/Oh, why not He? A Song at Easter. Charles Hanson Towne. BLRP

If Foe, our love shall conquer thee. Welcome over the Door of an Old Inn. Anonymous. PoToHe

If freedom be but there. O! Come to the Greenwood Shade. Alexander McLachlan. PeCV

If freedom was not more important/than even god or death/you could have me I would not escape. Prison. Paul David Ashley. LFAC

If from man's greater need beauty redound,/And claim his tears for homage of his peace. For Beauty Being the Best of All We Know. Robert Bridges. VLP

If given for the Saviour's sake,/They lose not their reward. Lord! Lead the Way the Saviour Went. William Croswell. AH

If giver could. Poem in Prose. Archibald MacLeish. LiTL; MoLP; PoPl

If goodness lead him not, yet weariness/May toss him to My breast. The Pulley. George Herbert. AtBAP; ATP; AWP; DiPo; EaLo; EBCP; ExPo; HAP; HBV 1-2; HeIP; InPK; InPo; InPS; LiTB; MePo; NOBE; NOCV; NoP; OAEL 1-2; OAEP; OBEV; OBS; OxBoCh; PAI; PPP; PrIm; SeCeV; SeCP; SeCV 1-2; TEP; TreFT; TrGrPo; ViBoPo; WHA

If grac'i, firme he stands, if not, easely falls. An Elegye. Thomas Campion. AAS

If grief should reach thee in thy heart of hearts. On a Picture by J. M. Wright, Esq. Robert Southey. FM

If Harry Wilmans who fought the Filipinos/Is to have a flag on his grave/Take it from mine! John Wasson. Edgar Lee Masters. LaNeLa

If he asks you wuz I running/Tell him no, tell him no. John Henry (E. vers.). Anonymous. ViBoFo

If he beats me ragged/he's got to rag it some Southern Blues. Ma Rainey. BluL

If he believe not, let him note her eyes.' Sonnet: To Dante Alighieri (He Reports in a Feigned Vision). Guido Cavalcanti. AWP

If he can reign king over all dry land,/I can reign king o'er the sea. Andrew Bardeen. Anonymous. BFSS

If he could speak he would deny it. Three Epigrams. J.V. Cunningham. MoAmPo

If he could talk, I'll guarantee/He'd never speak to you or me. On Buying a Dog. Edgar Klauber. GDP; NTCP

If he'd only had a mammy/For to hold him on her knee. Old Adam (with music). Anonymous. AS

If he didn't set/To whistling first.   Whistling Boy.   John Robert Quinn. BiCB

If he dozed, it was leases of lands.   Shrovetide's Countenance.   Francois Rabelais.   FaBoNo

If he gets loose, he shows no pity.   Aeliana's Ditty.   Henry Chettle.   ALV; OBSC

If he handles me right who is my ruler.   Plow.   *Anonymous.*   AnOE

If he insures/Such friends to laugh regrets away with/As you–and yours?   Aetate XIX.   Herman Charles Merivale.   OBVV

If he is a student in France or America   Going to School in France or America.   Tom Clark.   ConAP

If he knew you had read this/he would murder you.   If You See This Man.   Thomas Lux.   AmPA

If he'll ask you: "Were you ever at sea?' tell him: "Three times/around Cape Horn.'   Paddy West.   *Anonymous.*   OBSS

If he married a woman with nothing to wear?   Nothing to Wear.   William Allen Butler.   HBV 1-2; OBAL; PoLf

If he's so reckless, he's my baby child   It's Cold in China Blues.   Isaiah Nettles.   BluL

If he sees it at all.   Love Lies Sleeping.   Elizabeth Bishop.   NYP

If he should move his massive paw,/Lo, what a cloud of flies!   The Lion at Noon.   Victor Hugo.   LiTW

If he were alive we could kill him again.   Jig Tune: Not for Love.   Thomas McGrath.   VGW

If he were I, he would do what I did.   The Hanging Man.   Sylvia Plath. HaCAP

If he weren't, we'd be in a mess.   The Monster.   Edward Lowbury.   AmMo

If he will prove/As true as I, shews fourscore years in love.   To His Mistris Confined.   James Shirley.   OBS

If he wins but ae mile to the Highland/hills,/He'll defy you Gordons a'.'   James Grant.   *Anonymous.*   ESPB

If he would dig it all up again they would not die.   In Nunhead Cemetery.   Charlotte Mew.   FaBoWP

If her inward Worth were known/She might ever live alone.   True Riches.   Isaac Watts.   OBEC

If her voice didn't carry, he might.   Autumn Song on Perry Street.   Lloyd Frankenberg.   GrPl

If here a ghost has ever been/then it has left this house and gone.   Etude.   Joseph Brodsky.   VWA

If human souls did never kiss and greet?   Endymion.   John Keats.   OBRV; ViBoPo

If husbands now should only deck their own,/Silk would make many by their backs be known.   Caelica, L.   Fulke, Lord Brooke Greville.   FCP

If I am a fool/Or have done what my/karma demands.   Four Poems for Robin.   Gary Snyder.   NOBA; SOTW

If I am not here for breakfast, geologize at will.   Goodnight.   John Ciardi. OBAL

If I am the Narcissus, you are free/To pine into a sound with hating me.   Lines to a Reviewer.   Percy Bysshe Shelley.   OBSP

If I but live/Enough millennial years.   A Song: "A song of grass."   Yehoash. TrJP

If I called It is not me would it reach/through the bells   The Old Room.   William Stanley Merwin.   NYBP

If I can, my Wife will hold almost a year,/this Riddle me Riddle nine months will clear.   The New Married Couple.   *Anonymous.*   CoMu

If I can only make twenty-eight.   Slightly Old.   Bob Rosenthal.   APU

If I can squeeze out of my eyes/enough water. Water.   Parade's End.   Barbara Guest.   PoM

If I can't find her on Philippine's Island/she must be in Ethiopia some where   I Believe I'll Dust My Broom.   Robert Johnson.   BluL

If I can't have the sunshine,/I can have the rainbow.   A Factory Rainbow.   Muslih-ud-Din Sa'di.   SaC

If I can't leave myself and find my friend.   Sonnet XVIII: "Kiss me again, rekiss me, kiss me more."   Louise Labe.   BoWoP

If I can tell you more of Pyretic/Saline manufactured by Lamplough.   A Drinking Song.   *Anonymous.*   FaBoUs

If I cannot carry forests on my back,/Neither can you crack a nut.   Fable: "The mountain and the squirrel."   Ralph Waldo Emerson.   OBCA

If I catch you, how I'll shake you,/Fal lal day.   The Quaker's Wooing. *Anonymous.*   BFSS

If I condemn you, blame Me not.   Thus Speaketh Christ Our Lord. *Anonymous.*   PGD

If I could, I would not so.   The Bracelet: To Julia.   Robert Herrick.   EG; HBV 1-2; OBEV; TrGrPo

If I could only die that way,/I'd say goodbye to the business of living.   Three Lyrics.   Petronius Arbiter (Caius Petronius Arbiter).   LiTW

If I could only make this broken top/Fit snug back on this casket   The City of Satisfaction.   Daniel Gerard Hoffman.   CoPo; Prf

If I could remember how/and if I had the tears.   Self in 1958.   Anne Sexton.   HaCAP

If I could speak,/I would sing.   Beneath the Mound.   R. T. Smith.   STE

If I could tell you, I would let you know.   Villanelle.   W. H. Auden. MoAB; MoBrPo

If I court moe women, you'll couch with moe men.   Othello.   William Shakespeare.   LoBV

If I cry to you then, will you hear or know?   The Triumph of Time. Algernon Charles Swinburne.   GTBS; MaVP; VLP

If I'd been a gander I'd a-went with her,/Ho-dee-ing-dong-doodle-all-a-day.   Sourwood Mountain.   *Anonymous.*   ABF; AS; GBP; TrAS

If I'd crow my hea-rt out.   Cock and Hen.   *Anonymous.*   OxNR

If i/'d/OH/n/lygawntueco/llege.   As Joe Gould Says In.   Edward Estlin Cummings.   FiBHP

If I didn't go now, I never would.   Deer Isle.   Philip Booth.   BiP; VGW

If I didn't hate gum/I wouldn't need valium.   Tea for Two.   Pat Nolan. APU

If I don't know who I am/the wind does   The Ten-Fifteen Community Poems (excerpt).   John Knoepfle.   MAT

If I don't strangely love her.   Carmina.   Caius Valerius Catullus.   OBVE

...If I ever/caught the American bull/I would die.   Buffalo.   Henry Dumas. PoBA

If I ever say another word when my mother wields the shingle!   The Patter of the Shingle.   *Anonymous.*   BLPA

If I find them, we will sit aside somewhere/and talk this over.   A Store-House.   Louis Dudek.   CaP

If I forget Thee/if I forget You   Willows in Alma-Ata.   Aleksander Wat. VWA

If I forget you, may my eyes/lose their Jerusalem.   No One Talks about This. Carl Rakosi.   GP

If I get through my 33rd year,/I'll live forever.   Strictly for Posterity. Charles Simic.   NNaP

If I had a hundred dollars to spend,/Or maybe a little more.   The Animal Store.   Rachel Field.   SoPo; TiPo

If I had a son I know he'd run/Like a brook away to sea!   Grandser.   Abbie Farwell Brown.   HBMV

If I had known.   If I Had Known.   Mary Carolyn Davies.   BLPA

If I had not forever, if there were time.   Mutations: Midsummer.   Robert Fitzgerald.   PoA

If I had to do the whole thing over again/I wouldn't.   Dream Songs.   John Berryman.   NaP

An' if I hadn't tuck dat, I wouldn' git none.   He Paid Me Seven (parody). *Anonymous.*   BPo

If I have but the kisses of his proud red mouth.   The Fairy Lover.   Moireen Fox.   AnIV

If I have spoken to the common sense,/It envy kills, and is a wise offense.   Caelica, LI.   Fulke, Lord Brooke Greville.   FCP

If I have the mock, ye shall have the loss.   To wet your eye withouten tear.   Sir Thomas Wyatt.   FCP; SiPS

If I have the time/and the inclination.   The Art of Picasso.   Salvador Dali. EAS

If I keep at a distance he'll do me no harm.   The Octopussycat.   Kenyon Cox.   SoPo; TiPo

If I knew you and you knew me.   To Know All Is to Forgive All.   Nixon Waterman.   BLPA; GoTF; TreFT

If I live/Or if I die.   The Fly.   William Blake.   BoLiVe; CBEP; DiPo; FM; NLV; TrGrPo

If I lose out that pal-loving feeling/Of a malemute's nose on my hand.   A Malemute Dog.   Pat O'Cotter.   BLPA

...If I lost you,/I'd have to ask the grass to let me sleep.   To Dorothy. Marvin Bell.   Psk

If I love you!   Madam and Her Madam.   Langston Hughes.   BALP

If I loved you fondly, madly;–/But I do not, Phoebe dear.   To Phoebe.   Sir William Schwenck Gilbert.   InMe; OLR

If I'm on your book, love, please blot out my name.   Rambling Gambler. *Anonymous.*   CoSo

If I may call Thee mine/Eternally.   Saviour, Who Died for Me.   Mary J. Mason.   BePJ

If I may, can, shall–still/I might, could, would, or should!   Lines by a Medium.   *Anonymous.*   NA

If I might find again/My hand upon her breast.   Love Song.   *Anonymous.* LiTW

If I move she quickly breaks,/and the splinters stab me.   Mother.   Nagase Kiyoko.   BoWoP

If i never do/anything/it will go on   My Poem.   Nikki Giovanni.   BOLo; PoBA

If I of Heaven may have my fill,/Take thou the world, and all that will.   The Flesh and the Spirit.   Anne Bradstreet.   AP; APA; LiTA; MAmP; NePA; NOBA; OxBA; SCAP; TAP

If I of love can.   When I See on Rood.   *Anonymous.*   OBSP

If I only had that one I love,/How happy, happy should I be.   The Willow Tree.   *Anonymous.*   OBET

If I only knew the language to say it in.   Suenos.   James Reiss.   FiCP

If I please you thus, forget not to tell me.   The Songs of Bilitis.   Pierre Louys.   UnTE

If I prove false, it is the future errs. To Those Who Reproved the Author for Too Sanguine Patriotism. George Edward Woodberry. AmePo

If I really, really love Him,/Can I be afraid? A Question. *Anonymous.* BLRP

If I required it! Inscription of a Chemise. *Anonymous.* ErPo 06 64

If I said I regretted her, I should lie too. Epitaph: "Here lies my dear wife, a sad slattern and a shrew." *Anonymous.* FaBoEE

If I shall have the luck to be/The sort of man I like. Teddy's Wonderings. John Kendrick Bangs. BiCB

...If I should begin/To tell Thee all, the day would be too small/To tell it in. Ash Wednesday. Christina Georgina Rossetti. TrCP; VLP

If I should die before I wake/I pray The Lord my soul to take. Now I Lay Me Down to Sleep. *Anonymous.* FaFP; GBP; GoTF; OxNR; TreF

If I should play a minuet/Upon an old-time spinet. Picture People. Rowena Bastin Bennett. YeAr

If i should see you again, will you give me more/Yesterdays from your tomorrows? Where Have You Gone, Little Boy. Patty L. Harjo. VoR

"If I smell just as sweet to you/As you smell sweet to me!" In the Garden. Ernest Crosby. HBV 1-2; HBVY

...If I stepped out of my body I would break/Into blossom. The Blessing. James Wright. AmPC; ConAP; GrPl; HeIP; InPK; InPS; LLLT; NaP; NoAm; NOBA; NoP; PPP; TwCP

If I suddenly decided to sell shrouds,/People would suddenly stop dying. My Stars. Abraham Ibn Ezra. OFD

If I take to burn or return this world which is each/man's work. On No Work of Words. Dylan Thomas. LiTB; OBSP

..."If I've got a telephone, a television,/my Bible, and room service, what more do I need." Room Service. John W. Moser. FAZ

If I was a mole in the ground. Mole in the Ground. *Anonymous.* FSW

If I were a Bee. I would Like to be–A Bee. Dorothy Walter Baruch. BiCB

If I were a young animal ready to turn home at dusk. Hunting Pheasants in a Cornfield. Robert Bly. ConAP

If I were a young man I'd hurry and pluck some. Hares on the Mountain. *Anonymous.* UnTE

..."If I were dead, were dead/What would you do?" Dancing Partners. Philip Child. CaP

If I were not a clumsy calf/And you a little girl. I Would Like You for a Comrade. Edward Abbott Parry. OxBChV

If I were not human I would not be ashamed of anything. Avoiding News by the River. William Stanley Merwin. NaP

If I were thou, I'd call me Us. The Octopus. Ogden Nash. MOS; NePA; SoPo; TiPo

If ich of love can. On the Passion. *Anonymous.* OxBM

...If in fact I have not been good to my friends/I will be so now to a stranger. Elegy. David Ignatow. NNaP

If in my heart all nymphs else be defaced,/Honor the shrine where you alone are placed. Caelica, III. Fulke, Lord Brooke Greville. FCP

If in the Schools or Porches should appear/The fierce Hyaena, or the foaming Bear? Solomon on the Vanity of the World. Matthew Prior. FM

If it be foe, Fondling, how dar'st thou trust it? Mundus Qualis. Joshua Sylvester. FaBoEE

If it be not of Death. Elizabeth. Sylvia Townsend Warner. MoAB; MoBrPo

...If it burns up the stain/of sweet desire, I'll die when it is gone. Sonnet I: "Not Ulysses, no, nor any other man." Louise Labe. BoWoP

If it could weep, it could arise and go. Grief. Elizabeth Barrett Browning. AnFE; FPL; GTBS; HBV 1-2; HeIP; InPK; LoBV; NOBV; OBEV; OBNC; OBVV; PoLf; SBG; TrGrPo; VLP

If it flew off one day/I'd drop down to the ground. Bird. Agnes Nemes Nagy. BoWoP

If it had not been killed, it would/surely have died. Upon a Cock-Horse to Market I'll Trot. *Anonymous.* OxNR

If it hadn't been for Grayson/I'd-a-been in Tennessee. Tom Dooley. *Anonymous.* FSW

If it hadna come o yoursell, my lord,/'T would neer hae come o me.' The White Fisher. *Anonymous.* ESPB

If it is her, I sincerely wish/Her papa won't drink any more. Willie's and Nellie's Wish. Julia A. Moore. FiBHP

If it is sometimes swift and strong. The Singer. Anna Wickham. HBMV; MoBrPo

If it isn't somewhat quieter in the city! The Grass, Alas. Dick Emmons. QQQ

If it lifts/And lowers/Common things,/It will do. To W. C. W. M. D. Alfred Kreymborg. PoA

If it look like jelly, shake like jelly/it must be gel-a-tine If It Looks Like Jelly, Shakes Like Jelly, It Must Be Gel-a-Tine. Charlie Lincoln (Hicks). BluL

If it opens a little, I shall blame the spring wind. Tzu Yeh Songs. *Anonymous.* BoWoP

If it's bad to have money, it's worse to have none. The Boat Sails Away. Kate Greenaway. MoShBr

If it's done for hire,/It is done the worse. For Hire. Morris Rosenfeld. LiTW

If it's General Grant inspecting the lines/Hereafter let him pass. Achilles Deatheridge. Edgar Lee Masters. AmFN; MaC

If it says that it marks the place of my burial. Epitaph of a Sailor. Leonidas of Tarentum LiTW

If it shall come, will find me on my knees. The Land-Mine. George MacBeth. OBWP

If it wasn't for your cold nose/I would kiss thee now-o. The Little Lady Lairdie. *Anonymous.* OxNR

If it wasna plenty,/Puir folk wadna get it. Kissing's No Sin. *Anonymous.* HBV 1-2; UnTE

If it were not reminded/By days when I forget to wind it. Parable. W. H. Auden. FaBoCo

If it were not so, I would have found another use for the/days of the year. Spring Song. Rayner Heppenstall. NeBP

If it were offered/I would take the same journey again. One More Time. Richard Shelton. GP

If Jesus came in person to spend some/time with you. If Jesus Came to Your House. *Anonymous.* STF

If Jesus don't help me I sho'ly will die. I'm Troubled in Mind. *Anonymous.* BoAN 1-2

If Jesus wept, and pray'd and died. Hymns for the Amusement of Children. Christopher Smart. NOCV

If jist you make friends with the Cat at the door./–Morgan Cat Morgan Introduces Himself. Thomas Stearns Eliot. NOBL

If lawyer's hand is feed, sir,/He steals your whole estate. The Beggar's Opera. John Gay. CEP; NOEC; TEP

If leaner viands are your choice,/You Pamela may eat. Epigram on Two Ladies. Sophia Burrell. ErPo; PoL

If life is battle and love/Then my blood is boiling hot. My Portrait. Moishe-Leib Halpern. TrJP

If Light can thus deceive, wherefore not Life? To Night. Joseph Blanco White. EBEV; GoBC; GoTF; HBV 1-2; OBEV; OBRV; RoGo; TreFS; ViBoPo; WGRP

If love be sponsor, none is lost despite/The faulty sending or receiving set. The Network. Robert Finch. CaP

If Love his moment overstay,/Hatred's swift repulsions play. The Visit. Ralph Waldo Emerson. NOBA

If love or fear would let me tell his name. A Nymph's Passion. Ben Jonson. EnLit; OBEV

If Maggie will have no rival, I'll have no Maggie for spouse! The Betrothed. Rudyard Kipling. HBV 1-2

If many worlds, as that fantastic framed,/In every one be her great glory famed. In Honour of That High and Mighty Princess Queen Elizabeth... Anne Bradstreet. SBG

If me wife don't quit drinking your cod liver ile. Cod Liver Ile. *Anonymous.* FSW; OuSiCo

If memory serve us, we propose to keep/His natal day. A Birthday Ode to Mr. Alfred Austin. Sir Owen Seaman. NOBL

If men be left and otherwise combine,/Mine epitaph's–I did no hurt to thine. Verses Found in Thomas Dudley's Pocket after His Death. Thomas Dudley. SCAP

If men were as much men as lizards are lizards/they'd be worth looking at. Lizard. D. H. Lawrence. BoAnP

If mine are really worse,/with my hands I'll kill myself. Jewish Ballad. *Anonymous.* BoWoP

If more from Earth and Sense refin'd/W' are patient, pray'rful, meek, resign'd. Another to Urania. Benjamin Colman. SCAP

If my baby doesn't live, it's his... We Women. Edith Sodergran. WPOW

If my bark sinks, 'tis to another sea. A Poet's Hope. William Ellery Channing AA; AnAmPo

If my dear father should call for me,/Tell him that I am dead. Sir Hugh; or, The Jew's Daughter (B vers.). *Anonymous.* ViBoFo

...If my/house burns down, open my face/& you will be amazed. Instructions to a Princess. Ishmael Reed. CNA; PoBA

If my wife should na win a penny a day/She's aye her will for me. John Grumlie. Allan Cunningham. HBV 1-2; PoLf

...If my wife/Was as white as those. I Went to the Sea. *Anonymous.* PBBP

If needs be, Christ, to set us free!/To set us free! The Poet Loosed a Winged Song. Joseph Campbell. OnYI

If neist my heart I dinna wear ye,/While BURNS they ca' me. To Terraughty, on His Birth-Day. Robert Burns. NAs

If no one has misjudged himself. Or lied. Reasons for Attendance. Philip Larkin. BiP

If no, thy tongue belies itself, for lo/Thou saidst thy heart was dressed from sin also. The Outward Man Accused. Edward Taylor. LiTA

If nobody care for me,/I'll care for nobody. Nobody. Robert Burns. LiTL

If not already, Armenian will/ring in one of your ears someday. With the Bait of Bread. Helene Pilibosian. AMV-81

If not, by any means get wealth and place.   Ambition.   Alexander Pope. DBV

If not enjoy'd, it sighing cries–/Heigh ho!   Love Is a Sickness.   Samuel Daniel.   CBEP; ELP; GoTF; LiTL; LoBV; NOBE; OAEP; OBEV; PG; PoEL 1-5; TreFS; ViBoPo

If not performed at last.   Now That the Truth Is Tried.   Thomas Whythorne.   EIL

If not, she's rich because she is content.   Contention between Four Maids... Sir John Davies.   SiPS

If not the holiest of powers, sustaining/Only if mastered.   Sapphics Against Anger.   Timothy Steele.   SM

If not, then live and speak for Jesus/And speak out like a man.   Speak Out for Jesus.   Anonymous.   STF

If not, 'tis I must be asham'd of You.   To James Craggs, Esq; Secretary of State.   Alexander Pope.   CEP

If not, we'll cut your throats, and burn your/town.   To the Boston Women. Anonymous.   PAH

If not, what resolution from despair.   Paradise Lost.   John Milton.   MyFE

If now we must give up Spain.   An Excellent New Song Called "Mat's Peace," or The Downfall of Trade.   Arthur Mainwaring.   APAS

If offered a crown, refuse.   A Bestiary.   Kenneth Rexroth.   OBAL

If on the next day Cynthia change and leave,/Would you trust your eyes, since her eyes deceive?   Caelica, XLVIII.   Fulke, Lord Brooke Greville.   FCP

If one shall say me no/Spring joy I will forgo/And banished dwell.   Lenten Is Come.   Anonymous.   EnLi 1-2

If one sweet maid is true.   Wild Eden.   George Edward Woodberry.   AA

If one were sure to be buried so.   My Grave.   Thomas Osborne Davis. ACV; OnYI

If only a magic way were found/To make us children the whole year round! The Whole Year Christmas.   Angela Morgan.   TRV

...If only by being/First in a lower state, you've to pay for grace.   No Accident.   Norman MacCaig.   PoSH

If only for a last time.   Holy Spring.   Dylan Thomas.   WaP

If only he could find the special role.   The Sleeper.   Edward Field.   LiSp

If only her bracelets jangled as she did it/or if we saw her face   Moon Mattress.   Diane Di Prima.   NMM

...If only his energy lasts.   His Plans for Old Age.   William Meredith. TAP

If only History were wired for sound.   Afternoons with Baedeker.   Osbert Lancaster.   NOBL

...If only/I were back home again/whispering words of love/to you.   A Foreign Country.   Natan Zach.   VWA

If only I were born.   By the Babe Unborn.   Gilbert Keith Chesterton. NAs

...If only I were less than human, not angry/like a beaten thing.   Flying Deeper into the Century.   Pier Giorgio Di Cicco.   CaPN; NOBC

If only life and death were an eggshell like Princess Eggshell/Indelible lust (for you).   From Malay.   David Shapiro.   APU

If only pigs could fly!   If Pigs Could Fly.   James Reeves.   OnUR

If only someone would crawl through my veins/To tear out your shoulders and head!   Jane Retreat.   Edwin Honig.   LiTL

If only that so many dead lie round.   Chuch Going.   Philip Larkin.   SCV

If only the eye could hold it.   The Road along the Thumb and Forefinger. Mark Hickey.   AMV-81

If only there were two,/she'd like to have them both.   Rachel Goes to the Well for Water.   Itzik Manger.   VWA

If only this were all it took/to live forever.   Immortality.   Ai.   MAYP

If only to Jesus you'll yield your all,/He'll give His best unto you. Resolutions?–New and Old.   Harvey E. Rolfe.   STF

If only we could leave the port.   The Port.   Bernadette Mayer.   ANYP

If only we could stop the moon/And June!   Stay, June, Stay!   Christina Georgina Rossetti.   YeAr

If now we had remembered.   Orchestra.   Reg Saner.   AMV-80

If only you were immortal as your fame.   To an Aging Charioteer. Scholasticus.   LiSp

If other news there be,/Or admirabler show–/I'll tell it you.   The Only News I Know.   Emily Dickinson.   BoLiVe; NOCV

If otherwise, then I shall not,/For you, be mute.   My Spirit Will Not Haunt the Mound.   Thomas Hardy.   MoBrPo; OBNC; QFR

If our courage could refuse/The present hour with "No."   No!   Eliza Cook. PoToHe

If our Lamps be extinguisht at midnight or noon.   Pastoral Dialogue Castara and Parthenia.   Thomas Flatman.   CEP

If our two loves be one, or thou and I/Love so alike that none do slacken, none can die.   The Good-Morrow.   John Donne.   AtBAP; AWP; BiP; BoLiVe; BoLoP; CABA; DiPo; EBEV; EG; EIL; EnL; EnLoPo; ExPo; FaBoBe; FaBV; FF; FPL; HBV 1-2; HoPM; InPo; InPS; InvP; JCP; LiTB; LiTL; LoBV; MBW 1-2; MeLP; MePo; NAWM 1-2; NIP; NoP; OAEL 1-2; OBS; OLR; PAI; PoEL 1-5; PoPle; PoRA; PPP; SCV; SeCeV; SeCP; SeCV 1-2; SoSe; TEP; TreFT; TrGrPo; UnTE; ViBoPo

If out of the starry Western land,/Should come my Lafayette!   Cuba to Columbia.   Will Carleton.   MC; PAH

If paradise is to be here/it will have to include her.   There She Is.   Linda Gregg.   NPGG

If Plymouth Rock/Had landed on the Puritans.   Thoughts for St. Stephen. Christopher Morley.   ShM

If, poet, thou toss not bowl for bowl,/Thou shalt not kiss a doxy.   Trip It Gipsies, Trip It Fine.   Thomas Middleton.   OAEP

If Poet thou tosse not bowle for bowle/Thou shalt not kisse a Doxie.   Song: "Trip it Gipsies, trip it fine."   William and Thomas Middleton Rowley. OBS

If Puss declines a meal or two,/To feel her pulse and make ado!   A Cat's Conscience.   Anonymous.   PoLf

If REASON's for me, GOD is for me too.   The Apology Addressed to the Critical Reviewers.   Charles Churchill.   LAuP

If Rosalind prove cruel and unkind.   Of Rosalind.   Thomas Lodge.   GoBC

If Ross wil be so kind as share in/Their pint at Drousty.   To Mr. Alexander Ross.   James Beattie.   OxBS

If, roused thereby, the world shall tread/The twin-born vampires down!   To Pius IX.   John Greenleaf Whittier.   TW

"If's, in, ss'd/shsh" erced/"ft/"isk   Narrative.   Russell Atkins.   PoBA

If Saints, and Angels fal down, much more thou.   Silex Scintillans.   Henry Vaughan.   AnAnS 1

If Satan fright our trembling souls,/Thy mercy may appear.   Within These Doors Assembled Now.   Oliver Holden.   AH

"If seven king's-daughters here ye hae slain,/Lye ye here, a husband to them a'."   Lady Isabel and the Elf-Knight (A vers.).   Anonymous.   BaBo; ESPB; ViBoFo

If she but live, what are the dead!   The Cyclamen.   Arlo Bates.   AA; HBV 1-2

If she could find herself, herself planting/instead of keeping.   Foxfire. Nancy Willard.   IHMS

If she'd have done as much for Adam.   Women's Degrees.   Alfred Denis Godley.   GLGT; NOBL

If she does not count this blessed/Let her change her religion.   Phyllidula. Ezra Pound.   FaBoTw

If she doesn't that I don't care.   Waiting for Her.   Alden Nowlan.   NeAC

If she don't love me, she won't/love nobody else.   98 Degree Blues.   Texas Alexander.   BluL

If she gets up, I'll just lie still.   Within This Grave Do Lie.   Anonymous. ShM

If she give me many,/God am I for the time.   Me Happy, Night, Night Full of Brightness.   Ezra Pound.   InvP

If she has any tears.   Cherry Robbers.   D. H. Lawrence.   MoAB; MoBrPo

If she has but Wit to take care of her T–, she may pass for a/Maid again. The Country Girl's Policy; or, The Cockney Outwitted.   Anonymous. CoMu

If she has to ask she'll never/know.   A Long Overdue Thankyou Note to the Girl Who Taught Me Loving.   Tom Schmidt.   NeAC

If she's a fool she'll wed the knave–/If she's a knave, the fool.   The Touch-Stone.   Samuel Bishop.   HBV 1-2

If she's a knave, the fool.   The Maiden's Choice.   Anonymous.   ALV

If she sins to escape her bondage/Is there room for wonder then?   The Factory Girl.   J. A. Phillips.   SaC

If she when I love, should love me.   Love's Deity.   John Donne.   ATP; AWP; DiPo; EIL; EnLit; EnRePo; GBL; InPo; LiTB; LiTL; OAEP; SeCePo; WHA

If she wishes to go I will not forgive her.   The River God.   Stevie Smith. BrRo; FaBoNo; FaBoTw; FaBoWP; PBWP

If Sir James Jeans/Knows what that means.   Apostrophic Notes from the New-World Physics.   E. B. White.   ImOP

If so a man we throw to the dickey-birds!   If So the Man You Are.   Percy Wyndham Lewis.   OBSV

If so,/at least no one can be hurt/by such slight deceptions.   No One in Particular.   John Perreault.   ANYP

If so, how do ye: you and I embrace!   The Accusation of the Inward Man. Edward Taylor.   LiTA

If so, the day that now is o'er/Has been a real success.   Measure of Success. Anonymous.   STF

If so, the whole system is vicious'.   Limerick: "There was a young man of Mauritius."   T. Lindsay.   FaBoCo

If Soldier-like, he may have termes to come/With flying colours, and with beat of drum.   Secret-Love.   John Dryden.   SeCV 1-2

If some big dog should swallow Tiny.   Disaster (parody).   Charles Stuart Calverley.   HBV 1-2; SpRo

If some loving friend is standing nigh.   Sweet Loving Friendship.   Peter Bellamy.   OBET

If some other gets "Don't Care"–/I'll take "Never Mind!"   "Don't Care" and "Never Mind."   John Kendrick Bangs.   FaFP

If something doesn't happen soon.   To a Junior Waiter.   Sir Alan Patrick Herbert.   FiBHP

If, spurning art's inexorable law,/In Ariel's prison-sphere he leave one flaw. The Sonnet.   John Addington Symonds.   HBV 1-2

If such as you don't like this world–/We'll pass you to the next.   Answer to Pauper.   Thomas Hood.   NBM

If such there were–with you, the moral of his/strain.   Childe Harold's Pilgrimage: Canto III.   George Gordon, Lord Byron.   EnRP

If such thy dawning beauty's power,/Who shall abide its noontide hour?   To the Younger Lady Lucy Sydney.   Edmund Waller.   CBEP

If summer were spring, and the other way round,/Then all the world would be upside down.   If Buttercups Buzz'd after the Bee.   Anonymous.   LoGBV

If tears/show him/to the/letter.   Reading and Talking.   Louis Zukofsky.   VGW

If that don't get you/Then the afters will.   School Dinners.   Anonymous.   WTO

If that for weight the body fail, this soul shall/to her flee.   In Spain.   Sir Thomas Wyatt.   FCP

If THAT'S the way he is/even yr GHOST/can take m.   Panther Man.   James A. Emanuel.   BPo

If that we waste, in vain walled town and/lofty tower!   The Decay of a People.   William Gilmore Simms   AA

If the basin had been stronger/My story would have been longer.   There Was a King.   Anonymous.   NLV; OxBoLi; OxNR

If the bowl had been stronger/My song had been longer.   Three wise men of Gotham.   Mother Goose.   FaBoBe; FaFP; HBV 1-2; HBVY

If the cricket were that far away/I'd never hear it night or day.   The Cricket and the Star.   Mary Effie Lee Newsome.   GoSl

If the fault be great, love, 'tis none of mine,/So don't speak so harshly of womankind.'   The Disappointed Sailor.   Anonymous.   OBSS

If the fish are to be drawn in at all.   Jerusalem Sonnets.   James Keir Baxter.   OCNZ

...If the girl insist/On love–must be a very pantheist.   The River Walk.   Padraic Fallon.   OxBI

If the heart of the minstrel is mute.   Poetry.   Lucius Harwood Foote.   AA

If the lady's not willing/She's just old fashioned!   On Being Told That One's Ideas Are Victorian.   Sara Henderson Hay.   InMe

If the lens winks, it winds them who knows where.   Some Negatives: X. At the Chateau.   James Merrill.   NePoEA-2

If the letter C showed up/Beneath the devil's checkerboard.   The Cowboy at Church.   Anonymous.   CoSo

If the odor of the roses and the better things were there.   The Blind Girl.   Nathalia Crane.   MCCG

If the pleasure/For the measure/Of my treasure goe.   I Sigh, as Sure to Wear the Fruit.   Anonymous.   NCEP

If the queer pair below/Will pay their lodging.   The Lodging.   George Mackay Brown.   BSV

If the sheriff pain/Had not evicted me.   Eviction.   Elizabeth Brewster.   CaP

If the soul that we live by never, For aught that a lie saith, fear.   The Lake of Gaube.   Algernon Charles Swinburne.   OAEL 1-2; VLP

If the spinning-wheel Time move slow or fast.   Spinning Song.   Edith Sitwell.   MoAB; MoBrPo

If the spirit was just,/Why did the maid weep?   Why?   Stephen Crane.   AA

If the Sun and Moon should doubt,/They'd immediately go out.   Auguries of Innocence.   William Blake.   EG

If the tax collector hasn't got it before I wake.   One from One Leaves Two.   Ogden Nash.   NLV

If the thesis has managed this climb.   I Want to One Morning.   Gordon Turner.   AMV-80

If the water of life should come to thee, it would not/stir thee from the flame.   A Beauty That All Night Long.   Julal ed-Din Rumi.   AWP; LiTW

If the wind means me,/I'm here!/Here.   Meditations of an Old Woman.   Theodore Roethke.   NaP

If there are bastions, let my love be walls!   Rant Block.   Michael McClure.   EAS

If there be none, never mind it.   For Every Evil under the Sun.   Anonymous.   EvOK; HBV 1-2; HBVY; OxNR

If there be one thing I can't talk of/That one thing do be love.   Song: "I can't be talkin' of love, dear."   Esther Mathews.   NePA

"If there is a gude woman in the world,/Your one sister is she."   Redesdale and Wise William.   Anonymous.   ESPB

If there is a hoss-heaven, please, God, rest his soul.   To Midnight.   Anonymous.   BPAW; CoSo

If there is any way to baffle death.   "Since There Is No Escape".   Sara Teasdale.   AnAmPo

If there is hope for me at all,/She must be blind like thee.   The Lover's Song.   Edward Rowland Sill.   AA; HBV 1-2

If there is nothing on the tree,/'Tis the Chameleon you see.   How to Tell the Wild Animals.   Carolyn Wells.   FaFP; FiBHP; HBVY; MaC; NLV; TiPo

If there is sovereignty in this world, it takes after/us.   Sovereign Queen.   Padeshah Khatun.   WPOW

If there were not, where would my neighbors go?   Theology.   Paul Laurence Dunbar.   AmePo; TRV

If these delights thy mind may move,/Then live with me and be my love.   Two Songs.   Cecil Day Lewis.   HAP

If these endure we have not fought in vain.   If These Endure.   Lilith Lorraine.   PGD

If these essayes shall raise some quainter pens/Twil to the Writer make a rich amends.   A Supplement.   Benjamin Tompson.   SCAP

If these fail to make thee weary,/Then I cannot help thee, dearie.   To a Lady Troubled by Insomnia.   Franklin Pierce ("F.P.A.") Adams.   InMe

If these good folks would keep within their tether!   On Clergymen Preaching Politics.   John Byrom.   SeCePo

If these gross faults his choice Pen does commit/Proceed from want of Judgement and of Wit?   An Allusion to Horace. The Tenth Satire of the First Book.   John Wilmot, Earl of Rochester.   OBS

If these I tine,/Can books, or fire, or wine be good?   A Winter Wish.   Robert Hinckley Messinger.   AA; ViBoPo

If these mad changes do make children gods,/Women and children are not far at odds.   Caelica, XXVI.   Fulke, Lord Brooke Greville.   FCP

If these, my loved ones, were not here with me.   Morning Prayer.   Anonymous.   PoToHe

If they all only had one neck...It's so/Unnecessary and out of date. We do.   To the Rulers.   Howard Nemerov.   OxBC

...If they ask me to run/for President, I might give in!   The Professor Waking.   James Tate.   FF

If they ask what we want say we do not remember.   Meeting of a Poetry Society.   Henry Rago.   AnAmPo

If they couldn't lean against/Black....   What Is Black?   Mary Devenport O'Neill.   NTCP

If they delight thee not, 'tis thou art dead.   Melancholia.   Robert Bridges.   CMoP

If they don't want them,/God rid me of both.   Two Gifts.   Anonymous.   BoWoP

If they ever find their way/back home   A Trip on the Staten Island Ferry.   Audre Lorde.   CNA

If they, from their waterless, intractable hearts, might stretch for pears.   The Fruit of the Tree.   David Wagoner.   NYBP

...If they live/in the Empire, it matters what they say.   America.   John Newlove.   NOBC

If they'll all go a-hunting today.   We'll All Go A-Hunting Today.   Anonymous.   OBET

If they relieve their bladders against some/crappy wall or other.   Meditation on the BMT.   Paul Blackburn.   CoPo

If they rise again,/Love folds them then.   Pity Not.   William Haskel Simpson.   HBMV

If they roam towards me/I enter into life.   Egyptian Hieroglyphics.   Anonymous.   BoWoP

If they were pheasants, they'd be in his pot/For breakfast, or if wrens he'd make them king.   The Reading Lesson.   Richard Murphy.   IPY

If this ain't a proper ending, then you can go to Hell.   Darky Sunday School.   Anonymous.   OxBoLi

If this be crime, the crime's confessed.   To Archinus.   Callimachus.   AWP

If this be error, and upon me proved,/I never writ, nor no man ever loved.   Sonnets, CXVI: "Let me not to the marriage of true minds."   William Shakespeare.   AWP; BoC; CBEP; DiPo; ExPo; FaBV; FaFP; FPL; GBL; GoBC; GoTF; GTBS; GTBS-P; HAP; HBV 1-2; HeIP; InPo; InPS; InvP; LiTB; LiTL; LoBV; MasP; MBW 1-2; MCCG; NIP; NOBE; NoP; OAEL 1-2; OAEP; OBEV; OBSC; PAI; PeHV; PG; PoEL 1-5; PoPl; PoRA; PPoe; PPP; PrIm; SCV; SeCeV; SoSe; TEP; TreF; TrGrPo; TRV; UnPo; ViBoPo; WHA

If this be love, if love in these be founded,/My hart is love, for these in it are grounded.   To Live in Hell, and Heaven to Behold.   Henry Constable.   AAS; InvP

If this be love! O I remember/Tempest, and abysm gone.   If This Be Love.   Richard Eberhart.   LiTL

If this don't please, old Nick is in you.   Advice to the Ladies of London in the Choice of Their Husbands.   Anonymous.   CoMu

If this goes on, I will believe in God.   The Weasel.   Robert Pack.   CoPo

If this is not the true/tomb of David, surely/that was one/of his sons.   Dawn.   David Shevin.   VWA

If this is true, an ass can sew a cap.   I Came A-Riding.   Reinmar von Zweter.   AWP

If this is where I die/I want someone to know.   Panic.   Lloyd Davis.   WOLT

If this should be, then how should we/Here make an end of singing?   If All the World Were Paper.   Anonymous.   CBEP; FaBoCo; FaBoNo; GBP; LoBV; NTCP; PoPle

If this vile practice is discarded.   A New Bundling Song.   Anonymous.   ErPo

If those eggs began to sing!   Eggs.   Herbert Asquith.   BrR

If thou be just, O wherefore doth thy dart/Wound mine alone, and not my lady's heart?   To Cupid.   Francis Davison.   EG

If thou be noyed night or day,/Say "Passio Christi conforta me."   Dread of Death.   John Audelay.   OxBM

If thou but follow me!   The Master's Invitation.   Anson Davies Fitz Randolph.   AA

If Thou callest can I answer,/"Here am I, send me, send me"?   Saved, but–. *Anonymous.* STF

If thou canst–be happy still.   Lady Byron's Reply to Lord Byron's Fare Thee Well.   *Anonymous.* BLPA

If thou canst Plant but there with like success.   To Sir William Davenant, Upon His Two First Books of Gondibert.   Abraham Lovelace.   AnAnS 2

If thou from glove do'st take away the g,/Then glove is love: and so I send it thee.   Sonnets, XIV: "Here, hold this glove."   Richard Barnfield.   PeHV

If Thou in my life hast pleasure,/Speak, and now my soul shall live.   Still, O LORD, for Thee I Tarry.   Charles Wesley.   OxBoCh

If thou'lt sleep as I bid thee, my own/little boy.   Lullaby.   *Anonymous.* TrJP

If thou shouldst e'er forsake the spring/I should not wish to live.   The Swallow (parody) (excerpt).   J. C. Squire.   BXAP

If thou so wilt, to serve thee whilst I live.   Of Mistress D.S.   Barnabe Googe.   EnRePo

If thou sowest with liberal hand.   Cast Thy Bread upon the Waters.   Phoebe A. Hanaford.   AH

If thou wert longer away.   When My Love Was Away.   Robert Bridges.   BrPo

If thou will do as we thee bid,/To shew us quar that cros is hid.'   Cursor Mundi: The Pound of Flesh.   *Anonymous.* OxBM

If Thou wilt be my Guide.   To the End.   John E. Bode.   BLRP

If thou wilt come to London, Lady But-/ler,/Thou shalt goe home Lady Gray.'   Sir John Butler.   *Anonymous.* ESPB

If thou wilt foil thy foes with joy,/Then flit not from this heavenly boy.   New Heaven, New War.   Robert Southwell.   AnAnS 1; EG; LoBV; MePo; NOBE; NoP; OBSC; SBVL

If thou wilt kiss me in such wise.   Deadly Kisses.   Pierre Ronsard.   AWP

If thou wilt let down thy milk to me.   Cushy Cow, Bonny.   *Anonymous.* GBP

If through centuries, clouded and dingy, this Day/can keep/Expectation alive.   Christmas Eve.   C. Day Lewis.   EaLo

If thus you shame our father's name/My curse go forth with you.   Noble Sisters.   Christina Georgina Rossetti.   CoBE

If to the human mind's imaginings/Silence and solitude were vacancy?   Mont Blanc.   Percy Bysshe Shelley.   EnRP; ERoP 1-2; InPS; NIP; NoP; OAEL 1-2; OBTV; PP; TEP

If, to their time, they reason had to know the truth of this.   Laid in My Quiet Bed.   Henry Howard, Earl of Surrey.   EnRePo; FCP; InvP

...If tongue and temper wander,/flesh stiffen and decay, why do you fear?/It is still I.   For Miriam.   Marjorie Oludhe Macgoye.   WPOW

If 'twere not for the minstrelsy/Of Hope that sings of Light.   Hope's Song.   Francis Carlin.   HBMV

–If 'twere proper, Scirocco should vanish/In black from the skies!   The Englishman in Italy.   Robert Browning.   ExPo; OBTV; PoEL 1-5

If Villon were the King of France!   If I Were King.   Justin Huntly McCarthy.   HBV 1-2

...If/want decides, let it be me.   For My Unborn & Wretched Children.   A. B. Spellman.   CNA; PoBA

If wanting sweet Jessie, the Flower o' Dunblane.   Jessie, the Flower o' Dunbane.   Robert Tannahill.   HBV 1-2

If we always would remember/That He means just what He says.   Believe the Bible.   A. B. Simpson.   STF

If we are both John Clare/why does he go away?/and where? and where?   John Clare.   Mark Halperin.   SM

If we come together let it turn red,/Not leaf-flat, lime-insipid.   Carved on an Areca Nut...   Ho Xuan Huong.   PBWP

If we do well,/Their death is justified.   Consolation in War.   Lewis Mumford.   NYBP

If we do what we should, may fly/Than Angels higher.   To a New-Born Child.   Cosmo Monkhouse.   HBV 1-2

If we don't it doesn't matter, but we'd better start to die.   Get There If You Can and See the Land.   W.H. Auden.   InPS; NAMP

If we get there we will all be real.   Some of Us Are Exiles from No Land.   Diana O Hehir.   NPGG

If we had stuck to epsom salts,/We'd not been a-lying in these here vaults.   Epitaph.   *Anonymous.* TreFT

If we had wings, roots, petals/we would not be men.   The Day of the Night.   James Scully.   LTB

If we hadn't a French Captain, boys, what could we do!   Paul Jones.   *Anonymous.* ViBoFo

If we harken to His word, that we go nowhere astray.   The Lion's Nature.   *Anonymous.* MeEV

If we have reasons, they lie deep.   The Nature of Man.   C. H. Sisson.   FaBoTw

If we him love with all oure might.   A Carol of St. George.   *Anonymous.* MeEL

If we live well, in heaven with Christ our souls shall dwell.   For Soldiers.   Humfrey [(or Humphrey)] Gifford.   CH; EIL

If we loved each other the better because we quarreled here.   Betsey and I Are Out.   Will Carleton.   PaPo

If we may not kiss the girls,/Drink while time's a-flying?   Lauriger Horatius.   John Addington Symonds.   HBV 1-2

If we must live only in meeting and/parting/The rest of our days.   Strange.   Stanley Burnshaw.   TrJP

If we only had plenty, like Larry M'Hale.   Larry M'Hale.   Charles James Lever.   OnYI

If we the roast have, they the smell.   Steam in Sacrifice.   Robert Herrick.   CaPo

If we then, too, can be such men as he!   The Better Part.   Matthew Arnold.   MCCG

If we three can agree in one.   The Peace of the Roses.   Thomas Philipps.   ACP

If we've promised them aught, let us keep our promise.   The Pied Piper of Hamelin.   Robert Browning.   BBV; BeLS; BiP; BLPL; FaBoBe; FaBoCh; FaFP; FaPo; GN; HBV 1-2; HBVY; LoGBV; OBNV; OxBChV

If we walk, we walk on graves.   The Shudder.   Donald Hall.   NYBP

If well; the pain doth fade, the joy remains.   The Church-Porch.   George Herbert.   AnAnS 1

If, what this said, I dared repeat at last!   Sonnets from the Portuguese, XXVIII.   Elizabeth Barrett Browning.   CoBE

If when I am sick, your heart/is calm?   Do you have a sweet thought, Cerinthus.   Sulpicia.   BoWoP

If when night comes, you bid me goe away.   Idea.   Michael Drayton.   FaBoEn; PoEL 1-5

If, when night falls, all is so changed, dear heart?   Evening.   Mary Matheson.   CaP

If, when you speak, your words are of no worth.   Sonnet: To Certain Ladies.   Dante Alighieri.   AWP

If Winter come to Winter,/When shall men hope for Spring?   Invocation to Youth.   Laurence Binyon.   OBEV; OBVV

If Winter comes, can Spring be far behind?   Ode to the West Wind.   Percy Bysshe Shelley.   AnEnPo; AWP; BiP; BoNaP; DiPo; EBEV; EnL; ERoP 1-2; ExPo; FaBoBe; FaBV; FaFP; FiP; ForPo; FPL; GTBS; GTBS-P; HAP; HBV 1-2; HeIP; InPo; InPS; LiTB; LoBV; MBW 1-2; MCCG; MOS; NAWM 1-2; NIP; NOBE; NoP; OAEL 1-2; OAEP; OBEV; OBNC; OBRV; OHFP; PAI; PoEL 1-5; PoLf; PoRA; PPoe; PPP; PrIm; SeCeV; TEP; TreFS; TrGrPo; ViBoPo; WHA

If winter hue them like a pall, or if the summer night/Fantasy them starry brede.   A Sunset.   Victor Hugo.   AWP

If wit were always radiant,/And wine were always iced.   If.   Mortimer Collins.   FiBHP

If with me you'd fondly stray/Over the Hills and far away.   The Beggar's Opera.   John Gay.   PoEL 1-5

If with our soul 'tis well.   A Heavenly Friend.   Paul Tucker.   BePJ

If wives were but half as alluring/After the act as before.   Husbands and Wives.   *Anonymous.* UnTE

If worn and patched the garments that/men view.   Walk in the Precepts.   Moses Ibn Ezra.   TrJP

If worthy of you to the world they'll come/down from the uplands.   Castile.   Miguel de Unamuno.   PoPl

If ye fetch him from the Moors!   The Song of the Galley.   *Anonymous.* AWP

If ye'll only gimme RUM!   The Convicts' Rum Song.   *Anonymous.* NOAV

If ye touch one o' their eggs,/Bad luck will sure to follow.   The Robin and the Redbreast.   *Anonymous.* PBBP

If you allow me a chance/I will gnaw your backbone half in two   Back Gnawing Blues.   Ramblin' (Willard) Thomas.   BluL

If you are a sensible man.   The Charming Woman.   Helen Selina, Lady Dufferin.   ALV; OBRV

If you are too feeble, you will be crushed.   Instructions of King Cormac.   Cormac Mac Cuilenan.   PoToHe

If you are wise, I think you are a fool.   I Hardly Ever Ope My Lips.   Richard Garnett.   HBV 1-2

If you be in search of beauty/Go where beauty dwells.   Song: "In the air there are no coral-reefs or ambergris."   Duncan Campbell Scott.   PeCV

If you beat a bush, you'll start a thief.   Buckinghamshire.   *Anonymous.* GBP

If you become the aliment and the wet they will become flowers, fruits, tall branches and trees.   Roots and Leaves Themselves Alone.   Walt Whitman.   NePA

(If you can find any way) that is/ the only way left now/for you.   The Injury.   William Carlos Williams.   AP

If you can see anything twice, it is not to be loved.   The Shepherd's House.   Alfred de Vigny.   NU

If you can't manage that, for honour's sake/outclimb all idiots to the peak of madness.   You That Are Jealous and Have a Wife.   *Anonymous.* NOBI

If you come with me/You'll have still more cakes.   The Peace: Midst the Free Green Fields.   Aristophanes.   HW

If you could only do as well at night.   A Game of Dice.   *Anonymous.* UnTE

If you could only keep quite still and wait.   Myxomatosis.   Philip Larkin.   CMoP; ELU; NMP; NoAm; NoP

...& If you could sing, the song/is all that wld go/anywhere. Bushed. Barry McKinnon. NOBC

If you crave it. The Faithful Shepherdess. John Fletcher. EG

If you cross the briny ocean/Without your fortune you must go.' Arise, Arise. *Anonymous.* OBET

If you'd make your city better/Boost it to the final letter. Boosting the Booster. *Anonymous.* WBLP

If you'd promise me to do/everything I'd want you to. Estat ai en greu cossirier. Beatriz de Dia. ErPo

If you dare come with us, be/Lost in love's great unity. Dare You? Edward Rowland Sill. AnNE

If you do/I'll fall on you./Sabe? Last Fall of the Alamo. O. (William Sidney Porter) Henry. BPAW

If you do love as well as I. The Thought. Edward, Lord Herbert of Cherbury. AnAnS 2; InvP

If you do not like a bit/You may mend it. Our Bow's Bended. *Anonymous.* OxNR

If you' don't-a come, I'm gwineter tell-a yo' Mammy./Oh, Water-Boy! Water-Boy. *Anonymous.* TrGrPo

If you don't come soon, gonna throw it all away. Wake Up, Jacob. *Anonymous.* FSW

If you don't talk, why, I must. Two Little Dogs. *Anonymous.* OxNR

If you drive it through the door,/By the window it returns. Cat into Lady. Jean de La Fontaine. PCat

...If you eat this fruit/you will die,/they didn't mean right away. Goodbye. Chana Bloch. MAYP

If you ever get there, think of me. Parting. Michael Hogan. GP

If you ever navigated on the Erie Canal. Erie Canal. *Anonymous.* ABF

If you ever see me coming back again I'll be with the gambling man. The Roving Gambler. *Anonymous.* ABF; AS; TrAS

If you fail to lock your liquor with a lock. If You Stick a Stock of Liquor–. Newman Levy. ALV

If you go to the right, you are wrong. The Rule of the Road. *Anonymous.* FaBoUs

If you growl too loud your head they'll bust./Oh, poor old man! Poor Old Man. *Anonymous.* ShS

If you had been salted and pephard. Limerick: "They tell of a hunter named Shephard." *Anonymous.* TDH

If you had known what I know/You would know why. Words Like Freedom. Langston Hughes. BPo

If you hate the R.U.C., clap your hands. Ballymurphy. *Anonymous.* FSW

If you have made gentler the churlish world. If You Made Gentler the Churlish World. Max Ehrmann. PoToHe

If you have to ask,/You can't afford it. Maples (parody). Philip Appleman. BXAP

If you haven't got a ha'penny,/God bless you! Christmas Is Coming. *Anonymous.* NTCP; OxNR; PCh; SoPo

If you hear it in the distance, do not scorn the herald's note. Rex Mundi. David Gascoyne. ChMP

If you hear that they seem my heart to move:/Not them, O no, but you in them I love. Astrophel and Stella, XCI. Sir Philip Sidney. AAS; SiPS

If you knock on my door/I may not even hear. I Taught Myself to Live Simply and Wisely. Anna Akhmatova. PBWP

If you know what I mean. Edith Sitwell Assumes the Role of Luna. Robert Francis. MOON

If you/know what/I mean. Persephone. Keith Abbott. APU

...If you know/What you want, do, do, do, do, do. To the Young Rebels. E. L. Mayo. FAZ

If you laugh you don't love me. Tickly, Tickly, on Your Knee. *Anonymous.* OxNR

If you lift a guinea-pig by the tail/His eyes drop out! A Garden Lyric. Frederick Locker-Lampson. HBV 1-2; PeD

If you live without work, you must live without food. The Ant and the Cricket. *Anonymous.* HBV 1-2; HBVY

If you'll stop with this neighbor and visit awhile. Your Neighbor. H. Howard Biggar. PoToHe

If you'll tell me this riddle, I'll give you a groat. Riddle: "As I went through a garden gap." *Anonymous.* HBV 1-2; HBVY

If you look at the crimson people/You look at the human heart. Strawberries in November. Shaw Neilson. PoAu 1-2

If you look closely/you can see it. Look Closely. Morton Marcus. FF

If you love it not, of night. Out in the Dark. Edward ("Edward Eastaway") Thomas. BrPo; CH; GTBS-P; LiTM; MoAB; MoBrPo; MoVE; NOBE; PoPle

...If you love me, all/of nature, let the wind blow. Backyard. Alice Notley. APU

If you love them, give them their way/For fear their love may lead astray. There Were an Old and Wealthy Man. *Anonymous.* AmFP

If you meet your child in heaven/You will find the missing head. Pearl Bryan. *Anonymous.* AmFP

If you must go, go ever so slowly/Into that dark and rippled sunshine lake! I Was the Child. Valerie S. Warren. Str

If you paint me the picture, and leave that out. An Order for a Picture. Alice Cary. BLPA

If you please you may, or let it alone,/'Tis all one. Gabriel John. *Anonymous.* CBEP

If you prove faithless thrice,/None then will woo ye. To His Mistress. Robert Herrick. ViBoPo

If you put Jesus first and His glory/All things will be added to thee. The Cost. Flora L. Osgood. STF

If you're not sent up you never get off the ground. The Fabulous Teamsters. Judith Johnson Sherwin. NYP

If you're so damn smart, why aren't you rich? The Rainy Season. William Meredith. NePoEA

If you rise in the mornin',/Set the world on fire. Go Down, Ol' Hannah. *Anonymous.* OuSiCo; TTY

If you scratch him will fester. On Dr. Keene, Bishop of Chester. Thomas Gray. FaBoEE

"If you seek for Eldorado!" Eldorado. Edgar Allan Poe. AP; APA; AWP; FaBoBe; FaBoCh; FPL; HBV 1-2; InPo; LaNeLa; LoGBV; NePA; NOBA; NoP; OxBA; TAP; WiR

If you sprinke me thickly with mustard. A Baker's Dozen of Wild Beasts. Carolyn Wells. OBCA

If you stop believing in us/we inherit everything Voices Answering Back: The Vampires. Lawrence Raab. AmPA

If you stopped short of thresholds, did it matter,/If Love leaned down and lifted you across? For Simone Weil. Sister M. Therese. MoRP

If you suffer in the grave,/you can kill from it. Pentecost. Florence Anthony ("Ai"). LTB

If you think I don't love her,/Got a foolish idea. Little Willie's My Darlin'. *Anonymous.* OuSiCo

"If you too licked grass, you'd be dead to-day." Poisoned Lands. John Montague. NMP

If you touched the Hippo,/Hippo-pot-a-mus. The Hippopotamus. Georgia Roberts Durston. TiPo

If you've forgotten my kisses/And I've forgotten your name. An Interlude. Algernon Charles Swinburne. ViBoPo

...If you wake soon, wake me. The Shore. David St. John. LCAP; MAYP

If you want a field of labor,/You can find it anywhere. Your Mission. Ellen M. Huntington Gates. BLPA; BLRP; GoTF; TreFT

If you want a good time, then give something away! A Good Thanksgiving. Annie Douglas Robinson. PoLf

"If you want any breakfast,/Just come here and scratch." The Chickens. *Anonymous.* MoShBr

If you want any just, just help yourself. Frog Went A-Courtin'. *Anonymous.* ABF; AmFP; BFSS; BLPA; BLSo; FSW; TrAS

If you want any more, you can sing it yourself, Willaby-wallaby now, now, now! Risselty-Rosselty. *Anonymous.* DiPo; FSW

If you want the Lord,/he's in Popayan. Four Christmas Carols (excerpt). *Anonymous.* PCh

If you want the older ones, you don't play/any more, but seek & answer back. Epigram: "I delight in the prime of a boy of twelve." Strato. PeHV

If you want to be a communist you'll have to go to Hell. H–y P–tt. *Anonymous.* CoMu

If you want to die you will have to pay for it. Charon. Louis MacNeice. FaBoIP; FaBoTw

If you want to find out, go look for yourself!/A-hmmm, A-hmmm. The Frog and the Mouse. *Anonymous.* WiR

If you/want your wall/whole, get/rid of this. Up against the Wall (parody). D. C. Berry. BXAP

If you were a man, I wonder if we'd be friends. Meditation. Joseph T. Shipley. ALV

If you were but a jingle/And I were but a rhyme. A Catch. Tom (Thomas Hood, Jr.) Hood. CenHV

If you were going to get a pet/what kind of animal would you get. If You. Robert Creeley. NeAP; NoAm; NOBA; SM

...If you were told/The sugar was salt, would the Bohea be Congo? The Poets at Tea. Barry Pain. Par

If you will any more, sing it yourself. The White Dove Sat on the Castle Wall. W. Wager. FaBoNo

If you will be my joy, my sweet and only dear,/And walk along with you anywhere. The Keys of Canterbury. *Anonymous.* AmFP

If you will but stay for/this moment of love. Stay, Time. James Wreford Watson. CaP

If you will have any more of bold Robin Hood,/In his second part it will be. Robin Hood Newly Revived. *Anonymous.* BaBo; ESPB

If you will have me,/I will have you. Lilies Are White. *Anonymous.* PoPle

If you will not when you may,/You shall not when you will, sir. The Baffled Knight. *Anonymous.* ViBoFo

If you wish to fare well, say farewell to the springs. Written at the White Sulphur Springs. Francis Scott Key. OBAL

If you won't work, I'll kill you dead.   Chain Gang Blues.   *Anonymous.*
  OuSiCo

If you work, if you wait, you will find the/place/Where the four-leaf clovers
  grow.   Four-Leaf Clover.   Ella Higginson.   AA; HBV 1-2

If you would come with me, brown girl, sweet.   Paistin Fionn.   Sir Samuel
  Ferguson.   OxBI

If you would have them safe abroad/Pray keep them safe at home.   Three
  Children.   *Anonymous.*   NA; NOBL; OxNR

If you would rise to the sun like a phoenix.   Evening in Camp.   Patricia
  Ledward.   WaP

If your heart is as kind/As your young eyes now.   To a Golden-Haired Girl
  in a Louisiana Town.   Vachel Lindsay.   MoAmPo; MoLP

If your nerves are all awry,/Lettuces and onions try.   Dietary Advice.
  Anonymous.   FaBoUs

If your soul's like a North Sea storm?   The Admiral's Ghost.   Alfred Noyes.
  BBV

If yours be wand'ring, quickly call it home.'   Robin. A Pastoral Elegy.   John
  Dobson.   NOEC

If Zimri dye in Peace that slew his Lord.   From an Elegy upon the Most
  Incomparable King Charles the First.   Henry, Bishop of Chichester King.
  OBS

Ignited this Abode/To put it out–   Though the Great Waters Sleep.   Emily
  Dickinson.   EaLo

Ignorant and wanton as the dawn.   The Dawn.   William Butler Yeats.
  MoVE

The ignorant heart of you.   To Myself, after Forty Years.   T. H. White.
  NYBP

Ignorant, innocent, instantaneous, free,/Unwelcomed, unrenowned.   Rivers
  Unknown to Song.   Alice Meynell.   HBMV

Ignorant of the fact this way of grief/is shared, unnecessary/and political
  Translations.   Adrienne Rich.   WPOW

...The ignorant policeman walks the yard.   The Comman Man.   A.J.M.
  Smith.   NOBC

Ignore thyself, and strive to know thy God!   Self-Knowledge.   Samuel
  Taylor Coleridge.   ERoP 1-2; SeCePo

Ignoring little things like that.   The Perfect Reactionary.   Hughes Mearns.
  NTCP

Ile love thee, serve thee, and adore.   Be Thou Then by Beauty Named.
  Thomas Campion.   AAS

Ile think on you, and by you think on heaven.   To Celia, upon Love's
  Ubiquity.   Thomas Carew.   AnAnS 2

Ilion, in a short hour, higher/He can build, and once more fire.   The Power
  of Love.   John Fletcher.   HBV 1-2; UnTE

Ilium toppled thunder his ears, what's left/Of Helen naked drag between his
  toes.   Legend.   Ralph Gustafson.   CaP; PeCV

Ilka thing pleases while Willie's at hame.   Here Awa', There Awa'.
  Anonymous.   OBS

Ill broken, heart broken, I sing to myself.   Eighteen Verses Sung to a Tartar
  Reed Whistle.   Ts'ai Yen.   BoWoP; PBWP; WPOW

Ill is the weather that bringeth no gain,/Nor helps good hearts in need.
  Cold's the Wind.   Thomas Dekker.   ViBoPo

Ill met still are warm and wintry weather,/Death and birth.   Death and
  Birth.   Algernon Charles Swinburne.   MaVP

Ill's the airt o the Word the day.   Idleset (2).   Thurso Berwick.   OxBS

Illuminate this dream/With a cold art.   The Winter Lightning for Paul.
  Howard Nemerov.   MoVE

Illumined Heaven, eternal Sea.   Teneriffe (excerpt).   Frederic William Henry
  Myers.   OBVV

An illusion the will cannot destroy.   The Progress of Photography.   Byron
  Vazakas.   MoPo

An illustration of the snow.   Shh! The Professor Is Sleeping.   John N.
  Morris.   CABA

An image made of lime or brass/That's cleaned with tamarind.   True
  Knowledge.   Panatattu.   WGRP

"An image of Jesus Christ approximately this high."   Anecdote from William
  IV Street.   D. J. Enright.   OxBC

The image of my error.   Song: "Dressed up in my melancholy."   M. Carl
  Holman.   PoNe

An image of that calm life appears/That won my heart in my greener years.
  Green River.   William Cullen Bryant.   AP; NOBA; OxBA

An image of the dead.   The Four.   Geoffrey Grigson.   WaP

An image of the dead on the fingernail/of a newborn child.   Dream Songs.
  John Berryman.   HaCAP

The image of thy mother's loveliness.   To Ianthe.   Percy Bysshe Shelley.
  ATP

Images cast against the eternally shifting/heavens.   Study Peace.   LeRoi
  (Imamu Amiri Baraka) Jones.   PoBA

Images fill their vacant eyes.   A Friend.   W. D. Snodgrass.   MAT

Images of Buddha placed/In shells, and later found encased in pearl.   Portrait
  of an Artist.   Barbara Howes.   IHMS

"The images ye have made of me!"   A Parable.   James Russell Lowell.
  PGD

An imaginary scarlet/stained glass.   The Poppy.   Cid Corman.   HoAn

The imagination hurts, like fear: or toothache.   A Meditation upon the
  Toothache.   Laurence Lerner.   NePoEA-2

Imagination is the proof of love.   For My Brother Who Died before I Was
  Born.   Baron Wormser.   GOYP

The imagination that we spurned and crave.   To the One of Fictive Music.
  Wallace Stevens.   AP; APA; CoBMV; MoAB; MoAmPo; MoVE; NoP

Imagine that your cap's on back to front.   On Seeing My Birthplace from a
  Jet Aircraft.   John Pudney.   NYBP

Imagine what you'll be at five.   For Maria at Four.   John Becker.   BiCB

Imagine your heaven, I cried, but do it without me!   The Antagonist.   David
  Ferry.   NePoAm-2

The imagined pine, the imagined jay.   The Man with the Blue Guitar.
  Wallace Stevens.   LiTA

...Imagined the slow passion/to that deliberate progress.   Considering the
  Snail.   Thom Gunn.   GrPl; LiTM; MP; NePoEA-2; TwCP

...Imagining's no shutter/against the absolute, incorrigible sunrise.   Berceuse.
  Amy Clampitt.   SUW

Imagining that curve/to this night.   Overnight Guest.   Ramona Wilson.
  VoR

Imagining that I was one of those peaceful stones.   What the Stone Dreams.
  James B. Hathaway.   GOYP

Immaculate of man's infirmities.   O Glorious Childbearer.   Joseph Campbell.
  OnYI

The immaculate stream, heavy, and swinging home again.   The River That Is
  East.   Galway Kinnell.   NYP

The Immediate arc, alone, of life, of love.   Horses Graze.   Gwendolyn
  Brooks.   CNA; GP

The immediate is past.   Expectancies: The Eleventh Hour.   Karla M.
  Hammond.   AMV-80

Immediately–that Anguish stooped/Almost to Jealousy–   So proud she was to
  die.   Emily Dickinson.   NOBA

Immense and dark, where broken galleys flee.   Antony and Cleopatra.
  Henri Coulette.   NePoEA

An immense fanfare/of the dog's yapping...   A Dog in the Quarry.   Miroslav
  Holub.   BoAnP; GDP

Immense on the marshes, stood...MRS. RAVOON!   Alternative Endings to an
  Unwritten Ballad.   Paul Dehn.   FiBHP

...Immense pinned butterfly/at the entrance of a motionless station.   The
  Manless Society.   Pierre Unik.   EAS

Immensity cloistered in thy dear womb.   Annunciation.   John Donne.
  AnAnS 1; ISi; OBS; TrCP

Immigrants!   Immigrants.   Stanley Nelson.   AMV-81

Immobile, terrified eyes.   The Patient: Rockland County Sanitarium.   Calvin
  C. Hernton.   PoBA

Immortal beings were not born/To waste their time in bed.   Morning.   Jane
  Taylor.   HBV 1-2

Immortal dandy, towards an immortal star.   Shaemus.   Conrad Aiken.
  OxBA

Immortal in a picture of an old grange.   Haymaking.   Edward ("Edward
  Eastaway") Thomas.   AnFE; BrPo; MoAB; MoBrPo; SeCePo

The immortal, incommunicable dream.   Space and Dread and the Dark.
  William Ernest Henley.   WHA

Immortal Liberty, whose look sublime/Hath bleached the tyrant's cheek in
  every varying clime.   Independence.   Tobias George Smollett.   OBEC

Immortal praise with one accord.   A Satire on London.   Henry Howard,
  Earl of Surrey.   SiPS

The immortal still I seek and follow on to Heaven!   Ideal Beauty.   Fernando
  de Herrera.   CAW

Immortal, they may rest sublime,/though beauty burns and love goes wrong.
  Ode to a Nightingale (parody).   Roy Kelly.   BXAP

Immortal through the lamp within/his hand.   Gifts.   Emma Lazarus.
  TrJP; WGRP

Immortality contented/Were Anomaly.   Satisfaction–Is the agent.   Emily
  Dickinson.   NOBA

Immortalized by his extinction.   The Dodo.   Edward Lucie-Smith.   PoL

–Immortalized for the cops, for his fares, for the world–/to be looking his best.
  The Cabdriver's Smile.   Denise Levertov.   NYP

Immutable as my regret.   The Grave of Love.   Thomas Love Peacock.
  CH; HBV 1-2

Immutable to rhyme,/Impossible to scan.   To a Photograph.   Parker Tyler.
  NePA

...Impalpable country/Of sleep, holding all of this back, drifting toward the
  unborn.   Remembering Fire.   Rodney Jones.   MAYP

Impart it to my solitary lyre?   The Solitary Lyre.   George Darley.   LiTB;
  OBEV

Impartial History dare not leave thee/out.   Wendell Phillips.   Amos Bronson
  Alcott.   AA

Impatiently casting glimpses of itself/Back toward time.   Awakening.   David
  Robinson.   AMV-81

Impenetrable hollow!   The Hollow at Ilbalintja Soak.   *Anonymous.*   NOAV

Imperceptibly they shut me out of/the world. Walls. Constantine P. Cavafy. TrJP

Imperial to save! National Song. William Henry Venable. MC; PAH

Imperious, dainty lily for a soul. A Bulb. Richard Kendall Munkittrick. AA; PoL

Impersonally, in a group, or maybe/personally,/one at a time. The Leather Bar. Ralph Pomeroy. PeHV

Implacable Drought. Drought (excerpt). Francis Carey Slater. ACV

Implacable, that sky-wanderer. Its name is Love. The Dark Planet. John Heath-Stubbs. OAEL 1-2

Implacably shod into the perfect street. Sale. Josephine Miles. PoL

Importune me no more!' When I Was Fair and Young. Queen of England, Elizabeth I. BoLoP; CBEP; CTC; EnLi 1-2; NIP; NoP; PoRA

Impossible for to recount/Or any way expresse. In Thankfull Remembrance for My Dear Husband's Safe Arrivall.... Anne Bradstreet. TrPWD

Impossibly close/To the rich destroying fire. Magma. G. J. F. Dutton. PoSH

Imprison it or it will thee. To His Little Son Benedict from the Tower of London. John Hoskyns. OxBChV

Imprison my two eyes in my two hands/and see no other thing than it I touch. Green Enravishment of Human Life. Sister Juana Ines de la Cruz. WPOW

Imprison to spend all springs with you. Song: "With whomsoever I share the spring." Jan Burroway. NePoAm-2

Imprisoned never, no not soot or rain. The Phantom Bark. Hart Crane. CMoP

The imprisoned souls of soldiers and of me. Homecoming. Karl Shapiro. MiAP

...Improvise/by you our colors in the winter sun. Max Schmitt in a Single Scull. Richmond Lattimore. EyDe; NePoAm-2

An impulse of fish, dashed with light,/toward whatever intersections. The Small. Don Welch. WOLT

The impulsive foam/of a spastic Phraseology. Jayne Cortez. BlSi

Impure and pure are all alike to him. The Unity of God. Panatattu. WGRP

Impute this idle talk to that I go,/For dying men talk often so. A Valediction: Of My Name in the Window. John Donne. EnRePo; QFR

In a bar on the Piccola Marina.' A Bar on the Piccola Marina. Noel Coward. NLV

...In a Baron Bishop you have both/Leviathan served up and Behemoth. The Loyal Scot (excerpt). Andrew Marvell. ViBoPo

In a beau language without a drop of blood. Repetitions of a Young Captain. Wallace Stevens. WaP

In a birth of forgetting your tears must die. Autumn Healing. Jean Ward. LaNeLa

In a blinding blaze, from the filth of the world's floor. Remarks of Soul to Body. Robert Penn Warren. NAs

In a blizzard of doves. Desert Gulls. Dan Gillespie. TAT

In a blushing blissful song/that echoes against heaven. Flavius, If Your Girl Friend. Caius Valerius Catullus. ErPo

In a book that is shining. Poems to a Brown Cricket. James Wright. NaP; NYBP

In a cafe last summer/in Barcelona. Poem: "In secret." Pablo Picasso. EAS

In a calm voice, I ask you if you want some bread. Death Is a Second Cousin Dining with Us Tonight. Geraldine Kudaka. BrSi

In a Catholic hospital of sheets white as his hair Grandfather. George Bowering. NOBC

In a coal cellar, on Ludlow Street/in Nineteen hundred. At the Jewish Museum. Linda Pastan. VWA

In a cradle of grass at the goalposts. Watching the Jets Lose to Buffalo at Shea. May Swenson. LiSp

In a defiant gesture, that's my girl! Clinic Day. Jo Barnes. BrRo

In a delirium with the strange prolixity/Of the talking called for, I fear. The Praise of Ben Dorain. Duncan Ban MacIntyre. GoTS

In a dream, in a probable volume, in a/probable volume of dreams, think so. Treetops. Marvin Bell. AmPA

In a field of alien corn a girl was reaped. Lifelines. Gavin Ewart. EAS

In a flock of virgins/She spread about her. Like the Honeycomb Dropping Honey. Hildegard von Bingen. WPOW

In a folding chair/Waiting for his father? Jim. Barbara Howes. GP

In a forest of frost, in a dawn of cornflowers. Poppies in October. Sylvia Plath. FaBoWP; HaCAP; LCAP; NoAm

In a garden where some cold-sober slug will celebrate/Your wake through the night. To the Fly in My Drink. David Wagoner. DFF

In a green/airy space, not/locked in About Marriage. Denise Levertov. NMM

In a green garden in mid month of May. Three Ballate. Angelo Poliziano. AWP

In a green melancholy/Of overblown summer. With Me My Lover Makes. Cecil Day-Lewis. OBMV

In a heaven where all we of longing lie, clinging together/as it gets dark. Fog. Kenneth Patchen. NaP

In a heaving ring returning the same regrets. Caterpillars. John Freeman. ChMP

In a heavy light like yellow onions. Yellow Light. Garrett Kaoru Hongo. HoAn; MAYP

In a house beneath a beechwood/In an acre of wild land. A World within a War. Sir Herbert Read. MoPo

In a Jungian search/for lost parents/their own age Lost Parents. Lawrence Ferlinghetti. AmC; GP; PoM

In a land that no man knows. The Wild Duck. John Masefield. BrPo

In a land where all the inhabitants are old. Schizophrenic. P. K. Page. HeIP

In a landscape without love. The Snowman. P.K. Page. NOBC

In a little rock pool that reflects the moon. Orkney Interior. Ian Hamilton Finlay. NMP

In a look of his own for thee. The Child on the Judgment Seat. Elizabeth Rundle Charles. BLPA

In a luminous sea of sense. When a Body. Gene Dawson. AMV-80

In a manner unbecoming to the successor/Of Edward the Confessor. William the Bastard. Lakon". FiBHP

In a more mild and temp'rate ray/We may again enjoy the day. Noon Quatrains. Charles Cotton. LoBV

In a murky dream, I see your face again. Parting is Hard. *Anonymous*. BoWoP

In a narrow grave, just six by three,/We buried him there on the lone prairie. The Dying Cowboy. *Anonymous*. BFSS; FaBoBe

In a net of fireflies. Peasant and Geisha Songs. *Anonymous*. LiTW

In a New (bloody) Army he couldn't understand. Sergeant-Major Money. Robert Graves. MMM; OBWP

...In a place/Of unapplauding hands and broken song. My Dark Fathers. Brendan Kennelly. BIrV; CIP

In a pumpkin-shell coach, with two rats for her team! The Pumpkin. John Greenleaf Whittier. PoSC

In a red Volkswagen you are a snail,/hunched and alien and terribly humble. Otoe County in Nebraska. William Kloefkorn. GP

In a restaurant/dealing with humanity Tripart. Gayl Jones. BlSi

In a scathing, scolding lecture he's too happy to resent. Cedar Waxwing. William H. Matchett. ELU

In a season of snow, they shall batter my door to/borrow/A sip of my wild sweet grape. On Laying up Treasure. Lois Smith Hiers. GoYe

...In a sense we have all survived/Our words depend on it, with each chance. A Chinaman's Chance. Alex Kuo. APU

(In a shimmer of melting winters/A breast that was never extinguished.) Journey: IV. Erik Lindegren. LiTW

In a silent boat. Seven Poems. Lorine Niedecker. VGW

In a single day I have seen all the flowers of Ch'ang-an. After Passing the Examination. Meng Chiao. GLGT

In a sinuous tango The Woman Who Thought She Was More Than a Samba. Jessica Hagedorn. BrSi

In a slumber sweet and cold. Refrigerium. Frederick Goddard Tuckerman. AP

In a small container/on the ledge where the light enters. What Good Poems Are For. Tom Wayman. NoP

In a somer sesun The Vision of Piers Plowman. William Langland. CoBE

In a sudden giving-withdrawing move, like a county judge/striking a match. Reincarnation (I). James Dickey. HoPM

In a suit with two pr. pantsk. Do You Plan to Speak Bantu? Ogden Nash. FiBHP

In a Sunday's violent idleness. Two Illustrations That the World Is What You Make of It. Wallace Stevens. NePoAm

In a thousand furnished rooms. Preludes. Thomas Stearns Eliot. AnAmPo

In a thousand years we shall all forget/The things that trouble us now. After the Quarrel. Adam Lindsay Gordon. OBVV

In a time of brain and desire/patience is the mental equivalent of running. Redo, 1-5. Lyn Hejinian. APU

In a tumultuous privacy of storm. Announced by All the Trumpets of the Sky. Ralph Waldo Emerson. TiPo

In a war for freedom, who were never free. Poem: "I burn for England with a living flame." Gervase Stewart. WaP

In a well order'd measure beat the ground. Pan Piping. Thomas Stanley. FaBoEE

In a whispering tree, like cedar, evergreen. Kentucky Mountain Farm. Robert Penn Warren. MoVE

In a wind from what were sand dunes Some San Francisco Poems. George Oppen. NNaP

In a world of gigantic cushioncovers,/and enormous bamboo fans. Elephants from the Sea. Ian Young. NeAC

In a world of wonders far away. Dream-Song. Walter De la Mare. PoPle

In a yellow petticoat/And a green gown. Daffadowndilly. Mother Goose. NTCP; SoPo; TiPo

In Adam's garden/he plants all his blood. The Kropotkin Poems (excerpt). Phyllis Webb. NOBC

In Aglaia's only eyes/All my worldly paradise. Shepherd and Shepherdess. Nicholas Breton. OBSC

An' in agony he prayed. Song: "Dark was de night an' col' was de groun'." *Anonymous.* NAMP

In ale and kisses they forget their cares,/And Susan Blouzelinda's loss repairs. Blouzelinda's Funeral. John Gay. OBEC

In all external grace you have some part,/But you like none, none you, for constant heart. Sonnets, LIII: "What is your substance, whereof are you made." William Shakespeare. CTC; EBEV; FaFP; LiTB; LiTL; MasP; OAEL 1-2; OAEP; OBEV; OBSC; PeHV; ViBoPo

In all his words most wonderful,/Most sure in all his ways. The Dream of Gerontius. John Henry, Cardinal Newman. NOCV

In all its Valley Forges/As resolute as he. George Washington. James S. Tippett. YeAr

In all my ranging and serenading/I met no equal to Castle Hyde. Castle Hyde. *Anonymous.* FaBoPP; IrPN

In all proportion/the outsized Men. The Closed System. Larry Eigner. VWA

In all that grows while the winter reaps/we will live again. Comanche Ghost Dance. Lance Henson. VoR

In all the drowsy, warm, Sicilian air. A Sleeping Priestess of Aphrodite. Robert Cameron Rogers. AA

In all the endless road you tread/There's nothing but the night. A Shropshire Lad. Alfred Edward Housman. NOBV

In all the land no women found so fair. The Beauty of Job's Daughters. Jay Macpherson. ACV; NOBC; PoCh

In all the level stare that met our stare. The Outlanders. Andrew Glaze. NYBP

In all the magnanimity of Thought/Resolves; and re-resolves: then dies the same. Procrastination. Edward Hilton Young. OBEC

In all the windows/of stone. The Book of Nightmares. Galway Kinnell. NNaP

In all the world no two things match/But the green eyes of Patsy. A Love for Patsy. John Thompson, Jr. LiTA; LiTL; NePA; WaP

In all their heaumes some yellow hair. Near Avalon. William Morris. CBEP; OAEL 1-2

In amang the rosy clouds, far ayont the sea. Wee Davie Daylicht. Robert Tennant. OxBChV

In ambush here that night the Akhaians lay. The Odyssey. Homer. CTC; NAWM 1-2

In an age which advances progressively backwards? The Rock. Thomas Stearns Eliot. TRV

In an 8-ball universe built for ivory. Rotation. Julian Bond. FF; NIP; NNP

In an everlasting gesture/to catch a white fish. Little Marble Boy. James Wright. EyDe

In an eye's wink/the kingdom of light Handicapped. Daniel Berrigan. FAZ

In an instant all the junk/will burst into a flame. On the Farm. Barbara Winder. PH

In an orchard soft with rot. Never May the Fruit Be Plucked. Edna St. Vincent Millay. CrMA; MoLP; OBSP; SBG

In an unknown sky. Haiku: "Autumn's bright moon." Kaga no Chiyo. PBWP

In an unscrupulous and deserved embrace. Money. C. H. Sisson. PoL

In ancient cryptic blessing/on our heads. In a Maple Wood. Pat Schneider. AMV-81

In and oot with diddle doddle/Tommie makes my tail toddle. Tommie Makes My Tail Toddle. Robert Burns. ErPo

In annote is hire name—nempneth it non!/Whoso right redeth roune to Johon. Annot and John. *Anonymous.* OxBM

In another being, at last. Words for the Wind. Theodore Roethke. AP; NoAm; NOBA; PoCh

In another health to Kian. The Cup of O'Hara. Turlough O'Carolan. AnIV; OnYI

In any case, I'm told, he has been shot/As a precautionary News of the Phoenix. A.J.M. Smith. ELU; PeCV

In any drawingroom (in civil i/zation) an incred/ib/ly/long time... The Web. Gregory O'Donoghue. BIrV

In any way the world knew how to speak. Paul's Wife. Robert Frost. AnAmPo

In argosies to shores of dawn. Bathed Is My Blood. Oliver La Grone. NNP

In Arizona, in darkness or in glittering rays/of flashlights, goes round and round and round. Rimrock, Where It Is. Hayden Carruth. NNaP

In Artois or Picardy they lie—free of useless fashions. The Bohemians. Ivor Gurney. MMM

In as august a sphere:/Perchance, far higher. Plato in London. Lionel Pigot Johnson. VLP

In ashes warms the hero's heart! Avran. James Clarence Mangan. SeCePo

In August away I must. To the Cuckoo. *Anonymous.* OxNR

In August,/Go I must. Cuckoo, Cuckoo. *Anonymous.* PBBP

In August, June,/July, or May. The Oyster. Ogden Nash. ALV

In Autumn God/Heeds how He drops/The golden fruit. The King of Ulster. *Anonymous.* KiLC

In Autumn's funeral train. Torch-Light in Autumn. John James Piatt. AA

In autumn we used maple leaves,/In winter, snow. The Settlers. Judith Hemschemeyer. SO

In Autumn when the woods are red/And skies are grey and clear. In Autumn When the Woods Are Red. Robert Louis Stevenson. NOBV

...In back of their hard, or veiled, or shining/unknowable gaze... Olga Poems. Denise Levertov. LCAP; NNaP

In balance with this life, this death. An Irish Airman Foresees His Death. William Butler Yeats. AnEnPo; CoBMV; EnL; FaBoCh; FaBoMo; GoJo; GTBS-P; HeIP; HoPM; LiTM; LoGBV; MMM; MoAB; MoBrPo; NoAm; NOBE; NoP; OBMV; OBWP; PoPl; PPP; SCV; TrGrPo; WaaP; WaP; WeW

In battle his shield never cried out. Colloquy of the Ancients (excerpt). *Anonymous.* OnYI

In beauteous Erin, that pleasant time. A Day in Ireland. *Anonymous.* AnIV

In beauty it is finished. A Prayer of the Night Chant. *Anonymous.* ExPo

...In bed/my sweet wife dreams of an old lover/whose name she cannot remember. Frost Warning. Ron McFarland. AMV-81

In bed we depend on nothing but bed. Bed Time. Peter Davison. UnPo

In Beit-She'an the people of Israel wait. Saul. Amir Gilboa. VWA

In Bethlehem town/When the light was done. A Carol. Lizette Woodworth Reese. HBMV

In between lies/embroidery. Embroidery. Maria Jacobs. AMV-80

In bitter bales she has me brought–/Alas that ever she was unkind!.... Fragment of a Love Lament. *Anonymous.* OxBM

In bitter mockery the cheated son. A Thought. Mikhail Yuryevich Lermontov. AWP

In blisse; Quia amore langueo. Quia Amore Langueo. *Anonymous.* ACP; AtBAP; CBEP; CoBE; EnLit; ISi; LiTL; MeEL; NOBE; NOCV; OBEV; OxBM; OxBoChV; PoEL 1-5

In body healthy, and composed in mind. Mira's Will. Mary Leapor. NOEC

In Bolivia, Peru and Ecuador! In Praise of Llamas. Arthur Guiterman. FiBHP

In boyhood I knew them, and still they call to me. The Old Home. Madison Cawein. HBV 1-2

In brass pans and cauldrons, said John the Red Nose. The Cutty Wren. *Anonymous.* CBEP; FSW; GBP; NCEP; OxBoLi; WiR

In Breughel's great picture, The Kermess. The Dance. William Carlos Williams. AmP; AmPP; CMoP; ExPo; GoJo; GrPl; HAP; HeIP; InPK; LiTM; LoGBV; NCSH; NIP; NoAm; NOBA; NoP; OxBA; PoL; PrIm; SoSe; TAP; WeW

In bright succession raise, her ornament and guard! The Cotter's Saturday Night. Robert Burns. BeLS; CEP; EiCP; FaBoBe; HBV 1-2; LAuP; MCCG; OAEP; PoLf; WGRP

In Britain none can fit you better/Than can your servant the Bootmaker. From the Caledonian Mercury. Gavin Wilson. FaBoUs

In Bronx Park when he's feeling so pleased with himself. Random Reflections on a Cloudless Sunday. John Hall Wheelock. NePoAm

In Bronxville, Chicago, Butte, Fond du Lac? Last Year's Discussion: The Nobel Russian. Phyllis McGinley. FaBoEE

In brough or land, wherever we meet,/A rank thief I'll call thee.' Jock the Leg and the Merry Merchant. *Anonymous.* ESPB

In burst of music, love, and light! The Christmas Silence. Margaret Deland. OHIP

In canvas, stone, or written pages. The After-Comers. Robert and Spence Traill Lowell. AA

In casual simplicity. Simplicity. Emily Dickinson. AnNE

In Ceaseless Rosemary– Essential Oils–are wrung–675. Emily Dickinson. AmPP; CBEP

In change whereof I leave my heart behind. Nature, that gave the bee so feat a grace. Sir Thomas Wyatt. FCP

In Charon's palm it pay the toll to Death. The House of Life. Dante Gabriel Rossetti. NoP; OAEP; ViBoPo

In cheerful sounds all voices raise/And fill the world with loudest praise. From All That Dwell below the Skies. Isaac Watts. EBCP; TRV

In chief, in this poetic liturgy. To His Kinswoman, Mistress Penelope Wheeler. Robert Herrick. CaPo

In childhood, manhood, age, and death,/To keep us still Thine own! By Cool Siloam's Shady Rill. Reginald Heber. ELP; NOCV; OxBoCh

In Christ confide. Exhortation. Thomas Hastings. AA

In Christ his birth this day rejoice. A Carol for Christmas Day. Francis Kinwelmersh. SBVL

In Christ, its comradeship with men. It Isn't Far to Bethlehem. Arthur R., Jr. Macdougall. PGD

In cittie nor on hill, but all the night must sleep alone. Idylls. Theocritus. OBVE

In clear summer midnight/Ever sees it alone. Thoughts in the Gulf Stream. Christopher Morley. EtS

In College cloister live and die. Snapdragon. John Henry, Cardinal Newman. GoBC

In common with the building, the monkey, land etcetera. Dance with Banderillas. Richard Duerden. NeAP

In confirmation, I hear sevenfold lark-songs pealing. The Wild Common. D. H. Lawrence. CoBMV

In constructing a workable still. Limerick: "At a modernist school in Park Hill." Morris Bishop. TDH

In converse with the mountains, moors, and fens. Prelude. John Millington Synge. AWP; BoNaP; FaBoPP; HBMV; MoBrPo; OBMV

In copious gulps of potent ale expires. The Birth of the Squire. John Gay. EiCP; NOEC; PoEL 1-5

In countless myriads stretched for many a league. Tecumseh. Charles Mair. OBCV

In dance, in song, in that little taste. The Ration Card. Liz Sohappy Bahe. CDW

In danger be ever nigh! I Am With Thee. Ernest Bourner Allen. BLRP

In danger with no room to turn,/Ease her, stop her, go astern. Useful for Avoiding Collisions at Sea. Anonymous. FaBoUs

In dark accidents the mind's sufficient grace. The Beautiful American Word, Sure. Delmore Schwartz. CrMA; LiTA; VGW

In darkness for the city luminous. Shadows To-Day. Christina Georgina Rossetti. OxBoCh

In darkness like undeveloped film. Stood-Up. Bruce Byfield. AMV-80

In dat great gittin' up mornin'/Fare you well, Fare you well. In Dat Great Gittin' Up Mornin'. Anonymous. AA; BoAN 1-2

In days not yours, through thoughts of you! Oxford Nights. Lionel Pigot Johnson. BrPo

In dead men breath. Two Fusiliers. Robert Graves. MMM

In death I would be near her,/And rise beside my Irish wife. The Irish Wife. Thomas D'Arcy McGee. HBV 1-2

...In Death's clime/There's no pen, paper, notion–and no Time. Here Lies... Stevie Smith. PoA

In death sings on–that days to come/Are sweet as the days that are over! Tomorrow. Florence Earle Coates. AA

In death the whip lies in his sunburnt hands. The Team. Furnley Maurice. CBAP

In death till now there is nothing but grief. Alarum. Urszula Koziol. WPOW

In deeps or shallows, all projections of the divine. On the Death of Karl Barth. Jack R. Clemo. NOCV

In defeat or victory! God to Thee We Humbly Bow. George Henry Boker. AH

In deference to the cloud parade. The Cloud Parade. Laura Jensen. LCAP

In Derry of the little hills. Lament for the Poets: 1916. Francis Ledwidge. AnIV; AWP; OnYl; OxBI

In different directions/down the imperturbable street. An Aspect of Love, Alive in the Ice and Fire. Gwendolyn Brooks. CAPP; TAP

In dirt and darkness hundreds stink content. The First Epistle of the First Book of Horace Imitated (excerpt). Alexander Pope. OBSV

In distant worlds, and in years on this world as distant. From All These Events. Stephen Spender. LiTB; NAMP

In doors and out, summer and winter, Mirth. To the Grasshopper and the Cricket. [James Henry] Leigh Hunt. EnLi 1-2; EnRP; GN; HBV 1-2; OBNC

In doubt we'll go together–thou and I. Soul and Body. Samuel Waddington. OBVV

In dreams doth he behold her/Still fair and kind and young. Lost Love. Andrew Lang. BSV; HBV 1-2

In dreams I see that rampant He, and tremble at that Miaow. Sad Memories. Charles Stuart Calverley. FM

In drinking unexcised gin,/And wooing fair poissardes, sir. A Radical War Song. Thomas Babington, Lord Macaulay. OBSV

In each the potential is realized, the two wires/Are crossing. On Autumn Lake. John Ashbery. LCAP

In earthly bulbs, spring flowers; in man, the Christ;/In years, eternity. A Prayer for the New Year. Violet Alleyn Storey. TrPWD

In ecstasy swirls and sways/To her stange tryst. The Moth. Walter De la Mare. BrPo; MoVE

In Eden every flower is blown: Amen. My Epitaph. David Gray. OBVV

In either case it's dead. The Centipede. Sir Alan Patrick Herbert. CenHV

In empty houses where old things take place. The Dispossessed. John Berryman. AP; PoCh; VGW

In endless evenings of making love. My husband is the same man. Sila. BoWoP

In endless hurry round the world. Elegy on the Dust. Thom Gunn. NoAm

In equal parts the pye divide,/As you may see on t'other side. A Was an Apple Pie, B Bit It, C Cut It. Anonymous. FaBoUs

In every case/you find yourself standing against the wall. The Wall Test. Louis Simpson. GP

In every clime, to every age. In Memory of General Grant. Henry Abbey. AA

In every difference/love decrees The Nicest Phantasies Are Shared. Brian Coffey. CIP

In every hole the sea came up,/Till it could come no more. At the Sea-Side. Robert Louis Stevenson. NTCP; OxBChV; SUS; TiPo

In every hope appears a grave/And leaves no hope for me. A Sea Boy on the Giddy Mast. John Clare. PPP

In every man that suffers, he, the Man of Sorrows, stands! The Man of Sorrows. Anonymous. PGD

In every place the very wasp of flowers. The Fear of Flowers. John Clare. NBM; OBRV; SeCeV

"In every room, my beloved!" Dinner at the Hotel de la Tigresse Verte. Donald Evans. AnAmPo

In every soul the soul of all our souls. Crass Times Redeemed by Dignity of Souls. Peter Viereck. HoPM; MiAP

"In every storm I hear them pass." People Who Went by in Winter. William Stafford. GP

"In every thing give thanks." In Every Thing Give Thanks. Anonymous. STF

...In everything we are sprung/Of earth's first blood, have titles manifold. Old Man Travelling. William Wordsworth. OBWP

In fact, my form's the Bloomin' Utter! Culture in the Slums. William Ernest Henley. CenHV; HBV 1-2; InMe

In fact there is no toucan who can/do what four or three or two can. Toucannery. Jack Prelutsky. OnUR

In factories, where the eyes see what they know?) The Eyes Have It. William Stephens. NAMP

In failing light, and the coming of cold. Forms of the Earth at Abiquiu. N. Scott Momaday. CDW

In faith that Christ is still alive. Facts. William Henry Davies. BrPo

In far corners of night/science's watcher sees/fly-spirals mimicked in the galaxies. The Swarm. Richard Moore. SUW

In fascination of her brightness. The Dome of Sunday. Karl Shapiro. AP; CMoP; CoAP; CoBMV; LiTM; MoAB; MoAmPo; MoPo; NePA; NoAm; OxBA; WaP

In faultless failing, raised by our own weight. Most Like an Arch This Marriage. John Ciardi. MoLP; PoPl; WeW

In feeding the hungry and cheering the sad,/Paddy O'Rafther! Paddy O'Rafther. Samuel Lover. HBV 1-2; StPo

In fell disease/I lie, and deathly fearing. L'Aura Amara. Arnaut Daniel. CTC

In final terror hung/the wrong face back. Was a Man. Philip Booth. NCSH; NePoEA-2; VGW

In fine, deliver Israel,/O Lord, from all his troubles fell. Psalm XXV. Sir Philip Sidney. FCP

In flame and a clamorous breath known to the eye-pecking gulls. Epitaphs of the War, 1914-18. Rudyard Kipling. BrPo; OBWP

In flame that never tires. Song: "Now that Fate is dead and gone." Edith Sitwell. MoAB; MoBrPo

In flight I grieve,/my fur matted by desire. Corn-Woman Remembered. Judith Mountain Leaf Volborth. TWSS

In forest shade they disappeared. The Brownies' Celebration. Palmer Cox. OBCA

In from the dark ivy hopped a/Wee small bird.And that was Me. The Little Bird. Walter De La Mare. BiCB; BrR; NAs

In front of the sink and said, "Kid, this is IT." High-Life Low-Down. Justin Richardson. PV

In Gaelic, as big as a tombstone/And appropriately black. Miss Grant. Freda Downie. FaBoWP

In gaining my crown, I'd gladly share His cross. Sharing His Cross. Gracia L. Fero. BePJ

In gay Vauxhall now saunter beaux and belles,/And happier cits resort to Sadler's Wells. A Description of the Spring in London. Anonymous. NOEC

In gentle eyes thou veilest,/My blueveined child. A Flower Given to My Daughter. James Joyce. OBMV; PoPl

In gentleness and constancy. Robin Redbreast. George Washington Doane. AA; HBV 1-2; HBVY

In gestures of invincible desire. Sonnet: "The winter deepening, the hay all in." Richard Wilbur. PoPl

In ghostlier demarcations, keener sounds. The Idea of Order at Key West. Wallace Stevens. AP; CMoP; CoBMV; FF; ForPo; HaCAP; HAP; HeIP;

MoAB; MoAmPo; MoPo; MOS; NAWM 1-2; NIP; NoAm; NOBA; NoP; OxBA; PP; PPP; PrIm; TAP

In giving Love his sight/And striking Folly blind.   Behold a Wonder Here! *Anonymous.*   ALV; TrGrPo

In gladness may thy will be done.   Creator of Infinities.   Chadwick Hansen. AH

In glitt'ring dust and painted fragments lie!   The Rape of the Lock. Alexander Pope.   ViBoPo

In gloomy grandeur o'er the hills and seas/Reigneth omnipotent.   The Winter Shore.   Thomas Wade.   ERoP 1-2; NBM; OAEL 1-2

In glorious hope their proud sorrowing Land/Commits her children to Thy gracious hand.   The Supreme Sacrifice.   John Stanhope Arkwright. WGRP

In God's bright mirror cleared from mortal/breath!   Life and Death.   Lilla Cabot Perry.   AA

In God's most holy sight.   O Paradise! O Paradise!   Frederick William Faber.   WGRP

In God's time cometh the thing God will,/For God is the Lord of all!   The Friendly Blight.   Aubrey Thomas De Vere.   IrPN

In God who was her salvation.   The May Magnificat.   Gerard Manley Hopkins.   AtBAP; ISi; VLP

In Gotham, than a band in Butte.   I'd Rather Listen to a Flute.   Samuel Hoffenstein.   FiBHP; PoL

In green grass silk/With wild-flower frills.   Rain Clouds.   Elizabeth-Ellen Long.   BrR

In grief the flood is bursting home!   Low Tide on Grand-Pre.   Bliss Carman. CaP; NOBC; OBCV; PeCV

In Harlem wandering from street to street.   Harlem Shadows.   Claude McKay.   BANP

In hasty praise/of lemon/light.   Lemons, Lemons.   Al Young.   HeIP

In health, they do abuse/Nature, who Physick use.   Proverbial Advice on Keeping Healthy.   *Anonymous.*   FaBoUs

In hearts all rocky now the late remorse of love.   Childe Harold's Pilgrimage: Canto IV.   George Gordon, Lord Byron.   FiP

In hearts at peace under an English heaven.   The Soldier.   Rupert Brooke. BBV; BoC; BrPo; ExPo; FaBV; FaFP; FaPoR; FF; FPL; GoTF; GTBS; HeIP; LiTB; LiTM; MaC; MCCG; MoBrPo; MoVE; NIP; NOBE; OBEV; OBWP; OxBTC; PoA; PoLf; PoPl; PoRA; TEP; TreF; TrGrPo; ViBoPo; WaP; WHA

In hearts there linger yet/Ashes of roses.   Ashes of Roses.   Elaine Goodale Eastman.   AA; HBV 1-2

In heaven above, where all is love,/There'll be no sorrow there.   O Sing to Me of Heaven.   Mary Stanley Bunce Dana.   AH

In heaven at last we bless Thee.   I Am the Rose of Sharon.   Catherine Winkworth.   BePJ

In heaven He caught my wings.   The Snares.   Nahab Koutchak.   CAW

"In Heaven meet me, Henry!" and she sweetly smiled and died.   Henry Green.   *Anonymous.*   BaBo

In heaven, once more to meet again,/Their own poor Little Jim.   Little Jim. Edward Farmer.   PaPo

In Heaven stands the ripened grain.   Ripe Grain.   Dora Reed Goodale. HBV 1-2

In Heaven, their earthy bodies left behind.   To Lucasta, on Going Beyond the Seas.   Richard Lovelace.   GTBS-P; LiTB; TreFT

In Heavenly leaves to play at tents/With all the Holy Innocents.   To Betsey-Jane, on Her Desiring to Go Incontinently to Heaven.   Helen Parry Eden. HBMV

In heavens where tomahawks are barred.   Fancy Dress.   Siegfried Sassoon. BrPo

In heavy drops perpetually flow, flow,/flow.   My Honeyed Languor. Edward (Edward Dzyubin) Bagritsky.   TrJP

In her eyes copper men living next to the earth for her sake.   Early Copper. Carl Sandburg.   HeIP

In her first communion dress.   The Pear Tree.   Edna St. Vincent Millay. MoAmPo

In her misery we know it.   This My Emissary.   Christopher Dewdney. CaPN

In her paramour's song, by intellectual nuptials/unclosed.   Taliessin's Song of the Unicorn.   Charles Williams.   FaBoTw

In her partition is the stairway of unhunched love,/a muscular mouth.   A Fixture.   Bill Berkson.   APU

In her solemn sepulcher, Me.   A Poe-'em of Passion.   Charles F. Lummis. BXAP; ShM

In her tiger's mouth/returning me, returning me.   The Train Runs Late to Harlem.   Conrad Kent Rivers.   IDB; PoBA

In her tomb by the side of the sea.   Annabel Lee.   Edgar Allan Poe.   AA; AP; AWP; BeLS; BLPA; DiPo; DL; EtS; FaFP; FPL; GoTF; HBV 1-2; HBVY; HeIP; InPo; LiTA; LiTL; LoGBV; MaC; MAmP; MCCG; NePA; NOBA; NoP; OBCA; OBVV; OnMSP; OxBA; PG; PoPl; PrIm; RoGo; SeCeV; SpRo; StPo; TAP; TreF; TrGrPo; ViBoPo; WBLP

In her true love's arms she fell fast asleep.   Sweet William.   *Anonymous.* OBET

...In her wake/No waters breed or break.   Next, Please.   Philip Larkin. EiCP; HeIP; MoBrPo; NePoEA

In her wet prints a pretty housemaid passes.   Rain.   William Ernest Henley. SyP

In her window, in her sky.   What It Was.   Robert Sward.   CoPo

In her you started first to burn!   Redondillas.   Sister Juana Ines de la Cruz. CAW

In heven ther to see His face,/Wher we shall mend and pair nought.   Amend Me.   *Anonymous.*   OxBM

In highest heav'n he was receiv'd,/To reign with God for evermore.   Hymns and Spiritual Songs.   Christopher Smart.   NOCV

In him he all things with strange order hurl'd;/In him, that full Abridgment of the World.   Davideis.   Abraham Cowley.   OBS

In him thy righteousness be found.   Though I Should Seek.   Henry Ustic Onderdonk.   AH

In Him who dreams in me and you.   Crest Jewel.   James Stephens.   AnIL; MoAB; MoBrPo

In Himself by grace we enter,/Where there is the mercy seat!   Attraction. *Anonymous.*   STF

In his arms he'll take and shield thee,/Thou wilt find a solace there.   What a Friend We Have in Jesus.   Joseph Scriven.   FSW; TreFT

In his deep thoughts the wonder did increase,/And he divined 'twas England or the Peace.   The Last Instructions to a Painter.   Andrew Marvell. OBS; OBSV

In his fabulous, rigid, eternal/Unlooked-for role.   For the Nightly Ascent of the Hunter Orion over a Forest Clearing.   James Dickey.   TwCP

In his fist, rose of infinity.   Midsummer.   Stephen Spender.   AtBAP

In His hands I leave tomorrow/As I walk with Him today.   Tomorrow. Della Adams Leitner.   GTBS; GTBS-P; STF

In his mode is no crookedness.   For Deep Deer-Copse Beneath Mount Han. *Anonymous.*   OBVE

In His name, who blessed the children,/This I humbly ask.   A Birthday Prayer.   John Finley.   TrPWD

In his own and greater being,/In the house of life.   Pax.   D. H. Lawrence. TrCP

In His own time "He shall speak peace."   He Shall Speak Peace Unto the Nations.   Lila V. Walters.   BePJ; WBLP

In his place that His hand hath made.   At the Place of the Sea.   Annie Johnson Flint.   BLPA; STF

In his right arm/he carries his head.   Waking in the Dark.   Dorothy Livesay.   NOBC

In His terrible mercy, world without end.   For a Christening.   Anne Ridler. MoPo

In his tub. in his water. wife.   The Bath.   Joel Oppenheimer.   NeAP

In His unwithering sheaves, O bind my heart!   Laus Mortis.   Frederic Lawrence Knowles.   HBV 1-2

In holiness on high, has opened by His Ascension.   Christ 2.   Cynewulf. AnOE

In hope, in faith, in patience, and in vain.   International Conference.   Colin Ellis.   FaBoEE

In hopes that they'd be detected.   Epitaph on a Career Woman.   William Cole.   PV

In hush of adoration see Thee there.   Do We Not Hear Thy Footfall?   Amy Carmichael.   TRV

In Indiana once, things grew in it.   Memo to the 21st Century.   Philip Appleman.   SOTS; TAT

In insecurity to lie/Is joy's insuring quality.   Go not too near a house of rose. Emily Dickinson.   BoLiVe; MoAB; MoAmPo

In Ireland of the white hedges.   Epigram: "Peace is made with a warlike man–."   *Anonymous.*   BIrV

In it he finds his own words.   Below Bald Mountain.   Janice Townley Moore.   AMV-80

In it will be a light the color of steel/& landscape, into which the traveler might set out.   John Clare.   Jon Anderson.   AmPA

In its turn will be re-painted.   For the Princess Hello.   David Shapiro. ANYP

In jest, to hide a heart that bled.   For Paul Laurence Dunbar.   Countee Cullen.   BALP; CDC; GoSl

In Jesus the Beloved thou didst place thy love.   The Life of St. Cellach: Dear Was He.   *Anonymous.*   OnYI

In Jesus we receive the best we have.   What Shall We Render.   *Anonymous.* BLRP

In jicarilla, the apaches run their own bar.   Indian america.   Mah-do-ge Tohee.   STE

In Jordan now set we our watch.   Zionist Marching Song.   Naphtali Imber. TrJP

In joy or pain for to endure.   Lo! how I seek and sue to have.   Sir Thomas Wyatt.   FCP; SiPS

In joy or sadness, weal or woe,/Jesus, I'll turn to thee.   Jesus, in Sickness and in Pain.   Thomas H. Gallaudet.   AH

In joye withouten ende.   Where Beeth They Biforen Us Weren.   *Anonymous.* EBEV

In June she beats upon the drum,/And then she'll fly away. The Cuckoo. *Anonymous.* OBET

In just such a manner might this being be illuminated during a time gambol. 2nd Light Poem: For Diane Wakoski. Jackson MacLow. PoM

In keeping us in hopes strange things to see/That never were, nor are, nor e'er shall be. Against Fruition. Sir John Suckling. ErPo

In kindling thought and glowing word,/Thy love to tell, Thy praise to show. For Every Day. Frances Ridley Havergal. BLRP

In Kugler's glass headdown dangling by yellow legs. The Avenue Bearing the Initial of Christ into the New World. Galway Kinnell. NMP

In labor, as in prayer, fulfilling the same law. Songs of Labor: Dedication. John Greenleaf Whittier. AnNE; OxBA

In Lady Lusher's drawing-room, one summer afternoon. The Martyred Democrat. C. J. Dennis. CBAP

In large fulfillment of our biggest hope! Reality. Angela Morgan. WGRP

In latitudes where storms are born. Reconnaissance. Arna Bontemps. AmNP; BPo

In life, in death, O Lord, abide with me. Amen. Abide with Me; Fast Falls the Eventide. Henry Francis Lyte. VLP

In life or death we still may be. With Thee to Soar to the Skies. *Anonymous.* BePJ

In like disturbance, poetry begins. The Contagiousness of Dreams. Diane Middlebrook. AMV-81

In loneliness, and know my worth too late. A Curse. Daughter of Ka'b, Rabi'a. LiTW

In love and flowers pick themselves Who knows if the moon's. Edward Estlin Cummings. LOW

In love and the enamelled flowers of song? Death Sweet. Thomas Lovell Beddoes. NOBV

In Love's lips my roses lie. Rococo. John Payne. OBVV

In Love there is society/She never yet could find with ye! Song: "I've taught thee Love's sweet lesson o'er." George Darley. OBRV

In love we work to live in America under our own wings. Under Our Own Wings. Nellie Wong. BrSi

In love with all, yet lov'd of none. Love Who Will, for I'll Love None. William Browne. CavP; HBV 1-2

In love with none, but me. A Conjuration, to Electra. Robert Herrick. AtBAP; GBL; PoEL 1-5

In love with your speed, your heaviness and breath. Ode: "An idea of justice may be precious." Frank O'Hara. NeAP

In love you some other wise,/Believe't, I will. Madrigal: "How should I love my best?" Edward, Lord Herbert of Cherbury. PoEL 1-5; SeCP; ViBoPo

In Loveland for me and my gal. For Me and My Gal. Edgar Leslie and E. Ray Goetz. BLSo

In lowliness of heart. Lines Left upon a Seat in a Yew-Tree... William Wordsworth. MCCG

In lunch-hour lunatics who face/amused indifference of the crowd. Macquarie Place. Robert D. FitzGerald. PoAu 1-2

In ma han', Lord,/Shoutin' wid a sword in ma han'. Singin' wid a Sword in Ma Han'. *Anonymous.* BoAN 1-2

In many a heart now dead in sin,/A living temple rear. O God, Though Countless Worlds of Light. James D. Knowles. AH

"In Marie mild and free/I shall be found, ac more in Crist." All Other Love Is Like the Moon. *Anonymous.* OxBM

In May I lost her to a troll,/a recent arrival from Brooklyn. The Toad. Gerald Locklin. GP

(In me, in me,)/two people live side by side. Two. Moishe Kulbak. VWA

In me there howls a lust/To finish you finally. Ares. Albert Ehrenstein. TrJP

In me they sing. Song in the Songless. George Meredith. ACV; GTBS

In mercy, each by each set free. Song for an Allegorical Play. John Ciardi. PoCh

In midwinter, my love for you always./February 14/Mike Prayer. Mike Newell. AMV-80

In mingled murder fluttering on the ground. Autumn. James (1700-48) Thomson. LoBV

...In miniature, restages/The Vandal and Saracen outrages. The Temple at Segesta. Raymond Henri. GLGT

In monotone daylight/is the sound/the sound/of healing bone. For Mabel: Pomo Basketmaster and Doctor. Wendy Rose. TWSS

...In/moon-black verdure of summer... Portrait of the Father. Lindy Hough. IHMS

In Mornigan's park she walks alone. Riddle: "In Mornigan's park there is a deer." *Anonymous.* GBP; MOON

In murder, make love with hate,/or simply stalk a local fly. The Hindoo: He Doesn't Hurt a Fly or a Spider Either. A. K. Ramanujan. OxBC

In music, praise Messiah's name. Our Kind Creator. Solomon Howe. AH

In music through/The songless land. Love in Age. Charles G. Bell. NePoAm-2

In music to her soul. Rosalie. Washington Allston. AA

...In my end is my beginning. East Coker. Thomas Stearns Eliot. ChMP; MoVE; NePA; PPP; VGW

In my Fidelia I'll find more. In Praise of Fidelia. Mildmay Fane, Earl of Westmoreland. OBSP

In my flight I stir. The Fir-Tree. Edith Matilda Thomas. OHIP

In my Golden House on high,/There they Shine Eternally. The Caverns of the Grave I've Seen. William Blake. NCEP

In my grandfather's barn/In the Ozarks. Freemon Hawthorne. Melvin B. Tolson. FAZ

In my hair glimmered ever/A nest, a nest of blue light. Exaltation. Franz Werfel. TrJP

In my hands, and my hands full of dust,/O my lady. Song: "O lady, when the tipped cup of the moon blessed you." Ted Hughes. LLLT

In my haste, in my haste. Shining. Kathleen Spivack. AMV-81

...In my head, I swear,/Eden flourishes. A Midrash (excerpt). David Meltzer. GP

In my heart there are many/unmarked graves. Malcolm. Welton Smith. BPo

"In my hous is swich a smeke–/Go under, and ye shall wete.'/With hey, how! An Old Man and His Wife. *Anonymous.* OxBM

In my knowing Him, I create Him. When My Beloved Appears. Ibn al-Arabi. ILwL

In my little cup. December. Ron Padgett. EAS

In my own glass I trim my snakey locks. The Dead Ride Fast. Richard P. Blackmur. MoPo

...In my prison men assert their/innocence, their significance as men. Confab. Kenneth Rosen. AmPA

"In my Provence, my rose." Ma Provence. Kenneth Koch. ANYP

In my rhyme but half-expressed. Bird and Brook. Sir Samuel Ferguson. IrPN

In my sleep flags of blackness/Are folded and put away. My Mother. Hayim Naggid. VWA

In naked sunlight, on a naked world. The Journey. Yvor Winters. MoVE

In Nine Decades/a Mad Queen shall be born. Firebrand. Harry Crosby. EAS

In no congenial gulf for ever lost! On the Ice Islands Seen Floating in the German Ocean. William Cowper. OAEL 1-2; PrIm

In no such winter can survive alone. Midcentury Love Letter. Phyllis McGinley. MoLP; ViBoPo

...In no war would I bleed. Warriors. Douglas Dunn. OxBC

...In no way shall death part us. In No Way. David Ignatow. AMV-81

In not the usual sense of company. Battle Problem. William Meredith. NoAm; NYBP

In Oaxaca I was loudly scolded for feeling pineapples too long. Natural Selection. Summer Brenner. APU

In obedience to/the pull & tug/of your great tides. Summer Storm. John Montague. IPY

In olden ages, long ago,/In Mexico. In Mexico. Evaleen Stein. AA

In older abyss where time slept stirless yet. Essay on Memory. Robert D. Fitzgerald. BoAV

In one good manners grant me all. A Pastoral Courtship (excerpt). Thomas Randolph. ViBoPo

In one illimitable/arc: to praise,/but not to prize. Instruction in the Art. Philip Booth. SD

...In one motion depart/From each other. Tommies in the Train. D. H. Lawrence. MMM

In one of them I sit with a dead shepherd/And watch his lambs. December among the Vanished. William Stanley Merwin. NaP

In one short hour's delay, is tyranny. Death Invoked. Philip Massinger. ACP

In one strange, silent, piteous gaze,/and dim/With bitter tears of agonized despair. Moses and Jesus. Israel Zangwill. TrJP

In one weak, washy, everlasting flood! What's My Thought Like? Thomas Moore. CBEP; FaBoEE; OBRV

In one wide zone of rest, glooms the gray evenfall. An Old Seaport. *Anonymous.* EtS

In open comradeship to all the world? Armistice. Eunice Mitchell Lehmer. PGD

In open country again watching an aching spargosis of stars. In the Fall. Hugh" (Christopher Murray Grieve) MacDiarmid. InPS

In order to blow what it's like being born. Lester Leaps In. Al Young. NPGG; SM

In order to catch another glimpse of my lover... Love Song: "I passed by the house of the young man who loves me." *Anonymous.* TTY

In others the defect we find,/But cannot see our sack behind. To Varus. Caius Valerius Catullus. AWP

In our cold beds we pursue/the endless fall of silences. Night opens like an almond. Yvonne Caroutch. BoWoP

In our dreams. Dust Bowl. Robert A. Davis. GoSl; IDB

In our dreams, in our rhymes,/how the whistle screams. Carried Away. Anne Elder. CBAP

In our every breathing Manong Benny. Virginia Cerenio. BrSi

In our hands/Will prove no trifle. The Riflemen at Bennington. *Anonymous.* FSW

In our hearts 'tis summer still.   The Heart's Summer.   Epes Sargent   AA

In our land/Bullets are beginning to flower.   Poem: "Come, brother, and tell me your life."   Jorge Rebelo.   WhB

In our own likeness, on the edge of it.   Rebirth.   Rudyard Kipling.   GTBS; LoBV; OBNC

In our record climate I look pleased or glum.   The Climate.   Edwin Denby.   ANYP

In paddocks of shadows and showers,/Far, far from here.   Upon a Row of Old Boots and Shoes in a Pawnbroker's Window.   Furnley Maurice.   CBAP

In patient love out watch the world.   Serenade.   Thomas Hood.   HBV 1-2

In peace, and yet at strife.   Dispraise of Love, and Lovers' Follies.   Francis Davison.   EiL; HBV 1-2; OBSC; TrGrPo

In peace the Eye of Horus liveth.   He Kindleth a Fire.   Book of the Dead.   AWP

In Pearse and Plunkett's graves./GOD SAVE IRELAND.   Easter Week.   *Anonymous.*   OnYI

In perfect, in poetic state she lies.   First Flight.   Dorothy Wellesley.   OBTV

In peril of his blood his ears incline/To drums whose loudness is their emptiness.   On the Danger of War.   George Meredith.   CoBE; PPON

...In place/of two is one who hurries down the stairs.   The End of a Meaningful Relationship.   Kurt J. Fickert.   AMV-81

In plainest Lodge room in the land–up over Simpkins' store.   The Lodge Room over Simpkins' Store.   Lawrence N. Greenleaf.   PoOW

In pocket or by hand!   Treasure.   Elizabeth-Ellen Long.   BiCB

In prickle-green, speed-lashed/Massachusetts.   Stun.   James Schuyler.   ANYP; MAT

In princes' hearts God's scourge yprinted deep/Might them awake out of their sunful sleep.   "The great Macedon, that out of Persia chased."   Henry Howard, Earl of Surrey.   AAS; FCP

In proud Stamboul they sleep their slumber.   Ben Allah Achmet.   Sir William Schwenck Gilbert.   VLP

In proving that one has had the experience/of carrying a stick?   Critics and Connoisseurs.   Marianne Moore.   AnAmPo; AnEnPo; CMoP; FaBoWP; NePA; NoAm; NOBA; OxBA

In public now to tear his shirt.   Portrait of a Poet.   Edgar Lee Masters.   ATP

In purgatory fire on Bardolph's nose.   On Donne's Poem "To a Flea."   Samuel Taylor Coleridge.   FM

"In Pusseyville, it's raining cats and dogs!"   Cats and Dogs.   Howard Moss.   OBAL

In quest of that one beauty/God put me here to find.   Roadways.   John Masefield.   GTBS; MCCG

In quiet/guiltless/sleep   Moon at Three a.m.   Lance Henson.   CDW

In quiet sleep she sealed his cherished eyes.   The Odyssey.   Homer.   NAWM 1-2

In quietness and confidence/Shall be the strength I know.   A Hymn of Trust.   Nettie M. Sargent.   BLRP

In race of life their feet to guide/Who be to God inclined.   Psalm XI.   Sir Philip Sidney.   FCP

In rain, in earth, in love, in all, in all.   The Cocks.   Boris Pasternak.   LiTW

In random rivalry they climb/The oddest pinnacles of Time.   Approaching America.   J. C. Squire.   HBMV

In real cities, real houses, real time.   The Noodle-Vendor's Flute.   D. J. Enright.   NoP

In real life it takes only one to make a quarrel.   I Never Even Suggested It.   Ogden Nash.   FiBHP; FPL; LiTA; LiTL; PoLf

In red and yellow/Heaps of rubble.   Villages Demolis.   Sir Herbert Read.   BrPo

In remembrance of me and my sorrow/And of the new wandering!   The Wanderer.   William Carlos Williams.   MAPA

In reparation for the days/Of empty grief–before I knew.   Mater Incognita.   Sister Mary Benvenuta.   ISi

In rest, in peace, his labor nobly done.   Wordsworth's Grave.   William Watson.   EnLit; GoTL; HBV 1-2; OBNC; VLP

In Resurrection he will surely live.   The Author to His Book.   George Alsop.   SCAP

In rev'rent love we guard thy memory.   Robert G. Shaw.   Henrietta Cordelia Ray.   BlSi

In roaring he shall rise and on the surface die.   The Kraken.   Alfred, Lord Tennyson.   AmMo; CABA; NoP; OAEL 1-2; OBNC; OBRV; PoEL 1-5; SyP; VLP; WiR; WSC

In root and sky we can discern the hand.   The Boy with a Cart (excerpt).   Christopher Fry.   LiTB

In, Rose, and in, Provence and La Palie.   Les Vaches.   Arthur Hugh Clough.   OAEP; PeD

In Russia they've got some ripping new rears.'   A Happy New Year (excerpt).   W. H. Auden.   OBSV

In sacred Embassies from pole to pole.   The Latin Tongue.   James J. Daly.   CAW; GoBC

In sands, in fens, they died–no mother near!   The Children Band.   Sir Aubrey De Vere.   OBEV

In Saronis the men are certain/Greece beat herself, not the Turks.   Across to the Peloponnese.   James Welch.   CDW

In secret sorrow and sad pensiveness.   Amoretti, XXXIV.   Edmund Spenser.   AAS; AnFE; CoBE; DiPo; EnLi 1-2; HBV 1-2; OBSC

In secrete so, my stomacke will I serve,/Wishing thee better than thou doest deserve.   Farewell with a Mischeife.   George Gascoigne.   AAS

In seed, stem, leaf, and fruit appear.   The Point, the Line, the Surface and Sphere.   Claude Bragdon.   ImOP

In separateness they turn, and to the cook-house go.   The Harvesters.   Mary Gilmore.   NOAV

In shades like these to live, is to be blest.   Clifton Grove (excerpt).   Henry Kirke White.   OBNC

In Sherwood, in Sherwood, about the break of day.   A Song of Sherwood.   Alfred Noyes.   BBV; HBV 1-2; HBVY; MCCG; TiPo

In shiny bits like ribbons,/Sweet, like lavender.   Silence.   Winifred Welles.   HBMV

In short, be as lewd as a strumpet.   An Imitation of Martial, Book II Ep. 105.   Captain H—.   NOEC

In short, I grow so long that I've a notion/I must be measured soon for a new ocean.   The Sea-Serpent.   Planche.   NA

In short, my deary, kiss me, and be quiet.   Good Advice.   Mary Wortley, Lady Montagu.   PoL

In short, of behaving like men.   Bad Example.   Isabella Fey.   BoAnP

In short, the Heav'ns must needs propitious be,/Because Lucasia was concerned in me.   A Sea-Voyage from Tenby to Bristol, Begun Sept. 5, 1652...   Katherine ("Orinda") Philips.   SBG

In short: the poet.   Lamentations of an Au Pair Girl.   Susan Feldman.   AmPA

In short, the rogues all fled for fear and/flew to dark corners.   The Vision of Piers Plowman.   William Langland.   CoBE

In short they both were turned to yews.   Baucis and Philemon.   Jonathan Swift.   GN; StPo

In short, 'tis that provoking Charm/Of Caelia all together.   The Je Ne Scay Quoi: A Song.   William Whitehead.   OBEC; SoSe

–In short, whichever has an instrument.   29th Dance–Having an Instrument–22 March 1964.   Jackson MacLow.   CoPo

In sic a sark o fire, I burn/Trowe Heevin an Aert an Hell!   Gallow Hill.   William J. Tait.   OxBS

In sickness as in health, bless you, my Own!   To Helen.   Winthrop Mackworth Praed.   NOBV

In silence and sweet temper, loving the world.   Reading Room, the New York Public Library.   Richard Eberhart.   GOYP; GP; NYP

In silence, back to Amst-/-Erdam.   The Salmon.   Christian Morgenstern.   FaBoNo

In silent sympathy.   Prayer for a Day's Walk.   Grace Noll Crowell.   PoToHe

In silver whiteness over Padua.   Countess Laura.   George Henry Boker.   BeLS

In simmer, whan aa sorts foregether/in embro to the ploy.   Embro to the Ploy.   Robert Garioch.   OxBS

...In/simple time to/all their graces.   Quick-Step.   Robert Creeley.   VGW

In sinne, in sorwe, in nede us wisse.   Snatches: "Marie, thou queen."   *Anonymous.*   OxBM

In six short months she was laid by the side/Of her love who gave her such a frightful ride.   The Farmer's Daughter.   *Anonymous.*   BFSS

In slow and silent, dim and deepening waves.   Progress of Evening.   Walter Savage Landor.   OBNC

In snow, in light,/we are about to become!   Poems for the New.   Kathleen Fraser.   IHMS; NMM

In solitude the musing mind/Must ever love the autumn wind.   The Autumn Wind.   John Clare.   BoNaP

In solitude to where the dunes abide.   Evening.   Victor van Vriesland.   TrJP

In some astonished dream of sailing....   Battery Park, High Noon.   Ben Belitt.   NYP

In some far-off land,/Oh, in some far-off land.   Jackie Frazier.   *Anonymous.*   BFSS

In some forgotten life, long time gone by.   An Old Tune.   Andrew Lang.   AWP; HBV 1-2

In some place darker than ours.   Crossing Raquette Lake at Night.   Greg Kuzma.   WOLT

In song be praised, let a rouse be raised for the name of Ben/Milam!   The Valor of Ben Milam.   Clinton Scollard.   HBV 1-2; MC; PAH

In Spight of his Deanship and Journeyman Waters.   An Excellent New Song on a Seditious Pamphlet.   Jonathan Swift.   CoMu

In spirit I'll soothe you and "rock you to sleep."   Call Me Not Back from the Echoless Shore.   *Anonymous.*   BLPA

In spite of thee, and by firm faith deserve her.   Phyllis.   Thomas Lodge.   EG

In sportive chase the last pursue.   Let Us Drink.   Alcaeus.   AWP

In square black boots/The cabman dances. The Dancing Cabman. J. B. Morton. MoShBr; NOBL

In stable love fixt, and not variant. The True Knight. Stephen Hawes. ACP

In starlight, by the three Hesperides. Endymion. John Keats. OBRV

In steady silent march, our hundred thousand dead. The March. J. C. Squire. HBMV; OHIP; PoSC

In stede of blew, thus may ye were al greene. Against Women Unconstant. Geoffrey Chaucer. NoP

In straits which no escape afford/The hand takes hold of the edge of the sword. The Gulistan. Muslih-ud-Din Sa'di. AWP

In streaks of light across the desert's heart. Deserts. Leigh Hanes. GoYe

In streams of pure perennial peace. The Well of Living Water. Charles Wesley. BePJ

In such a fix to be so fertile. Autres Betes, Autres Moeurs. Ogden Nash. GoTF; NAMP; TreFS

In such a moment I but ask/That you'll remember me. When Other Lips and Other Hearts. Alfred Bunn. TreF

In such an armor he cannot be slain. Bronzeville Man with a Belt in the Back. Gwendolyn Brooks. IDB; PoBA

In such an unhumble, contemptual gamie/How anyone plays together. Who Taught Caddies to Count? or; A Burnt Golfer Fears the Child. Ogden Nash. LiSp

In such clean qualities as time and space. Aspects. Norman MacCaig. BSV; OxBS

In such immobile art? To a Blue Hippopotamus. Ellen de Young Kay. ForPo; NePoEA

In summer's sun, in winter breath of frost,/Of your fair eyes whereby the light is lost. The Cornet. Henry Howard, Earl of Surrey. OBSC

In Summertime? At school? Sing a Song of Sunshine. Ivy O. Eastwick. SiSoSe

In sunless fields of Erebus forlorn. The Laborer. Jose-Maria de Heredia. AWP

In sweet Perfumes of Praise. Sincere Praise. Isaac Watts. CEP

In sweet rain and warm rain,/Blue violets grow. Rainy Day Song. Violet Alleyn Storey. YeAr

In swelling notes of ceaseless praise. Lo, What Enraptured Songs of Praise. Sebastian Streeter. AH

In teaching me the way to live,/It taught me how to die. My Mother's Bible. George Pope Morris. BLRP; PaPo; WBLP

"In teaching you are always dealing with the criminal/mentality." Pedagogy. Gerald Locklin. GP

In Tel-Aviv there was a poet./And now? Harangue on the Death of Hayyim Nahman Bialik. Cesar Tiempo. TrJP

In temperance their sacred beauty find. Christian Ethics. Thomas Traherne. OBSP; UnS

In Tennessee. Tennessee. Francis Brooks. AA

...In terms/of shade and colour, without apprehension or regret. The Spirit of the Cairngorms. Axel Firsoff. PoSH

In text and context, history, word? Jutaculla Rock. Robert Morgan. SUW

In th'heaven of Mary's eye, a tear. The Tear. Richard Crashaw. EnLi 1-2; LiTB; MasP; OAEP; SeCP

In that certitude I rest./In happiness. Lied in Crete. Alvaro Mutis. AMV-80

In that country... Mother Goose Up-to-Date. Louis Untermeyer. MoAmPo

In that dark morning street/of early April. The Worm. Raymond Souster. WHW

In that day/shall the Lord be One,/and His name one. The Kingdom of God. Rab. TrJP

In that faith I live or die. Tom the Lunatic. William Butler Yeats. OnYI

In that fatal night that deported/fifty-three women/to the plantations of Sao Tome? Mamano. Jose Craveirinha. WhB

In that greater mouth/nothing can still or fill. Mouths. Louis Dudek. PeCV

In that green solitude I'll dwell,/And praise Thee all day long. The Cell. George Rostrevor. TrPWD

In that home of the sweet by-and-by. The Great Round-Up. Anonymous. BPAW; CoSo

In that hound's arch dwarf-legged on boxing-gloves. Islet the Dachs. George Meredith. FM

In that it came from the beginnings/unlike ours In the first place of my life. Ray A. Young Bear. STE

In that it falls her sacrifice. That Distant Bliss. Henry, Bishop of Chichester King. TrGrPo

In that lacquer liquor locker which a liquor lackey locked. The Lacquer Liquor Locker. David McCord. FiBHP; InMe

In that long-tailed parrot you know all about... I Pull out of the Depths of the Earth. Etnairis Rivera. InW

In that mindless rip-tide that got the best of me/Once, when I ventured on your deeps, Piranha. An Old Malediction. Anthony Hecht. TW

In that one house which never has been built. Architect. Louise Townsend Nicholl. EyDe

In that one moment I would have caught/and held. The Turning. Philip Murray. NePoAm

In that one word alone I had paid more,/Than can be now, when plentie makes me poore. An Elegy on Ben Jonson. John Cleveland. MeLP; OBS

In that pent track of living death–the city's cruel street. Faces in the Street. Henry Lawson. CBAP

In that plague-spot heart, Death's last dust-heap. Gold Coast Customs (excerpt). Edith Sitwell. OBMV

In that river my blood flowed on. Ceremony. William Stafford. LCAP

In that roaring bus from a grey/nowhere to a green. Some Indian Uses of History on a Rainy Day. A. K. Ramanujan. OxBC

In that room he could never, never enter again. Because He Liked to Be at Home. Kenneth Patchen. NaP

In that soft contour/Of a shell in the water. The Roosters Will Crow. Cecilia Meireles. PBWP

In that, somehow,/one recognizes oneself. Mr. T. S. Eliot Cooking Pasta. Jozsef Tornai. GrPl

In that tall lovely legacy of wood. The Axe in the Wood. Clifford Dyment. ACV

In that they shrunk back, and clapped to their/doors.... The Fairies Feast. Charles M. Doughty. CH

In that trim cage, he might sing true. The Magic Flute. W. D. Snodgrass. NYBP

In that war, that crazy war. That Crazy War. Anonymous. FSW

In that you'll all the treasures find/That can content a noble mind. A Song: "Chloris, when I to thee present." Anonymous. OBS

In the absence of a shawl. Furchte Nichts, Geliebte Seele. Louis Untermeyer. ALV

In the air to aggravate the truly menacing. Chez Jane. Frank O'Hara. CoAP; NeAP; NoAm; NOBA; PoA

In the Antarctical Zonio. Antonio. Laura E. Richards. MoShBr; OBCA; SoPo; TiPo

In the arab getup, is yo man, rocky, makin/the whole thing/perfect. Horatio Alger Uses Scag. LeRoi (Imamu Amiri Baraka) Jones. FaBoCh; GP; LoGBV

In the arid desert of Phryne's life, where all was parched and hot. 'Ostler Joe. George R. Sims. BeLS; BLPA; HBV 1-2; TreF

In the assemblies, I will bless thy/Name! My Soul in the Bundle of Life. Anonymous. TrJP

In the autumn evening. Haiku: "On this road." Basho (Matsuo Basho). LiTW

In the autumn night, under the moon. Two Poems. Anonymous. LiTW

In the background shades/of Eliot and Hughes. Still Life. Randolph Outlaw. LFAC

In the beautiful world by the bright Lake of Horus,/Riseth the Day. He Cometh Forth into the Day. Book of the Dead. AWP

In the billow become you/Your nude jubilation Little Air. Stephane Mallarme. PoPl; SyP

In the bitter and formless/Light-engulfing/Pit of the desolate sea. Henley on Taieri. Charles Brasch. AnNZ

In the black of desire/we rock and grunt, grunt and/shine Song for Ishtar. Denise Levertov. NaP; NMM; NoAm; PoM

In the bland hedge thick as a mound. June in Wiltshire. Geoffrey Grigson. WaP

In the bleak mid-winter/Long ago. In the Bleak Mid-Winter. Christina Georgina Rossetti. SUS

In the blinding drift from the angry sea. At Sea. D.H. Rogers. AnNZ

In the body-and-soul stinking town of Cologne. On My Joyful Departure from the City of Cologne. Samuel Taylor Coleridge. FaBoCo; InVP; NLV; OBTV; TW

...In the bottomless black/Silence through which it fell. Roarers in a Ring. Ted Hughes. NePoEA-2

In the bracken, by starlight,/had found our peace. Hill Love. James Macmillan. PoSH

In the brewer's big pan, says everyone. The Wren Hunt. Anonymous. OxNR

In the bright new season. Image from d'Orleans. Ezra Pound. LOW

In the bright wild circus flesh. When I Went to the Circus. D. H. Lawrence. CMoP; LiTB; NoAm

In the burning bush of antiquity/With starry flowers. Cold. Dorothy Roberts. NOBC

In the calm and peaceable kingdom. One Step from an Old Dance. David Helwig. WHW

In the cars, to the stars, waves, wars, riding/And questing. Rides. Gene Derwood. LiTM; NePA

In the cell/of matter-of-fact. Your Voice on the Telephone. Donald Hall. FF

In the centre of the huge lone land and sky. Prairie Graveyard. Anne Marriott. CaP; NOBC; OBCV

In the chaff-strewn light of the stable lantern/Was something beautiful and new and strange. The Witnesses: The Innkeeper's Wife. Clive Sansom. PCh

In the chill'd heart by gradual self-decay. Love's Apparition and Evanishment. Samuel Taylor Coleridge. EnRP

In the chorus all join in,/there'll be a hot time in the old town tonight. A Hot Time in the Old Town. Joe Hayden. FSN; YaD

In the churchyard of Clonmel? In Clonmel Parish Churchyard. Sarah Piatt. AA

In the cicada's torture-point of song. The Quest of Silence: Fire in the Heavens, and Fire Along the Hills. Christopher John Brennan. CBAP; PoAu 1-2

In the city that a murderer designed? Cold Water Flat. Philip Booth. NePoAm

In the city under the sea. Veneta. Mary Elizabeth Coleridge. CBEP

In the clear October morning. Going A-Nutting. Edmund Clarence Stedman. GN

In the cold and changeless waters of the Irish sea so deep. The Mail Boat, Leinster. *Anonymous.* OBSS

In the cold revery of an idiot. The Subway. Allen Tate. AP; NoAm; NOBA; NYP

In the cold snows of a dream. Meditations in Time of Civil War. William Butler Yeats. BIrV; CABL; NOBE

In the cold syllables/of the tongue I love. Identity. Robert Friend. GP; VWA

In the confusions of our light. Signatures. Daniel Gerard Hoffman. VGW

In the cool green shade/Of the walnut tree. August Afternoon. Marion Edey. YeAr

In the cool light,/in the darkness. Contemporania: Tenzone. Ezra Pound. PoA

In the cool of the even/In front of a cafe in Heaven. On Heaven. Ford Madox Ford. CTC; ViBoPo

In the country I long for conversation–/Our happy croaking. Frogs. Louis Simpson. BoAnP; PAI

In the court of heaven, your only comfort/Must come from her that day. When Your Eyes. *Anonymous.* WTO

In the crowd that has pressed beyond the gates. Travelling Backward. Gene Baro. NYBP

In the cry of anguish/the child's first breath is born. Christmas Landscape. Laurie Lee. OBCP

In the crystal vase Haiku: "Sprayed with strong poison." Paul Goodman. InPK

In the curious phenomenon of your occipital horn. To a Snail. Marianne Moore. CMoP; FaBoMo; FaBoWP

In the dark of the moon, behold! the spouse. The One-Eyed Bridegroom. Constance Urdang. MOON

In the darkness under the searchlights. In Praise of Antonioni. Stephen Holden. NYBP

In the dawn, 'twixt him and me. Nightingale Weather. Andrew Lang. ACV

In the dead miles nothing explains or changes or relieves? Leafless Trees, Chickahominy Swamp. Dave Smith. MAYP

The, in the deathless days before she died. Change. William Dean Howells. AA

...In the deep/Conundrum of the dirt he speaks/The one word you will never hear. Epitaph for the Poet. George Barker. OBSP

In the deep flood she drowned her beamy face. Upon Some Alterations in My Mistress, after My Departure into France. Thomas Carew. CaPo

In the deep,/trick-filled mountains/overrun by cerise winds. Olive Grove. Lewis MacAdams. ANYP

In the deeps of the nursery dusk/To his mother saith. The Buried Child. Dorothy Wellesley. DTC; OBMV

In the delicate flesh/And the tooth that bruises. Pisces. R. S. Thomas. OxBC

In the dens of vice had died. The Statue of Liberty,. Thomas Hardy. LiTB

In the desert wind, in the wordless/emptied gnarling he had become. Hawktree. Dave Smith. HaCAP

In the dim and dewy loneness/Where the woodlark sings. Sheepbells. Edmund Charles Blunden. BrPo

In the diocese of Derry it's a reserved sin. The Cure. Mebdh McGuckian. FaBoIP

In the drawing back, the breathing in, I find my bones. Seal at Stinson Beach. Roberta Hill. VoR

In the dream songs of my Great Uncle,/Joseph, elder to hawk and sparrow. After the Death of an Elder Klallam. Duane Niatum. CDW

In the Drill cage at the zoo. Poems from Prison. J. J. Maloney. FAZ

...In the dull asylum/Of our own enslavements. But Bird was a junkie! Historiography. Lorenzo Thomas. APU

In the dull distress of our pitiful sphere. Small Paths. H. Roland-Holst. WPOW

In the dusk he sat a-smiling,/Smiling there alone. John Mouldy. Walter De la Mare. NCSH; OxBChV; PoPle

In the early spring rain that has turned to hail. Norway. Norman Dubie. GeTw

In the earth, in the air, in the rock. Father's Voice. William Stafford. RFM

In the earth of your eyes, in easy wonder building God. In Judgment of the Leaf. Kenneth Patchen. VGW

In the ebony of an ancient cupboard. My Cousin Agueda. Ramon Lopez Velarde. OBVE

In the editorial room/Of the New York Tribune. Poetry and Thoughts on Same. Franklin Pierce ("F.P.A.") Adams. HBMV

In the elfish night and green cool gloom of the day. Rainy Summer. Ruth Pitter. MoVE

In the end, at the end of a war. Between Two Prisoners. James Dickey. AP

In the end we do but sleep. Bags Packed and We Expected This. Ramona Wilson. VoR

In the evening the air sank with the weight of darkness. At the Appointed Hour They Came. Michael Smith. CIP

In the evening you were still valid.... Thou Shalt Surely Die...: No Ghost Is True. Leslie A. Fiedler. PoA

In the ever-changing network woven between stars. Water (excerpt). Kathleen Raine. ImOP

In the eyes beneath the collar. The Presence. Dana Naone. CDW

In the eyes of the woman/I'm about to love. Birthplace. Duane Big Eagle. STE

In the fall of this house all houses stand condemned. Packing a Photograph from Firenze. William H. Matchett. NePoEA

In the far day, a dumbfounded pine/(my emerald soldier!) still runs, attacks, and thrusts. Tammuz. Nathan Alterman. VWA

In the fast pale of boisterous thighs. Bathers. Terence Tiller. ChMP; NeBP

In the fern bar a hand tries a knee, as if unplanned. A History of Civilization. Albert Goldbarth. HaCAP; MAYP

In the fields, only the year's two/Solstices, and patience between. Aside. R. S. Thomas. OxBC

In the fight and the flight that shall hold us/long,/In tale and song. Reid at Fayal. John Williamson Palmer. PAH

In the fine land, the west land, the land where I/belong. The West Wind. John Masefield. EnLi 1-2; FaFP; FPL; GoTF; GTBS; LiTB; LiTM; MoAB; MoBrPo; PG; PoPl; TreF

In the first floating and rising of/water. Poem in Which My Legs Are Accepted. Kathleen Fraser. AmPA; LLLT; NMM

In the flower of fury, the folded poppy,/Night. The Sentry. Alun Lewis. DTC

In the fluted singing/of a voice like polished silver/gleaming from a heap of trash. The Food of Love. Mary di Michele. CaPN

In the forest of your hair. Hair. Remy de Gourmont. AWP; ErPo

In the forest, the uncharted/uplands of the spirit Geography. Michael Dransfield. CBAP

...In the form of a sailor/with a shopping bag/whom nobody notices. The Stillness of the Poem. Ron Loewinsohn. NeAP; PoM

In the foul rag-and-bone shop of the heart. The Circus Animals' Desertion. William Butler Yeats. BiP; CMoP; DiPo; FaBoMo; FaBoTw; LiTB; MAT; NAWM 1-2; NIP; NoAm; NOBE; NOBI; NoP; OAEL 1-2; OAEP; OxBTC; PP; PrIm; TEP

In the fourthe yere of King Richarde. Snatches: "The ax was sharp." *Anonymous.* OxBM

In the full-fugued song of the universe unending. In a Museum. Thomas Hardy. UnS

In the full heat of the sun. The Glass Eaters. George Jonas. NeAC

In the full sun-burst of Eternity! Easter. Robert Whitaker. PGD

In the future must thou battle/Till the strife is won! A Russian Cradle Song. David Nomberg. TrJP

In the game are felt no pains,/For in all the loser gains. Pleasures, Beauty. John Ford. LiTL; ViBoPo

In the garden, a swing, where night is deep and still. Spring Night. Su Tung-P'o. Prf

In the garden of my sleepless dream. My Nightingale. Rose Auslander. VWA

In the gasoline smell of the/dust and waiting 15 minutes/at the grocer's The Cariboo Horses. Al Purdy. HeIP; NOBC

In the ghosts' moonshine. Wolfram's Song. Thomas Lovell Beddoes. CBEP; OBVV

In the glare of such election, slap backs, call each other/Moses. Late Lunch, San Antonio. Vincent O'Sullivan. OCNZ

In the golden olden glory of the days gone by. The Days Gone By. James Whitcomb Riley. OBCA; TreF

In the grand decadence of the perished swans. Academic Discourse at Havana. Wallace Stevens. MoPo

In the great dawn, then lift up me, thy son. Adoration of the Disk by King Akhn-Aten and Princess Nefer Neferiu.. Book of the Dead. AWP

In the great flight of stars across the earth? Yet Vain, Perhaps, the Fruits. Frederick Goddard Tuckerman. AnNE

In the great night my heart will go out. Owl Woman's Death Song. *Anonymous.* BoWoP

In the great serenade of things,/am I the most cancelled passage? Hello. Gregory Corso. PoM

...In the green fables/Of the dogdays, in early youth. Lightly Like Music Running. Jean Garrigue. MoVE

In the green fields they'll be saying/Can never grow again. Orient Wheat. Adrienne Rich. NePoEA

In the green green wood/Of the greenwood fawn, O lovely! Song for the Greenwood Fawn. I. L. Salomon. GoYe

In the green warm opulence of summer, and the/inexhaustible vitality and immortality of the earth? The Deceptive Present, The Phoenix Year. Delmore Schwartz. BoNaP

In the grey desolation/the land was its stones. Indian Summer: Vermont. Anne Stevenson. NCSH

In the griefs of the old and the graves of the young. The Road to Nijmegen. Earle Birney. OBCV

In the grit gray light of day. Daylights. Rosanna Warren. MAYP

In the halls of ivy:/the barricades come down– Barricades. Michael S. Harper. PoBA

In the happy harvest-fields as the sun/sinks low. Adonais. William Wallace Harney. AA; HBV 1-2

In the harsh scything of the German sword,/And beautifies the world that saw it die! Edith Cavell. George Edward Woodberry. HBMV

In the havoc of their transgression/a whirlwind swallows me up. Lo, I Am Stricken Dumb. *Anonymous.* TrJP

In the heart of a country of gold. Lullaby. Seumas (James Starkey) O'Sullivan. OnYI

In the heart's temple his pure torch abides. You See the Worst of Love, but Not the Best. Walter Savage Landor. GBL

In the high reeds behind this world. A Love Song. Else Lasker-Schüler. BoWoP

...In the hills/Beyond them, the pig farmers are ready for the kingdom. This Town. James Paul. HoAn

In/the/hollow/wind Crazy Horse. Lance Henson. VoR

In the holly colour,/The everlasting green. The Holly and the Ivy. *Anonymous.* OBET

In the home of little while. The Scales of the Eyes. Howard Nemerov. CMoP; NMP

In the hot sands where the nightingale never sings! The Cat of the House. Ford Madox Ford. PCat

In the House in the Wood, the witch and her child sleep. The House in the Wood. Randall Jarrell. LCAP

In the house of my Love/I found a pen! Weapons. Anna Wickham. MoBrPo

In the house, the tower of the house. Iowa, June. Michael Dennis Browne. AmPA

In the hunger/of his blizzard Old Storm. David Phillips. NeAC

In the infinite/mirror of the breast? Reconciliation. D. Rosenmann-Taub. VWA

In the invaded womb of time. The Eye of Humility. Kay Smith. OBCV

"In the Irish Times,' sez she.... The Queen's Afterdinner Speech (excerpt). Percy French. OxBI

In the Irrawaddy. The Indian Elephant. C. J. Kaberry. FiBHP

In the jet swish of a swallow diving to her/eaves nest that I, intruder here, obstruct. From a Rise of Land to the Sea. Roald Hoffmann. SUW

In the jingle, jangle morning I'll come followin' you. Mister Tambourine Man. Bob Dylan. NIP

In the Ladies locker room/at Natural Bridge I'll Tell You What a Flapper Is. Anne Hobson Freeman. GrPl

In the land o' the leal. The Land o' the Leal. Carolina Oliphant, Lady Nairne. GTBS; GTBS-P; HBV 1-2; MCCG; WBLP

In the land of handsome women. Hiawatha's Wooing. Henry Wadsworth Longfellow. BeLS; GoTF

In the land of the evening mirage. The Land of the Evening Mirage. *Anonymous.* WGRP

In the Land of the Pshah of Psham. What Will You Learn about the Brobinyak. John Ciardi. EvOK

In the large and full assurance/Of its triumph,–I believe. A Creed. Norman McLeod. WGRP

In the last days of April IV. Joseph Bruchac. CDW

In the last lovely light/of the moon, the moon, the moon. Business as Usual. Mark Vinz. Str

In the lateness of it all/a numbing silence & the rhythm/of another word written,/and another. Hello Goodbye. Sharon Thesen. CaPN

...In/the layered silence let me hear the choir. Coal Miner's Grace. Jay Divine. AMV-80

In the leaves' self blows the efficient wind/That opens and bends closed those leaves. The Swan's Feet. E. J. Scovell. FaBoWP; OxBTC

In the leisurely land where everything's wrong. The Song-Maker. Anna Wickham. MoBrPo

In the licorice veins of my sensuality. My Winter Past. Eldon Grier. NOBC

In the light of the Sun, my grandmother. The Great Lakes Suite. James Reaney. WHW

In the "line of least resistance',/Flows the life of Afternoon. Afternoon. Louisa S. Bevington. NOBV

"In the line she draws?" Early Unfinished Sketch. Austin Clarke. ErPo

In the little cage of Song! Birds. Richard Henry Stoddard. AA; HBV 1-2

In the little garden-square/Pampas grass will rustle there. Suburb. Harold Monro. HBV 1-2

In the living snare of her own bright hair/I tied her hands together. Katharine. Heinrich Heine. UnTE

In the long noon of Eternity/Unveiled, Thy "bright reality"? Reality. Frances Ridley Havergal. BePJ; WGRP

In the long war grown warmer/The sun will strike him dead and strip his armour. Hard Frost. Andrew Young. BoNaP; MoVE

In the long way that I must tread alone,/Will lead my steps aright. To a Waterfowl. William Cullen Bryant. AA; AnFE; AnNE; AP; APA; AWP; BLPL; DiPo; EBCP; ExPo; FaBoBe; FaFP; ForPo; GN; GoTF; HBV 1-2; HBVY; HoPM; LiTA; MAmP; MCCG; NePA; NOBA; NoP; OBAL; OBRV; OHFP; OxBA; PB; PoEL 1-5; PoLf; PrIm; SeCeV; SoSe; TAP; TreF; TrGrPo; TRV; WBLP; WGRP

In the love his beauty bringeth. The Singing Cat. Stevie Smith. BoC; OxBTC; PCat

In the low-roofed room/That drips with tears! Sappho's Tomb. Arthur Stringer. CaP

In the meadows of the spirit/I kiss the Word.' The Other Voice. Tom Paulin. FaBoIP

In the memory/of a man who is hungry. Late Rising. Jacques Prevert. CAD

In the mere wilfulness, and sick despair of soul! Koskiusko. Samuel Taylor Coleridge. EnRP

In the middle of them/A creature with its terrified/Arms reaching out. Tarantula. Diana O Hehir. NPGG

In the middle watch of the night. Resemblance. *Anonymous.* WTO

In the midst of my love! O Cuckoo. *Anonymous.* AWP

In the midst of our happiness we were very pleased. The Watch on the Rhine. Gertrude Stein. AtBAP

...In the mist/stands/the crow. The Crow. P. K. Page. WHW

In the moment before it disappears. The Garden. Mark Strand. GeTw

In the moment's centrifuge of dying/becoming Richard Hunt's Arachne. Robert Earl Hayden. FB

In the monstrous outstretched arms/of cranes and wagons. This Night. Nathan Alterman. VWA

In the morning, afternoon, and/evening/be at ease in Zion. The Lamps Are Burning. Charles Reznikoff. TrJP

...In the morning, driving,/it disappears. The Road Back and Forth to Ryley. Monty Reid. CaPN

In the morning glad I see/My foe outstretched beneath the tree. A Poison Tree. William Blake. AWP; BoLiVe; DiPo; EnL; FaFP; HAP; HoPM; InPo; LiTB; NoP; PPoe; SCV; SoSe; TreFS; TrGrPo; TW

In the morning in the morning in the morning In the Morning. Jayne Cortez. BlSi

In the morning mist. Haiku: "So the spring has come?" Basho (Matsuo Basho). WeW

In the morning the fields were wet/and it was autumn. September. Linda Pastan. Psk

In the mountains north of Zuni,/I heard their cry... The Songs. *Anonymous.* WTO

In the muckle ha' they birled the wine,/And glowered on the heid o' Sir Halewyn. Sir Halewyn. *Anonymous.* OxBB

In the naked and outcast, seek Love there. Where to Seek Love. William Blake. TRV

In the name of God, whatever be wrought,/I shal say "Deo Gracias'... Deo Gracias. *Anonymous.* OxBM

In the name of sweete Jesus/I take thee from the ground. Old English Charm Song. *Anonymous.* CAW

In the name of the Father and the Son/And the Holy Gost, Amen. Prayer for the Journey. *Anonymous.* OxBM

In the name of the Father, Son, and Holy Ghost. Charm for Burns. *Anonymous.* FaBoUs

In the noise of the birds/as they burst from the trees. Sound. Jim Harrison. VGW

In the noplace where all the nothings never are. Contra Mortem. Hayden Carruth. PoA

In the northern country far, in the placid pastoral region. The Ox-Tamer. Walt Whitman. CBEP

In the office is Mrs. Apostolacos; the bus driver is Ray.   The Questions. Robert Pinsky.   NPGG

In the offing scatterest foam, thy white sails crowding.   A Passer By. Robert Bridges.   BoC; CMoP; CoBMV; EtS; ForPo; GTBS; HBV 1-2; LiTB; LiTM; MoAB; MoBrPo; MOS; NBM; OAEL 1-2; OAEP; OBEV; OBNC; OBVV; OxBTC; PoPle; SeCeV; WiR

In the old house to which one will return.   Diaduminius.   Pierre Benoit. CAW

In the old Virginia lowlands, lowlands low,/In the old Virginia lowlands low! The Big Five-Gallon Jar.   *Anonymous.*   ShS

In the one depth/Without levels, deepening for us.   Deborah as Scion. James Dickey.   SV

In the orchard by the shore!   The Orchard by the Shore: a Pastoral.   Elinor Sweetman.   OBVV

In the ovens/of sophisticated fiends.   On Reading Mr. Ytche Bashes' Stories in Yiddish.   Lester Ehrlichman.   AMV-80

In the pale light that each upon the other throws.   Re-Statement of Romance. Wallace Stevens.   MoLP

In the pale splendour of the winter sun.   Schoolboys in Winter.   John Clare. CBEP; InvP; NBM; PoEL 1-5; VLP

In the palms of both soiled hands.   Preludes.   Thomas Stearns Eliot. AnAmPo

In the Parliament of man, the Federation of the world.   Locksley Hall. Alfred, Lord Tennyson.   PoLf

In the parlor after midnight making sheep's-eyes at a/statue.   Pygmalion. Albert G. Miller.   InMe

In the pentameter aye falling in melody back.   The Ovidian Elegiac Metre, Described and Exemplified.   Samuel Taylor Coleridge.   FaBoUs

In the place I am meant for/where air collapses.   Homing.   P. C. Bowman. AMV-81

In the plaza we walk/under tangerine moons.   In the Plaza We Walk. Nephtali De Leon.   FIA

In the pledge of fellowship./Skoal!   Dartmouth Winter-Song.   Richard Hovey.   AA

In the prism of dew and the cool of/dawn.   New Every Morning. *Anonymous.*   STF

In the pulse of my ruin/I make my cure.   In the Hospital of the Holy Physician.   Nancy Willard.   IHMS

In the pure light, my tears fall: a poem.   Spring Thoughts Sent to Tzu-an. Yu Hsuan-chi.   BoWoP

In the pure light of ever-present Heaven.   To Prote.   Simmias.   AWP

In the quiet glades of Eden.   The Quiet Glades of Eden.   Robert Graves. BoLoP; ErPo

In the quiet of your hands,/sparks of compassion,/in the stream, at night. Treason of Sand.   Hemda Roth.   VWA

In the red front of War.   Roses of Memory.   Armistead Churchill Gordon. AA

In the red rose's way!   The Betrayal of the Rose.   Edith Matilda Thomas. AA

In the red vase behind you.   History and Abstraction.   Thomas Lux. AmPA

In the resurrection and judgment/And world without end. Amen.   The Mediatix of Grace.   Francis Burke.   ISi

In the revolving world's unfathomed morrow,/Will blossom and bear fruit. The Sower.   Mathilde Blind.   SBG

In the right with two or three.   A Stanza on Freedom.   James Russell Lowell   AA

In the roads and the lanes of El Hums.   Limerick: "There was an old man of El Hums."   Edward Lear.   FaBoNo

In the roads outside a Jonah century/You paused, and smelled the darkness we know well.   To S. T. C. on His 179th Birthday, October 12th, 1951. Maurice Carpenter.   FaBoTw

In the rooms with pale blue walls,/Pale green, pale rose?   Construction. Virginia Schonborg.   QQQ

In the round/hill of the peacock, in the resounding hill.   Apples.   Donald Hall.   LCAP

In the Royal Victoria Dock.   Limerick: "An old East End worker called Jock."   Victor Gray.   NOBL

In the rubbish dumps, a concrete dam far off in the mountain....   Summer Holiday.   Robinson Jeffers.   CrMA; MoAmPo; MoVE; OxBA

In the Russian Orthodox steeple/a bell sings, "Goodnight, goodnight."   A Bell in the Orthodox Steeple.   Thomas Waltner.   LFAC

In the sacred bulb/the sea cave.   Musica No.   Richard Duerden.   NeAP

In the safety of the hills of Tsa gi.   The Hills of Tsa la gi.   Robert J. Conley.   STE

In the sails of their wings.   Beachhead Preachment.   Ahmos Zu-Bolton. AMV-81

In the same sweet eternity of love.   Love What It Is.   Robert Herrick. AnAnS 2; FaBoEE; GBL

In the scent of the sea...!   Alien.   Donald Jeffrey Hayes.   AmNP

In the School of Coquettes/Madame Rose is a scholar.   Circle.   Henry Austin Dobson.   CenHV

In the sea-roads of the moor.   The Seasons in North Cornwall.   Charles Causley.   ACV

In the sea's blue snow.   Sailor's Carol.   Charles Causley.   AtBAP; OBCP

In the sea that is salty like our blood.   Someplace Else.   Marge Piercy. NeAC

In the section of the niggers/Where a nickel costs a dime.   Prime.   Langston Hughes.   PoBA

In the seventh year a blossom.   The Celebration.   Robert Mezey.   FAZ

In the shade of my tree/in an autumn puddle.   A Bird Comes.   Yosano Akiko.   WPOW

In the shade of the down/Eucalyptus on the hill.   All through the Rains. Gary Snyder.   ConAP

In the shade where the coolibahs grow.   The Dying Stockman.   *Anonymous.* PoAu 1-2

In the shelter sweet of the juniper tree!   Juniper.   Eileen Duggan.   ChBR

In the sick and soundless air?   From Summer Hours.   Albert Samain. AWP

In the silence beyond right and wrong.   At It.   R. S. Thomas.   OxBC

...In the silence/many feathers.   A Hollow Tree.   Robert Bly.   GP; NNaP

In the silence of webs Abiku moans/Shaping mounds from the yolk.   Abiku. Wole Soyinka.   PBA

In the silence, "Who cares/ Who cares?"/Wailed to and fro.   Echo.   Walter De la Mare.   MoVE; OBMV; SeCeV

In the silent world/of black and white....   Black and White.   Leonard Adame.   SoSe

In the singular print of her palm,/anointing aloneness.   Mercedes, Her Aloneness.   Colette Inez.   IHMS

In the sky at the end of the beam of light...   Lament.   Rainer Maria Rilke. PoPl; TrJP

...In the sky the unsullied sun lake.   Beata L'Alma.   Sir Herbert Read. FaBoMo

In the slow autumn air, the still fountains.   Elegy.   Robert Fitzgerald. AnAmPo

In the small lock of a recording brain.   Millom Old Quarry.   Norman Nicholson.   ChMP; HaMV

In the small pools of our words, its business is radiance.   Portrait of the Artist with Hart Crane.   Charles Wright.   GeTw

In the smell of cabbages from fields/nobody has seen.   The Fields.   William Stanley Merwin.   HaCAP

In the snowmarsh, staring/at snowmoon!   One A.M.   Denise Levertov. CAPP

In the soft, cool mud. Quack! Quack! Quack!   Who Likes the Rain?   Clara Doty Bates.   TiPo

In the softened bitterness/of his heart.   Breakfast in a Bowling Alley in Utica, New York.   Adrienne Rich.   CoPo

In the solemn midnight/Centuries ago.   A Christmas Hymn.   Alfred Domett.   GN; HBV 1-2; OBVV; PGD; WGRP

In the Soul's sweet song to me.   The Voice of Thought.   Thomas Holley Chivers.   AnAmPo

In the source of that woodland, the improvident flood.   The Clovers.   Jean Garrigue.   MoPo

In the South be drooping trees.   Chou and the South.   Confucius.   CTC

In the sparkling whorls/Of living light.   Mother Earth: Her Whales.   Gary Snyder.   LCAP

In the Spring a young man's fancy lightly turns to/thoughts of love.   In the Spring.   Alfred, Lord Tennyson.   BoNaP

In the spring rain.   Sushi-Okashi and Green Tea with Mitsu Yashima.   Al Robles.   BrSi

In the spring up the trail on his bucking bronco.   Bucking Bronco. *Anonymous.*   ABF; AmFP; BPAW; CoSo; FSW

In the squalor of oxen the mien of the Mother of God.   Ox-Bone Madonna. John Duffy.   ISi

In the star-chamber of the Wild.   Nocturne.   Crosbie Garstin.   CH

In the starlit night.   The Old and the New.   Queenie B. Mills.   SoPo

In the starlit world above us, call me thine–forever thine!   Is It a Sin to Love Thee?   *Anonymous.*   BLPA

In the starry gloom of the canyon.   The Train Stops at Healy Fork.   John Haines.   TAT

In the still glory of the morning star.   Leiroessa Kalyx.   Maurice Baring. OBVV

In the still hour when my mind was free/To walk alone–yet wish I walked with thee.   To Mary: It Is the Evening Hour.   John Clare.   BoLoP; GBL

In the still of this rose/he dreams his bright dream.   To the Newborn.   Judit Toth.   WPOW

In the stir of the forces/Whence issued the world.   Switzerland.   Matthew Arnold.   OAEP; VLP

In the stones, bread, and life in the blank mind.   Dipsychus.   Arthur Hugh Clough.   OBVV

In the street of the sky night walks scattering poems   The Hours Rise Up. Edward Estlin Cummings.   CAD; OxBA

In the stunted remains of last summer's silk forest.   Modern Love.   Gerald Stern.   AMV-80

In the sulphur-yellow sun/of the unforgivable landscape.   The Mouth of the Hudson.   Robert Lowell.   AmFN; CAD; CoPo; NaP; NYP

In the sun of your white & laughing face.   Susan.   Robin Magowan.   EAS

In the sunlight that shone long ago on the shields/Of the Gaels, on the fair hills of Eire, O!   The Fair Hills of Eire, O!   James Clarence Mangan.   IrPN; OBVV

In the sunlit hall/Of Ideal America?   Snapshots of the Cotton South.   Frank Marshall Davis.   PoBA

In the sweat of his brow man lives and loves and sings/His ultimate hymn to God.   Testament.   Sister M. Therese.   MoRP

In the sweet green meadow land,/Sleep, little one, sleep.   Schlof, Bobbeli.   *Anonymous.*   TrAS

In the sweet hay yet dry the hay folks cower/& some beneath the waggon shun the shower   The Thunder Mutters Louder and More Loud.   John Clare.   NOBV

In the tea rooms of our revolution.   For the Truth.   Edward S. Spriggs.   BP

In the teashop's ingle-nook.   In a Bath Teashop.   Sir John Betjeman.   BoC; ELU; EnLoPo

In the teeth of all winds blowing.   At the Crossroads.   Richard Hovey.   BBV; HBV 1-2

In the tenement's highest casement.   A Pitcher of Mignonette.   Henry Cuyler Bunner.   AA; HBV 1-2

In the new year twelve hundred and ninety-one.   Sonnet: Of the 20th June 1291.   Cecco da Siena Angiolieri.   AWP

...In the thing/Itself, until, at last, the cry concerns no one at all.   The Course of a Particular.   Wallace Stevens.   ForPo; HaCAP; PPoe; QFR

In the third phase/of the moon.   Returning at Night.   Jim Harrison.   VGW

In the three names of Love, Light, and your/Divine Humanity I name you–   Ceremony for Birth and Naming.   Ridgely Torrence.   MoRP

...In the timehonored/tradition of what they are trying/to do to the universe   The Woodchuck Who Lives on Top of Mt. Ritter.   John Oliver Simon.   NeAC

In the tiny person/looking at me out of his eyes.   A Wife Talks to Herself.   Stephen Berg.   NaP

In the tiny world of lovers' arms and/challenge time.   To His Coy Mistress (parody).   John Flood.   BXAP; FaBoPa

In the tower that is left the tale to tell/Of Gabriel, the Archangel.   The Bells of San Gabriel.   Charles Warren Stoddard.   ACP; CAW; HBV 1-2; OBEV; OBVV

In the tranced dancing of men.   The Bear on the Delhi Road.   Earle Birney.   BoAnP; HeIP; NOBC; NoP; NYBP; PoCh; PrIm

In the treasonable night; by a kind of broken habit.   West End Blues.   John Hollander.   NYP

In the tricksy pomp of fairy pride.   The Culprit Fay.   Joseph Rodman Drake.   GN

In the unatonable guilt/of the executioner.   You Move Forward.   Thomas Sessler.   VWA

In the unwinding prose of our days.   Give Us This Day Our Daily Day.   Robert J. Levy.   AMV-81

In the velocity of rest.   Happiness in the Trees.   Joseph Ceravolo.   ANYP

In the void branches/of a tree, beside/a cold kettle.   The Moon.   Donald Hall.   NCSH

In the wake of a woman who's just swept past you on her way/Home/& you remain.   Iris.   David St. John.   LCAP

In the wall of a bar at night.   A Bar at Night.   Sakutaro Hagiwara.   LiTW

In the warm wonder of winter sun.   Miramar Beach.   J. V. Cunningham.   PoA

In the waters of Galilee.   Fishing.   Dorothy Wellesley.   BoC; OBMV

In the waves' minutes, or did the land advance?   Le Livre Est sur la Table.   John Ashbery.   EAS

In the way Sartre says that Giacometti "...takes/the fat off space."   Poem: "Some who are uncertain compel me."   Art Lange.   APU

In the wealth of the richest bloods of earth.   Scum o' the Earth.   Robert Haven Schauffler.   HBV 1-2

In the weather factory/Things begin to hum.   The Weather Factory.   Nancy Byrd Turner.   SUS

In the Whirlwind of our Rising in the West!   Tauhid.   Askia Muhammad Toure.   PoBA

In the white arms/hugging the black city.   The White Man Pressed the Locks.   James C. Kilgore.   InPK

In the wide vacant sky/The spring rains are falling.   The blossoms have fallen.   Princess Shikishi.   BoWoP

In the wind a part of April, now.   Poem for Good Friday.   D. G. Jones.   PeCV

...In the wind/Clatter the banners.   The Half of Life.   Friedrich Hoelderlin.   LiTW

In the wind/I hear her cry still.   Lindedi Singing.   Innocent Banda.   WhB

In the Wobbly hall.   Hitch Haiku.   Gary Snyder.   LCAP

In the wonder of the sea.   The Sea Gypsy.   Richard Hovey.   AmePo; BBV; GoTF; TreFS

In the worship of that child,/Gloria tibi domine.   Three Christmas Carols: I.   *Anonymous.*   ACP

In the/wrong/direction.   Assassination.   Don L. Lee.   BOLo; BP; FF; NeAC; OFD; PoBA

In the xiiii yere of Kyng Richarde.   Epigram on the Year 1390-1.   *Anonymous.*   NIP

In the yard where nothing English ever grows.   The Emigres.   Ted Walker.   OBTV

In the Year of a Hundred Years.   The Revenge of Rain-In-The-Face.   Henry Wadsworth Longfellow.   BBV; BPAW; PAH

In the year of many springs/my father was dead.   Spring Death.   Russell Marano.   AMV-81

In Thee my spirit learns its utmost might.   To Our Lord.   Francisco Galvam.   CAW

In Thee, O ultimate power, who art/Our victory and our vision.   All-Souls' Day.   Siegfried Sassoon.   MoRP

In thee poor Sapho lives, for thee she dies.   Sapho's Song.   John Lyly.   OBSC

In thee, the toilers cease their weary/quest.   Fragrant Thy Memories.   *Anonymous.*   TrJP

In their ageless, safe oblivion.   Album.   Carol Papenhausen.   AMV-81

In their big Mother Hubbards and their stockin' feet.   Duncan and Brady.   *Anonymous.*   OuSiCo

In their effervescent youth/And for indifferent seasons.   Poems: Birmingham 1962-1964.   Julia Fields.   PoBA

In their effervescent youth/And for indifferent seasons.   Birmingham.   Julia Fields.   PoNe

In their first radiance,/through what a fire you passed!   Epitaph of a Courtesan.   Asclepiades.   LiTW

In their grand anthem discord has no place.   Harmony.   Thomas Grant Springer.   PoToHe

In their interlocked rhythms, the pulse/In your thigh caressing my cheek.   Quiet.   Quietly.   Kenneth Rexroth.   ErPo

In their long coats/Running over the fields.   Days.   Philip Larkin.   EBEV; FaBoMo; OBSP; OxBC

In their prostituting mutual sight.   Sockeye Salmon.   Ronald Hambleton.   CaP; OBCV

In their shining innocence seeing/in him only another human being.   Two Girls...   Charles Reznikoff.   PCP

In their soft slippers and their bravery.   Juan Belmonte, Torero.   Donald Finkel.   NePoEA

In them the snows, in me the fires abide.   The Sonnet of the Mountain.   Mellin de Saint-Gelais.   AWP

...In these/cafes were contained the suffering and/shattered hopes of my orphaned people.   For My Father: Two Poems.   David Kherdian.   GP

In these deep, bright ashes.   The Storm.   Robert Wallace.   NYBP

In these dumb solitudes.   The Founts of Song.   Fiona Macleod.   WGRP

In these respects I may myself intrude/Among the poets' thickest multitude.   Fatales Poetae.   Henry Parrot.   FaBoEE

In these ways, and more, you tell on yourself.   You Tell On Yourself.   *Anonymous.*   PoToHe

In thick mundungus clouds he hides his head.   The Bowling-Green (excerpt).   William Somervile.   NOEC

In this book are heaped the ashes/Of my love as in an urn.   Ashes.   Heinrich Heine.   LiTW

In this dark place I am still with God.   Bordello.   Lewis Turco.   SM

In this desolate country's/Cadaverous clay.   Winter Nightfall.   Sir John Collings Squire.   OxBTC

In this emptiness only the singing sometimes almost fills.   Brother of My Heart.   Galway Kinnell.   FAZ

In this forgotten place?   To Faustine.   Arthur Colton.   AA

In this in which the wild deer/Startle, and stare out.   Psalm.   George Oppen.   NNaP

In this light and this like-weeping as we run on now, over the/sand that in wet places keeps...   Shore.   Jean Garrigue.   TAP

In this mirror, the world itself is another color.   Another Color.   Frank Stewart.   AMV-81

In this most Christian of worlds/all poets are Jews.   The Daughter of Jairus.   Marina Tsvetayeva.   BoWoP

In this most vile and sinful cast/Which I will still abhor.   The Gambler's Repentance.   Baron of Offaly, Gerald.   AnIV

...In this/my last summer of loneliness.   Above the Pool.   John Montague.   NOBI

...–In this/not recognize a sister?   The Eel.   Eugenio Montale.   WeW

In this odd life will tarnish or pass away.   Moonrise.   D. H. Lawrence.   LiTM; MOON; PoA

In this, or in some other spot,/I know they'll shine again.   Resignation.   Walter Savage Landor.   HBV 1-2; TreFT

In this other summer,/summer twice come.   Vermont: Indian Summer.   Philip Booth.   NePoEA

In this quiet corner, to fold your hands and sit.   Rest.   *Anonymous.*   PoToHe

In this room of the profane and holy bargain. Soaping Down for Saint Francis of Assisi: The Canticle of Sister Soap. Gibbons Ruark. MAYP

In this scene nothing serious can go wrong. Garage Sale. Karl Shapiro. Psk

In this, season of their loss. Thanksgiving at Snake Butte. James Welch. STE

In this shew Mercie, as I ever lov'd thee. The Epistle of Rosamond to King Henry the Second. Michael Drayton. AnAnS 2

In this sweet guise, so placid and/so young? For Lucas Cranach's Eve. Adelaide Crapsey. QFR

In this the brothel where we ply our trade. Ballade of Villon and Fat Margot. Francois Villon. UnTE

In this tweeny little, cosy little house of mine! The Shiny Little House. Nancy M. Hayes. SUS

In this wholly improvised conviction Fraudulent Days. Michael Benedikt. PoA

In this wide world I ain't got no place at all. Woman Blues. *Anonymous.* OuSiCo

In this world he hath no pleasure/That will none thereof. Love in May. Jean Passerat. AWP

In this world now, litle prosperity,/And coin to keep as water in a sieve. Satires. Sir Thomas Wyatt. EnRePo; FCP; SiPS

...In this world of/yes live/(skilfully curled)/all worlds Love Is a Place. Edward Estlin Cummings. OLR

In this worould now, little prosperite,/And coyne to kepe as water in a syve. To Sir Francis Brian. Sir Thomas Wyatt. EnPo

In thoughts' weave rest unrest. Bought. Francis Douglas Davison. NeBP

In three great jumps, he bounded to the shade,/And disappeared among the greenery! The Crackling Twig. James Stephens. ELU

In three weeks it stood alone. Bird Riddle: "One day I went down in the golden harvest field." *Anonymous.* GBP

In thy Boat, O Traveler! He Embarketh in the Boat of Ra. Book of the Dead. AWP

In thy clear crystal. Evening on the Moselle. Decimus Magnus Ausonius. AnEnPo; LiTW

An in Thy pardon and Thy care/The heaven of heavens is won. Friend of Souls. *Anonymous.* BePJ

In Tilbury Town, we look beyond/Horizons for the man Flammonde. Flammonde. Edwin Arlington Robinson. AnAmPo; CMoP; LiTA; LiTM; MAPA; NoAm; SeCeV

In time fused with divine breasts, buttocks, arms. Mythological Sonnet XVI. Roy Fuller. ErPo

In time I loath'd that now I love,/In both content and pleas'd. Doralicia's Song. Robert Graves. LoBV; OBSC

In time may prove a Rose, and be your owne. On a Rosebud Sent to Her Lover. *Anonymous.* AtBAP

In time she would be rid of all her books. A Fountain, a Bottle, a Donkey's Ears and Some Books. Robert Frost. VGW

In time the wound healed, but a scar was left–a long, white scar/across the prairie's breast. The Western Trail. Robert V. Carr. PoOW

In too full winde draw in thy swelling sailes. Odes. Horace. OBVE

In touch, it is the nearest thing to bone. Gravestones. Floyd C. Stuart. AMV-80

In transport sing/The Saviour's praise. Hail to the Joyous Day. Royall Tyler. AH

In triumph through the needle's/Microscopic arch. The Needle. Grace Cornell Tall. GoYe

...In tune with the sentence that confines/Gentile and Jew to the ghetto of this world. In the Old Jewish Cemetery, Prague, 1970. Edward Lowbury. VWA

In twenty minutes he forgot the sirens. The Sirens. John Streeter Manifold. LiTB; LiTM; MoBrPo; WaP

In twenty years, the whole wide world/May look and see and know. Labor Not in Vain. *Anonymous.* STF

In twilight square of port antonio Jam Fa Jamaica. Charles Lynch. LTB

In two-faced Janus' hour a deele of swyvinge Burialle of the Dede (parody). Martin Fagg. BXAP

In union with the communion of angels. Ludwig's Death Mask. Ted Hughes. NoAm

In vain are all the charms I can devise;/She hath an art to break them with her eyes. Love-Charms. Thomas Campion. NOBE

...In vain doth Valour bleed/While Avarice, and Rapine share the land. On the Lord Gen. Fairfax at the Siege of Colchester. John Milton. OBS

In vain in vain the/moment/gone Monoagram 23. Martina Werner. BoWoP

In vain, "This Lowell, who was he?" In an Album. James Russell Lowell. OBAL

In vain we build the work, unless/The builder also grows. Man-Making. Edwin Markham. PGD

In vain we call to them/Or entreat them to open their wings. The Birds of Tin. Charles Madge. EAS; NeBP

In vain we grant, if she refuse. Advice to the Old Beaux. Sir Charles Sedley. CEP; FaBoUs; SeCV 1-2

In Vallombrosa, where th'Etrurian shades/High overarcht imbowr. Paradise Lost. John Milton. FaBoPP

In vice we dwell, in sin that hath no end. Marius Victor. Sir Walter Raleigh. FCP

In view of which our momentary bereavement/Outshapes but small. After the Last Breath. Thomas Hardy. VLP

In Vishnu-land what Avatar? Waring. Robert Browning. PoEL 1-5; VLP

In wanting to silence any song. A Minor Bird. Robert Frost. CMoP

In water cold enough to break your ankles. There Were Some Summers. Thomas Lux. LCAP

In waves still as the skillful yachts pass over. The Yachts. William Carlos Williams. AmPP; BiP; CMoP; CoBMV; ExPo; HeIP; InPo; LiSp; LiTA; LiTM; MasP; MoAB; MoAmPo; MoPo; MOS; MoVE; NAMP; NePA; NoAm; NOBA; NoP; OxBA; SeCeV; ViBoPo

In ways of Love and Truth and Right. The Mother's Hymn. William Cullen Bryant. OHIP

In ways that I know and know not,/His labor of love I share. This Moment. Annie Johnson Flint. BLRP

In weak winter sun. Haiku: "An empty sickbed..." Richard Wright. FAZ

In wedlock she was tied/To the farmer's son. A Farmer's Son So Sweet. *Anonymous.* OBET

In Wee-John-Boo, in "Boo-Boo' by John Greenleaf Whittier. Orange Jews. Ron Padgett. EAS

In what age and what country you will come,/That I may meet you there. Rendezvous. Robert Hillyer. MoLP

In what ethereal dances,/By what eternal streams. To One in Paradise. Edgar Allan Poe. AA; AP; APA; BLPL; BoLiVe; BoLoP; HBV 1-2; LiTA; LiTL; NePA; OBEV; OBRV; OBVV; OxBA; PG; PoLf; TAP; TrGrPo; ViBoPo; WHA

In what fond flight, how many ways and days! The House of Life. Dante Gabriel Rossetti. VLP

...In what measure/Do you more than we? Is It Nothing to You? May Probyn. GoBC; OBEV; OBVV

In what they used to call Man, now not. A Woman I Mix Men Up... Bernadette Mayer. APU

In which a thousand birds had built their bowers. The Faerie Queene. Edmund Spenser. GN

In which being there together is enough. Final Soliloquy of the Interior Paramour. Wallace Stevens. HaCAP; HAP; LCAP

In which Dachau is maintained in something of/greater degree. Safari West. John A. Williams. NBP; PAI

In which Death he lies content. Epitaphs of the War, 1914-18. Rudyard Kipling. BrPo; OBWP

In which I walked, now clouded and confused. My Books. Henry Wadsworth Longfellow AA

In which if they turn and twist, it is neither with volition nor con-/sciousness. A Grave. Marianne Moore. AnAmPo; CABA; CMoP; CrMA; ExPo; FaBoWP; ForPo; HAP; HeIP; LiTA; MoPo; MOS; MoVE; NoAm; NOBA; PPoe; SeCeV; TAP; UnPo

In which the purse she would deposit,/As safely as in nurse's closet. The Daughter's Rebellion. Francis Hopkinson. PAH

In which there is no room for us. Walking Song. William E. Hickson. OxBChV

In which they have chosen to make their homes. The Poetry Reading. Bill Manhire. OCNZ

In which this other world of theirs grows dank, decays,/And founders and goes down. A House of the Eighties. Edmund Wilson. AnFE

In which to live is death, to die is Hell. Lewd Love is Loss. Robert Southwell. ACP

In which to take a dip. The Uses of Ocean. Sir Owen Seaman. ALV; FiBHP

In which we swam, two dreams now, tolling/against time, on the squares. In Prague. Paul Celan. VWA

In whom all saints are one for evermore! Iona. Frederick Tennyson. GoBC

In whom, save death, naught mortal was at all. Sonnet: "A passing glance, a lightning long the skies." William, of Hawthornden Drummond. ViBoPo

In whom the Lord of Hosts did pitch his tent! Ana(Mary-Army)gram. George Herbert. CABA; OAEL 1-2

In whom the rainbow's covenant is fulfilled. Infant Noah. Vernon Watkins. NeBP

In whose arms she will flourish/Or else will die. Looking On. Anthony Thwaite. NePoEA-2

In whose black sex/Our ancient culpability like a pearl is set. Eve. David Gascoyne. GTBS-P

In whose chief part your worths implanted be? Arcadia. Sir Philip Sidney. SiPS

In whose dear look thou shalt be satisfied. Satisfied. Samuel Valentine Cole. BLRP

In whose dim glades each hunter finds/his own torn spirit in his mesh. The Cascade. Edgell Rickword. ChMP; FaBoTw

In whose each part all tongues may dwell. Arcadia. Sir Philip Sidney. SiPS

In whose limbs there is latent flight Simile. N. Scott Momaday. CDW

In whose sweet praise/I all my days/Could gladly spend. My Song Is Love Unknown. Samuel Crossman. OxBChV

In winter grey as her eyes. Soft White. Lee Harwood. EAS

In wishing you herewith a Merry Christmas. Christmas Trees. Robert Frost. BiP

In woods so long time bare. Cuckoo! Hilaire Belloc. MoVE

In word or deed deception abounds/Do not believe your eyes. To a Cactus Seller. Anwar Shaul. VWA

In work done squarely and unwasted days. Unwasted Days. James Russell Lowell. MCCG

"In yonder grave your Druid lies!" Ode Occasioned by the Death of Mr. Thomson. William Collins. NOEC

...In you I love/All that our faith must find, or wisdom give. Girl in a White Coat. John Malcolm Brinnin. SaC

In your arms I'll/survive death./It's a dream. In Your Arms. Miklos Radnoti. VWA

In your army of lovers/I am a private soldier. Love Song. Gavin Ewart. OxBTC

In your brain will die/(1/2 a brain) Three Car Poems, III. Richard Jones. FAZ

In your eyes my sorrow. Ballad. Marjorie Allen Seiffert. HBMV

In your eyes/of the leopard/only the forest is seen. In the Forest of Your Eyes. Arlindo Barbeitos. WhB

In your far-off sunny southland/Do you dream of me tonight? The Spanish Needle. Claude McKay. GoSl

In your hair, at night/in the hotel of the world. Following Van Gogh (Avignon, 1982). Marla Puziss. PoDr

In your laughing eyes. Mouth of the Amazon. R. P. Gira. AMV-80

In your little corral/Asleep with mother again. Buckaroo Sandman. Anonymous. BPAW

In your name poems begin. Largo. Dunstan Thompson. LiTA; MoPo; WaP

In your new-fashioned world! The Skies Cant Keep Their Secret! Emily Dickinson. DiPo

In your own secret sins and terrors! In the Churchyard at Cambridge. Henry Wadsworth Longfellow. AP; PoEL 1-5; TAP

In your photograph of no survivors, I'm smiling. Before the Mountain. Elizabeth Libbey. AmPA

In your remembrance let it lie/That ons I was. What Once I Was. Sir Thomas Wyatt. EnPo; MeEL

In your solitude of bruises in/your arson of alert/beautiful Under the Edge of February. Jayne Cortez. BlSi

In your wheat-strewn bed's the planetary gust/of your people's victory! Love Pictures You as Black and Long-Faced. Lance Jeffers. FB

In your wicked/stride... Pachuco Remembered. Tino Villanueva. FIA

In your work,/And even in your rest. Beauty. E.-Yeh.-Shure (Louise Abeita). TiPo

In youre herte stedefastly/Notate. Lines from Love Letters. Anonymous. OBEV

In youth is pleasure, in youth is pleasure. In an Arbour Green. Robert Weever. ELP

In youth thou enter'dst on glass-bottled wall. On Mrs. Reynolds's Cat. John Keats. FM

In youth thou enter'dst on glass-bottled wall. To a Cat. John Keats. BoC; FaBoCh; PCat

Inalienable And Then There. Frantisek Halas. LiTW

The inarticulate brute/finds names for them all. The Naming of the Beasts. Francis Sparshott. NOBC

Inasmuch as ye did it not to them/Ye did it not to Me. Inasmuch! William E. Brooks. PGD

Inbred deformities of loneliness? Lonely. Bloke Modisane. PBA

Inbringing, inbringing the March's wild weather. Wild March. Constance Fenimore Woolson. YeAr

Incarnadine, the carnage of the swans. A High-Toned Old Fascist Gentleman (parody). William Zaranka. BXAP

Incense of summer flowers, and acrid tang/Of autumn's burning leaves. January. John Heath-Stubbs. OBCP

An inch of nothing for your soul. If i should sleep with a lady called death. Edward Estlin Cummings. BoLoP; VGW

Incidents in c-sharp/minor as a virgin scatter/and the poets will write. Of the Confident Stranger. Clark Coolidge. APU

Incline the wayward prow to front the sea. Shortening Sail. William Falconer. EtS

Inclines to think there is a god,/Or something very like Him. "There Is No God," the Wicked Saith. Arthur Hugh Clough. GoTF; NBM; NOBV; TreFS

...Including stash/of LSD, Peyote, Psilocybin, Amanita, Benzedrine, Valium/and aspirin. Destruction. Joanne Kyger. APU

Including the amazing/dissolution of walls between rooms. One of the Boys. Philip Dacey. Str

The incomparable presence of man. Presences. Zoe Karelli. PBWP

Incomprehensible/Promise of joy! Harold at Two Years Old. Frederic William Henry Myers. HBMV

Increase the deepening harvest here before/It snows again. Child of My Winter. W.D. Snodgrass. MoAmPo

Increases itself/Where it belongs. January. Richard A. Hawley. AMV-80

Incredible,/Inedible,/Salad of Greens! The Universal Favorite. Carolyn Wells. InMe; NLV

Incredible wampum Impossibly, motivated by midnight. Edward Estlin Cummings. NAMP

Incumbent steps ahead/to winter. Greedy Seasons. Eileen Myles. APU

"Indeed, I have not any." Simple Simon. Mother Goose. SoPo

Indeed, indeed, great Pan is dead. On the Death of the Great Chef Alexis Soyer. Anonymous. FaBoEE

...Indeed it is to be lamented. Concerning Unnatural Nature: An Inverted Form. Hollis Summers. ErPo

...Indeed our sweet/foods leave us cavities. Heart's Needle. W.D. Snodgrass. NePoEA; NoAm

"Indeed!' said Mr. Jones, "and please/Send me the half that's got my keys.' Some Ruthless Rhymes. Harry Graham. CenHV

Indeed/they are pure,/but they are also/broken. On the Margins of a Poem. Jiri M. Langer. VWA

...–Indeed,/they look like huge bouquets! Autumn Fashions. Edith Matilda Thomas. YeAr

Indeed will I, quo' Findlay! Wha Is That at My Bower-Door? Robert Burns. ErPo; InvP; UnTE

An Indian in me, toward that hill,/Conceives himself divinity. Shasta. Witter ("Emanuel Morgan") Bynner. BPAW

Indian pipe and moccasin flower/Scattered among our hills. Indian Pipe and Moccasin Flower. Arthur Guiterman. BrR; SUS

An Indian Summer comes at last! Equinoctial. Adeline D. T. Whitney. HBV 1-2

An indian with nothing to lose. One chip of human bone. Ray A. Young Bear. STE

Indianola, iowa Amazing Grace. Anselm Hollo. PoM

The Indians caught the wagon master/And burned him on a wagon wheel. Oliver Wiggins. Stanley Vestal. BPAW

Indians know how to wait. Lines for Marking Time. Roberta Hill. BoWoP; CDW; TWSS

Indicate a world into which I can dissolve. Ightham Woods. C. H. Sisson. FaBoTw

Indicated what? That I stood/in his light? I left the spot. News from the Cabin. May Swenson. NMP; NYBP

Indifference and success had crowned them all. On First Looking into Loeb's Horace. Lawrence Durrell. FaBoMo; LiTM

Indifferent to, unaware of us. Darkening Hotel Room. Alfred Corn. MAYP

Indispensable,/Old black billy. My Old Black Billy. Edward Harrington. PoAu 1-2

Indolent Housewife–in Daisies–lain! How many times these low feet staggered. Emily Dickinson. AmPP; HAP; PoEL 1-5

Indoors a purposeful man who talks at cross/Purposes, to himself, in a broken sleep. House on a Cliff. Louis MacNeice. NOBI

The Indwelling God, proclaimed of old. God, through All and in You All. Samuel Longfellow. TrPWD

Inestimably naught! All Flesh. Francis Thompson. BrPo

Inexorable gaffer in an old hat/Croaking our names. Who Was It Came. Daniel Gerard Hoffman. CoAP

Inexorable murmurs/of the ice machines. Star Motel. Bill Berkson. APU

The infant child is not aware/He has been eaten by the bear. Infant Innocence. Alfred Edward Housman. DTC; EnLi 1-2; FaBoCh; FaBoCo; FaBoNo; FaFP; LiTB; LoGBV; NOBL; OxBoLi

An infant flyaway; but now/We make a man of it. From Feathers to Iron. C. Day Lewis. ViBoPo

...The Infant/Knuckles the generous breast, and feeds. The Flight in the Desert. William Everson. VGW

An infant, the soul, springing from his head. The Wisdom of Insecurity. Richard Eberhart. NePA

Infant wiles and infant smiles/Heaven and Earth of peace beguiles. Sleep! Sleep! Beauty Bright. William Blake. CBEP

The infantry of rain and the strong wind. Hide in the Heart. Lloyd Frankenberg. AnFE

"Infected minds infect each thing they see." In Wonted Walks. Sir Philip Sidney. CABA

Infected sutures/and ill-knit bone? A Northern Hoard. Seamus Heaney. CIP

The infinite army marches on its remorseless way. Great Nature Is an Army Gay. Richard Watson Gilder. HBV 1-2

Into the stream/into the stream   In the Ravine.   W. W. Eustace Ross. PeCV

Into the sun, come out, come in.   Come Out into the Sun.   Robert Francis. NYBP

Into the sunless land they went,/Into the starless land.   Ballad.   May Kendall.   HBV 1-2

Into the terrible water & walk forever/under it out toward the island. Henry's Understanding.   John Berryman.   CAPP; NoAm; NOBA

Into the vast spiral that will throw up others.   A Mantelpiece of Shells. Ruthven Todd.   NYBP

Into the waste we know not, into the night?   The Wayfarers.   Rupert Brooke.   MoLP

Into the web of being, both radiant and/somber.   For the Sun Declined. Yitzhak Lamdan.   TrJP

Into the windlessness/Of our house in Taos.   A House in Taos.   Langston Hughes.   CDC

Into the wonderful world.   In Hospital.   William Ernest Henley.   BrPo

Into the world/again.   The Cat.   William Matthews.   AmPA

Into their true gentleness,/even with us.   Into Their True Gentleness. Pearse Hutchinson.   CIP

Into this being, half yours, I creep.   Before Sleep.   Anne Ridler.   NeBP

Into this realm so young ane King.   The Complaynt of Schir David Lindesay: The Childhood of James V.   David Lindsay.   AtBAP

"Into thy hands," and he was dead.   My God, My God, Look upon Me. Chad Walsh.   TrCP

Into Thy hands I give my soul!   Columbus Dying.   Edna Dean Proctor. MC; PAH

Into untraveled spaces of the stars.   Lute Music.   Kenneth Rexroth.   TAP

Into which the leaves push out/And fall away.   Of All Plants, the Tree. Mary Jane White.   AMV-80

Into your cup of always/oceanic water.   The Well-Aimed Stare.   Hugo Margenat.   InW

Into your mouth/&/swallow for dear life   Yes, the Secret Mind Whispers. Al Young.   PoBA

Intoning the blessing/Blessed be the Lord...   Holocaust 1944.   Anne Ranasinghe.   VWA

Intoxication of final loneliness.   Medlars and Sorb-Apples.   D. H. Lawrence. OAEL 1-2

The intransmutable verity.   Proof.   Bessie Calhoun Bird.   BlSi

Intreat her to excuse mee toe.   Pure Simple Love.   Aurelian Townsend. AnAnS 2; SeCP

An intricate maze of thin-sown poppyheads.   Vincent Van Gogh.   William Jay Smith.   EyDe

Introduce me to your friend.   Love-Songs, At Once Tender and Informative. Samuel Hoffenstein.   OBAL

The Intuition of the News–/In just a Country Town–   There's been a death, in the opposite house.   Emily Dickinson.   BoLiVe; InPS; NCEP; PAI; SoSe

Invades, and drowns them all in tears.   A Foren Ruler.   Walter Savage Landor.   PV

Invading Vietnam like a woman/whose neck snaps and breaks/before rape. Vision of 400 Sunrises.   Ruth Lisa Schechter.   SOTS

Invent the age! Invent the metaphor!   Hypocrite Auteur.   Archibald MacLeish.   AmPP; MoVE; NePA

Inventing translations.   Translations.   Patricia Y. Ikeda.   BrSi

(The inventor of the pinstripe suit)?   Gladstone Gave His Name to the Gladstone Bag.   Christopher Reid.   PoL

Invert their current, and the heart regain.   The Circulation of the Blood.   Sir Richard Blackmore.   FaBoUs

Invested money in a pet/That didn't misconduct itself.   'Twas Ever Thus (parody).   Anonymous.   BXAP

Investeth and ingirds all other lives.   The Mystic.   Alfred, Lord Tennyson. OAEP; VLP

Invincible fore-runner.   Baby Tortoise.   D. H. Lawrence.   BoAnP; CMoP

Invisible/as anyone.   Moontan.   Mark Strand.   NYBP

Invisible behind enormous trees,/in an incredible calm,/appraches the great horror.   The Journey to the Insane Asylum.   Alfred Lichtenstein.   VWA

Invisible fingers will mould/Palaces of gold.   Palaces of Gold.   Leon Rosselson.   OBET

Invisible & in complete control of everything.   Take I, 4: II: 58.   Philip Whalen.   NeAP

Invisible in itself,/Seen only by its movement.   The Hill Burns.   Nan Shepherd.   PoSH

Invisible ink.   The Jest.   Austin Clarke.   BIrV

Invisible insects dwelling uncomfortably/in the margins, in the white spaces around words.   Elegy.   Sandra M. Gilbert.   PoA

Invisible invisible invisible   The Widow.   William Stanley Merwin.   NYBP; UnPo; VGW

..Invisible judges/sit, wrapped in their knowledge,/taking terrible notes. Close-Ups of Summer.   Norman MacCaig.   OxBC

An invisible spirit/Watching.   Death.   Patty L. Harjo.   VoR

The invisible things/arming themselves/in your throat.   St. Julien's Eve: For Dennis Cross.   James (Olumo) Cunningham.   JB

...The invisible throng,/Beating the accent of their wrong.   We Whom the Dead Have Not Forgiven.   Sara Bard Field.   PGD

Invisibly clear, the only love.   The Woman in Sunshine.   Wallace Stevens. BiP; MoVE

Invite/you in, to spend the night.   I Say.   Malka Tussman.   VWA

Invited him to paradise.   Comrade Jesus.   Sarah N. Cleghorn.   NAMP

...Invited visitor/Lifted his claws above them, holes for eyes.   Santa Claus. Dom Moraes.   NoAm

Inviting yet, and waiting thy command.   An Infant's Eye.   Thomas Traherne.   CoBE

Involved like them in the not unhearing air.   Monologue of a Deaf Man. David Wright.   MP; NoAm

Inward as all the creatures/Drawn through my bone.   Ark to Noah.   Jay Macpherson.   NOBC

Io to Hymen, &c.   The Songe: "Drinke and be merry, merry, merry boyes." Thomas Morton.   SCAP

Ionian isles are thine, and all the fairy/shores!   Outward Bound.   Thomas Bailey Aldrich.   AA; EtS

Ipsey Wipsey spider/Climbing up again.   Ipsey Wipsey.   Anonymous.   OxNR

Ireland, Ireland, green and sad.   Ireland, Ireland.   Sir Henry Newbolt. FaPoR

"Ireland shall get her freedom and you still break stone."   Parnell.   William Butler Yeats.   CMoP

Iris, jonquil, fragile, spare,/pricked on silk and champagne air.   Lalique. Hal Porter.   PoAu 1-2

Irised by the gleam/Of tears, as it does now.   At Bungendore.   James Philip McAuley.   PoAu 1-2

The Irish wind on old St. Patrick's/Day/Is magical and surely full of blarney. An Irish Wind.   Zelma S. Dennis.   AMV-80

Iron-hearted man-slaying Achilles/Who would not live long.   The Shield of Achilles.   W. H. Auden.   EBEV; FaBoMo; FaBoPV; GTBS-P; HAP; NePA; NOBE; NOCV; NoP; OAEP; PoA; WeW

The iron mask of freedom.   Karl Heinrich Marx.   Hans Enzensberger. FaBoPV

The iron master,/sweaty,/breathless,/fierce.   The Indomitable.   Carl Rakosi. GP

Iron out of Calvary is master of men all!'   Cold Iron.   Rudyard Kipling. OnMSP

An iron ship glides into the deserted horizon.   Riding Double.   Peter Wild. AmPA

An iron spider waits for his successes.   Pepys Bar, West Forty-Eight Street, 8 a.m.   L. E. Sissman.   NYP

...The iron spike/of the sun is all he remembers.   Sea Owl.   Dave Smith. HaCAP

Irreconcilables, their treaty signed.   The Trophy.   Edwin Muir.   LiTM

The irresolvable mystery/of the human heart.   Assignment: Descriptive Essay. Gary Willis.   AMV-81

Irrevocable judgments/Of the parliament of trees.   On Entering a Forest. Elinor Lennen.   PGD

Irritating the natural contours of the earth.   Insomnia.   Joyce Carol Oates. DFF

Is a change for the worse, and not for the better.   Surnames to Be Avoided in Marriage.   Anonymous.   FaBoUs

Is a debt unpaid.   A Promise Made.   Anonymous.   FaFP

Is a derned sight better business/Than loafin' around The Throne.   Little Breeches.   John Milton Hay.   AA; FaBoBe; HBV 1-2; PaPo; TreFS

Is a keen, enormous, haunting, never-sated thirst for God.   God.   Gamaliel Bradford.   TRV; WGRP

Is a pure wonder, I must say, to me.   Columbus.   Arthur Hugh Clough. AmFN; MC; PoSC

Is a stately thing.   The Stranger.   Jean Garrigue.   LiTA

Is a/thread of pearls.   Hanging from the branches of a green willow tree. Lady Ise.   BoWoP

Is a well in Asia.   Hebrews.   James Oppenheim.   TrJP

Is all overrun with rue?   The Seeds of Love.   Anonymous.   GBP; OxBoLi

Is all that any body knows.   Men Say They Know Many Things.   Henry David Thoreau.   AnNE; ImOP; PoPl

Is all that is left of his wide domain.   Don Juan.   Lucius Harwood Foote. AA

Is all we make each other when we love.   Identity.   Elizabeth Jennings. NePoEA

Is allowed, considering   Play.   Archie Randolph Ammons.   PoA

Is also that of harmonies/That have made one's life and art for evermore off-key.   The Unremarkable Year.   Roy Fuller.   OxBC

Is also the ready roadway, running into heaven.   Love.   William Langland. BoC

Is always polite on principle.   Principal and Principle.   Anonymous. FaBoUs

Is always walcum.   Reflection on Babies.   Ogden Nash.   FaBoUs; NLV

Is least, and yet the proudest, for it is the last. Karl. Charles Spear. AnNZ

Is left to muse upon the solemn scene. A Night-Piece. William Wordsworth. EnRP; MOON

Is liberty of the mind,/Rather than of the belly? Jacob Godbey. Edgar Lee Masters. LiTA

Is lift you to where this illumination/overfills with space. Jerusalem. Jon Silkin. VWA

Is like a barrier round about us,/A barrier we may neither branch nor overpass. The Barrier. Louis Lavater. NOAV

Is like the brushing together of thin wing-tips of silver. The Skaters. John Gould Fletcher. MoAmPo; SD

Is like the cat, that purrs/To ape the rage of lions. Pretences. Ibn Rashiq. TTY

Is, Listen, listen, I am a man like you. The Hill Farmer Speaks. H. S. Thomas. GTBS-P; HaMV

Is love that ever seems of life a part,/And understand?/Try to.–One day? Will You, One Day. Marian Ramie. HBMV

...Is made a hotel by her/very absence alone. Dispatch Number Sixteen. Doug Fetherling. NeAC

"Is magic of love less powerful at your Court/Than at this green well-head?" The Frog and the Golden Ball. Robert Graves. DFT; NoP

Is more comfortable/than standing/on pedestals. Monument to Pushkin. Joseph Brodsky. VWA

Is more private than thought is, or upstairs sleeping. Standing on the Streetcorner. Edwin Denby. ANYP

Is more to me than any meal/Or banquet that I ever went to. Marble-Top. E. B. White. FiBHP; OBAL

Is moulded with the myriads of his foes. The House of Night. Philip Freneau. AA

Is much better far/Than a careful chair/And a wreath of thorns without. My Limbs I Will Fling. William Strode. CBEP

Is my calmness to be a tight calmness? That's All? Anna Hajnal. PBWP

Is my eye open? Henry Miller: A Writer. Carol Lem. AMV-80

Is nature, which is larger and more still. Solar Creation. Charles Madge. FaBoMo; OBMV; OxBTC

Is neither knowledge nor device/Nor thirteen pence a day. Grenadier. Alfred Edward Housman. EG; OBMV; OBWP

Is never at his best. Edgar Guest. Oscar Williams. PP

Is never for a moment dried. Like a Great Rock, Far out at Sea. Lady Sanuki. AWP

Is noise/is news The Print-Out. Howard Nemerov. AMV-80

Is not always too deuced/Lucid. Henry James. Clifton Fadiman. FiBHP

Is not death but the door to life begun/To those who hear far Heaven cry, "Well/done!" To America, on Her First Sons Fallen in the Great War. E. M. Walker. PAH

Is not soothed by the prospect of flowers. Crack in the Wall Holds Flowers. Adam David Miller. PoBA

Is not that pastoral instruction sweet/Which says who shall be eaten, who shall eat? Improvisations on Aesop. Anthony Hecht. OBAL

Is not that slight tossing dead Leander? A Private Letter to Brazil. Gloria C. Oden. AmNP; NNP; PoNe

Is not thy reason all these pow'rs in one? An Essay on Man. Alexander Pope. NU

Is not to be buried, and the boulders will drift. Bucyrus. John Holmes. NePoAm

Is now lit up alone over the fountain. Shooting at the Moon. Kim Yo-sop. MOON

Is of the slightest bondage made aware. The Silken Tent. Robert Frost. AmPP; ExPo; InPo; MoPo; MP; NePA; NOBA

Is offering too little and asking too much. The Dutch. George Canning. DBV; OxBoLi

Is one, always the same, one life, one fire? Lollingdon Downs. John Masefield. LiTB

Is one clear trumpet call to Faith and Will. Columbus the World-Giver. Maurice Francis Egan. PGD

Is one poynt of husbandry rye land do like. A Hundreth Good Poyntes of Husbandry. Thomas Tusser. FaBoUs

Is only who's a knave of the first rate. Wretched Man. John Wilmot, Earl of Rochester. SeCePo

Is order all, and all is right. On the Uniformity and Perfection of Nature. Philip Freneau. AmePo; AmPP

Is our De Tea Fabula. Sir Arthur Thomas ("Q") Quiller-Couch. CenHV

"Is out at elbows, why should I repine?" Shall I Repine? Jonathan Swift. NCEP; OBSP

Is plain as is the nose on your/Face. A Disagreeable Feature. Edwin Meade Robinson. HBMV

Is plunged into the depths, and we lie still. Consummation. *Anonymous.* UnTE

Is prettier far than these. The Rainbow. Christina Georgina Rossetti. OxBChV; SoPo

Is rife with excitements of the world's beginning/And its end. The Old One and the Wind. Clarice Short. IHMS

Is set in brass on the swart thumb of Doom. Epitaph for the Race of Man. Edna St. Vincent Millay. MoPo

Is Seymour really her first name,/And has the printer spelt it right? Mrs. Seymour Fentolin. Oliver Herford. HBMV

Is she not tenderer far than when she allures/Man on his pilgrimage? Asian Desert. Dorothy Wellesley. OBMV

Is shunned, we must admit it,/Like an adversity. Drowning is Not so Pitiful. Emily Dickinson. CMoP; ExPo; OBSP

Is sleeping a melody sweeter/Than ever on earth was made. Spring Whistles. Lucy Larcom. OBCA

Is solace to the pensive ear:/"Pewee! pewee! peer!" The Pewee. John Townsend Trowbridge. HBV 1-2

"Is something bothering you?" In spite of my efforts. Taira no Kanemori. LiTW

Is something i ain t/got anything but Time Time Said Old King Tut. Don (Donald Robert Marquis) Marquis. FiBHP

Is something more precious still. Charlotte Bronte. Susan (Sarah Chauncey Woolsey) Coolidge. OBCA

Is something we shall learn. After Reading a Child's Guide to Modern Physics. W. H. Auden. NYBP

Is spring not hard enough to bear/For one at autumn of his year? The Scarecrow. Andrew Young. BSV; FaBoTw

Is strangely like the folk in my dream,/And would flourish in Turvey Top. Turvey Top. *Anonymous.* NA

Is supported by layman and cleric. Limerick: "All hail to the town of Limerick." Langford Reed. TDH

Is sure to come true, be it never so old. Friday Night's Dream on a Saturday Told. *Anonymous.* HBVY

Is surely home, and home, sweet home,/For there the soul can rest. Home. Henry Van Dyke. STF

Is swallowed by the dark before dawn. Daybreak. Frank Lamont Phillips. CNA

Is sweet as yearling's blood/in the corners of your lips Lion. May Swenson. LiTM; SoSe

Is sweet or is bitter/Which makes it stand up. The Crab Tree. Oliver St. John Gogarty. OxBI

Is swiftly, surely preparing for you. Turn O Libertad. Walt Whitman. AmePo

...Is telling/to the very end a tale about Razin/and his most beautiful Persian girl. We Are Keeping an Eye on the Girls. Marina Tsvetayeva. PBWP

Is terribler than wearing it/A whole existence through. While we were fearing it. Emily Dickinson. NCEP; NIP; PPP

Is thair sic greif in hevinlie myndis hie? The Aeneid. Virgil (Publius Vergilius Maro). OBVE

...Is/that all, is/that all. The Gift. Robert Creeley. NOBA

Is that bower on the banks of the calm BENDEMEER! Bendemeer. Thomas Moore. FSW; OBRV

Is that dead woman's upturned face. The Pond. William Henry Davies. ChMP

Is that great water in the west/Termed Immortality. We thirst at first. Emily Dickinson. NOCV; WGRP

Is that how it was? One hopes so. Orpheus. Donald Davie. TEP

Is that other, her bridegroom,/here in the room? An Embroidery. Denise Levertov. DFT; NMM; NU

Is that perfectly clear? Circuit Breaker. Sid Gary. QQQ

Is that the crossing to the other side is mine. The Trestle Bridge. Carolyne Wright. AMV-80

Is that thin sound I hear/Your applause?... Letters Found near a Suicide. Frank Horne. CDC

...Is that thing alive? I hear a famisht howl. Homage to Mistress Bradstreet. John Berryman. AmP; FF; MoVE; NAs; NoAm

Is that what he/wanted back/or what? Beryl. Lyn Lifshin. NeAC

Is that why Lisette dislikes me? A Possibility. Carolyn Wells. ALV

Is that you have your slaves, and the Greek had his helot. A Fable for Critics. James Russell Lowell. AnNE; NOBA; OxBA

Is the bonny bowl/They breakfast in. Little Lad. *Anonymous.* BiCB; OxNR

Is the deed ever really done/For Heaven and the future's sakes. Two Tramps in Mud Time. Robert Frost. AnNE; AP; BLPL; CMoP; CoBMV; LiTA; LiTM; MasP; MoAB; MoAmPo; NAMP; NePA; NoAm; PrIm; TrGrPo

Is the excesse of sadnesse. Beauty Is But A Painted Hell. Thomas Campion. AtBAP; BiP

Is the glance softened?/Bowed the face? On the Photograph of a Man I Never Saw. Hyam Plutzik. VWA

Is the heart's design utmost. Shao and the South. Confucius. CTC

Is the infinite, tenderest, passionate love/Of one dead drunk for another. Love. *Anonymous.* SoSe

Is the joy around your footsteps, my own Cailin Donn! My Own Cailin Donn. George Sigerson. FaBoBe; HBV 1-2

Is the joy of being/Rude to it! Tee-Vee Enigma. Selma Raskin. QQQ

Is the leafy oak sapling/moving and restless! Bellower with the Antlers.
Suibne Geilt. NOBI

Is the only depth I'll sound/That may save me from myself. Rescue.
Dabney Stuart. NYBP

Is the pride of thus dying for thee. Pro Patria Mori. Thomas Moore.
GTBS; GTBS-P

Is the rich music of a summer bird/Heard in the still night, with its passionate
cadence. The Spirit of Poetry. Henry Wadsworth Longfellow. PP

Is the safe-kept memory/Of a lovely thing. The Coin. Sara Teasdale.
HBMV; TiPo

Is the slim curved crook of the moon tonight! Winter Moon. Langston
Hughes. DuDa

...Is the structure of the suggestive,/the space flowing between the lines.
Arriving. Gabriel Preil. VWA

Is the way to feel stupid and have red eyes. New Proverb. Shirley Brooks.
FaBoNo

Is there a book that I/Would not burn for the truth? Scholar I. Seamus
Deane. NOBI

Is there a hand-rail to the stairs? Epigram: "Had we two met, blythe-hearted
Burns." Walter Savage Landor. FaBoEE

Is there any plummet or flight as sheer as the fledgling's? Fledglings.
William Meredith. GLGT

–Is there anything/praiseworthy in that? The Women's Jail. Miriam
Waddington. NOBC

...Is/there anything you won't forgive/her/him. Landscape with Next of Kin.
Olga Broumas. BoWoP

Is there indeed, or is there not a shore/That is our home? Come Home,
Come Home! Arthur Hugh Clough. HAP

Is there no word to tell to me? The Tree Stands Very Straight and Still.
Annette Wynne. SoPo; SUS

Is there not sumptuous palace nor any inn at all/To lodge His heav'nly mother
but in a filthy stall? Christmas Day Is Come. Luke Wadding. OxBI

Is there nothing more soluble, more gaseous, more imper-/ceptible?/Nothing.
The Ecliptic: Cancer, or, The Crab (excerpt). Joseph Gordon ("Adam
Drinan") Macleod. NeBP

Is there nothing to be said about the cockroach which is good? Cockroach.
Mary Ann Hoberman. OBCA

Is there peace within like the peace without? Only the/darkness knows.
Rainy Season Love Song. Gladys May Casely Hayford. CDC

...Is there someone/you would like to invite no one. Christmas Eve. Bill
Berkson. ANYP

Is there something finished? And some new beginning on the/way? Falltime.
Carl Sandburg. PoA

Is this a life? Nay, death you may it call,/That feels each pain and knows no
joy at all. Death in Life. Thomas, Lord Vaux. OBSC

Is this, baby, what you were born to feel, and do, and be? American
Rhapsody. Kenneth Fearing. MoAmPo

Is this faire excusing? O no, all is abusing. Though Your Strangenesse Frets
My Hart. Thomas Campion. AAS

Is this home/There's fog over the harbor/And I can't see Not That Far.
May Miller. BlSi

Is this my hand in yours? Am I/So close? Wait till the insinuant wind's gone
by... Spring Air. Gene Derwood. FaFP; LiTL

Is this my mother/this rain wind touch of sound? Hanabi-ko. Wendy Rose.
TWSS

Is this not too a temple,/A Holy Place? Gentlemen. Geoffrey Taylor.
FaBoEE

Is this the dream that wakes us? It Comes during Sleep. Philip Dow.
NPGG

Is this the object, end and law,/And purpose of our being here? To Spend
Uncounted Years of Pain. Arthur Hugh Clough. NOBV; OBNC; OBSP;
WeW

Is this what you meant by "waves", Li Po? On the Subject of Waves...
Eldon Grier. PeCV

...Is to be nibbled/to death by small fish. Haiku: "To write too many."
Robert Phillips. GrPl

Is to call yourself "Doctor," and so be allowed/To specialize only on Man.
The Vet. Guy Boas. BoAnP

Is to-day official sinning,/And shall be for evermore! A General Summary.
Rudyard Kipling. HBV 1-2

Is to have another baby/while the real one dies. The 29th Month. Stan
Rice. NPGG

Is to keep that beloved's other face/clasped in your hands. Saddle and Cell.
The Three (Maria Isabel Barreno and Maria Teresa Horta and Maria Velho
da Costa) Marias. BoWoP

Is to see that we grow Nearer the sky. A Little Song of Life. Lizette
Woodworth Reese. BrR; GoTF; HBMV; OBCA; TiPo; TreFT

Is to take a dip from the side of a ship, in the trough of the rolling/sea.
Pater's Bathe. Edward Abbott Parry. OxBChV

Is tremulous, half dead with fright. The Tiger Stalking in the Night.
Edward Newman Horn. ELU

Is up and about, as is her custom,/drunk with child. The Vestal Lady on
Brattle. Gregory Corso. NoAm

Is vast creation's deathless theme. Long as the Darkening Cloud Abode.
George Richards. AH

Is wakeful for its melting images. Olive Grove. James Merrill. NePoAm

Is walking away in his/father's hands in the form/of four sticks. The Place
of V. Ray A. Young Bear. VoR

Is warm under Maisie's bedcover? Evening Star. George Barker. ELU;
ErPo; PoCh

Is what I've been always wanting. My Death. A. J. M. Smith. OBCV

Is what to make of a diminished thing. The Oven Bird. Robert Frost.
AP; AWP; CoBMV; CrMA; ForPo; HeIP; InPo; MAPA; NoAm; NOBA;
NoP; OxBA; PPP; TAP; UnS

Is when some heart indignant breaks,/To show that still she lives. The Harp
That Once through Tara's Halls. Thomas Moore. ACP; AnIL; BLPL;
EnRP; FaPoR; FSW; GN; OAEP; OBNC; OnYI; OxBI; PG; PoLf; RoGo;
TreF; ViBoPo

Is with me at thy farewell, joyous Bark! Sonnet: Where Lies the Land.
William Wordsworth. ChRP

Is woman giving as she loves. Turn of the Moon. Robert Graves. BoC;
TEP

Is won with flesh, not drapery. Clothes Do But Cheat and Cozen Us.
Robert Herrick. ALV; CaPo

Is worth an age without a name. Epigram: "Sound, sound the clarion, fill the
fife! Sir Walter Scott. FaBoEE

Is worth enough to soil this word or mar this world. Definition. Edwin
Rolfe. NAMP

Is woxen so deformed, that he has quight/Forgot he was a man, and Gealosie
is hight. The Faerie Queene. Edmund Spenser. NoP

Iscariot washes the Bridegroom's feet,/And dries them with his hair. Judas
Iscariot. Robert Williams Buchanan. OBVV; OxBoCh

Ise bound to leave this world. Hard Trials. Anonymous. ABF

Isis and Orus, and the dog Anubis haste. Hymn on the Morning of Christ's
Nativity. John Milton. WHA

An island in dishonored grass,/Whom none but daisies know. Of bronze and
blaze. Emily Dickinson. MAmP; MAPA; MoPo

Islanders too who of necessity/made disconnectedness a daily act. Trader's
Return. Sylvia Lawson. PoAu 1-2

Islands of night against their downward/drift. Island of Night. Galway
Kinnell. NePoAm

Isle of Man is the true explanation. Limerick: "There was a young lady of
station." Lewis (Charles Lutwidge Dodgson) Carroll. CenHV; FaBoNo

ISLITTLEFUN. A Cubic Triolet. Anonymous. PV

Isn't all the truth I've told ye,/Lots of fun at Finigan's wake? Finigan's
Wake. Anonymous. BLPA

Isn't it a blooming shame?' Poor but Honest. Anonymous. NLV; OxBoLi

"Isn't it a lovely day?" The Shopman. Eleanor Farjeon. HBVY

Isn't it an oppressive spring! I told you: Don't smoke. On the Hazards of
Smoking. Leah Goldberg. AMV-81

Isn't it better have luck than gold?/As the man long ago said. The Tramp's
Song. Mary Devenport O'Neill. AnIV

Isn't it delicious/To be a birthday child? The Birthday Child. Rose
Fyleman. BiCB; SiSoSe

Isn't it strange/how being near you/makes/me/happy too? Janna. King D.
Kuka. VoR

Isn't mamacita's heart going to/kiss mom/good night/no/no/no. Mom I'm
All Screwed Up. Frank Lima. ANYP

Isn't that a mighty storm/That blew the people away! Wasn't That a Mighty
Storm? Anonymous. AmFP

Isn't that juist like oor Scottish weather! The Day of the Crucifixion.
Hugh" (Christopher Murray Grieve) MacDiarmid. PV

Isn't there the child, beneath the presents/We heap upon him, that we are
fond of? Christmas Tree. Stanley Cook. OBCP

"Isola d'oro! Fior di Levante!" Sonnet–To Zante. Edgar Allan Poe.
MAmP

...The isolate, slow faults/That kill, that kill, that kill. Elm. Sylvia Plath.
NoAm

Israel glowed that day, God's Ten/Commandments receiving. Precepts He
Gave His Folk. Elijah Hazaken. TrJP

It added lustre to the view/Of Mr. Rockefeller, too. Mr. Rockefeller's Hat.
Helen Bevington. OBAL

It admitted no final/solution the ambiguity/they called my will. Construction
13. Judith Johnson Sherwin. NoAm

It ain't no fine for you/Get ready for the electric chair My Crime.
Barefoot Bill. BluL

It all happened just this way/In truth and in a Breton lay. The Two Lovers.
Marie de France. BoWoP

It also gives its length and breadth/And what's the price of coal. Scientific
Proof. James W. Foley. QQQ

It and its increase, and the crown and dignity thereof!' Congal: The Land Is
Ours. Sir Samuel Ferguson. IrPN

It appears the gift could not be refused.   In Dispraise of Poetry.   Jack Gilbert.   PP

...It, at least,/Knows exactly why it laughs.   The Laughing Hyena, by Hokusai.   D. J. Enright.   MP; TwCP

It be a Temple, but without a Saint.   Loves End.   Edward, Lord Herbert of Cherbury.   AnAnS 2; SeCP

"An it be true that Lillie's dead,/The sun shall nae mair shine on me."   Earl Crawford.   Anonymous.   BaBo; ESPB

It bears all away.   Lover's Reply to Good Advice.   Richard Hughes. MoBrPo

It beat the shapes of harps into the air.   Shopping for Meat in Winter. Oscar Williams.   LiTM; NePA

"It beats–God knows for whom!"   The Beating Heart.   Heinrich Heine. UnTE

It beats me. I feel it done to me, and ache.   Carmina.   Caius Valerius Catullus.   OBVE

It became mine too.   I Came to the New World Empty-Handed.   Hildegarde Hoyt Swift.   AmFN

It becomes cold and hardened/and only slightly shrunken.   The palm of my hand.   Fumi Saito.   BoWoP

...It begins where we are.   The "Portland" Going Out.   William Stanley Merwin.   NYBP

It behooves us/Yah, to do/What Yatu, Du/Craved for.   The Chisizas I. Guy C. Z. Mhone.   WhB

...It blesses/as it moves toward your own.   Conversation with God.   Jeanine Hathaway.   AMV-80

It blows like a spouting whale.   Song: The Railway Train.   Anonymous. NOAV

It boots me not that for my wrath I should disturb the same.'   Of a Lady That Refused to Dance with Him.   Henry Howard, Earl of Surrey.   SiPS

It bottoms ups.   The Duck.   Ogden Nash.   MoShBr

It braks like Fate throu Time's wanchancy reek.   Haar in Princes Street. Alexander Scott.   BSV

It breaks my bliss,–it breaks my heart.   The Day Returns.   Robert Burns. HBV 1-2

It brings the Glory that all men may share.   Pentecost.   John Bennett. EBCP

It broke about even, made no sense.   As in Their Time.   Louis MacNeice. PoL

It broke, and I emit one final fart.   Epitaph for G. B. Shaw.   Max Beerbohm.   FaBoEE

It brought me back my Mary's grave, the moon behind the hill.   The Moon behind the Hill.   Anonymous.   WTO

It buds and blows,/Delightful fragrance breathing.   I Know a Flower So Fair and Fine.   Nicolai Grundtvig.   AH

It burns the breasts of those who drink it and sends their souls to hell.   The Rowan County Crew (Tolliver-Martin Feud Song).   Anonymous.   AmFP; OuSiCo

It burns the thing/inside it. And that thing/screams.   An Agony. As Now. LeRoi (Imamu Amiri Baraka) Jones.   AmPP; BALP; BPo; LiTM; PPP

It burrowed back with never a sound,/And awoke the thaw.   Immortal. Mark Van Doren.   MoAmPo

It came from nowhere,/luckily for you.   Have you heard? The troubles of the road.   Sulpicia.   BoWoP

It can blame this limitless trait in the hearts of men.   There Are Roughly Zones.   Robert Frost.   CMoP; PPP

It can endure and suffer much.   The Hem of His Garment.   Anna E. Hamilton.   TrPWD

It can kill a man.   Poetry Is a Destructive Force.   Wallace Stevens.   OxBA

It can never be satisfied, the mind, never.   The Well Dressed Man with a Beard.   Wallace Stevens.   BiP

It can never be so clear again.   Home in Indianapolis.   Richard Pflum. AMV-80

It can never fly from you.   A Riddle: The Vowels.   Jonathan Swift.   GN

...It can only be the end/of the world ahead.   Childhood, IV.   Arthur Rimbaud.   PoPl

It can't be done.   Man, I Felt Like Running All Night.   Salomon R., Jr. Baldenegro.   FIA

It cannot be all you assert of it.'/And obviously...   In Memoriam James Joyce (excerpt).   Hugh" (Christopher Murray Grieve) MacDiarmid.   FaBoPV

It cannot be nothing else.   The Man with the Blue Guitar.   Wallace Stevens. CMoP

It cannot be/That I am he/On whom thy tempests fell all night.   Who Would Have Thought?   George Herbert.   EG

It cannot go into the fever: you cannot go down to the Spring.   You Cannot Go down to the Spring.   Shaw Neilson.   CBAP

It carries me with it,/so I shake with joy.   A Woman Shaman's Song. Uvavnuk.   WPOW

It carries your memory effortless–/like a sure thing.   Victorian Grandmother. Margo Lockwood.   Psk

It caught his image as he flew.   L'Oiseau Bleu.   Mary Elizabeth Coleridge. CH

An' it caused me to leave my happy home.   Prison Moan.   Anonymous. OuSiCo

It centres, Mary, still with thee.   What Is Love?   John Clare.   NCEP

It chokes the nostrils of cowards.   Six Sunday.   Hart Leroi Bibbs.   NBP

It christens and blinds.   The First Test.   Susan Fromberg Schaeffer.   IHMS

It comes at last to cancel time,/And waken unavailing tears.   What Winter Floods, What Showers of Spring.   Emily Bronte.   NOBV

It comes from Pompi, the round-house, from Kgobola-diatla.   The Train. Anonymous.   TTY

It comes incarnate rarely to the rare.   The Tapestry,   Stefan George. LiTW

It comes off the bow gravely,/Rephrases itself into the air.   The Given Note. Seamus Heaney.   FaBoIP; NCSH

It comes to a point. It comes and it goes.   Skins (excerpt).   Charles Wright. HaCAP

It comes to let one know/Of what has had an end.   To My Infant Daughter (II).   Yvor Winters.   VGW

It comes together like a fan.   The Cornfield.   Elizabeth Madox Roberts. GoJo; SUS

It comforted him.   The Life of Lincoln West.   Gwendolyn Brooks.   FB

It commands vacancy.   More Foreign Cities.   Charles Tomlinson. NePoEA-2

It conquers all men, like her,/And still for a Union flies.   The Rejected "National Hymns".   Robert Henry Newell.   InMe

It cost the king ten thousand pounds/to have a dash at Stonington.   The Battle of Stonington on the Seaboard of Connecticut.   Philip Freneau. PAH

It costs thee more in whips than hay.   Epigram: "Thy nags (the leanest things alive)."   Matthew Prior.   FaBoEE

It could be happening to you.   Get Up.   Philip Levine.   NYP

...It could be thought,/ours the older world.   A Quality of Air.   Henry Chapin.   FAZ

It could hardly be otherwise.   The Man Who Finds That His Son Has Become a Thief.   Raymond Souster.   NOBC; OBCV

It couldn't help/itself.   Close-Up.   Archie Randolph Ammons.   PoA

It covers the windows, her eyes.   Sleeping Beauty.   Laurie Sheck.   DFT

...It cries/as it circles, away out from Port Bradshaw.   The Djanggawul Cycle, 11.   Anonymous.   WTO

It cries in my ears and it urges my heart/To the path of the whale and the plunging sea.   The Seafarer.   Anonymous.   AnOE; EtS; MOS

It curves in a rush to the heart of the vast/Flower: the day has begun. Bombardment.   D. H. Lawrence.   MMM

It cut him–it cut him in two!   Limerick: "A railway official at Crewe." Anonymous.   TDH

It'd have been just too bad,/If he had.   Massenet/Never wrote a Mass in A. Antony Butts.   FiBHP

It dawns! It dawns!   Magpie Song.   Anonymous.   OBVE

It depends on us.   Us.   Jiri Wyatt.   LTB

It did not condemn–   The Bible is an antique volume.   Emily Dickinson. NoP

It didn't have CANDLES on top of it!   Un-Birthday Cake.   Aileen Fisher. BiCB

It does not even hate me with its eyes.   The Caged Bird.   Arthur Symons. BrPo

It does not mean/A single thing.   Blum.   Dorothy Aldis.   MoShBr

It does not scatter the heart,/but gathers the branches tenderly/into a slender, dark woman.   The Blood-Letting.   Joy Harjo.   TWSS

It doesn't become you/to refuse Buthayna, O Jamil.   Shall I Come There, or You Here?   Hafsa bint al-Hajj.   WPOW

It doesn't look so bad.   Up & out.   Nila NorthSun.   STE

...It doesn't mean I'm petty and it doesn't mean I want to/get caught.   Think Small.   Elaine Equi.   APU

It don't do/to wake up/quick...   The Alarm Clock.   Mari E. Evans.   BOLo

It don't hurt no more.   Tricked Again.   Ridhiana.   NBP

It don't seem to me like we're getting anywheres at all.   A Communication to Nancy Cunard.   Kay Boyle.   NMM; PoNe

It don't snow like that no more. Too bad.   Lester Tells of Wanda and the Big Snow.   Paul Zimmer.   FAZ

It doth suffice she doth me wrong.   Spite hath no power to make me sad. Sir Thomas Wyatt.   FCP; SiPS

..."It draws more near/Daily; and here shall it be in the end–or here?"   A Dream.   Charles Williams.   OBEV

It drowned in blood that amber-coloured skin.   The Jewels.   Charles Baudelaire.   BoLoP; ErPo

It dwindles in the west.   Aeroplane.   Pudjipangu.   NOAV

It [The wood] is a stranger from Bralgu, from the source of the/Star's shine. The Djanggawul Cycle, 10.   Anonymous.   WTO

It ends with a gasp.   Stormpetrel.   Richard Murphy.   IPY

It ends with skies and wings.   Our History.   Catherine Cate Coblentz.   BrR

...It/Enthralled me, Don Quixote.   How to Tell Juan Don from Another. Gardner E. Lewis.   FiBHP

It exposes each silk thread and rumple in the carpet.   Out of the Sea, Early.   May Swenson.   RFM

It fades, and the wounds of all we had accepted open.   The Homecoming of Emma Lazarus.   Galway Kinnell.   NaP

It faints and withers, and is done.   Evening Primrose.   John Clare.   TrGrPo

It fairly makes my blood run co-o-old.   Calliope (with music).   *Anonymous.*   AS

It falls and, falling, feels how terror chokes/The gullet, throttling, with two iron fists.   Famine.   Georg Heym.   LiTW

It falls and riseth quite beside my reach.   The Author, of His Own Fortune.   Sir John (1561-1612) Harington.   FaBoEE

It fill the sky to beat on an airy shell.   Bell Tower.   Léonie Adams.   AmLP; MoAB; MoAmPo; PoPl

It fills/The darkening room with light.   Where the Slow Fig's Purple Sloth.   Robert Penn Warren.   NoP

It finds him walking in his sleep again/balanced on his supplicating hands.   The Blind Man.   James Lewisohn.   LFAC

It finds no rest on earth, makes no abode,/In any Object, but his heav'n, his God.   On the Needle of a Sun-Dial.   Francis Quarles.   OBS; TrGrPo

..It flows/through the city of America/without fish.   Detroit.   Donald Hall.   AmFN

...It foams beryl green/in the sunset, and at every bend, leaves something behind.   Steps.   Roberta Hill.   VoR

It forbids us to approach it.   Le Musee Imaginaire.   Charles Tomlinson.   NePoEA-2

It fucking gets you fucking down/evidently chicken town.   Evidently Chicken Town.   John Cooper Clarke.   FaBoPV

It garris him oft-tymes leif foly,/And all murning of musardy.   Prologue to the Avowis of Alexander.   John Barbour.   OxBS

It gave them something to write about.   Success Story.   Bruce Bennett.   LTB

It gets harder to love/the things/you kill.   The Fish Come in Dancing.   Kevin Roberts.   WOLT

It gets late. But we make a mistake/in thinking it late for others.   The New Formalists.   Marvin Bell.   AMV-81

It gives a light to every age-/It gives, but borrows none.   The Spirit's Light.   William Cowper.   BLRP

It gives a lovely light!   First Fig.   Edna St Vincent Millay.   AmP; FaBoWP; FaBV; FaFP; FF; FPL; NoAm; NoP; PoLf; TAP

It gives, but borrows none.   The Light and Glory of the World.   William Cowper.   TRV

...It gives me something/to look forward to.   Finding You.   Virginia Gilbert.   IHMS

It gives me the impression of meeting/An unknown old gentleman.   When.   Hitomaro.   AWP

It gives no pleasure–learn it now or later–/To be on heat in the incinerafor.   To His Coy Mistress (parody).   W. J. Webster.   BXAP

It gives such divine materials to men, and accepts such/leavings from them at last.   This Compost.   Walt Whitman.   AWP; CABA; LiTA; MAmP; MoAmPo

It gives tho' bound, tho' bound 'tis free!   Christ Crucified.   Richard Crashaw.   GoBC; OBEV

It goads me, like the Goblin Bee–/That will not state–its sting.   If You Were Coming in the Fall.   Emily Dickinson.   AmePo; DiPo; LaNeLa; NOBA; OxBA; PoRA

It goes on ending/toward another/new ending.   Removal: Last Part.   Carroll Arnett.   VoR

It gots to beeeEEE, yeah. yeah. yeah.   Don't Wanna Be.   Sonia Sanchez.   CNA

It grieved him a damned sight more./With a fa la la la la la la...   The Greenland Whale.   *Anonymous.*   GBP

...It/grows extinct,/is not.   The Beach.   Robert Peters.   GP

It had better be soon.   Time's Mutability.   Bertolt Brecht.   ELU

It had my eyes and my hair.   The Pear-Tree.   Mary Gilmore.   PoAu 1-2

It had not done so then, and could not now.   Love Songs in Age.   Philip Larkin.   PPP

It had spots. And the little/hooves were soft and white.   Two Fawns That Didn't See the Light This Spring.   Gary Snyder.   HaCAP

It had turn'd wonder to Idolatry.   To the Right Honourable the Countesse of C.   William Habington.   AnAnS 2; SeCP

It happens over and over, me in/your body and you/in mine.   Together.   Maxine W. Kumin.   BoWoP; NMM

It hardly now enjoys a greater rest.   A Quiet Soul.   John Oldham.   OBEV

It has a mouth, but never eats.   Riddle: "Runs all day and never walks."   Mother Goose.   TiPo

It has become meat.   Transubstantiation.   Gary Geddes.   NOBC

It has been accomplished.   View by Color Photography on a Commercial Calendar.   William Carlos Williams.   LCAP

It has been aching many a day with measures/full of sadness!   Sing On, Blithe Bird!   William Motherwell.   GN; HBV 1-2; HBVY

It has been months, in spite of how the wind/Has beaten its dumb drum.   The Mill.   John Taylor.   FAZ

It has begun to snow.   Around the Rough and Rugged Rocks the Ragged Rascal Rudely Ran.   John Ashbery.   InPS

It has brought its flute it is a long way.   Dusk in Winter.   William Stanley Merwin.   NaP

It has done its work–I toss it carelessly to fall where/it may.   Spontaneous Me.   Walt Whitman.   OxBA

It has grown, it is/hungrier than ever   Feeding the Fire.   Donald Finkel.   VWA

It has its palace as it had before.   Onion Skin in Barn.   Kenneth Slade Alling.   NePoAm

It has itself the old disease of thought.   Out of Doors.   Walter Conrad Arensberg.   AnAmPo

...It has never been confined to one locality.   England.   Marianne Moore.   CrMA; FaBoWP; LiTA; MoAB; MoAmPo

It has to stop obligingly/If you but raise your hand.   B's the Bus.   Phyllis McGinley.   SoPo; TiPo

It has two horns, an' a hantle o' feet,/An' a forkie Tailie.   The Horny-Goloch.   *Anonymous.*   AmMo; FaBoCh

It has woven its simple nest among my bones.   The Defeated.   William Stanley Merwin.   AmPC

It hasn't happened often.   Not Often.   Ray Fraser.   NeAC

It hath made the whole day sweet.   Wild Eden.   George Edward Woodberry.   AA

It haunts me as it haunted then,/A flash from fire of hellbound men.   A Casual Song.   Roden Noel.   HBV 1-2

It held the heavens, shores, waters and all their brood.   The Swan.   W. R. Rodgers.   NeBP; NMP; NoAm

It hides from the eagle, and joins with the dove:/In beautiful green solitude.   Evening.   John Clare.   NOBV; VLP

It hurries down to wither on the strand.   Memory.   Walter Savage Landor.   EBEV; NOBV; OAEL 1-2

It hurts my pride.   Take This Hammer.   *Anonymous.*   FSW; OuSiCo

It hurts the health, it makes bad breath,'/Said Little Robert Reid.   I'll Never Use Tobacco.   *Anonymous.*   FaBoUs

It hurts to explain the reason/Grandma didn't snore.   Eclipse.   William Carson Fagg.   LFAC

It indicates the Whelk is out.   The Elk. The Whelk.   Robert Williams Wood.   NLV

It is a beacon ever lit/By One identified with it.   The Cross.   Charles Nelson Pace.   BePJ; BLRP

It is a Being of warmth I think; at heart/A house of mercy.   A House of Mercy.   Stevie Smith.   FaBoWP

It is a blast of light/from a full moon/that grips me in/this tiny room tonight.   Moon Blast.   Michelle Roberts.   LFAC

It is a blood red ruby/in a naked belly of gold.   Buddha.   Arno Holz.   AWP

It is a British soldier, armed for war!   The Horse and His Rider.   Joanna Baillie.   NOEC

It is a Christ drained of all blood.   Gothic Landscape.   Irving Layton.   TrJP

It is a comfort that the Sphinx took such an answer.   Four Legs, Two Legs, Three Legs.   William Empson.   MoPo

It is a corpse; or dust; a shadow; naught.   To Her Portrait.   Sister Juana Ines de la Cruz.   LiTW

It is a design.   The Orchestra.   William Carlos Williams.   HAP

It is a false spring this year.   Private Pain in Time of Trouble.   Kathleen Spivack.   AmPA

It is a flower. On this mountainside it is dying.   Flower Herding on Mount Monadnock.   Galway Kinnell.   ConAP; HeIP; LCAP; NaP; NOBA

It is a ghaist that walks the hoose/And casts its shadow on the wa'.   Nocht o' Mortal Sicht.   Bessie J. B. Macarthur.   OxBS

It is a gift/Which I am no longer afraid/to open.   Poverty.   Charles Simic.   MAT

It is a great day.   Today Is a Day of Great Joy.   Victor Hernandez Cruz.   TTY

It is a happy thing, I say,/To be alive on such a day.   April Showers.   James Stephens.   TiPo

...It is/a head from another century, the last one or the next.   Baudelaire Series (excerpt).   Michael Palmer.   APU

It is a known spot on an unknown star.   Scene with Figure.   Babette Deutsch.   TrJP

It is a land of poverty!   Is This a Holy Thing to See.   William Blake.   SCV

It is a lily-light she bears/For England up the ladder-stairs.   Jump-to-Glory Jane.   George Meredith.   VLP

It is a night passage/for WE/who know this.   Owl.   Rokwaho.   STE

It is a pain that most I rue.   Is It Not Sure a Deadly Pain.   *Anonymous.*   CBEP; EnLoPo

It is a praise to praise, when thou art prais'd.   Astrophel and Stella, XXXV.   Sir Philip Sidney.   AAS; CABA; SiPS

It is a sound/Cain will remember/till he dies   Cain's Song.   Donald Finkel.   VWA

...It is a tale/Told by an idiot, full of sound and fury,/Signifying nothing.   Macbeth.   William Shakespeare.   LiTB; PG; TreF; TRV

It is a time of water, a time of trees.   Three Green Windows.   Anne Sexton.   NYBP

It is a trap to catch us two.   Traps.   Mary Carolyn Davies.   HBMV

It is a trick/anyone can learn.   The Magician.   Gary Miranda.   SM

It is a vain matter about which I ask.   Who Will Buy a Poem?   Mahon O'Heffernan.   AnIL

It is a very/Zen/experience / this death   La Misere (parody).   Philip Appleman.   BXAP

It is a wasting zeal and, well observed,/is corpse, is dust, is shade, is nothingness.   She Attempts to Refute the Praises That Truth...   Sister Juana Ines de la Cruz.   BoWoP

It is a witty madness, or mad wit.   This Definition Poetry Doth Fit.   Thomas Randolph.   FaBoEE

It is a year to-day that thou art gone.'   La Vita Nuova.   Dante Alighieri.   AWP

It is about to die.   Upon a Dying Lady.   William Butler Yeats.   UnPo

It is again ourselves that we defeat.   Defeat.   Witter ("Emanuel Morgan") Bynner.   PoNe

It is all beauty, perilous and grave–/It is not you.   Infidelity.   Louis Untermeyer.   TrJP

It is all I have. I give it all to you. Yours,   Letter.   Mark Strand.   NoAm

It is all in vain that I ask.   I Ask, Who Will Buy a Poem?   Mathghamhain O Hifearnain.   NOBI

...It is all right, you can come/out now, god is sorry about the wrong wrapper.   Errore.   Pier Giorgio Di Cicco.   NOBC

...It/is all shit/for the flowers anyhow.   Poem: "What's the balm."   Alan Dugan.   CAPP; SM

It is almost easy/to keep going.   Night Fishing.   Greg Kuzma.   WOLT

It is also good to be poor, and listen to the wind.   Poem against the British.   Robert Bly.   ConAP; PAI

...It is always/A god being crucified.   Compulsive Qualifications (excerpt).   Richard Howard.   PoA

It is always heavier than you thought.   November.   Margaret Atwood.   NOBC

It is always modern times.   Always Modern Times.   Bradford Stark.   LTB

It is an ample fame.   Rome.   Thomas Hardy.   EnLi 1-2; MoAB

It is an army blanket and the sleeper/slept too near the fire.   Broken Sky.   Carl Sandburg.   PCP

It is an ill wind turns none to good.   The Winds.   Thomas Tusser.   WiR

It is an interesting/place to begin in.   At Kirk Yetholm.   Dave Calder.   PoSH

It is, as I am, sir, yours, very truly.   Another Letter to Lord Byron.   David R. Slavitt.   SM

It is as if I have come to an open window.   How.   S. J. Marks.   NYBP

It is as if you had never been.   As If You Had Never Been.   Richard Eberhart.   EyDe

It is at the corner of the terrace where the pot/of the tulsi plant stands.   Fairyland.   Rabindranath Tagore.   WSC

It is because I hear a man climb stairs/and clear his throat outside our door.   Poem: "I heard of a man."   Leonard Cohen.   ELU

It is best so, sith so it was to be.   Dialogue: Lover and Lady.   Ciullo d'Alcamo.   AWP

It is boundless! Love.   Immanuel Di Roma.   TrJP

It is bright as a garden,/and with no fence around it!   An Ivied Tree-Top.   Anonymous.   NOBI

It is building music.   Then.   Muriel Rukeyser.   LCAP

It is but for an hour," said the Spirit.   This Corruptible.   Elinor Wylie.   AnFE; CoAnAm; MoAB; MoAmPo; MoRP

"It is, but hadn't ought to be."   Mrs. Judge Jenkins.   Bret (Francis Bret Harte) Harte.   BXAP; CABA; FiBHP; HBV 1-2

...It is but lost time to/converse with you whose works are only Analytics.   The Marriage of Heaven and Hell.   William Blake.   NU

It is but that my soul is sighing,/To go and rest with thee.   Stanzas.   Emily Bronte.   LoBV

...It is calm seas/bring the sharp warriors from the North.   The Wind Is Wild Tonight.   Anonymous.   NOBI

It is Captain Mansfield of Bristol town,/And the Marigold a ship of fame.   Captain Mansfield's Fight with the Turks at Sea.   Anonymous.   OBSS

It is Christ with His Cross, conqueror of Christdom.   The Vision of Piers Plowman.   William Langland.   CAW

It is cold, and there is no mail service.   Reflections.   David R. Pichaske.   AMV-80

It is creation's morning–/Now is the world begun.   Now.   Harriet Monroe.   HBV 1-2

It is cruel and hard to be real.   Ellora.   Leonard Nathan.   GP

It is daybreak everywhere.   The Bells of San Blas.   Henry Wadsworth Longfellow.   AmP; OxBA

It is Dewey's glory to-day, as Nelson's/A hundred years ago!   A Ballad of Manila Bay.   Sir Charles G. D. Roberts.   PAH

It is done.   Dayak Man Making Fishtrap.   Carol Rubenstein.   WOLT

It is done: they are asleep.   The Djanggawul Cycle, 174.   Anonymous.   WTO

It is enough and as good as a feast.   Gascoigne's Memories.   George Gascoigne.   EnRePo

...It is enough/if present faith mend partial proof.   Enough.   Marianne Moore.   NOBA

It is excellent weather for a holiday.   The Unwilling Guest: An Urban Dialogue.   Horace Gregory.   CrMA

It is far from just between us.   It Is Far from Just between Us.   Anonymous.   NOBI

It is Fear, not Death that slays.   Epitaphs of the War, 1914-18.   Rudyard Kipling.   BrPo; OBWP

...It is filled/with presences. He says, I am.   A Solitude.   Denise Levertov.   NePoEA-2

It is fitting that you be here.   On Seeing Two Brown Boys in a Catholic Church.   Frank Horne.   BANP; CDC; PoBA; PoNe; TTY

It is flowing, ever flowing, further down.   Song of the Artesian Water.   Andrew Barton ("Banjo") Paterson.   ACV

It is for beauty only.   Yucca Is Yellowing.   William Haskel Simpson.   BPAW

..."It is for ever/washing the substance of the land into the sea."   Rain.   Anselm Hollo.   PoM

"It is for the Lord of Liddesdale/That I let all these teares downe fall."   The Knight of Liddesdale.   Anonymous.   ESPB

It is for youth the meetest play.   Youth.   Anonymous.   OBSC

It is four times as big as the bush!   Limerick: "There was an Old Man who said, "Hush!"   Edward Lear.   FaBoCo; GoJo; HBV 1-2; NA; NBM; NOBL; OxBChV; OxBoLi; TEP

It is God body and no mo.   The Sacrament of the Altar.   Anonymous.   MeEL

It is God's victory! Independence.   Anonymous.   WTO

It is going to be a good dance.   Tiger People.   Geary Hobson.   STE

It is good to descend, to rake in the remnants of honey/and the white milk–in the final place.   On the Pole.   Uri Z. Greenberg.   VWA

It is good we have the Old Repair Man.   The Old Repair Man.   Fenton Johnson.   AmNP

It is hard as diamonds; it wants to destroy us all.   The Unbeliever.   Elizabeth Bishop.   LiTA; NoAm

It is hard to guess.   Guessing.   Anonymous.   PBWP

It is her laughter on the slopes/at night.   Hyena.   Carol Muske.   AmPA

It is his singing/Outshines the noise/Of leaves clashing in the wind.   Metric Figure.   William Carlos Williams.   MoAmPo

"It is I, be not afraid!"   It Is I, Be Not Afraid.   A.B. Simpson.   BePJ; STF

It is I who am the lonely one/In Inse Carriganane.   Dirge on the Death of Art O'Leary.   Anonymous.   AnIV

It is in Danny's life and runs in the blood of him...a lean gray-ghost/car.   Portrait of a Motorcar.   Carl Sandburg.   AmC

It is in giving, not in getting,/our lives are blest.   Success.   Anonymous.   PoToHe

It is in the Winter that we dream of Spring.   It Is in the Winter That We Dream of Spring.   Robert Burns Wilson.   AA; AmLP

It is Isis the mystery/Must be in love with me.   Don Juan.   D. H. Lawrence.   PoA

It is July.   July.   Susan Hartley Swett.   GN

It is like a jagged stone/Flying toward them out of the darkness.   Romans Angry about the Inner World.   Robert Bly.   NoAm; NOBA; PPoe

...It is/like himself, only visible.   The Three Movements.   Donald Hall.   NePoEA-2

...It is like the wind–nor is it quite like the/wind–but more powerful.   The Story of a Well-Made Shield.   N. Scott Momaday.   CDW; GrPl

...It is/made of stone, round, and very ugly.   Audubon, Drafted.   LeRoi (Imamu Amiri Baraka) Jones.   PPP; TTY

It is Margaret you mourn for.   Spring and Fall.   Gerard Manley Hopkins.   AnFE; BiP; BrPo; CMoP; DiPo; EBEV; ELP; ExPo; FaBoUs; FF; GoJo; GTBS-P; HAP; HeIP; HoPM; InPS; LiTB; LiTM; MAT; MoAB; MoPo; MoVE; NIP; NOBE; NoP; OAEP; PAI; PoEL 1-5; PoPl; PoPle; PoRA; PPoe; PPON; PPP; SCV; SeCeV; SOTW; TEP; VLP; WeW

It is May, and the conceited cuckoo toots and whoots his name.   Larches.   Ivor Gurney.   FaBoPP

It is monstrous/and does not die.   Poem of Pathos.   Tadeusz Rozewicz.   FaBoPV

It is more/than enough.   Enough!   James Scully.   LTB

It is morning now. The light whitens her face more than ever.)   The Chorus Speaks Her Words as She Dances.   Linda Gregg.   NPGG

It is most pleasing for a chap/To bounce his Aunt upon his lap!   My Aunt.   Peggy Wood.   PoL

It is much too late.   My Mother on an Evening in Late Summer.   Mark Strand.   FYAP; GeTw

It is my father who keeps stumbling/Behind me, and will not go away. Follower. Seamus Heaney. FaBoIP; IPY

It is my fist you hear/Beating against your ear. The Distant Drum. Calvin C. Hernton. BOLo; CTBA; FF; NNP; TTY

It is my heart that makes my songs, not I. What Do I Care. Sara Teasdale. VGW

It is my helth eke and my sore. What Wourde Is That That Chaungeth Not. Sir Thomas Wyatt. AAS

...It is my/mother. Looking at a Dry Canadian Thistle Brought in from the Snow. Robert Bly. NNaP

It is my right: I stand here in your stead. Before Sentence Is Passed. Richard P. Blackmur. LiTA

It is my spirit that kisses your mouth lightly. Canoe. Keith Douglas. NeBP

It is my victory over meanness. Your Animal. Gerald Stern. AMV-81

It is night & already there are stars. Witness. Jon Anderson. MAYP

It is no Armour for the heart. Song: "Ladies, though to your Conqu'ring eyes." Sir George Etherege. HBV 1-2; OBS; OBSP

It is no fault of mine! Dream Land. Frances Anne Kemble. OBVV

It is no wonder & it was/in good taste too. Fifteenth Raga/for Bela Lugosi. David Meltzer. NeAP

It is noontide, and the fishes leap in the pool. By Loe Pool. Arthur Symons. VLP

It is not a taunt. Settling In. Floyd C. Stuart. TAT

It is not always from devotion. On the Use of Jayshus. Oliver St. John Gogarty. FaBoEE

It is not easy to adjust/The body to a severed head. The Submarine Bed. John Peale Bishop. LiTA

It is not from human grief, or any other. The Will to Live. Mekeel McBride. MAYP

It is not good/For water/To be so still that way. Sea Calm. Langston Hughes. LOW

It is not gunfire I hear but a hunting horn. Aristocrats. Keith Douglas. FaBoMo; NePoEA; OBWP

It is not heresy, but reformation. When Doctrines Meet with General Approbation. David Garrick. HBV 1-2

It is not I, ever or now. The Pebble. Elinor Wylie. MoAmPo; MoRP

It is not like a lawyer serving a writ Epigram: "Some people admire the work of a Fool." William Blake. OAEL 1-2

It is not manna/falls on them from these livid clouds. Twilight at the Zoo. Alex Rodger. NCSH

It is not meant for you. Herman Moon's Hourbook. Christopher Middleton. NePoEA-2

It is not mine. Heliodore. Andrew Lang. OBVV

It is not necessary any more. Stanzas in Meditation. Gertrude Stein. PBWP

It is not pain we fear, but triviality. 3 A. M. Lauris Edmond. OCNZ

It is not safe to walk on the sand or through the trees. Collaboration. Tony Towle. ANYP

It is not she! We Poets Speak. Francis Thompson. FaBV

It is not the key alone that can throw open the gate. The Walker. Arturo Giovannitti. AnAmPo

It is not the ones left that are keeping me going/But the new ones they are making me do.' The Old Munro Bagger. Anonymous. PoSH

It is not the plunder,/but "accessibility to experience." New York. Marianne Moore. NYP

(It is not the stuff of poetry.) Diary. The Deer Break Their Horns. Charlotte De Clue. TWSS

It is not they who give the life, it is you who give the life. The Sum of All Known Reverence. Walt Whitman. MoRP

It is not well to mention names. The Fall of J. W. Beane. Oliver Herford. OBAL; StPo

It is not words could pay you what I owe. Apology for Understatement. John Wain. NePoEA-2; OxBTC

"It is not yet so bad with us!" On the Death of Doctor Swift. Jonathan Swift. ViBoPo

It is nothing, nothing at all,/for the cabbage down the hall. Nocturn at the Institute. David McElroy. Psk

It is now I long to hear you,/before the summer begins. When the fifth month comes. Lady Ise. BoWoP

...It is old earth's groping towards the steep/Heaven whom she childs us by. Not of All My Eyes See. Gerard Manley Hopkins. OBSP

It is on the battlefield that you will find him. You Stand and Hold the Post of My Small House. Auvaiyar. WPOW

It is one that most people should be prepared to be blank upon. Ignorance of Death. William Empson. CMoP; CoBMV; LiTM; NoAm

It is only a door. Prospective Immigrants Please Note. Adrienne Rich. VGW

It is only because you are short. The Painted Ceiling. Amy Lowell. OBAL

It is only the genuflection that survives. For Paddy Mac. Padraic Fallon. CIP

It is only the men who are hungry. The pigeons are fed. Trinity Place. Phyllis McGinley. MoAmPo; OBSP; SaC

It is only the wind that you hear sighing. Now That the Flowers. Cullen Jones. GoYe

It is only this, my darling,/That you'll love me when I'm old. Will You Love Me When I'm Old? Anonymous. BLPA; BLPL; FaBoBe

It is only you, moon, the old cold stone of consolation. Absence. Kathy Mangan. AMV-81

It is Oosa who gave honour to Tiger,/Animal created to have honour. Tiger. Anonymous. WTO

It is our helplessness they choose/And our refusals that they haunt. Ghosts. Elizabeth Jennings. NePoEA-2; PPJ

It is our only friend. Earth Dweller. William Stafford. LCAP

It is our shadow that slides in between. The Child and the Shadow. Elizabeth Jennings. NePoEA-2

It is possible to use, to this/purpose, only certain postures. Notes to the Reader. Robert Bringhurst. NOBC

It is quiet and it is delightful./Delightful. Columcille's Greeting to Ireland. Saint Columcille. OnYI

& It is raining/in the prison yard. The Artist. Stewart Brisby. LFAC

It is rough/like my edges Poem about a Seashell. Ranice Henderson Crosby. NMM

It is sad–it is all we have/To remember him by... Ballad of the Golden Bowl. Sara Henderson Hay. OnMSP

It is she shall be my bride. A Strappado for the Devil: Of Maids' Inconstancy. Richard Brathwaite. EIL

It is silent now. What Were They Like? Denise Levertov. HeIP; NIP; OBWP; PPON; VGW

...It is snowing everywhere. Elizabeth at the Piano. Horace Gregory. UnS

It is so far from these my Roman regions! Triumph. John Crowe Ransom. HBMV

It is so massive, so incomplete. Choosing the Devil. Linda Gregg. NPGG

"It is so nice to go to bed!" How the Leaves Came Down. Susan (Sarah Chauncey Woolsey) Coolidge. HBV 1-2; HBVY

It is so that spiritual messengers/Deliver their meaning. The Laurel Tree. Louis Simpson. NNaP

It is so thin a splinter of singing. Splinter. Carl Sandburg. OBCA; SoSe; SUS; TiPo

It is some picture on the margin wrought. The Book of the World. William, of Hawthornden Drummond. HBV 1-2

It is something different, something/Nobody counted on. The Unhistoric Story. Allen Curnow. AnNZ

It is spring, the pear tree/filming with weak, white blossoms. Poem: "In the early evening, as now, a man is bending." Louise Gluck. HaCAP

It is St. George's Day. St. George's Day–Ypres, 1915. Sir Henry Newbolt. GTBS

It is strange to me/and strange, I think, even to themselves. American Dreams. Louis Simpson. CAPP; GP

It is such sound as death; and, after all,/'Tis but the forest letting dead leaves fall. November. Mahlon Leonard Fisher. HBV 1-2

...It is summer and/vacation there. Open Casket. Sandra McPherson. GeTw

It is sweeter and dearer to me. The Praise of Derry. Saint Columcille. CAW

It is swollen/to full flood! Look Out There. Anonymous. NOBI

It is that height of fortune doth undo/Both her own quietness and others' too. Philotas: Chorus. Samuel Daniel. OBSC

It is that knave who answers in my heart. Between the Acts. Stanley Jasspon Kunitz. ELU

It is that they together/Share deeply one distress. The Hard Lovers. George Dillon. AnAmPo; PoA

It is the answer of thy sons,/Carolina! Carolina. Henry Timrod. MC; PAH

It is the answer that no question asked. You Went to the Verge, You Say, and Came Back Safely? Conrad Aiken. LiTA

It is the beginning of survival. Poem after a Speech by Chief Seattle, 1855. Charles Brashers. AMV-81

It is the business of the wealthy man/To give employment to the artisan. Lord Finchley. Hilaire Belloc. DTC; ELU; FaBoCo; FaBoEE; FiBHP; NLV; NOBL; OxBLi

It is the call to labor,–not to death. The Sunrise to the Poor. Robert Burns Wilson. AA

...It is the calm/of the earth itself. Goodbye Nkrumah. Diane Di Prima. PoM

It is the child of all eternity. Athanasia. Oscar Wilde. BrPo

...It is the city consciousness/Which sees and says: more: more and more: always more. America, America! Delmore Schwartz. NYP

It is the darkest night of the year, and starless. A Walk in March. Tim Reynolds. MAT

It is the day of trouble. For the Earth God. Anonymous. EaLo

It is the deep skin/of an undeciphered presence Song for a Transformation (excerpt). Francisco Arrivi. InW

It is the greatest among herbs/and becometh a tree.   The Flowering of the Rod.   Hilda ("H. D.") Doolittle.   FaBoMo

It is the honey 'gainst a waspish wife.   The Honest Whore, I, 1604.   Thomas Dekker.   ViBoPo

It is the "Inn of Care'.   The Inn of Care.   Samuel Waddington.   OBVV

It is the last commends the play.   The Plaudite, or End of Life.   Robert Herrick.   CaPo

It is the last day and the first.   Poem for Roslyn.   James Lewisohn.   LFAC

It is the lightening, fading star of morning.   Nothing.   Barrie Reid.   BoAV

...It is the long-awaited.   Concerning the Awakening of My Soul.   H. Roland-Holst.   WPOW

"It is the Lord! It is the Lord Most High!"   Nocturne.   Victor Hugo.   CAW

It is the melancholy of ancient death/The harpsichord dreams of, sighing in the room.   On an Air of Rameau.   Arthur Symons.   OBNC

It is the milkman bringing milk/While I am still in bed.   The Milkman.   Jane W. Krows.   SoPo

"It is the most expensive picture, yes,/But only in the world."   The Most Expensive Picture in the World.   Howard Nemerov.   EyDe

It is the music of the soul.   Old English Prayer.   Anonymous.   GoTF; TreFT

It is the mute partner of her waltz.   The Wedding Coat.   Harriet Rose.   BrRo

It is the normal excellence, of long accomplishment.   The Abnormal Is Not Courage.   Jack Gilbert.   CoAP; NPGG

It is the octopus in every soldier's eye/In still deep waters calm, O calm.   Terror.   Thomas O'Brien.   NeIP

It is the old who must give what they have,–to a dove.   The Pigeon-Feeders in Battery Park.   Julia Cooley Altrocchi.   GoYe

It is the only art.   Light Showers of Light.   Kathryn Lindskoog.   AMV-80

It is the only science.   Even Though.   John Stone.   AMV-81

It is the past's supreme italic/Makes the present mean.   Glass was the street.   Emily Dickinson.   OxBA

It is the physicians' love heals the patient.   Tempora Mutantur.   Charles Brasch.   OCNZ

It is the reed, it is the reed that sings.   It Is the Reed.   Sister Maris Stella.   GoBC

It is the route you took through winter light/that falls across the pane again tonight.   Tracking the Sled, Christmas 1951.   Jeanne Murray Walker.   AMV-81

It is the same way there.   Come Back.   William Stanley Merwin.   NaP

It is the sea/that gives life to the rivers.   Requiem after Seventeen Years.   Dahlia Ravikovich.   VWA

It is the season, it is harvest time!   Harvest Time.   Star Powers.   GoYe

It/is the song you have been singing/all your life.   Afterword: Song of Song.   James Richard Broughton.   GP

"It is the stream! it is the stream!"   The Brook.   William Wilberforce Lord.   AA

It is the things we have that go.   Wisdom.   Sara Teasdale.   AmLP; MoAmPo

It is the thunder at dawn!   The Everlastings.   Norman Dubie.   GeTw

It is the tongue's easy wag that is deceptive.   The Stammerers.   Margaret Kent.   AMV-80

It is the tune to travel to.   A Song of the Road.   Robert Louis Stevenson.   BrPo

It is the universe he kills.   The Carpenter's Real Anguish.   Stephen Gardner.   AMV-81

It is the unpastured sea hungering for calm.   Prometheus Unbound.   Percy Bysshe Shelley.   ChRP

It is the vague of the soul that I know.   Vast Light.   Richard Eberhart.   CMoP; NMP

It is the water that bubbles up in the fountains in our studies.   The Old Age Home.   Theodore Holmes.   CoPo

It is the whole earth   The Blanket around Her.   Joy Harjo.   TWSS

It is the wife, it is the home.   Who Drags the Fiery Artist Down?   Clarence Day.   FaBoCo

It is the worst world that ever was known.   The Best and the Worst.   Anonymous.   TreFT

It is their triumph, and a true emblem of honour.   The Train Will Fight to the Pass.   Ruth Pitter.   HaMV

It is then you will see the flash shearers/Making johnny-cakes round in the bend.   The Springtime It Brings on the Shearing.   E. J. Overbury.   NOAV

It is there for anyone to take.   Siege at Stony Point.   Horace Gregory.   FAZ

(It is this clock that later falls/in wheels and chimes of leaf and cloud).   The Colder the Air.   Elizabeth Bishop.   MiAP

It is this fear/that now devours/desire.   Threatened.   Alice Walker.   LTB

...It is through you/That beauty lives, you make the midnight sing!   Nocturne.   Richard Church.   ChMP

It is time for us to leave her!   Time for Us to Leave Her.   Anonymous.   ShS

It is time it were time./It is time.   Corona.   Paul Celan.   VWA

It is time now to splash through/the thawed ice   Raccoon Poem.   Miriam Palmer.   NMM

It is time that I pour out the batter/and bake up a few hundred more.   The Pancake Collector.   Jack Prelutsky.   OBCA

It is time to live by a different light.   Night Light.   Nancy Willard.   LCAP

It is time to prepare/Another ambush.   Marcus Antoninus Cui Cognomen Erat Aurelius.   Burns Singer.   OxBS

It is to be enough for us that we are together–We never separate/again.   Long I Thought That Knowledge Alone Would Suffice.   Walt Whitman.   NOBA

It is to girls' voices he listens and not his own.   Girls' Voices.   Brendan Gill.   PoL

It is to me a verry dedly woo.   Subject to All Pain.   Anonymous.   MeEL

It is to this that everybody listens.   The Agents.   Robert Conquest.   EAS

It is to you that I have turned for help!   Prayer for Rain.   Aqib Abdullahi Jama.   WTO

...It is too dark/to prove that I have ever seen him.   Too Dark.   Mark McCloskey.   PoA

It is too difficult a Grace–/To justify the Dream–   I Reckon When I Count at All.   Emily Dickinson.   MAmP; MoAmPo; PP

It is too early to reveal itself.   Japan That Sank under the Sea.   Satoru Sato.   PoPl

"It is too late for laughter,–or for love."   An Old Street.   Virginia Woodward Cloud.   AA

...It is uncertain what they are. We go on.   The Continuance.   William Bronk.   GP

It is useless to say to the pulsating heart,/"Yankee-doodle ker-chuggety-chug!"   To Marie.   Anonymous.   NA

It is waiting for its terrible moment!   The Leopard.   Lorenzo Thomas.   APU

It is waving its arms/in a thousand different parodies.   The Scythe.   Henry Kanabus.   APU

It is well–it is well with the child!   A Nativity.   Rudyard Kipling.   NAs

...It is well spent/Easing a saviour's birth.   The Magnetic Mountain: Condemned.   C. Day-Lewis.   EnLit; PoA; PoPle

It is what I shall be when you are there no more.   The Lady of the Pearls (excerpt).   Alexandre Dumas.   TTY

...It/is what is about to happen,/not/what is already here.   Waiting for IT.   May Swenson.   BoAnP

It is what we mistake for love.   Luck.   Elaine Epstein.   AMV-81

It is when hiving brain-cells in us breed/Homage to change.   Rondeau: "Homage to change that scatters the poppy seed."   Ronald Bottrall.   MoVE

It is winter.   Alone.   Walter De la Mare.   EnLoPo

It is written "King of Kings, Lord of Lords.'"   The Veteran of Heaven.   Francis Thompson.   HBV 1-2

It is you I look for/in the slate face of the water.   Jug Brook.   Ellen Bryant Voigt.   MAYP

It is you who are my cap and tale/Not Paris.   Homage to Max Jacob.   Ron Padgett.   ANYP

It is your life that stands beyond the glass.   If You Will.   Josephine Miles.   GP

It is your own son about to be born.   Out of Our Shame.   Norman Rosten.   TrJP

It is yours.   The House.   William Carlos Williams.   VGW

It is yours to take.   To the Last Wedding Guest.   Horace Gregory.   NYBP

It isn't raining rain to me,/It's raining violets.   Rain Song.   Robert Loveman.   GoTF; TreFT; WBLP

It isn't snowing snow you know/it's snowing buttercups.   Than(By Yon Sunset's Wintry Glow.   Edward Estlin Cummings.   VGW

It isn't that he's better,/it's that Harvey always cheats.   Harvey Always Wins.   Jack Prelutsky.   NTCP

It isn't the church–it's you.   It Isn't the Church–It's You.   Anonymous.   BLPA; WBLP

It isn't the fact that you're dead that counts,/But only how did you die?   How Did You Die?   Edmund Vance Cooke.   BLPA; OHFP; PeD

It isn't your church, it's you.   It's You.   L. A. McDonald.   STF

It isn't your town–it's you.   It Isn't the Town, It's You.   R. W. Glover.   BLPA

It keeps its highest, holiest tone/For our beloved Jane alone.   With a Guitar, to Jane.   Percy Bysshe Shelley.   ERoP 1-2; HBV 1-2; OAEL 1-2

...It keeps on filling your room.   Virgo Descending.   Charles Wright.   LCAP

It landed me over on Canaan's shore,/And I'll never come back any more.   Didn't My Lord Deliver Daniel.   Anonymous.   AH

It lasts.   The Magician.   Joan Colby.   PoDr

It lay dead in their grasp till nonchalantly/He gripped expectant wrists.   The Diviner.   Seamus Heaney.   FaBoIP

It lay in your power to slay me/All on the mountains high.'   Young Barnswell.   Anonymous.   OBET

It lays a scarlet, outstretched wing.   Sunset.   Herbert Bashford.   AA

It leaves its moisture thick and thin.   A Candle.   Sir John Suckling.   ErPo

It leaves no stain upon the shrine.   Art Thou Afraid the Adorer's Prayer. Walter Savage Landor.   GBL

It leaves on a film/is immortal.   The Cloud Chamber.   Arthur Sze.   BrSi

It lies so deep, I know not why.   I Know Not Why.   Morris Rosenfeld. AA

It lifts again its spotless star.   A Snowdrop.   Harriet Prescott Spofford. GN

It liketh me," quod she, "to have heard your question,/But longer time doth ask resolution."   Mine old dear enemy...   Sir Thomas Wyatt.   FCP

It listened to all the jokes and it laughed.   Periphery.   Ruth Stone.   GP

It listens now, and practices at night.   The Animal That Drank Up Sound. William Stafford.   VGW

It lit, like a struck match, everything by.   Flighting for Duck.   William Empson.   MoPo

It lit on my fingers/As though they were grass.   A Dragonfly.   Eleanor Farjeon.   OnUR

IT lives./Enormous breathings/& compressions/of IT   Pindar's Revenge. Edward Sanders.   PoM

It lives for those who once upon a time had a dream.   There Is a Woman in This Town.   Patricia Parker.   BlSi

It'll be by means of a telescope from here to Arkansaw!   The Arkansaw Traveler.   *Anonymous.*   ViBoFo

It'll take the strongest angel to hold the old fellow in.   "Flash:" The Fireman's Story.   Will Carleton.   BBV

It looked down in serene repose/On its own realm of buried woe.   A Dream. Emily Bronte.   NBM

It looked like Eaton Square–but pink.   Air Travel in Arabia.   Sir Charles Johnston.   OBTV

An' it looks lak my cotton dress,/Dyed wid copperse an' oak-bark.   I'll Wear Me a Cotton Dress.   *Anonymous.*   BPo

It looks like the witchcraft of Papa John.   Papa John.   Jorge De Lima. TTY

It looks that way. But I dunno.   To Be or Not to Be.   *Anonymous.* FaBoCo; FaFP; MoShBr

It loves not, nor grieves.   Clear Eyes.   Walter De la Mare.   MoVE; ViBoPo

It made its man, and it may rest/Forever from the plow.   Where I Took Hold of Life.   Robert P. Tristram Coffin.   BiCB

It made me feel like letting off some air for decoration.   Column A. Michael Silverton.   PV

It made no signal, nor demurred,/But dropped like adamant.   'Twas Warm at First, Like Us.   Emily Dickinson.   CMoP; ExPo; ForPo; LiTA; NAWM 1-2; QFR; SoSe

It made us jump and laugh to see/The little new moon above the tree. Crescent Moon.   Elizabeth Madox Roberts.   SUS

It make this woman want to/run out and find her man.   Steam Song. Gwendolyn Brooks.   GP

It makes his children cry.   The Bird.   Louis Simpson.   NePoEA-2

It makes me think of your disgrace.   Dear Companion.   *Anonymous.*   FSW

It makes one wonder if they really care.   Dirge.   Hazel Townson.   PV

It makes poor servants' wages low,/And keeps them in subjection.   The New-Fashioned Farmer.   *Anonymous.*   OBET

It makes sense for me to die for Barbara.   Exit Lines.   George Jonas. NeAC

It maketh even the little child with heavy sighs complain.   The Sale of the Pet Lamb.   Mary Howitt.   CH

It mkait maydenys wombys to swelle,/Thereof I have a quantyte.   We Bear about No Cats' Skins.   *Anonymous.*   NCEP

...It mattered once,/If only to him. And before he turned into paper. Sensationalism.   Larry Levis.   MAYP

It matters not, since thou art chosen one/Here of my great and good foundation.   To His Kinsman, Master Thomas Herrick, Who Desired to Be in His Book.   Robert Herrick.   CaPo

It matters not to me/If sheep or tiger, man or worm/Earth's victor-captain be. Cupid.   Bernard O'Dowd.   NOAV

It matters not, we shall one day obtain/Our native and celestial scope again. To His Friend–.   Henry Vaughan.   OBS; PP

It may be, and yet be not.   Is It True, Ye Gods, Who Treat Us.   Arthur Hugh Clough.   VLP

It may be that only in Heaven/I shall hear that grand Amen.   A Lost Chord. Adelaide Anne Procter.   CAW; FaFP; GoTF; HBV 1-2; PaPo; TreF; VLP; WBLP; WGRP

It may be they shall give me greater ease/Than your cold Christ and tangled Trinities.   Look, You Have Cast Out Love!   Rudyard Kipling.   OBSP

It may behold thy holy face/And all its radiance truly.   On Earth There Is a Lamb So Small.   Nicolaus Zinzendorf.   AH

:It may chance that he/Will find no gift, where reverence is, unmeet. Tennyson.   Thomas Bailey Aldrich.   AA

It may fall out some honest Lover/The rest hereafter will discover.   Loves World.   Sir John Suckling.   SeCV 1-2

It may know age, but not decay.   To the World the Perfection of Love. William Habington.   AnAnS 2; JCP

It may rain–but, say,/Ain't it fine today!   Ain't It Fine Today!   Douglas Malloch.   WBLP

It may well be. I do not think I would.   Fatal Interview.   Edna St. Vincent Millay.   AmLP

It means everything.   Not-Knowing.   Dawn Hinshaw.   AMV-81

It means gathon ihn don....tomorrow.   Healing.   Charlotte De Clue.   TWSS

It means I shall see you soon.   I dreamed I held.   Lady Kasa.   BoWoP; LiTW; WPOW

It merges into the funeral/Cloud-continent of night/As if it belongs there.   A Departure.   Derek Mahon.   CIP

It might as well be smoke and ashes–it isn't worth a/farthing.   And All the While the Sky Is Falling...   Lora Dunetz.   NePoAm

...It might be heaven,/or hell   The Present Tense.   Joyce Carol Oates. AMV-81

It might be so forever, someone fears,/Or for days.   Derry.   Seamus Deane. CIP

It might be worse. Be glad with what you've got.   The Frogs Who Wanted a King.   Aesop.   MaC

It might give us–what?–some flowers soon?   What Is Poetry.   John Ashbery. LCAP

It might have been/A great deal worse.   The Saddest Words (Addendum). *Anonymous.*   PoToHe

It might have drawn from after-heat.   In Memoriam A.H.H., LXXXI. Alfred, Lord Tennyson.   VLP

It might look like he is guilty of something.   Being with Men.   Linda Gregg. NPGG

It mus' be now de kingdom comin',/an' de year of Jubilo!   Kingdom Coming. Henry Clay Work.   BLSo; PSoN

It must acknowledge the spiritual forces which have made it.   When I Buy Pictures.   Marianne Moore.   EyDe; OxBA

It must always be the animal who dies.   Lion Hunts.   Patricia Beer. OxBTC

It must be because of a/certain/strait jacket/i feel.   Between Me and Anyone Who Can Understand–.   Sharon Scott.   JB

It must be for them and changed by them all.   What Is Terrible.   Roy Fuller.   WaP

It must be older than the moon, older than salt.   Being Born Is Important. Carl Sandburg.   NAs

It must be that they are coming from the garden to the garden.   The Drunkards.   *Anonymous.*   NU

It must find refuge with the wolves/if such motherly wolves/still exist.   On the Death of Sylvia Plath.   Judith Herzberg.   VWA; WPOW

It must flow and scald.   Morning Glory Pool.   Sandra McPherson.   LCAP

It must forget/nothing   From the Prison House.   Adrienne Rich.   NNaP

It must have been the gravy/and vegetables/and ham.   Tummy Ache. Aileen Fisher.   SoPo

It must proceed from You alone.   The Fortune-Teller To a Young Lady in Search of Her Destiny.   Matthew Prior.   CEP

It must've been lousy   The Elizabethans Called It Dying.   James Schuyler. NeAP

It need not spend itself on fancy and the empty air.   Bedtime Story for My Son.   Peter Redgrove.   NePoEA-2

It needs just a little hypocrisy/To make the world safe for democracy.   The Prairie Dog.   Arthur Guiterman.   BPAW

It never hath been/Nor ever shall be.   Nimium Fortunatus.   Robert Bridges. MoAB; MoBrPo

It never shall flutter again.   Oh, Lovely Appearance of Death.   *Anonymous.* OuSiCo

It never should from thence depart.   The Glorious Gift of God.   Benjamin Beddome.   BePJ

It never touched down.   For the El Paso Weather Bureau.   Peter Wild. MAT

It never will be far.   Night.   Sara Teasdale.   BrR; SoPo; SUS; TiPo

It no longer needs you/but it misses you.   Yiddish.   Judith Herzberg. VWA

...It obliterates all tracks/leaving, clearly, nothing to go on.   A White Wall under the Wallpaper.   Brian Henderson.   CaPN

It often likes to be alone.   Cats.   Marchette Chute.   SoPo

It often makes the world go flat.   I Stand Corrected.   Margaret Fishback. PoPl

It only said its cussed hair was inclined to be red.   Joe Bowers.   *Anonymous.* ABF; AmFP; BaBo; BFSS; CoSo; FSW; TrAS; TreFS; ViBoFo

It pales and passes, fading when it came.   Most Quietly at Times.   Casar Flaischlen.   AWP

It passes for me   Cinderella Liberated.   Anne Hussey.   DFT

It pays to advertise!   Advertisement.   *Anonymous.*   FaBoUs

"It perfectly true is/Thet slavery's airth's grettest boon," sez he.   The Debate in the Sennit.   James Russell Lowell.   HBV 1-2; PAH

It picks up one person and knocks down a couple.   Hell's Bells.   Margaret Fishback.   ShM

It pits hiz laddies sair aboot.   A Schule Laddie's Lament on the Lateness o' the Season.   James Logie Robertson.   NOBV

It pounced my peace away.   One Careless Look.   John Clare.   AnFE; EG; LiTL

It poureth out as purest wine.   The Miracle.   Caelius Sedulius.   CAW

It prints silence   Fossil.   E. D. Blodgett.   NOBC

It rained and I cried and daddy bought me a gun.   Old Emily.   Hyacinthe Hill.   GoYe

It rained and it hailed and a storm o'ercame them,/Both a watery grave all in the sea.   The Jealous Brothers.   *Anonymous.*   AmFP

It rains across the country I remember.   Mnemosyne.   Trumbull Stickney.   AmePo; AnFE; CoAnAm; CrMA; LiTA; NCEP; NOBA; OxBA; ViBoPo

It rehearses death.   The Sleeper.   Sydney Clouts.   PeSA; VWA

It remains in me some/Sadnesses beyond belief.   A.M.–P.M.   Theodore H. Hirschfield.   AMV-81

It remains to orbit the earth/only occasionally reminded it is outranked.   Lunar Eclipse.   Diane Glancy.   STE

...It repeats the same word/Again and again, but not too loudly...   Evening.   Charles Simic.   GeTw

It rescued a reader/from being driven mad by a scold.   Tell Me, Tell Me.   Marianne Moore.   LiTM; NYBP

...It resembles/a crimson asparagus tip.   The Accident.   Len Gasparini.   NeAC

It results in a permanent slo.   Limerick: "When you think of the hosts without No."   *Anonymous.*   FaBoUs; NLV

It revives all the boarders at Stirling's Hotel.   Stirling's Hotel.   *Anonymous.*   AmFP

...It rimes with tiger/and the gallow tree.   The Kiss.   Ned O'Gorman.   FYAP

It rises from, and makes up things again.   De Rerum Natura.   Lucretius (Titus Lucretitus Carus).   OBVE

It run until the break of day.   The Midnight Train (with music).   *Anonymous.*   AS

It runs a naked stream, cold and chill.   Remembrances.   John Clare.   NBM

An it's a big lees/Frae the heid tae the tail.   Fower-an-Twenty Hielandmen.   *Anonymous.*   FaBoNo

It's a cozy sound at night.   The Clock.   Jean Jaszi.   SoPo

"It's a dark and dreary season–/Christmas trees are in the gutter."   Triolet on a Dark Day.   Margaret Fishback.   PoSC

It's a day like any other.   February.   James Schuyler.   ANYP; NeAP

"It's a double sestine," says he, lookin' mean, "and/they're hard as the deuce, that's what!"   The Protest of the Illiterate.   Gelett Burgess.   FiBHP

It's a fine day.   Armstrong Spring Creek.   Lloyd Davis.   AMV-81

It's a fine, fine thing to join a union,/For it will help you.   Its a Good Thing to Join a Union.   *Anonymous.*   FSW

It's a' for love of thee.   A Lyric.   Algernon Charles Swinburne.   HBV 1-2

It's a hard times in the country,/Out on Penney's farm.   Hard Times in the Country.   *Anonymous.*   OuSiCo

It's a heavenly jam-pot, the Promised Land/Which with other milk and honey overflows!   Sonnet: To the Asshole.   Arthur Rimbaud.   PeHV

It's a minute or two to 2.02.   Limerick: "There was a young lady named Sue."   *Anonymous.*   TDH

It's a picture from life's other side.   A Picture from Life's Other Side.   *Anonymous.*   FSW

It's a pretty good plan to forget it.   Forget It.   *Anonymous.*   PoLf; WBLP

It's a pretty thing!   Haiku: "Death it can bring."   Issa.   LiTW

It's a project that's sponsored by ANTA.'   Limerick: "A large, colored dyke from Atlanta."   *Anonymous.*   PeHV

It's a Public Enemy–to me, you, and Venus a complacent traitor.   From V.C. (a Gentleman of Verona).   Gavin Ewart.   OxBC

It's a queer time.   It's a Queer Time.   Robert Graves.   MCCG; MoAB; MoBrPo

It's a regular brute of a bee!   Limerick: "There was an Old Man in a tree."   Edward Lear.   FaBoNo; HBV 1-2; InvP; LBN; LiBL; NoP; OxBChV; TEP

It's a second nature to that class/Of lads called Cousin Jacks.   Cousin Jack Song.   Charley Tregonning.   AmFP

It's a son-of-a-bitch of a life on a destroyer.   Destroyer Life.   *Anonymous.*   ABF

It's a stiff, black world/you left behind.   Mandelstam.   David Young.   AmPA

(It's a terrible thing!)   It's a Terrible Thing!   Everett Hoagland.   BPo

It's a wonder I don't die.   Muskrat.   *Anonymous.*   FSW

It's a wonder I'm alive to tell the tale.   Household Remedies.   *Anonymous.*   OBET

It's about washing up,/entwining/It's about flowering   Tree Planting.   Endre Farkas.   CaPN

It's all-containing cry.   Spring.   W.R. Rodgers.   AnIL

It's all for my true love I never more shall see.   The Tri-Coloured Ribbon.   Peadar Kearney.   OnYI

It's all I've got.   Snail.   John Drinkwater.   GoJo; OnUR; SoPo

It's all one.   Civility a Bogey; or, Two Centuries of Canadian Cities.   Margaret Avison.   NOBC

It's all out and about!/Keep it dark!   Keep It Dark.   *Anonymous.*   PBA

It's all over over over   Nocturne.   Richard Murphy.   IPY

It's all that cursed duff!' "I'm sinking too,' says he,/"And fast enough.'   The Duff.   David McKee Wright.   AnNZ

"It's all the men, the dirty bastards!"   Unhappy Bella.   *Anonymous.*   ErPo

It's all the same/to Captain Arthur.   Captain Arthur Phillip and the Birds.   Lex Banning.   PoAu 1-2

...It's almost night.   Nymphing through Car Windows.   Greg Keeler.   WOLT

It's almost tender,/The way it's done.   Focus.   Kathleen Norris.   GP

It's almost time to get the cows and milk.   The Flowing Summer.   Charles Bruce.   CaP

It's alright. You're almost there.   Night Mare.   Anita Endrezze-Danielson.   STE

It's also greater/than before/we came/It's also later.   Changes around the Bay.   Michael Palmer.   NPGG

It's also the only reliable/Device for producing a chicken.   Eggomania.   Felicia Lamport.   NLV

It's always ourselves we find in the sea   Maggie and milly and molly and may.   Edward Estlin Cummings.   LOW; NePoAm-2; NOBA; PoSC

...It's an act/Of generosity–in point of tact.   Roman Presents.   Martial (Marcus Valerius Martialis).   OBCP

"It's an ill wood wind no one blows good."   Oboe.   Laurence McKinney.   NLV

It's an old soldier's button, says/Moll-in-the-Wad.   Moll-in-the-Wad and I Fell Out.   *Anonymous.*   OxNR

"It's an uncle you need, not an ant."   Limerick: "Once a grasshoper (food being scant)."   Oliver Herford.   TDH

It's been a trying day.   Important Matters.   Charles Mungoshi.   WhB

It's been ten years/since I missed/my last/rodeo   For Carole.   Diane Burns.   TWSS

It's bery difficult to try/To be like God, up in the sky!   A Child's Thought.   Bertha Moore.   PaPo

It's best to be best/right?   Best?   Siv Widerberg.   NTCP

It's better to be honest if ever so poor,/For he's made her his lady instead of his whore.   Squire and Milkmaid.   *Anonymous.*   CoMu; OxBB

It's better to live single than bound.   The Grey Cock.   *Anonymous.*   FaBoBa

"It's beyond all my expectorations."   Limerick: "He received from some thoughtful relations."   *Anonymous.*   TDH

It's bitter to be a man, while the knife is the brother of man.   Mother of Man.   Vesna Parun.   PBWP

It's break of day, and here I am once more.   Foolish Proverb.   *Anonymous.*   UnTE

It's Buklies joy that Christ his sons new making,/Hath placest in's churches for to shine as Stars.   Onely the Reverend Grave and Godly Mr. Buckly Remaines.   Edward Johnson.   SCAP

It's called "Pillow Talk"   Four Heads & How to Do Them.   John Forbes.   CBAP

It's chop-a-nose day.   Chop-a-Nose.   *Anonymous.*   OxNR

It's convenient, but certainly funny!   Limerick: "My name's Mister Benjamin Bunny."   Frederic Edward Weatherly.   CenHV

It's curious when to die   Fleche...   Larry Eigner.   VGW

It's cushy enough.   In Parenthesis.   David Jones.   FaBoMo

It's damned good land Judge you/got a bargain.   The Judge.   Karl Kopp.   TAT

It's doing your noblest–that's Success!   That's Success!   Berton Braley.   PoToHe

It's dreadful your life to a dog to owe.   A Terrible Thought.   Eliezer Steinbarg.   TrJP

It's dreams like these/that burn holes in the sky.   The Far North.   Terry Savoie.   AMV-80

It's due on swop, for pie-bald mare.   Anacreontic to Flip.   Royall Tyler.   OBAL

It's 1893. Sarah dies. My father's born.   Gas Lamp.   Willis Barnstone.   VWA

It's for my lips they're clay, clay-cold,/And my breath smells earthlye strong.   The Unquiet Grave.   *Anonymous.*   AmFP

It's full as opera!   I cannot dance upon my toes.   Emily Dickinson.   UnS

It's fun to go shopping for shoes.   It's Fun to Go out and Buy New Shoes to Wear.   Mary Ann Hoberman.   TiPo

It's funny/my puppy/knows such a great deal.   My Puppy.   Aileen Fisher.   OnUR

It's galling, though, when girls omit/To switch the set on first.   Sight Unseen.   Kingsley Amis.   ErPo; NePoEA-2

It's getting so you can't even take a military jet/home to hunt ducks.   The Keepsake Corporation.   David Fisher.   NPGG

–It's gey an' easy spierin', says the beggar-wife to me.   The Spaewife.   Robert Louis Stevenson.   BrPo; OxBS

It's giving us so much trouble/I wonder: what shall we do?   High Price Blues.   Roosevelt Sykes.   BluL

It's good-bye, dear heart, good-bye to you all.   Song for the New Year.   W. H. Auden.   EnLi 1-2

It's good enough for me.   Give Me That Old Time Religion.   *Anonymous.* FSW

"It's good to be at home," you said.   The Blue Bowl.   Blanche Bane Kuder. BLPA; FaBoBe

It's got Solomon beat–and no sweat.   Go to the Ant.   Stanley J. Sharpless. NOBL

...It's great,/but not for me.   History.   Art Lange.   APU

It's growed over with soapbushes and huckleberries now.   First Carolina Said-Song.   Archie Randolph Ammons.   OBAL

It's guilt!   Echo Poem.   M. Allan.   FiBHP

It's Hallowe'en!   Hallowe'en.   Harry Behn.   PoSC; SiSoSe; TiPo

It's hard on we po' farm(ers),/It's hard.   It's Hard on We Po' Farmers. *Anonymous.* OuSiCo

It's hard times in the country, out on Roberts' farm.   Robert's Farm. *Anonymous.* FSW

It's hard times, po' boy.   Po" Boy.   *Anonymous.*   ABF

It's hard to keep it up, he said)   The Bumper Sticker on His Pickup Said, "I'm a Lover, I'm a Fighter..."   Eldon Ray Fox.   LiSp

It's hard to know which life is sleep/Or where the door is with my real name on it.   The Banjo.   Robert Winner.   FF

It's hooping and yelling and cursing those dogies/To our misfortune but none of your own.   As I Walked Out.   Anonymous.   BPAW

It's horrid on the staircase/Going up to bed.   On the Staircase.   Eleanor Farjeon.   SiSoSe

...It's I who say/the words like "I love you' or "thank you.'   Long Lines. Paul Goodman.   PeHV

It's Independence Day.   I've Got a Rocket.   *Anonymous.*   SiSoSe; TiPo

It's just a Beau going in.   When a Beau Goes In.   Gavin Ewart.   OBWP; OxBTC; WaP

...It's just a matter of common sense.   Against Surrealism.   James Wright. LCAP

It's just a very blue sky I'm looking at   Strawberries in Mexico.   Ron Padgett.   ANYP; EAS

It's just as well that now you save your breath.   To an American Poet Just Dead.   Richard Wilbur.   HaCAP; NLV; NoP

It's just beginning to be dark.   Somewhere Else.   Paula Rankin.   MAYP

It's just for me.   My Bed.   Lucy Sprague Mitchell.   SoPo

...It's just/one more secret you got to live with.   Cleaning the Well.   Paul Ruffin.   Str

...It's just that at the Sacred/Moment they are always thinking of something else.   That Reminds Me.   Ogden Nash.   FiBHP

It's just that Lares is a rifle in the hills.   Why I Can't Write a Poem about Lares.   Ivan Silen.   InW

It's just the sort of news that gets around.   Ellie Mae Leaves in a Hurry. Peter Klappert.   SM

It's justifiable matricide,/Isn't it, Bess?'   The Widow's Plot; or, She Got What Was Coming to Her.   William Plomer.   NoAm

It's knowing what to do with things that counts.   At Woodward's Gardens. Robert Frost.   ImOP; PoA

It's layin' in the grave so long.   Hang Me, O Hang Me, and I'll Be Dead and Gone.   *Anonymous.*   AmFP

It's leaving thee, my bonnie Mary.   The Silver Tassie.   Robert Burns. NOBE; OBEC

...It's less than/Three weeks' shopping time to Christmas.   December.   John Heath-Stubbs.   OBCP

It's like a lovely fairy/Dropped in to say good-night.   Mother.   Rose Fyleman.   SiSoSe

It's like a piece of thread on which our days hang,/To fall away, one after another, wasted.   Song of a Prison Guard.   Lupenga Mphande.   WhB

It's like a thousand years ago,/Now, this evening.   Mediterranean.   Israel Pincas.   VWA

It's living blood at the bushes' roots/That feeds them in its flood.'   The Banded Cobra.   C. Louis Leipoldt.   PeSA

It's lots of fun–just try it some day/When it rains too hard to go out to play. Fun in a Garret.   Emma C. Dowd.   SUS; TiPo

It's me, it's me, it's me O, Lord,/An I'm standin' in the need of prayer.   It's Me, O, Lord.   *Anonymous.*   BoAN 1-2; FSW

It's me O Lord–or rather, it is I.   Study in Blue.   Evan Jones.   NOAV

It's moving that counts.   Chesapeake.   Gerta Kennedy.   NYBP

It's my favorite sort of meeting.   Meeting Mary.   Eleanor Farjeon.   BiCB

It's myself, not my getup that's weird.   Limerick: "There was a young man with a beard."   Norman R. Jaffray.   TDH

It's nearly evening now or morning.   The Sea Wind.   Harry Martinson. NU

It's nearly time for dinner!   Get Up, Get Up.   *Anonymous.*   FiBHP; NTCP

It's never enough.   Graffiti for Lovers.   Joan Joffe Hall.   AMV-80

It's never good weather when you're on the land.   The Sea-Gull. *Anonymous.*   GBP

"It's no cinch to become a dad."   Becoming a Dad.   Edgar A. Guest. BLPL; PoLf

It's/not a Herod's oath that cannot change.   The Mind Is an Enchanting Thing.   Marianne Moore.   AP; CMoP; CoBMV; CrMA; HeIP; InPK; InvP; MoAB; MoAmPo; MoPo; OxBA; PPP; WPOW

It's not a tent, it's not a tree,/A knee and nothing more.   The Knee on Its Own.   Christian Morgenstern.   FaBoNo

It's not a year only,/But a world/For You!   A New Year.   Mary Carolyn Davies.   YeAr

It's not all as evil as you think.   Sunflower.   Rolf Jacobsen.   NU

"It's not an old beast, but a gnu."   Limerick: "There was a sightseer named Sue."   *Anonymous.*   TDH

It's not slaves who die, but people.   Rosh Pina.   David Knut.   VWA

It's not the booze or pick-ups/that will kill me/on this road   Road Hazard. Rayna Green.   TWSS

It's not the first one in the family.   The Pulkovo Meridian: Leningrad: 1943. Vera Inber.   WaaP

It's not the joystick now, but the control column.   The Dream of Flying Comes of Age.   Howard Nemerov.   BiP

It's notes yield sweet delight.   Riddle: "Close in a cage a bird I'll keep." *Anonymous.*   CoBE

It's November/and I'm waiting   The Song of This House.   Stephen Vincent. NeAC

It's now He offers pardon/And gives joy where grief has been.   Joy to the World.   *Anonymous.*   STF

It's off in the woods for me.   It's Spring Returning, It's Spring and Love. *Anonymous.*   HAP

It's only a pain in the ass.'   Limerick: "A well-buggered boy named Delpasse."   *Anonymous.*   PeHV

It's only a shantih in old/Shantih town.   Shantih shantih shantih (parody). Edward Pygge.   BXAP

"It's only a tin full of people."   A Baby Sardine.   Spike Milligan.   OnUR

It's only by our lack of ghosts/we're haunted   Can. Lit.   Earle Birney. NOBC

"It's only peace'/he prophesies across my years.   Firebell for Peace.   Joyce Lee.   NOAV

It's only two devils, that blow/Through a murderer's bones, to and fro,/In the ghosts' moonshine.   Death's Jest Book.   Thomas Lovell Beddoes.   EnRP

It's only you, you April fool!   April Fool's Day.   Marnie Pomeroy.   PoSC

It's our misfortune we ever did roam.   Run along, You Little Dogies. *Anonymous.*   OuSiCo

It's over the river to Charlie.   Charlie, He's a Young Man.   *Anonymous.* LaNeLa

It's part of his head–it's grown!   The Elephant's Trunk.   Alice Wilkins. SoPo; TiPo

It's playing with your thought in/heaven's blue.   The Swallow's Flight. Louis Levy.   TrJP

It's prized more than my best dancing.   The First Tooth.   Charles and Mary Lamb.   OxBChV

It's prudenter–to dream–   We dream–it is good we are dreaming.   Emily Dickinson.   BoWoP

...It's quite a rarity/For the writing of philosophy/To exhibit clarity.   On Philosophy.   Jonas Goldstein.   AMV-81

It's raining, it's snowing, the old man is growing.   It's Raining, It's Pouring. *Anonymous.*   TrAS

It's raining violets.   April Rain.   Robert Loveman.   HBV 1-2; HBVY; SUS; TrJP

It's really quite a splendid beak/In quite a splendid size.   The Reason for the Pelican.   John Ciardi.   PoPl; SoPo

It's really quite an honor to be held up by Black Bart.   Black Bart. *Anonymous.*   BPAW

It's really/too far/to/the/moo....   The Pinwheel's Song.   John Ciardi.   SO

It's rest enough for anyone.   After Frost.   Brian Patten.   EBEV

It's sad kind words are seldom said/Until a rake is safely dead.   Obituary. Anthony Brode.   FiBHP

It's sky and brook and bird/And tree.   Father and I in the Woods.   David McCord.   SO

It's small bones,/and heel and toe forever and ever.   Two Stories.   Charles Wright.   FYAP

"It's so hard to raise a daughter."   Little Willie.   *Anonymous.*   ShM

It's so little, and yet it's all.   All.   Antoni Slonimski.   TrJP

It's so simple, so very simple/That only a child can do it!   New Maths. Tom Lehrer.   FaBoUs

...It's so/Untenable, but such a quiet place to rest.   The Visit.   Jim Gauer. AMV-81

It's somewhere else/Instead!   Halfway Down.   A.(lan) A.(lexander) Milne. FaPON; SO; TiPo

It's soon gonna carry me away.   New River Train.   *Anonymous.*   FSW

It's Spring. And no one's told Clorinda.   Thenot Protests.   C.N." S." InMe

It's spring at Mrs. Appleby's!   At Mrs. Appleby's.   Elizabeth Upham McWebb.   BrR; SiSoSe; TiPo

It's Spring, Spring, Spring!   Spring Wind.   Nancy Byrd Turner.   SiSoSe

It's still in Longman's shop, and oh!/The difference to him!   He Lived amidst th' Untrodden Ways.   Hartley Coleridge.   FaBoCo; Par

It's tasteless and so hard/I can chew it for hours.   Alone.   Jonathan Holden. Psk

It's ten to one she had had to make shift/With rickets instead of rockets!   Miss Kilmansegg's Birth.   Thomas Hood.   OxBoLi

It's ten to one you'll find the shell of the wonderful crocodile.   The Crocodile. *Anonymous.*   CBEP

It's that confounded cucumber/I ate, and can't digest.   The Confession. Richard Harris Barham.   FiBHP

It's the candy man   Candy Man Blues.   Mississippi John Hurt.   BluL

It's the city.   Disclaimer of Prejudice.   Eli Siegel.   PV

It's the cocaine talkin', and street-baby dreams.   My Street Baby's Lament. William Franklin.   LFAC

It's the coffin/They carry you off in.   It Isn't the Cough. *Anonymous.* FaFP; ShM

"It's the day before the races out at Tangmalangaloo."   Tangmalangaloo. Patrick Joseph Hartigan.   PoAu 1-2

It's "The full of the house" of Irish love is Mary Ann Malone.   The Agricultural Irish Girl. *Anonymous.*   OnYI

It's the greatest/Old folks home in the country.   The Geriatric Whore.   Pete Winslow.   PV

It's the name that goes with me/back to earth/no one else can touch.   Song for My Name.   Linda Hogan.   STE; TWSS

It's the people in front get the jar!   My Face.   Anthony Euwer.   FaFP; PoLf

It's the president of the country, scowling.   Trumpet Voluntary.   Paul Hoover.   APU

...It's the question/of male domination that makes everybody/angry.   A History of Lesbianism.   Judy Grahn.   PeHV

It's the stillness that fills me with peace.   The Spell of the Yukon.   Robert W. Service.   BLPA; BLPL; FaBoBe; FaFP; PoPl; TreF

It's the very devil that you and he/Ride, ride together, forever ride.   The Last Ride Together (From Her Point of View) (parody).   James Kenneth Stephen.   BXAP; FaBoCo; Par; UnPo

It's the whole show.   Fat Cat.   John Ronan.   AMV-81

It's the worst darn stuff I've ever seen:/I like it.   Tobacco.   Graham Lee Hemminger.   FPL; PoLf

...It's then/I must scream out my misery through the night.   Sonnet V: "White Venus limpid wandering in the sky."   Louise Labe.   BoWoP

It's then you will find that she's your best friend.   Speaking of Cowboy's Home.   *Anonymous.*   CoSo

It's thus he does it of a winter night.   An Old Man's Winter Night.   Robert Frost.   AnNE; AWP; HAP; HBMV; MoAB; MoAmPo; MoVE; NoAm; OxBA; VGW

It's time for us to leave her!   Time to Leave Her.   *Anonymous.*   AmSS

It's time I crowed. The sun will be waiting.   Cock before Dawn.   Norman MacCaig.   OxBC

It's time I got my valor to grow big.   Sonnet: Of Becchina in a Rage.   Cecco da Siena Angiolieri.   AWP

It's time I got off my arse.   High Wonders (parody).   Naomi Marks. BXAP

It's time it is time to straighten up and fly right tonight   It Is Time.   Ted Joans.   NNP

It's time to leave.   Reunion.   Heather Cadsby.   AMV-81

It's to one system the onion/and time curving in the onion's peel belong. Remembering.   Judit Toth.   VWA

It's too close to call.   Fish Story.   P. L. Jacobs.   LFAC

An' it's too nigh Chris'mus mo'nin' now fu' me.   Soliloquy of a Turkey. Paul Laurence Dunbar.   BPo

An' it's trunch, trunch, truncheon does the trick!   Police Station Ditties. Max Beerbohm.   NOBL

It's twice dead not to see!   Done For.   Rose T. Cooke.   AA

It's under-sized; for God's sake throw it back!   Farewell to New Zealand. Wynford Vaughan-Thomas.   DBV; NOBL; OBTV

It's up, by Jove, and away we go: it's all right, Jack.   I Am an Ancient Mariner.   *Anonymous.*   OBSS

It's void and empty,/and lonely,/and terribly boring,/brrr!...   I Just Walk around, around, around.   Moishe Kulbak.   VWA

It's watered by a spring, that makes it grow so fast.   Buxom Lass. *Anonymous.*   ErPo

...It's what I wanted,/If not what I want.   Poems from a Greek Anthology (excerpt).   Decimus Magnus Ausonius.   NNaP

It's when things seem worst that you mustn't quit.   Don't Quit.   *Anonymous.* BLPA; STF

It's where it is because it is/and not because it isn't.   Those Old Zen Blues. James Richard Broughton.   GP

It's where they ain't no matches and they don't need kerosene.   Boomer Johnson.   Henry Herbert Knibbs.   BPAW

It's worth a million dollars, and it doesn't cost a cent.   Let Us Smile. Wilbur D. Nesbit.   WBLP

It's worth a try. You never know.   Prospero Dreams of Arnaud Daniel Inventing Love in the Twelfth Century.   Jack Gilbert.   NPGG

It's your "good taste' that prefers/A bastard God!   To the Christians. Francis Lauderdale Adams.   OxBS; WGRP

It's your oyster–yours to open if you will.   Observe the Whole of It. Thomas Wolfe.   TreFT

It's yourself you should scrutinize to see/Whether you're center or periphery. True Enough: To the Physicist (1820).   Johann Wolfgang von Goethe. SUW

It said–"Dream on!" and "Dream no/more!"   Ebb and Flow.   George William Curtis.   AA; HBV 1-2

It said "Once more."   The Daemon.   Louise Bogan.   NYBP

It sails,–ah! quaint little bird indeed/Is the thistle-down.   Thistle-Down. Clara Doty Bates.   AA

...It says here/Picasso produces fourteen hours a day.   The Quarrel.   Diane Di Prima.   NMM

It scowls into my glasses at itself.   Falling Asleep Over the Aeneid.   Robert Lowell.   AP; CoBMV; CrMA; MoAmPo; NoAm; OxBA

It seemed as if she trod on holy ground.   The Sinner.   Margaret E. Bruner. PoToHe

It seemed as if the little horse had won.   The Long Race.   Edwin Arlington Robinson.   CrMA

It seemed better that we kept alive.   Old Apple Trees.   W. D. Snodgrass. CAPP; FYAP; SV

It seemed the sun had made them mad.   The Greeting of the Roses. Hamlin Garland.   AA

It seemed to us all a stupid trick.   The Inflatable Globe.   Theodore Spencer. LiTA; NePA; WaP

It seems bloody queer.   The Thinker.   Anthony Delius.   PeSA

It seems, for a moment, the river ceases flowing.   Summer Near the River. Carolyn Kizer.   CoAP; VGW

It seems I had the best o' him/And him the best o' me.   Reminiscence. Wallace Irwin.   FiBHP; NOBL

...It seems important not to hurt the land.   Rosebud.   Jon Anderson. MAYP

It seems me speaking all the lonely time.   Soliloquy: South Africa.   Arthur Nortje.   WhB

It seems the way to talk about old men.   Old Men.   Alicia Ostriker. AMV-81

It seems to be just what they want.   Limerick: "A Clergyman out in Dumont."   Morris Bishop.   LiBL

It seems to me I may be capable/Once I'm a skeleton, of love and wars.   The Knowledge That Comes Through Experience.   Jane Cooper.   NMM

It seems tonight all Closing bells are tolling/Across the Duchy shire wherever I turn.   The Thermal Stair.   W. S. Graham.   FaBoMo

It seems we haven't traveled far enough/let's sail sail on....   Anti-Nostalgia. Henryk Grynberg.   VWA

It sets the sand a-blowing,/And the blackberries a-growing.   What's the Railroad.   Henry David Thoreau.   ELU; MAmP; PoEL 1-5; TAP

It shakes its wondrous plumes of thought/And trails the stars along with them.   Unity.   George William Russell.   MoRP

It shall be buried in excelsior.   Japan.   Anthony Hecht.   CrMA; LiTA; LiTM

It shall be freed from foreign injury.   On the Death of a Prince: A Meditation.   Thomas Philipott.   JCP

It shall be Thy royal throne.   Take My Life and Let It Be.   Frances Ridley Havergal.   BLRP; GoTF; TreFT

It shall be witty, and it shan't be long.   Impromptu Lines on Being Asked by Sir Thomas Robinson...   Philip Stanhope, Earl of Chesterfield.   FaBoEE

It shall reach you yet.   Adam.   Anthony Hecht.   CoPo

It shall stay and cheer the end!   My Picture.   Adelaide Anne Procter.   PeD

It shall suffice that they were breathed and died for her delight.   Devotion. Thomas Campion.   NOBE; OBEV

It shall yet stand up the soldier of ultimate victory.   Ah, Poverties, Wincings, and Sulky Retreats.   Walt Whitman.   CBEP; OBSP

It shines and you ride its shining.   Sometimes Heaven Is a Mean Machine. William Pitt Root.   MAYP

It shook itself and was all green.   Spring Oak.   Galway Kinnell.   BoNaP; ELU; NePoAm

It should a been tauld for mony a lang/year,/The slaughter o the laird of Meller-/stain.'   The Slaughter of the Laird of Mellerstain.   *Anonymous.* ESPB

It should be better bred.   The Sunset.   Gelett Burgess.   FaBoNo; HBVY

It should be courted, ne'ertheless/In one who must, like me, be feared. Stanzas.   Pierre Corneille.   LiTW

It should be my wishing/That I might die kissing.   Song: "O, that joy so soon should waste!".   Ben Jonson.   LiTL; ViBoPo

It sings of its needles of ice, sings because of the scars.   Leap in the Dark. Roberta Hill.   WPOW

It sinks, and I am ready to depart.   On His Seventy-Fifth Birthday.   Walter Savage Landor.   AnEnPo; AWP; BLPL; BoLiVe; EBEV; GoTF; InPo; LiTB; OAEL 1-2; OAEP; SeCeV; TreF; TrGrPo; WHA

It sinks there into the place of the white gum trees, at Milin-/gimbi.   The Moon-Bone Cycle: The Evening Star.   *Anonymous.*   CBAP; WTO

It skims the earth/but always rises.   Epithalamion.   Grace Schulman.   FAZ

It sleeps as it's always slept, without/Shadow, waiting for nothing.   Northhanger Ridge.   Charles Wright.   HaCAP

It slides into a cloud over Point Lobos.   Phenomena.   Robinson Jeffers.   NoAm; NOBA; OxBA

It slips over it as shadows do, without hurting itself.   Sea-Weed.   D.H. Lawrence.   BoNaP; MOS

It smells as if a town/Was being burnt down.   Clerihews.   Edmund Clerihew Bentley.   FiBHP

It soared on golden pinions free!   Psyche.   Jones Very.   AP

The, it sort o' rests your face–/Just smiling.   Try Smiling.   *Anonymous.*   BLPA; FaFP; WBLP

It speaks of fruits that could not be.   The Flowering Urn.   Laura Riding.   LiTA

It speeds the parting guest.   Youth and Age.   William Butler Yeats.   ELU; FaBoEE

It spins to a rest and sighs, "I'm done."   Wash-Day Wonder.   Dorothy Faubion.   QQQ

It spoils the singing of the Nightingale.   Epistle to John Hamilton Reynolds.   John Keats.   ERoP 1-2

It spread to galleried naves and antique quires.   Barthelemon at Vauxhall.   Thomas Hardy.   UnS

It stands still on the water, rocking, blinking.   Downwards.   C. K. Williams.   GeTw

...It stands tall/between me and those yellow fields.   I Look at My Hand.   Angel Gonzalez.   AMV-81

It stares beyond the glass.   Three Poems, II.   Rosario Castellânos.   BoWoP

It starts with G, like God.   Guns.   John Woods.   GP

It Sticks to my Head!   My Legs Are So Weary.   Gelett Burgess.   LBN

It still exists in some dim way/While I remember it," she said.   My Mother's House.   Eunice Tietjens.   HBMV

...It still survives/Only in ashes, ashes of our lives.   To My Fellow-Mariners, March, '53.   Thomas Whitbread.   NYBP

It stirs the willow trees.   Willows.   Laura Schreiber.   AMV-81

...It stops for the one/who knows him whom the Brahman-knowers/call Eternal.   Upanishads: Third Adhyaya.   *Anonymous.*   ILwL

It strikes where it doth love.   She wakes.   Othello.   William Shakespeare.   BiP

..It sucks what/warmth was left today when wings hung fire.   House and Shutter.   Lewis Turco.   PoPl

It suddenly flies, unwavering, away.   On the Lawn at Ira's.   Gregory Orr.   GeTw

It suffers from brainstorms/And hangs upside down in a tree.   The Manatee.   Carey Blyton.   AmMo

It sure does it for me.   Hills Brothers Coffee.   Luci Tapahonso.   STE

It sure is raining hard today.   Prayer.   Isabella Maria Brown.   NNP; PoNe

...It sure was pleasant to spend a day in the country.   Farm Implements and Rutabagas in a Landscape.   John Ashbery.   CoAP; GP; SM

It swoops, and fires the sky wall.   The Energy of Light.   John Hay.   NePoAm-2

It takes a heap o'livin' in a house t' make it home.   Home.   Edgar A. Guest.   BLPA; BLPL; FaBoBe; GoTF; NIP; OBAL; OHFP; TreF; YaD

It takes a long time to forget an iron man.   Washington Monument by Night.   Carl Sandburg.   CMoP; OFD; OHIP; PoSC

It takes a shadowy stand/That shames a groping hand.   Yucca in the Moonlight.   Glenn Ward Dresbach.   BPAW

It takes all kinds/To make a Heaven.   The Thunderer.   Phyllis McGinley.   EaLo

It takes life to love Life.   Lucinda Matlock.   Edgar Lee Masters.   CMoP; FaBV; FF; HAP; LaNeLa; LiTA; LiTL; LiTM; MCCG; MoAmPo; MoVE; NoAm; NOBA; OxBA

It takes little to loose a link never made,/our gladness together.   Eadwacer.   *Anonymous.*   PBWP

It takes the mote out of the eye.   Bestiary for the Fingers of My Right Hand.   Charles Simic.   AmPA; LCAP

It takes three days and nights to tell it.   The Meanings in the Pattern.   Judy Grahn.   APU

...It takes two lines to make/an angle but only one lime to make/a Margarita.   Of Time and the Line.   Charles Bernstein.   APU

It taught me how to die.   Near the Lake.   George Pope Morris.   AA

It teaches how/not to be afraid of/finding new places/and building in them/all over again.   Advice to the Young.   Miriam Waddington.   NOBC

It teches 'em so light–one's still/A gal at forty year!   The Borrowed Child.   Howard Weeden.   AA

...It tells us what we mean.   The Speaking Tree.   Muriel Rukeyser.   VGW

It thrives without the moon, it thrives alone.   Epitaph for a Negro Woman.   Owen Dodson.   PoNe

It tolls for thee.   For Whom the Bell Tolls.   John Donne.   PoLf; TRV

An' it took on her fair body;/She burnt like holly gren.   Young Hunting.   *Anonymous.*   BaBo; OxBB; ViBoFo

It touched, it struck, it clattered and went out.   The Fear.   Robert Frost.   BeLS; MAPA; NAMP

It troubles my sleep.   Cantico del Sole.   Ezra Pound.   OBAL

It turns and turns in my mind, over and over.   The Mill.   Richard Wilbur.   Psk; SoSe

It unclenches its fist inside her heart.   Death of a Hind.   Alasdair MacLean.   PoSH

...It used to be/a plumber always had a place to wash/when he was through to tally up the costs.   The Plumber Arrives at Three Mile Island.   Robert Stewart.   AMV-81; FAZ

It vanished from history, as from legend.   Not Being Oedipus.   John Heath-Stubbs.   OxBC; TEP

It wanted to forget.   Two Poems.   Tsurayuki.   LiTW

It wants to shiver with the passion/of the earth/and feel its wings of weakness.   Iron Heaven.   Betti Alver.   BoWoP

It was a bow-legged conductor of a twopenny bus.   Polly Perkins.   *Anonymous.*   DTC; OxBoLi

It was a Chinese who/imagined this masterpiece.   Nine Nectarines and Other Porcelain.   Marianne Moore.   OxBA

It was a dance.   There Was a Dance, Sweetheart.   Joy Harjo.   TWSS

It was a drop too much.   Tim Turpin.   Thomas Hood.   WiR

It was a funky deal.   It Was a Funky Deal.   Etheridge Knight.   BOLo; BPo; PoBA

It was a great treat/To his lofty New-England nose.   A Hawthorne Garland.   Richard Harter Fogle.   OBAL

..."It was a/green mist, seemed/to lift and choke/the town."   The Pressures.   LeRoi (Imamu Amiri Baraka) Jones.   BPo

It was a hard thing to undo this knot.   At a Welsh Waterfall.   Gerard Manley Hopkins.   FaBoPP

It was a horrid thing to do!   A Low Trick.   Gelett Burgess.   OBCA

"It was a pretty rough trip, but it could have been worse."   The New-Chum's First Trip.   *Anonymous.*   FaBoBa

It was a simple world.   Hen Woman.   Thomas Kinsella.   CIP; IPY

It was a steep, slow climb.   Notes from a Journey.   Sam Hunt.   OCNZ

It was a thing of beauty and was sent/To live its life out as an ornament.   A Young Birch.   Robert Frost.   BoNaP; LiTA

It was a thrust of light restored him here.   Restoration.   Woodridge Spears.   GoYe

It was a wasp.   The Wasp.   Daryl Hine.   NYBP

It was all about that Battleship of Maine.   Battleship of Maine.   *Anonymous.*   FSW

It was all I had left to do.   Eddie and Eve.   Charles Bukowski.   GP

It was all very British.   Political Intelligence.   A. J. M. Smith.   EAS

It was all very tidy.   It Was All Very Tidy.   Robert Graves.   OxBTC

It was always a buyer's market, always.   Royalties.   D. J. Enright.   NOBL

...It was always winter/and a dark snow.   In the New Sun.   Philip Levine.   NNaP

It was an accident.   The Dolls.   William Butler Yeats.   BrPo; CMoP

It was an All-American day.   A Modern Romance.   Paul Engle.   PoPl

It was an ordinary tree/in an old garden-square.   Invisible, indivisible Spirit.   Hilda ("H. D.") Doolittle.   BoWoP

It was and was not she, a shape alone,/Impaled on light, and whirling slowly down.   Four for Sir John Davies.   Theodore Roethke.   NOBA

It was bitter at the core,/That was all I knew.   Black and White.   Esther Lilian Duff.   HBMV

...It was/Both land and morning, and the light/Was loud and everywhere, like bells.   The Summer Countries.   Henry Rago.   VGW

...It was bought by the/highest bidder for 5.2 million dollars.   An Open-Letter-Poem-Note to Vincent Van G.   Bernadine.   LTB

It was done long ago by a common old cow.   Same Old Trick.   William W. Pratt.   QQQ

It was enough to stop a man from girling.   It Was in Vegas.   J. V. Cunningham.   UnTE

It was five in the shadow of the afternoon!   Lament for Ignacio Sanchez Mejias.   Federico Garcia Lorca.   OBVE

It was general conflagration.   The Devil's Thoughts.   Samuel Taylor Coleridge.   FaBoCo; OBSV; OxBoLi

It was good for the virgin mary/its good enough for me   Poem for Unwed Mothers.   Nikki Giovanni.   OBAL

It was good to labour, and after labour/It is good to rest.   Jacob.   Charles Reznikoff.   VWA

It was hard to tell which smelt the worst./Tu rolly day.   Fod.   *Anonymous.*   AmFP

It was he who flew that lay/Stretched upon the desert sand.   Life and Death.   Walter James Turner.   FaBoTw

It was Heaven, it was Heaven,/Come before its time to thee.   The Expectation.   Frederick William Faber.   ACP

It was his first alphabet.   Lucky.   Cathy Song.   BrSi

It was his fort, he said, and he would make it strong.   Boy with a Hammer.   Russell Hoban.   PCP

...It was his happy song, happy with me, it was 1942 or 4,/and he was 53.   Cranston near the City Line.   Ted Berrigan.   APU

...It was his parents' fault. They/called him Dirk.   A Name.   Maxine Chernoff.   APU

It was I, it was I.   Who Killed Poor Robin?   *Anonymous.*   AmFP

...It was in the air!   Epitaphs of the War, 1914-18.   Rudyard Kipling. BrPo; OBWP

It was in the washrag I buried/For my father/To cure a wart.   Washrags. Vern Rutsala.   GP

...It was like/A new knowledge of reality.   Not Ideas about the Thing but the Thing Itself.   Wallace Stevens.   HaCAP; HAP; LCAP; TAP; ViBoPo

It was like feasting upon air.   Morels.   William Jay Smith.   BoNaP; MAT; NYBP; RFM

"It was love–sweetest love–led that soldier away."   The Deserter.   Bayard Taylor.   PaPo

It was,/My beloved/It was–   Vainly.   Nelly Sachs.   NYBP

It was my self you hauled/back from my despair.   The Rescue.   John Logan.   CoAP; NYBP

It was myn hert. I pray you hertely/Helpe me to seke.   Helpe Me to Seke. Sir Thomas Wyatt.   AAS

It was myself that sang in me.   On the South Downs.   Sara Teasdale. MoAmPo

It was not curious so much/As it was wicked of them.   Was It Not Curious? Stevie Smith.   NoAm

...It was/not fishing.   Fishing.   Philip Dow.   WOLT

It was not foolish women's talk/What those four sang.   Alexander the Great. *Anonymous.*   CH

It was not given me to sing/The song as yet unsung.   A Song as Yet Unsung. Yehoash.   TrJP

It was not in their power to stop what the rabble they designed.   The Boyne Water.   *Anonymous.*   AnIV; FaPoR; NOBI; OnYI

It was not love but fear that made him tame.   Ecclesiastes.   Joseph Langland.   NePoEA; PoPl

It was not my hands on the reins/the horse had obeyed/but his voice. Riding.   Florence Grossman.   PH

It was not my heart; it was this poor sorrow alone which broke.   Desolation Is a Delicate Thing.   Elinor Wylie.   MoAmPo

It was not so when Bess did reign and this old hat was new.   When This Old Hat Was New.   *Anonymous.*   OBET

It was not time to sing.   Whittier.   Margaret E. Sangster.   AA

It was only a mouth with a border of Jack.   The Sad Story of a Little Boy That Cried.   *Anonymous.*   BBGG

It was only that snow had fallen!   The Plum-Blossom.   Akahito (Yamabe no Akahito).   AWP

It was only three weeks after/Sarah became the captain's wife.   William Taylor.   *Anonymous.*   OBET

"It was Poverty who went!"   Love and Poverty.   Elisabeth Cavazza Pullen. AA

It was primitive, I its proselyte.   The Aging Poet, on a Reading Trip to Dayton...   Richard Snyder.   Psk

It was sad when that great ship went down.   The Titanic.   *Anonymous.* AmFP; FSW

It was searching for something else.   Casida of the Rose.   Federico Garcia Lorca.   NU

It was simple in the deep earth/and brief.   Nothing but a man.   Nadia Tueni.   BoWoP

It was so long ago...   So Long Ago.   Morris Rosenfeld.   TrJP

It was so quiet we could hear the birds.   Myths and Texts.   Gary Snyder. CAPP; NaP

It was something that you said.   Hartico.   Anna Walters.   VoR

It was terrible for me all over again   A Woman Came to Me.   Michael Silverton.   PoL

It was the breath of change/That breathed them apart.   The Feather.   Lilian Bowes Lyon.   ChMP

It was the dead who groaned within!   The Sleeper.   Edgar Allan Poe   AA; AP; APA; LiTA; NePA; NOBA; OBVV; OxBA; PoEL 1-5; TAP; TrGrPo

...It was the distance/Was savory.   Undue significance.   Emily Dickinson. LiTA; LiTM

It was the great Columbus/Dragging his prize to land.   The Discovery of America.   James Logie Robertson.   NOBV

It was the herbs and the haze.   Memory.   Michael Hamburger.   OxBTC

It was the hour of inquisition, when darkness/wasn't strange to those who dwelled there.   Dark Room.   Fredrick Zydek.   AMV-80

It was "The Irresistable" I read!   Sea Irony.   John Langdon Heaton.   AA

An' it was the last of that bully of this town.   Lookin' for the Bully of the Town.   *Anonymous.*   BaBo

It was the Lord that saved us.   The Armada, 1588.   John Wilson. OxBChV

It was the only thing he ever shoved down my throat.   A Man of Action. Charles Stetler.   GOYP

It was the purest light of heav'n for whose fair love they fell.   Icarus. *Anonymous.*   OBEV

It was the reddest rose in all the world.   Farewell to Juliet.   Wilfrid Scawen Blunt.   BoLoP; EnLoPo

...It was the/song he made which made her/happy, so she lived.   Air: "The Love of a Woman."   Robert Creeley.   VGW

It was the statue in the somnolence/of noon, the cloud, the soaring hawk. Life's Evil.   Eugenio Montale.   AMV-81

It was the thrush who, as the sun appeared,/Held up the Monstrance, a dew-circled leaf.   David Ap Gwillam's Mass of the Birds.   Padraic Colum. CAW

It was the world-memory alone/When I was dead and gone.   Words. Richard Eberhart.   NePA

It was their duty, and they did.   Captain Reece.   Sir William Schwenck Gilbert.   CenHV; EvOK; FiBHP; GN; HBV 1-2; MaC

It was their shining made us stay.   Explanation, on Coming Home Late. Richard Hughes.   ELU

It was then I spun her little ball of yarn.   Little Ball of Yarn.   *Anonymous.* FSW

It was then, of course, they knew she was pregnant.   Long History of the Short Poem.   Paul Hoover.   APU

It was there, I think, we finally met.   The Meeting.   Howard Moss. GOYP; HoAn; NYBP

It was they who girt me with gold and silver...'   The Dream of the Rood. *Anonymous.*   NOCV

It was turning/to the right/and folding into itself.   Hunchbacked and Corrected.   Ken Belford.   NeAC

...It was 2 o'clock and Miriam was quite white/With sorrow. Very well then, Goodnight.   Goodnight.   Stevie Smith.   FaBoWP

It was two sticks.   The Candid Man.   Stephen Crane.   MoAmPo; NLV

It was what she was used to.   Happy Endings.   Gail White.   DFT

It was Willie what got drowned in the deep blue sea.   Deep Blue Sea. *Anonymous.*   FSW

It was you berievt me o my life,/An wi the bishop playd the w   Hughie Grame (C version).   *Anonymous.*   ESPB

It was you who understood; it is we who change.   The Emancipators. Randall Jarrell.   PoA; WaP

It was your blundering mercies kept me alive/when heaven was a luckless dream.   Breasts.   Tess Gallagher.   AmPA

It watches for the dawn.   The Stars Are Lit.   Hayim Nahman Bialik.   TrJP

It well may be. I do not think I would.   Fatal Interview.   Edna St. Vincent Millay.   HAP

It went and cut a pigeon's-wing!   A Few Muddled Metaphors by a Moore-ose Melodist.   Tom (Thomas Hood, Jr.) Hood.   FaBoNo

It went to buy butter/When butter was dear.   Jack Sprat's Cat.   *Anonymous.* OxNR

It were a most delightful thing/To live in a perpetual spring.   Dismissal. Thomas Campion.   OBSC

It were a thing to which one might aspire.   Sonnet: Of Why He Would Be a Scullion.   Cecco da Siena Angiolieri.   AWP

It were better to die,/And soon!   Out of Tune.   William Ernest Henley. MoBrPo

It were in vain,–for Time hath long been knelling,–/"Sad one, depart!"   Last Verses.   William Motherwell.   HBV 1-2

It were in vain/To say again/Fortune's will.   A Lover Left Alone. *Anonymous.*   MeEL

It weren't a thing but the women/trying to run me down   Talking to Myself. Blind Willie McTell.   BluL

It weren't nothing that she knowed of/just something she had heard   Stack o' Dollars.   Sleepy John Estes.   BluL

It whips us whips us whips us dazed.   And "I Know Why the Caged Bird Sings": A Villanelle.   George, Jr Mosby.   LFAC

It who feels nothing It who answers prayers.   The Powerline Incarnation. Les A. Murray.   CBAP

It will be a larger one.   Was He Married?   Stevie Smith.   NoAm

It will be a prairie schooner/With the tongue a-pointing west.   The Prairie Schooner.   Edward Everett Dale.   BPAW

It will be as a heap of ruins with us workers beneath it.'   A Letter from Aragon.   John Cornford.   OBWP

It will be enough.   Baldpate Pond.   E. F. Weisslitz.   NYBP

It will be found, I say to thee/By one who yearneth deep as we.   The Quiet Kingdom.   Carl Busse.   AWP

It will be he/who hangs up first.   The Obscene Caller.   Philip Dacey. AmPA

It will be known I died a constant lover!   Sonnet: "It shall be said I died for Coelia!"   William Percy.   ElL

...It will be news/If you tell me I am saved.   At First.   C. H. Sisson. OxBC

It will be Spring. So: this/Is what it feels like.   Before the Cashier's Window in a Department Store.   James Wright.   CoAP; NYBP; NYP

It will be the day when we remember.   Note from an Intimate Diary. Emanuel Litvinoff.   NeBP

It will be the loveliest song we know.   Autumn.   Itzik Manger.   TrJP

It will be the seethe and drag of the river/That I will hear longer than any mortal song.   River Sound Remembered.   William Stanley Merwin.   SM

...It/will be there/ahead of me, long/before I am. Something for Supper. Carroll Arnett. VoR

It will be through a telescope from here to Arkansas. The State of Arkansas. *Anonymous.* BFSS; CoSo; FSW; TrAS

It will be told/That you are old/By those true tears y'are weeping. Age Not to Be Rejected. *Anonymous.* OBS

It will be torn from your chest/and will emigrate/to the sky. Draft of a Reparations Agreement. Dan Pagis. VWA

It will be word enough of praise. A Poet. Thomas Hardy. NoAm

It will be your body that will fall. Colloquy at Peniel. William Stanley Merwin. NePoEA

It will drift into this room/In an hour..... Night. Donald Jeffrey Hayes. CDC

It will land you, without doubt,/Upside down and wrong side out. Zephyr. Eugene Fitch Ware. PoLf

It will last long enough Letting Go. Richard Shelton. AMV-81

...It will last through the autumn days. Winter Sign. Loren C. Eiseley. SUW

It will look as though I am flying into myself. Death. Bill Knott. EAS

It will make a splendid pie for your/Thanksgiving Spread. Riddle: "First it was a pretty flower." Christina Georgina Rossetti. SoPo

It will matter less/what token we pay/for change One Year to Life on the Grand Central Shuttle. Audre Lorde. CNA

It will mean me. Everybody but Me. Margaret Goss Burroughs. BlSi; FB

It will merge into the splendors/Of the City of the Light. Hail! The Glorious Golden City. Felix Adler. AH; WGRP

It will not be able to help us. The New Poem. Charles Wright. GeTw; HaCAP

It will not be as far away,/as unfamiliar. Dulcimer Maker. Carolyn Forche. SaC

It will not be in our time. May-June, 1940. Robinson Jeffers. LiTA; MoAB; MoAmPo; NePA; WaP

It will not be long/Before I come and visit you. The Corpse-Keeper. *Anonymous.* BoWoP

"It will not be long, love, till our wedding day." She Moved through the Fair. Padraic Colum. InvP; NOBI

It will not be that the eye obeys not. The Giver of Life. Unknown. EaLo

...It will not bring me knowledge/of my hunger. Harvest Song. Jean Toomer. NoP

It will not come. It will not come. Baby-Sitting. Gillian Clarke. FaBoWP

It will not hurt me when I am old. Moonlight. Sara Teasdale. GOYP; VGW

It will not melt but must be chewed.) New Jersey White-Tailed Deer. Joyce Carol Oates. GeTw

It will rustle all night, darling. The Flower. Robert Penn Warren. PoPl

It will slide to the floor in a blue heap. Waiting. Yevgeny Yevtushenko. LLLT

It will smooth life's dull passage, 'twill slope/the descent,/And strew the way over with flowers. A Song: "Hark! 'tis Freedom that calls, come, patriots, awake!" *Anonymous.* PAH

It will snow fiercely enough to fill all these open graves. The Retrieval System. Maxine W. Kumin. FaBoWP

It will take a good scholar/To riddle me that. Riddle: "The land was white." *Anonymous.* OxNR

It will take shape in the end. Walk Past Those Houses on a Sunday Morning. Kendrick Smithyman. AnNZ

It will touch holy letters/I am forbidden. The Scholar's Wife. Susan Mernit. VWA

It will undo him. The Plot against the Giant. Wallace Stevens. CMoP; FF; OxBA

It will vanish forever/Just as A. did. Midpoint. Charles Simic. GeTw

It winna let a poor body/Gang about his biziness! Love Is Like a Dizziness. James Hogg. InMe

It wiz for me ye grat! The Deean Tractorman, Clear. Edith Anne Robertson. OxBS

"It won't be all right in the end, it just won't." Americans in an Orange Grove. Arthur Vogelsang. MAYP

It won't be changed with words. Repetition of Words and Weather. Ruth Stone. BoWoP

It won't be long till/back up this road I'm gone Out on Santa-Fe–Blues. Arthur Petties. BluL

It won't be long till he'll die. The Gambler. *Anonymous.* ViBoFo

It won't go down. Song of the Farmworker. T. R. Jahns. AMV-80

It won't help God/for me to be a nun. Song: "Since I'm a girl." *Anonymous.* BoWoP

It would be agreeable to be this Chinese gentleman. Dreaming in the Shanghai Restaurant. D. J. Enright. OBTV

It would be hard to say what brought them there,/commerce or contemplation. Large Bad Picture. Elizabeth Bishop. EyDe; MiAP; NoP; NYBP; OxBC

It would be I who kept on living here/and kept forgetting. The Keeper. William Carpenter. Psk

It would be impossible/to lose a key here. Keys. Glen Rockwell. AMV-81

It would be painful to interfere Memo. Charles G. Ballard. VoR

It would be such funny rigs/Of good and tender-hearted masters. Funny Rigs of Good and Tender-Hearted Masters. *Anonymous.* OBET

It would break with the weight of a thought! A Hot-Weather Song. Don (Donald Robert Marquis) Marquis. HBMV; YaD

It would confirm, alas! those harsh opinions/Which some men think I always have deserved. To the Frivolous Muse. George Meason Whicher. InMe

It would give me a cough, and a rheumatise too... A Reply to Lines by Thomas Moore. Walter Savage Landor. ChTr

It would give me rheumatics, and so it would you. A Sensible Girl's Reply to Moore's. Walter Savage Landor. FaBoEE

It would have been better than this. Waiting for Icarus. Muriel Rukeyser. NNaP

It would have burned, or rolled/Away, I said.... The Sword. Abu Bakr. TTY

It would like to light up expanses/And to chase away apparitions. The European Night. Stanislav Vinaver. VWA

It would not let the darkness heal/About my heart. My Song. Hazel Hall. HBMV

It would perish of dry-rot. Tamerlane. Victor J. Daley. PoAu 1-2

It wraps itself in silence/closing in on death Like an Ideal Tenant. Ruth Daigon. AMV-81

It writhes. It writhes in awful/waves of brooding. My Arkansas. Maya Angelou. BlSi

Ith woe too vast for being! The Voyage. Heinrich Heine. AWP

Its acute and terrible attritions. Summer Holidays. W. R. Rodgers. LiTB

Its apotheosis, at last–the hurricane! The Air Plant. Hart Crane. MoAB; MoAmPo; NoP

Its beauty is found/In the bombing of this ship. Mr. Kurtz. Robert McGovern. SOTS

Its birth and rebirth and decay. Semele Recycled. Carolyn Kizer. InPS

...Its blundering/stumbling days, again and again, to find my hand. Things That Happen. William Stafford. NNaP

Its body brevity, and wit its soul. What Is an Epigram? Samuel Taylor Coleridge. HBV 1-2; NIP; PV

Its body in a rag-tag army. Autumn Journal. Louis MacNeice. OBWP

...Its brightness/creaks under our shoes. Snow. David Malouf. CBAP

Its brightness harsh as bloodstained swords. Tour 5. Robert Earl Hayden. PPP

Its caves come out and carry us inside. Sleep. Bill Knott. EAS

Its coat-of-arms in my dream: BACH PLAYS BACH! Dream. Marianne Moore. NYBP

...Its colour/glows in the room where I have closed the door. Coming and Going. Louis Johnson. OCNZ

& its colour green. Grass, Grass. George Bowering. NeAC

Its constancy, its peace, be mine. On the Smooth Brow and Clustering Hair. Walter Savage Landor. GBL

Its continuous creation, dangling akimbo/amongst inaudible explosions. Space Fiction. Norman MacCaig. TEP

Its cries a sea/of darkness I do not know my name The Dwelling. Moshe Dor. VWA

Its cry still strung between us like a fine line. Running the River Lines. David Baker. MAYP

Its drop comes from my heart, that's all. May and Death. Robert Browning. FaBoRV; MBW 1-2; NOBE

Its earth bursts like a watermelon/and it's finished. The Body Is the Victory and the Defeat of Dreams. Katrina Anghelaki-Rooke. WPOW

Its ebbing surges in the "sestet" roll/Back to the deeps of Life's tumultuous sea. The Sonnet's Voice. Theodore Watts-Dunton. EtS; HBV 1-2

Its echoes speak/From vale to vale. Song of Longing. *Anonymous.* WTO

Its eyes clouded with sun, its face a death mask. Hunting for Blueberries. Thomas James. AmPA

Its fair Course still begun/By Her and by the Sun. Her Window. Robert Leigh. CavP

Its fathomless love, like the salt mill/at the bottom of the sea. Dinosaur Spring. Marilyn Waniek. MAYP

...Its finish and sharp weight/Flashing in his own hand. The Country of a Thousand Years of Peace. James Merrill. PoCh

Its flight strikes a root in me./A cow beneath it lies down. Trees and Cattle. James Dickey. NePoEA-2

Its flowers are bluish. Song of the Closing Service. Aliza Shenhar. VWA

Its God shall be the God of all the/earth. Seder-Night. Israel Zangwill. TrJP

Its grief, its scorn, can but be broken/By thee, thee, only thee. Thee, Thee, Only Thee. Thomas Moore. GBL; OBNC

Its harsh dance, its grave eccentric song. Alone by the Road's Edge. Diana O Hehir. NPGG

Its head which like your fist/Is large, bald, beakless and blind. Fork. Charles Simic. AmPA; GP; HaCAP; LCAP; PCP

...Its high, obstinate/Hulk more shadowy than the night.   Human Things. Howard Nemerov.   BoNaP

Its King a servant, and its sign/A gibbet on a hill.   In Hoc Signo.   Godfrey Fox Bradby.   TRV

Its light extinguished by a breath of night,/glows with a radiance that is the moon's.   In the Discreet Splendor.   Avner Strauss.   VWA

...Its light/rages, illiterate, until they leave.   The Good Beasts.   Willis Barnstone.   VWA

Its load of ripe Edam upon the quay.   Dutch April.   Daniel Halpern.   GrPl

Its lonely, yearning years,/Shall vanish in the moment of that meeting.   Some Day or Days.   Nora Perry.   HBV 1-2

Its love from living.   The Decoys.   W. H. Auden.   CMoP; SyP

Its lovelessness a deeper sort/Of illness than the womanliness/Of tulips with their bee-dark hearts   Tulips.   Mebdh McGuckian.   FaBoIP

Its main utility and pride/To be your prop, support, and guide.   To a Lady, with a Present of a Walking-Stick.   John Hookham Frere.   FaBoUs

...Its me being music/in kulu se & karma land   Me, in Kulu Se & Karma. Carolyn M. Rodgers.   PoBA

Its me next.   Rape.   Tom Pickard.   FaBoTw

Its mother was a cow.   What Is Veal?   *Anonymous.*   FaBoUs

Its movement/& the void   The Seed of Nimrod.   De Leon Harrison. PoBA

Its music moves, as if always back to a first love.   The Rocking Chair. Abraham Moses Klein.   CaP; HeIP; NoP; PeCV

Its naked arms were black as night,/And grim with prophecy.   Red Sky at Morning.   Gilbert Thomas.   TreFS

Its occasional cries of despair/A function of the furniture.   The Studio. Derek Mahon.   FaBoIP

Its odour quickens all my brain.   The Angel in the House.   Coventry Patmore.   VLP

...Its orange and yellow grasp/on the reality of the idea of apples.   Apples. Lisel Mueller.   NePoAm-2

Its panting tenant is not mine.   Emma.   Oliver Goldsmith.   OnYI

Its passion for its kind, the alder calls/To alder, and the plane to whispering plane.   Epithalamium for Honorius and Maria: Palm Tree Mates with Palm.   Claudian.   HW

Its pieces flash now in the crown/of the tallest oak.   The Trees.   Adrienne Rich.   CoAP; CoPo; NOBA

Its poems appear as nameless synonyms/In the faint collective effort of our art.   Essay on Rime (excerpt).   Karl Shapiro.   PP

Its proof is–to die!   Nydia's Song.   Edward Robert Bulwer, Earl of Lytton. OBVV

Its race of men long flown.   A Prehistoric Camp.   Andrew Young.   CBEP

Its reign will be/diamond/S U N   Vitality.   Maria Amalia Fonte Boa. BoWoP

Its ritual and secret life/Where I wish to be anointed.   Second Avenue Winter.   Charles Simic.   NYP

Its rooms, its chambers every one.   House Blessing.   Arthur Guiterman. BrR; PoToHe; TiPo; TrPWD

Its screendoor screeching,/endlessly screeching.   Euclid Avenue.   Charles Simic.   LCAP

Its secret with the dead.   The Stranger.   Walter De la Mare.   BrPo; MoVE; OxBTC

Its shadow falls alike on thee and me!   To a Rose.   John Banister Tabb. CAW

...Its shadow/on all fours, shaggy, limping at his heel.   Wolf-Boy.   David Malouf.   CBAP

Its shady branches spreading...   Sunrise Sequence.   *Anonymous.*   NOAV

Its silence I hear and obey/That I may lose my way/And myself.   Lights Out.   Edward ("Edward Eastaway") Thomas.   BrPo; MMM; NOBE

Its silence sings a dusty song of dust.   Eagle Sonnets.   Clement Wood. HBMV

Its skull keeps nodding and nodding/Crazily under the moon.   A Maiden Lies in Her Chamber.   Heinrich Heine.   AWP

Its soggy documents retain/your rights in rooms of falling rain.   Squatter's Children.   Elizabeth Bishop.   NePoAm-2; NoP

Its source he cannot know.   The Sign of the Cross.   John Henry, Cardinal Newman.   GoBC

Its stainless glory spreads its snowy blooms.   Dogwood Blossoms.   George Marion McClellan.   BANP

Its sunshine, or its dew?   The Blossom of the Soul.   Robert Underwood Johnson.   AA

Its surface glittering, the dawn, glancing from its glaze, ob-/lique, relentless, unadorned.   From My Window.   C. K. Williams.   SV

Its torrent is immersing/The blue globe at her feet.   Symphony in Blue. Raymond F. Roseliep.   ISi

Its tracings firm as when they first were set.   Like to a Coin.   Arlo Bates. AA

Its trembling echoes wing him to rebirth.   Countee Cullen.   Eugene T. Maleska.   PoNe

Its trunk and silk mesh of kirtle showed evening.   For You I Have Emptied the Meaning.   Louis Zukofsky.   NoAm

Its value in eternity...   Weighing the Baby.   Ethel Lynn Beers.   PoToHe

Its very courage stagnates to a vice.   Invocation.   George Gordon, Lord Byron.   LoBV

Its wheels in need of grease.   Tat for Tit.   Walter De la Mare.   FM

Its. "Why, my God, have I forsaken thee?"   False Gods.   Walter De La Mare.   EaLo

Its windows suddenly gold.   Anxiety Pastorale.   Ted Schaefer.   FAZ

Its worth was less than anything I saw,/But I observed it keeped most in awe.   A Dream, or the Type of the Rising Sun.   Jean Adams.   NOEC

Its youthful dreams, its secret bliss.   The Heart.   Jakov Steinberg.   TrJP

Itself crumbled and became sand like salt and legends   Sunny.   Robert Vander Molen.   FAZ

Itself in a flower, a child,/or another old man.   Distortions.   Pearse Hutchinson.   CIP

...Itself/Is the reader leaning late and reading there.   The House Was Quiet and the World Was Calm.   Wallace Stevens.   HAP; NoP; VGW

Itself more sheer and naked out of the green/In stark-clear roses, than I to myself am brought.   I Am Like a Rose.   D. H. Lawrence.   OBSP

Itself the more intact.   Chiefly to Mind Appears.   C. Day-Lewis.   MoAB; MoBrPo

Itself, too great, for interrupting–more–.   I Got So I Could Hear His Name. Emily Dickinson.   AmePo; CMoP

(Ivory was her breast!)   Confession.   Donald Jeffrey Hayes.   CDC

Iwis, powle-hachet, she blered thine I!   The Sleeper Hood-Winked.   John Skelton.   MeEL

J

Jack and I got see-double drunk.   Rank.   Lincoln Kirstein.   OBWP

Jack Baker he whacked his own father,/And thus ended Wednesbury Cocking. Wednesbury Cocking.   *Anonymous.*   FaBoBa

Jack Frost, the artist's name.   The Fairy Artist.   Nellie M. Garabrant. PoPl

Jack making a touchdown for the winning team.   Dream.   Harold Witt. SM

Jack o' Diamonds is a hard card to play.   Jack o' Diamonds.   *Anonymous.* OuSiCo

Jack Satan smelts the dead to make new bullets.   The Devil's Dictionary: Lead.   Ambrose Bierce.   OBAL

...Jackels attend/The offal. And new cities raven and distend.   A Lion Named Passion.   John Hollander.   NePoEA-2

"Jackson and victory!"   On the Death of Jackson.   *Anonymous.*   PAH

Jade was never what I wanted.   These Labdanum Hours.   Kathleen Fraser. NPGG

Jailors and Jailees/Within us,/Struggling to disprove/Either/Position.   Those Not Confused Are Prisoners of War...   Noah Mitchell.   LFAC

Jane, do be careful.   Jane, Do Be Careful.   Irene Page.   BBGG

Jane in the morning.me tarzan.   Arroyo.   Tom Weatherly.   PoBA

Jane Jane Jane Jane.   Monday Morning Back to School.   David McCord. TiPo

Janis in d'new house/she' glad/she' glad.   Daufuskie.   Mari E. Evans.   BlSi

January snow falls, listen...   Wild Strawberry.   Maurice Kenny.   STE

Jason–sham–too.   Finding is the first act.   Emily Dickinson.   MoVE

Jawbones find new way with meats, loins/Raking and blind, new way with women.   Heroic Heart.   Charles Donnelly.   CIP

Jazz June. We/Die soon.   We Real Cool.   Gwendolyn Brooks.   CAPP; FF; HAP; HeIP; HoPM; IDB; InPK; NoP; PoBA; PrIm; SM; SoSe; TAP; TTY; WeW

Jealousy when it strikes/Sticks in the marrowbone.   Jealousy.   *Anonymous.* KiLC

Jeannette! Jeannette! Jeannette.   Otto Julius Bierbaum.   AWP

Jeez! wha'ld use ale for Athol Brose?   Epistle to John Guthrie.   Sydney Goodsir Smith.   OxBS

Jehovah has triumphed–his people are free!   Sound the Loud Timbrel. Thomas Moore.   GoBC

Jehovah, my God, makes my darkness bright.   In the Distress upon Me. Henry Ainsworth.   AH

Jehovah's final name is deep I AM.   By the Salt Margin.   Abbie Huston Evans.   NePoAm

Jehovah the Blind Oculist/saying/You shall be borne.   Germination.   Arlene Stone.   VWA

Jekkel, and Jessop and one-eyed Jill.   Five Eyes.   Walter De la Mare. PCat

& Jennifer is the daughter of Willie Blake.   We Love You the Way You Are. David McFadden.   NeAC

Jenny came home with an empty can.   Hie to the Market, Jenny Come Trot. *Anonymous.*   OxNR

Jenny kiss'd me. Jenny Kiss'd Me. [James Henry] Leigh Hunt. ALV; BiCB; BLPA; EnLi 1-2; FaBoBe; FaFP; FPL; GoTF; HBV 1-2; InMe; LiTL; NLV; NOBE; NTCP; OBEV; OBVV; PoPl; PoRA; SpRo; TreF

Jenny, you know the city now. Jenny. Dante Gabriel Rossetti. NBM

& Jeremy, where are you/all these scams seem orphaned. Jeremy. Jeffrey Miller. APU

A jerking/whipping bow/and stillness Arabesque. Fred Johnson. PoBA

Jerusalem is the Venice of God. Jerusalem, Port City. Yehuda Amichai. VWA

Jerusalem, next year! Next year, Jerusalem! The Still Small Voice. Abraham Moses Klein. OBCV; PeCV

Jerusalem 1967,/The former address of God. Jerusalem. Shlomo Vinner. VWA

Jerusalem of the future/Which the glare/Of the summer snow unveils. Light of Judea. Claude Vigee. VWA

Jes a-lookin' for a home. Ballit of De Boll Weevil. Anonymous. ABF; NOBA

Jes' jump my bob here and be pardners with him! The Man in the Moon. James Whitcomb Riley. HBV 1-2; HBVY; InMe; NA

Jessie is a little child! Jessie. Bret (Francis Bret Harte) Harte. GN

Jessie Whitehead told me they sometimes choose a tree/and kill it, they so mire the branches. The Park. Robin Blaser. CoPo

Jest a-wearyin' fer you! Wearyin' fer You. Frank Lebby Stanton. HBV 1-2

Jest because it's June! June! June! June Is Bustin' Out All Over. Oscar, II Hammerstein. BLSo

Jest 'fore Christmas be as good as yer kin be! Jest 'Fore Christmas. Eugene Field. ChBR; FaBV; FaFP; FPL; HBV 1-2; HBVY; OHFP; PoLf; TreF

An' jest let me ketch you chasin'/Aft' them white trash any mo'. Mrs. Johnson Objects. Clara Ann Thompson. BlSi

Jest so it might been,/Then ag'in— Then Ag'in. Sam Walter Foss. HBV 1-2

"Jesu Domine!" Little Gregory. Theodore Botrel. CAW

Jesu, gif us grace as Thou wel may to luf Thee/withouten ending. A Song of the Love of Jesus. Richard Rolle. PoEL 1-5

Jesu give us grace, as Thou well may, to love Thee without/ending. Love is Life. Richard Rolle. ACP; CAW

Jesu have mercy of me,/That all this world honoures./Amen. The Penitent Hopes in Mary. Anonymous. MeEL

Jesu, honoured in high degree,/Yet may your grace be ours! Harley Lyrics: Now fade the rose and lily-flower. Anonymous. NOCV

Jesu! how the Jews and harlots/Welcomed Morgan the Buccaneer! Morgan. Edmund Clarence Stedman. AA; HBV 1-2

JESU! may we ever be/Grafted, rooted, built in Thee. Amen. Bread of Heaven, on Thee We Feed. Josiah Conder. TrCP; VLP

Jesu, me underfong! Amen. Of Jesu Christ I Sing. Anonymous. OxBM

Jesu, Thou art found: my God I hail,/My Lord, my God! Where the Blessed Feet Have Trod. Michael (Katherine Bradley and Edith Cooper) Field. OxBoCh

Jesukin is on our breast. Jesukin. Saint Ita. CAW; OnYI

"Jesus absent on vacation, heaven closed till his return.'" The Preacher's Vacation. Anonymous. BLPA; BLPL

Jesus, as He foresaid,/Is risen from the dead. Ye Heavens, Uplift Your Voice. Anonymous. OHIP

Jesus be with you. Columbus Reaches Juana, 1492. Ralph Gustafson. NOBC

Jesus' birthday/Comes again! Round and Round. Dorothy Brown Thompson. BiCB; ChBR

Jesus borned in Bethlea, and in the manger lay. Jesus Borned in Bethlea. Anonymous. AmFP

Jesus Christ is marching at their head. The Twelve. Alexander Blok. LiTW

Jesus Christ of Bethlehem. Let Christian Hearts Rejoice Today. Jean de Brebeuf. AH

Jesus gave him leave to drink,/He drank and fled to glory. Zion's Sons and Daughters. Anonymous. AmFP

Jesus gonna make up my dyin' bed. Tone de Bell Easy. Anonymous. ABF

Jesus, good Paragon, thou Crystal Christ? The Crystal. Sidney Lanier. AmePo; AmP; TrPWD; TRV

Jesus, Good Paragon, thou Crystal Christ? From the Crystal. Sidney Lanier. BePJ

Jesus is born;/In Excelsis Gloria! Jesous Ahatonhia. Jesse Edgar Middleton. CaP

JESUS is our Brother now,/And GOD is All our own! The Incarnation. Charles Wesley. NOCV

Jesus is the Christian's Trust. Jesus Lives, and So Shall I. Chr. Furchtegott Gellert. BePJ; PGD

Jesus, keep me sweet. Keep Sweet. Anonymous. STF

Jesus led me all the way. All the Way My Savior Leads Me. Robert and Fanny J. Crosby Lowry. FSW; STF

Jesus, little brother. To the Lighted Lady Window. Marguerite Wilkinson. CAW; ISi

Jesus, live rock, so that whenever I wish/I can return to port. When the Troubled Sea Swells and Surrounds. Vittoria da Colonna. PBWP

Jesus, look with pitying eye. Evening Contemplation. George Washington Doane. BLPA; BLPL; FaBoBe

Jesus, Lord, at thy birth, Jesus, Lord, at Thy birth. Silent Night. Joseph Mohr. FSW; GoTF; TreF

"Jesus, lover of my soul,/Let me to Thy bosom fly!" Singing My Doubts Away. Anonymous. BePJ

Jesus, my Lord, sent from above. Thy Nail-Pierced Hands. Kathryn Bowsher. STF

Jesus, my Saviour, abides with me still. Moment by Moment. Daniel W. Whittle. BLRP

Jesus, my Saviour, come. The Spirit in Our Hearts. Henry Ustic Onderdonk. AH; BePJ

"Jesus of Nazareth passeth by." Jesus of Nazareth Passeth By. Lydia Sigourney. BePJ

Jesus only, I will, joyous,/Through eternal ages sing. Jesus Only. Elias Nason. BePJ

Jesus our glorious King. Quiet from Fear of Evil. M'K." S.C. BLRP

Jesus receive me hence:/farewell sweet England. Sir Walter Rauleigh His Lamentation. Anonymous. CoMu

Jesus said, "I'll never leave thee,/But will guide while passing through." Have Faith in God. Joe Budzynski. STF

Jesus saves–S & H Green Stamps. In the Interest of Black Salvation. Don L. Lee. BP

Jesus shines brighter, Jesus shines purer,/Then all the angels heaven can boast. Fairest Lord Jesus. Anonymous. TRV; WGRP

Jesus, they run into millions. Soldiers. Anonymous. FaBoEE; GBP

Jesus, Thou canst not pray in vain. Graven on the Palms of His Hands. Charles Wesley. BePJ

Jesus waited long to know thee,/But he knows thee not. In the Silent Midnight Watches. Arthur Cleveland Coxe. AH

Jesus walked into the sun. Stones. William Jeffrey. OxBS

Jesus will be a Father to you–/through pains and sorrow lead you through. Motherless Children. Anonymous. FSW

Jesus your King is born. The Huron Carol. Jesse Edgar Middleton. OBCP

A jet black woman make a rabbit hug a hound/Won't he, baby? All Out and Down. Leadbelly. BluL

A Jew, a Jew, a common vulgar Jew! An Evil Man. Richard Beer-Hofmann. TrJP

A Jew has risen for Midnight Prayer. Midnight Prayer. Hayim Nahman Bialik. TrJP

Jewel, from each facet, flash your laugh at/time! Magical Nature. Robert Browning. VLP

A jewel set,/Unnumbered yet,/In our Republic's coronet! Ulric Dahlgren. Kate Brownlee Sherwood. PAH

Jewel-winged, a weld of blue fire and air. Blue Flag. Dorothy Donnelly. NYBP

Jewels of dew! Play about, Do. Basho (Matsuo Basho). SoPo

The Jews. The Chosen People. W. N. Ewer. ALV; DBV

Jill must have her pair of Jacks. Old Stuff. Bert Leston Taylor. HBMV

Jim Barnes is crawling through the underbrush. These Damned Trees Crouch. Jim Barnes. CDW

Jim crack corn I don't care,/Ole Massa gone away. Jim Crack Corn. Anonymous. PSoN

"Jim Lukus has drowned her and then run away." Pretty Molly. Anonymous. BFSS

Jimmie sees me all the time,–/But Georgie stays away. Georgie Porgie (parody). Franklin Pierce ("F.P.A.") Adams. HBMV

Jimmy crack corn and I don't care,/My master's gone away! The Blue Tail Fly. Anonymous. BLSo; FaFP; FSW; TreFT; ViBoFo

Jimmy doesn't understand much of it either. A Bouquet for Jerry Ford. Mordecai Marcus. SOTS

A jingle in a broken tongue. The Poet. Paul Laurence Dunbar. BPo

...Jingling golden/in otherwise empty pockets. Hubert Horatio Humphrey (1911-1978). Martin Galvin. SOTS

Jingling,/like the smallest,/cowbell/on the junkman's wagon,/in the distance. Masochistic Tendencies. Carolyn Baxter. LFAC

Jingling/on the rusty-green/of yesterday's/fire-escapes. Inventory–to 100th Street. Frank Lima. ANYP

Jinn, take her away. I Am Aladdin. Robert Carlton Brown. AnAmPo

Jist tell them 'twas from Paddy Blake,/Of Bally Blarney College. The Irish Schoolmaster. James A. Sidney. FiBHP

Jitterbugging/in the streets. Jitterbugging in the Streets. Calvin C. Hernton. PoBA

Jo'burg City, you are dry like death,/Jo'burg City, Johannesburg, Jo'burg City. City Johannesburg. Mongane Wally Serote. WhB

Joan as my lady is as good i' th' dark. No Difference in the Dark. Robert Herrick. CaPo

Job's patience or Solomon's wisdom, and I love attributes./Whoop!!! Jack and Jill (parody). Charles Battell Loomis. BXAP

Jocond his Muse was; but his Life was chast. The Pillar of Fame. Robert Herrick. AnAnS 2; JCP; SeCP

...Joe beat its brain out on the wheel. Sheet Lightning. Edmund Charles Blunden. HaMV

John, and the wings, and healing. Janitor Working on Threshold. Margaret Avison. PeCV

John, bid the Coachman drive. Lady M. M—'s Farewell to Bath. Mary Wortley, Lady Montagu. CEP

"John Blunt, ye hae spoken the fore-/most word,/Ye maun rise up and bar the door." Get Up and Bar the Door (B version). Anonymous. ESPB

John Brown is filling his last cavity. Epitaph on a Dentist. Anonymous. FaBoEE; GoTF; OxBoLi; TreFS

John Brown's soul not a higher joy can crave,/Freedom reigns to-day! John Brown. Edna Dean Proctor. PAH

John Case yet lives, though Saffold's dead. To Saffold's Customers. John Case. FaBoUs

John Deere, Farm-All, Oliver, Massey-Ferguson. On the Land. Ray Lindquist. TAT

John died, of no complaint,/With owl-eyes too. Glaucopis. Richard Hughes. OBMV

John Dory at length, for all his strength,/Was clapt fast vnder board-a. John Dory. Anonymous. BuBa; ESPB; OBSS

John Hardy, that's the last of you. John Hardy. Anonymous. AmFP

"John Henry I've been true to you." John Henry (B vers.). Anonymous. BaBo

The John Jacob H. Limerick: "An amorous M. A." Anonymous. LiBL

"John Jacob Jingleheimer Schmidt!"/Dah, dah, dah, dah, dah, dah, dah. John Jacob Jingleheimer Schmidt. Anonymous. FSW

"John Jones, you have spoken the first word,/Now get up and shut the door." Get Up and Bar the Door. Anonymous. AmFP

John Keats, keep revel with me, too. To John Keats, Poet, at Springtime. Countee Cullen. BANP; CDC

John saw the holy number sitting on the golden altar. John Saw the Holy Number. Anonymous. BoAN 1-2

John saw the island. Biddy, Biddy. Anonymous. OuSiCo

John Thomson's gay lady they took,/And hangd her on yon greenwood/tree. John Thomson and the Turk (A version). Anonymous. ESPB

John Winter coiled the anchor ropes/Among his mates once more. John Winter. Laurence Binyon. MOS

Johnnie eats them like a man. Little Fishes in a Brook. Anonymous. OxNR

...Johnny Damnation, that's me! John without Heaven. John Malcolm Brinnin. NoAm

Johnny get your gun, get your gun! Johnny Get Your Gun. F. Belasco. PSoN

Johnny get your hair cut, hair cut short. Hey Betty Martin. Anonymous. FSW

Johnny has gone for a soldier. Buttermilk Hill. Anonymous. FSW

Johnny Pringle he, Betty Pringle she,/and Piggy Wiggy. Betty Pringle's Pig. Anonymous. OxNR

Johnny's got the sweetest girl,/Mrs. Vickers' daughter. Mrs. Vickers' Daughter. Anonymous. AmFP

Johnny's so long at the fair. Oh, Dear! What Can the Matter Be? Anonymous. CH; FaBoNo; FSW; LiTL; PoPle

..."Join heir/With Christ make hast to ask him for thy share." My Legacy. Helen Hunt Jackson. HBV 1-2

Join in the chorus, my hookabadar. Cossimbazar. Henry Sambrooke Leigh. NA

Join in the chorus, sound the right sour note. Winter Coming On. Martin Bell. FaBoMo; OxBTC

Join in the shout, Noel, Noel. Carol of the Birds. Bas-Quercy. OHIP

Join in their anthems immortal. When Shall My Pilgrimage, Jesus My Saviour, Be Ended? Andrew Rudman. AH

Join your right hands, this broom step over,/And kiss the lips of your own true lover. The Chimney Sweeper. Anonymous. AmFP

Joined to its clearness, of their force! Courage. Matthew Arnold. OAEL 1-2

Joining with freedom's deathless song thy/deathless name. John Bright. Francis Barton Gummere. AA

Joint-heirs with Christ, because they bled to save/His weak ones, not in vain. The Loss of the Birkenhead. Sir Francis Hastings Doyle. HBV 1-2

A joke on his doctor, who'd thought that he was well. Hardly a Man Is Now Alive. Ring Lardner. OBAL

...A joke their daughters learn/From their new husbands. Home on the Range, February 1962. Edward Dorn. ConAP

The joke they wouldn't understand—/'Twould pain them very much!' The Bishop of Rum-ti-Foo. Sir William Schwenck Gilbert. CenHV

Joking on the fabulous mountain-side. On Looking into E. V. Rieu's Homer. Patrick Kavanagh. NOBI

Jolly good, I said. I Saw a Jolly Hunter. Charles Causley. BoAnP; OnUR

A jolly good Pipe of Tobacco! The Pipe of Tobacco. John Usher. HBV 1-2

Jonah's thoughts flying through his being. Jonah and the Whale. Viola Meynell. EtS

Jones Very above all. Irrational. Philip Lamantia. APU

A jonquil, not a Grecian lad. Look Not in My Eyes, for Fear. Alfred Edward Housman. PeHV; PoEL 1-5

A Joseph did betroth/Them both. To Our Blessed Lord upon the Choice of His Sepulchre. Richard Crashaw. ACP

Joseph, i shine, oh joseph, oh/illuminated night. Holy Night. Lucille Clifton. GeTw

Josephs all, not tall enough to try'. Mana Aboda. Thomas Ernest Hulme. FaBoMo

Jou be to you, who do enjoy/Your hearts with clearness armed. Psalm XXXII. Sir Philip Sidney. FCP

The journey, and the struggles of the moon. Ajanta. Muriel Rukeyser. LiTA; LiTM; MiAP; MoAB; MoAmPo; NNaP

The journey through life begins. The Hunter Sees What Is There. Edgar Jackson. LFAC

Jove built Arcady again, and so today I love/the white round shoulder of the distant sky. Merits of Laughter and Lust. Eli Mandel. PeCV

Jove send me more such after-noones as this. Elegies. Ovid (Publius Ovidius Naso). OBVE

Jove would leap down to surfeit here. A Serving Men's Song. John Lyly. ALV; NOBE; OBSC

Joy and pleasure is there none. Pluck the Fruit and Taste the Pleasure. Thomas Lodge. EIL

A joy as cleansing as the wind that fills/The open spaces on the sunny hills. If I Had Ridden Horses. Theodore Maynard. HBMV

Joy comes late. New Words for an Old Song. Babette Deutsch. NePoAm

Joy fill'd the brook, and comfort cheer'd the/field. Summer Rain. Hartley Coleridge. VLP

Joy! for Christ the Lord is come. Hills of God, Break Forth in Singing. John Wright Buckham. AH

The joy for the tear—the peace for the pain. The Aloe Plant. Henry Harbaugh. BLPA

Joy from the mingling of their misty limbs! Possession. Richard Aldington. MoBrPo

Joy is everywhere, funiculi, funicula! Funiculi, Funicula. Luigi Denza. TreFT

Joy nor sorrow knows not from each other/Birth and death. Birth and Death. Algernon Charles Swinburne. MaVP

Joy of joys for an hour to-day; then away, farewell! The Days of Our Youth. Anonymous. AWP

The joy of the boundless future—nay, God himself is/thine! Forward. Edna Dean Proctor. HBV 1-2

Joy out of strife by sparing/O'ercamest the sources of terror/In love with all that remains. Roma. Rutilius. CTC

Joy shall be theirs in the morning!' Wind in the Willows (excerpt). Kenneth Grahame. PCh

The joy she gives is true. Song: "Tell me no more I am deceived." Sir George Etherege. CavP

Joy, shipmate, joy! Joy, Shipmate, Joy! Walt Whitman. AmP; GoTF; HBVY; MCCG; MoAmPo; MOS; OHIP; TAP; TreFT

Joy sure shall come behind. Resignation. Santob De Carrion. TrJP

Joy, Temperance and Repose/Slam the door on the doctor's nose. Health Counsel. Sir John (1561-1612) Harington. GoTF; TreFT

The Joy that isn't shared, I've heard,/dies young. Welcome Morning. Anne Sexton. CAPP

The joy that only Jesus gives/Makes life worth living here below! A Gift of God. Anonymous. STF

Joy, the whole creation sings,/"Jesus is the King of Kings!" Wake the Song of Jubilee. Leonard Bacon. AH

The joy to be here/for one more spring. Spring Song. Katharine O'Brien. GoYe

Joye and blisse were ere, were ere me newe. Bird on Briar. Anonymous. OxBM

Joyful and gathering thirst for joy/throughout Unending Day. The Cool Gold Wines of Paradise. Robert Farren. AnIV; SeCePo

Joyful at length may be my fate. Consolation. Henry Howard, Earl of Surrey. NOBE; OBSC

A joyful, blessed life for aye to last. Whoso Would See This Song of Heavenly Choice. John Wilson. AH

"Joyful, joyful, we adore Thee...." Water and Worship: An Open-Air Service on the Gatineau River. Margaret Avison. HAP

Joyful mother of the bravest of the/brave! Albemarle Cushing. James Jeffrey Roche. PAH

Joyful music lifts us sunward/In the triumph song of life. Hymn of Joy. Henry Van Dyke. TRV

Joyfully, joyfully, safely at home.   Joyfully, Joyfully Onward I Move.
William Hunter.   AH

Joys ebb and flow within my tender heart.   A Sonnet of the Moon.   Charles
Best.   CH; HBV 1-2

Joys seldom yet attained by humankind!   To an Unborn Pauper Child.
Thomas Hardy.   CoBMV; FaBoRV; GTBS-P; LiTB; NAs; ViBoPo

Jubilate, Amen.   Hark! The Vesper Hymn Is Stealing.   Thomas Moore.
EnRP

JUDGE GIVES NEGRO 90 DAYS IN COUNTY JAIL.   Ballad of the
Landlord.   Langston Hughes.   HaCAP; NOBA

Judge if we do not love each other well.   An International Episode.
Caroline Duer.   AA; PAH

Judge tenderly–of Me   This Is My Letter to the World.   Emily Dickinson.
AmePo; AmPP; AnNE; GoTF; NoAm; NOBA; OxBA; SCV; TAP; TreFT

Judge then what debtor can keep touch truly.   A Secret Love or Two I Must
Confess.   Thomas Campion.   AAS; ErPo

Judge Thou us then, O Judge of men, if we deny them thrice!   If We Break
Faith–.   Joseph Auslander.   TRV

The judge tol' Dupree, "I believe you quit too late,/Because it is already your
fate."   Dupree (B vers.).   Anonymous.   ViBoFo

Judge when you hear.   A Midsummer Night's Dream.   William Shakespeare.
GDP

Judge whether I am happy, yea or no.   The Deformed Mistress.   Sir John
Suckling.   BXAP; ErPo

Judgement must come, and water then will be/A heaven to thee in hellish
misery.   On King Richard the Third, Who Lies Buried under Leicester
Bridge.   Sir John Suckling.   CaPo

Judges so just, so knowing, and so kind.   Epilogue Spoken at Oxford by Mrs.
Marshall.   John Dryden.   ATP

Judging that theft of fire from which they died.""   Prometheus Unbound.
A. D. Hope.   OxBC

The judgment of your peers!   The White Man's Burden.   Rudyard Kipling.
EnLi 1-2; FaBoPV

Juicy cherries tremble and fall on my lips.   Adjectives.   Moishe Nadir.
TrJP

Julia, roll! Roll! Julia, roll!/The Liverpool girls they've got us in tow!   Roll,
Julia, Roll.   Anonymous.   ShS

Juliet appears, and changes earth to heaven.   Epigram: "First in his pride the
orient sun's display."   Hilaire Belloc.   FaBoEE

Juliet has her hand on my door   Two Poems on the Emotions.   David
Shapiro.   ANYP

Juliet was next me and I do not know.   Juliet.   Hilaire Belloc.   BoLoP;
ELU; EnLoPo

July and June have slipped away/And August's here again.   August.   Helen
Maria Winslow.   YeAr

...July comes, and she/More wealth brings in, then all those three.   The Four
Sweet Months.   Robert Herrick.   WiR

July is born.   Weekend Stroll.   Frances Cornford.   BoNaP

July is just in the nick of time!   The Mowers.   Myron B. Benton.   YeAr

Jump back, honey, jump back.   A Negro Love Song.   Paul Laurence
Dunbar.   BANP; PoNe

Jump forward into the past/to bring back/goodness.   To Be Quicker...   Don
L. Lee.   JB

Jump–he went over.   Leg over Leg.   Anonymous.   OxNR

...Jump into focus/like true events under a microscope.   Stopping by
Shadows.   Robin Fulton.   PoSH

Jump into the thistledown/Sleep all night!   The Fairies.   Patricia Hubbell.
WSC

Jump stop shake.   Blackberry Sweet.   Dudley Randall.   BOLo; HAP; InPS;
NBP; NCSH; PAI; WeW

Jumpety-Bumpety-Hop!   The Kangaroo.   Anonymous.   SoPo

June, fuchsia and ear-lobe,/Snapdragon and bee.   June Song of a Man Who
Looks Two Ways.   Leslie Daiken.   NeIP

June in her eyes, in her heart January.   The Spring.   Thomas Carew.
AnAnS 2; CaPo; NoP; PoEL 1-5; PPoe; TrGrPo; WiR

June's ecstacy are these/That men call aspen trees!   Spring Song of Aspens.
Lilian White Spencer.   PoOW

A junkie with a flute in the rain   A Junkie with a Flute in the Rain.   David
Fisher.   NPGG

Juno's peacock screamed.   Meditations in Time of Civil War.   William
Butler Yeats.   CABL

Jupiter! What's the difference? Let/them go!   Classical Criticism.   George
Lynde Richardson.   AA

Jure divino, whip and spur again.   Dr. Wild's Ghost.   Anonymous.   APAS

The jury correctly the murder did tell.   Naomi Wise.   Anonymous.   ViBoFo

The jury hangs o'er/The rose marie.   The Two Sisters.   Anonymous.   MAT

Just a bad man, a thief.   Five Lyrics from "Good for Nothing Man".
Kenneth Pitchford.   CoPo

Just a-janglin' for old Santa Fe.   The Santa Fe Trail.   Anonymous.   CoSo

Just a knife-edge/this side of the horizon.   Blackfish Poem.   Milton Acorn.
NeAC

Just a little bit of loving,/And then you can be gone   Brown Skin Girl.
Tommy McClennan.   BluL

Just a little wee bunch of hair.   The Squirrel.   Anonymous.   FSW

Just a little white with the dust.   Break of Day in the Trenches.   Isaac
Rosenberg.   BrPo; FaBoMo; GTBS-P; MMM; MoBrPo; NIP; NOBE; NoP;
OAEL 1-2; OBWP; PoA; SeCePo; ViBoPo; VWA; WaaP; WaP

Just a minute while I write that down!   Testament.   Bill Zavatsky.   APU

Just a nickel–here you are!   Lemonade Stand.   Dorothy Brown Thompson.
SiSoSe

Just a portable, washable, lovable pup!   Dog Wanted.   Margaret Mackprang
MacKay.   GDP

Just a rain-washed track and an empty gun–/and the old home trail ahead.
The Desert.   Henry Herbert Knibbs.   BPAW

Just a small break,/from this war/on earth.   Woman Guard.   Pancho
Aguila.   LFAC

Just a soldier,/In the army.   I'm a Soldier in the Army of the Lord.
Anonymous.   AmFP

Just a wearyin' for you.   Just a Wearyin' for You.   Frank Lebby Stanton.
GoTF; TreF

Just a word from you and my dime/will be flying through the mails.
Dynamic Tension.   Steve Sanfield.   SOTS

...Just able/still to swiftly flow/it goes, it goes.   Poem: "This beauty that I
see."   James Schuyler.   PoA

Just about the time the morning broke.   Just Then the Door.   Merrill
Moore.   AnEnPo

Just an orange!   What Is Pink?   Christina Georgina Rossetti.   GoJo;
OnUR; OxBChV; SUS; TiPo

Just as a gesture/of good faith.   How to Change the U.S.A.   Harry
Edwards.   NBP; TW

Just as if bottled velvet tipp'd over one's lips.   The Fudge Family in Paris
(excerpt).   Thomas Moore.   BIrV; OBSV

Just as if there'd been a ball/with a magic wand and all.   Cinderella Grass.
Aileen Fisher.   DFT

Just as it will for evermore.   The Rose Still Grows beyond the Wall.   A. L.
Frink.   BLPA

Just as that monkey would, poor Polly, have done for you.   Poor Poll.
Robert Bridges.   EBEV; MoPo; OxBoLi; OxBTC

...Just as the El burst overhead/like a thunderclap.   On Hot Days.   James
Reiss.   AmPA

Just as the harvesters have said.   The Harvest Elves.   Wilfrid Thorley.
BrR

Just as the screening room door slams shut.   Western Movies.   Jeffry Jensen.
AMV-80

Just as the tall round moon arose.   Honey Dew Falls from the Tree.   John
Clare.   AtBAP

Just as the twig is bent, the tree's inclined.   Moral Essays.   Alexander Pope.
GoTF

Just as they did a thousand years ago/In morning meadows when the world
was young.   Clonard.   Thomas S. Jones, Jr.   HBMV

Just ask him about the time we all went up the trail.   John Garner's Trail
Herd.   Anonymous.   CoSo

Just barely/Beginning to walk.   The Spoon.   Charles Simic.   NNaP

Just because He loved me so.   Oh, No Cross That I May Carry!   Alice
Mortenson.   BePJ

Just because it perished?   Passer Mortuus Est.   Edna St. Vincent Millay.
CMoP; FaBoWP; MoAmPo; OxBA

Just because it's there.   The Baby Hilary, Sir Edmund.   Kathleen Leland
Baker.   NLV

Just bury it/and hide its face–/for shame.   Death.   William Carlos Williams.
OxBA; VGW

Just by dropping a kind word.   The Difference.   Anonymous.   STF

Just California stretching down/The middle of the world.   Just California.
John S. McGroarty.   BPAW

Just call it weathergrams.   Weathergrams.   Lloyd J. Reynolds.   FAZ

Just call the driver aboard and hitch a lantern on his back.   Raging Canawl.
Anonymous.   AS

Just controls their operations: the Napoleon of Crime!   Macavity: the Mystery
Cat.   Thomas Stearns Eliot.   BiP; CenHV; EnL; FaBoCo; HaMV; InPS;
NLV; NOBL; OBCA; OnUR; OxBChV; PAI; PoRA

...Just cram her/stocking with goodies, from the top/clean down to the toe!
Hang up the Baby's Stocking!   Anonymous.   OBCP

Just dreamin' about her. Havin' a good time.../two other women...   Talking
Blues.   Anonymous.   FSW

Just dump trucks in the distance/raising dust.   Driving through Coal Country
in Pennsylvania.   Jonathan Holden.   GOYP

–Just empties coming back.   Empties Coming Back.   Angelo De Ponciano.
BLPA

Just fetch your Jim another quart/To wet the other eye.   I Have No Pain.
Anonymous.   FaBoCo

Just find something good to do.   When Things Go Wrong.   Anonymous.
STF

Just for the birth long ago of a boy.   Christmas Day.   Roy Fuller.   OBCP

Just for the right to crawl after my children. The Eighties Becoming. Bob Rosenthal. APU

Just for you the colours filter through,/Just for you. Still He Sings. Allan Taylor. OBET

"Just give till the Master stops giving to you." How Long Shall I Give? *Anonymous.* BLRP

Just go on being a poor man. Sure a Poor Man. *Anonymous.* WTO

Just grief, heart tears, plaint worthy A Funerall Song (Lamenting Syr Phillip Sidney). *Anonymous.* CH

Just hands, hands, hands, lad,/Hands, hands, hands. Hands. Alex Glasgow. OBET

Just how hard I'd resist if a Vamp should insist,/On working the Vamp stuff on me! The Vamp Passes. James J. Montague. HBMV

Just in the happy Minute. A Song to Cloris. John Wilmot, Earl of Rochester. ErPo

...Just just barely not wringing/The swan's neck. Venice. James Wright. AMV-81

Just laying off, for evidence,/An overcoat of clay. Death is a dialogue. Emily Dickinson. WGRP

Just leap and die along her polished sides. On Seeing a Fine Frigate at Anchor in a Bay off Mount Edgecumbe. N. T. Carrington. FaBoPP

Just like being/awake/ain't it/frederick. Dreams. Charles Cooper. PoBA

"Just like Daniel Boone, coming back to/Work these bears." Percy/68. Glenn Myles. NBP

Just like I do,/Oh my Lord, just like I do. Look over Yonder. Lawrence Gellert. TrAS

Just like the ocean/carries the light on its back/for miles and miles and miles. A Field Poem. Laura Valaitis. GOYP

Just like the Travels of Captain Cook. The Pedlar's Caravan. William Brighty ("Matthew Browne") Rands. OxBChV

Just like these idle waves, son Cotton! Izaac Walton, Cotton, and William Oldways. Walter Savage Landor. NBM; PoEL 1-5

Just locking up–to Die. She dealt her pretty words like blades. Emily Dickinson. HAP

"Just looking at the Indian dance." Indian Dance. Frederick Niven. CaP

Just looking round to see how far/It is–Occasionally– We do not play on graves. Emily Dickinson. MoVE; NIP; PoEL 1-5

...Just missed him! On a Squirrel Crossing the Road in Autumn, in New England. Richard Eberhart. HeIP; LiTM; NePA; PoCh; Psk

Just one more cheer for her, Kady Brownell! The Daughter of the Regiment. Clinton Scollard. PAH

Just one of God's creatures, a creature fair. Guard. Michael C. Martin. WaP

Just one of the crowd lunching on Calvary. Santa Claus. Howard Nemerov. HAP

Just one wife for one man! One Wife for One Man. Frank Aig-Imoukhuede. PBA

Just passing through, you'd say/it looks like foolishness. In a Country Cemetery in Iowa. Ted Kooser. DFF

Just platoons of Scouts/planting flags. Memorial Day. Laureen Ching. AMV-80

Just pull an honest load, and then/There'll be no time for kicking. Horse Sense. *Anonymous.* BLPA; GoTF; TreFT; WBLP

Just push back the coffin lid,/Look down on a gambling man. Wild Bill Jones. *Anonymous.* AmFP

Just pushing For deLawd. Lucille Clifton. CNA; PoBA; TAP; TwCP

Just Quartering a Tree– The wind begun to knead the grass. Emily Dickinson. HAP

Just reeling off the names is ever so comfy. Lakes. W. H. Auden. NePA; NePoAm

Just remember the Red River Valley/And the cowboy who loves you so true. Red River Valley. *Anonymous.* BPAW; CoSo; FSW; TreFS

Just saddle your horse, young John/Forsyth,/And whistle, and I'll come soon.' Eppie Morrie. *Anonymous.* ESPB; OxBB

Just shrugs and says, "I never axter." Limerick: "A vigorous matron of Baxter." Jr, Blount Roy. TDH

Just so, I am grateful to be singled out though I am of low birth. The clear water of the imperial pond. Ise Tayu. BoWoP

Just so long and long enough As Freedom Is a Breakfastfood. Edward Estlin Cummings. AnFE; CMoP; CoAnAm; LiTA; LiTM; MAT; NOBA; OxBA; TAP; VGW

Just so much honor, when thou yeeld's to mee,/Will wast, as this flea's death took life from thee. The Flea. John Donne. AnAnS 1; BiP; BLPL; BoLoP; CABA; CBEP; EBEV; FF; FM; ForPo; HoPM; InPS; JCP; LiTB; LiTL; MAT; MePo; NIP; NLV; OAEL 1-2; PoPle; PPoe; SeCP; SeCV 1-2; SoSe; TEP; TrGrPo

Just so that my evil spirit won't be/hanging around your door no more Six Week Old Blues. John Henry Barbee. BluL

Just so the sallow trunk/Divides, and the branches/Are pale and smooth. Birch. Louis Simpson. ELU

Just spare me over/another year. Death Is Awful. Reed, Doc Hall, Vera. BluL

Just start to sing as you tackle the thing/That "cannot be done," and you'll do it. It Couldn't Be Done. Edgar A. Guest. BLPA; FaBoBe; FaFP; FPL; GoTF; STF; TreFS; WBLP; YaD

Just such enactments, just such daybreaks seen. A Bird-Scene at a Rural Dwelling. Thomas Hardy. FM

...Just the great wings spreading wide. Lilith: Adam to Lilith. Christopher John Brennan. PoAu 1-2

Just the muffled clink of your chains. To Song. Olga Berggolts. BoWoP

Just the same as if/They was people. Friends. Ray Durem. PoBA

Just the way the world began. Dawn of the Space Age. John Ciardi. OBAL

Just then the dearest of wives is a joyless problem. Andante, Ma Non Assai. Rufinus Domesticus. ErPo; LiTW

Just think of Jack Haggerty and the Flat River girl. Jack Haggerty. *Anonymous.* AmFP; ShS; ViBoFo

Just think, that She'll be eighty-one/When I am forty-nine! My Rival. Rudyard Kipling. OxBTC

Just this side of stillness and of death. The Morning Track. Edward Parone. NYBP

Just thought of one–and naturally died. The Greek Anthology (excerpt). *Anonymous.* ShM

Just through the woods we'll run, brave boys,/Just through the woods we'll run. Bold Rangers. *Anonymous.* BFSS

Just to feel like those who met/In the graceful minuet–long ago. The Minuet. Mary Mapes Dodge. OHFP

Just to keep her from the foggy, foggy dew. The Foggy Dew. *Anonymous.* AS; DTC; FSW; GBP; LiTB; OxBoLi; UnTE

Just to meet me over yonder/On that bright and golden shore. The Dying Mine Brakeman. Orville J. Jenks. AmFP

Just too late to save the stamp. Waste. Harry Graham. FaBoCo

Just try to be the fellow that/Your mother thinks you are. If I Only Was the Fellow. Will S. Adkin. BLPA

Just turn your back on her with scorn and disdain. The Range Riders. *Anonymous.* CoSo

Just under the water/It usually goes. The Flight. Theodore Roethke. TrGrPo

Just up and down and up and down. The Liftman. H. A. C. Evans. PoL

Just watch Melissa sweep a room! When Young Melissa Sweeps. Nancy Byrd Turner. NTCP

Just what it means I do not understand. Felo Da Se. Thomas Blackburn. OxBTC

Just when it meets his hopes, and proves the heav'n/He wanted, for a wealthier to enjoy! Capability Brown. William Cowper. SaC

Just when the water was settled and at home. Plans for Altering the River. Richard Hugo. FYAP

Just where the world begins–/Under my eyes. Song: "How do I love you?" Irene Rutherford McLeod. HBV 1-2

Just whisper if you get a chance to mother dear, and say,/I love her as I did long, long ago. Just Tell Them That You Saw Me. Paul Dresser. FSN; GoTF; TreFS

Just who cares to come with me. A Poem on Inter-Uterine Device. A. Rasheed Ghazi. PeD

Just you go down to Derby,/And you'll see the same as I! The Derby Ram, I. *Anonymous.* AmFP

Just your foot upon my hand/Softly bids it understand. To a Cat. Algernon Charles Swinburne. PCat

Justice has bid the World adieu,/And dead Men have no Friends. A Ballad. Sir Charles Sedley. CoMu

...Justice is/reason enough for anything ugly. It balances the beauty in the /world. Justice Is Reason Enough. Diane Wakoski. AmPA; CoPo

Justice may nocht have Dominatioun,/Bot quhare Peace makis habitatioun. The Dreme: Of the Realme of Scotland. Sir David Lindsay. OxBS

Justice we love, and next to justice peace. America to England. George Edward Woodberry. AA

Justice will soon prevail. I can tell lies in prose. Self-Criticism in February. Robinson Jeffers. AmPP

The justified mother of men. The Justified Mother of Men. Walt Whitman. OHIP

Justine, you love me not! Justine, You Love Me Not! John Godfrey Saxe. HBV 1-2

K

Ka-la-kaua, the illustrious! Praise Song for King Kalakaua. *Anonymous.* WTO

Kabir says: "As the river enters into the ocean, so my/heart touches Thee." Two Songs, II. Kabir. LiTW

"Kachoo, kachoo, kachoo, sir." Jump-Rope Rhyme. *Anonymous.* NTCP

The Kafir"s Fiery Cross illumes the midnight skies.   The Landing of the British Settlers of 1820 (excerpt).   Alex Wilmot.   ACV

Kafka tilts his telescope/and bursts out laughing.   The Jews in Hell.   Isaac Goldemberg.   VWA

Kalatalustchuk/Mischtaribusiclup-/Bulgari-/Dulbary -/Sagharimsing. e e n / i /   Russian and Turk.   *Anonymous.*   NA

Karen can stand still, Karen can/Pose like a weather vane.   Horse-Girl. Henry Petroski.   PH

Kase dose two locomotives is boun' to bump.   Casey Jones (A vers.). *Anonymous.*   ViBoFo

Kase he's been on de cholly so long.   Casey Jones.   *Anonymous.*   ABF

The Kearsage won. Alabama so brave/Sank to the bottom to a watery grave. Roll, Alabama, Roll.   *Anonymous.*   OBSS

Keats wrote in water that engulfed the world.   Piazza Di Spagna.   Willard M. Grimes.   GoYe

Keen execrations on this plate inscrib'd/Shall reach a judge who nevr can be bribed.   Unhappy Boston.   Paul Revere.   PAH

A keen-eyed brown earth-lover.   Father.   Frances Frost.   SiSoSe; TiPo

Keening a music like distant surf breaking/Within the very heart of the mountain.   Below Mount T'ui K'oy, Home of the Gods....   Joseph Stroud. NPGG

Keep a-inchin' along like a po' inch worm,/Massa Jesus is comin' bye an' bye. Keep A-Inchin' along.   *Anonymous.*   BoAN 1-2

Keep a wing over your heart.   Beware the Cuckoo.   Ernest G. Moll. BoAV; NOAV

...Keep all from every hurt, and deliver from/all wrath to come those who cry to thee:/ALLELUIA.   The Akathistos Hymn.   *Anonymous.*   ISi

Keep an eye on aged beggars/Lest they strike him in disgust.   Once for Candy Cook Had Stolen.   W. H. Auden.   PV

Keep Christ in your minds, my men, and let your cry re-echo.   A Boat Song. Saint Columcille.   NOBI

Keep clean, bear fruit, earn life and watch/Till the white winged reapers come! The Seed Growing Secretly.   Henry Vaughan.   OxBoCh; SeCV 1-2

Keep count of only shining hours.   Lessons.   Louis Untermeyer.   TiPo

Keep driving, boy, get your ass home/where you've got children of your own. Stopping by Home.   David Huddle.   GOYP

Keep him, Lord/As you made him,/Big, and strong, and black.   My Lord, What a Morning.   Waring Cuney.   TTY

Keep his lover waiting.   A Model for the Laureate.   William Butler Yeats. CMoP

Keep house, make love, wreak vengeance.   Yellow Woman Speaks.   Merle Woo.   BrSi

Keep it! for I cannot keep it for Thee.   Take My Heart.   Saint Augustine. TRV

Keep it out of your voice.   The Tone of Voice.   *Anonymous.*   PoToHe

Keep it simple. Down or up.   Grandfather's Heaven.   Naomi Shihab Nye. Str

Keep it. Someday you will understand.   Why Stone Does Not Sing by Itself. Anita Endrezze-Danielson.   STE

Keep love in your life alway.   Keep Love in Your Life.   Thomas Curtis Clark.   WBLP

Keep me ever, by Thy Spirit,/Pure and strong and true.   The Camp Hymn. Mary S. Edgar.   TRV

Keep me f'om sinkin' down f'om sinkin' down.   Keep Me f'om Sinkin' Down. *Anonymous.*   BoAN 1-2

Keep me free/Eternally/As in this hour.   Sung on a Sunny Morning.   Jean Starr Untermeyer.   TrPWD

Keep me in hunger through eternity.   The Taste of Prayer.   Ralph W. Seager.   TrPWD

Keep me in remembrance, long leagues apart.   Ireland.   Stephen Lucius Gwynne.   HBV 1-2

Keep me, Jesus, keep me.   Keep Me, Jesus, Keep Me.   Waverly Turner Carmichael.   BANP

Keep me perpetual in grace and fire!   To the Lord Love.   Michael (Katherine Bradley and Edith Cooper) Field.   OBMV

Keep more than the memory/Of a wolf's head, of eagles' feet.   Crag Jack's Apostasy.   Ted Hughes.   EaLo

...Keep moving till then.   End of the Line.   John Taylor.   FAZ

Keep on building Men!   Ballad of the Common Man.   Alfred Kreymborg. PAL

An' keep on keepin' on.   Just Try This.   *Anonymous.*   WBLP

Keep on tramping, that's the best thing you can do.   The Tramp.   Joe Hill. FSW

Keep open, oh, keep open/My mind, my heart!   Prayer during Battle. Hermann Hagedorn.   TrPWD

Keep sinners in thy maiden mantle gently furled.   Dedication.   Pope Eugenius III.   ISi

Keep the house frae reif and wear.   The Nativity Chant.   Sir Walter Scott. FaBoCh; LoGBV; NAs

Keep the old tryst, sweetheart, and thou/shalt know/If spirits walk.   If Spirits Walk.   Sophie Jewett.   AA; HBV 1-2

Keep the way clear! Let nothing between!   Nothing Between.   C.A. Tindley. BePJ

Keep their feet, mount their tails, and away!   An Appeal to Cats in the Business of Love.   Thomas Flatman.   EnLoPo; GBL; HAP; PCat

Keep thinkin' I won't be lonely/By and by.   Hope.   Langston Hughes. OBCA

Keep thou thine heart close fasten'd, unreveal'd,/A fenced garden and a fountain seal'd.   Retirement.   Richard Chenevix Trench.   OBVV

Keep too busy at your own to want "the other fellow's job."   The Other Fellow's Job.   Strickland Gillilan.   WBLP

Keep us from invaders by land and by sea,/And from all who'd deprive us of our liberty.   On Independence.   Jonathan Mitchell Sewall.   PAH

Keep us strong/to meet the/coming days.   Our Smoke Has Gone Four Ways. Lance Henson.   CDW

Keep vigil on your shores.   The Battle of the Jarama.   Pablo Neruda. WaaP

Keep we must, if keep we can,/These foreign laws of God and man.   Last Poems.   Alfred Edward Housman.   OAEP

Keep your eye on the grand old flag.   You're a Grand Old Flag.   George M. Cohan.   FSN

Keep your eyes on the prize,/Hold on.   Keep Your Eyes on the Prize. *Anonymous.*   FSW

Keep your hand on that plow, hold on.   Hold On.   *Anonymous.*   FSW

Keep your hands upon your wages/And your eyes upon the scale.   A Miner's Life.   *Anonymous.*   FSW; OBET

Keep your head. Remain a virgin.   Caution.   *Anonymous.*   UnTE

Keep your lamp trimmed and burning,/For this old world it is almost gone. Keep Your Lamp Trimmed and Burning.   *Anonymous.*   FSW

"Keep your manners but play for keeps."   Croquet.   David Huddle.   Str

...Keep your/Mouth shut and don't volunteer.   A Bestiary.   Kenneth Rexroth.   OBAL

Keep yourselves well in hand/And work hard for the State.   A Satirical Poem about Drink.   Chimedin Jigmed.   WTO

Keepand his herd under a heuch,/Amangis the holtis hair.   Robene and Makyne.   Robert Henryson.   BoLoP; BSV; GoTS

Keepers of the lean clean breeds.   For You.   Carl Sandburg.   MoAmPo; MoRP

...Keeping back/in the wet shade where no one can see me.   Black Hawk in Hiding.   George Keithley.   NPGG

Keeping close to the rock.   Another Face.   Ray A. Young Bear.   CDW

Keeping their proper seasons.   Prayer for Fish.   Ronald Wallace.   AMV-80

Keeping to round his holiday/The netted bird, the futile beast.   The Zoo in the City.   Sara Van Alstyne Allen.   GoYe

...Keeping trying in one or two nations/to put his boat back to sea.   Dream Songs.   John Berryman.   CAPP

Keeps him from walking on the snow/And printing it with stars.   The Snow-Bird.   Frank Dempster Sherman.   SiSoSe; SoPo; TiPo

Keeps pleading, "I don't know."   Their height in heaven comforts not. Emily Dickinson.   NePA

...Keeps/sleep from the eyes, to listen to her/otherwise unheard, at least now. Listening to Her.   Natan Zach.   VWA

Keeps the bones of man from lying/On the bed of earth.   Twice a Week the Winter Through.   Alfred Edward Housman.   LiSp

Keeps the sleeping child from harms.   Charm: "Let the superstitious wife." Robert Herrick.   WSC

Keeps the whole woodland echoing to the fall.   Dissonance.   Cedric Whitman.   AMV-80

Kellenberger Road announces itself.   Blessing at Kellenberger Road. Maxine Kent Valian.   AMV-80

Keno! Promenade to seats!   At a Cowboy Dance.   James Barton Adams. BPAW; HBV 1-2; PoOW

Kentucky-born, into the wilderness.   Out of the Wilderness.   Ulrich Troubetzkoy.   GoYe

Kept it from me/Whatever she saw.   Burning the Tomato Worms.   Carolyn Forche.   AmPA

Kept juist eneuch underneath us to ken/That a warl' used to be.   In the Hedge-Back.   Hugh" (Christopher Murray Grieve) MacDiarmid.   BSV; NeBP

Kept safe until they died/And handed on unbroken.   The Old Ladies.   Colin Ellis.   OxBTC

Kept the mighty Mudjekeewis.   The Song of Hiawatha.   Henry Wadsworth Longfellow.   AnNE

Kept the poison and lost the cure.   Song for a Lost Art.   Virginia Brasier. AMV-81

Kept them healthy.   The New Doctor.   Parmenas (Andrew J. Kelley) Mix. DBV

Kept time to the tune of "Dixie."   Wheeler's Brigade at Santiago.   Wallace Rice.   MC; PAH

Kept vigil o'er the sacred spoils of death.   Shakespeare's Mourners.   John Banister Tabb.   AmP

Kerrigan's wife was brought from Cross/home to Inishbofin/and she's buried there.   Pat Cloherty's Version of the Maisie.   Richard Murphy.   IPY

A kerry pipin and the crack and crunch,/And on the table a jug of punch. The Jug of Punch. *Anonymous.* FSW

...The key/Of wisdom and of might through all eternity. The Eternity of Nature. John Clare. EBEV

Keys lids acid and speed. Street Song. Thom Gunn. HeIP; NoP; OxBC

...Keys of either home,/Earth and the world to come. The Elements. John Henry, Cardinal Newman. GoBC

...Keys upon/which fingers recapitulate and learn. Suppose... Lewis B. Horne. AMV-81

Khvum, Khvum, come in answer to our call! Death Rites II. *Anonymous.* TTY

...Kick dust with all the force/Of shoes still hammered to a living horse. Old Men Pitching Horseshoes. X. J. Kennedy. AMV-81˙

Kick outer the Litany. Clerihew. Edmund Clerihew Bentley. NOBL

Kicked Mrs. Kickabout/Round about our coal fire. Three against One. *Anonymous.* OxNR

Kicking in frenzy, a swimmer enmeshed in weeds. Above These Cares. Edna St. Vincent Millay. NoP

Kicking their crowns off whilst they kiss their toes... A Copy of the Last Verses Made by Dr. Wild... (excerpt). Robert Wild. DBV

Kid Stuff/born two thousand years ago. Kid Stuff. Frank Horne. AmNP; PCh; PoBA; PoNe

Kiddies and grown-ups too! The Camel's Hump. Rudyard Kipling. EvOK

Kiddies and grown-ups too! The Hump. Rudyard Kipling. OxBChV

Kidnapped from Odeliseluse/To a New World in air.... Korf's Enchantment. Christian Morgenstern. WSC

Kill it at once or let it go. Plea for a Captive. William Stanley Merwin. NePoEA-2; NoAm; NYBP

Kill not the Moth nor Butterfly,/For the Last Judgment draweth nigh. Auguries of Innocence. William Blake. FaBoCh; LoGBV

Kill the white eel. Song for a Girl on Her First Menstruation. *Anonymous.* BoWoP

Kill those that live, and dead things animate. Celia Singing. Thomas Stanley. AnAnS 2

The Killaspuglonane graveyard/is wet to the bone. The Cold Irish Earth. Knute Skinner. InPK

Killed and redeeming, shines from all pale girls. Now Kindness. Peter Viereck. LiTA

Killed/Festubert, May 9, 1915–R.I.P. In Memoriam. Lewis MacAdams. ANYP

Killing care and grief of heart/Fall asleep or hearing, die. King Henry VIII. William Shakespeare. GN; OAEP; OBS

& Killing/like crazy Vietnam. Clarence Major. PoBA

Kilroy/Is/Here. Pacific Epitaphs. Dudley Randall. NoAm

Kin stay with that bronk when he makes/that high dive. The Strawberry Roan. Curley W. Fletcher. BPAW

"Kind God!" was the last he said. The Child-Musician. Henry Austin Dobson. GN

...Kind Heaven send/Me such a cook or coachman, but no friend. To Julius. Sir Charles Sedley. FaBoEE

The kind little feet of the rain ran by my side. The Comforters. Dora Sigerson Shorter. CH; HBMV

A kind of grace it is to slay with speed. Astrophel and Stella, XLVIII. Sir Philip Sidney. AAS; NoP; SiPS

A kind of insurance a kind of end I Promessi Sposi. Cid Corman. HoAn

A kind of ownership/not to care The North. Barry McKinnon. NOBC

...A/kind of small/nothing. Fancy. Robert Creeley. NOBA

Kind Robin lo'es me. Kind Robin Lo'es Me. *Anonymous.* BSV

A kind sweetheart o' mine, O. The Wren She Lies in Care's Bed. *Anonymous.* PBBP

Kind to Gypsy Jane. Gypsy Jane. William Brighty ("Matthew Browne") Rands. SoPo; TiPo

The kind with falsehood to destroy,/The cruel with despair! Song: "Ye happy swains, whose hearts are free." Sir George Etherege. HBV 1-2; LiTL; ViBoPo

Kind words can never die, no, never die. Kind Words Can Never Die. Abby Hutchinson. AH

Kindliest creature in ould Donegal. Father O'Flynn. Alfred Perceval Graves. HBV 1-2; OnYI

The kindliness of food. He Who Has Never Known Hunger. Elizabeth Jane Coatsworth. TiPo

Kindling floor of your dreaming Mayday. Ed Roberson. PoBA

Kindness fadeth away, but vengeance endureth. Verses in the Style of the Druids (excerpt). Sir Walter Scott. TW

Kindness to animals should be/Attuned to their brutality. Jack and His Pony, Tom. Hilaire Belloc. BoAnP; PH

The kindred rapture of the heart! Incognita of Raphael. William Allen Butler. AA

Kindred to angels on high. Woman. Thomas O'Hagan. CAW

...A king complete/Within thyself, much more an empire joined. Paradise Regained. John Milton. ViBoPo

King Domcome, Lord Howlong, and Baron Fig-tree. An Aristocratic Trio. Judson France. PV

The king had been an hour asleep. Mazeppa. George Gordon, Lord Byron. EnRP; OBRV

A King has come today. A Child Is Born. *Anonymous.* STF

King Herod of the Autumn massacred hundreds/of leaves with his words. Of Autumn. Veronica Porumbacu. BoWoP; VWA

A king. I know he is a king. Whenever the Snakes Come. Hedva Harkavi. VWA

The king is dead. No Swan So Fine. Marianne Moore. AmLP; AP; CoBMV; EyDe; NoP; OxBA; PoA; PrIm; UnPo

The King is drinking deep. Under the Pondweed. *Anonymous.* AWP

The King–is–duller than–the Queen. Ballade Tragique a Double Refrain. Max Beerbohm. OBSV

The King o' Scots, and a' his power/Canna turn Arthur O'Bower. The Wind. *Anonymous.* FaBoCh; LoGBV

King of all kings. Praises of the King of Oyo. *Anonymous.* WTO

A King of Bliss that hight Jesus. Miracle Play. *Anonymous.* ACP

King of Europe, King of Asia! Epiphany. Eileen Duggan. ISi

The King of Heven's Sonne.' Mary Is with Child. *Anonymous.* MeEL

The King of Kings he is so sweet and small. Carol: "We saw him sleeping in his manger bed." Gerald Bullett. HBVY

King over men who have learned all that it/costs to be free. The Surrender of Spain. John Milton Hay. AA

The king rides like a ghost on exhibition/To feed the faithful eye with superstition. A Ribbon Two Yards Wide. Alfred Kreymborg. HBMV

The king's dog! what's a man to do? Dilemma. Bhartrihari. LiTW

King's X–no fairs to use it any more! U.S. 1946 King's X. Robert Frost. NIP

King-walking hill after hill. Hedge Life. James Dickey. LCAP

The King you look for here/you won't find unless you bring Him. Getting to Rome. *Anonymous.* NOBI

The Kingdom come, the Sovereign State of Man! The Quest Eternal (excerpt). Brajendranath Seal. ACV

A kingdom, or a cottage, or a grave. Epigram: "Were I a king, I could command content." Edward, Earl of Oxford De Vere. FaBoEE

The kingdoms are less by three. A Song in Time of Order 1852. Algernon Charles Swinburne. VLP

Kings and crown-princes at her feet. Circumstance. Thomas Bailey Aldrich. AA

Kings are in war but cards: they're gods in peace. The Second Advice to a Painter. Andrew Marvell. APAS

The kings begoud their singin'. The Kings From the East. Alexander Gray. ACV; GoTS

Kings, entirely urban, whom the artist/Paints as such. Gallery Shepherds. Patricia Beer. OxBC

Kings even in captivity. Crossing the Plains. Joaquin Miller. AA; AmePo; AmLP; BPAW; GN

Kings fall with their crowns, poets sink with their laurels. Europe. Louis Dudek. OBCV

Kings from the earth and pirates from the waves. Freedom. Joel Barlow. AnNE; PAL

The Kings kneel to the trinity/And Christ is come again. Epiphany. Eileen Shanahan. NeIP

Kings ought to shear, not skin their sheep. Moderation. Robert Herrick. FaBoEE

Kings passed in the dark barge which Merlin dreamed. Hospital Barge at Cerisy. Wilfred Owen. CBEP; OBTV

The kings raised their voices in song. Three Holy Kings from Morgenland. Heinrich Heine. PCh

The Kirk without the people. Eighteen-Forty-Three. *Anonymous.* FaBoCo

Kised him up, and eased his pain. Rondelay. John Dryden. ALV; CavP; DiPo; ViBoPo

The Kiss alone./So 'tis enough. Kissing. Edward, Lord Herbert of Cherbury EnLoPo; LiTL; ViBoPo

Kiss'd him up and eas'd his pain. Kiss Me, Dear. John Dryden. UnTE

Kiss Endimion, kiss his eyes,/Then to our midnight heidegyes. A Fairy Song. John Lyly. OBSC

A kiss for him! Love Song. *Anonymous.* AnIL

Kiss her and call her honey. Old Lady Sitting in the Dining Room. *Anonymous.* AmFP

Kiss her from me and say unto her sprite/Till her eyes shine I live in darkest night. Arcadia. Sir Philip Sidney. SiPS

Kiss her slow and let her know/How you come to love her so. Here We March All Around in a Ring. *Anonymous.* AmFP

Kiss her to death, says this pig. Let's Go to the Wood, Says This Pig. *Anonymous.* OxNR

Kiss her, you crook; it is your life-work: Sweat! Savage Portraits. Don (Donald Robert Marquis) Marquis. HBMV

Kiss him twice and hug him, too. Negro Reel (with music). *Anonymous.* AS

Kiss his weef, wife, woaf. Did You Ever, Ever, Ever. *Anonymous.* AS; FaBoNo

The kiss I never had. Midsummer. Sydney King Russell. BLPA; FaBoBe

Kiss me again! Kiss Me Again. Henry Blossom. BLSo; GoTF; TreFT

Kiss me and take my soul in keeping,/Since I must go, now day is near.' The Wakening. *Anonymous.* OBEV

Kiss me, Jessica! Once for all. A Priest's Prayer. Martha Gilbert Dickinson. AA

Kiss me, love! for who knoweth/What thing cometh after death? Ogier the Dane: Song. William Morris. OAEP; ViBoPo

Kiss me softly and speak to me low. To My Love. John Godfrey Saxe. HBV 1-2

Kiss me, then,/Every moment–and again! To Lesbia. John Godfrey Saxe. HBV 1-2; UnTE

Kiss me, you desecration of a man. Mannequins. Daniel Mark Epstein. MAYP

The kiss my mother left there when she died. Sonnets from the Portuguese, XVIII. Elizabeth Barrett Browning. HAP

Kiss of our agony Thou gatherest,/O Hand of Fire/gatherest– The Tunnel. Hart Crane. AmP; AP; MoVE; NePA; OxBA

Kiss through your laughter, kiss again–and go. Pause. Ann Hamilton. HBMV

Kiss ye, to kill ye. Upon Love, by Way of Question and Answer. Robert Herrick. CaPo

Kiss your bride and come out of the ring. Kiss in the Ring. *Anonymous.* OxBoLi

Kiss your darlin' honey. Ladies in the Dinin' Room. *Anonymous.* OuSiCo

Kisse me sweete love, this favour doe for me:/Then Crownes and Kingdomes shall I scorne for thee. I Wish Sometimes, Although a Worthlesse Thing. Giles the Elder Fletcher. AAS

Kissed by the wind/And caressed by the rain. Scotland. Sir Alexander Gray. BSV; GoTS; OxBS

Kissed her as the down was floating/On the phlogisticated air. Tom Wedgwood Tells. Brian W. Aldiss. NOBL

The kisses are bitter. Haiku: "Hardly Spring, with ice." Chiyo. BoWoP

Kisses make men loth to go. Kisses. Thomas Campion. ElL; OBSC

Kisses that bleed and lips as hard as steel. Two Sonnets from a Sequence. Edgar Holt. BoAV

Kisses the terror;/for you see an empty chair. Terror. Robert Penn Warren. LiTA; MoPo; NePA; PoA; WaP

Kissing in her kitchenette/The minuets of memory. The Anniad. Gwendolyn Brooks. BlSi

A-kissing of Kafoozalum. Kafoozalum. *Anonymous.* BeLS

Kissing, still unable to speak. All Legendary Obstacles. John Montague. BIrV; CIP; FaBoIP; IPY; NOBI

Kissing the lover in the mouth of bread:/lip to lip. Song of the Taste. Gary Snyder. CAPP; LCAP

Kissing the queen-bee, Life! Edmund Pollard. Edgar Lee Masters. AnFE; APA

"The kiver's favoring your face to-day!" Kivers. Ann Cobb. AmFN

Klippity-klip, Klippity-klip, Klippity-klip. The Milkman's Horse. *Anonymous.* SoPo

The knack is this, to fasten and not let go. Women in Love. Donald Justice. SM

Knee-deep within the stream. Cattle. *Anonymous.* SoPo

Kneel and gather those bits of/thread which dropped from your hand/to the bare, bare floor. Departure. George Hitchcock. GP

Kneel, and thank Heaven they are not yours. William Gifford. Walter Savage Landor. GTBS-P

Kneel down, and take her pardon at her feet. Elegies. Andre Marie de Chenier. AWP

Kneel in the latter grass to pray again,/Ere the night cometh and she may not work. The House of Life. Dante Gabriel Rossetti. VLP

Kneel to your overlord,/Children of night! Night. William Rose Benet. MoAmPo

A kneeling enters them. Poem: "At your light side trees shy." Bill Knott. EAS

Kneeling upon the floor, absorbed in silent prayer. Tales of a Wayside Inn. Henry Wadsworth Longfellow. AnNE

Kneels, kisses hands, and shines again in place. The Statesman in Retirement. William Cowper. OBEC

Knew her themselves, through all her vailes. Ingratefull Beauty Threatned. Thomas Carew. AnAnS 2; CaPo; EG; EnLi 1-2; HBV 1-2; InvP; MeLP; OBEV; OBS; SeCP; SeCV 1-2

Knew nothing but the wind, the cold, the pain. Dauber. John Masefield. AnFE; EtS; MoAB; MoBrPo; WHA

Knew on the hunter's breast her refuge lay. Refuge. George William Russell. HBV 1-2; OnYI

Knew the arsonist/Of the church? In These Dissenting Times. Alice Walker. PoBA

The knife-edge at the throat of darkness. Edge. Robert D. Fitzgerald. CBAP

The knight, his grandson, and the judge, his son. Bucolic Eclogues: Waking, Child, While You Slept. Ethel Anderson. PoAu 1-2

The knight who came was Launcelot at/good need. The Defence of Guenevere. William Morris. OAEP; TEP; VLP

Knit, smiling in the sun. La Tricoteuse. George Walter Thornbury. BeLS

"Knit to my soul for ever thou remain/"With me, nor quit my regal roof again." Goliath of Gath. Phillis Wheatley. BALP

...Knitted a pair of thoughtful brows. Poems, VI. Philip O'Connor. EAS

Knock as you please, there's nobody at home. Epigram: "You beat your pate, and fancy wit will come." Alexander Pope. FaBoEE

Knock at a star with my exalted head. The Bad Season Makes the Poet Sad. Robert Herrick. AnAnS 2; CABA; CaPo; LiTB; OAEP; PrIm; SeCeV

Knock down their daughters to the noblest bid! Epigram: The Mother's Choice. *Anonymous.* OxBoLi

Knock him on the head and feed him to the crows. How to Choose a Horse. *Anonymous.* FaBoUs

KNOCK/KNOCK/KNOCK Fragment of an Agon. Thomas Stearns Eliot. LiTB

Knock when you will,–he's sure to be at home. The Housekeeper. Vincent Bourne. GN; HBV 1-2; PoLf

Knock when you will,–he's sure to be at home. The Snail. Charles Lamb. MoShBr

Knocked and heard no knock unfasten from his/knuckles? The Sleeping Beauty. Mary Hutton. DFT

Knocked down a fence, tore up a field of clover. On the Skeleton of a Hound. James Wright. LiTM; NePoEA

Knocking at the castle-gates. The Norman Baron (excerpt). Henry Wadsworth Longfellow. PeD

Knocking them down with a stick,/Leaving the broken stems. Icicles. Robert Pinsky. SM

Knot knit in the cup canst thou. Hey-ho Knave: A Catch. *Anonymous.* GBP

The knotted hands/That set us high! Old Botany Bay. Mary Gilmore. PoAu 1-2

Knotted with love/the quilts sing on. My Mother Pieced Quilts. Teresa Acosta. FIA; WPOW

Know a chaaaaaaanj gonna shur-lee/cooooooom.... Newark, for Now. Don L. Lee. PoBA

Know faces seen long before. Fate. Louis James Block. AA

Know how I comment,/solve my name in a moment. A Riddle. Cynthia Ozick. VWA

Know, I have prayed to Fury that some wind/May blow my ashes up and strike thee blind. The Curse: A Song. Robert Herrick. CaPo

Know I was a mother once. Epitaphs of the War, 1914-18. Rudyard Kipling. BrPo; OBWP

Know, man is sure of three, and never more. Eagle Sonnets. Clement Wood. HBMV

Know that I watch, and that I wake. London Spring. Antoni Slonimski. TrJP

Know that its dumbness riots more than sound. Pilgrimage. Eileen Duggan. AnNZ

Know that one soldier has not died in vain. Elegy for a Dead Soldier. Karl Shapiro. AP; CoBMV; HAP; LiTM; MiAP; OBWP; OFD; OxBA; WaP

Know that Spring has come? O Nightingale. Nakatsukasa. LiTW

Know that which makes them as forgot/As Dawn forgets them now. The moon upon her fluent route. Emily Dickinson. QFR

Know the spring? If It Were Not for the Voice. Nakatsukasa. AWP

Know the worth of humble servants, foolish-faithful to their gun. Gun Teams. Gilbert Frankau. OxBTC

Know then your selves, that Christ you so will use. R. B. Samuel Gorton. SCAP

Know this was meant a Poem not a Tract. A Poem, in Defence of the Decent Ornaments of Christ-Church..(excerpt). *Anonymous.* OBS

Know what I list, this all can not me move,/But that, oh me, I both must write and love! Poems. William, of Hawthornden Drummond. JCP

...Know what love has known, this shifting image. A Sestina for Cynthia. David Lougee. NePA

Know when to let go/Learn how to fall. Sky Diving. Ishmael Reed. APU

Know where its roots began./O my dear, O my dear. The Three Bushes. William Butler Yeats. DTC; LiTL

Know you not that lovely river? Know Ye Not That Lovely River. Gerald Griffin. OnYI

Know ye 'tis his word we hear. Hark, and Hear My Trumpet Sounding. *Anonymous.* AH

Know yu mean business and know where th business lies Christ i wudint know normal if i saw it when. Bill Bissett. NOBC

Knowe that it will my greatest comfort bee/T'acknowledge all the rest to Come from thee. Francis Beaumont's Letter from the Country to Jonson. Ben Jonson. SeCP

Knoweth most of sorrow? I am/whom thou seekest.   On My Sorrowful Life. Moses Ibn Ezra.   TrJP

Knowing a part of me is with you still.   Codicil.   Mabel MacDonald Carver. GoYe

...Knowing/after all you have been somewhere.   First of All.   Kenneth O. Hanson.   GP

Knowing, as you say it, that this is one/who won't take no.   Love.   Gerald Jonas.   PV

Knowing better than to blame anyone.   Shapes, Vanishings.   Henry Taylor. AMV-81; MAYP

Knowing each painful step I trod/Hath brought me daily home to God. Pisgah.   Willard Wattles.   WGRP

Knowing her union holier and more fond.   Spiritual Passion.   George Barlow.   OBVV

Knowing his tears/will turn to dew.   Yahrzeit.   Dan Jaffe.   VWA

Knowing how they will rise again/separately through water.   Marriage. Myra Sklarew.   AmC

Knowing how well on earth your love sufficed me,/A lamp in darkness.   The Lamp.   Sara Teasdale.   MoLP

Knowing I can swim but not/knowing for how long.   Under.   George Bowering.   NeAC

Knowing I was as far away and as near to it as I would ever come.   Sleeping in a Cave.   Naomi Shihab Nye.   AMV-81

Knowing, in a sense, there is no such thing/as the wrong man.   On Hearing the Airlines Will Use a Psychological Profile...   Stephen P. Dunn.   AmPA

Knowing in life no lovelier thing than death.   And If at Last.   Louise Labe. LiTW

Knowing myself a born doubter.   Old Mountain Road.   Charles Simic. FYAP

Knowing no bliss, save to toil and abide/Weeping by thee.   Margaret to Dolcino.   Charles Kingsley.   HBV 1-2

Knowing no magic ever can set free/That part of you that is a part of me. You Are a Part of Me.   Frank Yerby.   AmNP

Knowing nothing of you save/A final servant functioning.   Pause en Route. Thomas Kinsella.   OxBI

Knowing only the moment.   White.   Marguerite Bouvard.   AMV-81

...Knowing our pain/is not theirs or caused by them.   The Negatives.   Philip Levine.   NePoEA-2

Knowing she went to rest/This cross upon her breast.'   The Cross of Gold. David Gray.   AA

Knowing so many things they never have told.   Old Houses.   Jennie Romano.   PoToHe

Knowing that he has wings.   Wings.   Victor Hugo.   TRV

Knowing that His hand will lead you/Up the way that saints have trod. Keeping Victory.   Walter E. Isenhour.   STF

Knowing that it has not passed.   Trains Made of Stone.   Ray A. Young Bear.   CDW

Knowing that they are life, and they alone.   Epitaph for the Poet V.   Arthur Davison Ficke.   HBMV

Knowing that this/was holy ground, that no pursuing ghost/could claim us now.   Meeting.   Sam Harrison.   NeIP

Knowing the sand hills were near.   Evening.   King D. Kuka.   VoR

Knowing the slow mutations of the soul.   Lines for the Hour.   Hamilton Fish Armstrong.   HBMV; MC

Knowing the ways of Wisdom well/and in all names, the Name.   The Child. Ivor Popham.   EaLo

Knowing those cared for whom they love.   The Due of the Dead.   William Makepeace Thackeray.   OBWP

–Knowing too well my hopeless love.   Lesbia loads me night & day with her curses.   Caius Valerius Catullus.   BoLoP

Knowing, untold, he cannot need it now.   The Sprig of Lime.   Robert Nichols.   GTBS-P

Knowing what autumn mischief lurks/behind this April weather.   Weather Vanes.   Frances Frost.   SiSoSe

Knowing when to respect the anguish of timeless/time.   Lamentation. Harold LaMont Otey.   LFAC

Knowing worlds pass ere she enough can find/Of such heaven-stuff to clothe so heavenly a mind.   Astrophel and Stella, CI.   Sir Philip Sidney.   AAS; SiPS

Knowing yet the strong content/From answering the high event.   Comrade in Arms.   T. Inglis Moore.   PoAu 1-2

The knowledge of peace,/True happiness.   The Shepherd's Dog.   Leslie Norris.   OBCP

...The knowledge/that you would have wrought them so much better.   Ode to the Medieval Poets.   W. H. Auden.   PoA

Known/As Joan.   Careless Talk.   Mark Hollis.   FiBHP; NLV

The known is old and we are new.   Remove the Predicate.   Clark Coolidge. APU

...Known only/To lookouts watching high and lonely.   Crow's Nest. Richard F. Armknecht.   GoYe

Knows, in refined retirement, to possess/By friendship hallow'd–rural happiness!   He May Be Envied, Who with Tranquil Breast.   Charlotte Smith.   SBG

Knows not when we pass by.   Song.   Henry Killigrew.   CH

Knows of/no water unstirring   The Nike of Samothrace.   Hilda Morley. FAZ

Knows the flowers' speech and the speech of silent things!   Elevation. Charles Baudelaire.   AWP

Knows this the hardest thing to learn.   An Unsaid Word.   Adrienne Rich. NMM

Ko Rauru ko Tama rakei ora, ko, &c.   The Six Periods of Creation. *Anonymous.*   WTO

The Kremlin was on fire.   Frost.   Edwin John Pratt.   WHW

Ku Kluck Klan, Ku Kluck Klan,/Lowest down creeper in de lan'.   Ku Kluck Klan.   Lawrence Gellert.   TrAS

Ku, they ku.   Thang ku.   The Traditional Grammarian as Poet.   Ted Hipple. PoL

Kuan-yin/Deliver us.   The Discriminations: Virtuous Amusements and Wicked Demons.   Jim Bogan.   PoDr

Kyrie, eleyson!/Christe, eleyson!   Midnight Mass for the Dying Year.   Henry Wadsworth Longfellow.   GoBC

...Kyrie of a chainsaw drifting down off Wheelock Mountain.   Getting the Mail.   Galway Kinnell.   UnPo

Kysse me yn my way,/Onys ar y wend.   Gracius and Gay.   *Anonymous.* SeCePo

L

La la la la la la la la la la.   Yeah yeah yeah.   Joy Sonnet in a Random Universe.   Helen Chasin.   HeIP; NIP

A la-mode de francois, you're a bit for his grace.   The Beau's Receipt for a Lady's Dress.   *Anonymous.*   CoMu

Labor and love! then fade without a sigh,/Submerged beneath the inexorable wave.   Labor and Love.   Sir Edmund Gosse.   AMV-81; HBV 1-2

...Labor/for my mad heart, and be/my ally.   On your dazzling throne, Aphrodite.   Sappho.   BoWoP

A laborer but in heart, while bound my hands/Hang idly down still waiting thy commands.   The Idler.   Jones Very.   AA; HBV 1-2

Laborers that shall not fail, when man is/gone.   Quiet Work.   Matthew Arnold.   EnL; FaBoBe; HBV 1-2; MaVP; MCCG; OAEP

Labour for me; love rest in prince's bower.   Menaphon.   Robert Greene. LoBV; OBSC

The labyrinth, as a kind of school/for heroes, artificers, and mice.   The Bush on Mount Venus.   Donald Finkel.   CoPo

The lace fell like swans' feathers over the lake   The Sisters.   Nicki Jackowska.   BrRo

...The lack/Of a singular green is what we mean by black.   Jefferson Valley. John Hollander.   PPP

...Lacking even/the body of a shadow/to share.   Early Morning.   Philip Dow.   DFF

Lacking itself, in its essence, a future.   Ax.   Charles Simic.   GP

Lacking that word, you shall be poor in-/deed.   Reserve.   Lizette Woodworth Reese.   AA

The lacquefaction of her toes.   Whenas in Jeans.   Paul Dehn.   FiBHP

The lad that hopes for heaven/Shall fill his mouth with mould.   Ho, Everyone That Thirsteth.   Alfred Edward Housman.   OAEL 1-2

Laddy tell I day, tell I do, laddy laddy tell I day.   The Crafty Farmer (The Oxford Merchant).   *Anonymous.*   AmFP

Laden with motes, on the boards of a floor.   The Barn.   Stephen Spender. CMoP

Laden with our lonely love.   Meeting in Winter.   William Morris.   EnLi 1-2

The ladies all are dying for the Dandy O.   The Dandy O.   *Anonymous.* CoMu

..."Ladies and gentlemen,"/the stewardess says, "we have landed in Boston." Flight 539.   John Malcolm Brinnin.   HoAn

Ladies, help me for to sing,/Victoria, Queen of England.   Queen Victoria. *Anonymous.*   CoMu

"Ladies, if not plucked, we die."   Love's Emblems.   John Fletcher.   BoLoP; EG; EiL; HBV 1-2; NIP; NOBE; OBEV; UnTE

Ladies rule where hearts obey.   My Lady Nature and Her Daughters.   John Henry, Cardinal Newman.   GoBC

The ladies that ride in their carriage/Might envy my marriage to me.   O, the Marriage!   Thomas Osborne Davis.   OBVV

Ladies, this blind boy that ran from his mother/Will ever play the wag with one or other.   Caelica, XIII.   Fulke, Lord Brooke Greville.   FCP

Lads like Barry will free Ireland,/For her sake they'll live and die.   Kevin Barry: Died for Ireland,/1st November, 1920.   *Anonymous.*   AS; FaBoBa; FSW

The lads playing snow-snake in the stinging cold. Watkwenies. Duncan Campbell Scott. PeCV

The lads that will die in their glory and never be old. The Lads in Their Hundreds. Alfred Edward Housman. ATP; CoBMV; MasP; MoBrPo; OxBTC; VLP

Lads whose job is still to do/Shall whet their knives, and think of you. What, Still Alive. Hugh Kingsmill. BXAP; DBV; FaBoCo; InPK; NLV; SpRo

The lady and the knight. The Castle in the Fire. Mary Jane Carr. BrR

The Lady Anne came home. Birth by Anesthesia. George Scarbrough. GoYe

Lady Cabstanleigh's back in Berkeley Square. Epitaph: "Let poets praise the softer winds of spring." J. B. Morton. FaBoEE

A lady from her carriage leant,/And murmured softly, "It was Spohr." The Violinist. Archibald Lampman. CaP

Lady, giver of Bread,/Christ-bestowing. Litany to Our Lady. Caryll Houselander. ISi

"Lady, I love but thee!" Ad Finem. Heinrich Heine. AWP

Lady, I trust you come not to do harm. A Volume of Chopin. James Picot. PoAu 1-2

The lady in gratitude grants him the favor. An Excellent New Ballad, Called The Brawn Bishop's Complaint. Arthur Mainwaring. APAS

Lady in purple/you're it. Dark Phrases. Ntozake Shange. BlSi

Lady, lady, better run! Social Note. Dorothy Parker. FaBoUS; InMe

Lady love, lady love, welcome me home. Gaily the Troubadour. Thomas Haynes Bayley. BLSo

The lady loves her will. Hart and Hare. Anonymous. CBEP

Lady Moon, Lady Moon, whom are you loving?/"All that love me." Lady Moon. Richard Monckton, Lord Houghton Milnes. MoShBr; OxBChV

Lady Nancie died for pure, pure love,/Lord Lovel for deep sorraye. Lord Lovel (D version). Anonymous. ESPB

...Lady no parasol. Be gay! By the Beautiful Sea. Thomas Cole. NePoAm-2

Lady, not thou but she was glorified. The Moonstar. Dante Gabriel Rossetti. MaVP

Lady of the shortest day/watch over our daughter/whom we commit to the grass Prayer for the Little Daughter between Death and Burial. Diana Scott. BrRo

The lady of the spotted muff began. The Hind and the Panther. John Dryden. CEP; CoBE; FiP; PoEL 1-5; SeCV 1-2; TrPWD

A lady's invitation to her pillow.' The Instructions of King Cormac (excerpt). Anonymous. BIrV

Lady, that peace which none but He can send/Be thine. Even so. Canzone: Of His Dead Lady. Giacomino Pugliesi. AWP

Lady, the Holbein type wears well! Fancy Dress. Dorothea Mackellar. NOAV; PoAu 1-2

Lady, this is my sonnet to your eyes. Modern Love, XXX. George Meredith. HAP; NBM; NoP; OAEP; PoEL 1-5; ViBoPo; VLP

Ladybird! Ladybird! haste! fly away! Ladybird! Ladybird! Emily Bronte. OnUR

Ladybug, ladybug, I'll see you home. Fly, Ladybug. Annette Burr Stowman. AMV-80

"The ladys of Edinburgh city,/They neither milch goats nor kie." Lizie Lindsay (A version). Anonymous. ESPB

"Lafayette, we are here!" Pershing at the Tomb of Lafayette. Amelia Josephine Burr. PAH

The laggard body soon will waft to Heaven. Red o'er the Forest. John Keble. OxBoCh

The laggen they hae clautet/Fu' clean that day. A Dream: "Guid-mornin to your majesty." Robert Burns. NAs

"Laid I on him no condition,/Fixed no ways and means; so I/Wonder not my olive thriveth... The Olive Tree. Sabine Baring-Gould. GN

Laid like weights on the table. The Garden. Louise Gluck. AmPA; FiCP

...Laid low/and still blossoming/under the snow. Moss. Nancy Willard. HoAn

Laid low by a trumpet, or a dream. Logic. Calvin Murry. LFAC

Laid on by your merchants of the romantic. Epigram: "Long hair, endless curls." Strato. PeHV

...Laid open/to the weather of hard words. Southern Exposures. G. E. Murray. AMV-81

Lais can no longer see/Lais in Lais herself. Poems from the Greek Anthology (excerpt). Johannes Secundus. NNaP

A lake/Is a river curled and asleep like a snake. A Lake. Thomas Lovell Beddoes. NOBV

The lake is a wide silence/Without imagination. Voyage a L'Infini. Walter Conrad Arensberg. AnAmPo

–Lake, mountain, tree,/sings Harry. Lake, Mountain, Tree. Denis Glover. AnNZ

Lake sweat, sperm-wet from that first/renewal, thoughtless, paphian. Girl in a Black Bikini. Allan Brown. AMV-80

The lake was covered with gloom. Enna plunged into it/screaming. Geography. Kenneth Koch. AmPC; NoAm

Lakes faintly shine through/like white stones/or fish. Low Tide. Warren Woessner. WOLT

Laly, Laly,/So young were we. Laly, Laly. Mark Van Doren. SO

The lamb and the dove/Were preachers sent from God. Did any bird come flying. Christina Georgina Rossetti. EG

Lamb of God for sinners slain. The Coming and the Appearing. Anonymous. STF

Lamb of the shepherds, Child, how still you lie. The Holy Innocents. Robert Lowell. ATP; ConAP; InPo; InvP; MoAB; MoAmPo; NePoEA; OBCP; OxBC; SBVL

The Lamb who lay beneath the clay/Was slain for thee. A Fragrant Prayer. Biddy Crummy. WTO

Lambent and vast and ruthless as in thine/Incertitude! Flood. James Joyce. MoBrPo

Lambs bleat my lullaby. Daisy's Song. John Keats. BoNaP

Lambs who got their just deserts. A Bestiary. Kenneth Rexroth. OBAL

Lament the loss and fall/Of the poor "Benjamin', O. The Benjamins' Lamentation for Their Sad Loss at Sea, by Storms... Anonymous. OBSS

Lamented for the dead that slept below. The House of Night. Philip Freneau. PoEL 1-5

Lamenting all her fallen sons! The High Tide at Gettysburg. Will Henry Thompson. AA; BeLS; BLPA; FaBoBe; HBV 1-2; MC; PAH; PAL; PaPo; TreFS

Lamenting sore for those no more on board the Amphitrite. Loss of the Amphitrite. Anonymous. OBSS

Lamenting thru gipsies his fast suicide. Political Poem. LeRoi (Imamu Amiri Baraka) Jones. CoAP; NoAm

The lamp post seems tuned to your key. For Walter Lowenfels. Wendy Rose. CDW

The lamps fade; and the stars. We are alone. The Night Journey. Rupert Brooke. BrPo

The lamps of Heaven and earth's buried dream. Speaks the Whispering Grass. Jesse Stuart. FYAP

Lampshine blurred in the steam of beasts, the spirit's right/Oasis, light incarnate. A World without Objects Is a Sensible Emptiness. Richard Wilbur. ConAP; LiTM; NoAm; NOBA; PoA

A land apart, to dust, to clay. Prelude. Conrad Kent Rivers. PoBA

The land barely speaks. Gull Lake Reunion. Kelly Ivie. AMV-81

"Land ho!" Columbus cried. The Sea-Weed. Elisabeth Cavazza Pullen. AA

Land, ho! Eternity!/Ashore at last! On this wondrous sea. Emily Dickinson. AA

The land is laid in snow. The Idle Flowers. Robert Bridges. BoNaP

The land of love,/Where all unknown are tears. God's Trails Lead Home. John R. Clements. BLRP

The land of my heart. The Road. Nikolay Platonovich Ogarev. AWP

A land of shadows. On Eastnor Knoll. John Masefield. CH; MCCG

The land of spices; something understood. Prayer: "Prayer, the Church's banquet." George Herbert. NOBE

Land of the forest. "America, My Country..." Ralph Waldo Emerson. AmePo

Land of the new and lordlier race! Hymn of the West. Edmund Clarence Stedman. HBV 1-2; PAH

Land of the true, where we live a-new/Beautiful Isle of Somewhere! Beautiful Isle of Somewhere. Jessie B. Pounds. FSN; TreFT

A land that rides at anchor, and is moored/In which they do not live, but go aboard. Description of Holland. Samuel (1612-80) Butler. OBTV

The land unknown, to rest and comfort me. O Powers Celestial, with What Sophistry. Barnabe Barnes. EnLoPo

The land wants me to come back. Dust Bowl. Langston Hughes. PoA

The land will be yours How to Own Land. Susan Farley. AMV-80

...Landing gear/Needed for the interval between flight and flight. Dialectics of Flight. John Hall Wheelock. NePoAm-2

The lands I was to travel in/Or the death I was to die! The Queen's Marie. Anonymous. OBEV; PoPle

The lands lay fallow, but the wife was till'd. Epigram: "Milo's from home; and, Milo being gone." Martial (Marcus Valerius Martialis). OBVE

...The landscape drained/Of everything but its own light Escape and Return. Elizabeth Jennings. NePoEA

...Landslides of/bodies, all bigger than any one of us. After Peckinpah. Barry Dempster. CaPN

Lang may aw shout, ma' canny bairn! Ma Canny Hinny. Anonymous. FaBoPP; GBP

Language which met and dovetailed the event. A Different Speech. Louise Townsend Nicholl. ImOP

Lank camels lounge against transparent skies. Internal Firesides. Mathilde Blind. FM

Lapping up his dripping iron. The Worker. Richard Thomas. PoBA; PoNe

Large fire from smallest spark has many times been brought. A Century of Couplets (excerpt). Richard Chenevix Trench. OBRV

A large man living and dead is flying over the water with wings/spread, a wound on his chest. Christmas Eve Service at Midnight at St. Michael's. Robert Bly. NNaP

The largest town in west Michigan/Is the city of Grand Rapids. Grand Rapids. Julia A. Moore. OBAL

A lark arose.... Dawn. P.S.M". MCCG

A lark bursts up all dew. In Fields of Summer. Galway Kinnell. BoNaP; RFM; VGW

...The lark's beak neatly pierces his eye. Hot Day at the Races. Tom Raworth. EAS

...Larks at/Portiuncula singing when you died,/Pray for us,/AMEN A Little Litany to St. Francis. Philip Murray. NePoAm

Larks thrill the waste with a rapture of song. The Heather. Steen Steensen Blicher. LiTW

Lascars tiptoe, spit,/and await orders. Tanker. Christopher Middleton. NMP

Lascivious grace, in whom all ill well shows,/Kill me with spites; yet we must not be foes. Sonnets, XL: "Take all my loves my love, yea take them all." William Shakespeare. CBEP; InvP; OBSC

The lass o' Patie's mill,/Shou'd share the same with me. The Lass o' Patie's Mill. Allan Ramsay. BSV

The lassie thought it day, when she sent her lover away,/And it was but a blink of the moon. Saw You My True Love John? *Anonymous*. BFSS

A last, a last farewell! Stanzas in Memory of the Author of "Obermann'. Matthew Arnold. MaVP; VLP

...The last act crowns the play. Epigram: Respice Finem. Francis Quarles. OBEV

The last affirmation, the only deed of glory? Meditation of a Mariner. Dorothy Auchterlonie. CBAP

The last and greatest art, the art to blot. The Ideals of Satire. Alexander Pope. FiP

Last at the cross and earliest at the grave. Woman. Eaton Stannard Barrett. HBV 1-2; OnYI; OxBI

...The last chamber/of wolf- and bear-heart, where/all arrows wait, rot, and fly. Arrows. William Heyen. SM

The last coil of wire/was gone, flushed down/a thousand prison toilets. Passive Resistance. Joseph Bruchac. SOTS

Last comfort in Gethsemane. For Jim, Easter Eve. Anne Spencer. AmNP; PoNe

A last dressing. Grave Clothes. Karen Swenson. AMV-80

...The last gasp of time/Is thy first breath, and mans eternall Prime. The Evening-Watch. Henry Vaughan. NCEP

...The last girl/cradling several globes/in her bare arms/yellow and blue and rose. To Bring Spring. George Keithley. NPGG

The last god dies/With the last believer. Faith. Victor J. Daley. PoAu 1-2

The last grand holocaust of Liberty. The Foe at the Gates. John Dickson Bruns. PAH

...The last green field/That Lucy's eyes surveyed. Lucy. William Wordsworth. OBEV; TrGrPo

A last groan of the drum, panting she drops/into the darkness of past love. Egyptian Dancer. Terence Tiller. OBTV

Last I heard, she went to a college upstate. Eastside Chick with Drive. Albert Spector. CTBA

Last is the thumb. How Do You Spell "Missile"?: Preliminary Instructions... George Uba. BrSi

–The last laugh's mine!–and so escape forever. The Dark Cat. Audrey Alexandra Brown. CaP

...Last line the truth that's not/beauty but bone. bone. bone. bone. There Is No Balm in Birmingham. Ann Deacon. NIP

The last man couldn't, can you? Woman. Ai. GP

...The last/Marches of that giant Past/Faint upon the intense invisible. Celestine. Robert Fitzgerald. MoVE

Last month of the year. Tell Me What Month Was My Jesus Born in. *Anonymous*. FSW

A last moon is packing its bags. For Lerida. David St. John. AmPA

Last night I dreamed my lilies/Were twined about a cross! Premonition. Laura Goodman Salverson. CaP

Last night I were with her, but to-night she is gone. Old Smoky. *Anonymous*. BaBo

Last night should add/Your voluntary love. Song: "Fish in the unruffled lakes." W. H. Auden. MoAB; MoBrPo

Last night we had our first snow of the season. Miss Ada. Christophr Fahy. TAT

Last night–we parted. Last Night. George Darley. HBV 1-2; OnYI

Last of all last words spoken is Goodbye. Goodbye. Walter De la Mare. NoP

"The last of the heroes was Kleomedes." Kleomedes. David Wright. NoAm

Last of the Pagan race,/Lieth king Dathi. The Fate of King Dathi. Thomas Osborne Davis. OnYI

The last of the voice/the last. The Last. Ezra Zussman. VWA

The last piece flames up the draft and out/into the night, and I give you the rain. Around You, Your House. William Stafford. NPAW

The last pound of the drum. Bird of Power. Jim Tollerud. VoR

The last release, the rush,/the blunt completion The Spring. Ellen Bryant Voigt. MAYP

The last sad words she breathed upon earth/Were these simple ones, "Oh, poet, do hush!" In Memorial. J. Gordon Coogler. OBAL

Last Saturday we saw him at the horizon/screaming like a hawk as he fell into the sun. Minotaur Poems. E. W. Mandel. OBCV

Last seen losing altitude in the Sea of Cortez. Christ. Greg Forker. LFAC

"The last shall be first and the first shall be last." St. Peter at the Gate. Joseph Bert Smiley. BLPA

The last snow of this year's late slow thaw/dribbles as spring saliva down his jaw. Prague Spring. Tony Harrison. OBTV

The last still loveliest,–till–'t is gone–and all is gray. Childe Harold's Pilgrimage: Canto IV, XXIX. George Gordon, Lord Byron. AnFE

The last strong rival for his food. The Truth. William Henry Davies. FaBoTw

Last summer in Princes Street. For Ann Scott-Moncrieff. Edwin Muir. GTBS-P

The last thing/I want to hear before going to sleep/Is that man/Splashing ashore. Woods Night. Tom Hennen. GP

The last thing, the very/Last thing, I am afraid, is death. Mountain Creed. Hugh C. Rae. PoSH

The last time blues/with no hesitations... Do Nothing till You Hear from Me. David Henderson. CNA

...Last time I go diving/alone, I promised myself, though I lied. Nurse Sharks. William Matthews. FiCP

"The last time I saw her was in the arms/of another sky." Moonlight. Joy Harjo. TWSS

Last time the brown slave wore it garlanded. On a Lute Found in a Sarcophagus. Sir Edmund Gosse. GTBS

Last time together we bathed each other, chaste. I remember as I masturbate. Letter. Philip Dow. NPGG

The last to come will make his little tune,/And think it new–about the weary moon! Poets. Hortense Flexner. HBMV

The last to let go and fall/into the water and on the ground. Willow Poem. William Carlos Williams. NCSH

The last trees take them. Boy Riding Forward Backward. Robert Francis. LCAP; NePoAm-2

The last triumphant wonder of the world! Graffito Inscribed on a Wall of the Taj Mahal. *Anonymous*. OBTV

The last twist of the knife. Rhapsody on a Windy Night. Thomas Stearns Eliot. ACV; CMoP; ExPo; HeIP; InPo; InPS

The last wall down, look heavenward. We have wings. The Double Fortress. Alfred Noyes. GoBC

The last/waters go on rocking/in the conch of the ear. Noah. Chana Bloch. VWA

The last way out that leads not out but in. Alcohol. Louis MacNeice. LiTM

The last word I heard them say,/Was about Jerusalem, the saints' delightful home. The Traveler. *Anonymous*. AmFP

The last words that poor Georgie said was, "Nearer, my God, to thee." George Allen. *Anonymous*. AmFP

Lasting life and long enjoyment/Are not here, and are not yet. All the Scenes of Nature Quicken. Christopher Smart. ELP

Lastly, safely buried. Divination by a Daffadil. Robert Herrick. CaPo; CavP; OBS; SeCV 1-2

Lastly, that JESUS is a Deed/Of Gift from God: And here's my Creed. His Creed. Robert Herrick. SeCeV

Lastly, with friends t' enjoy our days. Four Things Make Us Happy Here. Robert Herrick. CaPo

Lasts the better part of a day. Another Stone Poem. Philip Dacey. AMV-81

The latch-string's hanging at the door/For you! For you! Christmas Singing. Elsie Williams Chandler. ChBR; SiSoSe

"A late apple's good," I say,/laying down the core. Hillside Pause. Catharine Morris Wright. GoYe

Late autumn was an oriental child. Skykomish River Running. Richard Hugo. PoA

Late, late in a gloamin' Kilmeny came hame! Bonny Kilmeny Gaed up the Glen. James Hogg. BSV; GoTS

Late may the second pass from earth to heaven! The English Succession. *Anonymous*. OxBChV

Late of the jungle, dim and wild. Billiards. Walker Gibson. LiSp; NePoAm

Late, or too soon, let it not rule the gain/Wherewith free will doth true desert retain. The Answer that Ye Made to Me, My Dear. Sir Thomas Wyatt. FCP; SiPS

A late-thirties couple in a roadside motel/on a second, desperate, honeymoon. The Children Grown. Haywood Jackson. SOTS

Lazily she lingered/Cradling a dream.   The Vengeance of Finn: The Awakening of Dermuid.   Austin Clarke.   AnIV

Laziness takes nine, and wickedness eleven.   Hours of Sleep.   *Anonymous.*   NLV

Lazy Elsie Marley.   Elsie Marley.   *Anonymous.*   BBGG; OxNR

Lazy to others, but be long to me.   Long and Lazy.   Robert Herrick.   FaBoEE

Lead at last to heaven above!   A Prayer.   George F. Chawner.   BLRP

Lead in hand to Crown thy Dear Embraces.   An Acrostick on Mrs. Elizabeth Hull.   John Saffin.   SCAP

Lead her flambeau boy the dark way home.   Mardi Gras / Grandmothers Portrait in Red and Black Crayon.   James Nolan.   Str

Lead me gently, lead me sweetly/To Thy home. Lead all the way!   Take My Hand, O Blessed Master.   Connie Calenberg.   BePJ

Lead me, Oh Lord–till perfect Day shall shine,/Through Peace to Light.   Per Pacem ad Lucem.   Adelaide Anne Procter.   TrPWD

Lead me until I reach the shore of Your covenant./Amen   Noah's Prayer.   Carmen B. Gastold.   TrCP

Lead the Republic as a bride/Up to God's side.   Siena.   Algernon Charles Swinburne.   VLP

Lead them–a happy household band–/Forever near to thee.   By Vows of Love Together Bound.   Eleazar Thompson Fitch.   AH

Lead us to our Sabbath rest.   Jesus, Thou Divine Companion.   Henry Van Dyke.   AH

Lead you back home again!   Roads.   Rachel Field.   BrR; SoPo; TiPo

A leaden rapier in a golden sheath.   Against Gaudy-Bragging-Undoughty Daccus.   John, of Hereford Davies.   FaBoEE

Leadeth them forth again./Gently, by death.   To O.S.C.   Annie Eliot Trumbell.   AA

Leading him into friendship unawares.   To the Memory of Yale College.   Howard Phelps (Phelps Putnam) Putnam.   AnAmPo

Leading to that wellspring true/Where old souls their age renew?   Ponce de Leon.   Edith Matilda Thomas.   PAH

Leads is through the grave to thee.   Rearrange a Wife's Affection?   Emily Dickinson.   AnNE; PoEL 1-5

Leads straightway to an old immortal wine/Pressed from God's vine.   The Thousand and One Nights: The Wazir Dandan for Prince Sharkan.   *Anonymous.*   AWP

Leads them through the sweet green shadows,/Far away in slumberland.   The Dustman.   Frederic Edward Weatherly.   HBV 1-2

Leads with its left and not the chin.   Mantis.   David McCord.   OBAL

Leaf after autumnal leaf/break off,/descend–/descend–   Quaker Hill.   Hart Crane.   LiTM

Leafl don't be neurotic/like the small chameleon.   Les Etiquettes Jaunes.   Frank O'Hara.   CAPP

Leaf from her brow, light from her torched hand.   Questing.   Anne Spencer.   CDC

...The leaf repeats the lesson.   The Lesson.   Robert Lowell.   CMoP; LCAP; NMP

Leaf, stem and cup, but could not last the night.   Indian Pipes.   Winifred Welles.   AnAmPo

The leafage of years is brown, our hair is not brown.   Your Hand Full of Hours.   Paul Celan.   OBVE

Leafless there by my door, trembled a sense of the rose.   In Earliest Spring.   William Dean Howells.   AA; FaBoBe

A leafy luxury, seeing I could please/With these poor offerings, a man like thee.   To Leigh Hunt, Esq.   John Keats.   EnRP

Leafy the boughs–they also hide big fruit.   Do Not Expect Again a Phoenix Hour.   C. Day-Lewis.   CMoP; FaBoMo; LiTB; LiTM; MoAB; MoBrPo; NoAm; OxBI; OxBTC; PoRA

A lean bird circles.   Legacy: My South.   Dudley Randall.   NNP; PoBA; PoNe

Lean is the ghost of Molly Means.   Molly Means.   Margaret Walker.   AmNP; BlSi; NMM; PoNe; StPo

Lean out of the window,/Goldenhair.   Chamber Music.   James Joyce.   LOW

Lean, provincial, burning/In their plot.   Carta Canadensis.   Ralph Gustafson.   PeCV

Lean to labor and to wait.   A Psalm of Life.   Henry Wadsworth Longfellow.   FaFP

The lean wolf unmolested made her lair.   Unguarded Gates.   Thomas Bailey Aldrich.   AA; AnNE; MC; PAH

Leanbhain O, Leanbhain O!   Lullaby.   Seumas MacManus.   AnIV

Leander hastened to his Hero's bed.   The Naturalist's Summer-Evening Walk.   Gilbert White.   NOEC; PBBP

Leander should have stood in bed/Or bought himself a rowboat.   Hero and Leander.   Joseph S. Newman.   FiBHP

Leaned close and drew them near.   Winter Dusk.   Walter De La Mare.   AnEnPo

Leaned from the admiral's walk and watched them drown.   Noah.   Roy Daniells.   PeCV; WHW

...Leaning gently/against the cupboard doors.   To an Estranged Wife.   Gary Young.   AMV-81

Leaning over graves like old men lamenting their age.   Wrestling Angels.   David Bottoms.   MAYP

Leap from the universe and plunge in Thee!   Surrender to Christ.   Frederic William Henry Myers.   OxBoCh

Leap girl upon his back/And he will race for ever.   The Invitation.   Donagh MacDonagh.   OnYI

Leap mountains laugh at walls?   The Leaping Laughers.   George Barker.   OBMV

Leap, plashless, as they swim.   A bird came down the walk.   Emily Dickinson.   AmePo; AmLP; AmPP; AnFE; APA; BiP; BLPL; CMoP; DiPo; FF; FM; GoJo; InvP; LiTA; LiTM; MAmP; MAPA; MoAmPo; MoShBr; MoVE; NAWM 1-2; NOBA; NoP; NTCP; OBAL; OBCA; OxBA; PB; PG; PoLf; PoRA; SeCeV; SoPo; SoSe; TiPo; TreFT

The leap the only faith that's left.   Hotel Fire: New Orleans.   Paul Ruffin.   AMV-81

Leap then, and come down on the line that draws to the earth's deep, heavy/centre.   Kangaroo.   D. H. Lawrence.   EBEV; InPS; MoVE; OBTV; OxBTC; PAI

Leaped and made shine the dark face in its sleep.   Made Shine.   Josephine Miles.   NoAm

Leaped like the roe when he hears in the woodland the voice of the huntsman?   Evangeline.   Henry Wadsworth Longfellow.   WBLP

Leaping from the bus to scurry home, intact/one time again   Bus Ride.   Lenore Kandel.   NMM

Leaping, full-mouthed, in murderous pursuit!   Barrage.   Richard Aldington.   BrPo

Leaping/Sweetly/your voice   Your Little Voice.   Edward Estlin Cummings.   LLLT; OLR

A Lear at last come to his own.   Old Age Pensioner.   Joseph Campbell.   AnIL

Learn, for who of us can ever make a sterile land a/lagoon?   The Lagoon.   Ashton Greene.   NePoAm

Learn that the man of straw has had his hour.   Beggar to Burgher.   A. R. D. Fairburn.   AnNZ

Learn to be Black men   The True Import of Present Dialogue: Black vs. Negro.   Nikki Giovanni.   BPo; PoBA

Learn to conform the order of our lives.   A Forest Hymn.   William Cullen Bryant.   AA; AnNE; AP; TAP; TrPWD

Learn to ease her, and stop her, and back her astern.   A Longford Legend.   *Anonymous.*   OnYI; StPo

Learn to labor and to wait.   A Psalm of Life.   Henry Wadsworth Longfellow   AA; AnNE; DiPo; FaBoBe; FPL; GoTF; HBVY; OBCA; OHFP; PoLf; PoPl; PrIm; WBLP; YaD

Learn to take one's lumps.   Lump.   Robert Phillips.   AMV-80

Learn to write well, or not to write at all.   An Essay upon Satire.   John Sheffield.   APAS

Learn, too, how God's own angels keep/Your ways by day, your dreams, asleep.   To a Child.   Norreys Jephson O'Conor.   DFT; HBMV

Learn what it means/To be up high.   Get Up, Blues.   James A. Emanuel.   AmNP; BOLo; PoBA

Learn with my hands the length of naked lines.   A Simpler Thing, a Chair.   Robert Mezey.   NePoEA

Learning from these, take back my banished pen.   Sonnet: "Sweet, when I think how summer's smallest bird."   Irene Rutherford McLeod.   HBMV

Learning is the business of the boy and girl in school.   Pedagogical Principles.   Harry Amoss.   CaP

...Learning to touch her wounds comes first.   My Daughter Considers Her Body.   Floyd Skloot.   SM

Least of all in the day of falling fruit.   Lancelot.   Arna Bontemps.   CDC

Leather and wood by his side smell like/A summer he'll knock clear out of the park.   Spring Rites.   Martin Robbins.   AMV-81

...A leather belt made/upon which he perched to enjoy her.   The Monstrous Marriage.   William Carlos Williams.   MoPo

Leather breeches to his toes.   Well I Never.   *Anonymous.*   FaBoCh

Leave a dime for beer   Alabama Bound.   Mance Lipscomb.   BluL

Leave but a filamentous line or two?   Thumbprint.   Celeste Turner Wright.   Psk

Leave but the withered heath and barren thorn.   The Gossamer.   Charlotte Smith.   ViBoPo

Leave by my dethe well rendred unto the.'   The Aeneid.   Virgil (Publius Vergilius Maro).   OBVE

Leave Her Devoted at Minerva's Shrine   One Presenting a Rare Book to Madame Hull Senr: His Vallintine.   John Saffin.   SCAP

Leave him at last to sea-dark sleep, with one clear Har-/bour light/Bright as the pole star over him   Sea Burial.   Robina Monkman.   EtS

Leave him spreadeagled on Rubicon Wall!   The Lost Leader.   Douglas Fraser.   PoSH

Leave him–still loftier than the world suspects,/Living and dying.   A Grammarian's Funeral.   Robert Browning.   BoLiVe; DiPo; HBV 1-2; LoBV; MaVP; NOBV; OAEP; VLP; WGRP

Leave, little darlin', I don't mind.   Columbus Stockade Blues.   *Anonymous.* FSW

Leave me but love and sherry.   A Loose Saraband.   Richard Lovelace. CaPo; CavP; PoEL 1-5

Leave me not a stone in thine enemies' hand!   The Mason.   Robert Farren. OnYI; OxBI

Leave me, O sky-born powers,/Brother to grass and stones.   A Mountain Wind.   George William Russell.   AWP

Leave me to my quiet rest/In the region of the blest.   A Happy Man. Carphyllides   AWP; LiTW

Leave no trace on the snow.   Soho.   Joseph Brodsky.   VWA

Leave not a groat behind!   Our Parodies Are Ended.   Horace Twist.   Par

Leave off, or paint her with a voice.   To the Painter Preparing to Draw M. M. H.   James Shirley.   CavP

An' leave our litty childern's tooes/To leap an' run in play.   When We That Now Ha' Childern Wer Childern.   William Barnes.   NOBV

Leave reason, faith, and conscience, all our own.   Happiness Dependent on Ourselves.   Oliver Goldsmith.   OBEC

The leave-taking in the dust/Binds us together with you.   Chorus of the Rescued.   Nelly Sachs.   VWA; WPOW

Leave tears, sweet, for to-morrow!   The King of the Cradle.   Joseph Ashby-Sterry.   HBV 1-2

Leave that sir Phip, least off your necke be wroong.   Astrophel and Stella, LXXXIII.   Sir Philip Sidney.   AAS; SiPS

...Leave the bars lying.   Fall.   Robert Francis.   VGW

Leave the Britons rough and free.   To Signora Cuzzoni.   Ambrose Philips. CEP; LoBV; OBEC

Leave the Fates to-morrow;/Give Love to-day.   Give Love To-Day.   Ethel Talbot.   HBV 1-2

...Leave the house-door wide/Until they had lit the lamp inside.   House Fear. Robert Frost.   WSC

Leave them all there/Old lover. Live on.   Morning Worship.   Mark Van Doren.   NePoAm-2

Leave unadorned by needless art/The picture as it came.   To the Muse. Robert Louis Stevenson.   EBEV

Leave us religion.   Leave Us Religion.   Blanaid Salkeld.   NeIP

Leave us to-night/Round the old tree.   The Mahogany Tree.   William Makepeace Thackeray.   HBV 1-2

Leave warm 'mid the gray grass their dusky bed.   Serenade.   Aubrey Thomas De Vere.   HBV 1-2; OBEV

Leave we all this worldly mirth,/And follow we this joyful birth/Transeamus. Two Carols to Our Lady: II.   *Anonymous.*   ACP

Leave what you die for and be safe to die.   The Teasers.   William Empson. OxBTC

Leave you to rock cradles, sing "Bye-o-babee.'"   The Wild Rippling Water. *Anonymous.*   CoSo; FaBoBa

Leave your arrows in the quiver,/And let the dead depart in peace.   Let the Dead Depart in Peace.   *Anonymous.*   WTO

Leaves are all my darker mood.   Leaves Compared with Flowers.   Robert Frost.   NOBA

The leaves are falling over the town.   Down! Down!   Eleanor Farjeon. NTCP; SoPo; SUS; TiPo

The leaves are leaves again no tree forgot.   Reflection in a Green Arena. Gregory Corso.   VGW

Leaves at last on a hillside to rot away with the seasons.   The Burden of Junk.   John Glassco.   OBCV

The leaves burgeon.   The Watchers.   Paul Blackburn.   NMP; NYBP

The leaves combing slowly the mild sea-air.   Evening Refrain.   Sherod Santos.   MAYP

The leaves do not mind at all/That they must fall.   The Leaves Do Not Mind At All.   Annette Wynne.   SoPo

Leaves fall. Blood runs cold in the wrist.   L'Aurore Grelottante.   Peter Levi. NePoEA-2

Leaves flung from his flanks/In terrible unknowing!   Lion.   Mary Elizabeth ("E") Fullerton.   PoAu 1-2

The leaves, frost-crisp'd, break from the trees/And fall.   November Night. Adelaide Crapsey.   AnAmPo

Leaves her to her radiant rest/Guarded by an angel-guest.   Annunciation Night.   Abby Maria ("Mary Josephine") Hemenway.   ISi

Leaves, lines, and rymes, seeke her to please alone,/whom if ye please, I care for other none.   Amoretti, I.   Edmund Spenser.   AAS; ATP; EBEV; OAEL 1-2

An' leaves me frontin' South by North.   P.S.   James Russell Lowell   AA

The leaves move away/falling on all but the/unmarked path no one can find. Ways of Seeing.   William Stafford.   SUW

Leaves must be green in Spring.   Malvern Hill.   Herman Melville.   AP; FPL; MAmP; MC; PAH; TAP

The Leaves of Life keep falling one by one.   The Rubaiyat of Omar Khayyam.   Omar Khayyam.   FF

The leaves of the Arabah are struck/thrice.   O Hark to the Herald.   Eleazar Ben Kalir.   TrJP

...Leaves/spearshaped/in the falling snow   Winter.   William Carlos Williams. NCSH

Leaves/ten/thousand/corpses/to rot!   The War Year.   Ts'ao Sung.   PPON

The leaves, the quenching leaves that drown upon the flesh.   Autumnall. Joseph Bennett.   NePA

The leaves twist, sighing, and the grass/rattles as harsh as brittle glass. Midsummer.   Hermann Hesse.   LiTW

Leavin the perils o the Arctic nicht.   Arctic Convoy.   J. K. Annand. OxBS

Leaving a handful of kisses/on their billboard smiles.   Animation and Ego. Jody Swilky.   AMV-80

Leaving all/The weeds.   In These Dissenting Times.   Alice Walker.   PoBA

Leaving behind him only foot-prints.   A Song of White Snow.   Ts'en Ts'an. LiTW

Leaving behind low, rippling laughter.   Evening Songs.   John Vance Cheney. AA

...Leaving/behind: me, wag.   Dream Song.   John Berryman.   CAPP; HaCAP; HAP; HeIP; LiTM; NaP; NoAm; PrIm; TAP; TwCP

Leaving behind them the dead on the shore, and the village in ruins. Evangeline.   Henry Wadsworth Longfellow.   AnNE

Leaving but a sprinkle,/As of tears.   Blowing Bubbles.   William Allingham. GN

Leaving darkly bruised, the man.   Black Fear.   Elizabeth Woody.   STE

Leaving each branch sprung/taut, alive like wires.   Composition in Black and White.   Katha Pollitt.   GrPl

Leaving fops and fogies/A thousand feet below.   The Invitation.   Charles Kingsley.   NOBV

Leaving for Baltimore.   Learning.   Earl Simpson.   GrPl

Leaving George and Liz the Second.   The Kings and Queens of England. *Anonymous.*   FaBoUs

Leaving her eyes/to the east.   Celebration.   Ray A. Young Bear.   CDW

Leaving him only motion, only speech.   Ghost.   Witter ("Emanuel Morgan") Bynner.   AnFE

Leaving luckless Charinus still panting/For pleasures he's no power to grasp. To Charinus, a Catamite.   Martial (Marcus Valerius Martialis).   PeHV

Leaving me despoiled of my glorious hours.   Often when alone I liken my lord.   Gaspara Stampa.   BoWoP

Leaving me in a daze of shameless desire.   Dancing-Girl's Song. Kshetrayya.   BoWoP

...Leaving me to decide whether/to steal, borrow, or merely adore it. Shopping for Midnight.   G. E. Murray.   MAYP

Leaving mine empty, the clean scythe in my hands.   Family Outing–A Celebration.   Nicki Jackowska.   BrRo

Leaving never a trace of their gay little selves/Or the winter-night dance of the fairies and elves.   The Dance.   Rudolph Chambers Lehmann.   HBMV

Leaving no footprints.   This Version of Love.   Dorothy Hewett.   CBAP

Leaving no purer, nobler soul behind.   Mulford.   John Greenleaf Whittier AA

Leaving our bodies beached/but unbruised,/white and firm like shells.   Blue Lantern.   Cathy Song.   MAYP

...Leaving red trails/for a hearse   Alabama.   Judy Dothard Simmons. CNA

Leaving the body desolate as a staircase.   Somebody's Gone.   Charles Henri Ford.   EAS

Leaving the gouty merchant in the dark.   The Gouty Merchant and the Stranger.   Horace (or Horatio) Smith.   BeLS

Leaving the old, both Worlds at once they view,/That stand upon the threshold of the New.   Of the Last Verses in the Book.   Edmund Waller. AnAnS 2; EBEV; FaBoRV; HAP; HBV 1-2; MePo; NoP; OAEP; OBS; SeCP; SeCV 1-2; ViBoPo

Leaving the rough hedge-cheeks long-strawed and streaked/with their weeping. Autumn.   W. R. Rodgers.   NeBP

Leaving the sleeping scaffolding in the port.   Song about My Father. Elizabeth Smither.   OCNZ

Leaving the stations of her body there/As a whip maps the countries of the air.   Transit.   Richard Wilbur.   LCAP

...Leaving the wet green curly/sod to the six o'clock vultures hovering nearby. Garden Party.   Mary Mills.   NePoAm

Leaving the world like a kitten outside!   When a Man Turns Homeward. Daniel Whitehead Hicky.   PoToHe

Leaving their brightness on dead moons/As suns less heavenly do. Reflection.   Walter James Turner.   OBMV

Leaving their names/on our mantles/at waking   Wood Floor Dreams. Lance Henson.   VoR

Leaving thine outgrown shell by life's unresting sea.   The Chambered Nautilus.   Oliver Wendell Holmes   AA; AnNE; AP; DiPo; EtS; FaBoBe; FaFP; FPL; GN; HBV 1-2; HBVY; HoPM; LiTA; MCCG; MOS; NePA; NOBA; NoP; OBVV; OHFP; PoEL 1-5; PoLf; PrIm; TreF; TRV; WGRP

Leaving those holes, a never/before known emptiness,/behind.   Some Knots. Edwin Honig.   NoAm

...Leaving those who look through to/guess about what is seen during a moment.   Ten Definitions of Poetry.   Carl Sandburg.   MoAmPo

Leaving to God/His own task for them. Mother-Prayer. Margaret Widdemer. HBMV

Leaving us all behind like a skimming tambourine/brittle with music. Near the School for Handicapped Children. Thomas W. Shapcott. CBAP

Leaving us stark naked there as for making love or art. First Reunion in New Orleans: The Father as King of Revels. John Logan. CAPP

Leaving us with old sonnets and our own uncertain wrists. Roses, Revisited, in a Paradoxical Autumn. J. W. Cullum. AMV-81

& Leaving, wherever she smiled, a flowering/longing for that clear, heavy fullness. The Leaves. Ron Loewinsohn. GP

Leaving, worldling, of thine own/Neither fruit nor leaf behind thee. Autumnus. Joshua Sylvester. ElL; OBS; SoSe

Leaving you alone to bend like the reed. Indian Rock, Bainbridge Island, Washington. Duane Niatum. CDW

...Leaving you/with stomach cramps on the black streets of Cranston? A Pizza Joint in Cranston (parody). Craig Weeden. BXAP

Led by a blind and teachit by a bairn. Fra Bank to Bank. Mark Alexander Boyd. ExPo; NoP; PPoe; QFR

Led by our battle-loving Andrew Jackson,/Blest of Jehovah. Jackson at New Orleans. Wallace Rice. PAH

Led not into stupid old Farmerville/But straight into Fairyland. Conversation with an April Fool. Rowena Bastin Bennett. SiSoSe

Led on th' eternal Spring. Paradise Lost. John Milton. PPP

Leddy and the day, day good day. A Rich Old Miser. *Anonymous.* AmFP

Lee felt the impulse of a sighted end. The Flowing Summer. Charles Bruce. CaP

The lee-lang night, and weep. It Was a' for Our Rightfu' King. Robert Burns. EnRP; GoTS; PoEL 1-5

Leer and Pinch Me and their kind/Are taking possession of/Our crowded rooms, our empty persons. Party. Donald Justice. GP

Leese but their show: their substance still lives sweet. Sonnets, V: "Those hours, that with gentle work did frame." William Shakespeare. TEP

Left a great poem, praise of his God. Wmffre the Sweep. Rolfe Humphries. EaLo

Left captive in rapidly dwindling/Rainforests. Once the Striped Quagga. Mary Tallmountain. TWSS

Left free from boys and dogs and noise and men The Martin Cat Long Shaged of Courage Good. John Clare. FM

Left from even/The most casual touch? New Potatoes. Ken Belford. NeAC

Left her garment in the tide. The Water-Lily. John Banister Tabb. AA; HBV 1-2; ViBoPo

Left, like a noble deed, to grace/The memory of an ancient race. The Rose of May. Mary Howitt. HBV 1-2

Left me at home deserted, alone, and took,/And took you, my child, away. The Little Lost Child. Edward B. Marks. TreFS

Left me here to sing this song. Poor Howard. *Anonymous.* FSW

Left nothing behind but the birds to mourn. Pretty Polly. *Anonymous.* AmFP

Left only the cloven print of hooves/In mud beside a stream. Stags. William Montgomerie. PoSH

Left only the fragments found in the grass,/From his project, as finally magnified. Two Illustrations That the World Is What You Make of It. Wallace Stevens. NePoAm

Left other elements, held this so rare,/That since he never feeds on ought but air. Britannia's Pastorals. William Browne. OAEL 1-2

Left, right, that's correct. Marching. *Anonymous.* OxNR

Left to God the calf and his mother. Birth of Rainbow. Ted Hughes. NAs

Left us this empty chair. Lillian's Chair. Olga Cabral. GP

Left you to grieve to heights again. Little Lover. Leonora Speyer. HBMV

The Legend of Love no couple can find/So easie to part, or so equally join'd. Mercury's Song to Phaedra. John Dryden. OBSP; SeCV 1-2

A legend's shadow shall not move you so! Andromeda. Thomas Bailey Aldrich. AA

Legends and lights; and return is out of the question. A View of Montreal (excerpt). Francis Webb. BoAV

The legion now is lost. None will follow. A Northern Legion. Sir Herbert Read. SeCePo

Legions of worms (who knows how soon?)/Shall feast on me, and mine. To a Worm Which the Author Accidentally Trode Upon. William Hawkins. FM

The legions who have suffered and are dust. The Troops. Siegfried Sassoon. CMoP

The legs are locked; the sky is dead. The Distant Runners. Mark Van Doren. LiTA; LiTM; LoGBV; MoAmPo; NePA

Legs dust shoes and/we keep still. Dry July. Arnold Adoff. CAD

Legs fluttering like blue hands/of old tired men. Mountain Oysters. Patrick Lane. NeAC

Legs up, la la, legs down, la la,/Back to sleep again. A Song for the Middle of the Night. James Wright. SM; WeW

A lemon/etc Esther K. Comes to America: 1931. Jerome Rothenberg. NNaP

A lemon is a proof of faith, of faith in the sun. Lemon. Mario Satz. VWA

The lemon-scented girl, the long green bed? Count Orlo in England. Jon Manchip White. NePoEA

The lemon sun again, and the scent/And magenta of cyclamens. Meeting by the Gjulika Meadow. Geoffrey Grigson. WaP

Lend All, submitted, to thy drad Command. Homeric Hymn to Neptune. George Chapman. EtS

A length of ribbon, my name, my number,/the holes in my suitcase. Possessions. Ken Smith. EAS

Lent him a pocky whore. She hath paid him. On Lieutenant Shift. Ben Jonson. OBSV

...The leonine faces/snuffed without a cry, dead as all day. The News Stand. Daniel Berrigan. CAD

Leper scales fall always from his eyes. Bacchus. William Empson. PoA

"A leper white as snow!" Father Damien. John Banister Tabb. ACP

Lesbia! I must love you still. Carmina. Caius Valerius Catullus. OBVE

Less actual, more magical, as shadow horses in some/awed dreaming. Horse. Gerard Benson. PH

Less alive/than dolls &/dream Dominic Has a Doll. Edward Estlin Cummings. PoPl

Less an age of senseless matter/Than an hour of love and tears! To Pikes Peak. Elijah Clarence Hills. PoOW

The less chance we have of being killed. The Tay Bridge Disaster. William McGonagall. EvOK; PeD

Less dead than deadly. Waiting for you, perhaps. A Warning to My Love. David Wagoner. NePoEA-2

Less greedy I will be. The Sweet Tooth. Katharine Pyle. BBGG

The less I want to squeeze your middle. To Chloe. Earnest Albert Hooton. UnTE

Less in the flutes than in those feet we heard/The pride that lifts men far above their fate. Elegy on the Death of Mme. Anna Pavlova (excerpt). E. H. W. Meyerstein. UnS

Less oft is peace in Shelley's mind,/Than calm in waters, seen. To Jane: The Recollection. Percy Bysshe Shelley. ChRP; OBNC; OBRV

Less shelter, more fear Packing in with a Man. Judith McCombs. LTB

Less than the sound of its blade/Dipping the stream once more. To Be Sung on the Water. Louise Bogan. MoVE; PrIm; VGW

Less than the wind that runs to the flamy call! The Enkindled Spring. D. H. Lawrence. NoAm

Less than total is a bucketful of radiant toys. Cut the Grass. Archie Randolph Ammons. HAP; PPP; TAP

Less yearning for the friendship fled,/Than some strong bond which is to be. In Memoriam A.H.H., CXVI. Alfred, Lord Tennyson. VLP

Lesse by their own jemms, then those beams of thine. To Master Denham, on His Prospective Poem. Robert Herrick. AnAnS 2

A lesser than the large. Love is that later thing than death. Emily Dickinson. LiTA; NePA

The lesson never learned. The Death of Fathers. Theodore Weiss. SV

A lesson taught by Him who loved all humankind. The Wind-Flower. Jones Very. AnNE

A lesson which shall be re-taught them, wake/Upon the thrones of earth; but let them quake!' George the Third. George Gordon, Lord Byron. FiP

Lessons that leave no time for prizes. A Young Man's Epigram on Existence. Thomas Hardy. BrPo; NoAm

Lest anybody spy the blood/And "You're hurt" exclaim! A wounded deer leaps highest. Emily Dickinson. AWP; InPo; TAP

Lest anyone cast a spell on Amanda. Amanda Is Shod. Maxine W. Kumin. PH

Lest Christ and man be forced to climb stark Calvary again. Soldier, What Did You See? Don Blanding. BBV

Lest Death shall greet and claim me ere/I keep Life's rendezvous. I Have a Rendezvous with Life. Countee Cullen. CDC

Lest death should vanquish love. Poem: "The haven and last refuge of my pain." Niccolo Machiavelli. AWP

Lest eyes well-seeing thy foul faults should find! Sonnets, CXLVIII: "O me! what eyes hath Love put in my head." William Shakespeare. GTBS; GTBS-P

Lest flesh at length lay waste the soul/In its sick heat. Those Not Elect. Léonie Adams. MoVE

Lest, flinching or lethargic,/Man slides into his past.' A Dream. Mary Elizabeth ("E") Fullerton. BoAV

Lest for a present paltry sport, you kill a future joy. To George Pulling Buds. Adelaide O'Keeffe. FaBoUs

Lest four tears from two eyes fall. Duality. Dannie Abse. NoAm

Lest from out my singing/Leaps my heart upon you! Come Not near My Songs. *Anonymous.* AWP; PG

Lest from out my singing/Leaps my heart upon you! Song of a Passionate Lover. Mary Austin. BPAW

Lest God with such like misery/Your wicked minds requite. The Babes in the Wood. *Anonymous.* HBV 1-2; HBVY; OBNV

Lest, haply, we be found/(Ah, dread no brave hath drowned!)/Fighting against Great God. Bury Them. Henry Howard Brownell. PAH

...Lest he believe you say more than an ingenuous alpha-/bet, a cruel child of a language. Page. Sandra McPherson. PoA

Lest he kill you with his cunning! The Song of Hiawatha. Henry Wadsworth Longfellow. SpRo

Lest horrid Cummerbunds should come,/And swallow you outright. The Cummerbund. Edward Lear. CenHV; OBTV

Lest I, discovered, perish as a spy. November 2 A.M. Conspiracy. Sara Bard Field. AnEnPo

...Lest I drunkenly sing/Of wattles, wars, childhoods, being at last home. Airliner. Francis Webb. CBAP; NOAV

Lest, if thou slip, thou fall to hell. On the Meetings of the Scotch Covenanters. *Anonymous.* FaBoEE

Lest in that world their cry/Of woe thou hear. The Effect of Example. John Keble. HBV 1-2; HBVY

Lest it be said, "With him New England fell!" An Elegie upon the Death of the Reverend Mr. Thomas Shepard (excerpt). Urian Oakes. NOCV

Lest joy so poignant slay a soul so weak. Joy May Kill. Buonarroti Michelangelo. AWP

Lest man sail, or woman row. Sail and Oar. Robert Graves. MOS

Lest moss take all our names when Old Mortality's gone. Surviving a Poetry Circuit. William Stafford. FAZ

Lest my brain turn, and the deficient sight/Topple down headlong. King Lear. William Shakespeare. FaBoPP

Lest my poor dust should dream of you. Requiescat. Rosamund Marriott Watson. HBV 1-2

Lest now I learn nothing, again. Pledge. Avraham Shlonsky. VWA

Lest of his kind intent some human cry/Interpret not the Messenger aright. Ex Libris. Arthur Upson. HBV 1-2

Lest once more those mad Merchants come/chanting from Cathay! Merchants from Cathay. William Rose Benet. HBMV; MoAmPo

Lest one imperfect gesture make demands/As troubling as the touch of human hands. Love in the Museum. Adrienne Rich. NePoEA; NYBP

Lest one touch of this heart convey its grief. Sonnets from the Portuguese, XIII. Elizabeth Barrett Browning. BrRo

Lest our children/go so fast/they go. The Child Bearers. Anne Sexton. BoWoP

...Lest pity/Shall bow low thine head while the salt tears fall. Regret. *Anonymous.* WTO

Lest rocks and stones should rise and break/Their silence into songs. Hosanna to Christ. Isaac Watts. NOCV

Lest seeking selfish ease/Thy best I lose. I Would Not Ask. Grace E. Troy. STF

Lest she should lie awake and tremble/When the great storm-winds blow. The Sailor. Sylvia Townsend Warner. OBMV

Lest she that stole it to his shame reveal it. Peter Hath Lost His Purse. *Anonymous.* FF

Lest some fine canting pen/Should be at him again. Thomas Logge. Walter De la Mare. FaBoEE

Lest soon, they whom thou holdest/dearest/Be past thy need. Kindness. *Anonymous.* STF

Lest that your husbands you entrap, and send you to Virginny. A Net for a Night Raven. *Anonymous.* OBSS

Lest the mind open/with intuitions and imaginings. Rogue Pearunners. Ronald G. Everson. PeCV

Lest the strings should break, and the music be done. My Heart Is a Lute. Lady Anne Barnard. HBV 1-2

Lest the wise world should look into your moan/And mock you with me after I am gone. Sonnets, LXXI. "No longer mourn for me when I am dead." William Shakespeare. AWP; CBEP; EBEV; FaBoRV; GBL; GoTF; GTBS; GTBS-P; HAP; HBV 1-2; InPo; LiTB; NoP; OAEP; OBSC; PoRA; PPoe; SeCeV; TEP; TreFT; TrGrPo; ViBoPo; WHA

...Lest the wrath of that Other/Should reach to him there! A Mother in Egypt. Marjorie Pickthall. CaP; HBV 1-2

Lest thence his wizard eyes might peep/To mark the things we do. Say Who Is This with Silvered Hair. Robert Bridges. VLP

Lest they falle down into thy ey/The spones that above thee be. How Should I Rule Me? *Anonymous.* OxBM

Lest they fly on those wild ways/And life be undone. The Gay. George William Russell. OBMV

Lest they say we are lacking in taste,/Or that there is no caste in this family. Lustra, III: Further Instructions. Ezra Pound. PoA

Lest they should parch too swiftly, where she passes. Ballatetta. Ezra Pound. VGW

Lest this same warrior-drover, Wayne,/Should ever catch the poet. The Cow-Chace. John André. PAH

Lest, too, thou have his wings. Conceits. Arlo Bates. AA

Lest we should ever fear the lust/Of earthly man, a lord of dust. Psalm X. Sir Philip Sidney. FCP

Lest we should neglect/But one of these fine things. For the Cultural Campaign. Chimedin Jigmed. WTO

Lest with thee henceforth ever, night and day,/Regret should walk. Counsel. Mary Evelyn Moore Davis. HBV 1-2

Lest you come to hell with me, for I must die. Captain Kidd. *Anonymous.* AmFP; TrAS; ViBoFo

Lest you should find me some tempestuous June,/Crying my mad white hunger to the moon. Two Married. Helen Frazee-Bower. HBMV

Let a race of men now rise and/take control! For My People. Margaret Walker. AmNP; BALP; CNA; IDB; MoRP; PoBA; PoNe

Let age approve of youth, and death complete the same! Rabbi Ben Ezra. Robert Browning. BBV; BLPL; FaFP; FiP; GTBS; HBV 1-2; MasP; MaVP; MBW 1-2; OAEP; OBNC; OBVV; TEP; WGRP

Let air fly through the body, let all women dance/Into kingdoms of where loving is not getting even I Want to Tell You. Sandra Hochman. GP

Let all be dumb. The Witches' Charm. Ben Jonson. ElL; FaBoCh; LoBV; LoGBV; NOBE

Let all be well, be well. Maud. Alfred, Lord Tennyson. NOBV

Let all else go to roof within your heart. Wild Cherry. Lizette Woodworth Reese. AnAmPo

Let all men believe it,/as you have taught me also/to believe it. To a Dog Injured in the Street. William Carlos Williams. LCAP; LiTM; MoAB; NePoAm; PP; SeCeV

Let all men pass who come in love. Panama. Amanda T. Jones. PAH

Let all our conquered wealth be gathered there. Preparing for the Wedding. Claudian. HW

Let all our people be free. Independence. Adebayo Faleti. PBA

Let all people live/In peace.../Peace. Pleading Voices. Shalom Katav. VWA

Let all stand by the ballot box,/For fair and free elections. Fair and Free Elections. *Anonymous.* FSW

Let all the nation judge it. I'll Sail upon the Dog-star. Thomas Durfey. CBEP; FaBoCh; LoGBV; OxBoLi

Let all the people worship Thee. Hymn of Gratitude. *Anonymous.* BLRP

Let an angel come and dwell to-night/In this dear double-heart, and teach! Wedding-Hymn. Sidney Lanier. TrPWD

Let angels speak, and heavens thy praises tell. An Epitaph upon the Right Honorable Sir Philip Sidney... Sir Walter Ralegh. FCP

Let appetite refrain from flesh, take only/A gentler nourishment. Metamorphoses. Ovid (Publius Ovidius Naso). NAWM 1-2

...Let apples/Overflow between her breasts. I shall call her Peace. Peace. Michael Longley. CIP

An' let Balfour/Gang through your Hielan' hills, man. The Battle of Glentilt (1847). Sir Douglas Maclagan. PoSH

Let be, or else consume me quite. Egg. Jay MacPherson. WHW

Let be these poppies, not for you/Cut down and spread. The Prince's Progress: Bride Song. Christina Georgina Rossetti. OBEV; ViBoPo

...Let be/what is gone. The Charge. Denise Levertov. NePoEA-2

Let Britons paint their bodies blue/As formerly, but touch not you. Observing a Vulgar Name on the Plinth of an Ancient Statue. Walter Savage Landor. EyDe

Let but another world-war kill/The rest, it will be safer still. Safe for Democracy. Leonard Alfred George Strong. HBMV

Let but their lids fall, and it will be night. Song: "Turn, turn thy beauteous face away." Beaumont, Francis and John Fletcher. PoEL 1-5

Let Buz bless with the Jackall–but the Lord is the Lion's provider. Jubilate Agno. Christopher Smart. NCEP

Let casuists tell us, if they can,/Is England's welfare furthered? On the Frequent Review of the Troops. M". NOEC

Let Christan Lyndesay wryt our epitaphis. To R. Hudson. Alexander Montgomerie. OxBS

...Let Christmas Day/Have a tear as well as a smile. How Grand and How Bright. *Anonymous.* GBP

Let compassion breathe in and out of you/filling you with poems. Waiting. Jane Cooper. TAP

Let de Midnight Special shine its ever-lovin' light on you. Midnight Special. *Anonymous.* ABF; AS; BFSS; FSW

Let down your hair! Rapunzel. Louis Untermeyer. DFT

Let each "I" look at "Me." What I See in Me. *Anonymous.* STF

Let each one and his brother turn up his scrubbed, gleaming/face to the sun, and yell. A Joyful Noise. Donald Finkel. CoAP

Let earth wide with glory flame,/Forever, ever and amen. Unto Our God Most High We Sing. John Vance Cheney. AH

Let Einstein be! restored the status quo. It Did Not Last. J. C. Squire. FaBoCo; InPK; QQQ

Let 'em find there's men meant to be men! The Strike. *Anonymous.* OBET

Let 'em pound drugs, they have no brains to beat. A Satire against Wit. Sir Richard Blackmore. APAS

Let 'em take heed, they do not speed as they did they know/when-a! Sir Francis Drake; or Eighty-Eight. *Anonymous.* GBP; OBSS

Let Erin's voice proclaim/In bardic praise on ev'ry hill/Columbia's glorious name. The War Ship of Peace. Samuel Lover. PAH

Let eternal morning rise,/And shadows end. The Day Is Dying in the West. Mary Artemisia ("Aunt Mary") Lathbury. WGRP

Let every knee to Jesus bow. Draw Near, O Son of God. Charles Wesley. BePJ

Let fall their heavy tears/gaunt music for lost ears. Ship-Building Emperors Commanded... Peter Levi. NePoEA-2

Let fall this day Thy dew! Song of the Dew. *Anonymous.* TrJP

Let fate and courage now conceal,/When truth could bring remorse alone. Shadows. Richard Monckton, Lord Houghton Milnes. HBV 1-2

Let flesh swing open! Let the ghost abide! Judges, Judges. Gene Baro. NePoEA-2

Let Folly be the guide of Love,/Where'er the boy may choose to go. Love and Folly. Jean de La Fontaine. AWP

Let gardeners too remember sowing-time. Bee-Master. Victoria Mary (Vita) Sackville-West. HaMV

Let glory from the Church arise/Through Jesus Christ our Lord. Lord, At This Closing Hour. Eleazar Thompson Fitch. AH

Let glory o'er these scenes be shed,/And smile on us today. Down to the Sacred Wave. Samuel Francis Smith. AH

Let go of a bat if he bites your ear. The Bat and the Scientist. J. S. Bigelow. QQQ

Let go the reef a-tayckle,/My sheets, they are jammed! Let Go the Reef Tackle. *Anonymous.* ShS

Let go, when drunk with wine your head into the gutter/sinks. On the Way. Georg Trakl. LiTW

Let God do that which He wills. Let his servants endure/and adore! The Three Woes. Aubrey Thomas De Vere. AnIV

Let God through! Give Way! Charlotte Perkins Stetson Gilman. WGRP

Let guilty man compassion find! Dies Irae. Thomas of Celano. WGRP

Let half-heard echoes of an Oread's song/Breathe on the drowsy lyre of my sleep. The Silent Ranges. Stephen Moylan Bird. HBMV

Let heathens know weak men they be. Selah. With All My Heart, Jehovah, I'll Confess. Henry Ainsworth. AH

Let Hell afford/The pavement of her Heaven! Non Nobis. Henry Cust. OBEV; OBVV

Let Hellicon, Pindus, Parnassus hill/Sound Isabella, Isabella still. Orlando Furioso. Lodovico Ariosto. OBVE

...Let her alone/Bemoan those broken lips with kisses from her own. Spring Offensive, 1941. Maurice Biggs. PoAu 1-2

Let her go to the devil!–there's no more to be said. Drinking Song. *Anonymous.* NOBL

Let her hear not sigh nor groan.' The Roman Earl. *Anonymous.* OBVE

Let her not be out of favour. Britannia's Pastorals. William Browne. EIL; ViBoPo

Let here his eyes be raised/On Nature's sweetest light! Song: "Who hath his fancy pleased." Sir Philip Sidney. OBEV; SiPS

Let herring school through heaven's hot July. The Fisherman's Son. Charles Bruce. CaP

Let him be brought to wait on us at table. Jupiter and Ganimede. Thomas Heywood. PeHV

Let him be still himself; and let him live. To Antenor. Katherine ("Orinda") Philips. SBG

Let him believe you're from my farm. From the Epigrams of Martial. James Michie. FaBoEE

Let him climb the rigging like his daddy used to do. Bell-Bottomed Trousers. *Anonymous.* AmSS; FSW; UnTE

Let him come. Nat Turner. Samuel ("Paul Vesey") Allen. CNA; FB

Let him come as her answer. Orphan Boy, Fishing. Albert Goldbarth. WOLT

Let him come, the Brigand! let him come! He Said That He Was Not Our Brother. John Banim. OnYI

Let him compare the two Tune: Magnolia Blossom. Li Ching-chao. PBWP

Let him fall asleep,/Locked in her arms, a second Endymion! A Lover's Curse. Meleager. LiTW

Let him go to the devil and seek his offense./Let 'em rip! Fa-lo, fa-larie, fa-la. Arizona Boys and Girls. *Anonymous.* BFSS

Let him in to feel your fire,/And toss him of your crumbs. The Wind of January. Christina Georgina Rossetti. YeAr

Let him look fixedly on Myrrha's eyes. Three Ballate. Angelo Poliziano. AWP

Let Him not lose what He so dear hath bought. Consider. Giovanni Pico della Mirandola. CAW

Let him prosper who bends his back/To sow a new idea. Fighter. Musaemura Bonus Zimunya. WhB

Let him rest on the buffalo-hide bed,/where his forefathers repose. Weep Not for a Warrior. Mbuyiseni Oswald Mtshali. WhB

Let him revise/His insolent ontology/Or teach himself to pray. Lives. Derek Mahon. FaBoIP

Let him sit down and pick the meaning out. A Copy of Non Sequitors. *Anonymous.* FaBoNo

Let him slumber, sweetly slumber,/Till God calls him from the tomb. A Departed Friend. Julia A. Moore. FiBHP

Let him stand as a monument raised to himself. A Serio-Comic Elegy. Richard Whately. ShM

Let him suck his thumb. Commercial Traveller. Lauris Edmond. OCNZ

Let him thank God and let him not provoke/To have the like of this my painful stroke. The flaming sighs that boil within my breast. Sir Thomas Wyatt. FCP

"Let him who may sight glory before death." The White Rainbow. Starr Nelson. GoYe

...Let him within/Wear all his beard, and none upon his chin. A Lady's Prayer to Cupid. Thomas Carew. CaPo; OBSP

Let him wonder if I lie;/Let him half believe me. Threnody. Dorothy Parker. InMe

Let his renowne be cleare as mine, equall his strength in warre.' The Iliad. Homer. OBVE

Let Holly have the mastery as the manner is. Nay, Ivy, Nay. *Anonymous.* CBEP; CH

Let Honor's self to thee grant highest place! Astrophel and Stella, CIII. Sir Philip Sidney. AAS; HBV 1-2; SiPS

Let Horace blush, and Virgil too. Epitaph for One Who Would Not Be Buried in Westminster Abbey. Alexander Pope. FaBoEE

Let it all be seen in your light, blushing drops. Trickle Drops. Walt Whitman. PeD

Let it all stand as it is. Zimmer in Fall. Paul Zimmer. PPJ

Let it be summer. Let it be Williamsburg, Iowa. Grandmother Grace. Ronald Wallace. GOYP; SM

Let it but be the tarrying of the sun. Youth. George Cabot Lodge. AA

Let it go on forever. Night Poem. Wayne Dodd. AMV-80

Let it hail or rain or snow. Cuckoo, Cherry Tree. *Anonymous.* OxNR

Let it in at one ear and out at the other. Advice to Young Children. Stevie Smith. ELU

Let it not grieve you,/if the following day is slow to arrive. Saturday Night in the Village. Giacomo Leopardi. OBVE

Let it run on now: I know what it is. The Examination of His Mistress' Perfections. Francis Beaumont. GoBC

Let kneeling faith adore thy will. My God, I Thank Thee. Andrews Norton. AH

Let law be father of our peace. Let There Be Law. Mark Van Doren. MoRP

Let learned Macclesfield say what he will,/Spite of New Style, we'll keep old Christmas still.' The Daventry Wonder. Agricola. NOEC

Let Light attend me to the grave! Prayer. Theodore Roethke. MP; TwCP

Let linger this reproach: behold the child. A Viet Cong Sapper Dies. Stephen Sossaman. AMV-81

Let living psalms of praise be heard. Mysterious Presence! Source of All. Seth Curtis Beach. AH

Let loose thy scorn on him, nor cease/Till thou hast cover'd him with shame. Tolerance. Sir Lewis Morris. OBVV

Let love be/at the end. Let There Be New Flowering. Lucille Clifton. GP; PPJ

Let love be kind, or else ye'll break her. Treat the Woman Tenderly, Tenderly. *Anonymous.* PoL

Let Love Divine through human hearts/Compel them to the fold. Compel Them to Come In. Leonard Dodd. BLRP

Let Love's beginning expiate Love's end. Remember Not. Helene Johnson. BANP; PoNe

...Let Lucy Lily. Four Saints in Three Acts: "Pigeons on the grass alas." Gertrude Stein. CrMA; TAP

Let 'm pocket-pool. Rapunzel. Faye Kicknosway. APU

Let maggots befoul her alive in bed,/and dibble thorns in her tongue. God Sour the Milk of the Knacking Wench. Alden Nowlan. PeCV

...Let marge up only/long enough to get food & drink occasionally. Wasp Sex Myth (Two). Anselm Hollo. PoM

"Let me alone, alas, and drive him back to London." Thyrsis, Sleep'st Thou? *Anonymous.* InvP; OBSP

Let me answer, unrepining,–/Father, "Not my will, but Thine." Disappointment. *Anonymous.* TRV; WBLP

Let me be as a tune-swept fiddle-string/That feels the Master Melody–and snaps! Let Me Live Out My Years. John G. Neihardt. GoTF; HBMV; TreFS; YaD

Let me be dumb! Evelyn. Rossiter Johnson. AA

Let me be joy, be hope! Let my life sing! A Prayer for Every Day. Mary Carolyn Davies. BLPA; FaBoBe; PoToHe

Let me be king, diddle diddle,/You be the queen. The Country Lovers. *Anonymous.* UnTE

Let me be loved, or else not loved be. Arcadia. Sir Philip Sidney. SiPS

Let me be my brother's friend. Anything God, but Hate. *Anonymous.* TreFT

Let me be Naught! The harp-strings tell me plain/That "unto Him do we return again!" Resurgence. Jalal ed-Din or al-Din Rumi. LiTW

Let me be severed/O Christ, from your sweetness! Sweetness. *Anonymous.* BIrV

Let me be the great nail holding a skyscraper through blue/nights into white stars. Prayers of Steel. Carl Sandburg. AnAmPo; AP; CMoP; MoAmPo; TrCP; TrPWD; YaD

...Let me be where it is. Psalm Concerning the Castle. Denise Levertov. TwCP

Let me burn in the hellfire/Of that sin At One Glance. Mihri Hatun. PBWP

...Let me/buy a love potion, a gin, a double. Gone Are the Days. Norman MacCaig. OxBC

Let me call to her! Appeal to the Moongod Nanna-Suen to Throw Out Lugalanne... Enheduanna. BoWoP

Let me carefully bear the cup of myself to Thee. Keep Hidden from Me. Rachel Korn. PBWP

...Let me carry the pangs/of this sorrow in my dreams and in my wakeful hours. If It Is Not My Portion. Rabindranath Tagore. BoC; OBMV

Let me die. Love, I Marvel What You Are. Trumbull Stickney. HBV 1-2

Let me die ere I see/That I'm forsaken. Long Betwixt Love and Fear. John Dryden. LiTL; ViBoPo

Let me die there when I'm old. Take Me Back to Old Montana. *Anonymous.* CoSo

...Let me/discover my home. I drag a boat over the ocean. Lal Ded. BoWoP

Let me drink wine, palm wine/and fuddled by my drunkenness forget/– Monangambeeee... Monangamba. Antonio Jacinto. TTY; WhB

Let me face the summons calmly/When Death beckons me away. A Creed. *Anonymous.* STF

Let me feed full, till that I fart, sayes Jill. Upon Jack and Jill. Epigram. Robert Herrick. AnAnS 2; CaPo

Let me follow your scent. Prowling the Ridge. Judith Minty. GeTw

...Let me gather gold. Nothing Gold Can Stay. Norma Farber. AMV-81

Let me give two, that doubly am got free/From my disease's danger, and from thee. To Doctor Empirick. Ben Jonson. DBV; FaBoEE; NoP; SeCP

...Let me give you an illusion of not/grieving. Structure of Rime. Robert Duncan. CAPP

"Let me go, mother, let me go/To my wife's country." Let Me Go. *Anonymous.* WTO

"Let me go you fool!" and "Hot dog!" The Mad Rapist of Calaveras County. Pete Winslow. PV

Let me have light at least one day! Burn out Burn Quick. Abraham Reisen. TrJP

Let me have power to do. Two Prayers. Charlotte Perkins Stetson Gilman. WGRP

Let me have those which are most red and white. In Yellow Meadows I Take No Delight. Sir Thomas Browne. FaBoEE

...Let me hear thy voice, as/thou passest, when mid-day is silent around. Fragments of Ancient Poetry (excerpt). James Macpherson. NOEC

Let me help you, daughter, wife/lover, will you Beautiful Black Women... LeRoi (Imamu Amiri Baraka) Jones. BPo; PoM

Let me hide myself in Thee. Rock of Ages. Augustus Montague Toplady. BLRP; BLSo; FaFP; FaPoR; FSW; GoTF; HBV 1-2; NOCV; OxBoCh; TreF; WGRP

Let me jump out o' waggon and go back and drown me/At Pummery or Ten-Hatches Weir. The Curate's Kindness. Thomas Hardy. CoBMV

"Let me kiss my Celin, ere I die!–Alas! alas for/Celin!" The Lamentation for Celin. *Anonymous.* AWP

Let me know it now while living; I can own and treasure it. If You're Ever Going to Love Me. *Anonymous.* BLPA

Let me know something when I'm dead. The Things That Matter. Edith Nesbit. OxBTC

Let me lie down exhausted, content with that. Eleven Addresses to the Lord. John Berryman. OxBC

Let me lie till Thine Own Springtime with the pines be-/side my bed! Returning. Ruth Guthrie Harding. HBV 1-2

...Let me live with you/and dig your blazing. Ballad of the Morning Streets. LeRoi (Imamu Amiri Baraka) Jones. CNA; SOTW

Let me my wishes on them Spend/That they poor Souls may live and mend. On the Decease of the Religious and Honourable Jno Haynes Esqr.... John James. SCAP

Let me narrow in on my night/with that effortless certainty. Leaf. John Hewitt. NeIP

Let me never know myself apart from the living God! The Hands of God. D. H. Lawrence. MoRP

Let me not dread pale death,/though the horror come when I am alone. Alone up Here on the Mountain. *Anonymous.* NOBI

Let me not love Thee, if I love Thee not. Affliction. George Herbert. LiTB; MeLP; MePo; NOBE; OBS; OxBoCh

Let me not stray again, but keep/Me folded fast amid Thy little sheep. The Holy Eclogue. Sister, Francisca Josefa del Castillo. CAW

Let me out in the dark, let me go, let me go! Divorce. Anna Wickham. MoBrPo

Let me out,/Let me out! Gratitude. Annette Lynch. FF

Let me play you/fresh on my guitar! The Tape. Myra Cohn Livingston. NTCP

Let me remember then the name I bore! He Holdeth Fast to the Memory of His Identity. Book of the Dead. AWP

Let me repentant work for thee! A Last Prayer. Helen Hunt Jackson. AA; TrPWD; TRV

Let me return to a safe harbor; like the waves'/Slate-sheets, crash in the jetties of your arms. Burn Down the Icons. Grace Schulman. GP

Let me sit here by this adobe wall/And lean against summer! Summer Comes. Edith Agnew. SiSoSe

Let me sleep now till the Judgment Day.' The Poor Ghost. Christina Georgina Rossetti. GBL

Let me sleep on, dear God, if I but dream. Mother. Max Ehrmann. PoToHe

Let me sleep through his blinding reign,/And only wake with you! Ah! Why, Because the Dazzling Sun. Emily Bronte. BrRo

Let me so read thy life, that I/Unto all life of mine may die. The Flaming Heart. Richard Crashaw. AnAnS 1; AtBAP; CAW; CoBE; GoBC; HAP; LiTB; LoBV; NOBE; OBS; OxBoCh; PoEL 1-5; SeCePo; SeCV 1-2; TEP; TrGrPo; WHA

Let me so swim in this Sea, that I may/With thee live happy in another day. Meditation. Philip Pain. NOBA

Let me stay in Grants Pass, Oregon, forever. Poem Composed in Rogue River Park... Tom Wayman. PoL

Let me steer close to touch YOUR BIG WHISKERS. The Voice of America 1961. James Liddy. CIP

...Let me still glow. To the Mercy Killers. Dudley Randall. DL

Let me/stroke your sweet hair. Perversity. Susan Griffin. LLLT

Let me take off my Arabian shawl. Two Nocturnes. Katherine Mansfield. HBMV

Let me think more of my neighbor/And a little less of me. My Daily Creed. *Anonymous.* TRV

Let me thy Angell bee, bee thou my Lord. Meditations. Edward Taylor. AP; LiTA; TAP

Let me tumble at your feet. My Childhood's Bedroom. Charles P.R. Tisdale. AMV-80

Let me unclench my being/to stroke the yellow flowers1 At Least. Don Mattera. WhB

Let me wind up with my rhyme/And I'll sing some other time. Lilliputian's Beer Song. Septimus Winner. OBAL

Let me wonder. Orders. Abraham Moses Klein. WHW

Let me work and be glad. A Prayer. Theodosia Garrison. TrPWD

Let men inquire, and gods obscurely know. Little Eclogue. Elinor Wylie. NMM

Let Men look to't, least Women wear the Spurrs. Mercury Shew'd Apollo, Bartas Book. Nathaniel Ward. SCAP

Let mine eyes see Thee and then see death. Let Mine Eyes See Thee. Saint Theresa of Avila. AWP; CAW

Let mother be in a tiny boat,/And that boat float on a moonlit sea. The Spring Waters. Ping Hsin (Hsieh Wang-ying). WPOW

Let music sound, and flowers be laid/Upon each resting-bed. Memorial Day. Emma A. Lent. WBLP

Let my child sleep,/hold back the branches. A Little Carol of the Virgin. Felix Lope de Vega Carpio. PCh

Let my descent and fall, O Lord,/Be into Paradise. Ambition. William Henry Davies. MoBrPo; TrGrPo

Let my future radiant shine/With sweet hopes of thee and thine. Hymn. Edgar Allan Poe. ISi

Let my gap be shut Pull My Daisy. Jack Kerouac. PoM

Let my heart your garden be/Give the seeds of love to me. Hearts and Flowers. Mary Dow Brine. FSN

Let my life help the other lives it touches by the way! My Prayer. *Anonymous.* BLRP

Let my life no longer be/Than I am in love with thee. Philarete Praises Poetry. George Wither. OBS

Let my life show forth thy praise. Hymn. Francis Scott Key. TrPWD

Let my love be heard/Whispering in your wings. A Prayer. Alfred Noyes. PoPl

"Let my people go!" Go Down, Moses. *Anonymous.* BoAN 1-2; BPo; EaLo; EBCP; FSW; NOBA; TrAS; TreF

Let my release be soon. Song: "If I had only loved your flesh." Victoria Mary (Vita) Sackville-West. HBMV

Let my women mourn for days/in flight. If Blood Is Black Then Spirit Neglects My Unborn Son. Conrad Kent Rivers. PoBA

Let neither winds nor stromy main,/Force back my shattered bark again. Temptation. William Cowper. EiCP

Let never man after me have will/For to make him frere! Against Friars. *Anonymous.* OxBM

Let never the fiend with false fending/Cumber us in no shame. The "Pater Noster". *Anonymous.* ACP; CAW

Let no blasphemer till the sacred earth/Or scatter seed upon it. Benediction. Mark Turbyfill. PoA

Let no man steal your thyme. Thyme. *Anonymous.* AmFP

...Let no one/tell you otherwise, we've never had it so good. The Fifties. Ira Sadoff. AmPA

Let no poet empty-handed/Leave the dwelling of his lord. Childless. Giollabhrighde MacConmidhe. BIrV; KiLC

...Let no slack lips dispel my charm. Prince Charming. John N. Miller. DFT

Let no such man be my friend! Medea: Chorus. Euripides. LiTW

Let no sunrise' yellow noise/Interrupt this ground. Ample make this bed. Emily Dickinson. AtBAP; MoAB; MoAmPo; OxBA; PoEL 1-5

Let no ungentle cold destroy,/All taste we have of heavenly joy! Song on a Young Lady Who Sung Finely. Wentworth Dillon, Earl of Roscommon. CavP

Let no unkind no fair beseechers kill;/Think all but one, and me in that one Will. Sonnets, CXXXV: "Whoever hath her wish, thou hast thy Will." William Shakespeare. OAEL 1-2

Let non don him offence, lest ille befalle. Ye Clerke of Ye Wethere (parody). *Anonymous.* BXAP

Let none look at me! Mother and Poet. Elizabeth Barrett Browning. HBV 1-2; SBG

Let none regret my end who called me friend. Last Poem. Ted Berrigan. APU

Let none with Thee have part! Give Me Thy Heart. Adelaide Anne Procter. ACP; CAW; GoBC

Let not a whisper fall/That we have died in vain! The Unreturning. Clinton Scollard. PAH

Let not its mockery hurt you. Ah, sing low. The Heart Has Its Reasons. *Anonymous.* GoBC

Let not old age disgrace my high desire. Arcadia. Sir Philip Sidney. SiPS

Let not our hearts be troubled/Close to and beside the giver of life! In Vain Was I Born. Nezahualcoyotl. ILwL

Let not our naive labours have been in vain! A Disused Shed in Co. Wexford. Derek Mahon. CIP; FaBoIP; FaBoPV; NOBI; OxBC

Let not the bullet go through one before the other. From My High Love. Kenneth Patchen. MoAmPo

Let not thine own inheritance/Be sold away for nought. O Thou Most High Who Rulest All. Anne Bradstreet. AH

...Let our black ashes/celebrate his necessary darkness. His Necessary Darkness. Nancy Sullivan. TAP

Let our brave sons know no fear! The Rigveda: Indra, the Supreme God. *Anonymous.* AWP

Let our enemies go blind. Love Songs. *Anonymous.* BoWoP

Let our firm hearts pray to be orphaned! The New Sun. John Wain. NePoEA-2

Let our loving mindes then meete,/For pure meetings are most sweet. Are You What Your Faire Lookes Expresse? Thomas Campion. AAS

Let our occident stream bear the young hero's/name,/Who taught him his path to the sea. On the Discoveries of Captain Lewis. Joel Barlow. AmPP; MC; PAH

Let our tears for the dead earn the Cwmrhydyceirw Elegiacs. Vernon Watkins. PoA

Let peace lie on lulled lips: I will not say. The Contretemps. Thomas Hardy. CMoP; LiTM

Let pilot Love the rudder guide,/And steer by Chloe's eyes. The Temple of Venus. Soame Jenyns. NOEC

Let poetry's too throbbing vein/Lie quiet in your breast. Advice. Walter Savage Landor. HBV 1-2

Let praise to Him arise. Trusting Jesus. Grace B. Renfrow. BePJ

LET PURE BLACK WORDS MOVE FROM THOUGHT/BEHIND. Oh Ease Oh Body-Strain Oh Love Oh Ease Me Not! Wound-Bore. Michael McClure. CoPo

Let Reason rule the hearts that she hath wonne. To His Love That Sent Him a Ring. George Turberville. EnPo; EnRePo

Let rhyme be my conclusion. The Chances of Rhyme. Charles Tomlinson. FaBoMo; PoA

Let rigid Cato read these lines of mine. When He Would Have His Verses Read. Robert Herrick. CaPo; EnL; NOBE; OAEP; OBS; SeCV 1-2

Let's both to kiss begin;/To kiss freely: if not, you may go spin. Westminster Drollery, 1671. Aphra Behn. SBG

Let's celebrate his birth! The Shepherd's Tale. Raoul Ponchon. OBCP

...Let's dance/the dance of feathers, the dance of birds. Kopis'taya. Paula Gunn Allen. STE; TWSS

Let's do it, let's fall in love. Let's Do It. Cole Porter. OBAL

Let's drink to the splendor of not being our bodies. Nothing. Julia de Burgos. BoWoP

Let's get our things and leave the dance. Leaving the Dance. Alexander Whitaker. NIP

Let's go down to the crawfish hole. Sweet Thing. *Anonymous.* OuSiCo

Let's go home,/you can't see a thing. My Son Doesn't See a Thing. Tomas Rivera. FIA

Let's go in and see if there's any jelly left,'/Jack said. And we did that. Ghost Story. Dylan Thomas. OBCP

Let's go to California O California. Alejandro Murguia. FIA

Let's go to sleep...good-night...an' see ye/Frid'y. Cell-Mates. Louis Untermeyer. HBMV

Let's go to the movies/just the 2 of us/love/peter. Dear Reader. Peter Meinke. Psk

Let's grow in love. Poem/Ditty-Bop. Carolyn M. Rodgers. JB

Let's hash the hush. The Inner Source. Andrei Codrescu. APU

Let's have a look at another five. In Dives' Dive. Robert Frost. VGW

Let's have a rouse that will ring round the earth. Men of the High North. Robert W. Service. ACV

Let's hope, at least, the Fount may last/Until our Generation's past. The Cow. Oliver Herford. NA

Let's hope she has no sense of smell. The Goat. Roland Young. BoAnP

Let's hope you won't think me too vicious. The Song of the Mischievous Dog. Dylan Thomas. FaFP; GrPl

Let's in: for the dark Hemisphere/Does now like one of them appear. Upon Appleton House, to My Lord Fairfax. Andrew Marvell. FaBoPV; SeCP; SeCV 1-2

Let's just send her back right where she came from! The Subversive. Merle Woo. BrSi

Let's keep sticking and be true. The Postage Stamp Lesson. *Anonymous.* STF

Let's kisse before you goe. There Was a Wyly Ladde. *Anonymous.* ErPo

Let's let my heavenly lostness overwhelm me. Lost in Heaven. Robert Frost. MoAmPo

Let's lie down somewheres/baby. Funny fantasies are never so real as oldstyle. Lawrence Ferlinghetti. ErPo

Let's lock our wealth out-doors! Rune of Riches. Florence Converse. SUS

Let's make a noise, Hey!...Hey!...Hullo!/Hullo! Silence. Walter James Turner. MoBrPo

Let's not forget now we're come home/Each bold sailor's pretty lass. The Lucky Sailor. *Anonymous.* OBSS

Let's not say dull things about her. Epitaphium Citharistriae. Victor Plarr. AnEnPo; EnLoPo; HBMV; NLV; ViBoPo

Let's pray God that so it be/Amen, for holy Charity. The Land of Cokaygne. *Anonymous.* BIrV; NOBI; OAEL 1-2; OnYI

Let's remember our glorious dead. Jarama Valley. *Anonymous.* FSW

Let's repeat the song of the rain. Auditory Hallucinations. Joyce Mansour. PBWP

Let's sing and dance down Brighton Pier/And fly the skull and crossbones here. The Blue Flag (parody). Chris Miller. FaBoPa

Let's smile and smile, and not forget/That smiles go everywhere! Growing Smiles. *Anonymous.* PoLf

Let's speak/as the bees do. April. Jean Valentine. TAP

Let's spread the greatcoat on the ground. Hops. Boris Pasternak. BoLoP

Let's still remain but one, till death divide. Another Letter to Her Husband, Absent upon Publick Employment. Anne Bradstreet. SCAP

Let's talk of change and come to no conclusions. Interim. Frank Ormsby. CIP

Let's talk of Relativity. Newton to Einstein. Jeannette Chappell. GoYe

Let's tango together/down to the clear/glad river. Conjuring Roethke. James Tate. OBAL

Let's tipple round; and so 'tis here. The Royalist. Alexander Brome. CavP

Let's to the Prado and make the most of time. How It Strikes a Contemporary. Robert Browning. CABL; CTC; FaBoPV; GTBS-P; MaVP; MBW 1-2; OAEL 1-2; PP; VLP

Let's touch the tankard while we can,/In memory of that day. The Battle of Trenton. *Anonymous.* MC; PAH

Let Samson/Be coming/Into your mind. How Samson Bore Away the Gates of Gaza. Vachel Lindsay. MoRP

Let sing again the velvet sonneteers! The Velvet Sonneteers. Tom MacInnes. CaP

Let slumber wrap them round, nor fear that Heaven/Will suffer any sprite to do thee wrong. Epigrams. Theocritus. AWP

Let some thee end that here remain behind. To the Translation of Palingenius. Barnabe Googe. EnRePo

Let some wild/Eclipse of reason build in me/The overthrow of Hagar'schild. Sarah. Robin Hyde. AnNZ

...Let somebody else/run their little way into the future. Now and Again. Roo Borson. AMV-81

Let someone get hurt good. Maybe get killed. The Rasslers. William D. Barney. LiSp

Let Sorrow string my heavy lute. The Virgin Mary to Christ on the Cross. Robert Southwell. ViBoPo

Let spare no treasure/To live in pleasure. Madrigal: "Sing we and chant it." Thomas Morley. EnRePo

Let spendthrifts' heirs inquire of yours–who's wiser? Don Juan. George Gordon, Lord Byron. UnPo

Let suppling grace, to crosse his art,/Drop from above. Grace. George Herbert. JCP; SeCV 1-2

Let thanks to God be said/That Old Years are not dead. New Years and Old. Maud Frazer Jackson. PGD

Let that cord be love; and some day make my narrow/Hallow'd bed according to Thy Word. Amen. A Prayer. Christina Georgina Rossetti. OBVV

Let that King deign to hear,/When as to Him our prayers do appear. Psalm XX. Sir Philip Sidney. FCP

Let that mob be the upper ten thousand or lower. A Fable for Critics. James Russell Lowell. TAP

Let the blind way shine out. The Scales of the Eyes. Howard Nemerov. NoAm

Let the book close. The Flight. Sara Teasdale. WHA

Let the cane fields bloom into white wands. At the Beginnings of the Andes. Barbara Ras. AMV-81

...Let the constellations/look at me before I disappear! To the Angel. Rainer Maria Rilke. LiTW

Let the crystal clasp them/When you drink your wine, in autumn. After the Persian. Louise Bogan. NePoAm; NYBP; PoA

Let the darkness race across your body. Last Rites. David Citino. AMV-80

Let the day perish, let the day come. Love in Particular. John Malcolm Brinnin. NYP

Let the earth suck at roots and discover the emblems of weather. From a Litany. Mark Strand. PPP

Let the far and the near, all unite with a cheer,/In defence of our Liberty Tree. Liberty Tree. Thomas Paine. MC; PAH

Let the fire not be quenched in the forge. The Rock. Thomas Stearns Eliot. EBCP

Let the harmonious spheres in music roll! The Amorous War: Time. Jasper Mayne. EG

Let the heart rest a measure/Before what was coming came. A Glance at the Album. Gray Burr. CoPo

Let the jar be filled with wine! The Jar. Richard Henry Stoddard. AA

Let the leaves fall. A Farewell. Harriet Monroe. AA; HBMV; PoA

Let the man in the city sleep. Milking Before Dawn. Ruth Dallas. ACV; AnNZ

Let the mill, let the mill go round. Pining for Love. Francis Beaumont. PoL

Let the monkeys at the Zoo/Make a monkey out of you! The Monkeys. Edith Osborne Thompson. TiPo

Let the moon shine ne'er so bright. The Jolly Beggar. King of Scotland James I, CoMu

Let the new cycle shame the old. Centennial Hymn. John Greenleaf Whittier AA; MC; PAH; PAL

Let the night be. Close the window, beloved...Come/here. Waters of Babylon. Louis Untermeyer. AnAmPo

Let the Old Year out and the New/Year in. New Year. Anonymous. OxNR

Let the paper remain on the desk unwritten, and the book on the shelf/unopen'd! Song of the Open Road. Walt Whitman. FaFP

Let the perfect one among you/Be the first to throw a stone. First to Throw a Stone. Anonymous. STF

Let the poets, one and all,/To his genius victims fall. Namby-Pamby. Henry Carey. FaBoNo; FaBoPa; NOEC; OBSV; Par

Let the prison dove call in the distance/and the boats go quietly on the Neva. Requiem 1935-1940. Anna Akhmatova. BoWoP

Let the rain wash/our hearts into one heart. Charm. Miklos Radnoti. LLLT

Let the same hand that gives the seed,/Provide a fruitful place! The Sower. William Cowper. SaC

...Let the sounding loom/Mix with the melody of ev'ry vale. The Wool Trade. John Dyer. OBEC; SeCePo

Let the storm wash the plates Strawberries. Edwin Morgan. BoLoP; LLLT

"Let the Whales Live." Genocide. Nora Dauenhauer. TWSS

Let the wind blow, for many a man shall die. Nostalgia. Karl Shapiro. AP; CMoP; CoAP; CoBMV; MP; NePA; TrJP; TwCP; WaaP

"Let the wind rip and the rain pelt. This'll keep." The Thatcher. Brendan Kennelly. CIP

Let the winged Fancy roam,/Pleasure never is at home. To Fancy. John Keats. HBV 1-2

Let them be burnt with fire/Those bamboos that make the flute. Flute Player. Anonymous. WTO

Let them buckle and drop. If the Stars Should Fall. Samuel ("Paul Vesey") Allen. IDB; NNP; PoBA

Let them cant about decorum/Who have characters to lose. The Jolly Beggars. Robert Burns. NLV

Let them come. The blue heron/Is awake and on guard. A Sentinel's Song. Rarawa Kerehoma. WTO

Let them enjoy the gain,/That thinks it worth the pain. Full well it may be seen. Sir Thomas Wyatt. FCP; SiPS

Let them ever flourish! Gaudeamus Igitur. Anonymous. GLGT

Let them fire over me when I lay low. The Buck's Elegy. Anonymous. OBET

Let them hang free. Hang out the Flags. James S. Tippett. SiSoSe

Let them lie perilous and beautiful. The Equilibrists. John Crowe Ransom. AP; CMoP; CoBMV; HAP; LiTM; MoAB; MoPo; MoVE; NePA; NIP; NoAm; NOBA; OxBA; PPP; TAP

Let them lie, then gently wake. Now through Night's Caressing Grip. W. H. Auden. PoRA

Let them listen to Galilee. The Gates, VI: The Church of Galilee. Muriel Rukeyser. GP

Let them loaf if they will, for the railroad's in sight. The Railroad Corral. Anonymous. TrAS

Let them not arise!' The Combat of Ferdiad and Cuchulain. Anonymous. OnYI

Let them perish and go to hell, never to return,/Who wish to have tender youths as spouses. A Perverse Custom. Anonymous. PeHV

Let them prevail to save us too! While O'er Our Guilty Land, O Lord. Samuel Davies. AH

Let them say more that like of hear-say well;/I will not praise that purpose not to sell. Sonnets, XXI: "So is it not with me as with that Muse." William Shakespeare. InvP; OBSC

Let them shine serene and still,/And with light my being fill. The Light of Stars. William Henry Furness. TrPWD

Let them sort out their bullroarers! The Great Beam of the Milky Way. Anonymous. NOAV

Let them speak. Winter Twilight. Jeff Schiff. AMV-81

Let there be a perpetual coming and going/Between your house and mine.' Things. Louis Simpson. OxBC

Let there be commerce between us. A Pact. Ezra Pound. AmPP; ELU; LiTA; NePA; NoAm; NOBA; OxBA; PoPl; TAP

Let there be light again, and set/Thy judgments in the earth. O Day of God, Draw Nigh. Robert B. Y. Scott. AH

Let there be only the earth and the seeds/and the harvests thereof. The Roots of Revolution in the Vegetable Kingdom. Constance Urdang. GP

Let there be peace between us ere we/die! Reconciliation. Caroline Atherton Briggs Mason. AA

"Let these poor colliers have their rights, and give them better pay."' The Collier Lad's Lament. Anonymous. OBET

Let thinking of you be enough! The Newlyweds' Separation. Tu Fu. HW

Let this a warning be to all/to be prepared when God does call. Springfield Mountain. Anonymous. AmFP

Let this be a sad and woeful warning/To all true lovers that have to part. The Silver Dagger. Anonymous. BaBo

Let this one have an end! Good Night! Good Night! John Holmes. PoToHe

...Let this poem/be the asp, diminutive,/but biting you. I write to make you suffer. Anne-Marie Kegels. BoWoP

Let those have neither right,/Nor part/In this night's art. Apollo's Song. Ben Jonson. LoBV

Let thy good sprite conduct/Me to the land of right. O Hear My Prayer, Lord. John Craig. AH

Let Thy love and Thy grace/Shine upon our dwelling place. Prayer for the Home (excerpt). Edgar A. Guest. TRV

Let thy old smile greet us well. In Memory of James T. Fields. John Greenleaf Whittier. OBVV

Let thy servant depart,/Having seen thy salvation. A Song for Simeon. Thomas Stearns Eliot. BoLiVe; EaLo; EBCP; LiTB; NAs; NOCV; OxBoCh

Let unremembrance only be your lot. To Celio. Sister Juana Ines de la Cruz. LiTW

Let us adore Pan, god of the world! Pan and the Cherries. Paul Fort. AWP

Let us await the late American novel! Critical Observations. Archibald MacLeish. OBAL

Let us be Children of the Light,/And tell the ages what we are! The Children of the Night. Edwin Arlington Robinson. NePA; OxBA

Let us be evil could we enter in/Your grace, and falter on the stony path! Last Days of Alice. Allen Tate. AmP; AtBAP; NoAm; NOBA; OxBA; UnPo

Let us be merry/Before we go! The Deserter's Lamentation. John Philpot Curran. FaBoRV; IrPN; SeCePo

...Let us be named/The constant swain, the virtuous maid. The Constant Swain and Virtuous Maid. Anonymous. HBV 1-2

"Let us be one!" The Deep-Sea Cables. Rudyard Kipling. VLP

Let us bury her alongside all other lovers. What the Animals Said. Peter Serchuk. HoAn

Let us cheer the weary traveler,/Along the heavenly way. Weary Traveler. Anonymous. BoAN 1-2

Let us commit a mortal sin/so we can deserve our death.   Equality, Father! Edith Bruck.   VWA

Let us count/into/the Darkness.   Mahler (excerpt).   Jonathan Williams. VGW

Let us do or die!   Scots Wha Hae.   Robert Burns.   ATP; CEP; CoBE; EnPE; FaPoR; FSW; OAEL 1-2; OAEP; OBEC; OxBS; SeCeV; TEP; WHA

Let us drink anew to the time when you/Were a tadpole and I was a fish. Evolution.   Langdon Smith.   BeLS; BLPA; FaBoBe; FaFP; HBV 1-2; TreF; YaD

Let us eat a peach after supper.   The Peaches.   Joel Oppenheimer.   CoPo

Let us ever honor Thee as Thou/Didst ever honor toil.   The Young Workman.   Mary Dillingham Frear.   TrCP

Let us fill our glasses/To our falls and risings.   A Simple Pastoral.   George Alexander Stevens.   NOEC

Let us find/A new location.   Bleat of Protest.   Mildred Weston.   FiBHP

Let us fly across to Lyons/And lay our tubers down.   Giving Potatoes. Adrian Mitchell.   NLV

Let us forget tomorrow,/This one day!   O Mors! Quam Amara Est Memoria Tua Homini Pacem Habenti ...   Ernest Christopher Dowson.   BrPo; GTBS; OBMV; PG

Let us get back our childlike faith again.   Let Us Keep Christmas.   Grace Noll Crowell.   TRV

Let us give thanks for the things of the north.   The Things of the North. Rennie McOwan.   PoSH

Let us go, and face it, and bear the shame.   In the Restaurant.   Thomas Hardy.   BrPo

...Let us go,/And hold close our loves.   The Lost Children.   Richard Eberhart.   NePoAm-2

Let us go then to Durban/Where we shall get a better woman.   My Money! O, My Money!   Mavimbela.   WTO

Let us go up and embrace him/And keep him here all day long.   Egyptian Hieroglyphics.   Anonymous.   BoWoP

Let us have a moment of silence/for the woman who cleans the floor.   Three Poems for Women.   Susan Griffin.   NPGG

Let us have a solid roof over our head/And bless one another.   Moving In. Karl Shapiro.   NAs

Let us have peace!   Let Us Have Peace.   Nancy Byrd Turner.   PoToHe

Let us have plenty of milk!   To a Sacred Cow.   Anonymous.   WGRP

Let us hear no sound of strife/In our band of brothers.   Every Christian Born of God.   Anonymous.   AH

Let us hope that they'll make your grandchildren smile.   The Caledonian Market.   William Plomer.   ChMP; HaMV

Let us hope they'll go better to-morrow.–/Ri-tol-de-rol, etc.   Song: Hamlet. "When a man becomes tired of his life (parody).   John Poole.   BXAP

Let us join the choral song,/And the heavenly notes prolong.   Swell the Anthem, Raise the Song.   Nathan Strong.   AH

Let us lay down on it and rest.   Tryst.   Derek Butler.   LFAC

...Let us learn to live swaying/As in a rocking boat on the sea.   All the Fruit...   Friedrich Holderlin.   NU

Let us maintain a stony silence/on the St. Lawrence Seaway.   The Only Tourist in Havana Turns His Thoughts Homeward.   Leonard Cohen. NoAm

Let us make them such cheer,/As will keep out the wind and the weather. Now Christmas Is Come.   Anonymous.   PCh

Let us never again be torn apart.   Friend, how can I meet my lord?   Mira Bai [(or Mirabai)].   BoWoP

Let us not lose this present minute.   Persuasions to Love.   Thomas Carew. LiTL; ViBoPo

Let us not use them ill.   What Is the Use? (excerpt).   Erastus Wolcott Ellsworth.   AA

Let us part, ere the season of passion forget us,/With a kiss and a tear on thy drooping brow.   The Falling of the Leaves.   William Butler Yeats.   VLP

Let us pray.   Powers and Times Are Not Gods.   W. H. Auden.   MoRP

Let us precede ourselves/across new thresholds.   The Future and the Ancestor.   Andrée Chedid.   WPOW

Let us reap, love's gains dividing!   Turn Back, You Wanton Flyer.   Thomas Campion.   EnLi 1-2; UnTE

Let us remember life, the salt, the sweet,/And make of that our tireless testament.   Testament.   John Holmes.   MoRP

Let us remember You as one who died/For love of every comrade at his side. Mary's Son.   Lucia Trent.   PGD

Let us renown the King of Kings!   Sing a Song of Joy!   Thomas Campion. UnS

Let us revel in parades, lowering the emblem/Of precious bones long laid asleep./Amen!   A Marching Litany to Our Martyrs.   Jack A. Mapanje. WhB

...Let us rise up and live!   Let Us Rise Up and Live.   Francis Sherman. CaP

...Let us say/how our lives have changed.   Outside Every Window Is a Flowering Thing.   Anita Skeen.   AMV-81

Let us se nowe, if th'one be wourth th'othre.   What Nedeth These Thretning Wordes and Wasted Wynde?"   Serafino.   OBVE

Let us see Thee, and adore.   Jesus First and Jesus Last.   Thomas MacKellar. BePJ

Let us show that twice-sent desolation/On every true heart in the nation/Has conquest achieved.   Boston.   John Boyle O'Reilly.   PAH

Let us sing merrily, merrily, merrily.   The Pleasant Comedie of Old Fortunatus.   Thomas Dekker.   AtBAP

Let us sing the sacred songs.   Carriers of the Dream Wheel.   N. Scott Momaday.   CDW

Let us sit and not break the silence.   Untitled: "Words do not grow on the landscape."   Jean Malley.   PoA

Let us sleep now....   Strange Meeting.   Wilfred Owen.   AnFE; AtBAP; BrPo; CMoP; CoBMV; DTC; EnLi 1-2; ExPo; FaBoMo; FaBoRV; GoTF; GTBS-P; HeIP; HoPM; LiTB; LoBV; MMM; MoAB; MoBrPo; MoPo; MoVE; NAMP; NoAm; NOBE; NoP; OAEL 1-2; OAEP; OBWP; SCV; SeCeV; TreFT; TrGrPo; WaaP; WaP

Let us so join our hearts that nothing may/Estrange them.   To Ask for All Thy Love.   Anonymous.   EIL

Let us spare no treasure/To live in pleasure.   Songs Set by Thomas Morley: "Sing we and chant it."   Anonymous.   OBSC

"Let us steal softly out of town,/Oisin, until we reach my place."   History. James Liddy.   CIP

Let us still pull together, and we/Shall still rob the dear British nation.   The Four Dears.   Ebenezer Elliott.   SaC

Let us take them into pity.   A Song for the Ragged Schools of London. Elizabeth Barrett Browning.   SBG

Let us talk, lean on each other's voices/in this long season of killing.   The Long Season.   James Haug.   AMV-81

Let us thank God for the Saxon grit.   Saxon Grit.   Robert Collyer.   HBV 1-2

Let us to Daffadill.   Shepherd's Garland,.   Michael Drayton.   FaBoEn; ViBoPo

Let us to the end dare to do our duty/as we understand it.   Let Us Have Faith That Right Makes Might.   Abraham Lincoln.   TRV

Let us try again!   War.   Anthony Ostroff.   FAZ

Let us try to save the babies.   The Babies.   Mark Strand.   GeTw; NYBP

Let us two a burden try.   Robin Hood.   John Keats.   AWP; EnLi 1-2; EnLit; InPo

Let us wait for the morrow.   The Child.   Reginald Massey.   ACV

...Let us walk/Close to the earth.   Poem to My Father.   Joseph Stroud. NPGG

Let us wax on and wane.   Easter Monday.   Christina Georgina Rossetti. NOCV

Let us who live/try.   The Death of Europe.   Charles Olson.   NeAP

Let us with Angels share.   Finis.   An Evening Thought.   Jupiter Hammon. PoNe

Let what rises live with what descends.   Poor Angels.   Edward Hirsch. MAYP

Let what will be, be.   Acceptance.   Robert Frost.   CMoP; MoRP; OxBA

Let who will thinke us dead, or wish our death.   A Celebration of Charis. Ben Jonson.   AtBAP; OAEP; SeCP

Let who would meet the beauty of the sky.   Sylvia.   Samuel Croxall. NOEC

Let wind polish the bones./It is done.   Preparations.   Leslie Marmon Silko. VoR

Let words, and sense, be set by thee.   To Mr. Henry Lawes.   Edmund Waller.   AnAnS 2; CTC; PP; SeCP; SeCV 1-2

...Let Y stand for yes.   A Bestiary.   Kenneth Rexroth.   OBAL

Let Your angels waken me/On Your birthday morn.   A Child's Christmas Song.   Thomas Augustin Daly.   BiCB

Let your breath fill my crumbled walls.   Woman in an Abandoned House. Michael Bily-Hurd.   AMV-81

Let your eyes just once/Fasten upon mine.   The Mistress Addresses the Wife. Naomi Replansky.   GP

Let your very bloodbeat drag/The lush world to the bars!   Bill.   Peter Kocan.   CBAP

Let your words/tread lightly on this earth of Europe/lest my people's bones protest.   To T. S. Eliot.   Emanuel Litvinoff.   VWA

Let youth take fire!–Sir Paul takes snuff.   The County Ball (excerpt). Winthrop Mackworth Praed.   OBNC

...The lethal weapon of/The gift of things and not the gift of love.   Luchow's and After.   L. E. Sissman.   NYP

Lethe had passed those lips, and he knew all.   Modern Love, XLIX. George Meredith.   EnLi 1-2; HBV 1-2; NoP; OAEL 1-2; OAEP; VLP

Lets down his hook and hoicks him in.   The Fisherman.   Jay Macpherson. NOBC; PeCV

Lets fly the shaft that is/Himself, and splits/The first arrow at the centre of the gold.   The Zen Archer.   James Kirkup.   EaLo

Lets go your pear-/shaped breast/to reach for?   Pears.   Linda Pastan. VWA

Lets itself be born over again.   Dog in the Fountain.   Raymond Souster. GDP

Letters that we ought to burn.   After Emerson.   Anonymous.   NOBL

Letters, trips and love in/every circling clay hollow. Tea Poems: Afternoon Tea. George Mackay Brown. OxBC

The letting go, the spilling. Any Time, What May Hit You. T. R. Hummer. MAYP

Letting in just as much world as I can stand. Mountain Born. Marcia Inzer Bost. AMV-80

Letting it pass away, becoming myth,/And memory, and finally this sleight. Indian Summer. Gray Burr. AMV-80

Letting the gone/years hug her/with his long wool arms. The Gone Years. Alice Fulton. Str

...Letting the hollow/students count off and break up and blow away/over the frozen ground. Accountability. William Stafford. LCAP; NoP; NPAW

Letting them go The Prophets. Richard Shelton. NYBP

The leve I'll keep to your sister Jane,/For tocher she gat nane.' Fair Annie. *Anonymous.* ESPB

Levedy, bring us to thine bolde/And shild us from helle wrake./Amen. In Praise of Mary. *Anonymous.* MeEL

Level across the face/Of Brennbaum "The Impeccable." Hugh Selwyn Mauberley, VIII: Brennbaum. Ezra Pound. NOBA

The leveled walls of Jericho,/Jericho, Jericho, Jericho.... Jericho. Willard Wattles. HBMV

A li'l lew corner o' airth to lie in. Man's Days. Eden Phillpotts. HBV 1-2; OBEV; OBVV; OxBTC

Liars are not believed, forsooth,/Even when liars tell the truth. The Boy and the Wolf. Aesop. MaC

Lias and Trias and that is enough. Rhyme for a Geological Baby. Joseph Cook. QQQ; SpRo

Liberty And Justice–/Huh!–For All? Children's Rhymes. Langston Hughes. BOLo; BPo

Liberty! Fraternity! Children of the Sun. Fenton Johnson. BANP

The liberty to die. The Heart Asks Pleasure First. Emily Dickinson. AmPP; AnNE; CMoP; InPo; MoAB; MoAmPo; NOBA; NoP; OxBA; PPP; PrIm; SBG; TrGrPo

Libido/ergo sum. Progress. Peter Meinke. PoL

The licensed fools who travel far/To gaze upon these simple folk. The Amish. John Updike. OBAL

Lichen of the blue American nights/from which we come. Driving By. Robert Wallace. LiSp

Lichens in frond with their dim arms adore. The Font in the Forest. Léonie Adams. CrMA

The licht that bends owre a' thing/Is less ta'en up wi't. Empty Vessel. Hugh" (Christopher Murray Grieve) MacDiarmid. BSV; FaBoTw; OxBS

Lick the juice from your fingers/and watch your step. Flipochinos. Cyn Zarco. APU

...Lick the salty leg of the/sea with my own grateful tongue. Finisterra. Bayla Winters. AMV-81

Lids sinking, darkness unconscious. Canto XV. Ezra Pound. MoPo

Lie cursed between the stale sheets of/paupered monogamy. Epigram: "Kissing Hippomenes." Paulus Silentiarius. PeHV

Lie deep 'neath a silence pure and smooth,/Like burnt-out craters healed with snow. Now Is the High-Tide of the Year. James Russell Lowell. TreFS

Lie down again beside me. Another Return. Winfield Townley Scott. ELU

Lie down in your corner of darkness till I return,/till I return from him. Revolt. Rachel (Rachel Blumstein). VWA

Lie down, lie down, lie down La, La, La! Thomas M. Disch. NLV

Lie for lie! The Goddess. Denise Levertov. AP; LiTM; PoCh

Lie gently and wide to the light-year/stars, lie back, and the sea will hold you. First Lesson. Philip Booth. BiP; LiSp; MP; SD; SM; TwCP

Lie heavy on him, earth! for he/Laid many heavy loads on thee. On Sir John Vanbrugh, Architect. Abel Evans. FaBoCo; FaBoEE; FiBHP; OBEC; PV

Lie in security–as this Dog lies. Epitaph: On the Favourite Dog of a Politician. Hilaire Belloc. CoBE; OBSV

Lie like the seed within the flower. Spell of Creation. Kathleen Raine. FaBoCh; LoGBV; OxBS

Lie long, high snowdrifts in the hedge/That will not shower on me. 'Tis Time, I Think. Alfred Edward Housman. PoPle

Lie mouldering away in the cold ground. Lonesome Dove. *Anonymous.* AmFP

Lie not light on the filth of your monstrous groom. Sepulchral Imprecation. Crinagoras. LiTW

Lie on young cheeks, young lips. Prothalamium. Edith Sitwell. HW

Lie one night in my arms and give me peace. News of the World. George Barker. AtBAP; FaBoTw; LiTB; LiTM

Lie still and peaceful there. I'll think no more on't. Cleopatra and Antony. John Dryden. FiP

Lie still; and rise not up to lie. Why Grudge Them Lotus-Leaf and Laurel. Algernon Charles Swinburne. NOBV

Lie the bleak and forever capacious tombs of the sea Pacific Door. Earle Birney. PeCV

Lie the soldiers and chiefs of The Irish Brigade. The Battle Eve of the Brigade. Thomas Osborne Davis. AnIV; OnYI

Lie to me. And lie to me. The Lie. Howard Moss. AtBAP; LiTM; MoAB; NePoAm

Lie two in a grave, and to bed, to bed! Wake All the Dead. Sir William Davenant. CBEP; ELP; FaBoCh; HAP; LoGBV; SeCePo

The lie upon his lips!... Rebels. Ernest Crosby. MC

Lie you must, and not with me. When the Eye of Day Is Shut. Alfred Edward Housman. NOBV; OAEL 1-2

Liefer would I turn and love/The ox in the by-path, the barn-yard dove! Deranged. Padraic Fiacc. NeIP

Lies a Sovereign/High and Holy! Above the Stable. Nona Keen Duffy. BrR; ChBR

Lies all that golden hair undimmed in death. The House of Life. Dante Gabriel Rossetti. HAP

Lies always at the bottom of thy warm and limpid waters. O Friendship! Friendship! the Shell of Aphrodite. Walter Savage Landor. GBL

Lies, and lies, and lies. Of Man and Nature. Horace Mungin. BOLo

Lies dead beneath the death-white moon. Flight. Madison Cawein. AA

Lies defeated and buried deep/Three or four hours unconscious there. Milk for the Cat. Harold Monro. FaBoBe; FaFP; HBVY; MoBrPo; OBMV; PCat

Lies her head/by oaks and roses/deliberated.) When Life Is Quite Through With. Edward Estlin Cummings. CrMA

Lies hid the pebble for the fatal sling. Danger. Helen Hunt Jackson. AnFE; APA

Lies in flawed words and stubborn sounds. The Poems of Our Climate. Wallace Stevens. AmP; MoPo; MP; NoP; OxBA; PP; TrGrPo; TwCP

Lies–lies, again–and still, they lie! The Confessional. Robert Browning. ViBoPo

Lies lost in a strength of jasmine down a summer beach. Malaga. Pearse Hutchinson. BIrV

Lies open onward to eternal day. Somewhere. Mrs. Major Arnold. PoToHe

Lies rusting, mouldering. The Dismantled Ship. Walt Whitman. AmPP; MOS; NoAm; NoP; OxBA

Lies sabbin' noo! The Love-Sick Lass. Hugh" (Christopher Murray Grieve) MacDiarmid. BSV

Lies sheltered only in her shift below him. The Ploughman, in Imitation of Milton. Samuel Jones. NOEC

Lies the gipsy's only child. The Gipsy's Warning. *Anonymous.* BeLS

Lies the night he shut down/machine number nine/to pull out his boy. The Boss Machine-Tender after Losing a Son. Paul Corrigan. AMV-81

Lies the queen-heart in sovereign overthrow. Supreme Surrender. Dante Gabriel Rossetti. MaVP

Lies where no man will steer,/No maiden land. Love at Sea. Theophile Gautier. AWP; HBV 1-2

Lies withered where the violets blow. Under the Violets. Oliver Wendell Holmes AA

Lieutenant-Colonel to the Earl of Mar. And Thou, Dalhousie, the Great God of War. *Anonymous.* FaBoCo

Life: a lighted window/And a closed door. I Pass a Lighted Window. Clement Wood. HBMV

Life and I are old! Age. William Winter. HBV 1-2

Life and Sacrament to me. The Holy Eucharist. Pedro Calderon de la Barca. CAW

Life and sweet earth are young, God grows not old! June. Theodore Harding Rand. CaP

Life and the weather mending worse,/Or worsening better. Old Man at a Cricket Match. Norman Nicholson. HaMV

Life, as a windmill grinds the bread of Life. The Windmill. John Byrne Leicester Warren, Lord De Tabley. NBM

Life bears Love's cross, death brings Love's crown. Lettice. Dinah Maria Mulock Craik. HBV 1-2

Life breeds a throng; and Death must come/To thrust some out, to make more room. On the Death of Squire Christopher, a Remarkably Fat Sportsman. John Wigson. OBSP

Life chambers and vessels/full cycle joy. Last Generation. Michelle Roberts. LFAC

A life–complete in death–complete to/die. The Bubble. John Banister Tabb. AA

Life death does end and each day dies with sleep. Sonnet: "No worst, there is none." Gerard Manley Hopkins. MoVE; OBNC

Life did her leave, and thus transform'd she was. The Statue of Medusa. William, of Hawthornden Drummond. EyDe

Life escapes defiantly/From the old, sleek tyrannies of earth. Poem: "O men, walk on the hills." Maxwell Bodenheim. TrJP

Life facing; death pursuing it. As with Heaped Bees at Hiving Time. Robert Louis Stevenson. NOBV

The life for which I long. At Last. John Greenleaf Whittier. AP; TreFS

Life has no need of reasons. The Quiet Glen. Douglas Fraser. PoSH

Life/he/tries/to/tell. The Birth of the Poet. Quandra Prettyman. BOLo

The life I shall ever adore. The Conjuror. Edward Verrall Lucas. BiCB

Life in captivity/Among inhuman foes.   Samson Agonistes.   John Milton.
   FaBoPV; ViBoPo; WHA

Life is a pilgrimage, they say.   Cockle-Shell and Sandal-Shoon.   Herbert T.
   J. Coleman.   CaP

Life is a scourge, a curse/It is tremulous like a drop of water on a mophane
   leaf.   A Protest from a Bushman (Masarwa).   Albert G.T.K. Malikongwa.
   WhB

Life is a waste and windless Sea.   Written in a Copy of The Earthly Paradise.
   William Morris.   VLP

...Life/is becoming moment by moment/unbearable.   Beaver Moon–The
   Suicide of a Friend.   Mary Oliver.   GOYP

Life is but a bubble on the water that is broken by the wind.   Shoes Are
   Made to Fit the Feet...   *Anonymous.*   WTO

Life is but a dream.   Row, Row, Row Your Boat.   *Anonymous.*   FSW

Life is fading fast away.   Silver Threads among the Gold.   Hart Pease and
   Eben E. Danks.   BLSo; FaFP; FSW; GoTF; PSoN; TreF

Life is fine!   Life is Fine.   Langston Hughes.   BP; NLV

Life is (I think) a blunder and a shame.   In Hospital.   William Ernest
   Henley.   VLP

Life is no more.   Mortality.   James Devaney.   BoAV; PoAu 1-2

Life is precious.   Poem Ending with an Old Cliche.   Paul Zimmer.
   AMV-81

Life is redoubled.   The American Hero.   Nathaniel Niles.   WaaP

Life is the jailer; Death the angel sent/To draw the unwilling bolts and set us
   free.   'Tis Sorrow Builds the Shining Ladder Up.   James Russell Lowell.
   WGRP

Life is the test of us!   Life, A Question.   Corinne Roosevelt Robinson.
   HBV 1-2

Life, is there more for me?   Two Questions.   William Stanley Braithwaite.
   BALP

...Life is too long and always too short.   In a Mist.   Al Young.   AMV-80

The life it asks of us is a dog's life.   The Victor Dog.   James Merrill.   NoP

Life knew a deadlier death; the blighting smart/Which only kills the heart.
   Love in Exile.   Mathilde Blind.   OBNC

Life licks and burns at me.   Evensong.   Judith Moffett.   LTB

Life, Life, Life! cries the bird/As if he had heard....   Let Us God, Then,
   Exploring.   Virginia Woolf.   BoNaP

Life, life, you will not let me die.'   The Innocent.   Gene Derwood.   NePA;
   WaP

Life like a cinder fading black at last.   Prisoners.   Frederick William Harvey.
   MMM

A life-line, how it chooses to run obscurely/In her hand, before her.
   Housewife.   Josephine Miles.   PCP

Life, looking out attentive from the eyes of the doe.   The Buck in the Snow.
   Edna St. Vincent Millay.   AmLP; BoANP; CrMA

Life, love and tears to fill my eyes.   To Madame A. P. Kern.   Alexander
   Pushkin.   LiTW

Life must go on;/I forget just why.   Lament.   Edna St. Vincent Millay.
   DL; PoPl

Life never knows the return of Spring.   The Beggar's Opera.   John Gay.
   CEP

...The life not yet/invented.   The Meeting.   Nicki Jackowska.   BrRo

Life! O give us this life!   The Water of Kane.   *Anonymous.*   WTO

The life of a man is a single and continuous journey of blood.   O.   Salvador
   Villanueva.   InW

The life of God must blood this cross for love.   A Quintina of Crosses.
   Chad Walsh.   TrCP

The life of hard times   The Life of Hard Times.   Joshua Tan Pai.   VWA

Life of his life, and soul of all his song!   How to the Singer Comes the Song?
   Richard Watson Gilder.   WGRP

Life of me, Miriam, my child–sleep on!   Lullaby for Miriam.   Richard Beer-
   Hofmann.   VWA

The life of significant soil.   Four Quartets.   Thomas Stearns Eliot.   ATP

A life on the ocean wave!   A Life on the Ocean Wave.   Epes Sargent   AA;
   EtS; FaBoBe; FSW; GN; HBV 1-2; TreFS

...Life rolleth on in fleetness/To finished loss or finished gain.   The Half
   Moon Shows a Face of Plaintive Sweetness.   Christina Georgina Rossetti.
   MOON

"Life ruled by Love nor dies nor dissi-/pates."   The Tutelage.   Robert
   Mowry Bell.   AA

Life's a very funny proposition, after all.   Life's a Funny Proposition after
   All.   George M. Cohan.   PoLf

...Life's cache/is flesh, flesh, and flesh.   The Lull.   Molly Peacock.   MAYP

Life's chords all answer from the wind-/swept wheat!   The Wind-
   Swept.Wheat.   Mary Ainge De Vere.   AA

Life's everwidening circles run/Revealing God to man.   Communion.   John
   Banister Tabb.   WGRP

Life's high adventure is its own reward....   The Tide of Life.   Watson
   Kirkconnell.   CaP

Life's iron heart, even Love's Fatality.   Love's Fatality.   Dante Gabriel
   Rossetti.   MaVP

Life's life and strikes my your our blossoming sphere   Might These Be
   Thrushes.   Edward Estlin Cummings.   CrMA

Life's loneliness of dreaming ecstasy.   The Poet.   Amy Lowell.   WGRP

Life's long, slow, sordid story.   Dreams.   Israel Zangwill.   TrJP

Life's more amusing than we thought!   Ballade of Middle Age.   Andrew
   Lang.   HBV 1-2

Life's pulse throbbing like a boy's.   Village and Factory.   A. Bezymensky.
   TrJP

Life's voyage to the world unknown.   On Even Keel.   Matthew Green.
   OBEC

Life-shaped and perfected,/So to remain.   Still Life.   Kathleen Raine.
   NeBP

Life, sweet savage life, goes on.   Assynt.   Alan Gilchrist.   PoSH

,The life/That is fluent in even the wintriest bronze   The Sense of the Sleight-
   of-Hand Man.   Wallace Stevens.   AP; CABA; CoBMV; HAP; LiTM;
   MoAB; MoAmPo; MoPo; MP; NOBA; PoA; TwCP

The life that maketh all things new.   O Life That Maketh All Things New.
   Samuel Longfellow.   AH

A life that will endure for evermore!   If Thou Wouldst Know.   Hayim
   Nahman Bialik.   TrJP

The life, the force, that binds us each to each.   The Eternal Kinship.
   Maurice E. Peloubet.   GoYe

The life today with me and mine to share.   Today.   Jones Very.   TAP

Life touching lips with immortality.   For a Venetian Pastoral by Giorgione.
   Dante Gabriel Rossetti.   ViBoPo; VLP

"Life was a dream, Oh, may this death be sleep."   The Drunkard.   Philip
   Levine.   NePoEA-2

Life, when thou putt'st the helmet on.   On the Sultan Mahmud.   Firdausi.
   LiTW

Life will be sweeter and more worth the living,/Because of you.   Because of
   You.   Sophia Almon Hensley.   HBV 1-2

Life with remorseless forceps beckoning–/Pangs and betrayal of harsh birth.
   Sleep.   Kenneth Slessor.   BoAV

Life would be disenchanted.   The Joy of Incompleteness.   Albert Crowell.
   PoToHe

...–Life would be sublime!   The Trees.   Lucy Larcom.   OHIP

Life would have paid.   My Wage.   Jessie B. Rittenhouse.   BLPA; PoToHe

The life yet of his lines shall never out.   Shakespeare Dead.   Hugh Holland.
   ACP

The lifeboats poised in wait!   Calm.   Stanton A. Coblentz.   EtS

The lifeless atmosphere....   The Recollection.   Percy Bysshe Shelley.   CH

A lifeless Deity.   Truth is as old as god.   Emily Dickinson.   MoAmPo

A lifelong love to this dear saint of mine.   A Valentine to My Mother.
   Christina Georgina Rossetti.   OFD; OHIP

A lifetime membership to his own private club/where there is just membership
   for one.   To Ellen.   Charles Stetler.   PPJ

Lift, in bereaved acknowledgment/Of their unthinking Drums–   I dreaded
   that first Robin, so.   Emily Dickinson.   AmPP; CBEP; HAP; MoAmPo

Lift me! Lift me!   Dragon Skate.   Gladys Cardiff.   CDW

Lift thou the soul to spheres that gave her birth!   Night.   John Addington
   Symonds.   HBV 1-2

Lift up a living nation,/A single sword to thee.   A Hymn–O God of Earth
   and Altar.   Gilbert Keith Chesterton.   GoTF; TreFT

...Lift up/sober toward truth a scared self-estimate.   A Prayer for the Self.
   John Berryman.   PPP

Lift up the latch–walk in.   Brow Bender.   *Anonymous.*   HBV 1-2; HBVY

Lift up the Standard of thy cross,/Draw all men unto Thee.   The Horrible
   Decree (excerpt).   Charles Wesley.   NOCV

Lift up thine hands to Him,/to Him implored.   Dirge for the Ninth of Ab.
   Anonymous.   TrJP

Lift up thy heart! Exult that it is so!   My Old Counselor.   Gertrude Hall.
   AA

Lifted our perished hearts toward you.   Mary Lifted from the Dead.
   William Alfred.   AH

Lifting a deathless Christ, the cross stands/At Calvary!   Consecration.
   Patrick F. Kirby.   GoBC

Lifting a mute and horrible face still towards you.   Look, I Have Thrown All
   Right.   L. A. MacKay.   PeCV

Lifting her horn in pleasant meads.   Lament for Thomas MacDonagh.
   Francis Ledwidge.   AnIV; BIrV

...Lifting the lid on/atom, He says: "Choose life or death, but choose!"
   We Who Are About to Die.   Harold E. Fey.   PGD

...Lifting/their hooves through the moonlight.   Herbert Street Revisited.
   John Montague.   CIP; FaBoIP; IPY

Lifting them gently through strange delight/To a clearer light.   Folded
   Power.   Gladys Cromwell.   HBMV

Lifting up, dear, upon you/The light of His countenance.   Atlantis.   W. H.
   Auden.   PoPl

Lifting us higher than fear.   The Planets Line Up for a Demonstration.
   Josie Kearns.   SUW

Lifting your red lips up to me,/Ettarre, and kiss, with no man to see!   Alone
   in April.   James Branch Cabell.   HBMV

Lifts her pale eye unjoyous.   A Winter Night.   James (1700-48) Thomson.
   NOBE
Lifts it heavy and wonderful in her hands and with triumphant/tenderness.
   Three American Women and a German Bayonet.   Winfield Townley Scott.
   NMP
The light above the mountain is/Now beyond sight.   Notes on a Life to Be
   Lived.   Robert Penn Warren.   NYBP
Light/against my skin.   I Have Seen.   Kathleen McCracken.   AMV-80
Light and the clear day and so simple a goal.   The Face of the Waters.
   Robert D. Fitzgerald.   BoAV; CBAP; PoAu 1-2
The Light, and Truth, and Love of Heaven!   The Moral Warfare.   John
   Greenleaf Whittier.   AnNE; PAL; TreFT
Light as that bird wandering beyond my shore.   The Unknown Bird.
   Edward ("Edward Eastaway") Thomas.   ACV; DTC
Light at the opening,/dark at the closing.   The Rhythm.   Robert Creeley.
   CoPo; LiTM
The light becomes me.   Praise to the End!   Theodore Roethke.   InPS
...A light comign steadily/through an interstellar mist?   Early Fall: The
   Adirondacks.   Carolyne Wright.   AMV-81
Light-footed trip,–the feast, the feast of blood!   The Art of War (excerpt).
   Joseph Fawcett.   NOEC
...The light/From the lighthouse that protects as it pushes us away.   Down by
   the Station, Early in the Morning.   John Ashbery.   HaCAP
...The light/from the ring on your finger darkens...   The Lake in the Sky.
   John Haines.   LCAP
A light growth of green dreams drying.   Losing Track.   Denise Levertov.
   HeIP; NaP; NoAm; NOBA; PoM
Light-hearted Circe!   Barine, the Incorrigible.   Horace.   UnTE
The light her love o'er mine is throwing!   To Helen.   Winthrop Mackworth
   Praed.   HBV 1-2
A light I knew not till my soul was dark.   Lost and Found.   George
   Macdonald.   TRV; WGRP
Light in them your fires.   A Hymn to Night.   Max Michelson.   TrJP
...The light is different. And they are alone.   Toro.   William Stanley Merwin.
   NePA
Light leaps on his face.   The Old Jockey.   Frederick Robert Higgins.
   AnIV; OBMV; OxBI; OxBTC
Light/light light light.   Claritas.   Denise Levertov.   VGW
Light! Light like the deathless past remains.   The Heart Flies Up, Erratic as a
   Kite.   Delmore Schwartz.   PoA
Light listened when she sang.   Light Listened.   Theodore Roethke.   BiP;
   MoAmPo; UnTE
The light of a firefly.   Going Back.   Salvatore Quasimodo.   AMV-81
Light of day held darkness back like the whole Atlantic.   Kennedy.   Michael
   Heffernan.   AMV-80
The light of little children, and their love.   On the Deaths of Thomas Carlyle
   and George Eliot.   Algernon Charles Swinburne.   HBV 1-2
The light of the Captain's faith!   Light in the Darkness.   Aileen Fisher.
   YeAr
The light of 2 x 2 is raining down on me.   Letter to My Wife.   Miklos
   Radnoti.   VWA
Light-plumed Irises, where are they now?   Irises.   Padraic Colum.   BoNaP
...Light-search of leaf/can bring to this dead beauty some fragment of
   meaning?   The Fallen Tree.   Patrick Maybin.   NeIP
Light strikes the face of the sleeper.   Piano.   Lisa Russ.   PPJ
Light that draws from him/like a poultice/some essence of himself.   The
   Photographer.   Roger Pfingston.   PoDr
A light that loves them both.   The Wedding.   Sandra Kohler.   AMV-80
The light that shone when Hope was born.   In Memoriam A.H.H., XXX.
   Alfred, Lord Tennyson.   VLP
The light, the cries, and the willow dim,/And the dark tide are one with him.
   The Fish.   Rupert Brooke.   FM; MOS
Light the dark with their gleam!   Bring Torches.   A. M. Stephen.   CaP
Light, the first creature, softly went.   God's First Creature Was Light.
   Winifred Welles.   ImOP
Light the path below, above, and lead us on to love!   Glow Worm.   Lila
   Cayley Robinson.   BLSo
Light torn from/Within a cold glassy fire.   The Mirrors.   Sophia de Mello
   Breyner Andresen.   PBWP
Light/twelve/Candles/In/My/Head.   Poem.   Frank Lima.   ANYP
Light up, light up your homes!   Illumination for Victories in Mexico.   Grace
   Greenwood.   PAH
Light was my love and better dead!   My Love Was Light.   Thomas Lanier
   Williams.   PoA
–A light wave,/That breaks, and whispers of its Maker's might.   The Fall of
   Niagara.   John Gardiner Calkins Brainard.   AmePo
The light went wading on its own.   Fishing Blue Creek.   Roy Scheele.   PPJ
A light white, a disgrace, an ink spot, a rosy charm.   A Petticoat.   Gertrude
   Stein.   NMM
A light wind rises: I become the wind.   Meditations of an Old Woman.
   Theodore Roethke.   NaP

A light would pass over her face.   Those Who Love.   Sara Teasdale.
   MoLP
Light-years away, one farewell image/burns and fades and burns.   Veracruz.
   Robert Earl Hayden.   AmNP
Lighted her soul in sleep with the glory of regions ce-/lestial.   Evangeline.
   Henry Wadsworth Longfellow.   PoEL 1-5
Lighting the doorway of the pioneer!   Suggested Device of a New Western
   State.   John James Piatt.   AnAmPo
Lighting this one, that one/to a flaming illumination.   Flannery O'Connor.
   Dorothy Walters.   IHMS
Lighting up from within/with the real thin/bones of the rainbow/body.
   NHR.   Jack Hirschman.   VWA
Lighting up the ridge of the world.   The World Looks On.   Louis I.
   Newman.   PoNe
Lighting up the steps of glory/With Salvation's radiant beam.   I Am with
   You Alway.   Edwin H. Nevin.   BePJ
Lightly as drifted leaves on an endless plain.   Commemoration.   Sir Henry
   Newbolt.   FaBoTw; OBVV
Lightly, gentle earth!   I Died True.   Francis Beaumont and John Fletcher.
   CH
Lightness, don't; being gamboge or magenta.   I Love...   Stevie Smith.
   FaBoCo
...Lightning brilliant as a sword/Should blaze the path of thunder.   Tableau.
   Countee Cullen.   AmFN; BANP; PoBA
A lightning-flash the wretch to smite/Who shields his license with thy name!
   The Bartholdi Statue.   John Greenleaf Whittier.   PAH
Lightning in one hand,/the unthinkable/stone in the other.   Junction.   John
   Pass.   WOLT
Lightning striking all the way.   Initial Response.   Katherine Soniat.
   AMV-80
The lights are cruel.   Birthday Party.   Patti Patton.   AMV-80
Lights flash, teeth clash–I fear the latter./Ouch!...Ouch!...   Roast Swan Song.
   Anonymous.   LiTW
...Lights/In quiet rooms/Left on for hours,/Burning, burning.   Bus Stop.
   Donald Justice.   FYAP
The Lights of England sent you and by silence shall/ye speak.   The Coastwise
   Lights.   Rudyard Kipling.   EtS
The lights of God draw nigh!   The Three Bells.   John Greenleaf Whittier.
   EtS
Lights up like a chandelier/in a flash of opals and amber.   Glass World.
   Dorothy Donnelly.   NCSH
The lights/Were MY CAT'S EYES/In the dark.   Cat.   Dorothy Walter
   Baruch.   SoPo; SUS; TiPo
The lights were out and the blood/had been wiped off the table.   The Blood.
   Nina Cassian.   VWA; WPOW
Lik' doves a-vlee-en to their nest,/In leafy boughs a-swayen.   Uncle an' Aunt.
   William Barnes.   NOBV
Like a bad dream on memory's ebbtide drifting.   Ode to Freedom.   Aaron
   Zeitlin.   VWA
Like a baked glistening afternoon/But only for a minute.   Death and the
   Maiden.   Dick Gallup.   ANYP
Like a beautiful butterfly/leaving a/lonely smile.   Jackie.   King D. Kuka.
   VoR
Like a bee in a wet spring bloom.   Identity Card.   Susan Tichy.   MAYP
Like a bird in flight under your tongue.   Saying Dante Aloud.   James
   Wright.   InPK
Like a blaze of summer straw, in winter's nick.   The Auroras of Autumn.
   Wallace Stevens.   CMoP
Like a blind man eating fish in an empty room.   An Ordinary Evening in
   Cleveland.   Lewis Turco.   NYBP
Like a boy searching for his dog?   The Haunted Garden.   Henry Treece.
   NeBP
Like a cat's tongue tastes/its whiskers/matter-of-factly.   Woman Par
   Excellence.   Rochelle Owens.   CoPo
Like a chieftain's frowning tower.   'Tis Merry in Greenwood.   Sir Walter
   Scott.   OHIP
Like a child who is laughing/because it's winter's last night.   A Day of
   Notes.   J. Charles Green.   LFAC
Like a clump of unwinding seaweed/And perhaps some grains of salt.   Here
   She Stands.   Jean Rabearivelo.   PBA
Like a clutch of startled/Debutantes, the flamingos/Lift a foot and stare.
   Animal Pictures.   Lawrence Locke.   GrPl
Like a cry for God's justice born!   News from Yorktown.   Lewis
   Worthington Smith.   MC; PAH
Like a dead fruit, a useless fruit/that rots,/and falls....   Per Amica Silentia
   Lunae.   Ronald de Carvalho.   LiTW
Like a devil in a saint's book.   The Tyrant Apple Is Eaten.   Norman
   MacCaig.   NeBP
Like a diamond in the sky.   The Star.   Jane Taylor.   NTCP; OxNR; SoPo;
   TiPo
Like a door-click after no one's there.   Displacement.   Horace Hamilton.
   AMV-80

Like a dream that all years had moved to.   Swimming in the Pacific.   Robert Penn Warren.   AMV-80

Like a fading allegory,/like doves,/like our own far-blood on forgotten altars.   Doves.   Joachim Neugroschel.   VWA

...Like a faithless brother/You take and drop my hand.   The Meeting.   Louise Bogan.   NePoAm-2; NYBP

Like a fine old salt-sea scavenger, like a tarry Buccaneer.   The Tarry Buccaneer.   John Masefield.   MCCG

Like a fire, like a poem/written on a wall.   Dawn.   Alejandra Pizarnik.   VWA

Like a flock of snowflakes drifting/towards a down bank of snows.   O Bird, So Lovely.   Louis Golding.   TrJP

Like a flower that seems too precious to be picked?   People Hide Their Love.   Emperor Wu-Ti.   LiTW; OLR

Like a French word, the one for nursery, the one for brine.   For Janice and Kenneth to Voyage.   Frank O'Hara.   ANYP

Like a fresh sacrifice.   Sleep and Poetry.   John Keats.   AtBAP

Like a fresh turd just dropped on snow.   Dick, a Maggot.   Jonathan Swift.   NLV; TW

Like a giant heart toying with my bones.   Soft Answers.   Robert Bagg.   FF; UnTE

Like a gift/that explained the waiting.   Waiting.   Liz Stout.   AMV-81

...Like a god/for whose deed/there is no parallel in the natural world.   Dedication to Hunger.   Louise Gluck.   FaBoWP

Like a handgrenade set to explode,/like goldenrod ready to bloom.   The Woman in the.   Marge Piercy.   NMM

Like a hard, white root.   Drinking Cold Water.   Peter Everwine.   NNaP

Like a hidden spring/Murmurs my blood.   My Love-Song.   Else Lasker-Schüler.   TrJP

Like a hole in the ice/where a child fell in.   Nechama.   Shirley Kaufman.   LCAP

Like a hooded nun telling her beads/In the twilight of a vast cathedral.   Pastorale.   Robert A. Davis.   GoSl

Like a house in Nebraska that suddenly explodes.   Watching Television.   Robert Bly.   BiP; CoAP

Like a hunter who in his return/recognizes his wasted shells in the woods.   Amen.   Alvaro Mutis.   AMV-81

Like a hushed village underneath a hill.   The Giantess.   Charles Baudelaire.   ErPo; OBVE

Like a lean knife between the ribs of Time.   The City of the Soul.   Lord Alfred Bruce Douglas.   HBMV

Like a light out of our heart,/You are gone.   Hymen: Never More Will the Wind.   Hilda ("H. D.") Doolittle.   TrGrPo; ViBoPo

Like a limitless reservoir for the ages to come.   Burial.   Paulin Joachim.   TTY

...Like a lonely hunger/for the hours when you love me.   Beyond Labelling Me.   Pier Giorgio Di Cicco.   CaPN

Like a long-legged fly upon the stream/His mind moves upon silence.   Long-Legged Fly.   William Butler Yeats.   CMoP; FaBoMo; FaBoTw; ForPo; InPS; LiTM; NoAm; NOBE; NoP; PAI; PPoe; TEP

Like a louch look in a lass's een.   By Wauchopeside.   Hugh" (Christopher Murray Grieve) MacDiarmid.   EBEV

...Like/A luminous choice.   The Green Afternoon.   Henry Rago.   VGW

Like a magnet's keeper/Closing the round.   Kisses in the Train.   D. H. Lawrence.   MoAB; MoBrPo

Like a man in a book on a book on a book.   Literary Gruk.   Piet Hein.   LiTW

Like a marvellous dream in his face?   The Last of His Tribe.   Henry Clarence Kendall.   CBAP; PoAu 1-2

Like a medieval bazaar   14th St./new york.   Patricia Jones.   NYP

Like a mild and patient prisoner/pecking through granite with a teaspoon.   Of Difference Does It Make.   Tom Paulin.   FaBoIP

Like a minute we pity ourselves/cancel our myths   The Membrane.   Mei-mei Berssenbrugge.   LTB

Like a morning flower/before the first light.   Unter der Linde.   George Ellenbogen.   AMV-81

Like a mother knaas hor young 'uns.   Jowl, Jowl and Listen.   Anonymous.   OBET

Like a mouth to open wider After Hours.   209 Canal.   Richard Howard.   NYP; TAP

Like a mouth/yawning and never closing.   The Return.   Dennis Saleh.   NeAC

Like a muslin-trapped bumble bee/Buzzing away its life force.   Meditation.   Blanaid Salkeld.   OnYI

Like a net to catch the delicate and plummeting bodies.   The Delicate, Plummeting Bodies.   Stephen Dobyns.   FYAP

Like a Nightingale in spring, Welcome home, my dearest.   The Sailor's Return.   Anonymous.   OxBoLi

Like a peacock throne/or the sigh of peaches.   Another Sunset.   John Minczeski.   PoDr

Like a persistent rumor/that will get us yet.   The Road Back.   Anne Sexton.   NYBP

Like a poor man finding a poorer, and each at the other stare!   Our Lady, Help of Christians.   Paul Claudel.   ISi

Like a pressed melodeon/across this forgotten/Northern landscape.   Last Journey.   John Montague.   FaBoIP

...Like a/punchline of a black joke   Scenery.   Ted Joans.   PoBA

Like a quavering, feverish laugh/Softened in a long-forgotten cradle.   Negroes.   Maxwell Bodenheim.   PoNe

Like a raiment of victory.   Waking an Angel.   Philip Levine.   NaP

Like a revealed mineral, a new earth.   In Piam Memoriam.   Geoffrey Hill.   NePoEA-2; OxBC

Like a revolving door/on a ten-day cycle/and belching.   The Giant Squid of Tsurai.   Kirk Robertson.   GP

Like a rich man who's made a galley-slave.   Sonnet: He Argues His Case with Death.   Cecco da Siena Angiolieri.   AWP

Like a root growing–   Eleven.   Archibald MacLeish.   HAP; NCSH

Like a root pulled from the water/like a heartroot torn free.   Birth.   George Ella Lyon.   Str

Like a rose-leaf I will crush thee,/Fairy Lilian.   Lilian.   Alfred, Lord Tennyson.   HBV 1-2; PeD

Like a rose that blooms in the morning/And in evening dies away.   There She Stands a Lovely Creature.   Anonymous.   AmFP; OLR

Like a shamed schoolboy then I mumbled low,/"We,/Lord."   Pronouns.   Karle Wilson Baker.   TreFT

Like a shot star, which doth repair/Upward, and rarify the air.   The Snail.   Richard Lovelace.   CaPo; OAEL 1-2

Like a slim brook the gamesome maid/Sparkled, and ran into the shade.   Defiance.   Walter Savage Landor.   HBV 1-2; VLP

Like a smoking traction engine/Puffing smoke from nose and ears.   Man Has No Smokestack.   Anonymous.   STF

Like a snipe scratching its feathers.   In My Heart's Depth.   Akazome Emon.   WPOW

Like a soul passing over, to the debit side.   Racing, Reckoning Fingers Flick.   Palladas.   OBVE

...Like a star,/Beacons from the abode where the Eternal are.   Lumen de Lumine.   Percy Bysshe Shelley.   GoBC

Like a state Janus or a church spread-eagle.   The Character of a Trimmer.   Anonymous.   APAS

Like a stockrider in a crowded restaurant/Homesick for a mirage.   The Inglorious Milton.   Francis Letters.   NOAV

Like a stripp'd child fain in the sea to dip.   Sent from Egypt with a Fair Robe of Tissue to a Sicilian Vinedresser.   Thomas Sturge Moore.   OBEV; OBVV

Like a sulphur yellow factory of chemical plenty/dyes every tongue.   Why the Soup Tastes Like the Daily News.   Marge Piercy.   MAT

Like a sweet nun in holy-day attire?   Epistle to George Keats (excerpt).   John Keats.   ChRP

Like a tea-tray in the sky./Twinkle, twinkle–   The Mad Hatter's Song.   Lewis (Charles Lutwidge Dodgson) Carroll.   FaBoNo; SpRo

Like a tear/flows down the folds/heavy as a stone.   A New Dress.   Rachel Korn.   VWA

Like a tear that has changed its mind.   January Wraps up the Wound of His Arm.   Charles Henri Ford.   EAS

Like a thousand girls with golden hair/Are singing at his side!   The Sod-Breaker.   Arthur Stringer.   CaP

Like a trace of a vanished breath.   Curtains for a Spinster.   Walter H. Kerr.   NePoAm-2

Like a traveler.   Haiku: "Even in my village..."   Kyorai.   FAZ

Like a tree that drips with gold you flow.   The Sleeping Beauty.   Edith Sitwell.   OBMV

Like a tree that fissures/Out of the center of all things.   Breasts.   Barbara Unger.   DFT

Like a Trojan true she made a vow/she would have one should mend it.   Walking in a meadow green.   Anonymous.   BoLoP; ErPo

Like a twig stuck into a snowman   I'm not here never was.   Constanta Buzea.   BoWoP

Like a war-like hero that never was afraid.   The Female Smuggler.   Anonymous.   AmSS

Like a water lily/gnawed by a beetle.   My Lover Capable of Terrible Lies.   Kaccipetty Nannakaiyar.   WPOW

Like a wedding/of Heaven and Earth.   Snow in the City.   Danny Siegel.   VWA

Like a well-conducted person,/Went on cutting bread and butter.   Sorrows of Werther.   William Makepeace Thackeray.   ALV; BLPA; FaBoCo; FiBHP; FPL; HBV 1-2; InMe; LiTL; NA; NBM; NLV; NOBL; NOBV; PoPle; ShM; TreF; VLP

Like a whisper before the fall/of the thin baton.   Retreat.   Martha Collins.   AMV-80

Like a white candle through a shuttered hand.   The Sisters.   Roy Campbell.   BoLoP; ChMP; FaBoTw; MoVE; OBMV

Like a white cemetery exposed by the Bosphorus...   Poem on Azure.   Anna de Noailles.   WPOW

Like a White Rhinoceros. The Thing Made Real. Ron Loewinsohn. NeAP

Like a wildman/kissing flowers Wash Day. Larry Mollin. NeAC

Like a wind-bell/On a porch where no wind ever blows? The Poet at Night-Fall. Glenway Wescott. PoA

Like a/Wind-blown autumn flower/That never lifts its head/Again. Troubled Woman. Langston Hughes. CTBA; PCP

Like a woolly caterpillar pinned on its back–man, that would/be sweet. I Wish My Tongue Were a Quiver. L. A. MacKay. TW

Like a worried spirit/waiting for love. Hanging Scroll. Gerald Stern. PoDr

...Like a wounded/dove out through scrub and leaves to the creek. Horace Kephart. Robert Morgan. MAYP

Like a yellow water-lily. The Song of Hiawatha. Henry Wadsworth Longfellow. OHIP

Like Abraham's faith, was counted righteousness. The Mother's Sacrifice. Lydia Sigourney. PaPo

Like air rising through thin ice, feed themselves forth/To inherit the earth. The Native. William Stanley Merwin. NePoEA-2

Like all God's good animals/any time any place. Seventh Georgic. George Economou. PoL

Like all other impropagandula? Limerick: "Animula vagula blandula." Conrad Aiken. FaBoNo

Like an emptied world, its grasses charged by great/shadows. Polo Match. John Ciardi. LiSp

Like an indifferent child/Too sleepy to undress. Song: "Life with her weary eyes." Marya Zaturenska. NMP

Like an old bold mate of Henry Morgan. Captain Stratton's Fancy. John Masefield. MoBrPo; OBEV

Like an old leaf/on a path, in winter. Scraps. Susannah Fried. VWA

Like an old proud king in a parable. Like an Old Proud King in a Parable. A. J. M. Smith. OBCV

Like an owl staring into the eyes/of a hawk. A Reflection of Night. T. Walking Eagle Marietta. LFAC

Like an undiscovered new world. Sugar Daddy. Elizabeth Smither. OCNZ

Like an unemployed idea/pretending it's a drop of rain. A Blue Jeaned Rock Queen in Search of Happiness... A. K. Redwing. VoR

Like any party/they photograph each other but forget/to develop the film. Punk Party.[They Told Me It Was Literary...] Wendy Rose. TWSS

Like any summer day. The Voice. Theodore Roethke. AmLP; VGW

Like ashes in the winds of God. For St. Bartholomew's Eve. Malcolm Cowley. NAMP

Like atoms, are exempt from blows. Directions for Making a Birth-Day Song: "To form a just..." Jonathan Swift. NAs

Like Axis Sally herself,/on out of town tires. Loony, 51: During the War. William Kloefkorn. GP

Like bees that haunt the lavender/Of some walled garden! In an Old Nursery. Patrick Reginald Chalmers. HBMV

The like before was never seen,/A serving-man to be a queen. The Famous Flower of Serving-Men. *Anonymous.* ESPB; OBET; OxBB

Like beggars gathering in the dust. The Great Depression. Patricia Goedicke. GP

Like blood,/in the air an apple/rusts. The Apple. Bruce Guernsey. PPJ

Like blood, like good, and like age/Make the happiest marriage. Proverbial Advice on Marriage. *Anonymous.* FaBoUs

Like brothers died, and their expiring breath/Was Freedom's breath of life! Hymn of the Alamo. Reuben M. Potter. BPAW

Like buckshot, changing/wine to blood. Twilight in California. Philip Dow. AmPA

Like building dream houses–/no one knows what you mean. Nails. Gary Gildner. TAP

Like burnt-out craters healed with snow. The Vision of Sir Launfal. James Russell Lowell. LiTA

Like cat down cellar wit' nohole mouse. Scottsboro. *Anonymous.* InPK

Like Chicken Little's, do not tumble down/And crash upon his crown. Truth. Jessica Nelson North. HBVY

Like cobwebs in the sky. Trip: San Francisco. Langston Hughes. AmFN; GoSl

Like coins between a dying miser's fingers. Maple Leaves. Thomas Bailey Aldrich. AnNE; GN

Like Coney island in winter Ladies and Gentlemen This Little Girl. Edward Estlin Cummings. CMoP

Like Costumes Grandsires wore. We outgrow love, like other things. Emily Dickinson. NOBA

Like daisies from a clover field in summer. Consolations of Philosophy. Derek Mahon. BlrV; CIP

Like David with washed face who ceased to weep. To Manon. Wilfrid Scawen Blunt. NBM

Like death, but seeing it, affects a soul/Of gentleness, if sweet death seek that goal. Pale Is Death. Joachim Du Bellay. LiTW

Like dews that drop on hills unknown,/To feed a lordly river. Koina ta ton Philon. John Addington Symonds. OBVV

Like dipped, dark candy. These Trees Are. Susan Strayer Deal. AMV-81

Like drifting foam upon the endless sea's/indifferent and listless sursurration. Greek Transfiguration. Kimon Friar. HoAn

Like dry-breasted hags/Welcoming their children to their withered arms. Ghetto Twilight. Alter Brody. VWA

Like earth-stained roots of squill The Storm. Imr el Kais. LiTW

Like empty parachutes/these ballads/without men. And Jesus Don't Have Much Use for His Old Suitcase Anymore. Tom Kryss. NeAC

Like every January first,/Brand-new in your old name. January 1. Marnie Pomeroy. PoSC

Like far-off conflagrations: roses of Anjou. The Lilacs and the Roses. Louis Aragon. OBWP

Like fishes for ever, so take it to heart. Jig. C. Day-Lewis. OxBI

Like flags that linger on/The sky when king and queen are gone. Epithalamion. Michael Longley. CIP

Like folded dove wings,/his black leather gloves. The Spirit of 34th Street. Peggy Shriver. AMV-80

...Like fossil rain-pits in/shale, equally beautiful. Calm and Full the Ocean. Robinson Jeffers. WaP

Like foul birds over the dead, and none to drive them away. Crash at Leithfield. Allen Curnow. AnNZ

Like freezing founts, where all that's thrown/Within their current turns to stone. I Wish I Were by That Dim Lake. Thomas Moore. NBM

Like fresh, sweet nosegays in the/dusky night. Morning and Evening. Antoni Slonimski. TrJP

Like funny people in a pantomime. Daddy. Rose Fyleman. SiSoSe

Like garden gods–and not so decent either. Don Juan. George Gordon, Lord Byron. WHA

Like glistering stones in the congealing air. Orion. Richard Henry Horne. VLP

Like gods in commune, formless, divine and dire. Sonnets, III: "Regions of soft clear air, of cold green leaves." Thomas Caulfield Irwin. IrPN

Like golden flowers/envy withered the last stars. Birth of the Foal. Ferenc Juhasz. BoANP; PH

Like gossip, or the smell of lilacs, or an overheard song: soon/everyone has caught it. Netting. Jorie Graham. NPGG

Like gravity, like weight Science as Art. Hugh Seidman. AmPA

Like grit caught on a wheel, like shining freight. Brooding Likeness. Louise Gluck. MAYP

Like groom, like peer! like peer, like groom! At Newmarket. Samuel Bishop. PV

Like grotesque question marks Archaeologists. Real Faucher. AMV-80

Like hardened rock that force nor power can move. Love's Labour Lost. Robert Tofte. EIL

Like,/he was really/nowhere. A Poem for Speculative Hipsters. LeRoi (Imamu Amiri Baraka) Jones. NoAm; NOBA

Like heavy honey out of hollow combs. Ballad of the Outer Life. Hugo von Hofmannsthal. AWP; LiTW; TrJP

Like her - because they love him. In School-Days. John Greenleaf Whittier AA; AnNE; BLPA; FaBoBe; FPL; GLGT; OBCA; OxBChV; PoPl; TreF

Like his hand, in fever, on my forehead. Out-of-the-Body Travel. Stanley Plumly. AmPA; GeTw; LCAP

Like his immeasured selfe, are infinite and great. Polyolbion. Michael Drayton. OBS

Like his, may love be thy reward,/But not thy hapless fate the same. Stanzas to a Lady, with the Poems of Camoens. George Gordon, Lord Byron. FaBoUs

Like horses use ne for the negative sound. Aids for Latin. Gordon Perry. FaBoUs

Like hunger that feeds on its own hungriness. Esthetique du Mal. Wallace Stevens. CMoP

Like imaged worlds and creatures–need/nurturing always. Song (2). Edwin Rolfe. TrJP

Like in the/poems/let's/pretend. Love U.S.A. Kathleen Spivack. BoWoP

Like it done in days of old. Winter is Coming. Waverly Turner Carmichael. BANP

Like its leader, free and grand,/Beauregard! Beauregard. Catherine Ann Warfield. MC; PAH

Like Jesus, humble, truly meek,/From self-applauses free. To Show How Humble. *Anonymous.* AH

Like kissing my kitten in the belly/The softness of our reward Mexico City Blues. Jack Kerouac. NeAP

...Like knowing the sound of the sea when you/live under the sea. The Two Selves. Margaret Avison. NoAm

Like lash marks, or rows of uncut wheat. Talking across Kansas. Paula Kwon. AMV-80

Like lazy mastodons/going from here to there. Riding in the Rain. Maxine W. Kumin. RFM

Like lifted clouds, reach on. The Departed. John Banister Tabb. AA

Like lips the hand has not wiped dry,/Are glistening, are glistening. Three Variations. Boris Pasternak. TrJP

Like little shreds of crimson silk. Impressions. Oscar Wilde. SyP

Like lizards on rocks. Haiku: "Eastern guard tower." Etheridge Knight. NeAC; SM; TAP

Like love & family romance, has neither beginning, middle nor end. My Guardian Angel Stein. Philip Schultz. MAYP

Like love or any other stubborn itch. Crabs. Marge Piercy. NLV

Like love we seldom keep. Law Like Love. W. H. Auden. CMoP; CoBMV; FaBoMo; NoP

Like love, wherefor I am so dumb to you. Songs. Babette Deutsch. HBMV

Like lovers. Or brothers. Brothers, if you like. Into the Dark. Paul Monette. AmPA

Like lyre strings I'd pluck the elastic laces/Of my battered shoes, one foot against my heart. The Strolling Player. Arthur Rimbaud. GrPl

Like magic to the tapping cane of thought. To a Blind Student Who Taught Me to See. Samuel Hazo. GOYP

Like Mallarme who had the good fortune/to find a style that made writing impossible. Shifting Colors. Robert Lowell. HaCAP

Like mama leaning out the window/calling her children home When Brothers Forget. Jill Witherspoon Boyer. CNA

Like man/we are/eternal in one sense/vulnerable in the next I Am Stone of Many Colors. Tauhindauli. STE

Like men lost in the heart/of New York, in an almost memorable past. Nothing but Image. Jody Swilky. AMV-81

Like morning singing in the heart of Man. Lyttelton Harbor. D'Arcy Cresswell. AnNZ

Like Moses, you will lead our people over/And through. Black Pride. Margaret Goss Burroughs. BlSi

Like moss upon a stone at a brook's edge. Baal Shem Tov. Abraham Moses Klein. CaP; TrJP

Like my Beaver-Spirit who takes–deep/In his Eskimo ear–much wisdom from a Loon. Talking to Animals. Barbara Howes. GrPl

Like my dead grandmother/loved her steins of Star beer. Old Dubuque. Dave Etter. AmFN

Like myrrh, or musk, or amber, that excite/The ecstasies of sense, the soul's delight. Correspondences. Charles Baudelaire. NAWM 1-2

Like myths/awaiting an occasion. Landscape Workers. Harley Elliott. LTB

Like night falling piece by piece. Figure and Ground. Elton Glaser. AMV-80

Like nightingale in spring,/welcome my dearest. The Valiant Seaman's Happy Return to His Love... *Anonymous.* GBP

Like nothing else in Tennessee. Anecdote of the Jar. Wallace Stevens. AP; CMoP; CoBMV; ExPo; HaCAP; HeIP; HoPM; InPK; LiTA; MoAB; MoVE; NAWM 1-2; NePA; NIP; NoAm; NOBA; NoP; OBSP; OxBA; PoA; PPP; PrIm; SOTW; TAP; UnPo

Like nursing mothers, to their babes/that croon. Love-Songs. Moses Ibn Ezra. TrJP

Like old Valrennes, be ready with/"I'm here to answer you!" The Battle of La Prairie. William Douw Schuylr-Lighthall. MC; PAH

Like old women knitting, breathless/to tell their tales. Necessities of Life. Adrienne Rich. HaCAP; NIP; NoAm; NOBA

Like one that loves thee nor will let thee pass/Ungreeted, and shall give its light embrace. Inscription for the Entrance to a Wood. William Cullen Bryant. AmLP; AnNE; AP; BiP; MAmP; MCCG; OxBA; TAP

...Like one who at a play/Finds himself all alone, and will not stay. The Fountains. W. R. Rodgers. MoVE; PoL

Like one who wraps the drapery of his couch/About him, and lies down to pleasant dreams. Thanatopsis. William Cullen Bryant. AA; AmLP; AnNE; AP; APA; AWP; BLPL; BoLiVe; BoNaP; DiPo; DL; FaBoBe; FaFP; GoTF; HBV 1-2; HBVY; LaNeLa; LiTA; MAmP; MCCG; NePA; NOBA; OBEV; OBRV; OBVV; OHFP; OxBA; TAP; TreF; TrGrPo; TRV; ViBoPo; WBLP; WGRP; WHA

Like orthodoxy, is a reticence. The Truest Poetry Is the Most Feigning; or, Ars Poetica for Hard Times. W. H. Auden. NYBP

Like other dreams must fade! Memories. George Denison Prentice. AA

Like our hope of success it has passed. Lines on the Back of a Confederate Note. Samuel Alroy Jonas. BLPA

Like ours at what their strange captivities/Invisibly engender. The Petty Officers' Mess. Roy Fuller. ChMP

Like painted idols seen to stir/By the idolators in a magic grove. Javanese Dancers. Arthur Symons. VLP

Like Paris and the Grecian chiefs/And the three Ulster brothers! Three Old Brothers. Frank O'Connor. OnYI

Like Paris at once give it to thee. Epigram. Thomas Moore. ALV

...Like pea/-nut butter on bread. Haiku: "The cat spreads herself." Robert Phillips. GrPl

...Like piers/rocking and trembling in my current. Balinda's Dance. Louise Erdrich. TWSS

Like pigeon in quest of a mate that is lost. The Lost. *Anonymous.* WTO

Like planets submerged and rising. Pumpkin. Robert Morgan. GeTw

...Like plastic spoons/being worked in a hardening cheese dip. All-Nite Donuts. Albert Goldbarth. GeTw; MAYP

Like pollen from the stamens of a flower. Lambs Frolicking Home. Fred Lape. BoAnP

Like priceless treasures sinking in the sand. America. Claude McKay. AnAmPo; BALP; CDC; NIP; NoAm; PoBA; PoNe; TAP; TTY

Like puffs of snow. White Season. Frances Frost. TiPo

LIKE/RAINING/SWORDS! Terror Conduction. Philip Lamantia. NeAP

Like red fire,/Like gold,/Like blood. Isaac Leybush Peretz. Moishe Leib Halpern. VWA

Like ripe fruit bruised/his dreaming mouth. Poem: something broke the dream. John Gill. NeAC

Like Rome's bold chief, he came and saw,/but neither/Awed us, nor conquer'd. Fort Bowyer. Charles L. S. Jones. PAH

Like roses that were loveliest. The Rose. Pierre Ronsard. AWP

Like rustic maids that meekly stand/Below the ladies of their land! Wild Roses. Edgar Fawcett. HBV 1-2

Like salmon on a heavenly fishing line. Goldfish. Harold Monro. BrPo

Like Samson, I'm in the dark,/and continue to ride the bus. In a Remote Cloister Bordering the Empyrean. Joel Sloman. VGW

Like Samson, Tranquil-souled,/Who remained strong, though blind. A Prayer. Vernon Watkins. MoRP; PoPl

Like seeing in the rain at night a woman's face. Old Iron. Douglas Stewart. BoAV

Like setting suns or music at the close! Man's Going Hence. Samuel Rogers. OBNC

Like she rolls her dough. Reason I Stay on Job So Long. *Anonymous.* ABF; GBP

Like sheep from the rains and thunders. Rhapsody. William Stanley Braithwaite. BALP; BANP

Like silence into music, opening a way through time. Air. Kathleen Raine. MoAB; MoBrPo

Like silhouettes against the sky. Les Silhouettes. Oscar Wilde. BrPo; MOS

Like sleep, like the valley's continuous sleep. Staying Up on Jack's Fork Near Eminence, Missouri. Albert Salsich. AMV-80

...Like smoke at great height/above the earth and sees it all. Ashes. Philip Levine. AMV-80

Like so many cows, Chagall's, in a shaken world? Boy in the Lamont Poetry Room, Harvard. D. G. Jones. PeCV

Like some ancient and magnificent tribe. The Enormous Aquarium. Sherod Santos. MAYP

Like some drenched truant, cower. The Rain-Crow. Madison Cawein. AA

Like some great colored wall of sudden lightning! The Painted Hills of Arizona. Edwin Curran. BPAW; HBMV

Like some hawk caught/in fingers of a foreign tree. Blessed and Resting Uncle. Harley Elliott. NeAC

Like some sweet singer's, when her sweetest strain/From the heaved heart is gradually dying! Song: "Sing the old song, amid the sounds dispersing." Aubrey Thomas De Vere. HBV 1-2

Like somebody the police have come for. In Laughter. Ted Hughes. PAI

Like someone waiting at a rendezvous. West Fifty-Seventh Street. Byron Vazakas. FAZ

Like something religious. Hansel and Gretel. Anne Sexton. InPS

Like something that's cut out/and won't ever go away. As a Child Seeing a Cardinal. John Gill. NeAC

Like songs/my mother/sang–happy/& betrayed. Maine. Elinor Nauen. APU

Like sores that grow and burst/no matter what. Poet Woman's Mitosis: Dividing All the Cells Apart. Wendy Rose. TWSS

Like sorrow or a tune. The Night Will Never Stay. Eleanor Farjeon. CH; HBMV; NTCP; OxBChV; SiSoSe; SoPo

Like sparks snapping through the foam of a fire. Death of a Cat. James Schevill. NMP

Like speaking of his love too little, or of love too much. What Does a Man Think About. John Holmes. CrMA

Like spilled cream/into a wild wind. Mares of Night. Virginia Long. AMV-81

Like spindrift flinging, in great joy or pain/Pass on and come no more. Beyond Feith Buidhe. Hamish Brown. PoSH

Like spines of air, frozen in an ice cube. The Patient Is Rallying. Weldon Kees. NaP

Like stars blinking at the dawn Pinay. Virginia Cerenio. BrSi

Like stars for words for doing something terrible. Photograph at the Cloisters: April 1972. Helen Chasin. NMM

Like still seas, to vacant skies. Betty by the Sea. Ronald McCuaig. BoAV; NOAV

Like stones of the road, like trees. Plainness. Jorge Luis Borges. NYBP

Like suppliants pleading. Good-By. Margaret E. Bruner. PoToHe

...Like taking/candy from a baby.   On the Edge.   Frank Dwyer.   AMV-81

Like tales of fairies often told/By doting age that dies for cold.   I thought that Love had been a boy.   *Anonymous.*   EnLoPo

Like tapers burning through the windy night.   Immortalis.   David Morton.   HBV 1-2

Like tatters of the Morpho butterfly.   Under the Window: Ouro Preto.   Elizabeth Bishop.   NYBP

Like that blind Homer kicked upon the shore, seaweed.   Extreme Unction in Pa.   David Ray.   AMV-81; FAZ

Like that long gold which wiped the feet/of God?   To St. Mary Magdalen.   Benjamin Dionysius Hill.   AA

Like that part of the fire that remains longest.   The Red Room.   Judith Berke.   PoDr

Like the algae in its sea–   Life of Life.   Johannes Edfelt.   LiTW

Like the animal shapes that sing at the gates of sleep.   Song of Reasons.   Robert Pinsky.   HaCAP

Like the backbone of an ass.   This Island.   Archilochus.   OBVE

Like the bicycle rider/irrationally dropping his books.   The Bicycle Rider.   David Shapiro.   ANYP

Like the birds who build and sing.   Easter Week.   Charles Kingsley.   OHIP

Like the bound crowds who sigh, who sigh.   Houdini.   Eli Mandel.   NIP; NOBC

Like the boy who goes whistling by.   Whistling Boy.   Nixon Waterman.   PoLf

Like the bubble on the fountain,/Thou art gone, and for ever!   The Lady of the Lake.   Sir Walter Scott.   BSV; OBRV; TreFS; TrGrPo; ViBoPo; WHA

Like the candle the priest offers/for the sinner humming/in his ear.   The Telephone Operator.   Saint Francis of Assisi.   AMV-80

...Like the city dump, at night/Outside Norwalk, Conn.   Commuter's Entry in a Connecticut Diary.   Robert Penn Warren.   AMV-81

...Like the coastguard's/windlight/In the tarted-up houses, widows' row.   Tobacco Hole.   Mebdh McGuckian.   FaBoIP

Like the created poem,/Or faceted crystal.   What I Expected.   Stephen Spender.   CoBMV; MoAB; MoBrPo; MoPo; NoAm; NOBE; OAEP

Like the dazzle on the sea, my darling.   Leaving Barra.   Louis MacNeice.   EBEV

Like the dead husks that rustle through her hands.   The Corn Husker.   [(Emily)] Pauline Johnson.   CaP

Like the dead moon she still shines on.   The Church Today.   William Watson.   WGRP

Like the empty words of a dream/Remembered on waking.   I Love All Beauteous Things.   Robert Bridges.   BrPo; CMoP; EBEV; ExPo; HBMV; HBVY; TrCP

Like the eye of a violet.   Nothing to Save.   D. H. Lawrence.   SOTW

Like the eyes of a girl who is buried alive.   After Visiting a Home for Disturbed Children.   Lou Lipsitz.   LTB

Like the eyes of a mild savior.   The Blue Booby.   James Tate.   AmPA; EAS; NoAm; NoP

Like the fireflies dragging among the trees/their separate, discontinuous lanterns.   Blue Ridge.   Ellen Bryant Voigt.   MAYP

Like the green life it did wither and down it did fall.   What's the Life of a Man?   *Anonymous.*   OBET

Like the ground I might at any moment/Choose to lie down upon.   Duty to Death, LD.   Dick Roberts.   WaP

Like the halo of light of.../Samuel.   The Return.   Shmuel Moreh.   VWA

Like the head of an adder,/Black with veins, a fist...   Paris.   Gertrud Kolmar.   PBWP

Like the helpless nightingale/you locked in a cage.   Love Songs.   *Anonymous.*   BoWoP

Like the hoola hoop dream dance/for singles only   As the World Turns.   Larry Mollin.   NeAC

Like the incestuous points/of burning stars.   Triad.   Donald Foster.   AMV-80

Like the Indians now, and God,/and everyone.   My Dog Jock.   Hayden Carruth.   FAZ

Like the last Gazette, or the last Address.   Epilogue to the Satires.   Alexander Pope.   OBSV

Like the leaping goat-footed waterfalls/Singing their cold, forlorn madrigals.   Spring.   Edith Sitwell.   OAEP

Like the little wind that laughing/Across the water blows.   The Sedges.   Seumas (James Starkey) O'Sullivan.   AnIV

Like the mother of the Gracchi,/Folds her jewels to her heart.   California.   Lydia Huntley Sigourney.   MC; PAH

Like the names of the ancients, like Hayman, Halevi.   Language of Ancients.   Hayim Lenski.   VWA

Like the nymphs dancing together/In the "Allegory of Spring'.   Autobiographies.   Derek Mahon.   FaBoIP

Like the one voice of multitudinous rills.   Sonnet: A sound of many waters!– now I know."   Richard Chenevix Trench.   OBRV

...Like the ones/she polished every week for twelve/pounds per annum and her keep.   Contre Jour.   Elizabeth Bartlett.   FaBoWP

Like the pages of a book coming together/for the last time.   The Thumb.   Dennis Saleh.   MAT; NeAC

Like the peace of summer noons/Beside the sea.   The Birth of Galahad: Ylen's Song.   Richard Hovey.   AA

Like the pear/when it grows ripe.   Song: "Dress me in green."   *Anonymous.*   BoWoP

Like the pile upon/a mountain pony's coat.   Windharp.   John Montague.   CIP; FaBoIP

...Like the plume/Of a warrior returning, under the low hills,/Into his own kingdom.   Fern.   Ted Hughes.   NYBP

Like the quiver of a Negro woman's eye-lids cupping/tears.   Negro Woman.   Lewis Alexander.   CDC; PoBA

Like the rest but still for thee.   Sept. 1957.   Edward Marshall.   CoPo

Like the retreat of water from sea-caves.   Through Binoculars.   Charles Tomlinson.   OAEL 1-2

Like the same body in another place.   Inconstancy's the Greatest of Sins.   Edward, Lord Herbert of Cherbury.   OBSP

Like the sea in which I floated.   Before.   Ann Stanford.   GP

...Like the search-beam/Of my father's flashlight, at every swing discovering/Death.   Elegies for the Hot Season.   Sandra McPherson.   AmPA

...Like the shadow/Of a flight, pass Storms and Time, Life and Death.   From Far away.   Delmira Agustini.   PBWP

Like the shovelfull over/the gravedigger's shoulder.   We Must Make a Kingdom of It.   Gregory Orr.   MAYP

Like the sight of a Royal with its Rights and Crockets,/Its Pearls, and Beam, and Span.   The Royal Stag.   Hugh" (Christopher Murray Grieve) MacDiarmid.   FaBoMo

Like the skin of the old man/I have become,/from a single/bite.   A Symposium: Apples.   Linda Pastan.   NIP

...Like the smallest/of cities we slipped through.   Departure.   Carolyn Forche.   AMV-80

Like the snout of a white-eyed pig.   Learning the Spells: A Diptych.   Anita Endrezze Probst.   CDW

Like the snowbank/Behind which it blooms.   Three Songs from the Haida, II: Queen Charlotte's Island, B.C., 2.   *Anonymous.*   BPAW

Like the sound of horns, the sound of thousands of small/wings.   The Executive's Death.   Robert Bly.   CoAP; NaP

Like the splume of a wave/Into the eye of the void.   A Mourning-Song for Rangiaho.   Te Heuheu Herea.   WTO

Like the starling/in its wicker cage   Mineral Point.   Robert Patrick Dana.   FAZ

Like the sweet sleep of the butterfly/In thin silk.   After the War.   Hayim Naggid.   VWA

LIke the swell of Summer's ocean.   For Music.   George Gordon, Lord Byron.   CBEP; PoPle

Like the things we give each other:/A ring, a word,/Some space in the light.   The Dragon of Red Lights.   David Swickard.   AmC

Like the tombs of nameless kings.   County Sligo.   Louis MacNeice.   OnYI

Like the tree apples, from me/I cast my songs around.   When I See Another's Pain.   Mani Leib.   TrJP

Like the tucked sleeve of a one-armed boy.   When You Go Away.   William Stanley Merwin.   LCAP

Like the ugly duckling at a high school dance.   An Untitled Poem, about an Uncompleted Sonnet.   Sanford Pinsker.   AMV-81

Like the white man you hate/in your dreams.   Pulling Weeds.   Eric Chock.   BrSi

Like the wind/That stirs but slightly the ancient dust.   Auschwitz from Colombo.   Anne Ranasinghe.   VWA

Like the woman waiting for me tonight/does to mine.   The Most Beautiful Woman at My Highschool Reunion.   Ellen Marie Bissert.   PeHV

...Like theirs arise/On callous earth and careless skies.   Birds.   Llywelyn.   PoAu 1-2

Like theirs that from an Ostian window gazed/Beyond the bastions of eternity.   Silentium Altum.   Blanche Mary Kelly.   CAW

Like them the meek and lowly,/On high may dwell with Thee.   The Church's One Foundation.   Samuel John Stone.   TreFT; WGRP

Like this calico cat/asleep, curled up in a bread basket,/on a sideboard where the sun falls.   A Man in Blue.   James Schuyler.   ANYP

Like this one.   The Flower.   Robert Creeley.   CAPP

Like this poem/that is already inside you.   The Rapist.   Stephen P. Dunn.   PoL

Like this, to the end of eternity.   Egyptian Hieroglyphics.   *Anonymous.*   BoWoP

Like this . . . You wouldn't hang me?/I thought not.   How Annandale Went Out.   Edwin Arlington Robinson.   AmP; AP; CoBMV; HBMV; MoAB; MoAmPo; NoAm; NOBA

Like those favored before me, hand-picked each one/for her joyful heart.   Cinderella.   Olga Broumas.   DFT

Like those girls.   Lovely Girls with Flounder on a Starry Night.   Anselm Parlatore.   SUW

Like those slow-moving treasures of the sky.   Clouds.   John Jay Chapman.   EtS

Like thoughts whose very sweetness yieldeth proof/That they were born for immortality. Inside of King's College Chapel, Cambridge. William Wordsworth. EnLi 1-2; GoBC; OAEP; OBNC; OBRV; OxBoCh

Like thousands of waving hands. The Inside Chance. Marge Piercy. LTB

Like to a man who stands with smoking knife/Above his dead, and sees the rising moon. Judgment. William Rose Benet. AnAmPo

Like to a slumbering bride, awake again. To Music, to Becalm a Sweet-Sick Youth. Robert Herrick. CaPo

Like to the heralds of old, stepped the Ser-/geant-at-Arms and the Speaker. The Fight over the Body of Keitt. Anonymous. PAH

Like to thee, faire cruell May. Song: "Shephard loveth thow me vell?" Jean Passerat. OBVE

Like tombs of pilgrims that have died/About the Holy Sepulchre. The Portrait. Dante Gabriel Rossetti. MaVP; OAEP; VLP

Like tothers–tothers–/Come–a–ran–tan–e–o. The Yorkshire Bite. Anonymous. BaBo

Like treble clefs they resound after/the departed train. To I. Lavrentevaya. Natalya Gorbanyevskaya. BoWoP

Like trees in lonely places. The Odd Ones. Ruth Suckow. MCCG

Like trees they murmur or like blackbirds sing/Courtesies of good-morning and good-evening. On Dwelling. Robert Graves. CBEP; CMoP; FaBoMo; MoVE; OBSP

Like trees waiting for leaves in the/spring. To Life I Said Yes. Chaim Grade. TrJP

Like trout among their grim stony gazes. An Irish Lake. W. R. Rodgers. BIrV

Like twinkling Starres before the rising Sunne. The Authour's Dreame. Francis Quarles. OBS

Like two black birds in flight. Painlessly out of Ourselves. William Page. AMV-81

Like two hands about to touch. The Cows near the Graveyard. Howard Nelson. NU

...Like, ugly is beautiful. Fashion in the 70's. May Swenson. NYP

Like unto the clasp of an old pocketbook. A Barefoot Boy. James Whitcomb Riley. FaFP

Like us he is holy and sinful. An Election. Mordecai Marcus. SOTS

Like violets by Durer;/even darker. Then the Ermine. Marianne Moore. NePoAm; PoA

Like vivid sunburst on some crystal sphere. On the Annunciation of Fra Angelico. Manuel Machado. CAW

Like voices on the gale. Stanzas. John Clare. EnLoPo

Like water falling under the night's drum. The Lovers. Alex Comfort. NeBP; PoA

Like we call it/home In the Inner City. Lucille Clifton. CNA; HeIP

Like weary trees,/interlaced,/shadowy we fell asleep. Like Weary Trees. Jacob Glatstein. VWA

Like whispers round the body of the/dead. I Know Not Why, but All This Weary Day. Henry Timrod. AmP

Like white thoughts smiling through gray memory. White Dusk. Marion M. Boyd. HBMV

Like widow'd turtle, still her loss complain. To His Lute. William, of Hawthornden Drummond. GTBS; GTBS-P; UnS

Like wine,/Aged and tart. Chickory. Zerubavel Gal'ed. TrJP

Like wings in waiting on the darkling lake. This Unimportant Morning. Lawrence Durrell. BoLoP; NeBP; OxBTC

Like winter pools at night/or appetite put a fine finish on. For Musia's Grandchildren. Irving Layton. NOBC

Like wintry weather–Why?–It blows its nose. A Child That Has a Cold We May Suppose. Thomas Dibdin. FaBoNo; PV

Like women. On Growing Old. Srinavas Rayaprol. ACV

Like worms through an apple The Foreman's Wife. Jeff Tagami. BrSi

Like Yellowstone National Park. Further Notice. Philip Whalen. PoM; VGW

Like yonder land. Perhaps–perhaps–/perhaps! Hope. William Dean Howells. AA; MOS

Like you–a bird! A Blackbird Suddenly. Joseph Auslander. TiPo

Like you a while, they glide/Into the grave. To Blossoms. Robert Herrick. BoNaP; CaPo; EG; GTBS; GTBS-P; HBV 1-2; JCP; LoBV; OBEV; OBS; SeCP; SeCV 1-2

Like you and me who, to sustain our pose,/Need wine and conversation, colour and light. Warning to a Guest. John Holloway. NePoEA

Like you, my iron-hearted friend! Dagger. Mikhail Yuryevich Lermontov. AWP

...Like you, we are alone. An Evening Walk. William Stafford. NPAW

Like young leaves in a forest place. Winter Night. A. R. D. Fairburn. AnNZ

Like your dreams,/it never was quite there. Exodus. Anita Endrezze Probst. CDW

Like yours, may sweeten and perfume my death. A Contemplation upon Flowers. Henry, Bishop of Chichester King. BoNaP; CBEP; EG; ELP; HBV 1-2; LoBV; MeLP; MePo; NoP; OBEV; OBS; PG; SeCP; TrGrPo

A likeness, one of the race of fathers: earth/And sea and air. The Irish Cliffs of Moher. Wallace Stevens. LCAP; NOBA; VGW

Likewise the parents of the seamen brave/Who in the Royal Charter met a watery grave. The Wreck of the Royal Charter. Anonymous. OBSS

Likewise those kind old people we left in Gaspereaux. The Banks of Gaspereaux. Anonymous. BaBo

Lil' Johnny Castro was two years old when/they collected. Did Ya Hear? Yasmeen Jamal. LFAC

Lilac was found in his hand. The Dream Songs. John Berryman. LCAP

Lilacs blowing across his face glad he brought you The Tennis Court Oath. John Ashbery. NoAm; TAP

Lilies of death-pale hope, roses of passionate dream. The Travail of Passion. William Butler Yeats. TrCP

The lilies of his love appear! The Revival. Henry Vaughan. BoLiVe; NOCV; OBS; OxBoCh; PoEL 1-5; PoPle; TrGrPo

Lilies that fester smell far worse than weeds. Sonnets, XCIV: "They that have power to hurt, and will do none." William Shakespeare. BLPL; ExPo; FaBoEn; GTBS; GTBS-P; InPS; LiTB; MasP; NOBE; NoP; OAEL 1-2; OBEV; PAI; PeHV; PoEL 1-5; PPoe; PPP; SCV; TEP; TrGrPo; ViBoPo

The lilies, the luminous lilies of France. Yorktown Centennial Lyric. Paul Hamilton Hayne. PAH

Lilli burlero, bullen a la. Lilli Burlero. Anonymous. FSW; NOBI

Lily bright and shine-a. Here Comes a Wooer. Anonymous. OxNR

Lily may deeper see than I. A Trifle. Henry Timrod. HBV 1-2

The lily, the rose, the rose I lay. The Maidens Came. Anonymous. AtBAP; CBEP; EG; GBL; ViBoPo

A limber tree, a timber tree,/And resinous with tar! The Trees. Christopher Morley. OHIP

Limbo! Limbo! Now and forever! Curtain Speech. Michael Braude. AMV-81

The limitless sun of Truth shines more and/more. Work. Louis James Block. AA

Limned in excuse your face. Conceits. Arlo Bates. AA

Limned in his blood across your clearing skies/Look up and read: Parnell! Parnell. Thomas Michael Kettle. AnIV

Limp,/simply A Little Tumescence. Jonathan Williams. ErPo; NeAP; PoM

Limp throatless words/dancing in shadows of snow Travels With the Band-Aid Army. Lance Henson. VoR

Lincoln, come back, rebuild our broken world. Lincoln, Come Back. Thomas Curtis Clark. PGD

Lincoln kept on growing. Abraham Lincoln. Rosemary and Stephen Vincent Benét. NAMP; PoSC; TiPo; YeAr

The Line that never was drawn. Too Much Coffee. Edwin Arlington Robinson. MoAmPo

A line without position/has brushed a stroke with its return. Painting by Chimes. Bernadette Mayer. ANYP

The lineage of Romulus! Hymn to Diana. Caius Valerius Catullus. AWP

The lineaments of a plummet-measured face. Statues. William Butler Yeats. AnIL; NoAm; WeW

The lineaments of Gratified Desire. The Question Answer'd. William Blake. ELU; ErPo; FaBoEE; GBL; NoP; OBSP; ViBoPo

Lined up, ready to fly. Of Oystermen, Workboats. Dave Smith. MAYP

The lines of strength that here had their beginning. Their Beginning. Constantine P. Cavafy. PeHV

The lines will be fulfilled–this is all they're saying. The Letters of Summer. Christopher Buckley. AMV-80

...Linger/And ponder whither has flitted his sitter impassioned. The Image. Richard Hughes. OBMV

Linger longer, Olga, prolong your vulgar conga. One-Line Poems from a New Statesman Competition. Molly Fitton. PoL

Lingered like incense from a censer/thrown. To Rosina Pico. William Wilberforce Lord AA

Lingering death with teares invoked. Live Not, Poor Bloom, but Perish. Anonymous. NCEP

Lingering like an unlov'd guest,/I sigh'd for thee. To Night. Percy Bysshe Shelley. EG

The lingering scent. Haiku: "The bride puts them away." Anonymous. HW

Lingering/to sniff at a green plum Tune: Crimson Lips Adorned. Li Ching-chao. PBWP

Linked here by bonds of love, now let us feed/Upon Thy grace and find it meat indeed. Prayer before Meat. Una W. Harsen. TrPWD

Linked on an unseen leash like gravity/To earth, and death still virgin on the sheet. A Prisoner Freed. Geoffrey Dutton. BoAV

Linked, than Death himself/With everything else.... Two Garden Scenes. Charles Burgess. NePoAm-2

The links are chance, the chain is fate. Mathematics of Love. Michael Hamburger. NePoEA-2

Linten, lowrin, lowrin, lowrin,/The barnyards of Delgaty. Barnyards of Delgaty. Anonymous. FSW

The lion and the serpent and the man/Watched her the while with each his own desire.   Black Marble.   Arthur William Edgar O'Shaughnessy.   SyP

The Lion and the Sovereign Leech also.   King Arthur's Dream.   *Anonymous.*   ACP

Lion! Eagle! Serpent!...Eve!   Lord of Eden.   Marie de L. Welch.   AnAmPo

Lion-hunger, tiger-leap.   The Way of Cape Race.   Edwin John Pratt.   CoBE; EtS; WHW

Lion,/Lamb–/hang on to my soul.   Not to March.   Kris Hackleman.   AMV-80

The lion of our Motherland!   Lexington.   John Greenleaf Whittier.   MC; PAH

Lioness/with cub.   Julia.   Wendy Rose.   STE; TWSS

Lions as symbol of sovereignty.   Leonardo Da Vinci's.   Marianne Moore.   NYBP

LIONS IN LOVE/FOREVER   LOVE TIGHT.   Ted Joans.   CNA

Lions stalk–/But–I walk!   Jump or Jiggle.   Evelyn Beyer.   SoPo; TiPo

Lions terrify most men/Who buy meat at the butcher's.   A Bestiary.   Kenneth Rexroth.   OBAL

Lions to be golden must be painted gold.   Venice.   Howard Moss.   MoAB

Lip and eye are bale and bliss.   Beauty's Queen.   Kisa'i of Merv.   LiTW

...Lip-serve the Cross, and keep/The working-classes carrying it.   After Two Thousand Years.   Hugh'' (Christopher Murray Grieve) MacDiarmid.   DBV

The lips are made to taste with/but the body is firmly held.   Reply to a Marriage Proposal.   Irihapeti Rangi te Apakura.   PBWP

Lips, breasts–led me to rooms/Where trumpets play all night.   Penny Trumpet.   Raphael Rudnik.   MAT; NYBP

The lips have curled up. The bright eye shines.   Lines I Told Myself I Wouldn't Write.   Paul Mariani.   MAYP

Lips his swords are,/The field his arms.   Song: "O come, soft rest of cares! come, Night!"   George Chapman.   ViBoPo

The lips of that Evangelist.   In Memoriam A.H.H., XXXI.   Alfred, Lord Tennyson.   VLP

Lips pressed against my heart.   Evening Song.   Jean Toomer.   BPo; CDC

The lips that falsely kissed, shall kiss but Death.   The Betrayal.   Alice Furlong.   AnIV

Lips unseen–and kissed me there.   Mistletoe.   Walter De la Mare.   SO

The lipstick stain/I could not wipe away/tells me and tells/joy of the marble/ is in the waiting.   Misdemeanor.   Eve Triem.   GP

Liquid as butterflies, with nothing to do.   The Second Dream.   Jean Valentine.   LCAP

A liquid hand.   Lapis.   Shawn Wong.   BrSi

List "a la vie," Tamia.   From the Beaumont Series.   Dick Gallup.   ANYP

List'ning with eager ears that understand.   The Poet.   Angela Morgan.   TrPWD

A list of doors that Truth had left unlatched.   Morning.   Patrick Kavanagh.   GLGT

List to a Tale of Love in Acadie, home of the happy.   Evangeline.   Henry Wadsworth Longfellow.   GoTF; TreF

Listen a moment–! Sh! Listen–!/that hurrying as of a shore of/fugitives!   At War.   Russell Atkins.   AmNP

Listen and save.   A Masque Presented at Ludlow Castle (Comus).   John Milton.   ViBoPo

Listen awhile ye nations, and be dumb.   Addressed to Haydon.   John Keats.   CBEP; EnRP

Listen, dear lady! You shall hear the last/Of the strange prayers Humanity has wailed.   Prayer to the Virgin of Chartres.   Henry Adams.   AmePo

Listen for that old command/dreaming of authority.   The Negatives.   Philip Levine.   NePoEA-2

Listen! I'll drink to that.   Raftery's Dialogue with the Whiskey.   Padraic Fallon.   DTC

Listen; it has a faint voice even so.   What Rider Spurs Him from the Darkening East?   Edna St. Vincent Millay.   TrCP

Listen! my web is what you hear.   Spider.   Norma Farber.   PCh

(Listen o how clever it thinks it is outside our windows coming down/the street again...   Fate in Incognito.   Michael Benedikt.   OBAL

Listen on to the world's tiny flutters and yelps.   Rain Falls. It Dries...   Miklos Radnoti.   AMV-81

Listen! that murmur is of angel's wings.   In Tesla's Laboratory.   Robert Underwood Johnson.   AA

Listen! That song that shakes my feathers/Will thong the leather of your satchels.   The Blackbird of Derrycairn.   *Anonymous.*   BIrV

Listen! The dust is humming a song to the men.   Return to Ritual.   Mark Van Doren.   MoVE

Listen: the river, like riders, approaches from nowhere.   To Her Dead Mate: Montana, 1966.   Elizabeth Libbey.   AmPA

"Listen!" the wind/Said to the children, and they fell asleep.   My Father in the Night Commanding No.   Louis Simpson.   CoAP; ConAP; HeIP; LCAP; MP; NePoEA-2; NoAm; NOBA; NYBP; SM; TAP; TwCP; VGW

Listen./The words/sure as a scream.   Poem.   Robin Blaser.   NeAP

Listen. There is another voice that speaks.   The Green Lake.   Michael Roberts.   ChMP

–Listen:there's a hell/of a good universe next door;let's go.   Pity this busy monster, manunkind.   Edward Estlin Cummings.   AmP; AmPP; AP; CoBMV; CrMA; LiTA; LiTM; MoVE; NePA; NOBA; OxBA; PPP; TAP

Listen/To John.   Sopranosound, Memory of John.   Sharon Bourke.   CNA

Listen to the mocking bird,/Still singing where the weeping willows wave.   Listen to the Mocking Bird.   Alice Hawthorne.   BLSo; FSW; PSoN; TrAS; TreFT

Listen to the pen of the Commissioner/As it goes "hihi', scratch, scratch.   We Object.   *Anonymous.*   WTO

Listen to the roar of your liberation...   On Death (excerpt).   Anghelos Sikelianos.   LiTW

Listen to the shamans roam through stars.   On Hearing the Marsh Bird's Water Cry.   Duane Niatum.   CDW

Listen. You can hear the river rising.   Widow to Her Son.   R. T. Smith.   Str

Listening for a human voice/our names.   Silences: A Dream of Governments.   Jean Valentine.   LCAP

...Listening for listeners.   Maxims of a Park Vagrant.   Nicholas Swift.   AMV-80

...Listening hard for voices/to come out of them. And they do.   Poetry.   Greg Kuzma.   PoA

Listening to a child crying in the night/On a chance, the remote chance,/It will hush.   Unintelligible Terms.   Charles Simic.   NoP

...Listening to a/woman breathing, just an ordinary/woman/breathing.   The Death of Marilyn Monroe.   Sharon Olds.   MAYP

Listening to Aunt Sue's stories.   Aunt Sue's Stories.   Langston Hughes.   DuDa

Listening to God/make the barley grow around his house.   To Trust.   Antonia Pozzi.   PBWP

...Listening/to the hum of the world's wood.   The Novices.   Denise Levertov.   NaP

Listening to the neighbours/Offering her more money.   Contemporary Nursery Rhyme.   *Anonymous.*   PV; SpRo

Listening to the strange melody of poised lilies.   Trees, Who Are Distant.   Bertram Warr.   CaP

Listening to the thin vowel sounds of the lighthouse foghorn.   A Day in France.   David Holbrook.   OBTV

Listening to your white hair wailing for the sea's dark sake.   For Her on the First Day Out.   Robert Bagg.   NePoAm-2

Listens to/the/heart.   The Mechanic.   Diane Wakoski.   AmPA

Listens well pleas'd.   Italian Music in Dakota.   Walt Whitman.   AmePo; AmP

Lit by a lonely wing, gliding small as snowflake and as silently.   In a Valley of This Restless Mind.   Ewart Milne.   NeIP

Lit by no skill of mine.   Milton's Prayer for Patience.   Elizabeth Lloyd Howell.   TRV; WGRP

Lit by the heart's exploding sun/Bursting from night to night.   The Edge of Day.   Laurie Lee.   NYBP

Lit by the sky's unfailing grace.   A Wish.   Hamlin Garland.   AA

Lit'le David play on yo' harp, halleluja.   Lit'le David Play on Yo' Harp.   *Anonymous.*   BoAN 1-2

Lit up the night of Jerusalem and the smoke of nonexistence.   Like a Young Levite.   Osip Mandelstam.   VWA

A litany of thanks to you/For flowers they know.   Thanksgiving.   Louise Driscoll.   YeAr

The litany that climbs and grows/upon the lattice of the Rose.   Lines for a Feast of Our Lady.   Sister Maris Stella.   ISi

Litel therof he shal distraine.   Snatches: "What shul these clothes thus manifold."   *Anonymous.*   OxBM

The literati will raise the cry:/Ewart's a genius!   2001: The Tennyson/Hardy Poem.   Gavin Ewart.   FaBoCo

Literature will make the ultimate touchdown.   Settling Some Old Football Scores.   Morris Bishop.   LiSp; SD

Lithe poppies ran like torchmen with the wheat.   Poppies on the Wheat.   Helen Hunt Jackson.   BPAW

A little crumpled, but lovely still.   Autumn Leaves.   Janie Screven Heyward.   HBMV

...Litter of day/Is gone from sight.   Twilight.   D. H. Lawrence.   OBMV

The litter of pop rhetoric blows down Terry Street,/Bounces past their feet, into their lives.   The Clothes Pit.   Douglas Dunn.   OxBTC

A litter of tiny Suilvens, each one/the dead spit of his father.   Above in Inverkirkaig.   Norman MacCaig.   PoSH

Litterbox.   Concrete poem: Concrete Cat.   Dorthi Charles.   InPK

Littering the waters with the chips/Of whale-boats and vainglorious ships.   The Cachalot.   Edwin John Pratt.   OBCV

Little Annie Rooney is my sweetheart!   Little Annie Rooney.   Michael Nolan.   FSN; GoTF; TreF

Little ash ascensions/of the Word.   Old Bibles.   Marilyn Waniek.   MAYP

Little avails that coinage to the old!   Modern Love, IV.   George Meredith.   OAEP; VLP

Little baby dear, good-night.   Good-Night.   Jane Taylor.   HBV 1-2; HBVY

...A little bird/May cause a lot of trouble by/Repeating what he's heard.   A Hint to the Wise.   Pringle Barret.   HBVY

Little bitty boy/Derby on/Wooooo-ooooo.....   Smokestack Lightnin'. Howlin' Wolf.   BluL

Little blood-brother of the Crucified.   The Mantle of Mary.   Patrick O'Connor.   ISi

The little blue flower everywhere.   Exile.   Ellen Bryant Voigt.   MAYP

A little blush-rose wet with dew.   Envoy.   Sarah Piatt.   AA

The little boat at anchor/in black water sat murmuring/to the tall black sky. Fourth of July Night.   Carl Sandburg.   OFD

Little boy blue/Blows a blue tune/On a wicked afternoon.   Abracadabra. Dorothy Livesay.   WHW

A little boy came along/Put it in his pocket,/Pocket, pocket.   Itiskit, Itaskit. Anonymous.   TrAS

The little boy I used to kiss is dead.   Tired Mothers.   May Riley Smith. HBV 1-2

The little boy would get to see, in time.   Cages.   Marvin Solomon.   NYBP

Little brown baby of mine, go to sleep.   Lullaby of the Iroquois.   [(Emily)] Pauline Johnson.   ACV

Little brown baby wif spa'klin'eyes!   Little Brown Baby.   Paul Laurence Dunbar.   BANP; NoP; PoNe

Little brown brother, good-bye.   Baby Seed Song.   Edith Nesbit.   HBV 1-2; HBVY

"A little brown-eyed fawn was born today!"   In Cool, Green Haunts. Mahlon Leonard Fisher.   WeW

The little bud was a whole bouquet.   A Scandal Among the Flowers. Charles S. Taylor.   BLPA

Little buried one!/Aa mihoya!   Hopi Lament.   Charles Beghtol.   BPAW

Little child.   Song.   Alfred Noyes.   CH

The little Child Jesus/Is come to be our King!   A Carol.   Frederic Edward Weatherly.   YeAr

A little child she bore us/E'en in the deepest night.   A Lovely Rose Is Sprung.   Anonymous.   AWP

Little Christ Jesus/Our Brother is born.   Now Every Child.   Eleanor Farjeon.   BiCB; SUS

A little coat of straw.   The Monkey's Raincoat.   Basho (Matsuo Basho). SoPo

Little creatures, everywhere!   Little Things.   James Stephens.   AnEnPo; MoBrPo; SiSoSe

Little crooked-legs, gwenxe, gwenxe!   Teasing Song.   Princess Magogo. WTO

Little David, play on yo' harp, Hallelu!   Little David.   Anonymous.   FSW; GoSl; TrAS

The little dog-angel's eager bark/Will comfort his soul in the shivering dark. A Little Dog-Angel.   Norah M. Holland.   PoLf

Little dreaming their souls they would lose.   Limerick: "A camel, with practical views."   Oliver Herford.   TDH

...Little else to do/But gaze and gaze on a splendid view.   Robben Island. Robert Dederick.   PeSA

Little face, quite as usual, in its place on my/wrist.   The Watch.   May Swenson.   HAP

Little faded grass-tufts, root and stalk.   The Stranger's Grave.   Emily Lawless.   OnYI

A little faith: the swimmers here don't know/where the next breath is coming from   Memorandum / The Accountant's Notebook.   Kathleen Norris. OBAL

Little faith were the angels keeping/All the years.   In the Carpenter's Shop. Sara Teasdale.   HBMV

A little fellow follows me.   The Little Chap Who Follows Me.   Anonymous. PoToHe

The little finger on the right.   One, Two, Three, Four, Five.   Anonymous. OxNR

A little folding of the hands to sleep.   The End.   Wallace Rice.   AA

A little further than I had thought/To go, a stream with a singing sound. Poetry is Death Cast Out.   Sydney Clouts.   PeSA

Little girl skipping the owl's hushed way.   Ballad.   Charles Simic.   LCAP

The little grasses/Crack through stone, and they are green with life.   Three Women.   Sylvia Plath.   NAs

A little grave that has no name.   Soliloquy.   Francis Ledwidge.   EnLit; HoPM

A little group above the foreign wood.   The Byrnies.   Thom Gunn. NePoEA-2; NoAm; OxBTC

...Little/has been said/of our coming through and leaving by them.   The Door.   Charles Tomlinson.   PoA

Little head and no eyes.   Riddle: "Long legs, crooked thighs."   Anonymous. GBP; HBV 1-2; HBVY; OxNR

A little here is best: because much more/Of poetry, perhaps, would make you poor.   To My Nephew, J.B.   Clement Barksdale.   OBSP

Little hoppy cottontails,/come and see tonight.   The Outdoor Christmas Tree. Aileen Fisher.   SiSoSe

...Little I care/To live myself, my dear,/Lone-labouring here!   Looking at a Picture on an Anniversary.   Thomas Hardy.   EyDe

A little is the sum of all.   Deservings.   Anonymous   HBV 1-2

Little Jack-a-Dandy.   Thumb He.   Anonymous.   OxNR

The little Jesus supped with me.   Bible Stories.   Lizette Woodworth Reese. BrR

Little Jewish poem/come sing to me.   What Is a Jewish Poem?   Myra Sklarew.   VWA

Little Johnny wants to play.   Rain, Rain, Go Away.   Mother Goose.   TiPo

Little Katy bit his head off.   Little Katy.   Anonymous.   ShM

A little kindness for insects, a little pity for the dead.   Baja.   Gerald Stern. SV

The little labourer at his task/Is worthy of his hire.   Praise.   Christopher Smart.   OxBChV

Little Lamb, God bless thee!   The Lamb.   William Blake.   BLPL; BoLiVe; CAW; DiPo; EaLo; EBCP; EnPE; ExPo; FaBoBe; FaBoCh; GoJo; GoTF; HBV 1-2; HeIP; InPS; LiTB; LoBV; LoGBV; NAWM 1-2; NIP; NoP; OAEL 1-2; OBEC; OxBChV; OxBoCh; PAI; PoPl; SBVL; SeCeV; SoSe; SUS; TEP; TrCP; TreF; TrGrPo; TRV; UnPo; WGRP; WHA

The little lark knows all her loveliness.   Over Saleve.   George Herbert Clarke.   CaP

The little lass who blushed to see!   Riding Down.   Nora Perry.   HBV 1-2

A little less a little more/add here detract there/.lonely.   Poem for Some Black Women.   Carolyn M. Rodgers.   BlSi

"Little lion in the corner,/Mama, isn't gettin' any!"   Misplaced Sympathy. Charles Follen Adams.   OBAL

Little long necks stretching to the sun.   Neighbor.   Charles Waterman.   GP

Little voice, my love, come to me.   Mendacity.   Alfred Edgar Coppard. LiTL; OBMV

A little lovely dream.   Cradle Song.   Sarojini Naidu.   BrR

Little master, this is why/In the pleasant fields I lie.'   The Sheep.   Ann and Jane Taylor.   OxBChV

Little matters though the door/Be a workhouse grave.   Little Willie.   Gerald Massey.   PaPo

Little men lack/the consolation of history.   The Visit.   William J. Rewak. AMV-80

The little moon my cargo is.   A Caravan from China Comes.   Richard Le Gallienne.   BrR

Little one! Oh, little one!/I am searching everywhere.   The Snare.   James Stephens.   CH; CMoP; HBMV; OxBI; TiPo

Little palm, white neck, bright eye,/I shall not die for you.   I Shall Not Die for Thee.   Douglas Hyde.   OxBI

Little papoose, we die!   Little Papoose.   Arthur Chapman.   BPAW

The little path, forgotten,/Winds on in beauty still.   The Path of the Padres. Edith D. Osborne.   AmFN

A little pig on a string/Cost him five shilling.   Little Jack Dandy-Prat. Anonymous.   OxNR

The little Plumpuppets plump-up it!   The Plumpuppets.   Christopher Morley.   TiPo

The little red ribbon, the ring and the rose!   The Little Red Ribbon.   James Whitcomb Riley.   HBV 1-2

The little road that has led/Thousands to sleep.   Will You Be as Hard? Augusta Gregory, Lady Gregory.   OBMV

The little rooster went cock-a-doodle doo,/Dee doodle-dee, doodle-dee, doodle-dee doo.   I Had a Rooster.   Anonymous.   FSW

The little silver crucifix/That keeps a man from harm.   The Ballad of Fisher's Boardinghouse.   Rudyard Kipling.   PoRA

A little sound it utters, and its cries are faintly heard.   Jerusalem.   William Blake.   OBRV

A little south the sunset in the Islands of the Blest.   A Ballad of John Silver. John Masefield.   EvOK

The little star-crossed boy at play/A continent of years away.   Fern House at Kew.   Paul Dehn.   ChMP

A little swank/And glide.   Some Scribbles for a Lumpfish.   Thomas Johnson.   AMV-80

Little tables around the world.   Nations.   Michael Brownstein.   ANYP

Little tea and sugar-bag/Lookin' nice and plump.   The Shearer's Song. Anonymous.   PoAu 1-2

Little they wis that the barefoot lass/Is the only millionaire.   A Song of Riches.   Katharine Lee Bates.   AA

A Little thing, this church? Remove its roots/Ossa upon Pelion would not fill the pit.   The Church.   Edwin Ford Piper.   WGRP

The little things creep out to patch themselves hovels/in the marred shadow/ Of your gift.   To S.A.   T. E. Lawrence.   PeHV

Little thou'lt love, or not at all.   Not to Love.   Robert Herrick.   CaPo; OAEP

A little thumb of flame.   Curses.   Joseph Duemer.   AMV-80

The little toil of love, I thought,/Was large enough for me.   The Little Toil of Love.   Emily Dickinson.   LiTL

Little Tom Tinker's dog,/Bow, wow, wow.   Tom Tinker's Dog.   Anonymous. OxNR

Little Tommy Nowadays, canny little man,/Buys some plastic roses as a present for his mam.   Little Tommy Yesterday.   Alex Glasgow.   OBET

Little Tommy Tinker's dog./Bow, wow, wow! Bow, Wow, Wow! Mother Goose. TiPo

A little touch of Harry in the night. King Henry V. William Shakespeare. FaBoRV

Little Treasure,/Little Boy. Mary's Lullaby. Ivy O. Eastwick. ChBR

The little trees die. Piney Woods. Malcolm Cowley. NYBP

Little wanderer, hie thee home.' A Dream. William Blake. CBEP; CH; PoPle

A little wastefulness to end the day. To Whom It May Concern. J. V. Cunningham. FYAP

A little water singing as little waters do. Singing Water. Rudolph Chambers Lehmann. HBMV

Little Wee-wee-wee. Tommy Tibule. Anonymous. OxNR

A little while/And thou shalt sail back heavenwards. Woe is me! The Falcon. Wilfrid Scawen Blunt. ACP

A little while I still would linger here. A Little While I Fain Would Linger Yet. Paul Hamilton Hayne. AA; HBV 1-2

A little while weep on,/Only a little while. The Summer Is Ended. Christina Georgina Rossetti. HBV 1-2

The little white cat, snowy white/That was drowned in a trench. The Little White Cat. Anonymous. OnYI

Little White Lily is happy again. Little White Lily. George Macdonald. HBV 1-2; HBVY

Little white moon, look down, look down. Canoe Song at Twilight. Laura E. McCully. CaP

The little white-skinned stranger who is in Geography! Geography. Eleanor Farjeon. BrR

Little wild baby, lie still! Lie still and sleep.) Little Wild Baby. Margaret Thomson Janvier. AA; HBV 1-2

Little wind, blow off the rain. Little Wind. Kate Greenaway. GoJo; SUS

Little winged Dandelion/Soareth away. Little Dandelion. Helen Barron Bostwick. HBV 1-2; HBVY

Little wonder the eye, healing, sees/for a long time through a mist of blood. The Knot. Adrienne Rich. CAPP

Little wotteth the Gosling/What the Goose thinketh. When the Rain Raineth. Anonymous. GBP

Littleman, he can dance alone. Finger Dance. Anonymous. OxNR

Live and learn, Jubilee. Jubilee. Anonymous. FSW

The live bread for the starved folk. Bread. R.S. Thomas. BoC

Live but to light your passing feet. He Gives His Beloved Certain Rhymes. William Butler Yeats. EG

...Live, dangerous/Gray bark of the street. The Street. Robert Pinsky. MAYP

Live day by day. Day by Day. Julia Harris May. BLRP

Live for Him, with Him you reign–/Pass it on. Pass It On. Henry K. Burton. BLRP

Live greatly; so shalt thou acquire/Unknown capacities of joy. The Angel in the House. Coventry Patmore. VLP

Live happily, and in your marital duty/Employ your vigorous youth. Hymn to Marriage, for Manlius and Junia. Caius Valerius Catullus. HW

Live in a happy anonymous town, your lawn,/green, your hair, a bit grey. Song for Healing. Roberta Hill. CDW

Live in a house/At the edge of a wood. Old Log House. James S. Tippett. BrR

Live in her page, and stink to after-times. The Author. Charles Churchill. OBSV

Live in the love of doves, and, having told/The raven's years, go hence more ripe than old. Connubii Flores, or the Well-Wishes at Weddings. Robert Herrick. HW

Live, lads, and I will die. A Shropshire Lad. Alfred Edward Housman. SpRo

Live large, man, and dream small. Lore. R. S. Thomas. OxBC

Live like wild Arab in a tent,/Before Bob Sowden's house you rent! I Want a Tenant: A Satire. John O'Keefe. NOEC

Live oak and madrone. The Truth Like the Belly of a Woman Turning. Gary Snyder. NNaP

Live on elevations/gravity can't reach. Mountains and Other Outdoor Things. Ruth Good. PoDr

Live/on the edge,/looking. Here. Robert Creeley. NOBA

...Live/Part invalid, part baby, and part saint? Waiting for Breakfast, While She Brushed Her Hair. Philip Larkin. NoAm

Live, pluck the roses of the world to-day. Four Sonnets to Helen, 4. Pierre de Ronsard. LiTW

Live says the Law–I sit here doing my best,/Relishing meat, listening to music. The Wandering Jew. Robert Mezey. NePoEA-2; VWA

Live somewhere yonder in the starlit/sphere? The Soul in the Body. Edith Matilda Thomas. AA

Live there at least, when any are at home. First Travels of Max. John Crowe Ransom. MoAmPo

Live things. Self-Portrait with Hand Microscope. Lucille Day. SUW

Live thou a Selden, that's a Demi-god. To the Most Learned, Wise, and Arch-Antiquary, M. John Selden. Robert Herrick. SeCV 1-2

Live truly, and thy life shall be/A great and noble creed. Be True. Horatius Bonar. FaBoBe; GN; HBV 1-2; TRV

Live without sex, and die without a name. The Rosciad. Charles Churchill. NOEC

Lived for a hour–then for all time were dead. Resurrection. Lady Margaret Sackville. HBMV

Lived in the world, that to the world now die. An Epitaph. Thomas Heywood. OBSP

Livelier than elsewhere, Stella's image see. Astrophel and Stella, XXXIX. Sir Philip Sidney. AAS; GoTF; HBV 1-2; NIP; OAEP; OBSC; SCV; SiPS; TEP; TreFS; TrGrPo; ViBoPo

Lives dimly on alone. Ninety. Mary Elizabeth ("E") Fullerton. CBAP

Lives in eternity's sun rise. Eternity. William Blake. AnFE; AWP; DiPo; FaBoEE; HW; InPo; LAuP; LoBV; NOBE; NoP; OBNC; OBSP; TrGrPo

The lives' long war, lost war–the pilot sleeps. The Dead Wingman. Randall Jarrell. MiAP

...Lives/must know the meaning of If. Thanksgiving for a Habitat. W. H. Auden. EyDe

Lives not, aged though he be,/Half a span, compared with thee. The Cricket. Vincent Bourne. HBVY; PoLf

Lives of all that ever breathed most worthy the envying. First Love. Thomas Campion. OxBoLi

The lives of our dear friends to take. The Brooklyn Theater Fire. Anonymous. AmFP

Living and dying, thou art near. O Love Divine, That Stooped to Share. Oliver Wendell Holmes. AH

...The living/awakened at last like the dead. Awakening. Robert Bly. ConAP; NaP

The living come back slowly from the dead. Dawn on the East Coast. Alun Lewis. OBWP

Living for a hating,/Dying of a love? The Dark Girl's Rhyme. Dorothy Parker. InMe

The living have so much to do. On Looking at a Copy of Alice Meynell's Poems. Amy Lowell. SBG

The living jewels of the spring! The Pageant. John Greenleaf Whittier. AmLP

A living Nyorai. Haiku: "The young bride's present." Anonymous. HW

Living relations, evidently Trine. On Trinity Sunday. John Byrom. PeD

Living, remembering, to eternity. To Ausonius. Paulinus of Nola. PeHV

The living seem more shadowy than they. The New Faces. William Butler Yeats. GTBS-P; MoVE

Living simply day by day. Day by Day. A. G. Fisher. STF

The living succeed, and the dead remain dead. Sunday Review Section. Baron Wormser. MAYP

Living things are lovely things,/And lovely things must die. Golden Falcon. Robert P. Tristram Coffin. CAW

The living things/that are going out of my life Things Going out of My Life. Robert Adamson. CBAP

A living tribute to that love–/A faithful memory. Love's Tribute. Lorena W. Sturgeon. PGD

Living with my brother and my sister-in-law. The Orphan. Anonymous. PoA

The living wound of love. Seasons of the Soul. Allen Tate. NePA; OxBA

Living, you break my heart, so would you dead! Tell Me Some Way. Lizette Woodworth Reese. PG

The lizard's tongue licks angrily/The shattered membranes of the fly. The Range in the Desert. Randall Jarrell. NOBA

A lizard sleeps in the sun. Abandoned Copper Refinery. Dan Gillespie. TAT

Lizards will want their parasols/To shade them from the sun. When Fishes Set Umbrellas Up. Christina Georgina Rossetti. FM

Lo, a new people rises from the sea. Public Beach (Long Island Sound). Christopher Morley. NLV

Lo! all is for the best for all! Rejoice. Joaquin Miller. PAH

Lo, all things can be borne! Endurance. Elizabeth Akers Allen. PoToHe

Lo! brightsome fruits to feed a mighty folk. The Old Santa Fe Trail. Richard Burton. BPAW; PAH

Lo! Every soul is Calvary,/And every sin a Rood. The Question. Rachel Annand Taylor. HBV 1-2

Lo, God shall strengthen all the feeble knees. Easter Communion. Gerard Manley Hopkins. BrPo; OFD

Lo, he is a twin brother of mine. For Those Who Fail. Joaquin Miller. PoToHe

Lo, her choice crown–its flowers are also/stone. To Guerdon. John James Piatt. AA

Lo! here my hert. See! Here, My Heart. Anonymous. MeEL

Lo, here they lie whom scorn defaced. Strive No More. George Peele. CoBE

Lo, I follow thee. May-Music. Rachel Annand Taylor. HBV 1-2

Lo, I myself then of thy dream/The interpreter will be. Awake, My Fair. Judah Halevi. TrJP

Lo I, somehow,/Am Thou. How Infinite Are Thy Ways. William Force Stead. OBMV

Lo! In due time she returned to the clod./She was missed. A Love Affair. Arnold Bennett. OxBTC

Lo, my Master/Was the Guest that supped with me! The Guest. Harriet McEwen Kimball. AA

Lo!–Nothing but some sarcenet/Deep-buried in a pile of dust. The End of Desire. Hugh McCrae. BoAV

Lo, prince and princess stir in their sleep! Love by the Water-Reeds. *Anonymous.* WTO

Lo, such is hap! Mark well my song! The Lover in Liberty Smileth at Them in Thraldom. *Anonymous.* EiL

Lo, ten times I have recited the/Honorable Name. Mingling My Prayer. Saigyo Hoshi. AWP

"Lo! The Fruit of Favours long Preserved." Epigram: "And now I, Meleager..." Meleager. PeHV

Lo! the shadow of the belfry crossed the sun-illumined/square. The Belfry of Bruges. Henry Wadsworth Longfellow. HBV 1-2

Lo! the Son of God is come! Watchman, Tell us of the Night. John Bowring. TreFS

Lo! the world is born again. A Pair. Karl Gjellerup. PoPl

Lo, there 'tis Death! How piteously he goes,/Wearily swinging. The Foiled Reaper. William Kean Seymour. HBMV

Lo! They were standing by His side! A Judgment in Heaven. Francis Thompson. MoAB; MoBrPo

Lo! this is she with whom are few on earth. A Virgin Declares Her Beauties. Francesco da Barberino. AWP; ErPo

Lo, thou shalt hear it. Song: "Under the Winter, dear." Eugene Lee-Hamilton. OBVV

Lo, what it is to love! Lo, what it is to love! Sir Thomas Wyatt. FCP

Lo! where the toil of a lifetime lies/In a winding-sheet! The Spinner. Mary Ainge De Vere. AA

Lo! while thou sleep'st they haste away! Wake, Lady! Joanna Baillie. HBV 1-2

"Lo! with this lady dwells the counterpart/Of the same Love who holds me weeping now." Mine Eyes Beheld the Blessed Pity. Dante Alighieri. LiTW

"Lo! you can kill me/but you'll never rule this land!" The Birth of Shaka. Mbuyiseni Oswald Mtshali. WhB

Load again, rifleman, keep our hand in! Civil War. Charles Dawson Shanly. HBV 1-2; PAH

A load of wine will lighten your despair. Enjoyment. Theognis. AWP

The loaded dice were thrown for me/Upon the night that I was born. The Dice Were Loaded. Mary Gilmore. BoAV

A loaf of new bread Rainpoem. Michael Dransfield. CBAP

Loathing each other's carrion company. The Glutton. Robert Graves. CMoP; TW

The locomotives stood against the prairie sky. A Siding Near Chillicothe. Richmond Lattimore. AmFN

Loccoli. Against Broccoli. Roy, Jr. Blount. NLV; OBAL

A lock full of rust on the door. Abandoned House in Late Light. Chase Twichell. MAYP

Lock the trap-windows, and patiently wait/Till the wee Darling grows wise. Sweeping the Skies. Elizabeth Anna Hart. CenHV

Locked in God's dream, wistful as man. New York City. George Abbe. GoYe

Locked into rooms, alone. Triolet against Sisters. Phyllis McGinley. OBCA

Locked up in mother's chamber. The Yankee's Return from Camp. Edward Bangs. MC; PAH

Lodged in the crinkles/of the human cerebrum. Warty Bliggins, the Toad. Don (Donald Robert Marquis) Marquis. FiBHP

Lodged in the vague vast valley the village sleeps. Hunters in the Snow: Brueghel. Joseph Langland. LiTM; NePoEA

The loftiest star of unascended heaven,/Pinnacled dim in the intense inane. Prometheus Unbound. Percy Bysshe Shelley. ChRP; FiP

Lofty poet! touch the sky! Ode to Quinbus Flestrin. Alexander Pope. OAEP

Logic is logic. That's all I say. The Deacon's Masterpiece Or, The Wonderful "One-Hoss Shay." Oliver Wendell Holmes. AnNE; AP; BeLS; FaBoBe; FaFP; FaPo; FPL; GoTF; HBV 1-2; InMe; LiTA; LoGBV; MCCG; MoShBr; NePA; NOBA; OBAL; OBCA; OHFP; OxBA; PaPo; PoLf; PoRA; StPo; TAP; TreF; WBLP; YaD

The logic of hatred. The Stone Orchard. Joyce Carol Oates. GeTw

The logic of the poem is not ours. The Poem. Babette Deutsch. PoA

Loin packed with moist, golden coin. Nude Kneeling in Sand. John Logan. ErPo

Loky moky poky stoky/Smoky choky chee! The Baby Goes to Boston. Laura E. Richards. TiPo

Lolly trudom, trudom, trudom, a lolly day. Lolly Trudom. *Anonymous.* BFSS

London burnt like rotten sticks. Four Dates. *Anonymous.* OxNR

London is a milder curse. Slaves to London. Peter Anthony Motteux. OAEP

London, thou art the flour of Cities all. To the City of London. William Dunbar. EBEV; FaBoPP

A lone, a steadfast eye/Silently looks in. The Reminder. Léonie Adams. MoVE

The lone and level sands stretch far away. Ozymandias. Percy Bysshe Shelley. AWP; BeLS; BiP; DiPo; DL; ERoP 1-2; ExPo; FaBoBe; FaBoCh; FaBoRV; FaFP; FaPo; FaPoR; FF; FiP; ForPo; FPL; GoTF; GTBS; GTBS-P; HAP; HBV 1-2; HBVY; HeIP; HoPM; InPK; InPo; InPS; LoBV; LoGBV; MBW 1-2; MCCG; MyFE; NIP; NOBE; NoP; OAEL 1-2; OAEP; OBNC; PoLf; PoPle; PoRA; PrIm; RoGo; SCV; SeCeV; SoSe; SpRo; SyP; TEP; TreF; TrGrPo; WeW; WHA

Lone as the blessed Jew. Shakespeare. Ralph Waldo Emerson. AnNE

A lone dog barks. A child cries. All of winter night. Last Look at La Plata, Missouri. Jim Barnes. CDW

Lone man! Lone man!/Dead broke! Ten Thousand God-Damn Cattle. *Anonymous.* CoSo

A lone voice whispers, "Blasphemy!"/The Lord. But Him they fail to hear. The Unbidden Wedding Guest. Kurt Marti. HW

The loneliness that I was drowning in. Dreamscape in Kummel. Harold Witt. NYBP

Loneliness, wings for my flight! Measure Me, Sky. Leonora Speyer. BiCB; HBMV; PG

Lonely and sweet longing/On her burning bank of sand. Song: "There stands a lonely pine-tree." Heinrich Heine. TrJP

A lonely darkness winds about/My soul like death, and shuts you out. Isolation. Arthur Symons. OBSP

The lonely-flowing waters, the secret-/Keeping stones, the flowing sky. Life from the Lifeless. Robinson Jeffers. CMoP

Lonely like a spectre's love,/Earth beneath, and stars above. Alpine Spirit's Song. Thomas Lovell Beddoes. OBNC; OBTV

Lonely, like crying. To-ta Ti-om. Peter Blue Cloud. STE

The lonely of heart is withered away! Fairy Song. William Butler Yeats. MoBrPo; OnYI

A lonely pool, and let a tree/Sigh with her bosom over me. The Kingfisher. William Henry Davies. MoVE; NOBE; OBEV

A lonely pseudopodium I wandered on my course. Ere You Were Queen of Sheba. Sir Arthur Shipley. FaBoCo

A lonely shell in place/Of that unrivalled grace. He Praises His Wife When She Had Gone from Him. Robin Flower. OxBI

Lonely, sleepless and dumb. Night-Piece. Raymond Richard Patterson. CAD; PoBA; WSC

...Lonesome man, wanted the trains/to speak for him. Seems Like We Must Be Somewhere Else. Denise Levertov. NePoEA-2

Long after me, is the wind. Councils. Marge Piercy. NeAC

Long after Nabara's passion was quenched in the sea's/heart. The Nabara. C. Day Lewis. HaMV; OBNV

Long after the ride/has ended. Emergency Poem 1973. Cyn Zarco. APU

Long after this and many another dream. A Dream in Early Spring. Fredegond Shove. MoVE

Long ago! In the Twilight. James Russell Lowell AA; HBV 1-2

Long ago, I moved my couch to face the mountain. For Hidden Mist Pavilion. Yu Hsuan-chi. BoWoP

Long ago..in a dream...O never again! The Enchanted Heart. Edward Davison. HBMV

Long ago, riding a crude wave in. Tahola. Richard Hugo. WOLT

Long ago the waves/were saltier/and the People strong. Eye of God. Jim Tollerud. VoR

Long ago there were white-trembling blossoms/upon the boughs where full fruit hangs now. Under the Boughs. Gene Baro. BoNaP

Long ago was buried here–/Long ago, with you! In the Fall o' Year. Thomas S. Jones, Jr. HBV 1-2

...The long and lonely learning/How to pray. The Tree of Silence. Vassar Miller. NePoEA-2

The long and lonely winter will be here. The Long and Lonely Winter. Dave Goulder. OBET

Long as the spear of Arnon, twice as long,/What time he hurled it at King Pharaoh's feet. A Classic Ode. Charles Battell Loomis. NA

Long as the stars do gleam upon it,/Shall memory come to dream upon it. Dirge. Thomas William Parsons. GN; HBV 1-2; PAH

Long before the shadow and/sun's accomplice, the tree./Maurice. Dusting. Rita Dove. HaCAP; MAYP

Long dead reminders/That the sea/Can wait. Beach House. Mary Rita Hurley. PoPl

The long, deep shiver. Long-Distance. Carol Burnes. AMV-81

The long-established colony of rooks/Their num'rous, ceaseless, varied cawings blend. The Life of Hubert, I (excerpt). Thomas Cole. NOEC

The long-extended arms/Of the dead, stretched wide. Exile. Audrey Beecham. NeBP

Long forgotten comme tout le monde je les en accuse. J'Accuse. Peter Klappert. AMV-81

Long, frilly/Palaver is silly.   Air: Sentir Avec Ardeur.   Marie Beauveau. CTC; WPOW

Long gone song/for Langston Hughes   Langston Blues.   Dudley Randall. CNA; FB

A long half-hour together I have stood/Mute–looking at the grave in which he lies!   There Was a Boy.   William Wordsworth.   ChRP; FaBoRV; MCCG; MyFE; OBRV; PoEL 1-5

Long in Kensal Green and Highgate silent under soot and stone.   Middlesex. Sir John Betjeman.   OxBTC

Long in the woods I drank remembered bliss.   Two Married.   Helen Frazee-Bower.   HBMV

The long incredible anguish/of questioning childless arms.   We Who Are Left.   George Whalley.   CaP

Long is th' impris'ment of the dead.   The Leaves Come Again.   Thomas Stanley.   FaBoEE

The long Kiang, reaching heaven.   Separation on the River Kiang.   Li Po. SOTW

A long lean lap-eared dog sitting on a roof/Blinks wet eyes at me. Investigator.   Miriam Waddington.   CaP

Long-legged Jim.   Jim.   Bret (Francis Bret Harte) Harte.   AA

Long Life and Success to the Farmer!   The Rewards of Farming. *Anonymous.*   PoPle

"Long life to jobbing; may the days/Of Peculation shine again!"   Tory Pledges.   Thomas Moore.   FaBoCo; OBSV

Long lines, clean and syllabic as knotted bamboo. Yes!   Poetics against the Angel of Death.   Phyllis Webb.   NOBC

Long live fair Oriana.   As Vesta Was from Latmos Hill Descending. *Anonymous.*   OAEP

Long live fair Oriana.   Come, Blessed Bird.   *Anonymous.*   NCEP

Long live great Washington!/Huzza! Huzza!   Old Song Written during Washington's Life.   *Anonymous.*   OHIP

Long live the gay servant that laughs for us all!   Ode for a Social Meeting (With Slight Alterations by a Teetotaler).   Oliver Wendell Holmes. OBAL; OxBoLi

"Long live the Republic,' said Master McGrath.   Master McGrath. *Anonymous.*   OBET

Long live the revolution   Get Stuffed.   Alurista.   FIA

Long live the weeds and the wilderness yet.   Inversnaid.   Gerard Manley Hopkins.   ACP; BLPL; BrPo; CMoP; FaBoMo; FaBoPP; GTBS-P; LiTB; LiTM; LoBV; MoAB; MoBrPo; NoAm; NoP; OAEL 1-2; PoRA; PoSH; UnPo

Long-living worthies, commerce, wealth.   Prince Alfrid's Itinerary (excerpt). *Anonymous.*   BIrV

The long, lone days, O Time, speed on!   In Old Tucson.   Harrison Conrard. BPAW

Long, long ago one hot summer day.   Cornfield Myth.   Mary Goose.   STE

Long, long ago someone had loved./Oh, whom? and who?   A Withered Rose. Yehoash.   TrJP

Long, Long before his Debts are Pay'd.   Poets' Corner.   Robert Graves. FaBoEE

Long, long I heard both voices/blending,/Uncomprehending.   Mystery. Yehoash.   TrJP

Long, long, long are de years!   Big Jim.   *Anonymous.*   ABF

The long, long patience of the plundered poor.   The Third Wonder.   Edwin Markham.   FYAP

A long long sigh to the darling tree.   Wild Cherry Tree.   Edmund Charles Blunden.   BrPo

A long, long time ago/petunias/adorable, sticky flower.   Roof Garden. James Schuyler.   ANYP

A long, long while in the butterbean tent.   The Butterbean Tent.   Elizabeth Madox Roberts.   GoJo; SUS

Long, louder, sweeter, fuller still–/Love to my Lord!   Love to My Lord. Louisa Van Plettenhaus.   BePJ

...The long low croon/Of the steady Trade Winds blowing.   Trade Winds. John Masefield.   FaBoCh; OBMV

Long may I live so, and my wreath of bays/Be less another's laurel than thy praise.   To His Honoured and Most Ingenious Friend, Master Charles Cotton.   Robert Herrick.   CaPo

Long may it stand!   The Church of the Revolution.   Hezekiah Butterworth. PAH

A long metallic cry of dung and dew/And the unearthly dead.   Daybreak. Frances Cornford.   FM

The long pain in my head.   Edwardian Hat.   Betty Parvin.   PoL

The long, perfect loveliness of sow.   Saint Francis and the Sow.   Galway Kinnell.   FYAP

The long ripple in the swamp grass/is a skunk/he shuns the day   Maps. Robert Hass.   NPGG

Long rollers wrinkling the dark bay.   Only Years.   Kenneth Rexroth.   TAP

The long seas of Brazil.   Summer's Early End at Hudson Bay.   Hayden Carruth.   NYBP

Long shall the British rue that march/And Emily Geiger's ride.   Emily Geiger.   *Anonymous.*   BLPL; PAL; PoLf

Long silences/Are of old words and ways/Full valleys.   Full Valleys.   F. R. Scott.   CaP

The long, silvery roar/Of Mal Bay.   Recessional.   Thomas MacGreevy. CIP

Long since forc'd by thy beames, but stone nor tree/By Sences priviledge, can scape from thee.   Astrophel and Stella, XXXVI.   Sir Philip Sidney. AAS; SiPS

Long since,–I know not when.   Oasis.   Edward Dowden.   OxBI

The long streets were still and the snow/swirled where I lay down to rest. Zaydee.   Philip Levine.   NNaP; VWA

Long summer day.   Long Summer Day.   *Anonymous.*   OuSiCo

Long they listen,/Deep in fancies of a fairy bride.   Emilia.   Sarah N. Cleghorn.   HBV 1-2

Long they'll roll it on the tongue–/Cumberland! Cumberland!   The Cumberland.   Herman Melville.   PAH

Long time ago.   Long Time Ago.   *Anonymous.*   ABF; AmSS

A long time yet, because you're strong as a mule.   George.   Dudley Randall. BP; BPo; ConAP; NoAm

Long, too long our seamen's jailors,/Dacre and the Guerriere!   On the Capture of the Guerriere.   Philip Freneau.   PAH

A long, unclouded, glorious day.   The Coracle Fishers.   Robert Bloomfield. OBNC

The long wait for the angel,/For that rare, random descent.   Black Rook in Rainy Weather.   Sylvia Plath.   LiTM; NePoEA-2; NIP; NoP; SM

The long walk back to winter, leagues away.   Holiday.   Adrienne Rich. MoLP

Long way he traveled, before he heard of ought.   The Faerie Queene. Edmund Spenser.   ExPo

A long ways from home.   Sometimes I Feel Like a Motherless Child. *Anonymous.*   BLSo; BoAN 1-2; FSW

The long-winged storm-gulls burning/Seaward when day is done,/Are like thee, young Desire.   Song of Eros.   George Edward Woodberry.   AA; HBV 1-2

The long winter/under foreign stars.   Chorus for Survival (excerpt).   Horace Gregory.   AtBAP

Long years after the once tall trunk is down.   Ravenglass Railway Station, Cumberland.   Norman Nicholson.   NYBP

Longed to see the sun again, so he sailed from Birkenhead.   Liverpool John. *Anonymous.*   OBSS

Longer I could not stay, and so/I fled back to your feet.   A Love Symphony. Arthur William Edgar O'Shaughnessy.   HBV 1-2

The longest life is brevity.   Ad Leuconoen.   Horace.   AWP

The longest of their lives, the men are free.   The Lines.   Randall Jarrell. CrMA

LONGFELLOW!   You're a poet.   *Anonymous.*   FaFP

Longing for each homesick heart/To make a pilgrimage among all men?   The Decision.   Owen Dodson.   PoNe

Longing for freedom on the moor.   The Shepherd's Calendar.   John Clare. OBRV

...Longing/For the red spider who is God.   The Lights in the Hallway. James Wright.   CAPP

Longing for the white/Frozen bough.   Autumn, Crystal Eye.   Margot Ruddock.   OBMV

Longing for women in windows.   Window.   Anne Cherner.   AMV-80

The longing in each breast/Some day to know a home like hers,/Wherein their hearts might rest.   The Dreamers.   Theodosia Garrison.   HBMV

A longing throbs against the planet/On which we must die.   End of the World.   Else Lasker-Schüler.   BoWoP

Longing to clear the hurdles/That ring the Point of Stoer.   Moorings. Norman MacCaig.   OxBTC

The longing world waits for Thee:/Arise, arise and shine!   Thy Kingdom Come.   Saint Bernard of Clairvaux   CAW

Loo-wit sings and sings and sings.   Loo-Wit.   Wendy Rose.   STE

A look, a moan, like that on ocean's/shore.   The Strong.   John Vance Cheney.   AA

Look/among the oppressors for his dad.   While Cecil Snores: Mom Drinks Cold Milk.   James (Olumo) Cunningham.   JB

Look angrily then if you must–but look at me!   Madrigal: "Eyes that are clear, serene."   Gutierre de Cetina.   LiTW

Look at me. Do not speak. But this is love.   Dogma.   Babette Deutsch. MoLP

"Look at me! Look at your mother!"   Extracts: from the Journal of Elisa Lynch.   Maura Stanton.   AmPA

Look at my contained continent.   Human Geography.   Gloria Fuertes. BoWoP

Look at some baseball/On TV.   May.   John Updike.   OBCA

Look at the snow, the girl, look at the day!   The Insomniac Sleeps Well for Once and.   Hayden Carruth.   NNaP

Look at you and wish you ill.   A Shropshire Lad.   Alfred Edward Housman.   BrPo

Look at your light, does it shine out/clear?   Christ in You.   *Anonymous.* STF

"Look at yourself," she said,/"You're disgusting." What She Wanted. Ronald Koertge. GP

Look away, Dixieland, from the smokehouse door. Notes for a Southern Road Map. Phyllis McGinley. NLV

Look away, look away over Yandro. He's Gone away. *Anonymous.* FSW; TrAS

Look away quick; you are watching the birth of song. Some Lines in Three Parts. Peter Viereck. MiAP

Look beyond the stormy skies,/And they see the beacon light. The Face against the Pane. Thomas Bailey Aldrich. TreFS

Look! Billy the Kid comes a-galloping down! When Billy the Kid Rides Again. Squire Omar Barker. BPAW

Look'd up in perfect silence at the stars. When I Heard the Learn'd Astronomer. Walt Whitman. AmePo; BoLiVe; DiPo; FF; FPL; GoTF; HAP; HeIP; InPK; LoGBV; MCCG; MoAmPo; NoP; OxBA; SoSe; SUW; TAP; TreFT; TrGrPo; TRV; WHA

Look down upon Captivity–/And laugh–No more have I– They shut me up in prose. Emily Dickinson. InPS; MAmP; NOBA; PAI; SBG

Look down upon your narrow house,/Old friend, and miss you! A Gentleman of the Old School. Henry Austin Dobson. EnLit; HBV 1-2

Look down upon Your serving-maid/Lord of unmeasured mercies. Sticheron for Matins, Wednesday of Holy Week. Kassia. WPOW

Look down with gracious mien. The Poplars. Theodosia Garrison. HBMV; OHIP

Look for my fist in the burst of your bright leaves. Vittoria Colonna. Roy Marz. PoA

A look half miserably wise,/Half heedlessly ironical. At the Cavour. Arthur Symons. NOBV; OBSP

Look, He is fast asleep! The Sleeping Beauty: Variation of the Prince. Randall Jarrell. DFT; PoA

Look how beautiful are all the things that He does. His signature/Is the beauty of things. Look, How Beautiful. Robinson Jeffers. MoRP

Look how the golden children/Are climbing the silver poplars to the sky! New Leaves. Juan Ramon Jimenez. PoPl

...Look,/if you dare, on your mind's eternal mate. I Am Your Mother, Your Mother's Mother. Jalal ed-Din or al-Din Rumi. OBVE

"Look in my face and see." A Denial. Elizabeth Barrett Browning. GBL; OBNC

Look in my heart, kind friends, and tremble,/Since there your elements assemble. In Me, Past, Present, Future Meet. Siegfried Sassoon. OBEV; OBSP

Look in the fire-light/and a phoenix may come to rest. The Phoenix. Robert Fisher. AmMo

Look in the harness cask and you'll find a horse and shoe! The Sailor's Grace. *Anonymous.* ShS

...Look in your/face and curse you by/pitying your tomish ways. Black People! LeRoi (Imamu Ameer Baraka) Jones. BPo

Look into the pewter pot/To reduce the world as the world's not. The Power of Malt. Alfred Edward Housman. HBV 1-2

Look! It is there! "Not Marble Nor the Gilded Monuments". Archibald MacLeish. AP; BoLoP; CMoP; CoBMV; HoPM; LiTL; MoAB; MP; NIP; PoRA; TwCP; ViBoPo

Look lady just don't/you interfere. Town Ghost. Lauris Edmond. OCNZ

Look like pearls upon a string. The Rains of Spring. Lady Ise. SUS; TiPo

Look like somewhere else today. First Snow. Marie Louise Allen. SoPo

Look! Both those/mice are watching you/from behind the kind bars. The Fury of Hating Eyes. Anne Sexton. TW

Look lovingly, look long, on what there is. The Mask the Wearer of the Mask Wears. William Bronk. GP

Look ma a virgin. Euch, Are You Having Your Period? Alta. NMM

Look, nor would they thank you if you said/you were. The Managers. W. H. Auden. EnLit

The look of April, after this,/When it, too, is hypothesis. Nature Study, after Dufy. Helen Bevington. NYBP

Look on dispassionate–critical–something 'mused. In the Dials. William Ernest Henley. BrPo

Look on her face; mine eyes dazzle; she died young. The Spoils of War. Vernon Watkins. WaP

Look/on me and be/renewed I Am a Black Woman. Mari E. Evans. CNA; NMM

Look on my leafy boughs, the Crown/Of living song and dead renown! Tapestry Trees. William Morris. BoNaP; OHIP

Look on our broken hands, our withered wings,/And pity, Lord, our poor humanity. To God. Furnley Maurice. BoAV

Look onely; for to love thee, who can be,/What angel fit? Dulnesse. George Herbert. AnAnS 1

Look out for the battle that's yet to come/Down there on Morris' Island! The Battle of Morris' Island. *Anonymous.* PAH

Look out how you use proud words. Primer Lesson. Carl Sandburg. MoAmPo; MoShBr; PoPl

Look out the dusty window/and make love to death Cold Feet in Columbus. William Heath. TAT

Look out with those round wondering eyes,/and squirm, and gurgle–and grow wise! The Bacchante to Her Babe. Eunice Tietjens. HBMV

Look out your back door/see me leave this town Slow Mama Slow. Sam Collins. BluL

Look proudly to Heaven from the deathbed of/fame. Lochiel's Warning. Thomas Campbell. EnRP

Look quite cross, and wonder how/They shall have their dinner now. The Story of Fidgety Philip. Heinrich Hoffmann. OxBChV

Look, reader, how we stare at an abyss! Look, in the Labyrinth of Memory. Delmore Schwartz. TrJP

Look sour, and hum a Tune, as you may now. Epistle to Miss Teresa Blount, on Her Leaving the Town... Alexander Pope. EBEV

The look that seemed reproach was only death. Salmon Draught at Inveraray. R. W. Nunley. WOLT

Look! the long road and the sky!.../Merrily! Merrily! The Turn of the Road. Fannie Stearns Gifford. HBMV

"Look," the ocean said (it was tumbled, like our sheets), "look in my/eyes" The Crystal Lithium. James Schuyler. PoM

Look then on me, thus shrouded, as I cry. The Search. John of the Cross. BoC

Look, they say, see how gracefully we are dancing. The Window. Stephen Dobyns. MAYP

Look to heaven, and find it there! Refuge. William Winter. HBV 1-2

Look to thy self/Or not look to thy self,/the self-same thing will be.' As I Walked By My Self. *Anonymous.* OBSP

Look up! and oh how glorious/He has restored the roof! Hymn: "The Church's Restoration. (parody). Sir John Betjeman. FaBoPa

Look up, and swear by the green of the Spring that you'll never forget! Aftermath. Siegfried Sassoon. AnFE; AP; BrPo; MCCG; MoBrPo; TrJP; ViBoPo; WaP

Look up beneath those folded wings,/And find them lined with gold. Azrael. Robert Gilbert Welsh. HBV 1-2

...Look up–It is I! It is I! Morning Star Man. George Keithley. NPGG

Look up now, softly: break it with your eyes. The Turning of the Leaves. Vernon Watkins. NeBP

Look up! See, there he flies! Song for December Thirty-First. Frances Frost. YeAr

"Look what I have!–And these are all for you." Fatal Interview. Edna St. Vincent Millay. VGW

Look, where the gray is white! Roll On, Sad World! Frederick Goddard Tuckerman. AnNE; TreFS

Looke down great Master of the feast; O shine,/And turn once more our Water into Wine! Silex Scintillans. Henry Vaughan. AnAnS 1

Looke on the following leaves, and see him breathe. Upon Bishop Andrewes His Picture before His Sermons. Richard Crashaw. OBS

Looke that you love your old loves best,/For infaith they are best companye.' Christopher White. *Anonymous.* ESPB

Looke well about they are not to stoute,/Or you may have worst of the blowes. Robin Hood and the Pedlars. *Anonymous.* ESPB

Looked at our world; and the dark/Grew dawn. Dawn and Dark. Norman Gale. HBV 1-2

...Looked like its spine would split through skin,/yet didn't in this master's hands. Watching Jim Shoulders. Leo Connellan. TAT

Looked prodigiously/like a tree. Hazlitt Sups. Katharine Day Little. GoYe

Looked up and wished he were the bird/To whom such doubts must seem absurd. The Labyrinth. W. H. Auden. LiTA; NePA

Lookee, lookee, lookee, lookee there now!/Don't you see? The Owl and the Jay Bush. *Anonymous.* BFSS

A-lookin'for a home, a-lookin'for a home. The Boll Weevil Song. *Anonymous.* AS; BLSo

Lookin' for the woman/Lord, that'll love me the best. Long-Line Skinner. *Anonymous.* FSW

Looking at ourselves. Fishing, at Coot Shallows. Don Welch. WOLT

Looking at paper roses, how they bloom./And ceilings crack. The Boarder. Louis Simpson. PoPl; SM

Looking at the earth, the wildwood/where the split began. Waking in the Dark. Adrienne Rich. FaBoWP

Looking at the sea and wondering what its name is. On First Looking into Chapman's Homer (parody). W. S. Brownlie. BXAP

...Looking/back over his shoulder, the quiet street/behind him. Twin Aces. Keith Wilson. Psk

Looking down upon us, all/Wish us joy. Epithalamion. W. H. Auden. HW

Looking each his own way to find the golden/river. The Klondike. Edwin Arlington Robinson. PAH

–Looking for breakfast or a little peace. The Avenues. David St. John. AMV-80; MAYP

...Looking for fools/Who want to hold even the lights of Main/Street, and the sweetness of a face. Dragging the Main. David Ray. TAT

Looking for you and me, my dear, looking for you/and me.   Refugee Blues. W. H. Auden.   InPo; LiTA

Looking from their eyes like sad dachshunds/As their long bodies float by.   Small Aircraft.   Bella Akhmadulina.   BoWoP

Looking in at the windows/the real faces of angels.   For the Altarpiece of the Roseau Valley Church, Saint Lucia.   Derek Walcott.   NoP

Looking on me, let him know, love's delights/Are treasures hid in caves, but kept with sprites.   Caelica, V.   Fulke, Lord Brooke Greville.   FCP

Looking out of their eyes/With their eyes, looking before us.   The Fathers. John N. Morris.   GP

Looking out the corner of his eye.   Fear and Anger in the Mindless Universe. Hayden Carruth.   NNaP

Looking things over/On his way home.   The Gnome.   Harry Behn.   SoPo; TiPo

Looking through a spring rain and imagining love.   On the Danube.   Robert Conquest.   NMP

Looking through the empty/limbs.   Brain.   Coleman Barks.   PPJ

Looking to Jesus and turning not back–/That's faith.   That's Faith.   S. N. Leitner.   STF

Looking towards heaven, yet seeing no more than they.   Easter Island. Frederick George Scott.   OBCV

Looking twice my age.   La Belle Dame sans Merci (parody).   T. Griffiths. BXAP

...Looking up at us,/asking for their legs.   Bullfrogs.   David Allan Evans. Psk

Looks at me.   Silent Hour.   Rainer Maria Rilke.   AWP

Looks betray all that the heart would be at.   Song: "When the heart's feeling."   Thomas Moore.   OBSP

Looks inward to his heart and sees/The objects that must ever please.   Sonnet. The Cell.   John Thelwall.   NOEC

Looks like rain–my Lawd!/Looks like rain–hanh!   Goin' Home.   Anonymous. ABF

Looks on and marvels,–'t is the soul of/man.   Soul and Sense.   Hannah Parker Kimball.   AA

Looks on your feats with a pleasure that's genuine.   To William (Whom We Have Missed).   P. G. Wodehouse.   NOBL

Looks once on life and goes his wordless way.   Brevities.   Siegfried Sassoon. PoLf

Looks, through men's eyes, on His own children then.   A Hospital.   Alfred Noyes.   PoPl

Looks up into the yellow sun each mirror-yellow flake.   Yellow.   Kenton Kilmer.   GoYe

Looks upon life as upon cast-off trials.   Homecoming.   Wislawa Szymborska. AMV-81

The loom stands like a skeleton/across the Aztec sky.   In the Flight of the Blue Heron: To Montezuma.   Anita Endrezze Probst.   CDW

A looming bastion fringed with fire.   In Memoriam A.H.H., XV.   Alfred, Lord Tennyson.   BiP; GTBS-P; NAWM 1-2; NOBE; OAEL 1-2; OAEP; OBNC; PoEL 1-5

Loops, billion-hookt principles undreamed-of.   Upon Looking at a Book of Astrology.   David McFadden.   NeAC

The loose behavior of the bone/And the immodest thigh.   The Man Who Married Magdalene.   Louis Simpson.   NePoEA; NoAm; SM; TAP

Loose ghostly mouths/Breathing.   Orchids.   Theodore Roethke.   CMoP; NMP; PPoe

Loose my braid to fly my hair.   Indian.   Laura Jensen.   AmPA

Loose skin over each/knuckle of my hand.   Watts.   Shirley Kaufman. NMM

Loosen our bonds/that we may live!   The Vedic Hymns: Varuna. Anonymous.   ILwL

A loosened spirit brings!   Precious Words.   Emily Dickinson.   BBV

A looseness.   Movies.   Clark Coolidge.   ANYP

Loosens her stays/pretending she's alone.   Kimono.   Jorie Graham. MAYP

Lope toward your own dark shelter.   The Strange People.   Louise Erdrich. TWSS

Lord Alcohol, the drunken fay,/Lord Alcohol alway!   Lord Alcohol. Thomas Lovell Beddoes.   WiR

Lord an Alabama boy but I don't wanna ride   Alabama Bus.   Brother Will Hairston.   BluL; FaBoPV

Lord! an insect's an insect at most,/Though it crawl on the curls of a Queen. The Toad-Eater.   Robert Burns.   PoL; TW

Lord, as thou givest me more hours to live,/So with it, Oh do thou thy grace me give.   Meditations for July 25, 1666.   Philip Pain.   SCAP

...Lord, before I die/Let me a better kingdom far espy.   Whilst in This World I Stay.   Philip Pain.   AH

Lord bless that woman/that: put that thing on me   Future Blues.   Willie Brown.   BluL

Lord, blow the coal, Thy love enflame in me.   Meditations.   Edward Taylor. AnNE

Lord, but how much beauty was there/Back in 1955!'   Betjeman, 1984. Charles Causley.   FaBoCo; NOBL; OxBTC

The lord chamberlain shivers/a moment sped by   Four Questions Addressed to His Excellency, the Prime Minister.   James P. Vaughn.   AmNP

Lord, choose for me,/The road that runs to Thee.   At Cockcrow.   Lizette Woodworth Reese.   TrPWD

Lord, come. Let her see you.   I can't break with the Dark One.   Mira Bai [(or Mirabai)].   BoWoP

The Lord doth guard, I have no fear!   Adon 'Olam.   Anonymous.   EaLo

The Lord everlasting,/almighty God.   Coedmon's Hymn.   Anonymous. EBEV

Lord, for thy mercy, lend us might/To see that joyful day!   Gascoigne's Good Morrow.   George Gascoigne.   AAS; EnRePo; NOCV

Lord, from this horror of iniquity,/And hellish grave, thou wouldst deliver me. Sonnet XCVIII.   Fulke, Lord Brooke Greville.   QFR

Lord, give them back when at thy holy altar/We feed on thee, who are the living bread.   Hymn.   Andrew Young.   EaLo

Lord God, I am slow to learn!   Rendez-vous Manque dans la Rue Racine. John Millington Synge.   BIrV

Lord God of Hosts, we give Thee thanks!   A Song of Thanks.   Edward Smyth Jones.   BANP

The Lord God's jealous of yourself and me.   Dread.   John Millington Synge. BoLoP; MoBrPo; OBSP

Lord god, what will become of us!   Truth Has Perished.   Ulma Seligman. TrJP

Lord, guard me from those Pirats that would catch/My Soul, do thou (Lord) be there over-match.   Meditation.   Philip Pain.   NOBA

Lord, have mercy on us.   The Black Death.   Philip Dacey.   GP

Lord, have mercy on us.   Summer's Last Will and Testament: Adieu, Farewell Earths Blisse.   Nashe [(or Nash[) Thomas.   AtBAP; DiPo; LO

Lord have mercy upon/Her sweet white bones. Amen.   A Cautionary Tale. Anne Wilkinson.   OBCV; PeCV

Lord have mercy while we gwine   Floating Bridge.   Sleepy John Estes. BluL

Lord, help me to be true;/For I am just beginning, too.   Prayer of a Beginning Teacher.   Ouida Smith Dunnam.   TrPWD

Lord, help Thou mine unbelief!   Oberammergau.   Leonora Speyer. AnAmPo; HBMV

Lord, here is darkness. Yet this heart unwise,/Bruised in Thy service, take in sacrifice.   How Shall I Build.   Wilfrid Scawen Blunt.   CAW

The Lord Himself will give you up/If you should drop a willow cup! Washing the Dishes.   Christopher Morley.   PoLf

The Lord holds fast my hand.   Walking with God.   Anonymous.   BLRP

Lord, Holy One! if thou who knowest worse/Should loathe us too!   Lord, Many Times.   Richard Chenevix Trench.   BePJ; OBRV

Lord, how much can we bear?   Song for the Infant Judas.   Thomas Blackburn.   NAs

Lord, I go softly all my years!   The Quiet Pilgrim.   Edith Matilda Thomas. AA

Lord, I long to be with thee!   The Christian Pilgrim's Hymn.   William Williams.   WGRP

Lord, I'm done!   Rondeau.   William Jay Smith.   FiBHP

Lord I'm gonna quit my bad way of living/And visit the Sunday school   Street Car Blues.   Sleepy John Estes.   BluL

Lord, I've hammered my insides in two.   John Henry (A vers.).   Anonymous. BaBo

Lord, I walked all last night/and all last night before.   No More Women Blues.   Texas Alexander.   BluL

Lord, I wan'ta go to heaben when I die.   Lis'en to de Lam's.   Anonymous. BoAN 1-2

Lord, I want to be a Christian,/In-a my heart.   Lord, I Want to Be a Christian.   Anonymous.   AH; BoAN 1-2

Lord, if I go, tell me what to say,/Dey won't believe in me.   You Go, I'll Go wid You.   Anonymous.   BoAN 1-2

Lord, if I loved her, count it not my shame.'   Canzone: Of the Gentle Heart. Guido Guinicelli.   AWP; CTC; LiTW; OBVE

Lord if she don't come on the big boat/I mean she better not land   Levee Camp Moan.   Texas Alexander.   BluL

Lord, if that were enough?   Songs of Travel.   Robert Louis Stevenson. OBNC

The Lord incline his countenance unto/thee and give thee peace: Amen./Selah. Blessing of the Priests.   Anonymous.   TrJP

The Lord indeed is here.   Lord, In thy Presence Here.   Jesse L. Holman. AH

The Lord is King, the Lord was King,/the Lord shall be King for ever and/ever.   The Terrible Sons.   Eleazar Ben Kalir.   TrJP

Lord, is there nothing left for a horse/but a daily quota of intercourse? Monologue of the Rating Morgan in Rutherford County.   C. F. MacIntyre. PH

Lord Jesus, bless us now!   Christ Is All.   Horatius Bonar.   BePJ

Lord JESUS receive my soule this night.   A Lamentable New Ballad upon the Earle of Essex Death.   Anonymous.   CoMu

De Lord knows de world's gwine to end up,/Jesus, won't you come b'm-by? Jesus, Won't You Come B'm-By?(with music).   Anonymous.   AS

Lord, let me die but not die/Out. For the Last Wolverine. James Dickey. LiSp

Lord, let me wake up dead, but not bored. Archetypes. Neal Bowers. AMV-81

Lord, let thy mercy come. O Lord, Turn Not Away Thy Face. John Marchant. AH

Lord, let thy Terrours every day cause me/To prepare for my end, and ready be. Meditations for July 26, 1666. Philip Pain. SCAP

Lord, look at the state you're in! A Man of Experience. Laoiseach Mac an Bhaird. KiLC

The Lord looks down contentedly upon a/willing mind. The Quaker Widow. Bayard Taylor. AA

Lord, Lord, gonna get on a rinktum. Ducks in the Millpond. Anonymous. OuSiCo

Lord, Lord, got those Brown's Ferry Blues. Brown's Ferry Blues. Anonymous. FSW

Lord, Lord, I got them coal loadin' blues. Coal Loadin' Blues. Anonymous. AmFP

Lord Lord Lord caw caw caw Lord Lord Lord caw caw caw Lord Kaddish. Allen Ginsberg. NeAP

Lord, Lord! was "I want to go to heaven when I die." John Hardy (B vers.). Anonymous. ViBoFo

Lord, make a regular man out of me. Lord, Make a Regular Man Out of Me. Edgar A. Guest. BLPA; BLPL

Lord, marching up to freedom land. Ain't Gonna Let Nobody Turn Me Round. Anonymous. FSW

Lord Maxwell has te'n his last good-night. Lord Maxwell's Last Goodnight. Anonymous. BaBo; OxBB

Lord, may a love replying,/Within my soul awake. O Son of God, Afflicted. Anonymous. STF

Lord, may I in thy bosom rest,/The bosom of thy love. The Day Is Past and Gone. John Leland. AH

Lord, may my life help others lives,/It touches by the way. My Influence. Anonymous. STF

Lord, may we live to spend next year/In Copenhagen! Non Sum Qualis Eram in Bona Urbe Nordica Illa. John Hollander. ErPo

The Lord Most High, at his home at last. The Dream of the Rood. Cynewulf. EnLi 1-2

Lord, now let our crying reach Thee. His Hand Shall Cover Us. Isaac Ben Samuel. TrJP

Lord of earth, and God of heaven,/Evermore–Thy will be done. Thy Will Be Done. Anonymous. BePJ

Lord of himself, an inborn gentleman! Lincoln. George Henry Boker. MC; OHIP

Lord of himself, though not of lands,/And having nothing, yet hath all. The Happy Life. Sir Henry Wotton. MyFE; WGRP

The Lord of Hosts! thrice holy is His/name! God, Whom Shall I Compare to Thee? Judah Halevi. TrJP

"The Lord of Life be praised! I, too,/have died." At Last. Katrina Trask. AA

The Lord of life has died. Credo. Seumas (James Starkey) O'Sullivan. OnYI

The Lord of Love is whole again. Mathematics or the Gift of Tongues. Anna Hempstead Branch. ImOP

The Lord of Love was standing there! The Search. Thomas Curtis Clarke. WGRP

Lord of Mercy, the dead still need bus fare & salvation! Balance. Philip Schultz. MAYP

Lord of my days, how thankful I/For a thankful heart, as life goes by! Common Blessings. Thomas Curtis Clark. TrPWD

Lord of my life, work Thou Thy perfect will. Prayer to God. Placido (Gabriel de la Conception Valdes). CAW; TTY

Lord of our hand and lord of head. Amen. Lord of Each Soul. Paul Engle. AH

The Lord of the children had heard her, and Emmie had/passed away. In the Children's Hospital. Alfred, Lord Tennyson. HBV 1-2

Lord of the days new and olden,/Shine on and gladden the earth. Deirdre's Song at Sunrise. Sister Maura. CaP

"Lord of the Land! but men have named me Death." At the Top of the Road. Charles Buxton Going. HBV 1-2

Lord of the world's elation,/Thou breath of things unseen. Lord of My Heart's Elation. Bliss Carman. AH; HBV 1-2; NOBC; OBCV; TrPWD

Lord of the worlds, make all the lands Thine own! A Hymn for Canada. Albert Durrant Watson. CaP

Lord of tomorrow,/Lover of me! Sheer Joy. Ralph Spaulding Cushman. TRV

The Lord our God is One God!' The Last Words of Don Henriquez. Zalman Schneour. TrJP

Lord, pardon, for thy sonne makes good/My want of tears with store of bloud. Grieve Not the Holy Spirit. George Herbert. AnAnS 1

Lord, pray forgive me–I did wrong. The Thrush. Timothy Corsellis. WaaP; WaP

The Lord shall be my righteousness;/The Lord for ever mine. Jehovah Our Righteousness. William Cowper. NOCV

The Lord shall raise me up, I trust. Even Such Is Time. Sir Walter Ralegh. BLPL; ElL; ExPo; FCP; ForPo; GoTF; HAP; LiTB; OBSP; PoRA; SeCeV; SiPS; TreF; WHA

The Lord shall reign for evermore. All the Hosts of Heaven. Simeon Ben Abun. TrJP

Lord she break in on a dollar/oh most anywhere she goes Walking Blues. Robert Johnson. BluL

Lord, show me how. My Daily Prayer. Grenville Kleiser. BLRP

Lord soe I am, if heare my thoughts may rest. Upon the Crucifix. William Alabaster. PoEL 1-5

The Lord survives the rainbow of His will. The Quaker Graveyard in Nantucket. Robert Lowell. AP; CMoP; CoBMV; HAP; LiTA; LiTM; MiAP; MoAB; MoPo; MOS; MoVE; NePA; NoAm; NOBA; NoP; OxBA; TAP; UnPo; ViBoPo

Lord, tarry not, but come. Beyond the Smiling and the Weeping. Horatius Bonar. HBV 1-2

Lord! teach us how to pray! What Is Prayer? James Montgomery. BLRP; STF; TRV; WGRP

The Lord that bought free and thrall/Is found in an ass's stall/By his moder Mary. A Cause for Wonder. Anonymous. MeEL

Lord, then said I, On me one breath,/And let me dye before my death! Silex Scintillans. Henry Vaughan. AnAnS 1

Lord thrust me deeper into dust/That thou may'st raise me with the just. Hymn to Charity and Humility. Henry More. OxBoCh

Lord, 'tis my All, and due to Thee. Dedication. Sir James Chamberlayne. CavP

Lord told John, "Don't you write no more." John Was A-Writin'. Anonymous. OuSiCo

"Lord turn us again, confer on us victory." Now as Then. Anne Ridler. WaP

Lord unto thee: even so shall I./Jo: Fiske. Upon the Much-to-Be Lamented Desease of the Reverend Mr. John Cotton.. John Fiske. SCAP

Lord, we beg, for Jesus' sake/A sweet refreshing shower. Help Thy Servant. Andrew Broaddus. AH

Lord, we cannot guess or believe,/We can only know. The Third Day. Edith Lovejoy Pierce. MoRP

...Lord, what a mess/Of beer and beef and bitterness. Timocreon. Simonides (of Ceos). DBV

Lord, what must she be/to other men? Outbreak. Bill Anderson. VGW

Lord, who am I that they should stoop–these holy folk of/thine? Good Company. Karle Wilson Baker. HBV 1-2; WGRP

Lord, who can live to see such love again? Wondrous Love. Mary Herbert, Countess of Pembroke. BePJ

The Lord will say, "Oh, go to h—." Steal Not This Book for Fear of Shame. Anonymous. FaBoUs

The Lord will see us through some day. We Shall Overcome. Anonymous. AH; EaLo

The Lord with me,–no fears my soul/can shake. Lord of the World. Anonymous. TrJP

Lord, with my reckoning half told/I know that I am rich indeed. I Have a Roof. Ada Jackson. TrPWD

Lord you know I want a friend/like the one what Adam had No Woman No Nickel. Bumble Bee Slim. BluL

The lordliest, earthward bending, hail/The Light of Bethlehem! The Light of Bethlehem. John Banister Tabb. CAW

Lords of the lonely deep. Kearsarge. Silas Weir Mitchell. PAH

The lore of Christ and his apostles twelve/He taught, but first he followed it himself. The Good Parson. Geoffrey Chaucer. WGRP

Lorn, bold, as if saluting with her fist. Iron Landscapes (and the Statue of Liberty). Thom Gunn. FaBoPV; OBTV

Lose myself in her warm caress/Intervolving earth, sky and flesh. Agbor Dancer. John Pepper Clark. PBA

Lose their umbrageous choice within your eyes. Grove and Building. Edgar Bowers. NePoEA

Lose thir defence distracted and amaz'd. Samson Agonistes. John Milton. OBEV

Lose yourself again/On the island of Calypso. Calypso's Song to Ulysses. Adrian Mitchell. GBL

Loses each day what never will return/to us. Today Is Armistice, a Holiday. Delmore Schwartz. TrJP

Losing its gust, and my ambition blind! I cry your mercy–pity–love!–aye, love! John Keats. BoLoP

Losing Mass, Cross, Faith, Truth–followeth damnation. Swearing. Henry Fitzsimon. ACP

Losing ourselves/finding For My People. Wendy Rose. CDW

Losing still, that I may find/This bounded self in boundless Mind. The Questionings. Frederic Henry Hedge. HBV 1-2

...Losing,/your eyes, once, made you beautiful. A Snapshot for Miss Bricka Who Lost in the Semifinal Round... Robert Wallace. LiSp; SD

The loss of beauty if not always loss! November. Elizabeth Stoddard AA

The loss/Of the dream/Leaves nothing/The same. Beale Street. Langston Hughes. PPP

The loss of toy balloons. The Cyclone. Stewart Brisby. LFAC

The loss of what is born, the lapse of what is old. Poem on Hampstead Heath. Louis Adeane. NeBP

"A loss', say others, "to the Cafe Royal'. Epitaph: Jacob Epstein. *Anonymous.* FaBoCo

Loss were thrice loss that thus their faith/should mar. The Watchers. Arlo Bates. AA

The loss whereof leaveth the man's face shabby and dull. The Testament of Beauty. Robert Bridges. EBEV

Lost, alas! I've lost–MY SKYE. I've Lost My––. Henry Cholmondeley-Pennell. CenHV

Lost, and all mine, all mine, forever. Dear Men and Women. John Hall Wheelock. NYBP; Prf

Lost and found, in sunset land. The Vanishers. John Greenleaf Whittier AA

Lost beyond roads in a sea of mist. Answering Li Ying Who Showed Me His Poems about Summer Fishing. Yu Hsuan-chi. BoWoP

...Lost finally/in that absence whose trace is silence. I Have Come Far to Have Found Nothing. Cid Corman. VGW

Lost in a pale orbit/somewhere/(late at night) Solitary Visions of a Kaufmanoid... James (Olumo) Cunningham. JB

Lost in a sundering throb and a shower of spray. Departure. Leonard Alfred George Strong. HaMV

Lost in a wound, not even questioning. Address to an Absolute. Roy McFadden. NeIP

Lost in day-dreams and vain desires of bliss. Love's Longing. *Anonymous.* UnTE

Lost in error lives and dies. Song: "Man's a poor deluded bubble." Robert Dodsley. OBSP

Lost in God, in Godhead found. Threnody. Ralph Waldo Emerson AA; AmePo; AnNE; AP; MAmP

Lost, in the heart's worship, and the body's sleep. Love Poem. Kathleen Raine. LiTB; MoAB; MoBrPo; MoPo; NeBP

Lost in the moment 'tis possessed. Love. George, Baron Lano Granville [(or Grenville(]. BoLoP

Lost in the sedge to watch the centuries. By Rail through the Earthly Paradise, Perhaps Bedfordshire. Denise Levertov. NNaP

Lost in wonder, love, and praise! Love Divine, All Loves Excelling. Charles Wesley. NOCV

Lost/inside/the/house. When My Grandmother Died. Sam Cornish. Psk

A lost key is found;/storm windows are stacked on the beams of the garage. An Almanac. James Schuyler. ANYP

Lost leaves–why, it is your dead selves/I mean! My Babes in the Wood. Sarah Piatt. AA

Lost, lost, all lost, between Hell and Heaven!) Sister Helen. Dante Gabriel Rossetti. BeLS; MaVP; OAEP; VLP

Lost, lost, lost. Wakeful in the Township. Elizabeth Riddell. NOAV; PoAu 1-2

Lost minerals colouring/The initial letter, the stance. Irish Poetry. Michael Longley. CIP

...The lost/Moment that stopped to grieve and moved on... Invisible Landscape. Charles Wright. LCAP

...The lost/Room is locked, my heart is attuned to frost. Summerhouse. Melvin Walker La Follette. NePoEA

Lost so long ago–/In the Heart of the Woods. Heart of the Woods. Wesley Curtright. GoSl; PoNe

Lost to this thin-clouding/sky of today. Casual Meeting. Sam Bradley. AMV-81

The lost traveller's dream under the hill. For the Sexes: The Gates of Paradise. William Blake. LiTB; NoP; PoEL 1-5

A lost tribe is singing "Abide With Me'. Nostalgias. Derek Mahon. FaBoIP

...The lot/Are all dressed up the same as/The Hottentot tot. Midsummer Fantasy. Newman Levy. PoSC

A lot of love along the way. A Day. William L. Stidger. PoToHe

Lot's daughters with no Lot and no wine-cup/To get them a son. On the Bridge of Athlone: A Prophecy. Donagh MacDonagh. OxBI

Lots of history. Let's go. H. S. Beeney Auction Sales. David R. Pichaske. AMV-81

Lots of more men sorry will be,/If they dont try to keep away from this/Poor little country maid. The Streets of Cairo. James Thornton. FSN

Lots of people had justice, they'd be in the penitentiary too Judge Harsh Blues. Furry Lewis. BluL

Loud as the ultimate loud clarion/Or the first murther. Doomsday. Elinor Wylie. CrMA

Loud cries for "Author"...but he doesn't come. Sonnet: "The world's a stage." Hilaire Belloc. DBV

Loud hallelujahs let us sing,/And praise his name on every chord. Let Tyrants Shake Their Iron Rod. William Billings. AH

A loud "Kerchoo!"–what would he do,/the pompous Pekinese? The Extraordinary Dog. Nancy Byrd Turner. TiPo

Loud kite in a remembered sky. Holding On. Richard Jackson. AMV-80

Loud with blk/nation/hood/builden. Listenen to Big Black at S.F. State. Sonia Sanchez. BPo

Louder, Yanni, louder! Two Communist Poets. Irving Layton. AMV-81

...Louise/in the dream. in the sunrise in the sunset. Alma to Her Sister. Linda Gregg. NPGG

A lousy parson, a nitty clerk, and a shabby congregation. Acton Beauchamp, Herefordshire. *Anonymous.* FaBoPP; GBP

Lousy shirts, the pocked forearm, and scarred wrist. Et Quid Amabo Nisi Quod Aenigma Est. Stephen Sandy. NYBP

The lousy son of a gun! We Pity Our Bosses Five. *Anonymous.* FSW

"Lousyana was my home. so scram!" The Birth of John Henry. Melvin B. Tolson. BPo

Love. Love. Norman Henry Pritchard, II. PoBA

Love, a childish game thou art! A Childish Game. Reinmar von Hagenau. AWP

Love all the people they love. Token. Peggy Bacon. PV

Love alone to Him is ever pleasing. Heart's Music. *Anonymous.* CAPP; OBEV

Love–and chains are broken. Alabama Earth. Langston Hughes. AmFN; GoSl

Love, and Faith, and true devotion,/For our Saviour, God, and King. The Adoration of the Wise Men. Cecil Frances Alexander. HBVY

Love–and let love. Toleration. John Barford. PeHV

Love and Liberty allied. Cuba Libre. Joaquin Miller. MC; PAH

Love and life are for to-day. Quid Sit Futurum Cras Fuge Quaerere. Matthew Prior. FaBoEE

Love and pity dare not cease/For a lifetime, at the least. The Coward. Stephen Spender. NoAm

Love and silence watch a hastening breath. Sonnet of Departure. J. R. Hervey. AnNZ

Love and tears for the Blue,/Tears and love for the Gray. The Blue and the Gray. Francis Miles Finch. AA; BLPA; BLPL; FaBoBe; GoTF; HBV 1-2; MC; PAH; PAL; PaPo; TreF; WBLP

Love, and the glad sweet face of her. Ike Walton's Prayer. James Whitcomb Riley. AA

Love, and the thoughts that yearn for human/kind. Fears in Solitude. Samuel Taylor Coleridge. EnRP; FaBoPP; OBNC; OBWP

Love and Truth can ride it out,/Come bridal song or battle shout. Women Singing. Sir Henry Taylor. OBVV

Love as you please–I owe you nothing back. From a Woman to a Greedy Lover. Norman Cameron. ELU; FaBoEE; GTBS-P

Love at its best/Is Heaven. Love. John Oxenham. BLRP

Love being placed above these middle regions/Where every passion wars itself with legions. Love's Glory. Fulke, Lord Brooke Greville. OBSC

Love being/the unnamed/the unnameable. For Whitman. Diane Wakoski. SUW

Love bridled me so forcefully/What good is now my reining in? What Helps It If of Love I Sing. Hadewijch. PBWP

Love! broken should have been thy bow/One year ago. One Year Ago. Walter Savage Landor. EnLi 1-2

Love buries itself in me, up to the hilt. A Renewal. James Merrill. OBSP; PoPl; SM

Love came so lightly/I knew not that he came. Love's Coming. Shaw Neilson. PoAu 1-2

Love can but last in us here at his height/For a day and a night. At Parting. Algernon Charles Swinburne. HBV 1-2; ViBoPo

Love, can this beauty in our hearts/End? June Twilight. John Masefield. GoYe

Love closed our lives' triumphant overture. Epithalamium. Sir Edmund Gosse. OBVV

Love comes back to his vacant dwelling. The Wanderer. Henry Austin Dobson. HBV 1-2

Love comes laughing up the valleys,/Hand in hand with hoyden Spring. The Call. Reginald Wright Kauffman. HBV 1-2

Love comes without bounds. A Spring Song of Tzu-Yeh. Hsaio Yen. LLLT

The love conceals/the care. Photographs. William Peskett. AMV-81

Love costs us nothing, satire costs a lot!' The Contemporary Muse. Edgell Rickword. OBSV

Love could not fill it full of cheer! I Never Knew a Night So Black. John Kendrick Bangs. PoToHe

Love dances, smiles. Oh, how he sings! The Serpent. Joseph Langland. MP

...Love, deep and kind,/Shall watch around, and leave good gifts behind,/Little Bell, for thee. Little Bell. Thomas Westwood. GN; HBV 1-2

Love did ever hoard up in his treasure. Song Set by Robert Jones: "O! How my thoughts do beat me. *Anonymous.* OBSC

Love, don't give me up! Yes? Henry Cuyler Bunner. HBV 1-2

Love from that days courting Burns my heart/to a coal.　We Passed by Green Closes.　John Clare.　VLP

The love, from which began/My question sad and vain,/Justifies thee to man.　The Affliction of Richard.　Robert Bridges.　QFR

Love give me all for all.　Love's Votary.　George Augustus Simcox.　NOBV

Love give me more such nights as these.　The Vision to Electra.　Robert Herrick.　ALV; SeCP

Love had won, and heaven pardoned her.　Curse of the Cat Woman.　Edward Field.　WeW

Love has a faith to keep/With past felicities/That weep for this.　A Lost World.　Robert Graves.　NYBP

Love has been good to you.　Congratulations: Two Versions.　Sappho.　HW

Love has found out a way to live by dying.　No, No, Poor Suffering Heart.　John Dryden.　LiTB; LiTL; LoBV; QFR; ViBoPo

Love hates the too-ripe fruit that falls alone.　Cupid's Revenge.　Francis Beaumont and John Fletcher.　EiL; FaBoEn

...Love hath wings,/And flies away from aged things.　Dear, Do Not Your Fair Beauty Wrong.　Thomas May.　ViBoPo

Love he must, or flatter me.　Young and Simple Though I Am.　Thomas Campion.　EnL; FaBoEn; SeCeV

Love, he said,/will eat away the Empire/until chaos remains.　Hero Song.　Robert Duncan.　CrMA

Love he to morrow, who lov'd never;/To morrow, who hath lov'd, persever.　Venus Vigils (excerpt).　*Anonymous.*　OBVE

Love her:/For her mistiming, for her longings, for her early death.　Fifth Sunday after Easter.　Thomas Kinsella.　NMP

Love, honie yeelds; but never stings.　The Kisse: A Dialogue.　Robert Herrick.　CavP

The love I dare not–to thy face–/I offer to thy feet.　To Jessie's Dancing Feet.　William De Lancey Ellwanger.　AA

...Love I hope (since wit/Becomes a clog) will soon ease me of it.　Astrophel and Stella, LIX.　Sir Philip Sidney.　AAS; GBL; OAEP; SiPS

Love in a test-tube he knew was a dangerous thing.　Scientia Vincit Omnia?　Merrill Moore.　AnAmPo

Love, in himself and diet spare,/Grows fat by contradiction.　Husbandry.　William Hammond.　JCP

Love in his heart, his empty hands, his eyes.　The Coffin-Worm.　Ruth Pitter.　MoBrPo

Love in his season/Had moved me with that song.　Musical Shuttle.　Harvey Shapiro.　VWA

The love in my life.　A Spring Day on Campus.　Gilbert Schedler.　AMV-80

...Love in the heart/That trembles only when the heart trembles.　Compline.　Duncan Campbell Scott.　GoBC

Love in your fullness of flesh and heart and humor.　Marriage.　Robert Lowell.　NAs

Love inconstant I forbear.　Love, Whose Month Was Ever May.　Ulrich von Liechtenstein [(or Lichten Stein)].　AWP

Love indeed is any thing, yet indeed is nothing.　Blurt: Master Constable: Song: Love Is Like a Lamb.　Thomas Middleton.　AtBAP

Love is a holy, holy, holy thing.　Ditty.　Sir Robert Chester.　EiL

Love is a jest and vows are wind.　To a Young Gentleman in Love: A Tale.　Matthew Prior.　TEP

"Love is a keeper of swans."　Love Is a Keeper of Swans.　Humbert Wolfe.　MoBrPo

Love is a naked shadow/On a gnarled and naked tree.　Song for a Dark Girl.　Langston Hughes.　AmPP; CDC; IDB; PoBA

Love is a terrible thing!　Love Is a Terrible Thing.　Grace Fallow Norton.　HBV 1-2

Love is always waiting there.　What a Friend We Have in Mother.　Charles E. Roat.　FSW

Love is aweary now.　Chamber Music.　James Joyce.　MoLP; OLR

Love is best.　Love Among the Ruins.　Robert Browning.　BoLiVe; EnLit; FaBV; HAP; HBV 1-2; MBW 1-2; MCCG; NOBE; OAEL 1-2; OAEP; OBEV; OBVV; PoEL 1-5; PrIm; VLP

Love is but desire and thy purpose fulfillment;/I, thy King, so say!　Before the Feast of Shushan.　Anne Spencer.　BANP; BlSi

Love is forever over all.　On an Old Sun Dial.　*Anonymous.*　GoTF; TreFT

Love is God, and sex conversion.　History of Ideas.　J. V. Cunningham.　NIP

...Love is like a dizziness,/Wont let a poor man go about his business.　A Love Song.　Royall Tyler.　TAP

Love is like the lion's tooth.　Words for Music Perhaps.　William Butler Yeats.　AtBAP

Love is not his that raves; hope is untrue.　Caelica, XXXVII.　Fulke, Lord Brooke Greville.　FCP

Love is that liquour sweet and most divine,/Which my God feels as bloud; but I, as wine.　The Agonie.　George Herbert.　AnAnS 1; MePo

Love is that one waking light/That leads now when all others darken.　Pole Star for This Year.　Archibald MacLeish.　AP; CoBMV; NAMP; NePA; OxBA

Love is the dearest thing that our Lord demands/And also the shortest pasth that points to heaven.　The Vision of Piers Plowman.　William Langland.　CoBE

Love is the end.'　Resurgam.　Marjorie Pickthall.　OBCV; TrCP

Love is the fury/To love and find/A single name.　Freud: Dying in London, He Recalls the Smoke of His Cigar...　James Schevill.　TAP

Love is the hardest where all things are hard.　Sonnets.　Muna Lee.　HBMV

Love is the lesson which the Lord us taught.　Amoretti, LXVIII.　Edmund Spenser.　AAS; BoC; HAP; HBV 1-2; InPS; NOCV; NoP; OxBoCh; SeCeV; TrPWD

Love is the pity that we feel for one another.　The Sounds of Dawn.　Efrain Huerta.　LiTW

Love is the whole and more than all　My Father Moved through Dooms of Love.　Edward Estlin Cummings.　AmP; AtBAP; CMoP; CoBMV; CrMA; FYAP; HAP; LiTA; MoAB; MoPo; MoVE; NoAm; NOBA; NoP; OxBA; PoCh; TAP; UnPo

Love is twice warm in a cold place.　North.　Philip Booth.　NePoEA; PoPl

Love is ugly, and the child, born wet.　Dragging in Winter.　David McElroy.　AmPA

Love is unjust: justice is loveless.　Sarah.　Delmore Schwartz.　VWA

Love is unreturning.　Counsel.　Roselle Mercier Montgomery.　HBMV

Love, it is love that gives me strength,/Averting the perils of the river.　Love Song: "The little sycamore."　*Anonymous.*　TTY

Love itself shall slumber on.　To –.　Percy Bysshe Shelley.　AtBAP; AWP; ExPo; FiP; HeIP; InPo; NoP; OAEP; OBNC; OBSP; PoEL 1-5; SeCePo

Love itself would, did they not.　Death.　Percy Bysshe Shelley.　DiPo

Love killed this man. No more but so.　The Cruel Maid.　Robert Herrick.　CaPo

The love-knot and the ruth.　To Demeter.　Maybury Fleming.　AA

Love laughs glad in the paths aside.　The Highway.　Louise Driscoll.　HBV 1-2

The love-lawns of the light.　Frolic.　George William Russell.　GTBS; MoBrPo

Love lights me up the ruddy glare/Of fire in Burncombe hollow.　Burncombe Hollow.　William Barnes.　OBNC

Love lights the evening star.　O Love That Lights the Eastern Sky.　Louis F. Benson.　AH

Love lives in gardens–/God and lovers know!　The Garden.　Caroline Giltinan.　HBMV

Love'll warm me as I go through the snow, among the/heather.　Among the Heather.　William Allingham.　IrPN

...Love-longing/mists the windshield, soothes the eye with milk.　Long Summer (excerpt).　Robert Lowell.　CAPP

Love looketh faire, but Lovers are accurst.　What Sugred Termes, What All-Perswading Arte.　Richard Lynche.　AAS

Love, love, it is as death were past!　Crossing the Tropics.　Herman Melville　AA

Love, love, my season.　The Couriers.　Sylvia Plath.　LCAP

Love loveth best of all the year/October's bright blue weather.　October's Bright Blue Weather.　Helen Hunt Jackson.　AmePo; BLPA; BLPL; FaBoBe; GN; GoTF; HBVY; PoSC; TreFT

Love lures life on.　Lines to a Movement in Mozart's E-Flat Symphony.　Thomas Hardy.　ELP

The love, lust, longing: reasons, but not the reason.　The Beauty of Things.　Robinson Jeffers.　PoA

Love made these poems. I don't know why.　Love's Own Form Is Sufficient Unto.　R. G. Vliet.　PoL

Love may not delay too long–/Is the burden of their song.　Chorale.　A. D. Hope.　ErPo; UnTE

Love may return, but never Lover.　Il Pastor Fido.　Giovanni Battista Guarini.　OBVE

Love me, and I'll love you.　The Dove Says.　*Anonymous.*　OxNR

Love me and save me, take me or waive me; death/takes one so soon!　At the Piano.　Algernon Charles Swinburne.　FaBoNo

Love me, and the world is mine.　Love Me, and the World Is Mine.　David Reed, Jr.　TreFT

Love me at last–I am but sliding water/Over a stone.　Love Me at Last.　Alice Corbin.　HBMV

(Love me for ever!)　Love.　Robert Browning.　EnLoPo

Love me freely, seal my peace,/And bid me sin no more.　Bid Me Sin No More.　Charles Wesley.　BePJ

Love me little, love me long,/Is the burden of my song.　Love Me Little, Love Me Long.　*Anonymous.*　BLPA; EiL; FaBoBe; FaFP; LiTL; TreF

Love me no more! for I am grown/Too dead and dull for thee to own.　Upon Absence.　Katherine ("Orinda") Philips.　PBWP

Love melts before a newer flame.　You Drop a Pearl...　*Anonymous.*　WTO

Love mocks us all!　Albi, Ne Doreas.　Horace.　AWP

The love-moon that must light my soul to Love?　The Love-Moon.　Dante Gabriel Rossetti.　MaVP

Love must ever yet return.　Marigolds.　Robert Graves.　BrPo

Love never lets you go. An Ever-Fixed Mark. Kingsley Amis. ErPo; NoAm; PeHV

Love not transcending the person but incarnate/As in his own hand given you in greeting. The White-Haired Man. May Sarton. MoRP

Love, O my God, to call Thee Love and Love. Let Me Be to Thee as the Circling Bird. Gerard Manley Hopkins. VLP

Love-of-God eternally/Keep your heart a-flower. To a Carmelite Postulant. Michael Earls. CAW

The love of Him overcometh al thing, in love we live/and dye. Love Is Life. Richard Rolle. OxBM

The love of life and death The Shock. Larry Eigner. CoPo

The love of my poor heart. My God, How Wonderful Thou Art. Frederick William Faber. GoBC

The love of the Father eternal/Is over us all the way. The Love of the Father. Anonymous. BLRP

Love, oh love, oh careless love/Has broke this heart of mine. Careless Love. Anonymous. BFSS

Love on, and turn to love again? If Lord Thy Love For Me Is Strong. Saint Theresa of Avila. AWP; CAW; LiTW; PBWP

Love on the Cross and in our star-crossed faces. Petition. Harold McCurdy. AMV-81

Love! on their lost repose. Ode to Fanny. John Keats. ChRP

The love once ours, but ours long hours ago. A New Year's Burden. Gerard Manley Hopkins. AtBAP

Love only on the cheek, which is to me most fair. L'Envoi. Thomas Lovell Beddoes. OBNC

Love only reading unto me this art. Astrophel and Stella, XXVIII. Sir Philip Sidney. AAS; OAEL 1-2; SiPS

Love only reigns in death; though art/Can find no comfort for a broken heart. Dirge. John Ford. LoBV

Love or Death should set me free. Ode to Chloris. Charles Cotton. CavP

Love played at Find-me-for-you-May/In Mary's breast. A Pastoral. Norman Gale. HBV 1-2

Love poured her beauty into my warm veins. Fragment of a Sonnet. Pierre Ronsard. AWP

Love reasons much better than Reason. Dear Fanny. Thomas Moore. HBV 1-2; InMe

Love's death, & body's end. Maybe Love. Allen Ginsberg. PeHV

Love's essence, like a poem's, shall spring/From the not saying everything. On Not Saying Everything. C. Day-Lewis. NoP

Love's long sustaining, and wept impatience here. For Peter. Lee Gerlach. HoAn

Love's martyr, when his heat is past,/Proves Care's confessor at the last. The Sea Hath Many Thousand Sands. Anonymous. EiL; LiTB; ViBoPo

Love's Martyrs must be ever, ever dying. Love's Martyrs. John Ford. NOBE

Love's monuments like tombstones on our lives. The Broken Bowl. James Merrill. PoA

Love's need becomes not cease. The War God. Stephen Spender. MoRP

Love's proverb is set down transliterate. Counsel to Unreason. Léonie Adams. PoA

Love's self outdo, dear Lovelace! hold/The pinnacles of song. A Footnote to a Famous Lyric. Louise Imogen Guiney. AA

Love's sharp pain encircles my heart. Then I said to the elegant ladies. Sappho. BoWoP

Love's sigh its harginber? What was/my dream? What Was My Dream? Joseph O'Connor. AA

Love's signature cementing faith. Melchior Vulpius. Marianne Moore. AP

Love's single moment is eternity:/Eternity, a thought in Shakespeare's brain. Since Cleopatra Died. Thomas Wentworth Higginson. AA

Love's solid land is everywhere! Love's Land. Isabella Valancy Crawford. CaP

Love's standard on the battlements of song. Endymion, II (excerpt). John Keats. OBNC

Love's the high fever of the mind. Heat. Anacreon. UnTE

Love's triumph must be Honour's funeral. Loving and Beloved. Sir John Suckling. CaPo; OBS

Love's very Heart, wherein all Loves shall live. Gautama. Thomas S. Jones, Jr. AnAmPo

Love's wilful potion/Veils the ensuing,/And brief, commotion. Ars Amoris. J. V. Cunningham. QFR

Love's worth love. Child's Song. Algernon Charles Swinburne. GTBS; OBVV

Love's zeal in Love's own glory. Hymn to Love. Lascelles Abercrombie. OBEV; OBVV

Love sees how vilely it must live/And smiles? String Quartet. Babette Deutsch. UnS

Love shall live, although he die! Love's Horoscope. Richard Crashaw. HBV 1-2

Love shattered my heart. Like a mountain whirlwind. Sappho. BoWoP

Love should intend realities: good-bye! Exit Line. John Ciardi. WeW

Love so amazing, so divine,/Demands my soul, my life, my all. Crucifixion to the World by the Cross of Christ. Isaac Watts. NOCV; NOEC; OBEC

Love so sweet bestows in all men's sight his own true/wife! His Own True Wife. von Eschenbach, Sir Wolfram AWP

Love, solitude, and the face of death. Pain. Edith Sodergran. PBWP; WPOW

Love, some day they'll print it, because it/Was written to You. A Nice Correspondent. Frederick Locker-Lampson. HBV 1-2

Love somebody, but I won't tell who. Love Somebody, Yes I Do. Anonymous. FSW

Love somebody, yes I do,/'Tween sixteen and twenty-two. Love Somebody, Yes I Do (with music). Anonymous. AS

The love-spent youth, and love-sick maid,/Come to weep out the night. To the Willow Tree. Robert Herrick. CaPo; HBV 1-2; OBEV

...Love/Strength/Light/and Dark/spring to blossoms. Canticle. Michael McClure. NeAP; PoM

A LOVE SUPREME.... JuJu. Askia Muhammad Toure. PoBA

A love supreme, a love supreme– Dear John, Dear Coltrane. Michael S. Harper. AmPA; GeTw; NIP

Love surfeits with rewards, his nurse is scorn. Disdain Me Still. William Herbert, Earl of Pembroke. EiL

Love that endures, from Life that disappears! Sonnets from the Portuguese, XLI. Elizabeth Barrett Browning. CoBE

...–Love that gives them each a name. Fire: The People. Alfred Corn. MAYP

Love that is born of the deep coming/up with the sun from the sea. Duet. Alfred, Lord Tennyson. GBL

The love that makes us one with thee. Thou One in All, Thou All in One. Seth Curtis Beach. AH

"The love that moves the sun and the other stars." The Vision. Dante Alighieri. BoC

Love that never quite touched earth,–/They...and thou and I. White Violets. Benjamin R. C. Low. HBMV

Love, that our love be this! Mummia. Rupert Brooke. BrPo

Love that's fragile,/Love that's old. Little Things. Marion Strobel. HBMV

Love that's true, is Love for ever. Amphitrion. John Dryden. CavP

A love that should have lasted years. For No One. John Lennon and Paul McCartney. WTO

Love, the door is open Absence. Peter Meinke. PPJ

Love the lore/you would one day change/the slow years for. Apology for Youth. Sister Mary Madeleva. PoPl

Love the men who can serve as hawk, spaniel or hound. Polly. John Gay. NOEC

Love, the real,/terrifies/the dreamer in his riot cell. Gold and Black. Michael Ondaatje. NoP

...Love,/The sole necessity of Earth and Heaven! Among the Hills: Prelude. John Greenleaf Whittier. OxBA; PoEL 1-5

Love them or hate, 'twere little matter then. Of Women No More Evil. Anonymous. AnIL

Love, these are you and I–enter this portal. Snowflake on Asphodel. Conrad Aiken. CMoP

Love they would learn full soon without/my teaching! A Plain Man's Dream. Frederick Keppel. AA

Love, thou breakest mine heart a-two. Christ's Gift to Man. Anonymous. ACP

Love, thou wilt break my heart! Knights Errant. Sister Mary Madeleva. CAW

Love-time would bring me back to you/And build our happy nest again. Child's Talk in April. Christina Georgina Rossetti. GN

Love to be saved for it, proffer'd to, spent on! Misconceptions. Robert Browning. AtBAP; OBEV; OBVV

Love to Death is gathered in. As Lambs into the Pen. Dorothy Wellesley. FaBoTw

Love told me all these things. I Know. Elsa Barker. HBMV

Love tunes my Heart just to my strings. Anacreontea: Love. Anonymous. OBVE

"Love was dead all day." Threnody. Alfred Kreymborg. MAPA

"Love, we have lost/a year!" Feminine. Henry Cuyler Bunner. AA

Love will awake again/That lay so long asleep. Muse and Poet. Robert Bridges. OBMV

Love will find out the way. Love Will Find Out the Way. Anonymous. CBEP; FaBoCh; GBL; GN; HBV 1-2; LiTL; LoGBV; OBEV; TreFS; WiR

Love will return with all its olden fire. Cynthia, Cynthia. Sextus Propertius. LiTW

A love-wing'd spirit glide in glory by,/Striking the tent of its mortality! Her, A Statue. Thomas Stoddart. OBNC

Love with all my death. Messages. Francis Thompson. CH

The love with which your great hearts overflow! Women Damned. Charles Baudelaire. PeHV

Love withheld.../...restrained If There Be Sorrow. Mari E. Evans. NNP; PoNe

Love would be merely you.　Song: "Oh! Love," they said, "is King of Kings." Rupert Brooke.　HBV 1-2

Love would die a sterile death,/did not music lend her breath.　Love. Johann Ludwig Tieck.　LiTW

LOVE YOU　Two Variations: All about Love.　Philip Whalen.　NeAP

Love,/your mother'/which is Naomi–　Kaddish.　Allen Ginsberg.　AmPC; HaCAP

...Love/your Statues, love their names.　Paul and Virginia.　John Wheelwright.　CrMA

Love, youth, and the sound of wings.　Autumn.　Humbert Wolfe.　PoLf

Loved her better, and forgave her.　Rebecca's After-Thought.　Elizabeth Turner.　HBV 1-2; HBVY

A loved immortal rose/All glorified!　Lincoln's Birthday.　John Kendrick Bangs.　PGD

Loved the tiger; and she bore him/Little Mimshi-tiger mixtures.　The Mimshi Maiden.　Hugh McCrae.　NOAV

The loveliest lynchee was our Lord.　The Chicago Defender Sends a Man to Little Rock, Fall, 1957.　Gwendolyn Brooks.　AmNP; PoBA

...The loveliness/of her gold rains down.　The Graveyard Road.　Tom McKeown.　HoAn

Lovely as pansies or a bluebird's wings!　A Prayer after Illness.　Violet Alleyn Storey.　TrPWD

A lovely Beauty in a summer grave!　Methought I Saw the Footsteps of a Throne.　William Wordsworth.　SyP

The lovely changing moon!　By Moonlight.　May Sarton.　MoLP

...Lovely day.　Three Fitts.　Stewart Parker.　CIP

Lovely fa-de-little-aro, sing tooral all day.　Moosehead Lake.　*Anonymous.* OuSiCo

Lovely human selves.　Breakthrough.　John Sinclair.　NBP

Lovely, like this.　The Dark Way Home: Survivors.　Michael S. Harper. CNA

Lovely Major Hoople.　A Classic Case.　Gilbert Sorrentino.　NeAP

A lovely nutbrowne face is best of all.　A Sonet Written in Prayse of the Browne Beautie.　George Gascoigne.　AAS; EnPo

Lovely the dead tree lies.　This Way Only.　Lesbia Harford.　PoAu 1-2

Lovely the leap, explosion into light.　As One Who Wanders Into Old Workings.　C. Day-Lewis.　FaBoMo; LiTM

The lovely vision of naked Helen.　Troy.　Robin Flower.　SeCePo

Lovely with a high-bridged nose.　Song of the Unloved.　*Anonymous.* PeSA

The lover lingers and sings/And the maid remembers.　Songs of Travel. Robert Louis Stevenson.　OBNC

The Lover of my soul for evermore!　I Love Thee, Lord.　Connie Calenberg. BePJ

A lover of Renoirs who has forgotten her name?　L'Apres Midi d'une Fille aux Cheveur de Lin.　Ronald McCuaig.　PoAu 1-2

The lover of the grave, the lover/That hanged himself for love.　A Shropshire Lad.　Alfred Edward Housman.　NOBV

Lover to lover, no kiss,/no touch, but forever and ever this.　At Baia.　Hilda ("H. D.") Doolittle.　AnFE; APA; LiTA; MAPA; NOBA

The lover who was a guest leaves.　Chicago: Near West-Side Renewal. Dennis Schmitz.　AmPA

...The lover/With a valley full of wheat.　Questions and Answers.　Diana O Hehir.　NPGG

Loverd Godd of sothfastheedd.　In Manus Tuas, Domine.　*Anonymous.* CoBE

Lovers alone lovers protect.　Prelude.　Patrick Kavanagh.　FaBoIP; IPY; NoAm

Lovers, continual lovers, only repay me.　City of Orgies.　Walt Whitman. NYP

(The lovers think of death.)　Blindman's Buff.　Peter Viereck.　LiTM; MiAP; MoAmPo

Lovers under the hemlock lie.　Pastoral.　Robert Hillyer.　MoAmPo

Loves Martyrs must be ever, ever/dying.　The Broken Heart.　John Ford. AtBAP

Loves she like me?　Loves She Like Me?　Samuel Woodworth.　AA

The loves that from his hand proud Youth lets fall,/Even as the beads of a told rosary!　The House of Life.　Dante Gabriel Rossetti.　OBNC

...Loves that seize/Man's soul, and waft her on storm-melodies!　Venice. John Addington Symonds.　HBV 1-2

Lovesong is the dry aftersound/of your long nails clicking.　Life's Work. Maxine W. Kumin.　GP

The loving are the daring.　The Song of the Camp.　Bayard Taylor.　AA; BeLS; GN; HBV 1-2; HBVY; WBLP

...Loving her I shall learn/My own secret at last from the words of her song. The Other.　Ruth Fainlight.　BrRo

Loving, I shall attain Love's perfect fee.　To Our Saviour.　Agostinho da Cruz.　CAW

A loving languor, which is not repose.　Don Juan.　George Gordon, Lord Byron.　MOON

Loving not me alone.　His Farewell to His Unkind and Unconstant Mistress. Francis Davison.　ElL; OBSC

Loving the smell and the houses/so completely it leaves my heart empty. Summer in a Small Town.　Linda Gregg.　MAYP

Loving Thee, find Thee; love Thee, finding Thee.　Lord, If Thou Art Not Present.　John Gray.　CAW; TrPWD

Loving what he beheld and will behold.　History.　Robert Fitzgerald. FYAP; MoVE

Loving what was not, might not be, nor is.　Not That, If You Had Known. Trumbull Stickney.　NCEP

Low flying crows.　Fallow Land.　Eunice Clark.　NAMP

Low in her grave.　The May Sun Sheds an Amber Light.　William Cullen Bryant.　AA

Low laughters and the lamp-lit room.　My Jack.　John Francis O'Donnell. IrPN

Low love fulfilled of low success?/(Ah me! ah me!/Hey diddle dee!)　A Ballad of High Endeavor.　*Anonymous.*　NA

Low over clarinet and flute/Hung heaven upon a single note.　At the Symphony.　Robert Nathan.　HBMV

Low places where the rock-fish feed.　Evening by the Sea.　Algernon Charles Swinburne.　FaBoPP; SyP

Low sinks the sun–and all is gone!　What Triumph Moves on the Billows So Blue?　Matthew Gregory Lewis.　OBTV

Low soft aerial chimes, unknown/Save 'mid these silences alone.　Australian Transcripts, IX: The Bell-Bird.　William Sharp.　FM

Low speech they murmur, in tones that bear no secrets/abroad: they gain their ends without toil...　Old Age.　Son of Ya'fur Al-Aswad.　AWP

Low twittering underneath the thatch/At the gray dawn of day.　The First Swallow.　Charlotte Smith.　HBV 1-2

...Lowell/struck down in his cab.　This Year.　Joseph Hutchison.　AmC; AMV-81

Lower, to swim secretly.　Niagara.　Richard Emil Braun.　NoAm

Lowering his head for a moment/He starts to step.　A Dawn Horse. William Harmon.　FYAP

The lowering lute lamenteth now therefore/Phillips her friend that can her touch no more.　On the Death of Phillips.　*Anonymous.*　OBSC

The lowest savages on earth.　A Suggestion Made by the Posters of the "Globe."　J. E. Thorold Rogers.　FaBoEE

Lowlands, lowlands, away, my John.　Lowlands.　*Anonymous.*　TrAS

The lowliest duties on herself did lay.　England, 1802.　William Wordsworth.　OBEV

The lowliest weed could tell at what terrible cost.　Invocation.　Carleton Drewry.　MoRP

The lowly Uncle Tomming/and Aunt Jemimas' smiles.　Song for the Old Ones.　Maya Angelou.　SaC

A loyal eye that stares/for years at the speedometer/waiting for it to turn over. 1948 Plymouth Abandoned on the Ice.　Bill Meissner.　AmC

–Luanda, you are here!　Song for Luanda.　Luandino Vieira.　WhB

Luandinha seconded it.　The Riverman.　Elizabeth Bishop.　NYBP

Lubov moya, otstoopnika prostee.　An Evening of Russian Poetry.　Vladimir Nabokov.　NYBP

The lucid outline of the Swan.　Canticle.　James Philip McAuley.　PoAu 1-2

Lucifer teareth me–/Jesu! Maria! liberate nos ab his diris tentationibus/Inimici. Hypochondriacus (parody).　Charles Lamb.　BXAP

Lucille/we are/the Light　Incandescence.　Lucille Clifton.　GeTw

...Luck is/shaking a cup of ice, I want/to drink that water.　Late Afternoon on a Good Lake.　Dara Wier.　MAYP

Luck is something I do not understand.　The Lover Remembereth Such as He Sometimes Enjoyed...　Leon Stokesbury.　SM

Luck loves him longest who can crack/this kind of lash on omens.　Favour. Robert D. Fitzgerald.　CBAP

Luckily for us.　Humming-Bird.　D. H. Lawrence.　CMoP; InPS; LiTB; LiTM; PAI; PPP; SeCePo

Lucky flute: what more could you wish?　Tree to Flute.　Anna Hajnal. VWA

The lucky lad was me!　Shy Geordie.　Helen B. Cruickshank.　ACV; BSV; GoTS; OxBS

The lucky ones with their shadows.　The Last One.　William Stanley Merwin.　LCAP; NoAm; VGW

Lucky the lad who from trouble can fly!　The Maiden Hind.　*Anonymous.* LiTW

Lucky with day approaching, with leaning dawn.　Something Is Bound to Happen.　W. H. Auden.　CoBMV; OAEP; PoRA

Lucy has survived this night/And has one created days hard grace　Lucy Taking Birth.　Diana Scott.　BrRo

Lucy, you brightnesse of our spheare, who are/The Muses evening, as their morning-starre.　To Lucy, Countesse of Bedford, with Mr. Donnes Satyres. Ben Jonson.　AnAnS 2; OBS; SeCV 1-2

Lug us back lifeward–bone by infant bone.　National Winter Garden.　Hart Crane.　AmP; ErPo; LiTM; OxBA

Lugubrious ending,/new lives pending?　Outlook Uncertain.　Alastair Reid. NePoEA-2

Lukewarm soup/is my second favorite. The Soup of Venus. James Tate. AmPA

Lukewarm to the blood... My America. Oliver La Grone. NNP

Lull and annul me–and become monstrously the mirrors/Of my insensate errors! The Music. Charles Baudelaire. SyP

Lull thee or lure, more fond thou wilt not find. Erotion. Algernon Charles Swinburne. PoEL 1-5

Lullaby..... Nocturne. Donald Jeffrey Hayes. CDC

Lullaby and lullaloo; sleep, lammie, noo. East Coast Lullaby. Lady Anne Lindsay. EtS

Lullaby, Lilibrow. Lie asleep;/Blest be thy rest. Lullaby. William Barnes. VLP

Lullay, my dear Heart, mine own dear Darling. I Saw a Maiden. *Anonymous.* ISi

Lulled her asleep, and then grew drunk. Grecian Kindness. John Wilmot, Earl of Rochester. OBSP

Lulling him to downy slumbers/With remembrances of Heaven. Two Angels. Richard Moncton, Lord Houghton Milnes. OBRV

Lulling the year, with all its cares, to rest! The Trosachs. William Wordsworth. EnLi 1-2; GTBS; HBV 1-2; OBEV; OBRV; SeCePo

Lulls the grim, drowsy cobra on her arm. The Bayadere. Francis Saltus Saltus. AA

Lumbered off to his eight o'clock/Gladly to teach– A Teacher. Reed Whittemore. GLGT

Luminescence all around. Female Rain. Laura Tohe. STE

Luminous horizon/where you are. Steady Rain. Lynn Merrill. AMV-80

Luminously indiscreet;/complete; continuous. The Sermon on the Warpland. Gwendolyn Brooks. BPo; LiTM; NOBA; PoBA

Lump in my throat growing harder. Coming Home in March. Harold Littlebird. STE; VoR

Lumpety, lumpety, lump! A Farmer Went Trotting upon His Gray Mare. Mother Goose. TiPo

Lumpety, lumpety, lump! The Mischievous Raven. *Anonymous.* OxNR

"Lunch is over!" says she. A Thin Facade for Edith Sitwell. John Malcolm Brinnin. FiBHP; NYBP

Lunging your beak down like a spear/To fetch them home again. Return of the Goddess Artemis. Robert Graves. PoA

..Lure and sadden/My heart with futile bounds. Home-Thoughts from France. Isaac Rosenberg. MMM

The lure, wherat the soaring hawk did strike. Madrigal: "The greedy hawk with sudden sight of lure." *Anonymous.* PBBP

Lures to the longed-for and regretted joys. This Little Vigil. Charles G. Bell. MoLP; NePoAm

The lurid snow-cloud on the down/Can scarcely hide the winter's head. Epilogue. John Meade Falkner. FaBoPP

Luscious to lick on the lips. Golden Gate: The Teacher. Lilyan S. Mastrolia. AMV-80

Lust it comes out, that gluttony went in. On Gut. Ben Jonson. AnAnS 2; JCP

Lustrous eyes 'neath Eastern skies, and a woman's veiled face. Drifting Sands and a Caravan. Yolande Langworthy. BLPA

A luxury diminishing death. Dancing the Shout to the True Gospel. Rita Mae Brown. NMM; PeHV

Lycoris–Let me introduce my wife. Epigram. Pott and Wright. ALV

Lye too-lye ring-dee-ring. Katy Dorey. *Anonymous.* OuSiCo

Lye ye here, a husband to them a'.' Lady Isabel and the Elf-Knight. *Anonymous.* FaBoBa; OAEP

Lying/by chance/on the kitchen floor. Alcoholic. F. D. Reeve. NYBP

Lying down in the frugality of sleep. Marchenbilder. John Ashbery. LCAP; NOBA

...The lying famous corrupt/Senators mine our lives for another war. Remembering That Island. Thomas McGrath. NePoEA; PPON

Lying in my arms asleep. Love. Toyohiko Kagawa. TRV

Lying like broken sticks among the stones. Wiltshire Downs. Andrew Young. ChMP; GTBS-P; OxBTC

Lying on her back waiting, fuck yes, waiting. Travis, the Kid Was All Heart. Terry Stokes. AmPA

Lying on/her exaggerated belly/lies/"Lying There." Pregnant Image of "Exaggerating the Village." Nora Dauenhauer. TWSS

Lying on their backs/thinking of the sea. The Distances. William Stanley Merwin. NOBA

Lying so primly propped. Bells for John Whiteside's Daughter. John Crowe Ransom. AmP; AP; CMoP; CoBMV; CrMA; DTC; FF; HAP; HeIP; HoPM; InPo; InPS; LiTA; LiTM; MoAB; MoAmPo; MoVE; NePA; NIP; NoAm; NOBA; NoP; OxBA; PAI; PPON; PPP; PrIm; SoSe; TAP; TreFT; UnPo; VGW; WeW

Lying still, always facing the constant motion. Death Looks Down. Linda Gregg. NPGG

...Lying trampled on the earth/yet blooming purple. Like a sweet apple reddening on the high. Sappho. BoWoP

Lying under the olive trees, O world, O death? Ultima Ratio Regum. Stephen Spender. BBV; CMoP; FaFP; LiTB; LiTM; OAEL 1-2; OBWP; SeCePo; WaaP; WaP

Lying, with face upturned and grim,/On the Llano Estacado. Tantalus–Texas. Joaquin Miller. HBV 1-2

Lyke co(n)stansie till death/and in heaven be our end! Here Followeth the Songe of the Death of Mr. Thewlis. *Anonymous.* CoMu

Lyre, my lyre, are your swanlike curve and hiss. Ars. Marina Tsvetayeva. BoWoP

M

M. Anantanarayanan. I Missed His Book, but I Read His Name. John Updike. OBAL

Ma foi! Chez Brebant ces choses sont rares! Chez Brebant. Francis Alexander Durivage. AA

Ma-ha-mee! My Mammy Was a Wall-Eyed Goat. *Anonymous.* FaBoNo

Ma sleepan reid Robin. For My Newborn Son. Sydney Goodsir Smith. ACV

Mab will pinch her by the toe. The Fairies. Robert Herrick. OBS

Mabbie or Mabbie to be. A Street in Bronzeville: The Ballad of Chocolate Mabbie. Gwendolyn Brooks. CAPP

Mabel–when is the bomb set to An Anarchist's Letter. Harald Wyndham. PoL

""MacDonald lost his life for love of Irish Molly O!" Irish Molly O. *Anonymous.* HBV 1-2

Machine, make me fingers to manage the dangerous keys. Learning to Type. Diana O Hehir. NPGG

Machines and morning fixed upon/The starting spectrum of the dawn. Goodmorning with Light. John Ciardi. WaP

Mad as the mist and snow. Words for Music Perhaps. William Butler Yeats. AtBAP

Mad as the polar moon, decipherable by none. Rocket Show. James Keir Baxter. AnNZ

Mad girls do love mad men. Song: "He that will court a Wench that is coy." *Anonymous.* ErPo

The mad in absolute power. Golgotha. X. J. Kennedy. NYBP

Mad monsters of no kind? Hide and Seek. Robert Graves. NTCP

Mad Queen Windmills and Weathervanes . Hurricane . 0164. Telephone Directory. Harry Crosby. EAS

..."Madam," I pleaded, "wouldn't you rather/See for yourself?" Telephone Conversation. Wole Soyinka. SoSe; TTY

Madam to you. Madam's Past History. Langston Hughes. NoAm

Madam, your humble servant, Samuel Sewall. Samuel Sewall. Anthony Hecht. ConAP; LiTM; MP; NePoEA; NLV; PoPl; TwCP

Madame Maynard has been ground down to a grey pebble/of strong Breton dignity Stranded in My Ontario. Ronald G. Everson. NOBC

Madame, regent/I may you call/Of vertuows all. To Mistress Margaret Tilney. John Skelton. MeEL

Made by adversity sublime,/By faith and hope immortal. Not Ours the Vows. Bernard Barton. HBV 1-2

Made by Contact, as Men get Meazles. Presbyterian Church Government. Samuel (1602-80) Butler. OBS

Made by God's providence the Anointed/One. To Abraham Lincoln. John James Piatt. AA

Made for man's dwelling. Caedmon's Hymn. Caedmon. EBCP; TEP

Made for my kisses,/made for my soul. The Fickle One. Pablo Neruda. FF; OLR

Made glory shine in her humility. To God the Son. Henry Constable. OBSC

...Made her heart rejoice/That she was almoner. When She a Maiden Slim. Maurice Hewlett. OHIP

Made him take up his shirt, lay down his sword. Upon Pagget. Robert Herrick. CaPo; FaBoCh

Made His own bed ere He was born. In the Holy Nativity of Our Lord: Shepherds' Hymn. Richard Crashaw. TrGrPo

Made in Sweden: carts are my trade. A Carriage from Sweden. Marianne Moore. HAP; LiTA; LiTM; MoAB; MP; NePA; TwCP; WeW

Made like fire by the rubbing of two sticks? To Ping-Ku, Asleep. Lawrence Durrell. ChMP; NeBP

Made/love made/children. The Children. Constance Urdang. CoAP; IHMS

Made me think just now of you untangling/blueberries, carefully, from their dense branches. Love Poem. Gary Miranda. SM

Made o' stone? Wake Cry. Waring Cuney. BANP

Made of my/palm a nest/for the dead. The Container. Cid Corman. VGW

Made of nothing/except loneliness. No Time Ago. Edward Estlin Cummings. OBSP

...Made of the bent bodies/of fabulous, elongate beasts   The Library.   John Logan.   AMV-80

Made of the world a hushed transfigured place.   Prayer.   Amos N. Wilder.   TrPWD

Made one now with the nameless multitude.   New York.   John Hall Wheelock.   NYP

"Made," quoth the fellow, with a smile,–"to sell."   The Razor-Seller.   John Wolcot.   HBV 1-2; InMe

Made so by destiny or by ourself.   The Broom.   Giacomo Leopardi.   LiTW

Made the boy dream/that he had rubbed his hands/against the sky.   In Dream: The Privacy of Sequence.   Ray A. Young Bear.   CDW

Made them all shrieke, it lookt so ghastly black.   Hero and Leander.   George Chapman.   AtBAP

Made up of all these halves, thou canst not pass/For anything entirely but an ass!   On the Supposed Author of a Late Poem "In Defense of Satire."   John Wilmot, Earl of Rochester.   APAS

Made young by joys that live from ours.   California.   Thomas Lake Harris   AA

The madman of Glen Balcain am I....   Sweeney the Mad (excerpt).   *Anonymous.*   OnYI

The madman saith He said so: it is strange.   An Epistle.   Robert Browning.   CABL; VLP

The madonnas at noon....   Poem: "So many pigeons at Columbus Circle."   Arthur Gregor.   VGW

The maggots of corrupted texts...   Religion.   Samuel (1602-80) Butler.   DBV

Magic hath stolen away.   The Truants.   Walter De la Mare.   MoBrPo

The magic of her cry.   Home Thoughts.   Odell Shepard.   HBMV

Magic words I mumbled all the way.   Hunger.   *Anonymous.*   WTO

The magician waved and bowed, showed us his/empty sleeves and she was gone.   Death's Blue-Eyed Girl.   Linda Pastan.   PPJ

Magicians bartered for.   Erige Cor Tuum Ad Me In Caelum.   Hilda ("H. D.") Doolittle.   CMoP

Magnific Fame! And let fat Plenty/Marry one Poet out of Twenty!   The Petition of Tom Dermondy to the Three Fates in Council Sitting.   Thomas Dermody.   AnIV

Magnificently unprepared/For the long littleness of life.   Youth.   Frances Cornford.   ELU; PCP

Magnified and sanctified be His great/Name!   Kaddish.   Levi Yitzhok.   TrJP

Magog, looming at the gate,/When music sounds, forgets his hate.   Missa Papae Marcelli.   James Philip McAuley.   BoAV

"Magpie"–signed Hokusai.   Camden Magpie.   Hugh McCrae.   PoAu 1-2

Mah 'ittle Touzle Head.   'Ittle Touzle Head.   Ray Garfield Dandridge.   BANP

A maid, a child, God young.   Meditation on the Nativity.   Elizabeth Jennings.   NAs

A maiden I will die.   The Two Magicians.   *Anonymous.*   OxBoLi

The maiden jewels of the rain/Sit in your dabbled locks again.   To K. de M.   Robert Louis Stevenson.   OBNC

De maiden mit nodings on.   Ballad by Hans Breitmann.   Charles Godfrey Leland.   BXAP; CenHV; NOBL; PaPo

Maiden, not to be greeted unbenignly.   Hendecasyllabics.   Alfred, Lord Tennyson.   EBEV; FaBoCo; NOBL; VLP

The maiden wept,/Beside the bright/Waukulla.   The Legend of Waukulla.   Hezekiah Butterworth.   PAH

Maids often lose their maidenhead/Ere they set foot in nuptial bed.   Love's Courtship.   Thomas Carew.   UnTE

The mailbox in which we'll mail this/Is slightly lighter than the sky.   To Robert Lowell and Osip Mandelstam.   Frederick Seidel.   AMV-81

..Maine trades/in staying power, not shiftless drives.   Maine.   Philip Booth.   AmFN

Maintain on one sun porch, in one mild/Summer, one dismay unreconciled.   Dolor.   Josephine Miles.   FaBoWP

Maintaining, both in sun and shade,/The semblance of a smile!   Duck in Central Park.   Frances Higginson Savage.   GoYe

Maintains its own life and its powers, peeking at us as it does.   Waiting and Peeking.   V. R. Lang.   NePA

The mair shame on't.   Pont and Blyth.   *Anonymous.*   GBP

Mak ay true honesty your law/An' safest shield.   An Address to the Plebeians.   John Learmont.   FaBoPV; NOEC

Make a most infernal clatter, here the dinner comes!   Going in to Dinner.   Edward Shanks.   OBMV; OxBTC

Make a sea of mud.   Dream.   Solomon Edwards.   NNP; PoNe

Make a very pretty face.   Patience Is a Virtue.   *Anonymous.*   OxNR

Make a wide dreaming pansy of an old pond in the night.   Nocturne in a Deserted Brickyard.   Carl Sandburg.   MoAmPo

"Make a wish, Tom, make a wish."   Drifters.   Bruce Dawe.   CBAP

Make all that is, and can delight,/from every atom run.   All That Is, and Can Delight.   Robert Farren.   OxBI

Make bloom the lily in the ash/Of this neglected urn.   To One of Little Faith.   Hildegarde Flanner.   HBMV

Make bold to write upon my telltale cheek/In a clear hand the things I dare not speak.   A Letter.   King of Seville Mu'tamid.   LiTW

Make but the dear Amanda mine!   To Fortune.   James (1700-48) Thomson.   BSV

Make every bargain clear and plain/That none may afterwards complain.   Proverbial Advice on the Conduct of Business.   *Anonymous.*   FaBoUs

Make every day a Pentecost.   Pentecost.   Adelbert Sumpter Coats.   TrPWD

Make for their uses out of flesh and blood.   Sonnet: "Flesh, I have knocked at many a dusty door."   John Masefield.   MoBrPo; SeCePo

Make friends forever/& go away   Things to Do in New York (City).   Ted Berrigan.   NoAm

Make game of that which makes as much of Thee.   Worldly Wisdom.   Omar Khayyam.   EG

Make glad the English, and the Indian.   Mans Restlesse Soule Hath Restlesse Eyes and Ears.   Roger Williams.   SCAP

Make haste, therefore, sweet love, whilest it is prime;/For none can call again the passed time.   Whilst It Is Prime.   Edmund Spenser.   OBEV

Make haste and run/to light up the dark fields of France.   Be Swift O Sun.   R. A. K. Mason.   AnNZ

Make haste away together.   An Invitation to Lubberland.   *Anonymous.*   CoBE; FaBoNo; GBP

Make haste! Before it is too late!/For Death stands knocking at the gate!   The Children's Ghosts.   Winifred M. Letts.   HBMV

Make her as much more base by loving me.   Arcadia.   Sir Philip Sidney.   SiPS

Make him stand up and fight.   Hare.   Molly Holden.   TEP

Make holes in theirs/to hang presents.   Song for Seven Parts of the Body, 7.   Maxine W. Kumin.   PoL

Make hunger-bread of/Beauty and tears.   Poet's Bread.   Sister Mary Philip.   GoBC

Make it a difficult world...for practical people.   Practical People.   Robinson Jeffers.   NAMP

Make it by steamboat/I likes to take it real slow   The Reactionary Poet.   Ishmael Reed.   CNA

Make it enough/make it enough/or eat/suffering without end   Minutes.   Denis Johnson.   MAYP

...Make it sweet again!   But What Is the Reader to Make of This?   John Ashbery.   InPS

Make its path smooth–then shall it travel/beyond the four hills!   Ho! Ye Sun, Moon, Stars.   *Anonymous.*   PrIm

Make known him Master, and for what good reason.   What's This of Death.   Edna St.Vincent Millay.   BoLiVe

Make lesser mornings, when the great are done.   After the Storm.   Henry Vaughan.   BoC

Make light of love, and check the trembling tears.   At Swindon.   Reginald, Viscount Esher Brett.   PeHV

Make love at home, and go to bed betimes.   Fatal Love.   Matthew Prior.   FaBoCo; NLV

Make Love in Tune, or thro' the Gamut rant.   Italian Opera.   James Miller.   OBEC; UnS

Make lullaby!   Sea-Sleep.   Thomas Lake Harris   AA

Make me a humble thing of love and tears.   "Multum Dilexit.'.   Hartley Coleridge.   EnRP; HBV 1-2

Make me an animal/who loves its own tongue.   The Seduction.   Suzanne Berger Rioff.   NMM

Make me anything but neuter/When the sap begins to stir!   Spring Song.   Bliss Carman.   HBV 1-2

Make me by thy answer blessed.   O Divine Star of Heaven.   John Fletcher.   GBL

Make me chaste, Lord, but not yet.   The Love Feast.   W. H. Auden.   ErPo

Make me content, O Lord, with daily bread.   Prayer for Contentment.   Edwin McNeill Poteat.   TrPWD

Make me cool and humble./Bless me.   Hunger in New York City.   Simon J. Ortiz.   MAYP

Make me doubt if heaven will gather/Roses hence, or lilies rather.   Upon the Infant Martyrs.   Richard Crashaw.   NoP; OAEL 1-2

Make me forget her tears.   At Casterbridge Fair.   Thomas Hardy.   EnLi 1-2

Make me immoderately wise.   Invocation.   John Drinkwater.   HBMV; PoA

Make me jealous while I angle in my ingle 'neath the/trees.   Midsummer Jingle.   Newman Levy.   BoNaP

Make me like thee, then shall I be/Prepared to see thy face.   The Morning Bright, with Rosy Light.   Thomas O. Summers.   AH

Make me recognize myself,/compose me.   Leit.   Marcos Rodriguez Frese.   InW

Make me, Saviour, what Thou art;/Live Thyself within my heart.   Gentle Jesus.   Charles Wesley.   OxBChV; OxBoCh; TreFS

Make me Thy fuel, Flame of God.   Deliver Me.   Amy Carmichael.   STF

Make me thy torch to burn out swiftly, Lord.   The Torch.   Theodosia Garrison.   BLPA

Make me your wife, that's all I ask of you. Take Back Your Gold. Louis W. Paitzakow. FSN; GoTF; TreF

Make merry, sing an thou canst, take heed to thy geer, that/thou lose none. Memorial Verses for Travellers. Sir Anthony Fitzherbert. FaBoUs

Make my bed, mammie, now! The Croodin Doo. *Anonymous.* OxNR

Make my dull spirit glow/This Silent Night! Come, Holy Babe! Mary Dickerson Bangham. PGD

Make my last breath a bugle call, carrying/Peace o'er the valleys and cold hills for ever! Valley of the Shadow. John Galsworthy. OHIP; TrPWD

Make my lone bed hard--/Would 'twere underground! Bereft. Thomas Hardy. BoLoP; NoAm

Make new friends, but keep the old;/Those are silver, these are gold. New Friends and Old Friends. Joseph Parry. BLPA; BLPL; GoTF; PoToHe; TreFT

Make Nones the 7th, Ides the 15th day. The Roman Calendar. Benjamin Hall Kennedy. FaBoUs

Make of it what you will. The Enlightenment. Patricia Sheppard. AMV-81

Make of me Thy darling/That I Thee love over all thing. Jesu Dulcis. Saint Bernard of Clairvaux CAW

Make of my Faith/a Black Star. I am Beckoning. Boys. Black. Gwendolyn Brooks. CNA

Make once more my heart thy home. Song: "Rarely, rarely, comest thou." Percy Bysshe Shelley. ERoP 1-2; HBV 1-2; OAEP; OBNC; OBRV; TrGrPo

Make one still music to the heart of God. There Is a High Place. Edwin Markham. AH

Make peace therefore, and graunt me timely grace./That al my wounds wil heale in little space. Amoretti, LVII. Edmund Spenser. AAS

Make pictures of themselves. An Aestuary. George Croly. IrPN

Make pleasing music, and not wild uproar. How Many Bards Gild the Lapses of Time! John Keats. EnRP

Make ready my grave-clothes to-morrow. Thekla's Song. Friedrich von Schiller. AWP

Make rich the winds with minstrelsy. Nepenthe. George Darley. OBNC

"Make room, make room for a faithful heart/In the House of Love, to-night." Song: "I came to the door of the House of Love." Alfred Noyes. HBV 1-2

Make some muscle/in your head, but/use the muscle/in yr heart Young Soul. LeRoi (Imamu Amiri Baraka) Jones. BPo; CNA

Make subjects love, and enemies to quake?/This is the time. The Advice. *Anonymous.* APAS

Make summer with their wide-eyed gold. Kingcups. Sacheverell Sitwell. MoBrPo

Make sure that they are thoroughly cremated. Shipment to Maidanek. Ephim G. Fogel. OBWP; TrJP

Make sweet May of Winter weather. A Glee for Winter. Alfred Domett. HBV 1-2

Make that what. I Have Been Thinking. Artie Gold. CaPN

Make the mighty ages/Of eternity. Little Things. Julia A. Fletcher Carney. FaFP

"Make the ocean free." The Ship Canal from the Atlantic to the Pacific. Francis Lieber. PAH

Make the will of the world your trumpet, the heart/of the world your drum! Toward a True Peace. Ralph Cheyney. PGD

Make thee another self for love of me,/That beauty still may live in thine or thee. Sonnets, X: "For shame! deny that thou bear'st love to any." William Shakespeare. MasP

Make them aware/it can be done. The red road. Nila NorthSun. STE

Make this memorial due. Memorials: On the Slain at Chickamauga. Herman Melville AA

Make this the emblem, for cloud-shadows/stumble vaguely across the moor like ghosts. More Than People. Robin Fulton. PoSH

Make this thing plain! Clean Hands. Henry Austin Dobson. TrPWD

Make Thou it perfect with Thy perfect life. It Is Toward Evening. *Anonymous.* BePJ

Make Thou the harvest of our days/To fall within Thy ways. Harvest. Ellen Mackay Hutchinson Cortissoz. AA; HBV 1-2

Make thy love larger to enlarge my worth. Sonnets from the Portuguese, XVI. Elizabeth Barrett Browning. OAEP

Make tiger-like retaliation;/But 'tis true! War! James Gilchrist Lawson. WBLP

Make-up, muslins, brazen talk/Go hand-in-hand with modern days.' Other Fabrics, Other Mores! Anna Maria Lenngren. PBWP

Make us learn that we must die. Lines on a Bill of Mortality, 1790. William Cowper. OxBoCh

Make us see. Diver. Robert Francis. LiSp

Make use of ev'ry friend--and ev'ry foe. An Essay on Criticism. Alexander Pope. OxBoCh

Make way for Brotherhood--make way for Man! Brotherhood. Edwin Markham. BBV; PGD

Make we merry as we may. Hay, Ay, Hay, Ay. *Anonymous.* SBVL

Make what you will thereof: to me/It has no sense at all. Allegro. McM" InMe

Make your best bow to her and bid adieu,/Then, if she likes it, she will follow you. On Fame. John Keats. CBEP; EnLit

Make your mocks and sly grimaces/At Love's self, and do not fear it. Song: "Down the dimpled green-sward dancing." George Darley. OnYI

Make your mouth into an "O."/That's right. Apostrophe to a Pram Rider. E. B. White. InMe

Make your own music. The Trumpet Shall Sound. John V. Hicks. AMV-81

Maken pilgrimage to herself. walken. Present. Sonia Sanchez. CNA; WPOW

The maker of a house, of a real human house, is God him-/self, the same who made the stars and ... Your House. *Anonymous.* PoToHe

Maker of Gods in lands beyond the sea. Evarra and His Gods. Rudyard Kipling. MoBrPo

The maker of the sea. Still-Life. Ted Hughes. NYBP

Makes a break, too (for us/Not Sisyphus). Aviemore. Janet Waller. PoSH

...Makes a feast,/And bids the greatest and the least. The Feast-Time of the Year. *Anonymous.* OHIP

...Makes a glass so true/As I therein no other's face but yours can view. Verses Made the Night before He Died. Michael Drayton. NOBE

Makes a man healthy/And wealthy and wise. The Cock Crows in the Morn. *Anonymous.* HBVY; OxNR; PBBP

Makes a meal you'll all remember. If You Want to Write Me. *Anonymous.* FSW

Makes David Logan crown his head with bays. L'Art poetique. Nicholas Boileau-Despreaux. EnLi 1-2

Makes glad the life,/And brings Death low! Wine. Micah Joseph Lebensohn. LiTW; TrJP

Makes it glad to come back to me through the screens. The Absence. Denise Levertov. NaP

Makes it seem sweeter to be hers! Monna Lisa. James Russell Lowell. AmLP

Makes lime for Mammon's tower. The Ravaged Villa. Herman Melville. AP; CTC; MAmP; NOBA; PoEL 1-5

Makes me falter at your feet, sweet Marie. Sweet Marie. Cy Warman. TreFS

Makes me think about that song my/Baby used to sing/Mmmmmm mmmm, Lord have mercy on me I'll Go with Her Blues. Robert Wilkins. BluL

Makes mirrors vague. It is the mist that I most favour. Autumn. Vernon Scannell. OxBTC

Makes of her eyes the simple grace. The Fire. Robert Creeley. NOBA

Makes soft the couch and calms the final rest. Epigram: "No charm can stay, no medicine can assuage." Walter Savage Landor. FaBoEE

Makes summer's welcome thrice more wish'd, more rare. Sonnets, LVI: "Sweet love, renew thy force." William Shakespeare. CBEP; PoLf

Makes summer when the lady lies/In ceaseless rosemary. Essential Oils Are Wrung. Emily Dickinson. AmPP; CBEP; SBG

Makes the circle endless/and godless. Lament. Yehuda Amichai. VWA

Makes the four-poster of a dream. All Animals Like Me. Raymond Souster. WHW

Makes the golden guesses what they are. Evening Songs. John Vance Cheney. AA

Makes the world nothing, pouring in oil and wine.' The Song of the Good Samaritan. Vernon Watkins. LiTM

Makes Time so vicious in his reaping. George Crabbe. Edwin Arlington Robinson. LiTM

Makes us prophets, priests, and kings. The Covenant of His Grace. Charles Wesley. BePJ

Maketh a mannes here to gorw through his hood. Snatches: "Gret hunting by rivers and wood." *Anonymous.* OxBM

"Makeum-Tell-It Squad." Dialect Quatrain. Marcus B. Christian. AmNP

& Making a cup/of coffee that's all   Good Morning Love! Paul Blackburn. NMP; NoAm

Making a sound like some other planet's machinery. Sects. Jack Gilbert. NPGG

Making a third, to round the simple moral. Scylla and Charybdis. Thomas Kinsella. OxBTC

Making a wind among the flowers. Beauty and Love. Andrew Young. GBL

...Making clear/His might and love in saving sinful man. Festus: Proem to the Third Edition. Philip James Bailey. VLP

Making click click, spin/spin noises, clearing his throat. The Boar. Robert Kelly. CoPo

Making down the roads of earth/Endless detour. Local Habitation: On Inhabiting an Orange. Josephine Miles. PoA

Making faces at heaps of people on a black heath. Poem: "The walls of the maelstrom are painted with trees." Charles Madge. EAS

Making garlands of their own/not of iron and of stone. Stanzas for My Daughter. Horace Gregory. MoVE

Making ice another burn,/Whilst itself doth harder turn! The Miracle. Sir John Suckling. CaPo

Making it good/to feel you/among us. Child Poem. Annette Arkeketa West. TWSS

Making its song against the sun. The Days. Paul Blocklyn. AMV-80

Making love to everything/Before it moves on/Yet returning. When Spring Came. *Anonymous.* RFM

Making music for her I love. Not All Sweet Nightingales. Luis de Gongora y Argote. CAW

Making my heart in its sorrow rejoice. Whispering Hope. Alice Hawthorne. PSoN

Making my senses' darkened fields/A theatre of war. In Me Two Worlds. C. Day Lewis. AnFE

Making no outcry, no matter/Who may be straining to hear. Listening to Foxhounds. James Dickey. LiSp; PAI

The making of a poem shall profit not. My Son, Forsake Your Art. Mahon O'Heffernan. BIrV

Making off with the flour and beans. Elf Night. Ron Rogers. STE

Making our pillows either down, or dust. Death. George Herbert. AnAnS 1; JCP; MePo; NoP; OBS; SeCP; SeCV 1-2

Making ourselves at home. Driving North from Kingsville, Texas. Naomi Shihab. TAT

Making out the menus of tasteless meals/You'll choose to devour, that'll devour you. Schedules. John Dean. AMV-81

Making ready the subjects/for the long afternoon. A Minor Victorian Painter. John Hewitt. CIP

Making ready to forget, and always coming back/To the mooring of starting out, that day so long ago Soonest Mended. John Ashbery. HaCAP; Prf

Making some passionate part of you/Faithless to me down there. Chartivel: Song. Marie de France. WPOW

Making the batter understand too late. Pitcher. Robert Francis. LiSp; NePoAm; OBSP; PP; SD; SoSe

...Making the breasts both flaccid/and firm. Gita Govinda. Jayadeva. AWP; ErPo

Making the children laugh./making butterflies sing. The Beautiful Woman Who Sings. Paula Gunn Allen. TWSS

Making the heart of God rejoice. Cock-Crow. Ralph Nixon Currey. PeSA

Making the owl in the Douglas fir turn his head... Asian Peace Offers Rejected without Publication. Robert Bly. CAPP; NaP; NoAm

Making the people happy, monarch great. The Parliament Dissolved at Oxford. John Ayloffe. APAS

Making the sound of heavy keys/along a thin brass ring. Nocturne of Birth and Water. Don Domanski. CaPN

Making the taste of death/Medicinal, preservative.' The Gifts. John Heath-Stubbs. OxBC

Making the wild/Heats of our blood an offering. A Calvinist in Love. Jack R. Clemo. ChMP

Making the woods reecho with his song. The Fair Morning. Jones Very. NOBA

...Making/their woodland way/much brighter,/und so/weit-/er. The Funnels. Christian Morgenstern. FaBoNo

Making thus my ditty/Of fair love lost for ever and a day. Song: "Oh fly not, Pleasure, pleasant-hearted Pleasure." Wilfrid Scawen Blunt. ViBoPo

Making unwearable golden shoes. Enamoured of the Miniscule. Michael Hartnett. BIrV

Malawi, your name means tomorrow! Malawi. Innocent Banda. WhB

Malcolm X told both of us the TRUTH....../now didn't he? My Ace of Spades. Ted Joans. BOLo

Male seeks, in the area around Berkeley,/another male whose fetish is corderoy... Billings and Cooings from "The Berkeley Barb." Mona Van Duyn. GP

Male spiders must not be too early slain. Arachne. William Empson. InvP; MoVE; OBMV

Male supremacy/never fattened me at its table. Birthplace. Tahereh Saffarzadeh. WPOW

Mally's every way complete. O Mally's Meek, Mally's Sweet. Robert Burns. GN; HBV 1-2

Mam, we're playing funerals now. Take One Home for the Kiddies. Philip Larkin. ELU; OxBTC

Mama, don't cry. Without Benefit of Declaration. Langston Hughes. AmNP; TTY

Mama don't 'low no singin' round here. Mama Don't 'Low. *Anonymous.* FSW

Mama, how long–how long! Epilogue to Rhymes and Rhythms. William Ernest Henley. ViBoPo

Mama's got to go down and join the union for herself. You Gotta Go Down (And Join the Union). *Anonymous.* FSW

Mamma, but it's so many bullies don't go at all. Mamma, Mamma. *Anonymous.* OuSiCo

Mamma felt quite irritated. Our Polite Parents. Carolyn Wells. BBGG

Mamma raised her eyebrows slightly. Our Polite Parents. Carolyn Wells. BBGG

Mamma's gone to the mail boat,/Bye. Mamma's Gone to the Mail Boat. *Anonymous.* OuSiCo

Mamma said, "Why, Moses, dear!" Our Polite Parents. Carolyn Wells. BBGG

Mammie's wee man. Thumb Bold. *Anonymous.* OxNR

Mammy's little baby loves short'nin' bread. Short'nin' Bread. *Anonymous.* BLSo

Man a fancy, earth a coral,/Dualism double zero. The Epistemological Rag. Gray Burr. CoPo

A man, a man alive. The Reply. Theodore Roethke. NoP; NYBP

...The man ain't alive/That can stay with old Strawberry when he makes that high dive. The Srawberry Roan. *Anonymous.* CoSo

Man alive! It comes round again! Garland Sunday. Padraic Colum. GoYe

Man and his greatness survive, lost in the greatness/of God. Hymn to the Sea. William Watson. EtS

Man and the universe shall both grow old,/But not the forms her pencil drew! To My Friends. Friedrich von Schiller. AWP; LiTW

Man and the woman, piggee! Tale of a Little Pig. *Anonymous.* ABF

...Man and woman are a she-/camel and her baby/Who take their radiance from one another. Women and Men. Hassan Sheikh Mumin. WTO

Man be my metaphor. If I Were Tickled by the Rub of Love. Dylan Thomas. FF

Man, blade of grass, pebble, squirrel and great forest. You Can Get Despondent. Maurice Careme. AMV-81

Man blows the golden horn of mind/And hunts beside his elements. The Elements. Oscar Williams. NAMP

Man by himself goes down into the/deep,/Certain, and unbefriended, and alone. Sonnet: "Because my grief seems quiet and apart." Robert Nathan. TrJP

Man can picture the Absent/and Non-Existent. Progress? W. H. Auden. SUW

...A man cannot live by bread/Alone. In the Night Field. William Stanley Merwin. AP; PoCh

The man coming at you may be armed. Give Way. Donald Finkel. NePoEA-2; PPON

The man coming toward you is marching forward on all fronts. The Man Coming Toward You. Oscar Williams. AnAmPo

A man earns strength to war only by dying. Strength to War. Stephen Stepanchev. WaP

Man eats the Dead/From pole to pole. On the Eve of the Feast of the Immaculate Conception: 1942. Robert Lowell. WaaP

Man enters hell without a golden bough. For the Word is Flesh. Stanley Jasspon Kunitz. AnAmPo; VGW

Man, equal and one with me, man that is made of/me, man that is I. Hertha. Algernon Charles Swinburne. EnLi 1-2; MaVP; OAEL 1-2; OAEP; VLP

"Man, everything is so profound..." At Rochdale. Ian Young. NeAC

Man fall'n shall be restor'd, I never more. Paradise Regained. John Milton. OBS

The man forlost, that wot not where he goth.' Lost. Charles, duc d' Orleans. OxBM

The man from above, from Yenan. The Landlord's Wife. Marilyn Chin. BrSi

The man from the country After Shiki. Larry Eigner. FAZ

A man grows old and indolent. But I am Growing Old and Indolent. Robinson Jeffers. AP; NoAm; NOBA; TAP

Man has created death. Death. William Butler Yeats. ChMP; OBSP

The man has found no comfort in the grave. The Man Who Dreamed of Faeryland. William Butler Yeats. CMoP; NoAm; NoP; OAEP; PoPle

The man has passed, the shade has vanished, the prisoner/is free!.... The Animal Runs, It Passes, It Dies. *Anonymous.* WeW

Man, I know your need,/But not your mind. Ark Astonished. Jay Macpherson. NOBC; PoA

Man in dust is lain/And exile wins hame. Hamewith. Sydney Goodsir Smith. BSV

A man in love I was, and I/Could not speak and could not move. Epithalamium. Walter James Turner. OBMV

A man in prison can whisper songs. Ulises Torres did. To Speak of Chile. Margaret Gibson. MAYP

...A man in red/Will blood his boy and carry home the brush. Birdwatcher. Henry Treece. WaP

A man in the moon. Orbiter 5 Shows How Earth Looks from the Moon. May Swenson. SUW

...Man/in this cloud spots/a common man. Where/nothing is familiar. Cloud Spots. Steven Lavoie. APU

Man is a spirit,/Let the bells ring. Holes in the Sky (excerpt). Louis MacNeice. TRV

Man is ever weary, weary,/Waiting for the May! Summer Longings. Denis Florence MacCarthy. HBV 1-2

Man is facing the rising sun! Song of the New World. Angela Morgan. HBMV; HBVY

Man is God, and God is Man. The Animals' Carol. Charles Causley. NAs

Man is mad as the body/Is sick, by nature. A Far Cry after a Close Call. Richard Howard. NYBP; UnPo

...Man is one world, and hath/another to attend him. Man. George Herbert. SeCV 1-2

The man is sick in his heart./that's what I call it. Euch, Are You Having Your Period? Alta. NMM

Man is sin, and flesh is grass. The Penitent Palmer's Ode. Robert Greene. LoBV; OBSC

Man is the judgment of the world. Variations. Randall Jarrell. MiAP; VGW

Man is vicious. We forgive you. The Soviet Union. John Berryman. FaBoPV

The man Jane loved! Janes's Marriage. Rudyard Kipling. BoC

Man kills his children. But the birds endure. The Sounding. Conrad Aiken. CrMA

Man-kind/white/kind/of man Dedication to the Final Confrontation. Djangatolum. PoBA

Man, kneel down, look after me and sing. On the Death of Mary. Rainer Maria Rilke. ISi

Man lives by love, and not by metaphor. The Body Politic. Donald Hall. MP; NePoEA; TwCP

& A man lurches out/coughing puke. Soft-Man 1. Ed Sanders. ANYP

Man made like his roads,/with somewhere to go. Stars Climb Girders of Light. Bert Meyers. MAT

Man makes himself. Each crest out-tops the last. Gordon Childe. David Martin. PoAu 1-2

Man, manwart, manimal. Cherries: "So when the hammers of the witnesses of heaven.." Edward Kamau Brathwaite. NAs

Man may conquer, a girl surrender her sweet The Love Song. Ivor Gurney. EnLoPo

Man may not see that innocence again. The Missal. Ruth Pitter. CAW

...The man may now resume/His journalistic prose. An Ode: "I sing a song of sixpence, and of rye." Anthony C. Deane. NOBL

Man may securely sinne, but safely never. Epode. Ben Jonson. SeCP

...Man must have his wonder. Autosonic Door. Dorothy Brown Thompson. GoYe

A man must make his living while he may. Said the Innkeeper. Myles Connolly. TRV

Man my mate and counterpart. Thee, God, I Come from, to Thee Go. Gerard Manley Hopkins. VLP

A man of action dials the telephone. Bachelor. William Meredith. NoAm

A man of rain/lies dead on the ground of decayed leaves. A Man of Rain. Arlindo Barbeitos. WhB

Man or not Pico della Mirandola. Mason Jordan Mason. PoNe

...The man picks up the/corpse & exits. Gorg, a Detective Story. John Nichol. NOBC

The man replied;; "It figures JESUS CHRIST." Love-Joy. George Herbert. OAEL 1-2

The man revealed himself to me. A Man Was Drawing Near to Me. Thomas Hardy. InPo

Man rises/from the kiss/and answers Yes. Woman. Carl Rakosi. TAP

Man rock the mountain with his two bare hands! Prayer in Time of War. Henry Treece. WaP

A man's a bit of English stuff,/True from head to heel! England's Heart. Martin Farquhar Tupper. PaPo

Man's a fool if he thinks/he's got a whole woman by hisself Married Man Blues. Blind Willie (Joe) Reynolds. BluL

A man's a man today! The Poor Voter on Election Day. John Greenleaf Whittier. PAL

The man's an ass for a' that. For A' That and A' That (parody). Shirley Brooks. FaBoCo; NOBL; Par

A man's body, or a memory, either one a whip. In the Silks. Diane Ackerman. MAYP

Man's but a temple of a shorter date. Sonnet Written in Tintern Abbey, Monmouthshire. Edmund Gardner. NOEC

A man's face as weathered as straw/By the summer's flare and winter's flaw. Conrad in Twilight. John Crowe Ransom. OxBA

Man's fate is a drum! Panic. Archibald MacLeish. MoAmPo

...Man's forgiveness give–and take! The Rubaiyat of Omar Khayyam. Omar Khayyam. ILwL; SeCeV

–De man's immortal, but de poems is baad. Ode: "Mistah Berrybones, you daid? (parody). William Zaranka. BXAP

Man's inhumanity to man,/Makes countless thousands mourn. Man's Inhumanity to Man. Robert Burns. BLPA; FaFP

Man's relationship with man. Friendship. Anonymous. PoToHe

Man's spirit comes with thine in peace to dwell. Wilt Thou Not Visit Me? Jones Very. AH

A man should seeke great glorie, and not broad. To John Donne. Ben Jonson. AnAnS 2; JCP; NoP; SeCP; SeCV 1-2

–Man, so soon hushed–the silence which endures/To bear in mind, and bless. Building in Stone. Sylvia Townsend Warner. MoBrPo

Man spread abroad, man was here now/It was Day The Kumulipo: The Dawn of Day. Anonymous. WTO

The man standing upright in the dream. Poem for My Twentieth Birthday. Kenneth Koch. PoA

A man that hath hem in his clos,/Reste shal he wrothe. Snatches: "An old wif and an empty cup." Anonymous. OxBM

A man to guide the strength in a boy's hands. Nemean Ode: VI. Pindar. LiTW

The man turns to his breakfast again, but sees it's been wounded, the yolk of/ one of his eggs... The Wounded Breakfast. Russell Edson. LCAP

A man were as good to be dede/As smell thereof the stynk! The Pilgrims' Sea Voyage and Seasickness. Anonymous. OBTV; OxBM

The man who comes up from the crowd. The Man from the Crowd. Sam Walter Foss. PoLf

The man who died in the market and woke up in the house Shango I. Anonymous. TTY

The man who has just crossed himself out. Metamorphoses. Howard Nemerov. EyDe; HaCAP

The man who hews the coal to feed my fire. Proem. Wilfrid Gibson. HBMV

Man, who is made more terrible far than they,/Dreams he is otherwise! Pumas. George Sterling. BPAW

A man who made machines to gain an hour/Shall lose himself before their ruthless power. Say This of Horses. Minnie Hite Moody. PoLf

The man, who once against thee fought. The Reprisall. George Herbert. AnAnS 1

A man who's untrue to his wife. Note on Intelligence. W. H. Auden. FiBHP; PoPl

The man who stomps into the heart of this/forest. You, Letting the Trees Stand as My Betrayer. Diane Wakoski. NoAm

The man who takes it to forget/Must know how little will suffice. Bottle Should Be Plainly Labeled Poison. Sara Henderson Hay. GoYe

The man who wears the high-crowned hat and patent-leather boots. The Journal of Society. Godfrey Turner. NOBL

Man will arise and spit his brackish soul/Out of himself and be a god again. The Second Iron Age (1939-1945). Michael Harrington. CaP

...Man with a hearing-aid walks/without aim, happy just to be alive. Lines. Heather McHugh. MAYP

...A man with no head/has a packet of chocolate and a souvenir of Tripoli. Cairo Jag. Keith Douglas. NePoEA

A man without courtesy/might quite as well cease to be. Yung Wind. Confucius. CTC

Man, you can't even/hear them; bats,/are they? Bats. George Macbeth. NoAm

The man you may be tonight/If you turn to the Valley of Light. Anastasis. Albert E. S. Smythe. CaP

The Manchester Railway great progress denoted. English History in Rhyme...(excerpt). Edward B. Goodwin. FaBoUs

Manhattan faces and eyes forever for me. Give Me the Splendid Silent Sun. Walt Whitman AA; HAP; MoAmPo; NOBA; NYP

Manhattan Manhattan Manhattan Manhattan The Penn Central Station at Beacon, N.Y. Ed Ochester. TAT

"Manhood's stronger far than storms, and Love is mightier than Death!" The Story of a Stowaway. Clement Scott. PaPo

...The mania/of waters above torpedoes. Resigning from a Job in a Defense Industry. Sandra McPherson. LCAP

"Manibus o date lilia plenis!" Divina Commedia: Purgatorio. Dante Alighieri. CAW

Manicured fingers shuffling/the same stakced deck/with the ante/raised On Watching Politicians Perform at Martin Luther King's Funeral. Etheridge Knight. NNaP

Mankind, like miserable frogs,/Is wretched, kinged by storks or logs. The History of Insipids. John Freke. APAS

...Mankind/Seemed elsewhere gone–to Fall– From Emily Dickinson in Southern California. X. J. Kennedy. NLV

Mankind shall cease.–So let it be,'/I said to Love. I Said to Love. Thomas Hardy. GBL; NoAm

Mankind their country–Israel but the grave! Oh! Weep for Those. George Gordon, Lord Byron. AnEnPo

"Mankind was ever far from well." Lines on a Certain Friend's Remarkable Faculty... Max Beerbohm. PV

The manly droop of marble./And its vein. David Homindae. Marjorie Stamm Rosenfeld. AMV-80

...Manned every speech with check-/points and reported back to nobody. England's Difficulty. Seamus Heaney. CIP

The mannerly word hiding its wilderness root. The Dusting of the Books. Dorothy Hughes. GoYe

Manomin on blackened tongue. Manomin. Phyllis Wolf. STE

The manticors of mountains/Might feed upon thy brains! A Curse on the Cat. John Skelton. EvOK

The mantle of self-righteousness? Oh, If They Only Knew! Edith L. Mapes. BLRP; WBLP

Manwolf, worse; and their packs infest the age. Tom's Garland. Gerard Manley Hopkins. FaBoPV; VLP

Many a blue eye of Clan Colman the turf covers,/Many a swan-white breast. The Dead at Clonmacnois. Angus O'Gillan. AnIL; FaBoPP; HBV 1-2; IrPN; OBEV; OnYI

Many a foul-footed thing/In the salt sea. Wash Well the Fresh Fish. Anonymous. PoPle

Many a note and many a lay. The Faithful Shepherdess. John Fletcher. OBS

Many a person who will never be a poet/Is tempted by: calypsos to show it. Calypsomania. Anthony Brode. FiBHP

Many a soldier, Lawd, is dead and gone,/Hey, hey, hey, hey. Trench Blues. Anonymous. OuSiCo

Many a soldier's kiss dwells on these bearded lips.). Drum-Taps. Walt Whitman. AP

Many a swan-white breast. Dead at Clonmacnois. Angus O'Gillan. AnIL; OnYI

Many a young lad singing a ship away. Shore Roads of April. Bill Adams. EtS

Many bones they must pike/While they lay adowne.' The Fox and the Goose. Anonymous. OxBM

The many-coloured images imprest/Upon the bosom of a placid lake. Characteristics of a Child Three Years Old. William Wordsworth. ERoP 1-2; OBRV

...Many corridors of the soul/that are dark also./Shalom.' Shalom. Denise Levertov. NoAm

Many dames with footfall light.... An Ancient Castle. William Morris. SeCePo

...The many doors/That many friends had opened long ago. Mr. Flood's Party. Edwin Arlington Robinson. AmP; AnNE; AP; AWP; BiP; BLPL; CMoP; CoBMV; CrMA; EvOK; FaFP; FF; HAP; HeIP; HoPM; InPK; InPo; LiTA; LiTM; MAT; MoAB; MoAmPo; NePA; NIP; NoAm; NOBA; NoP; OxBA; PoPl; PoRA; PPoe; PPP; PrIm; SeCeV; SoSe; TAP; TreFT; TrGrPo; UnPo; ViBoPo

Many green-lipped cavern mouths/Where the hills are blue. Song: "Christ keep the Hollow Land." William Morris. NBM

Many houses crumbling, step by step,/while I, thank God, am still on my feet. A Roman Roman. Crescenzo Del Monte. VWA

Many leaders fell at his hand/but his shield on the day of need was silent.' Creide's Lament for Cael. Anonymous. NOBI

...Many men/for whom the world is neither oyster nor pearl. The Perspective and Limits of Snapshots. Dave Smith. MAYP

...Many mysterious,/thin, wise lines change/in your cool palm. Hesitating Ode. Miklos Radnoti. LLLT

Many of the nicest people do. Deny Yourself. Christopher Morley. YaD

Many's the hopes that have vanished, after the ball. After the Ball. Charles K. Harris. BLSo; FSN; FSW; GoTF; TreF

Many selves, your life, many lives, your people. You Growing. Milton Acorn. NOBC

A many tendrilled vine. American Vineyard. Mildred Cousens. GoYe

Many things, as I sit quite still,/With Eternity in my hand. Is Love, Then, So Simple. Irene Rutherford McLeod. HBMV; WHA

Many thousand gone. Many Thousand Gone. Anonymous. ABF; FSW

Many thrive on frugal fare/Who would perish of excess. Promises Like Pie-Crust. Christina Georgina Rossetti. NOBV

Many ways to go, the best wall is the wind. In the Morning All Over. William Stafford. FAZ

A map cut in my skin/on forehead, elbow, palm. Signature. Carol Orlock. AMV-81

The map of all the wide world doth containe. Antiquitez de Rome. Joachim Du Bellay. OBVE

A map/with/no/corresponding/geographical/landmarks Coelacanth. Christopher Dewdney. CaPN

The maple-leaves lie deep. The Dream House. Marjorie Allen Seiffert. HBMV

The maple tree wept down. Mason Jar. David Steinberg. AMV-81

Marble hides nothing. Pentimento. Lori Fisher. PoDr

A marble one so warm'd would speak. Of a Fair Lady Playing with a Snake. Edmund Waller. PoEL 1-5

Marble smooth by flowing waters grown. Fragmenti. Ezra Pound. PoA

March and fight for our one common right,/CITIZENS TO BE! The Purple, White and Green. L. E. Morgan-Browne. BrRo

March, march you toilers, the world will be free. Whirlwinds of Danger. Anonymous. FSW

March on in the worker's united front,/For you are a worker too. United Front. Hans and Bertolt Brecht Eisler. FSW

March on! march on! all hearts resolved/On victory or death. The Marseillaise. Claude Joseph Rouget de Lisle. FSW; HBV 1-2; TreFS; WBLP

March with us, heroes! Pagan Prayer. Alice Brown. WGRP

Marchin' doun the Broomie-Law. The Forty-Second. Anonymous. GBP

The marching melody of stars and suns. Night. Victor J. Daley. PoAu 1-2

Marcia's Long Blonde Beauty/A+! Gee, You're So Beautiful That It's Starting to Rain. Richard Brautigan. WeW

The mares drinking it in drinking it in. When I Was Young I Tried to Sing. Donald Finkel. GP

Mareseatoats. Construe. Anonymous. OxNR

Marian Pyszko, hominaticum. Homage to Marian Pyszko. Richard Snyder. SOTS

Marianne, Madeline, Alys. Three Little Girls. Richard Aldington. BrPo

Marie! the Chanel model for Modom! Ha! Original Sin! Ogden Nash. FaBoCo; NLV

Mariner, Swineherd, King,/and set one free. A Pride of Ladies. Anne Halley. NMM

The mariners sleep by the sea. The Mariners. Margaret Louisa Woods. OBVV

Mark'd with most flimsy mottos, and in large/The name of one Boileau! Sleep and Poetry. John Keats. ChRP

A mark it left, intense and cold. Five Serpents. Charles Burgess. NePoAm-2

The mark of an old car/accident beating on his/ghostly forehead. The Cage. John Montague. CIP; FaBoIP

The mark we leave, by word or deed,/Cuts deep in someone's heart. Mistakes. George W. Swarberg. STF

Mark well his human prototype,/The fierce Apache fettered there. Geronimo. Ernest McGaffey. AA; BPAW; PAH

Mark yon shadow on the dial! The Fifteen Days of Judgement. Sebastian Evans. NBM; NOBV

Mark you whose badge and livery he wears. The Last Chapter. Walter De la Mare. CMoP; MoBrPo

Marke, the king with croun,/Seyd that feir him thought. Sir Tristrem: Tristrem and the Hunters. Thomas of Erceldoune OxBS

Marke well this–that lovers will be/Must nedes have oone of thes thre. Three Things Jeame Lacks. Anonymous. MeEL

Marked by bases I must run all night/for everything I should/by now/be worth. Double-Header. John Stone. TAT

Marked forever as her creature and her fool. Another Full Moon. Ruth Fainlight. BrRo

Marked with a flitch of bacon! The Dunmow Flitch of Bacon. Anonymous. OBET

...Marked/with well-earned, golden stars! School Is Out. Frances Frost. SiSoSe

The marker split for kindling a kitchen fire. Remembering Nat Turner. Sterling A. Brown. PoBA; PoNe

Market for salt; and dance to tinkly music. Discretions of Alcibiades. Robert Pinsky. NPGG

Marking our beginning/marking our end? Ronas Hill. Hamish Brown. PoSH

Marking the bed they'd shared, with a great stone. The Anatomy of Angels. Alden Nowlan. PeCV

Marking the cards in the new deck. Animal Acts. Charles Simic. LCAP

Marking the dead/landmen who ran the woodland/out of breath Seven Woodland Crows. Gerald Vizenor. VoR

The markings are for hope. Verse for Vestigials. Elizabeth Allen. AMV-80

The marks have sunk of Dante's mind. On a Bust of Dante. Thomas William Parsons AA; AnAmPo; HBV 1-2

The marks of that which once hath been. Christabel: Friendship. Samuel Taylor Coleridge. MCCG

The marks of the war-blades double and deepen. Shield. Anonymous. AnOE

Marriage is even so. Haiku: To Her Husband, at the Wedding. Kaga no Chiyo. LiTW

...Marriage/of the river's dark soul/with our endless thirst When We Are Like Two Drunken Suns. Yvonne Caroutch. LLLT

Married in haste, we may repent at leisure. The Mourning Bride. William Congreve. GoTF; TreF; ViBoPo

Married in pink, your fortune will sink. Wedding Signs. Anonymous. GoTF; TreFT

Married unwisely, yes, but died quite well. Poggio. Lawrence Durrell. OxBTC

Marry an artist,/If you can say:/I don't. Never Marry an Artist. Raymond Filip. CaPN

Marry another and prosper well,/But not, but never Ishmael. Song for Unbound Hair. Genevieve Taggard. PG; PoRA

Marry Saturday, no luck at all. Marry Monday, Marry for Wealth. Anonymous. HBV 1-2; HBVY

...Marry the long loved/and christen babies and the mended living into spring. Those Trees That Line the Northway. Ellen Perreault. AMV-81

A/mars/bar? Windfall. David Mitchell. OCNZ

The marsh hawks float on another water,/made fragile in the failing light. Dingman's Marsh. John Moore. NCSH

De Marster, de young Marster's done/come back! Uncle Gabe's White Folks. Thomas Nelson Page. AA

Martha I paint, and dream of Hera's brow,/Mary, and think of Aphrodite's form. The Young Glass-Stainer. Thomas Hardy. CTC; EyDe; SaC

Martin, you'll ask your wife about the songs/When you go in at dinner-time?"/"Not I." Child and Boatman (excerpt). Jean Ingelow. FM

The martins and the swallows/Are God Almighty's bows and/arrows. Praise. *Anonymous.* OxNR

Martyr all o'er, and meet to trace/The lines of Jesus' death. St. Stephen's Day. John Keble. CoBE

The martyrs of the Maine! Half-Mast. Lloyd Mifflin. PAH

Marvel in man and glory in the worm. You. John Masefield. MoRP

The marvellous animal blood go thin? Underwood. Howard Moss. MP; NePA; NePoEA-2; PP; TwCP

Marvellous is Thy love! A Love Song. Judah Halevi. TrJP

Marvelous to his marvelous eyes. The War of the Secret Agents. Henri Coulette. NePoEA-2

Marvelously catching my flight; containing me. Promise Your Hand. Henry Rago. NMP

"Mary, chile, kiss ma'han'." Conception. Waring Cuney. BANP

Mary, do you remember? Pleasant Memories: The Meadow-Field. Charles Sangster. OBCV

Mary Felton was her name. Tombstone Epitaphs. *Anonymous.* PeD

Mary had a baby:/Sing Whose, Whose! Crooked Carol. Norma Farber. PoL

(Mary, helper of heartbreak, send him to me to-night!) Mary, Helper of Heartbreak. Margaret Widdemer. HBMV

Mary, I'm sad for your Son and you. Under the Wood. *Anonymous.* HAP

Mary Immaculate, guide them home. In Memoriam. Padraig De Brun. WTO

Mary, it is the same with me," she said. She Said... Jonathan Henderson Brooks. PoNe

Mary, Joseph, lend your aid,/While our hearts in love we raise. Angels We Have Heard on High. *Anonymous.* TreFS

Mary leads him home at last. Mariale (excerpt). Bernard of Cluny. CAW

Mary Mother spake unto Granuaile. The Two Mothers. Shane Leslie. ISi

Mary puts round him/Her mantle of blue. A Cradle Song. Padraic Colum. CAW; GoBC; ISi; OnYI; OxBI

A Mary's cloistered prayer. The Sisters. John Banister Tabb. AA

Mary Star of the Sea! Cadgwith. Lionel Pigot Johnson. CoBE; ISi; OBVV

Mary that is most wise,/Bring us to thy Son's eyes. Amen. A Christmas Carol. Algernon Charles Swinburne. SBVL

Mary was a red bird/All day long! Mary Was a Red Bird. *Anonymous.* OuSiCo

Mary would not punish men--/If Mary came again. A Penitent Considers Another Coming of Mary. Gwendolyn Brooks. NoAm; PCh

Maryland, My Maryland! My Maryland. James Ryder Randall. AA; AnAmPo; FaBoBe; FaFP; HBV 1-2; MC; PAH; TreF

Mask'd with such violet disallow their green? The Rainbow. Gerard Manley Hopkins. FaBoPP; OBSP

The masked men are a spangle of leaves in the/suns crown A Tryptych for Jan Bockelson. John Oliver Simon. NeAC

The mass of my burnt bricks/crumbles/and turns back to clay. The Tower. Dan Pagis. VWA

Massing for action on the cold horizon. The Old Story. Louis MacNeice. GBL

Massive and taciturn years, the Age of Ice. The Strings' Excitement. W. H. Auden. MoAB; MoBrPo

"Master, I was the second mate!" The Second Mate. Fitz-James O'Brien. AA

Master of Life take me, Thy Cup am I. The Living Chalice. Susan Mitchell. HBMV

Master of Life, we thank Thee/That they were what they were. The Fallen. Duncan Campbell Scott. TrPWD

The Master of the Centuries Who will not be denied! The Voice of Christmas. Harry Kemp. HBV 1-2

Master, show Thy face. In Memoriam, A.C.M.L. (excerpt). Cecil Arthur Spring-Rice. TrPWD

The Master that you seek in Rome/You find at home, or seek in vain. A Word of Warning. *Anonymous.* KiLC

A master-touch!--its sweet soul wakes/and sings. The Old Violin. Maurice Francis Egan. AA

Master who crown'st our immelodious days/With flower of perfect speech. Lacrimae Musarum. William Watson. HBV 1-2

The masterful units of his siesta, and always did. The Perfection of Dentistry. Marvin Bell. AmPA; CoAP

Masterly at making songs,/Skilled at playing chess. The Hosts of Faery. *Anonymous.* OnYI

A masterpiece of God. The Masterpiece. Walter Malone. PGD

Masters of the Seven Seas, O, love and understand! The Flowers. Rudyard Kipling. OBVV

The masters quite omitted/The lore we care to know. April. Ralph Waldo Emerson. ViBoPo

Mastery, but be adored, but be adored King. Wreck of the Deutschland. Gerard Manley Hopkins. BoC

Masturbating in the twilight as though they were landing a 747. Some Boys. Chuck Ortleb. PeHV

Match the steel stillness. Haiku: "The falling snow flakes." Etheridge Knight. NeAC; SM; TAP

Matches the fine content/of what we do together. Sublimation. Alex Comfort. ErPo; UnTE

Matchless Christ, Oh, wondrous story. Easter, Day of Christ Eternal. Maurice Moore. STF

Material needs a life of fact/to make a spectacle of/one of these days. Passing Strange. Alan Bernheimer. APU

Material things must answer and obey. Attainment. Ella Wheeler Wilcox. WGRP

Maternal love, filial love/in the old place, desecrated by barbarians. Mother. Aldo Camerino. VWA

A mating call of sound/rises to pleasure me, Dives,/hoarder of common ground. Gifts of Rain. Seamus Heaney. IPY

Matisse breathes above his reed brush, while the paint clots and/dries unused. Ghazal: Japanese Paintbrush. Randy Mott. PoDr

Matisse preferred to paint this scene, not I. L'Art. Frederick Feirstein. SM

The matron will not be a maiden, now. Two Weeks after an April Frost. Steven Helmling. AMV-80

Matters that are judged and cleanly cut/like the severed head of Goliath. Perhaps It's Only Music. Natan Zach. VWA

Matting on my chamber floor. Ravin's of Piute Poet Poe (parody). C. L. Edson. BXAP

Maturior vis, quid moror alterna. ad Meunatem/Sicflevit Upon the Death of His Much Esteemed Friend Mr Jno Saffin Junr.... Grindall Rawson. SCAP

The mausoleum, the wax house. Stings. Sylvia Plath. NaP

The maut's aboon the meal the nicht/Wi' some. My Auld Wife. *Anonymous.* GBP

Max and I know this too: it will be night. Crepuscular. Richard Howard. TwCP

Maxima, maxima,/Gloria Dei maxima Through the Dark the Dreamers Came. Earl Bowman Marlatt. AH

May all our glory be in Thee! A Hymn: "A hymn of glory let us sing." The Venerable Bede. WGRP

May all your ramblin' bring you joy. My Ramblin' Boy. Tom Paxton. FSW

May all your stolen bones be sweet. Big Dog. Philip Booth. BoAnP; GDP

May all your valleys be fat/With wine, and full be every vat. Summer Journey. W. R. Rodgers. OBTV

May also come to like him too! First Impressions. Alfred Grant Walton. PoToHe

May at his perill further go. The Temple. George Herbert. AnAnS 1

May be as far off as a moral. LLewellyn and the Tree. Edwin Arlington Robinson. BeLS; HBMV

May be ashamed of your actions, and thus I bid you adieu. The Seamen's Wives' Vindication. *Anonymous.* OBSS

May be changed to a reed or a laurel. Exorcism. Oliver St.John Gogarty. AnIL

May be conditioned by traces/Of a derivative of phenanthrene! The Kind of Poetry I Want (excerpt). Hugh" (Christopher Murray Grieve) MacDiarmid. PAI

May be if the gas holds out we'll get there soon. Tumbling Mustard. Malcolm Cowley. AmFN

May be nothing but a cipher/With its rim rubbed out. Trouble. David Keppel. FaFP; FPL; GoTF; PoLf; TreF; WBLP

May be seed for ploughed up soil,/May help humanity/Grow. To the Mothers. Ernst Toller. TrJP

May be the dwelling place of peace. Our Father, by Whose Name. F. Bland Tucker. AH

May bring him life/or/drown his misery. A Personality Sketch: Bill. Ronda Davis. JB

May catch his last thoughts, whole life foul or fair,/Glassing it--where? Moments of Vision. Thomas Hardy. OAEL 1-2

May come unto the general dance. My Dancing Day. *Anonymous.* OxBoLi

May cross and cross above your hands. Flight. Hazel Hall. AnAmPo

May crown thy Feet, that could not crown thy Head.   The Coronet.
Andrew Marvell.   AnAnS 1; LoBV; MeLP; MePo; NCEP; NOCV; NoP;
OBS; OxBoCh; PoPle; PP; SeCV 1-2

May darkness when it unfolds/presage only a field of stars.   To My Father.
Ralph Pomeroy.   DFF

A May Day in the morning.   Alibazan.   Laura E. Richards.   OBCA

May de Devil preach 'is funer'l song.   Promises of Freedom.   *Anonymous.*
BPo

May each repeat, in words of bliss,/We're all–all here.   The Family Meeting.
Charles Sprague.   HBV 1-2

May enjoy our filets of mackerel, our dishes of cream.   Intruder.   Susan
Feldman.   AmPA

May ev'ry hour new woes reveal/That Hell reserves for Doneraile.   The
Curse of Doneraile.   Patrick O'Kelly.   TW

May every holy, happy, hearty tear/Help me to run to Heaven, as thou dost
there.   So Have I Spent on the Banks of Ysca Many a Serious Hour.
Thomas Vaughan.   FaBoPP

May every ill that bites or smarts/Perplex him in his hinder parts.   To His
Book.   Robert Herrick.   JCP

May give us life before it gives us death.   The Task.   Robert Bhain
Campbell.   MoPo

May God bless you always.   An Irish Wish.   *Anonymous.*   GoTF; TreFT

(May God defend us!) to shield from/ harm.   The Graveyard Rabbit.   Frank
Lebby Stanton.   AA

May God forgive him wholly.   An Autograph.   John Greenleaf Whittier
AA

May God grant that you, Philaenis,/Will yet learn to suck a penis.   To
Philaenis.   Martial (Marcus Valerius Martialis).   PeHV

May God have mercy on your death, tho' you are with/the Devil!   Epitaph
for a Tyrannous Governor Who Choked on Wine.   Adib-i Sabir.   LiTW

May God in heaven above protect them from all the perils of the sea.   The
Wreck of the Northfleet.   *Anonymous.*   OBSS

May God love thee, my beloved,–may God love thee!   A Valediction.
Elizabeth Barrett Browning.   HBV 1-2

May God stream down upon your land/refreshing, fertile rain.   To Ibn
Zaidun.   Wallada.   WPOW

...May God us keep/From Single vision & Newton's sleep!   With Happiness
Stretched Across the Hills.   William Blake.   EnRP

May Goddes body fede us everichoon!   Here Begins the Continuation of the
Cook's Tale (parody).   William Zaranka.   BXAP

May grateful hearts rejoice to see/The bonny harvest moon.   The Bonny
Harvest Moon.   John Barr.   AnNZ

May great success attend them/Till they return again.   Lisbon.   *Anonymous.*
AmFP

May grow to clubs and naked swords,/To murder and to death.   Love
between Brothers and Sisters.   Isaac Watts.   FaBoUs

May have a gentle sigh for him,/As one of the departed.   In These Fair
Vales.   William Wordsworth.   CBEP

May have been a dream.   For a Moment.   *Anonymous.*   PBWP

May have more of King Richard than Moses and Co.   A New Order of
Chivalry.   Thomas Love Peacock.   CenHV

May he continue making love to the mother.   Epigram: Lucilius.   Howard
Nemerov.   OBAL

May He find a place for the tears!   The Fountain of Tears.   Arthur William
Edgar O'Shaughnessy.   OBVV

May He have mercy on a fish's soul.   Flying Fish.   Katherine Kelley Taylor.
EtS

May he have more than he bargained for.   A Curse against the Owner.
Barton Sutter.   TW

May He show forth His might in saving Kathaleen Ny-Houlahan.   Kathaleen
Ny-Houlahan.   James Clarence Mangan.   NOBI; VLP

May He that was crowned with thorn/Bring all men to His bliss! Amen.   Sir
Gawain and the Green Knight.   *Anonymous.*   MeEV; NAWM 1-2

May hear the lonely leagues/Of the kittiwake and the fulmar.   The Dark
Dialogues, II.   W. S. Graham.   OxBS

May hear your dancing fainter than the drift/Of the last petals falling from the
rose.   The Dance of the Daughters of Herodias.   Arthur Symons.   BrPo

May Heaven assist them in their worke, and/thus our newes is done.   Newes
from Virginia.   Richard Rich.   PAH

May heaven bless the husbandman.'   The Husbandman and Serving-Man.
Anonymous.   OBET

May heaven defend its own cushla ma chree!   Cushla Ma Chree.   John
Philpot Curran.   HBV 1-2

May heaven forbid the Parting Glass!   The Parting Glass.   Philip Freneau.
AA; AmP

May heaven help that Dixieite wherever he may be!   Once I Lived in
Cottonwood.   *Anonymous.*   AmFP

May Heaven smile down on my infant and me.   The Isle of Man Shore (The
Desolate Widow).   *Anonymous.*   AmFP

May hell seize the villain/That smiles to betray.   Village-Born Beauty.
Anonymous.   PaPo

May her honor bright gain high estate and her offspring rise to fame.   Willie
Riley.   *Anonymous.*   BaBo

May her soul rest in the radiance of the/Shekhina!)   Epitaph.   Leone Da
Modena.   TrJP

May here be perfected and left behind.   The Sermon in the Hospital (excerpt).
Harriet Eleanor Hamilton King.   BoC

May His praise be fitly sung!   The Works of God.   Moses Ibn Ezra.   TrJP

May huge holes hex his hull.   Curse of a Fisherman's Wife.   Lila Chalpin.
AMV-80

May I again turn Wanderer,/And never settle more.   Fair Sylvia.
Anonymous.   OBS

...May I/Also survive its meanings, and my own.   After Greece.   James
Merrill.   ConAP; NOBA; NYBP

May I ask for a job/As headwaiter/Of this hotel?   In This Hotel.   Emanuel
Carnevali.   AnAmPo

May I be able to take horses!   A Dance Chant.   *Anonymous.*   WGRP

May I be dull enough to grow/Most miserably wise.   Song: "Phillis, for
shame let us improve."   Charles, Earl of Dorset Sackville.   SeCV 1-2

May I blow it out?   Translations from the Chinese.   Christopher Morley.
EvOK

–May I fall in feast on your moist locks!   Mighty Mary, Hear Me.
Muireadhach Albanach O Dalaigh.   NOBI

May I find a peaceful new birth,/Transcending the state of the wild beast.
The "Word" of an Antelope Caught in a Trap.   Sandag.   WTO

May I fly back as a yellow crane to visit my home!   Song of Grief.   Liu Hsi-
Chun.   HW

May I go with you? Aye, by-and-bye.   An Old Woman.   *Anonymous.*
OxNR

May I handle her well down tomorrow's sea-road.   The Last Galway Hooker.
Richard Murphy.   IPY

May I never from the fair with life return!   Pearl of the White Breast.
Anonymous.   AnIV; OnYI

May I not lie with evil,/And may evil not lie with me.   Four Prayers, III.
Anonymous.   OnYI

& May I praise God always/as a dog.   Jubilate Canis.   Erica Jong.   MAYP

May I say, "It is Nestus Gurley."   Nestus Gurley.   Randall Jarrell.   MP;
TwCP

May it be his for many a long year!   My Fiddle.   Leib Kwitko.   VWA

May it be with understanding that we live!   Understanding.   H. W. Bliss.
PoToHe

May it not be amongst the sons of Men.   To a Young Gentle-Woman,
Councel Concerning Her Choice.   Richard Crashaw.   AtBAP; OBS

May Jesus with His apostles/Be for our help against danger!   Hymn Against
Pestilence.   Saint Colman.   OnYI

May joy come from God above,/To all those who Christmas love.   Lordings,
Listen to Our Lay.   *Anonymous.*   OHIP

May know how my heart went with them/After the red-rose-bordered hem.
To Ireland in the Coming Times.   William Butler Yeats.   NoAm; NOBI;
OxBI

May know nothing whatever about Thee.   Limerick: "O God, inasmuch as
without Thee."   *Anonymous.*   LiBL

May know what sweet majestic face/The gentle Prince of Players wore!
Sargent's Portrait of Edwin Booth at "The Players".   Thomas Bailey
Aldrich.   AA

May live and grow and laugh and play.   I Come and Stand at Every Door.
Nazim Hikmet.   FSW

May Love defend thee from Oblivion's curse.   Our Casuarina Tree.   Toru
Dutt.   ACV

May means remembering you!   Rhyme for Remembrance of May.   Richard
Burton.   HBMV

The May month oystercatcher flights/Were madly piping still.   Change and
Immutability.   Syd Scroggie.   PoSH

May move thee to sigh once more.   Lise.   Rose T. Cooke.   AA

May Mrs. Maecenas object to your kiss,/And lie at the foot of the bed!   A
Counterblast against Garlic.   Roswell Martin Field.   NLV

...May my soul her nimble journey take/Into the regions of eternity.   Praise
Ye the Lord, O Celebrate His Fame.   Peleg Folger.   AH

May my soul learn at the turn of a corner/that one step back it still lived.
The Unforeseen.   Conrado Nale Roxlo.   LiTW; MoRP

May never come/This side the tomb.   A Great Time.   William Henry
Davies.   AnFE; ExPo; LiTB; MoBrPo; MoVE; WHA

May never hope to have her company.   La Vita Nuova.   Dante Alighieri.
AWP

May no grisliche gost glide ther hit shadeweth.   The Vision of Piers
Plowman.   William Langland.   PoEL 1-5

May no man for bren-wateres on night han his rest.   Blacksmiths.
Anonymous.   CABA; OxBM; WiR

May none armure hit lette, ne none hye walles.   The Vision of Piers
Plowman.   William Langland.   PoEL 1-5

May not gape sheer under you/As he does for me.   Ark Apprehensive.   Jay
Macpherson.   NOBC

May not know in whom they be.   Come, my sweet, whiles every strain. William Cartwright.   EG

May not make merry, when they heare me cry.   Caelica, XXXV.   Fulke, Lord Brooke Greville.   AtBAP; FCP

May not the two of us be parted long!   Prayer of Any Husband.   Mazie V. Caruthers.   PoToHe

May o'ercome the bent to evil/By Thy purity.   Thou Who Taught the Thronging People.   Henry S. Minde.   TRV

May one day swear that he's my friend.   A Serious Danger.   R. A. Davenport.   PV

May pause and look back/to toss their bouquet.   Plans.   Helen Morgan Brooks.   NNP; PoNe

May plead for they poor shade in days/to come.   Ave! Nero Imperator. Duffield Osborne.   AA

May please his neighbors round a common fire.   Tellers of Tales.   Chester Kallman.   DFT

May raise a thrush/Would put down all our waits.   To Cheer Our Minds. William Ronksley.   OxBChV

May reach His throne of glory,/Who is mercy, truth and love.   Secret Prayer. John Cross Belle.   STF

May read them not without some bitter tears.   Epitaph: "O flower of all that springs from gentle blood."   Gabriello Chaibrera.   AWP

May rest in the fleet with you, Lord Collingwood.   The Death of Nelson. *Anonymous.*   OxBoLi

May rise when thou art gone.   To a Departing Favorite.   George Moses Horton.   BALP

May say Alas but cannot help or pardon.   Spain 1937.   W. H. Auden. CABL; FaBoPV; LiTB; OBWP; WaP

May say, their lords have built, but thy lord dwells.   To Penshurst.   Ben Jonson.   AnAnS 2; AtBAP; AWP; CABA; FaBoEn; FaBoPP; FaBoPV; FM; JCP; LoBV; NIP; NoP; OAEL 1-2; OBS; PoEL 1-5; PPP; SeCP; SeCV 1-2; TEP

May search successfully as well/For truth in whores and ease in hell. Wedlock. A Satire.   Hetty Wright.   NOEC

May set its simpler meaning over mine.   Naples Again.   Arthur Freeman. NYBP

...May she by these songs/Know it was love I looked for at her hands.   The Gift of Song.   Anthony Hecht.   NYBP

May she drop her dung down stupidly into the porridge!   A Shrewish, Barren, Bony, Nosy Servant.   Daibhi O Bruadair.   NOBI

May she grow to her right powers/Unperturbed by passion of ours.   For a Child Expected.   Anne Ridler.   LiTM; MoVE; NeBP; SeCePo

May she like the fathers by the desert broken/In her own desert find at last salvation.   Lines: I Praise God's Mankind in an Old Woman.   Wilfred Watson.   NOBC

May she rest at home contented now, the female sailor bold.   The Female Sailor.   *Anonymous.*   OBET

May she rest in heaven!   Legacy.   Nancy Byrd Turner.   BrR

May sigh to think he still has found/The warmest welcome, at an inn. Written at an Inn at Henley.   William Shenstone.   AWP; CEP; HBV 1-2; LoBV; NOBE; NOEC; OBEC; OBEV; ViBoPo

May slugs jam every turnstile slot/If I forget thee not.   A Curse.   Irving Feldman.   TW

May, some day, bear a rose for Him/It took my life to grow.   Overnight, a Rose.   Caroline Giltinan.   HBMV

May some fruit from the tree of thy passion/Fall on us this night!   Epigram: "O King of the Friday."   *Anonymous.*   BIrV

May some kind angel clear thy path,/And break the hidden snare.   The Mouse's Petition.   Anna Laetitia Barbauld.   FM

May spend itself - what thrice-mocked/fools are we!   Parrhasius.   Nathaniel Parker Willis   AA

May'st sing thy song, soar skyward, make thy nest.   Accidia.   Henry Charles Beeching.   OBVV

May still thy soil be generous as its lord!   Mully of Mountown (excerpt). William King.   FaBoPP; OBTV

May storm-clouds change the gold of too much sun.   A Prayer for a Marriage.   Mary Carolyn Davies.   TrPWD

May such a spot, so wild, so sweet, be mine!   Sonnet upon a Swedish Cottage. Sir John Carr.   OBTV

May taste in its reproachful roar/The ancient relish of her sun.   Paphos. Lawrence Durrell.   NYBP

May that "Greenwood" of soul be in sight.   The Isle of the Long Ago. Benjamin Franklin Taylor.   FaFP; HBV 1-2; WBLP

May that vast motive wash and wash our own.   On the Marginal Way. Richard Wilbur.   CAPP; CoAP; NOBA

May the beneficent rains besought by the poor/Never forsake you.   The Palm Tree.   Abd-ar-Rahman I.   AWP

May the best church win . shake hands now and come/out conjuring.   Black Power Poem.   Ishmael Reed.   BPo

May the blood on the sails all be fishermen's tales.   Blood on the Sails.   Phil and June Colclough.   OBET

May the brightest and the best.   May.   *Anonymous.*   AnIL; KiLC

May the Father, the Son, and the Spirit all Three/Beneath thy protection praised be.   Welcome O Great Mary.   Alice O'Gallagher.   WTO

May the good God Almighty help them!" And they both said, "Amen."   The Soldier and the Sailor.   *Anonymous.*   ShS

May the land rest easy/without your step.   An Irish Blessing.   Joan Murray. LTB

May the little ones gather around me,/To bid me good night and be kissed! The Children.   Charles Monroe Dickinson.   AA; HBV 1-2

May the Lord in His mercy be kind to Belfast.   Ballad to a Traditional Refrain.   Maurice James Craig.   SeCePo

May the Man above/Give him a crown!   For C. K.   D. L. Kelleher.   NeIP

May the morn in heaven awake us,/Clad in bright, eternal bloom.   An Evening Blessing.   James Edmeston.   BePJ

May the peace of Allah abide with you.   Salaam Alaikum.   *Anonymous.* PoLf

May the Prince be King, we want no other,/And take the steps of his father and mother.   Prince of Wales' Marriage.   *Anonymous.*   CoMu

May the stain of sorrow the deepest one,/That I bear with me to Heaven. The Weaver.   Fanny Forrester.   BLPA

...May the taste of salt/recall to us the great depths about us.   The Depths. Denise Levertov.   NaP; NU

May their filaments last till true morning.   Fragment for the Dark. Elizabeth Jennings.   FaBoWP

...May there be nothing known/Of this rotten Brain which was the Earth, one day.   Winter Sunset.   Jules Laforgue.   SyP

...May there be sons/of your sons, nurtured, Queen Mother, from thee.) Austriad.   Juan Latino.   TTY

May they advance defeated–as today.   The Vanquished.   Charles Eglington. AA; HBV 1-2; PeSA

May they be strong to keep hate out/And hold love in.   Prayer for a New House.   Louis Untermeyer.   BLPL; PoLf; PoToHe; TrPWD

May they come, may they come/The days which enchant us.   Song of the Highest Tower.   Arthur Rimbaud.   AWP

May they find naught but joy and peace/And happiness therein.   A Kitchen Prayer.   M. Petersen.   STF

May they lie low in waves of woe,/And tortures slow each day!/Amen!   Evil Prayer.   Douglas Hyde.   TW

May they never eat of her bread!   Here's a Health to Them That's Awa'. Robert Burns.   HBV 1-2

May they never see no more such trials/And never know the like again.   The Ship in Distress.   *Anonymous.*   OBSS

May this the same kind welcome find with you,/As yours did here, and ever shall; adieu.   A Letter from the Country to a Friend in Town.   John Oldham.   PP

May this turn the heart of our enemy./Huzza, my brave boys.   Nelson's Death and Victory.   *Anonymous.*   OBSS

May thy dear Body ne're be Mine.   The Soul.   Abraham Cowley.   AnAnS 2

May thy good-will be equal to thy pow'r!   Daphne and Apollo.   Matthew Prior.   NOEC

May Thy love, O Father, bind this place about.   Hymn of Dedication. Elizabeth E. Scantlebury.   BLRP

May trouble you more than ever, when you've nailed his/coffin down!   How Old Brown Took Harper's Ferry.   Edmund Clarence Stedman.   HBV 1-2; MC; OnMSP; PAH; PoNe

May use my Needle at a pinch,/And do themselves great Pleasure.   The Jolly Trades-Men.   *Anonymous.*   CoMu

May view John Knox in paradise.   Partial Comfort.   Dorothy Parker. FaBoCo; OBAL

May we, as he spins us in the cool gloom,/Be forever in his keeping. Bacchanal.   Irving Layton.   OBCV

May we become the lords of many treasures!   The Vedic Hymns: To the One God.   *Anonymous.*   ILwL

May we follow/In the same delightful way.   Gracious Saviour, We Adore Thee.   Sewall Sylvester Cutting.   AH

May we fulfil the works of love.   Dear Lord, Behold Thy Servants.   Hosea Ballou I.   AH

May we greet with joy another year.   Reconsecration.   Dorothy Gould. PGD

May we humans/Flourish like the flowers of spring.   Benediction for the Tent.   *Anonymous.*   WTO

May we, Lord, remember thee.   Jesus Spreads His Banner O'er Us.   Roswell Park.   AH

May we not err of layman sort,/When priests and parsons fall?   Invitation. *Anonymous.*   WTO

May we now venture to be kind.   Exit.   Edwin Arlington Robinson. MoAmPo; OBSP

May with God's love shine bright/All thro' the year.   All Thro' the Year. *Anonymous.*   BLRP

May wound her heart deeper than any.   The Dainty Young Heiress of Lincoln's Inn Fields.   Charles, Earl of Dorset Sackville.   PoL

May wound the Man no more. Christmas Mourning. Vassar Miller. CoPo; MoAmPo

...May you be fond/Of me and these forever, and wood fire. Good Appetite. Mark Van Doren. OBSP

May you ne'er stir from out your threshold's door,/Save at the heels of some damned one eye'd whore To Lygdus. Martial (Marcus Valerius Martialis). PeHV

May you not be long on the way! Thoughts of a Young Girl. John Ashbery. ConAP; TAP; VGW

May you slip back through your arsehole and break your fucking/neck!' The Bastard from the Bush. *Anonymous.* NOAV

May your channels never break. Long Person. Gladys Cardiff. CDW; STE; TWSS

May your love follow my face/as the cow follows her calf/from today till the day I die. A Charm for Love and Lasting Affection. *Anonymous.* NOBI

"May your wish and my wish never be broke." Children's Runes and Omens. *Anonymous.* MAT

Mayakovsky's hat worn by a horse Answer to Voznesensky & Evtushenko. Frank O'Hara. HoAn; NNaP; PoM

Mayan sub-flowers in/the shade. Dangers of the Journey to the Happy Land. Joseph Ceravolo. ANYP

...Maybe, a little baby,/By and by to nestle within your arm. Youghall Harbor. *Anonymous.* OnYI

Maybe earlier in Ur! The Modernists. Tom MacInnes. CaP

Maybe–"Eden" a'nt so lonesome/ As New England used to be! What Is– "Paradise". Emily Dickinson. CMoP; DiPo

Maybe God has a house./But not here. Where Knock Is Open Wide. Theodore Roethke. HAP; VGW

Maybe I'll forget what could've been Forget about It. Robert Currie. Str

"Maybe I'm a king." A Story That Could Be True. William Stafford. GOYP; NTCP

Maybe I shall not die at all. The Wicked Hawthorn Tree. William Butler Yeats. WSC

Maybe it would be better/to go back to the angels. Back to the Angels. William Walter De Bolt. AMV-81

Maybe just listen to my voice. Loneliness. Sandra McPherson. AMV-80

Maybe's both ways, be simpler catching a bucket. In the Orpheum Building. Kit Robinson. APU

Maybe she's never seen you either. Discoveries in America. James Wright. NoP

...Maybe she was a witch from foreign lands! The Turn of the Road. James Stephens. SO; WSC

Maybe that's the best. Five Short-Shorts. Hayden Carruth. VGW

Maybe the earth herself had a good belly laugh/the era that she first gave birth to pigs. The Laughing Faces of Pigs. Fred Lape. BoAnP

Maybe the English too will have their day. Hope. Frank O'Connor. CIP; KiLC

–Maybe the water itself,/the message its salt. Before. Albert Goldbarth. MAYP

Maybe there'll be work for riggers,/In the Port, beyond the blue. Old Ship Riggers. H. A. Cody. EtS

Maybe they're Wally Pipp's And You Are There. Tom Clark. LiSp

Maybe we shall know each other better/When the tunnels meet beneath the mountain. Coda. Louis MacNeice. FaBoIP

Maybe you're not ready/yet, she says to herself,/to face them. Dogs. Susan Griffin. NPGG

Maybe you see it all, whiteman, or maybe you blind. For Dan Berrigan. Etheridge Knight. NeAC

Mayde milde, moder es/Effecta. Hymn to the Blessed Virgin. *Anonymous.* CAW

Mayest find thy darling in an urn. Epitaph on the Lady Mary Villiers. Thomas Carew. FaBoEE

Mayflower! Foremost and best of our/ships! Mayflower. John Boyle O'Reilly. AA; PAH

...Mayst thou more miscarry/Than ever hasty Clement's did with bloated Harry! Black Bull of Aldgate. Alfred, Lord Tennyson. TW

The maze in the onion Wonders of the World. Richard Shelton. DFF

Mbombo/silence Ndaaya's Kasala (excerpt). Citeku Ndaaya. PBWP

Me an' my God's gwinter do as we please! Hell and Heaven. *Anonymous.* OxBoLi

Me and a couple a sonsabitches we done got equal yestiddy. All Things Being Equal. J. Lee Humphrey. AMV-81

Me and my dog/don't care whether/we get any work/or not. Me and My Dog. *Anonymous.* PoAu 1-2

Me and my Doney-gal a-bound to go. Doney-Gal. *Anonymous.* BPAW; CoSo

Me, and my dreams, and my life,/All into a worsted stocking. Lachesis. Victor J. Daley. CBAP

Me and willie play togetherin/and we don't miss Knock on Wood. Henry Dumas. CNA; PoBA

Me back to my mountain and far, far, west. August on Sourdough, a Visit from Dick Brewer. Gary Snyder. SOTW

Me best of all, Maude Clare. Maude Clare. Christina Georgina Rossetti. BeLS

Me he disdains, and mocks me from her eyes! Great Is My Envy of You. Petrarch (Francesco Petrarca). NAWM 1-2

Me: I won't even let them/take my blood/pressure/now. On the Latest Crisis of Confidence. Haywood Jackson. SOTS

Me list no longer rotten boughs to climb. A Renouncing of Love. Sir Thomas Wyatt. EnLi 1-2; Enlit; EnPo; FaBoEn; GBL; LiTL; OAEP; SiPS

Me! made after the image o' God–/Jings! but it's laughable, tae. The Image o' God. Joe Corrie. OxBS

(Me memory's sich that I can't recall which,/Though at figgers I've seldom been beat). The Sea Serpent. Wallace Irwin. FiBHP

Me no care fe fum-fum/come Juju come... A Juju of My Own. Lebert Behune. PAI; PoBA; PoNe

Me onward to my home! Where Hudson's Wave. George Pope Morris. AA

Me reweth, marie, thi sone and the. Now Goeth Sun under Wood. *Anonymous.* CBEP; NCEP

Me such a cook, or coachman: but no such friend. Epigram. *Anonymous.* ALV

Me that/had a/weed in it. Reflective. Archie Randolph Ammons. HaCAP

Me then to love all thing above/Thou ought be fain. O Man Unkind. *Anonymous.* OxBM

Me thought I heard one calling, "Child";/And I replied, "My Lord." The Collar. George Herbert. AtBAP; ATP; AWP; BiP; BLPL; CBEP; CoBE; EaLo; EBEV; EnLi 1-2; ExPo; ForPo; HAP; HBV 1-2; HeIP; InPo; InPS; JCP; LiTB; LoBV; MasP; MeLP; MePo; NIP; NOBE; NOCV; NoP; OAEL 1-2; OAEP; OBS; OxBoCh; PAI; PoEL 1-5; PoPle; PoRA; PPoe; PPP; SCV; SeCePo; SeCeV; SeCP; SeCV 1-2; TEP; TrGrPo; ViBoPo; WHA

Me to strike for your life's blood, and you to strike for/mine. D.G.C. to J.A. Emily Bronte. BrRo

Me to take for aye/For her owne man. As I Lay Sleeping. *Anonymous.* EG; TrGrPo

Me, who am also, Dearest! scarred with/years. Post-Meridian. Wendell Phillips Garrison. AA

Me with only one word left;/survive. Words from a Bottle. Deborah Lee. BrSi

Me you shall not mock. I can wait. The Angel in the House. Coventry Patmore. VLP

...The meadow leaped, and took/The leaning mountain in a close embrace. Attraction. Ella Wheeler Wilcox. PeD

Mean less to the wanderers pressing towards them/Than to me the homelight as I look backward. Migrants. Ethel Anderson. BoAV

Mean mean mean to be free. Runagate Runagate. Robert Earl Hayden. BALP; BP; BPo; CNA; IDB; InPS; LCAP; PoBA; PoNe

Mean Sundown Blues! Song: "I've put some/ASHES in my sweet papa's bed." *Anonymous.* NAMP

Mean while what warms me I have blest. A Praefatory Poem to the Little Book, Entituled, Christianus per Ignem. Nicholas Noyes. SCAP

Meandering his weary way/On the green and golden hills of Africa. The Lonely Traveller. Kwesi Brew. PBA; TTY

Meanest old devil in the world. Where Are You Going, My Good Old Man? *Anonymous.* FSW

...Meaning/Being a virtue of shape and order. A Virtue of Shape. Thomas Swiss. AMV-80

The meaning shows in the defeated thing. The "Wanderer." John Masefield. BrPo; CABL; MCCG

Meaning/the movement of the sea. Reasons for Music. Archibald MacLeish. NePA

Meaning–you just/numbly dont get there Mexico City Blues. Jack Kerouac. NeAP

Meaningless–/buried mouths. The Old Pines. Cid Corman. GP

Meanings in search of a world. Found in a Storm. William Stafford. RFM

The means by which I waken into light. The Gateway. A. D. Hope. BoLoP; ErPo; UnTE

Means that we're that much nearer to slow-coming spring. High Wind at the Battery. Ralph Pomeroy. NYBP

Means to praise the earth and those we love? Hiking up Hieizan with Alam Lau/Buddha's Birthday 1974. Garrett Kaoru Hongo. BrSi

Meantime,/let them leave my heart alone! Exile in Nigeria. Ezekiel Mphahlele. PBA

Meanwhile a young frog/takes her for a little mirror. Half Moon. Federico Garcia Lorca. RFM

Meanwhile God keeps him whole and me i' the/ditch. Sonnet: Of Why He Is Unhanged. Cecco da Siena Angiolieri. AWP

Meanwhile, his loved banks now dry/The Muses with their tears supply. An Epitaph upon Doctor Brook. Richard Crashaw. WeW

Meanwhile, I'll buy it back again. Good day. Hattage. Sir Alan Patrick Herbert. FiBHP

Meanwhile I seek with some avid:/The fav: of your polite consid:. The Conversational Reformer. Harry Graham. InMe; YaD

Meanwhile I stand/And wait the event. The Hound. Robert Francis. SoSe

Meanwhile, I stand with/The free-falling ones/Who believe the parachutes/Will open some day. Free Fall. Don Gordon. AMV-81

Meanwhile I will smoke my canaster/And tipple my ale in the shade. Odes. Horace. OBVE

Meanwhile, move off, yielding the forest floor/As carefully as your honor. Meeting a Bear. David Wagoner. HAP

Meanwhile, my sweet Perrette, adieu! To Promise Is One Thing, To Perform Is Another. Jean de La Fontaine. UnTE

Meanwhile the distant Gnu with grateful eyes/Observes his opportunity and flies. The Gnu. Hilaire Belloc. BoAnP

Meanwhile we sit absorbed and precious to each/Other, for the time being where we want to be. August 13, 1966. Daryl Hine. GP

A measure effective though cruel. Limerick: "A patriot, living at Ewell." Langford Reed. TDH

...A measurement/of astral bodies. The Chalk Angel. Dennis Schmitz. NPGG

Measuring always this moment. Horas Tempestatis Quoque Enumero: The Sundial. John Hollander. NePoEA

Measuring mileposts of eternity. The Atlas. Kenneth Slessor. PoAu 1-2

Measuring off the careful square/Of someone else expected there. The Measuring. Jared Carter. AMV-80

Meat and sweat: my/whole life. This Shirt. Arturo Trias. InW

...Meat bleeding/on th silk of the seas and the arctic flowers/that do not exist. Enueg. Samuel Beckett. CIP

Meat! Meat! Meat! Meat! Cat's Meat. Harold Monro. OBMV

Meat, wine and ale. The Muse. D. H. Davies. BrPo

Mechanically, I followed with the rest. God's Funeral. Thomas Hardy. WGRP

Medallions of the sunken sun/glimmer on our lean shoulder.) Emblems of Evening. Robert Horan. CrMA

The/medicine/is all/in/her long/un-/braided/hair. Medicine. Alice Walker. NMM

...Medusa sleeps once/more. The Execution of Madame du Barry. J. J. Bray. NOAV

Mee thinks mount Aetna with his force is closed in my brest. Metamorphoses. Ovid (Publius Ovidius Naso). CTC; OBVE

The meek are haloed by thy light. Hymn. John Haynes Holmes. TrPWD

The meek-eyed senorita, the Maid of Monterey. The Maid of Monterey. Anonymous. AmFP

Meek got a word in edgewise after all. Japanese Beetles. X.J. Kennedy. HoAn; OBAL

Meekly composed awaited the fulfilling. Paradise Regained. John Milton. ISi

...Meet again,/Where dead men meet, on lips of living men. These Things to Come. Samuel (1835-1902) Butler. GLGT

...Meet him and stand by him in/toil and in the sweat of thy brow. Gitanjali. Rabindranath Tagore. WGRP

Meet me at the fair. Meet Me in St. Louis. Andrew B. Sterling. FSN; FSW; GoTF; OBAL; TreFT

Meet me in the green glen. Love, Meet Me in the Green Glen. John Clare. ELP

Meet me there   Perhaps It's as You Say. Peter Everwine. NNaP

Meet, meet me, by the thorn upon the hill! An Even-Song. Sydney Thomas Dobell. OBVV

Meet neighbourly and mingle without question. The Anti-Symbolist. Sidney Keyes. MoPo

Meet to adore some Calf of Gold. Retirement, an Ode (excerpt). Thomas Warton, Sr.. ViBoPo

Meeting in depths of the sea. The Good Dream. Denise Levertov. NNaP

Meeting the Gulf, hosannas silently below. The River. Hart Crane. AP; OxBA; PrIm

Meets its own coarse kind. March. William Everson. ErPo

Meets our bouquet of death–and turns sharp right. Unseen Fire. Ralph Nixon Currey. OBWP; OxBTC

Mehercle! You're gratus to that! Malum Opus. James Appleton Morgan. FaBoCo; NA

Mek' you think that heav'n/Is comin' clost ter you! Mighty Lak' a Rose. Frank Lebby Stanton. BLSo; FSN

Mellow as the glory roses. Gloire de Dijon. D. H. Lawrence. BrPo; CMoP; ELP; EnLoPo; GBL; NoAm; OAEP

Melody resigns to fate. Lines by a Person of Quality. Alexander Pope. InMe; NA

Melpomene! assist me, please,/To somewhat higher heights to climb. Rhymes (?). Henry Sambrooke Leigh. NOBL

Melt down my spirit, Lord, and mould/Into Thy perfect love. Now Is the Accepted Time. Charles Wesley. BePJ

Melt down their Sejanus to pots and brass kettles. On the University of Cambridge's Burning the Duke of Monmouth's... George Stepney. APAS

Melted down/and/ready/to/explode. The Nuclear Family. Melvin Douglass Brown. LFAC

Melted the hammer of his heart to fire. The North Sea Undertaker's Complaint. Robert Lowell. NePoEA

Melting all thought, the southward cloud withdrew into the air. The Great Scarf of Birds. John Updike. NYBP

Melting, flowing into one. Gnosis. Christopher Pearse Cranch. AnAmPo; HBV 1-2

Melting, flowing into one. Thought. Christopher Pearse Cranch. WGRP

Melting melodious words, to Lutes of Amber. Upon Julia's Voice. Robert Herrick. AtBAP; BoW; CABA; ExPo; JCP; MyFE; NOBE; SeCePo; SeCP; SoSe

Members, don't git weary for de work's mos' done. Members, Don't Git Weary. Anonymous. BoAN 1-2

The memoirs–/canvas, cable, chain, tar, paint. The Memoirs. Carl Rakosi. PoA

Memorable as the skin/Of a fierce animal. Lilies of the Valley. Jon Silkin. NoAm

A memorandum/That I am dying. Memorandum. Rudy Bee Graham. PoNe

Memories of old games/whose scores are lost forever. The Smell of Old Newspapers Is Always Stronger... Mike Lowery. Psk

Memories of the plunging sea. A Son of the Sea. Bliss Carman. EtS

Memories raise of joyous days/Upon the mountain side. The Scottish Mountaineering Club Song. John G. Stott. PoSH

The memories that follow! O Gather Me the Rose. William Ernest Henley. MoBrPo

Memory, committed to the page, had broke. Passage. Hart Crane. CMoP; ExPo; MoVE; NoAm; NOBA

Memory finds beyond that last/Improvidence, their mad remains. Respectable People. Austin Clarke. CMoP; NMP

A memory floating up from a dark water,/Can be more beautiful than the thing remembered. Winter Sunrise (excerpt). Laurence Binyon. ChMP

Memory has power as real as thine. All Hushed and Still Within the House. Emily Bronte. FaBoCh; NOBV; VLP

The memory of her kissing mouth/Burns me to gladness. Her Mouth. Richard Aldington. BrPo

A memory of light removed,/Behold in me! To a Photograph. John Banister Tabb. AmP

The memory of what has been,/And never more will be. Lucy. William Wordsworth. GN; OBEV; TrGrPo

The memory of your gentleness/remains/with promise. A Friend's Passing. Barclay Sheaks. AMV-80

Memory! set the tide a-swing. Cities Drowned. Sir Henry Newbolt. CH

The memory shall be ours. Decoration Day. Henry Wadsworth Longfellow. MC; OHIP; PoSC

...Memory,/Sowed my deep-furrowed thought with many a name,/Whose glory will not die. The Balloon. Alfred, Lord Tennyson. RoGo

The memory/spilling out/into the world. Where Mountain Lion Lay down with Deer February 1973. Leslie Marmon Silko. STE; VoR; WPOW

Memory that leads me now/and then back to that pure place. That Pure Place. Daniel J. Moriarty. WOLT

...Memory that works in gilt/And stucco to restore a fallen day. It Is Becoming Now to Declare My Allegiance. C. Day-Lewis. LiTM

Men all eating lunch. Hitch Haiku. Gary Snyder. LCAP

Men are each other. The whale was Moby Dick... The Whale and the Essex. A. M. Sullivan. EtS

Men are singing and drumming/Heartbeat. Black Hills Survival Gathering, 1980. Linda Hogan. STE; TWSS

Men are we, and must grieve when even the/shade/Of that which once was great is passed away. On the Extinction of the Venetian Republic. William Wordsworth. BoLiVe; EnL; FaBoRV; FaPo; GTBS; GTBS-P; HBV 1-2; LoBV; MBW 1-2; MCCG; NOBE; NoP; OAEP; OBEV; OBNC; OBRV; TrGrPo; ViBoPo

Men, be correct! And women, purr and smirk! For the Book of Love. Jules Laforgue. AWP; ErPo; LiTW

Men began to reign. Rhyme for a Chemical Baby. Joseph Cook. QQQ; SpRo

...Men cannot mock us in the clay.' Away, Delight. Francis Beaumont and John Fletcher. EiL; NOBE; OBEV; ViBoPo

Men clepen them sirens in France. The Romaunt of the Rose. Anonymous. PBBP

The men come in from the field/and don't notice. Spring Ease. Monty Reid. CaPN

Men creep like thoughts...The lamps are like pale flowers. Impression de Nuit: London. Lord Alfred Bruce Douglas. OBVV

Men cry when they hear stories of someone rising from the dead. Hurrying away from the Earth. Robert Bly. NaP; PoA

Men dance on deathless feet.' Mohini Chatterjee. William Butler Yeats. MoRP; NoAm

...The men/did not talk to them much, and neither time/nor that fine place gave them a sweetness.   Not Saying Much.   Linda Gregg.   NPGG

...Men do not celebrate in rhyme/Their daily bread.   Mother.   Theresa Helburn.   OHIP

Men do not so.   When Thou Didst Think I Did Not Love.   Ayton [(or Aytoun)] Sir Robert.   EIL

Men eat of it and die.   Fame is a fickle food.   Emily Dickinson.   TAP

Men have all these resources, we but one,/To love again, and be again undone.   Don Juan.   George Gordon, Lord Byron.   GoTF; TreF

Men have invented several/Thousand ways of killing them.   A Bestiary.   Kenneth Rexroth.   OBAL

Men heed them not–they only make/My soul unto herself more fair.   Poet Songs.   Karle Wilson Baker.   HBMV

Men hunt upon the hills of time/A nobler quarry to devour.   Scatheless.   Marguerite Wilkinson.   HBMV

Men led me to him, blindfold and alone.   Epitaphs of the War, 1914-1918.   Rudyard Kipling.   BrPo; FaBoEE; OAEP; OBWP

Men love in haste, but they detest at leisure.   Don Juan.   George Gordon, Lord Byron.   TW

Men loved: but hope they deemed to be/A sweet Impossibility!   Love's Spite.   Aubrey Thomas De Vere.   HBV 1-2

Men marry what they need. I marry you.   Men Marry What They Need. I Marry You.   John Ciardi.   MoLP

Men may take over the world!   Univac to Univac.   Louis B. Salomon.   FF; QQQ

Men most of all enjoy, when least they do.   Upon A. M.   Sir John Suckling.   CavP

Men must be men, and women women still.   Vain Men, Whose Follies.   Thomas Campion.   NCEP

"Men name me Death."   The Two Spirits.   James Benjamin Kenyon.   AA

...Men never can be still/But in their graves.   Daily Trials.   Oliver Wendell Holmes.   PoEL 1-5

The men of old time.   O Pine-Tree Standing.   Hakutsu.   AWP

Men of the Second Empire, I mean you!   Eighteen-Seventy.   Arthur Rimbaud.   FaBoPV; OBWP

Men's hammers break. God's anvil stands.   Hammer and Anvil.   Samuel Valentine Cole.   PoLf

Men's hungry souls have called that great Heart, GOD!   Life.   Margaret Deland.   WGRP

Men's strife with men is quiet/And the world lusts no more.   The Day of Wrath.   Helen Waddell.   OxBI

Men saw the blush and called it Dawn.   Dawn.   Paul Laurence Dunbar.   AmNP; GoSl; PoLf; PoNe

...Men seemed to be fatigued by the/whole question.   Original Child Bomb (excerpt).   Thomas Merton.   NAs

Men shul finde unnethe a frere/In Englonde within a while.   A Friar Complains.   Anonymous.   MeEL

The men that rode by Sarsfield's side, the roving Rapparees!   The Irish Rapparees.   Charles Gavan Duffy.   AnIV

Men to prevent foul conterfeit.   American Change.   Allen Ginsberg.   CABL; HaCAP

The men turn away and the boy's death grows.   Rape.   Thomas Rabbitt.   MAYP

Men walk in peace, like sleepwalkers,/in fields of vines and pine trees.   Forty Years Peace.   Arye Sivan.   VWA

Men who march away.   Men Who March away.   Thomas Hardy.   MMM; OBWP

Men who perish if they love.   The Azra.   Heinrich Heine.   AWP

Men who ride broomsticks with a mesmerist/Mock the typhoon. So, too, it was with Cook.   Five Visions of Captain Cook.   Kenneth Slessor.   BoAV; PoAu 1-2

Men who watch and fast and pray.   Give Us Sober Men.   Walter E. Isenhour.   STF

The men whose might made strong the height on the eve of/Bunker Hill!   The Eve of Bunker Hill.   Clinton Scollard.   MC; PAH

Men will be men when mony is gone.   The Rising in the North.   Anonymous.   BaBo; ESPB

...Men will go singing still/Of little dawns of springtime above an English hill.   Little Songs.   Marjorie Pickthall.   CaP

"Men work together," I told him from the heart,/"Whether they work together or apart."   The Tuft of Flowers.   Robert Frost.   AP; AtBAP; AWP; CBEP; CoBMV; GoYe; HBV 1-2; HBVY; LaNeLa; LiTA; MoAB; MoAmPo; OxBA; SeCeV

Mend your clothes.   Hold up Your Head.   Anonymous.   OxNR

La mer, la terre, le monde est seulement ces choses!   Acadian Lane.   David St. John.   SM

Merciful and gracious/Bang Bang Bang Bang.   The History of the Flood.   John Heath-Stubbs.   MoBS; OxBTC

Merciful One and All-holy,/Praised for ever and ever.   Light and Rejoicing to Israel.   Anonymous.   TrJP

Mercy asketh but Godes wille.   Mercy.   Anonymous.   OxBM

Mercy for the body burning in the wind of time!   The Journey to Golgotha.   K. Raghavendra Rao.   ACV

Mercy, how unpleasantly they–Smelt!   At the Zoo.   William Makepeace Thackeray.   NTCP; OxBChV

Mercy of irreverence.   Satie, at the End of Term.   Simon Curtis.   NOBL

The Mercy of My God.   The Wants of Man.   John Quincy Adams.   PoLf

Mere hunger cannot urge him from this drowse.   Pit Viper.   N. Scott Momaday.   CDW

"Mere local wind: no messenger of mine!"   Sirocco at Deya.   Robert Graves.   MoVE

Mere men, old boys, lost, the last hole a horror.   Golfers.   John Updike.   LiSp

A mere performance for your microphone.   The Bedbug.   Tony Harrison.   PV

"Merely a Negro"–in a day like this!   At the Closed Gate of Justice.   James David Corrothers.   BANP

Merely condemn the herd of narrow censors/and the hate they bear my people, O my God.   On Hearing It Has Been Ordered in the Chapterhouses of Ireland...   Padraigin Haicead.   NOBI

Merely in living as and where we live.   Esthetique du Mal.   Wallace Stevens.   LiTM

The merely nasty alters into vile.   An Adminsitrator.   Geoffrey Grigson.   FaBoEE

...Merely to be mere, ly to be   Song Form.   LeRoi (Imamu Amiri Baraka) Jones.   CTBA; SOTW

Merging Traffic Ahead/Yield./Yield.   Yield.   Ronald Gross.   InPK

Merit will live, though parties disagree!   To Wordsworth.   John Clare.   ERoP 1-2; OAEL 1-2

Mermen lay him in his tomb!   The Sea-Ritual.   George Darley.   BIrV; OBNC; OBRV; OnYI; OxBI; WiR; WSC

Merrily danced the Quaker.   Merrily Danced the Quaker's Wife.   Anonymous.   OxNR

Merrily, merrily, to welcome in the Year.   Spring.   William Blake.   FaBoCh; LoGBV; MoShBr; PoPl; SUS; YeAr

Merry, and Nought, and gay, and numb–/Than this smart Misery.   Of course–I prayed.   Emily Dickinson.   BoWoP; MoAmPo

Merry heart, go buy thy portion of the treasure!   The Bargain.   Reuental Neidhart von   LiTW

A merry heart goes twice the way/That tires a sad one.   The Wisdom of Folly.   Ellen Thorneycroft Fowler.   HBV 1-2

Merry may the keel row,/The ship that my love's in.   Merry May the Keel Row.   Anonymous.   GBP

The merry, merry bells of Yule.   In Memoriam A.H.H., XXVIII.   Alfred, Lord Tennyson.   NAWM 1-2; NOCV; OAEL 1-2; OAEP

A merry merry Christmas, and many may you see!   An Alphabet of Christmas.   Anonymous.   ChBR

Merry mites,/Welcome.   School's Out.   William Henry Davies.   BoC; OBMV

A merry monarch, scandalous and poor.   A Satire on Charles II.   John Wilmot, Earl of Rochester.   OBSV

The merry wave mutters.   Winter Has Come.   Anonymous.   AnIL

The Mesabi is young, my county an ocean.   Spawning in Northern Minnesota.   David McElroy.   AmPA

Meseems I hear sonorous lines/Of Iliads that the woods are dreaming.   The Wind in the Pines.   Madison Cawein.   AA

Meseems your "Garden" never could have grown.   Eve.   Oliver Herford.   OBAL

Mesh with dark plots implicit in the sun.   The Woolworth Philodendron.   Stephen Sandy.   CoPo

A message I sent to/the beetles of Japan.   On the Twenty-Fifth of July.   David Cornel DeJong.   NYBP

...The message is the world.   A Message from Space.   William Stafford.   SUW

The message unclear.   The Epistemologist, over a Brandy, Opining.   Robert Sargent.   AMV-80

Messenger, go, and think me not low breed/If to my lady I'm afraid to speed.   Canzo: "Can l'erba fresch'elh folha par."   Bernard de Ventadour   LiTW

Messenger to the mixed things/of your making, tell them I am.'   The Hand.   R. S. Thomas.   NOCV; OxBC

The messengers, of faces and names known/Or of forms familiar, are innocent.   To My Daughter.   Hyam Plutzik.   BiP

Messiah, when will you come?   The Field of Night.   Miriam Waddington.   VWA

Messing aroun' to make/one month's dirt be a day!!   Personals.   Leatrice W. Emeruwa.   PCP

A mesurabulle meane Way is best for us alle.   The Alphabet of Aristotle.   Mayster Benet.   FaBoUs

Met in the fierce breast of the eagle/The arrows of Gisli and Brynhild!   Gisli, the Chieftain: The Song of the Arrow.   Isabella Valancy Crawford.   OBCV

Met in the milder shades of Purgatory.   To Mr. H. Lawes on His Airs.   John Milton.   AWP; InPo; LoBV; NoP

Met, reaching to great fame by Fortitude. Johnny, I Hardly Knew Ye: Miltonese (parody). Oliver St. John Gogarty. OnYI

Met Stetson and gave him an earful. Limerick: "In April one seldom feels cheerful." Wendy Cope. FaBoWP

Metal for an elemental forge. To Earth. James Applewhite. PoA

...The metallic/feel of the silver flute. The Persistence of Memory, the Failure of Poetry. Robert Phillips. GeTw

Metallic, painted, solitary,/with New York plates. The Bus. Leonard Cohen. CAD; HeIP

The meteor of the war. The Portent. Herman Melville. AP; ExPo; InPK; MAmP; NOBA; NoP; OBWP; OxBA; PoEL 1-5; PrIm; TAP; WiR

Methinks I hear son Tom reply,/"I'll be a bishop by and by." A Familiar Epistle to J.B. Esq.. Robert Lloyd. NOEC; OBSV

Methinks I owe thee much, my little boy,/For this new duty, and its quiet joy. To a Tenting Boy. Charles Tennyson Turner. OBNC

Methinks it is no journey. Tom O'Bedlam. Anonymous. CH; FaBoCh; LoGBV; PoPle; TrGrPo

Methinks sometimes she pales the/stars/That have in heaven their dwelling. The Earth in Spring. Judah Halevi. TrJP

Methinks the birds will scarce be home/To wake our wedding-day! A Pastoral. Theophile Marzials. HBV 1-2

Methodically tearing small holes/with her fingernails, sharp/as crocodile teeth. Crocodiles. Mira Teru Kurka. APU

Methought I heard her very voice,/Rending the clouds asunder. Upon a Notorious Shrew. Anonymous. FaBoEE

"Mi amor, mi corazon!" Mi Corazon. Gordon W. Norris. BPAW

Michael, row the boat ashore, Alleluya. Michael, Row the Boat Ashore. Anonymous. BLSo; FSW

Micht maist as weel been spared. The Auld Man's Mear's Dead. Patrick Birnie. GoTS

Mickle said, little wrought. Cuckoo, Scabbed Gowk. Anonymous. PBBP

'Mid cannon's roar and rifle's peal,/We'll chant a soldier's song. The Soldier's Song. Peadar Kearney. OnYI

Mid lavedy, mid wive, mid maide, mid quene. Love Is Weal, Love Is Wo. Anonymous. OxBM

Mid-ocean deep to the sheer mountain walls. The Sonnet. Richard Watson Gilder. AA

'Mid such a sea of troubles blind and/dire! To Retirement. Luis Ponce de Leon. TrJP

Mid the sound of the speed of the worlds, the rushing/worlds, and the peal/Of the thunder of Life. Dawn on the Headland. William Watson. HBV 1-2

Middle of the first/line maybe no one/will notice Living in the Boneyard. John Oliver Simon. NeAC

The middle's best, and that give me. Song: "In a maiden-time professed." Thomas Middleton. OBSP

The middle Tree and highest there that grew,/Sat like a Cormorant... Paradise Lost. John Milton. ExPo

Middleton luck it's done and dead. The Bees of Middleton Manor. May Probyn. GoBC

Midnight is not time for Poetry No Time for Poetry. Julia Fields. AmNP

The midnight moon/Is covered with clouds. The Tale of Genji (excerpt). Lady Murasaki Shibiku. BoWoP

The midnight never tells. The Elm. Odell Shepard. HBMV

The midsummer moon? Haiku: "Sandy shore: and why." Shiki. WeW

Might and honor, glory and praise to God,/Only Giver of all that is good. Amen. Amen. On a Papyrus of Oxyrhynchus. Anonymous. CAW

Might as well pray for her/That she sleep sound.... Maumee Ruth. Sterling A. Brown. CDC

Might be once more the worm, the rock, the/tree? Genesis. John Hall Ingham. AA

Might can hardly keep from grinning. Might and Right. Clarence Day. InMe; NLV

Might fancy-fit his brows, silk-pillowed at his ease. Lamia. John Keats. SeCePo

Might gag their giggling through an endless sermon. Memorandum for Minos. Richard Kell. ELU

Might I but moor–Tonight–/In Thee! Wild nights–wild nights! Emily Dickinson. NIP; NOBA; NoP; OLR; OxBA; PBWP; SBG; TAP; UnTE; WeW

Might knock my darling off her unpriceable pivot. If, My Darling. Philip Larkin. EBEV; LiTM

Might live a memory and perish not. Epigrams. Theocritus. AWP

Might live invisible and dim. Night. Henry Vaughan. BoC; LiTB

Might lock their limbs, and in the sweat embrace!... Doric. Anghelos Sikelianos. ErPo

Might meet their Christ in sleep. In Dream. John Millington Synge. SyP

"Might of the night, unfleeing, sight unseen." Timon of Archimedes. Charles Battell Loomis. NA

Might'st let me breathe myself into thy breast. Epigram: "Would I were air that thou with heat opprest." Thomas Stanley. FaBoEE

Might startle this dull pain, and make it move and live! Dejection. Samuel Taylor Coleridge. SeCePo

Might they not be his green gay eyes. While Someone Telephones. Elizabeth Bishop. NMP

Might verse not best confuse itself with fate? St. Valentine,. Marianne Moore. NYBP; OFD

Mightn't be half so wicked for me. Limerick: "With a conscience we're able to see." Anthony Euwer. HBMV

The mighty Bush with iron rails/Is tethered to the world. The Roaring Days. Henry Lawson. BoAV

A mighty chorus to thy praise/World without end! Amen. Battle Hymn. Gustavus Adolphus. WGRP

A mighty, glorious, dazzling sea,/Stretching into infinity.' Tell Me, Tell Me, Smiling Child. Emily Bronte. LoBV; OAEP; TEP; ViBoPo; VLP

Mighty mountains loom before me and I won't stop now. Midway. Naomi Long Madgett. BlSi; BPo; NNP; PoNe

...Mike called me,/nigger,/hurt. Cathexis. F. J. Bryant, Jr., PoBA

The mikes that hung upon your lips/when you were at the Albert Hall. A Poem about Poems about Vietnam. Jon Stallworthy. NoAm

Mildest, most gentle, most eager for fame. Beowulf. Anonymous. AnOE

A mildewed hulk above the nations squatting? The Legion of Iron. Lola Ridge. NAMP

A mile or two from my first love. The Retreat. Henry Vaughan. LO

"Miles", and "John Alden" were Synonyme– God Is a Distant–Stately Lover. Emily Dickinson. AmePo; SoSe

...Miles and miles of water/That tilts to the North Pole. Island Moment. Ian Hamilton Finlay. NMP

Miles of pipeline. Steps. Bernadette Mayer. ANYP

The milestones into headstones change,/'Neath every one a friend. Sixty-Eighth Birthday. James Russell Lowell. OBSP; PCP; PoEL 1-5

The milk-white tooth of passion/is between us. Second Honeymoon. Anonymous. BIrV

The milkers lace their boots up at the farms. Cock-Crow. Edward ("Edward Eastaway") Thomas. GTBS-P; MoAB; MoBrPo; OBSP

Milking cows crying out/(off he goes)/Looking for them! Two Tongue-Pointing (Satirical) Songs. Anonymous. NOAV

...The Milkman brings a quart for my despair. The Milkman. Isabella Gardner. NePA

The milkwhite tooth of passion/is between us–or should be. Woman, Don't Be Troublesome. Augustus Young. CIP

"The mill cannot grind/With the water that is past." The Lesson of the Water-Mill. Sarah Doudney. HBV 1-2; PoToHe; TreFS

A mill-race for an unglimpsed fish? Return to Hinton. Charles Tomlinson. CMoP

A million billion trillion stars. A Man Who Had Fallen Among Thieves. Edward Estlin Cummings. AP; CoBMV; HAP; LiTM; MoVE; NoAm; NOBA; OxBA; TAP

Millions are learning how. Millions Are Learning How. James Agee. NAMP; PoPl

Millions of birds and worlds will God,/Sooner than His forsake. If Birds That Neither Sow Nor Reap. Roger Williams. AH

Millions of years shall come. Thou art above the years! The Dead Man Ariseth and Singeth a Hymn to the Sun. Book of the Dead. AWP

Millions will find you asleep. The Sweetest Thing. Anonymous. TTY

"The Mills of the Gods grind slowly,/Yet they grind exceeding small." The Mills of the Gods. Anonymous. BLPA; FPL

The milner said: "Shew, henne, shew!/I may not shake my bagge for you." Nonsense. Anonymous. OxBM

Milor's good food all fits the season. Fine Fish to Net. Anonymous. OBVE

Milton, thou should'st be living at this hour. Hippopotamothalamion. John Hall Wheelock. FiBHP; FYAP; NePoAm-2

Milwaukee on the bluff. Cities and Science. David McCord. AmFN

Mimic your mother's lovely face. Cradle Song. Lawrence Durrell. NAs

The mince pie that Min spied was Min's pie. Limerick: "A heathen named Min, passing by." Oliver Herford. TDH

A mind content, a conscience clear. A Contented Mind. Joshua Sylvester. HBV 1-2

A mind content both crown and kingdom is. Maesia's Song. Robert Greene. CTC; HBV 1-2; OBSC; UnPo

The mind downed in the dark may dream them on. A Balcony with Birds. Howard Moss. NePoEA

The mind entering the ground/more easily in pieces,/and all the richer for it. Mind. Jorie Graham. HaCAP

The mind has its own level to find. Alpine. R.S. Thomas. BoNaP; LiSp; PoL; RFM

Mind how I sell them while the merry, merry bells do ring. Three Jolly Fishermen. Anonymous. OBSS

The Mind is his Wife./so be it. Prayer for the Great Family. Gary Snyder. HAP; OFD

The mind is still. The Mind Is Still. Ursula K. Le Guin. AMV-80

A mind more pure, a form more fair.   Where Is She Now?   *Anonymous.*
LO

Mind's aim or what bright beings fill/The corries of the heart and will.   Glen
Rosa.   William Jeffrey.   PoSH

The mind's immortal, but the man is dead.   Time and the Garden.   Yvor
Winters.   MoAmPo; NoAm; QFR; VGW

The Mind's internal heaven shall shed her dews/Of inspiration on the humblest
lay.   The Inner Vision.   William Wordsworth.   GTBS; GTBS-P; HBV 1-2

Mind's unrest and soul's disease.   Madrigal: "What is life."   William Byrd.
EnRePo

...The mind/that directed the pride that the/hand killed.   At Cambridge.
Audrey McGaffin.   NePoAm

A Mind, that triumphs over Vice and Fate,/Esteems it mean to court the
World for Praise.   The Resolve.   Mary Lee, Lady Chudleigh.   OBEC

Mind the music and the step./And with the girls be handy.   The Yankeys'
Return from Camp.   *Anonymous.*   OxBoLi

Mind thee in Paradise/Of our's!   Jesus! Thy crucifix.   Emily Dickinson.
MoVE

Mind you keep your rifle an' yourself jus' so!   The 'Eathen.   Rudyard
Kipling.   OxBTC

Mindful the while that thus time flies for you.   Idyll of the Rose.   Decimus
Magnus Ausonius.   AWP

Minding true things, by what their mockeries be.   King Henry V.   William
Shakespeare.   WaaP

Mine, a swift pleasure-pain/None other knows.   In the Lilac-Rain.   Edith
Matilda Thomas.   HBV 1-2

Mine alone is made of stone–/Gotta work too hard.   Us Potes.   Franklin
Pierce ("F.P.A.") Adams.   PoPl

Mine and the mill's form/were written in water.   The Mill.   William Heyen.
EyDe

Mine angry and defrauded young?   Epitaphs of the War, 1914-18.   Rudyard
Kipling.   BrPo; FaBoEE

Mine are broken!   The Lyre.   George Darley.   OBVV

Mine are white with swans from Galway.   Snow Storm.   Sister Mary
Madeleva.   GoBC

Mine be as lowly and as green a tomb!   On the Death of a Young and
Favorite Slave.   Martial (Marcus Valerius Martialis).   AWP; LiTW

Mine be such faith, mine such a foe as he,/That, when my hour strikes, I, as
he, may dare!   To D'Annunzio: Lines from the Sea.   Robert Nichols.
OBMV

Mine be thy love, and thy love's use their treasure.   Sonnets, XX: "A
woman's face with nature's own hand painted."   William Shakespeare.
InvP; MasP; OAEL 1-2; PeHV

Mine but in flame refigures/your image lit in me.   Epigram: "At 12 o'clock in
the afternoon."   Meleager.   PeHV

Mine by the chain of love with links unbroken,/Dear Saviour, Thine and mine.
The Firstborn.   John Arthur Goodchild.   HBV 1-2

Mine eye says no to slumber all night long.   Hamasah: His Children.   Hittan
of Tayyi.   AWP

Mine eyes have seen the guru live, by cunning, like a lord.   One-Line Poems
from a New Statesman Competition.   *Anonymous.*   PoL

Mine eyes the tail that wagg'd contempt at Fate.   An Epitaph.   William
Watson.   NOBV

Mine eyes twain/From sore weeping!   To His Wife.   John Skelton.   CBEP

Mine eyes would never yearn to look/beyond.   Longing.   Judah Halevi.
TrJP

Mine has opened its soul to me; therefore I love it.   My Star.   Robert
Browning.   BoLiVe; EvOK; HBV 1-2; MBW 1-2; OAEP; SoSe; TrGrPo

Mine heart is desolate.   Il Pleut Doucement sur la Ville.   Paul Verlaine.
AWP; BrPo; EnLi 1-2; PG

Mine heart, Zepheria, then became thy fee.   Sonnet: "When, from the tower
whence I derive love's heaven."   *Anonymous.*   ElL

Mine is, that dozy flies can travel here without restraint/in the gentlest of
hatchures.   View from a Window.   Eldon Grier.   PeCV

Mine is the heart at your feet/Here, that must love you to live.   The
Oblation.   Algernon Charles Swinburne.   EnLit; GTBS; HBV 1-2; VLP

Mine is the saner attitude.   Remarks from the Pup.   Burges Johnson.
GDP

Mine is the sin, and justice fair demands/That I accept the guilt of bloody
hands!   If I Go Not, Pray Not, Give Not.   *Anonymous.*   STF

Mine is through/the flesh   Paths to God.   Musa Moris Farhi.   VWA

Mine–long as Ages steal!   Mine–By the Right of the White Election!   Emily
Dickinson.   MAmP; NoP

Mine must walk when dead.   Crazy Jane and Jack the Journeyman.
William Butler Yeats.   CMoP

Mine, O thou Lord of life, send my roots rain.   Sonnet: "Thou art indeed
just, Lord, if I contend."   Gerard Manley Hopkins.   MoVE

Mine only died.   In Obitum M.S., X Maii 1614.   William Browne.   JCP;
NOBE; SeCeV

Mine own, embraced, sought, knot, fire, disease.   Arcadia.   Sir Philip Sidney.
FCP

Mine own enough betray me.   Song: "O, do not wanton with those eyes."
Ben Jonson.   HBV 1-2

...Mine own self, are changed/For a dream's sake.   Mirage.   Christina
Georgina Rossetti.   BoLoP; EnLi 1-2; LLLT; PoRA

Mine would walk being dead.   Words for Music Perhaps.   William Butler
Yeats.   AtBAP

Minerva's snow-white marble eyes/Without the gift of sight.   Stars.   Robert
Frost.   MAmP

Mingle human bliss and woe.   Guy Mannering. Chapt. 4: Twist Ye, Twine
Ye! Even So.   Sir Walter Scott.   EnRP

Mingled with yours shall through the ages last.   To Italy.   Giacomo
Leopardi.   AWP

Mingling in one glow her ringlets/And her rings.   All Gold.   *Anonymous.*
KiLC

The mingling serenade looks.   Soul's Kiss.   Samuel Greenberg.   LiTA

Mingling their lives with its treacherous spray!   The Rapid.   Charles
Sangster.   CaP; WHW

"De minimis non curat lex."   Limerick: "Whenever a fellow called Rex."
Anonymous.   NOBL

A ministering angel fair,/In answer to my faithful prayer.   God Knows the
Answer.   F. B. Whitney.   STF

A ministering angel thou!   Marmion.   Sir Walter Scott.   TreFS

Miniver coughed, and called it fate,/And kept on drinking.   Miniver Cheevy.
Edwin Arlington Robinson.   AnNE; AWP; CMoP; CoBMV; FaBoCh;
FaBV; FaFP; FaPo; FF; ForPo; FPL; GoTF; HBV 1-2; HeIP; InMe; InPo;
LiTA; LoGBV; MaC; MCCG; MoAB; MoAmPo; NAMP; NePA; NIP;
NLV; NoAm; NOBA; NoP; OBSV; OxBA; PoEL 1-5; PoLf; PoPl; PoRA;
SCV; SeCeV; SpRo; TAP; TreF; TrGrPo; WHA; YaD

Miniver sighed, and read some more/F. Scott Fitzgerald.   Miniver Cheevy, Jr.
(parody).   David Fisher Parry.   BXAP; SpRo

Minnesota is what I mant to say,/And they may never know.   Depressed by
the Death of the Horse... (parody).   Henry Taylor.   BXAP

"Minnie lou had OUR boychild this morning!"   To our First Born.   Ebon.
BP

The Minster rings.   On Christmas-Day.   Thomas Traherne.   OBS; OxBoCh;
PoEL 1-5

Minstrels and maids, stand forth on the floor.   Outlanders, Whence Come Ye
Last?   William Morris.   OxBoCh

...A minuscule crack/in the great black wall/of the universe   Terra Cotta.
K. Curtis Lyle.   CNA

Minutes I lay awake to hear my joy.   The Song of the Tortured Girl.   John
Berryman.   CoAP

Mira belongs to Girdhar Nagar,/a slave at his feet.   At the Holi festival of
color.   Mira Bai [or Mirabai].   BoWoP

Mira has her lord Girdhar,/who turns poison into nectar.   Rana, why do you
treat me.   Mira Bai [or Mirabai].   BoWoP

Mira is lost,/her senses are dead.   I don't sleep.   Mira Bai [or Mirabai].
BoWoP

Mira's Lord acknowledges/her as his servant.   O King, I Know You Gave
Me Poison.   Mira Bai [or Mirabai].   PBWP; WPOW

Mira's lord knows she is his servant.   Rana, I know you gave me poison.
Mira Bai [or Mirabai].   BoWoP

Mira says: Lord Girdhar Nagar,/let our fires unite.   Yogi, don't go away.
Mira Bai [or Mirabai].   BoWoP

Mira says: Prince Girdhar,/help me.   Hari helps his people.   Mira Bai [or
Mirabai].   BoWoP

The miracle again is wrought,/And water changed to wine.   Dear Friend,
Whose Presence in the House.   James Freeman Clarke.   AH

The miracle and magic of the deed.   Dedication to the Generation Knocking
at the Door.   John Davidson.   BrPo

Miracle/Of their brilliance Miracle/of   Exodus.   George Oppen.   GP

Miracle, this massive, drab constant of experience.   The Constant.   Archie
Randolph Ammons.   HAP

Miriam the Prophetess will dance before us/at that Festival   The Morning
Prayers of the Hasid, Rabbi Levi Yitzhok.   Phyllis Gotlieb.   VWA

The mirror carries on/the family tradition:/that she was beautiful.   From My
Mother's Home.   Leah Goldberg.   VWA

Mirror in March my human face.   March, Upstate.   William Bronk.
NYBP

...The mirror is her open door.   The Importance of Mirrors.   Helga
Sandburg.   IHMS

...A mirror/tall as childhood/reflecting/nothing.   The Quiet Fog.   Marge
Piercy.   UnPo

Mirrored/calcined/futile/tough   Semen.   Martha Paley Francescato.
BoWoP

Mirth with thee, I mean to live.   L'Allegro.   John Milton.   AnFE; AWP;
BoLiVe; EnL; FaBV; FaFP; FiP; GN; GTBS; GTBS-P; HAP; HBV 1-2;
HoPM; InPo; InPS; JCP; LiTB; LoBV; MasP; MBW 1-2; MCCG; MyFE;
NoP; OAEL 1-2; OBEV; OBS; PoPle; PPP; SeCePo; SeCeV; TEP; TreFS;
TrGrPo; ViBoPo; WHA

The misbirth touches the surface/And glistens like quicksilver.   Ballydavid
Pier.   Thomas Kinsella.   BIrV; FaBoIP

...Mischief, thou art afoot./Take thou what course thou wilt! Julius Caesar.
William Shakespeare. GoTF; TreF

The miserable little Bitch! The Game of Cricket. Hilaire Belloc. DBV;
FiBHP

Miserere Domine! A Voice Sings. Samuel Taylor Coleridge. CAW; CH

Miserere, miserere, I am dying. Miserere, My Maker. *Anonymous.*
NOCV

Misery multiplied into infinity–and no door. Unplanned Design. Neal
Bowers. AMV-80

...Misery's love,/O, come to me! King John. William Shakespeare. TreFT

Misprize thou not these echoes that belong/To one in love with solitude and
song. Echoes. Emma Lazarus. SBG

Miss Amanda Burr/goes out into the bright eclipse. Two Ladies Bidding Us
"Good Morning." James P. Vaughn. NNP

Miss Beale and Miss Buss. Miss Buss and Miss Beale. *Anonymous.*
CenHV; PoPle

Miss half of the potato's joy,/And that's to dig it up. Vegetables. Eleanor
Farjeon. TiPo

Miss Lucy to Ringwood, the very next day,/Was given in a matrimonial way.
The Lover's Leap. A Tale. Andrew Macdonald. NOEC

Miss R. looks at the mantel-piece, which must mean something. Evening in
the Sanitarium. Louise Bogan. FaBoWP; FYAP; IHMS; MP; SBG;
TwCP

Miss Universe, for Thy Name's Sake, Amen. Boom! Howard Nemerov.
LiTM; MP; NIP; NLV

..."Miss Unknowable, 1964." On Rape Unattempted. Alan Dugan.
NoAm

Miss Wagnalls! Look! It's me! The Girl I Took to the Cocktail Party.
Trevor Williams. FiBHP

Miss Wray who adores you/And loves you, is true to you/Affectionately,
YOUR QUEEN. FayWray to the King. Judith Rechter. NMM

Missed in the commonplace of miracle. The Cathedral. James Russell
Lowell. AmePo; MAmP

The missing bridegroom and the midnight hag. Hurdy-Gurdy Man in
Winter. Vernon Watkins. NYBP

...The missing white frost-face of that slim yellow mountain lion! Mountain
Lion. D. H. Lawrence. AtBAP; BoAnP; HaMV; OBTV; OxBTC; RFM

Missing you/in Air Canada. Love. Ted Berrigan. APU

Mission in spite of all this/Accomplished. Reindeer Report. U. A.
Fanthorpe. OBCP

Missles stand ready/to empty the world of us. Us. David Ignatow. PPJ

Misstrums me, or tries a new tune. Player Piano. John Updike. WeW

The mist looms and shines. Surely My Soul... Jacob Cohen. TrJP

The mistake was made in teaching me/How not to be BLACK. Education.
Don L. Lee. BALP

Mistakes me for where I've been. From. Richard Terrill. AMV-81

Mister, you can rely on us/To execute your will. Overtures to Death. C.
Day Lewis. CMoP

Mistook him/for a former Macon waiter. Robert Whitmore. Frank
Marshall Davis. BPo; NoP; PoBA; PoNe

Mistress Mary is dead and gone! Telling the Bees. John Greenleaf Whittier.
AnNE; AP; AWP; BLPL; HBV 1-2; InPo; LaNeLa; NOBA; NoP; TAP

Mistress o' th' world and me, and Laura is her name. Female Glory.
Richard Lovelace. MyFE

Mistress Penelope Penwick, she,/Called by her father, "My Sweet P." The
Ballad of Sweet P. Virginia Woodward Cloud. PAH

Mistrust of GOD's good providence/Doth daily vex their wearied sense.
Resolution. Henry More. OxBoCh

"Mitchell's still in there, hob-nobbing with the officers." Class Incident from
Graves. Alan Brownjohn. OxBTC

Mite nigh the awkerdist thing/I seen. Uncle IV Surveys His Domain from
His Rocker.... Jonathan Williams. NLV; OBAL

The mither beneath the mools knows that. It Was Far in the Night and the
Barnies Grat (parody). Gerry Hamill. BXAP

Mithridates, he died old. A Shropshire Lad. Alfred Edward Housman.
OAEP

Mitigates the battles of salt and/gold. Nightingales Are Not Singing.
Moshe Dor. VWA

Mix a' thegither. The Poets at Tea. Barry Pain. Par

Mix'd with the murmur of the moving Nile. Mycerinus. Matthew Arnold.
MaVP

...Mix him with my swallowed/pearls and coins and whiskey and days. Fat
Tuesday. W. S. Di Piero. MAYP

Mix me this zone with that. Mechanophilus (excerpt). Alfred, Lord
Tennyson. FaBoCo

Mix them. Boil them. Swallow. Soup on a Cold Day. Nellie Hill.
AMV-81

Mix with the foam of pleasure tears of pain. Condemned Women. Charles
Baudelaire. SyP

Mix with thy name/As morning-star with evening-star/His faultless fame. In
Memory of Walter Savage Landor. Algernon Charles Swinburne. HBV
1-2; PoEL 1-5

Mixed in mad tumult and discordant joy. The Seasons. James (1700-48)
Thomson. FM

Mixed in my soul with the song the mariner sings. Parfum Exotique.
Charles Baudelaire. AWP

Mixed in with the other smells. Explaining about the Dachshund. John
Stone. NIP

Mixed with Soda's carbonate... Sunset in the Sea. Tom (Thomas Hood, Jr.)
Hood. FaBoNo

The mm/wind/ells/b/ells/b Night and a Distant Church. Russell Atkins.
PoBA

Mmm, mistreat me, baby,/And I swear I don't mind dying. Ragged and
Dirty. *Anonymous.* AmFP

Mo mange, mange mais pou' boi' do l'eau. Ou Som Souroucou.
Anonymous. ABF

The moaning of the sea of change/Between myself and thee! My Playmate.
John Greenleaf Whittier. AP; APA; HBV 1-2; NOBA; OBVV

The moaning rain, nor wind-embattled sea. The House of Falling Leaves.
William Stanley Braithwaite. PoLf; PoNe

Moans in the South by the ghost of a sea. Beyond Kerguelen. Henry
Clarence Kendall. NOAV; PoAu 1-2

Moans, shuns the light, and gulps tomato juice. Country Club Sunday.
Phyllis McGinley. CrMA

A mob collects: thank Phoebus, I am freed. The Bore. Horace. ATP;
EnLi 1-2

The mob–the crowd–the mass–will arrive then. I Am the People, the Mob.
Carl Sandburg. AmPP; OxBA; TAP

The mob turns Tory/And preacheth up Passive Obedience. To the Tune of
"Ye Commons and Peers Pray Lend Me Your Ears..." *Anonymous.*
APAS

Mocking the charm of death. O God, it knows! A Dying Viper. Michael
(Katherine Bradley and Edith Cooper) Field. FM

Mockingbirds do not kill/they mock... Wire Monkey. Paul D. Shiplett.
LFAC

The Modern Man I sing. One's-Self I Sing. Walt Whitman. AnAmPo;
DiPo; FaBoPV; NOBA; OxBA

The modern style, sir, with respect, has really come to stay. Executive. Sir
John Betjeman. NOBL

The modesty of fame conceals the rest. The Hind and the Panther. John
Dryden. OBSV

Moeliades sweet courtly nymphs deplore/From Thule to Hydaspes' pearly
shore. Lament. William, of Hawthornden Drummond. LoBV

Mofukuzela, son of Dube, hero of heroes! Lament for Mafukuzela.
Anonymous. WTO

Moisten thy holy dust with wet cheeks/streaming free. Longing for
Jerusalem. Judah Halevi. TrJP

Molded orchards in the concrete Holiday Inn at Bemidji. Gerald Vizenor.
STE

Molly Ban she shone above them like a mountain of snow. Young Molly
Ban. *Anonymous.* FaBoBa

Molly's ghost will stand before you like a mountain of snow. Molly Bond.
Anonymous. BFSS

"Molodyets, ti–moyo mat'!" An Incident of the Occupation. Ira Gershwin.
OxBoLi

"Molotov Cocktail," and Enola Gay. Formal Application. Donald W.
Baker. FF; SoSe

A molten gong–whose full/Resonance an artist/Brocades upon the soul. A
Conversation. Barbara Howes. IHMS

A moment ago I felt so sick/and so cold/I could hardly move. Child
Naming Flowers. Robert Hass. MAYP; NPGG

A moment, amazed at its size. Clear Night, Small Fire, No Wind. Reg
Saner. NPAW

A moment, as for breath, and then with free/And usual tone said,–"O yes,
certainly." The Story of Rimini. [James Henry] Leigh Hunt. EvOK

A moment held/in our empty hands. The Bread Hot from the Oven. John
Thompson. NOBC

Moment I can't forget, eternity I can't comprehend. Twelve Lines About the
Burning Bush. Melech Ravitch. VWA

A moment of the conscience of mankind! On the Founding of Liberia.
Melvin B. Tolson. UnPo

A moment's glance hath made/Our souls forever one. To a Wood-Violet.
John Banister Tabb. HBV 1-2

A moment's memory to that laurelled head. Coole Park, 1929. William
Butler Yeats. MBW 1-2; OAEL 1-2; OBMV; OxBI

A moment stood. Then wondering turned,/And speechless walked ashore.
The Aged Pilot Man. Mark (Samuel Langhorne Clemens) Twain. OBAL

A moment that had turned to gold! Magic Lariat. Glenn Ward Dresbach.
BrR

The moment that would force the world to love. Hiroshima. Margaret
Rockwell. PPON

Momentary, soon quenched, like a strangled flame. The Divers. Peter
Quennell. MoBrPo; MoVE

The moments neglected return not again. Amynta. Gilbert Elliot. HBV 1-2

Moments of clarity we also share. An Aftermath. Thomas Blackburn. NMP

Monarch of cloudland–yet a ghoul at prey. The Vulture of the Plains. Hamlin Garland. BPAW

A monarch's smile can set his subjects free! To the King's Most Excellent Majesty. Phillis Wheatley. TAP

Monarchs, whom Cities and Kingdoms obey,/Are not half so contented, or happy as they. How Pleasant Is This Flowery Plain. *Anonymous.* OBS

Money isn't everything/As long as you have dough! Money Isn't Everything! Oscar, II Hammerstein. OBAL

Money's the still-sweet-singing nightingale. Money Makes the Mirth. Robert Herrick. CaPo

Money will make the mare to go. Wilt Thou Lend Me Thy Mare? *Anonymous.* CBEP; ELU; OBS

The Mongol of the Monastery of Shan. The Llama. Hilaire Belloc. EvOK; FaBoCh; FiBHP; LoGBV

'Mongst all the earthly kings, there's none/Contented with one Crown alone. The Variety. John Dancer. CavP

'Mongst whom the more I seek to settle peace,/The more I find their malice to increase. Amoretti, XLIV. Edmund Spenser. AAS; CABA

An' monie jobs that day begin,/May end in houghmagandie/Some ither day. The Holy Fair. Robert Burns. CEP; EiCP; EnRP; LAuP; OAEP; OBSV

Monk, step further off.' Monk, Step Further Off. *Anonymous.* NOBI

The monkey doesn't jump around since little Willie died. In Memoriam. Max (Charles Heber Clark) Adeler. DTC; FaBoCo

The monkeys gibbering by our bridal bed. The Puritan on His Honeymoon. Robert Bly. FF; NePoEA

Monny an halled that gay lady,/But fue halled Richerd Storry. Richie Story (B version). *Anonymous.* ESPB

Monoglot, that you would speak Welsh. Jackdaw. Tom Earley. BoAnP

The monopolies banded together/To beat a poor hayseed like me. The Hayseed. Arthur L. Kellog. FSW

Monseigneur plays his new gavotte. Monseigneur Plays. Theodosia Garrison. HBMV

"Monster!" I cried. And "Monster!" cried the mouse The Monster. Henry Rago. PoA

A monster whom no vice can bigger swell,/Abhorred by Heaven and long since due to Hell. The Character of a Certain Whig. William Shippen. APAS

Monsters of thought through earth we stray/And how remission comes, God knows. The Avengers. Robert Graves. HBMV

Monstrous against the marshes of the night. Mending the Bridge. Douglas Stewart. AnNZ

Monstrous with stillness, yonder Alpine range. Perhaps. Stephen Spender. NoAm

Montana Rubens, wept for dead not long since,/Has turned herself into a delightful garland. Weather. Mary Ursula Bethell. AnNZ

Months, years, an echoing, garnish'd house–but dead, dead, dead. The City Dead-House. Walt Whitman. AmePo

Montreal, a city, it seems,/of dangerous joys. Dispatch Number Nine. Doug Fetherling. NeAC

A monument, that needs no scroll,/For those beneath the wave! On Board the Cumberland. George Henry Boker. PAH

The mood of men, the world's career. Imagination. John Davidson. MoBrPo

The Moods have drawn swift fingers through my heart. The Moods. Fannie Stearns Davis. HBV 1-2

The mooly cow only said, "Moo-o-o!" The Cow-Boy's Song. Anna Maria Wells. OBCA

Moon. Concrete Poem: Moon. Raymond Federman. MOON

The moon arose up in the murky East,/A white and shapeless mass–. The Moon. Percy Bysshe Shelley. BoLiVe

...The moon/bares the garden. Winter. Princess Shikishi. PBWP

The moon comes misty white. Deserted. Madison Cawein. MCCG

...The moon comes: terrain Terrain. Archie Randolph Ammons. ConAP

A moon drifting, light, alive. Dead Girl. Anna Hajnal. VWA

The moon, grand, not fanciful with clouds. The Climate of Thought. Robert Graves. MoAB; ViBoPo

The moon has no language. The Madwomen of the Plaza de Mayo. Eli Mandel. NOBC

The moon has stepped back like an artist gazing/amazed at a work/That points at him amazed. Full Moon and Little Frieda. Ted Hughes. OBSP; OxBC

The moon in a silver bag. Words for Music Perhaps. William Butler Yeats. AtBAP

The moon in truth, proud of its brilliance, doth lead/astray all this world. The Moon. Bhasa. LiTW

The moon is anchored/like a ghost/in heavy chains. Snowy Night. John Haines. NCSH

The moon is in the folds of the cloak. Of the Surface of Things. Wallace Stevens. ELU

The moon is so bright/the light bursts within me. Summer. Ramona Wilson. VoR

The moon is the mother of pathos and pity. Lunar Paraphrase. Wallace Stevens. MOON

The moon lays a hand on my forehead,/Blank-faced and mum as a nurse. Barren Woman. Sylvia Plath. OBSP

The moon light gets an un-/earthly white Belfast man. Haemorrhage. Padraic Fiacc. CIP

The moon like a thousand lanterns. The Winter Moon. Tagaki Kyozo. LLLT

Moon, Mr. Moon/When you comin' down? Mr. Moon. Bliss Carman. SUS

Moon on the edge of the mountains. I Go out of Darkness. Izumi Shikibu. WPOW

...The/moon rattles like a fragment of angry candy The Cambridge Ladies. Edward Estlin Cummings. HeIP; MoVE; NoAm; NOBA; NoP; OBAL; OxBA; PPON; TAP; ViBoPo

Moon rising without him/might be its suitable title. The Wolfman. Greg Kuzma. GP

The moon's dropped child! Fame. Charlotte Mew. BrRo; PBWP; SBG

Moon's left town. Moon's clean gone. Arizona Nature Myth. James Michie. NOBL

The moon's slow wonder with her hand. Home-Coming. Léonie Adams. HBMV; MoAmPo

The moon? She shines through the blood/& clouds. Where Fled. John Wieners. CoPo

The moon; then turns about, and earthward, too, is clear. On the Ineffable Inspiration of the Holy Spirit. C Greiffenberg. PBWP

A moon to her sun and his star Mother. Keith Sinclair. AnNZ

The moon turns them to chalk and they collapse. Elegy. Tony Towle. ANYP

Moon upon Moon, and year by year. Melhill Feast. William Barnes. CBEP; OBNC

A moon-warmed world of discontinuance. The Second-Fated. Robert Graves. NoAm

The moon was only a smile, your white smile congealed. Fantasy Under the Moon. Emmanuel Boundzekei-Dongala. TTY

The moon went on to her setting/And covered them with shade. On the Way to the Mission. Duncan Campbell Scott. CaP; NOBC

The Moon will not shine on your beauty again! The Flattered Flying Fish. Emile Victor Rieu. ShM; SO

The moonfish, quiet, lighting the darkness of the tea. Fish. Mario Satz. VWA

The moonlight is laid/Like a drawn sword. End of the Comedy. Louis Untermeyer. PoA

Moonlight: lead me over. After the Movement. Peter Oresick. LTB

...The moonlight/Means nothing to the soldiers/Camped in the western desert. Moon Festival. Tu Fu. NaP

The moonlight of a perfect peace/Floods heart and brain. The White Peace. William Sharp. FaBoBe; HBV 1-2

A moonlit snow slope. Haiku: "A bare pecan tree." Etheridge Knight. NeAC; SM; TAP

Moonshine'd not print me then, as it is printing now. To a Bicycle (parody). *Anonymous.* BXAP

The moonshine seemed dishevelled.... A Vision of Poets (excerpt). Elizabeth Barrett Browning. PeD

Moonstruck we staggered there. Tarras Moon. James Keir Baxter. AnNZ

Moor in my little boats vigilantly! Inland City. John Crowe Ransom. CMoP

Moor Swan Moor Swan Moor Swan. Three Poems on Morris Graves' Paintings. John Logan. PoDr

The moorland broke lose. Heptonstall Old Church. Ted Hughes. InPS

MORAL: "Behave." Rules and Regulations. Lewis (Charles Lutwidge Dodgson) Carroll. FaBoUs; NOBV

A moral climbs whose name should be a wreath. Mr. Pope. Allen Tate. AP; CABA; MoAB; MP; NoAm; NOBA; TwCP; VGW

THE MORAL: Everybody knows/How ill a wind it is that blows. The Arrogant Frog and the Superior Bull. Guy Wetmore Carryl. StPo

The moral is–Take care how you light. Darius Green and his Flying-Machine. John Townsend Trowbridge. BeLS; BLPL; FaBoBe; HBV 1-2; HBVY; InMe; MoShBr; OBAL; OBCA; OxBChV; PoLf; YaD

The moral is that little Boys/Should not be given dangerous Toys. George. Hilaire Belloc. FiBHP

Moral: Never stew your sister. Brother and Sister. Lewis (Charles Lutwidge Dodgson) Carroll. BBGG; FaBoNo; ShM

The moral of every great deed is–/The virtue of slandering the doers. Summing Up in Italy. Elizabeth Barrett Browning. VLP

The moral of this tale I could not guess/Till Mr Landor sent his works to press. A Fable. John Hookham Frere. FaBoCo

Moral of this woful poem:/Frequent oil your safety-clutch. The Devil's Dictionary: Safety-Clutch. Ambrose Bierce. OBAL

The moral says; mix water with your wine. Great Bacchus: from the Greek. Matthew Prior. FaBoCo

...A moral truth is a hollow tooth/Which must be propped with gold. Sexsmith the Dentist. Edgar Lee Masters. NePA

Moral: "You mustn't." My Fairy. Lewis (Charles Lutwidge Dodgson) Carroll. FaBoNo

More about the rose. The Rosebush and the Trinity. Alfred Joseph Barrett. GoBC

More alone/than if I were by myself. Anticipation of Sharks. Diane Wakoski. MAT

More amorous than Solomon. A Worm Fed on the Heart of Corinth. Isaac Rosenberg. AtBAP; BrPo; MoPo; OAEL 1-2

More and more from the first similitude. Aurora Leigh. Elizabeth Barrett Browning. TRV; WGRP

More and more./More! Since When As Ever More. Lawson Inada. BrSi

More and more thyself display,/Shining to the perfect day. Morning Hymn. Charles Wesley. CEP; NOEC; OBEC; PoEL 1-5; TrPWD

More beautiful songs as you climb/In splendour above the eternal rose. This Poem Will Never Be Finished. Raymond Souster. CaP

More beautiful than summer once had been. September Afternoon. Margaret Haley Carpenter. GoYe

More brave than me:more blond than you. I Sing of Olaf Glad and Big. Edward Estlin Cummings. AmP; HeIP; LiTA; LiTM; NePA; NoAm; NOBA; NoP; OBSV; OBWP; PPON; VGW; WaP

More cartridges, sir,–calibre fifty-four! Before Vicksburg. George Henry Boker. PAH

More conscious of the Love that glorifies/The common ways and makes them holy ground? More Lovely Grows the Earth. Helena Coleman. CaP

More dead than upright post or fence or chair. The Fallen Tree. Andrew Young. BoNaP

More dear, both for themselves and for thy/sake! Tintern Abbey. William Wordsworth. BLPL; LiTB; TRV; ViBoPo

More dear, more intimtely nigh/Than e'en the sweetest earthly tie. My Prayer. *Anonymous.* BePJ; BLRP

More delicate than the historians' are the map-makers' colors. The Map. Elizabeth Bishop. LoGBV; NOBA

More dreaded than the Bor, and frighten worse/Than damning Pope's Anathema's, and curse. Satyrs upon the Jesuits: Prologue. John Oldham. CEP; SeCV 1-2

"More English than the English'–if I may. It Always Seems (parody). A. M. Sayers. BXAP

More envied Phoebus for his western flying. A Country Song. Sir Philip Sidney. OBSC; SiPS

More flowers I noted, yet I none could/see/But sweet or colour it had stol'n from/thee. Sonnets, XCIX: "The forward violet thus did I chide." William Shakespeare. OAEP; OBSC

More for the Pleasure than the Vice. On the Loss of U.S. Submarine S4 (excerpt). Harry Clifford Canfield. FaBoCo

More form and more fair stateliness/than heretofore between us two. The Angel in the House. Coventry Patmore. FaBoPP

More fruits and fairer flowers/Will bear,/While I droop here. Sic Vita. Henry David Thoreau. AmPP; NePA; OxBA

...More full of pity/and gentleness than snow falling on a burning city. Epithalamium. A. R. D. Fairburn. AnNZ

More geese than swans do live, more fools than wise. Madrigal: "The silver swan." Orlando Gibbons. EnRePo; PBBP

More glad than they had done before. The Beggar Man. Lucy Aiken. OxBChV

More good they had taught him. To Cupid. Michael Drayton. ElL

More happy I, might I in bondage bide! Like as the Dove. Sir Philip Sidney. SiPS

More hard than any ghost there is or any man there was! The Looking-Glass. Rudyard Kipling. EvOK; FaBoTw; GTBS; OBMV

A more harmless vanity? On an Infant Dying as Soon as Born. Charles Lamb. GTBS; GTBS-P; OBEV; OBRV

The more he laughs, the more he may! The Knight of the Burning Pestle. Francis Beaumont and John Fletcher. TrGrPo

More Heaven than Earth was here no winter and no/night. Contemplations. Anne Bradstreet. PBWP

The more I give you gives me the more pleasure. Direct Song. Eve Merriam. UnTE

The more I think of this/The more I beat my wife. When Adam Day by Day. Alfred Edward Housman. ELU; FiBHP; PoPl

The more I thought: I too one day will create/Beauty from cruel weight. Notre Dame. Osip Mandelstam. OBVE

More Indian that we are it makes my stomach want/to turn. Where Have All the Indians Gone? Janet Campbell Hale. STE

The more it needs Thee, and the more I love. And Art Thou Come, Blest Babe? *Anonymous.* OxBoCh

More Jews are killed/to restore the general complacency. Scraps. Rodger Kamenetz. APU

More leaves on the surface of the pool than dixie cups/Fall is come The Sign. Paul Blackburn. TAT

More light and light: more dark and dark our woes! Romeo and Juliet. William Shakespeare. GBL; TreFT

More light, ye spheres/in concord sound/And with your music fill this round! Microcosmus. Nashe [(or Nash(] Thomas. UnS

More lik'd by her, or lov'd by mee. To the Most Fair and Lovely Mistris, Anne Soame, Now Lady Abdie. Robert Herrick. AtBAP; CaPo; NOBE; ViBoPo

More like a child's lost in woods at night/Than the eyes of a big brown bear. The Dancing Bear. Rachel Field. NTCP

More like a Stock than like a Vine. The Vine. Robert Herrick. CaPo; CavP; ErPo; NoP; UnTE

...More like clouds/than those which farmers see. When Silence Divests Me. Henry Birnbaum. GoYe

More like the Being that he enter'd in. The Vicar. George Crabbe. OBNC

More litter, less clutter. The Master of the Golden Glow. James Schuyler. ANYP

More love in woe's despite,/More hope to perish soon. The End of May. William Morris. NOBV

More love, O Christ, to thee,/More love to thee. More Love to Thee, O Christ. Elizabeth Payson Prentiss. AH

More love or more disdain I crave. Against Indifference. Charles Webbe. HBV 1-2; OBEV

More meek, more natural than a third-hand version. Lives of the Poet. Ron Miles. AMV-81

More mild in beastly kind, then that her/beastly foe. The Faerie Queene. Edmund Spenser. OAEP

More, more than wisdom understands/And love, love only knows. Little Hands. Laurence Binyon. HBV 1-2

The more of age the nearer heavenis bliss.' The Praise of Age. Robert Henryson. BSV

More of Thy love and truth, Incarnate Word. More of Thee. Horatius Bonar. BLRP

The more of your heart's possessing/Returns to make you glad. The Joy of Giving. John Greenleaf Whittier. ChBR

More open space, more roads! Give me my stick./I am going. Man Is Nothing But. Saul Tchernichovsky. VWA

More painful to sift the grains of hope/Than gold out of that stream. Madrigal: To His Lady Selvaggia Vergiolesi... Cino da Pistoia. AWP

More peasant in the soul of one,/More poet in the other. Poet and Peasant. R. H. Long. PoAu 1-2

More playfully/sapp'd of seminal rheum. Sic et Non. Sir Herbert Read. FaBoTw

More pleasing, too, than ever was/The lap of Proserpine. The Apron of Flowers. Robert Herrick. CaPo; SeCV 1-2

More precious than wealth or renown. Be Kind. Margaret Courtney. PoToHe

More profit than he ever hoped to gain–/The increment of immortality. Nicolas Gatineau. Arthur Stanley Bourinot. CaP

More pure, more true, more nobly wise. Before Thy Throne. William Boyd Carpenter. TRV

More rapturous far were their delight/Could all partake the common right! Ode to the Lake of Geneva. William Parsons. OBTV

More readily the more my years require/Help, and forgiveness speedy and entire. Eternal Lord! Eased of a Cumbrous Load. Buonarroti Michelangelo. TrPWD

More real and more inconclusive/for being/totally inhabited. Stopping the Heart. Murray Edmond. OCNZ

More rich than Cleopatra's tomb. The Amber Bead. Robert Herrick. CaPo

More sacred than the pleasing of a friend. Invocation. Max Eastman. WGRP

...More sensuous than broiling flesh spread dumb. Afternoon at Cannes. Paul Davis. AMV-81

More sound in France–that, too, he secret keeps. A Private. Edward ("Edward Eastaway") Thomas. GTBS-P; MMM

More spectral than November eve could mix/With sunset, to blaze on her pale crucifix. The Rooftree. Allen Tate. PoA

More sure in this, my full devotion's done–With spirit and sense, by love annealed, at one. Love Redeemed. William Baylebridge. BoAV

The more suspicious you are, the longer I've known you. Testimony to an Inquisitor. William Stafford. NePoAm-2

More sweet than Nectar or Ambrosiall meat,/Seemd every bit, which thenceforth I did eat. Amoretti, XXXIX. Edmund Spenser. AAS

More sweeter than the blossoms/that bloom upon the tree. Simon and Susan. *Anonymous.* OxBoLi

More than a thousand others blest. My Happy Life. Mildmay Fane, Earl of Westmoreland. CavP

More than his medals are to Sloane. On a Halfpenny Which a Young Lady Gave a Beggar... Henry Fielding. CBEP

The more than likely in an unlikely world/Of dogs and people and stone shells and roses. Nude in a Fountain. Norman MacCaig. OxBS

More than man's spoken word. Rain in Summer. Henry Wadsworth Longfellow. GN

The more than thanks of always merest me. Faithfully Tinying at Twilight Voice. Edward Estlin Cummings. NYBP

More than the wisest know your heart shall preach to me. My Owen. Ellen Mary Patrick Downing. HBV 1-2

More than this I scarce can die. Fare Thee Well! George Gordon, Lord Byron. BLPA; EnLit; FaFP; FPL; GoTF; HBV 1-2; OBNC; PoEL 1-5; TreFS

The more the better,–as it tells and pays,/Like bread on waters–after many days! Carrier's Address. *Anonymous.* PoOW

More then a thousand sunnes disburse in light,/In heav'n above. The Glance. George Herbert. AnAnS 1

More this grand sadness tells, than forms of fairest life. On the Picture of the Three Fates in the Palazzo Pitti, at Florence. Arthur Henry Hallam. OBRV

More thundering than that of worms. Conflict. Lincoln Fitzell. AnAmPo

More vainly turn and stretch to you my hands. The Unloved to His Beloved. William Alexander Percy. HBMV

More vent'rous is than he that sleeps/With twenty mortal foes! Let Not the Sluggish Sleep. *Anonymous.* OBSP; OxBoCh

More venturous is than he that sleeps/With twenty mortal foes. Song: "Let not the sluggish sleep." William Byrd. GoBC

More ways to set the selfsame welkin ringing? The Canadian Authors Meet. F. R. Scott. ACV; NOBC; OBCV

The more we climb the further we have to go. The Mountaineers. Dannie Abse. PP

The more we see of you, the less we like you? On Noman, a Guest. Hilaire Belloc. DBV; FaBoEE; PV

More wicked already than ever my uncle was. My Wicked Uncle. Derek Mahon. FaBoIP; OxBC

The more you beat them, the better they'll be. Proverbial Advice to Gentlemen. *Anonymous.* FaBoUs

Moreover, I have got the upper hand,/And mean to keep it. Do you understand? The Justice of the Peace. Hilaire Belloc. NOBV; OBSV

Moreover, when you've turned your tail,/Won't hesitate to follow. The Run from Manassas Junction. *Anonymous.* PAH

The Moril of My peese depend upon it./is good so here i End my odd or sonit. Odd to a Krokis. *Anonymous.* NA

The Morn approaches, and his fiery steeds are fleet. The St. Lawrence and the Saguenay. Charles Sangster. PeCV

Morning and evening in the corn. Country Summer. Léonie Adams. AnEnPo; GoJo; LiTM; MoAB; MoAmPo; MoPo; MoVE; TrGrPo; ViBoPo

The morning apples clanged as they fell. Through the Whole Long Night. Halper Leivick. VWA

A morning-glory at my window satisfies me more than the/metaphysics of books. I Dote Upon Myself. Walt Whitman. AnEnPo

...Morning glory/glowedthe only spot of color/over his shoulder. Why I Am Afraid to Have Children. Bin Ramke. MAYP

Morning is with me, and the breath/Of schoolgirls hastening down the way. Schoolgirls Hastening. John Shaw Neilson. BoAV; NOAV

The morning light creaks down. Aubade. Edith Sitwell. CMoP; ExPo; MoAB; MoBrPo; NoAm; PoRA

Morning, noon, and night. George III. Robert Lowell. FaBoPV

Morning repeats the malice and the light. Variation on a Line by Emerson. William Stanley Merwin. NePA

A morning's work of carpentry,/A miracle enough for me. Softening to Heaven. Raymond Filip. CaPN

The morning so early gone. Spring Morning: Waking. Emily Seelbinder. AMV-81

...The morning/spreads over him like a stain. The Wakening. Sam Hamill. AMV-80

Morning sun and smilingly, to wait for the bearers. In Parenthesis. David Jones. FaBoMo

Morning to all things that ever/Were and will be, and that are. Good Morning. Mark Van Doren. DuDa

Morning warning:/Red sun,/Rains come. Weather Rhymes. Hamish Brown. PoSH

Morning Wisdom, Kathy. It is no dream. With Kathy at Wisdom. Richard Hugo. FAZ

Morning would find me gone. Sam. Walter De La Mare. FaBV; MoAB; MoBrPo; OnMSP; TiPo

Mornings always bring/The blues. Blues. Quandra Prettyman. BOLo

Mornings naked on a rock. Pittsburgh. Witter ("Emanuel Morgan") Bynner. AmFN

Morris Graves has given you/the sudden awful wings of a mirror! Three Poems on Morris Graves' Paintings. John Logan. PoDr

Mors mihi aerumnarum Requies. Epitaph. Cotton Mather. SCAP

Mors omnibus communis. On a Man Run over by an Omnibus. Henry Luttrell. FaBoEE

A morse signal sounds the end of transmission. Dog Fight. Eric Rolls. NOAV

A mortal, a dutiful son. The Celebration. James Dickey. VGW

Mortal! Love that Holy One!/Or dwell for aye alone. Reality. Sir Aubrey De Vere. WGRP

A mortal man becomes a God! The Night of Marvels. Sister Violante Do Ceo. CAW

Mortality. And it makes our world stone. After Plotinus. William Stafford. PoA

Mortality is there. In the Taxidermist's Shop. Siv Cedering Fox. AMV-81

Mortality's ground floor/Is immortality. If my bark sink. Emily Dickinson. TRV

...Mortals can/not justify the ways of God to man When Any Mortal. Edward Estlin Cummings. PoPl

A mortgage over hearth and home. Tall Hat. Victor J. Daley. CBAP

The mosaic of a common light. Poem for a Neighbor. Pat Therese Francis. AMV-81

Moses, what a smash! How We Drove the Trotter. W. T. Goodge. NOAV; PH

The moss-covered bucket which hangs in the well. The Old Oaken Bucket. Samuel Woodworth. BLPA; BLSo; FaBoBe; FaFP; FPL; FSW; PaPo; PSoN; TreF; WBLP

The moss-covered buncombe we all love so well. The Old Hokum Buncombe. Robert E. Sherwood. InMe; NLV

Mossed gate, or farmyard hay-stacks tanned and/yellow. Sonnets, XIII: "I walk of grey noons by the old canal." Thomas Caulfield Irwin. IrPN

Most any soul with God's Good Will. A Poem for Christmas. C. A. Snodgrass. PoToHe

The most beautiful creature that ever was seen/Was the Blind Beggar's daughter of Bethlem Green. The Blind Beggar of Bednall (Bethnal) Green. *Anonymous.* BaBo

Most books, indeed, are records less/Of fulness than of emptiness. Writing. William Allingham. NOBV

Most comforting and gentle thoughts I had. The Lover and Birds. William Allingham. OBVV

The most corruptible metaphor/of a faltered humanity Myths. Daniel L. Klauck. LTB

The most effectual way to balk/Their malice, is–to let them talk. On Censure. Jonathan Swift. CBEP

The most Eve did was to display/Contributory neglige. Eve. Oliver Herford. HBMV; YaD

Most foul, most foul, the future in your face. Freshmen. Barry Spacks. NYBP

"Most gracious advocate, turn thine eyes this way." Our Lady of Mercy. Sister Mary Bertrand. ISi

Most happy she that most assured doth rest,/But he most happy who such one loves best. Amoretti, LIX. Edmund Spenser. AAS

Most justly damned to everlasting fame! Caries. Solyman Brown. FaBoUs

Most loved though most bare,/at the end of a rich season. For My Mother. Iain Crichton Smith. OxBS

Most noble company of saints and sages. House in Springfield. Gail Brook Burket. PGD

Most, O maid's child, thy choice and worthy the winning. Spring. Gerard Manley Hopkins. ACV; BoLiVe; BoNaP; BrPo; DiPo; EBCP; FaBV; ForPo; HAP; InvP; LiTM; MoAB; MoBrPo; MoVE; NoAm; NOBE; NOBV; OAEL 1-2; OAEP; OBMV; OBNC; OxBoCh; SoSe; TrCP; VLP

Most of all to the grey-eyed daughter of Zeus. The Odyssey. Homer. NAWM 1-2

Most of the people were eating already. Against the Grain. Michael Brownstein. ANYP

The most rapt god-drunken,/drawing to our dockyards eternal keels. Anabasis. St.-John (Alexis Saint-Léger Léger) Perse. AtBAP

Most ree-markable old party. Old Moll. James Reeves. WSC

Most rich endowed whose infant mind/Guesses not yet there is the rose. The Babe. Monk Gibbon. OxBI

Most useful is the modest ass. The Burro. J. J. Gibbons. PoOW

Most venerable Poverty! to thee all hail! Poverty, in Imitation of Milton. Samuel Jones. NOEC

The most vital thing in life. The Most Vital Thing in Life. Grenville Kleiser. PoToHe; SoSe

The most who die, the more we live. What If a Much of a Which of a Wind. Edward Estlin Cummings. AP; BLPL; FaFP; LiTA; LiTM; MasP; MoAmPo; MoPo; MoVE; NePA; NOBA; NoP; OxBA; PoA; PoRA; PPP; SoSe; ViBoPo; WaP

Most wrecked and longest of all histories. China. William Empson. OBTV

A mot's good-night to one and all! Villon's Good-night. William Ernest Henley. CenHV

A mote on the horizon, a silent O. Green Island. William Logan. MAYP

The moth-wing soul of Jane. Dulce Ridentem. Stephen Vincent Benét. LOW

Mothball, snowflake,/dead child. The Doll. Gregory Orr. AmPA

A mother, a mother was born. One Wept Whose Only Child Was Dead. Alice Meynell. AnFE; GoTF; TreFT

Mother and child!–your tears are past–/Surely your hearts have met at last. The Memorial Pillar. Felicia Dorothea Hemans. SBG

Mother and father sit at a small, round table. Kitchen Tables. David Huddle. Str

Mother and mistress, one. A Spark of Laurel. Stanley Jasspon Kunitz. NoAm

Mother and Virgin, Jesus born of thee/Is guardian of thine intact purity. How of the Virgin Mother Shall I Sing? Saint Ennodius. ISi

Mother, blessed among all women may you be! Promenades and Interiors. Francois Coppee. CAW

A mother cries for the murder her child's done/and spring has hardly begun. Poem Written before Mother's Day for Mrs. Lopez from the South. R. Wayne Hardy. LFAC

Mother don't just lie there say something please Mother the Wardrobe Is Full of Infantrymen. Roger McGough. MAT

Mother, farewell! The pilgrimage begins. Farewell to My Mother. Placido (Gabriel de la Conception Valdes). TTY

Mother I am monarch of all I survey. Lord of All I Survey. Keith Sinclair. AnNZ

Mother, I cannot whistle,/But I'll do the best I can. Inducements. Anonymous. OxNR

Mother–I saw/my life/in your pain. Visit. Randolph Outlaw. LFAC

"Mother, I strove with God, and was hard prest." The Struggle. Sully Prudhomme. AWP; PoPl

Mother, let me go! A Frosty Night. Robert Graves. CH; MoAB; MoBrPo; MoBS; OxBTC

Mother, let me pass. A Very Old Song. William Laird. HBV 1-2

Mother mine: loved Winchester! Winchester. Lionel Pigot Johnson. OBVV

Mother, never mourn. Mater Dolorosa. William Barnes. CH; HBV 1-2; OBEV

Mother o' mine, O mother o' mine! Mother o' Mine. Rudyard Kipling. FaFP; TRV; WBLP

The Mother of Fair Love has come to dwell/In God–O, angels, praise the glory of her face! The Assumption. John Gilland Brunini. ISi

The Mother-of-God will spread/a white shroud over these great sorrows. July 1914. Anna Akhmatova. WPOW

Mother of men, this bleeding face/Awaits the wonder of your love's embrace. Cry from the Battlefield. Robert Menth. ISi

Mother, oh, mother, it's Hell for you. The Cruel Mother. Anonymous. FSW

"Mother's kiss–Mother's kiss." Strange Lands. Laurence Alma-Tadema. HBVY

Mother's runaway daughter. Rosy Apple, Lemon, or Pear. Anonymous. CH; PoL

Mother said check/with her next/time we got to/feeling commercial-/minded. My Brother, Beautiful Shinault, That Goat. David Huddle. GrPl

...Mother said, "Well, he had thirty-four good/years..." Blind Adolphus. Angela McCabe. AmPA

The mother sees nought: the bride shall see/The Herald and Death-flag far off– not thee. The Dirge of Kildare. Aubrey Thomas De Vere. IrPN

Mother, so maybe they sent her away and made up the rest. Suicid/ing Indian Women. Paula Gunn Allen. TWSS

Mother takes by calculation/The angle of its inclination. Rhyme for Astronomical Baby. Joseph Cook. QQQ; SpRo

The Mother takes her child again. The Place of Rest. George William Russell. WGRP

Mother, the fading wall, the dream,/The drowsy bed. Many a Mickle. Walter De La Mare. FaBV

The mother then must suck the Son. Luke 11: "Blessed be the paps which Thou hast sucked'. Richard Crashaw. JCP

Mother, what hast thou done, what hast thou/done! San Francisco. John Vance Cheney. PAH

Mother, what more? What more? From an Asylum: Kathy Chattle to Her Mother, Ruth Arbeiter. Anne Stevenson. BrRo

The mother will not fail to keep/Where we can "lay us down to sleep." Down to Sleep. Helen Hunt Jackson. GN

A-mothering on Sunday. Mothering Sunday. Anonymous. OxNR

The mothers of Angola/died together with their sons. Fourth Poem. Jorge Carrera Andrade. WhB

The Mothers of the Generations of Life/we the/libation. Ceremony. Johari M. Kunjufu. BlSi

Mothers pray, and pray, and pray. Mothers–and Others. Amos R. Wells. WBLP

The moths/Lie in the black grass waiting The Moths. William Stanley Merwin. HeIP

Motion denied mother-fucker! Mother's Day. Sandie Castle. APU

The motion was passed. Wilfred Owen's Photographs. Ted Hughes. FaBoPV; OxBC

Motionless/as a lizard in the sun. Alfred Corning Clark. Robert Lowell. NoAm

Motionless sit the bridegroom and bride/On the Dead-Sea-shore. A Mammon-Marriage. George Macdonald. BoLoP; CBEP; NBM; OBVV

Mought them awake out of their sinful sleep. In Praise of Wyatt's Psalms. Henry Howard, Earl of Surrey. SiPS

Moulded by God, and temper'd with the tears/Of angels to the perfect shape of man. To–. Alfred, Lord Tennyson. VLP

Moulding from the burning voice a phoenix day. Poem from London, 1941. George Woodcock. NeBP

A mound of earth and naught beside,/There let me lie. When I Am Dead. James Edward Wilson. PoLf

Mount and go to Northumberland,/There a countess thou shall be.' The Duke of Gordon's Daughter. Anonymous. BuBa; ESPB

A mount that has no need of friends. The Island Cemetery. W. H. Auden. NePoAm-2

The mountain-cairn might mark my burial-place. Prospect of a Mountain. Andrew Young. PoSH

The mountain is his. The Time We Climbed Snake Mountain. Leslie Marmon Silko. VoR

Mountain/of short grass and subtle shadows. With Eyes at the Back of Our Heads. Denise Levertov. AmPP

A mountain people dwelling among moun-/tains. In Time of War. W. H. Auden. EnLit

...The/mountain shakes us very gently. The Hike. Neil Weiss. SD

A mountain stone–clear, like water. Words Spoken by Pasternak during a Bombing. Bella Akhmadulina. BoWoP

The mountain, wailing/in a terrible voice. To Xanadu, Which Is Beth Shaul. Arye Sivan. VWA

The mountain waves run o'er their graves on the banks of/Newfoundland.] The Banks of Newfoundland (I). Anonymous. OBSS

Mountains and houses, may be also men. In Time of War. W.H. Auden. CMoP

...The mountains/rising up like fists, surround the town. Christmas at Vail: On Staying Indoors. Patricia Monaghan. AMV-80

...Mountains/sing to each other across the cold valleys. A Common Ground. Denise Levertov. PoM; PP

Mountains/women/fish Codes. Diana Chang. BrSi

Mounting, mounting still, triumphant, on his torn and broken wings! Winged Man. Stephen Vincent Benét. MoAmPo

Mourn'd by the desert when she dies. The Phoenix. George Darley. EG; LoBV; WiR

Mourn, England, mourn, mourn and complain,/For the loss of Lord Nelson who died on the main. A New Song Composed on the Death of Lord Nelson. Anonymous. CoMu

"Mourn, hapless Caledonia, mourn,/"Thy banish'd peace, thy laurels torn.' The Tears of Scotland. Tobias George Smollett. NOEC; OBEC

Mourn not!–yield only happy tears/To deeper beauty than appears! Grieve Not for Beauty. Witter ("Emanuel Morgan") Bynner. PoA

Mourned by scholars who dream of the ghosts of Greek boys. The Funeral. Stephen Spender. CMoP; MoAB; MoBrPo; NAMP; NoAm

Mourned by the desert where she dies! O Blest Unfabled Incense Tree. George Darley. AtBAP; FaBoCh; FaBoRV; LoGBV

Mourned for the dear one mourning. The Song of Jed Smith (excerpt). John G. Neihardt. FYAP

Mourned too, for more to come. The Child at Winter Sunset. Mark Van Doren. NCSH

A mourner still, though friend and lover/Have both forgotten thee! The Wanderer from the Fold. Emily Bronte. EnLit

The mourners in the alien street/At their own doorways mourn. Revelation. William Soutar. HaMV

The mournful beauty of this land. In Louisiana. Albert Bigelow Paine. AA; AmFN

The mournful strain was in thyself alone. The Pines and the Sea. Christopher Pearse Cranch AA; AmLP; HBV 1-2

Mourning and weeping in this valley of tears. Ave, Vita Nostra! Clifford J. Laure. ISi

Mourning the first and last to love me I Would Like My Love to Die. Samuel Beckett. BIrV; CIP; NOBI

Mourns Lea Mogha, ruined too! Lament for Corc and Niall of the Nine Hostages. Torna. OnYI

Mourns o'er the beauty of the Cyclades. Don Juan. George Gordon, Lord Byron. CoBE; FiP

Moused in the dark for what she once had been. Innocence. Norman MacCaig. NMP

Mouth of dark spaces/the valley waits for the mountain. Cardrona Valley. Ian Wedde. OCNZ

...The mouth of one/Just dead. Triad. Adelaide Crapsey. PoPl

The mouth of the river/turns into smoke/and becomes the city City. Joseph Bruchac. CDW

...The mouth/of winter.　Lynx.　Ben Howard.　GrPl

Mouth open to these syllables of praise.　In Search of a Short Poem for My Grandmother.　Louise Hardeman.　AMV-81

The mouth takes food.　Russians Breathing.　Philip Hammial.　NOAV

...Mouthing our own sad psalms.　Nobody Lives on Arthur Godfrey Boulevard.　Gerald Costanzo.　MAYP

Move a' the miseries o' his flesh...　Love.　Hugh" (Christopher Murray Grieve) MacDiarmid.　CMoP

Move about, lighting the stove.　Two Lines from the Brothers Grimm. Gregory Orr.　AmPA

Move, child, move/if we don't get there/nobody must...　Heat and Sweat. Mongane Wally Serote.　WhB

Move her to pity, stay her from disdain,/Let never man love worthiness in vain.　Caelica, IX.　Fulke, Lord Brooke Greville.　FCP

Move, honey baby, where they don't 'low you.　Kansas City Blues. *Anonymous.*　FSW

Move not thy heavy grace, thou shalt in me,/Livelier than elsewhere, Stella's image see.　Astrophel to Stella, XXXIX.　Sir Philip Sidney.　AnFE

Move slowly, turn, return, and bring once more/Your lights and music. It will be good to talk.　When the Tree Bares.　Conrad Aiken.　MoAmPo

Moved from us like a moving crowd.　The Mountebanks.　Charles Henry Luders.　AA

Moved him maist to sla his eme.　Macbeth's Dream.　Andrew of Wynton. BSV

Moved on–and, thank God, forever at/rest/In the last reservation.　The Last Reservation.　Walter Learned.　AA; PAH

Moved through the summer night/crushing the patchouli.　Love Lifted Me. Paris Leary.　CoPo

Moved to the tune/of a different/even Blacker band...　Query.　Ebon. PoBA

Moveless with joy, to know you near once more.　Homecoming in Storm. Bernice Lesbia Kenyon.　EtS

Movement alone is his great honor.　Aesthetic.　Norman Rosten.　PoA

...The movement of a prehistoric fish/dredged up and exposed to light for the first time.　Waltz.　Heather Tosteson Reich.　AMV-80

The movement of benediction/does not turn back/the cold wind.　The Hounded Lovers.　William Carlos Williams.　MoLP; NYBP; TrGrPo

Movements following the eternal blueprint.　Saturday Night.　Antigone Kefala.　CBAP

Moves its arms like a giant Swedish drill whose/Mind is a vacuum. Christmas Shopping.　Louis MacNeice.　OBCP

Moves the calm spirit, but disturbs it not.　When Winds That Move Not Its Calm Surface Sweep.　Moschus.　OBVE

Moves with the numbers which she hears.　The Dancer.　Edmund Waller. TrGrPo

Movies you wouldn't let them see when they were young　Ave Maria. Frank O'Hara.　ANYP; HaCAP; NNaP; NoP; PoM

Moving along the white keys as men go/heavily through deep drifts of snow. From a Childhood.　Rainer Maria Rilke.　TrJP

Moving and childish as an ancient rhyme.　A Bagatelle.　James Reeves. PoL

Moving at all as all men, because you must.　The Awakening.　Robert Creeley.　NeAP

Moving at night like a diver among the bare branches/silently lying on the floor.　Silence.　Robert Bly.　NaP

Moving at summer's pace.　Cut Grass.　Philip Larkin.　OxBC; PrIm

The moving grass, the Indian in his glade.　The Auroras of Autumn. Wallace Stevens.　CMoP

Moving in a cloud of dust toward the theater marquee.　Stumptown Attends the Picture Show.　David Bottoms.　GP

Moving is the great earth of Kane...　Old Creation Chant.　*Anonymous.* WTO

Moving like women: Justice, Truth, such figures.　Another September. Thomas Kinsella.　BIrV; CIP; FaBoIP; PoCh

Moving on towards death. But sometimes standing still is also/life.　The Bungalows.　John Ashbery.　CoAP

Moving over all the floor/moving/threshing/sowing.　Zeimbekiko.　Robin Magowan.　EAS

Moving to the hidden rhythm of the real　The Exchanges II.　Robert Kelly. CoPo

Moving together through time to all good.　Time's Dedication.　Delmore Schwartz.　VGW

...Moving,/we will/move, and then/stop.　The Turn.　Robert Creeley. LCAP

...Moving where the wood of the boat/moves, merely floating, looking back. Return, Starting Out.　Daniel Halpern.　MAYP

Moving with wonder/through the antechamber/of a waking world.　Lagoons, Hanlan's Point.　Raymond Souster.　NOBC

Moving yet and never stopping,/Pioneers! O Pioneers!　All the Past We Leave Behind.　Walt Whitman.　AH

The mowers are all gone, and I go too.　Lying in the Grass.　Sir Edmund Gosse.　OBVV

Mown from the harvest's middle floor.　August.　Algernon Charles Swinburne.　AtBAP; WiR

Mox-pooh. Mox-pooh.　Ascending Red Cedar Moon.　Duane Niatum. CDW

Moyst, with one drop of thy blood, my dry soule.　Crucifying.　John Donne. AnAnS 1; OBS

Mozart's barber Figaro could never/cut the gold thread of the suffocating curtain.　Robespierre and Mozart as Stage.　Robert Lowell.　FaBoMo

Mr. and Mrs. Dukes, and Oscar Baer/Of 17 West 4th St., Oyster Bay. Ozymandias Revisited.　Morris Bishop.　NLV

"Mr. Billings of Louisville touched me for ten."　Mr. Billings of Louisville. Eugene Field.　NLV

–Mr. Bones: there is.　Dream Song.　John Berryman.　CAPP; HaCAP; HAP; NoP; OBAL; WeW

–Mr Bones, we all brutes & fools.　Dream Song.　John Berryman.　TwCP

"Mr. Cobbler, stick to your last."　Limerick: "An amateur, driving too fast." Frederick A. Wright.　LiBL

Mr. E. C. Bentley/just smiles gently.　Clerihew: "Instead of blushing cherry hue."　Allan M. Laing.　PV

Mr. Gilbert does a handspring in his grave.　The Belle of the Balkans. Newman Levy.　ALV; FiBHP

Mr. Hughes smiled like a tiger from the rug.　Mr. Hughes.　David Campbell.　CBAP

(A Mr. Hutton had pressed the wrong button/On the coast of Maine.)　A Leaden Treasury of English Verse.　Paul Dehn.　DBV; QQQ

Mr. Moon, does he make you hurry?　Moon Song.　Hilda Conkling.　TiPo

Mr. Moses Levy departed this Life/June the 14th. 1728.　Epitaph for Mr. Moses Levy.　*Anonymous.*　TrJP

"Mr. Nowlan, are you asleep?"　Semi-Private Room.　Alden Nowlan. NeAC

Mr. Orlimpit imagines his daybreak, its limpid, purely/Crystalline virtue.　O Rose, O Rainbow.　Nicholas Moore.　NeBP

Mr. Purvis on his mansion/He doesn't pay no mind　High Sheriff Blues. Charlie Patton.　BluL

"Mr. Roosevelt regrets......"　Mr. Roosevelt Regrets.　Pauli Murray.　PoBA

Mr. Someone/Or yourself/Should take a book down from the shelf.　If Someone Asks You.　Mitchell Donian.　PoSC

Mr. South burnt his mouth/With eating a cold potato.　Mr. East's Feast. *Anonymous.*　OxNR

Mrs Albion you've got a lovely daughter.　Mrs. Albion You've Got a Lovely Daughter.　Adrian Henri.　OxBTC

Mrs. Brown's dresses still button to my chin.　Dresses.　Kathleen Fraser. NMM

Mrs. Curtis says she smoked cigars!　Dear Wordsworth.　William Hathaway. APU

Mrs. Peck-Pigeon/Goes picking for bread.　Mrs. Peck-Pigeon.　Eleanor Farjeon.　NTCP; OnUR; SoPo; SUS; TiPo

"Mrs. Simpson's pinched our King."　Abdication Street Song.　*Anonymous.* PV

Much as we search now for ourselves in a fogbank of hope　Infants of Summer.　Lennox Raphael.　NBP

Much as you do about streptocucci.　Tallyho-Hum.　Ogden Nash.　PH

Much blood the Monsters lost, and they their Arms.　The Battel of the Summer-Islands.　Edmund Waller.　AnAnS 2; SeCV 1-2

Much Doctrine lyes under this little Stone.　A Great Favorit Beheaded. Luis de Gongora y Argote.　OBVE

Much faith; and, carefully laid by,/A little crutch.　The Widow's Mite. Frederick Locker-Lampson.　HBV 1-2

Much is lost each hour you delay!　Choose.　Verna Bishop.　STF

Much more ought they to God obey,/And serve but Him alone.　The Nut-Brown Maid.　*Anonymous.*　LiTL; MeEV; OBEV

Much more our Father seeks/To do us good.　Consider.　Christina Georgina Rossetti.　GN; TRV

Much nicer place to be–/for a worm.　Christmas Dinner.　Michael Rosen. OBCP

Much of greatness has passed,/still-born...　Action.　James Oppenheim. TrJP

Much quicker than you could say "Scat!"　Limerick: "Said the mouse with scholastical hat."　A. B. P.　TDH

Much rather let me die.　Canzonetta: He Will Neither Boast Nor Lament to His Lady.　Jacopo da Lentino.　AWP

Much sorwe I walke with/For best of bon and blod.　Snatches: "Foweles in the frith."　*Anonymous.*　OxBM

Much that well may be thought cannot wisely be/said.　The Priest and the Mulberry Tree.　Thomas Love Peacock.　GN; OnMSP; StPo

Much were it better for to be plain/Than to say abide, and yet shall not obtain.　Sonnets, VI: "I abide and abide and better abide."　Sir Thomas Wyatt.　SiPS

Much will be missing still, and much will be amiss.　The Profane.　Horace. AWP

Mud chokes his mouth, and plasters o'er his eyes.　Of Pick-Pockets.　John Gay.　EnLi 1-2

Must carry his own coffin and believe,/In dread, all that the clergy teach the young. The Straying Student. Austin Clarke. AnIL; BIrV; CIP; IPY; MoAB; NeIP; NOBI; OxBI

Must cure the harp's distress. That Harp You Play So Well. Marianne Moore. HBMV; MoAB; MoAmPo; PoA

Must die by the breath of Kate Kearney. Kate Kearney. Lady Morgan. BLPA; FaBoBe

Must end in dust and silence here. Sermon in a Churchyard. Thomas Babington, Lord Macaulay. OBRV

Must everything resolve itself to two? Threes. Henry Chapin. FAZ

Must fall aswoon, feeling all life grow weak. La Vita Nuova. Dante Alighieri. AWP

Must get some friend to stand a treat. One Fish Ball. Anonymous. FSW

Must gird his marble loins and follow me. The Royal Mummy to Bohemia. Charles Warren Stoddard. AA

Must hear that whisper when his hour has come. Je Ne Veux de Personne aupres de ma Tristesse. Henri de Regnier. AWP

Must I confess my weariness/At facing stringent mistresses/And head for haven? Here I come. Safety at Forty; or, An Abecedarian Takes a Walk. L. E. Sissman. Prf

Must I die now? Is this a part of life? A Cut Flower. Karl Shapiro. BoNaP; HAP; WeW

Must I endure your amorous cries? He Thinks of His Past Greatness... William Butler Yeats. DTC; OAEP; PoEL 1-5

Must I go on feeding these?/Says the Shan Van Vocht? The Irish Council Bill, 1907. Anonymous. OnYI

Must I keep on buying lovebirds, Miss Dix, or do you think it would/be all right to buy a cat? Two and One Are a Problem. Ogden Nash. FiBHP

Must lay his heart out for my bed and board. Words for Hart Crane. Robert Lowell. AP; CABA; CMoP; NMP

Must lean out into time to catch, and die in seeing. Ursa Major. James Kirkup. ImOP

Must learne in life to dye like Thee. In Memory of the Vertuous and Learned Lady Madre de Teresa. Richard Crashaw. AnAnS 1

Must make an end of something–even change. Like a Whisper. Ethan Ayer. GoYe

Must not be numbred in the year. Christ's Nativity. Henry Vaughan. AtBAP

...Must now love/The passage of time. In Autumn. Jon Anderson. AmPA

Must out and make way for the bold Fenian Men! The Bold Fenian Men. Anonymous. FSW

Must quench the lamps and pass/Alive into the house. Missing. W. H. Auden. OxBTC

Must ramble, and thin out/Like milk spilt on a stone. Spilt Milk. William Butler Yeats. OBSP

Must really be a sort of fish/not to be caught just with a wish. The House I Go to in My Dream. George Barker. OnUR

Must serve their masters, though they damn their souls. A Panegyric. John Grubham, and Henry Hall. Howe. APAS

Must shout to be heard above/the October wind The Chestnut Vendor. Karl Szelki. PCP

Must slay to live, but what excuse had I? Bete Humaine. Francis Brett Young. CH; HBMV

Must wait a year now to remember/Another fifth of November. November the Fifth. Leonard Clark. OnUR

...Must wait till/sunlight wakes/Knowledge of what was known, and/then descend.' The Homeward Journey. Leonard Aaronson. TrJP

Must we both fumble not to show our fears/Of holding back our pain, our kindness too? To My Mother at 73. Elizabeth Jennings. NAs

...Must we forever,/dear friends, die in our sleep? The Sun Wields Mercy. Charles Bukowski. MAT

Must we, to flatter her, be made/To wither, envy, pine and fade? Fable XLV: The Poet and the Rose. John Gay. EiCP

"Must worship Him in spirit/"And in truth." Malachi. Earl Bowman Marlatt. MoRP

Must you deny me a bite of your raisin? Brief Autumnal. Anonymous. LiTW; WeW

Must you find only at the end/That who has nothing has no friend? The Old Story. Marcus Argentarius. AWP; LiTW

Must you have a part in everything? Smell. William Carlos Williams. MoAB; MoAmPo; TAP; WeW

Mute and mean,/perceptible–/that is all. Comparatives. N. Scott Momaday. SM

Mute history stands on wooden wheels and aims at Woolworth's Five and Ten. Cannon Park. Mark St. Germain. PCP

Mute, remembered alone by him who made it. Fingernail Sunrise. Vernon Watkins. NYBP

Mute to the strange rumbling of demons/inside you Visiting Father. Genny Lim. BrSi

Mutely astonished to rehearse/The unutterable simple verse. Opening of Eyes. Laura Riding. NoAm

A mutilated structure, soon to fall. The Task. William Cowper. FiP

Mutter the Voices–the Guns. The Voices. Anonymous. MCCG

Muttering and poking spears/At every fish he found. Historical Incidents. Clarence Day. InMe

Muttering through cold spring air. Poem ("Woke This A.M."). Jim Brodey. ANYP

Mutters in sleep: "Bridegroom, behold your bride." The D Minor. E. L. Mayo. MiAP

The mutual rescues, quiet, understood. Poem to Negro and Whites. Maxwell Bodenheim. PoNe

My accent's improving. A Letter to Wilbur Frohock. Daniel Gerard Hoffman. CoPo

My act, in the onward press of business and/consequence. An Act. Kenneth Rosen. AmPA

My address will be unknown except to god and the/Boogaman. If I Ride This Train. Joe Johnson. PoBA

My air is as solid as the inside of a honeydew melon. The Old Lady under the Freeway. Diana O Hehir. NPGG

My Ale was tunn'd when I was young,/and a little above my knee. The Merry Hoastess. Anonymous. CoMu

My all–if you were ever home! Love-Songs, At Once Tender and Informative. Samuel Hoffenstein. OBAL

My all of you birchwood in lightning. Glanmore Sonnets. Seamus Heaney. IPY

My Amy is the only leaf/In all that forest sear. Amy. James Matthew Legare. AA

My analyst hints at amnesia impending.' A Right-of-Way: 1865. William Plomer. DTC

My arms around you to-night would banish/That stripling out of your delicate head. Braggart! Denis Wrafter. OnYI

...My arms/paddle into a field of lightning. Ethan Boldt. Roger Weingarten. AmPA

My auld calamitie!' The Deil o' Bogie. Sir Alexander Gray. BSV

My avarice cooled/Like lust in the chill of the grave. Hamatreya. Ralph Waldo Emerson. AmPP; AnNE; AP; HeIP; MAmP; MAT; NOBA; NoP; OxBA; PoEL 1-5; PrIm; SeCeV; TAP

My avenging ghost will wipe out/Your city and state. English Thornton. Edgar Lee Masters. OxBA

My awful dearth just as one pumpkin mocks,/In clownish glee, this frosted field! A Prayer in Late Autumn. Violet Alleyn Storey. TrPWD

My awful stamp will bury all names still unsung. Rumplestiltskin Poems. William Hathaway. DFT

My awn true love she is,/That loves her paramours. Sweethairt, Rejoice in Mind. Alexander Montgomerie. BSV

My baby, my dear son. Cradle-Song. Adelaide Crapsey. HBMV; ISi

My baby, she gone and left me/She left me all a lone Little Boy Blue. Robert Lockwood. BluL

My back to the wall, taking my cue from a/grinning disc-jockey between commercials. I Am Raftery. Derek Mahon. CIP

My bairn sleep softly now. O Jesu Parvule. Anonymous. ISi

My bait of pearls and gold was well devised! Columbus. Percy Adams Hutchison. EtS

My bar is somewhat further down the street. Third Avenue in Sunlight. Anthony Hecht. CoAP; NePoEA-2; NYP; PPP

My bare poles dip, through sun and spray,/The dim marge of God's outer sea. A Life. George Edward Woodberry. EtS

My barn is to build,/and my babe is unborn.' Bonnie James Campbell. Anonymous. ESPB

My battered ego will reply/With (-1) subscription. The Sub-Average Time Reader. Ernest Wittenberg. FiBHP

My bears, who keeps you now, in pride and fear? Bears. Adrienne Rich. NCSH; NePoEA; NYBP

My beautiful face is dust. Banishment from Ur. Enheduanna. BoWoP

My beautiful Georgian rose! Her Lips They Are Redder Than Coral. Anonymous. FaBoCo

My beauty broke her ankle./Hey nonny, nonny, etc. A Winter Madrigal. Morris Bishop. InMe

My beauty do I give to you–/Tsucroo, Tsucroo, Tsucroo. The Birds. Anonymous. PCh

My bells shall then thy praises bravely chime. Meditations. Edward Taylor. NoP

MY BIRTHDAY CAKE! The Miracle. Elsie Melchert Fowler. BiCB

My black self. America. Bobb Hamilton. BOLo

My blessing on the patient cows. A Blessing on the Cows. Seumas (James Starkey) O'Sullivan. BoAnP

My blood has adopted a child/who shuffles through my chest/carrying a doll. Organ Transplant. J. D. Reed. PoL

My blood is for thy ransom paid,/I die that thou mayest live. I Saw One Hanging. Anonymous. STF

My blood is redder for your loveliness. Song for the Passing of a Beautiful Woman. Anonymous. LiTA

My blood/yet more your blood/shall irrigate our victory. Your Pain. Armando Guebuza. WhB

My blue dress is dreaming of you. The Clothes. Rayzel Zychlinska. VWA

My boat should be her arms–/Mother's arms. The Boat. Caroline Gilman. OBCA

My body blue and wan,/Woefully arrayed. Woefully Arrayed. John Skelton. CABA; CBEP; LoBV; OxBoCh

My body is full of windows. Manhattan. H. R. Hays. EAS

My body shakes with the will to endure. The Necessity of Rejection. James Schevill. FAZ

My body shall be glorified/And shall be made like His. Discerning the Lord's Body. Carrie Judd Montgomery. STF

My bones began/beating and/beating the heart-drum/to shreds. Covenant. Paul Auster. VWA

My bones feel small. I am lifted easily. Under the Shawl. Rose Drachler. VWA

My bones turn to dark emeralds. The Jewel. James Wright. CAPP; CoAP

My bonnie dearie. Ca' the Yowes. Robert Burns. EnRP

...My books piled/beside me, wiping blue mold from the spines. End of August. Gregory Orr. MAYP

My books sleep, pretending to forget me. The Sofa. Mebdh McGuckian. FaBoIP

My brandy bottle's my best friend. Bachelor Bold and Young. Anonymous. AmFP

My breath is mixed into his breath. The Heart of the Woman. William Butler Yeats. GTBS

My breath,/my clay,/my open hand. Child. Tom MacIntyre. CIP

My bright and beauteous Bride. Love. Samuel Taylor Coleridge. BeLS; EnRP; GTBS; OAEP

My broken heart thy piteous fingers bore. In the Face of Grief. Sister Juana Ines de la Cruz. CAW

My brother, good morning: my sister, good night. The Early Morning. Hilaire Belloc. BoNaP; HBMV; HBVY; OBSP

My brother/is that one/at my side/who fights. My Brother. Frelimo. WhB

My brother's a knight o wealth and/might,/He'll wed nane but he will for me.' Thomas o Yonderdale. Anonymous. ESPB

My brother, the angel, has fallen. The Second Angel. Philip Levine. NaP

My budding heart swells,/ready to burst clusters/of yellow flame against/the clear sky. Broccoli. Tom Schmidt. GP

My burning Bull the first do try. The Dissembler. Abraham Cowley. AnAnS 2

My butter's melting in the sun. Donkey, Donkey, Do Not Bray. Anonymous. OxNR

My cabin never leaks when it doesn't rain! The Arkansas Traveler. Anonymous. FSW

My camera cannot shoot. Roll Call: A Land of Old Folk and Children. Isaac J. Black. CNA

(My crane–light, my hair/turning white). A Message to the Photographer Whose Prints I Purchased. Beryle Williams. PoDr

My car, a thundering shepherd, coaxed/him over the hill, and I went on. Jack Rabbit. Adrien Stoutenburg. BoAnP

My cat and I grow old together. The White Cat of Trenarren. A. L. Rowse. OxBTC; PCat

My cat met me/and licked my fins/till they were hands again. On Reading Poems to a Senior Class at South High. D. C. Berry. SoSe

My champion, Death! Life. Alice Brown. AA

My chief contentment I will entertain. Platonick Love. Edward, Lord Herbert of Cherbury. AnAnS 2; OBS

My child and I, together, to the sun. The Woman with Child. Freda Laughton. OnYI

"My child," He said, "what could I do?/You never did let go!" Reproof. Anonymous. STF

My choicest model thou hast ta'en. On William Graham, Esq., of Mossknowe. Robert Burns. DBV

My Christ, who reigns in heaven above,/Receive us to his breast of love! The Invitation (abridged). Gronwy Owen. LiTW

My city is a murmur of voices coming out of a pit. The Lame One. Sherwood Anderson. AnAmPo

My clever little eyes/raisins! Phantasus. Arno Holz. LiTW; PCh

My close of earth's experience/May prove as peaceful as his own. Tiresias. Alfred, Lord Tennyson. VLP

My clouds rain curtains, my vision's jewel is his. Third Madrigal. Gene Derwood. NePA

My conquering spirit sails and will not die. The Spirit of the "Bluenose." Claire Harris MacIntosh. CaP

My consecrated Vessel hangs at last. Odes. Horace. OBVE; WiR

...My consent/Is immediate. Ladies and gentlemen, my wife. Proposal. Robert Sward. ELU

My constant physic make it. Epigram: "Fair Ursly, in a merry mood." Anonymous. FaBoEE

My corn's unshorn,/my meadow grows green.' Bonnie James Campbell. Anonymous. ESPB

My crazy friend Fernando. Fernando. Marci Ridlon. NTCP

My crazy green kitchen gets a cloud of white dust./Hello. A Daughter's House. Norma Hope Richman. GOYP

My cries and weeping. O Grief! Anonymous. EIL

My cry caught in my throat, while the thin walls/thicken like distance, I am most alone. The Cell of Himself. Arthur Freeman. TwCP

My dad had done the same. Epitaph on a Pessimist. Thomas Hardy. FaBoEE; FF

My Dad he said a lot of things/you wouldn't tell your Mother. Two Hopper. Ron Ikan. Str

My Dad must never know I care/It's hard enough for him to bear. Otto. Gwendolyn Brooks. PCh

"My Daddy's just a cod." I Caught a Fish. Bertram Murray. OnUR

My Damon, I am sick. Ipecacuanha. George Canning. FaBoNo

My dank and dropping weeds/To the stern God of Sea. For Whom, Pyrrha? Horace. LiTW

My dark and sultry/love. The Invention of Comics. LeRoi (Imamu Amiri Baraka) Jones. AmNP; CAPP; LiTM; PoBA

My dark chateau. The Dark Chateau. Walter De la Mare. BrPo

My dark Rosaleen! Dark Rosaleen. James Clarence Mangan. ACP; CH; EnRP; GTBS; HBV 1-2; IrPN; NOBI; OBEV; OBVV; OxBI; ViBoPo

My darling daughter, pretty Puff,/And you'll be mine. Ad Persephonen. Franklin Pierce ("F.P.A.") Adams. InMe

My darling house among houses! Good Night. Joel Dailey. APU

My darling, thou shalt rest! Boy Brittan. Forceythe Willson. MC; PAH

My darling, what would'st thou/more? Thou Hast Diamonds. Heinrich Heine. TrJP

My daughter! O, my daughter! The New Arrival. George Washington Cable. AA; HBV 1-2

My dauntless spirit mutely stands/With eagle wings outspread for flight. Dawn. Frederick George Scott. CaP; PoPl

My days to his glory I'm bound for to spend. Mr. Davis's Experience. Anonymous. AmFP

My dead child's face look out at me. My Mirror. Aline Kilmer. AnAmPo

My dead friend's face as well. Requiem. Ivor Gurney. FaBoEE; FaBoTw

My dead lips breathe and into utterance wake/The thoughts I never knew. Prayer. Clive Staples Lewis. TrCP

My dead, my living child! The Gray Swan. Alice Cary. BeLS; GN

My dear lady. My Dear Lady. Anonymous. EIL

My dear, let me buy a red painted boat/And carry you away. For the Courtesan Ch'ing Lin. Wu Tsao. WPOW

"My dear, may we put on our new Sunday breeches?" Socrates Snooks. Fitz Hugh Ludlow. BLPA

My dear mother, lullay. As I Lay upon a Night. Anonymous. SBVL

–My dear, where have you been? On Lending a Punch-Bowl. Oliver Wendell Holmes. AA

My dear, my dearest dust; I come, I come. Epitaph on the Monument of Sir William Dyer at Colmworth, 1641. Lady Catherine Dyer. EnLoPo

My dears, 'twas the cabby deceived me–/the beast! Frustrate. Louis Untermeyer. HBMV; InMe; YaD

My death has become a necessary myth. Empedocles on Etna. H. B. Mallalieu. PoA

My death must be a simply enormous death. The Space Eater Camps at Fifth Lake. Reg Saner. GP

My death, or life with liberty. If Chance Assign'd. Sir Thomas Wyatt. FCP; SiPS

My desire dying/as I desire The Pentecost Castle (excerpt). Geoffrey Hill. HAP

My desk to find/And put it safe away. This Book Is Mine. Anonymous. FaBoUs

My desperate fears, in love, had seen/Mine execution. Upon Love. Robert Herrick. BoLiVe; TrGrPo

My devotion more secure/Woos thy spirit high and pure. Spiritual Love. William Caldwell Roscoe. OBVV

My digent self is sertive, choate, loof. Gloss. David McCord. OBAL

My ditty must come to a finish,–/Because all the liquor is out! St Patrick of Ireland, My Dear! William Maginn. InMe

My doings be as they were not,/And gone all trace of me! Tess's Lament. Thomas Hardy. FaBoTw; TEP

My door shall close on none tonight. Starry Sky. Anonymous. AnIL

My dove, but once let loose, I doubt/Would ne'er return, had not the flood been out. The Welcome. Abraham Cowley. BoLoP; SeCV 1-2

My dream a drink with Ira Hayes we discuss the code of the west. The Sonnets. Ted Berrigan. NoAm

My dream is what the hillside dreams! Howard Lamson. Edgar Lee Masters. NAMP; ViBoPo

My dreams to the wind everliving,/My song to the sea.   By the North Sea. Algernon Charles Swinburne.   PoEL 1-5; VLP

My dried and flattened heart.   Friendship.   Lucien Stryk.   GP

My dust fills the darkness I became.   Epitaph.   Julio Marzan.   InW

My early home was this.   My Early Home.   John Clare.   HBV 1-2; PoLf

My early love–and you–and you!   Possessions.   Lizette Woodworth Reese. HBMV

My ears fill and empty with the hiss! of snake.   Yetzer ha Ra.   Edward Codish.   VWA

My empty mosquito net/Is too large.   Haiku: "Whether I sit or lie." Ukihashi.   WPOW

My English blood condemns the cause/In which our soldiers die.   Mr. Gunman.   Vin Garbutt.   OBET

My entire shell will crack and bust.   Miss Crustacean.   Robert Phillips. GeTw

My every thought, Eternal God of/Heaven,/Ascends to Thee, to whom all praise/be given.   God Everywhere.   Abraham Ibn Ezra.   TrJP

My eye is fixed on you.   Baseball Pitcher.   Mabel M. Kuykendall.   LiSp

My eyes dry like stones/and my two hands–broken.   Song: "I placed my dream in a boat."   Cecilia Meireles.   WPOW

My eyes find only my own sorrow.   I let the incense grow cold.   Li Ch'ing-chao.   BoWoP

My eyes have seen what my hand did.   Dolphin.   Robert Lowell.   NOBA

My eyes, my wide eyes of eternal light!   To Beauty.   Charles Baudelaire. EnLi 1-2

My eyes tear and I really do reach for the switch.   Feeling That Way Too. Arthur Vogelsang.   MAYP

My eyes were blind with stars and still/I stared into the sky.   A Song of Honor.   Ralph Hodgson.   AtBAP; CAW; GTBS; LiTB; MCCG; MoBrPo

My eyes were closing and I may have dreamed.   Summer Storm.   Louis Untermeyer.   UnTE

My eyes were staring at the far horizon....   Ecstasy.   Walter James Turner. CH

...My face a stony skull staring in/yellow surprise at the sun....   Between the World and Me.   Richard Wright.   AmNP; IDB; LiTM; NoAm; PoBA

My face is like the face of one dead.   The Pillory.   Renee Vivien.   PeHV

My face once glowed in the dark.   The Old Biograph Girl.   Margaret Benbow.   AMV-81

My faire bryd, my sweete cynamone.   Young Woman.   Geoffrey Chaucer. BoW

My faith in God was sure and strong/When I had need of Him.   When I Had Need of Him.   S.E. Kiser.   BLRP

My faith's frail candle/Before the night.   Twilight.   Hazel Hall.   AnAmPo; HBMV

My falling tears wet the double gates.   Cold, cold the year draws to its end. Anonymous.   BoWoP

My fancy fled to the South again.   The Daisy.   Alfred, Lord Tennyson. EnLoPo; NOBV; OBNC; OBVV; PoEL 1-5

My fathe turns, with tears on his young face.   The Return.   George MacBeth.   NYBP

My Father hath made his Will.   Song: "Hang sorrow, cast away care." Anonymous.   OBS

My father is showing me the greater world/that I might find my resemblance in it.   Hunting with My Father.   Tom Absher.   AMV-80

My father loves good ale,/And so do I.   Counting Out Rhyme.   Anonymous. SpRo

My father met my mother on the road, in Donegal.   A Road of Ireland. Charles L. O'Donnell.   HBMV

My father's eyesight, my oldest child's talent, the key to/my house, the short way home.   Lost Objects.   Diana O Hehir.   AMV-80

My father's frown divides my face.   An Inheritance.   Naomi Replansky. GP

My Father's hand appointing me/My days and ways, so I am free.   Faith. Margaret E. Sangster.   TRV

My father's hands, my mother's eyes.   At Night.   Richard Eberhart.   Str

My father's voice in prayer.   My Father's Voice in Prayer.   Mary Hastings Nottage.   BLRP

My father was an employee/of the Atlantic-Richfield Corporation.   A Funny Joke.   Leon Stokesbury.   MAYP

My father was exceedingly rich.   A Post Card out of Panama.   William D. Barney.   LiSp

...My father/who was a tailor and a communist.   My Father, Who's Still Alive.   Jose Kozer.   VWA

My father would read on,/while we lay, listening, smiling/on either side. Sunday Funnies.   Anne Keiter.   DFF

My fathers followed theirs before Christ was crucified.   Last Lines.   Egan O'Rahilly.   KiLC

My fears walled in his body/must come to a certain stop.   Out of Body. Janice Townley Moore.   AMV-81

My feast was in the easy blood that flowed.   From Another Room.   Gregory Corso.   NeAP

My feeling sinks, as if standing on fishes.   Moving Ahead.   Rainer Maria Rilke.   NU

My feelings like a knifeblade's wound.   Failing the Examination.   Meng Chiao.   GLGT

My feet gag my heart/they're cold.   Pudgy.   Frank Lima.   ANYP

My feet take root against tomorrow.   Green Song.   Philip Booth.   BoNaP

My feet two hundred years old   Montgomery.   Sam Cornish.   CNA; PoBA; Psk

My feet were nourished on her breasts all night.   Modern Love, XXIII. George Meredith.   NOBV; VLP

...My fens shall with more shapes be/stored/Than Germany, or France, or Thuscan can afford.   Poly-Olbion.   Michael Drayton.   FaBoPP

My few sincerer friends detain,/And keep false friends away.   Lines Written on a Window at the Leasowes at a Time of Very Deep Snow.   William Shenstone.   OBSP

My fiddle and I have had.   Jacky, Come Give Me Thy Fiddle.   Anonymous. OxNR; UnS

My fiftieth year has come.   Fifty.   Kenneth Rexroth.   TAP

...My figure has led you to briars.   Poem for L. C.   Peter Klappert.   AmPA

My fingers are healing,/The pain is all gone.   Spinning Song.   Anonymous. UnTE

My fingers plait the same grasses, over and over.   Weaving Love-Knots. Hsueh T'ao.   BoWoP

"My," fish say, "he eats a lot-of-us!"   Hippopotamus.   Joanna Cole.   NTCP

My fists hardened many days/in the last ovens.   Entering the Body: The Survivor.   Stephen Berg.   NaP

My fixed canoe, its chain eternally drawn down/deep in this edgeless eye of water–to what slime?   Memory.   Arthur Rimbaud.   LiTW

My flesh be consigned to the tomb.   Ah! Lovely Appearance of Death! Charles Wesley.   AH

My flesh lives tenderly/inside its bone.   Living Tenderly.   May Swenson. BoAnP; OBCA

...My flesh would perish/there,/Before that dread apocalypse of soul.   The Soul's Expression.   Elizabeth Barrett Browning.   VLP

My foamless heart, the bloodleap at my wrist.   Rattler, Alert.   Brewster Ghiselin.   HAP; WeW

My foe came on, and beat the air for me,/Till that her blush taught me my shame to see.   Astrophel and Stella, LIII.   Sir Philip Sidney.   SiPS

My follies ten thousand times over I see.   The Irish Lady.   Anonymous. OuSiCo

My follies ten thousand times over I see.   A Rich Irish Lady.   Anonymous. FSW

My foot finds your lintel.   Invocation.   Vassar Miller.   NCSH

My forehead aching with stars.   David.   Eli Mandel.   PeCV

My forehead was mistaken for the moon./But now   What She Said. Maturai Eruttalan Centamputan.   BoLoP

My fortune in hand/and ready to go.   Remember That Night.   Anonymous. NOBI

My frail progeny will fade and die/as her brood grows rosier.   Lilith.   Ruth Feldman.   VWA

My freehold of thanksgiving.   My Triumph.   John Greenleaf Whittier. AnNE; NOBA

My friend, come speedily/To fare afield.   Song.   King of Portugal Dinis. CAW

–My/friend, I succeeded. Later.   Dream Songs.   John Berryman.   NaP

My friend, oh, my friend.   All Morning.   Terry Stokes.   AmPA

My friend Priapus with myself shall rise?   Quaere.   George Farewell. NOEC

My friends are real, though very few.   Money.   William Henry Davies. OBEV; OBMV; OBVV

My friends whose deaths have slowed my heart stay with me/now.   People Who Died.   Ted Berrigan.   APU

My fumbling voices clap their hands & shout.   Earthly.   Ian Wedde. OCNZ

My furs grow stiff around my shoulders.   Marceline, to Her Husband. Elizabeth Libbey.   AmPA

My future is not one of my concerns.   The Poet's Simple Faith.   Victor Hugo.   TRV; WGRP

My garden, full of fruits in harvest time.   Thy Garden.   King of Seville, Mu'tamid.   AWP

My gentle daughter.   Song for Naomi.   Irving Layton.   WHW

My ghostly fader, I me confesse,/First to God and then to you.   Confession of a Stolen Kiss.   Charles, duc d' Orleans.   MeEL

My ghostly father, I me confess/First to God and then to you.   My Ghostly Father.   Anonymous.   BoLoP; CBEP; EnLoPo; GBL

My girl advances and glances: my chance is to fall in/the trap!   A Dance Song.   Burkhard von Hohenfels.   LiTW

My girl and I/Sleep arm in arm.   Gossip Grows Like Weeds.   Hitomaro. OLR

My girl, I say be on your guard.   Death and the Maiden.   Anonymous. KiLC

My glass lies shattered at your feet. Resolve.   New Year's Eve.   H. B. Mallalieu.   WaP

My glimpse, this town, our time.   Right Now.   William Stafford.   NaP

(My God, consider dust!).   Hymn Written after Jeremiah Preached to Me in a Dream.   Owen Dodson.   AmNP

My God! do you wonder at crime!   The Poor Working Girl (with music).   *Anonymous.*   AS

My God, how the money rolls in.   How the Money Rolls In.   *Anonymous.*   GoTF; TreFT

My God; I'm going to croak without once being able/To hold you close to my cock and my heart!   The Man Sentenced to Death.   Jean Genet.   PeHV

My God, I mean my self.   Miserie.   George Herbert.   PoEL 1-5

My God, I mean my sinful heart.   The Dwelling-Place.   Henry Vaughan.   MeLP; OBS; OxBoCh; TrPWD; WGRP

My God is, and there's none but HE.   The Cherubim (excerpt).   Thomas Heywood.   WGRP

My God...my Brother-Man.   Real Presence.   Ivan Adair.   WGRP

My God, my Father, Maker, and my King!   Prayer of St. Francis Xavier.   Alexander Pope.   TrPWD

My God, my God, my God for more.   Ballad of Badmen.   Owen Dodson.   FB

My God, my God! Why hast thou forsaken me?   Calvary.   William Dean Howells.   AmePo

My God, O make no stay.   Psalm XL.   Sir Philip Sidney.   FCP

My God! perhaps I am!   The Moron.   *Anonymous.*   CenHV; GoTF; TreFT; YaD

My God, relieve me!   Sighs and Groans.   George Herbert.   AtBAP; PoEL 1-5

...My God shall lead me by the hand/to heaven's shining hills, my fatherland.   The Greater Country.   Grace V. Watkins.   AMV-80

My God shall raise me up, I trust.   The Conclusion.   Sir Walter Ralegh.   EG; EvOK; HBV 1-2; OBEV; WGRP

"My god–this is GOD..."   Instantaneous.   Vivian Ayers.   NNP

My god, what are ears for?   Ears.   Sonja Akesson.   WPOW

My God, who dies for me, for me.   O Thou Eternal Victim Slain.   Charles Wesley.   NOCV

My God would give a Sun-shine after raine.   Silex Scintillans.   Henry Vaughan.   AnAnS 1

My gold-bright maid, her dark-browed shepherd,/Enfolded in the hills of God.   The Hills of God.   A. A. Buist.   PoSH

My good Egnatius! for what's half/So silly as a silly laugh?   Carmina.   Caius Valerius Catullus.   OBVE

My good girl said, "Honey,/I hate to see you go."   Coal Diggin' Blues.   *Anonymous.*   AmFP

My gown, the wonder of beholders,/Hangs like a footnote from my shoulders.   The Masque of Balliol (excerpt).   Henry Charles Beeching.   GLGT

My grade book is ashamed/and my soul is/a sentence fragment.   Basic Writing 702.   John Paul Minarik.   LFAC

My grandfather knew this.   My Grandfather Was a Quantum Physicist.   Duane Big Eagle.   STE

My grandmothers were strong./Why am I not as they?   Lineage.   Margaret Walker.   BlSi; BOLo; CNA; NMM; PBWP; PoBA

My gray-haired style would have broken a stone/With words, and made it weep from tenderness.   The Amorous Worms' Meat.   Petrarch (Francesco Petrarca).   LiTW

My great grandam–She was a Witch.   The Little Creature.   Walter De La Mare.   EvOK

My greater, guiding star!   A Hymn.   Paul Laurence Dunbar.   TrPWD

My griefs been all too long.   The Linden Tree.   Aist, Dietmar von.   PoPl

My gristle-breasted, slack-jawed zealot, kiss me again.   Muse.   David Wagoner.   PoA

My grown uncertain way from life to death.   The Children.   Clifford Dyment.   ChMP

My guardian angel will speak out/In that high place, and tell thee all.   In Memoriam A.H.H., XLIV.   Alfred, Lord Tennyson.   VLP

My hair, and as it were divine/This peruked prettiness.   Peruke of Poets (parody).   William Zaranka.   BXAP

My hair coming down in the middle of a conversation.   Slips.   Mebdh McGuckian.   FaBoIP

My hair lifting beautifully, because we were/Coming home to the arms of brown people.   Black Hair.   Gary Soto.   NPGG

My hand/in yours,/Walt Whitman-/so–   Cape Hatteras.   Hart Crane.   InPS

My hand is at the door.   Wandering.   Hortense Flexner.   HBMV

My hand like an animal/that can not see or feel.   I Have Been My Arm.   Margo Taft.   NMM

My hand strays out and picks off one sick leaf.   The Secret Garden.   Thomas Kinsella.   IPY; TwCP

...My hand will want the exact/shape of his head, and my house will cry.   Wedlock.   Bink Noll.   GP

My hands are made to grasp.   Sisyphus Angers the Gods of Condescension.   Calvin Murry.   LFAC

...My hands/Invent another body for your body.   Touch.   Octavio Paz.   BoLoP

My hands on you, I seek your/knowledge, find your/longing.   Lines to a Tree.   Teller. J. L.   VWA

My hands were blades and it was murder murder/all over the place.   At Last We Killed the Roaches.   Lucille Clifton.   GP; NIP

My happiness came with you,/It fled again with you.   Long May.   Rosalia de Castro.   PBWP

My head full of the smell my nostrils smelt.   Manhood End.   Anthony Thwaite.   NMP

My head may twitch for itself, and those kings die.   On Being Invited to a Testmonial Dinner.   William Stafford.   NePoAm-2

My head unturned lest my dream should fade.   The Shadow on the Stone.   Thomas Hardy.   QFR

My head upon His breast.   Dark Was the Night.   *Anonymous.*   AmFP

My Health, my Life, my God!   Submission in Affliction.   *Anonymous.*   STF

My hearing suffers/no more sorrowing music   9 Verses of the Same Song.   Wendell Berry.   LLLT

My heart, a dark swan/confused in that vastness.   Farewell.   Chao Li-hua.   BoWoP

My heart, a hero, chafes and breaks/its bonds.   Night.   Solomon Ibn Gabirol.   TrJP

My heart a pleasure that do leave noo sting.   The Young Rhymer Snubbed.   William Barnes.   VLP

My heart, alas! must be divided.   Song Set by Michael Cavendish: "Faustina hath the fairer face."   *Anonymous.*   OBSC

My heart, and the sea and the heaven/Are melting away with love!   The Sea Hath Its Pearls.   Heinrich Heine.   AWP

My heart break, I loved on the same.'   Bad Dreams.   Robert Browning.   OAEP; OBSP

My heart, depressed and longing,/Revives when I see you./O, my dearest Siilen.   The Speckled Horse...   *Anonymous.*   WTO

My heart dies inch by inch; the time grows old,/Grows old in which I grieve.   Memory.   Christina Georgina Rossetti.   OBNC

My heart echoes to it "I love it!"   Song.   Frances Sargent Osgood   AA

My heart fell dead before.   "All in green went my love riding".   Edward Estlin Cummings.   AmLP; CMoP; FaBV; GoJo; HeIP; InPo; LiTA; LiTM; NePA; NoAm; NoP; OxBA; PoRA; SD

My heart fell dead before.   Song: "All in green went my love riding."   Edward Estlin Cummings.   ViBoPo

My heart finds rest, my heart finds rest in Thee.   Felixstowe, or The Last of Her Order.   Sir John Betjeman.   OxBTC

My heart gives you love.   Dirge for Two Veterans.   Walt Whitman.   BoLiVe; MoAmPo; PoEL 1-5

My heart goes sighing after swallows flown/On sometime summer's unreturning track.   From Sunset to Star Rise.   Christina Georgina Rossetti.   SBG

My heart groweth heavy, and whispereth/–"Gone."   Song.   Francis Howard Williams.   AA

My heart has left its dwelling-place/And can return no more.   First Love.   John Clare.   BoLoP; EnLoPo; GBL; HAP; NOBV; NoP

My heart has so long been/Calmed by dispassion.   Poema Morale.   Charles Gullans.   NePoEA

My heart in which her smile still blooms.   I Saw My Darling.   Frederick Morgan.   UnPo

My heart is a clot of blood/From this day till Doom.   The Mothers' Lament at the Slaughter of the Innocents.   *Anonymous.*   OnYI

My heart is aflame to be right.   The Cry of the Age.   Hamlin Garland.   WGRP

My heart is beating with an expectation/Of horrid joy.   The Cenci.   Percy Bysshe Shelley.   TW

My heart is breaking in the snow?   Love Song from New England.   Winifred Welles.   HBMV

My heart is clumsy, and my speech,/But, brother, hear my cry!   Imprisoned.   Eunice Tietjens.   HBMV

My heart is cold/And dark and lone.   The Nima.   Jorge Isaacs.   TrJP

My Heart is cold, my Quill grows dry,/And must a while in silence lie.   A Judicious Observation of That Dreadful Comet.   Ichabod Wiswall.   SCAP

My heart is colder than the clay!   Romance.   Andrew Lang.   HBV 1-2

My heart is comforted in Thee.   Comforted.   Amy Carmichael.   TRV

My heart is consumed in fire.   This Night of No Moon.   Ono no Komachi.   PBWP

My heart is darkened/With love./Alas, my husband!   Laieikawai's Lament after Her Husband's Death.   *Anonymous.*   WTO

My heart is dead in me.'   Ballata: He Reveals, in a Dialogue, His Increasing Love for Mandetta.   Guido Cavalcanti.   AWP

My heart is empty, O sons of Barmak.   The Thousand and One Nights: Abu Nuwas for the Barmacides.   *Anonymous.*   AWP

My heart is in my/pocket, it is Poems by Pierre Reverdy.   A Step Away from Them.   Frank O'Hara.   ANYP; ConAP; HaCAP; HoAn; InPS; NYP; VGW

My heart is in your hands: mind it well.   Sacrifice.   Thomas Kinsella.   IPY

My heart is love, for these in it are grounded.   Diana.   Henry Constable.
   HBV 1-2; OBSC

My heart is staggering somewhere in between.   Indian Guys at the Bar.
   Simon J. Ortiz.   STE

My heart is still, as time will tell.   Father Death Blues.   Allen Ginsberg.
   SM

My heart is stone. I will not budge.   Ballywaire.   Tom Paulin.   FaBoIP

My heart is thirsty, water-girl.   Water-Girl.   *Anonymous.*   WTO

My heart is with her altogther/Though I live not where I love.   I Live Not
   Where I Love.   *Anonymous.*   OBET

My heart is with them there.   Tadoussac.   Charles Bancroft.   BLPA

My heart is with you, and I understand/The lion turning in his living grave.
   At the Zoo.   Israel Zangwill.   TrJP

My heart it broke in half.   The Princess and the Gypsies.   Frances Cornford.
   StPo

My heart, just to have held it till it died,/Will be the better!   Embryo.   Mary
   Ashley Townsend.   AA; HBV 1-2

...My heart laughed/when the bird raised his soft wings.   The Owl.
   Thorkild Bjornvig.   NU

My heart lays down its load.   The Morning Glory.   *Anonymous.*   AWP

My heart of love, that heart Thou gavest/me,/Shall beat on in the dark.
   Cloistered.   Alice Brown.   AA

My heart, once by thy plowshare broke,/Will entertain thy word.   My Heart,
   How Very Hard It's Grown!   Cotton Mather.   AH

My Heart remains (deare Paradise) in thee.   Henry to Rosamond.   Michael
   Drayton.   AnAnS 2

My heart remembered then–does yours forget?   The Rainbow.   Vine Colby.
   HBMV

...My heart's a little fast. Otherwise everything's fine.   The First Psalm.
   Bertolt Brecht.   NU

My heart's in the Highlands, wherever I go.   My Heart's in the Highlands.
   Robert Burns.   AnEnPo; AWP; CoBE; FaBoBe; FaBoPP; FaFP; GN; HBV
   1-2; InPo; LiTL; PoPl; PoPle; SD; TreFT

My heart's keel slides to rest among the meadows.   Home from Abroad.
   Laurie Lee.   OBTV

My heart's loved Lord to me desertless given!   Waiting in Faith.   Buonarroti
   Michelangelo.   ILwL

My heart's own darling's face.   Es Stehen Unbeweglich.   Heinrich Heine.
   AWP; TrJP

My heart shall not forsake him; so/By-low, lie low.   By-Low, My Babe.
   Anonymous.   TrGrPo

...My heart/soars with that intrepid flyer.   Levitation.   Alvin Aubert.   GP

My heart still loves, will break.   Words for Love.   Ted Berrigan.   ANYP

My heart still walks a thing apart,/my heart is restless as of old.   My Heart
   Was Wandering.   Christopher John Brennan.   BoAV; PoAu 1-2

My heart takes pride to show how poor it is.   The Lamp's Shrine.   Dante
   Gabriel Rossetti.   MaVP

My heart that slept so still, so spent,/Awoke last night,–to break anew!
   Rencontre.   Jessie Redmond Fauset.   CDC

My heart toward heaven flies.   Chanson Mystique.   *Anonymous.*   CAW

My heart will keep the courage of the quest,/And hope the road's last turn
   will be the best.   Let Me Live but from Year to Year.   Henry Van Dyke.
   GoTF; TreFT

My heart will sink whenever I think/Of the journeywork I'm leaving.   The
   Journeyman.   *Anonymous.*   KiLC

... My heart would bedded clover become/to blossom beneath your form
   Pride and Hesitation.   Cerise Farallon.   UnTE

My heav'n, my home forevermore.   Beulah Land.   John R. and Page. Edgar
   Sweeney.   FSW

My heavy hoe/That earthward bows me to foreshow/A mattock heavier than
   the hoe.   In the Pauper's Turnip-Field.   Herman Melville.   OBSP; PoEL
   1-5

-My helpless paradox–because   Reading a Medal.   Terence Tiller.
   FaBoTw; GTBS-P

"My hen has laid an egg, I know;/And only hear the noise she's making!"
   Motherhood.   Charles Stuart Calverley.   FM

My heritage of storm.   The Disinherited, IX.   Mary Gilmore.   PoAu 1-2

My hert alone wel worthie she doth staye,/Without whose helpe skant do I
   live a daye.   If Waker Care, If Sodayne Pale Coulor.   Sir Thomas Wyatt.
   AAS; FCP

My hert, my will, my nature, and my mynd/Was changit clene rycht in ane
   other kind.   The Kingis Quhair: The Coming of Love.   King of Scotland
   James I,   GoTS

A! my herte,a! what aileth thee?   A! My Herte, A! What Aileth The.   Sir
   Thomas Wyatt.   AtBAP

My high with fontella takin care of much business in the/rhythm of the blues
   The Sound of Afroamerican History Chapt I.   S. E. Anderson.   PoBA

...My history/Stiffening with the tea towels/Hung outside the door to dry.
   Caravan.   Michael Longley.   FaBoIP

My home is in the bivouac.   Christmas Night of '62.   William Gordon
   McCabe.   AA

My home, my Zlotchev.   Zlotchev, My Home.   Moishe Leib Halpern.
   VWA

My honey, my love!   The Plough-Hands' Song.   Joel Chandler Harris.   AA

My honey my love, my heart's delight–/My honey, my love!   My Honey, My
   Love.   Joel Chandler Harris.   FaBoBe

My hope and treasure lie above.   Some Verses Upon the Burning of Our
   House, July 10th, 1666.   Anne Bradstreet.   AP; NOBA; TAP

My hope is but in song to show/How honored and how dear you are.   The
   Masters.   Laurence Hope.   HBV 1-2

My horse a thing of wings, myself a god.   St. Valentine's Day.   Wilfrid
   Scawen Blunt.   EnLoPo; NBM; OBVV; ViBoPo

My horse is not sure he can make it/to the next star. You are free.   To
   Women.   Richard Hugo.   NIP

My horse, my horse is galloping,/My horse, my horse goes on and on.   Mi
   Caballo Blanco.   *Anonymous.*   FSW

My hour of rest had fleeted by,/And back came labour, bondage, care.   A
   Little While, a Little While.   Emily Bronte.   OAEP

My house is quiet at this time. My mother holds the phone.   Emergency at 8.
   Geof Hewitt.   NeAC

...My huge/peach paper rose, or lavender sea-laced fan?   The Painted Lady.
   Margaret Danner.   BPo

My human heart on Thee!   The Eternal Goodness.   John Greenleaf Whittier
   AA; AmePo; AnAmPo; AnNE

My Human Snake, my Angeline!   My Angeline.   Harry Bache Smith.
   InMe; NLV

My hungry pulse beats to the rhythm of your rhythm,/to the tempo of your
   gait.   A Dedication.   Karin Boye.   PBWP

My husband and children saw me leaving.   For My Mother, Feeling Useless.
   Paula Rankin.   MAYP

My husband coming to pick me up.   The Mikveh.   Blu Greenberg.
   AMV-80

My husband got no courage in him/O dear O!   O Dear O.   *Anonymous.*
   ErPo

My husband says not a word and my mind is withering.   Love Songs.
   Anonymous.   WTO

My image was not on the cloud nor anywhere else.   The Same Dream.
   Shlomit Cohen.   VWA

My Irish cockatoo.   For the Marsh's Birthday.   James Wright.   NYBP

My jealous breast holds him for ever.   The Thousand and One Nights:
   Inscription at the City of Brass.   *Anonymous.*   LiTW

My Jesus relieved me and bid me not fear.   O Jesus, My Saviour, I Know
   Thou Art Mine.   Caleb J. Taylor.   AH

My joy, it rose,/a new-found land.   Dusk of the Gods (excerpt).   S.
   Funaroff.   NAMP

My joy to see thee near/Will fill me with new breath.   Song to Death.   Joan
   Escriva.   LiTW

My joyous soul no more on earth can wander to and fro.   Epigram: "At even,
   when the hour drew nigh."   Strato.   PeHV

My King can only captivate my mind.   Loyalty Confin'd.   Sir Roger
   L'Estrange.   OBS

My Kyng, my Contry, alone for whome I lyve,/Of myghty love the winges for
   this me gyve.   Tagus, Fare Well, that Westward with Thy Stremes.   Sir
   Thomas Wyatt.   AAS

My lady and love to be.   A Lady of High Degree.   *Anonymous.*   AWP

...My lady came not/in blue jeans & a sweater. I sat down & wrote.   Sonnet.
   John Berryman.   FaBoMo

My lady cometh, that all this may disteyne.   Hyd, Absolon, Thy Gilte Tresses
   Clere.   Geoffrey Chaucer.   ExPo; HAP; WeW

My lady, I love you because of the dark/Over which your glass slippers so
   ignorantly danced!   On the Way to the Island.   David Ferry.   NePoAm-2

My lady moving graciously./Beata mea Domina!   Praise of My Lady.
   William Morris.   HBV 1-2

My lady sleeps?/Sleeps!   Serenade.   Henry Wadsworth Longfellow.
   FaBoBe; HBV 1-2; LoBV; ViBoPo

My lady sweet, arise:/Arise, arise!   Cymbeline.   William Shakespeare.
   ATP; AWP; BoLiVe; DiPo; ElL; EnL; ExPo; FaBoCh; FaBV; FaFP; FiP;
   GN; HBV 1-2; HeIP; InPo; LiTB; LoBV; LoGBV; NIP; NoP; OBEV;
   OBSC; PrIm; SeCeV; TreF; TrGrPo; ViBoPo; WHA

My Lady wrapped in beauty Inanna be praised!   Inanna Exalted (excerpt).
   Enheduanna.   WPOW

My lamp, and life, both shall in thee abide.   The Morning Watch.   Henry
   Vaughan.   BoC; LiTB; LoBV; MePo; OBS; OxBoCh; SeCePo; ViBoPo

My landscape is grey rain/Aslant on bent seas.   Renewal by Her Element.
   Denis Devlin.   CIP

My Lawd, down in the valley one day.   Dem Bones.   *Anonymous.*   OuSiCo

My left hand asking my right/a question I could never answer.   Return.
   Richard Tillinghast.   MAYP

My left hand/leaks on the Chinese carpet.   The Alligator Bride.   Donald
   Hall.   ConAP; EAS

My legs ache & I feel lonely.   Comfortable Strangers.   Terence Winch.
   APU

My letter always went alone/to where/I never knew you reading. Two Presentations. Robert Duncan. PAI

My letter chases Conroy's sheep along the Castlereagh. The Travelling Post Office. Andrew Barton ("Banjo") Paterson. CBAP; NOAV

My life in thee, Thy life in me,/Makes heaven forever mine. Jesus, I Live to Thee. Henry Harbaugh. AH

My life is done,/And so I think to leave it. A Last Will and Testament. John Winstanley. OBSV

...My life/Is just about over. Postscript. Sandra Hochman. NMM

My life is lifeless till it live in Thee! L'Envoi. Frederic Lawrence Knowles. TrPWD; TRV

My life is like a music-hall. Prologue. Arthur Symons. BrPo

My life. My life. From Sand Creek (excerpt). Simon J. Ortiz. STE

My Life, my Strength, my Joy, my All. A Hymn to My God in a Night of My Late Sicknesse. Sir Henry Wotton. AnAnS 2; MeLP; MePo; OBS

My life, my strength, my joy, my all! It Is Finished. Sir Henry Watson. BePJ

...My life/pulses close to a huge heart, always within. I Am Sitting Here. Yehuda Amichai. VWA

My life to deepest holiness to lead. The Inward Light. Henry Septimus Sutton. WGRP

My life would grow divine! To My Dog Blanco. Josiah Gilbert Holland. PoLf

My light, my life, my God, my Saviour see,/And rival angels in the praise of thee.' The Day of Judgement. Edward Hilton Young. OxBoCh

My light's thy shadow's shadow, or 'tis done. St. Peter's Shadow. Richard Crashaw. ACP

My light–the Lamb of their Apocalypse. The Blessed Virgin Mary Compared to a Window. Thomas Merton. ISi

My lightning lord,/my home. The Elm's Home. William Heyen. MAYP

...My lips/are sealed/like sour artichokes. Elevator Landscapes. Stephen Vincent. NeAC

My lips are sweet, inspired by Stella's kiss. Astrophel and Stella, LXXIV. Sir Philip Sidney. AAS; CABA; EnRePo; SiPS

...My lips/half-parted, steady as the mouths/of antique statues. Attention. Adrienne Rich. TAP

My lips pressed upon stone. The Song. Theodore Roethke. AP; CrMA

...My lips seal the dead,/keep their secret from you. Canopic Jar. Rika Lesser. MAYP

...My lips touched/Its faultless agent. The Poet's Prothalamion (Excerpt). J. W. Scholl. PeD

My little boy–who ran away. Haiku: On Her Child's Death. Kaga no Chiyo. LiTW

My, little girls were surely clever/When great-grandmother was ten years old! The Sampler. Nancy Byrd Turner. BiCB

My little grey sister, Gampta,/I see you! The Desert Lark. Eugene Marais. PeSA

...My little halves who bear/Across an autumn freezing everywhere. What Shall I Give My Children? Gwendolyn Brooks. BPo

My little lambs shall play/Beneath the sun. A New Year. Dora Sigerson Shorter. YeAr

My little prayer-book at my right side,/And sound will be my sleep.' Sir Hugh, or, The Jew's Daughter (N version). Anonymous. AmFP; ESPB

My liver scorned by the vultures./And self-devoured! Chandler Nicholas. Edgar Lee Masters. NAMP

My long life, my long life. The Mother of Us All: "We cannot retrace our steps." Gertrude Stein. CrMA

My long scythe whispered and left the hay to make. Mowing. Robert Frost. AnNE; APA; BLPL; CMoP; DiPo; ExPo; HBMV; HoPM; LiTA; MAmP; NOBA; OxBA; PPP; VGW

My longest body is learning. News from the House. Michael Dennis Browne. NYBP

My loom you have got pretty square.' The New Bury Loom. Anonymous. OBET

My lord, adjudge my strength, and set me where/I bear a little more than I can bear. House Sonnet. Elinor Wylie. LiTL

My Lord must have the most–because/His name is at the top! His Name Is at the Top. Anonymous. STF

My Lord's a-writin' all de time yes, all de time. My Lord's A-Writin' All de Time. Anonymous. BoAN 1-2

My Lord sittin' in his Kingdom, Got his eyes on me. I Don't Want to Be a Gambler (with music). Anonymous. AS

"My Lord, Thy will be done." My Jesus, As Thou Wilt. Benjamin Schmolck. BePJ

My Lord,/we are quite ready. Well, 'tis very well. The Cenci. Percy Bysshe Shelley. EnRP; FiP

My lord white as jasmine. Till You've Earned. Mahadevi (Mahadeviyakka). PBWP

My Lords the Judges laugh, and you're dismissed. First Satire of the Second Book of Horace. Alexander Pope. OAEL 1-2; PPP; PrIm

My Love. The Street of Named Houses. Robert David Cohen. NYBP

My love a shadow that passes... Bird-Song. Mary Dixon Thayer. CAW

My love affects no fame, nor 'steems of art. To Delia. Samuel Daniel. OBSC

My Love and I are living now in May! In November. Anne Reeve Aldrich. AA

My love and I must part. A Chaste Maid in Cheapside: Parting. Thomas Middleton. EiL

My love–and nothing more! At Such a Time, in Such a Spot. Emily Bronte. VLP

My love doth wax more pure by your more trying,/And yet increaseth in the purifying. Sonnets to Philomel. Sir John Davies. SiPS

My love for the Lord/Is about ready to die. Too Busy. Anonymous. STF

My love for thee shall never, never die. Sweet Evelina. Anonymous. FSW

My love gave me a passion-flower. The Passion-Flower. Margaret Fuller. HBV 1-2

My love goes lightly, holding up/Her dress with dainty hand. Chamber Music. James Joyce. LOW

My love had walked there and 'twas holy ground! Sonnets, I: "Deep in a vale where rocks on every side." Gustav Rosenhane. AWP

My love has died for me to-day,/I'll die for him to-morrow. Barbara Allen. Anonymous. EnSB; FaBoBe; ForPo; MaC; ViBoFo

My love I gave for hate. My Love I Gave for Hate. Anonymous. BIrV

My love, I love, I love. Bedtime. Ian Hamilton Finlay. BSV

My love is in all you do,/Yours with me wherever I go. Platform Goodbye. H. B. Mallalieu. WaP

My love is still the same. Growing Old. Anonymous. ErPo; KiLC

...My love is/strong now / you really gotta hold on me... Motown/Smokey Robinson. Jessica Hagedorn. APU; BrSi

My love is Thine, and e'er shall be,/Because, my King, Thou reign'st o'er me! I Love Thee, Gracious Lord. C. C. Cox. BePJ

My love, like the vast majority,/lives touching poetry. Erotic Suite (excerpt). Jose Luis Vega. InW

My love makes death and death makes everything serious. Signals. Keith Waldrop. AMV-81

My love, my love, my love, why have you left me alone? I Hear an Army. James Joyce. AnIV; AWP; ExPo; LiTL; LiTM; MoBrPo; NAMP; NoAm; NOBE; OxBI; OxBTC; PoRA; PrIm; SyP; ViBoPo

My love of you was life and not a breath. Monna Innominata. Christina Georgina Rossetti. OBNC; ViBoPo; VLP

My love! Oh, God! Do not look back! To Tomas Costello at the Wars. Tomas O'Higgins. AnIV; KiLC

My love remains immortal though, as mortal, I must die. Buthaina. Jamil. LiTW

My love's under-rated Holy water. Judith Fitzgerald. CaPN

"My Love shall enfold them!" the answer came. Calvary. Mary Hallet. PGD

My love shall hover round thee! To the Lady in the Chemisette with Black Buttons. Nathaniel Parker Willis. OBAL

My love shall in my verse ever live young. Sonnets, XIX: "Devouring Time, blunt thou the lion's paws." William Shakespeare. AWP; DiPo; EBEV; InPo; MAT; OAEL 1-2; OBSC; PoEL 1-5; TrGrPo; WHA

My love to you in my desire to learn. Rich Mine of Knowledge. George Chapman. SeCePo

My love to yours shall reach, then one deep moan/Of joy, and then our infinite Alone. Reunited. Sir Gilbert Parker. OBEV; OBVV

My love wept. Armorial. Ralph Gustafson. ACV; PeCV

My love, what more can happen/To you and to me? The Bride. Bella Akhmadulina. BoWoP; PBWP

My love (who loves me not) and I. A May Song. Violet Fane. OBVV

My loved! My long-lost breeches! The September Gale (excerpt). Oliver Wendell Holmes. FiBHP

My lover, childbride. Lilly's Song. Evan Zimroth. AMV-81

My lover comes to watch. Gig at Big Al's. Heather McHugh. GeTw

My lover loves me,/And I am proud of my young beauty. The Bare Branches Tremble. Tzu Yeh. WPOW

–My lover's shoulder/still smells to me of pine shavings. And there is nothing at all–neither fear. Natalya Gorbanyevskaya. BoWoP

My lover's skin forms/stars in the morning. Woman Made of Stars. Earle Thompson. STE

My loves you cannot touch. They're buried deep. A Gentleman of Fifty Soliloquizes. Don (Donald Robert Marquis) Marquis. HBMV

My loving heart to thee would bear,/My Valentine. Valentine. C. T. YeAr

My Lowlands a-ray. Lowlands. Anonymous. AmSS; FSW; GBP; OxBoLi

My luck will turn when I'm a ghost. Optimism. Blanaid Salkeld. NeIP

My lungs are thick with the smoke of your absence. Hello, Hello. William Matthews. PCP

My lute and I/Continually/Shall us apply/To sigh and moan. At most mischief. Sir Thomas Wyatt. FCP; SiPS

My lute, be still, for I have done. The Lover Complaineth the Unkindness of His Love. Sir Thomas Wyatt. AtBAP; EiL; EnPo; FaBoEn; GBL; OAEP; PoEL 1-5; TrGrPo; ViBoPo

My lyfe shall everlastingly bee lengthened still by fame.   Metamorphoses. Ovid (Publius Ovidius Naso).   CTC; OBVE

My maid is so stupid that she/Offers me plum blossoms for my hair.   Morning.   Chu Shu-chen.   BoWoP

My mamma will kiss my red rosy lips,/When you have gone to the far-off land.   The Lass of Roch Royal (B vers.).   *Anonymous.*   ViBoFo

My man is a bone ringed with weed.   First Woman's Lament.   Brenda Chamberlain.   NeIP

My man is a bone ringed with weed.   Lament.   Brenda Chamberlain.   NeBP; WPOW

My man/you way behind the set   Nigger.   Sonia Sanchez.   BPo

My mansion and my crown.   While I Am Young.   Silas Ballou.   AH

My Mary, mavourneen, the Moon of Mobile!   The Moon of Mobile.   Thomas Holley Chivers.   OBAL

My master he did cudgel me,/For kissing of my dame.   Sing Jigmijole.   *Anonymous.*   OxNR

My master's son will clasp them/with a heavy, broken, sigh.   Even though my hands.   *Anonymous.*   BoWoP

"My master would that he were I."   Go Little Ring.   *Anonymous.*   CBEP

My masters all, Good day to you.   The Bellman.   Robert Herrick.   CaPo; CBEP

My Mide brothers,/The otters.   Song: "Now and then there will arise."   *Anonymous.*   OBVE

My mind goes no further.   Love Poem for Lin Fan.   Marilyn Bowering.   CaPN

My mind has murdered my suffering.   Why Do You Want to Suffer Less.   David Fisher.   NPGG

My mind is melancholic,/I cannot praise my maker.   Latter Day Psalms.   Cliff Ashby.   NOCV

...My mind's indicted by all I've taken.   Plunder.   Archie Randolph Ammons.   NoAm

My mind was often far away/Aboard the Ships of Yule.   The Ships of Yule.   Bliss Carman.   BiCB; CaP; HBVY; WHW

...My miniscule/Part in the swaying and tranquil grandeur here.   Colorado.   Robert Fitzgerald.   MoPo

My mistress and at th' instant he/Should steal her quite from me.   Platonic Love.   Abraham Cowley.   NoP; SeCV 1-2

My mistress, mind you, was not born.   Entwined.   *Anonymous.*   WTO

My mistress said I'd robbed her. I was straightway sent to gaol.   The Sheffield Apprentice.   *Anonymous.*   OBET

My mochiness tae ye wad thow an' get/Mair dwamin' than empires, an' mair switherin' yet.   To His Coy Mistress (parody).   Gerry Hamill.   BXAP

"My Mohawk's pure white star, Ojistoh, still am I."   Ojistoh.   [(Emily)] Pauline Johnson.   NOBC

My mood was shattered with its calm explosion.   The Wild Swan.   D. S. Savage.   NeBP

My most true mind thus maketh mine eye untrue.   Sonnets, CXIII: "Since I left you, mine eye is in my mind."   William Shakespeare.   WeW

My mother–ah! whom should I see/Within, save ever only thee?   The Shrine.   Digby Mackworth Dolben.   GoBC; HBV 1-2

My mother and aunts nearby/let him finish with no visible intervention.   Insight.   Mary Goose.   STE

My mother, combing her long hair, looking/curiously at the white, shrouded branches.   Palinode.   Maura Stanton.   MAYP

My mother dials and says,/"Here he is."   He.   Ronald Koertge.   Str

My mother's chastening love I own.   My Trust.   John Greenleaf Whittier.   OHIP; PGD

My mother's hollow sockets fill with tears.   Mother Marie Therese.   Robert Lowell.   CoPo

My mou was never even/Since I cam by Johnshaven.   Johnshaven.   *Anonymous.*   GBP

...My mouth frozen/round the sound of your name.   Like Wings.   Philip Schultz.   MAYP

My mouth, steer our lost bodies carefully downward)   Who's Most Afraid of Death?   Edward Estlin Cummings.   CMoP; SeCeV; VGW

My murdered body and your body's ghost.   God! How I Long for You...   Kenneth Mackenzie.   CBAP

My Muse bad, Bedford write, and that was shee.   On Lucy Countesse of Bedford.   Ben Jonson.   AnAnS 2; EnRePo; OAEP; OBS; SeCP; SeCV 1-2

My Muse had slept, and none had known my mind.   To Delia.   Samuel Daniel.   EnRePo; HBV 1-2; NOBE; NoP; OAEP; OBEV; OBSC; TrGrPo

My muse is rightly of the English straine,/That cannot long one fashion intertaine.   Idea.   Michael Drayton.   AAS

My nakedness the mask itself.   Masks.   Elizabeth Fenton.   NMM

"My name, ho-ho. You'll never know my name!"   Rumplestiltskin Poems.   William Hathaway.   DFT

My name is falcon.   Affirmations: I, II, III.   Peter Viereck.   MiAP

My name is "I am living." I am here.   I Have Bowed before the Sun.   Anna Walters.   WPOW

My name is known to all the village, and her name is/Ranjana.   The Yellow Bird Sings.   Rabindranath Tagore.   OBMV

My name is love.   Envoi.   Charles Causley.   FF

My name my naked virtue/for your tribes.   Rachel's Lament.   Linda Zisquit.   VWA

My name shall mount upon eternity.   Sonnet: "Whilst thus my pen strives to eternise thee."   Michael Drayton.   ViBoPo

My name to thine in words they'll bind/Of love inseparable.   Inseparable.   Philip Bourke Marston.   BoLoP

My name was Mellisandra which flowed once from his lips/like laughter/and now seems unsuitable.   Mellisandra.   Harriet Rose.   BrRo

My namesake, and the last Caligula.   Caligula.   Robert Lowell.   CoPo

My native land forever!   The American Flag.   Charles Constantine Pise.   CAW

My nest of mercies in the rude, red tree.   Altarwise by Owl-Light.   Dylan Thomas.   CMoP; CoBMV; FaBoMo; LiTM; MasP; NoAm

My new eyes searched the passion of the stars.   Passion.   Galway Kinnell.   NePoAm

My new mistress, My Lady Death.   Cavalier.   Richard Bruce.   CDC

My new shoes wait by the door./They are gleaming.   Looking for Work.   Raymond Carver.   GeTw

My next companion shall be flesh and bone.   Letter to Statues.   John Malcolm Brinnin.   EyDe

My night shaped by grief–/for whom? for whom?   Grief Plucked Me out of Sleep.   Jill King.   PeSA

"My noble lord, just as ye please./But supper is na ready."   Suppertime.   Robert Burns.   UnTE

My nothingness, my wants,/My sins, and my contrition.   Lord! Who Art Merciful as Well as Just.   Robert Southey.   TrPWD

My old, gray father celebrating this rite curled up like a fetus.   Bar Mitzvah.   Isaac Goldemberg.   VWA

My one point of rest/is the orange and black/oriole's swinging nest!   Fall 1961.   Robert Lowell.   OBWP; VGW

My only glory be thy cross!   Jesu, to Thee My Heart I Bow.   Nicolaus Zinzendorf.   AH

My only respite of the day/Is this wild ride–with God.   On a Subway Express.   Chester Firkins.   YaD

My only tribute, Christ, my King.   The Three Kings.   Eugene Field.   GN

My only wish is to forget/In endless sleep of death.   Sleep Brings No Joy.   Emily Bronte.   ViBoPo

My outside Woman, and your inside Man.   The Change.   Abraham Cowley.   AnAnS 2; CoBE; MeLP; MePo; OBS; SeCP; SeCV 1-2

My own and yet, how very far from me!   My Child Came Home.   Stefan George.   LiTW

My own Araminta, say "No!"   A Letter of Advice.   Winthrop Mackworth Praed.   HBV 1-2; NOBL; OBRV; OxBoLi

My own body spoke/from its long shyness.   An Artist Draws a Peach.   Patricia Hampl.   PoDr

My own face lay like a white pebble,/Waiting.   Dreams in War Time (excerpt).   Amy Lowell.   BoWoP

My own heart knocking/at my ribs, demanding/to be let out.   Dido's Farewell.   Linda Pastan.   GOYP

My own music/creaks from the loving saddle/under me.   Evening Ride.   Jill Hoffman.   PH

My own reflection in wide-opened eyes.   Narcissus.   John Press.   UnTE

My own seduced Heart to me,/Accompani'd with thine.   The Souldier Going to the Field.   Sir William Davenant.   MePo

My own voice silent in the morning air.   To a Friend.   Charles Gullans.   NePoEA

–My pain it is not beneath my head!   Last Night My Soul Departed.   Muireadhach Albanach O Dalaigh.   NOBI

My painted person crouched in his painted heart.   The Twins.   Mona Van Duyn.   GP

My palace builded is, and lo now here I lie.   A Rueful Lamentation on the Death of Queen Elizabeth.   Sir Thomas More.   AAS; FaBoRV; LiTB; OBSC

My past rose up and mocked at death.   The Last Fight.   Lewis Frank Tooker.   AA; FaBoBe

My paths are in the fields I know/And thine in undiscover'd lands.   In Memoriam A.H.H., XL.   Alfred, Lord Tennyson.   VLP

My peace because the trail is good.   The Pioneer.   Arthur Guiterman.   TiPo

My peace I leave with you!   The Peace of Christ.   John Antes La Trobe.   BePJ

My pen, I prithee write no more.   To His Pen.   Sir Thomas Wyatt.   OBSC

My pen, though frail and slim of figure,/Has a serpent's tooth and a lion's/vigour.   The Song of the Pen.   Judah Al-Harizi.   TrJP

My people,/Cry out to God.   The Rock Crumbles.   Else Lasker-Schüler.   TrJP

My plans are coming true. Nothing can stop me now.   The Mugger.   Robert Pack.   GP

My plate's empty.   1,2, Buckle My Shoe.   *Anonymous.*   OxNR

My pocket full of empty shells.   Trinidad, 1958.   Bob Mondy.   WOLT

My poems then I would really live!   The Caucasus.   Boris Pasternak.   PoPl

My poor soul, forever.   A Soul.   Randall Jarrell.   CMoP

My poor true heart, all comfortless.   Treizaine.   Sir Thomas Wyatt.   OBSC

My prayer, keep dew and anthem in my heart!   The Lord in the Wind. James Picot.   PoAu 1-2

My prayer was answered.   Prayer Answered.   *Anonymous.*   STF

My precious mother is with me.   My Mother.   Josephine Rice Creelman. OHIP

My precious one, you'll step to shore/On Mother's knee.   An Irish Lullaby. Alfred Perceval Graves.   HBV 1-2

My present Past, my root of piety.   Brother and Sister.   George Eliot. NOBV

My pretty little blue-eyed babe.   Gypsy Davey.   *Anonymous.*   AmFP; AS; FSW

My prisoned mind would fain be out/of chains and fetters of the flesh.   A Prisoner's Song of Jerusalem.   *Anonymous.*   ACP

My Pulses all would beat, I should not be/Drown'd in this Deluge of Security. Meditation.   Philip Pain.   NOBA; OBSP; QFR

My quarter-inch of cigarette/Goes flaring down to Baggot Street.   Baggot Street Deserta.   Thomas Kinsella.   CIP; CMoP; FaBoIP; IPY; NMP

My ransomed soul shall be,/Through all eternity,/Something for thee. Saviour, Thy Dying Love.   Sylvanus D. Phelps.   AH

My reason shall obey, my wings shall be/Stretch'd out no farther than from me to thee!   To His Mistress.   John Wilmot, Earl of Rochester.   OBEV

My reference is to Ezra .   Literary Criticism.   Myles Na Gopaleen.   DBV

My refuge is the mercy seat,/My hope within the vail.   O Lord! My Hiding Place.   Raffles.   BePJ

My rhyme is written, my work is done.   Courtesy.   Hilaire Belloc.   ACP; BoC; HBMV

My rose was gone, and nought but prickles left me.   Madrigal: "I always loved to call my lady Rose."   *Anonymous.*   ElL

My rosy red lips will never be kissed till you return again.   My Old True Love.   *Anonymous.*   OuSiCo

My ruin of a sad morning that I was not married to you.   From a Lament for Una.   Tomas Costello.   WTO

My ruth my righte, my trappe my styll advaunced/From woe to weale, from hell to heavenly raigne.   At Fotheringay.   Robert Southwell.   PoEL 1-5

My sadness sits around me   My Sadness Sits Around Me.   June Jordan. BPo

My salvation is in Thee.   Psalm XXXVIII.   Sir Philip Sidney.   FCP

...My sandaled/feet began to itch.   Seven Mexican Children.   Tom Schmidt. NeAC

My saule with sanctes, Salviour resaif,/Sen that thy Passioun purged my trespas.   The Passion of Jesus.   *Anonymous.*   MeEL

My saving might, Lord, in Thy sight,/Receive good acceptation!   Psalm XIX. Sir Philip Sidney.   FCP

My scolding wife has gone among the rest.   All's Well That Ends Well. *Anonymous.*   FaFP

My second in the sea.   Phenomenal Survivals of Death in Nantucket. Louise Gluck.   AmPA; SM

My self.   Game Resumed.   Richmond Lattimore.   LiSp; NYBP

(My selves dissolving, old whore petticoats)–/To Paradise.   Fever 103. Sylvia Plath.   CMoP; FaBoWP; NMP; NoAm; NOBA; VGW

My semely lorde, for your sake:/Good day!   In Honour of Christmas. *Anonymous.*   MeEL

My senses leave me.   Goodbye.   Bella Akhmadulina.   BoWoP

My service thus is growne into disdayne.   In Cipres Springes (Wheras Dame Venus Dwelt).   Henry Howard, Earl of Surrey.   AAS

My shadow darkens without/Lengthening ever, ever.   Under Cancer.   John Hollander.   CoAP

My shadow,/in your dark boat.   A Defeat.   Denise Levertov.   PBWP

My shadow walks before.   The Clouds Have Left the Sky.   Robert Bridges. CH

My ship and me Caribdid wol devoure.   Troilus and Criseyde.   Geoffrey Chaucer.   DiPo

My ship is on de ocean,/Po' sinner, fare-you-well.   My Ship Is on de Ocean. *Anonymous.*   BoAN 1-2

...My shoulder bag with 10,000 dollars/full of poetry left on the broken floor– Mugging (excerpt).   Allen Ginsberg.   HaCAP

My shoulders prick, as though they were half-fledged.   Field-Glasses. Andrew Young.   CBEP; GTBS-P

My sign: Mobility–and damn the cost!   The Summing-Up.   Stanley Jasspon Kunitz.   ELU; OBAL; PoPl

My silent soul howls like the jackals,/and cries out like the sea!   The Monasteries Lift Gold Domes.   Yocheve Bat-Miriam.   VWA

My silvery tail   So to Tell the Truth.   Janet Dube.   BrRo

My sister, heralded by no moan, no sound.   Epithalamium.   Leo Kennedy. OBCV

My sister, hidden/In Bessarabian evenings.   Plain, Humble Letters.   David Vogel.   VWA

My sister married a gambling man,/And I have gone astray.   As I Set down to Play Tin-Can.   *Anonymous.*   OuSiCo

My sister's nothing but a great big crow.   My Sister Jane.   Ted Hughes. OnUR; SO

My sister was quicker at everything than I.   The Paper Lantern.   Tennessee Williams.   CTBA

My sister wrote that.   Cats Climb Trees.   Tom Veitch.   ANYP

My sky is full of the dreadful sound/Of the wings of unsuccesses.   Glyph. *Anonymous.*   LiTA

My small black dog lies there...   Mycenae.   David Fisher.   NPGG

My son has birds in his head.   Daedalus.   Alastair Reid.   NCSH; NYBP

My son! my father! guide me there.   On the Death of My Son Charles. Daniel Webster.   AA

My son or my daughter.   Miscarriage.   Michael Longley.   PoL

My son puzzled by the grown-up fun/beyond the ken of Mrs. Roybal   Manly Diversion.   Karl Kopp.   GP

My song is now ended, I'll bid you farewell,/To enjoy a heaven instead of a cell.   Adieu to the Stone Walls.   *Anonymous.*   OuSiCo

My Song, my All in All,/That's JESUS.   That's Jesus.   Grace B. Renfrow. BePJ

...My song will speak in your living heart.   My Song.   Rabindranath Tagore. OHIP

...My songs will be softer/and lightly weight the air.   Three Modes of History and Culture.   LeRoi (Imamu Amiri Baraka) Jones.   NoAm

"My sons, I've told you many times that signs are naught," said she.   Marm Grayson's Guests.   Mary E. Wilkins Freeman.   OBCA

My sons'll see the land I am leaving/As barren as her deck.   The Complaint of the Morpethshire Farmer.   Basil Bunting.   CTC

"My sons! My sons! My sons!"   Prodigal's Return.   Ralph D. Eberly. AMV-80

My sons were faithful, and they fought.   The Mother.   Padraic Pearse. OnYI

My sorrow! Flood after ebb comes not to me.   The Triad of Things Not Decreed.   Alice Furlong.   AnIV

My sorrow for that might-have-been-a-hippopotamother.   I Had a Hippopotamus.   Patrick Barrington.   CenHV

My sorrow must be laid/On your head like a crown.   Any Human to Another.   Countee Cullen.   MoRP

My soul against your song?   To a Wasp Caught in the Storm Sash...   Peter Cooley.   MAYP

...My soul and yo' soul will meet in de day/When I lay dis body down.   I Know de Moonlight.   *Anonymous.*   BPo

My soul awaits–imprisoned here on earth.   What Guardian Counsels? Auzias March.   CAW

My soul basks on for hours.   When I Would Image.   George Meredith. NOBV

My soul exults before the Art, the magian Art of old.   The Joys of Art. Rachel Annand Taylor.   OBVV

My soul from a mother's old arm-chair.   Old Arm-Chair.   Eliza Cook. ATP; BrRo; InPK; PaPo; WBLP

My soul got happy/and i stayed all day.   I Went to the Valley.   Lucille Clifton.   TAT

My soul grows darker, and I cannot spare thee.   On a Rose in December. Ebenezer Elliott.   FaBoEE

My soul has grown deep like the rivers.   The Negro Speaks of Rivers. Langston Hughes.   AmFN; AmNP; BANP; BPo; CDC; GoSl; HaCAP; HAP; HeIP; IDB; NIP; NoAm; NOBA; NoP; OBCA; PoBA; PoNe; TAP; TTY

My soul I'll pour into thee.   The Night-Piece, to Julia.   Robert Herrick. AnFE; AtBAP; ATP; CaPo; ELP; HBV 1-2; InvP; JCP; LiTB; LiTL; LoBV; NoP; OAEL 1-2; OAEP; OBEV; OBS; PoEL 1-5; PoPle; PoRA; SeCeV; SeCP; SeCV 1-2; TreFT; WHA

My soul is a witness for my Lord.   Who'll Be a Witness for My Lord? *Anonymous.*   BoAN 1-2

My soul is all but out of me,–let fall/No burning leaf; prithee, let no bird call. God's World.   Edna St. Vincent Millay.   BLPL; CMoP; FaBoBe; FaBV; HBV 1-2; MCCG; MoAmPo; MoRP; PoPl; PoSC; TrCP

My soul is blest, sense joy'd, and fortune raised.   Night.   Sir Philip Sidney. SiPS

..."My soul is rent and torn,/like yours, but it is also beautiful,/like lace." On the Wide Stairs.   Yehuda Amichai.   VWA

My soul like a dismasted wreck went driving/Over a monstrous sea without a bourn.   The Seven Old Men.   Charles Baudelaire.   OBVE

My soul may sit, that cries upon thee now.   Litany to Satan.   Charles Baudelaire.   AWP; SyP

My soul more love than you can make my soul forget.   More Strong Than Time.   Victor Hugo.   AWP

My soul, my weary soul...   Shadows.   Yehoash.   TrJP

My soul, oh, keep it by Thy Word.   The Three Enemies.   Christina Georgina Rossetti.   CoBE; TrCP; VLP

My Soul retire,/Get free, and so thou shalt even all Admire.   The Preparative.   Thomas Traherne.   AnAnS 1; OxBoCh

My soul's dark offspring, willing it should die/To loves, to passions, and society.   Repentance.   George Chapman.   OBSC

My soul's so happy,/Dat I cain' set down.   Set Down, Servant.   *Anonymous.* ABF

My soul shall detonate on high/And plant itself in cracks of sky. Rockferns. Norman. Nicholson. MoBrPo

My soul shall float, friend Sun,/The day being done. Hymns of the Marshes: Sunrise. Sidney Lanier. PoEL 1-5

My soul shall spurn them evermore. The Holy Office. James Joyce. FaBoTw; NoAm; OxBTC

My soul stands up and knocks at God's own temple-gates. Sonnet: "Blest Spirit of Calm that dwellest in these woods!" Charles Sangster. PeCV

My soul still flies above me for the quarry it shall find. The Falconer of God. William Rose Benet. CAW; HBMV; PG; TreFT; WGRP

My soul that lingers sighing/About the glimmering weirs. Far in a Western Brookland. Alfred Edward Housman. AWP; NBM; PoEL 1-5

My soul this day hath tasted death! A Child's Question. Elias Nason. AA

My soul to keep in its resolved course.' Endymion. John Keats. SeCePo

My soul will be a-dry before;/But after, it will thirst no more. The Pilgrimage. Sir Walter Ralegh. ViBoPo

...–My soul with One/For whom no envy can make dim the truth. A Tribute to Dante. Giovanni Boccaccio. GoBC

My soul withdraws into itself, and seeks/The peaks and isles and eagles of the mind. Eagles and Isles. Wilfrid Gibson. PoSH

My soule imparadis'd, for 'tis with her. Upon Castara's Absence. William Habington. AnAnS 2

My sovereign is as sweet and fair. Give Beauty All Her Right. Thomas Campion. ViBoPo

My spirit and my God shall be/My seaward hill, my boundless sea. My Doves. Elizabeth Barrett Browning. VLP

My spirit feeleth noght of swich matere/But if yow list, my tale shul ye here. The Canterbury Tales: The Franklin's Prologue. Geoffrey Chaucer. OAEL 1-2; OAEP

My spirit follows her, and loves. Wild Eden. George Edward Woodberry. AA

My spirit had been fed? The Beggar. Margaret E. Bruner. PoToHe

My spirit I resign. At Day's End. Anonymous. GoTF; TreFT

My spirit is God. He Walketh by Day. Book of the Dead. AWP

My spirit is great," said the cat. "Who Are You?" Asked the Cat of the Bear. Elizabeth Jane Coatsworth. TiPo

My spirit it was that fell. A Mood. Winifred Howells. AA

My spirit loves with thine in peace to dwell. The Prayer. Jones Very. EBCP; OxBA; TrCP; TrPWD

My spirit must lose itself in Thee,/Crying a name–Life, Light, or Love. Love's Lord. Edward Dowden. HBV 1-2

My spirit sank and I was left to woe. First Vision. Tadhg Dall O'Huiginn. AnIL; BIrV

My sportin' Oul' Grey Mare! The Oul' Grey Mare. Anonymous. AnIV

My star and my religion here! To a Friend. James Fenimore Cooper, Jr. PeHV

My star dust melody,/The memory of love's refrain. Star Dust. Michell Parish. BLSo

My starved lips play'd the vampyre with her hand. An Utter Passion Uttered Utterly (parody). John Todhunter. BXAP

My state still dark, my dream too long to tell. Across Kansas. William Stafford. CAPP

My stock of wisdom I'll improve,/Nor be a butterfly. The Butterfly. Adelaide O'Keeffe. HBV 1-2; HBVY

My story's ended. Little Tee-Wee. Anonymous. OxNR

My strength is as the strength of ten,/Because my heart is pure. Sir Galahad: The Pure Heart. Alfred, Lord Tennyson. GoTF; TreF

My strength is in Thy might, Thy might alone. This Do in Remembrance of Me. Horatius Bonar. STF; TrPWD

My strength is yet my own. Thanksgiving. Robert Nichols. MMM

My strong son,/My prince,/My star. Even the Best. Gary Allan Kizer. LFAC

My subtle and proclamant song. My Subtle and Proclamant Song. Sean Jennett. NeIP

My sucking star-child dead./Lambleddian. Song: "I kept neat my virginity." Glyn Jones. NeBP

My sweet respected woman, get up! Song to Imogen (parody). Richard Leighton Greene. BXAP

My sweetheart keeps a warmer white. Song: "This peach is pink with such a pink." Norman Gale. HBV 1-2

My sweetness drips from that spire/Of dry stone to impregnate/Regions of no desire. St. Stephen's Word. Rayner Heppenstall. ChMP

My sword that will not save. As I Gird on for Fighting. Alfred Edward Housman. CMoP

My taste will not have turned insensitive/To honey and bread old purity could love. My Dreams, My Works, Must Wait Till after Hell. Gwendolyn Brooks. NoP

My tears brim over the Melmac of decorum. Funeral Song for Mamie Eisenhower. Nellie Wong. BrSi

My tears shall mingle with his blood. O Saviour of a World Undone. Leonard Withington. AH

My tears well forth. Although I Do Not Know. Saigyo Hoshi. AWP

My thanks to Thee, God, tonight. I Give Thee Thanks, My King. Mael Isu O Brolchain. NOBI

...My thighs/half-eaten by the raging twilight. The One Whose Reproach I Cannot Evade. George Hitchcock. EAS

My thing is my own, and I'll keep it so still,/Until I be Marryed, say Men what they will. My Thing Is My Own. Anonymous. CoMu

My thirst to bite where she had bit. O briar-scents, on yon wet wing. George Meredith. EG

My thought is disordered. The Dark-Red Shadow-Spots. Yumei Kanbara. LiTW

My thought is like the stream; and flows and follows you/on forever. I Am a Peach Tree. Li Po. OLR

My thoughts and actions are, and shall be free. A Satire Addressed to a Friend (excerpt). John Oldham. AnAnS 1; NoP; OBS; OBSV

My thoughts are dancing flowers/And joyful singing birds. Thunderstorms. William Henry Davies. HBV 1-2

My thoughts be bloody, or be nothing worth! Hamlet. William Shakespeare. BiP; HoPM; WaaP

My thoughts grow keen and clear. Heat. Archibald Lampman. CaP; NOBC; OBCV; PeCV

My thoughts have been fixed. Since I Heard. Mitsune (Oshikochi no Mitsune). AWP

My thoughts the guests, which would thereon have fed. Was It a Dream. Edmund Spenser. NIP

My thoughts were far above it. On Seeing a Lady's Garter. Anonymous. ErPo

My thread for the new wick/Of freedom's torch,/Oh world! My Thread. David Hofstein. TrJP

...My throat filled/with a rank, Arab bloodstain. A Hand of Solo. Thomas Kinsella. NOBI

My thunderbolt has eyes to see/His way home to the mark. Boston Hymn. Ralph Waldo Emerson. AnNE; LaNeLa; MC; PAH; PAL; TRV; WGRP

My tie becomes crooked but do not/be alarmed i am well mannered. Othello Jones Dresses for Dinner. Ed Roberson. PoBA; PoNe

My time is loosely spent, and I undone. A Palinode. Robert Greene. OBSC

My toil is for man's joy, his joy my own. I Will Be What God Made Me, Nor Protest. Robert Bridges. VLP

My toilette, patches, all the world, adieu!' Six Town Eclogues (excerpt). Mary Wortley, Lady Montagu. NOEC

My toils after a boy/Were as water on desert sand. Epigram: "Cease your labours, lovers of boys." Anonymous. PeHV

"My token expression for the day,"/I said. With dignity. Death Row. Charles Culhane. LFAC

My tongue a poisoned arrow/To pierce him through the heart. Song of Hate. Jacob Frances. TrJP

My tongue/clacked a few prayers. Chomei at Toyama. Basil Bunting. OxBTC

My tongue's none the wiser/for death's uninteresting taste. Deadsong. Don Domanski. NOBC

My tragedy a speck/in your radiant hand! Poem from "The Revolution." Ilya Rubin. VWA

My treadmill memory draws from you yet. Crystals Like Blood. Hugh" (Christopher Murray Grieve) MacDiarmid. HAP; NoP; PAI

My trees lean into summer. Poem in June. Milton Acorn. WHW

My tribute from the lustrous barons of the sky. Like the Prime Mover. Mehdi Ali Seljouk. ACV

My trouble merged in wonder and in love. The Comfort of the Stars. Richard Burton. AnAmPo

My true love died the other day/I believe I'll die tomorrow. Make Me a Garment. Anonymous. OuSiCo

My true love hath my hart and I have his. Arcadia. Sir Philip Sidney. AtBAP; FCP

My true-love is dead and in her grave, and it's there I long to be. The Fair Beauty Bride. Anonymous. AmFP

My true love's in her grave and I wish I was there. A Lover's Lament. Anonymous. AmFP

My true love! she cried, and sank down by his side/Never to rise again, O! O, Open the Door to Me, O! Robert Burns. FaBoCh; LoGBV

My truest friends, a loyal set,/Are all the folks I've never met. Me. Hughes Mearns. InMe

My twine dissolve beneath its weaver's hand. Fishing Season. Val Vallis. PoAu 1-2

My twisted mouth around your fear. Drive Imagining. Arthur Vogelsang. MAYP

My uncle Jack Fenwick/He kissed my aunt Peg. Call the Horse, Marrow. Anonymous. OBET

My uncles fill/my mouth with ashes. The Garlic. Bert Meyers. VWA

My Venus My Venice I cannot forget/my lake of desire I dip my oar The Love-Making: His and Hers. Eve Merriam. UnTE

N

Nachel-born easman ev'ywhere I go.   Nache-born Easman.   *Anonymous.*
ABF

Nae, by the hert.–Sae tae yere grief I will.   Sonnet: "Beckie, my luve!–What is't, ye twa-faced tod?–".   George Campbell Hay.   OxBS

Naebody cares for me,/I care for naebody.   I Hae a Wife O' My Ain.
Robert Burns.   EiCP; LAuP

Naething but you, and nicht nocht else concealed.   Milk-Wort and Bog-Cotton.   Hugh" (Christopher Murray Grieve) MacDiarmid.   BSV; NeBP

Naiad changes–/Quick as these.   Gardener Janus Catches a Naiad.   Edith Sitwell.   MoAB; MoBrPo

...The Naiad 'mid her reeds/Prest her cold finger closer to her lips.   The Fall of Hyperion.   John Keats.   EnRP

Nail ourselves to/crosses he must be there,/pinioned,/because/atlanta, georgia/november 20, 1966.   In the Time of Revolution.   Julius Lester.   PoBA

Nailed like illegible bronze on the futureless future.   Fishnet.   Robert Lowell.   HaCAP

A naked child jumps over the threshold,/waving a green spray of leaves of vine.   The Thousand Things.   Christopher Middleton.   NePoEA-2

Naked enough to keep its dignity/Though it eye God askance.   Few Things Can More Inflame.   Cecil Day-Lewis.   OBMV

The naked eye of truth/Bears the stain of a lonely tear.   Beale Street, Memphis.   Thurmond Snyder.   NNP

...Naked feet have rubbed/thigh-deep in a limestone cliff.   Haitian Suite.
Gregory Orr.   MAYP

Naked I can see again the limbs I loved.   The Next Table.   Constantine P. Cavafy.   PeHV

Naked in all their beauty, dancing round the Wine-presses.   Milton.
William Blake.   EBEV; OBRV

Naked in that black blast of his love.   Mortmain.   Robert Penn Warren.
NOBA; PoCh; Prf

Naked, it goes in search of you/to fall on the lap of light.   To the Elephants.
Nathan Alterman.   VWA

A naked nun clasping the crucifix!   Old Maid.   J. U. Nicolson.   HBMV

Naked...the morningstar is born(e)...   (...Prelude).   Rokwaho.   STE

"Naked the soul goes up to God,/Brother, my brother."   Stains.   Theodosia Garrison.   HBV 1-2; WGRP

Naked thou liest in an unknown grave!   The Helmsman: An Ode.   J. V. Cunningham.   MoVE

Naked to the naked moon.   In Bertram's Garden.   Donald Justice.   BoLoP;
ErPo; NePoEA; VGW

Naked under a summer cotton dress.   Four Poems for Robin.   Gary Snyder.
NOBA; SOTW

Naked we come hider and bare/And poore, swa shal we hethen fare.   The Newly Born.   *Anonymous.*   OxBM

A naked woman.   Three Poems.   Stephen Crane   AP

Naked you'have odds enough of any man.   The Dampe.   John Donne.
SeCP

The nakedness of woman is the work of God.   The Marriage of Heaven and Hell.   William Blake.   FF

Name-alert, hand-alert/forever,/from the unburiable.   Just Think.   Paul Celan.   VWA

The name and date and sad, sad fate/Of foreman, young Monroe.   The Jam at Gerry's Rock.   *Anonymous.*   BFSS

A name either English or Yankee,–just Irving.   A Fable for Critics.   James Russell Lowell.   AnNE

Name me broadleaved woods.   Changeling VIII.   Kristjana Gunnars.
CaPN; NOBC

Name my mistress, and 'tis done!   Song: "Would you know what's soft?"
Thomas Carew.   EG; EnLi 1-2

A name not to be worn out with the years.   Homage to Sextus Propertius, I.
Ezra Pound.   OxBA

The name of Business Man; Amen!   Beyond the Profit of Today.
Anonymous.   PoToHe

The name of fair Liberty's bold Buccaneer.   Paul Jones.   *Anonymous.*   PAH

The name of HALE shall burn!   Nathan Hale.   Francis Miles Finch.   MC;
PAH; PAL

The name of Robert Burns?   Burns.   Fitz-Greene Halleck.   AA

The name of young Napoleon will enshrine the Bonny Bunch of/Roses, O.'
The Bonny Bunch of Roses.   *Anonymous.*   FaBoBa; OxBoLi

The name stands:/Scottsboro.   The Trial.   Muriel Rukeyser.   PoNe

Name–you Muse of Music, you, Euterpe!   New Chitons for Old Gods (excerpt).   David McCord.   UnS

...Named after just one/dead Spaniard who wanted to live forever   Ponce de Leon: A Morning Walk.   Al Young.   HoPM; NPGG

Named me his heir–and promptly rallied.   From the Epigrams of Martial.
James Michie.   FaBoEE

A nameless and eternal thing/Forgetting what it was to die.   The Immortal Mind.   George Gordon, Lord Byron.   WGRP

A nameless "him' my eyes in vain salute.   Overripe Fruit.   Kasmuneh.
TrJP

The names creeping out everywhere.   Lying Awake.   Thomas Hardy.
FaBoRV

Names over your name, and mourns/under the dry rafter.   Crime.   Robert Penn Warren.   AmP

Naming's over.   Day is done.   Adam's Task.   John Hollander.   NIP; NoP;
PPP

Naming the instruments we all must hold.   Ives (excerpt).   Muriel Rukeyser.
UnS

Nana, I paid/My dowry for you,/Nana, Nana Kru.   Nana Kru.
Anonymous.   PBA

Nancy Hanks had the loveliest face!   Nancy Hanks, Mother of Abraham Lincoln.   Vachel Lindsay.   CMoP

Nane, nane on earth that wander.   The Ochil Hills.   *Anonymous.*   PoSH

Nane suld fra that exemptit be/Except the Queenis Majesty.   Ane Supplication in Contemptioun of Syde Taillis.   Sir David Lyndsay.   GoTS

"Nantucket's sunk, and here we are/Right over old Marm Hackett's garden!"
The Alarmed Skipper.   James Thomas Fields.   EtS; HBV 1-2; NLV; YaD

Nap perished at Saint Helena.   Song: "When working blackguards come to blows."   Ebenezer Elliott.   EBEV; NBM

Napoleon, thou wast island-born!   A Ballade of Islands.   Lucy Robinson.
AA

The narcissi look up like children, quickly and whitely.   Among the Narcissi.
Sylvia Plath.   FaBoMo; FaBoWP; SCV

Narcissus! and a pail of water!   Fancy.   Jonathan Smedley.   OBSP

Narcissus, clear and set free, shall force his way.   Sonnets to Orpheus.
Rainer Maria Rilke.   SOTW

"Narcissus, shan't miss us, and be by our side!"   Narcissus, Come Kiss Us!
Anonymous.   ErPo

Narcissuses their eyelids close.   On a Blind Girl.   Baha Ad-din Zuhayr.
AWP

Narcotics cannot still the tooth/that nibbles at the soul–.   This World Is Not Conclusion.   Emily Dickinson.   AmePo; EaLo

Narmada in/the Vindhya mountains.   He Who Stole My Virginity.
Silabhattarika.   WPOW

Narrow as the cracks/on the handball court.   Tugs.   Jose Y., Jr. Teran.
LFAC

A narrow place, sultry and dark.   The Turkish Bakery.   *Anonymous.*
PBWP

The narrow way to love and power.   I Bless Thee, Lord, for Sorrows Sent.
Samuel Johnson.   AH

Naso, you are many men's man: "To let–/You Queen!"   To Naso.   Caius Valerius Catullus.   ErPo

Natella! a voice answered.   The Names of Georgian Women.   Bella Akhmadulina.   BoWoP

Nathan,/Take this down!   The Bratzlav Rabbi to His Scribe.   Jacob Glatstein.   TrJP

The Nation Lincoln died for cannot fail!   He Leads Us Still.   Arthur Guiterman.   OHIP

A Nation's Cross to a new Calvary!   Lincoln.   Corinne Roosevelt Robinson.
OHIP

A Nation's freedom won.   The Settler.   Alfred Billings Street.   AA;
FaBoBe; MC; PAH

A nation's problems has to face.   Our Presidents.   *Anonymous.*   BLPA

A nation saved, a race delivered!   Mr. Hosea Biglow to the Editor of "The Atlantic Monthly."   James Russell Lowell   AA

Nation/Strength/People/(now)   Nation.   Charlie Cobb.   PoBA

Nationless bones, under the still ground.   Song for the Heroes.   Alex Comfort.   MoBrPo; NeBP

A nations's growth from sea to sea/Stirs in his heart who plants a tree.   The Heart of the Tree.   Henry Cuyler Bunner.   OHFP; OHIP; PGD

Nations shall learn war no more.   Vine and Fig Tree.   Shalom Altman.
FSW

The natives by the name of Lakers call.   The Lakers: Prologue (excerpt).
James Plumptre.   NOEC

Natural as the veronica and the verbena,/In agricultural health.   In the Proscenium.   Gene Derwood.   LiTA

Natural as the veronica and the verbena,/In agricultural health.   War's Clown in the Proscenium.   Gene Derwood.   NePA

The natural fatality of existence.   Drought.   Oumar Ba.   PBWP

The natural history of the human wish.   In the Garden: Villa Cleobolus.
Lawrence Durrell.   ChMP

Nature and Silence passed in solemn guise.   Evening.   Charles Sangster.
ACV; CaP

Nature and the Poet's mind.   Songs.   Richard Henry Stoddard.   AA

Nature before hand hath out-cursed mee.   The Curse.   John Donne.
CBEP; OAEP; TW

Nature forswears/Antiquity.   Pink, Small and Punctual (Arbutus).   Emily Dickinson.   FaBV

Nature herself would yield the ghost.   Epigram on Sir Roger Phillimore and His Brother, George Phillimore.   *Anonymous.*   FaBoCo; NLV

Nature, instinct, creative force,/Fanned to a living flame.   Creative Force.
Maude Miner Hadden.   GoYe

Nature is always wise in every part.   The Heron.   Edward Hovell-Thurlow.
HBV 1-2

"Nature is evil," Midas said. The Ungrateful Garden. Carolyn Kizer. NePoEA-2

...Nature, it seems, can afford/Such wastefulness–not we. A Meeting. C. Day Lewis. NYBP

Nature, it seems, the greatest Healer,/Is even greater as Congealer. Second Half. David McCord. SD

Nature, like liberty, is but restrain'd/By the same laws which first herself ordain'd. An Essay on Criticism. Alexander Pope. TreFT

Nature, like us, is sometimes caught/Without her diadem. The sky is low, the clouds are mean. Emily Dickinson. AA; BoNaP; DiPo; ELU; FaBV; MoAmPo; OxBA; PoEL 1-5

Nature must call her gold but dross,/If she would gain this heav'nly land. Windham. Anonymous. AmFP

Nature, my nurse, had me to bed betimes. On the Deputy of Ireland's Child. Sir John Davies. FaBoEE

Nature no med'cine can impart/When age once snows upon your heart. Cupids Call. James Shirley. ErPo

Nature's glee/Is in every mood and tone/Eternity. Song's Eternity. John Clare. CBEP; FaBoCh; LoGBV; NCEP; PG

Nature's most noble offspring–yet her worst! Microcosm. Bertram Dobell. OBVV

Nature's philosophy/in the snow. Snow Crystals on Meall Glas. Elizabeth A. Wilson. PoSH

Nature's primest Punchinello. The Monkey. Mary Howitt. GN

Nature's universal song/Echoes to the rising day. Morning. John Cunningham. NOEC

Nature's white spirits of the spring. The Winter's Spring. John Clare. AtBAP

Nature, take care! Prayer for a Play House. Elinor Lennen. TrPWD

Nature thy muse like Lucan's did create. To the Translater of Lucan's Pharsalia (1614). Sir Walter Ralegh. SiPS

Nature was in an opal apron,/Mixing fresher air. It sounded as if the streets were running. Emily Dickinson. NePA; OBSP; PBWP

Nature without check with original energy. Song of Myself. Walt Whitman. AA; NePA

Naught but truth have I told–/–And now make I ending.' The Elder Edda: The Short Lay of Sigurd (excerpt). Anonymous. OBVE

Naught helpeth time, humbleness, nor place. Process of time worketh such wonder. Sir Thomas Wyatt. FCP; SiPS

Naught left to mark the mother's name,/Save–immortality of shame! Butler's Proclamation. Paul Hamilton Hayne. PAH

Naught see I permanent or sure in thee! Rondel: "Love, love, what wilt thou with this heart of mine?" Jean Froissart. AWP

Naught so damn'd as Melancholy. The Authors Abstract of Melancholy. Richard Burton. OBS

Naught so sweet as is true love. Ideals. Robert Greene. PoToHe

A nauseous brood that fills your senate walls,/And in the chambers of your viceroy crawls. Verses Occasioned by the Sudden Drying up...(excerpt). Jonathan Swift. OBSV

Navies fed to the fish in the dark/Unbridled waters. Beasts. Richard Wilbur. CrMA; LCAP; MP; NePoAm; NU; PPoe; PPP; TwCP

The Navy of Old Spain! Phantoms All. Harriet Prescott Spofford. AA

Nay, a box on the eare hath no smell at all. All Things Have Savour. Anonymous. FaBoCo

Nay, and though all men seeing had pity on me,/She would not see. A Leave-taking. Algernon Charles Swinburne. CH; EG; HBV 1-2; MaVP; NOBE; NOBV; OAEP; OBNC; OBVV; PoEL 1-5; PoLf; ViBoPo; VLP

...Nay, death you may call/That feels each pain and knows no joy at all. No Pleasure Without Some Pain. Thomas, Lord Vaux. EiL; EnRePo

...Nay, depart not against my will!/never shouldst thou depart with it! A Reproach to Morvyth. Dafydd ap Gwilym. LiTW

Nay, e'en by wells of cream shall sullen swear,/Since PATTON, her lov'd mistress, is not there. A Favourite Cat's Dying Soliloquy. Anna Seward. FM

Nay ev'n the hopes I form'd: and on them fell/E'en in mid way, like some arm'd foe in wait. The Jealous Enemy. Petrarch (Francesco Petrarca). LiTW

"Nay, farther must I go." Babushka. Edith Matilda Thomas. OnMSP

Nay, force thy bud to blow; their tyrant breath/Anticipating life, to hasten Death. A Rose. Sir Richard Fanshawe. CavP; HBV 1-2; OBEV; OBS; PoEL 1-5; SeCePo

–Nay, give me any love, so it be love of thee. On the Nature of Love. Wilfrid Scawen Blunt. ViBoPo

Nay, God is witness, gave the names. The Miracle. Ralph Waldo Emerson. FM

Nay–God my Christ–I pass but shall not die. Idylls of the King. Alfred, Lord Tennyson. TreFS

Nay! here my children/fold/Their exiled hands in prison, and long for me. Our Lady of France. Lionel Pigot Johnson. ISi

Nay! I was cast in pitiful distress/By brown eyes wide with truth and tenderness. Omnia Vincit. Alfred Cochrane. HBV 1-2

Nay, more than this, I hold it still/Profoundly confidential. A Dialogue from Plato. Henry Austin Dobson. HBV 1-2

Nay, nay! She is my baby girl. Alice. Herbert Bashford. HBV 1-2

Nay, rather I laugh that I thought to own it/For more than a day. The Cynic. Theodosia Garrison. HBMV

Nay, rush not: time serves: we are going,/Gentlemen. An Ancient to Ancients. Thomas Hardy. CMoP; CoBMV; GTBS-P; LiTM; MoPo; MoVE; OxBTC

Nay, start not at the name–America! Tribute to America. Percy Bysshe Shelley. PAL

...Nay still/Bends desire but to my/Creating will. Frustration. Elizabeth Daryush. QFR

Nay, surely Thy name I will worship, while breath in/my nostrils be. I Have Sought Thee Daily. Solomon Ibn Gabirol. LiTW

"Nay, Sweet, now nay, now nay!/I am not ready." All in a Garden Green. William Ernest Henley. OBMV

Nay then, he said, do thus and I am done. Destroying Angel. Hilary Corke. NYBP

Nay, thou maist prove/That mans most Noble Passion is to Love. The Call. John Hall. MeLP; MePo; OBS; ViBoPo

Nay, 'tis confessed/That fools please women best. Mother Bombie: Fools in Love's College. John Lyly. TrGrPo

"Nay, 'twas the whip that spoke." The Beasts Are Very Wise. Rudyard Kipling. BoAnP

Nay, white as the angel of a child/That looks into God's own eyes! White Azaleas. Harriet McEwen Kimball. AA; HBV 1-2

Naylit full sore/Upon a tree. Ah My Dere. Anonymous. AtBAP; BoW

Nazarius, Celsus, Victor, Innocent! A Prayer for St. Innocent's Day. Helen Parry Eden. CAW

'Nd I havin' my opinyin uv him. Our Two Opinions. Eugene Field. AA

Ne derer is none in Goddys hurde/Than a chaste womman with lovely worde. Praise of Women. Robert Mannyng [(or Manning)]. OBEV

Ne'er flee the hateful spell. Tacita. James Benjamin Kenyon. AA

Ne'er love him as ye did me. Clerk Saunders. Anonymous. AnFE; OBEV; SeCeV

Ne'er paused, till he lighted in St. Stephen's lobby.) Fum and Hum, the Two Birds of Royalty. Thomas Moore. OBSV

Ne'er walked the earth a greater man than he. Dante. Buonarroti Michelangelo. AWP

Ne fort after Michelmasse hi ne come namore ther. Town against Gown at Oxford. Robert of Gloucester OxBM

Ne in al the welkin was a cloude. The Book of the Duchesse. Geoffrey Chaucer. FiP

Ne is this Love a god in deed,/But lies and bitter bane. Of Love. James Sandford. EiL

Ne'r may Prophetique Daphne crown my Brow. The Welcome to Sack. Robert Herrick. AnAnS 2; CaPo; SeCP; SeCV 1-2

Ne rested till she came without relent/Unto the land of Amazons, as she was bent. The Faerie Queene. Edmund Spenser. OAEL 1-2

Ne swik thu naver nu! Cuckoo Song. Anonymous. EnLit; NoP

Ne truste no man to this wele, the wheel it turneth so. The Lady Fortune. Anonymous. HeIP; NIP

Ne wish for death, ne fear his might. The Means to Attain a Happy Life. Henry Howard, Earl of Surrey. EiL; EnLi 1-2; FaBoEE; HBV 1-2; OBEV; ViBoPo

Near a patch of grass. It Moves Across. Bernadette Mayer. ANYP

The near approach a bed may show/Of human bliss to human woe. Translation of Lines by Benerade. Samuel Johnson. CABA

Near brandy, and my mouth that calls you, calls you. Summer, 1970. Daniel Halpern. AmPA

Near by Dundee and the bonnie Magdalen Green. An Address to the New Tay Bridge. William McGonagall. PeD

Near Cedar on Lake Street, where the used cars live. The Poet's Final Instructions. John Berryman. SM; VGW

Near death now, she accepts/the child who never left. Return. Mark Vinz. GOYP

Near one more and makes its final surge TIME: 4:25:9 400-Meter Freestyle. Maxine W. Kumin. LiSp; SD; SoSe

Near the blue spruce whose needles/knit and ravel darkness. Bell Weather. Lewis Turco. AMV-80

Near the nice little man in blue goggles. That's me. A Lost Illusion. George Du Maurier. CenHV

Near the opening which is the way in for you/and was the way out for me, my love. Eurydice. Linda Gregg. NPGG

Near the Ransom of the World. Mary Tired. Marjorie Pickthall. ACV; PeCV

Near the sea,/a new poem/for new men. Poem near the Sea. Frelimo. WhB

Near, there and/gone. Almost Everybody Is Dying Here: Only a Few Actually Make It. Daniel Berrigan. LFAC

Near things: Friend, here's my hand. Friends. William Stafford. PPJ

Near to Thine awful Feet let reach/This broken spikenard of my speech! Spikenard. Laurence Housman. TrPWD

Neared to the hour when Beauty breathes her last/And knows herself in death. The Great Breath. George William Russell. MoBrPo; OBEV; OBMV; OxBI; WGRP

Nearer, my God, to thee,/Nearer to thee. Nearer, My God, to Thee. Sarah Flower Adams. FaBoBe; FaFP; GoTF; HBV 1-2; PoLf; TreF; VLP; WBLP; WGRP

Nearer my home today, today,/Than I have been before. One Sweetly Solemn Thought. Phoebe Cary. AH

Nearer, nearer, oh, I fear/Murderous advances. Terror. Yehoash. TrJP

The nearer the sweet, the meeter the Beaune. Red Wine. Justin Richardson. PV

...Nearing/the shore where we will be reborn, ecstatic and black. A Small Bird's Nest Made of White Reed Fiber. Robert Bly. CAPP; NNaP

Nearing the town of Nimitybell,/Nimitybell on Monaro. The Coachman's Yarn. Edwin James Brady. PoAu 1-2

Nearly ripe for worms. Face. Jean Toomer. CDC; NoP

Nears its nest/over the porch door. Elegy. Philip Dow. NPGG

...Neat as a child's football lying under the/tree, waiting for whose hands to pick it up. The Bourgeois Poet–7. Karl Shapiro. PP

Neath stars, thy new uprising, from the East. Hymn to the Sun. Charles M. Doughty. FaBoTw

Necessity drives me, say I. I Sit With My Toes in the Brook. Anonymous. FaBoNo

The neck of God. Any Saint (excerpt). Francis Thompson. MoBrPo

Necklaced in/A coral toy. Emmett Till. James A. Emanuel. CNA; NIP; PoBA

Nectar more worthy of the halls/Where pontiffs hold high festivals. To Postumus. Horace. LiTW

Need any man be told what flowers are,/that hold a star? Bloom. Alfred Kreymborg. HBMV

Need I that you exist and show yourself any more than in these songs. Not Heaving from My Ribb'd Breast Only. Walt Whitman. NePA

...The need/Which grows from the arms' want through desolation. Letter to R. Willard Maas. WaP

Needing no other symbols of His love. Candle and Book. Nina Willis Walter. TRV

Needing no self beyond a self I know. Argent Solipsism. Howard Blake. PoA

The needle directed by beauty and art. The Needle. Samuel Woodworth. GN; HBV 1-2

Needle in the haystack. Going to Boston. Anonymous. ABF

The needle to the north degree/Wades so, through polar air. Through the Straight Pass of Suffering. Emily Dickinson. MoRP

Needless to say, I mean your Maxim Book. The Man and His Image. Jean de La Fontaine. OBVE

The needlessness of shedding human blood. Asking for It. Siegfried Sassoon. MoRP

Needs likewise its duality. Duality. Kenneth Slade Alling. AnAmPo; CAW

Needs no medicine High-Cool/2. James (Olumo) Cunningham. JB

Needs no other proof/Than its own fire. Desire Is a Witch. C. Day-Lewis. CMoP

Needs not to feare that engineer/Whose bottoms on the sand. The Whore That Rides in Us Abides. Anonymous. SCAP

Negation is equal to love. Sans Souci. Lisel Mueller. NePoAm-2

...A negative print/of a spider, a stopped moment. White Spider. Marita Garin. AMV-80

Neglected by the young,/Because of these reveries. Hugh Selwyn Mauberley, VII: Siena mi fe'; disfecemi maremma. Ezra Pound. NOBA

Neglected cars on the si–/ding, ding, ding. Tank Town. John Atherton. NYBP

Neglected heaps we in bye-corners lay,/Where they become to worms and moths a prey. The Art of Poetry. John Dryden. PP

Neglected, leaves a dreary waste behind. A Comparison. William Cowper. OBSP

Neglected virtue, seasons go and come,/While thine forgot lie closed in a tomb. Spring Bereaved. William, of Hawthornden Drummond. OBEV

Negro and a white man/picketing together! Street Scene–1946. Kenneth Porter. PoNe

Neigh to the pastured mothers of the race. A Prairie Ride. William Vaughn Moody. AnEnPo

The neighbors all to this thrice blessed stall. Corydon and Tityrus. Anonymous. CAW

A neighbour to stones am I, a sister to a priceless gift. The Woman and the Aloe. Perseus Adams. PeSA

Neither a love where may not be/Ever so little falsity. Though I Thy Mithridates Were. James Joyce. NoAm

Neither aging nor desire/makes enough time. Make Way. Steven Lavoie. APU

Neither can reach you, great and innocent. To the Countesee of Bedford. John Donne. ATP; MeLP; OBS

Neither can you crack a nut. The Mountain and the Squirrel. Ralph Waldo Emerson. BeLS; FaBoBe; GoJo; LaNeLa; TreFT

Neither does he, the spellbound one. Progress Report. Charles Simic. GeTw

Neither father nor lover. Elegy for Jane. Theodore Roethke. AP; CAPP; FF; NoP; PAI; TwCP

Neither for God, nor for his enemies. Theoretikos. Oscar Wilde. BrPo; VLP

Neither her peevishness annoy me. Song: "If I freely may discover." Ben Jonson. EiL

...Neither moves toward us/nor falls into watery wastes as we pass? History. Arthur Gregor. TAP

Neither of them had ever met. Quiescent, a Person Sits Heart and Soul. Ring Lardner. OBAL

Neither one, nor the two together. The Indigo Glass in the Grass. Wallace Stevens. PoA

Neither start nor finish, only at best/This strangely split unending Now. The Sea Dike. M. Vasalis. LiTW

Neither thorn nor thistle do I grow;/I grow the white rose. Simple Verses. Jose Marti. TTY

Neither to rule nor die? to change, to change! The Marchen. Randall Jarrell. CMoP; DFT

Neither what is nor what was, but the flat light rising. Low Fields and Light. William Stanley Merwin. ConAP; LCAP

Neither will it give out its rich sad secrets/To halfhearted tokens of transparent love. Tourists. Kizito Z. Muchemwa. WhB

Neither wish death, nor fear his might. Martial's Quiet Life. Henry Howard, Earl of Surrey. OBSC

Nelle ich speke no more with the! Riddles Wisely Expounded. Anonymous. BaBo; ESPB

"The nere the cherche, the firther from God." The Dancers of Colbek. [(or Manning)] Robert Mannyng. OxBM

Nere was't thou in a sence so sadly true,/The well of living Waters, Lord, till now. On the Bleeding Wounds of Our Crucified Lord. Richard Crashaw. SeCV 1-2

Nerves and follicles and arteries/ablaze in the suaveness of night. America the Beautiful. Stan Rice. NPGG

Nerves pulled/like autumn/strings across/an empty gourd. Summer 1970. Lindiwe Mabuza. WPOW

Nervous, earthy woman, you are reaching now/to the marrow of my bone. From: First Aspen. Lynn Strongin. IHMS

Nervy, glowering, your daughter/wipes the teaspoons, grows another way. Snapshots of a Daughter-in-law. Adrienne Rich. NCSH

A-ness never/Had a chance. The Negro. James A. Emanuel. BPo; HoPM

The nest is full of snow. The Snow-Filled Nest. Rose Terry Cooke. OBCA

...Nest of twigs so few/that both the sky and the eggs show through. Mallee in October. Flexmore Hudson. PoAu 1-2

The net/will still/be be/tween them. 40–Love. Roger McGough. LiSp; NoAm

Nets delicate as/the webs of spiders. The Sirens. Lou Lipsitz. LTB

Nettles, docks, thistles;/Praeterea nihil. The Cheerful Chilterns (parody). Frank Sidgwick. BXAP

...The neural/Web, the self-true mind, the trusty reflex. Speech for the Repeal of the McCarran Act. Richard Wilbur. CMoP; NePoAm

The neutered terraces subside beneath us. Flight to Italy. C. Day-Lewis. OxBTC

Nevah mine Scarman/will bring a blam-blam. Di Great Insohreckshan. Linton Kwesi Johnson. FaBoPV

Never a husband will marry us then. Lysistrata. Aristophanes. WaaP

Never a ploughman. Never a one. Ha'nacker Mill. Hilaire Belloc. FaPoR; HBMV; MoBrPo; OxBTC

Never a Worm so confident/Bored at so brave a Root   And This of All My Hopes. Emily Dickinson. ForPo

Never able to come alongside. The Admiral's Daughter. E. G. Burrows. HoAn

Never again remember the deep green hollow/Or the top of the kind old tree! Saturday Market. Charlotte Mew. HBMV

Never again to leave Chile/never in exile again. On the Death of Neruda. Olga Cabral. SOTS

Never again to the top came he/(By the water's edge, the water's edge) Isabel. Anonymous. WHW

"Never anything happens you can't wear jeans." The Lesson. Elizabeth Peterson. AMV-80

...Never be another like that great race between Ralph/and Peggy   The True Ballad of the Great Race to Gilmore City. Phil Hey. Psk

Never be chid. Come When You're Called. Anonymous. HBVY; OxNR

Never be it said that my thoughts are his thoughts. Antigone. Sophocles. LiTW

Never can take the mask to be a face.   Tonight the City.   R. L. Cook.
AMV-81

...Never/Can this decay, but is beginning ever.   Fragmentum Petronius
Arbiter, Translated.   Ben Jonson.   HeIP

Never caught him/and never/understood.   Wili Woyi, Shaman, also known as
Billy Pigeon.   Robert J. Conley.   STE

Never come home.   News of the World.   George. Barker.   LiTB

Never did Contraries soe well agree,/for th'one without th'other will not bee.
Sonnet XVI.   William Alabaster.   AnAnS 1

Never did look back.   Danville Girl.   *Anonymous.*   FSW

Never doth thy beauty flourish/More than in my reason's sight.   Voices at
the Window.   Sir Philip Sidney.   OBEV; PoPle

...Never for a moment suppose that they understand.   The Ram's Horn.
John Hewitt.   BIrV

Never forget. For there was none like you.   Memory of a Scholar.
Richmond Lattimore.   GLGT

Never forgetting him that kept coming constantly so near.   The World as
Meditation.   Wallace Stevens.   AP; HeIP; LCAP; MoAB; NIP; PPP

Never forgetting the hill, I wonder,/does the stream cry as it leaves?   The
Blue Hill Is My Desire.   Hwang Chin-i.   PBWP

Never gave, not even after a light rain.   First Winter.   Gail N. Harada.
BrSi

Never get a lickin' till I go down to Bimini.   Never Get a Lickin' Till I Go
down to Bimini.   *Anonymous.*   OuSiCo

Never giving up on living/without a brilliant battle.   Reflections of a Trout
Fisherman.   Andrew Demon.   AMV-80

Never have I wished more/Not to die.   In a Field.   Robert Pack.   MAT;
NePoEA-2

Never have they travelled but in each other's com-/pany.   The Song of
Mystic Unity.   Jami.   LiTW

Never hot with doubt nor faith nor reverence for tears?   Big Crash out West.
Peter Viereck.   AmC; PoPl

Never, I own, expected I/That life would all be fair.   Well, World, You Have
Kept Faith with Me.   Thomas Hardy.   SCV

Never imaginable mystery)/descend.   Enter No (Silence is the Blood Whose
Flesh.   Edward Estlin Cummings.   AP

Never, in field or tent,/Scorn the black regiment!   The Black Regiment.
George Henry Boker.   GN; HBV 1-2; PAH

Never kam sea-rovers/Seekan back tae Rackwick.   Shore Tullye.   Robert
Rendall.   OxBS

Never knew the smile of beauty,/Nor the blessing of a wife.   Farewell, Peace.
Anonymous.   MC; PAH

"Never know now," said the jay. "Never know."   Riley.   Charles Causley.
SO

Never like this a lass of them all.   Unique Among Girls.   *Anonymous.*
WTO

Never lipped the wine o Living to the lees!   Wine O Living.   Matt Marshall.
PoSH

NEVER MAKE FUN OF BABIES!).   A Bestiary.   Kenneth Rexroth.
OBAL

Never Mark Anthony/Dallied more wantonly/With the fair Egyptian Queen.
Mark Anthony.   John Cleveland.   ALV; EG; InvP; OAEL 1-2; SeCP;
ViBoPo

Never mind/the complete turn.   The Dog Yelped.   Larry Eigner.   CoPo

Never mind what he said.   When Alexander Pope.   Edmund Clerihew
Bentley.   FiBHP

Never more to find her where the bright waters flow.   Jeanie with the Light
Brown Hair.   Stephen Collins Foster.   FaFP; FSW; GoTF; TrAS; TreF

Never, never would she wear out.   Vocation.   Judith Herzberg.   WPOW

Never no more, never no more.   Never No More.   James Keir Baxter.
AnNZ

Never, O never!   Marmion.   Sir Walter Scott.   OBRV; ViBoPo

Never old/ever gold/lives.   Siasconset Song.   Philip Booth.   NePoAm

...Never one/Belonged to the House of They.   They Say.   Ella Wheeler
Wilcox.   WBLP

Never our lips, our hands.   Evening Song.   Sidney Lanier,   AP; GoTF; PG;
TreFT; UnPo; WHA

Never prosper, boy or man.   Kill a Robin or a Wren.   *Anonymous.*   PBBP

Never said how.   The Indian Graveyard.   Ramona Weeks.   TAT

...Never see me where/I hang, huge teardrop on the cheek of night.   Judas.
Vassar Miller.   MoAmPo

Never seen death, yet, Dickie? ...Well, how is your time to learn!   The "Mary
Gloster."   Rudyard Kipling.   BeLS

...Never send to know/for whom the bell tolls; it tolls for thee.   Devotions.
John Donne.   PoPl

Never serve a rabbit stew before you catch the rabbit.   Morals.   James
Thurber.   FaBV

Never "sha'n't,"/Never "won't."   Seldom "Can't."   *Anonymous.*   HBVY

...Never shall I see the U–/–niversity of Gottingen/–niversity of Gottingen.–
The Rovers: Rogero's Song.   George Canning.   CEP; NOEC

Never shall lingering honour quit/Thy heart sincere.   An Ode to Myself.
Thomas Dermody.   OnYI

Never, she cries, shall Pity soothe Love's thirst,/Or foul hypocrisy for truth
atone!   Modern Love, XLIV.   George Meredith.   VLP

Never show your face again.   Rain, Rain, Go to Spain.   *Anonymous.*
OxNR

Never sick, never old, never dead/From itself never turning.   "As you came
from the holy land of Walsingham."   Sir Walter Ralegh.   AAS; AtBAP;
EII; EnLoPo; FaBoEn; FCP; GBL; HAP; InPS; LiTL; LoBV; NoP; PAI;
PoEL 1-5; PrIm; TrGrPo; ViBoPo

Never so glad as we're going to be!   Morning Song.   Karle Wilson Baker.
HBMV

Never, somehow, could I seem to cotton/To another as I did to you!   First
Love.   Charles Stuart Calverley.   FiBHP; InMe

Never stain its bosom more.   Off from Boston.   *Anonymous.*   MC; PAH

Never strike a pleasing strain/Till she come abroad again!   Aglaia.   Nicholas
Breton.   OBSC

Never such innocence again.   MCMXIV.   Philip Larkin.   EBEV; OBWP

Never surrender!   Triumphalis.   Bliss Carman.   HBMV; PG

Never taking/Further vengeance on his people of Tirawley.   The Welshmen
of Tirawley.   Sir Samuel Ferguson.   OBVV; OnYI

Never tell/never tell/never tell.   Secrets.   Linda Pastan.   AMV-80

Never the connection, the return.   Route 29.   Catharine Savage Brosman.
AMV-81

Never the dream alone.   The First Reader.   Winfield Townley Scott.   PoA

Never! though I die thirsting. Go thy ways!   Modern Love, XXIV.   George
Meredith.   VLP

...Never through me/Shall you be overcome.   Conscientious Objector.   Edna
St. Vincent Millay.   WPOW

Never to carry a corpse/Again, to my dying day.   Corpse-Bearing.   Thomas
Ashe.   NOBV

Never to her dying day/Knew one from the other.   It's a Fib.   Elspeth.
ALV

Never to part more.   Meeting.   Christina Georgina Rossetti.   GBL

Never to rise again, O!   Open the Door to Me, O.   Robert Burns.   AtBAP;
PoEL 1-5

...Never/to wait! Now they were free.   The Children's Crusade.   Philip
Levine.   NaP

Never treat a British sailor/Like they did young Andrew Rose.   Andrew
Rose.   *Anonymous.*   OBSS

Never trust a girl on the greenbriar shore.   The Girl on the Greenbriar Shore.
Anonymous.   FSW

Never turning away/again   And That Will Be Heaven.   Evangeline Paterson.
EBCP

Never tyrannical,/But ever true.   A Maiden's Ideal of a Husband.   Henry
Carey.   HBV 1-2

Never wake early enough to pull the/Words out of this dream and make/
Them work for me in daylight.   Waking, the Love Poem Sighs.   Jim Hall.
GOYP

Never was grief like mine.   The Sacrifice.   George Herbert.   AtBAP; PoEL
1-5

Never was wine so red or bread so white.   Mass at Dawn.   Roy Campbell.
PeSA

Never were days yet called two,/But one night went betwixt.   Kind Are Her
Answers.   Thomas Campion.   AnFE; BoLoP; EG; ELP; FaBoEn; HBV
1-2; LiTL; SeCeV; TrGrPo

Never were stamps so well employed as they.   The Printer, to Her Majesty.
Leon Lichfield.   HW

Never will this poor lady come home.   The Small Lady.   Stevie Smith.
TEP

Never will we break our troth/Till the sea run dry in Malacca Bay.   Till the
Sea Runs Dry.   *Anonymous.*   WTO

Never would be man enough for me.   The Boys Brushed By.   Catherine
Gonick.   AMV-80

NEVER YOUR CAPTIVE!   How High the Moon.   Lance Jeffers.   CNA;
PoBA

Nevertheless I'd like to know/what you are doing and where you are going.
Letter to N. Y.   Elizabeth Bishop.   LiTL; MP; NoP; NYP; TwCP

Nevertheless I have put in a basket/The coins for the ferry.   Being Called
For.   Rosemary Dobson.   CBAP

Nevertheless it is good, though there is better than it.   Hope Evermore and
Believe.   Arthur Hugh Clough.   WGRP

Nevertheless my name/is being bandied like dust.   Because we suspected.
Lady Ise.   BoWoP

Nevertheless the cry is musical to me./A beagle's cry.   The Beagle's Cry.
Anonymous.   OnYI

Nevertheless, the praiseful, graceful soldier/Shouldn't be fired by his gun.
Grace.   Richard Wilbur.   LiTA

Nevertheless yes   Some San Francisco Poems.   George Oppen.   NNaP

New and different, but not less.   Our Coming Countrymen.   Henry Parkes.
NOAV

A new and singular sex?   Polar Exploration.   Stephen Spender.   ChMP;
MoAB; MoPo; NoAm

The next time you go sailing/Beyond enamel shore. The Voyage of Jimmy Poo. James A. Emanuel. AmNP; NNP

Next to a puddle,/next to the sun. Poem to the Sun. Morty Sklar. FAZ

Next week I will discuss:/Life and the Liver in Sibling Kidney Transplant. Dr. Dimity Lectures on Unusual Cases. Cynthia Macdonald. SUW

...Next week/She will be one year old. A Living Pearl. Kenneth Rexroth. LiTM

Next week, the pearl grey mist of early fall/will mute like Abishag the few leaves left. Fall Colors. Jerome Mazzaro. AMV-81

Next winter, the oranges/Will bloom on another hill. Still-Life. Ronald Perry. NePoEA-2

Next year I'll hang you on the rack,/And end the date of snaps. Snaps for Dinner, Snaps for Breakfast, and Snaps for Supper. George Moses Horton. OBAL

Next year I shall see no meadow, no horse. Omens. Michael Hamburger. NMP

Next year in...where?/Fie, fie! Lullaby for an Emigrant. Benjamin Fondane. VWA

Next year it will be flies. Calendar. Cecil Bodker. BoWoP

Next year the trees will rest and apples will be few. Apples in New Hampshire. Marie Gilchrist. BoNaP

"Next year," we cry, "next year,/Jerusalem." Theodor Herzl. Israel Zangwill. TrJP

Next year we'll come back with some more,/Heave O! Windlass Song. William Allingham. GN

Neyther wisshe death, nor fear his might. Epigrams. Martial (Marcus Valerius Martialis). OBVE

Niagara or Vesuvius is deferred. Modern Love, XXXIV. George Meredith. NOBV; VLP

"Niatum! Niatum!" No One Remembers Abandoning the Village of White Fir. Duane Niatum. CDW

A nice little star, but not very bright. When Last Seen. Hortense Flexner. QQQ

Nice mice to an untimely death. Cruel Clever Cat. Geoffrey Taylor. FaBoEE

Nice pallats hardly judge, if it be flesh or fish. Poly-Olbion. Michael Drayton. FM

Nice, though. Ode on a Grecian Urn Summarized. Desmond Skirrow. NIP; NOBL

Nice to be God... The Convent. Jeanne D'Orge. AnAmPo

The nicest in the town. Mrs. Hen. Anonymous. OxNR

The nicht is neir gone. The Nicht Is Neir Gane. Alexander Montgomerie. AtBAP; BSV

Nick through your flesh and creak into the block. The Last Word. Peter Davison. InPK

Nickety, nackety, now, now, now. Married Me a Wife. Anonymous. OuSiCo

Nicolay mah lun dee. Jingle Mammy Song (with music). Anonymous. AS

Nigger Christ/On the cross/Of the South. Christ in Alabama. Langston Hughes. PoBA

Nigger...nigger...nigger... Nigger. Frank Horne. BANP; CDC

Nigh a shattered drum and a king-post rotting/Are the bleaching bones of the old grey horse. The Old Whim Horse. Edward Dyson. CBAP

Night absorbs them/With the sponge of her silence. Fireworks. Babette Deutsch. NYBP; OFD

Night after night/the drunks and the dancers/hold still/in the ruined walls. October. Greg Pape. AmPA

The night after tonight. A Dream of Fair Women. Kingsley Amis. FF; MP; NMP; NoAm; OAEL 1-2

Night and day, I feel the trouble/Of the Wanderer in my soul. Song for the Wandering Jew. William Wordsworth. ERoP 1-2

Night and day, regret should walk. Parting. Coventry Patmore. PoToHe

Night and her thousand eyes and gleaming seas. Owning. Wilmot B. Lane. CaP

Night and night clouds/fold dark on the stars. The Mountain Afterglow. James Laughlin. VGW

The night and the field glitter. Sports Field. Judith Wright. LiSp

Night, argues/with certain houses Paris: This April Sunset Completely Utters. Edward Estlin Cummings. NAMP; SOTW

The night around tempers to another shade. Elver Fishers. Ivor Gurney. FaBoPP

The night before he swung, he sang/To his mandolin. Spanish Johnny. Willa Cather. ABF; BPAW; HBMV

Night begins to fall, the atmosphere is electric. Saying One Thing. Robert Long. AMV-81

Night behind me with the dim/vocabulary of rocks and stream ahead. Casting at Night. Allen Hoey. AMV-80; WOLT

The night-blooming moon opens its pale corolla. Falling Asleep in a Garden. David Wagoner. AMV-81

Night comes and reads the stars. Text. Aaron Zeitlin. VWA

Night comes; that is the mystery of day. Burial of a Fisherman in Hydra. Grace Schulman. BoWoP

Night coming tenderly/Black like me. Dream Variation. Langston Hughes. BALP; CDC; HAP; IDB; NOBA; PoBA; PoNe; PoPl; WeW

The night cries of birds drown in the surf's roar. Listening to Beethoven on the Oregon Coast. Henry Carlile. Psk

Night dark as leopard-flower. When My Love Becomes. Ono no Komachi. PBWP

Night–darkness–alone with the sea. Thalatta. Willis Boyd Allen. EtS

Night deepens, and I sit in cheerless doubt, alone. Watching. Emily Chubbuck Judson AA

Night floods us suddenly as history/that has sunk many islands in its good time. Nigger's Leap, New England. Judith Wright. NOAV

Night fluid like a smooth sea. Night. Aldo Camerino. VWA

The Night follows close with millions of suns, and sleep and/restoring darkness. Youth, Day, Old Age, and Night. Walt Whitman. AnAmPo

Night funeral/in Harlem. Night Funeral in Harlem. Langston Hughes. InPS; PAI

Night, good, good/night, has come. The End of the Day. Robert Creeley. AmPC

The night has come. By the Pool. Allen Grossman. AMV-80

Night has fallen. Earth sleeps wrapped round/with the sure purpose of eternity. Looking Down on Mesopotamia. Mary Ursula Bethell. AnNZ

A night-heron's screech. Haiku: "The lightning flashes!" Basho (Matsuo Basho). SoSe

The night is come at last. Break not the splendid dream. Drake. Alfred Noyes. CAW

The night is come. The land is wrapt in sleep. The Storm Is Over. Robert Bridges. BrPo; GTBS-P; LiTB; LiTM; MoPo; OBMV

The night is gone. As the Day Breaks. Ernest McGaffey. AA

The night is good; because, my love,/They never say good-night. Good-Night. Percy Bysshe Shelley. HBV 1-2; LiTL; ViBoPo

The night is near gone... Hey! Now the Day Dawns. Alexander Montgomerie. CH

Night is over and done. Watchman, What of the Night? Algernon Charles Swinburne. WiR

The night is past, our King is on His/way. Stir Me. Anonymous. STF

The night is stiller than the dark is dead. The Day's No Rounder Than Its Angles Are. Peter Viereck. AmP

Night, let me be part of you/but in my own dark way. For Bill Hawkins, a Black Militant. William J. Harris. PoBA

Night letter, leave us/for daylight. Compline. Debora Greger. AMV-81

Night-Moth, Change-Moth, Time-/Moth, eaters of dreams and of me! Moth-Terror. Benjamin De Casseres. TrJP

The night, New York, sardonic and alert,/Offers a soul to your reluctant dirt. New York City. Maxwell Bodenheim. HBMV

Night might sleep tight. Child's Game. Judson Jerome. DuDa

A night of memories and sighs/I consecrate to thee. Rose Aylmer. Walter Savage Landor. AWP; BoLiVe; BoLoP; CABA; CH; ELP; EnLoPo; ExPo; FaFP; GoTF; GTBS; HAP; HBV 1-2; HeIP; HoPM; InPo; LiTB; LiTL; LoBV; NOBE; NoP; OAEL 1-2; OAEP; OBEV; OBNC; OBRV; OBVV; PoEL 1-5; RoGo; SeCeV; TEP; TreFS; TrGrPo; WHA

A night of stars and God–and then/A workman's toil with working men. The Carpenter. Mary Brent Whiteside. TrCP

The night of torment cannot grow/into a liberated dawn Gethsemane, Illinois. Martin Samuel Allwood. LiTW

...The night on which I fell off my horse/in the shadows. That was really useful. Thank You. Kenneth Koch. NeAP; PoM

Night rests like a ball of fur on my tongue. Adolescence–II. Rita Dove. AmPA; HaCAP

Night's hymn of the rock, as in a vivid sleep. The Rock. Wallace Stevens. AP

Night's moonlight lake was neither water nor air. Reality Is an Activity of the Most August Imagination. Wallace Stevens. AmC

...A night's wild loving/With that young one I saw at the crossroads dance. The Poet Loves from Afar. Desmond O'Grady. NoAm

Night, sleep, death and the stars. A Clear Midnight. Walt Whitman. HAP; OBSP

Night slowly staggers away/And then the day. Dawn Patrol: Chicago. Richard V. Durham. GoSl

The night snows stars and the earth creaks. The Howling of Wolves. Ted Hughes. OxBTC

Night speaks, the artificer, beating out gold.' Poet and Goldsmith. Vernon Watkins. PoCh

Night stares down with her great bruised eye. Suite to Fathers. Jim Harrison. AmPA

A night, surrounded by such cries. Gulls. E. A. Muir. NCSH

The night that Peter said, "I know Him not." A Cock Crowing in a Poulterer's Shop. John Ferguson. BoAnP

The night the mother should have died,/The young son shall be born. Stratton Water. Anonymous. OxBB

The night their eyes burn two by two. Pondy Woods. Robert Penn Warren. MoAmPo

Night, Thunder, Lightning, Rain, and raging Wind,/To make a Storm had all their forces joyn'd. On a Sea-Storm Nigh the Coast. Richard Steere. SCAP

...Night to crawl/into folds and crevices,/haired cracks,/to stay. Tick Picking in the Quetico. Don Johnson. MAYP

Night to your voice belongs. Song for a Lyre. Louise Bogan. LiTA

Night, tragedy, the veiled, the end prefer? The Beautiful Negress. Ruth Pitter. MoVE

The night utter ripe unspeaking girls. La Guerre. Edward Estlin Cummings. MoAmPo

...Night was on the ridge/Of twilight, as the party crossed the bridge. Don Juan. George Gordon, Lord Byron. InPS

The night was opening/like a cotyledon. Walden in July. Donald Junkins. NYBP

The night was pain. The Night. Al-Khansa. BoWoP

The night was with you as you searched,/Without a hat, sawn-off binoculars. Horizon without Landscape. Tom Lowenstein. VWA

The night will be dark/Outside. Interlude. Amy Lowell. NMM

Night will be fading and moonlight dying. Dance on Pushback. James Still. GrPl

Night will be good; and Morning will be better. Convent Cemetery: Mount Carmel. Sister Mary St. Virginia. GoBC

Night will come my soul is ready Debout (excerpt). Tchicaya U Tam'si. PBA

...The night-wind veering, the smell/of the spilt wine drifted down hill from the house. Roan Stallion. Robinson Jeffers. BeLS; NAMP

A night wind woman/who burns/with every breath/she takes. Fire. Joy Harjo. TWSS

The nightfall a step on the path to/Thee. The End of Sorrow. Edmond Fleg. TrJP

—Nightfall of nations brilliant after war. Troop Train. Karl Shapiro. OxBA; WaaP; WaP

A nightingale in the sycamore. Go, Little Book. Robert Louis Stevenson. MoBrPo; PoRA

The nightingale's rapturous song is an ode that/ceases not. His Delight. Meilir ap Gwalchmai. LiTW

The nightingale sings. Spring. *Anonymous.* SUS

The nightingales, the nightingales! Bianca among the Nightingales. Elizabeth Barrett Browning. BrRo; GTBS-P

Nightingales with/Pearly tails. Christmas Ornaments. Valerie Worth. PCh

A nightlight turns its seashell back to the room. Parachute. Dwight Okita. BrSi

Nightlong at its tongs and bones. In the Round. Theodore Weiss. NMP

Nightly this repast go take,/Get to relief from thy brake. The Relief on Easter Eve. Thomas Pestel. CBEP; OxBoCh

Nightmare begins responsibility. Nightmare Begins Responsibility. Michael S. Harper. GeTw; HaCAP; LCAP; TAP

...Nights/Are kept smooth for dark promenades. Wandsworth Common. David Bromwich. PoA

"The nights are very damp!" The Mad Gardener's Song. Lewis (Charles Lutwidge Dodgson) Carroll. GoTF; TreFS

The nights come after me/low & polished like limousines. Industrial Size. Jeff Wright. APU

Nights in his corrugated harem he had so many lovers/it was nearly impossible to choose. The Man Who Owned Cars. Elliot Fried. GOYP

Nights of insult let you pass/Watched by every human love. Lullaby. W. H. Auden. CMoP; HAP; OAEL 1-2

Nights the mirror shines west/And directly receives the sun Master Canterel at Locus Solus. David Shapiro. ANYP

The nightwind storms and shivers through the reeds. Nocturne in G Minor. Karl Gustave Vollmoeller. AWP; LiTW

"Nikki,/isn't this counterrevolutionary...?" Seduction. Nikki Giovanni. NMM

Nikos loves you. Nikos Painting. Kenneth O. Hanson. FAZ

The nimble-footed rain doth rush! Before the Rain. Amelie Troubetzkoy. AA

The nimble piper and the strutting drummer/Putting the valley's herbivores to flight. Switzerland. Anthony Thwaite. OBTV

The Nimbleness of God. The Theology of Bongwi, the Baboon. Roy Campbell. PeSA

9. Bringer of woe; by whimsical etymological deriva-/tion from woe + man. Obs. The Dictionary Is an Historian. Judith McCombs. IHMS

Nine days old. Pease Porridge Hot. Mother Goose. OxNR; SoPo

A 9-lb. load to cart in and out of next year's bed. Waiting for the Doctor. Colette Inez. IHMS

Nine-o'clock/Bell! School-Bell. Eleanor Farjeon. BrR; SiSoSe

Nine pounds avoirdupois is added to my weight. Plantation Bitters. *Anonymous.* FaBoUs

The nine steps to the bottom of the sea. The Man Whom the Sea Kept Awake. Robert Bly. NePoEA

Nine, ten,/A good fat hen. One, Two, Buckle My Shoe. Mother Goose. SoPo; TiPo

Nine years have made you my master still. In a Copy of Browning. Bliss Carman. HBMV

1982 Employed as a salesman. Rap Sheet. Paul D. Shiplett. LFAC

Nineteen, twenty,/My stomach's empty. One, Two, Buckle My Shoe. *Anonymous.* HBV 1-2; HBVY

Ninety days on the county road, and the judge didn't even smile. Chain Gang Blues. *Anonymous.* WTO

Ninety-eight point six? Collapsars. Sandra McPherson. LCAP

Nip in the blossom all our hopes and thee. The Picture of Little T. C. in a Prospect of Flowers. Andrew Marvell. AnAnS 1; CBEP; ExPo; GTBS; HBV 1-2; JCP; LiTB; MeLP; MePo; NOBE; NoP; OAEL 1-2; OBEV; OBS; PPP; PrIm; SeCeV; SeCP; SeCV 1-2

Nip, Johnny Ringo. Who Goes Round My Pinfold Wall. *Anonymous.* GBP

Nipee off her nose! Song: "Singee songee sick a pence. (parody). *Anonymous.* BXAP

Nipped by winter/Stay in bed. Winter Days. Gareth Owen. OBCP

The nirds eat out one's hands! In the Churchyard. Eleanor Ross Taylor. UnPo

Nirvana! absorb us in your skies,/Annul us into thee. Buddha. Herman Melville. HeIP

Nirvana was their lovely happy gait! Nirvana. Ali Sedat Hilmi Torel. PeD

Nita! Juanita! Be my own fair bride. Juanita. Carolina Elizabeth Sarah Norton. FSW

An' niver spok' sin. Riddle: "Fatherless an' motherless." *Anonymous.* GBP

No ablative is ever absolute. Classroom in October. Elias Lieberman. GoYe

...No/Aches which are not yours. I too call myself I. An Introduction. Kamala Das. WPOW

No agony/as if/my mind had eaten death Poem by the Charles River. Robin Blaser. NeAP

No alien unthought breath corrupts/This decorously airless air. The Party. Margaret Avison. PoA

No angry hand shall rise to brush thy wings. To a Mosquito. William Cullen Bryant. AnNE

No answer, hand in hand, we cross the bridge. Over the Bridge. Li Kwang-T'ien. LiTW

No answer; this, at least, was as before. New Wine, Old Bottles. Colin Newbury. AnNZ

...No ark, though the sea/fall back from Ararat, can land/him. The Imbecile. Donald Finkel. NePoEA-2

No assassin's bullet. Stopped in Memphis. Steven Bauer. AMV-80

No Atoms casually together hurl'd/Could e'er produce so beautiful a world. What Is the World? John Dryden. TRV

No baby in the house! No Baby in the House. Clara Dolliver. HBV 1-2

No beast so hapless as a man. The Tigress. Ruth Pitter. HaMV

No beauty I can ever find/Can match the beauty of your mind. To My Mother. Louis Ginsberg. PoSC

No belly and no bowels,/Only consonants and vowels. Survey of Literature. John Crowe Ransom. FaBoCh; LiTA; LoGBV; MP; NLV; OBAL; TAP; TwCP; VGW

No belly,/no cry. The Starry Night. Anne Sexton. NMP; NoAm

No better a musician than the wren. The Merchant of Venice. William Shakespeare. PB

No better work can state- or church-man do. Aecclesiae et Reipub. William Strachey. OBTV

No bigger than a rat, with all dumb silence/In your little old woman hands. Bullfrog. Ted Hughes. NYBP; RFM

No birds sings/But notes of misery. Now the Earth, the Skies, the Air. *Anonymous.* EIL

No birth, no death, no time nor sun/In answer. North Labrador. Hart Crane. CMoP; FaBoMo; PoL

No blame lies with the rat for what it did. The Man from Changi. Graeme Hetherington. NOAV

No bomb that ever burst/Shatters the crystal spirit. The Italian Soldier Shook My Hand. George Orwell. OBWP

No bounds to human woe. Ode to Winter. Thomas Campbell. GTBS; GTBS-P

No bow is strung forever A Translation from.... Fred Levinson. AmPA

No brains, no sense–just gall. The Quarrelsome Trio. L. G. WBLP

No bread to eat! The Tailor. S, (Solomon Rapport) Ansky. TrJP

No! Bring them home! The Martyrs of the Maine. Rupert Hughes. PAH

No, but lovely in that way. Part of Plenty. Bernard Spencer. ErPo; GBL; LiTB; LiTL; LiTM; MoLP

No! by the Rood, we will not join your ballet. The Truant. Edwin John Pratt. NoAm; NOBC; NoP; OBCV

No captain, and the charts dead wrong. Open Country. Richard Hugo. LCAP; NPAW

No carrack ever bore to Thames or Tiber.   Social Science.   Thomas Edward Brown.   PeD

No cause, no cause.   King Lear.   William Shakespeare.   Prf

No chance could sever, nor the grave divide.   To the Earl of Warwick. Thomas Tickell.   CEP; HBV 1-2; NOEC; OBEC

No Charm will force unwilling Souls to love.   Sea Eclogue.   William Diaper. LoBV

No child is found sufficiently indiscreet/To whisper "No Majesty's inside." Epigram: An Old Story.   Howard Nemerov.   OBAL

No church on earth can be replaced/By "service"–on the air!   That Radio Religion.   William Ludlum.   WBLP

No clay-born lilies of the world/Could blow as free/As those wild orchids of the sea.   Sea Gulls.   Edwin John Pratt.   EtS

No concurrence of bone.   Landscapes.   Thomas Stearns Eliot.   BiP; LoGBV

...No constant moon/Sustains the hill's lost granite surge.   Watershed. Robert Penn Warren.   PoA

No country hath so short a night,/As England hath in summer.   To the Nightingale.   Sir John Davies.   OBSC; PBBP; TrGrPo

No creature comes to nourish her,/Wherefore she hunts and grieves.   The Huntress.   George Johnston.   WHW

...No cunning curse/Can mend that Night-peece: That is, Make her worse. Madam Gabrina, or the Ill-Favour'd Choice.   Henry, Bishop of Chichester King.   CavP

No curse, no care.   The Future.   Edward Rowland Sill.   AnNE; HBV 1-2

No dark can ever hide this dear loved land from me.   If I Were Old.   Will H. Ogilvie.   PoSH

No, de blues ain' nothing/But a good man feelin' blue.   De Blues Ain' Nothin'.   Anonymous.   AS; TrAS

No deals this time though/it's all/or nothing.   Coosaponakeesa (Mary Mathews Musgrove Bosomsworth)...   Rayna Green.   TWSS

...No death for you. You are/involved.   The Smiles of the Bathers.   Weldon Kees.   NaP

No death, no birth relieves or lunar pulses drown.   At Dead Low Water. Allen Curnow.   AnNZ

No deep ravine or dizzy fall/To scar and shock: but they were lovers.   The Last Ascent.   John Lehmann.   ChMP

...No defending/The cause against that murderous fire-engine.'   A Full and True Account of a Horrid and Barbarous Robbery.   John Byrom.   NOBL

NO DEPOSIT/NO RETURN.   A Charm for Our Time.   Eve Merriam. QQQ

No different then from them.   At the Trough.   Arthur Gregor.   FAZ

No, do not underrate the dachsie!   The Dachshund.   Edward Anthony. GDP

No; do the work you know, and tarry where you are.   Epistles.   Horace. OBVE

No dog, however mean or rude,/Is guilty of ingratitude.   The Dog. Anonymous.   WBLP

NO DOGS ALLOWED AT LARGE IN THIS PARK   Sunday in the Park. William Carlos Williams.   CrMA

No doom should make man's heaven become his hell.   Astrophel and Stella, LXXXVI.   Sir Philip Sidney.   AAS; SiPS

No doubt but the jury their minds they could tell.   Naomi Wise. Anonymous.   BaBo

No doubt he's at home in hell.   Where He Takes Tea with Cromwell. Anonymous.   DBV

No doubt in fable, as the unforgiven/Fire which Prometheus filch'd for us from heaven.   Don Juan.   George Gordon, Lord Byron.   OBRV; PoEL 1-5; PPP; ViBoPo

No dwelling in London, no biding in London, for Conscience and/Love. Simplicity's Song.   Robert Wilson.   CTC

No echo, and no shadow, and no reflection.   Morning.   Henry Reed. MoVE; NeBP

No empty space in life be found,/But one continued joy go round.   Let Some Great Joys Pretend to Find.   Thomas Shadwell.   OAEP

No enemy/But winter and rough weather.   As You Like It.   William Shakespeare.   ELP; ExPo; FaBoBe; FaFP; FiP; GN; GTBS; HBV 1-2; HeIP; HoPM; InPo; InPS; MCCG; NoP; OAEL 1-2; OAEP; OBSC; PAI; SeCeV; TiPo; TreFS; UnPo; ViBoPo; WHA; WiR

No, even if the harvest of our kissing/Were richer than the ripe gold ears of the corn.   If I Could Go On Kissing Your Honeyed Eyes.   Caius Valerius Catullus.   PeHV

No even/me.   Black Sketches, 9.   Don L. Lee.   NeAC

"No excuses, now"   Ode to Michael Goldberg's Birth and Other Births: "I don't remember."   Frank O'Hara.   NAs; NeAP

No face of all can ever seem the same.   The Cello.   Richard Watson Gilder. AA

No faintest sigh of story lisps the wave.   The Nameless Doon.   William Larminie.   AnIL; BlrV; IrPN; NBM; OxBI

No farmer, he turned in the dark and lay there, sighing.   Harvest.   Gene Shuford.   GoYe

No fault in womankind at all,/If they but slip, and never fall.   No Fault in Women.   Robert Herrick.   HBV 1-2

No fears for the brave; no fears for the/brave.   Nathan Hale.   Anonymous. PAH

No fetters in the Bay State–no slave upon our land!   Massachusetts to Virginia.   John Greenleaf Whittier.   AnNE

...No fierce/monstrous attack can find unsuffering parts.   Sonnet III: "O interminable desires, O futile hope."   Louise Labe.   BoWoP

"No, fool, this is not death."   This Is Not Death.   Humbert Wolfe. MoBrPo

No forebay, just water in a hard, thin line.   American Falls.   Greg Keeler. SM; WOLT

No friendly shade thy shade shall company!   Achtung.   Sappho.   CTC

No fruits, no flowers, no leaves, no birds,/November!   No!   Thomas Hood. FiBHP; HBV 1-2; NBM

No fuchulain!   The Pronunciation of Erse.   A. D. Hope.   PV

No garlic wreath can catch me,/nor your cold, cold cross.   When I Was Nine.   Raymond F. Roseliep.   FAZ

No gazer in the crystal ball can see/The future as we see the now and here. Here and Now.   Catherine Cater.   AmNP; PoNe

No generation was so gay as the lost.   For the Lost Generation.   Galway Kinnell.   NePoAm; PPON

No ghost ever had, immured in his hall.   Oh young men oh young comrades. Stephen Spender.   NAMP

No Gift shall bribe it, and no Pray'r persuade.   The Iliad.   Homer.   OBVE

No girl had loved unless she chose!   Summer Lightning.   Thomas Sturge Moore.   BrPo; SyP

No god shall crown the board, nor goddess bless the bed.   Eclogues.   Virgil (Publius Vergilius Maro).   AWP

No goddess of her bed'   Five Poems about Poetry (excerpt).   George Oppen. NNaP

No good to me, no good to me.   What the Earth Asked Me.   James Wright. NYBP

No government appointed him.   An Appointment.   William Butler Yeats. AnEnPo

No grace to me from the there may procede,/As but rewarded deth for to be my mede.   Resound My Voyse, Ye Wodes That Here Me Plain.   Sir Thomas Wyatt.   AAS; FCP; SiPS

No greater excellence the sun encloses.   One of the Regiment.   Douglas Le Pan.   CaP

No hand will reach into the obscure depth/to argue with me over your handful of bones.   Death Sonnet I.   Gabriela (Lucila Godoy Alcayaga) Mistral. BoWoP

No harm in kisses, I know.   Tom Jones's Plum Tree (The Juniper Tree). Anonymous.   AmFP

No hawk or hickory to true my run.   O.   Richard Wilbur.   LiTA; MoPo

No, he repeated, I never ordered/Jam, God damn you, leave me alone.   Il Piccolo Rifiuto.   Louis MacNeice.   CMoP

No heat like science and poetry when they kiss.   The Observatory Ode. John Frederick Nims.   SUW

No,–heaven forfend!–I would not kill thy soul.   Othello.   William Shakespeare.   EBEV

No home is broken by an unsaid word!   The Muscovy Drake.   E. A. S. Lesoro.   PeSA

No hopeful answer came–a Price more rare/Already shed in vain.   Judaism. John Henry, Cardinal Newman.   ACP

No hospital beds, but a lifting of metal wings.   Memorial.   Robert Pinsky. HaCAP; SM

No hush can drown a word once spoken.   Archaic Apollo.   William Plomer. ChMP

No, I admit–not necessarily of heaven...   Because Going Nowhere Takes a Long Time.   Kenneth Patchen.   NaP

No, I am not anything that is anything I am not.   I, Too, Know What I Am Not.   Bob Kaufman.   NBP

No? I could if I had time.   Pennsylvania Places.   Thomas Augustin Daly. OBAL

"No, I'm a poet," I said. "Fuck me again."   A Sailor at Midnight.   E. N. Sargent.   NMM

No, I really don't care for a drink.   Though You Serve Richest Wines. Martial (Marcus Valerius Martialis).   DBV

"No," I said. No.   A New Story.   Simon J. Ortiz.   STE

No–I warrant she'll like me the better.   My Wishes.   Patrick Healy.   OnYI

No ill can be felt but pain,/And that happy men disdain.   Whether Men Do Laugh or Weep.   Thomas Campion.   EnRePo; NCEP

No ill intent?   Stupidity.   Mary Elizabeth ("E") Fullerton.   CBAP

No imagination to forestall woe.   Charleston in the 1860s.   Adrienne Rich. CoAP

No instinct has survived in her/Older than those her grandmother/Told her would fit her station.   Hugh Selwyn Mauberley, XI.   Ezra Pound. CoBMV; NOBA

...No/insurance, no brakes/the whole way!   Untitled.   Herman Nibbelink. AMV-80

...No invasion is worth/such tears and foolishness.   The War of the Worlds.
  Vern Rutsala.   Psk

...No irony/Seeps through to move the pity of her shade.   Charlotte Corday.
  Charles Tomlinson.   OxBC

No is the genius of the world.   No.   E. M. Schorb.   AMV-80

No/It's a gift I made her   Love.   Patrick Lane.   NeAC

No, it's Bill, my friend.   Lost in a Blizzard.   Arthur W. Monroe.   PoOW

No it's when still others are boiling delicate things,/keeping up that process till
  the end.   37th Dance–Banding–22 March 1964.   Jackson MacLow.   CoPo

No Joan ivy, no Zacheus tree,/Were to the world so great a losse as he.
  Christs Sleeping Friends.   Robert Southwell.   AnAnS 1

No joy-dazzled shepherds crowd.   Death Swoops.   Kenneth Pitchford.
  CoPo

No joy to this!...   Wonder.   Thomas Traherne.   CH

No joys are above/The pleasures of love.   How Happy the Lover.   John
  Dryden.   LoBV; ViBoPo

No. Just say/Helloworm!   Glowworm.   David McCord.   NTCP

No key-hole will be fairy-proof,/When green leaves come again.   Oh! Where
  Do Fairies Hide Their Heads?   Thomas Haynes Bayly.   HBV 1-2; HBVY

No kind of balm. You look, though. Let me know.   Go Ahead; Goodbye;
  Good Luck; and Watch Out.   William Bronk.   GP

No King shall owne my verses for his Tombe.   An Ode: "Awake, faire Muse;
  for I intend."   William Browne.   OBS

No kings be crown'd but they some covenants make.   Astrophel and Stella,
  LXIX.   Sir Philip Sidney.   AAS; SiPS; TrGrPo

No lady is so fair as mine.   Ballade of My Lady's Beauty.   Joyce Kilmer.
  HBV 1-2

...No laughters/of sons, no wife from my bone, can drown your voice.
  Waiting for Lilith.   Jascha Kessler.   VWA

No legacy of sin annuls/Heredity from God.   Heredity.   Lydia Avery
  Coonley Ward.   HBV 1-2

No Les/No More.   At Boot Hill in Tombstone, Arizona.   Anonymous.
  ShM

No less true of course, no matter/how you look at it.   Something to Eat.
  Tom Veitch.   ANYP

...No life without our dying.   1944–On the Invasion Coast.   Jack Beeching.
  WaP

No light, being themselves obscure.   The Sensitive Plant.   Percy Bysshe
  Shelley.   EnRP; ERoP 1-2; GoTL; OAEL 1-2

No lip has touched it since his and mine/In turns therefrom sipped lovers'
  wine.   Under the Waterfall.   Thomas Hardy.   BoLoP; CTC; LiTB

No little doors at twilight/We may not enter in.   The New Freedom.   Olive
  Dargan.   HBMV

No, Little Margaret's in her cold black coffin/With her pale face to the wall.
  Lady Margaret.   Anonymous.   FSW

No, live up to thy mighty Mind;/And be the Mistress of Mankind.   Upon His
  Leaving His Mistress.   John Wilmot, Earl of Rochester.   EnLoPo; GBL;
  TEP; ViBoPo

No living man in any western room /But sits at amber sunset round a tomb.
  This Amber Sunstream.   Mark Van Doren.   GoYe; LiTA; MoPo; MoVE

No longer caring if we drift or go straight.   After Drinking All Night with a
  Friend...   Robert Bly.   NaP

No longer do I listen for the scrape of a keel/On the blank stones of the
  landing.   The Colossus.   Sylvia Plath.   CAPP; FaBoWP; HaCAP; LiTM;
  MP; NePoEA-2; NoAm; NOBA; NoP; TAP

No longer frightened because they don't care   Survivor.   Judy Dothard
  Simmons.   CNA

No longer I,/But, We!   Communion.   P. M. Snider.   PoToHe

No longer quite sure of his gender.   Limerick: "A young Harvard man, sweet
  and tender."   Anonymous.   PeHV

No longer the keeper/of what he was.   November Twenty-Sixth Nineteen
  Hundred and Sixty-Three.   Wendell Berry.   LiTM

No looks proceed/From those fair eyes but to me wonder breed.   Love's
  Insight.   Anonymous.   GTBS

No, Lord: Thou wilt accept a broken heart.   On Off'rings.   Francis Quarles.
  FaBoEE

...No loud/Voice (though innocently loud).   Doctor Faustus.   Geoffrey Hill.
  NMP

No louder now than falling leaves.   Hillcrest.   Edwin Arlington Robinson.
  AP; CoBMV; MAmP; MoAB; OxBA; PPoe

"No love," quoth he, "but vanity, sets love a task like that."   The Glove and
  the Lions.   [James Henry] Leigh Hunt.   BeLS; GN; GoTF; HBV 1-2;
  HBVY; MaC; TreF; WBLP

No love sweet but honesty.   Sitting by a River Side.   Robert Greene.   TEP

No love toward others in that bosom sits/That on himself such murd'rous
  shame commits.   Sonnets, IX: "Is it for fear to wet a widow's eye."
  William Shakespeare.   MasP

No lover peaceful while the rival weeps.   Old Age.   Anonymous.   WTO

No lover rests but that his rival weeps.   Love Is Bitter.   Anonymous.   PeSA

No maiden was by her side!   The Castle by the Sea.   Ludwig Uhland.
  AWP

No man alive nor I/Of double death can die.   At last withdraw your cruelty.
  Sir Thomas Wyatt.   FCP; SiPS

...No man can ever be/The friend of that poor queen.   Deirdre.   James
  Stephens.   AWP; CMoP; GTBS; HBMV; NoAm; OBMV; PG; PoRA;
  ViBoPo

No man can print a kiss; lines may deceive.   Caelica, XXII.   Fulke, Lord
  Brooke Greville.   AtBAP; EG; EnRePo; FCP; HAP

No man can read the time in me or you.   Cat's Eyes.   Francis Scarfe.
  PCat

No man could think base thoughts who looked on/her.   Sonnet: He Will
  Praise His Lady.   Guido Guinicelli.   AWP

...no man is our master,/nor can any ever be, at any time in time to come.
  To My Son Parker, Asleep in the Next Room.   Bob Kaufman.   PoBA;
  TwCP; VGW

No man shall mock me after this my day.   I Do Not Look for Love That Is
  a Dream.   Christina Georgina Rossetti.   GBL

No man will I remember. It is done.   Regret and Refusal.   Anonymous.
  WTO

No Marchioness, but now a Queen.   An Epitaph on the Marchioness of
  Winchester.   John Milton.   CavP; OBS

No mark of her late time as dame in her dwelling, whereby/I may picture her
  there.   Thoughts of Phena.   Thomas Hardy.   NOBV; NoP; OxBTC

No matter by what hand or trick.   Sonnet: "Of thee (kind boy) I ask no red
  and white."   Sir John Suckling.   MeLP; MePo; OxBoLi

No matter how, if only sin/Die out in me.   One Thing I of the Lord Desire.
  Anonymous.   STF

No matter how little it is.   The Mountain That Got Little.   William
  Stafford.   FAZ

No matter how much they consume.   To a Baked Fish.   Carolyn Wells.
  FiBHP

No matter how old I get,/She'll always be older.   Hard Lines.   Tom
  Robinson.   BiCB

"No matter; I'll die like a Briton."   Limerick: "There was a young man who
  was bitten."   Walter Parke.   LiBL; NA

No matter what birth, or what race, or what creed.   At Fredericksburg.
  John Boyle O'Reilly.   MC; PAH

No matter what heavy/traffic was coming down/on them   Untitled I.
  Ishmael Reed.   CNA

No matter what his contract was,/HE'D DO HIS LEVEL BEST.   He Done
  His Level Best.   Mark (Samuel Langhorne Clemens) Twain.   BPAW

No matter what I might say/she is not bored.   The Design.   Clarence Major.
  PoBA

No matter what pain that brings you.   My True Love Makes Me Happy.
  Beatrice de Dia.   WPOW

No matter what they style us, it's all about the same,/For all are talking of
  Utah.   Marching to Utah.   Anonymous.   AmFP

No mayde, nor honour, sure noe honesty.   On a Maide of Honour Seene by a
  Schollar in Sommerset Garden.   Thomas Randolph.   JCP; MePo

No memory/of shade,/of leaf,/no pollen.   Gathered at the River.   Denise
  Levertov.   SV

No monarch more blest than the man of the mill.   The Miller.   John
  Cunningham.   CEP; OBEC

No Money in Art!   No Money in Art.   Jim Gustafson.   APU

No moral to this tale has further been found out.   The Portraits.   Anna
  Maria Lenngren.   WPOW

No more a servant, nor yet a child.   Doris: A Pastoral.   Arthur Joseph
  Munby.   HBV 1-2

No more be tears in moon or mist/For thee, sweet sentimentalist.   What
  Counsel Has the Hooded Moon.   James Joyce.   MOON; OnYI; OxBI

–No more begrudge their freedom than his tears.   Mr. Whittier.   Winfield
  Townley Scott.   CrMA; VGW

No more beneath my head will lie.   On the Death of His Wife.
  Muireadhach Albanach O Dalaigh.   BIrV; CIP

No more change or death, no more/Salt sea-shore.   Luscious and Sorrowful.
  Christina Georgina Rossetti.   PoEL 1-5; SeCePo

...No more changed in fact in ten/thousand years than the beaks of eagles.
  The Beaks of Eagles.   Robinson Jeffers.   NOBA

No more, dear love, for at a touch I yield;/Ask me no more.   The Princess.
  Alfred, Lord Tennyson.   OAEP; PoEL 1-5; TrGrPo; UnTE

No more death.   Incanto.   Stan Rice.   NPGG

No more destructive flame but light.   No More Destructive Flame.   Francis
  X. Connolly.   ISi

No more distressed,/Shalt thou find rest.   Some Day, Some Day.   Cristobal
  de Castillejo.   AWP

No more driver's lash for me,/Many thousand gone.   No More Auction
  Block.   Anonymous.   BPo

No more dying   Ode to Joy.   Frank O'Hara.   NeAP; PPP

No more for sin's dark stain the debt of death to pay.   The Garden.   Jones
  Very.   AP; MAmP; OxBA; TAP

No more green water and blue hills.   Regretful Thoughts, I.   Yu Hsuan-chi.
  BoWoP

No more have I the power to enforce/Thy constancy, for lust will have its course. To Barba. Edward May. FaBoEE

No more he comes, who this way came and went. London Poets. Amy Levy. OBVV

No more I watch the last snows fade/On a dark hill above Glen Doll. Foxgloves and Snow. Marion Angus. PoSH

No more, mortal death,/Shalt thou deceive me. Farewell for a While. Elizabeth Daryush. QFR

No more, no more, don't go to sea no more. Off to Sea Once More. *Anonymous.* OBSS

No more, no more green land for you. When De Whale Get Strike. *Anonymous.* OuSiCo

No more no more no more. On Clark Street in Chicago. George Keithley. NPGG

No more–O never more! A Lament. Percy Bysshe Shelley. AtBAP; EG; EnLi 1-2; GTBS-P; NOBE; OBRV; WHA

No More! O solemn sound: This night I may/Be struck by Death, and never see the day. Meditations for August 1, 1666. Philip Pain. SCAP

No more of bangle, scarf or feather. The Power of Silence. William Henry Davies. BrPo

...No more/Shall deprive honest workmen of bread. General Ludd's Triumph. *Anonymous.* OBET

No more shall wars thy land divide,/Wert thou as good as great. Written in Ireland. Mary Alcock. NOEC; OBTV

No more than a nod/or a leaning away. David in April. Betty Booker. PPJ

No more than a thumbprint/on the edge of the sky Moon. Frances Horovitz. BrRo

No more than bluets, blown when April takes/Millions of them to make one meadow blue. Sonnets. Muna Lee. HBMV

No more than can be, and Thy Will Be Done. Old Man of Tennessee. John Hay. NePoAm-2

No more than money that's called in. Ballade of the Fair Helm-Maker. Francois Villon. UnTE

No more than the father knows of the child, or the sailor of/chartless isles. Sailor, What of the Isles? Edith Sitwell. ChMP

No more than those, that love do feign,/Give judgement of true lovers' pain. The Shipmen. William Hunnis. OBSC

No more the singer, but the song. The Makers. Nan McDonald. ACV

No more the trifles of my care. To Clio. From Rome. John Dyer. NOEC

No more to feel man's wrath or dread his chain. The Fugitive Slaves. Jones Very. AP; TAP

No more to visit vale or shade,/Some barbarous virgin's captive made. Ode: To the Nightingale. Joseph Warton. PBBP

No more we'll go a-roving on the banks of the Nile.' The Banks of the Nile. *Anonymous.* OBET

No more we'll have to sigh and sob beneath the willow tree. The Lady of the Lake. *Anonymous.* ShS

No more will I roam but contented stay at home/With a smiling and a charming little wife. A Shantyman's Life (II). *Anonymous.* AmFP; ShS

No more will make mankind subdue/The work of devastation. Song: "Whilst landmen wander, though controlled." *Anonymous.* OBSS

No more with wonted humour gay,/But pallid, cheerless, and forlorn. Hadrian's Address to His Soul When Dying. Emperor (Publius Aelius Hadrianus) Hadrian. OBVE

No mortal troth dare I trust home/Except He help that sits above. Moon-Like Is All Other Love. *Anonymous.* NOCV

No mother has a sweeter one! Bartholomew. Norman Gale. BiCB; HBV 1-2; HBVY

No murmuring streams her grief assuage. The Mother. Sara Coleridge. OBVV

No music in me to fit that great life-in-flood awakening. Dawns I Have Seen. Ivor Gurney. FaBoPP

No music like a bell. On the Clerk of a Country Parish. William Shenstone. FaBoEE

"No, my lad, I cannot come." Say, Lad, Have You Things to Do? Alfred Edward Housman. VLP

No name can fit him, therefore, let him be/The grumbling ghost of old Presbytery. The Tragi-Comedy of Titus Oates. *Anonymous.* APAS

No nearer home. Rondeau in Wartime. James Bertram. AnNZ

"No need," he said. Uncle Death. Walter Clark. NCSH

...No need to fear/the proud sea-coursing warrior. The Vikings. *Anonymous.* BIrV

No need to leave home,/sir, so suspicious. Sir, So Suspicious. *Anonymous.* NOBI

No need to weep Lament. Joseph Stroud. NPGG

No net, no ball, no game–/and still playing/to win. The Old Pro's Lament. Paul Petrie. LiSp; TAP

No New World to mankind remains!' Clarel. Herman Melville. OxBA

"No, next!" The Man of O. Marina Rivera. FIA

No night would be too dark, no death too long. Bird at Night. Marion Ethel Hamilton. GoYe

No, no! Desire both lives and dies/A thousand times a day. Of the Birth and Bringing Up of Desire. Edward, Earl of Oxford De Vere. FaBoEE; OBSC

No, no, no, no, my Dear, let be. Only Joy! Now Here You Are. Sir Philip Sidney. EIL; EnRePo; GBL; HAP; InvP; UnTE

No no? No such thing as no. Mexico City Blues. Jack Kerouac. NeAP

"No, no," said the Doc, "that's Teutonic." Limerick: "A man to whom illness was chronic." *Anonymous.* LiBL

...No, no, thy fair smooth/haunches. The Author to His Wife, of a Woman's Eloquence. Sir John (1561-1612) Harington. BoLoP; ErPo

No! nor fetter'd Love from dying/In the knot there's no untying. Freedom and Love. Thomas Campbell. BSV; GTBS-P

"No, not at first." From Ancient Fangs. Peter Viereck. MiAP

No, not even in death. Elegy. John Hall Wheelock. NYBP

No, not if she speaks to me.' Post Mortem. Arthur Joseph Munby. NOBV

No, not one shift–to rid me of this shame. Prometheus Bound. Aeschylus. LiTW

No, not the bulldozer. The Bulldozer. Robert Francis. PPJ

No, not the house–the lovely maid/Who lives there quiet and serene. I Love the Woods. Leib Neidus. VWA

...No. Not this pig. Animals Are Passing from Our Lives. Philip Levine. CoAP; NoAm; NOBA; SM; TAP; TW

No! Once again the harsh, the ugly city. The Tired Worker. Claude McKay. BANP; BPo

No one/bears witness for the/witness. Ash-Glory. Paul Celan. VWA

No one believes the booming old bore. With What Conviction the Young Man Spoke. W. H. Auden. PV

No one but him. Swimmer in the Rain. Robert Wallace. FiCP; LiSp

No one but him can see the good he's done. Trying. Leonard Nathan. Str

No one but Night, with tears on her dark face,/Watches beside me in this windy place. Fatal Interview. Edna St. Vincent Millay. HAP

No one can drown in it. Skycoast. Samuel Hazo. GrPl

No one can picture the worst. Reflexes. Marvin Bell. Str

No one can sleep in the arms of an enemy, however charming. The Lovesleep. Gavin Ewart. OxBC

No one comes to visit us for a week. In a Mountain Cabin in Norway. Robert Bly. RFM

No one could sum them up. Brightness. Heather McHugh. GeTw

No one ever finds them all. Happiness. Priscilla Leonard. BLPA; PoToHe

No one ever know–/Riding in the Park. Driving in the Park. *Anonymous.* OxBoLi

No one ever there when you need them. A Man All Grown Up Is Supposed To. Terry Stokes. AmPA

No one fears me/except Error,/who is everywhere. Knowledge. Nina Cassian. BoWoP

(No one feels half of what we know). Pick a Fern, Pick a Fern, Ferns Are High. *Anonymous.* OBVE

No one felt a tug. The Last Resort. Robert Willson. FAZ

No one guesses you are weak. Pick a Quarrel, Go to War. W. H. Auden. PV

No one has ever loved but you and I. The Ragged Wood. William Butler Yeats. BoC; GBL

No one has left; no one returns. Stepping Outside. Tess Gallagher. AmPA

No one has power to alter these heavenly lights... Song of Nexahualcoyotl. *Anonymous.* DL

...No one hears them among the talk and laughter. Wolves. Louis MacNeice. NoAm; OxBTC

No one is above the law. A Barbed Wire Fence Meditates upon the Goldfinch. Don McKay. NOBC

No one is drowning. Paul Klee. John Haines. LCAP

No one knows our name until our last breath goes out. The Name. *Anonymous.* NU

No one knows the rhyme. How Many Seconds in a Minute? Christina Georgina Rossetti. SiSoSe

No one knows why he came, or why he turned away, and did not climb the hill. Snowbanks North of the House. Robert Bly. LCAP

No one lays flowers/on the grave/of water,/for it is not/here,/it is/gone. Mourning Pablo Neruda. Robert Bly. LCAP

...No one left over/to eat up all the weird abundance. The Black Art. Anne Sexton. PoA

No one nearby, no wood on the way. A Cabin in Minnesota. Marvin Bell. HoPM

No one, no one at all, reveals. Open to Visitors. E. V. Milner. ELU

"No One, No One, No One." People of the South Wind. William Stafford. NNaP

No one, not even you. Lullaby. Robert Hillyer. DuDa; LOW

No one remembers us. Cradle Song for Miriam. Louis MacNeice. NAs

No one's dancing here tonight—wouldn't you know it. The Dance. Daniel Halpern. MAYP

...No one/says anything much. No one leaves anyone. Fidelities. Jean Valentine. NYP

No one shall now unwrite or right their time. Retreat. Amy Bushnell. AMV-80

No one sheds a tear. Jungle. Mary Carter Smith. PoNe

No one speaks a word. Off from Swing Shift. Garrett Kaoru Hongo. MAYP

No one that visited this fiery hive/Ever alive/Came out but me—I, I alone, survive. The Aztec City. Eugene Fitch Ware. AA; HBV 1-2

An' no one there to see! The Fairy Lough. Moira O'Neill. OBVV

No one to comfort my desolate heart. The Seafarer (excerpt). *Anonymous.* PBBP

...No one to drive the car To Elsie. William Carlos Williams. NOBA

No-one to touch. Story from Another World. Paul Petrie. AMV-81

No one was there to tell us where to leave the signs. Peace Walk. William Stafford. Psk

No one/will believe this/of vast import to the nation. Pastoral. William Carlos Williams. AmPP; OxBA

No-one will call me insane-/but God's great sibyl. The Hebrew Sibyl. Ruth Fainlight. VWA

No one will herald our return. While Waiting for Kohoutek. Christopher Erb. SOTS

No one will see,/no one will hear/anything. I Will Go Away. Zvi Shargal. VWA

No-one yet wove more sweetly than you for me. The Shirt. Jon Silkin. NoAm

No other heaven shall I ask than these! Canto Espiritual. Juan Maragall. CAW

No other high redeeming name wherein we must be saved. The Glorious Name. Amos R. Wells. BePJ

No other land/Nor East nor West/Attracts me so–/My Africa. My Africa. Michael Dei-Anang. PBA

No other name but thine. Olney Hymns. William Cowper. CEP

No other new years gift/Doth he require from us. On the Circumsision: New Years Day. Luke Wadding. NOBI

No other rock/but this to/build upon. The Faith Came First. Sydney Carter. EBCP

No other service would I ask/Than this my blessed, blessed task. The Blessed Task. Harriet McEwen Kimball. BePJ

No outward harm need to be sough,/Where en'mies be within so near. That Each Thing Is Hurt of Itself. *Anonymous.* EiL

No palace too great, no cottage too small. Christmas Everywhere. Phillips Brooks. BLRP; FaFP; OHFP; WBLP

No part besides must of thyself be known,/But by the topaz, opal, chalcedon. To Julia. Robert Herrick. CaPo

No part of them can have now with me here? Sonnet: "What doth it serve to see sun's burning face." William, of Hawthornden Drummond. EiL

–No past is mine, no future: look at me! Orpheus and Eurydice. Robert Browning. CTC

No penny, no Pater Noster.' The Peter-Penny. Robert Herrick. CaPo

...No permanent bond/between the passive watchers & moonglow. Apollo 8. John Berryman. MOON

No pity for you and for me no blame! A Storm of Love. Hilary Corke. NYBP

No place to go. The Gulf. Denise Levertov. NNaP

No place to go, no reason to remain. Coming to This. Mark Strand. HaCAP

No planet in your sunken house. Lady Day. Padraic Fallon. NeIP

No pleasure could be tasted/If flowery sommer always lasted. Why Are Our Summer Sports So Brittle? *Anonymous.* NCEP

No pois'nous tyrant on thy ground shall live. Britannia and Raleigh. John Ayloffe. APAS

No portion, but a being. Ortus. Ezra Pound. LiTA; NePA

No power from you my heart can ever wean. God and the Soul. John Lancaster Spalding. AA

No prick will bore your flabby arse again! To Bellinus. *Anonymous.* PeHV

No primal star is half so bright. Perspective. Coventry Patmore. FaBoEE; GBL

..."No problem. Everything touches everything." Ballade of the Back Road. Ron Block. SM

No question is ever settled/Until it is settled right. An Inspiration. Ella Wheeler Wilcox. WGRP

No rain, no crop, no feed, no faith, only/wind. The Wind of Our Enemy (excerpt). Anne Marriott. CaP

No reason aske of Love. O Love, How Strangely Sweet. John Marston. AtBAP

No reason at all, he declares, just a fine/Jersey bull, such a beautiful bull, goddamn! Valley Blood. Barry Sternlieb. SM

No refuge from the elements, no fixed address. Fire. William Carpenter. Psk

No remedy for our split mind. No Remedy. Drummond Allison. OxBTC

"No report (save that hell is dark, and we have just been there). The Patrol. J. H. Knight-Adkin. MCCG

No resurrection in the minds of men. Death. Thomas Hood. EG; OBEV

No rhyme can be said./where reason has fled. Poem from the Empire State. June Jordan. BPo

No rhythm. No melody./No words. Noh Play. Jim Brodey. APU

"No Right! No Wrong! All's perfect, evermore." The Planster's Vision. Sir John Betjeman. PoPl

No right ones either. Fugue. Kathleen Spivack. AMV-80

No road in or out. Fishing in Air. Lorna Crozier. CaPN

No room for chains. The Thousand and One Nights: The Beautiful Boy. *Anonymous.* LiTW

No rose has been original. Originality. Thomas Bailey Aldrich. AnNE

No rust corrodes,/What Pain has forged. Blacksmith Pain. Otto Julius Bierbaum. AWP

No sad relation/Can melt our frozen hearts into compassion,/Into compassion. Oh, Who Regards. *Anonymous.* EiL

No sadder smile/to reflect sorrow,/can dissolve no further. Inertia. Vivienne Finch. BrRo

No sadder sound salutes you than the clear,/Wild laughter of the loon. Seaward. Celia Thaxter. AA

No saddle yaps, I know, could fill/The noble boots of Braggin' Bill. Braggin' Bill's Fortytude. C. Wiles Hallock. BPAW

"No," said Mother. Social Studies. Mary Neville. PoL

"No," said the little girl, "no, no, no, no, no." Only One. Ralph Burns. PoDr

No savior,/rises still to fill/our vacant eyes. The Charge. Jay Wright. FB

No,/says the closing door. Bonner's Ferry Beggar. Duane Clark. AMV-81

...No secular wall will safely stand. Vespers. W. H. Auden. FaBoMo

No see before/come down on him. The Man. Robert Creeley. OBAL

No–seven young icicles taking leave/on their eave. Mistakable Identity. Elaine V. Emans. AMV-80

No shade on the golden ground. Aria. Rolfe Humphries. NYBP

No shame-faced outcast ever sank so deep/But yet might rise and be again a man! Opportunity. William Malone. HBV 1-2

No shameful price for peaceful years/Shall ever part this heritage. Our Heritage. Joseph Mary Plunkett. OnYI

No sights of despair for to-day. Engine Failure. Timothy Corsellis. WaP

No sin so great, but Christ's dear love shall more prevail. The Debate of the Body and the Soul. *Anonymous.* MeEV

"No, sir! In thee!" To Hear an Oriole Sing. Emily Dickinson. AnFE; APA; MAmP; PB; PoEL 1-5; UnS

No, Sir! we'll to the Mitre: Frank! my wig. Doctor Major. Lionel Pigot Johnson. BrPo

No sleep so sweet as thine, no rest so sure. A Good Night. Francis Quarles. OBS; TrGrPo

No slight news out of Niall's people. A Poem in Praise of Colum Cille. Dallan Forgaill. NOBI

No soil, nor token of the tomb's disgrace! On Some Humming-Birds in a Glass Case. Charles Tennyson Turner. FM

No soldier could sniff it without having an erection. A Yankee View. *Anonymous.* OBAL

No! Something more is needed for a home. Home. *Anonymous.* HBV 1-2

...No son, Big Novelist said/it's lonely up here A Morning to Remember; or, E. Pluribus Unum. Edward Dorn. NoAm

No sound is dissonant which tells of Life. This Lime-Tree Bower My Prison. Samuel Taylor Coleridge. CBEP; ERoP 1-2; FaBoPP; HeIP; LoBV; NIP; PoEL 1-5

No sound,/no/grove. Honestly I wish I were dead! Sappho. BoWoP

No spot is so dear to my childhood/As the little brown church in the vale. Little Brown Church in the Vale. William S. Pitts. TreFT

No spotless white on this earth– The Sleepwalker. Nelly Sachs. BoWoP; NYBP

No square poet's job. Haiku: "Making jazz swing in." Etheridge Knight. NeAC; SM; TAP

No stab the soul can kill. The Lie. Sir Walter Ralegh. AAS; AtBAP; CBEP; CTC; EBEV; ExPo; FaBoPV; FCP; ForPo; HAP; HBV 1-2; InvP; LiTB; MasP; NOBE; NoP; OAEP; OBSC; PoEL 1-5; PPoe; PPON; QFR; SCV; SeCeV; SiPS; TEP; TreFT; TrGrPo; ViBoPo

–No Stars shall be/In that Heaven but such as Thee. Home. Joseph Beaumont. GoTL

No straddler of winged horses, no budding centaur,/But a man biting the dust. The Trail Horse. David Wagoner. PH

No such lovely flowers as grow/In the South! Fanny. Anne Reeve Aldrich. HBV 1-2

No sudden weariness that thou art young? Written at Florence. Wilfrid Scawen Blunt. OBVV

No sunbeams rest on a prairie grave. The Lone Prairie. *Anonymous.* ViBoFo

No, sweet Mrs. Chloris–pray excuse me for that. A Solitary Canto to Chloris the Disdainful. John Smith. NOEC

No syllable that may be said or sung./Close, mortal eyes. Close, Mortal Eyes. Ruth Pitter. BoC

No talisman, tongue-sinew, signet-ring? Nothing? Lost Explorer. Edmund Pennant. GoYe

...No tapers here/Were lit but for the spirit's eye and ear. San Marco Museum, Florence. Sister Maris Stella. GoBC

No tempests of commotion shall disquiet/The calmes of my composure. The Broken Heart. John Ford. PoEL 1-5

No tenderer creature/Beneath the sky. Ladybird. Clive Sansom. GrPl

No the doolfu' that dreeps his head. Larikie, Larikie, Lee! *Anonymous.* PBBP

No theory that does not grow sick/at the odor escaping. No Theory. David Ignatow. NNaP

No, there's just your cruelty circling/my head like a bright stinking halo. Lady of Miracles. Nina Cassian. WPOW

...No, there's no risk/Of damage. They pack the cuckoo separately. Santa Claus in a Department Store. Christopher Hassall. OxBTC

No, they are moving. Open and Closed Space. Tomas Transtromer. EAS

No, they do not forget me so Awee'. Nia Francisco. STE

No, they might not be there at all/But that one sees the flames go out. Lost. Millen Brand. NYBP

No thief will ever steal thereof, God wot. Sonnet: He Jests Concerning His Poverty. Bartolomeo di Sant' Angelo. AWP

No thine, no mine, may other call,/Now all is one, and one is all. No Love, to Love of Man and Wife. Richard Eedes. InvP

No, things don't count till you're really old–/A witch told Jeremy. He's not told! Jeremy's Secrets. Barbara Euphan Todd. BiCB

No, this song ain't nothin'/But a poor man singin' the blues. Poor Man Blues. *Anonymous.* FSW

...No thought but of the strong/Sea, whence their food, their crisp hair, and their song. On the South Coast of Cornwall. John Gray. NOBV

No thought can think, nor tongue of mortal tell. Love's Labour's Lost. William Shakespeare. EIL; InvP

No thought of them, save in a lower room/To leave a light for them when they should come. The Insusceptibles. Adrienne Rich. ConAP; HeIP; SM

No ticket for the body to travel on. The Traveler. David Bottoms. AMV-80

No time for any–/thing but his painting. Pictures from Brueghel. William Carlos Williams. LCAP

No time is lost–/Wait on! Wait On! *Anonymous.* STF

No touch that brings such perfect peace as Mother's hands. Mother's Hands. W. Dayton Wedgefarth. PoToHe

No tree, but in it/A cooing cushat. Or Wren or Linnet. Samuel Taylor Coleridge. PBBP

No tribute's laid on Castles in the Air. What Is't to Us? Charles Churchill. SeCePo

No triste no man to his wele, the wheel it turneth so. Snatches: "The lovedy Fortune is bothe frend and fo." *Anonymous.* OxBM

No true Malayan maid is she,/But just an arrant little cheat. A Little Cheat! *Anonymous.* WTO

No use...No use... No Use. W. D. Snodgrass. BoLoP

No vale kissed by laughing waters,/Can be lovely as Ouray. Rivers of the West. Sunset Joe". PoOW

No victory for glutton such as you. The Song of Roland, CUV. *Anonymous.* WaaP

No victory, no grace, no sprig of laurel. Basic Communication. Thomas Hornsby Ferril. NePoAm-2

No voice availeth/To call back these. Song: "Love, Love today, my dear." Charlotte Mew. MoBrPo

No voice can answer from the dead again. The Gulistan. Muslih-ud-Din Sa'di. AWP; LiTW

"No" waits to be said. Pause between Clock Ticks. James Hearst. AMV-81

No want of conscience hold it that I call/Her "love" for whose dear love I rise and fall. Sonnets, CLI: "Love is too young to know what conscience is." William Shakespeare. BiP; CBEP; EBEV; HeIP; PoEL 1-5

...No way/but by its sting to know/we live and live together. Man and Wife Is One Flesh. Ann Deacon. NIP

No, we'll be wits, and then men must be fools. The Emulation. Sarah Fyge Egerton. NOEC

No wealth is like the quiet mind. The Quiet Mind. *Anonymous.* OBSC

No? Well, then the next time you're passin'; and ask after/Dow,–and thet's me. Dow's Flat. Bret (Francis Bret Harte) Harte. FaBoBe; HBV 1-2

No! When I want a pet, I want it dry! Ode of Odium on Aquariums. Arthur Guiterman. BoAnP

No will, no purpose/But their own. Wilderness Rivers. Elizabeth Jane Coatsworth. AmFN

"No wind at all, and the street stone-deaf with a cold in the/head." Weather Ear. Norman Nicholson. OBSP

No wine but the rich garnet pour of time/Tasting of pain and danger as you will. Prayer by Moonlight. Roberta Teale Swartz. TrPWD

No winter shall abate the spring's increase. Love's Growth. John Donne. JCP; MBW 1-2; NoP

No wisdom from our berries went? Berrying. Ralph Waldo Emerson. AtBAP

...No witch hath brewed/The drug that might avert my martyrdom. Sonnet: "When I was marked for suffering, love forswore." Miguel de Cervantes Saarvedra. AWP

No woman ever seemed to me more fair. Medieval Norman Songs. *Anonymous.* AWP

No wonder, Child, we prize the Hen,/Whose Egg is Mightier than the Pen. The Hen. Oliver Herford. LBN; NA

No wonder his eyes were/noticeboards saying/Private. Keep out. Flooded Mind. Norman MacCaig. OxBC

No wonder I am tired/all the next day. Rain-in-the-Face. Mary Crow. PH

No wonder if he wish he ne'er had learn'd to eat. The Two Boys. Mary Ann Lamb. CBEP; OBRV

No wonder such heroes and noblemen many/Should cross the blue ocean to kneel at her shrine. The Geraldine's Daughter (excerpt). James Clarence Mangan. IrPN

No wonder, that th' experienc'd Hebrew sage,/Of Man, pronounc'd it the extremest Rage. Jealousie is the Rage of a Man. Anne Finch, Countess of Winchilsea. FM

No wonder to look at the world is to go blind in it Tricks. Erin Moure. CaPN

No wonder you came/looking for me Ghazal XII. Mirza Ghalib. LLLT

No woodlot bloomed in spring without song...' I Have Had Not One Word from Her. Sappho. PeHV

No words are made for it. There is no way. Unison. John Hall Wheelock. MoRP

No words can ever express the thought–/It's "God's Unspeakable Gift." God's Unspeakable Gift. Macey P. Sealey. BePJ

No words from a woman/I loved were strong enough to make me stop. My Father's Leaving. Ira Sadoff. AmPA

No words, no tears can mend. Father and Child. Gwen Harwood. CBAP

...No wriggling Eel/Expresses half the Pangs I feel. To Miss * * * * * on the Death of her Goldfish. Mr. Meredyth. FM

No' yirdit thaim. The Eemis-Stane. Hugh" (Christopher Murray Grieve) MacDiarmid. BSV; NeBP

Noah had a Home in that Rock, don't you see? Home in That Rock. *Anonymous.* FSW

Nobilities, light, light and air. Written in a Copy of Swift's Poems, for Wayne Burns. James Wright. NOBA

The nobility of labor,–the long pedigree of toil. Nuremberg. Henry Wadsworth Longfellow. AmPP; HBV 1-2

A noble daughter is blessed forever. Wasn't your mother a woman? Honnamma. BoWoP

Noble hearts Love only joynes. A Dialogue betweene Araphill and Castara. William Habington. AnAnS 2

Noble six hundred! The Charge of the Light Brigade. Alfred, Lord Tennyson. BeLS; BLPA; FaBoBe; FaBV; FaFP; FaPo; FaPoR; FPL; GN; GoTF; HBV 1-2; HBVY; HoPM; MaC; MaVP; MCCG; NIP; NOBV; OBWP; OHFP; PaPo; PoPl; PrIm; TEP; TreF; WBLP

The noble ward he loves. Verses Intended to Be Written below a Noble Earl's Picture. Robert Burns. HoPM

A nobler feat than Inkerman. Words. Charles Harpur. PoAu 1-2

Nobler the conquered than the/conqueror's end! Bar Kochba. Emma Lazarus. TrJP

"Nobody asked you, sir," she said. Where Are You Going, My Pretty Maid. *Anonymous.* HBVY; NLV

Nobody can explain this:/That's the way it was. Magic Worlds. Nalungiaq. NU

...Nobody can tell me/The old dogs don't know. The Old Dog in the Ruins of the Graves at Arles. James Wright. NNaP

Nobody can touch them Pulling Out. Lyn Lifshin. NeAC

Nobody else can do the work/That God marked out for you. Get Somebody Else. Paul Laurence Dunbar. BLRP; TRV

Nobody feels sorry/For the lifetime man. Go Down, Old Hannah. *Anonymous.* AmFP

...Nobody/Has ever seen it fall, except in dreams... The Terror by Night. Giacomo Leopardi. MOON

Nobody is ever missing. Dream Songs. John Berryman. CAPP; HaCAP; HAP; NoP; SM

Nobody knows, and nobody cares. On Sir John Guise. *Anonymous.* FaBoEE

Nobody knows but Mother. Nobody Knows But Mother. Mary Morrison. BLPA

Nobody knows de trouble I see, Glory, hallelujah! Nobody Knows de Trouble I See. *Anonymous.* AH; BLSo; BoAN 1-2; FSW

Nobody knows for sure what is left of him. The Avenue Bearing the Initial of Christ into the New World. Galway Kinnell. NePoEA-2; NMP

Nobody knows my name. Po' Boy. *Anonymous.* TrAS

Nobody knows where she's gone. Gone. Carl Sandburg. AmP; APA; NOBA

Nobody living knows. The Mouse Whose Name Is Time. Robert Francis. LOW

Nobody must be sad or sorry/In the spring-time of flowers. Spring Song. Hilda Conkling. PoSC

Nobody, nobody ever can/count them all...if he counts all day. January Snow. Aileen Fisher. YeAr

Nobody, not even the rain, has such small hands. Somewhere I Have Never Travelled, Gladly Beyond. Edward Estlin Cummings. AtBAP; BoLoP; CoBMV; InPS; LiTA; LiTL; LiTM; MoAB; MoAmPo; MoPo; MP; NoP; PAI; SOTW; TrGrPo; TwCP; VGW

"Nobody prays for me." When Nobody Prays. Merl A. Clapper. STF

Nobody's going to think you're good and sane and smart. Getting Experience. Miller Williams. GP; TAT

Nodding in her robes/On a roaring dromedary. Crimson Tent. John Dos Passos. PoA

Nodding, whether in agreement or sleep. Bucolic. William Stanley Merwin. NMP

Noding but China tea. For silver. Fif box.' Tea Poems: Smugglers. George Mackay Brown. OxBC

Noe bangen butte wampere inferled The Holloe Menne (parody). Harrison Everard. BXAP

Noel, Noel, Noel, Noel. Lines for a Christmas Card. Hilaire Belloc. TW

Noel, noel, noel, noel! Season's Greetings. Hilaire Belloc. DBV

Noel of twinkling blue eyes/and beard of streaming fleece. To Noel. Gabriela (Lucila Godoy Alcayaga) Mistral. PCh

...The noise/I taste and know nothing of/gripping at my ears The Great Nebula in Andromeda. Hugh Seidman. AmPA

The noise of the mad torrent in the vale/Is faint indeed–and how the dawn delays! Night up There. G.D. Valentine. PoSH

The noise/Of the village. The Noise of the Village. *Anonymous.* OBVE

"Noli me tangere, for Caesar's I am,/And wild for to hold, though I seem tame." The Hind. Sir Thomas Wyatt. EnPo; OBSC; SeCeV; SiPS; TrGrPo

Noll's soul and Ireton's live within him yet. An Acrostic on Wharton. *Anonymous.* OBSV

"Nom. But she/taught me not to/piss on my fingers." Anadarko John. Carroll Arnett. VoR

Non but the howlet that cry "How, how!" Holly and His Merry Men. *Anonymous.* OxBM

Non but the owlet/That creye, "How! how!" Holly and Ivy. *Anonymous.* MeEL

Non est dolor, sicut dolor meus. Wand'ring in This Place as in a Wilderness. *Anonymous.* GBL

Non illam preciptorum/Shal gar et his ain. Hic Liber Ad Me Pertinet. Robert Barclay. FaBoUs

Non ti scordar di me! Aux Italiens. Owen Meredith. TreFS

None alive will pity me. Philomel. Richard Barnfield. CH; GTBS; HBV 1-2; OBEV

None are like you, Shulamite. The Hebrew of Your Poets, Zion. Charles Reznikoff. VGW

None but a beast's remains lie buried here. Epitaph for a Horseman. Michael Hamburger. NePoEA-2

None but a better man shall part/What God has joined together. Love-Songs, At Once Tender and Informative. Samuel Hoffenstein. OBAL

None but has kill'd his man, or writ his play. To Sextus. Sir Charles Sedley. FaBoEE

None but his gods and he/Knew his humility. The Magnanimous. Ellen de Young Kay. NePoEA

None but I this lip must owe;/Hey nonny, nonny no! Song: "Love for such a cherry lip." Thomas Middleton. EIl

None but my Lely ever drew a mind. To My Worthy Friend Master Peter Lely... Richard Lovelace. CaPo

None but the brave deserves the fair! Alexander's Feast, or, the Power of Music. John Dryden. ATP

None can disclose the tale/Or even explain it in part. The First One Drew Me. Rav Abraham I. Kook. VWA

None can repeat you, none complete, nor annul you. Ezekiel. Laurence Binyon. ChMP

None can well behold with eyes/But what underneath him lies. Caelica, LVI. Fulke, Lord Brooke Greville. EnRePo; FCP; PoEL 1-5

None cares if he is left upon a shelf. To a Humble Bug. Linda Lyon Van Voorhis. GoYe

...None cares whether, alas,/Its wearer live or die! The Beauty. Thomas Hardy LO

None does more than Milton can/To justify the Met to man. Ill Met by Zenith. Ogden Nash. NYBP

None ever liv'd more just, none more abused. Where Are All Thy Beauties Now, All Hearts Enchaining? Thomas Campion. GBL

None has yet lost/The unpossessed. The Unpossessed. Adele Naude. PeSA

...None heeded, and few heard. Cassandra. Edwin Arlington Robinson. CMoP; ExPo; LiTA; LiTM; NePA; NoAm; OxBA; PPON; SeCeV

None, I say still, shall ruined be/Who Him their trust esteem. Psalm XXXIV. Sir Philip Sidney. FCP

None is revealed. The Moment. Kendrick Smithyman. AnNZ

None know what woman died when fell/Gil, the Toreador. Gil, the Toreador. Charles Henry ("John Paul") Webb. AA

None knows if his death will be hard or his flesh desire it. Woman of This Earth (excerpt). Frances Frost. AnAmPo

"None like Jehovah is holy." Bless Him. *Anonymous.* TrJP

None, living or dying, like those dead hearts that are/lying/Away in the West in the rain! A Wind from the West. Lauchlan MacLean Watt. PoSH

None'll come, and then a lot'll. On Tomato Ketchup. *Anonymous.* FaBoUs; NLV

None love us, trust us, welcome us, but Thou. Mundus Morosus. Frederick William Faber. ACP; CAW; NBM

None may drink except in dreams. Now the Leaves Are Falling Fast. W. H. Auden. CMoP

None named thee but to praise. On His Friend, Joseph Rodman Drake. Fitz-Greene Halleck. OBVV

None needs our pity half so much/As idlers,–always pity such. The Mistake. *Anonymous.* PaPo

None, none. Of Objects Considered as Fortresses in a Baleful Place. Hyam Plutzik. VGW

None, none peals now, deep bells of love and pity. Giotto's Campanile. Guy Butler. PeSA

"None of self, and all of Thee!" Christ Alone. Theodore Monod. STF

...None of them/cared to know in truth/what harbor they were in. The Incredible Yachts. Philip Booth. GP

...None of them come! Sir Beelzebub. Edith Sitwell. BoWoP; CoBMV; FaBoWP; HoPM; MoAB; MoBrPo; OxBTC; PrIm

...None of this prepares you for what you will choose to tell: tell,/and retell. Prelude. Traise Yamamoto. BrSi

None of us could remember who charlie was. Eulogy for a Tough Guy. Daniel L. Klauck. LFAC

None of you ases/Can condense gases. Clerihew. Edmund Clerihew Bentley. NLV

None of your voices is enough/to fill this woman up. Obscene Phone Call #2. Joy Harjo. TWSS

None other reason can ye lay/But as who saith: "I reck not how." I Have Sought Long with Steadfastness. Sir Thomas Wyatt. EnRePo; FCP; SiPS

None pleaseth like your Fa la la. Madrigal: "My mistress frowns when she should play." John Hilton. OxBoLi

None proves less grateful to His care/Or yields him meaner fruit than I. My Soul Thirsts for God. William Cowper. TrCP

None shall now tell it. The Secret. Mary Morison Webster. PeSA

"None shall pluck them from My Hands." Missing. *Anonymous.* WGRP

None shall undo what God hath done. Doom. Arthur William Edgar O'Shaughnessy. OBVV

None so tall/Stands in all/Arkansas! Great-Great Grandma, Don't Sleep in Your Treehouse Tonight. X. J. Kennedy. GrPl

None the less, I serve the Gods! Epitaphs of the War, 1914-18. Rudyard Kipling. BrPo

None to talk with–always single! Mrs. Kriss Kringle. Edith Matilda Thomas. OBCA

None will harm you, little mouse. The Fieldmouse. Cecil Frances Alexander. OxBChV

None with swift feet. Dance Figure. Ezra Pound. AnAmPo; AnFE; HeIP; HW; MoAB; MoAmPo

None writes love's passion in the world, like Thee. Upon Master Fletchers Incomparable Playes. Robert Herrick. OBS

A nook to cry in, and to die in,/'Mid the Ruin's gloom. Song: "He found me sitting among flowers." Aubrey Thomas De Vere. IrPN

Noon and the eagles–not one good word. The Renegade Wants Words. James Welch. CDW

...Noon day hums/with bees and water and the ghosts of psalms. Luss Village. Iain Crichton Smith. BSV

Noon is dead, and the day grows old. Apple Hell. Mark Van Doren. PoA

Noon keeps swallowing. Transit. Margaret Avison. FaBoWP

The noon whistle. Hitch Haiku. Gary Snyder. LCAP; SM

A noonday light and truth to thee. Duty. Ellen S. Hooper. BLPA; GoTF; TreFS

Noontime. I/ wonder why. Tom Poole. BOLo; NBP

Nor a bill of any bird; and no response accorded she. When Oats Were Reaped. Thomas Hardy. OxBTC

Nor a chair to sit doon. Buchlyvie. *Anonymous.* GBP; TW

Nor a foreign foe land on her shore. The Emigrant. Alexander McLachlan. NOBC; OBCV

Nor, after Caesar, skulk in Rome. Non Dolet. Oliver St. John Gogarty. OBMV; OnYI; OxBI

Nor all earth's flowers, how fair. Slim Cunning Hands. Walter De la Mare. ELU; FaBoEE; NIP; SeCePo

Nor all that glisters, gold. Ode on the Death of a Favorite Cat, Drowned in a Tub of Gold Fishes. Thomas Gray. CEP; EBEV; EiCP; FaBoBe; FaBoCo; FM; GTBS; HoPM; InPS; LAuP; NLV; NOBE; NOBL; NOEC; NoP; OAEP; OBEC; PCat; PoEL 1-5; PPP; TEP

Nor all your Tears wash out a Word of it. The Rubaiyat of Omar Khayyam. Omar Khayyam. PoPl

Nor antlers through the thickness of his curls. Arms and the Boy. Wilfred Owen. AnEnPo; BrPo; CMoP; FaFP; HAP; LiTB; LiTM; MoAB; MoBrPo; NAMP; OAEL 1-2; OAEP; OBSP; WaP; WeW

Nor any bird of the air. The Deserted House. Mary Elizabeth Coleridge. CH; MoVE

Nor any dare to take thy name in vain.' English Bards and Scotch Reviewers. George Gordon, Lord Byron. EnRP

Nor any grief so black as this! Adelaide Neilson. William Winter. AA

Nor any knows, save the bright watching moon. Losing a Slave Girl. Po Chu-i. AWP

Nor any road is mine that leads to rest. Sonnet: In Absence from Becchina. Cecco da Siena Angiolieri. AWP

Nor any the less a part of the question/Of what the drama means. Alfonso Churchill. Edgar Lee Masters. GLGT

Nor any time can make me cease to love. Time. Thomas Watson. FaBoRV; OBSC

Nor any waters flow. Ardan Mor. Francis Ledwidge. AnIV; AWP

Nor any wish to keep. Riddle; "Formed long ago, yet made today." *Anonymous.* HBV 1-2; HBVY; OxNR

Nor appear'st but in the light. Honour. Abraham Cowley. BoLoP

Nor are the titles any help. Spectator's Guide to Contemporary Art. Phyllis McGinley. OBSV

Nor ask amid the dews of morning/If they are mine or no. Tell Me Not Here, It Needs Not Saying. Alfred Edward Housman. CBEP; CoBMV; ELP; GTBS-P; InPS; LiTM; MoPo; MoVE; NOBE; OAEL 1-2; OBNC; OxBTC; PoPle; SCV

Nor ask for more above. Love Unchangeable. Rufus Dawes AA

Nor attempt the Future's portal with the Past's blood-rusted key. The Present Crisis. James Russell Lowell. AmePo; OHFP; TRV; WGRP

Nor be one brother by the other slain. Boston in Distress. *Anonymous.* NOEC

Nor be so dainty/Of that which you have plenty. Madrigal: "Ladies, you see time flieth." Thomas Morley. EnRePo

Nor be that lost which he so dearly bought. Consider Well. Sir Thomas More. ACP; CAW; GoBC

Nor be weary/Nor be left behind,/In days of war. Flathead and Nez Perce Sin-ka-ha. William S. Lewis. BPAW

Nor beauty's want my first good will remove. To His Friend, Promising That Though Her Beauty Fade... George Turberville. OBSC

Nor bend thy back to mow the weeds of praise. Epigram: "Neither in idleness consume thy days." Walter Savage Landor. FaBoEE

Nor by a mortal seen, save he/A Lycidas or Lycon be. Hymn on Solitude. James (1700-48) Thomson. NOEC

Nor call you back again? Yesterday. Hugh Chesterman. SiSoSe

Nor can her eyes go out. Dream-Tryst. Francis Thompson. AnFE; EnLit

Nor can I fall more low, mounting no higher. I Feed a Flame Within. John Dryden. InPo; QFR

Nor can Juno sweeter be,/When she lies with Jove, than she. Love Perfumes All Parts. Robert Herrick. UnTE

Nor can reclaim, though all the rest be/flown. To My Lady. George Henry Boker. AA

Nor can such happy fate be given us/as will make death pity us. When I See the Earth Ornate and Lovely. Veronica Gambara. PBWP

Nor can the might of Theseus rend/The chains of hell that hold his friend. Translation of Horace, Odes, IV, VII. Horace. LAuP

Nor canst thou hear the reeds and yews/That sigh to me from lands not thine. Florence MacCarthy's Farewell to Her English Lover. Aubrey Thomas De Vere. IrPN; NBM

Nor carve any from your wombs/Aught but coffins, and their tombs. Orpheus to Woods. Richard Lovelace. CaPo

Nor casts one pitying Look behind. Song: Ah Stay. William Congreve. AtBAP; LoBV; OBEC

Nor cease thou never now. Summer Is A-Coming In. *Anonymous.* FSW

Nor cease until there be no night/nor day. Israel's Duration. Judah Halevi. TrJP

Nor change lives with a King. The Anti-Politician. Alexander Brome. CavP

Nor chase from Zara's side/Dreams bright and pure as these. Serenade. John Gibson Lockhart. OBRV

Nor claim one smile for all the comfort, love,/It may bring to thee. From the Arabic. Percy Bysshe Shelley. CBEP; HBV 1-2; OBEV

Nor conquer art, and nature, to be rude. Characters of Women. Edward Hilton Young. OBEC

Nor could that jubilant song of day prevail/Like thine of tender grief, O nightingale. Thysia. Morton Luce. HBV 1-2

Nor creesh, nor blot, not rend, nor spoil it. Lines Written in the Front of a Well-Read Copy of Burns's Songs. *Anonymous.* FaBoUs

Nor crown your nakedness/With jewels of my elegant pain. The Race Question. Naomi Long Madgett. BPo

Nor crumple, dogsear and deface–boys' way. Development. Robert Browning. MaVP; VLP

Nor Crusoe's raft nor any imploring gesture/Of thoughtful love shall ever find him here. A Small Boy, Dreaming. Albert Herzing. NYBP

...Nor dare he view alone/His future doom which is but to awake. On Death. John Keats. SyP

Nor dare she look upon her winter face. Madrigal: "Lais now old." Orlando Gibbons. EnRePo

Nor dare we think on what we are. Stanzas for Music. George Gordon, Lord Byron. ForPo

...Nor dares venture/To wander far from you, the centre. An Excuse of Absence. Thomas Carew. CaPo; SeCP

Nor death like any shower room. Athletes. Walker Gibson. LiSp; SD

...Nor death's cold flood,/Should fright us from the shore. There Is a Land. Isaac Watts. ELP

Nor depart like the year tha's awa'. The Year That's Awa'. John Dunlop. HBV 1-2

Nor did the peach complain. The Blue-Fly. Robert Graves. CMoP; MoVE; NoAm

Nor did they know it, knowing as yet no shame. A Beginning and an End. Edouard Roditi. VWA

Nor do these gentle creatures wrong. Kindness to Animals. *Anonymous.* FaBoUs; HBV 1-2; HBVY; SoPo

Nor do they defile the dead man's name–/That is reserved for his kind. The Hyaenas. Rudyard Kipling. OBSV

Nor does the Father do, for/already He has done. Creation. Robin Gurr. NOAV

Nor down in my lonesome gyardin. Down in the Lonesome Garden. *Anonymous.* BPo

Nor dream beneath the clay/Of all our days that were. If You Were Here. Philip Bourke Marston. HBV 1-2

Nor dreamed to know, nor wished to learn thereof. Poems: Birmingham 1962-1964. Julia Fields. PoBA

Nor dreamed what beat within her blood/Was Robert Bruce and Bannockburn! The Call to a Scot. Ruth Guthrie Harding. HBV 1-2

Nor drop did he ever drink more. The King of Thule. Johann Wolfgang von Goethe. AWP

Nor drop feet foremost through the floor/Into an empty space. The Ballad of Reading Gaol. Oscar Wilde. NOBE

Nor earth, nor all her empty joys/Shall long detain me here. Come All Ye Mourning Pilgrims. John A. Granade. AH

Nor echo through our peace. Peace. Bhartrihari. AWP

Nor either mother could my soul resign. Our Madonna at Home. Rafael Pombo. CAW

Nor Elbruz cool his veins with all its snow. Propertian. L. A. MacKay. PeCV

Nor envy's blast, nor fortune's rage/Shall ever work you ill. On Her Coming to London. Edmund Waller. HBV 1-2

Nor equal, nor encrease his own. The Animalcule, A Tale. Richard Savage. PeD

Nor ev'n the greatest difficulties chafe at,/Whilst such an animal is near, to laugh at. Bozzy and Piozzi (excerpt). Peter Pindar. PoEL 1-5

Nor even, at last, the voice that I should have known. J. Milton Miles. Edgar Lee Masters. CrMA

Nor even old Rosin the beau. Old Rosin the Beau. *Anonymous.* PSoN

Nor ever again with vinegar will I accustom/my cursing throat to prayer. Buy Us a Little Grain. Christine Lavant. WPOW

Nor ever before had I been aware of the sky. Gift of Sight. Robert Graves. PCP

Nor ever chaste except you ravish me. Holy Sonnets, XIV. John Donne. BiP; DiPo; EBEV; ForPo; HAP; HeIP; HoPM; InPS; JCP; NoP; PPoe; PPP; TrCP

Nor ever did a wise one. Epitaph on Charles II. John Wilmot, Earl of Rochester. DBV; FiBHP

Nor ever drunken falls. The Bee and the Petunia. Katherine Hoskins. ErPo

Nor ever jump because you fear to fall. To D—, Dead by Her Own Hand. Howard Nemerov. PoA

Nor ever knew that any of them bore/Upon his belly any man before. The Odyssey. Homer. LiTW

Nor ever lose that child's despair. Tyne Dock. Francis Scarfe. NeBP

Nor ever shall be. Fortunatus Nimium. Robert Bridges. BrPo

Nor ever shall, until they lean/On Jesus' breast! Thankfulness. Adelaide Anne Procter. TrPWD.

Nor ever sigh for a strange land/And songs no heart can understand. The Sleeping Beauty. Edith Sitwell. MoVE

Nor ever vernal bee was heard to murmur there! The Stormy Hebrides. William Collins. NOBE

Nor fail'd old Scotland to produce,/At such high tide, her savoury goose. The Fire. Sir Walter Scott. OBCP

Nor fail to show the way/Which leads us home. The Open Door. Grace Coolidge. TRV

Nor fear'd, nor joy'd, at death or fate. Contentment. Owen Felltham. CavP

Nor feare thy latest day, nor wish therfore. Epigrams. Martial (Marcus Valerius Martialis). OBVE

Nor fears to tell, that MORTIMER is he. To Robert Earl of Oxford, and Earl Mortimer. Alexander Pope. CEP; OBEC

Nor feeble-willed like me. A Prayer for Recollection. *Anonymous.* KiLC

Nor feel the heart-break in the heart of things? A Lament. Wilfred Wilson Gibson. MMM; OxBTC

Nor feel the love that he knew all about. In Time of War. W. H. Auden. PoPl; SCV

Nor feel this death-valse to be/The portal/To realms of glory and Living Light. The Night Is Falling. James Clarence Mangan. IrPN

Nor fetter for her lips, to make them cease/From saying still she loveth me no more. Song: "I went to her who loveth me no more." Arthur William Edgar O'Shaughnessy. OBNC

Nor find, in cold, a home. Watercress & Ice. Chase Twichell. MAYP

Nor find one jewel but the blazing log. To Mrs. Will H. Low. Robert Louis Stevenson. NOBV

Nor find our bluebells honeyless. Derbyshire Bluebells. Sacheverell Sitwell. ChMP

...Nor,/for its purpose, does the sea adorn shags more. Cormorants. John Blight. CBAP

Nor forced him wander, but confined him home. On Scotland. John Cleveland. DBV; PV

Nor frae their ancient amplefeyst/Sall God's ain sel' them wile. The Sauchs in the Reuch Heuch Hauch. Hugh" (Christopher Murray Grieve) MacDiarmid. NoAm

Nor fret for few who die before I do. Many without Elegy. W. S. Graham. OxBS

Nor furies that in hell be execrable,/For that they hate, are made most msierable. Such is the course that nature's kind hath wrought. Sir Thomas Wyatt. FCP

Nor give a damn/whose wife/I am. And What About the Children. Audre Lorde. PoBA

Nor give an elephant a cuff,/To be repaid in kind. Tit for Tat: A Tale. John Aikin. OxBChV

Nor gives me anything I want but myself. Sentience. Sandra McPherson. PoA

Nor go when dust is gone to dust. Remain, Ah Not in Youth Alone. Walter Savage Landor. HAP; OAEP; OBNC

Nor God the rage or fire control. God from His Throne with Piercing Eye. Joseph Steward. AH

Nor Grace, nor Charm, is wanting/To set the Heart on Fire. Song: "Love in her Eyes sits playing." John Gay. OBEC

Nor grace to those that crave it. Phyllis. Thomas Lodge. ACP

Nor grief, nor reason to repine,/As there is now in this of mine. The Dead Marten. Walter Savage Landor. FM

Nor had that sweet fa-laing. Madrigal: "Since Bonny-boots was dead, that so divinely." Antony and William Holborne. OxBoLi

Nor hands nor cheeks keep separate, when soul is join'd/to soul. Inclusions. Elizabeth Barrett Browning. HBV 1-2; OBVV; UnTE

Nor harmless worms that creep. Hurt No Living Thing. Christina Georgina Rossetti. FM; SiSoSe; SoPo

Nor has ploughed earth enwrapped/historian more fine. Epitaph for Mael Mhuru. *Anonymous.* NOBI

Nor hath more scrapings, or more dressings borne. Kate Being Pleased. Sir John Davies. PoL

Nor have courted no other. False True Love. *Anonymous.* FSW

Nor have I come to see you hanging/On the gallows tree. The Hangman's Tree. *Anonymous.* ExPo

Nor have the sad gift of tongues. The War of the Secret Agents. Henri Coulette. NePoEA-2

Nor he awake to know she does not care. Epitaph. Sara Teasdale. PoA

Nor heaven have I, nor place to lay my head,/Nor home, but Thee. None Other Lamb, None Other Name. Christina Georgina Rossetti. OxBoCh; TrPWD; TRV

Nor heed the Eagle screaming o'er it! The Fugitive Slave's Apostrophe to the North Star. John Pierpont. AA

Nor heed they now the lone bird's flight/Round the lone spar where mid-sea surges pour. A Requiem for Soldiers Lost in Ocean Transport. Herman Melville. PoEL 1-5

Nor help good hearts in need. Troll the Bowl! Thomas Dekker. EIL

Nor her peevishness annoy me. The Poetaster. Ben Jonson. EG

Nor Herb of all the plain/Can heal! Ah, necromancy sweet! Emily Dickinson. NOBA

Nor hills a bar; whereso he stray'th/Ensue loss, terror, ruin, death. Survey of Cornwall. Richard Carew. FaBoPP

Nor home from the hunting woods/Ever, ever come? Beyond the Hunting Woods. Donald Justice. ConAP; NCSH; NePoEA; NYBP; PoPl

Nor honey an adequate theme? The Buzzing Doubt. Donald L. Hill. NCSH

Nor house nor heart shall know the Christmastide! Nor House Nor Heart. Elinor Lennen. PGD

Nor how far Temple Bar is/From the Seven Starres. Colin Clout. John Skelton. OBSV

Nor how that wounded spirit/Left blood on my sword hand. The Duel. Harold Trowbridge Pulsifer. HBMV

Nor hymn, nor prayer, nor church. The Bohemian Hymn. Ralph Waldo Emerson. WGRP

Nor I am not in number one of those/That list to blow retreat to every train. Within My Breast. Sir Thomas Wyatt. EnRePo; FCP

Nor if I answered could you hear. The Two Societies. John Hall Wheelock. PoCh

Nor, if they have finished work,/ are they afraid. Lincolnshire Remembered. Frances Cornford. HaMV

Nor imitate the restless mind,/And proud ambition of mankind. Fable IV: The Eagle, and the Assembly of Animals. John Gay. EiCP

Nor immortality immortal is. The Book of Day-Dreams. Charles Leonard Moore. AA

Nor in the poets/nor the songs.' Iphigeneia in Aulis: Chorus. Euripides. AWP; OBVE

Nor is it essential to be young. Late Sonnet. Hayden Carruth. SM

Nor is it less (all prudent wives can tell)/To lose a husband's than a lover's heart. The Advantages of Washing. John Armstrong. FaBoUs

Nor is of any creed, and dead/Can never rise again. Le Roi Est Mort. Agnes Mary Frances (Mme Emile Duclaux) Robinson. OBVV

Nor is the deepest shade, the keenest air,/Black as my fate, or cold as my despair. Montalbert (excerpt). Charlotte Smith. BoWoP

Nor is there any god can lay/On love the finger of decay. Gold Is the Son of Zeus: Neither Moth Nor Worm May Gnaw It. Michael (Katherine Bradley and Edith Cooper) Field. OBMV

Nor "It is blest," but only "It is here." John Brown's Body. Stephen Vincent Benét. WHA

Nor ivory nor gold the Crucifix. A Proem. Samuel Ward. AA; AmLP

Nor Jests wilt thou afford me more. Animula Vagula, Blandula. Emperor (Publius Aelius Hadrianus) Hadrian. FaBoRV

Nor kens hoo firm she heads b' siklike toil/Man's aald inheritance o' sea and soil. The Planticru. Robert Rendall. OxBS

...Nor knew, although not less/Alone than thou, their loneliness. Switzerland. Matthew Arnold. OAEP; VLP

Nor know, for longing, that which I should do. The House of Life. Dante Gabriel Rossetti. OAEL 1-2

Nor know great Death is kind! Love and Death. Margaret Deland. AA; HBV 1-2

Nor know that what disturbs our blood/Is but its longing for the tomb. The Wheel. William Butler Yeats. GTBS-P; MoVE

Nor know they play Life's Comedy of Tears. The Play. James Benjamin Kenyon. HBV 1-2

Nor laurel him reward/Who hath his Maker's nod. Inspiration. Henry David Thoreau. AmPP; AP; NOBA; OxBA

Nor laurel wreaths against the sultry heat. To Summer. William Blake. CEP; ERoP 1-2; LAuP; WiR

Nor leaves his dry house though we come so near. Sudden Shower. John Clare. CBEP; OBRV; PoSC

Nor leaves nor orioles nor you. Dream. Witter ("Emanuel Morgan") Bynner. MoLP

Nor let his eye/see sin, but through my tears. Drop, Drop, Slow Tears. Phineas Fletcher. NOBE

Nor let me preach for ever and in vain! Phoebe Dawson. George Crabbe. EBEV; GoTL

Nor let the pow'rs of darkness boast/That I am foiled, and thou art grieved! The Valley of the Shadow of Death. William Cowper. EiCP

Nor let them punish me with loss of rhyme,/Who plainly say, My God, my King. Preparations. George Herbert. PoPle

Nor let thy wisdom make me wise. In Memoriam A.H.H., CIX. Alfred, Lord Tennyson. VLP

Nor let Thy Zion be forgot,/Where once Thy glory stood. Mear. *Anonymous.* AmFP

Nor let us lose our heaven here–/Dry be that tear. Dry Be That Tear. Richard Brinsley Sheridan. OnYI

Nor lets the type grow pale with age,/That first spoke peace to man. To the Rainbow. Thomas Campbell. HBV 1-2

Nor live curiously,/Cheating providence. A Moral Poem. J. V. Cunningham. VGW

Nor longer in my false love's eye/Remain'd the tear of parting sorrow. The Violet. Sir Walter Scott. EnRP

Nor Love her body from her soul. Love-Lily. Dante Gabriel Rossetti. AtBAP

Nor love's own kiss shall wake those eyes/To lift their silken lashes. The Maid of Neidpath. Thomas Campbell. GoTS; GTBS-P

Nor make the watch-dog bark/Under my lattice dark. Maytime. *Anonymous.* AWP

Nor Mediterranean– They called me to the window. Emily Dickinson. MoVE

Nor Medlar, Fruit delicious in Decay. The Thirsty Poet. John Philips. OBEC

Nor men/in caps/waiting. There Is No. Faye Kicknosway. GeTw

Nor mock the tears you have to hide. Vern. Gwendolyn Brooks. TiPo

Nor mortal minds aspire to know,/The universal loveliness. Gulls and Dreams. Lionel Stevenson. CaP

Nor mortals know a sympathy more rare. Lately, Alas, I Knew a Gentle Boy. Henry David Thoreau. AP; MAmP; PeHV

,Nor must I think it now,/In you, a work less pious. The Renegado (Act V, Scene I). Philip Massinger. ACP

Nor my dark face dishonor any song. The Negro Singer. James David Corrothers. BANP

Nor my titanic tears, the seas, be dried. The End. Wilfred Owen. CH; FaBoRV; HBMV; MMM

Nor my unseasoned step disturbs/The sleeps of trees or dreams of herbs. Parks and Ponds. Ralph Waldo Emerson. PoEL 1-5

Nor never could endure that we should taste/Of those delights which they themselves are past. Madrigal: "My dearest mistress." William Corkine. EnRePo

Nor Night, within its black Arms hide/A silent Beauty, half so fair. Sleeping on Her Couch. Richard Leigh. MePo

Nor none was found to bless the ground/Beneath the old oak tree. The Old Oak Tree. *Anonymous.* ShS

Nor note the glass/That shows Thy Face. The Mirror. Blanche Mary Kelly. GoBC; TrPWD

Nor numbed sense to steal it,/Was never said in rhyme. December. John Keats. GN

Nor oblique eyesight deciding other objects were there. The Heavenly Foreigner. Denis Devlin. CIP

Nor old heart's wisdom yet to know/The signs that mock me as I go. Bahnhofstrasse. James Joyce. NoAm

Nor one of all thy plants that grow/But Rosemary will with thee go. The Dying Man in His Garden. George Sewell. GTBS-P

Nor other hand could give so true a/touch. To Delia. Samuel Daniel. OAEP

Nor our weak orbs look through immensity. Jesus. Theodore Parker AA

Nor part in seed-time nor in harvesting. The Garden of Shadow. Ernest Christopher Dowson. HBV 1-2; OBNC

Nor pause, nor heed, till I behold/The happy, happy Hills of Rest. The Hills of Rest. Albert Bigelow Paine. HBV 1-2; WGRP

Nor pay but one, but come for many,/Many and many a happy year. To the Rev. F. D. Maurice. Alfred, Lord Tennyson. FaBoPP; GTBS-P; NOBV; VLP

Nor perceive that our ever-revered Thirty-Nine/Were made, not for men to believe, but to sign. Scene from a Play, Acted at Oxford, Called "Matriculation." Thomas Moore. NBM; OBSV

Nor pierce any bright eye,/That wandreth lightly. Hot Sunne, Coole Fire, Temperd with Sweet Aire. George Peele. GBL; NoP; PoEL 1-5; TEP

...Nor pine with noting/All the fever of some differing soul. Self-Dependence. Matthew Arnold. GoTF

Nor Pirate, though a Prince he be. Upon Kinde and True Love. Aurelian Townsend. CavP; EG; MeLP; MePo; OBS

...Nor pity the/Man imprisoned for stealing/Fire from heaven. He, too, is guilty. The Killing. George MacBeth. FaBoMo

Nor plagues that haunt the rich man's door/Embittering all his state. Moderation: Odes. Horace. PoToHe

Nor poured out quite when the life-blood has run. The Rooftree. Allen Tate. PoA

Nor quit the woods till oaks can yield no more. The Farmer's Boy. Robert Bloomfield. OBRV

Nor, quitted once, can it be quite recalled–/Not even with pity. Portrait of a Girl with Comic Book. Phyllis McGinley. CrMA; CTBA

Nor read the glowworms' constellations when they glisten. The Companions. Howard Nemerov. NYBP

Nor realizing that without life/there is no rhythm The Room. De Leon Harrison. PoBA

Nor rough, nor barren, are the winding ways/Of hoar Antiquity, but strown with flowers. Sonnet Written in a Blank Leaf of Dugdale's Monasticon. Thomas Warton, Jr.. CEP; OBEC

Nor round my heart's leg tie his galling chain. No More Will I Endure Love's Pleasing Pain. *Anonymous.* FaBoCo

Nor rush nor bush of broom was near,/To hide a bonnet or a spear. The Lady of the Lake. Sir Walter Scott. OBRV

Nor save together Thine are we. To the Christ. John Banister Tabb. TrPWD

Nor say alas that I can only rhyme on/Censures of, not praises of, Saint Simon. Lines on Being Refused a Guggenheim Fellowship. Reed Whittemore. TW

Nor see his smile distort/in the hundred hanging moons. Every Saturday He Stands. Albert Drake. AmC

Nor see the Angel at the helm/Who steers the Ship of Death! The Dead Ship of Harpswell. John Greenleaf Whittier. EtS

Nor seek impossibilities. The Retreat. Charles Cotton. CBEP

Nor seeks the idle eye to tell its power. The Rose. Angelus Selesius (Johannes Scheffler). CAW

Nor shall effaced be,/once known, from memory. Songs of Cheng. Confucius. CTC

Nor shall I miss you...over-much. I Shall Not Weep. Belle MacDiarmid Ritchey. HBMV

Nor shall the lutes of Eden avail/To let them dream they are not dead. Pallor. Agnes Mary Frances (Mme Emile Duclaux) Robinson. NOBV

Nor shall we ever, if we're wise,/The meanest, or the least despise. The Lion and the Mouse. Jeffreys Taylor. HBV 1-2; HBVY; OnMSP

Nor sin nor Sorrow, Love nor Hate/Can touch me there. The Rubicon. William Winter. HBV 1-2

Nor sing for those who not yet/Have learned a poet's worth. Why Should I Wander Sadly. Von Trimberg Susskind. TrJP

Nor slaves nor cowards we will prove,/Great Britain soon shall see. Pennsylvania Song. *Anonymous.* PAH

Nor slavish systems grant admittance here. A Warning to America. Philip Freneau. TAP

Nor slay Love's tree, nor plant instead/Another tree, save this alone. Arbor Amoris. Francois Villon. AWP

Nor sleep upon its side. Elfer Hill. *Anonymous.* AWP

Nor so little room for the crew. Close Quarters. John Banister Tabb. OBAL

–Nor sorrow darker than her night of leaves. A Song of Morning. Edith Sitwell. CMoP

Nor sorrow take/His endless look. This Lunar Beauty. W. H. Auden. MoAB; MoBrPo; OBMV; OxBTC; SOTW

Nor sought in me much more than thou couldst find. Epitaph: "I never cared for Life: Life cared for me." Thomas Hardy. FaBoEE

Nor speak it, knowing Death has made/His darkness beautiful with thee. In Memoriam A.H.H., LXXIV. Alfred, Lord Tennyson. LiTB; VLP

Nor spire may rise nor bell be heard therefrom. Secret Parting. Dante Gabriel Rossetti. MaVP

Nor spread them as distract with feares,/Mine owne enough betray me. A Song: "Oh do not wanton with those eyes." Ben Jonson. SeCP

Nor stand as one unsought and uninvited! The Seaside and the Fireside: Dedication. Henry Wadsworth Longfellow. MAmP

Nor stir the slimy slug that sprawls/Along thy dead indifference of walls. The Berg. Herman Melville. AmPP; AtBAP; LiTA; MAmP; NOBA; NoP; PoEL 1-5; TAP

Nor stronger, eager for a feast,/The fell constrictor boa. To Sally. Horace. AWP

Nor sweeter they'll slumber the green sod beneath,/Than we in the boisterous wave! The Whaleman's Song. *Anonymous.* EtS

Nor swim beneath the convict-hulks' appalling eyes! The Drunken Boat. Arthur Rimbaud. LiTW; SyP

Nor sword of angels could reveal/What they conceal. Merlin. Ralph Waldo Emerson. AA; AnNE; AtBAP; BoLoP; NOBA; OxBA

Nor symmetric/stillness prove/the finality/of love. Lines Written in a Mausoleum. Lillian Grant. GoYe

Nor the blue javelin-flame of thunderous noons strike fear. Thiepval Wood. Edmund Charles Blunden. AnFE; MMM

Nor the enemy forgiven,/Hans Beimler, our Comrade. Hans Beimler. Ernst Busch. FSW

Nor the eyes wear out, and the streets are filled with/beautiful breasts and words. The Art of Love: Life Is Full of Horrors and Hormones. Kenneth Koch. GP

Nor the fine nets, which oft we woven see/Of scorched deaw, do not in th' ayre more lightly flee. The Faerie Queene. Edmund Spenser. WHA

Nor the full moon more quick to chill. Voices from the Other World. James Merrill. GP; MP; TwCP

Nor the kiss of Caiaphas. The Ballad of Reading Gaol. Oscar Wilde. NOBV; OBNC; TEP; WHA

Nor the lions' growl. The Little Girl Found. William Blake. CBEP; DiPo

Nor the long, dreaming country lad who lies/Scorching his book before the dying brand. Gloriana Dying. Sylvia Townsend Warner. FaBoWP

Nor the meridian sun decline/Amidst those brighter skies. Ye Golden Lamps of Heaven. Philip Doddridge. OxBoCh

Nor the secret hoard up in his treasury.   Riches.   William Blake.   BoLiVe; TrGrPo

Nor the sublime/Fore-running of their time!   The Divine Tragedy: The Fate of the Prophets.   Henry Wadsworth Longfellow.   WGRP

...Nor the true form/of the prairie gathering in the dusk.   Saskatchewan Dusk.   C. M. Buckaway.   AMV-80

Nor the unseen certain hand/that kept it in its place.   Grandpa's Picture. Paul Ruffin.   Str

Nor then regret those scenes so gay/Where thou wert fairest of the fair?   O Nancy! Wilt Thou Go With Me?   Thomas Percy.   HBV 1-2

Nor they but vagrant melodies/Till harmonized by me.   Fraternity.   John Banister Tabb.   HBV 1-2

Nor they with their batteries,/Nor death, can move it.   Mortal Love.   Basil Dowling.   AnNZ

Nor thine nor others' praise shall unremembered be.   Hymn to Athena. Anonymous.   AWP

Nor this nor that man's crooked ways/One sordid doubt within me raise/To injure human kind.   Benevolence.   Mark Akenside.   OBEC

Nor thou nor other songs shall unremembered be.   Hymn to Earth the Mother of All.   Anonymous.   AWP

Nor time conveniently to draw your breath.   The Hurrier.   Harold Monro. MoBrPo

...Nor tip/Me out o' cart agean, nor slip/Cut hoss-heair down my neck. Polly Be-En Upzides Wi' Tom.   William Barnes.   NOBV

Nor torn from out my heart the old, cold sense/Of your misprision and my impotence.   On the Threshold.   Amy Levy.   NOBV

Nor travel swifter through the sky,/Nor with a zeal so warm.   The Comparison and Complaint.   Isaac Watts.   TrPWD

Nor trouble what we do when we do it; nor would have/it otherwise.   A Dog's Death.   J. C. Squire.   FM

Nor trusteth man to this weal, the wheel it turneth so.   Fortune. Anonymous.   ACP

Nor truthfully, those presidents that sat upon the shining dimes.   Mulberry Street.   Ruth Herschberger.   HoAn

Nor upon a cold stove lid.   Don't Copy Cat.   Mark (Samuel Langhorne Clemens) Twain.   GoTF; TreFT

Nor used this complaint, nor have thought the day to be so long.   Constant Penelope Sends to Thee, Careless Ulysses.   Ovid.   GBL

Nor veil, with restless film, his staring eyes.   The Stuffed Owl.   William Wordsworth.   Par

...Nor walk by moon,/Or glittering starling, without thee is sweet.   With Thee Conversing.   John Milton.   WiR

Nor, walking in the winter, woo the sun.   Jephthah's Daughter.   Charles Heavysege.   CaP

Nor was, like theirs, his bosom cold,/But always in a flame.   Epitaph on a Free but Tame Redbreast.   William Cowper.   PBBP

Nor was sun, sun; rose, rose; smoke, smoke; limb, limb.   He Liked the Dead. Malcolm Lowry.   OxBTC

Nor was there when his stroke came around.   Old Doc.   Mark Vinz.   Psk

Nor was your vision long enough to see US,/predators,/with disappearing prey.   The Undreamed.   Elaine V. Emans.   AMV-81

Nor waste your lips to count them.   Old Song.   Louis Dudek.   ACV

Nor water in the sieve!   The Sieve.   Muslih-ud-Din Sa'di.   LiTW

Nor what God blessed once, prove accurst.   Apparent Failure.   Robert Browning.   NOBE

Nor what I thought. I slept and woke alone.   Under the Arc de Triomphe: October 17.   Marilyn Hacker.   PoA

Nor what I "wished to say" a while ago.   A Grievance (parody).   James Kenneth Stephen.   BXAP; FaBoPa; HBV 1-2; Par

Nor, when we meet with evil, let us fall.   The Lord's Prayer in Verse. Aaron Hill.   FaBoUs

...Nor whether/To share, or to beware.   The Sympathizers.   Josephine Miles. CrMA

Nor why he was cut down and thrown here before his time.   The Grave. Saul Tchernichovsky.   VWA

Nor will the carvings on the granite last.   Epilogue.   H. B. Mallalieu.   PoA

Nor will under stormy sky/Laughter's airy music ring.   Laughter.   Isabella Valancy Crawford.   CaP

Nor wish nor will/can strike a fingerling of fire from one/who died for your too acquiescent sake.   Alcestis.   Isabel Williams Verry.   GoYe

Nor with anyone/of ox ancestry.   Imperious Ox, Imperial Dish: The Buffalo. Marianne Moore.   PoA

Nor with the Muse's laurel unbestowed.   Sonnet, to the River Loddon. Thomas Warton, Jr..   CEP; NOEC; OBEC; ViBoPo

Nor wonder, if you find that none/Prefers your eyesight to his own.   The Chameleon.   James Merrick.   HBV 1-2

Nor worth the forty years I died.   Phineas Pratt.   Gloria MacArthur. GoYe

Nor would I indulge my passion.   To a Lady in a Garden.   Edmund Waller. NCEP

Nor would kings rule the world but for love and good drinking.   Love and Wine.   Thomas Shadwell.   UnTE

Nor would she understand my reference.   Sidewalk Orgy.   Richard O'Connell.   PV

Nor would those fall, nor these shine forth to me.   A Valediction.   William Cartwright.   EG

...Nor yet can point a hope/To good, whereof itself is destitute.   Epitaph. Gabriello Chiabrera.   AWP

Nor yet his own benignity/Turned away from me.   Come Harken unto Me. Anonymous.   AH

Nor yet so ugly half can be/As is the inward suspicious mind.   Written in Her French Psalter.   Queen of England, Elizabeth I.   PBWP

Nor yet was such redemption granted us/That we should ever know her perfectly.   Sonnet: A Rapture Concerning His Lady.   Guido Cavalcanti. AWP

Nor yet, whilst we his wit commend,/Despise his want of sense.   Upon an Ingenious Friend, Over-Vain.   Thomas Fitzgerald.   OBSP

The north and nature taught me to adore/Your scenes sublime, from those beloved before.   The Highlands' Swelling Blue.   George Gordon, Lord Byron.   OBRV

North and South and every way/Every day.   My Horses.   Jean Jaszi.   SoPo

The North, as a deed, and forever.   To Hold in a Poem.   A. J. M. Smith. ACV

(North wind blowing.)   Snowgoose.   Paula Gunn Allen.   TWSS

North...Wind...eats...again!   The Moon's the North Wind's Cooky.   Vachel Lindsay.   BrR; EvOK; FaFP; NTCP; OBCA; SoPo; SUS

The north wind is tender after all.   The Spring Waters.   Ping Hsin (Hsieh Wang-ying).   WPOW

Northwest in the direction/Of his cosmic section.   A Baby Ten Months Old Looks at the Public Domain.   William Stafford.   NYBP

The Nortons' ancyent had the cross,/And the five wounds our Lord did bear. The Rising in the North.   Anonymous.   ACP

The nose of a healthy dog always is cold!   The Dog's Cold Nose.   Arthur Guiterman.   GDP; StPo; TiPo

The nose of the machinegun tilted up.   Two Summers in Moravia.   Roger McDonald.   CBAP

Nose uplifted to signal/your passing.   Out in the Country, Back Home.   Jeff Daniel Marion.   PPJ

...Noses/have stopped their incessant running and it is quiet here.   A Winter Scene.   Reed Whittemore.   NCSH

Nostalgia's throat from ear to ear.   Gary Gotow.   George Uba.   BrSi

Nostrils/like/devil's feet   Devils.   Norman Mailer.   OBAL

Not a beggar maid but a gay lady,/Your daughter comes back to thee.   The Jolly Beggar.   Anonymous.   BFSS

Not a bland refraction of sweet mirrors.   Departure.   Kingsley Amis. NePoEA

Not a brook that is limpid and clear,/But it glitters with fishes of gold.   Hope (excerpt).   William Shenstone.   BoNaP

Not a creature lingers by,/When clumping Two-boots comes to pry.   The Intruder.   James Reeves.   OnUR

Not a friend to bury.   Communion.   David Ignatow.   CAPP

Not a lake in the land like the Sneep.   Derwent: An Ode.   John Carr. NOEC

Not a lily on the land,/Or lily on the water.   Winter Rain.   Christina Georgina Rossetti.   BoNaP; WiR

Not a man in all England/Can mend that.   Riddle: "As I was going o'er London Bridge."   Anonymous.   OxNR

Not a man that you can mention/Can live without the plough.   The Painful Plough.   Anonymous.   OBET

Not a mother's fondest wishes/Can to greater joys aspire.   A Cradle Hymn. Isaac Watts.   CEP; LoBV; OBEC; OxBoCh; PoEL 1-5; SBVL

Not a one/for sale.   Utopia.   Johari (Jewel C. Latimore) Amini.   BPo

An' not a one will lead me now to Sheskinbeg, or near it.   Sheskinbeg. Elizabeth Shane.   HBMV

Not a poem, but the marks of talons.   A Decision.   Edith Sodergran. PBWP

Not a reproach/But a song....   Love.   Mary Carolyn Davies.   TRV

Not a roof but a field of stars.   Rent.   Jane Cooper.   FYAP; TAP

Not a rose in a walled garden!   Prisoners.   Nancy Barr Mavity.   HBMV

Not a stag, not a suitor in jealous weeds/but optimistic & boosting speech. Goddess of Wisdom Whose Substance Is Desire.   Anne Waldman.   APU

Not a streak that low of any sun or longed surprise.   Forecast.   Josephine Miles.   CrMA; NoAm

Not a word, not a word, not a word.   Crucifixion.   Anonymous.   BoAN 1-2; BPo; TAP; TrGrPo

Not a word of Laughing Water.   The Song of Hiawatha.   Henry Wadsworth Longfellow.   AnNE

Not all can nick it that will, heigho!   Ballad of Ladies' Love, Number Two. Francois Villon.   ErPo

...Not all our striving/Can do as much as one small word with/Him.   Take Time to Talk with God.   Helen Frazee-Bower.   STF

Not all Scotland can recall/What the eagles eat.   Rumba of the Three Lost Souls.   Charles Madge.   NeBP

Not all snowy frills—or hills—are nice.   The Harlot.   Hamish Brown.   PoSH

Not all the cream is clotted. Book Review. Russell Davies. FaBoEE

Not all the gold of Araby/Or Frisia would pay that fee. The Romance of the Rose: Love vs. Marriage. Jean de Meung. EnLi 1-2

Not all writers, yet all conscious/of the gift of the living word. Letters to Live Poets. Bruce Beaver. CBAP

Not always nothing to a pair;/But pretty nearly. The Law of Averages. Troubadour". FiBHP; InMe

Not always: there may not be room. No Laws. Brian Allwood. WaP

Not and tries less once tries tries AH, GOD– Falling. James Dickey. LCAP; NYBP

Not anger enough left–no, nor despair–/To break his teeth on the bars. Circus Lion. C. Day-Lewis. BoAnP; PoPle

Not another ship could make that trip but the Balena, I declare. The Balena. *Anonymous.* OBSS

...Not any of the/stars hide and seek. Bird Shadows Mounting. Larry Eigner. CoPo

"Not as I do, not as I do. Wait."/"Till when?" Wait Till Then. Mark Van Doren. SO

...Not/as one might have wished. After the Revolution. Marilyn Hacker. AmPA

Not as she is, but as she fills his dream. In an Artist's Studio. Christina Georgina Rossetti. EnLi 1-2; NoP; OAEP

Not as Slaves, but as Free men our money we'll give. The Liberty Song. John Dickinson. BLSo; TrAS

Not bad, my bargain! Price one dime! The Autocrat of the Breakfast-Table. Oliver Wendell Holmes AA

Not be the ash of memory in print/but cold mountain water Round Valley Reflections. William Oandasan. STE

Not beautiful or rare in every part,/But like yourself, as they were meant to be. The Confirmation. Edwin Muir. OxBS

Not beca'se we was dishonest, but indignant, sah. Dat's all. An Indignation Dinner. James David Corrothers. BANP; PoNe

...Not because he/Has no feeling but because he has so much. The Student. Marianne Moore. MP; TwCP

Not because he loved them, but only through fear. The Bold Soldier. *Anonymous.* FSW

Not because that dream's/A falsehood, but because it's/Truer than it seems. Thyme Flowering among Rocks. Richard Wilbur. LCAP

Not before/or after November Snow. E. J. Carson. AMV-81

...Not believe that human art/Can fail to make reality its heart. Spring 1943. Roy Fuller. LiTB; LiTM; WaP

Not bones but the shape of bones. The Recognition. Denise Levertov. VGW

Not Bran, the favorite dog of Fin,/Could rival John MacDonnell's hound. The Irish Wolf-Hound. Denis Florence McCarthy. GDP

Not caged, my bird, my shy, sweet bird,/But nested–nested! Nested. Habberton Lulham. HBV 1-2

Not chequered with rare blessing as of yore. Sonnet: "Time and the mortal will stand never fast." Luîs de Camoens. AWP

Not die of famine, amid dreams of gold. Idylls. Theocritus. AWP

...Not eating/Himself, or speaking, just taking the air. The Beak. Elizabeth Smither. OCNZ

Not elsewhere–if in Paradise/Its Tantamount be found–. Behold This Little Bane. Emily Dickinson. AmePo

"Not End of World,' says Well-Known Red. Headline History. William Plomer. FaBoCo

Not enough! Let me see it/once again–and as it was. News of the palace. Lady Ise. BoWoP

Not even a girl there. Longface Mahoney Discusses Heaven. Horace Gregory. ExPo; VGW

Not even an eye/do we need to take with us/into the light The Initiate. William Stanley Merwin. NNaP

Not even I–would undo me so! The Going. Thomas Hardy. EBEV; ELP; LiTB; NOBE; UnPo

Not even if the/flowers turn to moss and/loose sensations for their stems. A Song of Autumn. Joseph Ceravolo. ANYP

Not even if the weather be good. Buffalo Boy. *Anonymous.* AmFP; FSW

Not even Lois Lane knows for sure. Of Human Bondage. Miller Williams. NYP

Not even,–luckier than this other–/His sorrow in a marble face. A Likeness. Willa Cather. HBMV

Not even my mother knew, when she could see. Jack, Afterwards. Philip Dacey. SM

Not even nightfall, whose gold we are, can find us. Hematite Lake. James J. Galvin. AMV-80

...Not even the cat, who sleeps/between our sets of feet, will be/disturbed. Genius Loci of the Morning. Doug Fetherling. NeAC

Not even the knife-hot sun/that hangs overhead/like a spotlight on the fair. State Fair Pigs. Roger Pfingston. TAT

Not every time, but now and then? Market Day. Abigail Cresson. HBMV

Not excluding mr u. Mr U Will Not Be Missed. Edward Estlin Cummings. VGW

Not failure, but low aim, is crime. For an Autograph (excerpt). James Russell Lowell. MCCG

...Not/far, the pusher lurks. Mainline. John Ditsky. AMV-80

Not finding that the additions much encumber. Don Juan. George Gordon, Lord Byron. ErPo

Not flags of sex even can brag such sport. Games, Hard Press and Bruise of the Flesh. R. G. Vliet. WeW

Not for a seat upon the dais/but at the common table. Te Deum. Charles Reznikoff. TrJP; VWA

Not for forever, only a day. The Importance of Poetry; or, the Coming Forth from Eternity into Time. Hyam Plutzik. PP

Not for me! Bat. D. H. Lawrence. BrPo; GTBS-P; HAP; OAEL 1-2; OBTV

& Not for sale at all. They Sometimes Call Me. Wendy Rose. CDW

Not for the broken bodies,/Dear Lord–the broken hearts! Broken Bodies. Louis Golding. HBMV

Not for the knowledge in thy mind. Sweet Stay-at-Home. William Henry Davies. AtBAP; CH; HBMV

Not for their sake, but His who grants them or denies them. Human Life. Aubrey Thomas De Vere. HBV 1-2; OnYI

Not for you anyway, Peter. Required of You This Night. Peter Redgrove. NMP

Not free from faults, nor yet too vain to mend. An Essay on Criticism. Alexander Pope. ATP; MBW 1-2; PoEL 1-5

Not from her tongue/but from her mind. Eureka. Ruth O. Maunders. AMV-80

Not from sin, not from sin,/but from weariness. Fall. Gabriela Melinescu. AMV-80

Not from the heart, life's crystal/stream,/But from the depths of Love. Reliance. Henry Van Dyke. FaFP

Not fur from young Ashcake's side. Ashcake. Thomas Nelson Page. AA

Not God the Father or the Son/But God the Holy Terror. The Theology of Jonathan Edwards. Phyllis McGinley. MoAmPo

Not grudging any his share of it. The Lament for Yellow-Haired Donough. *Anonymous.* KiLC

Not half so much for what they said/As for the jolly way they said it. In Praise of Commonplace. Sir Owen Seaman. InMe

Not her, not her, but a voice. Maud. Alfred, Lord Tennyson. AtBAP

Not here he lives: but here he dies. Of the Loss of Time. John Hoskyns. FaBoEE

Not here, old shadows–I know you, all too well! Not Here. Edmund Wilson. PoA

Not Him. Thine Infant dies to save. Dei Genitrix. Aubrey Thomas De Vere. IrPN

Not/hing had,ever happ/ene/D (Im)c-a-t(mo). Edward Estlin Cummings. HAP; WeW

Not hunger, not heart–just a matter/of my not being wise in the ways of water. Not Being Wise. Virginia Elson. AMV-80

Not I, but Christ/In every thought and word. Not I. *Anonymous.* BLRP

Not I, my dear, not I. Song at Night. Norman Nicholson. FaBoTw

Not I, nor even Fate. The Dead. C. Day-Lewis. MP; TwCP

Not I, some child, born in a marvellous year,/Will learn the trick of standing upright here. Attitudes of a New Zealand Poet. Allen Curnow. AnNZ

Not I, sweet soul, not I! Young Love. Gerald Massey. OBVV

...Not in any days/This journey shall be done. Budding Spring. Jack Lindsay. PoAu 1-2

Not in sunlight, not like a blessing. No. Natan Zach. VWA

Not in the hope of a resplendent future/But with a sure sense of its intrinsic nature. A Garage in Co. Cork. Derek Mahon. FaBoIP

Not in the quarrel, but the flight. To the Mutable Fair. Edmund Waller. AnAnS 2; SeCP

Not Jew, nor Jewess was there found,/Who would commit a traitor's crime. Elegy. Baruch of Worms. TrJP

Not Jordan's stream, nor death's cold flood,/Should fright us from the shore. A Prospect of Heaven Makes Death Easy. Isaac Watts. NOCV; NoP; OBEC

Not knowing a word for zebra. Koko. Ann Downer. SUW

Not knowing himself nor how he should him guide. The Ship of Fools. Alexander Barclay. ACP

Not knowing how they wait, at the node, the/Curious encounter. Meeting Together of Poles & Latitudes: in Prospect. Margaret Avison. NOBC; OBCV

Not knowing it will some day move with wings. The Gully. Furnley Maurice. BoAV

Not knowing that I walk in cloistered ways/Bearing within one rapt, still thought of you. Transformation. Jessie B. Rittenhouse. HBMV

Not knowing the God's wonder, or His woe? On the Sale By Auction of Keats' Love Letters. Oscar Wilde. AnEnPo

Not knowing what thunder collects in the center of Caesar. Caesar. Paul Valery. WaaP

Nothing–except thirty-three. On My Thirty-Third Birthday January 22, 1821. George Gordon, Lord Byron. FaBoEE; MBW 1-2; NAs; OBRV

Nothing explains my eating alone Things of Late. David Phillips. NeAC

Nothing for sale in/Stupidity Street. Stupidity Street. Ralph Hodgson. AtBAP; BrPo; GoTF; HBV 1-2; LiTM; LOW; MoAB; MoBrPo; OxBTC; SiSoSe; TreFS

Nothing gold can stay. Nothing Gold Can Stay. Robert Frost. BoLiVe; GrPl; MoAB; MoAmPo; NCSH; NOBA; SoSe; TAP; VGW; WHA

Nothing half so good can'st bring,/Though men say, Thou bring'st the Spring. The Swallow. Abraham Cowley. CoBE; FM; PBBP

Nothing has changed! Did We Laugh or Did We Cry? Patu Simoko. WhB

Nothing has saved me./I live. The Flood. Ewa Lipska. VWA

Nothing I/can't get/but bad news. Chain Gang Trouble. Charlie Lincoln (Hicks). BluL

Nothing. I depart. Distances. Jeremy Kingston. NYBP

Nothing in it/but my hand. Seven Poems. Lorine Niedecker. VGW

Nothing in Nature's aspect intimated/That a great man was dead. The Warden of the Cinque Ports. Henry Wadsworth Longfellow. AA; HBV 1-2; WHA

Nothing in our beginnings knows our ends. Homecoming–Massachusetts. John Ciardi. NYBP

Nothing in us could explain. Irreconcilables. Arthur Gregor. NYBP

Nothing is bitter and is very deep. Nearing La Guaira. Derek Walcott. TTY

Nothing is certain, only the certain spring. The Burning of the Leaves. Laurence Binyon. ChMP; DTC; GTBS-P; MoVE; NOBE; OxBTC

Nothing/is clear to me except the smell of you/& the feel/of your skin. The Shirt. Hilda Morley. AMV-81

Nothing is different here. The Survivors. S.S. Gardons. AmPC

Nothing is enough! Nothing Is Enough. Laurence Binyon. MoBrPo

Nothing is here of the life, the joy, the loving,/Before a war was won. Silent Testimony. Catherine Parmenter. PGD

Nothing is innocent now but to act for life's sake. In the Heart of Contemplation. C. Day-Lewis. MoPo; MP

Nothing is left/But space and stars, and song! Bitter Bread. Osip Mandelstam. VWA

Nothing is left but to stay devastation by tribute. An Interlude. John Peale Bishop. LiTA

Nothing is lost, nothing has blown away. A Letter from the Caribbean. Barbara Howes. CoAP; UnPo

...Nothing is lovely,/Not even in poetry, which is not the case. Plains. W. H. Auden. NePA

Nothing is more bestial/than a clear conscience/on the third planet of the Sun. In Praise of a Guilty Conscience. Wislawa Szymborska. AMV-81

...Nothing/is perfect in the world. Whatever Is, Is Right. Frank Gaik. AMV-81

Nothing is real/But Here and Now. Song for a Blue Roadster. Rachel Field. TiPo

"Nothing is sacred now but Villany." Epilogue to the Satires. Alexander Pope. OBSV

"Nothing is unwilling to be born." Great Spaces. Howard Moss. TwCP

Nothing just now would seem to be/So certain as the unexpected. England Expects? Sir Owen Seaman. NOBL

Nothing like it ever heard in this valley. Mririda. Mririda n'Ait Attik. WPOW

Nothing like it in the British Museum. Take It from Me. Kenneth O. Hanson. CoAP

"Nothing, like something, happens anywhere." I Remember, I Remember. Philip Larkin. FaBoPP; NOBL

Nothing like us ever was. Four Preludes on Playthings of the Wind. Carl Sandburg. AmLP; AnAmPo; NePA; SeCeV

...Nothing more. View. Christian J. Van Geel. AMV-81

Nothing more/Need be said. Finis. Sir Henry Newbolt. TiPo

Nothing more than writing/which is silent Mouth. Clarisse Nicoidski. VWA

Nothing much happens and/Nobody screws. The Lower Criticism. John Hollander. DBV; PV

Nothing-much-matter-day-night! Saturday Night. Sir Alan Patrick Herbert. NLV

Nothing needs to be said. Here and Now. Philip Levine. PoA; VWA

A nothing no one need believe is there. The History of Truth. W. H. Auden. FaBoMo

Nothing, nothing, nothing happens here. Epistolary Briefs to Proclus. Jose I. de Diego Padro. InW

Nothing now shall leave, now nothing/more shall enter. Farewell to Narcissus. Robert Horan. NYBP

Nothing of me, when you are done, my friends. Nightmare of a Cook. Chester Kallman. CrMA

Nothing of theirs is ours. Fathers and Sons. *Anonymous*. KiLC

"Nothing of this is beautiful as you." After Storm. David Morton. HBMV

Nothing of this world belongs to me/any more Questions. Dagmar Hilarova. VWA

...Nothing on earth is free. A Wish. Laurence Lerner. FF

Nothing ours or what made earth seem ours to bless/Ever seemed ours less. Snow Fell with a Will. Richard Gillman. NePoAm-2

Nothing–plashing water, wind in the moorings. In the Turkish Ward. Peter Balakian. MAYP

Nothing proved can be,/Quoth Elizabeth prisoner. Written with a Diamond on Her Window at Woodstock. Queen of England, Elizabeth I. PBWP

Nothing really exists This little bride & groom are. Edward Estlin Cummings. AmPP; HW

...Nothing/Remains to us of all that was our own. Inis Fal. Egan O'Rahilly. BIrV; OBMV

Nothing's changed Love Poem. Yuri Kageyama. BrSi

Nothing's changed, Andrew Young;/nothing's changed. Status Symbols. Anne Sostrom. SOTS

Nothing says the third hand/will work together. Alluding to the One-Armed Bandit (parody). D. C. Berry. BXAP

Nothing sits on nothing in a nothing of many nothings/a nothing king. Notes after Blacking Out. Gregory Corso. NeAP

Nothing so active is, as that which least seems so. Contemplation. Francis Thompson. OBNC

Nothing so daintie sweet as lovely Melancholy. Song: "Hence all you vaine Delights." Francis Beaumont and John Fletcher. PoEL 1-5

Nothing so good as water? Ale is. On a Quaker's Tankard. Walter Savage Landor. FaBoEE

Nothing that is not there and the nothing that is. The Snow Man. Wallace Stevens. AP; CMoP; CoBMV; CrMA; ForPo; GoJo; HaCAP; HAP; HeIP; MAT; NoP; NU; PrIm; QFR; SoSe

Nothing; the nothing for which there's no reward. Thinking of the Lost World. Randall Jarrell. NoAm; NOBA

Nothing to atone for but the cold/And blurred perspectives of the dead. · To Philip Levine, on the Day of Atonement. Robert Mezey. AmPC

...Nothing to do/but scald it with milk until it stops. This Cold Nothing Else. Dara Wier. MAYP

Nothing to dream(come on kid/Let's go to sleep). If You Can't Eat You Got To. Edward Estlin Cummings. CMoP; PrIm

Nothing to know that is not she/Nor she know anything but me. Eve in My Legend. Denis Devlin. IPY

...Nothing/to relieve on principle/now this intense thickening. Je Suis une Table. Donald Hall. EAS

Nothing trembles/but the memory of us. On the Wallowy. Laura Chester. NPGG

Nothing will be lost. In Computers. Alan P. Lightman. SUW

Nothing will change them, let them not change you. To Lucia at Birth. Robert Graves. NAs

Nothing will cure it. ...And Mr. Ferritt. Judith Wright. MoBrPo

Nothing will escape her. Elegy for a Woman Who Remembered Everything. David Wagoner. DFF

Nothing, window,/weep. Words. Jean Burden. AMV-81

Nothing worse that the cold cry of snow. In Memory of Kathleen. Kenneth Patchen. MoAmPo

Nothing, yet all, she went down the pier,/wrapped in her glittering shroud of air. Eliza Telefair. Jocelyn Macy Sloan. GoYe

Nothing you have to give can equal these! Admonition. Philip Stack. BLPA

The notice to the startled grass/That darkness is about to pass. Presentiment. Emily Dickinson. AmePo; CBEP; ELU; InPo; OxBA

Notice what this poem has not done. Notice What This Poem Is Not Doing. William Stafford. LCAP

...Noting the boarded windows,/the drawn blinds. The Bomb Disposal. Ciaran Carson. CIP

...Notion/Of the lemmings moving in unison toward the ocean. The Lemmings. Donald A. Stauffer. WaP

The notion of using/cockroaches for bait Certain Maxims of Archy. Don (Donald Robert Marquis) Marquis. InMe; OBAL

Nou in saagin my weird rocks. Saagin. Sydney Goodsir Smith. AtBAP

Nought but religion is sincere. At Length the Busy Day Is Done. Francis Hopkinson. AH

Nought may endure but Mutability. Mutability. Percy Bysshe Shelley. BoLiVe; CoBE; ERoP 1-2; TEP

+ November 1974, just about/midnight, give or take a few minutes. An Excellent Memory. Allen Curnow. OCNZ

Now. In the Pocket. James Dickey. LiSp

Now a fastball, now a slow/curve hanging/like a model's smile. Mantle. William Heyen. MAYP

Now a new splendor quivers in the cold/Gray shadows overhead; still you are late. To One Who Denies the Possibility of a Permanent Peace. Lady Margaret Sackville. HBMV

Now, a'nt that a blinkin' shyme! It's the Syme the Whole World Over. *Anonymous*. AS; BeLS; FSW; GoTF; TrAS; TreFS; UnTE

Now a slimy brown harpsichord slapped ashore/November 25, 1970.   Albert Ayler: Eulogy for a Decomposed Saxophone Player.   Stanley Crouch.   PoBA

Now after all my hard trav'ling,/Things about comin' my way.   Things About Comin' My Way.   *Anonymous.*   FSW

Now Agnes, pull yourself together./You and your friends.   The Persian.   Stevie Smith.   FaBoWP

Now, alas, their days are ended; they died on Newgate's gallows/high.   Execution of Five Pirates for Murder.   *Anonymous.*   OBSS

Now all is one, and one is all.   Of Man and Wife.   Richard Eedes.   EIL

Now all the permanent and real/Furies are settling in upstairs.   During a Bombardment by V-Weapons.   Roy Fuller.   OBSP

Now all the spring and autumn trees   Poem: "The tiny new emotions."   Tom Clark.   ConAP

NOW all we want/is another one!   A Picnic.   Aileen Fisher.   SoPo

Now am I haunted by that taste! that sound.   Modern Love, XVI.   George Meredith.   EnLi 1-2; HBV 1-2; NOBV; VLP

Now and forever.   Vivaldi.   Delmore Schwartz.   NYBP

Now, and forever, my love, she says with the puppet master/making her voice with his falsetto...   The Little Lady.   Russell Edson.   GP

Now and forever, our hearts become one.   Anke von Tharau.   *Anonymous.*   HW

...Now and forever, sing Diana!   Dianae Sumus in Fide.   Caius Valerius Catullus.   MOON

Now and in the houre of my dede,/And bring my soule to requied.   Prayer to St. Helena.   *Anonymous.*   OxBM

Now and then to take breath in irregular/measure.   Six Variations (part iii).   Denise Levertov.   HeIP; InPK

Now are not her, but especially hers.   Bones of a French Lady in a Museum.   Richard Gillman.   NePoAm

Now are the forests dark and the ways full.   Southern Summer.   Francis Stuart.   NeIP

Now aren't you, honestly? Ye-es," she said.   Candor.   Henry Cuyler Bunner.   HBV 1-2

Now as we journey Westward into Connacht/old friends we'll leave behind us in their grief.   Exodus to Connacht.   Fear O Meallain.   FaBoPV

Now be clay in the ground.   For John Chappell.   Gary Snyder.   NNaP

Now be still, and I'll begin.   The Canterbury Tales: Prologue to the Pardoner's Tale.   Geoffrey Chaucer.   EnL; NAWM 1-2

Now begin, on Christmas day.   Moonless Darkness Stands Between.   Gerard Manley Hopkins.   OBCP

Now beneath the sod they're sleeping till the final Judgement Day.   The Sherman Cyclone.   *Anonymous.*   AmFP

Now blithe, effulgurant majesties.   I Saw My Life as Whitest Flame.   Christopher John Brennan.   PoAu 1-2

Now, boys, put yo' guns on yo' shoulders an' get back in the shade.   Sis Joe.   *Anonymous.*   OuSiCo

Now but a vague dream, circling, flies.   World-Secret.   Hugo von Hofmannsthal.   LiTW; TrJP

Now, but tell 'em if they be good they'll come to see me/People, on the Resurrection Day   Bad Luck Blues.   Sonny Boy Williamson.   BluL

Now close your mouths, children, and listen.   Teeth.   Miroslav Holub.   SUW

Now coaxing midnight gentle midnight no escape   Pressure.   Anne Waldman.   PoM

Now come to your senses./LO AND BEHOLD.   Fata Morgana.   Summer Brenner.   APU

Now constrewe ye what is the resydewe.   The Bowge of Courte.   John Skelton.   AAS

Now cover it in earth, - her earth no more.   Mary Booth.   Thomas William Parsons   AA

Now cut the cord/climb the wind/toughen your heart   I Hear You've Let Go.   Rosario Ferre.   BoWoP

"Now, Danny, we'll tell/A small word to the priest."   Danny's Wooing.   David McKee Wright.   PoAu 1-2

Now darkness is upon the face of the earth.   Good Friday: The Madman's Song.   John Masefield.   ACV

(Now, David, mind I'm not at home/In future to the Skinners!)'   Domestic Asides; or, Truth in Parentheses.   Thomas Hood.   EnRP

Now do a choir of chirping minstrels bring/In triumph to the world the youthful Spring.   Now That the Winter's Gone.   Thomas Carew.   PoSC

Now do I see in my head!   Skating.   Rudyard Kipling.   SD

Now do you prefer the blue?   Sentimental Lines to a Young Man Who Favors Pink Wallpaper...   Margaret Fishback.   FiBHP

..."Now do you still say you cannot choose/the road?"   The Origin of the Praise of God.   Robert Bly.   NU

Now don't you think that I can live a noble gentleman?   The Crooked Gun.   *Anonymous.*   OuSiCo

Now, don't you think that Scratchaway/Is a nice name for a cat?   Choosing Their Names.   Thomas Hood.   PCat

Now drops that floated on the pool/Like pearls, and now a silver blade.   Going for Water.   Robert Frost.   HBMV

Now e'n John Lilburn take 'em for't.   The General Eclipse.   John Cleveland.   AnAnS 2

"Now ended is God's high and pitiless joke."   Last Judgment.   John Gould Fletcher.   AWP

Now endeth our roundelay.   A Roundelay.   Edmund Spenser.   EIL

Now ever since, my bat and I/Walk every time we bat.   The Abominable Baseball Bat.   X. J. Kennedy.   WSC

Now falls the evening light. God give thee peace!   The Old House.   George Edward Woodberry.   HBMV

Now, farewell forever,/My Bonnie Black Bess.   Bonnie Black Bess.   *Anonymous.*   BFSS; BPAW; CoSo

Now Fight Cancer is there.   Sunny Prestatyn.   Philip Larkin.   NoAm

Now floats upon the air, and sends from far/A wildly-wailing note.   Sea-Ward, White Gleaming through the Busy Scud.   Samuel Taylor Coleridge.   BiP; PBBP

Now for the Union let's give three rousing/cheers,/As we go marching on./Hip, hip, hip, hip, Hurrah   Glory Hallelujah! or John Brown's Body.   Charles Sprague Hall.   PAH

Now forever fare thee well!   Lines by a Fond Lover.   *Anonymous.*   NA

Now forever flourishing,/As long as heaven is lasting.   To the Spring.   Sir John Davies.   EIL

Now & forever I praise your skill.   Elegy for a Diver.   Peter Meinke.   Psk

Now free me/quickly/before I destroy us.   Oya.   Audre Lorde.   CNA

Now from unfathomable distances/God's shadow has fallen on me.   From the Depths.   Otakar Fischer.   VWA

Now Georgie's a free man in this town,/By the loving of a lady.   Georgie Wedlock.   *Anonymous.*   AmFP

Now get to hell; I want to dress.   The Everlasting Mercy.   John Masefield.   NoAm

Now go quickly to your shelters.   Your Attention Please.   Peter Porter.   OBWP; OxBTC

Now go upstairs and take a nap.   Nothing to Do?   Shel Silverstein.   BBGG

Now God bless you, now God bless you,/If I don't see you more.   Good-Bye, Brother (with music).   *Anonymous.*   AS

Now God's great grace assoil the soul/That went out in the wood!   The Ride to the Lady.   Helen Gray Cone.   AA

Now God's sent Elizabeth:/All of us love her.   Kings and Queens: "First William the Norman."   *Anonymous.*   OxNR

Now, good men of the law, who is at fault,/The one who begins or resists the assault?   Epigram.   *Anonymous.*   PAH

Now grates upon the gravel of my grave.   In Rainy-Gloomy Weather.   Sir John Davies.   CBEP

Now Great-Heart is gone.   Great-Heart.   Rudyard Kipling.   HBV 1-2

Now green is blown and every gold gone sallow.   Croesus in Autumn.   Robert Penn Warren.   AnAmPo

Now ha, ha, ha, full well is me,/For I am nowe at libretye.   Tanglid I Was Yn Loves Snare.   Sir Thomas Wyatt.   AAS

Now hate returns no news, O heart, now die!   When He Thought Himself Contemned.   Thomas Howell.   EIL

Now have good day!   Here Have I Dwelt.   *Anonymous.*   MeEV

Now, have you such to spare?   To Mother Fairie.   Alice Cary.   OBCA

Now, having died, thou art as Hesperus, giving/New splendor to the dead.   Aster.   Plato.   LiTW

Now He again is born.   Milford.   *Anonymous.*   AmFP

Now he calls thee to his arms.   Now Behold the Saviour Pleading.   John Leland.   AH

...Now he can see/The sweetness of the fruit, his hand eats hers.   Love for a Hand.   Karl Shapiro.   CoAP; MoLP; NYBP

Now he comes! Will he come? Alas, no, no!   Complaint of the Absence of Her Lover Being Upon the Sea.   Henry Howard, Earl of Surrey.   EIL; ELP; GBL; OBEV

Now he flies straight in the face of his Father   The Man in That Airplane.   Oscar Williams.   WaP

Now he has his chance to choose/between the devil and the Jews.   Hilaire Belloc.   Humbert Wolfe.   FaBoEE

Now he is forced to fiddle-scrape,/And I am forced to beg.   Oh Cruel Was the Press-Gang.   *Anonymous.*   GBP

Now he is gone, he gets a stone instead.   An Epitaph.   Isaac Benjacob.   TrJP

Now he is only sound.   Ballad in Blonde Hair Foretold.   Robert Bagg.   NePoAm-2

...Now he is/The most implacable of my enemies.   Expect No Thanks.   Caius Valerius Catullus.   DBV

...Now he tries to lift/The insulting weight that stays and breaks his heart.   The Enchanted Knight.   Edwin Muir.   MoVE

Now he will defer to the house and to her.   Master's in the Garden Again.   John Crowe Ransom.   NoAm

Now hear the house become/A drum.   Rain on a Cottage Roof.   Freda Laughton.   OnYI

Now heaven conduct thee with a parent's love!   To Mr. S. T. Coleridge.   Anna Laetitia Barbauld.   NOEC

Now heaven protect your booze. Your wife. Your ears. Visiting Poet. John Frederick Nims. DBV; PV

Now heaven's bright harbor opens to thy gaze! To a Cloistress. Juan de Tassis. CAW

Now his head resembles heaven,/For there is no parting there. The Dying Fisherman's Song. *Anonymous.* TreFT

Now home, we have our trees and seasons'/Change and our own, unmixed, midwest prayers. Honolulu and Back. John Logan. AmPC

Now, I am four./ There's nothing more. Sophisticate. Barbara Young. BiCB; SiSoSe

Now I am laying a bridge back to you. Grandfather. Mary Joan Coleman. AMV-80

Now I am lost in the blinding/One./The sun roars at the prayer's end. Vision and Prayer. Dylan Thomas. LiTM; MoPo

...Now I am mistaken, often,/seeing his wraith in faces passing. The Lover. Robert Duncan. PeHV

...Now I am myself,/counting this row and that row of moccasins/waiting on the silent shelf. You, Doctor Martin. Anne Sexton. MoAmPo

...Now I am named,/As these six letters clearly say. Riddle 24 (Jay: Higora). *Anonymous.* PBBP

Now, I am stirring like a seed in China. The Pruned Tree. Howard Moss. NYBP

Now I call that meaness!" That's all Jim said. The Ghost That Jim Saw. Bret (Francis Bret Harte) Harte. ShM

Now I can mention it briefly in a poem. To Christian Montpelier. George Jonas. NeAC

Now I can no longer/give you birth. Pieta. Rainer Maria Rilke. OFD

Now I can see the pebbles/at the bottom of Heaven. Nevada. Lawrence Gurney. GoYe

...Now I find a coil of serpents there. Epigram: "A golden casket I designed." John Swanick Drennan. BIrV

Now I have turned again to Nature and Freedom. Returning to the Fields. T'ao Ch'ien. LiTW

Now I hear you clearly. Old Woman, Old Woman. *Anonymous.* OxNR

(Now I hereby bequeath to you/A life supply of CO2.) Have You Thanked a Green Plant Today. Don Anderson. QQQ

...Now I keep company/Only with seasons and the cold crazy moon. Plowman. Sidney Keyes. MoAB; PoRA

Now I know it's mad. There Is No Place to Hide. Gwendolyn MacEwen. NOBC

Now I lie silent here. Pacific Epitaphs. Dudley Randall. NoAm

Now I'm as well as him! It Happens, Often. Edwin Meade Robinson. HBMV

Now I'm borrowed./Now I'm numb. The Addict. Anne Sexton. CTBA

...Now I'm cold like him/Cold and untameable. Will have to be put down. Mourning and Melancholia. Alfred Alvarez. VWA

Now I'm in your tum! The Last Cry of the Damp Fly. Dennis Lee. NTCP

Now I'm on fire too! The Wooing. *Anonymous.* UnTE

Now I'm the sweet child/and no longer the bitter woman. Love Which Frees. Gloria Fuertes. WPOW

...Now I may ride him/Every land my imagination knew. A Glut on the Market. Patrick Kavanagh. OnYI

Now I may wither into the truth. The Coming of Wisdom with Time. William Butler Yeats. DiPo; FaBoEE; PoL; SoSe

Now I no longer need anything. Letter to a Dead Father. Richard Shelton. DFF; GP

Now I should be extremely loath,/Not to be thought expert in both. Alma: or, The Progress of the Mind. Matthew Prior. EiCP; NOEC

Now I sike and mourne stille,/For he is far. He Is Far. *Anonymous.* OAEL 1-2; OxBM

...Now I thank you,/depressed, down on my knees. Dream Songs. John Berryman. TAP

Now I've got two minor convictions/and a kiss from time to time. Autobiography. Gloria Fuertes. PBWP

Now I want to be a dog. A Dog in San Francisco. Michael Ondaatje. GOYP

Now I will melt the pearl that was my tears,/And pledge you in Love's sweet and bitter wine. Consummation. Elsa Barker. HBMV

...Now I woo/The footprints that you make across November. Pursuit of an Ideal. Patrick Kavanagh. FaBoIP

Now if now only. June Thunder. Louis MacNeice. CMoP; MoPo

Now if of God both these have but the name,/What mortal idol then can equal fame? Caelica, CIV. Fulke, Lord Brooke Greville. FCP; OxBoCh

Now in another world he hops about. Tombstone Epitaphs. *Anonymous.* PeD

Now in completeness/We wait. The Christmas Trees. Mary Frances Butts. OHIP

...:Now in God's ken/I stand unsoiled again. The Burnt Bush. Jack R. Clemo. FaBoTw

Now in the evening/There is rain. Then and Now. Anne B. Murray. PoSH

Now in the last estrangement judge the truth! The True, the Good and the Beautiful. Delmore Schwartz. MiAP

Now in the place another thought doth rest,/In eternum. In eternum I was once determed. Sir Thomas Wyatt. AAS; FCP; NOBE; SiPS

Now in the watry light wave after wave/Rolls overhead, crests, passes, and subsides. The Day the House Sank. Constance Urdang. MAT

Now in this age should them succeed,/And reign in more sweet manner. To the Rose. Sir John Davies. OBSC

Now is a raging fire, then is like ice,/Then breaks, and it is dawn. The Nightingale near the House. Harold Monro. HBMV; MoBrPo

Now is he dede and lies law/Was wont to blaw thaim ay. Snatches: "Wela! qwa sal thir hornes blau." *Anonymous.* OxBM

Now is the time when such as I/Must set down rhymes on sheets of paper! Spring Signs. Rachel Field. InMe

...Now it is a street beside the park. Central Park South. Donald Revell. NYP

Now it is coming, now it is here. Waiting for Winter. George Keithley. NPGG

Now it is night; come, let us both rest. With My God, the Smith. Uri Z. Greenberg. VWA

Now it's a slow consumption, and it's/killing you by degrees Milkcow Blues. Sleepy John Estes. BluL

Now it's green. Now it isn't. Green Revolutions. Barbara Guest. FaBoWP

Now it's killing me. Latin. *Anonymous.* ChTr; PoPle

Now it's my humbler hope just to outlive thee. To My Least Favorite Reviewer. Howard Nemerov. TW

Now it screams closer, and he flags it down. The Railway Stationery. Kenneth Koch. ANYP; NoP

Now–Italy or London, which you will! To Maria Gisborne in England, from Italy. Percy Bysshe Shelley. NOBE

Now Jane is mine without a doubt, a sweet and lovely wife. Sweet Jane. *Anonymous.* AmFP

Now Jesu, that wore the crown of thorn,/Bring us all to heaven's bliss! The Brome Abraham and Isaac. *Anonymous.* EnLi 1-2

Now Jesus travels Britain through,/But who the stranger knows? Jacob's Well. *Anonymous.* OBET

Now Jimmy and Diana both lie in one grave. Villkins and His Dinah. *Anonymous.* BaBo

Now joy to the house of fair Ellen of Lorn! Glenara. Thomas Campbell. HBV 1-2

Now just you learn a lesson,/Or you'll finish up alone. Prince Sumiya. *Anonymous.* WTO

Now kept it flat, and raked the walks and shrubs. Sonnets. Frederick Goddard Tuckerman. AP

Now leading to the empty room of night. The House-Wreckers Have Left the Door and a Staircase. Charles Reznikoff. WeW

Now let me die, for I indeed was slain/With my three sons. Saul. Charles Heavysege. PeCV

Now let me fly unto Mount Zion, Lord, Lord. Let Me Fly. *Anonymous.* FSW

Now let me over/To go where I will. The River Dart. *Anonymous.* GBP

Now let's go back and get another one... Unloading Rails. *Anonymous.* AmFP

Now let the pain I planned begin. This Love. Judith Hemschemeyer. GOYP

Now let them be your elegy. An Aged Writer. Roy McFadden. NeIP

Now let them gaze at your great constellation. It Is the Stars That Govern Us. Michael Magee. PoA

Now let them kill me,/That will be better. The Bhagavad-Gita: Considerations of Murder. *Anonymous.* LiTW

Now lies as though beneath a paperweight. Last Lines. X.J. Kennedy. OBAL

Now, life's so deadly slow.' Subalterns. Elizabeth Daryush. OBWP

Now like lovers stumbling because of their locked fingers/And their gaze Initial. Arthur Boyars. NePoEA-2

Now listen! McKissen is missen. Limerick: "A careless young driver, McKissen." Lee Blair. TDH

Now little General Monk is dead. Little General Monk. *Anonymous.* OxNR

Now lock the chest, for we/Are dead, and lose the key! An Italian Chest. Marjorie Allen Seiffert. HBMV

Now Love and Truth will end in man. Assurance. George Herbert. OxBoCh

Now love hits lover, in loathing, in fright of criticism. The Summer Ending. Glenway Wescott. PoA

Now Lubin is away. My Mother Bids Me Bind My Hair. Anne Hunter. CBEP; HBV 1-2; OBEC

Now make good chere,/And welcome everychone. A Mery Gest How a Sergeaunt Wolde Lerne to Be a Frere. Sir Thomas More. AAS

Now/make of our hearts a field/to raise your praise May 20: Very Early Morning. Luci Shaw. EBCP

Now make your unwavering last stand. Old Argonaut. Sara Saper Gauldin. AMV-81

Now, mamma, couldn't you? A Lesson for Mamma. Sydney Dayre. OBCA; OxBChV

Now masseur's in the cold, cold ground. Health and Fitness. J. B. Morton. FaBoCo

Now may I have/all these things. O dream from the blackness. Sappho. BoWoP

Now may my lord spare me! The "Word" of a Wolf Encircled by the Hunt. Sandag. WTO

Now mine eyes have seen her glory! After Death. Fanny Parnell. AnIV; OBVV; OnYI; OxBI

Now more admir'd in being understood. The Copernican System. Thomas Chatterton. FaBoUs

Now, Mr. Wind, just come along/And blow me if you dare. The Wind. Dorothy Graddon. OnUR

Now must I rise and go to him, the Dead who calls on me. The Warnings. Alice Furlong. AnIV

...Now my fingers eagerly/toward the machine In One Battle. LeRoi (Imamu Amiri Baraka) Jones. BPo

Now, my friends, attend, and hear the/end/Of honest Robin Hood. Robin Hood and the Golden Arrow. Anonymous. ESPB

Now my hair has turned grey/and I'm not what I was.' There Once Was a Time. Anonymous. NOBI

Now new old first day jump. The Fire. Robert Duncan. VGW

Now newly born, and now/Hastening to die. Spring. Christina Georgina Rossetti. OBNC

Now, now,/Just take it easy./Aha! Love in a Warm Room in Winter. James Wright. OBAL

Now, now, now, is the day we should be/Not waiting but mating. To His Coy Mistress (parody). Edward Bird. BXAP; FaBoPa

Now of the wave's blade. Decks Awash. Archilochus. OBVE

Now of what place could such strange tales/Be told with truth save New South Wales? There Is a Place in Distant Seas. Richard Whately. NOAV

Now Paris, our black classic, breaking up/like killer kings on an Etruscan cup. Beyond the Alps. Robert Lowell. NOBA

Now play out the game! No More Words. Franklin Lushington. PAH

...Now rain cleans the air, and falls,/and falls, and will be falling. Geography. Michael Dransfield. CBAP

Now return, my children, to your pastures green/And your fellow shepherds. May your life be serene. Pastoral Song for the Nuptials of Charles, Duke of Lorraine... Pierre de Ronsard. HW

Now, rewarded, I submit to his transfiguration. Mythics. Helen Chasin. DFT

Now's the time for hide and seek. Bo-Peep. Anonymous. OxNR

Now save and keepe our noble king,/And maintaine good yeomanry! Durham Field. Anonymous. ESPB

Now seated by your tattered tent she broods/On timeless heights, eternal solitudes. Autumn, Dark Wanderer. Elizabeth Daryush. QFR

...Now sent back/Swift to their sources, never more to rise;... Xantippe. Amy Levy. BrRo

Now, servent, please set down. Set Down, Servant. Anonymous. FSW

...Now shall a new thing be,/by which the world shall spread in wider circles. Annunciation over the Shepherds (excerpt). Rainer Maria Rilke. PCh

...Now shall I gently seize in my/Desperate soldier's hands which kill all things. Place Pigalle. Richard Wilbur. HeIP

Now she advances: now she brings her vestal/lamp to the tomb, with nameless consolation. Urania. Ruth Pitter. MoVE

Now she hangs her weapon in/The midst of your golden gate. Poems from the Greek Anthology (excerpt). Asclepiades. NNaP

Now she held on to Deborah, looked her steadily/in the empty eye. Through a Glass Eye, Lightly. Carolyn Kizer. BoWoP

Now she is striding/although she had lain. Africa. Maya Angelou. NIP

Now she knows her lover's fate! Mercedes. Elizabeth Stoddard AA

Now she's at rest, and so am I. Epitaph Intended for His Wife. John Dryden. DBV; InMe

Now she's gone on that raging canal. I Sent My Brown Jug Downtown. Anonymous. FSW

Now she sits with the Sun. The Assumption. Sir John Beaumont. ACP; CAW

Now shines from the eyes of the President/in the swollen head of the nation. Up Rising. Robert Duncan. NNaP

Now shout in universal song/The crowned Lord of all. All Hail the Power of Jesus' Name. Edward Perronet. NOCV

Now, since my love is tongueless, know me/such,/Who speak but little, 'cause I love so much. To His Mistress Objecting to Him Neither Toying or Talking. Robert Herrick. EnLit

(Now sleep, and may you dream just what/the GAWNOSE WATT was doing.) Ballad of the Icondic. John Ciardi. OBAL

Now slightly pink,/and never to be used. Photographs: A Vision of Massacre. Michael S. Harper. PoBA

Now snug in their oiled paper below the floors/Of sundry kirks and tabernacles in that county. Settlers. Tom Paulin. FaBoIP

Now speed alone is king, romance is dead. Ballade of the Old-Time Engine. Eda H. Vines. QQQ

Now start whistling/and lead her into/the barn. Catching a Horse. Barbara Winder. PH

Now step right up and take a little swig/And you'll soon see a Boothbay whale. The Boothbay Whale. Anonymous. FSW

Now stored away our thirst to stay/In ever-dewy pages. The April of the Ages. Digby Mackworth Dolben. GoBC

Now sucklings at her milkey papps they been. An Almanack for the Year of Our Lord, 1657. Samuel Bradstreet. SCAP

Now—sweet singing. Blue Tanganyika. Lebert Bethune. PoBA

Now take my word for jewel in the open light. Coal. Audre Lorde. BlSi; CNA; NoP; PoBA

Now takes form our children's food. Rain Magic Song. Anonymous. WTO

Now tell me if you can. Round and Round the Rugged Rock. Anonymous. OxNR

Now terror touches me when I/Dream I am touching a butterfly. The Enamel Girl. Genevieve Taggard. HBMV; MoAmPo

Now that death has fled these quiet corridors Another Poem for Me. Etheridge Knight. NNaP

Now that death is gone. Come with Me into Winter's Disheveled Grass. Karen Swenson. GrPl

Now that I am dead I must submit to an epitaph/Graven by a fool! Cassius Hueffer. Edgar Lee Masters. NoAm; OxBA

Now that I am yours/yours and saved Saved. Maria Teresa Horta. PBWP

Now that I can teach Upjohn. Journey to a Parallel. Bruce McM. Wright. PoNe

Now that I have your heart by heart, I see. Song for the Last Act. Louise Bogan. AmLP; NePoAm; NoP; NYBP; UnPo

Now that is the reason why/I believe I'll make a change Moonshine. Sonny Boy Williamson. BluL

Now that Sophia has crossed the sea. The Loving Ballad of Lord Bateman. Charles Dickens. BeLS; BLPA; CoBE

Now that the grapes are withering and dry. Grapes. Anonymous. AWP

Now that the marrying wrens are in/Setting up house? The Stack. Stanley Snaith. ChMP

Now that the two are one again! The Eagle's Song. Richard Mansfield. HBV 1-2; HBVY; MC; PAH

Now/that was/revolutionary. The Revolutionary Screw. Don L. Lee. GP

Now that we call the little/we remember of it "the past"? Cows Grazing at Sunrise. William Matthews. AMV-81; NPAW

Now that we've been round the village,/Let's go home again. Marching Song. Robert Louis Stevenson. TiPo

Now the breeches are put on. Going into Breeches. Charles and Mary Lamb. OxBChV

Now the brown hands of mother earth will mind him/All through the night. Epitaph. Robert Nathan. MoLP

Now the crinkled spice-bush/in flower. An Elegy for D. H. Lawrence. William Carlos Williams. NoAm

Now the dark does his longing enfold. A Man's Love. Tove Ditlevsen. LiTW

Now the dead bury us/with their final falling. The Death of Friends. Adele Levi. GoYe

Now the deer falls; hark, how they ring! Haymakers, Rakers. Thomas Dekker. ELP; ViBoPo

Now the dude of the ballroom./Promenade to seats. Rhymed Dance Calls. Anonymous. CoSo

Now the eyes of my eyes are opened) I Thank You God for Most This Amazing. Edward Estlin Cummings. BiP; EaLo; ILwL; MoAB; MoRP; TAP; TrCP

Now the first tutoyers of tragedy/Speak softly, to begin with, in the eaves. The Beginning. Wallace Stevens. VGW

Now the forest is red/and the hanged men still laugh,/but do not burn. Song of the Trees of the Black Forest. Edmond Jabes. VWA

Now the grave lies buried. Upon the Holy Sepulchre. Richard Crashaw. FaBoEE

Now the illusions of grace must be invented once again. Night Clouds. Tom McKeown. HoAn

—Now the long silence. Now the beginning again. About My Poems. Donald Justice. PoA

Now the men will follow,/In Virginia,/In Virginia! Virginiana. Mary Johnson. HBMV

Now the moral of this long story,/Is to drink while you're still alive. Chevaliers de la Table Ronde. Anonymous. FSW

Now the owls hoot/at the fearful night A Version of a Song of Failure. Larry Eigner. FAZ

Now the pier is his, now the tide. The Fisherman. George Bruce. BSV

Now the summer air is sweet with the rose's fragrant breath/That conquered Death. Love and Death. Rosa Mulholland. HBV 1-2

Now the thing the Negro has GOT to do–! View from the Corner. Samuel ("Paul Vesey") Allen. BP

Now the wild rose blossoms o'er her little green grave,/'Neath the trees in the flow'ry vale. Lilly Dale. H. S. Thompson. BLSo

...Now/the wood is dark/with old pleasures. The Long River. Donald Hall. ConAP; LCAP; NePoEA-2; SM

Now there is a memory on paper To Shima sani. Laura Tohe. STE

Now there is nothing new. Departure Platform. Kenneth Allott. NeBP

Now there is nothing there. Burial. Mark Van Doren. MoBS

Now there is nothing/to say. Deceased. Cid Corman. PCP; VGW

Now there lays the lonely three,/Old man, old woman, and little piggy, uh-uh-huh! The Old Woman Who Bought a Pig. *Anonymous.* BFSS

Now there's nothing. I'm dead, and I want to die. The State. Randall Jarrell. LiTM; MiAP

"Now therefore go," He said, "and I will be with thy mouth." Spit. C. K. Williams. VWA

Now they are both cut off in the height of their/prime. The Bermondsey Tragedy. *Anonymous.* VLP

Now they are but a trace of that fury:/An axed forest, a couple of trees. They. Leib. VWA

Now, they are gone! The Passing of the Buffalo. Hamlin Garland. BPAW

Now they are married Nature breathes once more. Summer Storm. Louis Simpson. ErPo; OxBC; WeW

Now they are old and brown and all but dead! Spinners at Willowsleigh. Marya Zaturenska. HBMV

Now they are scattered over the pavements–/the delicate skeletons of the leaves. Lament of the Jewish Women for Tammuz. Charles Reznikoff. VWA

Now they are waving/to each other/with rags,/not smiling. Neighbors. David Allan Evans. Psk

Now they can see you, they know/The open meadows are safe. To the Evening Star: Central Minnesota. James Wright. NaP

Now they're fishing the fissure for Fisher. Limerick: "When a jolly young fisher named Fisher." *Anonymous.* LiBL

...Now they're hers. The Golden Spurs. *Anonymous.* UnTE

Now they stand still. Riddle: "Thirty white horses." Mother Goose. SoPo; TiPo

Now they were strong they could reach it, and they must go. The Garden of Ships. Douglas Stewart. CBAP; PoAu 1-2

Now think on this widow and on her distress,/And make her a present, and God will you bless. Henry K. Sawyer. *Anonymous.* AmFP

...Now this keyhole shows him/My conquest of Amore Vincitore. Caravaggio Dying, Porto Ercole, July 1610, Aged 36. Edward Lucie-Smith. PeHV

Now thou, too, mayst persecute/Those poor wretches, like a brute. El Ropero. Antonio de Montoro. TrJP

Now thou which erst despised children small/Shall wax a child again and be my thrall. Venus and Cupide. Sir Thomas More. EnRePo

Now throw the dice/and tell me, Joseph,/Where is paradise? Machupuchare. What the Mountain Said. Shaking the Dead Bones... Joseph Stroud. NPGG

...Now, to finish my rhyme,/I'll start it properly: Once upon a time– After Ever Happily. Ian Serraillier. SO

Now to the sweet and many-mingling sounds/Of kindliest human impulses respond. The Trackless Deeps. Percy Bysshe Shelley. EtS

Now truly are your haunts their home/Eternal, whom with tears I name. Fresh Spring. Elizabeth Daryush. QFR

Now turn from each: so fare our sever'd hearts/As the divorced soul from her body parts. A Renunciation. Henry, Bishop of Chichester King. OBEV

Now two are one and one is you:–/Which one? Which one? What the Serpent Said to Adam. Archibald MacLeish. NePA

Now up, my knee, to keep on top of another year of snow. A Leaf-Treader. Robert Frost. MoAmPo

Now us to God goes our appeal. Had I Been Mindful of My High Descent. Hadewijch. PBWP

Now voyager sail thou forth to seek and find. The Untold Want. Walt Whitman. MoAmPo

Now walk through me Through You. Edwin Honig. TAP

Now was that not a wrong? Money and a Friend. *Anonymous.* BLPA

"Now, wasn't she a darned old fool, to think that I was blin'." The Wife of Kelso (The Wily Auld Carle). *Anonymous.* ShS

...Now we are all sitting here strangely/On top of the sunlight. A Winter Daybreak above Vence. James Wright. InPS; LCAP

Now we are going where God knows. Possession. Marie Ponsot. VGW

"Now we are up in heaven to dwell,/And you are doomed to hell." The Cruel Mother (Down by the Greenwood Side). *Anonymous.* AmFP

Now we begin another day together. Prayer at Dawn. Edwin McNeill Poteat. TrPWD

Now we have to buy a filter. Sister Nell. *Anonymous.* BBGG

Now we'll never gang doun to the/brume onie mair. Sheath and Knife . *Anonymous.* CH; ESPB; ViBoFo

...Now we,/Mother, yet once more/come home to thee. O Strong to Bless. Elizabeth Daryush. QFR

Now we sing: "Bless the king."/Let us drink to every English tar.' The Sea Fight in '92. *Anonymous.* OBSS

An' now we've went an' fixed it so she'll never go away. Romance of the Range. Robert V. Carr. PoOW

...Now we wake up to mutual delight,/as priests and presidents wither into indefinite night. To Marie Osmond. Jack Skelley. APU

..."An now/we will go and see what happened to your father." Inside History. Angela McCabe. AmPA

Now what about this pain/what about this ecstasy. Renaissance/A Triptych. John Minczeski. PoDr

Now what do you think of that! Catkin. *Anonymous.* TiPo

Now what had chanced, to spoil the tale? The Wooing Frog. James Reeves. SO

Now what was the name of this scholar? Riddle: "As I was a-walking on Westminster Bridge." *Anonymous.* OxNR

Now what would you give for a pig like that? Mary Middling. Rose Fyleman. SUS

Now when shall we see such a wedding in town? A Country Wedding. *Anonymous.* HBV 1-2

Now when the good Lord set me free You Shall. Frank Stokes. BluL

Now, where in the world to go. Journey through the Night. John Holloway. NePoEA

Now whispered and revealed/To wood and field. Snow-Flakes. Henry Wadsworth Longfellow. AnNE; AP; FaBoRV; FPL; MAmP; NOBA; PoEL 1-5; TAP; UnPo; WiR

Now who'll replace this old coal miner/When I've paid God my fare? The Old Miner. *Anonymous.* OBET

Now,Willie dear, don't scratch the paint. Careless Willie. *Anonymous.* BBGG

Now wol ye vouche-sauf, my lady dere?'/"Gladly,' quod she, and seyde as ye shal/here. The Canterbury Tales: The Prioress's Prologue. Geoffrey Chaucer. OAEP

Now woone by woone the trees do die,/An' vew of all the row do stand. The Zilver-Weed. William Barnes. NOBV

Now wouldn't it be much more fun/If shoppers carried things undone? Bundles. John Farrar. BrR; ChBR; TiPo

Now wrapt in the gross clay, bereft of life's breath. The Revenant. Walter De la Mare. GBL

"Now ye'r my ain, I have ye win,/An we will walk the green woods/within." Erlinton (A version). *Anonymous.* ESPB

Now, years too late, my voice quavers:/Can I help? Night Letter. Marge Piercy. NMM

Now, yields you, with some sighs, our explanation. To R. B. Gerard Manley Hopkins. CBEP; CMoP; CoBMV; OAEL 1-2; VLP

Now you are a bit of foam that sizzles/Upon the peak of a wave in mid-ocean. To a Courtesan a Thousand Years Dead. Paul Eldridge. PoA

Now you are dancing. Wolf. Peter Blue Cloud. VoR

Now you are dead... Lines for an Interment. Archibald MacLeish. CMoP; NOBA

Now you are heavier than earth, everything/has become lighter than the air. My Olson Elegy. Irving Feldman. Prf

Now you bleed the desire to tear this maze down/and these segments of rock you know/own you. Survival in a Stone Maze. George Rachow. LFAC

Now you can call all your lungs with song/Of another man's bold hunting. Walrus Hunting. Aua. WTO

...Now you can tell/Exactly what's wrong. The Engine: A Manual. Michael Dobberstein. AMV-81

...Now you conclude or never. Now or Never. Judith Moffett. SM

Now you have seen all that is here/Have patience till another year. Hounslow Heath. *Anonymous.* APAS

Now you know it too/we both know it/while we wait to be reborn. In Memoriam. Franco Fortini. VWA

Now you know why my heart/does not beat under your hand. There Is In Human Closeness a Sacred Boundary. Anna Akhmatova. WPOW

Now you look down. The waters of childhood are there. Where Are the Waters of Childhood? Mark Strand. HaCAP; LCAP

...Now you may drop/Your money in my hat. The Beggar on the Beach. Horace Gregory. NMP

Now you must work on Beelzebub's black flies for Me. Christiana. Peter Redgrove. OxBC

Now you're a fading woman–and not a goddess. Without Me You Won't Be Able to See Yourself. Chaim Grade. VWA

Now you're gone for good...say,/Wasn't they no other way? Two Ways. John V. A. Weaver. HBMV

Now you're nearly out of date, says the fine old hag. The Gay Old Hag. *Anonymous.* BIrV; IrPN

Now you roll/in your sleep, seasick/on your own breathing, poor old convict. For God While Sleeping. Anne Sexton. CABA; NePoEA-2

Now you see him every hour on the hour. Limerick: "There once was a man, named Power." John White. ShM

...Now you think/your way out of this Red Light. LeRoi (Imamu Amiri Baraka) Jones. SOTW

Now you trying to give me the jive, baby, but you/you got to help ourself. Charleston Blues. Chippie Hill. BluL

Now you want your car super serviced/Get your super right there/ (Talking 'bout the Conoco station) Hottest Brand Goin'. Smoky Babe. BluL

Now you will go and look at the fish upstairs. The Fish Upstairs. William Dickey. Psk

Now young and old, a warning take,/And shun the bite of a rattlesnake. Springfield Mountain (C vers.). *Anonymous.* ViBoFo

...Now your hands/Are on the mysteries of the commonplace. Piano Practice. Howard Moss. NYBP

Now your little daddy's gone/Now who you gonna get to chop your wood? Awful Fix. Buddy Boy Hawkins. BluL

Now your poppy is your cousin/And your mama do's the lawdy lawd. The Dirty Dozens. Speckled Red. BluL

...Now your voice/weighs nothing though/you sing. Rabbits. Dennis Schmitz. FiCP

Nowadays, I observe, poetry is chiefly lyrical. Childe Roland, etc. Elder Olson. OBAL

...Nowhere beneath the gray/Sky would be much safer seemed very plain. Hobbes, 1651. John Hollander. NoAm

Nowhere blossoms Miracle. O Heavy Step of Slow Monotony. Ernst Toller. TrJP

Nowhere is there an ointment sweet/enough to heal the wounds/of my shattered Sabbath. Shattered Sabbath. Roberta B. Goldstein. AMV-81

Nowhere on earth so sad a man you'd found. The Song of Roland, CL. *Anonymous.* WaaP

Nowhere to come but back. The Pessimist. Ben King. NLV

A nucleus of a pearl, in a hailstone/inside a cloud. The Burial. Mark Thalman. AMV-80

Nude ghosts seeking each other out in the silence. Love Poem on Theme by Whitman. Allen Ginsberg. CAPP; NaP

The nudity of a Lawrence nude! Gross, Coarse, Hideous. D. H. Lawrence. FaBoEE

Nuflo de Olano/I called Nuflo de Olano (Who Sailed with Balboa). Antar S. K. Mberi. LTB

A number one guy, Louie Rodriguez. Louie. Jose Montoya. FIA

Number seventy, Simmery Axe! The Sorcerer: Mr. Wells. Sir William Schwenck Gilbert. WSC

Numbered but twenty that answered/"Here!". Roll-Call. Nathaniel Graham Shepherd. AA; HBV 1-2; OHIP

Numberless noisy weathercocks rattled and/sang of mutation. Evangeline. Henry Wadsworth Longfellow. AA

A nun among drunks. Lust. William Matthews. PCP

Nursing flowers of sweet affection/In the valleys of the heart.... Woman (excerpt). Alexander McLachlan. CaP

Nursing the tough skin of figs. This Life. Rita Dove. AmPA

Nurslings of immortality! Prometheus Unbound. Percy Bysshe Shelley. ViBoPo

A Nut, a World, a Squirrel, and a King. Night: an Epistle to Robert Lloyd. Charles Churchill. FaBoRV; OBSV

Nutmeg, the glory of the British toast. The Art of Making Puddings. William King. FaBoUs

Nuts and grapes of several sorts are here,/If you will take the pains them to seek for. New England's Growth. William Bradford. PAH

Nuzzles confinement from my hand. Shetland Pony. Maurice Lindsay. BSV

An' nwone o' comely height like her/Went by; but all my grief agean awoke. The Wind at the Door. William Barnes. AtBAP; CBEP; ELP; GBL; GTBS-P; NBM; PoEL 1-5

The nymph died more quick, and the shepherd more slow. Whilst Alexis Lay Prest. John Dryden. ErPo; FF; PrIm; UnTE

The Nymph fled fast away. A Pastorall Dialogue. Thomas Carew. AnAnS 2

A nymph took root, and here and there a laurel. Corrib. An Emblem. Donald Davie. PoCh

Nymphs and satyrs/Copulate in the foam. News for the Delphic Oracle. William Butler Yeats. CMoP; CoBMV; FaBoMo; LiTB; LiTM; MoPo; NoAm; OAEP

O

O! a Dieu, que vous gard;/Valete! To the One I Love Most. *Anonymous.* MeEL

O' a' the trades that I do ken,/Commend me to the ploughman. The Ploughman. *Anonymous.* CoMu

O Absalom, my son! The Chamber Over the Gate. Henry Wadsworth Longfellow. AP; MAmP

O accept the song of praise. Now from Labor and from Care. Thomas Hastings. AH

O all come green again. Come Green Again. Winfield Townley Scott. PoPl

O american rhyme is yours is mine is ours. Instruction from Bly. Cynthia Macdonald. NMM

O and maybe he will take me away. At Kresge's Diner in Stonefalls, Arkansas. Edward Hirsch. SM

O animation! O liberty! The Nursery. Fanny Howe. APU

...O answer us/on the day that we call. O Lord, Save We Beseech Thee. *Anonymous.* TrJP

...O Aphrodite,/Fight by my shoulder! Ode to Aphrodite. Sappho. AWP; EnLi 1-2

O ashen admiral of the hale, hard blue... Statue against a Clear Sky. Wallace Stevens. EyDe

O Atthis, how I loved thee long ago/In that fair perished summer by the sea! I Loved Thee, Atthis, in the Long Ago. Bliss Carman. CaP

O Babylon! O Carthage! O New York! Storm on Fifth Avenue. Siegfried Sassoon. MoVE

"O, bairnies, cuddle doon." Cuddle Doon. Alexander ("Surface man") Anderson. GN; HBV 1-2; OHFP

"O barren daughters of the fruitful night." Guided Missiles Experimental Range. Robert Conquest. OxBC

O be as others are to me,/Or let me be more to thee. Song: "Why canst thou not, as others do." *Anonymous.* LiTL

O, be my friend, and teach me to be thine! Forbearance. Ralph Waldo Emerson. AA; AnNE; GN; GoTF; HBV 1-2; HBVY; LaNeLa; LiTA; MCCG; TAP; TreFT; TrGrPo; ViBoPo; WGRP

O be thy bowers still fild with serpents' hisses,/That sought by treason to betray our kisses. Thanks, Gentle Moon, for Thy Obscured Light. *Anonymous.* NCEP

O, bear me away on your snowy wings/To my immortal home. My Latest Sun Is Sinking Fast. Jefferson Haskell. AH

O, bear me safe above,/A ransomed soul. My Faith Looks Up to Thee. Ray Palmer. AH; BLSo; WGRP

O bear me safe o'er death's cold wave/To heaven, my blissful home. Keep Thou My Way, O Lord. Fanny J. Crosby. TrPWD

O bear me to the spirit's haunts! O Thought! Von Trimberg Susskind. TrJP

O, bear/O, turtle/I sing. Death Chant. Peter Blue Cloud. VoR

O beauteous Queen of second Troy,/Accept of our unfeigned joy! The Ditty of the Six Virgins. Thomas Watson. OBSC

O' beauty, then is still in bud/In Blackmwore by the Stour. Blackmwore Maidens. William Barnes. HBV 1-2

O believe this! America Was Promises. Archibald MacLeish. AmFN; PAL

O belle femme qui ca voule mo fai. Remon. *Anonymous.* ABF

O bid BRITANNIA rival GREECE! Ode I. To Fancy. Joseph Warton. CEP

"O binna feared, mither, I'll maybe no dee." Glenlogie. *Anonymous.* HBV 1-2

O bitterly beloved! and all her gain/Is but the pang of unpermitted prayer. Broken Music. Dante Gabriel Rossetti. MaVP

O black men, simple slaves of ruthless slaves. In Bondage. Claude McKay. PoBA

O blessed Solitude. Woman Alone. Denise Levertov. WPOW

O bow to his scepter while it's called today. You That Have Been Often Invited. *Anonymous.* AH

O boy, O boy! I call that Spring! Kite Days. Mark Sawyer. BrR; SiSoSe; TiPo

O break it not, lest all the leaves/Shall scatter like the dust. Family. *Anonymous.* STF

O broken and blind may be the eyes/Of any girl that looks at him. My Love Is Playing... *Anonymous.* WTO

O broncho that would not be broken of dancing. The Broncho That Would Not Be Broken. Vachel Lindsay. BBV; BPAW; LaNeLa; NePA; PH; RoGo

O brother Death,–I knew you when you smiled. The Dying Reservist. Maurice Baring. HBV 1-2

O brother, take my sword and spear,/For I have seen the false mermaid.' Clerk Colvill (B version). *Anonymous.* BaBo; ESPB; FaBoBa; GBP; OxBB; ViBoFo

O brother, what brought love to them or thee? Hedro's Lamp. Dante Gabriel Rossetti. MaVP

O Buddha, when will he depart? Translations from the Chinese. Christopher Morley. EvOK

O, but life went gaily, gaily,/In the house of Idiedaily! In the House of Idiedaily. Bliss Carman. OBVV

O but Log was too heavy to dance it. The Masque of Christmas. Ben Jonson. OxBoLi

O buttercups, buttercups,–/Rooted birds! Buttercups. Louis Ginsberg. HBVY

O buy it, pray, for me! The Coconut. Angela Milne. FiBHP

O, by an' by, by an' by,/I'm gwinter lay down my heavy load. By an' By. Anonymous. BoAN 1-2

O' Cheetie-Poussie-Cattie, O.' Cheetie-Poussie-Cattie, O. Anonymous. FaBoCh

O Child, come to our hour of dearth/And bid the dead heart live. In Time of Need. Katharine Tynan Hinkson. TrPWD

O childhood, o images slipping from us/Whither? Whither? Childhood. Rainer Maria Rilke. SOTW

O chillen, run, de Cunjah man! De Cunjah Man. James Edwin Campbell. BANP

O Christ and Mary, pity your wretched one. I Read, or Write. Sedulius Scottus. NOBI

O Christ our King, in mercy bring/Us thither we implore thee! Wayfarers in the Wilderness. Alexander R. Thompson. AH

O Christ, our King, our Lord whom we adore. Have We Not Seen Thy Shining Garment's Hem. Amy Carmichael. TRV

O Church of God, awake! The Clarion-Call. Anonymous. BLRP

O city of gypsies, game of moon and of sand. Ballad of the Spanish Civil Guard. Federico Garcia Lorca. LiTW

O clemens! O pia! O dolcis!/Maria! For Eleanor and Bill Monahan. William Carlos Williams. VGW

O come, let us adore Him, Christ the Lord. Adeste Fideles. Saint Bonaventure. CAW; WGRP

O come Lord Jesus quickly! Buriall. Henry Vaughan. SeCV 1-2

O come quickly, glorious Lord, and raise my sprite to thee. Never Weather-Beaten Sail. Thomas Campion. BoC; EIL; GoBC; OAEL 1-2; OBSP; OxBoCh; PoEL 1-5

O come that hour, when I shall never/Sleep again, but wake for ever. A Colloquy with God. Sir Thomas Browne. OBS

O, come to me again, dear love. To the Parted One. Johann Wolfgang von Goethe. AWP

O come to us, abide with us,/Our Lord Emmanuel! O Little Town of Bethlehem. Phillips Brooks. AA; AH; AmePo; BLRP; FaFP; GN; HBV 1-2; OHIP; TreF; WBLP; WGRP

O commemorate me with no hero-courageous/Tomb–just a canal-bank seat for the passer-by. Lines Written on a Seat on the Grand Canal, Dublin. Patrick Kavanagh. BIrV; CIP; CMoP; InPS; IPY; NOBI

O communication!/O rapid transit! Tourist Time. F. R. Scott. PoPl

O comrades, let us one and all/Join in to get Him back His ball! Out of Bounds. John Banister Tabb. TRV

O cool and pleasant is the valley/And there, love, will we stay. Chamber Music. James Joyce. HW

O cool, grey city of love! The Cool, Grey City of Love. George Sterling. BPAW

O costly valor never won! Guilty. Marguerite Wilkinson. TRV

"O could I love!" and stops, God writeth "Loved." A True Hymn. George Herbert. InvP; NOCV; OxBoCh

O, could the word/so speak,/reply,/be heard! Poet to Dancer. Bernice Kavinoky. UnS

O Cupid, so thou pity me,/Spare not, but play thee. Love in My Bosom Like a Bee. Thomas Lodge. LiTL

O cursed effects of Honourable Peace! An Epistle from a Half-Pay Officer in the Country. Richardson Pack. NOEC

"O cursed mother! hell is deep,/And there thou'll enter step by step." The Cruel Mother. Anonymous. ViBoFo

O cut the sweet apple and share it! Sharing Eve's Apple. John Keats. ChRP; ErPo; NLV

"O! Cynthia, thou hast angel's eyes,/But yet a woman's heart." Cynthia. Sir Edward Dyer. OBSC

O da quod jubes, Domine. New Year Letter. W. H. Auden. FaBoRV; NoAm

O dame Romulus, oh!/How could you be cruel to me? Remon. Anonymous. TrAS

O damned vacillating state! Supposed Confessions of a Second-Rate Sensitive Mind. Alfred, Lord Tennyson. VLP

O dark! I leave you to oblivious night! The Hours. John Peale Bishop. MoVE; OxBA

O darlin', you can't love five. Darlin'. Anonymous. ABF

O daughter, so far, you've only had a taste of icing,/are you eady now for some cake? Child Beater. Florence Anthony ("Ai"). BoWoP

O dead, to the dying/Come home! The Dead Feast of the Kol-Folk. John Greenleaf Whittier. PoEL 1-5

O dear divine old Giant, at thy feet. After Reading Homer. Digby Mackworth Dolben. GoBC

"O, dear! I didn't know 'twas you!" The Retort. George Pope Morris. HBV 1-2

O dear my doctor, love, be still/Hush, surgeon, little friend, come fast. O Doctor Dear My Love. Anne Halley. NMM

O dearest life! joy's sweet! O sweetest love! And Is It Night? Anonymous. EIl; GBL

O Death, be gracious to my dying suit!' Hero and Leander. Thomas Hood. EnRP

O Death in Life, the days that are no more. The Princess. Alfred, Lord Tennyson. AtBAP; AWP; DiPo; ELP; FaBoRV; FaPoR; FiP; GoTF; GTBS; GTBS-P; HAP; InPo; InPS; InvP; MasP; NIP; NOBE; NoP; OAEL 1-2; OAEP; OBNC; OBVV; PoEL 1-5; PoLf; PPoe; PPP; SeCeV; TreF; TrGrPo; ViBoPo; WHA

O death, that gave my life to me! The Sense of Death. Helen Hoyt. HBMV

O Death, the loveliness that is in thee,/Could the world know, the world would/cease to be. In Death. Mary Emily Bradley. AA

O Death! where is thy sting? The Dying Christian to His Soul. Alexander Pope. CAW; GoBC; GoTF; HBV 1-2; OBEV; TreF

O death, where is thy sting! Dying Hymn. Alice Cary. HBV 1-2

O Death, where is thy sting?/Thy victory, O Grave? Lines Written after the Discovery ... of the Germ of Yellow Fever. Ronald Ross. ImOP

O deepening spring. 18 West 11th Street. James Merrill. NYP

O DELUSIVE DREAM! The Red-Breast of Aquitania. Francis Sylvester ("Father Prout") Mahony. OnYI

O Desdemona, Desdemona! dead!/O! O! O! Othello. William Shakespeare. BiP

O do not let thy temple be destroy'd! Astrophel and Stella, XL. Sir Philip Sidney. AAS; SiPS

O, do thou kindly lay me low/With him I love at rest. A Mother's Lament for the Death of Her Son. Robert Burns. HoPM

O doctor, where's my lily? The Maiden and the Lily. John Fraser. HBV 1-2

O dog my god, how can I cease to praise? Dog, Dog in My Manger. George Barker. LiTM

O don't flinch!–it is over./You are grateful. The Wasp. Joyce Carol Oates. GeTw

O! don't you wish that you were me? Foreign Children. Robert Louis Stevenson. GoJo

O drank ones, I wold drink yet. At the Tavern. Anonymous. OxBM

O Dream undying,/Chrysola! The Knights to Chrysola. Rachel Annand Taylor. OBVV

O drink to thirst, and thirst to drinke that treasuer,/where the onely danger is to keepe a measuer Sonnet XXXII. William Alabaster. AnAnS 1

O earth and heaven not made with hands! Elected Silence. Siegfried Sassoon. MoBrPo

O Earth! art thou not weary of thy dead? O Earth! Art Thou Not Weary? Julia Caroline Ripley Dorr. AA

O earth, break open and take me in. Once I Played and Danced in My Parents' Kingdom. Anonymous. WTO

O Earth, O Sky, you use is done,/Take care of me. The Butterfly. Alice Archer (Sewall) James. AA

O Echo, Echo. Narcissus. Alistair Campbell. AnNZ

O emigrant ships stoked/wi misery. No Voice of Man. Raymond Falconer. PoSH

O'er all miracles preceding/His inestimable death. Hymns and Spiritual Songs. Christopher Smart. NOCV

O'er all the house-tops and through heaven above/Proclaim the elevation of the Host! Divina Commedia. Henry Wadsworth Longfellow. AmPP; OxBA

O'er battles that made us a nation. The Flag of the Constellation. Thomas Buchanan Read. EtS

O'er blackened ridges crawls. Dalmatian Nocturne. Aleksa Santic. LiTW

O'er Cahir O'Dogherty/Red in his tomb. The Gray Plume. Francis Carlin. HBMV

O'er every sea and every land. Sing to the Lord Most High. Timothy Dwight. AH

O'er grief and wrong. Overflow. John Banister Tabb. CAW; HBV 1-2

O'er his white banes when they are bare,/The wind sall blaw for evermair. The Twa Corbies. Anonymous. AWP; BoLiVe; BSV; ELP; EnL; ESPB; ExPo; FaBoBa; FaBoCh; GoTS; GTBS; GTBS-P; HAP; HBV 1-2; InPK; InPo; LiTL; LoGBV; NoP; OBEV; OxBS; PBBP; PoPle; PPP; SeCePo; SeCeV; StPo; UnPo

O'er life's dark lough my course I still pursue. Ways of Pronouncing "Ough'. Anonymous. FaBoUs

O'er my pretty lad so young/Now ceased growing. The Trees So High. Anonymous. OxBoLi

O'er sea and shore and continent,/To all the sons of men.   O'er Continent and Ocean.   John Haynes Holmes.   AH

O'er the land of the free, and the home of/the brave.   The Star-Spangled Banner.   Francis Scott Key.   AA; BBV; BLPA; BLSo; FaBoBe; FaFP; FaPo; FaPoR; FSW; GoTF; HBV 1-2; HBVY; MC; NePA; PAH; PAL; TAP; TreF; WBLP; YaD

O'er the little green apple boy's green little grave.   Verdancy.   *Anonymous.* ShM

O'er the Unknown Sea to the Unseen Shore.   Some Time at Eve.   Elizabeth Clark Hardy.   HBV 1-2; PoLf

O'er thee the sun doth pine/And angels mourn.   Since to Be Loved Endures. Robert Bridges.   GTBS

O'er those we love, we drop it in their grave.   Procrastination.   Doctor Edward Young.   AnEnPo

O'erlooking a superior spectre–/Or more–.   One Need Not Be a Chamber–To Be Haunted.   Emily Dickinson.   AmePo; SyP

O even in Paradise/the mind would make its own winter.   The Climate of Paradise.   Louis Simpson.   NOBA

O evermore great Psalm spring forth! spring forth/ anew!   The Psalm. Robert Bridges.   FaBoTw; LiTB

O everything each and everyone so pitiful.   Madness.   Sachiko Yoshihara. BoWoP

O evil Angel, set me free!   A Clever Woman.   Mary Elizabeth Coleridge. BrRo

O fading loves of the old green earth–/Good-bye,–good-bye–good-bye!   Song of Maelduin.   T. W. Rolleston.   HBMV

O fair, full-bosomed, passionate weeping sea.   Sea-Grief.   Dowell O'Reilly. PoAu 1-2

O, fair the breaking day in Ireland now!   A Bird from the West.   Dora Sigerson Shorter.   OBVV

O faith of mine, be big! be big!   The Awakening.   Angela Morgan.   OHIP

O faithless thorn.   O Faithless Thorn.   *Anonymous.*   WTO

O far too long, and poisoned through!   Spirit's Song.   Louise Bogan. NYBP

O fare you well, my mother dear,/I leave you all compleatly.   Bonny Lizie Baillie.   *Anonymous.*   BaBo; ESPB

O farewell, my life's treasure!   Your Fair Looks Inflame My Desire. Thomas Campion.   UnTE

O farther, farther, farther sail!   Passage to India.   Walt Whitman.   AmePo; DiPo; MoRP; PoEL 1-5; TrPWD; TRV; WGRP

O Father, gently lead all hearts/That hardly come to sorrow!   In the Time of Trouble.   Leslie Savage Clark.   TrPWD

O Father! touch the east, and light/The light that shone when hope was born. Rise, Happy Morn.   Alfred, Lord Tennyson.   BePJ

O fayrest fayre let never it be named,/That so fayre beauty was so fowly shamed.   Amoretti, XLI.   Edmund Spenser.   AAS; OAEP

O fearful thought–a convict soul.   The Singer in the Prison.   Walt Whitman. BeLS

O fie on her and him and Love and HER and me!   Round Robin. Bhartrihari.   LiTW

O finer far, not gems/But their eternal parts.   Here Too the Spirit Shafts. Mechtild of Magdeburg.   WPOW

O fireman! save my child!   No More Booze.   *Anonymous.*   TrAS; TreF

O flashing Orion,/your stars are muscled like the lion.   Baseball and Writing. Marianne Moore.   BoWoP; LiSp

O flower having reached your fruition!   Tuberose.   Louis James Block.   AA

O Flower of flowers, our Lady of the May!   Our Lady of the May.   Lionel Pigot Johnson.   ISi

O flowers on the coffin,/While the burial's carried on.   Those Gambler's Blues (with music).   *Anonymous.*   AS

O fly away home fly away   O Daedalus, Fly Away Home.   Robert Earl Hayden.   BiP; HAP; IDB; NCSH; PoBA; PoNe; WeW

...O folly of a child who dreams/Of heaven, and, waking in the darkness, screams.   Nerves.   Arthur Symons.   BrPo; FaBoTw; SyP

O foolish woman, dost thou set/Thy pride upon a ring?   Variations on Sappho.   Michael (Katherine Bradley and Edith Cooper) Field.   PeHV

O! foolishe Mayd to be soe sadde/The Momente that her Care was drownd! The Carelesse Nurse Mayd.   Thomas Hood.   FaBoNo; VLP

O for that night! where I in him/Might live invisible and dim.   Silex Scintillans.   Henry Vaughan.   AnAnS 1

O Fortune's darling, dowered with rest!   Sleep.   Alice Brown.   AA

–O friend, nought happens twice thus; why,/I cannot tell!   On the Departure Platform.   Thomas Hardy.   NOBE; OBNC; OxBTC

O Full of Grace, we pray!   Inscription on a Shrine Near Ischl.   Empress of Austria-Hungary Elizabeth.   CAW

O gentle Death, how dear thou makest the dead!   Incompatibility.   Aubrey Thomas De Vere.   IrPN

O gentle, gentle summer rain!   Invocation to Rain in Summer.   William C. Bennett.   GN

O gentle Mary! Our lovely Mother in heaven!   The Evening of the Visitation. Thomas Merton.   ISi

O gentle, O tender, O gracious Virgin Mary.   Salve Regina.   *Anonymous.* ISi

O gentle Saviour, leave me not to die.   Deeply Repentant of My Sinful Ways. Gaspara Stampa.   WPOW

...O gently silent forms/Of the last spaces.   The Naked Land.   Kenneth Patchen.   EAS

O, give me all!   Props.   John Oxenham.   TRV

O give me health, expel this foul disease,/because my heart sincerely honors you.   Prayer against Love.   Caius Valerius Catullus.   LiTW

O give me the sweet shady side of Pall Mall.   Country and Town.   Charles Morris.   NOEC

O give us now repose.   The Shadows of the Evening Hours.   Adelaide Anne Procter.   TreFS

O Giver of Life, O God!   Thanksgiving.   Angela Morgan.   TrPWD; TRV

O glorious day, eternity/With Him, the blessed One in Three.   It Was for Me.   Eva Gray.   STF

O glorious Sun! imagine me the West,/Shine in my Arms, and set thou in my Breast.   In Praise of His Loving and Best-Beloved Fawnia.   Robert Greene.   PoEL 1-5

O God, a sweet good-will/To all mankind.   Sir Marmaduke's Musings. Theodore Tilton.   AA

O God, forgive me my shortcomings.   Modern Love Poems.   *Anonymous.* WTO

O God, give me words to make my dream-children live.   A Prayer.   Joseph Seamon, Jr Cotter.   BANP

O God, give us the strength to build/With Christ that city here!   Outside the Holy City.   James G. Gilkey.   AH

O God! have mercy on the mariner!   O God! Have Mercy in This Dreadful Hour.   Robert Southey.   MOS; TrPWD

O God, have Thou no mercy upon me!/Poor Child!   If I Were Dead. Coventry Patmore.   ACP; CAW; GoBC; HBV 1-2

O God, how embraced we have been!   Birth.   Amir Gilboa.   OFD; VWA

O God, I kneel before the art,/Of this great lyrist, earth.   Rain.   Kenneth Slade Alling.   HBMV

O God! I would there were no life for me.   On His Love.   Daqiqi.   LiTW

O God in Your Heaven give ease to my pain!   It Is Well for Small Birds That Can Rise up on High.   *Anonymous.*   NOBI

O God, make this lively, mischievous boy/A power for Thee, to Thy heart a joy.   The Teacher Sees a Boy.   Margaret Morningstar.   STF

O God,–not, not for death!   In Youth.   Evaleen Stein.   AA

O God! O Montreal!   O God! O Montreal!   Samuel (1835-1902) Butler. FaBoCo; NBM

O God of Freedom, stir us in our night/That we set forth, for justice, truth and right!   The Call.   Thomas Curtis Clark.   PGD

O God of strength, be thou to us/Our fathers' God again!   O God, in Whose Great Purpose.   James G. Gilkey.   AH

"O God, save us!"   Hymn.   Stephen Crane.   MoAmPo

O God, set thy kiss on the cloud!   Remember Thy Covenant.   Edith Lovejoy Pierce.   MoRP

O God, that I were dead!   Mariana.   Alfred, Lord Tennyson.   AWP; BiP; CABA; CBEP; CH; ChRP; GTBS; HBV 1-2; InPo; InPS; LiTL; MaVP; MBW 1-2; MyFE; NOBE; NoP; OAEL 1-2; OAEP; OBEV; OBNC; OBRV; OBVY; PAI; PoEL 1-5; PoPle; TEP; TrGrPo; UnPo; ViBoPo; VLP; WiR

O God, that men will be so blind!   From Beyond.   Lucia Trent.   PGD

O god/the dreaming   It's Comforting.   Judy Dothard Simmons.   CNA

O God! the lonely hillside,/The passionate wind of spring!   The Birch-Tree at Loschwitz.   Amy Levy.   TrJP

...O God, the only summer/Is on her lips, and even they have lied.   Une Idole du Nord.   Francis Stuart.   NeIP

O God, the Powerful, save us from the roaring thunderbolts!   The Suez Crisis.   *Anonymous.*   WTO

O God! to us may grace be given/To follow in their train!   The Son of God Goes Forth to War.   Reginald Heber.   HBV 1-2; TreFS

O golden child the world will kill and eat.   Mary's Song.   Sylvia Plath. CAPP; FaBoMo; FaBoWP

O good Shepherd, feed my sheep.   The Blood-Strained Banders.   *Anonymous.* AmFP; OuSiCo

O gracious Mary, lend thine aid.   Hail to the Queen.   *Anonymous.*   AH

O grant him light to see himself as foe!   Prayer for Light.   Stanton A. Coblentz.   TrPWD

O grant us in our souls to see/The living flame that comes from Thee.   The Burning Bush.   Henry Van Dyke.   TRV

O graunt that of my love at last I may not misse!   Address to Venus. Lucretius (Titus Lucretitus Carus).   AnEnPo; AWP

O grave! I would have thy gates were wide.   Under the Violets.   Edward Hilton Young.   AA

O grave, keep shut lest I be shamed.   C. L. M.   John Masefield.   BoLiVe; HBV 1-2; LiTM; MoBrPo; OxBTC

O grave, where soundeth thy triumph? O death, where/hideth thy sting?   If to Die–.   Myrtle Romilu.   BLRP

O great, just, good God! Miserable me!   The Ring and the Book.   Robert Browning.   OAEP

O green as goslinshit, and fertile/to the poorest Muse! The Bitch-Kitty. Jonathan Williams. PoM

O green, beneath which all of them shall drown! Fresh Air. Kenneth Koch. CAPP; NeAP; NNaP; NoAm; PP

O guide me through the shoals of fear–/"Furchte dich nicht, ich bin bei dir." An Exequy. Peter Porter. OxBC

O had thou suck'd thy thumb! The Woman's Wish. Matthew Prior. FaBoEE

O hairlips pooping speech. O men and women. Cripples. J. D. Reed. NeAC

O halfmoon man, my scars ache. Leda Forgets the Wings of the Swan. Diane Keating. CaPN

O Hallelujah!...Kindly pass the milk. Tennyson at Tea. Barry Pain. HBV 1-2

O hame cam' his gude horse,/But never cam' he! Bonny George Campbell. Anonymous. BSV; GoTS; OxBoLi; PoPle; ViBoPo

O happy England, and oh great glory of self-laudation. Amours de Voyage. Arthur Hugh Clough. OBSV

O happy field wherein this fodder grew,/Whose taste doth us from beasts to men renew. The Nativity of Christ. Robert Southwell. EBCP

O happy hands–an angel's fee!/That clasp the Lord of Majesty! The Young Priest to His Hands. Edward F. Garesche. CAW

O happy Israel in America,/In such a Moses such a Joshua. Upon the Tomb of the Most Reverend Mr. John Cotton... Benjamin Woodbridge. SCAP

O happy Love, where such delights consorteth! A Very Phoenix. Thomas Lodge. CBEP

O happy Mother, to possess/So loving-kind a boy! Mother and Child. Ivy O. Eastwick. SiSoSe

"O have me commended to your wife/at home;'/So Robin went laughing away. Robin Hood and the Butcher. Anonymous. BuBa; ESPB

O! he gave the snakes and toads a twist,/And bothered them forever! St. Patrick Was a Gentleman. Henry Bennett. SiSoSe

O he's a rider, but she'll leave that rail some time. Payday at Coal Creek. Anonymous. AmFP

O, he was good, if e'er a good man lived! Written after the Death of Charles Lamb (excerpt). William Wordsworth. CoBE

O hear us, our handmaid unheeding,/And take it away! Swinburne at Tea. Barry Pain. HBV 1-2

O heart! for all thy griefs and pains/Thou shalt be loth to die. Riding Adown the Country Lanes. Robert Bridges. VLP

O heart, in the great dawn! Second Best. Rupert Brooke. MoBrPo; OBVV

O heart! O heart! if she'd but turn her head,/You'd know the folly of being comforted. The Folly of Being Comforted. William Butler Yeats. AnIL; AnIL 019; AnIV; BrPo; GBL; GTBS; HeIP; MBW 1-2; VLP

O hearts that hunger through the world! Hungering Hearts. Anonymous. PoToHe

O heaven of music, absolve us from this hell/Unto unmechanized mastery over life. A Prayer from 1936. Siegfried Sassoon. TrPWD

O, heaven was in His sight, I know,/That little Child of long ago. A Child's Song of Christmas. Marjorie Pickthall. YeAr

O heavy breast of the dead horse! The Dead Horse. Cecilia Meireles. PBWP

O, help many of them to come unto You. To Whom Shall They Go? Anonymous. STF

O hermitage well found/Whatever hour it be!' The First Solitude. Luis de Gongora y Argote. OBVE

O highest of the gods! The Birds. Aristophanes. HW

O him she stores, to show what wealth she had,/In days long since, before these last so bad. Sonnets, LXVII: "Ah wherefore with infection should he live." William Shakespeare. PeHV

O hold me to Thy Heart once more,/And hide me from the past. Prodigal. Ellen Gilbert. GoBC

O honey, your hair grows too long, O honey, your hair grows too long. Levee Moan (with music). Anonymous. AS

"O hoppy-toad," he cried. Ballad of the Hoppy-Toad. Margaret Walker. BlSi; FB; HoPM

O horrible enchantment, that him so did blend! The Faerie Queene. Edmund Spenser. EBEV; OBSC

O House of love! O desolate/Pale flower beaten by the rain! La Bella Donna Della Mia Mente. Oscar Wilde. UnTE

O house them in the home of God! Requiescant. Frederick George Scott. OHIP

...O how deep into fear must I wedge/The strangeness I follow fools! Waterchew! Gregory Corso. VGW

O how I hope this lovely fire will spread! Honesty at a Fire. J. C. Squire. FiBHP

O how much wiser you would be/To play at Indian wars with me! The Gardener. Robert Louis Stevenson. HBV 1-2; HBVY; TreFS

O how should that God worship be,/who is but One and True? God Gives Them Sleep on Ground, on Straw. Roger Williams. SCAP

O, how sweet/Is the touch of a child's hand! Oshun, the River Goddess. Anonymous. WTO

O how that glittering taketh me! Upon Julia's Clothes. Robert Herrick. AnFE; AtBAP; AWP; CaPo; EnLi 1-2; EnLoPo; ExPo; FaBV; FaFP; FF; GBL; GoTF; GTBS; HAP; HBV 1-2; HeIP; HoPM; InPo; InPS; JCP; LiTB; LoBV; NIP; NLV; NOBE; NoP; OAEL 1-2; OAEP; OBEV; OBS; OBSP; PAI; PoEL 1-5; PoPle; PPoe; PPP; SeCeV; SeCP; SeCV 1-2; SpRo; TreF; TrGrPo; ViBoPo; WeW

O how the commonwealth doth need/Such justices as you! Farewell to the Fairies. Richard Corbet. EvOK; HBV 1-2; MoShBr

O Hunter, your own shadow stands/Within your forest lair! In the Caves of Auvergne. Walter James Turner. HBMV

...O, I'd rather be/A living mouse than dead as a man dies. No Coward's Song. James Elroy Flecker. OBSP

O I had a future. I Had a Future. Patrick Kavanagh. BIrV; NoAm

"O I have deserted my house carpenter,/For a grave in the depths of the sea." The House Carpenter's Wife. Anonymous. FSW

O I say now these are the soul! I Sing the Body Electric. Walt Whitman. CTC; ErPo; MasP

O I shall surely win thee,/Beloved, again! If Grief for Grief Can Touch Thee. Emily Bronte. EnLoPo; OBNC

O Illuminatio mea, I wait/For your entering smile. Bibliotheca Bodleiana. Geoffrey Grigson. GBL

O inconsolable friend, I lay my hand/Upon this page, and hear it, though you sleep. Ernest Dowson. John Hall Wheelock. HBMV

O indoctrinated cattle of an illusion. O White Mistress. Don Johnson. NNP

O ineffable Lady of O. Lady of O. James J. Galvin. ISi

O innocent throat! O human ear! A Thrush before Dawn. Alice Meynell. HBMV; MoBrPo

O io kalunga ua mu bangele.../We are. Friend Mussunda. Agostinho Neto. WhB

O Ireland! O my country! he comes to/break thy chain! Andromeda. James Jeffrey Roche. AA; HBV 1-2

O irritant, iterant, maddening bird! Owl against Robin. Sidney Lanier. LaNeLa

O, is this sleep, or waking where/Lie hush'd the Valleys of Dream? Dream Fantasy. Fiona Macleod. WGRP

O Isis, mother of God, hear my prayer. Prayer to Isis. Christina Walsh. BrRo

O it is terrible to dream of angels. The Gardener. Sidney Keyes. ChMP; MoAB; MoBrPo

O it's captain, I don't want to go. Yonder Comes the High Sheriff (with music). Anonymous. AS

O, it would grieve me utterly, to find them on my bier! When I Am Dead. Georgia Douglas Johnson. CDC

O Jean, look out the window at the trees! Heresy for a Class-Room. Rolfe Humphries. GLGT

O Jesu, Jesu, will it be/That Thou wilt turn away from me? What No Man Knoweth. Hugh Francis Blunt. CAW

O Jesu, my Savior, I languish for thee! Prayer before Execution. Queen of Scots Mary. CAW; TRV; WGRP

O Jesus, drink of me. A Better Resurrection. Christina Georgina Rossetti. EBCP; HBV 1-2; NOBV; OxBoCh; TrPWD; VLP

"O Jesus, Hasbrouck, am I drunk or dead?" Hasbrouck and the Rose. Howard Phelps (Phelps Putnam) Putnam. CoAnAm; MoVE; OxBA; ViBoPo

O jolly are we! for love, you see,/Fetters a heart and sets it free. The Flitch of Dunmow. James Carnegie. HBV 1-2

O joy, and joyful happy day, when wretches want their will. Lulla La, Lulla Lulla Lullaby. William Byrd. SBVL

O junius bird/who excavated. Evolution. Rochelle Owens. CoPo

O keep me from falling deeper/And deeper away. O King of the World. Anonymous. WTO

O Keith of Ravelston,/The sorrows of thy line! The Ballad of Keith of Ravelston. Sydney Thomas Dobell. HBV 1-2; OBEV; OBVV

O King, in my hour of danger,/Wilt thou be strong for me? Nativity Song. Jacopone da Todi. OHIP

...O King of/kings, alone and speechless shall I stand before thee to/face? Day after Day. Rabindranath Tagore. OBMV

O King of the Zulus, consecrate me! New Orleans. Hayden Carruth. AmFN

O la, o la. Thinking Twice in the Laundromat. Harley Elliott. NeAC

O Ladder of heaven. The Gaelic Litany to Our Lady. Anonymous. CAW; ISi

O lady full of guile. O Lady Full of Guile. Seathrun Ceitinn. NOBI

O lady hear me. I have no/other/voice left. Air: Cat Bird Singing. Robert Creeley. Prf

O Lady Moon. Minnie. Thomas Caulfield Irwin. IrPN

O lady, slumbering be thine/alone where the cold couch is dressed? Love Song. Luis Ponce de Leon. TrJP

O Lamb, I praise/the perfect whiteness of your shirt. Salesman. Ruth Roston. AMV-80

O Lamb of God, I come! Just As I Am. Charlotte Elliott. HBV 1-2; VLP

O Lamb of God! was ever pain–Was ever love like Thine? The Saviour. Samuel Wesley. BePJ

O lambs! The whole wolf-world sits down to eat/and cleans its muzzle after. How It Goes On. Maxine W. Kumin. FAZ; FiCP

O last belated love, thou art/a blend of joy and of hopeless surrender. Last Love. Fyodor Tyutchev. BoLoP; LiTW

O Lawd, my woman's down in Cummins, I love her just the same. O Lawd I Went Up on the Mountain. Anonymous. OuSiCo

O, learn to read what silent love hath writ:/To hear with eyes belongs to love's fine wit. Sonnets, XXIII: "As an unperfect actor on the stage." William Shakespeare. BiP; HBV 1-2; InvP; OAEP

O leave me, Creator, Tormentor, alone! Saul. Charles Heavysege. OBCV

O leave me easy, leave me alone. The Libertine. Louis MacNeice. DTC; NoAm

O leave thy cares and follies! go this way,/And thou art sure to prosper all the day. Fragment. Henry Vaughan. TRV; WGRP

O Leerie, see a little child and nod to him to-night! The Lamplighter. Robert Louis Stevenson. FaFP; OxBChV; SaC; TreF

O lei, O lei, O lei.... My Indian Girl. Ali Sedat Hilmi Torel. PeD

O, let me be at peace with it. Life's Testament. William Baylebridge. BoAV; PoAu 1-2

O let me feel the biting strokes/That I may fight again! Prayer for Pain. John G. Neihardt. HBV 1-2; TrPWD; WGRP

...O let me live/To love, and flush, and thrill-or let me die! A Life-Drama (excerpt). Alexander Smith. VLP

O let me not die a maid, take me for pitty. The Wooing Maid. Martin Parker. CoMu

O let me serve Thee now! He Doeth All Things Well. Anne Bronte. TRV

O, let my eyes no more see such a sight! Visions. Petrarch. EnLi 1-2

O let my joyes, have some abiding. Lullaby: "Come sleep, and with the sweet deceiving." Francis Beaumont and John Fletcher. FaBoEn

O! let my Wish be crown'd,/And send it from above! The Desponding Soul's Wish. John Byrom. OBEC; TrPWD

O let that dying, piercing cry,/Melt and reclaim my wand'ring soul. Calvary's Cry. Cunningham. BePJ

O let the heart's tough riggings salvage him,/Only whose lengths can grapple with these dead. S.S.R., Lost at Sea–The Times. Ralph Gustafson. OBCV

O let the Midnight Special shine its everlovin' light on me. Midnight Special. Kenneth Patchen. VGW

O let them all thy love receive,/And saved, with us, for ever live! On Sympathisers with the American Revolution. Charles Wesley. NOCV

O let they power cleer/Thy gift once more, and grind this flint to dust! Silex Scintillans. Henry Vaughan. AnAnS 1

O let thy mercy interpose/And set thy captives free. Far from Our Friends. Jeremy Belknap. AH

O, let us hope a little ere we die. Antigone and Oedipus. Henrietta Cordelia Ray. BlSi

O, let us think of those/Whose lives are lost in woes,/Whose cup of grief runs o'er. Moan, Moan, Ye Dying Gales. Henry Neele. HBV 1-2

O Liberty! my spirit felt thee there. France: An Ode. Samuel Taylor Coleridge. ATP; ERoP 1-2; OAEP

O Life! O Sun! Escape. Robert Graves. BrPo; MoBrPo

O Light Invisible, we give Thee thanks for Thy great/glory! The Rock. Thomas Stearns Eliot. ILwL; OxBoCh

(O little Lord of Christmas, let us keep the day with Thee!) Christmas at Babbitt's. Henry Hallam Tweedy. TRV

O little lost poet with/many fine doctors and one celestial pillow. Lost. David Fisher. NPGG

O little sad sardine, I fear/Our world is full of woe! Reverie. Don (Donald Robert Marquis) Marquis. FPL; PoLf

O little town of bedlam in the beginning/Of the end as it was, as it is to all, good night. Canticle for Xmas Eve. David Wagoner. SM

O living pine, be still! Sleep. Yvor Winters. PoL

O longings irrepressible! O I will go back to old Tennessee/and never wander more. O Magnet-South. Walt Whitman. LaNeLa

...O, look we like a pair/Who for fresh nuptials joyfully yield all else? Modern Love, XLI. George Meredith. HBV 1-2; VLP

O Lord All-Merciful, be merciful to me. Before the Beginning. Christina Georgina Rossetti. OxBoCh

O Lord, be lost with us,/And then we shall be found. In the Wilderness. Edith Lovejoy Pierce. TrPWD

O, Lord, have mercy on me'/An' I hope I'll jine de ban'. Gwineter Ride Up in de Chariot Soon-a in de Mornin'. Anonymous. BoAN 1-2

O Lord, how long? Heaven Is Not Far. Christina Georgina Rossetti. OxBoCh

"O Lord, I thank thee ('tis not scorn)/That I was not a woman born." The Unfortunate Male. Ben Kalonymos. TrJP

O Lord, in thee have I trusted; let me never be confounded. Te Deum Laudamus. Anonymous. WGRP

O Lord in your odd way please do not desert me Prayer. Gavin Ewart. OxBC

O Lord, Kum ba yah. Kum Ba Yah (Come By Here). Anonymous. FSW

O Lord my God, my Lover, and my Friend. Prayer. George Villiers. TrPWD

O Lord, no longer be my days/Than I may fruitful be. Deliverance from a Fit of Fainting. Anne Bradstreet. TAP

O Lord of life! am I forbid/To cross the room? The Room's Width. Elizabeth Stuart Phelps Ward. AA

O Lord, our hearts we lift to thee./For everything give thanks! For Everything Give Thanks. Helen Isabella Tupper. GoTF; TreFT

O Lord, remember me. 'Tis Sweet to Rest in Lively Hope. Anonymous. AmFP

O Lord, remember us. Litany. Charles Angoff. TrPWD

O Lord! speak soon to me-"Lo, here am I!" Doubt. Margaret Deland. TrPWD

O Lord that rulest our mortal line,/How through the world Thy name doth shine. Psalm VIII. Sir Philip Sidney. FCP

O Lord, the shield and buckler/of my need. Lo, Who Could Stand. Anonymous. TrJP

O Lord, Thou art my Master/And I Thy slave. I Know That I Am a Great Sinner. Purohit Swami. OBMV

O Lord! When in Thy winepress I am/cast/Shall I e'er find rebirth? Grape-Gathering. Abraham Shlonsky. Abraham TrJP

O lord white as jasmine. Like a Silkworm Weaving. Mahadevi (Mahadeviyakka). PBWP

O Lord, won't you help-a me! Blind Man Lay Beside the Way (with music). Anonymous. AS

O lose it not! look up, wilt Change those Lights/For Chains of Darkness, and Eternal Nights! Silex Scintillans. Henry Vaughan. AnAnS 1

"O lost Jerusalem." The Wandering Jew Comes to the Wall. Edmond Fleg. TrJP

O lost to the bliss of any more remembering. Long Since Last. Ruth Miller. PeSA

O love-inspiring Spring! To Spring: On the Banks of the Cam. William Caldwell Roscoe. OBVV

O love is passing by! Three Rimas, 1. Gustavo Adolfo Becquer. LiTW

O love! O wonder! Conquered. Zoë Akins. HBMV

O love that turns to stone! Medusa. Robert Kelley Weeks. AA

O Love, thou art the pearl my heart hath made,/And I am sore afraid. The Pearl. Hans Christian Andersen. LiTW

"O love,/where are you/leading/me now?" Kore. Robert Creeley. ConAP; CoPo; InPS; NMP; PAI

O Love, who dost with goodness crown/The moments and the ages down! O Love, That Dost with Goodness Crown. John Chadwick. TrPWD

O loved for ever, evermore! Serenade. Oscar Wilde. HBV 1-2

O lovely April rich and bright. Song: "O lovely April, rich and bright." Gustave Kahn. TrJP

O Lover! drive me through a stilly land/With the compelling of your open hand. The Tired Woman. Anna Wickham. MoBrPo

O'Luve sends it plungin'/A'else into nicht!.... Moonlight among the Pines. Hugh" (Christopher Murray Grieve) MacDiarmid. OAEL 1-2

O Magistrates, take heed, lest ye be found/As fighters against God! The Proclamation. Henry Wadsworth Longfellow. PAH

O Mahsr! call yo' chillen soon, an' take 'em home! Amen. Blessing the Dance. Irwin Russell. AnAmPo

O Maiden of the Maronites! On Lebanon. David Gray. AA

O maister, maister, God thy soule reste! Lament for Chaucer. Thomas Hoccleve. OBEV

O! maistres mine, till you I me commend. O! Mistress Mine. Anonymous. GoTS; MeEL

O make them white, that they may singing die! Hoc Cygno Vinces. Henry Hawkins. ACP

O Maker of the hills and sea and wind! To the Western Wind. Judah Halevi. TrJP

"O Man! from tyrannous war release/Our troubled hearts and grant our children peace." War. J. C. Hall. HaMV

O Man of Nazareth, be our guest! Hymn for a Household. Daniel Henderson. HBMV

O man, what fools are we/In prison-walls to dwell! Early Morning at Bargis. Hermann Hagedorn. HBV 1-2

O man who follow English ways. Civil Irish and Wild Irish. Laoiseach Mac an Bhaird. AnIL

O Mary, Christ, have mercy on your man. Apologia Pro Vita Sua. Sedulius Scottus. BIrV

O Mary don't you weep. O Mary, Don't You Weep, Don't You Mourn. Anonymous. AH

O Mary, don' you weep, don' you mo'n. Pharaoh's Army Got Drownded (with music). *Anonymous.* AS

O Mary, if you let me I/Will wrap him warmly in my own. Christmas Night. Hugh MacCawell. KiLC

O Mary Virgin, full of grace! Ave. Dante Gabriel Rossetti. GoBC; ISi; OxBoCh

O master let us go again/and play beside the sea Pete at the Seashore. Don (Donald Robert Marquis) Marquis. GDP

O Master of our many lives,/In thee our life is one. One in Christ. Henry Van Dyke. TRV

...O may he never/answer my one with three. The Shade-Seller. Josephine Jacobsen. TAP

O, may her choice be fixed on me!/Mine's fixed on her alone. The Lass of Richmond Hill. James Upton. HBV 1-2

O May, in purity outshone. Author's Entreaty for His Lay. Eysteinn Asgrimsson. ISi

O may thy hand conduct me home! To Thee, O God. Abiel Holmes. AH

O may we all the loving mind/That was in Thee receive. The Loadstone of His Love. Charles Wesley. BePJ

O may we in Thy bosom rest,/The bosom of Thy love. Evening Shade. *Anonymous.* AmFP

O, may we meet together there and dwell in endless peace! The Gale of August, '27. *Anonymous.* ShS

O maybe you think there's another verse,/But there isn't. The Three Ravens (C vers.). *Anonymous.* ViBoFo

...O me, that eye/Doth make my heart give to my tongue the lie. The Yoke of Tyranny. Sir Philip Sidney. TrGrPo

O men of earth, that wandering voice/Still goes the upward way: rejoice! The Poet. Edwin Markham. WGRP

O men of the Marmion class, sons of the free. Mythology. Lawrence Durrell. DTC; OxBTC

"O mercy!' to myself I cried,/"If Lucy should be dead!' Strange Fits of Passion Have I Known. William Wordsworth. CBEP; CoBE; EBEV; EnL; ERoP 1-2; FiP; GBL; LiTB; LiTL; MBW 1-2; OAEL 1-2; OAEP; OBNC; OBRV; PPP; TEP; ViBoPo

O merry, merry sing for joy,/Ut hoy! 'Twas Jolly, Jolly Wat. Charles William Stubbs. OHIP

O Messiah, he stands grimy in his/tank! Ballad of the Days of the Messiah. Abraham Moses Klein. TrJP

–O might our children find ere death/The far land that we have died to find! The Far Land. John Hall Wheelock. WGRP

O might we live to him alone,/And nevermore transgress. O Heaven Indulge. Stephen Tilden. AH

O mighty charm! which makes men love theyr bane,/And thinck they dy with pleasure, live with payne. Trust Not the Treason. Edmund Spenser. BoLiVe

O mighty Jove the windes for this me geve. Of His Returne from Spaine. Sir Thomas Wyatt. EnPo; FaBoEn

O miseries and appetites of the world. The Hermit. Howard Moss. NePoAm

O Mission bells of Monterey! The Mission Bells of Monterey. Bret (Francis Bret Harte) Harte. PeD

O mistress mine, my kindling wood. Hearthside Story. X. J. Kennedy. CoPo

O moon above the mountain crest. From Darkness. Izumi Shikibu. PBWP

O moon-white maid! On a Nightingale in April. William Sharp. HBV 1-2; OBVV

O moonlight, bear my message of love to the heart that beats/for me. In the Moonlight. David McKee Wright. AnNZ

O most noble king./Consider well this thing. Vox Populi, Vox Dei (excerpt). *Anonymous.* FaBoPV

"O mother dear, when I was thine,/You did no prove to me sae kind." The Cruel Mother (A vers.). *Anonymous.* BaBo; ESPB; FaBoBa

O mother, hath one grave room for two? Ballade de Marguerite. *Anonymous.* AWP

O mother of lakes and glaciers save us gamblers/whose wagon is perilously rapt. Santa Fe Trail. Barbara Guest. NeAP; PoM

O move in mercy among us. Grant accepted grace. The Need. Siegfried Sassoon. TrPWD

O Mr Cromek, how do ye do? Cromek. William Blake. FiBHP; PV

O muddy grandeur!–ignominy ironic and sublime! You'd Take the Entire Universe to Bed with You. Charles Baudelaire. NAWM 1-2

O muse immortal, singer true,/What harmonies unite the two! An Old-Fashioned Poet. Ada Foster Murray. HBV 1-2

O music through my clay,/When will you sound again? A Mystic as Soldier. Siegfried Sassoon. WGRP

O my babe, my honey babe. Harvey Logan. *Anonymous.* OuSiCo

O my Belov'd, a smile of Thine/Is heav'n enough for me. Consecration. Anna Hoppe. BePJ

O my companions, Wind, Water, Stars, and Night. The Full Heart. Robert Nichols. BoNaP; HBMV

O my dahlin', I love you. O My Honey, Take Me Back (with music). *Anonymous.* AS

O my dear and only. Cressida. James Keir Baxter. AnNZ

O my friend has brought me five o'clock/and the sign of impending snow. The Composition of Distances. Pien Chih-lin. LiTW

O my God, let it be thine! Silex Scintillans. Henry Vaughan. AnAnS 1

...O my heirs,/You of the equal sadness, give him your prayers. In All the Argosy of Your Bright Hair. Dunstan Thompson. WaP

O my Hornby and my Barlow long ago! At Lord's. Francis Thompson. LiSp; OBSP

...O my husband, what is this/strange land I have no desire to explore? Urgency. Betsy Sholl. AMV-80

O my lady, wife of An, I have told your fury! Antiphonal Hymn in Praise of Inanna. Enheduanna. BoWoP

O, my little breath, now I go there alone in sorrow. The Willows by the Water Side. *Anonymous.* WTO

O, my Lord, I'm gwinter see my mother again,/Hallelu. Death Come to My House He Didn't Stay Long. *Anonymous.* BoAN 1-2

O, my Lord! Jubalee, Jubalee,/O, Lord! Jubalee. Jubalee; or, What Is de Matter wid de Mourners. *Anonymous.* BoAN 1-2

O, my Lord, Save-a me/De blin' man stood on de road an' cried. De Blin' Man Stood on de Road an' Cried. *Anonymous.* BoAN 1-2

O my Lord, what shall I do to be saved? Soon One Mornin' Death Come Creepin'. *Anonymous.* OuSiCo

O my love, my life, my queen. Since We Loved. Robert Bridges. VLP

O my much praised but-not-altogether-satisfactory lady. The Bathtub. Ezra Pound. NIP

O my poor darling O My Poor Darling. Wilfred Watson. EnLoPo

O my red phoenix from the south! Welcome My World. Denis Devlin. AnIV

O my river's complex course. The Call of the River Nun. Gabriel Okara. PBA

O my son! O my son! David's Lamentation. *Anonymous.* AmFP

O my sweet my sweet The Test. Rachel McAlpine. OCNZ

O nebber you fear, if nebber you hear/De driver blow his horn! At Port Royal: Song of the Negro Boatman. John Greenleaf Whittier. GN

O needy sinner, come, O come. Just As Thou Art. Russell Sturgis Cook. AH

O neighbors, O dogs. O porcupines! Porcupines. Robley Wilson, Jr. AMV-81

...O neither these verses/Nor my prudence, love, can heal your wounded stare. A Dream of Jealousy. Seamus Heaney. CIP; FaBoIP

O never again/will anyone be anonymous and all our graves/will be national shrines! Fame. Vern Rutsala. GP

O never be faint hearted. O Earnest Be. *Anonymous.* AH

O never could be found garments too good/For thee to wear, but these, of thine own blood. On Our Crucified Lord, Naked and Bloody. Richard Crashaw. CABA; HoPM; OAEL 1-2; OBSP; SeCV 1-2; TrCP

O never I turned, but let, alack,/These less things hold my gaze! Overlooking the River Stout. Thomas Hardy. FaBoPP

O never you will, said she The Juniper Tree. Wilfred Watson. WHW

O night betrayed by darkness not its own. Night, Death, Mississippi. Robert Earl Hayden. FF; LCAP; VGW

O night! O doubly-happy night! The Wedding Night. Johannes Secundus. UnTE

O night, O eyes of love! The Thousand and One Nights: Drinking Song. *Anonymous.* LiTW

O night of love and beauty, all the years/Shall pay for thy brief ecstasy with tears. Sonnets. Robert Hillyer. HBMV

O night so clear, so fair to see!– Night of the Immaculate Conception. Juan Maragall. CAW

O no, I would rather work hard all the day,/My little blue apron to fill.' The Gleaner. Jane Taylor. OxBChV

O no, John! No, John! No, John! No! O No, John! *Anonymous.* ErPo; UnTE

O, none, unless this miracle have might,/That in black ink my love may still shine bright. Sonnets, LXV: "Since brass, nor stone, nor earth, nor boundless sea." William Shakespeare. AWP; DiPo; FaFP; FF; FiP; GTBS; GTBS-P; HAP; InPS; LiTB; LiTL; MasP; MCCG; NOBE; NoP; PAI; PoRA; SeCeV; UnPo

O, Omega, violet ray of Her Eyes! Vowels. Arthur Rimbaud. SOTW

O only universe we know, forgive us. On Frozen Fields. Galway Kinnell. CAPP

O our Mother the Earth, O our Father the Sky! Song of the Sky Loom. *Anonymous.* WTO

O oxygen, pinkness, protein, hair, and bone,/a stump in the meadow, river, and stone. Girls. Kenneth Rosen. AmPA

O, P, Q, R, S, T, U, V, W, X, Y, Z. Great A Was Alarmed at B's Bad Behaviour. *Anonymous.* FaBoUs; OxNR

O past that is! Two Lovers. George Eliot. HBV 1-2

O peevish and uncertain soul! obey/The law of life in patience till the Day. In the Shadows. David Gray. OxBS

O, sweet relief from faces that are white!   Negro Servant.   Langston Hughes.
VGW

O sweet shepheard, hie thee,/For methinks thou stay'st too long.   Madrigal:
"Crabbed age and youth."   William Shakespeare.   GTBS; GTBS-P

O sweet song.   Lovesong.   Rainer Maria Rilke.   OLR

O SWEETEST WATER O GLORIOUS/WHEELING/BIRD   Song of the
Turkey Buzzard.   Lew Welch.   PoM

O sweetheart! waht is this/Lieth there so cold?   What the Bullet Sang.   Bret
(Francis Bret Harte) Harte.   AA; CBEP; OBEV; OBVV; PeD

O Swine that takest away our sins/That takest away   Pig.   Anthony Hecht.
OxBC

O syllables of light...O dark cathedral...   There Is.   Louis Simpson.   ConAP

O teach our love to grow/Up to thy heavenly light, and reap what Thou hast
sown.   Balaam.   John Keble.   OBNC; OBVV

"O, tell her I'm dead and lying in my grave,/Way out in Idaho."   Two Little
Boys.   *Anonymous.*   BaBo

O tell me, tell me soon.   Is It No Dream That I Am He.   Walter Savage
Landor.   GBL

O that fair Winifred would once say so.   A Dialogue between the Lovelorn
Sir Hugh and Certain Ladies....   Thomas Deloney.   UnTE

O that great Sabbaoth God, graunt me that Sabaoths sight.   The Faerie
Queene.   Edmund Spenser.   OAEL 1-2; PoEL 1-5

...O that I could fly/From my self you, or from your own self I!   Idea.
Michael Drayton.   TrGrPo

O that I too were attired in such dun colours!   Dun Colour.   Ruth Pitter.
FM; MoVE

O! That I were a glove upon that hand,/That I might touch that cheek.
Romeo and Juliet.   William Shakespeare.   BoC; LiTB; LiTL; MaC; MasP;
MOON; TreF; TrGrPo; WHA

O that I were blind!   Japanese Hokku.   Lewis Alexander.   CDC

O that mine eyes sent forth a blaze of/light,/To be a beacon in another's night.
Psalm.   Yehoash.   TrJP

O that our hearts were all a heaven,/Forever fill'd with God.   Come, Lord
Jesus.   Charles Wesley.   BePJ

O, that that earth, which kept the world in awe,/Should patch a wall t' expel
the winter's flaw!   Hamlet.   William Shakespeare.   DL

O that was me, said the madman.   Song: "A little onion lay by the fireplace."
Nicholas Moore.   EAS

"O that we were pumpkins too!"/Their glances seemed to say.   Coach.
Eleanor Farjeon.   DFT

O that we were there! O that we were there!   In Dulci Jubilo.   *Anonymous.*
CAW

O the ash and the oak and the willow tree/And that's an end of the infantry!
The Ash and the Oak.   Louis Simpson.   ConAP; NePoAm

O the broken ranks and the trumpets ringing/On the sunny side of
Slievenamon!   Slievenamon.   *Anonymous.*   KiLC

O the darling!   Little Brother's Secret.   Katherine Mansfield.   NAs; TiPo

O the Earl was fair to see!   The Sisters.   Alfred, Lord Tennyson.   InvP

O the fair nymph born to do women honour,/Lady my Treasure.   Lady My
Treasure.   Sir Philip Sidney.   GBL

O, the farmer is the man who feeds them all!   The Farmer (with music).
Anonymous.   AS

O the nutbrown tresses nodding interlaced!   Love in the Valley.   George
Meredith.   ErPo

O the sun and the moon, mother,/shall both rise with me.   The Cherry-Tree
Carol.   *Anonymous.*   BaBo; BoLiVe; CBEP; DiPo; ELP; EnSB; ESPB;
FaBoBa; GBP; HeIP; LoBV; OAEL 1-2; OAEP; OFD; OnMSP; OxBB;
OxBoCh; OxBoLi; SBVL; SeCeV; ViBoFo

O the sun and the moon, mother,/shall both rise with me.   Joseph Was an
Old Man.   *Anonymous.*   OBCP

O the sweeping past of the ruined sky!   The Bracelet of Grass.   William
Vaughn Moody.   AP

O, the Temeraire no more!   The Temeraire.   Herman Melville.   WaaP

O the tidings be sad that I bring.   Henry Martyn.   *Anonymous.*   CBEP

O, then give me cold water.   Come, Happy Children.   *Anonymous.*   AH

O then I clap aloft my brave broad wings,/And make the wide air tremble
while it rings!'   The Plea of the Midsummer Fairies.   Thomas Hood.
OBNC

O then let every orphan breast/With grateful transport beat.   Chilled by the
Blasts of Adverse Fate.   Jacob Duche.   AH

...O then the unloosen'd ocean,/Of tears! tears! tears!   Tears.   Walt Whitman.
AnAmPo; NePA

O then we'll wed and then we'll bed,/But not in our Alley.   The Ballad of
Sally in our Alley.   Henry Carey.   CEP; NOEC; OBEC

O, then! with what rapture/Will it fill dean and chapter!   A Receipt for
Stewing Veal.   John Gay.   FaBoUs

O there above the little grave,/We kiss'd again with tears.   As Thro' the Land
at Eve We Went.   Alfred, Lord Tennyson.   LiTB; LiTL

O, there be players that I have seen play, and heard others praise, and that
highly, not to speak..   Hamlet.   William Shakespeare.   TreFS

O there's a terrifying innocence in my face/drenched with the silver salvage of
the mornfrost.   History.   Robert Lowell.   CAPP; HaCAP; TAP

O there's love all day   What There Is.   Kenneth Patchen.   LLLT

O, there's naught to compare wi' ane's ain fireside.   My Ain Fireside.
Elizabeth Hamilton.   FaBoBe; HBV 1-2

O there's peace, peace, ev'rywhere!   In My Father's House (with music).
Anonymous.   AS

O they be rightly blessed.   Psalm II.   Sir Philip Sidney.   FCP

O they're all like sweet Mistress Malone!   The Widow Malone.   Charles
James Lever.   HBV 1-2; TreFS

O think I then, what paradise of joy/It is, so fair a virtue to enjoy!   Astrophel
and Stella, LXVIII.   Sir Philip Sidney.   AAS; OBSC; SiPS

O think of Jane and me.   The Emigrant's Dying Child.   G. W. Patton.
BPAW

O think on Morris, in a lonely chamber,/Dabbling in Sapphic.   Sapphics.
Thomas Morris.   NOEC

O thou, enthron'd with Cherubs in the realms of day.   On Virtue.   Phillis
Wheatley.   TAP

O Thou Kitchi Manito, hear us!   Indian Prayer.   Chief Joseph Strongwolf.
TRV

"O thou my Voice, the word was thine.' "Was thine.'   The Two Poets.
Alice Meynell.   OBVV

...O Thou, our works/To happiest end address.   In Pilgrim Life Our Rest.
Edwin Sandys.   AH

O thou that art my light, my life, my way.   Why Dost Thou Shade Thy
Lovely Face?   Francis Quarles.   OxBoCh

O Thou, who openest graciously/Thy hand to all that live.   The Living God.
Abraham Ibn Ezra.   TrJP

O thou, whom my soul Loves, and feares!   Silex Scintillans.   Henry
Vaughan.   AnAnS 1

...O thou whose cheeks and body were as/jasmine, how art thou?   On the
Death of His Child.   Faydi.   LiTW

O thou whose deeds and dreams were one.   Dear Master, in Whose Life I
See.   John Hunter.   TRV

O, 'tis pretty Picking/With a tender Chicken.   Asparagus.   Jonathan Swift.
NCEP

O to abide in the desert with thee!   The Skylark.   James Hogg.   ATP; BSV;
GN; HBV 1-2; HBVY; PBBP

O to be happy–to be kind–/Sure never is too late!   The Reconcilement.
John, Duke of Buckingham Sheffield.   CEP; LiTL; OBEV

O to haste firm holding–to haste, haste on with me.   Starting from
Paumanok.   Walt Whitman.   AtBAP; PAI; ViBoPo

O to send to a friend my last love.   Articles of War.   Dunstan Thompson.
WaP

O to what height of horror are they come/Who dare pull down a crown, tear
up a tomb!   Upon the Double Murther of King Charles I...   Katherine
("Orinda") Philips.   SBG

O'Toole, Hodain, ye Bruthers Dogg.   Ye Bruthers Dogg.   Jon Anderson.
NLV

O traveler, abiding not/Where he pretends to be!   The Traveler.   Vachel
Lindsay.   MoAmPo

...O tree, sing through her hair/As she sways into dark!   A Star.   George
MacBeth.   NYBP

(O Troy's down,/Tall Troy's on fire!)   Troy Town.   Dante Gabriel Rossetti.
MaVP

O tuck my baby in.   Tucking the Baby In.   Curtis May.   HBV 1-2

O turn once more.   O Turn Once More.   Duncan Campbell Scott.   CoBE

O twilight bell,/flower of the wonga vine.   Wonga Vine.   Judith Wright.
PoAu 1-2

O-U-T, and in again.   Intery, Mintry, Cutery, Corn.   *Anonymous.*   OxNR

O–U–T, etc.   Dips or Counting Out Rhymes: "Ex and squary."   *Anonymous.*
GBP

O unchanging Truth.   In a World of Change.   Joseph Awad.   AMV-80

O under grass, O under grass, the secret.   Yeats' Tower.   Vernon Watkins.
NeBP

O unspeakable passionate love.   Song of Myself.   Walt Whitman.   AtBAP

O! Violated.../O! Murdered...   Corpses in the Wood.   Ernst Toller.   TrJP

O Virgin blest!   Cantiga.   Gil Vicente.   CAW; ISi

O voices all! like you I die!   In Immemoriam.   Cuthbert (Edward Bradley)
Bede.   NA

O walk not in the wind!   To the Maids Not to Walk in the Wind.   Oliver
St.John Gogarty.   AnIL

O, was it you?   A Bowl of Roses.   William Ernest Henley.   EnLi 1-2;
MoBrPo

O, was no deny.   Love's Secret.   William Blake.   EnLoPo

"O wasted kisses! O too happy child!"   When I Was Small.   Andre Marie de
Chenier.   ErPo

O we must start back t'night!   Goin' Back T'morrer.   Hamlin Garland.
OBAL

O we who hew, build, deck, shall we not also/The happiness that we have
given partake?/Hallelujah!'   Evening Hymn in the Hovels.   Francis
Lauderdale Adams.   OxBS

O wear your tribulation like a rose.   Song for St. Cecilia's Day.   W. H.
Auden.   FaBoTw; MP

(O weary mother, drive the cows to roost). Rossetti at Tea. Barry Pain. HBV 1-2

O weep no more; thou art all wan with sighs.' Sonnet: To the Same Ladies; with Their Answer. Dante Alighieri. AWP

O welcomes forever here!/Eivlin a ruin! Eileen Aroon. Carrol O'Daly. OnYI

O, what a plague is an obstinate daughter. Song. Richard Brinsley Sheridan. CEP

O, what a round of applause! Coup de Grace. A. D. Hope. DFT; PPP

O what a savoury supper/For my old dame and me.' A Croon on Hennacliff. Robert Stephen Hawker. NOBV

O what endless Hydrox cookies! High. John Perreault. ANYP

O! what is praise, pomp, glory, joy, but so/As shine by fountains, bubbles, flowers, or snow? A Palinode. Edmund Bolton. EIL; InvP; OBSC; PoEL 1-5; PrIm

O what is there like love. The Powers of Love. George Moses Horton. BALP

–O what made fatuous sunbeams toil/To break earth's sleep at all? Futility. Wilfred Owen. AtBAP; CBEP; ChMP; CMoP; CoBMV; FaBoMo; GTBS-P; MMM; MoAB; MoBrPo; NoAm; NoP; OAEP; OBWP; SeCePo; TrGrPo

"O what matter, when for Erin dear we fall!" God Save Ireland. Timothy Daniel Sullivan. OnYI

O what shall I do/to this dump of a town! Shall I Charge Like a Bull. Auvaiyar. WPOW

O what weeps is the love that hears, an/Accident occurring in his substance. Spring 1940. W. H. Auden. OAEP

O when will the morning rise? The Golden Net. William Blake. ERoP 1-2

O when will they ever learn?... Where Have All the Flowers Gone? (excerpt). Pete Seeger. WeW

O, where is all our love? When Love Meets Love. Thomas Edward Brown. OBVV; PeD; UnPo

O where is my boy tonight? Where Is My Wandering Boy Tonight? Robert Lowry. FaFP; FSW; TreF

O, where's Polly? A Midsummer Song. Richard Watson Gilder. BoNaP; HBV 1-2

O where was I, that was not where I am? Sonnet XXXIII. William Alabaster. AnAnS 1

O who can tast thy Good, and not Thanksgiving Raise. A Monumental Memorial of Marine Mercy &c. Richard Steere. SCAP

O, who dat a comin' ovah yonder, Hallelu. Who Dat A-Comin' ovah Yondah? Anonymous. BoAN 1-2

O, who hath heard what I have heard, or seen what I/have seen? The Story of the Shepherd. Anonymous. OHIP

O, who would not be/He, he, he? Nano's Song. Ben Jonson. BoLiVe; LoBV

O why did she linger and why did she stay? A Night Full of Nothing. Keith Sinclair. AnNZ

O why do you walk through the fields in gloves/Missing so much and so much? To a Fat Lady Seen from the Train. Frances Cornford. BLPA; ELU; FaBoWP; GoJo; MoBrPo; OBMV; SpRo; WeW

O, why should Heavenly God to men have such regard! The Faerie Queene. Edmund Spenser. GoBC; NOCV; SMC

O wild, waste lands that await/The harvest exceeding great,/Break forth into praise of God! On the Big Horn. John Greenleaf Whittier. PAH

O, Wilderness were Paradise enow! Rubaiyat of Omar Khayyam. Omar Khayyam. LiTL; TEP

O wildest of untouched dreams. Another Cross. Stephen Gardner. AMV-80

"O Wind, hae maircy, haud yer whisht, for I daurna listen mair!" The Wild Geese. Violet Jacob. BSV

O wind, that sings so loud a song! The Wind. Robert Louis Stevenson. GN; HBVY; SoPo; SUS; TiPo

O wings that beat at dawning, ye return/Out of the desert to your young at eve! Epitaphs of the War, 1914-18. Rudyard Kipling. OBWP

O wise and travelled souls,/Before I go.' From Disciple to Master. Monk Gibbon. AnIV

"O! Wise Sun above,/will you ever guide/me into school?" The Shepherd and His Flock. Mbuyiseni Oswald Mtshali. GrPl

O! woful wretche! O! wretche, lesse ones thy speche! Come, Death–My Lady Is Dead. Charles, duc d' Orleans. MeEL

O woman full of wile! O Woman Full of Wile. Geoffrey Keating. OnYI

O woman, love of my soul, do not pursue me of/all men. Do Not Torment Me, Woman. Anonymous. AnIL

O women shut up, yelling for baby meat more. Flashback. Allen Ginsberg. CAPP

O World, be nobler, for her sake! O World, Be Nobler. Laurence Binyon. GTBS; HBV 1-2; MoBrPo; OBEV

O world, be not so fair. O World, Be Not So Fair. Grace Fallow Norton. HBV 1-2

O World–dost thou not know Me even yet? Still Thou Art Question. Anonymous. PGD

O wretched man, the throne of tyranny! Here Pause: The Poet Claims at Least This Praise. William Wordsworth. EnRP

O, write my name,/De Angels in de heab'n gwineter write my name. De Angels in Heab'n Gwineter Write My Name. Anonymous. BoAN 1-2

O yikes/o yikes. Death. Jeffrey Miller. APU

O you! Hybrid! Roar, bitch! Blast! Make me–pure! The Nightmare. Jascha Kessler. AmPC

O you unquiet heart! Sleep Now, O Sleep Now. James Joyce. GBL

O you who like a woman/are so full of jealousy. Animal Songs: Zebra Stallion. Anonymous. PeSA

O Zion, When the bridgroom come. Don't You Be Like the Foolish Virgin. Anonymous. AH

O Zobo bird! The Zobo Bird. Frank A. Collymore. AmMo; GoJo

The Oak now resembles which lightning hath blasted. Chloris and Hilas. Made to a Saraban. Edmund Waller. SeCV 1-2

Oak sky. Drunken Winter. Joseph Ceravolo. ANYP

The oaks go down with thunder in the singing air. Clabe Mott. James Still. GrPl

Oaks have entered the places of the poets/and taken the light of the schools from everyone. Epigram: "Loss of our learning brought darkness, weakenss and woe." Anonymous. NOBI

Oar blues demon shun Simfunny of Thee Hold Whorl. Charles Lynch. LTB

The oars we spent years to learn/Push air by us in tight bundles. Desert in the Sea. Brian Swann. AmPA

Oasis of my dreams, and gourd from whence/Deep draughted wines of memory will flow. Her Hair. Charles Baudelaire. NAWM 1-2

Oates being to this happy nation/The mystic emblem of salvation. A Panegyric upon Oates. Richard Duke. APAS

Obedient to the last command/Thine eye impose on me– The Moon Is Distant from the Sea. Emily Dickinson. DiPo

Obedient to the living God,/His judgment and his laws. Poem, 1972. Syd Scroggie. PoSH

Obelisk of a beard admonishes the heavens. For Malcolm X. Nanina Alba. PoBA

Obey and thank thy God of all.' The Abbey Walk. Robert Henryson. BSV

...Obey/The law of life in patience till the Day. Sonnet I: "If it must be; if it must be, O God!" David Gray. BSV

The object floating at his side/Made no distinct reply. The waters chased him as he fled. Emily Dickinson. PoEL 1-5

,An object like a throne/Under a shining canopy of state/Stood fixed.... The Excursion. William Wordsworth. BoLiVe

Oblige me in a more obliging way,/Or know such over-acting spoils the play. Air: "So full of courtly reverence." Dudley, Lord North. OBSP

Oblivion–the shroud and envelope of happiness. Oblivion. Jessie Redmond Fauset. BANP; PoNe

Oblivious of its transparent silence. Away from You. Cecilia Meireles. AMV-81

Oblivious to apricot-tree death. Vegetable Destiny. Nina Cassian. PBWP

Obscurity has another tale to tell. Focus. Adrienne Rich. FaBoWP

Observe enduring life in you/And start to die together. My Son, My Executioner. Donald Hall. InPK; SM

"Observe," she said, "the action/Of mustard on Mamma." Amelia Mixed the Mustard. Alfred Edward Housman. DBV; FaBoNo

Observe the curving wake of our boat on the slate bay. Visit by Water. Floris Clark McLaren. OBCV

Observe/the jasmine lightness/of the moon. To a Solitary Disciple. William Carlos Williams. PP; VGW

Observe the tremble of the weeping willows. Vernal Equinox. Ruth Stone. MoAmPo

Observe well my rules and you'l say so too. Methods of Cooking Trout. Thomas Barker. FaBoUs

The observer, the mincing flag. An unendurable age. A Boy. John Ashbery. NeAP

Obstructors of distribution. Canto XIV. Ezra Pound. MoPo

Obtained the chariot for a day,/And set the world on fire. The Female Phaeton. Matthew Prior. HBV 1-2

The occasion and expediency determines the form. The Past Is the Present. Marianne Moore. PP

Occupied, without self-importance, in the thousands-/of-millions-of-sea. Boat Poem. Bernard Spencer. FaBoTw; OxBTC

Ocean and light the proof, the pact. Ark of the Covenant. Louise Townsend Nicholl. ImOP

The ocean is a dish of water carried by a woman,/where the worry of our lives lies down. As the Window Darkens. Laura Jensen. LCAP

The ocean lifted, stirred,/Leaving no word. Missing. John Pudney. HaMV; OxBTC

An ocean of salt/Rubs in our wounds. Slick. Daniel Gerard Hoffman. SOTS

An ocean rushes into my throat/but my thirst remains unquenched. Meditation. Carl Rakosi. VWA

...The ocean's utmost rim/Burned yet a moment: then the world grew dim. Urania.   Aubrey Thomas De Vere.   IrPN

Ocean will lie on the horizon, a destination.   Nostalgia for 70.   Jim Wayne Miller.   AmC; AMV-81

The ocean/with fierce courage?   There Is Something I Want to Say.   Alex Kuo.   BrSi

Och, Johnny, I hardly knew ye.   Johnny, I Hardly Knew Ye.   *Anonymous.* AnIV; BIrV; ELP; FaBoBa; GBP; OnYI; OxBoLi; WaaP

Och, then, for the glens and the heather!/And all that the Gael holds dear. The Return.   Pittendrigh Macgillivray.   GoTS; OxBS

October, like a King resigned to fate,/Dies in his forests with their sunset fire. October in Tennessee.   Walter Malone.   AA

The October reality, the image of spring.   Evergreen.   Ewart Milne.   OxBI

October would look no different than it looks.   Going.   James Schuyler. ANYP

Oculus me tamen ardens et iniquae flagra linguae/agitant exanimatum. "Horace: Book V, Ode III.'.   Ronald Arbuthnott Knox.   CenHV

'Od, lassie, what mair wad you hae?   Lassie, What Mair Wad You Hae? Alexander Gray.   GoTS; OxBS

The odd, friendless boy raised by four aunts.   Thumb.   Philip Dacey.   PoL; PPJ

Odds are on rape.   Lost Contact.   Sylvia Wheeler.   FAZ

Odor of earth/Enriches azuring air.   Morning Workout.   Babette Deutsch. LiSp; NePoAm-2; SD

...Odorless horses/spring onto the screen below waving flags.   Bijou.   Vern Rutsala.   DFF

An odorous Chaplet of sweet sommer buds/Is, as in mockery, set. Midsummer's Night Dream.   William Shakespeare.   BoW

Odors of challenge bright motives   Rainier.   Jim Tollerud.   VoR

Odours of bread...   Domestic Scene.   Michael Hartnett.   BIrV

Odyssey turned to Iliad/in parked cars   The Sea and Ourselves at Cape Ann. Lawrence Ferlinghetti.   PoM

Of a bisexual built for two.   Limerick: "A hermaphrodite fairy of Kew." *Anonymous.*   PeHV

Of a brave horse that could untie knots.   Unseen Horses.   Joan Byers Grayston.   PH

Of a color, of a bell/of yourself, torn   The Maximus Poems.   Charles Olson. NOBA

Of a dark dial in a sunless place.   The Sea of Death.   Thomas Hood.   CH; ERoP 1-2; LiTB; LoBV; OBNC; PoEL 1-5

Of a demon in my view.   From Childhood's Hour.   Edgar Allan Poe. NePA; PoEL 1-5

Of a flying strophe, a splendid sheath/of thunderbolts and flowers!   Make Way!   Ada Negri.   PBWP

Of a full feast; And the Out Courts of glory.   Son-Dayes.   Henry Vaughan. AtBAP; SeCP

Of a gust that kept insisting/and swept toward you.   The Bat.   Roberta Spear.   AmPA

Of a large heron ready at the first/touch to spring into bluest air.   Days of 1956.   Robin Magowan.   EAS

Of a long-forgotten stream?   Circus Elephant.   Kathryn Worth.   BrR

Of a love or a season?   Reluctance.   Robert Frost.   CMoP; ExPo; MoAB; MoAmPo; NOBA; OxBA

Of a love that could not redeem/But maimed her, Aimee.   Dostoievsky's Daughters.   Michael Hamburger.   NAs

Of a man that plays a blue guitar.   The Man with the Blue Guitar.   Wallace Stevens.   CMoP; UnS

Of a man who sits among his dead/like me, here, now.   In Jerusalem Are Women.   Arye Sivan.   VWA

Of a ride on horseback over the forehead.   Your Air of My Air.   Hugo Margenat.   InW

Of a rush of fourteen thousand miles/for the chance of a bitter fight!   The Rush of the Oregon.   Arthur Guiterman.   PAH

Of a sad game of Grab-bag–a sad game to see!   Grab-Bag.   Helen Hunt Jackson.   OBCA

Of a spot (or a leopard) was seen.   Limerick: "A leopard when told that benzine."   Oliver Herford.   TDH

Of a sylphish shellfish weeping/By a selfish shellfish' cell.   Idyll.   Stoddard King.   NLV

Of a white face framed in our avid gunsight.   Reply to the Committed Intellectual.   Francis Sparshott.   NOBC

Of Abdullah Boul Boul Ameer.   Ye Ballade of Ivan Petrofsky Skevar. *Anonymous.*   ABF

Of al this world ne give ich a pese!   All Too Late.   *Anonymous.*   OAEL 1-2; OxBM

Of all feeling bereft.   Winter Dawn.   D. H. Lawrence.   BrPo

Of all he loved: thy living Truths are/left.   On the Late S. T. Coleridge. Washington Allston.   AA

Of all his dear domain to live forgot.   Martyr's Memorial.   Louise Imogen Guiney.   AA

Of all senses magnificent.   A Hymn of Touch.   Gordon Bottomley.   BrPo

Of all that is, that has been, and will be!   To Sleep.   Frances Sargent Osgood AA

Of all that's sacred, first comes motherhood.   Essay in Defense of the Movies. Walker Gibson.   NePoAm

Of all that waste me, no thrust as my own/Is half so dire.   Sextains. William Baylebridge.   BoAV

"Of all the actors in this town, I loved Wilkes Booth the best."   Booth Killed Lincoln.   *Anonymous.*   AmFP; OFD

Of all the husbands in the land/There's none so fierce as Jessie's.   Jessie. Eugene Field.   InMe

Of all the pleasant flowers in June/The red rose hath no peer.   The Rose. Thomas Howell.   ElL; OBSC

Of all the things he should do, to do one.   Epitaph: "Nor practising virtue nor committing crime."   Geoffrey Taylor.   FaBoEE

Of all the things that happened there/That's all that I remember.   Incident. Countee Cullen.   BiP; BPo; CDC; CTBA; FF; GoSl; IDB; NoAm; NTCP; OBCA; PoBA; PoNe; SoSe; VGW

& Of all these/the greatest is the last/by far.   The World Is with Me Just Enough.   Sam Abrams.   APU

Of all those fools that will have all they see.   Arcadia.   Sir Philip Sidney. SiPS

Of all thy blameless Life the sole return/My Verse, and QUEENSB'RY weeping o'er thy Urn!   Bufo.   Alexander Pope.   OBEC

Of all thy kith dare sleep thee with a night under thy/shete.   With I and E. *Anonymous.*   OxBM

Of all which past.   Farewell to the Court.   Sir Walter Ralegh.   LO

Of all which speak our English tongue, but those/of thy device.   Another of the Same.   Sir Walter Ralegh.   FCP

Of an age we had long believed/outgrown.   112 at Presidio.   Virginia Long. AMV-80

Of an unfinished singlemindedness/about something which no longer seemed/ to matter.   Lynched.   Stephen Todd Booker.   LFAC

Of an unvisited garden in Mexico.   Dream Record: June 8, 1955.   Allen Ginsberg.   ConAP; NOBA

Of angry nostrils webbed with leaping veins,/The stallions come.   Ambuscade. Hugh McCrae.   BoAV; PoAu 1-2

Of Anne, of Phyllis do they talk,/Of Lydia not at all.   Lydia Is Gone This Many a Year.   Lizette Woodworth Reese.   CH; GoJo; HBV 1-2

Of ardent eye, who, with fraternal love,/Sweetens his solitude.   Lines Written at Bridgewater, 27 July 1797 (excerpt).   John Thelwall.   NOEC

Of aromatic larch below/The breast of Broad Cairn, long ago.   Long Ago. Syd Scroggie.   PoSH

Of Auschwitz, Dachau, Treblinka...   Golda.   Adrienne Wolfert.   AMV-80

Of bare fields,/In Spain.   Eisenhower's Visit to Franco, 1959.   James Wright. CAPP; NaP

Of bearing rearing the troublesome sons of men.   All Over the World. Geoffrey Johnson.   HaMV

Of being Daughter, Mother, Spouse of God?   The Ghyrlond of the Blessed Virgin Marie.   Ben Jonson.   ISi

Of being relative to nothing; isolated;/responsible?   The Sea Fog.   Josephine Jacobsen.   NYBP

Of Bessie at her spinning-wheel?   Bess and Her Spinning-Wheel.   Robert Burns.   BSV

Of bins for the fruit/And death for the flower.   Mid-August.   Louise Driscoll.   YeAr

Of birds that, waking in the heart of rain,/Would just as boldly start to mate again.   The Moon Pond.   Mebdh McGuckian.   FaBoIP

Of births and deaths and bridal nights.   In the Room.   James (1834-82) Thomson.   NOBV; OBVV

Of blackness, of blackness, of emptiness.   The Starry Night.   George Starbuck.   NYBP

Of blood dripped, piteous friend, who seekest me in vain?   God Has Spoken. Paul Verlaine.   SyP

Of bluff, bold men who dared and died/In foremost battle, quite aside. Westward Ho!   Joaquin Miller.   AA; FaBoBe

Of bonnie Jeanie Melville, who was scarce/sixteen years old.   Glenlogie, or, Jean o Bethelnie (B version).   *Anonymous.*   BuBa; ESPB

Of both, can ride me. Bellerophon, I am yours.   Pegasus.   Lewis, Cecil Day. AtBAP; PoPle

Of breaking to a sacred, bloodier speech.   Ruins under the Stars.   Galway Kinnell.   RFM

Of bride and groom, of outcast, and the fatal wedding night.   The Fatal Wedding.   W. H. Windom.   GoTF; TreFS

Of Cahal Mor of the Wine-red Hand!   Vision of Connaught in the Thirteenth Century.   James Clarence Mangan.   AnIL; IrPN; NOBI

Of captives, vanquished...and of many more.   The Swan.   Charles Baudelaire.   SyP

Of carnal being, blind and glorified.   The Virgin Mary.   Edgar Bowers. NePoEA; QFR

Of Chaos planted, all our trash to cinders bring.   September Sun: 1947. David Gascoyne.   AtBAP

Of chatter from the reasonable young/Who love each other so. The Poet at Fifty. Laurence Lerner. PeSA

Of cherry, apricots and plums/To be imbrued. Ode on His Majesty's Proclamation, Commanding the Gentry... Sir Richard Fanshawe. NOBE

Of chiselled boughs against the winter night! Misericordia. Margaret Mead. PoA

Of Christian should more have been wrecked/on shore/Than ever lost at sea! With a Nantucket Shell. Charles Henry ("John Paul") Webb. AA

Of cities insane/ Psychedelic Firemen. David Henderson. NBP

Of city for city and land for land. The Base of All Metaphysics. Walt Whitman. NePA

Of country wine, divinely sup. To a Gardener. Robert Louis Stevenson. AnEnPo

Of course I'd/be gone by then I'd/be far away The Key to Everything. May Swenson. IHMS; NePoEA

Of course it shows. Cathleen. Anonymous. BIrV

Of course, screamed the king and queen, are you blind, can't you see that/our mouths... Out of Whack. Russell Edson. LCAP

Of course they kill. Why did I ever/delude myself they do not kill? Epistle to the Gentiles. Alfred Hayes. TrJP

Of course, we tell him what we can. David. Walker Gibson. CrMA; NePoAm

Of course you can keep spring, says the invisible bush. Mollesse. Josephine Jacobsen. NePoAm-2

Of creatures going about their business among the equally/Earnest elements of nature. Boats in a Fog. Robinson Jeffers. MOS; NoP; OxBA

Of daddy's big rough cows. Wild Roses. Mary Effie Lee Newsome. CDC

Of darker nights a day. A Serenade. Edward Coate [(or Coote)] Pinkney. AA; AmLP; AnFE; APA; HBV 1-2

Of David Our Lord and Savior Jesus Christ was born of her. Weddase Maryam. Anonymous. ISi

Of Death and Fortune, Growth and Strife. The Undersong. Ralph Waldo Emerson AA

Of Death, of Life, those inwound notes are mine. A Ballad of Past Meridian. George Meredith. OAEL 1-2; VLP

Of, Delilah Aberyswith and most mean Ulysses Gunne! Delilah. Rudyard Kipling. BrPo

Of Denise combing her hair. The War of the Secret Agents. Henri Coulette. AmPC; NePoEA-2

Of divine Nature of his God,/And blest eternall Maker. The Pagans Wild Confesse the Bonds. Roger Williams. SCAP

Of Dragons, Hydraes, Sphinxes, fill the Grove. Sospetto d'Herode. Richard Crashaw. SeCV 1-2

Of dumb meek things and/golden hay. She Walks. Joseph Joel Keith. ISi

Of Earth's first blood, have titles manifold. England, 1802. William Wordsworth. OBEV

Of Egyptian? Indian? Persian? Akkadian?/In Eighteen-hundred-and-forty-two... Wandering Jews. Nancy Keesing. VWA

Of empty blowing prairie/on the coldest winter day. ESP. Carter Revard. VoR

OF ETERNALLE. Lines for a Sundial. Thomas Herbert Warren. OBVV

Of every man and wife. Wedlock. Anonymous. ABF

Of every sailor who threw his/Bag down on deck, sucked in/Salt and signed himself whole. One Year After. Gary Allan Kizer. LFAC

Of everything, alas, save thee. Spleen. Paul Verlaine. AWP; EnLi 1-2; SyP

Of evils on the watching shore. A Monument. Charles Madge. FaBoMo

Of Fancy, Reason, Virtue, nought can me bereave. Indifference to Fortune. James (1700-48) Thomson. OBEC

Of far away B. C./From us of Anno Domini. Lay of Ancient Rome. Thomas Russell Ybarra. HBV 1-2; InMe

–Of feeling no pain? Painkillers. Thom Gunn. AMV-81

Of ferns & flowers & butterflies Amber the Sky. Rokwaho. STE

Of finite space and mortal discipline. Not for Its Own Sake... Hazel Littlefield. GoYe

Of first, and last, and midst, and without end. The Simplon Pass. William Wordsworth. InPo; SyP

Of fishes that wander slowly out to the far waves. Father Fisheye. Peter Balakian. MAYP

...Of folly he made beauty. Johnson on Pope. David Ferry. PP

Of food, man's keen and elemental need/Of fire. Peat-Cutters. Geoffrey Johnson. HaMV

Of fruit boughs whitening, a foam of time. To the South. Brewster Ghiselin. LiTA; NePA

Of gains unsought your apple brought, to stagger a re-/vivalist!) Ode to Eve. Edwin Meade Robinson. InMe

Of God in Christ their chiefest good,/And from all troubles rest. For Just Men Light Is Sown. Michael Wigglesworth. AH

Of going to Heaven I've heard him boast,/But down in Hell he'll surely roast! Rufus's Mare. Anonymous. ShS

Of good and bad the tryers are these twain. Speak Thou and Speed. Sir Thomas Wyatt. EnRePo; FCP

Of grasshoppers and dragonflies/That go with us, that do not live again. Powwow. W. D. Snodgrass. GrPl; NYBP

Of greater wonders heard we never tell,/Than for the dumb to speak, the dead to live. Diana. Henry Constable. OBSC

Of having discovered sodium. Sir Humphry Davy. Edmund Clerihew Bentley. FaBoCo; ImOP

Of healing herbs to just men's fields. Mist. Henry David Thoreau. AA; AmePo; AmLP; AWP; InPo; OxBA

Of Heaven, and hope to have it after all. The Argument of His Book. Robert Herrick. AnAnS 2; AtBAP; SeCePo

Of her familiar animals/Indifferent or unaware. Cortege. Paul Verlaine. AWP; OBVE

Of her make yourself/new love,/until nothing's left. Advice. Yehuda Amichai. VWA

Of her mind and his, digesting this wild good fortune. Clancy. David Wagoner. PH

Of her we had, but praise our living Queen,/Who brings us equal, if not greater, bliss. Petition to the Queen. Sir Walter Ralegh. FCP

Of her wonderful wonderful snout. Reversion. Barry O. Higgs. PeSA

Of here kinde and of here colours to carpen hit were/to longe. The Vision of Piers Plowman. William Langland. PoEL 1-5

Of high with low, celestial with terrene! Sonnet to the Virgin. William Wordsworth. ISi

Of him whose grief was fatally sincere. Convicted (excerpt). Harry Edward Mills. PeD

Of hireling wolves, whose Gospel is their maw. Cromwell, Our Chief of Men. John Milton. CABA

Of His gret goodnesse and His gras,/Sende us such warning to be ware. A Warning to Beware. Anonymous. OxBM

Of his halo or harp like enough. Limerick: "G is a grumbler gruff." Oliver Herford. TDH

Of his impeded soul would through his bosom eat. Childe Harold's Pilgrimage: Canto III. George Gordon, Lord Byron. OBRV

Of his morsel a morsel will give,/Well-a-day. Gaffer Gray. Thomas Holcroft. HBV 1-2; NOEC

Of his penans God do him mede!/Careful is my hart therfore. Care Away! Anonymous. OxBM; OxBoLi

Of his raven color of hair. They Were Welcome to Their Belief. Robert Frost. AtBAP

Of his strange language all I know/Is, there is not a word of fear. Death Stands above Me. Walter Savage Landor. LiTB; NOBE; NoP; OAEL 1-2; OAEP; OBNC; OBSP; PoEL 1-5; SoSe

Of hopes and fears, being himself alone. Political Greatness. Percy Bysshe Shelley. EnRP

Of horses and horses of the sea, white horses. Oedipus at Colonus. Sophocles. OBVE

Of human and angel face. The Grave's Cherub. Sydney Clouts. PeSA

Of human bliss to human woe. A Son Lit. Samuel Johnson. FaBoEE

Of human joy &/sorrow... Pan-Asian Holiday Tour. Luis Syquia. BrSi

Of humble quietness. Pastoral Poesy. John Clare. ACV; ERoP 1-2; OAEL 1-2

Of Idle Tales, and foolish Riddles. On Beauty. A Riddle. Matthew Prior. CEP

Of Ilion, Paris, sunlike all in arms/Glittering. The Iliad. Homer. OBVE

Of Inami Moor? Shall We Make Love. Anonymous. AWP

Of joy to his widow and pride to himself. Undertakers. Ambrose Bierce. DBV

...Of Joys departed/Not to return, how painful the Remembrance! Friendship. Robert Blair. OBEC

Of Learning is its own/Inscrutable old Bar. An Ode on the Despoilers of Learning in an American University (1947). Yvor Winters. ExPo

Of leaves and lamps and traffic mingled before me. Brooding Grief. D. H. Lawrence. CMoP; LoBV

Of leisurely tensions between them/and private silence. The Rainwalkers. Denise Levertov. CAD; CTBA; NePoEA-2; PPP

Of lesser force, and less prevail. To the Winds. A Song. Philip Ayres. CEP

Of Life reborn of Death. The Key. John Oxenham. BePJ

Of life the mingled wine and brine/I sit and sip pipslipsily. Indifference. Anonymous. NA

Of lips, arms, and hidden charms. A Poem of Privacy. John Addington Symonds. ALV

Of Living, attention, please pay attention, greeniness and/mountains, oh this is the art of love! The Art of Love: Happy the Man Who Has Two Breasts to Crush. Kenneth Koch. GP; NNaP

Of Lord Christ's heart, and Shakespeare's strain. The Informing Spirit. Ralph Waldo Emerson. AWP; InPo; WGRP

Of lost stars and suns forlorn/And moons bereft. The Celtic Lyric (parody). J. C. Squire. BXAP

Of love and lovers' ecstasy/At dawn or evening. Man to Man. John McClure. HBMV

Of love, of loneliness, of life being death.　Sonnet: You Were Born; Must Die. Stephen Spender.　EnLit; MoAB; MoBrPo

Of love's stars, thou'lt meet her/In eastern sky.　Death's Jest-Book.　Thomas Lovell Beddoes.　OBRV

Of lovers' hearts, when newly blest,/Too newly to be quite at rest!　Lalla Rookh.　Thomas Moore.　OBNC

Of lovers they are onely true/Who pay their Hearts where they are due. Chang'd, Yet Constant.　Thomas Stanley.　AnAnS 2

Of lovers, who so nearly err'd,/And yet who–did not!　Quantum Est Quod Desit.　Thomas Moore.　EnLoPo

Of Lydia not at all.　Lydia is Gone This Many a Year.　Lizette Woodworth Reese.　CH; GoJo

Of magic music wild and sweet,/Anemones and clarigolds.　Christmas Eve. John Davidson.　OHIP

Of man, beast, worm, and bird.　Eternity's Low Voice.　Mark Van Doren. EaLo

Of martial truth, that must prevail,/To lay on all the eternal law.　Ways of War.　Lionel Pigot Johnson.　AnIV

Of me a grain!　A Pedlar.　*Anonymous*.　OBEV; WiR

Of memory of things before, confirm/After-life's ludicrous reality.　The Other Side.　Roy Fuller.　OxBC

Of men escaping/From the mind of man.　To flee from memory.　Emily Dickinson.　FaBoEE

Of men grown old.　St. Anthony's Township.　Gilbert Sheldon.　CH

Of mighty love the wings for this me give.　In Spain.　Sir Thomas Wyatt. OBSC; SeCePo

Of Mods, of Greats, of Weekly Dues,/And yet he is an Andrew Lang. Ballade of Andrew Lange.　Dugal Sutherland MacColl.　CenHV

Of more than victory the monument.　Inscription for Marye's Heights, Fredericksburg.　Herman Melville.　UnPo

Of moving worlds to this eclipse/Not returning.　Is Love Not Everlasting? Ronald McCuaig.　BoAV

Of my fond heart, hath made me poor.　A Complaint.　William Wordsworth.　ATP; CBEP; NOBE; OBRV; PoEL 1-5

Of my grief Thou makest glory,/Of my labor greatest gain.　The Blessings of Surrender.　Mary J. Helphingtine.　STF

Of my iron will, my fear of love, my itch for money, and/my madness.　The Dead Shall Be Raised Incorruptible.　Galway Kinnell.　GP

Of my Lord who is going to deign to come.　O Boy Cutting Grass. Hitomaro.　AWP

Of my own spirit let me be/In sole though feeble mastery.　Mastery.　Sara Teasdale.　HBV 1-2; WGRP

Of my pure faith, I'd give the whole.　No Marvel Is It.　Bernard de Ventadour　AWP; LiTW

Of my soveraigne I have redresse,/And I content me with my hire.　The Lover Rejoiceth the Enjoying of His Love.　Sir Thomas Wyatt.　FaBoEn

Of my sufferaunce I have redres,/And I content me with my hiere.　Ons as Me Thought Fortune Me Kyst.　Sir Thomas Wyatt.　AAS

Of my work lessen, yet some wise man shall,/I hope, esteem my writs canonical.　Satire.　John Donne.　OBSV

Of mystic beauty, day by day, to be/Diadem for the Queen of the Rosary. The Rosary.　Sister Maura.　ISi

Of Necco Wafers, Nibs, and Juju Beads.　Ex-Basketball Player.　John Updike.　CTBA; LiSp; NYBP; SM

Of new steel and sulphur and coal/and grey trains/and home.　Looking Down on West Virginia.　John Dickson.　AMV-81

Of night stirred with light and the rush of wings.　Diretro al Sol.　Charles G. Bell.　NePoAm

Of nobleness alone a noble mind is proud.　The Maid of Orleans.　Friedrich von Schiller.　AWP

Of nothing, nothing, nothing–nothing at all.　The End of the World. Archibald MacLeish.　AP; BLPL; CMoP; LiTM; MAT; MoAB; MoAmPo; NCSH; NePA; NoAm; NOBA; OBAL; OxBA; TAP; TrGrPo; VGW

Of nothings in their tuneful/prime.　In Robin Hood Cove.　Marsden Hartley.　AnFE; CoAnAm

Of now done darkness I wretch lay wres-/tling with (my God!) my God. Carrion Comfort.　Gerard Manley Hopkins.　AtBAP; CoBE; HeIP; LiTB; MoVE; NoAm; NoP; OAEL 1-2; OAEP; OxBoCh; PoEL 1-5; PPP; TEP

Of of　The Needless Alarm.　John Ruskin.　FM

Of old "Cats" and young "Kits."　Epigram on the Toasts of the Kit-Kat Club, Anno 1716.　Alexander Pope.　CEP

Of older things than fairy-folk will talk.　Western Magic.　Mary Austin. AmFN

Of one they can still recognise, though scarcely understand.　Spring MCMXL. David Gascoyne.　MoVE

Of one who, decision taken, darkly plunged/deep into water.　Water-Images. Mary Elizabeth Osborn.　NePoAm-2

Of one who died of growing pains.　Epitaph on a Young Poet Who Died before Having Achieved Success.　Amy Lowell.　OBAL

Of one who makes you sing again/When all the songs were mute?　Debts. Jessie B. Rittenhouse.　HBMV

Of orchis in the pasture/Or rhododendron worn.　There is a flower that bees prefer.　Emily Dickinson.　MoAmPo

Of other bells than those that give us pause.　The Anthill.　Donald Campbell Babcock.　NePoAm

Of other husbands, lovers, wives.　Agatha.　Nadine Major.　PoL

Of our great Lord and King.　At Length There Dawns the Glorious Day. Ozora S. Davis.　AH

Of overlanding mates of old,/If stirring yet or slain.　Moreton Miles, LIV. William Baylebridge.　BoAV

Of pangs more grievous, sufferings more/fell,/Than Dante or his master dared rehearse!　To an Imperilled Traveller.　Nathan Haskell Dole.　AA

Of passions rivalling the sculptured tomb!　The Ancestors.　John Peale Bishop.　PoA

Of peace and purity in all men's sight/For the unfolding age!　Song for Memorial Day.　Clinton Scollard.　OHIP

Of Peace and yielding who would doubt,/When the white Flag he sees hung out?　Clad All in White.　Abraham Cowley.　SeCV 1-2

Of Pedro-Pablo-Ignacio-Juan-/Francesco Garcia y Gabaldon.　A Feller I Know.　Mary Austin.　AmFN

Of people in perpetual memory.　Fame.　Sir Thomas More.　EnRePo

Of photon-jets bannering your martyred name.　Tulips from Their Blood. Edwin Brooks.　NBP

Of Pisa's leaning miracle.　Snow-Bound.　John Greenleaf Whittier　AA

Of precious jewels like to those that grace/The Babylonian Kaiser, Prester John.　Sonnets of the Months.　Folgore da San Geminiano.　AWP

Of proselytes of one another's trade.　Epigram: "The greatest saints and sinners have been made."　Samuel (1612-80) Butler.　FaBoEE

Of quean Earth and her fancy-fellow Heaven.　The Marriage of Earth and Heaven.　Jay Macpherson.　OBCV

Of repentance for the false day that's fled.　White Christmas.　William Robert Rogers.　ChMP; LiTM; MoAB; MoBrPo; PPON; SeCePo

Of riders who still hold the fraying reins/Of horses with their hooves raised in mid air.　The Last Campaign.　Geoffrey Lehmann.　PoAu 1-2

Of rising again from the dead: through the same Jesus Christ our/Redeemer. Amen.　Last Antiphon: To Mary.　James J. Donohue.　ISi

Of rivets nosing in like bees.　On Watching the Construction of a Skyscraper. Burton Raffel.　PCP

Of rocks in the desert/Is mad as a dervish.　Jars.　Paul Raboff.　VWA

Of roses dying like Petronius/a seemly death.　The Vase.　Terence Tiller. ChMP

Of roses hammered from gold and dyed with his own blood.　Beachcomber. W.H. Oliver.　AnNZ

Of running feet from every side was heard/Bent on the　The Spooniad. Edgar Lee Masters.　OBAL

Of Saint Theresa in her wild lament.　The Groundhog.　Richard Eberhart. AmLP; CMoP; DTC; ExPo; FaBoMo; FaFP; LiTA; LiTM; MasP; MiAP; MoAB; MoAmPo; MoPo; MoVE; NePA; NoAm; NoP; NU; PPoe; SeCeV; TAP; UnPo; WaP

,Of seed pearls dropping/down the well of the fecund plantation.　Florida Hillocks.　Kenward Elmslie.　ANYP

Of setting her plants before the shroud came round her.　A Dream.　Victoria Mary (Vita) Sackville-West.　MoVE

Of sexless love, and strange unreached kisses.　A Sapphic Dream.　George Moore.　SyP

Of shadow and/light.　Hard Country.　Philip Booth.　CoAP

Of shadow in the slew.　A Prairie Water Colour.　Duncan Campbell Scott. OBCV

Of shaping danger they go–and widen their eyes/Innocent and voluptuous. The Eyes of Children at the Brink of the Sea's Grasp.　Josephine Jacobsen. NePoAm-2

Of sharpening one's nails with a file!　Limerick: "There was an old man of the Nile."　Edward Lear.　TDH; VLP

Of showers of meteorites.　Limerick: "There's a lady in Washington Heights." Morris Bishop.　QQQ

Of simple tastes and mind content!　Contentment.　Oliver Wendell Holmes. AmPP; AnNE; AP; HBV 1-2; InMe; OxBA; TreF

Of singing thy perfumed grace,/and queenly beauty of thy face.　Homage. Gustave Kahn.　TrJP

Of skin the broken interdiction/of touch　Paradigms of Fire.　Brian Swann. AmPA

Of sleep, our peacefullest sea–save blessed death.　In Pace In Idipsum Dormiam Et Requiescam.　Patrick O'Connor.　CAW

Of small black shadows on roads/that trail off into the back country and are lost.　When We Drive at Night.　Katha Pollitt.　AmC

Of some blank world where dawn for ever wept.　We Woke Together. Christopher John Brennan.　BoAV

Of someone coming/To your aid.　To a Lady Holding the Floor.　Mildred Weston.　FiBHP

Of sorrow unfeigned, and humiliation meek.　Paradise Lost.　John Milton. OAEL 1-2

Of spheres with lead/under their wings.　The Windmill of Evening.　Shlomo Reich.　VWA

Of the time and reign/Of Cahal Mor of the Wine-red Hand.　King Cahal Mor of the Wine-Red Hand.　James Clarence Mangan.　AnIV; GoBC

Of the unknown sheltering palm.　The Candle Flame.　Janet Lewis.　CrMA

Of the wide world I stand alone, and think/Till Love and Fame to nothingness do sink.　The Terror of Death.　John Keats.　GTBS; GTBS-P

Of the wind in her hair will be stopped much too soon.　Descending.　Valentin Iremonger.　EnLoPo

Of the windy bishop who'd preach our dust home.　The Windy Bishop.　Wilfred Watson.　OBCV

Of the wrong of worshipping the blood's terror of sacrifice.　Isaac.　Stanley Burnshaw.　VWA

Of their own charity, may envy thee.　On the Death of a Favourite Old Spaniel.　Robert Southey.　FM

Of their woven acres and their linen fields.　The Spinning Wheel.　Abraham Moses Klein.　CaP

Of them that do not have the faith/And will not have the fun.　The Song of the Strange Ascetic.　Gilbert Keith Chesterton.　HBMV

Of these shall my songs be fashioned, my tales/be told.　A Consecration.　John Masefield.　EnLit; HBMV; MCCG; MoAB; MoBrPo; NoAm; WHA

Of these your words the other's sense denies.　Sonnet: To Dante Alighieri (On the Last Sonnet of the Vita Nuova).　Cecco da Siena Angiolieri.　AWP

Of things both high and low/God hideth His intention.　The Gate of the Year.　M. Louise Haskins.　GoTF; TreFS

Of things exactly as they are.　The Man with the Blue Guitar.　Wallace Stevens.　CMoP; NoAm

Of things invisible to mortal sight.　Paradise Lost.　John Milton.　AtBAP; ExPo; MBW 1-2; OAEL 1-2; OAEP; SCV; WHA

Of this and that, and Antony,/And the laugh that will not die.　Queen Cleopatra.　Conrad Aiken.　HBMV

Of this delicious stuff!　Soliloquy of a Tortoise on Revisiting the Lettuce Beds...　Emile Victor Rieu.　FiBHP

Of this great Land in which we live!　The Land Where Hate Should Die.　Denis A. McCarthy.　PGD

Of this regular army of ants!'　Limerick: "There was a young curate of Hants."　Edward Valpy Knox.　CenHV

Of those calm solitudes, is there.　O Fairest of the Rural Maids.　William Cullen Bryant.　AA; AmLP; AnAmPo; LaNeLa

Of those that stood with Dan/On Mullach-Maist!　A Fighting-Man.　Joseph Campbell.　OnYI

Of those that under grim oppression groan.　The Seasons.　James (1700-48) Thomson.　SeCePo

Of those who left humanity/and barred the door.　Alma Mater.　Mary Elizabeth Osborn.　NePoAm

Of those who list to waggonere,/And keepe bad companye.　The Rime of the Auncient Waggonere (parody).　William Maginn.　BXAP

Of thy departure, when thou wentest forth, it went out/after thee.　Parting.　Judah Halevi.　AWP

Of thy desire, and to the land of thy true belonging.　Parted Lovers.　Judah Halevi.　LiTW

Of Thy Glory makes us bright. Amen.　Hail, Mother of the Savior.　Adam of St. Victor.　ISi

Of time and change and mortal life and/death.　To My First Love, My Mother.　Christina Georgina Rossetti.　OHIP

Of time past and time future.　Four Quartets.　Thomas Stearns Eliot.　AtBAP

Of touch they are, and poor I am their straw.　Astrophel and Stella, IX.　Sir Philip Sidney.　AAS; SiPS

Of travelling through the world that lay/Before me in my endless way.　Stepping Westward.　William Wordsworth.　CH; EnLi 1-2; EnRP; ERoP 1-2; ExPo; HBV 1-2; InPK; OBRV; PoEL 1-5; SeCeV

Of trees that have added another ring of growth.　Protective Colors.　William Logan.　AMV-81

Of trust and strength and calmness from above.　Father, in Thy Mysterious Presence Kneeling.　Samuel Johnson.　AH

Of twice ten thousand warriors slain.　Three Poems.　Basho (Matsuo Basho).　LiTW

Of under me you so quite new　I like my body when it is with your.　Edward Estlin Cummings.　BoLoP; ErPo; LLLT; VGW

Of unkept promises and broken hearts.　Norfolk.　Sir John Betjeman.　ChMP

Of up-rearing billows that come hither from Kahiki.　Ending.　Anonymous.　WTO

Of vermin and of lice/And of all manner vice?　How the Doughty Duke of Albany Like a Coward Knight...(excerpt).　John Skelton.　OBSV

Of very little use,/And execrably plain.　England and America.　James Kenneth Stephen.　InMe

Of violets and love and death.　Her Music.　Martha Gilbert Dickinson.　AA

Of violets, and my soul's forgotten gleam.　Sonnet: "I had no thought of violets of late."　Alice Dunbar Nelson.　BlSi; PoBA; PoNe

Of waking up, and finding it Home.　Heaven.　Anonymous.　PoLf

Of warmth and love abounding.　Around Thanksgiving.　Rolfe Humphries.　OFD

Of water-pipes antiphonal, and the dome,/Round-arched, goes up to God in lapis lazuli?　To K. H.　Thomas Edward Brown.　OBNC

Of wedlock, love, and youth is Hymen king.　Bridal Song.　Thomas Dekker.　OBSC; TrGrPo

Of what Abe Lincoln said/One time at Springfield.　The Hill.　Edgar Lee Masters.　AmLP; AmP; CMoP; ExPo; FYAP; LiTA; LiTM; NePA; NoAm; NOBA; OxBA; SeCeV; TAP; ViBoPo

Of what happened so long before that/In some small town, one indifferent summer.　Syringa.　John Ashbery.　HaCAP

Of what inexorable cause/Makes Time so vicious in his reaping.　For a Dead Lady.　Edwin Arlington Robinson.　AnFE; AnNE; APA; CMoP; CoBMV; DL; ForPo; FYAP; GoTF; HeIP; HoPM; InvP; LiTA; MAmP; MAPA; MoAB; MoAmPo; NOBA; OxBA; PoEL 1-5; PoRA; TreFT; ViBoPo; WHA

Of what is done far better by a watch.　On a Sundial.　Hilaire Belloc.　FaBoEE; MoVE; PoL; PV; QQQ

Of what is he thinking/Between those wide ears?　The Elephant.　Herbert Asquith.　SoPo

Of what is past, or passing, or to come.　Sailing to Byzantium.　William Butler Yeats.　AnIL; AtBAP; BiP; CMoP; CoBMV; DiPo; ExPo; FaFP; FF; ForPo; FPL; GoTF; GTBS-P; HAP; HeIP; HoPM; InPK; InPo; InPS; InvP; LiTB; LiTM; MasP; MBW 1-2; MoAB; MoBrPo; MoPo; MoRP; MoVE; NAMP; NAWM 1-2; NIP; NoAm; NOBE; NoP; OAEL 1-2; OAEP; OBMV; OxBI; OxBTC; PAI; PP; PPoe; PPP; PrIm; SeCePo; SeCeV; SoSe; TEP; TreFT; UnPo; ViBoPo

Of what lay behind and before it.　Visitations: VII (excerpt).　Louis MacNeice.　EaLo

Of what makes her remain/The one woman.　Twentieth Century Love-Song.　Richard Church.　HaMV

Of what's eternal shake his grave of time.　Poem in the Matukituki Valley.　James Keir Baxter.　AnNZ

Of which once smelt, the gods thou wilt implore/Fabullus that they'd make thee nose all ore.　Carmina.　Caius Valerius Catullus.　OBVE

Of which our yearning hope is both/The prophecy and sign.　Refracted Lights.　Celia Parker Wooley.　WGRP

Of which you will not speak.　Speak.　Bea Opengart.　AMV-80

Of whos five woundes print in your hert a rose.　Like a Midsummer Rose.　John Lydgate.　OxBM

Of wintry wind...look up, and scent/The snow!　Snow.　Adelaide Crapsey.　QFR

Of wisdom esteemed/And chiefly required.　Of Perfect Friendship.　Henry Cheke.　ElL

Of wisdom infinitely calm.　Eastern Tempest.　Edmund Charles Blunden.　MoBrPo

Of woman or pebble/the body of the dark.　The Practice of Absence.　Robert Friend.　VWA

Of women, best/And loveliest.　Mother–a Portrait.　Ethel Romig Fuller.　PGD

Of wondrous things about Arthur the kind.　The Brut.　Layamon.　MeEV

Of wood-hung Meinai, stream of Druids old.　The Pleasures of Melancholy.　Thomas Warton, Jr..　CEP; EnRP; LAuP; NOEC

Of yon ice mountain hurled/Down this unfinished world.　Alaska.　Joaquin Miller.　PAH

...Of your childhood's/joy in its solitude.　The Quarry Pool.　Denise Levertov.　VGW

Of your fair eyes whereby the light is lost.　"I never saw you, madam, lay apart."　Henry Howard, Earl of Surrey.　AAS; FCP; SiPS

Of your/soul/upon/my lips.　As Is the Sea Marvelous.　Edward Estlin Cummings.　MOS

Of youth; without it life and death are one.　O Friends! Who Have Accompanied Thus Far.　Walter Savage Landor.　GBL

Off, before the Fool comes on!　Colophon.　Oliver St. John Gogarty.　OBMV

Off into darkness. Ask my name.　Riddle #14: A Horn.　Anonymous.　DiPo

Off lusty May upone the nynt morrow.　The Thrissil and the Rois.　William Dunbar.　HW

Off the map with Baiae, murderer of love–and its/waters.　The Watering Place.　Sextus Propertius.　LiTW

Off the tripes, he could pour us a sly drink, from the/cider jug.　These Obituaries of Rattlesnakes Being Eaten by the Hogs.　Roger Weingarten.　AmPA

...Offending will would still deny/Dependence, know denial too must/end.　Error Pursued.　Helen Pinkerton.　NePoAm

Offer a prayer–a tear.　The Passing of the Unknown Soldier.　Vilda Sauvage Owens.　MC

Offer varied attractions to Whistler.　Limerick: "There's a combative Artist named Whistler."　Dante Gabriel Rossetti.　CenHV

Offered from beyond the sea/has extinguished itself in my darkness.　Sister Zahava.　Edith Bruck.　VWA

Offering all its gold to me for nothing. Letter to a Mute. Thomas James. AmPA

An offering from Philocles. Philocles. of Tarentum Leonidas. AWP

An offering pure of love, where to/God leadeth me. O'er Waiting Harp-Strings of the Mind. Mary Baker Eddy. AH

...Offering you/drenched fields, nearly drowned in dew. An Expanded Want Ad. Brad Leithauser. MAYP

Offers herself, a rose, and craves of us/A rose's place among our memories. Paris. Arthur Symons. NOBV; SyP

Offers in shape and colour all I need/for sight to torch the mind with living light. The Glens. John Hewitt. NeIP

Offers the boon of death. Compensation. Paul Laurence Dunbar. AmNP; BPo; HBV 1-2; PoNe

The officers they all did shout:/"Why, kick him out of the army." Captain Jinks. *Anonymous.* FaFP; TreF

The officious touch that makes me droop again. Written in Very Early Youth. William Wordsworth. EnRP

Offspring of my loins. Ages and Ages Returning at Intervals. Walt Whitman. AP

Oft in the silent night. Oft in the Silent Night. Otto Julius Bierbaum. AWP

Oft won, oft lost, and O! too dear to lose! Conflict. Caroline Clive. OBVV

Often a woman drifts off down her long hair and is lost. Hair Poem. Bill Knott. EAS

Often am I by my husband/Always in the arms of man. A Woman Grows Soon Old. Larin Paraske. PBWP

Often my tears fall in a shower/Because of Anger's freeing power. Anger's Freeing Power. Stevie Smith. OxBC

Often, often, often/Goes the Christ in the stranger's guise. The Rune of Hospitality. *Anonymous.* CAW

Often we milk you and you brim our pail. Lesotho. B. Makalo Khaketla. PeSA

The Ogre stalks with hands on hips,/While drivel gushes from his lips. August 1968. W. H. Auden. OBSP

Oh, a day in the city-square, there is no such pleasure/in life. Up at a Villa–Down in the City. Robert Browning. CBEP; EnLit; FaBoPP; GTBS-P; HBV 1-2; InPS; MBW 1-2; NOBE; OBTV; PoRA; PPP; SeCeV

Oh, a far cry to Heaven! A Far Cry to Heaven. Edith Matilda Thomas. AA; WGRP

Oh, a leper may be a glorious thing to see/When one is beautiful, young, and free! The Vocation of St. Francis. Sister Mary Eleanore. CAW

Oh, Absalom, my son, my son. Oh, Absalom, My Son. *Anonymous.* FSW

Oh, ain't there some place in between them/Where this poor buffer can go? Wrap Me Up in My Tarpaulin Jacket. *Anonymous.* AS

Oh, Alice, good bye, I'm going! Tom Dixon. *Anonymous.* ShS

Oh alter ego, fluttered at the glass. A Child's Visit to the Biology Lab. Kathleen Spivack. AmPA

Oh, and sleeves are drenched. Through the thatched roof. Emperor Tenchi. LiTW

Oh, Arctic seas, what you have sealed/At the judgment-day will be revealed! Lady Franklin's Lament (II). *Anonymous.* ShS

Oh, at the gates, they move,/But–fear no evil. Security. Robert Tucker. PPON

Oh! Avalon! my son! my son! Avalon. Thomas Holley Chivers. APA

Oh, babes,/Oh, no-home babes. Two Hoboes. *Anonymous.* WTO

Oh, baby, telephone and tell me I'm your own. Hello, Ma Baby. Howard. Joseph E. Emerson. Ida. BLSo; FSN

Oh, be less beautiful, or be/A little less available. To His Girl. Martial (Marcus Valerius Martialis). UnTE

"Oh, best little blade of grass!" he said. The Blades of Grass. Stephen Crane. AmP; GoTF; MoAmPo; PoPl; TreFT

Oh! Birthday Cake/Is VERY nice! Birthday Cake. Ivy O. Eastwick. BiCB

Oh bitter drops will start–/O'er graves, when friends depart–/In life's maturer years. Anna Playing in a Graveyard. Caroline Gilman. OBCA

...Oh, bleeding feet!/In step with mine on the city street! Comrade Jesus. Ralph Cheyney. PGD

Oh blind hands, feel the toughness of the blades/And the cold ground beneath them as your friend. Apopemptic Hymn. Dorothy Auchterlonie. PoAu 1-2

"Oh, bother the flowers of spring!"/Tra la la-la la. The Flowers That Bloom in the Spring. Sir William Schwenck Gilbert. BLSo

Oh, bring again my heart's content,/Thou Spirit of the Summertime! Song: "O spirit of the Summertime!" William Allingham. IrPN

Oh! can it be that darkness/Is ever anywhere? November Morning. Evaleen Stein. YeAr

Oh, can it be, thine other name is Heaven? To Duty. Thomas Wentworth Higginson. AA; AnAmPo

Oh, can't you rise an' tell what de Lord has done for you. Rise, Mourner, Rise. *Anonymous.* BoAN 1-2

Oh, can't you see how happy we will be. Tea for Two. Irving Caesar. BLSo

Oh, Captain, that's been here and gone, oh, Lawd,/Oh, Lawdy, Lawd. Drive It On. *Anonymous.* OuSiCo

Oh, Cara!–does the infant live? To Cara, after an Interval of Absence. Thomas Moore. PeD

Oh, carry me away. The Old Lady of London. *Anonymous.* AmFP

Oh! Celia, Celia, Celia shits!' Cassinus and Peter. Jonathan Swift. OAEL 1-2; PPP

"Oh, cheetie-pussie-cattie, O!" There Was a Wee Bit Mousikie. *Anonymous.* MoShBr

Oh children think about the/good times. Good Times. Lucille Clifton. AmPA; BPo; CNA; FF; GrPl; InPS; NCSH; PAI; PoBA; TAP; TwCP

Oh Christ, why dost thou Shepheard take away,/In erring times when sheepe most apt to stray. Mr. Thomas Shepheard...Hee a Man of a Thousand. Edward Johnson. SCAP

Oh! clear and shining light! Hymn for Christmas. Felicia Dorothea Hemans. GN

Oh, close my hand on Beatitude!/Not on her toys. Deo Optimo Maximo. Louise Imogen Guiney. TrPWD

Oh, close, safe, warm sleep I and she,–I and she! Never the Time and the Place. Robert Browning. AnFE; EnLoPo; HBV 1-2; NOBV

Oh, come again! Summer Sunshine. Mary Artemisia ("Aunt Mary") Lathbury. YeAr

Oh, come let us welcome sweet/Sabbath, the Queen! Welcome, Queen Sabbath. Zalman Schneour. TrJP

Oh come to us, abide with us,/Our Lord Immanuel! Oh, Little Town of Bethlehem. Lewis H. and Philip Brooks Redner. FSW

Oh! come unto thy battle bed,/Savannah! O Savannah! Savannah. Alethea S. Burroughs. PAH

Oh, come, Unworldly, from the World within! The Passion of Christ. Denis Devlin. IPY

Oh, could I hide me under ground,/How thankful should I be! The Chimney-Sweeper's Complaint. Mary Alcock. NOEC

Oh! could that be a wonder, my boy? An Irishman's Christening. *Anonymous.* OnYI

Oh, cruel I, to intercept it! Kissing Helen. Plato. OBVE

Oh Cupid was that ploughing boy/Who caused me all my pain. Cupid the Ploughboy. *Anonymous.* OBET

Oh, curious fate that makes us live,/But will not teach us how to do it! Traveller's Ditty. Miriam Allen DeFord. HBMV

Oh, de black gal smell like a billy goat,/But he her smell jes' de same. De Black Girl. *Anonymous.* GBP

"Oh dear," he cried, "what burns me so?"/And held up the spoon with his little toe. The Story of the Wild Huntsman. Heinrich Hoffmann. NA

Oh dear! I fall adown, adown, adown! The Shepherd's Week. John Gay. CEP; PoEL 1-5

Oh, dear,–I guess if He were a Boy–/He'd–climb–if He could! Over the fence. Emily Dickinson. SBG

Oh dear, my heart was ready to burst! As I was going by Charing Cross. *Anonymous.* CH; FaBoCh; LoGBV

Oh, dear sister, do not weep. Little Rosewood Casket. *Anonymous.* FSW

Oh, dearest, remember me. Song. Gerald Griffin. BLPA

"Oh! deary, deary me, this is none of I!" There Was an Old Woman, as I've Heard Tell. Mother Goose. TiPo

Oh Death in Life, the lack of animation. Quand On N'a Pas Ce Que l'on Aime, Il Faut Aimer Ce Que l'on A– Stevie Smith. FaBoEE

Oh death please sting me,/and take me out of my misery. Death Sting Me Blues. Sara Martin. BluL

Oh devious miles/That stretch between! The Telescope. J. C. Hall. HaMV

Oh! didn't he ramble, ramble,/He rambled 'til the butchers cut him down. Didn't He Ramble. Will Handy. FSW

Oh, dinna, dinna droun the lowe/That lights a heaven here! They Speak o' Wiles. William Thom. HBV 1-2

Oh, do Lord, remember me. Do, Lord, Remember Me. *Anonymous.* AmFP

Oh, do, Lord, remember me. When My Blood Runs Chilly and Col'. *Anonymous.* ABF

Oh, do not weep for any lad/Lost among the flowers! The Runaway. Daniel Whitehead Hicky. BrR

"Oh, drat it! I've married a snorer!" Limerick: "There was a young man from Elnora." *Anonymous.* TDH

Oh dreadfully, our humanness must be achieved. Words in the Mourning Time. Robert Earl Hayden. CNA

Oh, drink not thou forgetfulness of me. This Stone. *Anonymous.* AWP

...Oh each poet's a/beautiful human girl who must die. World's Bliss. Alice Notley. APU

Oh, eager, clear-like love in eyes–/The soul of you. Due North. Benjamin R. C. Low. EtS; HBMV

Oh! Eliza, Li'l Liza Jane. Li'l Liza Jane. *Anonymous.* BLSo

Oh embassy of doves/you are late/flying! Late. Helen Salz. GoYe

...Oh, every child/hoped secretly to be stolen by gypsies.   Gypsies.   Alden Nowlan.   NeAC

Oh, experience, feeling, joy–enormous!   Sonnets to Orpheus.   Rainer Maria Rilke.   SOTW

Oh, fair to see!   Oh, Fair to See.   Christina Georgina Rossetti.   OHIP; TiPo

Oh, fare you well, my darling.   Callahan.   *Anonymous.*   OuSiCo

"Oh! Farewell to the end of my Nose!"   Limerick: :"There was a young lady whose Nose."   Edward Lear.   EBEV

Oh father, who am I?   Oh Father.   Wendy Rose.   CDW

Oh, fearsome hunter,/Your hidden bow.   Hidden Bow.   Mordecai Temkin.   VWA

Oh filthy tongue, you'd better far/Be what you were than what you are.   On a Slanderer.   Martial (Marcus Valerius Martialis).   PeHV

Oh find it–Sir–for me!   I Lost a World–the Other Day!   Emily Dickinson.   DiPo

Oh, for a bee's experience/Of clovers and of noon!   Like trains of cars on tracks of plush.   Emily Dickinson.   MoAB; MoAmPo

Oh for a life on the rolling sea!   Eddystone Light.   *Anonymous.*   FSW

Oh, for a Pentecost!   Oh, for a Pentecost!   *Anonymous.*   BLRP

Oh, for an Healed Soul!   O Glorious Christ of God; I Live.   Cotton Mather.   SCAP

Oh for grace to love thee more!   Lovest Thou Me?   William Cowper.   HBV 1-2; OBEC; TrPWD

Oh! for the dead let us all kneel to pray!   The Varuna.   George Henry Boker.   PAH

Oh, for the life at the speed of c!   The Asteroid Light.   *Anonymous.*   FSW

Oh, forgive my hardihood/If I speak offending.   Danae.   Simonides (of Ceos).   LiTW

"Oh fox come down from your lair/And steal our chickens."   A Call to the Wild.   Edward John, Lord Dunsany.   OnYI

Oh, girl of the low voice, love me!   Girl of the Red Mouth.   Martin MacDermott.   HBV 1-2; OnYI

Oh, git along, boys, git along, do,/Be handy, boys, be handy!   The Ebenezer.   *Anonymous.*   ShS

Oh, give me ale!   In Praise of Ale.   Thomas Bonham.   ALV; FaBoCh; OBS; TrGrPo; ViBoPo

Oh, give me some time to blow the man down!   The Black Ball Line.   *Anonymous.*   AmSS

Oh! give relief–and heaven will bless your store.   The Beggar.   Thomas Moss.   NOEC

Oh gladly, love, for you I bear!   Envoi.   Kathleen Raine.   NeBP; NOBE

Oh glory gone.   River Song.   Elizabeth Brewster.   CaP

Oh Glory! to the dying Lamb.   Everybody's Welcome.   *Anonymous.*   TrAS

Oh, God, forgive me when I whine.   Forgive Me When I Whine.   *Anonymous.*   STF

Oh god, how i love my music!   Manong Federico Delos Reyes and His Golden Banjo.   Al Robles.   BrSi

Oh, God! Oh, God! have pity on that one.   One of Us Two.   Ella Wheeler Wilcox.   PoToHe

Oh God, that I were far from here,/Or lying fast asleep!   The Visitor.   William Henry Davies.   GBL

Oh God, to us may grace be given/To follow in their train!   Who Follows in His Train?   Reginald Heber.   WGRP

Oh, God! You think I want to be a ghost?...   Ghost.   John V. A. Weaver.   HBMV

Oh, got her wedding band.   Single Girl.   *Anonymous.*   FSW

Oh grant, amang this warldis steir,/that I may florische in the sture.   On Seein an Aik-Tree Sprent Wi Galls.   Robert Garioch.   OxBS

Oh grant an honest fame, or grant me none!   Honest Fame.   Alexander Pope.   OBEC

Oh! grant me grace, O God, that I/My life may mend, sith I must die.   Upon the Image of Death.   Robert Southwell.   CH; CoBE; EiL; NOBE; OBSC

Oh grant that I may faithful be/To clearer light vouchsafed to me!   Old-Testament Gospel.   William Cowper.   TrCP

Oh, grant that of my love at last I may not miss!   Prayer to Venus.   Edmund Spenser.   EiL

Oh grief that Earth's best hopes rest all with Thee!   Sonnet: "England! the time is come when thou shouldst wean."   William Wordsworth.   ViBoPo

...Oh-h-h/Yes, the cock begins to crow.   And the Cock Begins to Crow.   Richard K. Avery.   AH

Oh, hame cam his guid horse,/but never cam he!   Bonnie James Campbell.   *Anonymous.*   ESPB

Oh, happy little ponds to be/So well deceived!   Little Ponds.   Arthur Guiterman.   HBMV

Oh, hark, hark, forward,/The wind's roaring, so we would say.   Southerly Wind.   *Anonymous.*   ShS

Oh, hasten, oh, hasten, oh, hasten away.   Il Janitoro.   George Ade.   OBAL

Oh, he could see what tears had done to stone.   Private Worship.   Mark Van Doren.   LiTL; MoVE

Oh, he died with his hammer in his hand.   John Henry (C vers.).   *Anonymous.*   ViBoFo

Oh, he fancies it QUITE THE CHEESE!   Quite the Cheese (parody).   H. C. Waring.   BXAP

Oh he is out of hiding now/and is drumming drumming/drumming my heart.   X-Ray.   David Ray.   NePoEA-2

Oh, hear me prayin',/I want to be more holy ev'ry day.   Oh, Hear Me Prayin'(Lord, Feed My Lam's).   *Anonymous.*   BoAN 1-2

Oh, hear us, our handmaid unheeding,/And take it away!   The Poets at Tea.   Barry Pain.   Par

Oh, heaven is where she stands!   Paean.   Jonathan Henderson Brooks.   CDC

Oh hell–he's throwed you a mile.   Ride 'Im Cowboy.   A. L. Freebairn.   PH

Oh! hoh! what Diff'rence between Ox and Ass!   Epigrams.   Francis Daniel Pastorius.   SCAP

Oh hold me, for I am afraid.   Woman to Man.   Judith Wright.   BoAV; CBAP; PoAu 1-2

Oh, honey, won't you have a little sniff on me,/Have a sniff on me.   Cocaine Bill and Morphine Sue.   *Anonymous.*   FSW

Oh, Horses have four!!!   Haiku: "Cherry-blossoms, more."   Onitsura.   LiTW

Oh, how can I endure you when ye shine?   Sleeping Beauty.   William, of Hawthornden Drummond.   LiTL

Oh how can such a body sinne-procuring,/Be slow to love, and quicke to hate, enduring?   Sonnets, XVII: "Cherry-Lipt Adonis in his snowie shape."   Richard Barnfield.   PeHV

Oh how hard is life for many! oh, how sweet it is for some!   The Ballad of Charity.   Charles Godfrey Leland.   InMe

Oh how he wishes he were there again!   The Mountains.   Walker Gibson.   SD

Oh how I love that girl.   Kitty Kline.   *Anonymous.*   AmFP

Oh, how I never want to part from him!   As If from Her Nest.   *Anonymous.*   HW

Oh! how I wish he'd go away!   I Met a Man.   *Anonymous.*   OnUR

Oh! how I wish I had the bread/That once I threw away!   The Crust of Bread.   *Anonymous.*   HBV 1-2; HBVY

Oh, how it stabbed, the stranger's/rose!   All through the Stranger's Wood.   Isaac L. Peretz.   TrJP

Oh how/marvelous, how/nice, how lovely to be/part of all this.   The Finest Thing.   Tom Weatherly.   ANYP

Oh how near thy happy state/Comes the Gods to imitate!   Anacreontea: The Grasshopper.   *Anonymous.*   OBVE

Oh how real to me you are!   Auburn.   Paul Verlaine.   ErPo

Oh, how that flopping floppeth me!   Upon Julia's Arctics.   Bert Leston Taylor.   NLV; OBAL

Oh, how the Commonwealth doth need/Such justices as you!   The Fairies' Farewell.   Richard Corbet.   LiTB; TrGrPo

Oh how the deluge of these many years/has driven us apart.   Exodus 1940.   Alfred Wolfenstein.   VWA

Oh, how the little muzzles squeaked.   Beautiful Youth.   Gottfried Benn.   PoL

Oh, how their likeness taketh me!   Upon Julia's Clothes (parody).   E. V. Knox ("Evoe").   BXAP

Oh, I am not like that at all!   The Evening Primrose.   Dorothy Parker.   ALV; InMe

Oh I burned my eyes and I filled up my head like a cage.   The Finches.   Philip Murray.   NePoAm

Oh I'd like for to change your name.   The Train Is off the Track.   *Anonymous.*   AmFP

Oh, I'd much rather have my mummy/Than all the gold in the world!   By the Klondike River.   Alan Coren.   OnUR

Oh, I'd rather sweep the streets than have/To burrow like a mole.   The Plodder Seam.   *Anonymous.*   ELP

Oh, I do appeal to the Justice of Time!   Poor Ellen Smith.   Peter Degraph.   AmFP

Oh I don't suppose it mattered;/But I happened to be there.   Civil Riot.   G. D. H. Cole.   OxBTC

Oh, I don't want you to weep after me.   Don't You Weep after Me.   *Anonymous.*   FSW

Oh, I hate men!   I Hate Men.   Cole Porter.   DBV

Oh, I have stood with only God/Between me and the sun.   Pioneer Woman.   Vesta Pierce Crawford.   BPAW; PoOW

"Oh I'll forswear all my lands and dwellin's/For the Turkish lady who set me free!"   The Turkish Lady.   *Anonymous.*   MaC

Oh, I'll NEVER come back any more, ma'am!   The Mouse.   Laura E. Richards.   OBCA

"Oh, I'll range no more in foreign lands,/Since Susie Pye has cross'd the sea."   Lord Beichan and Susie Pye.   *Anonymous.*   GN

Oh, I'm a gwinter sing, gwinter sing, gwinter sing all along de way all along de way.   Gwinter Sing All along de Way.   *Anonymous.*   BoAN 1-2

"Oh I'm so sorry,/officer, I broke your gun."   A Mother Speaks: The Algiers Motel Incident, Detroit.   Michael S. Harper.   AmPA; BPo

Oh, I think you had better go back to sea!   Light Lover.   Aline Kilmer.   HBMV

Oh, I wish I were a single girl again. Oh, I Wish I Were Single Again. *Anonymous.* AmFP

Oh I wish that I could be/Richard Cory. Richard Cory (parody). Paul Simon. InPK

Oh! I wish that young fellow was with me now,/On a May day morning early. I Want to Be Married and Cannot Tell How. *Anonymous.* OnYI

Oh! I would be wild and free/And with the shadow people be. The Shadow People. Francis Ledwidge. MCCG

"Oh, I would give the moon if I had heard/A thrush, or ever seen a hummingbird!" Unless We Guard Them Well. Jane Merchant. QQQ

...Oh, if/I could but find again/That stone called Kiph! Kiph. Walter De la Mare. TiPo

Oh, if I say I love you, can you know/It better, for my having told you so? Another Song. Marion Strobel. MoLP

Oh, if men were all like that wise bird! There was an old owl lived in an oak. *Anonymous.* CenHV

Oh, if my mother went away/Who would start the night and day? Night and Morning. Dorothy Aldis. PoSC; YeAr

Oh, in Death's garden be/Prime witness of the only Resurrection. Churchyard of St. Mary Magdalene, Old Milton. John Heath-Stubbs. NePoEA

Oh, in my arms, all her charms/were casted in the foggy dew. The Foggy Dew. *Anonymous.* FSW

Oh! islanders of Ithaca, we will return no more. The Lotos-Eaters. Alfred, Lord Tennyson. OBRV

Oh, it's about ship, stations, boys, be 'andy./All raise tacks, sheets, and mainsl' 'aul! Mainsail Haul. *Anonymous.* ShS

Oh it's lots of fun at Finnigan's wake. Finnigan's Wake. *Anonymous.* FaBoBa; FSW; TrAS

Oh, it's Love, Love, Love, LOVE,/That makes the world go 'round! The Work of Love. Margaret Sangster. BLRP

Oh! it's perfectly true you can beat a tattoo,/But you can't beat a tattooed man. The Tattooed Man. Harry Bache Smith. InMe

Oh! it's then I'd be the dandy O. Peeler and the Goat. *Anonymous.* AnIL

Oh! it's there my soul shall wander, though it's here my/bones must lie. Hot Weather in the Plains–India. E. H. Tipple. HBV 1-2

Oh Jenny get your oat cake done. Whip Jamboree. *Anonymous.* OBSS

Oh, Jerry, go and ile that car-r-r! Jerry, Go an' Ile That Car (with music). *Anonymous.* AS

Oh, join me gentlemen, I beg,/In honoring our friend, the egg. The Egg. Clarence Day. NLV

Oh, Jordan is a hard road to travel, I believe. The Other Side of Jordan. *Anonymous.* FSW

Oh! joy it was for her, and joy for me! Among All Lovely Things My Love Had Been. William Wordsworth. GBL; MyFE

Oh, just as the chandler sat down to die. For-Ever Morning. Laura Riding. LiTA

Oh, Kafoozalum, the daughter of the Baba. Kafoozalum. *Anonymous.* BLPA

Oh Keats, the violet. The violet. The violet/was your favorite flower. On the Death of Keats. John Logan. Prf

Oh! keep it unharmed, dear London town! London. T. P. Cameron Wilson. HBMV

Oh, Keith of Ravelston,/The sorrows of thy line! A Nuptial Eve. Sydney Thomas Dobell. OBNC

Oh, Kentucky, the hunters of Kentucky. The Hunters of Kentucky. Samuel Woodworth. AS; BLSo; FSW; PAH; TrAS

Oh, Laddie–oh, Laddie,/Those red fields of France! They Who Wait. Charles Buxton Going. HBMV

Oh, lady, grant me time,/please, to finish my rhyme. Ballad of the Despairing Husband. Robert Creeley. AmPC; NeAP; NoP; OBAL; SM

Oh Lana Turner we love you get up Poem: "Lana Turner has collapsed!" Frank O'Hara. CAPP; VGW

Oh, lay the lily ho! Lily Munro. *Anonymous.* OuSiCo

Oh, lay those arms of yours aside. He Charges Her to Lay Aside Her Weapons. Pierce Ferriter. AnIL; LiTW; OnYI

Oh, lead me, lead me/with your pale hands/to the dark side/of the light. City of Light. Nahum Bomze. VWA

Oh, let it ring! Assembly: Harlem School. Eugene T. Maleska. GoYe

Oh, let me fly across the world/To where the Fairies are! In the Moonlight. Norreys Jephson O'Conor. HBMV; SoPo; SUS

Oh, let me join the faithful shades that throng that round/above. Italian Rhapsody. Robert Underwood Johnson. HBV 1-2

Oh, let me love with all my strength/Careless if I am loved again. A Prayer. Sara Teasdale. HBMV; TrPWD

Oh, let me 'mid my friends expire,/And with my fathers lie. The Wanderer's Grave. Rufus B. Sage. BPAW; PoOW

Oh, let me not be last to fall asleep! Insomnia. Edith Matilda Thomas. AA

Oh, let's build bridges everywhere/And span the gulf of challenge there. Interracial. Georgia Douglas Johnson. PoNe; TTY

...Oh let/the fierce goddess/come The Sibyl's Song. Michele Roberts. BrRo

Oh, let the little children see/A teacher leaning hard on Thee. The Teacher. Leslie Pinckney Hill. BANP; PoNe; TrPWD

Oh let there be one Abdication more. Of the French Kings Nativity, &c. Benjamin Harris. SCAP

Oh, let they spirit stay with me, sweet/vale! Evening in Tyringham Valley. Richard Watson Gilder. AA

"Oh, Life! Oh, Life!" I kept saying,/And the very word seemed sweet. Life and Nature. Archibald Lampman. PeCV

...Oh, life should give/Light till we understand they live, they live. Love's Immaturity. E. J. Scovell. GBL; LiTB

Oh, little body, do not die. A Child Ill. Sir John Betjeman. DTC

Oh, little cat beside my stool. Cinderella's Song. Elizabeth Madox Roberts. DFT

Oh, little Charlie Chipmunk was a very tiresome child! Little Charlie Chipmunk. Helen Cowles LeCron. SoPo; TiPo

...Oh Little Town, enveloped in unease. December Blues. Robert Pinsky. MAYP

Oh Liza, poor girl,/She died on the train. Goodbye 'Liza Jane. *Anonymous.* FSW

Oh, lonely Cross! Late Corner. Langston Hughes. NePoAm-2

Oh, Lord, have mercy if you please. Let Us Break Bread Together. *Anonymous.* AH; FSW

"Oh, Lord have mercy on me! Can this be I?"/Fol-lol, diddle, diddle, diddle, dol. The Old Woman Who Went to Market. *Anonymous.* BFSS

Oh, Lord, honey, take a drink on me. Take a Drink on Me. *Anonymous.* FSW

Oh, Lord! I see on reading this,/He is an awful sap! The Danger of Writing Defiant Verse. Dorothy Parker. InMe

Oh lord: my lord/Lord, lordy lord/(Oh lord). Frying Pan Skillet Blues. Bessie Tucker. BluL

Oh Lord, oh Lord/let me see a brand new year. 34 Blues. Charlie Patton. BluL; FaBoPV

...Oh Lord, the possible/bells ringing, to bring me out of here. When I Was Well into Being Savored. Joanne Kyger. PoM

Oh, Lordy, pick a bale a day. Pick a Bale of Cotton. *Anonymous.* ABF; FSW

...Oh, love, I would/never have seen that without you. Make Me Hear You. Reginald Gibbons. MAYP

Oh, love, take all the faithfulness/Of my unfaithful heart! Hymn. Louise Townsend Nicholl. EaLo

Oh lover man/Oh where can you be? For Lover Man, and All the Other Young Men Who Failed to Return... Mance Williams. NNP

Oh, low down the chariot, let-n me ride. Low down Chariot. *Anonymous.* OuSiCo

Oh Lucky Jim, how I envy him! Oh Lucky Jim. *Anonymous.* GBP

Oh mak my bed, mammy, now, now, oh mak my bed, mammy,/now! Lord Randal (C vers.). *Anonymous.* BaBo; ESPB; ViBoFo

Oh, make my sad heart sing anew;/make warm, make sweet, my camping/ground! My Camping Ground. Morris Rosenfeld. TrJP

...Oh, mammy! I'm not well! The Devil's Bag. James Stephens. WSC

Oh, Mary and the Baby, sweet Lamb. Mary and the Baby, Sweet Lamb. *Anonymous.* AmFP

Oh, Mary don't you weep. Oh, Mary Don't You Weep. *Anonymous.* FSW

"Oh, Mary loves the lamb, you know,"/The teacher did reply. Mary's Lamb. Sarah Josepha Hale. OxNR; SoPo; TiPo

Oh may my spirit still by memory share/The high serenity that blessed me there! The Old Mountaineer. W. K. Holmes. PoSH

Oh! may the earth on him lie lighter/Than did his quartos upon us! Epitaph on Robert Southey. Thomas Moore. FaBoCo; FaBoEE; PP

Oh, meet me at the river, I ask in Thy name./Amen. Prayer. *Anonymous.* OuSiCo

Oh, Mexico's the place I belong in,/Round the Bay of Mexico. Round the Bay of Mexico. *Anonymous.* OuSiCo

Oh, might it die or rest at last! Hellas: Chorus. Percy Bysshe Shelley. AtBAP; AWP; ChTr; EBEV; EnLit; ERoP 1-2; ExPo; FiP; HAP; HBV 1-2; HeIP; InPo; MyFE; NOBE; NoP; OAEL 1-2; OAEP; OBEV; PoEL 1-5; SeCePo; SeCeV; TrGrPo

Oh, miserie! All flesh is grass!/Unhappy I! A Rondeau of Remorse. Burges Johnson. HBMV

"Oh misery! must I lose that too?... Lalla Rookh. Thomas Moore. SpRo

Oh, Miss Bailey! unfortunate Miss Bailey! Unfortunate Miss Bailey. George the Younger Colman. DTC; FiBHP; FSW; GBP; ViBoFo

Oh! Mister Johnson made him good. Mister Johnson. Ben Harney. OBAL

Oh, moment where the lost is found! The Marriage of Heaven and Earth. Howard Nemerov. NYBP

Oh, Mona! that accounts for you now! Mews Flat Mona. William Plomer. FaBoTw

Oh, morning was a lovely thing to feel! Morning. Dorothy Hamilton Gallagher. SiSoSe

Oh, Mother, is there anyone to plead on our behalf? Mother. Anwar Shaul. VWA

Oh mother, mother, where is happiness? The Sonnet-Ballad. Gwendolyn Brooks. WeW

"Oh mother–oh mother–you never can know–/I loved him so!" Folk-Song. Louis Untermeyer. HBV 1-2

Oh Mr Tennyson, your dream of fair women,/how it echoes remotely, at this late date, a lemon! La Belle Dame sans Merci. A. R. D. Fairburn. AnNZ

Oh, music, oh, mine. Merry-Go-Round. Mark Van Doren. SO

Oh my boy Jesus: rest./Shushhh, you need the rest. The Confession Stone. Owen Dodson. TTY

Oh my bride, my bride. I Remember. Stevie Smith. BoLoP; BoWoP; FaBoWP; InPK; OxBC

Oh my brothers,/we will dwell by the altar,/our cattle and gold. Shechem. David Shevin. VWA

"Oh, my dark one,/tell of the coming of cold/and of Kings, ancient and ruined." Passing Out. Philip Levine. AmPC

...Oh my Father, it is time to go! Mignon. Johann Wolfgang von Goethe. NU

Oh my fine, my honey-colored Duke of Marmalade!? Elegy for the Duke of Marmalade. Luis Palés Matos. InW

Oh, my God! It ain't decent any more either way! Reaping. Amy Lowell. SBG

Oh, my good Lord, show me de way,/Enter de chariot, travel along. Oh, My Good Lord, Show Me de Way. Anonymous. BoAN 1-2

Oh, my li'l John Henry,/Godamighty know. My Li'l John Henry. Anonymous. ABF

Oh, my little breath, now I go there alone in sorrow. A Lover's Lament. Anonymous. AWP

Oh, my Lord, a manikin, not a man. The Bantam Husband. Anonymous. OuSiCo

Oh, my New England where true worth is valued yet! Praise of New England. Thomas Caldecot Chubb. GoYe

Oh my slender boy! Love Song. Anonymous. BoWoP

Oh, Nature–good! Oh, Art–no whit/Less worthy! Both in one–accurst! Bad Dreams. Robert Browning. OAEL 1-2; VLP

Oh never call it loving! A Woman's Shortcomings. Elizabeth Barrett Browning. BLPA; HBV 1-2

Oh, never in all the world was such a night as this! Prothalamion. Francis Brett Young. HBMV

Oh never mind her squalling/Or the rumpling of her gown. Blow away the Morning Dew. Anonymous. OBET

Oh, never mind–tomorrow,tomorrow! His Majesty the Letter-Carrier. Emanuel Carnevali. AnAmPo

Oh, never play this game with ugly clothes on. Frisbee. Rolfe Humphries. GrPl

Oh, no. By Jove! There comes the white hippocampus. The Mermaid. Ben King. OBAL

Oh no categories I pray. No Categories! Stevie Smith. NoP

Oh no it was not a pen/i wanted in my hand. The Lust for Murder. Gerda Penfold. GP

Oh no John, no John, no John, no. Oh No John. Anonymous. OBET

Oh no she hasn't marihuana for to smoke. La Cucaracha (The Cockroach). Anonymous. TrAS

Oh! no, they just sold them for bioux. The American Indian. Anonymous. FaBoCo; FiBHP; NLV

Oh, no! 'Twas the truth in her eye ever dawning,/That made me love Mary, The Rose of Tralee. The Rose of Tralee. C. Mordaunt Spencer. FSW; OnYI; TreFT

...Oh, noble/Pico Blanco, steep sea-wave of marble. Return. Robinson Jeffers. GoYe

...Oh noble/Ulysses! Oh Zeus! before the tumble. Youth. Barend Toerien. PeSA

Oh, not for me/Comes spring a-winging. Returning Spring. Baron Joseph von Eichendorff. CAW

Oh, not I,/not I,/not I. Night Enchantment. Eleanor Muth. SiSoSe

Oh, nothing matters but the longest journey. Ship of Death. D. H. Lawrence. DTC; MoAB; MoBrPo; NAMP; ViBoPo

Oh oh have none of it,/Blow it away, have done with it. Thoughts on the Christian Doctrine of Eternal Hell. Stevie Smith. PPON

Oh! Oh! Oh! The Ghost. O'Brien. NOEC

...Oh, on my/hands and knees, crawl-/ing forward. A Sight. Robert Creeley. NaP

Oh, one's the one that's left alone,/A-mourning to be alone. Come, Let Us Sing. Anonymous. BFSS

"Oh, Philemy Hyland, come back to me:/Och anee! Och anee!" Ballinderry. Anonymous. WTO

Oh photograph me thus! The Oneness of the Philosopher with Nature. Gilbert Keith Chesterton. FaBoNo

Oh please to give a little glee/To them that go without. For Them. Eleanor Farjeon. ChBR

Oh, poor Mary! oh, poor Jane! Mary Jane. Anonymous. NA

Oh, poor old horse! The Dead Horse. Anonymous. AmSS; AS

Oh, poor Paddy works on the railway. Paddy Works on the Railway. Anonymous. AmSS

...Oh, poor us, I begin. The Madman's Wife. Steve Orlen. MAYP

Oh! press it to thine own again,/Where it will break at last. The Indian Serenade. Percy Bysshe Shelley ATP; AWP; BLPL; BoLiVe; EnLi 1-2; EnLit; EnRP; ExPo; GoTF; GTBS; HoPM; InPo; LiTB; LiTL; LoBV; MCCG; OAEP; OBEV; OBRV; PG; PoPl; TreF; TrGrPo; UnTE; ViBoPo

Oh, pretty warbling from a sweet sweet throat! Pretty Wantons. Anonymous. EiL

Oh promise me! Oh promise me! Oh Promise Me. Clement Scott. BLSo; FaFP; FSN; GoTF; TreF

Oh, prove't a well-set song indeed, which shows/Sweet'st in the close! Epithalamium. Richard Crashaw. HW; NOCV

Oh punish us not! The Vedic Hymns: Forgive, Lord, Have Mercy. Anonymous. ILwL

Oh, puppy, I love you so. My Dog. Marchette Chute. SoPo; TiPo

Oh queen, as in thy chamber thou didst perish, so do/thou thyself make them ashamed. Lament to Nana of Erech. Anonymous. LiTW

Oh, rabbit a-hash. Rabbit Hash. Anonymous. ABF

Oh, rest in peace, for the Lord will care! He Careth. Marianne Farningham. WBLP

Oh rest ye, brother mariners. we will not wander more. The Lotos-Eaters. Alfred, Lord Tennyson. AtBAP; BoLiVe; EnL; ExPo; GoTL; GTBS; LiTB; MaVP; MBW 1-2; NoP; OAEL 1-2; OAEP; PoEL 1-5; SeCeV; TEP; VLP; WHA

Oh, rock-a my soul. Rock-a My Soul. Anonymous. FSW

Oh, rock me in de cradle all de day. Bright Sparkles in de Churchyard. Anonymous. AA

Oh, rock 'n' row me over,/One more day! Rock 'n' Row Me over. Anonymous. FSW

Oh, ROLL, Alabama, ROLL! The Alabama. Anonymous. ShS

Oh, roll the cotton down. Roll the Cotton down. Anonymous. AmFP; ShS

Oh! rum! tum!! tum!!! my Geraldine. Oh, My Geraldine. Sir Francis Cowley Burnand. NA

Oh, sable is my throat! Negro Spiritual. Perient Trott. PoNe

"Oh, save my Country, Heav'n!" shall be your last. Moral Essays. Alexander Pope. CEP

Oh! save the salary, and drink the sack! On the Candidates for the Laurel. Alexander Pope. FaBoEE

...Oh, say a prayer/for one only kid, son of Our Father/Avraham, who wandered like a gypsy. Hands up. Anthony Rudolf. VWA

Oh say I'm/all right it's/springtime. Mardi Gras. George Keithley. TAT

Oh! send us not despairing home,/Send none unhealed away. Jehovah-Rophi. William Cowper. EiCP

Oh, shall we wander into space/Or fall into the sun?' Taking Long Views. May Kendall. CenHV

Oh she mist her maiden-head. The Bard. James Shirley. ErPo

"Oh, sir! the flowers, they are wild," replied the timid/creature. Wild Flowers. Peter Newell. NA

Oh! so fickle, oh! so vain, oh! so false, so false, is she! A Song: "Hast thou seen the Down in the Air." Sir John Suckling. EnLoPo

Oh, so that's who you are, my Mother: Mother:/Father's-old-widow. Mother. Philip Dow. NPGG

Oh so white, oh so soft, oh so sweet is she! See the Chariot at Hand Here of Love. Ben Jonson. InvP

Oh, someone came and found me. Wanderer. Jessica Powers. AMV-80

Oh something's happening there this very minute! Home Thoughts. Claude McKay. GoSl

Oh, speed the blown chaff down the smoking sky! The Harvest of Time. Harold Trowbridge Pulsifer. HBMV

Oh, spring,/To maid of the flowering apple-breath/Clinging! The Apple-Tree. Brian Vrepont. PoAu 1-2

"Oh, stop your dodging, Mrs. C.!" Thomas Carlyle. Anonymous. FiBHP

Oh sure I am the wits of former days,/To subjects worse have given admiring praise. Sonnets, LIX: "If there be. William Shakespeare. FaBoEn

Oh! sweet is the anguish/Of death to me! Amor Mysticus. Sister Marcela de Carpio. AWP; CAW; LiTW

Oh, swing 'em 'round the green. Walking on the Green Grass. Anonymous. AmFP

Oh, take me away/To the country again! City Streets and Country Roads. Eleanor Farjeon. BrR; SoPo; TiPo

"Oh tell her I lie in fair Kirk-land,/And home will never come." The Two Brothers. Anonymous. EBEV

Oh tell if she were not designed/The eclipse and glory of her kind? On His Mistress, the Queen of Bohemia. Sir Henry Wotton. AnAnS 2; EG; EiL; EnLoPo; GBL; HAP; JCP; LoBV; MeLP; MePo; MyFE; NoP; OBS; SeCP; TrGrPo; ViBoPo

Oh thank you Drum/for bringing us home   For Drum Hadley.   Harold Littlebird.   VoR

An' oh! that happy hours should glide/Away so soon, an' never bide.   Sheep in the Sheade.   William Barnes.   FM

"Oh, that hushed forest! - soon may I/be there!"   Into the Noiseless Country. Thomas William Parsons   AA

Oh! that I were the happy dream that creeps/To her soft heart, to find my image there.   Night.   Hartley Coleridge.   NCEP

Oh that moment! Oh that breath of locust bloom!   Under the Locust Blossoms.   Frederick Goddard Tuckerman.   NOBA

Oh that my baa-ing nature would win thence/Some woolly innocence!   The Nativity.   Clive Staples Lewis.   EBCP; TrCP

Oh, that's "the man for Galway."   The Man for Galway.   Charles James Lever.   OnYI

Oh, that somehow I might contrive/My first night dead to be alive...!   Prescience.   Donald Jeffrey Hayes.   PoNe

Oh, that Strawberry Roan.   The Strawberry Roan.   Anonymous.   FSW

Oh, that with them I had fought my fill/And found like cover!   Happy Death.   John Freeman.   HBMV

Oh, the bears and the bulls/Are but corpulent gulls/To the valiant Shrove-tide martyr.   Cock-Throwing!   Martin Lluellyn.   PBBP

Oh, the blithest of sights in the world so fair/Is a gay little pup with his tail in the air!   Little Lost Pup.   Arthur Guiterman.   BBV; GoTF; TreFS

Oh, the blunder of it!   Love-Songs, At Once Tender and Informative. Samuel Hoffenstein.   OBAL

Oh, the dance of our sister!   The Dance of the Rain.   Eugene Marais. PeSA

Oh, the dust!/How it's cuss'd.   A Colorado Sand Storm.   Eugene Field. PoOW

(Oh, the embers black and cold!)   Cottonwood Leaves.   Badger Clark. TiPo

"Oh, the farther the better, kind sir," she said.   Mary Jane, the Milkmaid. Anonymous.   BFSS

Oh! the fiddles and the flutes were the finest in the land.   The Ceremonial Band.   James Reeves.   OnUR

Oh, the grizzly, grizzly, grizzly bear.   Grizzly Bear.   Anonymous.   FSW

Oh, the ingle-side for me!   The Ingle-Side.   Hew Ainslee.   HBV 1-2

Oh, the joy to see you come!   Safely Home.   Anonymous.   STF

Oh the oak and the ash and the bonnie ivy tree,/They flourish at home in my own country.   The Oak and the Ash.   Anonymous.   FaBoCh; FSW; LoGBV

Oh the Poor Workhouse Boy.   The Workhouse Boy.   Anonymous.   GBP; VLP

Oh the/professionals what we/should fear.   For the Barbers.   Joel Oppenheimer.   CoPo

Oh the Roast Beef of Old England,/And Old English Roast Beef.   A Song in Praise of Old English Roast Beef.   Richard Leveridge.   OBEC

Oh, the rustling, rustling of that autumn night by the/pools!   Folk Song. Anonymous.   LiTW

Oh the sad fate of/The babes in the wood!'   The Babes in the Wood. Anonymous.   OxBChV

Oh, the scent of mint was plain!   After.   Lizette Woodworth Reese.   HBV 1-2

Oh, the shadows which seek each other in nights of sad-/ness and tears! Nocturne–III.   Jose Asuncion Silva.   LiTW

Oh, the sound of all sounds is the hunter's horn!   The Hunter's Song.   Barry (Bryan Waller Procter) Cornwall.   GN

Oh, the stones not yet cut.   The Air of June Sings.   Edward Dorn.   NeAP; PoM

Oh, the wind blow the China/Right down in town.   The Wind Blow East. Anonymous.   OuSiCo

Oh the wine-cup/Elevates me to be one/Of the company of all the gods! Alcibiades to a Jealous Girl.   Arthur Davison Ficke.   HBMV

Oh! the withy it shall be the very first tree/That perishes at the heart.   The Bitter Withy.   Anonymous.   BaBo; FaBoBa; GBP; NOCV; NoP; OAEP; OBET; SBVL; ViBoFo

Oh the wold, the wold, the wold!   Wind.   Sydney Thomas Dobell.   PeD

Oh, the world is all before us!   There's Gowd in the Breast.   James Hogg. HBV 1-2

Oh, then, Mollidusta, I'll love thee no more.   To Mollidusta.   Planche. NA

Oh! then remember me.   Go where Glory Waits Thee.   Thomas Moore. OBNC; TreFS

Oh! then, to me.   Moorland Night.   Charlotte Mew.   ChMP; ViBoPo

Oh, there are many things to chew/While walking down the avenue.   Food. Marchette Chute.   BrR

Oh, there are things/Feet know/That hands NEVER will.   Feet.   Dorothy Aldis.   SUS

"Oh, there are things/Hands do/That feet NEVER can."   Hands.   Dorothy Aldis.   SUS

"Oh there! just there! Oh there! just there!"   The Nameless Maiden. Anonymous.   ErPo

Oh, there let me live till I die.   Oh, Give Me the Hills.   Anonymous. AmFP

Oh! there was loneliness in all of them together.   Cold, Sharp Lamentation. Augusta Gregory, Lady Gregory.   OBMV

Oh, there will need no porters/When all those doors open!   Ballad of Mistress Death.   Denis Devlin.   NMP

Oh, they lied in their teeth when they told me of her!   Fable.   Dorothy Parker.   ALV

Oh, things are up and comin', God bless the T.V.A.   The T.V.A. Anonymous.   TrAS

Oh! think me not a Prince of Troy,/By whom such treacherous deeds are done.   Young Paris.   George Crabbe.   OBRV

Oh, think not there is no judgment or/judge!   Believe Not.   Isaac L. Peretz. TrJP

Oh, think of His sorrow, that we may know/His wondrous love in His wondrous woe!   Behold Your King!   Frances Ridley Havergal.   BePJ

Oh, think what a joy/To look after a barge.   The Barge.   Rose Fyleman. BrR

Oh this is rest. Oh this is paradise.   The Oasis of Sidi Khaled.   Wilfrid Scawen Blunt.   OBTV

Oh, this tearful, snaky, smiling crocodile!   Limerick: "Oh, there once was a merry crocodile."   Gerturde E. Heath.   TDH

Oh! 'tis glorious,/To know we'll meet again.   When Our Earthly Sun Is Setting.   Edwin H. Nevin.   AH

Oh, 'tis lonely, lonely, by the little grave!   The Mother's Prayer.   Dora Sigerson Shorter.   HBV 1-2

Oh, 'tis my delight on a shining night/In the season of the year!   The Lincolnshire Poacher.   Anonymous.   CH; FSW; GBP; OnMSP; OxBoLi; SD

An' oh! 'tis the maid I'm a-hopen/to wed in the Spring.   In the Spring. William Barnes.   GBL

Oh, to remain on a broad flat rock/And cast my fishing-line forever!   A Green Stream.   Wang Wei.   SD

Oh, town and field will mind you/Till Ludlow tower is down.   The Recruit. Alfred Edward Housman.   FaPoR

Oh! 'twas light that ne'er can shine again/On life's dull stream.   Love's Young Dream.   Thomas Moore.   HBV 1-2; WBLP

Oh, venom I next gonna see you?   Limerick: "Said an asp to an adder named Rhea."   Joseph S. Newman.   TDH

Oh, Virtue always wins, I sing,/If Wisdom's mingled in it!   King Cophetua and the Beggar Maid.   Don (Donald Robert Marquis) Marquis.   HBMV; InMe

Oh visit thou my soothing dream!   Ode: "Tell me, thou soul of her I love." James (1700-48) Thomson.   OBEC

Oh, wait, good Lawd, 'twell ter-morrer!   A Plantation Ditty.   Frank Lebby Stanton.   AA; HBV 1-2

Oh, waltz me around again, Willie, a-round, a-round, a-round.   Waltz Me Around Again, Willie.   Will D. Cobb.   FSN; GoTF; TreFT

Oh, wash my eyes with tears that they may know the light of Thy/love!   A Psalm to the Son.   Marguerite Wilkinson.   TrPWD

Oh, wasn't that a bunch of hoodlums/For to take a ship around Cape Horn! Paddy, Get Back.   Anonymous.   AmFP; AmSS

Oh, we are given such a little while!   Protest.   Countee Cullen.   CDC

Oh, we'e the boys that'll do it once more!/Handy, me boys, so handy!   So Handy.   Anonymous.   ShS

Oh, we'll go home by boat, says Bryan O'Lynn.   Bryan O'Lynn. Anonymous.   GBP

Oh, we'll kill the old red rooster when she comes.   She'll Be Comin' Round the Mountain.   Anonymous.   BLSo

Oh! we might see as happy days as ever we did then.   The Times Have Altered.   Anonymous.   CoMu

(Oh! weary mother, drive the cows to roost.)   Oh! Weary Mother.   Barry Pain.   NA

Oh well/Done gone over/Make up my   Jesus Make Up My Dying Bed. Blind Willie Johnson.   BluL

Oh, wert thou here,/Or still the crimson roses glow.   Vigil.   Richard Dehmel.   AWP; LiTW

Oh, what a lesson for us all/To only eat at dinner.   The Vulture.   Hilaire Belloc.   HBVY; OxBChV

"Oh what a lovely slice of bread'.   Christmas 1970.   Spike Milligan.   OBCP

Oh! what a merry little fat grey man!   The Merry Man of Paris.   Stella Mead.   SUS

Oh, what a plague is an obstinate daughter!   The Duenna (excerpt). Richard Brinsley Sheridan.   DBV

Oh, what a proud mysterious cat/Mew...Mew...Mew.   The Mysterious Cat. Vachel Lindsay.   GoJo; OBCA; SoPo; TiPo

Oh what a Saturday night.   Linstead Market.   Anonymous.   FSW

Oh, what a scorching Jim will get when Gabriel blows his horn!   Sam Bass. Anonymous.   AmFP

Oh, what a sweet death I might have died this day three/years to-day!   He Wishes He Might Die and Follow Laura.   Petrarch (Francesco Petrarca). OBMV

Oh, what an effort it is/to love you as I do! It Is True. Federico Garcia Lorca. OLR

Oh, what beastesses/to make such feastesses! Three Ghostesses. *Anonymous.* OxNR

Oh, what CAN the package be? The Package. Aileen Fisher. SoPo

Oh, what despairing morrows,/If nought to us replies!– Nightfall. Antonio de Trueba. CAW

Oh! what fun it is to ride in a one-horse open sleigh! Jingle Bells. James S. Pierpont. BLSo; FaFP; FSW; GoTF; OxNR; PSoN; TreF; YaD

Oh, what know they of harbors/Who toss not on the sea! Plymouth Harbor. Mrs. Ernest Radford. HBV 1-2

Oh! what new Physics waits up there to teach/other matters to another ear...' Pyrargyrite Metal, 9. Cecilia Meireles. PBWP

...Oh what/Of a century at one glance? What of that fury? Sun-Up in March. Abbie Huston Evans. NePoAm

Oh, what shall be said/By the Angels who see Thee/And me visited?– Five Roses. Jacinto Verdaguer. CAW

Oh, what will you leave your sweetheart, my son?/A rope that will hang her. Lord Randall. *Anonymous.* FSW

Oh, what would I do when my life is through/If perchance my God should forget me? Forgetting God. J. E. Harvey. STF

Oh! whatever can that be? Riddle: "Higher than a house." Mother Goose. OxNR; SoPo; TiPo

Oh, when you counsel me, think what you/mean! Modern Love, XXXVIII. George Meredith. VLP

"Oh, where can I get a good sailor/To sail this ship of mine?" Sir Patrick Spens. *Anonymous.* AmFP

"Oh, where is All Sinners' if this is All Saints'?" All Saints'. Edmund Yates. HBV 1-2

"Oh, where is my darling gone?"/Salangadou, Salangadou. Salangadou. *Anonymous.* FSW; TrAS

Oh where, oh where is he? Where Is He? *Anonymous.* OxNR

Oh where shall I hide/from the stipples that peck? Fable of the Speckled Cow. D. J. Opperman. PeSA

...Oh, where/Shall I thee find to ease my Mind? Oh, where? Solitude. Thomas Traherne. OBS

Oh, while my brother with me played,/Would I have loved him more. The Child's First Grief. Felicia Dorothea Hemans. BLPA

Oh! who can guess the rest? Amyntas Led Me to a Grove. Aphra Behn. ErPo

Oh! who knows what the Clover thinks?/No one! unless the Bob-o'-links! A Song off Clover. Saxe Holm. GN

Oh! Who would inhabit/This bleak world alone? 'Tis the Last Rose of Summer. Thomas Moore. ATP; BLPA; BoNaP; ELP; FPL; GoTF; HBV 1-2; NOBI; PoEL 1-5; PoPl; TreF; WBLP; WHA

Oh! who would live if this be death!' The Geranium. Richard Brinsley Sheridan. BoLoP; ErPo; UnTE

Oh, who would not be/He, he, he? Fools, They Are the Only Nation. Ben Jonson. EIL; InvP

Oh who would not sleep with a snake? Eurynome. Jay Macpherson. NMP; OBCV; PV

Oh who would not sleep with the brave? Lancer. Alfred Edward Housman. EnLit; InPS; MoBrPo; OBWP

Oh why did I awake? when shall I sleep again? A Shropshire Lad. Alfred Edward Housman. AnFE; NOBV; OAEP

Oh why do you tremble, child, as I draw near? Homecoming. Anna Margolin. VWA

Oh, why should the spirit of mortal be proud? O Why Should the Spirit of Mortal Be Proud? William Knox. WGRP

Oh wide wide world I Am a Horse. Hans Arp. FaBoNo

–Oh, will I hear her calling/Over the sea again, over the hill? Will Beauty Come. Robert Nathan. HBMV

Oh, will soon fade away. Do Come Back Again. *Anonymous.* OuSiCo

Oh will the ships go down, go down,/In the windy sea? The Wind Has Such a Rainy Sound. Christina Georgina Rossetti. BrR; TiPo

"Oh willow, titwillow, titwillow!" The Suicide's Grave. Sir William Schwenck Gilbert. ALV; GoTF; LiTL; TreF; VLP

Oh whim, oh snowy interior,/rocks and hurt birds, we come. Winterward. William Stafford. SM

Oh, wise are the wild things, preparing for the winter! Remembering the Winter. Rowena Bastin Bennett. SiSoSe

Oh! with what a fire your page had glow'd! Waterspout. Luís de Camoens. EtS

Oh woe is me! oh misery!"' The Thorn. William Wordsworth. EnRP

Oh, Woe, woe, woe, etcetera.... Mr. Housman's Message. Ezra Pound. FaBoEE; FaBoPa

Oh, won't you come an' read it,/See what it say,/Dere's a han' writin' on de wall. Dere's a Han'writin' on de Wall. *Anonymous.* BoAN 1-2

Oh would the day had died first when you were born. Bye Baby Bother. Stevie Smith. TW

Oh, would they'd fight their friends no more,/And cease this bloody strife. Battle of Somerset. Cornelius C. Cullen. PAH

Oh, Yale, Eli Yale! Yale Boola March. Charles H. Loomis. FSN

Oh yes, and cucumbers in season,/and apples, and pears. Fragments. Praxilla. PBWP

"Oh yes!" if only they could rise and be there. To a Tyrant. Joseph Brodsky. VWA

Oh! yes, the soldier is home! The Soldier Is Home. Shaw Neilson. CBAP

Oh, yes, they must talk, you know. People Will Talk. *Anonymous.* GoTF; TreFS

Oh, yon's the way to Arcady,/Where all the leaves are merry. The Way to Arcady. Henry Cuyler Bunner. AA; InMe

Oh you are a whirlpool, you are a whirlpool,/And I am very nearly drowned. Nessa. Paul Durcan. FaBoIP

Oh you better watch out when the boat begins to rock,/Or you'll lose your girl in the ocean. Turn the Glasses Over. *Anonymous.* FSW

Oh, you canna spend a dollar when you're dead. Ding Dong Dollar. Hamish Henderson. FSW

Oh, you New York gals, can't they dance the polka! Can't They Dance the Polka! *Anonymous.* FSW; ShS

Oh, you pinks and poses,/Come down, you bunch of roses, come down. Come down, You Bunch of Roses, Come down. *Anonymous.* ShS

Oh, you're just as bad as we are, perhaps a damn sight worse. I Came to This Country in 1865. *Anonymous.* OuSiCo

Oh your tired mind starts to dream/Of the comforts at the trawler wharf/In the port of Aberdeen. Deep Sea Tug. *Anonymous.* OBSS

"Oh, Zooks!" says Nell, "we've acted well/In coming to Sledburn Fair." Sledburn Fair. *Anonymous.* CH

Oha! ohe! ohesa, hesa, he! Medieval Norman Songs. *Anonymous.* AWP

...The/Ohio river, that is no tomb to/Rise from the dead/From. Three Sentences for a Dead Swan. James Wright. NaP; NoAm; NOBA

Oho, sing I, oho! The Song of the Christmas Tree. Blanche Elizabeth Wade. OHIP

..The oiled machinery of nature shunts/Day down for repairs. Silently, the night's technicians hunt In New Ross. Valentin Iremonger. NeIP

"Okay; I'll help you build a raft." Forever Ambrosia. Christopher Morley. OBAL

Okay, you said, c'mon:/dominate the night for me. Iron Eyes. Terence Winch. APU

Oklahoma will be the last song/i'll ever sing. The Last Song. Joy Harjo. TAT; TWSS

De ol' ark's a-moverin',/An' I'm goin' home. De Ol' Ark's A-Movering' an' I'm Goin' Home. *Anonymous.* BoAN 1-2

Ol' Judge Bean, with all his snortin',/Made his court plumb self-supportin'! Fine! Squire Omar Barker. BPAW

De ol' sheep done know de road,/De young lam's mus' fin' de way. De Ol' Sheep Done Know De Road. *Anonymous.* BoAN 1-2

Ol' woes! Ol' Clothes. *Anonymous.* PoToHe

Old Abe Lincoln came out of the wilderness,/Many long years ago. Old Abe Lincoln Came out of the Wilderness. *Anonymous.* AS; FSW; TrAS

Old age is something they can never know. Whom the Gods Love. Margaret E. Bruner. PoLf

Old age, not Fairyland, was his delusion. The Broken Girth. Robert Graves. BIrV

Old Age with stealing pace/Casts up his nets, and there we panting die. The World a Hunt. William, of Hawthornden Drummond. NOBE; ORS

Old and unhappy, gazing out to sea. St Enda. Laurence Lerner. PeSA

The old ark's a-movin' and I thank God. The Old Ark's A-Moverin'. *Anonymous.* FSW

Old Bill will signal me. Bill the Whaler. Will Lawson. PoAu 1-2

An old birch tree. Hiking. Joseph Bruchac. CDW

An old bit of china with worn-off design. The Child's Power of Wonder. P. K. Saha. ACV

An old bitch, with a warm mouthful of game. Dowager. John Montague. IPY

Old bones upon the mountain shake. The Black Tower. William Butler Yeats. CMoP

Old Books are best. Old Books Are Best. Beverly Chew. HBV 1-2

The old bore stopped calling. Autobiographical Fragment. Kingsley Amis. NePoEA-2

...Old boy next door, and old me. Carry Me Back. John Holmes. AmFN; NePoAm-2

The old cathedral, to the years to be/Showing, with wounded arms, their own disgrace. The Cathedral of Rheims. Emile Verhaeren. CAW

Old Charley spit on his hands/and stood the drinks around. Desert Holy Man. John Beecher. TAT

Old climbers never die, they just run out of rope. Rock Leader. Dave Bathgate. PoSH

The old cow died, sail a-round. The Old Cow Died. *Anonymous.* FSW

Old daddy Skinflint, the father of me. Old Skinflint. Wilfrid Gibson. OBMV

Old Dan'l's out again. Old Dan'l. Leonard Alfred George Strong. ELU; MoBrPo; PoSC

Old Dan Tucker your to late to come to supper. Old Dan Tucker. Daniel Decatur Emmit. ABF; BLSo; FSW; PSoN; TrAS

...An/old deaf lady/burned to death/in South Carolina.) Leadbelly Gives an Autograph. LeRoi (Imamu Amiri Baraka) Jones. CNA

The old deceptive peace of God! The Snare. Patrick MacDonogh. NeIP

Old, departing,/can confer/nothing. Dark Song. Archie Randolph Ammons. MAT

"Old Dobbin" will wait/for this headless horseman/to take hold of his fate. Indecsion Means Flexibility. Elliot Abhau. PH

The old fighting and the old peace. A Drum for Ben Boyd. Francis Webb. PoAu 1-2

The old fire yet survives,/Here in our modern lives,/Of splendid chivalry and valor high! In Apia Bay. Sir Charles G. D. Roberts. PAH

...The old flicks/are followed by the news. The Late Show. William Heyen. GLGT

Old follies returning grow wise at last. Oh Light Was My Head. Cecil Day Lewis. OAEP

...Old foxes, rusty red like dried-up wounds,/and a G.I. escort. The Year of the Foxes. David Malouf. NOAV

Old garden walks, old roses, and old loves. Old Mothers. Charles Sarsfield Ross. PoToHe

Old gods sleep far away. Exile. Jennette Yeatman. GoYe

The old gray mare, she ain't what she used to be,/Many long years ago. The Old Gray Mare. Anonymous. AS; FSW; GBP

The old, gray monarch of Judah/Is a youthful Poet again! The Harp of David. Yehoash. TrJP

A old grey eye, weeping for lost renown,/Have made me a beggar before you, Valentine Brown. A Grey Eye Weeping. Egan O'Rahilly. FaBoPV; KiLC

The old, grey God my Polish boyhood/knew. There Is No Country. Julian Tuwim. TrJP

Old Hickory,/The pride of the frontier. Andrew Jackson. Stephen Vincent Benét. InMe

The old hills hunch before the north wind blows. A Spell before Winter. Howard Nemerov. LiTM

Old Honey-Paw sleeps in the wood. The Brown Bear. Mary Austin. PoSC

An old hope shivers far in the cold air. Decayed Time. Jean Wahl. VWA

An old house knew my mother's lovely face. Old Houses. Homer D'Lettuso. PoToHe

Old hulk Rocky Marsh. The River Map and We're Done. Charles Olson. CoPo

Old I am, and therefore may,/Like Silenus, drink and play. Old I Am. Thomas Stanley. AWP

An old Indian recites/meaningless words:/Topeka, Manhattan, Wichita. Moonlit Night in Kansas. Victor Contoski. TAT

"Old Ironsides" means victory,/Acrost the Western ocean. The Constitution's Last Fight. James Jeffrey Roche. MC; PAH

Old John Brown. John Brown. Vachel Lindsay. AnAmPo; MoAmPo

Old John, you do me good! John Skelton. Robert Graves. BrPo

The old Lie: Dulce et decorum est/Pro patria mori. Dulce et Decorum Est. Wilfred Owen. AnFE; CMoP; CoBMV; DL; FaBoPV; FaBoTw; FaBV; FF; HeIP; HoPM; InPK; InvP; LiTB; LiTM; MMM; MoAB; MoBrPo; NIP; NoAm; NoP; OAEL 1-2; OAEP; OBWP; PPON; PPP; PrIm; SoSe; TW; UnPo; WaP

...Old like rain/older than anything that dies can be. The Knife. Richard Tillinghast. MAYP

Old Liza told me so. Sal Got a Meatskin. Anonymous. FSW

Old love shall dwell with old delight. To a River in the South. Sir Henry Newbolt. CH

...Old lovers/Tossing again in a warehouse loft, straining free. On the Upside. G. E. Murray. MAYP

Old man Choska had died. Materialized into an owl. Louis (LittleCoon) Oliver. STE

The old man had loved more than he could say. Hospital. G. C. Millard. PeSA

An old man in May, a boy in December. Fool Song. Cornel Lengyel. GoYe

An old man lost in sleep and Time. Georgia Towns. Daniel Whitehead Hicky. AmFN

An old man may at least good wishes give you. Prologue to Love Triumphant. John Dryden. OxBoLi

Old man mumbling in his dotage, or crying child, unborn? For Malcolm X. Margaret Walker. BP; BPo; CNA; PoBA

An old man's eagle mind. An Acre of Grass. William Butler Yeats. CMoP; MBW 1-2; NoAm

Old Man, the last of my old men. Elegy for Jack Bowman. Joseph Bruchac. CDW

The old man was not used to visitors/And he might resent our curiosity. Post Mortem. Verna Loveday Harden. CaP

Old Memory's rich flood-tide. In Town. David McKee Wright. ACV

Old men cloaked in wisdom/stuttering their love. Better to Spit on the Whip than Stutter Your Love Like a Worm. Colette Inez. TW

Old men frighten love away/With cold frost and dry decay. Invitation to Youth. Anonymous. UnTE

The old men gather the vines for burning. Harvest Poem. David Fisher. NPGG

Old men, I shall grow older/Than you, when men look back! Joan of Arc to the Tribunal. Anthony Frisch. CaP

Old men speak of what they have to lose./Young men of taking. Warriors. Michael Hogan. LFAC

Old men that tap their way through worlds of dust/To find Man's path near the Sun. Elegy for Dylan Thomas. Edith Sitwell. PoA

Old Mis' Wind and Old Man Rain. Old Man Rain. Madison Cawein. PoSC

Old Missus went to the race track/and lost all-a her mon' Old Timbrook Blues. John Byrd. BluL

The old Moon dies to grow new again, to rise up out of the sea. The Moon-Bone Cycle: New Moon. Anonymous. WTO

Old Mother Doorstep had nursed him well. Mother Doorstep. Victor J. Daley. NOAV

...Old Mother Earth/Is come upon me. I am ready to give birth. The Annunciation. Amrita Pritam. WPOW

Old Mother Grumble clapped her hands/And said that she was very glad. Father Grumble. Anonymous. BaBo

Old Mr. Jones. The Corner. Walter de la Mare. BiCB

The old myth-makers, starting something over. Something Starting Over. Thomas Hornsby Ferril. AnAmPo

Old newspapers nobody's ever got to read again. Twenty-Year Marriage. Florence Anthony ("Ai"). BoWoP; GP; MAYP

Old Nicodemus' Phantom/Confronting us again! The Bone That Has No Marrow. Emily Dickinson. AmePo; TAP

Old Night and Death frail men appal,/Without dismaying you at all. The Force of Love. Samuel Jones. NOEC

–Old Noumenon, come true, come true! Socrates' Ghost Must Haunt Me Now. Delmore Schwartz. AnFE; LiTM

Old nuns in France who carve beads out of knuckle bones. On the Symbolic Consideration of Hands and the Significance of Death. Miller Williams. InPK

The old ones mourn themselves. Burial. Geoffrey Grigson. PoA

Old Proteus naps. On This Sea-Floor. Ralph Gustafson. PeCV

Old Ptolemy Copernicus/Flammarion McGower. A Marvel. Carolyn Wells. OBCA

Old Rat/And Flea/And Bird/And Me. Chez-Nous. A. G. Austin. PoAu 1-2

Old Rudiger sat, dead. The Baron's Last Banquet. Albert Gorton Greene. AA; BeLS

Old schoolhouse! a blessing on thee! The Old Brown Schoolhouse. Anonymous. TreF

The old sickness overcomes me. Poems from a Greek Anthology (excerpt). Palladas. NNaP

The old sixth/avenue/el;in the top of his head:to tell/him One Times One. Edward Estlin Cummings. CTC

Old soldiers never die,/They just fade away. Old Soldiers Never Die. Anonymous. FSW

Old solitary Whiff-Beard. Fast Ball. Jonathan Williams. NeAP

The old spider outside space/Runs down it–and where's raven? Or where's hill? High Up on Suilven. Norman MacCaig. PoSH

Old Spot's respectable and he/Won't stand fer no profanity. Enlightenment. Robert V. Carr. BPAW

The old stale bitter world plays new–/And the new world old. Brave New World. Archibald MacLeish. AmP; NOBA; OFD; OxBA

Old stems will rather break than yield. To His Child. William Bullokar. OxBChV

Old tales of life, of love and hate,/Of time and space, and will and fate. Dead Men Tell No Tales. Haniel Long. HBMV; MCCG

...Old Testament battleground/of warring shades whose weapons kill. Locus. Robert Earl Hayden. FYAP

...Old theories of/seem to work again. At least for now. Transducing. George-Therese Dickenson. APU

Old things are changed, and new revealed. Earth and Sky. Euripides. EaLo

Old Thomas Kelly/Thrusts his bit hands, for warmth,/'Twixt waistcoat and belly. Winter. Richard Hughes. OBMV

Old Tillie Turveycombe's/Floating by. Tillie. Walter De la Mare. TiPo

Old times unqueen thee, and old loves endear thee. To a Lofty Beauty, from Her Poor Kinsman. Hartley Coleridge. OBVV

The old tissue goes outside./Into the fire, she says. Tissue. Susan Griffin. NPGG

Old Uncle Fuerbringer and all. Time Like an Ever-rolling Stream. P. G. Wodehouse. FiBHP

Old Uncle Tom Cobley and all. Widdecombe Fair. Anonymous. BBV; CH; MoShBr; PH

Old violence is not too old to beget new values. The Bloody Sire. Robinson Jeffers. CMoP; LiTM; NePA; PoA

Old Virginny never tire. Clare De Kitchen. *Anonymous.* BLPA

Old volumes shake their Vellum Heads/And tantalize–just so– A Precious–Mouldering Pleasure–'tis–. Emily Dickinson. DiPo

Old Walt went seeking/And finding. Old Walt. Langston Hughes. HeIP

Old warships drowning in the raindrop. A Dream of Suffocation. Robert Bly. NaP

The Old we leave without a tear,/The New we hail without a fear. Confidence. *Anonymous.* BLRP

Old when these old walls were young,/"Manuela of La Torre." At the Hacienda. Bret (Francis Bret Harte) Harte. AA

The old white haired coot./Fucking dead. On the Death of Robert Lowell. Eileen Myles. APU

Old Wichet went a noodle out, a wise man he came home. Old Wichet. *Anonymous.* StPo

The old wind blowing up the land,/The old thoughts at our heart. The Road of Remembrance. Lizette Woodworth Reese. HBV 1-2

An old wives' tale, not ours. The Fallen Tower of Siloam. Robert Graves. WaP

An old woman in a sleep of voices. Evening Harbour. Tom Paulin. AMV-81

The old woman went off ti-hippity-hop, ti-hippity-hop,/Hey, hey, ti-hippity-hop, ti-hippity-hop. Old Humpy. *Anonymous.* AmFP

Old women, pitying all that age can kill,/Lie quiet, wondering that they are old. Old Women. Babette Deutsch. HBMV

The old world worshipped thee, O Lotus/flower/Then carved its sphinx and reared its pyramid. The Egyptian Lotus. Arthur Wentworth Hamilton Eaton. AA

Older than any hope I ever knew. Because. James Philip McAuley. CBAP; NOAV

Older than many a generation of men. The House That Was. Laurence Binyon. MoBrPo

Older than night, the silent stars, or death. Empedocles. Thomas S. Jones, Jr. AnAmPo

Older than this psalm I'm singing right to the end. Psalm. Charles Simic. AmPA; LCAP

The older, the dearer! To M.T. Bayard Taylor. AA

The oldest in the world?' "Yes, love.' I said. On the Ridgeway. Andrew Young. FaBoPP

The oldest soldier of the row. The Oldest Soldier. Robert Graves. DTC

Ole, Ole, Ole, Ole, Ole, Ole anna. Oleanna. *Anonymous.* FSW

The olive garden for the nightingales. Painted Head. John Crowe Ransom. AP; CoBMV; CrMA; LiTA; LiTM; MoAB; MoAmPo; MoPo; MoVE; NoAm; NOBA; NoP; OxBA

Olive oil! Good-bye! Funny Face: The Babbitt and the Bromide. Ira Gershwin. ALV

An' 'oller in ees yerole. Zeke. Leonard Alfred George Strong. MoBrPo

Oluto/oluto/aaaaaaaaaaah From the Narrator's Trance. James (Olumo) Cunningham. JB

Om, pom, push. Eenie, Meenie, Mackeracka. *Anonymous.* OxNR

'Ome an' friends so dear, Jenny, waitin' in the cold! The Liner She's a Lady. Rudyard Kipling. FaBV

"Omnia non omnibus"–no harm is meant! Parleyings with Certain People of Importance in Their Day. Robert Browning. VLP

Omnia qui tua vult sua gaudia semper habes. To the Rev'd Mr. Jno. Sparhawk on the Birth of His Son... Samuel Sewall. SCAP

...Omnibus/Bullies a passage through congested ways. Secret Idiom: Sanctuary. Clifford Dyment. PoA

"An Omnibus Guide to Chance and Superstition," by One Who Knows. The People vs. the People. Kenneth Fearing. MoAmPo

Omnipotence o' God than a fribble like me. Deep-Sea Fishing. Hugh" (Christopher Murray Grieve) MacDiarmid. SeCePo

The omnipotent Shade to meet/And flatter thus. Slain. T. W. H. Crosland. OBWP

Omstead of Bread, give only Stones. Epigram. *Anonymous.* PAH

On a beach, four males in brilliant weather Sant'Angelo D'Ischia. Edwin Denby. ANYP

On a bed of the Morgue...With his eyes wide open! Paris at Night. Tristan Corbiere. SyP

On a checkered table cloth, blue and white. Painting of a Lobster by Picasso. Hy Sobiloff. NePA

On a cut braid/on a cut/on a broken/neck. The Condemned. Edmond Jabes. VWA

On a damned continent without a name. Cheshire Cat. Kenneth Allott. NeBP

On a damp/stone/melt Rain. Lance Henson. VoR

On a dead hand/and a book fallen from it. In My Mind. Norman MacCaig. OxBC

...On a diningroom-table,/naked confronted her unanswering Lord. Mrs. Severin. Winfield Townley Scott. NePoAm

On a distant/empty beach. Home Again. Susan Petrykewycz. AMV-81

On a fine and frosty morning. Nuts an' May. *Anonymous.* EvOK

On a fine morning. Interior: The Suburbs. Horace Gregory. AnAmPo

On a flimmering floom you shall ride. On a Flimmering Floom You Shall Ride. Carl Sandburg. GoYe; OBAL

On a green wave's tow. Aran Islands. Irving Layton. NeAC

On a hazel twig. Bob Robin. *Anonymous.* OxNR

...On a hill a butterfly/makes a cup that I drink from, walking over a bridge of/flowers. Second Poem. Peter Orlovsky. NeAP

On a long shot at long odds, a black mare/By Hatred out of Envy by Despair. Trivial, Vulgar, and Exalted: 19. J. V. Cunningham. QFR

On a lost afternoon of fiesta. The Tale the Hermit Told. Alastair Reid. NePoEA-2

On a lost field and slept among/His neighbour men. Old I Am. Herman Charles Bosman. PeSA

On a May morning. Cheddar Pinks. Robert Bridges. ChMP; MoVE; SeCePo

On a nickel or a dime/Or hitchhiking or nonetheless Wheat Metropolis. Alfred Starr Hamilton. FAZ

On a night like this one Van Gogh dug in into his bla/and died It Is When the Tribe Is Gone. Duff Bigger. FAZ

On a perfectly good/chatty afternoon. Small-Scale Reflections on a Great House. A. K. Ramanujan. OxBC

On a silvery afternoon/talk is filled with light. Rest. Jacob Isaac Segal. VWA

On a single surmise that the owner is dead. Epitaph on Francis Atterbury, Bishop of Rochester. Matthew Prior. FaBoEE

On a summer night in Odessa. Dvonya. Louis Simpson. NNaP; NOBA

On a very fine gander. Mother Goose. *Anonymous.* SoPo

On a warm evening/in childhood. Elegy. Duane Big Eagle. STE

On a wound. You must have/come. Saturday Morning. Richard Howard. ErPo

On All Saint's Day with a simple ornament, a little moss. Poet's Wish. Valery Larbaud. GrPl

On all the gods who guard his home. Drowning of Conaing. *Anonymous.* AnIL

On all these living pages of God's book. To the Dandelion. James Russell Lowell. AP; HBV 1-2; HBVY

On an air-conditioned veranda. Limerick: "A lady who lived in Uganda." William Jay Smith. TDH

On an ancient wave/of dreams. Shabbat Morning. Bradley R. Strahan. AMV-81

On an autumn night we raised the light on the old head of Kinsale. The Yankee Man-of-War or The Stately Southerner. *Anonymous.* AmSS

On an invisible staff/To run up an allegiance! The Lovers Go Fly a Kite. W. D. Snodgrass. NYBP

On an old spider wrapping a fly in spittle-strings. Under the Williamsburg Bridge. Galway Kinnell. NYP

On any object for the chance/to breed. Life Story. J. Kates. AMV-81

On any sheet the least display of mind. A Considerable Speck. Robert Frost. AmP; MoAB; MoAmPo; OBAL; PPP

On Bennington and Bunker Hill. New England: For a Celebration in Kentucky of the Landing of ... George Denison Prentice. AA

On black curving thighs/thrusts love upward Wedding. Dorothy Livesay. PeCV

On boats with sail/And mast. Our Lady of Good Voyage. Lucy A. K. Adee. ISi

On Christ's Sunday at morn. I Saw Three Ships. *Anonymous.* ACP; BLPA; CAW

On Christmas day in the morning. Carol: "As I sat on a sunny bank." *Anonymous.* OxNR

On Christmas merry Jesus day. In Lord Carpenter's Country. Barry O. Higgs. PeSA

On Commonwealth, on Marlborough. Technologies. George Starbuck. NYBP

On coontless stars the Babe maun cry/An' the Crucified maun bleed. The Innumerable Christ. Hugh" (Christopher Murray Grieve) MacDiarmid. EaLo; EBEV; NoP; OxBS

On David's Throne, be propheci'd what will. Paradise Regained. John Milton. OBS

On death and beauty till a bullet stopped his song. All Day It Has Rained. Alun Lewis. GTBS-P; OBWP; OxBTC

On Delia's blushing lips I see/A thousand full as sweet as thee. To a Kiss. John Wolcot. HBV 1-2

On delusion my raptures arose! Lines Written Immediately after Parting from a Lady. Sir Samuel Egerton Brydges. NOEC

...On each side, the unreadable/fresco of my life... Another Life. Frank Bidart. HaCAP

On earth but love there is no other pleasure. Diana. Henry Constable. OBSC

On earth, good-will and peace. Sing, Sing for Christmas. J. H. Egar. OHIP

On Earth, in heaven, to God most high,/For Christ's great victory! The Morning Purples All the Sky. Roman Breviary. BePJ

On earth's far plains of sun and wind. The Poor. Emile Verhaeren. AWP

On earth. Sadly the angel watched them go. Adam and Eve: The Sickness of Adam. Karl Shapiro. AP; CoBMV; MoAB

On earth the good man base detraction bars/From thy fair name, and waters it with tears. Sonnet to Chatterton. John Keats. ERoP 1-2

On east street/in opelika bama   I Remember How She Sang. Rob Penny. CNA; PoBA

On eight poor groschens a day. Two Surprises. R. W. McAlpine. PoLf

On elder-spray by broken tile. Stormcock in Elder. Ruth Pitter. BoC

On every fall I feel a full year older! The Game. Walker Gibson. NePoAm-2

On every starry moorland loch, and every shadowy glen,/Hills o' my heart! Hills o' My Heart. Ethna (Anna Johnston MacManus) Carbery. HBV 1-2

On feet that still smell delicately/of withered ferns and mold. Calling in the Cat. Elizabeth Jane Coatsworth. BoAnP; PCat

On fif stedes on His body/The stremes ran o blode. White Was His Naked Breast. Anonymous. OxBM

On fire and sinking! From "The River-Fight." Henry Howard Brownell AA

On flowers, until the vision and the glory came! Sonnets. Frederick Goddard Tuckerman. AP

On flung hills/an eagle descends The Messenger. Frances Horovitz. BrRo

On freedom's broad basis that empire shall rise,/Extend with the main and dissolve with the skies. Star of Columbia. Timothy Dwight. TrAS

On gleams of star and depths of blue/The glaring sunshine never knew! All's Well. John Greenleaf Whittier. CBEP; OBSP; OBVV

On golden times to come our vision resting. To Liebig–7. August von Platen. PeHV

On ground he takes his rest. A Nosegay Always Sweet, for Lovers to Send for Tokens of Love... William Hunnis. EIL

On her breast a turtle dove/To signify she died of love. A Miner Coming Home One Night. Anonymous. GBP

On her broad breast hath dancing ever been. The Sea Danceth. Sir John Davies. EtS

On her lips familiar words become the words/Of an elevation, an elixir of the whole. The Woman That Had More Babies Than That. Wallace Stevens. LiTA

On her right hand it rides, and earth/Turns quietly on the spindle. Lakshmi. Padraic Fallon. NOBI

On her soft lap he sat, and caught the sounds. The Charms of Nature. Joseph Warton. OBEC; SeCePo

On her untiring wing my love shall follow! Godspeed. Harriet Prescott Spofford. EtS

On high, on high. Carol. W. R. Rodgers. ChMP; DTC

On Him we call, His creatures all,/Who heaven and earth sustains. Hail, Day of Days! In Peals of Praise. Saint Venantius Fortunatus. BePJ

On him who is burned up, yea, visibly. He Speaks of His Condition through Love. Folcachiero de' Folcachieri. AWP

On his axe hops across, and fiercely comes on.... Sir Gawain and the Green Knight. Anonymous. FaBoPP

On his great voyage, to the world unknown. An Address to His Elbow-Chair, New Cloath'd. William Somervile. CEP; OBEC

On his handlebars/a flower. Walking down Jalan Thamrin. R. F. Brissenden. CBAP

On his mangy back. Haiku: "The dog's violent sneeze..." Richard Wright. FAZ

On his new legs, between the stems of the white trees? The Fawn. Edna St. Vincent Millay. LaNeLa

On his right hand/and behind/the flag of his office hangs,/a wet 4th of July,/refusing to burn. Flag. Reg Saner. GP

On Huntly banks it is merry to be,/Where birds do sing both night and/day. Thomas of Erceldoune. Anonymous. MeEV

On incandescent clouds of spirit or rage. Under the Pot. Robert Graves. FaBoEE

& On into/Streets... Clear. Angelo Lewis. PoBA

On into supreme intimacies/of our household closed upon itself. Shutting the Curtains. Bink Noll. GP

On Jailhouse floor. Haiku: "Morning sun slants cell." Etheridge Knight. NeAC; SM; TAP

On light's reflected word. The Heron. Vernon Watkins. ChMP; GTBS-P; MP; TwCP; UnPo

On Little White Horses all speckled with foam. White Horses. Winifred Howard. BrR; SoPo; SUS

On me love's fiercer flames for ever prey,/By night he scorches, as he burns by day. Pastorals: Summer. Alexander Pope. CEP

On Meelin's mournful mountain where the magic harps make moan! The Fairy Harpers. James B. Dollard. CaP

On moon-washed apples of wonder. Moonlit Apples. John Drinkwater. BoNaP; OBMV; OxBTC; PoRA

On Moosehead Lake I saw no boats except/The rented one that carried me away. The View from Father's Porch. Celeste Turner Wright. Str

On my body there's no part/But bears a scar for every dart. Plea to Eros. Anonymous. UnTE

On my breast babe Jesu slumbers,/Yet in heaven his soft feet go. Saint Ita's Fosterling. Saint Ita. OnYI

On my new-born apple-trees. Merlin's Apple-Trees. Thomas Love Peacock. OBRV

On my own little horse of wind and fire. One Poet Visits Another. William Henry Davies. DTC; TW

On my third cast I hooked/the largemouth bass. No Idle Boast. Edward C. Lynskey. WOLT

On my way up to Sanctuary Wood. Zillebeke Brook. Edmund Charles Blunden. MMM

On New-Year's day in the morning. Three Ships. Anonymous. OxNR

On ocean's long reach, on parables of God? The Spider. Richard Eberhart. PoA

On&off bandwagons/(MEMORIAM. Epigram: "IN)/all those who got". Edward Estlin Cummings. FaBoEE

On one of these three I am resolved: make your choice! An Elder's Reproof to His Wife. Abdillaahi Muuse. TTY; WTO

On Orion, the mountain-tops. Thalamos. Peter Kane Dufault. ErPo

On our down trip to Buffalo from Milwaukee. The Bigler. Anonymous. AmSS; OuSiCo

On our meat, and on us all. Amen. Two Graces. Robert Herrick. PoPle

On our passage home from Liverpool to Philadelfiee. The Light on Cape May. Anonymous. ShS

On our side is Virtue and Erin!/On theirs is the Saxon and Guilt. The Song of O'Ruark, Prince of Breffni. Thomas Moore. OnYI

On pavements Saul and David go. To a Flea in a Glass of Water. D. A. Greig. PeSA

On phantom feet/He rushed into slumber. Boy's Day. Ruth Evelyn Henderson. BiCB

On planting the apple-tree. The Planting of the Apple-Tree. William Cullen Bryant. AA; AnNE; GN; HBV 1-2; HBVY; LaNeLa; OHIP; PoSC

On purpose for pure merriment. All Fools' Day. Anonymous. SiSoSe; SoPo

On reef and cave the sea's hexameter beating. Homecoming. James Keir Baxter. AnNZ

On rich particular beauty for their heirs. Citation for Horace Gregory. Muriel Rukeyser. NAMP

...On rows of yellow jars/In which the lemon trees were ripening. Saratoga Ending. Weldon Kees. NaP

On set wings, down/slowly, into the last light– The Duck Pond at Mini's Pasture, a Dozen Years Later. Philip Dow. AmPA; NPGG

On Sion hill may sing the praise of our most mighty Lord. A Joyful New Ballad. Anonymous. CoMu; OBSS

On slopes, on plains,/On mountains, or peaks. God's Blessing on Munster. Saint Patrick. OnYI

On so sweet an archipelago/As love on love. Poem: "O gentle queen of the afternoon." W. S. Graham. NeBP

On some high lonely hill/Before the cleansing's done. On Calvary's Lonely Hill. Herbert Clark Johnson. PoNe

On some red day in a burst of fists on a new horizon! I Have Seen Black Hands. Richard Wright. NoAm; PoBA

On stars that brighter beam when most we need their love. The Tree. Jones Very. AnNE; GN; HBV 1-2; OHIP; PoSC

On stealthy, mouselike feet she trod,/And tiptoed out again. The Sleeper. Walter De la Mare. MoAB; MoBrPo; SeCeV

On strong new worlds he planned/the king looks down. Tudor Portrait. Richmond Lattimore. EyDe

On such a ground, music 'twill be to die. On Christmas Day. Clement Paman. OxBoCh

On such a night as this is! The Sun Has Long Been Set. William Wordsworth. YeAr

...On sweetness through these kitchen/Odors and the stink backway? Aubade: The Desert. Frederick Bock. PoA

On Talladega Mountain in the likker raids. Kissie Lee. Margaret Walker. BlSi; NMM

On tears, and sighs, and groans, and brains, and blood. The Flying Tailor (parody). James Hogg. BXAP; Par

On that day's children, armistice and all. That Day. Mark Van Doren. WaP

On that first Christmas night through Christ, our Brother. Cause of Our Joy. Sister Maris Stella. ISi

On that moonshiny, Island-strand,/For ever and for evermore. The Dancing Seal. Wilfrid Gibson. HBMV; OnMSP

On that old self of yours that filled my heart/Only a little while! Song: "Only a little while since first we met." Brian Hooker. HBMV

On that precios perle wythouten spot. Pearl (excerpt). Anonymous. EBEV

On that small island they had looked with scorn/And in Great Britain thought the Thunderer born. Instructions to a Painter. Edmund Waller. APAS

..."On that subject I/am coy," said Aaron Burr. Colonel B. Constance Carrier. NePoAm-2

On that unfashionable gyre again. The Gyres. William Butler Yeats. GTBS-P; HAP; NoAm

On that vast ocean death conducts us to. Malvern Hills. Joseph Cottle. NOEC

On that water,/Which thy spirit blowes! Silex Scintillans. Henry Vaughan. AnAnS 1

On the autumn moor/young deer cry. In the gathering dew. Lady Sagami. BoWoP

On the bald street breaks the blank day. In Memoriam A.H.H., VII. Alfred, Lord Tennyson. GTBS-P; NAWM 1-2; NOBE; OAEP; OBNC; PoEL 1-5; PPoe; SCV

On the banks of Allan Water,/There a corse lay she. Allan Water. Matthew Gregory Lewis. HBV 1-2

On the banks of River Smile. The Town of Don't-You-Worry. I. Bartlett. BLPA

On the banks of the Ohio. Banks of the Ohio. Anonymous. FSW

On the banks of the Pamanaw. Banks of the Pamanaw. Anonymous. ABF

On the banks of the Wabash, far away. On the Banks of the Wabash, Far Away. Paul Dresser. BLSo; FSN; FSW; GoTF; TreFT

On the bare, sunlit stage the hungers could begin. Faust. John Ashbery. NoP; TwCP

On the beautiful trail am I, with it I wander. Dawn Boy's Song. Anonymous. FaBV

On the black horse of midnight I ride. Night Musick for Therese. Dachine Rainer. NePoAm-2

On the bonnie, bonnie banks of Loch Lomond. Loch Lomond. Lady John Scott. FSW; GoTF

On the bonnie braes o' the Silvery Tay. The Newport Railway. William McGonagall. PeD

On the bottom shelf/In the shoe shop? Question. Norma Craig. PoL

On the broad Garonne/Shed a wintry ray. L'Envoy to W. L. H. Ainsworth, Esq. Francis Sylvester ("Father Prout") Mahony. OnYI

On the brown dry/forest-bed. If Ice. W. W. Eustace Ross. NOBC; OBCV

On the bumper I sit, and I chew and I spit./All over my sweetheart's behind. My Sweetheart's the Mule in the Mines. Anonymous. AmFP; BPAW; FSW

On the chalk downland bare. Midnight. John Masefield. BrPo

On the child crying for the bird of the snow. Snow. Edward ("Edward Eastaway") Thomas. FaBoTw; MoVE

On the cobblestones of Pushcart Row. Pushcart Row. Rachel Feild. BrR; SoPo

On the cold earth lies th' unregarded King./A headless Carkass, and a nameless Thing. The Aeneid. Virgil (Publius Vergilius Maro). OBVE

On the cold granite slab that covers his bones. English Beach Memory: Mr. Thuddock. Osbert Sitwell. NYBP

On the cold morning/Of a cold day. Early in the Morning. Louis Simpson. ConAP; LCAP; PPoe

On the curved roof of the universe as a drum. The Destroyers (excerpt). Archibald Fleming. NAMP

On the dark distant flurry. Angle of Geese. N. Scott Momaday. CDW; QFR

On the day of Resurrection/May be opened for inspection. Epitaph for a Postal Clerk. X. J. Kennedy. NIP; PCP; ShM

On the dead oak tree bough. The Gallows. Edward ("Edward Eastaway") Thomas. ChMP; FM; HaMV; InPS; LiTB; MoAB; MoBrPo; NoAm; PAI; UnPo

On the earth, may still befriend/Thee, and this arbour. The Faithful Shepherdess. John Fletcher. OBS; ViBoPo

On the edge is best. Edge. John Montague. IPY

On the edge/of/rain Bay Poem. Lance Henson. VoR

On the empty way the hawk in his beauty went. Hawk's Way. Ted Olson. HoPM

On the evergreen youth/around the stone raised in remembrance. Augusto Ngangula. Jorge Carrera Andrade. WhB

On the fair hills of holy Ireland. The Fair Hills of Ireland. Sir Samuel Ferguson. AnIV; FaBoPP; IrPN; OBEV; OBVV; OnYI

On the familiar road/Galloped in dreams. Until the desert knows. Emily Dickinson. MoPo; NOBA

On the fire the cauldron bubbles/All the long dark day. Winter. Anonymous. KiLC

On the frontiers to eyes impenetrable,/Some soul is passing over.) Whispers of Heavenly Death. Walt Whitman. AnFE; APA; LiTA; NePA; NoAm

On the gasping red piazza/Where the young men play darts. Saint's Parade. Robert Layzer. NePoEA

On the grass, thinking of the sea always, of the ship plunging. Lament for Richard Rolston. Osbert Sitwell. ChMP

On the heart's secret altar is burning the same! Palestine. John Greenleaf Whittier. WBLP

On the heart slope,/tomorrow. Irish. Paul Celan. OBVE

On the high hills/A hint o' snaw. A Hint o' Snaw. William Soutar. PoSH

On the highways of your mind. For My Son on the Highways of His Mind. Maxine W. Kumin. MAT

On the Hill of Cucorb's Fate/High his Cromlech raise. The Lament of Maev Leith-Dherg. Anonymous. OBWP; OnYI

...On the hill/Of the blue breath, gray boulder, and my burial. Burial. Robert Francis. NCSH

On the hill where she, too, was once young. Thanksgiving. Philip Booth. Str

On the Horus throne of all the living, eternally like Re. The Obelisk Inscriptions (excerpt). Hatshepsut. WPOW

On the house, on a world of possibilities. A Winter without Snow. J. D. McClatchy. FYAP

On the infinite waves of skin smelly and crushed/and light and absorbed. Biotherm. Frank O'Hara. CoPo

On the last morn, on Cristmas Morn,/Umpteen hundred and eternity. Carol for the Last Christmas Eve. Norman Nicholson. OBCP

On the laugh of a child I am borne to the joy of the King. Reconciliation. George William Russell. MoRP; OBMV; OxBI; TrCP

On the leafwork of a continent axil and veins. From Le Havre. Charles G. Bell. NePoAm

On the length and breadth of the marvellous marshes/ of Glynn. The Marshes of Glynn. Sidney Lanier. AA; AP; ATP; EtS; HBV 1-2; MAmP; MCCG; NePA; NOBA; OxBA; PG; PrIm; TreFT; TRV; WGRP; WHA

On the menorah/the Pleiades pray– Hasidim Dance. Nelly Sachs. VWA

On the merry-go-round. At a Country Fair. John Holmes. MoShBr

On the merry morning of May. The Padstow Night Song. Anonymous. GBP

On the monster that murdered Nell Flaherty's drake. Nell Flaherty's Drake. Anonymous. OnYI

On the morning after...love./i walk. The Morning after...Love. Kattie M. Cumbo. BlSi

On the mountain top called "Going-To-The-Sun. The Apple-Barrel of Johnny Appleseed. Vachel Lindsay. AmFN; OxBA

On the night before/we go to war. Lesbian Poem. Robin Morgan. IHMS

On the now vanished past. Amagansett Beach Revisited. John Hall Wheelock. NYBP

On the ocean floor as the foraminifera die. On the Ocean Floor. Hugh" (Christopher Murray Grieve) MacDiarmid. FaBoMo; HAP

On the other shore. Other Shore. Anonymous. ABF

On the other side of ourselves, we live/in our times. Our Backs Are to the Cypress. Leah Goldberg. BoWoP

On the other side of the world. Exercise for the Left Hand. Constance Urdang. AMV-81

On the outcast majesty/They lean as a friend. The Outcast. George William Russell. OBSP; OxBI

On the paint/of a peeling wall. Outside White Earth. Gordon Henry. STE

On the parallel sides of the present/death watches Shores of Anguish. Magda Portal. PBWP

On the part of the painter named Scott. Limerick: "There was a painter named Scott." Dante Gabriel Rossetti. CenHV

On the path that leads to Nowhere/I have sometimes found my soul! The Path That Leads Nowhere. Corinne Roosevelt Robinson. BLPA; HBMV

On the Pennsylvania line! Ten Thousand Miles From Home. Anonymous. ABF

...On the Phoenix-Viewing/Terrace toasting their wienies. Forty-Five Years Since the Fall of the Ch'ing Dynasty. Philip Whalen. NeAP

On the porch, the fierce poet/Is chanting words to himself. A Poet's Household. Carolyn Kizer. PoL

On the promising young robber, the lieutenant of his/band. Gentle Alice Brown. Sir William Schwenck Gilbert. FaBoCo; FiBHP; InMe; NA

On the rampin', raw-boned, cast-steel-jawboned Army/Transport mule. Mules. Cecily Fox-Smith. BoAnP

On the rattling rail by the broomstick train! The Broomstick Train. Oliver Wendell Holmes. MCCG

On the rich man's table, rim to rim. The Two Glasses. Ella Wheeler Wilcox. BLPA; BLPL

On the ridgepole the running horse spins and spins. Leaving Mendota, 1956. Lawrence Locke. GrPl

On the right hand of God, that man/May come unto the general dance. To-Morrow Shall Be My Dancing Day. Anonymous. PoEL 1-5

On the road to Vagabondia that lies across the earth! The Road to Vagabondia. Dana Burnet. PoLf

On the rock of a living faith! Nearer Home. Phoebe Cary. AA; AnAmPo; BLRP; FaFP; HBV 1-2; TreF; WBLP; WGRP

On the screen of the Douglas Art Theatre. The Flicker. Lew Blockcolski. VoR

On the seat of his pants he wears patchez.　Limerick: "A careless young lad down in Natchez."　*Anonymous.*　TDH

On the secret, slate-dark, flowering, flooded sea.　On an Italian Hillside. Richard Weber.　NMP

On the shining girder's side/where he has passed his death.　Getting Across. Carter Revard.　VoR

On the sidewalk like flooded houses/wasted of time and touch　I Done Got So Thirsty That My Mouth Waters at the Thought of Rain.　Patricia Jones. BlSi

On the sightless horse, riding into the bottomless abyss.　Censorship.　Arthur Waley.　OxBTC; WaP

On the single cord of his violin/A cricket preludes his monotone.　Symphony in Gray Major.　Ruben Dario.　LiTW

On the sixth day we came.　The Animals.　Edwin Muir.　CMoP; EBCP; EBEV; HeIP; MoBrPo; NoP

On the snow!　Beauty.　Basho (Matsuo Basho).　SoPo

On the snowy plain.　Haiku: "The long, long river."　Boncho.　LiTW

On the soft white breast of the world.　The Falls.　F. D. Reeve.　NYBP

On the sunny side always, the sunny side of the/street.　The Songs.　Martin Bell.　FF

On the swift warm blade of a cutlass　Foreign Aid.　Lionel Kearns.　NOBC

On the third day./Man died.　The Second Coming.　Carl Clark.　JB

On the tip of each, waiting to be counted,/the fallen angels sit.　I Am Too Near.　Wislawa Szymborska.　BoWoP; PBWP

On the trunk of a haunted tree.　The Haunted Oak.　Paul Laurence Dunbar. BANP; UnPo

On the vast wave of life go by/That, reared, shall never reach the shore. Life's Testament.　William Baylebridge.　BoAV

On the verge of the infinite/In Jerusalem.　Jerusalem.　(or Molodovski) Kadya, (or Kadia) Molodovsky.　AMV-81

On the very tip-toe of his tail!　Tip-Toe Tail.　Dixie Willson.　NTCP

On the waves, that lend their gentle breast/In gladness for her couch of rest! Calm as the Cloudless Heaven.　John Wilson.　EtS

On the white sidewalks.　The Wives.　Donald Hall.　CoAP

On the whole, we conclude the Romans won't do it, and I/shan't.　Amours de Voyage.　Arthur Hugh Clough.　FaBoPV

On the wings of the buck and wing.　Buckdancer's Choice.　James Dickey. NoAm; NOBA; NoP; NYBP; PoNe

"On the wings of the cinnamon bee."　After.　Ralph Hodgson.　MoBrPo

On the withered leaves and the maiden dead.　The Rose and the Gauntlet. John Wilson.　BeLS

On the wood and the pool and the elder tree.　A Song of Enchantment. Walter De la Mare.　GTBS

On the wood's floor released/tangy dews and ozones.　Rain at Wildwood. May Swenson.　NYBP

On the wrong side of the mirror.　I Dream I'm the Death of Orpheus. Adrienne Rich.　NMM; NoAm

On their charms to a dull little varmint/Of seven or eight.　The Schoolmaster Abroad with His Son.　Charles Stuart Calverley.　NOBL

On their hills are strangely childlike.　Iowa.　Michael Dennis Browne. NYBP

On their knees at the last?　"C'est pas zaffaire a tou!"　Ballade des Belles Milatraisses.　Rosalie Jonas.　BlSi

On their way through town, on the way to my World.　After Tsang Chih. Alice Notley.　APU

On these, and make those gardens mine.　The Plea.　John Drinkwater. MoRP

On these honeycombs of light, the buildings of Manhattan.　Winter Sketches. Charles Reznikoff.　PoA

On these our hills.　Centennial Hymn.　John Pierpont.　AnNE; PAL

...On this a hot summer's day.　Descent to Bohannon Lake.　Jim Barnes. FAZ

On this bright Bicentennial morning.　The Tall Poets.　William Jay Smith. SOTS

On this high hill in a year's turning.　Poem in October.　Dylan Thomas. BiP; BoC; CoBMV; DiPo; LiTB; MoVE; NAs; NeBP; OAEP; PoA; PoPl; PoRA; PrIm; SeCePo; SoSe

...On this hill,/overlooking a river in Iowa,/it melts in its own sweet time.　A Child's Grave Marker.　Ted Kooser.　GOYP

On this ocean stammering with poverty and love.　Computer.　Otto Orban. VWA

On this perfectly normal Saturday morning.　Death Comes to the Salesman. Louis Daniel Brodsky.　AMV-81

On this same spot again I hinder you.　New World of Will.　David Shapiro. ANYP

On this sharp ridge dividing death from hell.　The Sharp Ridge.　Robert Graves.　FaBoEE

On those days of the week–just two, not counting/Sunday–when I was blank. A Week of Doodle.　Reed Whittemore.　NePoEA

On those that are thy people is/Thy benediction still.　Eternal God, How They're Increased.　Cotton Mather.　AH

On thoughts like these no man ever grew fat.　Words Made of Water. Burns Singer.　NePoEA-2

On Thy blessed making hand/Shall in endless pleasures stand!　Psalm XVI. Sir Philip Sidney.　FCP

On, to the City of God.　Rugby Chapel–November, 1857.　Matthew Arnold. CBEP; MaVP; OAEP; OxBoCh; PoEL 1-5; VLP; WGRP

On to the darknesses the eye caresses/In us and into us and ours.　For Euse, Ayi Kwei & Gwen Brooks.　Keorapetse Kgositsile.　PoBA

On to the walls, and over!　A Troop of the Guard.　Hermann Hagedorn. HBV 1-2; OHIP

On top of my head, I walked the rest of the night.　The Calculation.　David Wagoner.　NYBP

On voyage comme poisson, incog.　Sonnet with a Different Letter at the End of Every Line.　George Starbuck.　OBAL

On waspish men (who taking wing/Surround us) that they can not sting. Delight in Books from Evening.　Francis Daniel Pastorius.　SCAP

On water the Man-Fisher walks.　The Drunken Fisherman.　Robert Lowell. AP; CMoP; CrMA; LiTA; LiTM; MoPo; MoVE; NOBA; OxBA; SeCeV; VGW

On waves that shroud a thousand newly dead!　Mid-Ocean in War-Time. Joyce Kilmer.　MOS

On ways that end in evening and the waste.　Omnia Exeunt in Mysterium. George Sterling.　AnAmPo; WGRP

On went She, and due north her journey took.　With Ships the Sea Was Sprinkled.　William Wordsworth.　EnRP; HBV 1-2; MOS

On what does this shadow feed/And shall it not fade?　And on This Shore. M. Carl Holman.　AmNP; PoBA

On what pulsation do we stop?　The Call of the Eastern Quail.　George Hitchcock.　OBAL

On whether somebody marked the barrel where the glasses are.　Hiatus. Margaret Avison.　HAP

On which time/in luminous drops/is raining down.　Jacaranda.　Roo Borson.　CaPN; NOBC

On whose decision hangs Columbia's fate.　The Federal Convention. *Anonymous.*　PAH

On whose new margins children greet the swans.　The Made Lake.　Louise Townsend Nicholl.　NePoAm-2

On wild fruits of wonderment/I have nourished ever since.　Fancy's Home. William Henry Davies.　AtBAP

On William the Conqueror's nose.　Limerick: "Said the mole: "You would never suppose."　Oliver Herford.　TDH

On wind-swept uplands, yearning toward the dawn.　The Land of Dreams. Henry Martyn Hoyt.　HBMV

On with the Message! On, on, and on!　On with the Message.　Wesley Duewel.　STF

On wither'd goldenrod and snapdragon/and tarnisht marigold.　Load.　John Hewitt.　OnYI

On woman's word, but wisdom would mistrust it/to endure.　"Too dearly had I bought my green and youthful years."　Henry Howard, Earl of Surrey.　FCP; SiPS

On your bare heath to hang yourself in chains?　To One Who Quotes and Detracts.　Walter Savage Landor.　FaBoEE

On your forehead/While you dance?　Grotesque.　Amy Lowell.　BoWoP

On your hands are four green thumbs.　The Story of Two Gentlemen and the Gardener.　Christopher Logue.　CABL

On your harp of sighs/I hear your dirge.　Inanna and Ishkur.　Enheduanna. BoWoP

On your shadow, the one/that kisses back　The Lover to Himself.　David Phillips.　NeAC

Once again, I trace my signature in red.　The Pact.　Larry Rubin. AMV-81

Once and forever before the wave shut down.　Sonnet: "I watched the sea for hours blind with sun."　Winfield Townley Scott.　MiAP

Once dead, his sin/Men cannot expiate with tears.　Quoniam Ego in Flagella Paratus Sum.　William Habington.　ACP

Once for an endless moment turned on me.　The Three-Faced.　Robert Graves.　FaBoEE

Once for thin walls, once for the sound of time.　Fall Wind.　William Stafford.　PPJ

Once, forest leaves, they murmured round his soul.　Before Rereading Shakespeare's Sonnets.　Thomas Sturge Moore.　BrPo

Once fully enslaved, no nation, state, city of this earth, ever after-/ward resumes its liberty.　To the States.　Walt Whitman.　CTC

The once heard sound I know to be/Chirico's horses trampling on the shore. Forgotten Objects on a Beach.　Patricia Excell.　BoAV

Once home, we shall have a little supper of Lucie's fresh-/picked morels. Bonnard: A Novel.　Richard Howard.　CoAP; NYBP

Once I fancied 'twas starlings they built it for.　The Barn.　Edward ("Edward Eastaway") Thomas.　EyDe

Once I loved until I could not breathe.　Morning Star.　Thomas Hornsby Ferril.　VGW

Once. I will walk out into the day.　Elegy.　David St. John.　LCAP

Once in a life/such wonder.   Just after Noon with Fierce Shears.   Tram Combs.   MP; TwCP

"Once in a stall/In Bethlehem..."   The Mother's Tale.   Eleanor Farjeon.   BiCB

Once in a thousand days your voice/Has laid temptation low.   At Mass.   Vachel Lindsay.   VGW

Once, in a word, I was a fool,–/And then I was in love.   Once Did My Thoughts.   Anonymous.   EBEV; ELP

Once it lay upon her breast, and ages/Cannot make it old!   A Sigh.   Harriet Prescott Spofford.   AA; HBV 1-2

Once more arose that wailing, like a song,/Of one who called and called upon his friend.   The Shooting of the Cup.   John G. Neihardt.   PoOW

Once more be heavy; otherwise I die.   Chaucer's Complaint to His Empty Purse (modern version).   Geoffrey Chaucer.   TrGrPo

Once more I turn to greet/Ground that flees from my feet.   Return.   Seamus Deane.   BIrV

Once more in dying notes complain/Of slighted vows and cold disdain.   Song: "In vain you tell your parting lover."   Matthew Prior.   HBV 1-2

Once more, once more men gather in the hay.   Labor of Fields.   Elizabeth Jane Coatsworth.   TiPo

...Once/More ourselves in ourselves alone.   The Smell on the Landing.   Peter Porter.   NMP

Once more sweep through my brain.   Shapes and Signs.   James Clarence Mangan.   ACV; OnYI

Once more to my Juggy's labour.'   Juggy's Christening.   Anonymous.   NOEC

Once more to trust, once more his/God to love.   Eulogy for Hasdai Ibn Shaprut.   Anonymous.   TrJP

Once, now calm as earth whose only change is/Wind, and light, and wind, and cloud, and wind.   By the North Sea.   Algernon Charles Swinburne.   FaBoPP

"Once only can the miracle avail.–Be wise!"   Le Chevalier Malheur.   Paul Verlaine.   SyP

Once only the barbarian lyre calls.   The Scythians.   Alexander Blok.   AWP; WaaP

Once or twice a summer/old school bell   Haiku.   Gerald Vizenor.   VoR

...Once or twice/I touched at isles of Paradise.   Fair Isle at Sea.   Robert Louis Stevenson.   NOBV

Once our love is cemented/Let no parting break!   Poem #18.   Anonymous.   HW

Once seen, once kissed, once reft from me/Anigh the murmuring of the sea.   A Garden by the Sea.   William Morris.   NOBE; OAEL 1-2; OBNC; PoEL 1-5

Once sped the dance when the corn was on the floor.   A Deserted Home.   Sidney Royse Lysaght.   CH

Once the ivory box is broken,/Beats the golden bird no more.   Memorial to D.C.   Edna St. Vincent Millay.   OxBA

Once they were quick to follow/The shadow of golden Fionn.   Oisin.   Anonymous.   KiLC

Once to live,/Once to die.   What the King Has.   Ethel Romig Fuller.   PoToHe

Once to see the sun come up/across his fields.   Greener Grass.   Frank Steele.   Psk

Once Underwood–now under water.   In Memory of Captain Underwood, Who Was Drowned.   Anonymous.   FaBoEE

Once used to shimmer.   Haiku: "Green weeds of summer."   Basho (Matsuo Basho).   InPK

Once walked a thing that seemed, as it were, a burning cloud.   Fallen Majesty.   William Butler Yeats.   PoA

Once was champagne and laughter, Lunt and Fontanne!   Adam, Eve and the Big Apple.   Edward Watkins.   AMV-81

Once we have done our dance.   Nancy, You Dance.   Michael L. Johnson.   AMV-81

"Once we was slaves"   A Special Moment.   Frank Lamont Phillips.   FAZ

Once/when I was little, smaller, littler   Once.   Siv Widerberg.   NTCP

Once will I share thine ecstasy/With thee, O Death!   Surrender.   Ruth Guthrie Harding.   HBMV

Once you pass its borders, you can ne'er return again.   Toyland.   Glen MacDonough.   BLSo; FSN

Once you said it was in my eyes.   Eclipse.   Anita Endrezze Probst.   CDW

One a new world would seek, and one/Would save the old!   The Dead Tribune.   Denis Florence McCarthy.   ACP

One another in the vestibule of the heart.   Talking to Myself.   Vincent McHugh.   ErPo

One after the other shimmer boldly in the wind.   The Long Parenthesis.   Roberta Hill Whiteman.   TWSS

One among God alone knows/how many roads beneath my feet.   Buzzard.   Michael Daugherty.   PoSH

One and all cry out Amen!   The Jolly Beggars.   Robert Burns.   EnRP

One are we with the ever-living One.   The Invisible.   Richard Watson Gilder.   WGRP

The one-armed lift the wine to you,/McClellan,/And great Antietam's cheers renew.   The Victor of Antietam.   Herman Melville.   MC; PAH

One as a lonely shadow, one a star!   Mirthful Lunacy.   Thomas Stoddart.   OBNC

"One at the foot, and one at the head."   One and One.   Mary Mapes Dodge.   HBV 1-2; HBVY

One beam of love will soon destroy/And melt that ice to floods of joy.   A Looking-Glass.   Thomas Carew.   CaPo

...One beauty alone,/can give me life and deprive me of wits.   When before those eyes, my life and light.   Gaspara Stampa.   BoWoP

One black, and one white, and two khaki.   Limerick: "There was a young lady called Starky."   Anonymous.   CenHV

One blood-red petal stained the Baudelaire.   Hallucination: I.   Arthur Symons.   SyP

One bottle more of fizzy lemonade.   The Archaeological Picnic.   Sir John Betjeman.   EnLoPo

One brief "Good-night," for thee and me./Good-night.   Good-Night.   Silas Weir Mitchell.   HBV 1-2

One bright horn/that lifts the sky.   Mercado.   Greg Pape.   AmPA

...One/But one, are thrown away.   Three Poems about Children.   Austin Clarke.   CIP

The one by day and one at night have charmed me.   Song: "Do I venture away too far."   Keith Douglas.   NePoEA

One by one his white birds/Falter, and fall, out of the sky.   His Swans.   Geoffrey Grigson.   FaBoRV

One by one/I fill my heart with them.   Littoral.   Hjalmar Flax.   InW

...One by one/I should write them down. Now that can never be done.   Now That Can Never Be Done.   Sister Maris Stella.   GoBC

One by singular/one, so quiet,/so still.   The Figures.   Robert Creeley.   UnPo

One came and opened Michael's gate,/And Magdalen went in.   Magdalen.   Henry Kingsley.   HBV 1-2; OBVV

One can catch a cold so quickly/In the absence of a shawl.   Precaution.   Heinrich Heine.   UnTE

One can fancy a tear runs down his face/When the butcher wins, and he's driven from the place.   Bags of Meat.   Thomas Hardy.   BoANP; FM

One can only wonder/At so grotesque a blunder.   George the Third.   Edmund Clerihew Bentley.   DBV; FaBoCo; OxBoLi

One can't achieve/infrangible solutions/outside the rock.   The Rock.   Mary Fabilli.   AMV-81

One can't always be stirring the fire.   All in the Downs.   Thomas Hood.   ALV; CenHV

One cannot begin it too soon.   Brown Penny.   William Butler Yeats.   BoLoP; CMoP; ELP; ExPo; FaBoCh; LLLT; LoGBV; OLR

One cannot live in the same room twice.   Variation on Heraclitus.   Louis MacNeice.   NoAm

One cheerful moment to regain: The First Olympionique to Hiero of Syracuse.   Pindar.   ATP

One clear fixed star forever is denied me.../The light of home!   The Unwilling Gypsy.   Josephine Johnson.   HBMV

The one clear place given to us when we are alone.   A Morning.   Mark Strand.   GeTw; HaCAP

...One cold as ouse or ice/is not so nouse, is not so nice.   Singular Indeed.   David McCord.   OBCA

...One corner/of my mouth twitches–a fish on a hook!–/whenever you abandon me.   The Married Man.   Robert Phillips.   GeTw

One could do worse than be a swinger of birches.   Birches.   Robert Frost.   AnNE; BiP; CMoP; DiPo; FaBV; FPL; HaMV; HBMV; HeIP; LiTA; LiTM; LoGBV; MAPA; MCCG; MoAB; MoAmPo; MoVE; NIP; NoAm; NoP; OxBA; PoLf; PoPl; PoRA; TAP; TreF; TrGrPo

One could not prove that they had followed her.   The Woman Who Disapproved of Music at the Bar.   Horace Gregory.   MoPo

One could notice persons burrowing, hearts hammering,/Toward the risks of the wind.   The Day the Winds.   Josephine Miles.   FaBoWP

One crowded hour of glorious life/Is worth an age without a name.   Sound, Sound the Clarion.   Thomas Osbert Mordaunt.   FaPoR; NOBE

...One crumb doing for it/what heaped-up platters cannot do for Them.   As You Like It.   Theodore Weiss.   TAP

One dark as water, its root among the bones.   The Atoll in the Mind.   Alex Comfort.   LiTB; LiTM; SeCePo

...One dark more to coil/Around them, perfect still until the last.   The Lake.   Louis O. Coxe.   MoVE; NYBP

One day,/I will risk everything.   Conjugation of the Verb, "To Hope."   Lou Lipsitz.   FiCP

One day like the Luck of Edenhall!   The Luck of Edenhall.   Henry Wadsworth Longfellow.   AWP; StPo

One day of one September/I never can forget.   September.   Helen Hunt Jackson.   FPL; PoLf

...One day we'll/just have snow/to wear too.   Self-Pity Is a Kind of Lying, Too.   James Schuylr.   PoM

...One day, with life and heart,/Is more than time enough to find a world.   Columbus.   James Russell Lowell.   PGD

...One deed/Power shall fall short in, or exceed! Service. Robert Browning. TrGrPo

One died, one survived, two divorced, two beheaded. Henry VIII. *Anonymous.* FaBoUs

One dinner Mexico City Blues. Jack Kerouac. NeAP

One dislikes it of course: it is the seat of Me. Thoughts on One's Head. William Meredith. HAP

One door alone is shut, one chamber still. Gone. Mary Elizabeth Coleridge. HBV 1-2; OBEV; OBNC; OBVV

One doth not stroke me, nor the other strike. To Fool, or Knave. Ben Jonson. FaBoEE; NoP; SoSe

One dripping trophy! In a Garret. Herman Melville. OBAL

One driver, pinned beneath the seat,/Escapes from the machine at last. Highway: Michigan. Theodore Roethke. AmC

One drop of wine, wherewith wild rain has/mixed. And in the Hanging Gardens. Conrad Aiken. MAPA; MoAB; MoAmPo

One ear, seven teeth–and his life. Limerick: "There was a young fellow from Fife." Thomas Russell Ybarra. LiBL

One end is moo, the other milk. The Cow. Ogden Nash. CenHV; NLV; NoP

One equal, for Dame Venus' bowers. A Song of Pleasure. Philip Massinger. UnTE

...One face/that is mine, that is going to wheel at me the secrets of many. Photographic Plate, Partly Spidered, Hampton Roads, Virginia... Dave Smith. MAYP

One farewell kiss before we go. A Song of Dust. John Byrne Leicester Warren, Lord De Tabley EnLoPo

One favor before you go? Smile for me. Hello, Sister. Mark Saylor. AMV-80

One flake at a time teaches/grace, even to stone. Montana Eclogue. William Stafford. NYBP

One flick of a surgeon's knife/struck long-idle retinas/into perfect sight. The Unblinding. Laurence Lieberman. NYBP

One fog-walled island more. The Flying Dutchman. Edwin Arlington Robinson. MOS

One foot forever into the wastebasket. My Physics Teacher. David Wagoner. SUW

One foot near the Grail. The Five Feet. Ed Sanders. APU

One foot on 72nd Street, one foot in the river. One Foot in the River. Gerald Stern. NYP

One for each side of the tracks. Ethics for Everyman. Roger Woddis. DBV; NOBL

One for to grieve/When I am gone. Jane, Jane. *Anonymous.* FSW

One freeman more, America, to thee! Ode to Venice. George Gordon, Lord Byron. CABL

One from Ten Thousand! Title of a Swift Horse. *Anonymous.* WTO

One Gael, one Norman; both discrowned. In Ruin Reconciled. Aubrey Thomas De Vere. BIrV; IrPN

One ghostly Hasid/Out to greet me. A Visit Home. Joseph Glazer. VWA

One God and one faith all victorious! Our Nation Forever. Wallace Bruce. OHIP

One God in three Persons. Amen. Hymn for Laudes Feast of Our Lady of Good Counsel. *Anonymous.* ISi

One goes with me along the never-ending shore/and whispers–one alone.. One Goes with Me along the Shore. Manfred Winkler. VWA

One good bet, gone. Flight. Barbara Howes. NYBP

One grand sweet song. A Farewell. Charles Kingsley. HBVY

One had to be versed in country things/Not to believe the phoebes wept. The Need of Being Versed in Country Things. Robert Frost. NoAm; NOBA; OxBA; UnPo

One half Spanish,/the other African. Neither This Nor That. Luis Palés Matos. InW

One hand clutching your little nursebag/and the other the ripcord. Lispy Bails Out. David Barker. GP

One hard piece of metal flying off/might even topple a government. A Poem Like a Grenade. John Haines. EAS

One heart, one hope, one destiny, one flag/from sea to sea. Albert Sidney Johnson. Kate Brownlee Sherwood. MC; PAH

One Heaven, one Hell, one immortality,/And one annihilation... Epipsychidion. Percy Bysshe Shelley. OAEL 1-2

The one here/is accented by fur & fire Old Country Talk. Endre Farkas. CaPN

One holy light, one heavenly flame! A Sun-Day Hymn. Oliver Wendell Holmes. AnNE; TrPWD; TRV; WGRP

One hour with thee. An Hour with Thee. Sir Walter Scott. BoLoP

A one hundred and fifty ton, toothless blue whale. The Blue Whale. Robert Watson. MAT

One hundred will go/to school and IndoChina American Commencement. Aram Boyajian. NeAC

The one I'd give up my eyes/in order for you to hear. Gray Glove. Roo Borson. NOBC

The one immortal poem he had written. Lecture Note: Elizabethan Period. Geoffrey Grigson. PV

...One Indian guide/who returned them to this wild territory. California Dead. G. E. Murray. MAYP

One industrial union grand. There Is Power. Joe Hill. FSW

One inscrutable, black, bleeding feather. Black Humor. Archibald MacLeish. NCSH

The one integrity/Of soul is to be lone,/Inviolate, and free. Lovers. Mary Elizabeth ("E") Fullerton. BoAV; PoAu 1-2

One iota to abate/Of a pure impartial hate. Indeed Indeed, I Cannot Tell. Henry David Thoreau. TW

One is always nearer by not keeping still. On the Move. Thom Gunn. CMoP; ForPo; HAP; LiTM; MP; NePoEA-2; NIP; NMP; NoP; OAEL 1-2; OxBTC; PPP; TwCP

One is ignored/By so much cold suspended in so much night. Tramontana at Lerici. Charles Tomlinson. GTBS-P

One is nearer God's heart in a garden/Than anywhere else on earth. The Lord God Planted a Garden. Dorothy Frances Gurney. BLPA; FaBoBe; FPL; HBMV; WGRP

...One is not bored/In a world where everything happens at least once. The Chance. John Holmes. NePoAm-2

One is one and all alone/And ever more shall be so. The Dilly Song. *Anonymous.* GBP; OBET

One is one and all alone/And evermore shall be so. Green Grow the Rushes O. *Anonymous.* FSW; OxBoLi

One jail did all their criminals restrain,/Which, now, the walls of Rome can scarce contain. The Third Satire of Juvenal. John Dryden. OAEL 1-2

The one king's dochter has ridden awa,/But bonnie Lady Ann lay in the deed-/thraw. Sheath and Knife . *Anonymous.* ESPB

One kiss before I leave you,/For we have gained the day. Marching 'Round the Levee. *Anonymous.* AmFP

One knight loves both, and both in thee remain. To His Friend Master R.L., in Praise of Music and Poetry. Richard Barnfield. EIL; UnS

One lamp had flickered in the evening breeze and died. In the Dusky Path of a Dream. Rabindranath Tagore. OBMV

One last time? End of the Affair. Curtis W. Casewit. AMV-80

One Law for the Lion & Ox is Oppression. The Marriage of Heaven and Hell. William Blake. EnRP; ERoP 1-2; OAEL 1-2

One leaf lying underfoot/Speaks, though dead and fallen and deaf. Marsh Leaf. David Wagoner. PoA

One life I have lived for you. This one/is mine. The Ritual of Memories. Tess Gallagher. GeTw

...One life, or the faring stars. Tenth Elegy. Elegy in Joy. Muriel Rukeyser. MiAP

One life to lose, another to live. Epitaph: "Here lies the man that madly slain." John Hoskyns. FaBoEE

One little corner of thy light. Parting. Gerald Massey. HBV 1-2

One live as two, two live as one,/Under the bamboo tree. Under the Bamboo Tree. Bob Cole. BLSo; FSN

One look into those sad and haughty eyes/Tells me she never can be truly mine. Highland Region. Victor Price. PoSH

One looked up, grinning,/And said: "Comrade! Brother!" I Stood Upon a High Place. Stephen Crane. AmePo; AmP; LiTA; NePA

One loses patience with a bird like that. Cuckoo. R. P. Lister. BoAnP

One luck is not for all. Shao and the South. Confucius. CTC

One man as tall as any tower,/and one deep as stone. The Brigg. Robin Skelton. NMP

One may find on every side/Signs of Nature's wonder. The Month of the Thunder Moon. Marion Doyle. YeAr

One might not make of life and death/A pillow for love's feet! Song: "If love were but a little thing." Florence Earle Coates. HBMV

One might well open a vein/And decorate a bower for dying/With red rosettes. Rain Forest. Eric Rolls. NOAV

One moment, and that realm is ours. On, on, dark rolling stream! Indian Woman's Death-Song. Felicia Dorothea Hemans. SBG

One moment fills the amazed heart,/And never comes again. An Orchard at Avignon. Agnes Mary Frances (Mme Emile Duclaux) Robinson. HBV 1-2; NOBV; OBTV

One moment, what it is to love. Dust. Rupert Brooke. ALV; HBV 1-2; MoBrPo; OBVV; OxBTC

One more amazing arabesque/Of arms and legs. Nina. Alan Dienstag. ErPo

One more cheer for Massachusetts,/And one more for Michigan! The Crossing at Fredericksburg. George Henry Boker. PAH

One more day's work for Jesus,/One less of life for me. One More Day's Work for Jesus. Anna B. Warner. AH

One more drop of their sweat, one more drop of molten/steel. Women Transport Corps. *Anonymous.* WPOW

One more quadrille,–one more quadrille! One More Quadrille. Winthrop Mackworth Praed. OBRV

One more remains–just one per cent left. America's Wounded Knee. Phil George. VoR

One morning before Titan thought of stirring his feet.   Reverie at Dawn.
Egan O'Rahilly.   AnIL; FaBoPV; KiLC
One morning the world woke up and there was no news.   One Morning the
World Woke Up.   Oscar Williams.   FaFP; WaaP; WaP
...One moving voice touching whatever is present/or might be, even what I
cannot see when it comes.   For a Daughter Gone Away.   William
Stafford.   NPAW; SV
One must be very simple, dear,/To let it sting one–don't you think so?   The
Snake.   Thomas Moore.   HBV 1-2
One must die for love.   Love Song.   Bob Zmuda.   AMV-81
One must go trustful through the dark/To earn the friendship of the stars.
Wisdom.   Scudder Middleton.   HBMV
One name shall shine with splendor–WASHINGTON.   At Mount Vernon.
Thomas Curtis Clark.   PAL; PGD
One nearer to God's altar trod,/The other to the altar's God.   Two Went up
to the Temple to Pray.   Richard Crashaw.   ALV; CAW; HAP; TRV
One never knows the beauty round the bend!   Hope.   Anna Blake Mezquida.
TRV
One night he got upon the moon–and sailed away to Heaven!   The Story of
Samuel Jackson.   Charles Godfrey Leland.   StPo
One night of words/will not change/all that.   Summary.   Sonia Sanchez.
BPo
The one, no-one/that is us all.   Blue Black.   Bloke Modisane.   PBA
One nose is enough.   The Difference.   Laura E. Richards.   HBV 1-2;
HBVY
The one note, not lost, for nothing   In the Secret House.   Christopher
Middleton.   FaBoMo
One o'clock, two o'clock, three and away.   Bell Horses, Bell Horses, What
Time of Day?   Mother Goose.   OxNR; TiPo
One-of-a-kind machines fall silent.   The Hermit Wakes to Bird Sounds.
Maxine W. Kumin.   GrPl; Psk; WeW
..."One of ours; one of ours. Yes. Yes."   The Examination.   W. D.
Snodgrass.   CAPP; ConAP
"One of the most distinguished members of his race."   Mr. Z.   M. Carl
Holman.   SoSe
One of the neat ones in your awkward squad.   Forgive Me, Sire.   Norman
Cameron.   FaBoEE; GTBS-P; OBSP; OxBS
The one of the old forest/Seemeth the best of all.   Among the Beautiful
Pictures.   Alice Cary.   BLPA
One of these awakened me,/And I sped to succour thee.   On a Poet's Lips I
Slept.   Percy Bysshe Shelley.   ELP
One of those old-type natural fouled-up guys.'   Posterity.   Philip Larkin.
OxBC
One of us sleeping/One always/Awake.   Shira.   Howard Schwartz.   VWA
One of you is lying.   Unfortunate Coincidence.   Dorothy Parker.   ALV;
BXAP; FaBoUs; NoP; PoPl; SBG; TreF
One old convict ended up marrying the governor's mother.   The New
Warden.   Jimmy Santiago Baca.   LFAC
One only comprehending pair,/Unique, since first the world began.   Another
Generation.   J. C. Squire.   HBMV
One pair of trousers (which had died)   My Specialty Is Living Said.   Edward
Estlin Cummings.   MoVE; NOBA
One part papa,/one part Doppelganger.   Rumpelstiltskin.   Anne Sexton.
DFT
One plunge at once t' his death, his grave, his Hell.   Algernon Sidney's
Farewell.   Anonymous.   APAS
"The one pours out a balm upon the World,/"The other vexes it.'   The Fall
of Hyperion.   John Keats.   OBRV
One primrose from my Kentish home/Is worth all these to me.   The Memory
of Kent.   Edmund Charles Blunden.   HBMV
1 privet bush,/1 ivy plant,/1 radish.   Spring Arithmetic.   Anonymous.
FiBHP
One pye-meat spiced brave I see,/One which, I must not leave alone.   Old
Christmas.   Anonymous.   OHIP
One quick gust/They fountain into air.   Pigeons.   Richard Kell.   BoAnP
One reed will stay, though all the swamp fly off.   Heron in Swamp.   Frances
Minturn Howard.   GoYe
One regardeth her going forth abroad/Even as hers yonder, the Only One.   A
Love Song.   Anonymous.   LiTW
One river born of many streams/Roll in one blaze of blinding light!
Salutation.   George William Russell.   OnYI
One Roman,/Finis.   Tenuous and Precarious.   Stevie Smith.   FaBoNo;
OxBTC
One's enough, and twa's too mony.   A Scottish Proverb.   Anonymous.
FaBoUs
One's friends are one's sarcophagi.   Among the Anthropophagi.   Ogden
Nash.   CenHV
One saw her with the Master's eyes.   Transfigured.   Sarah Piatt.   AA
One: scattering the blind swarms that drink at the carcass.   Herman Moon's
Hourbook.   Christopher Middleton.   NePoEA-2
The one shoe,/Dissatisfied, perhaps, in the incomplete life.   On a Child with a
Wooden Leg.   Bertram Warr.   OBCV

One showing the eggs unbroken.   The Explosion.   Philip Larkin.   EBEV;
FaBoMo; HAP; OxBC; SCV
One shriek. The arm was gone.   Bad Dream.   Louis MacNeice.   FaBoIP;
NoAm
One side in death; the other burning.   Headsong.   Joseph Bennett.   NePA
One sinful wish would make a hell of heaven.   If I Have Sinn'd in Act.
Hartley Coleridge.   NCEP
One single symbol–/Flight.   Arctic Tern in a Museum.   Mary Effie Lee
Newsome.   PoNe
One sleepless soul among the souls that sleep!   Sea Dirge.   Archias.   AWP
One slit's enough to let Adultry in.   Upon Scobble. Epigram.   Robert
Herrick.   AnAnS 2; CaPo; FaBoEE; NoP; TW
One sliver of the moon.   The Short Night.   Buson (Taniguchi Buso).
MOON
One small grave is all he gets.   Cui Bono?   Thomas Carlyle.   HBV 1-2;
OBRV; WGRP
One solid San Francisco, one,/The fairest sight beneath the sun.   San
Francisco.   Joaquin Miller.   PAH
One stamps at heaven's portal.   Comrades.   Henry Ames Blood.   AA
One standing at each end.   A Dedication.   Gilbert Keith Chesterton.
FiBHP
One star that I loved ere the fields went brown.   A Winter Twilight.
Angelina Weld Grimke.   CDC; PoBA; PoNe
One still at heart, that so thyself beguilest.   The Book of Day-Dreams.
Charles Leonard Moore.   AA
One still chewing/picks up a copper strip/and runs his eye along it.   Fine
Work with Pitch and Copper.   William Carlos Williams.   OxBA
One, still one, while the world grows old.   Unity.   Alfred Noyes.   HBV 1-2
One still white face brings home the news I read.   News.   Marnie Pomeroy.
PoL
One sudden Coming? Many so believe./So not, without knowing anything, do
I.   Eleven Addresses to the Lord.   John Berryman.   OxBC
One sun, one moon, and called it heaven.   Western Town.   David
Wadsworth Cannon, Jr..   PoNe
One superb white cloud passes, dropping rain.   Sonnets, VII: "Upon an
upland orchard's sunny side."   Thomas Caulfield Irwin.   IrPN
One syllable of ecstasy/Confusing shame, confounding bone.   Your Chase
Had a Beast in View.   John Peale Bishop.   LiTA
–The one that courses through my veins   In the Barrio.   Alurista.   FIA
The one that sings was mine.   Night Song.   Lisel Mueller.   AMV-80
The one that stinks the most infests the rose.   To Poets.   Walter Savage
Landor.   FaBoEE
The one that wanted nothing/Took the most of me.   Prices.   Louis
Ginsberg.   TrJP
One the Appalachian range from Maine to Alabama.   Uncle Ambrose.
James Still.   AmFN
1. The Iliad and 2. the wife!   Poor Devil That I Am, Being So Attacked.
Palladas.   OBVE
One theirs, one ours. But as to which you wore,/No indication.   On the
Relative Merit of Friend and Foe, Being Dead.   Donald Thompson.   WaP
"One thing at a time, and that done well,"/Is wisdom's proven rule.   One
Step at a Time.   Anonymous.   WBLP
"The one thing I regret," he said,/"Is that it cannot speak!"   Sylvie and
Bruno.   Lewis (Charles Lutwidge Dodgson) Carroll.   NA
One this is done, and it bells/up in the throat.   Out from Lobster Cove.   J.
D. Reed.   NeAC
...One thinks of the small dangling/forelegs of the flesh-eating dinosaurs.   In
the Bistro.   Gwen Harwood.   FaBoWP
One thought: Good will to all–and charity!   Perpetual Christmas.   Arthur
Gordon Field.   PGD
One thought, one grace, one wonder at the least,/Which into words no virtue
can digest...   Tamburlaine the Great.   Christopher Marlowe.   ChTr;
ViBoPo
One thought soars like a hawk, in the heaven of my mind.   Solitudes.   John
Hall Wheelock.   MoLP
One to the Peaceful Sea!   The Two Streams.   Oliver Wendell Holmes.   AP
One to watch, one to pray,/And two to bear my soul away.   Prayer.
Anonymous.   OxBoLi
One truth is clear, WHATEVER IS, IS RIGHT.   An Essay on Man.
Alexander Pope.   CEP; EnL; EnLi 1-2; FaBoPV; MBW 1-2; NAWM 1-2;
NoP; OAEP; OBEC; PoEL 1-5
One twist of the ribbed knob/would set its nest of tiny/spiders crawling again.
The Gold Nest.   Robert Wallace.   PPJ
ONE TWO THREE you're dead.   Chair, Dog, and Clock.   Hilary Corke.
NYBP
...One/warm stone remains when the rest are washed away.   Hope.   F. D.
Reeve.   PoA
..:One was so like the other/That he mistook and took her for his mother.
The Compliment.   William Habington.   ACP
One white egret/Guards the harbor mouth.   Like a wave crest.   Emperor
Uda.   LiTW

...The one who bent/and petted you, and murmured–and went on. Stray Dog. Charlotte Mish. PoLf

...One who can see/no/beautiful element of unreason under it? Melancthon. Marianne Moore. AtBAP; CrMA

...One who creates/Sacramental relationships/That last always."/With love and admiration... A Letter to William Carlos Williams. Kenneth Rexroth. NNaP; PP

The one who is going to die in my place. Working the Skeet House. Jon Eastman. AMV-80

The one who is missing/was myself. My Father. Abraham Chalfi. VWA

The one who is not lying there/Could have been. Middle Age. Patricia Beer. FaBoWP

One who knows/Why we live–and die. The Flight of the Arrow. Richard Henry Stoddard. AA

...The one who left/and stopped screaming The Good Woman. Crystal MacLean. FAZ

One who lies prostrate from the blows of Envy. Pier delle Vigne. Dante Alighieri. HoPM

One who, past doubtings all,/Waits in unhope. In Tenebris. Thomas Hardy. OAEL 1-2

One who should drown him too. I Looked Up from My Writing. Thomas Hardy. MMM

One who sleeps/away reality. I'm a Dreamer. Kattie M. Cumbo. BlSi

...One who survives everything/Will shortly survive even himself. The Cost of Pretending. Peter Davison. TW

One will be leaving any minute now. Of Angels. E. L. Mayo. FAZ

One will walk today! I haven't told my garden yet. Emily Dickinson. AA

One, with its forepaws,/Wash its whiskered face. Rats. Walter De La Mare. BoAnP

The one with sad eyes who represents pleasure,/had a canvas to herself, entirely to herself. Against Botticelli. Robert Hass. AmPA; NPGG

One with the sunlit air and the calling wind/And the sea for ever. Fire Burial. Edgar McInnis. CaP

One wonders at her fate. Death of a Fair Girl. Alpheus Butler. PeD

...The one word/my mouth must open to is why. The Negatives. Philip Levine. NePoEA-2

One word, no more, to say. Merops. Ralph Waldo Emerson. AmePo; AnFE; APA; OxBA

One word not said through some old Roman helmet. Talk. Philip A. Stalker. FiBHP

One world have I–yea, no other/Than the world which lives in me. Throbs the Night with Mystic Silence. Hayim Nahman Bialik. TrJP

One would continue to contend with one's ideas. The Glass of Water. Wallace Stevens. AtBAP; CoBMV; MoAB; MoAmPo; MoPo; OxBA; TAP

One would have thought some influence/Their ravish'd spirits did possess. An Ode upon a Question Moved, Whether Love Should Continue For Ever? Edward, Lord Herbert of Cherbury. AnAnS 2; JCP; MeLP; MePo; OBS; SeCP; ViBoPo

One wrestler challenging–oh how unsafe–/Himself. Two Wrestlers. Robert Francis. LiSp

One youth we loved as tenderly as ye. Whom the Gods Love. Mark A. De Wolfe Howe. AA

Onely behold her rare perfection,/And blesse your fortunes fayre election. Amoretti, LXXXIV. Edmund Spenser. AAS

Onely let her abstaine from cruelty,/And doe me not before my time to dy. Amoretti, XLII. Edmund Spenser. AAS

Onely my paines wil be the more to get her,/But having her, my joy wil be the greater. Amoretti, LI. Edmund Spenser. AAS

Onely that of which Thou mak'st/Use in time, from time Thou tak'st. Time Recover'd. Girolamo Casone. OBVE

Onely the actions of the just/Smell sweet, and blossom in their dust. Dirge. James Shirley. ACP; AWP; InPo; OAEL 1-2; PoEL 1-5; TreFT

Onely true in shreds and stuffe. Upon Some Women. Robert Herrick. AnAnS 2; CaPo; DBV

Onerous to satiate souls, increased their buoyance. A Jog-Trot Pair. Thomas Hardy. PeD

...The ones where simple/crumbs over the forest/floor endure/to help us home? History. Jorie Graham. NPGG

...Only/a bony ghost the contemptuous wind makes light of. The Beautiful Ruined Orchard. Daniel Berrigan. FYAP

Only a brassiere salesman in his blue suede/shoes/could look on her face, long,/and not go blind. The Cross-Eyed Lover. Donald Finkel. Prf

Only a cloud or two hangs here and there. Another. Richard Lovelace. SeCP

Only a cup of tears waits at the end. The Stirrup Cup. Aline Kilmer. CAW

"Only a day, love,'/Murmurs the bee. Wood-Song. Eugene Lee-Hamilton. OBVV

Only a/dull/whining/ache/in the minds/of those who live. Attica Is. Stewart Brisby. LFAC; SOTS

Only a dusty statue lifts and drops its hand. Landscape. David Gascoyne. FaBoMo

Only a fable like all our strange and beautiful dreams. Elegy. Robert Hillyer. EtS

Only a fat man/Breaks the mirror, O, it is not I! The Fat Man in the Mirror. Robert Lowell. PoA

Only a hundred yards to go,/But not in distance, Syd–in time. Space and Time. Syd Scroggie. PoSH

Only a look and a voice, then darkness again and/a silence. Ships That Pass in the Night. Henry Wadsworth Longfellow. EtS; MOS

Only a moving/with no note/granite lips/a stone throat Old Song. F. R. Scott. PeCV

Only a pleading gesture/and the dark green of grass. A lake. Storm. Agnes Nemes Nagy. PBWP

Only a prairie child/Knows such sweet hours. Prairie Spring. Edwina Fallis. SUS

Only a signal-light of love for us, afar! Isolation. Josephine Preston Peabody. AnAmPo

Only a song, only a dream,/Only a blue dove. The Wedding (1957). Boris Pasternak. HW

Only a tattered rag/of blue hangs on a thorn. Lakeside Incident. Robin Skelton. NOBC

"Only a woman's hair." Swift. Thomas Caulfield Irwin. IrPN

Only a woman would think he could be shot. Iambic Feet Considered as Honorable Scars. William Meredith. OBSP; PoA

Only a word, sweet! Only a touch! Kate Temple's Song. Mortimer Collins. HBV 1-2

Only about what the people are doing. A Little More About the Brothers and Sisters. Sharon Scott. JB

Only above is found all with security. Contemplations. Anne Bradstreet. WPOW

Only afterwards don't anyone stand close/to an open window You Don't Know What Love Is (parody). Raymond Carver. BXAP

Only an avenue, dark, nameless, without end. Old Man. Edward ("Edward Eastaway") Thomas. ChMP; LiTM; MoVE; SCV; SeCeV

Only another island, quiet and simple, forming in another mind. Fishermen, Drowned beyond the West Coast. Vivian Smith. CBAP

The only answer I get is his back. If He Let Us Go Now. Shirley Williams. BoWoP

The only answer no one questioned,/a radiance that ripened. Catechism Elegy. Margaret Gibson. MAYP

The only ape in town who/uses yards and yards of/pink flowered toilet paper The Great Poet. Linda King. GP

Only as they were, if that is where you are. Movies for the Home. Howard Moss. NePoEA-2; NYBP

The only barrier which contrives/to keep us in our separate lives. To His Dear Friend, Bones. Jay Parini. MAYP

The only beautiful things on earth/turn into themselves. In the Distance. H. L. Van Brunt. FAZ

Only because to live thee it presumed. Sonnets to Philomel. Sir John Davies. SiPS

Only because you are her coin. To T. H., a Lady Resembling My Mistress. Thomas Carew. AnAnS 2; CaPo

Only behold her rare perfection,/And blesse your fortune's fayre election. Let Not One Sparke of Filthy Lustfull Fyre. Edmund Spenser. TEP

The only being that bears a heart/Not recreant to the wild. Wild Ass. Padraic Colum. MoBrPo

Only bitter and wise blood,/the shorn fleece of the womb. Locale. Penelope Shuttle. BrRo

Only blackpeople play it fair. One Sided Shoot-Out. Don L. Lee. BPo; PoBA

Only by its own cry. The Deer Which Lives. Onakatomi Yoshinobu. AWP

Only by the sound of his own voice. The deer on pine mountain. Onakatomi Yoshinobu. LiTW

The only cloud/on which I can rest/my head. Love Letter. Linda Pastan. DFF

Only content and we are here,/My baby dear. Oh, Baby, Baby, Baby Dear. Edith Nesbit. NOBV

Only crass grass should dance in the end. Epitaph. Theodore Spencer. LiTA

Only dark answering day? Judith of Minnewaulken: Judith Remembers. Maxwell Anderson. WHA

Only death's insect whiteness/crooks its neck in a tumbler/where I placed its sign by choice. The Corpse-Plant. Adrienne Rich. CoPo

Only death will taste bitter/In the shameful ointment. A Donkey Will Carry You. Jakov Steinberg. VWA

Only disenchanted people/Can be heavenly. The Frog Prince. Stevie Smith. DFT; HAP

Only do Thou lend me a hand,/Since thou hast both mine eyes. Submission. George Herbert. JCP

The only emperor is the emperor of ice-cream. The Emperor of Ice Cream. Wallace Stevens. AP; BiP; CMoP; CoBMV; FaBoMo; FF; HaCAP; HAP;

InPK; LiTA; MoPo; MoVE; NAWM 1-2; NePA; NIP; NoAm; NOBA; NoP; OxBA; TAP; ViBoPo; WeW

The only eyes that, near or far,/Can gaze on thine without despair.   To Amine.   James Clarence Mangan.   OBEV; OBVV

The only faint source of hope/is the snow on Kurakake mountain.   The Snow on Saddle Mountain.   Gary Snyder.   NoAm; NOBA

The only folks who give us pain/Are those we love the best.   Life's Scars.   Ella Wheeler Wilcox.   BLPA

Only for important weddings.   The Rock.   Thomas Stearns Eliot.   NAMP

Only for me, for me she cried.   Only for Me.   Mark Van Doren.   NCSH

Only free of the sea for five or six thousand years.   Looking at Some Flowers.   Robert Bly.   NaP; NOBA

Only fright can make it bristle.   Havdolah Wine.   Miriam Ulinover.   VWA

Only from time to time I hear the voice/Of an old liar/Laughing at my/Extinction.   The Akedah.   Matti Megged.   VWA

The only girl I ever did love,/Was on that train and gone.   Who's Gonna Shoe Your Pretty Little Foot?   *Anonymous.*   FSW

Only give you a drunken/Smile from under his tousled hair.   The Wild Flower Man.   Lu Yu.   NaP

Only glory restores.   You Who Were Made for This Music.   Louis Zukofsky.   CoPo

Only God can understand.   God Know What He's About.   *Anonymous.*   STF

Only happy for the winesaps/In tomorrow's applesauce!   A Ballad of Johnny Appleseed.   Helmer O. Oleson.   SiSoSe; TiPo

Only he hears, and farther away,/Some happy animal's slow, listless moo.   The Plum Tree.   James Reaney.   CaP

Only he/is her ultimate protector.   Mira is dancing with bells tied.   Mira Bai [(or Mirabai)].   BoWoP

...Only he is unknown/who is unknown to himself.   The Soldier.   Conrad Aiken.   WaaP

Only hide thee, Lost Enchantress!   The Rousing Canoe Song.   Hermia Fraser.   CaP; WHW

Only his fair, unshadowed face/Abides with me until tomorrow.   At Daybreak.   Siegfried Sassoon.   PeHV

Only his fearsome prints are seen.   The Snitterjipe.   James Reeves.   AmMo

The only home for me—/Ah me!   Songs of Seven.   Jean Ingelow.   HBV 1-2

Only hooves.   Celebrant.   David Mitchell.   OCNZ

Only I and then the sheet/and bulk dead   Alba.   Samuel Beckett.   BIrV

Only I have enough insolence for that.   Sunday Morning.   Christina Jenkins.   BrRo

Only I that mourn out.   The Courtier's Good-Morrow to His Mistress.   *Anonymous.*   EIL

Only immortal love, all-rich/In warmer wool than fleece, can stitch.   Apology.   Vassar Miller.   NePoEA

Only in hope of they redeeming grace/I live.   So Little and So Much.   John Oxenham.   BLRP

Only in love can life's true path be trod;/Love is self-giving; therefore love is God.   Thysia.   Morton Luce.   HBV 1-2

Only in this, that you both painted be.   Phryne.   John Donne.   FaBoEE

Only in you my song begins and endeth.   To Stella.   Sir Philip Sidney.   EIL; WHA

Only insofar as it is honest—/no more–no less.   Untitled.   Robert J. Conley.   STE

Only it is precisely this/That keeps us still alive.   Life is Struggle.   Arthur Hugh Clough.   EnLi 1-2

Only its quiet part shall live/When I am dead.   I Shall Be Loved as Quiet Things.   Karle Wilson Baker.   HBMV; MCCG; MoLP

Only Jesus will I know,/And Jesus crucified.   Only Jesus Will I Know.   Charles Wesley.   BePJ

Only joke-matches....Then I knew he was Richard.'   Identification in Belfast (I.R.A. Bombing).   Robert Lowell.   OxBC

Only jump over the wall and all delight shall be yours.   Come to Me.   *Anonymous.*   WTO

An only kid! An only kid!   Had Gadya–A Kid, a Kid.   *Anonymous.*   TrJP

Only kind and am'rous Spirits,/Kindle and maintain a flame.   When Aurelia First I Courted.   *Anonymous.*   OBS

The only kind of middle wife/My folks could beg or borrow.   Saturday's Child.   Countee Cullen.   LiTM; NAs; OFD; PoBA; SaC

"Only let it form within my hands once more."   The Brandy Glass.   Louis MacNeice.   FaBoIP

The only light on the block   Living in the World.   Alan Chong Lau.   BrSi

Only, like fate, sweet Myra never varies,/Yet in her eyes the doom of all change carries.   Caelica, VII.   Fulke, Lord Brooke Greville.   EnRePo; FCP

Only like heaven's own logic: hard to read.   Clock without Hands.   John Frederick Nims.   PoA

Only lovely youth.   The Singers in a Cloud.   Ridgely Torrence.   AnAmPo; HBMV; UnS

The only lover my mind has left/separates my mind, like milk.   Not Wanting Myself.   Linda Gregg.   NPGG

The only magic that kept us alive–/to believe in ourselves.   Magic Word.   Edgar Jackson.   LFAC

Only my beard, only my wrinkles/near thee!   Abishag.   Andre Spire.   TrJP

Only my being there is different.   The Nature of an Action.   Thom Gunn.   ACV; NePoEA

Only my franchised heart to fuel the fires/to suns.   I Served in a Great Cause.   Horace L. Traubel.   AA

Only my soul was tired and tame.   Love's Flight.   Else Lasker-Schüler.   TrJP

Only my two eyes and the wild skies to see.   Poem for Epiphany.   Norman Nicholson.   PoPl

Only myself how strange/to the strange present come!   On Leaving Ullswater.   Kathleen Raine.   NeBP

Only night heals again.   Songs from Cyprus.   Hilda ("H. D.") Doolittle.   MoAmPo

Only no one could stop her/From being improper.   Clerihew: "The Empress Poppaea."   *Anonymous.*   PV

Only, of course, they can't sustain the part.   Fireflies in the Garden.   Robert Frost.   OBSP

Only of waves/which come and go.   The New Notebook.   Maria Banus.   PBWP

Only one.   Beyond Belief.   Tom Luhrmann.   AMV-81

The only/one his returning master/actually to recognize.   On First Looking into Chapman's Homer II (parody).   Peter Peterson.   BXAP

Only one kiss. Good-bye, my dear.   Jenny.   Dante Gabriel Rossetti.   MaVP; PoEL 1-5

Only one more day!   One Day More.   *Anonymous.*   AmSS

Only one other in our life would know us.   Sadness, Glass, Theory.   Roy Fuller.   WaP

Only one snowflake(and we speak our names   When What Hugs Stopping Earth Than Silent Is.   Edward Estlin Cummings.   PoA

Only one span is all the life we borrow.   Three Score and Ten.   *Anonymous.*   OBSP

Only one weapon let us keep.   Preparedness.   Jean Grigsby Paxton.   PGD

The only one who understood the joke,/Who slipped out well before the first glass broke.   How Did It Seem to Sylvia?   Gjertrud Schnackenberg.   SM

Only–only call me thine.   I Asked My Fair, One Happy Day.   Samuel Taylor Coleridge.   HBV 1-2

The only open door/is the door to man   Don't Ask Me Who I Am.   James A. Randall, Jr.   BPo

Only our coats knew each other,/rubbing shoulders in the dark closet.   Walking through the Upper East Side.   Erica Jong.   NYP

Only our love and prayers.   Outward Bound.   Edward Sydney Tylee.   PAH

Only our shoulders still like butterflies/are playing.   Love-Song.   Else Lasker-Schüler.   TrJP

Only outside my body can I live/or else in exile like a fugitive.   Sonnet XVII: "I flee the city, temples, and each place."   Louise Labe.   BoWoP

Only owls have homes.   Notes for Albuquerque.   Roberta Hill Whiteman.   STE

The only place I really want to go.   Moving: New York–New Haven Line.   Alfred Corn.   MAYP

The only pontiff is the pontiff of candy bars.   Sunday Service (parody).   Michael Heffernan.   BXAP

The only proof that Caroline had bowels.   On Queen Caroline's Deathbed.   Alexander Pope.   TW

The only purpose of the earth.   Envoy.   Richard Hovey.   AA

Only remains the superscription.   On the Oxford Carrier.   John Milton.   NA

Only remember these words: we/are fucked.   For Nothing.   Andres Castro Rios.   InW

Only ribbon round it.   Lucy and Kitty.   *Anonymous.*   OxNR; TiPo

Only Robin/still is here!   Winter in the Wood.   Ivy O. Eastwick.   YeAr

Only sad hearts learn to wait.   Learn to Wait.   *Anonymous.*   PoToHe

Only seeking, seeking without finding.   In the Third Year of War.   Henry Treece.   WaP

Only seems like now, they ain't so/revolutionary anymore.   Just Taking Note–.   Sharon Scott.   JB

Only she on her knees, peeking into/Her own clasped hands.   Preface to a Twenty Volume Suicide Note.   LeRoi (Imamu Amiri Baraka) Jones.   AmNP; CAPP; InPS; NNP; PAI; PoBA; PoM; PoNe; PPP; TTY

The only sign of perfect Cure.   The Indifference.   Sir Charles Sedley.   CEP; SeCV 1-2

The only song that I can sing/Is bile them cabbage down.   Bile Them Cabbage Down.   *Anonymous.*   AmFP; FSW

The only sound is the fan stirring the heat.   A Kitchen Memory.   Roy Scheele.   Str

Only still bands of desolate mist/And a single fishing boat.   Seeking a Mooring.   Wang Wei.   BoWoP; WPOW

Only such proud restraining purity/Restores the else-betrayed, too-human heart.   At a Bach Concert.   Adrienne Rich.   NePoEA; NIP; SM

Only take thy fingers off me.'   Pain.   James Henry.   NOBV

Only ten ticks of the watch, but it makes/First, second, third, and the last. The Hundred-Yard Dash. William Lindsey. AA

Only that 'twas heaven/Just to be with You. Miss You. David Cory. BLPA; FaBoBe; GoTF; TreFS

Only that underlying sense/Of the look of a room on returning thence. The Walk. Thomas Hardy. CMoP; PoEL 1-5; PrIm

Only the actions of the just/Smell sweet, and blossom in their dust. Ajax and Ulysses: The Glories of Our Blood and State. James Shirley. TrGrPo; WaaP

Only the awful mother stirs stricken/with grief. The Awful Mother. Susan Griffin. NPGG

Only the bare bones/of a life remain. Ice Dragons. Diane Ackerman. SUW

Only the beauty is/real. The Rhododendron Plant. Allen Katzman. WeW

Only the best composed and worthiest hearts/God sets to act the hard'st and constant'st parts. Epistle to Henry Wriothesley, Earl of Southhampton. Samuel Daniel. EnRePo

Only the broken heart can sing/Not asking why...! Threnody. Donald Jeffrey Hayes. AmNP

...Only the cat,/who misses her,/licks it now and then. The Photograph the Cat Licks. Beatrice Walter. NMM

Only the creaking cart/Disturbing their sorrowful serenity. The Refugees. Sir Herbert Read. BrPo

Only the cry, "Abel, awake, awake!" The Discovery. Monk Gibbon. OnYI

Only the dead men know the tunes/The live world dances to. All Sung. Richard Le Gallienne. OBVV

Only the echoes, which he made relent,/Rung from their marble caves, "Repent, repent!" For the Baptist. William, of Hawthornden Drummond. BSV; GoTS; HBV 1-2; LoBV; OBS; OxBoCh

Only the English are really her own. The White Cliffs. Alice Duer Miller. BLPL

Only the eyes show through. You Refuse to Own. Margaret Atwood. NeAC

Only the faces and the names remain. A Warning to Conquerors. Donagh MacDonagh. CIP; OxBI

Only the falling dust of all the dead,/the sound of passing feet. Epithalamium. Edith Sitwell. HW

Only the fog-horn/that shroud-sails our hearts. No Fear. Mary Doyle Curran. AMV-80

Only the fugitive shapes are we,/Wrought in the web of eternity. The Hidden Weaver. Odell Shepard. WGRP

Only the Gold/Who is God ever will. Captain Kelly Lets His Daughter Go to Be a Nun. Thomas Butler Feeney. PoPl

Only the grace from simple stone. Elegy Before Death. Edna St. Vincent Millay. AnFE; APA; CMoP; LiTA; LiTM

Only the grave is warm, Granny,/isn't it. Lend me your arm. One Foot in the Door. Anne Elder. CBAP

Only the hawk moves, fain to kill,/Circling on high. On the Plains. Francis Brooks. AA

...Only the head/drags & the eyes roll/over, counter to the earth. The Man Who Buys Hides. Dennis Schmitz. LCAP

Only the heart knows its own despair! Only the Heart. Marjorie Freeman Campbell. CaP

Only the heart, with love afire,/Can satisfy the soul's desire. Not by Bread Alone. James Terry White. GoTF; PoLf; TreFT

Only the ivy and the wind/May tell of it at all. The Buckle. Walter De la Mare. BrR

Only the king of the land and the sea. Wishes. Norman Ault. HBMV; HBVY

Only the leaves come between us. Possible Love Poem to the Usurer. Octavio Armand. AMV-81

Only the leaves of autumn, the snows of winter/Knew where she lay. At Gull Lake: August, 1810. Duncan Campbell Scott. NOBC; OBCV

Only the little bones and the great ones, disarranged. Leukothea. Keith Douglas. NeBP

Only the lonely are free. Morning Song. Sara Teasdale. MOON

Only the mother, like God, forgives, and/comforts her heart with the past. Saturninus. Katherine Eleanor Conway. AA

...Only the muscles of her haunches appearing to move. Hmmmm, 10. Leslie Scalapino. NPGG

Only, the nations shall be great and free. Near Dover, September, 1802. William Wordsworth. EnLi 1-2; EnRP; MBW 1-2

Only the old home welcomes them again. The Farm on the Links. Rosamund Marriott Watson. OBVV

Only the poem I can never write is true. Apologia. David Gascoyne. ChMP

Only the ribbons. Concerning the Dead Women: The Munitions Plant Explosion: June, 1918. Elizabeth Libbey. AmPA

Only the rich have need of money. Home Is the Sailor. Phyllis McGinley. DBV

...Only the sand and wind forget to die. El Alamein Revisited. Roy MacNab. PeSA

Only the sea sings this legend. The Captain. Blanca Varela. WPOW

Only the skin remembers, swirling to clench/the archetypal wound: the center holds. Certified Copy. Ann Deacon. NIP

Only the sleep eternal/In an eternal night. The Garden of Proserpine. Algernon Charles Swinburne. AWP; BLPA; BLPL; BoLiVe; DiPo; ExPo; FaBoRV; FaBV; FaPoR; ForPo; HAP; HBV 1-2; InPo; LiTB; MaVP; NOBE; NOBV; NoP; OAEP; OBNC; PoEL 1-5; PoPl; PoPle; PoRA; SCV; SeCePo; SeCeV; TreFT; TrGrPo; VLP; WHA

Only the song of a secret bird. The Ballad of Dreamland. Algernon Charles Swinburne. HBV 1-2

Only the sound of a stream/Through the misty trees. Starting at Dawn. Sun Yun-feng. PBWP

Only the sound of washboards through silk curtains. Boudoir Lament. Yu Hsuan-chi. BoWoP

Only the steadfast and the true/Find that which is forever new. Solomon. Hermann Hagedorn. GoBC

Only the strong can know that. The Invisible Woman. Robin Morgan. IHMS; NMM

Only the thrush, the thrush that never spoke,/Sang from her bursting heart. The Thrush. Laura Benet. HBMV

Only the white statue and the darkness realize. Deaf-and-Dumb School. Anthony Delius. PeSA

Only the wind. Modern Grimm. Dorothy Lee Richardson. DFT

Only the wind continued/To call. White Bird. Matti Megged. VWA

Only Theatre recorded/Owner cannot shut– Drama's vitallest expression is the common day. Emily Dickinson. NOBA

Only then was I fit for human society. Matthew V: 29-30. Derek Mahon. CIP

Only then will the return/begin. Ourobouros. Jorge Plescoff. VWA

Only there wants an Adam on the Green,/Or else all Paradise might here be seen. To "Philomela." Benjamin Colman. SCAP

Only these blank, oracular/Headshakes or headnods. The Grandfathers. Donald Justice. NCSH

Only these lines remain! Lost Garden. Katherine"(Amelia Beers Warnock Garvin) "Hale. CaP

Only they not embrace,/We face to face. Love's Matrimony. William Cavendish, Duke of Newcastle. SeCePo

The only thing caught, a fish trapped inside the wind. Enigmas. Pablo Neruda. NU

The only thing I fear/Is the Almighty Face. A Song in Passing. Yvor Winters. VGW

The only things that concern me are the acts.' He Said the Facts. Merrill Moore. CrMA

The only things we ever keep/Are what we give away. Song. Harold C. Sandall. PoToHe

Only thirty years to come down human. A Picture of Okinawa. Dennis Schmitz. LCAP; NPGG

Only this alignment/should matter. Blue Tropic. Luis Cabalquinto. BrSi

...Only this stone,/Out in the fields, ever bring forth a tear. Poems from a Greek Anthology (excerpt). Martial (Marcus Valerius Martialis). NNaP

...Only those/that lie dead revealing/their rockgreen color and the bold/cut of the wings. The Dead Butterfly. Denise Levertov. NoP

Only those who brave its dangers/Comprehend its mystery!' The Galley of Count Arnaldos. Henry Wadsworth Longfellow. OBEV; OBVV

Only Thou our leader be,/And we still will follow Thee. Children of the Heavenly King. John Cennick. WGRP

Only through love will you enter heaven. Child, Child. Sara Teasdale. HBV 1-2

Only through time time is conquered. Four Quartets. Thomas Stearns Eliot. AtBAP

...Only time and loss, not/you and I, are the subject to be held. Dear Mrs. McKinney of the Sixth Grade:. David Kherdian. GLGT

Only to coo their songs to thee. To Little Renee on First Seeing Her Lying in Her Cradle. William Aspenwall Bradley. HBV 1-2

Only to feel this touching at my sleeve. Credo. Zona Gale. TrPWD

Only to kiss that air/That lately kissed thee. To Electra. Robert Herrick. ALV; BLPL; CaPo; CavP; EG; EnLit; HBV 1-2; HoPM; LO; LoBV; OBEV; OBS; SeCV 1-2

Only to lie so still. Haiku: "Why is the hail so wild..." Richard Wright. FAZ

Only to make a sound to last for ages. Untitled. John Crowne. BoC

Only to name the little stars, the pretty Pleiades. The Pleiades. Elizabeth Jane Coatsworth. ImOP

Only to say, Here I am in person. Stumpfoot on 42nd Street. Louis Simpson. NNaP; NYP; UnPo; VGW

Only to see him vanishing at the damp edge/Of the road. A Prayer to Escape from the Market Place. James Wright. NaP

Only to stand at last on the strand/Where just beyond lies God. The Mystic. Cale Young Rice. WGRP

Or a wall to lie by/myself there being/nowhere else to go. Drunk. Carroll Arnett. VoR

Or a word in the brain's ways. Soldier: Twentieth Century. Isaac Rosenberg. ChMP; MMM

Or all that we have left is empty talk/Of old achievements, and despair of new. England. William Cowper. OBEC

Or all that we have left is empty talk/Of old achievements, and despair of new. The Task. William Cowper. OAEP

Or am I a wrecker, who walks the town,/Content with the labor of tearing down. Which Are You? *Anonymous.* FPL; PoLf

"Or am I, too, a ghost?' and so/Turn once more to my task. Tudor Church Music. Sylvia Townsend Warner. UnS

Or an old horse. Nuances of a Theme by Williams. Wallace Stevens. CMoP; LiTA

Or an old man upon a winter's night. On Being Asked for a War Poem. William Butler Yeats. MoVE; NIP; OBWP; PP

Or an open book/lying next to me. Nights. Cyn Zarco. APU

Or any other reason why. Five Reasons for Drinking. Henry Aldrich. FaBoCo; GoTF; TreFT

Or any other thing that's false, before/You trust in critics. English Bards and Scotch Reviewers. George Gordon, Lord Byron. DBV

Or any style of any age or any place or name. And Through the Caribbean Sea. Margaret Danner. BPo

Or any thynge remove/His ardent mynde from God his hevenly/love. The Twelve Properties or Conditions of a Lover. Sir Thomas More. CoBE

Or any warm thing. Hunter's Moon. Stephen Sandy. NYBP

Or anything else remarkable,/Thou must follow me! All or Nothing (parody). Bayard Taylor. BXAP

Or anything, in fact,/That people ought to be. England and America. James Kenneth Stephen. OBTV

Or are they silenced by that silence out beyond?/Struck dumb? The Peepers in Our Meadow. Archibald MacLeish. NCSH

Or are you a leaner who lets others bear/Your portion of worry and labor and care? Lifting and Leaning. Ella Wheeler Wilcox. BLPA; WBLP

Or are you hunting me, or I pursuing? Valse Oubliee. John Heath-Stubbs. OxBTC

Or, art thou on fair angel lips a song? Whither. Philip Becker Goetz. AA

Or as in Jewellary Shops, do jems. Prologue. Edward Taylor AP

Or as the pearls of morning's dew/Ne'er to be found again. To Daffodils. Robert Herrick. BoLiVe; BoNaP; CaPo; CBEP; ELP; EnLi 1-2; ExPo; FaBoCh; GN; GTBS; GTBS-P; HBV 1-2; HBVY; InPo; InPS; JCP; LiTB; LoBV; NOBE; NoP; OBEV; PAI; PoRA; PPP; QFR; SeCeV; TrGrPo; ViBoPo; WHA

Or ask if you could see again. Tango. Elena Jordana. AMV-80

Or at the undying difference in the corner of a field. Father Mat. Patrick Kavanagh. MoAB; NMP

Or back outside you shall hang by a thread. Japanese Beetles. X.J. Kennedy. HoAn; OBAL

Or be a goat. Mating the Goats. Aliki Barnstone. AMV-81; BoWoP

Or—be shattered! To—? Richard Dehmel. AWP

Or bear his willing soul aloft. Blest Is the Man Whose Tender Breast. Abijah Davis. AH

Or beating against the black clouds of the storm,/Protecting the sea-cliffs. Her Longing. Theodore Roethke. NU

Or beauty's apparition so/Puts on invisibility. The Rainbow. Coventry Patmore. GTBS-P

Or because we have fallen so far. Survey. Paul Lawson. GP

Or been fit spoil for a centaur/Drunk with the unmixed wine. A Thought from Porpertius. William Butler Yeats. OAEL 1-2; OBSP

Or, being near the grave itself, it bent/Because of nothing more than gravity. The Sagging Bough (parody). Louis Untermeyer. BXAP

Or better, be with me,/Yours, Fly. Bee! I'm Expecting You! Emily Dickinson. BoAnP; SO; SOTW

Or, better still, complain direct to God. Any Complaints? Vernon Scannell. OxBTC

Or big waves, about to break over him. The Price of Paper. Lawrence Russ. AMV-81

Or bloom thy laurels o'er my winding-sheet? The Dying Prostitute, An Elegy. Thomas Holcroft. NOEC

Or, bold in faith, emerge, and walk, as He/Who lightly trod the Galilean sea. Adventure. Guy Mason. CaP

...Or, bones in/live flesh are better than scattered dry bones. Or/of course, all bones are bones. Discoveries of Bones and Stone. Geoffrey Grigson. OBTV

...Or born/Out of a strange and glorious darkness. DNA Lab. Michael Spence. SOTS

Or branches of a tall tree deep in the middle/of a forest. Peking Man, Raining. Katharine Auchincloss Lorr. SUW

Or break off what you can and cut it clean. Tree Ferns. Stanley Plumly. SM

Or breathe one breath of yours upon my verse,/And leave its odor there. Had I the Choice. Walt Whitman. PP; SoSe

Or bringe where eyes, nor tears, nor blood shall neede. Sonnet LXXI. William Alabaster. AnAnS 1

Or build thy house upon this grave. A Poet's Epitaph. William Wordsworth. EnRP; OBRV

Or by his grace I never more may love. Diana. Henry Constable. OBSC

Or by this hand I'll never draw thee, but against a post. Stand, Stately Tavie. *Anonymous.* ErPo; PV

Or call the tune to make the dancing throng/Free only as they aloof compose it and are strong. Letter. William Empson. LiTB

..,Or cared much like I/Do today whether it rained or not. Out-Dated Poem. Dick Gallup. ANYP

Or caught a rat/Requiescat! For a Little Girl Mourning Her Favorite Cat. John Greenleaf Whittier. PoL

Or cease to wonder why they fly you thus. Carmina. Caius Valerius Catullus. OBVE

Or censure what we cannot reach. To the Nightingale. Anne Finch, Countess of Wilchilsea. CEP; SBG

Or chant some line of cadenced, classic/hymn. Landor. John Albee. AA

Or Charon, seeing, may forget/That he is old, and she a shade. Pericles and Aspasia. Walter Savage Landor. AWP

Or Chloe in the morning. A Lamentable Case. Charles Hanbury-Williams. ErPo; UnTE

Or cling half-drunken to the rotting peach. Among the Orchards. Archibald Lampman. PeCV

Or come not my first looks again?' Odes. Horace. CavP

Or come upon the Savior's imaged face/Lost from a kindly padre's crucifix? Letter from the Vieux Carre. Ethel Green Russell. GoYe

Or conquer others was the only difference between us. Mirror for the Barnyard. Jack Myers. AmPA

Or corks afloat upon the sullen flood. On the Great Fog in London, December 1762. James Eyre Weeks. NOEC

Or crush her, like a vice of blood,/Upon the threshold of the mind? In Memoriam A.H.H., III. Alfred, Lord Tennyson. NAWM 1-2; OAEL 1-2; OAEP

Or, curled up in a car, her purr? See That One? Robert Bagg. ErPo

Or curtain'd close such Scene from ev'ry future View. Ode on the Poetical Character. William Collins. CEP; EiCP; EnPE; EnRP; ERoP 1-2; LAuP; NOEC; NoP; OAEL 1-2; OAEP; PoEL 1-5; TEP

Or death. Guyana. Fern Pankratz Ruth. AMV-80

...Or death's/Handshake, in gray gloves, hidden. Mr. Secretary. Karl Patten. SOTS

Or did they even dream, those specimen souls? And Did the Animals? Mark Van Doren. VGW

Or did you cradle in your arms a child/Which God and you were certain would be great? February 12, 1809. Gail Brook Burket. PGD

Or die by self-denial. The Greater Trial. Anne Finch, Countess of Winchilsea. TrGrPo

Or die in my bed, as a Christian should, is/all the same to me. The Two Friends. Charles Godfrey Leland. AA

Or die of a broken heart. For a Winnebago Brave. Joseph Bruchac. CDW

Or die? Or dance in the street the day that the world/goes crack? Behaviour of Money. Bernard Spencer. LiTB

...Or disdain the loving/that living alone, or else lonely in pairs, impairs? By the Boat House, Oxford. Anne Stevenson. FaBoWP

(Or do I, rather, live in hope/To see the red-necked phalarope?) A Bird in the Bush. Edward Hilton Young. PV

Or do you just belong? Do You Just Belong? *Anonymous.* STF

Or do you refer to my figure? Limerick: "A lady there was of Antigua." Cosmo Monkhouse. HBV 1-2

...Or do you want me to whisper/in your beautiful ear. The Magic Words. Ronald Koertge. AMV-81

Or doe you sporte at my calamitie? Piers Gaveston. Michael Drayton. PeHV

Or does in aught but Nature shine. A Song. Matthew Coppinger. CavP

Or does it explode? Lenox Avenue Mural. Langston Hughes. AmNP

Or does it make for death to be/Oneself a living armoury? The Dead Crab. Andrew Young. BSV; FaBoTw; FM; LoBV

...Or does know/and doesn't care, or neither. Existential. William Heyen. GeTw

...Or dont you yet/get what I'm saying? I'm a Baby. Cid Corman. GP

Or dreamed among the stars on some tall hill. Wooden Ships. David Morton. EtS

Or dried up in the bleak drought/of bitter thought. O Heart, Small Urn. Hilda. Doolithe. AtBAP

Or drink rice wine by moonlight with my former. Bone China. R. P. Lister. NYBP

...Or drives them wide-dispersed,/Wounded and wheeling various down the wind. The Seasons. James (1700-48) Thomson. PBBP

Or droont in a deep, deep sea. The Lark. *Anonymous.* GBP

...,Or/drown in despair when his days darken. The Answer. Robinson Jeffers. CMoP; GoYe; MoRP

Or dying, there at least may die.   In Memoriam A.H.H., VIII.   Alfred, Lord Tennyson.   VLP

Or e'er the Snowdrop die!   Saint Valentine's Day.   Coventry Patmore.   GoBC; OBNC

Or earth Thy humble footstool laid.   Stratfield.   *Anonymous.*   AmFP

Or Eden selfe, if ought with Eden mote compaire.   The Faerie Queene.   Edmund Spenser.   FiP

Or, egad, if you don't, there's an end of your credit:/Which nobody can deny.   A New Song of Wood's Halfpence.   Jonathan Swift.   OxBoLi

Or either Indies, East or West, do send us.   What Needeth All This Travail.   *Anonymous.*   EIL

Or elles your breth ys wonder strong,/Hum, ha, trill go bell.'   Hogyn cam to bower's dore.   *Anonymous.*   EnPo

Or ells with gret shame your game wylbe sene.   The Auncient Acquaintance, Madam, betwen Us Twayn.   John Skelton.   AAS; EnPo; PoEL 1-5

Or else a little Conservative!/Fal lal la!   Iolanthe.   Sir William Schwenck Gilbert.   EnLi 1-2

Or else be banished to some desert place,/And perish in each other's foul embrace.   A View of the Town (excerpt).   Thomas Gilbert.   NOEC

Or else from joy be ever banished.   Faint Heart.   Rufinus Domesticus.   ErPo

Or else he'll start to sleep much thinner.   Little Tiny Puppy Dog.   Spike Milligan.   GDP

Or else he would forego his mortal nature.   The Human Seasons.   John Keats.   CoBE; EnRP; FaFP; GTBS; GTBS-P; HBV 1-2; OBRV; WiR

Or else he wouldn't have gone so far from me,/Dog-gone it!   Song: "Ah hate to see de evenin' sun go down."   *Anonymous.*   NAMP

Or else his dear papa is poor.   System.   Robert Louis Stevenson.   TEP

Or else, how should we bless what we receive?   Natural Architecture.   John Hay.   NePoAm

Or else I'd never dared.   Under the Mistletoe.   Countee Cullen.   GoSl; PCh

Or else it will be.   Say Goodbye to Big Daddy.   Randall Jarrell.   LiSp; PoNe

Or else like scarecrows, that have been forgotten/In fields, when fall has preyed on everything.   That's Our Lot.   Moishe Leib Halpern.   VWA

Or else of thee this I prognosticate:/"Thy end is truth's and beauty's doom and date."   Sonnets, XIV: "Not from the stars do I my judgement pluck."   William Shakespeare.   MasP

Or else one that plaid his ape,/In a Hercules-his shape.   A Celebration of Charis.   Ben Jonson.   AnAnS 2; EnRePo; OAEP; SeCV 1-2

Or else quite extinguish mine.   A Prayer to the Wind.   Thomas Carew.   AnAnS 2

Or else remove me hence unto that hill,/Where I shall need no glass.   They Are All Gone into the World of Light.   Henry Vaughan.   BoC; InPS; JCP; MePo; NOBE; NoP; OAEL 1-2; OAEP; OBS; OxBoCh; PAI; PoEL 1-5; SeCP; SeCV 1-2

Or else the gift would be, however sweet,/Fragile and incomplete.   Absence.   Walter Savage Landor.   EnRP; OBRV

Or else the object lost,/Ere we can call it ours.   Song: "'Tis true our life is but a long dis-ease."   Katherine ("Orinda") Philips.   OBSP

Or else the poor sow's heart will down.   Hic, Hoc, the Carrion Crow.   *Anonymous.*   OxBoLi

Or else the snow.   In Winter.   Paul Blackburn.   NYP

Or else they nodded when their Master-Chance/Wound his one signal, and went on his way.   Failures.   Arthur Upson.   HBV 1-2; WGRP

Or else they take their ease.   The Fairies' Farewell.   Richard Corbet.   CBEP

Or else you'll complain/Of a stomach in pain.   To Sleep Easy All Night.   *Anonymous.*   OxNR

Or else your breath is wonder strong,/Hum, ha, trill go bell.   Hogyn.   *Anonymous.*   GBP

Or England breed again/Such a King Harry?   Agincourt.   Michael Drayton.   BeLS; EIL; FaBoBe; FaBoCh; FaPoR; GoTL; HBV 1-2; LoGBV; MCCG; OBEV; WHA

Or enough to suffer the relief and the pity.   A Dark Country.   Derek Mahon.   BIrV

Or ere I'll weep, O fool, I shall go mad!   King Lear.   William Shakespeare.   TreFT

...Or erect a/memorial they could not once afford.   Memo.   Charles Lynch.   PoBA

Or even a Report of Land–/To justify–Despair.   It Was Not Death, for I Stood Up.   Emily Dickinson.   AmePo; AtBAP; BiP; CBEP; MAPA; MasP; MoPo; NePA; NOBA; NoP

Or even a velvet-eyed lemur.   Something for My Russian Friends.   Edmund Wilson.   OBAL

Or even hated me.   I'm Black and Blue.   Heinrich Heine.   AWP

Or even in Rheims during the middle ages.   Ode.   David Lehman.   AMV-81

Or ever all who love, shall gain.   The Fading Rose: Epitaph.   Philip Freneau.   AA

Or ever be sorry/Of getting mud on my nice clean shirt.   I'd Like to Be a Worm.   Zhenya Gay.   TiPo

Or ever yet to young desire/Was told the mystic name of Love.   Natura Naturans.   Arthur Hugh Clough.   HAP; NOBV; VLP

Or fail to satisfy the urge/To hansel their untrodden snaw.   What Finer Hills?   J. K. Annand.   PoSH

Or feel some presence staring, glaring out at you/It's only me.   Beyond the Wall.   J. J. Maloney.   LFAC

Or felt awfully cut up, at least.   A Baker's Dozen of Wild Beasts.   Carolyn Wells.   OBCA

Or fetters she the free-born soul?   Owen of Carron.   John Langhorne.   FaBoCo

Or firm and silken as young peony flowers.   Baby Running Barefoot.   D. H. Lawrence.   NoP

Or float/freely/on the morning's filigree!   She Speaks the Morning's Filigree.   Philip Lamantia.   VGW

Or flowers creeping over Mojave!   Invocation to the Wind.   Joseph Kalar.   AnEnPo

Or foot, or face, or foolish hand.   If Fathers Knew But How to Leave.   *Anonymous.*   EG; EIL

Or for myself in my retreat/For yet another blow.   In Winter in the Woods Alone.   Robert Frost.   HeIP

Or forward to what they might become.   A Way of Speaking.   Gretel Ehrlich.   MAYP

Or fossilized into one set form–/Which alone after all is death.   The Stupid Old Body.   Edward Carpenter.   WGRP

Or gathers seaward, ebbing out of mind.   The Slow Pacific Swell.   Yvor Winters.   ForPo; HeIP; MOS; NoAm; NOBA; QFR

Or ghostly scarecrows walk his dream.   The Late, Last Rook.   Ralph Hodgson.   MoBrPo

Or girl's beauty–a Western spirit in a loved coloured dress of/flesh.   Epitaph on a Young Child.   Ivor Gurney.   FaBoEE

Or give me strength enough to bear/My load of misery.   If This Be All.   Anne Bronte.   TrPWD

Or give the mighty will, or give the good man power.   An Excelente Balade of Charitie.   Thomas Chatterton.   CEP; EBEV; EnPE; EnRP; GoTL; LAuP; LiTB; NOEC; OBEC; SeCePo

Or go about my business well abroad,/And naught to hinder...   A Looking-Glass for Smokers (excerpt).   Lawrence Spooner.   NOEC

Or go out of our single mind/to have another child.   Children.   Sandra McPherson.   FaBoWP

Or grief may pierce, or falling, seem to fall.   Walking to Dedham.   David Wright.   NeBP

Or–gulp–somebody else!   She Sees Another Door Opening (parody).   Firman Houghton.   Par

Or hate you but i will have you/have you have you.   Her Love Poem.   Lucille Clifton.   GP

Or have the mountains eaten me?   Nightmare on Rhum.   James Macmillan.   PoSH

Or have you been holding the end of a frayed rope/For a thousand years?   As I Step over a Puddle at the End of Winter.   James Wright.   CAPP; NaP

Or have you never suffered/And tasted misery?   The Reed.   Mikhail Yuryevich Lermontov.   AWP

Or have you, polyvowelled friends/conspired in brief white nights/to make a truly light champagne?   Finnair Fragment.   Roald Hoffmann.   SUW

Or hear old Triton blow his wreathed horn.   Sonnet: "The world is too much with us."   William Wordsworth.   LoBV; ViBoPo

...Or hear the tinkling knell/Of water-breaks, with grateful heart could tell.   The Unremitting Voice of Nightly Streams.   William Wordsworth.   NOBV

Or heart-shaped mulberry leaf.   Woman Without Fear.   George Dillon.   AnEnPo

Or help her old mother to wring 'em.   Limerick: "There was a young lady at Bingham."   *Anonymous.*   LiBL

Or help me soon, or cast me off for ever!   Diana.   Henry Constable.   OBSC

Or her kisses where a serpent hides.   Returning, We Hear the Larks.   Isaac Rosenberg.   BrPo; FaBoMo; MMM; OAEL 1-2; OBWP; VWA; WaaP

Or his mither take him frae cauld!'   The Queen of Elfland's Nourrice.   *Anonymous.*   FaBoCh

Or how beloved above all else that dies.   And You As Well Must Die, Beloved Dust.   Edna St. Vincent Millay.   FPL; PoLf; PoRA; TAP

Or how I dance for their frightened,/unawakened, sweet/women.   Belly Dancer.   Diane Wakoski.   NIP

Or howl like Lear, or laugh like a green child.   December Day, Hoy Sound.   George Mackay Brown.   OxBS

Or I a traitor turn.   Turtle Dove.   *Anonymous.*   FSW

Or I have spent the night in bed, and was it all a dream?   Night for Adventures.   Victor Starbuck.   HBV 1-2

Or I'll have to find you all over the place   Ben Plays Hide & Seek in the Deep Woods.   Geof Hewitt.   FAZ

Or I'll kill your father and mother tonight.   Crow, Crow, Get out of My Sight.   *Anonymous.*   PBBP

Or I'll ne'er draw thee, but against a post.   One Writing against His Prick.   *Anonymous.*   TW

Or I must goo to workhouse, I do fear. Eclogue. William Barnes. VLP

Or I shall "man' you both, horrible pair! I'll Have You by the Short and Curly Hair. Caius Valerius Catullus. PeHV

Or I shall quickly grow/To Frost or Snow. Upon a Delaying Lady. Robert Herrick. PoPle

Or I suppose I can. Self's the Man. Philip Larkin. NOBL

...Or I will/Come down to you. To the Muse. James Wright. NNaP

Or if all else has vanished into air,/Take me. The Constant One. George Dillon. AmLP

Or if all my love's been effaced. Human Soul. Rene Maran. TTY

Or if for me they rise and pass. Kitchen Window. J. E. H. MacDonald. CaP

Or if he hadn't just stepped out. Blue Max. Harvey Shapiro. GP

Or if he's only guessing. Chanticleer. John Farrar. SoPo; TiPo

...Or if I just wanted/to go nowhere at all. Rogation Days. Kenneth Rexroth. NaP

Or, if I strive, still must I blindly follow. An Invocation. John Addington Symonds. TrPWD; TRV; WGRP

Or if it must be ridden at last, let it bear a hero on its back. Wild Horse. Elder Olson. GrPl

Or if not that, prepared in fall to fall. Squash in Blossom. Robert Francis. FYAP

Or if the Act be good, yet maist thou plead/A second Freedome; for the flesh is dead. Emblems. Francis Quarles. AnAnS 1

Or, if the heart provide, a snake. Priapus and the Pool. Conrad Aiken. AnAmPo

Or if they ever found their Faith again. Charite Esperance et Foi. Earle Birney. OxBC

Or, if they sing, 'tis with so dull a cheer,/That leaves look pale, dreading the winter's near. Sonnets, XCVII: "How like a winter hath my absence been." William Shakespeare. ATP; AWP; CBEP; DiPo; FaBoEn; GTBS; GTBS-P; NOBE; OAEL 1-2; OBEV; OBSC; PoRA; TEP; TrGrPo

Or if, this night, happiness too is going. Arrivals, Departures. Philip Larkin. MoBrPo

Or, if thou bid me yet,/Then dost thou bid me die. Song: "Oh, bid my tongue be still." Richard Watson Dixon. VLP

Or if thou more cruell prove/Learne of steel and stones to love. The Magnet. Thomas Stanley. MePo; NOBE

Or if Virtue feeble were,/Heaven itself would stoop to her. A Mask Presented at Ludlow Castle (Comus). John Milton. ViBoPo

Or, if your fancy will be farther led/To find her woman, it must be abed. Prologue to The Tempest. John Dryden. EnL

Or in a blind man's cup. Old Joyce. Sean Jennett. NeIP

Or in a cave which only the dead inhabit. Cave. Jose Emilio Pacheco. AMV-81

Or in front, and I followed her just the same. Children of Adam. Walt Whitman. AP

Or in sea-song be drowned to death. Summer Afternoon. Elizabeth B. Harrod. NePoEA

Or in the glass come see your face. Anecdote of the Sparrow. Robert Pack. NePA

Or in the light of deeper eyes/Is matter for a flying smile. In Memoriam A.H.H., LXII. Alfred, Lord Tennyson. VLP

Or in the sea each watery spiritual sphere. In Him. James Vila Blake. WGRP

Or-in-tho-rhyn-chus Par-a-dox-us. The Platypus. Oliver Herford. FiBHP; NA

Or in your own breast place the suicidal blow. To a Very Beautiful Lady. Ruthven Todd. BSV; NeBP

Or is God a large rabbit? Tour de Force. Peter Kane Dufault. ErPo

Or is it a whirlpool/twitching with memory? Dorothy. Alfred Kreymborg. AnAmPo

Or is it because Secrecy/gains females loud applause To Nobodaddy. William Blake. DiPo; OAEL 1-2

Or is it mere sophistry, John "Doctor' Donne? Death Again (parody). T. Hope. BXAP

Or is it the ghosts/In silver hosts/Of birds that were drowned at sea? Flying Fish. Mary McNeil Fenollosa. AA

Or is my voice in a stranger's hands? Etude for Voice and Hand. Gabriel Levin. VWA

Or is the above to be our planet? Nuclear Land. Ellen Tuft. AMV-81

Or is the Caucasian played out? Further Language from Truthful James. Bret (Francis Bret Harte) Harte. FaBoCo; NOBL

Or is there blessedness like theirs? In Memoriam A.H.H., XXXII. Alfred, Lord Tennyson. VLP

Or is there still in those great eyes/That look of lonely hills and skies? Spirit of Sadness. Richard Le Gallienne. HBV 1-2

Or it brings the heart/Smart/And pain. Silent Love. Anonymous. LiTW

Or it goes to the backyard and stands like/an old horse cold in the pasture. Original Sin: A Short Story. Robert Penn Warren. AmP; CrMA; HoPM; LiTA; LiTM; MoVE; NOCV; PPP; SM; TAP

Or it is enough when what is wanted, unfortunately or not,/is more than enough. The Bells Are Ringing for Me and Chagall. Terence Winch. APU

Or it may be she's tricked by me/Wearing her grandpa's hat. Be a Monster. Roy Fuller. AmMo

Or just about/Like other folks. Professors. Harold A. Larrabee. InMe

Or just some human sleep. After Apple-Picking. Robert Frost. AnNE; CMoP; CoBMV; DiPo; ForPo; FPL; InPS; LiTA; MoAB; MoAmPo; MoPo; MoVE; NoAm; NOBA; NU; OxBA; PPP; PrIm; RoGo; TAP; UnPo; ViBoPo

Or kettle whispering its faint undersong. Personal Talk. William Wordsworth. InPo; MyFE; NOBE

Or kiss the lips you once betrayed. Fond Affection. Anonymous. AS

Or knew they had ridden a Magic Stair! Hump, the Escalator. Dorothy Faubion. BrR

Or knight of the shire/Lives half so well as a holy friar! The Friar of Orders Gray. John O'Keeffe. OnYI; OxBI

Or know what we can never act,/Or what we cannot say. For My Students, Returning to College. John Williams. NePoAm-2

Or lament that the pleasure is ended? To Papilus. Martial (Marcus Valerius Martialis). PeHV

Or lapse for ever into a classic fatigue. Consider This and in Our Time. W. H. Auden. FaBoMo; LiTB

Or lay behind them, maybe, in the ruined cities. Safe Places. Constance Urdang. GP

...Or lay your/life frail as a rose petal against my face. Orphans. David Ray. FiCP

Or lean together laughing to notice this wild haired madman who sits/weeping among you a stranger. Cafe in Warsaw. Allen Ginsberg. HAP

Or learn to bear with grace his tragic part. This Life a Theater. Palladas. NIP

Or leave the lover's state. Olden Love-Making. Nicholas Breton. DiPo; OBSC

Or lend my soul seraphic wings,/To get to Thee. The Invitation. Anonymous. OxBoCh

Or Lenin with his cry of Dare We Win. The Motive of All of It. Muriel Rukeyser. MiAP

Or lest the burly oarsman turn his prow/Within your guardian isle. A Passer-By. Robert Bridges. BrPo

...Or let it go/for life with its three possibilities! I Have a Terrible Fear of Being an Animal. Cesar Vallejo. EAS

Or let me be more to thee. The Appeal. Samuel Daniel. OLR

Or let us Glory gain, or Glory give! The Iliad. Homer. OBVE

Or, like my own Herrings, I soon shall be dead. Herrings. Jonathan Swift. NCEP; OnYI

Or like th' offended sky/Frown death immediately. A la Bourbon. Richard Lovelace. CaPo

Or like the lights/In quiet rooms/Left on for hours,/Burning, burning. Bus Stop. Donald Justice. LCAP

Or like the look some lovely she sends shining on our battery. Calligram, 15 May 1915. Guillaume Apollinaire. OBWP

Or like the tender struggle of a fan). Flags. Gwendolyn Brooks. AmNP

Or like walking/past shut doors/in a never quiet street and talking. He Met Her at the Green Horse... Peter Levi. NePoEA-2

Or link by precious link forge chains that hold/The wandering passions of men in one vast fold. The Gully. Furnley Maurice. BoAV

Or listen into silence, like a god. The Swan. Theodore Roethke. VGW

Or look in a gipsy's eye. Where Do the Gipsies Come From? Sir Henry Howarth Bashford. ALV

Or look tireless to the stars/and a ripped doorbell. I Walk in the Old Street. Louis Zukofsky. VGW

...Or looking/at the photograph of a dead lover. In a Cafe. Richard Brautigan. PCP

Or Love in a golden bowl? Thel's Motto. William Blake. ChTr; CLRP; DiPo

Or Love that swoons on sleep, or else delight/That is as wide-eyed as a marigold. The Green River. Lord Alfred Bruce Douglas. HBMV; OBEV; OBVV

Or made it an image of their heart. Poem: "Pity, repulsion, love and anger." Roy Fuller. NeBP

Or make a heart that's like our own! A Sonnet Made on Isabella Markham. John (fl. 1550) Harington. EIL; OBSC

Or make me unremember choirs/that sang for me in June. June. Wilson MacDonald. CaP

Or man a woman halfe so faire. There Is None, O None But You. Thomas Campion. AtBAP; EIL; HBV 1-2

Or, man, forsake thyself, to heaven turn thee,/Her flames enlighten nature, never burn thee. Caelica, LXXXVI. Fulke, Lord Brooke Greville. FCP; JCP

Or maybe hear the thunderan sea/...Wantan me. Leander Stormbound. Sydney Goodsir Smith. OxBS

Or maybe I will stay a child. The Question. Karla Kuskin. NTCP

Or maybe, manager for some liquor chain.   Support Your Local Police Dog. Carter Revard.   VoR

Or maybe yet–/Olivet?   Joy's Peak.   Robert Farren.   ISi

Or maybe you have wisely moved to the country/in your old age?   Walking Past Paul Blackburn's Apt. on 7th St.   Diane Wakoski.   TAP

Or Medway smooth, or royal towred Thame.   Rivers Arise.   John Milton. FaBoPP

Or meeting myself very suddenly/In a little-known part of any town.   Five Stanzas on Perfection.   George Jonas.   PeCV

Or memory would transfigure them, and show/Them always fair.   At Casterbridge Fair.   Thomas Hardy.   EnLi 1-2; NoAm; OBNC

Or men have mixt with Beasts and so,/Brought forth that monstrous Race. When Indians Heare That Some There Are.   Roger Williams.   SCAP

Or merely the pause/between monster and monster.   Rhinoceros.   Adrien Stoutenburg.   BoAnP

Or Mezz Mezzrow...   Paterson.   William Carlos Williams.   CMoP

Or mind nothing can slit her/free of.   At the Long Island Jewish Geriatric Home.   Jorie Graham.   NPGG

Or mocking winds whirl round a chaff-strown floor/Thee and thy years and these my words and me.   Memorial Thresholds.   Dante Gabriel Rossetti. MaVP

Or money, that connects with government everywhere.   The Shoulder. Edwin Denby.   ANYP

Or Montcalm, propped in the backstage/Ruin of battle.   Quebec.   Eldon Grier.   PeCV

Or mumble petulant inanities?   Danny.   Malcolm Cowley.   PoA

Or Muses that uses/At fountain Helicon.   The Cherry and the Slae (excerpt). Alexander Montgomerie.   GoTS

Or must you call me nigger?   Cap'n & Me.   Leon Baker.   LFAC

Or, "Nardoo is no fit food for white men."   Burke and Wills.   Ken Barratt. BoAV; PoAu 1-2

Or Nature's DARKLING of this mossy shed?   The Contrast: The Parrot and the Wren.   William Wordsworth.   FM

Or news of me cutting my throat/Would move you enough.   Stiles.   John Pudney.   NYBP

Or noon in mazarin?   Utterance.   Emily Dickinson.   AA

Or North America of yesterday today and tomorrow...   Birth.   Edith Bruck. BoWoP

...Or of the sad/corruption of their leaders.   12 O'Clock News.   Elizabeth Bishop.   GP; OxBC; WeW

Or on the struck tambour.   Song for a Slight Voice.   Louise Bogan.   AmLP

Or once presume to move, but as they move in thee.   Emblem.   Francis Quarles.   EBEV

Or one cell's shadow/in the great body of growing/we grow in.   Song: "What binds the atom together."   Philip Dow.   NPGG

Or one forgets the joy to which we were born.   A Mourning Letter from Paris.   Conrad Kent Rivers.   BPo

Or one vain wit's, that might a hundred tire.   An Essay on Criticism. Alexander Pope.   OBSV

Or only for what has been.   Owning a Dead Man.   Marcia Southwick. AMV-80; MAYP

Or only more intelligently mad?   After Reading a Book on Abnormal Psychology.   Ernest G. Moll.   ELU

Or only the delights, which you did give?   To a Lady Who Did Sing Excellently.   Edward, Lord Herbert of Cherbury.   AnAnS 2; OBS; SeCP

Or ope the sacred source of sympathetic tears.   The Progress of Poesy. Thomas Gray.   ATP

Or Orange golden as the breast.   Ward Two.   Francis Webb.   CBAP

Or overrated thy designs.   Prayer.   Henry David Thoreau.   AmePo; AnNE

...Or part of someone dead/Who thought that life was choice, not accident. Good People.   Maura Stanton.   SM

Or passing gale or hum of murmuring bees!   Inscription for a Fountain on a Heath.   Samuel Taylor Coleridge.   ERoP 1-2; MCCG; OAEP

Or passing through it, all signs/Of them vanishing into the hills.   Parish. Norman Dubie.   MAYP

Or perches in the branch her soul has chosen.   Salt.   Monk Gibbon.   OxBI

Or perhaps a joke we didn't quite hear.   Cain.   Irving Layton.   PeCV

–Or perhaps/like gunpowder.   Self-Portrait.   Cecil Bodker.   BoWoP

Or placed thy friends above her stern decrees?   The Complaint.   Mark Akenside.   OBEV

Or plant of wondrous powers of which we dream!   Soul-Sickness.   Jones Very.   AP

Or play the veins of their strong tender arms/with needles/to prove how proud we are.   A Dance for Ma Rainey.   Al Young.   NBP

Or playing at making designs.   Americans Are Afraid of Lizards.   Karl Shapiro.   AmFN

Or pleasures, seldom reach'd, again pursu'd.   A Nocturnal Reverie.   Anne Finch, Countess of Wilchilsea.   CEP; EBEV; FaBoEn; GoTL; LoBV; NOEC; NoP; OBEC; PBWP; PoEL 1-5; SBG; SeCePo

Or prepare for a hot but interesting tour/Through a tight personal corner of hell.   Shut Up, I Said.   Peggy Bennett.   ELU

Or prove as false as thou art now.   The Message.   John Donne.   EIL; EnLit; MBW 1-2; MeLP; OBS; ViBoPo; WHA

Or Queen Persephone's gaze/In the numb fields of the dark.   Stop.   Richard Wilbur.   LCAP

Or rather make no Thine and Mine.   Clasping of Hands.   George Herbert. ILwL; PoEL 1-5

Or reach for the sky/for the 500th time?   Identities.   Al Young.   NPGG

Or read the book. It's shorter.   To a Certain Most Certainly Certain Critic. David McCord.   OBAL

Or read to thyself alone/The songs that I made for thee.   When Death to Either Shall Come.   Robert Bridges.   HBV 1-2; OBEV; PoPl

Or relaxing on the train back to New York, the parachute as a/souvenir. The City in the Throes of Despair.   Tony Towle.   ANYP

Or remember how his poet took a girl to Saadabad?   Saadabad.   James Elroy Flecker.   SeCePo

Or remember that that fifteen-year campaign/Won seven years of peace?   The Cost.   Anthony Hecht.   OxBC

Or remove the eyelid/To see the end.   The Crystal.   George Barker. LiTM; OBMV

Or return the scolding promise/to wish me safe love again.   The Death of a Negro Poet.   Conrad Kent Rivers.   BPo

Or roaring of a fierce/lion given to/the wind.   Afternoon in the Tropics. Ruben Dario.   LiTW

(Or, roughly, the peace that passeth understanding.)   Make Love Not War. Howard Nemerov.   NAs; NoAm

Or, Round the world?   American Jump.   *Anonymous.*   OxNR

Or, sad-eyed lady, should I wait?   Sad-Eyed Lady of the Lowlands.   Bob Dylan.   BiP

Or sailed off on the broad back of a swan.   Hidden Valley.   E. G. Burrows. HoAn

...Or satisfy my itch/Upon some farmyard ass or common bitch.   Unto the Breach.   Andrea Poliziano.   PeHV

Or say, the foresight that awaits/Is the same genius that creates.   Fate. Ralph Waldo Emerson.   ForPo

Or scull him across that rough river to me!   The Waters of Tyne. *Anonymous.*   GBP

Or seeing, saw as deadly company   November Walk.   Susanne Doyle. AMV-81

Or seekest thou, in mouldering realms of night,/Rest, by the crumbling comrades, out of sight?   The Wilderness.   Gyula Juhasz.   LiTW

Or seems to deny, or in denying grants.   Providence.   Vincenzo da Filicaja. CAW

Or seen in the wind their glittering wild hair flow?   Of the Scythians.   Katha Pollitt.   SM

Or sees the eagles gathering, the farms afire?   The Garden.   George M. Brady.   NeIP

Or send some answer far more blest.   Prayer.   Eliza M. Hickok.   BLRP

Or shake his trust in God!'   The Last Man.   Thomas Campbell.   EnRP; OBRV

Or shall at last, it be mine to find/That all I'd worked for is left behind?   Out of This Life.   *Anonymous.*   STF

Or shall I marry old knives-and-scissors/Shouting through the town?   Mirror, Mirror.   Robert Graves.   HBMV

Or shall I pull it in/To rhyme upon a dish?   Word.   Stephen Spender. NYBP; PP

...Or shall some floating thing/Upon the river point me out my course?   Oh There Is Blessing in This Gentle Breeze.   William Wordsworth.   TreFT

Or share, what still is worse–old Charles's fate.   George the Third's Soliloquy. Philip Freneau.   NOBA

Or she'll kill you all e'en now.   Snail Hunters.   *Anonymous.*   OxNR

Or shipped on commodious sands whatever pleasure/Of the moment as august as sorrow burned.   Big, Fat Summer–and the Lean and Hard.   Frederick Bock.   NYBP

Or Silence lay her kiss on Music's mouth!   Music at Twilight.   George Sterling.   HBV 1-2

Or silks or gold.   The Ship.   J. C. Squire.   CH

Or sing at the Cytherean's shrine.   Home, Sweet Home.   Henry Cuyler Bunner.   CenHV

Or sink and merge forever/In that which bids them be.   Veni Creator.   Bliss Carman.   WGRP

Or sitting drunk in my coffin...   And Don't Bother Telling Me Anything. Cesar Vallejo.   EAS

Or sleep grunting all winter.   Rose Red to Snow White.   Joan Colby.   DFT

Or sleep is the golden goal.   Davis Matlock.   Edgar Lee Masters.   LiTA; LiTM

Or sleet sharp at a pane?   A Puritan Lady.   Lizette Woodworth Reese. AnAmPo; MoAmPo

Or snafu–if you know what we mean.   Limerick: "In this book every line has been clean."   *Anonymous.*   LiBL

Or so believes the Board of Ed.   Primary Education.   Phyllis McGinley. GLGT

Or so kind-hearted, any may procure them.   Are Women Fair?   Francis Davison.   HBV 1-2

Or so men think who like a different tree.   Aspens.   Edward ("Edward Eastaway") Thomas.   ChMP; InPS; PAI

Or so we say of three clear tones/That in eternal quiet lie.   Music God. Mark Van Doren.   UnS

Or some shy angel calling me/To follow far away?   Nightingales.   Grace Hazard Conkling.   HBMV

Or something curious in its place?   Curious Something.   Winifred Welles. TiPo

Or sour the sweetness that in thee I tasted.   Poietes Apoietes.   Hartley Coleridge.   OBNC

Or Southey, or Barrow.'   Who Kill'd John Keats?   George Gordon, Lord Byron.   EnRP

Or speed like arrows, swift and sure to the mark.   Envoy.   James Weldon Johnson.   TrPWD

Or spoor of pads, or a bird's adept splay.   Age.   Philip Larkin.   CMoP

Or spot lovely Melisande leaning out from an upper floor/to let down her long golden hair.   Looking at the Empire State Building.   Ralph Pomeroy. GP

Or stain a point with blood.   Ghostly Tree.   Léonie Adams.   MoAB; MoAmPo

Or stand a fisherman.   Fishermen.   James A. Emanuel.   BP

Or stand above some Eastern monarch's/throne.   The Scarlet Tanager.   Joel Benton.   AA; AmLP

Or stand all night watering roses, his feet blue/in rubber boots.   Old Florist. Theodore Roethke.   CTBA; NCSH; OBSP; PCP; SaC

Or stare at the right rondure of the wheel.   Form Was the World.   Maurice English.   NYBP

–Or starve yourself, and starve me, and be right.'   Plea.   John Ciardi. OBSP

Or stay!–because thou art/Only Myself.   Death Deposed.   William Allingham.   OnYI

Or still in night's dark prison stay.   He Came Unlook'd For.   Sara Coleridge.   OBRV

Or stop the four winds racing overhead/Nought/Waste/Eased/Sought Syrinx.   James Merrill.   HaCAP

Or strip away its gaudy facade/And let it die.   Allegory in Black.   Carl Clark.   JB

Or such as did in fury turn/Th' Assyrian's palace to his urn.   Marvell's Ghost.   John Ayloffe.   APAS

Or summer detonate in our heads.   These Apple Trees.   Valentin Iremonger. NeIP

Or sure I must envy the song.   A Pastoral Ballad in Four Parts.   William Shenstone.   CEP

Or surely the day after that/would be lighter/and bluer/and easier-/and less lonely.   Less Lonely.   Alfred Kreymborg.   AnAmPo

Or sweet the golden glue/That's built for by the bee.   On a Piece of Music. Gerard Manley Hopkins.   UnS

Or Tantalus, with streams that shone as golden.   On Lisa's Golden Hair. Roy Campbell.   AtBAP

Or tell me, tyrants, have you both agreed/That where one reigns the other shall succeed?   Jealousy.   Esther Johnson.   OBSP

Or th' innocence of children's plays,/Or lamps in ancient urns.   To Her Lover's Complaint.   Jane Barker.   OBSP

...Or that misfortune/placed these worlds in us.   The Lost Pilot.   James Tate.   CoAP; NoP; OBWP; TwCP; UnPo

Or that soft chain of spoken flowers/and airy gems,–thy words.   Song: "We break the glass, whose sacred wine."   Edward Coate [(or Coote)] Pinkney. HBV 1-2

Or that the languages of sap and blood/are only wood and word/and therefor good.   Morning Dialogue.   Conrad Aiken.   NoAm

Or that there is no caste in this family.   Further Instructions.   Ezra Pound. AnAmPo; MP; TwCP

..Or that these prayers be/For weariness of life, not love of thee.   To Heaven. Ben Jonson.   AnAnS 2; EnRePo; ExPo; ForPo; HAP; ILwL; JCP; LiTB; LoBV; NOCV; OBS; PPoe; QFR; SeCeV; SeCP; TrPWD; UnPo

Or the best of our pleasures may turn into pain.   The Mouse and the Cake. Eliza Cook.   OxBChV

Or the bosom it dwelt in, stone.   The River in the Meadows.   Léonie Adams.   AnAmPo; MoAB; MoAmPo

Or the burden of Atlas falling?   Street Song.   Edith Sitwell.   CMoP; CoBMV; MoPo; MoVE

Or the Chaplain (for 'tis his trade,) as in duty bound,/shall ever pray.   Mrs. Frances Harris's Petition.   Jonathan Swift.   CBEP; CEP; OxBI

Or the day's vanity, the night's remorse.   The Choice.   William Butler Yeats.   CMoP; NoAm; OBSP; OxBTC

Or the deer who shyly from afar/Peer through chinks in the forest.   Nones. W. H. Auden.   CoBMV

Or the doctrine of the Trinity.   Rillons, Rillettes.   Richard Wilbur.   NYBP

Or the features of the man/who should be bones.   On Learning That Certain Peat Bogs Contain Perfectly Preserved Bodies.   Susan Ludvigson.   MAYP

...Or the film/played backwards on his grandson's eyes.   Grandfather. Michael S. Harper.   FiCP; GeTw; LCAP; TAP

Or the first cloud so terrible and still/That bears the coming harvest in its breast.   The Zulu Girl.   Roy Campbell.   AtBAP; MoVE; OBMV; PoPl

Or the Great Santa Barbara Oil Disaster/OR: The Great Santa Barbara Oil Disaster OR:.   Conyus.   AmPA

...Or the hoarser tide/That parts fam'd Trachis from th' Euboic shore. Sonnet Suppos'd to Be Written at Lemnos.   Thomas Russell.   CEP; NOEC; OBEC

Or the home of the victor=folk, where He Himself dwells.   Cotton Manuscript: Maxims.   Anonymous.   AnOE

Or the hoot of a horned owl/On a glacial stone.   Come Not the Seasons Here.   Edwin John Pratt.   NoP; PeCV

Or the horrible beautiful kind?   Question in a Field.   Louise Bogan. NYBP; SBG

Or the King's young courtiers.   The Old and Young Courtier.   Anonymous. ViBoPo

Or the light/they wept at   Tale of Genji.   Hugh Seidman.   AmPA

Or the night-porter's knowledgeable smile.   The Small Hotel.   Michael Longley.   CIP

Or the old grasshopper molasses-mouthed.   Thin Little Leaves of Wood Fern, Ribbed and Toothed.   Frederick Goddard Tuckerman.   TAP

Or the one flower of ease in bitterest hell?   Memory.   Dante Gabriel Rossetti.   CBEP; OBSP

Or the outstretched arms of the crucified man.   Walking in London.   Wrey Gardiner.   NeBP

Or the Palace of Cyrus, cemented with gold.   The Seven Wonders of the Ancient World.   Anonymous.   EyDe; GoTF; TreFT

Or the Persians and Xerxes? His judges, or Socrates?/Pilate, or Christ?   Io Victis.   William Wetmore Story.   AA; HBV 1-2; WGRP

Or the red cup, when I am drunken yet.   Haroun al-Rachid for Heart's-Life. Anonymous.   AWP

Or the rest will be wanting one, too!'   Limerick: "An epicure, dining at Crewe."   Anonymous.   CenHV; LiBL; NLV; NTCP

Or the sand alone,/For the blank sand.   At Staufen.   Michael Hamburger. VWA

Or the songs of the butterflies be.   Eutopia.   Francis Turner Palgrave. OBVV

Or the sound of the water when it is flowing.   Rebirth.   Antonio Machado. NU

Or the stone heart probed of a Syrian tower.   Two Women.   Tania Van Zyl. PeSA

Or the strong hand reaching towards/you, about to make you famous/and pregnant.   Folds of a White Dress/Shaft of Light.   Deborah Keenan. PoDr

Or the sweet coming of the evening star.   True Love.   James Russell Lowell. LiTL

Or the tears of a girl remembering her dread.   Vaunting Oak.   John Crowe Ransom.   OxBA; VGW

Or the trees on a familiar street, repeating/and repeating.   Ruston, Louisiana: 1952.   Cleopatra Mathis.   AMV-80

Or the unimaginable touch of Time.   Mutability.   William Wordsworth. CABA; EBEV; ERoP 1-2; ExPo; HeIP; InPK; LiTB; NOBE; NoP; OAEL 1-2; OBEV; OBRV; PoEL 1-5; PrIm; SeCeV

Or Thebes half buried in the desert sand.   The Rock of Cashel.   Sir Aubrey De Vere.   IrPN; NBM

Or these sharp spangles trammelling the wind's beak.   Birdsong.   James Burns Singer.   FaBoTw

Or they'll lock us up like the apes, and control us forever.   Singing Aloud. Carolyn Kizer.   IHMS

Or they will be sand as you; and I, a shadow/Upon them, ever length-ening in the sun.   Epilogue of the Wandering Jew.   Colin Newbury.   AnNZ

Or they will not be catch'd, whate'er you do.   Neither Hook nor Line.   John Bunyan.   LiSp; SD

Or they will take thee for an owl.   On Himself.   Walter Savage Landor. FaBoEE

Or think it strange I often wish I warn't an inventor's wife?   The Inventor's Wife.   Mrs. E. R. Corbett.   PoLf

Or think me strange who long to be/Wrapped in their cool immunity.   The Wise.   Countee Cullen.   PoNe

Or Think We've Met subhuman rights Before   A Salesman Is an It That Stinks Excuse.   Edward Estlin Cummings.   AmP; DBV; NIP; NoAm; OxBA; TW

Or think you can bargain for/Wild flower grace.   Spring Market.   Louise Driscoll.   HBMV; HBVY

Or those fish spread flat on newspaper,/something for the eye.   Mountain Study.   Peter Van Toorn.   NOBC

Or those not seen, but understood,/That live in vinegar and wood.   Sidrophel, the Rosicrucian Conjurer.   Samuel (1602-80) Butler.   OxBoLi

Or thou alone, To tell what others were, came down?   An Epicurean Ode. John Hall.   EG; MeLP

...Ordinary air/on fire every blessed day I waken the world. On My Own. Philip Levine. FYAP

An organ grinder in Pine street. These Purists. William Carlos Williams. OBAL

The organ with the organ man/Is singing in the rain. Singing. Robert Louis Stevenson. SUS

The original great-mother,/who drove/harnessed scorpions/before her. The Walls Do Not Fall. Hilda ("H. D.") Doolittle. PBWP

Orion in a cobweb, and the World. Beloved, Let Us Once More Praise the Rain. Conrad Aiken. LiTA; UnPo

Orisha Orisha Satchmo Orisha. Orisha. Jayne Cortez. BlSi

Orlando is quite a philosopher. The Political Orlando. George Macbeth. NOBL

The ornamental water of the mind. Ornamental Water. Louise Townsend Nicholl. NePoAm

Orpheus' Sermon captivated–/It did not condemn–. The Bible Is an Antique Volume. Emily Dickinson. AmePo; MAmP; NoP

'Orse, foot an' guns, The Service Man/'Enceforward, evermore! The Service Man. Rudyard Kipling. Par

Oscar! my toby, and I'll sin a skinful,/So to bed gayly Persicos Odi. Charles Edmund Merrill, Jr. AA

...Ossian, last of all his race!/Lies buried in this lonely place. Glen-Almain, the Narrow Glen. William Wordsworth. GTBS

Other bells that we would ring. At the New Year. Kenneth Patchen. AnFE; LiTM

The other cast away, she only gave. The Widow's Mites. Richard Crashaw. OxBoCh

The other could not mate. The Primrose Bed. Robert Graves. TEP

...Other earths/rock this one, so queerly stuck in the sun's throat. Poem: "There is a Wailing Baby Under Every Stone." Norman MacCaig. EAS

The other, far on this side of the stars,/By men called home. Two Heavens. [James Henry] Leigh Hunt. GN

The other Florida/of patient Africanus. Florida. Carl Rakosi. TAP

Other graffiti of the prisoners of this world. Wall, Cave, and Pillar Statements, After Asoka. Alan Dugan. CoAP

The other great eye/closed Kathe Kollwitz. Muriel Rukeyser. NMM

Other help for him I know there's none. A Shepherd's Complaint. Richard Barnfield. OBSC

Other joys/Are but toys,/And to be lamented. The Angler. John Chalkhill. HBV 1-2

Other little children/Shall bring my boats ashore. Where Go the Boats? Robert Louis Stevenson. FaBoBe; FaBoCh; GoJo; NTCP; OxBChV; SoPo; SUS; TiPo; TreFT

The other marks them crumble, silently. An Old Thought. Charles Henry Luders. AA

The other meaning we're alone–apart. Alone. Carolyn Wells. PoToHe

The other never read. Epigram on One who Made Long Epitaphs. Alexander Pope. FaBoEE

The other one got away. Lulu. *Anonymous.* ABF; CoSo

The other open, ready for/His master coming through the door. My Dog. John Kendrick Bangs. BLPA; BLPL; FaBoBe

The other parts will richly please. Upon His Julia. Robert Herrick. SpRo

The other remains/passive today–– Classic Scene. William Carlos Williams. AmP; OxBA

The other's only nice. Two People. Emile Victor Rieu. BBGG

The other side of Nowhere/Led somewhere in the end. Sailor Man. H. Sewall Bailey. EtS

The other side of the mountain,/Was all that he could see! The Bear Went over the Mountain. *Anonymous.* BLSo

...Other strangers/Will put their mouths together. Reasons. Thomas James. PoA

The other sun, the jealous coursing of the unrivalled blood. On the Marriage of a Virgin. Dylan Thomas. EnLoPo; HW

The other swollen bellies. Epigram: "Poverty? wealth? seek neither." Kassia. WPOW

Other than all the love he can muster/and all the man he can be. Of an Old Con. George, Jr Mosby. LFAC

Other than this, my song of love to thee. The Camel-Rider. *Anonymous.* AWP

Other the flute craft. Snatches: "Levere is the wrenne." *Anonymous.* OxBM

The other voice in a silence of blood, 'neath the noise of/the ash. Discord in Childhood. D. H. Lawrence. CBEP; ELU

Other voices are also somehow dimly you. Autobiography, Chapter XII. Jim Barnes. AMV-81

Other wives. Business Trips. Laurie Taylor. AMV-80

Others are already descending through gates of ivory and horn. Scala Coeli. Kathleen Raine. NYBP

Others do otherwise/Maybe I Live Up Here. William Stanley Merwin. CAPP

...Others fight below/With gnats, and shaddowes, others nothing know. The Poetaster. Ben Jonson. PoEL 1-5

Others, one day nearer spring. February Thaw. G. J. F. Dutton. PoSH

Others sing clapping their hands. Assembly. William Stanley Merwin. GP

The others thought of tomorrow, but they/Only remembered yesterday. Late October. Sara Teasdale. PoSC; YeAr

Others trap in the snarl of frenzy.' Attis. Caius Valerius Catullus. OBVE

Others will be attracted/From darkness into light. Pray! Irene Arnold. BLRP; STF

Others will come. We make it so. Cairngorm, November 1971. Martyn Berry. PoSH

Others will punctually come for ever and ever. Song of Myself. Walt Whitman. BoLiVe

Otherwise I think I could/Dress in ermine, mink or sable. Poem for Mother's Day. Margaret Fishback. InMe

Otherwise kill me. Prayer before Birth. Louis MacNeice. FaBoIP; GTBS-P; LiTB; MP; NAs; OAEP; TwCP

Ou sont les neiges downtown? Les Chasse-Neige. Ralph A. Lewin. FiBHP

Ought to be told to come and take him in. The Runaway. Robert Frost. AnNE; AWP; FaBoCh; GoJo; HaMV; InPo; LoGBV; MCCG; MoAB; MoAmPo; MP; PH; TiPo; TwCP; VGW; CH

Ought to have a separate bomb for colored! You Know, Joe. Ray Durem. BOLo

Ought to have his lips cut off,/And never kiss another. Come, Landlord, Fill the Flowing Bowl. *Anonymous.* OxBoLi

Ought to inhabit nowhere but the reverence of/the heart. Lyrebirds. Judith Wright. BoAnP; GoJo

Oui, Miche, mo'oule rire. Criole Candjo. *Anonymous.* ABF

"Oui, oui–/Combien?" Comrades in Arms: Conversation Piece. *Anonymous.* ErPo

Our ancient boy (age seven)/Woke up and went to sleep. One Winter Night in August. X. J. Kennedy. OBCA

Our animal passion rooted in the city. Twenty-One Love Poems. Adrienne Rich. PeHV

Our answering spirits chime one/roundelay. The House of Life. Dante Gabriel Rossetti. OAEP

–Our anti-Horace/Of the nuclear American Imperium. Robert Lowell. Richard O'Connell. AMV-81

Our apples rotted, only His crosstree/Bears crimson fruit. But no hand plucks it down. No Return. Vassar Miller. CoPo

Our army was done for. The Soldier. Conrad Aiken. WaaP

Our babes toddle barefoot thru the cities of the universe. Revolutionary Letters. Diane Di Prima. GP

Our babie straight frae Heaven. The Babie. Jeremiah Eames Rankin. AA; HBV 1-2

Our beauty pure expertise. A Poem for Ed "Whitey" Ford. Jonathan Holden. MAYP

Our beauty's Spring, our Prince of Light! Shine Out, Fair Sun. *Anonymous.* ELP

Our beds by their leave lain in. The Eremites. Robert Graves. LiTB

Our beginning, our conveyance, and our journey's end. Open Your Hand. Dorothy R. Fulton. AMV-81

Our blood may seal the victory, but God will shield the Right! The Nineteenth of April. Lucy Larcom. MC; PAH

...Our blue carpet's/Fading evergreen, Pauli. Dayley Island. Frederick Seidel. CoPo

Our bodies turn into reeds, our eyes into nomads. Homage to Chagall. Duane Niatum. CDW

Our bodies twain shall be as one. Take Up the Pen... *Anonymous.* WTO

Our bodies two salt hills and our feet seaweed. Hills of Salt. Dahlia Ravikovich. WPOW

Our Bodyes, not wee move. Song (Attributed to the Earl of Pembroke). George Herbert. AnAnS 1

Our bounds shall be the girdling seas alone. The Dominion of Australia. Brunton Stephens. PoAu 1-2

Our brave and honored captain who died all in command. The Loss of the Cedar Grove. *Anonymous.* ShS

Our breasts are as crashing brass. Our March. Vladimir Mayakovsky. AWP

Our breasts are two inches of dust. Sister Pharaoh. Ruth Whitman. MAT

Our brother, friend, or a creature even of this flesh. On the Apparition of Oneself. William Burford. PoA

Our business is like men to fight,/And hero-like to die! The Cavalier's Song. William Motherwell. GN; HBV 1-2

Our children know and suffer the armed men. Litany For Dictatorships. Stephen Vincent Benét. AnEnPo; NAMP; OxBA

Our children turned to us & said/"umph! dig it!" And We Conquered. Rob Penny. PoBA

Our Christ hath brought us over/With hymns of victory. Resurrection. Saint John of Damascus. PGD

..."Our Christ is arisen, He comes to give a/sign from the Dead." Harvest. Edith Sitwell. CoBMV; OAEP

Our cigarettes so crazy in the dark. The Parents-Without-Partners Picnic. Ted Schaefer. FAZ

Our city tends to disappear in cold weather. How Was Your Trip to L.A.? Philip Whalen. TAT

Our cleanest Light is One! Stranger. Thomas Merton. EaLo

...Our coins/for the guardian of that last river which was the first. Limbo. Marieve Rugo. AMV-81

Our common sorrow, like a mighty wave,/Swept all my pride away, and trembling I forgave! Forgiveness. John Greenleaf Whittier. TrCP

Our country, in fenced areas, in cool shady streets. The One Thing That Can Save America. John Ashbery. NOBA

Our couple have embraced and done it well. The Villanelle. Donald Harington. AMV-81; FAZ

Our course is secret; it is a time of war. Concert at Sea. Hubert Creekmore. WaP

Our crookedness Thou canst make right,/Glory to Thee for aye. Amen. God Our Help. Anonymous. OxBoCh

Our cupboard is bare! Saturday Shopping. Katherine Edelman. SoPo

Our cynic cries—"How damned absurd/To take such pains to make a—-!" The Cynic. St. George Tucker. NLV; OBAL

Our daily lives a prayer. The Quaker of the Olden Time. John Greenleaf Whittier. AnNE

Our daily strength for thee be spent/With thought and loving care. Within the Shelter of Our Walls. Elinor Lennen. AH

Our dark disgrace atoned for by a glorious victory. The Dash for the Colors. Frederick G. Webb. BeLS

Our darkness which can make us think it dark. Sonnet of Black Beauty. Edward, Lord Herbert of Cherbury. AtBAP; MePo

Our darling's now completely frappe!' L'Enfant Glace. Harry Graham. FaBoCo; NLV

Our day is dying: let it die. Swan Song. Som Parkash Ranchan. ACV

Our day, not theirs, as new? Days of the Leaders, 1925: The Deaf. L. Lamprey. BBV

Our days were a joy, and our paths through flowers. After a Journey. Thomas Hardy. AtBAP; CMoP; DTC; EBEV; ELP; EnLoPo; FaBoPP; GBL; GTBS-P; MoVE; OBNC; OxBTC; PoEL 1-5

Our deepest devotion and homage we/bring. The Cradle and the Cross. Albert Simpson Reitz. STF

Our deepest need until...until...until... A Plea for Postponement. Petronius Arbiter (Caius Petronius Arbiter). UnTE

Our dog Fido/Et the pie-dough. The Diners in the Kitchen. James Whitcomb Riley. GDP; OBAL

Our doings have been done,/And that which shall be was. Passing and Glassing. Christina Georgina Rossetti. OBNC

Our door is the door of man. Through an Embrace. Paul Eluard. LiTW

...Our dreams/Flowed into each other's arms, like streams. Daybreak. Stephen Spender. BoLoP; DFF; LiTL

Our drowsy thighs touched and we/Were caught in bed by the dawn. We Dressed Each Other. Empress Eifuku. WPOW

Our Eden-glances follow us as well. After Vacation. Katherine Hanley. AMV-81

Our end is life. Put out to sea. Thalassa. Louis MacNeice. BIrV; FaBoMo; FaBoRV; NOBE

Our end is our own to be won by our own endeavor/And held on our own terms. Explorations. Louis MacNeice. ChMP; CoBMV

Our end nae end/But in thy Grace. The Ineffable Dou. Sydney Goodsir Smith. OxBS

Our enemies/who make us heroes. For a Man Who Learned to Swim When He Was Sixty. Diane Wakoski. FAZ

Our eyes could never see. The Unknown God. George William Russell. GTBS; MoBrPo; WGRP

"Our eyes have seen the living God,/And now—once more to die." The Southern Cross. Robert Stephen Hawker. OxBoCh

Our faces pale as dying men. Finally. Vittoria Pompili. PBWP

Our faith triumphant o'er our fears,/Are all with thee,–are all with thee! O Ship of State. Henry Wadsworth Longfellow. FaFP

Our Father calls, and all my fret is done! Are You There? Strickland Gillilan. PoToHe

Our father, from Thy children's plea/Turn not, we implore Thee! Hymn for Atonement Day. Judah Halevi. TrJP

Our Father, our King, do it for the sake/of thy great, mighty and awful/Name, by which we are called Our Father, Our King. Anonymous. TrJP

Our fingers touching the earth, like two Buddhas. The Fertile Muck. Irving Layton. NOBC; OBCV; PeCV

Our fire their fire surpasses,/And turns all our Lead to Gold. The Highwaymen. John Gay. WiR

Our flocks, upon the leas/May scatter far as wandering bees. Shepherd and Shepherdess. Thomas Hennell. FaBoTw

Our foes on the ocean have been forced/to yield,/And fresh laurels we now gather up in/the field. Capture of Little York. Anonymous. PAH

...Our folk thin/Lamentably. Frog Autumn. Sylvia Plath. OBSP

Our fontanelle, the trout's dimpled feet. The Flower Master. Mebdh McGuckian. FaBoIP

Our foot's in the door. Mushrooms. Sylvia Plath. BoNaP; FaBoWP; NePoEA-2; WeW; WPOW

Our four "hoss" team/Will soon be seen/Way out in Idaho. Idaho. Frank French. BPAW; GBP

Our friend, protector, strength, and trust,/Lies low and mould'ring in the dust. Mount Vernon. Anonymous. AmFP; OFD

"Our game is up, my covies, blow me tight!" The Thieves' Anthology (excerpt) (parody). Sir Theodore Martin. FaBoPa

Our glorious beauty for the upright/heart. Unto the Upright Praise: Chorus. Isaac Luzzatto. TrJP

Our glory at most/Is only that–tyrants recant. Lord North's Recantation. Anonymous. PAH

Our God can give songs in the night. The God of Comfort. Anonymous. STF

Our God, forever more. The Abiding Love. John White Chadwick. BLPA; FaBoBe

Our God hath sent another troop,/And means to carry on the war. Reinforcements. Thomas Toke Lynch. OBVV

Our God is marching on! From Age to Age They Gather. Frederick Lucian Hosmer. AH

Our God's forgotten, and our soldiers slighted. Of Common Devotion. Francis Quarles. FaBoEE; OBSP

Our God, the beginning and end! Johnny Appleseed's Hymn to the Sun. Vachel Lindsay. MoRP

Our God Who imprisons in coffin and grave/and unbinds the bound. New Year's. Charles Reznikoff. OFD

Our government firm, and our citizens free. The New Roof. Francis Hopkinson. PAH

Our Gracious Queen Elizabeth. Grace: "God bless our meat." Anonymous. OxNR

"Our grand old Army held the ridge, and/won that glorious day!" Gettysburg. Edmund Clarence Stedman. PAH

Our guilt is the heroin of Vietnam,/the best smack on the streets. Bring the War Home. William Matthews. GeTw

Our guns have pounded retreat to rout! The Last Lap. Rudyard Kipling. OxBTC

Our guts in love Cycles, Cycles. Suzanne Berger Rioff. NMM

Our hands icepicks and soft blood/Blood in our pockets. The Subway Witnesses. Lorenzo Thomas. PoBA

Our hands leaving little glittering pieces of feeling/behind us. The Dutchman. Don Welch. WOLT

Our hard bed of dreams, his sea flaw-/less. Irish Hotel. David Wevill. NYBP

Our harp is never silent. Harp in the Rigging. Hamish Maclaren. EtS

Our heads are grey from the foam...we are tired from/paddling. The Djanggawul Cycle, 18. Anonymous. WTO

Our headstrong spouses still will have their way! A City Eclogue. W." J. NOEC

Our hearts and lips together. The Blackbird. William Ernest Henley. HBV 1-2; MoBrPo; TrGrPo

Our hearts beat prouder for the blood we inherit. Memorial Wreath. Dudley Randall. CNA; IDB; NNP; PoBA; PoNe

Our hearts' charity's hearth's fire, our thoughts' chivalry's throng's Lord. The Wreck of the Deutschland. Gerard Manley Hopkins. AtBAP; BoC; BrPo; CMoP; CoBMV; DiPo; FaBoMo; LiTB; LiTM; MasP; MoVE; NoAm; NOBE; NOBV; OAEP; OBNC; OxBoCh; PoEL 1-5; SeCePo; SeCeV; TEP; VLP

Our hearts close knit shall feel no chilling/change. Blossom Time. Wilbur Larremore. AA

Our hearts sang together. Bab-Lock-Hythe. Laurence Binyon. MoVE; SD

Our hearts still listen for the landward bells. An Irishman in Coventry. John Hewitt. BIrV; CIP

Our hearts stood still in the hush/Of an age gone by. Martha. Walter De la Mare. GoTF; MoBrPo; TreFS

Our hearts were thwarted by so frail a fence,/And could not break the weak wall that divides. Comfort. May Doney. HBMV

Our hearts with fable gray. History. Robert Penn Warren. NoAm

Our heritage is rich and fair,/And this thy chosen land. To Thee, O God, the Shepherd Kings. John Gardiner Calkins Brainard. AH

Our heritage of hills. Our Heritage. Jesse Stuart. AmFN

Our heritage the sea. A Sea Song. Allan Cunningham. BBV; FaBoBe; FaPoR; GN

Our holding on/and our letting go/and our letting go. No-Kings and the Calling of Spirits. Nancy Willard. LCAP

Our holy and obsolete symbols. Elegy for the Giant Tortoises. Margaret Atwood. BoWoP

..."Our home was where you saw her/Standing in the quarry!" Green Slates. Thomas Hardy. FaBoPP

Our honeymoon lake, ignoring the lit-up land,/Shows blank Orion where to dip his hand. A Bride's Hours. Jean Valentine. FaBoWP

Our honeymoon was nothing more/than breakfast in bed. Niagara Falls Nocturne. Len Gasparini. NeAC

Our hope and stay along a war-worn way,/Whose end is–Christ! He Lifted from the Dust. Helen Rogers Smith. BePJ

Our horses neigh to each other/as we are departing. Taking Leave of a Friend. Li Po. AnFE; SOTW

Our houses need holes for new air and we will get them through/our heads. Elegy for the Silent Voices and the Joiners of Everything. Kenneth Patchen. NaP

Our human touch did on him pass,/And, with our touch, our agony. The Sea-Mew. Elizabeth Barrett Browning. HBV 1-2; VLP

Our humble prayer–/Forever free! Prayer of a Patriot. Henry J. Von Schlichten. BePJ

Our humble, thankful hearts. The Most Acceptable Gift. Matthis ("Asmus") Claudius. BLRP

Our inexperienced troops inspire,/And conquest's laurels gain! Ode to the Inhabitants of Pennsylvania. Anonymous. PAH

Our ingenuous dark demands of each other. Ashokan. Dachine Rainer. NePoAm

Our invisible tongues of silence/understand Earth Song. Thomas Love Peacock. VoR

..."Our island home/Is far beyond the wave; we will no longer roam." The Lotos-Eaters. Alfred, Lord Tennyson. CoBE; FiP; HBV 1-2; OnMSP; TreFT

Our island is full of comfortless noises. Triptych. Seamus Heaney. CIP

Our Jack's come home today! Our Jack's Come Home Today. Anonymous. ShS

Our jaunt must be put off to-morrow. Signs of Rain. Edward Jenner. BLPA; BoNaP; FaBoUs

Our Jesus all these years/keeps them burning out their lives. Cecil County. Ron Welburn. PoBA

Our Jesus Christ is born. Go Tell. Anonymous. EBCP

Our Joe, aged just 20, was killed in the mines. Only a Miner. Anonymous. AmFP

Our Johnnie's no that weel.' Rise Oot Your Bed. John Barr. AnNZ

Our journey is ended in the land of our dream. Sioux Indians. Anonymous. CoSo

Our joy, a rampart to the mind. The Passing Strange. John Masefield. BoLiVe; LiTB; MoAB; MoBrPo; MoPo; OBEV

Our Joy that hath no end. Amen. The Day of Resurrection. Saint John of Damascus. TrCP

Our kin are here./Were here. The Forgiveness Dream: Man from the Warsaw Ghetto. Jean Valentine. LCAP

"Our King was with us–yesterday!" The King. Rudyard Kipling. CABA; VLP

Our knowledge is historical, flowing, and flown. At the Fishhouses. Elizabeth Bishop. CoAP; FaBoWP; HaCAP; HAP; LCAP; LiTM; MoVE; NoP; NYBP

Our lady lived, fierce in each other's frown. Our Lady Peace. Mark Van Doren. WaP

...Our Lady/of Guadalupe and by her side Fidel. Aztec Figurine. John Beecher. GP

...Our Lady takes/Her cloak and, questing souls, goes out from Aix. Der Heilige Mantel Von Aachen. Benjamin Francis Musser. ISi

Our language is beautiful. Breaking Silence. Janice Mirikitani. BrSi

...Our laughs are/belts of Indian bells as we walk. What If Jealousy... Miriam Palmer. NMM

Our life as it is now. Exchanging Glances. William Pitt Root. MAYP

Our life is changed; their coming our beginning. The Horses. Edwin Muir. ACV; CMoP; HaMV; HAP; MoBrPo; NMP; NoAm; NOBE; NoP; OAEL 1-2; OxBTC; PPoe; TEP

Our life that brimmed over like diamonds in our light. Farewell and Good. Denis Devlin. IPY

Our life will be the same/held together by/the sinew of our dreams. The Sinew of Our Dreams. Edgar Jackson. LFAC

Our little child! Our little child! The Unborn. Julia Neely Finch. AA

Our little lane, what a kingdom it was!/oi weih, oi weih. The Avenue Bearing the Initial of Christ into the New World. Galway Kinnell. CoPo; NaP; NePoEA-2

Our little Way the dark/glitter in their sight. Fire Island. May Swenson. PoA; TAP

...Our lives and bodies/and all that we hope survives them. An Elegy for Bob Marley. William Matthews. MAYP

Our lives are a circular stair/and i am turning Perhaps. Lucille Clifton. GeTw

Our lives, in a slow quadrille, have intertwined. Head Couples. William H. Matchett. NYBP

Our lives shall not endure. The Man That Lives. Anonymous. OBET

Our lives, that angel-vision. Life Sculpture. George Washington Doane. BLPA; OHFP; WBLP

Our lives we consecrate to thee, our guide the Might of Right. Land of the Free. Arthur Nicholas Hosking. BLPA; PAL

Our long-wished Cynthia, the forest's queen! The Forest's Queen. Philip Massinger. GoBC

Our love calls tiny as a tuning fork. Summer Home. Seamus Heaney. FaBoIP; IPY

Our love can despise the world.) Years and Years I Have Loved You. Gabriel Gillett. PeHV

...Our love makes still more fair/Our friends on earth, fairer in death on high. Celestial Love. Buonarroti Michelangelo. AWP

Our love shall live, and later life renew. Amoretti, LXXV. Edmund Spenser. AAS; AnFE; AWP; EBEV; HAP; HBV 1-2; HeIP; InPS; NoP; OAEL 1-2; OAEP; SeCeV

Our love which had a thousand leaves. Winter. Sheila Wingfield. EnLoPo

...Our loves are brought/before us and followed securely into a new evening. Observation Car and Cigar. William Stafford. LCAP

Our men, as of old, are men in/truth! The Homing. John Jerome Rooney. AA

Our mind is full of sorrow, who will know of our grief? Song of the Bowmen of Shu. Anonymous. OBVE

Our minor zoos/Will love to mushroom/In this great zoo. In the Zoo. Solomon Mahaka. WhB

Our minuter intuitions–/Deem unplausible– Color–Caste–Denomination. Emily Dickinson. EaLo; TAP

Our moccasins do not mark the ground. Returned to Say. William Stafford. ConAP; NaP

Our modern bards! why what a pox/Are they but senseless stones and blocks? A New Simile in the Manner of Swift. Oliver Goldsmith. LAuP

Our morning hymn this is, and song at evening. Arcadia. Sir Philip Sidney. FCP

Our mystery of time, the only hopeful light. The Incomparable Light. Richard Eberhart. MoRP

Our natural steps and the earth and skies from harm. Oedipus. Edwin Muir. CMoP

Our night would last twice as long. All the while, believe me, I prayed. Sappho. BoWoP

Our notes to each other, always repeated, always the same. A Love Poem. John Ashbery. HaCAP

Our O'SULLIVAN Bear. Dirge of O'Sullivan Bear. Jeremiah Joseph Callanan. IrPN; NBM

Our oars we all will lay/Down, and desire will cease. Life's Circumnavigators. W. R. Rodgers. AnIV; GTBS-P; OxBI

Our one prayer, improbable in the nearest/quarter-mile, killing us with all we've got. Sheltering the Same Needs. Alex Kuo. APU

Our only enemy was gold,/And we had no arms to fight it with. The Castle. Edwin Muir. LiTB

Our own beyond the salt sea-wall. They Lie at Rest, Our Blessed Dead. Christina Georgina Rossetti. NOBV

Our own calm journey on for human sake. A Thought of the Nile. [James Henry] Leigh Hunt. ERoP 1-2; NBM

...Our own/mid-river laughter as the warmth begins again. Baptism. Dale Zieroth. NOBC

Our paddles! We drag them along, the flat and the narrow/paddles... The Djanggawul Cycle, 21. Anonymous. WTO

Our path emerges for a while, then closes/Within a dream. Vitae Summa Brevis Spem Nos Vetat Incohare Longam. Ernest Christopher Dowson. AWP; BrPo; FaBoRV; HAP; HBV 1-2; InPo; LoBV; NOBE; NOBV; NoP; OBEV; OBSP; TrGrPo; ViBoPo; VLP; WGRP

Our path lies–Father–thither, oh repair! Mignon. Johann Wolfgang von Goethe. PoPl

Our physicians all are men. Doctor Blenn. Ambrose Bierce. DBV

Our poor romantic daughter thinks he is. The Marriage. Sara Henderson Hay. DFT

Our prayer of thanks. Our Prayer of Thanks (excerpt). Carl Sandburg. TRV

Our present joy and our hopes increase. Puerperium. Edmund Waller. JCP

Our purchased souls Him first and last/Love, trust, obey, adore. His Plan. Anonymous. STF

Our puss is gray, so of course/She spins gray thrums. Gray Thrums. Clara Doty Bates. OBCA

Our rays united make one sun,/With fairest summer weather. Stanzas. Henry David Thoreau. AmLP

Our reality and its insupportable innocence. The Master. William Stanley Merwin. NePoEA

Our red mouths visible and the white sky full of clouds. From the Spanish. Tony Towle. ANYP

...Our rootlessness/a fragile bond that will not bear embrace. Anthropology: Cricket at Kano. Stewart Brown. OBTV

Our roots knotting themselves/in that dark world/that allows us our drunkenness. Drinking. Virginia R. Terris. FAZ

Our sacred earth in our day is our curse. The Dead in Europe. Robert Lowell. CMoP; DTC; LiTM; NePA; NePoEA; OxBA; OxBC

Our safety from the savage,/The guardian of our home. Here's to the Ranger! *Anonymous.* CoSo

Our sails are loosed and our anchor secure, so I'll bid you goodbye/once more. The Leaving of Liverpool. *Anonymous.* OBSS

Our scholar travels yet the loved hillside. Thyrsis. Matthew Arnold. EnLit; NoP; OBEV; OBNC; OBVV

...Our selves are lost lost/In a final fear which none understands. Murder in the Cathedral. Thomas Stearns Eliot. OxBTC

Our selves become our best sacrifice. In the Holy Nativity of Our Lord God. Richard Crashaw. PoEL 1-5; SBVL; SeCeV; SeCV 1-2

Our sense of how Active you've been. Limerick: "Wrote the clergy: Our Dear Madame Prynne:". Richard Harter Fogle. NIP

Our singing, our hands, our stream. Anasazi at Mesa Verde. Reg Saner. NPAW

Our skulls/much smaller than theirs/begin to shine. Looking at Henry Moore's Elephant Skull Etchings in Jerusalem... Shirley Kaufman. BoWoP; LCAP

Our small tireless names/murmured in their voices. A City Graveyard. Joyce Carol Oates. DFF

"Our soil's redeemed from hateful yoke,/We'll keep it pure or die." Sumter– A Ballad of 1861. *Anonymous.* PAH

Our Sorcerie dimmes the Morning faire, and darkes the Sun at/Noone. Metamorphoses. Ovid (Publius Ovidius Naso). OBVE

Our souls adore the eternal God/Who condescended to be born. Miracles at the Birth of Christ. Isaac Watts. NOCV

Our souls with God, our bodies clay. A Faithless Shepherd. John Clare. VLP

Our source, our center and our dwelling-place! Adoration. Jeanne Marie Guyon. STF; WGRP

Our species can be best and/blessed when we are most at play. Ode to Pornography. Jack Anderson. PoA

Our starry flag: red, white, and/blue. A Song for Our Flag. Margaret E. Sangster. FaFP

Our stepladder to the high places/our stairway/to the summits. Mountain Sculpture. James Will. PoSH

Our stories grow too dark to tell. Winter Watch. Jeff Daniel Marion. AMV-80

Our Streamlet curved, as now, through grass and wheat. Meadowsweet. William Allingham. OBNC

Our suffering life the dream. The Other World. Harriet Beecher Stowe. AA; HBV 1-2; WGRP

Our Summer made her light escape/Into the Beautiful. As imperceptibly as grief. Emily Dickinson. CMoP; DiPo; ExPo; ForPo; LiTA; LiTM; NOBA; NoP; PBWP; PoEL 1-5; QFR

Our Sundays with whatever is at hand/and Idries Shah's THE WISDOM OF THE IDIOTS. Canzone. Lorenzo Thomas. APU

Our supper is plain but we are very wonderful. Twenty-third Street Runs into Heaven. Kenneth Patchen. ErPo

Our sweetest memorial the first kiss of love. The First Kiss of Love. George Gordon, Lord Byron. HBV 1-2

...Our sympathy as real as silicone. Once in a While a Protest Poem. David B. Axelrod. InPK

Our teeth are hard/from the rocks we eat. Epilog (to Lost Copper). Wendy Rose. TWSS

Our thanks and our praises we'll render to thee. With God and His Mercy. Carl Olof Rosenius. AH

Our thoughts dusting the past. Autobiography. Mbella Sonne Dipoko. TTY

Our time, and each were as content and free/As I believe that thou and I should be. Sonnet: To Guido Cavalcanti. Dante Alighieri. AWP

Our tongues blunt as husks in our cheeks? The Real Thing. Ronald Wallace. AMV-81

Our tossing bark of Progress sunward/steers. John Brown. Harry Lyman Koopman. AA

Our tragedy, is it alive or dead? Modern Love, XXXVII. George Meredith. NOBV; VLP

Our tree will not light up for him/Another Christmas Day. The Sun Came Out in April. C. Day-Lewis. MoBS

Our tributes are resounding,/For the village we love best. Lines on Mountain Villages. Sunset Joe. PoOW

Our true and only destiny. The Way of Life. Joseph V. B. Danquah. ACV

Our tubs of hot water, the glue, and please,/remember me. Or we are lost. Changsha Shoe Factory. Willis Barnstone. SaC

Our two bloods in the membrane-severed sea. La Ci Darem La Mano. John Frederick Nims. MiAP

Our utmost wish possessing;/So may I always keep. Air XXIII: "Sleep, O sleep." John Gay. ViBoPo

Our vast disfigures cast/immediate on the wall. The Wall. Isidor Schneider. PG

Our very souls pass overseas. Flight of the Earls. *Anonymous.* AnIL

Our vessel, plunging deeper into night/To reach a land unknown. Song: "The boat is chafing at our long delay." John Davidson. OBEV; OBVV; PoPle

...Our voices join the birds who wait for/our eyes to freeze like berries in the face of winter. Blizzard. Patricia Garfinkel. AmC

Our voices the color of watching Anniversary Poem for the Cheyennes Who Fell at Sand Creek. Lance Henson. VoR

Our weather the invention of rain. Towards the Vanishing Point. David Lehman. SM

...Our weather/vanish altogether (all together). Views of Our Sphere. Ernest Sandeen. MOON

Our words/beat the air/like tarpaulins. The Wharf, May 1978. Carolyn Foster Segal. WOLT

Our words keep no faith with the soul of the world. The Ancient Speech. Kathleen Raine. PoSH

Our work is done; we have no heart/to mar our work, we cried. Paracelsus. Robert Browning. OBRV

Our world–the one thing truly/We in this world have builded. Home. Verner von Heidenstam. PoPl

Ours are the only natures/That you cannot give back. Weather. William Meredith. NYBP

Ours is to watch, with a living faith/In Him–the victorious One! What Though the Dark! Archie Edwards. BePJ

Ours the fruits of victory,/His the agony and strife. It Is Finished. Horatius Bonar. BePJ

...Ours the stuff sublime/To build Eternity in time! Earth Is Enough. Edwin Markham. GoTF; TreFS; TRV

Ours, then, be the watchword, "We conquer or die." We Conquer or Die. James S. Pierpont. MC; PAH

... Ourselves arranged,/Oddly, in one room, at a stranger's table. The Table. Michael Heffernan. PoA

Ouside, a stone forgets that it was born. Cockley Moor, Dockray, Penrith. Norman Nicholson. NeBP

Out across the bay to where the ice is thinnest and let yourself vanish. Bum's Rush. Michael Dransfield. CBAP

Out after what I had long thought I'd hate. Space. X. J. Kennedy. MOON

Out again to the blue! The Captive Ships at Manila. Dorothy Paul. PAH

Out among the rows of green onions Killing the Rooster. Sheryl L. Nelms. Str

Out break the tears again for pain and woe. The Twelve Properties or Conditions of a Lover. Sir Thomas More. EnRePo

Out dog!...And let me into/Sputnick Number Two. Bang Street. Livingston Welch. FaFP

Out, far out, by the Thunderer/To sea on a great white bull. Europa. William Plomer. MoBS

Out from this dripping cave/in the name of Love. Sirventes. Paul Blackburn. NeAP; PoM

Out - goes - he. Dips or Counting Out Rhymes: "Hickety pickety i sillickity." *Anonymous.* GBP

Out goes you. Inter, Mitzy, Titzy, Tool. *Anonymous.* OxNR

Out in the fields of God. Out in the Fields. *Anonymous.* GoTF; HBV 1-2; HBVY; TreFS; TRV

Out in the fields with God! Out in the Fields with God. Elizabeth Barrett Browning. BLRP; WBLP; WGRP

Out in the fields with God. A Song from Sylvan. Louise Imogen Guiney. BLPA

Out in the Night! Star of Ethiopia. Lucian B. Watkins. BANP

Out into sunlight. The Proof. W. H. Auden. OAEL 1-2

Out into the night, and down/The dazzling vista of streets! City Nights, I: In the Train. Arthur Symons. VLP

Out into traffic, dead or alive. Slipping out of Intensive Care. Florence Trefethen. AMV-80

Out of a bolle to plukke out the lining. Froward Maymond. John Lydgate. OxBM

Out of a continuous process of succession Crows. Tom Clark. DFF

Out of a dead man's grave, whom no one knows. Correspondent. Witter ("Emanuel Morgan") Bynner. AnFE

Out of commonplace lives makes His beautiful whole. Commonplace. Susan (Sarah Chauncey Woolsey) Coolidge. GoTF; TreFT

Out of dark and different time. The Ivory Dog of My Sister. Mary Tallmountain. TWSS

Out of dark night where lay/The crowns of Nineveh. Fragments. William Butler Yeats. NoAm; PrIm

Out of deep time have shelved this shallow ledge/Where the waves break– Signature for Tempo. Archibald MacLeish. MoVE; VGW

Out of fear of my voice to say yes/in the empty space. Document. Tuvia Ruebner. VWA

Out of heaven on your bugles blown! England, My England. William Ernest Henley. BLPL; EnLi 1-2; HBV 1-2; MoBrPo; OBEV; OBVV; PoLf; TreF

Out of her ashes let a Phoenix rise/That may outshine the first and be more wise. Chelmsfords Fate. Benjamin Tompson. SCAP

Out of her mouth came forth strawberry, strawberry froth. Hexameter and Pentameter. *Anonymous.* FaBoNo

Out of his pocket he played tune/After tune until they came up to him. The Reason for Skylarks. Kenneth Patchen. NaP

Out of ignorance not love. Past Time. Harvey Shapiro. PoL

Out of Nowhere, Nothing answered "yes." Tzu Yeh Songs. *Anonymous.* BoWoP

Out of revolving doors into the glorious anonymous streets. Girls Working in Banks. Karl Shapiro. WeW

Out of sand, barren sand. Moenkopi. Arthur Sze. BrSi

...Out of season, we watch/an owl, gone brown in the chest/drift soundlessly north. The Shorebirds. Monty Reid. CaPN

Out of sight, all that's left is/a clatter of leaves. Morgans in October. Suzanne Brabant. PH

Out of sight, beyond light, at what goal may we meet? The Song of the Bower. Dante Gabriel Rossetti. HBV 1-2

The out-of-sight, buried too deep for shafts. Always the Following Wind. W. H. Auden. MoBrPo

...Out of sight/Though not, in time's ruining stream, out of mind. The Sanctuary. Howard Nemerov. NePoEA

Out of that childhood country what fools climb/To fight with tyrants Love and Life and Time? Peace. Patrick Kavanagh. FaBoIP

Out of the big sky into Montana... Elegy to the Sioux. Norman Dubie. MAYP

Out of the books which Ezra Fink/Gave and controlled for Spoon River? Rhoda Pitkin. Edgar Lee Masters. NoAm

Out of the clouds, pomp of the air,/By which at least I am befriended. Idiom of the Hero. Wallace Stevens. OxBA

Out of the clutch of the Foe of mankind. Christ 1: Advent Lyrics, VIII. *Anonymous.* AnOE

Out of the dark ages of the sky. Snowfall: Four Variations. George Amabile. NYBP

Out of the dead, cold ashes,/Life again. Evolution. John Banister Tabb. AA; AnAmPo; GoTF; HBV 1-2; PoPl; TreF

Out of the desert, out of sight,/Into the solid sky. New Mexican Desert. Witter ("Emanuel Morgan") Bynner. BPAW

Out of the desert's pride and woe. Honey from the Lion. Leah Bodine Drake. NePoAm

Out of the Empress's bedroom furniture on the Phoenix-Viewing/Terrace roasting their wienies. 10:X:57, 45 Years Since the Fall of the Ch'ing Dynasty. Philip Whalen. PoM

Out of the eyes of a hundred flowers. Talking in Their Sleep. Edith Matilda Thomas. BoNaP; OHIP

Out of the finite dark,/Into the Infinite Light. In Memorium. Louisa May Alcott. AA

Out of the grave, get us all good end. The Finding of the Tain. Robert Farren. CoBE

Out of the hitherwhere into the yon. Out of the Hitherwhere. James Whitcomb Riley. BLPA; FPL

Out of the leaf-fall of its grove. Ascent. Wendell Berry AP

Out of the lives ye cast away/The coming race is born. The Settlers. Laurence Housman. HBV 1-2; OBVV

Out of the living word/Come flower, serpent and bird. The Book of Kells. Howard Nemerov. EaLo

Out of the long felt nights and days of yesterday. Ancestor. Jimmy Santiago Baca. LFAC

Out of the meadow he came to mow,/With nobody by to see him go.... Springfield Mountain (B vers.). *Anonymous.* ViBoFo

Out of the mouths of sons/Come mothers, creeping,/Dancing. Mothers of Sons. Lesley Saunders. BrRo

Out of the naked days. Giant's Tomb in Georgian Bay. Katherine"(Amelia Beers Warnock Garvin) "Hale. CaP

Out of the North, where life did freeze,/Into the haven where they would be. Love at Large. Coventry Patmore. NOBV

Out of the ripping pain of war/A new world nation... The New World. Paul Engle. AmFN

Out of the saddle, and roll in the clover. A Trot, and a Canter, a Gallop, and Over. *Anonymous.* OxNR

Out of the storm let us have one star. Prayer after World War. Carl Sandburg. VGW

Out of the tane there grew a birk,/And the tither a bonny brier. Fair Janet. *Anonymous.* BaBo; ESPB; OxBB

Out of/the unguarded/window/for the boys/upstate.... Cell-Rap #27. Raymond Ringo Fernandez. LFAC

Out of the whirlwind I came. Boolee, the Bringer of Life. Mary Gilmore. BoAV

Out of the Wilderness, Lord. Grant at Appomattox. Gertrude Claytor. GoYe

Out of the wind's and the rain's way. An Old Woman of the Roads. Padraic Colum. BoC; CAW; FaBoBe; FYAP; GoBC; GoTF; GTBS; HBMV; MoBrPo; NOBI; OBEV; PG; PoRA; TreFS; WHA

Out of the window the trees in the Square/Are covered with crimson may. Red May. Agnes Mary Frances (Mme Emile Duclaux) Robinson. HBMV

Out of this outside me, shall wing/Itself fair and free.' Old Age. E. Keary. NOBV

Out of those nights shall emerge/the blade of the flame that will rend the dark cloak! Those Makheta Nights. Frank Mkalawile Chipasula. WhB

Out of whatever we have been/We will make something for the dark. For Fran. Philip Levine. FF; PoCh; SM

Out of which I shall prevent/flowers from growing, your flowers. For James Dean. Frank O'Hara. NeAP; NNaP

Out on important business–back at 6. Poetry and the Poet. Henry Cuyler Bunner. OBAL

Out on the lonely prairie, where skies are always blue. Cowboy Jack. *Anonymous.* CoSo

Out our death and yours. Indian Mounds. Angela Peace. AMV-80

Out packed in the rain. Hitch Haiku. Gary Snyder. LCAP

Out pops itselve. The Phoenix. Ogden Nash. CenHV; NePA

Out there in the magic grass/of centerfield. Byron vs. DiMaggio. Peter Meinke. LiSp

Out there in the sun–in the rain. Rooms. Charlotte Mew. PBWP

Out through the end of a log/and into the sky. Breaking Ground in Me. Tom Kryss. NeAC

Out to Old Aunt Mary's. Out to Old Aunt Mary's. James Whitcomb Riley. FaFP; OHFP

Out to the lily-pond to feed the fish. Two Old Ladies. Siegfried Sassoon. OxBTC

Out where the wind/is free/of the branches. Three in Transition. David Ignatow. CAPP

Out-witted by a Country Girl/About his Pipe of Wine. The Fair Lass of Islington. *Anonymous.* OxBB

Out you get and/Walk the rest of the way. A Lighthouse in Maine. Derek Mahon. FaBoIP; OBTV

...The outflying spirit's/vertical trampoline. Movement. Denise Levertov. LLLT

Outpacing bargain, vocable and prayer. For the Marriage of Faustus and Helen. Hart Crane. AP; FaBoMo; LiTM; NePA; NoAm; NOBA; PAI

Outshines the noise/Of leaves clashing in the wind. Metric Figure. William Carlos Williams. MoAB

Outshining in brilliance the rays of the sun. Lake Chemo. James Wilton Rowe. AmFP

Outshone the sun in summer skies. To Harriett. John Clare. AtBAP

Outside, a nation/crowns its queen. Life of a Queen. Lisel Mueller. GP

Outside a rustling and twig-combing breeze/Refreshes and relents. Is cadences. Glanmore Sonnets. Seamus Heaney. IPY

Outside her window, behind the hive's/ungovernable hexagons, the queen bee stirs. Sleeping Beauty. Jane Shore. DFT

Outside.(it was New York and beautifully,snowing.... I Was Sitting in McSorley's. Edward Estlin Cummings. NoAm

Outside my perfect knowledge or my fate. A Wry Smile. Roy Fuller. WaaP; WaP

Outside, separate as minds,/the stars too come alight. Novella. Adrienne Rich. PPP

Outside the body, all things are encumbrances. Chinoiserie. Charles Wright. AmPA

...Outside the gemini kingdom/people are catching. Falling Out. Helen Chasin. IHMS

Outside the gods survive. The Hero Leaves His Ship. Barbara Guest. AmPC

Outside the lunchroom, tufts and air-sacs/swell to the size of fruits bursting with seeds. Feathered Dancers. Kenward Elmslie. ANYP

Outside the madhouse hung the yellow sun. Yellow. Josephine Jacobsen. GP

Outside the sky will clear./By noon/someone will be born. Labor. Lucille Day. VWA

...Outside the temple/a lone bird sounds its call,/waits for response. Yom Kippur. Lucille Day. VWA

Outside, the vast/calm of the hills beneath a vestal moon. At the Shelter-Stone. Brenda G. Macrow. PoSH

Outside, the water is moving/past in search of some/low place to lie down. Connais-Tu le Pays? Richard Shelton. NYBP

& Outside the women's blindness/lies ruined in the nightshade Monkshood XXIX. Kristjana Gunnars. CaPN

Outside/they start to shout obscene remarks. Friday. Wet Dusk. Christopher Logue. OxBTC

Outside, Toyko growls like a hunting tiger. In a Bar near Shibuya Station, Tokyo. Paul Engle. AmFN; CAD

...An outstretched arm offers me its hand.   Notes for Echo Lake 5.   Michael Palmer.   NPGG

Outstripped by queenly sauntering.   That Strain Again.   Ronald Hambleton.   CaP

Outvieing all the buds in Flora's diadem.   Imitation of Spenser.   John Keats.   EnRP

Outward forms, too beautiful, beget only sorrows.   The Naked World.   Rene Sully-Prudhomme.   ImOP

The outwarde countenance I made gladde and light.   The Pastime of Pleasure.   Stephen Hawes.   PoEL 1-5

Outworn, burnt out, exhausted–like the bard.   Gas and Hot Air.   Morris Bishop.   OBAL

Ov her bright feace, by mornen light.   The Rwose in the Dark.   William Barnes.   AtBAP; NOBV

...The oven door says: it says/Queen Clarion/Wood & Bishop/Bangor, Maine 1911 Stove.   Philip Booth.   FYAP

Over a sea with death acquainted, yet forever chaste.   Ragged Island.   Edna St. Vincent Millay.   NoP

Over all I place/a glass bell.   Woman Skating.   Margaret Atwood.   FaBoWP; IHMS

Over all the graves that lie between here and Illinois.   Between Here and Illinois.   Ralph Pomeroy.   Psk

Over and over again.   Before Dawn.   Horace Hamilton.   NYBP

Over and over and ever and along.   Driving.   Myra Cohn Livingston.   InPK

Over and over, biting and rending the night air.   Fear.   Stephen Dobyns.   AMV-80

Over and over, like a song.   The Child's Dream.   Susan Ludvigson.   AMV-80; MAYP

Over and over they must speak/The water's cadences alone.)   From the Righteous Man Even the Wild Beasts Run away.   David Bromwich.   PoA

Over and under and all ways/All days and always.   The Creditor.   Louis MacNeice.   EaLo

Over bank and over brae,/Hie away, hie away.   Gellatley's Song to the Deerhounds.   Sir Walter Scott.   OBRV

Over blackberries.   Hitch Haiku.   Gary Snyder.   LCAP

Over buried, drowned Santos, Hill/Town, a moon rises.   The Lake above Santos.   Keith Wilson.   GP

Over faces/carried in the/darkened stream.   Breathe on the Glass.   Raymond Stineford.   AMV-81

Over fields and over valleys/Flew his orphaned cry.   Birds Are Drowsing on the Branches.   Leah Rudnitsky.   VWA

Over grass and over stone,/And under mountains in the moon.   Roads Go Ever Ever On.   J. R. R. Tolkien.   TiPo

Over his pain my chaste, my disenchanted/And death-rebuking star.   Emily Bronte.   C. Day Lewis.   ChMP; GTBS-P

...Over it/stretches the red, starry sky.   Apple.   Nan Fry.   PPJ

Over lovers fornicating breathlessly in the fields   Agent of Love.   A. K. Redwing.   VoR

Over miles and miles of water just by dropping one kind word.   Drop a Pebble in the Water.   James W. Foley.   BLPA; PoToHe

Over, oh over/the thorn.   Psalm.   Paul Celan.   VoR

Over our harms, who's to know/Where their feet dance while their heads sleep?   Witches.   Ted Hughes.   GoYe

Over our head to sleep I bow.   Song: "The moth's kiss, first!"   Robert Browning.   HBV 1-2; TrGrPo

Over our naked guilt.   The Net.   W.R. Rodgers.   AnIL; BoLoP; CIP; ErPo; NMP; OxBI

Over & over, bamming it in while I cry out your name I do love you.   Please Master.   Allen Ginsberg.   PeHV

Over pine-tree tops and can no longer/be heard. Although we listen sadly.   Among the Pine Trees.   Moshe Dor.   VWA

Over Puerto Rican agony lawyers' screams in slums.   A Vow.   Allen Ginsberg.   OBWP

Over rips and tears and/thin places.   A Nameless One.   Margaret Avison.   HeIP; NOBC

Over that sea of frozen foam/Floats the white moon.   Winter.   Walter De la Mare.   OAEL 1-2; OBMV

Over the absence of/revival meetings/and/home.   Okay–.   Sharon Scott.   JB

Over the ashes of the future.   Reveille.   Ted Hughes.   PPP

Over the bay, and over the ship Mayflower.   The Mayflower.   Erastus Wolcott Ellsworth   AA; FaBoBe; HBV 1-2; MC; PAH

Over the body of your last slain sorrow.   Forgetfulness.   Maxwell Bodenheim.   MAPA

Over the Bridge and past Hay's Wharf!   Hay's Wharf.   Richard Church.   HaMV

Over the bridge water/under the street lamps.   Simply.   Laura Chester.   NPGG

Over the broken bodies of our youth!   Hialmar.   Roy Campbell.   CoBE

Over the cage floor the horizons come.   The Jaguar.   Ted Hughes.   LiTM; PoPl

Over the clean sea-beach.   The men of valor.   Akahito (Yamabe no Akahito).   AWP; LiTW

Over the cobbles, in a lost Spring.   Kings River Canyon.   Kenneth Rexroth.   NaP

Over the corridor.   Haiku: "The young wife's dreams."   *Anonymous*.   HW

Over the darkening waters.   The Death of the Sailor's Wife.   Fred Barton.   AMV-80

Over the earth brushing the eternal grass.   The Noise That Time Makes.   Merrill Moore.   MoAmPo; TrGrPo; YaD

...Over the East River/That loves them and drowns them.   A Poem of Towers.   James Wright.   CAPP

Over the fields. They come in Spring.   In the Fields.   Charlotte Mew.   BoNaP; MoAB; MoBrPo

Over the gambler and the bitch followed by the whole human pack.   Behold, One of Several Little Christs...   Kenneth Patchen.   NaP

Over the grasses of the ancient way/Rutted this morning by the passing guns.   August, 1914.   John Masefield.   HBV 1-2

Over the Great Divide I go.   Mountain Song.   Harriet Monroe.   HBV 1-2

Over the hill, among the burning worlds.   Autumn Journey.   Denise Levertov.   NeBP

"Over the hills and far away."   Captain Sword.   [(James Henry[) Leigh Hunt.   GN

Over the hills and far away.   Over the Hills and Far Away.   William Ernest Henley.   HBVY; TreF

Over the hills and far away.   Song: "Were I laid on Greenland's coast."   John Gay.   EnLoPo; OBEC; OxBoLi

"Over the hills and far away," and a crescent moon.   The Gypsy.   Edward ("Edward Eastaway") Thomas.   HeIP; NoAm; NoP

Over the hills of God, laddie, the beautiful hills of Home.   A Cry from the Canadian Hills.   Lilian Leveridge.   BLPA

Over the least fossil/day breaks in gold, frankincense, and/myrrh.   The Fossils.   Galway Kinnell.   NYBP

Over the line/to victory...   Letters Found near a Suicide.   Frank Horne.   BPo; PoNe

Over the loch/upon a golden/whin, a blackbird/stirred.   Belfast Lough.   *Anonymous*.   BIrV

Over the long drawer/they've closed in the earth.   Funeral.   Bert Meyer.   PCP

Over the lost empire of the peaks.   The Dying Eagle.   Edwin John Pratt.   ACV

Over the ocean blown!   Winds of the West, Arise!   George Darley.   AtBAP

Over the parapet, "spear in hand!"   The Storming of Stony Point.   Arthur Guiterman.   MC; PAH

Over the pass the voices one by one/Faded, and the hill slept.   He Fell Among Thieves.   Sir Henry Newbolt.   BBV; FaPoR; HBV 1-2; HBVY; OBEV; OBVV; OBWP; OnMSP; OxBTC

Over the past table I repeat this present grace.   January 1939.   Dylan Thomas.   EAS

Over the roofs go his eyes and outcry.   Esther's Tomcat.   Ted Hughes.   OxBC; PCat

Over the rushes/Of Inami Moor?   Three Poems.   *Anonymous*.   LiTW

Over the saddlehorn, he led/fall's last drive/across the hazy range.   The Rancher.   Keith Wilson.   GP

Over the salt and table at a friendly meal.   May He Lose His Way on the Cold Sea.   Archilochus.   OBVE

Over the scarred volcanic rock   Incipience.   Adrienne Rich.   CAPP

Over the sirens, knuckles, boots,/my sounds begin again.   The Sounds Begin Again.   Dennis Brutus.   WhB

Over the speechless needles/of pines which are dead or born again.   Cold Water.   Donald Hall.   NCSH

Over the static, light years away.   Stars Shine So Faithfully.   Jane Flanders.   AMV-80

Over the stile of pearl!   Arcturus Is His Other Name.   Emily Dickinson.   FaBV; NOBA; SUW

Over the tender, bowed locks of the corn.   Summer Dawn.   William Morris.   AtBAP; CBEP; GTBS; LoBV; NOBE; NOBV; OAEL 1-2; OBEV; OBNC; OBVV; ViBoPo

Over the tree tops to predestined mates.   The Lost Orchard.   Edgar Lee Masters.   CMoP

Over the veld broods Night.   Camp Fire.   Beatrice Marion Bromley.   ACV

Over the waves of the sea....   The Seafarer.   *Anonymous*.   EnLi 1-2

Over the whole wood in a little while/Breaks his slow smile.   Not Dead.   Robert Graves.   HBMV

Over them pour thy song, like a rich flood/of light.   To the Mocking-Bird.   Albert Pike   AA

Over there are faith, life, virtue in the sun.   Report on Experience.   Edmund Charles Blunden.   CBEP; FaBoTw; GTBS-P; NOBE; OBMV; OBWP

Over this vessel you sail on."/Tri-at-ling, tri-la, tri-lay.   The False Lover.   *Anonymous*.   BFSS

Over thresholds of welcome dream with wet and moonlit skin.   Elegy for Drowned Children.   Bruce Dawe.   NOAV

Over thyself I crown thee and mitre thee.' Virgil's Farewell to Dante. Laurence Binyon. FaBoTw

Over us on these silent beaches the bright/earth,/presence among us. Voyage to the Moon. Archibald MacLeish. MOON

Over wealthy in the treasure/Of her own exceeding pleasure! The Kitten and the Falling Leaves. William Wordsworth. HBVY; PBBP; PCat

Over which I constantly stumble like my pants at the age six–/embarrassed. Ignu. Allen Ginsberg. NaP

Over which nymphs and under which naiads dream. And to the Young Man. Merrill Moore. MoAmPo

Over white lakes of cotton, like moonfields on every side. Down the Mississippi. John Gould Fletcher. LiTA

Over whose unhungering marble there is no conquest. To a Greek Ship in the Port of Dublin. W. B. Stanford. NeIP

Over whose waves the insect pipes and drummers/Die in an afternoon. Ronsard. Miriam Allen DeFord. HBMV

Over willow trees. Haiku: "I would like a bell..." Richard Wright. FAZ

Over worn-out hands–oh! beautiful sleep! Beautiful Things. Ellen Palmer Allerton. BLPA

Over your folded wings, which will soar tomorrow. Nike. Adam Wazyk. VWA

Over your head to sleep I bow. In a Gondola. Robert Browning. BoLoP; GBL; GTBS; OBEV; OBVV; UnTE

Overboard into the dark river/Swift cold and deep Charon's Cosmology. Charles Simic. GeTw; HaCAP; NoP

"Overdue and must be considered lost..." Sounding. Doris Ferne. CaP

The overturn of her turnover. Limerick: "There was an old lady of Dover." Carolyn Wells. TDH

Overturning the bowl/with his trembling hands. It's Already Autumn. Elio Pagliarani. PCP

'Ow quick we'd chuck 'er! But she ain't! The Return. Rudyard Kipling. MoBrPo

Owed us nothing but the grace of God. A Cocker of Snooks. Phyllis Gotlieb. NOBC

Ower the croon,/And awa' wi' it. Tae Titly. *Anonymous.* OxNR

Owing himself only the need to go and go. Four Brothers. W. S. Di Piero. MAYP

Owl-blind in early sun/for what I had begun. Father and Child. Gwen Harwood. CBAP

The owl car blutters along in a sleep-walk. Blue Island Intersection. Carl Sandburg. MoAmPo

Owl-clawed, hooks to the heart. The Parthenon. John Heath-Stubbs. OBTV

The owl from the steeple sing/Welcome, proud lady! Madge Wildfire's Death Song. Sir Walter Scott. HAP; NOBE; OBNC

An owl rises/From the cutter-bar/Of a hayrake. A Message Hidden in an Empty Wine Bottle That I Threw into a Gulley ... James Wright. AmPC

The owl shall stoop from his turret, the rat cry out. Water Color of Grantchester Meadows. Sylvia Plath. NYBP

Owls who lived in tombs/And now inhabit a palace. Inscriptions at the City of Brass. *Anonymous.* AWP

Own, by neglecting sorrow's wound,/The consanguinity of sound. The Spleen. Matthew Green. NOEC

Owned/bi/esther feldman Childhood. Johari (Jewel C. Latimore) Amini. JB

Owning no rule save his can set men free! He Is Our Peace. Molly Anderson Haley. PGD

An ox/bound to God's yoke. What Am I? Abo Stoltzenberg. VWA

Ox-fed orating ominous octastichs. Salad. Mortimer Collins. CenHV

The Ox fought with the Humble Bee/And claw'd him by the face. A Fancy. *Anonymous.* FaBoNo

Oxford abounds in bird-watcher and fern. Views of the Oxford Colleges. Barbara Howes. GLGT

The oyster's churchyard, and the capon's tomb. The Triumph of Infidelity. Timothy Dwight. NOCV

An oyster will cover the irritant in him by coating it over and over. Hmmmm, 13. Leslie Scalapino. NPGG

P

P e o p l e. Imagine a World of People. Ronald James Dessus. LFAC

P–lease! P–lease! P–lease! Hotel Continental. William Jay Smith. WaP

P.S.–As to Trinity Hall/We say nothing at all. Satire upon the Heads; or, Never a Barrel the Better Herring. Thomas Gray. FaBoCo

P.S. I want to resign. Light, 4. Louis Zukofsky. NoAm

P. She cannot starve, if there was only CLIVE. The Farewell. Charles Churchill. CEP

Pa, Pa, build me a boat/To sail across the ocean. Pa, Pa, Build Me a Boat. *Anonymous.* AmFP

...Pa-/rishioners in Wells, England (1595), marked/with crosses. Numberous scattered... The Romance of Imprinting. Christy Sheffield Sanford. APU

Paces your burning thought,/For the delight of Whom? The Lion-House. John Hall Wheelock. HBMV

Pacing toward what I know. The Farm on the Great Plains. William Stafford. HAP; PoCh; VGW

The pack rats scurry home–and suddenly/Comes desert peace. Arizona Village. Robert Stiles Davieau. AmFN

Pack straps and belts, fading from their embarrassed bodies! The New Saddhus. Robert Pinsky. MAYP

Paddle weary feet. A City Song. John Hanlon Mitchell. CaP

The page is printed. The Thought-Fox. Ted Hughes. FaBoMo; HeIP; InPS; NCSH; NePoEA-2; NoAm; NoP; NYBP; SCV

Paid homage to them of unevent. A Love Story. Robert Graves. AtBAP; CMoP; FaBoTw; LiTB; MoVE

Paid me my precious wages–"Baby's Kiss." Bedtime. Francis Robert St. Clair Erskine. HBV 1-2; HBVY

Paid with pride of course. Epigrams. Martial (Marcus Valerius Martialis). OBVE

...A pain and fear/familiar in the love of the unreachable dead. Like Loving Chekhov. Denise Levertov. InPS

Pain and the dark must claim you,/and passion and the day. Woman's Song. Judith Wright. BoAV

The pain is life-like in that waxwork tear. The Place of Pain in the Universe. Anthony Hecht. CrMA; LiTA

Pain is only being born awake. Rino's Song. Lynne Lawner. IHMS

...Pain kept coursing through me like/life, like the gift of life. First Love. Sharon Olds. FYAP

...Pain not yet become grief. The Son. R. S. Thomas. NAs

The pain of loving you/Is almost more than I can bear. A Young Wife. D. H. Lawrence. BrPo; ChMP; ELP; MoBrPo

...Pain, teach thou/The god to love, let him learn how. The Dying Swan. Thomas Sturge Moore. OBMV; SeCePo; SyP

Pain, that unpurposed, matchless elemental/Stronger than fear or grief, stranger than, love. Surgical Ward: Men. Robert Graves. FaBoMo

Pain whistled in my blood. New Spring. Juan Ramon Jimenez. OLR

Paine and his "Rights of Man'/shall be my song. God Save Great Thomas Paine. Joseph Mather. FaBoPV; NOEC

Pains are worthy such a treasure. Madrigal: "Shall a frown." William Corkine. EnRePo

Paint me a Plea to My Sister Carolyn Cunningham: the Artist. James (Olumo) Cunningham. JB

Paint samples. Bruises. Coleman Barks. PPJ

...Painting quietly dissolved itself/into its surrounding clouds. The Final Painting. Lee Harwood. EAS

The paints are in their boxes: they have gone,/the fantoccini and the Chinese shades. Street Performers, 1851. Terence Tiller. GTBS-P

A pair of dark blue panties/among hairbrushes. Familiar Music. Bill Berkson. APU

A pair of eyes open and stare back. For Delphine. James Simmons. PoL

The pair of eyes that lay ready there as/tear-upon-/tear. ...Plashes the Fountain. Paul Celan. OBVE

...The pair/Score liquid Euclids in foolscaps of air. Tennis. Margaret Avison. NoAm

Paired in death, as paired in love. The Turtle Thus with Plaintive Crying. John Gay. PBBP

A palace fair for greatest king! The Neighbors of Bethlehem. *Anonymous.* OHIP

...Palate of my mind/Losing its gust, and my ambition blind! To Fanny. John Keats. EBEV; EnRP; ERoP 1-2; TrGrPo; UnTE

The palaver is finished. Landscapes. Thomas Stearns Eliot. BiP; LoGBV

The pale, amorphous masks of prisoners,/whose lack of freedom guar- antees their lives. Korea Bound, 1952. William Childress. AmFN

Pale bodies the sea's farness from their shore. Braemar. Galway Kinnell. PoA

Pale carnage beneath bright mist. April. Ezra Pound. CMoP

Pale cowards there must stand. Cogitabo Pro Peccato Meo. William Habington. CoBE

Pale faced, tight laced, ice chaste and undisgraced. One-Line Poems from a New Statesman Competition. Margaret Southgate. PoL

The pale lover I never knew. Two Poems. Sosei (Sosei Hoshi). LiTW

Pale ravener of horrible meat. The Maldive Shark. Herman Melville. AP; LoGBV; MAmP; MOS; NePA; NOBA; NoP; OxBA; PoEL 1-5; TAP; TW

Pale were the lips I kiss'd, and fair the form/I floated with, about that melancholy storm. On a Dream (after Reading Dante's Episode of Paolo and Francesca). John Keats. CBEP; ERoP 1-2

Pallas? Juno? Venus?–he/Should have chosen all the three! My Loves. John Stuart Blackie. OBVV

Pallid the leash-men! The Return. Ezra Pound. AP; APA; CMoP; CoBMV; HAP; MoAB; MoAmPo; MoPo; NAMP; NePA; NoAm; NOBA; OxBA; PPoe; VGW; ViBoPo; WeW

The palm gives of its wine/At the sacramental font.　Three Phases of Africa. Francis Ernest Kobina Parkes.　PBA

The palm is born by the bastard race.　The Midnight Court.　Brian Merriman.　BIrV

The Palo/Alto/bus schedule.　Three Portraits.　George Hitchcock.　VGW

Palpable as the smoke from your cigar.　Academic Affair.　Brenda S. Stockwell.　AMV-80

Pam and I, as the organ/Thunders over you all.　Potpourri from a Surrey Garden.　Sir John Betjeman.　CenHV; FiBHP

Pampering the spirit/With obscure, proud merit?　Certain Mercies.　Robert Graves.　CoBMV; GTBS-P

Pan, Pan is dead.　The Dead Pan.　Elizabeth Barrett Browning.　VLP

The pang which parts us from our weeping friends.　On Friendship. William Whitehead.　OBEC

Pangwangling was her pace.　Uffia.　Harriet R. White.　NA

Panic and war postponed another day.　Bookra.　Charles Dudley Warner. AA; HBV 1-2

Pannyra naked in a flash divine!　Pannyra of the Golden Heel.　Albert Samain.　AWP

Panorama of ghostly Indian battles/Re-fought in Canadian skies.　Indian Night Tableau.　Hyman Edelstein.　CaP

Pansy eyes/Of the noblest blue.　Song: "Like violets pale i' the spring o' the year."　James (1834-82) Thomson.　OBVV

The Panthers are surrendering/1 at a time.　Newsletter from My Mother. Michael S. Harper.　PoBA

The pants blown off his seat.　Jubilation T. Cornpone.　Johnny Mercer. OBAL

Pap by night, pap by night/Or such a Divel.　Epigrams.　Martial (Marcus Valerius Martialis).　OBVE

Papa's going to buy you another today.　Hush, Little Baby, Don't Say a Word.　Anonymous.　OxNR

"Papa's letter" was with God.　Papa's Letter.　Anonymous.　WeW

The paper folded like a napkin/other wings flew into the stone.　Red Lilies. Barbara Guest.　PoM

The paper windows of a soul.　Japanese Fan.　James Kirkup.　GrPl

The papers of the period/spoke of bloodless operations.　The Crusaders knew the Holy Places.　Jenny Mastoraki.　BoWoP

The papers of the period/spoke of bloodless operations.　Three Poems. Jenny Mastoraki.　PBWP

The papers on my blowing desk,/and my beast-haunted mind.　Ivory Paper Weight.　Adrien Stoutenburg.　GP

Papiol, be glad to go speedily to "Yea and Nay," and tell him there's/too much peace about.　Well Pleaseth Me the Sweet Time of Easter.　Ezra Pound.　InvP

Papist intellectuals/Can be very misleading.　A Bestiary.　Kenneth Rexroth. OBAL

The parable that time told in that room.　The Poolhall.　Don Burt. AMV-80

Parachutists gliding down to mined branches, all seen in/mirrors.　Flaming Creatures.　Kenward Elmslie.　ANYP

A paradise I planted see/On open Calvary.　The Garden.　Joseph Beaumont. JCP; OBS; OxBoCh

The paragon of animals!　Hamlet.　William Shakespeare.　TreF

A paragon of virtue.　Transformation.　Caius Valerius Catullus.　LiTW

...Paralysed with mere pity's peace?　Three Memorial Sonnets.　George Barker.　MasP

Paralyzed for eternity.　Walnut.　Jorge Carrera Andrade.　ELU

A Paramount Supreme.　Balder.　Sydney Thomas Dobell.　PeD

Parcel of columbines.　In Ampezzo.　Trumbull Stickney.　AnFE; APA; CoAnAm; CrMA; NCEP

Pardon at Thy people's cry,/As the closing hour draws nigh.　God That Doest Wondrously.　Moses Ibn Ezra.　TrJP

Pardon those erring prayers! Father, hear these!　Now and Afterwards. Dinah Maria Mulock Craik.　HBV 1-2; PoLf; WGRP

Pardoned in heaven, the first by the throne!　The Lost Leader.　Robert Browning.　EnL; FaBoPV; GoTF; GTBS; HBV 1-2; MBW 1-2; MCCG; TreFS; TrGrPo; ViBoPo; VLP

A parent-link to all that lies before.　Love Song to Lucy.　Helen Ehrlich. SUW

...Parents like the word "aver"/though they don't use it.　The Bourgeois Poet-67.　Karl Shapiro.　PP

Pariahs and saints–this song is for you.　Song: "This is the song."　William Justema.　NYBP

Paris avec us Boches, madame,/Ce n'est pas Paris.　Patrol: Buonamary. Bernard Gutteridge.　WaP

The paris peace talks, 1968.　Communication in Whi-te.　Don L. Lee.　BPo

Parked therein, numerous, timid, dumb/Musings retired or neared.　On Harting Down.　Thomas Sturge Moore.　OxBTC

The Parliament soldiers are all to be hang'd.　The Parliament Soldiers. Anonymous.　GBP

The parson knows enough who knows a duke.'　Tirocinium; or, A Review of Schools.　William Cowper.　OBSV

The parson says, "Contented be, and you will heaven gain."　A New Hunting Song.　Anonymous.　CoMu; OBET

The parson who came in his one-horse chaise.　Parson Allen's Ride. Wallace Bruce.　MC; PAH

The part called the calf with the toesiery.　Limerick: "The ankle's chief end is exposiery."　Anthony Euwer.　HBMV

Part eye, part tear, unwilling to recognize us.　Stone Canyon Nocturne. Charles Wright.　HaCAP; LCAP

Part for ever in the gape of hell.　Bunhill's Fields.　Anne Ridler.　NeBP

The part in her hair had a little bend/at the end.　No Complaints.　Anselm Hollo.　APU

Part looks into your light/And lives to tell you so.　Last Words.　James Merrill.　TAP

Part may be more than whole, least may be best.　Part for the Whole. Robert Francis.　PoA

...Part of a/bough of a juniper-tree,"/javelin-ed consecutively.　Walking-Sticks and Paperweights and Watermarks.　Marianne Moore.　PoA

A part of him is on my side.　Two in Bed.　Abram Bunn Ross.　NTCP; SoPo; TiPo

Part of his/Nativity.　Carol of the Brown King.　Langston Hughes.　PCh; SBVL

A part of life/begins　Last Quarter.　John Hollander.　MOON

A part of love, the heart of love, and center.'　Mandala.　Patrick Boland. LiTA

A part of mine may live in thee/And move thee on to noble ends.　In Memoriam A.H.H., LXV.　Alfred, Lord Tennyson.　VLP

The part of my eye/That is not golden, sees.　Felicia's Cafe.　Mebdh McGuckian.　FaBoIP

Part of our nation of our fanatic sun.　The Soul and Body of John Brown. Muriel Rukeyser.　MoAmPo

Part of something at last.　The Death of Janis Joplin.　Robert Phillips. SOTS

A part of that of which you were the known/part, Provence, he loved so well. To Ford Madox Ford in Heaven.　William Carlos Williams.　AmPP; NoAm; NOBA

Part of the dust of so worthy a college.　His Own Epitaph, When He Was Sick, Being Fellow in New College...　John Hoskyns.　FaBoEE

Part vulture, part wolf,/Part neither–for his blood was cold.　The Shark. Edwin John Pratt.　NOBC; WHW

...Part/With earth for heaven, and climb, and reach God's feet.　Turris Eburnea.　Anonymous.　GoBC

Parted me leaf and leaf, divided me, eyelid and eyelid of/slumber.　Moonrise. Gerard Manley Hopkins.　FaBoPP; MoAB; MoBrPo; MOON; NOBV; SeCePo

...Participate in the cosmos/like a peeping tom.　December Eclipse.　Margo Lockwood.　Psk

Particles scraping against an interior lining.　A Plan to Live My Life Again. Diana O Hehir.　NPGG

Particularly, I let you go. Sink, or float, or fly now,/Bad child.　To His Book. Leon Stokesbury.　SM

Parting be as parting may,/After all, we meet.　Morgan Stanwood.　Hiram Rich.　PAH

Parting is all we know of heaven,/And all we need of hell.　My life closed twice before its close.　Emily Dickinson.　AA; APA; AtBAP; BoLoP; BoWoP; DiPo; GBL; GoTF; HeIP; LiTA; LiTM; MAPA; MoAB; MoAmPo; MoVE; NePA; NIP; NoAm; NOBA; OBSP; OLR; OxBA; PoPl; PPP; SBG; SCV; SoSe; TreFT; TrGrPo; ViBoPo; WHA

Parting its beak to greet/Men long dead.　A Talisman.　Marianne Moore. AnFE; APA; GoJo; MoAB; MoAmPo; NCSH; ViBoPo

A partridge in a pear tree.　The Twelve Days of Christmas.　Anonymous. FaFP; GoTF; LiTL; OxNR

...Parts of me/are a woman who judges.　The Parts of a Poet.　Wendy Rose. TWSS

Party–HALT!　On the March.　Richard Aldington.　BrPo

Party pooper O hater of dance/vampire outlaw of the milky way　I Am a Cowboy in the Boat of Ra.　Ishmael Reed.　NBP; NoP; PoBA; PrIm

Pas de million until our singeing-day.　Mordent for a Melody.　Margaret Avison.　ACV

Pas on, and fend thy self amang thame.　The Sevin Seages: Epilogue.　John Rolland.　OxBS

Pass away so easily.　The mists rise over.　Akahito (Yamabe no Akahito). HoPM

Pass by, and curse thy fill; but pass and stay not here/thy gait.　Timon's Epitaph.　Callimachus.　AWP

Pass, Crow.　Examination at the Womb-Door.　Ted Hughes.　NAs; OxBC

"Pass in," our Saviour said.　Quatrains.　Charles J. Quirk.　CAW

Pass it along to Stand-to.　In Parenthesis.　David Jones.　NoAm

Pass on, weak heart, and leave me where I lie:/Go by, go by.　Go By. Alfred, Lord Tennyson.　OBNC

Pass rascal deer, strike me the largest doe.　La Bella Bona-Roba.　Richard Lovelace.　AtBAP; CaPo; CavP; EBEV; OAEL 1-2; PoEL 1-5; SeCP

Pass the pirogen/you/communist! Strawberries Mit Cream. Rochelle Owens. CoPo

Pass, then, into oblivion, sweet word The Winds of Change. Charles G. Ballard. VoR

Passed in light from the house of dust/To the Home of the Glorified! Albert Sidney Johnston. Francis Orrery [(or Orray)] Ticknor. PAH

Passed on: pure, round/Midnight Two Handfuls of Waka for Thelonious Sphere Monk (d. Feb. 1982). Walter Lew. BrSi

Passed out of record into renown. Read, Sweet, How Others Strove. Emily Dickinson. AH; NOCV

Passed roughly through,/and before it was time. The Wedding Night. Anne Sexton. PoA

Passers will wonder at my words,/But your dark dust will know. I'll Be Your Epitaph. Leonora Speyer. HBMV

Passing answers. Etudes. Laurence W. Thomas. AMV-80

The passing freight flutters the laundry hung out like cliches. Plaque. Bruce Ruddick. CaP

Passing over a park, flows into air. Instructions for a Park. Brad Walker. AMV-80; AMV-81

Passing overhead at night/on their way to the sea. To Be a Master in Your House. Natan Zach. VWA

Passing the time away/Till the night begins. Sunday Afternoons. Anthony Thwaite. OxBTC

Passing through one condition on its way to the next. Two Masks Unearthed in Bulgaria. William Meredith. EyDe

Passion comes flooding and thrilling again. In the Heart of the Hills... *Anonymous.* WTO

The passion of her white December? Ice. Stephen Spender. AtBAP; FaBoMo; GTBS-P; SeCePo

The passion of mine own infinity. The East Wind. George Cabot Lodge. AmePo

The passion-sadness of the soul of night. Night and the Pines. Duncan Campbell Scott. OBCV

Passion—that breath of Instinct, and the key/Of Thy dominions, untold Majesty! A Prayer. William Ellery Channing. TrPWD

Passionate beyond the will. The Alchemist. Louise Bogan. AWP; LLLT; MoAmPo

...The passionate failures,/the perfect despairs, these never fail us. The Moral. Theodore Weiss. Prf

...A passionate heaven rose no/God in heaven could create! On Listening to the Spirituals. Lance Jeffers. PoBA

Passionless, austere, afar,/Underneath the Polar Star. The Ice King. A. B. Demille. WHW

The passions flourish, the affections die. Regeneration. Walter Savage Landor. ViBoPo

Passions of love with love./Fortune, Adieu. Caelica, XXIX. Fulke, Lord Brooke Greville. EnRePo; FCP

Passive, observing with a steady eye. Intimate Parnassus. Patrick Kavanagh. MoBrPo

Past all chronometry. The Migrant. Donald Campbell Babcock. NePoAm

Past all endurance, existing. In the Half Light of Holding and Giving. John Wieners. CoPo

Past cliffs with stories and songs/painted on rock./700 years ago. Slim Man Canyon. Leslie Marmon Silko. VoR

The Past comes back in the mouth with blood. The Past. Ralph Hodgson. PoL

Past for ladies up like smoke in narrow wind. Lady in a Distant Face. James Welch. AmPA

The past hovering as it revisits the light. It Rains. Edward ("Edward Eastaway") Thomas. MoVE; OxBTC

Past innocence, beyond these aging bricks/To where the Charles flows in to join the Styx. A Walk by the Charles. Adrienne Rich. NePoEA; NYBP

The past is best forgotten. Custer Lives in Humboldt County. Janet Campbell Hale. STE; VoR

Past sunset they send up their shadows/to lean against the trees,/like holograms. October, Hanson's Field. Roo Borson. CaPN

...Past that/is relaxation, like a swimmer/climbing onto shore. Let Go: Once. Gerald Fleming. AMV-81

A past that redeems any future. Help from History. William Stafford. AMV-81

Past the energy of survival/In its sadness/The hard life of the young. Album. Josephine Miles. FaBoWP

Past the solace of the shade/Or the rescue of the sun. Song: "Poppies paramour the girls." Haniel Long. HBMV

Past things retold were to her as things existent,/Things present but as a tale. One We Knew. Thomas Hardy. VLP

The past unpiteous to your need! Inscription for a Mirror in a Deserted Dwelling. William Rose Benet. MoAmPo

Past your noble and desperate king/whose beard-lengths go down to the sea. The King of Harlem. Federico Garcia Lorca. NYP

A paste of yellows,/wading uphill. August. Roy Scheele. PPJ

...Pastime of a provincial winter. So through That Unripe Day You Bore Your Head. Philip Larkin. NoAm

The pasture is thy Word; the streams thy grace,/Enriching all the place. Shall I Be Silent? George Herbert. TRV

The pasture's frisky innocents bucked up. The Human Tragedy (excerpt). Alfred Austin. FaBoCo

Pasture to living beauty, life that was. Roses are Beauty, but I Never See. John Masefield. EnLi 1-2

A pasture to the shaggy goats of Pan,/Whence flee forever a woman and a man. Sonnet: "Not with Libations." Edna St. Vincent Millay. HBMV

Pastured with sheep, forever green. The Pentland Hills. *Anonymous.* GBP

Pasturing the stallions in the standing corn. Bacchus. William Empson. PoA

...The patched gate/You left open will never be shut again. Invasion on the Farm. R. S. Thomas. PoL

...Patches that you sewed/On my old battledress tonight, my sweet. Goodbye. Alun Lewis. OBWP

The path lies through Gethsemane. From Stone to Steel. Edwin John Pratt. NoP; PeCV

Path, motive, guide, original, and end. The Consolation of Philosophy. Boethius. OBVE

A path of hairpins, gentle arrows, leads to my room. Sea Legs. Susan Feldman. AmPA

The path of the light comes to you. Waiting for the Fire. Philip Appleman. SOTS

The path whereon his footsteps go. The Passing Bell at Stratford. William Winter. AA

The path which leads to heaven and thee! Defend Us, Lord, from Every Ill. John Hay. AH

Pathetic, this, the dark posture. All Hungers Pass Away. Arthur Nortje. WhB

The pathos of the past, the human creature. At an Exhibition of Historical Paintings, Hobart. Vivian Smith. CBAP; NOAV

Patience and the withered hands of toil. Widows. Edgar Lee Masters. MoAmPo

...Patience fills/His crisp combs, and that comes those ways we know. Sonnet: "Patience, hard thing! the hard thing but to pray." Gerard Manley Hopkins. OBNC

The patience of your tail? Fulani Cattle. John Pepper Clark. PBA

"Patience! that village shall hold ye all!" The Two Villages. Rose Terry Cooke. HBV 1-2

The patience that wears out the flesh/in order for the bone to shine. Patience. Bartola Cattafi. AMV-81

Patience, with a good will,/Is easy to fulfil. Patience for My Device. Sir Thomas Wyatt. FCP; SiPS

Patience without offence/Is a painful patience. Patience Though I Have Not. Sir Thomas Wyatt. FCP; NoP; OBSC; SiPS; TrGrPo

The patient beating of the animal heart. Epitaph for the Race of Man. Edna St-Vincent Millay. AmP

...The patient dandelion/should not remain at large in our terrible garden. Fear of the Earth. Alex Comfort. MoBrPo; NeBP

Patient, like thee, that prime of nature lies/T' imbibe the quintessence of flowing sweets. There's Life in a Mussel. A Meditation. George Farewell. NOEC

The patient, painted face of her, the little Teresina,/With its cowed, all-knowing eyes! Teresina's Face. Margaret Widdemer. HBMV

Patient to outwait these worst days that beat/Their crowns bare and dripped from their feet. November. Ted Hughes. CMoP; GTBS-P; NePoEA-2; NMP; NoP

Patiently ever, through the eternal night! Thoughts on the Shape of the Human Body. Rupert Brooke. BrPo

The patriarch he coost the sark/And up and till't like fire!!! The Patriarch. Robert Burns. CoMu

A patriot/Who would not lie. Episode of the Cherry Tree. Mildred Weston. PV

The patriotism of a pair of thieves. The Murder of William Remington. Howard Nemerov. CMoP; CoAP

Patriots drag the felon's chain. The Exile's Reveries. James Kennedy. NOEC

Patrolling the unconscious of Ted Hughes. A Policeman's Lot. Wendy Cope. FaBoWP

Patrols for God His private grounds. Wild Sports of the West. John Montague. CIP

Patter, chatter everywhere. To Beatrice Stuart Wortley: Aetat 2. Alfred Austin. PeD

The pattern and mirror of the acts of earth. To Christ Our Lord. Galway Kinnell. MP; NIP; PrIm; RFM; SM; TwCP

The pattern of Oedipus wrecks. Mother, Mother, Are You All There? Felicia Lamport. NLV

...The pattern of your/heart falling into my/soft and empty arms. Seasons. Barry Dempster. CaPN

Les pattes/Le cou Alouette. *Anonymous.* FSW

Paumonikides/So long! Narcissus in Camden (parody). Helen Gray Cone.
BXAP

Pause–"And it's never been." A Family Turn. William Stafford. CAPP

...The pause,/hand over eyes, the glare,/the desert sea. Winding down the
War. Philip Appleman. SOTS

...Pauses to wonder why he/alone breasts the wronging tide. Dream Songs.
John Berryman. CAPP; TAP

The Pavement boyling with the soules they reft. The Odyssey. Homer.
OBS

Pawing us who dealt them war and madness. Mental Cases. Wilfred Owen.
BiP; BrPo; CMoP; FaBoMo; MMM; NoAm; WaP

Pay homage to America and glorious Wash–/ington! The Trip to Cambridge.
Jonathan Mitchell Sewall. PAH

Pay me for them tobacco, boys,/And I will leave this place. Lynchburg
Town. *Anonymous.* OuSiCo

Pay me my money down. Pay Me My Money Down. *Anonymous.* FSW

Pay when th'art honest; let me have some hope. Upon Bunce: Epigram.
Robert Herrick. CaPo

Pay your debt of blood and tear/For those who died in the Alamo! Lament
for the Alamo. Arthur Guiterman. AmFN

A-payin' fer the chattels/What the cyclone blowed away. Cyclone Blues.
Anonymous. CoSo

Paying a price, at his right hand? Johannes Agricola in Meditation. Robert
Browning. MaVP; OAEL 1-2; OBVV

Paying back the sea. The Life. Philip Dow. AmPA

Paying coin/to gypsies–/maybe–. Dorothy. Alfred Kreymborg. AnAmPo

Paying you tribute with our wild applause! Nijinsky. Doris Ferne. CaP

Peace. The Bells. Antonio Fogazzaro. CAW

Peace and a comforter. Immortality. Lizette Woodworth Reese. AA

Peace and freedom and Ho Chi Minh. Ballad of Ho Chi Minh. Ewan
MacColl. FSW

Peace and happiness are Thine,–/Mine they are, if Thou art mine. Lord! It
Is Not Life to Live. Augustus Montague Toplady. OxBoCh

Peace and I are at home, at home! Snow. Elizabeth Akers. HBV 1-2

Peace and quiet/in this world. On Wearing Ears. William J. Harris.
BOLo

Peace, and this Cot, and thee, heart-honoured Maid! The Eolian Harp.
Samuel Taylor Coleridge. OAEL 1-2

Peace be upon thee, Israel! At the Pantomime. Oliver Wendell Holmes.
AnNE

"Peace!/Borso..., Borso!" Canto XX. Ezra Pound. MoPo

Peace both the duty and the prize/Of him that creeps and him that flies. The
Nightingale and Glow-Worm. William Cowper. HBV 1-2; OnMSP;
PBBP

Peace by the way, and port of noble fame! Echoes from Theocritus.
Edward Cracroft Lefroy. OBVV

Peace corps to/europe. Black Sketches, 3. Don L. Lee. NeAC

Peace, croaks the mother, Peace, the angelus! Battledore. John Gray.
NOBV

Peace drowning passion, and passion/Leaping from peace. Four Japanese
Paintings: III The Wave Symphony. Arthur Davison Ficke. PoA

"Peace I implore!" and this alone. Implora Pace. Charles Lotin Hildreth.
AA

Peace in themselves, which is their sole applause. At the Front. John
Erskine. HBMV

Peace is the man I love not/Marching away to be killed. Not Marching away
to Be Killed. Jean Overton Fuller. FF

"Peace! It is I!" Jesus, Deliverer. Saint Anatolius. BePJ

Peace laid upon her breast a child. Birth. Annie R. Stillman. AA

Peace lies profound on their forgotten acres. Meditation by Mascoma Lake.
Donald Campbell Babcock. NePoAm-2

A peace of Heaven with Hell. The Rose of Peace. William Butler Yeats.
OBVV

The peace of heaven within thy tranquil/breast. Winter Twilight. George
Tracy Rlliot. AA

The peace of the sky. At Carbis Bay. Arthur Symons. FaBoPP

Peace on eart' amids' huh sorrows, an' up yonder heavenly/res'! Black
Mammies. John Wesley Holloway. BANP

Peace on earth and mercy mild! Hark the Herald Angels Sing. Sir Thomas
Beecham. PV

Peace on earth, and mercy mild;/God and sinners reconciled. The Nativity.
Charles Wesley. BLRP

"Peace on earth, good will to men!" Christmas Carol. J. R. Newell.
BLRP

Peace on earth, good will toward men. God of Peace, in Peace Preserve Us.
Ernst W. Olson. AH

"Peace on earth, goodwill to men." Christmas Eve. Marion Edey. YeAr

Peace on earth, peace on earth, peace on earth. What A Grand and Glorious
Feeling. Bill Wolff. FSW

Peace on Israel. Blessed Is Everyone. *Anonymous.* AH

Peace, peace! I come. Dipsychus. Arthur Hugh Clough. VLP

Peace, Peace on Earth! The Prince of Peace is born! A Christmas Carol.
Samuel Taylor Coleridge. ISi; OxBoCh

Peace, remote in the morning star. Vigils. Siegfried Sassoon. CMoP

"Peace, Sheriff," said the hairy man, "I'm no hooper–I'm/from Dumas,
Arkansas." The Narrative Hooper and L.D.O. Sestina with a Long Last
Line. James Whitehead. HoPM; TAT

Peace, since you know not love. To the Harpies. Arthur Davison Ficke.
HBV 1-2

Peace that hallows rudest ways. Forerunners. Ralph Waldo Emerson
AA; AnNE; OxBA

The peace that "passeth knowledge"/reigns in the earth again. A Forest
Meditation. Bernice Hall Legg. PGD

Peace to ev'ry Christian Heart! The Soul's Tendency Towards Its True
Centre. John Byrom. CEP

Peace to his manes; and may he sleep/As soundly as his readers did! Epitaph
on a Well-Known Poet. Thomas Moore. DBV

Peace to the heart's rage. Solstitium Saeculare. Robert Fitzgerald. MoVE

Peace to the heart that can accept this cold! The Castle of Thorns. Yvor
Winters. NoAm

Peace to the world from ports without a gun! At Gibraltar. George
Edward Woodberry. AA; AnAmPo; GN

Peace war religion revolution/Will not help. This Tokyo. Gary Snyder.
NeAP

Peace will be yours, the greatest known. With Thee. Cora M. Pinkham.
STF

The peaceable kingdom/made by your hands. For Edward Hicks. David
Helwig. NOBC

The peaceful barracks where their bodies/sleep. For Decoration Day:
1861-1865. Rupert Hughes. AA

Peaceful dreams! Army Bugle Calls: Taps. *Anonymous.* TreF

Peaceful now that its peace/Lay busily hid. A Grasshopper. Richard
Wilbur. HAP; HoPM

...Peacefully continuing in his verse forever. The High Bridge above the
Tagus River at Toledo. William Carlos Williams. CTC

Peacefully pursue their war. Picasso and Matisse. Robert Francis.
NePoAm

Peacefully round him circling,/Pursued their Heavenly way. The Bible.
David Levi. TrJP

Peacefully upon its plantlike stem. Flowers By the Sea. William Carlos
Williams. AmLP; AnEnPo; CMoP; ExPo; GoJo; MoAB; MoAmPo;
NoAm; TAP

The peacock's tail is furthest from his sight! Pride. Barten Holyday.
FaBoEE

The peacock spreads his fan. Story of Isaac. Leonard Cohen. VWA

The Peak still glimmers: thrill, my/spirit, thrill! Martyrdom. Rufus Learsi.
TrJP

The peaks will be white and the leaves be gone. Blue Smoke. Frances
Frost. SiSoSe

:A peal of groans/Cry'd Egypt is no more... All for Love. John Dryden.
BoW

Peans to advaunce her name,/New Canaans everlasting fame. New Canaans
Genius: Epilogus. Thomas Morton. SCAP

"Peanuts or lollies!" sez a boy upstairs. The Play. C. J. Dennis. PoAu
1-2

Pearl in her tears, and in her hair/Offers thee gold. And She Washed His
Feet with Her Tears,... Sir Edward Sherburne. CBEP; MeLP; OBS;
OxBoCh

Pearl-shells and rubied star-fish they admire,/And will arrange above the
parlour-fire. The Borough. George Crabbe. FaBoPP

Pearls singly-whispering. The Moon Is Hiding in. Edward Estlin
Cummings. AtBAP

The pears are not seen/As the observer wills. Study of Two Pears. Wallace
Stevens. AP; InPK; InPS; NU; OxBA; PAI

The peasants watch them die. The Peasants. Alun Lewis. LiTM; PPP

A pebble wakens in a sleepy pond. Poem in May. John Hewitt. NeIP

Pebbles and grains will be modifed put in human form. Hmmmm, 14.
Leslie Scalapino. NPGG

Pecks at my heart/With pink and tender bill. White Swan. Glanz-Leyeles.
A. VWA

...A peculiar Jewish-Russian air.../Blessed be he who has breathed it. A
Woman from the Book of Genesis. Dovid Knut. VWA

A peculiar name flickers in the mirror, and then disappears. Picture of Little
Letters. John Koethe. AMV-81

Pedant, fool–lie/with what we make of need. Rainy Night at the Writers'
Colony. Josephine Jacobsen. TAP

Peddling joy/On the end of a string. Balloon Man. Jessica Nelson North.
SoPo

Pedigreed bitches pregnant with bloodhounds. The City Mouse and the
Garden Mouse. Christina Georgina Rossetti. FaPON

Pedlar arise a new day a new day/to be/hocked/in the streets Pedlar.
Sharon Nelson. VWA

Peek in the inky beauty of the roofs. Waking in New York. Allen Ginsberg. NYP

Peel peel/Peel off/The skin. Special Bulletin. Langston Hughes. PoBA

Peeling an apple somewhere far away. A Primer of the Daily Round. Howard Nemerov. NYBP; SM; WeW

Peeling peeling the onion skin/down to the nothingness within. Five Lyrics from "Good for Nothing Man". Kenneth Pitchford. CoPo

...Peeping at me, peeping/at him, peeping at me enjoying the rewards/of being without age-spots. On Youth, the Warden & Solitary! Leon Baker. LFAC

Peeps in fair fragments forth the full-orb'd harvest-moon! On a Ruined House in a Romantic Country. Samuel Taylor Coleridge. FaBoPa; Par

Peer at the rest, but cannot tell/How much is cut off by my Shell. From a Street Corner. Eleanor Hammond. HBMV

Peering from balconies for his tragic twist. Tales of the Islands, II. Derek Walcott. OxBTC

...Peering/near-sightedly down its furthest reaches. The Gnomes. Beth Bentley. SaC

Peerless, pre-eminent fruit, who dwellest apart/In noble solitude! The Lychee. Wang I. FaBoCh

The peerless splendors of thy soul by far/Outshine the glow of heaven's serenest star. Mary Immaculate. Eleanor C. Donnelly. CAW

Pell-mell let's to the battle fall,/And lofty music sound, a.' A Song of the Seamen and Land Soldiers. *Anonymous.* OBSS

...Pelted by the shit of the stars at last in flood/like a breath. Easter. Frank O'Hara. EAS

Penance, and standing so, are both but one. Upon Groins: Epigram. Robert Herrick. CaPo

Pendant for my lips, Maria! Mary. Fray Angelico Chavez. ISi

The penetrating Biblical cold. Haifa. Dovid Knut. VWA

Penitential low recall. Late Light. Edmund Charles Blunden. EnLoPo

The pennant.... Barbarian. Arthur Rimbaud. LiTW

The penny that usurps the poor. The Reckoning. Theodore Roethke. PoA

The pensive goat and sportive cow,/Hilarious, leap from bough to bough. 'Tis Midnight. *Anonymous.* NA; NTCP

A pentagram/cut in packed soil,/the bricks stacked ready. Symbolum. Johann Wolfgang von Goethe. FaBoPV

People all eating/Camp quiet again. Kilaben Bay Song. *Anonymous.* NOAV

The people are calling/South Africa, are you listening? Echo of Mandela. Zindzi Mandela. WhB

People are good to her On the Train. Rachel McAlpine. OCNZ

...People in tennis/whites who look so graceful from this distance. Old Dominion. Robert Hass. MAYP

People, it don't seem like to me/that God takes care of old folks and fools Fool's Blues. Funny Paper Smith. BluL

The people keep a-coming and the train done gone. Mary Had a Baby. *Anonymous.* BoAN 1-2; FSW

People; let us nourish & protect each other Elegy. Karoniaktatie. STE

People like to watch baseball games,/Where Things are not confused with Names. The Umpire. Walker Gibson. NePoAm; SD

People live here...you'd be amazed. A Friend of the Family. Louis Simpson. NNaP

People lived there. Now we live there... Lynching and Burning. Primus St. John. PoBA

The people move/in a fine thin smoke,/the people, yes. The People, Yes. Carl Sandburg. FYAP

The people nod and applaud. Love. Anthony Ostroff. FAZ

A people of love, a compassionate people. Out of the Strong, Sweetness. Charles Reznikoff. VWA

A people renowned in war and peace and faith. The Land Called Scotia. Donatus. NOBI

A people's dream that died in bloody snow. Dead in Bloody Snow. Meridel Le Sueur. GP

People's friends are people's sarcophagi. Funebrial Reflections. Ogden Nash. ImOP

...People said that/he was holding clean globes in his hands. Medgar Evers. Gwendolyn Brooks. NoP; PoBA

People shoot the Windigo, they/do not pray for him, or it. Windigo. Paulette Jiles. NOBC

The people strode, with step of hope,/To the music in their hearts. Vicksburg. Paul Hamilton Hayne. AA; MC; PAH

People tell/of the melting/man. Snowman. Andrew McCord Jones. LFAC

People think I drink, or something. Grotesques (excerpt). Don (Donald Robert Marquis) Marquis. FiBHP

The people, those by which it lives and dies. The Owl in the Sarcophagus. Wallace Stevens. FaBoMo

People turning into pullets, distributor caps, jackhammers. Triplets. Michael Brownstein. APU

The people wander forward now. And the world begins. Day Begins at Governor's Square Mall. Leon Stokesbury. MAYP

The people who own them seem rock-true and marvelously/self-sufficient. The Ongoing Story. John Ashbery. HaCAP

...People whose song/hearts break if there is no song mouth; these are my people. Work Gangs. Carl Sandburg. SaC

People you've seen somewhere? Bowwow! Dog. William Jay Smith. GoJo

Peopled with wolves and our lost, flower-gathering/sisters they feed on. Little Red Riding Hood. Olga Broumas. DFT

Pepe, Luis, Coyotito,/Ended not as they began. The Smugglers. Owen Wister. BPAW

Peradventure they foresaw the day/Now dawning in Californi-a. The Californian. Jesse Hutchinson. AmFP

Perchance a lurking tiger sleeps therein. The Gulistan. Muslih-ud-Din Sa'di. AWP; LiTW

Perchance an elfin choir is swarming nigh,/To whisper soft, sweet bridal melodies. To Schmidlein–2. August von Platen. PeHV

Perchance, beloved, when the years have lengthened–/They will remember us. The Nights Remembered. Harold Vinal. HBMV

Perchance I knew what I was about.... Night (excerpts). Charles Peguy. LiTW

Perchance I may return with others there/When I have purged my guilt. The Palace of Art. Alfred, Lord Tennyson. EnLi 1-2; MaVP; OAEP; VLP

Perchance it is of them the poet saith/"Dear as remembered kisses after death." Constancy. Minor Watson. HBV 1-2

Perchance the heart may keep its songs of spring/Even through the wintry dream of life's December. Omnia Somnia. Rosamund Marriott Watson. HBV 1-2

–Perchance upon that desolate quest again. Cling to Me. John Le Gay Brereton. PeHV

Perched on a rickety chair, he wipes his glasses/Watches the hours go by, and mourns his losses. Blues for an Old Blue. Walker Gibson. NYBP

Perched on your spray of speech. Silence Spoke with Your Voice. Ryah Tumarkin Goodman. GoYe

Le Pere, et le Fils, et le Pigeon. Limerick: "Il etait un jeune homme de Dijon." *Anonymous.* LiBL

Perennial tears descend in gems. The Valley of Unrest. Edgar Allan Poe. AP; PoEL 1-5; ViBoPo

Perfect amid the flames, like Cranmer's heart. The True Martyr. Thomas Wade. OBVV

The perfect and nonexistent obsequies. Pacific Sonnets. George Barker. LiTM; MOS

The perfect animal, the group animal. Skinning-the-Cat. Dennis Schmitz. NPGG

Perfect at last/In the image of Him! Beautiful Lily. Alice Mortenson. BePJ

Perfect. Beast, brute, bastared. O dog my God! Elegy V. George Barker. FaBoTw

The perfect body is itself the soul. Before a Statue of Achilles. George Santayana. HBV 1-2

Perfect distance from what is. The Map. Mark Strand. NYBP

A perfect grievance–rolled from off the tongue. The Precious Pearl. Pat Wilson. AnNZ

A perfect halo of rich golden light. A Serendipity of Love. Richard Aldridge. NePoAm-2

...Perfect law of love/Bids spheres and atoms in just order move. The Hand and Foot. Jones Very. TAP

Perfect love is Jesus only,/Come to dwell in you and me. Perfect Love. *Anonymous.* STF

Perfect most of all her song. She Was Young and Blithe and Fair. Harold Monro. HBV 1-2

The perfect order trusted to the dead. The Astronomers of Mont Blanc. Edgar Bowers. PoA; QFR

The perfect quiet that comes after rain. Evensong. Conrad Aiken. HBMV; PG

The perfect razor of my rage. Brothers (I). James Reiss. AMV-81

Perfect, without wound nor mark! The Stations of the Cross. Padraic Colum. GoBC

Perfected and casual as to a child's eye/Soap bubbles are, and skipping stones. Lion & Honeycomb. Howard Nemerov. PP

Perfected in the moment of his fall. Snowflakes. Howard Nemerov. HaCAP; PCP

Perfection The Maximus Poems. Charles Olson. CAPP; CMoP; NMP

Perfection in the final negative. And the Dead. Sean Jennett. NeBP

The perfection/Of the flight or death of a bird. One Last Word. John Glassco. NOBC

Perfectly beautiful, perfectly ignorant of it. Piazza di Spagna, Early Morning. Richard Wilbur. GrPl; InPS; OBSP; PAI; SM; VGW

The perfidious goblets, the theater's skull, and the bane. Unsleeping City. Federico Garcia Lorca. NYP

Perform the dance/of my own being.   Demonstration.   Margaret Finefrock. AMV-80

Performing once again, for you and for me.   Civilisation and Its Discontents. John Ashbery.   CAPP; LCAP; TwCP

...Perfumed/With gums of paradise and eastern air.   The Alchemist, 1610. Ben Jonson.   EBEV; ViBoPo

Perhaps a building, and whatever is holy.   What I Saw in October.   Warren Carrier.   PoDr

Perhaps a butterfly.   Shankill.   Eileen Shanahan.   NeIP

...Perhaps a few/even dancing, joyful with the knowledge/of what they missed. The Cat in the Box.   Ann Rae Jonas.   SUW

Perhaps a slice of wedding cake,/Perhaps a toy or two.   My Bed Is a Boat. Robert Louis Stevenson.   GoTF; TreFS

Perhaps, alas, these prophet tears foretell.   Sonnets: A Sequence on Profane Love.   George Henry Boker.   AmePo

Perhaps all will be well.   A and B.   C. H. Sisson.   OxBC

Perhaps Aunt Ellie smiles to see/What she had never, when alive.   A Poor Relation.   Audrey McGaffin.   NePoAm-2

Perhaps forgive the vast impertinence.   Diminutivus Ululans.   Francis MacNamara.   OxBI

Perhaps had someone written mine/I might have been as great as they are. By Deputy.   Arthur St. John Adcock.   CenHV

Perhaps he does...O Lord, that House in Stratford!   Ben Jonson Entertains a Man from Stratford.   Edwin Arlington Robinson.   APA; ATP; CoAnAm; MAPA; MoAB; MoAmPo; MoPo

Perhaps he'll hear her low at morn/Lifting her horn in pleasant meads. Thomas MacDonagh.   Francis Ledwidge.   NOBI; OnYI; OxBI

Perhaps he'll let me turn the sign/And make the people Stop! and Go!   The Policeman.   Marjorie Seymour Watts.   TiPo

Perhaps he was found at the Throne.   William Blake.   James (1834-82) Thomson.   CBEP; HBV 1-2; OAEP; OBVV

Perhaps he was your father.   On a Wag in Mauchline.   Robert Burns. ELU; FiBHP

Perhaps he will fall.   Wilderness Gothic.   Alfred W. Purdy.   NOBC; NoP; PeCV

Perhaps hoping if he keeps on playing/he can keep from dying.   Harmonica Man.   P. Wolny.   PCP

...Perhaps/I'll be able to find it before the mails are closed.   A Postcard to Send to Sumer.   William Bronk.   VGW

Perhaps I'll see the hearts of men.   High Resolve.   Anonymous.   PoToHe

Perhaps I will, on my way/down-town, look in to-morrow!   Thalia.   Thomas Bailey Aldrich.   AA; HBV 1-2; InMe

Perhaps...in the coming years...   The Sad Years.   Eva Gore-Booth.   HBMV

Perhaps is the child, perhaps the summer and sea.   The Mirror.   John N. Morris.   PoA

Perhaps it's unlikely, but I'd like to stay.   O'Reilly's Reply.   Richard Weber. NMP

Perhaps it should be clear why i am here.   Setting/Slow Drag.   Carolyn M. Rodgers.   JB

Perhaps it will look down on the thatch yet.   The Christmas Tree.   Patricia Beer.   OBCP

Perhaps it would make me vain.   The Sparrow's Song.   Anonymous.   STF

Perhaps large stars will burn above/Their camp within the West.   The Camp Within the West.   Roderic Quinn.   PoAu 1-2

Perhaps my mother murdered me.'   The Inquest.   William Henry Davies. CBEP; DTC; GTBS-P; NOBE; OxBTC

–Perhaps no further dare.   The Fall of Hyperion.   John Keats.   OAEL 1-2

Perhaps nothing dies but husks.   At the Natural History Museum.   William Meredith.   NYP

Perhaps of Heav'n, if there a Dog-star be.   On the Sicilian Strand a Hare Well Wrought.   Decimus Magnus Ausonius.   OBVE

Perhaps one day men would be more spiritual.   The Ghostly Father.   Peter Redgrove.   MoBS; NePoEA-2

Perhaps, perhaps, perhaps, Thou'llt not move me again?   The Hut.   Avigdor Hamameiri.   LiTW

Perhaps she's with you now.   What They Do to You in Distant Places. Marvin Bell.   Psk

Perhaps silence/already climbs up the hour/as the rain climbs upon/the lightning.   From Life.   Lazer Eichenrand.   VWA

Perhaps some day he will weep for me.   The Weeping Willow.   Anonymous. AmFP

...Perhaps some find/Stella's great powers that so confuse my mind. Astrophel and Stella, XXXIV.   Sir Philip Sidney.   AAS; SiPS

Perhaps that is what/Being a friend means,/After all.   Love.   Roy Croft. BLPA; FaBoBe; TreFT

Perhaps that is what love means.   Why Do I Love You?   Roy Croft. PoToHe

Perhaps that will instruct them to/Ravage a poet's favorite view. Malediction.   Phyllis McGinley.   DBV

Perhaps the lamp my love in heaven/Hangs out to light the way for me. Song: "There's one great bunch of stars in heaven."   Theophile Marzials. OBVV

Perhaps the little fairy folk/Will visit you to-night.   The Fairy Folk.   Robert Bird.   HBV 1-2; HBVY

(Perhaps the parson) is self-interest.   A Vulgar Error.   J. E. Thorold Rogers. FaBoEE

Perhaps these are not poetic/times/at all   For Saundra.   Nikki Giovanni. BPo; TTY

Perhaps to blossom soon again.   A Cure for the Spleen.   Matthew Green. OBEC

Perhaps we do not altogether either/who cannot touch him.   Eagle Plain. Robert Francis.   AmFN

Perhaps we shall be One at once.   On His Garden Book.   Francis Daniel Pastorius.   SCAP

Perhaps we will bring it down sometime/when we visit you at the prison.   A Letter from Home.   John Paul Minarik.   LFAC

Perhaps you have a birthday every week!   Tree Birthdays.   Mary Carolyn Davies.   BiCB; OHIP

...Perhaps you'll let us know/If anything happens in the world below?   Letter to Graham and Anna.   Louis MacNeice.   OBTV

Perhaps you're a goddess that bears a bright beacon.   Hollywood.   Don Blanding.   YaD

...Perhaps you should talk to them?   The Medium.   Elaine Feinstein.   BrRo

Perhaps you told me/you were not/dead.   The Night a Sailor Came to Me in a Dream.   Diane Wakoski.   TAP; VGW

Perhaps/You will recall/John Brown.   October 16: The Raid.   Langston Hughes.   BOLo; PoBA

Perianth recessing/as we watched.   The Night-Blooming Cereus.   Robert Earl Hayden.   HoAn; NU

The peril that His care permits/Is our defence where'er we go.   Sometimes. Annie Johnson Flint.   STF

Perilous is sweeping change, all chance unsound.   Blest Statesman He, Whose Mind's Unselfish Will.   William Wordsworth.   VLP

Perished so vast a multitude of men.   Salamis.   Aeschylus.   WaaP

The permanence of the young men/Who are not by his side.   The Permanence of the Young Men.   William Soutar.   NeBP; OxBS

Permanently, seriously/without thought.   At the Ball Game.   William Carlos Williams.   CMoP; ExPo; LiSp; NoAm; NOBA

Permeable world,–all man would come to.   Great God Paused among Men. Daniel Berrigan.   MAT

Permissive, smiling on our silliness You forged.   Lauds.   John Berryman. HAP

Permit me voyage, Love, into your hands.   Permit Me Voyage.   James Agee. MoAmPo

The perpetual struggle of Good and Evil.   The Rock.   Thomas Stearns Eliot. TiPo

Perplex him in his hinder parts.   Another.   Robert Herrick.   AnAnS 2

Perplexed, bewildered, languishing, an alien/Who was born to cherish all his world forgot.   To a Roman.   J. C. Squire.   HBMV

...Perplexed/to find you where it hid a bolted room.   Pin-Up Girl.   Louis O. Coxe.   WaP

Perplexing song/Impossible to write.   Melody.   Shmuel Moreh.   VWA

Perrie, merrie, dixi, domine.   The Tokens of Love: II.   Anonymous.   GBP

Persephoneous lutes/to be redeemed,/to swell the spring.   Sussyissfriin. Philip Dow.   NPGG

Perseverant in not doing what he need not do.   On Visiting Central Park Zoo.   Alan Dugan.   NYP

Persia's pale star: so empire passed away/From Harold's brow,–but He disdained to live!   Waterloo.   Aubrey Thomas De Vere.   HBV 1-2

The Persian on his throne!   The Vision of Belshazzar.   George Gordon, Lord Byron.   FaPo; GN; HBV 1-2

The person I have become now/Can be found.   On Going Home.   Marjorie L. Agnew.   GoYe

A person too, he must agree some love can be.   Sonnet: Kamikaze. Bernadette Mayer.   APU

A personal experience of the the body of Mrs. Boogry/before I pass from lust! Dream Song.   John Berryman.   FaBoMo

Personally, I have other things to do.   Serenade.   Kenneth Slessor.   PoL

Perspective leads us to admire is the brown calfskin of the/principal executioner's boots.   Coming Events.   John Montague.   FaBoIP

Persuade the world to trouble me no more!   The Sad Day.   Thomas Flatman.   OBEV

Peruked and stately for the final act.   Alceste in the Wilderness.   Anthony Hecht.   ConAP; PoA

The pessimist sees the hole.   Optimist and Pessimist.   McLandburgh Wilson. GoTF; TreFT

A petal falls from the Dreamland Rose.   Ballade of the Dreamland Rose. Brian Hooker.   HBMV

The petalled flesh of the human rose.   Good for Nothing Man.   Kenneth Ptichford.   CoPo

The petals from the plum turn brown/and blow/Down the dark driveway. Last Breath.   Laura Chester.   NPGG

Petals on a wet, black bough.   In a Station of the Metro.   Ezra Pound. AmP; AmPP; CAD; ExPo; ForPo; HAP; HeIP; InPK; MoAB; MoAmPo; NIP; NoAm; NOBA; OxBA; TAP; UnPo; VGW; WeW

Peter, go ring dem bells I heard f'om heav'n today,/I heard f'om heav'n today.   Peter, Go Ring Dem Bells.   Anonymous.   BoAN 1-2

The petrifactions of a plodding brain,/That, ere they reach the top, fall lumbering back again.   English Bards and Scotch Reviewers.   George Gordon, Lord Byron.   OBSV

Petrified like skeletons.   Drunken Streets.   Malka Locker.   VWA

Petrushka's valentine pivots on its pin.   The Wine Menagerie.   Hart Crane. AP; NoAm; NOBA; OxBA; VGW

Petticoats up/And trousers down.   Apples Be Ripe.   Anonymous.   GBP

The pettiness got him with metal.   Brother Malcolm: Waste Limit.   Clarence Major.   BP

Petting one another's love so it won't be sad.   Getting Serious.   Gary Soto. NPGG

A phallus going around a corner/carefully   Banana.   Adrian Mitchell.   PV

A phantom of departed splendour lone.   Satan.   Michael Madhusudan Dutt. ACV

Phantom or real,/I have looked on a noble animal.   Chimera.   Barbara Howes.   MP; TwCP

...A Pharaoh's portion of turkey and/pumpkin pie.   This Is the Life.   Louis MacNeice.   NoAm

The pheasant-shooter be himself the pheasant!   The Bofors A.A. Gun.   Gavin Ewart.   WaP

...Pheasants/Are waiting at the head of the stairs with robbers' eyes.   The Clear Air of October.   Robert Bly.   NaP; NoAm

"Phew! wow! pow! zat voss somsink!"   The Discovery of LSD a True Story.   Anselm Hollo.   PoM

Phil, Heb, James, Pet, Pet, John, John, John, Jude,/Revelations.   Memoria Technica for the Books of the Bible.   Braybrooke.   FaBoUs

Phil's not one of them there highbrows.   Brats.   X. J. Kennedy.   NLV

Philip will crie still: yet, yet, yet.   Of All the Birds That I Do Know.   Anonymous.   CH; NCEP

Philista's pomp and Art's pomposities!   Translator to Translated.   Ezra Pound.   FaBoEE

Phillis was loved, and she liked Coridon.   Coridon and Phillis.   Robert Greene.   OBSC

Phillis, without frown or smile,/Sat and knotted all the while!   Song: "Hears not my Phillis how the birds."   Sir Charles Sedley.   EnLoPo; SeCV 1-2

...The philosophy/of the saw, the theory of the nail/that holds my world in place.   The Ex-Poet.   Bill Zavatsky.   APU

Philosophy was wrong, and you may meet.   Parting at Dawn.   John Crowe Ransom.   AnAmPo

The phlegm of last rites/stains the sleeves of the survivors   North to Milwaukee.   Gerald Vizenor.   VoR

Phoebus forgets not his companion.   To the Noble Sir Francis Drake.   Thomas Beedome.   OBSP

Phoebus ordained: presenting, see,/The laurel never sere.'   Mercury. On Losing my Pocket Milton...   Robert Andrews.   NOEC

...Phoenixes/burning quietly, where the dew cannot climb.   Late Air.   Elizabeth Bishop.   PoPl

'Phoning the news/through a daffodil.   Hello!   Louise Ayres Garnett. SiSoSe

A photograph of the real thing.   Still Life.   Regina M. Austin.   AMV-80

Photographs still reflect a young girl/before an awkward car.   Mary Ackerman, 1938, Eugene Buechel Photograph Museum of Modern Art...   Diane Glancy.   STE

The Phryne whom he loved!   Praxiteles and Phryne.   James Russell Lowell AA; BeLS

Phyllida flouts me.   Oh, What a Plague Is Love!   Anonymous.   InvP

...Phyllida/Is all the world to me!   The Ladies of St. James's.   Henry Austin Dobson.   HBV 1-2; PoRA

Phyllis, without frown or smile,/Sat and knotted all the while.   Phyllis Knotting.   Sir Charles Sedley.   NOBE

Pianissississimo/Notes for the horn.   Wrath.   John Hollander.   PV

...The piano stood/For all that we wanted to do yet never would.   Piano Lessons.   Baron Wormser.   MAYP

Pibroch of Donuil Dhu,/Kneel for the onset!   Pibroch of Donald Dhu.   Sir Walter Scott.   EnLi 1-2; FaBoCh; FaPoR; HBV 1-2; InPo; NBM; OxBS; PoEL 1-5

"Pick on somebody your own size."   Way Down South...   Anonymous. EvOK; SoPo

Pick your speed, pick your steed.   Pony Girl.   Jane P. Moreland.   PH

Picked and plucked and put in a pie.   Riddle: "Higgledy-piggledy here we lie."   Anonymous.   OxNR

The picket's off duty forever!   All.Quiet along the Potomac.   Ethel Lynn Beers.   AA; PaPo; PSoN; TrAS

The picket's off duty forever.   The Picket-Guard.   Ethel Lynn Beers.   HBV 1-2; MC; PAH

Pickety/Pickety/Pick.   The Pickety Fence.   David McCord.   NTCP; TiPo

Pickin' on de old banjo.   Massa's in de Cold, Cold Ground.   Stephen Collins Foster.   TreF

Picking her way through a field/of imaginary violets.   Pliny Jane.   Mildred Luton.   PH

Picking off stragglers/with the garden hose.   Termites.   Eric Chock.   BrSi

Picking the horn of plenty's garbage can.   In the Year of Many Conversions and the Private Soul.   John Ciardi.   MiAP

Picking us up in one state and putting/Us down in a different one every time.   Climbing.   Tom Clark.   APU

The pickpockets move among the crowds.   Return of a Popular Statesman.   Vincent Buckley.   CBAP

The Pickwick, the Owl, and the Waverley Pen.   The Waverley Pen.   Anonymous.   FaBoUs

The picter's deed, and this is leevin'.   A Border Burn.   J.B. Selkirk.   PoSH

A picture keeps its eyes, somehow.   Faded Pictures.   William Vaughn Moody.   AP

Picture of their teacher crumbling/before a blackboard spattered with lessons.   The Unteaching.   Carole Oles.   SOTS

The pictures come, the pictures go,/Quick, quick, currente calamo.   Currente Calamo.   Arthur Hugh Clough.   LoBV

Pictures show us, the living, our true character, living/out of age....   The Church of the Sacred Heart.   Ashton Greene.   NePoAm

The piebald clouds spill down on us like a country woman's house-dress.   Sparrow Hills.   Boris Pasternak.   NaP

Piece the world together, boys, but not with your hands.   Parochial Theme.   Wallace Stevens.   LiTA

A piece would be missing/from my jigsaw-puzzle day.   Commitment in a City.   Margaret Tsuda.   CTBA

Pieces of a green/bottle   Between Walls.   William Carlos Williams.   HoPM; SOTW; TAP; VGW

Pieces of the puzzle of the night/that fit nowhere/and precisely where they are.   Benediction.   William Freedman.   VWA

Pierce with your eyes my heart, or pluck it out.   Give Me a Kiss.   Anonymous.   InvP; UnTE

Pierced by a brilliant nerve of sound.   New Music.   Gwen Harwood. CBAP

Pierced by the sounds of winter-crazed birds.   Hunger.   Ruth Stone.   InPS

Pierced on the cruel cross,/At peace shall never be.   Lauda.   Girolamo Beneveni.   CAW

Pierces me with "Alas/That the beloved must die!"   In the Egyptian Museum.   Janet Lewis.   NYBP; QFR

The piercing absence of one face/withdrawn for ever from my sight.   Last Meeting.   Gwen Harwood.   PoAu 1-2

...A piercing cry/That tears my heart. "Eloi...lama/Sabachthani!"   Symbols.   John Richard Moreland.   PGD

Piercing the darkness/for the slightest/wind and impulse.   Wind and Impulse.   Duane Big Eagle.   STE

Piercing through rotting bark for their food.   Written in Dejection near Rome.   Robert Bly.   NaP

Pierrot whistled down the wind–/And of course I went!   Resolution.   Wiolar".   InMe

A pigeon dreaming of red flowers.   Sightings I.   Jerome Rothenberg.   CoPo

...The pigeons were picking/up crumbs in the dark February wind.   February.   Bill Berkson.   ANYP

The pigment the genius of a world/artless but supreme...   The Last Turn.   William Carlos Williams.   NYP

...The pigmy plan/Is one note each and the tune goes out free.   Sonnet: "Not wrongly moved by this dismaying scene."   William Empson.   LiTM; WaP

Pile up, and fill my seedless eyes.   Avalanche.   Adrien Stoutenburg.   NYBP

...Piled high/with thick ivy and a bed of white reed.   Epigram: "I celebrate Rhegion."   Anonymous.   PeHV

The pilgrim sighs and sings for thee,/O miserere, Domine!   The Monks of Bangor's March.   Sir Walter Scott.   CAW

The pilgrim with the weary heart/Brings to the grave his tears.   At Delos.   Duncan Campbell Scott.   PeCV

Piling the golden fleeces at her feet.   Museum Piece.   Lawrence P. Spingarn. GoYe

Pilk lauds the verse of Jobble to the skies...   Perpetuum Mobile.   Edith Sitwell.   HBMV

Pillage to soldiers, prize-money to seamen.   Don Juan.   George Gordon, Lord Byron.   MCCG

A pillar of damp fire.   The Old Tree.   Andrew Young.   GoJo

A pillar of fire!   To Be Said at the Seder.   Karl Wolfskehl.   TrJP

A pillar of fire shall light the way/While you journey heavenward.   Trust in Me.   Anonymous.   AH

The pillar perking from the groin of me.   Epigrams on Priapus.   Anonymous. ErPo

A pin dropt in and turn'd the scale.   On a Certain Effeminate Peer.   John Winstanley.   FaBoEE

The pin men of madness in marathon trim/race round the track of the stadium pupil.   The Stenographers.   P. K. Page.   CaP; HeIP; LiTM; NoP; OBCV; PeCV

Pindar, forgetful of his pipes for you.	Pindar.	Antipater of Sidon.	AWP

A pine in solitude/Cradling a dove.	No One So Much As You.	Edward ("Edward Eastaway") Thomas.	ChMP; GBL

Pines and magnolias. Also, we have lately,/Certain uncertainties–.	Report from the Carolinas.	Helen Bevington.	AmFN

The pines dance on, the quick and dead together.	Dance of Death.	Aulus Persius Flaccus.	AnAmPo

...Pines sieving/air, the cleat ringing like small jewelry.	Looking for the Melungeon.	Dave Smith.	HaCAP

The pines, the patient stars,/And the new day.	The Pilgrim.	Richard Wightman.	WGRP

The pining body;/Just sleep.	Lullaby.	Shlomo Vinner.	VWA

–Pink/as the breasts of Botticelli's Venus–foretinting dawn.	Above the Arno.	May Swenson.	NYBP

Pink propaganda of annihilation.	Twentyseven Bums.	Edward Estlin Cummings.	OBAL

Pinning themselves to our sleeves/Like medals given the brave.	The Field Hospital.	Paul Muldoon.	CIP

Pinning you to me on a sword of tears.	Poem: "I do not want to be your weeping woman."	Alison Boodson.	NeBP

Pioneers! O pioneers!	Pioneers! O Pioneers!	Walt Whitman.	FaBoBe; WHA

A pious example of Christian peace!	A Message of Peace.	John Boyle O'Reilly.	OnYI

A pious, sordid, drunken scold.	On Delia.	Sir Hildebrand Jacob.	FaBoEE

A pious wish to whiteness gone over/or nothing.	Queen-Ann's-Lace.	William Carlos Williams.	AmPP; AP; BLPL; MoAB; MoAmPo; NoAm; NOBA; NoP; PrIm; TAP

Pipe of Pan was once its naming, now it/hath a name diviner.	World Music.	Frances Louisa Bushnell.	AA

Piping a magic of March,/Just as he did long ago!	Pan-Pipes.	Patrick Reginald Chalmers.	HBMV

Piping on reeds I had sat, and had lulled my sorrow to/sleep.	Idylls.	Moschus.	AWP

Piping one death was over.	The Nesting Ground.	David Wagoner.	PoCh

Pipperoo, pippera, pipperum...The rest is rot.	On an Old Horn.	Wallace Stevens.	LiTA

Pips holding Eve's promise here,/And Adam's grief.	Orchard Snow.	J. B. Goodenough.	AMV-81

Pirate and wrecker kept their revels then.	The Buccaneer: The Island.	Richard Henry Dana.	AnNE

The Pirate Don Durk of Dowdee.	The Pirate Don Durk of Dowdee.	Mildred Plew Merryman.	OnUR; SoPo; TiPo

A pismire, a conflagrations, a.......	The Clouds.	William Carlos Williams.	MoPo; VGW

Piss in the river beyond O'Ryan's bar.	Five for the Grace.	Winfield Townley Scott.	VGW

...Piss on sobriety, and take care. Dick.	Letter to Logan from Milltown.	Richard Hugo.	NNaP

Piss on this university.	Dog Prospectus.	Peter Redgrove.	OxBC

Pit my plum.	Song: Fie My Fum.	Allen Ginsberg.	ErPo

...The pit/that opens, toothed with dew.	Song of the Invisible Corpse in the Field.	Gregory Orr.	LTB

Pitch a tent in the pasture, and starve.	Pursuit from Under.	James Dickey.	HAP; PPP

(The pitcher walks), casual/in the space where the poem has happened.	The Double-Play.	Robert Wallace.	SD

...Pitches our pod/To the mouth of the death for which no one is ready.	Three Memorial Sonnets.	George Barker.	MasP

A piteous, reeking relic, where the clean, sweet winds/still blow.	The Last Gloucesterman.	Gordon Grant.	EtS

Pity a wretch like him should ever live!	The Monument.	Samuel Wesley.	OBSP

Pity and innocence his heart at rest.	In Memory of G. K. Chesterton.	Walter De la Mare.	GoBC

"Pity. Design."	Said J. Alfred Prufrock.	George Starbuck.	PV

Pity Inexorable, Remorseless Love.	Prayer.	John Hall Wheelock.	EaLo; NePoAm

Pity me, for here you see me/Persecuted, poor, and old.	Once I Was a Monarch's Daughter.	Anonymous.	PBBP

Pity me, lean to me,/Thou God above me!	A Woman's Thought.	Richard Watson Gilder.	HBV 1-2

Pity me, my darling/And carry me away.	Factory Girl.	Anonymous.	ABF; FSW; SaC

Pity me, too, who found so soon a tomb.	Upon a Young Mother of Many Children.	Robert Herrick.	CaPo

Pity rather the rabbit who even when free/Keeps trembling in his skin.	Lion and Rabbit.	Eliezer Greenberg.	BoAnP

Pity that every song he tried to teach her/Made it more diffifcult for her to sing.	Fisherman's Blunder off New Bedford, Massachusetts.	Annemarie Ewing.	NePoAm-2

Pity the fat, round, pretty, blushing thing/Should ere be thus condemned to counseling.	The Nine.	John, of buckingham Sheffield.	APAS

Pity the world, or else this glutton be,/To eat the world's due, by the grave and thee.	Sonnets, I: "From fairest creatures we desire increase."	William Shakespeare.	CTC; FaBoEn; LiTB; LiTL; MasP; OAEP; OBSC; PBBP; TrGrPo

Pity them, Mother,/the untaught/of earth.	The Black Madonna.	Albert Rice.	CDC

Pity this small and new/Bright soul on hands and knees.	A Prayer for My Son.	Yvor Winters.	CrMA; TrPWD

Pity us, pray for us, ye that will!	Wishmakers' Town.	William Young.	AA

A pity you cannot see your fault,/as you follow foreign ways.	Two Sons.	Laoiseach Mac An Bhaird.	NOBI

Pity your littleness from all my passion,/Leave you my sins to weep and whine away!	You Preach to Me of Laws.	Iris Tree.	HBMV

Place after place we touch no more than going.	Islanders, Inlanders.	Michael Mott.	PoA

Place before thy pardoning Son!	Lux Advenit Veneranda.	Adam of St. Victor.	CAW

Place de la Concorde/At noon August Fifteenth.	La Belle Saison.	Jacques Prevert.	CAD

...A place/I may go both in and out of.	Thanksgiving for a Habitat.	W. H. Auden.	NYBP

The place is Haunted!	The Haunted House.	Thomas Hood.	AnEnPo; EBEV; MyFE; NBM; SeCePo; WiR

The place my mother lies buried in/Is far too good for thee.	Jellon Grame (A version).	Anonymous.	BaBo; EBEV; ESPB; OxBB

A place of toil by daytime,/Of dreams when toil is done.	A Net to Snare the Moonlight.	Vachel Lindsay.	PoLf

...The place's spell/is lifted: the trunk bare, the frog elsewhere.	Between Leaps.	Brad Leithauser.	MAYP

PLACE STAMP/HERE	In Lucas, Kansas.	Jonathan Williams.	FAZ

The place that calls you hence is, at the worst,/Milk all the way.	To the Infant Martyrs.	Richard Crashaw.	NoP; OBSP; SeCV 1-2

A place that His hand has made.	The Red Sea Place in Your Life.	Annie Johnson Flint.	BLRP

The place that's broken my heart–the place where I've lived/my life.	The Old Place.	Blanche Edith Baughan.	AnNZ

The place that was you/changed to air.	Even There.	Lyn Lifshin.	IHMS

A place to be lonely for.	Taos Winter.	Patty L. Harjo.	VoR

A place to moor my bark.	Motto for a Dog House.	Arthur Guiterman.	GDP

A place to stand and love in for a day,/With darkness and the death-hour rounding it.	Sonnets from the Portuguese, XXII.	Elizabeth Barrett Browning.	AnFE; EnLi 1-2

A place to start.	Considerations.	David Helwig.	NOBC

The place where is ruled/its overwhelming–/white	Etat (excerpt).	Anne-Marie Albiach.	PBNaP

Place where passing souls can rest/On the way and be their best.	A Prayer.	Edwin Markham.	HBMV; HBVY; PGD; TrPWD; TRV; WGRP

The place where the Lord once lay,/Is empty forevermore.	The Sepulcher.	Annie Johnson Flint.	STF

...A place/Where there's nothing to eat and but little to steal.	The Indian Convert.	Philip Freneau.	TAP

Placed before the god with the handsome countenance.	Love Song: "My boat sails downstream."	Anonymous.	TTY

Placed him as Musagetes on their throne.	Shakespeare.	Henry Wadsworth Longfellow.	AWP; InPo; MAmP

Placed number four, with twenty-eight below.	Columbia College, 1796.	Joseph Shippey.	PeD

Placed out in the afternoon sun.	Meditation for a Pickle Suite.	R. H. W. Dillard.	HoPM

The places/In which we all begin.	History.	Gary Soto.	GP

The placid cows pensively/Wondering why they wondered.	Three Things.	Joseph Auslander.	HBMV; TrJP

Plague me no longer now, for I/Am listening like the Orange Tree.	The Orange Tree.	John Shaw Neilson.	BoAV; CBAP; PoAu 1-2

Plagues and miracles/sand snakes/The lamb the lamb	Passover.	Rose Auslander.	VWA

Plain men/come out of the ground.	Through the Smoke Hole.	Gary Snyder.	PoM

Plain of the noblest companies!	A Farewell to Fal.	Gerald Nugent.	OnYI

The plain virtue of the chosen few.	Jansenist Journey.	Denis Devlin.	IPY

Plain virtue, which shall one day vice outshine,/And truth in rags a diamond from the mine.	A Remonstrance.	John Gerrard.	NOEC

Plainly not knowing/Its symbolism.	Jig for Sackbuts.	Dominic Bevin Wyndham Lewis.	ErPo

Plaiting a dark red love-knot into her long black hair.	The Highwayman.	Alfred Noyes.	BeLS; FaBV; FaFP; FPL; GoTF; GTBS; HBV 1-2; HBVY; MaC; MCCG; OBNV; OHFP; PoLf; TreFS

Plaiting the generations.	Combing.	Gladys Cardiff.	CDW; STE

Plane clenched in insubstantial clouds tattering like cobwebs/on wings catching flame. In Grandfather's Glasses. Patricia Peters. Str

The plane for America is a sort of star Gertrude Stein at Snails Bay. Peter Porter. OxBC

The planeitis for to agif us licht. May Poems. *Anonymous.* OxBS

...The planet spins/and tips these acres further into night. When the Cows Come down to Drink. Allen Hoey. WOLT

A planet surges, plunging, and goes out. The Hourglass. Weldon Kees. NYP

Planning revolution/or salvation/without me. Saying Goodbye. Suzanne Juhasz. IHMS

Plant daisies at his head and feet. De Mortuis Nil Nisi Bonum. Richard Realf. HBV 1-2

Plant of an age of railways, for flowering into today! Before Invasion, 1940. Sir John Betjeman. MoVE

The plant of honour is her house. Hen Under Bay-Tree. Ruth Pitter. OxBTC

An plant Thy strong sword/In their livers at last. Hymn to Moloch. Ralph Hodgson. HBMV; OxBTC

Plant you forty acres of cotton/and try to do yourself some good Go back to the Country. Jazz Gillum. BluL

Planted bang upon the table/A lightly roasted rump of horse. The Flying Bum: 1944. William Plomer. DTC

Plastic Jesus is a holy bar. Plastic Jesus. *Anonymous.* FSW

Plated the residue of Adz/With Monotony. Not Any More to Be Lacked. Emily Dickinson. MAmP

Platted quite neat to catch applause, with a sliding noose at the end. Her Whole Life is an Epigram. William Blake. InPK; NIP

Plautus impennis, the extinct Great Auk. In the Local Museum. Walter De la Mare. HAP

Play by me, bathe in me, mother and child. The Water-Babies. Charles Kingsley. GN

Play chess, as then we played together! The Chess-Board. Edward Robert Bulwer, Earl of Lytton. HBV 1-2

Play cross-purpose fore and aft/By the moon and candle-light. Moon and Candle-Light. William Renton. NOBV

(Play it boy, play it, play it)/(Yes, yes) I Been Treated Wrong. Washboard Sam. BluL

...Play/it out, run with it. Pet Panther. Archie Randolph Ammons. NoP

Play? Play?—What should he play? Pan with Us. Robert Frost. OxBA

Play, poppy lady, play/the tunes that go with waiting by the way. Moment Musicale. Wallace Gould. AnAmPo

Play sweeter than pray, that the darkened be gay. Master's in the Garden Again. John Crowe Ransom. AP

"Play up! play up! and play the game!" Vitaï Lampada. Sir Henry Newbolt. BLPA; FaPoR; OBWP; PaPo; TreF

Play what I get until the break of day. Whist. Eugene Fitch Ware. PoLf

...Play/without bumping their heads/or losing their way. Fireflies. Aileen Fisher. SoPo

Played gently while the beauteous statue reconciled/The jarred generations, and Sicily and Bohemia. Last Sheet. Roy Fuller. TEP

Player with Railroads and Freight Handler to the Nation. Chicago. Carl Sandburg. AmPP; AP; CMoP; FaBV; GoTF; LiTM; LoGBV; MoAB; MoAmPo; MoVE; NePA; NOBA; NoP; PoA; PoPl; TAP; TreF; UnPo; ViBoPo; YaD

Playful killer/Whose loving embrace/Splits the antelope's heart. Leopard. *Anonymous.* WTO

Playing a flute! The Coyote and the Locust. *Anonymous.* AWP

Playing at Royal Welch Fusiliers. The Next War. Robert Graves. BrPo

A-playing music/Unto empty pockets. I Am Raftery. Anthony Raftery. LiTW; OnYI

Playing naked and dirty among the chickens. An Event. Edward Field. CoAP

Playing soundlessly in the/Circle of dancing gopis. On Flower Wreath Hill (excerpt). Kenneth Rexroth. GP

Playing the queen to nobler company. Theseus and Ariadne. Robert Graves. HAP

Playing with/bleeding/blue lips Energy. Victor Hernandez Cruz. PoBA

Playing your blue steel/guitar book-long song/crazy! The Music. Everett Hoagland. CNA

The plays here at Mort author of News Some Bombs (excerpt). Ron Padgett. ANYP

Pleaders, blend pray'r in./So we seek Erinn— The Incantation. Amergin. OnYI

The pleading image of his native land. Wellington. Charles Harpur. NOAV

Pleas'd with the slippery Surface, swift descends. Frost at Night. James (1700-48) Thomson. OBEC

The pleasant land of counterpane. The Land of Counterpane. Robert Louis Stevenson. BrPo; EBEV; FaBoBe; FaFP; NLV; OxBChV; PoPl; SoPo

The pleasant'st fruits in all God's Paradise. Thou Art the Tree of Life. Edward Taylor. AH

Pleasant to live with and blessed are they. Blessed Are They. Wilhelmina Stitch. PoToHe

The pleasant wave has started muttering. Toward Winter. *Anonymous.* NOBI

Pleasantplash! Spring, St. Stephen's Green. Leslie Daiken. OnYI

PLEASE... Whale Song. Francis Maguire. BoAnP; PoL

"Please adjust your dress before leaving." Sweeney in Articulo (parody). Myra Buttle. BXAP; Par

...Please ask the king of glory, when/you enter heaven, to join us once again. My Lady Carenza of the lovely body. *Anonymous.* BoWoP

Please be certain that it grows/Very, very much like Rose. To Rose. Sara Teasdale. BiCB; HBV 1-2

Please believe in me. Celebration for My Mother. Wendy Rose. CDW

Please bring the sunshine/Back again. Windshield Wipers. Dennis Lee. WHW

Please choose me. Ickle Ockle, Blue Bockle. *Anonymous.* OxNR

Please don't call us. You Understand the Requirements. Lyn Lifshin. NeAC

"Please don't let them make fun of my music." Bruckner. James Camp. MAT

Please, father, dear father, come home! Father, Dear Father, Come Home with Me Now. Henry Clay Work. FSW; TreF

Please/get me tobacco. The Way & the Way Things Are. Nila NorthSun. GP

Please give fresh courage, ease their load. Prayer for Shut-Ins. Ruth Winant Wheeler. PoToHe

"Please God, to-morrow!/Then we will work and play." Galway. Mary Devenport O'Neill. NeIP; OxBI

Please God we use, and not abuse/The land so hardly won! The Great Swamp Fight. Caroline Hazard. PAH

Please hear me I am alone. The Reason for Poetry. Nancy Morejo. WPOW

Please let it be in the far, far West. The Far, Far West. *Anonymous.* CoSo

Please make my secret sun return to me/and I'll be iridescent, blossoming. Sonnet XV: "To honor the return of sparkling sun." Louise Labe. BoWoP

Please omit/flowers. Coming and Going. Mitchell Goodman. VGW

Please send me money enough for at least three weeks. Baudelaire. Delmore Schwartz. MP; TwCP; VGW

Please take a letter: Dear Sirs, In reply— Any Man to His Secretary. Hilary Corke. ErPo

Please, therefore, cut that shit out. Don't Answer the Phone for Me the Same. Gerald Locklin. GP

Please to make pancakes/'Gin tomorrow morning. Shrovetide. *Anonymous.* OxNR

Please to take my daughter in. Three Brethren from Spain. *Anonymous.* OxNR

Pleases you conscious/And is put to print. To Stephen Spender. Timothy Corsellis. WaP

Pleasure and I yes I did enjoy our/conversation goodnightthankyou A Word in Edgeways. Charles Tomlinson. NOBL

The pleasure I cannot reveal,/It far surpast the Spinning-Wheel. As I Sat at My Spinning-Wheel. *Anonymous.* CoMu

Pleasure laughed sweet,/But Joy kissed me. The Best Friend. William Henry Davies. OBMV

Pleasure never is at home. Fancy. John Keats. EnLi 1-2; LoBV; OBEV

Pleasure of such a kind as truly is/A self-renewing vegetable bliss? Sonnet Made upon the Groves near Merlou Castle. Edward, Lord Herbert of Cherbury. JCP

A pleasure secret and austere. In November. Archibald Lampman. NOBC; OBCV

A pleasure without loss; a treasure without stealth. He Is a Path. Giles the Younger Fletcher. TRV

...Pleasures more refin'd/And better suited to th' immortal mind. To a Lady on the Death of Her Husband. Phillis Wheatley. TAP

Pledge deep our land in/Our land's own wine! In a Wine Cellar. Victor J. Daley. PoAu 1-2

A pledge of blessing to the world. Decoration Day. Julia Ward Howe. OHIP

Pledging my love to countless/surrenders and repeals. How Are You, Dear World, This Morning? Horace L. Traubel. TrJP

A plenitude of silver leaves. The Piper of Arll. Duncan Campbell Scott. PeCV

"A plenteous feast in field and fen,/Enough for all.–Amen, amen!" The Grasshopper's Song. Hayim Nahman Bialik. YeAr

"Plimsolls, plimsolls in the summer,/Oh goloshes in the wet!" Westgate-on-Sea. Sir John Betjeman. OxBoLi

Plod dumbly on, and dream. Snow. Archibald Lampman. PeCV

An' plough, in my sweet fancy, now do sheen. Lowshot Light. William Barnes. VLP

Ploughing, like a huge serpent from its ambuscade.   The St. Lawrence and the Saguenay.   Charles Sangster.   OBCV

A ploughing match with a guinea's prize/For the skill of your hands and eyes.   The Market Town.   Francis Carlin.   HBMV

Ploughs up the silvering surface of her plain.   Gebir.   Walter Savage Landor.   OBRV

The plover's piping note, now here, now there.   In June.   Nora Perry.   YeAr

Plow deep and straight with all your powers.   The Plow.   Richard Henry Horne.   HBV 1-2

...Plowing ever since,/for more than seven score years!   Ever Since.   Elizabeth Jane Coatsworth.   SiSoSe

Plowing life away/To make the cotton yield.   Share-Croppers.   Langston Hughes.   SaC

Pluck'd and placed in Annie's bosom,/Hums the bee!   A Merry Bee.   Joseph Skipsey.   OBVV

Pluck forth your heart, saltblood, a fruit of tears./Pluck and devour!   A Memory of the Players in a Mirror at Midnight.   James Joyce.   InvP; NoAm; ViBoPo

Pluck, pluck betime thy flower,/That springs, and perisheth in one short hour.   A Description of Beauty, Translated out of Marino.   Samuel Daniel.   OBSC

Pluck the rose, therefore, maiden, while 'tis May.   A Lyric: "Into a little close of mine I went."   Lorenzo de Medici.   AWP

Pluck the sun down/and go.   Words at Farewell.   Vahan Derian.   AMV-81

Plucked out by nervous crows.   A Foreigner Comes to Earth on Boston Common.   Horace Gregory.   EaLo

The plucking of hope from the hand, honor from the complexion,/Sprite from the spell.   Government Injunction.   Josephine Miles.   PoNe

Plucking the crowded vermin from their folds.   Thinking of Holderlin.   Christopher Middleton.   NePoEA-2

Plum-pudding, goose, capon, minced pies, and/roast beef.   Old Christmas Returned.   *Anonymous.*   GN; OHIP

Plum tree and moon.   Harbingers.   Basho (Matsuo Basho).   PoPl

Plunge and thrash salty hair.   An Invocation to the Goddess.   David Wright.   NMP; NoAm

The plunge forward, the awful/crashing and surging of the new.   The Work-Out.   Geoffrey Movius.   MAT

Plunged into the dark furrows/Of the sea again.   Stages on a Journey Westward.   James Wright.   AmPC; LCAP; NaP

Plunging into darksome tunnels with a roar.   In the Evening from My Window.   *Anonymous.*   SUS

Plunging into itself without me.   Between Us.   Stephen Berg.   NaP

The plural's what one damn well pleases.   What's the Plural?   *Anonymous.*   FaBoUs

...Plus everything/else in the world/going on here.   Today's News.   Ted Berrigan.   APU

Plus we see Peggy.   It Was Miss Scarlet with the Candlestick in the Billiard Room.   Bernadette Mayer.   APU

Plutonian, descendant, or beast in the stretching night–/there was light.   Vancouver Lights.   Earle Birney.   CaP

Ply them in prison souls to break the bars/And by me, Lord, pass in.   A Prayer for a Preacher.   Edward Shillito.   TrPWD

Plying our trades, in hopes of a good drowning.   Marginalia.   Richard Wilbur.   CMoP; NMP; PoA

Po', good Jesus.   Troubled Jesus.   Waring Cuney.   BANP; GoSl

Po' little lamb.   Lullaby.   Paul Laurence Dunbar.   GoSl

Po' mourner's got a home at las'.   Po' Mourner's Got a Home at Las'.   *Anonymous.*   BoAN 1-2

Po' nigger ain' got no show.   Ain't It Hard to Be a Right Black Nigger?   *Anonymous.*   OuSiCo

Pocket bright bits of obsidian and fragments/old potters left behind.   Recuerdo.   Paula Gunn Allen.   STE

A pocket full of money, and a cellar/full of beer.   Christmas Comes but Once a Year.   *Anonymous.*   OxNR

A pocket full of rocks bring home, so, brothers, don't you cry.   I Came from Salem City.   *Anonymous.*   AmFP

The pod that Duty locks!   Forbidden Fruit.   Emily Dickinson.   AnNE

The poem ascends.   The Jacob's Ladder.   Denise Levertov.   AmPP; CoPo; PoM; PPP

Poem in throat and hand, asleep,/and my storm beating strong!   This Place in the Ways.   Muriel Rukeyser.   MiAP

...The poem/is always too much after the fact.   For an Old Friend.   Norbert Krapf.   AMV-81

The poem is hunter.   Poet prey.   The Hunt of the Poem.   Richard Behm.   AMV-80

The poem is plain, final, able to please,/Clear of the hungers that made it what it is.   The Makers.   Richard Kell.   CIP

The poem/Is seen from all sides,/Everywhere,/At once.   As for Poets.   Gary Snyder.   CAPP

...The poem is you.   Paradoxes and Oxymorons.   John Ashbery.   NoP

A poem of remembrance, a gift, a souvenir for you   A Ballad of Remembrance.   Robert Earl Hayden.   AmNP; BPo; IDB; PoBA; PoNe

...The poem of the act of the mind.   Of Modern Poetry.   Wallace Stevens.   AmP; InvP; NePA; NIP; NoAm; OxBA; PP; PrIm; TAP

The poem on the summit of a high head/Crown of happiness   Crown of Happiness.   Anne Hebert.   BoWoP

A poem should not mean/But be.   Ars Poetica.   Archibald MacLeish.   AP; AWP; BiP; CMoP; CoBMV; DiPo; ExPo; FPL; HAP; HeIP; HoPM; InPK; InPo; LiTA; LiTM; MoAB; MoAmPo; NIP; NOBA; NoP; OxBA; PoA; PoPl; PP; SoSe; TAP

The poem sits/smiling/just/behind my lips.   Poem.   Pearl Cleage Lomax.   CNA

...The poem stays.   An Instance.   Alastair Reid.   PP

The poem that has stolen these words from my mouth/may not be this poem.   The Man in the Tree.   Mark Strand.   EAS

Poems are slingshot words, Goliath.   Stone Words for Robert Lowell.   Richard Eberhart.   AMV-80

Poems for ending,/And sleeping's for bed.   Things.   William Jay Smith.   TiPo

Poems force the lock of my throat.   Cancion.   Denise Levertov.   PoM

...Poems like these/you'll never understand.   Broads (parody).   David R. Slavitt.   BXAP

Poems that stick like blood/closing wounds   Blok Let Me Learn the Poem.   Aram Boyajian.   NeAC

Poems uniform, safe and pure.   The Line of an American Poet.   Reed Whittemore.   MoVE; PPON

...Poems will sometimes overcome them, or else stones.   Notes for Echo Lake 11.   Michael Palmer.   APU

The poet and the child walked hand in hand.   The Poet and the Child.   Winifred Howells.   AA

The Poet drew, in the thunderous blue in-/volved dread of those mounted pinions.   A Judgment in Heaven.   Francis Thompson.   CoBE

A poet in his joy.   The Peasant Poet.   John Clare.   ERoP 1-2; OAEL 1-2; OBNC; WGRP

The poet is playing the Habeas Corpus Blues.   The Habeas Corpus Blues.   Conrad Aiken.   NYBP

A poet now or never!   'Tis the Witching Hour of Night.   John Keats.   TEP

Poet, Professor, Autocrat of Wit's own Breakfast-Table.   Filling an Order.   John Townsend Trowbridge.   OBAL

The Poet's heart shall quiver in the brine.   Where Avalanches Wail.   *Anonymous.*   NA

Poet, see your sylvan view/Fresh with an eternal dew!   The Poet of Gardens.   Daniel Henderson.   HBMV

...A poet should be feared/When angry, like a comet's flaming beard.   The Rebel Scot.   John Cleveland.   PeD; TW

The poet vanished, in the vanished forest,/among his brightly tinted extinct birds?   Extinct Birds.   Judith Wright.   PBWP

The poet with a beat of words/Flings into time for time to keep.   Words in Time.   Archibald MacLeish.   CrMA; NePA; PoCh; PoRA

The poetics of such a situation/are yet to be found out   A Later Note on Letter #15.   Charles Olson.   CAPP

Poetry and letters/Persist in silence and solitude.   Night in the House by the River.   Tu Fu.   NaP

Poetry ends like a rope.   A Book of Music.   Jack Spicer.   PoM

Poetry, insanely sweet.   Asylum.   David R. Clark.   PPON

Poetry is life and life lies lazy in the sun.   Poetry Is Happiness.   Wrey Gardiner.   NeBP

Poets alone should kiss and tell.   Ballade of a Talked-Off Ear.   Dorothy Parker.   DBV

Poets are liars, and for verses sake/Will make the Gods of humane crimes partake.   Epigrams, CXVIII.   Decimus Magnus Ausonius.   OBVE

Poets. minor poets ruined by/minor fame.   An Afterword: For Gwen Brooks.   Don L. Lee.   JB

Pohutukawas endlessly/varied endlessly the same.   This May Be Your Captain Speaking.   C. K. Stead.   OCNZ

A point of agate reference.   Analogue of Unity in Multeity.   Richard Eberhart.   NoAm

A point on fire/with the friction of turning.   Turning Point.   W. L. Holshouser.   AMV-81

Point to one end, which is always present.   Four Quartets.   Thomas Stearns Eliot.   AtBAP

The point/to pull/the ripcord.   Paratrooper.   John Giorno.   ANYP

Pointed at, mocked again/By men for whom He shed His Blood–in vain?   Wednesday in Holy Week.   Christina Georgina Rossetti.   PGD; TrCP

...The pointed mountain, far away, unfamiliar?   Sestina from the Home Gardener.   Diane Wakoski.   NoAm

Pointing out for each other the brown faces in the leaves.   Reply to the Provinces.   Galway Kinnell.   NYBP

Pointing to these chained limbs, this blasted/forehead,/May mock your ruin, as ye mocked at mine!   South Carolina to the States of the North.   Paul Hamilton Hayne.   PAH

...Pointing/toward the factory/far down the hill.   1937 Ford Convertible. Tom McKeown.   PPJ

Pointing us Home to our own sun/The world's and his HYPERION.   In the Glorious Epiphanie of Our Lord God.   Richard Crashaw.   PoEL 1-5

Points to an eternal rest.   I Will Praise the Lord at All Times.   William Cowper.   EiCP

Poise of my hands reminded me of yours.   Villanelle.   William Empson. CMoP; EnLoPo; NoAm; OAEL 1-2

Poised on a curve of gusty autumn sky.   Let Him Return.   Leona Ames Hill.   PoToHe

Poised on a moving ladder in the sun.   For Marianne Moore's Birthday. Kay Boyle.   NMM

The poison of their own sweet country has brought them here.   Something Is Dying Here.   Thomas McGrath.   TAT

Poisonously green and bursting with the wet.   London.   J. R. Rowland. CBAP

Pokes its red head/Into the sun.   Inquisitive Barn.   Frances Frost.   BrR

Pokes through a musty sheath/Its pale tendrilous horn.   Cuttings.   Theodore Roethke.   HaCAP; LCAP; NoAm; NOBA; TAP

The poking finger to a nervous age.   Morvin.   John Fuller.   NePoEA-2

The polar currents close,/And stiffen, and remain.   Winter Holding Off the Coast of North America.   N. Scott Momaday.   CDW

Police lady or Lesbian/over there?/Where?   Cafe: 3 A.M.   Langston Hughes.   HaCAP

The policeman/is a pig./(oink/oink.)   Definition for Blk/Children.   Sonia Sanchez.   PoBA

A policeman's lot is not a happy one.   The Pirates of Penzance.   Sir William Schwenck Gilbert.   TrGrPo

...Polished women called/small girls to dream awhile toward the flashing & bursting tree!   Dream Songs.   John Berryman.   NaP

Politely each/greets his own face.   Fable.   D. J. Opperman.   PeSA

Polities that clock us safely/Over this dark; freighting us.   States.   Tom Paulin.   FaBoIP

The pollen-chambers of the infinite/Flower, and its petals only half uncurled. Caresses.   Elsa Barker.   HBMV

The pollen-dust of centuries!   Wild Honey.   Maurice Thompson.   AnFE; APA; HBV 1-2

Polly Ann hammered steel like a man.   Song: "John Henry tol' his Cap'n." Anonymous.   NAMP

Polly Vaughn is the fairest in a mountain of snow.   Polly Vaughn (Molly Brawn).   Anonymous.   AmFP

Pomp, pride, honor, riches and worldly lust,/Parrot saith plainly shall turn all to dust.   The Parrot.   John Skelton.   ACP

Pompilia, will you let them murder me?   The Ring and the Book.   Robert Browning.   OAEP

Pond'ring these things within my heart,/Surely, said I–life is a f–t!   A Solemn Meditation.   William Shenstone.   NOEC

Pond snails crying/in the saucepan.   After the Gentle Poet Kobayashi Issa. Robert Hass.   GeTw

Pondering on the matter,/St Martin bent and ate.   St. Martin and the Beggar. Thom Gunn.   MoBS

...Ponds of silver water/that shiver and can't understand their being here. Marriage.   Raymond Carver.   GeTw

Ponsonby smiled back. He was above her. Of that he was now sure.   Fiction: A Message.   Gavin Ewart.   OxBC

The pontiff washes in the silver bowl that saves.   Pacelli and the Ethiop. Turner Cassity.   GP

The pools lie flat and shallow and black/As death, the ultimate absence of qualities.   One Way Down.   David Craig.   PoSH

...The poor/Are naked as a pin.   Epigram: "Wealth covers sin."   Kassia. WPOW

Poor as a Salford child.   Carol.   John Short.   DTC; FaBoCh; LoGBV

(Poor beggars!–they'll never see 'ome!)   The Widow at Windsor.   Rudyard Kipling.   BrPo; NoP; OAEP

Poor Billy Rose. God, he could fight/Before my three sharp coins knocked out his sight.   The Ballad of Billy Rose.   Leslie Norris.   MoBS

Poor boy. Poor boy. Poor boy long way from home.   Poor Boy Blues. Ramblin' (Willard) Thomas.   BluL

Poor boy, you're bound to die.   Tom Dooley.   Anonymous.   BLSo

Poor, burnt, blinded Pache. I love him.../That's why.   Kit Carson's Ride. Joaquin Miller.   BPAW; TreFS

The poor can feed the birds.   The Poor Can Feed the Birds.   Shaw Neilson. PoAu 1-2

Poor ChinaMAN-child.   Disco Chinatown.   Yuri Kageyama.   BrSi

Poor clod–while you've parried and parleyed out there.   Halt and Parley. George Herbert Clarke.   CaP

The poor creature could scarce get her head in.   Limerick: "There was an old miser at Reading."   Anonymous.   OxBChV

Poor Cupid sits and blows his nails for cold.   Blame Not My Cheeks. Thomas Campion.   AAS; EG; UnPo

(Poor, dear, fat Jane! And now–poor, dear, fat You!)   Tea.   Jacqueline Embry.   HBMV; YaD

Poor dilapidated, broken,–/Old umbrella.   The Outcast.   Frank Elwood Sanford.   PeD

The poor do by submission/What pride by opposition.   The Priesthood. George Herbert.   AnAnS 1

Poor dusty leaf,/Whistled into a hall!   College of Surgeons.   James Stephens. AnIL; LOW

Poor fool! be not deceived, God is not mocked.   The Witch.   Lord Alfred Bruce Douglas.   HBMV

Poor furious girl, our voices sound/alike (your nurse told me), discreet and gentle.   El Sueno de la Razon.   Jane Cooper.   FaBoWP

Poor Jelly Jake and Butter Bill.   Jelly Jake and Butter Bill.   Leroy F. Jackson.   BBGG

Poor Jim Jay.   Jim Jay.   Walter De la Mare.   BrPo; CenHV; HBMV; SiSoSe; SO

Poor little creature she has but one eye.   Riddle: "I have a little sister, they call her Peep-Peep."   Anonymous.   OxNR

"Poor little devil! born without a chance!"   Born Without a Chance. Edmund Vance Cooke.   BLPA

Poor little lost baby, baby, poor little lost babe!   The Lost Baby. Anonymous.   AmFP

"Poor little pigs, they see the wind."   The Unknown Color.   Countee Cullen. GoSl; OBCA

The poor little thing hasn't got but one eye.   Riddle: "I have a little sister they call her Peep-peep."   Mother Goose.   TiPo

Poor little timid furry man.   The City Mouse and the Garden Mouse. Christina Georgina Rossetti.   FaBoBe; HBV 1-2; HBVY; NTCP; SUS; TiPo

Poor Lubin fears that he may die;/His wife, that he may live.   Cause and Effect.   Matthew Prior.   NLV

The poor man blessed the rich.   A Spider Danced a Cosy Jig.   Irving Layton.   WHW

The poor man's landlord leading down to/dine.   Vision.   William Dean Howells.   AA; AnAmPo

Poor man, thou searchest round/To find out death, but missest life at hand. Vanity (I).   George Herbert.   NoP

Poor me, I brood.   Poor Me.   Anonymous.   ErPo

Poor old horse, let him die.   Poor Old Horse.   Anonymous.   CH; OBET

Poor old man.   Johnny Come Down to Hilo.   Anonymous.   ABF

The poor old man.   A Note Left in Jimmy Leonard's Shack.   James Wright. HaCAP; NoP

Poor old Michael Finnegan.   There Was an Old Man Named Michael Finnegan.   Mother Goose.   TiPo

Poor old Michael, please don't begin ag'in.   Michael Finnigan.   Anonymous. FSW

Poor old Robinson Crusoe!   Robinson Crusoe.   Anonymous.   OxNR

A poor old Widow in her weeds.   A Widow's Weeds.   Walter De La Mare. AtBAP; FaBV

Poor Pilgrims needs must lose their way,/When all the shadowes do increase. O Fly My Soul.   James Shirley.   AtBAP; OBS; OxBoCh

Poor Polly Picklenose!   Polly Picklenose.   Leroy F. Jackson.   BBGG

(Poor,/poor/wolf.)   Night, Stars, Glow-Worms.   Halper Leivick.   LiTW

Poor savages who fought in France.   Song of the Dark Ages.   Francis Brett Young.   HBMV

A poor shawl for your perfect throat.   Gift.   Judith Hemschemeyer.   PCP

"Poor soul," He said.   There Was One I Met upon the Road.   Stephen Crane.   EaLo

The poor survivor may not weep and wake.   So Live, So Love, So Use That Fragile Hour.   Robert Louis Stevenson.   NOBV

Poor tired Tim! It's sad for him.   Tired Tim.   Walter De la Mare.   ALV; MoShBr; NTCP; SoPo; TiPo

Poor Tom.   Mr. Merry's Lament for "Long Tom".   John Gardiner Calkins Brainard.   AA

Poor Tom will injure nothing.   Tom o' Bedlam's Song.   Anonymous. AtBAP; EBEV; EvOK; InvP; LiTB; MOON; OAEL 1-2; OxBoLi; PoEL 1-5; SeCeV; ViBoPo

Poor wearied pilgrim–in this toiling scene!   To the Moon.   Charlotte Smith. MOON

Poor Wisdom's chance/Against a glance/Is now as weak as ever.   The Time I've Lost in Wooing.   Thomas Moore.   ALV; EnLi 1-2; GoTF; HBV 1-2; HoPM; LiTL; OAEP; OnYI; TreF

Poor, without work or friends.   A Dream.   Bella Akhmadulina.   BoWoP

Pop-a-da!   Be-Bop Boys.   Langston Hughes.   OBAL

Pop! goes the weasel.   Pop! Goes the Weasel.   Anonymous.   BLSo; FaBoNo; FSW; OxNR; PoPle; PSoN; SoPo; TreFT

Pop goes the weasel!   Up and Down the City Road...   Anonymous.   EvOK

Pop-gun, Popular and Unpopular!   Popular.   Alfred, Lord Tennyson. NOBL

The poplar plume belongs/to what enormous wing?   The Poplar's Shadow. May Swenson.   NYBP

Poplars are lonely. They must grow/Close to each other in a row.   Poplars. Edward Bliss Reed.   HBMV; HBVY; OHIP

The poplars in the fields of France,/Like glorious ladies come to dance.   In France.   Frances Cornford.   HBMV

Popped in our pouch of spit, a hot-cross bun.   Good Friday.   John Frederick Nims.   TW

The poppied sleep, the end of all.   Ilicet.   Algernon Charles Swinburne.   MaVP; NOBV

Poppies and cornsheaves on each laden arm.   Idylls.   Theocritus.   AWP

Poppies the last I shall see as they close/Over my sinful earth.   A Farewell Ballad of Poppies.   Eva Brudne.   VWA

The porcupine sips a quill of mercy.   News from Mount Amiata.   Eugenio Montale.   NaP

Porpoises plunging like the necks of horses.   Two Horses.   William Stanley Merwin.   NePA

Port Admiral, you be d—d.   Port Admiral.   Frederick Marryat.   MOS

The port was known—the reckoning was true.   Old Voyager.   Walter Blackstock.   GoYe

Portly pusher of waves, wind-slave.   Winter Ocean.   John Updike.   ELU; InPK; MOS; SoSe

Posed with his Knight astride, on the opposite wall.   The Spanish Lions.   Phyllis McGinley.   NYBP

Possessed and blessed by the power which flowers as a fountain/flowers! How Strange Love Is, in Every State of Consciousness.   Delmore Schwartz.   MoLP

Possessed of an echo but not a fate.   The Mirror Perilous.   Alan Dugan.   LiTM; MP; TwCP

Possessing what the owners can but own.   A Summer Morning.   Richard Wilbur.   FaBoMo; NLV

The possibility alone keeps me reaching.   Tending.   Paula Rankin.   AMV-81

...A possible extension bridge/extending from the more recent past/into the less/renamed the presen   The Classical Style.   Michael Palmer.   NPGG

The possible/Our modicum/for this spent life at last.   Spendthrift.   I. A. Richards.   PoPl

Possibly this is best to be/or not to be.   Salvos for Randolph Bourne.   Horace Gregory.   NAMP

The Possum that really was just playing possum/Gets up in a flash and scurries away.   Opossum.   William Jay Smith.   TiPo

Post-obits rarely reach a poet.   Epigrams.   Martial (Marcus Valerius Martialis).   OBVE

Posterity shall know/The cooling brooks that from thy nooks/Singing and dancing go.   To the Fountain of Bandusia.   Horace.   AWP

Postmen like doctors go from house to house.   Aubade.   Philip Larkin.   SoSe

Postpones his dying with a dish/Of several suffocated fish.   Hunting Season.   W. H. Auden.   LiSp

Postpones the end of the world: in which we live forever.   The End of the World.   Thomas McGrath.   SM

The pot began to play with the ladle.   Christmas Eve.   Anonymous.   OxNR

The potatoes sit quietly on top of each other growing eyes.   Potatoes.   David Donnell.   NOBC

Potent armies of the peace/Love takes from me.   Waters of the Sea.   Cecil Goldbeck.   EtS

Potent/as vineyards of deathless Cypris.   Epigram: "As honey in wine."   Meleager.   PeHV

Pothole the size of a wagon wheel in shade almost.   Trench.   Stephen Pett.   GrPl

Pound them to soup. Win! Win! Win! Die! Die! Die!   13 Ways of Eradicating Blackbirds (parody).   Mark DeFoe.   BXAP

Pounding them into mummy, Shoulder, hoop!   Sonnet to Britain.   Ayton [(or Aytoun)] Sir Robert.   FaBoCo

Pounds the tombs of the world into dust and loosens the dust/of Jan who sleeps...   Monument.   A. M. Sullivan.   GoYe

Pour down your unstinted nimbus sacred moon.   Look down Fair Moon.   Walt Whitman.   MOON

Pour no worry in the new world's making/Consider a host of giant's raking! Never, Never Can Nothingness Come.   Norma Keating.   GoYe

Pour on water, pour on water.   Scotland's Burning.   Anonymous.   FSW

Pour one more brandy, as it were, on me.   Lines Declining a Transatlantic Dinner Invitation.   Marilyn Hacker.   MAYP

Pour out with confidence their plaints,/And find celestial rest.   Tell Us, Ye Servants of the Lord.   William Staughton.   AH

Pour secrecy upon the dying page.   I Held a Shelley Manuscript.   Gregory Corso.   VGW

Pour through the lifted/Throat of a bird.   You That Sing in the Blackthorn.   Alfred Noyes.   GoBC

Poured from the hogsheads of the thunder.   Thunder Pools.   Robert P. Tristram Coffin.   LOW

Poured my hot tears upon the margin of the road.   The Bones of Chuang Tzu.   Chang Heng.   AtBAP; AWP

Poured one wine for the high invisible ones.   Introductory Lines (excerpt).   William Butler Yeats.   NU

Poured up one outward and widening wave/Of eager and extravagant anger. The Lovers.   W. R. Rodgers.   BIrV; OBSP

Pouring unto us from the heaven's brink.   Endymion.   John Keats.   MCCG; OBRV; TrGrPo

Pours down on every true believer/The mystic blood of martyrdom.   The Martyrdom of St. Teresa.   A. D. Hope.   CBAP

Pours forth its fragrant secret yet/Amidst the solitary shades.   Ill Luck.   Charles Baudelaire.   PoPl

Pours from the blood into ink.   Movie Actors Scribbling Letters Very Fast in Crucial Scenes.   Jean Garrigue.   TAP

Pours the confounding main.   Smooth between Sea and Land.   Alfred Edward Housman.   MoPo

Pours the whole forest from one tiny/throat!   The Mocking-Bird.   Ednah Proctor (Clarke) Hayes.   AA

Povert maketh pees.   Peace.   Anonymous.   MeEL

Poverty begs from none but Death/In my land.   The Princess of Scotland.   Rachel Annand Taylor.   BSV; GoTS

Poverty's fixed, archaic physiognomy/Projects only through masks where nothing else extrudes.   Winter Offering.   D. S. Savage.   LiTB; NeBP

The Poverty that was not Wealth–/Cannot be Indigence.   None Can Experience Stint.   Emily Dickinson.   MAmP

Powdered her nose/tip-/toe/in a badge.   Chic Freedom's Reflection.   Alice Walker.   NMM

Power and Peace to keep one throne.   Power and Peace.   Robert Herrick.   CaPo

The power and the heartbeat and male music of our being.   Of the New Prosody.   Brewster Ghiselin.   MoVE

Power may have knees, but Justice hath our hearts.   To Sir Thomas Egerton.   Samuel Daniel.   OBSC

Power of my life, let here thy grace be shown.   Madrigal: "Is Love a boy?"   William Byrd.   EnRePo

The power of the single/thrust, the pure/gesture of/self   Aleph.   Stuart Z. Perkoff.   VWA

The power of trains advancing/Further, advancing further.   For X.   Louis MacNeice.   BoLoP; EnLoPo

Power! Power! Power! To the people!   The Raging Generation.   Mbuyiseni Oswald Mtshali.   WhB

...Power that formerly came/from the use of Tamunoemi/your African name. Goodbye David Tamunoemi West.   Margaret Danner.   BPo

The power that kindles green in trees,/And light in star?   Hope.   Amy Carmichael.   TRV

The power, the pride, the reach of perished Rome.   In the Old Theatre, Fiesole.   Thomas Hardy.   OBTV

The power to be alone and vote with God.   The Need of the Hour.   Edwin Markham.   PAL

The power to bring birds and wheat/and gentle rain again.   Windmill in March.   Katharine Privett.   AMV-80

A power was his beyond the touch of art/Or armed strength–his pure and mighty/heart.   On the Life-Mask of Abraham Lincoln.   Richard Watson Gilder.   AA; HBV 1-2

Powerful almost as vocal harmony/To stay the wanderer's steps and soothe his/thoughts.   Airey-Force Valley.   William Wordsworth.   VLP

A pox upon the devil, boys! Why didn't you skid the road?   Tomah Stream.   Anonymous.   ShS

Practise the candor of our bones.   Fall in Corrales.   Richard Wilbur.   CoPo

Practise these rules, and more to them/I'll add/For thine instruction if my life endure!   A Father's Testament.   Judah Ibn Tibbon.   TrJP

Practising sands.   We Play at Paste.   Emily Dickinson.   CBEP

A prairie fire.   Plainview: 3.   N. Scott Momaday.   CDW

Praise be done to the Three in One,/Alleluia! Alleluia!   Cantemus Cuncti Melodum.   Notker Balbulus.   CAW

Praise Father, Son, and Holy/Ghost!   Morning Hymn.   Thomas Ken.   FaFP; GoTF; TreFS

Praise Father, Son and Holy Ghost.   Old Hundredth.   William Kethe.   BLSo

Praise God, give thanks tomorrow and tomorrow.   Ode on a Plastic Stapes.   Chad Walsh.   HoAn

"Praise God, may His Name be exalted!"   Isidor.   Louis Simpson.   GP; NNaP

Praise him all creatures!   Cantico del Sole.   Saint Francis of Assisi.   CTC

Praise him. He dances upon the whitecaps.   Praise Doubt.   Mark Van Doren.   EaLo; MoRP

Praise Him, the only good.   Praise Him Who Makes Us Happy.   Mark Van Doren.   AH

Praise him till he calls thee home;/Trust his love for all to come.   Sing, My Soul.   Anonymous.   AH

Praise him who sweetens/On a small hate.   The Mouse.   Jean Garrigue.   MP; TwCP

Praise His name forevermore.   Christ, My Salvation.   Eva Gray.   STF

Praise is comely   The Sequence of Generations.   Hayim Be'er.   VWA

Praise it who list, I like it not.   Give place all ye that doth rejoice.   Sir Thomas Wyatt.   FCP; SiPS

The praise of Neptune's empery.   In Praise of Neptune.   Thomas Campion.   BoNaP; CBEP; NOBE; WiR

Praise Saint Thomas, of Tocaima–none can question now or/doubt him! The Feast of Padre Chala. Thomas Walsh. CAW

...Praise the few/Who built in chaos our bastion and our home. The Great House. Edwin Muir. EyDe

Praise the Lord, and pass the ammunition/And we'll all stay free! Praise the Lord and Pass the Ammunition! Frank Loesser. YaD

Praise the Lord through endless days,/Him the wide creation sings. Hallelujah! Praise the Lord. Edwin Francis Hatfield. AH

"Praise this world/to the angel...Tell him things." Rilke Speaks of Angels. Susan Donnelly. PoDr

Praise to the cry that I cannot understand. A Loon Call. Richard Eberhart. AMV-80

Praise to the rock. Biographical Note. Gabriel Preil. VWA

Praise we our God again,/Lord of our Peace! Hymn to Christ the Saviour. Clement of Alexandria (Titus Flavius Clemens). CAW

Praise we today in sturdy chorus,/Mother of Men–Old Yale! Mother of Men. Brian Hooker. HBMV

Praise ye and bless the Lord, and give thanks to Him and serve/Him with great humility. Canticle of the Sun. Saint Francis of Assisi. BoC; WGRP

Praise ye the King that comes to reign. Bless the Blessed Morn. Horatius Bonar. BePJ

Praise you, "All these were lovely"; say, "He loved." The Great Lover. Rupert Brooke. BoLiVe; BrPo; FaFP; FPL; HoPM; LiTB; LiTM; MCCG; MoBrPo; NAMP; TreF; TrGrPo; WaP

Praised be my fellow man/For dwelling in milk Mexico City Blues. Jack Kerouac. NeAP

Praised be the Night. Hymn to Night. Melville Cane. MoAmPo

Praised Him with fervent breath/Who conquered death. Van Elsen. Frederick George Scott. HBV 1-2

Praises God exceedingly,/Exceedingly. The Least of Carols. Sophie Jewett. OHIP

Praising all the nipples. Geisha. Gary Gildner. GP; PoL

Praising my Saviour all the day long. Blessed Assurance, Jesus Is Mine. Fanny J. Crosby. AH

Pray be silent and not stir/Th' easy earth that covers her. Another. Robert Herrick. OBEV

Pray death to make my brightest day turn black. Sonnet XIV: "Although I cry and though my eyes still shed." Louise Labe. BoWoP

Pray for his soul's health, gentle brother. On a Contentious Companion. John Hoskyns. FaBoEE

Pray! for Jesus joins your prayer. Pray! Amos R. Wells. STF

...Pray/For men that lose their fairylands. Dedication on the Gift of a Book to a Child. Hilaire Belloc. EBEV; HBVY

Pray for the six skippers who are lost out at sea/In this ill-fated trawler, the Evelyn Marie. The Loss of the Evelyn Marie. Anonymous. OBSS

Pray for the soul of Maire Og at dawning of the day! The Love-Talker. Ethna (Anna Johnston MacManus) Carbery. AnIV; OnYI; OxBI

Pray for us now and at the hour of our birth. Animula. Thomas Stearns Eliot. LiTB; MoVE; NAs

Pray for us to the Father, alleluia. Regina Coeli. Anonymous. ISi

Pray go on, and don't mind me. Some Ruthless Rhymes. Harry Graham. CenHV

Pray go on living to a hundred yet! For Patrick, Aetat: LXX. Sir John Betjeman. NAs

Pray God, I'll get married next Sunday. I'll Be Fourteen Next Sunday. Anonymous. AmFP; OLR

Pray God my paper bundles hold together. The Eternal Return. Robert Hillyer. NYBP

Pray hard: you too can be a Superior/And squat, proud, on a lotus. A Buddhist Priest. Ho Xuan Huong. PBWP

Pray Heaven for a human heart,/And let the foolish yeoman go. Lady Clara Vere De Vere. Alfred, Lord Tennyson. HBV 1-2

Pray her, before I die she will come see me. Phyllis. Thomas Lodge. EIL

Pray Her remember! To a June Breeze. Henry Cuyler Bunner. AA

Pray, is there one who can count the unborn souls? Counting. Fenton Johnson. AmNP

Pray, Ladies, give me leave to show it. A Present to a Lady. Anonymous. ErPo

Pray leave me where you found me first. Horace, Epistle VII, Book I, Imitated. Jonathan Swift. CEP

Pray lightning's flash/be both hope's reins/and hope's light lash. If Love's a Yoke. D. C. Berry. AMV-81

Pray, Lord,/We are near. Tenebrae. Paul Celan. VWA

Pray, mamma, give us our/dinner. Hey Ding a Ding. Anonymous. OxNR

Pray, Mary, fill the teapot up,/And do not make it strong. Cowper at Tea. Barry Pain. HBV 1-2

Pray/or promise/or prophesy? Explanations. Lucille Clifton. GeTw

Pray'r a-bringen welcome rest/So softly to the troubled breast. Vo'k a-Comen into Church. William Barnes. OxBoCh

Pray rest on my shell as a pillow. Limerick: "There once was a kind armadillo." Oliver Herford. TDH

Pray, sir, tell me,–whose dog are you? I Am His Highness' Dog at Kew. Alexander Pope. HBV 1-2

Pray tell me, sir, whose dog are you? Epigram Engraved on the Collar of a Dog Given to His Royal Highness... Alexander Pope. FaBoCo

Pray tell me, what is that? Riddle: "Hoddy doddy." Anonymous. OxNR

Pray that my sun go down with meeker beams to bed. Astrophel and Stella, LXXVI. Sir Philip Sidney. AAS; CABA; SiPS

Pray that our pilgrimage may end like thine! To a Young Girl Dying. Thomas William Parsons AA

...Pray/the removal of what my troubled eyes have seen. Fair/Boy Christian Takes a Break. Jim Harrison. NoAm

Pray thee, young lady, creep under the bush. Draw a Pail of Water. Anonymous. OxNR

Pray there is that strength in me to bring him home If You Can Hear My Hooves. Harold Littlebird. STE; VoR

Pray think of us poor children/Who are wandering in the mire. Good Master and Mistress... Anonymous. EvOK

Pray Thou Thyself in me and cleanse my prayer. Prayer. Willem Bilderdijk. LiTW

Pray to God for the world that you discovered! To Columbus. Ruben Dario. TTY

"Pray, why did not your father make/A gentleman of you?" A Modest Wit. Seeleck Osborn. BLPA; HBV 1-2

Prayed like a preacher, save my soul. Ha Ha This-a-Way. Anonymous. FSW

The prayer and faith of seamen will not fail/O God, my God, as long as ships do sail. A Seaman's Confession of Faith. Harry Kemp. TrPWD

...-A prayer and the idea of prayer. Two Egrets. John Ciardi. PoPl

Prayer-Book revision time down Lambeth way. 1894 in London. Charles Spear. AnNZ

Prayer-crowned, on blessed bed. Exhortation to Prayer. Margaret Mercer. AA

...A prayer for the beloved/in your heart and a song of praise upon your lips. The Prophet. Kahlil Gibran. PoLf

A prayer for you, a poem for you, a time together. An Afternoon in the Garden. Murray Edmond. OCNZ

A prayer to the East/Before light–the sun later–/To get over even its chaos early. From the Head. Louis Zukofsky. VWA

Prayers to be said/With no sacrifice. Wisdom. Hy Sobiloff. VGW

Praying in tongues If I Stand in My Window. Lucille Clifton. BPo

Praying, "Lord, grant her/wings." On Measure. Keith Waldrop. InPK

The praying mantis in unending prayer. 25 December 1960. Ingrid Jonker. PeSA

Praying that Providence this Wind may use/To puff your Sails, and to confound your Views. Absolute and Abitofhell. Ronald Arbuthnott Knox. CenHV; FaBoCo

Praying to God that we may never meet. Faithless. Louis Lavater. PoAu 1-2

Preach the Word with holy fervor,–/Leave the miracle to Him! Leave the Miracle to Him. Thomas H. Allan. BLRP

...Preaching the truth of winter/To the fallen heart that does not cease to fall. Wild Bees. James Keir Baxter. AnNZ; NoP

Preceding their leaders behind them. The Space Child's Mother Goose. Frederick Winsor. QQQ

Precious stone of the Prophet/Pearl of God. I, Lord of All Mortals. Anonymous. WTO

Precious treasure, thou art mine. Holy Bible, Book Divine. John Burton. BLRP; WBLP

Precise as hell is, precise/as any words, or wagon,/can be made In Cold Hell, In Thicket. Charles Olson. PoM

Precise preparation (mercy!)/For the Academy of Hard Knocks. Love Necessitates. Eugene B. Redmond. CNA

Preferred to drown than visit it again. Hibernia. Stuart Howard-Jones. NOBL

Prepare, O troops, that are to fall to-day!/Prepare,prepare! A War Song. William Blake. OHIP

Prepare, prepare! A War Song to Englishmen. William Blake. CH; WaaP

Prepare to meet your God above,/And dwell beyond the sky. Fifteen Ships on George's Banks. Anonymous. AmFP; BaBo

Prepare your selfe new love to entertaine. Amoretti, IV. Edmund Spenser. AAS

Prepared by the Spouse-Emperor for His Bride. Our Lady with Two Angels. Wilfred Rowland Childe. ISi

Preparing for the Night. Reserved. Walter De La Mare. GTBS-P

A prescient tingling, a prophecy of sound. Morning Glory. Ruth Pitter. FaBoWP

The present hour was ever markt with shade! On Man. Walter Savage Landor. NBM; OBNC; OBRV

Present our meek escutcheon/And claim the rank to die! One dignity delays for all. Emily Dickinson. SoSe

Present pain never come to an end. The Ejected Wife. Anonymous. OBVE

Present to us their note for maintenance. Robins. George Bruce. BSV

Present us sanctified to God,/And perfected in love below. For the Peace of Jerusalem. Charles Wesley. BePJ

Present you with a perfect piece,/Form'd on the model of old Greece. The Critic's Rules. Robert Lloyd. OBEC

Presently when I follow if I may! The Old Pope is Comforted by the Thought of the Young Pompilia. Robert Browning. BoC

Presently will come the two welcome angels/Noise in the hall, the last supper served. The Death of General Uncebunke: A Biography in Little. Lawrence Durrell. FaBoMo

Presents a blue and scarlet ass–to what? Eighteen-Seventy. Arthur Rimbaud. FaBoPV; OBWP

Preserve and govern evermore! Vexilla Regis. Saint Venantius Fortunatus. CAW

Preserve us also/from the French Mood. The French Mood. Abo Stoltzenberg. VWA

Preserver of all things visible and invisible! A Dance Chant. Anonymous. WGRP

Preserver of whiteness. Prayer to the Snowy Owl. John Haines. BoAnP

Preserves us, not for specialists. April Inventory. W.D. Snodgrass. AP; BiP; CABA; CAPP; CoAP; HAP; LiTM; MP; NePoEA; NoAm; NoP; PoPl; PPoe; TAP; TwCP

Preserving remnants of a model ship. The Glass Blower. James Scully. MP; NYBP; TwCP

The President himself came in/Took one look around and said/We Resign. Tentative Description of a Dinner to Promote the Impeachment... Lawrence Ferlinghetti. CoPo

The President knows what I mean. News from Detroit. Judith Minty. SOTS

Press forward evry gallant man/With hatchet, pike and gun. The Cropper Lads. Anonymous. OBET

Press on, for victory's ahead. Be hopeful, friend, and win it. Be Hopeful. Strickland Gillilan. PoToHe

Pressed between two pages in this place? Crossing. Archibald MacLeish. PoL

Pressed by fear and hunger on both hands. O Mad Spring, One Waits. Merrill Moore. AnAmPo

Pressed shapes, thin, woven and uncertain/As white locks of tall waterfalls. Said the Canoe. Isabella Valancy Crawford. NOBC

Pressed to the wall, dying, but fighting back! If We Must Die. Claude McKay. AmNP; BALP; BANP; BP; BPo; FaBV; IDB; NoAm; PoBA; PoNe; PPP; TTY; UnPo

Presume not on thy heart when mine is slain;/Thou gavest me thine, not to give back again. Sonnets, XXII: "My glass shall not persuade me I am old." William Shakespeare. OBSC

A pretence of wit. The Hawk. William Butler Yeats. AtBAP; PoA

Pretend very dead. Crawl into Bed. Quandra Prettyman. BOLo

...Pretending/I would never go near the luncheonette again. Arrowhead Christian Center and No-Smoking Luncheonette. Janet Sylvester. MAYP

Pretending that he rode/the back of a bronco/as wild as thunder. The Journey. Henry Johnson. LFAC

Pretending the wind's/blown something/into my eyes. Mask of Stone. Henry Johnson. LFAC

...Prettie Redbreast, Sing,/What I would speake. The Robin. George Daniel. FaBoRV; FM; OBS

The prettiest doll in the world. The Lost Doll. Charles Kingsley. MoShBr; SoPo

Prettiest little girl in all this world,/Her name was Devilish Mary. Devilish Mary. Anonymous. AmFP

Pretty cow, go there and dine. The Cow. Ann and Jane Taylor. HBV 1-2; HBVY; OxBChV

Pretty girls when I'm lonesome and heaven when I die. Red Whiskey. Anonymous. AmFP

The pretty loxia weaves. Namaqualand After Rain. William Plomer. ACV

Pretty maid, be wise, beware,/O, take care! If a Maid Be Fair. Laura Goodman Salverson. CaP

Pretty, pretty Robin,/Near my bosom. The Blossom. William Blake. CBEP; GoJo; PB; PBBP

...Pretty redbreast, sing/What I would speak. Ode: "Poor bird, I do no envy thee." George Daniel. PBBP

Pretty Robin Redbreast, Come. Robin Redbreast. William Henry Davies. PB

Pretty woman has killed me stone dead. Darling Cora. Anonymous. TrAS

Prevailed upon the long forsaken peace/To verify my ultimate return. Return. M. L. Sussman. AMV-81

Prevent the wingy swarm and scorching heat. The Fleece. John Dyer. FaBoUs

The price of meat has made men rage/And always with abundant reason. The Same Old Story. James J. Montague. HBMV

The price of my poems is one hamburger! Poem. Jim Brodey. ANYP

The prices of despair/Range from a single human heart/To two–not any more. The auctioneer of parting. Emily Dickinson. PoEL 1-5

Prices reasonable. Floss won't save you. Emily Dickinson. LiTA; NePA

Pricked to the core of deep and restless thoughts. Madrigal: "The swans, whose pens as white as ivory (excerpt). Robert Greene. ViBoPo

Pricking the sky, shelled by the dirty sea. Room of Return. Galway Kinnell. NYP

Pricks up its yellow ears and stares through the mist. Mahony's Mountain. Douglas Stewart. PoAu 1-2; SeCePo

Pride, Envy, Malice, are his Graces. Around the Child. Walter Savage Landor. HBV 1-2

Pride is with me yet! Noblesse Oblige. Jessie Redmond Fauset. CDC

Pride, like a goldfish, flashed a sudden fin. The Lesson. Edward Lucie-Smith. NCSH; OxBTC; TwCP

The pride of many a father, likewise a mother's joy. Whalen's Fate (George Whalen). Anonymous. ShS

The pride of the Suckers so lucky,/For Lincoln and Liberty, too. Lincoln and Liberty. F. A. Simpson. AS; FSW; TrAS

The pride of the valley, the girl I adore. The Plain Golden Band. Anonymous. ShS

Pride, pomp, and circumstance of glorious war! Othello. William Shakespeare. WHA

Priding herself only in the shadows of yesterdays. The Political Prisoner. Raymond Mazisi Kunene. WhB

...Pries/Open finger after finger for the small change inside. Casino Beach. Thomas Rabbit. MAYP

The priest was a painter (panther), I've heard people say. Bear in the Hill. Anonymous. ABF

A priestly farewell to her: suddenly, woman. Pericles. William Shakespeare. EBEV

Priez pour lui.' Battlefield. Richard Aldington. MMM; OBWP

Prim ghost the evening light shone through. Ode to a Dressmaker's Dummy. Donald Justice. DFF

Primary among which will be the overwhelming need for a nice/hot drink/ And a fire, and a friend. For Them. Michael Brownstein. APU

Primeval leper, animal treading ponderously. Salute to the Elephant. Odeniyi Apolebieji. WTO

Primitive, convincing, disgustingly real. That Everything Moves Its Bowels (parody). David R. Slavitt. BXAP

The primitives the first men who evolve again to civilize the/world. Black People: This Is Our Destiny. LeRoi (Imamu Amiri Baraka) Jones. CAPP; CNA

The primrose of the later year,/As not unlike to that of Spring. In Memoriam A.H.H., LXXXV. Alfred, Lord Tennyson. VLP

The prince is again a frog. Song for Seven Parts of the Body, 3. Maxine W. Kumin. PoL

Prince of Orange Will., Mary, Anne, G.G., G. Billy/Victor. The Kings and Queens of England. Anonymous. FaBoUs

The Prince of Peace may found His home/In Africa at last. Who knows? Who knows? Who Knows? A. L. Milner-Brown. PBA; TTY

Prince, still humped like a frog in the slime of sex. A Fairy Tale. Phyllis Thompson. DFT

The princely eagle shrunk into a bat. The King's Disguise (excerpt). John Cleveland. JCP

Princes of courtesy, merciful, proud, and strong. Craven. Sir Henry Newbolt. HBV 1-2; HBVY; PAH

Princes, round his final bed/Be your great protection shed. Night Song for a Child! Charles Williams. OBEV

Princes would covet what they could not buy. Selling Ruined Peonies. Yu Hsuan-chi. BoWoP

The princess flings our halo, knife by knife. The Necromancers. John Frederick Nims. PoCh

The princess is rocked to sleep. The Sea Princess. Katharine Pyle. SoPo

Printed in blood on its wings. Love Songs. Mina Loy. AnAmPo

Printed on the immortal/Hydrocarbons of flesh and stone. Lyell's Hypothesis Again. Kenneth Rexroth. MoVE; NoAm

Printed the foot of Venus/Where bloomed this asphodel. Hymn to Her Unknown. Walter James Turner. LiTL; OBMV

Printing white sand, the fair skin–blue-veined and/curved, has pressed. The White Sand. Edmund Wilson. NePoAm

Prints of the gentle feet whose passing healed/All blight from Tabor unto Olivet? In His Steps. Katharine Lee Bates. PGD

The prints where first she trod, a child of mortal birth. Love. Jones Very. AP

...A prism will appear,/breaking the light to show its color? Prisms (Altea). Philip Dacey. Psk

Prismatic slidings/Underneath a windy sky. Dolphins in Blue Water. Amy Lowell. LaNeLa

The prison scene from Trovatore/Dies on a dozen radios. Afternoons with Baedeker. Osbert Lancaster. FaBoCo

A prison, with a friend, preferr'd/To liberty without. The Faithful Friend. William Cowper. FM

The prisoner to the free replied. The House Was Still–The Room Was Still. Charlotte Bronte. NOBV

A prisoner without number/or guard. Prisoner. Marguerite George. GoYe

Prithee, haunt my fireside still,/Voice of Summer, keen and shrill! To a Cricket. William C. Bennett. GN; HBV 1-2

Prithee know, my dear, that I've a/Scorn for him who watched Godiva. To a Lady across the Way. E. B. White. InMe; NLV

Prithee, love, play me/T'other little tune. I Won't Be My Father's Jack. *Anonymous.* OxNR; UnS

..."Privacy is only/contraction, heavy/body, dangle of shriveled nuts..." String. Dennis Schmitz. LCAP

Privileged prisoners in a haunted land. Picnic: The Liberated. M. Carl Holman. PoBA; PoNe

"Privy Councillors do not sleep in barns." Lodging with the Old Man of the Stream. Po Chu-i. AWP

The Prize contended was great Hector's Life. The Iliad. Homer. OBVE

The prize I have/given you for travelling/so closely with me. X, Oh X. Mark Simpson. GOYP

The prize they do aim at they do procure. Upon the Snail. John Bunyan. OBSP

Pro nobis Puer natus est. Rorate Coeli Desuper. William Dunbar. BSV; SBVL

...Probably/dead (the doctor said)/before he hit that board pile. Tom Ball's Barn. Ted Kooser. GP

Probe to the utmost plan,/here the sincerity to rest a man. Deer Song. Confucius. CTC

The problem is,/if you won't be your own friend/you may never find one. Face in a Mirror. Jack Anderson. LFAC

Problems beneath his Im-/Perial drag. Heliogabalus. John Hollander. NLV; OBAL

...The problems of action/And honesty are still unreconciled. Gladstone. Julian Symons. WaP

Proceeding soon a graduated dunce. The Task. William Cowper. CoBE

The process itself is too undignified to be worth description. Verse. Richmond Lattimore. PP

Proclaim the elevation of the Host! Three Sonnets on The Divina Commedia. Henry Wadsworth Longfellow. SeCeV

Proclaim, "The Lord is come." Daybreak. Samuel Francis Smith. BLRP

Proclaim the truth that makes men free. As Tranquil Streams. Marion Franklin Ham. AH

Proclaimed unrivalled in my song. The First Olympionique to Hiero of Syracuse. Pindar. ATP

Proclaims how Ruin rules with full content-/ment here. Blennerhassett's Island. Thomas Buchanan Read. PAH

Proclaims what's left unsaid/in Egypt of her dead. Birds in Snow. Hilda ("H. D.") Doolittle. PoA

Procuress to the Lords of Hell. In Memoriam A.H.H., LIII. Alfred, Lord Tennyson. VLP

A prodigal in promise now;/A miser in fulfilling! Gone! Gone! Forever Gone. Gerald Griffin. OnYI

–Profession/of his father: dealer in scent-bottles. Anabasis, IV. Saint-John Perse. AtBAP; OBVE

...Profession of writing,/where one needs one's brains all the time. The Lake Isle. Ezra Pound. CABA; CrMA; FaBoCo; HBV 1-2; OBSP; PoA

The professional mowers drone, clipping the inch-high/green. Examiner. F. R. Scott. PPON

The Professor, or his wife, or the young lady. The Modern Chinese History Professor Plays Pool Every Tuesday... James Baker Hall. TAT

...Profiles loomed high/Thrown by anger against a white sky. Dirge. Louis Aragon. WaaP

Profundities: tears. Yes, why the tears? Man and Woman. Robert Conquest. OxBTC

Profundity I cannot claim;/Respectability I can. An Election Address. James Kenneth Stephen. NBM

A program for aristocrats! Sitting Pretty. Margaret Fishback. PoLf

Progress takes its toll, I'm told–/But should it take the best? They're Tearing down a Town. Jud Strunk. QQQ

...Prolong/the whiteness of your body in the song. The Brahms. Herbert Morris. NePoAm-2

Prolonging flight into the night/Never reaching. Love Songs. Mina Loy. VGW

Prom'nade all, you know where. Bill Haller's Dance. Robert V. Carr. PoOW

Promenade around the Old Brass Wagon,/You're the one, my darling. Old Brass Wagon (with music). *Anonymous.* AS

Promise of ground below the sprawling flood. In Heaven, I Suppose, Lie down Together. C. Day-Lewis. MoPo

The promise of his spirit be/fulfilled. John Fitzgerald Kennedy. John Masefield. PAL

Promise to keep no diary of/Days when I fail, dear love, to love! Postscript to a Pettiness. Arthur Seymour John Tessimond. OBSP

...Promising as the sunlight, carefully/arranged, cutting her right arm in half. Sunlight in a Cafeteria. Criss E. Cannady. PoDr

Promising,/To take a shape. The Power to Change Geography. Diana O Hehir. NPGG

Promoter of Mutual Acquaintance/Of Peace and Good Will. The Meaning of a Letter. *Anonymous.* PoToHe

Prone on his face, where gasping he expir'd. The Iliad. Homer. OBVE

Pronounce the sweet well done? The Stately Structure of This Earth. Martha Brewster. AH

Proof is what I do not need. Proof. Brendan Kennelly. CIP

Proof that earth was made for man. On a Fine Morning. Thomas Hardy. VLP

Propagandistically/Knew how to die. Twilight's Last Gleaming. Arthur W. Monks. OFD

Propagandizing our projects for stability,/and silence O Realm Bejewelled. Forugh Farrokhzad. WPOW

Propelled him, all pallid and prayerless,/From attic to hall. Goosey Goosey Gander. William Percy French. CenHV

Proper, popular, popular, operette. Finale. Sir Alan Patrick Herbert. InMe

The proper study of mankind is man. On a Distant Prospect of an Absconding Bookmaker. George Rostrevor Hamilton. FaBoCo

Property's private as ever, ever. Gypsy. Josephine Miles. NoAm

Prophet and priestess! At one stroke she/gave/A race to freedom and herself to fame. Harriet Beecher Stowe. Paul Laurence Dunbar. AA; AmePo; BPo

The prophet Moses feeds the grape,/ and fruitful is the Promised Land. Bullocky. Judith Wright. BoAV; CBAP; PoAu 1-2; SeCePo

Prophetic Nature bares the secret of the story/That holds the spheres in song! Mother Carey's Chicken. Theodore Watts-Dunton. OBVV

Prophetic to have mourned of man the fall. The Nightingale. Edward Moxon. OBRV

...The prophets of Baal/Were aesthetically significant, while Elijah's were very plain. On Certain Wits. Howard Nemerov. HaCAP; OxBC

Proportioned to the groove. That love is all there is. Emily Dickinson. NOBA

...Propped up/by bayonets, forever falling. Crispus Attucks. Robert Earl Hayden. CNA

Props of the church, and pillars of the throne? The Paradox. *Anonymous.* APAS

Proputty, proputty, proputty–canter an' canter/awaay. Northern Farmer, New Style. Alfred, Lord Tennyson. BiP; BoLiVe; MBW 1-2; NOBV; OAEP; VLP

Prospero is translated to a place where it is/possible to distinguish between age and sorrow. Prospero on the Mountain Gathering Wood. Jack Gilbert. NPGG

The prosperous gleaming smelt. Opening the Season. Stephen Lewandowski. WOLT

The protean lenses turned to slime. Citizen. Louis Grudin. NePA

Protect and guard the whole world/from woe. Epigram: "Queen,/thou holdest in thine arms." *Anonymous.* ISi

...Protect them with thine influence. To the Evening Star. William Blake. BoNaP; CEP; ChRP; EnRP; ERoP 1-2; FaBoRV; FaBV; FPL; HW; LAuP; LoBV; MCCG; NOEC; NoP; OAEL 1-2; OAEP; PoLf; PPP; TEP; TrGrPo; WiR

Protect us by Thy might,/Great God, our King. America. Samuel Francis Smith. AA; BLSo; FaBoBe; FaFP; GoTF; HBV 1-2; HRVY; PAL; PoLf; PSoN; TreF; WBLP; YaD

Protect us from invading night/And the unbroken silence of the dead. Oreads. Kathleen Raine. PoSH

Protect us more than your sword! Pogroms. Andre Spire. VWA

...The protecting flesh/When it falls will melt away in a kind of mud. Landscape and Figure. Thomas Kinsella. IPY

Protecting, till the danger past,/With human love. A Prayer for My Son. William Butler Yeats. EBEV; NAs

Protects the lingering dewdrop from the sun. To a Child. William Wordsworth. HBV 1-2; HBVY; OBSP

The Protestant cause let's serve,/And give to the devil the pope. The Procession: A New Protestant Ballad. *Anonymous.* APAS

Proud are your Berkshire hearts to bleed/When drest with Goodman's prime Vale Sauce. Goodman's Sauce. *Anonymous.* FaBoUs

Proud beautiful black women/Could better make and use/Black bread. Naturally. Audre Lorde. BlSi; CNA

The proud cocks crow. Eerily Sweet. Elizabeth Jane Coatsworth. ChBR

Proud creature was she the next day,/The little orphan, Alice Fell! Alice Fell; or, Poverty. William Wordsworth. BeLS; OBNV; SpRo

The proud, false queen should fealty take/ of thee! To the Moonflower. Craven Langstroth Betts. AA

Proud inclination of the flesh/in honor of the secret wish. Villanelle. Dilys Bennett Laing. ErPo; NMP

Proud of her small victory/For the new, free generation! Silent Is the Night. Hirsch Glick. FSW

Proud of love's pain and humble to its healing.   The Altar.   Jean Starr Untermeyer.   HBMV

Proud remnants of a visionary race.   Cry Faugh!   Robert Graves.   CoBMV; MoBrPo

The proud stupidity of soldiers' wives.   Homage to Jack Yeats.   Thomas MacGreevy.   OBMV

Proud to have embraced/total beauty for a few moments.   The Mirror in the Front Hall.   Constantine P. Cavafy.   PeHV

...Proud–wise and savvy to the white man ways.   Geronimo: Old Man Lives On.   Ronald James Dessus.   LFAC

Proudly give the churl his own,/And forget me when I'm gone!   Love's Last Suit.   Thomas Davidson.   BSV

Proudly sailed the arrow-breasted/Ships of Cossack yeomanry.   Stenka Razin.   Anonymous.   FSW

Proudly the tangle/of the wind.   He Praises the Trees.   Anonymous.   BIrV

Proudly, under the lights/of Jerusalem.   When I Came to Israel.   Bert Meyers.   AMV-80; VWA

Prov'd, by ends of being, to have been.   Moral Essays.   Alexander Pope.   CoBE

Prov'd here on earth the joys of paradise.   Stolen Pleasure.   William, of Hawthornden Drummond.   EnLoPo

Prove every fool to be a poet.   Epigram: "Yes, every poet is a fool."   Matthew Prior.   FaBoEE

Prove grateful emblems of the lays he sung.   Wind, Gentle Evergreen.   Anonymous.   CBEP

Prove half humility that you/May bless, good Woolman and sweet Francis!   Trimming the Sails.   Vassar Miller.   NMM

Prove that your terrible ways are one.   O Love, Answer.   Anne Ridler.   SeCePo

The provender the asses left/So sweetly he slept on.'   The Carnal and the Crane.   OBET

Proving His love again and again!   Gently He Draweth.   Anonymous.   BePJ

Proving that double negatives mean "No."   Unrecorded Speech.   Anna Adams.   BrRo

Proving that one and one make One.   One and One.   Cecil Day Lewis.   OAEP; UnS

Proving to Death that Love is so and so.   Goodby Betty, Don't Remember Me.   Edward Estlin Cummings.   CMoP

Prowde tyme of welthe, in stormes appawld with drede–/Murdred hymself to shew some manfull dede.   Thassyryans King, in Peas with Fowle Desyre.   Henry Howard, Earl of Surrey.   AAS

...Prowess of such sort/is to all the city a boon, to all Hellenes.   The Breed of Athletes.   Euripides.   SD

Prowling along the desolate wharves/in the dead of night?   Waterfront.   Oliver Jenkins.   EtS

Prudence (her teeth were a/Carious green.)   Appearance and Reality.   John Hollander.   OBAL

A prudent dentist always fills/himself with gas before he drills.   Archy at the Zoo.   Don (Donald Robert Marquis) Marquis.   NLV; OBAL

Prune me/light me/tend me.   HOURLY   Why So Many of Them Die.   Susan Wallbank.   BrRo

The Prussian boundaries were drawn by Polish chaps.   Philatelic Lessons: The German Collection.   Lawrence P. Spingarn.   NYBP

A psalm-book, and a Presbyter.   O What's the Rhyme to Porringer.   Anonymous.   GBP

Pu-leeze! Mister Hemingway!   Abner Silver's "Pu-leeze! Mr. Hemingway!"   Ring Lardner.   OBAL

The public bar-lamb's worse!   The Inhuman Wolf and the Lamb Sans Gene.   Guy Wetmore Carryl.   ALV; AmePo

The publican is a cheat.   The War of the Secret Agents.   Henri Coulette.   NePoEA-2

Puddles are to plop.   What They Are For.   Dorothy Aldis.   SoPo

The puddles of parking lots/Cannot contain such rainbows   To Waken a Small Person.   Donald Justice.   NYBP

Puhtita bhavana si ta ram.   Ragupati Ragava Rajah Ram.   Anonymous.   FSW

Puir folk couldna' hae it.   Kissin'.   Anonymous.   FiBHP; GoTF; LiTL; TreF

The Pukwana of the Peace-Pipe!   The Song of Hiawatha.   Henry Wadsworth Longfellow.   AnNE

Pull down the house of cards.   Three-Handed Fugue.   Phyllis Gotlieb.   NOBC

Pull out your tongue,/And see what you can say.   Up Time.   Anonymous.   OxNR

Pull petals from the sun,/and atoms pick apart.   Joy of Knowledge.   Isidor Schneider.   TrJP

Pull the stars out/with their teeth.   Evening Ceremony: Dream for G.V.   Wendy Rose.   TWSS

Pull up the jellyfish. You know the rest.   Skip-Scoop-Anellie.   Tom Prideaux.   FiBHP

,Pulled by—here,/yowly hound.   Shirley Temple Surrounded by Lions.   Kenward Elmslie.   ANYP

Pulled down from the source, a cardboard bolt.   A Chinaman's Chance.   Marilyn Chin.   BrSi

Pulled me into it.   Infant.   Diana O Hehir.   NPGG

Pulled six months for selling snow.   The Season 'Tis, My Lovely Lambs.   Edward Estlin Cummings.   NIP; UnPo

Pulling all the sky over him with one smile.   May My Heart Always.   Edward Estlin Cummings.   MoRP; OBSP

Pulling an old woman downstairs to the toilet/among the red eyes of her cats.   Late Lights in Minnesota.   Ted Kooser.   TAT

...Pulling free/to the yearning pulse, the blood/and the final cleaving.   Razor.   Robert B. Smith.   LFAC

...Pulling/stiff clothes away from the weather, the back road, post-modern/literature   Post-Modern Literature.   Erin Moure.   CaPN

Pulling the leaves of pink and pearl/With pale green nails of polished jade.   Impression Japonais.   Oscar Wilde.   SyP

Pulls out a long blade,/Who slit his throat...   Who Shall Die?   James A. Randall, Jr.   BPo

...Pulls shabby tricks in the/guillotine hour/(don't worry baby)   Broken Heart, Broken Machine.   Richard E. Grant.   PoBA

Pulverable dunes of the Least Sandpiper.   Surrealism in the Middle Ages.   Philip Lamantia.   APU

A pulverized screen/of patience   The Pulverized Screen.   Edmond Jabes.   VWA

The pump don't work/'Cause the vandals took the handles.   Subterranean Homesick Blues.   Bob Dylan.   InPK

Pumping blood through the stillness of my arteries   Factories.   Edward Hirsch.   AMV-81

Pumpkin moon.   The Shape of Autumn.   Virginia Russ.   GoYe

Pumps up the roaring sap of vegetables through their veins.   The Glacier.   Louis MacNeice.   AnFE

Punch, boys, punch, punch with care,/All in the presence of the passenjare.   The Passenjare.   Isaac H. Bromley.   FiBHP

Punchdrunk, against the carbon, seeing stars.   Stars.   Howard Moss.   HoAn

Punches my heart, until it is too dark to see.   The Ikons.   James Keir Baxter.   OCNZ

...Punctual-/ity is not a crime.   Four Quartz Crystal Clocks.   Marianne Moore.   AmPP; ImOP; MP; TwCP

Punctually, at a certain hour, on a certain date.   The Lovers.   Conrad Aiken.   AP; NYBP

Punished bottoms interrupt philosophy.   Is 5.   Edward Estlin Cummings.   AnAmPo

Punished by crimes of which I would be quit.   Sonnets at Christmas.   Allen Tate.   HAP; LiTM; NoAm; NOBA; OxBA; PoNe; VGW

Punishing you like a common adulterer.   I Entrust My All to You, Aurelius."   Caius Valerius Catullus.   PeHV

The pupil, plays its liquid jet/To win a look of violet.   Mark You How the Peacock's Eye.   Gerard Manley Hopkins.   FM

"Purdy, how are you? How you doodle do?"   Lunch at the Coq D'or.   Peter Davison.   TwCP

Pure as a pane of ice. It's a gift.   Love Letter.   Sylvia Plath.   NOBA

The pure-bred animals crossed the/wood in the thundery evening.   Four Stories.   David Shapiro.   ANYP

Pure, Bright, and Glorious be/Whose wondrous works I see.   As Often as Some Where before My Feet.   Francis Daniel Pastorius.   SCAP

Pure, cold, diffuse and wayward like the snow.   Milk at the Bottom of the Sea.   Oscar Williams.   LiTA; MoPo

Pure flowing Joy, and Happiness sincere.   Winter.   James (1700-48) Thomson.   CABL; EnLit; NOEC

Pure genius at work. Darling, the composer has stepped/into fire.   The Kiss.   Anne Sexton.   NIP

Pure like her never grew in womb/nor will till the end of time.   Adoramus Te, Christe.   David O Bruadair.   NOBI

Pure peacock blue, brass glory, furious stone.   Things Kept.   William Dickey.   NYBP

The pure source poured altogether out and away.   History of My Heart.   Robert Pinsky.   NPGG

A pure spirit is growing strong under the bark of the stones!   Golden Lines.   Gerard de Nerval.   NU

The pure, the pure! will never live so long.   In Shame and Humiliation.   James Wright.   CAPP

The pure white flag of love and brotherhood.   On a World War Battlefield.   Thomas Curtis Clark.   PGD

Purer in heart, help me to be.   Purer in Heart.   Anonymous.   STF

The purer passion and the firmer faith.   Song.   George Meredith.   EnLit

A purer sky, where all is peace.   I Saw Two Clouds at Morning.   John Gardiner Calkins Brainard.   HBV 1-2; PoToHe

The purest fishing remained a dream.   Dream Fishing.   Jim Thomas.   WOLT

Purest light brilliant & ruddy/so/favorable!   Dance & Eye Me (Wicked)ly My Breath a Fixed Sphere.   Rochelle Owens.   NMM

Purge and disperse, that I may see and tell/Of things invisible to mortal sight. Hail Holy Light.   John Milton.   LoBV

Purged of the flames that loved the/wind/Is the pure glow that has not sinned. Beauty.   Isaac Rosenberg.   TrJP

Purging the spirits of the pure from grief.   The Defence of Night. Buonarroti Michelangelo.   CAW

...A purple billiard ball/explodes the color scheme.   Two Lean Cats... Myron O'Higgins.   PoBA; PoNe

A purple Flowre see of this Marble borne.   Ioolas' Epitaph.   William, of Hawthornden Drummond.   AtBAP; PoEL 1-5

The purple plumage of your respendence.   The Purple Blemish.   Par Lagerkvist.   AMV-81

...The purpose of the total was obvious/& uncompromising.   The "Utopia'. Lee Harwood.   EAS

Purposeless matter hovers in the dark.   The Annihilation of Nothing.   Thom Gunn.   NePoEA-2; NoAm

Purr, says the cat.   Dame Trot.   *Anonymous.*   OxNR

Purring and crooning:–"Lie in us, and dream."   Week-End Sonnet No. 1. Harold Monro.   BSV

The purring of the invisible antennae/Is both stimulating and delightful. Tame Cat.   Ezra Pound.   ELU; OBAL

Pursue after thy King in the intimate company/Of souls that flow unto the goodness of the Lord.   Asleep in the Bosom of Youth.   Judah Halevi. LiTW

Pursue downhill, half blind with my own laughter.   Old Dog, New Dog. Sydney Lea.   MAYP

Pursue the Bird of Jove, that sails along the Skies.   The Island of the Blest. Gilbert West.   OBEC

Pursue the wild game through thickets of irony.   Preliminary Poem.   John Heath-Stubbs.   OxBC

Push back the mountains and the stars.   Soul Lifted.   Albert Durrant Watson.   CaP

Pushed to the ultimate end/to leave the naked soul.   Pushed to the Scroll. Winifred Hamrick Farrar.   AMV-80

Pushing against it, I said: "Go away!"   Drinking.   Hsin Ch'i-chi.   LiTW

Pushing back into the dust.   Star Quilt.   Roberta Hill.   CDW; TWSS

Pushing me away but blue, so blue.   Marlow and Nancy.   Sandra McPherson.   AmPA

Pushing my hand deeper into the dog's/brilliant eye.   Black Dog.   Ray A. Young Bear.   CDW

Puss lizard will lunch on some other T-bone/sunset grand couturier.   Canto LXXX.   Ezra Pound.   PoA

Pussicat, wussicat, don't be too late.   Wedding.   *Anonymous.*   OxNR

Pussy-cat said naught but "Mew," and Robin flew away.   Robin Redbreast. *Anonymous.*   HBV 1-2

The pussycat fell on the dumpling./Said God,/"Oops."   Fielding Error. Robert Paul Smith.   CAD

Put all your beauty in your rhymes,/Your morals in your living.   The Origin of Didactic Poetry.   James Russell Lowell.   PoEL 1-5

Put back upon his jaws.   Seasons of the Soul.   Allen Tate.   NePA; OxBA

Put best foot forward/New Year, with a will.   Up the Hill, Down the Hill. Eleanor Farjeon.   PoSC

Put forward your best foot!   Respectability.   Robert Browning.   EnLoPo; MBW 1-2; ViBoPo

Put Heaven on a postal card.   To a Post-Office Inkwell.   Christopher Morley.   PoLf

Put it in cold/then bring to the boil   In the Case of Lobsters.   Petra von Morstein.   BoWoP

Put it in the oven for Tommy and/me.   Pat-a-Cake, Pat-a-Cake, Baker's Man. *Anonymous.*   OxNR

Put it into your left-hand pocket/And never look inside.   Parting Gift. Elinor Wylie.   LOW; OxBA

Put it through!   Put It Through.   Edward Everett Hale.   MC; PAH

Put me on Phaon's lips to rest,/And cheat the cruel day!   And on My Eyes Dark Sleep by Night.   Michael (Katherine Bradley and Edith Cooper) Field.   OBMV

Put not thy trust in such as use to feign,/Except thou mind to put thy friend to pain.   Accused though I be without desert.   Sir Thomas Wyatt.   FCP; SiPS

Put on a new skin of flame/and became/Vietnamese.   Norman Morrison. Adrian Mitchell.   FF

Put on the reins of love.   All These Birds.   Richard Wilbur.   NOBA; Prf

Put out my hand, and touched the face of God.   High Flight.   John Gillespie Magee, Jr.   BBV; FaFP; GoTF; MaC; PGD; TreFS; TRV

Put out their coloured lights of comfort and of hope.   The Single Woman. Frances Cornford.   ELU

..."Put out your lights,/children of earth. Sleep warm."   Night Plane. Frances Frost.   TiPo

...Put the roast on a hot dish after/having removed the grease–if there is any–, and serve.   A Dish for a Poet.   *Anonymous.*   OBCP

Put the witches to their speed.   Against Witches.   *Anonymous.*   GBP

Put up your caravan/Just for one day?   Time, You Old Gipsy Man.   Ralph Hodgson.   BoLiVe; BrPo; CH; GoTF; HBV 1-2; LiTM; MoAB; MoBrPo; MoShBr; PG; SiSoSe; TreF; TrGrPo; ViBoPo

Put up your wife, she's crosser than all four.   On a Window at the Four Crosses.   Jonathan Swift.   FaBoEE

Put your arms around me. Our winter is real.   Paradise.   E. N. Sargent. NYBP

Put your hand in his mouth! Do you feel? He can bite!   The First Tooth. William Brighty ("Matthew Browne") Rands.   HBV 1-2; HBVY

Puts down all drink when it is stale!   The Nut-Brown Ale.   John Marston. EIL

Puts each minute such as you/A dozen dozen to disgrace.   Sir Toby Matthews.   Sir John Suckling.   SeCV 1-2

Puts on a hard shell/for weathering this world.   Bricking the Church. Robert Morgan.   MAYP

Puts on his glasses, and resumes his reading   The Company of Scholars. Helen Bevington.   GLGT

Puts on rubber gloves when stealing a cookie.   Psychological Prediction. Virginia Brasier.   BBGG

Puts out her light, and turns away to sleep.   Curiosity: Fiction.   Charles Sprague.   AA

...Puts some/spit on it and then/sticks out the other foot/again.   74th Street. Myra Cohn Livingston.   CTBA

Puts up his pipe, and lids his moony eye.   Snakecharmer.   Sylvia Plath. NePoEA-2; PP

Putting our arms around the necks of the men, began kissing them. Hmmmmm, 22.   Leslie Scalapino.   NPGG

The putting-out of the candle in the blind man's room.   Bog and Candle. Robert D. Fitzgerald.   CBAP

Putting soup in his mouth with a spoon.   Soup.   Carl Sandburg.   NOBA; OBCA

A pyramid is strange to see,/Though only at its base you be.   The Story of Pyramid Thothmes.   *Anonymous.*   NA

Q

Qietly looking between the green trees.   Every One to His Own Way.   John Vance Cheney.   AA

Qu-ow wow, quall, wawl, moon.   A True Cat.   Anna Seward.   PCat

A quack, a honk, an oink, a moo.   The Answers.   Robert Clairmont.   SoPo

Quack! in the dark, says he.   Music in the Air.   George Johnston.   PeCV

Quadruped swoons into billiardBalls!   Space Being(Don't Forget to Remember)Curved.   Edward Estlin Cummings.   NoAm

Quail from your downward darting kiss.   The Kiss.   Siegfried Sassoon. MMM

The quaint, old, cruel coxcomb, in his gullet/Should have a hook, and a small trout to pull it.   And Angling, Too.   George Gordon, Lord Byron.   SD

Quan the mayden hayt that sche lovit,/sche is without longyng.   Love without Longing.   *Anonymous.*   OxBoLi

The quarry goes to Autumn, let Spring die.   The Hound.   Babette Deutsch. HBMV

A quarter's worth of nickel and aluminum.   In Galleries.   Randall Jarrell. EyDe

The quarter sounded from the steeple.   Pan in Wall Street.   Edmund Clarence Stedman.   AA; AnAmPo; HBV 1-2

Quarter twain.   Mississippi Sounding Calls, I.   *Anonymous.*   AmFP

Queen.   Lady...   *Anonymous.*   OxNR

The Queen and Prince Albert, and do it no more.   Old England Forever and Do It No More.   *Anonymous.*   GBP

The queen bee marries the winter of your year.   The Beekeeper's Daughter. Sylvia Plath.   IHMS

Queen both for beauty and for majesty.   With How Sad Steps, O Moon, Thou Climb'st the Sky.   William Wordsworth.   MBW 1-2

The Queen in silence is driving by.   The Queen's Last Ride.   Ella Wheeler Wilcox.   BLPA

The Queen is much distressed.   Much Distressed.   *Anonymous.*   CBAP

The Queen next morning fried.   King Arthur.   *Anonymous.*   NA; OxNR

The queen of faerie guarded by blue winged griffins/Untouched by.   The Faerie Queene.   Robin Blaser.   CoPo

Queen of Fragrance, lovely Rose.   The Rose-Bud To a Young Lady. William Broome.   CEP; LoBV; OBEC

Queen of my heart,/My Mother.   Mother.   Thomas Curtis Clark.   PGD

Queen of the pure hearts, do I love thee!   Nanny.   Francis Davis.   HBV 1-2

The queen of the world, and the child of the skies.   Columbia.   Timothy Dwight.   HBV 1-2; MC; PAH

Queen of them all, the red red rose, the flower which/lovers love.   A Garland for Heliodora.   Meleager.   AWP; EnLi 1-2

The queens you'll meet on any street in old New York. The Streets of New York. Henry Blossom. FSN

The queer bites on her voluptuous thighs. Hostia. Irving Layton. PV

Queer, what a dim dark smudge you have disappeared/into! The Mosquito. D. H. Lawrence. BoANP; PoPle

Queets Indian Reservation in the rain. Hitch Haiku. Gary Snyder. LCAP

Quelque chose tres deep, ma foi! Another Canto (parody). J. B. Morton. FaBoPa

Queme thee thenne, milsful King, oure offringe of this song. A Palm-Sunday Hymn. William Herebert. MeEL

Quench in my heart the flames of bad desire. To the Blessed Sacrament. Henry Constable. ACP; CAW

The quench in the west. Dog Yoga. Charles Wright. LCAP

The quenched sparks of our life. Our Children's Children Will Marvel. Ilya Ehrenburg. WaaP

The quenching of candles. The Dedicated. Philip Larkin. OxBC

Querying too, querying, my quiet kin? Preliminary to Classroom Lecture. Josephine Miles. NoAm

A question bangs in our heads like an old door/That will not stay closed, for all our knowledge. The Campus. David Posner. NYBP

Question me again. Casualty. Seamus Heaney. FaBoPV; IPY

Quhais hie plesance, Lord, lat ws neuer mys! Amen. The Aeneid. Virgil (Publius Vergilius Maro). OxBoCh

Quhen frostis doith ourfret baith firth and fald. The Aeneid. Virgil (Publius Vergilius Maro). OxBS

Quhilk wald ye waill to your wif, gif ye suld wed/one? The Tretis of the Tua Mariit Wemen and the Wedo. William Dunbar. EBEV; GoTS; OxBS

–Quhom I luve I dare nocht assay!' When Flora Had O'erfret the Firth. Anonymous. NoP; OBEV

Quhy sowld nocht Allane honorit be? The Gude and Godlie Ballatis: Quhy Sowld Nocht Allane Honorit Be? Anonymous. OxBS

Qui dabit eternam nobis pro munere vitam/In permansuro ponite vota deo. Pageant Verses. Sir Thomas More. AAS

Quick action is the main thing. A Cold Front. William Carlos Williams. NAs

The quick and dead together talked,/On Kingston Bridge. On Kingston Bridge. Ellen Mackay Hutchinson Cortissoz. AA

Quick! and see what he has done/Ere 'tis stolen by the Sun. Wizard Frost. Frank Dempster Sherman. YeAr

Quick as Aladdin rubbing his lamp, she would. Dance of the Abakweta. Margaret Danner. PoNe

The quick brief cry of memory, that knows/At the dark's edge how great the darkness is. Then Came I to the Shoreless Shore of Silence. Conrad Aiken. LiTA; NePA

Quick/children kiss us/we are growing through dream. Rites of Passage. Audre Lorde. CNA; PoBA

Quick, cool kisses. Snow-Dance for the Dead. Lola Ridge. AnAmPo

The quick-darting breath is/our portion of honesty. Herons. Robin Blaser. NeAP

Quick into ashes turned. Madrigal: "The gods have heard my vows." Thomas Weelkes. EnRePo

Quick jingling comes the cattle-bell. The Canadian Herd-Boy. Susanna Moodie. OBCV

Quick, let's hide him. How to Hide Jesus. Steve Turner. EBCP

The quick relics, the ministers of His Church. The Twelve Properties or Conditions of a Lover. Sir Thomas More. EnRePo

Quick, Rose, and kiss me. Is It Far to Go. Lewis, Cecil Day. AtBAP

Quick, tender, virginal, and unprofaned! The Angel in the House. Coventry Patmore. VLP

Quick, thy tablets, Memory! A Memory-Picture. Matthew Arnold. VLP

Quick trout dimple the pool.–Distance makes clean. Skunks (excerpt). Robinson Jeffers. BoANP

Quick, wake! The soul survives? eh? though life goes? Lines in Order to Be Slandered. Paul Verlaine. SyP

The quick whip of the wind, and the sting of rain. April 1940. Patrick Maybin. NeIP

Quick with game, heavy with the wind's wild mint. Four Things Choctaw. Jim Barnes. STE

Quicken our gratitude! A Thanksgiving. William Dean Howells. HBV 1-2; TrPWD

Quickened are they that touch the Prophet's bones. Michael Angelo: A Fragment (excerpt). Henry Wadsworth Longfellow. MAmP

Quickened with touches of transporting fear. Three Sonnets. [James Henry] Leigh Hunt. NOBL

Quicker with cards/than with a gun. Epitaph for a Man from Virginia City. Kenneth Porter. NePoAm-2

Quickly. Apocalypse. Francis Ernest Kobina Parkes. PBA

Quickly; do what you must do. Family Portrait 1933. Peter Oresick. LTB

Quickly, secretly, so the shop owner sitting at the back/wouldn't realize what was going on. He Asked about the Quality. Constantine P. Cavafy. PeHV

Quickly, she might say, unless she understands/that silence is itself a measure. Tatiana Kalatschova. William Logan. SM

...Quickly, too quickly, I am gone? Angel Surrounded by Paysans. Wallace Stevens. HaCAP; LCAP; PPP

Quickly tucked him away in his–"you know!" Limerick: "A jolly young artist called Bruno." Anonymous. TDH

Quickly we others Errors find,/But see not our own Load behind. Carmina. Caius Valerius Catullus. OBVE

Quickly we pray oh Lord! say thou Amen. Seaconk Plain Engagement. Benjamin Tompson. SCAP

A quickness which my God hath kissed. Quickness. Henry Vaughan. BoC; ELP; LoBV; MeLP; MePo; NOBE; NOCV; OBS; OxBoCh; SeCePo; SeCP; SeCV 1-2

(Quien sabe? Who really knows?) Havana Dreams. Langston Hughes. GoSl; PoNe

...Quiet/after the stroke, he rocked himself/through childhood and a second infancy. Rockingchair. Robert Morgan. PPJ

Quiet and love and peace/Be to this, our rest, our place. Evening Hymn. Elizabeth Madox Roberts. TiPo

...Quiet/At slammed door and smoker's cough in the hall. Docker. Seamus Heaney. NoAm; NOBI; TW

Quiet beyond recall,/Into irrelevance. To the Holy Spirit. Yvor Winters. ForPo; MoAmPo; MoVE; QFR; VGW

Quiet, fragrant, and relieved. The Dusk of Horses. James Dickey. AP; LiTM

...The quiet glow on the water. Documentary. Joseph Stroud. NPGG

Quiet in the yard where tree trunks do not lie/More quietly. Head and Bottle. Edward ("Edward Eastaway") Thomas. BrPo

The quiet kindness of the Angevin air. Heureux Qui, Comme Ulysse, A Fait Un Beau Voyage. Joachim Du Bellay. AWP

Quiet lakes and milking sheds; "Fares please, fares please." The Agricultural Show, Flemington, Victoria. Furnley Maurice. CBAP

The quiet like a curtain/when the piece is complete. The Offensive. Keith Douglas. NeBP

Quiet, my bride, till morning comes/and your voice shall sound in the caves of my heart. The Cage. Avner and Levenston. E. A. Treinin. VWA

A quiet passage to a welcome grave. The Angler's Wish. Izaak Walton. HBV 1-2

A quiet, pilfering, unprotected race. Gipsies. John Clare. CH; NBM; PoEL 1-5

Quiet, Quiet, Quiet. Nemea. Lawrence Durrell. ChMP; FaBoTw; GTBS-P

The quiet sands have run. Twilight Calm. Christina Georgina Rossetti. BoNaP; OBNC

The quiet shutting, one by one, of doors. Doors. Hermann Hagedorn. AnAmPo

A quiet small corner of your bedroom in which to hide. Submission. Anonymous. ErPo

The quiet (Thames' or Don's or Salween's) waters by. Whitmonday. Louis MacNeice. NYBP

The quiet that my dream fulfils/Of Quiet, aching tho' it be. Quiet. Ernest Radford. OBVV

The quiet that you seek is only found/Where heart beats not and hands are still. The Monks at Ards. Patrick Maybin. NeIP

Quieter now than he used to be, but listening still to the magpie chatter/Over his grave. Here Lies a Prisoner. Charlotte Mew. MoBrPo

Quietly Quietly Quietly Three Kings. James P. Vaughn. NNP; PoNe

Quietly shining to the quiet moon. Frost at Midnight. Samuel Taylor Coleridge. BoC; CABA; CBEP; EBEV; ERoP 1-2; FaBoRV; FiP; GLGT; HAP; LoBV; MBW 1-2; NAs; NOBE; NoP; OAEL 1-2; OAEP; OBNC; OBRV; PoEL 1-5; PPP; PrIm

Quietly they shine, covered up, for they are sacred... The Djanggawul Cycle, 166. Anonymous. WTO

Quietly you possess me. Variations (excerpt). Conrad Aiken. PG

Quince fragrance in hedges,/shadows on asphalt. A Serenade for Two Poplars. Esther Raab. VWA

Quit a', an' seek nae mair. Odes. Horace. OBVE

Quit me of stubborn death. A Thought for My Love. Bruce Williamson. NeIP

Quite beyond recall, but not forgotten quite. Love and Age. Walter Savage Landor. GBL

...Quite possibly this life of his/will land him in a devastating scandal. The Twenty-Fifth Year of His Life. Constantine P. Cavafy. PeHV

Quite sufficiently alone/For mine ownself's company. I Set Aside. Mary Morison Webster. PeSA

Quiu, qui, qui. The Thrush's Song. W. Macgillivray. CH

Quiver like a/heartbeat in the/air and are/no more. Song: "Where I walk out." Yvor Winters. BoANP; PoL

...A quivering of human steps/upon the banks among the tender canes. The Gentle Hill. Salvator Quasimodo. PoPl

Quivering, quiet, dumb,/Drinks up the lighted room. What Was Solomon's Mind? Geoffrey Scott. OBMV

Quivers and/breaks out in blue leaves.　Winter Scene.　Archie Randolph Ammons.　WeW

Quo life, the warld is mine.　The Flyting o' Life and Daith.　Hamish Henderson.　OxBS

Quo' the wee boy, and still he shude.　The Fause Knicht upon the Road. *Anonymous.*　OxBoLi

Quoth Echo (sotto voce),–"Take her!"　Echo.　John Godfrey Saxe.　AnNE

Quoth he, "There's never shepherd's boy/That ever was so blest."　Cassamen and Dowsabell.　Michael Drayton.　OBSC

Quoth the Reagan, "Nevermore!"　The Reagan (parody).　Richard Quick.　FaBoPa

Quoth the wee boy, and still he stood.　The False Knight on the Road. *Anonymous.*　AmFP; AtBAP; CBEP; EnSB; ESPB; GBP

Quoth Tom in Tatters.　Tom Tatter's Birthday Ode.　Thomas Hood. LoBV

Quoth Tom, "So they said at our marriage."　Too Candid by Half.　John Godfrey Saxe.　HBV 1-2

R

Rabbi Nachman blesses her with the gift/of good life/until it becomes day.　Love Song.　Hayim Be'er.　VWA

Rabbit, the drummer,/Straightens his ears/And marches with summer.　The Drummer.　Anne Robinson.　SUS

Rabbit tracks, deer tracks,/what do we know.　Pine Tree Tops.　Gary Snyder.　NOBA; Prf

The Rabbit with a sudden leap/is gone.　A Bestiary of the Garden for Children Who Should Know Better.　Phyllis Gotlieb.　WHW

Rabbits and chipmunks, clear the track!　Autumn!　Nancy Byrd Turner.　YeAr

The rabbits' ears, the birds' beaks/on call.　Rhyme for the Child as a Wet Dog.　Judith Johnson Sherwin.　TAP

The rabbits, the oak and the walnut trees.　Mr. Walter de la Mare Makes the Little Ones Dizzy (parody).　Samuel Hoffenstein.　Par; SpRo

...The rabbits/will bare their teeth at/the spring moon.　The Springtime.　Denise Levertov.　CoAP; ConAP

Rabble?" she groused.　Said Agatha Christie.　George Starbuck.　OBAL; PV

The race is to the swift,/The battle to the strong.　War Song.　John Davidson.　NBM; OBNC

Race up into fresh water.　Salmon-Fishing.　Robinson Jeffers.　AnEnPo; SD

The race will bear Field-Marshal God's inspection.　Inspection.　Wilfred Owen.　WaP

...Racers,/whips, cobras and kings wait, ready to weave/through all my dreams.　Dreams of Snakes, Chocolate and Men.　Christy Sheffield Sanford.　APU

...Rack of balls explodes,/running hard for the far green corners.　8-Ball at the Twilite.　David Baker.　MAYP

Racked carcasses make ill anatomies.　Love's Exchange.　John Donne.　LiTL

Racks with his famine, sucks marrow from the bone.　Hungry Grass.　Donagh MacDonagh.　BIrV; NeIP; OxBI

...Radiance/Which is engendered of its own!　O Virtuous Light.　Elinor Wylie.　NePA

The radiant blossom of English earth–is dead!　The Crowns.　John Freeman.　CH

Radiant Thammuz, risen anew!　Thammuz.　William Vaughn Moody.　AP

The radiant, white, hanging day?　The Yucca Moth.　Archie Randolph Ammons.　NOBA

A radio, a television set, and a bourgeois/prairie newspaper hang as accomplices　Two Hookers.　A. K. Redwing.　VWA

The radios hot/misery　On a Country Road.　Harley Elliott.　NeAC

The rag doll that was a child.　Epitaph for an American Bomber.　James Bertram.　AnNZ

Rage, rage against the dying of the light.　Do Not Go Gentle Into That Good Night.　Dylan Thomas.　ACV; BiP; CoBMV; DiPo; DL; FaFP; FF; GoTF; HAP; HeIP; HoPM; InPK; InPS; LiTM; MoAB; MoBrPo; MoVE; MP; NIP; NoAm; NOBE; NoP; OAEL 1-2; OxBTC; PAI; PPON; PrIm; SCV; SeCeV; SoSe; TEP; TreFT; TW; TwCP; UnPo; ViBoPo; WeW

The rage that sweeps my sons away,/My baneful gold shall well repay.'　The Revenge of America.　Joseph Warton.　OBTV

Rage warps my clearest cry/To witless agony.　Open House.　Theodore Roethke.　AP; CoBMV; NoAm; NOBA; NoP

Raggedy! Raggedy Man!　The Raggedy Man.　James Whitcomb Riley.　HBV 1-2; HBVY; OBCA; OxBChV; TiPo; TreFS

A raging dog, gnawing its way to pass out.　The Rain.　*Anonymous.*　WTO

A raging mimic of the universe's grand indifference.　A Curfew: December 13, 1981.　Amy Clampitt.　SUW

Ragnarok, twilight of the gods.　My Birth.　Minot Judson Savage.　AA; WGRP

A raided crapgame scrambling for its cash.　For the ERA Crusaders.　X. J. Kennedy.　SOTS

The railway cars are coming, humming/Through New Mexico.　The Railroad Cars Are Coming (with music).　*Anonymous.*　AmFN; AS; BPAW; BrR

Rain against a hidden sun,/the form plain　To Her Body, Against Time.　Robert Kelly.　CoPo

Rain beat against the window panes all night.　Gooseberries.　Stephen Berg.　NaP

The rain-clouds flash with April mirth,/Like Life on earth.　April Rain.　Mathilde Blind.　HBV 1-2

The rain comes sobbing to the door.　The Rain Comes Sobbing to the Door.　Henry Clarence Kendall.　ACV

...The rain/coming down in a distant orchard.　Raincoats for the Dead.　Albert Bellg.　FAZ

The rain dried us off.　The Day It Was Night.　Robert Desnos.　WeW

Rain glances off dots that divide the lanes/that contain the flow that issues from consummate waking　Up Early.　Kit Robinson.　APU

The rain hushes the surface of tin porches.　Rain.　Emanuel DiPasquale.　InPK; PoL

Rain in my heart, and at my window rain.　Night of Rain.　Bernice Lesbia Kenyon.　HBMV

The rain is over and gone!　Written in March.　William Wordsworth.　BoNaP; EnRP; GoJo; HBV 1-2; HBVY; NTCP; SUS; TiPo; UnPo; YeAr

Rain on the house-top,/But not on me.　Rain on the Green Grass.　*Anonymous.*　OxNR

Rain pastes the leather-black streets with large pale leaves.　Watershed.　Margaret Avison.　OBCV

Rain, rain in Cochiti!　A Dance for Rain.　Witter ("Emanuel Morgan") Bynner.　BPAW

Rain rain on the baby auctioneers.　Rain Rain on the Splintered Girl.　Ishmael Reed.　PoBA

The rain returns into their lives.　Closing Time.　James Michie.　NePoEA-2

...Rain/singing over the din of the/loneliest mornings.　Six Days.　Mario Petaccia.　LFAC

...The rain that gave/my eyes their vigilance.　Two Variations.　Denise Levertov.　NaP

Rain water now is falling!/Aha we ahe, aha we ahe,/Aha a a a, e e he e heye!　Songs in the Turtle Dance at Santa Clara.　*Anonymous.*　WTO

The rain, wherewith she watereth the flowers,/Falls from mine eyes, which she dissolves in showers.　Diana.　Henry Constable.　HBV 1-2; OBSC

Rain will come down.　Crow on the Fence.　*Anonymous.*　PBBP

Rain will never come to pass.　When the Dew Is on the Grass.　*Anonymous.*　OxNR

Rain, wind, and fire! The secret, bestial peace!　The Card-Players.　Philip Larkin.　OxBC

...Rain would confuse him,/or he would be reminded thereof.　By Hallucination Visited.　Robert Horan.　EAS

Rainbow at morning,/Sailors, take warning.　Weather Wisdom.　*Anonymous.*　HBV 1-2

A rainbow beauty passion-free/Wherewith was veiled Divinity.　The Immaculate Conception.　John Banister Tabb.　ISi

Rainbow colors/fade from sight,/come back to me/when I write.　Rainbow Writing.　Eve Merriam.　GrPl

The rainbow in its scattering grains of spray.　The Beautiful Lawn Sprinkler.　Howard Nemerov.　PCP

A rainbow stands and summer passes under.　I Hear a River.　Trumbull Stickney.　NCEP

...–Raindrops on the roof, no comment/On the matter of God.　Unitarian Easter.　Sandra McPherson.　MAYP

Rained violets upon his sleeping eyes.　Endymion.　John Keats.　SeCePo

Raining arrows of fire/into the great darkness.　Hebrew Script.　Tali Loewenthal.　VWA

Raise a slender stalk of words/From a root unseen.　New Life.　Amelia Josephine Burr.　HBV 1-2

Raise corn on the hillside an' the devil in the valley.　Sally Goodin.　*Anonymous.*　FSW

Raise from the excellent the better still.　To Yvor Winters, 1955.　Thom Gunn.　GTBS-P

Raise her marble heart i' th' room,/And 'tis both her corse and tomb.　To Lucasta.　Richard Lovelace.　CaPo

Raise him a tombstone of snow.　Last Rites.　Christina Georgina Rossetti.　OxBChV

Raise it again, man. We still believe what we hear.　The Singer's House.　Seamus Heaney.　CIP; EBEV

Raise the stone, and thou shalt find Me;/cleave the wood, and I am there.　They Who Tread the Path of Labor.　Henry Van Dyke.　TRV

"Raise the stone and thou shalt find me; cleave the wood, and/there am I."　A Lost Word of Jesus.　Henry Van Dyke.　TrCP; WGRP

Raise the world to my dream.　Tidying Up.　Nancy Weber.　AMV-80

Raise us in Thy dawn.　Evensong.　Clive Staples Lewis.　TrCP

Raise your bewildered eyes to the luminous hills of tomorrow.   Song for Tomorrow.   Lucia Trent.   PGD

Raised me to praise you from the crag where I cling.   From the Crag.   Mani Leib.   VWA

Raised up this bribe against their fate.   On a Replica of the Parthenon.   Donald Davidson.   MoVE

Raises a mist, that, glittering in the sun,/Runs with her all the way, wherever she doth run.   There Was a Roaring in the Wind All Night.   William Wordsworth.   GoTF; TreFT

Raises up both hands and shouts three times!   Meeting the Mountains.   Gary Snyder.   NoAm; TAP

Raising its radiance to the moon.   Bread.   William Stanley Merwin.   EAS

...The raising of the foot as much as the laying of it down.   Epigrams (excerpt).   Rabindranath Tagore.   PoA

Raising their braided heads,/their gold tongues whetted.   Yom Kippur.   Chana Bloch.   VWA

...Raising you/on my fork as all the dead shall be risen?   For the Eating of Swine.   Rodney Jones.   MAYP

Rajah, over, and out.   Some Questions to Be Asked of a Rajah...   Preston Newman.   FiBHP

Raking an iron rooster through the sky.   Traditional Red.   Robert Huff.   HoPM; NePoEA-2

Rally and cheer in freedom's holy name!   A Prophecy.   Maurice Thompson.   AA

...Rambling and singing in her hills and/open valleys, bathing in all her beauty Pennsylvania Winter Indian 1974.   Harold Littlebird.   VoR

The rampikes of the forest/attain a brittle silence.   Colonial Set.   Alfred Goldsworthy Bailey.   OBCV

Ran down the hill.   And Then the Sun.   Pradip Sen.   ACV

Ran into Mississippi and were drowned.   John Brown's Body.   Stephen Vincent Benét.   AmFN

Ran screaming from the mirror, and was mad.   The Madman.   Constance Urdang.   PoPl

Rancid goat-butter and the piss of cats.   Coptic Poem.   Lawrence Durrell.   FaBoCo

A random glance to see where next/Yon butterfly will go!   Spring Song.   Aubrey Thomas De Vere.   IrPN

A randomness, a darkness of one's own.   The Ice-Cream Wars.   John Ashbery.   PoA

Rang out loudly "INDEPENDENCE,"/Which, please God, shall never die.   Liberty and Independence.   *Anonymous.*   TreFS

...A range/of open time at winter's outskirts.   February Evening in New York.   Denise Levertov.   NoAm; PAI

Rank after rank, with even feet/And uniforms of snow.   To fight aloud is brave.   Emily Dickinson.   LiTA

Rank and tangled vine and jungle block our/pathway to the peak.   Rare Moments.   Charles Henry Phelps.   AA

The rank, primeval innocent smell of night!   After the Party.   Frances Cornford.   ELU

Rank with the sea, which crumbles evermore.   On a View of Pasadena from the Hills.   Yvor Winters.   QFR

A ransomed soul!   Faith.   Ray Palmer   AA; HBV 1-2

The rantin dog the Daddie o't.   The Rantin Dog the Daddie O't.   Robert Burns.   OxBoLi; PPP

Ranzo, boys, Ranzo!   Reuben Ranzo.   *Anonymous.*   AmFP; AmSS; ShS

Rap chose me   Detroit Conference of Unity and Art.   Nikki Giovanni.   HoPM

Raphael's Joys and Graces, and thy clear stars, Galileo!   A Letter from Rome.   Arthur Hugh Clough.   LoBV

The Rapids are near and the daylight's past.   A Canadian Boat Song.   Thomas Moore.   GoBC; HBV 1-2; OBRV

The raptures languish, and the numbers groan.   The Bastard.   Richard Savage.   CBEP; OBEC

A rare old plant is the Ivy green.   The Ivy Green.   Charles Dickens.   BoNaP; HBV 1-2; HBVY

Rarer than beauty–like genius a gift and equivocal.   I Think of Your Generation.   Charles Brasch.   AnNZ

The rarity, the odd go, the oddity,/the flaming cloth.   Arachne.   Judith Kazantzis.   BrRo

Rasping a bitter death-dirge through the August/night.   Katydids.   Amy Lowell.   PBWP

A rat could eat him,/Hat and all.   Jerry Hall.   *Anonymous.*   OxNR

The rat will have dragged it into his hole.   What Invisible Rat.   Jean-J. Rebearivelo.   TTY

...A rat with its tail down the body's back.   Children.   Russell Edson.   AmPA

Rat within or bird without.   Dawn Has Yet to Ripple in.   Melville Cane.   MoAmPo

The rath survives; the kings/are covered in clay.   The Rath in Front of the Oak Wood.   *Anonymous.*   NOBI

...Rather admiring/the look of suffering/in my middle-aged eyes.   Milne's Bar.   Norman MacCaig.   FaBoTw

Rather drink muddy water/go sleep in a hollow tree/Than to hear my kid gal/say she don't want me.   Depot Blues.   Charlie Lincoln (Hicks).   BluL

Rather hast Thou braced his spirit/to withstand affliction.   Though Mine Eye Sleep Not.   *Anonymous.*   TrJP

Rather rubbed in than off.   My Boots.   Henry David Thoreau.   PeD

Rather sweet Jesus, fill up time, and come/To yield the sin her everlasting doom.   Caelica, CIX.   Fulke, Lord Brooke Greville.   EnRePo; FCP; PoEL 1-5

Rather than hurting/openly/for still another/Hour.   Another Letter to Joseph Bruchac.   Jack Anderson.   LFAC

Rather than lead a sumpuous tinselled life/With twenty million dollars and a wife.   Epigram: "Me Polytimus vexes and provokes."   Martial (Marcus Valerius Martialis).   PeHV

Rather than live in snuff, will be put out.   On the Snuff of a Candle.   Sir Walter Ralegh.   FaBoEE; FCP; SiPS

Rather than making them happy/by giving to them.   Arc.   Tom Clark.   APU

Rather than mend, put out the light.   Upon Himself.   Robert Herrick.   OBSP

Rather than not for heavenly light/Wait on to show the truly right.   Come Back.   Arthur Hugh Clough.   NCEP

Rather than passing my time/Searching for "Simple Rurality."   Rural Simplicity.   H. J. Byron.   NOBL

Rather than time upon my wrist I wear/The dial, the four quarters of your death.   For My Grandfather.   Francis Webb.   BoAV

Rather to please us were the flowers she gave.   A Death.   Elizabeth Jennings.   NMP

Rather with blithe Adonis shall thou rove/And play the Ganymede to highest Jove.   Epigram: "Glad youth had come thy sixteenth year to crown."   Decimus Magnus Ausonius.   PeHV

Rats, bedbugs, blacks.   From Our Album.   Lawson Fusao Inada.   AmPA

...The rattler/Filmed his glinty eye, and found his hole.   The Making of the Cross.   William Everson.   VGW

Rattles them to scare off/foxes there in the dark.   Hiding in the Cucumber Garden.   Vidya.   WPOW

Rattling like dried leaves on a stunted tree.   Song of the Fucked Duck.   Marge Piercy.   BoWoP; NMM

The raven dies.   The Raven.   Nicarchos [(or Nicarchus)].   AWP; LiTW; UnS

The raven dies.   Variations of Greek Themes.   Edwin Arlington Robinson.   OBAL

Raven listens, whistling in stunted trees.   Raven/Moon.   Anita Endrezze-Probst.   VoR

Ravens crying out, ravens flying in.   What's worse than this past century?   Anna Akhmatova.   BoWoP

Ravens flourish, summer has come!   Summer Has Come.   *Anonymous.*   LiTW; OnYI

Raves in his windy heights above a cloud.   When Yon Full Moon.   William Henry Davies.   MoBrPo; MOON

A raving barracuda/took a bit of something tender.   Carravagio.   Janet Hamill.   APU

Ravished in that fair Via Lactea.   Upon Julia's Breasts.   Robert Herrick.   CaPo; NoP

A raw material   Aesthetics of the Moon.   Jack Anderson.   MOON

Raw towns of man, the pockmarked/sun.   The Insomniacs.   Adrienne Rich.   NYBP

Ray Charles is a dangerous man ('way cross town),/And I love him.   Blues Note.   Bob Kaufman.   CNA; NIP; PoBA

Re-echoing vales where every balm distils!   The Night Serene.   Luis Ponce de Leon.   CAW; TrJP

...Re-light/the tarnished mirrors and the flames blown to the night.   The Lovers' Death.   Charles Baudelaire.   SyP

Re-mold it nearer to the Heart's Desire!   Rubaiyat of Omar Khayyam.   Omar Khayyam.   BiP; EG; FaBV; LiTW; PoPl

Re-registration of the duple name.   Sea Side.   Robert Graves.   MoPo

Rea(be)rran(com)gi(e)ngly/,grasshopper;   R-P-O-P-H-E-S-S-A-G-R.   Edward Estlin Cummings.   AmPP; InPK; NoP; PPP

Reach back and bring me the firmness of her hand.   Request to a Year.   Judith Wright.   CBAP; FaBoWP

Reach for the light, for Pharaoh's daughter.   First Days.   Tuvia Ruebner.   VWA

Reach my soul building a nest against the wall.   Street Kid.   Duane Niatum.   STE

"Reached Cape Verde Islands, "Lusitania.""   S. S. "Lusitania."   Matthew Arnold.   CBEP

Reached no Alps: or, knows no Alps to reach.   But Can See Better There, and Laughing There.   Gwendolyn Brooks.   PoNe

The/reaches/of Africa where an actual/measure/exists.   El Camino Verde.   Paul Blackburn.   CoPo

Reaching blackened arms of the chimneys on the other.   Late Gothic.   Phyllis Gotlieb.   NOBC

Reaching out alone in words oh/peerless poesy.   Speeches at the Barriers (excerpt).   Susan Howe.   APU

Reaching righteously skyward!   Suzie Wong Doesn't Live Here.   Diane Mei Lin Mark.   BrSi

Reaching that seasoned door I can clasp and open.   The Longing.   William Goodreau.   AMV-80

Reaching toward eternity/All-unavailing antennae!   After Tempest.   Percy MacKaye.   FYAP

Read by whose hostile eyes, in what bed-sitting rooms,/in which rainy, dejected railway stations?   Public Library.   Dannie Abse.   OxBC

Read faith as on a lover's in their faces.   The Sacred Order.   May Sarton.   ImOP

Read his indictment, let him hear/What he's to trust to: Boy, give ear!   A Song of Diana's Nymphs.   John Lyly.   OBSC

Read, mark, and learn to obey.   God's Treasure.   A.M. N.   STF

Read, mouthing out his hollow oes and aes,/Deep-chested music, and to this result.   The Epic.   Alfred, Lord Tennyson.   VLP

Read my riddle, I pray.   Riddle: "What God never sees."   *Anonymous.*   OxNR

Read not, but first desire God's grace/To understand thereby.   Of the Incomparable Treasure of the Scriptures.   *Anonymous.*   TRV

Read the New Yorker; trust in God;/and take short views.   Under Which Lyre.   W. H. Auden.   MoAB; MoBrPo; NOBL

Read this/and count them   Ruth.   Colleen J. McElroy.   BlSi

Read this in the histories:/Newsweek, or Thucydides.   In Humbleness.   Daniel Gerard Hoffman.   NePA

Read this Song of Hiawatha!   The Song of Hiawatha.   Henry Wadsworth Longfellow.   AnNE; NOBA

Read this ye Statesmen now in Favour,/And mend your own, by True's Behaviour.   An Epitaph on True, Her Majesty's Dog.   Matthew Prior.   FM

Reader in fast pursuit/of summer transformations.   By a Rich Fast Moving Stream.   John Tagliabue.   ELU

The reader's rest and editor's colophon.   A Dream.   Charles Tomlinson.   OxBC

Reader! then make time, while you be/But steps to your eternity.   Caelica, LXXXII.   Fulke, Lord Brooke Greville.   FCP

Reader, think oft, and help thy thoughts thereby.   On the Following Work and Its Author.   Jonathan Mitchell.   SCAP

Reading between such covers he will likely/Prove his own disproportion and not laugh.   Ogres and Pygmies.   Robert Graves.   CABA; CMoP; FaBoMo; LiTB; LiTM; NoAm; SeCePo; SeCeV

...Reading/even humming, the one book.   Homing.   Reg Saner.   NPAW

...Reading some poetry/because he wants to have something to say.   To Hear My Head Roar.   Henry Taylor.   MAYP

Reading Thy Bible, and my Book; so end.   His Wish to God.   Robert Herrick.   AnAnS 2; OxBoCh

Reads my poems by his locker/instead of the sports page   Whom Do You Visualize as Your Reader?   Linda Pastan.   PPJ

Ready for rain, and the first, most vivid green/springing electric from the paddock's night.   Burning Off.   Geoffrey Dutton.   NOAV

Ready shield and swords/Beside his crumbling hand.   The Compasses.   George MacBeth.   NePoEA-2

...Ready/to be recruited by the night.   Seventeen.   Jonathan Holden.   Psk

Ready to crunch/if I hug him   Edwin A. Nelms.   Sheryl L. Nelms.   Str

Ready to leap, and sink, and disappear.   First Dark.   Joyce Carol Oates.   GeTw

...Ready to snap/My digits off if I gave him/Half a chance.   Zimmer and His Turtle Sink the House.   Paul Zimmer.   Psk

Ready to spend and be spent for your sake.   Monna Innaminata.   Christina Georgina Rossetti.   VLP

Ready with level gaze and quickened ears/To face Eternity at eighteen years.   Sonnet for My Son.   Melanie Gordon Barber.   GoYe

Real Bliss I then shall prove;/Heav'n below, and Heav'n above.   Happiness Found.   Augustus Montague Toplady.   TrPWD

...The/real breadth of where we move toward, the perfection/of space.   Plenty.   LeRoi (Imamu Amiri Baraka) Jones.   CAPP

The real brightness is the brightness of my child.   Invocation before the Rice Harvest.   *Anonymous.*   WTO

Real danger. gambles. and the edge of death.   What You Should Know to Be a Poet.   Gary Snyder.   NNaP; PoM

The real longing is for the irrecoverable,/Barely-forgotten, child's world.   Caterpillar.   R. E. Rashley.   CaP

Real pleasure and peace in her paths you may gain,/Nor will disappointment ensue.'   The Disappointment.   Jane Taylor.   FaBoUs

"Really, Will," said he, "what next?"   Willie the Poisoner.   *Anonymous.*   NTCP

The realm our tribes are crushed to get/May be a barren desert yet.   An Indian at the Burial-Place of His Fathers.   William Cullen Bryant.   HeIP

Reap what ye have sown!" saith God.   God and the Strong Ones.   Margaret Widdemer.   HBMV

...Reaps/A truth from one that loves and knows?   In Memoriam A.H.H., XLII.   Alfred, Lord Tennyson.   VLP

Reason and Madmen never could agree.   Reason.   John Tatham.   CavP

Reason I'm going home with you, sugar, I ain't much hard to be fooled   Rabbit Foot Blues.   Blind Lemon Jefferson.   BluL

The reason I'm leaving you/I don't like your dogging ways.   Doggin' Me around Blues.   Jenny Pope.   BluL

The reason is under "N."   A Bestiary.   Kenneth Rexroth.   OBAL

Reason, look to thyself! I serve a goddess.   Arcadia.   Sir Philip Sidney.   SiPS

Reason, Reason is my middle name.   Reason.   Josephine Miles.   AmC; InPK; NCSH; NoAm; NoP; PoCh; TAP

Reason's whole pleasure, all the joys of sense,/Lie in three words–Health, Peace, and Competence.   O Sons of Earth.   Alexander Pope.   TreFT

Reason shall steer, and skill disarm the gale.   Columbus to Ferdinand.   Philip Freneau.   OBCA; PAH

Reason thou kneel'dst, and offeredst straight to prove/By reason good, good reason her to love.   Astrophel and Stella, X.   Sir Philip Sidney.   AAS; SiPS

Reason to hate me–none at all/For loving you.   Dialogue.   John Erskine.   HBMV

The reason why I cannot tell.   Epigrams.   Martial (Marcus Valerius Martialis).   OBVE

Reason why I was mad/I didn't know what she done it for   Highway Blues.   Lightning Hopkins.   BluL

...Reason why so much/Should come to nothing must be fairly faced.   Pod of the Milkweed.   Robert Frost.   LiTM

The reasons/for our being/among them   Among Hawks.   Lance Henson.   VoR

Reawaken with the dawning soul.   In Memoriam A.H.H., XLIII.   Alfred, Lord Tennyson.   VLP

The rebel discords up the sacred mount.   The Promise in Disturbance.   George Meredith.   VLP

Rebel sinners, rebel sinners,/Glad the message will obey.   Sinners, Will You Scorn the Message?   Jonathan Allen.   AH

Rebelled not, loathing from the trodden heart/That thing which she had found man's love to be.   Words on the Windowpane.   Dante Gabriel Rossetti.   SyP

The rebellious angels play with fire.   In Praise of Music in Time of Pestilence.   Daryl Hine.   OBCV

Reborn in flames, pain cried its price.   The Second Life of Lazarus.   Gwen Harwood.   CBAP

Reborn may be as great as any.   The Field of Glory.   Edwin Arlington Robinson.   HBV 1-2; MoAmPo

Recall my wandering thoughts to mourn.   O God of My Salvation, Hear.   Joel Barlow.   AH

Recall the finished dead.   Suppose in Perfect Reason.   Howard Griffin.   CrMA

Recall the gods that die/To rule/In Parian o'er the sky.   Art.   Alfred Noyes.   OBEV

Recalled me to the love of song.   "I Broke the Spell That Held Me Long."   William Cullen Bryant.   AmePo

Recalling the nothing from the nothing gate.   Back Aways.   Clark Coolidge.   APU

Recalls some similar woman,/And thinks of his mouldering bones.   Bury Me Out on the Prairie.   *Anonymous.*   BPAW; CoSo

Recalls the scenes of Childhood to her view,/And lives those pleasing moments o'er anew.   Danebury.   *Anonymous.*   PeHV

Recalls your warmth, your smile, the grace and stir/That were its element.   As Well as They Can.   A. D. Hope.   GrPl

Receded as speechless and as wide as death.   A Death in the Desert.   Charles Tomlinson.   FF

Receiv'st the gift for more than mild content!   Sonnet: To–.   William Wordsworth.   ChRP

Receive him, like Peter, to dwell in THY HOUSE at last!   Lament of the Mangaire Sugach.   Andrew Magrath.   OnYI

Receive me, Lord.   An Evening Prayer.   Laura E. Kendall.   BLRP

Receive/me, Mother.   Snow White.   Olga Broumas.   DFT

Receive, O sweet Saviour, my spirit unto thee.   The Execution of Luke Hutton.   *Anonymous.*   OBET

Receive the Lamb of God to dwell/In England's green and pleasant bowers.   Jerusalem.   William Blake.   OBRV

Receive this vow, So fare ye well for ever.   His Tears to Thamasis.   Robert Herrick.   FaBoPP; OAEP

Received his blessing and then shot him dead.   In India.   Karl Shapiro.   NYBP

Received the full shock of the deadly West, and screamed.   Drama.   William Hart-Smith.   BoAV

Receives the tiny burden of her death.   The Death of the Bird.   A. D. Hope.   PoAu 1-2

Receiving a profit, before it holds a snare.   The Spring Equinox.   Anne Ridler.   NeBP

The/receiving/blackness/sigh   Into Blackness Softly.   Mari E. Evans. PoBA

Receiving my last breath in peace.   Ode to the Virgin.   Petrarch.   ISi

Receiving naught by elements so slow/But heavy tears, badges of either's woe. Sonnets, XLIV: "If the dull substance of my flesh were thought."   William Shakespeare.   CBEP

Receptacle of life's decay.   The Dead Sparrow.   Caius Valerius Catullus. EnLi 1-2

Receptacle, receive me.   Trees, Effigies, Moving Objects.   Allen Curnow. OCNZ

Recite her life back, (in the) same order.   Lower Court.   Carolyn Baxter. LFAC

Reckoning peoplehood,/shadowing the shadow-men.   If We Cannot Live as People.   Charles Lynch.   CNA; PoBA

Reclin'd us on a rightfull Monarch's Breast.   The Medal.   John Dryden. CEP

Recognise the five/That make the Muses sing.   Those Images.   William Butler Yeats.   CMoP; PP

Recompt the same to kesar, king, and/pere.   The Complaint of Henrie Duke of Buckinghame.   Thomas, Earl of Dorset Sackville.   PoEL 1-5

Recorder and hautbois only moan at a mouldering sky.   The Old Liberals. Sir John Betjeman.   ChMP

...Recording passage/on a brain so small how could it hurt?   The All-Night Waitress.   Maura Stanton.   AmPA

Recount the same to kesar, king, and peer.   The Induction to the Mirror for Magistrates.   Thomas, Earl of Dorset Sackville.   OBSC

A recreant, I needs must follow still.   God Leads the Way.   Cleanthes. EaLo

Red as dying, our quick bright blood.   The Watch.   Marge Piercy.   GeTw

Red as his guide-book grows, moves on, and offers up a prayer for/France. The Three Musicians.   Aubrey Beardsley.   NOBV; OBTV; VLP

Red bird, red bird soon in the morning.   Red Bird.   Anonymous.   FSW

The red blaze of freedom in Erin Go Braugh.   Erin Go Braugh! Anonymous.   FSW

The red blood of the people, warm, sincere,/Blending of Puritan and Cavalier. The Masterful Man.   Henry Tyrrell.   PGD

Red brick building/With many windows.   The Song of a Factory Worker. Ruth Collins.   SaC

Red China is not allowed in the league/unless she attacks...   It Is Not Enough.   David Henderson.   PPON

Red-currant red, a graceful/ornament or a merry smile.   The Victors. Denise Levertov.   NoP

Red drops of blood are falling.   A Night in Odessa.   Louis Simpson. NNaP

Red empty rooms/to measure long journeys.   Tour Guide: La Maison des Esclaves.   Melvin Dixon.   LTB

Red-eyed, foot-dragging, single-minded blunt-/Tusk, lugging his bones to the bones piled?   The Thrifty Elephant.   John Holmes.   NYBP

The red-faced ones are looking about intently.   Kangaroos.   Anonymous. NOAV

Red flamelets here and there reveal/a man, a woman there.   Andraitx– Pomegranate Flowers.   D. H. Lawrence.   NoAm; NoP

The red-haired dreamer wakens.   Nightmare.   Isabella Gardner.   CoAP

The red-hot, pot-bellied furnace raging/inside me, when, leaving me,/you turn up stairs?   The Eel.   Eugenio Montale.   NaP

Red in the light the dying sun is bleeding.   Evening Landscape.   Pol de Mont.   LiTW

Red Jack and Mephistopheles/Went all their ways alone.   Red Jack.   Mary Durack.   PoAu 1-2

Red label on a little butterfly.   On Discovering a Butterfly.   Vladimir Nabokov.   NYBP

The red lamp hissing through the midnight air.   The House of Night.   Philip Freneau.   AP

Red leaves that fall.   Maple Leaves.   Shiko.   SoPo

The red mouth darts a dizzy sting,/And clenches the eternal ring.   The Snake-Charmer.   Thomas Gordon Hake.   VLP

Red, orange, yellow, green, eternal blue, eternal violet.   Homage to the Philosopher.   Babette Deutsch.   ImOP; TrJP

Red oranges in May.   May.   John Shaw Neilson.   NOAV; PoAu 1-2

Red Rahab and white Maid!   Winds.   Hugh McCrae.   CBAP

Red river, river, river.   Landscapes.   Thomas Stearns Eliot.   LoGBV

Red Rose, proud Rose, sad Rose of all my days.   To the Rose upon the Rood of Time.   William Butler Yeats.   NoAm; OAEP; TEP; VLP

Red roses within roses within roses.   Southern Gothic.   Donald Justice. NIP

The Red Sea running down the heart of God.   Jeremiad.   Oscar Williams. LiTA

Red seamed are the ends of my days and nights.   The Valley of Men.   Uri Z. Greenberg.   VWA

A red shadow of steel mills.   Twilights.   James Wright.   LCAP; NaP

A red/Shred in his little fist.   Balloons.   Sylvia Plath.   FaBoWP; NCSH

Red sky at night,/Shepherd's delight.   Proverbially Useful for Weather Forecasts.   Anonymous.   FaBoUs

Red specks that are the tiniest spiders/if you look real close   The Detail. Cid Corman.   PCP

Red-spotted black beast of Nobamba/That goes about causing trouble. Senzangakhona.   Anonymous.   WTO

...The red sunset flare/Was blood about his head as he stood there.   The Last Post.   Robert Graves.   MMM

Red thunderbolts to purify the world.   The Flaming Terrapin.   Roy Campbell.   MoBrPo

The red-tiled towers of the old Chateau/Burn in the western evening glow! Chateau Papineau.   S. Frances Harrison.   CaP

Red, too, is the hollow in which I am resting.   Ankotarinya.   Anonymous. CBAP

A red votive candle withering/an Argentine jungle.   The Interrogations. Michael Knoll.   LFAC

The redcaps have murdered my dear loving wife.   The Fair Lady of the Plains.   Anonymous.   BFSS

Reddening, and disappears.   Mask of Love.   Thomas Kinsella.   CMoP; NMP

Redder than coral round Calypso's cave?   To My Child Carlino.   Walter Savage Landor.   NoP; OBRV

The rede rose an te lilye flowr.   Maiden in the Mor.   Anonymous.   AtBAP; BuBa; LoBV; MeEL; NCEP; PoEL 1-5

Redeem itself through deed and sacrifice.   Mi Y'Malel.   Anonymous.   FSW

Redeem the evil time!   The Church Universal.   Samuel Longfellow. WGRP

Redeem us by Thy hope, lest Thy disgust/Makes future empires violate our dust.   To God.   Furnley Maurice.   BoAV

Redeemer, King, Creator,/In bliss returns to reign.   From Greenland's Icy Mountains.   Reginald Heber.   FaPoR; HBV 1-2; TreF; VLP; WGRP

Redefinition of structures/no one has yet looked at.   Beach Glass.   Amy Clampitt.   FaBoWP

Redemption–Brittle Lady–/Be so–ashamed of Thee–   What soft–cherubic creatures.   Emily Dickinson.   AnNE; HAP; MoAB; MoAmPo; PPON; SoSe

Redemption draweth nigh.   Lift Up Your Heads, Rejoice.   Thomas Toke Lynch.   TrCP; VLP; WGRP

Redemption hangs upon the nails.   He.   Stanley Jasspon Kunitz.   CrMA; VGW

Redemption's problem unto thee well solved.   Milton.   Henrietta Cordelia Ray.   BlSi

A redgold salmon/flowed into her/at full of evening.   Sunset.   John Montague.   FaBoIP

Reduce me now to ashes Night, like a black sun.   Insomnia (excerpt). Marina Tsvetayeva.   PBWP

Reducing the stubbornest beauty to nakedness.   Old Crabbed Men.   James Reeves.   ErPo

A reed mat on dark nights/enough for him to die on/thankfully/and of hunger.   Western Civilization.   Agostinho Neto.   WhB

The reed's lost shadow.   Elegy for Chief Sealth (1786–1866).   Duane Niatum.   CDW

The reeds are shivering (one clump of them/nestling a lark's eggs, I know, in a hoof-print).   Touching the River.   Thomas Kinsella.   FaBoIP

Reeds whisper to the lake below.   Upon the Lake.   Hayim Lenski.   VWA

Reel back from him. The dust is drinking wine.   The Shooting of Werfel. Vernon Watkins.   WaP

The reel unrolling towards the river.   The Three Fates.   Rosemary Dobson. BoWoP

Refine my Heart; and that it be/Kept Pure, O Lord, I give it Thee.   My Mind Keeps out the Host of Sin.   Edmund Elys.   NCEP

Refined by bile as yellow as a lump of gold.   For George Santayana.   Robert Lowell.   CMoP; VGW

Refining still, the social passions work.   The Seasons.   James (1700-48) Thomson.   NoP; SeCePo

Reflected/in a macrocosmic I.   Cell.   Dennis Shady.   LFAC

Reflecting what cannot be/onto what cannot stay nameless forever.   The Monkish Mind of the Speculative Physicist.   Bin Ramke.   SUW

Reflecting where our scaly heart is/Some skyey grace.   The Poet and the Wood-Louse.   Helen Parry Eden.   HBV 1-2

Reflection losing itself in the dark globes of/his eyes.   Reflections on the Death of a Parrot.   Jaime Jacinto.   BrSi

Reflections, at night, from the reflected light of the moon.   A Deserted Barn. Larry Woiwode.   WeW

Reflects little credit on God.   On the Painter Val Prinsep.   Dante Gabriel Rossetti.   FaBoEE

Reflects the setting sun/And becomes the Sea of Gold.   Spring Waters (excerpt).   John Wolcot.   BoWoP

Reflects the white Autumn/sky.   Three Tanka, 3.   Yosano Akiko.   LiTW

Reforms each error, and refines the whole.   English Bards and Scotch Reviewers.   George Gordon, Lord Byron.   OBRV; OBSV

Reforms the laws, or builds an aqueduct. Quantum. Martin Johnston. CBAP

Refresh myself; ere that I go,/And I no more shall be. Fire in My Meditation Burned. Henry Ainsworth. AH

Refresh us from thy wells of peace. O Risen Lord upon the Throne. Louis F. Benson. AH

Refreshed but tired by the weekend. On a Seven-Day Diary. Alan Dugan. OBAL

Refreshing us to face our lost world's pain. Elegy for a Dead Confederate. Robert McGovern. SOTS

...A refuge find/From the rude napkin's irreligious touch. On a Young Lady's Going into a Shower Bath. Francis Scott Key. UnTE; YaD

Refuse such fruitless toil, and present pleasures choose. Behold, O Man. Edmund Spenser. EIL

Refuse us not an alms, for love of God! Our Poets' Breed. Luis, Montoto y Rautenstrauch. CAW

...Refusing the/only thing that will/comfort him at all. Mother Poem. Joel Oppenheimer. PoM

Refut overt to wreches in distresse,/And al comfort of mischief and misese. God, the Port of Peace. John Walton. OxBM

Refutes the ancient axiom/That Nothing has no use. From a Cheerful Alphabet. John Updike. FaBoCo

Regain'd in heav'n, or what more lost in hell? Paradise Lost. John Milton. MyFE

Regain our precious metal. Free Silver. Anonymous. AmFP

Regard with such pity, disgust, absorption, crabs? Crustaceans. Roy Fuller. NeBP; NoAm

Regarding still what heaven should do,/And not what earth deserveth. The Return of Astraea. Ben Jonson. NOBE

Regards, Lois. From Lois in London. Angela McCabe. AmPA

Regent of Nature's will, in heart, in head, in hand. Woman Free (excerpt). Elizabeth Wolstenholme-Elmy. BrRo

The regions of unclouded light–Where joy forever reigns. The Only Name Given Under Heaven. Steele. BePJ

Regret pour a poison in the ear of memory. Seven South African Poems. David Wright. PeSA

Regrets she made her dear husband go to win a fief. In Her Boudoir, the Young Lady,–Unacquainted with Grief. Anonymous. OBVE

...A regularity from which the clouds drift/into their wet embankments. Medusa's Hair Was Snakes. Was Thought, Split Inward. Kathleen Fraser. NPGG

...Rehearsing behind/The screen of the world for another audience. Evening Ebb. Robinson Jeffers. NoAm

The reign of Christlike brotherhood. Day Dawn of the Heart. Anonymous. PGD

Reign over all. Curfew. Henry Wadsworth Longfellow AA; MCCG; OxBA

The reindeer lift their heads to hear/The happiest laugh of all the year. Mrs. Santa Claus' Christmas Present. Alice S. Morris. PoSC

The reins still taut in that armored fist. The Middle Ages. John Haines. LCAP

Reinvent it on earth/as song. Last Songs. Galway Kinnell. CAPP

Reject Him not lest He reject thee then,/And bid thee from His glory to depart. The Christ of God. Russell E. Kauffman. BePJ

Reject me not! Suppliant. Florence Earle Coates. TrPWD

Rejecting vain delights/For quiet nights. Choice. J. V. Cunningham. VGW

Rejoice a moment–then/Remember. On Such a Day. Mary Elizabeth Coleridge. MoVE

Rejoice; for Light was slain to-day, yet did not die. Good Friday. Anonymous. BoC

Rejoice! for the Lord brings back His own. There Were Ninety and Nine. Elizabeth Cecilia Clephane. VLP; WGRP

Rejoice, for thou art near to thy possession. Elegy: On a Lady, Whom Grief for the Death of Her Betrothed Killed. Robert Bridges. OBEV; OBVV

Rejoice! He liveth, heaven's risen King! Rejoice! He Liveth! Kathryn Blackburn Peck. BePJ

Rejoice in Thee, O blessed Lord, in Thee. O Blessed House, That Cheerfully Receiveth. Karl J. P. Spitta. TrPWD

Rejoice! let me dream of your felicity. May Time. Sir Thomas Wyatt. OBSC

Rejoice, oh my heart! For I Have Done a Good and Kindly Deed. Franz Werfel. TrJP

Rejoice or mourn, and let the world swing on/Unmoved by cricket song of thee or me. The Cricket. Frederick Goddard Tuckerman. FM; MAmP; NOBA; QFR

Rejoicing find amid the joy of thee/returned unto thine olden youthful/time. Ode to Zion. Judah Halevi. TrJP

Rejoicing is where we are from. Chant. Oscar Williams. MoRP

Rejoined to life/In time and space. For Kinte. Oliver La Grone. FB

...Rekindle a/pentecost in Trafalgar Square. The National Gallery. Louis MacNeice. EyDe

Rekindle here the torch of love for Him. Thou Light of Ages. Rolland W. Schloerb. TrPWD

Relax, and wander off to pass the holy day. Base Chapel, Lejeune 4/79. Archie Hobson. AMV-81

Relax; they're not for you. Donne Redone. Joseph Paul Tierney. ShM

Relax until your heart/is vulnerable, wide open. You Are Reading This Too Fast. Ken Norris. CaPN

Released them to their parents, on probation. Juvenile Court. Sara Henderson Hay. DFT

Releases smoke like grey stone/and old hair. The Old. George, Jr Mosby. LFAC

...Releasing now/loved women locked in you/and hungering to be found. The Source. Jon Stallworthy. NoP

Relent not for my feeble prayer, nor dim/The burning of thine altar for my hymn. O Martyred Spirit. George Santayana. TrPWD

Relentless caper for all those who step/The legend of their youth into the noon. Legend. Hart Crane. CABA; InPo; InPS; MoVE; NoAm; OxBA; SyP

Relentlessly she understands you. The Adversary. Phyllis McGinley. DBV; FaBoEE; OBCA; OBSP

A relic and a shrine! Jefferson Davis. Walker Meriwether Bell. PAH

A Relick fam'd by all Posterity. To My Dead Friend Ben: Johnson. Henry, Bishop of Chichester King. AnAnS 2; SeCP

The relics of a mystery men forget. Football Field: Evening. J. A. R. McKellar. LiSp

The relics of generals and kings/still abdicate Malcom, Iowa. Charles Itzin. FAZ

...Relief is the word. Mahabalipuram. Louis MacNeice. NoAm; OBTV

...Relieved/of their secrets, are as honestly/miserable as they look. Losers. Jonathan Holden. MAYP

An relieved sall she never be,/Till St. Mungo come oer the sea.' Kemp Owyne (B version). Anonymous. ESPB

Religion stands, the church blocking the sun. The Landscape Near an Aerodrome. Stephen Spender. AnEnPo; CoBMV; LiTM; MoAB; MoBrPo; MoVE; NoAm; OAEP; OxBTC

Religion took her flight, sir,/And ne'er was heard of since. The Battle Royal between Dr. Sherlock, Dr. South, and Dr. Burnet. William Pittis. APAS

Relishing life, sucking the honeycomb. On the Curve-Edge. Abbie Huston Evans. NYBP

Reloading a gun/that doesn't work/and praying for a war. James Gerard. Paul D. Shiplett. LFAC

Reluctant, tho' at first you'll find him grow/Ev'n fond, when round your Neck his Arms he'll throw. Odes (excerpt). Albius Tibullus. PeHV

Reluctantly, as if it had too often/reached its destination. Among Commuters. Jon Swan. NYP

Reluctantly surrender every height. Sunset. Arthur Bayldon. PoAu 1-2

Remain my pledge in heaven, as sent to show/How to this port at every step I go. Of My Dear Son, Gervase Beaumont. Sir John Beaumont. GoBC; JCP; NOBE; OBS; ViBoPo

Remain, O Dionysian, in our heart. A Skater's Waltz. Gray Burr. CoPo

Remain there; do not fool around. A Moral Alphabet (excerpt). Hilaire Belloc. NOBL

Remain thou as thou art. Two lengths has every day. Emily Dickinson. MoPo

Remain unspoken. I Would That Even Now. Princess Shoku. AWP

Remain your only cause for tears. From the Epigrams of Martial. James Michie. FaBoEE

Remained for her–of rapture/But the humility. A bee his burnished carriage. Emily Dickinson. NOBA

The remaining years are disappointing. Poem. Tony Towle. ANYP

Remains a fool his whole life/long. Who Does Not Love Wine, Women and Song. J. H. Voss. FaFP

Remains but one oak/broader/than six/men in a ring. Ancient of Days. Anthony Rudolf. VWA

Remains of face or feet when visitors have gone home. The Strand. Louis MacNeice. AnIV

Remaking chaos into an intimate order/Where sometimes light flows through a windowpane. Dutch Interior. May Sarton. SM

Remanded to a ballad's barn/Or clover's retrospect. A faded boy in sallow clothes. Emily Dickinson. PoEL 1-5

Remark in dance on the shaven lawn/Rustics, Death and Sin. Lady Sara Bunbury Sacrificing to the Graces, by Reynolds. Daryl Hine. EyDe

A remarkable thing in Aberdeen. Epitaph from Aberdeen. Anonymous. DBV

Remarked how ill we all dissembled. Song: "The merchant, to secure his treasure." Matthew Prior. HBV 1-2; LiTL; OBEV; TrGrPo

Remember Afric's woes–and save your destined land.' Ode on Lord Macartney's Embassy to China. William Shepherd. NOEC

Remember Bob the Swagman, and the old bark hut. The Old Bark Hut. Anonymous. PoAu 1-2

Remember, Christians, Negroes, black as Cain,/May be refin'd, and join th' angelic train. On Being Brought from Africa to America. Phillis Wheatley. BALP; FF; HeIP; NOBA; NOEC; SBG; TAP; TTY

"Remember, daughter," she bleats, "you and I go halves!" Rumoresque Senum Severiorum. Marcus Argentarius. ErPo; LiTW

Remember each unto the end. A Nameless Epitaph. Matthew Arnold. VLP

Remember, even this, shall pass away! This, Too, Shall Pass Away. A. L. Alexander. PoToHe

Remember exactly why one was happy/There is no forgetting that one was. Good-Bye to the Mezzogiorno. W. H. Auden. OxBTC

Remember Gascoigne's lullaby. Gascoigne's Lullaby. George Gascoigne. NoP; PoEL 1-5; TrGrPo

...Remember his two hands, his laugh,/His craftsmanship. They are his epitaph. At His Father's Grave. John Ormond. FaBoTw

Remember how you always bore me! Villeggiature. Edith Nesbit. NOBV

Remember I must go home. Brandy Leave Me Alone. *Anonymous.* FSW

Remember Lorca, who died only for being Lorca. Poem for Garcia Lorca. George Woodcock. NOBC

"Remember me?" Museum Piece No. 16228. Elaine Watson. AMV-81

Remember me to Pa-/ulette when you see/her, will you please? Clipping. Tom Veitch. ANYP

Remember me when I am dead/and simplify me when I'm dead. Simplify Me When I'm Dead. Keith Douglas. NePoEA; OxBTC

Remember old Jack Palmer/And the Old Keg of Rum. The Old Keg of Rum. *Anonymous.* PoAu 1-2

Remember only, for your own salvation,/Your brotherhood, and give it to the world. Man, Not His Arms. Selden Rodman. WaP

Remember only when her babe first smiled. Remembrance. John Henry Boner. AA

..."Remember our life together," she whispers,/as she falls asleep. Widow. Felix Pollak. FAZ

...Remember? Phaidros went that way too. Epigram: "All I said was–Alexis is gorgeous." Plato. PeHV

Remember, Phyllis? Honeymoon. Samuel L. Albert. GoYe

"Remember, remember the Maine!" Battle Song. Robert Burns Wilson. MC; PAH

Remember Tam O'Shanter's mare. Tam O'Shanter. Robert Burns. BeLS; BoLiVe; BSV; CABL; CEP; EnLi 1-2; GoTL; GoTS; HBV 1-2; NoP; OAEL 1-2; OAEP; OBEC; OBNV; OxBS; SeCePo; TrGrPo; ViBoPo; WHA

Remember that Aldebaran is blind. Exquisite Lady. Mary Elizabeth Osborn. NePoAm-2

...Remember that/civilization is a transient sickness. New Mexican Mountain. Robinson Jeffers. InPS; NoAm; PAI

Remember that men loved him for his heart. Abraham Lincoln. Mildred Plew Meigs. PAL; TiPo

Remember that you live by permission of the police. Homage to Our Leaders. Julian Symons. NeBP

Remember that young lips were meant to kiss,/And hold that laughter is a seemly noise. Retractions. James Branch Cabell. HBMV

Remember that your birth was mortal. To a Book. Elinor Wylie. LiTA

...Remember the child who wanted never/To grow up? The child has gone and found his way. The Biplane. Steve Orlen. GOYP

Remember the dance that language is, that life is./Remember. Remember. Joy Harjo. STE

Remember the faith of the earth and the holy burden of man. Hymnal. Harold Vinal. TrPWD

Remember the Giver fading off the lip. A Drink of Water. Seamus Heaney. FaBoIP; OxBC

Remember the loss is her own if she lose it. Nonsense Verses. Charles Lamb. NA

Remember the Maine! The Word of the Lord from Havana. Richard Hovey. HBV 1-2; PAH

Remember the pathway that leads to our door! Brother Jonathan's Lament for Sister Caroline. Oliver Wendell Holmes. HBV 1-2; MC; PAH

Remember the seed of my sires, Queen,/in this distress. To the Queen of Dolors. Sister Maura. ISi

Remember the shriek/Of the frail ballerina in the book Fear. Peter Schjeldahl. ANYP

Remember the widow's fat rump,/And see how I'm served thro' her mutton. Mutton and Leather. *Anonymous.* CoMu

Remember thee. Doria. Ezra Pound. MoAB; MoAmPo; MoVE; ViBoPo

Remember this and let the world be lost. Remember, Though the Telescope Extend. George Dillon. ImOP

Remember this, how true it is, bushranging hath no charms! The Death of Morgan. *Anonymous.* FaBoBa

Remember this, though I tell no more. The Natives of America. Ann Plato. BlSi

Remember through the night. Remember. Georgia Douglas Johnson. PoNe

Remember to be thankful for the same. G. Hilaire Belloc. FiBHP

Remember/to remember. Remember. Joy Harjo. TWSS

Remember...Tom...and...Aunt Jemima/Bent low to pay your dues. The Generation Gap. Fareedah Allah. BlSi

Remember us in our low dell,/Who love thee well!/Farewell! Vale! Roden and Wriothesley Berkeley Noel. OBVV

Remember us with no familiar name. The Largest Life. Archibald Lampman. CaP

Remember well, good Christians all,/Not one whit worse the coal. Two Hundred Men and Eighteen Killed. James Henry. NOBV

Remember what else there was,/and warm your lightened body in it. And If I Turn. Marilyn Bowering. CaPN

Remember what old nurse has sung/Of busy Lady Wind. My Lady Wind. *Anonymous.* HBV 1-2; HBVY

Remember where you walked you smoothed the way/That those who follow may discover day. To a Negro Boy Graduating. Eugene T. Maleska. PoNe

Remember? You were glad that I did it once before! The Circus Ringmaster's Apology to God. Norman Dubie. MAYP

Remember your lovers who gave you more than love. Remember Your Lovers. Sidney Keyes. WaP

Remembered barks form a discourse that still perforates the common silence. Lily, Lois & Flaubert: The Site of Loss. Kathleen Fraser. NPGG

Remembered cinnamon and lime/Will fructify a bleaker time. Lovemusic. Carolyn Kizer. ErPo

Remembering/as something stirred. The Quickening. Stella Weston Tuttle. GoYe

Remembering distance leaves a haze/On all that lies below. The Men of Old. Richard Monckton, Lord Houghton Milnes. GTBS

Remembering he looked last into the sun/that was a golden gabriel and sang him home. The Green Family. Colleen Thibaudeau. NOBC

Remembering snow as I remember sun. Remembering Snow. Ralph Nixon Currey. PeSA

Remembering that once it sheltered love. Old House Place. Velma Sanders. AMV-80

Remembers our meeting. Her eyes moisten. Riddle: "I'm a strange creature, for I satisfy women." *Anonymous.* PV

Remembrance of a torn world well forgot. Sleep: and between the Closed Eyelids of Sleep. Conrad Aiken. LiTA

...Remind me/Of castles I used to build in air. The Kitchen Chimney. Robert Frost. EyDe

Remind ya of women,don't they' Of Flowers. Alan Loney. OCNZ

Reminding him that he is in it. Travelling Companions. Richard Armour. GrPl

Reminding what is soft/of what is hard. Broken Treaties: Teeth. Victor Contoski. GP

Remnant face/rubber/the pucker. Fed Drapes. Clark Coolidge. ANYP

Remnants of/My poetic eye Honeysuckle Was the Saddest Odor of All, I Think. Thadious M. Davis. BlSi

Remodels the little cottage in the woods/with gingerbread. Snow White. Ed Ochester. GP

Remote and lonely, dim, divine. Iphione. Thomas Caulfield Irwin. EnLoPo; IrPN

Remote as the sweet apple swinging/–Ah me!/At the end of the bough! Sweet Apple. James Stephens. CMoP

Remote serenity of something/gray. Gray Days. Joanne Lawlor. AMV-80

A renaissance of wonder I Am Waiting. Lawrence Ferlinghetti. CAPP; PoPl

Renal calculus and gastritis. Only the Wholesomest Foods You Eat. Samuel Hoffenstein. TrJP

A rendable tissue of sea lanes, there is the heart. Merchant Marine. Josephine Miles. TAP; VGW

Rendering toward that goal/Thy separate mind. The Continuing City. Laurence Housman. WGRP

...Rending them with their bloody teeth crunching on his/hollow bones. I Saw Them Lynch. Carol [(or Carole)] Freeman. NMM; PoBA

The rending veil shall thee reveal,/All-glorious as thou art. Jesus, These Eyes Have Never Seen. Ray Palmer. AH

Renew the patriot's vow! Washington's Statue. Henry Theodore Tuckerman. AA

Renounce its ragged petals one by one. A Tough Generation. David Gascoyne. LiTM

The rent is up and the cat/is dead: we ought to go home. The Square at Dawn. James Tate. NoAm

Rent money/in one pocket and/my heart/in another... Where Have You Gone. Mari E. Evans. BPo; NNP; PoNe; TTY

...repair/My heart with gladness, and a share/Of thy meek nature! To the Daisy. William Wordsworth. CoBE; EnRP; GTBS; GTBS-P; HBV 1-2

Repairing her small wounds. Matinal. Cilla McQueen. OCNZ

Repeat the only/word you know Wish. Lance Henson. CDW

Repeat/The robins, nested over. A Spring Lilt. *Anonymous.* HBV 1-2

Repeat this day. Raking Leaves. Robert Pack. CoPo; NYBP

ATP; DiPo; EnRePo; ExPo; InPS; JCP; MePo; NOCV; NoP; OAEL 1-2; OxBoCh; PPP; SeCP; SeCV 1-2; TEP

...Restore us,/And sanctify us as thine own.　Slain Lamb of God.　Nicolaus Zinzendorf.　AH

Restores those pains which that sweet folly lost.　The Conquest of Granada. John Dryden.　FiP

Restraining reckless middle-age?　On Hearing That the Students of Our New University Have Joined...　William Butler Yeats.　NoAm

Rests and expatiates in a life to come.　An Essay on Man.　Alexander Pope. GoTF

Rests in the earth, absolute and complete.　Revelation.　Nancy Keesing. PoAu 1-2

Resuming the suffering flesh/by which we are daily grieved.　Could You Once Regain.　Kenrick Smithyman　AnNZ

A resurrection of a sort for a non-believer!　Sitting in Bib Overalls, Workshirt, Boots on the Monument to Liberty.　Louis Daniel Brodsky.　AMV-81

The resurrection will be/Finding myself yours again.　A Pair of Lovers. Jeanne Robert Foster.　HBMV

Retain the sorrow of my night again/there behind the stone steps.　Cricket. No Ch'on-myong.　PBWP

Retaining tears, but there are no more words.　The Return.　Arna Bontemps.　CDC; PoBA; PoNe

Retire to my penitential madness.　Abelard at Cluny.　Grover, III Rees. AMV-80

Retired, a lonely figure, to lay eggs at Bordighera.　I Had a Duck-billed Platypus.　Patrick Barrington.　CenHV; FiBHP

The retired heart/where the wind glitters　Suddenly.　Robin Blaser.　PoM

Retouch in memory, with sentiment relive,/April and May.　The Veterans. Donagh MacDonagh.　CIP; OnYI

Retreat/and all our loving/we'll take/and leave you.　Tambourine Song for Soldiers Going into Battle.　Hind bint Utba.　WPOW

The retreat of tide from shore　Liberation.　Diane Mei Lin Mark.　BrSi

...Retreats/through ruined squares,/desolate streets.　The Horse.　Jose Maria Eguren.　WSC

Return, and back into your Sun subside.　The Sun of My Perfection Is a Glass.　Samar Attar.　ILwL

Return by many a different road.　Spring.　Caius Valerius Catullus.　PoPl

The return is certain.　Pine Barrens: Letter Home.　Cleopatra Mathis. TAT

Return my mother to me.　Footpath.　Stella Ngatho.　WPOW

The return of the dream that will be only the arrival of/145/the nova:/. . . . . Sphere (excerpt).　Archie Randolph Ammons.　HaCAP

Return, return.　Return!　Sydney Thomas Dobell.　OBVV

Return the exiles, the people oppressed/and humble.　Jewish Arabic Liturgies. *Anonymous.*　TrJP

Return the mirage on a coin that spells/Something of sand and sun the Nile defends?　The Urn.　Hart Crane.　PoA

Return to peaceful dreaming dearly bought.　The Close of Day.　Wesley Curtwright.　CDC

Return to the terrible menace of love/and to our children.　The Soldiers Returning.　Richard Shelton.　GOYP

Return unto they native land again.　To a Young Child.　Eliza Scudder. AA

Return with honey on our drunken feet.　16. ix. 65.　James Merrill.　NAs

Return with me where I am crying out with the/gorilla and the bird!　The Song of the Militant Romance.　Percy Wyndham Lewis.　FaBoTw; OxBTC

Return with pleasant warblings.　Ye Little Birds That Sit and Sing.　Thomas Heywood.　ElL; ViBoPo

Returned back,/From not one third their number.　The Modern Jonas. *Anonymous.*　PAH

...Returning, and/To kill.　Again!　Sacrifice of a Virgin in the Mayan Ball Court.　Norman Dubie.　GeTw

Returning light to the light, come to be?　Hall of Ocean Life.　John Hollander.　PoA

Returning, masterless and twisted.　The Men's Room in the College Chapel. W. D. Snodgrass.　GP; MoAmPo; PPP; TW

Returning wings promise/one more day/one more day.　Pigeons in Prison. Derek Butler.　LFAC

Returns no more, no more.　My Wind Is Turned to Bitter North.　Arthur Hugh Clough.　OAEP; VLP

Returns the whispered message of the leaves.　Oak.　Philip Child.　CaP

...Returns to/grizzled craniums, in uncertain days.　Edmond Halley.　Roy Fuller.　OxBC

Reveal/and veil/a peacock-tail.　Arthur Mitchell.　Marianne Moore.　PoNe

Reveal thyself in every law,/And gild the towers of truth with holy awe.　The Builders (excerpt).　Henry Van Dyke.　TrPWD

Reveal to me thy serene knowledge.　O Brother Tree.　Max Michelson. TrJP

Revealed the truth/That they had been/The slaves of fools.　The Search. Kwesi Brew.　PBA

Revealing, not God's radiant throne,/But the fires of wrath and agony. Doors of the Temple.　Aldous Huxley.　HBMV

Revealing something hidden.　Renaming the Evening.　Eric Pankey. AMV-81

Revealing with it God's great providence.　The Light of Faith.　Edgar Dupree.　BLRP

Reveals a well-honed and deliberate edge/to mutilate your awkward charity. Perpetuum Immobile.　Bruce Dawe.　CBAP

A revelation! Just a speck/Of friendship, love and light!　To G.R.　Samuel Elsworth Cottam.　PeHV

Revels in night's ancient cloud.　Night's Ancient Cloud.　Thomas Keohler. AnIV

Revenge and pride shall spur them?　What Is Truth? (excerpt).　James Harold Manning.　CaP

Revenge, revenge, revenge,/Shall appease my restless sprite.　I'm like a skiff on the Ocean tost.　John Gay.　EnLoPo

Revenges there the Brass-bound Man his long-enforced truce!　Poseidon's Law.　Rudyard Kipling.　MOS

Revere me for his sake, and love me for my own.　Full Well I Know. Hartley Coleridge.　NCEP

Revere the sacred spot, however low,/Which form'd to martial acts a Hawke, a Howe.　The Midshipman.　William Falconer.　MOS

Revered by friends, and far frae faes,/We'd live in bliss on Logan Braes. Logan Braes.　John Mayne.　OxBS

The revery alone will do,/If bees are few.　To make a prairie it takes a clover and one bee.　Emily Dickinson.　AmePo; BoWoP; DiPo; HBVY; HeIP; MAmP; NLV; OBCA; PoPl

Revised and corrected/by/The Author.　Epitaph.　Benjamin Franklin. TRV

The revisited soul is wrapped in the aura of familiarity.　I Have Folded My Sorrows.　Bob Kaufman.　PoBA

Revive the embrace in that melted glow.　Chicago.　Galway Kinnell. NePoAm

Revive us again.　Hallelujah, Bum Again.　*Anonymous.*　ABF; GBP

The revolution it will go on　My Poem.　Nikki Giovanni.　BPo

Revolves a once rectumistic joyous reminder　Identikit.　Jim Brodey. ANYP

Revolving across Kansas.　The Center of America.　Robert Siegel. AMV-81

Reward and release,/Of Rannoch, Schiehallion and Mamore.　The Climber Surveys His Mountain.　Hugh Ouston.　PoSH

Reward your servant liberally.　The heart and service to you proffered.　Sir Thomas Wyatt.　FCP

Rewarding a crowd of 200 persons/standing vigil for the event.　The American Book of the Dead: Six Selections.　John Giorno.　ANYP

Rewards me with a kisse,/and thanks me for my paine.　A Pleasant New Court Song.　*Anonymous.*　CoMu

Rewards me with variety/Which men who change can never know.　The Angel in the House.　Coventry Patmore.　VLP

REX DISPOSAL CO.　The Trash Men.　Charles Bukowski.　NoP

The Rhine, the Rhine, the German Rhine!　The Watch on the Rhine.　Max Schneckenburger.　HBV 1-2

Rhinoceros-black (a flowing sea!).　Four in the Morning.　Edith Sitwell. NoAm

Rhou shalt be judge how I do spend my tyme.　Satires.　Alamanni.　OBVE

Rhyme it with Noel.　Man. matron, maiden.　Sir Robert Baden-Powell. CenHV

Rhymes of battle for the Right!　Juanita.　Joaquin Miller.　AA

The rhymes of Leaning.　The Blackstone Rangers.　Gwendolyn Brooks. BALP; NoAm; PoBA

The rhymes were befriended/and my poem is ended.　Rhymes.　Y. Y. Segal. WHW

(The rhythm of tradition.) goodbye.　The Discovery of Tradition.　Lawson Fusao Inada.　LTB

A rhythm's maker catch, by words uncaught.　To a Young Lady Swinging Upside Down on a Birch Limb...　James H. Koch.　GoYe

...The/rhythm will keep me awake, changing.　Late Spring.　Robert Hass. GeTw; MAYP

Rhythms of casting–that slow dance.　The Ritualists.　William Carlos Williams.　NYBP

Ribs, the salt desert, and crazy religion.　Salt Lake City.　Hayden Carruth. AmFN

The rice and fish taste better dat way.　Manong Jacinto Santo Tomas.　Al Robles.　BrSi

A rich cape/woven of many loves/swept recklessly/about his shoulders.　At Midnight.　Ted Kooser.　GOYP

Rich in the simple worship of a day.　Fragment of an Ode to Maia.　John Keats.　EnRP; ERoP 1-2; OAEL 1-2; OAEP; OBEV; OBRV; PoEL 1-5

The rich juice will gush and stain your hands.　The Jackfruit.　Ho Xuan Huong.　PBWP

The rich man eats them with a fork,/The poor man with a knife.　The Gourmand (parody).　Harry Graham.　FaBoPa

Rich meat to princes and kings. The Land of Cokaigne. *Anonymous.* CAW

Rich queen of mist and vapors! The Fleece. John Dyer. TrGrPo

The rich too much,/Enough not one. Enough Not One. Benjamin Franklin. TRV

Rich with that flowering, rich with repeated song. The Lyre-Bird. Roland Robinson. PoAu 1-2

Rich Words! Heav'n will make amends/For all. Go Then, My Dove, but Now No Longer Mine. Cotton Mather. SCAP

Richard, thah thou be euer trichard,/tricchen shalt thou neuermore. The Song of Lewes. *Anonymous.* OxBM; OxBoLi

The richest harvest reaped on earth/Crowns the last century's closing year. Dante. William Cullen Bryant. ViBoPo

The richest one that ever such a load/could find but that was not to be. The Man with the Hollow Breast. Tania Van Zyl. PeSA

Rid de veloc'pede in de vestibule,/Ah, vimmens! Ah, mens! In De Vinter Time (with music). *Anonymous.* AS

A riddle is here no man tells, no woman. Mist Forms. Carl Sandburg. CMoP; HBMV

The riddle nature could not prove/Was nothing else but secret love. Secret Love. John Clare. CBEP; ERoP 1-2; FaBV; LiTL; LO; NBM; OAEL 1-2; OBNC; PoEL 1-5; TrGrPo; VLP

...Riddled/with rationale,/like vaudeville. Confirmation. Art Lange. APU

Ride away to the heaven that mornin'. If I Got My Ticket, Can I Ride? *Anonymous.* OuSiCo

Ride him to Rocky Island, on a long summer day. I'm Going to Rocky Island. *Anonymous.* AmFP

Ride on, King Emanual,/I want to go home in de mawnin'. Ride On, Moses. *Anonymous.* BoAN 1-2

Ride on with all white Omens; so, that where/ Your Standard's up, we fix a Conquest there. To the King, Upon His Comming with His Army into the West. Robert Herrick. AnAnS 2

Ride on, young lord, ride on! Compensation. James Edwin Campbell. BANP

Ride over them with love! Love and Liberation. John Hall Wheelock. MoAmPo

Ride, ride together, for ever ride? The Last Ride Together. Robert Browning. BoLiVe; BoLoP; CenHV; FiP; GTBS; HBV 1-2; LiTB; LoBV; MaVP; OAEP; OBEV; OBVV; PoEL 1-5; UnPo; VLP; WHA

An' ride ter Hebben up de Glory Road? De Glory Road. Clement Wood. HBMV; YaD

Ride valiant through the celestial arch of his arms. Choral Symphony Conductor. Carol Coates. CaP

Rider and horse, friend, foe, in one red burial blent. Don Juan. George Gordon, Lord Byron. FaBoBe

The rider grasps his steed again. Burial of the Minnisink. Henry Wadsworth Longfellow. LaNeLa

Rider on the bat-winged horse. The Bad Habit. Charles Henri Ford. EAS

The rider on the skyline/Is scouting to the east. The Horseman on the Skyline. Henry Lawson. CBAP

Rides, and earth rests as silently. Two Pewits. Edward ("Edward Eastaway") Thomas. CH; FM

Rides in the whirlwind, and directs the storm. The Campaign. Joseph Addison. OBWP

Ridges white to the north, and islands in the sea. Theme and Variations. W. P. Ker. PoSH

Ridiculous the waste sad time/Stretching before and after. Four Quartets. Thomas Stearns Eliot. AtBAP

Ridin' the brake beams close to the wheels. A. R. U. (with music). *Anonymous.* AS

Riding at anchor, by a Meeting-house. The Captain. John Gardiner Calkins Brainard. EtS

Riding on a little jackass. On Seeing Francis Jeffrey Riding on a Donkey. Sydney Goodsir Smith. FaBoEE

Riding the palest days/Its perfect blaze. My Father Paints the Summer. Richard Wilbur. NCSH; NOBA

Riding the springy branches of an elm. Sleep and Poetry. John Keats. GoTF; OBRV; TreFT

Riding the wind/And screaming bitterly? Homing. Arna Bontemps. CDC

Riding through the jungles,/On the Wabash Cannonball. The Wabash Cannonball. *Anonymous.* BLSo; FSW; TreFT

Rifle the air to make farewell forever. Angel Eye of Memory. John Malcolm Brinnin. PoA

Rifles and tables explode/pretty much the same. Ballad of an Empty Table. Tom Kryss. NeAC

Right again: Eight...Nine...and...! Someone. John Ciardi. BiCB

"Right as a Ribstone Pippin!" But it lied. The False Heart. Hilaire Belloc. FaBoCh; FaBoEE; HBMV; LoGBV; OBSP

Right back on in My Mama Moved among the Days. Lucille Clifton. BlSi; PoBA

Right down/right down here Happy Day. James (Olumo) Cunningham. JB

Right good is rest. Inscription for an Old Bed. William Morris. OBEV; OBVV; WiR

The Right hand keep, if Hell on Earth you fear! Warning to Travailers Seeking Accomodations at Mr. Devills Inn. Sarah Kemble Knight. SCAP

Right in the neck–THERE! College Yell. *Anonymous.* ExPo

Right in the water Long Song. Yityangu ("New") Ejong. CBAP

Right now, just you and me, Ben, and the species. Letter to Ben, 1972. Paul Durcan. FaBoIP

The right of his wife against Partholan. The First Lawcase. *Anonymous.* BIrV

The right of way to Tripoli/A more essential thing. The pedigree of honey. Emily Dickinson. BLPL; NOBA

"RIGHT ON/MOTHERS/MOTHER,/DYNAMITE..." A Grandson Is a Hoticeberg. Margaret Danner. BlSi; CNA; FB

...The right place to be/where we start again. The Spring Offensive of the Snail. Marge Piercy. TAP

Right seldom would I fail. It's up Glenbarchan's Braes I Gaed. Sir Walter Scott. PBBP

Right so, madam, the roses red of hue/With lilies white your beauty doth renew. To My Lady Mirriel Howard. John Skelton. LoBV

Right then we'd be in heaven. What You See Is Me. Barbara Gibbs. NYBP

Right thou me, right thou me, Harold the/King! The Appeal to Harold. Henry Cuyler Bunner. AA

–Right through into Czechoslovakia. My Return to Czechoslovakia. Murray Edmond. OCNZ

A right tur-a-naddy, mish-n-darn tur-nan. Oh, It's Nine Years Ago I Was Digging in the Land. *Anonymous.* AmFP

Right was the pathway leading to this. Afterwards. Frances Ridley Havergal. BLRP

"Right you are, my Brigadier." Brigadier. A.J.M. Smith. NMP

Righted the stagger of the earth. Childbirth. Ted Hughes. NAs

...A rigid crust/Of icy crystals coats the ground, for nights. Larch Hill. Leslie Daiken. OnYI

Rigid with it Each Found Himself at the End of... Ebbe Borregaard. NeAP

The Rigiment's flatthered to own ye, me/spark! The Recruit. Robert William Chambers. AA; HBV 1-2

Ring-a dat big bell,/In Ab'ham's breas' at last. Dives and Laz'us. *Anonymous.* TTY

Ring compass, gentle joy! Drinking Song. Thomas Dekker. TrGrPo

Ring down the abyss of twice ten thousand years. Almighty God, Whose Justice Like a Sun. Hilaire Belloc. TrPWD

The Ring has no beginning, middle, end. Time and Eternity. John Bunyan. WiR

Ring in the Christ that is to be. In Memoriam A.H.H., CVI. Alfred, Lord Tennyson. HBV 1-2; NAWM 1-2; OAEL 1-2; OAEP; OFD; TreF; TrGrPo

Ring, my bawnjer, ring! Uncle Eph's Banjo Song. James Edwin Campbell. BANP

Ring not your bells ye fools, but wring your hands. Upon the King's Return from Flanders. Henry Hall. APAS

Ring out the false, ring in the true. Ring Out, Wild Bells. Alfred, Lord Tennyson. TiPo

Ring out the silence I am nourished by. Sonnets at Christmas. Allen Tate. HAP; LiTA; NePa; NoAm; NOBA; OxBA; VGW

Ring peace and freedom in. The Battle Autumn of 1862. John Greenleaf Whittier. MC; PAH

Ring ring ring ring ring!/Catholic bells–! The Catholic Bells. William Carlos Williams. CMoP; NOBA; OxBA

The ring that serves/to identify corpses. Foreign Woman. Rosario Castellânos. WPOW

Ring the bell, the calf is dead. Johnny Armstrong. *Anonymous.* OxNR

Ring the bells of Heaven! Sound the gladsome chimes! John L. Sullivan Enters Heaven (parody). Robert Frost. BXAP

Ring the saints'-bell to affright/Far from hence the evil sprite. The Spell. Robert Herrick. CaPo; WSC

Ringing at dawn ringing all afternoon ringing up midnight/ringing now forever. I Am a Victim of Telephone. Allen Ginsberg. GP; NLV; NYP

Ringing like cymbals. Night Hymns on Lake Nipigon. Duncan Campbell Scott. CoBE; OBCV

Ringleader, tom-boy, and chum to the weak. Myfanwy. Sir John Betjeman. BoLoP

Rings in his darkness that we cannot heed? Crotalus Rex. Brewster Ghiselin. MoVE

The rings of a winter sunrise. Epithalamium. Anne Cluysenaar. HW

...Rings/stamped/from mattress buttons/all over/my body Signature. Larry Mollin. NeAC

Rinsing the choked mud, keeping the colours new. In Carrowdore Churchyard. Derek Mahon. CIP; FaBoIP

"Rio Bravo"–"Roncesvalles,"/Ye are names blent evermore.　Rio Bravo–A Mexican Lament.　Don Jose de Saltillo.　PAH

A riot among friends.　The Day Glo Question of Identity.　Jeffrey Miller.　APU

Riot–that bloodies every porch,/Hurls justice down/And burns the town.　The Draft Riot.　Charles De Kay.　PAH

Ripe and golden, from the spirit's tree.　How Could We, Beforehand, Live in Quiet.　Nikolai Gumilev.　WaaP

Ripe cherries and a honeycomb must make my bread and wine.　Cherry Tree.　Sacheverell Sitwell.　AtBAP

...Ripe pears of wintry brown/Waiting for dusk to shake them down.　Daydreamers.　Norma L. Davis.　PoAu 1-2

Ripen within me, O vine of the world!　After the Annunciation.　Eileen Duggan.　ISi

Ripening by the black wall.　Human Geography.　Ruth Whitman.　AMV-80

The ripening clusters hang) rivaled the deep mid-/night....　The Assignation.　Imr el Kais.　LiTW

Ripening the transient under her veil.　Daisies of Florence.　Kathleen Raine.　NYBP

The ripest fruit you must eat from the spray.　Keepsake from Quinault.　Dorothy Alyea.　GoYe

Ripping its way through the denim air　The Garden at St. John's.　May Swenson.　NePoEA; PoPl

A ripple in his reverie.　The Giant Tortoise.　Edward Lucie-Smith.　BoAnP; PoL

A ripple widening from a single stone/Winding around the waters of the world.　The Far Field.　Theodore Roethke.　NaP; NoP; PrIm

The ripples from my stones/will circle/long after I have let you go　Morgain Le Fay.　Lorna Crozier.　CaPN

Ripples its waters in a sinuous curve,/And dives again in safety.　At Her Step the Water-Hen.　Dante Gabriel Rossetti.　FM

...Rippling and responsive lies the water/For him to contemplate, then powerfully to enter.　High Diver.　Robert Francis.　LiSp; NePoAm; SD

The rippling notes of his song, which are clear and sweet.　Water Ouzel.　William H. Matchett.　CoAP; NePoEA; NYBP; PoCh

Rise and deride this sepulchre of crime.　On Passing the New Menin Gate.　Siegfried Sassoon.　AnEnPo; OBMV

Rise and shake your skirts/to the buttercups, yellow as polished/gold　The Words, the Words, the Words.　William Carlos Williams.　BiP

Rise and sleep, and leave/just once.　To Summer.　Alan Nadel.　AMV-80

Rise and sweep past me, spinning threads of fear.　The Minute.　Karl Shapiro.　ATP; LiTA; MiAP; MoVE

Rise–Arch of the Ocean, and Queen of the West!　Eire.　William Drennan.　OnYI

Rise at that hour and hear my name.　They Found Him Sitting in a Chair.　Horace Gregory.　MoAmPo

Rise black angels in white robes/riding bicycles.　A Dawn of Jaffa Pigeons.　Eli Bachar.　VWA

Rise, in God's name, Shane O'Neill.　Shane O'Neill.　Seumas MacManus.　OnYI

Rise in the new creation/Which springs from love and Thee.　Light of the World.　John S. B. Monsell.　TrPWD

Rise me up from down below.　Rise Me up from down below.　Anonymous.　ShS

Rise, O Muse!　Green Sunday.　Katue Kitasono.　LiTW

Rise odors of ploughed field or flowery/mead.　Chaucer.　Henry Wadsworth Longfellow　AA; AmePo; AmLP; AP; AWP; CBEP; DiPo; HeIP; InPo; InvP; MAmP; NePA; NOBA; NoP; OBEV; OBVV; OxBA; PoRA; PP; PrIm; TAP; TrGrPo

Rise tacks 'n' sheets, 'n' main s'l haul!　Paddy, Get Back.　Anonymous.　ShS

Rise to a longer course more bright and brave.　The Waterfall.　Henry Vaughan.　ViBoPo

Rise to all eternity.　Jesus, Lover of My Soul.　Charles Wesley.　HBV 1-2; WGRP

Rise to greet you, Willow Sunday,/Holy day.　Little Catkins.　Alexander Blok.　EaLo; OFD

Rise to one brimming golden, spilling cry!　The Road.　Helene Johnson.　BANP; BlSi; CDC; GoSl; PoNe

Rise to the meaning of True Brotherhood.　True Brotherhood.　Ella Wheeler Wilcox.　WBLP

Rise toward the dam's lip too much for flood gates.　The Desire of Water.　Mark Jarman.　PoA

Rise up an' choose de one dat's suitable to yo' min'.　Way Over in the Blooming Garden.　Anonymous.　ABF

Rise up and choose another love,/All on this summer's day.　All on a Summer's Day.　Anonymous.　PoPle

Rise up, O men of God!　Rise Up, O Men of God.　William Pierson Merrill.　AH

"Rise up out of your grave, for now the Judge is come."'　Bethinking Hymself of His Ende.　Thomas, Lord Vaux.　EnPo

Rise up shepherd and follow.　Rise Up, Shepherd, and Follow.　Anonymous.　BoAN 1-2; FSW

Rise, wing'd with music, from the o'er-labored heart.　The Flute: A Pastoral.　Jose-Maria de Heredia.　AWP

...Rise with passion/in an echoing spring burn every day.　You within Love.　Norman MacCaig.　NeBP

Risen, He liveth,/And liveth to God.　Christ Is Arisen.　Johann Wolfgang von Goethe.　TrCP

Rises a conflagration of peace, a bloody dawn.　Apollo and Daphne.　W. R. Rodgers.　ErPo; LiTB

Rises a silken ladder/into the depthless air.　The Ladder.　Gene Baro.　NePoEA-2

Rises/as only stunted structures can.　The City Rises.　James (Olumo) Cunningham.　JB

Rising and falling back and rising.　Delta Traveller.　Charles Wright.　AmPA; LCAP

Rising and setting he fills all my dreaming.　How Well for the Birds.　Anonymous.　KiLC; WTO

Rising, forever, rising!　Elegy on a Nordic White Protestant.　John Gould Fletcher.　PoNe

Rising gently to receive our thrusting feet.　Aircraft, Landing.　Colin Thiele.　ACV

Rising past the boundaries we know, past the season/of our own deaths.　Celebrating the Mass of Christian Burial.　Cleopatra Mathis.　LTB

Rising to the surface/without a single fish.　Useless Day.　Rosario Castellânos.　WPOW

...Rising toward our crest of dawn.　Two Poems Based on Fact.　Frank J. Lepkowski.　AMV-81

Rising up from deep waters.　The Deep Calling.　John Rothfork.　WOLT

Rising up in prayer/along the horizon.　Three Songs from the Temple.　Don Domanski.　NOBC

Rising up to heaven?　Haiku: "The halo of the moon."　Buson (Taniguchi Buso).　MOON

Rising within a circle of light/like a star.　The Linebacker at Forty.　Jon Wallace.　AMV-81

The risk itself cries out to be possessed.　A Boon.　William Meredith.　NePoEA

...Risk yours, or you're not going to make/it.　Quatrain: "Unless you can dance through a common bar."　Mahsati.　WPOW

...A rite/Reflecting in the burning windows.　Walls Breathe.　Paul Mariah.　LFAC

The rites of the Church bestow on me.　King Arthur's Death.　Anonymous.　ACP

The rites uninterrupted by our arrival/Or departure.　Keraunograph.　Hayden Carruth.　NMP

The rituals of our humanity.　Against the False Magicians.　Thomas McGrath.　NePoEA; PP

The river and all that it contains,/Including my own reflection.　Paris by Night.　Joseph Milbauer.　VWA

The river bears me through the fragrant darkness,/And so I cannot sleep.　The River.　Mary Sinton Leitch.　HBMV

The river contains no map. All's over with me.　A Chinese Mural.　Carlos Baker.　EyDe

The river creeps, choked with weeds, through the lower/grounds.　Supervising Examinations.　Sean Lucy.　CIP

River echoes of the women who fled.　Slow Dancer That No One Hears but You.　Duane Niatum.　CDW

The river has splashes,/The sky hasn't any.　The River Is a Piece of Sky.　John Ciardi.　PoPl; SoPo

River, I am passing.　River Afram.　Andrew Amankwa Opoku.　PBA

The river is always going home.　River.　Lawrence Locke.　GrPl

The river leaning like a wave towards the emptiness.　Poems of Night.　Galway Kinnell.　NaP

The river smoothly slides away to sea.　Waitaki Dam.　Denis Glover.　AnNZ

The river that flows nowhere, like a sea.　The River of Rivers in Connecticut.　Wallace Stevens.　HaCAP; HAP; NOBA; VGW

...The river/tossing a shoe up, a handful of hair.　Orpheus and Eurydice.　Jean Valentine.　FaBoWP; LCAP

The rivers bridged, and new towns named.　Conquest.　Elizabeth Jane Coatsworth.　AmFN

The rivers of time/and/space　Sometimes I Go to Camarillo & Sit in the Lounge.　K. Curtis Lyle.　PoBA

Rivers of wings surround us and vast tribulation.　Glazunoviana.　John Ashbery.　LCAP

Ro-ly-bo-ly sho-ly hog-eye!　Hog-Eye (with music).　Anonymous.　AS

Road and tree and house are one.　Softly, White and Pure.　Dorothy R. Fulton.　AMV-80

The road from Adonoi? I just don't know.　The Three Towns.　Howard Nemerov.　AMV-81

The road goes on ahead, it is all clear.　After Working.　Robert Bly.　NaP

The road leads on.　The Way.　Edwin Muir.　LOW

The road of life/around/my memories Remembering. Clarisse Nicoidski. VWA

The road one treads to labour/Will lead one home to rest,/And that will be the best. A Shropshire Lad. Alfred Edward Housman. AnFE

Road that is right entirely. Entirely. Louis MacNeice. CMoP; LiTB

The road to Bethlehem runs right through/The homes of folks like me and you. How Far to Bethlehem. Madeleine Sweeny Miller. BLPA; FPL

The road to Christmas is clear. The Road from Election to Christmas. Oscar Williams. NAMP

The road was invisible in the dark. Crazy Movie. Gregorio Barrios. FIA

The Road would serve you well enough for bed. The Road. Siegfried Sassoon. MCCG

Roaming through a fenceless world. Ten Poems. Stephen Crane. DBV

Roar when the pumping heart, bop, stops for a beat. The Silence at Night. Edwin Denby. ANYP

Roaring on under the tenements of Harlem. To a Fighter Killed in the Ring. Lou Lipsitz. LiSp

Roaring pirate tunes/On down the dunes. Nor'Easter. Bianca Bradbury. EtS

Roaring to the sunset on the Oregon Trail! Oregon Trail: 1851. James Marshall. BPAW

Roars of a million tongues, and none knows what/they mean. Fragment. John Clare. BoNaP

Roars on the coast at Ise I love and fear him. Lady Kasa. BoWoP

Roars to miraculous heat and turbulence. Golden Bough. Elinor Wylie. MoAmPo; PBWP

Rob Roy, he pulled some clover/as we crossed the field, I told her. The Centaur. May Swenson. FaBoWP; GrPl; MP; NePoAm-2; NMM; PH; SO; TwCP

Rob was never seen again! The Story of Flying Robert. Heinrich Hoffmann. SpRo

The robber rich, a yet more hateful band! William Wallace. Francis Lauderdale Adams. OxBS

Robbing from us the sun, robbing the moon From behind the Bars. Fadwa Tuquan. WPOW

A robe of honor and a harnessed steed/I send to thee. Odes, VII. Hafiz. AWP

...Robert Fulton/praised it as an instrument/for true liberty and peace. Robert Fulton. Ann Stanford. GP

Robert Rowley rolled round? Robert Rowley Rolled a Round Roll Round. Anonymous. OxNR

Robes and garbs/of the Kali-yuga/end of days. LMFBR. Gary Snyder. PoM

Robes of bright scarlet, horns that were never blown. Before the Carnival. Thom Gunn. NePoEA

Robin Hood, Robin Hood,/He will fret full sore. Robin Hood, Robin Hood. Anonymous. OxNR

Robin lyeth in greenwood bounden. Robin and Gandelyn. Anonymous. BaBo; EnSB; ESPB; OxBB

The robin pensive autumn cheer,/In all her locks of yellow. The Humble Petition of Bruar Water to the Noble Duke of Athole. Robert Burns. PBBP

The robin pipeth low. Song: "The feathers of the willow." Richard Watson Dixon. GTBS-P; LoBV; LoGBV; NOBE; OBNC; OBVV; YeAr

A robin shrills/His lonely tune. Snow. Walter De la Mare. OnUR

Robin was a rovin boy,/Rantin rovin Robin! Rantin, Rovin Robin. Robert Burns. OxBS

Robins on the roof, sing/Awaken the dead imprisoned in skin. Summons for the Undead. Diane Keating. CaPN

Robs me of that which not enriches him/And makes me poor indeed. Othello. William Shakespeare. FaFP; GoTF; TreFS

Rock-a-by, baby! wake by-and-by!/Rock-a-by! In the Tree-Top. Lucy Larcom. OBCA

Rock, be my dream, a burning fulfilled. Rock, Be My Dream. MacKnight Black. PoSH

Rock'd in the cradle of the deep. Rock'd in the Cradle of the Deep. Emma Hart Willard. PSoN

The rock finds a path, a path that sings, any path for all paths sing. Stone Song (Zen Rock) the Seer & the Unbeliever. Karoniaktatie. STE

Rock him again and his fair Queen asleep. The Lark. Anonymous. OBS

The rock loved and laboured; and all is lost. Sea Holly. Conrad Aiken. AP; LiTM; MAPA; NePA

Rock me to sleep, mother,–rock me to/sleep! Rock Me to Sleep. Elizabeth Akers Allen. AA; BLPA; BLPL; FaBoBe; FaFP; HBV 1-2; OBCA; PaPo; TreF; WBLP

The Rock of Ages chose thee for His/rest. Crown of Days. Anonymous. TrJP

The rock respects your stable towers. Brooklyn Bridge. Sir Charles G. D. Roberts. PAH

Rock, rock, rock the casket here in the moonlight. The Pale Blue Casket. Oliver Pitcher. NNP; PoBA; TTY

Rock-shores of the world and the secret waters. Birds. Robinson Jeffers. AP; CoBMV; VGW

Rock shutting out the sky, the old life done. The Walking Tour. W. H. Auden. CMoP

The rock sunders. Anniversary. Daniel Weissbort. VWA

Rock them, rock them, lullaby. Golden Slumbers. Thomas Dekker. CH; ELP; HBV 1-2; ViBoPo

The rock will wear washed with a winter's rain. Sonnet: "Fair is my love, for April is her face." Robert Greene. ViBoPo

Rocked on this dreamy and indifferent tide. The Absinthe-Drinker. Arthur Symons. BrPo; FaBoTw; NOBV

Rockes turn to Rivers, Rivers turn to Men. Dean-Bourn, a Rude River in Devon, by Which Sometimes He Lived. Robert Herrick. SeCV 1-2

The rocket molten into flakes/Of crimson or in emerald rain. In Memoriam A.H.H., XCVIII. Alfred, Lord Tennyson. VLP

Rocking and distant the islands slept. Incident at Matauri. Kendrick Smithyman. AnNZ

The rocks and nodding groves rebellow to the roar. The Progress of Poesy. Thomas Gray. ATP

...Rocks and skies/Unchanged from what they were when I was young. I Shall Go Back. Edna St. Vincent Millay. AnNE; MoAmPo; NePA; UnPo

Rocks mesas cactus blood. Black Mesa. Ron Rogers. STE

Rocks on the tide, tugs at the anchor chain. Arrival and Departure. Charles Eglington. PeSA

Rocks turn to rivers, rivers turn to men. To Dean Bourn, a Rude River in Devon, by Which Sometimes He Lived. Robert Herrick. AnAnS 2; CaPo; FaBoPP

A rockslide of agate. Llanberis Summer. Marianne Loyd. AMV-81

The rod doth sleep, while vigilant are men. The Rod. Robert Herrick. LiTB

A rod from the leader's nose. Stampede. Anonymous. ABF

...The rod/that nods like an innocent stalk of wild rice. The Cedar River. Reginald Gibbons. MAYP

"Roderigh Vich Alpine dhu, ho! ieroe!" The Lady of the Lake. Sir Walter Scott. EnRP; PoEL 1-5; ViBoPo; WHA

A Rodney and a Nelson may/Without him not have won the day. Daniel Defoe. Walter Savage Landor. NCEP

Rogi-rogbe!/Terror in battlement. Praise of Ibikunle. Anonymous. WTO

The rogues rule and ruin, while honest men/swing. The Burning of Jamestown. Thomas Dunn English. PAH

De Rohan staked a name to gain. Winter Days. Henry Abbey. AA

Roll'd round in earth's diurnal course,/With rocks, and stones, and trees. Lucy. William Wordsworth. AnFE; HBV 1-2; LiTL; OBEV; TrGrPo

Roll de ol' chariot along,/Ef you' don't hang on behin'. Roll de Ol' Chariot Along. Anonymous. BoAN 1-2

Roll, Jinnie Jinkins, roll! Jinnie Jinkins. Anonymous. AmFP

Roll, Missouri, roll. Little White Schoolhouse Blues. Florence Becker Lennon. PoNe

Roll on!/It rolls on. To the Terrestrial Globe. Sir William Schwenck Gilbert. FaBoNo; HBV 1-2; NLV; PoPl; TrGrPo

Roll on, little dogies, roll on. The Cowboy's Dream. Charles J. Finger. BPAW

...Roll on, reels of celluloid, as the great earth rolls on! To the Film Industry in Crisis. Frank O'Hara. CAPP; NoAm; NOBA; OBAL; SOTW

"Roll on, thou deep and dark blue Ocean, roll!" John Horace Burleson. Edgar Lee Masters. CrMA

Roll them overboard and sleep. The Sea and the Mirror. W. H. Auden. FaBoTw

Roll this golden chariot along,/And I won't stand back behind. Holy Ghost. Anonymous. OuSiCo

Roll up your mattresses, ye nightly-dead, and neglect/not prayer! Night. Jami. LiTW

Rolled effortless and mammoth through the night. Just as the Small Waves Came Where No Waves Were. Pamela Millward. NU

Rolled in the spray as I strolled up the beach. Tales of the Islands, I. Derek Walcott. OxBTC

Rolled round in earth's diurnal course,/With rocks, and stones, and trees. A Slumber Did My Spirt Seal. William Wordsworth. ELP

The roller, pitch, and stumps, and all. Brahma (parody). Andrew Lang. BXAP; CenHV; FaBoCo; NOBL

Roller-striped fields, and smooth cow-shadowed pond. The Elm Beetle. Andrew Young. LoBV

A rollerskate collides with a lunchpail. It's Not the Heat So Much as the Humidity. James Tate. NoAm

Rolling himself together like a blanket. Animal Songs: Springbok. Anonymous. PeSA

Rolling home, dear land, to thee! Rolling Home. Charles Mackay. FSW

Rolling home to dear New England,/rolling home, dear land, to thee. Rolling Home. Anonymous. AmSS; ShS

A-rolling in the dew makes the milkmaid so fair. The Milkmaid. Anonymous. AmFP

Rolling John attend my prayer:/Hi ho my bonny boy!   Rolling John (excerpt).   A. J. Wood.   PoAu 1-2

Rolling 'ome to Merry England,/Where kind friends do await for me.   Rolling Home.   Anonymous.   ShS

Rolling through leaves, in some perpetually loving motion.   Leaving One of the State Parks after a Family Outing.   Elizabeth Macklin.   AMV-81

Rolling up, under, over&over o whee.   I Never Saw a Man in a Negligee.   Alta.   GP

Rolling with the breakers.   Seal Pups.   Nora Dauenhauer.   TWSS

Rolls the dirge of thy last and thy bravest–O'More!   Dirge of Rory O'More.   Aubrey Thomas De Vere.   IrPN

Rolly-trudum, trudum, trudum-rolly-day.   Rolly Trudum.   Anonymous.   AmFP

The Roman eagles never flew.   Horace.   John Osborne Sargent   AA

The Roman Road.   The Roman Road.   Thomas Hardy.   AWP; BrPo; FaBoPP; GoJo; MoBrPo; NOBE

Romance, expected once to stay,/has left a note saying GONE AWAY.   Ending.   Gavin Ewart.   NLV; OBSP

Rome bound with oak her patriots' brows,/As Albyn shadows Wogan's tomb.   To an Oak Tree.   Sir Walter Scott.   OBNC

Rome fell/not having grasped the phrase: darkmotherscream.   Darkmotherscream.   Andrei Voznesensky.   NU

...Rome, the armpit of the universe.   All Tropic Places Smell of Mold.   Karl Shapiro.   VGW

Romeo, Macbeth, Cleopatra, Caesar, Coriolanus.   Memoria Technica for the Plays of Shakespeare.   Anonymous.   FaBoUs

The Ronin, the Wave-Men, camp in the ruined door.   If So the Man You Are.   Percy Wyndham Lewis.   OBSV

A roof with a pig under it/Means home.   Pigs.   John Cotton.   BoAnP

Rooks are homing, says.   Our Bodies.   Denise Levertov.   NaP; PPP

Rooks circle in the sun.   Park Pigeons.   Melville Cane.   CAD

Room by room like a shabby genteel boarding house, age.   Letters to Live Poets.   Bruce Beaver.   CBAP

The room everywhere filled with light!   Mrs. Applebaum's Sunday Dance Class.   Philip Schultz.   AMV-81; MAYP

Room for Him–Room!   Song of Hope.   Mary Artemisia ("Aunt Mary") Lathbury.   BLPA

The room sleeps dreamlessly...   Tenement Room: Chicago.   Frank Marshall Davis.   GoSl

Room to start again.   The Homes.   Anne Pitkin.   AMV-80

Roosevelt, Roosevelt, where them catfish be?   Roosevelt Considers Catfish Stew.   R. T. Smith.   WOLT

The rooster lifting his legs/high in the wet grass.   Reading in Fall Rain.   Robert Bly.   GP; GrPl

A rooster the winter wind sliced/Through a red fence   The Firstborn.   Gary Soto.   NPGG

Root hog or die.   Bull-Whacker.   Anonymous.   ABF

Rooted and blowing beyond sense or touch.   This Measure.   Léonie Adams.   MoAB; MoAmPo

...Rooted by his lightning/sheathed and unsheathed.   Late Spring.   John Gill.   NeAC

Rooted deep in the hearts of millions.   The Tree of Hatred.   Shmuel Moreh.   VWA

Rooted in rock beyond the eye,/Their giant forms emerge.   Girl Athletes.   Haniel Long.   HBMV

Rooted they/grip down and begin to awaken.   Spring and All.   William Carlos Williams.   AP; CABA; ExPo; ForPo; InPK; InPS; MoVE; NoAm; NOBA; QFR; TAP

Rooting/backwards/in their eyes.   Awakening–.   Nelly Sachs.   PBWP

Roots and dry meat, enough to last fifty years.   Invasion North.   Richard Hugo.   GP

The roots of life are deep and dearly won.   Duality.   Katherine Thayer Hobson.   GoYe

The roots of the tiniest grasses curl toward one another/like secret smiles.   Where Children Live.   Naomi Shihab Nye.   MAYP

The roots of the tree were dead.   MACV Advisor.   Patrick Worth Gray.   SOTS

The roots shaken with water and dirt/Torn from a long sleep.   A Late Spring.   James Scully.   NYBP

"A rope and a gallows for to hang him on."   The Cruel Brother.   Anonymous.   AmFP

The rope burns still/hot on his neck   Rope and Drum.   Robert Currie.   Str

...The rope,/That lands you at the Station Hope–/Get a transfer.   Get a Transfer.   Anonymous.   BLPA; WBLP

Rosa, let us get married, O Rosa sweet!   Rosa.   Anonymous.   TrAS

De Rosa y Ribera.   Tamales.   O. (William Sidney Porter) Henry.   BPAW

Rose and grape, pear and bean/are bad to keep.   Song: "Rose and grape, pear and bean."   Anonymous.   BoWoP

Rose bay willow herb.   Rose Bay Willow Herb.   Judy Ray.   AMV-81; FAZ

Rose came by with a smile for me,/Just as I thought I was getting old.   The Prime of Life.   Walter Learned.   HBV 1-2

Rose, desert–mirage too.   Marriage of Two.   C. Day Lewis.   ChMP

The rose forever doomed to globe but as it bleeds.   Spring Song.   George Brandon Saul.   GoYe

Rose in the morning/full of spermatic words.   Translating.   Ruth Whitman.   VWA

The Rose in Wood Street kill'd me.   His Own Epitaph.   Thomas (Tom) Brown.   FaBoEE

Rose, lily, violet, marigold, pink, pansies.   The Garden.   Joshua Sylvester.   CBEP

The rose-lipt girls are sleeping/In fields where roses fade.   With Rue My Heart Is Laden.   Alfred Edward Housman.   AWP; BLPL; CMoP; EnL; FaFP; GoTF; GTBS; HAP; HeIP; HoPM; InPK; LiTB; LiTL; LiTM; MasP; MoAB; MoBrPo; NoAm; NoP; PG; PrIm; SoSe; TreFT; TrGrPo; UnPo

Rose-mouth, russet-eyes!   A Letter to Elsa.   Grace Hazard Conkling.   HBMV; HBVY

Rose of the world, that sweetened so the same.   The Complaint of Rosamond.   Samuel Daniel.   OBSC

Rose once redly glowing.   The Rose.   Johann Wolfgang von Goethe.   AWP

The rose one leaves in some forgotten book.   Her Horoscope.   Mary Ashley Townsend.   AA

A rose-red city half as old as Time.   Pedra.   John William Burgon.   BLPA

A rose, say, or an old man's humiliation.   The Desolate Rhythm of Dying Recurs.   Michael Smith.   CIP

The rose, that draws the touch, and stings.   To Himself.   Richard Aldridge.   NePoAm

The rose, the little wind and you/Have gone so far away.   The Little Rose Is Dust, My Dear.   Grace Hazard Conkling.   HBV 1-2

The rose tree's thread of scent draws thin–/and snaps upon the air.   Field of Autumn.   Laurie Lee.   LiTM; NCSH

A rose unopened,/blackened by the cold.   Separation.   P. Wolny.   DFF

Rose, were you not extremely sick?   A True Maid.   Matthew Prior.   ALV; FaBoCo; FaBoEE; NIP; NOEC; PV

The rose will die, and a skull/Gives back no caresses.   Tattooed.   William Plomer.   ChMP

A rose will fade in a day!   A Rose Will Fade.   Dora Sigerson Shorter.   HBV 1-2

–Rosemary, Rosemary, let down your bright hair!   A Nonsense Song.   Stephen Vincent Benét.   OBAL

Roses are her cheeks,/And a rose her mouth.   Go Not, Happy Day.   Alfred, Lord Tennyson.   LiTL

The Roses first came red.   How Roses Came Red.   Robert Herrick.   CaPo; CavP; EnL; SoSe

The roses lie upon the grass/Like little shreds of crimson silk.   Le Jardin.   Oscar Wilde.   SeCePo

Roses must live and love, and winds must blow.   The Rose and the Wind.   Philip Bourke Marston.   OBVV

Roses of death– Simple Things.   Paul-Jean Toulet.   CAW

The roses of the Past!   Temple Garlands.   Agnes Mary Frances (Mme Emile Duclaux) Robinson.   HBV 1-2

The roses raced around her name.   Missing My Daughter.   Stephen Spender.   AtBAP; GTBS-P; Str

Roses, you are not so fair after all!   Garden Fancies.   Robert Browning.   ACV; VLP

A rosy air washes his absence.   Mediterranean.   Ruth Whitman.   VWA

Rosy and Colin and Dun.   The Old Woman's Three Cows.   Anonymous.   OxNR

Rosy, rust-red, Orange, white!   The Breech.   Michael McClure.   NeAP

A rosy warmth from marge to marge.   In Memoriam A.H.H., XLVI.   Alfred, Lord Tennyson.   VLP

Rot on the vine: in that land were we born.   The Mediterranean.   Allen Tate.   AP; ExPo; FaBoMo; HAP; InPo; LiTA; LiTM; MoAB; MoAmPo; MOS; MoVE; NePA; OxBS; PoCh; SeCePo; SeCeV; VGW; WeW

Rot which makes us prolific as the sun on white unfastened/clouds.   Thanksgiving.   Kenneth Koch.   VGW

Rots, stinks, and dies, and is trod under feet.   The Beggar's Opera.   John Gay.   TEP

Rottin crok, dirtin dok, cry cok, or I sall quell the.   Flyting of Dunbar and Kennedy.   William Dunbar.   TW

...Rotting caps/gave off a musky smell of loam.   Fall.   Robert Hass.   AmPA

The rough and ready roving boys, like Rory of the Hill.   Rory of the Hill.   Charles Joseph Kickham.   OnYI

Rough as th' Adratick sea, yet I/Will live with thee, or else for thee will die.   Odes.   Horace.   OBVE

...Rough boards,/spotted horses in the frame.   Crepes Flambeau.   Tess Gallagher.   AMV-81; MAYP

...The rough deck/Inhabited, and what it always was.   Population.   George Oppen.   PoA

Roughly per specimen, space/sufficient for decent burial.   Rehabilitative Report: We Can Still Laugh.   Daniel Berrigan.   LFAC

Roun' dat po' ol' cabin do'.   The Old Cabin.   Paul Laurence Dunbar.   PoLf

Roun the pinnacles/mak kythans.   Kythans.   Stewart McGavin.   PoSH

Round about your path the ranks encroach,/Bannered with the grace of angel splendor. Saint. Kersti Merilaas. LiTW

Round again, round again, round/they go. Hush-a-Bye, Baby, They're Gone to Milk. *Anonymous.* OxNR

Round an Egyptian wound. Passover Dachau. B. Z. Niditch. AMV-81

A round animal, nameless. Poem: "After your death." Bill Knott. EAS

Round by the lilac bushes back to you! In the Orchard. James Stephens. LOW; RoGo; SO; WSC

"Round Cape Horn." Round Cape Horn. *Anonymous.* EtS

A round full-orb'd eidolon. Eidolons. Walt Whitman. AmePo

Round her trusting child she fondly/flings. Why Thus Longing? Harriet W. Sewall. AA

Round Howie's impotence drew in the night. The Desertion of the Women and Seals. George Mackay Brown. OxBC

Round our restlessness, his rest. Round Our Restlessness. Elizabeth Barrett Browning. TRV

Round pictures of the moon. Euclid. Vachel Lindsay. ImOP; MAPA; NAMP; YaD

"Round, sir, on Sundays, square on other days." The Snuff-Boxes. *Anonymous.* StPo

A round tear/drops from your eye. Round. Rachel Boimwall. VWA

Round the black headlands/Streaming with rain. Rain. Seumas (James Starkey) O'Sullivan. OnYI

Round the light of the burning glow-worm, steady and clear. The Glow-Worm. Edward Shanks. WHA

Round the Palace and up over the walls crows and/magpies are flying. Cock-Crow Song. *Anonymous.* LiTW

Round the wild witch-hazel tree. The Culprit Fay. Joseph Rodman Drake. AA; GN

Round the world and home again.' Last Journey. John Davidson. PoSH

Round the world and home again,/That's the sailor's way! Homeward Bound. William Allingham. FaBoBe; HBV 1-2; HBVY

Round twists old Earth, and round,/Stillness not yet found. The Walking Road. Richard Hughes. OBMV

Round up their flocks and shout/and scour the land. Glory, Glory to the Sun. John Alford. HBMV

The round-up waits another call. The Round-Up. Sarah Elizabeth Howard. PoOW

Round which revolves the Sages' Wheel. The Gravel-Pit Field. David Gascoyne. NeBP

A routh o' donnert feckless fules/Wha dinna coont a dang! Comfort in Puirtith. Helen B. Cruickshank. OxBS

...Routine/as the river I cross over. In the Hellgate Wind. Madeline Defrees. NYP

Rouz'd like a huntsman to the chace, and, with/Thy buskin'd feet, appear upon our hills. To Morning. William Blake. EnRP; ERoP 1-2

The roving spirit/stay her and return. November. Elizabeth Daryush. QFR

Row boat for catfish, row boat. Ol' Hag, You See Mammy? *Anonymous.* OuSiCo

Row, brothers, row, to the blue of the verge, where the low/sky mates with the sea. The Coromandel Fishers. Sarojini Naidu. BBV; EtS; MCCG

...A row of books suggests the art. I/have little access to myself. Alogon. Michael Palmer. APU

Row on, row on, to catch the gold/In dripping fleece, as they of old. Young Argonauts. Sheila Wingfield. SD

Rowing and football I'll forswear, and join the Volunteers! Football and Rowing–An Eclogue. Alfred Denis Godley. CenHV

& roy wilkins on/the mod squad. Black Sketches, 11. Don L. Lee. NeAC

Le Roy, you're earning too much money now. Songs for a Colored Singer. Elizabeth Bishop. FaBoWP

Rub his face in, real, and warm, and nubbled lovely. Pleasures. Albert Goldbarth. GeTw

Rub/Me/Out. An Indignant Male. Abram Bunn Ross. BrR

Rubbed her hips and sang/of a country, like this, far off. Verifying the Dead. James Welch. CDW

The rubbish must be cleared away! A Bargain Sale. S. E. Kiser. PoToHe

A ruby sequin/over his heart. Ladybug's Christmas. Norma Farber. PCh

Ruddy as a hard nut, hair in his ears, clear sea lights in his eyes. The Old Flagman. Carl Sandburg. YaD

Rude and ragged rascals run. Jumbled in the Common Box. W. H. Auden. PoRA

Rudel sing the Lady of Tripoli. March Thoughts from England. Margaret Louisa Woods. OBVV

Rudely composed in this tempestuous sea. The Ship of Fools. Alexander Barclay. ACP; CAW

Rue on my life; or else your cruel wrong/Shall well appear, and by my death be seen. The Restless State of a Lover. Henry Howard, Earl of Surrey. GoTL

–A rueful, chaste,/Unshaven kiss. Developers at Crystal River. James Merrill. AMV-81

Rugged and resolute, a man of men! A Man of Men. Leonard Charles Van Noppen. PGD

Rugged canyons smooth into valleys/while shards reform their urn. In Mutual Time. Steven Lavoie. APU

Ruin–bitter dawn: you not wed to your dark beloved. Una Bhan. Tomas ""Laidir" Mac Coisdealbhaigh. NOBI

The ruin of the world. I Breathed into the Ash. Roland Robinson. BoAV

Ruin yer health and kill yer baby,/Poor little innocent child. Cigarettes Will Spoil Yer Life (with music). *Anonymous.* AS

The rule of the place is Eat and Walk. Eat and Walk. James Norman Hall. BLPA

Rule over myself He has taken away from me. Jerusalem Sonnets. James Keir Baxter. OCNZ

Rule well v and come to hevyn. Ten Commandments, Seven Deadly Sins, and Five Wits. *Anonymous.* FaBoEE

Ruled by a mighty lust. Three Lyrics. Petronius Arbiter (Caius Petronius Arbiter). LiTW

Rules all of God's creatures/In peace and love! A Christmas Carol. Harry Behn. BiCB; PCh

Rules he who notes the sparrow's fall. Old and New. *Anonymous.* BLRP

Ruleth all England under a Hog. Snatches: "The Cat, the Rat, and Lovel our dog." *Anonymous.* OxBM

...The ruling laws of the globe in reference to its veins of water. Landscape I. Charles Madge. EAS

A-rum-a-tee-tum-a-tee-tum-/a-tee-tum. A Parade. Mary Catherine Rose. SoPo

Rumbling on stone that will run us out tomorrow. Envoi. E. L. Mayo. FAZ

Rumination cannot tell her what to say/to hecatombs of a Shakespearean play. Rehearsal. David Fisher. NPGG

Rumney and Rye, the five ports be. The Cinque Ports. *Anonymous.* FaBoUs

Rumors of home like oceans in a shell. The Urn. Malcolm Cowley. AnAmPo; MoVE

Rumour has it she's taken to rouge again. The Aphrodisiac. Mebdh McGuckian. FaBoIP

Run come see Jerusalem. Run Come See. *Anonymous.* FSW

"Run for your lives to the mountain side!" The Man Who Rode to Conemaugh. John Eliot Brown. PAH

Run, Great Excursioner. Run if you can. To William Wordsworth from Virginia. Julia Randall. NMM

Run in circles, scream and shout. Sound Advice. *Anonymous.* FaBoUs; NLV

Run, nigger, run, it's almos' day. Run,Nigger, Run! *Anonymous.* ABF

Run out your measured arcs, and lead/The closing cycle rich in good. In Memoriam A.H.H., CV. Alfred, Lord Tennyson. VLP

Run swiftly to escape/the rape of the hunter Alpheus. O Artemis and your virgin girls. Telesilla. BoWoP

Run, tailors, run,/Or she'll kill you all e'en now. The Snail. *Anonymous.* GBP

Run to bed children/Before it gets dark. Down with the Lambs. *Anonymous.* OxNR

Run, uncle, run/And see what has happened! The Fox Rhyme. Ian Serraillier. ELU

Run yeh! Run yeh! 'Fo' do link o' day. Link O' Day. *Anonymous.* TrAS

Rung from their flinty caves, "Repent! Repent!" The Baptist. William, of Hawthornden Drummond. TrGrPo

Rung from their marble caves "Repent! Repent!" Saint John the Baptist. William, of Hawthornden Drummond. CBEP; EaLo; GTBS; GTBS-P; NOBE; OBEV; TrCP

Running/coyote/song/done. Sweat Song. Peter Blue Cloud. STE; VoR

A running fire in my breast/That turns my heart to ashes. No Moon, No Chance to Meet. Ono no Komachi. WPOW

Running from Grandmother's hands/Down to God's listening ears.... For Mattie & Eternity. Sterling D. Plumpp. CNA

...Running in wild dread/Toward Arcturus–and returning as suddenly... The Mind Is an Ancient and Famous Capital. Delmore Schwartz. TAP

A running lake, a flock of sheep,/And one who sings her child to sleep. An Old Song. Yehoash. AWP; LiTW

Running my whole family off a cliff. All Quiet. David Ignatow. BeLS; CAPP; ConAP; FaBoBe; FaFP; TreFS

Running on forever, down the long road west. The Long Road West. Henry Herbert Knibbs. BPAW

Running over the bright/Green mould of an apple-tree. Garden Party. Sir Herbert Read. BrPo

Running with the red stag through fields. Wolves for Company. *Anonymous.* BIrV

Runs down, a brook o' laughter, thru the air. The Biglow Papers. James Russell Lowell. FaBV

Runs on the standing windows and away. Storm Windows. Howard Nemerov. ConAP

Runs out, and streams away behind. Karoo Town. Robert Dederick. PeSA

Runs the great bull, the dogs upon his heels. The Bull. Judith Wright. GrPl; PoAu 1-2

The rural letter box said Toffile Lajway. The Witch of Coos. Robert Frost. AP; AtBAP; CMoP; CoBMV; DiPo; ExPo; InPK; InPS; MoAB; NePA; NoAm; NOBA; ViBoPo

Rush'd forth with Hector to the Fields of Fight. The Iliad. Homer. OBVE

The rush of their charge is resounding still,/That saved the army at Chancellorsville. Keenan's Charge. George Parsons Lathrop. AA; HBV 1-2; MC; PAH

Rush, the swoln flood of bitterness I pour,/And knock, and knock, and knock– but none replies. Sonnet: Addressed by a Father Mourning... Jacopo Vittorelli. LiTW

Rushed to my arms and spat upon your/face! Recrimination. Ella Wheeler Wilcox. AA

Rushing down singing inside this breast of mine. Wenberi's Song. *Anonymous.* CBAP

The rushing sounds of a river/under our house. Rushing. Ray A. Young Bear. CDW

Rushing through the vast astonishment. His Legs Ran About. Ted Hughes. LLLT

Rushing up his green ungoverned hillside. I Remember Galileo. Gerald Stern. FYAP

Russet/amber/and gone. Fickle in the Arms of Spring. Susie Fry. AMV-81

A Russian freighter bound for home/Mourns to the city in its gloom. Derry Morning. Derek Mahon. NOBI

Russian shades out of old slow novels,/Lengthened the afternoon. A Meeting of Cultures. Donald Davie. OBTV; OxBC

Rust at the muscle. Canto 5. Tom Weatherly. PoBA

A rusted plow filling with snow. Abundance. Roo Borson. CaPN

The rustle of a tree, a bell's peal,/smoke.... Restless as a Wolf. Moishe-Leib Halpern. TrJP

Rustles the song of my pain–in the insomniac nights. To the Jews in Poland. Jozef Wittlin. VWA

Rustling, zoro-zoro, like a lady's/train. Colts. *Anonymous.* SUS

Rusty ingot, bleak paralyzed blob! The Word. Basil Bunting. PoA

The rusty smith her leman was,/For a' her muckle pride. The Twa Magicians. *Anonymous.* BaBo; ESPB; GBP; OxBB

The ruthless one/whose eye is in the sun! The Return. Conrad Aiken. NePA

Rye, flax, horses, platinum, timber, and fur. The Monkeys. Marianne Moore. CMoP; LiTA; NAMP; NoAm; NOBA; OxBA; SeCeV

S

S'all full o' mud, I tossed it away. Kitty, Kitty Casket. *Anonymous.* OuSiCo

S'en vont y fair' leurs nids. Aupres de Ma Blonde. *Anonymous.* FSW

S(oon & there's/a m oo/)n. I Will Be. Edward Estlin Cummings. VGW

Sa lang as I may gear get to steill/Will I never work. How the First Hielandman of God Was Made of Ane Horse Turd... *Anonymous.* FaBoCh; GBP; OBSV

Sa that I may thi mercy syng/in thi blys with-owten ende. Mercy Is Most in My Mind. *Anonymous.* CoBE

Sabe Dios si volvere. Yo Soy de la Tierra. *Anonymous.* OuSiCo

Sack beside the fragrant apple/bushel under my back stoop! Parable: November. Stephen Tapscott. FAZ

The sack of rich great London. Picture of Loot. Alan Sillitoe. OxBTC

The sacramental host of God's elect. The Task. William Cowper. CoBE

Sacred and murderous from your sanctuary? Moon-Man. Dorothy Hewett. CBAP

A sacred city of the mind. Toledo. Roy Campbell. MoBrPo

Sacred despite disgust, protective, real. For an Egyptian Boy, Died c. 700 B.C. Mary Baron. HoAn

Sacred, his plumage as purple as waves, and his heart/never burdened. No More, O Maidens. Alcman. LiTW

The sacred pendants, the feathered strings... The Djanggawul Cycle, 144. *Anonymous.* WTO

The sacred spaces of the sea. Songs Before Sunrise: Prelude. Algernon Charles Swinburne. MaVP; VLP

The sacred spirit, labourers refreshing,/Still be renowned. Amen. To the Trinity. Richard Stanyhurst. OxBoCh

Sacred to Poseidon are both the/nimble dolphin and the stiff pine tree. On a Horse Carved in Wood. Donald Hall. EyDe

Sacred to Scudder's shells and Dr. Griscom. Fanny. Fitz-Greene Halleck. OBAL

A sacrificing swift night-shade. In Memoriam S.C.W., V.C. Charles Hamilton Sorley. MMM

The sad advice/of your ugly friend/archy. The Hen and the Oriole. Don (Donald Robert Marquis) Marquis. EvOK; FiBHP

Sad Aziola! from that moment I/Loved thee and thy sad cry. The Aziola. Percy Bysshe Shelley. CBEP; EBEV; PBBP

Sad Bell-wether to the rest. The Passing Bell. James Shirley. ACP

The sad bones of my hands descend into a valley/Of strange rocks. Rain. James Wright. NaP

A sad but excusable/Slip of the tong. Lapsus Linguae. Keith Preston. NLV; OBAL

Sad disappointment waits for ever Love's Memories Haunt My Footsteps Still. John Clare. NOBV

Sad every dungeon where earth's hosts/Lie hidden from the light of day. Under Sorrow's Sign. Gofraidh Fionn O'Dalaigh. BIrV

Sad-eyed conquerors,/drink your coffee,/think of home. Truck Drivers. Terri Haag. CTBA

...Sad friend, you cannot change. North Haven. Elizabeth Bishop. HaCAP

Sad is Eros, builder of cities,/And weeping anarchic Aphrodite. In Memory of Sigmund Freud. W.H. Auden. AtBAP; CoBMV; HAP; LiTB; OAEL 1-2; OxBA

Sad lingerer, that gave to thee/His heart, his hope, his melody. Elegy for Lucy Lloyd. Llewelyn Goch. LiTW

Sad Memory brings the light/Of other days around me. Oft, in the Stilly Night. Thomas Moore. AnFE; BLPL; CBEP; FaBoBe; GoBC; LiTB; LoBV; MCCG; OAEP; OBNC; OBRV; OxBI; PoEL 1-5; Prf; WHA

Sad, sad, that bitter wail–/"Almost–but lost!" Almost Persuaded. Philip Bliss. AH

Sad songs of Autumn mirth. Digging. Edward ("Edward Eastaway") Thomas. BrPo; MoAB; MoBrPo; OxBTC

Sad study, grammar! Its whole content's/one long string of accidents! Grammar Commences with a 5-line Curse. Palladas. OBVE

Sad tree, whose perishing boughs/So few birds house! A Fallen Yew. Francis Thompson. BrPo; MoAB; MoBrPo

Sad true love never find my grave/To weep there! Twelfth Night. William Shakespeare. CBEP; CTC; DiPo; EiL; ELP; ExPo; FiP; GBL; GTBS; GTBS-P; InPo; NOBE; NoP; OBEV; OBSC; PoPle; PoRA; SeCeV; ViBoPo; WHA

Sad Willy's pipe shall bid his friend farewell. Britannia's Pastorals. William Browne. EiL

A sadder and a wiser man,/He rose the morrow morn. The Rime of the Ancient Mariner. Samuel Taylor Coleridge. AtBAP; ATP; BeLS; DiPo; EBEV; ERoP 1-2; ExPo; FaBoBe; FaBoCh; FaBV; FaFP; FiP; GoTF; HAP; HBV 1-2; HoPM; InPS; LiTB; LoGBV; MasP; MBW 1-2; MCCG; MOS; NOBE; NoP; OAEL 1-2; OAEP; OBEV; OBNC; OBNV; OBRV; PAI; PoEL 1-5; PrIm; RoGo; SeCeV; TEP; TreF; TrGrPo; ViBoPo; WHA

Sadder, wiser, and plumb dead! Little Boys of Texas. Robert P. Tristram Coffin. ShM

Sadly he rides the elevator down/and starts again at the foot of the blind wall. Climbing. Daniel Mark Epstein. AMV-80

A sadly-pleasing, melancholy joy. Morna's Hill: A Distant Prospect of the the City of Armagh. James Stuart. IrPN

Sae ald Carl Hood was not the dead o ane,/But he was the dead o hale seeventeen. Earl Brand (A vers.). *Anonymous.* BaBo; ESPB

Sae Jock maun to his flail again,/And Jenny to her wheel. Yule's Come, and Yule's Gane. *Anonymous.* GBP

Sae laith as she was her true-love to be-/guile,/Because he brocht mony men frae the/West Isle. Charlie Macpherson. *Anonymous.* ESPB

Sae Lawty says I shou'd na hae him. The Carle He Came O'er the Croft. Allan Ramsay. OxBS

Sae let the Lord be thankit. Grace at Kirkudbright. Robert Burns. OBSP

Sae slicht was the Gaelic he built on. Limerick: "There was an auld birkie ca'ed Milton." Andrew Lang. CenHV

Sae you and I maun tak the gate/Before it's lang. To My Auld Dog Dash. John Barr. AnNZ

Safe Cornish holidays before the storm! Summoned by Bells: Cornwall in Childhood. Sir John Betjeman. FaBoPP; OxBTC

Safe from death, I keep them in endless summer. My Father's Country. Joyce Lee. NOAV

Safe from hurt and free from harm. A Prayer for a Sleeping Child. Mary Carolyn Davies. OHIP

Safe from the canting band. The Cavalier's Escape. Walter Thornbury. FaBoBe; GN; HBV 1-2

Safe from the wolves black jaw, and the dull Asses hoofe. Underwoods. Ben Jonson. AtBAP

Safe harbor from the whistling gale! Love at the Door. Meleager. AWP

Safe in a world you do not need to know. Teaching Swift to Young Ladies. William Dickey. PoA

Safe in firelight sit. Safe. James Walker. OBCP

Safe in my jar. I shall have ten more yet. The Boy Fishing. E. J. Scovell. FaBoWP; HaMV

Safe in my room, beside the pier,/I find my vessel fast. My Bed Is a Boat. Robert Louis Stevenson. HBV 1-2; HBVY

Safe in Paradise with Thee. Stabat Mater. Jacopone da Todi. WGRP

...Safe in the arc cut/by the rope swing/thirty years ago. The World. Vern Rutsala. Psk

Safe in the promised land. Where Are the Hebrew Children? Peter Cartwright. AH

Safe moored in haven skies above our fold. New Horizons. Sidney Royse Lysaght. HBMV

Safe now in the Promised Land. Where, Oh Where Are the Hebrew Children? *Anonymous.* BLPA

Safe on the perilous heights of power and wealth,/As in the straitness of the ancient ways. Columbus and the Mayflower. Richard Monckton, Lord Houghton Milnes. MC; PAH

Safe temples, quiet graves! The Covenanter's Lament for Bothwell Brigg. Winthrop Mackworth Praed. OBRV

Safe to its home in thy presence above. To the Child Jesus. Henry Van Dyke. TrPWD

Safely rest, all is well! God is nigh. God Is Nigh. *Anonymous.* TRV

Safely she takes her way and drops to rest,/Peace-filled and unafraid. The Ship. Louise A. Doran. EtS

Safely the gentle Shakespeare slept and smiled. On Shakespeare and Voltaire. Thomas Holcroft. NOEC

The safety of the world was lying there,/And the world's danger. I Saw a Stable. Mary Elizabeth Coleridge. EBCP; OBCP; OBSP; OxBoCh; PCh; TRV

...A sage fool trapped/by music in a copper net of hair. Prize-Giving. Gwen Harwood. CBAP

Said E. P. Roe to Opie Read. To Be Continued. James M. Flagg and Julian Street. FiBHP; InMe; PV

Said Eddie, "Yeah, mebbe." The Newlyweds. John Updike. PV

Said Ford, "I agree;/It's the same thing with me." Mutual Problem. William Cole. OBAL; PoL

Said, "He passed to be with Jesus in the singing of that hymn." The Last Hymn. Marianne Farningham. BLPA

Said he wouldn't have another drink, he couldn't take it. Yes Please Gentlemen. A. R. D. Fairburn. ACV

Said her Pater Noster. The Wee May o'Caledon. Lewis Spence. ACV

Said, "I knew that the angels were whispering with thee." The Angel's Whisper. Samuel Lover. OnYI

Said, "I'm going to ride the scoundrel to Niagra Fall." Casey Jones (C vers.). *Anonymous.* ViBoFo

Said, "I really can't tell, for I rent 'em!" Limerick: "There was an old man of Tarentum." Cosmo Monkhouse. HBV 1-2; InvP; LBN; LiBL

Said, "It's never too late to begin." Limerick: "There was an old fellow of Lynn." *Anonymous.* LiBL

Said it's train time now/Hear that ring I do adore Squabbling Blues. Barefoot Bill. BluL

Said it was going/over to your place. The Poem You Asked For. Larry Levis. AmPA; GOYP

Said Kelly and Burke and Shea. The Fighting Race. Joseph Ignatius Constantin Clarke. AA; AmePo; BLPA; BLPL; HBV 1-2; MC; OnYI; PAH; YaD

Said, "Ladies, don't you know we are all in Hell?" Mother Goose Rhyme. Kenneth Rexroth. ErPo

Said Life:—"Here's grief." Love and Life. Julie Mathilde Lippmann. AA; HBV 1-2

Said little old mouse./Squeak-cak-eak-eak-eak. Little Black Bug. Margaret Wise Brown. NTCP

Said our Lady of the Snows. Our Lady of the Snows. Rudyard Kipling. ACV

Said, Pull up your boots and take the air:/We climbers have to die. The Emergency Maker. David Wagoner. NePoEA-2

Said that the fall might come and whirl of leaves,/For summer was done. The Quest of the Orchis. Robert Lee Frost. AmePo

Said the antipodes, and twice spring chimed. Altarwise by Owl-Light. Dylan Thomas. CMoP

Said the gamey black-maned wild boar/Tusking the turf on Mal Paso Mountain. The Stars Go over the Lonely Ocean. Robinson Jeffers. LiTA; LiTM; NePA; WaP

Said the Great Dane to Peter the Great. Peterhof. Edmund Wilson. GoJo

Said the guy, "If you fellows St. Whouis?" Limerick: "A guy asked two jays at St. Louis." Ferdinand G. Christgau. TDH

Said the infant's mother: "No." A Father Does His Best. E. B. White. ALV

Said the lobster with grasping claws. Sea Shanty. Clifford Dyment. PoL

Said the people in the cities dying/Counta their wicked ways Jesus Is Coming Soon. Blind Willie Johnson. BluL

Said the tree, while he bent down his laden boughs/low. The Tree. Bjornstjerne Bjornson. OHIP; PoSC

Said Wisdom to Folly,/"I thought to ask you." On the Road. Tudor Jenks. NA

...Sail a million years/In nothing, not even Death, not even tears. I Could Not Sleep for Thinking of the Sky. John Masefield. LiTM

The sail on the mast flaps, dancing, and "talks' in the wind... Sail at the Mast Head. *Anonymous.* WTO

A sail, that for a day/Has cheered the castaway. Thou Didst Delight My Eyes. Robert Bridges. ELP; MoAB; MoBrPo

Sail through the past, nor heed the strife to be,/Scrolled on the Teacher's fan. Tao. Alfred Goldsworthy Bailey. CaP

Sail Westward ho, and away! Ballad. Charles Kingsley. GN

Sailing away/Like a toy/Balloon. Flying. J. M. Westrup. OnUR

"Sailing down along the coast/Of the High Barbaree." The High Barbaree. Laura E. Richards. BaBo; SUS

Sailing down the coast of High Barbary. The Pirate of High Barbary. *Anonymous.* EtS

Sailing down the river on the O-Hi-O. Boatman's Dance. Daniel Decatur Emmett. FSW

The sailor's wife his star shall be! Nancy Lee. *Anonymous.* AmSS

"Sailor, what is your will of me?" The Drowned Seaman. Maude Goldring. HBMV

Sailors and Satyrs, Cupid's knights, and I,/Fear women that swear, nay, and know they lie. Caelica, XXI. Fulke, Lord Brooke Greville. FCP

Sailors, take warning. Rainbow at Night. *Anonymous.* FaBoBe

The sails swell full. To sea, to sea! Death's Jest-Book. Thomas Lovell Beddoes. OBRV

The sails swell full: To sea, to sea! To Sea. Thomas Lovell Beddoes. CH; EtS

The sails that are blown by the strength of/your will. Convention. Alfred Kreymborg. MAPA

A Saint–a Saint was there! The Discovery. John Henry, Cardinal Newman. OBRV

Saint Bridget? Or her near and dear? The Giveaway. Phyllis McGinley. PoRA

Saint Christopher, be with me still. In My End Is My Beginning. Rosemary Dobson. BoAV

Saint Francis preaching to the birds. Saint Francis. John Peale Bishop. EaLo

Saint George of mery England, the signe of victoree. The Faerie Queene. Edmund Spenser. FaBoPV

The saint heaven hath, the mother once they had. On the Death of a Pious Lady. Olof Wexionius. AWP

Saint-like to Canonize you to the Sky. To My Cosen Mrs. Ellinor Evins. George Alsop. SCAP

The Saint of the Pit is holier in my eyes! Artemis. Gerard de Nerval. LiTW

Saint Paul ne'er saw but one such day before. The Spanish Descent. Daniel Defoe. APAS; OBWP

The saint Pygmalion, saint, beggar and thief. Hagiograph. Rayner Heppenstall. NeBP

Saint's grove, my rest at night. Gardens Are All My Heart. Eve Triem. GoYe

Saint Simon the Cyrenean shall lead you forth to feed. The Murmur from the Stable. Ruben Dario. CAW

The Saint sustain'd it, but the Woman dy'd. Epitaph V On Mrs. Corbet, Who Dyed of a Cancer in her Breast. Alexander Pope. CEP

Sair fyel'd, hinny,/Sin' aw ken'd thou. Sair Fyel'd, Hinny. *Anonymous.* GRP

The salamander circus/followed like a hungry dog The Death Circus. John Tranter. CBAP

Salangadou? Salangadou. *Anonymous.* ABF

The sale of half-hose has/Long since superseded the cultivation/Of Pierian roses. Hugh Selwyn Mauberley, XII. Ezra Pound. CoBMV; NOBA

Sales, races, rabbits, and (still stranger!) pews. Love of Fame, The Universal Passion. Edward Hilton Young. OBSV

...Sallow virginal pools in/windy amber watercolor. Prewar Late October Sea Breeze. Robert Grenier. APU

Sally go round the chimney-pots/On a Saturday afternoon. Sally Go Round the Sun. *Anonymous.* OxNR

Sally, I was happy with you. Sally. Paul Durcan. FaBoIP

Sally, tell my Mother I shall never come back. Gypsies in the Wood. *Anonymous.* DTC; FaBoCh; OxBoLi

A salmon, a sow of solid silver,/Bulges to glimpse it. The River in March. Ted Hughes. OxBC

Salome comes in, bearing/The head of God knows whom. Night Club. Louis MacNeice. OBSP

Salome said, Baloney!/And kicked the chandelier. Salome. *Anonymous.* WTO

Salt end/of the sea dream's/seder/night. In a Dream Ship's Hold. Suzanne Bernhardt. VWA

A salt foot, too humble to have a voice,/thumps for representation, joy. Clams. Stanley Moss. GP

Salt from my weak moist hand/The strength of my religion   John Landless
Leads the Caravan.   Yvan Goll.   TrJP

Salt on the tongue I feel the smart/Of the blood of the fox that gnaws my
heart.   The Stars Go By.   Lilian Bowes Lyon.   ChMP

Salt'peanuts!/De-dop!   Children's Rhymes.   Langston Hughes.   InPS; PAI

Salt without tears.   Desert River.   Patricia Benton.   GoYe

Salus tua, Domine, sit semper nobiscum./Amen.   Deer's Cry.   Saint Patrick.
OnYI

Salute my garrulous old age, and be/Thine own what now thou honorest in
me.   Of Himself.   Meleager.   AWP

Salute the last, and everlasting day.   Resurrection.   John Donne.   AnAnS
1; OBS

Salute the mystery beyond their ken.   Idols.   Richard Burton.   TrPWD

Salute the stones that keep the limbs that held/so good a mind.   An Epitaph
upon the Right Honorable Sir Philip Sidney.   Fulke, Lord Brooke Greville.
FCP; Prf

Salvation in his grief's confession:/Memento mei.   Prayer to the Crucifix.
Mossen Juan Tallante.   CAW

Salvation is of Christ the Lord.   The Breastplate of St. Patrick.   Frances
Alexander.   OxBI

The salvation of the world lies in a deserted garden–/in a blind worm's crawl.
Blind Steersmen.   Francis Ernest Kobina Parkes.   PBA

Salvation to all that will is nigh.   La Corona.   John Donne.   OBS

The same again but different.   Nuts in May.   Louis MacNeice.   MoAB;
MoBrPo

The same arts that did gain/A power, must it maintain.   An Horatian Ode
upon Cromwell's Return from Ireland.   Andrew Marvell.   AnAnS 1;
EBEV; FaBoPV; FaBoRV; GTBS; GTBS-P; HAP; HBV 1-2; InPS; JCP;
LoBV; MePo; NOBE; NoP; OAEL 1-2; OBEV; OBS; OBWP; PAI; PoEL
1-5; SeCP; SeCV 1-2; ViBoPo

The same as a big wooden god or a brass/Or dough-face god with golden ear-
rings.   Manufactured Gods.   Carl Sandburg.   WGRP

The same as ever and the last as always.   Emeritus, n.   Henri Coulette.   FF

The same as ever to the sight.   The Mill.   Edwin Arlington Robinson.
AmP; CMoP

The same as from the start?   Common Dust.   Georgia Douglas Johnson.
AmNP; PoBA; TTY

Same cicadas.   Haiku: "Once my parents were older."   Chiyo.   BoWoP

The same dear winsome lass.   To a Child of Fancy.   Sir Lewis Morris.
HBV 1-2

The same dream that then flared before intelligence/When light went forth
looking for the eye.   The Painter Dreaming in the Scholar's House.
Howard Nemerov.   PoDr

The same fence we pass through by opening the gate.   Fishing on a Lake at
Night.   Robert Bly.   LCAP

The/same/first/dust   Curtain.   Lance Henson.   VoR

The same gesture as/eased your snowbound/heart and flesh.   The Same
Gesture.   John Montague.   BIrV

The same look which she turned when he rose.   Believe Me, If All Those
Endearing Young Charms.   Thomas Moore.   AnFE; BLPA; CBEP; ELP;
EnRP; FaBoBe; FaBV; FaFP; FPL; FSW; GoTF; HBV 1-2; LiTB; LiTL;
MCCG; OBNC; OBRV; OnYI; PoEL 1-5; PoPl; TEP; TreF; WBLP

Same old names and same old faces; M.P.'s strike for/higher pay.   Rhyming
Prophecy for a New Year.   Leonard Cooper.   FaBoCo

The same's the drones is livin' on the beeses honey.   The Parsons.   Thomas
Edward Brown.   DBV

The same shawl/Wraps them around.   Indian Sky.   Alfred Kreymborg.
BPAW

The same since I was born, the same to be/When all my children's children
grow old men.   A Glimpse.   Frances Cornford.   OBMV

The same, that mocks the memory/With sweet, not sour.   Blackberry Winter.
Peter Huggins.   AMV-81

The same then in our selves we are.   To Her Questioning His Estate.
William Hammond.   JCP

"The same to yourself," says I.   Differences.   Paul Laurence Dunbar.
GoTF; TreFS

Same train be back tomorrer,/Same train, same train.   Same Train.
Anonymous.   BoAN 1-2

The same Village–our Village.   The Village.   Meridel Le Sueur.   GP

The same weed managing/its brood of minute stars/in the cracked flagstone.
Continuum.   Denise Levertov.   LCAP

...Same words/that began love/end it/with changed emphasis.   And the
Same Words.   David Ignatow.   NNaP

The same, yet ever new.   My Beautiful Lady.   Thomas Woolner.   OBVV

A Samson at the mill with slaves.   Edward Millington.   Richard Church.
HaMV

San Sabas, ample as a tree,/Giving his paternal shade.   San Sabas.   Luis
Palés Matos.   CAW

Sanctuary against the malice of the world.   Twenty-One Sonnets.   C. K.
Stead.   OCNZ

Sand earth song sand of the earth afternoon sand earth.   Poem: "Hasten on
your childhood to the hour."   Pablo Picasso.   EAS

Sand I was, and now am dust.   Epitaph: Iohannis Sande.   Thomas Bastard.
FaBoEE

...Sand/Is the beginning and the end/Of our dominion.   Shoreline.   Mary
Barnard.   PoA

The sand smooth because soft.   Little Father Poem.   Marvin Bell.   LCAP

Sand starts to blow.   Tumor.   Lucille Day.   SUW

The sand whispers to developers/money, money, money.   The Development.
Marge Piercy.   NLV

The sanderlings were crying.   The Time I Went to See My Sister.
Tsurayuki.   AWP

"Sandman steal Thee, little One!"   Lullaby: "Dormi, Jesu, mater ridet."
Anonymous.   ISi

The sands are dry, the ocean filled.   The Ocean Spills.   Samuel Hoffenstein.
ALV

Sands of our darkening great ills.   From Venice Was That Afternoon.   Jean
Garrigue.   NOBA

Sands run through the children in their sleep.   Love Poem.   Miller Williams.
MAT

The sands upon the shore, I keep/And name my lovely nights of sleep.   The
Quiet Nights.   Katharine Tynan Hinkson.   HBV 1-2

Sandy bottom, sandy lan'.   Sandy Lan'.   Anonymous.   ABF

Sane men have worshipped stranger Gods than these.   Inscription for Arthur
Rackham's Rip Van Winkle.   James Elroy Flecker.   BrPo

Sang in my veins/That summer day.   The Waking.   Theodore Roethke.
RFM

Sang little Ah Sid, this Chinese kid,/As he played the long summer day.
Little Ah Sid (with music).   Anonymous.   AS

Sang to the light and the kiss of love was peace.   Canticle of Darkness.
Wilfred Watson.   ACV

Sang unmeaning down the stream.   Orpheus.   Yvor Winters.   MoVE;
NOBA; VGW

Sang unnoticed like a bird.   The Three Hermits.   William Butler Yeats.
AtBAP; CMoP

...Sanity/is colorblind.   Colors for Mama.   Barbara Mahone.   CNA; PoBA

Sans duchies of leaves,/Sans baronies of blooms.   Catalpa Tree.   Padraic
Colum.   NePoAm

Sans teeth, sans eyes, sans taste, sans every thing.   As You Like It.   William
Shakespeare.   AWP; BoLiVe; BoNaP; CTC; DiPo; EIL; ELP; FaFP;
FaPoR; FF; FiP; GoTF; GTBS-P; HBV 1-2; HeIP; InPo; InPS; LiTB; MasP;
MCCG; NIP; NOBE; OAEL 1-2; OAEP; OBEV; OBSC; OHIP; PAI; PoEL
1-5; PoLf; PPoe; PrIm; SeCeV; TreF; TrGrPo; ViBoPo; WHA; WiR

Sans Wine, sans Song, sans Singer, and–sans End!   The Rubaiyat of Omar
Khayyam.   Omar Khayyam.   NOBE; OBNC; OxBI; SeCeV; WGRP

––Sap in your mouth/terror/in your member   Conversation between the
Chevalier de Chamilly and Mariana Alcoforado.   The Three (Maria Isabel
Barreno and Maria Teresa Horta and Maria Velho da Costa) Marias.
BoWoP

Sappho was singing.   Sappho Rehung.   LeRoy Smith, Jr.   NePoAm

Sappy and gabby, just like a cadet,/Comes Spring.   Spring.   Vladimir
Mayakovsky.   CAD

Sarapodo no flo ro.   An Island in the Moon.   William Blake.   FaBoNo

A sarcophagus, a crown.   Hoot Owl Shift.   Robert Stricklin.   AMV-80

Sarpedon of the mighty war.   A Dirge for McPherson.   Herman Melville.
AP; PAH; PoEL 1-5

Sashes are chosen.   Haiku: "Plum-viewing..."   (Taniguchi Buso) Buson.
FAZ

Sat the little drummer, fast asleep,/With his rat-tat-too.   The Little Drummer.
Richard Henry Stoddard.   PAH

Sat with you there.   Whither Away?   Mary Elizabeth Coleridge.   CH

Satan exalted sate.   An Afternoon in Artillery Walk.   Leonard Bacon.
AnAmPo

Satan has enough in hell.   For a Mouthy Woman.   Countee Cullen.
OBAL; PoBA; ShM

Satan's deep voice–O thou unhappy God!   What the Devil Said.   James
Stephens.   CMoP

Satan trembles when he sees/Bibles sold as cheap as these.   From a London
Bookshop.   Anonymous.   FaBoUs; NLV

Sate like a beggar upon Heaven's threshold,/Muttering its wrongs.   Death's
Jest Book.   Thomas Lovell Beddoes.   CTC

Sated with thy summer feast,/Thou retir'st to endless rest.   The Grasshopper.
Abraham Cowley.   AWP; EnLi 1-2; FM; HBV 1-2; HBVY; OAEL 1-2;
WiR

Sathan shall nout spede,/With wrenches ne with crok. Amen.   The Devout
Man Prays to His Relations.   William Herebert.   MeEL

Sathan sittes wher our Lord did swaye/Walsingam oh farewell.   In the
Wracks of Walsingham.   Anonymous.   NCEP

Satisfied the way He taketh/Must be always best.   God Knoweth Best.
Anonymous.   WBLP

The Satrap smiles, and on his finger turns/The all-envied emerald.   Amasis.
Laurence Binyon.   OBVV

Saturday no luck at all.   Propitious Days for Weddings.   Anonymous.
FaBoUs

Saturday's light, delicate/membrane still intact. Sadness and Still Life. Bin Ramke. MAYP

Saturday, Sunday, Monday. How Many Days Has My Baby to Play? Mother Goose. OxNR; TiPo

"Saturn, sleep on! while at thy feet I weep." Saturn Fallen. John Keats. AnEnPo; LoBV

The saucy subjects will bear the sway. The Power in the People. Robert Herrick. CaPo

The saups are on the heather and the white birds on the sea! For Summer's Here. Ratcliffe Barnett. PoSH

Sautez, mignonne Cecilia,/Ah! Ah! Cecilia! Cecilia. *Anonymous.* WHW

Sav'd by his Love, incessant we shall sing/Of Angels, and of Angel-Men, the King. Hymn for Christmas Day. John Byrom. NOCV; OBEC; PoEL 1-5; SBVL

Savage and sidelong. The Pine Tree for Diana. Horace. AWP

A savage servility/slides by on grease. For the Union Dead. Robert Lowell. AmPP; CoAP; FaBoPV; FYAP; HaCAP; HAP; HeIP; InPS; LCAP; LiTM; MP; NaP; NMP; NoAm; NOBA; NoP; OBWP; PAI; PPoe; PPP; SCV; TwCP; UnPo

A savage sun consumes its hidden day. Winter Garden. David Gascoyne. ChMP; GTBS-P

Save as it serve the many, mysteriously made One. The Holy Earth: In the Immense Cathedral. John Hall Wheelock. MoRP

Save breed, to brave him when he takes thee hence. Sonnets, XII: "When I do count the clock that tells the time." William Shakespeare. AWP; DiPo; InPo; InPS; OAEL 1-2; TEP

Save doing nothing, to undo a heart. Killing No Murder. Sylvia Townsend Warner. MoBrPo

...Save exactly/as you would wish it done. A Woman Mourned by Daughters. Adrienne Rich. IHMS; NCSH

Save for a quiet unbroken as we stood/Each in his solitude. Birds in the Flax. Stanley Snaith. HaMV

Save for the little rodent cares that make/Me small as they. If Some Grim Tragedy. Ninna May Smith. HBMV

Save for the soft hiss of the rain that falls impartially on/both the sleeping armies. The Dynasts. Thomas Hardy. OAEL 1-2

Save for this trivial/Idiosyncrasy,/Didn't do much. Historical Reflections. John Hollander. DBV; NIP; OBAL

Save he who reigns above, none can resist. Paradise Lost. John Milton. DL

Save her? What for? To act this wedded lie! Modern Love, XXXV. George Meredith. VLP

Save just a dream of amethyst. A Dead Calm and Mist. William Sharp. SyP

Save laughter and the love of friends. They Say, and I am Glad They Say. Hilaire Belloc. ALV

Save, Lord, by Love or Fear. Whitsunday. John Keble. OBRV

Save love, for love is all in all... The Convent Threshold. Christina Georgina Rossetti. LO

Save marks he well what the mystical woods disclose... Melampus. George Meredith. BoC; EnLi 1-2; OBVV; PoEL 1-5; VLP

Save me from the awful blast/and this high tempest out of Hell! A Great Tempest on the Plain of Ler. *Anonymous.* NOBI

"Save me from what,/a flock of sheep?" Dusk Chant. Judith Mountain Leaf Volborth. TWSS

Save of peace alone. To My Brother. Louise Bogan. NYBP

Save, or we perish, Son of God! The Agony in the Garden. Felicia Dorothea Hemans. TrCP

Save, save, oh! save me from the Candid Friend! The Candid Friend. George Canning. GoTF; TreFT

Save the love we have shown to the children of men? Service. Georgia Douglas Johnson. CDC

Save the squadron, honor France, love thy wife the Belle Aurore! Herve Riel. Robert Browning. BeLS; FaBoBe; GN; HBV 1-2; HBVY; MCCG; MOS; OnMSP

Save the Weasel' from "Pop Goes the King.'" Limerick: "There was an Old Person of Tring." *Anonymous.* LiBL; TDH

Save thou a soul, and it shall save thy own! The Two Rabbins. John Greenleaf Whittier. AmePo

Save three wild violets among the grass. Down a Woodland Way. Mildred Howells. AA

Save to the Lampads Seven,/That watch the throne of Heaven! Ne Plus Ultra. Samuel Taylor Coleridge. ERoP 1-2; OAEL 1-2

Save us and send us some drink or we dey! Marvels. *Anonymous.* OxBM

...Save us/by the grace He gave/to the herb,/rosemary. Good Frend. Hilda ("H. D.") Doolittle. NOBA

Save us, Lord, from this second fall when the weary spirit crumbles! Seventh Station. Paul Claudel. CAW

Save us, O Father, Son,/And Spirit, ever one! The Canon for Apocreos. Saint Theodore of Studium. CAW

Save your heart for the deathless brave. Song of the Brave. Laurence Altgood. PAL

Save yourself. Leave me. I must go back. Epigrams and Epitaphs, VI. Clive Staples Lewis. EBEV

Saved from extinction by a puff at the last possible/moment. Nights Passed on Ward's Island, Toronto Harbour. Doug Fetherling. NeAC

Saved the life of the fellow in front. Limerick: "A young engine-driver called Hunt." Victor Gray. NOBL

Saves me from unearned/mysteries. Aunt Melissa. R. T. Smith. Str

A saving grace and its dividends. Suite for Celery and Blind Date (parody). Philip Dow. BXAP

The saving Wisdom that mankind adores!– The Secret. Jose Joaquin Casas. CAW

Savior–I've seen the face–before! A Wife–at Daybreak I Shall Be. Emily Dickinson. AmePo

The Savior of men, he answered, "Why?" Why. Robert Freeman. PGD

Savior, who indeed would never think of saving herself. Modern American Nursing. Lucy Hricz. AMV-80

Saviour, show Thyself to me! Show Me Thyself. Margaret E. Sangster. TrPWD

Saviour, teach us so to rise! Christ Our Example in Suffering. James Montgomery. HBV 1-2

Saviour, Thou who thus hast loved me,/Give me love like this. Few Wholly Faithful. *Anonymous.* BePJ

"Saviour!" with my last parting breath,/I'll cry, "Remember me!" Remember Me! Thomas Haweis. BePJ

Saw a lamb being born! Lamb. Michael Dennis Browne. NU

Saw a long-legged sailor/Kiss his long-legged wife! Hand-Clapping Rhyme. *Anonymous.* NTCP

Saw, and carried the big bird off, a pardon/For no crime, for which there is no name. The Broken One. John Holmes. MiAP

Saw beauty vanished away/And love gone by. The Star. Grace Hazard Conkling. HBMV

Saw him cool from fire to bronze,/to aluminium,/To water,/And vanish. The Alchemist. Richard Church. OxBTC

Saw his bright hand send signals from the suns. Revelation. Edwin Markham. WGRP

Saw how remote were the dead asleep. Majuba Hill. Roy MacNab. PeSA

Saw it grow dark around him, the air fill with death. For Adolf Eichmann. Primo Levi. VWA

Saw now and then how a few last sparks would rise/To their brief ecstasy among the stars. The Fire. Charles G. Bell. MoLP

Saw the great beast fall and lie/With muzzle deep in mire. The Ageing Hunter. Avane. WTO

A saw wails over my head. Root. Miklos Radnoti. VWA

Saw white. Critter. W. M. Ransom. CDW

Saw with his human eyes a wild white maid,/And gazing, died. The White Women. Mary Elizabeth Coleridge. BrRo

Saweste not you mine oxen, you litill pretty boy? The Twelve Oxen. *Anonymous* CH

Sax troop o horsemen they hae beat,/And chased them into Glasgow town. Loudon Hill, or, Drumclog. *Anonymous.* ESPB

Saxifrage is my flower that splits/the rocks. A Sort of a Song. William Carlos Williams. BiP; FAZ; HoPM; NoP; OBSP; PP; SeCeV; TAP

Say, a flippant communication under the moon. The Auroras of Autumn. Wallace Stevens. HaCAP

...Say again/how the cramped world turns, say again. Space Shuttle. Diane Ackerman. MAYP; SUW

Say all, and all, well sayd, still say the same. Astrophel and Stella, XCII. Sir Philip Sidney. AAS; SiPS

Say all the bells about the Throne. Before the Anaesthetic; or, A Real Fright. Sir John Betjeman. EBCP; SeCePo

Say all the sea's grave names, and build/with words this beach that is the world. Adam. Philip Booth. MoLP

Say, are not women truly, then,/Styled but the shadows of us men? The Shadow. Ben Jonson. NOBE; OBEV

(Say, big boy, what did the elephant say to the cat?) Hip Shakin' Strut. Hokum Boys: Georgia Tom. BluL

Say, but my father's a wonderful man! A Wonderful Man. Aileen Fisher. SiSoSe

Say butt won word–"Neigh, let us weight/Until 'tis settled whether." A Tail of the See. Elizabeth T. Corbett. OBCA

Say, "Drat it,' to the parlour-maid,/But never, never "—!' Ponjoo. Walter De La Mare. ShM

Say, Gringo, come an' see the Injuns race/The cowboys, come an' watch me take first place. The Pinto. Owen Wister. BPAW

"Say I am designing St. Paul's." Clerihew. Edmund Clerihew Bentley. FiBHP; NLV; PV

Say, I come to-morrow. Westphalian Song. *Anonymous.* AWP; LiTW; OBVE

Say I'm looking in his eyes/Though my eyes are dim.' An Old Song Ended. Dante Gabriel Rossetti. BoLoP

Say I'm young and strong, but Lord/Gerald kissed me! Another Cynical Variation. Helen". InMe

Say I've had a filthy cold/Since Jenny kiss'd me. Jeny Kiss'd Me When We Met. Paul Dehn. FiBHP

Say, is it possible...to love too much? Male and Female Created He Them. Aldous Huxley. ALV

...Say it again and again, the names are/lying down to sleep together. Praise. William Matthews. AmPA

Say it and speak it loud, United, free... Written in a Time of Crisis. Stephen Vincent Benét. PAL

Say, Jesus Christ of Nazareth–/Hast thou no Arm for me? At Least–To Pray–Is Left–Is Left. Emily Dickinson. AmePo

Say, light proceeding edgewise, like a sword. Gardens No Emblems. Donald Davie. LiTM; NePoEA-2; OAEL 1-2

Say me no villainy/In lands where we go.' Holly and Ivy. Anonymous. CBEP

Say nay! say nay! The Lover's Appeal. Sir Thomas Wyatt. GTBS; GTBS-P

Say naytheless "my heart is hers'/When life and all is past. To His Ring, Given to His Lady. George Turberville. ElL

Say nothing yet./Prepare. It Is the Season. Josephine Jacobsen. TAP

Say "Now" and "Here", and are in our own house. The West. Edwin Muir. MoVE

Say Oliver: "Now is our battle grand." The Song of Roland, XCVII. Anonymous. WaaP

Say only "Eatherly, we have your message." A Song about Major Eatherly. John Wain. CABL; OxBTC

Say proudly yet–"'Twas hers who loved me well!" Properzia Rossi. Felicia Dorothea Hemans. SBG

Say, "Pure, sweet lady, please do give them back." Hendecasyllables, Help! Caius Valerius Catullus. DBV

"Say, Sarge, who the hell was that Clara Bell Lou/we fell out for?" Snapshot. George Garrett. NePoAm-2

Say she doesn't think at all. Love-Songs, At Once Tender and Informative. Samuel Hoffenstein. OBAL

Say, "She was happy." Say, "She knew it." Biography. Jan Struther. InMe

Say, soul,–are songs of Death no heaven to thee,/Nor shames her lip the cheek of Victory? Death's Songsters. Dante Gabriel Rossetti. MaVP

Say that's true now, and I'll believe it then. Her Faith. Hilaire Belloc. GoBC

Say that you do no work/and that you will live forever. Salutation the Second. Ezra Pound. NOBA; OxBA

Say, there's a lamb in the daisies. For a Lamb. Richard Eberhart. CMoP; LiTM; MiAP; OBSP

Say this, and her sweet pity will approve,/And bind yet closer her dead bond of love. Thysia. Morton Luce. HBV 1-2

Say thou instead, "I am not as these are." The House of Life. Dante Gabriel Rossetti. VLP

...Say to him drawn back/like an arrow on a bow Athlete. Don Maynard. PoAu 1-2

Say to Patrick, I wait. Ossian (excerpt). John Francis O'Donnell. IrPN

Say to their pals and wives now: I see by the papers Anna/Held is dead. An Electric Sign Goes Dark. Carl Sandburg. HBMV

Say to what ye have betrayed me. Eyes So Tristful. Diego de Saldana. AWP

Say, wasn't them heroes the sillies? Limerick: "There was a young man named Achilles." Edwin Meade Robinson. HBMV

Say well is good,/Do well is better. Say Well and Do Well. Anonymous. OxNR

Say, what is the gospel/According to you? Your Own Version. Paul Gilbert. BLRP

Say, what was your name in the States? What Was Your Name in The States? (with music). Anonymous. AS

Say, what would many do? To Oenone. Robert Herrick. CaPo; OBEV

Say what you did for me, too, only last Christmas Day. Christmas Day in the Workhouse. George R. Sims. BeLS; BLPA; TreF

Say what you will about a T.V.–/at least it isn't alive. The Day the T.V. Broke. Gerald Jonas. QQQ

Say, who shall welcome thee? The Indian's Welcome to the Pilgrim Fathers. Lydia Huntley Sigourney. AA

Say who you are and where you're going. Advice to Travelers. Walker Gibson. NePoAm-2; NLV; PPJ

Say, wilt thou, my dear?" And she wilted. Old-Fashioned Love. Anonymous. MaC

Say: Wisdom is a silver fish/And Love a golden hook. Go Take the World. Jay Macpherson. OBCV

Say woman. Song of the Fisherman's Lover. Roseann Lloyd. WOLT

Say yes. Be nice. Love. Dick. Letter to Scanlon from Whitehall. Richard Hugo. NNaP

Say Yes, if you please. Sukey, You Shall Be My Wife. Anonymous. OxNR

Say you'll be mine forever:/I love you. The Story of the Rose. Alice". FSN

Saying as the earth says after rain/this one is on me. The Anniversary. Roberta Spear. MAYP

Saying blackberry, blackberry, blackberry. Meditation at Lagunitas. Robert Hass. MAYP; NoP; NPGG

Saying, "Come on, Blue, finally got here too." Old Blue. Anonymous. GDP; OuSiCo; SD

Saying Dear child, and all time has disproved. Faith Healing. Philip Larkin. NoAm

Saying forever to the spirit, "Sigh!" La Vita Nuova. Dante Alighieri. AWP

Saying, "Give your heart to Jesus,/For He's comming, coming soon!" Christmas Bells. Alice Mortenson. BePJ

Saying, "Go down, you murderer, go down." Go Down You Murderers. Ewan MacColl. FSW

Saying goodbye/to himself Vision song (cheyenne). Lance Henson. STE

Saying: "He's late–he's late." Wishes for William. Winifred M. Letts. OnYI

Saying, "Here is the prize that you have won." Lady of Carlisle. Anonymous. AmFP; FSW; OuSiCo

Saying, "Here lies the body of Georgie.'" Geordie (Georgie). Anonymous. AmFP

Saying "I wish, Willie Brennan, in your cradle you had died." Brennan on the Moor. Anonymous. BaBo; FaBoBa; ViBoFo

Saying, "If ever our daughter gets wed,/It will help to enlarge her portion." The Crafty Farmer. Anonymous. BaBo; ESPB

Saying, "If I had staid there seven years longer,/No girl but you could have married me." The Love Token. Anonymous. BaBo

Saying, "Is this my little single soldier,/Returning home to marry me?" A Sweetheart in the Army (B vers.). Anonymous. BaBo

Saying, "Leave this as a dreadful token/To those that keep me and Julie apart." The Silver Dagger. Anonymous. AmFP

Saying–Man is distant, but God is near! Afar in the Desert. Thomas Pringle. HBV 1-2

Saying "Oh my son my son" La Llorona. Greg Pape. AmPA

Saying, Out upon you, fie/upon you,/Bold faced jig! Ungrateful Jenny. Anonymous. OxNR

Saying, "See, I am your own true cowboy,/Who has seven long years been gone from thee." The Cowboy's Return. Anonymous. BFSS

Saying she had buried somebody/into the earth with her red/hands. In Missing. Ray A. Young Bear. CDW

Saying something for us. And Now Farley Is Going to Sing While I Drink a Glass of Water! Albert Goldbarth. GeTw

Saying the black man living with the white/Had given more than white men could requite. Upstairs Downstairs. Hervey Allen. HBMV; PoA; PoNe

Saying: "The red rose of England shall flourish no more!" Jane Was a Neighbor. Anonymous. BaBo

Saying, "The Stars are beautiful tonight!" Star-Fear. Leonora Speyer. AnEnPo

Saying, "There goes an unfortunate lad to his home.'" Young Man Cut Down in His Prime. Anonymous. FSW

Saying, "There Mary died, once the gay village bride,/From the winds that blew across the wild moor .Mary of the Wild Moor. Anonymous. BaBo; BFSS

Saying, this is the moment,/Here, now. Green Apples. Ruth Stone. InPS

Saying, "This tastes so good!" or, "This smells so sweet!" Old Men and Old Women Going Home on the Street Car. Merrill Moore. MoAmPo

Saying, "Thou art mine ain, I have/bought thee dear,/An we will wauk the wuds our lane." Erlinton (B version). Anonymous. ESPB

Saying through the scary opposites to death. Viable. Archie Randolph Ammons. TAP

Saying to her too, "Ease and peace thou art." Sonnet: Death Is Not without but within Him. Cino da Pistoia. AWP

Saying, "To the Lord be all honour and praise/For his defence both now and always!" A Prayer to Be Said When Thou Goest to Bed. Francis Seager. OxBChV

Saying we cannot waste time/only ourselves. Movement Song. Audre Lorde. CNA

Saying, "When next you want a beating,/Write "No Irish need apply.'" No Irish Need Apply. Anonymous. FSW

Saying, "Would our son but rise again,/We would send for Betsy over the main." The Betrayed Maiden. Anonymous. OBET

Saying, "You write to your sweetheart and I'll write to mine." Green Grow the Lilacs. Anonymous. BFSS

Says Advertising Mr. Hyde. The Double Standard. Franklin Pierce ("F.P.A.") Adams. OBAL

Says de day is done. A Corn-Song. Paul Laurence Dunbar. AA

Says far more than I am saying. The Penny Whistle. Edward ("Edward Eastaway") Thomas. MoAB; MoBrPo

Says, "Good -by, honey," that's all. My Lulu (with music). Anonymous. AS

Says Greedy-gut,/Let's sup before we go. Come, Let's to Bed. Anonymous. GBP; OxBoLi

The scrimmage of appetite everywhere. The Repetitive Heart. Delmore Schwartz. MoVE

The script not altered by a breath/Of perhaps meaning otherwise? The Wind, the Clock, the We. Laura Riding. LiTA

(Scripture seith thus)/Nunc natus est Altissimus. Now the Most High Is Born. James Ryman. MeEL

Scriv'ners and clarks, and lawyers and atturneys. Orlando Furioso. Lodovico Ariosto. OBVE

A scroll of crystal, blazoning the name/Of Adonais! On Keats Who Desired That On His Tomb Should Be Inscribed–. Percy Bysshe Shelley. FaBoEE

...Scroppo's dog forlornly/yodels in time to the village siren sounding noon. Scroppo's Dog. May Swenson. GDP

Scrubbed/Them as you smiled and I lowered my eyes from despair. Far from Africa. Margaret Danner. AmNP; NNP; PoBA

A scullion fleeing with a bloody knife. Marlowe. Arthur Bayldon. PoAu 1-2

The sculpture of these granite seams/Upon a woman's face. Erosion. Edwin John Pratt. CaP; CoBE

Scurrying back to realities and glories on the wane As I Look Out. Laura St. Martin. FF

...Se if you can find/the one flea which is laughing. The Book of Nightmares. Galway Kinnell. NNaP

...The sea/Across daubed rock evacuates its dead. Requiem for the Plantagenet Kings. Geoffrey Hill. NoAm

The sea-beat scorns the minster clock/And breaks the glass of Time. Nahant. Ralph Waldo Emerson. AmPP

The sea beneath my feet. The Cliff-Top. Robert Bridges. BoNaP

Sea-birds' shelter, our shelter and ark. Ireland. Francis Stuart. NeIP

Sea-born and wind-wayward/Child of the sun. Song: "Love, by that loosened hair." Bliss Carman. HBV 1-2

A sea breathes in and out/upon a shore. Until I Saw the Sea. Lilian Moore. NTCP

The sea creaked with worked vessels. Of Commerce and Society. Geoffrey Hill. PPoe

Sea-dead, having died so without even hate. Prey to Prey. David Rowbotham. CBAP

The sea decent again behind walls. Of Commerce and Society. Geoffrey Hill. PPoe

...The sea, desperate,/will proffer wave after wave. Cootchie. Elizabeth Bishop. FaBoWP; NIP

The sea grows old in it. The Fish. Marianne Moore. AnFE; APA; FaBoWP; MoAB; MoAmPo; MOS; MoVE; NoAm; OxBA

(The sea hath no King but God alone.) The White Ship. Dante Gabriel Rossetti. OBNV; VLP

The sea is breeding night. Sea Island Miscellany. Richard P. Blackmur. MoVE

The sea is/fat. Waking from a Nap on the Beach. May Swenson. NTCP; PCP; RFM

The sea is His; He made it. Enoch Arden (excerpt). Alfred, Lord Tennyson. TRV

The sea is lulled to rest, flowers cover the earth. The Ossianic Cycle: The Song of Finn. Anonymous. OnYI

The sea is no sea. Loved/Without lover is not all. Islands. Ralph Pomeroy. CoPo

The sea is steadfast in its laws–/time too, as it crumbles. I Am Like a Book. David Rokeah. VWA

The sea; its pearls, seeds, children. Diving for Pearls. Traise Yamamoto. BrSi

The sea must know more than any of us. The Sea Hold. Carl Sandburg. MOS

Sea-parted, share/This quickening fear. Islands: A Song. John Malcolm Brinnin. AnFE

The sea-rocks dolphin-dark the green wave frays. Headland. Brewster Ghiselin. PoA

The sea's in flood! The Sea. Anonymous. KiLC

The sea ship sinking and the waves were dashing,/They were both drowned in the deep. The Bramble Briar. Anonymous. BFSS

The sea sparkles with the sperm/Of his rejected light. Resurrection. Robert Pack. NePoEA-2

The sea that fled this hovering vengeance. Horned Lizard. Charles Molesworth. GrPl

The sea that soon should drown them all,/That never yet drowned me. Our Bog Is Dood. Stevie Smith. FaBoNo; NLV; WeW

The sea, the gulls, the narrow land. Provincetown, Mass. Harvey Shapiro. PoA

Sea Thetis bore may hear its dirge of the sea. Epitaph on Achilles. Anonymous. AWP

The sea unfurled and what was blue raced silver. The Return. John Peale Bishop. LiTA; MoPo; MoVE; OxBA; WaP

The sea unrolls and rolls itself into the low room. Fiascherino. Charles Tomlinson. NoAm

...The sea, unstained,/Haunts what it cannot fill. Urban History. Chester Kallman. CrMA

The sea-wash repeats, repeats. Sea-Wash. Carl Sandburg. BrR; OBCA

A sea-wave full of sand and sound and foam. Tears of the World. King of Seville, Mu'tamid. AWP

The sea whisper'd me. Out of the Cradle Endlessly Rocking. Walt Whitman. AA; AP; APA; AWP; DiPo; ExPo; ForPo; GoTF; HAP; HeIP; InPo; MAmP; MoAmPo; NAWM 1-2; NePA; NOBA; NoP; OxBA; PB; PoEL 1-5; PPoe; PrIm; SeCeV; TAP; TreFS; ViBoPo; WeW; WHA

The sea will carry us where tides run and currents flow. The Fall. Kathleen Raine. MoPo

"Sea-Woman–slim-fingered-water-thing..." Appoggiatura. Donald Jeffrey Hayes. AmNP; PoBA; PoNe

The sea worth living for. Winter Mask. Allen Tate. AmLP; NePA; OxBA; Prf

The sea you saw/Is not the same sea/You see. The Sea. Ken Noyle. MOS

Sea, you shadow of all things, now mock us to death with/your shadowing. The Sea. D.H. Lawrence. BoNaP; MOS; NAMP

The seal of your mind borrowed and not returned. Scroll-Section. Robert Finch. PeCV

The seal's wide spindrift gaze toward paradise. Voyages. Hart Crane. AmLP; CoBMV; DTC; ExPo; ForPo; HAP; LiTM; MoAB; MoAmPo; MoPo; NAMP; NePA; NU; PPP; UnPo; VGW; ViBoPo

...Sealed thick and tight and safe/with paint and piss and lemonade. The Painters. Judith Hemschemeyer. Psk

Sealed up till on some doomsday morrow/The sun arise! The Sleepers. Frederick William Harvey. MMM

The sealing unction from above/The breath of life, the fire of love. Come Holy Spirit, Dove Divine. Adoniram Judson. AH

The seals/Have the best deals? A Question. William Cole. BoAnP

Seals of love, but sealed in vain, sealed in vain. Measure for Measure. William Shakespeare. AWP; BiP; BoLiVe; DiPo; EBEV; ElL; ELP; EnLoPo; ExPo; Fip; ForPo; GBL; GTBS; HBV 1-2; HeIP; InPS; LiTB; LiTL; MCCG; OAEL 1-2; OAEP; OBEV; OBSC; PAI; SeCeV; TrGrPo; ViBoPo; WHA

Seals with thy mouth his immortality. Love's Lovers. Dante Gabriel Rossetti. MaVP

A seaman's body! There'll be more tonight! The Winter Storm at Sea. George Crabbe. EtS

Seamews and curlews/In a brisk brine? Voyage. Josephine Miles. LiTM

Search/and find. Evening in a Lab. Miroslav Holub. SUW

Search for one doubt, and whisper: "Truly, we are not dead." Jews at Haifa. Randall Jarrell. MoAmPo

...Searching a place/in my arm. The Planting. Harley Elliott. NeAC

Searching for something she's hidden there. House. Diana O Hehir. NPGG

Searching for the current/before heading upstream. Feeling the Quiet Strike. James Minor. WOLT

...Searching/for what's missing/in both of us. Girl. A. W. Purdy. NoAm

...Searching/in stillness for jewels of sight. At the Smithsonian. Vanessa Haley. AMV-81

Searching its fault for your secret. Fan. Walter Lew. BrSi

Searching out our time from his heathen place Monkshood XXIII. Kristjana Gunnars. CaPN

Searching, searching something/That had been lost... The Mad Lover. Speer Strahan. CAW

Searching the darkness for a landing place. Downstream. Thomas Kinsella. FaBoIP

Seas gliding with swans/In the seal-barking moon. A Conversation. Dylan Thomas. RFM

The seas shine, and anigh/Flashes above the sunny reef some snowy wing. Song: "My dreams were doleful and drear." Thomas Caulfield Irwin. IrPN

Seas suck at the shore's breast/With rhythmic sound. Far in the West. Douglas Fraser. PoSH

Seasick, I drop into the sea. The Demon Lover. Adrienne Rich. IHMS

Season'd with sage and onions, and port wine. To a Goose. Robert Southey. BXAP; FM; NOBL

The season drowns me. Midwestern Man. Paul Giandi. AMV-81

Season of ice–these are my tidings. Summer is Gone. Anonymous. FaBoCh; LoGBV; OnYI

Season of sudden storms and brilliant suns. Autumn Change. John Clare. VLP

The season's right/The distance slight/Upon the Road of Anthracite. The D.L. and W.'s Phoebe Snow. Anonymous. TreF

The seasons hammer. I no more remember. Apoem I. Henri Pichette. LiTW

The seat beside me is empty.' I, Pluto. Tilottama Daswani. ACV

The seat of bliss, and last retreat of man. Western Emigration. David Humphreys. AnAmPo

Seated alone and in peace till God bids it arise. Wisdom. Christina Georgina Rossetti. OBVV

Seated beside me, like an obedient child? Interior. Joseph Milbauer. VWA

Second Avenue or any other/blueprint of the future. Where I Hang My Hat. Dick Gallup. APU

The second best's a gay goodnight and quickly turn away. Oedipus at Colonus. William Butler Yeats. OBMV

The second bounding snow. A Mill. William Allingham. FaBoEE; IrPN; NBM; OBSP; PoL; SeCePo

Second came she whom he begot us by. Lilith. X. J. Kennedy. UnTE

A second century not half-way run/Since the new honours of her blood begun. The Hind and the Panther. John Dryden. OBS

A second crop thine acres yield,/Which I gather in a song. The Apology. Ralph Waldo Emerson. AmePo; AP

"The Second Evening and the Fourteenth Psalm." Sunday Afternoon Service in St. Enodoc Church, Cornwall. Sir John Betjeman. MoVE; NOCV

The second glory of the Heavens?–Thou hast. Address to My Infant Daughter. William Wordsworth. EvOK; Par

Second growth and second growth. An Old Field Mowed. William Meredith. NYBP

Second in order of felicity/I hold it, to have walk'd with such a soul. Epigram: "'Tis human fortune's happiest height." William Watson. GoTF

The second lesson was long. Music. Naomi Shihab Nye. Str

The second Love, she is so like to me. La Vita Nuova. Dante Alighieri. AWP

The second thing they say when they sit down/Is "Madam, your Johnny cake is baking brown." Kansas Boys. *Anonymous.* AS

The secret anniversaries of the heart. Holidays. Henry Wadsworth Longfellow. PoToHe

A secret chord that mine will bear. Trembling Before Thine Awful Throne. Augustus Lucas Hillhouse. AH

The secret each alone must learn. The Poet's Secret. Elizabeth Stoddard. AA

Secret fates guide our states,/Both in mirth and mourning. What If a Day. Thomas Campion. AAS; BiP; EBEV; ElL; EnRePo; PrIm

Secret imperfections/kept virginal for a lover? Blackheads. Knute Skinner. GP

A secret, kept from all the rest,/Between yourself and me. She's All My Fancy Painted Him. Lewis (Charles Lutwidge Dodgson) Carroll. ALV; CenHV; FaBoNo; LiTL; NA

A secret!/Know this. Manifesto of the Soldier Who Went Back to War. Angel M. Queremel. WaaP

The secret lords, whom only death can change. Lovers Relentlessly. Stanley Jasspon Kunitz. UnTE

The secret of an ordered peace/Is in the rule Christ taught. Peace Is the Tranquillity of Order. Robert Wilberforce. GoBC

The secret of flight is hidden from those who fly. Becoming Is Perfection. Tom Johnson. AMV-81

The secret of Heather Ale. Heather Ale. Robert Louis Stevenson. AnEnPo

The secret of poetry is cruelty. The Secret of Poetry. Jon Anderson. MAYP

The secret of secrets is inside me again. A Land Not Mine. Anna Akhmatova. NU

The secret's out. Squeal. Heather McHugh. GeTw

The secret that had wrought the spell. The Waiting Chords. Stephen Henry Thayer. AA

The secret this of Rest below. We Need Not Bid, for Cloistered Cell. John Keble. HBV 1-2

The secret worth/Of all our human worthlessness. Homage to Theodore Dreiser on the Centennial of His Birth (excerpt). Robert Penn Warren. GP

Secretly bathed the world, that now flows out of flesh. The Pomegranate. Louis Dudek. OBCV; PeCV

Secretly I am envious of everyone,/And with everyone secretly in love. A Reed. Osip Mandelstam. VWA

Secur'd from Conquest by Captivity. The Bracelet. Thomas Stanley. AnAnS 2

Secure from violent and harmful fates. To Mars. George Chapman. LoBV

Secure in dullness, madness, want, and age. On Dennis. Alexander Pope. FaBoEE

...Secure that God/Will come in thunder from the stars to save her. Andromeda. Robert Browning. OBRV

Securely shall my ashes lie,/And wait the summons from on high. Asleep in Jesus. Margaret Mackprang MacKay. BePJ

Securer lives the silly swain! Fortunati Nimium. Thomas Campion. GTBS

Securing Wall Street/against the striking students. The Workers Rose on May Day or Postscript to Karl Marx. Audre Lorde. GP

...Sed hunc Corn-greivus heros/Nout-headdum vocavit, et illum forcit ad arma. Polemo-Middinia (excerpt). *Anonymous.* OxBS

Sed miles, sed pro patria.' Clifton Chapel. Sir Henry Newbolt. OBEV; OBVV

See a man who so loves you as your fond S. T. COLERIDGE Lesson for a Boy. Samuel Taylor Coleridge. FaBoUs

...See a/ripple-topped stream in its best suit, in the ground. Mi Abuelo. Alberto Rios. MAYP

See, above the starry clime/God a great reward preparing. Ode to Joy. Friedrich von Schiller. LiTW

See all! say nought! hold thee content! Look or You Leap. Jasper Heywood. ElL

See all, say nought, hold thee content. The Lookers-On. Jasper Heywood. ACP

See by the loch-side ye come to the Bothie of Tober-na-/vuolich. The Bothie of Tober-Na-Vuolich. Arthur Hugh Clough. FaBoPV

See Cromwell damned to everlasting fame! An Essay on Man. Alexander Pope. ViBoPo

See Fire itself in ice beshrouded,/And Ice in joy ablaze! Christmas Carol. Sister Francisca Josefa del Castillo. CAW

See from it what a world may still be wrought! The Dead Water. Wen I-to. LiTW

See God's own radiance in a tranquil star. Sonnets: A Sequence on Profane Love. George Henry Boker. AmePo

See! He is hushed in sweet repose! Babyhood. Josiah Gilbert Holland AA

See, hear, and am silent. Leaves of Grass. Walt Whitman. TRV

"See here. See here. See here." Tribute to Kafka for Someone Taken. Alan Dugan. CAPP; NoAm; WeW

...See him raise his/arms to the sun, hear him say/"Thank you father"/...again Can I Say. Dolly Bird. WPOW

See His face, and sing His praise! A Cradle Hymn. Isaac Watts. HBV 1-2; OBEV; OxBChV; TreFS

See his mane! The Cock Again. *Anonymous.* SoPo

See, how gorgeous the world is/Outside the door! Spring Morning. D. H. Lawrence. BrPo; CMoP; MoAB; MoBrPo

See how He watches? He snatches the bad ones. Fraulein Reads Instructive Rhymes. Maxine W. Kumin. NYBP; Psk; SpRo

...See how it will fit/so sweetly, sweetly in the infant's glove. Man with One Small Hand. P. K. Page. OBCV

"See how our works endure!" Cities and Thrones and Powers. Rudyard Kipling. GoJo; MoVE; NOBE; OBNC; OxBTC; PoEL 1-5; SeCeV; VLP

'See how she's cock her head!' The Axe-Helve. Robert Frost. CABL; OxBA

See how she tosses/the mutton, mutton bone. Puss in the Pantry. *Anonymous.* OxNR

See how the East flames up,/An eternal candle. Celan. Asya (Asya Gray). VWA

See how the lily grows! Consider the Lilies. William Channing Gannett. WGRP

See how you wrote it once in sand/And soon no trace of it remains. The Lamp Now Flickers. Alfred Grunewald. VWA

See if you can apply this/To your history lessons. A Bestiary. Kenneth Rexroth. OBAL

See it at the Eastwood Theatre, friends,/next time 1930 rolls around. This One's on Me. Phyllis Gotlieb. NOBC

...See it lie/Apart–a cold moon, barren entity. The Fault. Edward Lucie-Smith. NePoEA-2

See, it smiles as it is sleeping/Mocking your untimely weeping. Dirge for the Year. Percy Bysshe Shelley. GN

See, my hand fits it like a glove. The Flesh-Scraper. Andrew Young. ELU

See my ship come sailin' home. Standin' on the Walls of Zion (with music). *Anonymous.* AS

See, now, man gazes into the outer deeps. Stonefish and Starfish. John Blight. BoAV

See! Shining still the sweet star's holy fires. Oh, Day of Days. Leroy V. Brant. AH

...See that he is living somewhere in the middle/of the twentieth century, and leave him there. Five Ways to Kill a Man. Edwin Brock. DL

See the boss man comin' down the line. Hammer Man (with music). *Anonymous.* AS

...See the clouds/become deeper as they pass the rise. Rolling Thunder. Phyllis Wolf. STE

See the drivers roll. Jay Gould's Daughter. *Anonymous.* FSW

See, the fire's by: Farewell. To His Book. Robert Herrick. CaPo

See, the lark quivers! May. Edward Hovell-Thurlow. HBV 1-2; OBEV

See the lean tree of their arms/spread/out and could hear each color they/said. Division. John Ratti. NYBP

See the north-south horizon parting like a string. Lent in a Year of War. Thomas Merton. EAS

See, the old rustic porch, with its roses so sweet,/Lies scatter'd and fallen to the ground. Ben Bolt. *Anonymous.* PSoN

See the plum redden, and the beurre stoop. Gardener. Ralph Waldo Emerson. OxBA

"See the pretty shooting star!" If This Little World Tonight. Oliver Herford. ShM

See the real magician's hammer. An Arctic Vision. Bret (Francis Bret Harte) Harte. MC; PAH

See the stubble turn gold and the wormwood bear roses/of song? Nonsense. Robert Haven Schauffler. HBMV

See Thee truly as Thou art! Nothing Fair on Earth I See. Angelus Selesius (Johannes Scheffler). BePJ

See! there is lifted the hand of a baby—Marthy Virginia's/hand! Marthy Virginia's Hand. George Parsons Lathrop. MC; PAH

See to it, then, that all your seed/Be such as bring forth noble deed. Influence. John Oxenham. STF

See Us, and Clouds below. The Motto. Abraham Cowley. AnAnS 2; SeCePo

See what careless love has done. Careless Love. Anonymous. UnPo

See what they chiseled: "Contessa Navigato/Implora eterna quiete." Dora Williams. Edgar Lee Masters. HAP

...See–what thirst/We have we can quench from the sky. The Water Tower. James Paul. AMV-81

...See/what you see. How to See Deer. Philip Booth. Psk

"See what your greed for money has done." The 1913 Massacre. Woody Guthrie. FSW

See, when you have stopped, that the journey is/completed. Baedeker for Metaphysicians. Brian Higgins. FaBoTw

See where they blur, and die, and are outsoared. Camping Out. William Empson. CMoP; FaBoMo; MoVE; OxBTC

See: with the voice of my past and the face of my soul. The Future. Vahan Tekeyan. AMV-81

See, with what proud hearts we advance/To France! The Road to France. Daniel Henderson. HBV 1-2; MC; PAH

See you in London: there's a lot to do. To Pete Atkin: A Letter from Paris (excerpt). Clive James. OBSV

See you in nineteen and forty-fo'. Mississippi Blues. Anonymous. AmFP

See you not where my red heart's blood/Runs trickling down my knee? Young Johnstone (A version). Anonymous. ESPB

See you soon. love, fay 1/17/78. A Letter to Peter. Fay Chiang. BrSi

See you sweep clean. Welcome to the New Year. Eleanor Farjeon. YeAr

Seed dazzled over the footbattered blaze of the earth. Vapor Trail Reflected in the Frog Pond. Galway Kinnell. CAPP; NoP; OBWP; VGW

Seed falls there now, birds build, and life takes over. The Builders. Judith Wright. SeCePo

Seed, leaf, flower, fruit, herb, bee, and tree, and more, then I may sing. The Garden. Nicholas Grimald. OAEL 1-2

The Seed o' the woman bruise the serpent's head. For the Holy Family by Michelangelo. Dante Gabriel Rossetti. GoBC

A seed patient as time. Last Letter to Pablo. Pat Lowther. NOBC

Seed pods wait/With their sealed order. A Warm Winter Day. Julian Cooper. BoNaP

The seed within the husk. The Blue Gift. David Perkins. NCSH

Seeds are falling everywhere. Rorschach. Laura Fargas. SUW

The seeds of life and everlasting good. Trust and Obedience. Anonymous. BLRP

The seeds of Spring lie swelling in their soaking house. February. D. S. Savage. NeBP

(Seeing, at last, she could never know why)/And never could understand! The Vampire. Rudyard Kipling. BLPA; BLPL; EnLit; HBV 1-2; NOBV

Seeing death/in their eyes/when they smirk/at you/as you/pass. Slow Drivers. Gerald William Barrax. AmC

Seeing, feeling and hearing the things which are hidden. Red Cross Nurses. Gervase Stewart. WaP

Seeing in the firelight the brightness of snow. The Fire in the Snow. Vernon Watkins. LiTM; MoVE

...Seeing/just ahead the tall grasses/part. Auguries for Three Women. Jacquelyne Crews. AMV-81

Seeing me in my wish, free from self-wrongs. Prothalamion. Delmore Schwartz. OxBA

Seeing more harmony/In her bright eye,/Than now you hear. Orpheus to Beasts. Richard Lovelace. CaPo

Seeing that death, a necessary end,/Will come when it will come. Julius Caesar. William Shakespeare. FF

Seeing that thou, beloved, art so sweet! Che Sara Sara. Vicor Plarr. HBV 1-2

Seeing that true love walked beside her/All of the way, all of the way. The Road's End. Theodosia Garrison. HBMV

Seeing the full moon/loaded on an ox cart. Starlight Scope Myopia. Yusef Komunyakaa. MAYP

Seeing the lake through the small doorway... Seven Dreams. John Bayliss. EAS

Seeing the world outside with eyes that shun/The greater glasshouse round his smaller one. Brother Ass. Eric Irvin. BoAV

Seeing this season of the world's despair. Wet Summer: Botanic Gardens. Nan McDonald. BoAV

Seeing we were your servants to this last. Epitaphs of the War, 1914-18. Rudyard Kipling. BrPo; OBWP

Seek God, my soul–God shall thy/portion be! Time-Servers. Judah Halevi. TrJP

Seek in all things that you can/To be a little gentleman. The Little Gentleman. Anonymous. HBV 1-2; HBVY

...Seek/No happier state, and know to know no more. Their Wedded Love. John Milton. SeCePo

"Seek, nor abandon yet your quest, the way/Still upward goes–in content still the same." A'Chuilionn. A. G. Hutchison. PoSH

Seek not for him,–he is with thee. Thoreau's Flute. Louisa May Alcott. AA; HBV 1-2

Seek out the lives/with a rifle/for a bulldozer?/to the death? Dangerous Condition: Sign on Inner-City House. Russell Atkins. CNA

Seeking a loveliness she scarcely knows,/Whose meaning is beyond the reach of Time. After the War. Richard Le Gallienne. MC; PAH

Seeking the long-lost children of his God. Marquette on the Shores of the Mississippi. John Jerome Rooney. CAW

Seeking the shores forever. I Stand as on Some Mighty Eagle's Beak. Walt Whitman. RFM

Seeking the thing no man has ever found. Sonnets from a Sequence. Shirley Barker. AnAmPo

Seeking their way to love once more. Shelley's Arethusa Set to New Measures. Robert Duncan. CMoP

Seeks God, although an Atheist. Perfection. Francis Carlin. FaFP; HBMV

Seeks investment anyhow,/Anywhere. The Peau de Chagrin of State Street. Oliver Wendell Holmes. AP

Seem'd that which fell along your flow'ry ways. With you first shown to me. William Barnes. EnLoPo

Seem'd to have brought the Gold-smiths World againe. Song II: "It Autumne was, and on our Hemispheare." William, of Hawthornden Drummond. OBS

Seem like a golden court-way of the Sun! Quatorzain. Henry Timrod. AA

Seem then a golden court-way of the Sun! Sonnet: "Most men know love but as a part of life." Henry Timrod. HBV 1-2

Seem with their quiet to have stilled in/life's dream/All sorrowing now. The Ghost. Walter De La Mare. OAEP

Seemed almost a personal loss. When Daddy Died. Duane Ackerson. PoL

Seemed as I dreamed the only things/That had ever stirred. Supper. Walter De La Mare. NYBP

Seemed like the right time/to disappear. A Trip to Four or Five Towns. John Logan. AmPC; CoAP; ConAP; NNaP

Seemed to lead me brightly,/Toward the throne of God. M-Y T-E-M-P-E-R. Anonymous. STF

The seeming-desperate task whence our new/nation rose. The New-Come Chief. James Russell Lowell. PAH

Seems a fleeting sunbeam's gift, whose peace/The sufferance only of a breath of air!' The Excursion. William Wordsworth. EnRP

Seems ever with us whispering love and truth. Fragment: "Some pretty face remembered in our youth." John Clare. VLP

Seems of a brighter world than ours. March. William Cullen Bryant. GN

Seems the music made when God's own hands His mighty/harpstrings sweep. Music of the Dawn. Virginia Bioren Harrison. HBV 1-2

Seems yon low lily-vale of peace and rest! Two Points of View. Lucian B. Watkins. BANP

Seen and unheard-of constellations wheel. Refugees. Louis MacNeice. LiTB; WaP

...Seen/dawn arrive in gold, there along the crest,/the way it does for us. Ducks down in the Meadow. William Stafford. NPAW

Seen love make bright our yearning faces. A Conjecture. Charles Francis Richardson. AA

...Seep/slow pain on our joy and stain our sleep. Juncture. Rea Lubar Duncan. PoNe

Sees also from a height/Some secret goal. Once in an Ancient Book. Marya Zaturenska. GP

Sees dark birds pass, then us,/and is himself again, staring, blessed. The Collector of the Sun. Dave Smith. SM

Sees far below the steadfast lands. On the Heights. Lucius Harwood Foote. AA

Sees his foule inside through his whited skin. Tetrachordon (excerpt). John Milton. NCEP

Sees the grave and is silent and restrains himself within his heavens. The World Is Not a Fenced-Off Garden. Jakov Steinberg. VWA

Sees through the untuneful bough the wingless skies? Winged Hours. Dante Gabriel Rossetti. MaVP

A segment of Eternity! I Am Still Rich. Thomas Curtis Clark. PoToHe

Seigneur, again we/resurrect and the judges come. Domaine Public. Geoffrey Hill. OxBC

...Seize at once/The roving thought, and fix it on themselves. The Task. William Cowper. EnRP

Seize me ere I die! I am the Life of Life. The Testament of Beauty. Robert Bridges. MoVE

Seize our tongues, and strike us dumb! Invocation of Silence. Richard Flecknoe. OBSP

Seize this maid, and strike her dumb. Silence Invoked. Richard Flecknoe. GoBC

Seized by the boy, falling upwards to some height above the earth. Falling Upwards. David Shapiro. AMV-81

Seizes the prey with more voracious bite,/To satisfy his hungry appetite? The Wounded Man and the Swarm of Flies. William Somervile. FM

Seizing my forelock...it was gone. Poems, CXL: "The burden of an ancient rhyme." Walter Savage Landor. PG

Seldom it comes, to few from heaven sent,/That much in little, all in naught– Content. Risposta. John Wilbye. HBV 1-2

Seldom would trees have anything to wear! The Leaf-Makers. Harold Stewart. PoAu 1-2

Selects his Single, and stands out to sea. In and Out: Severance of Connections, 1946. L. E. Sissman. TwCP

The self is never lost. Coming Home. Rolfe Humphries. MoRP

Self-love is not a fault of Joe's. Epigram. *Anonymous.* ALV

A self outside himself, and again a man,/Spent and cleansed in a chaos not his own. The Diver. Ben Howard. SM

Self-proclaimed poets who, to wow an/audience, utter some resonant lie. Ode to Terminus. W. H. Auden. HAP

Self's the long exile we appear to choose. The Documentary on Brazil. Alfred Corn. MAYP

The self's unnameable and shaping home. The Cavern. Charles Tomlinson. CMoP; NMP

The self same doctrin of the Sacred Page/Convey'd to ev'ry clime, in ev'ry age. The Hind and the Panther. John Dryden. OBS

The self-same power in yonder sunset glows/That kindled in the words of Holy Writ. Immanence. Richard Hovey. TRV; WGRP

The self-same Power that brought me/there brought you. The Rhodora. Ralph Waldo Emerson AA; AnNE; AP; APA; AWP; BoNaP; FaBV; FaFP; GN; HBV 1-2; HBVY; HeIP; InPo; LiTA; MAmP; MCCG; NOBA; NoP; OHFP; OxBA; SeCeV; TAP; TreFS; TrGrPo; TRV; WHA

The self-same thing will be. King William the Third to Himself. *Anonymous.* FaBoEE

Self-singing, solid, megalithic poem. Stonetalk. Jacques Hamelin. AMV-80

...The self/sought for the purpose that had brought it there. Selah. R. S. Thomas. FaBoMo

Self-sufficing as gods, never heeding the woe of the/maiden. The Nereids. Charles Kingsley. NBM

Selfless,/that pearl-of-great-price. There Is a Spell, for Instance. Hilda ("H. D.") Doolittle. MoPo

The selfsame breath can blow it out. A Breath. Mary Ainge De Vere. AA

Sell in May/And go away. Stock Exchange Wisdom. *Anonymous.* FaBoUs

Sell your eggs, and buy shoes. Hen and Cock. *Anonymous.* GBP

Selling of pigs' tails. Johnny Morgan. *Anonymous.* OxNR

Selling the feathers a penny a piece. Snow, Snow Faster. *Anonymous.* PBBP

Semper in coelestibus,/Ecce lignum crucis! A Rime of the Rood. Charles L. O'Donnell. GoBC

Sen scho is deid, I speik of hir no moir. The Testament of Cresseid. Robert Henryson. BSV; CABL; EBEV; GoTS; MeEV; OxBS; PoEL 1-5; SeCePo

Sence you went away. Sence You Went Away. James Weldon Johnson. BALP; BANP

Send all the children to the Dogget Gap. Dogget Gap. *Anonymous.* AmFP

...Send an ode or elegy/In the old way and raise our heritage. Poem from Llanybri. Lynette Roberts. NeBP

Send back my other Me! My Other Me. Grace Denio Litchfield. AA; HBV 1-2

"Send back our lovers whom you stole/away." The Women at the Corners Stand. Louis Golding. TrJP

Send down the peace Thou holdst above! To Holy Jesus. Princess Philipa. CAW

Send every giglot of this town such another lemman/Even as he was. Draw Me Nere, Draw Me Nere. *Anonymous.* EBEV

Send from above harmonious love/And joy and consolation. Yoke Soft and Dear. John C. Kunze. AH

Send him off to sleepy-o. Prettiest Little Baby in the County-o. *Anonymous.* FSW

Send him to Blank the oculist. The Better Way. Walter Leaf. FaBoCo

Send me no flowers, man, send me no flowers Junglegrave. S. E. Anderson. PoBA

Send me only some little line of comfort/Though it be as sad as Simonides' tears. Your Catullus Is Depressed. Caius Valerius Catullus. PeHV

...Send/Me such a cook or coachman, but no friend. The Mistaken Resolve. Martial (Marcus Valerius Martialis). PV

Send me the half that's got my keys.' Mr. Jones. Harry Graham. FaBoCo; FaFP; MaC

Send mee it back as free from smart/As it was free from wrong. Upon a Diamond Cut in Forme of a Heart... Ayton [(or Aytoun)] Sir Robert. EIL; OBS

Send peace and contentment to all British tars. Second of August. *Anonymous.* OBSS

Send round your bottles, Hal–and set your night. Saint Peray. Thomas William Parsons. HBV 1-2

Send such a chief, with men like these,/On such a ship! The Brooklyn at Santiago. Wallace Rice. PAH

Send the rain! Prayer for Rain. Herbert Palmer. HaMV

...Send thee grace/To rule thy realm in unity and peace. Complaint of the Common Weill of Scotland. Sir David Lyndsay. BSV; GoTS

Send thou thy light, thy love, thy word. To Thee, Eternal Soul, Be Praise. Richard Watson Gilder. AH

Send trials–tears! but give me strength to bear them–/This is a Christian's prayer. The Christian's New-Year Prayer (excerpt). Ella Wheeler Wilcox. TrPWD

Send up the strict articulation of your throats,/And say His name. A Canticle to the Waterbirds. William Everson. NeAP; PoM

Send us blessings free! Sir Launfal. Thomas Chestre. ATP

Send us new nymphs with each new moon. The Progress of Beauty. Jonathan Swift. CABA; ForPo; NCEP

Send us one such morning to grow on. Poem at Thirty. John Woods. CoPo

Send ye for the wee cooper o' Fife. The Wee Cooper of Fife. *Anonymous.* FSW

Send you back to your mama some old day. Red Apple Juice. *Anonymous.* FSW

Sending our hearts racing to shore. Open Heart. Michael Salcman. AMV-80

Sending our messages over the mountains and waters. Amusing Our Daughters. Carolyn Kizer. VGW

Sending tiny slivers of straw into his eyes. Hangman. Florence Anthony ("Ai"). AmPA

Sending us back to our lath and dowel. The First Lesson. Thomas Reiter. WOLT

Sends a little of His heaven/To every living thing. Each a Part of All. Augustus Wright Bamberger. WBLP

Sends a song up/reed and wind rise to. Bay Bank. Archie Randolph Ammons. DFF

Sends a thrilling pulse through me. The Secret of the Sea. Henry Wadsworth Longfellow. AnNE; EtS

Sends rich aroma through the house. Winter Fairyland in Vermont. Francis P. Osgood. WeW

Sense now steadying/hears spirit crying. Legerdemain. Kenneth MacKenzie. BoAV; PoAu 1-2

A sense of doom, a dread to see/The Rock of Ages cleft for me. Matlock Bath. Sir John Betjeman. NYBP

A sense of flowers drifting down the wind. Elizabeth. George Brandon Saul. HBMV

Sense of new joy ineffable diffused... Paradise Lost. John Milton. ATP

The sense of worship into uttered praise. Moonlight in Italy. Elizabeth Clementine Kinney AA

...The senses crawl slowly/over the surface not heavy/enough to sink. The Name of Our Country. Dennis Schmitz. AmPA

The sensitive approach of body to body,/hands joined, lips meeting. The Window of the Tobacco Shop. Constantine P. Cavafy. PeHV

Sent a White politician/A green sprig of simile. Footnote. Anthony Delius. PeSA

Sent forth an angel flying through it. The Penalties of Baldness. Sir Owen Seaman. FiBHP

...Sent forth from hearts contrite, in sign/Of sorrow unfeigned, and humiliation meek. Paradise Lost. John Milton. NAWM 1-2

Sent forth the beams which made so fair my race. Astrophel and Stella, XLI. Sir Philip Sidney. AAS; CoBE; EG; HAP; OAEP; OBSC; SiPS

Sent to his slumber by the lightning's stroke. Without the Herdsman. Diotimus. AWP

The sentence without appeal, the sentence without appeal remains a/dead letter! Beyond Memory. Monny De Boully. VWA

Sentinel of the grave who counts us all! Ode to the Confederate Dead. Allen Tate. AP; FaBoMo; HeIP; InPo; LiTA; LiTM; MoAB; MoAmPo; MoPo; MoVE; NoAm; NOBA; NoP; OBWP; OxBA; PrIm; SeCeV; TAP; UnPo; ViBoPo

Separate but equal where it counts.   A Negro Cemetery Next to a White One.   Howard Nemerov.   OBSP

SEPTEMBER BLACKBERRIES!   With Tendrils of Poems.   Michael McClure.   PoM

A sepulchre for its eternity.   Epipsychidion.   Percy Bysshe Shelley.   ChRP

A sequence carried down through many captains/In a long line from the founding of the race.   The Aeneid.   Virgil (Publius Vergilius Maro).   NAWM 1-2

"Sequence, consequence, and again/consequence."   Reflection by a Mailbox.   Stanley Jasspon Kunitz.   TrJP; WaP

Sere of the sun exploded in the sea.   O Carib Isle!   Hart Crane.   AP; MoPo; NePA; NoAm; PoA; VGW

Serene, grotesque Olympian.   A Smiling Demon of Notre Dame.   Sophie Jewett.   AA

Serenely gay, and strict in duty,/Jack finds his wife a perfect beauty.   The Double Transformation.   Oliver Goldsmith.   OBNV

Serenely, our visionary heritage has flowered.   Poets in Time of War.   Bertram Warr.   CaP

–A series of Chinese tortures of prisoners.   From a Museum Man's Album.   John Hewitt.   OxBTC

Series of little silver waterfalls in the moon.   Nocturn Cabbage.   Carl Sandburg.   DuDa

Seriously debating/the intention of the gods/towards their civilization.   Certain Maxims of Archy.   Don (Donald Robert Marquis) Marquis.   NLV

Seriously, I am fascinated by the way a seal moves.   Hmmmm, 9.   Leslie Scalapino.   NPGG

Seriously running.   A Picture.   Howard Nemerov.   OxBC

Sermons in stones and good in every thing./I would not change it.   As You Like It.   William Shakespeare.   GoTF; LiTB; PoToHe; TreFS; TrGrPo

The serpent bright: but now must I sink.   Voluspo.   Anonymous.   AWP

The serpent fled, and round the Angels wheeled,/Up to their stations flying back alike.   Divina Commedia: Purgatorio.   Dante Alighieri.   CAW

The serpent with the eagle in the boughs.   The Dance.   Hart Crane.   AnAmPo; LiTM; OxBA

The serpent/wrings him in the pit and calls him guilty.   The Dreamers and the Sea.   Eithne Wilkins.   NeBP

Serve at once. It does not keep.   Recipe for an Ocean in the Absence of the Sea.   Richard Howard.   TAP

Serve at six, and then devour.   To Stew a Rump-Steak.   Anonymous.   FaBoUs

Serve Thee through all this coming year.   A Prayer for the New Year.   Anonymous.   BLRP

Serve up in a clean dish, and throw the whole out of the/window as fast as possible.   To Make an Amblongus Pie.   Edward Lear.   FaBoNo

The servers attend to each other, forever.   The Grief of Cafeterias.   John Updike.   PPJ

Serving and blessing till the close of day.   There Is a Love.   Philip Jerome Cleveland.   TRV

Serving high God with useful good.   Camoens in the Hospital.   Herman Melville.   ViBoPo

A-serving out my twenty-one years in the penitentiary.   The Boston Burglar.   Anonymous.   CoSo; FSW

Sestina order,/Austere master,/BE GONE!!!   A Fit of Something against Something.   Alan Ansen.   PP

Set all her blood astir/And glittered in her eyes.   To a Young Girl.   William Butler Yeats.   EBEV; OLR

Set free, or outlawed, now I walk the sand/And search this rubble for the promised land.   Variations on a Time Theme.   Edwin Muir.   NoAm

Set him a grinning/and see how he grins!   Teapots and Quails.   Edward Lear.   GoJo

Set in a cheap but perfect ring.   Sunday in South Carolina.   Robert Parham.   AMV-80

Set in a ring of mountains, a hard cold ring.   Not Thinking of America.   Judith Kroll.   AmPA

Set matters right will I.   That Woman Down There beneath the Sea.   Anonymous.   WSC

Set me to these, or any other trial,/Except my Mistress' anger and denial.   The Last Trial.   Anonymous.   OBSC

Set on my skull their black flags, in the wind's scope.   Spleen.   Charles Baudelaire.   SyP

...Set the bright/Scales in the sky until that judgment's done.   Feast of the Ram's Horn.   Harvey Shapiro.   VGW

Set the tune and I will follow you.   Fallen Leaves.   Anonymous.   LiTW

Set them into the earth to sprout and blossom.   Rite of Spring.   Leo Kennedy.   CaP

Set your dainty hand awhile/On my shoulder, Dear, and I'll/Put them on.   My Mistress' Boots.   Frederick Locker-Lampson.   HBV 1-2

Sets the withered leaves fluttering to and fro.   The Twilight People.   Seumas (James Starkey) O'Sullivan.   OnYI

Sette on youre brest, yourself t'assure,/A mighty shelde of doublenesse.   The Duplicity of Women.   John Lydgate.   MeEL

Settin' in corner,/Smokin' my seegar.   Ol' Mother Hare.   Anonymous.   ABF

Setting them free from the manacles/that couple them to this desperation, this life.   Jailhouse Lawyers.   Robert B. Smith.   LFAC

Setting up the flag!   In a Moonlit Hermit's Cabin.   Allen Ginsberg.   MOON

Seven days and/she has abandoned me.   Conversations in Courtship (excerpt).   Anonymous.   CTC

...The seven/dead stars in your sky.   Two Chorale-Preludes.   Geoffrey Hill.   OxBC

The seven dwarfs were singing these mystical motifs.   Lines.   Gavin Ewart.   EAS

Seven for a secret ne'er to be told.   One for Sorrow, Two for Joy.   Anonymous.   OxNR

Seven little streets with dolls in each one,/and not one child in the town.   Toys.   Abraham Sutzkever.   VWA

7. Name the prima donnas who have appeared in the operas of/Virgil and Horace since...   Entrance Exams.   Cuthbert (Edward Bradley) Bede.   FaBoNo

Seven slum children from/Wooloomooloo!   Dusk in the Domain.   Dorothea Mackellar.   PoAu 1-2

Seven the de'il's ain sell.   One Is Sorrow, Two Mirth.   Anonymous.   PBBP

Seven up and six to play.   Some Ruthless Rhymes.   Harry Graham.   CenHV

Seven years ago that sailor set forth for Antarctica.   Ramon.   E. A. Lacey.   PeHV

Seven years since, of seven times seven.   Seven Years Old.   Algernon Charles Swinburne.   HBV 1-2

The seventeen days till Christmas.   Making It Simple December 8, 1969.   David McElroy.   AmPA

The seventh was her comfort, for he in time/Will surely avenge his father's crime.   The Lady and the Dwarf-King.   Anonymous.   BaBo

Seventy being our span, then thirty years/Of idleness are still left to live.   The Temple.   Po Chu-i.   OBMV

...Seventy years and three/lived I,–then yielded to a slow disease.   Epitaph.   Gabriello Chiabrera.   AWP

Sever me not from Thy sweetness!   The Sweetness of Nature.   Anonymous.   KiLC

Several swatches of verbena near bloom.   Periphery.   Archie Randolph Ammons.   NOBA

Sew up/her bleeding hole.   The Dead Lady Canonized.   LeRoi (Imamu Amiri Baraka) Jones.   CAPP

Sewing a new/button my last year/ragdoll.   Christmas Morning I.   Carol [or Carole] Freeman.   PCh; PoBA; TTY

Sews the seams/And shines their faces.   The Cobbler.   Eleanor Alletta Chaffee.   SoPo; TiPo

Sexless, seducible, deeply disguisable!   Motley.   Peter Davison.   NLV

Sez the world'll go right, ef he hollers/out Gee!   The Biglow Papers.   James Russell Lowell   AA; AnNE

Sforzando Suilven reared on his ground base.   Moment Musical in Assynt.   Norman MacCaig.   PoSH

Sh'as no more wit to ask than to deny.   Resolution in Four Sonnets.   Charles Cotton.   PoEL 1-5; Prf

Shabby old Dad!   Shabby Old Dad.   Anne Campbell.   PoToHe

Shade fading within the shadows, lost to me, to herself,/To the world: lost and looking back.   Vanessa Vanessa.   Ewart Milne.   BIrV; NeIP

Shade for a sleeping child/Stirring in safety, smiling at being/a Jew.   The Wall.   Eve Merriam.   TrJP

Shade of Leigh Hunt! Oh, guide this laggard pen/To write of one who loved his fellow men!   A Dirge.   William Augustus Croffut.   InMe

The shade of the noble Roland is still forlorn!   The Sound of the Horn.   Alfred de Vigny.   AWP

Shade that was Elizabeth...immortal completeness!   Life-Long, Poor Browning...   Anne Spencer.   CDC; PoNe

The shades of the dead through the ages lie/dreaming.   Little Big Horn.   Ernest McGaffey.   PAH

A shadow and caress-/ing a disguise!   An Image of Leda.   Frank O'Hara.   HaCAP

A shadow empties the bottom of the moon.   Mexico City: 150 Pesos to the Dollar.   Jim Mitsui.   BrSi

...A shadow is a man/when the mosquito death approaches.   How to Kill.   Keith Douglas.   ChMP; FaBoMo; NOBE

Shadow makes more noise.   Time.   Ralph Hodgson.   BrPo; GTBS-P

(The shadow of a great bird falls on my face.)   Anabasis.   St.-John (Alexis Saint-Léger Léger) Perse.   AtBAP

The shadow of the black bee.   How the Invalids Make Love.   Susan Feldman.   AmPA

The shadow of the great White Throne/Falls broader, deeper, year by year.   Resurgam.   Anonymous.   WGRP

The Shadow of the night comes on...   You, Andrew Marvell.   Archibald MacLeish.   AnEnPo; AP; APA; AWP; BoLiVe; CMoP; CoAnAm; CoBMV; FaBV; FYAP; HAP; HeIP; HoPM; InPo; LiTA; LiTM; MoAB;

MoAmPo; MoVE; MP; NoAm; NOBA; NoP; OxBA; PoRA; PPP; PrIm; SoSe; TreFT; TrGrPo; TwCP; ViBoPo; WeW

The shadow of this lip, an abyss.   Gulliver.   Sylvia Plath.   NOBA

The shadow of thy beauty over me.   Shadows.   Victor Plarr.   NOBV

The Shadow sits and waits for me.   In Memoriam A.H.H., XXII.   Alfred, Lord Tennyson.   VLP

A shadow smiling/Back to a shadow in the night.   La Melinite: Moulin-Rouge.   Arthur Symons.   SyP

The shadow still of what hath been,/Which fashion yearly fades away.   December.   John Clare.   OBCP

A shadow that steps to meet us in the dark.   Vivaldi on the Far Side of the Bars.   Michael Knoll.   LFAC

Shadowing the snow-limb'd Eve from whom she came.   Maud.   Alfred, Lord Tennyson.   BoNaP; ELP; PoEL 1-5

Shadowless, free, I'm lost/in these splinters.   Summer Solstice.   Diane Keating.   CaPN

Shadows are bodiless shapes, yet they have a song.   Transaction.   Archie Randolph Ammons.   HaCAP; PoA

Shadows deep into a black night.   Night Fishing.   Stephen Lewandowski.   WOLT

The shadows fade and now the bay is still.   Boats at Night.   Edward Shanks.   CH; MCCG

The shadows gather...what comes after/No man knows!   A Little While.   Don (Donald Robert Marquis) Marquis.   HBV 1-2

...Shadows known to them/in parting only, and all flesh ravaging.   Such Comfort as the Night Can Bring to Us.   Peter Cooley.   MAYP

...Shadows leave the hills/And bring to the fields the quiet night.   Vacation Song.   Edna St. Vincent Millay.   YeAr

...Shadows long and straight and spare/As of young trees, new-leaved.   Baucis and Philemon.   Katherine Hoskins.   PoA

Shadows my noontime still/And haunts my night.   Love Was Once Light as Air.   Cecil Day Lewis.   OAEP

The shadows of a king and queen/Will darken on the daffodils.   Three Children near Clonmel.   Eileen Shanahan.   OnYI; OxBI

Shadows of Calvary.   A Christmas Carol.   Fred Cogswell.   ACV

The shadows of ringdoves chanting, but easing nothing.   Winter Trees.   Sylvia Plath.   CAPP; HaCAP; LCAP; NMM; SBG

The shadows stoop over like guests at a christening.   Candles.   Sylvia Plath.   NMM

A shaft of glory from the throne of God.   Hospital.   Wilfred J. Funk.   PoToHe

The shaft of light/thru a chink in roof/falls at your feet.   The Gifts.   Charles Levendosky.   TAT

The shaft we raise to them and thee.   Concord Hymn.   Ralph Waldo Emerson   AA; AmFN; AmP; AP; AWP; BLPA; BLPL; ExPo; FaBoBe; FaFP; FaPo; FaPoR; GN; GoTF; HAP; HBV 1-2; HBVY; HeIP; InPo; LiTA; MC; MCCG; NePA; NOBA; NoP; OBWP; OHFP; OxBA; PAH; PAL; SeCeV; TAP; TreF; TrGrPo; WaaP; YaD

Shaggy at evening, to drink among the shadowy lakes.   Among the Finger Lakes.   Robert Wallace.   GrPl

Shake hands, good-bye, and have no fear/To welcome well another year.   Older Grown.   Kate Greenaway.   BiCB

Shake hands with elder brother, Doom,/Nor bawl, nor scurry from the room.   A Prayer.   William Laird.   HBMV

Shake, Mulleary and Go-ethe.   Shake, Mulleary and Go-ethe.   Henry Cuyler Bunner.   ALV; AnAmPo; FiBHP; InMe

Shake'nbake their envy-schooled tongues.   Shake'nbake Ballad.   Peter Van Toorn.   NOBC

& Shake the shit out of them.   A Dance for Militant Dilettantes.   Al Young.   PoBA

Shake the table!/That's the fun.   The House of Cards.   Christina Georgina Rossetti.   PoPl

Shake them 'simmons down.   The Persimmon Tree.   Anonymous.   GBP

Shake violently in the wind.   Moving.   Barbara Crooker.   AMV-80

Shake walls, floors, windows, brain and bone.   Standard Forgings Plant.   William Stephens.   NAMP

Shake yer spurs and make 'em rattle. Kino! Promenade to seats!   Idaho Cowboy Dance.   Anonymous.   ABF; BPAW

Shake your fingers down your throat/and gag yourself awake.   Advice.   Emanuel Di Pasquale.   AMV-81

Shake yourself a little, and turn yourself about.   Looby Loo.   Anonymous.   SoPo

Shakes all together, and produces–You.   Heaven's Last Best Work.   Alexander Pope.   OBEC

The shaking earth will wreck/Its cities: I am greatest. I am all.   The Jewish Woman.   Gertrud Kolmar.   VWA

Shaking the air around me   Letters from Kazuko (Kyoto, Japan–Summer 1980).   Alan Chong Lau.   BrSi

Shaking the snow off his coat/his rifle glistening.   The Victory of the Battle of Wounded Knee.   Tom Parson.   SOTS

Shaking will not tell.   Do Not Open Until Christmas.   James S. Tippett.   ChBR

Shal pay for thy charges thou spendest abrode.   A Hundreth Good Poyntes of Husbandry.   Thomas Tusser.   FaBoUs

Shall ask God's self, incredulous, some day,/Why in the name of Christ He let you come!   Sonnets.   Muna Lee.   HBMV

Shall be lifted - nevermore!   The Raven.   Edgar Allan Poe   AA; AnFE; AP; APA; BeLS; BLPA; FaBoBe; FaBoCh; FaBV; FaFP; FPL; GN; GoJo; GoTF; HBV 1-2; LiTA; LoGBV; MCCG; NePA; NOBA; OBCA; OBNV; OHFP; OxBA; PaPo; PoRA; RoGo; TAP; TreF; ViBoPo; WBLP; WHA

Shall be made friends in a left handed trance.   Nonsense.   Anonymous.   FaBoNo; NA

Shall be the psalms sung forth in gracious lays.   Meditations.   Edward Taylor.   AnNE

Shall break thy Edwin's too.   Edwin and Angelina. A Ballad.   Oliver Goldsmith.   CEP

Shall brighten evermore.   Iona.   Arthur Cleveland Core   AA

Shall brithers be for a' that.   A Man's a Man for A' That.   Robert Burns.   BoLiVe; CoBE; EnLi 1-2; EnPE; FSW; InPo; LoBV; MasP; OxBS; TrGrPo; ViBoPo

Shall burn rose-red while stars be sped; tho' stars dropt/dead would burn.   Christmas Rede.   Jane Barlow.   OBVV

Shall Churchill reign, and shall not Gotham sing?   Gotham.   Charles Churchill.   NOEC

Shall cleanse the stain and expiate all.   A Plea for Flood Ireson.   Charles Timothy Brooks.   PAH

Shall climb their shining cars.   To the Soul.   Frederick Napier Broome.   ACV

Shall come no scarlet-coated fool/To tease my foxes from their haunts.   To Any M.F.H.   Victoria Mary (Vita) Sackville-West.   SBG

Shall come the city of our God.   Where Cross the Crowded Ways of Life.   Frank Mason North.   AH

Shall conclude a happy peace.   Die Not, Fond Man.   Anonymous.   ElL

Shall dawn the glory of eternal light.   A New Year's Wish.   S., J. H..   BLRP

,Shall delight for ever/In the grace of the King and glory with God.   Christ 3: The Last Judgement.   Anonymous.   AnOE

Shall die, at the last, by his sword, as a sea woman/dies.   Figurehead.   Dorothy Paul.   EtS

"Shall dip their flag to a slaver's rag–to show that his trade is fair!"   The Rhyme of the Three Captains.   Rudyard Kipling.   BeLS

Shall drag me back from my immortal path!   He Maketh Himself One with the Only God, Whose Limbs Are the Many God.   Book of the Dead.   AWP

Shall draw the Thing as he sees It for the God of Things as They Are!   L'Envoi.   Rudyard Kipling.   FaFP; HBV 1-2; OHFP; PoPl

Shall dream a dream crept from the sunless pole/Of how her end shall be.   November.   Robert Bridges.   NBM; OBNC; PBBP; PoEL 1-5

Shall feast on the corpses that float by the ferry.   Horsey Gap.   Anonymous.   FaBoPP; GBP

Shall fill the vale of Dussindale/With slaughtered bodies soon.   The Norfolk Rebellion: The Slaughter of the Rebels.   Anonymous.   GBP

Shall flock about thee, and keepe time with kisses.   On the Death of a Nightingale.   Thomas Randolph.   AnAnS 2; PBBP

Shall fly, the feathered arrow of the foam.   Choosing a Mast.   Roy Campbell.   BoC; FaBoTw; PeSA

Shall foam and freeze no more.   The Pilgrim Fathers.   John Pierpont.   AA; HBV 1-2; MC; PAH

Shall fold their tents, like the Arabs,/And as silently steal away.   The Day Is Done.   Henry Wadsworth Longfellow.   AmePo; AnNE; BLPA; FaBoBe; FaFP; FPL; GoTF; HBV 1-2; MCCG; NOBA; OHFP; OxBA; PG; PoPl; PoRA; TreF; TrGrPo

Shall forge for fetter on the seas/Tally of his tormented days.   Magellan.   Allen Curnow.   AnNZ

Shall give Thee a scepter, a crown, and/a throne.   Cradle and Throne.   Anonymous.   STF

Shall give to Venus offerings rich enow,/Her maiden zone, her arrows, and her bow.   Atalanta's Race.   William Morris.   DTo

Shall grow to manhood in a world at war.   The Quick.   Sean Jennett.   NeBP

Shall have the cunning skill to break a heart.   Cupid and Death: Victorious Men of Earth.   James Shirley.   TrGrPo

Shall have the cunning skill to break a heart.   Death, the Conqueror.   James Shirley.   GoBC

Shall he grin like the Gorgon and rule?   The New Ancient of Days.   Herman Melville.   OBAL

Shall hear us murmur ever above his sleep.   The Thousand and One Nights: Dates.   Anonymous.   AWP; LiTW

Shall her smile breed that mouth, behind the mirror,/That burns along my eyes.   Not from This Anger.   Dylan Thomas.   LiTB; PoA

Shall I a virgin die? Fie no!   Poor Is the Life That Misses.   Anonymous.   ElL; UnTE

Shall I be refused your bed?   Love's Torment.   Anonymous.   UnTE

Shall I come at last/To the lost beginning? Two Invocations of Death, II. Kathleen Raine. OxBTC

Shall I come away? Buckee Bene. *Anonymous.* CH

Shall I complain, who still this Bliss may know? Shall I Complain? Louise Chandler Moulton. PoToHe

Shall I find that little chamber as of old! An Upper Chamber. Frances Bannerman. HBV 1-2; OBEV

Shall I find you south of the Gulf?–or are you dead in my heart? The Lost Shipmate. Theodore Goodridge Roberts. CaP

"Shall I go with you? Aye, by-and-bye." Sweeping the Sky. *Anonymous.* SoPo

Shall I, with backward-streaming hair,/Outfly my bleeding feet? She Bewitched Me. Thomas Burbidge. EnLoPo

Shall journey onward in perpetual peace. An Evening Revery. William Cullen Bryant. AA

Shall lead his horsemen headlong on the foe,/In victory careering! Obsequies of Stuart. John Randolph Thompson. PAH

Shall lead man up through happy realms of/light/Unto his goal sublime. Commemoration Ode. Harriet Monroe. AA

Shall live for evermore. Christmas Eve in France. Jessie Redmond Fauset. BANP

Shall long keep his memory green in our souls. Oh, Breathe Not His Name. Thomas Moore. AnIL; CoBE; HBV 1-2; TreFS

Shall love you always. Modern Declaration. Edna St. Vincent Millay. MoLP

Shall lull both terror and innocence to rest. Send Forth the High Falcon. Léonie Adams. InPo

Shall make us sad next morning, or affright/The liberty that we'll enjoy tonight. Inviting a Friend to Supper. Ben Jonson. AnAnS 2; AWP; BiP; EnRePo; JCP; LiTB; LoBV; NIP; NOBE; NoP; OAEL 1-2; OAEP; OBS; OxBoLi; PoEL 1-5; PPP; SeCP; SeCV 1-2

Shall meet again as heirs of His eternal love. On Our Thirty-Ninth Wedding Day. Jonathan Odell. CaP

Shall memory come to dream upon us. Dirge: For One Who Fell in Battle. Thomas William Parsons AA

Shall move without all Night/Of Excentricity. The Stone. Thomas Vaughan. OBS

Shall never cease to praise. A Joyful Sound It Is. George Strebeck. AH

Shall never compass, leaving thee behind. The Waning of Love. Arthur Lyon Raile. PeHV

Shall no man know her name for me. A Secret. *Anonymous.* OBSC

Shall not perish from the earth. The Gettysburg Address. Abraham Lincoln. TRV

Shall not touch them with his blind all-canceling fingers. Elegy on Herakleitos. Callimachus. LiTW

Shall one day mark the Port which ruled/the Western seas. The Cotton Boll. Henry Timrod. AA; MAmP

...Shall our white feet gleam/In the dim expanses? Where Shall Wisdom Be Found. Euripides. UnS

Shall outlive garlands, stol'n from the chaste tree. To the Learned Critic. Ben Jonson. PP

Shall own our independence of "Yankee-Doodledom." Death of the Lincoln Despotism. *Anonymous.* PAH

Shall pass away. The Soul's Defiance. Lavinia Stoddard. AA

Shall pause at the song of their captive and weep! Oh! Blame Not the Bard, If He Fly to the Bowers. Thomas Moore. NOBI; OnYI

Shall permeate the heavens at your feet! To William Stanley Braithwaite. Georgia Douglas Johnson. BALP

Shall pour such splendour as your heart to me. Most Lovely Shade. Edith Sitwell. AtBAP; FaBoTw; GTBS-P

Shall raise the choral hymn from eve till morn. The Marriage of Pocahontas. M. M. Webster. MC; PAH

Shall reap from our glad sowing. A Good Creed. *Anonymous.* PoToHe

Shall rise the glorious thought–I am with Thee. Still, Still with Thee. Harriet Beecher Stowe. AH; BLRP

Shall 'scape Oblivion's broom so long. An Autograph. James Russell Lowell AA

Shall see almost a forest. Solitude. Philip Henry Savage. AA

Shall see His glorious face–perhaps/today! Perhaps Today. *Anonymous.* STF

Shall see this, and bless Heaven. King Henry VIII. William Shakespeare. WGRP

Shall sleep and sleep for ever. From the Antique. Christina Georgina Rossetti. EnLoPo; NOBV

Shall still revive and flourish in the dust. Childhood. Thomas Traherne. TrGrPo

Shall survive the then of then,/the now of now. In Defense of Black Poets. Conrad Kent Rivers. BOLo; BPo

Shall take a full glass, shall take a full glass/To his passage o'er the ferry. The Sailor's Complaint. *Anonymous.* OBSS

Shall the retreat/Of fierce brother from lost sister/End, and they meet. Sun and Moon. Jay Macpherson. SoSe

Shall the very last woman obey. The Lords of Creation. *Anonymous.* PoLf

Shall the voice of peace bring sweet release to the men be-/hind the guns! The Men behind the Guns. John Jerome Rooney. AA; BLPA; EtS; FaBoBe; HBV 1-2; MC; PAH; YaD

Shall then the virgins rejoice? Saul's Song of Love. Saul Tchernichovsky. VWA

Shall Then with Just Confusion, bow/And break before thee. To the Name Above Every Name, the Name of Jesus A Hymn. Richard Crashaw. SeCV 1-2

Shall through Thee call on men to rejoice and/adore! The Irish Language. James Clarence Mangan. VLP

Shall throw open the gates of new life to thee! See/the Christ stand!' Saul. Robert Browning. ILwL; TRV

Shall throw their arms around thy lintels poland/& begin to crow Poland/1931.The Wedding. Jerome Rothenberg. PoM; Prf

Shall thus forespeak Thy secret works in sight/of Adam's race. Psalm LXXIII. Henry Howard, Earl of Surrey. FCP

Shall true hearts be fancies fuell? Rosalynde. Thomas Lodge. AtBAP; EG; PoEL 1-5; TrGrPo

Shall turn and welcome me at the door. The Wizard's Funeral. Richard Watson Dixon. ELP; LoBV; NOBV; VLP

Shall turn marble, and become/Both her mourner and her tomb. Epitaph. William Browne. HBV 1-2

Shall us apply/to sigh and mone. My Lute and I. Sir Thomas Wyatt. MeEL

Shall we be able to die according to the rules? Now When So Much Has Passed. George Seferis. LiTW

Shall we be thus for ever? Memory of Brother Michael. Patrick Kavanagh. FaBoIP; MoAB; OnYI; OxBI

Shall we ever again be heart to heart? The Wind's Way. Richard Le Gallienne. HBMV

...Shall we/ever dare to be parted! Marriage Vow. *Anonymous.* HW

...Shall we fight? America. Sydney Thomas Dobell. OBVV

Shall we leave it unabated in its place? Mesopotamia. Rudyard Kipling. MMM

Shall we not be as wise as they/Though love live but a day? This Heart That Flutters Near My Heart. James Joyce. AnIV

Shall we play barley-break./Fa la la! Now Is the Month of Maying. *Anonymous.* EBEV

Shall we ride/To the blue star/Or the white star? Baby Toes. Carl Sandburg. LaNeLa; SUS

Shall we stick by each other as long as we live? Song of the Open Road. Walt Whitman. MoAmPo; NePA; NOBA; TreFT; ViBoPo; WHA

Shall whisper, "Hark! who sang that love-/song? Hark!" Recollection. Amelia Walstein Carpenter. AA

Shall wholly do away, I ween,/The marks of that which once hath been. The Scars Remaining. Samuel Taylor Coleridge. OBNC

Shall you wash your hands of me? I Am Your Loaf, Lord. David Ross. GoYe

ShallIshellIshallIshellIshallI...? The Snail's Monologue. Christian Morgenstern. BoAnP

Shallo, Shallo Brown! Shallo Brown. *Anonymous.* ShS

Shallow oppressor, intruder,/insister, you have here a resister. Apparition of Splendor. Marianne Moore. NePoAm

Shalom Aleichem! Shalom Aleichem. *Anonymous.* FSW

Shame and ruin wait for you! Boadicea. William Cowper. BeLS; FaPo; FaPoR; HBV 1-2

Shame on us/for the doubled wounds of/Jamila. Jamila. Nazik al-Mala'ika. WPOW

Shame, shame, the Johnson boys. The Johnson Boys. *Anonymous.* FSW

Shame upon us, shame upon us, should the/nation e'er forget! The Men of the Merrimac. Clinton Scollard. PAH

Shame will bar the only way/to all you want to do. Epigram: "If you see someone beautiful." Adaios. PeHV

Shame ye not that all things are gold but you. Ad Henricum Wottonem. Thomas Bastard. FaBoEE; FaBoPP

Shameful to own and scandalous to hear. A Journey to Hell. Edward Ward. NOEC

Shamrock, Westward, Lulworth, Britannia. Lament for the Great Yachts. Patric Dickinson. HaMV

Shantih shantih shantih The Waste Land. Thomas Stearns Eliot. CMoP; CoBMV; HAP; LiTA; LiTM; MasP; MoAB; MoAmPo; MoPo; NAWM 1-2; NePA; NoAm; NOBE; NoP; OAEL 1-2; OAEP; OxBA; PPoe; TAP; UnPo

Shape for us holier lives to live/And nobler work to do! Our Father! While Our Hearts Unlearn. Oliver Wendell Holmes. AH

Shape from that thy work of art. Gaspar Becerra. Henry Wadsworth Longfellow. AnNE

The shape he had made himself of himself. Rothko. James Moore. AMV-81

...The shape of it tilting/at me crushed under the sun. Beetle on the Shasta Daylight. Shirley Kaufman. NYBP

The shape of the land/Takes form.　Listen to the Bird.　Laya Firestone. VWA

...The shape/you had to leave behind/to grow away from here.　Sweetheart. Phil Hey.　GOYP

Shaped happily beneath my cheek,/Hollow and beautiful.　A Song for My Mother–Her Hands.　Anna Hempstead Branch.　OHIP

Shaped like a tear but/Not falling for anyone.　The Indigestion of the Vampire.　William Stanley Merwin.　NaP

Shaped like a Tiffany lamp and shining.　Over the Phone.　Mekeel McBride. MAYP

Shaped otherwise, and fashioned for you only?　For Any Member of the Security Police.　Josephine Jacobsen.　NePoAm

A shapeless mass of wreck and rubbish lies.　The Warning.　Henry Wadsworth Longfellow.　AmePo

Shaping immortality.　Brief History.　Olga Hampel Briggs.　GoYe

Shaping our burrows in the sand.　Assignation with a Somnambulist.　John Streeter Manifold.　CBAP

Shaping the matter of all energies/to our one energy　Moonshot.　Robert Kelly.　MOON

Shaping the weasel's jaw in His leap/And the staggering rush of the bass.　In All These Acts.　William Everson.　NoP

Sharako, Hokusai!　Japanese Print.　Austin Clarke.　IPY; NOBI

Shards of reasonable nights.　The Meeting.　Ramona Wilson.　VoR

Share my harvest and my home.　Ruth.　Thomas Hood.　BoLoP; EnLoPo; EnRP; GN; GoTF; HBV 1-2; LiTL; LoBV; NOBE; OBEV; OBNC; OBRV; OBVV; TreFS

Share your wisdom with us, your learning, art!　Praises of King George VI. A. Z. Ngani.　PeSA

Shared with the adder and the mole.　World, Defined.　Edward Weismiller. AnAmPo

A sharer in Thy dying love,/A follower of thine.　Bless, Dear Saviour, This Child.　Beck.　BePJ

...Sharing our/desires and lack of faith in desire.　The Orotava Road.　Basil Bunting.　NoAm

Sharing something which you had no right to share.　Apparitions Are Not Singular Occurrences.　Diane Wakoski.　CoPo

The shark/Glides white through the phosphorus sea.　Commemorative of a Naval Victory.　Herman Melville.　AP; HAP; MOS; UnPo

The shark will swim away.　The Spirit of Wrath.　William Heyen.　AmPA; WOLT

A sharp caught cry.　Fragment.　Jessie Redmond Fauset.　CDC

Sharp enough to stick a pig with.　The Boasting Drunk in Dodge City. Anonymous.　CoSo

Sharp on the hard ground/in the hard cold　Big Man.　Mason Jordan Mason.　PoNe

A sharp taste in the mouth.　The Truth Is Blind.　David Gascoyne.　EAS

The sharp-toothed father/Of our fathers/Who was wont to gore in the past The Letters of the Book.　Rose Drachler.　VWA

...Sharply on my mind/Presses the sorrow: fern and flower are blind.　Noon. Michael (Katherine Bradley and Edith Cooper) Field.　NOBV

Shatter the night with fear.　Death Songs.　L.V. Mack.　PoBA

Shattered obsidian.　Hitch Haiku.　Gary Snyder.　LCAP

The shattered ship that sails tonight!　On the Verge.　William Winter.　AA

Shaun O'Dwyer of the Valley/Your pleasure is no more.　Lament for the Woodlands.　Anonymous.　KiLC

The Shay's man with the green branch in his hat,/Or silent sagamore, Shaug or Wassahoale.　Elegy in Six Sonnets.　Frederick Goddard Tuckerman. QFR

An' she, a-smilen wi' her bow/O' blue, look'd roun' an' nodded, No.　Jenny's Ribbons.　William Barnes.　VLP

She Abigail turned out of doors,/And hanged up Machiavell.　A New Ballad. Arthur Mainwaring.　APAS

She abruptly rises, knowing well/How to stalk off in wise indifference. Apartment Cats.　Thom Gunn.　GrPl

...She adds a spring of/mint and bruises the leaves lightly against the rim of/ the glass.　Traveling through Ports That Begin with "M".　Christy Sheffield Sanford.　APU

She aint sold out yet & her tongue's still flapping　Not Her, She Aint No Gypsy.　Al Young.　GP

...She alas is poor,/Which caus'd her thus to send thee out of door.　The Author to Her Book.　Anne Bradstreet.　AP; InPK; MAmP; NePA; NOBA; NoP; OxBA; SCAP; TAP

She alone burns none to prove her Sleep.'　The Galliass.　Walter De la Mare.　FaBoTw

She, alone in her tower.　The Return of the Greeks.　Edwin Muir.　CMoP; NoP

She alone/Knew from her birth the mystic Avalon.　The Grail.　Sidney Keyes.　FaBoTw

She alone unfolds the town-plan,/sculling away on water.　Matronita. Dennis Silk.　VWA

She also will turn middle-aged.　The Tea Shop.　Ezra Pound.　HeIP

She alwayth returned a thoft anth'er!　Limerick: "Here's sweet little Sarah Samantha."　Anonymous.　TDH

She, and comparisons are odious.　The Comparison.　John Donne.　ErPo; TEP

She and he lie(undead)　Why from This Her and Him.　Edward Estlin Cummings.　NoAm

She and I are two,/Three with the rustle of sea-spray.　The Glory of Hanalei Is Heavy Rain.　Alfred Alohikea.　WTO

She and I, we walked and talked/Half an hour after our heads were cut off. She and I.　Norman Cameron.　OBSP

She answered: "Then what about kilts?"　Limerick: "There was a young lady of Wilts."　Cosmo Monkhouse.　HBV 1-2; TDH

She bathes her knees in the blood of attendants,/her smock in the entrails of the ministrants...　Distances (excerpt).　Christopher Okigbo.　TTY

She began again/and named the sky/plate.　The Renaming.　Valerie Sinason. BrRo

She begins to wash the water from the fish.　Wash.　Eilean Ni Chuilleanain. BIrV; WPOW

She, being hopeless, did not weep/As the grey dawn came in.　At Dawn. Arthur Symons.　OBNC

She boasts a Race,/To ev'ry nobler virtue bred,/And polish'd grace.　The Vision.　Robert Burns.　OxBS

She bore one cub, one only, but it wears/the lion's mane!　The Lion's Cub. Maurice Thompson.　AA

She bore the vicious bird away.　The Bee, the Ant, and the Sparrow. Nathaniel Cotton.　OxBChV

She both loved you and hurt you/In her only way.　In Her Only Way. Robert Graves.　OBSP

She breathes! She burns! She'll come! She'll come!/Maryland, my Maryland! Maryland, My Maryland.　James Ryder Randall.　FaPo

She brews and bottles, unfermented,/The stupid and abiding jelly.　Beth Appleyard's Verses.　Peter DeVries.　OBAL

She brings me from Knock shrine/John Kennedy's head on a china dish. Green Martyrs.　Richard Murphy.　NOBI

She brings out her broom at six o'clock.　Clean Clara.　William Brighty ("Matthew Browne") Rands.　HBVY

She brings the distant briefly close/above his dreamy abstract stare.　The Ex-Queen among the Astronomers.　Fleur Adcock.　FaBoWP

She brings the silver olive-leaf.　The Stockdove.　Ruth Pitter.　HaMV; SeCePo

She buys a cotton gown.　Trot, Trot!　Mary Frances Butts.　HBV 1-2; HBVY

She buys them black, they therefore need/No subsequent immersion.　On an Old Woman.　Lucilius [(or Lucillius)].　AWP; LiTW

She calls and calls each vagabond by name.　A Vagabond Song.　Bliss Carman.　GN; HBV 1-2; HBVY; MCCG; PoSC

...She came; God's work was done.　To the Authoress of "Aurora Leigh". Sydney Thomas Dobell.　PeD

She came in such still water, and so nursed/In Silence, beauty blessed and beauty cursed.　The Bathers.　Hart Crane.　SyP

She came, she loved, and then she went away.　To Keep the Memory of Charlotte Forten Grimke.　Angelina Weld Grimke.　BlSi

She came to gued by grait misgiding,/By the follouing of her laddie.　The Beggar-Laddie.　Anonymous.　ESPB

...She came to her father's house/One hour before it was day.　Pretty Polly. Anonymous.　UnTE

She can always tell.　My Mother and My Sisters.　Simon J. Ortiz.　GP

She can conquer hell and a husband too,/To-i-lu, and a husband too.　Farmer Jones's Wife.　Anonymous.　BFSS

She can ease the heart of the old, old aching,/And put away regret.　Virgilia (excerpt).　Edwin Markham.　EtS

She can leave him alone.　Dick & Jane.　Judith Kroll.　AmPA

She can't care. She loves us each like a friend.　The Dancing Sunshine Lounge.　Thomas Rabbit.　MAYP

She can wage a gallant war,/And give the peace of Eden.　Marian.　George Meredith.　HBV 1-2

She can whup out the devil and her husband too.　Tee Roo.　Anonymous. OuSiCo

She cannot love, and therefore thou must die!　Corydon to His Phyllis.　Sir Edward Dyer.　EIL

She cannot reach me.　Parting.　Gabriel Preil.　VWA

She carried Him till Christmas morn/When Jesus Christ the Lord was born. The Annunciation.　Anonymous.　ISi

She cast her violets underneath his feet.　The Passing of March.　Robert Burns Wilson.　HBV 1-2

She changes my moccasins/as she pleases.　Sunflower Moccasins.　Phil George.　VoR

She chanted, till along the sea/The feet of Morn came whisperingly.　Three White Birds of Angus.　Eleanor Rogers Cox.　HBMV

She checks the Flame, but cannot quench the Fire.　I sighed and owned my love.　Anonymous.　EG

She chose her bearers before she died/From her fancy-men. Julie-Jane. Thomas Hardy. MoVE

She cleaves the earth–a silver brook. Sleeping Beauty. Elinor Wylie. DFT

...She/climbs the dusty path home. Deja Vu. Shirley Kaufman. LCAP

She comforts them; and wraps it in a paper/featuring: Tasty dishes from stale bread. Suburban Sonnet. Gwen Harwood. CBAP

She conjures the snow softly into bloom. Duchess. Lilian Bowes Lyon. HaMV

She consenting, I withstood. Requirements. Rufinus Domesticus. ErPo

She could borrow him for rent. Epitaph for Jean Maillard. Anonymous. PeHV

She could never show him–never,/That swan's nest among the reeds! Romance of the Swan's Nest. Elizabeth Barrett Browning. GN

She could not live a maid. The Old Wife's Tale. George Peele. ALV; OBSC

She could not love Him more,/But loved Him just the same./Lullee, lullee, lullay. A Lullaby. Janet Lewis. NOCV

She counts the alien seed. The Gardens of Proserpine. Turner Cassity. PoA

She crashed through the glass Unhappy Diary Days. Gerald Vizenor. VoR

She crawls toward him, not away,/bound by habits not yet broken. The Victim. Ellen Bryant Voigt. MAYP

She cried out with a thrilling cry:/"O Lord, O Lord, I'm ruined." Trooper and Maid, II. Anonymous. AmFP

She cries on his stairs. The Demolition. Anne Stevenson. OBSP

She cull'd suspicious–lo! she starts, she frowns/With indignation at a negro's nail. How to Cure Hops and Prepare Them for Sale. Christopher Smart. FaBoUs

She cunningly powders the breast that nourished you. The Injured Moon. Charles Baudelaire. MOON

She cut me off, ay me, and answered,/You cannot conquer and be conquered. Relent, My Deere, Yet Unkind Coelia. William Percy. AAS

She'd be so proud she'd dance and sing/To see herself tonight. A Brown Girl Dead. Countee Cullen. BP; TAP

...She'd fondle a diseased/Hangman and lick him anywhere he pleased. So Help Me God. Caius Valerius Catullus. DBV

She'd for no angels' conduct stay,/But fly, and love-on, all the way. The Aspiration. John Norris. LoBV; OxBoCh

She'd found a Father for her Child,/Hye, Marry and thank him too. The Lass of Lynn's New Joy, for Finding a Father for Her Child. Anonymous. CoMu

She'd saved them for her lover who is far, far away. Round Her Neck She Wore a Yellow Ribbon. Anonymous. FSW

She'd scarce have shown such little wit/As to let Adam taste of it! The Apple. Lady Margaret Sackville. OBVV

She'd turn her head/to the side. Takes All Kinds. R. P. Dickey. PoL

She daily ventures at the same,/And shuts and opens like an Oyster. As Oyster Nan Stood by Her Tub. Anonymous. CoMu

She dances Henry away. Dream Songs. John Berryman. CAPP

She did not give a single dam. Six-Year-Old Marjory Fleming Pens a Poem. Marjory Fleming. TreFT

She did not know. Two Lips. Thomas Hardy. BoLoP

She did not suffer the pig to escape,/And never became breathless. The Hunt of Sliabh Truim (excerpt). Anonymous. OnYI

She did not want it, but she stole. Kleptomaniac. Leonora Speyer. AnAmPo; HBMV

She didn't come back at all. I'm Leery of Firms with Easy Terms. C. S. Jennison. QQQ

She died a maid, the more the pity. Upon One of the Maids of Honour to Queen Elizabeth. John Hoskyns. FaBoEE

"She died as she lived, sniffing cocaine." Cocaine Lil and Morphine Sue. Anonymous. AS; GBP; MAT; OxBoLi; TrAS

She died full long agone! Meg Merrilies. John Keats. BoLiVe; ELP; FaBoCh; FiP; LoGBV; OxBChV; PoPle; TEP; TiPo

She died in the mill-pond/Standing on her head. Aunt Rhody. Anonymous. FSW

She died, of course. Poor Old Lady. Anonymous. OBCA; SoPo

...She died/"of malaria." Elmira would. Her Apron through the Trees. Roger Weingarten. AmPA

She died on the train. Liza Jane. Anonymous. ABF; AS

She died–they wept about the room,/And showed the coats she made. Dorcas. George Macdonald. OBVV

She dies of a distant death/she who loves the wind. Who Will Stop His Hand from Giving Warmth. Alejandra Pizarnik. VWA

She does not beg for anything, who knew/The change of tone, the human hope gone gray. Arrangements with Earth for Three Dead Friends. James Wright. NIP

She does not know she is the one/survivor. Time-Travel. Sharon Olds. AMV-80

She does not know what/the deer dreams or desires. The Pet Deer. James Tate. EAS

She does not turn to watch/where he, unmoving now,/is drowned, subsumed, in light. The Woman's Dream. Frances Horovitz. BrRo

She does the work that no man can. Riddle: "Little bird of paradise." Anonymous. OxNR

She doesn't come home till she dies. Five Songs. David Shapiro. ANYP

She drawled, When Ah itchez, Ah scratchez! Limerick: "There was a young belle of old Natchez." Ogden Nash. LiBL; NLV; NoP

She dreamed her question and we lay alone. Anecdote of 2 A.M. John Wain. NMP

She dreamed she had me in her arms,/And she was not deceived. I Dreamed My Love. Anonymous. UnTE

She dreams of marvelous worlds/Marvelous worlds/Where her son will be able to live. Dream of the Black Mother. Marcelin Dos Santos. WhB

She dreams she writes this poem. There's Been Some Sort of Mistake. Caroline Gilfillan. PeHV

She dreams; till now on her forgotten book/Drops the forgotten blossom from her hand. The Day-Dream. Dante Gabriel Rossetti. SyP

She drew a kerchief from her pocket/And wiped his eyes, though they were blind. Bruton Town. Anonymous. EnSB

She drew an angel down! Alexander's Feast, or, the Power of Music. John Dryden. ATP; BoLiVe; CEP

She drives with all her magic down a/different route to darkness where/all life begins. The Bad Mother. Susan Griffin. NPGG

She dropped the light and she fainted quite,/"Twas Chin-ti, the Chinese cook! The Boss's Wife. Anonymous. CBAP

She endures this for three weeks/before running away/forever The Snake. Andrew Suknaski. NOBC

She ever since has kept her word. Meddlesome Matty. Ann Taylor. HBV 1-2; HBVY; LaNeLa; OnMSP; OxBChV

She expunges evil/by creating missiles. Jezebel: Her Progress (excerpt). Gillian E. Hanscombe. BrRo

She fades into the wrinkling heat. The Spirit of the Wheat. Edward A.U. Valentine. AA

She faints and quits her hold. The Consolation of Philosophy. Boethius. OBVE

She fed me cartridges, she clicked my safety off. Monologue through Bars. Nelson Hubbell. AMV-81

She fell between two stools, and broke her neck. R. I. P. Jan Struther. InMe

She fell, she felt the water, and forgot/All, save the drowning agony of breath. The Abandoned. Arthur Symons. SyP

She finds the fountain where they wailed "Mirage!" The Ancient Sage. Alfred, Lord Tennyson. WGRP

She fished him out with a ten-foot pole/and sent him off to school./Singing tra la la la la la la.. .The Bulldog on the Bank. Anonymous. FSW

She fled, and left the moonlight there. The Hare. Walter De la Mare. TiPo

She fled from the county of Limerick. Limerick: "There was a young lady of Limerick." Andrew Lang. CenHV

She flickers out to bone and calcium. Shells. Medb Mahony. AMV-80

She flies into the night, and with one draught drinks/All the sighs of a thousand miles. Drinking the Wind. Tan Ying. WPOW

She flings to her head a leg, bobs, all is well,/she dances Henry away. Dream Songs. John Berryman. NoP

She flourisheth fresh and new/In beauty and virtu. Maystress Jane Scroupe. John Skelton. EG

She folds her wings about her sleeping child. Bats. Randall Jarrell. BiP; GrPl; NTCP; NU; OBCA; RFM

...She forgets it easily,/Who never speaks of losing. Games. Sandra McPherson. LCAP

She found him drown'd in Yarrow. Rare Willy. Anonymous. OxBB

...She gallops night by night/Through lovers' brains, and then they dream of love; Romeo and Juliet. William Shakespeare. BoW; FiP; LiTB; MaC; TreF; TrGrPo; WSC

She gave an armful of strawberries on rushes. Son of the King of May. Anonymous. AnIL

She gave, and did not know she gave. A Girl in a Window. James Wright. ErPo

She gave her father forty-one. Lizzie Borden. Anonymous. GoTF; ShM; TreFS

She gave me a diamond,/As big as my shoe. Gift for the Queen. Anonymous. OxNR

She gave me these two secrets–/but don't ask why. Oh moon, oh moon! Anonymous. BoWoP

She gently touched him with her hand. The Iliad. Homer. PoPl

She gestures inward, inward,/The cabbage (vegetable). Cabbage. Rosemary Norman. BrRo

She glances back with bashful eyes. A Moral in Sevres. Mildred Howells. AA; HBV 1-2

She glides along–the solitary-hearted. The Solitary-Hearted. Hartley Coleridge. HBV 1-2

SHE GOES REAL SMOOTH Carmen. Victor Hernandez Cruz. CAD; PoBA

She got slowly boiled to death in the copper. The Fox and the Hare. *Anonymous.* OBET

She got the same jelly roll/She had/forty years ago Hambone Blues. Ed Bell. BluL

She had a bad face, which did always molest her. Epitaph on Dr. Keene's Wife. Thomas Gray. FaBoEE

...–She had/Another morn than ours. The Death Bed. Thomas Hood. EnRP; GTBS; GTBS-P; HBV 1-2; MCCG; NOBE; OBEV; OBNC; OBRV; OBVV; PG; TreFS

–She had been asleep! The Declaration. Nathaniel Parker Willis. OBAL

She had been talking all the while. A Dancing Girl. Frances Sargent Osgood AA

She had better be there than be John Ford's wife. Epitaph at Potterne, Wiltshire. *Anonymous.* FaBoCo

She had fewer in spite of all she had done. Riddle 9 (Cuckoo). *Anonymous.* PBBP

She had found a rock to keep,/and I went down. At White River. John Haines. FiCP

She had misunderstood what I had said. Joe Brainard's Painting "Bingo". Ron Padgett. ANYP

She had never heard the great Wind blare. The Wind and the Moon. George Macdonald. GoJo; HBV 1-2; HBVY; MoShBr; OnMSP; SUS; TreFS

She had not died today. An Elegy on the Glory of Her Sex, Mrs. Mary Blaize. Oliver Goldsmith. OnYI

She had, she said, embraced Philosophy. They Meet Again. Mary Aldis. HBMV

She had the fewer for what she did. Cuckoo. *Anonymous.* AnOE

She had to be Milked by a Man and his Wife. The Cow. Theodore Roethke. FiBHP; OBAL; OBCA

She had to sit down on the floor. Limerick: "There was a young girl of Lahore." Cosmo Monkhouse. HBV 1-2

She had to step it up and go! Step It Up and Go. *Anonymous.* FSW

...She has/a policeman and a wrong sonnet in fifteen lines. To a Red-Headed Do-Good Waitress. Alan Dugan. CAPP

She has at heart a certain dawn. Now She Is Like the White Tree-Rose. C. Day-Lewis. CMoP; FaBoTw; MoBrPo

She has brown breasts and the mouth of no other country. Landscape as a Nude. Archibald MacLeish. CMoP

She has gone weeping away. The Lover Mourns for the Loss of Love. William Butler Yeats. WeW

She has lain down/with the lord, white as jasmine,/and has lost caste. O Brothers, Why Do You Talk. Mahadevi (Mahadeviyakka). WPOW

She has lain in the church-yard full many a year. Down Hall. Matthew Prior. MyFE

She has made the grass grener even here with her grave–/My Kate. My Kate. Elizabeth Barrett Browning. OBVV; OHFP; WBLP

An she has marred Dugall Quin,/An lives belou Strathbogy. Dugall Quin (A version). *Anonymous.* ESPB

She has no bosom and no behind. This Englishwoman. Stevie Smith. FaBoEE

She has no honour and she has no fear. Invasion Summer. Laurie Lee. OBSP

She has not put her face on. On a Painted Woman. Percy Bysshe Shelley. FaBoCo; NLV

She has taken back into her flesh,/and made light, the dark seed of her pain. Poem for J. Wendell Berry. GeTw

She has the self-same eyes too/That wrought me such misery. I Met by Chance. Heinrich Heine. AWP

She has well chosen silence/With her hands crossed. Requiescat. Katherine Anne Porter. HBMV

She hath an art to break them with her eyes. Thrice Toss These Oaken Ashes in the Air. Thomas Campion. AnFE; AtBAP; EBEV; EiL; EnLoPo; FaBoCh; HAP; LoBV; LoGBV; MAT; OAEL 1-2; OBSP; PoEL 1-5; PoRA; ViBoPo

She hath her reward. The Man Who Married Magdalene... Anthony Hecht. CoPo

...She hears/someone crying, then her father's voice raised in anger. Girl in White. Stephen Dobyns. MAYP

She hears the caustic ticking of the clock. Cinderella. Sylvia Plath. DFT

She hears the infantry of eyes advance. The Retreat of Ita Cagney. Michael Hartnett. CIP

She heeds them not (poor Bird) her soul's with him. The Beggar's Opera. John Gay. PoEL 1-5

She held it as her dying creed/That she would grow again. For My Grandmother. Countee Cullen. CDC; GoSl; VGW

She her Endymion, I'll my Phoebe kiss. Madrigal: "Stay, nymph." Francis Pilkington. EnRePo

She hers, he his, pursuing. The Dalliance of Eagles. Walt Whitman. AA; AmPP; BiP; BoAnP; FM; HAP; HeIP; NoP; PoL; PPoe; PPP; PrIm; TAP

She hit her mother forty-one. The Crimes of Lizzie Borden. *Anonymous.* FaBoCo; FaFP

She holds the cat so close to her he pants. Moving. Randall Jarrell. DFF

She holds you up. The Accomplice. Ron Slate. AMV-80

She hopes that he never will do it again. Young Sammy Watkins. *Anonymous.* BBGG

She hugs the dart that wounded her, and dies. After the fiercest pangs of hot desire. Richard Duke. BoLoP

She hurries through the night to a far lover. The Runner in the Skies. James. James Oppenheim AnEnPo; TrJP

She, I think, will tell no tale. Song: "Under the lime-tree, on the daisied ground." Walther von der Vogelweide. OBVE

She is a lo'esome wee thing,/This sweet wee wife o' mine. My Wife's a Winsome Wee Thing. Robert Burns. HBV 1-2; LiTL

She is a mistress to my mind. Yes, I Could Love if I Could Find. *Anonymous.* ALV

She is a poet/she don't have no sense Admonitions. Lucille Clifton. BPo; NMM; PAI

She is a tree in spring/Trembling with the hope of leaves,/Of which the leaves are tongues. First Love. Stanley Jasspon Kunitz. GOYP

...She/Is all of darkness in the dark. The Landscape of Love. Thomas Cole. NePoAm

She is all these, and ten times more. On a Mistress of Whose Affections He Was Doubtful. Thomas Nabbes. EG

She is blind... Spirit, Silken Thread. Margot Ruddock. OBMV

She is breaking tradition. Breaking Tradition. Janice Mirikitani. BrSi

She is caught. Captive. Marion Strobel. ErPo

She is changing back again to spring's. May Is Building Her House. Richard Le Gallienne. HBVY; OHIP; YeAr

She is Death enjoying Life,/Innocently,/Lasciviously. Autumn Night. Evelyn Scott. AnAmPo

She is great,/we measure her by the pine-trees. Moonrise. Hilda ("H. D.") Doolittle. PoA

She is happy and I am contented. On a Shrew. *Anonymous.* FaBoEE

She is her God's ideal. God's Ideal Mother. Cora M. Pinkham. STF

She is his slave for many lives. My eyes are thirsty. Mira Bai [(or Mirabai)]. BoWoP

She is living all alone/In this old house. Sadie and Maud. Gwendolyn Brooks. NoAm; NOBA; TAP

She is looking so lovely today. A Spring Song. *Anonymous.* PoLf

She is more strong than death,/Being strong as love. Madonna Mia. Algernon Charles Swinburne. HBV 1-2

She is my cenotaph. I Am the Blood. Isaac Rosenberg. MoBrPo

She is my mother: you will agree/That all the rest may be thrown away. Her Mother. Alice Cary. OHIP

She is my soverene and serene,/Off womanheid the flour delice. Off Womanheid Ane Flour Delice. *Anonymous.* OxBS

She is no woman, but a senseless stone. Of This World's Theater in Which We Stay. Edmund Spenser. NIP

She is noiseless on the stones. The Street. Gene Baro. NYBP

She is not on good terms with my wife. I Hear That Lycoris Has Buried. Martial (Marcus Valerius Martialis). DBV

She is now water and air,/Who was earth and fire. Sea Burial from the Cruiser "Reve." Richard Eberhart. NYBP

She is only unseen, unseen? To Clarissa Scott Delany. Angelina Weld Grimke. AmNP

She is our first attempt at victory, our final/painted desert of defeat. The Pro. Karen Swenson. AMV-81

She is possessed by time, who once/Was loved by men. Portrait. Louise Bogan. HBMV

She is such an unrivalled goddess in appearance. Love Song: "My loved one is unique, without a peer." *Anonymous.* TTY

She is teck'wi:/Taboo. The Taboo Woman. *Anonymous.* WTO

She is the best dressed. A Fixture. May Swenson. NYBP

She is/The constellation/Of all creation. A Little Girl. Charles Angoff. GoYe

She is the fairest of her days. The Fairest of Her Days. *Anonymous.* EiL

She is the queen of all the rest. The Kinkaiders. *Anonymous.* CoSo

She is the seed and the eye and the Moon-That-/Diminishes,/the counting memory of space. The Lunar Games. Eeva-Liisa Manner. WPOW

She is the Sunshine of Paradise Alley. The Sunshine of Paradise Alley. Walter H. Ford. FSN

She is the thing that she despises. Amoret. William Congreve. ViBoPo

She is with-out longing. The Tokens of Love: I. *Anonymous.* GBP

She is worth her weight in gold/Tell her so! Tell Her So. *Anonymous.* PoToHe

She is worthy to be enrolled/With letters of gold./Car elle vault. The Commendations of Mistress Jane Scrope. John Skelton. OBSC

She kicked old Crumbly on the chin,/And blood ran to his toes. Old Crumbly Crust. *Anonymous.* BFSS

She kindly kissed his cheek with lips of roses. Within a Greenwood Sweet of Myrtle Savour. *Anonymous.* GBL

She kissed me for good-night. So you'll not tell. A Match with the Moon. Dante Gabriel Rossetti. NCEP; NOBV; VLP

She kissed me through her tears, and set/On high this spangling comb. The Comb. Walter De la Mare. FaBoRV

She kist, and wip'd their dove-like eyes;/And gave the bag between them. The Bag of the Bee. Robert Herrick. OAEP

She knew him—by his appetite! The Recognition (parody). Frederick William Sawyer. HBV 1-2

She knew what it meant—but she went! Limerick: "There was a young lady of Kent." Anonymous. CenHV; LiBL

She knew what they alone can know/Who live above but dwell below. Our Sister. Horatio Nelson Powers. HBV 1-2

She knits the only warmth/she will receive all winter. The Old Woman Sits. Leasa Davis. CTBA

She knows it's there, it's there. Dame Liberty Reports from Travel. Dorothy Cowles Pinkney. GoYe

She knows my Wrongs, and will regard my Pray'r. Elegy: to Delia. James Hammond. CEP

She knows not I am beggar at her door. Ursula. Robert Underwood Johnson. HBV 1-2

She knows nothing about babies. The Cherry Tree. Thom Gunn. Psk

She knows so much that she did not know. Experience. Aline Kilmer. BiCB; HBMV

She knows there is a woman in each one. Another Poem about the Madness of Women. Tom Wayman. NOBC

...She knows you are running back into/yourself. Autobiography: Last Chapter. Jim Barnes. CDW

She'l never kiss you I dare swear. Epodes. Horace. OBVE

She laugh'd and danced—but not like them. The Time Hath Been. Joseph Skipsey. VLP

She laughed, he frowned; I turned and went my way. A Lawn-Tennisonian Idyll (parody). Anonymous. FaBoPa

She laughs to see his bobbing dance. The Waltzer in the House. Stanley Jasspon Kunitz. ErPo; NYBP

She lay before me small and still/And did not care at all. A Wind Rose in the Night. Aline Kilmer. HBMV

She lay beside me in the dawn. Alba. Ezra Pound. GBL; HAP; SOTW; WeW

She lay deid in her lover's airms,/Between that day and morrow. The Dowie Dens of Yarrow. Anonymous. FSW

She lay distracted in a ditch,/Considering how to run. Quandary. Mrs. Edward Craster. GoTF; TreFS

She lay down and died and was buried in dirt. The Housewife's Lament. Anonymous. MAT

She lays six eggs in colours dull,/Blotched thick with spots of burning red. The Missel-Thrush's Nest. John Clare. VLP

She leaned her face, her thick hair shut/Her from the stars and trees. Symbols. Vance Thompson. AA

She leaned over and whispered: "You go with me." Indian Macho. Louis (LittleCoon) Oliver. STE

She leans across the hilltop: see, the light! Dawn-Song to Waken the Lovers. Anonymous. LiTW

She leaves a little measle The honey bee. Don (Donald Robert Marquis) Marquis. BoAnP; FPL; PoPl

She leaves her soldier—famine and a name! The American Soldier. Philip Freneau. TAP

She leaves the clover standing/And the Queen Anne's lace! Portrait by a Neighbor. Edna St. Vincent Millay. LOW; MoShBr; OBCA; TiPo

She left a bit of her tail in a trap. Riddle: "Old Mother Twitchet had but one eye." Mother Goose. SoPo

She left a long-abiding curse/On the chiefs of the Red Branch... Dinnshenchas: The Story of Macha. Anonymous. OnYI

She felt lonely for ever/The kings of the sea.' The Forsaken Merman. Matthew Arnold. BeLS; BoLiVe; CBEP; EBEV; EtS; FaBoCh; FaPoR; FiP; ForPo; GN; GTBS; HBV 1-2; LoGBV; MaVP; MCCG; MOS; OAEP; OBNV; OBVV; PoPle; ViBoPo; VLP; WHA

...She left out/A large part of the story but told it well. Rubaiyat for Sue Ella Tucker. Miller Williams. SM

She left the bowl with me. And that is that. A Good Thing. Ray Mathew. CBAP

She left this world of sorrow and pain,/And return'd to the land of thought again. Kilmeny. James Hogg. CABL; HBV 1-2; OBEV; OBRV

She let her head be driven/against the stone, and made a mass of fragments of it, and she was dead. Exile of the Sons of Uisliu (excerpt). Anonymous. NOBI

She lies long in the sun/slides among the roots/and muses The Serpent Muses. Peggy Henderson. NMM

She lies where I cannot be. Variations on a Medieval Theme. Geoffrey Dutton. PoAu 1-2

She lifts attentively. That/will be all, I suppose. A Reliable Service. Allen Curnow. OCNZ

She lights on earth the New/Jerusalem! The Star. Willoughby Weaving. HBMV; HBVY

She lived long, till God gave her rest. A Cat. Edward ("Edward Eastaway") Thomas. BoAnP; BrPo

"She lives, but all her usefulness is past." Uselessness. Ella Wheeler Wilcox. TrPWD

She lives in glory—like the sun/Amid the blue of June. She Died in Beauty. Charles Doyne Sillery. HBV 1-2

She'll be comin' round the mountain, When she comes. She'll Be Comin' Round the Mountain (with music). Anonymous. AS

She'll be fruitful, never fear her. Oysters. Jonathan Swift. ErPo

She'll come to deem the Dragon dead/Has waked to life again. The Dragon of the Seas. Thomas Nelson Page. PAH

She'll cup no joy now in her palm,/But perch it on her knuckle.. A Lesson in Detachment. Vassar Miller. NePoEA-2

She'll do, my friend, whatever you desire. Ageless. Anonymous. UnTE

She'll dress like a lady,/And dance on the green. Washing Day. Anonymous. OxNR

She'll get/a ticket How to Walk in a Crowd. Robert Hershon. FF

She'll keep you buying rats all the time Short Haired Woman. Lightning Hopkins. BluL

She'll love to hear you mutter: "Damn that bird!" Unregenerate. Jacqueline Embry. HBMV

She'll make up her mind not to mind them. Rhyme for Botanical Baby. Joseph Cook. QQQ; SpRo

She'll never break this heart of mine. Hangman (with music). Anonymous. AS

She'll rise a star that fell a flower. On Eleanor Freeman. Anonymous. OBEV

She'll run to all adulteries. To His Book. Robert Herrick. OBSP

She long had wanted cause of fear. A Sonnet: "Weeping, murmuring, complaining." Oliver Goldsmith. NOBI

She looked like a stranger when she died. Another Death. D. E. Borrell. FF

She loved him with a feeling/Or she won't love at all You Got to Love Her with a Feeling. Tampa Red. BluL

She loved it before it was understood. The Causes of Color. Ann Rae Jonas. SUW

She loved the tarry sailor well,/And told the squire to go to hell. Jack the Jolly Tar. Anonymous. AmFP

"She loved you better than you knew." Left Behind. Elizabeth Akers. HBV 1-2

She loves, and loves for ever. Song: "Oh! say not woman's love is bought." Isaac Pocock. HBV 1-2

She loves him...and the frightening fact sinks in. Americanized. Bruce Dawe. CBAP

She loves you not; she never heard of love. Fatal Interview. Edna St. Vincent Millay. VGW

She low obeisance made, and disappear'd. Davideis. Abraham Cowley. OxBoCh

She made a Heaven about her here,/And took how much! with her away. In Memoriam. Richard Monckton, Lord Houghton Milnes. HBV 1-2

She made me weep. The Village Tudda. Kenneth Patchen. VGW

She made the little woods so ring,/They waked me from my sleep. Upon a Dainty Hill Sometime. Nicholas Breton. PBBP

She makes it glory, now, to be a man. America. Bayard Taylor. AA; PAL

She may become more kind to thee or me. To Delia. Samuel Daniel. OBSC

She may let me take/The bloom from my wild Irish rose. My Wild Irish Rose. Chauncey Olcott. BLSo; FSN; FSW; GoTF; TreFT

...She/May not exist. The Unknown. Edward ("Edward Eastaway") Thomas. GBL

She may rub so hard they will disappear! Going Too Far. Mildred Howells. OnMSP; TiPo

She may search this wide world over,/Never find as sweet a man as me. St. James Infirmary. Anonymous. TreFT

She meditates, a vision of repose. Cat on Couch. Barbara Howes. DFF; NCSH

She might be a mirage, and my long/Soliloquies part of the action. Desert Warfare. Michael Longley. CIP

She might have survived and he would have gotten out/of her bed. Radical Coherency. David Antin. APU

She might have to acknowledge her latest face. Evasion. Blanaid Salkeld. NeIP

She mourn'd in silence, and was Di-do-dum. On the Latin Gerunds. Richard Porson. FaBoUs

She moves like a she-tortoise/head tilted over/1983's Guide to Real Estate. Condo Girl. Elaine Equi. APU

She murmured "Homo"...and then added "Sap!" Afterthought. Justin Richardson. PV

She murmurs an old air/That she used to know!   The Blind Linnet.   Robert Williams Buchanan.   FM

She must be free, though I stand bound and still.   On a Pair of Garters.   Sir John Davies.   CBEP; SiPS

She must have known before she came/That it was Christmas Eve.   One Night.   Marchette Chute.   ChBR

She must have something heavy inside.   My Sister Laura.   Spike Milligan.   NTCP

...She must/have swept them from the corners of her studio–was full/of dead bees.   A Story About the Body.   Robert Hass.   GeTw; NPGG

She must make love slowly, the way/she climbs the stairs.   Last Night They Heard the Woman Upstairs.   Leslie Ullman.   AMV-80

...She must, of due,/Render for that a crown of life to you.   To Mistress Katherine Bradshaw, the Lovely, That Crowned Him...   Robert Herrick.   CaPo

She must show black and blue, or no divorce/Is granted by the Law of Physical Force.   As Proper Mode of Quenching Legal Lust.   Gerald Massey.   NOBV

She, my heart's friend.   The Heart's Friend.   Mary Austin.   BPAW

She needs good character indeed.   Women.   Anonymous.   WTO

She neither taught the Father to destroy//Nor promis'd any man, by dying, joy.   Mustapha.   Fulke, Lord Brooke Greville.   OBS

She nerved her heart with woman's pride,/And spurned his fickle love.   He Came Too Late.   Elizabeth Bogart.   AA

She never knew to call me Beast or Swan.   The Sleeping Beauty.   Leonard Cohen.   DFT

She never looks back.   29 (A Dream in Two Parts).   Ai.   MAYP

She never, no never, no never would tell.   Was She a Witch?   Laura E. Richards.   SoPo

She never was much given to literature.   Alas! for the South!   J. Gordon Coogler.   HBV 1-2; OBAL

She never will say "No!"   When We Court and Kiss.   Thomas Campion.   UnTE

She now may sit to Gavarni.   Spring in the Students' Quarter.   Henri Murger.   AWP

She, onely she, is ever chast,/That is with every looke outfact.   Gaze Not on Youth.   Anonymous.   NCEP

She, only she, can please the taste!   To an Author.   Philip Freneau.   AmPP; MAmP; NOBA; OxBA

...She/opened all the drawers and doors and windows–and a cool bay/breeze shot through.   Diagnosis.   Janine Canan.   APU

She opens her legs to your coming.   How You Get Born.   Erica Jong.   UnPo

She ought to sign it "Pinxit."   Artist.   Ernestine Mercer.   InMe

She passively nods. And they go that way.   By Her Aunt's Grave.   Thomas Hardy.   BrPo

She pets the wet neck/of her horse!   Two at Showtime.   Suzanne Brabant.   PH

She pictures her face and breasts/lit by that tin badge/flashing in the sun.   Calamity Jane Greets Her Dreams.   Kathleen Lignell.   AMV-80

She placed the rose behind her ear/& cried herself to sleep.   For Colored Girls Who Have Considered Suicide...(excerpt).   Ntozake Shange.   BoWoP

She played Bach so that/it was carved and fragrant.   I Know a Man.   Peggy Steele.   PPJ

She pricked hard, and made herself to bleed.   Epigram: "Who hath heard of such cruelty before?   Sir Thomas Wyatt.   SiPS

She promised to come hersel,/But she sent three men to slay me.'   The Duke of Athole's Nurse (A version).   Anonymous.   ESPB

She proved to be the King's daughter,/And he but a blacksmith's son.   The Knight and Shepherd's Daughter (B vers.).   Anonymous.   BaBo; ESPB

She pulled him by his twirly tail/All about the house.   C Was Papa's Gray Cat.   Edward Lear.   PCat

She put her arms around me and we cried.   The Truth.   Randall Jarrell.   OxBC

She quenched his spirit's motion.   Two Puritans.   Anonymous.   UnTE

She reads it/as a metaphor/for her   Generation Gap.   Bronwen Wallace.   AMV-80

"She reaped as she sowed, Lo! this is her son!"   To My Son.   Margaret Johnston Grafflin.   PoToHe; SoSe

She recognized the symptoms as her own.   How Jack Found that Beans May Go Back on a Chap.   Guy Wetmore Carryl.   ALV; HoPM

...She/records us in it, weeping, nearly mad.   In Lombardy.   Donald Revell.   SM

She replaces the packages under her arms/And walks through the door.   Doors.   Tom Clark.   ConAP

She returns to Andre with the sails.   Kites.   Michael Brownstein.   ANYP

She rights! she rights! Boys, we're off shore!   The Tempest.   Anonymous.   AmFP

She rode for exercise, and thus/Rhode Island every day.   Stately Verse.   Anonymous.   TiPo

She rode till she came to her father's hall,/Three hours before it was day.   The Outlandish Knight.   Anonymous.   ShM

She rose and from the bed-side crept/With cautious step away.   The Nurse Believed the Sick Man Slept.   Charlotte Bronte.   NOBV

She runs ahead, beyond the fallen horse.   Charioteer.   Witter ("Emanuel Morgan") Bynner.   AnFE

She runs & runs & runs.   A Day at the Races.   Louis Phillips.   PH

She rustles, rustles through the town.   November Wears a Paisley Shawl.   Hilda Morris.   YeAr

She rusts beneath the rolling sea.   The Sinking of the Graf Spee.   Anonymous.   OBSS

She's a bird in a gilded cage.   A Bird in a Gilded Cage.   Arthur J. Lamb.   BLSo; FSN; FSW; GoTF; TreFT

She's a fine looking fair brown/but she ain't never learned Lemon's rule.   Chock House Blues.   Blind Lemon Jefferson.   BluL

She's a greenhorn, you're another."/Fal tum a link tum, a tu rye day.   Madame, I Have Come A-Courting.   Anonymous.   AmFP

She's a young thing, and cannot leave her mother.   Billy Boy.   Anonymous.   ABF; AmFP; BLPA; HoPM; OxNR

"She's all my fancy painted her,'/But oh! how much besides!   Disillusioned.   Lewis (Charles Lutwidge Dodgson) Carroll.   CenHV

She's already figured me out.   Dinah.   Archie Randolph Ammons.   PV

She's as true as your mountains/And as pure as the dove.   Old Smoky.   Anonymous.   AmFP

She's built. Does she or doesn't she?   Untitled Poem. "Hands folded like napkins in my lap."   Robert Peterson.   NeAC

She's but to please herself the world to/please.   A Countrywoman of Mine.   Elaine Goodale Eastman.   AA

She's even afraid of the bark of a tree.   The Hero.   Leroy F. Jackson.   SiSoSe

She's fair, whose beauty only makes her gay.   To His Mistress.   Abraham Cowley.   EG

"She's got more gold on her little finger/Than you, new bride and all your kin."   The Turkish Lady.   Anonymous.   BaBo

She's here, installed amid the kitchen ware!   Song of the Exposition (excerpt).   Walt Whitman.   PP

She's hoy'd me out o' Lauderdale,/My fiddle and a' thegither.   She's Hoy'd Me Out o' Lauderdale.   Anonymous.   CoMu

She's left five little goslings/to scratch for their own bread.   The Old Gray Goose.   Anonymous.   GBP

She's mandarin of a cow beside the Golden Horn!   And When They Fall.   James J. Montague.   HBMV

She's mine till death shall set her free/Those bells shall not ring out!   Those Wedding Bells Shall Not Ring Out.   Monroe F. Rosenfeld.   FSN

She's my freckle-faced, consumptive Mary Jane.   She Promised She'd Meet Me (with music).   Anonymous.   AS

She's my little baby/love her just the same   She's Mine.   Lightning Hopkins.   BluL

She's my Nancy, please-my-fancy,/I'm her charming Billy boy.'   Billy Boy.   Anonymous.   OBET

She's my wife. Ther' ain't none better than ole Filkin's daughter Nell.   The Engineer's Story.   Eugene J. Hall.   PaPo

She's nodding her head at me!   Springtime.   Alfred Kreymborg.   MAPA

She's not and never can be mine.   The Angel in the House.   Coventry Patmore.   EG; VLP

She's not fit for heaven and she's too mean for hell.   The Bad-Tempered Wife.   Anonymous.   MaC

She's now yo' own. Salute yo' bride!   Slave Marriage Ceremony Supplement.   Anonymous.   BPo; PoL; TAP

She's o'er the Border, and awa'/Wi' Jock of Hazeldean!   Jock of Hazeldean.   Sir Walter Scott.   BeLS; BFSS; EnLit; GN; GTBS; GTBS-P; HBV 1-2; MCCG; OAEP; OBRV; OxBS; TEP

She's only been gone an hour.   The Fate of the Cabbage Rose.   Wallace Irwin.   FiBHP

She's really quite too old for me.   Time's Revenge.   Walter Learned.   HBV 1-2

She's resting in the bosom of Jesus.   Go Down Death.   James Weldon Johnson.   AnAmPo; DL; PoBA; TRV

She's sailed, and sailed, but she'll sail no more./She's a-sinking to the bottom of the sea.   The Ship A-Raging.   Anonymous.   BFSS

She's sitting on the garden bench/Listening to a bird!   Where's Mary?   Ivy O. Eastwick.   TiPo

She's the flag of our country forever!   Our Flag Forever.   Frank Lebby Stanton.   PGD

She's the mint in the julep of joy.   Have You Seen the Lady?   John Philip Sousa.   OBAL

She's the one I will marry on Red River shore.   Red River Shore.   Anonymous.   ABF

"She's the stilliest child I ever heard!"   Extremes.   James Whitcomb Riley.   HBVY

She's to me a paragon.   No Loathsomeness in Love.   Robert Herrick.   AnAnS 2; GBL

She's too loose if you get in.   Ignorant Men, Who Disclaim.   Sister Juana Ines de la Cruz.   PBWP

She said, - "Auf Wiedersehen!" Auf Wiedersehen. James Russell Lowell AA; HBV 1-2

She said farewell forever. Black Jack Davie. *Anonymous.* BaBo

She said, "Hello, and do please note/My lovely furry wolfskin coat." Little Red Riding Hood and the Wolf. Roald Dahl. DFT

She said, "I will go to Solomon." Balkis. Lascelles Abercrombie. HBV 1-2

She said, "it's history." The Silent Generation. Louis Simpson. CAPP; NePoAm-2

She said it was pear Robert, but non pear Jennet. The Pear-Tree. *Anonymous.* GBP

...She said, "That's what/you think." Myth. Muriel Rukeyser. FaBoWP; IHMS; NNaP

She said, "Yes, but not during vacation!" Limerick: "A schoolma'am of much reputation." Minnie Leona Upton. TDH

She saide I was a prety manne/And wel coude bere myn baselard! My Baselard. *Anonymous.* OxBM

She salaams down/on to, dear God, well trodden ground. In Memory, 1978. Judith Kazantzis. BrRo

She sang this "Song of the Shirt!" The Song of the Shirt. Thomas Hood. CABL; CoBE; EnRP; FaPoR; HBV 1-2; MaC; MCCG; OBVV; PaPo; PPON; SaC; TEP; TreF; VLP; WBLP

She sank into the moonlight/And the sea was only sea. Santorin. James Elroy Flecker. FaBoTw; GoJo; OBMV

She sank, thank God! unsoiled by foot of/traitor! The Attack. Thomas Buchanan Read. PAH

She sat by the fire/And told many a fine tale. My Little Wife. *Anonymous.* OxNR

She says I am her rain beau since/I kissed her in the rain. A Kiss in the Rain. Samuel Minturn Peck. OBAL

She says no word, but looks on the the crown He has worn... Fourth Station. Paul Claudel. ISi

She scrap'd her tripe, lick thou the knife. Three Blind Mice. *Anonymous.* FaBoNo; OBS

She searched in her basket/And fixed her ruffled sheet. The Laundress. Thomas Kinsella. IPY

She seemed to be a witch.... The Tunning of Elinor Rumming. John Skelton. AAS; EBEV; EnPo; OAEL 1-2; TrGrPo

She sees her image in the glass. The Shadow Dance. Louise Chandler Moulton. AA; HBV 1-2

She sees how much of me is rotten. Ode to a Dental Hygienist. Earnest Albert Hooton. FiBHP

She seized her time and made new. Looking at Quilts. Marge Piercy. SaC

...She/Sets up for love and gallantry. The Coquette. Aphra Behn. TrGrPo; ViBoPo

She shall have music wherever she goes. Ride a Cockhorse. Mother Goose. ExPo; FaBoBe; FaFP; HBV 1-2; HBVY; SoPo; TiPo

She shall live in the proud memorial of your arms! Appeal. Sousa, Noemia Da. TTY; WPOW

She shall my heart obtain. Love doth again. Sir Thomas Wyatt. FCP; SiPS

She shall sleep. Ginevra (excerpt). Percy Bysshe Shelley. ChRP

She shattered on the pavement. Woman, Gallup, N.M. Karen Swenson. NYBP

She, she herself, and only she,/Shone through her body visibly. Phantom. Samuel Taylor Coleridge. ERoP 1-2; OAEL 1-2; OBSP; PoEL 1-5

She shines intrinsically fair. The Lover's Choice. Thomas Bedingfield. HBV 1-2

She shines, the first white love of my youth, passionless and in vain. A White Blossom. D. H. Lawrence. MoBrPo

...She shook/Me saying I was talking in my sleep. East Texas. Leon Stokesbury. SM

She shook the world. The Poet. Alfred, Lord Tennyson. EnL; OAEP; PP

"She should have thought of the chance she took,/Making a pass at a poet's cook." Malice Domestic. Ogden Nash. DBV

She should ne'er be ruled by he. The Old Man Who Lived in a Wood. *Anonymous.* MoShBr

She–shrieking–turned and fled. Little Miss Muffet (parody). *Anonymous.* BXAP; FaBoPa

She sighed for the ruins of her country/As she strolled along Dixie's green shore. Dixie's Green Shore. *Anonymous.* BFSS

She sighed voluptuously, voice trailing into the night. I Turned On the Hot Water. Janine Canan. APU

She sighs, then tags a femur, pondering the remains. On Hearing a Beautiful Young Woman Describe Her Class... A. J. Hovde. AMV-81

She simply wasn't there! The Messed Damozel (parody). Charles Hanson Towne. SpRo

She sings and threads her antique tapestry. My Lady Takes the Sunlight for Her Gown. Thomas Cole. NePoAm

She sings some simple song. The Court We Live On. Bill Tremblay. TAT

...She sits to think/of tonight's dinner. Tomorrow's pressing. Days through Starch and Bluing. Alice Fulton. GOYP

She sleeps every afternoon. It Fell on a Summer's Day. Thomas Campion. ErPo; HAP; UnTE; WeW

She slipped through the straw and fell in. Limerick: "There was a young lady of Lynn." *Anonymous.* CenHV; SoSe

She smells exactly like hot buttered toast! Smells. Christopher Morley. TiPo

She smiled, and put a rose into her hair. Idyl. Alfred Mombert. AWP

She smiles like a victor, serene on the world! Lines Addressed to a Seagull. Gerald Griffin. OnYI

She smiles; she cannot quite forget/The mother overseas! Thompson Street. Samuel McCoy. HBMV

She smiles, she triumphs; but the Crucified/Falls off into the darkness with a cry. The Temptation of Saint Anthony. Arthur Symons. BrPo

She, sole of all the innumerous feathered tribes,/Passes a stranger's life, without a home. The Birds of Scotland (excerpt). James Grahame. PBBP

She spends her days looking for crows. Let me see you. Mira Bai [(or Mirabai)]. BoWoP

She spills/her last proposition/an abstraction lost in her moan. Rapist. Jose Y., Jr. Teran. LFAC

She stands on two hooves while the machine is on her,/And almost dances. The New Cows. Charles Waterman. GP

She stares into the night. The Storm. Heinrich Heine. AWP

She steals away./For awhile. To My New Mistress. Beverly Bowie. PoPl

She stole oranges,/I do believe. My Mammy's Maid. *Anonymous.* OxNR

She stood on a Member that cost as much/As a Member for all the County! Miss Kilmansegg and Her Precious Leg. Thomas Hood. NOBV

She stood on her head while Aunt Lily/Hung buckets full of water from her feet,/to no avail. The Old Girl. Gary Lenhart. APU

She stoops–to drink the meaning/At the still brink of song. Piano Recital. Babette Deutsch. NePoAm

She stript him and tore him, she tore him in three,/Because he had murdered her baby and she. The Gosport Tragedy (A vers.). *Anonymous.* BaBo

She survived–sadder, wiser and sloa. Limerick: "A lady track star from Toccoa." Jr, Blount Roy. TDH

She swallows the river/and mourns on down, a thin bellyful Madwoman at Rodmell. Michele Roberts. BrRo

She sweeps herself up into the line/Of darkness that is her discipline. The Lady in the Barbershop. Raphael Rudnik. NYBP

She swept the heavy rugs today/And hung them on the line. Signs. Beatrice M. Murphy. GoSl

She takes him inside. My love is in my house. Mira Bai [(or Mirabai)]. BoWoP

She takes the blues away and satisfies my mind One Way Gal. William Moore. BluL

She tasted/death. She Tasted Death. John Giorno. ANYP

...She tells me/it is spring and that means perfume. Smell My Fingers. David B. Axelrod. Str

She thanked God most cheerfully/The dangers she oercame. Lady Isabel and the Elf Knight (B version). *Anonymous.* ESPB

She that a clinquant outside doth adore,/Dotes on a gilded statue, and no more. Strive Not, Vain Lover, to Be Fine. Richard Lovelace. OAEP

She, that can this weapon use,/Fire and sword with ease subdues. Beauty. Thomas Stanley. AWP; PG

She that makes the humblest hearth/Lovely but to one on earth! Corinne at the Capitol. Felicia Dorothea Hemans. BrRo

She that, Oh, broke her faith, would soon breake/thee. A Jeat Ring Sent. John Donne. PoEL 1-5

She the insect in his brain,/Nor he her angry God. Titus and Berenice. John Heath-Stubbs. GTBS-P

...She then/exploded, killing ten. One Morning We Brought Them Order. Al Lee. FF

She thinks nothing was/Before she came. Birth. Constance Urdang. VWA

She throws a stone and laughs at the clug-clug. Three Spring Notations on Bipeds. Carl Sandburg. AWP; InPo

She tied it round "her' white hause-bane,/"And tint her life on Yarrow.' The Braes o Yarrow (A version). *Anonymous.* ESPB; ViBoFo

She ties a carbon ribbon in her hair and dreams,/longing for the missing text and the hard copy. Nude Reclining at Word Processor, in Pastel. Carl Conover. GOYP

She to heaven has passed. Dirge. Charles Gamage Eastman AA

The she-toad vetoed him. Tree Toad. *Anonymous.* NTCP

She, too, has wings. Warning to Cupid. *Anonymous.* UnTE

She took a good half-hour to loose and lay/Those locks in dazzling disarrangement so! Eve's Daughter. Edward Rowland Sill. AmePo

She took a million lives to pay the debt. Harpers Ferry. Selden Rodman. PoNe

She took and she did spank her most emphatic. There Was a Little Girl. Henry Wadsworth Longfellow. GoTF; LBN; NA; TreF

She took my sword from her side all bloody/And died for love. My Lady Has the Grace of Death. Joseph Mary Plunkett. OxBI

...She took the tax away/And built herself an everlasting name. Godiva. Alfred, Lord Tennyson. BeLS; HBV 1-2

She trades on broken English with success/And, disenchanted, I'm enamoured yet. Hearing Russian Spoken. Donald Davie. GTBS-P; NePoEA-2

She trembling, asked that I should leave./I stayed. At Early Morn. Binga Dismond. PoNe

She, trembling, creeps upon the ground away,/And looks back to him with beseeching eyes. Annus Mirabilis. John Dryden. FiP

She tried to kill her husband with a boomerang. Cassie O'Lang. Anonymous. ShM

She turn'd back at the last to wait/And say farewell once more. Song: "I made another garden, yea." Arthur William Edgar O'Shaughnessy. HBV 1-2; OBEV; OBVV

She turned/And made her slow way back to the house. Aunt Alice in April. William H. Matchett. CTBA

She turned and thinned away. The Woman I Met. Thomas Hardy. AtBAP

She turned back. Hardcastle Crags. Sylvia Plath. GoYe

She turned her back upon the day/But will not lie at night alone. Elegy Written on a Frontporch. Karl Shapiro. MoPo

She turns into corruption and disease. Sodom; or, The Quintessence of Debauchery (excerpt). John Wilmot, Earl of Rochester. PeHV

...She turns the necklace/kindly in her fingers, and soothes the beads. Blue Glass. Fleur Adcock. FaBoWP

She turns upon her other side. In Moncur Street. Dorothy Hewett. NOAV

She vanished, and was gone. Full Moon. Walter De La Mare. AtBAP; BoNaP; TiPo

She vanished, leaving fragrant breath/And warmth and chill of wedded life and death. Pontoosuce. Herman Melville. MAmP; NOBA

She vows that they shall lead/Apes in Avernus. Hark, All You Ladies That Do Sleep. Thomas Campion. AAS; EBEV; EiL; OAEP; PoEL 1-5

She waited,/and was good. My Mother's Childhood. Barry Spacks. GP

She waits for truth; and truth is with the dreamer,–/Persistent as the myriad light of stars! Dream the Great Dream. Florence Earle Coates. HBMV

...She waits/for your applause. Equestrienne. Joan Colby. PoDr

She waits, from earthly cares forever free. Remembrance. Margaret E. Bruner. PoToHe

...She waits in her surface, her name my speech's/mistress. Bordering Manuscript. James Applewhite. PoA

She waits the wizard that will never come/To wake the sleep-struck playground of the dead. Mimma Bella. Eugene Lee-Hamilton. HBV 1-2

She walked the deep fields of the sky. High-Tide. Jean Starr Untermeyer. MCCG; MoAmPo

She walks like a captive/in fetters. What Can You Expect. Maryam bint Abi. WPOW

She walks–the lady of my delight–/A shepherdess of sheep. The Shepherdess. Alice Meynell. ACP; AWP; GoBC; GoTF; HBV 1-2; HBVY; MoBrPo; NOBV; OBVV; PeD; SBG; TreFS

"She waltzed rather well! It's a pity she's dead!" An Epitaph. George John Cayley. ELU; FiBHP; HBV 1-2

She wants it to stop. An Old Lady Watching TV. Knute Skinner. SOTS

She wants the best for you/when you get out/of that pen Aunt Beulah's Wisdom. Earl Gene Box. LFAC

She warbles wildly as before! On Sivori's Violin. Frances Sargent Osgood AA

She was a beauty in the days/When Madison was President. She Was a Beauty. Henry Cuyler Bunner. AA; HBV 1-2

She was a child's purse, full of useless things. Death of an Irishwoman. Michael Hartnett. CIP

She was a nice girl, a decent girl,/But one of the rakish kind. The Fire Ship. Anonymous. AmSS

She was a phantom of delight Lines Where Beauty Lingers. Franklin Pierce ("F.P.A.") Adams. OBAL

She was a ringing tree of fragile glass,/shivering in a leaf storm. Denials 1. Jane Somerville. AMV-80

She was already floating in air. Orchids. Judith Minty. GeTw

She was already turning beautiful. Adam and Eve: The Recognition of Eve. Karl Shapiro. MoAB

She was always here, an obverse view in my land, in her land. Death; She Was Always Here. Yona Wallach. VWA

She was,/as Hesiod says/a "lover of dicks" Sheep-Fuck Poem. Ed Sanders. ANYP

She was best, but yet untrue. Change Thy Mind Since She Doth Change. Robert Devereux, Earl of Essex. EiL

She was buried an bemoaned,/But the birds waur Willie's companaie. Alison and Willie. Anonymous. BaBo; ESPB

She was dead herselfe ere even-song time. The Three Ravens. Anonymous. CABA

She was drinking down her troubles/With a low-down, sorry man. Darling Corey. Anonymous. OuSiCo

She was everyone's grandmother, I guess. Measles in the Ark. Susan (Sarah Chauncey Woolsey) Coolidge. OxBChV

She was fairest of all! Agnes. Henry Francis Lyte. GTBS

She was glad to be alone. What Grandma Knew. Edward Field. CoPo; Psk

...She was in NY forever and I, fishing and/drinking. Drinking Song. Jim Harrison. WOLT

She was in wretched case. Old Poulter's Mare. Anonymous. PeD

She was it pleasd, when she'd a son,/To hae a pap again. The Queen of Scotland. Anonymous. ESPB

She was more beautiful than thy first love,/But now lies under boards. A Dream of Death. William Butler Yeats. GBL

She was more than six feet tall. At ninety could/still chop and tote firewood. Beginnings (excerpt). Robert Earl Hayden. CNA

She was most exuberant. Dream about Sunsets. Annabelle Hebert. GrPl

She was mother, wife and partner–/Every inch a pioneer. The Home Winner. Gene Lindberg. PoOW

She was motion she was prairie. Consummation. Lorna Crozier. CaPN

She was never much given to literature. Poor South! Her Books Get Fewer and Fewer. J. Gordon Coogler. FaBoCo; FiBHP

She was no stranger, love. And none/can drive her out. Passage of an August. Eithne Wilkins. NeBP

She was not very lusty. Little Pretty Nancy Girl. Anonymous. OxNR

...She was on the bed/crying. Poem for Lorry. Gerald Hausman. CTBA

She was the Bee, the hive her sacred womb. The Bee. Henry Hawkins. ACP

(She was the daughter of Glubstein the Glover;/I wooed with poems–a lyrical lover.) Villanelle of a Villaness. Edwin Meade Robinson. HBMV

...She/was the stone at the center of/the pool whose circles/shuddered off around her. A Circle, a Square, a Triangle and a Ripple of Water. Jane Cooper. TAP

She was twice marriet in ae day,/Ere she keest aff her goon. Katharine Jaffray (B vers.). Anonymous. ESPB; OxBB; ViBoFo

She washed and washed the pity from her hands. The Intruder. Carolyn Kizer. BoWoP; GP; NePoEA-2

She washes her face, and forgets her neck. Nursery Rules from Nannies. Anonymous. FaBoUs

She wears it proudly/a black and grey/round head of hair Sam's World. Sam Cornish. CNA

She went about as fur as she could go! Kansas City. Oscar, II Hammerstein. OBAL

She went and let him in herself. Caprice. William Dean Howells. ALV

She went as though with a quick fear/Of the eternal winter here. June Night. Hazel Hall. HBMV

She went to tend her flock; while Daphnis ran/Back to his herded bulls, a happy man. A Countryman's Wooing. Theocritus. ErPo

She wept and could not tell him why. Two. Robert Canzoneri. HoPM

She wept, and made it deeper by a tear. Upon Julia Weeping. Robert Herrick. ExPo

She wept upon thy tomb. On the Death of a Lady's Owl. Moses Mendes. TrJP

She whipped them all soundly and put them/to bed. The Old Woman in a Shoe. Anonymous. OxNR

She who heard the songs first, was her pride like mine? David. Mary Carolyn Davies. HBMV

She who is dead brought sorrow to us all. To Heliodora, Dead. Meleager. LiTW

She who no equal has, must be alone. A Panegyric on Nelly (excerpt). John Wilmot, Earl of Rochester. UnTE

She, who's been old, is now a child again. The Ice. Wilfrid Gibson. OxBTC

She who sings her melodies/In the deep sea... My Father Is the Nightingale. Anonymous. LO

She who will be fused/with me/in life or death! Girls. Pablo Neruda. OLR

She whose eyes are open forever. Two Variations. Denise Levertov. PPoe

She will be bound with garlands of her own. On the Sonnet. John Keats. CABA; ERoP 1-2; NIP; NoP; OAEL 1-2

She will be stung to death with snakes, as Cleopatra was. In Praise of a Gentlewoman. George Gascoigne. EnRePo

She will be taken to a temple in ruins/she will be left/alone. The Mask and the Poem. Alejandra Pizarnik. VWA

She will come and be beside him as quiet as a stone. The Interpreter. Orrick Johns. AnAmPo; HBMV

...She will communicate with a number of friends/and relatives long deceased. Readings, Forecasts, Personal Guidance. Kenneth Fearing. MoAmPo

...She will/drive nails into my tongue. Mothers, Daughter. Shirley Kaufman. BoWoP; GP; NMM

She will embrace me for eternity I Am of the Earth. Anna Walters. VoR

She will ever hide her face/And elude my grasping hand!   I Sit and Wait for Beauty.   Mae V. Cowdery.   BlSi

She will feel his heartbeats in sun and air.   Where the Dropwort Springs up Lithe and Tall.   John Lyle Donaghy.   NeIP

She will make the dearest wife/In the world.   A Southern Girl.   Samuel Minturn Peck.   AA

She will neither stay in, nor come out.   Clara.   Ezra Pound.   DTC

She will not blame me,/But suffer it so.   I Need Not Go.   Thomas Hardy.   DTC; EG; NOBE; OBEV; OBVV; OxBTC

She will not dim her lucid peace/With bitterness.   Beauty's Hands Are Cool.   Karle Wilson Baker.   GoYe

She will not know.   Early Morning of Another World.   Tom McKeown.   AMV-80

She will not smile to-day, for she is dead.   The Dead Child.   George Barlow.   OBVV

She will not wake, mavrone, she will not wake.   Out of Hearing.   Jane Barlow.   HBV 1-2

She will not want this snake.   Mother Doesn't Want a Dog.   Judith Viorst.   NLV

She will sit and cry,/Fie fie fie fie fie!   Madrigal: "Ay me, alas, heigh ho, heigh ho!"   Thomas Weelkes.   OxBoLi

She will tread on a toad if she possibly can.   As into the Garden Elizabeth Ran.   Alfred Edward Housman.   NLV

She will us attend,/For the South Carolina we've lost.   The South Carolina.   *Anonymous.*   PAH

She woke sometimes to feel the daylight coming/like a relentless milkman up the stairs.   Living in Sin.   Adrienne Rich.   FF; IHMS; NePoEA; NoP; NYBP; SoSe; TAP; UnPo

She won't forget.   The Unknown.   E. O. Laughlin.   BLPA

She wonders how it happened to her   The Old Maid Factory.   Constance Urdang.   GP

She woos Reflection in the silent gloom,/And ponders on the world to come.   Written on a Sunday Morning.   Robert Southey.   OBEC

She would be gathered, though she grew on thorn.   Ah Were She Pitiful.   Robert Greene.   TrGrPo; ViBoPo

She would have seen in two dimensions, the knuckles of his toes,/The top of my head.   The Man Hidden behind the Drapes.   Pattiann Rogers.   MAYP

She would lie down among the clothes, mingle/with the refuse, wait for the weeds to rise to her.   The Disordering.   Lynda Yates.   AMV-81

She would not for a hundred pounds/Serve Holly so.   Holly Beareth Berries (excerpt).   *Anonymous.*   PBBP

She wove for him in darkness, day by day,/Out of the labor of a lovely loom.   Our Lady's Labor.   John Duffy.   ISi

She wraps me in her belly/From/Across the room.   Woman.   Jane Chambers.   IHMS

She wreathes the air with green/And weaves the stillness in.   The Clavichord.   May Sarton.   UnS

She writes, has bunions, and–Good God! her Nose!   Savage Portraits.   Don (Donald Robert Marquis) Marquis.   HBMV

The shearing naked absolute blade has torn/through false French roses to her foreign cry.   John Knox.   Iain Crichton Smith.   OxBS

Shearwaters, insatiable,/Stun themselves in the sea.   The Poet Is Dead.   William Everson.   NoP

A sheath to keep us pure of fear.   The Shape of Death.   May Swenson.   TAP

Sheathing speed in sleep.   Park Avenue.   Robert Fitzgerald.   NYP

Sheaves of drooping dandelions to the courts of/Kentish Town.   Parliament Hill Fields.   Sir John Betjeman.   FaBoTw; HaMV; NOBE

Shed a tear for the victims who're laid to their rest.   The Blantyre Explosion.   *Anonymous.*   OBET

Shed all the blood, felt all the smart.   Celia Bleeding, to the Surgeon.   Thomas Carew.   AnAnS 2; PeD

Shed for my sake–and how you wept alone.   The Dark Memory.   John Hall Wheelock.   LiTL

Shed milder rays, and daylight disappears/In low melodious music of still hours.   The Sonnet.   John Addington Symonds.   HBV 1-2

Shed no tears, that's the way it is.   On Dreams and Mexican Songs.   Tom Dent.   APU

Shed o'er the world thy holy light.   Jesus, Thou Joy of Loving Hearts.   Saint Bernard of Clairvaux.   WGRP

Shed that wisdom's guiding light.   Mighty One, Before Whose Face.   William Cullen Bryant.   AH

Shedding around themselves/five inches of limbo.   Five Poems for Dolls.   Margaret Atwood.   NIP

The sheds are noisy with packing.   In the Huon Valley.   James Philip McAuley.   CBAP

Sheds doubled darkness up the labouring hill.   The House of Life.   Dante Gabriel Rossetti.   PoEL 1-5; ViBoPo; VLP

Sheds holy blood as e'er the sod/Received on Freedom's field of honor!   The Brave at Home.   Thomas Buchanan Read.   HBV 1-2

Shee could not live a maid.   The Old Wife's Tale.   George Peele.   AtBAP

Shee hath more beauty then becomes the chast.   I Must Complain, Yet Doe Enjoy My Love.   Thomas Campion.   AAS

Sheepwalks. Trails. Uncertain rights of drift.   The Great Garret; or, 100 Wheels.   James McMichael.   AmPA

...Sheer/linen billowing/on the wind: Nile, Amazon, Mississippi.   Leda and Her Swan.   Olga Broumas.   PeHV

The sheet had dried.   Duo-tang.   Kenward Elmslie.   ANYP

Sheeting an old man's agony.   Hut Near Desolated Pines.   Alistair Campbell.   AnNZ

Sheets like sacraments on a holiday.   Shacked Up at the Ritz.   Doug Fetherling.   NeAC

Sheldon Jackson, evangel to that race/whose reprieve he read in the reindeer's face.   Rigorists.   Marianne Moore.   NU; SBG

Shells and animalcules/generally and so to man,/to Paterson.   Paterson.   William Carlos Williams.   CMoP; NoAm; NOBA

The shelter of th' eternal Rock.   When Thickly Beat the Storms of Life.   Gurdon Robins.   AH

The sheltered ways, the quiet ways of peace.   Quiet Things.   Grace Noll Crowell.   PoLf

Shema.   "Grandfather" in.Winter.   Frederick Feirstein.   NYP

The shepherd, all involved in wreaths of fire,/Now shows a shadowy speck, and now is lost entire.   An Evening Walk (excerpt).   William Wordsworth.   EiCP

The shepherd of the forest went.   The Indian Student.   Philip Freneau.   OxBA

Shepherd of things gone wrong,/Mend my broken mood.   Prayer for Song.   Fay Lewis Noble.   TrPWD

A shepherd's bliss nor stands nor falls to ev'ry tongue.   The Purple Island.   Phineas Fletcher.   ViBoPo

A shepherd's coat drawn over me.   A Shepherd's Coat.   Lilian Bowes Lyon.   ChMP

Shepherd's warning.   Red Sky at Night.   *Anonymous.*   OxNR

Shepherd, try me.   The Musterer.   Eileen Duggan.   CoBE

Shepherd, wash them clean.   Shepherd, Show Me How to Go.   Mary Baker Eddy.   AH

A shepherdess of sheep.   The Lady of the Lambs.   Alice Meynell.   GTBS; OBEV

Shepherdess, show me now where I may sleep.   Shepherdess.   Norman Cameron.   GBL; GTBS-P; OBSP; OxBS

The shepherds, satyrs, nymphs, and fauns/For thee will trip it o'er the lawns.   The Golden Age: Hymn to Diana.   Thomas Heywood.   EIL

The sheriff cuts off his black legs/And nails them to a tree   War and Silence.   Robert Bly.   CAPP

An' shet the shore out, an' the smell/Of sea-weed sweeter'n clover.   The Skipper-Hermit.   Hiram Rich.   EtS

Shield & fresh fountain! Manifester! Even mine.   Eleven addresses to the Lord.   John Berryman.   OxBC

Shield him with Thy smile.   Rest in Peace.   Wilfred J. Funk.   PoLf

A shield of safety o'er my head,/A spring of comfort in my heart.   The Doubter's Prayer.   Anne Bronte.   TrPWD

Shield us here./Farewell!   Rouge Bouquet.   Joyce Kilmer.   HBV 1-2; MC; PAH; PoPl; TreFS

Shielding the truth and giving birth to it.   Betweens.   Norman MacCaig.   EAS

Shifting about, grow less and less,/With here and there a pawn.   On the Young Statesmen.   Charles, Earl of Dorset Sackville.   APAS

Shifts in his soiled flesh/and remembers...   Awakening.   John Haines.   EAS

Shimmering on the quiet floor of our private world.   Dr. Coppelius.   Wrey Gardiner.   NeBP

Shine brightly upon us/When we leave behind us our withered bodies.   To Crinog.   *Anonymous.*   AnIL; OnYI

Shine down, O Light,/Illumine this night.   To the Unknown Light.   Edward Shanks.   TrPWD

Shine forth through darkness, Son of Man,/and give our conscience light.   Give Our Conscience Light.   Aline Badger Carter.   TrPWD

Shine, Hesperus, shine forth, thou wished star!   Masque of Cupid: Up, Youths and Virgins, Up, and Praise.   Ben Jonson.   HW

Shine in my arms, and set thou in my breast!   Fawnia.   Robert Greene.   EG; HBV 1-2; OBEV; OBSC

Shine in my Arms, and set thou in my Breast.   Pandosto: In Praise of his Loving and Best-Beloved Fawnia.   Robert Greene.   AtBAP

Shine/In the sun.   On the Porch of the Antique Dealer.   Paul Ramsey.   FAZ

...Shine, O shine/unfalsifying sun, on this sick scene.   Keeping Their World Large.   Marianne Moore.   WaP

Shine on, shine oh, Oh! Jerusalem.   Shine On.   Luke Schoolcraft.   TrAS

Shine out, and make this winter night/Our beauty's Spring, our Prince of Light!   Song: "Shine out, fair Sun, with all your heat."   *Anonymous.*   EIL

Shine out, O splendid stars, and light/Our thinning columns through the night!   The Battle-Flag.   Mary Evelyn Moore Davis.   BPAW

Shine, Poet! in thy place, and be content.   If Thou Indeed Derive Thy Light from Heaven.   William Wordsworth.   EnRP; OBRV; TrCP; VLP

Shine the names of Ethan Allen and his bold volunteers! The Surprise at Ticonderoga. Mary A. P. Stansbury. MC; PAH

Shine through a dark, benighted soul,/And bid a sinner live. My Soul Would Fain Indulge a Hope. Joseph Steward. AH

Shine to the trembling heart of me,/Light my soul to the mother-sea. Wind and Lyre. Edwin Markham. TRV

Shine 'twixt the Hills, or wander o'er the Plain. The Iliad. Homer. OBVE

Shine upon you all the way/Till Christmas comes again! As I Went Down to David's Town. George Craig Stewart. AH

Shining, being raised, where holy water shone. For a Christening. Vernon Watkins. MoRP

The shining fauna of that fire. Burning the Christmas Greens. William Carlos Williams. CoBMV; LiTM; MoPo; NePA; NoAm; NOBA

A shining Jacob's ladder of the mind. Between the Sunken Sun and the New Moon. Paul Hamilton Hayne. AA

The shining of the morning is most marvellous. That Way. Anne Welsh. PeSA

The shining stars pass silently from sight! The Dead Singer. Mary Ashley Townsend. AA

The Shining Strand who interlaced our/Grays/To lift, to hold and beautify always. The Father's Gold. Anonymous. STF

Shining they stare! Song: "Lovely hill-torrents are." Walter James Turner. MoBrPo

Shining through/The thing I wrought.) Petition for a Miracle. David Morton. ISi

Shining with time like any pilgrim? Spindrift. Galway Kinnell. NaP; NYBP

A ship condemned, like a lost soul. Derelict. Elisabeth Cavazza Pullen. AA

Ship-fed seas bring us/from colder waters. Underground. Ian Mudie. BoAV

The ship is your cradle, the sea is your home. An Ocean Lullaby. Charles Augustus Keeler. EtS

The ship my striving made/May see night fade. Truth. John Masefield. WGRP

Ship of the body, ship of the soul, voyaging, voyaging, voyaging. Aboard at a Ship's Helm. Walt Whitman. NePA; NOBA; OxBA

The Ship sinks found'ring in the vast Abyss. The Splendid Shilling (parody). John Phillips. BXAP; CEP; FaBoPa; NOEC; OAEL 1-2; Par

The ship that holds the straightest course/Still sails the convex sea. At Best. John Boyle O'Reilly. AA

A ship that meets all storms, rides out all gales. The Old Parish Church, Whitby. Hardwick Drummond Rawnsley. OBVV

Ship with Him! Ars Poetica About Ultimates. Tram Combs. MP; TwCP

Shipboard fire in an icy ocean not/shown on any chart. Dispatch Number Sixty. Doug Fetherling. NeAC

(Shipmate, my shipmate!) and the late dusk falling! Hastings Mill. Cecily Fox-Smith. HBV 1-2

Shipping/is the/most interesting thing in the world. Dock Rats. Marianne Moore. AnAmPo

The ships forever gone. Old Seawoman. Gordon LeClaire. CaP

Ships, which to day a storm did find,/are since becalm'd, and feel no wind. Chorus. Sidney Godolphin. LoBV

Shirts billow out over hair/No one will comb any more. O Night of the Crying Children. Nelly Sachs. VWA

Shirts can do no harm inside, but the oyster can. Mary Had a William Goat (with music). Anonymous. AS

...Shirts from which slow/dirty tears are falling. Walking around. Pablo Neruda. EAS

Shit, something happened. Poem Technology. Miroslav Holub. SUW

Shiver the porcelain fable to green shards. A Korean Woman Seated by a Wall. William Meredith. NePoEA

...Shivering and full like two cups of milk. Gift Hour. Maria Banus. BoWoP; VWA

Shivering I wait for him here. At Casterbridge Fair. Thomas Hardy. EnLi 1-2

Shlof-zhe, Yidele, shlof. Rozhinkes Mit Mandlen. Anonymous. FSW

"Sho-sho-ne Sa-ca-ga-we-a, who led the way/to the West!" Sa-ca-ga-we-a. Edna Dean Proctor. PAH

Shock and strain and ruin are/Friendlier than the smiling days. The Making of Man. John White Chadwick. AA

The shocking abandon of fertile and phallic bloom. Banana. Charles G. Bell. ErPo; NePoAm-2

Shone Bunny's twinkling eye! A Story in the Snow. Pearl Riggs Crouch. SoPo; TiPo

Shone foremost in action, and gave us command. Paul Jones. Anonymous. BaBo; PAH; PAL

Shone in the opening and shutting of your/ingenious blindness. Partial Resemblance. Denise Levertov. CoAP; NaP

Shone over it with a warm good-night. Barbara Frietchie. John Greenleaf Whittier. PaPo

Shone suddenly like the sun/before you died. Evening Dance of the Grey Flies. P.K. Page. NOBC

Shoo, old lady, shoo, my love,/And I'm going to Tennessee. Tennessee. Anonymous. AmFP

Shook down the shining shadow of her hair,/And nothing said. Perdita. John Swanick [(or Swanwick)] Drennan. IrPN

Shoot shot shout/ scup. Mangrove in Crome. Clark Coolidge. ANYP

Shoot these smartasses dead/Who thought this old life/Had no more to show them. Jane Seagrim's Party. Leonard Nathan. GOYP

Shoots fire into my bones. Girl's Song. Anonymous. LLLT

Shoots her barb/of guilt into my game heart. Lines on His Birthday. John Logan. CAPP

The shopkeepers have long lit up their stores. Shopkeepers. Mani Leib. AMV-81

The shopping cart. P. T. Barnum./The sky. Introduction of the Shopping Cart. Gerald Costanzo. MAYP

The shore a fading memory and the direction lost. Notes from a Slave Ship. Edward Field. PP

The shore repels it; it returns again. My Hopes Retire; My Wishes as Before. Walter Savage Landor. GBL; OBNC

Shores aglow under/Its receding inches. A Wet Night. Richard Ryan. CIP

Short and simple is the lore/Of the beasts and birds. Man Is but a Castaway. Clarence Day. ImOP

A short dark passage to Eternal Light. The Christians Reply to the Phylosopher. Sir William Davenant. MeLP

The short day turns toward a harsher season. Tree Tag. Mary E. Caragher. GoYe

Short Follies are the best. When One or Other Rambles. Francis Daniel Pastorius. SCAP

Short has my pleasure, long has my sorrow been. A Bird Was Singing. Sir Dietmar von Aist. AWP; LiTW

Short hymns of Bach/In Jewish/Moroccan. Beginnings. Erez Biton. VWA

Short, night, to-night, and length thyself to-morrow. A Night Watch. Anonymous. OBSC

Short pains can never grievous be,/Which work a blest eternity. An Anodyne. Thomas Ken. OxBoCh

Short, short is the time. The Poet. C. Day-Lewis. OxBI

The short way home... The Daily Manna. Sara Henderson Hay. GoYe

The short word "us' at a table. Genesis. Lotte Kramer. VWA

"Shorter hours and better pay." A Strike among the Poets. Anonymous. FaBoCo; FiBHP; PP

The shorter she grows. Riddle: "Little Nancy Etticoat." Mother Goose. OxNR; SoPo; TiPo

Shot a hundred times, tearing me apart. Sonnet XIX: "After having slain very many beasts." Louise Labe. BoWoP

Shot at a pigeon,/And killed a crow. All of a Row. Anonymous. PBBP

The shot goes in. The Poet Tries to Turn in His Jock. David Hilton. LiSp

Shot him through the keyhole/An' never touch a hair... Daddy Shot a Bear. Anonymous. OuSiCo

Shot in the chest, taken back to be questioned. Driving through Minnesota during the Hanoi Bombings. Robert Bly. NoP

Shot like a pellet from his own pop-gun. Past and Present. R. E. Egerton Warburton. NOBV

Shot to death by a scab/In the employ of Duke Power Co. For Laurence Jones. Gary Allan Kizer. CTBA

A Shot 'twixt Wind and Water,/Which won this fair Maids Heart. A Soldier and a Sailor. William Congreve. CoMu

Shots in my locker yet remain,/John Bull, Esquire, my jo! A New Song to an Old Tune. Anonymous. PAH

Should aid the first created things/To meet upon their day of rest. Sunday. Josephine Miles. PoA

Should always gild the philosophic pill! The Philosophic Pill. Sir William Schwenck Gilbert. GLGT

Should be/A little bit stupid Ar(chibald')s Poetica (parody). Alan Ribback. BXAP

Should be inscribed upon the air,/Or in the running stream. On the Inconstancy of Women: From the Latin of Catullus. George Lamb. PV

Should bring down curses on our heads/To think what he has missed. Catullus to Lesbia. James Reeves. ErPo

Should burst in bloom–should blossoms/bear. Fear. Langdon Elwyn Mitchell. AA

Should certain persons die before they sing. The Desired Swan-Song. Samuel Taylor Coleridge. UnS

Should find brief solace there, as I have found. Sonnet: "Nuns fret not at their convent's narrow room." William Wordsworth. OBEV; ViBoPo

Should find in Bethlehem/The Lamb of God! It Was Not Strange. Esther Lloyd Hagg. PGD

Should have/a name: Downy Hair in the Shape of a Flame Moving up the Stomach... Coleman Barks. PV

Should have his head upon one end,/His feet upon the other.   Poor Brother. *Anonymous.*   NA

Should he look up and laugh?   The Chickadees.   John Hay.   NePoAm-2

Should he send half the whole!   Sent with a Rose to a Young Lady. Margaret Deland.   AA

Should heed the boobook's warning: "Go back, go back, go back!"   Morgan. Edward Harrington.   PoAu 1-2

Should help a man, not drag him in the mire.   Ballade to His Mistress. Francois Villon.   WeW

Should I die tonight, let me be Thine.   Poem of the Son.   Gabriela (Lucila Godoy Alcayaga) Mistral.   PoPl

Should I have riz to what Potiphar is,/Hadst thou been mated to Me?   Study of an Elevation, in Indian Ink.   Rudyard Kipling.   InMe

Should I have warmed my poor old feet as well?   Envoi.   Dominic Bevin Wyndham Lewis.   FiBHP

Should I tell what a miracle she was.   The Relic.   John Donne.   CABA; EIL; GBL; HAP; LiTB; LoBV; MyFE; NOBE; NoP; OAEL 1-2; PPP; SeCeV; WHA

Should I think/of beauty/until it passes/away?   Riddle of Night.   Jiri M. Langer.   VWA

Should, in his mouth, be never without honey.   He Who in His Pocket Hath No Money.   *Anonymous.*   HBV 1-2

...Should it move/to life eternal, I could love.   Upon Julia's Petticoat. Robert Herrick.   UnTE

Should Jove descend, they could no more.   To the King, at His Entrance into Saxham.   Thomas Carew.   CaPo

Should keep her head up and her skirts down.   Advice to Country Girls. *Anonymous.*   UnTE

Should let itself be snuff'd out by an article.   Don Juan.   George Gordon, Lord Byron.   OBRV

Should love turn dowf, it will find/pleasure....   Give Me a Lass.   Allan Ramsay.   CEP; CoBE

Should make men Atheists, and not women Whores.   A Rapture.   Thomas Carew.   AnAnS 2; CaPo; CavP; JCP; OAEL 1-2; SeCP

Should notice, suddenly,/they had no ears?   Orpheus in Greenwich Village. Jack Gilbert.   NPGG; PoL; PP

Should one enter a caveat,/Or a monastery?   Unlawful Assembly.   D. J. Enright.   OxBTC

Should say: "Sleep in my bosom, O my/child!"   The Mother.   Catulle Mendes.   TrJP

Should smile like you, and perish as they smile!   Sonnet: "Evening, as slow thy placid shades descend."   William Lisle Bowles.   NOEC

Should'st thou be honest, thou'rt a dev'lish cheat.   To a Rogue.   Joseph Addison.   PV

Should still be tossing on the open sea.   Hic Me, Pater Optime, Fessam Deseris.   Lucy Robinson.   AA

Should suddenly see a chicken devouring a worm....   Treason.   Lora Dunetz. NePoAm

Should teach His brethren and inspire/To suffer and to die.   The Dream of Gerontius.   John Henry, Cardinal Newman.   NOBV; PoEL 1-5

Should think of me, who never thought of him.   Gaily I Lived.   *Anonymous.* ELU

Should understand me, little me. My name is William/Too.   The Tarantula. Reed Whittemore.   CoAP

Should we give our hearts to a dog to tear?   The Power of the Dog. Rudyard Kipling.   BLPA; BoAnP; GDP

...Should we have stayed at home,/wherever that may be?   Questions of Travel.   Elizabeth Bishop.   NOBA

Should we, her wiser sons, be less content/To sink into her lap when life is spent?   Leaf After Leaf.....   Walter Savage Landor.   TRV; ViBoPo

Should we two be severed, my death is sure.   Fish in River.   *Anonymous.* AnOE

Should you doubt what I say, take a bumper and try!   The Women All Tell Me.   *Anonymous.*   BLSo

Should you want, O lovely and divine Circe,/Another erection.   What Ulysses Said to Circe on the Beach of Aeaea.   Irving Layton.   ErPo

Shoulder the sky, my lad, and drink/your ale.   Last Poems.   Alfred Edward Housman.   OAEP

Shoulder them in to shore.   The Gravedigger.   Bliss Carman.   BoNaP

Shoulder to shoulder and friend to friend.   The March of the Women. Cicely Hamilton.   BrRo

Shouldering its way and shedding the earth crumbs.   Putting in the Seed. Robert Frost.   ErPo; NoAm; OxBA

Shouldn't I show my daughter how to get a man?   Epigram: "Do you not wish to renounce the Devil?"   Armand Lanusse.   PoNe; TTY

...Shouldst thou wake/The passion of a demon, be not afraid.   Modern Love, XXVII.   George Meredith.   VLP

Shout! for long shall Mexico mourn the wreck/Of her proud state at the siege of Chapultepec.   The Siege of Chapultepec.   William Haines Lytle.   MC; PAH

Shout! Shout! Columbia's name, Columbia's name.   Ode to the Fourth of July.   Daniel George.   TrAS

Shout "Thy Redeemer liveth, and calleth for thee!"   The Redeemer.   Fiona Macleod.   WGRP

Shouteth faint tidings of some gladder place.   The Excursion.   William Wordsworth.   OBRV

A-shoutin' "Hallelujah!" singing praises to de Lord.   Song: "Yes, the book of Revelations be brought forth dat/day."   *Anonymous.*   NAMP

Shouting, beneath the leaves' tumultuous green.   Here Is the Place Where Loveliness Keeps House.   Madison Cawein.   HBV 1-2

Shouting, Mammie! Mammie!/Mammie!   Tammy Tyrie.   *Anonymous.* OxNR

Shouting my own/Hallelujahs.   My Own Hallelujahs.   Zack Gilbert.   PoBA

Shouting stale slogans on the Liffey quays.   Afternoons with Baedeker. Osbert Lancaster.   NOBL

Shouts at the crows–and dreams of white gulls flying.   Kansas Boy.   Ruth Lechlitner.   AmFN

Shouts of salvation are rending the sky.   Hail to the Brightness of Zion's Glad Morning.   Thomas Hastings.   AH

...Shouts/threats and obscenities at no one we know   The Seventies.   Tony Beyer.   OCNZ

Shovel across the breast of earth and her/ragged history, home.   In Random Fields of Impulse and Repose.   Jeanine Hathaway.   AMV-81

Shovel earth in. We haven't got all day.   Last Lines.   X. J. Kennedy. OBAL

Show an affirming flame.   September 1, 1939.   W. H. Auden.   CMoP; CoBMV; ExPo; ForPo; InPo; LiTA; MasP; MoAB; MoBrPo; MoVE; NePA; OAEP; OxBA; PrIm; SeCeV; WaP

Show how Bath-waters serve to lay the dust.   The Abbey Church at Bath. Henry Harington.   FaBoEE

Show how they lived; the other where they lie!   Of Books.   John Florio. EIL

Show me a man more great.   Truly Great.   William Henry Davies.   HBV 1-2; OBMV; OBVV

Show me, and set me, I have one reply,/Which they that know the rest, know more than I.   The Answer.   George Herbert.   TEP

Show me more love, my dearest LORD!   Show Me More Love.   *Anonymous.* OxBoCh

Show me my mother now!   The Vision of the Snow.   Margaret Junkin Preston.   AA

Show me the other side of passing,/the other side of death.   Pictures on the Wall.   Zvi Shargel.   VWA

Show me Thy pierced side.   Prayer of a Modern Thomas.   Edward Shillito. PGD

Show me Thyself in all I see,/Thou Lord of all.   Prayer.   Robert Louis Stevenson.   TrPWD

Show me the lake all frozen over,/show the mound of snow   The Runner.   Gary Gildner.   TAP

Show the praise of your perfections.   Pretty Twinkling Starry Eyes. Nicholas Breton.   EIL

Show them this day you were on Calvary.   Father in Heaven.   Petrarch (Francesco Petrarca).   NAWM 1-2

Show there was one who held it in disdain.   Epilogue to the Satires. Alexander Pope.   OAEL 1-2

Show Thyself to me!   Hail, Thou Head!   Saint Bernard of Clairvaux.   BePJ

Show us there's chance at least of winning through.   To Whistler, American. Ezra Pound.   PoA

Show weakness speaks in prose, but power in verse.   English Poetry. Samuel Daniel.   OBSC

Show you the way? I will!   Spring.   Orrick Johns.   InMe

Showed me the virtues whose images/you destroyed.   To an Enemy. Maxwell Bodenheim.   TrJP

Shower blessings on my wife.   The Seasons.   Kalidasa.   AWP

Shower us with breath of pine/and freesia buds.   Wind Gardens (parody). Louis Untermeyer.   BXAP

Showing her child before it is born.   The Beautiful.   William Henry Davies. ELU

Showing himself as such, among his friends.   Shenandoah: Let Us Consider Where the Great Men Are.   Delmore Schwartz.   MoAB; MoAmPo

Showing in the autumn shade/That you moulder where you played.   Last Words to a Dumb Friend.   Thomas Hardy.   FM; OAEP; PCat

Showing no visible sign, for such things are untold.   The Battle of Waterloo. George Gordon, Lord Byron.   FaFP

Showing such weakness to a fallen foe?'   An Early Christian.   Robert Barnabas Brough.   OBVV

...Shows Death/Smilingly over the place,/Trusting this new face.   A Clear Shell.   Frances Bellerby.   FaBoWP

Shows thou wert mortal,–Mother,–yea, and more!   Mother Most Powerful. Giovanni Dominici.   CAW

Shrieking Bacchantes with their souls of wine!   Modern Love, XXXII. George Meredith.   VLP

Shrieking to the south/And clutching at the north.   Moriturus.   Edna St. Vincent Millay   AnAmPo; LiTA; NAMP

Shrieks and starts and laughter–/This is Halloween!   This Is Halloween.
Dorothy Brown Thompson.   BrR; TiPo; YeAr

The shrill, primeval hawk gazed down–and screamed.   The Automobile.
Percy MacKaye.   AnAmPo

The shrill quick sound that the insect makes.   Voices of the Air.   Katherine
Mansfield.   HBMV

The shrill sentence: God is love.   On the Farm.   R. S. Thomas.   OxBTC

The shrimp and cockle, when the tide is out.   The Town of Passage.
Anonymous.   OxBoLi

Shrimps, periwinkles, and a most/Voracious appetite.   A Very Odd Fish.
D'Arcy Wentworth Thompson.   OxBChV

Shrinking beneath the burden of the Flesh.   Rhotus on Arcadia.   John
Chalkhill.   OBS

The shrinking brain, sick of an inner war.   The Foreign Gate (excerpt).
Sidney Keyes.   OBWP

The shrivelled apples of the moon,/The cankered apples of the sun.   The
Hero (parody).   Roger Woddis.   FaBoPa

The shrivelled circle/Of magnetic fear.   How Still the Hawk.   Charles
Tomlinson.   LiTM

Shropshire may soon be known as the Deserted County.   Loveliest of
Counties, Shropshire Now (parody).   Ian Sainsbury.   BXAP

Shrugged at, abandoned/by a frivolous worldling,/does not abandon?   Amor
Loci.   W. H. Auden.   NOCV

The shrugged-up riches of deep darkness sang.   The Idea of Entropy at
Maenporth Beach.   Peter Redgrove.   FaBoMo

Shua-O! Shua-O!   Bird Scarer's Song.   Anonymous.   OxNR

Shucking lightly into dark.   Dismissal.   Peter Redgrove.   NMP

Shucks a'mighty. If you're an eagle, you just go.   One to Nothing.   Carolyn
Kizer.   OBAL

The shudder of total winter in whose/misshapened sun the Children bathe
Thesis.   Edward Dorn.   NOBA

Shuddering through the shuddering main.   Jigsaw III.   Louis MacNeice.
HaMV

Shuheen, sho, lulo lo!   The Fairy Nurse.   Edward Walsh.   OnYI

Shule, shule, shule, agrah!   Shule, Agrah!   William Sharp.   OBVV

Shun him from the start.   The Panchatantra: Fool and False.   Anonymous.
AWP

Shun my paws if you care to live.'   The Wolf and the Stork.   Jean de La
Fontaine.   FM; OBVE

Shun them as you would shun the devil.   Said the Whisky Flask.
Anonymous.   STF

Shupe with hait flambis to stem the freezing fell.   An Evening and Morning
in Winter.   Gavin Douglas.   BSV

Shut from the busy world of more incredulous.   Lamia.   John Keats.
CABL

Shut in my boyhood's years...   There Is an Old City.   Karl Bulcke.   AWP

The shut out of his eye.   3 a.m. in New York.   Jean Valentine.   NYP

Shut, shut, shut your eyes.   Down Dip the Branches.   Mark Van Doren.
DuDa

Shut your eyes, my darling, and slip back into our dream.   Bereaved Child's
First Night.   Frances Bellerby.   FaBoWP

"Shut your trap, you. The question is, what about Karl Marx?"   Cultural
Notes.   Kenneth Fearing.   CMoP

Shuts up her springs, and will no grace impart.   Sonnet: "If ever Sorrow
spoke from soul that loves."   Henry Constable.   EIL

Shuts up the story of our days.   Nature, That Washed Her Hands in Milk.
Sir Walter Ralegh.   CABA; FCP; NoP

The shy hearts of the wilderness.   Christmas in the Wood.   Frances Frost.
BrR; ChBR; TrCP

Shy penis, mostly/swirled white.   A Sheeprancher Named John.   Gretel
Ehrlich.   MAYP

"Si Mailligh mo stor.   Mailligh Mo Stor.   George Ogle.   IrPN

Sibyl always answered,/"Dribble."   Spectator's Guide to Contemporary Art.
Phyllis McGinley.   OBSV

Sic a man was never seen.   Insect Riddle: "Wee man o' leather."
Anonymous.   GBP

Sic blissing in kissing/I quit till we twa meet.   Adieu to His Mistress.
Alexander Montgomerie.   BSV

Sic counseils ye gave to me, O.   Edward (A vers.).   Anonymous.   HoPM;
ViBoFo

Sic favour get before a king/As did the Outlaw Murray of the for-/est frie?
The Outlaw Murray.   Anonymous.   ESPB; OxBB

Sic kindly kisses as he gae me.   Kiss'd Yestreen.   Anonymous.   ErPo; GBP;
PoL

Sic perrell lyis in paramouris.   Allace! So Sobir Is the Micht.   Mersar.
OxBS

The sick never get well.   Song of the Darkness.   John Bricuth.   SM

Sick of the tides of the heart.   Sex at thirty-one.   Artie Gold.   CaPN;
NOBC

Sick with memories.   Song of the Night at Day-Break.   Alice Meynell.   CH

Sicklestraw and all such glamourie.   A Suit of Nettles.   James Reaney.
OBCV

Sickly crept on, and, with complainings rude,/On nature seemed to call, and
bleat for food.   The Prophecy of Famine.   Charles Churchill.   OBSV

...Sickness for Eden was so strong.   In a Garden.   Elizabeth Jennings.
NOCV

Sickness is the hatred of a repentance/knowing there is nothing he wants.
The Crow.   Robert Creeley.   TW

Side by side, to a tinkling of bells.   News from Norwood.   Christopher
Middleton.   FaBoMo; NePoEA-2

Side by side we battle onward,/Victory will come.   Hold the Fort.
Anonymous.   FSW

Sideburns have been sapping my strength   Christchurch, N.Z.   Earle Birney.
OxBC

Sideward, the River turning like a wheel.   Sonnets.   Frederick Goddard
Tuckerman.   AP

Sidewards–moving–always moving–never resting.   From the Point.   Paul
Petrie.   AMV-80

The sideway watery dog's-glances I/Send fawning on you, thinking you will
not scold.   Old Man Pondered.   John Crowe Ransom.   MoAmPo

Siegfried lies in his red, red blood!   The Three Songs.   Bayard Taylor.
StPo

Sifting through hair as if through sand.   A Traveller.   J. R. Rowland.
CBAP

Sigh, breezes, sigh.   Blow, Bugles, Blow.   John S. McGroarty.   HBV 1-2

Sigh not for love,–the ways of love are/dark!   Sigh Not for Love.   Helen
Hay.   AA

A sigh of soft reflection   Stanzas to Mr. Bentley.   Thomas Gray.   NoP

Sigh out a groan, weep down a melting tear.   Hymn: Crucifixus Pro Nobis.
Patrick Carey.   OxBoCh

Sigh then beyond my song: whirl & rejoice!   Canto Amor.   John Berryman.
CoAP; MoAmPo; MoPo; MoVE; NePA; VGW

Sigh there thy last, and therewith break!   Comfort thyself, my woeful heart.
Sir Thomas Wyatt.   FCP; SiPS

A sigh within a dream!   Songs of the Sea-Children.   Bliss Carman.   OBCV

Sighed, and like Odysseus/wished for home.   Leda and the Swan.   Alice R.
Friman.   PoDr

Sighed o'er the ruin, and returned to heaven!   On the Death of Catarina de
Attayda.   Luîs de Camoens.   AWP

Sighed over the fields of wheat, "He is gone.../Forlorn."   The Youth with
Red-Gold Hair.   Edith Sitwell.   FaBoTw; MoVE

Sighing deeply, knowing that nothing/can save it now.   The Idea of Detroit.
Jim Gustafson.   APU

Sighing I murmur, "O mihi praeteritos!"   Eheu Fugaces.   Richard Harris
Barham.   FaBoEE; NBM; OxBoLi

The sighing of ferns/Half-asleep in their boxes.   Memory of a Porch.
Donald Justice.   NCSH

The sighing time, the sighing time.   The Sighing Time.   Edmund Charles
Blunden.   BrPo

Sighing you into sleep/Where peace prevails and only soft rains fall.   Moods
of Rain.   Vernon Scannell.   BoNaP

Sighs Nature an Alas? Or merely, Amen?   The Spotted Flycatcher.   Walter
De la Mare.   OBSP

Sighs; stares at the ocean–and hastens away.   False Dawn.   Walter De la
Mare.   FaBoNo

Sighs through the dews of evening peacefully/Falling, "Dream!"?   Voices.
Walter De la Mare.   UnPo

...Sighs will convey/Any thing to me. Harke, despair away.   The Bag.
George Herbert.   AnAnS 1; SeCP

A sight for kings, and still the soldier's love.   Soldier's Song.   Tobias Hume.
WiR

A sight not infrequently seen.   Green.   Walter De la Mare.   FaBoNo

The sight,/the touch,/or memory/of You.   That We Head Towards.
Stephany.   BPo

Sign it 'El Greco.' I'll/Slap on a frame."   High Renaissance.   George
Starbuck.   NLV; OBAL

The sign says/donations/will be appreciated   Old Trail Town, Cody,
Wyoming.   John Garmon.   TAT

A sign,/that your world moves still.   The Dead.   Jay Wright.   FB

Sign the warrant for its death.   The Lily of the Valley.   Thomas Lovell
Beddoes.   EG

Signed when our Redeemer died,/Sealed when He was glorified.   Come to
Calvary's Holy Mountain.   James Montgomery.   BePJ

The signet of love's distress.   Six Religious Lyrics: I (excerpt).   Karl Shapiro.
CMoP

Signing for Soul and Body, set to them my name...   Come, Said My Soul.
Walt Whitman.   NOBA

A signpost; pointing this way, pointing that.   The Fork of the Road.
William Renton.   NOBV

Signs for the distant and disconsolate heart.   Loving the Rituals That Keep
Men Close.   Palladas.   OBVE

The signs, the journeys of the night, survive.   Akiba.   Muriel Rukeyser.
VWA

Siklyke this Turnus semis, quhair he went...   The Aeneid.   Virgil (Publius Vergilius Maro).   OBVE

(Silence)   A Collage for Richard Davis–Two Short Forms.   De Leon Harrison.   PoBA

Silence and fierce cold.   Harsh Climate.   Charles Simic.   LCAP

Silence and sleep like fields/Of amaranth lie.   All That's Past.   Walter De La Mare.   AnFE; GoJo; MoAB; NOBE; OAEL 1-2; OAEP; OBMV; OxBTC; SeCeV; TreFT; TrGrPo; ViBoPo; WHA

A silence audible with growth.   Star of Eternal Possibles and Joy.   Peter Yates.   ChMP

The silence between drops of rain.'   Why Must You Know?   John Wheelwright.   CrMA; VGW

...The silence for which/the mouth slowly opens.   The Penalty for Bigamy Is Two Wives.   William Matthews.   AmPA

Silence has passed to speech/and back again to silence.   The Chinese Graves in Beechworth Cemetery.   Philip Mead.   AMV-81

Silence here–but, far beyond us, many/voices crying, Hail!   Tennyson.   Henry Van Dyke.   AA

Silence in the hall; dark in the hall; all's done.   The Don.   Barbara Howes.   GLGT

Silence is golden–St. John Chrysostom.   Rhapsody of the Deaf Man.   Tristan Corbiere.   LiTW

Silence is still a crown,/Courage a grace.   Never Admit the Pain.   Mary Gilmore.   PoAu 1-2

Silence like music flowed.   Helmet Orchid.   Douglas Stewart.   BoAV

Silence of a world asleep–/And...your breast.   Nocturne.   Amelia Josephine Burr.   HBV 1-2

The silence of books settled over the hills.   Impressions of My Father/I.   Country Ways.   Marcia Masters.   GoYe

Silence of love that cannot sing again.   Monna Innominata.   Christina Georgina Rossetti.   ViBoPo; VLP

The silence of my surroundings and go to sleep forever.   Poetry Paper.   Andrei Codrescu.   EAS

The silence of the heart.   The Lip and the Heart.   John Quincy Adams.   AA; AmLP

Silence only may adore thee!   So Far, So Near.   Christopher Pearse Cranch.   TrPWD

Silence) sky;   A Great.   Edward Estlin Cummings.   NYBP

Silence that shines, and speech that is proud/and tender!   King of the Belgians.   Marion Couthouy Smith.   PAH

Silence the even exchange of/the guilty.   The Triple Mirror.   Gloria C. Oden.   IHMS

Silence. We do not know.   A Night Piece.   Edward Shanks.   HBMV

Silence where hope was.   Autumn.   Walter De la Mare.   OxBTC

Silence within silence   Pedro.   Luis Omar Salinas.   FF

Silences rang for him, cage-eater greedy of snakes, abroad in the dawn.   The Catch.   Brewster Ghiselin.   HAP

...The silences that grew/within him for a life-time, intertwined?   The Death of an Old Man.   Michael Hamburger.   NePoEA

Silent and pouncing, ruinous and swift?   The Owl.   Victoria Mary (Vita) Sackville-West.   SBG

Silent as I, and lonesome as the land.   An Uninscribed Monument on One of the Battle-Fields of the Wilderness.   Herman Melville   AA; AmLP

Silent as light in old grey Galloway.   Grey Galloway.   Thomas S. Cairncross.   PoSH

Silent as we, but crazed, crazed as the flame.   The Lumberyard.   Ruth Herschberger.   LiTA; LiTL

Silent, athwart my soul, moves the symphony true.   After the Dazzle of Day.   Walt Whitman.   NePA

Silent be the singer who thinks of me/And how I was defeated.   William Yeats in Limbo.   Sidney Keyes.   MoBrPo

A silent beauty half so fair.   Thus Lovely Sleep.   Richard Leigh.   ELP

The silent cortege.   The Coming of War: Actaeon.   Ezra Pound.   CMoP; PoA

Silent hammers of decay.   The Hammers.   Ralph Hodgson.   GoJo; MoBrPo; NOBE; OxBTC

A silent messenger/Of infinite mysteries.   Hymn to the Night: II.   "Novalis."   LiTW

The silent sapphire-spangled marriage ring of the land?   Maud.   Alfred, Lord Tennyson.   SyP

The silent slain–   The Too-Late Born.   Archibald MacLeish.   AmP; APA; GoJo; MoAB; MoAmPo; NAMP; OxBA; SeCeV; WaP

Silent sliding silver waterfalls and stars.   Fireworks.   Valerie Worth.   NTCP

The silent soul declares/the glory of the world.   The Blade of Grass Sings to the River.   Leah Goldberg.   TrJP

...The silent, the indifferent sun.   Last Days.   Richard Hugo.   PoA

Silent the sea/the wind and the well.   Poetry Is...   Bruce Bennett.   AMV-81

Silent, they drift away, over the glimmering/sand.   A Concert Party.   Siegfried Sassoon.   EnLit; MMM

Silent, upon a peak in Darien.   On First Looking into Chapman's Homer.   John Keats.   BiP; BLPA; BoLiVe; DiPo; ERoP 1-2; ExPo; FaBoBe; FaBoCh; FaBV; FaFP; FaPo; FF; FiP; ForPo; FPL; GN; GoTF; GTBS; GTBS-P; HAP; HBV 1-2; HBVY; HeIP; HoPM; InPK; InPo; LiTB; LoBV; LoGBV; MBW 1-2; MCCG; NAWM 1-2; NIP; NOAV; NOBE; NoP; OAEL 1-2; OAEP; OBEV; OBNC; OBRV; PoEL 1-5; PPoe; PrIm; RoGo; SeCeV; SoSe; TEP; TreF; TrGrPo; ViBoPo; WHA

Silent upon a spike in Magpie Lane.   On First Looking into the Dark Future.   Roger Lancelyn Green.   CenHV

Silent with peace he had not understood.   Lao-Tse.   Thomas S. Jones, Jr.   AnAmPo

Silently and very fast.   The Fall of Rome.   W. H. Auden.   MAT; OAEL 1-2; OxBTC; PAI; UnPo

Silently rocking and rocking,/The moon-cradle out in the sky.   The Ballad of Downal Baun.   Padraic Colum.   SUS

Silently, slowly, the great clouds are piled/In pale straw-colored mows against the blue.   Bread the Holy.   Elizabeth Jane Coatsworth.   MoRP

The silhouetted pitcher waiting to be filled.   The Annunciation.   John Duffy.   ISi

Silk tatters, "Nec Spe Nec Metu."   Canto III.   Ezra Pound.   TAP

Silk under hatches, and stars in the shrouds!   Last Cargo.   Silence Buck Bellows.   EtS

Silky with oil of distilled experience.   When the Ripe Fruit Falls.   D. H. Lawrence.   CMoP

The siller road to Appin rinnin' a' the way to God!   For Love of Appin.   Jessie MacKay.   AnNZ

The sills of heaven would founder/Did such as I aspire.   Two Voices in a Meadow.   Richard Wilbur.   NePoAm-2; NLV; UnPo

The silly bard grows fat, or falls away.   Epistle to Augustus (excerpt).   Alexander Pope.   EBEV

"Silly boy, as if I cared,"/Petronilla said.   To Petronilla Who Has Put Up Her Hair.   Sir Henry Howarth Bashford.   HBV 1-2

A silly lad that longs and looks/And wishes he were I.   Oh Fair Enough Are Sky and Plain.   Alfred Edward Housman.   MCCG

"Silly little Johnny look,/You have lost your writing-book!"   The Story of Johnny Head-in-Air.   Heinrich Hoffmann.   BBGG; OxBChV; TiPo

The silly poor hoggs came hirpling hame.   The Borrowing Days.   *Anonymous.*   GBP

The silver answer rang,–"Not Death, but Love."   Sonnets from the Portuguese, I.   Elizabeth Barrett Browning.   AnFE; CoBE; EnLit; GBL; GTBS; HBV 1-2; NOBE; NoP; OAEP; OBEV; OBNC; TreFT; ViBoPo

The silver apples of the moon,/The golden apples of the sun.   The Song of Wandering Aengus.   William Butler Yeats.   BoLiVe; BrPo; CMoP; DiPo; EnLi 1-2; FaBoCh; GoJo; LoGBV; LOW; MAT; MoAB; MoBrPo; PG; PoEL 1-5; PoRA; SOTW; TiPo; VLP; WSC

Silver money/sobs in the pocket.   The Moon Rises.   Federico Garcia Lorca.   SOTW

A silver papoose, in the Indian West?   Early Moon.   Carl Sandburg.   BPAW; LaNeLa; PG

A silver penny shall be found/Within the compass of her shoe–/And so we bid you all adieu!   Ann Grenville, Countess Temple, Appointed Poet Laureate...   Horace Walpole.   OBEC

(The silver reaches of the estuary).   The Swimmer's Moment.   Margaret Avison.   NOBC

A silver soil bedeck'd with streams of gold!   The Art of Making Puddings.   William King.   FaBoUs

The silver spider living alone, and spinning.   Love.   Francis Jammes.   AWP

Silver the hills where the moon climbs over.   Gloaming.   Robert Adger Brown.   HBV 1-2

The silver wasp-nests hang like fruit.   Escape.   Elinor Wylie.   AnFE; APA; LiTA; MoAmPo

The silvery curtain is drawn, and he sees/The beautiful city no more!   The Sunset City.   Henry Sylvester Cornwell.   HBV 1-2

A silvery dream shunning red lips of morn.   The Sonnet.   John Addington Symonds.   HBV 1-2

Simmer sall set thy sorrow free!   Villanelle.   Margaret Winefride Simpson.   OxBS

The simple and the chambered eye.   Confrontation.   John Hart.   PoL

A simple bare room, no window, an empty book/Of white pages, and a bed for sleeping.   The Gold Country: Hotel Leger, Mokelumne Hill, Revisited.   Joseph Stroud.   NPGG

A simple drop alone.   Art.   Jose Asuncion Silva.   CAW

A simple farmer's lad, among the girls in the hay.   The City Clerk.   Thomas Ashe.   OBVV

The simple grandeur of thy life and death.   Samuel Hoar.   Franklin Benjamin Sanborn.   AA

The simple joys that Nature yields/Are dearer far to me.   The Midges Dance Aboon the Burn.   Robert Tannahill.   BoNaP; HBV 1-2

The simple, kindly man,/Lincoln, American.   Lincoln.   John Vance Cheney.   OHIP

A simple life or death.   Not in the Guide-Books.   Elizabeth Jennings.   LiTM; MP; NePoEA

A simple soul should breed so mixed woes. The Seven Wonders of England. Sir Philip Sidney. FaBoPP

"The simple things that we will always have." After Speaking of One Dead a Long Time. Padraic Colum. GoYe

A simple tune and great,/The fittest utterance of the voice of earth. In the Isle of Dogs. John Davidson. OBNC; VLP

Simplest of swains! the world may see/Whom Chloe loves, and who loves me. The Question to Lisetta. Matthew Prior. OBEV

Simplicities unlearned long since and left behind. My Past Has Gone to Bed. Siegfried Sassoon. AtBAP

Simply a human face and no more! By the Waters of Babylon. Benjamin Fondane. VWA

Simply because my fire is going out. My Muse and I, Ere Youth and Spirits Fled. George the Younger Colman. ELU

Simply to leave him out of the scene forever. Anonymous Drawing. Donald Justice. CoAP; EyDe; HeIP; NePoEA-2

...The sin/Against the Holy Ghost–What is it? The Blasphemies. Louis MacNeice. FaBoIP

Sin I am free, I counte him not a bene! Three Roundels of Love Unreturned. Geoffrey Chaucer. MeEL

A Sin! Its Ugly face/More Terror, then its Dwelling Place,/Contains,(O Dreadfull Sin!)/Within! The Third Century. Thomas Traherne. AnAnS 1

Sin, shame, and death; His life is ours/Whatever may befall! His Life Is Ours. Dorothy Conant Stroud. STF

The Sin still blithe on earth that sent them/there. The House of Life. Dante Gabriel Rossetti. VLP

Sin the blude of my Norse forebears/Melled the mountain dew and the brine. On the Croun o Bidean. J. K. Annand. PoSH

A sin, then fall to weeping when 'tis done. Cock-Crow. Robert Herrick. PBBP

Sin, then we knew thee not, and could not hate,/And now we know thee, now it is too late. Caelica, CII. Fulke, Lord Brooke Greville. FCP

Sin' they nailed him to the tree. Ballad of the Goodly Fere. Ezra Pound. CAW; CMoP; HBV 1-2; LiTA; LiTM; MoAB; MoAmPo; MoBS; NePA; NoAm; OFD; PoRA; TrCP; TrGrPo

...Since all the stars rain blind. Sonnet. John Berryman. NoAm

Since all these ease not, best ye hang awhile. Jack and His Father. John Heywood. DiPo

Since alone for sinners' sake/God on thee endured to die. The Cross. Pedro Calderon de la Barca. CAW

Since bones have caught their marrow chill. The Horn. Léonie Adams. InPo

Since Caesar will be sure to seek thee there. Pompey and Cornelia. Nicholas Rowe. OBEC

Since certainly it is mine. Lilacs. Amy Lowell. AtBAP; BLPL; LaNeLa; MoAmPo; MoVE; OxBA

Since Christ in all the ways of man hath trod. The Christ. John Oxenham. TRV

Since cruel seas and angry winds parted my love and me. The Lowlands of Holland. Anonymous. AmFP

Since death is close, and death is death for us. In a Museum. Babette Deutsch. HBMV

Since Deucalion's flood in no chronicle is/told. Speak, Parrot. John Skelton. CoBE; PoEL 1-5; ViBoPo

Since even her own self has forgotten her. The Merry Window. Francis Scarfe. EAS

Since every woe is joined with some wealth. Venomous thorns that are so sharp and keen. Sir Thomas Wyatt. FCP

Since excellence, in other form enjoyed,/Is by descending to her saints destroyed. Caelica, X. Fulke, Lord Brooke Greville. FCP

Since fate has designed her to Ley alone. There Was a Brisk Girle. Anonymous. CoMu

Since first I laboured with a wooden spade/Against the background of Etnity. Summer Beach. Frances Cornford. BrRo; ChMP

Since first it was my fate to know thee? How Great My Grief. Thomas Hardy. BrPo

Since for my truth she needeth no witness. What Dreamed I? Anonymous. CBEP

Since from my hair they fled. Heavy-Hearted. Judah Al-Harizi. TrJP

Since God had no Hand in his Lordship's Promotion. Epigram on Seeing a Worthy Prelate Go out of Church... Jonathan Swift. NCEP

Since God Himself played by her gown. Mater Dei. Katharine Tynan Hinkson. ISi

Since Grandad broke the council's regulation in the park.' West Paddocks. Arthur Davies. NOAV

Since he'd only one ounce in his pound. Limerick: "Once a pound-keeper chanced to impound." Oliver Herford. TDH

Since he kissed them and put them/there. Little Boy Blue. Eugene Field. AA; BeLS; FPL; GoTF; OBCA; PoLf

Since her heart was resurrected by/The smell of death. The Smell of Death Is So Powerful. Marguerite de Navarre. PBWP

Since I am free, I count him not a bean. Merciless Beauty. Geoffrey Chaucer. CBEP

Since, I ask, Ron, is that you? That Summer. Herbert Scott. PoL

Since I can face neither death nor a life any longer without you. Seventh Eclogue. Miklos Radnoti. VWA

Since I could never find her/Upon the mortal side. She died–this was the way she died. Emily Dickinson. AA

Since I do hold nothing too dear for thee. I Send Thee Here of Ribbon a Whole Yard. Anonymous. LO

Since I have lain with you/you have lifted my heart high. Egyptian Hieroglyphics. Anonymous. BoWoP

Since I have tasted the wine of paradise? I Planted My Bright Paradise. Alexandr Blok. HW

Since I looked on Death in Flanders/And he did not look at me. Songs from an Evil Wood. Edward J. M. D. Plunkett. HBV 1-2

Since I lost my heart's darling–my Draherin O Machree! Draherin O Machree. Anonymous. AnIV

Since I'm not to be granted/licence to run my life. Drat My Hateful Birthday. Sulpicia. PBWP

Since I may work with thee! Laborers Together with God. Lucy Alice Perkins. BLRP

Since I must go now, day is near. On a Time, the Amorous Silvy. Anonymous. GBL; ViBoPo

Since I renounced the whole wide world/For one beloved face. To a Vagabond. Constance Davies Woodrow. CaP

...Since I shall never have/children and since they are so far from my/mouth, kiss them for me.' The Breasts of Mnasidice. Pierre Louys. PeHV

Since I, to be a man, had taken one. Deer Hunt. Judson Jerome. RFM

Since I write oftener than you, I vow/Another letter twenty years from now. A Letter to Robert Frost. Robert Hillyer. MoAmPo

Since if my scent be good, I care not, if/It be as short as yours. Life. George Herbert. AnAnS 1; CBEP; EG; FaBoRV; HBV 1-2; JCP; LiTB; MeLP; MePo; NoP; OBS; PoPle; SeCeV; SeCP; SeCV 1-2

Since if ye list ye may my woe restrain. If with Complaint the Pain Might Be Express'd. Sir Thomas Wyatt. FCP; SiPS

Since in the gilt-age Saturn ruled alone,/And in this painted, planets every one. Caelica, XLIV. Fulke, Lord Brooke Greville. FCP; OAEL 1-2

Since in your Hoast that Coward nere was fed/Who to his Prostrate ere was Prostrated. Valiant Love. Richard Lovelace. SeCP

Since ista possum is a goner! Carmen Possum. Anonymous. BLPA; NLV

Since Joan in the dark is as good as my lady. Court and Country Love. Anonymous. UnTE

Since Knowledge is but Sorrow's spy,/It is not safe to know. The Philosopher and the Lover to a Mistress Dying. Sir William Davenant. MePo; NOBE; Prf

Since, like a fragrant grove, these boys all flower in thee. Epigram: "Gathering the bloom of all the fairest boys that be." Strato. PeHV

Since love, as before God, for ever shows/Before its object reverence and fear? Sonnets to Karl Theodor German. August von Platen. PeHV

Since love himself hath no part in her beauty/Nor findeth abode in her spirit? Forgotten Island. Radclyffe Hall. PeHV

Since love no doomsday hath, where bodies change,/Why should new be delight not being strange? Caelica, LXXII. Fulke, Lord Brooke Greville. FCP

Since love's broke through an iron door. The Servant Man (The Iron Door). Anonymous. AmFP

Since Mars and she played even and odd. What Thing Is Love. George Peele. ElL; ELP; EnRePo; NOBE; OAEP; SeCePo; UnTE

Since men prove beasts, let beasts bear gentle minds.' The Rape of Lucrece. William Shakespeare. PBBP

Since more him none shall see. A Lamentation. Thomas Campion. CH; OHIP

Since my exercise done, I am ever prepared,/And have leisure remaining for play.' Henry's Secret. Dorothy Kilner. OxBChV

Since my hart holdes not thee, hold thou my hart. Sonnet XIX. William Alabaster. AnAnS 1

Since my Love died for me. Fair Helen. Anonymous. FaFP; GTBS; GTBS-P; LiTL; ViBoPo

Since my love died for me today,/I'll die for him tomorrow. Bonny Barbara Allan. Anonymous. BiP; BoLiVe; EnLit; InPK; LiTL; TrGrPo

Since my parents are both so contrary–/You'd better ask me! Ask and Have. Samuel Lover. GoTF; HBV 1-2; TreFS

Since Nature's pride is now a withered daffodil. Cynthia's Revels. Ben Jonson. AtBAP; EG; TrGrPo

Since nature's works declare/God is there. Through All the World. Anonymous. TrAS

The since neglected and unwanted. In the Tub We Soak Our Skin. Edward Newman Horn. ELU

Since night has made me such a happy lover. Moonlight. Jacques Tahureau. AWP

Since none alive can truly tell/What Fortune they must see. Ah Cloris! That I Now Could Sit. Sir Charles Sedley. CavP; OAEP; OBS

Since not to feel what wrong I bear in this,/A senseless state, and no true patience is.   Caelica, XLVI.   Fulke, Lord Brooke Greville.   FCP

Since nought beside can bless thee/Return and dwell with me.   Shall Earth No More Inspire Thee?   Emily Bronte.   ELP

Since now we know how lucky we are.   March the 3rd.   Edward ("Edward Eastaway") Thomas.   NAs

Since observed by Yours faithfully, GOD.   Limerick: "Dear Sir, Your astonishment's odd."   *Anonymous.*   FaBoCo; LiBL; NLV; NOBL; PoPle

Since of all good you are the best alive.   The Cuckoo and the Nightingale.   Thomas Clanvowe.   MeEV

Since only he could utter the right curse.   Fragment.   Miklos Radnoti.   VWA

Since our Lord was nail'd t' ye.   The Elder, or Bourtree.   *Anonymous.*   GBP

Since outward wisdom springs from truth within,/Which all men feel, or hear before they sin.   Caelica, LXVI.   Fulke, Lord Brooke Greville.   FCP

Since Phoenix-like I from this fire/Both life and youth receive.   Song: "When I lie burning in thine eye."   Thomas Stanley.   ViBoPo

Since she, alas! hath left me,/Falero, lero, loo!   A Love Sonnet.   George Wither.   EIL; FaBoPP; GBL; LiTL; OBS; ViBoPo

Since she did herself resign/To my vows, for ever mine.   The Happy Swain.   Ambrose Philips.   EnLoPo

Since she found the bonnie laddie she adores.   The Jolly Plowboy.   *Anonymous.*   AmFP

Since she is plighted to me, a wilderness, and I to/The silver country of Canaan.   Canaan.   Muriel Spark.   NYBP

Since she joys in my death, I for her die.   A Maid Me Loved.   Patrick Hannay.   ALV

Since she was lovelier than any of you.   Blue Girls.   John Crowe Ransom.   AmP; AnFE; APA; CMoP; GBL; GoTF; LiTA; LiTL; MoAB; MoAmPo; MoVE; NoAm; PrIm; TAP; TreFT; VGW; WeW

Since that day I have had no pleasant nights.   Light, Light of My Eyes.   Sextus Propertius.   LiTW

Since that the tears of more and less/Right well declare his worthiness.   An Epitaph of Sir Thomas Gravener, Knight.   Sir Thomas Wyatt.   EnRePo; SiPS

Since the day I did the railroads for "The Rocky Mountain News."   Doing Railroads for the "Rocky Mountain News."   Cy Warman.   PoOW

Since the days of the snake.   Who Be Kind To.   Allen Ginsberg.   NNaP

...Since the mark was not/Your heart or mine, not this time, my companion.   Sometimes when Night...   Victoria Mary (Vita) Sackville-West.   SBG

Since the prime of life–that I might have spent as a boor.   O It's Best Be a Total Boor.   Daibhi O Bruadair.   NOBI

Since the voice of death must be His true voice.   At the End of Things.   Arthur Edward Waite.   WGRP

Since then, I have not met an officer/That I can call by name.   Officers.   Josephine Miles.   FaBoWP

Since then no desert bar/will serve a passing boar/even ginger-beer.   The Boar and the Dromedar.   Henry Beissel.   WHW

Since then they've called him Sunny Jim.   Force.   *Anonymous.*   FaBoUs

Since there is play in pleasant work?   Discovery.   Benjamin Keech.   PoToHe

Since this we feel, great loss we cannot find.   Why Fear to Die?   Sir Philip Sidney.   SiPS

Since thou art where the ills o live can/never reach thee more.   Lament of Anastasius.   William Bourne Oliver Peabody.   AA

Since thou hast left us–all alone with/sorrow/And blind with tears?   Not Changed, But Glorified.   *Anonymous.*   STF

Since thou, her more loved master, art not there.'   An Old Cat's Dying Soliloquy.   Anna Seward.   NOEC

Since, though they fostered man, they never loved him.   Wessex Guidebook.   Louis MacNeice.   HaMV

Since through a double mean nought right appears.   To the Same Man's Life.   William Hammond.   OBS

Since through its living semblance passed/The thought that bade a race be free!   The Hand of Lincoln.   Edmund Clarence Stedman.   AA; OHIP; PGD

Since 'tis my God that leadeth me!   He Leadeth Me.   Joseph Henry Gilmore.   AH; BLRP; WBLP; WGRP

Since upon night so sweet such awful morn could rise!   Childe Harold's Pilgrimage: Canto III, XXIV.   George Gordon, Lord Byron.   AnFE

Since we are ever ready to disburse,/If any one our Masters hand can show.   To All Angels and Saints.   George Herbert.   SeCV 1-2

...Since we are/Pure before life and since we love one another?...   Words to My Friend.   Renee Vivien.   PeHV

Since we kep' rakin' in the hay/Thon day–thon day!   Rosies.   Agnes I. Hanrahan.   HBV 1-2

Since we must part, let's part as heroes do.   Farewell in a Dream.   Stephen Spender.   MoAB; MoBrPo

Since we no Provocation want from you.   Sir Patient Fancy: Epilogue (excerpt).   Aphra Behn.   WPOW

Since we our Passion have subdu'd,/Which is the strongest thing I know.   Parting with Lucasia: A Song.   Katherine ("Orinda") Philips.   PeHV

Since well ye know this painful fit/Hath last too long.   The knot which first my heart did strain.   Sir Thomas Wyatt.   FCP; SiPS

Since what we think is never what we see.   What We See Is What We Think.   Wallace Stevens.   SyP

Since whatever pig-/latin we talked, none called it love.   Awkward Goodbyes.   Vassar Miller.   FAZ

Since when, his brain that had before been dry,/Became the well-spring of all Poetry.   Orchestra.   Sir John Davies.   EG

Since when it grows, and smells, I swear,/Not of itself but thee.   Song to Celia.   Ben Jonson.   AWP; CABA; DiPo; ELP; ForPo; GBL; GoTF; HeIP; InPo; NoP; OAEL 1-2; PoEL 1-5; PoPl; PrIm; SeCP; SeCV 1-2

Since when the dismal solace of their woe,/Has only been weak mankind to undo.   Davideis.   Abraham Cowley.   OxBoCh

Since while he pitches he waters the lawn.   Spitballer.   Fred Chappell.   LiSp

Since with these she must divide/Heaven's envy, here she died.   Epitaph.   Claudian (Claudius Claudianus).   AWP

Since woman is the helpmeet made for man?   Monna Innominata.   Christina Georgina Rossetti.   VLP

Since women use so much to feign.   Resignation.   Sir Thomas Wyatt.   OBSC

Since yee heare his falser play;/And that he is Venus' run-away.   Beauties, Have Ye Seen This Toy.   Ben Jonson.   OAEP

Since you into a hole did tumble.   The Last Will and Testament of Anthony, King of Poland.   *Anonymous.*   APAS

"Since you're up, try Channel Four."   Addict.   Jack Montgomery.   QQQ

Since you with these misfortunes meet,/For want of looking to your feet.'   The Stargazer.   *Anonymous.*   OxBChV

Sincerely yours,/The Boy in the Green Shirt.   Letter to a Substitute Teacher.   Gary Gildner.   Psk

Sine cloak, sine shirt, sine breeches.   Epitaph: "Hic jacet Tom Shorthose."   *Anonymous.*   FaBoEE

Sine, in the clifting of a craig,/She found him drownd in Yarrow.   Rare Willie Drowned in Yarrow, or, The Water o Gamrie (A version).   *Anonymous.*   BaBo; BSV; ESPB; GBP; GoTS

Sine on the path of right,/Show us the way!   Strength, Love, Light.   King of France Robert II.   WGRP

Sinew and breath and body; it would live.   A Football-Player.   Edward Cracroft Lefroy.   LiSp

...Sinewing from side to side,/as he passed us and vanished.   Tao and Unfitness at Inistiogue on the River Nore.   Thomas Kinsella.   FaBoIP

Sing a bit, be patient./Wait.   Crossing the Colorado River into Yuma.   Simon J. Ortiz.   TAT

Sing a little faster,/Sing a little faster!/Sing!   Song: "I am weaving a song of waters."   Gwendolyn B. Bennett.   BlSi

Sing a new note.   Lament of the Flutes.   Christopher Okigbo.   PBA

Sing again!   Sing Again.   Marie Van Vorst.   AA

Sing all ore heaven for aye. And that's but all.   Gods Determinations.   Edward Taylor.   AP

Sing and build inside my thin lips.   Byzantium Burning.   Jack Gilbert.   NPGG

Sing as quietly as love.   To Jann, in Her Absence.   C. J. Driver.   PeSA

Sing, birds in every furrow.   Pack, Clouds, away, and Welcome, Day!   Thomas Heywood.   EG; EIL; GBL; GTBS-P; SoSe; ViBoPo

Sing,/but not too loudly, so he will come.   Cuckoo, noisy among the Shenbaka flowers.   Andal.   BoWoP

Sing, care away, care away, let the world go!   On a Fair Morning.   *Anonymous.*   ViBoPo

Sing cuccu, Phye Betta Cappe, nu!   Baccalaureate.   David McCord.   BXAP; NLV; OBAL; SpRo

Sing cuccu, sing cuccu, nu.   Sumer Is Icumen In.   *Anonymous.*   AWP; BiP; EBEV; EnLi 1-2; FF; GBP; HeIP; InPo; InPS; InvP; MeEL; NIP; OAEL 1-2; OBEV; OxBM; PAI; PBBP; SeCePo; SeCeV; SpRo; TreFT; TrGrPo

Sing dum de whickerty, dum de way.   The Factory Girl's Come-All-Ye.   *Anonymous.*   AmFP; OBAL

Sing Ebenezer, Robert, sing Hallelujah!   Hallelujah: A Sestina.   Robert Francis.   PoCh

Sing fod-a-linky-day, sing, fod-a-linky-day.   The Dishonest Miller.   *Anonymous.*   AmFP

Sing, "Fol do ra dowdy, oh, fol do ra dowdy O day."   Johnny O Dutchman.   *Anonymous.*   BFSS

Sing for the world/has need of you.   Sing Little Bird.   Maria Hastings.   SoPo

Sing goddamm, sing goddamm, DAMM.   Ancient Music.   Ezra Pound.   BXAP; DBV; FaBoCo; FaBoPa; FF; HeIP; LiTM; NePA; NLV; OBAL; OxBA; PPON; SpRo; TW

Sing heigh! diddle-eye, diddle-eye, fie!/Diddle-eye, diddle-eye, day!   The Farmer's Curst Wife.   *Anonymous.*   AmFP

Sing hey, cock without a comb,/Cock-a-dle luddle.   Madrigal: "The white hen she cackles."   *Anonymous.*   PBBP

Sing hi,/Sing hey,/Sing ho!   Sweet Wild April.   William Force Stead.   HBV 1-2; HBVY

Sing ho! for the Hatteras whale!   A Song of the Hatteras Whale. *Anonymous.* EtS

Sing holly, go whistle, and ivy!   Three Acres of Land.   *Anonymous.*   NA; OxNR

Sing "Hymen, Hymen', sing/The god of marrying!   Hymeneal.   Caius Valerius Catullus.   PeHV

Sing hymns to Virtue's deity.   Fortune and Virtue.   Thomas Dekker. GoTL

Sing intimate songs/and pour the mead.   Lady of the Ferry Inn.   Gwerfyl Mechain.   BoWoP

Sing it high, sing it low,/Love me–I love you.   Lullaby.   Christina Georgina Rossetti.   PoPle

Sing loud the disgraces of exuberant love.   Psyche to Cupid: Her Ditty. James Richard Broughton.   ErPo

Sing loudly this my Lady-day.   On a Birthday.   John Millington Synge. GBL; OBMV

Sing lullaby, my life's Joy.   Our Lady's Lullaby.   Richard Verstegan.   ACP; CAW; GoBC; ISi

Sing, merry bird, the charm's complete,/"Witchery–witchery–witchery!"   The Maryland Yellow-Throat.   Henry Van Dyke.   HBV 1-2

Sing more will wonderfully birds than are   White Guardians of the Universe of Sleep.   Edward Estlin Cummings.   NYBP

Sing, O my home–sing, O my home, of thee.   The Wanderer.   Eugene Field. BPAW; PoOW; PoPl

Sing of the things you know so well.   The Sea Shell.   Amy Lowell.   BrR

Sing on, dear Thrush, amid the limes!   My Thrush.   Mortimer Collins. HBV 1-2

Sing on in the soul alway.   The Human Touch.   Spencer Michael Free. BLPA; FaBoBe; PoToHe

Sing our patroness's praise/In cheerful and harmonious lays.   Come Ye Sons of Art (excerpt).   Henry Purcell.   UnS

Sing patience, patience,/Only still have patience.   Carol of Patience.   Robert Graves.   OBCP

Sing, poet, thou–and sing thy best for May!   Spring.   Meleager.   AWP

Sing Polly-wolly-doodle all the day.   Polly Wolly Doodle.   *Anonymous.* FSW; GoTF; TreF; YaD

(Sing, sad nightingale!) is my Maid.   I Go by Road.   Catulle Mendes. AWP; TrJP

Sing. See no one.   Inside the River.   James Dickey.   PoA

Sing, sing with the hummingbirds.   Vision.   Richard Eberhart.   NYBP

Sing terribly afar in the lost lands.   Sonnets–Unrealities.   Edward Estlin Cummings.   AnAmPo; MoLP

Sing the blues/so pain will bleed and let the islands in.   A Poem.   Ezekiel Mphahlele.   WhB

Sing there! Sing there!   Ecstasy.   Duncan Campbell Scott.   CaP

Sing thou, my Soul–Love's face–yet this shall be!   Sing Thou, My Soul. Theodosia Garrison.   CAW

Sing to make the work go well,/Like the Scissor-man.   The Scissor-Man. Madeline Nightingale.   TiPo

Sing to my God a grateful Song.   An Evening Hymn.   Thomas Ken.   OBS; OxBChV

Sing to others if you'll tarry/Silent with your serving boy.   The Market-Square's Admiring Throngs.   Johann Wolfgang von Goethe.   PeHV

Sing tol-de-rol, sing tol-de-rol-de-ray.   Had a Little Fight in Mexico. *Anonymous.*   OuSiCo

Sing tu-re-lye laddie, I tu-re-lye-lay.   As I Went A-Walking down Ratcliffe Highway.   *Anonymous.*   ShS

Sing, "tura, lura, laur-e-ay," sing, "tura, lura, lum."   She Loved Her Husband Dearly.   *Anonymous.*   BFSS

Sing we in sight.   A Lyric from a Play.   *Anonymous.*   MeEL

Sing while he may, man hath no long delight.   Sestina.   Algernon Charles Swinburne.   VLP

Sing while you may.   Dark Wings.   James Stephens.   PoA

Sing yes Sing no   Seesaw.   Gerardo Diego.   LiTW

Sing yet another song, hoi!/chirry, birry, bin.   Light Another Candle. Miriam Chaikin.   NTCP

Sing yip, yip, yippy-doodle-do.   From the Ballad of Two-Gun Freddy. Walter R. Brooks.   SoPo

Singer of sweet Colonus, and its child.   To a Friend.   Matthew Arnold. EnLi 1-2; OAEP

The singer, the song, and the sung.   Blessed Lord, What It Is to Be Young. David McCord.   NTCP

...The singer wants applause/not criticism as he leaves the stage.   Goodbye, Sally.   James Simmons.   BIrV

Singin' all together!   The Song on the Way.   *Anonymous.*   BrR

Singin': "Come, shove in your heids and growl!"   With the Herring Fishers. Hugh" (Christopher Murray Grieve) MacDiarmid.   BSV; LiTM

Singin' fare-thee, O my honey, fare-thee-well!   Alice B. (with music). *Anonymous.*   AS

Singin' in the mornin',/Corrieneuchin' a' the nicht.   Water Music.   Hugh" (Christopher Murray Grieve) MacDiarmid.   GoTS

Singin' ya old Blue, you good dog you.   Old Blue.   *Anonymous.*   FSW

Singing, a grapevine climbs the sun!   The Grapevine.   Zoe Kincaid Brockman.   GoYe

Singing a winter song/For you and me.   Walk on a Winter Day.   Sara Van Alstyne Allen.   YeAr

Singing about her head, as she rode by.   Love without Hope.   Robert Graves.   BoLoP; ELU; FaBoEE; GBL; GTBS-P; OAEL 1-2; OxBI

Singing and caroling to meet the sun....   The Phoenix (excerpt).   *Anonymous.* OAEL 1-2

Singing and dancing all of my life,/Yea, father, yea.   Daughters Will You Marry?   *Anonymous.*   FSW

Singing and dancing we go!   Eternal Sabbath.   Isaac L. Peretz.   TrJP

Singing and singing and singing!   Prelude.   Josephine Preston Peabody. AA

Singing and sounding under the grumbling sea.   Two Musics.   Norman MacCaig.   NeBP

The singing and the silence of a bird?   The Bird at Dawn.   Harold Monro. MoBrPo

The singing begins.   Let Us Sing Unto the Lord a New Song.   Denise Levertov.   CAPP

Singing blood's syllables.   Walking.   H. L. Van Brunt.   LTB

The singing children of her brain.   The Mad Woman of Punnet's Town. Leonard Alfred George Strong.   MoBrPo

Singing/daddy/daddy/daddy   When Slavery Seems Sweet.   Ed Bullins. NBP

Singing fah-de-ing, ding/Dah-de-ing-ding/Di-di-um da-de ing ding/Didium da de ing ding/Di-di-um day.   .The Devil and the Farmer's Wife. *Anonymous.*   FSW; TrAS

Singing glory to the souls/Of the brave!–   The Battle of the Baltic.   Thomas Campbell.   CBEP; GN; GTBS; GTBS-P; HBV 1-2; NBM; RoGo

Singing in the darkness behind their own eyelids.   Singing in the Dark. Irma Wassall.   PoNe

The singing leaves began to sing.   The Singing Bush.   William Soutar. ACV

The singing Murrawal, the Voice-that-does-not-cease.   Song of the Captured Woman.   James Devaney.   PoAu 1-2

Singing of gods, and nations overthrown.   The Sea's Voice.   William Prescott Foster.   EtS

Singing of him what they could understand.   Beowulf.   Richard Wilbur. CrMA

Singing of home, death, a blossoming tree.   Grandfather.   Joseph Stroud. NPGG

The singing of my sisters/Whom the sea hath drowned so long.   Der Mond Ist Aufgegangen.   Heinrich Heine.   AWP

Singing of springtime.   Act II.   Katherine Davis.   PoPl

Singing: Ohe Oh, Ohe Oh!   St. Ursanne.   Michael Roberts.   LiTM

Singing on fine and shivering limbs/of spread and open trees.   Late in Fall. Ramona Wilson.   VoR

A singing page I'll be/Here, in Thy springtime,/Jesu.   A Page's Road Song. William Alexander Percy.   TrPWD; YeAr

Singing singing? What am I singing?   In Ancient December.   Alice Notley. APU

Singing their lives, yours and mine.   The Old Women Still Sing.   Charles H. Rowell.   CNA

...Singing/to our brother, singing to/our might.   Behold the Sea.   Aaron Kurtz.   PPON

Singing to the Father, Son and Holy Ghost,/Alleluia. Amen.   Funeral Hymn. William Walsham Howe.   WGRP

Singing together in the eternal morn.   Towards the Source: Let Us Go Down, the Long Dead Night Is Done.   Christopher John Brennan.   PoAu 1-2

Singing/"we/shall/over/come".   Black Taffy.   Peggy Susberry Kenner.   JB

Singing with glorious song as I speed/O'er field and flood, a ghostly wanderer. Riddle: The Swan: "Silent my robe, when I rest on earth."   *Anonymous.* CoBE

Singing with open mouths their strong melodious songs.   I Hear America Singing.   Walt Whitman.   AmePo; AmFN; AWP; FaBoBe; FaBV; FaFP; FF; FPL; HAP; LiTA; LoGBV; MoAmPo; PAL; PoPl; PoSC; SaC; TreFS; TrGrPo; WeW; YaD

Single am I amid the countless many.   From Country to Town.   Hartley Coleridge.   CBEP; OBRV

The single beam of all my life intense.   Vita Nuova.   Stanley Jasspon Kunitz.   VGW

Single body alone in the universe/against its own best time.   Sex without Love.   Sharon Olds.   MAYP

Single boy gonna talk about you,/Hi-li-li-lee-o.   Married Man Gonna Keep Your Secret.   *Anonymous.*   OuSiCo

The single chord the wild bar.   Publishing 2001.   Bob Rosenthal.   APU

A single crusty/or crustacean/word.   The Crab.   Conrad Aiken.   BoAnP

Single 'e bided, and 'e wished/'Is father done the same.   The Greek Anthology (excerpt).   Leonard Alfred George Strong.   DBV

A single geranium.   Lightning Rides.   P. Wolny.   PPJ

The single-minded/lovers of multiplication.   The Terrorist Smiles.   Anselm Hollo.   APU

A single mouth, friend, but a pair of/ears.   The Mouth and the Ears.   Shem-Tob Palquera.   TrJP

A single ripple starts from where he stood.   The Heron.   Theodore Roethke.   BoAnP; MiAP; RFM

A single soul that lacks a sweet crystalline cry.   Paudeen.   William Butler Yeats.   HAP; OBSP; PAI; PoEL 1-5

A single/specious need/to keep/what you have/never really/had.   As a Possible Lover.   LeRoi (Imamu Amiri Baraka) Jones.   AmNP

A single spirit never to return.   The Marriage.   Yvor Winters.   HW; MoVE

A single sword to thee!   Prayer.   Gilbert Keith Chesterton.   WGRP

Single to serve th' erron'ous throng,/Spite of themselves, be mine.   The American Patriot's Prayer.   *Anonymous.*   PAH

Single, unpropp'd, and nodding to my fall.   Sonnet On a Family Picture.   Thomas Edwards.   CEP; NOEC; OBEC

A single wild goose climbs into the void.   Clear After Rain.   Tu Fu.   PoPl

The singleness in every name.   Late Last Night.   Arthur Gregor.   VGW

Sings by himself a song.   In the Swamp in Secluded Recesses.   Walt Whitman.   RFM

sings for us two/especially.   The Blackbird.   Humbert Wolfe.   GoJo; GrPl; HBMV; HBVY; SUS; TiPo

Sings Harry in the wind-break.   Songs.   Denis Glover.   AnNZ

Sings its own seablown Te Deum,/In and out the slipping slates.   Ireland with Emily.   Sir John Betjeman.   GTBS-P; OxBTC

Sings to the lines/in her face.   Self-Portrait.   Judith Mountain Leaf Volborth.   TWSS

...A singular island where people may come/Together, as we have, making a singular place.   Discovering My Daughter.   Dabney Stuart.   SM

Sink lower, fade, as dark womb/Recedes creation will step clear.   Rest from Loving and Be Living.   C. Day-Lewis.   CoBMV; MoBrPo; OBMV

Sink reddening through the sullied shades–/From lost Oriskany.   The Battle of Oriskany.   Charles D. Helmer.   PAH

Sink sail! for such a dream as Love is lost before the/waking.   Barcarolle.   Arthur William Edgar O'Shaughnessy.   NBM

Sinking and fading as it nears the sun/In this relentless river of desire.   The Gulf Stream.   Henry Bellamann.   EtS

Sinking her teeth/into the cleft/of a voluptuous peach.   A Fine, a Private Place.   Diane Ackerman.   MAYP

The sinner now is born again,/To dwell with Christ above.   Waked by the Gospel's Powerful Sound.   Samson Occom.   AH

Sinner, please, don't let dis harves' pass,/An' die, an' lose you' soul at las' yo' soul at las'.   Sinner, Please Don't Let Dis Harves' Pass.   *Anonymous.*   BoAN 1-2

Sins first disliked, are after that beloved.   Sins Loathed, and Yet Loved.   Robert Herrick.   LiTB

The sins in her soul are seven,/The sin upon his is one.   The Dole of the King's Daughter.   *Anonymous.*   AWP

Sinuously it swims through the stars.   Outward.   Louis Simpson.   NYBP

Sion, had I not memory of thee!   Babylon and Sion (Goa and Lisbon).   Luís de Camoens.   AWP

Sipping clear rain/from a trumpet flower.   The Storm.   Elizabeth Jane Coatsworth.   OBCA

Sips it patiently/between his silver-mirrored teeth.   A Scholder Indian Poem.   Joy Harjo.   TWSS

Sir, God give you good-morrow!   Carol.   *Anonymous.*   FaBoCo

Sir Guy's tall phantom stoops to pat/His little phantom hound!   Hold.   Patrick Reginald Chalmers.   HBV 1-2

..."Sir, I do declare/everyone's sick! The soldiers poison the air."   From Trollope's Journal.   Elizabeth Bishop.   FaBoPV

Sir, I Ham a very Bad Hand at Righting.   On Not Being Milton.   Tony Harrison.   FaBoPV

Sir Isaac said nothing of.   Natural Law.   Babette Deutsch.   MoLP

Sir Menenius Agrippa's the friend of the/people.   Sir Menenius Agrippa, the Friend of the People.   Robert Barnabas Brough.   VLP

Sir! Quicken us again,/Spirit of Life within!   Invocation.   Gilbert Thomas.   TrPWD

Sir Rotherham Redde gathers bags of gold/Instead of the cherries ruddy and cold.   Evening.   Edith Sitwell.   MoBS

Sir,–taking cover.   Three Around the Old Gentleman.   John Berryman.   AP

Sir Thomas Plumtre is hanged on a tree.   A Ballad of the Rising in the North.   *Anonymous.*   ACP

Sir, you are sealed of the tribe of Ben.   An Epistle Answering to One That Asked to be Sealed of the Tribe...   Ben Jonson.   SeCV 1-2

The Siren waits thee, singing song for song.   To Robert Browning.   Walter Savage Landor.   EnLi 1-2; GTBS; MCCG; NoP; OAEP; ViBoPo

Sirocco, monsoon, khamsin, and chinook.   Weather Words.   David McCord.   ImOP

Sister and brother,/Grandsire, and sire.   A Catch by the Hearth.   *Anonymous.*   ChBR; OHIP

The Sister appears in autumn and black decay.   Rest and Silence.   Georg Trakl.   LiTW

Sister, brother,/We bespatter one another.   Like Birds of a Feather.   Ralph Schomberg.   TrJP

Sister by sister around the fire/that no one watches go out.   Hokkaido.   Jim Trifilio.   FAZ

Sister of every flag/In the wide world.   The Flag Speaks.   Emily Greene Balch.   PGD

Sister sister./another child has come.   Mississippi Born.   Pearl Cleage Lomax.   CNA

–The Sister, when she turned his pillow over,/Kissed "Treasure Island" on its well-worn cover.   Saint R. L. S.   Sarah N. Cleghorn.   HBMV

Sisters and sisters/brothers and brothers/together.   Christopher Street Liberation Day, June 28, 1970.   Fran Winant.   PeHV

Sisters in love, a love allowed to climb/Ev'n in this earth, above the reach of time.   To Lady Eleanor Butler and the Honourable Miss Ponsonby...   William Wordsworth.   PeHV

Sisters of Mercy, to love is delight!   Notre Dames des Champs.   John Millington Synge.   SyP

Sisters of Silence, in Our Mother's fold!–   You Are My Sisters.   Georges Rodenbach.   CAW

...Sit alone looking down at/evening on the ocean, drinking wine or not.   Trying to Believe.   Linda Gregg.   NPGG

Sit by the fire and spare shoe leather.   A Devonshire Rhyme.   *Anonymous.*   BrR; SiSoSe

Sit down, and I'll play you a snatch.   Limerick: "There was a young fellow named Hatch."   *Anonymous.*   LiBL

Sit down–and sleep, if so inclined.   Epitaph of Hipponax.   Charles Stuart Calverley.   FaBoEE

Sit down, with Shakespeare, to a P.E.N. Club supper.   Critics and Poets.   Geoffrey Grigson.   FaBoEE

Sit him on father's foot, jump him up high.   Rigadoon, Rigadoon, Now Let Him Fly.   *Anonymous.*   OxNR

Sit on the mushroom circles of the forest floor.   The Krankenhaus of Leutkirch.   Richmond Lattimore.   NYBP

Sit on their soft, fat, velvet bums,/To wriggle out of hollow flowers.   All in June.   William Henry Davies.   OBSP

Sit silent Nun–sit there and be/Comrade and Confidant to me.   The Autumn Day Its Course Has Run.   Charlotte Bronte.   NOBV

Sit there in plain glass jars/and worry about their parents' future.   Family Matters.   Gunter Grass.   ELU

Sit, thy hands wringing,/Whilst I go singing.   Madrigal: "No, no, Nigella!"   Thomas Morley.   EnRePo

Sit very still,/And wait God's will!   A Charm for Bees.   *Anonymous.*   CAW

...Sit with them/once in a while.   Anatomy.   Gilbert Sorrentino.   PoL

Sith for my truth she needeth no witness.   Benedicite, What Dreamed I This Night?   *Anonymous.*   NCEP

Sith I Her love'd ere on this Earth shee came.   Sonnet VII: "That learned Graecian (who did so exell)."   William, of Hawthornden Drummond.   OBS

Sith sighing zephyrs answer us again.   Madrigal: "Poor turtle, thou bemoans."   William, of Hawthornden Drummond.   PBBP

Sith sleepeth my child here/Stay ye the branches.   A Song for the Virgin Mother.   Felix Lope de Vega Carpio.   LiTW

Sith that is rich, and all her rareness shows?   Against Proud Poor Phryna.   John, of Hereford Davies.   FaBoEE

Sith Time hath conquer'd the world's conqueror?   Rome, Conqueror, Conquered.   Joshua Sylvester.   FaBoEE

Sith travel then, nor frost, can cool this fire,/From Moscow I thy friend will home retire.   Unable by Long and Hard Travel to Banish Love, Returns Her Friend.   George Turberville.   OBTV

Sits by your bed–and brings her knitting.   Good Fortune.   Heinrich Heine.   BLPA

Sits, statue-like, alone!   The Funeral of Time.   Henry Beck Hirst   AA

Sits, tight-lipped, quaking, eager-eyed and pale,/Beneath her purple feather.   On Hampstead Heath.   Wilfred Wilson Gibson.   HBV 1-2

Sits till evening and will not move from the place!   Planting Flowers on the Eastern Embankment.   Po Chu-i.   BoNaP

...A sitter on Boards/preparing to live for ever.   A Lifetime Devoted to Literature.   Judith Rodriguez.   NOAV

Sittin' down side ob de Holy Lam'.   Father Abraham.   *Anonymous.*   BoAN 1-2

...Sitting by a cottage/in a small country.   To Hugh MacDiarmid.   Edwin Morgan.   FaBoTw

Sitting by the golden sheaves on our wedding-day.   Like a Laverock in the Lift.   Jean Ingelow.   HBV 1-2

Sitting on a stool.   Sum, Es, Est.   *Anonymous.*   ChTr

Sitting quiet on the down/Grabbed the princess and the crown.   Peter.   Laura Benet.   HBMV

Sitting soft.   Ravens.   Ted Hughes.   InPS; NAs

Situation improving. Stop. They're using/our rifles.   Turista.   Mark Osaki.   BrSi

The six beggared cripples. O For Doors to Be Open. W.H. Auden. AtBAP; CoBMV; OAEP; ViBoPo

The six-day riders/Want a five-day week! Bicycalamity. Edmund W. Peters. SD

Six for father, hot and tired,/Knocking at the door. Mother Shake the Cherry-Tree. Christina Georgina Rossetti. TiPo

The Six-Horse Limited Mail was in! The Six-Horse Limited Mail. Ethel Romig Fuller. BPAW

Six hundred and eighty-five ways to dress eggs? French Cookery. Thomas Moore. OBRV

Six is the sign of a bastard bairn. One Is a Sign of Mischief. Anonymous. PBBP

Six islanders for a ten bob note/Rowed us out to the anchored boat. Letter to Derek Mahon. Michael Longley. FaBoIP

Six little, seven little, eight little,/nine little, ten little Injuns more. Ten Little Injuns. Septimus Winner. OBAL

Six long-headed jazzers play. Jazzonia. Langston Hughes. BANP; NIP

6. Man is a sun and his senses are the planets. Aphorisms. Novalis (George Friedrich Philipp von Hardenerg). NU

Six men dead at my shoulder/on an Autumn day. An Autumn Day. Sorley MacLean. AMV-81

6. Reduce two academical years to their lowest terms. Entrance Exams. Cuthbert (Edward Bradley) Bede. FaBoNo

Sixteen full branches a penny. Sweet Blooming Lavender. Anonymous. OxNR

Sixteen thousand miles I've come,/To march along with a blanket drum. Whaler's Rhyme. Anonymous. NOAV

Sixty forts at our gates last night–/To-day there is not one! A Ballad of Orleans. Agnes Mary Frances (Mme Emile Duclaux) Robinson. HBV 1-2

Size of the tick of the hospital's clock on the archway over the/white door– Kaddish. Allen Ginsberg. NeAP

Sizz.../Fizz.... The Kallyope Yell. Vachel Lindsay. BoLiVe

Ska-bibba-lala-boo and a slo-o-ow reel. Shoo, Shoo, Shoo-Lye. Anonymous. ABF

The skaters are gone home. All is dark. I leave you these hours. Adultery at the Plaza. John Thompson. WeW

Skeletons of birds/Fell like snowflakes./Fell continually. The Case. H. R. Hays. EAS

The Skies, and Stars, his Properties must seem,/And turn-spit Angels, tread the Spheres for him. Satires. Nicholas Boileau-Despréaux. OBVE

Skies, the aimless circles of joy. First Ice of Winter. Michael Shorb. AMV-81

The skilled musicians there,/Around him in the nimble air. Mother. D. L. Kelleher. NeIP

...Skims/this jagged distance without leaving sons. Sleeping with Foxes. Roberta Hill. CDW

Skims your fate o'er the moonlit grass! Father Coyote. George Sterling. BPAW

The skin and sinews of/something else that went before. The Presence. Maxine W. Kumin. RFM

The skin is history.the dark horse Poll. Ed Roberson. PoBA

...A skin of wood/as much the earth's as his. Farmer. Lucien Stryk. FAZ

Skinny and shining in the nighfall light. Of Kings and Things. Lillian Morrison. CAD; NCSH

Skip to my Lou, my darling. Skip to My Lou. Anonymous. ABF; AmFP; FSW; TrAS

The skirts of young girls on their way to church. Casanova. Richard Usborne. PoL

The sky above and the desert flood/Of silence all around. The Water-Hole. Charles Erskine Scott Wood. BPAW

The sky became a still and woven blue. Merlin Enthralled. Richard Wilbur. CMoP; NePoEA; NYBP

A sky-born form so beautiful as she. Of His Mistress. Robert Greene. EIL

The sky grows big. Father. Jean Lipkin. PeSA

The sky is always slipping back/And getting far away from me. The Sky. Elizabeth Madox Roberts. MoAmPo

The sky is clear and very patient overhead. Day on Kind Continent. Robert David Cohen. NYBP

The sky is clearer when I'm not in heat,/& the poems/are colder. Becoming a Nun. Erica Jong. MAYP

(The sky is falling, my son.) John Brown's Body. Stephen Vincent Benét. TreF

The sky is filled with stars, invisible by day. Morituri Salutamus. Henry Wadsworth Longfellow. MAmP; PoToHe

...The sky/is really something. Message at Sunset for Bishop Berkeley. Heather McHugh. GeTw

The sky looked faultless, empty. Hard Strain in a Delicate Place. Janet Sylvester. MAYP

The sky moves that quickly through the frame. Documentation. Michael Palmer. NPGG

Sky neither blue nor gray. A Discussion of the Vicissitudes of History under a Pine Tree. Katha Pollitt. MAYP

A sky scraper among skyscrapers less stellar. The Magistrate's Escape. Alice Fulton. PoDr

The sky, their chosen element, has abandoned them. The Jam Trap. Charles Tomlinson. MoBrPo

A sky-thrown torch has kindled me to flame. The April Earth. Max Eastman. AnEnPo

The sky-tree is ours. Interior Monolgue #666. Tom Marshall. NOBC

Slabs of jasper, crystals of mica. The Spring Festival on the River. John Peck. AmPA

Slag-wattled turkey-cock,/Dross-jabot? Turkey-cock. D. H. Lawrence. AnEnPo

Slain Lincoln, worthy found to die/A soldier of his Captain, Christ. A Tribute. Anonymous. PGD

Slammed the door and was off in flight,/Ridin' the parson's horse. The Raven Visits Rawhide. Anonymous. BPAW

Slant to the shore, and all their seamen land. Sonnet. J. C. Squire. CH

Slap-a-hand, lend-a-hand, main man? Main Man Blues. Eugene B. Redmond. GP

Slap. Drat the mosquitoes. Quick, Henry, the Flit! James Schuyler. NoAm

Slapping her thighs. The Return to Work. William Carlos Williams. CTBA; NYBP

Slaps hasps soon. The Hammer. Clark Coolidge. ANYP

Slaps, slaps, slaps/On the beach, and roars. Storm Tide on Mejit. Anonymous. RFM

The slats of my cage are rattling,/so loose I could brush them aside. Thaw. T. Alan Broughton. AMV-81

Slaughterman, overman, everyman,/time's eminent surgeon. Bring Your Own Victim. Allen Curnow. OCNZ

Slav'ry chain done broke at las',/Goin' to praise God 'til I die. Slav'ry Chain (Joshua Fit de Battle). Anonymous. TrAS

A slave hr touch could quicken or benumb. Virtuosa. Mary Ashley Townsend. AA

THE SLAVE PERIOD IS OVER Proclamation/From Sleep, Arise. Carolyn M. Rodgers. JB

The slave systems of Rome and Greece, and no one agreed. Sleet Storm on the Merritt Parkway. Robert Bly. ConAP; NOBA

The slavery and precipitancy of his days. Orlo's Valediction. Jon Manchip White. NePoEA

Slavery never did impress me. January 3, 1970. Mae Jackson. PoBA

Slavery's curse went out. Tolling. Lucy Larcom. OHIP

Slaves to their quiet and good name,/Are used like A Quiet Life and a Good Name. Jonathan Swift. CBEP

Slaying and slain; and I am all of these. The Summer Landscape; or, The Dragon's Teeth. Rolfe Humphries. NYBP

Sle thy fadre and jape thy modre and thay will thee assoile! Friars' Enormities. Anonymous. MeEL

The sleek silk vanishes into foaming shade. The Lost Parasol (excerpt). Sandor Weores. OBVE

Sleek with the bloom/Of health next week! Poor Henry. Walter De La Mare. HBMV

Sleekly, so blood ran like hot gold in his mouth. Oracle at Delphi. Robert Bagg. NePoAm-2

Sleep after our short light/One everlasting night. Lines from Catullus. Sir Walter Ralegh. EnRePo; FCP; SiPS

Sleep and Death differ, noe more, then a Carkasse/and a skeleton. A Serious and a Curious Night-Meditation. Thomas Traherne. SeCP

Sleep, as they sleep who find/Their heart's desire. How Far Is It to Bethlehem. Frances Chesterton. HBMV; HBVY; PCh

Sleep away, lad; wake no more. Wake Not for the World-Heard Thunder. Alfred Edward Housman. CMoP; NoAm

Sleep, baby mine,/Crabs are in the pot. Crabe dans Calalou. Anonymous. OuSiCo

Sleep, Beloved, safe for ever/From the one who loved too much. And When the Prince Came. Robert Silliman Hillyer. DFT

Sleep, Big Baby, sleep your fill. Lullaby. W. H. Auden. FaBoMo

Sleep, by a strange bed in the dark of dreaming. Hotel de l'Univers et Portugal. James Merrill. MoAB; NePoAm; NePoEA-2; PoA

Sleep by other means continues dialogue. Debora Sleeping. William Logan. MAYP

Sleep came instead, in a three-cornered skull/Shaped much like death's, and oddly beautiful. Narcissus in a Cocktail Glass. Frances Minturn Howard. GoYe

Sleep can I get nane,/For thinkin' o' my dearie. Aye Waukin' O! Anonymous. BSV; GoTS

Sleep close to me! Sleep Close to Me. Gabriela (Lucila Godoy Alcayaga) Mistral. PBWP

...Sleep comes. And with it my snails. The Spider's Nest. George MacBeth. NMP

Sleep comes at last, but sleep made rich with dreams.   Sonnets.   Robert Hillyer.   HBMV

Sleep comes to close the ears of/the mind to night sounds of this world.   Nocturnal Sounds.   Kattie M. Cumbo.   BlSi

Sleep does disproportion hide,/And, death resembling, equals all.   Say, Lovely Dream.   Edmund Waller.   OAEP

Sleep falls again on all the land.   The Twelve-Elf.   Christian Morgenstern.   WSC

Sleep, I beg you, you babbling women,/shut up!   Epigram: "Why all the racket."   *Anonymous.*   PeHV

Sleep I can get nane,/For thinking on my dearie...   Ay Waukin O.   Robert Burns.   NOEC

Sleep in a world your final sleep has woken.   Child of Our Time.   Eavan Boland.   CIP

The sleep is deep and long.   Poem without a Title.   Charles Simic.   GP; NNaP

Sleep is too short a death.   January.   Weldon Kees.   CoAP

Sleep, Jesu, sleep! ei, Jesu, ei.   Carol: "Mary, the mother, sits on the hill."   Langdon Elwyn Mitchell.   OHIP

Sleep, little one, sleep.   Norse Lullaby.   Eugene Field.   SUS

"Sleep, little tulip, sleep!"   Nightfall in Dordrecht.   Eugene Field.   AA

Sleep, love, sleep.   Lullaby.   Quandra Prettyman.   BOLo

Sleep, McKade./Yawn./Go to sleep.   Evening Song.   Kenneth Fearing.   EAS

Sleep, mouseling, sleep.   Lullaby.   Elizabeth Jane Coatsworth.   SiSoSe

Sleep, Mr. Speaker; sleep, sleep while you/may!   Stanzas on Seeing the Speaker Asleep...   Winthrop Mackworth Praed.   EnRP

Sleep, my darling son.   Door and Window Bolted Fast.   Mani Leib.   TrJP

Sleep, my little one.   Sleep, My Child.   Sholom Aleichem.   TrJP

Sleep, my little one, sleep, my pretty one, sleep.   The Princess.   Alfred, Lord Tennyson.   MOS; TrGrPo

Sleep on.   A Prayer to the Lord Ramakrishna.   James Wright.   NNaP

Sleep on, I lie at heaven's high oriels,/Who loved you so.   Nirvana.   John Hall Wheelock.   HBMV; MoAmPo

Sleep on my heart till Heaven the flower unfold.   Sonnet to Edgar Allan Poe.   Sarah Helen Whitman.   AnAmPo

Sleep on, sleep sound.   Parta Quies.   Alfred Edward Housman.   NOBE; TEP

SLEEP, ON WAKING, SAYS TO ME: YOU HAS SAWN ME APART.   Litany of Sleep.   Tristan Corbiere.   OBVE

Sleep, or only for this/Break your united repose!   Haworth Churchyard (excerpt).   Matthew Arnold.   FaBoPP

Sleep safe till tomorrow.   Peace on Earth.   William Carlos Williams.   LiTA; LOW; ViBoPo

Sleep shall outlast them all./Sleep.   Taps.   Lizette Woodworth Reese.   OHIP

Sleep, sleep again, my Lyre, and let thy Master dy.   Davideis.   Abraham Cowley.   SeCV 1-2

A sleep so plaisant and so wholesome/As he may never wholly waken from.   The Stones of Sleep.   E. L. Mayo.   FAZ

Sleep sweet! Good night! Good night!   Sleep Sweet.   Ellen M. Huntington Gates.   BLPA; BLRP; FaBoBe

Sleep, then kiss those blue eyes dry./Lullaby! O lullaby!   Lullaby, O Lullaby.   William C. Bennett.   HBV 1-2

Sleep Uncle Nathan, sexton in Narwhale's synagogue!   Ichthycide.   Joe Rosenblatt.   NOBC

...Sleep with the dead Ben Hall/Than go where that traitor went.   The Death of Ben Hall.   Will H. Ogilvie.   PoAu 1-2

Sleepily blinking snowflakes from his lashes.   First Snow.   Ted Kooser.   GrPl

The sleeping beauty wakes, immortal bride,/And holds you fast.   The Sleeping Beauty.   Robert Layzer.   NePoEA

Sleeping butterfly!   Wake Up! Wake Up!   Basho (Matsuo Basho).   SoPo

Sleeping on half a leaf, hoping the other half/isn't just earth.   The Minyan.   Jack Myers.   VWA

Sleeping on the cellar/Shelf like this/Empty/Jelly jar.   Haunted House.   Valerie Worth.   WSC

Sleeping peasants./Lovers of the same village.   Sleeping Peasants.   Phyllis Janik.   PoDr

Sleeping the lucklesse age out, till that she/Her resurrection ha's again with thee.   Upon M. Ben Jonson–Epigram.   Robert Herrick.   CaPo; OAEP

Sleeping together?...How tired you were...   Two Nocturnes.   Katherine Mansfield.   HBMV

Sleeping upon my shoulder/With all her hair unbound?   Hair-Dressing.   Louis Untermeyer.   UnTE

Sleepless with cold commemorative eyes.   The House of Life.   Dante Gabriel Rossetti.   PoEL 1-5

Sleeps!   The Spanish Student: Serenade.   Henry Wadsworth Longfellow   AA

Sleeps as thy lover for a little while.   Hymn to Earth.   Elinor Wylie.   AmLP; LiTM; MoAB; MoAmPo; MoPo; MoVE; NePA

Sleeps here the sleep that must be slept by all.   Crethis.   Callimachus.   AWP

Sleeps shelter'd there, scarce wrinkled by the gale!   To a Young Friend.   Samuel Taylor Coleridge.   ChRP

Sleeps with her kings, and dignifies the scene.   A Poem Sacred to the Memory of Sir Isaac Newton.   James (1700-48) Thomson.   CEP

Sleeps with his mate in his arms.   The Muddy Rat.   Horiguchi Daigaku.   LiTW

Sleet in the golden vein.   Death by Rarity.   Marguerite Young.   LiTA

The sleeve I pressed to it/would float back moist with foam.   Like a ravaged sea.   Lady Ise.   BoWoP

Slender and tall a Round Tower's pointed crest/Rose dimly black against the gorgeous west.   Ruins at Sunset.   William Allingham.   IrPN

The slender stem and radiant/Flower rise.   A Shallot.   Richard Wilbur.   GP

The slender trunks, to inward peeping sight/Thronged in dark pillars up the gold green light.   Places of Nestling Green.   [James Henry] Leigh Hunt.   OBRV

Slept mortal all morning.   Pre Domina.   Jean Lipkin.   PeSA

Slept, & woke alone, awhile serene.   Years.   Jon Anderson.   AmPA

Slice bullock's rumps–but spare the rump of man.   On Having Piles.   Sir Walter Scott.   FaBoEE

Slices of green pepper/on a bone-white dish.   Song: "Afternoon cooking in the fall sun."   Robert Hass.   AmPA

Slices star bright ice.   Haiku: "Under moon shadows."   Etheridge Knight.   NeAC; SM; TAP

...Slide/In the same blood you closed your eyes to.   The Morning They Shot Tony Lopez, Barber and Pusher Who Went Too Far.   Gary Soto.   MAYP

Slide right over in de Promise Land.   If You Want to Go to Heben.   *Anonymous.*   GBP

A slight but regrettable/Slip of the Tong.   He Shot at Lee Wing.   *Anonymous.*   ShM

The slightly simpering sparkle of the eye.   Dans l'Allee.   Paul Verlaine.   AWP

...Slime steps on stone,/I count them–not my own.   The Loss of Strength.   Austin Clarke.   IPY

Sling me...under the sea.   Bones.   Carl Sandburg.   MOS

A-slingin' pie-crust 'long the road/Forever an' forever!   An Impetuous Resolve.   James Whitcomb Riley.   BiCB

...Slinging cherry bombs/at all those tragic fools picking their way forward.   Laughing Backwards.   Jim Hall.   GOYP

Slip out of darkness, it is time.   The Second Life.   Edwin Morgan.   OxBS

Slip their snowy bands and run/Sparkling in the welcome sun.   Winter Streams.   Bliss Carman.   YeAr

Slip with the sky into the bay!   Contentment.   Laurence E. Estes.   AMV-80

The Slipper went off to the ball.   High and Low.   John Banister Tabb.   BrR

The slipper went off to the ball.   Limerick: "A boot and a shoe and a slipper."   John Banister Tabb.   TDH

Slippers and hatchet before the television.   The Last Refuge.   Augustus Young.   BIrV

Slippery sloppery, alumny calumny, raggery waggery, uttery/guttery trash!   Tattle.   Godfrey Turner.   NOBL

Slipping–is Crashe's law.   Crumbling is not an instant's act.   Emily Dickinson.   AmPP; DiPo; NOBA; PPP

...Slips of our mother tongue.   Lapsus Linguae.   Richard Howard.   NoAm

Slips silently down the river's winding way.   Shadow Dirge.   R. P. Dexter.   LiSp

Slithering in the/quiet water's wake.   Daysleep.   Virginia E. Smith.   AMV-81

Slitherum, slatherum, take her.   Ducks and Drakes.   *Anonymous.*   OxNR

Sloth, Dirt, and Theft, around her wait.   On an Ill-Managed House.   Jonathan Swift.   AnIV

Slouch three days later said, "Ouch!"   Limerick: "So tall was a cowboy called Slouch."   *Anonymous.*   TDH

A slouched back against the shoulders/of the world.   Light Baggage.   Alice Walker.   LTB

Slow?/????/???/??/?   Go Slow.   Langston Hughes.   LiTM

Slow as the tide/that moves great stones.   Stone Giant.   Joseph Bruchac.   CDW

...Slow, cumbersome,/elegant, coiffed with a headful of poison.   Quills.   Charlotte Gafford.   AMV-81

Slow horses and fast women.   Proust's Madeleine.   Kenneth Rexroth.   NoAm

A slow hot glare out on the lake/spreading over the water.   Crab Orchard Sanctuary: Late October.   Thomas Kinsella.   IPY

Slow into nothing, nothing but air.   Hiawatha.   Stephen Sandy.   CoPo

The slow light threads his hands/That thrashed the lost dragon.   The Frozen Hero.   Thomas H. Vance.   NYBP

The slow lives sank from being like a dream?   Port of Embarkation.   Randall Jarrell.   MiAP

Slow me down, Lord, so I can talk/With some of Your angels as they walk. Slow Me Down. *Anonymous.* STF

The slow night trawls its heavy net/And hauls the clerk to Surbiton. Sunken Evening. Laurie Lee. LiTM; NYBP

The slow pride/of a lament. A Graveyard in Queens. John Montague. IPY

...The slow-setting star/Bootes called, by some the Wagoner. The Odyssey. Homer. JCP

Slow–/slow–/slow–/slow. A Swing Song. William Allingham. BrR; MoShBr; SUS

Slow-smiling sloe-dark eyes/From hyacinthine hair. Bluebell. Geoffrey Taylor. NeIP

The slow suburban cars outside. Delaying Tactics. Christopher Wiseman. AMV-81

Slow tramp the Centuries,/And the Cycles wheel! Just Lost, When I Was Saved! Emily Dickinson. AA; AmePo; AnFE; APA; MoAmPo; NOBA; NOCV; Prf

Slow Vengeance, like a Blood-hound at his Heels. Odes. Horace. OBVE; WaaP

Slow winding silver tracks of slime/Showed bright where came back none. The Navigators. Walter James Turner. OBMV

Slow with air and atmosphere and desolate space. The Ghost of the Cargo Boat. Pablo Neruda. WSC

Slowly across the chequer'd shadows pass. Sweet Peas. John Keats. GN

Slowly away into the utmost dark. An Elegy. David Gascoyne. FaBoTw; MP

Slowly beginning to wake. The Kite. Mark Strand. NYBP

Slowly he dies and the battle is o'er! There She Blows! *Anonymous.* EtS

Slowly he drove up to the starting line Buffalo–Isle of Wight Power Cable. Anselm Hollo. PoM

Slowly I begin to rehearse it. Incident. Harvey Shapiro. FAZ

Slowly life is running out/like drops along a drainpipe. Morning. Tove Ditlevsen. PBWP

Slowly open their gorgeous, Carnaby wings. Angels. Dannie Abse. PoA

Slowly out into the sun-blackened landscape. Rivers and Mountains. John Ashbery. ANYP; CoAP; NoAm; NOBA

Slowly slipping away Out of You. Rodney Phillips. PoL

Slowly the darkness slides apart/And soundless, lets him in. Cat on the Porch at Dusk. Dorothy Harriman. GoYe

Slowly the old roads lose their grip. Old Roads. Eilean Ni Chuilleanain. CIP

Slowly the salt of the earth becomes salt of the sea. Salt of the Earth. D. H. Lawrence. NoAm

Slowly they settled/To the ocean floor/To be found in stone years after. Putting on My Shoes I Hear the Floor Cry out beneath Me (parody). Michael Heffernan. BXAP

Slowly, till scissors of cockcrow snip the air. The Afterwake. Adrienne Rich. NOBA; Prf

Slowly we lose our seabright colours/and wait to die. Time of Turtles. Grace Perry. NOAV

The slum man they killed, the mountain man lives on. Early Lynching. Carl Sandburg. MoAmPo

Slumber pours down... ...About the Cool Water. Sappho. OBVE

Slumbering by the young, eternal/river-voices of the western vale. The Grave of Rulry. T. W. Rolleston. AnIL; AnIV; IrPN; OnYI

Slumbers and dreams, devoid of fear. The Fringilla Melodia. Henry Beck Hirst AA

The sly, inviting smile into the labyrinth. Some Small Shells from the Windward Islands. May Swenson. FYAP

Sly naked damsels nodding their downy plumes. Cranach. Sir Herbert Read. BrPo; FaBoMo

Slynk first to me the can. Manere of the Crying of Ane Playe. William Dunbar. AtBAP

Small, and absurd, and hers: for once, not hers, unclassified. Underground System. Edna St. Vincent Millay. SBG

A small and little thing! News. Thomas Traherne. NOBE; OBEV; PoPle; SeCV 1-2

The small birds converge, converge/With their gifts to a difficult borning. The Manor Garden. Sylvia Plath. FaBoWP; LCAP

Small, but how dear to us,/God knoweth best. Only a Baby Small. Matthias Barr. HBV 1-2; HBVY; PaPo

Small change when we are to bodies gone. The Ecstasy. John Donne. ATP; BoLoP; CABA; DiPo; EnRePo; ExPo; FPL; HAP; InPS; JCP; LiTB; LoBV; NOBE; NoP; OAEL 1-2; OBEV; PAI; PPoe; PrIm; TEP; TrGrPo; UnTE; ViBoPo

Small cheek against her cheek, He/Sleepeth, three hours old. Christmas Carol. May Probyn. GoBC; HBMV; OBVV

Small division between the world and the spirit. La Crosse at Ninety Miles an Hour. Richard Eberhart. AmFN

...The small flakes/Inseparable from stars. Street Scene. Robert Mezey. LiTM

The small footprints of Nampti/that make my heart sing.' Heart-of-the-Daybreak. Eugene Marais. PeSA

Small gain I found to let her come,/Less loss to let her go. Content and Rich. Robert Southwell. OBSC

Small gardens and bright fish/too tender/for the air. Unclench Yourself. Marge Piercy. NeAC

The small ghosts flicker, whisper, unconsoled. S. S. City of Benares. G. S. Fraser. NeBP

Small girls to dream awhile toward the flashing & bursting tree! The Dream Songs. John Berryman. NoAm

The small, immediate candle in the prow/Burns brighter in the water than any star. On the Lake. Victoria Mary (Vita) Sackville-West. ChMP; MoVE; OBMV; SBG

A small imperfect replica of you. Havana Blues. Henry Carlile. SM

The small ironic silence of his claws. Vicissitudes of the Creator. Archibald MacLeish. NePA

Small-jawed, weak-chinned, big-eyed I stare/At the forgotten boy I was. Upon Shaving Off One's Beard. John Updike. OBSP

The small jeweled hunger in the seabird's eye. The Return of Robinson Jeffers. Robert Hass. AmPA

A small man/with a broken nose/angel of the annunciation. Annunciation. Sister Maura. TAT

"Small men never feel small." The People, Yes. Carl Sandburg. OBAL

A small milking vessel, when filled to the brim, soon overflows. To a Dictatorial Sultan. *Anonymous.* WTO

The small-mouth bass breaks water gorged/with spawn. After the Surprising Conversions. Robert Lowell. AmPP; AP; CoBMV; ConAP; HAP; NePoEA; NoAm; NoP; PPP; SeCeV

Small nuts fall/Mine too New York–Albany. Lawrence Ferlinghetti. PoCh

...Small ocean, small mercator. Note from an Exhibition. Albert Goldbarth. AMV-81

A small part of it will die if I'm not around/feeding it anymore. Chicago Poem. Lew Welch. NeAP; PoM

Small pathways idly tend/Towards no certain end. An English Wood. Robert Graves. BrPo

Small perfect Manhattan. Small Perfect Manhattan. Peter Viereck. MiAP

...A small purple cavern/that no one walks out of. This Is the Last Night. Roo Borson. CaPN

...The small rain spits/today. You smile in your grave. To a Print of Queen Victoria. James Keir Baxter. OxBC

The small remainder dies for want of Food. Metamorphoses. Ovid (Publius Ovidius Naso). OBVE

Small sparrows have left droppings to be remembered by. Powwow Remnants. Lew Blockcolski. VoR

...Small stars/in their sleepless flight. We Will Watch the Northern Lights. *Anonymous.* RFM

Small talk comes from small bones. Homage to Sextus Propertius, VI. Ezra Pound. OxBA

Small talk i said to myself/and went away from there. Small Talk. Don (Donald Robert) Marquis. StPo

A small thing,/Singing. A Light Breather. Theodore Roethke. NoP

The small tree outside, unfit for a man's dead weight, breathes,/hang on! A Typical 6:00 P.M. in the Fun House. Daniel Berrigan. LFAC

The small vocabulary/of love needs its own/thin blue dictionary. Discourse. Sharon Thesen. CaPN

The small welt of remorse subsides as side/By side we, murderer and murdered, sleep. Mosquito. John Updike. BoAnP

...A small wind sighed, colder than the rose/Blooming in desolation, "No one knows." The Sleeping Beauty. Edith Sitwell. OxBTC

Small wonder that the tree had cracked/Under their weight. Breaking Point. Sylvia Auxier. GoYe

Small wonder the smallest boy behaves! Graveyard. Robert P. Tristram Coffin. AmFN

Small wonder thou dost shudder at His kiss. Grief and God. Stephen Phillips. WGRP

Smaller and clearer as the years go by. Lines on a Young Lady's Photograph Album. Philip Larkin. EnLoPo; HAP; HeIP; OAEL 1-2

A smaller role for peanut butter. Being Adult. Bill Zavatsky. PoL

Smallpocks the oil-green water with a hurled/ten million wire nails. Woodyards in the Rain. Anne Marriott. CaP

The smart tale dogs the wag. The Durable Bon Mot. Keith Preston. HBMV

Smashed between two cars at midnight. Portrait. Gail Fox. NOBC

Smashed, mix his heart's blood with the mire of the land. The Hawk in the Rain. Ted Hughes. ACV

A smashed world whirl away in stinging snow. On the Death of an Emperor Penguin in Regent's Park, London. David Wright. NYBP

Smashes my forehead/the moon Hills picking up the moonlight. Nina Cassian. BoWoP

...Smeared/On the landscape, to make of us what we could. Street Musicians. John Ashbery. HaCAP

Smeared with the gold of the opulent sun.   A Postcard from the Volcano. Wallace Stevens.   AP; HaCAP; HAP; LiTA

Smears brandy on the trampling boot/And sends it sweeter on its way.   A Summer Commentary.   Yvor Winters.   LiTM; QFR

The smeddum intil her!   Cophetua.   Hugh" (Christopher Murray Grieve) MacDiarmid.   OxBS; PoL

The smell/comes from stone.   Nativity.   Linda Hogan.   TWSS

The smell of burning now seems sweeter than flowers.   The Hibakusha's Letter (1955).   David Mura.   BrSi

The smell of cedar wood and hickory on your clothes   The One Who Is Within.   Nia Francisco.   STE

...The smell of food raking/through its middle like a red hot fingernail.   Case. Phyllis Janowitz.   AMV-81

The smell of/oranges or/something growing.   The Murdered Girl Is Found on a Bridge.   Jane Hayman.   NYBP

The smell of popcorn and worn plush/lingers for weeks.   You Take My Hand And.   Margaret Atwood.   HAP

The smell of the wattle by Lichtenberg,/Riding in, in the rain!   Lichtenberg. Rudyard Kipling.   EnLit

Smell of wet heleniums. The rainbow of roses.   The Rain and the Rainbow. Leo Fredericks.   ACV

Smell sweet, and blossom in their dust.   Equality.   James Shirley.   AnEnPo

Smelling a pungent weed, noting a bird's/two notes.   The Letter.   Charles Reznikoff.   VWA

Smelling each Christmas smell.   Eighth Street West.   Rachel Field.   ChBR; SiSoSe

Smelling faintly/of Virginia/creepers.   Foxgloves.   Ted Hughes.   LOW

...Smelling/of soap, they lay at his sides/as though they were listening. Commanding Elephants.   Philip Levine.   NaP

Smiffkins, Pimple, and Jingle. Oh Lord! how long?   On the Oxford Book of Victorian Verse.   Hugh" (Christopher Murray Grieve) MacDiarmid. MoBrPo

Smile again on your children.   Chant for Reapers.   Wilfrid Thorley. OBEV; OBVV

A smile and kind word when we meet,/And a place in thy memory.   A Place in Thy Memory.   Gerald Griffin.   HBV 1-2

A smile as small as mine might be/Precisely their necessity.   They might not need me.   Emily Dickinson.   PoToHe; TRV

Smile as you say this who will be/Dust when these stones still mark the Sacred Way.   Morality.   Jean Garrigue.   ELU

Smile at discharge from care, and shut out light.   Alone in an Inn at Southampton, April the 25th, 1737.   Aaron Hill.   NOEC

Smile at us, pay us, pass us. But do not quite forget.   The Secret People. Gilbert Keith Chesterton.   FaPoR; OxBTC

A smile denotes the cheerless captive become the cheer-/ful guest.   The Cloisters.   Samuel Yellen.   NePoAm

Smile from the single exposure and shoulder out/One's own body from its instant and heat.   Six Young Men.   Ted Hughes.   OBWP

...Smile frozen at the North Pole/Might take pity on their tricks.   To Poets and Airmen.   Stephen Spender.   WaP

Smile on her waywardness,/Oh, if you love her!   Advice to a Lover.   S. Charles Jellicoe.   HBV 1-2

Smile on—nor venture to unmask/man's heart, and view the Hell that's there. Childe Harold's Pilgrimage: Canto I.   George Gordon, Lord Byron. MBW 1-2

A smile or kiss, as he will use the art,/Shall have the cunning skill to break a heart.   The Last Conqueror.   James Shirley.   GTBS; GTBS-P

The smile that bless'd one lover's heart/Has broken many more!   Fair Ines. Thomas Hood.   EnRP; HBV 1-2; OBEV; OBRV; OBVV

Smile Thou and I shall sing,/But shall not question much.   Twice. Christina Georgina Rossetti.   GBL; GTBS; NOBE; OBEV; OBNC; OBVV; TrCP; ViBoPo; VLP

Smile with those lips that never yet have spoken!   To Azrael.   Charles Baudelaire.   SyP

Smiles and brightens/before your eyes.   Bright Winter Morning.   Chris Klein.   AMV-81

Smiles from the Cross upon a conquered world.   The Peacemaker.   Joyce Kilmer.   CAW

Smiles her clear smile as sleep and tearing grief return.   Forza D'Agro. Edwin Denby.   ANYP

Smiles your forerunner drew,/Know what it knew!   This Summer and Last. Thomas Hardy.   OxBTC

Smilest Thou?   Song of a Shepherd Boy at Bethlehem.   Josephine Preston Peabody.   OHIP

...Smiling at her,/pleasantly, and, damn it, without/malice, even.   The Feeding.   Joel Oppenheimer.   NeAP

Smiling, dying.   Waiting, the Hallways under Her Skin Thick with Dreamchildren.   Lyn Lifshin.   NeAC

Smiling, faces pressed against the stone.   Salmon.   Jorie Graham.   MAYP

Smiling like an old man.   My Cow.   Howard McCord.   GP

Smiling now from a/Yellowed/Yearbook page.   Class of 19–.   Frederick Dec.   PCP

Smiling, "Now you have come."   Love among the Manichees.   William Dickey.   PoCh

Smiling sweetly like a well-fed baby.   Korf's Joke.   Christian Morgenstern. ELU

Smiling, the boy fell dead.   Incident of the French Camp.   Robert Browning. BeLS; EnLi 1-2; FaPo; FaPoR; GN; HBV 1-2; HBVY; MaC; MaVP; MBW 1-2; MCCG; OBWP; RoGo; TreF; TrGrPo

Smiling to hear/God's querulous calling.   Theology.   Ted Hughes. FaBoMo; NoAm

Smites with her stark immortal palimpsest/The green arcades of immemorial years!   The Exquisite Sonnet.   J. C. Squire.   HBMV

...Smith and/Wesson pistols and Winchester rifles".   The Dream about Junior High School in America.   Dick Lourie.   NeAC

Smoggy windows you clean with a squeejee–   Postcard to D–.   Allen Ginsberg.   InPK

Smoke and blood is the mix of steel....   Smoke and Steel (excerpt).   Carl Sandburg.   MoAmPo

Smoke Creek desert.   Hitch Haiku.   Gary Snyder.   LCAP

Smoke curls even higher/Like silvery doves.   Winter.   Mani Leib.   VWA

...Smoke drifting/past neon like dreams/into the night.   1939 Mercury. Albert Drake.   AmC

...Smoke of a cigarette/held to a bound woman's nipple.   Burning the Root. Margaret Gibson.   MAYP

The smoke of many a calument/Ascends to heaven again.   Indian Summer. John Banister Tabb.   AA

Smoke rises from the stones; no, it is mist.   An Airstrip in Essex, 1960. Donald Hall.   LCAP; LiTM; PAI; PoCh

The smoke should dry me well before I slept.   The Author Loving These Homely Meats...   John, of Hereford Davies.   EIL; FaBoNo

Smoking contented in the falling rain.   An Irish Picture.   J. Stanyan Bigg. NOBV

"The smoking flax before it burst to/flame/Was quenched by death, and broken/the bruised reed."   Keats.   Henry Wadsworth Longfellow.   AmP; AP; MAmP; TAP

(Smoking sawdust/cigarettes in the/middle of the night)   Is 5.   Edward Estlin Cummings.   AnAmPo

Smooth and fine, with beauty stored,/Shines the garment of the Lord!   The Cosmic Fabric.   Yakov Polonsky.   EaLo

Smooth as time and/love for you   Portrait of Malcolm X.   Etheridge Knight.   CNA; PoBA

...Smooth face might well perplex/A stranger to discern his sex.   Too Young for Love.   Horace.   UnTE

A smooth folder in a steel file.   Paper Men to Air Hopes and Fears.   Robert Francis.   LCAP

Smooth-visaged, while a seeming prude/Was marked for life.   Suppose. Anne Reeve Aldrich.   HBV 1-2

Smoother than river-rain/Falls chime on chime.   Men Fade Like Rocks. Walter James Turner.   OBMV

Smoothing the heads of the hungry children.   Prelude to an Evening.   John Crowe Ransom.   AP; CoBMV; EAS; MoAB; MoAmPo; MoPo; MoVE; NePA; OxBA; PoCh

Smoothly under to the dark,/And out the other side.   Bridges.   Rhoda Warner Bacmeister.   SoPo

Smouldering in a self-made cave, like a sold son.   Love Poem Investigation for A.T.   Frank Frate.   AMV-80

A smudge of blue dust on my hand.   Blue Ghosts.   Stanley Snaith.   ChMP

Smug in his power; watching me watch.   Corner.   Ralph Pomeroy.   CAD; CoPo; NYP

Smut if smitten/Is front-page stuff.   Invocation.   Ogden Nash.   OBAL

The snail drags his caution into the sun.   Rain.   Christopher Fry.   BoC

A snail/dreaming in the throat of an old wine bottle.   Drunk Last Night with Friends, I Go to Work Anyway.   Philip Dow.   NPGG

A snail or a stone under the lowliest leaf.   The Secret Garden.   Robert Nichols.   WGRP

...Snails are licking/the moon's full body, all the parts/we will never see.   The Blood Supply in New York City Is Low.   Terry Stokes.   NYP

Snails, their sound blowing overhead from among the bushes.   Snails. Liagarang.   WTO

The snake had often to go without/His breakfast, dinner, and tea, oh.   The Fastidious Serpent.   Henry, Lord Johnstone Johnstone.   HBV 1-2; HBVY

The Snake is living yet.   The Python.   Hilaire Belloc.   EvOK; HBVY; NA; OxBChV; ShM

Snakelike over the secret it hides.   In the Bayou.   Don (Donald Robert Marquis) Marquis.   AmFN

Snappity, crackity,/Out it fell.   The Squirrel.   *Anonymous.*   SoPo; SUS; TiPo

Snatch out of time the passionate transitory.   The Hospital.   Patrick Kavanagh.   BIrV; CIP; FaBoIP

The snazzy summer theatre takes us in.   In the Hamptons.   John N. Morris. NYP

Sneer'd, "What a Transcendentalist!"   The Flesh-Fly and the Bee.   Coventry Patmore.   FaBoEE

A sneer on four square wheels   Private Transport.   Adrian Mitchell. FaBoEE

Sneeze and warble, Tra-la-la!   Spring's Delights.   Joseph Ashby Sterry. CenHV

...Sneezing madly in the midst of that/life of theirs, weighed down by madness and sorrow.   Immensity.   Gerald Stern.   AMV-80

Sniff and stand back and proudly offer you/the celebrated Anglo-Irish stew. A Farewell to English (excerpt).   Michael Hartnett.   NOBI

Snites, Doppers, Sea-Larkes, in whole million flees.   The Princely Eagle, and the Soaring Hawke.   William Wood.   SCAP

Snodgrass is walking through the universe.   These Trees Stand...   W. D. Snodgrass.   NIP; NoAm; PPP

Snored out (as if some Clerk had given/His nose the cue) "Amen."   A Recent Dialogue.   Thomas Moore.   NBM

Snort kerchoo!   Winter Is Icumen In.   Bradford Smith.   PoSC

Snorting and bounding heavily before me.   Once More.   Hayden Carruth. NNaP

Snow and the threat of snow....   Landscape.   Alfred W. Purdy.   CaP

The snow and you, your stalking home.   Blue Like Death.   James Welch. CDW

Snow curls in on the cold wind.   Courtyard in Winter.   John Montague. IPY

The snow dissolves–and so must all!   Man's Mortality.   Simon Wastell. HBV 1-2

The snow-dusted face of the god.   Walking with Lulu in the Wood.   Naomi Lazard.   NYBP

The snow flakes drifting through green tops of pine.   My Land Is Fair for Any Eyes to See.   Jesse Stuart.   TiPo

The snow-flakes drop as lightly–snows on/snows.   The Snowing of the Pines. Thomas Wentworth Higginson.   AA; GN

The snow has melted.   Cold Fact.   Dick Emmons.   PoPl

...The snow has no voice.   The Munich Mannequins.   Sylvia Plath.   NaP

Snow is falling, the sun is late,/and someone goes out with a lantern/to search the roads.   Forest without Leaves (excerpt).   John Haines.   NPAW

The snow is falling. What shall I do/If he comes no more!   Forsaken. Zalman Schneour.   TrJP

...The snow is piling up all around the/car. Are you coming?   Violence on Television.   Louis Jenkins.   NU

The snow is still thick around/Your bamboo flute.   Boy and the Wandering Recluse.   Al Robles.   BrSi

Snow moves/like an ancient herd   Flock.   Lance Henson.   VoR

The snow poised on that bough.   The Watcher.   John Peck.   AmPA

The snow settles on his shoulders.   August/Fresno 1973.   Roberta Spear. AmPA

Snow, silver, ceruse, age, and a chaste breast.   Five Things White.   Edward May.   FaBoEE

Snow to play in getting soaked and frozen whenever outside.   My Christmas: Mum's Christmas.   Sarah Forsyth.   OBCP

Snow-trickles, feldspar, dirt.   For Nothing.   Gary Snyder.   NNaP

Snow us Under/Winter Over Nothing   Winter over Nothing.   Elliott Coleman.   FAZ

Snow-water violets, and distant moss turf.   Life in the Boondocks.   Archie Randolph Ammons.   HAP

The snowball/packed with rock/aimed at my face.   Back Road.   Bruce Guernsey.   AMV-81

Snowdrops a-shivering,/Winter dead.   Robin's Song.   E.L.M. King.   TiPo

The snowflakes fall...   No Sky At All.   Hashin.   SoPo

The snowy hosts of heaven arrive/To pitch their tents therein.   The Deserted Pasture.   Bliss Carman.   HBV 1-2

A snuff box has no right to sneeze.   The Humorist.   Keith Preston.   ALV; EvOK; HBMV

Snuff is a delicous thing.   Sneezing.   [James Henry] Leigh Hunt.   HBV 1-2

Snuffle No! No! to proffered hand and heart.   The Wood of the Self-Destroyers.   Samuel Yellen.   NePoAm-2

Snuffling the horizons of the justice of God.   To Julia de Burgos.   Julia de Burgos.   BoWoP; PBWP

Snug in my nest shall live, and snug shall/die.   The Smooth Divine. Timothy Dwight.   AA; AnAmPo; PPON; WGRP

Snugged in the arms of comfortable night.   Immolated.   Herman Melville. ViBoPo

So a man cannot fall asleep without a girl.   A Man's Need.   *Anonymous.* WTO

So a warning take by my sad state–beware of piracy!   The Flying Cloud (I). *Anonymous.*   AmSS; OBET; OBSS; ShS

So abhorrent of evil is the ever-righteous.   Cleanness (excerpt).   *Anonymous.* NOCV

So act in the way that will tickle/Belsnickel.   Belsnickel.   Arthur Guiterman. BBGG

So after all our fears and alarms/We all ended up in the Druid's Arms. Stormy Weather, Boys.   *Anonymous.*   OBSS

So again the miraculous thunder of discovering wings is/heard.   Death for the Dark Stranger.   Thomas McGrath.   VGW

...So air was reduced to water and we,/under strife, grew souls like Undines of the sky.   Apollo 113.   Diderik Finne.   AMV-80

So all night long endured, the wounds of day/Doubly are sorrow to the miserable.   We Are Such Stuff As Dreams...   Arbiter (Caius Petronius Arbiter) Petronius.   AWP

So all the world may plainly see/That they loved each other dear.   Prince Robert.   *Anonymous.*   ESPB

So all who hide too well away/Must speak and tell us where they are. Revelation.   Robert Frost.   InPo

So all within be livelier than before.   The Forerunners.   George Herbert. AnAnS 1; JCP; MePo; NoP

So alone in the cold I end.   Fortune's Wheel.   John Byrne Leicester Warren, Lord De Tabley.   OBVV

So am de ban'.   De Drum Majah.   Ray Garfield Dandridge.   BANP

So and no otherwise–so and no otherwise–hillmen desire their/Hills.   The Sea and the Hills.   Rudyard Kipling.   FaBV; MOS

So April's without flower, and no song heard.   A Street in April.   Louis Dudek.   OBCV

So are lilies, so are roses!   Evanescence.   Harriet Prescott Spofford.   AA

So are the loves they inflame.   Epigram: "I don't care for women." *Anonymous.*   PeHV

So as alike thou driv'st away/Both light and darkness, night and day.   A Beautifull Mistress.   Thomas Carew.   EG; OBS

So as my heart be pure and free my mind.   To the Evening.   John Codrington Bampfylde.   NOEC

So as to become a homesickness of the kind/That must bring to the world the Messiah!   In the Ghetto.   Hugo Sonnenschein.   VWA

So as you come, and as you do depart,/Joys ebb and flow within my tender heart.   The Moon.   Charles Best.   OBSC

So as you go round, kiss her one, two, three.   The Rich Widow. *Anonymous.*   AmFP

...So ashes breathe–Around me now.   Go Round.   Laura Chester.   NPGG

So at war dreamt a soldier for him I made this rhyme.   A Domestic Cat. Edwin Denby.   ANYP

So at you, ye bitches, here's give you Hot/Stuff.   Hot Stuff.   Edward Botwood.   PAH

So be gone; you are sped.'   The Merchant of Venice.   William Shakespeare. CTC

So be it: we can bear.   The Prophecy of Dante.   George Gordon, Lord Byron.   ERoP 1-2

So be it, without end!   No Occupation.   George Rostrevor Hamilton. FaBoEE

So be kind-hearted while you can/To the miner from Morea.   John J. Curtis. Joseph Gallager.   AmFP

So be merry, so be dead.   All the Hills and Vales Along.   Charles Hamilton Sorley.   EBEV; EnLit; FaBoCh; HBMV; MMM; MoBrPo; OBWP

So be reposed and praise, praise praise/The way it happened and the way it is. Question to Life.   Patrick Kavanagh.   MoBrPo

So be she got hir Pusheres into court.   The Probatioun Officeres Tale. Gerard Benson.   BXAP; NLV

So be the angels blinded in her new holiness.   O Terrible Is the Highest Thing.   Kenneth Patchen.   VGW

So, be wise, my lamb, and sleep.   Lullaby.   Samuel Hoffenstein.   TrJP

So be within as faire, as good, as true.   The Comparison.   Thomas Carew. AnAnS 2

So beautiful it hurts.   Cynthia in the Snow.   Gwendolyn Brooks.   TiPo

So beauty blemished once for ever lost,/In spite of physic, painting, pain, and cost.   Beauty.   *Anonymous.*   OBSC

So beauty thou, beauty is not in thee.   Diana.   Henry Constable.   OBSC

So Benjamin Franklin went to France.   The Truth about B. F.   Albert Stillman.   InMe

So beware! beware!   Asleep in the Deep.   Arthur J. Lamb.   FSN; TreFT

So, Billy, let's thank Providence/That you and I are sailors.'   The Sailor's Consolation (excerpt).   *Anonymous.*   PoPle

So bitter is the world I cannot live;–/I dare not die.   I.M.H.   Maurice Baring.   ACP

So bitter keen the sky/These dark December days.   Winter Noon in the Woods.   Thomas Caulfield Irwin.   IrPN

So bitter, yet so sweet!   Honey Dripping from the Comb.   James Whitcomb Riley.   AA

So bless'd as the Englishen Heer SECRETARIS.   The Secretary Written at the Hague, in the Year 1696.   Matthew Prior.   CEP

So blind are we, and selfish, too,/We crucify Him every day!   Crucifixion. Mrs. Roy L. Peifer.   STF

So, blind to Some-one/I must be.   All but Blind.   Walter De la Mare. FaPON; HBMV; MoAB; MoBrPo

...So blinding/bright that even Purdy couldn't see through it.   Coon Hunt, Sixth Month (1955).   Sydney Lea.   MAYP

So bloom the unfading petals five,/And verses that all verse outlive.   Solution. Ralph Waldo Emerson.   OBAL

So blow gently the winds on the ocean/And send back my Johnny to me. My Johnny.   *Anonymous.*   OBET

So fare you well my own true love/For ever. Still Growing. *Anonymous.* FaBoBa

So fares it when with truth falsehood contends. Paradise Regained. John Milton. CABL

So farewell—until tonight. Cherry Blossoms. Michael Lewis. UnTE

So fierce a fire thy eyes have on me played. Epigram: "Thy eyes are sparks, Lycines." Strato. PeHV

So, fill, for the day, your mission/By shining just where you are. Shine Just Where You Are. *Anonymous.* STF

...So filled/with such strength, such tenderness of love. Search. Raymond Souster. ELU; OBCV

So find me with you Christmas night, adoring, loving/Him. A Nun Speaks to Mary. Sister Mary Madeleva. ISi

So fine and clean and pure. The Translated Way. Franklin Pierce ("F.P.A.") Adams. FiBHP

So "finish it"/gets done, alone. Time. Robert Creeley. LCAP

So firm, so burdened, on such light gay feet. The Beautiful Train. William Empson. MoVE

So firmly stood the Greeks, nor fled for all the Ilians' ayd. The Iliad. Homer. OBVE

So: First pleasures after hard times,/Hello in time for goodbye. Untitled Poem. Alan Dugan. GP

So flourish these, when those are past away. The Iliad. Homer. OBVE

So fold thyself, my dearest, thou, and slip/Into my bosom and be lost in me. The Princess. Alfred, Lord Tennyson. AtBAP; BLPL; BoLoP; DiPo; EBEV; FaBoBe; FiP; GTBS-P; LLLT; LoBV; NIP; NOBE; NOBV; NoP; OAEP; OBNC; OBVV; PoEL 1-5; PPoe; PPP; SCV; SeCeV; TreFT; TrGrPo; UnTE; ViBoPo

So folks'll say, "He looks like sin/But ain't he beautiful within! Some Folks in Looks Take So Much Pride. *Anonymous.* PoToHe

So for God's sake lock/that kitchen door! Kitchen Door Blues. Tennessee Williams. GrPl; OBAL

So forth they went, the Dwarfe them guid-/ing euer right. The Faerie Queene. Edmund Spenser. CoBE; OAEP

So fortified with wit, stor'd with disdain,/That to win it is all the skill and pain. Astrophel and Stella, XII. Sir Philip Sidney. AAS; SiPS

So from his lips the crime returned/To haunt the spot where it was done. Screaming Tarn. Robert Bridges. ExPo

So from the eternal Light the soul doth spring,/Though in the body she her powers do show. The Soul and the Body. Sir John Davies. CTC; NOBE; OBSC

So, from this hour,/Be love's own flower. Go, Happy Rose. Martial (Marcus Valerius Martialis). PeHV

...So full of shapes is fancy,/That it alone is high fantastical. Twelfth Night. William Shakespeare. TreFS

So full so still/I cannot mend it. The Bush-Fiddle. Judith Green. PoAu 1-2

So gaily flew the flagstaff's bunting. Between Brielle and Manasquan. Oliver St. John Gogarty. OnYI

So gay, serene, supreme his power. News of the World. Anne Ridler. MoLP

So gentle and so beautiful, should perish/with the flowers. The Death of the Flowers. William Cullen Bryant. AA; AnNE; BLPL; BoNaP; GoTF; HBV 1-2; OBCA; PoLf; TreF; WBLP

...So gentlemen/Are made, not born, with infinite labor pains. Talking Union: 1964. L. E. Sissman. TW

So, Gentles, let us rest a bit./O miserie! A Legend of Camelot. George Du Maurier. CenHV

So get you gone—'tis too absurd/To come a-courting me!' The King-Fisher Song. Lewis (Charles Lutwidge Dodgson) Carroll. FaBoNo

So get you gone, Von Hugel, though with blessings/on your head. Vacillation. William Butler Yeats. MBW 1-2; MoVE; NoAm; OBMV

So get yourself/a little loving/in between. Advice. Langston Hughes. NLV

So give them the flowers now. Give Them the Flowers Now. *Anonymous.* WBLP

So gives He them by turn, to suffer or be blest. England. John Henry, Cardinal Newman. ACP; CAW; GoBC

So go to sleep,/My little buckaroo. My Little Buckaroo. *Anonymous.* BPAW

So go to your grave, you silly old man. The Silly Old Man. *Anonymous.* CoMu; TW

So God loves me! Meditation. Toyohiko Kagawa. TRV

So God made a cole-pit to put the devil in. Old Lesson. *Anonymous.* GoTF; TreFT

So God send to my foes all they have thought. Written on a Wall at Woodstock. Queen of England, Elizabeth I. PBWP

So good-by, an' let's let be! Whether or Not. D. H. Lawrence. MoBrPo

So, good night, with lullaby. A Midsummer Night's Dream. William Shakespeare. BoLiVe; CTC; EiL; FiP; GN; HBV 1-2; InvP; NOBE; OBEV; OBSC; PoRA; TrGrPo; ViBoPo; WHA; WSC

So good, they expect to be so good... Street. George Oppen. GP

So goodly wonne with her own will beguiled. Like as a Huntsman. Edmund Spenser. BoLiVe; GBL; SeCePo

So great a sweetness flows/I shake from head to foot. Friends. William Butler Yeats. NoAm; WeW

So great is their love for praise, their will to win. The Georgics. Virgil (Publius Vergilius Maro). SD

So growled the earth's revolving heap;/And will forever. Axle Song. Mark Van Doren. MoPo

So guard your own ranches, and mind the Comanches/Or surely they'll scalp you in less than a year. The Disheartened Ranger. *Anonymous.* BFSS; CoSo

So hail to Mira, the Inconstant Star! La Donna E Mobile. A. K.. FiBHP; InMe

So hallow'd and so gracious is the time. Hamlet. William Shakespeare. FaBoRV; GN; OFD; PCh

So handsomely she moved, so darkly as through glass. Sayre. Lynn Strongin. IHMS

So hang, boys, hang! Hanging Johnny. *Anonymous.* AmSS; FSW; GBP; ShS

So Happy New Year, anyway./You might as well pretend. Happy New Year, Anyway. Joanna Cole. NTCP

So hard a lot God lays upon the old. Youth and Age. Mimnermus. AWP

So has our love. Love Redeemed. William Baylebridge. BoAV; PoAu 1-2

...So hath Hylas/Now lost his heart but hath not won Volina. Count Filippo. Charles Heavysege. PeCV

So having no card, these poetical brayings,/Are the record I leave of my doings and sayings. Lines Left at Mr. Theodore Hook's House in June, 1834. Richard Harris Barham. FaBoUs

So he and she lies in one bed, and he lies next the wall. Six Questions (A vers.). *Anonymous.* BaBo

So he back to Bristol bolted,/For his heart was true to Poll. His Heart Was True to Poll. Sir Francis Cowley Burnand. HBV 1-2

So he can wait, and doze,/and get in nobody's way. Slow Waker. Thom Gunn. Str

So he clapped his wings and away he flew. A Little Cock Sparrow Sat on a Green Tree. *Anonymous.* OxNR

So he dashed up the ladder and had her. Limerick: "While Titian was grinding rose madder." *Anonymous.* NOBL

So he hippety-hopped away. Meeting the Easter Bunny. Rowena Bastin Bennett. SiSoSe; SoPo; SUS; TiPo

...So he/ornaments his with/fresh contempt. The Grace-Note. Denise Levertov. ConAP

So he puff'd himself out in his shirt,/Like a b'loon. The Bloated Biggaboon. Henry Cholmondeley-Pennell. NA

So he sha'n't have jam for tea! Impetuous Samuel. Harry Graham. NA

So he stood up and spat on the ceiling. Limerick: "There was an old man from Darjeeling." *Anonymous.* NTCP

So he thought it was night, and he went to bed. Nicholas Ned. *Anonymous.* NTCP

So he threw down his pitchfork and went to his work. The Riot; or, Half a Loaf is Better Than No Bread. Hannah More. NOEC

So he threw her in the river. Dicky Dilver. *Anonymous.* OxNR

So he touched pearblossom, appleblossom Avenue Y. Anita Barrows. VWA

So he very soon went back to Dover. Limerick: "There was an old person of Dover." Edward Lear. FaBoNo

So he wanted to throw something/And he picked up a baseball. The Origin of Baseball. Kenneth Patchen. LiSp

So he who has sorrow/Shall have rest. O Sweetheart, Hear You. James Joyce. FaBoRV; GBL; HBMV; MoBrPo

So he won't forget his darling he's left so far behind. The Sporting Cowboy. *Anonymous.* OuSiCo

So Hector Protector was sent back again. Hector Protector Was Dressed All in Green. Mother Goose. HBV 1-2; HBVY; MoShBr; OxNR

So help me God! An Easy Poem. Terry Kennedy. AMV-80

–So her song closes! Blanaid's Song. Joseph Campbell. OxBI

So here's to my lovely sweet Nan of the Vale. The Brown Jug. Francis Fawkes. CBEP; ViBoPo

So here we are by the sounding sea. Compromise. Laurence McKinney. InMe

So here, will you take it–hall-marked by a day/Over the hills and far away? The Boyne Walk. Frederick Robert Higgins. OxBI

So hiero the glyphics and poly the glot. Woolly Words. Robert N. Feinstein. NLV

So hight my trew love and non other. Snatches: "Garden wayes and comfort of flowres." *Anonymous.* OxBM

So his Immortal Soul should fled above,/With his Creator, Peace, Joy, Truth, and Love. Epitaph for Himself. Edward, Lord Herbert of Cherbury. AnAnS 2

So his lost land went with him, pulling/Its tatters close around. Foreclosure. Mark Van Doren. CrMA

So his pardon is lightly spoken. Goethe and Frederika. Henry Sidgwick. HBV 1-2

So, holla boys; God save the King. The Furniture of a Woman's Mind. Jonathan Swift. CEP; PPoe

So huge their numbers, and so numberlesse their nation. The Faerie Queene. Edmund Spenser. MOS

(So hush-a-by, weary my Dearie!) When the Sleepy Man Comes. Sir Charles G. D. Roberts. HBV 1-2; HBVY

So hush-a-bye, babby, lie still. Hush Thee, My Babby. *Anonymous.* OxNR

So hush-a-bye, baby, bye-bye. Hush-a-Bye, Baby. *Anonymous.* OxNR

So I ain't in no mood/For sin today. Madam and the Minister. Langston Hughes. NOBA

So i asked the guard to call me in about 20 minutes. Visits. Daniel L. Klauck. LFAC

So I awaked, as wise this while,/As when I fell a-sleeping. To Colin Clout. Anthony Munday. OAEP; OBSC; ViBoPo

So I awoke, to find me still Time's thrall,/Time's sport,–nor by thy warm, safe/presence stayed. The Inverted Torch. Edith Matilda Thomas. AA

So I believe and take it. Of the Holy Eucharist. *Anonymous.* ACP

...So I came by the name of Old Glory. Home Folks: The Name of Old Glory. James Whitcomb Riley. GN

So I can hear how pomegranates laugh. When You Laugh. Ingrid Jonker. WPOW

So I can stare/at the sugar white pillars/and black lace grills/of this pink house. Brazilian Fazenda. P. K. Page. FaBoWP

So I clik'd hod o' my gret club stick an' went whistlin' oot/again. The Wensleydale Lad. *Anonymous.* FaBoPP

So I cut the cords of the lift and down we went,/With nothing in our pockets. Song: Lift Boy. Robert Graves. DTC

So I did sit and eat. Love. George Herbert. AWP; EBCP; EBEV; ExPo; FaBV; ForPo; HBV 1-2; HeIP; ILwL; InPK; InPo; JCP; LiTB; MAT; MeLP; MePo; NOBE; NOCV; NoP; OAEL 1-2; OBEV; OBS; OxBoCh; PoEL 1-5; PoLf; PoPle; PPP; Prf; SCV; SeCePo; SeCeV; SeCP; SeCV 1-2; TEP; TreFT; TrGrPo; TRV; ViBoPo; WHA

So I didn't listen to him/As he sang upon a tree. The Rivals. James Stephens. InvP; MoVE; NoAm; OBEV; OBMV; PoPl

So I do none of this/in offices away from weather. Winter's Onset from an Alienated Point of View. Alan Dugan. FF

So I don't blame myself one iota. Limerick: "A Conservative, out on his motor." A. W. Webster. TDH

So I don't have to think/any/more How to Meditate. Jack Kerouac. PoM

So I, dressed in my idle dreams,/Will think myself the king of men. The Sluggard. William Henry Davies. OBMV

So I fish with a woman the whole year round. The Lure. John Boyle O'Reilly. HBV 1-2

So I guess that you had better/Go to sleep. Mexican Serenade. Arthur Guiterman. FiBHP

So I hand him half. Now. Christopher Gilbert. MAYP

So I have a coverlet for my narrow bed. The Patchwork Quilt. Dora Sigerson Shorter. HBMV

So I her absens will my penaunce make,/That of her presens I my meed may take. Amoretti, LII. Edmund Spenser. AAS

So I know I love you, dear,/Because you're you! Because You're You. Henry Blossom. BLSo

So I know not who came knocking,/At all, at all, at all. Someone. Walter De la Mare. MoBrPo

So I know really, I suppose,/As much as anybody knows. I Want to Know. John Drinkwater. FaPON

So I knowed I'd brung the joke too far/And we wasn't friends no more. Sensitive Sydney. Wallace Irwin. FiBHP

So I leave a note on your doorstep; alison, wake up–/the clouds can be beautiful! Alison. Artie Gold. CaPN

So I left her alone at her door. Song: "She spoke to me gently with words of sweet meaning." Patrick MacDonogh. NeIP

So I left it laying in the same position. As I Was Laying on the Green. *Anonymous.* FiBHP

So I let him go on his way. Grandmother, Rocking. Eve Merriam. GrPl; PCP

So I levelled my gun and I shot him dead. Ho, Brother Teig. *Anonymous.* GBP

So I lie awake & let my hands fight unfilled love. Epigram: "Great woe, fire & woe." Skythinos. PeHV

So I'll come singing home to tea/A poem in my pocket. Inspiration. Robert W. Service. WeW

So I'll dry up my milk as you shall plainly see,/And pass for a maid in my own country.' The Servant of Rosemary Lane. *Anonymous.* OBSS

So I'll fly to the tops of some tall tree/And there I'll sit and sing. Loving Henry. *Anonymous.* BaBo

So I'll go bite the crust of things and thrive/While hedgerows still are sunny. Transitional Poem. Lewis, Cecil Day. EnLit

So I'll not fear the judge or thee. To His Conscience. Robert Herrick. AnAnS 2; NoP; OxBoCh; PoEL 1-5

So I'll pray while I live. Mary Mild, Good Maiden. Colum Cille. NOBI

So I'll sing no more songs for the men that care nothing/for me. O Bruadair. James Stephens. BIrV; OxBI

So I'll sit down all broken-hearted/And try to pass my troubles by. Little Sparrow (Come All You Young and Handsome Ladies). *Anonymous.* AmFP

So I'll taste of joy, though I steal, beg, or borrow! The West-Country Lover. Alice Brown. HBV 1-2

So I'll trust Him, ever trust Him,/Since I know He cares for me. God's Eye Is on the Sparrow. Bertha Meyer. STF

So I'm a next-door beggar/With lilacs in my eye. With Lilacs in My Eye. Lucile Coleman. GoYe

So I'm gonna put my name down. Put My Name Down. Irwin Silber. FSW

So I'm through with you and I hope you don't feel hurt. I'm Through with You. *Anonymous.* WTO

So I makes for up the country at the old jig-jog. A Bushman's Song. Andrew Barton ("Banjo") Paterson. PoAu 1-2

So I may sleep, rest at night. The Visit. Phil George. VoR

...So I melt a ball of snow/From the hedge into their rusty tin before I go. Penal Rock: Altamuskin. John Montague. FaBoIP

So I might catch you to my heart, and prove/'Tis not your beauty only that I love! I Do Not Love to See Your Beauty Fire. John Hall Wheelock. HBMV

So I must carry his death about me/Like a large fly, like a large frail purpose. A Death to Us. Jon Silkin. NePoEA

So I on Fife wad glowr no more,/But gallop'd to Edina's shore. Auld Reikie. Robert Fergusson. CABL

So I quit. The Function Room. Patrice Phillips. MAT

...So I read books and bit/my thumbnails to the quick/in false despair: I am still here. On When McCarthy Was a Wolf among a Nation of Queer-Queers. Alan Dugan. GP

So I resigned myself, picked up my father,/And turned my face toward the mountain range. The Aeneid. Virgil (Publius Vergilius Maro). NAWM 1-2

So I return rebuked to my content,/And gain by ill thrice more than I have spent. Sonnets, CXIX: "What potions have I drunk of Siren Tears." William Shakespeare. CBEP; WHA

So I rode homeward, free of doubt. The Traveller. C. J. Dennis. NOAV

So I securely go. The Day–The Way. John Oxenham. TRV

So I sent the coming tears back with the/whispered word, "He knows." Not Knowing. Mary Gardiner Brainard. AA; TRV

So i shall offer up this bloody piece to her/and pause a while Bloody Pause. Astra. BrRo

So I shook my head/and just didn't look around. "Somedays now". Wendy G. Rickert. NMM

So, I think, God hides some souls away,/Sweetly to surprise us, the last day. The Petrified Leaf. Mary Bolles Branch. HBV 1-2

So I think I'll be six now for ever and ever. The End. A.(lan) A.(lexander) Milne. BiCB; SiSoSe

So I think I were lucky because I were shy. Because I Were Shy. *Anonymous.* StPo

So I think I will go there an' see./Me! Chant-Pagan. Rudyard Kipling. FaBoPV; OAEP; VLP

So I thought it both safest and best/To marry, for fear you should chide. Song: "Can love be controll'd by advice?" John Gay. LoBV; OBSP

So I thought the matter over/And I rather think I will. Common Bill. *Anonymous.* AmFP; AS; FSW

So I thrust my spear into its side. Bear Hunting. Aua. WTO

So I thy Martyr am, or never. The Contrary. Alexander Brome. CavP

So I trust, too. An Epilogue. John Masefield. FaBoEE; OxBTC

So I turn'd into a sty/And laid me down among the swine. I Saw a Chapel All of Gold. William Blake. CABA; EnRP; LAuP; LiTB

So I wait–bereft of 2,000 years and the bath of life. Marriage. Gregory Corso. CABA; CoAP; InPS; LiTM; NeAP; NoAm; NoP; OBAL; PAI; PPP; PrIm; TAP

So I want to warn you to be wary.' Limerick: "A Fire Island pixie called "Mary.'". *Anonymous.* PeHV

–So, I was afraid! Instans Tyrannus. Robert Browning. EBEV

So I was cryin'/On account of/You! Late Last Night. Langston Hughes. NoAm

So I was ready/When trouble came. I to My Perils. Alfred Edward Housman. EnLi 1-2; ViBoPo; WeW

So I went home/And lived in idleness. A Long Time Ago. T'ao Ch'ien. LoGBV

So I went on/counting my numberless fingers. Mountain Talk. Archie Randolph Ammons. HaCAP

So I will be your Mrs. Q./Horatius. The Reconciliation: A Modern Version Odes of Horace III, 9. Franklin Pierce ("F.P.A.") Adams. NLV

So I will catch the Cluricawne and you shall have them all.   Of Certain Irish Fairies.   Arthur Guiterman.   PoLf

So I will go down to the harbor soon/And stand around all afternoon.   A Ship Comes in.   Oliver Jenkins.   EtS

So I will stay in the background/where you will find me.   A Person, a Mexican.   Lorri Martinez.   LFAC

So I wish you a gude morning.'   Johnnie Cope.   Adam Skirving.   OxBS

So I won't have so long to lay?   Ella Speed.   *Anonymous.*   AmFP

So I would rather some time yet/Play on with you, my little pet!   According to eternal laws.   Walter Savage Landor.   EiCP

So if all do their duty they need not fear harm.   The Chimney Sweeper.   William Blake.   AtBAP; DiPo; EnPE; FaBoPV; FF; HeIP; InPK; NAWM 1-2; OAEL 1-2; OxBChV; PPP; SaC; SoSe; TEP

So if my spring had any flowers before,/Your breaths, Favonius, hath increased the store.   To Favonius.   Edmund Bolton.   OBSC

So, if we may not let the Muse be free,/She will be bound with garlands of her own.   If by Dull Rhymes Our English Must Be Chained.   John Keats.   PP

So if you must,/Pray standing.   Scroll.   Stanley Moss.   VWA

So if you want to do him in,/You must sneak up behind.   Eggs and Marrowbone.   *Anonymous.*   FSW

So if you will believe me now, it's the truth I did unfold.   Cockies of Bungaree.   *Anonymous.* ⁷   PoAu 1-2

So if you wish to marry, boys, I'll tell you what to do.   Wedding Song.   *Anonymous.*   OBET

So imagine her meaning of that.   Limerick: "A charming young woman named Pat."   *Anonymous.*   NIP

So impotent Our Wisdom is/To her Simplicity.   "Nature" Is What We See.   Emily Dickinson.   MAmP

So in her blood for you the bright bird sings.   To a Child Before Birth.   Norman Nicholson.   ChMP; NAs

So in love with you, my love am I.   So in Love.   Cole Porter.   BLSo

So in my song I bind them/For all to find them.   I Praise the Tender Flower.   Robert Bridges.   EG

So in one picture I have seen/An angel here, the Devil there.   To Lucasta: Her Reserved Looks.   Richard Lovelace.   CaPo; SeCV 1-2

So in seconds is his final, secret name.   Rumplestiltskin Poems.   William Hathaway.   DFT

So, in silence, slowly, they surrounded me/and tore me to pieces.   In the Garden of the Turkish Consulate.   Pinhas Sadeh.   VWA

So in spite of our virtue, it's hard to suppress/A sneaking affection for Frank and for Jess.   Crime at Its Best.   Stoddard King.   NLV

So in the eye of Nature let him die!   The Old Cumberland Beggar.   William Wordsworth.   CABL; ERoP 1-2; LaA; MBW 1-2

So in the sun, some say, there is no heat,/Though his reflecting beams do fire beget.   To His Lady.   Sir John Davies.   SiPS

So in which sea I swim my heart may know.   Epigram: "O Diodorus."   *Anonymous.*   PeHV

So inaccessible and cold,/That to be his is to be old.   A Song: "The nymph in vain bestows her pains."   Anne Finch, Countess of Winchilsea.   OBSP

So is a strain of music with pleasant/wine.   Music.   *Anonymous.*   TrJP

So is each man's spirit stirred by wine.   Song and Wine.   Bacchylides.   LiTW

So is my love, my passion/& my devotion/To him to whom I give them.   Love.   *Anonymous.*   BIrV

So is my love still telling what is told.   Sonnets, LXXVI: "Why is my verse so barren of new pride."   William Shakespeare.   EBEV; PP

...So is substantial God,/tuning in from abroad.   Dream Songs.   John Berryman.   TAP

So is the equal poise of this fell war.   King Henry VI.   William Shakespeare.   MOS

So it always was, so shall ever be!   De Gustibus–.   Robert Browning.   FaBoPP; HBV 1-2; MaVP; MBW 1-2; OAEP; OBTV; PAI

So it is just that you should give/your love in the same measure.   Do Not Torment Me, Lady.   *Anonymous.*   NOBI

So it is the soldier goes away!   Dirge for Fajuyi.   Arowa. *Omobayode*   WTO

So it is to be an Old Soldier.   Old Soldier.   Padraic Colum.   OBMV

So it is with the gods,/and with the halfgods,/and with the heroes.   Man Alone.   Denise Levertov.   CAPP

So it's all over, and the old woman's home again now.   The Old Woman Who Bought a Pig.   *Anonymous.*   OxNR

So it's better for to leave the town than go to gaol for debt.   The Carpet-Weaver's Lament.   *Anonymous.*   OBET

So it's God bless you all, both great and small,/And send you a joyful May.   A May Day Carol.   *Anonymous.*   PoSC

So it's move along, you dogies, 'fore th' devil brands you sure.   Cowboy's Salvation Song.   Robert V. Carr.   PoOW

So it shall be spoken./So it shall be done.   Martin Luther King Jr.   Gwendolyn Brooks.   BOLo; CNA; PoBA

So it was. And David heard.   Saul.   Nathan Alterman.   TrJP

So it wasn't a pleasure to smoke 'em.   Limerick: "There was a young lady of Oakham."   *Anonymous.*   TDH

So it went the common road to decay.   Remembrances.   John Clare.   CBEP; NCEP

So Jewellers no Art or Metal trust/To form the Diamond, but the Diamonds dust.   Upon the Death of My Ever Desired Friend Doctor Donne Dean of Pauls.   Henry, Bishop of Chichester King.   AnAnS 2; SeCP

So Jim never said anything.   Modern Ode to the Modern School.   John Erskine.   YaD

So Jockie had siller, and Sandy had pleasure.   Twa Bonny Lads.   Robert Burns.   OBSP

So John and I are more than quit.   Epigram: "To John I ow'd great obligation."   Matthew Prior.   FaBoEE

So, Johnny, how dost thou now?   John Jiggy Jag.   *Anonymous.*   OxNR

So just rhododendron, of course.   Limerick: "A major, with wonderful force."   *Anonymous.*   TDH

So keep a straight face and sit tight on yours.   Japanese Beetles.   X. J. Kennedy.   HoAn; OBAL

So kiss, kiss, kiss, and away.   Good Morning, Father Francis.   *Anonymous.*   OxNR

So kisses to a lover's guest/Are invitations, not the feast.   A Pastoral Courtship.   John Wilmot, Earl of Rochester.   UnTE

So know that when it is your intention/mine shall be to make believe.   I Can't Hold You and I Can't Leave You.   Sister Juana Ines de la Cruz.   PBWP

So lacks all picture of reproach it ends/Denying what it started up to say.   Song: "So large a morning, so itself, to lean."   W. H. Auden.   NePoAm-2

So Ladie, now to you I doo complaine,/Against your eies that justice I may gaine.   Amoretti, XII.   Edmund Spenser.   AAS

So LARGE a trunk before.   The Elephant.   Hilaire Belloc.   SoPo; TiPo

So lat us deiyen bothen isame.   Mary Suffers with Her Son.   *Anonymous.*   MeEL

So late emerged from, shall so soon expire.   The Rubaiyat of Omar Khayyam.   Omar Khayyam.   WGRP

So late in the century/in the 20th Century.   Au Bout du Temps.   Andrei Codrescu.   APU

So Laura's words be not unkind.   Ode to a Young Lady, Somewhat Too Sollicitous about Her Manner...   William Shenstone.   CEP

So lazy and hum-strumming.   Summer Stars.   Carl Sandburg.   LOW; RFM; YeAr

So leave but perfect to my eye/Thy columns set against thy sky!   Resignation–To Faustus.   Arthur Hugh Clough.   VLP

So leave they take of Coelia, and her daugh-/ters three.   The Faerie Queene.   Edmund Spenser.   OAEP

So left him here to shepherd us and battled back to jail.   Stir the Wallaby Stew.   *Anonymous.*   FaBoBa

So let him have the spurs, and the glory!   Crecy.   Francis Turner Palgrave.   BeLS; HBV 1-2

So let his name go down to fame,/Whatever it may be.   Stairs.   Oliver Herford.   FiBHP; InMe

So let it be.   A Clymene.   Paul Verlaine.   AWP

So let it be lost/Expectabo Argentum/As much as it cost (viz. 5s.).   To the Borrower of This Book.   Samuel Showell, Jr.   FaBoUs

So let it smite, such deeds shall be no more!   Abraham Lincoln.   Edmund Clarence Stedman.   PAH

So let me beware of cruel jealousy.   In Oxford City.   *Anonymous.*   OBET

So, let me render back again/This millionth of Thy gift. Amen.   Prayer of a Soldier in France.   Joyce Kilmer.   CAW; GoBC

So let me step westward; my shadow/is long.   Easter Sunday, 1945.   Giuseppe Antonio Borgese.   NePoAm

So let my solace be the breath/Of morning when I move to death.   Morning.   Philip Henry Savage.   AA

So let my soul, in life's last even,/Retire to glorious rest.   Hail, Tranquil Hour of Closing Day.   Leonard Bacon.   AH

So let our hopes to meet allay,/The fears and Sorrows of this day.   Lucasia, Rosania and Orinda Parting at a Fountain, July 1663.   Katherine ("Orinda") Philips.   PeHV

So let's go home to bed,/Renee, and dress and dress and dress.   Clothes Make the Man.   Theodore Weiss.   NoAm

So let them bide, burrowing in the dirt.   The Houses of Corr an Chait Are Cold.   Seamas Dall Mac Cuarta.   NOBI

So let us avoid all little sinnings,/Since such is the end of petty beginnings.   The Results of Stealing a Pin.   *Anonymous.*   FaBoUs

So let us dyen bothen isame.   Why Have You No Ruth?   *Anonymous.*   OBSP

So let us patients do our bit/To help the surgeons make us fit.   Cancer's a Funny Thing.   J. B. S. Haldane.   OxBTC

So let us welcome peaceful ev'ning in.   The Task.   William Cowper.   FiP

So light, so deep.   She lay as if at play.   Emily Dickinson.   LiTA

So like a ship the dead man comes to shore.   Epitaph.   Alex Comfort.   MoBrPo; MOS

So like that bird's, wherein I see myself/more than I see myself in thee, my father. The Bird. Lima, Jorge De. LiTW

So, like the ancients, I advise/You too should make this sacrifice. Epitaph on Pegasus, a Limping Gay. Antonio Beccadelli. PeHV

So like the smaller stars we rowed among. The Lotus Flowers. Ellen Bryant Voigt. MAYP

So like to this, nay, all the rest,/Is each neat niplet of her breast. Upon the Nipples of Julia's Breast. Robert Herrick. CaPo; ErPo; LiTL; UnTE; ViBoPo

So likewise love cheare you your heavy spright,/And chaunge old yeares annoy to new delight. Amoretti, LXII. Edmund Spenser. AAS; OBSC

So, little Master Wagtail, I'll bid you a good-bye. Little Trotty Wagtail. John Clare. CBEP; OnUR; PB; UnPo

So little/then it matters/what is treasured. The Rope. Tania Van Zyl. PeSA

So live each day that God shall say,/"Well done!" at last. Life. Edward Rowland Sill. BLRP

So live, yellow boy,/For your Blackness. From a Bus. Malaika Ayo Wangara. NBP

...:So live you free/From Fames black lips, as you from me. The Suspition upon His Over-Much Familiarity with a Gentlewoman. Robert Herrick. CavP

So lives desire which hope hath left,/As twilight shines when sun is reft. Hopeless Desire Soon Withers and Dies. A. W. OBSC

So long. Portmanteau Parodies: After Walt Whitman. Gilbert Keith Chesterton. FaBoPa

So long!–And I hope we shall meet again. Now Lift Me Close. Walt Whitman. DFF

So long as earth and heaven endure. I Shall Not Want: In Deserts Wild. Charles F. Deems. AH

So long as I can have my beer,/I'll glady miss the skittles. Chicago Analogue. Keith Preston. NLV

So long as I declaim with oratorical display. An Overworked Elocutionist. Carolyn Wells. BLPA; BLPL

So long as men can breathe, or eyes can see,/So long lives this, and this gives life to thee. Sonnets, XVIII: "Shall I compare thee to a summer's day?" William Shakespeare. ATP; AWP; BoLoP; CTC; DiPo; ExPo; FaBoBe; FaBV; FaFP; FiP; FPL; GBL; GoTF; GTBS; GTBS-P; HAP; HBV 1-2; HeIP; InPK; InPS; InvP; LiTB; LiTL; LoBV; MasP; MAT; MBW 1-2; MCCG; NIP; NOBE; NoP; OAEL 1-2; OAEP; OBEV; OBSC; OLR; PAI; PoEL 1-5; PoLf; PoPl; PoRA; PPoe; PrIm; SCV; SeCePo; SeCeV; TEP; TreFT; TrGrPo; ViBoPo; WHA

So long as the dikes of Holland/Divide the land from the sea! The Leak in the Dike. Phoebe Cary. FaFP; PaPo; TreF

So long as the Green Train thunders on into space? The Green Train. Emile Victor Rieu. SO

So-long, my fancy man! A Valediction (Liverpool Docks). John Masefield. OBMV

So long now these people were the only family he had. The Movies. Jack Gilbert. NPGG

So long shall Erin's pride/Tell how they lived and died. How Oft Has the Banshee Cried. Thomas Moore. AnIV; AWP

So long (though he from booke myche hope to desire)/Till without fewell you can make hot fire. Astrophel and Stella, XLVI. Sir Philip Sidney. AAS; SiPS

So long to love/so long So Long. Jayne Cortez. BoWoP

So look dumb, play poor, form car pools or walk. A Choctaw Chief Helps Plan a Festival... Jim Barnes. TAT

So looks and lyes the shepherd boy/The summer long his whole employ. The Shepherd Boy. John Clare. NOBV

So lost a thing as thou hadst been. Upon My Lady Carliles Walking in Hampton-Court Garden. Dialogue. Sir John Suckling. AnAnS 2; CaPo; NoP

So Love and Folly were in hell. A Barley-Break. Sir John Suckling. CaPo; SeCV 1-2

So love my loves of you. Variables of Green. Robert Graves. FaBoEE

So love will take between the hands a face... Moon Compasses. Robert Frost. DiPo; MOON; MoVE

So lovely, pure and fair. Du Bist Wie Eine Blume. Heinrich Heine. AWP

So lovers in their silence die. Silent Love. John Clare. EnRP

So low in hell your bed shall be. Shame. Coventry Patmore. OBVV

So made/Of their Red Sea, a Spring; I wash, they wade. Silex Scintillans. Henry Vaughan. AnAnS 1

So Madeleine serves the soldiers still in the Green Estaminet. The Green Estaminet. Sir Alan Patrick Herbert. HBMV

So, maids when you're young, never wed an old man. Maids When You're Young, Never Wed an Old Man. Anonymous. FSW

So make yourself content, my love,/Till God calls you away. The Unquiet Grave. Anonymous. AnFE; AtBAP; BaBo; DTC; ELP; ESPB; ExPo; GBP; HAP; HeIP; LoBV; NoP; OAEL 1-2; PoEL 1-5; PoPle; ViBoPo; WeW

So Man that dies, shall live again. Like as the Damask Rose. Francis Quarles. CBEP; LoBV

So man, the insect, stands on his defence/Against the very hand of Providence. The Bee-Wisp. Charles Tennyson Turner. FM

So man to his revenge supplies/The added terrors of surprise. Condone. Ambrose Bierce. DBV

So manners win our admiration/And the best manners are imitation. The Mother Crab and Her Family. L. T. Manyase. PeSA

So many a night in the olden years? The Quiet Night. Heinrich Heine. LiTW

So many Chinook souls, so many Silverside. The Fish Counter at Bonneville. William Stafford. AmFN

So many eyes and only one authority of paper. Household. Laura Jensen. LCAP

So many feathers i remember/Josephine Josephine So Many Feathers. Jayne Cortez. BlSi

So many goblins you shall see. Ceremony upon Candlemas Eve. Robert Herrick. OBCP

So many hearts already she hath slain,/As few behind to conquer shall remain. Of the Nativity of the Lady Rich's Daughter. Henry Constable. OBSC

So many of them and so small,/Suppose I cannot know them all. August Night. Elizabeth Madox Roberts. YeAr

So many people, not to speak of the dog.' The Taxis. Louis MacNeice. FaBoIP; OxBTC

So many times do I love again. Song: "How many times do I love thee, dear?" Thomas Lovell Beddoes. ERoP 1-2; LiTB; LiTL; NBM; OBRV; PoEL 1-5; TrGrPo; ViBoPo

So many ways they say death,/Up in the tennis tree, co-ki. Tennis in San Juan. Reuel Denney. SD

So many ways to be unsure or bold. The Young Ones. Elizabeth Jennings. OxBTC

So many words to speak that the tongue cannot utter. Tramp. Richard Hughes. MoBrPo

So many years/before the soft key of your tongue/unlocked my body. Like Any Other Man. Gregory Orr. FF

So marrily to life's house I sped:/And herein shape our double bed. Ballad of the Double Bed. Eve Merriam. UnTE

So may God direct you in your wise consultations,/To ruin these happy and flourishing nations. The Queen's Speech. Arthur Mainwaring. APAS

So may God give to them and all/The blessing of His lasting peace! The Old Woman Remembers. Lady Gregory, Augusta Gregory. OnYI

So may his high exploits at last make even/With earth his honor, glory with the Heaven. In Defiance to the Dutch. Anonymous. APAS

So may I always keep. Polly. John Gay. EG

So may the city that I love be great/'Till every stone shall be articulate. The City's Crown. Dudley Foulke. HBMV; WGRP

So may the relation of each man be clipped. The Comedian as the Letter C. Wallace Stevens. NePA; OxBA

So may we long continue thus,/Admiring you, you pitying us. To Stella. Jonathan Swift. NOEC

So may you handle Lagos with care. Mayor of Lagos. Anonymous. WTO

So may you, when the musick's done,/Awake and see the rising sun. Her Sweet Voice. Thomas Carew. LiTL

So me and my baby/To the workhouse must go. Rosemary Lane. Anonymous. OBET

So mean I. Waiting Both. Thomas Hardy. MoAB; MoBrPo; OxBoLi

So men shall God in Christ adore,/And worship idols vain no more. Once More, Our God, Vouchsafe to Shine. Samuel Sewall. AH

So men; some stiff, some loose, some firm: All earth! Mankind. Anonymous. FaBoEE

So men write poems in Australia. Five Visions of Captain Cook. Kenneth Slessor. BoAV

So merrily march the merchantmen. The Merchants of London. Anonymous. GBP

So merrily on our way we go, until we reach the valley-o. The Handcart Song. Anonymous. AmFP

So merrily the shepherds their pipes did blow. As I out Rode. Anonymous. SBVL

So merrily trip and go! A-Maying, A-Paying. Nashe [(or Nash()] Thomas. ElL

So midst the wither'd waste of life, those tears would flow to me! Youth and Age. George Gordon, Lord Byron. GTBS; GTBS-P

So, midst the withered waste of life, those/tears would flow to me. Stanzas for Music. George Gordon, Lord Byron. CoBE; EnLi 1-2; EnLit; HAP; HBV 1-2; OAEP

So might I find my loving spouse of course/Endued with all the virtues of a horse. Mary Gulliver to Captain Lemuel Gulliver. Jonathan Swift. OAEL 1-2

So mightiest powers by deepest calms are fed,/And sleep, how oft, in things that gentlest be. The Sea–in Calm. Barry (Bryan Waller Procter) Cornwall. EtS

So mine be your eyes! To Morfydd. Lionel Pigot Johnson. AnIV; MoBrPo; OAEL 1-2; OBMV

So mote he bere hir ful to Marlborrowe. The Hicche-Hykeres Tale (parody). W. F. N. Watson. BXAP

So much could stay a moment in so little. On a Child Who Lived One Minute. X. J. Kennedy. DFF; HoAn; HoPM; NYBP

So much depends on bed and board/They give them in the Hay Hotel. The Hay Hotel. *Anonymous.* BIrV

So much film and conjugation/depending on the angle Touch of zygosis. Judith Fitzgerald. CaPN

So much for Calvary!" He said. The Second Coming. Norman Gale. HBV 1-2

So much for idle wishing–how/It steals the time! To business now. The Italian in England. Robert Browning. FaBoPV; MaVP; OAEP; OBNV

So much for that. Ragout fin de siecle. Erich Kastner. ErPo; PeHV

So much for the Mothers Goose and Earth. From the Brothers Grimm to Sister Sexton to Mother Goose (parody). David Cummings. BXAP

So much grace, and so approve her,/That for everything I love her. The Complete Lover. William Browne. HBV 1-2

So much I love the most Unloving one. To Delia. Samuel Daniel. HBV 1-2; OBEV; OBSC

So much I think upon thee, that I wax all green. When the Nightingale Sings. *Anonymous.* CBEP

So much, so little space/between two faces/of a wall. Coloratura. Geoff Page. AMV-81

So much talk for/So close a relation. Husbands and Wives. Miriam Hershenson. NTCP

So much that was most dear to me. A Leaf. Ludwig Uhland. AWP

So must her dreams be... Nocturnal. Os Marron. NeBP

So must I sleep enchanted another hundred year. Barbarossa. Friedrich Rueckert. AWP; WSC

So must you too, haughty maid. The Lover's Posy. Rufinus Domesticus. AWP

So my course turns/Where I walk each day. Hawk's Eyes. Yvor Winters. PoA

So, my fond friends at home, all, goodnight. The Miner's Lament. *Anonymous.* AmFP

So my gallant Youths farewell. The Muses Elizium. Michael Drayton AnAnS 2

So–my Lord Tomnoddy went home to bed! Hon. Mr. Sucklethumbkin's Story. Richard Harris Barham. OBRV

So my old evil spirit/can get a Greyhound bus and ride Me and the Devil Blues. Robert Johnson. BluL

So my sad tears run/Like streams of Water, streams of/Water. Water Song. Solomon Ibn Gabirol. TrJP

So my storm-beaten heart likewise is cheered,/With that sunshine when cloudy looks are cleared. Amoretti, XL. Edmund Spenser. AAS; OBSC

So near to death, so far from God, forlorn. A Prayer for Purification. Buonarroti Michelangelo. AWP

So Nero once, with Harp in hand, survey'd/His flaming Rome, and as it burn'd, he play'd. Of My Lady Isabella Playing on the Lute. Edmund Waller. HAP; MePo

So night by night, my life has gone. Orpheus. W. D. Snodgrass. CABA

So nimbly with a marble heart. On Her Dancing. James Shirley. PoPle

...So no more now, from your loving husband, Wilfred. The Jungle Husband. Stevie Smith. FaBoWP; NLV

So, no more talk of funerals. Begin! A Boisterous Poem about Poetry (excerpt). John Wain. PP

So nobody arrived on shore but him. Don Juan. George Gordon, Lord Byron. MOS

...So nought/Be missed that makes a man's bed-furniture. Sonnets of the Months. Folgore da San Geminiano. AWP

So now be kind to unicorns. Inhuman Henry or Cruelty to Fabulous Animals. Alfred Edward Housman. BBGG; FiBHP; NLV

So, now for your blessin', sweet Father Molloy. Father Molloy or, the Confession. Samuel Lover. HBV 1-2

So now Godolphin is the Boy/Who blacks the Boots at the Savoy. Godolphin Horne. Hilaire Belloc. CenHV; DTC; FaBoCo

So now hard force my heart doth all to break. "The furious gun in his raging ire." Sir Thomas Wyatt. FCP

So now I languish, till he please,/My pining anguish to appease. Four Anacreontic Poems, 4. Edmund Spenser. AAS

So now in days of fevered fret and stress/Let Europe measure out our Irishness! Written on the Sense of Isolation in Contemporary Ireland. Robert Greacen. NeIP

So now my dear Mother, &c., &c., &c. The New Bath Guide. Christopher Anstey. CEP; NOEC

So now once more I'm bang up prime,/Ri tol de lol. Johnny Raw and Polly Clark. *Anonymous.* CoMu

So now that she's married, she lives at her ease;/She goes at her will and returns as she pleases. Pretty Polly. *Anonymous.* BFSS

"So now we know." The Lizard. Ruth Lechlitner. AMV-81

So now you'll please excuse me, for I'm nearly out of breath. The Schooner Blizzard. *Anonymous.* ShS

...So of the soul. By the Sea. Richard Watson Dixon. OBNC

So off to the Bishop, my Muse, and make my request. Request for Meat and Drink. Sedulius Scottus. NOBI

So old Nigger Add'll just brand her now. Whose Old Cow? *Anonymous.* CoSo

So, old truculence–our thundercloud, our rainbow. Pancho Villa. Lou Lipsitz. NCSH

So on (ad infinitum). Such is fame! 1886 A.D. George Lynde Richardson. AA

So on mine, my baby, thou./Puva...puva...puva. Lullaby. *Anonymous.* SUS

So on thy shore the fisher-boys shall sing/Sweet songs of peace to our sweet peace's King. Chromis. Phineas Fletcher. LoBV

So one might find a meteor from the sun/Or sound one trumpet ere the play's begun. Child with a Cockatoo. Rosemary Dobson. CBAP

So, only, the stain shall be razed–so, only, the great debt/be paid! To Spain– A Last Word. Edith Matilda Thomas. MC; PAH

So ope me the door when I tap by and by. Open the Door. *Anonymous.* WTO

So our English, I think you will all agree,/Is the trickiest language you ever did see. Why English Is So Hard. *Anonymous.* FaBoUs

...So passing forth she him/obaid. The Faerie Queene. Edmund Spenser. OAEP

So peace begins the winsome day. The Ivory Bed. Winfield Townley Scott. ErPo

So perfect was the silence Nature kept. On the Eclipse of the Moon of October 1865. Charles Tennyson Turner. OBNC

So perhaps I'd better drop it. Goosey Goosey Gander. William Percy French. CenHV

So perhaps you may charm/her tongue, tongue, tongue. The Dumb Maid. *Anonymous.* CoBE

So perish souls, which more choose men's unjust/Power from God claimed, than God himself to trust. Satire. John Donne. CABA; EBEV; JCP; MeLP; MePo; NoP; OAEL 1-2; OBS; OBSV; PoEL 1-5; SeCP; SeCV 1-2

So pimps grow rich, while gallants are undone. On Authors and Booksellers. Alexander Pope. FaBoEE

So pleasant a ground of no earthly man. The Flower and the Leaf. *Anonymous.* PBBP

So pleasant it is to have money. Dipsychus. Arthur Hugh Clough. FaBoPV; OAEL 1-2

So please, sir, let me be/With the good old engine I loved so well,/One Hundred Forty-three. Georgie Allen. *Anonymous.* BFSS

So plenteous nature shall inward virtue crown. Full Be the Year, Abundant Be the Grain. *Anonymous.* OBVE

So Porter proves himself a brave man's son. Running the Batteries. Herman Melville. PAH

So pray attend to what you hear./And a warning take I pray. A Ballad from the Seven Dials Press... *Anonymous.* CoMu; VLP

So pray for me, my friends, who have not strength to pray. The Dream of Gerontius. John Henry, Cardinal Newman. ACP

So prayer revives/The soule, by prayer it lives. Ensamples of Our Saviour. Robert Southwell. PoEL 1-5

So precarious but miraculous foothold? Copper-Beech and Butter-Fingers. Pearse Hutchinson. CIP

So precious to me are the fourscore words,/That each letter changes into a bar of gold. The Letter. *Anonymous.* LoBV

So purer light shall mark the road/That leads me to the Lamb. Walking with God. William Cowper. EiCP; EnPE; NOCV; NOEC; OAEP; OBEC; PoEL 1-5; TEP; TRV

...So quiet/Not a soul is wakened. Death and the Arkansas River. Frank Stanford. FiCP

So ran Sir Wolf, and runneth yet. The Wolf and the Dog. Jean de La Fontaine. LiTW; OBVE

So ran this river on. Britannia's Pastorals. William Browne. FaBoPP

So ran to regale on a new-taken fly. The Virtuous Fox and the Self-Righteous Cat. John Cunningham. OnMSP

So rare a Fleet, was never made nor man'd. John Smith of His Friend Master John Taylor. John Smith. SCAP

So rat and doctor may converse together. The Doctor Who Sits at the Bedside of a Rat. Josephine Miles. VGW

So ready is Heaven to stoop to him. Grace of the Way (excerpt). Francis Thompson. MoAB; MoBrPo

So red, so ripe, the roses burn'd! The Flowers. William Brighty ("Matthew Browne") Rands. OBVV

So remember, dear heart, whatever may come,/The Bethlehem Star shines on! The Bethlehem Star Shines On! Alice Mortenson. BePJ 033

So remember our journey. Remember us all. Southern Ships and Settlers, 1606-1732. Rosemary and Stephen Vincent Benét. AmFN

So rest in the arms of your mother/Who sings you a la ru. Duermete, Nino Lindo. *Anonymous.* FSW

So rewful ded was nevere non.'... At the Crucifixion. *Anonymous.* OxBM

...So ring/down the curtain, poor Carmen's at rest. Carmen. Newman Levy. ALV; FiBHP

So robs the sheep, in favour's fair pretence. Virgidemiarum. Joseph Hall. OBSV

So rock-a-bye, baby, mother is here. Rock-A-Bye Baby. Effie I. Canning. FSN

So run along now to your chamber Miss and rhyme with bliss. Admonition to the Muse. Geoffrey Taylor. FaBoEE

So runs my catalogue of lovely things. A Ballade-Catalogue of Lovely Things. Richard Le Gallienne. HBMV

So runs the world away. Hamlet. William Shakespeare. CoBE

So sad, and true, it may invite/My self to die, and prove mine owne. The Garden. James Shirley. CavP; OBS

So, saving you, does everything. Spleen. John Gray. NOBV

So says the love-song of Vusumzi. Vusumzi's Song. L. T. Manyase. PeSA

So see I Life within Death's shadowy/place. Death, Thou Hast Seized Me. Isaac Luzzatto. TrJP

So send it to Victoria that wears the British crown. The Bold Dragoon. Anonymous. OBET

So senses you, none breathes who's less alone! Love Redeemed. William Baylebridge. CBAP

So shall I compass peace on earth,/And endless bliss in heaven. A Morning Hymn. Christopher Smart. OxBChV

So shall I first begin, so last shall end thy will. Desiderium. Phineas Fletcher. OBS

So shall I live with Thee, and thy dear fame/Shall link my love unto thine honored name. Ad Matrem. Julian Fane. HBV 1-2

So shall my day that's doubtful yet be bright. Time Lags Abed. D'Arcy Cresswell. AnNZ

So shall my days be full of heavenly light! The Celestial Passion. Richard Watson Gilder. AA; AnAmPo

So shall the centuries drift, trailing like a caravan,/Coming for judgment, out of the dark, to me. "Garden of Gethsemane." Boris Pasternak. MoRP

So shall the Crown and Laurel, too,/Descend from Fool to Fool! An Ode for the New Year. John Gay. OxBoLi

So shall the land be truly blessed: he reign/For our protection; we his rights maintain. A Poem on England's Happiness. Anonymous. APAS

So shall the music of Thy name/Refresh my soul in death. The Precious Name. John Newton. BePJ

So shall the seventh be truly blest,/From morn to eve, with hallowed rest. Devotional Incitements. William Wordsworth. OxBoCh

So shall the wonders of thy power be seene,/And thou for euer liue the Planets Queene. The Shadow of Night. George Chapman. NCEP

So shall their freedome save them from extreames. How Collingbourne Was Cruelly Executed for Making a Foolish Rhyme. William Baldwin. NCEP

–So shall thy unfailing love/Guide, and support, and cheer me to the end!' The Excursion. William Wordsworth. EnRP; NoP

So shall we smoothly pass away in sleep. A Dialogue between Thyrsis and Dorinda. Andrew Marvell. SeCP

So shall ye have a man of the sphere,/Fit to grace the solar year. Alphonso of Castile. Ralph Waldo Emerson. AP; NOBA

So shall ye waste to dust. The Aged Lover Renounceth Love. Thomas, Lord Vaux. EIL; EnPo; EnRePo; OAEL 1-2; OAEP; PoEL 1-5

So shall you honor well the shades, from whom/Are thanks–and from the dead is gratitude. Cleitagoras. of Tarentum Leonidas. AWP

So shall you not be shent/But worthily praised,/As you have deserved. The Lover Exhorteth His Lady to Be Constant. Anonymous. OBSC

So shalt thou quench her fire, and mine. To Her Againe, She Burning in a Feaver. Thomas Carew. AnAnS 2; SeCP

So she fed a whipped cat on black cream. Limerick: "There was a young lady whose dream." David Starr Jordan. TDH

So she kept her eyes trained on the ceiling. Limerick: "There once was a spinster of Ealing." Anonymous. NIP

So she took his life and laid it by,/To keep her sisters compan-eye. The Bonnie Banks O Fordie (B vers.). Anonymous. BaBo; BuBa

So she took some paper and began as she used to/when there had been a sky, to write about the sky. Spring Street Bar. Mei-Mei Berssenbrugge. WPOW

So she went her love away,/And it proved but the blink of the moon. Saw You My Father. Anonymous. OBET

...So she went/upstairs, to have herself one last look. Direct Address. Amy Gerstler. APU

So shorten I the stature of my soul. Modern Love, XII. George Meredith. TEP; ViBoPo; VLP

So silent you vanished, so sweet you endure,/And never a word. Out of the Sea. Witter ("Emanuel Morgan") Bynner. MoLP

So silvered by the familiar moon. Personality. Archibald Lampman. PeCV

So singularly among/the thundering numbers. Tiny Catullus. Steve Levine. APU

So sleeps my Love, and yet my love doth wake. Madrigal: "Sleep, wayward thoughts." John Dowland. EnRePo

So small I could have drowned it with a tear. Interlude. Karl Shapiro. DFF; MoVE

So small is the applause of men,/So great the silence of the good. St. Simon and St. Jude's Day. Cecil Frances Alexander. IrPN

So smelling their sweetness would be no theft. Unharvested. Robert Frost. BoNaP

So smiles the spring, and so smiles lovely May. To the Lady May. Aurelian Townsend. GBL; MePo

So smooth, so soft, as this. My Mistress. William Warner. EIL

So soft it falls and slow. Quatrains. Gwendolyn B. Bennett. CDC

So soft that a mother that's nigh/Her still cradle, may hear her babe sigh. The Storm-Wind. William Barnes. NOBE

So softly down you'll think him the month of May. Farmer. Padraic Fallon. OxBI

So softly out of mine! A Living Memory. William Augustus Croffut. AA

So soon to slacken, too soon disappear/In sleep I know not why, you know not how. Evensong. Carleton Drewry. GoYe

So soon we vanish! Haiku: "Tow-head dandelions." Robert Phillips. GrPl

So sorrow still doth seeme too long to last,/But joyous houres doo fly away too fast. Amoretti, LXXXVII. Edmund Spenser. AAS

"So sorry, this my garden now." The Japanese. Ogden Nash. DBV; InMe

So sovereigne a Mastery/Has Grace to cure debauchery. Of John Bunyans Life &c. John James. SCAP

So space can pierce the crevice wide between/Fast hearts, skies deep-descended intervene. Twilit Revelation. Léonie Adams. MoAB; MoAmPo

So spends a summer's jasper century. Slug in Woods. Earle Birney. CaP; NOBC; OBCV; PeCV

So stand we, great in men's eyes: our ladies ne'er turn/aside whenso they travel from Khatt... The Mufadaliyat: Gone Is Youth. Son of Jandal, Salamah. AWP

...So stay alive/to carry on tradition:/we survive Generations. Judy Dothard Simmons. CNA

So stick close to your husband and keep clear of Berry's/drop. Penal Servitude for Mrs. Maybrick. Anonymous. OxBoLi

So still will be my heart when I/Am dead. Moon Shadows. Adelaide Crapsey. AnAmPo

So strengthen me, Lord, all the way,/That I may travel to thy Mount. Silex Scintillans. Henry Vaughan. AnAnS 1

So strong thy magic or so weak am I. Last Words on Greece. George Gordon, Lord Byron. ERoP 1-2

So strong you thump O terrible drums-so loud you bugles blow. Drum-Taps. Walt Whitman. AP

So subtly will the old be shed/That I'll dream on and never know I'm dead. Scene-Shifter Death. Mary Devenport O'Neill. NeIP

So succession passes, through strangest hands. The Country Fiddler. John Montague. FaBoIP

So sup'rabundant joy shall be/The executioner of me. To Dianeme. Robert Herrick. CaPo

So sweet a load as you. Farm Cart. Eleanor Farjeon. BrR

So sweet/and so cold. This Is Just to Say. William Carlos Williams. AmP; FF; ForPo; GoJo; HoPM; InPK; InPS; NIP; NOBA; NoP; PAI; PPoe; SOTW; SpRo; TAP

So sweet sounds straight mine ear and heart do hit/That I well find no eloquence like it. Astrophel and Stella, LV. Sir Philip Sidney. AAS; SiPS

So sweet, that joy is almost pain. Prometheus Unbound. Percy Bysshe Shelley. PBBP; ViBoPo

So sweet to live? Magnificent to die! Dulce et Decorum. T. P. Cameron Wilson. HBMV

So sweetly done in verse and paint. Cimabuella (parody). Bayard Taylor. BXAP

So sweets my paines, that my paines me rejoyce. Astrophel and Stella, LVII. Sir Philip Sidney. AAS; SiPS

So t'was better Betty Botter/Bought a bit of better butter. Betty Botter Bought Some Butter. Anonymous. OxNR

So takes their dole and leaves behind/The ice on lakes and rivers. The Beggar Wind. Mary Austin. BoNaP

So talks as it's most used to do. Christabel. Samuel Taylor Coleridge. ViBoPo

So talks as it's most used to do. A Little Child, a Limber Elf. Samuel Taylor Coleridge. LoBV

So tall as to unite/roots and/heavenly bodies. There Is Good News. Josephine Jacobsen. AMV-80

So tame and defenseless/even the air could kill us. Angels in Winter. Nancy Willard. FiCP; LCAP

So Tantalus am I, and in worse pain/Amids my help, and helpless doth remain. Epitaph: "The fruit of all the service that I serve." Sir Thomas Wyatt. SiPS

So tawdry and so dear! Sunday Evening in the Common. John Hall Wheelock. HBV 1-2; MoAmPo

So tenderly and sweetly dear/As my lost boyhood is to me?   The Song the Oriole Sings.   William Dean Howells.   AmePo; HBV 1-2

...So tentatively kneading/its claws into my temples.   Your Woods. Margaret Holley.   AMV-80

So that all the world rejoices/In a day when death was dear?   To Charlotte Corday.   Osbert Sitwell.   ChMP

So that alone her happy sight/Contains perfection and delight.   Rowland's Rhyme.   Michael Drayton.   OBSC

So that ere my life be spent/Thou'lt have sent and cleared my way.   In the Heart of Jesus.   Muireadhach Albanach O Dalaigh.   CAW

So that for them to be is to advance?   The Starry Host.   John Lancaster Spalding.   AA; HBV 1-2

So that good and evil may die in equal hope.   May, 1945.   Peter Porter. OxBC

So that I count me blest a certain while.   Sonnet: Of His Lady's Face. Jacopo da Lentino.   AWP

...So that I forgot/The sheer drop from the cliff's edge, just for a moment. The Sick Image of My Father Fades.   John Horder.   TEP

So that I have my lady in my arms.   Prayer to Venus.   Geoffrey Chaucer. LiTL

So that I understand it, ladies mine.   La Vita Nuova.   Dante Alighieri. AWP

So that, iron ringing in our bones, we shall seem/admirable killers!   The Technique of Power.   Jascha Kessler.   AmPC

So that is why I am glad that I/Am not a Goop. Are you?   Table Manners. Gelett Burgess.   BBGG; OBCA

So that many would come back/to me, come back/one by one.   A Young Deer/Dust.   Hemda Roth.   VWA

So that my children may survive   Watching Salmon Jump.   Simon J. Ortiz. CDW

...So that not even an artist, a Renoir,/could have told the difference. Another Mother and Child.   Joe-Anne McLaughlin.   FAZ

So that Prussia she'll disdain.   The Complaint of New Amsterdam.   Jacob Steendam.   PAH

So that's why God invented work.   Work.   James W. Thompson.   PoToHe

...So that she/Will listen and think of love, and I of you.   Retractions. James Branch Cabell.   HBMV

So that suddenly I might find you standing at my side!   Hearing That His Friend Was Coming Back from the War.   Wang Chien.   LiTW

So that the cheek blanches and then blushes.   At First Sight.   Robert Graves.   FaBoEE; OBSP

So that the dead shall outnumber the living!   The Epic of Gilgamesh (excerpt).   Anonymous.   Prf

So that their happiness may protect us/now and on other days.   God Has Pity on Kindergarten Children.   Yehuda Amichai.   VWA

So that they will forget nothing.   Eyes of Summer.   William Stanley Merwin. CAPP

So that thy brethren may see it and say, "Go thou and do likewise!" Nauvoo.   Bayard Taylor.   OBAL

...So that understanding/May begin, and in doing so be undone.   And Ut Pictura Poesis Is Her Name.   John Ashbery.   InPS

So that we stand/Like a bright flame/Over the plain.   The Joy of a Singer. Piuvkaq.   WTO

So that when they wore out she could singham.   Limerick: "A thrifty soprano of Hingham."   Ogden Nash.   TDH

So that you may see it trembling and cold over the/world.   Almeria.   Pablo Neruda.   LiTW; WaaP

So that you may share with me/a moment of morning silence.   Ode to a Homemade Coffee Cup.   Marine Robert Warden.   AMV-81

So that your heaven-given task/May be safe forever.   All That You Have Given Me, Africa.   Anoma Kanie.   PBWP

So the body of me to all I meet or know.   I Am He That Aches with Love. Walt Whitman.   LLLT

So the count's soul they bare to Paradis.   The Song of Roland: The Last Battle.   Anonymous.   LiTW

So the day begins—/If only it were done!   The Forsaken Girl.   Randall Jarrell.   OLR

So the faire Modell broke, for want/Of roome to lodge th'Inhabitant.   An Other.   Thomas Carew.   AnAnS 2; SeCV 1-2

...So the false Spirit shall fly/And leave to thee thy true integrity.   Sonnet: Guido Cavalcanti to Dante.   Guido Cavalcanti.   OBVE

So the fancy cools, till when/That brave spirit comes again.   Not Every Day Fit for Verse.   Robert Herrick.   PoRA

So the fight was won that our Sampson planned!   Santiago.   Thomas A. Janvier.   MC; PAH

So the green and the grey move in the early morning on the/downtown streets. Working Girls.   Carl Sandburg.   SaC

So the green grave shall ease me if I cannot have that man.'   Bushes and Briars.   Anonymous.   OBET

So the gulls could snap them up.   Homage to Hart Crane.   Peter Balakian. MAYP

...So the heart, that last/Bloom of conspiracy, would not be lost!   The Coming of Dusk upon a Village in Haiti.   Henry Rago.   HoPM

So the little children sing.   Christmas Song.   Lydia Avery Coonley Ward. OHIP

...So the lonely tutors keep saying.   The Learning Soul.   Reed Whittemore. GLGT

So the love I won so hardly/Has been shattered since you have betrayed me. The Shattering of Love.   Anonymous.   WTO

So the most recent/Is the least decent.   On Thomas Moore's Poems. Anonymous.   FiBHP

So, the next Parson stubb'd and burnt it.   Baucis and Philemon.   Jonathan Swift.   CEP; EiCP; GoTL; NOEC; OAEL 1-2; OBEC

So the people must root hog or die.   The California Stage Company. Anonymous.   CoSo

...So the regulars can make up/my story: Gone to find Tequila–   Tequila. Elizabeth Spires.   MAYP

"So the rigid hills had been forgot/In darkness, if God had wasted not."   Pro Sua Vita.   Robert Penn Warren.   MoAmPo

So the spirits dance/the devil's step, and are kept/from riding the winds to the sea.   Prison Graveyard.   Etheridge Knight.   LFAC

So the spread of infidelity was checked in camp that day.   Silver Jack's Religion.   John P. Jones.   BPAW; CoSo

...So the sun/Peoples all heaven, although he be but one.   The Telephone. Hilaire Belloc.   MoVE

So the touched needle courts the pole.   Great God, Thy Works.   Mather Byles.   AH

So the world woos its children back for an evening kiss.   Letters from a Father.   Mona Van Duyn.   FYAP

So their twa souls flew up to heaven,/And there shall ever remain.   Bonny Bee Hom.   Anonymous.   BaBo; ESPB

So then be their masters your son and mine.   Grace before Meat.   Robert D. FitzGerald.   NOAV

So then he slew that Eastmure king,/Beneath that garden tree.   Fause Foodrage (B version).   Anonymous.   ESPB

So then, let it be.   The Sinking of the Mendi.   S. E. K. Mqhayi.   PeSA

So then replies brave Wolfe, "I die with pleasure."   Brave Wolfe. Anonymous.   BaBo

So there entwined in a true lovier's knot,/For all true lovier's to admire, ire, ire...   Lord Lovel (A vers.).   Anonymous.   ViBoFo

So there was an end of Lily white Sand,/His ass, and the Ratcatcher's daughter!   The Ratcatcher's Daughter.   Anonymous.   GBP; OxBoLi

So there was no one left but me.   A Good Play.   Robert Louis Stevenson. MoShBr; TiPo

So therefore we say all.   I Have a Pretty Little Flow'r.   Francis Daniel Pastorius.   SCAP

So they beaved all day in a cozy wee den.   Over in the Meadow. Anonymous.   SoPo

So they can carry their dark glasses in their hand.   After They Put Down Their Overalls.   Lenrie Peters.   TTY

So they canonized him by the name of Jim Crow!   The Ingoldsby Legends: The Jackdaw of Rheims.   Richard Harris Barham.   PaPo

So they chased that man out of Toulon.   Limerick: "There was an old man of Toulon.   William Jay Smith.   TDH

So they closed their eyes to the earth and skies on India's burning shore.   The Paisley Officer.   Anonymous.   ShS

So they did, vanishing away off and shouting.   Summer.   Josephine Miles. FaBoWP

So they flew through a flaw in the flue.   Limerick: "A flea and a fly in a flue."   Anonymous.   LiBL

So they had to give up with Miss Hartley.   Limerick: "A lady whose name was Miss Hartley."   William Jay Smith.   TDH

So they just stood still and looked wise.   Beautiful Sunday.   Jake Falstaff. BoNaP

So they pause and from their distance/outside of time/They wait.   Horses at Valley Store.   Leslie Marmon Silko.   VoR

So they sent me down to Huntsville to wear my life away.   The Bad Boy. Anonymous.   CoSo

So they sipped it and ate honey/Beneath the maple tree.   The Five Little Fairies.   Maud Burnham.   HBVY

So they smashed that Old Man of Whitehaven.   Limerick: "There was an old man of Whitehaven."   Edward Lear.   EBEV; NBM; VLP

So they smashed that Old Man with a gong.   Limerick: "There was an old man with a gong."   Edward Lear.   GoJo; TDH

So they still are quick and well/Who should be, by rights, in hell. Frustration.   Dorothy Parker.   DBV

So they that suffered wrong and were upbraded/Shall be made friends in a left-handed trance.   Nonsense.   Anonymous.   FaBoNo; NA

So they that suffered wrong and were upbraded/Shall be made friends in a left handed Trance.   Odd but True.   Anonymous.   FaBoCo

So they toiled and were wise,/Where the men dig and delve.   Over in the Meadow.   Oliver A. Wadsworth.   MoShBr

So they would rest and understand. Ollie, Answer Me. Stephen Berg. NaP

So Thine the breath/That must continue it, till death/Be dead and cease to be. The Farewell. *Anonymous.* OxBoCh

So this religious rascal sure/is able to Stock a nation. The Lusty Fryer of Flanders. *Anonymous.* CoMu

So those who never marry may well be called wise./So, gentlemen, excuse me; goodbye. Fuller and Warren. Moses Whitecotton. AmFP; CoSo; ViBoFo

So Thou but mold the remnant clay/To shape not all unworthy of the Thee in me. Epilogue (excerpt). William Alexander Percy. TrPWD

So, Thou dear master God, look down and see/Whether I do Thy bidding heedfully. The Artisan. Alice Brown. TrPWD

So thou'lt leave him and goe with me. The Second Nimphall. Michael Drayton. AtBAP

So thou, with fencing art,/Feigning to wound mine eyes, hast hit my heart. Ah Cupid, I mistook thee. Francis Davison. EG

So, though thou hidden wert, my heart and eye/Did turn to thee by mutual sympathy. Sonnets to Philomel. Sir John Davies. SiPS

So through the Plymouth woods passed onward the bridal procession. The Courtship of Miles Standish. Henry Wadsworth Longfellow. BeLS

So through the streams Leander did enjoy her sight. Shall I Come, If I Swim? Wide Are the Waves, You See. Thomas Campion. EnLoPo

So thus you may well know by that/They were two lovers dear. The Lass of Roch Royal (A version). *Anonymous.* BaBo; ESPB

So Tiberius might have sat/Had Tiberius been a cat. Matthias (excerpt). Matthew Arnold. PCat

So tides will turn and sweep him, too, away. Lucy Answers. Helen Ehrlich. SUW

So, till the judgment that yourself arise,/You live in this, and dwell in lovers' eyes. Sonnets, LV: "Not marble, nor the gilded monuments." William Shakespeare. AWP; BLPL; CBEP; CTC; DiPo; ExPo; FaBoEn; FaFP; FF; ForPo; HeIP; InPo; LiTB; LiTL; LoBV; MasP; MBW 1-2; NIP; NOBE; NoP; OAEL 1-2; OAEP; OBSC; PeHV; PoEL 1-5; PoRA; PP; PPoe; SeCeV; TEP; TrGrPo; ViBoPo

So time is counted, so far back, so far ahead, in/measurements of sweet kisses. Counting. Carl Sandburg. MoLP

So tiny that I, weak and wretched, am able to contain Thee!... Psalm. Murilo Mendes. MoRP

So to conclude calamity in rest. The Lovers Melancholy. John Ford. PoEL 1-5

So to cut Holland's head from England's shoulders. On Sir John Fenwick. Henry Hall. APAS

So to deceive yourself until you move/into that house whose tenants do not love. The Things. Conrad Aiken. HAP

So to my heart brought full beatitude. Of Wonder. Mary Gilmore. BoAV

So to the height and nick/We up be wound,/No matter by what hand or trick. Song: "Of thee, kind boy, I ask no red and white." Sir John Suckling. LoBV

So to thee farewell. Love Me Little, Love Me Long. *Anonymous.* CBEP; NoP

So to Thy Pity, I commend/My self, and my afflicted Friend. To My Worthy Friend, Mr. James Bayley... Nicholas Noyes. SCAP

So too to extract false comfort from that word. Manchouli. William Empson. CoBMV

So tossing faction will o'erwhelm/One crazy double-bottomed realm. Verses Said to Be Written on the Union. Jonathan Swift. APAS

So touchly stood these to their taske and made their worke/as even. The Iliad. Homer. OBVE

So toyl the Nymphs, to snatch and to defend/The men of Lusus from a dismal end. The Luciad. Luís de Camoens. OBVE

So true a fool is love, that in your will/Though you do anything, he thinks no ill. Sonnets, LVII: "Being your slave, what should I do but tend." William Shakespeare. GTBS; GTBS-P; HAP; LiTL; OBEV; PeHV; PoEL 1-5; ViBoPo

So truly set all forth as now/'Tis writ within this book I trow. The Romance of the Rose. Guillaume de Lorris. EG; EnLi 1-2; OAEL 1-2; PoEL 1-5

So trustless is love's treasure. Come, You Pretty False-Eyed Wanton. Thomas Campion. ELP

So turn again, pony,/Turn again home. Trot along Pony. Dorothy and Marion Edey Grider. SoPo; TiPo

So turn the wheel round so bonny. The One-Horned Ewe. *Anonymous.* GBP

–So turn the World's bright joys to cold and blank disgust. The Glow-Worm. Charlotte Smith. FM

So turne they still about, and change in restlesse wise. The Faerie Queene. Edmund Spenser. PoEL 1-5

So Turnus, hasting headlong to the Town,/Should'ring and shoving, bore the Squadrons down. The Aeneid. Virgil (Publius Vergilius Maro). OBVE

SO UNCOY SOONEST ANDY Telegram One. Adrian Mitchell. PV

So undiscern'd she mov'd, that we/Perceiv'd she stirr'd, but did not see. Seeing Her Dancing. Robert Heath. OBS; OBSP

...So unimaginably young a star "Noone" Autumnal This Great Lady's Gaze. Edward Estlin Cummings. CrMA

So union members are we. Raggedy. *Anonymous.* FSW

So-up, so-up, they gave me a bowl of soup. Soup Song. Maurice Sugar. FSW

So useless and so void. Jean. Paul Potts. NeBP

So vale, vale; ho, ho, ho! Robin Good-Fellow. *Anonymous.* FaBoCh; ViBoPo

So vast a thing to plant a tree! Arbor Day. Dorothy Brown Thompson. SiSoSe

So verses start them on their way. Poem: "So they begin." Boris Pasternak. TrJP

So very sad his eyes from little boys and girls. Evening Music. Kendrick Smithyman. AnNZ

So very, very, very Vegetarian. The Logical Vegetarian. Gilbert Keith Chesterton. CenHV

So violent, yet long these furies be. The Storm. John Donne. CABL; EtS; NOBE; PoPle

So vivid that they take from keenest sight/The liquid veil that seeks not to hide them. Lyre! Though Such Power Do in Thy Magic Live. William Wordsworth. VLP

So wags the good old world away/Forever and a day. So Wags the World. Ellen Mackay Hutchinson Cortissoz. AA

So was I. On the Eve of a Birthday. Geoffrey Grigson. NAs

So was the first day/After the gentle birth. St. Stephen's Day. Patric Dickinson. OBCP

So was the friend that made this moan. An Elegy, or Friend's Passion, for His Astrophel (excerpt). *Anonymous.* PBBP

So was the high aspyring with huge ruine humbled. The Faerie Queene. Edmund Spenser. NoP

So we all fled on. The Cry-Bird Journey. Stan Rice. NPGG

So we all got down and walked,/as our good manners required. Manners. Elizabeth Bishop. CTBA; GOYP; NCSH; OxBC

So we are the cuckolds, boys, all in a row. A New Song, Called the Frolicsome Sea Captain, or Tit for Tat. *Anonymous.* OBSS

So we can count our lambing times as I am counting sheep. A Lincolnshire Shepherd. *Anonymous.* OBET

,So we can go/to see A NIGHT AT THE OPERA. Personal Poem #7. Ted Berrigan. ANYP

So we can snuff the candle out together. Cherry Blossoms. Michael Lewis. UnTE

So we clap on Dutch bottoms just 20 per cent. The Dutch. George Canning. OBTV

So we freeze on,/Until the grave increase our cold. Employment. George Herbert. JCP; OxBoCh

So we, grown penitent, on serious thinking,/Leave whoring, and devoutly fall to drinking. The Spanish Friar. John Dryden. OBSV

So we may identify/What we've ruined by and by. To Nature Seekers. Robert William Chambers. MoShBr

"So we may wear whatever we like,/Anything, everything!" Freaks of Fashion. Christina Georgina Rossetti. FM

So we moved out, sad in the vast offing,/having our precious lives, but not our friends. The Odyssey. Homer. NAWM 1-2; WTO

So we remitted to another day/The prosecution of Et Cetera. Et Cetera. John Wilmot, Earl of Rochester. UnTE

So we sat there all afternoon. On the Lawn at the Villa. Louis Simpson. CoAP; LCAP; OBAL; OxBC; PPP

...So we shall/Be one, and one another's all. Love's Infiniteness. John Donne. LiTL

So we shall meet! Again. Charlotte Mew. MoAB; MoBrPo

So we the Doom may pass,/And see Him in the Face. He Would Have His Lady Sing. Digby Mackworth Dolben. CAW; EBEV; GoBC

So we threw away our skins./Yiya wo! Was It All Worth While? *Anonymous.* WTO

So we tumble to bed. Tumbling. *Anonymous.* OxBChV

So wedg'd the helmets and boss'd bucklers stood... The Iliad. Homer. OBVE

So were his troubles small. A Dead Child. Lucian [(or Lucianus)]. EnLi 1-2; LiTW

...–So/Wert thou to me–and art thou to the world. Shelley. Robert Browning. OBRV

So what? Haiku Ambulance. Richard Brautigan. InPK

So what could I do but laugh and go? Called Away. Richard Le Gallienne. SoPo; SUS

So what do you think/Of my little old man? Hey Diddle Diddle. *Anonymous.* OxNR

So what, I think happily. So what! More Than Fifty. Jack Gilbert. NPGG

...So what/if it fades and dies? A Head. James Schuyler. NoAm; PoM

So what the hell are we fighting for? World War II. *Anonymous.* FaFP

So what was Heaven's gift we'll reckon thine. The Siege: Seal Up Her Eyes, O Sleep. William Cartwright. EG

A soft grass covers them and light falls. From. Tom Paulin. FaBoIP

Soft hope is the relique I bear,/And my solace wherever I go. Pastoral Ballad: Absence. William Shenstone. OBEC

A soft hot star hugged by the sea. Swamp. Roberta Hill. VoR

Soft I vow–'tis done–Oh, feel here! Shakespearean Soliloquy in Progress: "To shave, or not to..."(parody). T. F. Dillon Croker. BXAP

Soft putty to their strong demands. Cudworth's Undergraduate Ode to a Bare Behind. John Ower. AMV-81

A soft sleep, undisturb'd by love. Across the Sky the Daylight Crept. Coventry Patmore. GBL

Soft, soft, soft, and deep, deep, deep! Winter Sleep. Elinor Wylie. NePA

The soft, south wind of memory blows. A Painted Fan. Louise Chandler Moulton. AA

Soft white/Popcorn. The Popcorn-Popper. Dorothy Walter Baruch. BrR

The soft wind of summer blew in the light green trees. The Circus. Kenneth Koch. ANYP

...Softening the surprise/Of his rapt gaze on unfamiliar skies! Bayard Taylor. John Greenleaf Whittier. HBV 1-2

Softer music make–That my lover may not wake... Rain, Rain. Zoë Akins. HBMV

Softly an inch from your enchanted face. Gesture. Donald Finkel. InPK

Softly I set my foot/On the path to my long home. I Know That I Must Die Soon. Else Lasker-Schüler. TrJP

Softly, let the measure be/Unheard, but never wholly. Harp Music–. Rolfe Humphries. UnS

Softly my friend/softly Softly Softly. Richard Shelton. NPAW

Softly, now softly lies/Sleeping. Weep You No More. John Dowland. CH; EBEV; EIL; ELP; EnLoPo; ExPo; ForPo; GBL; HAP; LoBV; NoP; OAEP; PoPle; SoSe; TrGrPo; ViBoPo

Softly,/On a summer's day. Names. Dorothy Aldis. SUS

Softly ring, He comes to rest/In the quiet of my breast. Easter Song. Kenneth Leslie. MoRP

Softly rustling as He cometh o'er the far green hill. In the Cool of the Evening. Alfred Noyes. HBV 1-2

Softly she comes to me,/And goes to God again. The Invisible Bride. Edwin Markham. HBV 1-2

Softly sings where the columbines grow. Land Where the Columbines Grow. Arthur J. Fynn. PoOW

Softly, slowly: Minstrel, wake! Fairy Song. Winthrop Mackworth Praed. SeCePo

Softly, softly let him tread,/Nor disturb her narrow bed. On the Death of a Cat. Christina Georgina Rossetti. PCat

Softly swell the trembling air,/To complete our concert fair. Welcome Every Guest. *Anonymous.* TrAS

Softly the 'cellos sing:/"Colombine'.../"Colombine'... Colombine. Hugh McCrae. PoAu 1-2

Softly then, his footsteps. Skylights. Tess Gallagher. MAYP

Softly, too, by this most gentle/Rein of all, this drop of water. At a Child's Baptism. Vassar Miller. GoJo

Softly tracing the mortar with our fingers. Indian Summer, 1927. Anne Hussey. AMV-81

Softly will I drop beside thee like/the dew upon Hermon. Love Song. Judah Al-Harizi. LiTW; TrJP

The soggy small marsh, nutgrass and swordweed! Runoff. Archie Randolph Ammons. PPP

Soil glistens, the furrow rolls, sleet shifts, brightens. Boy Remembers in the Field. Raymond Knister. CaP; NOBC

Soirees at Saint Cloud...a bluish vapour. Eighteen-Seventy. Arthur Rimbaud. FaBoPV; OBWP

Solace hast thou for pain! The Dying Words of Stonewall Jackson. Sidney Lanier. PAH

Solace in the midst of woe. Hymn to the Holy Spirit. Stephen Langton. TrCP

Sold his wife for a minikin pin. Jack in the Pulpit. *Anonymous* OxNR

Soldier,beware of mrs smith In Heavenly Realms of Hellas Dwelt. Edward Estlin Cummings. NOBA; OBSV

The soldier dying dies upon a kiss,/The very kiss of Christ. Summer in England, 1914. Alice Meynell. BrRo; SBG

Soldier, I wish you well. The Street Sounds to the Soldiers' Tread. Alfred Edward Housman. PPP

A soldier of his Captain Christ. Lincoln. *Anonymous.* OHIP

Soldier, sit you down and idle/At the inn of night for aye. Soldier from the Wars Returning. Alfred Edward Housman. LiTB; OBMV; OBWP

Soldier, sleep sound! Requiem. Joseph Lee. OHIP

A soldier stalks before my door. Contrary Theses (I). Wallace Stevens. OxBA

Soldiers and poor, unable to rejoice. The Owl. Edward ("Edward Eastaway") Thomas. DTC; EBEV; FaBoRV; FaBoTw; FF; GTBS-P; LiTB; NoAm; NOBE; NoP; OAEL 1-2; PoPle; PPoe; SoSe; UnPo

Soldiers of the Cross. Jacob's Ladder. *Anonymous* FSW

The soldiers of World War Two. The End of World War One. Sharon Olds. AMV-81

Soldiers on his side. Jesu, Come on Board. Johann C. Pyrlaeus. AH

Soldiers, this solitude/Through which we go/Is I.' Napoleon. Walter De La Mare. FaBoCh; FaBoTw; LoGBV; MoVE; NOBE

Sole is for Sunday, swell me net full. Swell My Net Full. *Anonymous* OBSS

Sole mark on that huge-meadowed plain! Nepenthe. George Darley. OBNC; OBRV

The sole necessity of Earth and Heaven! Prelude. John Greenleaf Whittier. AP

Sole watchman of the wide & single stars. Eleven Addresses to the Lord. John Berryman. OxBC; UnPo

Solely because thou art my God,/And my eternal King. Hymn: "My God, I love thee, not because." Robert Francis. WGRP

...The solemn report of those/Who have done nothing and will never die. Brummell at Calais. John Glassco. PeCV

The solemn "Yea, I understand!" Fraternity. Anne Reeve Aldrich. AA

Solicitudes canine, four-footed amities. Sonnet: To Tartar, a Terrier Beauty. Thomas Lovell Beddoes. NOBV; OBNC

Solid in the/spring and serious/he walks away. April. Yvor Winters. ELU; RFM

Solid joys and lasting treasure/None but Zion's children know. Zion; or, the City of God. John Newton. NOEC

The solid man and the coxcomb. Words for Music Perhaps. William Butler Yeats. AtBAP

The solid sepulchre where lie all things that blight,/Both avaricious silence and the massive night Funeral Toast. Stephane Mallarme. LiTW

Solidarity Forever,/For the union makes us strong. Solidarity Forever. Ralph Chaplin. FSW

A solitary being begins/its slow dance... The Cave of Night. John Montague. CIP

...A solitary broken hand or two upon the scales/like butchers do... A Street in Kaufman-Ville: or a Note Thrown to Carolyn... James (Olumo) Cunningham. JB

Solitude walks one heavy step more near. Solitude. Harold Monro. BSV; MoBrPo; TrGrPo

A solo clarinet in western wind. Anabasis. Rodney Nelson. AMV-81

Solutions to the Problem,/Of course, wait. Dinner Guest: Me. Langston Hughes. BPo

...Solve/resolve the mystical dance. On the Birth of Dan Goldman. Daniel Berrigan. NAs

Solve them to unity. Einstein (1929). Archibald MacLeish. ImOP

Somber November in amber and umber embering out. The Dying Garden. Howard Nemerov. Psk

The sombre city that will never cease/its lost unhappy crying in the night. Chez Madame. Sam Harrison. NeIP

Some are born to endless night. Auguries of Innocence. William Blake. TreFT

Some are loud others/merely sick,/saddened. Inebriates. Philip Brasfield. LFAC

Some are written in green rain and stone. All Songs. B. Sanford Page. AMV-81

Some baked some fried/some burned/some blue White People. David Henderson. PoBA

Some bell-like evening when the May's in bloom. Almswomen. Edmund Charles Blunden. OBMV; OxBTC

Some black star climbing/the deep globe of his eye. Black Money. Tess Gallagher. GeTw; LTB

Some body (pleeease)/CALL/for help) Somebody Call (For Help). Carolyn M. Rodgers. JB

Some brown skin woman/gon' be the death of you Barbecue Blues. Barbecue Bob Hicks. BluL

Some buried theirs. The stones tell when and where. Despair. William Stanley Merwin. AmPC

Some call it Consecration,/And others call it God. Each in His Own Tongue. William Herbert Carruth. AmePo; BBV; BLPA; HBV 1-2; OHFP; TRV; WBLP; WGRP

Some call it love, some grace. Its Name Is Known. D. L. Kelleher. NeIP

Some can be poets, and some can't. De Senectute. Franklin Pierce ("F.P.A.") Adams. HBMV

Some cannot praise him: I am one of those. Three Epigrams. Theodore Roethke. NLV

Some chicken-bliss whereof he knows/And I am unaware. The Darkling Chicken (parody). Robert Peters. BXAP

Some compromise is possible with life. Couple. Walter Stone. NYBP

Some creature on the waste sea-floor/Is spinning a heavenly city/From its dreaming shell. Walking the Beach. Sarah Youngblood. IHMS

Some cursed him with Iscariot, that day in Baltimore. The Sack of Baltimore. Thomas Osborne Davis. IrPN

Some day.–Alas, alas! Near Lanivet, 1872. Thomas Hardy. AWP; CMoP; LoBV; NoAm

Some day ere shall perish my Little Dark/Rose! The Little Dark Rose. Owen Roe MacWard. OnYI

Some day, for all your arms can do,/The dust will hold you fast.   The Sweeper.   Agnes Lee.   HBMV; QFR

Some day mankind will be claiming/The world the dreamers made.   The Dreamers Cry Their Dream.   Lucia Trent.   PGD

Some day more kind I fate may find,/Some night, kiss thee.   The Wandering Knight's Song.   John Gibson Lockhart.   HBV 1-2

Some day–some day–I must cross that rim!   The Edge of the World.   Mary Fanny Youngs.   BrR

Some day thou shalt it view.   I Have Seen Higher, Holier Things Than These.   Arthur Hugh Clough.   OAEP

Some day we'll crown You our Lord and King.   God Incarnate.   Ruth M. Williams.   BePJ

Some day we meet the dwarf and force the answer.   The Bear.   Ann Stanford.   WSC

Some day when men have half their evens/we'll dare talk proudly of Old Thad Stevens.   Old Thad Stevens.   Kenneth Porter.   NePoAm-2

Some days, yes. We look up and follow.   At the Edge of Town.   William Stafford.   NNaP

...Some echo of that Song/Of Songs that was sung to the soul of the madman, Blake!   Mad Blake.   William Rose Benet.   HBMV

Some end is there, we indeed may gain?   Self-Deception.   Matthew Arnold.   MaVP

Some even stretch out their arms/To/Rest.   Chairs.   Valerie Worth.   NTCP

Some even to themselves seem strange/Thorough their own delay.   O Do Not Prize Thy Beauty.   Anonymous   LiTL

Some face and legs   Unusual.   Larry Eigner.   FAZ

Some fellows talk about New York,/But I shall stay at home.   A Country Boy in Winter.   Sarah Orne Jewett.   OBCA

Some find it in forgetting,/And some in memory.   To Each His Own.   Margaret Root Garvin.   HBV 1-2

Some flake of the dust is brushed away/That had settled over my heart.   A City Flower.   Henry Austin Dobson.   TEP

Some flowers of rhyme untouched by Time,/And songs that sing forever.   Recollections of "Lalla Rookh."   John Townsend Trowbridge.   OBAL

Some food, some sun, some work, some fun, some-one.   Human Needs.   E.M. Walker.   PoL

Some forlorn and henpecked brother,/When he sees, shall crow again.   A Parody on A Psalm of Life.   Oliver Wendell Holmes.   BLPA

Some games I aim to lose, not win.   Shooting Gallery.   Martin Galvin.   AMV-80

Some gas like helium must be innate.   Innate Helium.   Robert Frost.   ImOP

Some gave them plum cake,/And sent them out of town.   The Lion and the Unicorn.   Mother Goose.   EvOK; HBV 1-2; OxBoLi

Some go in by the door called "push,"/And some by the door called "pull."   Fame.   Anonymous.   TreFT

Some god looks/truly down/upon them.   The People.   Robert Creeley.   VGW

Some good old hermit of a horse that fed/With loud bite in his dark and tranquil field.   Country Wooing (parody) (excerpt).   J. C. Squire.   BXAP

Some good wine! and who would lack it,/Ev'n on board the Lisbon Packet?   Lines to Mr. Hodgson.   George Gordon, Lord Byron.   ERoP 1-2

Some high magnificence to last as long/As the clear vision of the summer child.   To the Ghost of a Kite.   James Wright.   NePoEA

Some hot, some cold.   Some Hot, Some Cold.   Thomas Campion.   LO

Some ill hap of Time is sure to meet him at morningtide.   This World.   Abu-l-Ala al-Maarri.   LiTW

Some just discovered face that once was ours.   In Front of the Seine, Recalling the Rio De La Plata.   Silvina Ocampo.   AMV-80

Some lamb/Says Death.   Some Lamb.   Stan Rice.   NPGG

Some like chaff;/Not I.   Not I.   Robert Louis Stevenson.   NA; NOBL

Some little bug is going to find you some day.   Some Little Bug.   Roy Atwell.   PoLf; ShM

Some living source, half-imagined and half-real/Pulses in the fictive water that I feel.   The Water Carrier.   John Montague.   FaBoIP

Some lonely soul to bless.   Let Me Be a Giver.   Mary Carolyn Davies.   PoToHe

Some may not be slain but live,/Forgotten in the thaw.   Victory.   Eileen Duggan.   AnNZ

Some Mrs. Hopkins, taking tea/And toast upon the Wall of China!   Rhymes on the Road (excerpt).   Thomas Moore.   OBSV; OBTV

Some musing seraph had let fall a flower.   Evening.   Edward Rowland Sill.   AnAmPo

Some new Equation, given–/But, what of that?   I reason, earth is short.   Emily Dickinson.   TAP

Some of husbands, some of lovers,/Which an empty dream discovers.   Queen Mab.   Ben Jonson.   HBV 1-2

Some of the stones are broken/but they are my friends   The Angel and the Anchorite.   Richard Shelton.   NPAW

Some one, entering in the dark,/Later on, may see it shine.   Candles.   Anonymous   GoBC

Some one may live in deeds we leave behind,/However unrecorded and unsigned.   The Stump Is Not the Tombstone.   Ralph W. Seager.   AMV-81

Some one unknown perhaps, and far away,/On bended knee.   Because We Do Not See.   Anonymous.   BLRP

Some other day we'll have lightning again.   Magic Lantern.   William Stafford.   FAZ

Some other Paris does to your fair Helen.   To a History Professor.   Anonymous   UnTE

Some other spirit feels it dying.   Favonius.   Hubert Church.   AnNZ

...Some part/of us forever gone on loan to hawks.   Spring Hawks.   Jim Thomas.   AMV-81

Some poems have no beginning and no end.   Smile.   D. M. Thomas.   AMV-81

Some poor old mother is waiting for her/Who has seen better days.   She May Have Seen Better Days.   James Thornton.   FSN

Some power in my revenge convey/That love to her I cast away.   Disdain Returned.   Thomas Carew.   AWP; CaPo; CavP; EnLit; HBV 1-2; InPo; OBS; SeCV 1-2; TEP; TrGrPo; ViBoPo

Some say both, all quote Torah.   Pilpul.   Rodger Kamenetz.   APU; VWA

Some say, moreover, that her tower is not of/ivory and that she is not even virtuous nor a/princess   The Princess of Dreams.   Ernest Christopher Dowson.   VLP

Some scarlet berries and a Christmas rose.   Strange, All-Absorbing Love.   Digby Mackworth Dolben.   GoBC; TrPWD

Some secret sense shall cry, 'Tis you and/–you!   Recognition.   John White Chadwick.   AA

Some seek in art–the Art of peace–   The martyr poets–did not tell–.   Emily Dickinson.   EyDe

Some shone like stars, and, as the chariot passed,/Bedimmed all other light.   Queen Mab.   Percy Bysshe Shelley.   GN

Some silver-fingered fountain steals the world.   This is the Garden.   Edward Estlin Cummings.   BoLiVe; MoAmPo

Some small grey fur is pulsing in its grip.   The End of the Weekend.   Anthony Hecht.   ConAP; FaBoMo; HAP; LiTM; NePoEA-2; SM; WeW

Some smile, I sigh, to see thy madness such/That that which stands not, stands thee in so much.   Against an Old Lecher.   Sir John (1561-1612) Harington.   FaBoEE

Some soul, poor soul, in its mute weeping,/Drags the specter of pain to asphodel prairies.   Your Passing, Fleet Passing.   Joseph Eliyia.   VWA

Some sparrows chirruped on a tree/Outside, and then they flew away.   Paul.   James Wright.   NePoEA; PoPl

Some specialness within.   Of Robert Frost.   Gwendolyn Brooks.   NoAm; NOBA

Some speck of fire the night eclipsed.   Firefly.   George Uba.   BrSi

Some spirit dies with the murdering of trees.   Mrs. Asquith Tries to Save the Jacarandas.   Harold Witt.   AMV-81

Some sticky coins/compose their prayers./He is not there.   Looking for Maimonides: Tiberias.   Shirley Kaufman.   VWA

Some stilly shaping thing that bides and broods?   A Man's Sliding Mood.   Mary Elizabeth ("E") Fullerton.   CBAP

...Some store/Of emmit's eggs; what would he more?   Oberon's Feast.   Robert Herrick.   ViBoPo

Some stormy council hold in the high trees.   The Garden in September.   Robert Bridges.   PoPle

Some sudden thought, some careless rhyme/Still floats above the wrecks of Time.   Of an Old Song.   William Edward Hartpole Lecky.   WGRP

Some surfaces responded to your touch?   Technique.   Burnham Eaton.   GoYe

Some taint by proxy prickles on my skin.   Amelia Street.   Frank Ormsby.   CIP

Some talent that is rare.   Envy.   Charles and Mary Lamb.   OxBChV

Some thanks for every lovely tree/That dead men grew for me.   Planting Trees.   Violet Helen Friedlaender.   BoNaP

...Some/things/are, even if no one comes.   In Winter.   Robert Wallace.   BoNaP

Some think it service in the place/Where we, with late, celestial face,/Please God, shall ascertain   Musicians wrestle everywhere.   Emily Dickinson.   UnS

Some, though they shun the Frying-pan,/Do leap into the Fire.   The Pilgrim's Progress.   John Bunyan.   EBEV

Some thought, much whim, and all a contradiction.   To a Young Lady.   Richard Savage.   CBEP; OBEC

Some three years before the war.   The Aged Stranger.   Bret (Francis Bret Harte) Harte.   AA; AmFN; MaC; TreFS

–Some time after/and in shallower water.   One Time.   Douglas Livingstone.   PeSA

Some time I think I'll live that way.   The Hippo.   Theodore Roethke.   VGW

Some tune they sang, but not,/Not the Old Hundred.   The Village Choir (parody).   Anonymous   FaBoPa

Some useful door–/somewhere–/up there.   Riding the Elevator into the Sky.   Anne Sexton.   NYP

Some Victorious answer/to everything.   Dog.   Lawrence Ferlinghetti.   HoPM

...Some/wait alone/for conspicuous men/to come.   Lines for the Planned Parenthood Clinic.   Linda Westfall Spurrier.   SOTS

...Some/Wander the world, and never find a home.   Bitter Sanctuary.   Harold Monro.   FaBoMo; LiTB; OBMV

Some wanness where, I think, thy foot may fall!   The Ring and the Book.   Robert Browning.   CoBE; FiP; OAEP; OBVV

Some were lame and some were blind/And some they could not hear.   The Beggar.   *Anonymous.*   OBET

Some whiskers, and four eyes!   Tuscaloosa Sam.   Robert Henry Newell.   OBAL

Some will rise that clear morning like the swallows.   Dream of Rebirth.   Roberta Hill Whiteman.   CDW; TWSS

Some woman that I used to have/gonna be my baby some day   Telephone Arguin' Blues.   J. D. (Jelly Jaw) Short.   BluL

Some women understand it.   Otis.   Lorenzo Thomas.   APU

Some word huge and black in my mouth.   The Word.   Neil Weiss.   NYBP

Some word/To tell.   Birth.   Langston Hughes.   NAs

Some would claim that I have succeeded/in this.   My Style.   Charles Bukowski.   AMV-81

...Some young lovers break in/& then we get ripped & then we get ripped.   Stay Beautiful.   Jeff Wright.   APU

Somebody asked me to marry him,/"Course I said, "All right."   Somebody (with music).   *Anonymous*   AS

Somebody bet on de bay.   Camptown Races.   Stephen Collins Foster.   FSW; PSoN

Somebody else has arrived. Somebody else is writing.   My Life by Somebody Else.   Mark Strand.   GP

Somebody else's photograph.   Hut.   G. J. F. Dutton.   PoSH

Somebody loves us all.   Filling Station.   Elizabeth Bishop.   AmC; FaBoMo; HaCAP; HAP; InPK; NoP; NYBP; WeW

Somebody muffed it? Somebody wanted to joke.   A Sunset of the City.   Gwendolyn Brooks.   FaBoWP; PBWP

Somebody's darling lies buried here.   Somebody's Darling.   Marie Ravenal de la Coste.   BLPA; HBV 1-2; TreF; UnPo; WBLP

Somebody's done for.   Death & Co.   Sylvia Plath.   CMoP; ConAP; FF; LCAP; PrIm

Somebody's dying way over yonder,/Way over in the new buryin' groun'.   Way Over in the New Buryin' Groun' (with music).   *Anonymous*   AS

Somebody stole my myths.   Song to the Tune of "Somebody Stole My Gal."   X. J. Kennedy.   CoPo

Somebody to stay with me always/And never to leave me alone.   New Jail.   *Anonymous*   AmFP

Someday he'll leave me: then what will I do?   How Lies Grow.   Maxine Chernoff.   APU

...Someday I'm going to ask/him why poets just get by and/what it means to be a pangolin.   Testing Ground.   Karla M. Hammond.   AMV-81

Someday I will show them this basket/filled with water/that sings.   Owl and Rooster.   Gladys Cardiff.   STE

...Someday, in due course,/I will find that it's still there.   Mementos.   W. D. Snodgrass.   FF; HeIP; MoAmPo; PPP

Someday it will return to trouble you.   The Revenant.   Robert Siegel.   GeTw

Someday no-one will march there at all.   The Band Played Waltzing Matilda.   Eric Bogle.   OBET

Someday we'll behold His face–/Wondrous Son of God.   Wondrous Son of God.   Berniece Goertz.   STF

(Somehow when Whatchmacallit and Whathisface are "out of/town.")   Your Friends Come and Go.   Jeffrey Miller.   APU

Somehow began the/measured rise.   The Diver.   Robert Earl Hayden.   AmPP; BPo; LiSp; MOS

Somehow, catch all the height and breadth of sky.   Horizontal World.   Thomas Saunders.   CaP

Somehow it seemed to me that God/Somewhere had just relieved a picket.   Relieving Guard.   Bret (Francis Bret Harte) Harte.   RoGo

Somehow, it would appear, we drifted right/On through it into the future, into the night.   Six Years Later.   Joseph Brodsky.   AMV-80

Somehow or other we have to find it.   We Let It Go That He Was a Perfect Man.   Nicanor Parra.   PoL

Somehow, the three of us.   Fly in December.   Robert Wallace.   NYBP

Somehow they are a lie.   Elemental.   D. H. Lawrence.   NoP

Somehow thickening their grace.   Spade Scharnweber.   Don Welch.   Psk

Somehow to protest death rather than merely/acquiesce.   Diseases of the Moon.   Doug Fetherling.   NeAC; PoL

Someone before him to see and to know.   Bouquet of Belle Scavoir.   Wallace Stevens.   MoAB; MoAmPo

Someone beside you (rather like "crying') weeping.   A Considered Reply to a Child.   Jonathan Price.   BoLoP

Someone had taken Mr. Hardy's place.   At Max Gate.   Siegfried Sassoon.   NoAm

Someone half in love with herself/and half in love with the world.   January 18, 1979.   John Yau.   APU

"Someone has to plant them,' she said.   Ross's Poems.   Geoffrey Lehmann.   CBAP

Someone is in charge of telling mother that she'll never see us again.   Addio a la Mamma.   Noe Jitrik.   VWA

...Someone is noticing you.   Middle of the Day.   Jack Driscoll.   WOLT

Someone is sinking today.   Throw out the Lifeline.   Edward Smith Ufford.   TreF

Someone is swimming to the surface/of our sleep.   Telephoning It.   Murray Edmond.   OCNZ

Someone is waiting and watching there,/In the little green orchard.   The Little Green Orchard.   Walter De La Mare.   EvOK

Someone is watching me./Look out./Keep quiet.   Leoun.   Jean Cocteau.   OBVE

Someone knows that time can't fly.   As Long as the Heart Beats.   Christine Zawadiwsky.   AMV-81

Someone must think/she is beautiful.   The Distant Orgasm.   James Tate.   AmPA

Someone of it is answering to/your name.   Mother, I Am.   Lucille Clifton.   GeTw

Someone's face at the window.   Another November.   Stanley Plumly.   LCAP

Someone's sent a valentine!   A Sure Sign.   Nancy Byrd Turner.   SoPo; TiPo

Someone should trace all those who/knew Will, to interview them.   The Death of Will.   Charles Tomlinson.   OxBC

...Someone who can't stop, can't stop wanting.   She Is Carefully Stepping over the Important Communications.   Janine Canan.   APU

Someone will tell him how to put it straight....   Love in a Cottage.   J. A. R. McKellar.   PoAu 1-2

The somethin like the somethin/u ain't suppose to be.   Positives for Sterling Plumpp.   Don L. Lee.   JB; PoBA

Something bad/is going to keep on/happening.   Look Back.   Carroll Arnett.   STE

Something below pushed up a knob of skull,/Feeling its way to air.   South Country.   Kenneth Slessor.   CBAP

Something died out by this river: but it seems/Less than a nightingale ago.   In Arcadia.   Lawrence Durrell.   MoBrPo

Something discovered vividly and sudden.   Lecture Hall.   Patrick Kavanagh.   FaBoTw; NoAm

Something forgets us perfectly   For E.J.P.   Leonard Cohen.   NoAm; NoP

Something frightening, even now, is here.   The Fear of Trembling.   John Hollander.   NePoEA

Something has just flown over the mountain!   White Pass Ski Patrol.   John Logan.   BiP; CAPP

Something he meant, who stumbled with a cross!   Dying.   Jessie Holt.   PGD

Something I had known in sleep.   The Night Hunt.   Thomas Macdonagh.   GDP; OxBI; RoGo

Something important above love, and about love's grace.   Revelation.   Robert Penn Warren.   AnFE; LiTA; MoPo; NePA; NoAm

...Something in the night/will touch us too from that other place.   Listening.   William Stafford.   RFM

Something is afraid.   Haiku: "Deep in a windless."   Buson (Taniguchi Buso).   WSC

Something is coming and wants to get by.   Something Is There.   Lilian Moore.   WSC

...Something/Is gone lonely/Into the headwaters of the Minnesota.   Lifting Illegal Nets by Flashlight.   James Wright.   NNaP

"Something is Groton in/Denmark, at least!"   Danish Wit.   John Hollander.   NLV; PV

Something is here that was not here before,/And strangely has not yet been crucified.   A Christmas Sonnet.   Edwin Arlington Robinson.   EaLo

Something/like a hint,/from an/Old Warrior.   Pass it on grandson.   Ted D. Palmanteer.   STE

Something like life's pure notations, being taken.   Pure Notations.   Steve Levine.   APU

Something like night moves through the weeds.   The Actor.   Thomas Snapp.   NYBP

Something like spoiled sweets.   The Voyeur.   Deanna Louise Pickard.   AMV-80

Something lying on the ground,/In the bottom of my mind.   The Goat Paths.   James Stephens.   AnIV; AWP; CH; GoJo; LiTB; OxBI; PG; UnPo; WHA

Something money or promises can buy.   Levant.   Lawrence Durrell.   OBTV

Something my former eyes had wept for/came asking to be pitied.   Intrusion.   Denise Levertov.   CAPP

Something new under the sun:/Another sun,/Where the earth was.   CANDU Can't Do.   Raymond Filip.   CaPN

Something nice/To make me sleepy.   Bedtime Stories.   Lilian Moore.   NTCP

Something no other soul will fit/Save hers for whom thou makest it.   The Clue.   Charlotte Fiske Bates.   AA

Something not known to anyone at all,/but wild in our breast for centuries.   Everything is Plundered.   Anna Akhmatova.   WPOW

Something of His love to last/Until next Christmas Eve!   After-Christmas Poem.   Elizabeth-Ellen Long.   ChBR

Something of that old love I feel/For this old Street before me.   St. James's Street.   Frederick Locker-Lampson.   HBV 1-2

Something of you in the mirror changes my face.   One Year Later.   Eric Torgerson.   PoL

–Something out of it, I think.   The Best.   Elizabeth Barrett Browning.   OBSP; OBVV

Something plans these things...   I Heard a Young Man Saying.   Julia Fields.   NNP

Something pleasing perhaps to former minds or eyes.   Old Crabbed Men.   James Reeves.   ChMP

...Something reminded/me of my own hand/at the other end of the line.   Spring Catch.   Greg Keeler.   WOLT

Something should break, the tunnel or his heart.   In Camus Fields.   Leonard Alfred George Strong.   DBV

Something silver and ancient and hungry/rising to swallow them from below.   Fishermen at Dawn.   William Meissner.   WOLT

...Something terribly/nimble-fingered/finding all of the stops   San Sepolcro.   Jorie Graham.   HaCAP

Something that can't breathe scratches/at the door.   We Are Leaning Away.   Gayle Elen Harvey.   AMV-80

Something that her moons/can waylay waylay waylay/in the dark.   Loose Woman Poem.   Sharon Thesen.   CaPN; NOBC

The something that infects the world.   Resignation.   Matthew Arnold.   MaVP; OAEP; VLP

Something that served me well,/And I am quite content.   Growing Old.   Douglas Fraser.   PoSH

Something that sounds like a thousand/transparent wings rising behind my eyes.   Judith Recalls Holofernes.   Maura Stanton.   AmPA

Something that swings the spirit to a star.   Our Dead, Overseas.   Edwin Markham.   MC

...Something that water blurs.   The Suicides.   George Macbeth.   NoAm

Something there is moves me to love, and I/Do know I love, but know not how, nor why.   Love's without Reason.   Alexander Brome.   OBS

Something there is that does not love a Bore.   Apocryphal Apocalypse.   John Wheelwright.   MoVE

Something to be tinkered with at their leisure.   Talk.   Roo Borson.   CaPN; NOBC

Something to build with, take a chisel to.   For an Age of Plastics.   Plymouth.   Donald Davie.   NePoEA-2

Something to cherish, though no words were said.   Casual Meeting.   Margaret E. Bruner.   PoToHe

Something to roll up and stow in my mind/against those odd moments of happiness.   View from My Window.   Alasdair MacLean.   PoSH

...Something to wear/Against the heart in the long cold.   A Day in Autumn.   R.S. Thomas.   BoNaP

...Something ugly/and eaten into. What a mess his eyes are.   Goethe's Death Mask.   Linda Gregg.   MAYP

Something very light and fragile to carry.   Love Poem.   Lauris Edmond.   OCNZ

Something we can take up in our hands and bear away.   The Brown Family.   Colleen Thibaudeau.   NOBC

Something we have lost.   Ross's Poems.   Geoffrey Lehmann.   CBAP

Something went wrong, they say.   Abandoned Farmhouse.   Ted Kooser.   DFF; GP

Something within me shall tower/When you are talus and dust.   To Lizard Head.   Clifford James Laube.   CAW

Sometime, someway, somewhere.   Ask, and Ye Shall Receive.   Annie Johnson Flint.   BLRP

Sometimes/A dime.   In These Dissenting Times.   Alice Walker.   PoBA

Sometimes a frog becomes a prince.../But often he does not.   Noblesse Oblige.   Celeste Turner Wright.   Psk

Sometimes a pale and cold surprise.   At the Aquarium.   Max Eastman.   AnAmPo; HBMV; WGRP

Sometimes a pencil tap.   Ghost Boy.   Mark Van Doren.   SO

Sometimes afraid to meet me with/their eyes   In Love with the Bears.   Greg Kuzma.   NYBP

Sometimes I almost wish I were alive.   Ennui.   Peter Viereck.   NYBP

Sometimes I don't like her at all.   Polarities.   Kenneth Slessor.   CBAP

Sometimes I make a strong gesture–a poem/and I record it.   Hymn to St. Geryon, I.   Michael McClure.   NeAP

"Sometimes I talk to a seagull," Joe said.   I'm 92, Joe Said.   Tom Weber.   CTBA

Sometimes I think without a name/of him whose name I don't know.   Nameless Journey (excerpt).   Leah Goldberg.   BoWoP

Sometimes I want to die because of this.   The Holes.   Stephen Berg.   NaP; NYBP

Sometimes I write/my poems for that/stone hammer.   Stone Hammer Poem.   Robert Kroetsch.   NOBC

Sometimes, in my sad breast,/I wish him dead, best.   Anchises.   Blanaid Salkeld.   OxBI

Sometimes in the great desert the Greeks imagined/Atlantis.   Western Ways.   Richmond Lattimore.   AMV-80

Sometimes in the sun today I glimpse that world in the blue.   Friend Who Never Came.   William Stafford.   FAZ; SM

Sometimes later, they zig-zag crazily back/in no decided direction.   On History.   Paul Hoover.   APU

Sometimes remember us. Love, fare you well.   Lament for the Cuckoo.   Alcuin.   PeHV

Sometimes the little muddler/can't stand itself!   Child's Song.   Robert Lowell.   NMP

Sometimes think of the stockman below.   The Dying Stockman.   *Anonymous*   ViBoFo

Sometimes when I have found a friend/I give a blade of corn away.   Real Property.   Harold Monro.   BoNaP

Sometimes when I'm deep in love/I don't know what I'm thinking of./Oh, don't I, though!   Evidence.   Arthur Kober.   InMe

...Sometimes,/you know, the snow never falls forever.   Going to Remake This World.   James Welch.   CDW

Somewhere, a city will take the train apart.   Western Town.   Karl Shapiro.   NYBP

Somewhere a door must be fanning the air,/someone practicing an exit,/a girl looking both ways.   Looking Both Ways.   Jane O. Wayne.   GOYP

Somewhere a hot roof waits/spine thrust into the sky/for your sound.   Robin.   Paula Gunn Allen.   TWSS

Somewhere a mother will rejoice.   Somewhere.   Ezekiel Mphahlele.   WhB

Somewhere afloat/Amid the spheres, as part of sick Life's antidote.   To Meet, or Otherwise.   Thomas Hardy.   OBNC

Somewhere among the purpling wild verbena.   Variations on Southern Themes.   Donald Justice.   SV

Somewhere down below me is a street/Where faintly can be heard the sound of feet.   Somewhere Down below Me Is a Street.   J. J. Maloney.   LFAC

...Somewhere in me, clues   More Clues.   Muriel Rukeyser.   IHMS

Somewhere in this sunny plain/Echo waits upon her lover.   Country Gods.   Cometas.   FaBoCh; LoGBV

Somewhere is a Great God of Thumbs who can tell the/inside story of this.   Personality.   Carl Sandburg.   CrMA

...Somewhere is an Eye/That weighs the world exactly as it pleases.   Man O'War Bird.   Derek Walcott.   TTY

Somewhere makes the black frog sing   If the Black Frog Will Not Ring.   Ed Roberson.   PoBA

The Somewhere meant for me!   Somewhere.   Walter De la Mare.   BrR; FaPON

Somewhere near/the volumed/dun?   Dark Area.   Russell Atkins.   FB

Somewhere or other doubtless/These make the blackthorn blow.   Endure Hardness.   Christina Georgina Rossetti.   NOBV

Somewhere, somewhere.   Whenever a Little Child Born.   Agnes Carter Mason.   AA; BiCB

Somewhere, somewhere it is so.   But for Lust.   Ruth Pitter.   FaBoTw; OxBTC

Somewhere, surely, a child was born.   Family Reunion.   Hollis Summers.   GoYe

Somewhere the country's saviour cries in his sleep..   Only the Beards Are Different.   Bruce Dawe.   PoAu 1-2

Somewhere the islands of the blest.   Nocturne.   Kathleen Raine.   ChMP

Somewhere to send your old blouses,/Or those wormy little windfalls.   Charity.   Connie Bensley.   FaBoWP

Somewhere under New York.   Train to Reflection.   Lawrence T. O'Neill.   AMV-80

Somewheres about if I took care/To strike a match and find out where.   A Philosopher.   John Kendrick Bangs.   HBV 1-2

Somme forty mile, and dam neere lyke to friz.   Aprilly.   Bert Leston Taylor.   OBAL

The son I did not have.   Things That Might Have Been.   Jorge Luis Borges.   AMV-80

Son...my work's done.   When I First Came to This Land.   *Anonymous*   FSW

Son-of-a-gun, Columbo!   Christofo Columbo.   *Anonymous*.   AmSS

A son of Adam is no name for thee.   Adam's Race.   Muslih-ud-Din Sa'di.   LiTW

The Son of God and Man.   The First Spousal.   Coventry Patmore.   OBVV

Son of God! 'tis Thou! 'tis Thou!   The Crucifixion.   Henry Hart Milman.   BePJ

The son of man goes forth to war/with trumpets clap and syphilis.   Come,Gaze with Me upon This Dome.   Edward Estlin Cummings.   NoAm; OxBA

Son of the darkness walker.   Hyena.   *Anonymous*   TTY

Son's head impaled on the stiff spear clutched/In her own hand soiled with dirt and blood. Essay on Psychiatrists. Robert Pinsky. HaCAP

...Son, when you clam,/Clam. Clamming. Reed Whittemore. NYBP; TAP

The son will date his love of the world, traveling swiftly past. Permission to Speak. Steve Orlen. MAYP

Sonabitch ran out of balls. The Pinball Queen of South Illinois St. Stephen Tietz. AMV-80

...The song, in a studio/Across town, in our throats, goes on. Honeysuckle. James Paul. HoAn

Song is so fair,/Love is so new! Song: "Song is so old." Hermann Hagedorn. HBV 1-2

A song more true/Than art or craft/Or history knew. Robin Hood. Gray Burr. NCSH

The song of a vast unrest. A Sea Lyric. William Hamilton Hayne. EtS

The song of ancient ways/turns in our blood again The Song of Ancient Ways. William Oandasan. STE

A song of faith and youth and love/He sings at the gates of death. The Poet. Mary Sinton Leitch. HBMV

The song of love,/the doublewind. Fugato (Coda). Gad Hollander. VWA

Song of my soul that will not forget/The sleeping body of me. Little Pagan Rain Song. Frances Shaw. HBMV

The song of the child/rings in the heart/of ancient men. Between Rivers and Seas. Lance Henson. VoR

The song of the seasons never grows old. Song of the Seasons. Blanche De Good Lofton. YeAr

A song of the swag and the swig. A Ballad in "G". Eugene Fitch Ware. PoLf

A song of us and Willow Street,/Tapping a heel all out of time... The Cobbler in Willow Street. George O'Neil. HBMV

The song responsive raise. Now Be the Gospel Banner. Thomas Hastings. AH

A song that lovers' heads/Ear to, and on ear foretell. Non Ti Fidar. Louis Zukofsky. VGW

A song that was of little worth,/And the song of a bird. As I Went Singing over the Earth. Mary Elizabeth Coleridge. UnS

The song! the green and the gold! Awakening. Margaret E. Sangster. AA

A song to stir the hearts of men/'Ere I shall pass them by! Give My Heart a Song. Anna M. Gilleland. STF

A song was singing me. What Black Elk Said. R. T. Smith. LTB

A song, we say, for the men of to-day, who have proved/themselves their peers. Deeds of Valor at Santiago. Clinton Scollard. HBV 1-2; MC; PAH

The song went up the stair. Larks. Katharine Tynan Hinkson. OnYI

A song with a man's face/That God holds up in his fingers. After Lorca. Ted Hughes. PoA

A song/yet to come The Unreal Song of the Old. James Koller. PoM

The songbirds in the public boughs. After the Last Bulletins. Richard Wilbur. CoAP; ConAP; MoAB; MoAmPo; NePoAm; NYBP; TrGrPo; ViBoPo

The songless fields of Eirinn? On Not Hearing the Birds Sing in Ireland. Padraic Colum. NePoAm

Songs and smiles of love return/To friends who love you truly. The Canary. Elizabeth Turner. OxBChV

The songs I've heard, the things I've done,/Make my unbirthdays not so un– Between Birthdays. Ogden Nash. OnUR

...Songs/in praise of the green brown river/flowing clean through the blue green world. Let Us Gather at the River. Marge Piercy. GeTw

Sons, and heirs of all thy lands! A Song of Handicrafts. Annie Matheson. OBVV

Sons asleep/in their workclothes. Crossing Kansas by Train. Donald Justice. NYBP

The sons of ignorance and night/May dwell in the Eternal Light,/Through the Eternal Love. Eternal Light. Thomas Binney. NOCV; WGRP

The sons of smut and scandal hurt me not. The Scurrilous Scribe. Philip Freneau. AA

Soon a single horse escaped out of the foam/Shall fill with fire all the ways of the world. House of the Living. Claude Vigee. VWA

Soon born to die, soon flourishing to fade. The Life of Man. Barnabe Barnes. OBSC

Soon brings another patient/Who loves her just as much. The Bed. A. D. Hope. NoAm; OBSP; OxBC

Soon come, soon gone! and Age at last/A sorry breaking-up! Ode on a Distant Prospect of Clapham Academy. Thomas Hood. BXAP; CBEP

Soon everything moving & the/hustle is on/toward busy new/early early. Mississippi Mornings. Tom Dent. APU

An' soon I'll dee for Peggy, O! Love Is Like a Dizziness. James Hogg. HBV 1-2

...Soon I shall risk the bed,/wriggling down among mute faces of bone. One-Night Expensive Hotel. Ronald G. Everson. NOBC

Soon i wear it as a wreath/around my neck and smile. Walking in the Rain. Dan Saxon. DFF

Soon, in faith, I'll be thy mate. To Edom. Heinrich Heine. TrJP

Soon it will be spring. Giving Up Butterflies. Geraldine Kudaka. BrSi

Soon it will be time for another job. Girl Friday. Elaine Equi. APU

Soon it will be time for the cradle to rock my boy.' Carpenter. George Mackay Brown. OxBC

Soon Jeremiah Job will be walking among men. Munich Elegy No 1. George Barker. SeCePo; WaP

...Soon kindled and soon spent, we that were the pick of many. Two Translatons from Villon. John Millington Synge. MoBrPo

Soon may be thus united/All Israel's hosts again! Marriage Song. Judah Halevi. TrJP

Soon, once more, all things shall be equal. Dr. Joseph Goebbels. W. D. Snodgrass. TW

Soon one more goes thither! Exeunt Omnes. Thomas Hardy. QFR

Soon pied flowers, sweet-breathing,/shall thy head be wreathing. Cyclops. Euripides. AWP

Soon shall proud Carilong be humbled low/Nor Montcalm's self, prevent th' avenging/blow. On the Defeat at Ticonderoga or Carilong. Anonymous PAH

An' soon she'll sing dat heavenly song-oh, Lord, how long? Oh, Lawd, How Long? Anonymous. ABF

Soon she shall ascend and sing/Your praise to th' eternal King. A Lark's Nest. Christopher Smart. FaBoCh; LoGBV

Soon, soon he sickened and then died. William Was a Royal Lover. Anonymous AmFP

Soon the pilgrims will be there! Watchman, Tell Me. Anonymous AH

Soon the world shall know/That all is grand in the western land;/Ho! westward Ho! Ho! Westward Ho!. Ossian E. Dodge. BLSo

Soon there will be nothing left/with which to compare myself. They are rebuilding. Lady Ise. BoWoP

Soon they'll play it in the nude! Nothing Sacred. Roger Woddis. NOBL

...Soon they/will be in the field again. Rural Lines after Breughel. Norbert Krapf. PoDr

Soon to the silence I come, soon in the shades to repose. Snowfall. Giosue Carducci. PoPI

Soon we die, embracing and alone–remember we have/lost nothing. The Technique of Laughter. Jascha Kessler. AmPC

Soon we'll be immortal, too. Immortality. Nicolai M. Minsky. TrJP

Soone on a tree uphang'd I saw her spoyle. The Visions. Joachim Du Bellay. AWP

The sooner he'll behold the Promis'd Day. Labour. M. Saint-Marthe. FaBoUs

Sooner my Lyre, than all Mount Palatine,/Mild Anjou's air, than all the salt sea spate. Returning Home. Joachim Du Bellay. LiTW

The sooner, the better for Roger and me! The Vagabonds. John Townsend Trowbridge. AA; BeLS; BLPA; TreFS

The sooner the better their bodies amende. A Hundreth Good Poyntes of Husbandry. Thomas Tusser. FaBoUs

The sooner the better they fill up a rome. A Hundreth Good Poyntes of Husbandry. Thomas Tusser. FaBoUs

Sooner to be food for ravens than to the funeral rites. The Lovely Youth. Aneirin. LiTW

Soothing themselves to sleep. Hearing the Wind at Night. May Swenson. BoNaP

The Sooty Slut replaces/her defeated dead. To His Chi Mistress. George Starbuck. NYBP

Sophisticated as hell. Matisse Tits. David Barker. GP

Sordid, unfeeling, reprobate, degraded,/Spiritless outcast!' The Friend of Humanity. J.H. Frere and George Canning. BXAP; CEP; FaBoCo; HBV 1-2; Par

...The sordidness/of your vicissitudes. To a Depraved Lying Woman. Sorley MacLean. NeBP

Soregh and murne and fast. Now Comes the Blast of Winter. Anonymous SeCePo

Sorer to Him was the grief/That was upon her for His sake. The Crucifixion. Kuno Meyer. OxBI

Sores in the city/that do not want to heal. The Blackstone Rangers. Gwendolyn Brooks. CAD

Sorrow and mourn and fast. Merry It Is. Anonymous HAP

Sorrow and sighing shall be swept away! The Garden That I Love. Florence L. Henderson. HBV 1-2

Sorrow follows the footsteps of crime,/And Sin is the consort of Woe. An Appeal to My Countrywomen. Frances E. W. Harper. BlSi

...Sorrow follows/this too long wait for one who is estranged. The Wife's Complaint. Anonymous BoLoP

...Sorrow for my sons/At the first notes pierces my heart's core. Eighteen Verses Sung to a Tatar Reed Whistle. Ts'ai Yen. WPOW

Sorrow ill shadow those he called "my/boys"! James McCosh. Robert Bridges. OxBI

The sorrow in my head/will wrench it through the roof. The Young Man. Lewis MacAdams. ANYP

Sorrow is the Only Faithful one.   Sorrow Is the Only Faithful One.   Owen Dodson.   AmNP; IDB; PoBA

Sorrow kills as oft as frost the leaf.   On a Grave in Christ-Church, Hants. Oscar Fay Adams.   AA

The sorrow of our sad mistakes.   Mistakes.   Ella Wheeler Wilcox.   PoToHe

The sorrow of the moments/of His creation.   Prologue.   Lazer Eichenrand. VWA

The sorrow of thee.   Farewell.   John Addington Symonds.   OBVV; PG

Sorrow's sauce for every kiss.   A Wish.   John Millington Synge.   FaBoEE

A sorrow to the housewife.   Ghost.   Christian Morgenstern.   WSC

Sorrow we could understand/And the mystery told in tears.   A Leader. George William Russell.   HBMV

A sorrowful strikeout victim/Of daily anticipation.   From the Batter's Box. David K. Harford.   AMV-80

Sorrows and hates, home to Hell's waste and wild.   Ireland.   Lionel Pigot Johnson.   HBV 1-2

...Sorrows come/To stretch out spaces in the heart for joy.   Victory in Defeat. Edwin Markham.   BLPL; GoTF; PoLf; PoPl; TreFT

The sorrows of thy former cup/In full fruition swallowed up.   The Finished Course.   Saint Joseph of the Studium.   WGRP

The sorrows of thy line!   Keith of Ravelston.   Sydney Thomas Dobell.   CH

Sorry I am, my God, sorry I am.   Sins' Round.   George Herbert.   ExPo; LoBV

Sorry there's no more space. But date your reply.   Letter from Pretoria Central Prison.   Arthur Nortje.   WhB

Sort of a/miracle.   Beer Bottle.   Ted Kooser.   SM

Soughing, soughing in the wind and rain of night/they startle dreams and compound the gloom.   Composed on the Theme "Willows by the Riverside."   Yu Hsuan-chi.   WPOW

Soul and body transcending I live in the soul of my/Loved One anew!   Not in India.   Jalal ed-Din or al-Din Rumi.   ILwL

The soul in all things born or framed,/Eros.   Eros.   Algernon Charles Swinburne.   MaVP

A soul in her to match thine own,/Though yet ungrown.   Song: "Wait but a little while."   Norman Gale.   HBV 1-2

The soul is freed froevermore from strife/And enters into rich abundant life. Disillusion.   Bessie B. Decker.   PoToHe

The soul is its own monument.   Song by Mr. Cypress.   Thomas Love Peacock.   ERoP 1-2; OAEL 1-2; OBNC; OBRV; Par

The Soul lies buried in the ink that writes.   Language Has Not the Power to Speak What Love Indites.   John Clare.   ELU; OBNC

The soul now turning to the Love Divine,/That oped, to embrace us, on the Cross its arms.   On the Crucifix.   Buonarroti Michelangelo.   CAW

The soul of Adonais, like a star,/Beacons from the abode where the Eternal are.   Adonais.   Percy Bysshe Shelley.   AtBAP; EBEV; ERoP 1-2; FaBoPP; FiP; GoTF; GoTL; HBV 1-2; HoPM; LoBV; MasP; MCCG; NoP; OAEL; OAEP; OBNC; OBRV; PoEL 1-5; SCV; TreFS; TrGrPo; ViBoPo; WGRP; WHA

The soul of Andrew Jackson/Shone forth in glory there.   The Battle of New Orleans.   Thomas Dunn English.   MC; PAH

The soul of Ireland seems to bend/Above her children there.   Cois na Teineadh.   T. W. Rolleston.   AnIV

The soul of Jesus is restless today,/But eternally undismayed.   The Soul of Jesus Is Restless.   Cyprus R. Mitchell.   TrCP

The soul of Lady Barbeque.   Ballade of the Harrowing of Hell.   Dominic Bevin Wyndham Lewis.   CoBE

The soul of man is cast.   A Creed.   Edwin Markham.   BLPA; BLPL; FaBoBe; FaFP; GoTF; PoPl; TreFS

The soul of our hero goes marching on.   Crispus Attucks McCoy.   Sterling A. Brown.   BPo

The soul of the sea.   Portmanteau Parodies: After Algernon Charles Swinburne.   Gilbert Keith Chesterton.   FaBoPa

"Soul of the vanished years,/O where! where! where!   The Wood-Dove's Note. Emily Huntington Miller.   HBV 1-2

Soul of you that comes by night, never goes away.   Paris: The Seine at Night. Charles Divine.   HBMV

The soul's something very sweet indeed.   Dishonor.   Edwin Denby.   ErPo

Soul's vague lily scents the void.   How on Solemn Fields of Space. Elizabeth Daryush.   NOCV

Soul said, Now come with me.   Two Trinities.   Kenneth Mackenzie. CBAP

The soul shall speak in tears of gratitude!   O, Thou Eternal One! Derzhavin.   WGRP

Soul, soul, there is a sequel to thy tale!   The Second Volume.   Robert Mowry Bell.   AA

The soul still catches sight of its faithful star.   O What Transparent Waves, What a Tranquil Sea.   Vittoria da Colonna.   PBWP

A soul that knew it well.   The Happiest Day, the Happiest Hour.   Edgar Allan Poe.   AmPP; LITA; NePA; OxBA

The soul that made that form so bright,/To Heaven had passed away.   The Dying Child's Request.   Hannah Flagg Gould.   OBCA

A soul that shall speak to my soul till I too pass afar,/And perchance, even then.   Perugia.   Amelia Josephine Burr.   HBV 1-2

The soul, through gates rolled open wide,/Passed into Paradise.   My Father's Child.   Gertrude Bloede.   AA

The soul to feel the flesh and the flesh to feel the chain!'   Julian M. and A.G. Rochelle.   Emily Bronte.   BrRo

The soul, uneasy, and confined from home,/Rests and expatiates in a life to come.   An Essay on Man.   Alexander Pope.   TreF; ViBoPo

...The soul would miss/Its footing, and fall headlong from to-day.   Mimma Bella.   Eugene Lee-Hamilton.   HBV 1-2

Soulfolk, think on that/A minute.   To Soulfolk.   Margaret Goss Burroughs. BlSi

A soulful tune/Salaam, salaam.   Al Fitnah Muhajir.   Nazzam Al Sudan. NBP

Souls immortal we descry.   In Common.   Gene Derwood.   NePA; PoPl

Souls in conflict, burdened, sighing,/Jesus came to save.   The Light Now Shineth.   *Anonymous*   STF

Souls of all the sea-dogs, lead the line today!   Sailing at Dawn.   Sir Henry Newbolt.   EtS

The souls of bluebells come to comfort me.   Bluebells.   Lucia Clark Markham.   HBMV

The souls of children will play with your long ears!   The Perfect Life.   Jorge Carrera Andrade.   LiTW

Souls, precious souls, my ceaseless cry.   A Heart That Weeps.   Oswald J. Smith.   STF

Sound, as the sacred poles are moved about with the rolling of/the canoe! The Djanggawul Cycle, 1.   *Anonymous*   WTO

The sound as when a time of singing willed it so!   In Grato Jubilo.   David McCord.   UnS

Sound dark's uttermost, stangely light-brimming, until/time be full.   The Dumbfounding.   Margaret Avison.   NOBC

The sound floats upward like a bird to me.   Autumn Scene.   Basil Dowling. BoNaP

Sound forth, my Brayers, and the welkin rend.   The Dunciad.   Alexander Pope.   AtBAP

The sound is forced, the notes are few!   To the Muses.   William Blake. AnFE; BoLiVe; ChTr; ERoP 1-2; GTBS; HAP; HBV 1-2; HeIP; LAuP; LiTB; LoBV; NOBE; NOEC; NoP; OAEL 1-2; OAEP; OBEC; OBEV; SeCeV; TrGrPo; ViBoPo; WHA

Sound like a sea to conceal the bone, the broken shell,/the broken ship. Radio.   Arthur Seymour John Tessimond.   HaMV

A sound like any other. It will end.   Bethou Me, Said Sparrow.   Wallace Stevens.   CrMA; NePA

Sound like my own.   Haiku: "winter midnight."   Otsuji.   LiTW

The sound now/is a direct, intense/sound of/direction.   The Resolve. Denise Levertov.   RFM

The sound of Brendan's bell, and the sloughed-off pelt of a wild/swan.   Erris Coast, 1943.   Hugh Connell.   NeIP

The sound of disaster and misery, the sound/Of passionate heartbreak at the centre of the world.   Sound of Breaking.   Conrad Aiken.   AnAmPo; AWP; InPo; MAPA

The sound of it/stayed in our ears...   ...And the Old Women Gathered. Mari E. Evans.   BlSi; NNP; PoBA

The sound of me watching, if I had been a bird.   The Bird's Nest.   John Drinkwater.   EvOK; SoPo

The sound of rain.   On Gay Wallpaper.   William Carlos Williams.   MoAB; MoAmPo; TAP

Sound of the sea from the Djanggawul's paddling!   The Djanggawul Cycle, 4. *Anonymous*   WTO

The sound of water.   The Old Pond.   Basho (Matsuo Basho).   SoPo

The sound of your voice/the feel of your shoulder.   Rain Journal: London: June 65.   Lee Harwood.   PeHV

Sound out aloud so rare a thing,/That all the hills and vales may ring. Constancy.   Samuel Daniel.   OBSC

Sound/over and/over.   For Kelley.   Ken Belford.   NeAC

Sound was the lament of/The poets for deciduous language.   Postscript.   R. S. Thomas.   FaBoMo; OxBC

Sounding like a strange season/sounding like you.   Dreamtime.   Don Domanski.   CaPN

The sounding motif of my heart,/The impetus and goal!   Proving.   Georgia Douglas Johnson.   CDC

Soundings on each other, each alone.   Owls.   W. D. Snodgrass.   BoAnP; Psk

Soundless as dots on a disk of snow.   Safe in Their Alabaster Chambers. Emily Dickinson.   AnFE; APA; MAmP; MAPA; MoPo; NIP; NOBA; NoP; OxBA

...Sounds/from the kitchen again are muffled, vague.   The Obscure Pleasure of the Indistinct.   Bin Ramke.   MAYP

...The sounds/he lets out when he crows with a will.   The Kangarooster. Kenyon Cox.   TiPo

Sounds, like shawls falling.   Friday Night.   Kendrick Smithyman.   OCNZ

Sounds make the song, not sense,/Thus I inhibit! Psycholophon. Gelett Burgess. CenHV; NA

Sounds of a horn they heard, and the distant/lowing of cattle. Evangeline. Henry Wadsworth Longfellow. AA

The sounds of joy once heard, and heard no more. Sonnet. At Ostend, July 22, 1787. William Lisle Bowles. NOEC; OBEC

Sounds of tents flapping/in the background. Last Night in Sisseton, S. D. Mary Goose. STE

Sour as social justice, on the wash-house wall. Her Garden. Freda Downie. FaBoWP

Sour is the wine, and harsh the mead,/Where such sad news is told. Ebbe Skammelson. Anonymous. BaBo

The source and origin of all life. Artorius. John Heath-Stubbs. EBEV

A source of innocent merriment!/Of innocent merriment! The Mikado. Sir William Schwenck Gilbert. LiTB

The source of the song will die away. The Reaper. Robert Duncan. CrMA

Sourness in the clay. The roots tear softly. Ritual of Departure. Thomas Kinsella. CIP; CMoP

South-bound wedge shatters/down the emerald sky. Fall Again. H. R. Coursen. AMV-81

The south is mistress of his grave. Scenes from Carnac. Matthew Arnold. FaBoPP; OBTV

The South will wear eternally a stain. Tuskegee. Leslie Pinckney Hill. BANP; PoNe

Southeast/Mazama nods/and waits. Mount Saint Helens/Loowit: An Indian Woman's Song. Wendy Rose. TWSS

...The sovereign Architect,/Has deigned to work as if with human Art! Cave of Staffa, I. William Wordsworth. VLP

Sow in our souls like living grass,/The laughter of all lowly things. Hymn for the Church Militant. Gilbert Keith Chesterton. OxBoCh

The sow took the measles and she died in the spring. The Sow Took the Measles. Anonymous. FSW

Sowed my deep-furrowed thought with many a name,/Whose glory will not die. As When a Man. Alfred, Lord Tennyson. ChRP

Sown whitely up and down its opposite slopes/With farms and villas. Aurora Leigh. Elizabeth Barrett Browning. OBTV

Space for his silences, and space for mine. I Hear It Said. Barbara Young. BLPA

Space for oceans to turn in, things that bend. Heron's Bay. Martin Galvin. AMV-81

Space in communion binds us in one thought. Another Spirit Advances. Jules Romains. AWP

A space in the lives of their friends Beware : Do Not Read This Poem. Ishmael Reed. BPo; CNA; NCSH; NIP; NoP; PoBA; WeW; WSC

Space is his grave. Lumumba's Grave. Langston Hughes. CNA

...A space/on this side, hut for clouds. Environ S. Larry Eigner. NeAP

The space you see is all. Stanky. Bill Berkson. ANYP

The spaces/between them, a distance/we must try to cover. The Runner. Jerah Chadwick. AMV-81

Spain, in her pride, has set/Honor above them. Cervera. Bertrand Shadwell. PAH

Spangled with fire/Warm over cold. Christmas Tree. Laurence Smith. OBCP

The spar/is in my hand. Here Be Dragons. Ginny Friedlander. AMV-80

Spare him the pity–he departed whole,/spitting the dear brown weed, owning his soul. Old Men's Ward. Elma Dean. GoYe

Spare, Lord, in that hour of terror! Dies Irae. Thomas of Celano. HBV 1-2

Spare me from the blast of Hell. Storm at Sea. Anonymous KiLC

Spare me the ingalenight! The Oocuck. Justin Richardson. BoAnP; FiBHP

Spare not, but play thee! Rosalynde. Thomas Lodge. ALV; EIL; EnLit; GoBC; GTBS; HBV 1-2; InvP; LoBV; NOBE; NoP; OBEV; OBSC; SeCePo; UnTE; ViBoPo

Spare not for her gay clothing,/But lay her body flat on the ground. The Baffled Knight. Anonymous BaBo; ESPB

Spare the culprit, God of Glory! Dies Irae. Anonymous CAW

Spare this one Jewel; I'll be Dives still! On Dives. Richard Crashaw. ACP

Spare, woodman, spare the beechen tree! The Beech Tree's Petition. Thomas Campbell. GTBS; HBV 1-2

Spareribs are too much for me. Folk Song. Anonymous ShM

...A spark/Lingers, then that, too, fades; then all is dark. Sonnet: "There, on the darkened deathbed, dies the brain." John Masefield. EBEV

A spark of life hath glistened and hath gone. On Music. Walter Savage Landor. GoJo; HBV 1-2

...The sparkle-crest/Seen spinning on the bracken-crook. Night of Frost in May. George Meredith. VLP

Sparkles from the wheel. Sparkles from the Wheel. Walt Whitman. BiP; DiPo; InPS

...A sparrow escaping from a boy's hand/resembles the morning. Cicada. Libero de Libero. LiTW

Sparrows ate the half of it, the gentry will eat the rest. Three Fields. Adolf Heyduk. LiTW

The Spartans on the sea-wet rock sat/down and combed their hair. Last Poems. Alfred Edward Housman. OAEP

The Spasm passed without detection. Sylvia. Alan Dienstag. ErPo

The spastic T-bars pivot and descend. T-Bar. P.K. Page. NOBC; OBCV

Spattered/with red rose petals. Blue Mason Jars. Keith Abbott. APU

Spawned in a different sea. Early. Bruce Bennett. WOLT

The spawnless salmon strike to kill! Around the Fish: After Paul Klee. Howard Moss. MoPo

Speak, and a taste of that old time restore! Modern Love, VIII. George Meredith. OAEP; VLP

Speak but the word, and cure me quite. His Ejaculation to God. Robert Herrick. SeCV 1-2

Speak! fairy Moon, interpret this! The Dawn of Love. Henrietta Cordelia Ray. BlSi

Speak for the comfort of the weary/Who weep to know. Adjuration. Charles Enoch Wheeler. AmNP; PoNe

Speak for the unreturning traveller. Silence. John Hall Wheelock. LiTM

Speak–for you must–you have no hour to lose. Reflections (excerpt). Philip Freneau. PPON

Speak, God of Visions, plead for me/And tell why I have chosen thee! Plead for Me. Emily Bronte. EnLi 1-2; PoEL 1-5

Speak, gracious Lord, oh speak; Thy servant hears. A Paraphrase on Thomas a Kempis. Alexander Pope. GoBC; OBEC; TrPWD

Speak in me now for all who are to die! Maple and Sumach. C. Day-Lewis. CoBMV; FaBoMo

Speak in that speech beyond reproach/The body's speech. The Body's Speech. Donal, Earl of Clancarty, MacCarthy. KiLC

Speak my name, call to me, call... To My Sister. Olga Berggolts. BoWoP

Speak not, ah, breathe not–there's peace on the deep. In Our Boat. Dinah Maria Mulock Craik. HBV 1-2

Speak not ill of woman kind. Against Blame of Woman. Gerald, Earl of Desmond. AnIL; BIrV

Speak, O dim traveller, speak: thy host/believes! The Book of Day-Dreams. Charles Leonard Moore. AA

...Speak/of those un-mountainous matters, in few words, without fraud. Alps. Rosanna Warren. MAYP

SPEAK,OR I FIRE! The Impetuous Lover. A. R. D. Fairburn. AnNZ

Speak out, and bid me blame no rogues at all. Epilogue to the Satires. Alexander Pope. OBSV

Speak, passing winds; ye torrents, with your/strong/And constant voice, protest against the wrong. On the Projected Kendal and Windermere Railway. William Wordsworth. VLP

Speak South African bloodstone speak! South African Bloodstone. Quincy Troupe. CNA

Speak, that my torturing doubts their end may know! Why Art Thou Silent! William Wordsworth. CBEP; HBV 1-2; OBRV

Speak Thou, availing Christ!–and fill this pause. Substitution. Elizabeth Barrett Browning. WGRP

Speak through the blighted chestnut: Was a lark. The Ventriloquist. Robert Huff. GP

Speak to dead walls, but those hear not my moans. My Body in the Walls Captived. Sir Walter Ralegh. CBEP; FCP; SeCePo; SiPS

Speak to me... Home Thoughts. Carl Sandburg. MoLP

Speak when I have nothing to say Lady Love. Paul Eluard. OBVE

Speaking a different language and forgetting/why it was so important/to go to a new country. My Polish Grandma. Edward Field. Prf

Speaking saying come awake it is spring now? The Tree Sleeps in the Winter. Norman H. Russell. STE

Speaking when you touch me. Boom. Julian Lee Rayford. AMV-80

Speaks, and in accents disconsolate answers the wail of the forest. Evangeline. Henry Wadsworth Longfellow. AnNE; SpRo

Speaks at this hour my name within her heart. Night. Hermann Hesse. AWP

Speaks in the still, small voice. Burning Bush. Louis Untermeyer. MoLP

Speaks of sequence, denies the absolute death. Beads from Blackpool. Anne Ridler. NMP

...The spears/That clank–but gently clank–but clank again! Business as Usual 1946. A.J.M. Smith. NMP

The Special Branch castled their plans,/Quicklimed the last Republicans. The Last Republicans. Austin Clarke. CIP

The special name of your love. Midway in the Night: Blackman. Eugene B. Redmond. GP

A special providence for fatherhood. The Ring and the Book. Robert Browning. PoToHe

A spectre-horde repeating without change. From One Who Stays. Amy Lowell. BoWoP

The spectres, the hawkers, the talkers, the damned are/all there. The Suicide. V. R. Lang. PoA

Speech as of powers whose uttered word laid bare/The world's great heart. The Death of Richard Wagner. Algernon Charles Swinburne. LoBV

Speech echoes from the canyon's wall/resonant/indubitable. Without Benefit of Tape. Dorothy Livesay. NOBC

...Speech/is a mouth. The Language. Robert Creeley. CAPP; CoPo; TAP

...Speech is death/who can but laugh and pipe a flute,/who loves you. Time; or, How the Line About Chagall's Lovers Disappears. Jane Miller. SM

Speech is silver and it never should be free! How a Girl Was Too Reckless of Grammar. Guy Wetmore Carryl. FiBHP; OBAL

Speech stumbles over lost/syllables of an old order. A Grafted Tongue. John Montague. BIrV; CIP

Speechless, I hold love to my breast/And listen to the clock! Too Soon the Lightest Feet. Amanda Benjamin Hall. HBMV

Speechless in the tide. The Waning of the Harvest Moon. John Wieners. CoPo

Speechless, inept, and totally unmanned. Double Sonnet. Anthony Hecht. SM

Speechless still, and never cry. Epitaph on the Earl of Strafford. John Cleveland. CavP; SeCePo; TrGrPo

Speechless while things forgotten call to us. A Day of Love. Dante Gabriel Rossetti. MaVP

A speed beyond my speed. The Gentled Beast. Dilys Bennett Laing. PH

Speed it, O Father! Let thy Kingdom come! Reflections. Samuel Taylor Coleridge. EnRP; OBEC

Speed last night upon its way. Soraidh Slan Don Oidhche Areir. Niall Mor Mac Muireadach. BIrV

Speed thanks to Him who swept death's yoke from every town. Salutations to Mary, Virgin. *Anonymous* ISi

Speed you, and good-morrow! Wood-Song. Josephine Preston Peabody. AA

Speeding happy hours/Till he comes at last! The Shoe Factory. Ruth Harwood. HBMV

Speeding through white water like a log. The Real Muse. Fred Muratori. AMV-81

Speeds through the land/The train. Song of a Train. John Davidson. BrPo

Speedy oblivion, rest for memory. Farewell to Juliet. Wilfrid Scawen Blunt. ViBoPo

Speir ye for Maggie Lauder.' Maggie Lauder. Francis Sempill. OBS; OxBS

Spell, "Come back." Driftwood. Trumbull Stickney. HBV 1-2

Spell Him with a capital. On Clinton Edward Dawkins, Commoner of Balliol. J. W. Mackail. FaBoEE

Spell me that without a P,/And a clever scholar you will be. Pease Porridge Hot, Pease Porridge Cold. *Anonymous* OxNR

The spell of the world is loosed, it is time to go. Light and Dark. Barbara Howes. MoVE

The spell that shall not fail. The Hills. Berton Braley. MCCG

...Spellbound I relax–/the knife steady, a precious bond. Journey. Rodney Hall. NOAV

Spend it, and render our mutual Christmastide/Happy! The Annual Solution. Edwin Meade Robinson. InMe

Spends his life in solitude,/Neither envied nor envious. On Leaving Prison. Luis Ponce de Leon. ILwL

Spent in the dream of thy life below. Absolution. Edward Willard Watson. AA

Spent my money on Sally Brown. Sally Brown. *Anonymous* AmFP; AmSS; FSW; ShS

Spent the day/burning gasoline. Tiempo Muerto. Ricardo Alonso. SaC

Spent with sane joy beyond the bees' numb drone. The Sundial. Jane Cooper. AmPC

Spent your childhoods in this house left almost/as she left it and kept for you. And her. Divorce. Bink Noll. MAT

The sperm of our long woes, our large disgrace. Prelude to Space. Clive Staples Lewis. HW

Sphinx-like untold, the ages hold/The tale of CRO-A-TAN! The Mystery of Cro-A-Tan. Margaret Junkin Preston. PAH

Spicy grove, cinnamon tree/What is Africa to me? Heritage: What Is Africa to Me? Countee Cullen. FaBV

Spider does not sing,/only sits, sees, eats, and weaves. Spider. Richmond Lattimore. PP

Spider recite his one sin. Self-Portrait in 2035. Charles Wright. LCAP

The spider with her web across our lips. Liberation. Ruth Stone. BoWoP

Spilled it on the grass The Moon. Ryuho. SoPo

Spilling all its starlight into yours. Migration as a Passage in Time. Jody Bolz. SUW

Spilt shattered gold about his back... Small Fountains. Lascelles Abercrombie. CH

Spin, Dame, spin. Spin Dame. *Anonymous* OxNR

The spindly sandpiper stopped short and leapt/To air, while time rose, circled and was gone. Madaket Beach. Isabel Harriss Barr. GoYe

The spine, the tail, the mercy/of dark clothing and work. The Animals. Stephen Berg. NaP

...The spinning globe/You wear, and the star running down his cheek. Swimming by Night. James Merrill. NYBP; SM; VGW

Spinning in silence. Child Bearing. Charles Ghigna. AMV-81

Spinning, she swathes herself again/In a fresh web of mist and rain. The Witch. Wilfrid Gibson. PoSH

Spinning thy sparkling wheel on high. Freya's Spinning Wheel. Adam Oehlenschlager. LiTW

(The spiral deep in the storm,/the world turning over) Significant Fevers. Alison Fell. BrRo

Spirit always gonna live on. President Roosevelt. Big Joe Williams. BluL; FaBoPV

...The spirit as a bird shall/flee to her mountain. To J. S. Collis. Ruth Pitter. OxBoCh

A spirit cries Be strong! and cries Be still! Dead. Lionel Pigot Johnson. BrPo; OBNC; PoEL 1-5

The spirit-crowded courts of solitude. In High Places. Harriet Monroe. PoA

Spirit flowers we are. Spirit Flowers. Della Burt. BlSi

A spirit form, till on the sight it dies. Dandelions. John Albee. AA

The spirit moves on/from within. For Both of Us at Fisk. Sharon Scott. JB

...A spirit must be free/To tread the upper air of day with him. The Man of Kerioth (excerpt). Robert Norwood. CaP

...Spirit/now less than bone The Old People Speak of Death. Quincy Troupe. CNA

The spirit of America today is marching by! Memorial Day. Theodosia Garrison. OHIP; PoSC

The spirit of June, here prisoned by his spell,/May cheer the herds with pasture memories. The Mowing. Sir Charles G. D. Roberts. ExPo; NOBC; OBCV

Spirit of the Mountain! Prayer to the Mountain Spirit. *Anonymous* WGRP

The spirit of the red man/Is welcomed by his fathers up on high. Ode to the Spirit of Earth in Autumn. George Meredith. TEP; VLP

Spirit of the rugged ranges,/Soul of the open West. The Man of the Open West. Arthur W. Monroe. PoOW

...A Spirit that strove/For truth, and like the Preacher found it not. Sonnet: "Lift not the painted veil which those who live." Percy Bysshe Shelley. OBNC; SyP

Spirit, Thou hast/Done thy best/To allay my fear. Hopi Prayer. Charles Beghtol. BPAW

Spit in his face, and pass him by. So Runs Our Song. Mary Eva Kitchel. PGD

The Spital, or the Gaol! The Lay of the Labourer. Thomas Hood. SaC

Spitalfields weaver, and that's all. Daniel Saul. *Anonymous* FaBoEE

Spitting–from lips once sanctified by Hers. To Edward Fitzgerald. Robert Browning. DBV; OBSP; TW

A splash quite unnoticed/this was/Icarus drowning. Pictures from Brueghel. William Carlos Williams. LCAP; PPP

Splashdown claptrap To the Moon and Back. William Plomer. MOON

Splashed with foam from far away on the wide sea, near the/Spirit Country. The Djanggawul Cycle, 182. *Anonymous* WTO

Splashes, and half recalls a waking dream. Cosmogony. Edgell Rickword. FaBoTw

Splashing about in the blue exhaust? Eclogue. David Bergman. AMV-80

Splendid. Please Excuse Typing. John Basil Boothroyd. FiBHP

A splendor greater yet while serving thee. We Thank Thee, Lord. Calvin W. Laufer. AH

The splendors of the sunrise in your heart. The Errand Imperious. Edwin Markham. PAL; PGD

Splendour, simplicity, joy–such as were seen/In one who now rests by his mountain road. New Guinea. James Philip McAuley. NOCV; PoAu 1-2

Splinters in their teeth and their eyes full of dust. Moon-Witches. Ted Hughes. WSC

Splishhhh. Haiku: "In the old stone pool." Basho (Matsuo Basho). InPK

Split as we are in twain,/With cloven core? Janus. Madeline Mason. GoYe

Splitting the board with a final hit. The Lion and O'Reilly. Richard Weber. PPON

Spoil his salvation for a fierce miscreed? How Fevered Is the Man. John Keats. EnL

...Spoil/what may be vision of a Pharaoh's face. In Time of Gold. Hilda ("H. D.") Doolittle. PoA

Spoiling the market value of the house. Corposant. Peter Redgrove. NePoEA-2; OxBTC

Spoken; even when your friend, the magnate, is/gone. X Minus X. Kenneth Fearing. AmLP

Spoken slightly through the nose,/With a whistle at the close.　What the Engines Said.　Bret (Francis Bret Harte) Harte.　BPAW

Spoken words/a wind has blown away.　Rain Has Fallen on the History Books.　David Rosenberg.　VWA

A sponge would do a better job.　To an Old Fraud.　Martial (Marcus Valerius Martialis).　LiTW

The spoor of feathers/and slight, pink bones.　Poem: "Form is the woods."　Jim Harrison.　VGW

Sport and folly are youth's own,/Tender youth and ruddy.　Invitation to the Dance.　Anonymous　UnTE

A spot like this would be her chosen home.　The Pettichap's Nest.　John Clare.　PBBP

The spot where the hot baths burst into air.　The Ruin.　Anonymous.　AnOE; PrIm

Spouse, Sister, Mother,' Jesus saith.　Herself a Rose Who Bore the Rose.　Christina Georgina Rossetti.　ISi

Spread like a field of death; gold on the sea.　Annual Legend.　Winfield Townley Scott.　CoAP; LiTM; WaP

Spread out, unbuttoned, grateful, under the trees.　The Wife's Tale.　Seamus Heaney.　IPY

Spread silence round Thee, and dwell there apart,/Awful, alone.　Seaward Bound.　Alice Brown.　TrPWD

Spread the great round promises of green morning.　Weeds.　Ann Stanford.　GrPl

Spreadeagled in the empty air/of existence　Constantly Risking Absurdity.　Lawrence Ferlinghetti.　CAPP; SoSe; TAP

...Spreading/a darker darkness/over the river.　When Howitzers Began.　Hayden Carruth.　Psk

The spreading wide my narrow Hands/To gather Paradise–　I Dwell in Possibility.　Emily Dickinson.　MAmP; NAWM 1-2; NIP; NoAm; NOBA; OxBA; PP

Spreads as a river.　Round about Me (fragment).　Sappho.　AWP

Spreads joy abroad and doubles all his own.　My Neighbor's Reply.　Anonymous.　PoToHe

Sprightly Rebecca, Anne,/And Adelaide.　Three Sisters.　Walter De la Mare.　FaBoEE

Spring came on forever,"/Said the Chinese nightingale.　The Chinese Nightingale.　Vachel Lindsay.　HBMV; MAPA; MoAmPo; NePA

Spring flowers!　Directions.　Onitsura.　SoPo

A spring gale/Eddying amidst the scrap iron.　Juxta.　Grover Jacoby.　GoYe

...Spring giggles/coating me with petals.　Epigram: "The breath of my life."　Meleager.　PeHV

Spring grass/Deer fawn/sun children.　Sun Children.　Leslie Marmon Silko.　VoR

Spring/Has come and I am alive/With the sense that I am still alive.　Julian Barely Misses Zimmer's Brains.　Paul Zimmer.　GOYP

The spring has come–has come to Florida,/With yellow jessamine.　Yellow Jessamine.　Constance Fenimore Woolson.　AA; HBV 1-2

Spring has flung forward an unringed hand.　February's Forgotten Mitts.　Raymond Knister.　NOBC

...Spring in bud, in brook,/in small grass through the thaw!　Spring in Hiding.　Frances Frost.　YeAr

Spring in the world when you fetch me/away!　So Might It Be.　John Galsworthy.　BLPL; PoLf

Spring is but a tiny child.　Infant Spring.　Fredegond Shove.　HBMV

Spring is the winner!'　The Fight of the Year.　Roger McGough.　OBCP

Spring laughing with a windy sound.　April.　Eunice Tietjens.　SoPo; YeAr

Spring/like all men living/will soon/grow old　Tune: The Butterfly Woos the Blossoms.　Li Ching-chao.　PBWP

The spring may find her still, and grow towards her.　The Dressmaker's Dummy as Scarecrow.　Barbara Howes.　DFF

Spring morning!　Galante Garden.　Juan Ramon Jimenez.　PoPl

Spring of the war, spring of the mighty yield,/That promised corn but ripened into men.　The Year 1812.　Adam Mickiewicz.　OBVE; OBWP

The Spring returns! O madness beyond sense,/Breed in bones thine own omnipotence!　The Spring Returns.　Charles Leonard Moore.　HBV 1-2

The spring's behavior here is spent/To make the world magnificent.　May Garden.　John Drinkwater.　HBMV

The spring's first dandelion shows its trustful face.　The First Dandelion.　Walt Whitman.　NePA

Spring's new odors flow in waves/Brilliant colors, scents and singing/Will arise above our graves.　Hope and Faith.　Isaac L. Peretz.　TrJP

Spring's whole delight bloom like a marvel there!　Spring Landscape.　Arthur Davison Ficke.　HBMV

Spring, the sweet Spring!　Spring.　Thomas Nash.　AtBAP; BoNaP; CBEP; EIl; GTBS; GTBS-P; HBV 1-2; MCCG; OBSC; OnUR; TrGrPo; WiR

Spring the sweeter past　I Looked & Saw History Caught.　A. B. Spellman.　NBP

The spring was late that year,/But the harvest early.　The Son.　Ridgely Torrence.　HBMV; InvP; WHA

Spring was rehearsing/Genesis.　Song in Spring.　Louis Ginsberg.　YeAr

Spring will be reborn under our bright steps.　The Vultures.　David Diop.　PBA; TTY

The Spring Wind is a gay lad/Who blows a silver whistle.　Winds A-Blowing.　May Justus.　BrR

Spring wine from their ivory/Or roses from their eyes?　A Responsory, 1948.　Thomas Merton.　VGW

Spring with triumph–and our old black hen/(Thank the Lord!) will begin to lay.　In Winter.　C. H. Bretherton.　BiP; InMe; MAPA; SeCeV

Spring would be springier, I think/If we could meet a pinkletink.　Pinkletinks.　Grace Elisabeth Allen.　GoYe

Springing from two such fires/May blaze the virtue of their sires.　A Nuptial Song, or Epithalamie, on Sir Clipseby Crew and His Lady.　Robert Herrick.　AtBAP; CaPo; HW; JCP; PoEL 1-5; SeCP; SeCV 1-2

Springing, full-grown, from your own head, Athena?　Pro Femina.　Carolyn Kizer.　NMM

Springs like a star to her milk, is not for the grave.　The Mother and Child.　Vernon Watkins.　NeBP

Springs, streams and water, the hills' own life.　Corries.　Janet M. Smith.　PoSH

Sprinkle here the twinkling shower/On each perfume-stifled flower.　Song: "Hither haste, and gently strew."　Thomas Lovell Beddoes.　EG

Sprinkles another's laughing face/With nectar, and runs on.　On Catullus.　Walter Savage Landor.　OBEV; ViBoPo

The sprouting of the meadow grass,/But churchyard weeds about our head.　We Hurry On, Nor Passing Note.　Digby Mackworth Dolben.　OBNC

Sprouting through scales in the new coolness of the weather.　Links.　Ricardo Pau-Llosa.　AMV-81

Spun from our impermanence/our celebration.　Looking for Buddha.　Jaime Jacinto.　BrSi

Spun in the current, swept toward no visible ocean.　No More the Slow Stream.　Floris Clark McLaren.　OBCV

Spurning, like a wild bird, whose home is on the tides.　The St. Lawrence and the Saguenay.　Charles Sangster.　NOBC

Spurning true genius prostrate at his feet.　The Mortified Genius.　James Graeme.　NOEC

Spurred by the furious heels of immortal horsemen?　A Frieze.　John Peale Bishop.　MoPo

Spurred, galled, and tired by jauncing Bolingbroke.　Richard II.　William Shakespeare.　PoPle

Spurs upon a chamber-pot I never saw before.　Shickered as He Could Be.　Anonymous　NOAV

Spurting the foam of your heart's blood.　Sleepless.　Al-Khansa.　BoWoP

Spy at their task even here the hands of chance and change.　Tantramar Revisited.　Sir Charles G. D. Roberts.　CaP; NOBC; OBCV

Squabbling and laughing as they pushed/And pulled a cart full of dung.　Signature.　Joseph Stroud.　NPGG

...Squandering in my love's amorous/vice longer than you wished it, marred but poignant.　Carmina.　Caius Valerius Catullus.　OBVE

Squandering transformation.　Cider and Vesalius.　John Peck.　AmPA

Square and oil-shambled, blue between elms, the caboose!　A Rune for C.　Barbara Howes.　NYBP; SM

Squashed his wife with a lemon-squeezer.　Julius Caesar.　Anonymous　InPK

Squat, little Josey!　Squat Down, Josey.　Anonymous　AmFP

Squeak! quo she, I'm weel awa.　The Puddy and the Mouse.　Anonymous　GBP

...Squinting/through the windshield of that cab, saying, Prosser.　Prosser.　Raymond Carver.　GeTw

...Squinting your eyes/against the sun that glints/too brightly off the hard-packed/snow.　Jealousy.　Rachel DeVries.　AMV-81

The squire of Newgate rock them on a sledge.　On Calamy's Imprisonment and Wild's Poetry.　Hudibras"　APAS

The squire will out-poll us and 'peach you again.　Death and the Cobbler.　Anonymous.　APAS

Squirrel, rain, grass, tree–which now the cat runs up.　Can-Opener.　David McAleavey.　AMV-81

The squirrel was not/one of those.　The Gray Squirrel.　Humbert Wolfe.　GoJo; MoBrPo

St. George ere long will be a place that everyone admires!　St. George.　Anonymous　AmFP

...St. George gives birth to The Dragon.　In Memory of David Archer (excerpt).　George Barker.　FaBoMo

St. Michael's victory in the purged and praising rain.　Michaelmas.　Norman Nicholson.　MoBrPo

Stab at the blue eyes of the murdered saints?)　Figure for an Apocalypse.　Thomas Merton.　CrMA

Stab to the guts in a rich battle-scene.　Uccello on the Heath.　Geoffrey Grigson.　WaP

Stabbed by the needles of the mind.　Crow Country.　Kenneth Slessor.　BoAV

Stabbed with the shadow light of wolves.　The One Who Grew to Be a Wolf.　Patricia Monaghan.　PoDr

Stabbing a dead leaf from below/Kills winter at a blow. Last Snow. Andrew Young. OxBTC

Stabbing those who lingered there/torn by screaming steel. Winter Warfare. Edgell Rickword. OBWP; OxBTC

The stable world itself is her great monument. The New Victory. Margaret Widdemer. WGRP

A stag dormant, antlered? In Autumn. Barbara Howes. LiSp

The stag, the runnable stag. A Runnable Stag. John Davidson. AnFE; BrPo; BSV; EvOK; FaPoR; FM; GoTS; GTBS; HAP; HBV 1-2; OBEV; OBVV; OxBTC; PrIm; SD; WiR

A stag with head held high!' An Old Man Said. Padraic Colum. OxBI

Stagger for stagger,/Star for star. East River (New York). Rosemary Thomas. AmFN

Stagnant, and green, and full of slimy things. October Journey. Margaret Walker. AmNP; IDB; PoBA; PoNe

The stain of blood that writes an island story. Landfall in Unknown Seas. Allen Curnow. AnNZ

Stain/red novae/from/my thighs. Nova. Charles Levendosky. SOTS

...A stained glass of surprise. Stained Glass. Willis Barnstone. AMV-81

Stained her rain-blue dress like tears. Chinoiseries. Amy Lowell. AnAmPo

Staining her fingers with the sweet juice. Pomegranate. Gail N. Harada. BrSi

Stakes with a smile the world against thy heart. Heart's Compass. Dante Gabriel Rossetti. MaVP; WHA

A stallion in the night. Song: "Sergei's a flower." Ruth Herschberger. FF

The stalls are put up around them. The Dusk of Horses. James Dickey. NYBP

The stalwart smash as putter meets ash/Where April holds the way. After Reading Twenty Years of Grantland Rice. Don Skene. InMe

Stammered in a dark dream of men and birds. But How It Came from Earth. Conrad Aiken. MoAB; MoAmPo

Stamp not upon it the Beloved's face. Odes, III. Hafiz. AWP

Stamping marigolds and parsley. Draw a Pail of Water. Anonymous. MoShBr

Stan' still Jordan,/Lord, I can't stan' still. Stan' Still Jordan. Anonymous. BoAN 1-2

...The stance of vague/Horror; paralysed with mere pity's peace? Pacific Sonnets. George Barker. LiTM

...Stand about my wraith,/And harbour me—almighty God. The Prophet Lost in the Hills at Evening. Hilaire Belloc. OxBoCh

Stand anywhere and you can be seen. Aran Islands. Irving Layton. NeAC

Stand by my side beneath the Southern Cross. Chant of Departure. Alfred Joseph Barrett. GoBC; ISi

Stand by us in the hour of need/And we shall stand by you. The Hands-Across-the-Sea Poem. J. C. Squire. HBMV

Stand by! Your humble servant owns/The Tenant of this Dark Apartment. The Skeleton in the Cupboard. Frederick Locker-Lampson. HBV 1-2

Stand, chin in hand,/suddenly vigilant. Climbing Zero Gully. David J. Morley. PoSH

Stand fast as often as thou recallest him,/O my heart, and do not flee. Stand Fast, O My Heart. Anonymous. LiTW

Stand in a row and learn. The Drunk in the Furnace. William Stanley Merwin. CAPP; LiTM; MAT; MP; NePoEA-2; NoAm; SM; TwCP

Stand "in HIm," in Him alone,/Gloriously "complete!" What Must I Do to Be Saved? Anonymous. STF

Stand lonesome, leaning on their staves. Old Men, White-Haired, beside the Ancestral Graves. Basho (Matsuo Basho). AWP

...Stand on a corner stiff/with rhetoric, promising nothing under the sun. Ecclesiastes. Derek Mahon. BIrV; CIP

Stand out the bright steamers/to kingdom come Away Above a Harborful. Lawrence Ferlinghetti. BoLoP; ErPo; NMP

Stand, stand firm, stop, sto-o-o-p! The Black Army. S. E. K. Mqhayi. PeSA

Stand-/;Still) She being Brand. Edward Estlin Cummings. AmC; ErPo; NOBA; OxBA

Stand still, I'll make Joan Hunter Dunn. To His Coy Mistress (parody). Stanley J. Sharpless. BXAP

Stand still, Time. The Unbeseechable. Frances Cornford. MoBrPo

Stand the ecstatic solitary pyres/Of unknown lovers, featureless with flame. Terra Australis. James Philip McAuley. NOAV

Stand tiptoe to touch the stars. Country Reverie. Carol Coates. CaP

Stand up and catch his mantle as it falls!' Dunciad Minor. A. D. Hope. BXAP

Stand up and clap Goosepimples. Coleman Barks. PV

Stand up and depart! Whispering Ghosts of the West. Anonymous. WTO

Stand up, ye bones. Your heaven is overhead. The Last Day. Daniel Sargent. CAW

Standeth God within the shadow, keeping watch above his own. Careless Seems the Great Avenger. James Russell Lowell. TreFT

Standing about the charmed root. The Hesperides. Alfred, Lord Tennyson. MBW 1-2; OAEL 1-2; SyP

Standing by an open grave. The Unscarred Fighter Remembers France. Kenneth Slade Alling. HBMV

Standing in a stillness that now is yours. Water Island. Howard Moss. CoAP; MP; NePoEA-2; NYBP; Prf

Standing in her two eyes, and will not call me with a word. A Translation from Petrarch. John Millington Synge. MoBrPo

Standing in ribbons, over our heads, for an hour. End of the Picnic. Francis Webb. NOAV

Standing like an old man/Cemented in the strong window. Clay and Water. Sandra Hochman. Str

Standing, like demigods, in light and triumph upon their own/Lookout! The Battle of Lookout Mountain. George Henry Boker. MC; PAH

Standing on end at echo even. Earth Psalm. Denise Levertov. PPP

Standing on my head makes swallowing this hot dog hard. Ingestion. Barry McDonald. PoL

Standing sentry for the avalanche. Strength through Joy. Kenneth Rexroth. FYAP; VGW

Standing slender on the tables in the dining-cars. Child of the Romans. Carl Sandburg. LaNeLa

Standing with held breath in the hall. Winter Night. Louis O. Coxe. NYBP

Standoffishness will kill the buff giraffe. The Giraffe. Marvin Solomon. NePoAm-2

Stands also, calm as glass. The Ice Skin. James Dickey. NYBP

Stands Brownie the cart-horse,/Whose labor is over. The Four Horses. James Reeves. PH

Stands forever the camp of that dead brigade. The Centenarian's Story. Walt Whitman. CTC

Stands in a drift of cabbage-leaves/And grieves. The Victoria Markets Recollected in Tranquillity. Furnley Maurice. BoAV

...Stands on a footstool/to observe the day. Haiku: "That early riser." Robert Phillips. GrPl

Stands steady the supple new growth/Beyond the strained stretch of the clutching tide. Sandstone. Anne Marriott. CaP

Stands the tall shadow of old John Burns! Night at Gettysburg. Don C. Seitz. OHIP

Stands with bowed and dewy head/That one little leaden Lad. The Sunken Garden. Walter De La Mare. HBMV

The star ascended in his nativity. At the Cannon's Mouth. Herman Melville. PAH

The star, burning the flowers in those gold cups,/held and exchanged by the children. Six of Cups. Diane Wakoski. CoPo

...A star comes/loose, slipping down like a sigh. Fall Song. Daniel David Moses. AMV-81

Star crack wings and raise dead. Star. Gene Derwood. NePA

The star-crowned solitude of thine oblivious hours! To One in Bedlam. Ernest Christopher Dowson. ACP; BrPo; MoBrPo; OBMV; VLP; WHA

Star in his casket. Play Ball! Robert Francis. AMV-80

A star in the Milky Way. In a China Shop. George Sidney Hellman. AA

The star is standing over the animal shed. Minstrel's Song. Ted Hughes. OBCP

The star laughs from its rotting shroud/Of flesh. O star of men! A Camp in the Prussian Forest. Randall Jarrell. AP; MiAP; MoAmPo; NMP; OBWP; OxBC; SM

A star nothing but a star lost in the fur of the night. Dreams. Andre Breton. PAI

Star of the Sea, shine for us. Our Lady of the Waves. George Mackay Brown. NePoEA-2

Star of the twilight, beautiful star. Star of the Evening. James M. Sayles. Par; SpRo

Star over star, a larger, lovelier unknown heaven beyond the/known! Day and Dark. George Cabot Lodge. AnAmPo; APA

The Star's shole Secret–in the Lake–/Eyes were not meant to know. The Outer from the Inner. Emily Dickinson. MAmP

The star that beams above the seas. Carlyle and Emerson. Montgomery Schuyler. AA

A star that has no parallax to speak of/Conduces to repose. Canopus. Bert Leston Taylor. ALV; FiBHP; HBMV; InMe; NOBL

The star that led to Bethlehem! O Years Unborn. John Richard Moreland. PGD

..."The star that moves–that's your father." Flying. Henry Carlile. AMV-80

Star, that points our high endeavor,/Whither Thou hast gone before! Via Crucis, Via Lucis. T. H. Hedge. BePJ

The star-ways must be won! Benediction. Georgia Douglas Johnson. GoSI

The star within the stone. Stone from the Gods. Irma Wassall. GoYe

The starch came raining down. Calamity. F. R. Scott. PeCV

Stare at him as if/he were the universe. Eichmann. Douglas Blazek. LTB

Steady, be ready,/Good luck! The Angler's Reveille. Henry Van Dyke. GN

Steady, boys, steady–/To give them our voices again and/again. A Song: "Come, cheer up, my lads, like a true British band." *Anonymous.* PAH

The steady journey due/To grief's ballast. Alone. Robert Finch. CaP; PeCV

Steady! Pull it thro-o-o-ough! Eight Oars and a Coxswain. Arthur Guiterman. SD

A steady, sturdy, staunch believer. A Dedication to G**** H******* Esq. Robert Burns. OBSV

Steal from the world, and not a stone/Tell where I lie. Ode on Solitude. Alexander Pope. ATP; AWP; DiPo; ExPo; FiP; GoBC; GoTF; HBV 1-2; HBVY; HeIP; InPo; NIP; OAEP; OBEC; PoPl; PoPle; PoRA; PPoe; Prf; SeCeV; TEP; TreFS; ViBoPo

Steal from the world, without a wife/To LAUGH–or CRY! The Widower. Royall Tyler. OBAL

Steal what you want,/not what the catalogue/says you ought to. Tutankhamen. William Dickey. Psk

A stealer of beef. A Laird, a Lord. *Anonymous.* OxNR; SaC

The steam rising wherever the edge may be? Tractatus. Derek Mahon. FaBoIP; OBSP

Steam rollers stay home, this year. Frost Heaves. Michael Dorris. AMV-80

Steaming and silent and standing straight,/sprouting leaves. Simultaneously. David Ignatow. GrPl; NCSH; PoL; TwCP; WeW

Steaming rakes and picking sacks! Raking Walnuts in the Rain. Monica Shannon. BrR; SiSoSe

The steel, if cold, is one, and strong and/pure. My Comrade. James Jeffrey Roche. AA

Steel plates and/long injections of pure oil. Oil. Gary Snyder. LCAP

Steep from an ocean where no landfall can be. Voyage West. Archibald MacLeish. VGW

The steep frowning glories of dark Loch no Garr. Lachin Y Gair. George Gordon, Lord Byron. OxBS

Steep rocks through the soaking ferns. Autumn Rain. Kenneth Rexroth. NU

Steep travel a-/head. Hitch Haiku. Gary Snyder. LCAP

Steeple and State!" said the Axe to the Sword. Ned Braddock. John Williamson Palmer. MC; PAH

The steeple gives a nod. Winwick, Lancashire. *Anonymous.* GBP

Stella behold, and then begin to endite. Astrophel and Stella, XV. Sir Philip Sidney. AAS; CoBE; OAEL 1-2; OBSC; SiPS

Stella looked on, and from her heavenly face/Sent forth the beams which made so fair my race. Astrophel to Stella, XLI. Sir Philip Sidney. AnFE

Stem of elder, tall and yellow/Twig of willow. Counting-Out Rhyme. Edna St. Vincent Millay. GoJo; InPK; MoShBr

Stemmed flower/at the cross's/foot A Very Old Woman. Clayton Eshleman. MAT

Stemming the wounds when they did bleed. The Corpus Christi Carol (from Scotland). *Anonymous.* GBP

A step is on the stairs. Hope. Randall Jarrell. MoAB; MoAmPo

Step lightly, strangers–also hold your noses. Beneath This Mound. Ambrose Bierce. DBV

Stepping in the twin moons of the dance Obon by the Hudson. Richard Oyama. BrSi

Stepping/on velvet Images. Alistair Campbell. MOON

Stepping out of the shells/of the only life it's never known. The Incubation. Al Zolynas. LTB

Stepping up to the adjoining window next in line. Fourth Street, San Rafael. Bill Berkson. APU

The steps I must stumble almost/fail me in his stride. Catching Up. David Walker. FAZ

Sterile and impotent and justified. Paradise Saved. A. D. Hope. OxBC

A stern and dreadful lesson learn/When, as you've read, they're cut in turn. How the Helpmate of Blue-Beard Made Free with a Door. Guy Wetmore Carryl. InMe

Stern truth will never write, "By hands unknown." "So Quietly". Leslie Pinckney Hill. BANP; IDB; PoBA

...Stick his bloody head on the battlements/on your way out, please. The Five-Minute Orlando Macbeth. George Macbeth. NOBL

Stick in the mud, old heart,/what are you doing here? The Marsh. W.D. Snodgrass. BoNaP; NePoEA

Stick one in the old man's crown. Tit, Tat, Toe. *Anonymous.* OxNR

Stick them up your asses lads/My Valentine to you. Valentine. Ernest Hemingway. OBAL; TW

Stickerum, stackerum, buck. One-ery, Two-ery, Ickery, Ann. *Anonymous.* OxNR

Sticking morphine in the arm and eating meat. Last Night in Calcutta. Allen Ginsberg. NoAm

Sticks, bones, or rags, or you! To a Lady Friend. William Henry Davies. MoBrPo

Stiff as nurses and slow as metaphysicians. Ode to the Protestant Poets. Paul Hoover. APU

The stiff locks squeaking/"I love I love." Rowing. Ed Ochester. Str

A stiff, naked, without a name. The Death of the Craneman. Alfred Hayes. LiTA; NAMP; NCSH; WaP

The stiff, still features. Canto VII. Ezra Pound. NoAm; NOBA

Stiff with weapons, fighting back over the same ground. Thistles. Ted Hughes. NoAm; OBSP; OxBTC

Stiffening of old men Mother, in the 45 cent Bottle. Paul Blackburn. NYP

Stil'd but the shaddowes of us men? Song: "That women are but men's shadows." Ben Jonson. FaBoEn

Still a memory we cherish though the recollection/pales. John Betjeman's Brighton (parody). Gavin Ewart. FaBoPa

Still a rover of the seas and glory's own! The Lost War-Sloop. Edna Dean Proctor. PAH

Still achieving, still pursuing,/Learn to labor and to wait. A Psalm of Life. Henry Wadsworth Longfellow. AA; FPL; HBV 1-2; TAP; TreF

The still air of the speechless night,/When lovers crown their vows. The True Lover. Alfred Edward Housman. ATP; BoLiVe; LiTL

The still air sparkled keen. A Frosty Morning. John Davidson. VLP

Still am I lord, and will in freedom/strive. Night-Thoughts. Solomon Ibn Gabirol. TrJP

...Still am I/The torch, but where's the moth that still dares die? Modern Beauty. Arthur Symons. EnLit; HBV 1-2

Still an Angel appear to each Lover beside,/But still be a Woman to you. Song: "When thy Beauty appears." Thomas Parnell. OBEC; OBEV; UnTE

Still are secret, unreach'd and untouch'd and not subject/to you. The Red-Haired Man's Wife. James Stephens. HBMV; MoBrPo; OBVV

Still as a sea-rock, sat a toad. Events. George O'Neil. HBMV

Still, as still as everness returning. Homage and Lament for Ezra Pound in Captivity. Robert Duncan. NOBA

Still at the prophets' feet the nations sit. Bibliolaters: God Is Not Dumb. James Russell Lowell. WGRP

Still base as when from earth it came. On True Worth. Muslih-ud-Din Sa'di. LiTW

Still be my vision, O Ruler of all. A Prayer. *Anonymous.* OnYI

Still be thou kind, for still thou wast most/dear. Invocation. Edmund Clarence Stedman. AA

Still be to my fond hope a friend. To Silence. Thomas Sturge Moore. BrPo

Still beaming bright and fair. That Wind. Emily Bronte. CH

A still black star/and drown Sea Island Miscellany. Richard P. Blackmur. MoVE

Still bringing all the pain they cost. Music and Memory. John Albee. AA

Still burning from their final touch of you. The Ending. Paul Engle. NYBP

Still calls that deep and dangerous ford/The Passage of the Scot. The Island of the Scots (excerpt). Ayton [(or Aytoun)] Sir Robert. VLP

Still coiled around the trunk of the tree of paradise. The Golden Fleece. Oscar Williams. PoA

Still cold, that should last us, and our grandchildren. Burning Mountain. William Stanley Merwin. NYBP

Still cramped and wet from the journey. May 10th. Maxine W. Kumin. BoNaP; NYBP; RFM

Still crying out for life!! This Hour. Oliver La Grone. NNP; PoNe

"Still do I love, still shed my innocent light, my Blood, for thee." Still Falls the Rain. Edith Sitwell. BoWoP; ChMP; CoBMV; DTC; EBCP; LiTM; MoAB; MoBrPo; MoPo; MoRP; MP; NoAm; NOBE; OBWP; SBVL; SeCePo; TEP; TrGrPo; TwCP; WaaP

Still, down the glades of Arden, dance/The feet of Rosalind. The Deathless. Ednah Proctor (Clarke) Hayes. AA

Still dreaming audibly. A Summer's Dream. Elizabeth Bishop. OxBC

Still drowsy with wine. Plum Blossoms. Chu Shu-chen. PBWP

Still Esau went on sawing. I Saw Esau Sawing Wood. *Anonymous.* FaBoNo

Still find my way back. Long Walks in the Afternoon. Margaret Gibson. AMV-81; MAYP

Still from care and thinking free,/Is a sailor's life at sea. Jack the Guinea Pig. *Anonymous.* AmSS

Still gather to a language without flaw/Our loves, and all the hours of our death. Bell Speech. Richard Wilbur. AP; CABA; MoAB; MoAmPo; MoVE

Still glides the swan across the mere of magic,/Dark under cypress. Program Note on Sibelius. Donald Campbell Babcock. UnS

Still greater wonders have occurred ere this. Hope for Miracles. Eschenbach, Sir Wolfram von. LiTW

Still guarding the peace it defends. Swedenborg's Skull. Vernon Watkins. FaBoTw

Still he dies,/one eye closed on the ground. One Eyed Black Man in Nebraska. Sam Cornish. PoBA

Still hell is an entrancing place/Because you're going there. Love Song. Samuel ("Paul Vesey") Allen. NNP

Still his remembering lips know her caress! Ulysses Returns. Roselle Mercier Montgomery. HBMV

Still holding and feeding the stem of the/contained flower. The Shape of the Fire. Theodore Roethke. AmP; CMoP; LiTA; MiAP; MoAB

Still, how nice for our egos. A Local Storm. Donald Justice. NCSH

Still I can't say to nurse the trumpet. Domestic Duties. Richard Emil Braun. NoAm

Still I can trust His love to give/What is best for me. The Best for Me. *Anonymous.* STF

Still I have you–so I am not afraid! Body of the Queen. Donald Evans. AnAmPo

Still, I keep my weapons handy, sitting here/Smoking and shaving and drinking the dry beer. A Way of Life. Howard Nemerov. NIP

Still I must go and weed/Hard in my garden. On an Old Muff. Frederick Locker-Lampson. CenHV

Still, I must try to think a little of it,/With so much winter in my head and hand. The Paperweight. Gjertrud Schnackenberg. SM

Still I needs must cook their dinner. The Ship's Cook, a Captive Sings. Hugo von Hofmannsthal. TrJP

Still/I/play,/trimming/the wick. Warm rain, sunny wind. Li Ch'ing-chao. BoWoP

Still, I search in these woods and find nothing worse/than myself,... Kind Sir: These Woods. Anne Sexton. GoYe

Still I swear, she's my loved one. She's My Love. Augustus Young. CIP

Still in New-England shall be my delight. God's Controversy with New-England. Michael Wigglesworth. SCAP

Still in the quiet o the hills. On Ellson Fell. William Landles. PoSH

Still innocent of us. The Lonesome Dream. Lisel Mueller. CoAP

Still is that fur as soft as when the lists/In youth thou enter'dst on glass bottled wall. To a Cat. John Keats. BoC; PCat

Still is the epiglottis–/The warrior is dead. Lines Written after a Battle. *Anonymous.* InMe

Still it flows on, and shall for ever flow. The Village. George Crabbe. CEP; LAuP

Still it's not deep enough/to drink the moon from. Adam's Complaint. Denise Levertov. BoWoP; NNaP; PP; SOTW; TEP

Still journeying toward the sunset and their rest. An Old-World Thicket. Christina Georgina Rossetti. SBG

Still knocks at my gate. Haiku: "I called to the wind." Kyorai. WSC

Still Lalage's sweet smile, sweet voice even there/I will adore. Integer Vitae. Horace. EnLi 1-2

Still, leagues beyond those leagues, there is more sea. The House of Life. Dante Gabriel Rossetti. HBV 1-2

Still leave their lower province to themselves. The Emigrant: Winter in Lower Canada. Standish O'Grady. OBCV

Still let me sleep, embracing clouds in vain;/And never wake to feel the day's disdain. To Delia. Samuel Daniel. HBV 1-2

Still let my thoughts, leaving the worldly roar/Like pilgrims, wander on thy haunted shore. Lough Bray. Standish O'Grady. IrPN

Still let the earth abide to set Thee forth,/Or vanish like a smoke to set forth Thee. Lord, Grant Us Calm. Christina Georgina Rossetti. OxBoCh

Still let us for his golden corn,/Send up our thanks to God! The Corn-Song. John Greenleaf Whittier. GN; OHIP

The still light of planets and the star-swarms whirled. Song: "Something calls and whispers, along the city street." Georgiana Goddard King. HBV 1-2

Still listening to the bee, still basking in the sun. The March Bee. Edmund Charles Blunden. PoPle

Still live I in thy thoughts, but as in heaven I live. Elisa, or an Elegy upon the Unripe Decease... Phineas Fletcher. ViBoPo

Still lovely and still fugitive? Unwritten Poems. William Winter. AA

Still loving, and ageing by centuries... Nocturne in the Women's Prison. Maria Beneyto. WPOW

Still loving Song, but loving more/Life, of which Song is made! Farewell. Harry Kemp. HBMV

Still master in his pyramid. With Metaphor. Sarah Wingate Taylor. GoYe

Still may meet again and together build/One house before we die. The Dual Site. Michael Hamburger. MP; NePoEA-2

An still my ghost sits at my eyes/And thirsts for their untroubled snows. The Mountains. Walter De la Mare. BrPo

Still my reputation/reaches to the skies/like a dust storm. Since "The Pillow Knows All." Lady Ise. WPOW

Still oh and the roaches are sleeping Aubade: N.Y.C. Robert Wallace. HoPM

Still on Israel's head forlorn,/Every nation heaps its scorn. The World's Justice. Emma Lazarus. HBV 1-2

Still over us, still in parenthesis. The Picture. Robert Lowell. NoAm

Still past their lashes–still, the treasure slips? Carmina Amico. Edward James. PeHV

Still Petrarch's Genius weeps o'er Laura's tomb. Sonnet to Valclusa. Thomas Russell. CEP; OBEC

Still pining for love of your tender white bodies O children of Wichita! Wichita Vortex Sutra, II. Allen Ginsberg. NaP

...Still pitifully gathering all/windfalls onto its damp lap of graves. In an Old Orchard. Peter Kane Dufault. NYBP

Still placed in the path/That winds to the spring. Leavetaking. Lisa Reape. AMV-81

Still quaffing, to my lip I place a finger,/Lest waking he should freshen my delight. The Poet to the Sleeping Saki. Johann Wolfgang von Goethe. PeHV

Still quiring to the young-ey'd cherubims. The Merchant of Venice. William Shakespeare. BoC; FaBoRV; FiP; GBL; GN; GoBC; GoTF; OHFP; PoPle; TreFS; TrGrPo; WHA

Still raised her yearning vision to the stars. Survival. Florence Earle Coates. AA

Still rubs his hands before him, like a fly,/In a queer sort of meditative mirth. Modern Love, XIX. George Meredith. VLP

Still sat and preened a common songless fieldfare. Illusion. Sir Edmund Gosse. SyP

Still shall the lustre of his name/Stand as his cenotaph! On a Bust of Lincoln. Clinton Scollard. OHIP

Still shall tremble/At a gray hair. Unbeliever. Dorothy Dow. HBMV

Still should I surely/Hear you call. Above the Wall. Susannah P. Malarkey. AMV-80

Still songs to be sung on the other side/of mankind. Thread Suns. Paul Celan. OBVE

Still, still the mild Madonna face will glow,/Although the lamp has darkened long ago. The Madonna's Lamp. Prince of Sweden, Wilhelm. CAW

Still, still the wild blue feather/brings my mild father. Blue Jay. Robert Francis. ELU; PCP

The still, strange land, unvexed of sun or stars,/Where Lancelot rides clanking thro' the haze. At Queensferry. William Ernest Henley. VLP

Still strove with his last ounce of courage,/To reach the unreachable stars. The Impossible Dream. Joe Darion. BLSo

Still such an Ethiope be. A Maske for Lydia. Thomas Randolph. AnAnS 2

Still talking when/the night had gone. Deep in Love. Bhavabhuti. LLLT

Still that his path may be worth pursuing,/And to bring peace thereto. The Haunter. Thomas Hardy. AtBAP; NOBE; PoPle; QFR

Still, the dust devils swirl, the old wind blows. High Wheat Country. Elijah L. Jacobs. AmFN

Still the may falls. Bright Clouds. Edward ("Edward Eastaway") Thomas. BrPo

...Still the old lady shakes her puff/In the well of the wind, and feathers fly from the rip. Snow. Ruth Stone. NYBP

Still the poor and weak and weary/Only, worship and believe. Flowers for the Altar. Digby Mackworth Dolben. GoBC

Still therefore of Thy graces shall be my/Song's ditty. Psalm XIII. Sir Philip Sidney. FCP

Still, though many an age be gone,/Round Killarney lingers. Killarney. William Larminie. AnIV

Still threaded with the mountain mist, the morn/Sat like some glowing conqueror satisfied. The Dawn on the Lievre. Archibald Lampman. CaP

Still to be wrangling in a noisy grave. Demos. Edwin Arlington Robinson. AP

Still to call forth a natural cupidity/In any native who's a byre to build. Boat-Haven, Co. Mayo. Geoffrey Taylor. NeIP

Still to survive in my immortal song. How Many Foolish Things. Michael Drayton. CBEP

Still to us at twilight comes love's old song,/Comes love's old sweet song. Love's Old Sweet Song. G. Clifton Bingham. BLSo; FaBoBe; FSN; GoTF; TreF

Still to us this strength and song/Through eternal days prolong. The First and the Last. Horatius Bonar. BePJ

Still trying to get their crisp/black fingers on our white throats Remembrance of Things Past. Horace Coleman. FAZ

Still trying/to steer things/his own way My Elbow Ancestry. Larry Mollin. NeAC

Still turning round the earth. Aridity. Clive Staples Lewis. BoC

Still 'twas me that went wid her right on to the end! The Road. Patrick Reginald Chalmers. HBV 1-2

Still undiscovered shore. The Long Harbour. Mary Ursula Bethell. ACV; AnNZ

Still visioning the stars! Oriflamme. Jessie Redmond Fauset. BANP; BlSi; PoBA

Still wandering in a City of the Dead! Naples. Samuel Rogers. OBTV

Still waters running deep/Along the embankment walk. Twice Shy. Seamus Heaney. NCSH; TwCP

Still we are the same,/Sideways Russian New Year. Bill Berkson. ANYP

Still, we need that adult help/If we are ever to develop.   An Underdeveloped Country.   D. J. Enright.   NOBL

Still we shout with voice emphatic,/Hi!   Roundel in the Rain.   *Anonymous.*   FiBHP

Still wearing her ancient/polka dot dress.   Red Riding Hood at the Acropolis.   Myra Sklarew.   DFT

Still wrestling with the father.   Still Wrestling.   Phil Boiarski.   AMV-81

Still you brood in the lake like wild rice.   Lament, with Flesh and Blood.   Sandra McPherson.   SM

The stillness is all in the key of that desolate sound.   Autumn Refrain.   Wallace Stevens.   LiTA; WeW

Stillness returns as of old. Desolate stretches the desert.   The Dead of the Wilderness.   Chaim Nachman Bialik.   AWP

Stillness was an eternity/long since begun   The Rose.   William Carlos Williams.   NOBA

A sting, and honey, and a body small.   Epigram: "Three things must epigrams."   *Anonymous.*   NIP

Stir not the blissful quiet of the night.   The Singer.   Edward Dowden.   IrPN

Stir not to-night till the sun whitens over you.   Lullaby of the Woman of the Mountain.   Padraic Pearse.   OnYI

The stir of the world, the music of the mountain.   Fawn's Foster-Mother.   Robinson Jeffers.   NoAm; NOBA

The stirred dust ankle deep/Steams up languid, to clog the struggling lamp flame.   Hero Entombed I.   Peter Quennell.   LiTB

Stirred with a spade/By an old maid.   Lemonade.   *Anonymous.*   GBP

Stirring ashes/from a sleeping fire/at night.   Grandmother.   Ray A. Young Bear.   STE

The stirring of a sonnet still unborn.   Quickening.   Christopher Morley.   HBMV

Stirring the curtain back and forth/soundless/into an unknown sky   Muse Poem.   Kathryn Van Spanckeren.   FF

Stirs proudly and secretly in my blood.   Dublin Made Me.   Donagh MacDonagh.   AnIV; NeIP

Stirs the culprit,–Life!   Surgeons Must Be Very Careful.   Emily Dickinson.   CBEP; DiPo; ImOP; TAP

The stock market went up 18 points...   White Weekend.   Quincy Troupe.   NBP

The stock-response still raging in the shroud?   Rites for a Demagogue.   Anthony Thwaite.   NePoEA-2

Stodole pumpa, pum, pum, pum.   Walking at Night.   *Anonymous.*   FSW

Stole my morning song!   Translation.   Anne Spencer.   BANP

Stole sixteen of the King's royal deer/And he sold them in Gilhooley.   Geordie.   *Anonymous.*   FSW

Stomp-dancing out there on the lawn/where the living room used to be.   Home Movies.   Carter Revard.   VoR

A stomp of feet. A bevy of swift hands.   Woman Me.   Maya Angelou.   BlSi

The stone and marsh and leaf and spray.   From My Thought.   Daniel Smythe.   GoYe

Stone cedes to blossom everywhere.   City of Monuments.   Muriel Rukeyser.   NAMP

STONE——COAL!   Southern Season.   Alice Moser Claudel.   TAT

Stone-for-a-statue waveworn pebble-round.   The Man in the Bowler Hat.   Arthur Seymour John Tessimond.   HaMV

Stone for the sake of the souls of the slain birds sailing.   Over Sir John's Hill.   Dylan Thomas.   CABL; DiPo; LiTB; MoAB

A stone is a better pillow than many visions.   Clouds of Evening.   Robinson Jeffers.   MoAB; MoAmPo

...The stone like stone/hit bottom and was obsolete.   Last Things.   Bill Manhire.   OCNZ

...Stone of considerable size/growing beneath one's/skin?/I see.   I Think of Housman Who Said the Poem Is a Morbid Secretion...   Judith Kroll.   UnPo

The stone of Sisyphus rushes/down.   Arrival in Hell.   Ricarda Huch.   PBWP

A stone remote in some bleak gully of the hills!   Jessie.   Thomas Edward Brown.   HBV 1-2

The stone the angel rolled away with tears/Is back upon your mouth these thousand years.   To Jesus on His Birthday.   Edna St. Vincent Millay.   TrCP; TrGrPo

...The stone/the builders had doubts about/has become the corner-stone   Prayer for Kafka and Ourselves.   Anthony Rudolf.   VWA

The stone, the stone parentheses of years.   Long Island Springs.   Howard Moss.   GP; HoAn; UnPo

The stone-walled fields are featureless.   Henry James at Newport.   Weldon Kees.   PoA

...Stones are like deaths./They uncover limits.   In Defense of Metaphysics.   Charles Tomlinson.   MoBrPo

Stones are tender, thorns are kind,/Where your piping goes before.   To William Blake.   Olive Dargan.   HBMV

The stones bow as the saddened armies pass.   Poem against the Rich.   Robert Bly.   NMP; NoAm; NOBA

Stones in the high weeds/mark where there was.   Gone.   Ralph Pomeroy.   DFF

The stones of cheerfulness, the steel of money, the father of/rocks.   A Busy Man Speaks.   Robert Bly.   ConAP

The stones of Gallowes Hill shall tread.   Salem.   Edmund Clarence Stedman.   AA; PAH

Stones of the river rising up/in the forms of women.   From the Other Shore.   William Pitt Root.   MAYP

The stones shall rise in towers to answer him.   In Memory of Bryan Lathrop.   Edgar Lee Masters.   PoA

Stones shall sing in ecstasy!   Psychometrist.   James Stephens.   NoAm

...Stoning, burning,/beheading, and strangling.   For the Sin–.   *Anonymous.*   TrJP

Stood Helva of Nesvek and Esbern Snare!   Kallundborg Church.   John Greenleaf Whittier   BeLS

Stood like the closed gate of your own backyard.   Returned to Frisco.   W.D. Snodgrass.   AP

Stood on their feet/This very morning.   Both My Child.   Teitoku.   OFD

Stood the black shako with its white death's-head.   The Last Evening.   Rainer Maria Rilke.   OBWP; WaaP

Stood the Giraffe beside a Tree.   Giraffe and Tree.   Walter James Turner.   CH; GrPl

Stood, transfixed,/by another fear.   The Tiger.   Robert Creeley.   GP

Stoop, and begin the ancient croaking.   The Poets Agree to Be Quiet by the Swamp.   David Wagoner.   CoAP; VGW

Stoop, but upon your back be ever conscious/Of sunlight, and a shadow that may grow.   Samadhi.   Conrad Aiken.   MAPA

Stop–docile and omnipotent/At its own stable door–   I like to see it lap the miles.   Emily Dickinson.   AmLP; BoWoP; CABA; DiPo; InPK; LiTA; LiTM; MoAB; MoAmPo; MoShBr; MoVE; NAWM 1-2; NOBA; OBAL; OBCA; OxBA; PrIm; SoSe

...Stop here, my Muse! forbear the/rest,/And veil that grief which cannot be exprest.   Mully of Mountown (excerpt).   William King.   FM

Stop I'll get/all of it published yet/I'll get them all   A Judezmo Writer in Turkey Angry.   Stephen Levy.   VWA

"Stop it," she says, "the hammering in the hall."   Beside My Grandmother.   Al Lee.   SM

...Stop it so they can/have some peace.   The Hostage and His Takers.   Sharon Olds.   SOTS

Stop! Kookaburra, stop! Kookaburra,/Leave some there for me.   Kookaburra.   *Anonymous.*   FSW

STOP! Lemme outa here! I still can't sleep!   Sleep, Madame, Sleep.   Annemarie Ewing.   NePoAm

Stop, Reader, and if not in a hurry, shed a tear.   Epitaph at Hadleigh, Suffolk.   *Anonymous.*   FaBoCo

Stop, stop and listen for the bough top/Is whistling...   The Blackbird of Derrycairn.   Austin Clarke.   NeIP

"Stop, stop," you/whisper,/"Lest you wake the pain."   Pomegranate Tree in Jerusalem.   Zerubavel Gilead.   VWA

Stop the courts in each county, and bully the/laws.   A Radical Song of 1786.   St. John Honeywood.   PAH

Stop the white man's mule stop/in his traces.   My Relatives for the Most.   Frederick B. Hudson.   AMV-80

Stop there, wringing our hands this time.   The Stranger Not Ourselves.   William Stafford.   NNaP

Stop thinking of the girl you love,/Bow down your head and cry.   Bow Down Your Head and Cry.   *Anonymous.*   CoSo; WTO

...Stop to tuck/Each sleepy blinking town in bed!   Trains at Night.   Frances Frost.   BrR; TiPo

Stop, traveller, and piss.   Epitaph.   George Gordon, Lord Byron.   FaBoEE; TW

Stop you my mouth with still still kissing me.   Astrophel and Stella, LXXXI.   Sir Philip Sidney.   AAS; SiPS

Stopped short - and closed his triumphs/in a jail.   On a Travelling Speculator.   Philip Freneau.   AA

(Stopping of course for ice cream popcorn 'n coke)/to watch the late movie.   Pacified.   Thomas G. Nickens.   LFAC

Stopping the breath with banner of a name.   Contact.   Dorothy Livesay.   CaP

Stoppt and swam and ate my lunch.   A Walk.   Gary Snyder.   NoAm; NOBA

Stops and starts and guides them,–is our Father's hand.   Our Father's Hand.   Annie Johnson Flint.   BLRP

An' stops dis ha't f'um sighin'!   Negro Serenade.   James Edwin Campbell.   BANP

The Storax, Spiknard, Myrrhe, and Ladanum.   Another on Her.   Robert Herrick.   SpRo

Store advice/in a cool, dry place.   A Manifesto for the Faint-Hearted.   Carole Oles.   SM

...Streaming over the/roof of this room, and I am deep in my comforter. Returning to the World. Laura Chester. NPGG

...A streaming wound which heals in evil. October 1942. Roy Fuller. WaP

...Streams ever repeat/Their senseless noise to perfect solitude. Delusions VI. Charles Madge. NeBP

The street and back to my brick house, my sleeping wife. Is There Life across the Street? Robert Watson. GP

The street lights are on/tony get the boys Tony Get the Boys. D. L. Graham. PoBA

Streets of an endless town. Night falls in rain. Elegy for an Estrangement. John Holloway. NePoEA

The streets will flicker, the asylums will be still. The Gothic Dusk. Frederic Prokosch. PoA

Streiket his length on the chuckie-stanes, houpan the Boss/wadna spy him. Sisyphus. Robert Garioch. PoSH

Strength and austerity/that this land has. This Land. Ian Mudie. NOAV

Strength and calm for every crisis/Come–in telling Jesus all. Tell Jesus. *Anonymous.* BePJ; STF

Strength ever lessening, hope grown/ever less. Remembrance. Antoni Slonimski. TrJP

The strength he gains is from the embrace he gives. Faith. Alexander Pope. WGRP

Strength in the struggle. Ask me my name! Anchor. *Anonymous.* AnOE

Strength'ning their arms to warfare glad and grim. The Christian Soldier (excerpt). G. Anketall "Woodbine Willie" Studdert-Kennedy. TRV

Strength of soul brings health/To the place of feasting. Spirit Song. *Anonymous.* WTO

The strength you sweat/Shall blossom yet/In golden glory to the sun. Go, Ploughman, Plough. Joseph Campbell. HBMV

Strengthen, my Love, this castle of my heart. Rondel: "Strengthen, my Love, this castle of my heart." Charles d'Orleans. AWP

Strengthen thee, in this sorrow, I pray the gods! A Roman Officer Writes. Charles M. Doughty. FaBoTw

The strenuous faithful buckled to their prayers. Last Night We Had a Thunderstorm in Style. Robert Louis Stevenson. NOBV

Stretch'd out, and bleaching in the northern blast. The Seasons. James (1700-48) Thomson. BSV; EBEV

Stretch forth Thy arm from out the ark,/And take me to Thy rest. O That I Had Wings Like a Dove. *Anonymous.* OxBoCh

Stretch hands, and bid ye welcome home! To the Thirty-Ninth Congress. John Greenleaf Whittier. PAH

Stretch out immense, and eddy all the Main. Halieutica. Oppian. OBVE

Stretch out those comrade hands to be/A shelter over land and sea! The Christ of the Andes (excerpt). Edwin Markham. TrPWD

Stretch themselves out and, like boats passing the boom/At sunset, reach open sea–a spiritual south Antwerp Musee des Beaux-Arts. Alan Ross. NYBP

Stretch toward me their indulgent, graven arms. Helen, the Sad Queen. Paul Valery. AWP; CAW

The stretched hawk fly. Summer Wish. Louise Bogan. AnFE; CoAnAm

Stretched mazily this way and that in perspective. The Song of the Spirits. Joseph Sheridan Lefanu. OnYI

Stretched out to all things, and with all content! Christian Ethics. Thomas Traherne. NOCV

Stretched up thin to catch the sun. A Gnarled Riverina Gum-Tree. Ernest G. Moll. PoAu 1-2

Stretching across the miles that sever you from me. In Death Divided. Thomas Hardy. DTC

Strewings need none, every flower/Is in this word, Batchelour. To His Tomb-Maker. Robert Herrick. SeCV 1-2

Striae of Grief by Grief by Grief. Bi-focal. Hal Porter. BoAV

Stricken at last Time's lonely Titans bend. Three Sonnets on Oblivion. George Sterling. HBV 1-2

The stricken silences,/When Thou art dumb! Loneliness. Edwin Essex. TrPWD

Strides through the windows and the doors/and the stone floors To Ultima Thule. George Dangerfield. CAW

...Strife shall cease/Upon the highway of the Prince of Peace. Heralds of Christ. Laura S. Copenhaver. AH

Strike a sad note, and fix 'em trees again. Song: "Music, thou queen of souls, get up and string." Thomas Randolph. OBSP

Strike at the truth of composition. Shakespeare, an Epistle to David Garrick, Esq.. Robert Lloyd. NOEC

Strike! for the brave revere the brave! The Banner of the Jew. Emma Lazarus. AA; TrJP

Strike for the crown of victory! Upon the Hill before Centreville. George Henry Boker. PAH

Strike for your country, "O'Donnell Aboo!" O'Donnell Aboo. Michael Joseph McCann. FSW; OnYI

Strike home thy pipe, Tom Long! Tom Long. *Anonymous.* EBEV

Strike! let every blaze and sinew/Tell on ages, tell for God. We Are Living, We Are Dwelling. Arthur Cleveland Coxe. TRV

Strike me unaware/And transfix my heart. Hunting. Yehoash. TrJP

Strike! Men of the North and West. Men of the North and West. Richard Henry Stoddard. PAH

Strike off your chains, and make your souls your own! Suave Mari Magno. Lucretius (Titus Lucretius Carus). AWP

Strike sayle! go soule! rest followes them that dye. Fly from the World. *Anonymous.* NCEP

Strike the blow! Strike the Blow. *Anonymous.* PAH

Strike through my breast and pour your courage in–/Enough to last this little way to night. Hymn to the Sun. William Alexander Percy. TrPWD

Strike ye our land/With curved horns! Buffalo Dance. Alice Corbin. BPAW

A striken deer, I seek the forest zones. O Spirit of Venus Whom I Adore. *Anonymous.* PeHV

Strikes her glorious flag at last/To the formless thing that builded Roncador. The Kearsarge. James Jeffrey Roche. AA; PAH

Strikes his thundering hoofs like a proud highbred racer. Metrical Feet. Samuel Taylor Coleridge. HBV 1-2

Strikes never moon or star. The Earth. Ralph Waldo Emerson AA

Striking their pensive bosoms–Here lies GAY. Epitaph XI On Mr. Gay. In Westminster Abbey, 1732. Alexander Pope. CEP

Striking two towns, and fed its flocks. The Children of Greenock. W. S. Graham. FaBoTw

String me up, Dave! Go dig my grave! I rode him across/the skies! The Horse Thief. William Rose Benet. BBV; BPAW; HBMV; MoAmPo; OnMSP

String of pearls with whose final link/their lives, as ours, are irreclaimably fated. Georges Bank. Julia Older. WOLT

The striped wasp/Confused by the Book/Can thrive on/The dark scent of prayer. The Dark Scent of Prayer. Rose Drachler. VWA

Stripes going round. The Ronan Robe Series. Jaune Quick-To-See-Smith. TWSS

Stripped of body's shame/and heart's modesty? Riding the Blue Sapphire Mountains. Mahadevi (Mahadeviyakka). BoWoP; PBWP

Stripped to the pants, we did advance at the Battle of Bull Run! The Battle of Bull Run. *Anonymous.* AmFP

"Strive and thrive!" cry "Speed,–fight on, fare ever/There as here!" Asolando. Robert Browning. EnLit; FaBV; FiP; GTBS; HBV 1-2; HBVY; OAEP; TEP; TreFT; TrGrPo; VLP

Strive for an honored name–/Do it Right; Do It Right. Samuel O. Buckner. WBLP

Strive in this, and love the strife. The Banquet. George Herbert. AnAnS 1

Strive not with Love; for if ye do, it will ye thus befall. Love's Rebel. Henry Howard, Earl of Surrey. OBSC

Strives to surpass herself, and still resumes the song. The Impious Feast. Robert Eyres Landor. OBRV

Striving to smoke a tear in Heaven's eyes. Mad Maid's Whim. Randolph Stow. ACV

Stroke and loll, loll and stroke, stroke, loll. Sea-Ruck. Richard Eberhart. MOS

The stroke of death is as a lover's pinch,/Which hurts, and is desired. Dost thou lie still? Antony and Cleopatra. William Shakespeare. FaBoRV

Stroking its dales with a tingling finger of peace. Carol for His Darling on Christmas Day. Derek Stanford. NeBP

Stroking the Melody–/Is this–the way? Title divine–Is mine! Emily Dickinson. NOBA; ViBoPo

Strolling arm in arm, perhaps with cigars/through our own American Beauties. Dykes in the Garden. Sharon Barba. PeHV

...Strolling down the/streets arm-in-arm / like tropical apparitions / only visible to a/few. Chiqui and Terra Nova. Jessica Hagedorn. APU

Strong and content, I travel the open road. Afoot and Light-Hearted, I Take to the Open Road. Walt Whitman. TiPo

Strong and content I travel the open road. Song of the Open Road. Walt Whitman. HBVY; MCCG; RFM

Strong arms and broad claymores, three hundred and ten! McLean's Welcome. James Hogg. OxBS

Strong as love when my woman calls me! Song of the Full Catch. Constance Lindsay Skinner. CaP

The strong demand, contend, prevail; the beggar is a fool! The Suppliant. Georgia Douglas Johnson. BALP; CDC; PoBA; PoNe

Strong enough/to encompass our lives. For all my Grandmothers. Beth Brant. STE

Strong eyes and brave,/Inexorable to save! The Daguerreotype. William Vaughn Moody. AnAmPo

Strong flakes of radiance on the tremulous/stream. An Evening Walk (excerpt). William Wordsworth. CoBE

Strong in faith, with mind subdued,/Yet elate with gratitude. Day by Day the Manna Fell. Josiah Conder. TrCP; VLP

Strong in thy strength, to anticipate/Rewarding Destiny!' Anticipaton. Emily Bronte. OBNC

Strong is your hold, O love.) The Last Invocation. Walt Whitman. AmP; AnFE; APA; BoLiVe; HBV 1-2; MoAmPo; OBSP; OxBA; PoEL 1-5; TreFT; TrGrPo; TrPWD; TRV

Strong men and lads are dwelling/In Denmark's island glades. There Is a Charming Land. Adam Oehlenschlager. AWP

The strong men gittin' stronger./Strong men..../Stronger.... Strong Men. Sterling A. Brown. BANP; BPo; CNA; FB; PoBA; PPON; TTY

The strong men keep coming on. Upstream. Carl Sandburg. HBMV; MoAB; MoAmPo; MoRP

Strong old North Wind from the branches/Shakes the nuts; 'tis nutting time! Nutting Time. Emilie Poullsson. BrR

Strong perfumes, and glaring light,/Oft destroy both smell, and sight. To My Cousin, (C.R.) Marrying My Lady (A.). Thomas Carew. AnAnS 2; SeCP

Strong scented with the summer's warm delight. Beans in Blossom. John Clare. VLP

Strong, sly, and painful, doubt inserts its knife. Crematorium. Sir John Betjeman. PoA

...A strong strong man/older, but no wiser than the defect of love. The New World. LeRoi (Imamu Amiri Baraka) Jones. NoAm; NoP

Strong, strong, strong! Lament for Sean. D. J. O'Sullivan. NeIP

Strong to obstruct, tenacious to delay. Buffalo. Roy Daniells. CaP

Strong trouble ariseth now already. The Elder Edda: Part of the Lay of Sigrdrifa. Anonymous. OBVE

The strong who, having wrought, can never/die. Commemoration Ode. Harriet Monroe. AA

Strong with its cryptic American,/Its dated beauty. Manhole Covers. Karl Shapiro. AmFN; GoJo; GP; NCSH

Strong with love's humility. Pilgrim Song. Florence Earle Coates. OHIP

A stronger soul within a finer frame. Baptism. Claude McKay. AnEnPo; PoNe

Stronger their clasp upon the wind-swept bough/When the birds sleep. That Which Hath Wings Shall Tell. Linda Lyon Van Voorhis. GoBC

...The stronger we our houses do build,/The less chance we have of being killed. The Albion Battleship Calamity. William McGonagall. BXAP; PeD

The strongest of the universe/Guarding the weakest! The Weakest Thing. Elizabeth Barrett Browning. HBV 1-2

Stronghold given by God to Thesele. The Birth of Moshesh. David Granmer T. Bereng. PeSA; TTY

Strow at thy door/That one poor Blossome. Silex Scintillans. Henry Vaughan. AnAnS 1

Struck by bass!/in the brain. The Big One. Luis Cabalquinto. BrSi

Struck free and holy in one Name always. A Name for All. Hart Crane. PP; VGW

...Struggle end/With the last kindness of a foe or friend? The Jungle. Alun Lewis. MoPo

Struggling to death and birth. What's Living? Linda Hogan. AMV-81

Strut your stuff, people–/I/won't/care! Trombone Solo. Stoddard King. NLV

Stub-tailed, short-haired, Biscuit Hound. The Dollar Dog. John Ciardi. GDP

Stubborn and selfish; hard inside.../That makes us even. Catalogue. Louis Untermeyer. HBMV

Stubborn as stone and set to wear out time. Green Mountain Boy. Florida Watts Smyth. GoYe

The stubborn humming sound that this instant is with us/upward into/The depths. Schubertiana. Tomas Transtromer. NU

Stubborn of heart/And stiffened of hair/Even then, even there. Donkey. Mark Van Doren. EaLo

A stubborn, undissolving vatican. I Woke Up Revenge. A. Poulin, Jr. TW

Stubbs butters Freeman, Freeman butters Stubbs. On the Historians Freeman and Stubbs. J. E. Thorold Rogers. FaBoEE

Stuck/at the foot of her head. Movie Queen. James P. Vaughn. NNP

Stuck deeply into the world's flesh,/each one at his place. A Painful Love Song. Yehuda Amichai. LLLT

Stuck in glass panes/cut from the Bible. African Day. Gloria de Sant'Ana. PBWP

Stuck to by drab threads of January. Saint-Henri Spring. Milton Acorn. NeAC

Stuck/Up/The/Tree! Dad and the Cat and the Tree. Kit Wright. OnUR

Study, cook oxtail stew, and walk on picket lines. New Romance. Nellie Wong. BrSi

Stuffing its heart with rags Running through Sleep. Kathleen Norris. IHMS

Stuffing my guts/With gingerbread nuts. To-Morrow's the Fair. Anonymous. GBP

Stuffs air down my throat. Mother. Seamus Heaney. NAs

Stumbles and cries like any lonely lover. The Snow. Sidney Keyes. NeBP

A stumbling block/Or a steppingstone. A Bag of Tools. R. L. Sharpe. BLPA; GoTF; PoToHe; TreFT; YaD

Stung silent in the martyr's blaze. Fragment. Hugh McCrae. BoAV

...Stunned, as the yellow of the mustard field,/we galloped beside that evening. The Good Time Is Now. Laura Chester. APU

Stupid cattle/mine cattle/cattle of Africa, marked and sold. Mamparra M'gaiza. Jose Craveirinha. WhB

The stupid fool! I've always hated birds... From a Letter from Lesbia. Dorothy Parker. DBV

...A stupid panic/when we drive so noiselessly/by. Test Drive. Monty Reid. CaPN

...The sturdy indifference of whatever/there is that rules us all? What Has Happened. Charles Angoff. AMV-81

Sturts quick as fear, and seeks its hidden lair. Hares at Play. John Clare. CBEP

Style's something else again. The Evans Country. Kingsley Amis. NOBL

The subject and object/should get together/more often. Foreplay of the Alphabet. Darrell Gray. APU

Subject to ev'ry mounters bended knee. The H. Scriptures. I. George Herbert. AnAnS 1

Sublime, from that valley of bliss to the world! Lalla Rookh. Thomas Moore. TEP

The submission to chance. Elementary Cosmogony. Charles Simic. NNaP

Submits that home and certainty/And sanctity are best. The Robin Is the One. Emily Dickinson. FaBV; HBVY

"Subside,' it begs and begs. From the Country to the City. Elizabeth Bishop. CrMA; NYP

A Substance, not a Qualitie. Science in God. Robert Herrick. ImOP

...Subvert/Our state with fears that do not touch the soul? Horatian Ode. Joseph Warren Beach. PoA

Succeeded by eternal Frost. Sweet Is the Budding Spring of Love. John Hippisley. BLSo

Success to fair America/And our good privateer. The Cruise of the Fair American. Anonymous. PAH

Success to North America,/Ye sons of liberty! Brave Paulding and the Spy. Anonymous. BFSS; MC; PAH

Success to our wives and sweethearts and God save the king. The Smuggler's Victory. Anonymous. OBSS

Success to the bawd and the whores of Kinsale. Captain Barton's Distress on Board the Lichfield. Anonymous. OBSS

Success to the brave Americans, the sons of liberty. Major Andre. Anonymous. BFSS

Success to the girl that will do so/Just as the tide was a-flowing. Just as the Tide Was A-Flowing. Anonymous. OBET

Successfully in business. Cheat. Don't Steal. Ambrose Bierce. NLV; PoL

Successive broods of little Hanks/Rise up to give their father thanks. The Crow and the Nighthawk. Watson Kirkconnell. CaP

Succour it from mine enemies' rage. Blessed Mary. Anonymous. OBSP

...A succulence/On which to feast, grinning ourselves, I fear. A View of the Burning. James Merrill. NePoEA-2

...;Such a church/Bears in its lines the trademark of the Kingdom. The Kingdom. Louis MacNeice. ChMP

Such a clear little jewel! A Tear. Henry Austin Dobson. CenHV

Such a garland wreath'd shall be/As shall crown both her and thee. To the New Year. Thomas Carew. CaPo

Such a golden store of honey! The Quest. Clinton Scollard. BrR

Such a lot of pleasant things. Some Things That Easter Brings. Elsie Parrish. SoPo

Such a moment came to pass/In Bethlehem! Five Carols for Christmastide. Louise Imogen Guiney. ISi

Such a quick answer to a prayer/Shakes one a bit. Louise. Stevie Smith. SBG

Such a result so soon–and from such a beginning! A Hand-Mirror. Walt Whitman. CBEP; MAmP; OxBA; TW

Such a rural queen/All Arcadia hath not seen. Arcades: O'er the Smooth Enamelled Green. John Milton. AtBAP; BoLiVe; InPo; OBEV; TrGrPo; ViBoPo

Such a sacred offering/God will not despise. Ellsworth. Anonymous. PAH

Such a ship as nevermore will be. The Brave Old Ship, the Orient. Robert and Spence Traill Lowell. AA; FaBoEe

Such a summer morning! Barefoot Days. Rachel Field. YeAr

Such a Vision to me/Appear'd on the sea. To My Friend Butts I Write. William Blake. EnRP

Such/agreeable monsters go/up and down Third Avenue. Agreeable Monsters. Amy Clampitt. AmC

Such another horrid fire,/See again I do not wish. The Miramichi Fire. Anonymous. AmFP

Such another leman/Even as he was! The Magician and the Baron's Daughter. Anonymous. MeEL

Such antediluvian ocean's stream,/Haunts shadowy my domestic mood. The Ivory Gate: Stanzas. Thomas Lovell Beddoes. EG; TrGrPo

...Such are The Fleeting Hues of Ice and The Fire/which we fear to touch. Prose Poem. Humphrey Jennings. EAS

Such are your seekers of virtue Philosophers. On Philosophers. *Anonymous.* TW

Such art of eyes I never read in books! The Art of Eyes. Edmund Spenser. LiTL

Such as do make a man but smart/For bearing them a faithful heart. The Lover Abused Renounceth Love. George Turberville. EIL

...Such as men smatter/When they throw out and miss the matter. The Metaphysical Sectarian. Samuel (1612-80) Butler. MeLP

Such as mine has been! May the Men Who Are Born. Hitomaro. AWP

Such as she was, such as she would become. The Gift Outright. Robert Frost. AmFN; AP; CMoP; CoBMV; CrMA; InPo; LiTM; LoGBV; MoAB; MoAmPo; NoAm; NOBA; NoP; OxBA; PAL; PPP; WaP

Such as that which I confess/Is my furnace of distress. None Is Happy. Hartmann von Aue. AWP

Such as the creation's dawn beheld, thou rollest now. By the Deep Sea. George Gordon, Lord Byron. OBNC

Such as to better men was never given. Confession. Kenneth MacKenzie. BoAV

Such as washing the dishes. Das Liebesleben. Thom Gunn. ErPo

Such as will drink, and drink again,/To treat about the matter. To His Friend J. H. Alexander Brome. CavP

Such attics cleared of me! Such absences! Absences. Philip Larkin. PoCh

Such brazen slatterns; but later, white-haired, genteel. Dandelions. Gerda Mayer. PoL

...Such/cackle as girls & boys will make/discomfit to their less demonstrative/fold. Special Pleading. Charles Bernstein. APU

Such Care to propagate the Male obtains,/And through each Species undistinguish'd reigns. How to Conceive Boys. Claude Quillet. FaBoUs

Such Cloe is, and common as the air. Cloe. [or Grenville], George, Baron Lansdowne Granville. FaBoCo; FaBoEE; NIP

Such closets to search, such alcoves to im-/portune! Love in a Life. Robert Browning. CBEP; HBV 1-2; InvP; LiTL; MaVP; NOBE; NOBV; OAEP; OBNC; OBVV

Such counsels ye gave to me, oh. Edward, Edward. *Anonymous.* AtBAP; ATP; BaBo; BBV; BiP; BSV; BuBa; CBEP; CH; EBEV; ELP; EnLi 1-2; ESPB; ExPo; FaBoBa; FaPoR; GoTS; HAP; HBV 1-2; HoPM; InPK; InPS; LiTB; MaC; NOBE; NoP; OAEP; OBEV; OxBB; OxBS; PAI; PoEL 1-5; PoRA; PPoe; PrIm; SeCeV; SoSe; TreFS; TrGrPo; TW; ViBoFo; WHA

Such deeds of valor, swelled their hearts with pride. Decoration Day. George Hurlbut Barbour. OHIP

Such desperate beauty they never had seen/before. The Door. Leonard Alfred George Strong. MoBrPo

Such dismal night, such heaps of slain,/Foe mix'd with foe promiscuously. The Battle of Bridgewater. *Anonymous.* PAH

...Such doom/Waits luxury, and lawless love of gain! Cyder, I: How to Catch Wasps. John Philips. FaBoUs

Such eyes, such hair, such wit, and such a hand? Conquest. Philippe Desportes. AWP

Such fierce attention to their tiny uproar. The Moths. Sean O Riordain. NOBI

Such fireballs dropping in the Temple Flame/Burns up the building: Lord, forbid the same. An Address to the Soul Occasioned by a Rain. Edward Taylor. AP; OxBA; PoEL 1-5

Such flesh such bones allow/the heart and hands to repeat. Afterbirth. Beryle Williams. PoDr

Such fools we women are who weep/For men not worth a tear! Joe Tinker. Amanda Benjamin Hall. HBMV

Such fortitude and grace/As grudging ocean yields a conquering race. Nantucket Whalers. Daniel Henderson. EtS

Such fragrant flowres doe give most odorous smell,/But her sweet odour did them all excell. Amoretti, LXIV. Edmund Spenser. AAS; OAEL 1-2

...Such fullness alone they tell/Who walk the unbounded waste! Across the Fens. Gilbert Thomas. HaMV

Such gaudy Tulips rais'd from Dung. The Lady's Dressing Room. Jonathan Swift. ErPo; NCEP; NoP; TEP

Such grace now to be happy, is before thee laid. The Faerie Queene. Edmund Spenser. FiP

Such grace, so self-contained, was the best escape to know. The Ballet of the Fifth Year. Delmore Schwartz. MoAB; MP; OxBA; TwCP

Such happiness as I have known today. 'Tis Said That Some Have Died for Love. William Wordsworth. EnRP

Such heate they caste as lifts the Spirit high. To Musicke Bent. Thomas Campion. AAS; CoBE; NOCV; OxBoCh; TrPWD; UnS

Such heavenly formes ought rather worship be,/Then dare be lov'd by men of meane degree. Amoretti, LXI. Edmund Spenser. AAS

Such his last pillow. Man's Pillow. Irving Browne. AA

...Such honey of that heavy rider. Burning and Fathering: Accounts of My Country. Jack Gilbert. NPGG

Such insight is one's own death rattling past. The Tobacconist of Eighth Street. Richard Eberhart. MiAP; NYP

Such is a Vision of the lamentation of Beulah/over Ololon. Milton. William Blake. EnRP

Such is religion. The Minister. Fenton Johnson. AnAmPo

Such is the death the soldier dies. Such Is the Death the Soldier Dies. Robert Burns Wilson. AA; HBV 1-2

Such is the end of all the sons of Earth. Upon a Funeral. Sir John Beaumont. FaBoRV

Such is the entertainment Home Cooking Cafe. Greg Field. FAZ; PPJ

...Such is the force/With which his frantic heart and sinews swell. The Seasons. James (1700-48) Thomson. FM

Such is the GREAT CREATOR'S glorious plan/Of veinous action in the frame of man! Watt's Improvements to the Steam Engine. Thomas Baker. FaBoUs

Such is the illusion of the stones that challenge air N. Hugh Seidman. PoA

Such is the power of love in gentle mind,/That it can alter all the course of kind. Amoretti, XXX. Edmund Spenser. AAS; FF; TrGrPo

Such is the sad disparity of time. So, So. William Clerke. ELP

Such is the Salutation of the Dawn! Salutation of the Dawn. Kalidasa. GoTF

Such is the song of the sea. Song of the Sea. Richard E. Burton. EtS

Such is their love/of flowers/& their pride/in honey-making Virgil: Georgics, Book IV. Dennis Schmitz. NPGG

...Such ivory/As elephants hold lofty, like champagne. Champagne. Mebdh McGuckian. FaBoIP

Such labour like the Spyders web I fynd,/Whose fruitlesse worke is broken with least wynd. Amoretti, XXIII. Edmund Spenser. AAS; CoBE 060

Such life should be the honor of your light,/Such death the sad ensample of your might. Amoretti, VII. Edmund Spenser. AAS

Such love is in my breast that I,/When winter is most frigid, fry. Love Laughs at Winter. *Anonymous.* UnTE

Such massive sweetness fills no smaller air. Rose. Lewis Thompson. AtBAP

Such matchless beauty with disdain,/Are all turn'd into stones again. Celia Singing. Thomas Carew. OAEP

...Such matters are as old/As sin and folly, rust and must and mould! The News. John Godfrey Saxe. NLV

Such men as thou are England's boast,/Oh, miller of the Dee. The Miller of Dee. *Anonymous.* GBP

Such men have lost all patriotic feeling. Lamentations. Siegfried Sassoon. OBSV

Such mercy shal you make admyred to be,/So shall you live by giving life to me. Amoretti, XLIX. Edmund Spenser. AAS

Such merit had music in hell. When Orpheus Went Down. Samuel Lisle. ALV

Such mocks of dreams do turn to deadly pain. The Lover, Having Dreamed of Enjoying His Love.... Sir Thomas Wyatt. AAS; CoBE; WHA

Such monsters huddle yet. Under Creag Mhor. Stewart Conn. PoSH

Such monstrous things, they say, now sleep/Within the caverns of the deep. The Sea-Deeps. Thomas Miller. EtS

Such moods as this, how many men know? In Early Summer Lodging in a Temple to Enjoy the Moonlight. Po Chu-i. LiTW

–Such my parting, in troubled tiredness,/from the partner of my heart. A Heart Made Full of Thought. Maghnas O Domhnaill. NOBI

...Such mysteries as men/do not conceive–let ocean grow again How Many Moments Must(Amazing Each. Edward Estlin Cummings. PoA

Such news to me was never new/whose honey's long been mixed with rue. Busy with love, the bumble bee. Meleager. BoLoP

Such nice machines. Spring Coming. Archie Randolph Ammons. HeIP; InPK

Such one vile Envy was, that fifte in row did sit. The Faerie Queene. Edmund Spenser. TW

Such outlaws as he and his men/May England never know again! Robin Hood and the Valiant Knight. *Anonymous.* ESPB

Such peace/has no need/to figure/out who pulled/the trigger. Light, 2. Richard Eberhart. NoAm

Such pitiless disharmony of shapes. Leviathan. Peter Quennell. MoBrPo

Such pleasures rife shall I obtain/When distance doth depart us twain. The Oftener Seen, the More I Lust. Barnabe Googe. InvP

Such power hath music in hell! The Power of Music. Thomas Lisle. NOBL

Such quiet as is lent/To stones in winter fields. The Quiet of the Dead. Mary Morison Webster. PeSA

Such resonance, such love. Upon Hearing His High Sweet Tenor Again. Joseph Langland. AMV-81

Such rich provision made. Some Murmur When Their Sky Is Clear. Richard Chenevix Trench. HBVY

Such rogues there can't be worser. The Jolly Sailor's True Description of a Man-of-War. *Anonymous.* OBSS

Such seeing hadst thou, as it once befel/To Dian, Queen of Earth, and Heaven, and Hell. Sonnet: To Homer. John Keats. ChRP

–Such seeming disarray/The more becomes the fairest face.   The Hairdresser's Art.   Claudian.   HW

Such shinings on water/are fact. Or sublime.   The Floating Candles.   Sydney Lea.   MAYP; SM

...Such skill in distribution-equally–/to every pocket of life.   The Coral Reef.   Laurence Lieberman.   CoAP

Such songs have been mine.   A Dedication.   Adam Lindsay Gordon.   PoAu 1-2

Such Stock of Wit unable to supply,/To spare herself, was glad to let him die.   On Mr. Hobbs, and His Writings.   John, Duke of Buckingham Sheffield.   PoEL 1-5

Such strange things did mother say to me.   In Childbed.   Thomas Hardy.   NAs

Such such is life–[The bitter and the sweet].   A Sonnet.   Edward Lear.   CenHV

Such, such is the Life of a Beau.   The Life of a Beau.   James Miller.   OBEC

Such the drear roar of battle when they mixt.   The Iliad.   Homer.   OBVE

Such the glorious vista Faith/Opens through the shades of death.   Deathless Principle, Arise.   Augustus Montague Toplady.   OxBoCh

Such the raiment of Sri Rama.   Sri Rama's Raiment.   *Anonymous.*   WTO

Such the tenor man told/When he had grown old.   The Choirmaster's Burial.   Thomas Hardy.   DTC

Such things as these best please his majesty.   Edward the Second (excerpt).   Christopher Marlowe.   ViBoPo

Such things made even half-real, 'twere not vain/To be a poet ministering to pain!   The New Physician.   Stephen Chalmers.   HBMV

Such things my mind continually amaze.   Summer Days.   Roy Daniells.   CaP

"Such things no longer are; this is today."   She Is No Liar.   Robert Graves.   OBSP

Such tink and tank and tunk-a-tunk-tunk.   Wallace Stevens Gives a Reading.   Harriet Zinnes.   AMV-81

Such understanding that it seems like love.   Celtic Cross.   Norman MacCaig.   OxBS

Such unequal distribution/Is part of Heaven's constitution.   Unequal Distribution.   Samuel Hoffenstein.   TrJP

Such vice avail more then their vertues can.   Elegy for Doctor Dunn.   Edward, Lord Herbert of Cherbury.   AnAnS 2

Such violence. And such repose.   Tywater.   Richard Wilbur.   CMoP; ConAP; LiTA; LiTM; MiAP; MoAB; NePA

Such walks may be our ruin.   I Pray You.   Thomas Moore.   OBRV

Such warmth, such light, such love, and so much fear.   Boy at the Window.   Richard Wilbur.   NoP

Such was th' end of this ambitious Brere,/For scorning eld.   The Oak and the Brere.   Edmund Spenser.   OBSC

Such was the custom in Lilliput-land.   Lilliput Levee.   William Brighty ("Matthew Browne") Rands.   CenHV

Such was their burial of Hektor, breaker of horses.   The Iliad.   Homer.   NAWM 1-2

Such were the judger and the judged   At the Dog Show.   Christopher Morley.   MoShBr

Such wind.   On Such a Windy Afternoon.   Theodore Enslin.   AMV-80

Such words fulfil their prophecy, and lack/But the full time to harden into things.   To John C. Fremont.   John Greenleaf Whittier.   MC; PAH

Such would be the greatest good for every Greek.   The Greek Athlete.   Euripides.   LiSp

Suck the sweet grapes out of their juicy blue/Pockets and let the sun pour down on you.   Grapes.   Sister Maris Stella.   GoBC

...Sucking the good water/between my teeth.   The Problem of Wild Horses.   Barbara Winder.   PH

Sucking the sweet grass of stubbornness.   Time Out.   John Montague.   BoAnP

Sucks the body dry.   Accommodation.   Anselm Parlatore.   SUW

...Sudden clank of his horse's hoof/Frightens the Wanderer aloof.   The Heath.   Thomas Boyd.   OnYI

Sudden dark as/if a swan/sang.   Swan and Shadow.   John Hollander.   NoP; PoA; WeW

...A sudden homage/To peace that penetrates and is not feared.   A World of Light.   Elizabeth Jennings.   NePoEA-2

Sudden light on earth and air.   April.   Remy Belleau.   AWP

A sudden madness seized him, and he tore/His hair and dashed the tea-cup to the floor.   Conversation.   Berenice C. Dewey.   InMe

A sudden movement shakes the crowd/Stampeded on the hooves of fate.   The Blue Horses.   James Philip McAuley.   BoAV

Sudden splashing breaks/stillness of morning.   Song: "Woman sits on her porch."   Earle Thompson.   STE

Suddenly a wet cold nose/nuzzles/my empty hand.   A Dog.   Charlotte Zolotow.   GDP

Suddenly am quite alone/With the beating of my heart.   At a Country Dance in Provence.   Harold Monro.   OBVV

Suddenly/bloody & beautiful/she is here   Poem Proud Papa.   Endre Farkas.   CaPN

Suddenly come alive/and jabber like/foreigners   Semen.   Coleman Barks.   PV

Suddenly I meet your face.   A Deep-Sworn Vow.   William Butler Yeats.   CMoP; ELU; OAEL 1-2; PCP; UnPo

...Suddenly I saw, looked again and saw/The merciful corn.   Full Moon in Malta.   Asphodel.   BrRo

...Suddenly, I thought/Of Elizabeth, frigidly stretched.   This Houre Her Vigill.   Valentin Iremonger.   CIP; NOBI; OxBI; OxBTC

(Suddenly in sunlight/he will bow,/& the whole garden will bow)   If There Are Any Heavens.   Edward Estlin Cummings.   DFF; MoAB; MoAmPo

Suddenly into it a lithe frog leaps.   A Lonely Pond in Age-Old Stillness Sleeps.   Basho (Matsuo Basho).   AWP

Suddenly into the arc a hummingbird flew/Miniature bird and bow–and the moment gone.   Suspended Moment.   Mariana B. Davenport.   GoYe

Suddenly leap out at the thought of white wings.   The Crow-Children Walk My Circles in the Snow.   Ray A. Young Bear.   CDW

Suddenly my tongue/floats in blood.   Hare in Winter.   Marge Piercy.   NeAC

Suddenly on Calvary all the olives wept.   Mary's Baby.   Shaemas O'Sheel.   CAW; HBV 1-2; HBVY

...Suddenly the color/Is intense. And he finds no defense.   Concert Scene.   John Logan.   NePoEA-2

Suddenly to become John Benbow...   Metempsychosis.   Kenneth Slessor.   NOAV; ViBoPo

Suddenly wait against the moon's face.   Portrait.   Edward Estlin Cummings.   AnNE

Suddenly will look up/with a pale, clear sadness.   Autumn.   Bella Akhmadulina.   BoWoP

Suddenly wise, I fight the dream:/Green screams enfold my night.   African Dream.   Bob Kaufman.   PoBA

...Suet and seed are cool and good.   Starlings.   Laura Jensen.   AMV-81

Suffer me thus secure, to his return.   My Love behind Walls.   Heather Spears.   OBCV

Suffer, poor Negro/Negro black as Misery!   Suffer, Poor Negro.   David Diop.   PBA

Suffer the heaven's children through my heartbeat.   Altarwise by Owl-Light.   Dylan Thomas.   CMoP; NoAm

"Suffer the little children,/And let them come to Me."   God, Who Hath Made the Daisies.   E. P. Hood.   OHIP

Suffering to find a world that matches/the freedom trapped inside our souls.   For Zorro.   Diane Bickston.   LFAC

Suffice the ageing man as once the growing boy.   Meditations in Time of Civil War.   William Butler Yeats.   CABL

Suffice, thou shalt be loved as well as she.   To Delia.   Samuel Daniel.   HBV 1-2; NOBE; NoP; OAEP; OBSC

Sufficient, clear, and for that use ordained.   Religio Laici.   John Dryden.   OBS; WGRP

"Sufficient for the day were the day's evil things!"   Vesperal.   Ernest Christopher Dowson.   OBMV

Sufficient is it just to live/On such a day as this.   An April Day.   Joseph Seamon, Jr. Cotter.   CDC

Sufficient to take Britain which they did.   Poems, II.   Philip O'Connor.   EAS

Suffre the paynes that I may; it is my fader wyll.   A god and yet a man?   *Anonymous.*   EnPo

A Sugar Crisp box dropped past their heads/From a few stories up, riling them.   Satellites.   Gary Lenhart.   APU

Sugar is sweet/And so are you.   You Shall Be Queen.   *Anonymous.*   OxNR

Sugar, the blues ain't on me, but things ain't going on right.   Black Horse Blues.   Blind Lemon Jefferson.   BluL

Sugared, colored, out of a jar, an ode.   Purchase of a Blue, Green, or Orange Ode.   Josephine Miles.   NoP

Suggest that where he was is where we are.   Progress.   David McCord.   ImOP

The suicide stream inching its way to the breakers.   Song from the Maker of Totems.   Duane Niatum.   STE

"Suit thy gree the stroke!" and I–"Suit thy gree!"   Poems of the Arabic (excerpt).   *Anonymous.*   ErPo

Suits me just fine.   Let Me Put This Way.   George Jonas.   NeAC

Sullen sounds and gloomy seeming/Soon shall mingle in thy dreaming.   Ancient Lullaby.   Gerald Griffin.   IrPN

The sum of my love for thee/Seems poor, scant, and unworthy.   Dear Lady, When Thou Frownest.   Robert Bridges.   LiTL

Sum souse or pork or chidlins, sum sphar-rib, or de chine.   Hog Meat.   Daniel Webster Davis.   BANP

Sum up his strength to perish with a /ship.   Ode for a Master Mariner Ashore.   Louise Imogen Guiney.   AA; GoBC

The summer air those wrinkled leaves forsook/Nor ever played in them.   Cut It Down.   Mary Elizabeth Coleridge.   MoVE

The summer dream beneath the tamarind tree? Sonnet—To Science. Edgar Allan Poe. AP; APA; MAmP; NePA; NoP; OxBA; TAP; TW
...A summer evening/Across the island below the sky The Island in the Evening. Fairfield Porter. PoA
Summer, farewell, farewell. Ode to the End of Summer. Phyllis McGinley. NLV
The summer holds me here. The Aspen's Song. Yvor Winters. PoL
The Summer is begun. A Song of Waking. Katharine Lee Bates. OHIP
Summer is gone. Summer Is Gone. Anonymous. AnIL; PoPl
Summer is over, summer is over. Moo! Robert Hillyer. OBAL
The summer's beauty yields to winter's blast. Winter. Thomas, Earl of Dorset Sackville. EIL; SeCePo
Summer's the time for fun. Grasshopper Green. Anonymous. FaPON; HBVY; SoPo
Summer sometime shall bless this spot, when I,/Hapt in the cold dark grave, can heed it not. Summer. John Clare. BoNaP
Summer sun was on their wings,/Winter in their cry. Something Told the Wild Geese. Rachel Field. BrR; NTCP; OBCA; OnUR; PoSC; SiSoSe; TiPo; YeAr
Summer-time,/With the hay, and bees achime. If It's Ever Spring Again. Thomas Hardy. OxBTC
Summer uncoiling in which we are/farther and farther apart. Lily. Rosanna Warren. MAYP
Summer vacation! Peace and Joy. Shel Silverstein. PoSC
The summer when our life was fair. Musings. William Barnes. HAP; NOBE; OBNC
The summer will not be dreadful. The Candles Draw Well after All. Laura Jensen. LCAP
Summer will return. Junker Schmidt. Kozma Prutkov. ELU
Summon one's powers Some San Francisco Poems. George Oppen. NNaP
Summoned the angels of Sodom down to earth. Upon the Heavenly Scarp. Abraham Moses Klein. PoA
...A summons has come and I am ready/for my journey. I Have Got My Leave. Rabindranath Tagore. OBMV
Summons the dead who sleep beneath thy shadow/Around the Crucified! The Crucifix. Alphonse Marie Louis de Lamartine. CAW
Sumptuous wreaths to the dead. A Rose to the Living. Nixon Waterman. HBV 1-2; PoToHe
A sun—a shadow of a magnitude. On Seeing the Elgin Marbles. John Keats. BLPL; BoLiVe; DiPo; ERoP 1-2; EyDe; LiTB; MBW 1-2; NIP; PrIm; SeCeV; TrGrPo; WHA
...The sun above/Laughed down on me, the fool of love. The Fool of Love. Anonymous. UnTE
Sun ain' gone down yit. Tie-Shuffling Chant. Anonymous. ABF
The sun already up A Sleep. Larry Eigner. CoPo
Sun an mune an the warld, ma dear? Can I Forget? Sidney Goodsir Smith. NeBP; SeCePo
Sun and moon, winter and summer/will come to you,/infinite treasures. Surely You Remember. Dahlia Ravikovich. VWA
The sun- and star-shaped killers gorge and play. The Face. Edwin Muir. ChMP; GTBS-P
The sun and the moon know nothing,/And between them I know less. Ballad of the Three Coins. Vernon Watkins. NoAm
"The sun and the moon shall dance on/the green/That night when I come hame." Lizie Wan. Anonymous. BaBo; ESPB; ViBoFo
The sun brightly beam'd, the birds/sweetly sang. Who Was It, Tell Me. Heinrich Heine. TrJP
The sun burns at love's two ends,/On the eternal launching pad. When We Hear the Eye Open... Bob Kaufman. CNA
Sun-coloured to the imperishable core/With sweet well-being of love and full heart's ease. Last Fire. Dante Gabriel Rossetti. MaVP
The sun comes out again in power/And the sky is washed and clean. The Storm. Edward Shanks. BoNaP
The sun directs the angle of their flight. The Beekeeper's Dream. Katharine Auchincloss Lorr. SUW
Sun-doped and happy, a gnawed twig in your paw like/a pen. Koala. Alan Ross. BoAnP; OBTV
The sun doth not contain him nor the sea. Transcendence. Richard Hovey. TRV; WGRP
The sun dries me as I dance Burning. Gary Snyder. NOBA
The sun drops red through a curtain of dust. The Sun Drops Red. Nellie Burget Miller. PoOW
The sun finishing, the car huddled,/watching, inert: silent as animals. As Animals. Kathleen Spivak. AmC
A sun-god in a temple of decay. Of Dying Beauty. Louis Zukofsky. PoA
The sun goes down. He sees nothing./It's calm. After. Michael Ryan. MAYP
The sun goes down, the wind's/Self says No. Intuition. Anthony Delius. PeSA
Sun gonna shine in my door some day. Sun Gonna Shine in My Door Some Day. Anonymous. OuSiCo

The sun had just begun its set-/ting you were my evening star. You Came as a Thought. James Laughlin. GOYP
The sun had risen. He could let her go. Jacob and the Angel. Stephen Mitchell. VWA
The sun has always been red Who Is My Brother? Pinkie Gordon Lane. BlSi
...The sun himself can give/But little colour to the desert sands. No, Thou Hast Never Griev'd but I Griev'd Too. Walter Savage Landor. GBL
The Sun himself cannot forget/His fellow traveller. Epigram: On Sir Francis Drake. Anonymous. OBTV
The sun in our eyes for ever covered/with black crows. I Drift in the Wind. Ingrid Jonker. PeSA; WPOW
A sun, in this wash, would run and fade on the sky. Wet Weather. Patricia Low. VGW
The sun is but a morning star Myths and Texts. Gary Snyder. NaP; NeAP; NoP; PoM
...The sun is but a morning star. Walden. Henry David Thoreau. NU
The sun is in eclipse. Debt. Anonymous. WTO
The sun is set, I wait the rise of starlight,/Starlight and—you! The Lover is Near. Johann Wolfgang von Goethe. LiTW
The sun-knot tightens to dark. Horizon Thong. George Abbe. GoYe
The sun leaves a virgin spot/of joy. Making Chicago. Dennis Schmitz. LCAP; NPGG
Sun moon stars rain. Anyone Lived in a Pretty How Town. Edward Estlin Cummings. AP; BiP; CABA; CMoP; CoBMV; DiPo; EvOK; FPL; HAP; InPK; LiTA; LiTM; MoAB; MoAmPo; MoPo; MP; NIP; NOBA; NoP; PoA; PrIm; TAP; TwCP; VGW; WeW
The sun of ancient dancers in my mouth. Tea. Ann Struthers. AMV-80
The sun of heaven, and the son of God. Twelfth Night. Laurie Lee. BoC
...Sun of October/Summery/On the hill's shoulder. October. Dylan Thomas. YeAr
...The sun outside/Has turned lead-colored lakes into pure gold. Twink Drives Back, in a Bad Mood, from a Party in Massachusetts. George Amabile. NYBP
...The sun paints/our bodies simple and shining. Love Poem. Susan Irene Rea. AMV-80
...The sun/Receives me in the questions which you always pose. To You. Kenneth Koch. CAPP
The sun refuses to set,/bright as a penny in a loafer. June Twenty-First. Bruce Guernsey. PPJ
The sun repeating/its tender warmth The Ladder Has No Steps. Jorge Plescoff. VWA
...The sun/Rises upon a world well-tried and old. Stealing Trout. Ted Hughes. NYBP
...The sun's bright finger/On a dead face. Map Reference T994724. John Pudney. WaP
The sun's first light pursued her flight/At the dawning of the day. The Dawning of the Day. Anonymous. OnYI
The sun's true sun, no vapour, but a ray. Don Juan. George Gordon, Lord Byron. OAEL 1-2
Sun shines and larks break forth from winter branches. An Anniversary of Death. John Wieners. PoM
The sun shines last in the West! In Spain. Emily Lawless. AnIV
The sun should choose those minutes to rise! Three Sunrises from Amtrak. Florence Dolgorukov. AMV-81
The sun smooths and shines your mouth. Spring in Virginia. Ramona Wilson. VoR
The sun still proved, the shadow still disdained. Song: "Follow thy fair sun, unhappy shadow." Thomas Campion. OBSC
The sun that I now cover for always/With black butterflies When You Write Again. Ingrid Jonker. PBWP
The sun, that others burn'd, did her but kiss. Astrophel and Stella, XXII. Sir Philip Sidney. AAS; OBSC; SiPS
Sun that whirls and glares in a mad dance. At dawn of the day the Creator. Gaspara Stampa. BoWoP
The sun, the big flower, looked at him through the leaves. The African Tramp. Geoffrey Haresnape. PeSA
Sun throat cut Zone. Guillaume Apollinaire. SOTW
The sun touches its image to the/ground. Going to School. Karl Shapiro. TrJP
...The sun/unaccustomed to anything else/goes all the way down. Lament. Anne Sexton. ConAP
The sun was up, the country woke! A July Dawn (excerpt). John Francis O'Donnell. IrPN
...The sun/Whose laurel a green summer wears. John Donne's Statue. John Peale Bishop. EyDe
The sun will rise, the winds that ever move/Will blow our dust that once were men in love. Sonnets. John Masefield. HBV 1-2
The sun with long legs wades into the sea. Gigha. W. S. Graham. NeBP
A sunbeam/flickering at twilight/on a wall in a courtyard. What Will Remain after Me? Mendel Naigreshel. VWA

A sunbeam giving the air a kiss. The Hummingbird. Harry Kemp. HBMV

"Sunday comes only once a week," they told each other. Elephants Are Different to Different People. Carl Sandburg. MoAmPo

Sunday drives meant looking for a lot. The House on Buder Street. Gary Gildner. TAP

The sundering ultimate kingdom of genesis' thunder. Ceremony after a Fire Raid. Dylan Thomas. CMoP; CoBMV; ExPo; MoPo; WaP

...A sundown/dance viewed from a cool veranda. There Were Fierce Animals in Africa. Alvin Aubert. GP

The sundown splendid and serene,/Death. In Memoriam. William Ernest Henley. GoTF; TreFT

Sunflower, swan, sandhill,/sprout hidden under the dress,/indescribable grave. To a Young Girl. D. Rosenmann-Taub. VWA

Sunk past its gleam/in the meal bin. Mossbawn: Two Poems in Dedication. Seamus Heaney. CIP

Sunken fourteen years in that aquarium. Elegy for William Soutar. William Montgomerie. NeBP; OxBS

The sunlight everywhere. Common Dawn. Guy Butler. PeSA

...Sunlight/hanging from the lips of the lightning. Sooner or Later. John Digby. EAS

The sunlight lays a streak upon the floor. London Interior. Harold Monro. BrPo

...Sunlight/sliding over ocean water a thousand miles from land. At Mid-Ocean. Robert Bly. LLLT

The sunlit air full of leaping chances. Green Frog at Roadside, Wisconsin. James Schevill. TAP

Sunny as a May-day dance, along that spectral avenue. An Infantryman. Edmund Charles Blunden. ViBoPo

Sunny sunlight on stony stone returning. Watching a Cloud. Dannie Abse. OxBC; TEP

Sunrise, please come!/Come! Come! Junior Addict. Langston Hughes. BPo; CNA

A sunrise. The snow. February: The Boy Breughel. Norman Dubie. LCAP

Sunrising and sunsetting evermore. Another and Another and Another. James Henry. NOBV

Suns before this morning. Indians. John Fandel. AmFN; NYBP

Suns of the world may stain when heaven's sun staineth. Sonnets, XXXIII: "Full many a glorious morning have I seen." William Shakespeare. ATP; AWP; EBEV; FaFP; GoTF; HAP; HBV 1-2; InPo; LoBV; MBW 1-2; NoP; OAEL 1-2; OAEP; OBSC; OHFP; PoRA; PPP; SeCePo; SeCeV; TEP; TreFS; TrGrPo; ViBoPo

...Sunset blazed on the windows. The Black Cottage. Robert Frost. VGW

Sunset like the grasshopper flying. Canto XVII. Ezra Pound. ExPo; InPS; LoBV; NAMP; OBMV

Sunshine, blinding as daybreak in Sahara glares. Noon Glare. Matthew Brennan. AMV-80

Sunshine came along with thee,/And swallows in the air. Aura Lea. W. W. Fosdick. BLSo; PSoN

Sunshine not yet through. Poem for Ben Barney. Leslie Marmon Silko. CDW; VoR

The sunshine of achievement/Ripens nothing there. In a Shoreham Garden. Laurence Lerner. NePoEA-2

The super-powers of those super-mammals/Beneath the eaves! The Circus-Postered Barn. Elizabeth Jane Coatsworth. MoAmPo

Super-super-superwho? Superman. John Updike. LiSp

Superabundant being/wells up in my heart. Duino Elegies. Rainer Maria Rilke. NAWM 1-2

Superbly, like Zenobia, wear/Thy chains,–Virginia Victrix still! Virginia Capta. Margaret Junkin Preston. PAH

Superfluous was the bite. Mir Traumte Wieder Der Alte Traum. Heinrich Heine. AWP

The superior lift of their wings lifts the heart. The Serious Merriment of Women. Patricia Goedicke. TAP

Supernal Wisdom only knows how much. George Levison. William Allingham. IrPN

Supple and green, these actions of the sun. Cloud Country. James Merrill. NePoEA

The supple definitions of his strength. No Snake in Springtime. Elizabeth Jane Coatsworth. AnAmPo

...Suppliants/in lime-specked groves/to dirty mysteries. City Pigeons. Helen Chasin. WeW

Supplicate with sweet gifts my heart your worshipper. A Song for Beauty. P. Lal. ACV

Supply the honest jester's place. The Kings of Europe A Jest. Robert Dodsley. CEP

Support the green entablature of boys and dogs and grass. Manly Ferry. John Philip. NOAV

Supports me like imperial drams/Afforded day by day. The stimulus beyond the grave. Emily Dickinson. OBSP

Suppose the sea should come back here/And gather up its shells. Shells in Rock. Elizabeth Madox Roberts. AnAmPo

Suppose those/who made/wars/had to fight you. Nigerian Unity/or little niggers killing little niggers. Don L. Lee. NeAC

Suppose you just stay where you are:/I'll be your jailer! To Heliodora: A Fretful Monody. Meleager. LiTW

Suppose your mother/Was a bullfrog's brother. For Those Who Always Fear the Worst. Anonymous. NLV

Supreme in state, and in three more decays. The Oak. John Dryden. OHIP

Supreme is God, and by His side is Love. One Immortality. Norbert Engels. CAW

The supreme poet who imagined God. The Masterpiece. Walter Conrad Arensberg. AnAmPo

Supreme the triumph on the cross! Green Plumes of Royal Palms. LeRoy V. Brant. AH

Supremely calm, though just a little late. On the Beach. Frances Cornford. BoAnP

Sure as steel/gathers in his back. A Fieldmouse. Robert Sund. BoAnP

Sure I can take my Bible oath/I've seen that face before. To the Portrait of "A Gentleman." Oliver Wendell Holmes. InMe

Sure I'm the man you don't meet ev'ry day! The First of the Emigrants. Anonymous. ShS

Sure never were seen such true lovers/before,/Nor eer will there be again. Lady Alice (A version). Anonymous. ESPB

Sure of the Father, Self, and Love, alone. The Cloud. Sidney Lanier. AmePo

The sure, small dream that kills,/that keeps. The Sixth Day. Betty Adcock. LiSp

Sure that what is voted for is just as good as done. Bears. Arthur Guiterman. PoRA

...Sure that your voice/will carry, clear that it will all come back in another form. Virginia Beach. Stanley Plumly. AMV-81

Sure there's a God (for else there's no delight)/One infinite. Insatiableness. Thomas Traherne. OxBoCh

Sure, thou wilt joy to see/Thy sheep with thee. Silex Scintillans. Henry Vaughan. AnAnS 1

Sure to be grateful, to be kind,/Can never be too late. Song: "Come, Celia, let's agree at last." John, of Buckingham Sheffield. HBV 1-2

"'Sure to catch you sooner or later. Who's the next?" The Undertaker's Horse. Rudyard Kipling. FaBoNo; FM

"Sure to, dear, but it's time for tea.'/Says Alice. Buckingham Palace. A.(lan) A.(lexander) Milne. OxBChV

Sure to win in his name victory. If You Happy Would Be. Abraham Fernandez. AH

Sure will he Saint her in his Calendere. Virgidemiarum. Joseph Hall. FaBoEn

Sure you wouldn't come hither if you didn't love me? By the Turnstile. John Francis O'Donnell. IrPN; NBM

...Surely a big man/now, votes this year for Smith or Hoover. Chicago Boy Baby. Carl Sandburg. NAs

Surely God is nigh. The Ancient Thought. Watson Kerr. TRV; WGRP

Surely God should have our service now and evermore./Amen. A Little Rhyme and a Little Reason. Henry Anstadt. BLRP

Surely it is so. The Caterpillar. Anselm Hollo. FAZ

....:Surely one always knew that cultures/decay, and life's end is death. The Purse-Seine. Robinson Jeffers. CMoP; HAP; NoAm; NOBA; NoP; OxBA; PrIm; WeW

Surely, some chieftain's soul! The Bells at Midnight. Thomas Bailey Aldrich. PAH

Surely. That's what we said. What We Said. W. D. Snodgrass. GP

"Surely the things he loved the best/Are his to-day." Ilicet. Theodosia Garrison. PoLf

Surely, the tide comes in twice a day. After I Had Worked All Day. Charles Reznikoff. PrIm; VGW

Surely these acres are Elysian Fields. The Mushroom Gatherers. Donald Davie. NePoEA-2

–Surely these claim eternity of tears! To Monsieur de la Mothe le Vayer. Jean-Baptiste Poquelin Moliere. AWP

Surely thou art come to betray me,/And to curtail my gift of life... The Life of St. Cellach: Hail, Fair Morning. Anonymous. OnYI

The surface flashes like a coat of mail. Uncertain Sonnets. Martin Johnston. CBAP

...The surface that the face/refuses to shine through. Night Catch. Heather McHugh. AmPA

...A surfing shout of love,/and blasts of flowers. When a Warlock Dies. Isabella Gardner. NePA

The surge and thunder of the Odyssey. The Odyssey. Andrew Lang. HBV 1-2; LoBV; OBEV; OBNC; OBVV; PoLf; PoRA; ViBoPo; WHA

Surge with the life-song of humanity. Prelude. W. W. Gibson. MoBrPo

Surges and tugs the dreaded undertow. Inheritance. Mary Thacher Higginson. AA

Surging, sweetening, shaking,/Lapping. Take away. Margot Ruddock. OBMV

Surly, use other arts, these only can/Style thee a great fool, but no great man. On Don Surly. Ben Jonson. FaBoEE

Surprised by softer footfall of our dream. The Skilful Listener. John Vance Cheney. AA

...Surprised/that children watched from the trees. The Woman Who Combed. Ruth Rankin. FAZ

Surprised when one/side smiles. After the Dentist. May Swenson. DFF; GP

Surrender to none the fire of your soul. Ruth. Pauli Murray. NMM

Surrendering to the wolves about her throat. Burial at Sea. Edwin John Pratt. CaP

Surrexi Dominus de sepulchro. Done Is a Battell on the Dragon Blak. William Dunbar. BSV; HAP; NoP

Surround thee quite, and style thy borders/The land redeemed from all dissorders! To the River Isca (the Usk). Henry Vaughan. FaBoPP

Surrounded by the familiar and the famous. The Forgotten City. William Carlos Williams. LiTA; NePA; PoPl

Surrounded in that played-out pose of age/By notes he was, but cannot be again. High Fidelity. Thom Gunn. PoA

Survey the pains my sick heart feels,/And wounds themselves have made discover. The Willing Prisoner to His Mistress. Thomas Carew. CaPo

Survival motion set to music. Soul. D. L. Graham. PoBA

Survive not Judgment that requires his own? Sonnets upon the Punishment of Death (excerpt). William Wordsworth. PeD

Survived, - its ruin and our peace to see. Garrison. Amos Bronson Alcott. AA

Survivors will be human. Deathwatch. Michael S. Harper. AmPA; PoBA

Suspend their dread and civil war. Aria. Delmore Schwartz. ErPo

Suspended on cold iron, branded on air. The Precision. Yvor Winters. EAS

Suspends her yet in immortality. Sappho's Death: Three Pictures by Gustave Moreau (excerpt). Thomas Sturge Moore. SyP

Sustained but for an hour. Caesar and Pompey. George Chapman. ViBoPo

Sustained in time astride the flying change. The Flying Change. Henry Taylor. MAYP

The sustained violence of her terpsichorean expertise. At the Hammersmith Palais... Alan Riddell. NOAV

Swallow family with pain. The Doll House. Darlene Button Kitzman. AMV-81

Swallow with no nest./Arrested flight./What now? Heavenly Jerusalem, Jerusalem of the Earth. Leah Goldberg. VWA

Swallow your stale saliva, and still sit. The Intellectual. Karl Shapiro. CMoP

Swallowed along the hidden road/Turning among the trees! Echoes of Wheels. Furnley Maurice. NOAV

...Swallowing/apples, swallowing her life. Apples. Shirley Kaufman. NMM

Swallowing old questions with a numbing tongue. Next. Tina Koyama. BrSi

Swallowing raindrops/clear from China. Prayer to the Pacific. Leslie Marmon Silko. CDW; NoP; VoR

"The swallows are flying by us." They've Come. Alfonsina Storni. BoWoP; WPOW

...Swallows, two/By two, nest under the painted eaves. Green Jade Plum Trees in Spring. Ou Yang Hsiu. NaP

A swami, a world,/seldom whole. "It's a Whole World, the Body. A Whole World!" David Young. FF

The swan has sung his dying lay. Es Fällt Ein Stern Herunter. Heinrich Heine. AWP

Swan of the waves, thin brow that will not bend/with gloom! To Mackinnon of Strath. Iain Lom. GoTS

The swan's near death; man's life is done! Man's Mortality. Simon Wastell. WBLP

The swan sail with her young beneath her wings. Modern Love, XLVII. George Meredith. AnFE; EnLoPo; GTBS; GTBS-P; NOBE; NOBV; OAEL 1-2; OBNC; SeCeV; ViBoPo; VLP

The swan saith. The Bereaved Swan. Stevie Smith. FaBoNo; FaBoTw

Swans call, river water falling/Is calling too. The Hermit's Song. *Anonymous.* KiLC

Swappin' yarns an' fishin' in a little River! Noah an' Jonah an' Cap'n John Smith. Don (Donald Robert Marquis) Marquis. LoGBV; PoLf

Sware what is felt with hand, or seen with eye,/As mortal, must feel sickness, age, and die. Caelica, XXVIII. Fulke, Lord Brooke Greville. FCP

A swarm of bees in July/Is not worth a fly. A Swarm of Bees in May. *Anonymous.* FaBoBe; HBV 1-2; OxNR

The swarms of extended wings. After Alcman. Dick Gallup. ANYP

Swathed by the red breath of the sun. The Angel in the House. Coventry Patmore. VLP

Sway again/And again, in the bright new clean rain. Twice. Ian Hamilton Finlay. BSV

Swayed in the air:– The Revolt of Islam. Percy Bysshe Shelley. ChRP

Swaying for her son who walks in sorrow. The Lonely Mother. Fenton Johnson. GoSl; PoNe

Swear that's true now, and I'll believe it then. Because My Faltering Feet. Hilaire Belloc. OxBoCh

Swearing, no greater mischief could be wrought/Than love united to a jealous thought. Love and Jealousy. Robert Greene. ElL

The sweat and sights and smells/of Haiti under my straw hat. Haitian Suite. Gregory Orr. MAYP

The sweat creeps out on his forehead, it scatters in the sun. The Bicycle Rider. Thomas W. Shapcott. CBAP

Sweat drips from my chin/into the uncivilized/crevasse. The Edge. Ann Chandonnet. AMV-81

Sweat of taffeta beaches without shelter/Lunacy of my lost flesh. The Sun in Capricorn. Joyce Mansour. PBWP

The sweat-stained garments, heavy with dust and destiny/Stacked at the feet of Saul. The Feast of Stephen. Kevin Nichols. OBCP

Sweating beneath encumbering rags. Apologue. Tony Connor. BoLoP

Sweats in frightened endurance of her own sudden emotions. Nightmares: Part Three. Lynn Moskowitz. AMV-81

The Swedish cart to be part of the heart. The Prejudice against the Past. Wallace Stevens. LiTM

Sweeping him bare of all opinion. The Independent. Phyllis McGinley. FaBoEE

Sweeping the shavings from his work-shop floor. When through the Whirl of Wheels. G. A. Studdert Kennedy. EBCP

Sweeps down and down and down into the pit. Let Me Not Die. Edith Lovejoy Pierce. TrPWD

Sweeps in with every force that stirs our souls/To admiration, self-renouncing love. The Tide of Faith. George Eliot. TRV; WGRP

Sweet Amoret in all her prime. Amoret. Mark Akenside. HBV 1-2; OBEV

Sweet and bitter January! January. Frank Dempster Sherman. YeAr

The sweet and smart from thence shall bring/Of the bee's honey and her sting. Upon a Mole in Celia's Bosom. Thomas Carew. AnAnS 2; CaPo

Sweet Angels come, and sing the rest. On the Glorious Assumption of Our Blessed Lady. Richard Crashaw. ISi; OBS

Sweet as the breath of roses blown,/The fragrance of her life. My Mother's Garden. Alice E. Allen. BLPA; BLPL; FaBoBe

Sweet beast, cat of my own stripe,/come and take my milk. Song: "Sweet beast, I have gone prowling." W. D. Snodgrass. LLLT; NYBP; SM

Sweet black mother of our food/you will have the rest. Kneeling Here, I Feel Good. Marge Piercy. NeAC

Sweet Catullus's all-but-island, olive-silvery Sirmio! "Frater Ave Atque Vale". Alfred, Lord Tennyson. ChTr; FaBoPP; GTBS-P; HAP; InPS; MBW 1-2; NoP; OBSP; OBTV; PAI

The sweet cheat gone. The Ghost. Walter De la Mare. BrPo; CMoP; ELP; EnLoPo; HaMV; HBMV; LiTM; MoAB; MoBrPo; MoVE; NOBE; OAEL 1-2; OxBTC

Sweet childish days, that were as long/As twenty days are now. To a Butterfly. William Wordsworth. EG; FM; HBV 1-2; SeCeV

Sweet clever acts/Like Wai-"ale"ale. Albatross. Lele-io-Hoku. WTO

Sweet Corrymeela, an' the same soft rain. Corrymeela. Moira O'Neill. AnIV; AWP; HBV 1-2

Sweet Daddy! Uh-huh! Trun me down! Uh-huh! Got Dem Blues (with music). *Anonymous.* AS

Sweet Daffadowndilly. Growing in the Vale,. Christina Georgina Rossetti. BrR; TiPo

Sweet daughter of Mendoza! The Daughter of Mendoza. Mirabeau Buonaparte Lamar. AA; BPAW; HBV 1-2

The sweet, dreamy night passed away. The Kansas Line. *Anonymous.* CoSo

Sweet Earth, we know thy dimmest mysteries,/But he is lord of his. In Early Spring. Alice Meynell. AnFE; HBV 1-2

Sweet especial rural scene. Binsey Poplars. Gerard Manley Hopkins. BoNaP; BrPo; CoBMV; ELP; FaBoPP; InPS; MoVE; NoAm; NoP; PAI; VLP

Sweet fair without, and stinking foul within. A Painted Whore, the Mask of Deadly Sin. William Lithgow. OBTV

...Sweet Farewell/Be to the Nymphs that on the old Hill dwell. Farewell to the Muses. John Hamilton Reynolds. OBRV

Sweet flavor/he's never tasted before. Persimmons and Plums. Elizabeth Hodges. GrPl

A sweet fore-warning? Hester. Charles Lamb. EnRP; GTBS; GTBS-P; HBV 1-2; LoBV; OBRV

Sweet friends at evening, and a The Seasons. Kalidasa. AWP

The sweet fruition of an earthly crown. Tamburlaine the Great. Christopher Marlowe. PoEL 1-5; TrGrPo

Sweet hallelujahs shall be sung/To welcome us to God. Courage. Stopford Augustus Brooke. WGRP

Sweet homes wherein to live and die.   My Love.   James Russell Lowell.
BLPL; FaBoBe; HBV 1-2

Sweet Hope! thy fragance pure and healing in-/cense steal!   Hope.   William
Lisle Bowles.   EnRP

Sweet instruments of music/And the firing of guns.   The Wagoner's Lad.
Anonymous.   AmFP

Sweet is boldness, shyness, pain.   Song.   Thomas Macdonagh.   ACP

Sweet is his death, that takes his end by love.   Complaint of a Lover
Rebuked.   Petrarch (Francesco Petrarca).   AWP; LiTW

Sweet is pleasure after pain.   Alexander's Feast, or, the Power of Music.
John Dryden.   ATP

Sweet is the death that taketh end by love.   Rime CXL: "Love that doth
raine and live within my thought."   Petrarch (Francesco Petrarca).   OBVE

Sweet Jesu, deliver/Thy servants ever.   A Prayer.   Digby Mackworth
Dolben.   GoBC

Sweet joy befall thee!   Infant Joy.   William Blake.   BiCB; GoJo; GTBS;
HBV 1-2; HBVY; LoBV; NAs; OBSP; PoLf; SiSoSe; TEP; ViBoPo

Sweet lady, tell me–can you make a pudding?   On Ladies' Accomplishments.
Anonymous.   FaBoUs

Sweet Lass of Richmond Hill.   The Lass of Richmond Hill.   Leonard
McNally.   BLSo

Sweet lip, you teach my mouth with one sweet kisse.   Astrophel and Stella,
LXXX.   Sir Philip Sidney.   AAS; SiPS

Sweet little babies in his damned freezer....   Faces.   Jack Anderson.   LFAC

The sweet little, green little, shamrock of Ireland!   The Green Little
Shamrock of Ireland.   Andrew Cherry.   HBV 1-2

A sweet lonesome goodbye   Last Impression of New York.   Mason Jordan
Mason.   PoNe

Sweet Love dead.   An Evening.   William Allingham.   EnLoPo; IrPN;
NOBV

Sweet Love has freed my eyes, but they are wet.   Love's Prisoner.   Mariana
Griswold Van Rensselaer.   HBV 1-2

Sweet lovers love the spring.   As You Like It.   William Shakespeare.
AWP; BiP; BoLiVe; CTC; ELP; EnLit; ExPo; FiP; GBL; GTBS; GTBS-P;
HBV 1-2; HeIP; InPo; InPS; LiTB; LiTL; LoBV; MCCG; NOBE; NoP;
OBEV; OBSC; OLR; PAI; PoRA; PPoe; TrGrPo; UnTE; ViBoPo

Sweet mama, won't you let it fall   Hang It on the Wall.   Charlie Patton.
BluL

Sweet mare: I never forget your name.   To a Horse.   Jill Hoffman.   PH

Sweet Marjorie's the word, and a fig for the vicar!   The Lady of the Lake.
Sir Walter Scott.   NBM; ViBoPo

Sweet Mary, keep our souls from harm!/Good night! good night!   Twilight
Song.   John Hunter-Duvar.   WHW

"Sweet Mary, weep no more for me."   The Banks of Dee.   *Anonymous.*
AmFP

Sweet moods of minds that sang to their sun, or sea/star low in the night.
Hours I Remember Lonely and Lovely to Me.   Thomas Caulfield Irwin.
IrPN

Sweet moon between her lighted clouds!   The Angel in the House.   Coventry
Patmore.   PeD; ViBoPo

Sweet mothers!–as they pass, one sees again/Old garden-walks, old roses, and
old loves.   Dear Old Mothers.   Charles Sarsfield Ross.   PGD

Sweet-mouth, honey paws, hairy one!   Black Bear.   Douglas Lepan.   WHW

"Sweet my child, I live for thee."   The Princess.   Alfred, Lord Tennyson.
BoLiVe; OAEP; TreFS; TrGrPo

The sweet, new smell which rose after the fall.   Although I Remember the
Sound.   Robert Huff.   SM

Sweet Nightingale! once more, my friends! fare well.   The Nightingale.
Samuel Taylor Coleridge.   EnRP; ERoP 1-2; FM; OBRV; PBBP

The sweet of Trinidado.   Come, Sirrah Jack, Ho!   *Anonymous.*   NCEP;
OAEP

Sweet of twigs and twine/My perennial nest.   Her breast is fit for pearls.
Emily Dickinson.   PeHV

Sweet Peg, thou shalt be my Summer's Queen.   Song: "O the month of May,
the merry month of May."   Thomas Dekker.   PBBP

Sweet Philip shall be my bird still.   The Praise of Philip Sparrow.   George
Gascoigne.   ViBoPo

Sweet Rosalie, "The Prairie Flow'r".   Rosalie, the Prairie Flower.   George
Frederick Root.   BLSo

Sweet saint 'tis true, you worthy be,/Yet without love nought worth to me.
Caelica, LII.   Fulke, Lord Brooke Greville.   AtBAP; FCP

The sweet Saints grant I live not long.   Riding Together.   William Morris.
NOBE; OAEL 1-2

Sweet silence after bells.   Sweet Silence after Bells!   Christopher John
Brennan.   BoAV; NOAV

Sweet silences abound, and all is peace.   Thy Sea So Great.   Winfred Ernest
Garrison.   TrPWD

Sweet silver trumpets,/Jesus!   When Sue Wears Red.   Langston Hughes.
CNA; GoSl; TTY

Sweet singing in the choir.   The Holly and the Ivy.   *Anonymous.*   FSW;
PCh

Sweet sixteen is shy and cold,/Calls mesir," and thinks me old.   Growing
Old.   Walter Learned.   HBV 1-2

Sweet smiling and sweet spoken.   To Sally.   John Quincy Adams.   AA;
ALV; OBAL

Sweet, soft, peaceful is thy note.   Blackbird.   *Anonymous.*   AnIL; OnYI

Sweet soul! not scorning honest sweat/And favouring virgin freshness yet.   On
St. Winefred.   Gerard Manley Hopkins.   SaC

Sweet Spirit comfort me!   Litany to the Holy Spirit (excerpt).   Robert
Herrick.   CoBE; OBEV; PoPle

The sweet spruce,/and the sweet hemlock.   The Saws Were Shrieking.   W.
W. Eustace Ross.   CaP; PeCV

Sweet Stella's image I do steal to me.'   Astrophel and Stella, XXXII.   Sir
Philip Sidney.   AAS; SiPS

A sweet surmise of grief of harassed corn?   Cornfield.   Leo Cox.   CaP

Sweet sweet love was,/Now bitter bitter grown to me.   Grown and Flown.
Christina Georgina Rossetti.   NOBV

Sweet sweet sweet sweet sweet tea.   Susie Asado.   Gertrude Stein.   SOTW;
TAP

Sweet Thames, run softly, till I end my song.   Prothalamion.   Edmund
Spenser.   AAS; AnFE; AtBAP; ATP; AWP; BoC; CABA; EBEV; EIL;
EnRePo; FaBoPP; GoTL; GTBS; GTBS-P; HAP; HBV 1-2; HW; InPo;
LiTB; LiTL; LoBV; MCCG; NIP; NoP; OBEV; OBSC; PBBP; PPoe; PPP;
SeCePo; ViBoPo; WHA

Sweet the death she shall crown/Under the stars.   Under the Stars.   Wallace
Rice.   AA; OHIP

Sweet thoughts I envy your so happy rest,/Which oft I wisht, yet never was so
blest.   Amoretti, LXXVI.   Edmund Spenser.   AAS

Sweet to myself that am so sweet to you!   The Azalea.   Coventry Patmore.
ELP; GBL; GoBC

Sweet to the chilled frame, nerves soothed were so sore shaken.   After War.
Ivor Gurney.   OBSP

The sweet, wild, poignant passion of thy song.   In Memoriam: John
Davidson.   Ronald Campbell Macfie.   GoTS

Sweet William died from the wounds that he received,/Fair Ellen died for
sorrow.   Earl Brand (Sweet William).   *Anonymous.*   AmFP

Sweet wind, sweet wind, where have you blown our past?   Failure.
Richmond Lattimore.   PCP

The sweet winds at their play.   Medieval Norman Songs.   *Anonymous.*
AWP

Sweet, you are praised in a silence,/Sung in a sigh.   Praise.   Seumas (James
Starkey) O'Sullivan.   HBV 1-2

Sweetened and re-dressed.   Dream Girl.   Karen Snow.   HoAn

Sweetened by the orchards of the earth.   Concert.   Michael Arvey.
AMV-81

A sweeter Christmas than we to ours/May you bequeath to yours.   A Carol
for Children.   Ogden Nash.   EaLo

A sweeter English rose?   A Colonist in His Garden.   William Pember
Reeves.   ACV; AnNZ

Sweeter than any apple I have known.   The Kiss.   Robert Pack.   AMV-81

Sweeter than the silver string.   The Faithful Shepherdess.   John Fletcher.
TrGrPo

The sweetest and sleepiest/Bird at this hour!   Serenade.   George Darley.
HBV 1-2

The sweetest bird that ever was,/In friendly sort, farewell.   The Blackbird.
Anonymous.   EIL

The sweetest meat should be/around the claws.   Nervous Miracles.   Jim
Gustafson.   APU

Sweetest mouth red as the rose.   Truelove.   *Anonymous.*   AWP

–The sweetest sea.   The Triangle Ladies.   Carol Artman Montgomery.
AMV-80

The sweetest solace is to act no sin.   Mirth.   Robert Herrick.   LiTB

The sweetest time in all my life/To deem in thinking spent.   Of a Contented
Mind.   Thomas, Lord Vaux.   CoBE; EIL; EnRePo; GoBC

Sweetheart, make much of him and shed/Tears on his taciturn dry head.   The
Sea Horse.   Robert Graves.   FaBoMo

Sweetly screaming to be fed.   The Happy Family.   John Ciardi.   DuDa

Sweetly to surprise us the last day.   The Petrified Fern.   Mary Bolles
Branch.   AA

The sweetness and the peace of real content.   Compensation.   E. M.
Brainard.   PoToHe

The sweetness of His face.   The Little Angels.   Jacopone da Todi.   CAW

...The swelling river/Winds his broad stream majestic, deep, and/slow.
Midnight.   Alfred, Lord Tennyson.   VLP

Swelling the song that my paddle sings.   The Song My Paddle Sings.   E.
Pauline Johnson.   BPAW; CaP; HBV 1-2

Swept along/and along.   Getting Started.   Janet Campbell Hale.   VoR

Swept away by winds. Eya-ya-ya...   Manerathiak's Song.   *Anonymous.*
WHW

Swept by the murmuring winds of ocean, join/The murmuring shores in a
perpetual hymn.   A Hymn of the Sea.   William Cullen Bryant.   MOS

Swetest of alle thinge?   Snatches: "Alas! how shold I singe?"   *Anonymous.*
OxBM

Swich appetit hath he to ete a mous.   Snatches: "Let take a cat." *Anonymous.* OxBM

Swich maner study was to him but game.   A Clerk Ther was of Cauntebrigge Also (parody).   Walter William Skeat.   BXAP

Swift feet the readiest aid supply.   The Song of the Four Winds.   Thomas Love Peacock.   OBRV; WiR

...A swift kick from a gentle/gust & our fears would all be gone.   Fire. 10/78. Bart Plantenga.   AMV-80

A swift steed–gift of the stranger–/or the lipped and lidded goblet!   Young Man of Alien Beauty.   Muireadhach Albanach O Dalaigh.   NOBI

Swift to Thy sons who in God rest/secure.   Open the Gates.   *Anonymous.* TrJP

Swiftly and out of sight is borne the brave corpse.   The Beautiful Swimmer. Walt Whitman.   PeHV

Swiftly flew the fingers fine/When the pen that motto drew.   Long Neglect Has Worn away.   Emily Bronte.   NOBV; NoP

Swiftly the darkness fell.   Twilight.   Heinrich Heine.   AWP

Swim like a fish toward Rome.   Cleopatra to the Asp.   Ted Hughes. EBEV

"Swim' she told me and I/did, I did.   In the Place Where Her Breasts Come Together.   Judy Grahn.   PeHV

...–The swimmer floats, the lover sleeps.   Swimmer.   Robert Francis. CrMA; DFF; NePoAm

Swimming pupils gazing up seraphical at the azure vault...   The Sun Spirit. Ralph Chubb.   PeHV

Swims into the deep humours of my eye/bringing this fish pale day.   A Suite of Six Pieces for Siskind.   John Logan.   LCAP

Swing it straighter and higher!   The Passionate Sword.   Jean Starr Untermeyer.   HBMV; TrJP; TrPWD

Swing, swing together/With your bodies between your knees.   Eton Boating Song.   William Johnson Cory.   ELP

...Swing to its strength,/and let it be the hill in you at length.   The Gatineaus. James Wreford Watson.   CaP

Swing up into the apple-tree.   Landscapes.   Thomas Stearns Eliot.   BiP; GTBS-P

Swing yo' ladies round and round/Ain't gonna rain no mo'.   Ain't Gonna Rain (with music).   *Anonymous.*   AS

Swingeth he as the moon goes down.   The Irish Franciscan.   Rosa Mulholland.   CAW

...Swinging our flashlights/Up and around our heads like holes in the night. Looking for Mountain Beavers.   David Wagoner.   VGW

Swinging there alone/As if to challenge you!   November Garden.   Louise Driscoll.   YeAr

Swings open & shut/like a gate.   A Heart That's Been Broken.   Maureen Owen.   LLLT

A swirl of black flags, white crescents, a language of swords.   Arabic Script. Anthony Thwaite.   OBTV

Swirling over everything alive.   Melancholia.   Robert Bly.   NoP

The sword by his side breaks into flame.   Looking at New-Fallen Snow from a Train.   Robert Bly.   NaP

The Sword-fish mightier than the Penguin.   The Pen-Guin. The Sword-Fish. Robert Williams Wood.   NLV

The sword of Meade and Lee!   Gettysburg.   James Jeffrey Roche.   MC; PAH

"The sword of the Lord and Gideon."   The Band of Gideon.   Joseph Seamon, Jr Cotter.   BANP; CDC

The sword of war may mow me down.   The Recruiting Sergeant. *Anonymous.*   OBET

The sword shall maintain me as long as I live.   A Copy of Verses Composed by Captain Henry Every.   *Anonymous.*   OBSS

Swore, but too late, he shouldn't catch him twice.   The Crow and the Fox. Jean de La Fontaine.   AWP; MaC

Swore he'd learned his last lesson as somebody's fool.   The Fox and the Crow.   Jean de La Fontaine.   OBVE; PPP

Swung back and forth in the sultry air like chandeliers.   The Man in Black. Mark Strand.   EAS

Swung in its orbit, bringing you, dark angel, down.   Dark Angel.   Elizabeth Bartlett.   NePoAm-2

Swung in the rope he found.   Exchange.   George Rostrevor Hamilton. FaBoEE

Syllable by syllable, language grows.   A New Genesis.   Avraham Schlonsky. VWA

Symbol of coming Springs!   Wild Geese.   Frederick Peterson.   HBV 1-2; HBVY

Symbol of life, me with such faith endow!   Ode to a Butterfly.   Thomas Wentworth Higginson.   AA; FaBoBe; HBV 1-2

The symbol of medicine.   The Staff of Aesculapius.   Marianne Moore. ImOP

Symbols, games, radiant, red, blonde, loving–so long ago.   Symbols.   Harry Roskolenko.   FAZ

Symbols of Peace, now war is ended.   The Unemployed.   LeVan Roberts. PGD

...A symmetry of any number/dancing.   Some Semblance of Order.   Charles David Wright.   FAZ

...A symphony/Of highest joy and deepest agony!   The Common Lot. Adelbert Sumpter Coats.   TrPWD

A symphony of praises loud we sing/In faithful memory of our Peaceful King. Elegy on Albert Edward the Peacemaker.   *Anonymous.*   CoMu

Syne rin like hell afore the result explodes!   Recipe: To Mak a Ballant. Alexander Scott.   BSV

T

T'devil tak t' pynot an' God save me.   Against the Magpie.   *Anonymous.* GBP

'T is all I know of weather.   Yuki.   Mary McNeil Fenollosa.   AA

'T is grown a Gettysburg or Waterloo.   Distinction.   Mark A. De Wolfe Howe.   AA

'T is more than one man's work to please you all.   All for Love.   John Dryden.   DiPo

'T is summer!'–and it melts away.   Snowflakes.   Henrietta Robins Eliot. AA

'T is we who dread the thunder, and not/they.   The Wild Geese.   James Herbert Morse.   AA

T' oblige the world, bright nymph, thou sure wast born.   Old Tityrus to Eugenia.   Charles Cotton.   ViBoPo

T'one's at God's finding; t'other at his owne.   On the Plough-Man.   Francis Quarles.   OBS

T, then, is a symbol for the plane earth.   The Plane: Earth.   Sun-Ra. PoBA

'T was a lucky escape for the stone.   On a Stone Thrown at a Very Great Man, but Which Missed Him.   John Wolcot.   NLV

'T was Clerk Saunders, that good earl's/son,/That pledgd his faith to marry me.'   Clerk Saunders.   *Anonymous.*   ESPB

'T were cruelty to tumble down.   Ode to Fortune.   Joseph R. and Halleck, Fitz-Greene Drake.   AA

'T were not so grave a thing to bear/The burden of a seed.   Silkweed. Philip Henry Savage.   AA

Ta-ta, pigeye.   Rip-off #1: Hippie Capitalism.   Geof Hewitt.   NeAC

The table made of stone.   Skara Brae.   Michael Longley.   FaBoIP

Tacking air, quicker and quicker/To rock, sea and star.   High Island. Richard Murphy.   CIP; NOBI

Taddle diddle dink dink, taddle diddle day.   Wunst I Had an Old Gray Mare. *Anonymous.*   OuSiCo

Tae win awa' tae Africa an' poach a rhinocerious.   Poaching in Excelsis.   G. K. Menzies.   FaBoCo

Taeping?/Ariel?   Cutty Sark.   Hart Crane.   FaBoMo

The tail-boards slam, and the trailers ram–and the great trucks/roll again. The City and the Trucks.   Dorothy Brown Thompson.   BrR

Tail bone raw, says Billy Barlow.   Billy Barlow.   *Anonymous.*   FSW; OuSiCo

Tail end of a dust storm/somehow battered up from Kansas.   The Hide of My Mother.   Edward Dorn.   NeAP

Tail, eyes...wings and from these letters flew.   Lament of a Last Letter. Janet E. Harrison.   AMV-80

A tail like a cat, but it isn't a cat.   Riddle: "It has a head like a cat, feet like a cat."   *Anonymous.*   NTCP

...The tailor fades/from all of us, forever, stitching sleeves.   Grandfather. Willis Barnstone.   VWA

A tailor's goose will never fly.   Hyder Iddle.   *Anonymous.*   NA; OxNR

Tailors and soutars, blest be ye.   Amends to the Tailors and Soutars.   John Skelton.   BSV; CBEP

Tails like vibrators/used to shock as a joke/when shaking hands.   Catching Soft Craws.   William J. Vernon.   WOLT

Tails set atilt for/Wagging!   Poetic Tale.   Grace Maddock Miller.   GDP

Tak tyme in tyme, or tyme will not be tane.   A Description of Tyme. Alexander Montgomerie.   OxBS

Take a drink most any time–whiskey clear with me.   The Roving Shanty Boy. *Anonymous.*   AmFP

Take a last turn/In the tang of possibility.   Linen Town.   Seamus Heaney. CIP

Take a later flight,/a later train.   Another look around.   Unsent Message to My Brother in His Pain.   Leon Stokesbury.   MAYP

Take a leaf and/come/just come   Invitation Standing.   Paul Blackburn. VGW

Take a long breath and let yourself go.   Plunger.   Carl Sandburg.   BoLiVe

...Take a look at yourself/and you'll say, "I'm not Stratophon."   Advice to a Prizefighter.   Lucilius [or Lucillius].   LiSp

Take a look. Let your eye cast its own bronze,/the bronze of pure occasion justify your eye.   Further Instructions.   Vincent O'Sullivan.   OCNZ

Take advice of present love.　A Plea for Promiscuity.　Edmund Waller.
UnTE

Take all of our family of rabbits/To bed with us just for tonight.　Birthdays.
Marchette Chute.　BiCB; SiSoSe

Take all the sun goes round beside.　On a Girdle.　Edmund Waller.　ALV;
AnAnS 2; AWP; CavP; GTBS; GTBS-P; HBV 1-2; HeIP; LoBV; NoP;
OBEV; SeCePo; TrGrPo; UnTE

Take back, MacJohn, thy matchless hound.　The Foray of Con O'Donnell,
A.D. 1495.　Denis Florence MacCarthy.　OnYI

Take back the gift of our separateness.　God of Mercy.　(or Molodovski)
Kadya, (or Kadia) Molodovsky.　WPOW

...Take care, Chief Boiling/Whiskey. Dick.　Letter to Welch from Browning.
Richard Hugo.　NNaP

Take care!/If she looks at you-/Tiggady Rue.　Tiggady Rue.　David
McCord.　TiPo; WSC

Take care of your pocket!-take care of your pocket!　Ye Tourists and
Travellers, Bound to the Rhine.　Thomas Hood.　OBTV

Take care you don't pousser trop/The one who gives you such jolis plats.
Monsieur Pussy-Cat, Blackmailer.　Stevie Smith.　PCat

Take care: your eyes still more than mine may weep.　Sonnet, XXIV: "Don't
scold me, Ladies, if I have loved."　Louise Labé.　PBWP

Take charge of me, and of my end!　Dies Irae.　Anonymous.　AWP

Take compassion all on us and never forget/Those poor pipeclay rangers, so
called of late.　The Fancy Frigate.　Anonymous.　OBSS

Take courage, man! and steal the rest.　To a Living Author.　Anonymous.
NLV

Take day and night for woman's love, what angels we should/be!　Venetian
Air.　Thomas Moore.　OBSP

-Take, divine one,/This vanity away, and to thy lover/Give what is needful:-
Odes.　George Santayana.　CoAnAm

Take drugs white men/are coming consciousness/& awareness are so different/
you wouldn't believe.　The United States of America We.　Sam Abrams.
APU

Take flesh of my tired bones.　A Clash with Cliches.　Vassar Miller.
AMV-80; FAZ

Take fright in his bewildering bower, and die.　Winter Will Follow.　Richard
Watson Dixon.　GTBS-P

Take from me all my trumpery lest I die.　The Apologist's Evening Prayer.
Clive Staples Lewis.　TrCP

Take from my heart this divine existence!　The Blind Singer.　Friedrich
Hoelderlin.　LiTW

Take from the glass that shone/The vintage that remains.　For a Wine
Festival.　Vernon Watkins.　OxBTC

Take from the lady what you yearn for every time you/can....　The Book of
True Love (excerpt).　Juan, Archpriest of Hita, Ruiz.　ErPo

Take half our heavens with a roar.　Ancient Lights.　Austin Clarke.　BIrV;
CMoP; IPY; NMP; OxBI

Take half thy canvas in.　To Licinius.　Horace.　AWP; EnLi 1-2

Take Heart of me, who by His Grace,/Slough'd off my Pris'n and won my
Race.　On Amaryllis A Tortoyse.　Marjorie Pickthall.　PeCV

Take heart then, poet!　Theory of Poetry.　Archibald MacLeish.　AP; DFF

Take Heed, all ye Swains, how you love one so fair.　A Pastoral.　John
Byrom.　OBEC

Take heed; take heed! believe me, girls; don't let this be your lot!　Pearl
Bryan.　Anonymous.　BaBo

Take hence my life an happier State,/More Heav'nly, more Sublime.　A
Hymn of Praise, on a Recovery from Sickness.　Benjamin Colman.　SCAP

"Take her, boy, and make her happy. Towser shall be tied tonight.　Towser
Shall Be Tied Tonight.　Anonymous.　BLPA; BoAnP

Take her, boy, you're mighty lucky,/When you marry a girl like Sue.　She
Was Bred in Old Kentucky.　Harry Braisted.　FSN

Take her down the river further, 'cause they ain't no mo'.　Roustabout Holler.
Anonymous.　OuSiCo

Take her in a ditch/Easy as a bat.　Easy as a Bat.　Anonymous.　WTO

Take her out and chop the head of her,/Early in the morning.　I Had a Wife.
Anonymous.　FSW

Take her, then, for evermore,-/For ever-evermore.　Softly Woo Away Her
Breath.　Bryan Waller Procter.　HBV 1-2

Take her to you.　Friend, don't be angry.　Mira Bai [(or Mirabai)].
BoWoP

Take her up and shake her.　Betsy Baker.　Anonymous.　OxNR

...Take/Him home with us, put him/Away, on a shelf, to keep.　Duck.
Valerie Worth.　NTCP

Take if thou canst this bitter cup from us.　Vicarious Atonement.　Richard
Aldington.　MoBrPo; WGRP

Take in a reef: haste is waste, proof doth find　The Golden Mean.　Henry
Howard, Earl of Surrey.　SiPS

Take in good part, from our poor poet's board,/Such riveled fruits as winter
can afford.　All for Love.　John Dryden.　DiPo

Take in the tangled slack!　Pitch Seven.　Hamish Brown.　PoSH

Take it and pass it on. That stuff won't kill you.　The Money Cry.　Peter
Davison.　FYAP

Take it at last for friend.　A Dream.　Hugh Connell.　NeIP

Take it. It is well spent/Easing a savior's birth.　Tempt Me No More.　C.
Day-Lewis.　AnFE; MoAB; MoBrPo; NAMP; OAEP; OBMV; PoPl

Take it like a man.　Male Rage Poem.　Pier Giorgio Di Cicco.　NOBC

Take it. No, give it back!　The Pedlar.　Charlotte Mew.　HBMV

Take it out/for a private airing.　Dissembler.　Charles Shaw.　GoYe

Take it up like a kite on a string.　Limerick: "Well, it's partly the shape of
the thing."　Anonymous.　SoSe; TDH

Take journey and return again,/Yet on her crystal couch still lie.　Song:
"Distil not poison in mine ears."　John Hall.　OBSP

Take Loire and Po, yet all may not compare/With English Thamesis for
buildings rare.　Rivers.　Thomas Storer.　EIL

Take love sublimely.　Ah, Be Not False.　Richard Watson Gilder.　AA;
HBV 1-2; HBVY

Take me, and brand me with thy cross,/Thy slave's proud sign.　Work.　G.
A. Studdert Kennedy　EBCP

Take me and break me, mould me to/The pattern Thou hast planned.　His
Plan for Me.　Martha Snell Nicholson.　STF

Take me and mine together!　To Aenone.　Robert Herrick.　HBV 1-2

Take me, and weep me on the desolate hills!　The Well.　Thomas Edward
Brown.　NOBV

Take me back before everything.　Being Aware.　Dennis Cooper.　APU

...Take me by the hand/And guide me onward to thy Promised Land!
Madonna Natura.　Fiona Macleod.　WGRP

Take me-make me next of kin/To your leafy brood.　The House of the Trees.
Ethelwyn Wetherald.　CaP

Take me to your clime.　All Things Are Current Found.　Henry David
Thoreau.　AnNE; ViBoPo

Take me up in a tarpauling jacket,/And fiddle and dance to my grave.
Tarpauling Jacket.　Anonymous.　DTC; OxBoLi

Take me when I die to heaven,/Happy there with Thee to dwell.　Jesus
Tender Shepherd.　Mary L. Duncan.　BLRP

Take me with you in your coach!　Shih Ching.　Anonymous.　BoWoP

Take my advice, don't try it twice/If you've got but fifty cents!　I Had but
Fifty Cents.　Anonymous.　BeLS; BLPA; NLV; TreF

Take my hand, and let us follow the great Captain to his/Queen.　The Last
Meeting of Pocahontas and the Great Captain.　Margaret Junkin Preston.
MC; PAH

Take my last gift; thy heart hath sung my/praise.　The House of Life.
Dante Gabriel Rossetti.　VLP

Take my spirit to Thee.　Prayers.　Henry Charles Beeching.　OBEV; OBVV

Take, O Friend, unseen, eternal,/Praises this Thanksgiving Day.
Thanksgiving.　Margaret E. Sangster.　BLRP

"Take of my feathers but not of my toe."　The False Fox Came into Our
Croft.　Anonymous.　GBP; OxBM; PBBP

Take off his hide and feed him to the crows.　On Buying a Horse.
Anonymous.　NLV; PH

...Take off that crucifix around your neck/And hang a corkscrew there?
Written on a Girl's Table-Napkin at Wiesbaden.　Ronald Duncan.　WeW

Take off your coat and free your throat/With the real old Mountain Dew.
Real Old Mountain Dew.　Anonymous.　FSW

Take, oh, take that heart from me.　Song: "Who has robbed the ocean cave."
John Shaw.　HBV 1-2

Take refuge-Of bad lines a centiane dose/Is sure enough-and so "here follows
prose."　Epistle to John Hamilton Reynolds.　John Keats.　OAEL 1-2

Take root like me, or give me life like thine!　The Sunflower to the Sun.
Mary Elizabeth (DeWitt) Stebbins　AA

...Take/Soon the mouth out of my very words.　Landed: A Valentine.
Richard Howard.　PoA

Take that bowl to chiny/stand a test just any where　Pigmeat.　Leadbelly.
BluL

Take the avenue and run, and I'll/be in Scotland before you.　Leave
Cancelled.　Bill Berkson.　ANYP

Take the extra coin. I only came/to see you living and the fountains run.
Napoli Again.　Richard Hugo.　LCAP

Take the laughter first of all.　Song: "Take it, love!"　Richard Le Gallienne.
HBV 1-2

Take the men, harness them by our side/And there obedient bid them bide.
The Midnight Court.　Brian Merriman.　LiTW

Take the pistol./Shoot.　The Huntsman.　John Wheelwright.　CrMA

Take the reins for me, will you?　To My Blood Sister.　Christine E. Hemp.
Str

Take the sap and leave the heart.　I Was Made Erect and Lone.　Henry
David Thoreau.　PoEL 1-5

Take the thanks of a boy.　A Boy's Prayer.　Henry Charles Beeching.　GN

...Take them down to the department secretary and have her put/them in the
mail.　Paschal Lamb.　Robert Hass.　NPGG

"Take them for what they were, they weren't so bad!"　Fantasia on a
Wittelsbach Atmosphere.　Siegfried Sassoon.　MoVE

Take them, lest the chain be broken/Ere the pilgrimage be done.　One by
One.　Adelaide Anne Procter.　GN; HBV 1-2

Take them, lest they disappear.　Lullaby.　Nohomaiterangi.　WTO

Take these lambs within thine arms,/Gently to thy bosom pressed. Jesus, Shepherd of Thy Sheep. George Washington Bethune. AH

Take this flyswatter and exterminate the angels. Adolph Hitler Meditates on the Jewish Problem. Oscar Hahn. AMV-81

Take this for your motto, "I can, will,"/And live up to it each day. The Town of Nogood. W. E. Penny. BLPA

Take this parting tear. John O'Dwyer of the Glen. *Anonymous.* AnIV

Take this stane aff my wame, and lay it on o' thine. On Jocky Bell. *Anonymous.* FaBoEE

Take Thou, at last, our souls to Thine eter-/nal peace. New National Hymn. Francis Marion Crawford. PAH

Take thou the heart with the heart's Paradise. At the Last. Philip Bourke Marston. HBV 1-2

Take to him thus the soul's food,/Through our Lord's own might. The Eagle's Nature. *Anonymous.* MeEV

Take two-o coo, Taffy! Take Two-O Coo, Taffy! *Anonymous.* PBBP

Take up thy life and go! A Cry from the Shore. Ellen Mackay Hutchinson Cortissoz. AA

Take us to the place for the new birth blood. Initiation. Jayne Cortez. PoBA

Take warning, spring, and stay/Or I might never turn to look your way. Stay, Spring. Andrew Young. FaBoTw

Take we our seats and let the dirge begin. On the Death of M. D'Ossoli and His Wife, Margaret Fuller. Walter Savage Landor. PAH

Take what the Friend gives as a bliss and joy. The Bustan. Muslih-ud-Din Sa'di. AWP

Take yo' net an' foller me. My Lord Says He's Gwineter Rain Down Fire. *Anonymous.* BoAN 1-2

Take yo' time, Miss Lucy Long. Take Yo' Time, Miss Lucy Long. *Anonymous.* GoSl

"Take your Eternity," he said. Epitaph for Any New Yorker. Christopher Morley. ShM

Take your own kisses, give me mine again. My Love and I for Kisses Play'd. William Strode. FaBoEE

Take your pick/While I take mine. Children, It's Time. Michael Brownstein. ANYP

Take your place! Take Your Place. *Anonymous.* STF

Take your time, sir, there's no hurry. Indictment. Margaret Tod Ritter. AnAmPo

Taken by storm, she is the girl you will marry. Courtship. Mark Strand. GP; HaCAP

Taken my mind away. Dreams in Progress. Richard Oyama. BrSi

Takes a young lettuce for a sallet. Epitaph: "See here, nice Death, to please his palate." Alexander Pope. FaBoEE

Takes aim at all the sky/And starts to ramify. Seed Leaves. Richard Wilbur. BoNaP; NCSH

Takes all them dogs to/run my women down Saturday Blues. Ishman Bracey. BluL

Takes all too long to lay asleep again. A Memory. Rupert Brooke. BrPo

Takes his boots off, has a dram, forgets the matter. Marry the Lass? Andrew Greig. PoSH

Takes his pen in tears and triumph, and he writes it down for them. Will Yer Write It Down for Me? Henry Lawson. CBAP

Takes its shirt dazzled/Off the glazier's back. The Glazier. Stephane Mallarme. OBVE

Takes off the prize, who is no more than ghost. Poem: "I take four devils with me when I ride." Gervase Stewart. WaP

Takes out a box, and peels away his face. Sunday Night in Santa Rosa. Dana Gioia. GrPl

Takes out a ring of brass keys/and opens every door. Daybreak. Bert Meyers. EAS

Takes soap and water/for to keep it clean. Keep It Clean. Charlie Jordan. BluL

Takes to her breast the sad ripe apples. Larch Tree. Laurie Lee. NeBP

Takes us a thousand miles from where we were before. The Motion of the Earth. Norman Nicholson. ImOP

Takes waving of the corn. The Waving of the Corn. Sidney Lanier. AP

...Taking/certain life from the wasting of my bones. Pocahontas to her English husband, John Rolfe. Paula Gunn Allen. STE

Taking his answer from the nested dove/That ever hymneth skies forever blue. Epigrams. Theocritus. AWP

...Taking/His sensible underclothes off, rolls into bed? Street Preacher. Norman MacCaig. BSV

Taking it in, traveling still. Cities behind Glass. Linda Hogan. STE

Taking my place among the small things of the world. The Window Frames the Moon. Laureen Mar. BrSi

Taking no notice of posted limits or/signs of treacherous soft shoulders,/frost heaves ahead. Minuet in a Minor Key. Phyllis Janowitz. AmC

...Taking over/The whole south of England at a blow. Painting of my Father. Padraic Fallon. NOBI

...A taking/pains: as though seeing the light. Passages. David Walker. AMV-80

Taking small comfort from our day as it is. The Last Moriori. Kendrick Smithyman. OCNZ

...Taking stock of/Monkey, Piggsy, Sandy's belt of skulls. Letters to Live Poets. Bruce Beaver. CBAP

...Taking sustenance/from animals of the ground. A Trial. Alan Dugan. NoAm

Taking the scissors/began to trim off the baby's fingers. My Face Is My Own, I Thought. Tom Raworth. EAS

...Taking/the step they will follow, Octobers and years from now. Kicking the Leaves. Donald Hall. GLGT

Taking this train/to visit miriam. Going Uptown to Visit Miriam. Victor Hernandez Cruz. FF; MAT; NYP

...Taking up/Upon his shoulders all the destined acts/And fame of his descendants. The Aeneid. Virgil (Publius Vergilius Maro). NAWM 1-2

...Taking what's not yours/but fits you & good luck. The Imagination of Necessity. Andrei Codrescu. EAS

The tale apocryphal. The Whale, His Bulwark. Derek Walcott. OxBC; TTY

A tale of the children who planted me. An Arbor Day Tree. *Anonymous.* OHIP

The tales of girls he used to have? De Produndis. Dorothy Parker. ErPo

Tales that are earnest, noble and gran'/Belong to the life of a railroad man. Casey Jones. *Anonymous.* AS; GoTF; TreF; ViBoFo

Talin glaring from that rising sickle moon. Babel. Gary Pacernick. AMV-81

The talk is getting mean. Unidentified Flying Object. Robert Earl Hayden. NCSH

Talk is her business; and her chief delight/To tell of Prodigies, and cause affright. The Aeneid. Virgil (Publius Vergilius Maro). OBVE

Talk is too unreal. On the Death of Lisa Lyman. Della Burt. BlSi

Talk to me. Talk to me. Talk to Me, Talk to Me. Hedva Harkavi. VWA

Talking and talking and talking and talking and talking. Old People. Myra Cohn Livingston. CTBA

...Talking/pleasantly, of the green wood and the dry. The Rick of Green Wood. Edward Dorn. NeAP; PoM

Talking to myself and would draw blood. My Mother Would Be a Falconress. Robert Duncan. PoM

A tall candle burning/In a shadowy room. Shadbush. Christina Rainsford. GoYe

Tall dames go walking in grass-/green Avalon. The Statesman's Holiday. William Butler Yeats. AtBAP; CMoP; OxBTC

The tall fin slid away and then the tail. Basking Shark. Norman MacCaig. BoAnP

Tall, foolish, furious; alone. Ballad of the Mouse. Robert Wallace. NYBP

Tall hotels ablaze with neon/Magnetise the sons of Dai. The Evans Country. Kingsley Amis. NOBL

Tall plumes surmount a painted mask of death. Atavism. Elinor Wylie. AnEnPo; HBMV; PoA; SBG

Tall, slim, amid the statues and the trees. A Pastel. Paul Verlaine. SyP

A tall, smooth candle white,/Walthena. Walthena. Elisabeth Peck. AmFN

The tall towers rise/Like Jacob's ladder/Into the skies. Building a Skyscraper. James S. Tippett. OnUR

The taller mastiff deems it aptest/To lift a leg and play the baptist. The Scribblers. Walter Savage Landor. OBSV

Tally-ho hark-away, Tally-ho hark-away, Tally-ho hark-/away/My boys, away, hark-away! Reynard the Fox. *Anonymous.* OnYI

A Tambourine made out of a riddle,/And that's the end of my song. The Monkey's Wedding. *Anonymous.* BLPA; NA

An, tan, toosh, Jock. Eenity, Feenity, Fickety, Feg. *Anonymous.* OxNR

...Tangle in the same old snare/saying the little lies again. At the End of the Affair. Maxine W. Kumin. TAP

The tangled swamp, through which a pathway strays/Becomes a garden with strange flowers and sprays. The Path. William Cullen Bryant. MAmP

Tansy for seed. Tansy for August. The Path. Theodore Enslin. CoPo

Tap dancing for my life The Poet. Lucille Clifton. DFF; GP

The tap-tap of a ringmaker is heard,/Beating his penny in a distant wing. Ideal and Reality. Joseph Campbell. BIrV

...The tape finishes again/and we sit on. Unable to find things to say. The Lord Sits with Me Out in Front. Jack Gilbert. NPGG

A taper in a rushing wind. I Am Not Yours. Sara Teasdale. VGW

The tapestries of paradise/So notelessly are made! A shady friend for torrid days. Emily Dickinson. NePA

Tapped out long ago/for a child. Playing the Bones. Elizabeth Brewster. AMV-81

"Tapping at your windowpane." Who Is Tapping at My Window. A. G. Deming. SoPo

"Tare-an-ages, girls, which o'yees own the child?" Pharao's Daughter. Michael Moran. BIrV

Tarred and feathered and carried in a cart/By the women of Marblehead! Skipper Ireson's Ride. John Greenleaf Whittier. AA; AmP; AnNE; AP;

BeLS; HBV 1-2; InMe; NOBA; OBAL; OBCA; OxBA; PAH; PoLf; StPo; TreFS; YaD

Tarried to share the human condition. A Letter to Auden. Robert Phillips. AMV-81

Tarry by that old garden of your delight. Rupert Brooke. Wilfrid Gibson. HBMV

Tarrydiddle, den. One-erum, Two-erum. *Anonymous.* OxNR

The Tartar horsemen shake their spears. The Wind Sprang up at Four O'Clock. Thomas Stearns Eliot. NePA

A taste of death, yet look! he has such hair!). Figures of Authority. Edward Watkins. NYBP

Taste of resignation, sweet! Men of the Rocks. Adam Drinan. OxBS

The taste/of rust. Some Good Things to Be Said for the Iron Age. Gary Snyder. HoPM; WeW

The taste of you will be/the first thing/to pass my lips. Breakfast. Robin Shectman. AMV-80

Taste thine immortal wine! Indian Summer. Emily Dickinson. AnNE; BoLiVe

Taste thine immortal wine! These are the days when birds come back. Emily Dickinson. AmePo; FF; ForPo; HBV 1-2; MAmP; MoAmPo

Taste with contempt beholds, nor deigns to place/Amongst the lowest of her favour'd race. On Himself. Charles Churchill. OBEC

Tastes sweet the water with such specks of earth? Pictor Ignotus. Robert Browning. CTC; TEP; VLP

Tasting all the secret bits of life. Dream Songs. John Berryman. NaP

Tasting bitters when they want/Sweets will make men grumble. The Confession of Golias (abridged). Archpoet of Cologne. LiTW

Tasting new pleasures in a far-off country/Sacred to beauty. Odes. George Santayana. AmePo

Tasting the Glories that shall crown/An endless Life when this is done. The Retirement. *Anonymous.* OBEC

Tasting the rain/singing/the world will change Anishinabe Grandmothers. Gerald Vizenor. VoR

The tattered/tapestry/hold/many/moths. Music in an Empty House. Hugh Sykes Davies. EAS

Taught babes in grace their grammar,/And struck the simple, solemn. One Word More. Robert Browning. OAEP

Taught by the vastness of God's pictured plan/In the big world how small a thing is man! How Small Is Man. John Stuart Blackie. PoSH

Taught in my Saviour's school of grace,/Have learn'd to be content. Olney Hymns. William Cowper. CEP

Taught to sit on his trainer's hand. The Fortunes of Men (excerpt). *Anonymous.* PBBP

Taught us all early justice, made us a race. The Murder of Moses. Karl Shapiro. EaLo

Taunts them and scampers off,/laughing as he goes. Kid. Robert Earl Hayden. CAD; NCSH

Taurus by nightfall. Logging (excerpt). Gary Snyder. NMP

Taut smiles stretched open as a hand. Temple of the Muses. Beth Bentley. EyDe

Tawny petticoats,/Silver lace. A Tawnymoor. *Anonymous.* OxNR

The tawny, shining coat! Candlemas. Alice Brown. AA

A Tayl well-furnish'd, but an empty Head. On a Peacock. Thomas Heyrick. PB

Te Deum laudamus O Thou Hand of Fire Ave Maria. Hart Crane. NePA

...Te Kare,/Is that you are not beside me. He Waiata mo Te Kare. James Keir Baxter. OCNZ

Te-quem-tem te-quem-tem te-quem-tem. Punishment for a Wayward Train. Antonio Jacinto. WhB

Te whit, te whoo, te whit, te whit. Madrigal: "Sweet Suffolk owl." Thomas Vautor. EnRePo; PBBP

Tea rooms teeter like kites. Non-Euclidean Elegy. John Frederick Nims. MoVE

Tea to the n–th. The Poets at Tea. Barry Pain. Par

Teach beauty, virtue, truth, and love, and melody. Nature and the Poets. James Beattie. OBEC; SeCePo

Teach despairing crags to number/Blue infinities of bliss. Blue Moonshine. Francis G. Stokes. NA

Teach him to hold it holy and high/For the sake of its sacred dead. The Old Flag. Henry Cuyler Bunner. PAL; PGD

Teach me a roaring like you to your creatures. Prayer. Avraham Schlonsky. VWA

Teach me how to repent; for that's as good/As if thou hadst sealed my pardon, with thy blood. Holy Sonnets, VII. John Donne. ATP; DiPo; HAP; HeIP; JCP; MBW 1-2; NoP; PPP

Teach me, my son, the ways of day. Notes on a Life to Be Lived. Robert Penn Warren. NoAm

Teach me of death, and for ever, and set my feet on the way! The River of Stars. Alfred Noyes. OnMSP

Teach me the way that I should die. A Sergeant's Prayer. Hugh Brodie. PGD

Teach me there/is/someone Marrow of My Bone. Mari E. Evans. BPo

Teach me to love Thy Sacred Word/And view my Savior here. O How Sweet Are Thy Words! Anne Steele. BLRP

Teach me to talk like a man! Intervals. Beatrice Ravenel. HBMV

Teach me to travel far and bear my loads. December Stillness. Siegfried Sassoon. CMoP; MoRP

Teach sulky lips to say, my Lord,/That flaxen hair is dust. Senex. Sir John Betjeman. DTC

Teach the fit wayes their fruitlesse scope t' obtaine. Greatness. *Anonymous.* OBS

...Teach this hate of mine/The patience and integrity of the steel. Camouflage. John Streeter Manifold. WaP

"Teach us, altho' we die, to stand." Conemaugh. Elizabeth Stuart Phelps Ward. PAH

Teach us the gesture and the glee/Of the world-love that is to be. O Mothers of the Human Race. Robert Whitaker. PGD

Teach us to sacrifice our best,/And every effort make. Call to Conflict. *Anonymous.* STF

Teach us to say: "I will arise." An Easter Hymn. Richard Le Gallienne. OHIP

Teach us to share thy ageless power. O Child of Lowly Manger Birth. Ferdinand Q. Blanchard. AH

Teach us who had forgot to pray:/"God give you peace!" Joculator Domini. Sister Mary John Frederick GoBC

Teach your grandmother egg suction. An Importer. Robert Frost. FaBoCo

...The teacher hides behind his fan. The Teacher. Helen Bevington. GLGT

The teacher knows success. Ways of Loving. Theodore Weiss. GP

Teacher said I never polish my shoes. The Good Shepherd. Keidrych Rhys. NeBP

The teachers themselves/stare out of windows,/remembering April. Schoolyard in April. Kenneth Koch. PoA

Tear away grief. Spell against Sorrow. Kathleen Raine. PBWP

Tear me apart with your holy, invisible hands. Guadalajara Hospital. Ai. MAYP

Tear off a satyr's periwig! The Satyr in the Periwig. Edith Sitwell. AnEnPo

A tear rolling down the cheek of/Long-suffering humanity! Legend of His Lyre. Aaron Schmuller. GoYe

The tear that would have soothed it all. Ianthe. Walter Savage Landor. EiCP; TrGrPo

A tear to his memory shed. Simpson's Rest. George S. Simpson. PoOW

...Tearing roses/and trampling the gooseberries and the strawberries. Ave Eva. John Wheelwright. MoPo

Tearing the hairy leeches from his throat. The Lost Man: A Crocodile. Thomas Lovell Beddoes. AnFE

The tearless/Who cannot/Weep. Vagabonds. Langston Hughes. SaC

Tears, and my earliest love, Elizabeth, and changeless art. For Elizabeth Madox Roberts. Janet Lewis. QFR

Tears are but Tears! Death Is but Death. Will Dyson. BoAV

Tears are but vain, so I will keep/The silence of the soul. Hora Christi. Alice Brown. HBV 1-2; TrPWD; WGRP

Tears are real tears while we can laugh to-morrow. Moments. Hervey Allen. HBMV

Tears are the gems of joy and misery. South-Wind. George Parsons Lathrop. AA

Tears are worlds not seen. Epithalamion. Olga Broumas. LTB

Tears at my flimsy dress. Cherry Blossoms. Michael Lewis. UnTE

Tears can no more affection win,/Than wash thy Aethiopian Skin. A Fair Nymph Scorning a Black Boy Courting Her. John Cleveland. AnAnS 2

Tears doth he weep, laments doth he pour forth. Penitential Psalm. *Anonymous.* WGRP

The tears fall down and wet my skirt. Ch'in Chia's Wife's Reply. *Anonymous.* BoWoP

Tears fill my eyes, for she is not for me. She Is Not for Me. *Anonymous.* WTO

Tears for such wrongs that only tears repair. To God. Furnley Maurice. BoAV

Tears have pressed white hair/to face. The Feral Pioneers. Ishmael Reed. PoBA; PoNe

Tears like a lover wept. In the Wilderness. Robert Graves. BoC; EaLo; MoAB; MoBrPo; OxBI; SeCePo

...The tears of those/Who live between the breaking and the broken leaf. Land-Fall. George M. Brady. NeIP

Tears on my pillow–tears against the moon. Tears against the Moon. Thomas Walsh. CAW

The tears ran down the poor girl's cheeks:/"I love this highway man." The Maid Freed from the Gallows (D vers.). *Anonymous.* ViBoFo

Tears, sighs, prayers fail, but true love lasteth ever. At Her Fair Hands. Walter Davison. EIL; WHA

Tears that streak the dusty firmament. To Redoute. John Ashbery. PoA

The tears, the sighs, the anguish/Came later–and to me. When Two Are Parted. Heinrich Heine. AWP

Tears, true as those, which, ere she found her grave,/The noble Lady to our sorrows gave.' The Lady of the Manor. George Crabbe. NOBE; OBNC

Teasingly, then closing in black/and sudden, with fierce jaws. March. William Carlos Williams. NCSH

Tech herte myn right love thee/Whos herte-blood was shed for me. World's Bliss, Have Good Day! *Anonymous.* OxBM

Teddy follows his feet/Like a sneaker. Foots It (parody). D. C. Berry. BXAP

A tedious tale in rime, but little reason. Gascoigne's Woodmanship. George Gascoigne. AAS; EnRePo; QFR

Tee hee. Naval Engagement. Tom Veitch. ANYP

A teenage plankton luminously twitch. Watching the Dance. James Merrill. NIP

Teeth gnashing like the chattering of storks Homage to Ezra Pound (parody). Gilbert Highet. Par

The teeth in order greet the wondering sight,/A theme of admiration and delight! Artificial Teeth. Solyman Brown. FaBoUs

A telephone number: yours. Love Poem. Gregory Orr. GeTw

Tell 'em it was me, and I sing it all day long. Worried Man Blues. *Anonymous.* FSW

Tell every one that you meet–/There is a man on the cross. There Is a Man on the Cross. Elizabeth Cheney. PGD; TRV

Tell her, Good faith, good faith, good faith–not I! Love's Limit. *Anonymous.* EG; TrGrPo

Tell her he nightly lodgeth in my heart. Love Vagabonding. William, of Hawthornden Drummond. EG

Tell her if e'er she prove unkind,/I never shall have rest. Bright Was the Morning. Thomas D'Urfey. OBS

...Tell her, if you can,/that I have seen her there, and know. Mother and Son. William Heyen. GeTw

Tell her to find her purse. The Ghost in the Martini. Anthony Hecht. OxBC

Tell him I'm a child of God. Child of God. *Anonymous.* FSW

Tell him not to keep trying, for I have left... I Am Going to Sleep. Alfonsina Storni. BoWoP

Tell him, O night. The Thousand and One Nights: Tell Him, O Night. *Anonymous.* AWP; LiTW

Tell him our ails, that he, wi' wonted skill,/May fleg the schemers o' the mortmain-bill. The Ghaists: A Kirk-Yard Eclogue. Robert Fergusson. OxBS

Tell him/That it is we who are important For a Coming Extinction. William Stanley Merwin. HaCAP; NNaP

& Tell if the days it/adds up to/is one. Suicide. Alice Walker. FF

Tell me again. Tell Me Again. Nigar Hanim. PBWP

Tell me, Apollo, tell me where/The Sunbeams go, when they do disappear. On a Sunbeam. Thomas Heyrick. MePo

Tell me/everything/just as it was/from the beginning. Against Still Life. Margaret Atwood. NMM

Tell me how lucky I was. Bringing Flowers. Roberta Spear. AmPA

Tell me how many T's there are in all THAT! Riddle: "Thomas a Tattamus took two T's." *Anonymous.* HBV 1-2; HBVY

Tell me I say, who contemplate, aghast,/sky bells now silent, and the channel lost. Sea Sonnet. Norma Lay. GoYe

Tell me I will live another year. Birthday. James Merrill. NAs

Tell me if I am not glad! Lines for an Old Man. Thomas Stearns Eliot. FaBoTw; TW

Tell me, if it followed you,/Would the world be better? The Question. *Anonymous.* WBLP

"Tell me, is there any part of me/That is not lovable?" It Is Night Again. Tzu Yeh. WPOW

Tell me lies about Vietnam. To Whom It May Concern. Adrian Mitchell. OBWP

Tell me, mother, which the best? When Your Cheap Divorce Is Granted. Robert Henry Newell. OBAL

Tell me, my heart, if this be love? Tell Me, My Heart, If This Be Love. George, Lord Lyttelton. HBV 1-2

Tell me, O Lord–tell me, O Lord, how long/Are we to keep Christ writhing on the cross! Calvary. Edwin Arlington Robinson. AnNE; GoTF; MoAmPo; OFD; TreFS; WGRP

Tell me! or don't even grown-ups know? Curiosity. Harry Behn. SoPo

Tell me, phoenix,/is rebirth such a beautiful bird? Epitaph. Wendy Rose. CDW

Tell me, Queen, am I irredeemably spoiled? In the Queen's Bedroom. Norman Cameron. GTBS-P; OxBTC

Tell me sister,/What color is lonely? What Color Is Lonely. Carolyn M. Rodgers. BPo

Tell me, tell me, sir/has the gruesome sight/of a mangled corpse/not begun to sit on your conscience Tell Me News. Sipho Sepamla. WhB

Tell me that you love me,/For that's the sweetest story ever told. The Sweetest Story Ever Told. R. M. Stults. BLSo; FSN; GoTF; TreFS

Tell me that you love me, Katy Cline. Katy Cline. *Anonymous.* FSW

Tell me the riddle and then hang me. Bird Riddle: "As I went out, so I came in." *Anonymous.* GBP

Tell me this riddle while I count eight. Riddle: "Purple, yellow, red, and green." *Anonymous.* OxNR

Tell me what that eruption on the sun/is. Before the War. Marilyn Hacker. AmPA

Tell me why, oh tell me why. Medieval Norman Songs. *Anonymous.* AWP

Tell Michael the truth, if we know what the truth is. Another Given: The Last Day of the Year. William Dickey. AMV-80

Tell my good gal I'm going but I'm/still a-standing pat Pneumonia Blues. Blind Lemon Jefferson. BluL

Tell none of your dream! The Dream-Teller. Padraic Gregory. HBMV; OnYI

Tell of the night that cometh nigh,/The brief day's close. On Recrossing the Rocky Mountains after Many Years. John Charles Fremont. BPAW; PoOW

Tell ole Pharoh,/Let my people go. When Israel Was In Egypt's Land. *Anonymous.* AH

Tell on ages–tell for God. The Present Age. Arthur Cleveland Coxe. BLPA

Tell on shaft and storied brasses/How he took the famed Manassas. How McClellan Took Manassas. *Anonymous.* PAH

Tell Rome!' Forty Days (excerpt). John Brooks Wheelwright. NOCV

Tell that same line to somebody else./Lord lord/lord lord lord. Searching the Desert for the Blues. Blind Willie McTell. BluL

Tell the darkness/Never to flee/When smitten at dawn/By the shafts of the sun. You Tell Me to Sit Quiet. A. C. Jordan. PBA

Tell the Gospel Truth, Rev. It's All the Same. Thadious M. Davis. BlSi

Tell the hour of Andrew's resting. Rest Hour. George Johnston. WHW

Tell the nations that He reigns,/Who alone is Lord and God! Laus Deo. John Greenleaf Whittier. AmP; AnNE; AP; MC; PAH

Tell the refrain, rain rustling lehua. Hilo, Hanakahi, Rain Rustling Lehua. *Anonymous.* WTO

Tell the world that time/will never mark your face. Theme Brown Girl. Elton Hill-Abu Ishak. NBP

Tell them, because our fathers lied. Epitaphs of the War, 1914-18. Rudyard Kipling. BrPo; FaBoEE; OBWP

Tell them, whate'er my morn had been,/My noon was penitent. An Epitaph. Samuel Wesley. NOEC

Tell them ye smile, for your eyes know Tomorrow. Envoy. Francis Thompson. MoBrPo

Tell thou their number, then, in cups/of wine! The Rosy Days Are Numbered. Moses Ibn Ezra. TrJP

Tell um 'bout the world I just come from. Hold the Wind. *Anonymous.* GBP

Tell us a real story. A Real Story. Linda Pastan. Str

Tell us alas, that cannot tell our grief,/Or hope relief. Elegy over a Tomb. Edward, Lord Herbert of Cherbury. AnAnS 2; AtBAP; EIL; OBS

...Tell us of their juju years/so ours will be that much stronger. Now Poem. For Us. Sonia Sanchez. CNA; PoBA

Tell us: Was it you who prayed? Who Prayed? *Anonymous.* STF

Tell where I lie. The Quiet Life. Alexander Pope. ALV; GTBS-P

...Tell you more lies/Than the cross-ties on the railroad and the stars in the sky. I Once Loved a Young Man. *Anonymous.* AmFP

Tell your dad that from me. New Approach Needed. Kingsley Amis. OxBTC; PPON

Tell your masters they were dreamers,/When they thought to cheat the brave. A New Song: "As near beauteous Boston lying." *Anonymous.* PAH

The tellers will be Jews and their speech Hebrew. Dew. Charles Reznikoff. VWA

Tellin' God about my troubles,/And to help me if He please. Slavery Chain Done Broke at Last. *Anonymous.* FSW

Telling of much that once had come to pass/With him, whose mother should have had no sons. Lost Anchors. Edwin Arlington Robinson. CMoP; MAmP

Telling of them is dear. In Praise of Three Young Men. Lochlann Og O Dalaigh. NOBI

Telling the bees. Telling the Bees. Lizette Woodworth Reese. AA

Telling them what are their identities. The Dolls Play at Hansel and Gretel. William Dickey. DFT

Tells all in his lusty crowing! The Vision of Sir Launfal. James Russell Lowell. OHFP; PoLf

Tells also of bright calms that shall succeed. Sonnet: Composed While the Author Was Engaged in Writing a Tract... William Wordsworth. ChRP

Tells how death can only be/A lovely thing we do not see. From the Parthenon I Learn. Willard Wattles. HBMV

...Tells me/Exactly where I can go, steering me, cutting me out of the herd. Being Herded Past the Prison's Honor Farm. David Wagoner. SoSe

Tells them this way is safety–this way home. A Desolate Shore. William Ernest Henley. SyP

Tells us that you are not buggered; what's then left for you but/sucking? To Phoebus. Martial (Marcus Valerius Martialis). PeHV

Telyouris and Sowtaris, blist ye. The Amendis to the Telyouris and Sowtaris... William Dunbar. OBSV

Temper a graver with a lighter song. Proem to Hellenics. Walter Savage Landor. ViBoPo

The temperate zones are yet more fully manned. N. B., Symmetrians. Gene Derwood. LiTA; NePA

The tempest smote them, and clouds drearily/Closed o'er the fleet upon the starless sea. Leaving Troy. Thomas Caulfield Irwin. IrPN

...The Tempest springs/In joy away on softly wafting wings. The Easter Song. Caelius Sedulius. OnYI

A temple of coloured sorrows and perfumed/sins! Orchids. Theodore Wratislaw. VLP

The temple of our purest thoughts–Is silence. Silence. Edgar Lee Masters. PoToHe

A temple the Father will own/In the city of light above? Building for Eternity. N.B. Sargent. BLPA

Temples, obelisks, the statued ages/were equaled in that democratic rock. Rushmore. Harold Witt. TAT

Ten bloody arrows in his straining fist! Goddwyn: Ode to Liberty. Thomas Chatterton. TrGrPo

Ten bright spikes nailed to the door! Man Is in Pain. Philip Lamantia. NeAP

Ten frozen parsnips hanging in the weather. Winter Remembered. John Crowe Ransom. AP; HAP; MoAB; NOBA; OxBA; PrIm; UnPo; VGW

Ten heads as well as two gryphons/drop their blessings on all who pass. 527 Cathedral Parkway. Rika Lesser. NYP

–Ten minutes before the invention of money... Letter to an Imaginary Friend. Thomas McGrath. NNaP

Ten mothers would weep at the sight/of those dancers hand in hand. Ballad of the Ten Casino Dancers. Cecilia Meireles. BoWoP

Ten others, "Jesus, I wish I had a job." Muckers. Carl Sandburg. CTBA; SaC

Ten thousand beautiful sensual/Ways we will make love. A Farewell to a Southern Melody. Huang O. BoWoP

Ten thousand got drowned that never were born. Nottamun Town. Anonymous. FaBoNo; NCEP; OxBoLi

Ten thousand suns explode. The Day after Trinity. Richard Oyama. BrSi

Ten thousand times over your Sally you'll see. A Rich Irish Lady (Sally). Anonymous. AmFP

Ten thousand Watchmen waited on this Mouse,/With Bills,and Halberds,to her Country-House. The Town Mouse and the Country Mouse (parody). Matthew Prior. BXAP

Ten thousand years. Above Pate Valley. Gary Snyder. CoAP; ConAP; LCAP; NaP; NoP

Ten thousand years ago! The Fossil Raindrops. Harriet Prescott Spofford. OBCA

Ten thousand years of knowledge were in her eyes/As first he cut her throat and then his own. Faustus. A. D. Hope. NOAV

Ten thousand yesterdays are gathered here. In an Old Library. Yuan Mei. LiTW

Ten tons of rice-balls tumbling/Into a pleased ringside geisha's lap. Sumo Wrestlers. James Kirkup. OBTV

Ten we spend fasting in sackcloth/and ashes. Simchas Torah. Morris Rosenfeld. TrJP

Tenants of a vision we rent out endlessly. Essay. Bernadette Mayer. APU

Tender, and averse to killing. To Miss Margaret Pulteney, Daughter of Daniel Pulteney, Esq. Ambrose Philips. CEP

Tender, blinks, and opens/face up to the skies. Love Should Grow Up Like a Wild Iris in the Fields. Susan Griffin. NPGG

The tender cluck of the hen pheasant urging them on. Random Reflections on a Summer Evening. John Hall Wheelock. NYBP

Tenderness is in the hands. Because One Is Always Forgotten. Carolyn Forche. MAYP

Tenderness only confuses/The children who wait in the dusk. There Are Children in the Dusk. Bertram Warr. PeCV

Tending sick and nervous old & cranky ship. The Sappa Creek. Gary Snyder. NCSH

Tengo que buscar/una linda mujer. The Way I Was... Carol Lee Sanchez. TWSS

The Tent is listening,/But the Troops are gone! Expanse Cannot Be Lost. Emily Dickinson. MAmP

The tenth visitor/Is not usually named. Ten Types of Hospital Visitor. Charles Causley. OxBC

Tenting on the old camp ground. Tenting on the Old Camp Ground. Walter Kittredge. FSW; PSoN

Terminat hora diem; terminat auctor opus. Doctor Faustus. Christopher Marlowe. BoLiVe; TrGrPo

...The termometers burning/in the mouths of the gone. This Is a Poem for the Fathers and for Michael Ryan. Thomas Lux. AmPA

The terribe Cape of Good Hope. The Day the Tide. Philip Booth. CoAP

Terribilis mors conturbat me. Fearful Death. Anonymous. MeEL

A terrible beauty is born. Easter, 1916. William Butler Yeats. BrPo; CABA; CMoP; CoBMV; DiPo; FaBoMo; FaBoPV; FaPoR; HAP; InPS; LiTM; MBW 1-2; MoAB; NAWM 1-2; NIP; NoAm; NOBE; NOBI; NoP; OAEL 1-2; OBWP; OxBI; OxBTC; PAI; PPoe; PPP; SeCeV

Terrible burghers in terrible lodgings. Lodgers. Julian Tuwim. VWA

Terrible children, comrades, enemies. Paper Anarchist Addresses the Shade of Nancy Ling Perry. George Woodcock. NOBC

The terrible robber men. The Terrible Robber Men. Padraic Colum. HBMV; LOW

Terribly like a swoop of water. The Sea and the Eagle. Sydney Clouts. PeSA

The terror and the splendor of the/Atomic Age. Trail Breakers. James Daugherty. AmFN

Terror does not belong to open day Counterpoint. Owen Dodson. PoNe

Terror for fat burghers in far plains below. Rocky Acres. Robert Graves. LiTB; NoAm; UnPo

Terror, like armaggeddon,/in the sky Nuclear Racial Lockdowns. Pancho Aguila. LFAC

The terror of his beak, and lightnings of his eye. The Progress of Poesy. Thomas Gray. ATP

Terror of his terror, nightmare of his nightmare. The Diver. Nikos Phocas. AMV-81

Terror reigns like a new crowned king. Enchantment. Lewis Alexander. PoBA

Testicles, testicles, said Daddy. A Man gets tired of testicles. The Snack (parody). L. L. Zeiger. BXAP

Testing her own lips then,/the coolness, till/she could taste the salt. His Wife. Shirley Kaufman. LCAP

...Testing/their diagonals, in common clothes. The Hands. Denise Levertov. NeAP; PoM

An' tether 'im out on the Bloomin'dale route/Like a loonytick goat! Whurroo!' Officer Brady. Robert William Chambers. InMe

A tether that held me to the hare/Here, there and everywhere. Beagles. W. R. Rodgers. FaBoTw; GDP; OnYI; SD

Tethering us all to our star. Unrelenting Flood. William Matthews. GeTw

Texas grew from hide and horn. Cattle. Berta Hart Nance. BPAW

Texas has passed the pistol stage,/The law has come to stay. Texas Types– "The Bad Man." William Lawrence Chittenden. PoOW

Th'Assembly having sat Four Years,/Has now brought forth a Whelp. The Four-Legg'd Elder. Sir John Birkenhead. CoMu

Th'effect and cause, the punishment and sinne. Holy Sonnets, III. John Donne. MasP; OBS

Th' in-dwelling God, proclaimed of old. God of the Earth, the Sky, the Sea. Samuel Longfellow. TRV

Th ride theyr taking/us all on Th Wundrfulness uv th Mountees Our Secret Police. Bill Bissett. NOBC

Th' Usurper Death will make thee lay it down. The Defiance. Thomas Flatman. OBS

Thaelmann Battalion. Ready, forward march. Freedom. Ernst. Karl Daniel. Peter FSW

Than a pound of Cheddar? The Grocer and the Gold-Fish. Wilfrid Thorley. BrR

Than a tall stone temple that may stand too long. Little Things. Orrick Johns. AnAmPo; PG

Than Adam was not adamant! A Reflection. Thomas Hood. FaBoEE; NBM; PV

Than all it holds more deep, more high.' Woodnotes. Ralph Waldo Emerson. NOBA; WGRP

Than all the burning words in lovers' songs! A Gazelle. Richard Henry Stoddard. AA

Than all the gold that leaden minds can frame. To the Lady Margaret, Countess of Cumberland. Samuel Daniel. FaBoEn; LoBV; OBSC

Than all the Muses with their pens can do. To the Prince. Sir John Davies. SiPS

Than all the sky which only/is higher than the sky. Love Is More Thicker Than Forget. Edward Estlin Cummings. AnFE

Than Angelos's hand could ever carve in stone. Soliloquy II. Richard Aldington. MMM

"Than any freedom in this world could be." Just To Be Needed. Mary Eversley. PoToHe

Than any pebble on the shore,/Or this indifferent moment as it dies. At Dieppe: Green and Grey. Arthur Symons. BrPo; FaBoPP; NOBV; OBNC; SyP

Than aught except its living years. Elegy on Thyrza. George Gordon, Lord Byron. GTBS; GTBS-P

Than be a man who walks with men,/But has a frozen heart! The Snow-Man. Marian Douglas. OBCA

Than be in a false woman's company. Early, Early in the Spring. Anonymous. OBET

Than be in love with you.   Song: "Dew on the bamboos."   *Anonymous.*
LLLT

Than be spitted by the many pins that bristle from your hat.   Cupid's Darts.
Sir Alan Patrick Herbert.   CenHV

Than be the ship that never sailed.   The Ship That Sails.   *Anonymous.*
PoToHe

Than boughs that comb swift heavens and shake/Rain upon rainy lakes.
Black Poplar-Boughs.   John Freeman.   HBMV

Than break one hair to gain her liberty.   So Fast Entangled.   *Anonymous.*
EG; TrGrPo

Than could a saint with fifty lives.   On the Death of a Journalist.   Roy
Campbell.   CoBE

Than count that day as worse than lost.   At Set of Sun.   George Eliot.
PoPl; PoToHe; TRV

Than crouch in a hypocrite's cloak.   Quatrain: "Better to live as a rogue and
a bum."   Mahsati.   WPOW

Than do high deeds in Hungary/To pass all men's believing.   An Immorality.
Ezra Pound.   CMoP; ForPo; GoJo; GrPl; HBV 1-2; LiTL; LiTM; MoAB;
MoAmPo; NePA; NOBA; OBAL; OLR; PoPl

Than dream more meagre and awful,/Reality.   Drugged.   Walter De la
Mare.   BrPo

Than dreaming of the things he'd do/If still he were a boy.   The Dreamer.
Thomas Nunan.   WBLP

Than ever got in through your guts.'   Limerick: "There was a young fellow
named Nutz.   *Anonymous.*   PeHV

Than ever I for him.   My Name and I.   Robert Graves.   NoAm; NYBP

Than fighting for something you know nothing of.   To Nearly Everybody in
Europe To-Day.   Hugh" (Christopher Murray Grieve) MacDiarmid.   DBV

Than go ambling with the ague.   Lines to Our Elders.   Countee Cullen.
CDC

Than go to church with oily Sue and afterwards to bed.   Correspondence
between Mr. Harrison in Newcastle and ...   Stevie Smith.   FaBoNo; NLV;
OxBC

Than granite remembered of man.   Lament of Granite.   David Ross.   PG

Than him that said, "Rejoice! rejoice!"   The Two Voices.   Alfred, Lord
Tennyson.   MasP

Than his Casella, whom he woo'd to sing/Met in the milder shades of
Purgatory.   Sonnet XIII: "Harry whose tuneful and well measur'd Song."
John Milton.   OBS

Than his charge on Stony Point in the heart of the murky/night.   Wayne at
Stony Point.   Clinton Scollard.   MC; PAH

Than his pale cheek should assign/A perpetual blush to thine.   Good Counsel
to a Young Maid.   Thomas Carew.   AnAnS 2; CaPo; CavP; CBEP; ErPo;
OBS

Than home or palace gardens/If she is there.   Revolution.   Lesbia Harford.
PoAu 1-2

Than I should keep a-livin' on an' seein' things at night!   Seein' Things.
Eugene Field.   HBV 1-2; HBVY; TreF

Than, in our veins, its keenest rage achieved.   The Magnolia Tree.   Hubert
Witheford.   AnNZ

Than light that left Andromeda/Nine hundred thousand years ago.   Parallax.
Maxwell Anderson.   NYBP

Than live a slave without a blow/For the Green!   After Aughrim.   Arthur
Gerald Geoghegan.   OnYI

Than live in pleasure far away.   Farewell to Cuba.   Maria Gowen Brooks.
AA

Than loafin' around The Throne.   Old Grimes.   Albert Gorton Greene.
BeLS

"Than may be proved here, anon,/That we three be agrede in on."   I Love a
Flower.   Thomas Philipps.   MeEL

Than mute bare splendors of the sun and moon.   Sur Ma Guzzla Gracile.
Wallace Stevens.   PoA

Than none at all. Provide, provide!   Provide, Provide.   Robert Frost.
AmP; AmPP

Than not have been at Monterey?   Monterey.   Charles Fenno Hoffman
AA; FaBoBe; HBV 1-2; MC; PAH

Than one whose truths all/always meet the eye.   Diehard.   Judith Moffett.
PoA

Than public faces in private places.   Epigram: "Private faces in public
places."   W. H. Auden.   FaBoEE; PV

Than put in a woman your trust and confidence.   Whan netilles in wynter
bere rosis rede.   *Anonymous.*   EnPo

Than read to you, and cannot keep you waking.   One Desiring Me to Read,
but Slept It out, Wakening.   George Daniel.   OBSP

Than rebels are without their head the King.   Strange Monsters.   Rowland
Watkyns.   FaBoEE

Than rise in the morning early.   Cold Blows the Wind.   John Hamilton.
CH

Than shit as they do, foully, and moistly give vent to their/asses   Hygiene
Sonnet.   Dick Gallup.   ANYP

Than stand in cool shadows by him forgot!   The Blazing Heart.   Alice
Williams Brotherton.   AA

Than still pursue a star as its light dims.   Ten Sonnets for Today.   Phil
Stanway.   AMV-80

Than streams of water in a desert place!   Praise.   R. H. Grenville.   PoToHe

Than teach ten thousand stars how not to dance   You Shall Above All
Things Be Glad and Young.   Edward Estlin Cummings.   NePA; NoAm;
NOBA; OxBA

Than that colder, lowly light.   Evening Star.   Edgar Allan Poe.   AmP; AP

Than that of growing grass/Or lambs or infant joys!   On Hearing a Broadcast
of Ceremonies in Connection with....   Denis Wrafter.   NeIP

Than that some object, passion, throb, or ache,/Has kept some solitary heart
awake.   Sonnet in the Mail Coach.   Henry Taylor.   TEP

Than that the largest heart is soonest broken.   No Truer Word.   Walter
Savage Landor.   GoTF; TreF

Than that the world should stay a stuffy room!   Prayer for Dreadful Morning.
E. Merrill Root.   TrPWD

Than that, which one day, Worms, may chance refuse.   Sonnets from
Walton's Life of Herbert, 1670.   George Herbert.   AnAnS 1

Than that which you/can do!   I, Maximus of Gloucester, to You.   Charles
Olson.   CAPP; LiTM; NeAP; NoAm; PoM

Than the bishop, hight Don Tello, has been hurt by hand of/mine.   San
Miguel De La Tumba.   Gonzalo de Berceo.   CAW

Than the extasy of falling like a fan/beyond our war.   Soldier's Dove.
James Forsyth.   WaP

Than the girl I raped.   Pacific Epitaphs.   Dudley Randall.   NoAm

Than the one world-embraceing look we shared.   Conversation in Black and
White.   May Sarton.   GoYe

Than the rocks in the bottom of the sea.   John Hardy (A vers.).
Anonymous.   BaBo

Than the two hearts beating each to each!   Meeting at Night.   Robert
Browning.   AWP; BoLiVe; BoLoP; CBEP; DiPo; ELP; FaBV; FF; FiP;
GBL; GTBS; HBV 1-2; HeIP; InPo; InPS; InvP; LiTL; MaVP; MBW 1-2;
MCCG; MOS; NOBE; NOBV; OAEP; OBEV; OBNC; OBSP; OLR; PAI;
PoPl; PoRA; SCV; SeCePo; SoSe; TreFT; TrGrPo; UnPo; ViBoPo; VLP;
WeW

Than thee, thy chosen Queen shall never find/A truer subject nor a firmer
friend.   To W.L.G. on Reading His Chosen Queen.   Charlotte Forten.
BlSi

Than this fair Park from what it was before.   On St. James's Park, as Lately
Improved by His Majesty.   Edmund Waller.   AnAnS 2

Than this vague peace, akin to nothingness.   Calm After Storm.   Frank
Yerby.   AmNP

Than those that to the earth with many/tears they give.   The Dead.   Jones
Very   AA; AnNE; AP; HAP; MAmP; NOBA; OxBA; TAP

Than to a tryst with a foolish woman.   Church Bell in the Night.
Anonymous.   AnIL

Than to drive saw-longs on the Plover,/And you'll never get your pay.
Driving Saw-Logs on the Plover (with music).   *Anonymous.*   AS

Than to fight the bloody In-ji-ans.   The Bloody Injians.   *Anonymous.*   CoSo

Than to give it in a moment, gloriously.   To Give One's Life.   Mary
Carolyn Davies.   PoToHe

Than to know I have to spend my days/With you all the time.   Trifling
Women.   *Anonymous.*   AmFP

Than under the whole damn range (he finds) of the/Big Horns   Oil Painting
of the Artist As the Artist.   Archibald MacLeish.   NAMP

Than waking with a stranger.   Daughter.   Kimiko Hahn.   BrSi

Than wearing horns hath caused an aching head.   Good Susan, Be as Secret
as You Can.   *Anonymous.*   ErPo

Than wed what I lov'd not, or turn one thought from thee.   Thro' Grief and
Thro' Danger.   Thomas Moore.   AnIV

Than when beside your brooks at noon I watch'd the/sallows gleaming!
Retrospect.   Agnes Mary Frances (Mme Emile Duclaux) Robinson.
OBVV

Than when I was a boy.   If I Had But Two Little Wings.   Thomas Hood.
CH

Than when they broke into a church to try and steal a rope.   How Paddy
Stole the Rope.   *Anonymous.*   BLPA

...Than when thou givest birth to thy love.   The Songs of Bilitis.   Pierre
Louys.   UnTE

Than where I loathed so much.   Discontents in Devon.   Robert Herrick.
AnAnS 2; CaPo; OAEP; OBSP; PoL; SeCV 1-2

Than with these horrid moods be left i' the lurch.   Epistle to John Hamilton
Reynolds.   John Keats.   OBNC

Than woo my body while my soul/Tips through the stars alone.   Star
Journey.   Naomi Long Madgett.   BPo

Than write such hopeless rubbish as thy worst.   A Sonnet: "Two voices are
there."   James Kenneth Stephen.   DBV; FaBoCo; FaBoPa; NOBL; SpRo

Than you who have eyes.   The Hands.   Daniel David Moses.   AMV-80

Than young Hope in his sunniest hour hath known.   Dreams.   Edgar Allan
Poe.   AmPP; OxBA; TAP

Thanan o'n dhoul, do ye think I'm dead?'   Finnegan's Wake.   *Anonymous.*
NLV

Thane shall erthe of erthe have a foulle stinke./Mors solvit omnia.   Earth out of Earth.   *Anomymous*   CBEP; MeEL

Thank God and dance merrily!   Chanuke, O Chanuke.   *Anonymous*.   FSW

Thank God, and there's an end of that.   A Portrait.   Robert Louis Stevenson.   SeCePo

Thank God for a feeble light, for our phantom youth,/for need and tenderness.   Thailand Railway.   Randolph Stow.   CBAP

Thank God for every sunrise/In the circuit of the year.   Sunrise.   Margaret E. Sangster.   TRV

Thank God for peace! Thank God for peace, when/the great gray ships come in!   When the Great Gray Ships Come in.   Guy Wetmore Carryl.   AA; EtS; FaBoBe; HBV 1-2; MC; PAH

Thank God for the splendor of work!   Work: A Song of Triumph.   Angela Morgan.   PoLf

Thank God for you!   Song: "Let my voice ring out and over the earth."   James (1834-82) Thomson.   GoTF; HBV 1-2; OBVV

Thank God from whom all blessings flow!   King William's Dispatch to Queen Augusta...   Coventry Patmore.   FaBoEE

Thank God! Here comes a man.   The Sheep-Herder.   Charles Badger Clark, Jr.   BPAW

Thank God, I am not as these rigid fools,/Even as this Pharisee.   The Newer Vainglory.   Alice Meynell.   MoRP

Thank God, I'll always find,/Dat a little talk wid Jesus, makes it right.   A Little Talk wid Jesus Makes It Right.   *Anonymous*.   BoAN 1-2

Thank God I'm not/That poor old man.   The Poor Old Man (parody).   J. C. Squire.   HBMV

Thank God, thank God, for Christ was born/Ages ago, as on this morn.   A Christmas Carol.   Christina Georgina Rossetti.   PCh

Thank God,–thank God for rain!   Reprieve.   Barbara Villy Cormack.   CaP

...Thank God,/the bar should be open when we land.   The Usual Exquisite Boredom of Patrols.   Hugh Popham.   OxBTC

Thank God the silly bastard is extinct.   The Critic on the Hearth.   L. E. Sissman.   TW

Thank God the Stars and Stripes still wave above Virginia's soil.   Virginia's Bloody Soil.   *Anonymous*.   AmFP

Thank goodness, old October's here!   Old October.   Thomas Constable.   HBV 1-2

...Thank goodness/they're both of them over!   The Chancellor's Nightmare.   Sir William Schwenck Gilbert.   FaBoNo

Thank Lufe that list you to his merci call!   Spring Song of the Birds.   King of Scotland James I   OBEV

Thank my God I will,/Sure aid, present comfort.   Psalm XLIII.   Sir Philip Sidney.   FCP

Thank with their Tongues, but curse you with their Heart.   The Art of Love. (Publius Ovidius Naso) Ovid.   ErPo

Thank-worthiest yet when you shall break my heart.   Astrophel and Stella, XCV.   Sir Philip Sidney.   AAS; SiPS

"Thank you."   The Piano Tuner.   W. Atmar Smith, II.   AMV-80

...Thank you all for the best performance by a male   Up.   Bill Kushner.   APU

...Thank you, anyway,/colorful individuals.   Ode to Bohemians.   Ron Padgett.   APU

Thank you, Aunt Libby,/from a failed beach girl,/out of the West.   Ode to a Lebanese Crock of Olives.   Diane Wakoski.   GP

Thank you. Even though the nights are never danger-/ous, I have one of everything.   A Practical Program for Monks.   Thomas Merton.   CoPo

Thank you for my tea.   Visitor.   *Anonymous*.   OxNR

Thank you for this happy day,/This happy day!   This Happy Day.   Harry Behn.   TiPo

"Thank you for your milk,/Mrs. Good Moolly Cow."   The Good Moolly Cow.   Eliza Lee Follen.   OBCA

Thank you, God, for all it brings.   Thank You, God.   Nina Stiles.   PoToHe

Thank you, Grandam.   Little Girl.   *Anonymous*.   OxNR

"Thank you, I prefer the bottle."   Said Aristotle Unto Plato.   Owen Wister.   PoPl

Thank you, my friend./thank you.   Paperweight Escape.   Stephen Todd Booker.   LFAC

Thank you, Prescott.   Ascot Waistcoat.   David McCord.   FiBHP; NLV

...Thank you sincerely/For giving me my madness back, or nearly.   Come Dance with Kitty Stobling.   Patrick Kavanagh.   FaBoIP; NoAm

Thank you very much.   Liberace.   Jonathan Holden.   MAYP

Thank you. You are too.   My Erotic Double.   John Ashbery.   LCAP

Thanked it, and let it go.   A Fairy Went A-Marketing.   Rose Fyleman.   OxBChV; SoPo; SUS

Thanked me for water thru a straw/During the long hot prison summer.   Grey Him.   Paul Mariah.   LFAC

Thankful to work for all the seven,/Trusting the rest to One in heaven!   Which Shall It Be?   Ethel Lynn Beers.   BLPA; TreF

Thankful to you, or friends, for me.   To the Yew and Cypress to Grace His Funeral.   Robert Herrick.   QFR

Thankfully I consent/To my estrangement/From me in you.   To Whom Else?   Robert Graves.   FaBoMo

Thanks a heap for the rocks.   Only a Little Litter.   Myra Cohn Livingston.   QQQ

"Thanks be unto God for His unspeakable gift!"   Suppose That Christ Had Not Been Born.   Martha Snell Nicholson.   BePJ

...Thanks/for the gift of corn.   "Among the Savages..."   Ralph Salisbury.   STE

Thanks his animals, ev'ry one,/For the work that has been done.   The Barnyard.   Maud Burnham.   TiPo

Thanks–joyful thanks!–a soldier's, traveler's thanks.   Thanks in Old Age.   Walt Whitman.   MCCG

Thanks/rubin/for givin' us/fun   Rubin.   Charles Cooper.   PoBA

"Thanks.–So fine a time! Good night."   A Parting Guest.   James Whitcomb Riley.   HBV 1-2; TreFT

"Thanks, teacher dear," the scholars cried, and awe crept/darkly o'er 'em.   The Original Lamb.   *Anonymous*.   InMe

Thanks through all eternity.   Thanks to God.   J. A. Hultman.   STF

Thanks to the generous vine/Invites fresh grapes to fill his press with wine.   An Ode to Master Endymion Porter, upon His Brother's Death.   Robert Herrick.   CaPo

"Thanks to the gracious God of heaven,/Quhilk send this summer day."   Of the Day Estivall.   Alexander Hume.   BSV; FaBoPP; NOCV; OxBS

Thanks you as much as if he did.   The King's Answer.   John Wilmot, Earl of Rochester.   FaBoCo

Thanksgivings for the golden hours,/The early and the latter rain!   Harvest Hymn.   John Greenleaf Whittier.   OHIP

Thannhauser said, "Oh, is that so!'/And died. I think it's some fool show.   Tannhauser.   Newman Levy.   OBAL

Thar was more in the man than thar was in the land.   Thar's More in the Man Than Thar Is in the Land.   Sidney Lanier.   AP; NOBA

Tharfor is neidfull that yhe be/Worthy and wicht, but abaysyng.   The Bruce.   John Barbour.   OxBS

That a certain FIRE made him a danged millionaire!   The Little Johnny Mine.   Daisy L. Detrick.   PoOW

That a dead man lay on the road.   The Stab.   William Wallace Harney.   AA

That a friend is near and feels.   A Friend.   Sir Thomas Noon Talfourd.   PoToHe

That a little dab/of color, aptly mixed,/makes all the difference.   A Dab of Color.   Theodore Weiss.   VGW

That a man was the cause of it all.   She Is More to be Pitied than Censured.   William B. Gray.   BeLS; BLPA; FSN; GoTF; TreF

That a man who has many children/Shall never die without a trace.   Death Killed the Rich.   *Anonymous*.   WTO

That a negro boy would tell the golden Whites/of the coming of the reign of the ears of corn.   Ode to Walt Whitman.   Federico Garcia Lorca.   PeHV

That a rat is not an elephant.   The Rat and the Elephant.   Jean de La Fontaine.   OBVE

That a songster may be fed.   To the Swallow.   *Anonymous*.   OBVE

That a word you don't sound could send awry.   3rd Migration, Third Series.   Brian Henderson.   CaPN

That act of mine the ultimate stars/Shall look on sprang in primal ooze.   Life's Testament.   William Baylebridge.   BoAV; PoAu 1-2

That Actia, Arlotte, and Mandane dreamed?   Sonnets.   Frederick Goddard Tuckerman.   AP

That Adam was not Adam-ant!   When Eve upon the First of Men.   Thomas Moore.   HBV 1-2

That adds to English statesmen Pitt, to/English arms Duquesne!   Fort Duquesne.   Florus B. Plimpton.   PAH

That, after all, concerns no one.   All for Love.   *Anonymous*.   UnTE

That after deth ful often have I gapid.   The Regimen of Princes (excerpt).   Thomas Hoccleve.   PoEL 1-5

That after my great sleep I may/Awake to thy eternal day! Amen.   A Child's Evening Prayer.   Samuel Taylor Coleridge.   OxBChV; TrPWD

That after your life, fraile and transitory,/You may than live in joye perdurably.   The Pastime of Pleasure.   Stephen Hawes.   PoEL 1-5

That age, ache, penury, and impisonment/Can lay on nature is a paradise/To what we fear of death.   Measure for Measure.   William Shakespeare.   FaBoRV; FiP; TreFT

That agony is our triumph.   Last Speech to the Court.   Bartolomeo Vanzetti.   NAMP

That aims me/where I will go/and will arrive,/my dears.   And Yet.   (or Molodovski) Kadya, (or Kadia) Molodovsky.   VWA

That all beyond is not Oblivion.   The Undiscovered Country.   Thomas Bailey Aldrich.   AA

That all but VIRTUE's solid joys,/Are vanity and woe.   Ode to Wisdom.   Elizabeth Carter.   OBEC

...That all death and all/life may seem to you strange and/new.   Moments.   Marcel Schwob.   TrJP

That all fruit that follows/Belongs to the new year/To come.   The New Year for Trees.   Howard Schwartz.   VWA

That all hir first laubour was in vane...   The Aeneid.   Virgil (Publius Vergilius Maro).   OBVE

That all is love which brings my Lord to me. Revelation. Warren F. Cook. BLRP

That all it moves, or is inclin'd,/Comes from the motions of your mind. The First Meeting. Edward, Lord Herbert of Cherbury. AnAnS 2

That all its folded hands may stretch with love. To the Spring Sun. Freda Laughton. NeIP

That all may form a wreath of beauty, meet/To deck my Heliodora's tresses sweet. I'll Twine White Violets. Meleager. NIP

...That all my days/with that persistent search were full. Wilderness Theme. Ian Mudie. PoAu 1-2

That all my life must change and fall away. Time Will Not Grant. Sidney Keyes. SeCePo

That all my Powers, with all their might,/In Thy sole Glory may unite. A Morning Hymn. Thomas Ken. OBS

That all my trust and travaill is but wast. Rime LVII: "Ever myn happe is slack and slo in commyng." Petrarch (Francesco Petrarca). OBVE

That all night had been strengthened by/Heaven's purer flood. Songs of Joy. William Henry Davies. MoBrPo; OBVV

That all that see this wonder maye expresse/Upon this grounde how well growes barrennes. On the Reed of Our Lord's Passion. William Alabaster. PoEL 1-5

That all the flowering was meant for them. Bermuda Suite. Winfield Townley Scott. MiAP

That all the glories formerly I knew/Shone from the cloudy splendour of your name. The Claim That Has the Canker on the Rose. Joseph Mary Plunkett. OxBI

That all the jealous little birds/Went off from me completely. Before I Stumbled. Francis Carlin. HBMV

That all the spices of the East/Are circumfused there. Of Her Breath. Robert Herrick. EG

That all the world/May enter in. Mary's Song. Charles Causley. OBCP

That all the world may see how false of love/False Paris hath to his Oenone been. Oenone's Complaint. George Peele. EIL; OBSC

That all these dyings may be life in death. Mortification. George Herbert. AnAnS 1; MePo; OAEP; SeCP; ViBoPo

That all things may be resolved correct and dead . Hot Afternoons Have Been in West 15th Street. Paul Blackburn. VGW

–That all we love is born again. Christmas in Freelands. James Stephens. TrCP

That all your labours will be vain. Hence, Away, You Sirens! George Wither. EIL

That already you will have understood these Ithacas,/and what they mean. Ithaca. Constantine P. Cavafy. LiTW

That always was from out of heaven's wall. The Spirit Craft. Charles G. Ballard. VoR

That America may always boast/That we are brave Virginians. The Battle of Baltimore. Anonymous. PAH

That amiable Man of Dumbree. Limerick: "There was an Old Man of Dumbree." Edward Lear. NBM; OxBChV

That 'amper an' 'inder an' scold men/For fear o' Stellenbosch! Stellenbosch. Rudyard Kipling. OBTV

That an Arthur shulde yete com Anglen to fulste. The Brut. Layamon. OxBM

That an empty, cruel burst of wind rubs out. Winter Moon. Maria Spaziani. PBWP

...That an' mai's the dirdit/Word–Sumburgh, Sumburgh Heid. Sumburgh Heid. George Bruce. OxBS

That and the Child's unheeded dream/Is all the light of all their day. The Angel in the House. Coventry Patmore. EG; GTBS-P; LO

That angry mood engendered rooted hate,/War to the knife, and an untimely fate. Epistles. Horace. OBVE

That April's due to saunter by. Spring Cricket. Frances Rodman. SiSoSe

That aquatic old person of Grange. Limerick: "There was an old person of Grange." Edward Lear. FaBoNo

That are echoing from star to star. Gitanjali. Rabindranath Tagore. ILwL

That are now seen sitting on any Cliff like the/Title above a Poem. You. John Tagliabue. GP

That are trodden upon are your own or your foes'. A Fable for Critics. James Russell Lowell. AnNE; NOBA

That are under the mound/In Prairie-Dog Town. Prairie-Dog Town. Mary Austin. BPAW; TiPo

That assume a willing suspension of despair. Hollandaise. Sharon Bryan. MAYP

That at any moment I could put my head in her lap and weep. Making Contact. John Streeter Manifold. CBAP

That at least once a week you dine with the Squire. Bishop Blomfield's First Charge to His Clergy. Sydney Goodsir Smith. FaBoEE

That at our given work we do our best. The Common Tasks. Grace Noll Crowell. PoToHe

That, at this moment, the violins would emerge/in a struggle with the loud, combatant horns... The Composer's Winter Dream. Norman Dubie. LCAP

That at threescore and ten I'll from the picture/Be even more distant than I was at six. Old Man. James Henry. NOBV

That awful stranger Consciousness/Deliberately face– I never hear that one is dead. Emily Dickinson. MoVE

That balked our eager rushers beneath their very goal. Under the Goal Posts. Arthur Guiterman. BBV

That battle-fit we lived, and though defeated,/Not without glory fought. Lessons of the War. Henry Reed. OBWP

That beams which pass/Through black cannot but be divine. To Her Eyes. Edward, Lord Herbert of Cherbury. JCP; OBS

That beautiful, beautiful, beautiful God/Was breathing His love by a cut-away bog. The One. Patrick Kavanagh. MoBrPo

That beauty does not count. The Isles of Greece. Demetrios Capetanakis. GTBS-P

That bellies and drags in the wind/Into its narrow shed. The Balloon of the Mind. William Butler Yeats. PoL

That beyond all expressing,/her joys did abound. The Wandering Maiden; or, True Love at Length United. Anonymous. CoMu

That beyond the Chagres River/All paths lead straight to hell! Beyond the Chagres. James Stanley Gilbert. PoLf

That bids me go. The Day Will Soon Be Gone. Fujiwara-No- Michinobu. AWP

That bird wasn't black, he was yellow! Limerick: "There once was a guy named Othello." Edwin Meade Robinson. HBMV

That black forest and the fire in earnest. Gretel in Darkness. Louise Gluck. AmPA; DFT; GP

That black man is me. To Strike for Night. Lebert Bethune. NBP

That blame is just as dear as praise/And praise as mere as blame. Dear March, come in! Emily Dickinson. YeAr

That blends the scope/of lion, horse,/and antelope. Motorcycle. Benjamin Sturgis Pray. GoYe

That blessed gods in servile masks/Plied for thee thy household tasks. Saadi. Ralph Waldo Emerson. AmP; OxBA

That blind and deafen you to compromise. Directions to a Rebel. W. R. Rodgers. LiTM

That blood-red wakening. Ripening. Noelle Caskey. DFT

That bloody stain/Shall not be seen upon thy hand again. Thy Brother's Blood. Jones Very. AP; MAmP; NOBA; PoEL 1-5; QFR; TAP

That blossomed at last, red geranium, and mignonette. Red Geranium and Godly Mignonette. D. H. Lawrence. GTBS-P

That blue September day. Biftek aux Champignons. Henry Augustin Beers. AA; AmLP; HBV 1-2

That board–you'd rave and rend them with your teeth. A Question. John Millington Synge. MoBrPo; NOBI; OBVV

That boatman am I. In the Past. Trumbull Stickney. NOBA; OxBA

That body, soul, and spirit be/Forever living unto thee! The God of the Living. John Lodge Ellerton. WGRP

That both the Vicar and the Squire/Were still unrescued from the fire. The Nimble Stag. E.G.V. Knox. HBMV

That bows and disappears. "Whole gulfs of red and fleets of red". Emily Dickinson. AmLP

That boys shall kiss their share. Holly and Mistletoe. Eleanor Farjeon. PCh

That brains are sometimes northward found/as well's in C. S. A. The C. S. A. Commissioners. Anonymous. PAH

That brave man. The Brave Man. Wallace Stevens. SOTW

That, braving the rain of bullets,/Comforts the fresh bones. The Spring Waters. Ping Hsin (Hsieh Wang-ying). PBWP

That breaks,but calls a million birds to/flight. Mystic River. John Ciardi. AmP; NYBP

That breath is what I give them when I send my love. Breath. Mark Strand. HaCAP

That breathed the living breath of spring. The Resurrection. Jonathan Henderson Brooks. AmNP; CDC; PoNe

That breathes on earth the air of paradise. Love's Justification. Buonarroti Michelangelo. AWP

That broke up our Society upon the Stanislow. The Society upon the Stanislow. Bret (Francis Bret Harte) Harte. AA; BeLS; BPAW; HBV 1-2; InMe; MaC; OBAL

That, brought from cold, it never will desire/To rest with me, which am more hot than fire. Come, Gentle Death! Thomas Watson. EIL

That buds, and spreads, and withers in an hour. Love Is a Law. Anonymous. EIL; GBL

That burn from year to year with unextinguished/light. To Mary. Percy Bysshe Shelley. EnRP

That burn unnoticed, quietly. The Little Things. Elizabeth Isler. PoToHe

That burnt the temple where she was ador'd. A Cruell Mistris. Thomas Carew. AnAnS 2

...That by it our devotion may with greater zeal prepare a/temple for the Lord. Sequaire. Godeschalk. CTC

That by sharp proofs the heathen themselves may see/But men to be. Psalm IX. Sir Philip Sidney. FCP

That by snow were set on fire. The Snow-Ball. Thomas Stanley. CavP

That by some strange miracle/May reach them yet. Pawnshop Window. R. H. Grenville. GoYe

That by that time the Hat/came he had no head. Cardinal Fisher. John Heywood. ACP

That by thine aid this work may have good speed. Dedication of the Chronicles of England and France. Robert Fabyan. ISi

That cage of wizardry. Come Wary One. Ruth Manning-Sanders. CH

That called him so briefly/from his deep/deep sleep? In the Old House. Joan Aiken. WSC

That calls itself/knife/(cuchillo). Cuchillo. Joy Harjo. TWSS

That calm seems certainly safe to last tonight. On Looking up by Chance at the Constellations. Robert Frost. CMoP; NePA

That calm tranquillity of soul/Is thine? The College Cat. Alfred Denis Godley. CenHV

That came like lightning shattering my heart! Sonnets. Muna Lee. HBMV

That can happen at any time of the day or night. This above All Is Precious and Remarkable. John Wain. LiTM

That cannot long one fashion entertain. Sonnet: "Into these loves who but for passion looks." Michael Drayton. ViBoPo

That casts upon the heart, as it recedes,/Splinters and spars and dripping, salty weeds. Fair Weather. Dorothy Parker. SBG

That Cat awaits the Judgment. May I go? Supplication of the Black Aberdeen. Rudyard Kipling. BLPA

That cautious old person of Dean. Limerick: "There was an old person of Dean." Edward Lear. MoShBr

That central black, the ringed and targeted grave. The Archer. A. J. M. Smith. OBCV; PeCV

That change in thee, if not thyself, I claim. Appreciation. George Meredith. ViBoPo

That chant the chant of the Whole. Ode in May. William Watson. OBEV; OBVV; WGRP

That characteristic POP of a burst balloon/followed by no crying. Pop. David McFadden. NeAC

That cheerful Old Man in a pew. Limerick: "There was an Old Man in a pew." Edward Lear. MoShBr

That chickens had been miss'd at Syllabub Farm. Wanderers. Charles Stuart Calverley. CenHV

That child, never touched by the rays of the sun,/Might rise, because of love. The Landfall. James Dickey. PoA

That Christ is not ashamed of me! Ashamed of Jesus. Joseph Grigg. BePJ

That Christ may draw in His spread net the living and the dying. Hymn to the Virgin Mary. Conal O'Riordan. ISi

That Cibber may serve both for fool and for poet. On the New Laureate. *Anonymous.* FaBoCo

...That clapping of hands/before which we may not speak or sing or ever stop. Rain Forest. Dave Smith. HaCAP

That clean white paper waiting under a pen/is the gift beyond history and hurt and heaven. The Gift. John Ciardi. BiP; LiTM; MP; NMP

That cod!/O God!/O God! High Overhead My Little Daughter. Thomas Edward Brown. NOBV

That comes a model New Year's Day! A Vow for New Year's. Mary Carolyn Davies. PoToHe

That comes into and steadies my soul. The Pangolin. Marianne Moore. AP; CoBMV; CrMA; FaBoWP; HAP; NoAm; NOBA; PBWP

That comes unsought to bird and boy. Interlude. Eileen Duggan. AnNZ

That continues to last These Crossings, These Words. Quincy Troupe. LTB

That converse bone to bone? Sixteen Dead Men. William Butler Yeats. FaBoPV; OBWP

That, cooling, moves from room to room. The Wake. Wyatt Prunty. AMV-80

That could be heard ten miles or/more. The Devil. *Anonymous.* OxNR

That could laugh only–after His murder. Saw God Dead but Laughing. Jose Garcia Villa. AnFE

That cows are very useful creatures. The Cow. *Anonymous.* FaBoUs

That crawls to the cool shadows of the pillars/To die. A Row of Thick Pillars. Stephen Crane. AmePo

That cries far out and calls us to partake/in his great tidal movements round the earth. Ireland. John Hewitt. CIP; FaBoPP

...That cries: You shall try strange fruit. Strange Fruit. Randolph Stow. PoAu 1-2

That crimson thread was twined. The Red Thread of Honor. Sir Francis Hastings Doyle. BBV

That cross, that thorn, and those five wounds bear witness. The Choice of the Cross. Dorothy L. Sayers. TrCP

That cures like smoke. Shelby County, Ohio. November 1974. G. E. Murray. FAZ

That Curtain'd grave, though sleep, like ashes, hide/My lamp, and life, both shall in thee abide. Silex Scintillans. Henry Vaughan. AnAnS 1

That dares not write things false, nor hide things true. To Sir Henrie Savile. Ben Jonson. NoP; OBS; SeCV 1-2

That day and night of his destruction/wait!... Paradise Lost. John Milton. CoBE

That day, even the lilacs/Were borne down/By the diamonds on their backs. For My Son, Born during an Ice Storm. David Jauss. Str

That day (for come it will) that day/Shall I lament to see. When None Shall Rail. David Lewis. CBEP; OBEC

That day I kissed a woman of my people/ice cold, stretched out in her box. Ice Cold. Sean O Riordain. NOBI

...That day in Cork/Had scarcely time for knife and fork. Irish-American Dignitary. Austin Clarke. BIrV

That day, the last of my youth, on the last of our mountains. David. Earle Birney. CaP; NOBC

That day they read no more. The Story of Rimini. [James Henry] Leigh Hunt. EnRP

That dead, as living, she may be with roses. His Lady's Tomb. Pierre Ronsard. AWP

That, dead unto myself, in you I live. In health and ease am I. Francis Davison. EG

That death himself brings nothing to an end. Letter VIII. Randall Swingler. WaP

That death may not cleave to us. The Creation. *Anonymous.* WTO

That death should spare perfection so complete? The Doom of Beauty. Buonarroti Michelangelo. AWP; LiTW

That Death should turn her thoughts on me,/Who never thought of her at all. Epitaph on Himself. Mathurin Regnier. LiTW

That debt thou left'st to us, which none but he/Can truly pay, Fletcher, who writes like thee. Upon the Dramatick Poems of Mr. John Fletcher. William Cartwright. OBS

That deluded Old Man of The Hague. Limerick: "There was an Old Man of The Hague." Edward Lear. EvOK; TDH

That depressing old person of Crowle. Limerick: "There was an old person of Crowle." Edward Lear. FaBoNo

That describe the voyages of the body and soul. Intimate Associations. Charles Baudelaire. NU

That despair came any closer than ash to being total. Hope's Okay. Archie Randolph Ammons. HaCAP

That devasted childhood's realm,/So easy to repair. Softened by time's consummate plush. Emily Dickinson. NOBA

That devours everything/endlessly If night takes the form of a whale. Isabel Fraire. BoWoP

That did alone defeat Publicity. To the Unknown Warrior. Gilbert Keith Chesterton. MMM

"That did be fun!" the youngest shouted, and/ate pies/With wild surmise. The Party. Reed Whittemore. CAD; CoAP; ConAP; NCSH

...That dip/Their wings in tears, and skim away. In Memoriam A.H.H., XLVIII. Alfred, Lord Tennyson. VLP

That disdains both me and you. Song: "Fool, take up thy shaft again." Thomas Stanley. EnLoPo

That distressing Old Person of Burton. Limerick: "There was an old person of Burton." Edward Lear. EBEV

That Doctor Emmanuel's head contains. Doctor Emmanuel. James Reeves. PV

That does not know it knows/there's an end to dreaming. To My Daughter Riding in the Circus Parade. Joan Labombard. GOYP

That does not need a spear-torn side/Or sight of body crucified/To teach me not to be unkind. A Prayer for Charity. Edwin O. Kennedy. TrPWD

That dog, and that bare bitter place. At the Fishing Settlement. Alistair Campbell. AnNZ

That dogs may dig him up, for what he's worth. Last Lines. X.J. Kennedy. OBAL

That doing it, the boy should look away. The Fish. Ralph Gustafson. OBCV

That dolorous Man of Cape Horn. Limerick: "There was an old man of Cape Horn." Edward Lear. EBEV

That dolphin-torn, that gong-tormented sea. Byzantium. William Butler Yeats. CABA; CMoP; CoBMV; DiPo; EBEV; FaBoMo; HAP; InPS; LiTM; LoBV; MoAB; MoBrPo; MoPo; NAWM 1-2; NIP; NoAm; NOBE; NoP; OAEL 1-2; OAEP; OnYI; OxBTC; PAI; PPP; SeCePo; SeCeV; TEP

"That don't give 'em/much of a chance, does it!" Ladybug. Robert Sund. BoAnP

That don't seem right, does it, Joe? Ultimate Equality. Ray Durem. PoNe

That doubtful old man of Spithead. Limerick: "There was an old man of Spithead." Edward Lear. FaBoNo

That doubts as fervently as it believes. Ourselves we do inter with sweet derision. Emily Dickinson. FaBoEE

That doutfull hope, that certaync woo, and sure dispaire of/helthe.   Suche Waywarde Wais Hath Love.   Henry Howard, Earl of Surrey.   AAS

That drag down sheep and cattle between the rivers.   Growing Wild.   Jim Wayne Miller.   GP

That draws all waters toward/Its live formality.   Looking into History.   Richard Wilbur.   VGW

That Dread can darken not, nor Death destroy.   Wood-Pigeons.   John Masefield.   ChMP

That dreaded word of gloom!)   The Cloth of Gold (excerpt).   M. Krishnamurti.   PeD

That dream was written long ago.   I Gazed Within.   Emily Bronte.   ViBoPo

That dreams are dreams?   Since I Am Convinced.   Saigyo Hoshi.   AWP

That dreams, the eye has known,/May trouble souls to-night.   The Young Woman of Beare.   Austin Clarke.   NoAm

That drinking and the women/Would be my ruin at last.   Tom Dooley.   *Anonymous.*   AmFP; ViBoFo

That drop from the angels' shoon.   Excelsior.   Ralph Waldo Emerson.   PeD

That drop into the slanted suns of love?   Harvest.   Jeannette Maino.   AMV-80

That drop untasted might be somehow/spilled.   If.   William Dean Howells.   AA

That dull assignment/of being the world's/most sober animal   Dromedary.   Francois Dodat.   BoAnP

That dun, worn, airy to-be-bounced/Treasurable and humble dweller in closets.   Adulescentia.   Robert Fitzgerald.   SD

That each kind of grain may grow for men.   Charm for Unfruitful Land.   *Anonymous.*   AnOE

That each may have a blessing/From Thee to take away. Amen.   Table Graces, or Prayers for Adults: Morning Meal.   *Anonymous.*   BLRP

That each subscriber's eyes might freely range/O'er clown so clever! spectacle so strange!   The Life and Lucubrations of Crispinus Scriblerus (excerpt).   James Woodhouse.   NOEC

That each tail should be properly placed.   Little Bo-Peep.   Mother Goose.   HBV 1-2; HBVY

That earnest little/rooster off again.   Rocking.   Archie Randolph Ammons.   GP

That Easter on the first Sunday after the full moon/following the vernal equinox doth fall.   Rhyme for Remembering the Date of Easter.   Justin Richardson.   FaBoUs

That ebs from pittie lesse and lesse.   Upon Moon.   Robert Herrick.   MOON

That Edward Taylor's Paradise was seen/By other light than day?   Having No Ear.   Donald Davie.   AMV-81

That even his hopes became a part/Of earth's eternal heritage.   At the President's Grave.   Richard Watson Gilder.   PAH

That even in death they shall be one.   Epitaph: "Daniel and Abigail."   Miguel de Barrios.   TrJP

That even recording angels find it best/To keep us alphabetical.   Holy Order.   John Basil Boothroyd.   FiBHP

That even the creators of soundtracks/could understand.   Graffiti in a University Restroom...   Jim Mitsui.   BrSi

That even the moonlight/cannot put out.   The Owl.   Sue Owen.   AMV-81

That even the Toucan he can too.   The Pecan. The Toucan.   Robert Williams Wood.   NLV

That even the unopened future lies/like a love-letter, full of sweet surprise.   Still-Life.   Elizabeth Daryush.   FaBoWP; QFR

That even the verie losse of them did move hir more to teares.   Metamorphoses.   Ovid (Publius Ovidius Naso).   OBVE

That even the weariest river/Winds somewhere safe to sea.   The Garden of Proserpine.   Algernon Charles Swinburne.   ViBoPo

That even to die is somehow to invent.   Seferis.   Lawrence Durrell.   EBEV

That ever since my hart did greve,/now endeth our roundelay.   Perigot and Willye.   Edmund Spenser.   LoBV

That ever went over Tipple Tine.   Riddle; "As I was going o'er Tipple Tine."   *Anonymous.*   OxNR

That evere I lovede hir so!   Snatches: "Ich have a love untrewe."   *Anonymous.*   OxBM

That every educated feller ain't a plumb greenhorn.   The Zebra Dun.   *Anonymous.*   AmFP; CoSo; FSW; PH; StPo; ViBoFo

That every eye may here commend/The kind delights you breed.   Song: To the Masquers Representing Stars.   Thomas Campion.   LoBV

That every fool is not a poet.   Epigram: "Sir, I admit your gen'ral rule."   Alexander Pope.   FaBoEE

That every Hyacinth the Garden wears/Dropt in her lap from some once lovely Head.   The Rubaiyat of Omar Khayyam.   Omar Khayyam.   SeCePo

That every ocean smells alike of tar.   The Beach.   Robert Graves.   OBSP

...That every shirt needed/ironing is being forgotten.   What Is Being Forgotten.   Eloise Klein Healy.   GP

That everywhere poke from the roadside.   The Mirrors of Jerusalem.   Barbara F. Lefcowitz.   AMV-80; VWA

That evil ended. So also may this!   Deor's Lament.   *Anonymous.*   AnOE; EBEV; EnLi 1-2; EnLit; OAEL 1-2; TEP

...That execrable conjunction/of gasoline and desert air.   At Barstow.   Charles Tomlinson.   NoAm; TwCP

That expensive Young Lady of Corsica.   Limerick: "There was a young lady of Corsica."   Edward Lear.   CenHV; FaBoNo

That face of the Sun and Mist begotten,/Its singing lips and death-cold eyes.   The Dream of Aengus Og.   Eleanor Rogers Cox.   HBMV

That failing would incense her more/Than all his trespasses before.   The Penance.   Nahum Tate.   CavP

That fall without cease,/from a sky with never a rift in the clouds.   The Farmer's Clothes Are Soaked Through and Never Dried.   Ise Tayu.   WPOW

That fame of thy divorce may spread as far/As of thy marriage!   Medea. (Lucius Annaeus Seneca)   Seneca.   HW

That fate, that dear fate.   Dear Possible.   Laura Riding.   LiTA

That, fearing God's Wrath only, firm may/stand the State they made.   The Sudbury Fight.   Wallace Rice.   PAH

That feeds the living, thousand-lighted stream/up which we toiled into this timeless dream.   The Ancestors.   Judith Wright.   BoAV

That field of ponies.   Love Song.   Anne Sexton.   NCSH

That fierce dying of humans consumed/In raging fires of Love.   Walking Parker Home.   Bob Kaufman.   PoBA

That fill Edina's street/Sae thrang this day.   My Winsome Dear.   Robert Fergusson.   SeCePo

That fills with farewell notes the dark'ning plain.   Ode to Evening.   Joseph Warton.   ATP

That finds no object worth its constancy?   To the Moon.   Percy Bysshe Shelley.   AnFE; BoNaP; ERoP 1-2; GTBS; GTBS-P; MBW 1-2; MCCG; MOON; PPP; TrGrPo; ViBoPo

That fire that eats what it illuminates.   Style.   Howard Nemerov.   NoAm

That first act of our own/is still the best act left. Let's go to bed.   After Shakespeare.   Alex Comfort.   ErPo

That first had this heart of mine.   The Seeds of Love.   *Anonymous.*   CBEP

That first Lord Cozens Hardy,/The Master of the Rolls.   Lord Cozens Hardy.   Sir John Betjeman.   OxBTC

That fixed the tilt of the wings.   Perfect.   Hugh" (Christopher Murray Grieve) MacDiarmid.   NeBP

That Flesh and Blood can't bear it.   Two Monopolists.   John Byrom.   FaBoEE

That floats like a shell to the shore,/Both given and found.   The Event.   Thomas Sturge Moore.   OBMV

That flower had fallen,–that crimson blossom.   The Nativity of Christ.   Luis de Gongora y Argote.   CAW

That flowing beards are all the go way up in Ironbark.   The Man from Ironbark.   Andrew Barton ("Banjo") Paterson.   PoAu 1-2

That flows not every day, but ever.   Song: "When, dearest, I but think of".   Owen Felltham.   CavP; MePo; SeCeV

That fluttering things have so distinct a shade.   Le Monocle de Mon Oncle.   Wallace Stevens.   AP; APA; CoBMV; LiTM; MAPA; MoAB; NoAm

That folks may see that she died for love.   Died of Love.   *Anonymous.*   OBET

That folks you like will sure like you.   Folks and Me.   Lucile Crites.   WBLP

That foolish sleep transfers to thee.   In Memoriam A.H.H., LXVIII.   Alfred, Lord Tennyson.   VLP

That fools please women best.   Song: "It is all one in Venus' wanton school."   John Lyly.   SeCePo

That for a little space some wandering dream/May come and lock Rhodanthe's arms about me.   The Swallows.   Agathias.   LiTW

That for a little while we were so sad.   He Will Give Them Back.   George Klingle.   BLRP

That for him too the Savior once did bleed.   Tannhauser.   William Morton Payne.   AA

That for long pain makes brief complete amends.   New York * December * 1931.   Babette Deutsch.   ImOP

That for one moment she at least/was not utterly alone.   Declaration at Forty.   Judson Crews.   UnTE

That for thair reird they micht nocht heir the sound.   King Hart: Hart's Castle.   Gavin Douglas.   AtBAP

That for thy sake my youth decayed is.   Sonnet: "I have not spent the April of my time."   Bartholomew Griffin.   ElL

That forever we would keep if but we could.   The Wrestling Match.   Robert Penn Warren.   AnAmPo

That forming on a cigarette covers the red.   Morning Sun.   Louis MacNeice.   MoAB; MoBrPo; MP

That fountain other streams/forever.   A Short History of the Teaching Profession.   Sister Maura.   AMV-80

That fountains of the heart run dry.   Vanity.   Robert Graves.   GTBS-P

That he hadna either killd or taen/Ere his heart's blood was cauld.   The Battle of Otterburn (C ver.).   *Anonymous.*   ESPB

That he left his lonely caw/Behind in the fields.   Hokku Poems.   Richard Wright.   AmNP; PoBA

That he may boast around his grove/A visit from the BIRD OF JOVE.   A Card of Invitation to Mr. Gibbon, at Brighthelmstone.   William Hayley.   OBEC

That he may choose which are the pure in heart.   The Witnesses.   X.J. Kennedy.   PCh

That he may harvest for the better time.   Prayer to the Blessed Virgin.   Rodriquez de Padron.   CAW

That he may hear the devil and his wife/In bed, talking secrets.   Fragment.   Thomas Lovell Beddoes.   ELU

That He may lose Dinant next Year,/And so be Constable of France.   An English Ballad, on the Taking of Namur by the King...   Matthew Prior.   PoEL 1-5

That he may reign king of the merry/dryland,/But that I will be king of the sea.'   Henry Martyn (E version).   *Anonymous.*   ESPB

That he may share/Our Christmas cheer.   Christmas Chant.   Isabel Shaw.   ChBR; SiSoSe

That he may sleep upon his hill again?   Abraham Lincoln Walks at Midnight.   Vachel Lindsay.   AmLP; CMoP; FaBV; FaFP; GoTF; HBV 1-2; LaNeLa; LiTA; MC; MCCG; MoAmPo; MoRP; MoVE; NAMP; NoAm; NOBA; OFD; OHFP; OxBA; PAH; PAL; PoPl; PPON; TAP; TreF; VGW

That he never again shall commit/the crime/Of diggin' two-cent coal.   Two-Cent Coal.   *Anonymous.*   AmFP

That he's the kind of a man it takes for the work here in the West.   The Stampede.   Freeman E. Miller.   BPAW

That he sees more than all the world beside.   On a Proud Fellow.   *Anonymous.*   PV

That he slept with plenty of quilts to keep him warm.   Angina Pectoris.   W. R. Moses.   LiTA; NCSH

That he sublimed defeat.   A Hero.   Florence Earle Coates.   OHIP

That He uses with Hadley and Dwight!   On the Democracy of Yale.   Frederick Scheetz Jones.   HBV 1-2; YaD

That he wald gae to see his luve,/By the le licht of the mune.   Brown Adam (B version).   *Anonymous.*   ESPB

"That he was a Kosmos is a piece of news we were/hardly prepared for..."   The Adhesive Autopsy of Walt Whitman.   Jonathan Williams.   PoM

That he was bred a poet whose selfish trade is/To keep no beauty to himself.   Mary Hynes.   Padraic Fallon.   AnIV; OxBI

That he was gone, and I discerned not how.   La Vita Nuova.   Dante Alighieri.   AWP

...That He who designed/all simple wonderers, may have had me in mind.   The Groundhog.   Luci Shaw.   TrCP

That he who hath not endured to the death, from his birth he hath never/ endured!   The Old Men.   Rudyard Kipling.   OBSV

That he who lived on the first may rise on the last day.   Isis Wanderer.   Kathleen Raine.   OxBS

That he who once has been my slave/Should ever be my king.   Phillis's Resolution.   William Walsh.   OBSP

That He Whose might shaped heavenly glory/In His safe-keeping held you close.   St. Andrew's Voyage to Mermedonia.   *Anonymous.*   AnOE

That he will grant us of his grace/In heaven high to have a place!   Fair Maiden, Who Is This Bairn?   *Anonymous.*   ISi

That heard me whisper, "I am she!"   The Other Side of a Mirror.   Mary Elizabeth Coleridge.   BoWoP; CBEP

That Heaven itself came down, and bled/To win a mortal's love.   Sweet Muse.   Isaac Watts.   NOBE; OxBoCh

That hell is but a single room of mirrors.   I Go to Whiskey Bars.   Raymond Thompson.   LFAC

That hem hath holpen, whan that they were seke.   The Canterbury Tales: The Influences of Breezy April.   Geoffrey Chaucer.   DiPo; GoBC; TrGrPo; ViBoPo

That her English is painfully weak!   Limerick: "I know a young girl who can speak."   Mary A. Webber.   TDH

That her heart was a cinder instead of a coal?   Disappointment.   John Boyle O'Reilly.   ACP; OnYI

That her image must always abide in my heart.   Geraldine's Daughter.   Egan O'Rahilly.   AnIL; OnYI

That here obedient to her laws we lie.   On the Spartan Dead at Thermopylae.   Simonides (of Ceos).   WeW

That here we cannot live or love the same again.   Narrative.   Louis Dudek.   CaP

That hides for shelter from the summer heat.   Summer.   John Clare.   CBEP

That them you love, is also loved by me.   To a New Daughter-in-law.   *Anonymous.*   PoToHe

That hint of a solemn pity: and are gone.   Christmas 1942.   Eric Irvin.   BoAV; PoAu 1-2

That his daddy once tied up my garter for me!   The Dark-Eyed Gentleman.   Thomas Hardy.   MoAB; MoBrPo; NLV; UnPo; VLP

That his heart may not be lifted up in pride.   Sorrow Shatters My Heart.   Moses Ibn Ezra.   LiTW

That his heart trembles and his sight growns dim?   La Vita Nuova.   Dante Alighieri.   AWP

That his pants flew out of his pocket.   Limerick: "There was a young person named Crockett."   William Jay Smith.   TDH

That his sweet day augurs a sweeter morrow,/With smiles, not sorrow.   Time to Go.   Susan (Sarah Chauncey Woolsey) Coolidge.   GN

That His true weight is heavy on your back.   Jerusalem Sonnets.   James Keir Baxter.   OCNZ

That his wife could do more work in a day/Than he could do in seven.   Old Man in the Wood.   *Anonymous.*   FSW

That his young shepherd has outwitted me."/Lolli-doll-lay, Lolli-doll-luddy-tri-ol-de-dum-day.   The Bishop of Canterbury (King John and the Bishop).   *Anonymous.*   AmFP

That history pauses still upon their noble names.   In the Annals of Tacitus.   Philip Murray.   NePoAm

That history would ultimately justify/the Dorians   The Vandals.   Jenny Mastoraki.   BoWoP

That holds the splendor though the days depart.   Riverton.   Edmund Wilson.   AnFE

That holds the summer in its green concave.   To a Friend in the Wilderness (excerpt).   A. R. D. Fairburn.   AnNZ

That holy fire being fed/By the compost heap.   The Compost Heap.   Vernon Watkins.   NYBP

That horrid dream of marble halls!   The Palace of Humbug.   Lewis (Charles Lutwidge Dodgson) Carroll.   FaBoNo

That House is narrow, and dark, and small–/But the only Peaceful House of all.   Rest Only in the Grave.   James Clarence Mangan.   BIrV

That howsoever taste may veer/I'll be in the swim, sir.   The Poet of Bray.   John Heath-Stubbs.   NOBL

That hurts my pride.   Tamping Ties.   *Anonymous.*   AmFP

That I almost received her heart into my own.'   The Pet Lamb.   William Wordsworth.   OxBChV

That I am as I am and so will I be.   I Am As I Am.   Sir Thomas Wyatt.   CBEP; FCP; SiPS

That I am glad to die for love of her.   Canzone: He Perceives His Rashness in Love, but Has No Choice.   Guido Guinicelli.   AWP

That I am guiltless of your innocent blood.   Summa Contra Gentiles.   Paris Leary.   CoPo

That I am lovelier without my dress/Gave me sweet wanton happiness.   Vanity.   Anna Wickham.   FaBoTw

...That I am not/inferior to those I despise.   At One O'Clock in the Morning.   Charles Baudelaire.   SyP

That I am yielded fully to Thy power/Dynamic and serene.   Let Me Lift Jesus, Lord.   Jo Gardner.   BePJ

That I am your man.   To Mistress Anne.   John Skelton.   EnRePo

That i am yr soil, come/& build here   Before/and After...   Johari (Jewel C. Latimore) Amini.   JB

That I an accessary needs must be,/To that sweet thief which sourly robs from me.   Sonnets, XXXV: "No more be grieved at that which thou hast done."   William Shakespeare.   CBEP; PeHV

That I bought for a halfpenny, yesterday.   A Maudle-In Ballad (parody).   *Anonymous.*   BXAP; FaBoPa

...That I can be any/shape I want, even pudding-shaped and/nobody can stop me.   The Pot-Bellied Anachronism.   Ann Darr.   GP

That I can live my life/by this single creek.   Cascadilla Falls.   Archie Randolph Ammons.   NIP; NOBA

That I can no longer tell/Dream from reality.   I am so lost.   Narihira (Ariwara no Narihira).   LiTW

That I can think away from thee and live!'   Endymion, III.   John Keats.   EnRP

That I could be a boy again,–/A happy boy,–at Drury's.   School and Schoolfellows.   Winthrop Mackworth Praed.   OBRV

That I could be the princess whose kiss will change you/into a man.   Frog Prince.   Phoebe Pettingell.   DFT

That I'd be led to a scaffold high to meet a fatal doom.   Charles Guiteau, I.   *Anonymous.*   AmFP; FSW

That I'd disdain to breathe or be,/If Nancy was not born for me.   On My Wife's Birth-Day.   Christopher Smart.   NAs

That I die, that I die, though my breath/Prolongs this space of lingering death.   Song Set by Robert Jones: "Life is a poet's fable."   *Anonymous.*   OBSC

That I gave you my last, I have none other.   Elegy for a Cricket.   J. V. Cunningham.   NoAm

That I had alighted there!   Faintheart in a Railway Train.   Thomas Hardy.   CTC; EnLoPo

(That I had never been made of this–/The angel's prayer, or the gipsy's kiss!)   I Was Made of This and This.   Gertrude Robison Ross.   HBMV

That I have kept the divine Form and the Essence/Of my festered loves inviolate!   A Carrion.   Charles Baudelaire.   AWP; LiTW; NAWM 1-2

That I have known no day/In all my life like this.   The Idle Life I Lead.   Robert Bridges.   EG; LiTM

That I haven't been born with a breign.   Limerick: "A king, on assuming his reign."   *Anonymous.*   TDH

That I'll have the strength to believe that/What happened–really happened.   The Author's Apology.   T. Carmi.   VWA

That I'm happier than they are sittin' on my porch at night.   Sittin' on the Porch.   Edgar A. Guest.   TreFS

That I'm not quite so handsome now.   Rotten Row.   Frederick Locker-Lampson.   ALV

That I'm the sole survivor of/The famous Forty Thieves!   My Recollectest Thoughts.   Charles Edward Carryl.   HBV 1-2; HBVY; NA

That i'm to die/or she's to leave me   My Love Is Young.   Earle Birney.   NOBC

That I may also learn to grow/In sweet humility.   The Violet.   Jane Taylor.   GoTF; HBV 1-2; HBVY; TreF

That I may be a child again this blissful/morn of May.   May Morning.   Celia Thaxter.   AA

That I may be/Faithful to God and thee.   Song: "Beloved, it is morn!"   Emily Henrietta Hickey.   OBVV

That I may be forgiven/For following loveliness!   A Prayer.   Clinton Scollard.   TrPWD

That I may be free from the worm at my heart's root.   The Princess in the Ivory Tower.   Joy Davidman.   DFT

That I may drowne me in you?   Weepe O Mine Eyes.   *Anonymous.*   AtBAP; PoEL 1-5

That I may fold it round me and in comfort lie.   The Embankment.   Thomas Ernest Hulme.   EBEV; ELU; FaBoMo; GTBS-P; OBSP; OxBTC

That I may give for every day/Some good account at last.   How Doth the Little Busy Bee.   Isaac Watts.   GoTF; HBV 1-2; HBVY; HoPM; TreF

That I may have the power to sing of thee,/And sound thy praises everlastingly.   To the Supreme Being.   Buonarroti Michelangelo.   AWP; LiTW; TrPWD; TRV

That I may laugh at her in equall sort,/As she doth laugh at me and makes my pain her sport.   Amoretti, X.   Edmund Spenser.   AAS; NoP

That I may lean my elbow on your knee.   Idea of a Swimmer.   Jean-Richard Bloch.   TrJP

That I may leave both love and life, & thereby purchase/rest./Haud ictus sapio.   The Divorce of a Lover.   George Gascoigne.   AAS

That I may let alone my toil/And rest with thee?   Weary in Well-Doing.   Christina Georgina Rossetti.   SeCePo; TrPWD

That I may live, and feel, and speak again!   Absent Creation.   D. S. Savage.   NeBP

That I may live because I hope no more!   To His Mistress in Absence.   Torquato Tasso.   AWP

That I may live in some disport.   Meditation in Winter.   William Dunbar.   BSV; CEP; NCEP

That I may meet you in the heavens,/where I do hope to rest.   John Rogers' Exhortation to His Children.   *Anonymous.*   OBCA

That I may meet you there.   Nocturne.   Robert Hillyer.   FYAP

That I may run, rise, rest, with thee.   Trinity Sunday.   George Herbert.   OBSP

...That I may see and tell/Of things invisible to mortal sight.   Light.   John Milton.   OBEV

That I may seek thee, the wide world around?   Childhood Fled.   Charles Lamb.   EnRP

That I may sing my one specific song?   Pervigilium Veneris.   Suzanne Noguere.   PoA

That I may write into the north/I have wone the life o Geordie'?   Geordie (D version).   *Anonymous.*   ESPB; OBET

That I met her in the garden/Where the praties grow.   I Met Her in the Garden Where the Praties Grow (with music).   *Anonymous.*   AS

That I might die kissing!   The Kiss.   Ben Jonson.   HBV 1-2; UnTE

That I might know all things.   Take Your Accusation Back!   Kittaararter.   WTO

That I might know the passion of this day!   June Rapture.   Angela Morgan.   HBMV

...That I might lose/Myself in finding Thee!   Hymn from the French of Lamartine (excerpt).   John Greenleaf Whittier.   TrPWD

That I might maiden come again/To my mother and to thee.   The Three Captains.   *Anonymous.*   AWP

That I might there present it:–O, to whom?   The Question.   Percy Bysshe Shelley.   CH; EnRP; FiP; HBV 1-2; MyFE; OBEV; OBRV; PoPle

...That I must breed/alive unique love from her wax and his steel.   49th & 5th, December 13.   Josephine Jacobsen.   NYP

That I must journey on.   Supplication.   Joseph Seamon, Jr Cotter.   BANP; CDC; PoNe

That I must run, who in the end am caught.   The Contemplative Quarry.   Anna Wickham.   HBMV

That I my Best-Beloveds am; that He is mine.   Canticles II. XVI.   Francis Quarles.   MeLP

That I nam thine and thou art mine,/To don all they wille.'   A Cleric Courts His Lady.   *Anonymous.*   MeEL

That I no more may feel/A want and ache not yet appeased.   Give Me My Infant Now.   Te-whaka-io-roa.   NAs; WTO

That I rode on. Am still riding.   White Horse of the Father, White Horse of the Son.   William Pitt Root.   MAYP

That I say: "Lady, I am wholly thine."   Ballata: Of a Continual Death in Love.   Guido Cavalcanti.   AWP

That I shall be past making love/When she begins to comprehend it.   To a Child of Quality.   Matthew Prior.   CBEP; CEP; CoBE; EiCP; ExPo; GN; HBV 1-2; LiTB; NIP; NOBE; NOEC; OBEC; OBEV; PoEL 1-5; SeCeV

That I should be making haste for ever.   Laura Waits for Him in Heaven.   Petrarch (Francesco Petrarca).   OBMV

That I should go to Strawberry Fair.'   Strawberry Fair.   *Anonymous.*   OBET

That I should render for my part/A thankful heart.   A Thankful Heart.   Robert Herrick.   PoToHe

That I should such a life destroy,–/Yet live by Him I kill'd!   In Evil Long I Took Delight.   John Newton.   OxBoCh

That I sit so much by myself alone.   Long Are the Hours the Sun Is Above.   Robert Bridges.   EG

That I, though bruised, may fearlessly ascend/High sorrow's ladder, singing, to the end!   Sorrow's Ladder.   Gertrude Callaghan.   CAW

That I thy love so dere have bought,/And I aske thee nought elles.   Christ's Plea to Mankind.   *Anonymous.*   OxBM

That I thy purpose did not know,/Or overrated thy designs.   My Prayer.   Henry David Thoreau.   HBV 1-2; HBVY; PoPl

That I too may let my light shine through the dark.   Night.   Sam Duby R. Sutu.   PeSA; TTY

That I've been borne away to bed.   Dum Vivimus Vigilemus.   Charles Henry ("John Paul") Webb.   AA

That I've finally managed my A.   A Hawthorne Garland.   Richard Harter Fogle.   OBAL

That I was never blest.   The Repulse.   Thomas Stanley.   AnAnS 2; MeLP; MePo; OBS

That I was the one waiting for the miracle.   Twilight Thoughts in Israel.   Melech Ravitch.   VWA

That I who was, would shrink to be/That happy child again.   The Deserted Garden.   Elizabeth Barrett Browning.   HBV 1-2

That I with more delight may share/My native meads again.   To Miss L.F.... (parody).   J. C. Squire.   BXAP

That I wou'd rather kip my staddle.   Liady-Day an' Ridden House.   William Barnes.   OBRV

That I would wish me thus to dream and die.   The Ivory, Coral, Gold.   William, of Hawthornden Drummond.   ELP

That ich habbe in the bowre/Y-don almyn wille, wille.   Snatches: "Ne shalt thou never, levedy."   *Anonymous.*   OxBM

That if I dipped my hand the spawn would clutch it.   Death of a Naturalist.   Seamus Heaney.   HAP; NCSH; OxBC

That, if I then had wak'd after long sleep,/Will make me sleep again.   The Tempest.   William Shakespeare.   UnS

That if water were my prison strong/I would swim for libertie.'   Broughty Wa's.   *Anonymous.*   ESPB

That if you found its size among the swellings and diminishings it would be/calm and shine.   Tall Windows.   Robert Hass.   NPGG

That ilka ane might plainly see/They war twa lovers sweet.   Lord Lovel (B version).   *Anonymous.*   ESPB

That illusive old person of Woking.   Limerick: "There was an old person of Woking."   Edward Lear.   NA

That image nearest borders on the blest/Creations of pure art that never dies.   The Gypsy Girl.   Henry Alford.   HBV 1-2

That imprudent old fellow named Woodin.   Limerick: "There was a queer fellow named Woodin."   Cuthbert (Edward Bradley) "Bede.   CenHV; TDH

That in black ink my love may still shine bright.   Since Brass, Nor Stone, Nor Earth.   William Shakespeare.   BoLiVe

That in death as in life thy body may be roses.   Roses.   Pierre de Ronsard.   LiTW

That in fighting as in love/The true British tar is the dandy O!   Chesapeake and Shannon.   *Anonymous.*   PAH; ViBoFo

That in her heart would be content/To be at his commandement.   Little Lute.   Richard Corbet.   FaBoEE

That in his final act our old friend Malory/Was obviously playing to the gallery.   The Passing of Arthur (parody).   J. C. Squire.   BXAP

That in it all, save she, there is no good.   Sonnet: "Let others of the world's decaying tell."   William Alexander, Earl of Stirling.   EiL

That in loving you I've almost/Oft forgot my God of yore!   Crusader's Song.   *Anonymous.*   CAW

That in Majorca Alfonso watched the door.   In Honor of St. Alphonsus Rodriguez.   Gerard Manley Hopkins.   EBEV; ForPo

That in my age as cheerful I might be/As the green winter of the Holly Tree.   The Holly Tree.   Robert Southey.   EnRP; HBV 1-2

That in my glowing embers he might see/The burning bird and tree.   E Questo Il Nido in Che la Mia Fenice?   A. D. Hope.   OxBC

That in my woes for thee thou art my joy,/And in my joyes for thee my only annoy. Astrophel and Stella, CVIII. Sir Philip Sidney. AAS; SiPS

...That in one draught, Mortality/May drinke it self up, and forget to dy. An Apologie for the Precedent Hymnes on Teresa. Richard Crashaw. AnAnS 1

That in rearing such a school,/Was the founder. A Fit of Rime against Rime. Ben Jonson. AnAnS 2; InvP; MAT; OAEL 1-2; PoEL 1-5; PP; SeCP; SeCV 1-2; TEP

That–in short, that's why I'm grandma,/and you children all are here! Grandmother's Story of Bunker-Hill Battle. Oliver Wendell Holmes. PAH

...That in such places little/girls must be afraid. Woman and Nature. Susan Griffin. NPGG

That in the deepest pit of Hell/He smoorit them with smuke. The Dance of the Seven Deadly Sins. William Dunbar. BSV; GoTS; OxBS

That in the dreariest places peace will be/A dweller and a joy. To the Snipe. John Clare. FaBoPV; NCEP; OBNC

That in the living Creature find on earth a/place. Suggested by a Picture of the Bird of Paradise. William Wordsworth. VLP

That in thy arms, for ever, I/May lie. My Soul Doth Pant towards Thee. Jeremy Taylor. TrPWD

That in thy house for evermore/My dwelling place shall be. My Shepherd Is the Living Lord. Thomas Sternhold. AH

...That in time one comes/to be a stranger to nothing. The Cemetery at Academy, California. Philip Levine. NaP; NYBP

That in your very/arms I still/can think of you. The Act of Love. Robert Creeley. GP; HAP

That inlet to severe magnificence/Stood full blown, for the God to enter in. Hyperion. John Keats. OBRV

That innocuous Old Man of Hong Kong. Limerick: "There was an Old Man of Hong Kong." Edward Lear. FaBoCo; NBM

That intrinisic Old Man of Peru. Limerick: "There was an old man of Peru." Edward Lear. EBEV; TDH

That is a convention/I cannot attend. Hypnopompic Poem. William Cole. PoL

That is a game that two can play. A Children's Don't. Harry Graham. BBGG

That is a haunted town to me! Almae Matres. Andrew Lang. BSV; OBVV

...That is all/anyone can ever ask. Crimes of Passion. Terry Stokes. AmPA

That is all that God/gave us to hold. On a Drawing by Flavio. Philip Levine. VWA

That is all the world has:/A Cross on a Hill. A Cross on a Hill. Carl S. Weist. BePJ

That is because it would be hard to find/A tongue so loosely allied to a mind. On Mrs. W–. Nicolas Bentley. DBV; FiBHP

...That is enough. Rural Lines after Breughel. Norbert Krapf. PoDr

That is fit home for thee! To the Cuckoo. William Wordsworth. BoLiVe; CBEP; CoBE; ELP; EnLit; FaFP; FiP; GTBS; GTBS-P; HBV 1-2; LoBV; MCCG; OBRV; PB; PBBP; PoLf; TreFT; TrGrPo

That is how we have learned, the embrace is all. Goodbye. Galway Kinnell. Str

That is, I hope, how I'm to you. The Passionate Encyclopedia Britannica Reader to His Love. Maggie". InMe

That is just the time to trust. The Time to Trust. *Anonymous*. BLRP

That is love, that is love! Love, Sweet Love. Felix McGlennon. PaPo

That is more kind, but not so fair. To His Young Mistress. Pierre Ronsard. AWP

That is my soul, my darling! A Bathing Girl. Johannes V. Jensen. PoPl

That is not all unworthy of/The God I mourn? Good Friday. A. J. M. Smith. CaP

That is not love, she said rightly. These Poems, She Said. Robert Bringhurst. NOBC

...That is nothing/when put next to the last crucial fact/of who is doing the crying. Gemwood. Marvin Bell. FiCP; LCAP

That is one of the soul's windowed habitations. Windowed Habitations. Charles G. Bell. NePoAM-2

That is our Queen, the Marigold. The Marigold. Thomas Ford. ACP; CAW

That is Outdoor's valentine! A Valentine. Eleanor Hammond. TiPo; YeAr

That is passed from sweet Jesus Christ.' The Holy Well. *Anonymous*. OBET

That is postally known as E.C. The Cannibal Flea (parody). Tom (Thomas Hood, Jr.) Hood, SpRo

That is raging in my soul? Communism. Ella Wheeler Wilcox. PeD

That is so deadly/but so cruel to withhold. Over to God. Stephen Harrigan. FAZ

That is stade in perplexite. When Alexander Our King Was Dead. *Anonymous*. GoTS

That is, that each shall understand. Lines for a Wedding Gift. Wesley Trimpi. NePoEA

...That is the fullest possible/account I can give, of the encounter. Cole's Island. Charles Olson. PoM

That is the life that counts. The Life That Counts. A.W. S. FaFP; WBLP

—That is the look/on the little duck's face. The Little Duck. Joso. SoPo

That is the measure of Muirland Meg. Muirland Meg. Robert Burns. ErPo

That is the message of "Desert Bloom." Desert Bloom. Gertrude Thomas Arnold. BPAW

That is the only after-life I need. My Own Hereafter. Eugene Lee-Hamilton. WGRP

That is the place–that is the place–that is the place for me! Scotch Rhapsody. Edith Sitwell. MP; TwCP

That is the precious, the/long-looked-for Love. A Sonnet to My Mother. Heinrich Heine. TrJP

That is the root of my profound aversion. Lord Barrenstock. Stevie Smith. FaBoNo; NLV

That is the substance of this shortness. Friends. John Perreault. ANYP

That is the thing that I should do/If I had little hands like you.' The Boy and the Parrot. John Hookham Frere. OxBChV

That is the way to London town. See-Saw, Sacradown. *Anonymous*. OxNR

"That is the world where yesternight you/died." The Flight. Lloyd Mifflin. AA; AnAmPo; HBV 1-2

"That is the wraith/Of Victor Galbraith!" Victor Galbraith. Henry Wadsworth Longfellow. PAH

That is their quality: not mind, not goodness, but the beauty of/God. Birds and Fishes. Robinson Jeffers. NoP

That is their whole devotion! Colin Clout. John Skelton. TrGrPo

That is to all this land enlumining. To Chaucer. Thomas Occleve. ACP

That is to say, for service true and fast,/Too long delays, and changing at the last. Sonnet: "To rail or jest, ye know I use it not." Sir Thomas Wyatt. SiPS

That is to say which makes/soda pop. You Too? Me Too–Why Not? Soda Pop. Robert Hollander. NIP

...That is unable/to hate, therefore to love. Merced. Adrienne Rich. NOBA

That is, unless the Yankees happen also to be playing. The New Hellas. Irwin Edman. InMe

That is what I want to teach my son. Juanita, Wife of Manuelito. Simon J. Ortiz. MAYP

That is what love is all about After Verlaine. Anselm Hollo. FAZ

...That is what they were like/Before we agreed to be friends. The Cats. Samuel Exler. GOYP

That is why I say "cold"! Song of Winter. *Anonymous*. AnIL; OnYI

That is why my hand has pain! My Hand Has a Pain. Saint Columcille. BIrV

That is why the joyful body-music/of old Vienna/puzzled me to blindness/and left him starved. Two Refugees. Mordecai Marcus. VWA

That is why this circumstance of energy/is recorded as glory and passes into study. New Students. Marvin Bell. GLGT

That is why we take such care,/Lest some one run away with her. Songs for Fragoletta. Richard Le Gallienne. HBV 1-2

That it blunt the edge of seeing. Sunday Morning. Judith Fitzgerald. CaPN

That it could be worse there after all. The Chosen. Carl Dennis. AMV-81

That it dothe stincke before the face of God. Against the Court of Rome. Petrarch (Francesco Petrarca). LiTW

That it had/4,269 specks/of dust on/its wings. Confusion. Victor Hernandez Cruz. APU

That it hardly becomes any of us/To talk about the rest of us. Good and Bad. Edward Wallis Hoch. GoTF; TreFS

That it just went and gone and burst. Melancholia. *Anonymous*. NA

That it killed that Old Man of Madras. Limerick: "There was an Old Man of Madras." Edward Lear. FaBoNo

That it killed that Old Man of the East. Limerick: "There was an old man of the East." Edward Lear. EBEV

That it may be our highest joy,/Our Father's work to do. O Master Workman of the Race. Jay T. Stocking. AH; TRV

That it may break beneath my feet/And let a lover in! Thy Heart. *Anonymous*. NA

That it might bind on my face the mask of birds. The Hydra of Birds. Nikos Engonopoulos. LiTW

That it receiv'd too large a share/From Nature's rich perfumes... Lines. Michael Drayton. LoBV

That it return to us when we return. Invocation. Denise Levertov. PoA

That it's your disappointment that drives me. Wood Butcher. Norman Hindley. AMV-81

That it the temple of the Spirit may prove. To God the Father. Henry Constable. GoBC

That it was as you had wished. Everglade. Anne Cherner. AMV-81

That it will be a piteous thing/In one small grave to lie. The Wanderer. Zoë Akins. HBMV

That joynt to ashes sho'd be burnt,/Ere I wo'd love at all. Upon Love. Robert Herrick. SeCV 1-2

That joys for the harvest done. I Will Go with My Father A-Ploughing. Joseph Campbell. AnIL; GoBC; OFD; OnYI; SiSoSe; TiPo

That judgement soothes, thy dusty heart-speck's tear. The Philosophic Apology. Samuel Greenberg. MoPo; NePA

That kingdom he had left his debtor,/I wish it soon may have a better. On the Death of Doctor Swift. Jonathan Swift. EiCP; OnYI; ViBoPo

That kings for such a tomb would wish to die. An Epitaph on the Admirable Dramatic Poet, W. Shakespeare. John Milton. FaBoEE; HBV 1-2

That kissed in some forgotten May... The Dust. Gertrude Hall. AA

That knit hills closer than loose stones. The Lane. Andrew Young. HaMV

That laconic old person of Wick. Limerick: "There was an old person of Wick." Edward Lear. FaBoNo; NA

That land thy country, and that spot thy home. There Is a Land. James Montgomery. PAL; PGD

That lap like tidepools/the walls of its cave Night Watch. Margo Magid. NMM

That laughter sweeps across our pompous brains. To the Memory of Yale College. Howard Phelps (Phelps Putnam) Putnam. AnAmPo

That law may fulfil herself wholly, to darken man's face/before God. The Death of Meleager. Algernon Charles Swinburne. OBVV

That law preserves the earth a sphere,/And guides the planets in their course. On a Tear. Samuel Rogers. HBV 1-2

That lay in the house that Jack built. The Domicile of John. Alexander Pope. InMe

That lay in the house that Jack built. The House That Jack Built. Anonymous. FaBoBe; HBV 1-2; HBVY; NLV; OxBoLi; OxNR; SoPo; SpRo

That leads him to the grave unblest,/And drops him, hopeless, in? The Spider. Hannah F. Gould. OBCA

That leaves me stunned/by your survival. Daughter. Ellen Bryant Voigt. AMV-80

That Liberty may greet you all, her shields of/land and wave. To the Returning Brave. Robert Underwood Johnson. PAH

That lies behind night/and draws you into its silence. Blue Owl Song. Alfred Kittner. VWA

That lies in the house of Bedlam. Visits to St. Elizabeths. Elizabeth Bishop. CoAP; VGW

That lies on th' other side Death's Rubicon. A Thought of Death. Thomas Flatman. CEP; OBS

That life could stir in me/Like first free laughter. Waterfall. Anne Welsh. PeSA

That life, if nothing else,/is something he knows. In Blanco County. Russell T. Fowler. AMV-80

That life is but one long caress/Of gentle words and gentle hands. In Memorium—Leo: A Yellow Cat. Margaret Sherwood. BLPA

That life be all poetry,/And weariness a name. A Health. Edward Coate [(or Coote)] Pinkney. AA; AmePo; AnAmPo; GoTF; HBV 1-2; TreFS

That life renewed whereof the Florentine/Sang ere he wrote the Comedy Divine! Incipit Vita Nova. William Morton Payne. AA

That lifts the world to realms divine. O Thou Whose Gracious Presence Shone. Marion Franklin Ham. AH

That light, reflected, but makes darkness plain. In Dispraise of the Moon. Mary Elizabeth Coleridge. BoNaP; CH; MOON; NBM

That lights the wreaths for soldiers/In Bedford Avenue. The Moon of Brooklyn. Nathalia Crane. AnAmPo

That, like a skewer of flame,/Impales the heart. Love. Gordon LeClaire. CaP

That line of rose no more be drawn/Above the ocean's spray! The Miracle of Dawn. Madison Cawein. HBV 1-2

That little Bess had planted ere they laid her by his side. Bill Venero. Anonymous. CoSo

That little brown ball, the earth? Ego's Dream. Alfred Kreymborg. MAPA

That little Irish cailin in her ould plaid shawl. The Ould Plaid Shawl. Francis A. Fahy. HBV 1-2

That Little Jack Frost was glad to go. Little Jack Frost. Anonymous. SoPo

That little old woman was/Surely a mouse! The Old Woman. Beatrix Potter. GoJo; NTCP

That little room I showed you is not made of perspex. Naming of Private Parts (parody). John Lloyd Williams. BXAP; FaBoPa

(That liv'd so sweetly) dead, so sweet a/grave! Music's Duel. Richard Crashaw. CoBE; GoTL; OBS; PBBP; SeCP; SeCV 1-2

That lively Old Person of Blythe. Limerick: "There was an old person of Blythe." Edward Lear. EBEV

That living idly without taking paine/(Like to the first) made every man a Caine. Noah's Flood. Michael Drayton. PBBP; PoEL 1-5

An' that'll keep up int'rest some/In my poor thumb! My Sore Thumb. Burges Johnson. HBVY

That lone heath and its melancholy pond. The Sand Martin. John Clare. PBBP; TEP

That long face, in a place of graves/With nettles overgrown. The Tin-Whistle Player. Padraic Colum. UnS

That long have watched for light, and wept in vain. Sonnet: "As when, to one who long hath watched, the morn." John Codrington Bampfylde. NOEC

That long lonesome train whistling down. 900 Miles. Anonymous. FSW

That longs to burst a frozen bud/And flood a fresher throat with song. In Memoriam A.H.H., LXXXIII. Alfred, Lord Tennyson. NOBV; VLP

That Lord that for us all did die/Save all these shires. Amen say I. The Properties of the Shires of England. Anonymous. FaBoPP; GBP

That Lord us grant now our prayere,/To dwel in heven that we may.' What Tidings? John Audelay. OxBM

That love had triumphed over death. His Mother's Joy. John White Chadwick. AA

That love hath set aloft/And casten in the dust. "O loathsome place..." Henry Howard, Earl of Surrey. FCP; SiPS

That love in all seasons/is false, but the same. And Fall Shall Sit in Judgment. Audre Lorde. NNP

That Love is ever nigh. God the Omniscient. James Cowden Wallace. BLRP

That love is ripening while they surmise/Escapes their eyes! As on the Heather. Reinmar von Hagenau. AWP

"That love is scarce worth the repose it will cost!" Ill Omens. Thomas Moore. PoEL 1-5

That love lacks surveillance/On sweet Killen Hill. On Sweet Killen Hill. Tom MacIntyre. CIP; NCSH

That love might come to life. Evolution. Israel Zangwill. TrJP

That love, or none, is fit for one/Man-shaped like thee. Song: "Seek not the tree of silkiest bark." Aubrey Thomas De Vere. OBVV

That Love, this art in every part might show. The Dance of Love. Sir John Davies. ElL; SeCePo

That Love would prove so hard a master. Triolet. Robert Bridges. BrPo; HBV 1-2; OBSP; PV; SeCePo

That lovers' tears in lifetime shed/Do restless run when they are dead. The Hour-Glass. Robert Herrick. CaPo

That lowland smell. The Elwha River. Gary Snyder. NoAm

That maddened me, until I laughed and wept. The Barber. John Gray. NOBV; SyP

That made of wood and hill a market-square. Wood and Hill. Andrew Young. HaMV

That madonna womb. The Frog Prince. Anne Sexton. DFT

That magic was for yesterday,/And not for our enchanting? Fairy Story. Barbara Euphan Todd. BoC

That maids make not half such a tumult, as wives. Another True Maid. Matthew Prior. FaBoEE

That make life worth the fight. Little Things. Anonymous. PoToHe

That make our longing's mutual glow/As if it had not been? If You Are Fire. Isaac Rosenberg. ChMP

That makes a chimney of your nose. Tobacco. Anonymous. FaBoEE

That makes life blessed. A Wish for the New Year. Phillips Brooks. STF

That makes me miss my mark. Prayer to the Hunting Star, Canopus. Anonymous. PeSA

That makes poetry/and moves stars. Five Words for Joe Dunn on His 22nd Birthday. Jack Spicer. PoM

That makes the wind change and the grasses. Les Hiboux. Charles Baudelaire. AWP

That makes their broo' baith thick and fat. The Wives of Spittal. Anonymous. GBP

That makes words empty and the senses dumb. A Venetian Night. Hugo von Hofmannsthal. AWP

That man alone may speak the word - Farewell. Last Days. Elizabeth Stoddard AA; AnAmPo

That man from chains of wrath be freed,/Eternal peace to win. Give Peace, O God, the Nations Cry. John W. Norris. AH

That man, I wish him well. I wish him grass. A Removal from Terry Street. Douglas Dunn. FaBoMo; OxBC; PoL

That man in terror may learn once more to be/child of that hour when rock and ocean meet. Hatteras Calling. Conrad Aiken. BoNaP; NoAm; NOBA; TAP

That man is dead in sin, and life a gift.' Truth. William Cowper. NOCV

That man is God, however low-/Is man, however high. Young Democracy (excerpt). Bernard O'Dowd. PoAu 1-2

That Man is ready to defend/With Life his Country, or his Friend. Part of the 9th Ode of the 4th Book of Horace... Horace. OBVE

That man is you.   The Next Time You Were There.   Samuel Hazo.   FAZ

That man's long journey through the night/May not have been in vain.   Ecce Homo.   David Gascoyne.   ChMP; LiTM; NeBP; OBWP

That man's unwise will search for ill,/And may prevent it, sitting still.   To His Muse.   Robert Herrick.   OAEP

That man shall be both proud and happy to obey.   The Rights of Women.   William Cowper.   CBEP

That man to man the warld o'er,/Shall brothers be for a' that.   For a' That and a' That.   Robert Burns.   AnFE; CABA; CoMu; EnLit; FaBoBe; FaBoPV; FaFP; FaPoR; HBV 1-2; HBVY; LAuP; LiTB; MCCG; OAEL 1-2; OAEP; OHFP; TEP; UnTE; WBLP

That man will decipher/As an omen of his final hunger.   Cattle.   Peter Skrzynecki.   CBAP

That man will win some other day,/Who loses with a smile.   A Smile.   Anonymous.   BLPA; WBLP

That many a glorious age their captives were.   The Muses Elizium.   Michael Drayton.   AnAnS 2; OAEL 1-2

That many a life hath cost.   Arm, Arm, Arm, Arm!   John Fletcher.   EIL

That many people nowadays/Like hugaboo/To read.   When We Were Very Silly.   J.B. Morton.   FaBoPa

That mark thee now but pander to the/crowd!   El Blot Til Lyst.   William Morton Payne.   AA

That Marrowbone itch, it's a sight;/You have to scratch it day and night.   The Marrowbone Itch.   Anonymous.   OuSiCo

"That may be so, but you don't come in!"   Six Little Mice Sat Down to Spin.   Mother Goose.   HBV 1-2

That may breed love's delights?...   The Happy Countryman.   Nicholas Breton.   CH

That may breed true love's delights?   Pastoral.   Nicholas Breton.   ELP

That mean mean black snake/He won't bother/me no more/Mmmmmmmmmmmmmmmmmmm.   Black Snake.   John Lee Hooker.   BluL

That measures and is of itself the measure/Of works and hope and faith.   The Three Taverns: Out of Wisdom Has Come Love.   Edwin Arlington Robinson.   MoRP

That melodious old person of Bradley!   Limerick: "There was an old person of Bradley."   Edward Lear.   UnS

That men are gods, the blessed and the unblessed.   At the Museum.   John Malcolm Brinnin.   EyDe

That men make hotter hells than ever he did.   Lament of an Idle Demon.   R. P. Lister.   DBV; FiBHP; NOBL

That men may know we've been at Jesus' feet.   At His Feet.   Lis R. Carpenter.   BePJ

That men might not live?   The Known Soldier.   Kenneth Patchen.   WaaP

That men weep hearing it, and have no choice.   La Vita Nuova.   Dante Alighieri.   AWP

That men will get the toil and sweat, and the Ladies' Aid the Rest.   The Ladies' Aid.   Anonymous.   PoLf

That mendacious Old Person of Gretna.   Limerick: "There was an Old Person of Gretna."   Edward Lear.   OxBChV; VLP

That merges into the empty twinkling/Of the air and of the bright wallpaper.   Vuillard: "The Mother and Sister of the Artist."   W. D. Snodgrass.   CoAP

That mighty bulk of brain boiled when they burned him!).   The Fishes and the Poet's Hands.   Frank Yerby.   AmNP; PoNe

That millennia ago/had disappeared.   A Farewell to the Moon.   Ed Ochester.   MOON

That mind where thoughts float round/As geese do round a pond/And never get out.   The Upper Canadian.   James Reaney.   NOBC

That ministered to thee, is open still.   The Conqueror's Grave.   William Cullen Bryant.   AA

That mock the faded blue/Of your remoter heaven.   Children's Song.   R.S. Thomas.   BoC

That mock yir thrawan with their peace.   Whan the Hert Is Laich.   Sidney Goodsir Smith.   NeBP

That mocking tyrant in an instant rears/A wall between the sickle and the ears.   Hope.   Sir Richard Fanshawe.   CBEP; OBS

That moment when my soul/And body part!   Closing Prayer.   Johnstone G. Patrick.   TrPWD

That money makes the man.   There's Nae Place Like Otago Yet.   John Barr.   AnNZ

That money was all he had ever earned.   What's In It For Me?   Edgar A. Guest.   PoToHe

That month thereafter I am gay.   Medieval Norman Songs.   Anonymous.   AWP

That moonlight makes/so beautiful.   Birch Trees.   John Richard Moreland.   HBMV; HBVY; OHIP

That moony Old Person of Ickley.   Limerick: "There was an Old Person of Ickley."   Edward Lear.   CenHV; EvOK

That morbid Old Man of Vesuvius.   Limerick: "There was an Old Man of Vesuvius."   Edward Lear.   FaBoNo; GLGT; LiBL

That more than what they seem, they are.   Tribute on the Passing of a Very Real Person.   Anonymous.   PoToHe

That more things move/Than blood in the heart.   Night.   Louise Bogan.   UnPo

That morning ere Titan had thought to stir his feet.   The Vision.   Aogan O Rathaille.   NOBI

That Morning Herald that he'd bought/Forth from his breast, and read it through.   Peace.   Charles Stuart Calverley.   NBM

That morning when the storm winds swept the town.   Mighty Day.   Anonymous.   FSW

That mortifies and saves us.   Wellington Letter: XI.   Lauris Edmond.   OCNZ

That most ancient Briton of English beasts.   The Combe.   Edward ("Edward Eastaway") Thomas.   FM; GTBS-P

That most of all he wished himself John Doe.   Richard Roe and John Doe.   Robert Graves.   CMoP

That mounted morn and noon and eve on that first Thanks-/giving Day!   The First Thanksgiving.   Clinton Scollard.   MC; PAH

That mourns a man like thee.   On the Death of Joseph Rodman Drake.   Fitz-Greene Halleck.   AA; AmLP; GoTF; HBV 1-2; PAH; PoEL 1-5; TreFS

That mourns its joy and its joy's minister.   La Vita Nuova.   Dante Alighieri.   AWP

That move unceasing toward the gate of/Death.   Power.   Thomas Stephen Collier.   AA

That move unvexed to their mysterious end.   Suppliant.   Alan Sullivan.   CaP

That moves, is born,/& leads a life,/& gives it on.   The Language.   Anselm Hollo.   APU

"That moves the sun and the other stars."   At Dante's Grave.   Ezra Zussman.   VWA

...That much/I can take. It's all I want.   Lines to a Friend in Trouble.   W. S. Di Piero.   MAYP

That Mushroom—it is Him!   The Mushroom Is the Elf of Plants—.   Emily Dickinson.   DiPo; NePA

That music, remote, forlorn.   The Old Summerhouse.   Walter De la Mare.   CMoP; FaBoPP; FaBoRV; GTBS-P; MoPo

That must be said to them, to me/or anyone alive? What?/Love,/Abraham.   Letter.   Alexander Bergman.   TrJP

That mute as a moth with a torn wing,/lurches a path across the table.   The Quarrel.   Karen Swenson.   GrPl

That my friends may weep as much as they like.   Epitaph: "I was buried near this dyke."   William Blake.   FaBoEE

That my good lorde accept this ventrous verse,/Until my braines may better stuffe devise.   The Steele Glas.   George Gascoigne.   AAS

That my last sigh in peace may in His arms, be breathed!   To the Virgin Mary.   Petrarch.   CAW

That my life may please Him/Everywhere I go.   Holy Spirit, Lead Me.   Anonymous.   STF

That my love Marie/Might love me yet.   Lost For a Rose's Sake.   Anonymous.   AWP

That my particular current soon will reach/The unfathomable gulf, where all is still!'   The Excursion.   William Wordsworth.   OBRV

That my poor name may have the glory/To live remembered in your story.   To Groves.   Robert Herrick.   CaPo

That my proud life should be/Acceptable, delightful, to his ways.   Ballata of Love's Power.   Guido Cavalcanti.   LiTW

That nane can be sae dear to me/As my sweet lovely Jean!   Jean.   Robert Burns.   GTBS; GTBS-P; MCCG

That Nature wrought must unto dust be brought.   A Remembrance of My Friend Mr. Thomas Morley.   John Davies.   OBSP

That ne'er did wrang to thine or thee.'   Lament for Culloden.   Robert Burns.   CBEP; GTBS; GTBS-P; HBV 1-2; OBEV

That ne'er returns us to the fields of light.   The Spirit-Land.   Jones Very.   AmLP; HAP

That need endless talk-talk/To make them out.'   An Empty Threat.   Robert Frost.   RFM

That neither present time, nor years unborn/Could to my sight that heavenly face/restore.   Desideria.   William Wordsworth.   BLPL; GTBS; GTBS-P; OBEV

That nervous conscience amid the concessions/Is a haunting, haunted moon.   Far Rockaway.   Delmore Schwartz.   NoAm

That never again we could find each other.   We Cared for Each Other.   Heinrich Heine.   AWP

That never fails, nor stops to count the/cost.   Invocation for the New Year.   Margaret D. Armstrong.   STF

...That never had been robbed/But for our sloth and hesitancy.   Defeat of the Rebels.   Robert Graves.   WaP

That never really led to tomorrow.   Broken Home.   William Stafford.   NNaP

That night at Trafalgar!   The Dynasts.   Thomas Hardy.   MOS; WaaP

That night he slept—within the/Railway Arms!   Burglar Bill.   Christopher Anstey.   CenHV

...That night I eat them, boiled, with oil and vinegar. Early Discoveries. David Malouf. CBAP

That night of fever fierce and calamitous! The Ideal. Charles Baudelaire. SyP

That night she kissed his coral lips/How could she know the rest? Mary, Mother of Christ. Countee Cullen. PCh

That night which makes us all lie down the same? Ballade of the Grindstones. Judith Johnson Sherwin. SM

That ninety million think the same–including Eddie Guest. Mother Goose Up-to-Date. Louis Untermeyer. MoAmPo

That nobody roweth or steereth. Erith, on the Thames. *Anonymous.* FaBoPP; GBP

That none or all/Might disappear. The Leaf. John Williams. NePoAm-2

That none should mow the grass there/While so confused with flowers. Rose Pogonias. Robert Frost. MAmP

That not one grief remaineth. Of Death. Mary Herbert, Countess of Pembroke. EiL

That not the sun can wither; no,/Nor any tempest overthrow. St. Michael's Mount. John Davidson. HBV 1-2

That nothin' happens down this way. In Hardin County, 1809. Lulu E. Thompson. PoSC; StPo

That nothing but love/Can quite identify for sure. Some Tips on Watching Birds. Deatt Hudson. NYBP

That nothing, nothing will happen. Sleeping with One Eye Open. Mark Strand. NYBP; SM

That nothing there is ever killed or sold. Letter to the City Clerk. Frederick A. Wright. FaFP

That nought which lives should wholly lack/The things that are more excellent. The Things That Are More Excellent. William Watson. OHFP

That now are fall'n, Kate's known to have the pox. Of Kate's Baldness. John, of Hereford Davies. FaBoEE

That now, at any moment,/you may come, come, come. Longing. Rachel Korn. VWA

That now do seem as in a reace/Wi' air-birds to ha' vled. Slow to Come, Quick A-Gone. William Barnes. NOBV; VLP

That now grows brutal and heavy as a burned out star. The Peaceable Kingdom. Marge Piercy. TwCP

That now he sees him face to face, in hell. On a Puritan. Hilaire Belloc. FaBoEE

That now is tamed, and once was wild. Rapid Transit. James Agee. AnAmPo; MoAmPo; NAMP

That now to them dost all thy substance give. The Lost. Jones Very. MAmP; NOBA

That now your mouths are stopped and streaked with earth./Ho-o-wi-na, a-ye-a-a. The next scalp! Scalp Dance Song. *Anonymous.* WTO

That nun was Smaylho'me's Lady gay,/That monk the bold Baron. The Eve of Saint John. Sir Walter Scott. EnRP; PoEL 1-5

That of the heavens and earth is the maker. Except the Lord, That He for Us Had Been. Henry Ainsworth. AH

That old movie, your lives, while/mumbling here in the sun? Eclipses. Nancy Sullivan. TAP

That old night life, that sportin' life is killin' me. Sporting Life Blues. *Anonymous.* FSW

That old Sir J., in the kindest way,/Made me his Secretarry? Pink Dominoes. Rudyard Kipling. CenHV

That old starlight/On the earth again. Words and Music (excerpt). Samuel Beckett. BIrV

That ombliferous person of Crete. Limerick: "There was a young person of Crete." Edward Lear. FaBoNo

That on his shoulders he might carry him! Because He Is Young. Okura. AWP; LiTW

That on the banks of this delightful stream/We stood together. Lines Composed a Few Miles above Tintern Abbey. William Wordsworth. Prf

That on the seaventh, he can nor preach, or pray. Upon Parson Beanes. Robert Herrick. AnAnS 2

That once she cherished anything so fair. Dreaming of Cities Dead. Eleanor Rogers Cox. CAW

That once was mock turtle turned turtle. Limerick: "There was a young waitress named Myrtle." Oliver Herford. TDH

That once you had opened the valley's singing day. The Valley's Singing Day. Robert Frost. UnS

That one has children in order/to be forgiven! A Child's Christmas without Jean Cocteau. David Fisher. NPGG

That one is right whose natal faith/Doth guide him to the blest abode. Apostasy. Aus of Kuraiza. TrJP

That one is your dear mother. Mother's Love. Ross B. Clapp. WBLP

That one of all the rest shall be/The glory of my work and me. His Prayer for Absolution. Robert Herrick. AnAnS 2; EnL; EnLi 1-2; OxBoCh; SeCV 1-2; TrPWD; TRV

That one same Will which chooses the elect. Calvin in the Casino. Turner Cassity. NIP

That one small head could carry all he knew. The Deserted Village. Oliver Goldsmith. GLGT; TrGrPo

That only a halter/can alter/the middleclrass assitude. The Ass. Edwin Allan. PoPl

That only children listen to and ponder. World's Centre. Ruth Dallas. AnNZ

That only come out at night. The Girl with 18 Nightgowns. Gregory Orr. PoL

That only Death can earn! Now. Mary Barker Dodge. AA

That only the slightest repugnanace of our bodies/we no longer control could drag us back. July in Washington. Robert Lowell. LCAP; NaP; Prf

That only thine, thine is the saving name. Eternall Mover (excerpt). Sir Henry Wotton. TrPWD

That open on the day, fresh and willing/from having studied the heart. The Heart. David Ignatow. VWA

That other April,–/How far away! She Sews Fine Linen. Julia Johnson Davis. HBMV

That other does not smile. The Sunlit Vale. Edmund Charles Blunden. CBEP; MoVE

That other sun, the jealous coursing of the unrivalled/blood. The Marriage of a Virgin. Dylan Thomas. ErPo

That our own houses show as strange when we come back in the dawn! The Dykes. Rudyard Kipling. OBWP; VLP

That our quick day, from error free,/May live in Thine eternity. Hymn. John Haynes Holmes. TrPWD

That our thought may take her immediate in its embrace. Sonnetto VII: "Who is she that comes." Guido Cavalcanti. CTC

That out of thirty thousand men but few of you returned. The Battle of New Orleans. *Anonymous.* AmFP

That outside this store/Is another door Hiroshima Exit. Joy Kogawa. BrSi

That painting is no idol, 'tis too like. Don Juan. George Gordon, Lord Byron. ISi

That paints with gold the flowery mead,/Which blossoms in our way. Mother Dear, O! Pray for Me. *Anonymous.* AH

That pair have gone into the cave. Nishikigi: The Love-Cave. Seami Motokiyo. LiTW

That parched dry Lip, that fading Face,/That Thirst were all for me. His Are the Thousand Sparkling Rills. Frances Alexander. OxBI

That pardons poor drunkards, and crowns them above. John Adkins' Farewell. *Anonymous.* AmFP

That parts fam'd Trachis from th'Euboic shore. Philoctetes. Thomas Russell. LoBV

That pass through the cedars where/our old ones sleep/to tell us of their dreams We Are a People. Lance Henson. VoR

That Peggy and I agree. To couple is a custom. *Anonymous.* EG

That peine vs helpe ay to fle,/The wikkede fendes lore. Amen. Lullay, lullay. *Anonymous.* OxBoCh

That perfect pardon which is perfect peace. Divina Commedia. Henry Wadsworth Longfellow. AmPP; OxBA

That perhaps one day i can unfold/for my grandchildren Scrapbooks. Nikki Giovanni. CNA

That Phillida with Love's content/Is sworn the shepherds' queen. A Supplication. Nicholas Breton. OBSC

That picks out the climbing/Hidden Way. A Silver Lantern. Karle Wilson Baker. HBMV

That placid old person of Bar. Limerick: "There was an old person of Bar." Edward Lear. FaBoNo

That plain, that modest structure, promising/Bread to the hungry, to the weary rest. The Great St. Bernard. Samuel Rogers. OBTV

That Pobbles are happier without their toes. The Pobble Who Has No Toes. Edward Lear. AmMo; FaBoCh; FaBoCo; FaBoNo; HBV 1-2; HBVY; LBN; LoGBV; MaC; MoShBr; NA; OxBChV

That poetry always was/& always will be/as long as we live. Meanwhile. Joel Dailey. APU

...That/poetry, by which I lived? The Bear. Galway Kinnell. CAPP; CoAP; InPS; NNaP; RFM; TAP; VGW

That poets are not/sensible. Behaviorally. Anselm Hollo. APU

That point on the far/horizon, the last stop. No Signal for a Crossing. Rhoda Donovan. AMV-80

That ponderous, murderous burden of everyday. The Burden of Everyday. Buddhadeva Bose. LiTW

That poor Cupid have his vision/Back again? Love-Songs, At Once Tender and Informative. Samuel Hoffenstein. OBAL

That poor stutterer will disappoint/who gave him birth Elegy. Alan Loney. OCNZ

That power was once our torture and our lord. The Passions That We Fought With. Trumbull Stickney. NCEP

That prompts the passions of this strutting world. The Rustic at the Play. George Santayana. HBV 1-2; OBVV

That puts it not unto the Touch,/To win or lose it all. Montrose to His Mistress. James Graham. OxBS

That quiet waitcth for His Voice.   Aridity.   Michael (Katherine Bradley and Edith Cooper) Field.   BoC; OBMV; OxBoCh; TRV

That radiance illumines all this world.   Upanishads: Second Khanda.   *Anonymous.*   ILwL

That rather had to die in troth than live forsaken so.   The Lady Prayeth the Return of Her Lover Abiding on the Seas.   *Anonymous.*   EIL; GBL

That re-enters as the children spill from the open car doors.   Remembering the Automobile.   Deirdra Baldwin.   AmC

That read the corporate virtue strumpeted.   On a Baltimore Bus.   Charles G. Bell.   NePoAm

That red jag of a headland, to harbor.   Offshore Breeze.   Milton Acorn.   NeAC

That remarks the wider movement of its actual thought.   Venice Recalled.   Bruce Boyd.   NeAP

That ripens on the branches of my horns.'   The Bull.   Freda Laughton.   NeIP

That rise and glitter o'er the ambient tide.   The Alliance of Education and Govenment.   Thomas Gray.   CEP

That risk/is all there is.   Waiting.   Robert Creeley.   VGW

That romantic old person of Putney.   Limerick: "There was an old person of Putney."   Edward Lear.   TDH

...That rope/may now hang from some rotted fence.   Dobbin.   George Bowering.   NOBC

That rose slowly towards me, watching.   Pike.   Ted Hughes.   CMoP; FaBoMo; HAP; HeIP; InPS; LiTM; MAT; NCSH; NePoEA-2; NMP; OxBTC; SoSe

That's a lying woman/and a monkey man./Mmmmmmmmmmmmmmmmm.....   Pistol Slapper Blues.   Blind Boy Fuller.   BluL

That's a man's business!.../If I ever get it....   Drug Store.   John V. A. Weaver.   HBMV; YaD

"That's a moon."   Sketches of Harlem.   David Henderson.   NNP; PoNe

That's a poor share of wisdom, but it's all.   The Counsels of O'Riordan, the Rann Maker.   T. D. O'Bolger.   AnIV

That's a task far beyond him, methynx.   Limerick: "Consider the lowering Lynx."   Langford Reed.   CenHV

That's about the best-looking colt we ever had.   Unclaimed.   Florida Watts Smyth.   PH

That's all.   Death.   Mildred Jeffrey.   AMV-80

That's all right, mama/your troubles will/come some day   My Black Mama.   Son House.   BluL

That's all the explanation I find necessary.   Hunger.   Charles Simic.   NNaP

(That's all the spanish i know.)   Skirt Dance.   Ishmael Reed.   APU; FF

That's all you need to know.   Epigram: "Boys' cocks, Diodore."   Strato.   PeHV

That's also why I'm quiet/as an old shoe/happily wrinkled   Quiet.   Brian Swann.   AmPA

"That's certainly the case," said he.   Words for Music Perhaps.   William Butler Yeats.   AtBAP

That's corked with an old corn-cob.   Molasses River.   Richard Kendall Munkittrick.   OBCA

That's good. The sun will soon be rising.   Old King Cole.   Edwin Arlington Robinson.   HBV 1-2

That's heart-break, heart-break!   The Inverted Torch.   Edith Matilda Thomas.   AA

That's how he felt–that's how I feel.   Plain Talk.   William Jay Smith.   DBV; FiBHP; MoAmPo

That's how it goes with us.'   The Old Lady's Lament for Her Youth.   Francois Villon.   BoLoP

"That's how it is,' says Pooh.   Us Two.   A.(lan) A.(lexander) Milne.   OxBChV; TiPo

That's how they did it to her.   How They Killed My Grandmother.   Boris Slutsky.   VWA

That's how we got the microscope.   The Microscope.   Maxine W. Kumin.   QQQ

...That's it, just/the sound, and the imagination of the sound–a place.   Triphammer Bridge.   Archie Randolph Ammons.   NOBA

That's just the way with asses, just the way.   The Ass in the Lion's Skin.   Aesop.   AWP; LiTW

That's May Bennett, that's my baby.   Baby May.   William C. Bennett.   HBV 1-2

That's much too difficult. I quit.   Some Opposites.   Richard Wilbur.   OBCA

That's my best friend, my kid man,/the one that's kicking in my stall   Three Men.   Alice Moore.   BluL

That's my son! That's my son!   Elsa Wertman.   Edgar Lee Masters.   NoAm; OxBA

That's my song: a couple of mouthfuls of air,/a serenade, by bulblight.   O'Connor the Bad Traveler.   Peter Klappert.   FiCP

That's not my point, and where are we at.'   Liberal or Innocent by Definition.   James Philip McAuley.   NOAV

That's not/what/will calm me/no/that's not it.   Cradle Song.   Yona Wallach.   VWA

That's nothin', I'm thinkin', kin foller them things/In the way of surprisin' inventions but wings.   Broncho Versus Bicycle.   John Wallace (Jack) Crawford.   BPAW

–That's odd.   Short Song: "There was an old crow."   *Anonymous.*   OxNR

That's odd. I can hear you quite distinctly.   The After-Thought.   Stevie Smith.   OxBC

That's one of earth's most blessed things/They can't monopolize.   My Sort o' Man.   Paul Laurence Dunbar.   AmNP

That's one thing I never got enough of/In my business,/Or I wouldn't be here.   Birdie McReynolds.   Samuel Hoffenstein.   BXAP; NLV

That's our Fourth of July.   Listen to the People: Independence Day, 1941 (excerpt).   Stephen Vincent Benét.   PoSC

That's our style of funeral.   Ross's Poems.   Geoffrey Lehmann.   CBAP

That's she alone kind shepherd's boy,/Let us to Daffadill.   Gorbo and Batte.   Michael Drayton.   LoBV

(That's something I find hard to swallow.)   Limerick: "A big bull-dyke, surly and sallow."   *Anonymous.*   PeHV

That's the best cure for a little pussy cat.   Visitor.   *Anonymous.*   OxNR

That's the dream denied us in one-night stands of first/names only.   Homosexual Sonnets.   Kenneth Pitchford.   GP

That's the end of O'Donnell and forever say a prayer for him.   Clonmel Jail.   *Anonymous.*   BIrV

That's the fault of the puppy to whom it is tied.   A Wife.   Matthew Gregory Lewis.   DBV; PV

That's the First and Second Law of Thermodynamics.   First and Second Law.   Michael Flanders.   FaBoUs

That's the lady's corset string.   Street Chants: "Mother, mother what is that."   *Anonymous.*   ExPo

That's the life for a man!   Young Washington.   Arthur Guiterman.   OHIP; PoSC

That's the Marna of my soul,/Wander-bride of mine!   The Wander-Lovers.   Richard Hovey.   AA; HBV 1-2

That's the meaning of love in the soul.   The Meaning of Love.   *Anonymous.*   WTO

That's the new fatigue.   The Wall.   David Jones.   PoA

That's the price you pay raising the kind of bird/that flies.   Poem for My Mother.   Lowell Jaeger.   AMV-80

That's the sort they'll buy.   Choosing Shoes.   ffrida Wolfe.   BrR; SoPo; SUS; TiPo

That's the tale of the Moth and the Flame!   The Moth and the Flame.   George Taggart.   FSN; TreF

That's the tid i fa la truth.   The Derby Ram.   *Anonymous.*   FaBoNo; GBP

That's the true pathos and sublime/Of human life.   Epistle to Dr. Blacklock.   Robert Burns.   OBEC

That"s the way for Billy and me.   A Boy's Song.   James Hogg.   BSV; CH; FaPoR; HBV 1-2; HBVY; MoShBr; OBEV; OnUR; OxBChV; PoPle; WiR

...That's the way it is/with friends. We make certain choices.   Certain Choices.   Richard Shelton.   Psk

That's the way of June.   June.   Nora Hopper.   YeAr

That's the way the Polka goes.   My Cousin German Came From France.   *Anonymous.*   FaBoCh; LoGBV

That's the way they are.   Kindly Unhitch That Star, Buddy.   Ogden Nash.   LiTA; PoPl

"That's the way they eat soup in New York."   Limerick: "There was a young lady from Cork."   Ogden Nash.   TDH

That's the world.   Questions and Answers.   Doris Muhringer.   AMV-80

That's their story.   Freely Espousing.   James Schuyler.   ANYP; NeAP; NoP

That's to grow to a man/That's to lay me.   Song of the Cauld Lad of Hylton.   *Anonymous.*   GBP

That's to lay me.   The Ghost's Song.   *Anonymous.*   FaBoCh; LoGBV

That's to make him pace weel, pace/weel, pace weel.   John Smith, Fellow Fine.   *Anonymous.*   OxNR

That's very nice. He'll bless our enterprise.   Temporary Problems.   Larry Rubin.   AMV-80

That's what corruption does for you.   Honi Soit Qui Mal y Pense.   Ian Young.   PeHV

That's what gave me/This jolly red nose.   Prevarication.   *Anonymous.*   OxNR

That's what goes into a birthday cake!   The Birthday Cake.   Victoria Chase.   BiCB

That's what got me–to/face into the wind's teeth.   The Manoeuvre.   William Carlos Williams.   LOW; PCP

That's what happens when Blue Nuns/bail out./It's that simple.   With a Bottle of Blue Nun to All My Friends.   Madeline De Frees.   GP

That's what I'd do!   What Will You Do, Love?   Samuel Lover.   OnYI

That's what I said.   The Song of the Mad Prince.   Walter De La Mare.   AtBAP; EBEV; FaBoCh; GoJo; LoGBV; MoVE; NoAm; NOBE; OAEP; OxBChV

That's what I say,/love,/Mother   My Mother.   Robert Mezey.   NaP; SM

That's what it means, the flag we fly.   The Flag We Fly.   Aileen Fisher.   YeAr

...That's what it's come back for,/to set you on your way, gladly, with a hum– An approval. In a Motion. Laura Chester. NPGG

That's what little boys are made of. Snips and Snails and Puppydog Tails. *Anonymous.* TW

That's what perplexes me. A Tiger's Tale. John Bennett. TiPo

That's what Robin told me. What Robin Told. George Cooper. TiPo

That's what shepherds listened to in Arcadia/Before someone invented the radia. The Carnival of Animals (excerpt). Ogden Nash. UnS

–That's what they tell the eggs. A War. Randall Jarrell. DFF; OBSP

That's what we'd do,/When the moon came out. That's What We'd Do. Mary Mapes Dodge. OBCA

That's what we'll do with the baby-o. What'll We Do with the Baby-O? *Anonymous.* FSW

"That's what you get for scabbing on the S.P. Line." Casey Jones (Union). Joe Hill. FSW

That's what young women are made of. Natural History. *Anonymous.* OxNR

That's where I'd like to be. It Is Raining. Lucy Sprague Mitchell. BrR; SoPo; TiPo

That's where I'm a-goin' to be. Tom Joad. Woody Guthrie. TrAS

That's where we'll all be/One hundred years from now. On to the Morgue (with music). *Anonymous.* AS

That's why all our/lies and/covering over/are all so/very very/good. Mama Knows. Sharon Scott. JB

That's why he turns to you now for advice,/to your deep wisdom and understanding. I Have a Big Favor to Ask You, Brothers. Ziche Landau. VWA

"That's why I brought you home." The Little Road. Nancy Byrd Turner. TiPo

(That's why I have not traveled more.) The Unexplorer. Edna St. Vincent Millay. LOW; MoShBr; SUS

That's why I love the secret place,/The secret place of prayer! The Secret Place of Prayer. Georgia B. Adams. STF

That's why I'm writing this poem,/to sell for money. Writing for Money. Edward Field. PPJ

That's why I say, an American classic. American Classic. Louis Simpson. AmC

That's why the lady is a tramp! The Lady Is a Tramp. Lorenz Hart. OBAL

...That's why/they're all crusades. Quintana Lay in the Shallow Grave of Coral. Karl Shapiro. VGW

That's why we/ain't got nuthin He Cool, Baby. Rob Penny. PoBA

That sang this song of ours/with pistols and grenades. Tell Us No More. *Anonymous.* FSW

That sat with thy white lap full of nuts/Beneath the hazel tree. The Lapful of Nuts. Sir Samuel Ferguson. IrPN; VLP

That savage trinity warily watching. Patroling Barnegat. Walt Whitman. CBEP; LoBV; MOS; NePA; NoP

That says "yes" to the coming winter and a summoning odour of/balsam. Himalayan Balsam. Anne Stevenson. FaBoWP

That scarce his loosed limbs he able was to weld. Winter. Edmund Spenser. GN

That Science should skilfully mend what it skilfully shatters. Charing Cross. Cecil Roberts. HBMV

That scorn which is but a dream/Of the shepherd prouder than a king. It May Be. Max Jacob. PoPl

That search all the province, you'd find no man there is/So blessed as the Englishen Heer SECRETARIS Verses Written at The Hague. Ano 1696. Matthew Prior. OBTV

...That secret interior/In which all aging gods become their sons. The Sleeping Saint. Melvin Walker La Follette. CoPo

That seemed like a soft moon entrapped in the branches of/the forest. The Childhood of an Equestrian. Russell Edson. AmPA

That seems for all the world/as though in celebration. High Summer. Guy Rotella. AMV-80

That seems so hot, but is so hard and cold. The Jazz of This Hotel. Vachel Lindsay. ATP; PoPl

That sees things and not people. Dear Mother,/good-bye... Ballad: "Mother mine, Mother mine, what do you see?" Annemarie Ewing. NePoAm

That seize the spirit and the senses exquisite. Correspondences. Charles Baudelaire. SyP

That selfish, callous woman whom the English call "the Queen'. The English Queen. Henry Lawson. NOAV

That sent him out of the chandler's/shop. Tommy's Shop. *Anonymous.* OxNR

That separate rights are lost in mutual love. The Rights of Women. Anna Laetitia Barbauld. NOEC

That serene ardent glory/Which distinguishes the gods from mortals. Dionysus. Sophia de Mello Breyner Andresen. PBWP

That sets the soul on fire. Beauty. Peter Hille. AWP

That sets the wooden workhorse working here below. New York 1962: Fragment. Robert Lowell. NYP

That seven times the moon had come/And you were gone from me. Seven Times the Moon Came. Jessie B. Rittenhouse. HBMV

That sex does Venus most befriend,/That party best obtains its end.' The Judgement of Tiresias. Hildebrand Jacob. NOEC

That shakes the blossoms of my hoary hair!' Children of a Future Age. William Blake. CBEP

That shall be created from our chaos! Song for These Days. Patrick F. Kirby. GoBC

That she, a woman,/dared take on Pindar. Fragments. Corinna. PBWP

That she has a son, who has a friend/Who knows when the war is going to end! Source of News. *Anonymous.* GoTF; TreF

That she hath done, the motive of my paine;/Who whilst I love, doth kill me with disdaine. If So It Hap, This Of-Spring of My Care. Samuel Daniel. AAS

That she in peace may wake and pity me. Sleep, Angry Beauty. Thomas Campion. ElL; EnRePo; ErPo; FF; GTBS; HBV 1-2; NCEP; OBSP; TrGrPo

That she is thine, what can proclaim it more. To Sergius. Sir Charles Sedley. FaBoEE

That she may hark to love, and read this lesson often. The Faerie Queene. Edmund Spenser. OBSC

That she may sing Cuckoo!/Three months in the year. The Cuckoo Is a Merry Bird. *Anonymous.* PBBP

That she's your tootsey wootsey in The good old summer time. In the Good Old Summer Time. Ren Shields. BLSo; FSN; GoTF; TreF

That she should come to Oxford Street, and I be there to see! Yesterday in Oxford Street. Rose Fyleman. TiPo

That she that makes me sin awards me pain. Sonnets, CXLI: "In faith, I do not love thee with mine eyes." William Shakespeare. PoEL 1-5; TrGrPo

That she was sleeping and he was merciless. Girl Betrayed. Hedylos. LiTW

That she were mine, and might be sure/She should be while that life doth dure. That Time That Mirth Did Steer My Ship. Sir Thomas Wyatt. FCP; SiPS

That she will move from mourning into morning. Sonnet to My Mother. George Barker. FaFP; LiTB; MoAB; SeCePo; ViBoPo; WaP

That she will return in Love's low tongue/My vows as we wheel around. The Night of the Dance. Thomas Hardy. BrPo

That she wished me a wound far worse to staunch–/And not in the hand! One of the Principal Causes of War. Hugh" (Christopher Murray Grieve) MacDiarmid. OBSP

That she would have smiled and said, "Yes,"/if I had asked; and I didn't know. He Runs into an Old Acquaintance. Alden Nowlan. GOYP

That shede His blode for my redempcion! The Cherry Fair. *Anonymous.* FaBoRV

That shepherded the moonlit sheep/A hundred years ago. On Moonlit Heath and Lonesome Bank. Alfred Edward Housman. CMoP; SoSe

That shin'st thus in thy counterfeit! The Transfiguration. Robert Herrick. CaPo

That ship, that tree, and that same beast am I,/Whom ye doe wreck, doe ruine, and destroy. Amoretti, LVI. Edmund Spenser. AAS

That shoot great drops of gism through the sky. Graffiti. Edward Field. CoPo

That show, contain, and nourish all the world. Love's Labour's Lost. William Shakespeare. GBL

That sikerly it were my deth/Thy companie to lete. Snatches: "Me thinketh thou art so lovely." *Anonymous.* OxBM

That silence here is music there. A Soldier Poet. Rossiter Johnson. AA

That simple duty hath no place for fear. Abraham Davenport. John Greenleaf Whittier. AnNE; NoP

That since you would save none of me, I bury some of you. The Funeral. John Donne. ATP; AWP; BiP; BoLoP; CBEP; CoBE; DiPo; EBEV; EnLoPo; HeIP; InPo; LiTL; MBW 1-2; NAWM 1-2; NoP; OAEL 1-2; OBEV; PoPle; PoRA

That sit on tombstone for your mats. My Cats. Stevie Smith. FaBoNo

That sleep indeed were endless, even as death. Living Marble. Arthur William Edgar O'Shaughnessy. VLP

That sleeps and sleeps and won't wake up/when you need it. Morning Fog. Quinton Duval. AMV-81

That slew so cruelly/My lytell pretty sparowe. Anathema of Cats. John Skelton. PCat

That slid from the ocean without a sound. The Jellyfish. William Pitt Root. BoAnP

That "slow and sure goes far at last'. The Horse and the Mule. John Huddlestone Wynne. OxBChV

That slowly made me dry again. Ba Cottage. Andrew Young. OBSP

That small twinkling star/Is your little baby. The Moon. Eliza Lee Follen. HBV 1-2; HBVY

...That smile/we rode all the way to/Albuquerque on. She Was a Pretty Horse. Joy Harjo. TWSS

That so hath judged Babylon,/Immortal praise with one accord. London, Hast Thou Accused Me. Henry Howard, Earl of Surrey. AAS; FCP; OAEP

That so many rivers at once/Washed over you. The Stringer. James Brasfield. AMV-81

That so to-day what might have been,/To-morrow may appear. Evening Hymn (excerpt). George Macdonald. TrPWD

That softly, effortlessly/Slips the catch that opens the soul to love. The Contemplative. Sister M. Therese. MoRP

That solace to Thy last, worn steps on Calvary/Gently to give. The Unpetalled Rose. Saint, of Lisieux Therese. CAW

That some are like my own. I measure every grief I meet. Emily Dickinson. MoAB; MoAmPo

That some day would be today. I knew quite well that some day. Narihira (Ariwara no Narihira). LiTW

...That some delicious stew/Is cat instead of rabbit, you must answer, "Tant mi-eux"! To Henrietta, on Her Departure for Calais. Thomas Hood. OBTV; OxBChV

That some have grown prodigious fat,/That were prodigious lean! To a Noisy Politician. Philip Freneau. TAP

That some men, early or late, may listen? Letters to Live Poets. Bruce Beaver. CBAP

That some old peace I had forgotten/Is crying to come back again? By the Pool at the Third Rosses. Arthur Symons. FaBoPP

That some wool in our ears/Would really be more apropos. You Read Us Your Verse. Martial (Marcus Valerius Martialis). DBV

That someone could love us,/seeing us. To the Man Who Watches Spiders. Siv Cedering Fox. LTB

That someone is condoning lust,/drugs, and a merry life. Marking Time. Peter Steele. NOAV

That something left behind in their rooms/Won't look the same when they return. The Band. Carl Dennis. AMV-80

...That something needs saving.../And the book dissolves. The Gypsy Bible. Julian Tuwim. VWA

That sometimes show what's left of me! Narcissus: To Himself. David Galler. PoA

That soothing fountain/outpouring/from her side. This Child Is the Mother. Gloria C. Oden. BlSi

That sought our Pearles, and div'd to find/Such pretious perils for mankind! The Consolation of Philosophy. Boethius. OBVE

That sours a doubtful earth,/the stars commemorate. A Time to Dance: The Flight. C. Day-Lewis. MoVE

That sparkles warm in Sansovine. Bacchus in Tuscany (excerpt). Francesco Redi. AWP; OBVE

That speaks the words of life so pure and fair! The Quiet Hour. Louise Hollingsworth Bowman. BLRP

That spits on night's/conditioned surrender. Higher Love. Jeff Wright. APU

That Spring is dead, that Love is slain? Anticipation. John Byrne Leicester Warren, Lord De Tabley. ELP

That springs and parches in the self-same hour. Fading Beauty. Giambattista Marino. AWP

That springs and parcheth in one short hour! Enjoy Thy April Now. Samuel Daniel. EIL; ELP

That stad is in perplexite. Quen Alysandyr Our King Was Dede. Anonymous. AtBAP

That sticks to my bosom/Like you? Susan Van Dusan. Anonymous. ABF

That stiffens quietly to quartz,/Upon her amber shoe. I know a place where summer strives. Emily Dickinson. NePA

That still I praised with all my might/The wondrous works of God. The Epitaph. Katharine Tynan Hinkson. WGRP

That still my Syrinx' lips I kiss. Pan's Song. John Lyly. ELP; OBSC; ViBoPo

That still the reason was not. There Was a Crimson Clash of War. Stephen Crane. UnPo

That stonge myn hert ful stray atount,/And ever the lenger, the more and more. Pearl. Anonymous. OxBM

That stop, stop, go. Twentieth-Century Blues. Kenneth Fearing. CMoP

That stores a childhood/crushed to smithereens. Glenn Miller's Music Is a Trunk. Carmen Valle. InW

That story. Cinderella. Anne Sexton. InPS

That Strangest is of all, yet brought to pass. The Salutation. Thomas Traherne. AtBAP; InvP; NOCV; NoP; OBS; OxBoCh; SeCP; SeCV 1-2

That strike mine eyes, but not my heart. Clerimont's Song. Ben Jonson. BoLiVe; LoBV; OAEL 1-2; PAI; PPP; SeCP; SeCV 1-2

That strike mine eyes, but not my heart. The Silent Woman: Clerimont's Song. Ben Jonson. PoPle; TrGrPo

That, struggling through the western sky, have won/Their pensive light from a departed sun! Decay of Piety. William Wordsworth. TrCP

That Studebaker. Mothers-in-Law. Robert Sward. CoPo

That such have lived,/Certificate for Immortality. That such have died enable us. Emily Dickinson. AA

That suggestive young lady of Milton. Limerick: "There was a young lady of Milton." Anonymous. NA

That suits me, I'll do it for free. Smoking Drugs with Strangers. George Bowering. NeAC

That sullen mixture shall at once declare/Winds, rain, and storms, and elemental war. Georgics. Virgil (Publius Vergilius Maro). FaBoUs

That sum tyme ressoun may yow bind,/For to To the Merchantis of Edinburgh. William Dunbar. FaBoPP; OxBS

That summer evening long ago/A-sitting on a gate. The White Knight's Song. Lewis (Charles Lutwidge Dodgson) Carroll. EnLi 1-2; FaBoCh; FaBoCo; FaBoNo; HAP; InPS; LoGBV; NOBE; NOBL; NoP; OAEL 1-2; PAI; VLP

That Summer seemed in love with idle days. Loch Ossian. Syd Scroggie. PoSH

That surrounds Montecito like the echo of a scream. In Montecito. Randall Jarrell. CoAP; MAT; NoP; NYBP; VGW

That surrounds us,/singing. Letters to Walt Whitman. Ronald Johnson. VGW

That susceptible man of Girgenti. Limerick: "There was an old man of Girgenti." Edward Lear. FaBoNo

That sway from mood to mood the willing/mind. The Poet. William Cullen Bryant. AA; AP; MAmP

That swayed and sang/when the wind passed through. A Sacred Grove. Fran Winant. BrRo

That sweeps the grass and is gone. Two Clouds. Lawrence Raab. AMV-80

That sweet accord is seldom seen. Throughout the World. Sir Thomas Wyatt. CBEP; ELU; FCP; MAT; OBSP

That sweetly soothe the Saviour's woe. 'Tis Midnight and on Olive's Brow. William B. Tappan. AH

That switched his slim legs like a hula skirt. The Huckster's Horse. Julia Hurd Strong. GoYe

That takes at last the bitter sting/Of day's keen pain away. A Winter Twilight. Arlo Bates. AA

That takes his ayse/As he surveys/This Cristial Exhibition. The Crystal Palace. William Makepeace Thackeray. InMe

That takes the cake/For a grand gigantic thunderous tragic exit. The Great Lakes Suite. James Reaney. WHW

That takes those dangerous chances/For this little lump of coal. That Little Lump of Coal. Anonymous. AmFP

That takes us all and under like that/grass. A Walk in the Country. Galway Kinnell. NePoAm

That talk shifts the cycle of the scenes of kings? Converstion with Three Women of New England. Wallace Stevens. NePA

That taste like dust. The Magical Mouse. Kenneth Patchen. LOW; SO

That tell us solemn secrets of ourselves. Dreams. Henry Timrod. AmePo

That the bird has roused the god-with-pointed-/ears? Rural Legend. Mary Elizabeth Osborn. NePoAm

That the bishops, the bishops did throw out the bill. Upon the King's Voyage to Chatham.... Anonymous. APAS

That the block of ice which binds us/binds us both. The Jungle. Diane Di Prima. PoM

That the crown of love is...to be in at the death. Wisdom. Padraic Fallon. OnYI

That the cry FIRE burst from its heart/as its speech. The Offended. Anne Hebert. BoWoP

That the Dawn and the Day is coming, and forth/the Banners go. The Day is Coming. William Morris. EnLi 1-2; OAEP; WGRP

That the Devil had been ordered to let Andy Regan out/For the steeplechase on Father Riley's horse! Father Riley's Horse. Andrew Barton ("Banjo") Paterson. NOAV

That the dogs may have no trouble in dragging him out. Epitaph of Nearchos. Ammianus. WeW

That the earth falls asunder, being old. On Refusal of Aid between Nations. Dante Gabriel Rossetti. CoBE; EBEV; LoBV; VLP

That the end has happened to all/Of the whole of the Clan Discobbolos? Mr. and Mrs. Discobbolos. Edward Lear. BLPL

That the Female of Her Species is more deadly than the Male. The Female of the Species. Rudyard Kipling. BLPA; FPL; HBV 1-2; TreFS

That the German is not a Hun. The Labors of Hercules. Marianne Moore. AnAmPo; OxBA

That the grasshopper feeds on dew. Thinking of a Master. Richard Church. HaMV

That the great work not falter but go on. A Fable of the War. Howard Nemerov. NePoEA; OBWP

That the guy's only doing it for some doll. Guys and Dolls. Frank Loesser. OBAL

That the home in which we dwell is hers. The Angora. Jim Gerard. AMV-80

That the king enjoys his own again. When the King Enjoys His Own Again. Martin Parker. FaBoCh; OxBoLi

That the lady of light is lovely and returns/regardless, uncaring, like the grass. Winter Solstice Poem. Diana Scott. BrRo

That the lines of their lives/were sewn from a tougher fabric/than the son had previously known. That Day. David Kherdian. SaC

That the Lord He was born in a dark and cold byre. The Feast o' Saint Stephen. Ruth Sawyer. OBCP; OHIP

That the lore of comrades, the honor of arms,/Have not yet perished from earth. Miles Keogh's Horse. John Milton Hay. PAH; PoOW

That the moon shines. Two Figures in Dense Violet Light. Wallace Stevens. MoAB; MoAmPo

That the music had somehow got mixed with the whole. A Fable for Critics. James Russell Lowell. AnNE; NOBA

That the night is to long. Snatches: "The nightingale singes." Anonymous. OxBM

That the poor Babe in homely rags and stable/Is the Lord God. For Us No Night Can Be Happier. Nicolaus Zinzendorf. AH

That the rage had gone out of/their bones in one mad dance. The Horse. Philip Levine. CoAP

That the right man lay in the dust. After Goliath. Kingsley Amis. NePoEA-2; NOBL; OxBTC; PoCh

That the risen Christ should be risen. Don'ts. D. H. Lawrence. LiTB; LiTM; NoAm; OxBoLi

That the rocks will harp on for ever, and my Love me never be/heard. Love Me! Stevie Smith. OBSP

That the rush hour/of their birth/is over,/over,/over!/? Out of Question & Mind... Noah Mitchell. LFAC

That the salt winds which scattered us blow softer. Elegy on My Father. Allen Curnow. AnNZ

That the sun rose in the west. Come All You Fair and Tender Ladies. Anonymous. FSW

That the time is bringing in with the bills. Christmas Bills. Joseph Hatton. OBCP

That the time is nearing/Which will see/All men free,/Tyrants disappearing. Hanukkah Hymn. Anonymous. GoTF; TreFT

That the uttermost peoples, hearing,/Shall hail Thee crowned King. All the World. Anonymous. TrJP

That the vain, the ambitious and the highly sexed/Are the natural prey of the incarnate Christ. A Letter to John Donne. C. H. Sisson. NOCV

That the waters of Babylon should no longer flow,/And men see light. Super Flumina Babylonis. Algernon Charles Swinburne. AnFE; MaVP; OBVV; PoEL 1-5; VLP

That the way of this clay be upward/above the dust. To Our Lady, the Ark of the Covenants. Raymond E. F. Larsson. ISi

That the will to survive/Is a pivot of pain. Return. Adele Naude. ACV

That the word the vessel brings/Is the word they wish to hear. Letters. Ralph Waldo Emerson. OBSP

That the world may be blest in the Saxon Race! The Anglo-Saxon Race. Martin Farquhar Tupper. PeD

...That the young behold/With envy, what the Old Man hardly feels. An Old Man. William Wordsworth. FaBoCh; LoGBV

That their cheeks got a permanent puff. Limerick: "There was an old cat named Macduff." J. G. Francis. TDH

That their descent from such a calorie/Accounts for their genius and love of drink. Pride of Ancestry. Robert Frost. OBAL

That them two bucks will grow up wild as/sassafras patches? In the Corn Land. Quentin R. Howard. TAT

That there are fifty roads to Town,/And rather more to Heaven. The Chaunt of the Brazen Head (excerpt). Winthrop Mackworth Praed. OBSV

That there dorg had got that inseck in the bottle. Daley's Dorg Wattle. W. T. Goodge. GDP; PoAu 1-2

That there is more to life/Than increasing its speed. Slow Me Down, Lord! Orin L. Crane. GoTF; TreFT

That there my heart and joy may rest,/though here in flesh I be. Though Here in Flesh I Be. Philip, Earl of Arundel Howard. CoBE

That there shall be a day of Dome. The Sea Marke. John Smith. SCAP

That there shall neuer be open warres/kept in my land/Whilest peace kept that there may/bee.' Hugh Spencer's Feats in France (A version). Anonymous. ESPB

That there Thou hast more fully then requir'd/Or understood could bee whilst sin annoy Upon the Decease of Mrs. Anne Griffin... John Fiske. SCAP

That there was my/Immortality! The Crib. Christopher Morley. BiCB

That there was not a single hour/We might have kissed, and did not kiss! Heart of My Heart. Anonymous. HBV 1-2

That there was somewhat in their way of going/Put doom upon my tongue and bade me utter. Tales from a Family Album. Donald Justice. NePoEA-2

That these are whose–but whose are these?/On Friday– Lines Written by a Bear of Very Little Brain. A.(lan) A.(lexander) Milne. FaBoNo

That these be brought into the fold/In Jesus' Name we pray. Prayer for Neighborhood Evangelism. Annetta Jansen. STF

That these may be thy Praise, and my Joy too. Silex Scintillans. Henry Vaughan. AnAnS 1

That these things shall/Be added unto thee. Work. Kenyon Cox. PGD

That these will not be needed/By those who are properly in love. Some Kisses from the Kama Sutra. Hugo Williams. BoLoP

That they can hardly gather one plum more. O Love, how thou art. Margaret Cavendish, Duchess of Newcastle. EnLoPo

That they have no heavenly Father/Such as cares for you and me. Overheard in an Orchard. Elizabeth Cheney. BLRP; TRV

That they may have, in sweetly-breathed/air,/Their immortality! Sweets That Die. Langdon Elwyn Mitchell. AA

That they may say, when I am dead/Here lies bold Robin Hood.' Robin Hood's Death. Anonymous. FaBoBa; ViBoFo

That they may think they see in me/Another crop of golden corn! Flying Blossoms. William Henry Davies. BrPo

That they may upset the words which have been spoken. Eastward I Stand, Mercies I Beg. Anonymous. EaLo

That they may weep. The Thousand and One Nights: Her Rival for Aziza. Anonymous. AWP

That they might sing with mery hert/This song with us in fere. Sometime I Loved. Anonymous. OxBM

That they never in the world would make a pile. The Fools of Forty-Nine. Anonymous. CoSo

That they our light may share. A Cry for Light. Anonymous. BLRP

That they settled it by blows. A Rub. John Banister Tabb. OBAL

That they shall be in touch with thee. Pray for the Dead. Arthur Wentworth Hamilton Eaton. AA

That they should harbour where their lord would be.' The Two Gentlemen of Verona. William Shakespeare. CTC

That they would look at one another. The Grand Guignols of Love. Michael Benedikt. AmPA

That they would not attack after dark. The Indians on Alcatraz. Paul Muldoon. CIP

"That things are xo worse, O my sire!" That Things Are No Worse, Sire. Helen Hunt Jackson. OHIP

That things with no legs should pretend to be frogs. Some Fishy Nonsense. Laura E. Richards. SoPo; TiPo

...That this/Accused thing, this Achan in our camp,/May be removed. Lines. Mary Ada, Sister. BlSi

That this eye not be folly's loophole/But giver of due regard. The Eye. Richard Wilbur. FiCP

That this foul deed shall smell above the earth/With carrion men, groaning for burial. Julius Caesar. William Shakespeare. TreFS

That this is a land/which has been bright with magic Three Poems for the Indian Steelworkers in a Bar... Joseph Bruchac. CDW

That this is an ocean because there isn't any land on any/other side. Eight Miles South of Grand Haven. Dave Kelly. AMV-80

That this is blessing, this is life. The Kingdom of God. Richard Chenevis Trench. WBLP

That this is the way/we live now The Way We Live Now. Robert Patrick Dana. AMV-80

That this my life may be as short to me/As are the days of sweet Zenocrate. The Bloody Conquests of Mighty Tamburlaine (excerpt). Christopher Marlowe. WHA

That this, our holy matin light,/May guide us thrugh the busy day. Thou Bounteous Giver of the Light. Saint Hilary of Arles. BePJ

That this sette on youire booke behinde. Snatches: "Who that lust for to looke." Anonymous. OxBM

That this thy WANT may be prepared/To meet the Judgment Day. The Wants of Man. John Quincy Adams. OBAL

That those conditions must endure,/Which, wanting, I myself should miss. The Angel in the House. Coventry Patmore. VLP

That those who know her, know her less/The nearer her they get. What Mystery Pervades a Well! Emily Dickinson. MAmP

That those who loved you best despised you most. Discovery. Hilaire Belloc. DBV; OBSP; ViBoPo

That those who mock might find a better way! The Negro Soldiers. Roscoe Conkling Jamison. BANP

That those who shook them must be dancing. Sleigh Bells at Night. Elizabeth Jane Coatsworth. SiSoSe

That thou again the same severe/Revenge for the same Crime would'st prove. Basia, VIII. Johannes Secundus. OBVE

That thou alone in sleeplessness wast found/To comfort me. Insomnia. John Banister Tabb. TrPWD

That thou and I henceforth may be at peace! He Asketh Absolution of God. Book of the Dead. AWP

That thou be beryd in my brest and bryng me to blysse. A Song of the Passion. Richard Rolle of Hampole. OxBoCh

That thou doo runne no longer at large. Charm for Bleeding. Anonymous. FaBoUs

That thou hast had, lo causeless,/To Cupido the recheless. The House of Fame: Jove's Eagle Carries Chaucer into Space. Geoffrey Chaucer. OxBM

That thou hast sweetness to bestow!   A Spray of Honeysuckle.   Mary Emily Bradley.   AA

That thou may come to everlasting life,/Take to thy minde revertere.   Turn Again.   *Anonymous.*   OxBM

That thou mayest feel Him near alway,/For this is bliss!   A New Year Wish.   *Anonymous.*   BLRP

That Thou mayst answer all my need–/Yea, every bygone prayer.   That Holy Thing.   George Macdonald.   HBV 1-2; OBEV; OBVV; TrPWD; TRV

That thou mayst fit thy self against thy fall.   Church-Monuments.   George Herbert.   AnAnS 1; CABA; ForPo; HAP; JCP; NOCV; NoP; OAEL 1-2; QFR

That thou mayst shake the superflux to them,/And show the heavens more just.   King Lear.   William Shakespeare.   PPON

That thou might'st but tread on me.   The Wish.   Thomas Stanley.   AWP

That Thou, my Lord, my God, art love.   Hope Springing Up.   John Wesley.   BePJ

That thou remember them, some claim as debt,/I think it mercy, if thou wilt forget.   If Poisonous Minerals.   John Donne.   LiTB; UnPo

That thou shalt be a fitting messenger/To carry hope to all the sons of men.   Land of My Heart.   William Dudley Foulke.   PAL

That though I wake or sleep/I turn and toss?   Songs of Ch'en.   Confucius.   CTC

That, though we saw–we saw not her.   Zalka Peetruza.   Ray Garfield Dandridge.   BANP; PoBA

That thoughts enflamed with such heavenlie muse/the coldest ice of feare may not refuse.   Sonnet I.   William Alabaster.   AnAnS 1

That threats my eyeballs with extinction dire!   On a Piece of Unwrought Pipeclay.   John Frederick Bryant.   NOEC

That thrills the wanderer of that trackless way?   Song of the Corsairs.   George Gordon, Lord Byron.   EtS

That through long winter nights swings in the storm.   Metamorphoses of the Vampire.   Charles Baudelaire.   ErPo

That through my grassy grave/Will rack my haunted brain.   In a Dream.   John Millington Synge.   SyP

That through the darkness quivered/with those perceiving eyes.   On the Threshold.   Karl Kraus.   TrJP

That through the hall bemocked the lost year's/wrong!   The Earthly Paradise.   William Morris.   VLP

That thu hast slawe good Robin/And Gandelin his knave.'   Robin and Gandelein.   *Anonymous.*   OxBM

That thus the watery realm cannot contain/The joy they breathe?   The Mysterious Music of Ocean.   *Anonymous.*   EtS

That tie up my bonny brown hair.   What Can the Matter Be?   *Anonymous.*   OxNR

That Time and Space are both Acute/When dropping in a parachute!   Relativity.   Kathleen Millay.   QQQ

That time frames miniatures on every hill.   These People.   Howard McKinley Corning.   AnAmPo

That time leave us/Words, loves.   Graphemics (excerpt).   Jack Spicer.   VGW

That time's whole later hush would speak farewell?   Sonnets of a Portrait Painter.   Arthur Davison Ficke.   AnAmPo

That time (when truly understood)/Is the most precious earthly good.   Fable XIII: Plutus, Cupid, and Time.   John Gay.   EiCP

That tinkle in the wither'd leaves below...   The Robin in Winter.   William Cowper.   BoAnP

...That tiny image/could smash the atom of space and time.   A Backwards Journey.   P.K. Page.   WHW

That 'tis a house, but not a dwelling.   On Blenheim House.   Abel Evans.   CBEP; OBEC

That to both kingdoms we might/then/Say Amen.   Carol: "Now is the world withdrawn all in silence and night."   Howard Nemerov.   TrCP

That to hear him speak all degrees do disdain.   The "Gloria Patri."   John Heywood.   ACP

That to hirself she sayde: "Who yaf me drinke?"   Troilus and Criseyde.   Geoffrey Chaucer.   OxBM

That to sit alone with my conscience/Will be judgment enough for me.   Conscience.   Charles William Stubbs.   BLPA

That to the cottage, as the crown/Brought tidings of salvation down.   Marmion.   Sir Walter Scott.   GN

That to which we link ourselves must/die.   Strangers Are We All upon the Earth.   Franz Werfel.   TrJP

That to yourself ye most assured are?   Amoretti, LVIII.   Edmund Spenser.   AAS; EnRePo

...That toad you heard is I.   The Toad.   Tristan Corbiere.   SyP

That tomorrow a new walk is a new walk.   Corsons Inlet.   Archie Randolph Ammons.   CoAP; NoAm; NOBA; NoP; PPP

That, too,/was white.   Song in White.   Anne Le Dressay.   AMV-80

That took a morning's work/Were waste of time.   Forebears.   Monk Gibbon.   NeIP

That tough luck has sunk me/and the rats is getting in my hat   Tin Cup Blues.   Blind Lemon Jefferson.   BluL

"That train's quite like an old familiar friend," one feels.   A Local Train of Thought.   Siegfried Sassoon.   AtBAP

That tranquil old person of Hove.   Limerick: "There was an old person of Hove."   Edward Lear.   FaBoNo

...That truth should defer/To beauty. It was not granted.   Petition.   R. S. Thomas.   FaBoMo

That truth to keep, that life to win,/Whose joys eternal flow.   Thou Art the Way.   George Washington Doane.   AH

That turned all five fingers/to grease or black ink or ashes.   Something Has Fallen.   Philip Levine.   LCAP

That turns slowly, triumphantly, swiftly to God.   The Triumph of Doubt.   John Peale Bishop.   EaLo

That turns the natural/Into supernal.   Lilies.   Padraic Colum.   NePoAm

That two Eds are better than one?   Limerick: "When twins came, their father, Dan Dunn."   Berton Braley.   TDH

That under the enfeebled stars/They may feel happy and at home.   Various Wakings.   Vincent Buckley.   PoAu 1-2

That understanding will flash through the arrested mind.   Rededication.   Emanuel Litvinoff.   WaP

That undoubtedly are heard unconfused through/thin walls.   Man and Woman.   Don L. Lee.   NeAC

That uneasy Old Man of the West.   Limerick: "There was an old man of the West."   Edward Lear.   EBEV

That unfortunate Man of Peru.   Limerick: "There was an old man of Peru."   Edward Lear.   EBEV

That unhappy Old Man in a boat.   Limerick: "There was an old man in a boat."   Edward Lear.   EBEV; FaBoNo; HBV 1-2; WiR

That unpleasing Old Person of Bromley.   Limerick: "There was an Old Person of Bromley."   Edward Lear.   NBM

That unseen, still, as from above,/Gives love.   The Strongest.   Yehoash.   TrJP

That unto us and others it may be/Honour hereafter to be laid by thee.   Elegy on Shakespeare.   William Basse.   CBEP

That upward goes, shows Rose knows those bows' woes!   A Nocturnal Sketch.   Thomas Hood.   FaBoCo; FiBHP; NBM

That vagrant never so transparent staggering around the/neighborhood.   Washing Windows.   Peter Wild.   Str

That vainly weeping lovers call/Repentance, or Regret.   The Three Arrows.   Edward Fitzgerald.   OBVV

That vampire Conger eel.   The Conger Eel.   Patrick MacGill.   OnYI

That verdant hill, and silver stream,/Divide my love and me.   Song: "How pleas'd within my native bowers."   William Shenstone.   OBEC

That very retiring old oyster.   Limerick: "There was an exclusive old oyster."   Laura A. Steel.   TDH

That Virtue but that body grant to us.   Astrophel and Stella, LII.   Sir Philip Sidney.   NoP; SiPS

That, Virtue, thou thyself shalt be in love.   Astrophel and Stella, IV.   Sir Philip Sidney.   AAS; SiPS

That wait upon the car of noiseless Night.   Idylls.   Theocritus.   AWP

That waiteth for me.   A Summer Night.   Elizabeth Stoddard   AA

That walked among the ancient trees.   The Bard.   William Blake.   TRV; WGRP

That wand'reth lightly.   David and Bethsabe.   George Peele.   AtBAP; ATP; ExPo

That warms the hands of a cold God.   About an Allegory.   Walter Conrad Arensberg.   AnAmPo

That wars to finish hatreds have undone!   Rain Inters Maggiore.   Alfred Kreymborg.   AnAmPo

That was a child; and he was/Change.   City Songs.   Mark Van Doren.   NYBP

"That was a Piedmontese! and this is the Court of the King."   A Court Lady.   Elizabeth Barrett Browning.   BeLS; HBV 1-2

That was all the "Thank you"/He knew how to say.   Baby's Breakfast.   Emilie Poulsson.   HBV 1-2; HBVY

That was an evil thought that her death she wrought.   The Brut.   Layamon.   MeEV

That was blac and that was broun.   Snatches: "Ich wille bere to washen doun i the toun."   *Anonymous.*   OxBM

...That was done in the Dark Ages.   Hi-Fashion Girl.   Elaine Equi.   APU

That was in summer, some time before he died.   The Soldier in the Park.   Elizabeth Riddell.   CBAP

That was love but I kept on traveling   Mary Desti's Ass.   Frank O'Hara.   ANYP

That was my first disappointment with the US Mails.   Backing into the Fan Mail (Unreceived).   Dick Gallup.   APU

That was my first experience on the Miramichi.   The Winter of '73.   *Anonymous.*   ShS

That was my heart you heard/Leaping under the willows.   Neither Spirit Nor Bird.   *Anonymous.*   AWP; PG

That was my ticket to come in.   Back to Dublin.   R. A. D. Ford.   CaP

That was not a reminder of the end.   Sonnet: Death Warnings.   Francisco Gomez de Quevedo y Villegas.   AWP

(That/was someone else's idea).   It's No Good.   Ian Young.   NeAC

That was summer.   That Was Summer.   Marci Ridlon.   NTCP

That was the black winter when I came/Into my own.   Tarantula or the Dance of Death.   Anthony Hecht.   CoAP

...That was the end, and/what a crazy image of love.   Kirk Lonegren's Home Movie Taking Place Just North of Prince George...   Sharon Thesen.   NOBC

That was the end of his work in the world.   Beowulf.   *Anonymous.*   AnOE

That was the place he was really moving from.   1614 Boren.   Richard Hugo.   LCAP

That was the righteous Virgin, which of old/Lived here on earth, and plenty made abound.   August.   Edmund Spenser.   GN

That was the Song–the Song for me!   O Nightingale! Thou Surely Art.   William Wordsworth.   AtBAP; HBV 1-2; PBBP

That was the way/He used to play.   Liszt.   Edmund Clerihew Bentley.   UnS

...That was then.   That Was Then.   Isabella Gardner.   GP

"That was Theodore Roosevelt..."   Zolgotz.   *Anonymous.*   AmFP

That was thy mistress, best of gloves.   The Glove.   Ben Jonson.   ElL

"That was young owl. He don't know!"   Alibi.   Zoe A. Tilghman.   BPAW

That we again may quaff his wine,/Again collect our jovial crew.   Stanzas Occasioned by the Ruins of a Country Inn.   Philip Freneau.   OxBA

That we, all children of the Spouse,/May live as brethren in Thy house.   England's Prayer.   William Blundell of Crosby.   GoBC

That we all may sing for aye,/Hallelujah!   Resurrection Hymn.   Michael Weiss.   BePJ

That we are ruined by the thing we kill.   Australia 1970.   Judith Wright.   CBAP

That we are soldiers for our Lord/Beneath His flag unfurled.   It's Wonderful.   Walter E. Isenhour.   STF

That we are to you all as the manifest Godhead that/speaks in prophetic Apollo?   The Birds.   Aristophanes.   AWP

That we ARE to you all as the manifest godhead that/speaks in prophetic Apollo?   Grand Chorus of Birds.   Algernon Charles Swinburne.   PoEL 1-5

That we both safely saw and lived thy Scene.   To the Memory of Ben Johnson (excerpt).   Jasper Mayne.   OBS

That we by easy steps may rise/Through all the joys on earth to those above.   Written in a Lady's Prayer Book.   John Wilmot, Earl of Rochester.   BoLoP

That we cannot pause to thank Him/For the blessings of today.   Are We Thankful?   *Anonymous.*   STF

That we climb the swaying ladder/to God's house.   The Hours.   Susan Tichy.   MAYP

That we commend your spirit to His care.   To Scott.   Winifred M. Letts.   PoLf

That we could not flee from Thee anywhere,/We fled to Thee.   God Our Refuge.   Richard Chenevix Trench.   EBCP; GoTF; OxBoCh; TreFT

That we do not know what is.   Letter to a Young Poet.   George Barker.   ChMP

That we escape, Redemption comes by thee.   To Julia, the Flaminica Dialis, or Queen-Priest.   Robert Herrick.   CaPo

That we had rather not with Him/But with each other play.   God is indeed a jealous God.   Emily Dickinson.   NOBA

That we have wrought him, stone-deaf and stone-blind.   February Afternoon.   Edward ("Edward Eastaway") Thomas.   NoAm

That we his Priests should all absolve.   The Masque of the Inner-Temple and Gray's Inne.   Francis Beaumont.   OBS

That we love and need her/World without end.   Identity.   Sister Mary Helen.   GoBC

That we may a' gang in gladness to our ain countree.   My Ain Countree.   Mary Lee Demarest.   HBV 1-2; TRV; WGRP

That we may finde the same Powers on the Main,/Secure three Kingdoms in the Oak again.   An Essay on the Fleet Riding in the Downes.   *Anonymous.*   CoMu

That we may grow as we would be.   In a London Terminus.   John Lehmann.   AtBAP

That we may lick their hinder parts and/thump their heads.   Power to the People.   Howard Nemerov.   PoL

That we may look unflinchingly on death/As the greatest good, like philosopher should.   Grace to Be Said at the Supermarket.   Howard Nemerov.   SoSe

That we may love so with other mo/To kepe the cold wind away.   To Keep the Cold Wind away.   *Anonymous.*   OxBM

That we may meet with dear Jesus–that is our prayer–hail!   Prayer to the Virgin.   *Anonymous.*   OnYI

That we may praise thee, year by year,/With angel-hosts above.   The Opening Year.   *Anonymous.*   BLRP

That we may see!   Europa.   Stephen Henry Thayer.   AA

That we may spare this hour's term/To practice for eternity.   Bearded Oaks.   Robert Penn Warren.   AmP; LiTM; MoAmPo; MoVE; MP; NoAm; NOBA; PoA; TAP; TwCP

That we may sport our fill/And love continue still.   Madrigal: "The spring of joy is dry."   Martin Peerson.   EnRePo

...That we maye never try/More griefe in parting, but growe olde and dye.   Britannia's Pastorals.   William Browne.   LO; OBS

That we might have riches eternal,/And with Him forever abide.   A Christmas Thought.   Mrs. Frank A. Breck.   BePJ

That we moten ay and o/Habben the eche blisse.   A Prisoner's Prayer.   *Anonymous.*   OxBM

That we moten comen till him,/In luce.   A Hymn to Mary.   *Anonymous.*   MeEL

That we moten thy sone iseen/In joye withouten ende./Amen   Contempt of the World.   *Anonymous.*   MeEL

That we mow there singe, "Nowel',/Nowel!   Man Exalted.   *Anonymous.*   MeEL

That we must either be on edge/or not at all, or not at all.   The Voice.   Judith Herzberg.   VWA

That we, obedient to Thy word,/May weep with those that weep.   And Jesus Wept.   Sir Samuel Egerton Brydges.   BePJ

That we ratepayers have to keep paying the/burdensome interest.   The Firm of Happiness, Limited.   Norman Cameron.   FaBoTw

That we're apt to leave behind us/Letters that we ought to burn.   Lives of Great Men.   *Anonymous.*   FaFP; GoTF; TreFT

That we shall conquer/without a doubt!   Last Letter to the Western Civilization.   D. T. Ogilvie.   NBP

...That we survive by hearing.   Woman and Nature.   Susan Griffin.   NPGG

That we think of him sometimes,/Sometimes and always, with mixed feelings?   At North Farm.   John Ashbery.   HaCAP

That we were born of those, unflinching,/loyal,/Who wore the gray.   The Rear Guard.   Irene Fowler Brown.   PAH

That we were never/here   Crossing Portsmouth Bridge.   Alan Chong Lau.   BrSi

That we were unwilling to trade for this?   The Refugees.   Randall Jarrell.   MoAB; MoAmPo

That we with merth mowe savely sing/"Deo gracias."   The Agincourt Carol.   *Anonymous.*   OAEL 1-2; OBET; OxBM

That we would know from what heights it fell.   Mules.   Paul Muldoon.   CIP

That weariness which makes us love the/night?   Death and Night.   James Benjamin Kenyon.   AA

That weary-laden mourn!   Man was Made to Mourn, A Dirge.   Robert Burns.   CEP

That wedding and hanging is destiny.   The proverb reporteth, no man can deny...   *Anonymous.*   ElL

That were bare as the rock and the sea and the sand.   Sea Dirge.   Tom Scott.   ACV

That were not born to die.   Marco Bozzaris.   Fitz-Greene Halleck.   AA; BeLS; GN; HBV 1-2; HoPM; TreF; WBLP

That what counts in a poem is brevity.   Paradox.   Benjamin K. Bennett.   PoL

That–what else could I do?   In Explanation.   Walter Learned.   AA; HBV 1-2

That what was good enough for Aeschylus is by no means/Good enough for me!   The Eumenides at Home (parody).   James Agate.   BXAP

That what we hope for cometh with the morn!   Faith for Tomorrow.   Thomas Curtis Clark.   PoToHe

That what we intended and failed/could never have happened–/and must be done better.   For Sheridan.   Robert Lowell.   HaCAP

That whatsoever king shall reign,/I'll be the Vicar of Bray, Sir.   The Vicar of Bray.   *Anonymous.*   CEP; DBV; FaBoPV; FSW; GBP; HBV 1-2; NOBE; NOBL; OBSV; OxBoLi; ViBoPo

That when a lady lifts her shift she's killing off a Yankee.   An Appeal to John Harralson.   *Anonymous.*   OBAL

That when He calls I'll worthy be/To wear a crown of light.   He Wore a Crown of Thorns.   Alice Mortenson.   BePJ

That when I fall–if fall I must–/My soul may triumph in the dust.   A Soldier: His Prayer.   Gerald Kersh.   TreFS

That when I rise again/I may shine bright/As the sky after rain,/Day after night.   For Sleep, or Death.   Ruth Pitter.   TrPWD

That, when I wake, clear eyed may be/My soul's desire.   The Mystic's Prayer.   William Sharp.   HBV 1-2; TrPWD; WGRP

That when my spirit won above/Hers could not stay for sympathy.   It Is Not Beauty I Demand.   George Darley.   ERoP 1-2; HBV 1-2; LiTL; OAEL 1-2; OBRV

That when we lifted out of sleep, there was/Life with its dark, and love above the laws.   Ascension.   Denis Devlin.   BIrV

That when we live no more, we may live ever.   To My Dear and Loving Husband.   Anne Bradstreet.   AmPP; AP; BLPL; BoWoP; FF; ForPo; HAP; HeIP; HW; MAmP; NePA; NOBA; NOCV; OBSP; OxBA; PoEL 1-5; PoLf; PrIm; SBG; SCAP; TAP

That when we stabbed Thy heart it was our own real hearts we/slew.   For Our Sakes.   Oscar Wilde.   PGD

That when ye love, the like return ye prove not. Pan Loved His Neighbour Echo–but That Child. Moschus. OBVE

That when you cut it/in the box you never press/as hard. The Answer. Chuck Wachtel. APU; FaBoRV

...That where Britain's pow'r/Is felt, mankind may feel her mercy too. Slaves Cannot Breathe in England. William Cowper. OBEC

That where I love best I dare not discure. Unfriendly Fortune. John Skelton. MeEL

That, where so much is doubtful, certainly is good. For My Wife. Julian Symons. NeBP; WaP

That whereso'er My face/Is hidden, none may grope/Beyond eternal Hope. Christ and the Pagan. John Banister Tabb. CAW; TrCP

That whi/te man with/that/cross on his back. Wake-Up Niggers. Don L. Lee. PoBA

That which an Angel's touch hath blest/Is meet, my love, for thee! Are They Not All Ministering Spirits? Robert Stephen Hawker. CoBE; GoBC; HBV 1-2

That which Death takes is ours forever-/more. Immustabilis. Alice Learned Bunner. AA

That which has quelled me, lives with me,/Accomplice in catastrophe. Theme and Variations. Edna St. Vincent Millay. SBG

That which his eyes alone to thee unfold! A Dedication. Mary Elizabeth Coleridge. TrPWD

"That which I have myself seen and the fighting'... Conquistador. Archibald MacLeish. NAMP

That which is fairer than all song–the grace/That takes the world into captivity. Sonnets to Miranda. William Watson. HBV 1-2

That which is felt but may never be told. The Whole Duty of a Poem. Arthur Guiterman. PoToHe

That which is firme doth flit and fall away,/And that is flitting, doth abide and stay. Rome. Joachim Du Bellay. LiTW

That which is in part, finding its whole again throughout the universe. Tortoise Shout. D. H. Lawrence. LiTM; NoAm

That which kind and harmless is,/None can deny us. What Harvest Half So Sweet Is. Thomas Campion. EG; PBBP; UnTE

That which lives there/Is coming, and makes a noise. The Approach of the Storm. Anonymous. OBVE

That which the fountain sends forth returns again to the/fountain. Evangeline. Henry Wadsworth Longfellow. PoToHe

That which was never thought in any season. Canzone: To the Lady Pietra, of Sienna. Dante Alighieri. LiTW

That which was poised already in the ah! of praise. Relearning the Alphabet. Denise Levertov. NOBA

That which when said/becomes a little/of what is not said. I'm Going to Break Out. Carmen Valle. InW

That while he lived never thought of death. Sonnet LXXXVII. Fulke, Lord Brooke Greville. OBS

That while I lay them on the shrine/Of your white hand, they are mine. On Mr. G. Herbert's Book. Richard Crashaw. AnAnS 1; OxBoCh; SeCV 1-2

That whilest I thus in pleasures lappe did lye,/I might refresh desire, which else would die. I Would in Rich and Golden Coloured Raine. Thomas Lodge. AAS

That who is not still for conformity bill/Will be surely a rogue on occasion. A Health to the Tackers. Anonymous. APAS

That who so joys such kinds of life to hold,/In prison joys, fetter'd with chains of gold. The Courtier's Life. Sir Thomas Wyatt. FaBoEE

That who so trusteth ere he know/Doth hurt himself and please his foe. Driven by desire I did this deed. Sir Thomas Wyatt. FCP

That who would travel here might know/The little world in folio. What need I travel, since I may. John Hall. EG

That widens to meet an opening world? A Book of Verses. Mordecai Marcus. AMV-80

That wikked tunges fro you falle,/That ye mowen to hevne go. Wicked Tongues. Anonymous. OxBM

...That/will be that. December 18th. Anne Sexton. CAPP

That will destroy you and your race? Too Loud. R. S. Thomas. NMP

That will not fade or vanish/While the arch of Heaven stands. Gabriel. Willard Wattles. HBMV

That will not mix with our mortality. Upper Air. Frank Ernest Hill. AnAmPo

That will set those lands on fire. I Know a Name! Anonymous. BLRP

That will speake what this can't tell/Of his glory. So farewell. Upon Ben Johnson. Robert Herrick. CaPo; FaBoEE; NoP; OAEP; OBS; SeCV 1-2

That wind is carrying the world away. Against the Age. Louis Simpson. NePoEA-2

That winter's had its day. The Coming of Spring. Nora Perry. HBVY; SoPo; YeAr

That wisdom is the folly of the wise. A Word to the Wise. Caroline Duer. AA

That with my life you gave me no apology,/and hear them whence they come. The Dove Apologizes to His God for Being Caught by a Cat. Anthony Eaton. PeSA

That with the morn I may awake/Unto the perfect day. The Twilight Shadows Round Me Fall. Ernest Edwin Ryden. AH

That with the Son of His dear love,/In heav'n we have a place. We'll Never Know. Alma Hoellein. STF

That woman likes a slave–but loves a/master. Philomel to Corydon. William Young. AA

That woman's hand–can it be true?–/No more beneath my head will lie. On the Death of His Wife. Frank O'Connor. BIrV; CIP

That woman–she only complains/in her sleep. Mother. Jose Montoya. FIA

That word and life thy truth may tell/And praise thee evermore! O Lord of Life. Washington Gladden. AH

That word begins that ends a true love ditty. A True Love Ditty. Thomas Middleton. EIL

That word kills grief, and through the dark-boughed tree/Gives to each dead his resurrection day. The Yew-Tree. Vernon Watkins. EaLo; LiTB

That worldly weeds needs must be loath/that can these flowers find. Seek Flowers of Heaven. Robert Southwell. TrCP

That worms should have their sun and I want mine. Astrophel and Stella, XCVIII. Sir Philip Sidney. EnLoPo; SiPS

That worst of tyrants in the noblest cause. Tribute to Washington. Anonymous. OHIP

That would add up only/to this one: that would be/without years. Unposted Birthday Card. Norman MacCaig. NAs

That would be Christine, his novel, and/Christine be him. The Author of Christine. Richard Howard. CoAP

...That would have been a hell of/A way to make a living. A Way to Make a Living. James Wright. NNaP

That would not take it in her hand. Riddle: "Stiff standing on the bed." Anonymous. GBP; PoL

An' that wuz the last of po' Railroad Bill. Railroad Bill. Anonymous. ABF

That ye may love in spite of beaver hats. Modern Love. John Keats. CBEP; OBNC

That ye wore round your necks what you hold in your/hand! On Bell-Ringers. Voltaire (Francois Marie Arouet). ShM

That years to come, if they get home,/They'll make their boasts and brags, Sir. British Valor Displayed. Francis Hopkinson. PAH

That you and I are sailors. The Sailor's Consolation. Charles Dibdin. BeLS; FaBoCo; HBV 1-2; TreFS

That you are as much a Canadian as they are. Riverdale Lion. John Robert Colombo. PeCV

That you are so oppressed/you even laugh at yourself. Drink from My Empty Cup. Zindzi Mandela. WhB

That you are you, and I am me? In former days we'd both agree. Bhartrihari. BoLoP

...That you claim/stains my Celtic soul. The Secret Irish. Allen Hoey. AMV-81

That you'd all of you know, as you sped,/Where a bullet of sense ought to hit. A Pastoral Ballad. By John Bull. Thomas Moore. BIrV; OBSV

That you, dear Plant, have birth. After Annunciation. Anna Wickham. MoBrPo

–That you did it/And do it yet. Tanist. James Stephens. OnYI

That you have forgotten that/you will forget. Death Songs. L. V. Mack. PoBA

That you have left to darken and fail,/Was cut out of the grass. The Ballad of the White Horse. Gilbert Keith Chesterton. ACP; MoVE

That you'l Confess the Comfort such, as even/Brings to, and comes from Heaven. Silex Scintillans. Henry Vaughan. AnAnS 1

That you learn from your mother at home. Mother's Advice. Anonymous. AmFP

That you long for but deny, in your chaste North. 104 Boulevard Saint-Germain. Kenneth Pitchford. NYBP

That you love me in December as you do in May? Will You Love Me in December as You Do in May? James J. Walker. FSN; GoTF; TreFT

That you made me that pallet/Down upon your floor Make Me a Pallet on Your Floor. Ma (and Jimmy) Yancey. BluL

That, you may know, is only a fragment/of my own splendor. Bhagavadgita: The One. Anonymous. ILwL

That you may ne'er offend my ear. An Epigram upon a Young Gentleman Refusing to Walk with the Author... David Garrick. FaBoEE

That you may not be here a thousand years. Glass Houses. Edwin Arlington Robinson. MoRP

That you met in the morning early.' A Kiss in the Morning Early. Anonymous. GBP

That you shall never suffer the half I do today. Over the Hill to the Poor-House. Will Carleton. BeLS; BLPA; FaFP; PaPo; TreF

That you two often agreed on in bygone days. The Husband's Message. Anonymous. AnOE; EnLit

That you will know/the instant you are really kissed. Dornroschen. Hayden Carruth. DFT

That you will swear her body by this law/Is but its shadow, as this its–now draw.   Upon the Curtain of Lucasta's Picture It Was Thus Wrought.   Richard Lovelace.   CaPo

That you woon't vind the fellow to thik there/wold yew.   Dobbin Dead.   William Barnes.   VLP

That your honour aye savit be.   Bruce Addresses His Army.   John Barbour.   GoTS

That your lives are not thus/Prevented, but made strong!   Man and Nature.   Robert Kelley Weeks.   AA

That your substance never may decay.   The Maunding Soldier.   Martin Parker.   CoMu; WaaP

Thata by his powre & might/he may give them a right/For the welth of all christen landes.   Songe betwene the Quenes Majestie and Englande.   *Anonymous.*   CoMu

An' the bigger bugs have other bugs/An' so–ad infinitum.   Bugs.   Will Stokes.   MoShBr

An' the captain's worst of all!   Army Bugle Calls: Reveille.   *Anonymous.*   TreF

An' the dawn comes up like thunder outer China 'crost the Bay!   Mandalay.   Rudyard Kipling.   ATP; BrPo; EnLit; FaBV; FPL; GoTF; HBV 1-2; LiTB; MoBrPo; NOBE; OBTV; TreF; TrGrPo

An the last bonfire that I come to,/Mysel I will cast in.'   Lady Maisry (A version).   *Anonymous.*   BaBo; ESPB; OxBB; ViBoFo

An' the memory's fairly spoilt on me/Wid mindin' to forget.   Forgettin'.   Moira O'Neill.   HBV 1-2

An' The Screamer put his tongue out, and he won/by half-a-tongue.   Grog-an'-Grumble Steeplechase.   Henry Lawson.   PH

"A' the smiths that lives on land/Will neer bring such a sheath and knife/to my hand."   Leesome Brand (B version).   *Anonymous.*   ESPB

An' the thyme it is wither'd and rue is in prime.   Kellyburnbraes.   *Anonymous.*   OxBB

An' the tongue of the woman that owns him.   The Grand Match.   Moira O'Neill.   HBMV

Thea very walls echo with cheer!   The Walls of Jericho.   Blanche Taylor Dickinson.   CDC

Thee, God's own Mother, we would magnify.   Maid, out of Thine Unquarried Mountain-Land.   *Anonymous.*   ISi

Thee may I serve and follow all my days,/Whose thorns are sweet as never roses are!   Quid Non Speremus, Amantes?   Ernest Christopher Dowson.   HBV 1-2

Thee, O Mary, will I praise,/Love and serve thee all my days!   Song of Praise to Mary.   Angelus Selesius (Johannes Scheffler).   CAW

Thee, sacred Spirit, labourers refreshing,/Still be renowned.   A Prayer to the Trinity.   Richard Stanyhurst.   CoBE; ElL

–Thee sitting to behold/On the hills of God.   Songs of Seven.   Jean Ingelow.   HBV 1-2

Thee the prompt waiter to a jolly toper/Hous'd in an arbour.   Odes.   Horace.   OBVE

Thee thyself we could not lose.   After St. Augustine.   Mary Elizabeth Coleridge.   TrPWD; TRV

Thee to adore thy God, the first of all.   God to Be First Served.   Robert Herrick.   OxBChV

Theer then! theer! No, I'll have none of your/goodnights.../Congergal rights! conjergal rights!   In the Coach: Conjergal Rights.   Thomas Edward Brown.   VLP

Thehorizonofholland.   Concrete poem: The Horizon of Holland.   Ian Hamilton Finlay.   InPK

Their ancient, glittering eyes, are gay.   Lapis Lazuli.   William Butler Yeats.   CMoP; CoBMV; DTC; FaBoMo; FaBoTw; FF; ForPo; InPK; InPS; LiTB; LiTM; MAT; MoPo; MoVE; NAWM 1-2; NoAm; NOBE; NoP; OAEL 1-2; OAEP; PAI; PP; PPoe; TEP

Their arrows are found in trees.   The Insular Celts.   Ciaran Carson.   BIrV; CIP

Their astronaut may choose to settle/Down upon the farthest star.   Astronaut's Choice.   M. M. Darcy.   QQQ

Their barges built from fear you never know.   The Barge Horse.   Sean Jennett.   PH

Their blood ran on in silence.   Losing the Straight Way.   Ian Wedde.   OCNZ

Their blue tails as whip-sharp as a March wind.   Blue Horses: West Winds.   Anita Endrezze-Danielson.   STE

Their blurred faces, caught up in one wish,/Are blurred into one face: a child's set face.   A Hunt in the Black Forest.   Randall Jarrell.   CoAP; LCAP

Their blurred smiles meant for no one.   Old Photographs.   David Harsent.   PoL

Their bodies scatter type as if block letters make/the news.   The Cubistic Lovers.   Charles Edward Eaton.   AMV-81

Their bones not even picked for souvenirs.   From Colony to Nation.   Irving Layton.   NOBC

Their boredom real, and reassuring.   To the Shore.   May Swenson.   NePoAm-2

Their breath smells as sweet as the good old moonshine.   Kentucky Moonshiner.   *Anonymous.*   AS; OBAL; TrAS

Their bright, unhollowed eyes.   The Curse.   John Hollander.   UnPo

Their bush cast a shadow like a bell.   Birds and Roses Are Birds and Roses.   William Heyen.   GeTw

Their cannon and blue flares/pumping fear into the night.   The Invaders.   John Haines.   TAT

Their carpet-bag.   Contentment.   Charles Stuart Calverley.   ALV; NOBV

Their children's children shall say they have lied.   He Thinks of Those Who Have Spoken Evil of His Beloved.   William Butler Yeats.   CTC; ELU; NOBV

Their children. The horn is blown, but I do not hear it.   The Green Valley.   Sylvia Townsend Warner.   MoBrPo

Their circle is complete.   Celebration.   Elizabeth Newton Sachs.   AMV-81

Their clattering feet–/their clattering feet!/to the slaughterhouse.   Eau-Forte.   Frank Stewart Flint.   OxBTC

Their coming down again.   At the Airport.   John Malcolm Brinnin.   MoAB

Their country don't love them.   Love Rejected.   Lucille Clifton.   BPo

Their crests tousled by the fight,/Like your unruly hair.   Lines for My Father.   Patrick Worth Gray.   AMV-81

Their crowns and purples in this light/Are shoddy when compared with yours.   For Tu Fu.   Feng Chih.   LiTW

...Their/dark sorority/exempts them from.   A Comfort Stop.   Tony Beyer.   OCNZ

Their dark veins/bruise-blue.   A Day Begins.   Denise Levertov.   DFF; NaP

Their day was dark, and dim.   The Shepherds.   Henry Vaughan.   SBVL

Their days are spent, whose minds are bent/To follow the useful plow.   The Useful Plow.   *Anonymous.*   HBV 1-2

...Their delicate mouse-like tread/printed in tracks of snow over my mind.   Years Later.   Ruth Stone.   BoWoP

Their disclosure, in nature,/Reminds me of you, of blending.   Four Fawns.   Barbara Howes.   AMV-80

Their doctrine could be held by no sane man.   Cleon.   Robert Browning.   MaVP; MBW 1-2; OAEL 1-2; OAEP; VLP

Their dower the yoke their sires have worn/Through snug and sheeplike generations.   With Freedom's Seed.   Alexander Pushkin.   TTY

Their dream of happiness is his smile/And his skilful way with the hardest rod.   Still Century.   Tom Paulin.   FaBoIP

Their dual disciplines of tenderness.   Woodtown Manor.   John Montague.   IPY

Their eyes are calm/surviving smoothly/in a monstrous environment....   On Falling.   Andrew Greig.   PoSH

Their eyes shining, grave with a perfect pleasure.   The Little Dancers.   Laurence Binyon.   CH; MoBrPo; MoVE; OBVV; OxBTC

Their faces dead, turned towards Italia.   The Gauls Sacrifice.   Charles M. Doughty.   FaBoTw

Their faces gleam through the marriage canopy/Like stars through a braiding of clouds.   To the Choice Bridegroom.   Judah Halevi   HW

Their faces glowing with disaster.   The Snowbound City.   John Haines.   EAS

Their faces that/Of men whose wound/Was mortal, and/Who knew it not.   The Lost Tribe.   Robert Finch.   CaP

Their fathers' mothers, daughters, and wives.   Parable.   Peggy Bennett.   ELU

Their fierceness tempered/By the air that flows between.   The Rio Grande.   Sacheverell Sitwell.   SeCePo

...Their five long toes trembling in the soaked earth.   Johnson's Cabinet Watched by Ants.   Robert Bly.   NoAm; NOBA

Their footsteps borrow silence from the snow.   Persephone.   Michael Longley.   FaBoIP

Their frenzy's spell unbroken/defines the topgallant soul.   In the Beginning.   Daniel Gerard Hoffman.   PP

Their freshest linen/and their cleanest smile.   Sleep Only with Strangers.   George Jonas.   NeAC

Their frozen stream flowing/from Mantua to Amsterdam.   A Late Manuscript at the Schocken Institute.   Gabriel Preil.   VWA

Their generals are already poring over maps.   When Statesmen Gravely Say "We Must Be Realistic."   W. H. Auden.   FaBoCo; PV

Their ghosts illume my lurid West.   By the Pacific Ocean.   Joaquin Miller.   AA; AnAmPo

Their good, ill, health, wealth, joy, or discontent,/Being, end, aim, religion–rent, rent, rent!   The Age of Bronze: Rent, Rent, Rent!   George Gordon, Lord Byron.   OBSV

...Their great-grand-uncles/Were kicked by me in passing....   Rainuv: A Romantic Ballad from the Early Basque (parody).   Margaret Widdemer.   BXAP

Their greatest curse has been removed,/John Barley-Corn, my foe!   John Barley-Corn, My Foe.   Charles Follen Adams.   OBAL

Their green indifference barbarous at its panes.   The Chestnut Avenue at Alton House.   Charles Tomlinson.   FaBoTw

Their groans and whispers down the village street/Soon soured his nature, which was never sweet.   The Villagers and Death.   Robert Graves.   HeIP

Their hand is put away.   Medea: Chorus.   John Byrne Leicester Warren, Lord De Tabley.   OBEV

Their hands in the dusk, their frail hair in the sun.   Song for September.   Robert Fitzgerald.   VGW

Their heads for signs shall hang up high,/Upon that hill call'd Beacon.   The Battle of Bunker Hill.   *Anonymous.*   PAH

Their hearts are high, their might is great,/Who will endure.   Behold the Meads.   Guillaume de Poitiers.   AWP

Their hearts, as well as inn's, are made of clay.   Upon Christ His Birth.   Sir John Suckling.   NCEP

Their hearts, contemptuous of death, shall dare/His roads between the thunder and the sun.   The Black Vulture.   George Sterling.   AmLP; BPAW; HBV 1-2; PB

...Their hearts each the flame of a candle/That his breath can extinguish at will.   The Invitation in It.   Kay Boyle.   NMM

Their hearts the flowers from whence the honey sprung.   The Lovers.   George Gordon, Lord Byron.   LiTL

Their heels make sober solitary/sounds appropriate to Sunday.   Aside.   Alan Dugan.   PoA

Their hinges fold in on mortality.   Figures in a Ruined Ballroom.   George Hitchcock.   VGW

Their hopes are retinal.   Poem: "Love being what it is, full of betrayals."   Ruth Herschberger.   HoAn

Their hopes have come to rest/in the radiant roses of Queens.   The Roses of Queens.   Claire Nicholas White.   NYP

Their images I loved I view in thee,/And thou, all they, hast all the all of me.   Sonnets, XXXI: "Thy bosom is endeared with all hearts."   William Shakespeare.   NOBE; OBEV; OBSC; PoEL 1-5

Their journey still when his boughs shrink with age.   The Trees of the Garden.   Dante Gabriel Rossetti.   MaVP

Their joy the joy of heaven.   The Head That Once Was Crowned with Thorns.   Thomas Kelly.   TRV

Their lips stiff from an imaginary trumpet.   The Bands and the Beautiful Children.   P. K. Page.   PeCV

Their lips together.   "April's amazing meaning".   George Dillon.   AmLP

Their little lives are fun to them/in the sea.   Little Fish.   D. H. Lawrence.   OxBTC; SOTW

Their little sky-time is over.   Sky Diving.   Richmond Lattimore.   LiSp

Their lives have parallels, but thine has none.   Plutarch.   Agathias.   AWP

Their loneliness/given away in poems, only their solitude kept.   The Correspondence School Instructor Says Goodbye...   Galway Kinnell.   NOBA; NoP; TAP

Their long yellow fingers kissing the holy waters.   The Poor in Church.   Arthur Rimbaud.   LiTW

Their looks are incidental, monumental, sweeping.   Gargoyle.   Thomas Rabbit.   MAYP

Their Lord entombed in the blazing hill.   For Mao Tse-Tung: A Meditation on Flies and Kings.   Irving Layton.   NOBC

Their love makes them forget all time.   Ancient Quatrain.   *Anonymous.*   HW

...Their loves, joys, persons, voyages.   Memories.   Walt Whitman.   PCP

Their machines humming/like locusts in a swarm.   Into the Book.   Martin Grossman.   VWA

Their Master and Maker, drunkards of the sky.   Jerusalem Sonnets.   James Keir Baxter.   OCNZ

Their middle-aged children from the new estates.   The Patricians.   Douglas Dunn.   OxBC

Their mingled strokes tell over again.   Belfast: High Street.   Padraic Colum.   NePoAm

Their momentary cries before it is dawn/Would carry it away to blasphemous men.   Ego Dominus Tuus.   William Butler Yeats.   CMoP

Their moon-led waters white.   The Palace of Art.   Alfred, Lord Tennyson.   FaBoPP

Their mouths full of one another.   Their Mouths Full.   David Ignatow.   GP

Their music marvelous, though sad, and strange.   The Town Dump.   Howard Nemerov.   BiP; CMoP; MAT; NIP

Their mysteries so perfect even their undoings/seem as planned as way signs on a map   Looking for a Country under Its Original Name.   Colleen J. McElroy.   BlSi

Their name unknown, their praise unsung.   The Lay of the Last Minstrel.   Sir Walter Scott.   OBRV

Their names are spoken/Somewhere at world's end.   The Constant Bridegrooms.   Kenneth Patchen.   CrMA; LiTM; NaP

Their names erased, in an unfrequented way.   If I Could Walk out into the Cold Country.   Elizabeth Brewster.   NOBC

Their nature uniformly base is.   The Human Races.   R. P. Lister.   FiBHP

Their newborn eyes pale and soft.   At Wonder Donut.   Laureen Mar.   BrSi

Their noses drip with snow in flight/O'er Aughty in the twilight.   Murrough Defeats the Danes, 994.   *Anonymous.*   KiLC

Their number last he sums.   Paradise Lost.   John Milton.   MyFE

Their ochre clings to the stone.   Ts'ai Chi'h.   Ezra Pound.   NoP

Their old, disordered dance.   Unalterables.   Arthur Gregor.   NYBP

Their only monument the asphalt road/And a thousand lost golf balls.   The Rock.   Thomas Stearns Eliot.   TRV

Their own delusive shadows slow and part.   The Storm.   Elizabeth Jennings.   NePoEA-2

Their peerage is from God!   Aristocrats of Labor.   W. Stewart.   PGD

Their perfect tribute to Perfection paid.   For Nijinsky's Tomb.   Frances Cornford.   UnS

Their pinions, in short flights their strength to prove,/And venturous, trust the bosom of the air.   Spring (excerpt).   Thomas Gisborne.   PBBP

Their plain attire such glorious gallantry/Disdains so much, that none them in doth call.   Colin Clout at Court.   Edmund Spenser.   OBSC

Their power is gone, and my life is the token.   The Death of the Gods. An Ode.   L. Ker.   NOEC

Their power still to mar/known only from inside.   To a Young Poet.   Paula Bennett.   AMV-81

Their prayers have gone down in the holy river.   Homesick.   Else Lasker-Schüler.   PBWP

Their promises are like smoke,/like smoke, like smoke, like smoke.   Like Smoke.   Mririda n'Ait Attik.   PBWP

Their pure, unwavering, deep disdain.   Urania.   Matthew Arnold.   HBV 1-2

Their ransom, their rescue, and first, fast, last friend.   The Lantern out of Doors.   Gerard Manley Hopkins.   CMoP; LiTB; OxBoCh; TrCP; VLP

Their raptur'd tongues do tell/Their joys great.   A Poem Containing Some Remarks on the Present War.   *Anonymous.*   PAH

Their real loves waiting,/indifferent, in far off towns.   Explanation.   Geof Hewitt.   NeAC

Their red coats and the swift whimpering hounds.   Childhood.   Sir Herbert Read.   BrPo

Their rill-like voices called and cried/Until the dawn began.   April.   Dora Sigerson Shorter.   HBMV; HBVY

Their scanty truth, their lies beyond a joke.   Sonnets of the Months.   Folgore da San Geminiano.   AWP

...Their sermons/Ending in the air.   Clonfeacle.   Paul Muldoon.   CIP

Their shadows grow monstrous.   Poems.   Antonio Machado.   LiTW

Their shimmering voices/singing.   In Populated.   Lucille Clifton.   GeTw

Their ships were shatter'd in our sight/Or swiftly driven from our coast.   Chester.   William Billings.   TrAS

Their side of the glass, water is everywhere.   Aquarium.   George T. Wright.   NYBP

Their silence all these years/doesn't fool anyone   Nanye'hi (Nancy Ward), the Last Beloved Woman of the Cherokees...   Rayna Green.   TWSS

Their silence shall be interpreted/As we approach them.   Silence.   Edgar Lee Masters.   LaNeLa; MoAmPo

Their silences burn like pine knots/campfire on a cold night.   The Heart Mountain Japanese Relocation Camp: 30 Years Later.   Charles Levendosky.   TAT

Their sin-sick souls by him shall be recured.   Out of My Soul's Depth.   Thomas Campion.   OxBoCh

Their sinuous silhouettes serve/as barometers, define like mirrors.   How to Measure a Cat.   Louis Johnson.   OCNZ

...Their skirts/flared out around them, open and burning.   Spring in the Old World.   Philip Levine.   FAZ

Their slimy embryos came in youthful Lottery's brain.   Marvellous Martin.   Charles Harpur.   CBAP

Their soft wings whirr, they dream that they are flying.   The Silkworms.   Douglas Stewart.   CBAP; PoAu 1-2

Their sons' proud feelings here/Their noblest monuments.   The Field of the Grounded Arms.   Fitz-Greene Halleck.   PoEL 1-5

Their sorrow sings through the cracked tenement walls.   To a Gone Era.   Irma McClaurin.   BlSi

Their sparkle's on his broomstraws.   The Museum of the Second Creation.   Sandra McPherson.   LCAP

Their speech torn to bits in the torrent.   The Imprisoned.   Robert Fitzgerald.   MP; TwCP

Their strong foundations laid and held by God's right hand.   The New World.   Jones Very.   AA; AnNE; AP

Their swords less danger carry than their gifts.   The Destruction of Troy: Aeneid II.   Sir John Denham.   SeCV 1-2

Their tails were thirty feet in length.   Riddle: "I saw five birds all in a cage."   *Anonymous.*   CoBE; GBP

Their tears, their late regrets I curse.   When in My Arms.   Alexander Pushkin.   ErPo

Their ten fingers idle,/while clothes fill the hamper.   Weaving at the Window.   Wang Chien.   SaC

Their thurst unto him bring.   Living Water.   Ruth M. Williams.   BePJ

...Their time most happy is,/If, to their time, they reason had, to know the truth of this.'   How No Age Is Content.   Henry Howard, Earl of Surrey.   LiTB; LoBV

Their tongue was directed to heaven,/Now it lies in the dust.   Duel with Verses over a Great Man.   *Anonymous.*   TrJP

Their town first heard his babbling word.   To W.B.Yeats Who Says That His Castle of Ballylee Is His Monument.   Oliver St.John Gogarty.   AnIL

...Their tyrant breath,/Anticipating life, to hasten death.   The Rose of Life. Luis de Gongora y Argote.   AWP

Their very memory is fair and bright,/And my sad thoughts doth clear. They Are All Gone into the World of Light.   Henry Vaughan.   FaBoRV

Their violet velvet shadow robes/Beside them on the grasses.   Little Birches. Mary Effie Lee Newsome.   PoNe

Their visions mountain-clear, their needs immodest.   Spring.   Philip Larkin. ACV; MoBrPo

Their voices choked/In suspicious silence.   Gods in Vietnam.   Eugene B. Redmond.   NBP; PoBA

–Their voices drown in the hiss of steam.   Cressida.   James Keir Baxter. AnNZ

Their voices upon the wind/are in my ear   Song: "The sun is mine."   Robert Hogg.   WHW

Their watchword is thy memory!   Sumter's Band.   J. W. Simmons.   PAH

...Their will/Grinds on their fate. So was, so shall be still.   Whether There Is Sorrow in the Demons.   John Berryman.   LiTM

Their work be my employ.   Hard Heart of Mine.   Henry Alline.   AH

Their work is done–the camp's asleep.   Silhouette in Sepia.   Robert V. Carr. PoOW

Theirs, who shall hurt themselves or me, refrain.   The Temple.   George Herbert.   AnAnS 1

Them am I yours, and what you feel, I share.   To a Republican Friend. Matthew Arnold.   VLP

Them drow to Dumbar!   The Battle of Dunbar.   *Anonymous.*   OxBM

Them ez will, kin.   A Baker's Duzzen Uv Wize Sawz.   Edward Rowland Sill.   FaBoBe; FaFP; GoTF; HBV 1-2; HBVY; InMe; TreFS

Them knuckles was talking.   720 Gabriel St.   Randolph Outlaw.   LFAC

"Them poets, goddam 'em, always/in school with their white hands." Mending Crab Pots.   Dave Smith.   GeTw

Them string up undecayed and stellify.   O Sheriffs.   Drummond Allison. OBSP

Them uge great vings balls up his plates, yer see.   The Helbatrawss. Kingsley Amis.   NOBL

Them were the days, my fel-/Low bards!   That Did in Luve So Lively Write. Georgine M. Adams.   InMe

Themself, should come to me–   'Twas Just This Time, Last Year, I Died. Emily Dickinson.   DiPo

...Themselves the only/shelter they have found   Furniture.   Phyllis Harris. NYBP

Themselves, they marry, they raise their kind.   The Sheep Child.   James Dickey.   CAPP; GP; HaCAP; NoAm; NOBA; Prf; TAP

Themselves they wisely could bestow,/Lest any should espy them. Nimphidia, the Court of Fayrie.   Michael Drayton.   ViBoPo

Then a cornerboy borrows my pencil/to keep track of his sale of newspapers. The Continuity.   Paul Blackburn.   CAD; NeAP

Then a Drinking we will go.   Hunting Song.   Henry Fielding.   CEP; OBEC; OxBoLi; ViBoPo

Then a 2-hour drive/to her sheep.   Sheepherder blues.   Luci Tapahonso. STE

Then acts in Nature's office, brings to pass/The glad espousals, and ensures the crop.   The Task.   William Cowper.   FaBoUs

Then after, who plowgheth, plowgh thou with the/furste.   A Hundreth Good Poyntes of Husbandry.   Thomas Tusser.   FaBoUs

Then again bow that way.   Sur le Pont d'Avignon.   *Anonymous.*   FSW

Then all are pleased, for Coleman's in his grave.   Elegy on Coleman. *Anonymous.*   ALV

Then all at once in Air dissolves the wondrous Show.   A Wondrous Show. James (1700-48) Thomson.   OBEC

Then all men else, then Thy selfe onely lesse.   To Ben. Johnson. Upon Occasion of His Ode of Defiance.   Thomas Carew.   AnAnS 2; CaPo; MePo

Then all of heaven's blessedness/Into your heart He'll bring!   He Lives! He Lives to Bless!   Dorothy Conant Stroud.   STF

Then all swim out to wait until/The right waves gather.   From the Wave. Thom Gunn.   NoP

Then all the egg yolks will bear/The dreaded blood spot.   In the Courtyard. Miriam Ulinover.   VWA

Then, all the hours left I'd go/A-SPREADING out-of-doors.   Rudolph Is Tired of the City.   Gwendolyn Brooks.   TiPo

Then all those young men would go bang those bushes.   Hares on the Mountain.   *Anonymous.*   CBEP

Then all young sailors pray beware,/And never sail with a murderer! William Glen.   *Anonymous.*   BaBo

Then am I ready like a palmer fit,/To tread those blest paths which before I writ.   The Pilgrimage.   Sir Walter Ralegh.   EBCP; SiPS

Then an old friend kindly/Chopped off his head.   Mysterious East.   William Cole.   OBAL

Then answer no and I, and I and no.   Nothing but No and I, and I and No. Michael Drayton.   GBL

Then are these songs I sing of thee/Not all ungrateful to thine ear.   In Memoriam A.H.H., XXXVIII.   Alfred, Lord Tennyson.   VLP

...Then arise,/Sagest Greek...   Son of Erebus and Night.   William Browne. ViBoPo

Then arm in arm along the path/Silent they saunter away.   September Evening, 1938.   William Plomer.   SeCePo

Then arms pine up and up/Like worship.   Diver.   R. A. Simpson.   CBAP

Then art thou safe forever.   God Bless You.   *Anonymous.*   PoToHe

Then as now, a coral city/is rising from the hardest parts of us.   Coralville, in Iowa.   Marvin Bell.   FAZ

Then Asaph's song shall be like Doeg's rhyme.   Old England.   Nahum Tate. APAS

...Then, at least for Flo,/begins the long and painful process of letting go. Meet the Supremes.   David Trinidad.   APU

Then at night in the confidence of their homes/rip out their apology-tongues and steal their poems.   I Am 25.   Gregory Corso.   CoPo

Then awake from thy slumbers, my Bessy, awake.   Song: "Awake thee, my Bessy, the morning is fair."   Jeremiah Joseph Callanan.   IrPN; OnYI

...Then awake me,/Morning of eternal rest!   Tarry with Me, O My Saviour. Caroline Sprague Smith.   AH

...Then awakes once more/His song, ecstatic with the May.   The Canadian Rossignol.   Edward William Thomson.   CaP

Then back to Henry, the English king,/Restored the stately Wanton Brown. The Lochmaben Harper.   *Anonymous.*   BaBo

Then be an age! that we may never try/More grief in parting, but grow old and die.   Memory.   William Browne.   HBV 1-2

Then be blessed with light, more light.   Let the Light Enter.   Frances E. W. Harper.   PoNe

–Then be life's locht, my wife!...   The Light of Life.   Hugh" (Christopher Murray Grieve) MacDiarmid.   CMoP

Then be thou kind–bestow them free on me.   O say, dear life, when shall these twinborn berries.   *Anonymous.*   EG

Then, before he is immersed,/he calls me by my Jewish name.   Blessing. Melvin Wilk.   VWA

Then, beneath your poet's head/Be a downy pillow spread.   The Storm. Alcaeus.   AWP

Then, Bill, let us thank Providence/That you and I are sailors!   Sailor's Consolation.   William Pitt.   EtS; LBN

Then birds of ill omen, and women no more.   An Ape, Lion, Fox and Ass. *Anonymous.*   OBET

Then blank and gone and still, and utterly lost.   Yonnondio.   Walt Whitman.   MCCG

Then bleak and cold is the silent spot/Where the lilies used to spring!   Where the Lilies Used to Spring.   David Gray.   OxBS

Then bless thee, and beware, and let us pray/We part not with thee at this meeting day.   Sir Walter Ralegh to His Son.   Sir Walter Ralegh. EnRePo

Then blow ye winds westerly, westerly blow,/We're bound to the southward, so steady we go.   Song of the Fishes.   *Anonymous.*   AmSS

Then blue night, and the day was ended/That never will come again.   A June Day.   Sara Teasdale.   YeAr

Then both to bed together creep,/And join the general troop of sleep. Description of a Summer's Eve.   Henry Kirke White.   OBRV

Then brag not on thy cannon shot/as though there were no mo.   To the Roving Pirate.   George Turberville.   EnRePo

Then break your heart when Cloe dies.   Epistle to a Lady: Of the Character of Women.   Alexander Pope.   OBSV

Then brought him gently to the beach,/And wiped the briny moisture from his breach.   Don Leon (excerpt).   *Anonymous.*   PeHV

Then, buzzing 'round her snowy breast,/He crept into the hive.   As on Serena's Panting Breast.   *Anonymous.*   UnTE

Then by a sunne-beam I will climbe to thee.   Mattens.   George Herbert. AnAnS 1; TrPWD

Then by my threatenings rest still innocent.   The Apparition.   John Donne. AnAnS 1; AtBAP; CBEP; EnLoPo; ExPo; GBL; HeIP; LoBV; MePo; NAWM 1-2; NLV; NOBE; OAEL 1-2; OBEV; OBS; SCV; SeCP; ViBoPo

Then call'd the happy Composition Floyd.   On Mrs. Biddy Floyd Written in the Year 1707.   Jonathan Swift.   CEP

Then call the lost dream back.   Dream Song.   Lewis Alexander.   PoBA; PoNe

Then call their darkness–Thee.   For All Sorts and Conditions.   Norman Nicholson.   EaLo

Then call your neighbors in.   Cross Patch.   Mother Goose.   BrR; EvOK

Then calmly smiled at him before they kissed.   The Corner of the Field. Frances Cornford.   ELU

Then came Longeus with a spere and cleft His hart in sonder.'   My Heart Is Woe.   *Anonymous.*   OxBM

Then can it be my eyes, with love afire,/Can flatter him who is my soul's desire.   Epigram: "One boy alone."   Meleager.   PeHV

Then cast once more your heightening spell. Sancta Silvarum. Lionel Pigot Johnson. BrPo; VLP

Then cease, fair ladies, why weep ye? why weep ye? Hark, All Ye Lovely Saints. *Anonymous.* OAEL 1-2

...Then ceased from bearing evermore. Nature's Travail. *Anonymous.* AWP

Then ceased, like these. This quiet dust was gentlemen and ladies. Emily Dickinson. CMoP; DL; EG; MoAB; MoAmPo; OxBA; ViBoPo

Then, chances are, you should be prepared to burrow/Deep for a deep winter. Staying Alive. David Wagoner. BoNaP; CoAP; NYBP; RFM; SM

Then cherish pity, lest you drive an angel from your door. Holy Thursday. William Blake. BoC; CBEP; DiPo; EnPE; HBV 1-2; InPS; NAWM 1-2; NOBE; NoP; OAEL 1-2; OBEC; OFD; PAI; SCV; TEP; TrCP

"Then chiefly lives." On Reading the Metamorphoses. George Garrett. NePoAm-2

Then Christmas and his train are here. Signs of Christmas. Edwin Lees. OHIP

Then claps his well fledg'd wings and bears away. The Grave. Robert Blair. EnRP

Then clean us to the bone. Bait Shop. Thomas Reiter. WOLT

Then close the valves of her attention/Like stone. The Soul Selects Her Own Society. Emily Dickinson. AmP; AnNE; APA; AWP; BLPL; BoWoP; CMoP; DiPo; GoTF; InPK; InPo; InPS; MAmP; MoAB; MoAmPo; NAWM 1-2; NePA; NoAm; NOBA; NoP; OxBA; PAI; PoEL 1-5; SBG; TAP; TreFT; TrGrPo; UnPo; WHA

Then close your ears with dust and lie/Among the other cheated dead. Reprisals. William Butler Yeats. OBWP

Then closed the sad career,/Of the most celebrated "Englishman"/Of the nineteenth century. Sketch of Lord Byron's Life. Julia A. Moore. OBAL

Then closes the eyes that dare no longer see/Save hooded, their erratic destiny. For a Child's Drawing. Anton Vogt. AnNZ

Then come, and to my hero bend/Upon the grass your knee! The Hero. Robert Nicoll. HBV 1-2

Then come away, turn/Countryman with me. Coridon's Song. John Chalkhill. HBV 1-2; ViBoPo

Then Come, deare bridgrome, Come away! As Weary Pilgrim, Now at Rest. Anne Bradstreet. AnNE; PoEL 1-5; SCAP

Then come to us slowly, out of nowhere and anywhere/risen,/Breathlessly bright. Breath. James Dickey. SM

Then comes the sound as of abundant rain. Transfigured Life. Dante Gabriel Rossetti. MaVP

Then count that day as worse than lost. Count That Day Lost. George Eliot. GoTF; TreFT

Then crave not of the night my vanished flame. Give Me Not Tears. Rose Hawthorne Lathrop. AA

Then crown her Queen of the World! Queen of the World. *Anonymous.* PGD

Then cut your throat with a barlow knife–/For it's easier done that way. The Horse Wrangler. D. J. O'Malley. CoSo

Then dangle from the Housewife's Broom–/His Boundaries–forgot– The spider holds a silver ball. Emily Dickinson. FM; WPOW

Then day surrounds us like an empty room. New World. Brewster Ghiselin. MoVE

Then, Death, please turn my day to night. Sonnet, XIII: "As long as I continue weeping." Louise Labé. PBWP

...Then Death's his Epilogue. De Morte. Sir Henry Wotton. OBS

Then Death that changes happy things/Damned his soul to water springs. Epitaph: "If fruits are fed on any beast." John Millington Synge. PV

Then Delicate pasticios/Say Travel a little higher The MJQ. Joyce Carol Thomas. CNA

Then depart, but see ye tread/Lightly, lightly, o'er the dead. Upon a Maid. Robert Herrick. CaPo; FaBoCh; FaBoEE; LoGBV; OxBoLi

–Then died before her feet. Windle-Straws. Edward Dowden. HBV 1-2

...Then do I add a slice/Of tender tripe; and a snout soak'd in vinegar. Sausage. Axionicus. FaBoUs

Then do I wear the crown/Without a cross! Beer. George Arnold. AA; OBAL; TreFT

Then do it like this, cocky doodle doodle doo. Cocky Doodle Doodle Doo. *Anonymous.* OuSiCo

Then, down fall butler, and bowl and all. Wassailer's Song. Robert Southwell. OHIP

Then downe shee Layd, & since tis sayd,/shee quencht his spirits motion. Off a Puritane. *Anonymous.* CoMu

Then draw me close, and hold me fast! A Seeker in the Night. Florence Earle Coates. TrPWD

Then draw your curtains, and begin the dawn. The Lark Now Leaves His Wat'ry Nest. Sir William Davenant. AnEnPo; InvP; LO; PoRA; ViBoPo; WHA

Then drop into his grave; and then;– The Story of Life. John Godfrey Saxe. PoToHe

Then drop into thyself, and be a fool! An Essay on Man. Alexander Pope. ExPo; FiP

Then drop once more into centuries or dreams. Paiute Ponies. Jim Barnes. CDW

...Then drops in/dread/And cannot cover his despair. Hate! Antokolsy. TrJP

Then each fell back, limp as a sack,/Into the world of men. The Sensualists. Theodore Roethke. ErPo; NePoAm-2; UnTE

Then each on a leg or thigh fastens. On Oxford (parody). John Keats. Par

Then earth in earth had of earth its fill. Earth Took of Earth. *Anonymous.* HAP

Then ebbed back into the horizon/and back of the stars. Buffalo Trace. Robert Morgan. GeTw

Then–eddies like a Rose–away–/Upon Vermilion Wheels– The name–of it–is "Autumn." Emily Dickinson. InPS; PAI

Then even sin contrives your greater glory. Poem for a Christmas Broadcast. Anne Ridler. NeBP

Then every minute count–as I do now. To Miss Lucy F––, with a New Watch. George, Lord Lyttelton. FaBoUs

Then every voice of wisdom joins/To bid you leave them in your loins. Summum Bonum. Abu-l-Ala al-Maarri. LiTW

Then everything was darkness/In a great...big...night. Sylvester's Dying Bed. Langston Hughes. NoAm; UnPo

Then fade as doth a silenced song. The Long Night. Harry Bache Smith. AA

Then, far away, the thudding of the guns. The Death-Bed. Siegfried Sassoon. LiTM; MMM; MoVE; PoPle

Then farewell, fairest age, the world's best days,/Thriving in ill, as it in age decays. The Olden Days. Joseph Hall. OBSC

Then farewell, O farewell! Welcome, my Love, welcome my joy/for ever! Farewell, Unkind! Farewell! to Me, No More a Father! *Anonymous.* EnLoPo

Then farewell parsonage! I shall ne'er be poor. A Poem upon the Imprisonment of Mr. Calamy in Newgate. Robert Wild. APAS

Then fears not the eye to show the heart. And if an eye may save or slay. Sir Thomas Wyatt. FCP; SiPS

Then fight, brave captains, that these joys may fly/Into your bosoms with sweet victory. David and Bethsabe. George Peele. ViBoPo

Then first the lightning broke. Before the Storm. Richard Dehmel. AWP

Then flap at last/in black circles sunward. Trout Fishing: A Sign. Richard Behm. WOLT

Then fling me back to the battle where/men labor the peace of God! Wild Eden. George Edward Woodberry. AA

Then flit not from this heavenly Boy. Come to your Heaven, You Heavenly Choirs! Robert Southwell. EG; OxBoCh

Then, flooded with foreknowledge, knelt and prayed. The Return. Leonard Alfred George Strong. HaMV

Then folded to his heart his boy,/And fainted on the deck. The Main-Truck; or, A Leap for Life. George Pope Morris. BLPL; PoLf

Then for all time, O love, God give thee joy! To His Friend in Absence. Wilafrid Strabo. LiTW; PeHV

Then for his subjugation, ah,/There was the total Julia. Herrick's Julia (parody). Helen Bevington. BXAP; SpRo

Then forget Phelim Brady, the Bard of Armagh. Bold Phelim Brady, the Bard of Armagh. *Anonymous.* OnYI

Then from her Eyes, with fresh supplies, down trickles many a/brinish Tear. The Dutchess of Monmouth's Lamentation for the Loss of her Duke. *Anonymous.* CoMu; FaBoBa

Then from the craven fear of death/Good Lord, deliver me. A Litany for Old Age. Una W. Harsen. TrPWD

Then from the shoes they slipped her feet,/And the little shoes died. The Little Shoes That Died. Mary Gilmore. NOAV

Then from the swinging lantern's light/Runs to his Mother in the night. Four-Paws. Helen Parry Eden. HBMV

Then gather up the splinters,/and love the ruins,/my God. Love the Ruins. Malka Tussman. VWA

Then gaze again to sea–and sigh. The Master Mariner. George Sterling. HBV 1-2

Then gently shoo the flocks away,/Before the winter comes to stay. October Winds. Virginia D. Randall. YeAr

Then get the hell out, fast. Directions to the Nomad. James Welch. CDW

"Then give me a handful of pepper-seed!" Elms of the Eastern Gate. *Anonymous.* LiTW

Then give me leave to die,/And show thy power thereby. Give Me Leave. "A. W." TrGrPo

Then give me welcome, next my heaven the best,/Even to thy pure and most most loving breast. Sonnets, CX: "Alas! 'tis true I have gone here and there." William Shakespeare. EBEV; OAEP; OBSC; PeHV; ViBoPo

Then give three cheers, and one cheer more,/For the well-bred Captain of the Pinafore! I Am the captain of the Pinafore. Sir William Schwenck Gilbert. TreFT

Then gladly will I leave my all/To follow Christ my Lord. Discipleship. C. O. Bales. STF

Then gladly would I end my mortal days. Personal Talk. William Wordsworth. CABA

Then go out and burn the file. On File. John Kendrick Bangs. PoToHe; WBLP

Then go rolling home to Hades,/Roses round each lovely brow. Anacreon to the Sophist. B. H. InMe

Then go sailing with his heart still free. Jack Is Every Inch a Sailor. *Anonymous.* FSW

Then go sidewise for all you are worth. Limerick: "Said the crab: "'Tis not beauty or birth." Oliver Herford. TDH

Then go up the trail every chance in the spring. Jess's Dilemma. *Anonymous.* CoSo

Then goats were the wisest of creatures/on earth. Epigram. Joseph Solomon Del Medigo. TrJP

...Then gropes/Back on itself and begins/To eat its own leaf. Leaf-Eater. Thomas Kinsella. FaBoIP

...Then, Hail to Mary! spring/Of so much safety to the realm, and King. An Epigram to the Queen, Then Lying In. Ben Jonson. SBVL

Then halter up this Cur that is so Curst. God's Determinations. Edward Taylor. PoEL 1-5

Then hang me, Ladies, at your door,/If e'er I doat upon you more. Verses. Sir John Suckling. CavP

Then hatched/And lives! Easter Egg. Alan Kieffaber. AMV-80

Then hatred is in head. Of Drunkenness. George Turberville. NLV; NoP

Then haul'd our wind and stood again for/Freedom's happy shore. The General Armstrong. *Anonymous.* PAH

Then have we missed the bus? Or are we sure/which way the wind is blowing? Waiting for the Bus. D. J. Enright. OxBTC

Then he became his truck again, and I my car/to cross a river–that's where the highway was going. Who's in Charge Here? Marvin Bell. AmC

Then he can be my little boy/Yes I'll treat him good Me and My Chauffeur Blues. Memphis Minnie. BluL

Then he closed his eyes, no more to rise on the banks of the Sweet and Dee. The Banks of Sweet Dundee. *Anonymous.* AmFP

Then he closes his fist and there is nothing there. A Magus. John Ciardi. MAT

Then he gave me sixpence/To kiss him on the stairs. Eight O'Clock Bells. *Anonymous.* PoPle

Then he'll raise us our wages to ninepence a day. Fourpence a Day. *Anonymous.* OBET

Then he may commit suicide, then/He may go. Exeat. Stevie Smith. NoAm

Then he puts the yellow horn to his ear/and listens. I Show the Daffodils to the Retarded Kids. Constance Sharp. DFF

Then he runs away–/And joins the Arab Army! The Gofongo. Spike Milligan. AmMo

Then he's the finest boy I've ever seen alive. Fishing for Sticklebacks, with Rod and Line. Sir Francis Cowley Burnand. PV

Then he stuffs his black bag/with our lives and is gone/in his alphabet auto. Reservation Special. Lew Blockcolski. VoR

Then he turned on his side and died. The Miller and His Sons. *Anonymous.* OBET

Then he went out; and as he went, he wept. La Vita Nuova. Dante Alighieri. AWP

Then he will crown a tranquil life/By becoming a Cabinet Minister. On the Birth of His Son. Su Tung-p'o. AWP; LiTW; OBVE; OFD; TRV

Then he would sway and shiver as he walked. May the man who gained my trust yet did not come. Ryojin Hisho. BoWoP

Then heave up the anchor! To the westward we go! A Trip to the Grand Banks. Amos Hanson. AmFP; ShS

...Then Henry/will heft the ax once more, his final card,/and fell it on the start. Dream Songs. John Berryman. HaCAP

Then her white knife,/Her closing eyelid./Her darkness. The Death of the Moon. David Wagoner. PoA

Then here conclude/Fair Daphnis' praise. In Praise of His Daphnis. Sir John Wotton. EiL

Then here perhaps I'd own the perfect good. I live on this depraved and lonely cliff. Vittoria da Colonna. BoWoP

Then hey noney, noney: hey noney, noney. Pleasant Comedie of Patient Grissill. Thomas Dekker. AtBAP

Then his shadows are deep and not gray. Else a Great Prince in Prison Lies. Denise Levertov. NaP; PPP; VGW

Then hold thee still, my heart,/For I shall wait His lead. Be Still, My Heart. *Anonymous.* STF

Then hold thy hand, Spencer,/I dearly thee pray. Hugh Spencer's Feats in France (B version). *Anonymous.* ESPB

...Then home in chastened/pride,/With aching heads, our slaughter satisfied. An Idler's Calendar: January. Wilfrid Scawen Blunt. VLP

Then–hope and happy skies/Are thine forever! Sit Down, Sad Soul. Barry (Bryan Waller Procter) Cornwall. CAW; TreFT

Then hope for a prosperous autumn that year. Proberbially Useful Dates for Weathermen. *Anonymous.* FaBoUs

Then hot-foot some of them Spanish magistrates Robert's Rules of Order. Robert Peterson. FAZ

Then hugs her huge body to sleep. Not Quite Spring. Lyn Lifshin. NeAC

Then hush, forevermore. The Song of the Spanish Main. John Bennett. HBV 1-2

Then Huzzah! Huzzah! Huzzah! Huzza!/For the British Grenadier! The British Grenadier. *Anonymous.* CBEP; FSW; HBV 1-2; OBEC; OxBoLi; PAH

Then–I am ready to go! Tie the strings to my life, my Lord. Emily Dickinson. TrCP

Then I answer'd: Yea. Passing Away. Christina Georgina Rossetti. GoBC; NoP; OAEL 1-2; OBVV

Then I bust out laughing/and let the woman live. Women's Locker Room. Marilyn Waniek. MAYP

"Then I'd cry my eyes out, my kind old husband,/The best old fellow in the world." The Best Old Fellow in the World. *Anonymous.* AmFP

Then I do when I'm well. A Health Note. Walter Hard. AnNE

Then I felt peculiar/And found that I couldn't! Faith. Marjorie Dunkels. PH

Then I found myself a stranger/In my own town. Finite. Power (Haold Caleb Dalton) Dalton. HBMV

Then I got 300 miles to go/traveling through the mud and clay/ Mmmmmmmmmmmmmm Whoopee Blues. King Solomon Hill. BluL

Then I leave thee lord and master, latest lord of/Locksley Hall. Locksley Hall Sixty Years After. Alfred, Lord Tennyson. EnLi 1-2

Then I'll be twelve and won't that be fine! Growing Up. Arthur Guiterman. BiCB

Then I'll fall to my loving and drinking amain. Drinking Song. Alexander Brome. PoPle

Then I'll give you half a crown. Cobbler, Cobbler. *Anonymous.* OxNR

Then I'll go with him. The Husband. Donald Finkel. ELU

Then I'll leave aff where I began,/And tak' my auld cloak about me. Tak' Your Auld Cloak about Ye. *Anonymous.* OxBS

An' then I'll leave thee an' Lochaber no more. Lochaber No More. Allan Ramsay. HBV 1-2

Then I'll leave/you in your tower/and over the world/will a glow spread. Sermon on the Mount. Jeff Wright. APU

Then I'll no more to Greenland sail, no, no, no. Cordial Advice. *Anonymous.* OBSS

Then I'll rise and fight again. Johnny Armstrong. *Anonymous.* MaC

Then I'll tak back my word again,/And the Coutts will come and see me.' The Laird o Drum. *Anonymous.* ESPB

Then I'll understand that all is well/again for the human and leave,/content with my condition. I'm Here. David Ignatow. GP

...Then I'm allowed/to be accepted as human–and even beautiful. Self-Portrait. Nina Cassian. VWA

–Then I must fold thee closer still! The Flight from the Convent. Theodore Tilton. AA

Then I must weep–and bitterly. I Love but Thee. Heinrich Heine. AWP

–Then I remember that I once was young/And lived with Esther the world's gods among. Esther. Wilfrid Scawen Blunt. OBMV

Then I return to her/with panic in my throat. Prisoner's Song. Horace Gregory. OLR

Then I saw him,/the childhood friend I loved. Apricot Tree. Magda Isanos. BoWoP

Then I shan't be dead,/but waiting for something to come in. The Cup. Judith Wright. FaBoWP

Then I should joy, as thou dost now,/and thou shouldst wail thy case. Once Musing as I Sat. Barnabe Googe. NoP

Then I simply sleep in peace, until you come to me. Danny Boy. *Anonymous.* FSW

Then I the mark of ingratitude stand/For betraying the church and enslaving the land. The False Favorite's Downfall. *Anonymous.* APAS

Then I walked on and crossed the bridge. An Advancement of Learning. Seamus Heaney. NCSH

Then I will be sane again, I will/sit in a room free of flies and write superbly of snow. Fall Letter. Dave Kelly. FAZ

Then I will prove my indebtedness/By blowing the candle out. Blow the Candle Out. *Anonymous.* FaBoBa; FSW

...Then I will travel the Great Northern Railways/and we can talk things over, sitting down. Arches and Shadows. Annie Dillard. CTBA

Then I would vastly hold/and embrace you. Phallic Root. Shiraishi Kazuko. WPOW

Then if in dreaming so, I so did speede,/What should I doe, if I did so indeede? Sonnets, VI: "Sweet Corrall lips, where Nature's treasure lies." Richard Barnfield. PeHV

Then if others share with me,/Farewell her! whate'er she be! His Further Resolution. *Anonymous.* HBV 1-2

Then if thy victims pause, prepare th' eternal chain. Ode to Moderation (excerpt). Annabella Plumptre. NOEC

Then, in another time. White Notes. Donald Justice. LCAP

Then in gigantic glory, fade/Sunward through the western glade... Giardino Pubblico. Osbert Sitwell. ChMP

Then, in justice, take my book. Dedication for a Book of Criticism. Yvor Winters. GLGT

Then in Mount Jerome I will lie, poor wretch,/With worms eternally. To the Oaks of Glencree. John Millington Synge. ELU; MoBrPo; NOBI; OxBI

Then in peace I'll abide when I take my final ride/On a caisson that's rolling along. The Caisson Song. Edmund L. Gruber. BLSo; PAL; TreF

Then in requite, sweet virgin, love me! Damelias' Song to His Diaphenia. Henry Constable. ELP; HBV 1-2; OBSC; PoEL 1-5; ViBoPo

Then in the heaven my God. Composed while Under Arrest. Mikhail Yuryevich Lermontov. AWP

Then is priest savage, or Red Indian priest? Brebeuf and His Brethren. F. R. Scott. NOBC

Then it grew into a kite/and flew far out of sight... Catch a Little Rhyme. Eve Merriam. OBCA

Then Johnny walk along to Hilo,/Oh, poor old man! Johnny Walk along to Hilo. *Anonymous.* ShS

Then, journey on, if not elate,/Still never broken-hearted! Sympathy. Emily Bronte. OAEP

Then judge not thou thy fellows what they are. Sonnet: Of Moderation and Tolerance. Guido Guinicelli. AWP

Then keep your apple–wait, and watch it rot. Apple Offering. *Anonymous.* UnTE

Then kiss her dear, sweet lips for me,/And break the news to her. Break the News to Mother. Charles K. Harris. FSN; TreFS

Then knit, and passed/In seamless company. Of All the Sounds Despatched Abroad. Emily Dickinson. AnFE; APA; MAPA

Then knocked their tea-cups over, and scampered through the door. The Cats' Tea-Party. Frederic Edward Weatherly. TiPo

Then know all ye whom it concerns,/Subscripsi huic, The Inventory. Robert Burns. CABL; FaBoUs

Then know Thy sheep, which knows his Shepherd's voice. O Gracious Shepherd. Henry Constable. OxBoCh

Then laconically scribbled, "I'm forum." Limerick: "A senator, Rex Asinorum." *Anonymous.* TDH

Then lady, by green Erin's wave,/I'll gladly wake my harp for thee. To * * * * *. Jeremiah Joseph Callanan. IrPN

Then, Lady, take your own,/That lives for you alone. Where His Lady Keeps His Heart. A. W. CTC; EIL; OBSC

Then lastly to his holy shrine,/Exalt amind the tapers' shine/At Venice,– The Eve of St. Mark. John Keats. EnRP

Then laws are made to keep fair play. Blind-Man's Buff. William Blake. WiR

Then lean again to scoop up the swill. Feed. Raymond Knister. OBCV; PeCV

Then learning is most excellent. When Land Is Gone and Money Spent. *Anonymous.* OxNR

Then leave all this for smaller men to do. Work for Small Men (excerpt). Sam Walter Foss. PoToHe

Then leave it with Him; He has everywhere/Ample store. Divine Abundance. *Anonymous.* BLRP

Then leave nae mair my heart to break/'Mang Scotland's hills behind. The Mariner. Allan Cunningham. EtS

Then leave the room to you, my sleeping lover. Waking Early. R. L. Barth. AMV-81

Then, lest we like not these, in Dark's bazaars/She nightly tempts us with her store of stars. As an Old Mercer. Mahlon Leonard Fisher. HBV 1-2

Then let me love thee more than they,/And try to serve thee best. Praise for Mercies Spiritual and Temporal. Isaac Watts. NOEC

Then Let my Muse for Thee this Trophy raise. A Satyreterricall Charracter of a Proud Upstart. John Saffin. SCAP

...Then let the Lyre/Sound, whilst his Altars endlesse flames expire. The Sacrifice to Apollo. Michael Drayton. OBS

Then let the stalwart skipper drown/And the little child go free! Alec Yeaton's Son. Thomas Bailey Aldrich. EtS; MOS

Then let them change. Under the Catalpa Trees. Gary Young. AMV-81

"Then let us all reflect with pleasure,/That labour is the source of treasure." The Father and His Children. *Anonymous.* OxBChV

Then let us all rejoice amain! I Saw Three Ships. *Anonymous.* EBCP; OxBoCh

Then let us bless the Lord. Grace after Meals. *Anonymous.* TrJP

Then let us call for grace/That we may shun this wicked vice/And mend our lives apace. Little Mousgrove and the Lady Barnet. *Anonymous.* OxBB

Then let us hold the bliss of peaceful/mind,/Since this we feel, gret loss we cannot/find. Since Nature's Works Be Good. Sir Philip Sidney. OAEP

Then let us play at queen and king/As down the garden walks we go. Henry and Mary. Robert Graves. BrPo; GoJo; LOW; SO

Then let us sit and watch the while/The blue ice curdling on the stream. How Still, How Happy! Emily Bronte. NOBV; OBNC; VLP

Then lighted strength; and then the letting go. History Lesson. Mark Van Doren. NYBP

Then lightly tripping, ran away. The Boy and the Snake. Charles and Mary Lamb. OxBChV

Then, like a creature with a mortal hurt,/She fell, and wept away the afternoon. The Mountain Woman. DuBose Heyward. AnAmPo

Then like a foaming torrent, pouring down/Precipitant, we smoke along the vale. The Chase (excerpt). William Somervile. NOEC

Then like a lily drooping/She bowed her head, and died. 'Twas when the Seas Were Roaring. John Gay. HAP

Then like a new Jill/Toiling up a hill/Life scrambles after. Art and Life. Lola Ridge. HBMV

Then, like an alligator, drags him in. To a Fly, Taken out of a Bowl of Punch. John Wolcot. NOEC

Then like, and love, and never fear. Never Love. Thomas Campion. AAS; EG; EIL; LoBV; TrGrPo; ViBoPo

Then like the brown fox of copperplate/Made exit over the lazy dog. Idyll. Francis Webb. PoAu 1-2

Then live with me and be my Love. The Passionate Shepherd to His Love. Christopher Marlowe. AAS; AnEnPo; AWP; BiP; BoLoP; CTC; DiPo; EIL; ELP; EnL; ExPo; FaBoBe; FaFP; FCP; FF; FPL; GoTF; GTBS; GTBS-P; HAP; HBMV; HBV 1-2; HeIP; HoPM; InPK; InPo; InPS; LiTB; LiTL; LoBV; NIP; NLV; NOBE; NoP; OAEL 1-2; OAEP; OBEV; OBSC; OLR; PAI; PG; PoLf; PoRA; PPoe; PPP; SCV; SeCePo; SeCeV; TreF; TrGrPo; UnTE; ViBoPo; WHA

Then living men ask how he left his breath,/That while he lived never thought of death. Caelica, LXXXVII. Fulke, Lord Brooke Greville. FCP; PoEL 1-5

Then loafs all winter upon his hoard,/With the mercury at zero. A More Ancient Mariner. Bliss Carman. OBAL

Then loiter homeward, slow as we please. Hal's Birthday. Lucy Larcom. BiCB

Then long too late we falconers cry hey lo! For the Hern and Duck. *Anonymous.* PBBP

Then look around, and choose thy ground,/And take thy rest. On This Day I Complete My Thirty-sixth Year. George Gordon, Lord Byron. AnFE; CABA; CoBE; ERoP 1-2; FiP; HBV 1-2; MBW 1-2; MCCG; NAs; NoP; OAEL 1-2; OAEP; OBWP; TreFT; TRV; ViBoPo

Then lose in time thy maidenhead! Then Lose in Time Thy Maidenhead. *Anonymous.* ErPo

Then lose no time, for Love hath wings,/And flies away from aged things. The Old Couple, III, i: Love's Prime. Thomas May. EG

Then love is sin, and let me sinful be. Astrophel and Stella, XIV. Sir Philip Sidney. AAS; NoP; OAEL 1-2; SiPS

Then, Lydia, then...I still shall stay,/And firmly answer–No. To Lydia Languish. Henry Austin Dobson. NBM; VLP

Then Lytle turned with an oath–By God it's true! The Oath. Allen Tate. FaBoMo; LiTM; NoAm; OxBA; VGW

Then make my reservation/On a rocket to the moon. Space Travel. Jane W. Krows. SoPo

Then make/our move./a-men. Black Lotus/a Prayer. Alicia Loy Johnson. NBP

Then man my soul with firm resolves/To bear and not repine. Prayer under the Pressure of Violent Anguish. Robert Burns. TrPWD

Then many little children's feet/Go hippity across the street. I'm the Police Cop Man, I Am. Margaret Morrison. SoPo

Then Mary went home/with her heavy load. The Cherry-Tree Carol. *Anonymous.* AnEnPo; TrGrPo

Then may be proved here anon/That we three be agreed in on.' Roses. *Anonymous.* OxBM

Then may I too find words to voice your praise–/But oh, not yet, not yet. Some Day. Medora C. Addison. HBMV

Then may it leap and catch a heart/And set it burning bright. Little Sticks. Eric Rolls. PoAu 1-2

Then may remorse, in pitying of my smart,/Dry up my tears, and dwell within her heart. Sweet Violets. *Anonymous.* EIL; NoP

Then men will say thereafter/That "A gentleman was here." Manners at Table When away from Home. *Anonymous.* OxBChV

Then met my Fanny with a borrow'd smile. The Sad Lover. George Crabbe. OBNC

Then might our pretty modern Philomels/Sustain our spirits with their roundelays. Whither Is Gone the Wisdom and the Power. Hartley Coleridge. HBV 1-2

Then might the Voice that is law have said "Cease!' and the ending have come. In Tenebris. Thomas Hardy. OAEL 1-2

Then mine apparel shall display before ye/That I am clothed in holy robes for glory. Housewifery. Edward Taylor. AnNE; DiPo; LiTA; NePA; NIP; NoP

Then,/more funny nazis! T.V. (2). Anselm Hollo. APU

Then mount and ride away/To any dream deserving the sensible world. Always Begin Where You Are. Thomas Hornsby Ferril. PrIm; VGW

Then mourn no less/The living glory of/Each Gaelic word! The Little Clan. Frederick Robert Higgins. OBMV

Then move not while my prayer's effect I take. Romeo and Juliet. William Shakespeare. BiP; SoSe

Then muse not Cupids sute no better sped,/Seeing in their loves the Fates were iniured. Hero and Leander. Christopher Marlowe. PoEL 1-5

Then muse not (Licia) if my Muse be slacke,/For when I wrote, I did thy beautie lacke. Lyke Memnons Rocke Toucht, with the Rising Sunne. Giles the Elder Fletcher. AAS

Then must I needs advance myself by skill,/And live to serve, in hope of your goodwill. "Sweet are the thoughts where hope persuadeth hap." Sir Walter Ralegh. FCP

Then my cat and i go back inside/And talk about the past. My cat and I. Roger McGough. OxBTC; PoL

Then my dear may I drink a fond deep health to thee! The Girl I Love. Jeremiah Joseph Callanan. IrPN; OnYI

Then my finger taps on your throat/groping like a blind man's cane. Observation at Dawn. Abba Kovner. VWA

Then my joys shall never end. The Satisfying Portion. Anonymous. BLRP

Then my lyfes Leach doe you your skill reveale,/And with one salve both hart and body heale. Amoretti, L. Edmund Spenser. AAS

Then my sorrow would never leave me,/Until the earth should cover me. Two Folk Songs, 2. Anonymous. LiTW

Then, Myra give me leave for Cupid's sake/To kiss thee oft that I may court'sy make. Caelica, XLIX. Fulke, Lord Brooke Greville. FCP

Then name this bloody ground/firm underfoot/home, however homely. Accepting. Vassar Miller. FiCP

Then ne'er let the gentle Norman blude/Grow cauld for Highland kerne.' Harlaw. Sir Walter Scott. EnLi 1-2

Then never blush Cupid (quoth I)/For many have err'd in this beauty. Four Anacreontic Poems, 3. Edmund Spenser. AAS

Then never break your heart when Cloe dies. Characters of Women. Alexander Pope. NOBE; OBEC

Then never take a second one,/To spoil the first impression. To His Saviour, a Child; a Present, by a Child. Robert Herrick. OxBoCh; SeCP; TrCP

Then nobody will buy. Poem by a Perfectly Furious Academician. Shirley Brooks. FiBHP; NOBV

Then none but slaves shall bend to tyranny. Reparation or War. Anonymous. PAH

Then, not despised, I'll not complain,/But cherish Autumn in her stead. Autumn. Anonymous. NOEC

Then O as he kittled me–/But I forgot to cry. Johnie Cam to Our Toun. Anonymous. GBP

Then off behind the plough afield/He goes, the whalebone whip to yield. The Ploughboy. John Clare. PoEL 1-5

Then–off like a shot he'll go. Road Runner. Sharlot M. Hall. BPAW

Then, oh Come, in pious Laies,/Sound we God-Almighties praise. Haleluiah; or, Britain's Second Remembrancer: Hymne I. George Wither. SeCV 1-2

Then oh, the glory we shall know/Which cannot wane or dim! No Room. Dorothy Conant Stroud. STF

Then, on Man's earthly peak, I might behold/The unearthly self beyond, unguessed, untold. Sonnet: "If I could get within this changing I." John Masefield. WGRP

Then, on my slab, while stars put on their white/Uniforms, yield myself to absolute night. On Having Grown Old. Ernest G. Moll. BoAV

Then on my tongue the taste is sour/Of all I ever did. When the Bells Justle in the Tower. Alfred Edward Housman. NOBV

Then, on the anvil of Thy wrath, remake me, God, that day! A Wanderer's Litany. Arthur Stringer. WGRP

Then on to blisses manifold. Niplets. Anonymous. ErPo

Then once again/Vesture my every vein. Arbor Vitae. Siegfried Sassoon. PoPle

Then once so merrily hop't she,/Heigho,heigho, heigho! Hop't She. Anonymous. GBP

Then only numbers sweet/With endless life are crowned. To Live Merrily, and to Trust to Good Verses. Robert Herrick. AnAnS 2; AWP; CaPo; InPo; InvP; LoBV; MyFE; OBS; PP; SeCP; SeCV 1-2

Then, only then, shall my dear Tysey be/Forgotten by his fond Penelope. The Fatal Dream; or, The Unhappy Favourite. Emanuel Collins. NOEC

Then only, thought may grind/A harder sharper lens. Eye. Gray Burr. WeW

Then open time's doors and let loose/Your misery and awaken deaf mute men Listen. Charles Patterson. NBP

Then opened wide.../In ecstasy. Young Shepherd Bathing His Feet. Peter Clarke. PBA

Then our entire twisted nature will turn/And run when a single secret word is spoken. When Geometric Diagrams... Novalis (George Friedrich Philipp von Hardenerg). NU

Then out a-shin-shan-shining/In the bright, blue day. The Barber's. Walter De la Mare. GoJo; SoPo; SUS

Then outdoors is Out West,/But indoors is Home. New Mexico. Polly Chase Boyden. TiPo

Then, Pallas, take away thine Owl,/And let us have a lark instead. To Minerva. Thomas Hood. FaBoCo; FaBoNo; FiBHP; HBV 1-2; InMe; NLV; NOBL; OxBoLi

Then parts his crust and hobbles on. The Soldier That Has Seen Service. Anonymous. NOEC

Then pass into the shadowy night,/Where formless shades blindfold the light. The Camera Obscura. John Addington Symonds. NOBV

Then, perhaps, in the morning my love will remain. Four Folk-Songs in Hokku Form, 4. Anonymous. LiTW

Then, perhaps then, God Bless America. God Bless America. John Fuller. OBSV

Then place this stone rose here/on this grave, just to mark a love? One Rose of Stone. Keith Wilson. GOYP

Then practise dumbly staring at your plight. The Double Autumn. James Reeves. OBSP

Then pray, Christian, pray! Pray, Christian, Pray! Anonymous. STF

Then pray to God to cast that wish away. Prayer. Hartley Coleridge. GoTF; TreFT

Then prove but kind, and thou shalt see/Love hath more power then Destinie. The Farewell. Thomas Stanley. CavP

Then pushed her over the edge into the river. Traveling through the Dark. William Stafford. AmC; BiP; BoAnP; CAPP; CoAP; GrPl; HAP; HeIP; InPK; LCAP; LiTM; NCSH; NMP; NoP; SM; SoSe; WeW

Then pushing out her shapely bow she braves/The next tall sea, and, leaping, onward goes. The Clipper. Thomas Fleming Day. EtS

Then put it back again with a slight frown. Grotesque. Robert Graves. DTC

Then put women in trust and confidence. Trust in Women. Anonymous. NA

Then quick I seized my husband's hand while he stared at his/bride. In the Museum. Isabella Gardner. ELU; NYBP

Then quickly choose the prudent/part,/Or else you break a faithful heart. To a Lady on Her Passion for Old China. John Gay. FaFP; LiTB; LoBV; OBEC

Then quite quickly her portcullis closed. The Oracular Portcullis. James Reaney. ErPo; PeCV

...Then rats ate his thumbs. Trench Poets. Edgell Rickword. DBV

Then reading, then sinking into slumber, too does Trastevere. Edwin Denby. ANYP

Then, remembered or not, these touchings were the start. Midnight, Walking the Wakeful Daughter. Joseph Meredith. AMV-81

Then rest a little; and in sleep/Forget to weep, forget to weep! Lines for a Drawing of Our Lady of the Night. Francis Thompson. ISi

Then rested in/Bliss of calm and quiet. The Creation of Man. Anonymous. WTO

Then return and linger not! To My Distant Beloved. Alois Jeitteles. TrJP

Then rides away leaving/his enemy behind Male Rain. Laura Tohe. STE

Then ripe cucumbers and apples and pears. Most beutiful of things I leave is sunlight. Praxilla. BoWoP

Then rise with his ascending Lord/To realms of endless day. Christ's Resurrection and Ascension. Philip Doddridge. NOCV

Then rises up anew, to take/The desert road... And So Should You. Anonymous. STF

Then Roger, go saddle my horse,/For I will be there tonight. The Newmarket Song. Thomas D'Urfey. APAS

Then rose, girded himself, and o'er the bleak/Hills fled from our sight; but left his golden load. To Autumn. William Blake. BoNaP; ERoP 1-2; WiR

Then roused from this reality I saw/Nothing, anywhere, but snow. Nature Be Damned. Anne Wilkinson. NOBC; OBCV; PeCV

Then, safe until the matinee. Playwright. John Woods. CoPo

Then sall they savit be/Through Thy mercy alone. All My Love, Leave Me Not. Anonymous. BSV; GoTS

Then sang the shepherds and Nymphs of Diana:/Long live fair Oriana. Thus Bonny-Boots the Birthday Celebrated. Anonymous. NCEP

Then saw the cow well served, and took a groat. The Shepherd's Week. John Gay. NOEC

Then say, my dears: "It's old Lizette–/She's turning in her sleep." Old Lizette on Sleep. Agnes Lee. HBMV

Then says oure maister "que vos ren ne vaut".' Choristers Training. Anonymous. OxBM

Then says Rollant: "Great power in that thrust." The Song of Roland, XCIX. Anonymous. WaaP

Then says this brave youth, "I quit this earth with pleasure." Montcalm and Wolfe. Anonymous. AmFP

Then seal your lips until the sun/Discovers one as fair. A Song of Praise. Countee Cullen. BiP

Then see them home in a baruig. Balearic Idyll. Frederick Packard. FiBHP

Then see us safe home to the boss. To G. K. Chesterton. Joseph Mary Plunkett. OnYI

Then seek the place where heaven pours/Her wealth on humankind. Some Things You Cannot Will to Men. Walter E. Isenhour. STF

Then send for me with speed. The Maids Conjuring Book. *Anonymous.* CoMu

Then sent, too late, for her litter. Portrait of a Married Couple. Margaret Scott. NOAV

Then shakes his powdered coat and barks for joy. The Woodman's Dog. William Cowper. ELU; GDP

Then shall come back to me with Him/my youth. Song of Loneliness. Judah Halevi. TrJP

Then shall earth of earth have a foul stink./Mos solvit Omnia. Memento Homo quod Cinis Es Et in Cinerem Reverteris. *Anonymous.* FaBoRV

Then shall I chaunge for no newe. Love Undeclared. *Anonymous.* OxBM

Then shall i turn my face, and hear one bird/sing terribly afar in the lost lands. It May Not Always Be So. Edward Estlin Cummings. BoLoP; FaBV

Then shall I, wistful, try to trace/The child you once were in your face? To My Little Son. Julia Johnson Davis. HBMV

Then shall my Ghost not walk about, but keep/Still in the coole, and silent shades of sleep. To Perilla. Robert Herrick. AtBAP; CaPo; OBS; SeCP; SeCV 1-2

Then shall my soul her conflict cease,/And find a heaven within. Peace. *Anonymous.* STF

Then shall our people all be thine,/Our church, like that above. O for the Happy Hour. George Washington Bethune. AH

Then shall this atom of the Eternal Soul/Encompass thee in its benign control! O Solitary of the Austere Sky. Sir Charles G. D. Roberts. CaP

Then shall Venuku eat men/Till none remain. Lament for Taramoana. Makere. WTO

Then shall we know full surely, quick or dead,/Death, if thou be. A Dialogue. Algernon Charles Swinburne. PoEL 1-5

Then shall Wilson and Gautier/Never sing or play more here. A Lyric to Mirth. Robert Herrick. CaPo

Then shall you see a cinder, not a man,/Beneath the lightnings of the Vatican. The Lost History Plays: Savanarola (parody). Max Beerbohm. BXAP

Then shalt thou see her virtue risen in heaven. Ballata V: "Light do I see within my Lady's eyes." Guido Cavalcanti. CTC

Then shatter the mirror. It was made to shatter. Gift of a Mirror to a Lady. David Wagoner. NePoAm-2

Then shave myself with Uncle's full-dress sabre. Revised Notes for a Sonnet (parody). Edward Pygge. BXAP

Then she appeared to say, "I am at peace." La Vita Nuova. Dante Alighieri. AWP

Then she closed her eyes and died. The Jealous Lover. *Anonymous.* ShS

Then she had rest. The Forsaken. Duncan Campbell Scott. CaP; NOBC; WHW

Then she'll lie still, asleep, who now lies ill, awake. Rough Winds Do Shake. Louis Simpson. ErPo

An' then she made the lasses, O. Green Grow the Rashes. Robert Burns. ALV; CABA; CEP; CoMu; CTC; EiCP; EnLi 1-2; EnPE; ErPo; FaFP; FSW; HBV 1-2; LAuP; LiTB; LiTL; NoP; OAEL 1-2; OBEC; PPoe; PPP; SeCePo; UnTE; ViBoPo; WHA

Then she sang down a down, Hey down derry. The Courteous Knight. *Anonymous.* OxBB

Then she, too, would have been an old maid! My Grandmother Green. *Anonymous.* AmFP

...Then she was in darkness/crying. She didn't know what she wanted. The Feast. Robert Hass. GeTw

Then shield me, heavens, from such a subtle thing. Madrigal: "When younglings first." William Byrd. EnRePo

Then shield me in the woods again. Hymn on Solitude. James (1700-48) Thomson. CEP; OBEC

Then shudder away with cries of rapture diminishing/sadly. Singing on the Moon. Ted Hughes. WSC

Then, since to heaven ye likened are the best,/Be like in mercy as in all the rest. Amoretti, LV. Edmund Spenser. AAS; HBV 1-2; TrGrPo

Then sing. Mockingbird, Copy This. Jack Myers. AMV-81

Then sink them together–the ship and the name! The Sinking of the Merrimac. Lucy Larcom. MC; PAH

Then sinks untimely, and defrauds the chase. Elegy XI. William Shenstone. NOEC

Then sit for half an hour and drink our mocks. Portrait of a Lady. Thomas Stearns Eliot. AnAmPo

Then sit on the lid and laugh. Then Laugh. Bertha Adams Backus. BLPA; PoToHe; TreFT; WBLP; YaD

Then sith to heaven ye lykened are the best,/Be lyke in mercy as in all the rest. So Oft As I Her Beauty Do Behold. Edmund Spenser. BoLiVe

Then slept, with their swords, and died. Abraham Lincoln. Henry Howard Brownell. GN

Then slowly lift so frail a fame,/Or softly drop so poor a shame. Died. Elizabeth Barrett Browning. NOBV

Then slowly turned his pinto horse/And rode away again. Death Rode a Pinto Pony. Whitney Montgomery. BPAW

Then smile on it, so that it may not die. Epipsychidion. Percy Bysshe Shelley. ISi

Then smiled as she thought that there had been one/And that Peeping Tom was better than none. Lady Godiva. Edward Shanks. HBMV

Then soared away a captive queen set free. The Wasp. John Davidson. FM

Then solitude flows onward with the/rivers... Solitude. Rainer Maria Rilke. TrJP

Then/something/stacks/up/pushes/forward/and/happen s. d How Everything Happens (Based on a Study of the Wave). May Swenson. HAP; RFM

Then sound sleep to you till the day be wide. Sonnets of the Months. Folgore da San Geminiano. AWP

...Then splitting skull and dream, there come/Blotting our lights, the Trumpeter, the sun. Beethoven's Death Mask. Stephen Spender. OxBTC; UnS

Then stills its artisans like ghosts,/Denying they have been. It sifts from leaden sieves. Emily Dickinson. DiPo; PoPl; SoSe

Then stoop so swift unto our Sence,/As thou wert sent Intelligence. The Falcon. Richard Lovelace. PB

Then straight air, sea, and earth are hushed at once. The Seasons. James (1700-48) Thomson. OAEL 1-2

Then, stretched on the faithless ground, spill/Libations of cold tea, scatter crusts. At a Potato Digging. Seamus Heaney. IPY

Then stretches out my golden wing,/And mocks my loss of liberty. How Sweet I Roam'd. William Blake. CBEP; SeCePo; TreFT

Then striking boldly seaward, reach/The smooth-stoned slope of heaven's beach. Earth-Canonized. Henry Morton Robinson. CAW

Then substitute a little hope/And lots of faith in God. Worry. George W. Swarberg. STF

Then sudden heart to heart was wildly/pressed. But Once. Theodore Winthrop. AA

Then suddenly he reels. The Satirist. Harry Lyman Koopman. AA

...Then suddenly/I saw You with my heart. Sight and Insight. Eleanor Slater. TrPWD

& Then suddenly wonderfully/soaring/ultimately away/ A Documentary on Airplane Glue. David Henderson. MAT

Then supperless he laid him down/That night, and slept beneath the stars. The Mendicants. Bliss Carman. HBV 1-2

Then sure thou'lt like, or thou wilt envy me. Upon the Same. Robert Herrick. CaPo

Then sure 'tis right, in time of trouble,/That our good rulers should see double. Porson on His Majesty's Government. Richard Porson. FaBoCo

Then swallowed up to view. I've Known a Heaven Like a Tent. Emily Dickinson. BoLiVe

Then, Sweet Saint Francis, make me mad. A Franciscan Prayer. Enid Dinnis. CAW

Then take Julia de Burgos by force. Pentachromatic. Julia de Burgos. InW

Then take me to thyself above. Here, Lord, Retired, I Bow in Prayer. Matthew Bolles. AH

Then teach desire, hope, not rage, fear, grief,/Powers as unapt to take, as give relief. Caelica, LIV. Fulke, Lord Brooke Greville. FCP

Then tell, O tell, how thou didst murder me. When Thou Must Home. Thomas Campion. AWP; InPo; LoBV; OBSP; SeCeV; ViBoPo

Then tell, O tell, how thou didst murther me. Carmina, II, 28. Sextus Propertius. OBVE

Then tenderly your eyes will let it go... Initiation. Rainer Maria Rilke. TrJP

Then terror took his soul by storm:/So he decided to reform. The Reformed Pirate. Theodore Goodridge Roberts. WHW

Then thank the Lord, O thank the Lord,/For all his love. We Plough the Fields. Jane M. Campbell. FaPoR

Then thank thyself, wild fool, that would'st not be/Content to know–what was too much for thee! To His Books. Henry Vaughan. QFR

...Then/The Birthday shines, when logs not burn, but/men. Another Birthday. Ben Jonson. WiR

Then the devil should have no power. Dives and Lazarus. *Anonymous.* BaBo; ELP; ESPB; FaBoBa; OxBB

Then the Dispenser I beheld,/His fleshfork on his back. A Vision That Appeared to Me. MacConglinne. OnYI

Then the dog sat on the tucker-box/Five miles from Gundagai. Bullocky Bill. *Anonymous.* PoAu 1-2

Then the dreadful night shall break. Cradle Song. William Blake. FPL; GTBS; HBV 1-2; HBVY; OBEV; PoLf; PoPl

Then the droll recommencement of the search. Egg-and-Dart. Robert Finch. OBCV

Then the dubious smell/of flowers placed under circling flies. Minor Elegy. Henriqueta Lisboa. BoWoP

Then the face of sleep must be the one face you were looking/for. Mammy Hums. Carl Sandburg. PoNe

Then the fly. The Pets. Robert Farren. CoBE; OxBI

Then the hard side, cold side, skinside's, beyond all question,/inside outside. The Sleeping-Bag. Herbert George Ponting. CenHV

Then the hunger wakens in me–/For the glittering sensations of the night! Trumpet and Flute. Gunnar Hernaes. LiTW

Then the laurel shall lie on the crumpet/And crown of my head! A Song of Renunciation. Sir Owen Seaman. CenHV

Then the living fleece of her long bright hair, she combed with a/golden comb. I Love My Love. Helen Adam. NeAP; NMM; WPOW

Then the mill stops. When the Wind Blows. Anonymous. OxNR

...Then the monster, then the man. The Princess. Alfred, Lord Tennyson. ImOP

Then the moon goes crocus. Crocus Night. James Schuyler. PoM

...Then the noblest breast first felt/Itself for its own proper object melt. Love's Force. Thomas Carew. CaPo

An' then the noise of the crowd began. The Mountain Whippoorwill. Stephen Vincent Benét. StPo; TrGrPo; YaD

...Then the rest/of us pitched in and hit. Why We Bombed Haiphong. Jonathan Holden. MAYP

Then the sky filled with tears of blood, and snakes sang. A Temple. Kenneth Patchen. EAS

Then the slimy son of a gun, he gaives us double time. The Sergeant, He Is the Worst of All (with music). Anonymous. AS

Then the souls you've cheered will/know/Who ye be, an' say "Hullo!" "Hullo!" Sam Walter Foss. PaPo

...Then the steps towards the lighted town Dieppe. Samuel Beckett. NOBI

Then the unwilling Marble must/Surrender all this Saint's sweet dust. Epitaph. Sir William Davenant. ACP

Then the warrior son of my father has become a witless fool. Battle Pledge. Anonymous. WTO

Then the weather will be warm. If the Robin Sings in the Bush. Anonymous. PBBP

...Then the whole bloody business starting all over/again. Watt (excerpt). Samuel Beckett. BIrV

Then the whole land is lost indeed in night. The Rejected "National Hymns". Robert Henry Newell. InMe

Then the whole secret will be out. The Secret. Anonymous. SoPo; TiPo

Then there is hope that you may see/Her love me once, who now hates me. Impossibilities, to His Friend. Robert Herrick. OBSP; OLR

Then there lies a Lady of pleasure. The Ranting Wanton's Resolution; 1672. Anonymous. CoMu

Then there's a dim/smell of moose, an acrid/smell of gasoline. The Moose. Elizabeth Bishop. FaBoWP

Then there's the road to go/And the stranger's bed. The Home Fire. Orrick Johns. HBMV

Then these delights my minde might move,/To live with thee, and be thy love. The Nimphs Reply to the Sheepheard. Sir Walter Ralegh. AAS

Then these fat, foul, unbreathing, moving/things/Droop back to stagnant immobility. The Andante of Snakes. Arthur Symons. VLP

Then they are satisfied! The Limits of Submission. Faarah Nuur. TTY; WTO

Then they'll see me and the darling day/Footing it over the Hill together! The Bride. Ruth Comfort Mitchell. HBMV

Then they put my beauty in the ground. The Hairdresser. David Hopes. AMV-81

Then they remember their calves/let's go Evening. Tristan Tzara. VWA

Then they sank once more and were washed ashore/At the Point of Interrogation. Metaphysics. Oliver Herford. NA

Then think at last I too am such an one. A Sonnet. Conrad Aiken. AnEnPo

Then think I love more than I can express,/And would love more, could I but love thee less. Song: "No, no, fair heretic." Sir John Suckling. AtBAP; CaPo; LiTL; LoBV; OBS; PrIm

Then thinke not long in taking litle paine,/To knit the knot, that ever shall remaine. Amoretti, VI. Edmund Spenser. AAS

Then thinke not that my heat can dye,/Til you burne as well as I. To My Mistris, I Burning in Love. Thomas Carew. AnAnS 2; SeCP

Then this land will be for you and me. Is This Land Your Land? Anonymous. FSW

Then thou the hours of dark shalt spend/Out there, where is no wrong. Days and Nights. Thomas Sturge Moore. HBMV

Then–thou then–mayst heed me! Smile and Never Heed Me. Charles Swain. HBV 1-2

Then, though kings, player-like, act glory's part,/Yet all within them is but fear and art. Caelica, CI. Fulke, Lord Brooke Greville. FCP

Then, though we do not know, we love. Lord, When the Wise Men Came from Far. Sidney Godolphin. HAP; MeLP; NOCV; OBS

Then thought I, Oh there is a Judge above/Will all this wrong with one true sentence move. Satyrus Peregrinana. William Rankins. OBSV

Then 'tis at the very best. When the Wind Is in the East. Anonymous. OxNR

Then to fall back exhausted into the unconscious, molten life! Dreams Old and Nascent. D. H. Lawrence. WGRP

Then to increase thy Triumph, let me rest,/Since by thine Eye slain, buried in thy Breast. The Tombe. Thomas Stanley. OBS

Then to injoye what others misse/Laridon, tan, tan, Tedriton teight.' The Judgement of Desire. Edward, Earl of Oxford De Vere. EnPo

Then to our fifth French Suite. Considerations on Certain Music of J.S. Bach (excerpt). J. C. Beaglehole. AnNZ

Then to sea, boys, and let her go hang! The Tempest. William Shakespeare. FF; MOS; NOBL; OBSP; ViBoPo

Then to still sing to thee, how great thou art. Then Sings My Soul. Paul Mariani. GeTw; MAYP

Then to the church they both did hie. Coridon's Song. Thomas Lodge. UnTE

Then to the Maker selfe they likest be,/Whose light doth lighten all that here we see. Amoretti, IX. Edmund Spenser. AAS

Then to the poor she freely gives the milk. Upon Sybilla. Robert Herrick. CaPo

Then too late the scorn of youth by age shall be repented. Underneath a Cypress Shade, The Queen of Love Sat Mourning. Anonymous. GBL

Then took he the wound, smiling,/And died, content. Content. Stephen Crane. AA

"Then trust on Mon, whose yerde can talke." Imitation of Chaucer (parody). Alexander Pope. FaBoPa; Par

Then turn aside and leave my dust in earth. Requiem. Theodore Maynard. GoBC

Then turn it off and go on reading. Growing Up. Linda Gregg. NPGG

...Then turne/O pensive soule, to God, for he knowes best/Thy true griefe, for he put it in my breast Holy Sonnets, VIII. John Donne. MasP

...Then turned and looked once more/Upon her sky-blue cloth, and closed the door. Blue Homespun. Frank Oliver Call. CaP

Then turned to his sizzling,/And sank him back. Alas, Alack. Walter De La Mare. EvOK; FaPON; OxBChV; TiPo

Then turning slides his saddle off,/An' quickly disappears. Ol' Dynamite. Phil Le Noir. BPAW

...Then turning they/drift out like heavy clouds into the meadow. The Wheelbarrow. Russell Edson. LCAP

Then Uddalaka Aruni was silent. Upanishads: Seventh Brahmana. Anonymous. ILwL

An' then, vor all I can but way my hat/An' thank en, I do veel a little shy. False Friends-Like. William Barnes. NOBV

Then walked to me and touched me, as if she knew/Something neither of us would ever say. Brief Encounter. Winfield Townley Scott. GOYP

Then waltzed me off to bed/Still clinging to your shirt. My Papa's Waltz. Theodore Roethke. AmP; CAPP; CMoP; CrMA; CTBA; FF; HaCAP; HAP; HeIP; HoPM; InPK; InPS; LCAP; LiTM; MiAP; MoAB; NCSH; NIP; NLV; NoAm; NOBA; NoP; PAI; PPoe; PPP; PrIm; SM; TAP; VGW; WeW

Then was his Father King Henry,/Who (men thought) did the same. The Journey into France. Anonymous. CoMu; FaBoBa; OBTV

Then wastes and crumples it to dry brown sorrow. Prognostic. Samuel Yellen. NePoAm

Then watch and labour while time is. Awake, Awake! Thomas Campion. ELP

Then Waterford true shall never decrease–/Quam diu vere intacta manes. The Praise of Waterford (excerpt). Anonymous. NOBI

Then we are nearest to the dreamed-of gods. Epilogue. Richard Aldington. BrPo

...Then we go looking. Origin of Dreams. Marvin Bell. LCAP

...Then we have nightmares/even the huge storms of the prairies cannot overcome. Paths They Kept Barren. John Garmon. AMV-81

...Then we heard them, every word. Charles Carville's Eyes. Edwin Arlington Robinson. CMoP; NePA; OxBA; TAP

Then we knew that earth to earth had called. What We Listened for in Music. Gray Burr. HW

Then we'll believe in that incredible/unanimal mankind(and not until) When Serpents Bargain for the Right to Squirm. Edward Estlin Cummings. MP; PrIm; SoSe; TwCP

Then we'll land on the shore and we'll shout forever more! Now Our Meeting's Over. Anonymous. ABF

Then we'll surely have a soak. If the Oak Is out before the Ash. Anonymous. OxNR

Then we sail o'er yellow waves. The Fairies in New Ross. Anonymous. OnYI

...Then we/shall call her worthy; and for destroyers perfect.   New Construction: Bath Iron Works.   G. Stanley Koehler.   NePoAm-2

Then we shall turn to the evening,/We two on our own,/To rest.   When I Was Growing Up.   David Vogel.   VWA

Then we weep for ourselves, and wish thee good-/bye.   Dirge Written for a Drama.   Thomas Lovell Beddoes.   EnRP

Then we will be safe, and rich, and happy here forever.   Discovery of the New World.   Carter Revard.   VoR

...Then we will dance/to the music/of his flute.   Woman Painter of Mithila.   Erika Mumford.   PoDr

Then weigh against a grain of sand the glories of a throne.   Mary, Queen of Scots.   Henry Glassford Bell.   BeLS; BLPA; FaBoBe

Then welcome day, and farewell mortal night!   We Would See Jesus.   *Anonymous.*   AH; BePJ

Then welcome, hail! damnation.   On James Grieve, Laird of Boghead, Tarbolton.   Robert Burns.   DBV

Then were the natural charites exhaled/Afresh, from out the blessed love of Mary.   Our Lady in the Middle Ages.   Frederick William Faber.   ACP; CAW; ISi

Then what have I to do with thee?   To Tirzah.   William Blake.   EnRP; NOBE; OxBoCh

Then what is? I ask. What is?   Consider a Move.   Michael Ryan.   MAYP; SM

Then what odds 'twixt you and Joan?/Truly in my judgment, none.   Joan to Her Lady.   *Anonymous.*   UnTE

Then what we sow/With our lips let's reap, love's gains dividing.   Basia.   Thomas Campion.   GTBS

Then, wheesht man. Sae it is wi me.'   Still Gyte, Man?   George Campbell Hay.   BSV

Then when my sunne is absent from my sight/How can it chuse (with me) but be dark night?   Sonnets, IV: "Two stars there are in one faire firmament."   Richard Barnfield.   PeHV

Then, when the trumpet's holy Yes/rings clear,/We shall be here!   And Yet We Are Here!   Karl Wolfskehl.   TrJP

Then which of us will not lie last at crossroads?   To the Thoughtful Reader.   William Meredith.   NoAm

Then while we live, in love let's so persevere/That when we live no more, we may live ever.   Another.   Anne Bradstreet.   SBG

Then whipped them all soundly and put them to bed.   There Was an Old Woman Who Lived in a Shoe.   Mother Goose.   FaBoBe; FaFP; HBV 1-2; HBVY

Then, whirr! she was over, a mile at a flight.   Hunting Song.   Robert Burns.   PBBP

Then who a jolly fisherman,...   The Fisherman"s Song.   Thomas D'Urfey.   ALV

Then, who knows/Rose-footed swan from snow, or girl from rose?   The Swans.   Edith Sitwell.   ACV; CMoP; MoVE

Then why art thou silent, Kathleen Mavourneen?   Kathleen Mavourneen.   Louisa Macartney Crawford.   FaBoBe; FSW; HBV 1-2; TreF

Then why do they sneer at me?   The Jew.   Isaac Rosenberg.   MoBrPo; VWA

Then why does your reflection seem/So lonely in the moving night?   Corner Seat.   Louis MacNeice.   MoVE

Then, "Why, no,"/I thought, "Why should I, if the rest are so?"   Company.   William Dean Howells.   AmePo

Then why such haste? so groan'd and dy'd.   Fables: The Sick Man and the Angel.   John Gay.   CEP

Then, why the dickens don't you go and do it?   Our Traveller.   Henry Cholmondeley-Pennell   InMe

Then wi a sigh his heart it brast,/An his soul to heaven has flown.   The Lass of Roch Royal (D version).   *Anonymous.*   AmFP; ESPB

Then will be cleared up all mystery.   Constance Kent.   *Anonymous.*   OBET

Then will Christ and Christmas be/The hope of all humanity.   Christmas Still Lives.   Clarence Hawkes.   BePJ

Then will His angels come and lead/thee in/To Paradise.   O Soul, With Storms Beset.   Solomon Ibn Gabirol.   TrJP

Then will I crave with sured confidence./And thus begins the suit of his pretense.   De Profundis.   Sir Thomas Wyatt.   FCP

Then will I laugh and clap my hands,/As they do now at me.'   A Farewell.'   George Gascoigne.   LoBV; NOBE; OBSC

Then will I rise and dress me lord for thee/Who did'st by death undress thee lord for me.   The Resurrection.   Nathaniel Wanley.   LoBV

Then will I surely overcackle thee.'   The Cock and the Hen.   John Heywood.   PBBP

Then will I swear beauty herself is/black,/And all they foul that thy complexion/lack.   Sonnets, CXXXII: "Thine eyes I love, and they, as pitying me."   William Shakespeare.   OAEP; OBSC

Then will no more such sport be found.   Sweet Cupid, Ripen Her Desire.   *Anonymous.*   OBSP; ViBoPo

Then will she greet the new world with her cry?   The Idiot.   Adele Naude.   PeSA

Then will such bright candles as these/Be not held hostages too soon.   So?   James P. Vaughn.   AmNP

Then will we, when labour's o'er,/At harvest-home our catches roar.   The Seasons.   Thomas Holcroft.   NOEC

Then will your hidden Pride/Raise greater fires in men.   The Lilly in a Christal.   Robert Herrick.   AnAnS 2; AtBAP; NoP; PoEL 1-5; SeCePo; SeCP

Then willing let my spirit go/To work or wait elsewhere or here!   A Wish.   Matthew Arnold.   HBV 1-2

Then wilt thou too achieve thy destiny and redeem!   The Messiah.   David Frishman.   LiTW

...Then winds up his line/and continues to walk, looking down.   The Subway Grating Fisher.   Louis Simpson.   CAPP

Then, winter, do I cry, "Thy greed/Is great, ay, thou art cold indeed!"   Winter.   Charles Mair.   OBCV; PeCV

Then with a head erect, but without a sound,/"Rake" Windermere stepped out.   "Rake" Windermere.   Leonard Pounds.   PaPo

Then with a shuddering heart no more I/read.   I in the Grayness Rose.   Stephen Phillips.   EnLit

Then, with lowered head, came back to the Ants' Nest.   Having Climbed to the Topmost Peak of the Incense-Burner Mountain.   Po Chu-i.   SD

Then worth, love, reason, beauty be content/In Myra only to be permanent.   Caelica, XIV.   Fulke, Lord Brooke Greville.   FCP

Then would I decke her head with glorious bayes,/And fill the world with her victorious prayse.   Amoretti, XXIX.   Edmund Spenser.   AAS

Then would I set as little by him/As my master doth set by me.'   The Jolly Pinder of Wakefield (A version).   *Anonymous.*   BaBo; ESPB

Then yef I little of kith or kin,/For ther is alle gode./Amen.   Crucified to the World.   *Anonymous.*   MeEL

...Then you are interested/in poetry.   Poetry.   Marianne Moore.   AmP; AP; APA; ATP; BiP; BLPL; BoWoP; CoAnAm; CoBMV; ExPo; FaBoWP; FF; HAP; HeIP; InPo; LiTA; LiTM; MoAB; MoAmPo; NAMP; NePA; NIP; NoAm; NOBA; NoP; OxBA; PP; TAP; TreFT; UnPo; ViBoPo

Then you blow it rough.   Jeremiah, Blow the Fire.   *Anonymous.*   OxNR

Then you came forth, and all the earth was light!   The Meeting.   Jocelyn Hollis.   AMV-80

Then you have finished/Being small/And started/Being Big.   Then.   Dorothy Aldis.   BiCB

Then you in the twilight will long for my burning voice/to praise your black beauty.   Songs for a Three-String Guitar.   L. Sedar-Senghor.   PBA

Then you know that the poor boy's in the ground   Two White Horses in a Line.   Two Poor Boys.   BluL

Then you may tell the tale, nor fear/What the result of speech may be.   Three Gates.   Beth Day.   BLPA; GoTF; PoToHe; TreFS

Then you must fly and I must run,/Shu-a-O! Shu-a-O!   O All You Little Blackey-Tops.   *Anonymous.*   PBBP

Then you must, please,/Fall on your knees.   The Snowdrop.   Anna Bunston de Bary.   HBMV

Then you will slowly kiss me.   Notice the Convulsed Orange Inch of Moon.   Edward Estlin Cummings.   VGW

Thence came Jesus to release us,/Favored Bethlehem.   Lowly Bethlehem.   Nicolaus Zinzendorf.   TrAS

Thence falling on her garment's hem/For greife it freez'd into a gem.   On a Gentlewoman Walking in the Snowe.   William Strode.   BoC; OBS

Thenk well who me rente on the Rode.   Jesus Bids Man Remember.   *Anonymous.*   MeEL

Thenne woweth he wurs.   Snatches: "Whenne bloweth the brom."   *Anonymous.*   OxBM

An ther came never on back/Bat Young Allan alive.   Young Allan.   *Anonymous.*   ESPB

Ther fore we mown syngyn/Deo Gracias.   Adam Lay I-Bowndyn.   *Anonymous.*   AtBAP; BoW; CBEP; CTC; EG; EnPo; GoBC; HAP; InPS; MeEL; NOBE; NOCV; OAEL 1-2; OAEP; OxBM; OxBoCh; OxBoLi; PAI; PoEL 1-5; PPoe; SeCeV

Ther mideers went up and doun the water,/Saying, Clayd's water din us wrong!   The Mother's Malison, or, Clyde's Water.   *Anonymous.*   ESPB

Ther's dool i the kitchin, and mirth i/the ha,/The baronne o Braikley is dead and/awa.   The Baron of Brackley (A version).   *Anonymous.*   BaBo; ESPB; OxBB

Ther's hemp, and flax and tow to to to,/Tow to to to to tero.   Whipping Cheare.   *Anonymous.*   FaBoBa

Ther's lesse to be Applauded then forgiven.   The Appology.   Anne Finch, Countess of Winchilsea.   SBG

Ther shall I be,/Man to restore,/Naylit full sore/Uppon a tre.'   Mary Weeps for Her Child.   *Anonymous.*   OxBoLi

Ther wakeneth in the world wondred and wee-/As good is swinden anon as so for to swinke!   The Farmer's Complaint.   *Anonymous.*   OxBM

Ther was Adam sore aferd,/For labour coude he werken non.   Adam Driven from Eden.   *Anonymous.*   OxBM

Theras Saint Jeorge y-named was,/St. George. St. George. St. George.   For the Night-Mare.   *Anonymous.*   OxBM

There a very little girth/Can hold round what once the earth/Seemed too narrow to contain.   The Bourne.   Christina Georgina Rossetti.   ELP; HBV 1-2; LoBV; NOBV; OBNC

There ain't a body livin' in the land/As I "swop" for my dear old Dutch!   My Old Dutch: A Cockney Song.   Albert Chevalier.   VLP

There ain't no fig.   No Fig.   Stephen Todd Booker.   LFAC

There all the year/Love's nightingales shall sit and sing.   Love's Nightingale.   Richard Crashaw.   LoBV

There alone, at last, I rest.   For Them All.   John Hall Wheelock.   HBMV

There alway, alway something sings.   Music.   Ralph Waldo Emerson.   AnNE; FaBV; WGRP

There are a lot better ways to have a ball/Than scraping the hair off your own head.   Because Sometimes You Can't Always Be So.   Kenneth Patchen.   NaP

There are always new words/new books he can turn to/till the breath becomes natural.   Davening.   Rochelle Ratner.   VWA

There are as many tastes as tongues!   Food and Drink (excerpt).   Louis Untermeyer.   MoAmPo

There are better things to do/With it than make a home of it.   A Bestiary.   Kenneth Rexroth.   OBAL

There are birds summoned by words.   Sophia Nichols.   Robin Blaser.   CoPo

...There are bones at the hearth.   Abel's Bride.   Denise Levertov.   FaBoWP; VGW

There are butterfly wings on a gypsy's loving./Gorgio lad, good-bye.   Gorgio Lad.   Amelia Josephine Burr.   HBMV

There are courses in log-rolling/and a shortage of trees.   University Curriculum.   William Price Turner.   OxBS; PoL

There are doors of tissue gold...   May Morn.   Michael McClure.   EAS

...There are dozens of wood ducks on the/slough!   The Mad Farmer Stands Up in Kentucky for What He Thinks Is Right.   James Baker Hall.   TAT

There are few such noblemen here to be found.   The Jolly Thresherman.   *Anonymous.*   AmFP

..."There are five or six lunatics,/one of them a woman."   Berthe Morisot.   Anne Waldman.   APU

...There are ghosts/on the island of Yorrick.   The Island of Yorrick.   N. M. Bodecker.   WSC

There are gold heelprints on the fading/staircases of the stars.   Love in Labrador.   Carl Sandburg.   VGW

There are holes in his face.   Flowers.   Roo Borson.   CaPN; NOBC

There are hundreds and thousands/of advantages   Sharks in Shallow Water.   Fred Levinson.   AmPA

There are many things/I wish he would never learn.   First Holes Are Fresh.   Vivian Shipley.   AMV-81

...There are mines/Far down, whose sacred fee/And golden hold can not trammelling can bind.   Rosa Nascosa.   Maurice Hewlett.   OBVV

There are more women here than men.   Poetry Reading.   Vernon Scannell.   NOBL

"There are no birds in last year's nests"?   To Miguel de Cervantes Saavadra.   Richard Kendall Munkittrick.   AA

There are no butterflies, here, in the ghetto.   The Butterfly.   Pavel Friedmann.   VWA

...There are no echoes.   A San Diego Poem: January–February 1973.   Simon J. Ortiz.   CDW

There are no horses we will use/the dogs. they will do.   Mathematics.   Joel Oppenheimer.   CoPo

There are no kings or poison,/Are laws but no more reason.   The Tribes.   Roy Fuller.   LiTM

There are no mails in a city of the dead.   I Will Write.   Robert Graves.   PCP

There are no more songs but his stirring.   Man Holding Boy.   Melvin Dixon.   LTB

There are no rent days on the sea!   The Fisher's Life.   *Anonymous.*   EtS; GBP

There are no sunsets now, and I am cold.   The First Day of the Hunting Moon.   Patricia Low.   VGW

There are no two exactly alike.   Limerick: "In the wax works of Nature they strike."   Anthony Euwer.   HBMV

There are no violets here.   War Is Kind.   Stephen Crane.   AP

There are no words for "love" or "death."   Rissem.   Sandra M. Gilbert.   AMV-81

There are none like me here, only/companions and marvels.   Prospect Beach.   Lou Lipsitz.   VGW

There are not many better/Things than a unicorn horn.   A Bestiary.   Kenneth Rexroth.   OBAL

There are old-fashioned folk still like it.   To an Ungentle Critic.   Robert Graves.   HBMV; InMe

...There are only/Cypress moments lingering and the long tray of the sky.   The Cats of Campagnatico.   Peter Porter.   OBTV

There are records.   The Business.   Robert Creeley.   CAPP

There are riches far greater/Than his he can know!   True Riches.   Bessie June Martin.   STF

...There are seasons no longer acceptable.   Counterparts.   Stephen Dobyns.   PoA

There are seekers of wisdom no less absurd,/son Hang, than thy fish that would be a bird.   The Flying Fish.   John Gray.   NOBV

There are so many little dyings that it doesn't matter which of/them is death.   And What with the Blunders...   Kenneth Patchen.   NaP

There are so many people/More clever than I am.   From Greenland to Iceland.   *Anonymous.*   FaFP

There are so many things admirable people/do not understand.   Passing Remark.   William Stafford.   GP

There are some things, it seems,/you just can't get close to.   Mysterious Britain.   Amy Clampitt.   AMV-81

There are some thoughts that are my own/I do not wish to share.   Where Have You Been Dear?   Karla Kuskin.   NTCP

...There are the Alps,/fools! Sit down and wait for them to crumble!   On the Fly-Leaf of Pound's Cantos.   Basil Bunting.   FaBoTw; NoAm; OxBTC

"There are the useful stars, and here am I."   Sonnet: "The understanding of a medical man."   Rex Warner.   ChMP

There are the wings of a thousand biplanes.   The Old Pilot.   Donald Hall.   LCAP

There are too many monuments of broken hearts.   There's No Place to Sleep in This Bed, Tanguy.   Charles Henri Ford.   EAS

...There are/twice as many stars as usual.   The Two-Headed Calf.   Laura Gilpin.   FYAP

There are two moons on the horizon/and for you/I have broken loose.   Two Horses.   Joy Harjo.   TWSS

There are two of us here. Touch me.   The Blind Leading the Blind.   Lisel Mueller.   IHMS

There are words that must be written,/Songs that must be sung.   Flail.   Power (Haold Caleb Dalton) Dalton.   HBMV

There beams above a manger/The child-face of a star.   The Kings of the East.   Katharine Lee Bates.   WGRP

There beauty walks, wherever it may be,/And paints the sunset on the quiet sea.   Beauty Is Ever to the Lonely Mind.   Robert Nathan.   HBMV

...There being such need/of loaves and fishes everywhere.   Ants and Others.   Adrien Stoutenburg.   BoAnP; FYAP; NYBP

...There blooms a deathless flower,/That breathes on earth the air of paradise.   To the Marchesana of Pescara.   Buonarroti Michelangelo.   CTC

There breaks in every Gloucester wave/A widowed woman's heart.   Gloucester Harbor.   Elizabeth Stuart Phelps Ward.   AA

There breaks this day their dawn of liberty.   Sonnet to Negro Soldiers.   Joseph Seaman Cotter, Jr.   PoBA

There but for the grace of God speak I.   Oh, Stop Being Thankful All Over the Place.   Ogden Nash.   NePA

There came a day when Adam turned his back upon Eve,/and gardened.   I Thought I Saw Stars.   R. P. Lister.   PV

There came a little blackbird,/And snapped off her nose.   Sing a Song of Sixpence.   *Anonymous.*   HBV 1-2; OxNR; PoPl; SpRo

...There came a red robin/To sing of the buttercups and dew.   Sleepyhead.   Walter De la Mare.   TiPo

There came a wave and stood above your mast.   The Death of Peter Esson.   George Mackay Brown.   NePoEA-2

There Caron Cerberous and the rout of/feinds,/Had lap enough and so their pastims ends.   The Poem: "I sing th' adventures of mine worthy wights."   Thomas Morton.   SCAP

There comes a sound of marriage bells.   The Letters.   Alfred, Lord Tennyson.   HBV 1-2

There comes no wanderer to the tree/And for himself she is not there.   The Tree in the Desert.   Friedrich Hebbel.   LiTW

There crackles in the hearth/The holly's fusillade.   Winter.   Maurice James Craig.   OnYI

There creeps upon my inward ear/The creak of hidden wires.   To Cynthia, Not to Let Him Read the Ladies' Magazines.   P. M. Hubbard.   FiBHP

There'd be no Hell, there'd be no grief,/there'd be no terror, but for me.   Eve Am I, Great Adam's Wife.   *Anonymous.*   NOBI

There dwells thy loved Santa Claus.   Santa Claus.   Walter De la Mare.   PCh

There ends the whole tale of Nell Flaherty's drake.   Nell Flaherty's Drake.   *Anonymous.*   TW

There falls the shadow of an eagle's breast.   Timber Line Trees.   Jamie Sexton Holme.   PoOW

There, far away, between sky and wave, alone,/would they believe Moishe Leib.   Memento Mori.   Moishe Leib Halpern.   VWA

There fayth doth fearlesse dwell in brasen towre,/And spotlesse pleasure builds her sacred bowre.   Amoretti, LXV.   Edmund Spenser.   AAS

There fix their stings, and leave their souls behind.   Georgics.   Virgil (Publius Vergilius Maro).   FaBoUs

There fixed till the last thunder's sound/Shall bid thy prisoners be unbound.   The Genius of Death.   George Croly.   HBV 1-2

There flames the first gay daffodil/Where winter-long the snows have lain!   Daffodils.   Ruth Guthrie Harding.   HBMV

There for an hour on that lean/threshold, neither outside nor in. The Porch. R. S. Thomas. NOCV

There for ever may we sing/Alleluyas to our King. As with Gladness Men of Old. William Chatterton Dix. FaPoR

There from the burning light of you/The world and I am laid. Who Is It Talks of Ebony? Manmohan Ghose. OBMV

There go a wild and wicked youth. The Rambling Boy. *Anonymous.* OBET

There God is dwelling too. The Divine Image. William Blake. CEP; EBCP; EnL; EnPE; EnRP; NOBE; NoP; OAEL 1-2; OBEC; OBNC; OxBoCh; PPP; TEP; TRV; ViBoPo; WGRP

"There goes another girlie,/That's being led astray." When I Was Young and Foolish (with music). *Anonymous.* AS

"There goes Jack Rack, poor sailor lad, he must go to sea once more!" Off to Sea Once More. *Anonymous.* ShS

There goes the kettle, I'll make the tea. Departure. Edna St. Vincent Millay. MoAmPo

"There goes the milk,"/As the hoofs went by! The Strangers. Audrey Alexandra Brown. WHW

"There goes the Riley." I Never Saw the Train. Jean Roberts. AMV-80

There grateful to heaven, with transport shall bring. As Down a Valley. Timothy Dwight. AH

There grows one in the Human brain. The Human Abstract. William Blake. BiP; DiPo; EnRP; PPP

There guarded from the wolf and–sheared. By Plain Analogy We're Told. Ambrose Bierce. DBV

There had been at least ere this/A dozen dozen in her place. Song: "Out upon it, I have lov'd." Sir John Suckling. MeLP; MePo; SeCP; WHA

There has been enough tears. Flash. Stephen Todd Booker. LFAC

There has been no greater sinner than yourself. To a Pope. Pier Paolo Pasolini. PeHV

There! have them all! Choosing. Eleanor Farjeon. TiPo

There he changed into a man again/And carried her off like a sack of hay. How Our Forefather Got His Wife. Eda Lou Walton. BPAW

There heavenly splendors shine. And Have the Bright Immensities. Howard Chandler Robbins. AH

There I'll meet Mary and my Jane. The Little Dove. *Anonymous.* AmFP

An' there I'll meet ye a' soon/Frae my ain countrie! The Sun Rises Bright in France. Allan Cunningham. BSV; HBV 1-2; OBRV

There I saw her. The Death of Venus. Robert Creeley. AmPC; NOBA

There I stand. There I be. A Living. W. S. Di Piero. AMV-80

There I would be at dawn. When Dawn Comes to the City: New York. Claude McKay. GoSl

There in the beginning. Loss. Alex Kuo. BrSi

There in the flower garden/they will kill me. Song: "There in the flower garden." *Anonymous.* BoWoP

There in the fragrant pines and the cedars dusk and dim. Drum-Taps. Walt Whitman. AP

There in your teeth much Leprosie. To Women, to Hide Their Teeth, if They Be Rotten or Rusty. Robert Herrick. FaBoUs

There is a balm in Gilead, to heal the sin-sick soul. Balm in Gilead. *Anonymous.* FSW

There is a calm for you when men and women/Unroll the chill precision of moving feet. Death of Little Boys. Allen Tate. LiTA; MoAB; MP; TwCP

There is a chance he will swim towards me./Will he take it? The Possibility That Has Been Overlooked Is the Future. Michael Hartnett. NOBI

There is a dignity in silence. Memorial to the Great Big Beautiful Self-Sacrificing Advertisers. Frederick Ebright. WaP

There is a face which you shall see/And wish for nothing more. Wind Me a Summer Crown. Menella Bute Smedley. HBV 1-2; OBVV

...There is a fire/"raging" throughout a house, and a company–No. 7–/pulling a hose toward it. Careers. Marjorie Welish. APU

There is a great deal to be said/For being dead. Clerihew. Edmund Clerihew Bentley. NOBL

There is a memory in the forest. Not unto the Forest. Margaret Widdemer. HBMV

There is a mirror for our transparent sadness The Tree of Diana. Alejandra Pizarnik. VWA

There is a part which can't decay. Hymns for Infant Minds (excerpt). Jane Taylor. PaPo

There is a picture of the incident. Lord Abbott. Hilaire Belloc. FaBoNo

There is a place where love begins and a place where/love ends–and love asks nothing. Explanations of Love. Carl Sandburg. LiTL; MoLP

There is a sign of His foot/On Marblestone where He stood. Domine, Quo Vadis? *Anonymous.* ACP; CAW

There is a single hole/in the clouds through which/time is escaping. The River. Don Welch. Str

There is a spirit, shifting around from foot to foot. Thoughts. Michael Benedikt. ConAP

...There is a tear/in my blue eyes for her sake. Saint Harmony My Patroness. Paul Goodman. VGW

There is a Tide/stronger than/death/Which Humankind/is carried/on. Hunger Strike. William Franklin. LFAC

There is always a time/for retribution/and that time/is beginning. I Like to Think of Harriet Tubman. Susan Griffin. NMM

There is always a wicked secret, a private reason for this. At Last the Secret Is Out. W.H. Auden. InPS; SeCePo

There is an Alexandria for every age. To Theon from His Son Theon. C. A. Trypanis. NCSH

There is an ear that may incline/Even to words so dull as mine. I Know Not Whether I Am Proud. Walter Savage Landor. EnRP

"There is an end to even the worst career!" Elegy in the Cemetery of Spoon River...(parody). J. C. Squire. BXAP

There is an heirloom somewhere. Heirloom. Leonard Cohen. NOBC

There is another kind of/Eagle on flags and money. A Bestiary. Kenneth Rexroth. OBAL

There is but little Latin in my maw. The Shipman. Geoffrey Chaucer. ACP

There is but one, and that one ever. Easter. George Herbert. AtBAP; FaBoCh; LoGBV; NOBE; OBS; OHIP; SeCV 1-2; TrGrPo

There is but time for prayer. Christian, Be Up. Robert Nathan. AH

There is dule in the kitchen, and mirth/i the ha,/But the Baron o B The Baron of Brackley (B version). *Anonymous.* ESPB

There is far more sea than land./Yo...ho, yo...ho. The Sea Serpent Chantey. Vachel Lindsay. AmMo; WSC

There is grey in your hair. The Aged Woman to Her Sons. Babette Deutsch. AMV-81

There is honey in the groin/Billy. Billy the Kid. Jack Spicer. CoPo

There is just time enough for that.' The Barber. Roy Fuller. NoAm

There is life. White Fox. Elizabeth Alsop Shepard. GoYe

There is life, still/unbelief is left. Still. Aila Meriluoto. PBWP

There is mony a man and mother's son/That was at my love's burial.' The Coble o Cargill. *Anonymous.* ESPB

There is more if there is any. To a Child with Eyes. Mark Van Doren. LOW

There is more of the same,/Especially,/today... Today: The Idea Market. Michael Nicholas. NBP

There is more than glass between the snow and the huge roses. Snow. Louis MacNeice. BiP; CIP; CMoP; ExPo; FaBoIP; FaBoMo; FPL; LiTM; NoAm; NOBE; OBSP; OxBTC

There is more than half left. Vital Message. Robert Phillips. GeTw

...There is/Much more of it than something. A Bestiary. Kenneth Rexroth. OBAL

There is my bed, table and dish,/And all things. A Collection of Hymns...of the Moravian Brethern (excerpt). *Anonymous.* NOEC

There is my Lord self-revealed: and the scent of sandal and/flowers dwells in those deeps. Songs of Kabir. Kabir. WGRP

There is naught but anguish ev'rywhere/As on through life we go. Oh, My Liver and My Lungs. *Anonymous.* OuSiCo

There is naught can amaze me,/Dislike can not daze me,/'Cos I don't care. I Don't Care. Jean Lenox. FSN

There is no answer other to this mystery. Psyche with the Candle. Archibald MacLeish. MoLP; PCP

There is no ball. Baseball. Tom Clark. ANYP; LiSp

...There is no/barrier between his thought and you. Yom Kippur: Fasting. Ruth Whitman. OFD

There is no being alone again. The Changing Wind. Julian Orde. NeBP

There is no black. Is no white./No guilt./All/Are right. Rabbi Yussel Luksh of Chelm. Jacob Glatstein. TrJP

There is/no cart/moving Poeti-c Art. Arudra. PCP

...There is no choice among the voices/Of love. Even a carp sings. The Talking Fish. Ruth Stone. BoWoP

There is no conclusion to this poem. Ever. Drunken Poem. David Helwig. NOBC

...There is no cure/Nor antidote but tears. Time! Where Dist Thou Those Years Inter. William Habington. OxBoCh

There is no dark, nor death. Nightsong. Philip Booth. MoLP

There is no death–there's immortality. There Is No Death. *Anonymous.* BLPA; FPL

There is no doubt of that. Night Thought of a Tortoise Suffering from Insomnia... Emile Victor Rieu. FiBHP

There is no escape–/no escape. The Sacrifice. Moshe Yungman. VWA

There is no face tonight that is not alien. Sonnet: "The crumbled rock of London is dripping under." Roy Fuller. PoA

"There is no failure save in giving up!" Don't Give Up. *Anonymous.* FaFP; PoToHe

There is no fishing to the sea, nor service to the king. The Mariner's Song. Sir John Davies. OBSC

There is no game/like one that creates/its own good geometry. Billiards. Laurie Blauner. AMV-81

There is no God, but we, who breathe the air,/Are God ourselves and touch God everywhere. Sonnet: "There is no God, as I was taught in youth." John Masefield. WGRP

...There is no guilt in love   Numbers, Letters.   LeRoi (Imamu Amiri Baraka) Jones.   BPo; NOBA

There is no holier spot of ground/Than where defeated valor lies,/By mourning beauty crowned!   Ode to the Confederate Dead in Magnolia Cemetery.   Henry Timrod.   PAL; TreFT

There is no hope to take it in.   The Triumph of Beautie Song (excerpt).   James Shirley.   ErPo

...There is no hope unless/I give in and never go back.   Herdsman.   Michael Pettit.   MAYP

There is no ideal time for canning.   The Joy of Cooking: Conserves.   David Mus.   PoA

There is no jungle, sighed the striped mind.   The Known World.   Brewster Ghiselin.   MoVE

There is no king can rule the wind,/There is no fetter for the sea.   A Song of Freedom.   Alice Milligan.   AnIV; OnYI

There is no King more terrible than Death.   The Dance of Death.   Henry Austin Dobson.   HBV 1-2

There is no knob on the door. Or there is no door.   Why God Permits Evil: For Answers to This Question of Interest...   Miller Williams.   SM

...There is no law which says/That men must imitate their images.   Five Epigrams.   Donald Hall.   NePoAm-2

There is no light but Thine: with Thee all/beauty glows.   Third Sunday in Lent.   John Keble.   VLP

There is no living with thee nor without thee.   Temperament.   Martial (Marcus Valerius Martialis).   AWP; ELU

There is no love/Without leaves falling   Tree Poem on My Wife's Birthday.   Tom Hanna.   FAZ

There is no luck out there beyond earshot.   A Play of Opposites.   Gray Burr.   CoPo

There is no man on earth who must not face this task now.   Ultimatum.   Peggy Pond Church.   TRV

There is no mask to hide a lonely soul.   The Clown.   Margaret E. Bruner.   PoToHe

...There is no more giving in/when there is no more sin.   The Kind of Act of.   Robert Creeley.   NeAP

There is no more life for me!'   Rajpoot Rebels.   Sir Alfred Comyn Lyall.   OBTV

There is no music now in all Arkansas.   Variations for Two Pianos.   Donald Justice.   NYBP

There is no need for you to answer.   The Fever.   Rosemary Dobson.   FaBoWP

There is no need of Hell, while Earth shall last.'   There Was No Place Found.   Mary Elizabeth Coleridge.   OxBoCh

There is no need of other sound/To soothe my Lady's dreams.   The Linnet in the Rocky Dells.   Emily Bronte.   BrRo; VLP

There is no one but that will play/At up-tails all.   Up-Tails All.   Anonymous.   UnTE

There is no one like me.   Meditations of a Tortoise Dozing under a Rosetree...   Emile Victor Rieu.   FiBHP

"There is no one more beautiful than I."   Leaves.   Frank Asch.   NTCP

..There is no one/to hear. The water is red.   Wounds.   Judith Minty.   GeTw

There is no one to keep her from leaving.   Memory, a Small Brown Bird.   Rich Ives.   AMV-81

There is no one to share my thoughts.   Alone.   Chu Shu-chen.   BoWoP

There is no other hope.   Tomorrow the Heroes.   A. B. Spellman.   CNA; PoBA

There is no other life.   Why Log Truck Drivers Rise Earlier Than Students of Zen.   Gary Snyder.   NNaP; SOTW

There is no other Viverols.   Viverols.   David Starr Jordan.   AA

...There is/no other way, academically, to settle their likenesses/but by brutal dislocation.   The Old Stories.   Gene Frumkin.   AMV-80

There is no pain for me. I am your heart.   Funeral.   Murray Bennett.   GoYe

There is no peace with you/Nor ever any rest!   Enigma.   Jessie Redmond Fauset.   PoNe

There is no perfect record standing by/Of God's reply.   Conversation in Avila.   Phyllis McGinley.   EaLo

There is no pity in the flesh.   Young Woman.   Howard Nemerov.   ErPo

There is no prize for loving, but there's laurel in a rhyme!   Daphne and Apollo.   George Macy.   InMe

There is no reason you should read,/And much less understand, this rhyme.   To a Poet a Thousand Years Hence.   John Heath-Stubbs.   OxBC

There is no remedy.   O Death, Rock Me Asleep.   Anonymous.   CBEP; TrGrPo

There is no respite from day, no furlough from dying.   No Furlough.   Stephen Stepanchev.   WaP

There is no rest upon the earth, peace is with/Death and thee–/Barbara!   Barbara.   Alexander Smith.   BSV; GoTS; HBV 1-2; OBVV

There is no room for pupils any more.   Ballata: Of True and False Singing.   Anonymous.   AWP; UnS

There is no siding for the brain.   Listening to a Broadcast.   John Streeter Manifold.   WaP

There is no sorrow and no sadness here!   A Calm Sea.   Robert Southey.   EtS

...There is no sound but a window/opened wide to show more air.   Beginning by Example.   Christopher Gilbert.   FYAP

There is no thing which love may not achieve.   Love much. Earth has enough of bitter in it.   Ella Wheeler Wilcox.   PoToHe

There is no time now for my dream of hawks.   I Have Exhausted the Delighted Range...   Michael Hartnett.   CIP

There is no time to ask–he knows not what.   Conscious.   Wilfred Owen.   MMM

There is no waking, not anywhere.   Breath.   Reginald Gibbons.   MAYP

There is no way that is so just/As truth to lead, though t'other fail,/And thereto trust.   It Was My Choice.   Sir Thomas Wyatt.   EnRePo; FCP; QFR; SiPS

There is no wind can mark his place/Here, or hence.   Twenty Stars to Match His Face.   William Stanley Braithwaite.   HBMV

There is no word for goodbye.   There Is No Word for Goodbye.   Mary Tallmountain.   STE

There is none in this world like a pitboy for me.   Brave Collier Lads.   Anonymous.   OBET

There is none like the Boy that sold Broom, green Broom.   Green Broom.   Anonymous.   ALV; StPo

There is none that knows.   My Love.   Ono-no-Yoshiki.   AWP; LiTW

There is not a single believer/Who went up into the sky!   You Are Lying, O Missionary.   Raymond Mazisi Kunene.   WTO

There is not much else that we dare to praise.   Courage Means Running.   William Empson.   LiTB

There is nothing.   A Day for Anne Frank.   C. K. Williams.   GeTw

There is nothing at all but Me.   Illusion.   Ella Wheeler Wilcox.   WGRP

There is nothing at all I can do except hold your hand/and not go away   Poem: "You are ill and so I lead you away."   Al Purdy.   NOBC

There is nothing between us.   Jealousy.   Stephen Vincent.   NeAC

There is nothing between us.   Medusa.   Sylvia Plath.   CAPP

There is nothing but sand/where I go.   Water.   Edmond Jabes.   VWA

There is nothing/expected nor/leaving   Untitled Requiem for Tomorrow.   Conyus.   PoBA

...There is nothing/for you.   Death Songs.   L.V. Mack.   PoBA

There is nothing in a hole in the ground/That continues being dry.   Bob Stanford.   Anonymous.   CoSo

There is nothing in books, only a few words.   There Is a Box.   Uri Z. Greenberg.   VWA

There is nothing more beautiful/Than memory.   Our Angels.   Howard Schwartz.   VWA

There is nothing more to say.   The House on the Hill.   Edwin Arlington Robinson.   AA; AnNE; GoJo; GoTF; HBMV; LaNeLa; MoAmPo; PG; PrIm; TreFT; TrGrPo; WHA

There is nothing new in new york.   There Is Nothing New in New York.   Miguel Pinero.   NYP

There is nothing one man will not do to another.   The Visitor.   Carolyn Forche.   FYAP

...There is nothing/sorrier than the marriage of two deaths.   Black Spring.   Annensky.   NaP

There is nothing that He cannot do.   The Saviour Can Solve Every Problem.   Oswald J. Smith.   BePJ

There is nothing to be afraid of. Nothing at all.'   Brother and Sisters.   Judith Wright.   FaBoWP

There is nothing/To comfort me but you.   When I Am Not With You.   Sara Teasdale.   MoLP

...There is nothing to/Say about them. Nothing at all.   Time Is the Mercy of Eternity.   Kenneth Rexroth.   VGW

There is nowhere a land more loved/Than bonnie Nidderdale.   The Song of Nidderdale.   Dorothy Una Ratcliffe.   HBMV

There is one voice between us.   No Difference.   Beverly Lawn.   AMV-81

There is only one flaw in the window/of his sleep: Nothing on the other side.   Man Asleep in the Desert.   Thomas Lux.   LCAP

There is only one To-day.   The Voice of the Dove.   Joaquin Miller.   AA

There is only one wave/in the universe and Hokusai is/master of it.   Hokusai's Wave.   Olga Cabral.   PoDr

There is only one way, to be sure/There is a way   The Fourth Option.   Henry Rasof.   AMV-80

There is only the grass to fight!   Dandelion.   Hilda Conkling.   TiPo

There is openness/wind/trees/children running/To keep appointments I kept long ago.   Getting Out.   J. J. Maloney.   LFAC

"There is really no circumstance of human life,/in which He has not at times been our forerunner."   These Past Years: Passages 10.   Robert Duncan.   PoM

There is silver in the wind.   Silver in the Wind.   Ian Strachan.   PoSH

There is singing of morals in Latin and Greek.   A Dream of Judgement.   Douglas Dunn.   OxBC

There is so little time/even for the finest/of watches. There Are Delicacies. Earle Birney. NoP

There is so much that shames me/Before Thy saints in radiant light. This Flock So Small. Anna Nitschmann. AH

There is someone who understands why.../we do the things we do. The World's Last Unnamed Poem. A. K. Redwing. VoR

There is something/being said April 68. Sam Cornish. CNA

There is something between us. Breasts. Donald Hall. OBAL

There is something down there and you want it told. Dark Pines under Water. Gwendolyn MacEwen. NOBC

..."There is something/Far wrong, certainly, somewhere. But with me or the world?" Crisis. G. S. Fraser. NeBP

There is something in your throat that wants/to get out and you won't let it. Your Back Is Rough. Margaret Atwood. NeAC

There is the child's voice/Of a coyote's crying. There Are Places. Myra von Riedemann. OBCV

There is the gaunt power/That sucks men for their marrow. Northern Ireland: Two Comments. Seamus Deane. CIP

There is the sea. Space. The wind blowing. East Coast–Canada. Elizabeth Brewster. CaP

There is the sound of the balalaika waking in heaven. Balalaika. Norman Dubie. AmPA

There is the tarnish; and there, the imperishable wish. Armour's Undermining Modesty. Marianne Moore. AP; CoBMV

There is the westrn gate, Luke Havergal–/Luke Havergal. Luke Havergal. Edwin Arlington Robinson. MAmP

There is this look of love Throne Silent look of love Still Poem 9. Philip Lamantia. NeAP

There is thy glorie, riches, force, and Art. Shadow of Night: Hymnus in Noctem. George Chapman. AtBAP

There is, to be named one with her, no woman born. No Woman Born. Robert Farren. OxBI

There is too much sun on the lids of my eyes to be listening Frescoes for Mr. Rockefeller's City. Landscape as a Nude. Archibald MacLeish. UnPo

There is white quiet at the end. Elegy, Montreal Morgue. Goodridge MacDonald. CaP

There is yet time. There Is Yet Time. Arvel Steece. PGD

There isn't any/Three-l lllama. The Lama. Ogden Nash. FaBoCh; FiBHP; PV

There isn't any/where to go. Outside. Phyllis Beauvais. IHMS

There isn't very much to do. James Wetherell. Edwin Arlington Robinson. MoAmPo

There it comes, then it comes, and it comes. Santo Domingo Corn Dance. R. P. Dickey. TAT

There it is: I give you my gift. The Gift. Dick Lourie. NeAC

There lay the wind at their feet like a pathway. The Land behind the Wind. David Wagoner. NPAW

There least amusement where he found the most. The Task. William Cowper. FiP

There–leaving out a Man–. It's Easy to Invent a Life. Emily Dickinson. AmePo

There let Faith beget on Love/The angel thou shalt be Above! Fall of the Year. Henry Ellison. OBVV

There let men hear thee, O my song, until/Thy tears are ended and my pain is stilled. Night. Chaim Nachman Bialik. AWP; LiTW

There lies a fair young maiden/All silent in the tomb. Florella. *Anonymous.* AmFP

There lies the body of Ellen Adair!/And there the heart of Edward Gray!' Edward Gray. Alfred, Lord Tennyson. OBVV

"There lies the George E. Corbitt! She's a handsome barkentine!" Corbitt's Barkentine. *Anonymous.* ShS

...There lies/Upon its head of thorns a crown of beads. Autumnal Consummation. Patric Stevenson. NeIP

There lingering till time and tides/Shall surge no more. To William Sharp. Clinton Scollard. HBV 1-2

There! little girl, don't cry! A Life-Lesson. James Whitcomb Riley. AA; FPL; HBV 1-2; PoLf; TreFS

There lived a certain man and he had three sons. The Western Approaches. Howard Nemerov. HaCAP; TAP

There lives not, never did, nor will,/one who more gravely stole my love. No Sickness Worse Than Secret Love. *Anonymous.* NOBI

There'll be A Hot Time/In The Old Town/Tonight. My Grandaddy Mostly with His Knife. David Huddle. GrPl

There'll be a lively mix-up down there among the coals. Sam Bass. *Anonymous.* ViBoFo

There'll be no second helpings/When you get to the Nine Springs. Clear Bright. Li Ch'ing-chao. BoWoP

There'll be two losses for one winter. The Plowman. *Anonymous.* APAS

There'll never coal nor candle-light/Shine in my bower nae mair.' Clerk Saunders. *Anonymous.* FaBoBa; ViBoFo

There Love in very presence seemed to be. Ballata: Concerning a Shepherd-Maid. Guido Cavalcanti. AWP

There Mary hath kissed her Child. A Christmas Carol. May Probyn. ACP; CAW; ISi

There may be hidden meaning in his grin. The Menagerie. William Vaughn Moody. AP; YaD

There may be smoke and a thin sound. The Depot. Lewis Turco. GrPl

There may be still one left for you. The Yacht. Walter Savage Landor. OBVV

...There may be then/No resurrection in the minds of men. Sonnet: "It is not death, that sometime in a sigh." Thomas Hood. LoBV; OBNC; ViBoPo

There may emerge the green and tender shoots/Of two or three bright stanzas. Translations from the Chinese. Christopher Morley. EvOK

There, most of all, thou art. Not Only Where God's Free Winds Blow. Shepherd Knapp. AH

...There must be/other tigers about Sad Day in Berlin. Sarah Kirsch. PBWP

There must be some such place somewhere/But I never heard of it Where? Kenneth Patchen. LiTM

...There must be/something else. Silence. Someone else? A Short Treatise upon Our Failures. Ken Norris. CaPN

There must be somewhere work to do. Habeas Corpus. Helen Hunt Jackson. AA; AnAmPo; WGRP

There must be sorrow if there can be love. Canzone. W. H. Auden. LiTA; MoVE

There never was such taxes in Ireland before. A New Song on the Taxes. *Anonymous.* WTO

There never will be room for walls to rise! A Bridge Instead of a Wall. *Anonymous.* PoToHe

There/No flower. In the Grave No Flower. Edna St. Vincent Millay. CrMA

There, now and then, are found/Life-loyalties. The Woodlanders: In a Wood. Thomas Hardy. PoPl

There, O there, where'er I go, I'll leave my heart behind me. Since First I Saw Your Face. *Anonymous.* CBEP; ELP; LiTB; OBEV; OBSP

There of thy master keep that sign./And this plain stave. Kaiser Dead. Matthew Arnold. FM

There, on a winter dawn, thy corse I found,/Lone Spirit of the Fall. The Spirit of the Fall. Danske Dandridge. AA

There on the happy tree they hung/The Savior of mankind. The Happy Tree. Gerald Gould. WGRP

There one; on earth alone/I lie, you free. Eudaimon. Kathleen Raine. PBWP

There only came to her forlorn/Butterflies all black. Butterflies. John Davidson. HBV 1-2

There Paradise is found! Forbidden Fruit. Emily Dickinson. AnNE

THERE'RE PLENTY OF SOLDIERS. Dead Soldier. Nicolas Guillen. TTY

There read the fable, time is always now. Fable. Mary Mills. NePoAm

There, rigid as death and unforgiving, stand/the mountains–and close at hand. Benicasim. Sylvia Townsend Warner. OBWP

There's a better home a-waiting/In the sky, Lord, in the sky. Can the Circle Be Unbroken? *Anonymous.* FSW

–There's a bit on stone, a bit on bone/and a bit on this withered hand.' My Hands Are Withered. *Anonymous.* NOBI

There's a circus in the sky/every snowy winter day! Winter Circus. Aileen Fisher. YeAr

There's a curley headed girl just a-roaming in the world,/I'll always call her mine. The Mournful Dove (The False True-Lover). *Anonymous.* AmFP

There's a fire under the moon. Driftwood. Witter ("Emanuel Morgan") Bynner. FYAP

There's a great camp meeting in the Promised Land. Walk Together Children. *Anonymous.* BPo

There's a hush in the deeps beyond deeps/That is kin to the hush within you! Taos Drums. William Haskel Simpson. BPAW

There's a joke there somewhere./Get it? Autograph Book/Prophecy. Anne Halley. NMM

"There's a Land that is Fairer than This." Nelson Street. Seumas (James Starkey) O'Sullivan. OxBI

There's a little black train a-comin',/An' it may be here tonight. The Little Black Train. *Anonymous.* AmFP; OuSiCo

There's a little death in every body. Horror Movie. Howard Moss. NePoEA-2

There's a loss for every gain! An Old Song Reversed. Richard Henry Stoddard. AA

There's a man going 'round taking names. The Angel of Death. *Anonymous.* AmFP

There's a-many a river that waters the land. The Brazos River. *Anonymous.* PrIm

There's a puff–and so good night! Good Night. Thomas Hood. SiSoSe; SoPo

There's a red light on the track for Bolsum Brown.　Bolsum Brown (with music).　*Anonymous.*　AS

There's a ring around the world/Made of children's friendly faces.　Ring around the World.　Annette Wynne.　TiPo

There's a roarin' in my head, O Lord,/There's a roarin' in my head.　John Henry (A vers.).　*Anonymous.*　ViBoFo

There's a scad o' things that to make a house a home it takes not only a/heap, or a peck, but...　Lines to a World-Famous Poet...　Ogden Nash.　OBAL

There's a scorpion under every stone.　Fragments.　Praxilla.　PBWP

There's a sound of gentle sobbing in the South.　Anzac Cove.　Leon Gellert.　PoAu 1-2

There's a stagnant pool that wants to be fed/New bodies, every day.　At the Center of Everything Which Is Dying.　Patricia Goedicke.　FAZ

There's a sweet, soft page of mine/Does the trick worth forty wenches.　Song: "Love a woman? You're an ass!"　John Wilmot, Earl of Rochester.　GBL; NLV; NOBL; PeHV; TW

There's a voice telling me I'm he, the good little egg you meant.　Parodies of Cole Porter's "Night and Day".　Ring Lardner.　OBAL

There's a welcome above for a Moneyless Man!　The Moneyless Man.　Henry T. Stanton.　BLPA

There's a word for my praise–if there's a rhyme for/cantos!　Published Correspondence: Epistle to the Rapalloan.　Archibald MacLeish.　PoA

There's also no place comfortable to sit.　Windy Trees.　Archie Randolph Ammons.　PPJ

There's always hot water/in this house　Ming the Merciless.　Jessica Hagedorn.　BrSi

...There's always something new.　The Body.　William Bronk.　VGW

There's always the self same mind to lead us home at/night.　Little Roads to Happiness.　Wilhelmina Stitch.　PoToHe

There's an awful shrug and, suddenly,/you're beautiful for as long as you live.　Poem for People Who Are Understandably Too Busy to Read Poetry.　Stephen P. Dunn.　GOYP

There's an end of old John Brown!　The Battle of Charlestown.　Henry Howard Brownell.　PAH

There's an end to all misery.　The Smile.　William Blake.　OBRV

There's Banbury Cakes, and Lollipops/For me, me, me.　The Cupboard.　Walter De la Mare.　BrR; FaPON; NTCP; SoPo; TiPo

There's barley there, and water there,/And stabling to your mind.　Come Ride and Ride to the Garden.　Gregory Lady.　SUS

There's been a great change since I been bohn.　Things I Used to Do (with music).　*Anonymous.*　AS

There's bread and cheese upon the shelf,and if you want any just help yourself.　Mister Frog Went A-Courting (with music).　*Anonymous.*　AS

There's but one white violet.　To Miss Arundell.　Walter Savage Landor.　OBVV

There's comfort for the comfortless,/There's nane but you for me.'　The False Lover Won Back (B version).　*Anonymous.*　ESPB

There's danger in crossing to Twickenham Town.　Twickenham Ferry.　Theophile Marzials.　HBV 1-2

There's few enough as it is.　The Betrothal.　Edna St. Vincent Millay.　PG

There's five black swine and never an odd one.　Pigs o' Pelton.　*Anonymous.*　GBP

There's hardly a baby that hasn't been born.　In Spring in Warm Weather.　Dorothy Aldis.　BiCB

There's just one Book.　Just One Book.　*Anonymous.*　BLRP

There's light for us above!　The Watcher.　Sarah Josepha Hale.　AA

"There's light upon it still."　Lincoln.　Nancy Byrd Turner.　TiPo

There's little coin and less devotion.　The Voice of Ardent Zeal Speaks from the Lollard's Tower of St. Paul's.　Henry Farley.　FaBoEE

There's little comfort in the wise.　Tiare Tahiti.　Rupert Brooke.　BrPo; SeCeV

...There's little nourishment in ashes.　Earth Buried.　Kenneth Mackenzie.　CBAP

There's little pleasure in the house/When our gudeman's awa'.　The Sailor's Wife.　William Julius Mickle.　BeLS; BSV; GN; GTBS; GTBS-P; HBV 1-2

There's logs to run, there's peavy fun/To break the timber loose!　When the Drive Goes Down.　Douglas Malloch.　AmFN

"There's magic, too, at home."　Vacation Time.　Rowena Bastin Bennett.　SiSoSe

There's many a man killed on the railroad,/An' cast in a lonely grave.　Ther's Many a Man Killed on the Railroad (with music).　*Anonymous.*　AS

There's many another Inn in town.　Quits.　Thomas Bailey Aldrich.　AA

There's more grief at my heart than my poor tongue can tell.　Johnny Dyers.　*Anonymous.*　AmFP

There's more pretty girls than one.　There's More Pretty Girls Than One.　*Anonymous.*　AmFP

There's more–there's more!　God's Love.　*Anonymous.*　BLRP

There's Mother. There's Sister.　A Guide to Familiar American Incest: Inventing a Family.　Dennis Saleh.　NeAC

There's music in the old bones yet.　Song for the Clatter-Bones.　Frederick Robert Higgins.　LiTB; OBMV; OnYI; OxBI

There's nae luck about the house,/When our gudeman's awa.　The Mariner's Wife.　William Julius Mickle.　ViBoPo

There's nane again sae bonnie!　Bonnie Lesley.　Robert Burns.　AtBAP; CTC; GTBS; GTBS-P; NOBE; OBEC; OBEV

There's neer a man lie by my side/Since Willie's drowned in Yarrow.　The Water O Gamrie.　*Anonymous.*　BaBo

There's never a man will lose his can/Till he hears the mighty Tom.　Christchurch Bells.　*Anonymous.*　OBET

There's newer, nearer crucifixion/Than that.　One Crucifixion is Recorded Only.　Emily Dickinson.　AnNE

An' there's no discharge in the war!　Boots.　Rudyard Kipling.　BLPA; FaPoR; FPL; MoBrPo; WHA

There's no good day to die/in these wars.　Another Dying Chieftain.　Rayna Green.　TWSS

There's no hiding place down here.　No Hiding Place.　*Anonymous.*　FSW

...There's no mirth/Which is not truly season'd with some madness.　The Lovers Melancholy.　John Ford.　PoEL 1-5

There's no more to be said.　On Prince Frederick.　*Anonymous.*　FaBoEE; GoTF; NOBL; TreFS

There's no' much pleasure livin' aff'n ten and nine.　The Jute Mill Song.　*Anonymous.*　OBET

There's/no one/person/to send/it to.　Rattan bed, paper netting.　Li Ch'ing-chao.　BoWoP

There's no place/anymore for me to go now/except home.　A Folded Skyscraper (excerpt).　William Carlos Williams.　AnAmPo

There's no place like home, oh, there's no place like home!　Home, Sweet Home.　John Howard Payne.　AA; BLPA; BLSo; FaBoBe; FaFP; GoTF; HBV 1-2; PaPo; PSoN; TreF; WBLP

There's no recipe like laughter–/Laugh it off.　Laugh It Off.　Henry Rutherford Elliot.　WBLP

...There's no right name/for how it was. The farm's never looked the same.　One-Night Fair.　Nancy Price.　GOYP

There's no saving you.　Lightness Remembered.　Nancy Willard.　LCAP

There's no sense making earnest out of game.　The Canterbury Tales: Prologue to the Miller's Tale.　Geoffrey Chaucer.　EBEV; NAWM 1-2; OAEL 1-2; TEP

There's no vexation that can make thee prime.　To a Weak Gamester in Poetry.　Ben Jonson.　JCP

There's no vice now but has his president.　Nothing New.　Robert Herrick.　CaPo

There's no Vitality.　There is a languor of the life.　Emily Dickinson.　BoWoP

There's none but a madman will fling about fire,/And tell you, "'Tis all but in sport."　Innocent Play.　Isaac Watts.　NOEC

There's none like the Skoodawabskooksis/Excepting the Skoodawabskook.　Sweet Maiden of Passamaquoddy.　James De Mille.　WHW

There's not a bird of day that dare/Extinguish that delight.　A Last Confession.　William Butler Yeats.　BoLoP; CMoP; ELP; HAP; LiTL; OAEL 1-2; WeW

There's not a bonie bird that sings,/But minds me o' my Jean.　Of A' the Airts the Wind Can Blaw.　Robert Burns.　AWP; EiCP; EnLi 1-2; GoTS; InPo; LoBV; NoP; OAEP; OBEC; OxBS; ViBoPo

There's not a boy in a thousand/That a young girl can trust.　My Love, She Passed Me By.　*Anonymous.*　AmFP

There's not a flower in Erin's bower/Can match the Orange Lily O.　The Orange Lily O.　*Anonymous.*　GBP; IrPN

There's not a man in Highland dress/Can face the cannon's fire.　Bonny John Seton.　*Anonymous.*　BaBo; ESPB

There's not a peal in England sounds so well.　Mole Catcher.　Edmund Charles Blunden.　OBMV

There's not a thing but love can make/The world a narrow pound.　Solomon to Sheba.　William Butler Yeats.　CMoP; ELP

There's not a wish the heart can have/Which Thou dost not fulfill.　He Satisfies.　Frederick William Faber.　BePJ

There's not one blade that does not long to fall.　Counter-Serenade: She Invokes the Autumn Instant.　Peter Viereck.　CrMA

There's nothing at all that will make them respect us.　Heredity.　Arthur Guiterman.　OBAL

There's nothing but our own red blood/Can make a right Rose Tree.　The Rose Tree.　William Butler Yeats.　CMoP; DiPo; ELP; FaBoPV; OBMV

There's nothing calm but Heaven!　This World Is All a Fleeting Show.　Thomas Moore.　HBV 1-2

There's nothing here to salvage, and yours is another problem.　Dwarf of Disintegration.　Oscar Williams.　LiTM; MoPo; NePA; PoCh

There's nothing left but Lord, have mercy on us!　Truth Brought to Light; or, Murder Will Out.　Stephen College.　APAS

There's nothing left for us to say of us.　Thirtieth Anniversary Report of the Class of '41.　Howard Nemerov.　HaCAP

There's nothing like a woodpile/At one's back door!　A Word About Woodpiles.　Nancy Byrd Turner.　BrR

There's nothing like the sun till we are dead.　There's Nothing Like the Sun.　Edward ("Edward Eastaway") Thomas.　FaBV

There's nothing of value here for a man/but the heavy word from everyone's tongue.　If I Went Away.　Desmond O'Grady.　CIP

There's nothing on earth can help you/So much as a kindly deed!　Do Something.　*Anonymous.*　STF

There's nothing this planet can show him!　Jim the Splitter.　Henry Clarence Kendall.　PoAu 1-2

There's nothing to do but to set the teeth/And plough it in.　A Failure.　C. Day-Lewis.　NOBE

There's nothing to fear but life and death--as far as/we know today.　Song, on Reading That the Cyclotron has Produced Cosmic Rays...　Samuel Hoffenstein.　ShM

There's nothing to him like thy ding, dong, Bell.　Upon a Ring of Bells. John Bunyan.　CH

There's nothing we can do to help him now.　On a Dying Boy.　William Bell.　NePoEA

There's nothing worth the wear of winning,/But laughter and the love of friends.　Dedicatory Ode: They Say That in the Unchanging Place.　Hilaire Belloc.　PoLf

There's nought but hum-drum, hum-drum, hum-drum.　Song: "When maidens are young, and in their spring."　Aphra Behn.　FF

There's one amongst them shall not fail/To join the Bos'n's Crew.　Bos'n Hill.　John Albee.　AA

There's one in my bosom,/t'other one in my heart.　Bye Bye Baby Blues. Blind Boy Fuller.　BluL

There's one more river, just one more river to cross.　One More River to Cross.　*Anonymous.*　FSW

There's only room in poetry/for one of us!　S. T. Colerige Dismisses a Caller from Porlock.　Gerard Previn Meyer.　GoYe

There's other fifty pounds in my left/pocket,/Divide it from door to door.' Lord Derwentwater (A version).　*Anonymous.*　BaBo; ESPB

There's plenty all around the chair.　Old Grandpaw Yet.　*Anonymous.* AmFP

There's plenty of bones, so I've been told,/On the banks of the Sacramento. The Banks of Sacramento (with music).　*Anonymous.*　AS

There's plenty of gold in the world, I'm told,/On the banks of the Sacramento shore.　California (with music).　*Anonymous.*　AS

There's quiet in the deep.　The Deep.　John Gardiner Calkins Brainard. AA; EtS

There's room for another/One, Mrs. Malone.'　Mrs. Malone.　Eleanor Farjeon.　OxBChV

There's room for many a more.　Get On Board, Little Children. *Anonymous.*　FSW

There's something in their attitude/That taunts her bayonet.　My country need not change her gown.　Emily Dickinson.　AmFN

There's still more cause why I the more should love.　When I Thy Parts Run O'er.　Robert Herrick.　UnTE

There's such a little way to go.　Be Patient.　George Klingle.　PoToHe

There's tew ways o' remittin'?　Widow Brown's Christmas.　John Townsend Trowbridge.　BeLS

There's the Bodleian!　Cubes.　Mary Elizabeth ("E") Fullerton.　PoAu 1-2

There's this little street and this little/house.　Ashes of Life.　Edna St. Vincent Millay.　BLPL; FaBoBe; HBV 1-2; LiTL

There's werm air tae lave you and bield fae the storm/Wi its cheated scream. Rothiemurchus.　Colin Lamont.　PoSH

There's where the old darkey's heart am longed to go.　Carry Me Back to Old Virginny.　James A. Bland.　BLSo; FaBoBe; FaFP; GoSl; PSoN; TreF

There's where we'll meet and we'll never part no more.　Old Virginny. James A. Bland.　FaBV

There's whiskey in the car.　Bad Day on the Boulder.　Lloyd Davis. WOLT

...There's/work yet, for the living.　Ron Mason.　Hone Tuwhare.　OCNZ

There's your fried egg　A Trueblue Gentleman.　Kenneth Patchen.　SO

...There settling down/Upon the reedy bosom of the water.　A Flight of Wild Ducks.　Charles Harpur.　NOAV

There shall be no more land, say fish.　Heaven.　Rupert Brooke.　AnFE; BrPo; EBEV; ExPo; HoPM; LiTB; LiTM; MoBrPo; NOBE; PoPle; PoRA; SeCeV; WGRP

There shall be no more of you...　The Still Voice of Harlem.　Conrad Kent Rivers.　CNA; IDB; NNP; PoBA

There shall be no more sin to hate.　Taliesin: A Masque: Voices of Unseen Spirits.　Richard Hovey.　AA

There shall be peace between us two.　Reconciliation.　J. U. Nicolson. HBMV

There shall I sing in bliss amid angelic lyres,/The eternal, glad today!　My Song of Today.　Saint, of Lisieux Therese.　CAW

There she sits in the picture,/Daughter of foam and fire.　Laus Veneris. Louise Chandler Moulton.　AA; HBV 1-2

There she was before.　Snatches: "A man may a while."　*Anonymous.* OxBM

There should be Joy!　A Bell.　Clinton Scollard.　AA

There should be reassuring voices,/Silent, in the flutters of the heart.　The Fate of Birds.　Kenneth Seib.　AMV-80

There should our hearts be--Christ, how/far!　Shop.　Robert Browning. VLP

There showed small semblance of a missing link!　At the Zoo.　Walter De La Mare.　BoAnP

There, sick with deaths, the sword/Sighs back into the sheath.　Deus Noster Ignis Consumens.　Laurence Housman.　HBMV

There sleeps that fair Florilla,/So silent in her tomb.　The Jealous Lover (A vers.).　*Anonymous.*　BaBo; ViBoFo

There soon would be nothing but trees.　Kind Lovers, Love On.　John Crowne.　InvP

There stands bird-haunted Lehua.　O Thirsty Wind.　*Anonymous.*　WTO

There, still in murderer's guise, two stand embraced, embalmed.　Packet of Letters.　Louise Bogan.　GrPl; LiTL; PCP

There still will be too much for me/To hold in one glad heart.　God, You have Been Too Good to Me.　Charles Wharton Stork.　TrPWD; WGRP

There still would seem to be a way.　The Unforgiven.　Edwin Arlington Robinson.　CMoP

There stood that little Elvish man/And smiled to see her, too!　The Man Who Hid His Own Front Door.　Elizabeth MacKinstry.　TiPo

There sure was a lot of noisy conversation at Pawirra Pool.　Dark Mountains. Milton Lockyer.　CBAP

There the Larks are, and we shall/See them, when the sky doth fall.　The Commonwealth of Birds.　James Shirley.　GoBC

There the miners are a-digging, digging in the cold, damp ground.　The National Miner.　*Anonymous.*　AmFP

There the nuggets see,/In the Golden Gullies of the Palmer.　The Golden Gullies of the Palmer.　*Anonymous.*　PoAu 1-2

There the Spring-goddess cowers in faint attire/Of frightened fire.　The Palm Willow.　Robert Bridges.　VLP

There the true silence is, self-conscious and alone.　Silence.　Thomas Hood. CBEP; CH; EBEV; GTBS; NOBE; OBEV; OBRV; PoEL 1-5; ViBoPo

There the whole Chore/With one accord/Shall praise the Lord/For evermore. A Psalm of Praise (excerpt).　Richard Baxter.　NOCV

There, there, O there lies Cupid's fire.　Beauty, Since You So Much Desire. Thomas Campion.　ErPo; OAEL 1-2

There they shall cry "All hail!"　Carroll's Sword.　Dallan MacMore.　KiLC

There they twined in a true-lover's knot,/For all true lovers to admire. Bonny Barbara Allen (B vers.).　*Anonymous.*　BaBo

There thou shalt finde my faults are thine.　Judgement.　George Herbert. AnAnS 1; SeCP

...There through a tangent of ice,/his face and hands ashimmer.　Cold Glow: Icehouses.　David Wojahn.　AMV-81; MAYP

There Time shall be/Marshal to Eternity.　Life's Testament.　William Baylebridge.　PoAu 1-2

There to another friend, whom we shall find/As glad to have my body as my mind.　The Blossom.　John Donne.　AWP; InPo; LiTB; UnPo

There to live an Anchorite.　The Muses Elizium.　Michael Drayton. AnAnS 2

There to love our God most glorious.'/Ecce virgo, radix Jesse.　Mary, Queen of Heaven.　*Anonymous.*　MeEL

There to pass over the river and rest/Under the shade of the trees!　Under the Shade of the Trees.　Margaret Junkin Preston.　MC; PAH

There to remain, and there to reign/With him Eternally.　The Day of Doom. Michael Wigglesworth.　SCAP

There to weep and weep, and weep/My whole soul out to thee.　Maud. Alfred, Lord Tennyson.　NOBV; SyP

"There, too, the simple wench will follow after."　Jack and Jill (parody). Charles Powell.　BXAP

There, Victor of his health, of fortune, friends,/And fame, this lord of useless thousands ends.　The Duke of Buckingham.　Alexander Pope.　NOBE; OBEC

There waits the peace thy spirit dwelleth in.　Vain Questioning.　Walter De la Mare.　MoVE

There wanted yet the master work...　Paradise Lost.　John Milton.　FM

There wants no marble for a tomb/Whose breast hath marble been to me. To Roses in the Bosom of Castara.　William Habington.　AnAnS 2; EnLoPo; GoBC; HBV 1-2; LoBV; MeLP; NIP; OBEV; SeCP; UnTE; ViBoPo

There was a deeper gloom around.　The Dead and the Living One.　Thomas Hardy.　MMM

There was a Helen before there was a War,/but who remembers her?　Winter Love.　Hilda ("H. D.") Doolittle.　FaBoWP

There was a navy went into Spain,/When it returned, it came again.　There Was a Monkey.　*Anonymous.*　NA; OxNR

There was a shout about my ears,/And palms before my feet.　The Donkey. Gilbert Keith Chesterton.　BoC; EBCP; FaBV; FaPoR; FPL; GoBC; HBVY; InPK; MoBrPo; OBEV; PoLf; TreFT; WGRP

There was a time/when you were not a loafer.　Will you sleep forever. Korinna.　BoWoP

There was/a woman like a departure in a fragment of/landscape.　More Distant Than the Dead Sea.　Nadia Tueni.　PBWP

There was a year when twice I lost a love/And have not touched that music again. Antigone I. Herbert Martin. PoBA

"There was a youth, once on a time,/Who dearly loved a maid." Once on a Time. Kendall Banning. HBV 1-2

There was an empty place,–they were but three. The Young Gray Head. Caroline Bowles Southey. BeLS

There was an end of their Rilloby-rill. Rilloby-Rill. Sir Henry Newbolt. HBVY

There was an enormous sight of the sea,/A silent water beyond society. Inishkeel Parish Church. Tom Paulin. FaBoIP

There was–and then no more of Thee and Me. Rubaiyat of Omar Khayyam. Omar Khayyam. HoPM

There was many a hearty fisherlad did find a watery grave. Three Score and Ten. Anonymous. OBSS

There was Marie Seton, and Marie/Beton,/And Marie Carmichael, and me.' Mary Hamilton (A version). Anonymous. AmFP; BaBo; ESPB; FaBoBa; NoP; OAEP; ViBoFo

There was my road, and nothing more to say. The Road. John Gould Fletcher. HBMV

There was neither knight, lord, nor earl/Could make him yield before. Robin Hood and the Curtal Friar. Anonymous. BaBo; ESPB

There was never bairn born of a woman/That was born mair bitterly. Duriesdyke. Anonymous. OxBB

There were never three lovers that ever met/More sooner they did depart. Lord Thomas and Fair Annet (B vers.). Anonymous. BaBo; ESPB

There was never winter/But brought the spring. Force. Edward Rowland Sill. AA

There was no authority above them. Lamentations. Louise Gluck. MAYP

There was no girl, there were no cattle, and it was day. The Island and the Cattle. Nicholas Moore. EAS

There was no heart to break if death/For me had made demanding. On the Moor. Cale Young Rice. HBV 1-2

–There was no light; there was no light at all. The Shimmer of Evil. Theodore Roethke. NePoAm-2

There was no Malady–. They Say That Time Assuages. Emily Dickinson. AmePo; OBSP

There was no more talking. The Intellectuals. Dudley Randall. PoBA

...There was/no one here who could play it. Legacy. Gena Ford. IHMS

There was no-one of Dover/With a sister in Deal. The Eel. Walter De La Mare. ShM

There was no other way for mending the breed! An Excellent New Ballad Called the Prince of Darkness. Anonymous. APAS

There was no road except the smothering grove. The Grove. Edwin Muir. LiTM; MoPo

There was no woman in all her mountains/Wonderful as thou! Song at Santa Cruz. Francis Brett Young. HBMV

There was not. The Lobster Pot. John Arden. ELU

There was not any yearning in his eye,/But on his lips and nostril infinite scorn. The Dromedary. A. Y. Campbell. HBMV

There was not one who did not think of home. Conquerors. Henry Treece. GOYP

There was nothing. Glove Glue. Ken Belford. NeAC

There was nothing I could do. Wind Secrets. Diane Wakoski. AmPA

There was nothing more fun than a man! The Little Old Lady in Lavender Silk. Dorothy Parker. InMe; NLV; YaD

There was silence in heaven; as if for half an hour/No angel breathed. Mary's Assumption. Alfred Joseph Barrett. ISi

There was the yellow chalk sign/the factory's "X." The Factory. Olga Cabral. GP

There was this rest for him and her. On Seeing Swift in Laracor. Brinsley MacNamara. AnIV; OxBI

There we'll meet, my ain dear Jean, down by yon burn/side. By Yon Burn Side. Robert Tannahill. HBV 1-2

There we shall meet, when life is o'er,/In that blest Home, to part no more. Mother, Home, Heaven. William Goldsmith Brown. FaBoBe; HBV 1-2

There we two, content, happy in being together, speaking little, perhaps not a word. A Glimpse. Walt Whitman. AmPP; NePA; OxBA; PeHV; PPP

There were a thousand, more or less! The Goatherd. Grace Hazard Conkling. TiPo

There were all of us–all together–and we came. Discovery of This Time. Archibald MacLeish. LiTA; WaP

There were always towns like that Soap (II). Jerome Rothenberg. NNaP

There were arms that, clinging,/Would not let me go. An Autumn Road. Glenn Ward Dresbach. HBMV

There were four recorders sweet upon the wind. Recorders in Italy. Adrienne Rich. UnS

...There were many slain/In the dark fields. The Riders Held Back. Louis Simpson. ConAP

There were no loose ends/to dangle in our dreams. On a Friend's Suicide. Michael Yots. AMV-81

There were thirteen traitor hulls/On fire and sinking! The River Fight. Henry Howard Brownell. AA; EtS

There were thousands of poor people/didn't have no place to go. Back Water Blues. Anonymous. FSW

There were three wold be beten, three wold be/beten there were:/A myll, a stokfish, and a woman. This Pretty Woman. Anonymous. OxBM

There where he sits in Heaven's high/sphere. A Love-Song. Hales Thomas of. MeEV

There where no thought may follow me,/Nor stillest dreams whose pinions plume the way. The Inner Silence. Harriet Monroe. HBMV

There where the grass can grow nearly/four times yearly. Cezanne. Gertrude Stein. TAP

There where the Lord of all/Doth hold His hall. Psalm XXIII. Sir Philip Sidney. FCP

There where there is no grief, nor shall be sadness. Planh for the Young English King. Bertrand. LiTW

There, where we still stand talking in the quad. One More New Botched Beginning. Stephen Spender. CMoP; NoAm; NYBP

There will be found no stays/To stop a thing so clear. Your Looks So Often Cast. Sir Thomas Wyatt. EnRePo; FCP; SiPS

"There will be hundredes today in the Garden of Paradise!"/M'ochon agus m'ochon, O! The Keening of Mary. Anonymous. ISi

"There will be moonlight again!" Whaup o' the Rede: The Blades of Harden. Will H. Ogilvie. GoTS

There will be no pain/but in thirty seconds/the poison will reach your heart. Money. Victor Contoski. GP

There will my eyes have sight. Allah. Siegfried August Mahlmann. AWP

There will never be/enough crying between us. For Anne, Who Doesn't Know. Gail Fox. IHMS

There with His arms stretched wide– The Lord. Jose Maria Gabriel y Galan. CAW

There won't be a drop when you're dead and gone. The Yellow Bittern. Cathal Bui Mac Giolla Ghunna. NOBI

There would be far more goats on the Karroo/And far less in the Senate and the House. A Veld Eclogue: The Pioneers. Roy Campbell. OBSV

There would be no agents. Horae Canonicae (excerpt). W. H. Auden. SaC

There would be no fear, if it were not for me. Eve's Lament. Anonymous. OnYI

There would be no need for tinkers. If "Ifs" and "Ands." Anonymous. FaBoBe; HBV 1-2

There would it live/Close to your flock, nor ever errant wander. About the Heavenly Life. Luis Ponce de Leon. ILwL

There would ye all await, and humble homage do. Easter Morn. Giles the Younger Fletcher. EIL; NOCV

An' there ye saw your picture. The Keekin' Glass. Robert Burns. FaBoEE

There you are, Primrose! I see you, Black Wing! Fairies. Hilda Conkling. TiPo; WSC

Thereafter I sat me against a tree. The Demiurge's Laugh. Robert Frost. OxBA

Thereby denying to this hour of grace/A full-up measure of felicity. The Minute before Meeting. Thomas Hardy. VLP

Thereby to make frail mortal man immortal. Du Bartas: His Divine Weeks...Fifth Day of the First Week (excerpt). Joshua Sylvester. PBBP

Therefor of the bounty of thy Lord be thy discourse. The Morning Hours. Anonymous. PoPl

Therefore give now, that the season of giving may be yours and not/your inheritors'. The Prophet. Kahlil Gibran. PoPl

Therefore, I agree/night in the south/is different from the north/but silent/no. Tennesse Crickets. Randolph Outlaw. LFAC

Therefore, I am immeasurably grateful/To you, for proving shallow, false and hateful. Sonnet for the End of a Sequence. Dorothy Parker. DBV

Therefore I lie with her and she with me,/And in our faults by lies we flattered be. Sonnets, CXXXVIII: "When my love swears that she is made of truth." William Shakespeare. AWP; BiP; EBEV; InPo; NoP; OAEL 1-2; OAEP; PoEL 1-5; PPP; SoSe; TEP; TrGrPo; ViBoPo

Therefore I render of her the memory/Unto the legend of fare Laodomi. To Maystres Jane Blenner-Haiset. John Skelton. AAS

Therefore I stir my inmost heart to worship fervently. My Morning Song. George Macdonald. TRV

Therefore, if Myra change as others do,/Free her; but blame the son, and mother too. Caelica, XXXII. Fulke, Lord Brooke Greville. FCP

Therefore, if thou wilt prove thyself a god,/In thy sweet fires, let me burn this fair rod. Caelica, XXXIV. Fulke, Lord Brooke Greville. FCP

Therefore in all the world, Thy glories, Lord, they own. Hymn for the Lighting of the Lamps. Saint Athenogenes. CAW

Therefore, let every man give Him Thanksgiving/For all that His mercy may allot for men. The Exeter Book: Fates of Men. Anonymous. AnOE

Therefore, like her, I sometime hold my tongue,/Because I would not dull you with my song. Sonnets, CII: "My love is strengthen'd." William Shakespeare. AWP; LiTL; OAEP; OBEV; OBSC; ViBoPo

Therefore little children sing.   Christmas Song.   Eugene Field.   YeAr

Therefore mend, mend! whilst young and fresh.   Learn, Lads and Lasses.   Francis Daniel Pastorius.   SCAP

Therefore my notes on this feast,/These poems,/I, Wang Hsi-chih.   Colophon for Lan-t'ing Hsiu-Hsi.   John Peck.   AmPA

Therefore, now is to me/Eternity!   Song: "Because the rose must fade."   Richard Watson Gilder.   HBV 1-2

Therefore O love, unless she turn to thee/Ere cuckoo end, let her a rebel lie.   Amoretti, XIX.   Edmund Spenser.   AAS; OBSC

Therefore release me and depart on your way.   Whoever You Are Holding Me Now in Hand.   Walt Whitman.   InvP; PoEL 1-5

Therefore take heed!   "Take heed betime lest ye be spied."   Sir Thomas Wyatt.   FCP; SiPS

Therefore that he may raise, the Lord throws down.   Hymn to God My God, in My Sickness.   John Donne.   CABA; DiPo; DTC; EBEV; EnL; GoBC; InPS; LoBV; NIP; NoP; OAEL 1-2; OAEP; OxBoCh; PPP

Therefore the doom is, wherein thou must rest,/Myra that scorns thee shall love many best.   Caelica, XLI.   Fulke, Lord Brooke Greville.   FCP

Therefore, the thing being unavoidable,/Thou shouldst not mourn.   Bhagavad Gita (excerpt).   Anonymous.   DL

Therefore, to-day the singer/Turns beggar once again.   Rhymes to Be Traded for Bread: Prologue.   Vachel Lindsay.   LaNeLa

Therefore we must singen/Deo Gratias.   "O Felix Culpa!"   Anonymous.   ACP; CAW

...Therein lies crushed/Thy heart–to smithereens.   Smithereens.   Dante Gabriel Rossetti.   NOBV

Therein the patient/Must minister to himself.   Macbeth.   William Shakespeare.   TreFT

Thereof God send them part.   Mistrustful Minds Be Moved.   Sir Thomas Wyatt.   FCP; SiPS

Theres no willy in th blues theres no you.   Canto 7.   Tom Weatherly.   PoBA

Therewith she laught, and did her earnest end in jest.   The Faerie Queene.   Edmund Spenser.   MOS

Therfore on thy firme hand religion leanes/In peace, and reck'ns thee her eldest son.   So Sr. Henry Vane the Younger.   John Milton.   OBS

Therfore this song sing I may,/Timor mortis conturbat me.'   The Sparrow-Hawk's Complaint.   Anonymous.   OxBM

"Thermoplylae left one alive–the Alamo/left none."   The Men of the Alamo.   James Jeffrey Roche.   BPAW; PAH

Therof I have a quantyte.   We ben chapmen lyght of fote.   Anonymous.   EnPo

Therwith to trayn the Grekish host/From Troyes return where they wer lost.   The Lover Accusing Hys Love for Her Unfaithfulnesse...   Anonymous.   EnPo

These accents seem their own defence.   Some Trees.   John Ashbery.   CAPP; ConAP; HaCAP; SM

These acts of attention to fill in/all the gaps/where his body keeps going away   Locations.   Kathleen Fraser.   NPGG

These afternoons are rare.   Amores.   Jay Parini.   MAYP

These are a type of the world of Age.   Ballade of Youth and Age.   William Ernest Henley.   VLP

These are certain signs to know/Faithful friend from flattering foe.   Ode: "As it fell upon a day."   Richard Barnfield.   OBSC

...These are flowers/Of middle summer.   The Winter's Tale.   William Shakespeare.   YeAr

These are her gifts which all mankind may use,/And all refuse.   In a Meadow.   John Swinnerton Phillimore.   OBEV; OBVV

These are his wounds,/made whole in a cloud of grey feathers.   The Cloud Factory.   John Haines.   EAS

These are imaginations. We are free.   The Usurpers.   Edwin Muir.   CMoP

These are Imperial Works, and worthy Kings.   Moral Essays.   Alexander Pope.   CABL; PoEL 1-5

...These are men!/Men!   Ol' Bunk's Band.   William Carlos Williams.   NOBA

"These are my body. Sister, take and eat."   To L.H.B.   Katherine Mansfield.   AnNZ; HBMV

These are not lost.   These Are Not Lost.   Richard Metcalf.   PoToHe

These are private words addressed to you in public.   A Dedication to My Wife.   Thomas Stearns Eliot.   BoLoP; FF

These are prosperity and vital wealth!   America's Prosperity.   Henry Van Dyke.   PGD

These are the arrows that murder sleep.   The Song of Crede.   Anonymous.   BIrV; LiTW; OnYI

...These are the better notions.   More Sonnets at Christmas.   Allen Tate.   LiTA; SBVL

These are the bulwarks of the State.   God Send Us Men.   F. J. Gillman.   TRV

These are the city's earliest and tenderest loves.   South End.   Conrad Aiken.   CMoP; HoPM; MoVE; OxBA

These are the features only futures know.   Winter Term.   John Malcolm Brinnin.   GLGT

These are the fellows who keep the salt in the blood.   Words Are Never Enough.   Charles Bruce.   CaP; OBCV

These are the first to die in the shock and terror of war.   Epitaph (Inscription from Anticyra).   Anonymous.   WaaP

These are the homosexual elk cruising each other in/Angel's Meadow.   12 Photographs of Yellowstone.   Ronald Koertge.   GP

...These are the interrupted.   The Interrupted.   Josephine Jacobsen.   GP

These are the joys of the open road–/For him who travels without a load.   The Joys of the Road.   Bliss Carman.   HBV 1-2; HBVY; OBVV

These are the knotty Riddles, whose darke doubt/Intangles his lost Thoughts, past getting out.   The Massacre of the Innocents: The Devil's Doubts.   Giambattista Marino.   OBVE

...These are the last/words I shall write.   The Postman's Bell Is Answered Everywhere.   Horace Gregory.   MoAmPo; MoVE; NYBP

These are the mainsprings, after all.   Trifles.   Anonymous   HBV 1-2

These are the obsequies I think on most.   Half-Tide Ledge.   Richard P. Blackmur.   AnFE; MOS

These are the only sweets of love.   The Platonic Lady.   John Wilmot, Earl of Rochester.   UnTE

These are the small gold buttons/On earth's green, windy coat.   Dandelions.   Frances Frost.   TiPo

These are the sounds that murder.   Daily the Drum.   Anne Wilkinson.   NOBC

These are the summer days, and these our walks.   Modern Love, XLV.   George Meredith.   NBM; PoEL 1-5; VLP

These are the things/God meant.   To Search Our Souls.   Jane McKay Lanning.   TRV

These are the things that we have learned to do/Who live in troubled regions.   Storm Warnings.   Adrienne Rich.   GOYP; NIP

These are the things we can keep.   Mary and Martha.   Annie Johnson Flint.   STF

These are the things we mean by saying, Peace.   Peace Is the Mind's Old Wilderness.   John Holmes.   AH

These are things it revolts me to wear.   Limerick: "I don't give a...."   Gelett Burgess.   FaBoNo

These are things we must remember now our duty shall begin.   An Armoury.   Alcaeus.   WaaP

These are tombs and memorials and temples and altars sun-kindled/for me.   Green Symphony.   John Gould Fletcher.   AnFE; APA; MAPA; MoAmPo; MoVE

These are unchanging: man must still explore.   The Birds.   J. C. Squire.   HBMV

"These Armageddons weary me much," he said.   Armageddon.   John Crowe Ransom.   LiTA

These autumn nights I think that he/Imagines he's the ocean.   Autumn Squall–Lake Erie.   Lola Ingres Russo.   AmFN

These axioms of light/repeat their lessons to a failing world.   The Balcony Poems.   Douglas Smith.   AMV-81

These be rewards for such/As live and love too much.   The Uncertain State of a Lover.   Anonymous.   EIL

These be the watchers still/Over her stone.   Dirge.   Madison Cawein.   AA

These be thy verities, to have, to hold!   Companionship.   Mary Elizabeth Coleridge.   NBM

These beauties make me die.   White and Red.   Edward, Earl of Oxford De Vere.   OBSC

These, benign, shall drive afar/To Persia's plains or Britain's sea.   Odes.   Horace.   OBVE

These bounties bless and grant that we/May feast in Paradise with Thee.   Table Graces, or Prayers for Adults: Noon Meal.   Anonymous.   BLRP

These bright dews once were mixed with blood and sweat.   Peace.   Walter De la Mare.   MMM; MoAB; MoBrPo

These bronze, unbarbered heads are not our kings/But subjects of our thought.   The Junk Shop.   Henri Coulette.   NYBP

These bubbles mark/o/o/o/Where Ezra sank.   Ezra Shank.   Anonymous.   ShM

These buildings come as close to heaven now/As I myself would ever want to go.   Mr. Frost Goes South to Boston (parody).   Firman Houghton.   Par

These can yet sting the patriot thoughts which turn/To Erin's past, and bid them weep and burn.   Irish History.   William Allingham.   IrPN

These chains that now are become as garments to me.   The Prison House.   Alan Paton.   PeSA

...These characteristics he shares/With the body politic.   A Bestiary.   Kenneth Rexroth.   OBAL

These children/eating/themselves.   Encounter with Hunger.   Brian Vanderlip.   AMV-81

These cold blue hills/sometime.   A Song.   Edward Dorn.   ConAP

These constitute a State...   What Constitutes a State?   William, Sir Jones.   BLPA; MCCG; PGD

These curls of their soft hair.   We Put the Urn Aboard Ship.   Sappho.   PBWP

These dark days toward spring.   November.   Samuel S. Turner.   AMV-80

These days I slide off without batting an eyelash.   I don't have the energy...
Artie Gold.   CaPN; NOBC

–These discover/What fainting hopes are in a lover.   The Primrose.   Robert
Herrick.   HBV 1-2; OBEV; ViBoPo

These done, I'll only cry/God's mercy, and so die.   To Death.   Robert
Herrick.   CoBE; InPo

These events are intelligible. Interpret. You cannot enjoy.   Sunday, July 14th:
A Fine Day at the Baths.   Julian Symons.   WaP

These eyes at last leak out their dying stare?   Pearl Perch.   John Blight.
CBAP

These facts I know but find it difficult to understand.   The Invisible Man.
T. S. Matthews.   PoL

These fade. All fade. Let us honor them with our own fading/sight.   Movie-
Going.   John Hollander.   CoAP; NYP; PPP

These fatuous, ineffectual Yesterdays!   Under a Stagnant Sky.   William
Ernest Henley.   SyP

These few are sacred moments. One More Day/Drops in the shadowy gulf of
bygone things.   After Sunset.   William Allingham.   IrPN

These few is all it takes to be/A cowboy an'...a man!   Code of the Cow
Country.   Squire Omar Barker.   PoOW

These foetal-/Voiced people lack eloquence to blow a sick/Maggot off a dead
beetle.   A Simplification.   Richard Wilbur.   CMoP

These fools of time/Who know no distance.   Escape.   Andrew McCord
Jones.   LFAC

"These for their country fought and bled."   On the Departure of the British
from Charleston.   Philip Freneau.   PAH

These for you, so small and young,/In your hand and heart and tongue.
Wishes for My Son.   Thomas Macdonagh.   AnIV; HBMV

These genuine sons of mother Britain?   M'Fingal.   John Trumbull.   AnNE

These giants are more constant than evergreens/By being never green.
Telephone Poles.   John Updike.   FYAP; Psk; SaC

These glories now are turned to bays.   Apollo's Song.   John Lyly.   HBV
1-2

These had their joy/of dance and song, as day waned into evening.   The
Odyssey.   Homer.   NAWM 1-2

These have crimes accounted been.   Come, My Celia.   Ben Jonson.
CABA; EiL; FaBV; FF; HeIP; NIP; NLV; NoP; TEP; TrGrPo; WHA

These hearts of living fire that beat below!   Fireflies.   Edgar Fawcett.
AnAmPo; HBV 1-2

These hills bear human scars.   Burma Hills.   Bernard Gutteridge.   WaP

These honours, Homer, had been just to thee.   Mr. Pope's Welcome from
Greece.   John Gay.   EBEV; OBEC; OxBoLi; PoEL 1-5

...These huge/animals of the ocean came.   Up out of the African.   Ted
Joans.   GP

These Indians tilt the odds/in a lottery/you can't buy tickets for   Mexico
City Hand Game.   Rayna Green.   TWSS

These kill her embryo, and preserve her honour.   The Progress of a Divine
(excerpt).   Richard Savage.   OBSV

These knitters at their doors.   The Knitters.   Padraic Colum.   SaC

These large-eyed mournful lovers in the rain.   Yugoslav Cemetery.   Celeste
Turner Wright.   DFF

These last pretenders of an innocence they know is vain.   In a London
Schoolroom.   James Kirkup.   GLGT

These laws, O Lord, write in my heart, that I,/May in thy faithful service live
and die.   The Ten Commandments.   *Anonymous.*   OxBChV

These leaves that autumn branches bear/Are an autumnal bore.   Autumn
Leaves.   Charles Henry ("John Paul") Webb.   OBAL

These let her feel!...nor these too oft!   So Late Removed from Him She Swore.
Walter Savage Landor.   OBRV

These lights flung like farfel./These golden girls.   For the Yiddish Singers in
the Lakewood Hotels of My Childhood.   Harvey Shapiro.   VWA

These lines file it for a while.   The Final Fall.   Alexandre L. Amprimoz.
AMV-81

These lines I use, t'unburthen mine owne hart;/My love affects no fame, nor
steemes of Art.   These Plaintive Verse, the Postes of My Desire.   Samuel
Daniel.   AAS

These lips and these eyes of the loved and the lover.   Love Is Enough.
William Morris.   AnEnPo; FaBV; LiTL; OBEV; OBVV; ViBoPo; VLP

These loans are canceled forever.   Dividends.   Hubert Creekmore.   WaP

These lowly numbers for the House of Fame!   Chaucer.   Benjamin Brawley.
BANP

These magnets draw my heart their way.   Magnets.   Countee Cullen.
BALP

These make a town.   People.   Lois Lenski.   SoPo

These many grasses and these many snows.   The Death of Crazy Horse.
John G. Neihardt.   BPAW

These many summers you and me.   Ianthe.   Walter Savage Landor.
TrGrPo

These marshes pale and meadows by the sea.   The Salt Flats.   Sir Charles
G. D. Roberts.   CaP

These massacre the grass along...   Appleton House (excerpt).   Andrew
Marvell   AtBAP

These men are the game.   Line-Up for Yesterday.   Ogden Nash.   SD

These men/(How vainly!) turn towards me again.   Fred Apollus at Fava's.
Nicholas Moore.   ErPo; NeBP

These men who through the centuries grew gaunt.   The Settled Men.
George M. Brady.   NeIP

These miracles to be so true,/That are impossible.   To cause accord or to
agree.   Sir Thomas Wyatt.   AAS; FCP; SiPS

These Mississippi towns ain't/Fit fer a hoppin' toad.   Bound No'th Blues.
Langston Hughes.   AmNP; BiP

These momentary pleasures, fugitive delights.   Chorus.   Samuel Daniel.
LoBV

These/mosquitoes/on the buffalo's hide?   Would a circling surface vulture.
Mahadevi (Mahadeviyakka).   BoWoP

These, nay, and more, thine own shall be/If thou wilt love, and live with me.
To Phyllis, to Love and Live With Him.   Robert Herrick.   AnEnPo;
CaPo; LiTL; OAEP

These near, immediate thickets where we hide?   Location.   Knute Skinner.
MAT

These new battalions/–The blue battalions–.   When a People Reach the Top
of a Hill.   Stephen Crane.   AmePo

These old tears in the chopping-bowl.   Peeling Onions.   Adrienne Rich.
BoWoP; CAPP; HaCAP; TAP

These only with our Law best form a king.'   Paradise Regained.   John
Milton.   OAEL 1-2; OBS

–These, our streets of gold.   Revelation.   Jerald Bullis.   AMV-81

These outstretched feverish hands, this restless heart?   November.   William
Morris.   GTBS

These people live here.   Gauley Bridge.   Muriel Rukeyser.   NNaP

These places I have known.   Places I Have Been.   Joyce M. Volk.
AMV-80

These pleasures, Melancholy, give,/And I with thee will choose to live.   Il
Penseroso.   John Milton.   AWP; BoLiVe; EiCP; EnL; FiP; GTBS; GTBS-
P; HAP; HBV 1-2; HoPM; InPo; JCP; LiTB; MasP; MBW 1-2; MCCG;
MyFE; NoP; OAEL 1-2; OBEV; OBS; PPP; SeCeV; TEP; TrGrPo; ViBoPo;
WHA

These poor daily rags we wear/Shine brighter than the silks of kings.   As for
Me, I Delight in the Everyday Way.   Joseph Stroud.   NPGG

These purblind Doomsters had as readily strown/Blisses about my pilgrimage
as pain.   Hap.   Thomas Hardy.   AWP; CABA; CMoP; CoBMV; EaLo;
InPo; MoBrPo; NIP; NoAm; NoP; OAEL 1-2; OAEP; PPON; PPP; TEP;
VLP

These Ravens have fed me.   Course Bread and Water's Most Their Fare.
Roger Williams.   SCAP

These remain.   Egypt's Might is Tumbled Down.   Mary Elizabeth Coleridge.
CH

These rules will render thee a king complete/Within thy self, much more with
empire joined.   Paradise Regained.   John Milton.   OBTV

...These scarred years that are/journeying and pity, of myself.   The Dance
Called David.   Theodore Weiss.   CoPo

These shape the creature that is I.   Long Live the Weeds.   Theodore
Roethke.   NoAm; NOBA; PoA

These shepherds, and these nymphs do know,/Thy Sylvia is as chaste, as fair.
Sylvia.   Michael Drayton.   LoBV

These shine to aftertimes; each sacred name/Stands still recorded in the books
of fame.   Tarquin and Tullia.   Arthur Mainwaring.   APAS

These so, these irretrievable.   Battle of the Bonhomme Richard and the
Serapis.   Walt Whitman.   UnPo

These songs I sing are a tribute that I bring/And make me a link in your
chain.   Women of My Land.   Frankie Armstrong.   BrRo

These soothing hands of light will never/Massage oblivion into your bones.
Love Poem–1940.   Miriam Hershenson.   GoYe

These stanzas are done.   Stanzas in Meditation.   Gertrude Stein.   PoA

These stars, these nightingales, these scents: then shame would cease.   Bagley
Wood.   Lionel Pigot Johnson.   AnFE; VLP

These stones remain their monument and mine.   Meditations in Time of Civil
War.   William Butler Yeats.   CABL

These strewn rocks belong to the wind/If it could use them.   The Gods.
William Stanley Merwin.   NaP

These stripes as well as stars/Lead after Him.   In the Hospital.   Mary
Woolsey Howland.   HBV 1-2

These Strong and Fair shall be as I.   Once.   Eric N. Batterham.   CH

These tears had never flowed.   Had There Been Falsehood in My Breast.
Emily Bronte.   NOBV

These Tears, these Tears shall mend thy Way.   On His Mistress Drown'd.
Thomas Spratt.   ATP; EnLoPo

These, that the wind removed, in memory remain.   The Death of a Snake.
William Plomer.   ELU

...These the mental eye/Suffice to charm, and all it sees is good.   Picturesque;
a Fragment.   John Aiken.   NOEC

...These, the Prince said,/when I was in love/were always with me where I
was.   Dream Data.   Robert Duncan.   NeAP

These therefore and their journey now do come/For to be treated on, and Coacht along. God's Determinations. Edward Taylor. PoEL 1-5

These, these are joyes the Gods for Youth ordain. Odes. Horace. OBVE

(These things are all available to salvation they say). Eyewash. Niall Montgomery. EAS

These things are August's own. The Month of Falling Stars. Ella Higginson. YeAr

These things/astonish me beyond words. Pastoral. William Carlos Williams. MP; TwCP

These things considered make me, in despite/Of idle rumor, keep at home and write. An Epistolary Essay from M.G. to O.B. upon Their Mutual Poems. John Wilmot, Earl of Rochester. APAS

These things we never show/and children suffer. My Child. Susan Griffin. NPGG

These things were death. I Was Always Fascinated. Alma Villanueva. WPOW

These things were made beautiful by sleep. Do You Not Hear? James Picot. BoAV

...These things who knows/With joy and praise he goes! Thanksgivings for the Beauty of His Providence. Thomas Traherne. FaBoCh; LoGBV

These thoughts we have, walking among our ruins. The Good Town. Edwin Muir. CMoP

These three times thirteen lines I'll write down for/Fun, some May morning between five and six. Tomorrows. James Merrill. OBAL

These thy foundations are, O firm-set State! My Country (excerpt). George Edward Woodberry. AA

These tombstones,/by the rest. At a Chinaman's Grave. Wing Tek Lum. BrSi

These too would Fionn have given away. Generosity. *Anonymous.* KiLC

These twenty threadbare men with frost-bit ears/And canvas bags and little chests of gears. The Crowd. John Masefield. OxBTC

These unseen gravestones, and the darker dead. In a Churchyard. Richard Wilbur. HeIP

These veins/And those latitudes. Survival Kit. Robert Slater. FAZ

These vows, these perfumes, and those countless kisses? The Balcony. Charles Baudelaire. AWP; NAWM 1-2

These waifs from the deep, cast high and dry,/Wash'd on America's shores? As Consequent, etc. Walt Whitman. MAmP

These walls, this bed/do/not/grow. Screw Spring. William M. Hoffman. FF

These waterie villagers with thousands more,/Do passe and repasse neare the verdant shore. The Kind of Waters, the Sea Shouldering Whale. William Wood. SCAP

These weeping Eyes, those seeing Tears. Eyes and Tears. Andrew Marvell. MePo

These were his right; he never questioned it. Murgatroyd. Celeste Turner Wright. Str

These were men, who the well-aimed arrow/Let fly in the eyes of a girl. The Faun Tells of the Rout of the Amazons. Thomas Sturge Moore. AnFE

These were our footprints, seven lives ago. The Caves. Michael Roberts. ChMP

These were the same horses. She Had Some Horses. Joy Harjo. STE; TWSS

These were thy charms–but all these charms are fled. The Deserted Village. Oliver Goldsmith. TrGrPo

These were truth,/And a memorable thing. I've Worked for a Silver Shilling. Charles W. Kennedy. HBMV

These were whispered/to have dull authority. Nausicaa with Some Attendants. Tom Lowenstein. VWA

These who go home at dusk,/Along the lane. French Peasants. Monk Gibbon. HaMV; NeIP; OxBI

These winter nights are blue and cold! Sugar in the Cane. Tennessee Williams. OBAL

These words, Donald, are vanity's. Five Epigrams. Donald Hall. NePoAm-2

These Words soft Pity in the Chief inspire,/Touch'd with the dear Remembrance of his Sire. Priam and Achilles. Alexander Pope. OBEC

These would be first to fall. A Portrait in the Guards. Laurence Whistler. GTBS-P

Thether resortes, and laying his sad dartes/Asyde, with faire Adonis playes his wanton partes. The Faerie Queene. Edmund Spenser. PoEL 1-5

They agreed that it had been a most/unusual conversation. Chocolates. Louis Simpson. InPS; LCAP; OxBC

They ain't no place for a poor old girl to go. Rock Water Blues. Bessie Smith. BluL

They ain't no sound that gits me/Like horsus chawin' hay! Horses Chawin' Hay. Hamlin Garland. OBAL

They ain't playing for no secret/they playing it a wide open hand. Bad Girl Blues. Memphis Willie Borum. BluL

They all are dancing in the morn/Because a little child is born. Christmas Song. Bliss Carman. PeCV; PoSC

They all belong to me. They All Belong to Me. Eliza Cook. PGD

...They all belong/To Mr. Nobody. Mr. Nobody. *Anonymous.* HBVY

They all bring rest in a nothingness/From where no road returns. Song for a Suicide. Langston Hughes. PoNe

They all came down again. The King of France. *Anonymous.* OxNR

They all did declare, and solemnly swear,/They'd conquer, or die by his side. Robin Hood and the Ranger. *Anonymous.* ESPB

They all drew back/into themselves,/and immediately/began building walls. The Color. John Haines. GP

...They all,/passengers and crew, the dream/and the artist alike, dissolve/into sepia fractions. The Chauffeur of Lilacs. George Hitchcock. GP

They all together go ahead and do those things/That I never believed they would. Song of Resignation. Yehuda Amichai. NYBP

...They all want to play Hamlet. They All Want to Play Hamlet. Carl Sandburg. NOBA

They almost put me off my game. I Was Playing Golf That Day. *Anonymous.* FiBHP; PV

They almost try to dig, they need/So much to plant their thistle-seed. Thistledown. Harold Monro. BrPo; OxBTC

They also have good bread. The Geraniums. Genevieve Taggard. VGW

They also live/Who swerve and vanish in the river. The Snowflake Which Is Now and Hence Forever. Archibald MacLeish. NoP

They also serve who only stand and wait. Sonnet on His Blindness. John Milton. BBV; FaBoBe; LoBV; OHFP; WGRP

They also speak my own. Dear Maiden. Heinrich Heine. AWP

They also, then, shall hear the Sabbath's cry. Cleansing. Heinrich Suso Waldeck. CAW

...They always land on their own or somebody/else's feet. England Expects. Ogden Nash. DBV

They always must be with us, or we die. Endymion. John Keats. BLPL; BoC; GoTF; LiTB; PG; TreF; ViBoPo

They always talk, who never think. When You with Hogh Dutch Heeren Dine. Matthew Prior. OBTV

They and my mind may chime,/And mend my rhyme. Denial. George Herbert. AnAnS 1; EnL; InPo; JCP; LoBV; MePo; NOBE; NoP; OAEL 1-2; PoEL 1-5

They answer, knowing all. Epicedium. J. Corson Miller. HBMV; PAH

They answered, "Mr. Toad." The Song of Mr. Toad. Kenneth Grahame. FiBHP; GoJo; NOBL

...They appear more/like intensely dedicated politicians. The Crows. Zulfikar Ghose. BoAnP

...They appear wrenched awry/From the scheme Nature planned for them,–wondering why. Horses Aboard. Thomas Hardy. BoAnP; FM

They are all beautiful too. Hamlet. Emmett Jarrett. NeAC

They are all crying. Paddling Song. *Anonymous.* PBA

They are all dead now. And. Robert Creeley. LCAP

They are all gone, and thou art gone as well! Thyrsis. Matthew Arnold. FaBoPP

They are all in Pennsylvania this morning! Philadelphia. Rudyard Kipling. OBTV

They are all on secret missions for Montgomery the/Tops. Montgomery. H.A.C. Evans. GDP

They are allies courting in the bloodstreams/welcome them and dance with them. The Fairies Are Dancing All over the World. Michael Rumaker. PeHV

They are always/inside The Recluses. Stuart Z. Perkoff. NeAP

They are as light as upper air! The Garden Seat. Thomas Hardy. GoJo; HAP

They are both hard and marred,/If thou not read'st them well. To My Ill Reader. Robert Herrick. CaPo

...They are brothers of cinders. Psalm of Those Who Go Forth before Daylight. Carl Sandburg. AnAmPo; MoShBr; OxBA

They are cast down, and never shall/Have power again to raised be. Psalm XXXVI. Sir Philip Sidney. FCP

They are conjoyn'd in Man, as well as Me! On the Crocodile. Thomas Heyrick. FM

They are divine, all-comprehending Death. Death. George Pellew. AA

They are engaged. To be married. Prothalamium for Bobolink and His Louisa A Poem. Gertrude Stein. HW

...They are face to face/With the Eternal Father! Raphael's San Sisto Madonna. George Henry Miles. CAW

They are gay sons-of-bitches. French Poets. Aram Saroyan. ANYP

They are going in one direction, and know it. Nino Leading an Old Man to Market. Leonard Nathan. CTBA; NCSH

They are going to some point true and unproven. Geometry. Rita Dove. HaCAP

They are GONE like the cracking of a bubble. The Atlas. Kenneth Slessor. PoAu 1-2

They are gone to the wedding, and so/to bedding,/And so I bid you good night. Robin Hood and the Prince of Aragon. *Anonymous.* ESPB

They are grinding the mortar/between straw-thin teeth/and broken families. Conversations between Here and Home. Joy Harjo. TWSS

They are humble, with a creeping humility, being parasites/or carrion creatures. Proper Pride. D. H. Lawrence. FaBoEE

...They are/its remembrance of what it is. The Wild. Wendell Berry. VGW

They are made for you. Condemning the Moongod Nanna. Enheduanna. BoWoP

They are made to be thrown away. The Legend of Paper Plates. John Haines. GP

They are my battle. Looking Out. Helen Chasin. NMM

They are my sisters' lovers in other days and years. Daughters of War. Isaac Rosenberg. BrPo

They are needed somewhere! Ducks. Robert Bly. PV

They are neither fickle nor inconstant–not as I am. On the Flightiness of Thought. *Anonymous.* OnYI

They are no more, the old houses of Flanders. The Old Houses of Flanders. Ford Madox Ford. CTC

They are no trophies of the sun. Praise for an Urn. Hart Crane. AP; ATP; AWP; CMoP; CoBMV; HAP; InPo; LiTM; MoAB; MoAmPo; MoVE; NoAm; NOBA; OxBA; PPP

They are not allowed to drink. Forty Pounds of Blackberries Equals Thirteen Gallons of Wine. Robert D. Hoeft. AMV-80

They are not half so fair as she I love. Similes. Edward Moxon. OBRV

...They are not in the City. The Rock. Thomas Stearns Eliot. TiPo

...They are/not listening, not listening. Tenebrae. Denise Levertov. NoP

They are not resigned. Homage to Robert Bresson. Jon Anderson. MAYP

They are not those who used to feed us/When we were young–they cannot be! The Puzzled Game Birds. Thomas Hardy. PBBP

They are not to be found/Neither in East nor in West. Prayers to Liberty. Anwar Shaul. VWA

They are not wasted,/they are thrown away. The Old Man Said. Carroll Arnett. STE

They are not wonder. Kochia. Thomas Hornsby Ferril. NePoAm-2

...They are only bees that moan in/the quarries now. Quarries in Syracuse. Louis Goldberg. TrJP

They are our friends. Spirits. Victor Hernandez Cruz. PoBA; WSC

They are our steady progress and the lack of it. Dinosaurs. Carolyn Stoloff. NYBP

They are peaceful; they have great things; who are they? Who Are They? *Anonymous.* NIP

They are pregnant Tracks. Joseph Torain. FAZ

They are really scared! Wardance. Phil George. VoR

They are resting and saving themselves to be right/For the Jellicle Moon and the Jellicle Ball. The Song of the Jellicles. Thomas Stearns Eliot. FaBoCh; FaBoNo; LoGBV; OxBChV; PCat; PoPle

They are ringing in the mountains. Songs of the Ghost Dance. *Anonymous.* WSC

...They are round and ready. Upland. Archie Randolph Ammons. NOBA

They are running to arrive. The Rescue. Robert Creeley. CAPP

They are seeking out a way/For to blow the candle out. Blow the Candle Out (The Jolly Boatsman). *Anonymous.* AmFP

They are singing Emmanuel's birth. After Trinity. John Meade Falkner. OxBTC

They are slaves who dare not be/In the right with two or three. Stanzas on Freedom. James Russell Lowell. GN; MC; OHIP; PGD; PoNe

They are so silent they are in another world. The White Horse. D. H. Lawrence. SOTW

They are speaking of you at home. Winds of Africa. Dorothy S. Obi. WPOW

They are spread wide that each/May rend what comes in reach. The Crazed Moon. William Butler Yeats. MOON

–They are taller than their cars. Do It Yrself. Larry Eigner. NeAP; PoM

They are tangibly covered with mold. Limerick: "These places abound in the old." George Libaire. LiBL

They are teased/By fear/And snickering death. When They Grow Old. Nathan Ralph. CaP

They are that City's shining spires/We travel to. God's Saints. Henry Vaughan. TRV

They are, that we may know. Statues. Kathleen Raine. NYBP

They are the D-Day Dodgers who stay in Italy. The D-Day Dodgers. Hamish Henderson. FSW

They are the things which I regret! Would I Be Shrived? John D. Swain. BLPA

They are the tongue's wrangle,/the world's pottage, the rat's star. With Mercy for the Greedy. Anne Sexton. CAPP; HaCAP

They are there. Friends Come. Lucille Clifton. GeTw

They are Thy tears which fall. Lachrymae. David Gascoyne. AtBAP; BoW

They are too big for toys. Dance. Lula Lowe Weeden. CDC

...They/are touching hips and shifting on the single-footing waves. Notes Made in the Piazza San Marco. May Swenson. CoAP

They are ungrateful. What a relief/Never to find expected grief! The Ladybirds. Edward Lucie-Smith. BoAnP

They are waiting for me. Why won't they call my name? A Cemetery in New Mexico. Alfred Alvarez. VWA

They aren't small-/time haters/that joined up. Pit Viper. George Starbuck. NYBP; SUW

They ask how we are. It is this year. Now. William Stafford. NNaP

They at his pleasure lie to stuff his glutt'nous maw. Polyolbion. Michael Drayton. PBBP

They bark at the ice-fanged killer/Who leaves no footstep in the night. Central Heating System. Stephen Spender. GrPl

They batter the winds with great hands,/And are happy again. The Equinox. Dubose Heyward. PoA

They bear Count Roland's soul to Paradise. The Song of Roland. *Anonymous.* NAWM 1-2

They bear the glory of Washington! The Rivers Remember. Nancy Byrd Turner. AmFN

They beautify any room in your house. Readymade. John Perreault. ANYP; EAS

They being, like the stars "preserved from wrong." The Herd. Frances Cornford. FM

They bigget a bower on yon burn brae/And theekit it o'er wi' rashes. Bessy Bell and Mary Gray. *Anonymous.* BSV; ESPB; OxBB; ViBoFo

They blest the wedding/Of a pure colleen! The Faery Reaper. Robert Williams Buchanan. OBVV

They blow beyond the headland, to the sea. Wings. Judith Wright. CBAP; NOAV

They bore over sea-paths back to the Danes/Back to her home, and her own dear people. Beowulf: The Lay of Finn. *Anonymous.* AnOE

They both grew friends, and drank their liquor off. On a Young Man and an Old Man. Edward May. OBSP

They both kept their promises. Marrying the Hangman. Margaret Atwood. NOBC

They both licked their plates clean. Jack Sprat (parody). Henry Hetherington. FaBoPa

They bound thy holy limbs, Andromeda. Ibant Obscurae. Thomas Edward Brown. OBNC

They boys they did dance and the girls they did sing. The Silk Merchant's Daughter (I). *Anonymous.* ShS

They breathe the wind of other nebulas... The Struggle with the Angel. Claude Vigee. VWA

...They breathe their light/into the mind, year after year. The Lilies. Wendell Berry. GeTw

They bring the telephone and telegraph. The Line-Gang. Robert Frost. OBSP

They brought us here–/to drive us mad./(like them) The Primitive. Don L. Lee. BPo

"They build these 'ere churches too narrow." Limerick: "There was an old lady of Harrow." *Anonymous.* TDH

They buried him there in the deep, deep sea. The Ocean Burial. *Anonymous.* PSoN; ShS; ViBoFo

They buried him there on the Wingate Road. Two Bits. Sharlot M. Hall. BPAW

They burn a path through timeless sleep. Behold This Dreamer. Elizabeth Bartlett. NePoAm-2

...They/burn, or don't burn, in their own/strange way, when you say them. Report from a Far Place. William Stafford. CAPP

They but yield the passing stranger/Wild-flower wreaths for Beauty's hair. To a Lady. Sir Walter Scott. OAEP

An' they caal hor Cushie Butterfield,/An' aa wish she wes heor. Cushie Butterfield. George Ridley. VLP

They call it not "climbing,' but "doing the Dubhs.' Doing the Dubhs. *Anonymous.* PoSH

They call it the thing of things, essence/of essences: great northern snowy owl; whiteness. "Now you have burned..." John Thompson. NOBC

They call me the Gull Decoy. The Gull Decoy. *Anonymous.* ShS

They call us Janna and Carolina, those two mad straniere. For Jan, in Bar Maria. Carolyn Kizer. VGW

They called her Diana Fitzpatrick Mauleverer James. Miss James. A.(lan) A.(lexander) Milne. MoShBr

They called the eldest Young Etin,/Which was his father's name. Hynd Etin. *Anonymous.* BuBa

They came as good as ours, or better,/And are not spent a whit... A Ballad upon a Wedding: The Bride. Sir John Suckling. TrGrPo

They came at Bessie's call. Chicken. Walter De la Mare. TiPo

They came to plumo with the Kynges trusty towne. Fragment of an Anti-Papist Ballad. *Anonymous.* CoMu

They came to the old house. Tamar: Part III. Robinson Jeffers. AnAmPo

They can add little unto blisse/who cannot wish. On New-Years Day 1640 to the King. Sir John Suckling. SeCV 1-2

They can bring no heart to me/Evermore, evermore. Ships at Sea. Barry Gray. EtS

They can but listen at the gates,/And hear the household jar within. In Memoriam A.H.H., XCIV. Alfred, Lord Tennyson. VLP

...They can dance/on and on as long as the music lasts. Golden Oldie. Paul Mariani. GeTw

They can shake their bodies but they can't shake you. The Blues Don't Change. Al Young. NPGG

They can suit whomever man's intestines can. Summer. Edwin Denby. ANYP

They can't do without the labouring man. The Labouring Man. *Anonymous.* OBET

They can't/have lasted long Ashkelon. Anthony Rudolf. VWA

They can't hear the clicking/of the gun/inside my head I Am a Dangerous Woman. Joy Harjo. TWSS

They can't resist the charm. London Is a Fine Town. *Anonymous.* CoMu

They cannot find a priest. Epigram. Robert Dodsley. ALV

They cannot make us ope His wounds again–/"Next time"! Next Time. Laura Simmons. PGD

They cannot spread nets where a harvest yields. O Lapwing, Thou Fliest around the Heath. William Blake. PBBP

They cannot steal, thou giv'st so much. To Saxham. Thomas Carew. AnAnS 2; CaPo; JCP; NoP; OBS

They carry with them diadem and sceptre/And move from throne to throne. Exiles. George William Russell. BIrV; MoBrPo

They cast lots between blood and blood./Both are for Azazel. Lament for Azazel. Francis Landy. VWA

They casually shoot every general/and strip the laughing ladies Hot Springs. Earle Birney. OxBC

They change, and pass,/and are the same. But Still in Israel's Paths They Shine. Carter Revard. VoR

They charge us with the improbable. Death As History. Jay Wright. PoBA

...They chase dragonflies/without caring what people will say. Making Feet and Hands. Benjamin Peret. EAS

They chase me everywhere I go–/Melchizidek, Ucalegon. Two Men. Edwin Arlington Robinson. LaNeLa

They churn the ancient wall-stones to a dust. Barnfire during Church. Robert Bly. NePoEA

They circle their rose on my rose tree. Women and Roses. Robert Browning. ViBoPo

They clatter back in the hanging dark. Homing Pigeons. Ted Walker. NYBP

They climb the stairs to the city. The Flood. Lev Mak. VWA

They cling to their long-standing fallacies. Limerick: "The young things who frequent picture-palaces." *Anonymous.* NOBL

They combine into words held together by a string of plot,/words tha are, words that are not. Life of the Letters. Emily Borenstein. VWA

They come–and they go, captain. The Anathemata. David Jones. EBEV

They come here to see! They come here to see!/Mbe'e a-ha we-o-'e. Rains for the Harvest. *Anonymous.* WTO

They come on wool-soft sandals/But they strike with iron hands. The Avengers. Edwin Markham. MoAmPo

They commenced to break their rollways and I knew it must be Spring. Turner's Camp on the Chippewa. *Anonymous.* AmFP

They construct anew/not merely their own/truncated lives/but the language of the tribe. Finders Keepers. Donald Finkel. VWA

They could not choose but to return in blue. October Maples, Portland. Richard Wilbur. CoPo

...They could not escape/the crops even in sleep. The Farm Hands. Dilys Bennett Laing. SaC

They could not guess, at midnight lone/How she would weep the time away. She Dried Her Tears. Emily Bronte. NOBV

They could not see/Who had gained/The victory. Peace. Langston Hughes. BPo

They couldn't hide tigers/Or me any more. Growing Up. Harry Behn. BiCB; SiSoSe; SoPo

They cover the stains of my presence with clear dust Room Poems. Eli Bachar. VWA

They covered him, and none knew where/To find him when the storm was done. The Wakeupworld. Countee Cullen. GoSl

...They crawl below the oceans of air/that smell of lilacs and roses, and do not get involved. Ants. Lewis Hyde. AMV-80; FAZ

They cried: Depart! let us be/murdered! Be Not Silent. *Anonymous.* TrJP

–They crossed hard times to the Comstock Lode! American Laughter. Kenneth Allan Robinson. AmFN; TreFS

They crowd in a dense baffled throng and the sun does not shine/through. Civil Elegies (excerpt). Dennis Lee. NOBC

They crown my daily intent. Girl to Woman. Nixeon Civille Handy. AMV-80

They cruise the ocean of an alien dream. Goldfish. Howard Nemerov. BoAnP

They cry their ink was faulty, and their pen;/We, "The corn threshes bad, 'twas cut too green." The Thresher's Labour. Stephen Duck. NOEC

They cup their heads in prodigal idleness. Au Jardin des Plantes. John Wain. NePoEA-2; OxBTC

They curl round you, lie at your feet, swing and wing through the/dark air. Murder in the Cathedral. Thomas Stearns Eliot. OxBTC

They curse; they strike; they break the wall/Which buries them beneath its fall. Parable. William Soutar. HaMV

They cut back all the flowery mass/In the morning. The Lodging-House Fuschsias. Thomas Hardy. OBSP

They cut them off with sharpened shears. The Dust of Time (fragment). Sappho. AWP

They'd deplore even more than before. Limerick: "A is the autograph bore." Oliver Herford. TDH

They'd rather eat than study butter. Butter's Etymological Spelling Book, &c. Hartley Coleridge. GLGT

They'd run like hell from in the slums. An Old Woman, outside the Abbey Theater. Leonard Alfred George Strong. DBV; FiBHP; MoBrPo

They'd spend one night, or two or three./But... They Went Home. Maya Angelou. IHMS

They dance together, and are truly gay. Gay Boys. James Kirkup. PeHV

They dance together then till dawn/and a single shadow make. Shadow-Bride. J. R. R. Tolkien. SO

They dance wi' nae sic unco man. The Mer-Man and Marstig's Daughter. *Anonymous.* AWP

They danced by the light of the moon. The Owl and the Pussy-Cat. Edward Lear. BeLS; FaBoBe; FaBoCh; FaBoNo; FaFP; FPL; GoJo; GTBS-P; HBV 1-2; HBVY; LBN; LoGBV; MoShBr; NA; NLV; NOBE; NoP; NTCP; OxBChV; OxBoLi; PCat; PoLf; PoPl; PoRA; SoPo; SUS; TiPo; TreFS; TrGrPo

They did it by hand. A History of Photography. Albert Goldbarth. MAYP

They did not disgrace you... Los Cuatro Generales. *Anonymous.* FSW

They didn't plan it that way. Happy Birthday. Frank Bidart. HaCAP

They disappear again/into the fading trees/& fields & light/upstream. Poem for Hemingway & W. C. Williams. Raymond Carver. WOLT

They do all the work for your fat arms Some Pieces. Calvin Forbes. MAYP

They do it bind/In cloudy errors. When Stars Are Shrouded. I. T. EIL

They do like to spend a time in a soldier's company. The Royal Light Dragoon. *Anonymous.* OBET

They do not eat, they do not drink;/They do not even try to think. The Inefficacious Egg. Roy Bishop. HBMV

They do Not Have Much Fun! The Lazy Roof. Gelett Burgess. NA

They do not know it is the new-mown hay smell calling/and the wind of the plain praying... Population Drifts. Carl Sandburg. OxBA

They do not know/Life from its ghost. He Knoweth Not That the Dead Are Thine. Mary Elizabeth Coleridge. ELU; OBNC

They do receive, but you Sir make the Gift. A New-Years-Gift to Brian Lord Bishop of Sarum... William Cartwright. MePo

They do say only the lun-/atic stares at the bare moon. On Aesthetics, More or Less. Peter Kane Dufault. NYBP

(They do those things so well in France). George Sand. Dorothy Parker. FiBHP

They don't blame you–long as you're funny! The Family Fool. Sir William Schwenck Gilbert. ALV; InMe; NLV

They don't care for that in Bolivia. Limerick: "O's Operatic Olivia." Isabel Frances Bellows. TDH

They don't come by twos/But they come by tens. Old Lem. Sterling A. Brown. BPo; FB; IDB; PoBA; PoNe; TTY

They don't have it. The Moment. William Stafford. NNaP

They don't need my candle/But I do. Old Age Compensation. James Wright. NNaP

They don't recognize each other. Strange Meetings. Harold Monro. MoBrPo

They don't want/to/no Listen. Edward Estlin Cummings. WaaP

An' they done it, the Jollies–'Er Majesty's Jollies–soldier an' sailor too! Soldier an' Sailor Too. Rudyard Kipling. MOS

They drank his health in ice-cold beer that/night! Paddy Murphy. *Anonymous.* PV

They draw but what they see, know not the heart. Sonnets, XXIV: "Mine eye hath play'd the painter, and hath steel'd. William Shakespeare. EyDe

They draw my life, my life, out of my heart. After a Parting. Alice Meynell. NOBV

...They dream of California/as tho from here/there is no where else to go. Reno, 2 a.m. Sam Hamill. TAT

They drew a figure of an angel/braiding daisies in the hair of God. Hippies. Barry Dempster. CaPN

They drop asleep on sofa, chair or floor. Analysands. Dudley Randall. BPo

They dug out a lot from that Ol' Jinny mine. The Ol' Jinny Mine. Daisy L. Detrick. PoOW

They dwell and dream together,/The kin of court and wild. Unguarded. Ada Foster Murray. HBV 1-2

They each and all betoken–love. Love. Samuele Romanelli. TrJP

They each took one and left four in it. Riddle: "Elizabeth, Lizzy, Betsy and Bess." Anonymous. HBV 1-2; HBVY; OxNR

They endure and, freezing, find/A clear sustaining stream. Sierra Kid. Philip Levine. PoA

They even has the poor boy/all/hobbled down Aberdeen, Mississippi Blues. Booker White. BluL

They ever should be. People. D. H. Lawrence. BrPo

...They exist/Beyond your grief; they have their own/Quiet reality. These Trees Are No Forest of Mourners. D.G. Jones. NOBC

They expect him to live/On the food of a canary. Some Bird. Anonymous. STF

They extend farther than a man can see. The Bones. William Stanley Merwin. ConAP; LiTM; NePoEA-2

They faded away; and they never came back! The Nutcrackers and the Sugar-Tongs. Edward Lear. ALV; BLPL; PoLf; PoPle

"They fail, and they alone, who have not striven." The Arrow. Clarence Urmy. HBMV

They fail, and they alone, who have not striven. Enamored Architect of Airy Rhyme. Thomas Bailey Aldrich. AnNE; APA; HBV 1-2; MCCG

They fall, and leave their little lives in air. Field Sports. Alexander Pope. OBEC; SeCePo

They fall apart. When You Speak to Me. Tess Gallagher. LTB

They fall,/Flutter,/Fall. The City of Falling Leaves. Amy Lowell. MAPA

They fall to dreaming of the days long past. Old Ships. Louis Ginsberg. HBMV

They feed they Lion and he comes. They Feed They Lion. Philip Levine. LCAP; MAT; NNaP; NoAm; NOBA; Prf

They fell to work like husbandmen. The Scarecrow. H. L. Doak. OnYI

They fell together by the ears,/And ne'er were fond again. In the Sprightly Month of May. Sir John Vanbrugh. UnTE

They felt God is, though inconceivable. Evening in Gloucester Harbor. Epes Sargent. EtS

They fight, they fall, they sink into/the night. A Cry from the Ghetto. Morris Rosenfeld. TrJP

They fill me with new joy–this is my dream. Poetry and Science. Walter James Turner. SeCePo

They fill the waiting room with striding feet. Port Authority Terminal: 9 A.M. Monday. Chad Walsh. PPON

They fit & fit & fit... Lines. Brian Swann. AMV-81

...They flake and snow/down on us lost, unrecoverable lives. News. Dennis Schmitz. NPGG

They fled with blush, which guiltie seem'd of love. Astrophel and Stella, LXVI. Sir Philip Sidney. AAS; SiPS

They flew away. The Empty Cradle. Jose Selgas y Carrasco. CAW

They flitted/Through the palace walls. The Ordinary Women. Wallace Stevens. OxBA

They flutter there/And poise in air. The Ocotillo in Bloom. Marilla Merrimar Guild. BPAW

They fluttered off like withered souls of/men. The Pity of the Leaves. Edwin Arlington Robinson. AA; MoAmPo

They fly into my Head. The Birdcatcher. Ralph Hodgson. MoBrPo

They fold their forests round their feet/And bolster up the sky. The Mountains Are a Lonely Folk. Hamlin Garland. GoTF; TreFT

They forget me for a little pride of old time. Running Vines in a Field. Robert Carlton Brown. AnAmPo

They form men's thoughts, and the obedient clay/Takes disagreeing tempers from their ray. The Times. Marcus Manilius. LiTW

They found his wayward wife's sweet hair. The Witch in the Glass. Sarah Piatt. AA

They from its ruins build their own. Vanbrug's House. Jonathan Swift. PP

They fuck for their lives/in heatless rooms. Who Then Is Crazy? Barry Spacks. GP

They fused into a single stone that struck/sparks, the leaping green of cottonwood. The Gathering. Dwayne Thorpe. AMV-81

They gained a better Peace than ours. Peace. Phoebe Cary. PAH

They gallantly sail out &/shoot them as if the Pacific/were a Chicago garage on/St. Valentine's day Al Capone in Alaska. Ishmael Reed. TW

They gather themselves up... Eden. D. M. Thomas. NCSH

They gave its splendor to our fall. The Sumach Leaves. Jones Very. NOBA

They gave the calf my name. The Naming. Terry Hummer. AMV-81

They gave their lives that November day,/Those heroes of the Jervis Bay. The Jervis Bay. Anonymous. OBSS

They gave us guilt and the past,/and we sing what we know best. The Music of the Spheres. Marvin Bell. PoA

They gave us six fishhooks/and two blankets embroidered with smallpox. Meeting the British. Paul Muldoon. FaBoPV

They gaze into a dream. Hope. Phillips Stewart. CaP

They gaze upon him with a/most/satiric eye. All Goats. Elizabeth Jane Coatsworth. BoAnP

They get along–and we'll get along. Caboose Thoughts. Carl Sandburg. AnAmPo; CMoP

They get excited by dismembered chickens and dance up and/down Two Poems on the Emotions. David Shapiro. ANYP

They get up/at once/and go. Birthdays. Hilde Domin. BoWoP

They give a man a taste for death. Epigram: "Some can gaze and not be sick." Alfred Edward Housman. FaBoEE

They give me more hard luck and trouble/than I The First Time I Met You. Little Brother Montgomery. BluL

They give the drafts to others. The Origins of Life. Titus Lucretius Carus. LiTW

They glide most gracefully. The Ducks. Alice Wilkins. TiPo

They glorify the spell of light on/water. Hermann Ludwig Ferdinand von Helmholtz. Peter Meinke. SUW

They go. And the day The Lordly and Isolate Satyrs. Charles Olson. CABL; CoAP; NeAP; PoM

They go in search of life. Farewell at the Hour of Parting. Agostinho Neto. WhB

...They go out/on a little breath, they do not care. Illi Morituri. Mary Morison Webster. PeSA

They go out when they like and come in when they please. The Boys of the Island. Anonymous. ShS

They go so clad with lovely awe/None but the noble dares desire. The Angel in the House. Coventry Patmore. EG

They got so much/to be hot about Weeksville Women. Elouise Loftin. PoBA

They got this poet/only by flashlight/they got this poet. Nights Primarily III. Ed Lipman. LFAC

They got womens in the camp don't/mean no man no good New Minglewood Blues. Noah, Jug Band Lewis's. BluL

They grew till they joind in a true/lover's knot,/And then they died both together. Fair Margaret and Sweet William. Anonymous. BaBo; ESPB; OBET; ViBoFo

...They grip and flex/like small animals, restless/at the ends of his arms, waiting.) Because Our Past Lives Every Day. Ed Lipman. LFAC

...They/grip down and begin to awaken. Poem: "By the road to the contagious hospital." William Carlos Williams. UnPo

They grow smoother/and smoother A Stone Diary. Pat Lowther. NOBC

They grow through daily exercise/to all iniquity. The Image of Irelande (excerpt). John Derricke. OBTV

They had changed their throats and had the throats of birds. Cuchulain Comforted. William Butler Yeats. CMoP; LiTM; OAEL 1-2

They had each other–God was Good! For Sale or Rent. Anonymous. PoToHe

They had given him back to her, but not to keep. Not to Keep. Robert Frost. AnAmPo; CMoP; OxBA

They had my paper clip too tight. The Perforated Spirit. Morris Bishop. FiBHP; QQQ

They had no poet, and are dead. The Immortality of Verse. Horace. AWP

They had run in twenty puddles/Before I regained them. The Legs. Robert Graves. HaMV; LiTB; LiTM; NoAm

They had taken his all, and REVENGE it was sweet! The Raven. Samuel Taylor Coleridge. WiR

...They had to break her/before she would lie down in her coffin. The Grandmother. Wendell Berry. DFF; GP; SaC

They hail the ever-coming dawn/Though all the nations darkly grope. The Message of the Bells. Thomas Curtis Clark. PGD

They hand in hand with wandering steps and/slow,/Through Eden took their solitary way. Paradise Lost. John Milton. EnL; FaBoRV; FiP; HeIP; MyFE; NAWM 1-2; NOCV; OAEL 1-2; PoEL 1-5; SCV;

They hang'd the proud Sheriff on that,/And releas'd their own three men. Robin Hood and the Widow's Three Sons. Anonymous. BuBa; EnLi 1-2; ESPB; OnMSP; ViBoFo

They hang the cross upon the thief. On a Nomination to the Legion of Honour. Anonymous. FaBoEE

They hanged the proud sheriff on that,/And released their own three men. How Robin Hood Rescued the Widow's Sons. Anonymous. StPo

...They harbor/no hostilities Some have great gifts. Decks. Robert Phillips. GeTw; NYP

They hardly take God by surprise. Acceptance. Langston Hughes. NePoAm-2

They hate bright ribbons tying wooden shoes. Epigram: "Why do the Graces now desert the Muse?" Walter Savage Landor. FaBoEE

They hate for hate's sake. There Will Be No Peace. W. H. Auden. NePoAm-2

They have a cheerful warmth–those ashes on the stone. Salve! Thomas Edward Brown. HBV 1-2; OBEV; OBVV

They have accomplished nothing! The Long War. Li Po. WaaP

They have become a bridge/that arches toward the other shore. Gathering the Bones Together. Gregory Orr. AmPA; GeTw; Psk

They have become a new underworld. Freethinkers. Deborah Eibel. VWA

They have but changed one for another woe. Elegies. Andre Marie de Chenier. AWP

They have carried me in their branches. Trees. William Stanley Merwin. GP; PPJ

They have cast their burden upon the Lord, and–the/Lord He lays it on Martha's Sons! The Sons of Martha. Rudyard Kipling. HBV 1-2; WGRP

They have given me back the bliss of my senses The Child's Sight. Hy Sobiloff. VGW

They have left her The Seven Hells of the Jigoku Zoshi (excerpt). Jerome Rothenberg. NNaP

...They have left/the snow falling inside/the earth. Before the Actual Cold. Ray A. Young Bear. VoR

They have my lollypops. Little Johnny's Confession. Brian Patten. CAD

They have never been christianized. Pig Poem. Cary Waterman. GP

They have never forgotten. Country Landscape. Sherod Santos. AMV-80

They have no graves as yet. Elegy in a Country Churchyard. Gilbert Keith Chesterton. DBV; GoTF; MMM; MoBrPo; OBSP

They have no Heavenly Father/To care for them like you and me. Feathered Faith. Anonymous. STF

They have not changed! Ancestral Faces. Kwesi Brew. PBA

They have not come down yet! Timothy Boon. Ivy O. Eastwick. SoPo; TiPo

They have not forgotten/even if I did. The Book. William Carson Fagg. LFAC

They have not sown, and feed on bitter fruit. A Black Man Talks of Reaping. Arna Bontemps. BANP; BPo; CDC; FB; IDB; PoBA; PoNe

They have play and pleasure,/But not love like ours. Evening Song. Cecil Frances Alexander. OHIP

They have sat a long time/In one of our highest courts. The Grand Canyon. James Merrill. TAP

They have set my heart more cock-a-hoop,/Than could whole seas of crawfish soup. To a Young Lady, with Some Lampreys. John Gay. FaBoUs; NOEC

They have slipped away into the mists... Thomas and Charlie. Peter Wild. AmPA

They have still higher notes of fire/LIke cardinals upon the wing. Carolina Spring Song. Hervey Allen. HBMV

They have stolen his wits away. Arabia. Walter De la Mare. HBMV; WHA

...They have taken the cities/who were no enemies. The Inundation. Howard Sergeant. EAS

They have taken your name. Suicid/ing Indian Women. Paula Gunn Allen. TWSS

They have the faces of/no-one. The Animals in That Country. Margaret Atwood. NoP

They have to be. Sheep in the Rain. James Wright. AMV-80

They haven't left an atom there/Of my anatomie. Mary's Ghost. Thomas Hood. FiBHP

They, he and I know incense from dead ash. To the Muse. X. J. Kennedy. InPK; NoP

They hear from strands eternally unknown/The pulse of chords tremendous and remote? Sonnets on the Sea's Voice. George Sterling. EtS

They heare, & see, and sigh, and then they breake. Lowest Trees Have Tops. Sir Edward Dyer. FaBoEn

They held their venom behind wide-open eyes. Snake Hunt. David Wagoner. GP

They hide the dirt on father's shirt,/They're always in the way. Father's Whiskers. Anonymous. FSW

They hold the mirror up to you. On the Fly-Leaf of Manon Lescaut. Walter Learned. AA

They hold up my temples with their tusks. Birth. Gabriela Melinescu. BoWoP

They hop because they do not choose/To run. Nature Note. Arthur Guiterman. SUS

They hunt, the velvet tigers in the jungle. India. Walter James Turner. MoBrPo

They in the sea being burnt, they in the burnt ship drowned. A Burnt Ship. John Donne. EBEV; InPK; OBWP; WaaP

They in the thickest fight shall stand and/proudly answer, "Here!" Thomas at Chickamauga. Kate Brownlee Sherwood. PAH

They inch forth for heat and light,/waiting for their time slot to expire. Filling Station. Edward Morin. SOTS

They joined in stabbing frogs in the river. Praises of the King Dingana (Vesi). Anonymous. PeSA

They joined their hands in wedlock bands, long looked for, but come at last. Two Lovers Discoursing. Anonymous. ShS

They jostle white-armed down the tent-bordered/thoroughfare/Praising my Lady. First Praise. William Carlos Williams. VGW

They jumped BONG into bed like a bull at a gate. William I–1066. Eleanor Farjeon. BBV

They just need me & maybe you Poet-Tree. Earle Birney. OxBC

They just tumble into bed, in Kansas. In Kansas. Anonymous. FSW

"They keep me out of the bars". Dialog outside the Lakeside Grocery. Ishmael Reed. APU

They keep their men from going in/With muddy feet to God. Door-Mats. Mary Carolyn Davies. HBMV; YaD

They kiss the Rod with filial submission. By Mrs. Hopley, on Seeing Her Children Say Goodnight to Their Father. Gerard Manley Hopkins. FaBoEE

They knew He was God the Almighty/Come love to seek. In the Stable. Elizabeth Goudge. ChBR

They knew that sorrow her heart had broke. The Song of the Ghost. Alfred Perceval Graves. AnIV

They knew that when you die you lose your name. The Church on Comiaken Hill. Richard Hugo. LCAP; Prf; SM

They knew you once, O beautiful and wise. Discordants. Conrad Aiken. LiTM; NOBA; PG; PoA

They know a softer, stranger thing–/That there are children to be borne. A Woman of Words. Amanda Benjamin Hall. HBMV

They know and hate it–for it is lofty. A Degenerate Age. Solomon Ibn Gabirol. TrJP

They know Earth-secrets that know not I. An August Midnight. Thomas Hardy. BrPo; NOBV

They know for them I lived and died. The Good Shepherd. J. Harold Gwynne. BePJ

They know how to spin a gossamer web in the void. Song of the Weaving Woman. Yuan Chen. SaC

They know me not, but mourn with me. In Memoriam A.H.H., XCIX. Alfred, Lord Tennyson. VLP

They know more trucks are coming/As surely as the moon. Country Trucks. Monica Shannon. BrR; TiPo

They know not how to rate us. The Human Touch, 2. Helen King. PoToHe

They know not what–but surely something great. National Presage. John Kells Ingram. OnYI

They know not what they do! The Star of Calvary. Nathaniel Hawthorne. AA

They know the lion's power. Killed in Action. Terence Tiller. NeBP

They know the worthy General as "that most immoral/man'. A Code of Morals. Rudyard Kipling. FaBoCo

...They know/Us better than we know ourselves, and rightly so. King Midas Has Asses' Ears. Donald Finkel. NePoEA-2

...They know/what's going on/inside us. The Old Nudists. Joan Colby. AMV-80

They know who work, not they who play,/If rest is sweet. A Roundel of Rest. Arthur Symons. HBV 1-2

They labour to find an entrance without stairs Proceedings of the Wars. Erin Moure. CaPN

They laid the Index on his grave. Epitaph on the Proofreader of the Encyclopedia Britannica. Christopher Morley. ShM

They landed low by Barwicke side;/[There Douglas] landed Lord Percye. Northumberland Betrayd by Dowglas. Anonymous. ESPB; OxBB

They laugh at wiser men. The Gipsies. Richard Scrace. CaP

...They laze/neglected in corrals, or pace/at tether, shabby and unkempt. Mules. Ted Walker. NYBP

They lead their charges down the street, and some-/times to the curb. The Dog Parade. Arthur Guiterman. BoAnP; GDP

They lean over and touch the rose dead. B-52s. Arnold Kenseth. PPON

They leap on shafts of sunlight/through the mind's/shutters. The Children's Letters. Dorothy Livesay. NOBC

They learned to leave the house-door wide/Until they had lit the lamp inside. The Hill Wife. Robert Frost. VGW

They leave me strictly vertical. Apologia. Herbert Farjeon. PV

They leave me their keys which they never use. The Students of Justice. William Stanley Merwin. NaP

They leave so green, so jungle green. Animal Fair. Philip Booth. NePoAm-2

–They leave/The skull of Pharaoh staring at the sky. Three Sonnets on Oblivion. George Sterling. HBV 1-2

...They left/behind their notes, partially erased, like snow around a plane/crash. Instant Coffee. John Yau. APU

They left him–dead. The Jester in the Trench. Leon Gellert. PoAu 1-2

They licked the platter clean. Jack Sprat Could Eat No Fat. Mother Goose. FaBoBe; FaFP; HBV 1-2; HBVY

...They lie against the ship's side, and will nudge the hole open that/lets the water in at last. August Rain. Robert Bly. LCAP

They lie apart at the mother-heart of God's eternal sea.   The Shannon and the Chesapeake.   Thomas Tracy Bouve.   MC; PAH

...They lie forever, each in a forgotten grave.   In North Great George's Street. Seumas (James Starkey) O'Sullivan.   BIrV

They lie there now,/feeding your country's dwindling soil.   Certain Dead. John Haines.   LCAP

They lift their skirts like blinds across your eyes.   In Memoriam.   Michael Longley.   FaBoIP

"They lightly serve who serve us best,/Nor know they how the task was done!"   The Muses.   Edith Matilda Thomas.   HBV 1-2

They, like the dew, drop trembling from their/thorn.   There Are Sweet Flowers.   Walter Savage Landor.   EnRP

"They little think my real name's/V. Stuyvesant De Vere!"   What's in a Name?   Richard Kendall Munkittrick.   InMe

They live somewhere.   Aphrodite Metropolis.   Kenneth Fearing.   CAD

They live, they live in blest eternity.   Eternal Life.   Henry More.   TRV

They'll be damned like the sinners in hell.   The Gresford Disaster. *Anonymous.*   GBP; OBET

They'll be fine ships on that eternal sea.   Stowaway.   Bill Adams.   EtS

They'll be selling each other I do declare.   Kentucky Bootlegger. *Anonymous.*   FSW

They'll call you/a minor poet.   When (parody).   Philip Appleman.   BXAP

They'll Carry-Him!   I can wade grief.   Emily Dickinson.   NOBA

They'll cheenge folks' talk but no' their nature, fegs!   Sic Transit Gloria Scotia.   Hugh (Christopher Murray Grieve) MacDiarmid.   CMoP

They'll come down by the mills.   When the Clouds Are upon the Hills. *Anonymous.*   OxNR

They'll double-cross you and leave you with them empty bed blues.   Empty Bed Blues.   Bessie Smith.   UnPo

They'll find that their religion has been one.   Love of Fame, The Universal Passion.   Edward Hilton Young.   OBSV

They'll get a chance to meet/The female police/& eat Chicken McNuggets. Laundry & School Epigrams.   Bernadette Mayer.   APU

They'll give you frogs instead of fish,/And do you foul, foul play.'   Katherine Johnstone.   *Anonymous.*   BuBa

They'll have something to think about.   What the Sixties Were Really Like. Sam Abrams.   APU

They'll lay another by tomorrow's sun.   I'm Thankful That My Life Doth Not Deceive.   Henry David Thoreau.   PoEL 1-5

They'll let you play anybody but you,/that's pretty much what they will do. A Poem for Players.   Al Young.   GP

They'll make a sweet Bishop when Gentlefolks sup.   Oranges.   Jonathan Swift.   NCEP

They'll make their boasts and brag, Sir.   The Battle of the Kegs.   Francis Hopkinson.   OBAL

They'll meet us ere we leave the narrow way.   The Country Lovers.   George Smith.   NOEC

They'll not meet/The apex of his self-conceit.   Epitaph for George Moore. Thomas Hardy.   FaBoEE

...They'll not use/The gold but hold it as a memorial/To Chance and their own abstinence.   Boys in October.   Irving Layton.   OBCV

They'll pension me off to go fishing.'   Off Brighton Pier.   Alan Ross.   OBWP

They'll put your name on a list; then visitors/Will have to imagine you for years and years.   The Visiting Hour.   David Wagoner.   HoPM

They'll send you to jail, you bad gahlia.   Limerick: "A maiden caught stealing a dahlia."   *Anonymous.*   TDH

They'll shave his beard, nose, ears and hair/To look like everyone else. Tapestry.   Charles Simic.   LCAP

They'll simply call him names.   The Umpire.   Milton Bracker.   SD

They'll soon see who was left at home.'   The Rat.   William Henry Davies. OxBTC

They'll stand up for his right,/And their own, to the tight little Island.   The Island.   Robert Southey.   CoBE

They'll take you to Australia! Slide, Kelly, slide!   Slide, Kelly, Slide.   J.W. Kelly.   FaFP; TreFS

They'll thraw ye frogs instead o fish,/An steal your bride away.   Katharine Jaffray (C version).   *Anonymous.*   ESPB

They'll use us then they care not how-/Balow, la-low!   Balow.   *Anonymous.* OBEV

They'll weep for the Maiden who sleeps in this wave.   Lalla Rookh. Thomas Moore.   OBNC

They'll yet regret they sent Jim Jones in chains to Botany Bay.   Jim Jones. *Anonymous.*   CBAP; GBP; PoAu 1-2

They long for the easy diversion, but that is gone.   American History.   W. R. Moses.   LiTA

They look at stars, and think they are/Denominational.   Creeds.   Willard Wattles.   HBMV

...They look at us through reach for us through/the open windows   Sharks. Dick Lourie.   NeAC

They look like bunny shoes./Love,/T.   Roethke Plain.   John Malcolm Brinnin.   NoAm; TAP

They look like shepherds moving on a plain.   The Inca Tupac Upanqui. William Hart-Smith.   NOAV

They look more fair within the depths below.   The Trees of Life.   Jones Very.   NOBA

They lose most who are afraid.   Faint Heart.   William James Linton. OBVV

They love no more strawe they had rather to fast.   A Hundreth Good Poyntes of Husbandry.   Thomas Tusser.   FaBoUs

They love, and cover me/For the squares of bread I give.   St. Ciaran and the Birds.   Ciaran Carson.   CIP

They love indeed who dare not say they love.   Astrophel and Stella, LIV. Sir Philip Sidney.   AAS; InPS; OAEP; OBSC; SiPS; TrGrPo

...They love the songs/of joyous saints whose tongues are holy dust.   Saints. George Garrett.   EaLo

They loved to walk bare-headed in the rain.   Epigram: April.   Howard Nemerov.   OBAL

...They made a little mirth/Until the great moon rose upon the earth.   The Earthly Paradise.   William Morris.   VLP

They made her a coffin o the gowd sae/yellow,/And buried her deep on the high banks/o Yarrow.   Bonnie Annie (B version).   *Anonymous.*   ESPB

They made the back part shabby.   The Building of a New Church. *Anonymous.*   EyDe

They make me remember the one whom I adore!   I Took Leave of My Beloved One Evening.   At Taliq.   PeHV

They make me sick, they make me tired.   Men.   Dorothy Parker.   DBV

...They make the anthill/bearable of course the price is blood.   Portrait of the Autist as a New World Driver.   Les A. Murray.   CBAP

They make the greatest sacrifice.   Hymn for the Slain in Battle.   William Stanley Braithwaite.   BALP

They make the stars of bone   Some Last Questions.   William Stanley Merwin.   CAPP; HaCAP

They make the world light when the moon is out of sight.   Ballad of Davy Crockett.   *Anonymous.*   ABF

They make up 52% of the collective farm workers and/48% of the factory workers   Women Called Bossy Cowboys.   Beth Jankola.   AMV-80

They makes me feel just right.   Greens (with music).   *Anonymous.*   AS

They march on Halloween.   Skeleton Parade.   Jack Prelutsky.   NTCP

They march us out with, from one/to the next lost place.   The Ancestors. Christopher Middleton.   NMP

They may carve monuments yet lack all understanding.   Needle and Thread. Pan Chao.   WPOW

They may look, they may wait till the cold water rise,/They may look to the bottom of the sea.   The Mermaid.   *Anonymous.*   AmFP

They may rejoice today–while I resign/Life, to be numbered 'mongst the feeling swine.   The Sow of Feeling.   Robert Fergusson.   NOEC

They may serve Eight, instead of serving Four.   Be Just (Domestick Monarchs) unto Them.   George Alsop.   SCAP

They may still be there,/may still be there.   A Poem to Delight My Friends Who Laugh at Science-Fiction.   Edwin Rolfe.   NePA; NePoAm; PPON

They mean absolutely nothing to me.   A Vase of Flowers.   John Ashbery. ConAP

They meant there were griefs involved–though kept on saving.   The Accountings.   Albert Goldbarth.   GeTw

They melt.   At Liberty.   Anne S. Perlman.   SUW

They merge from your ears and infect love.   A Poem for Diane Wakoski. Ray A. Young Bear.   CDW

They might as well.   Untitled.   Humbert Wolfe.   BoC

They might chart out that voyage to a shore/On which with confidence a nation would arise.   The Tempest.   William Jay Smith.   MoAmPo

They miss your flashing wings,/Your splendorous flying.   White Dove of the Wild Dark Eyes.   Joseph Mary Plunkett.   HBMV

They mix in one another's arms/To one pure image of regret.   In Memoriam A.H.H., CII.   Alfred, Lord Tennyson.   PoEL 1-5

They moan and I'm there/and it's still like that.   Pigeons.   Bert Meyers. EAS

They mock their anxious mothers/With their mothers' eyes.   Mothers and Daughters.   David Campbell.   PoL

They mount the lonely street.   The Lonely Street.   William Carlos Williams. MP; PoA; TwCP

They mourn for you, your sons who never were.   The Lament of the Voiceless.   Laura Bell Everett.   PGD

They move into the future and are gone.   The Twins.   Judith Wright. PoAu 1-2

They move into the trackless cover of the night.   The Uninvited.   William D. Mundell.   NYBP

They move like melting mountains.   The Whales off Wales.   X. J. Kennedy. OBCA

They munch along their quiet search.   Pastoral.   Alan Creighton.   CaP

They must be muzzled in the dog days for fear they might/go mad. Alphabetical Song on the Corn Law Bill.   *Anonymous.*   OxBoLi

They must be seen to," says little Prince Tatters.   Prince Tatters.   Laura E. Richards.   HBV 1-2; HBVY

They must be very precious to/The blessed Prince of Peace. The Faithful Few. Chester E. Shuler. STF

They must learn to stay in their graves. That is what graves are for. Natural History. Robert Penn Warren. FF

They must obey... When the God Returns. Russell Edson. GP

They must strive to be as good/Alive; or 'tis impossible. Epitaph on Mistress Mary Draper. Charles Cotton. CavP

...They must turn to blood inside you. Dispossessions. Jane Cooper. FaBoWP

They neither care, nor care not, they are only dead. Agamemnon's Tomb. Sacheverell Sitwell. LiTB; MoBrPo; OBMV

They never began and great hunks of the world will fit Sorting, Wrapping, Packing, Stuffing. James Schuyler. NoAm

They never came back to me. Calico Pie. Edward Lear. CBEP; FaBoCh; LoGBV; SoPo; TrGrPo

They never danced on any heath/As when the time hath been. The Fairies' Farewell. Richard Corbet. FaBoCh; LoGBV; ViBoPo

They never knew where they were at,/Till the old Ark bumped on Ararat. One More River. Anonymous. TreFS

They never let him any deeper in. Epigram: "You ask me how Contempt who claims to sleep." J. V. Cunningham. ELU

They never more would slam the Door,/–As often they had done before. Rebecca, Who Slammed Doors for Fun and Perished Miserably. Hilaire Belloc. NOBL; SO

They never regarded your warm feet,/But I regarded. English Girl. Edward Powys Mathers. OBMV

They never talk who always think. They Never Taste Who Always Drink. Matthew Prior. GoTF

They never told me I might turn back Lullaby in Auschwitz. Pierre Morhange. VWA

They never told me that I was/White-armed and amber-eyed. Discovery. Hildegarde Flanner. HBMV

They never were heard of again. Captain Spud and His First Mate, Spade. John Ciardi. OBCA

They of your song sublime! The Celts. Thomas D'Arcy McGee. OnYI; OxBI

They oft decline into the worst of ill/That act the people's wish without law's will. On the Duke of Buckingham, Slain by Felton... Owen Felltham. JCP

They only ask and pray to God to make John hold his base. The Indian Ghost Dance and War. W. H. Prather. PoOW

They only ask the wind to blow,/And that his will be ever done. Epitaphs: For a Fickle Man. Mark Van Doren. ViBoPo

They only find a Med'cine for the Itch. No Platonique Love. William Cartwright. CABA; GBL; InvP; JCP; LiTB; OAEL 1-2; PoEL 1-5

They only sing who are struck dumb by God. Poets. Joyce Kilmer. AnAmPo; WGRP

They only study the disease,/Alas, who live not to detect. It Is Not Sweet Content, Be Sure. Arthur Hugh Clough. VLP

They order things so damnably in Hell. To Dives. Hilaire Belloc. CAW; HBMV; OBSV

They owned their passiveness. The Subalterns. Thomas Hardy. CMoP; MoAB; MoBrPo; NoAm; NOBV; OAEL 1-2; PPP

They packe them thence, to place of richter haunt: Donec Eris Felix Multos Numerabis Amicos. Anonymous. EnPo

They pale,/They turn white. Invocation. Nakasuk. WTO

They parted aff careerin/Fu' blythe that night. Halloween. Robert Burns. OBEC

They parted with a kiss quite cold and sad. Once. George Ives. PeHV

They pass, they pass, and know not whither. All Lovely Things. Conrad Aiken. PoRA

They pause and smile, at peace,/each in his own condition. Washing Windows. Barry Spacks. NCSH

They perchance may make you tumble,/So respect them. Q. E. D. The Domineering Eagle and the Inventive Bratling. Guy Wetmore Carryl. OBAL

...They persuade me/all will be well. Photograph in a Stockholm Newspaper for March 13, 1910. Don Coles. NOBC

They pinch for it as it rolls/out of the therapist's hands, very small. Coma. Dennis Schmitz. NPGG

They pluck blanched flowers in the valley of the moon,/Sarah Lorton and her death together. Sarah Lorton. Mary Finnin. BoAV

They pray the insignificance/of most private behavior. Adultery. Alan Dugan. CAPP

They Pu'd down the steeple, and drunkit the bell. Ech, Sic a Pairish. Anonymous. FaBoCo; FiBHP

They purge the aire without, within the breast. The Storm. George Herbert. AnAnS 1

They put Lord Roden in the van. Irish Antiquities. Thomas Moore. FaBoEE

They quite forgot their quarrel. Dum and Dee. Anonymous. OxNR

They'r very fine! sais my deluded eye. Pleasent Delusion of a Sumpteous Citty. Sarah Kemble Knight. SCAP

They raced into the wood! The Centaurs. James Stephens. AmMo; AnEnPo

They raced the wild boar to his den,/And found the bones of a thousand men. Old Bangum. Anonymous. BaBo

They're a' flown frae me! Here's a String o' Wild Geese. Anonymous. PBBP

They're a one-man dog/And, once broken, will bite another. Jeans. J. V. Brummels. GP

They're all a-growin' green in my own countree. Home, Dearie, Home. Anonymous. AmSS

They're all crooked. Journal, Part IV. Gayl Jones. BlSi

They're all growing green in the old countrie. Home. William Ernest Henley. GN; HBV 1-2; PoLf

They're all the same to your behind. A Bestiary of the Garden for Children Who Should Know Better. Phyllis Gotlieb. WHW

They're apt/to grow up/hostile. The New Calf. Frances Downing Vaughan. AMV-80

–They're bringing them home, now, too late, too early. Homecoming. Bruce Dawe. CBAP

They're dead...for God's sake stop that gramophone. Dead Musicians. Siegfried Sassoon. BrPo

They're falling through the atmosphere/And also through the air. The Autumn Leaves. Anonymous. NA

They're funny, sir./They are. Ants. Alfred Kreymborg. MAPA

They're gettin' together and layin' a plan/For buildin' the city again! Barriers Burned. Charles K. Field. BPAW

They're going to hang me up in the air/Between the earth and sky. The Oxford Girl (Expert Town). Anonymous. AmFP

They're holding hands/By holding tails. Holding Hands. Lenore M. Link. MoShBr; NTCP; SoPo

They're liars all. Medieval Norman Songs. Anonymous. AWP

They're living together, doing well. John Riley. Anonymous. OuSiCo

They're preachin' Corey's funeral,/In the lonesome graveyard ground. Darlin' Corey. Anonymous. FSW

They're pretty revolting. The Canary. Ogden Nash. DFF; FiBHP

They're pulled from the green ground of the sea,/Big as a six pound rose. Off Molokai. Norman Hindley. WOLT

They're said to us in consolation/From the window of a railroad car)... Words from the Window of a Railway Car. Anatoly Steiger. VWA

...They're shifting/monuments, take no risks, are true. The School for Objects. Paul Hoover. APU

They're sick. Commissary Report. Stoddard King. ALV; ShM

They're slaves with slaves' morals,/all these slaves within me. All the Slaves. Thomas Lux. SM

They're stifled by the pressure of his chain. To a Golden Heart, Worn Round His Neck. Johann Wolfgang von Goethe. AWP; LiTW

They're such a solid comfort to a poor old bum. Erie Canal Ballad. Anonymous. ABF

They're the spirit of our times–the pollstergeist. Poll Star. Felicia Lamport. NLV

They're too real to be a dream. Songs for a Colored Singer. Elizabeth Bishop. PoNe

They're up there now, if anybody'd look. Wild Pigs. Ted Kooser. SM; TAT

They're with O'Leary in the grave. September, 1913. William Butler Yeats. BrPo; CMoP; CoBMV; FaBoPV; GTBS-P; HAP; NoAm; PoRA; PPoe

They're worse to get on. Horses. Richard Armour. PoPl

They recognize his color and his greed. Lullaby for Ann-Lucian. Calvin Forbes. PoBA

...They refuse/to be blessed, throat, eye and knucklebone. The Truth the Dead Know. Anne Sexton. MoAmPo; NePoEA-2; NIP; NoAm; PBWP; TAP

They rejoiced on their way. The Pastor. William C. Summers. STF

They remind me of good friends, old letters,/and of her who gave me my life. Parts. Ziche Landau. VWA

They return to clothe you/in their dreams and their hopes. Dry Your Tears, Africa! Bernard Dadie. TTY

...They returned safe. The three/went home. The Difference. Winfield Townley Scott. NePoAm

They, returning, bring us back/Absence, winter, what we gave. The Way Down: They Return. Jay Macpherson. PoA

They ride against the mothering earth. The Automobile. James Lewisohn. AmC

They Ride me Everywheres. My Feet. Gelett Burgess. NA

They rightly were mine–instead. Borrowed. Anonymous. BLRP

They rise above a vault into the air. Doctrinal Point. William Empson. AtBAP

They rise and fall; and all the seething plain/Bubbles a cauldron vast of many-coloured pain. Sonnet: The Army Surgeon. Sydney Thomas Dobell. NCEP

They rise, they walk again. The Heaven of Animals. James Dickey AP; CAPP; CoAP; HeIP; LiTM; NCSH; NoAm; NOBA; TAP

They riveted my youth to an insulting repose. Les Salaziennes (excerpt). Auguste Lacaussade. TTY

They roam together now, and wind among/Its bye-streets, knocking at the dusty inns. The House of Life. Dante Gabriel Rossetti. NoP; VLP

They rocked the infant Time! Along Shore. Herbert Bashford. AA

They rode him to his grave. I Once Knew a Man. Lucille Clifton. GeTw

...They rose then to join/in praise of Shivaji's shrewd sense of politics. The Rise of Shivaji. Zulfikar Ghose. MoBS

They rule themselves they'll be as good,/Almost, as Englishmen! The Native Irishman. Anonymous. OnYI

They run, they run, until they wake again. Two Sonnets from a Sequence. Edgar Holt. BoAV

They's nary angel 'bout the place with "curv'ture of/the spine." The Little Hunchback. James Whitcomb Riley. PeD

They safe arriv'd at Dunstable, thirteenth/day of May. Lovewell's Fight. Anonymous. BaBo; HBV 1-2; PAH

They said he was dry-footed. And he was. Biography. Charles Bruce. CaP

They said it might just save the world. For James Baldwin. Kay Boyle. NMM

They said that I had given it thee. Popular Songs of Tuscany. Anonymous. AWP

They said, "To die is glorious."/They lied. Battle Won Is Lost. Phil George. GrPl

They sat, she laughing at a quiet joke. Modern Love, VI. George Meredith. NOBV; ViBoPo; VLP

They saw Apollo come again, and heard/His name cried in the porches of the sun! The Lord of All. Edwin Markham. CAW

They saw that I fell more than twice./I'm grateful for that. The Chums. Theodore Roethke. NoAm

They say...A drink? I don't believe I would. You Serve the Best Wines Always, My Dear Sir. Martial (Marcus Valerius Martialis). InPK

They say about loving, about riding/a bicycle: you never forget how. Why Not? Linda Pastan. FAZ

They say, "Glad may this child's friends be/To have a child so mannerly as he." A Goodly Child. Anonymous. OxBChV

They say I've burned all my brown sticks/for telling time/and still it passes away. Leaving. Linda Hogan. TWSS

They say, interpret it your own way, Christ is born. An Eclogue for Christmas. Louis MacNeice. FaBoMo; MoPo; MoVE; NoAm; OBMV

They say it's a child. But/I ain't quite so sure. For Hettie. LeRoi (Imamu Amiri Baraka) Jones. NeAP; NoAm; NOBA

They say, mothers of the dead are never alone. Hopi Woman. Lillian White Spencer. BPAW

They say only those pipes are real. The Pipes. Lou Lipsitz. LTB

They say/Spring is icummen in– The Sea-Elephant. William Carlos Williams. LiTA; NU

They say such different things at school. Michael Robartes and the Dancer. William Butler Yeats. OAEL 1-2

They say the balloon/Is gone up to the moon. What's the News? Anonymous. OxNR

They say the largest catfish wait. Fools. Glenn Hardin. AMV-81

They say the spring air comes without much intention. War Walking Near. Ray A. Young Bear. CDW

They say their master is a knave–/And sure they do not lie. Epigram: The Parson's Looks. Robert Burns. OxBoLi

They say there is no end to it. Prologue. Archibald MacLeish. MoAmPo

They say they feel unfathered, left alone,/Hurt by the indifference of His tone. Our Father. Roberta Teale Swartz. MoRP

They say 'twas a case of consumption. Limerick: "A certain young man of great gumption." Anonymous. ShM

They say what makes him flee so fast/Is fleas–because he's got 'em! Jackrabbits. Squire Omar Barker. BPAW

They scatter all their stuff abroad,/And tumble down their tools. The Tower of Babel. Nathaniel Crouch. OxBChV

They scattered our bones/in the heart of the gulag. Green Haven Halls. Charles Culhane. LFAC

They scorn to yield their ancient sway to man. Lords of the Wilderness. John Leyden. OBRV

They see a little dark-eyed girl at play. Romance. Mildred Howells. AA

They see with living eyes/How long they have been dead. Through These Pale Cold Days. Isaac Rosenberg. TrJP

They seek a solution; they have it,/And they know it not. World Planners. Arvel Steece. PGD

They seek the mountain and the tumbling flood. Goats. Charles Erskine Scott Wood. AnEnPo

...They seem/to be mourning Some San Francisco Poems. George Oppen. NNaP

They seem worthy of His Hand. The Birds. Blossius Aemilius Dracontius. CAW

They, self-thought saints, a dissolution dread. True and Joyful News. Anonymous. APAS

They sell the best wedging and ebbing. Tie Your Tongue, Sir? Robert Paul Smith. CAD

They settled to the slot and disappeared. The Quarry. William Vaughn Moody. AnAmPo

They severally promote or hinder,/Unknown. Four trees upon a solitary acre. Emily Dickinson. PoEL 1-5

They shake their own two hands, and then/Ask, "Have you eaten rice?" How Do You Do? H. Bedford Jones. WBLP

They shall be guests at the secret/wedding of form and content. A Question of Form and Content. Jon Stallworthy. OxBC

They shall be thick and cloudie to my breast. Confession. George Herbert. AnAnS 1; JCP

...They shall come to you for ever/with their desire, and you shall bleed for them in return. The Woman. R. S. Thomas. OxBC

They shall find him ware an' wakin', as they found him long ago. Drake's Drum. Sir Henry Newbolt. AnFE; EtS; FaBoCh; FaPoR; GTBS; HBV 1-2; HBVY; MCCG; OBMV; OBVV; PaPo; PoRA; TreF; VLP

They shall lie there, together. The Old Churchyard of Bonchurch. Philip Bourke Marston. HBV 1-2; NBM; OBNC; OBVV

They shall never rest in peace. International Brigade Dead. Thomas O'Brien. NeIP

They shall never sound in slavery. The Minstrel-Boy. Thomas Moore. ACP; AnIL; CoBE; FaBoBe; FaFP; FSW; GN; GoBC; GoTF; HBV 1-2; OAEP; OnYI; PrIm; RoGo; TreF

They shall now also march obediently eastward for your sake/Libertad. A Broadway Pageant. Walt Whitman. NYP

They shall rise up from this knowledge. On the Death of Parents. Alfred Barson. AMV-80

They shall to children's children make notorious/His righteousness, and this His doing glorious. Psalm XXII. Sir Philip Sidney. FCP

They shaped our minds and morals/With switches on the seat! America Was Schoolmasters. Robert P. Tristram Coffin. PAL

They shed our pale voices, crying for time. They Grow Up Too Fast, She Said. Diana O Hehir. NPGG

They shone like the gleaming/Stars in the sky. Kings Came Riding. Charles Williams. OBCP

They shot him for folding/An IBM card. Epitaph: "Here he lies moulding." Leslie Mellichamp. ShM

They should be bitten and boiled like spoons. Clouds. Philip Levine. LCAP

They should let it go by. Women. Louise Bogan. HBMV; MoAB; MoAmPo

They shoulder one another to be taken first. Bridesmaid. Robley Wilson, Jr. AMV-80

They shout and gunning motors roar/into the parking lot of the Dairy Queen. Heroes of the Strip. Sheila Cudahy. TAT

They shove your anger in your face. Diary. Black Bear's Moon. Charlotte De Clue. TWSS

They show them to you sometimes at a terminus. La Bete Humaine. James Kirkup. NeBP

...They showed me/the way Djanbun went across the mountain range. The Platypus. Anonymous. NOAV

They showed the tartar on their teeth,/scratched and grinned. The Gorilla at Twenty Nine Years. J. D. Reed. NeAC

They shriek beneath the sod,/"There is no God!" A Common Inference. Charlotte Perkins Stetson Gilman. AA; AnAmPo; WGRP

They sing and sing like all the birds of the desert. The Retarded Children Find a World Built Just for Them. Diana O Hehir. NPGG

They sing their songs,/and carry on. Floodtide. Askia Muhammad Toure. PoBA; PoNe

They sink to their deaths,/the haul beside them still theirs. The Escapade. David Ignatow. PP

They sit in their white lawn sleeves, as cool as history. King's College Chapel. Charles Causley. BoC

They sleep, and wait for dawn. Mountain Evenings. Jamie Sexton Holme. PoOW

They sleep from midnight till eight in/a little bed a mile behind their meat. The Age of the Butcher. Stuart Friebert. AMV-80

They sleep on two too little feet. Pelicanaries. J. Patrick Lewis. PPJ

They slept for the waiting day. The Animals' Arrival. Elizabeth Jennings. PBWP

...They slew me because I slept. Epitaphs of the War, 1914-18. Rudyard Kipling. OBWP

They slide into the ear of a corpse/and listen to his great sigh. The Fury of Flowers and Worms. Anne Sexton. BoWoP

They slide to us and Air. The Indian Queen: Song of Aerial Spirits. John Dryden. AtBAP

They slump in booths like rags, not even drunk. Drug Store. Karl Shapiro. CMoP; MoVE; MP; OxBA; TwCP

They smile (while purring the refrains),/At little thoughts that cross their brains. My Uncle Paul of Pimlico. Mervyn Peake. OnUR

They smoke awhile,/& then they make structure with a roof or under a roof. 3rd Dance–Making a Structure with a Roof or under a Roof... Jackson MacLow. CoPo

...They smoke Lucky Strikes. They buy Wonder Bread. You Owe Them Everything. John Allman. SaC

They sneak into your dreams/just before the world ends. Training for the Apocalypse. Gloria Frym. APU

They sought, O Albion! next thy sea-encircled coast. The Progress of Poesy. Thomas Gray. ATP

They splash ashore, pretending to feel buoyant. Lament for the Non-Swimmer. David Wagoner. DFF

They spring together in this fertile air/Loud with thunder. Rain on the Cumberlands. James Still. GrPl

They stalk on Newbury Street. The Beasts of Boston. Betty Lowry. AMV-80

They stand and twirl their moustaches. A Ballad of the Mulberry Road. Ezra Pound. LOW

They stand hesitating in the lonely road and their tears fall like/rain. The Little Cart. Arthur Waley. AtBAP; LoBV

They stand most straight/who learn to walk beneath a weight. Sindhi Woman. Jon Stallworthy. OxBC

They stand together. The future comes. In Fur. William Stafford. RFM

They stare, a sheet loose-folded round their knees,/Off into space, as from Etruscan tombs. The Lovers. William Jay Smith. MoAmPo

...They stare,/fouling our acts of love. Concerning the Dead. Mark Halperin. FAZ

They stare into their coffee cups. Crazy Horse Returns to South Dakota. Harley Elliott. NeAC

They started the fuss/And left it to us! Ancient History. Arthur Guiterman. OBCA

They stay puckered and promise to laugh again. Tongues. Sharon Berg. AMV-80

They steal your stores and clothes away,/Across the Western Ocean. Across the Western Ocean. Anonymous. AmSS; AS; FSW

They steam in wine & anise,/are eaten with butter. Nantucket / Mussels / October. Stephen Lewandowski. WOLT

They stept into the boat, and launch'd from land. Endymion, I. John Keats. EnRP

They still will clamour for a sign! An Argument–Of the Passion of Christ. Thomas Merton. CrMA

They strain out wide and wounded,/Like arms upon a cross. Gesture. Winifred Welles. HBMV

They stretched until they seemed/to converge where we began. Outer Space, Inner Space. Gladys Cardiff. TWSS

They strike mine eyes, but not my heart. Simplex Munditiis. Ben Jonson. GoBC; HBV 1-2; HoPM; InPo; NOBE; OBEV

They stubbornly show the hour/it occurred. Clocks. Malka Locker. VWA

...They sway/In one black phalanx towards the day. The Rookery at Sunrise. William Sharp. FM

...They swim forward to greet me. Tokyo West. Alfred Corn. NYP

They take to filtering the water. Postscript to Die Schone Mullerin. R. P. Llster. PoL

They talk. They dip snuff./They are happy. Old Men Working Concrete. Phil Hey. FiCP

They taste and die: what likelier can ensue? Paradise Lost. John Milton. ATP

They taste good to her To a Poor Old Woman. William Carlos Williams. OBAL; SOTW; TAP

They tell how much I owe/To thee and Time! The Poet's Song to His Wife. Bryan Waller Procter. HBV 1-2

They tell me time is time,/And only heaven mature. In Rama. George Alfred Townsend. AA

They tell me we shall win the bloody war. And the World's Face. Julian Symons. WaP

They tell of the heavens to me. To a Skylark. George Meredith. EnLit

They tell of the little mer-men! Sea Shells. Clinton Scollard. BrR

They tell stories. Street Window. Carl Sandburg. PCP

They tell the clattered trees that I/Should weep? Night Winds. Adelaide Crapsey. QFR

They tell you to go. And you do. Ringing the Bells. Anne Sexton. BiP; CAPP; FF; HaCAP; NMP; TAP; VGW

They tend the fire, and wait. Native Origin. Beth Brant. STE

They terrify my soul! They tear/My heart asunder! In the Night. James Stephens. OBMV

They that are rich in words, in words discover/That they are poor in that which makes a lover. The Silent Lover. Sir Walter Ralegh. LiTB; OBEV

They that do change old love for new,/Pray gods they change for worse. Song of Oenone and Paris. George Peele. OBSC

They that have seen thy look in death/No more may fear to die. Dirge. Felicia Dorothea Hemans. OBEV

They that will boast of Bigness,/Naught can they boast besides! Ephraim the Grizzly. Arthur Guiterman. BPAW

They that would look on her must come/to me. The House of Life. Dante Gabriel Rossetti. VLP

They think by this/Us men to overreach. Song Set by Robert Jones: "A woman's looks." Anonymous. OBSC

They think him, all around,/The mildest curate going. The Rival Curates. Sir William Schwenck Gilbert. CenHV; VLP

They think their knowledge far exceeds his own. The Rising Village. Oliver Goldsmith. CaP

They thought it best to disappear. Blossoms. Frank Dempster Sherman. OBCA

They throw coconuts at us. A Bestiary. Kenneth Rexroth. OBAL

They thus become a model of true love. The Love Suicides at Sonezaki (excerpt). Chikamatsu Monzaemon. DL

They, too, have done the same! At Casterbridge Fair. Thomas Hardy. EnLi 1-2

They too ignored the bird's half-baffled cry. Half-heard. Christopher Koch. PoAu 1-2

They took a cage with stout bars/And shut it up inside. The Red Cockatoo. Po Chu-i. LiTW

They took away his crotch. Dream Songs. John Berryman. CAPP

They took my soul, lord,/they gonna kill me dead Canned Heat Blues. Tommy Johnson. BluL

They touch you. People Trying to Love. Stephen Berg. NaP

They trembled and ador'd. The Bonhomme Richard and Serapis. Philip Freneau. PAH

They trod the stained flute where it lay. The Flute. Joseph Russell Taylor. AA

They trot the field, lofty as horses' asses. Busby, Whose Verse No Piercing Beams, No Rays. Richard Moore. TW

They troubled not the little Jesus' sleep... On Christmas Eve. Edith Lovejoy Pierce. MoRP

They truly live who truly share!/Give, children, give. The Song of the Lilies. Lucy Wheelock. OHIP

They trust it, dear, because they must. One Way of Trusting. Hannah Parker Kimball. AA

They try revolving,but the wheels/give way, they will not bear the weight. Wading at Wellfleet. Elizabeth Bishop. AmP

They tumbed in Twede/That woned by the see. The English Retort. Anonymous. OxBM

They turn and croak over our harvests Mothers. Tristan Tzara. VWA

They turn slowly/especially in public/when one must be polite. Dressed to Kill. Clarence Major. APU

They turn the light out and they go to sleep. Once More. George Jonas. NeAC

They turn to tread the impetus/that moves about their feet. Ad Infinitum. Joan Aronsten. NOAV

They turned them into water! Alpheus and Arethusa. Eugene Howell Daly. AA

They turned to bed and took the gift of sleep. The Odyssey. Homer. NAWM 1-2

They twist and turn all in your air-blue sky. Song for Ireland. Phil and June Colclough. OBET

They understood each other pretty well. Two Englishmen. Douglas Stewart. CBAP

They understood that wisdom comes of beggary. The Seven Sages. William Butler Yeats. NOBI

They utter the heart in me. Joy-Month. David Atwood Wasson. HBV 1-2

They vanished one by one! Jack Frost. Helen Bayley Davis. SoPo

They've all disappeared with the passing of the summer. End-of-Summer Poem. Rowena Bastin Bennett. SiSoSe

They've all grown up ugly, and nobody cares. John, Tom, and James. Charles Henry Ross. NLV; OxBChV

They've been alike as a pair of pins/Since they could scarcely toddle. Betwixt and Between. Hugh Lofting. BiCB

They've cut them up since those days. School Days. Will D. Cobb. GoTF; TreFT

They've descended from something, but/not from us. Three Monkeys. Anonymous. STF

They've got to stop kicking my dog around! Stop Kicking My Dog around. Anonymous. GDP

They've made God of his carrion/And labelled it "Christ!" Jesus. Francis Lauderdale Adams. OxBS

They've no more use for us in Wardour Street. Wardour Street. Humbert Wolfe. OxBTC

They've rustled my pile, my pile away. Ten Thousand Cattle. Owen Wister. BPAW

They've sense to get, what we want sense to keep. The Prophecy of Famine. Charles Churchill OBSV

...They've snowed their gold/to Ikhnaton and stand/tracking stations with nothing to behold. Wintered Sunflowers. Richard Snyder. PPJ

They wad get grist eneugh. Manor Water. *Anonymous.* GBP

They wail a curse against their fate. Prairie Wolves. Robert V. Carr. BPAW; PoOW

They wait and touch and watch their dreams/eat the morning. Like Rousseau. LeRoi (Imamu Amiri Baraka) Jones. PoA

...They wait upon a sign/That promises no future but their name. The Wise Men. Edgar Bowers. NePoEA

They walk uncertainly,/That is all. Healing Song. *Anonymous.* OBVE

They watched the waning moon. Scenes de la Vie de Boheme. Arthur Symons. BrPo; OBTV

...They watched/The white man approach, shaking/His rattles. At Grand Canyon's Edge. David Ray. TAT

They wear the gowns of Gibson. In Philistia. Bliss Carman. ALV

They weigh salt, coffee and the souls of men. The Child Reads an Almanac. Francis Jammes. AWP

They well are fitted: both are but a span. On the Death of Mistress Mary Prideaux. William Strode. JCP

They went a-hog-huntin' hard as they could stave. Groun' Hog. *Anonymous.* ABF

They went about their gravest deeds/As noble boys at play. The Men of Old. Richard Monckton, Lord Houghton Milnes. OBEV; OBVV

They went and told the sexton, and/The sexton toll'd the bell. Faithless Sally Brown. Thomas Hood. HBV 1-2; NOBL; OBNV; TreFS

They went inland to paint/the idea of storms. Studies from Life. Martha Dickey. FAZ

They went off socks Strawberry Blond. Bill Berkson. ANYP

They went to a tavern, and there they/dined,/And bottles cracked most merrilie. The Bold Pedlar and Robin Hood. *Anonymous.* AmFP; BaBo; ESPB

THEY WEPT UPON THE STOCK EXCHANGE. Headlined in Heaven. Paul L. Grano. NOAV

They were all there; the clock ticks spoke with castanet clicks. Moist Moon People. Carl Sandburg. MoAmPo

They were as invisible/as the true stars at daybreak. Daybreak. Galway Kinnell. LCAP

They were buried on Easter Monday. Bonnie Barbara Allen (C vers.). *Anonymous.* BaBo

They were buried side by side. Love Me and Never Leave Me. Ronald McCuaig. BoAV; PoL

They were by winged souls/Entred for both, farre above their desert! Obedience. George Herbert. AnAnS 1

...They were caught/by their instincts, unable to end their flight. Marriage and Midsummer's Night. Linda Gregg. NPGG

They were fine horses–/See their shoes fit. Daniel Webster's Horses. Elizabeth Jane Coatsworth. AmFN; AnNE; MoAmPo; OBCA; PH

They were gone. Another One for the Devil. David C. Childers. AMV-80

They were introduced in a green grave. The Introduction. Louis MacNeice. FaBoIP

They were launched into eternity, and may God grant them rest. George Jones. *Anonymous.* OBSS

They were love's characters come face to face. We Reason of These Things. Wallace Stevens. CrMA

...They/were neither necessary nor always present. Temperature. Gerard Malanga. NYBP

They were neither up nor down. The Brave Old Duke of York. *Anonymous.* OxNR

They were never sad enough/In burying the dead man dragged from the sea. The Dead Man Dragged from the Sea. Carl Gardner. PoBA

They were never/seen no more. Mr 'Gater. N. M. Bodecker. NTCP; OnUR

They were off–down the Gila Monster Route. Gila Monster Route. L. F. Post. ABF

They were (perhaps) lesse faire then Poets write./But he is fairer then I can indite. Sonnets, XII: "Some talke of Ganymede th' Idalian Boy." Richard Barnfield. PeHV

They were putting in the poles: bringing the electric light. Men Working. Edna St. Vincent Millay. SaC

They were said to be wishing us well in Scranton. The Missionary Visits Our Church in Scranton. Jay Parini. MAYP

They were smote, they were fallen,/And had melted for ever. When Banners Are Waving. *Anonymous.* GN; HBV 1-2

They were so bad I cried. My Father, My Son. John Malcolm Brinnin. NYBP

They were still going to town in/novels she never had time to finish In Spite of His Dangling Pronoun. Lyn Lifshin. IHMS

They were the helpless lips that long ago/Kept me from being born. Years Later. Laurence Lerner. PeSA

They were the one I always had! Andre. Gwendolyn Brooks. TiPo

They were the Yiddish speaking socialists/of the Lower East Side. Yiddish Speaking Socialists of the Lower East Side. Ed Sanders. APU

They were very thick in places where 'twas root hog or die. Root Hog or Die. Floyd B. Small. PoOW

They were writers, and they wrote. A Note on The Hunted City, 1939-1967. Kenneth Patchen. NaP

They whisper, "She's been asleep." Adventure. Laura Benet. HBMV

They who, in life were wedded,/Through hallowed death are reunited. Although Tormented. Kalonymos Ben Judah. TrJP

...They who know the sound of/surf have blood tempestuous as wind/yet ever bound. They Who Possess the Sea. Marguerite Janvrin Adams. EtS

They who one another keep/Alive, ne'er parted be. Sweetest Love, I Do Not Go. John Donne. BiP; TEP; TreFT; TrGrPo

They who to the Saga listened/Heard the name of Thorberg Skafting/For a hundred year! The Building of the Long Serpent. Henry Wadsworth Longfellow. EtS

They wich have tasted of the muses spring,/I hope will smile upon the tunes they sing. Collin My Deere and Most Entire Beloved. William Smith. AAS

They will be a libation/To our cupidity/In our pursuit of happiness. Recessional for the Class of 1959... Joseph R. Cowen. PoNe

They will be covered and gone. Chinoiseries. Amy Lowell. AnAmPo

They will be cut/or silenced or raped. The Pueblo Women I Watched Get down in Brooklyn. Wendy Rose. TWSS

They will be done; and let discussion cease. A Fragment. Yvor Winters. OBSV

They will be no more to me then/Than mine are now to you! The Dying Lover. Richard Henry Stoddard. HBV 1-2

They will be proud a while of something death/Still seems to need. Memories of a Lost War. Louis Simpson. NePoAm; OBWP; VGW

They will blaw out the caunnles, and guid-nicht. Judgment Day. Giuseppe Belli. OBVE

They will bury you at last. At Last. Syd Scroggie. PoSH

They will concoct a scripture explaining this. The Copulating Gods. Carolyn Kizer. Prf

They will find the sign/we took care to leave behind. Gone Fishing. Mark Sanders. WOLT

They will find the streets are guarded/By United States Marines. The Marines' Hymn. *Anonymous.* BLSo; GoTF; PAL; TreF; YaD

...They will keep on, lowering/their barred visors against the setting sun. The King's Men. William Heyen. PoA

They will knock hard to be born. Getting Through. Maxine W. Kumin. SUW

They will leave you behind, love, in grief and in pain. Fare Ye Well, Lovely Nancy. *Anonymous.* OBSS

They will make us wash the green/From our hands and our knees. Peter Rabbit. Sandra McPherson. LCAP

They will not blame me for anything. Sleep in the Heat. Laura Jensen. AmPA

They will not love you so. Shadowy Swallows. Gustavo Adolfo Becquer. LiTW

They will not need them: in due time one dies. All in Due Time. J. V. Cunningham. NIP

They will not shine, they will not shine. Apple Blight. Paul Zimmer. VGW

They will only know me The Promise. Johari M. Kunjufu. BlSi

They will people your mind. You will never touch/their hands. Imagine the South. George Woodcock. NeBP; NOBC

They will remain, and so thou canst not die. To Delia. Samuel Daniel. EnRePo

They will ruin a good ship-carpenter,/His little one and his wife. The Carpenter's Wife. *Anonymous.* OBET

They will sing softly to each other/softly For the Coming Year. Peter Everwine. OFD

...They will sound/in the dreams of your children's children. The Names. Lauris Edmond. OCNZ

They will tell us the old story over again. The Old Story over Again. James Kenney. OnYI

They win the gold, they must keep the girl. Dragon Lesson. James Hearst. AMV-80

They wish again to be a/falling tree When These Old Barns Lost Their Inhabitants.... David Kherdian. TAT

...They wish to be/A Catholic, Madonna fair, to worship thee. Maternal Lady with the Virgin Grace. Mary Ann Lamb. ISi

They with no past/And fire their only future The Asians Dying. William Stanley Merwin. CAPP; CoAP; HaCAP; NaP; NOBA; NYBP

They won't look/they will just say/no one died. Celebration 1982. Terri Meyette Wilkins. LFAC

They woo'd and vow'd, and that they keep,/And go contented to their sheep. From his flock stray'd Coridon. Robert Greene. EG

THINK BLACK. Awareness. Don L. Lee. BOLo; PoBA

THINK/don't/be/like/me. The Steelworker. Melvin Douglass Brown. LFAC

Think how our anguish must make/Some meaning for your sake. A Small Thought Speaks for the Flesh. Carleton Drewry. MoRP

Think how the roots of the roses/Are kept alive in the snow. November. Alice Cary. OBCA

Think I am waving "Good morning; goodbye." Morning from My Office Window. John A. Wood. AMV-81

"Think I'll roll in,/good-night, boys, and.../well...Damn the Sheep!" Eighteen-Ninety. E. Richard Shipp. PoOW

Think it enough for me to have had thy love. On His Mistress. John Donne. AnAnS 1; BoLoP; LiTB; PoEL 1-5; SeCeV; ViBoPo

Think nae mair of gauin back,/But tak it for your hame, lady.' Rob Roy. *Anonymous.* ESPB

Think no more; 'tis only thinking/Lays lads underground. Think No More, Lad. Alfred Edward Housman. CABA; CMoP; InPo

Think, O think, it worth Enjoying. Alexander's Feast. John Dryden. GoTF; TreFS

Think of Hans and Katrina and the big bologna sausage. Villkins and His Dinah (B vers.). *Anonymous.* BaBo

Think of heaven's bliss, and give the sign/To parting friends;–such death be mine! Night. James Montgomery. HBV 1-2

Think of him as uninjured, barely disturbed. Little Exercise. Elizabeth Bishop. CoAP; CrMA; MoAB; MoAmPo; NCSH; NYBP; UnPo

Think of me, and know the worth you've lost. My Wish for You. Rabi'a of Balkh. WPOW

Think of my fate, and shun her snares. Come, All Ye Youths. Thomas Otway. OAEP

Think of that only when they think of me. When the Sword of Sixty Comes Nigh His Head. Firdausi. NAs; OBVE

Think of the blood which Jesus spilt,/And let that blood my pardon buy! Forgiveness. Henry Francis Lyte. BePJ

...Think of the forty million/families of the hungry.... Rusia en 1931. Robert Hass. MAYP

Think of the things we used to say! Words! Words! Jessie Redmond Fauset. CDC

Think of this and you'll understand,/sweet friend. Go, Then. Edith Bruck. VWA

Think of Villikins and Dinah and the cup of cold pizen./Singing tu la lol la rol lal to rol lal la. Villikins and His Dinah. *Anonymous.* FSW

Think of wheatfields/rippling like oceans/and spreading/in the flat Kansas sun. Kneading. Barbara Crooker. SOTS

Think of your roots. The Palace for Teeth. Abigail Luttinger. AMV-80

Think on the grave where He was laid,/And calm descend to yours. On a Similar Occasion for the Year 1792. William Cowper. NOCV

Think on vengeance for my ruin,/And for England–shamed in me. Admiral Hosier's Ghost. Richard Glover. HBV 1-2; NOEC; ViBoPo

Think, perhaps, the title of your latest painting/another name for liar. The Politics of Rich Painters. LeRoi (Imamu Amiri Baraka) Jones. CoPo; VGW

Think: poems fixed this landscape: Blake, Donne, Keats. Homage to Literature. Muriel Rukeyser. NAMP

Think: spring is coming soon The Women in Old Parkas. Mary Tallmountain. STE

Think that he is right, young and right. Autumn. Douglas Ridley Beeton. PeSA

Think that I am not so torrid. Neighbors. "Lennox." InMe

Think that the sunrise left the door ajar! Lonely House. Emily Dickinson. AnEnPo

Think the blod fro Jesu ran,/Whan he deyed, withouten nay. Remember the Day of Judgment. *Anonymous.* MeEL

Think, think...Oh, think... Crucifixion. Waring Cuney. BANP; GoSl

Think, think what a heaven she must make of Cashmere! Lalla Rookh. Thomas Moore. EnRP

Think upon that fatal morning,/Frederick Manning and his wife. Life of the Mannings. *Anonymous.* FaBoBa

Think well, your youth is ended. O Little Well. *Anonymous.* WTO

Think what a lovely hand, O Rose,/Shall place your body in the tomb! To a Rose. Frank Dempster Sherman. AA

Think what a lovely time they had! Elegy. Arthur Guiterman. InMe

Think what, and be adviz'd, you are but young yet. A Masque Presented at Ludlow Castle (Comus). John Milton. AtBAP; PoEL 1-5

Think what those feel who'r stung by thee. The Bee. *Anonymous.* TrAS

Think, wilt thou let it/Slip useless away. To-Day. Thomas Carlyle. GN; HBV 1-2; HBVY

Think ye awful lucky in the town-e-o. The Fox Walked Out, B vers. *Anonymous.* BFSS

Think you, had Been Petrarch's wife,/He would have written sonnets all his life? Don Juan. George Gordon, Lord Byron. UnTE

Think you that I could let a beggar enter/Where a king stood before? The Kiss. Sara Teasdale. HBV 1-2

Thinkblink/blink/think/blink Neuteronomy. Eve Merriam. QQQ

Thinking barbed thoughts in stanza form/after shafting's a right sweat. Time for a nap. What about You? (parody). Edward Pygge. BXAP; FaBoPa

Thinking deceit and friendship and malice/By the river at Richmond. Mr. Symons at Richmond, Mr. Pope at Twickenham. Julian Symons. WaP

Thinking hard. Poems, V. Philip O'Connor. EAS

Thinking, in lines as long as a camel's stride, of Kipling. The Virgin Warrior. Gwendolyn MacEwen. FaBoWP

...Thinking it might mean/Love. The Bear That Came to the Wedding. Howard McCord. GP

Thinking it to be only/the grave of an animal. The Week-End Indian. Anita Endrezze-Probst. VoR

Thinking of happiness, I think of that. Running. Richard Wilbur. NCSH

Thinking of my father's fathers/And of my own will. The Ballad of the Children of the Czar. Delmore Schwartz. MiAP

Thinking of saints and of Petronius Arbiter. Her Courtesy. William Butler Yeats. LiTB

...Thinking of the good king/who lies there, long with a broken heart/for the sweet day of peace. War in Chang-An City. Wang Tsan. PPON

Thinking of the old days upon the shoogy-shoo. The Shoogy-Shoo. Winthrop Packard. HBV 1-2

Thinking she might come to life again. The Nobleman's Wedding. *Anonymous.* AnIV

Thinking that many Christs could hang there, crying. The Deer and the Snake. Kenneth Patchen. MoAmPo

...Thinking/the honor of Empire/is saved. Peace with Honor. Philip Appleman. SOTS

Thinking thereon I swoon away. Medieval Norman Songs. *Anonymous.* AWP

Thinking they are gone. The Dead of the World. Jeanne Finley. AMV-81

Thinking to save all, we cast all away. The Ant. Richard Lovelace. CaPo

Thinking upon this barn His gentle doom! Elegy for the Monastery Barn. Thomas Merton. CoPo; VGW

Thinks the heavenly guide/Trembles on its cotton thread. Starlight. Freda Downie. FaBoWP

The thinner she, the closer I/Can press against her heart. True Love. *Anonymous.* UnTE

The thinnest deer-track prints,/Or a midwood trail ahead. Woodlore. Kim Kurt. NePoAm-2

Thir are the bewteis of the fute-ball. The Bewteis of the Fute-Ball. *Anonymous.* BSV; FaBoCo; GoTS

...Thir songs/Divide the night, and lift our thoughts to Heaven. Evening in Paradise. John Milton. LoBV

The third for a warming-pan,/Doctress, and nurse. My Three Wives. *Anonymous.* FaBoEE

The third lifts himself/into a sky of smoke,/chanting his black chant. The First Hunt. Gordon Anderson. PPJ

The third said 'twas an old man,/And his beard growing grey. There Were Three Jovial Welshmun. *Anonymous.* GBP

The third sat by the glowing hearth and smiled into/his glass. Wayfarers. Dana Burnet. EtS

The thirst for peace a raving world/Would never let us satiate here. Switzerland. Matthew Arnold. OAEP; VLP

A thirstier minstrel drew in me! Nepenthe. George Darley. ERoP 1-2; NOBE; OBRV; PBBP

The thirsty Dipper on the arc of night. The Death of the Sheriff. Robert Lowell. MoAB; MoAmPo

Thirsty without me Other. Lance Henson. VoR

Thirteen years of life/and your heart on fire/Nely Silvinova! Theresienstadt Poem. Robert Mezey. NaP; VWA

30 g/kg (3%) Metaldehyde, in the form of a pellet. A Balanced Bait in Handy Pellet Form. Allen Curnow. OCNZ

Thirty-one camels/make their way/without a leader,/without a guide. The Thirty-One Camels. Rachel Korn. VWA

"Thirty Rattvik fiddlers in skinpants!" After Illness. Vi Gale. GP

...A thirty year old woman/is waiting for her name. Naming Power. Wendy Rose. TWSS

This air will kill us all/ere long. Chronicle. Edward Dorn. TAT

This alone is certain:/Not a light was lit. By Moonlight. *Anonymous.* UnTE

This ample and opulent bosom/That must some day nurse us all! There Is Strength in the Soil. Arthur Stringer. OHIP

This answer then she made to me,/"Kind sir, I've sold my barley." The Maid that Sold Her Barley. *Anonymous.* OnYI

This apparent clumsiness is far from true. The Words. Lee Harwood. EAS

This architecture will stand. Now I Have Come to Reason. C. Day-Lewis. CMoP

This arduous earth. This Earth. Phillip Yellowhawk Minthorn. STE

This astonishing delay, the everyday, takes place. The Geese. Jorie Graham. HaCAP

This Atlas who fell down under a bubble.   The Neurotic.   Lewis, Cecil Day.   ACV

"This Bairn is Lord of life and death."   The Purification.   Saint Cosmas.   ISi

...This beame/Will guide him In.   Joy of My Life!   Henry Vaughan.   OBS; SeCV 1-2

This beauteous form assures a piteous mind.   Holy Sonnets, XIII.   John Donne.   EBEV; HeIP; JCP; MBW 1-2; NOCV

This beauty's kinder, yet for a reason/I could weep that the old is out of season.   The Arrow.   William Butler Yeats.   EG

This bed thy center is, these walls, thy sphere.   The Sun Rising.   John Donne.   BiP; BoLiVe; BoLoP; CABA; DiPo; ExPo; FF; GBL; HAP; HeIP; InvP; JCP; LiTB; LiTL; LoBV; NIP; NOBE; NoP; OAEL 1-2; OAEP; PAI; PoPle; PPP; SCV; SeCePo; SeCeV; SoSe; TEP; TrGrPo; UnTE

"This beggar maid shall be my queen!"   The Beggar Maid.   Alfred, Lord Tennyson.   BeLS; HBV 1-2; OnMSP

This being they have shut out/Of their houses, their thoughts, their lives?   They.   R. S. Thomas.   OxBTC

This belief damned him, and damned, what's harder,/The heavy stone.   Sisyphus.   Josephine Miles.   NYBP

This Bell bids thee, Beware!   Upon a Passing Bell.   Thomas Washbourne.   FaBoRV

This blazoned flag and ghostly sail/Stream out upon a spectral gale.   The Spectre Ship.   Thomas Stephen Collier.   EtS

This blessed Christ of Calvary!   This blessed Christ of Calvary.   Anonymous.   STF

This blessing love gives again into our arms.   After Making Love We Hear Footsteps.   Galway Kinnell.   InPS

This Book, and I/Will tell thee so; Sweet Saviour thou didst dye!   H.Scriptures.   Henry Vaughan.   AnAnS 1

This bottle has been in the cave all the time/we have been together.   The Hosts.   William Stanley Merwin.   GP

This, boys, shall be our doom, in spite of malice.   The Boatswain's Call.   Anonymous.   OBSS

This Bridge of wonders is the paramount.   Of London Bridge, and the Stupendous Sight, and Structure Thereof.   James Howell.   FaBoPP

...This brightness/which comes to us from across the world.   Vigil.   Michael Knoll.   LFAC

This brings a happiness so sweet,/And springs up from within!   Happiness.   Walter E. Isenhour.   STF

This bubble here is always ready, for you.   Look.   William Stafford.   FAZ

This bubble world. What than this bubble? Nought.   Epigram: "My soul, what's lighter than a feather? Wind."   Francis Quarles.   FaBoEE

This call to you goes forth today/To rally to the man.   Operation–Souls.   Anonymous.   STF

This calm-flowing river.   The River.   Patrick MacDonogh.   NeIP

This causes a very peculiar sensation,/difficult to describe.   Light in the Open Air.   Annie Dillard.   SUW

This charming old woman of Lynn.   Limerick: "There lived an old woman at Lynn."   Anonymous.   OxBChV

...This child in you, this half-assed gesture of an/angel leaving the earth.   The Explosion of Thimbles.   Pier Giorgio Di Cicco.   CaPN

This child is no more than a child.   The Magus.   James Dickey.   NAs

This children's world of skyward twisting/poles of peppermint   Haircut.   William Packard.   CAD

This city razed,/This my son dead.   Aftermath.   Margaret McCulloch.   PGD

This clock that can be wound/only with a silver "M" shaped key.   Thank You for the Valentine.   Diane Wakoski.   HoPM

This close-companioned inarticulate hour/When two-fold silence was the song of love.   The House of Life.   Dante Gabriel Rossetti.   PoEL 1-5

This cold steel slowly burns to be a gun.   Scrap Iron.   Raymond Durgnat.   PCP

This conscious world with guarded men.   Four Walls.   Blanche Taylor Dickinson.   CDC

This cordial take.' I drank. Urania flew.   Urania.   Robert Andrews.   NOEC

This corpse will not stop burning!   The Dead Shall Be Raised Incorruptible.   Galway Kinnell.   NOBA

This country kills you slowly   Camoes and the Debt.   Sophia de Mello Breyner Andresen.   BoWoP

This country looks grey, hunted and murderous.   Morgan's Country.   Francis Webb.   BoAV

This couple they got married, and why not you and me?   Jack Monroe (Jackie's Gone A-Sailing).   Anonymous.   AmFP

This courageous Young Lady of Norway.   Limerick: "There was a young lady of Norway."   Edward Lear.   EBEV; TiPo

This crazed retainer/Who seeks no coins in my bed?   Complaint of the Fisherman's Wife.   Sheila Nickerson.   WOLT

This crazy puzzle, even/Spinoza could not solve.   A Vilna Puzzle.   Sasha Chorny.   VWA

...This creature/at last come home to me.   The Beast.   Brian Patten.   AmMo

This crisis can't shake England's nerves./It's playing hell with mine.   Nerves.   Sagittarius (Olga Katzin).   OxBTC

This crucial day, whose decapitate joke/Languidly winds into the inner ear.   More Sonnets at Christmas.   Allen Tate.   LiTA; NePA

...This cruel and absolute/jewel of your life.   Now, My Usefulness Over.   Edwin Honig.   NoAm

This crying and spying young sister for sale?   For Sale.   Shel Silverstein.   CTBA

This curse should be a blessing. Fare thee well!   To the Lord Chancellor (excerpt).   Percy Bysshe Shelley.   DBV; ViBoPo

This "damned Yankee jade"/Who had run the blockade!   Running the Blockade.   Nora Perry.   PAH

This dance, this life is not very charming.   Anthropology in Fort Morgan, Colorado.   Sam Hamod.   TAT

This dangled day, the fabulous country/That lies between us and futurity.   The Day.   George M. Brady.   NeIP

...This dark/Ceiling without a star.   Child.   Sylvia Plath.   HaCAP; PBWP

This day is born mans only saviour, Christ the King.   A Poem, upon the Caelestial Embassy Perform'd by Angels...   Richard Steere.   SCAP

This day is for Israel light and/rejoicing,/A Sabbath of rest.   A Sabbath of Rest.   Isaac Luria.   TrJP

This day is our last!   Jamaican Bus Ride.   Arthur Seymour John Tessimond.   OBTV; OxBTC

This day is past; but tell me, who can say/That I shall surely live another day.   Meditations for July 19, 1666.   Philip Pain.   SCAP

This dead moist smell of rain!   Jack.   Louis Goldberg.   TrJP

This dead street never stops!   Crossing the Atlantic.   Anne Sexton.   MOS; NoAm

This dear, dear, dear old lady,/And the boy who was half-past three.   One, Two, Three!   Henry Cuyler Bunner.   HBV 1-2; PoLf

This death, this fitful dark declaring light.   John Donne's Defiance.   J. R. Hervey.   AnNZ

This done, thou hast no more, but leave the rest/To virtue, fortune, time, and woman's breast.   Truth Doth Truth Deserve.   Sir Philip Sidney.   HBV 1-2; LiTL

This downhill path is easy, but there's no turning/back.   Amor Mundi.   Christina Georgina Rossetti.   NBM; NoP; PoEL 1-5

This dream, this drowning in your sleep.   To a Defeated Saviour.   James Wright.   NePoEA

This dumb/woman, this/buried/force/in you.   Field.   Susan Griffin.   NPGG

This early May morn when there is none to wed.   The Cherry Trees.   Edward ("Edward Eastaway") Thomas.   OBWP; PoPle

This earth the tomb was./HOME.   Home.   Stephen Chalmers.   HBMV

This earth we possess has cost us ten heavens.   Twilight of Freedom.   Osip Mandelstam.   VWA

This ends by going over things.   12th Dance–Getting Leather by Language–21 February 1964.   Jackson MacLow.   CoPo

This ends my carol with care away.   Now Is Yule Come.   Anonymous.   OxBM

This England, Old already, was called Merry.   The Manor Farm.   Edward ("Edward Eastaway") Thomas.   ExPo; HaMV; SeCeV

This epitaph which here you see,/Supplied the epithalamy.   That Morn Which Saw Me Made a Bride.   Meleager.   NIP

This epitaph, which here you see,/Supplied the epithalamy.   Upon a Maid That Died the Day She Was Married.   Meleager.   AWP; OBVE

This existence is real only with respect/to its origin, but whatever is derived/has no reality.   Quatrain.   Sarmed the Yahud.   TrJP

This exultation when I consummate/The passion of my body for the sea.   Early Summer Sea-Tryst.   Frederick T. Macartney.   CBAP

This fabulous shadow only the sea keeps.   At Melville's Tomb.   Hart Crane.   AP; CoBMV; HAP; InPo; MoAmPo; MOS; NePA; NoAm; NoP; PoA; TAP; UnPo; VGW

This face, the face of Jesus Christ.   The Face of Jesus Christ.   Christina Georgina Rossetti.   BePJ

This finger's length above reality.   While I Have Vision.   Peter Quennell.   ChMP

This fire, limpid and mysterious.   Ode Written in 1966.   Jorge Luis Borges.   AMV-81

This first snow of winter,/This gentle newcomer.   First Snow.   Ivy O. Eastwick.   TiPo

This fitted him to teach Creative Writing.   For an Early Retirement.   Donald Hall.   TW

...This flax is spun.   Oberon's Palace.   Robert Herrick.   CaPo

This flower I give you, beloved.   The Flower.   Henrik Wergeland.   LiTW

This foirsaid flour that wes so fair.   May Poems.   Anonymous.   OxBS

...This for thy sake/Shall honor all my life.   Madrigal: "Flow forth, abundant tears."   John Attey.   EnRePo

This Foreign Country speaks to You.   Young Heroes.   Frank Horne.   BPo

This formula for drawing comic rabbits made.   Epitaph on an Unfortunate Artist.   Robert Graves.   FaBoEE; NOBL

This fort of your fair self, if't be not won/He is repulsed indeed–but you are undone.   To the Noblest and Best of Ladies, the Countess of Denbigh.   Richard Crashaw.   JCP; MeLP

...This from thee/Will I to mine leave as 'tis left to me.'   A Quotation from Shakespeare with Slight Improvements.   Lewis (Charles Lutwidge Dodgson) Carroll.   FaBoNo

...This gallant soul,/Divinely guided, reached the goal.   Balboa.   Nora Perry.   PAH

This gave me that precarious Gait/Some call Experience.   I Stepped from Plank to Plank.   Emily Dickinson.   AmePo; CMoP; MAmP; NOBA; NOCV; OBSP

This ghoul-haunted woodland of/Weir.   Ulalume.   Edgar Allan Poe   AA; AmP; AnEnPo; AP; APA; AWP; BLPL; DiPo; GoTF; LiTA; MAmP; NePA; NOBA; OxBA; TAP; TreF; ViBoPo; WHA

This/gives us/wings.   Wings.   Miroslav Holub.   SUW

This glad time has no returning–/Need you burn so fast away.   Six Birthday Candles Shining.   Mary Jane Carr.   BiCB

This grace is gravity.   The Gift of Gravity.   Wendell Berry.   GeTw

This grand conversation on brave Nelson arose.   Grand Conversation on Brave Nelson.   *Anonymous.*   OBET

This grand conversation was under the rose.   Under the Rose.   *Anonymous.*   OBET

This grave a father's hopes doth hide.   His Son.   Callimachus.   AWP

This grown-up man, with pluck and luck,/Is hoping to outwit a duck.   The Hunter.   Ogden Nash.   EvOK; LiSp; PPJ; SD

This halt and blasted gang? Yes, you would.   Bathing the Aged.   Paul Monette.   AmPA

This happy failure, this is Art.   Art.   Lilla Cabot Perry.   AA

This happy harmony would make them none.   Sonnet: "Oh, if thou knew'st how thou thyself dost harm."   William Alexander, Earl of Stirling.   EIL

This harp still makes my name its voluntary.   Passion and Worship.   Dante Gabriel Rossetti.   MaVP

This has been the poetry reading.   Before the Poetry Reading.   Louis Simpson.   OxBC

...This has gone on ten years.   Waking.   Hugh Maxton.   BIrV; CIP

This has not happened before.   The Hollow Thesaurus.   Roger McDonald.   CBAP

This hath a relish of eternity.   The Sovereign Poet.   William Watson.   WGRP

This hath pleas'd, doth please, & long will please; never/Can this decay, but is beginning ever.   Foeda Est In Coitu.   Petronius Arbiter (Caius Petronius Arbiter).   LiTW

This have I done for my true love.   My Dancing Day.   *Anonymous.*   CBEP

This hayseed was strictly dead in it.   Hayseed (with music).   *Anonymous.*   AS

This heart of mine, that, albeit young/in years,/Is none the less rich in deep, keen-eyed experience   Defiance.   Solomon Ibn Gabirol.   TrJP

This heathen bit of the world lies warm in my palm.   Of Thomas Traherne and the Pebble outside.   Sydney Clouts.   VWA

This here prison stew......   Dopefiends Trip.   Hector Angulo.   FIA

This holiday, personal,/exotic, paid, is our last one.   End of the War in Merida.   Anthony Ostroff.   FAZ

This holy land, our faith itself, to share again/with our godfathers, Will and Ben.   Mayflower.   Conrad Aiken.   MP

This Holy Night and make His rule your own.   And Lo, the Star!   Molly Anderson Haley.   PGD

This home we consecrate to-day/Will be a Holy Place.   O Thou Whose Gracious Presence Blest.   Louis F. Benson.   TrPWD

This Honour have,/to make my grave.   This Crosse-Tree Here.   Robert Herrick.   OFD

This horror that I writhe in–is my soul!   The Octopus.   Hugh" (Christopher Murray Grieve) MacDiarmid.   TW

This horsefly hovering above the pear.   Still Lives.   Emilie Buchwald.   PoDr

...This house I live in/has pockets of magic.   Reflections on a Womb Which Is Called "Vacant."   Jeanine Hathaway.   IHMS

This huge passion, this small breath.   Definition.   May Sarton.   MoLP

This hurts most, this...that, after all, we are paid/The worth of our work, perhaps.   Aurora Leigh.   Elizabeth Barrett Browning.   TEP

This I can say, O lad,/I am fitted to lie my lone.   The Poor Girl's Meditation.   Padraic Colum.   BIrV; OBMV; OLR

This I have learned/from my daughter.   For Refugio Talamante.   Ed Ochester.   LTB

This, I protest, is all my own.   Oxford Barber's Verses on the Queen's Death.   *Anonymous.*   APAS

This if thou canst; then shew me Him/That rides the glorious Cherubim!   To Finde God.   Robert Herrick.   WGRP

This incomprehensible blue.   Did You Not See.   Alex Kuo.   BrSi

This indolent, this all but evermore/October such as never came before.   When the World Ends.   Mark Van Doren.   GoYe

This instigates an appetite/Precisely opposite.   That it will never come again.   Emily Dickinson.   NOBA

...This intellectual, this rich American, this/fascist boss!   Near Barbizon.   Galway Kinnell.   NePoAm-2

This is a beautiful way)   Who Are You, Little I.   Edward Estlin Cummings.   NYBP

...This is a dainty breed.   Pigeons.   Marianne Moore.   PoA

"This is a darn'd clever bunch!"   Soiree.   Ezra Pound.   DTC

This is a dream of Winter, sweet as Spring.   Swedes.   Edward ("Edward Eastaway") Thomas.   BrPo; MoVE; OAEL 1-2

This is a dream. Where is your lost beloved?   The Insult.   Robert Layzer.   NePoEA

This is a duel to the death, and when/We part as friends we meet as foes again.   The Duel.   Theodore Maynard.   CAW

This is a house of unwritten poems,/this is where I am unborn.   Stray Animals.   James Tate.   NoAm

This is a hymn.   Pig Song.   Margaret Atwood.   NoP

This is a lonesome world, and WEBSTER/dead!   Webster: An Ode (excerpt).   William Cleaver Wilkinson.   AA

...This is a message from an atom in my hand.   The Life of Particles.   Michael Benedikt.   SUW

This is a night to be out/Whoring with the wind.   Street-Walker in March.   Samuel L. Albert.   NePoAm-2

This is a pause/for love. It is only/a brief pause.   The Convoy.   Juan Antonio Corretjer.   InW

This is a poppy,/this an epilogue   The Village of Reason.   Michael Palmer.   NPGG

...This is a portrait/of a woman who is trying to tell the truth.   Portrait in Available Light.   Sara Miles.   NYP

This is a scar upon the year.   Age in Youth.   Trumbull Stickney.   NCEP

This is a sin-tryin' world.   This Is a Sin-Tryin' World.   *Anonymous.*   TrAS

This is a soul, a possible proud Florence.   Hollywood.   Karl Shapiro.   LiTM; OxBA

This is a stormy day; yesterday was the calm day.   A Stormy Day.   *Anonymous.*   WTO

This is all my song,/I will love only hate.   Love and Hate.   Frank O'Connor.   KiLC; TW

This is all we ask, from thee,/Hermione, Hermione!   Hermione.   Bryan Waller Procter.   OBVV

This is alone Life, Joy, Empire, and Victory.   Prometheus Unbound.   Percy Bysshe Shelley.   FaBoRV; OAEL 1-2; OAEP; OBRV; SeCeV

This is an accident of hourly proof,/Which I mistrusted not.   Much Ado about Nothing.   William Shakespeare.   TrGrPo

This is an end, and yet another start.   Merlin in the Cave: He Speculates without a Book.   Thom Gunn.   NePoEA

This is Ancona, yonder is the sea.   The Guardian Angel.   Robert Browning.   GoBC; HBV 1-2

This is art.   Collages and Compositions.   Richmond Lattimore.   PP

This is better than cutting of broom.'   Broom, Green Broom.   *Anonymous.*   LiTB; OxBoLi

...This is but an Afghan youth/Shot by the stranger on his native hills.   In Snow.   William Allingham.   IrPN

This is delirium,/please say this bridge cannot/end/as it ends.   The Poem of the End (excerpt).   Marina Tsvetayeva.   BrRo; OBVE; PBWP

This is early morning in a world of kings.   A Morning Letter.   Robert Duncan.   PoA

This is eterntiy! Eternity is now!   Holderlin.   Delmore Schwartz.   MoRP

This is for beasts, and that for men the spring.   The Spring.   Abraham Cowley.   HAP; JCP; MeLP; OBS

This is God's will, for you and me.   God's Will for Us.   *Anonymous.*   BLRP; SoSe; WBLP

This is heaven, its peace, its beauty,/Radiant with the love of God.   Heaven Is Here.   John G. Adams.   AH

This is how birds are made.   Arbeit Macht Frei.   Dennis Schmitz.   NPGG

This is how he grows: by being defeated, decisively,/by constantly greater beings.   The Man Watching.   Rainer Maria Rilke.   NU

This is how we finish it.   Once There Were Three Fishermen.   *Anonymous.*   FSW

This is idle fyno.   Fara Diddle Dyno.   Thomas Weelkes.   CBEP; EIL; FaBoCh; LoBV

This is indeed a battle worthy of our weapons.   The Hunted City, V.   Kenneth Patchen.   NaP

This is Invasion Morning!   D-Dawn.   Margaret McGarvey.   GoYe

This is known/as genealogy.   Hymn for Lanie Poo. 4. Each Morning.   LeRoi (Imamu Amiri Baraka) Jones.   NNP

This is life; to do less would be nothing but dis-/honesty.   Peter.   Marianne Moore.   AnAmPo; CMoP; NoP; OxBA

...This is living art,/Which thus presents and thus records true life.'   Aurora Leigh.   Elizabeth Barrett Browning.   PBWP

This is London! How d'ye like it?   A Description of London.   John Bancks.   NOEC

This is London. I lie, and twine in the roots of things.   London.   Manmohan Ghose.   ACV

This is long and deep and wide,/And has–rockers at the side.   Katie Lee and Willie Grey.   *Anonymous.*   BeLS; BLPA

This is me knowing, this is what I know.   Walter Jenks' Bath.   William Meredith.   HoPM

This is mortality,/this is eternity.   What Are Years?   Marianne Moore.   AmP; AP; BLPL; CMoP; CoBMV; EaLo; ForPo; LiTA; MoAB; MoAmPo; MoPo; NoAm; NOBA; OxBA; TrGrPo

This is my face.   Sure You Can Ask Me a Personal Question.   Diane Burns.   STE

This is my farewell of love to thee.   The Mist over Pukehina.   *Anonymous.*   WTO

This is my last affair   Last Affair: Bessie's Blues Song.   Michael S. Harper.   GeTw; HaCAP; LCAP

"This is my last/Worst pain, the bitter enlightenment that buys peace."   Woodrow Wilson.   Robinson Jeffers.   FaBoPV

This is my love for you...   This Is My Love for You.   Grace Fallow Norton.   HBV 1-2

This is my page for English B.   Theme for English B.   Langston Hughes.   BALP; HaCAP; NoAm; NOBA; NoP

This is my rotting-place, and that is thine.'   The Dream.   *Anonymous.*   NOEC

This is my song/for the North/coming toward us.   Erosion.   Jorie Graham.   MAYP

This is my space/i am not movin   Nappy Edges (A Cross Country Sojourn).   Ntozake Shange.   BlSi

This is my will.   When I Am Dead.   George Macbeth.   OxBTC

This is, naught else is, certainty.   Sarasvati.   James Stephens.   NoAm

This is none of I!   The Little Woman and the Pedlar.   *Anonymous.*   OxNR

This is not done by Jostling in the Street.   Great Things.   William Blake.   OBSP; PV

This is not it   Instructions.   Anita Skeen.   IHMS

This is not mere personification.   Moon, Son of Heaven.   Miyazawa Kenji.   MOON

...This is not tardy.   A Time to Eat.   Gertrude Stein.   NMM

THIS IS NOT THE END.   One Flight Up.   Bob Holman.   APU

This is not the end of the island, or the tablets this life has been/scribbled on, or the song.   Hugging the Jukebox.   Naomi Shihab Nye.   MAYP

This is not your harvest, these are not your fields!   In Your Arrogance.   Lynne Lawner.   ErPo

This is one of the best compliments he ever had.   Epigram: To Hunt.   William Blake.   OxBoLi

This is only a most piteous pretense of sleep!   Beside the Bed.   Charlotte Mew.   AnEnPo; MoAB; MoBrPo; OBSP; TrGrPo

This is plenty. This is more than enough.   September Song.   Geoffrey Hill.   NoP; OBWP

This is prettiest of all, it is very pretty.   Pretty.   Stevie Smith.   NoP; TEP

This is pure Platonicke Love.   Pure Platonicke.   George Daniel.   CavP

This is quite the best use for my ribbon.'   Limerick: "There was an old man with a ribbon."   Edward Lear.   FaBoNo

This is that other music, to which/I embrace your shadow.   Girl Sitting Alone at Party.   Donald Justice.   DFF

This is the Abomination. This is the wrath of God.   If, on Account of the Political Situation.   W. H. Auden.   LiTA; WaP

This is the card that reads as seven.   Le Chariot.   John Wieners.   VGW

This is the country.   Dolls.   David St. John.   LCAP

This is the country faith/And best of all!   The Country Faith.   Norman Gale.   HBV 1-2; OBEV; OBVV; WGRP

This is the cry of the peoples/That rang in the empty sky!   The Cry of the Peoples.   Alter Brody.   TrJP

THIS is the curse. Write.   A Curse for a Nation.   Elizabeth Barrett Browning.   SBG; WPOW

This is the dawn/The beginning/Again.   In the Beginning.   Rachel Fishman.   VWA

This is the divine repose, that watches/The ever-changing light and shadow, rock and ksy and ocean.   Seventh Day.   Kathleen Raine.   ChMP

This is the end for which we twain are met.   Ballad Written for a Bridegroom.   Francois Villon.   AWP

This is the end,/in peace,/as it was found.   Hymn to Amen Ra, the Sun God.   *Anonymous.*   WGRP

This is the end of all the songs man sings.   Dregs.   Ernest Christopher Dowson.   HBV 1-2; NCEP; OBMV; SeCePo

This is the end of every man's desire.   A Ballad of Burdens.   Algernon Charles Swinburne.   EnLi 1-2

This is the end of good breeding.   A Study in Aesthetics (parody).   Robert Peters.   BXAP

This is the end of him, here he lies.   Epitaph: "This is the end of him, here he lies."   Amy Levy.   NOBV

This is the end of/Solomon Grundy.   Solomon Grundy.   Mother Goose.   HBVY

This is the end of the world   At the Roadside.   John Knoepfle.   FAZ

...This/Is the exciting part, do not interrupt me.   My Children's Book.   John N. Morris.   AMV-80

This is the fall o' the year!   Chant for Skippers.   Katharine Gallagher.   SiSoSe

This is the fault they may not/Absolve nor remedy.   The Great Magicians.   C. Day Lewis.   EaLo

This is the first action.   Cartography.   Joel Oppenheimer.   CoPo

This is the flower of the World.   In Back of the Real.   Allen Ginsberg.   AmPP; HeIP

..."This is the gift/I was going to give you forever."   Happiness of 6 A.M.   Harvey Shapiro.   NYBP

This is the Gnat that mangles men–.   Wonder–Is Not Precisely Knowing.   Emily Dickinson.   AmePo; MoPo

This is the happy warrior; this is he/That every man in arms should wish to be.   Character of the Happy Warrior.   William Wordsworth.   EnLit; EnRP; FaBoBe; FaFP; HBV 1-2; HBVY; LiTB; LoBV; OBRV; TreF

This is the House of History.   The Seven Houses.   George Mackay Brown.   NAs

This is the key of the kingdom.   This Is the Key of the Kingdom.   *Anonymous.*   OxNR

This is the Landlords' Circle, built by me.   Inferno: A New Circle.   Frank Ormsby.   CIP

This is the last curve/in the last curve home   Driving Home.   Jonathan London.   AMV-81

...This is the last/lesson in the first book.   First Reader.   Paris Leary.   CoPo

This is the last news that I can write to you./To England's coast from Barbary.   The George Aloe and the Sweepstake.   *Anonymous.*   BaBo; ESPB; ViBoFo

"This is the last of wars–this is the last!"   This Is the Last.   Gilbert Waterhouse.   PGD

This is the legeand of my lif, thought Latine it be/nane.   The Book of Two Married Women and the Widow.   William Dunbar.   PoEL 1-5

This is the man whom I must get to know.   Things to Come.   James Reeves.   OBSP

This is the meaning of "no god but He!"   Six Rubaiyat.   Abu Sa'id Ibn Abi'l-Khayr.   LiTW

...This is the/meaning of the music of the spheres.   Structure of Rime.   Robert Duncan.   CAPP

This is the most beautiful flower/Of the Partisans who died for freedom.   Bella Ciao.   *Anonymous.*   FSW

This is the most generous contribution I can afford.   The Tragic Condition of the Statue of Liberty.   Bernadette Mayer.   APU

This is the peaceful Mecca all men know!   At Chappaqua.   Joel Benton.   AA

This is the place I love. Here I belong.   Mountain Creed.   Medora Addison Nutter.   GoYe

This is the place where human harvests grow.   God's-Acre.   Henry Wadsworth Longfellow.   HBV 1-2

This is the poet and his poetry.   On a Portrait of Wordsworth by B. R. Haydon.   Elizabeth Barrett Browning.   HeIP

This is the Profession, that never will alter.   The Careless Good Fellow Written March 9, 1680.   John Oldham.   APAS; CEP; SeCV 1-2

This is the road of life!   On the Meadow.   Katri Vala.   PBWP

This is the room, hands oarlocked,/in which you will work.   Car Episode.   Coco Gordon.   AmC

...This is the route I take/each time I walk home.   The Southeast Ramparts of the Seine.   Judit Toth.   VWA

This is the saddest news...and I/am nearer to death...   Father to the Man.   John Knight.   EaLo

This is the shadow of the vast madrone.   The Manzanita.   Yvor Winters.   VGW

This is the Shepherds Holy-day.   Pans Anniversarie.   Ben Jonson.   OBS

This is the ship of treasure,/laden with gold, silver, and jade.   Treasure Boat.   Seiki Fujino.   HW

This is the silence of astounded souls.   Crossing the Water.   Sylvia Plath.   HaCAP

...This is the stalk/True Power doth grow on; and her rights are these.   I Grieved for Buonaparte.   William Wordsworth.   EnRP

This is the summe of my desire,/Until I come unto heaven's quire.   The Wish.   Rowland Watkyns.   CavP

...This is the time of loves.   An Easter Carol.   Christina Georgina Rossetti.   OHIP

This is the ultimate steel!   The Mainspring.   Martha Eugenie Perry.   CaP

This is the way it is, get used to it.   You Want to Go Back.   Margaret Atwood.   NeAC

...This is the way she seems/walking on into East St. Louis .)   Number 29.   Wesley Wallace.   BluL

This is the way the farmers ride,/Hobbledy-hobbledy-hoy!   This Is the Way the Ladies Ride.   Mother Goose.   FaBoUs; OxNR; TiPo f10]

This is the way things go,/hard or soft,/swift or slow.   The Cloud-Mobile.   May Swenson.   SO

..."This is the/way to the back country."   Journeys.   Gary Snyder.   NU

This is the week when Christmas comes.   In the Week When Christmas Comes.   Eleanor Farjeon.   ChBR; PCh; SiSoSe

This is the Will of the Yukon–Lo! how she makes it plain!   The Law of the Yukon.   Robert W. Service.   CaP; HBV 1-2; TreFS

This is the Year that for you waits/Beyond To-morrow's mystic gates.   The Year Ahead.   Horatio Nelson Powers.   WBLP

This is thy life-insurance, I'm thy Pru-man.   New Improved Sonnet XVIII (parody).   Peter Titheradge.   FaBoPa

This is thy sheath; there rust, and let me die.   Romeo and Juliet.   William Shakespeare.   DL

This is today! Today!   Wedding Day at Nagasaki.   Rodney Hall.   CBAP

This is true bliss, and I confess/There is no other happiness.   The Second Rapture.   Thomas Carew.   CaPo; UnTE

This is true taste, and whoso likes it not,/Is blockhead, coxcomb, poppy, fool, and sot.   The Man of Taste.   James Bramston.   FaBoCo

This is what a guy must come to/Ere you yield!   Reflections in a Hospital.   Emanuel Eisenberg.   ALV

This is what comes of snapshots. Of talking in bed.   A Family Man.   Maxine W. Kumin.   IHMS; TAP

This is what I have learnt from America–it is the amount, and it I teach again.   The Poet.   Walt Whitman.   MoAmPo

₍This is what I think of the international situation–very/lucid, is it not).   Letter to Robert.   Mary Fabilli.   IHMS

This is what is called the brotherhood of man.   Family.   Josephine Miles.   FaBoWP; FYAP; GP; GrPl

This is what we are now.   Mill at Romesdal.   Richard Hugo.   AMV-80

This is what you are to me.   Priapus and the Pool.   Conrad Aiken.   CMoP; NOBA; TrGrPo

This is what you will/come back to, this is your hand.   You Begin.   Margaret Atwood.   NOBC; NoP

This is where babes bow down.   Pibroch.   Ted Hughes.   FaBoMo; NePoEA-2; OAEL 1-2; PoCh

"This is where the white man and the red man know/nothing."   Circles.   Carl Sandburg.   AmFN

This is where you/begin   Starting over.   Shirley Kaufman.   VWA

This is your plan.   A Woman.   Mary Dixon Thayer.   HBMV

This it is to be Learned and Witty.   Sir T. J.'s Speech to his Wife and Children.   Anonymous.   CoMu

This Jack, joke, poor potsherd, patch, matchwood, immortal diamond,/Is immortal diamond.   That Nature Is a Heraclitean Fire...   Gerard Manley Hopkins.   AtBAP; BiP; BoW; CoBMV; DiPo; FaBoMo; GTBS-P; LiTB; MoAB; MoPo; MoVE; NoP; OAEL 1-2; OAEP; PoEL 1-5; TEP; VLP

...This Jason/of the vacuum   Strange Kind (II).   J. D. Reed.   MOON

"This Jasper was slow with a gun."   The Cowboy's Lament (I).   Anonymous.   CoSo; FaFP; TreFS

This joker god with a spastic/Twitch said away with the bitch/And gave his snake a break.   Oil and Blood.   Gary Allan Kizer.   LFAC

This jolly little king!   The King of Yvetot.   Pierre Jean de Beranger.   AWP

This jolly old pedagogue, long ago!   The Jolly Old Pedagogue.   George Arnold.   HBV 1-2; TreFS

...This joy/between our daughter and the neighbor boy.   Eighteen.   Sister Mary Honora.   NePoAm-2

This kiss, father, from him who was your son.   The Gardener.   John Hall Wheelock.   NYBP

This Kiss, my Dear,/Is sweeter far/Than Strawberries, Cream and Sugar.   Song: "Smooth was the Water, calm the Air."   Sir Charles Sedley.   SeCV 1-2

...This knelling/for green bones as well as brittle.   Decoration Day.   Bennie Lee Sinclair.   TAT

This knife/I hold against your throat.   Hieroglyph.   Paul Auster.   VWA

This lady, curled like a shell.   The Shellpicker.   Ronald Perry.   NePoEA-2

This lady of the West Country?   An Epitaph.   Walter de la Mare.   BoLiVe; CoBMV

This land's salvation.   My Blackness Is the Beauty of This Land.   Lance Jeffers.   NBP; PoBA

This language wants both tongue and voice.   In Allusion to the French Song, N'entendez Vous Pas ce Language.   Richard Lovelace.   CaPo

This last disguise, himself.   The Missing Person.   Donald Justice.   NYBP

This laud as for a conqueror.   Hymn to Night.   Anonymous.   LiTW

This legend I have told you.   The Legend of the Admen.   Everett W. Lord.   BLPA

This lethal water, sister/of death?   Slow Rain.   Gabriela (Lucila Godoy Alcayaga) Mistral.   PBWP

This life I'm livin' is very hard.   Oh, Babe, It Ain't No Lie.   Elizabeth Cotton.   FSW

...This life, I would not live,/For all, the King and Parliament could give.   The Tired Petitioner (excerpt).   George Wither.   SeCV 1-2

This life is most jolly.   As You Like It.   William Shakespeare.   BoLiVe; GTBS; NoP

This life was not a dream that passes/To Ock, but like the summer flower.   Reynard the Fox (excerpt).   John Masefield.   CMoP

This life will never be what once it was!   Starlight Like Intuition Pierced the Twelve.   Delmore Schwartz.   AmP; MiAP; MoRP; NMP; PoCh

This lily trampled underfoot/Not for the last time dare not fade.   Fleur de Lys.   Rayner Heppenstall.   WaP

This little battery without a spark.   Camera.   Ted Kooser.   Psk

This little one shall make it Holy-day.   King Henry VIII.   William Shakespeare.   NAs

This little pig cried wee, wee, all the way home.   This Little Pig Went to Market.   Anonymous.   HBV 1-2; HBVY

This little Pipkin fits this little Jelly.   A Ternarie of Littles, Upon a Pipkin of Jelly Sent to a Lady.   Robert Herrick.   ALV; FaBoCh; FaBoUs; GoJo; HBV 1-2; HBVY; LoGBV; PoEL 1-5; PoRA

This little song of foam which silver rang/Through worlds a-drowse.   The Ark and the Dove.   Daniel Sargent.   EtS

This little while, oh, Thou art mine,/Jesukin.   Cradle Song.   James L. Duff.   ISi

This live-long minute true   Love and Life.   John Wilmot, Earl of Rochester.   BoLoP; CavP; CEP; ELP; EnLoPo; GBL; HAP; HBV 1-2; LiTL; LoBV; MePo; NIP; NOBE; OBEV; OBS; PoEL 1-5; SeCV 1-2; TrGrPo; ViBoPo

This loaf is my son's bread.   Nationality.   Mary Gilmore.   BoAV; CBAP; PoAu 1-2

This long and lonely month.   The Lonely Month.   Ruthven Todd.   NeBP

This long distance moan/about to worry me to death this time   Long Distance Moan.   Blind Lemon Jefferson.   BluL

This love is not so hard to smutch.   Old Love.   William Morris.   PeD; VLP

This loved Philology.   A Word Made Flesh Is Seldom.   e d.   MAmP

This luck is something all of us must share.   The Surprise.   Anonymous.   UnTE

This lyfe is best whan all is done.   To Master Henrye Cobham, of the Most Blessed State of Lyfe.   Barnabe Googe.   EnPo

This made him comfortable, and though she died/He should not know how bitterly she lied.   She Remembers.   Mary Aldis.   HBMV

This maiden is as young and pure and fair/As Eve agaze on Adam sleeping there.   Sunday up the River.   James (1834-82) Thomson.   OAEP

This makes my arm your prisoner, that my heart.   Upon a Ribband.   Thomas Carew.   AnAnS 2; CaPo; OAEL 1-2

This makes no sense?   Buzz.   Jim Tollerud.   VoR

This man ain't got nobody to/take his troubles to   Roberta.   Leadbelly.   BluL

...This man hath travail'd well.   To William Roe.   Ben Jonson.   OBS; SeCV 1-2

"This man/"is immortal'   The Mice at the Door.   Vincent McHugh.   NePoAm-2

"This man loved me," tears upon the pages!   Mind Flying Far.   Edgar Lee Masters.   PoA

"This man loved me!" then rise and trip away.   Ianthe.   Walter Savage Landor.   EnLoPo

This man with the shy smile has left behind/Something that was intact.   The Suicide.   Louis MacNeice.   FaBoIP

This many a year–this many a year!   Memories.   Arthur Stringer.   HBV 1-2

This mass is his salt/his girl/his sky/his work/his floor.   Moon Man.   Jean Valentine.   MOON

This meal will never end.   Thanksgiving.   John N. Morris.   OFD

This measuring hand. We are beholden all.   Drinking Song.   Anthony Hecht.   NMP

This medieval miracle of song!   Three Sonnets on the Divina Commedia.   Henry Wadsworth Longfellow.   SeCeV

This melodious hymn with great solace,/O lux beata Trinitas.   Devotions of the Fowls.   John Lydgate.   PBBP

This message is a conviction/from someone sprung into the joy of not knowing The Know.   Kathleen Fraser.   NPGG

This moment/is not enough?–then/eternity won't be either.   Glimmers.   Jack Marshall.   APU

This moonlight/is the perfect/human touch.   Rigmarole.   William Carlos Williams.   AnAmPo

This morning I looked into the pale/raisin of Harry's face.   The Raisin.   Donald Hall.   TAP

This morning i wept.   Diary. Solitary Moon.   Charlotte De Clue.   TWSS

This morning my thoughts are as tangled/as my black hair.   How Long Will It Last?   Lady Horikawa.   WPOW

This morning, this evening, so soon.   Tell Old Bill.   Anonymous.   FSW

This morning, waking the world away/in the violent day.   This Morning.   Muriel Rukeyser.   NMM

This most beautiful Moscow night.   Moscow Nights.   Anonymous.   FSW

This music cannot leave me.   Sugarfields.   Barbara] Mahone.   CNA; PoBA

This music was made entirely of silence.   The Silent Piano.   Louis Simpson.   CAPP

This must have been a pretty garden once.'   Time.   Mary Ursula Bethell.   FaBoWP

This my heart so flowing and so lasting! Poem of the Intimate Agony. Julia de Burgos. InW

This my poor and small request:/Rejoice not at my pain. Tho' I Can Not Your Cruelty Constrain. Sir Thomas Wyatt. SiPS

...This myriad I/Tingles, not knowing how, yet wondering why. What Am I, Life? John Masefield. ImOP

This Negro laughs and prays to God for Light! The Negro's Tragedy. Claude McKay. BPo

This Neutral British Gentleman, one of the modern time. The Neutral British Gentleman. Robert Henry Newell. OBAL

This night, and the world, unfinished. The Middle of the World. Kathleen Norris. GP

This night was born for love, my Phaon./Come. Summer Matures. Helene Johnson. BlSi; CDC; PoNe

This night we all must start/To heaven or else to hell. The Mermaid. *Anonymous.* OuSiCo

This night you have given me much happiness to carry/within an empty heart. To an Indian Poet. Patty L. Harjo. VoR

This "no' with griefs both prove/Report oft turns to love. Song: "Four arms, two necks, one wreathing." *Anonymous.* EIL

This noble mind, even in a clown,/Is more than to possess a crown. Content Thyself with Thy Estate. *Anonymous.* EIL

This noble young knight of Lorraine. Limerick: "There was a brave knight of Lorraine." Mary Mapes Dodge. TDH

This now has winter's black and/measured tread. Sonnet: "Afterwards there are dogends in the ashtray." Maureen Duffy. PeHV

This nurse, this teeming womb of royal kings. Richard II. William Shakespeare. FaBoPP

This nymphomaniac enjoys/Inexhaustibly is boys. Careless Love. Stanley Jasspon Kunitz. WaP

This observ'd, the Manes shall be/Of your horses, all knot-free. Another Charme for Stables. Robert Herrick. WSC

This old hammer weighs forty pounds, sah,/Can't kill me, Baby, can't kill me. Drivin' Steel (with music). *Anonymous.* AS

This old witch can still/Make a furious scene! To the Tune "The Fall of a Little Wild Goose." Huang O. WPOW

This once to live. Glad World. Robert D. FitzGerald. ACV

This oncoming traffic with your hah, hah, hah. My Father's Martial Art. Stephen Shu Ning Liu. BrSi

This one, beside it, is a slum. Epitaph: "Here, time concurring (and it does)." John Ciardi. BiP

This one makes a perfect pipe,/That a perfect cup. Fall Days. Marion Conger. SiSoSe

This one remaining rebel/is the sparrow-camel. He "Digesteth Harde Yron". Marianne Moore. CMoP; NoAm

This one solid moral teach us--/That a pile of paradoxes are expected to result! Federation. W. T. Goodge. NOAV

This only true:/E = mc2 Crossedroads. Martin Staples Shockley. FF

This open book...my open coffin. Reading Myself. Robert Lowell. HaCAP; TAP

This, or a kindred rapture, let me own,/I covet ceaselessly! Invention. William Watson. HBV 1-2

This ordeal has almost nothing to do with love. The Recovery Room: Lying-in. Helen Chasin. IHMS

This organ vast shall play his symphony! The Organ Cactus. Dorothy Scarborough. BPAW

This paine thu put away,/And if it possibil be may. This Yonder Night I Sawe a Sighte. *Anonymous.* NAs

This paradise of pleasure and ennui. Don Juan. George Gordon, Lord Byron. NOBL

This pasta, green and garlicky/made with my own hands. Having Replaced Love with Food and Drink. Diane Wakoski. NAs

This pen into magic, this paper to dance. Next Door to Monica's Dance Studio. Barbara Smith. AMV-81

This perfect night could never be/Were we not mated each to each. The Reason. James Oppenheim. HBV 1-2

This permits him time to consider/what he wishes to say to me. Four Translations from the English of Robert Hershon. Robert Hershon. NeAC

This perpetual ecstasy denies. Mythics. Helen Chasin. DFT

This picture, once, resembled thee. To Miss Charlotte Pulteney in Her Mother's Arms. Ambrose Philips. CEP; ELP; NOEC; OBEC

This piece of knotted rope/still blowing. Treehouse. Ted Kooser. PPJ

"This place isn't for you," he says, "I am/their host.") Penelope. Monique Laederach. BoWoP

This place rumord to have been Sodom is blessd/in the Lord's eyes. This Place Rumord to Have Been Sodom. Robert Duncan. NeAP; NOBA; PoM; PPP

This place's curvature precludes its end. The World's End. William Empson. CoBMV; MoVE

This place shall I remember. Be Wise, and Fly Not. Thomas Campion. UnTE

This plain announcement, nicely read,/Iambically runs. On the Imprint of the First English Edition of.... Max Beerbohm. InPK; PV

This playmate sweet,/This child of twelve years old. The Revolt of Islam. Percy Bysshe Shelley. GN

This poem, for your ear,/My dear Monseer,/Of their blue continual hell. The Great Lakes Suite. James Reaney. WHW

This poem has slant eyes. Nine Years after Viet Nam. Leroy V. Quintana. AMV-80

...This poem is an ancient form. Poem Called Poem. James Whitehead. GrPl

This poem/Is for whoever/Had the light on Poem to Be Read at 3 a.m. Donald Justice. HoPM

This poem isn't for you/but for me/after all Your Phone Call at Eight A.M. Joy Harjo. TWSS

(This poem took fourteen years to write--/'Cause I'm just one inch tall). One Inch Tall. Shel Silverstein. OBCA

This poor poem that doesn't begin to give you/what i feel about you, my little friends... Song for My Little Friends. Leonard Adame. FIA

This portion thou wert born for? why should we/Vex at the time's ridiculous misery? To His Retired Friend, an Invitation to Brecknock (excerpt). Henry Vaughan. FaBoRV; ViBoPo

This progress to completion moves like death. Autumn: An Ode. Charles Gullans. NePoEA

This proud usurper and walk free as they. I Will Enjoy Thee Now. Thomas Carew. LiTL; UnTE

This rapture, clear and pure,/my soul to dream induces/of her secret architecture. Pomegranates. Paul Valery. LiTW

...This red should have been much duller. Vlamertinghe: Passing the Chateau. Edmund Charles Blunden. MMM; OBWP

--This relic saved/face, to face the bald-faced sun. Mussel Hunter at Rock Harbor. Sylvia Plath. NYBP

This restless life I may not lead. So unwarely was never no man caught. Sir Thomas Wyatt. FCP; SiPS

This Resurrection field, with sheaves in glory like risen souls. Edlesborough. Anne Ridler. NeBP

"This Ring the Bridegroom did for none provide,/But for his bride." The World. Henry Vaughan. AtBAP; ATP; AWP; CABA; CoBE; DiPo; EnL; ExPo; FaBV; GoTL; HAP; HBV 1-2; HeIP; ILwL; InPo; JCP; LiTB; LoBV; MasP; MePo; NOBE; NOCV; OAEL 1-2; OAEP; OBS; OxBoCh; PoEL 1-5; PPoe; PPP; SeCeV; SeCP; SeCV 1-2; TEP; TrCP; TreFS; TrGrPo; ViBoPo; WGRP

This room would not confine us as before/Since cyclones and tornadoes had begun. Physical Geography. Louise Townsend Nicholl. ImOP

This said--he seized the prize, while round the ring/High soared applause on acclamation's wing. The Gymnasiad, or Boxing Match (excerpt). Paul Whitehead. NOEC

This satire, perhaps, else had looked like sense. On Tobacco. Charles Cotton. OBSV

This Saviour who still lives today,/The Christ of Calvary. My Companion. Joyce Ramage. BePJ

This Sculker I shall never find. Carmina. Caius Valerius Catullus. OBVE

This selfsame cold abstract/So ancient town. Above the High. Geoffrey Grigson. EnLoPo

This separation curse embraced in war. To My Wife. James Forsyth. WaP

This shall be called the laying on of hands/And a farewell. A Necessary Miracle. Eda Lou Walton. NYBP

This shall my love doe, give thy sad death one/Teare, that deserves of me a million. Upon His Spaniell Tracie. Robert Herrick. FM

This shame of so many was mine;/humble, it's my lot to remember. Fear. Aldo Camerino. VWA

This sharp and sudden pain in the side/the compositor's error. Want of Want of. Anne Szumigalski. FaBoWP

This she'll remember, when off the foggy banks/The clammy cod lie quivering on her planks. Escapade. Kenneth Leslie. EtS

This Sheet that brought thee in shall lay thee out. Ad Librum. Samuel Danforth II. SCAP

This should be the Prince of Whales. The Triumph of the Whale. Charles Lamb. ImOP; OBRV

This siege of a shore that no misgivings have steeled,/No doubts defend? Time Passing, Beloved. Donald Davie. BoLoP; NePoEA-2

This sight it caused his aged mother's heart then for to bleed. A Copy of Verses on Jefferys the Seaman. *Anonymous.* OBSS

This sign of a god's ownership/Can make me feel uneasy still. At the Roman Baths, Bath. Edward Lucie-Smith. NePoEA-2

This silken thread of verse/Closely binds the departing sun and me. Three Poems. Ping Hsin (Hsieh Wang-ying). PBWP

This singing-bird's a lad, a lad. The October Redbreast. Alice Meynell. MoBrPo

This sinne of yours, hath no excuse, nor end. Eves Apologie. Emilia Lanier. BoWoP

...This sir is what I do,/Not learning from recipes or books of cookery. A Banquet. Sotades. FaBoUs

This sister knows/and waits. To All Brothers. Sonia Sanchez. BPo

This slow one. Tortoise-Shell. D. H. Lawrence. CMoP; ExPo; FM; OAEL 1-2

This small son of Euclid's own. The Spider. Robert P. Tristram Coffin. ImOP

"This smell is Crist, clepid the plantynge of the Rose in Jerico."' The Canticle of the Rose. Edith Sitwell. NoAm

This smile encouraged young and old–was it you? Was It You? Stewart I. Long. WBLP

This snow, unsaying itself on the pavement. Still. Lisa Zeidner. SM

This snowy mantle for her robe of bloom. The April Snow. Jones Very. AP

This solitude's my home. Now all that sound of laughter, sound of singing. Rosalia de Castro. BoWoP

...This son/with sculpin, coin, and bone,/become the dark he must explore. Elegy for a Diver. Philip Booth. LiSp

This song for mariners and all their ships. In Cabin'd Ships at Sea. Walt Whitman. MOS

This song is isaid of me,/Ever iblessed mote ye be. A Satire on the People of Kildare. Anonymous. OnYI

–This song is secret. Mine ear it pass'd/In a wind o'er the stone plain of Athenry. Song: "The little Black Rose shall be red at last!" Aubrey Thomas De Vere. IrPN

This song is sung and sung not, and its words are sealed. The After Woman. Francis Thompson. ISi

This song is y-said of me;/Ever y-blessed mot ye be! An Irish Satire. Anonymous. OxBM

This soul may see thy face, O Lord of death! The Heart of the Night. Dante Gabriel Rossetti. MaVP

This spark that crackles in the void/As between fate and fate. Come Up, Methuselah. Cecil Day-Lewis. OBMV

This spinner's wheel onfleeing/Outside perception's range. According to the Mighty Working. Thomas Hardy. CMoP

This spray of Western pine! Dickens in Camp. Bret (Francis Bret Harte) Harte. BPAW; HBV 1-2

This spring day. Haiku: "Things long forgotten–". Shiki. FAZ

This spring these plants our rings On the Eve of Our Anniversary. Gary Margolis. Str

...This stone/of yours, which is not you. Which is. To Laura Phelan: 1880-1906. Leon Stokesbury. MAYP

This stone on the mouths of the silent? In This Hour. Josephine Winslow Johnson. MoRP

This story ends with me still rowing. Rowing. Anne Sexton. BoWoP; CAPP

This strip of sand, with hedge on every side... Lawrence: The Last Crusade (excerpt). Selden Rodman. NAMP

This struggle is our miracle new found. Epilogue to the Outrider. Dorothy Livesay. CaP

...This sweet alto-man/wickered in vestibule, drifting away. Cannon Arrested. Michael S. Harper. CNA; FAZ

This tender girl and I/were married in rain-water. Sensibility. Louis Simpson. GP

This test for love:–in every kiss sealed fast/To feel the first kiss and forbode the last. True Woman. Dante Gabriel Rossetti. MaVP

This that urges through the surges beneath you to-day is queen/On the tide-top, the tide-top. Boatman's Hymn. Andrew Magrath. OnYI

This the fays gave him, and thus the child thrived. The Brut. Layamon. MeEV

This the fellow/made the world/what it is O Dirty Bird Yr Gizzard's Too Big & Full of Sand. James Koller. PoM

This the lips we will permit/For to tell, not publish it. Lips Tongueless. Robert Herrick. CaPo

"This the wine, and this the bread." Au Tombeau de Mon Pere. Ronald McCuaig. NOAV; PoAu 1-2

This the Wine & this the Bread My Spectre around Me Night & Day. William Blake. CBEP; NCEP; OAEL 1-2; OxBoCh

This the word that brake his heart–/Yet it brake mine, too! Love Came Back at Fall o' Dew. Lizette Woodworth Reese. HBV 1-2

...This then you may know/as the hero. Part of a Novel, Part of a Poem, Part of a Play: The Hero. Marianne Moore. PoA

This therapy works with amazing success. At the Treatment Center. Jerome Sala. APU

This thing will run at you/And scare itself to spasms.' The Faun. Ezra Pound. FaBoCh; FaBoTw; LoGBV

This, this is my grand recreation! O'Tuomy's Drinking Song. John O'Tuomy. OnYI

This, this, my poor own! Casualty. Robert Nichols. MMM

This thought is as a death, which cannot/choose/But weep to have that which it fears to lose. Sonnets, LXIV: "When I have seen by Time's fell hand defaced." William Shakespeare. AWP; BLPL; FaFP; GTBS; GTBS-P;

HAP; HeIP; InPo; LiTB; LiTL; MCCG; NOBE; NoP; OAEL 1-2; OBSC; PoRA; PPoe; SeCeV; ViBoPo

This 300 year poem/To our suffering. For you, you this atheist. Untitled. James A. Randall, Jr. BPo

This thunder, growing. Direction. Roberta Hill. CDW

...This time/I am going to win. Basketball. Stephen Vincent. LiSp; NeAC

...This time I feel/a wind I never knew blow through my bones. For Nicholas, Born in September. Tod Perry. NYBP

This time tomorrow I'll be gone gone gone. Soliloquy in a Motel. Walker Gibson. GrPl

This time, unless I feed you with my heart? The Grey Wolf. Arthur Symons. BrPo; FaBoTw

This time we'll see her tip her head and sing. Recollection. Marilyn R. Mumford. AMV-80

This time, you completely beside me,/riverfrost on your hair, and on mine. A Prayer for Rivers. Keith Wilson. GOYP

This Tinme forgets and never heals, far less transcends. In Railway Halls. Stephen Spender. EnLit; FaBoMo

This tomb nor wife nor children raised, but we/His fellow-toilers, fishers of the sea. The Fisherman. of Tarentum Leonidas. AWP

This tomb, this dungeon: O castrated trees! Palm House, Botanic Gardens. George Hetherington. NeIP

"This, too, shall pass away." This, Too, Shall Pass Away. Lanta Wilson Smith. BLPA

This too was in the savvy of the Chaldeans. Crapshooters. Carl Sandburg. VGW

...This touching/home goes far. This fishing in the air. We Manage Most When We Manage Small. Linda Gregg. AmPA; NPGG

This tower then only falls when treason undermines. The Purple Island. Phineas Fletcher. JCP

This Town of Hell/Where between sleep and sleep I dwell. In Procession. Robert Graves. MP; TwCP

This tranquil roof where jib-sails hunt in flocks. The Cemetery by the Sea. Paul Valery. LiTW

...This tranquil strength/is better than the thing she's waiting for. Narrative. Elisabeth Eybers. PeSA

This treasure which no death can filch away/My soul to God shall bear. Souvenir. Alfred de Musset. AWP

This turning away, this longing to be there. Nights in Hackett's Cove. Mark Strand. GeTw

This turning world, the which like grains we fill. Georgiques Chretiennes (excerpt). Francis Jammes. CAW

This underpass is endless. Father. Paul Carroll. NeAP

This vast treasure of content/That is mine to-day! Love's Prayer. James Whitcomb Riley. AA

This Verse is lost, his PILL embalmes him safe/To future Times without an Epitaph. Epitaph on One Lockyer, Inventor of a Patent Medicine. Anonymous. FaBoUs

This was a dream– In Winter in my Room. Emily Dickinson. AmPP; BiP; ErPo; LiTA; NoAm; NOBA; OxBA

This was a fiddle, and thus it spoke,/and now it speaks no longer. The Dead Fiddle. Humbert Wolfe. TrJP

...This was a game, when it began. Portrait. Judith Wright. OBSP

....This was a kingly thing! The Ruin. Anonymous. EnLit

This was George Washington. George Washington. Anonymous. OHIP

This was I taught by th' swan. Whilst I Beheld the Neck o' th' Dove. Patrick Cary. JCP

This was/Icarus drowning. Landscape with the Fall of Icarus. William Carlos Williams. NIP

This was Montana fifty years ago. Montana Fifty Years Ago. J. V. Cunningham. Prf

This was no playhouse but a house in earnest. Directive. Robert Frost. MoAmPo

This was no world of rest for thee! Eleventh Sunday after Trinity. John Keble. VLP

This was once a tortured lover,/Sick to death of hot despair. Epitaph in Sirmio. David Morton. PoLf

This was our peace, this was our war. The Sick Nought. Randall Jarrell. OxBA

This was the bed of forgotten seas; this wheat is/blossoming. Nebraska. Jon Swan. RFM

This was the parting that they had/Beside the haystack in the floods. The Haystack in the Floods. William Morris. BeLS; CABA; EBEV; ExPo; HAP; LiTL; LoBV; NBM; NoP; OAEL 1-2; OAEP; OBNC; OBNV; PoEL 1-5; PoRA; SeCeV; VLP; WHA

This was the Pompadour's Fan! On a Fan That Belonged to the Marquise De Pompadour. Henry Austin Dobson. ALV; HBV 1-2; OBVV; ViBoPo

"This was the time agreed upon?" Time's Fool. John Updike. DBV

...This was the very first wall/that you had to have passed through. Comes Winter, the Sea Hunting. Norman Dubie. MAYP

This wasted chance, and with celestial rage/Cry "O what fools were we!" The Future Verdict. Ada Cambridge. NOAV

This way he settled us into a savagery   What Pablo Picasso Did in "Les Demoiselles d'Avignon'.   John Robert Colombo.   PeCV

...This way of grief/is shared, unnecessary/and political   The Ninth Symphony of Beethoven Understood at Last as a Sexual Message.   Adrienne Rich.   NoP; TAP

This way, this way, seek delight!   Song in the Wood.   John Fletcher.   EIL

This way we experience both/without knowing either of them.   We Separate the Days.   Henrik Nordbrandt.   AMV-81

This way were all reproved/Who dig old customs up.   The Priest of Coloony.   William Butler Yeats.   OnYI

This were to be new made when thou art old/And see thy blood warm when thou feel'st it cold.   Sonnets, II: "When forty winters shall besiege thy brow."   William Shakespeare.   BLPL; FF; LiTB; MBW 1-2; OBSC; TEP

This wet evening, in a lost age.   The Mountain Over Aberdare.   Alun Lewis.   ACV

This whole Experiment of Green–/As if it were his own!   A little madness in the spring.   Emily Dickinson.   MAmP; TAP

, This will be about all.   Balloon Faces.   Carl Sandburg.   CMoP

This will be true a hundred million years from now,/As it is now, at this moment.   Death.   James Oppenheim.   WGRP

This will change.   The Dust Will Settle.   Luci Tapahonso.   STE

This will ensure thee/A Happy New Year.   New Year's Wishes.   Frances Ridley Havergal.   BLRP; STF

This winter/is so beautiful to me.   Aging.   Diane Wakoski.   AMV-81

This woman beside me murmuring My God! My God!   Lough Derg.   Denis Devlin.   BIrV; CIP; IPY

This wonder to the vulgar prove,/Our bodyes, not wee move.   Song: "Soules joy, now I am gone."   George Herbert.   OBS

...This wood/is for you.   The Wilding.   Philip Booth.   NePoEA

This work and it was not finished?   The View from the Window.   R.S. Thomas.   BoC

This work shall shine, and walkers bless my name.   Of Watchmen.   John Gay.   EnLi 1-2

This world is all too wide for thee.   On Fanny Godwin.   Percy Bysshe Shelley.   ChRP; OBNC

This world it should end as begun.   The Rural Lass.   Catherine Jemmat.   NOEC

This world may lose its motion, love/If I prove false to thee.   The Storms Are on the Ocean.   Anonymous.   FSW

This world of beauty, color, and perfume;/Hoary with age, yet of unaging bloom.   Above Salerno.   Ada Foster Murray.   HBV 1-2

This world's use will have been ended.   Cristina.   Robert Browning.   MaVP; MBW 1-2; OAEP

...This world shines,/rings and shines, like his dream of heaven.   The Armorer's Daughter.   Debora Greger.   MAYP

This world should wake and be a soul   Wild Eden.   George Edward Woodberry.   AA

This world so many have left.   Luminous Night.   Louis Simpson.   CAPP

This would I buy.   Dream-Pedlary.   Thomas Lovell Beddoes.   AtBAP; FaBoBe; GoTF; OBEV; OBVV; TreFS

This wounds me most (what can it less) that Man,/Man fallen shall be restored, I never more.   Paradise Regained.   John Milton.   LiTB

This wretched life.   Quick-Falling Dew.   Basho (Matsuo Basho).   AWP

This year draws up whose belly sings/with some three hundred ruinous days.   New Year's Eve in Troy.   Adrienne Rich.   NePoEA-2

...This year we haven't/seen the hummingbird.   What the Light Was Like.   Amy Clampitt.   FaBoWP

This yearning, yearning, this ending/Of the heart and its ache.   Water Music.   Alun Lewis.   ChMP

This your one wrynecked woedealing/world   World Winter.   Earle Birney.   GrPl

This your threefold mystery?   Clover.   John Banister Tabb.   AA; AnAmPo; APA

Thither by death-tides borne, as ye full soon/have been.   On Disbanding the Army.   David Humphreys.   PAH

Thither we all, alas! must go,/Where death will quickly end my woe.   Modern Midnight Conversation: Between an Unemployed Artist...   Anonymous.   NOEC

Tho' but now the spirit of a flower.   Hermontimus.   Ayton [(or Aytoun)] Sir Robert.   OBVV

Tho hard, yet proper for a vig'rous Strain.   The Best Time for Conception.   Claude Quillet.   FaBoUs

Tho havede erthe of erthe erthe ynogh.   Snatches: "Erthe tok of erthe erthe with wogh."   Anonymous.   OxBM

Tho' he be nae mine, as I am his.   Mary's Song.   Marion Angus.   BSV

Tho' he's sair pock brocken,/And he's blind of an e'e.   The Waggoner.   Anonymous.   GBP

Tho Llull remain a lover.   Night Song for Two Mystics.   Paul Blackburn.   NeAP

Tho' love was kind, why should we fear,/But holy death is kinder?   Reply.   Hartley Coleridge.   OBRV

Tho' men say thou bring'st the Spring.   Anacreontics.   Abraham Cowley.   OBEV

Tho' rich in Tongues, Arts, Parts, and Fame/And every Thing that's High.   On My Lord Bacon.   John Danforth.   SCAP

"Tho' shortest the day is–the night, sir, is longest."   A Bon Mot.   Anonymous.   PoL

Tho' stack to the cunt of a Queen.   Epigram: "No more of your titled acquaintances boast."   Robert Burns.   FaBoEE

Tho the cradle it be full spread up,/the bride-bed is left bare.   Fair Mary of Wallington.   Anonymous.   ESPB

Tho' thou art all unconscious of thy Might.   To Poesy.   Alfred, Lord Tennyson.   VLP

Tho' very chaste people, to die of a clap.   Epitaph: "Here lie two poor lovers, who had the mishap."   Alexander Pope.   FaBoEE

Thocht lufe be sweit, oft syis it is full sour.   King Berdok.   Anonymous.   OxBS

The thocht o my true-luve/Continuallie.   Cokkils.   Sydney Goodsir Smith.   OxBS; PoA

Thocht verse be vaine,/Composit heir.   To His Darrest Freind.   of Baldynnis John Stewart.   OxBS

Thogh tumbd bee carcasse in towne of martyred Alban.   Sometime Lively Gerald.   Richard Stanyhurst.   NCEP

The thong and point of rain.   Good Friday and the Present Crucifixion.   Vincent Buckley.   CBAP

The thorn and the storm your eyes have shed/and they are in me and you are dead.   Lullaby.   Max Harris.   BoAV

The thorn has pierced her heart.   The Rose and the Thorn.   Paul Hamilton Hayne.   AA; FaBoBe; HBV 1-2

Thorow sight of thy shining,/In Heven withouten ending./Amen.   A Song of Love for Jesus.   Richard Rolle.   MeEL

Thorrow that falsenese of that lither ladd/These three liues werne all gone.   Glasgerion (A version).   Anonymous.   BaBo; ESPB

Thorrow that falsenese of that lither ladd/These three lives werne all gone!   Glasgerion.   Anonymous.   ViBoFo

Thos the damselle spake, and dyed.   Mynstrelles Songe.   Thomas Chatterton.   AnFE; EnLoPo; OBEC

Those abject, who together have partaken/These Sacraments of Nature–and in vain.   The Sacraments of Nature.   Aubrey Thomas De Vere.   ACP; CAW

Those are my best days, when I shake with fear.   Devout Fits.   John Donne.   SeCePo

Those are my best days when I shake with fear.   Fear Test: Integrity of Heroes.   James Simmons.   CIP

Those are the D-Day Dodgers who'll stay in Italy.   Ballad of the D-Day Dodgers.   Anonymous.   WTO

Those are the tears of morning,/That weeps, but not for thee.   The Sigh That Heaves the Grasses.   Alfred Edward Housman.   MoVE; NOBV

Those be favourable hours/Hymned by Pan beneath the shepherd star.   Summer Storm.   Lionel Pigot Johnson.   BrPo

Those best and most poetic days/When all the hills were young!   Mountain Days.   Barclay Fraser.   PoSH

Those bosom chums to whom you're known as "Who?"   Japanese Beetles.   X.J. Kennedy.   HoAn; OBAL

Those boy-scouts practicing again!   Solo for Ear-Trumpet.   Edith Sitwell.   MoAB; MoBrPo

Those children, charred in Cavan,/Passed straight through Hell to Heaven.   Three Poems about Children.   Austin Clarke.   CIP

Those creatures walking without pain or love.   The Giraffes.   Roy Fuller.   ChMP; NeBP; NoAm

Those cut-throat bandits in the paths of fame.   Second Epistle to Robert Graham.   Robert Burns.   DBV

Those dark mountains have never wavered.   Holding the Sky.   William Stafford.   RFM

Those darkened eyes.   He is the Lonely Greatness.   Madeleine Caron Rock.   CAW; CH

Those darling rags.   Haiku: "Don't dress for it."   Chiyo.   BoWoP

Those dear, well-meant, unsatisfactory/approximations of the eventual me?   Out in the Cold.   George Starbuck.   NYBP

...Those/died after for no reason, or/for want of a Spanish imperative.   Miss Lavender.   Jon Stallworthy.   OxBC

Those empty spaces. It has found them.   For a Child Gone to Live in a Commune.   William Stafford.   CAPP

Those facets of copiousness which I proposed/Exist, do so when we have silenced ourselves.   Observation of Facts.   Charles Tomlinson.   NePoEA-2

Those for a moment lie still and sun themselves.   These Days the Papers in the Street.   Charles Reznikoff.   VGW

Those for whom some central thing has vanished.   Bernie's Quick-Shave (1968).   Sydney Lea.   MAYP

Those gilded trees, those statues green and white.   Ideal Landscape.   Adrienne Rich.   NoAm

Those glaring lamps were set, that made a dreadful shade.   The Faerie Queene.   Edmund Spenser.   SeCePo

Those goldnails and their gaylinks that hang along a lime   Cherry Beggar.   Gerard Manley Hopkins.   FaBoPP

Those hands to greet,/Us, where love needs no speech.   In Memory.   Lionel Pigot Johnson.   OBNC; PoEL 1-5

...Those he loves, he deceives.   A Christmas Message.   Gavin Ewart.   FaBoMo

Those hidden rocks that wrecked him into song.   A Child Accepts.   Michael Hamburger.   NMP

Those I loved best died of it–/the fool's disease.   Flee on Your Donkey.   Anne Sexton.   NYBP

Those Infant-Days, when I did see/Wisdom and Wealth couch'd in Simplicity.   Right Apprehension.   Thomas Traherne.   PoEL 1-5

Those ladies giving those monkeys nuts will injure their constitution.   Van Amburgh's Menagerie.   *Anonymous.*   BLPA

Those lives are over. All their hopes and/ fears/Are lost like shadows in the morning-break.   Stone Walls.   Julie Mathilde Lippmann.   AA

...Those many marriages/That life on each live thing bestows.   Upon a Second Marriage.   James Merrill.   HW; NoP

Those melancholy thoughts we'll flee,/And cheerful lovers always be.   A Song: "If for a woman I would die."   Anne Finch, Countess of Winchilsea.   ViBoPo

Those mighty whisperers/Missouri Mississippi.   Like Ghosts of Eagles.   Robert Francis.   LCAP

Those moments when you say of beauty: "Be"?   To a Poet.   Walter Conrad Arensberg.   AnAmPo

Those names which in immortal strains/Angelic choirs have sung.   Upon the Feast of St. Simon and St. Jude.   Samuel Johnson.   EiCP

Those old, unyielding eyes may flash,/And flinch–and look the other way.   The Wandering Jew.   Edwin Arlington Robinson.   MAmP; QFR

Those other countries of the mind,/So tousled, dark and undefined!   The Atlas.   Kenneth Slessor.   PoAu 1-2

Those others will die at this or the next year's turn/And find the resurrection encased in sleep.'   Knole.   C. H. Sisson.   NOCV

Those parks, those paintings in which I live.   Crossing the Park.   Howard Moss.   NYBP

...Those pealing Stedman caters kept/Time with their own time, ringing for whatever reason.   The Ringers.   John Peck.   AmPA

Those places, almost the exact same places.   The Exact Same Places.   Charles Vandersee.   AmC

Those powerful, clear hoofprints on the path.   The Origin of Centaurs.   Anthony Hecht.   NePoEA

Those righteous unrueful ruthless men/On a May day in Washington.   Watergate.   Ruth Herschberger.   FAZ

Those silver lanes of liquid ran like a dawn?   The Flood.   Charles G. Bell.   GrPl

...Those that survive/Their infancy, black cat, will make some man their slave.   Black Cat.   Lora Dunetz.   NePoAm-2

"Those that want learning, he that seeks to teach,/Himself (though most unlearned) may all outreach   A Schoolmaster's Precepts.   John Penkethman.   OxBChV

Those the great days, and that the heroic/age.   The Heroic Age.   Richard Watson Gilder.   AA; OHIP

Those they did buy at such a costly rate,/That it was able to subvert a State.   The Moone-Calfe.   Michael Drayton.   PoEL 1-5

Those things which me most terrify/I neither can hear nor touch nor see.   Upon Being Awakened at Night by My Four Year Old Daughter.   Dachine Rainer.   NePoAm-2

Those thoughts too fleet/For any save the soul's swift feet!   When as a Lad.   Isabel Ecclestone Mackay.   HBV 1-2

"Those trees were planted by Apple-Seed John."   Apple-Seed John.   Lydia Maria Child.   OHIP

...Those trips/Which I no longer take/And only partly took.   Abroad Thoughts from Home.   Donald Hall.   NePoEA

Those two little mules on the road to Cook's Peak.   The Road to Cook's Peak.   *Anonymous.*   CoSo

Those unknown things or these things overknown.   From Dawn to Noon.   Dante Gabriel Rossetti.   MaVP

Those webs were filled with words/that tumbled meaning into wind.   Snow Country Weavers.   James Welch.   CDW

Those were the days when first it was we learned/Words bitter, beautiful and harsh.   Fire, the Rope...   Nikolay Tikhonov.   LiTW

Those whispering leaves behind the slit/on the cabin wall of childhood's/dreaming and becoming.   Palm Leaves of Childhood.   G. Adali-Mortti.   PBA

Those whistling knives of his/are kitchened at night.   On a Professional Couple in a Side-Show.   Alan Dugan.   GP

...Those white teeth only show/How much you've swallowed from your chamber pot.   Egnatius, Because His Teeth Are White.   Caius Valerius Catullus.   DBV

...Those who can move need not/dance.   Of Dancing.   Alan Brownjohn.   FaBoMo

Those who deny it, though they cannot live,/Possess, but finally, a life to give.   Sonnets for a Dying Man.   Burns Singer.   NePoEA-2

...Those who dwell/Near these great beacons are instructed well.   The Needles' Lighthouse from Keyhaven, Hampshire.   Charles Tennyson Turner.   FaBoPP

...Those/Who err each other must respect.   Courtesy.   Coventry Patmore.   OBVV

Those who have driven me into the dusty sands of the desert...   A Denunciation.   Mahammed A. Hassan.   WTO

Those who have killed the dream and left me poor.   The Dean.   Alan Porter.   AnAmPo

...Those who held them, not until, but so/they gave.   Women's Tug of War at Lough Arrow.   Tess Gallagher.   MAYP

Those who pity them for their chaste lives and troubled/fortunes.   Crowds.   Charles Baudelaire.   SyP

Those who rode with Kilpatrick can never/forget!   Riding with Kilpatrick.   Clinton Scollard.   PAH

Those who were never meant/to survive?   Anchorage.   Joy Harjo.   STE; TWSS

Those who win heaven, blest are they!   One Way of Love.   Robert Browning.   HBV 1-2

Those who would have the whole loaf,/let alone the house,/had better throw away their breadcrumbs.   The Two Gretels.   Robin Morgan.   DFT

Those who write not, and yet all Writers nick,/Are Bankrupt Gamesters, for they damn on Tick.   Secret-Love.   John Dryden.   SeCV 1-2

...Those whom you saw were those whom you saw and/So understood, not trying to understand.   Seeing St. James's.   Ray Mathew.   NOAV

Those wicked, heartless married men who ridicule their/wives.   The Legend of the First Cam-u-el.   Arthur Guiterman.   ALV; CenHV

Those wild flowers stand the bl   An Anecdote of Love.   John Clare.   NOBV

Those willow cats that ran away/And left their toes behind!   The Willow Cats.   Margaret Widdemer.   BrR

Those windless flags you see,/Alone in the dying glare.   For a Very Old Man, on the Death of His Wife.   Jane Cooper.   NePoEA-2

Those wondrous secrets which it knows–/and keeps.   Duality.   Arthur Sherburne Hardy.   AA

Those years and years by of world without/event/That in Majorca Alfonso watched the door.   St. Alphonsus Rodriguez.   Gerard Manley Hopkins.   VLP

Those yet unborn shall offer up their Vows.   Cloris and Mertilla.   Michael Drayton.   LoBV

Thou a slight thing, thou in access of cunning/dar'dst to assume this?   Apparuit.   Ezra Pound.   AnFE; APA

Thou answerest/them only with/spring).   O Sweet Spontaneous.   Edward Estlin Cummings.   AnNE; NoAm; NoP; OxBA; PrIm; TrGrPo

Thou are a whore, despite of grace,/Good counsel and an ugly face.   Madrigal: "To be a whore, despite of grace."   Charles Cotton.   FaBoEE

Thou art able to make this water calm/Until we have safely passed over.   A Voyager's Prayer.   *Anonymous.*   WGRP

Thou art able to make this water calm/Until we have safely passed over.   Voyagers' Prayer.   *Anonymous.*   TRV

Thou art all my treasure thou.   The Island Boatman's Love-Croon.   Robert Farren.   CoBE

Thou art alone, fond lover.   The Evening Darkens Over.   Robert Bridges.   CMoP; HAP; NBM; NOBV; PoEL 1-5

Thou art already on the wing!   The Blackcock.   Joanna Baillie.   PBBP

Thou art avenged, my first-born, sleep in peace!   Yussouf.   James Russell Lowell.   BBV; BeLS; BLPA; BLPL; FaBoBe

Thou art but shadow with a broken glaive,/Within thy futile hands His winding-sheet.   Christus Triumphans.   Conde B. Pallen.   CAW

Thou art content and sleepest well.   Passiontide Communion.   Katharine Tynan Hinkson.   TrPWD

Thou art lost and gone forever,/Dreadful sorry, Clementine.   Clementine.   Percy Montrose.   BLSo; FSW; OBAL

Thou art mine–and fast I hold Thee,/Baby dear.   Lullaby in Bethlehem.   Sir Henry Howarth Bashford.   HBV 1-2; HBVY

Thou art my ever-living judgment-day.   Count My Time by Times That I Meet Thee.   Richard Watson Gilder.   AA

Thou art my Monument, and this my last farewell./Echo Well.   Echo to a Rock.   Edward, Lord Herbert of Cherbury.   AtBAP; PoEL 1-5

Thou art my pennon that will not go down.   Canzone: To Love and to His Lady.   Guido delle Colonne.   AWP

Thou art my Wit, and thou my Vertue art.   Astrophel and Stella, LXIV.   Sir Philip Sidney.   AAS; HBV 1-2; OBSC; SiPS

Thou art no more immortal than I.   Epitaph: "When you look on my grave."   *Anonymous.*   FaBoEE

Thou art so long away!   Chanson de Rosemonde.   Richard Hovey.   HBV 1-2

Thou art still my consolation/In all tribulation.   Peace and Joy in Jesus Christ.   Johann Franck   BePJ

Thou art the Channel my soul seeks,/Not this with Cataracts and Creeks.   Silex Scintillans.   Henry Vaughan.   AnAnS 1

Thou art the God that worketh wondrously.   I Minded God.   Henry Ainsworth.   AH

Thou art the harlot, now thy time is done,/Of all the mighty nations of the sun.   Africa.   Claude McKay.   BALP

Thou art the man, and thou alone will make/A Felix tremble, and a David quake!   A Model Sermon.   *Anonymous.*   FaBoUs

Thou art the ocean, too, and thine,/That ever deepening roll!   From Heart to Heart.   William Channing Gannett.   AH

Thou art the Proclamation; and I am/The Trumpet, at whose voyce the people came.   The Second Anniversarie.   John Donne.   AnAnS 1; FaBoEn; OAEL 1-2; OxBoCh

Thou art the worn memorial, Baker Street.   The Metropolitan Railway. Baker Street Station Buffet.   Sir John Betjeman.   EBEV; OxBTC

Thou art these tears–wilt flow from my lids away/from me?   The Ecstasy.   Al-Hallaj.   ILwL

Thou art, thyself, thy one unopened book.   To Shakespeare.   Richard Edwin Day.   AA

Thou art weighed in the scales and found/wanting, the balance of God, O Spain!   Mene, Mene, Tekel, Upharsin.   Madison Cawein.   PAH

Thou art what thou art.   To a Lark in War-Time.   Franz Werfel.   TrJP

Thou art within me like a sea at dawn.   O Christ, Thou Art within Me Like a Sea.   Edith Lovejoy Pierce.   TrPWD

"Thou art worse than a fool, O head!"   Retort.   Paul Laurence Dunbar.   AA

Thou askest nothing, evermore at home/In thy own self's perennial masterdom.   At Sainte-Marguerite.   Trumbull Stickney.   LiTA; MoVE; NCEP; OxBA

Thou bare the Lamb of Innocence.   Hail, Queen of Heaven.   *Anonymous.*   OBSP

Thou bark divine!   My Brigantine.   James Fenimore Cooper.   AA; EtS; MOS

Thou be oure helpe we be not forsake,/Amice Christi, Johannes.   A Song to John, Christ's Friend.   *Anonymous.*   MeEL

Thou bear'st the arrow, I the arrow-head.   Astrophel and Stella, LXV.   Sir Philip Sidney.   AAS; SiPS

Thou berest thy love behind thy back',/In every place whereso he go.   A Bachelor's Life.   *Anonymous.*   OxBM

"Thou best humour'd man with the worst/humour'd muse."   Retaliation.   Oliver Goldsmith.   OAEP

Thou bidest wall nor floor, Lord!   The Hurricane.   Hart Crane.   AP; CMoP; CoBMV; MoAB; MoAmPo; OxBA; TrCP

Thou blowest forgotten things into my mind,/From long ago.   Song: "Bring from the craggy haunts of birch and pine."   John Todhunter.   OBVV

Thou break'st all thy girdles, and break'st forth a god.   Hymn to Comus.   Ben Jonson.   EIL; OAEP

Thou breath of things unseen!   Veni Creator.   Bliss Carman.   MoRP

Thou bring us into Hevene light./Amen.   The Mother and Her Son on the Cross.   *Anonymous.*   MeEL

Thou but of all the kingly Tribute take.   Astrophel and Stella, LXXXV.   Sir Philip Sidney.   AAS; SiPS

Thou but preserv'st a Form, and I a name.   To Mr. Jervas, with Fresnoy's Art of Painting, Translated by Dryden.   Alexander Pope.   OBEC

Thou call'st me madman, but I call thee blockhead.   To Flaxman.   William Blake.   FaBoEE

Thou cam'st to kindle, go'st to come; then I/Will dream that hope again, but else would die.   The Dream.   John Donne.   InvP; LiTB; LiTL; LoBV; OBEV

Thou canst inflame and quench the kindled fire.   "If he that erst the form so lively drew."   Henry Howard, Earl of Surrey.   FCP; SiPS

Thou canst not come too soon; and I can wait/If Thou come late.   When.   Susan (Sarah Chauncey Woolsey) Coolidge.   HBV 1-2

Thou canst not lose thy way, thy king with all hath peace.   Christ's Victory and Triumph.   Giles the Younger Fletcher.   FaBoPP

Thou canst not see, for countless tears/Are ever streaming here below.   A Star There Fell.   Zalman Schneour.   TrJP

Thou canst not then be false to any man.   Hamlet.   William Shakespeare.   FaFP; GN; GoTF; LiTB; OHFP; PoPl; TreF; TrGrPo; TRV

Thou Chame, and Chamish nymphs, bear witness of my vow!   Lines Written at Cambridge, to W. R., Esquire.   Phineas Fletcher.   EIL

Thou chosen sister of the Spirit/That gazes on thee till in thee it pities...   To the Moon.   Percy Bysshe Shelley.   LoBV

Thou com'st and dost relieve.   A Parodie.   George Herbert.   AnAnS 1; OBS

Thou comest with tired limbs to sink be-/side/The ashes of his fire and find them cold.   Doubt.   Robert Cameron Rogers.   AA

Thou crocodile, who when thou hast me slain,/Lamentest my death, with tears of thy disdain.   Idea.   Michael Drayton.   EnRePo

Thou dar'st not face the godlike sun.   The Legend of Montrose. Chapt. 6: Annot Lyle's Song: "Birds of Omen".   Sir Walter Scott.   EnRP

Thou didst provide, e'en for this nameless bird,/Home, and a natural love, amid the surging seas.   Pater Vester Pascit Illa.   Robert Stephen Hawker.   CAW; CoBE

"Thou didst thy best–that is success!"   Judgment.   *Anonymous.*   AnAmPo; GoTF; TreFT

Thou died'st an envious wonder, whose high fate/The world must still admire, scarce imitate.   Conjectured to Be upon the Death of Sir Walter Ralegh.   Henry, Bishop of Chichester King.   EG

Thou dog, don at once/The grand Khizzilbash turban!   To the Ingleezee Khafir, Calling Himself Djann Bool Djenkinzun.   James Clarence Mangan.   OnYI

Thou dost all terrors quell.   To Mary.   Gottfried von Strasburg.   ISi

Thou dost loth me,–I love thee, though cause of my death.   The Complaint of a Lover Forsaken of his Love.   *Anonymous.*   CoMu

Thou dost not know it, and I do.   To a Cat.   Hartley Coleridge.   FM

Thou dost punish us with blessing!   The Poet's Journal (excerpt).   Bayard Taylor.   TrPWD

Thou dost waive disease and pain/And resume new life again.   To a Marsh Hawk in Spring.   Henry David Thoreau.   PB; PoEL 1-5

Thou dravest love from thee, who dravest Me.   The Hound of Heaven.   Francis Thompson.   ACP; ATP; BLPL; BrPo; CAW; FaBV; FaFP; GoBC; GoTL; GTBS; HBV 1-2; ILwL; LiTB; LiTM; LoBV; MasP; MCCG; MoAB; MoBrPo; OAEP; OBMV; OxBoCh; PoEL 1-5; SeCePo; SeCeV; TreF; TrGrPo; TRV; ViBoPo; VLP; WGRP; WHA

Thou dread'st and hop'st Thou know'st not what.   Adriani Morientis ad Animam Suam.   Matthew Prior.   CEP; OBSP; OBVE

Thou dreamest still which way my life to wast.   Thou Sleepest Fast.   *Anonymous.*   EIL; OBSP

Thou'dst better part with Flesh and Blood,/Than be, where Life's not understood.   Not to sigh and to be tender.   Aphra Behn.   BoWoP

"Thou'dst spit upon me less, thou sibilant sot!"   Tudor Aspersions.   R. A. Piddington.   FiBHP

Thou fail not in a world of sin,/And ev'n for want of such a type.   In Memoriam A.H.H., XXXIII.   Alfred, Lord Tennyson.   VLP

Thou false to him, thou fiend to me!   Remember thee! remember thee!   George Gordon, Lord Byron.   BoLoP; MBW 1-2; OBSP; ViBoPo

Thou first and worst disturber of man's rest.   On a Cock at Rochester.   Sir Charles Sedley.   FaBoEE; PoL; TW

Thou first-fought field of freedom–/Alamance.   Alamance.   Seymour W. Whiting.   PAH

Thou flatter'st thine, mine cannot flat-/ter'd bee.   To the Ghost of Martial.   Ben Jonson.   OAEP

"Thou fool, tomorrow thou must die."   Though You Are Young.   Thomas Campion.   EnRePo

Thou givest all things, take our praise!   Thanksgiving.   Arthur Ketchum.   STF

Thou goest about to slay me.   Shall I Abide This Jesting?   *Anonymous.*   GBL

Thou gushest forth! O, hail! Fount of salvation!   To Our Lord in the Sacrament.   Saint Anselm.   CAW

Thou hadst better disband,/For old Bully, thy doctors are gone.   Jack Frenchman's Defeat.   William Congreve.   APAS; CoMu

An thou hadst not come to my bed.   Hamlet.   William Shakespeare.   UnTE

Thou hadst the peace and I the undying pain.   Not Thou But I.   Philip Bourke Marston.   BLPA; BLPL

Thou hast a name, a name, a name,/To make the stars thine own.   Though Fatherland Be Vast.   Allen Eastman Cross.   AH

Thou hast all seasons for thine own, O Death!   The Hour of Death.   Felicia Dorothea Hemans.   HBV 1-2; LoBV; OBNC

"Thou hast begun to love one of my works/Almost enough."   Femina Contra Mundum.   Gilbert Keith Chesterton.   MoRP

Thou hast brave health and fortitude/To live and die alone!   Knapweed.   Arthur Christopher Benson.   HBV 1-2

Thou hast brought him a pardon from good King/John.   King John and the Abbot of Canterbury.   *Anonymous.*   GN; HBV 1-2

Thou hast feitched vs home good Iohn/oth Side,/That was now cleane ffrom vs gone.   Jock o the Side (A version).   *Anonymous.*   ESPB; ViBoFo

Thou hast not kissed her silver feet.   Song from the Story of Acontius and Cydippe.   William Morris.   EG

Thou hast put an upward reach/Into the heart of man.   God the Architect.   Harry Kemp.   HBMV; TRV; WGRP

Thou hast slighted the critical minute of love.   Oh! the time that is past.   *Anonymous.*   BoLoP

Thou hast the lips that should be kissed!   Endymion.   Oscar Wilde.   HBV 1-2

Thou in my name/Must hold the same,/Until thou bring it to the grave.   Sorrow.   Samuel Daniel.   OBSC

Thou in those groves, by Dis above,/Shalt live with me and be my love.   The Jew of Malta: The Song of Ithamore.   Christopher Marlowe.   WHA

Thou innocent! He lingers in the breast,/Of our humanity.   To the Mother of Christ, the Son of Man.   Alice Meynell.   ISi

Thou it is that wakest me.   To My God.   George Macdonald.   TrPWD; TRV

Thou know'st its use—it hides—no matter whom.   An Epitaph: "My name—my country—what are they to thee?"   William Cowper.   FaBoEE

Thou know'st the proverb: Nothing due for naught.   To That Most Senseless Scoundrel, the Author of Legion's Humble...   Thomas (Tom) Brown.   APAS

Thou knowest, eternal God, and thou alone!   As Some Mysterious Wanderer of the Skies.   Henry Jerome Stockard.   AA

Thou knowest the chase useless, and again/Turnest to follow it.   A Pause of Thought.   Christina Georgina Rossetti.   NOBE; OBNC

Thou knowst its use. It hides—no matter whom.   No Matter.   Paulus Silentiarius.   AWP; EnLi 1-2

Thou last great prophet of tautology.   MacFlecknoe.   John Dryden.   FiP

Thou leadest me by unsought ways,/And turn'st my mourning into praise.   The Christian Life.   Samuel Longfellow.   WGRP

Thou leadest, O God! All's well with/Thy troopers that follow.   The Wild Ride.   Louise Imogen Guiney.   AA; CAW; HBV 1-2

Thou lentest Thy rod and staff to comfort me—/Lord, I give thanks!   Thanksgiving.   Susie M. Best.   TrPWD

Thou let me live a day/In my new world.   My New World.   Irving Browne.   AA

Thou lightest the peaks with Thine eternal beam.   The Conversion of the Magdalene.   Pedro Malon de Chaide.   CAW

Thou livest singing, but I singing die.   Madrigal: "Dainty sweet bird."   Thomas Vautor.   EnRePo

Thou, Lord of all within!   Sun.   Henry Rowe.   OBEV

Thou, lovely thing.   The Birthnight: To F.   Walter De la Mare.   NAs

Thou'lt find me dressed and on my way/Watching the break of thy great day.   The Dawning.   Henry Vaughan.   MePo; NOCV; OxBoCh; TrPWD

...Thou'lt meet her/In eastern sky.   Wolfram's Dirge.   Thomas Lovell Beddoes.   NOBE; OBEV

Thou mad'st my soul embrace/Jesus as mine.   Now I Have Found a Friend.   Henry Hope.   BePJ

Thou maist thinke life, a thing but lent.   To Sir Robert Wroth.   Ben Jonson.   SeCV 1-2

Thou mak'st the heaven thou hop'st indeed/thy home.   East London.   Matthew Arnold.   OAEP; WGRP

Thou may'st repent that thou hast scorned my tears,/When Winter snows upon thy golden hairs.   When Men Shall Find.   Samuel Daniel.   LiTL

Thou mayst control her limbs, but not begin/To know what planet rules the tides within.   The Book of Day-Dreams.   Charles Leonard Moore.   AA

Thou mayst love on, through love's eternity.   Sonnets from the Portuguese, XIV.   Elizabeth Barrett Browning.   CTC; GTBS; NOBE; OBEV; PG; UnPo; ViBoPo

Thou murth'rer which hast kill'd, and devil which/wouldst damn me.   Beauty.   Abraham Cowley.   LiTB; PoEL 1-5

...Thou must,/this erstwhile youth replies, I just can't.   Kind of an Ode to Duty.   Ogden Nash.   TrGrPo

"Thou, my dear, wert born to-day."   On My Birthday, July 21.   Matthew Prior.   OBEV

Thou, my everlasting life!   The Joys of Paradise.   Saint Augustine.   CAW

Thou my meaning, Thou my death.   Prayer in Mid-Passage.   Louis MacNeice.   EaLo

...Thou my Minde dost raise/To Ayres of Spheares, yes, and to Angels Layes.   To a Nightingale.   William, of Hawthornden Drummond.   OBS

Thou ne'er took such a bleth'ran bitch/Into thy dark dominion!   On a Noisy Polemic.   Robert Burns.   FaBoEE

Thou needst not fear no other ill/Than Turtles suffer when they Bill.   On His Mistris that Lov'd Hunting.   Anonymous.   OBS

Thou not thoughtless nor fickle,/unlike to myself.   I'm Ashamed of My Thoughts.   Anonymous.   NOBI

Thou only, O Christ, with the Holy Ghost, art most high in/the glory of God the Father.   Gloria in Excelsis.   Anonymous.   WGRP

Thou, our shepherd, go in peace.   The Death of Moses.   Anonymous.   TrJP

Thou pin'st, to hear by wood or lawn/Apollo's nightingale.   The Blackbird.   Henry Charles Beeching.   OBVV

"Thou poor blind spinner, work is done."   Spinning.   Helen Hunt Jackson.   HBV 1-2

Thou powerful one, help me to bring also a scalp of my foe, that/my people may rejoice at my coming.   .Blackfoot Sin-ka-ha.   William S. Lewis.   BPAW

Thou Prince and Saviour, come. Amen.   Ten Thousand Times Ten Thousand.   Henry Alford.   VLP

Thou'rt gone for evermore!   The Maniac.   Thomas Russell.   OBEC

Thou'rt our faith in nights darkness and love in morns light.   Hymn to the Creator.   John Clare.   NOBV

Thou'rt present with assistance.   I Love My Jesus Quite Alone.   Johannes Kelpius.   AH

Thou'rt welcome my fancy, welcome home to me.   Hallo My Fancy.   William Cleland.   CH; OxBoLi

Thou rul'st the waves; my task's to waive the rules.   The Lost History Plays: King Canute (parody).   Stanley J. Sharpless.   BXAP

(Thou's ower lang in thy bed),/Bonny at morn.   Bonny at Morn.   Anonymous.   GBP

Thou seemest wreathed, by some immortall Hande.   Sonnet: "Innumerable Beauties, thou white haire."   Edward, Lord Herbert of Cherbury.   PoEL 1-5

Thou shalt be, and thou art!   The Celestial Country.   John Mason Neale.   GoBC

Thou shalt be and thou art.   Jerusalem, the Golden.   Bernard of Cluny.   CAW; WGRP

Thou shalt be call'd, the Cap of Fugitive.   Lines on a Purple Cap Received as a Present from My Brother.   George Alsop.   SCAP

Thou shalt be judge how I do spend my time.   Satires.   Sir Thomas Wyatt.   FCP; PoEL 1-5; SiPS

Thou shalt be/Mine Eternal heaven.   During His Courtship.   Charles Wesley.   NOCV

Thou shalt be served thyself by every sense/Of service which thou renderest.   Reward of Service.   Elizabeth Barrett Browning.   BLPA; FaBoBe

Thou shalt bruise them with rod of iron,/and break them like vessels of clay.   The Reed.   Henry Bernard Carpenter.   AA

Thou shalt find help to bear thy daily lot/Which is not elsewhere found.   Unanswered Prayers.   Ella Wheeler Wilcox.   WGRP

Thou shalt have no displeasure/By knocking at my breast.   The Constant Lover.   Aurelian Townsend.   OxBoLi

Thou shalt hear so sweet a song/Never shepherd sung the like.   A Pastoral.   Nicholas Breton.   EIL

Thou shalt hear the Master calling.   Christmas Eve.   Eugene Field.   OHIP

...Thou shalt in me,/Livelier than elsewhere, Stella's image see.   To Sleep.   Sir Philip Sidney.   NOBE

Thou shalt lie still and ebb no more.   Sea-Way.   Ellen Mackay Hutchinson Cortissoz.   AA

Thou shalt no pleasure comparable find/To the inward gladness of a virtuous mind.   The Twelve Weapons of Spiritual Battle.   Sir Thomas More.   EnRePo

Thou shalt non harm have, trewely.'   The House of Fame: The Eagle Converses with Chaucer.   Geoffrey Chaucer.   OxBM

Thou shalt not covet, but tradition/Approves all forms of competition.   The Latest Decalogue.   Arthur Hugh Clough.   CABA; EBEV; ExPo; FaBoCo; FF; GoTF; HoPM; InMe; LoBV; NBM; NIP; OBVV; PPP; TreFT; WGRP

Thou shalt not live at Shackley-hay.   Shackley-Hay.   Anonymous.   GBP

Thou shalt not steal from Samuel Rogers, nor/Commit-flirtation with the muse of Moore.   Don Juan.   George Gordon, Lord Byron.   FiP

Thou shalt rest, thou shalt rest.   Come, O Sabbath Day.   Gustav Gottheil.   AH

Thou shouldst murder with a kisse.   To Death, Castara Being Sicke.   William Habington.   AnAnS 2

Thou shouldst not, gentle roachling, be/Forlorn and gaunt and weak and sad.   A New Year Idyl (excerpt).   Eugene Field.   PoSC

–Thou silly worm, gnaw not/Yet thine intricate cocoon.   Felo de Se.   Richard Hughes.   OBMV

..."Thou single wilt prove none."   Sonnets, VIII: "Music to hear, why hear'st thou music sadly?"   William Shakespeare.   PoEL 1-5; ViBoPo

Thou sleepest too long, thou art beguiled.   My Darling Dear, My Daisy Flower.   John Skelton.   HAP

Thou Son of God! Thou Son of Man!   The Master of Laborers.   George Edward Day.   PGD

Thou sovereign gift of God most sweet, most blest,/O happy Sleep!   Sleep.   Ada Louise Martin.   HBV 1-2

"Thou'st reckoned thy chickens before they were hatched."   A-Begging Buttermilk I Will Go.   Anonymous.   OBET

Thou strikest, like Olympian Jove, but once.   Pericles and Aspasia.   Walter Savage Landor.   OBRV

Thou struckst her arme, but 'twas my heart/Shed all the blood, felt all the smart.   Celia Bleeding, to the Surgeon.   Thomas Carew.   AnAnS 2; PeD; SeCP

Thou the bridegroom, I the bride!   The Sun-Witch to the Sun.   George Howe.   NYBP

Thou, the Man Christ JESUS,/Strength in flesh made weak.   Come to Me, Beloved.   Digby Mackworth Dolben.   OxBoCh

Thou then mayst smile while all around thee weep.   The Baby.   Sir William Jones.   GoTF

Thou, thou, thou shalt rule our queen, and share our monarch's throne!   Ode to Mercy.   William Collins.   EiCP; LAuP

Thou–Thou wilt help us, dearest Friend,/In nature's last infirmity.   The Last Hour.   Henry Augustus Rawes.   CAW

Thou to the darker bars art blind.   Any Father to Any Son.   Francis Burdett Money-Coutts.   OBVV

Thou to their teeth hast proved Thy Deity. On the Miracle of Loaves. Richard Crashaw. ACP; OBSP

Thou to thy crucifix, I to my mother. Thoughts in Separation. Alice Meynell. ACP; GoBC

Thou too hast kept thy plight full well,/As many a baffled Heart can tell. Ode to a Lady Whose Lover Was Killed by a Ball... George Gordon, Lord Byron. ERoP 1-2

Thou too shalt groan at heart that all thy spending/Cannot repay the dead, the hungry dead. From Generation to Generation. Sir Henry Newbolt. FaBoTw

Thou too shalt rest. Wanderer's Night Song. Johann Wolfgang von Goethe. AWP; PoPl

Thou trumpet set for Shakespeare's lips to blow! Fabien Dei Franchi. Oscar Wilde. BrPo

Thou visor'd, vast, unspeakable show and lesson! Broadway. Walt Whitman. NYP

Thou wander'st in the Labyrinth of Life. De Rerum Natura. Lucretius (Titus Lucretitus Carus). OBVE

Thou war worn soul communing with thy God! To Borglum's Seated Statue of Abraham Lincoln. Charlotte B. Jordan. OHIP

Thou wast the Instrument! And thy huge limbs/Cover nine kingdoms as thou lie'st asleep. Lines on the Death of Bismarck. John Jay Chapman. PoEL 1-5

Thou waterful land. Farewell to Ireland. Saint Columcille. AWP; LiTW

Thou who art the Life, continue to live in us and love us. The Way; The Truth; The Life. Samuel Judson Porter. BLRP

Thou whose charms all art transcend! Madrono. Bret (Francis Bret Harte) Harte. AA

Thou, whose face at the fighting blanched,/Out of the battle I bring thee–rest. Comrades. Laurence Housman. HBV 1-2

Thou wilt abide with me,/And I with Thee! Abide with Us. Horatius Bonar. BePJ

Thou wilt accept my sheaves. Bringing Our Sheaves. Elizabeth Akers. HBV 1-2

Thou wilt avail me in the lonely end. In the Dark. Sophie Jewett. TrPWD

Thou wilt be my confidence! Ye Shall Live Also. Arthur Cleveland Coxe. BePJ

Thou wilt find a solace there. The Unfailing Friend. Joseph Scriven. BLRP

Thou wilt, God's holiest gift, thou woman pure,/Yet pray for me. To His Wife. Daniel Henry Deniehy. BoAV

Thou wilt not break thy heart, dear,/No more, I think, shall I! If. James Jeffrey Roche. HBV 1-2

Thou wilt not ever see her weep. On a Child. Walter Savage Landor. OBVV

Thou wilt not hear at all,/My dear, my dear. Dirge. Adelaide Crapsey. HBV 1-2

Thou wilt not love to live, unless thou live to love. Song: "Fond men! whose wretched care the life soon ending." Phineas Fletcher. ElL

Thou wilt peace around diffuse,/Gently as the evening dews. In the Morning I Will Pray. William Henry Furness. AH

Thou wilt perform unto the end the work thou hast begun. Light Shining Out of Darkness. Jane Borthwick. BLRP

Thou wilt sink to sleep on thy mother's breast. On the Picture of a "Child Tired of Play." Nathaniel Parker Willis. HBV 1-2

Thou wilt stand stark and dumb/At the first question asked. Te Judice. Frederick George Scott. PeCV

Thou wilt to us Thy word of promise keep. The Coming of the Lord. Jones Very. BePJ; MAmP

Thou wilt weep all thy life. Esthonian Bridal Song. Johann Gottfried von Herder. AWP

Thou winged bloom! thou blossom–butterfly! The Mariposa Lily. Ina Donna Coolbrith. AA; BPAW

Thou winnest the heart of thy laboring man. A Digression from Husbandrie: To a Poynt or Two of Huswifrie. Thomas Tusser. FaBoUs

Thou winnest the name, of a right husband man. A Hundreth Good Poyntes of Husbandry. Thomas Tusser. FaBoUs

Thou with the spring wouldst wander there. With Garments Flowing. John Clare. GBL

Thou wolt fursake me thrien ar the coc him crowe. Judas. Anonymous. ViBoFo

Thou wouldst be scorched and drowned again! A Fly about a Glass of Burnt Claret. Richard Lovelace. CaPo

Thou wouldst have pity on me this day. Medieval Norman Songs. Anonymous. AWP

Though a pauper, he's one whom his Maker yet owns. The Pauper's Drive. Thomas Noel. PaPo

Though aa his feres were fremmit men/wha cry: Owre late, owre late. The Makar. William Soutar. OxBS

(Though ain't no vision visited my cell). The Sun Came. Etheridge Knight. NeAC; PoBA

Though all of them were George. Which Washington. Eve Merriam. NTCP

Though art, and care, and cost/Do promise nature's help in vain. Albinovanus. Anonymous. FCP

Though as Jesukin he sits at my breast. Vision of Ita. Anonymous. AnIL

Though ash lay on the altar stone. Lines for the Ancient Scribes. Harvey Shapiro. VWA

Though ask'd, I know not how she would resist. Resolution in Four Sonnets. Charles Cotton. PoEL 1-5

Though at night there is the smell of morning. Neither Here Nor There. W. R. Rodgers. LiTB; LiTM; MoAB; MoBrPo; NeBP; ViBoPo

Though bare as rifted paradise. The Quest. James Wright. NYBP

Though big with art, they Cannot Overtopp/the spirits teaching in a Coblers Shopp. On How the Cobler. Anonymous. SCAP

Though black and bitter and unsavoury meat. The Hedgehog. John Clare. SeCeV

Though boots, though knife shall fail us, fear no death. My Head on My Shoulders. Jeremy Ingalls. GoYe

Though born in snow, it died in flame. On Burning a Dull Poem. Jonathan Swift. TW

Though but a cat lies buried here. Epitaph for a Cat. Margaret E. Bruner. PoLf

Though church-bells must have been its symbol then. Childhood Church. Pat Wilson. AnNZ

Though death is in the healing, it will heal. The Slip. Wendell Berry. NOCV

...Though dressed in metaphor,/abstract celebration's still a bore. Coming Down to It (parody). Malcolm Glass. BXAP

Though driftin's hard, plumb hard! Last Drift. Arthur Chapman. BPAW

Though dull and ancient, I still gleam,/like worn cloth, not like a woman's eyes. Now It Can Be Told. Philip Levine. VWA

Though dust return to dust/And all our striving vain. Nevertheless. Gustav Davidson. GoYe

Though dust to dust return, I think I'll scarcely mourn,/If I may change into green things growing. Green Things Growing. Dinah Maria Mulock Craik. FaFP; HBV 1-2; HBVV; OHIP

...Though each oblivious night/Shoulders aloft your golden epaulets. Admiral. John Alexander Allen. NYBP

...(Though each upset/makes me considerably more/concrete than I was before.) For the Poet Who Said Poets Are Struck by Lightning Only... Peter Klappert. NLV

Though Earth has rolled beneath her weight/The bones that cannot bear the light. Genesis. Geoffrey Hill. ACV; HAP; NePoEA; OAEL 1-2; OxBC

Though even now she is sleeping. The Stories in the Light. Michael Waters. GeTw

Though faded their glory as fadeth the flower of the grass! The Fancy. William Rose Benet. SD

Though far from these, and Irwan's vale! A Farewell Hymn to the Valley of Irwan. John Langhorne. CEP

Though far off it be. Spring Quiet. Christina Georgina Rossetti. BoNaP; CH; EG; GTBS-P; InPS; LoBV; PoEL 1-5

Though few can write, yet fewer can refrain. What Frenzy Has of Late Possess'd the Brain! Sir Samuel Garth. NLV

Though 50 years and more/have passed/dry-sapping this older tree. On Corwen Road. Jay Ames. AMV-80

Though flaming like a werewolf in the night. Wellfleet Harbor. Paul Goodman. CoAP

Though got by Beauty, kept by Love. La Belle Ennemie. Thomas Stanley. CavP

Though gravity-held,/I lie unselved. The Sun-Bather. Kim Kurt. NePoAm-2

...Though he flings/His soul to the winds that whirl his songs away. Sonnets to Miranda. William Watson. HBV 1-2

Though he is a servant he is a gentleman. Pet Crane. Anonymous. AnIL

Though he know 'twas our due, 'twould help to increase his store. The Sailor's Lamentation. Anonymous. OBSS

Though he should offer fifty fold. A New Song Called the Gaspee. Anonymous. PAH

Though he stand in the shambles of death. Wishmakers' Town. William Young. AA

Though he told me he never saw/the same one twice. The Other Side. Thomas Reiter. AMV-80

Though heaven and earth prove both to me untrue,/Yet am I still inviolate to you. Idea. Michael Drayton. EnRePo; PoEL 1-5

Though heaven and earth shall pass away! Dies Irae. Sir Walter Scott. GoBC

Though her lips are redder than the raspberries. Berry Picking. Irving Layton. NoP

...Though his face is also a map/of Israel, his eyes are tiny/dead seas. Approaching Washington Heights. James Reiss. NYP

Though his record be dark, is the man-eating shark/Who will eat neither woman nor child.　The Rhyme of the Chivalrous Shark.　Wallace Irwin. ShM

Though I am but clay and dust,/Yet thy grace can lift me high.　View Me, Lord, a Work of Thine.　Thomas Campion.　OxBoCh; TrPWD

Though I am doomed to endless flames.　Young People Who Delight in Sin. *Anonymous.*　AmFP

Though I am God–to see thee so submit!)　The Breaking.　Margaret Steele Anderson.　HBV 1-2

Though I am/no woman.　Death.　Sean O Riordain.　NOBI

Though I am theirs to kill.　For Masturbation.　Alan Dugan.　CAPP; NoAm

Though I be hers, she makes of me no treasure.　Arcadia.　Sir Philip Sidney. SiPS

Though I come to it with a broken head/In the cat-house of the dishevelled dead.　Dark Thoughts Are My Companions.　J. V. Cunningham.　TW

Though I consent like him to go on claws.　Colloquy with a King-Crab. John Peale Bishop.　LiTA; MoPo

"Though I die, I shall live; though I fall, I shall rise."　I Have Fought the Good Fight.　Jared B. Waterbury.　AH

Though I/do not know you.　The Gods.　Dennis Lee.　NOBC

Though I don't suppose/You'll believe it's true.　The Man from the Woods. John Ciardi.　SO

...Though I finally/realized those songs/were no longer my feelings.　Monday, Monday.　David Trinidad.　APU

Though I forget their name!　Arac's Song.　Sir William Schwenck Gilbert. FiBHP

Though I go loose, tied am I with a lune.　The World So Wide. *Anonymous.*　OxBM

Though I had one already and the other came.　The Evil Eye.　John Ciardi. AtBAP; MoBS; NAs

Though I'm a Weaver of low degree,/Ile teach them to read their A.B.C. Wil the Merry Weaver, and Charity the Chamber-Maid.　*Anonymous.* CoMu

Though I'm so old I scarce know what.　The Old Man's Complaint. *Anonymous.*　OBSP

Though I may but trail a verse/Languider than Lamartine's.　Bourbons. Walter Savage Landor.　OBSV

Though I must bear the blame/Because he bore my name.　Back.　Wilfred Wilson Gibson.　GTBS; TreFT

Though I sang in my chains like the sea.　Fern Hill.　Dylan Thomas. AtBAP; BiP; CMoP; CoBMV; DiPo; EvOK; FaBoPP; FaBV; FPL; GoJo; GTBS; HAP; HeIP; InPK; InPS; LiTB; LiTM; LoGBV; MasP; MoAB; MoBrPo; MoPo; MoVE; MP; NIP; NoAm; NOBE; NoP; OAEL 1-2; OAEP; OxBTC; PAI; PoLf; PoPl; PoRA; PPoe; PPP; RoGo; SoSe; TrGrPo; TwCP; ViBoPo; WeW

...Though I wonder what it means/to own my father's name.　The Desk. David Bottoms.　MAYP

Though in life I used to kiss her, now she's dead, I draw the line. Clementine.　*Anonymous.*　AmFP

Though in my life I never thought of death,/Death thought of me.　Epitaph on a Vagabond.　Alexander Gray.　HBMV

Though in pain cannot complain./No, no, no, no.　Song: "No, no, no, no, I cannot hate my foe."　Sir Philip Sidney.　SiPS

Though in rock rooted like an oleaster.　The Oleaster.　Robert Graves. OBTV

Though, indeed, neither started as a fish.　The P'eng That Was a K'un.　Lao Tse [or Lao Tzu].　AmMo

Though it be burning for evermore.　On the Death-Bed.　Thomas Hardy. BrPo

Though it be cold, hard, foul, from loving man/Withhold thee.　Sepulchre. George Herbert.　AnAnS 1

Though it be winter, I would break/Into spring blossoms white and blue. Impression de Paris.　Oscar Wilde.　SyP

Though it beat in a low-backed car!　The Low-Backed Car.　Samuel Lover. HBV 1-2

Though it crawl on the locks of a queen.　Addressed to a Gentleman at Table Who Kept Boasting...　Robert Burns.　DBV; PV

Though it may look like (Write it!) like disaster.　One Art.　Elizabeth Bishop.　HAP; SM; SoSe

Though it was he who foolishly proud/Started the quarrel with stupid words. Accusation.　Utahania.　WTO

Though it were ten thousand mile.　My Luve's Like a Red, Red Rose. Robert Burns.　BoLiVe; FaBoBe; FPL; GTBS-P; HoPM; PoSC; TrGrPo

Though justly we will serve our king,/We'll try a tug with Rome.　The Sentiments.　*Anonymous.*　APAS

Though life be dead, and my joys gone.　Silex Scintillans.　Henry Vaughan. AnAnS 1

Though light forsake thee, never fall/From fealty to light.　The Enthusiast. Herman Melville.　MAmP

Though love and all his pleasures are but toys,/They shorten tedious nights. Winter Nights.　Thomas Campion.　CBEP; NOBE; OBEV

Though love appears far off,/you will move into its depth.　Love has seven names.　Hadewijch.　BoWoP

(Though love be a day/and life be nothing, it shall not stop kissing).　Song: "Thy fingers make early flowers."　Edward Estlin Cummings.　MoAmPo

Though love be sweet, learn this of me/No love sweet but honesty. Philomela's Ode in Her Arbour.　Robert Greene.　OBSC

Though lyre's tamed to tintinnabulum.　Lyre.　Patrick White.　AMV-80

Though men by knowledge wiser grow,/Yet here 'tis wisdome not to know. To One That Desired to Know My Mistris.　Thomas Carew.　AnAnS 2; SeCP

Though mine own sepulchre can see/A paradise reserved for me.　Meditations on the Sepulchre in the Garden.　Philip Doddridge.　NOCV; NOEC

Though more than Hope can claim, could Friendship less require?　To Ianthe.　George Gordon, Lord Byron.　OBNC

Though my life thou drav'st away,/Maugre thee my love shall stay.　Marie Magdalen's Complaint at Christ's Death.　Robert Southwell.　AnAnS 1; MePo

Though my mother will stand in her doorway/and pass half an hour away. A Northern Spring.　Gene Baro.　NePoEA-2

Though never claimed by us within my hearing.　The Swimmers.　Allen Tate.　AP; MoAmPo; MoVE; NOBA; PAI

Though never, never can thyself, ah me, be mine!　Hopeless Love.　Sir Samuel Ferguson.　IrPN

Though no more than a hair/discovered in a gravy.　Old Road Song Poem. Artie Gold.　CaPN

Though not a Pallace, it will prove/the most wisht monument.　Constancye. Sidney Godolphin.　MePo

Though not so virtuous as the horse.　On a Horse and a Goat.　R. P. Lister. PV

Though nothing can bring back the hour/Of splendour in the grass, of glory in the flower;　Intimations of Immortality from Recollections of Early Childhood.　William Wordsworth.　ATP

Though nothing I touch can save me.　Flights.　Roger McDonald.　CBAP

Though now we muffle our souls/our very darkling selves ourselves　Winter's Dregs.　George Bowering.　PeCV

Though now you mourn, 't had lessened much your woe/Had Sorrel stumbled thirteen years ago.　The Mourners.　Bevil Higgons.　APAS

Though of course you may think what you wish.　The Concept of Force. Robert Sargent.　SUW

Though on the plains the winds of March blow wild.　March Winds.　Cecil Francis Lloyd.　CaP

Though once we lay and waited for a death.　Lines to Accompany Flowers for Eve.　Carolyn Kizer.　BoWoP

Though one lies still, the heart and mind can grow.　Quiet Days.　Mildred T. Mey.　PoToHe

(Though only if you feel you must)/begin your walk again....　Lady and Crocodile.　Charles Burgess.　NePoAm-2

Though others may perhaps forget,/I give my all to Thee.　In Memory of Two Sons.　Russell Stellwagon.　STF

Though our ancestors are dead we still remember/them.　Those Were the Days.　*Anonymous.*　WTO

Though pious but with meal and crackling salt.　To Phidyle.　Horace. AWP

Though poor and plain his diet,/Yet merry it is and quiet.　The Herdman. *Anonymous.*　NOBE; OBSC

Though proud once as Juno!　Going or Gone (parody).　Charles Lamb. BXAP

Though Ranzo was no sailor,/He's first mate of that whaler.　Reuben Ranzo. *Anonymous.*　FSW

Though ruffled once, would soon appear/The same as ever to the sight.　The Miller's Wife.　Edwin Arlington Robinson.　TAP

Though scarce this Spring could my body leap four yards.　Health.　Edward ("Edward Eastaway") Thomas.　SeCePo

Though Scipio should wait upon Cremorne.　Twelve O'Clock Boat.　J. A. R. McKellar.　BoAV

Though set like dough, they shall be drawn like bread.　Epitaph in Christ Church, Bristol, on Thomas Turner.　Francis, Lord Jeffrey Jeffrey. OxBoLi

...Though she left them behind/To seek for them suitable food.　The Bird's Nest.　Elizabeth Turner.　OHIP

Though she look at us forever, silent,/from out of the cave of her eyes.　This Child.　Norman Rosten.　TrJP

Though she sometimes gets angry like a nail.　Country Pastor.　Mitsuko Inoue.　LiTW

Though silent as your sandals, danced undone.　To Potapovitch.　Hart Crane.　UnS

Though silent your tongue, you can speak with your pen.　How to Write a Letter.　Elizabeth Turner.　MoShBr; OxBChV

Though some have complained of tenuity.　A Hawthorne Garland.　Richard Harter Fogle.　OBAL

...Though stall'd/In Somewhere, yet a piece of the Everywhere.　The Fools' Adventure: The Seeker.　Lascelles Abercrombie.　WGRP

Though still she kept the form and voice of Mentor. The Odyssey. Homer. NAWM 1-2

Though suddenly neglectful of one another. The Adventurers. John Thompson. PoAu 1-2

Though surrounded by care,/While possessing this blessing Divine. My Old Bible. *Anonymous.* BLRP; STF

Though th' error of my youth in them appeare,/Suffice, they shew I lov'd and lov'd thee deere. Let Others Sing of Knights and Palladines. Samuel Daniel. AAS

Though that was not what Berkeley meant at all. The Fountain. Donald Davie. GTBS-P; OxBTC

Though the alternate stars were there/To watch all history? The Ballad of Banners. John Lehmann. MoBS

Though the bird were long since slain,/though the song had died in the/ dark. Youth. Virginia Woodward Cloud. AA

Though the cage fret kings, you may make free with it. The Sparrow in the Zoo. Howard Nemerov. NoAm

Though the dead to our dead bid welcome, and we farewell. In Memory of "Barry Cornwall." Algernon Charles Swinburne. HBV 1-2

Though the feet halt and the heart ache. Dawn. John Masefield. BrPo

Though the gold of the dice has been lost. The Gold-Seekers. Hamlin Garland. AA; FaBoBe; MC; YaD

Though the shadows still linger behind. The Shepherd's Despair. Thomas Dermody. OnYI

Though the sun at Little Saling/Lies warm upon the leads. Little Saling. Olaf Baker. HBMV

Though the toil of Vainamoinen. Prayer for Rain. Kalevala. WGRP

Though the twigs crackling under a light foot/Declare her immanence. The Clearing. Robert Graves. NYBP

Though the way with fire be strewn. The Unknown. John Davidson. MoBrPo

Though the wintry winds reprove you,/And the snow is on the hill. To a Sparrow. Francis Ledwidge. HBMV

Though the world fall apart, surely ye shall/prevail. Carthusians. Ernest Christopher Dowson. VLP

Though the worst cold's to come. New Year's Song. Ted Hughes. OBCP; OFD

Though then I smile and speak no words at all. To His Lovely Mistresses. Robert Herrick. CaPo; CTC; OAEP; SeCP

Though there be nothing new beneath the sun. Monna Innominata. Christina Georgina Rossetti. VLP

Though there, forgotten and alone,/The Bard may draw his parting groan. The Lay of the Last Minstrel. Sir Walter Scott. EnRP; FaBoPP; OBRV

Though there was nowhere I had to go/and nothing I had to do Yesterday. William Stanley Merwin. FYAP

Though they could see, those other guys,/The guys who used white turnip filler. Consumer's Report. X. J. Kennedy. FiCP

...Though/they/Have long been dead, haunt now the world, is it we mean to/ say. The Fate of Narcissus. William Warner. OBSC

Though they're lords of the sea, we'll be/lords of the lakes. The Battle of Erie. *Anonymous.* PAH

Though they were not always the same A Weekday. Larry Eigner. CoPo

Though this might take me a little time. The More Loving One. W. H. Auden. HoPM

Though this was but a death among ruined stones/Of one who knew them with the intimacy of children. With a Posthumous Medal. John Malcolm Brinnin. SaC

Though thou art coveted by some,/Who're destined to be poor. The Blasted Herb. Mesech Weare. PAH

Though thou hast won to Paradise! In Paradise. Arlo Bates. AA

Though thou shalt drive me hence, I love thee so/That I shall watch thee when thou dost not know. Sonnets. Robert Hillyer. HBMV

Though time is the heart of music. The Enigma Variations. Paul Petrie. NYBP

Though top and tackel all be torne,/Yet I aloft the surge am bourne. The Pine to the Mariner. George Turberville. EtS

Though touching far from her true body,/make the loveliest of maps. Her True Body. Jerred Metz. VWA

...Though trees, you/write, have not had much to say to your work,/the happiness is pure. At Torrey Pines State Park. Jerome Mazzaro. FiCP

Though Venice proudly wears a robot/As a child a birthday watch. From a Venetian Sequence. Adele Naude. PeSA

Though waves climbed upward o'er her shining face. Martyr. Mary Elizabeth ("E") Fullerton. CBAP

Though we are broken, they are whole. Restricted. Miriam Waddington. CaP

Though we choose chocolate, will the world suspect/Genius undying? A Girtonian Funeral. *Anonymous.* FaBoCo; Par

Though we may thank him for the plough,/We'll not forget the sword! Tubal Cain. Charles Mackay. WBLP

Though we take separate pathways evermore. No Less Than Prisoners. Frederick T. Macartney. CBAP

Though what we can is but a lisp, we pray/Accept thereof. We have no better pay. Our Insufficiency to Praise God Suitably for His Mercy. Edward Taylor. LiTA

Though with no Lilie, stay with me! Cock-Crowing. Henry Vaughan. AtBAP; MePo; OAEL 1-2; PBBP; SeCV 1-2

Though with patience He stands waiting, with exactness/grinds He all. Retribution. Friedrich von Logau. BLPA; PoToHe

Though wrote with care, are wrote with ease. Letter from Smyrna to His Sisters at Crux-Easton, 1733. Thomas Lisle. OBTV

Though ye to me ne do no daliaunce. To Rosamond. Geoffrey Chaucer. CBEP; NoP

Though yet we do not know/Who called, or what marks we shall leave upon the snow. The Call. Charlotte Mew. ChMP

Though you've a-lost em, zunny woodlands. The Woodlands. William Barnes. BoNaP; OBVV

Though your pulseless clay may moulder/In the Forest of Argonne! On an American Soldier of Fortune Slain in France. Clinton Scollard. MC

Though your sleep be deeper/Than the depth of Night/Waken from your sleep! The Summons. W. W. Eustace Ross. CaP

Thought and reflection must begin again/To fit the image and to make it true. A Way of Looking. Elizabeth Jennings. NePoEA; PP

Thought Burbank, meditating on/Time's ruins, and the seven laws. Burbank with a Baedeker: Bleistein with a Cigar. Thomas Stearns Eliot. HBMV

A thought can glide through stone,/and steel, and iron chain. The Power of Thought. Von Trimberg Susskind. TrJP

Thought Clitheroe, with precision, as he poured. Professor Drinking Wine. Alasdair Clayre. PV

A thought had blossomed, and shaken/free/One sheath of its innermost soul for me. A Drifting Petal. Mary McNeil Fenollosa. AA

...Thought I knew I built it/And led you there./Was it you? Dream Sequence, Part 9. Naomi Long Madgett. BPo

Thought I on no gile. A Night with a Holy-Water Clerk. *Anonymous.* MeEL

Thought little of by those around,/But satisfying Thine Heart. An Intercessor. *Anonymous.* STF

Thought must length it in the heart. Are They Shadows That We See? Samuel Daniel. ATP; ElL; ExPo; InvP; LoBV; NoP; SeCeV

The thought o' Mary Mary Morison. Robert Burns. AnFE; BoLiVe; CEP; EG; GTBS; GTBS-P; HBV 1-2; InPo; MCCG; OAEP; OBEC; OBEV; OxBS; TreFT; TrGrPo; WHA

"A thought of Brougham."–/And that is Fame! J.B. Henry Cuyler Bunner. AA

The thought of my attempting such a stay! A Hillside Thaw. Robert Frost. CMoP; DiPo; ExPo

The thought of that same chariot, and the strange/Journey it went. Sleep and Poetry. John Keats. SeCePo

The thought of this curious mistake/Often kept him awake. The Younger Van Eyck. Edmund Clerihew Bentley. FiBHP

Thought on it, and filed suit for libel. Apocrypha. X. J. Kennedy. PV

Thought proper to reward my flame/With two black eyes! Rondeau: "By two black eyes my heart was won." *Anonymous.* FaBoCo

Thought, reason, sense, time, you, and I, maintaine. In Wonted Walks. Sir Philip Sidney. PoEL 1-5

Thought the little black-eyed rebel, with a/twinkle in her eye. The Litttle Black-Eyed Rebel. Will Carleton. PAH

The thought, the soul, the grief of you. Rondeau for You. Mario De Andrade. TTY

Thoughtless as Monarch Oakes that shade the plain,/And, spread in solemn state, supinely reign. MacFlecknoe. John Dryden. OBS

Thoughtless of Beauty, she was Beauty's Self,/Recluse amid the close-embowering Woods. Lavinia. James (1700-48) Thomson. OBEC

Thoughts, hopes, and love, return to me no more,/Till Cynthia shine as she hath done before. To Cynthia. George, Earl of Cumberland Clifford. OBSC

The thoughts may not have risen that so keep/This new-built city from both work and sleep. A Brook in the City. Robert Frost. OxBA

Thoughts of a dry brain in a dry season. Gerontion. Thomas Stearns Eliot. AP; APA; CMoP; CoBMV; DiPo; EBEV; ExPo; ForPo; GTBS-P; HAP; InPS; LiTA; LiTM; LoBV; MAPA; MoPo; NAMP; NePA; NoAm; NOBA; OAEL 1-2; OAEP; OxBA; PAI; PPP; SBVL; SeCePo; SeCeV; TAP

Thoughts that do often lie too deep for tears. Intimations of Immortality from Recollections of Early Childhood. William Wordsworth. ATP; BoLiVe

Thoughts that tongue can tell no word of! The Aeolian Harp. Herman Melville. AP; MAmP

The thoughts that we thought when young. Early Thoughts. William Edward Hartpole Lecky. OnYI

Thoughts that were once her own. In Wicklow. Rhoda Coghill. NeIP

Thoughts which, at last, shall lead/To some clear, firm assurance of a satisfying creed. The Beginnings of Faith. Sir Lewis Morris. WGRP

A thousand cranes curtain the window,/fly up in a sudden breeze. The Youngest Daughter. Cathy Song. MAYP

A thousand dreams of joy, or power,/Gone in the splendor of an hour. San Francisco Falling. Edwin Markham. BPAW

A thousand lines shall all be sung in four! A Quatrain. Frank Dempster Sherman. AA

A thousand tanagers will glow. The Scarlet Tanager. Mary Augusta Mason. AA

A thousand thanks then thou shalt have./Is the opinion of a false/Jacobite loon. A Jacobite Scot in Satire on England's Unparalleled Loss. *Anonymous.* APAS

A thousand thanks to GOD I paid,/That my sad Never was delay'd. Now. Thomas Ken. OxBoCh

A thousand times have we been crucified. The Jew to Jesus. Florence Kiper Frank. HBMV; TRV; WGRP

A thousand times I measured it! Allalu Mo Wauleen (The Beggar's Address to His Bag). *Anonymous.* AnIV

Thousand torments, thousand kisses.' Love's Arithmetic. Sir Edward Sherburne. CavP

...Thousands/and thousands of cars/driving men to work. Marin-An. Gary Snyder. TAT; WeW

Thousands have lived without love, not one without water. First Things First. W. H. Auden. NePoAm-2; NYBP

Thousands may enter through the gates of death. An Epistle to a Lady. Mary Leapor. NOEC

Thousands of new-born loves with your chaste eyes. An Anniversary on the Hymeneals of My Noble Kinsman, Thomas Stanley... Richard Lovelace. CaPo

Thousands of new selves/Rose joyously out of those deaths. Autumn Song. Stephen Stepanchev. FAZ

Thousands of years, thousands of years,/If all were told. A Faery Song. William Butler Yeats. ViBoPo

Thousands this glad night, ere turning bedward,/Will, with us, drink "Victory to Charles Edward!" Welcome to Prince of Ossory. James Clarence Mangan. IrPN

Thr-ree thr-reads in the thr-rum,/Pr-rrum! What the Gray Cat Sings. Arthur Guiterman. MoShBr

Thrashing back and forth, a swimmer/going under. Zoe and the Ghosts. Dieter Weslowski. PPJ

...The thread rose and floated/through the open window. The Tailor. Patricia Garfinkel. AMV-80

A thread to bind the heart of man! Eve-Song. Mary Gilmore. CBAP; PoAu 1-2

Threading dances light? Angel Spirits of Sleep. Robert Bridges. CH

Threading my dazzling way within my night. Too Much. Edwin Muir. LiTB

Threads of the flowerprints/coming loose from her sky of wool. The Child in the Rug. John Haines. DFF; GP

Thready moss grows on the high hill between us. Rhyming with a Friend. Yu Hsuan-chi. BoWoP

...Threatening eyes/When thou shalt to thy noon arise! To a Very Young Lady. Sir George Etherege. CEP; ViBoPo

Three a penny fire shovel,/Hot cross buns. Good Friday. *Anonymous.* OxNR

Three bowers of love/Won Christ from Heaven above. God's Mother. Laurence Housman. ISi

Three cheers for John,/Eating his bread and butter! The Birthday-Cake Glockenspiel. Elizabeth Henley. BiCB

"Three cheers for old Ireland,' says Master McGrath. A Ballad of Master McGrath. *Anonymous.* FaBoBa

Three cheers for the red, white and blue. The Red, White and Blue. David T. Shaw. WBLP

Three children stand around in silence. Repose. Alfred Lichtenstein. VWA

Three cyclists, like a school of delicate fish,/sway in your lights, darting home. Airwaves. Warren Woessner. TAT

Three days later he is transferred to another class. Change of School. Elizabeth Smither. OCNZ

Three dead men have I loved,/And thou art last of the three. In the Garden at Swainston. Alfred, Lord Tennyson. GoBC; OBEV; OBNC; OBVV; VLP

...Three dwarves in search/of tobacco. The Cook. Ray A. Young Bear. CDW

Three elements of recognition become new numbers. Poem: "I keep feeling all space as my image." Sanders Russell. EAS

3. Energy is Eternal Delight. The Marriage of Heaven and Hell. William Blake. NU

3/4 man and the Parthenon is crumblin' Judeebug's Country. Joe Johnson. PoBA

...Three frozen idols of a speechless muse. The Great Hunger. Patrick Kavanagh. IPY; MoAB

Three future lights defend me. Three Darks Come down Together. Robert Francis. LCAP

Three hundred able-bodied men are wanted on the Pelican drive. The Shanty Boys and the Pine. *Anonymous.* AmFP

Three in One confess thee. Ave Maris Stella. *Anonymous.* ISi

...Three jaguars are eating his entrails and he is/watching. Spring Drawing II. Robert Hass. MAYP

Three-legged stray? You're Sorry, Your Mother Is Crazy, & I'm a Chinese Shiksa. Deborah Lee. BrSi

The three of them went down the road/and never glanced behind. The Young Calves. Robert P. Tristram Coffin. TiPo

Three old ladies sat in a tree. The Three Ladies. Robert Creeley. NeAP

...Three pairs of eyes/on him. It's a Different Story When You're Going Into the Wind. David McFadden. NeAC

Three persons and one god. The Happy Man. Gilbert Keith Chesterton. EBCP

Three Persons in God likewise, and but the one God. To the Holy Trinity. *Anonymous.* NOBI

Three Persons in God; to one God alone we make prayer. Four Prayers, IV. *Anonymous.* OnYI

Three Persons in God, yet only one God is there. The Rann of the Three. *Anonymous.* CAW

Three roguish chaps fell into mishaps,/Because they could not sing. Old Colony Times. *Anonymous.* BLSo

Three scarcities that are better than abundance: a scarcity/of fancy talk, a scarcity of cows... The Triads of Ireland (excerpt). *Anonymous.* OxBI

Three seraphim watch three years through. Song: "Three little maidens they have slain." Maurice Maeterlinck. AWP

Three services, the worst that a man can serve: serving a bad/woman, a bad lord, and bad land. From the Triads of Ireland. *Anonymous.* OnYI

...Three syllables/rose from the corners of my skull. Axioms. Gad Hollander. VWA

Three times! four times! Then leave us now! Dead on the War Path. *Anonymous.* WTO

Three times he kissed her cold corpy lips,/And he fell in her arms asleep. Fair Margaret and Sweet William. *Anonymous.* AmFP

Three times I've named his name. Riddle: "There was a man rode through our town." *Anonymous.* OxNR

Three to make ready,/And four to go. One for Money. *Anonymous.* OxNR

Three wars later, as well as I can. Three Migrations. Ralph Salisbury. STE

Threepence on the railway—out goes she. Out Goes She. *Anonymous.* PoPle

Threescore summers, when they're gone,/Will appear as short as one! On a Fly Drinking out of His Cup. William Oldys. EG; FaFP; OBEV; TrGrPo; ViBoPo

Threshing the salt green sea. Sailors. Louis Simpson. NYBP

Threw in the sponge and was/Scraped off the tracks. The Russian Soul II. John Hollander. NLV

Threw the basin on the bricks. Mrs. Mason's Basin. *Anonymous.* OxNR

Threw them amongst the lilies there to fade. Upon a Gloomy Night. Roy Campbell. AtBAP; BoLoP; OBVE; PeSA

Threw up his arms, shivered, and fell and died. An Allegory. Barcroft Henry Boake. CBAP

Thrice blessed they who cleave until/Death do them part! To the Polyandrous Lydia. Franklin Pierce ("F.P.A.") Adams. HBMV

Thrice blest! in being seldom seen. To a Lady: With a Head of Diana. Thomas William Parsons AA

Thrice gladly will I turn away,/And bid these scenes adieu! Summer on the Great American Desert. Rufus B. Sage. BPAW; PoOW

Thrice happy they that leaving mandring wayes/Sloe duely walk to their Creator's praise. Time Tryeth Truth. *Anonymous.* SCAP

Thrice happy youth! thrice happy maid! Epithalamium. Johannes Secundus. HW

Thrice so merrily hopped she,/Heigh O, heigh O, heigh O! A Pie Sat on a Pear Tree. *Anonymous.* PBBP

Thrice sounded "Nineveh'. The Impious Feast. Robert Eyres Landor. OBRV

Thrice the age of a deer is that of an eagle. The Age of Animals. *Anonymous.* FaBoUs

Thrice-threefold walled with emerald from our mortal morn-/ings grey... The Mistress of Vision. Francis Thompson. CH

Thrice we bow to Thee alone. Hark, My Soul. John Austin. OxBoCh

The thrill of your gayest young years! Limerick: "The S & M bar, oh my dears." *Anonymous.* PeHV

The thrill that shook you at your child's/first cry. Memories. Thomas Bailey Aldrich. AA

Thrilled to the roots for very happiness. The Creek of the Four Graves (excerpt). Charles Harpur. CBAP; PoAu 1-2

Thrills every male groin while he swings there/and, helpless, spills the fire of his urine. The Picador Bit. Bink Noll. LiSp

Thriving in ill, as it in age decays. Virgidemiarum. Joseph Hall. OBSV

Thro' which the living Homer begg'd his bread.   A Cure for Poetry. *Anonymous.*   FaBoEE

Thro' your eternal or your finite day/Give us your prayers!   A Solis Ortus Cardine.   Ford Madox Ford.   ViBoPo

The throb of cilia with cilia.   Celia.   Ellen Bass.   NMM

...The throb/Of concrescence could give it no/thought.   Definition of the Soul.   Boris Pasternak.   TrJP

The throb of the unborn summer/Under her bare, brown breast.   March. Charles Henry ("John Paul") Webb.   AA

Throbbing, beneath the wound, the whole world's pain.   Cozzo Grillo.   H. B. Mallalieu.   WaP

Throbbing, the pulse, the divine heart of man.   Zola.   Edwin Arlington Robinson.   AmePo; MoVE; NePA; OxBA

Throbbing through you, and sobbing, unsubdued.   Song of Songs.   Wilfred Owen.   NAMP

Throbs the dissolving call/of the beachball players.   The Skin Divers. George Starbuck.   NYBP

The throe of Second Manassas Share.   The March into Virginia.   Herman Melville.   AmP; AP; BLPL; HAP; LiTA; NoP; TAP; TrGrPo; ViBoPo; WaaP

The throne is now vacant, and no one can tell/The name of the next, so I'll bid you farewell.   Kings of France.   Mary W. Lincoln.   BLPA

Throned in my heart I see thee still.   A Remembrance.   Willis Gaylord Clarke   AA

Thrones of the continents! Isles of the sea!   Welcome to the Nations.   Oliver Wendell Holmes.   PAH

The throng go crowned with blue.   November Blue.   Alice Meynell. MoBrPo

Throng the brief word. The maelstrom has us all.   Watch Long Enough, and You Will See.   Conrad Aiken.   CMoP; NePA

...Thronging in the/membrane of a scuffy space.   Muscae Volitantes.   Lewis B. Horne.   HoAn

Through a confession of the Oneness/Of the Creator of creation.   The Deer's Cry.   Saint Patrick.   AnIL; CAW; WGRP

Through a second youth of a hundred years.   Dorothy Q.   Oliver Wendell Holmes   AA; AnNE; AP; HBV 1-2; InMe; NOBA; TreFS

Through a world politely turning/From the loutishness of learning.   Gnome. Samuel Beckett.   BlrV; OBSP

Through aeons it remains as right/As birth and dying are.   The Starfish. Robert P. Tristram Coffin.   ImOP

Through all eternity–NOW!   God Is in Every Tomorrow.   Laura A. Barter Snow.   BLRP; STF

Through all eternity,/Something for Thee.   Something for Jesus.   Sylvanus D. Phelps.   BLRP

Through all my wounds to thee I cry!   Thou Who Createdst Everything. *Anonymous.*   NOCV

Through all our absences the long tide surges.   North of Berwick.   Sydney Tremayne.   BSV

Through all the circles seven come,/To fetch the Torah down!   The Angels Came A-Mustering.   Israel Zangwill.   EaLo

Through all the coiling passages of/(Curled ear) my prison!   The Dark Morning.   Thomas Merton.   PoA

Through all the darkness, unto the dawning,/To his beloved he giveth sleep. A Prayer for Peace.   Edward Rowland Sill.   TrPWD

Through all the days Thy name we raise/Who made our nation great. America Prays.   Arthur Gordon Field.   PGD

Through all the universal frame.   Ye Realms Below the Skies.   Hosea Ballou II.   AH

Through all the years,/Immutable stands this event.   Autumn Burial: A Meditation.   Charles Gullans.   QFR

Through battle climbed to battle, free/To grapple God up there.   Life's Testament.   William Baylebridge.   PoAu 1-2

Through blurred and glazing eyes to see/A Female Figure with a Child. Ballade of Illegal Ornaments.   Hilaire Belloc.   ACP

Through Calvary's clouds they seek the light that led Him to the/dawn. From Bethlehem to Calvary.   Meredith Nicholson.   PGD

Through Christ, the Way–the Truth–the Life.   The Pilgrim.   Emma Catharine Embury.   OBCA

Through clouds of fleecy white, laughs the coerulean sky.   Imitation of Spenser.   John Keats.   ATP

Through clumped stars dangling all the way.   Presence of an External Master of Knowledge.   Wallace Stevens.   NePA

Through crowds of almost-men and almost women/Howl for their lost immediacy.   The Wedding.   Robert Graves.   HW

Through crystal prisms in a falling rain.   Psittachus Eois Imitatrix Ales Ab Indis.   Sacheverell Sitwell.   AtBAP; MoBrPo

Through darkness/of the bald horn of the moon.   Wart Hog.   Robin Skelton.   NOBC

Through dusty Time its beauty shall make plain/Man, and, Without, a spirit scattering grain.   Drop Me the Seed.   John Masefield.   MoRP

Through each rent wall their feeble works in-/vade/Once shamed all such in power of pier and/groin.   Rome.   Thomas Hardy.   VLP

Through earth and heaven exalted be,/Beloved, obey'd, adored.   Our Ever-Present Guide.   *Anonymous.*   BePJ

Through endless fields of changeless peace.   The Capitals Are Rocked. Nikolai Nekrasov.   AWP

Through Father, Son, and Holy Ghost/And Christ Eternity.]   The Joys of Mary.   *Anonymous.*   AmFP

Through fits of thought or raptures of disease.   Sonnet against the Too-Facile Mystic.   Elizabeth B. Harrod.   NePoEA

Through force or fraud, look westward to your child!   To England.   George Henry Boker.   AnAmPo; HBV 1-2

Through frost and snow, when winds do blow,/To carry the milking-payl. The Innocent Country-Maid's Delight.   *Anonymous.*   CoMu

Through hate we come to love,/No other means is known.   For One Who Would Not Take His Life in His Hands.   Delmore Schwartz.   NAMP

Through heaven, the very spheres,/As men, turn all to ears.   A Canticle to Apollo.   Robert Herrick.   CaPo

Through her holy truth/she goes about.   Puberty Rite Dance Song. *Anonymous.*   BoWoP

Through her I weep, at her I smile.   Whereat Erewhile I Wept, I Laugh. Robert Greene.   ElL

Through high still air.   Mid-August at Sourdough Mountain Lookout.   Gary Snyder.   HAP; MAT; NaP; NCSH; NoP; TAP

Through hornleaved holly.   Description of Elysium.   James Agee.   CrMA

Through it I see the days ahead open/like a path to a sepulchre.   Absence. Elizabeth Knies.   GOYP

Through its deep night, that kindled as he/fell.   Ode to England.   William Wilberforce Lord   AA

Through Jesus Christ our Lord. Amen.   Until the Shadows Lengthen.   John Henry, Cardinal Newman.   TRV

Through leafy lights I see a nymph's face beam,/Which fades not when in daylight dies my dream.   Sonnets, VI: "Awakened, I behold through dewy leaves."   Thomas Caulfield Irwin.   IrPN

Through life and death, a chainless soul,/With courage to endure!   The Old Stoic.   Emily Bronte.   EnLi 1-2; EnLit; FaPoR; FPL; GoTF; NOBE; OAEP; OBEV; OBNC; OBVV; OxBI; PoLf; PoPl; TreFT; TrGrPo; ViBoPo

Through life I have heard you, in death I shall hear.   Chamonix.   George Hookham.   OBVV

Through life, in death, eternally,/Thou art my All.   Jesus, My Saviour, Look on Me!   John MacDuff.   BePJ

Through life, through death, beyond the sun,/On heaven's eternal shore. Satisfied.   Edgar Cooper Mason.   BLRP

Through marble pastures overflow/And do not run to waste.   On a Bas-Relief.   Wesley Trimpi.   NePoEA

Through miles of glass and cloud, I thought of you.   England.   Mary Jo Salter.   AMV-80

Through open window like a voice/You love says let's dance.   In Like a Lion.   Geof Hewitt.   PPJ

Through Peter the Flame,/Peter the Rock.   Father Malloy.   Edgar Lee Masters.   OxBA

Through rafters,/roof, belfry/and beyond.   For Wilma.   Don Johnson.   GOYP

Through scepters create emotional resist.   Essence.   Samuel Greenberg. MoPo; NePA

Through sin, at least, thine Eden is not lost.   Baby.   Elaine Goodale Eastman.   AA

Through slippery space, and past the floating stars.   Bathtubs.   Richmond Lattimore.   NYBP

Through so many different countries...   Little Political Poem.   Edward Hirsch.   AMV-81

Through some closed corner of my heart,/Should laugh to find you there. The Wife.   Theodosia Garrison.   HBV 1-2

Through steel it breath'd, and blew as it would burst.   The Odyssey. Homer.   EnLi 1-2

Through such snow falling, and so far from help.   Variations on a Theme by Sidney Keyes.   Eithne Wilkins.   NeBP

Through the backs of things lost.   Morning.   Alberto Rios.   MAYP

Through the bending twigs of the coral/grove.   The Coral Grove.   James Gates Percival.   AA; AnNE; EtS; GN

Through the bright, busy, and eternal day.   Paradisi Gloria.   Thomas William Parsons   AA

Through the cambered flesh of clover and wild carrot.   The Flitting.   Mebdh McGuckian.   FaBoIP

Through the dark stony desert.   Hitch Haiku.   Gary Snyder.   LCAP

Through the day and time and war and history.   The Wayside Station. Edwin Muir.   FaBoTw; MoVE

...Through the dazzling/lives of the planets and stars. I am. sings.   Planetary Exchange.   LeRoi (Imamu Amiri Baraka) Jones.   CAPP

Through the deep litter of the years.   River Road.   Stanley Jasspon Kunitz. NoAm

Through the dry leaves of last autumn.   At Night.   Bella Akhmadulina. BoWoP

Thus am I Beauties bounden thrall,/At hir commaunde when shee doth call./ Ever or never   The Arraignment of a Lover.   George Gascoigne.   AAS

Thus am I still provoked to every evil,/By this good-wicked Spirit, sweet Angel-Devil.   Idea.   Michael Drayton.   HBV 1-2; OAEP

–Thus answered Johnny in his glory,/And that was all his travel's story.   The Idiot Boy.   William Wordsworth.   OBNV

Thus are all dreams made true/Ever to last!   Dream-Pedlary.   Thomas Lovell Beddoes.   AnFE; EnRP; HAP; LiTB; LoBV; NOBE; OBNC; OBRV; PoEL 1-5; TrGrPo; ViBoPo; WiR

Thus, at least, its mouldering corpse will nourish/That from which it sprung– Eternity.   Death.   Emily Bronte.   OBNC; VLP

Thus at the height we love and live,/And fear not to be poor.   Fair Iris and Her Swain.   John Dryden.   ViBoPo

Thus blest, I scarce one thought should cast away/On heav'n's eternal happiness, or you!   The Rapture.   Sir Henry William Baker.   NOEC

Thus brought from wealth, alas, to endless pain,/That undeserved, causeless to remain.   The Joy So Short Alas, the Pain So Near.   Sir Thomas Wyatt. SiPS

Thus by design or chance did he/Drop anchors to posterity.   A Hint from Herrick.   Thomas Bailey Aldrich.   HBV 1-2

Thus chamber'd here, may not kings envy me?   Night on the Prairie.   Rufus B. Sage.   PoOW

Thus could I sing & thus rejoice: but it is not so/with me.'   The Four Zoas. William Blake.   EnRP; OAEL 1-2; Prf

Thus Death made way for Liberty!   Make Way for Liberty.   James Montgomery.   TreFS

Thus departed Hiawatha.   Hiawatha's Photographing.   Lewis (Charles Lutwidge Dodgson) Carroll.   CenHV; FaBoCo; FiBHP; NOBL

Thus did the battle vary to and fro...   The Faerie Queene.   Edmund Spenser. HoPM

Thus did this ancient poet look.   The Description of Sir Geoffrey Chaucer. Robert Greene.   AnFE; CTC; OBSC

Thus dividing the part which loved/from the mind not worthy.   The Poor Shammes of Berditchev.   Rochelle Ratner.   VWA

Thus do I wilfully increase my load.   All This Sunday Long.   B. S. Johnson. ELU

Thus doth she traine and teach me with her lookes,/Such art of eyes I never read in bookes.   Amoretti, XXI.   Edmund Spenser.   AAS

Thus down the tide of Time shall flow/My dreams forevermore.   It's a Long Way.   William Stanley Braithwaite.   GoSl

Thus Earth from flames and Ice repreev'd,/E're since hath in her Sun-shine liv'd.   Lucasta's World.   Richard Lovelace.   CaPo; SeCP

Thus, either Time his sickle brings/In vain, or else in vain his wings. Persuasions to Enjoy.   Thomas Carew.   CaPo; HBV 1-2; MePo; NOBE; SeCP; SeCV 1-2

Thus ended at length a most delicate chase,/That held us five hours and ten minutes' space.   The Kilruddery Hunt.   Thomas Mozeen.   BIrV

Thus ended his career in the violent jaws of death.   Charles Gustavus Anderson (II).   Anonymous.   ShS

Thus ended the fight, and with mickle/delight/To Sherwood they hasted away. Robin Hood and the Scotchman.   Anonymous.   ESPB

Thus ended they their Song, and off th'assembly brake.   Poly-Olbion. Michael Drayton.   AtBAP

Thus endeth been these homicides two,/And eek the false empoisoner also. Death and the Three Revellers.   Geoffrey Chaucer.   OBNV

Thus endeth the song of great sweettness,/Veni, coronaberis.   Neni, Coronaberis.   Anonymous.   BoW

Thus ends the First part of the Ballad of DOWN./Derry down, down, hey derry down.   Down-Hall.   Matthew Prior.   CEP

Thus ends this sad and tragic tale. And Mark? He keeps on/singing.   Tristan and Isolda.   Newman Levy.   InMe

Thus even by Rivals to be Deifide.   Obsequies to the Lady Anne Hay. Thomas Carew.   AnAnS 2

Thus far was right, the rest belongs to heav'n.   An Epistle from Mr. Pope to Dr. Arbuthnot.   Alexander Pope.   NOEC

Thus far was right, the rest belongs to Heaven.   The Maimed Debauchee. Alexander Pope.   CABA

Thus fareth many and many an one.   The Complaint of the Fair Armoress. Francois Villon.   AWP; CTC; OBVE; UnTE; VLP

Thus fools and bravoes kindred pranks pursue;/As savage quite, and oft as fatal too.   The Farmer's Boy.   Robert Bloomfield.   PBBP

Thus for her sake/To be undone!   With Serving Still.   Sir Thomas Wyatt. EG; ElL; FCP; InPK; LoBV; SiPS; WHA

Thus, from the Night, Dawn's sunlit beauty/breaks.   Laura Sleeping.   Louise Chandler Moulton.   AA

Thus frozen shall we ever stay/Locked in this paradise.   Boy in Ice.   Laurie Lee.   NYBP

Thus God and Nature link'd the gen'ral frame,/And bade Self-love and Social be the same.   An Essay on Man.   Alexander Pope.   CEP; MBW 1-2

Thus graciously the war I wage,/As witnesseth my hand,–TOM GAGE. Tom Gage's Proclamation...   Anonymous.   PAH

Thus grant my suit, as grant unhurt you may,/Your chaplain, and without your groats, shall pray!   A Sea-Chaplain's Petition.   J. T.   NOEC

Thus great Pan is ever sung.   The Faithful Shepherdess.   John Fletcher. TrGrPo

Thus hath his death raised up this soul of mine.   Sonnet XCIX.   Fulke, Lord Brooke Greville.   QFR

Thus have I achieved...a permanently bad reputation.   The Complaint of Tarpeia's Door.   Sextus Propertius.   LiTW

Thus have I gained.   Caelica, VI.   Fulke, Lord Brooke Greville.   FCP

Thus have I had thee as a dream doth flatter,/In sleep, a king; but waking, no such matter.   Sonnets, LXXXVII: "Farewell! thou art too dear for my possessing."   William Shakespeare.   EBEV; GTBS; GTBS-P; InPS; InvP; LiTB; MasP; NOBE; OAEL 1-2; OAEP; OBEV; OBSC; PAI; PeHV; PoEL 1-5; QFR; TrGrPo; ViBoPo

Thus have I made the woman of my dream.   Dawn of Womanhood.   Harold Monro.   HBV 1-2

Thus have we heard.   Smokey the Bear Sutra.   Anonymous.   MAT

Thus having been, that thou shouldst cease to be.   To Wordsworth.   Percy Bysshe Shelley.   EnRP; ERoP 1-2; FiP; MCCG; NoP

Thus having said, the vision disappears,/Leaving the trembling princess drowned in tears.   The Duchess of York's Ghost.   Anonymous.   APAS

Thus he may to that land win.   The Land of Cockayne.   Anonymous. MeEV

Thus Hiamovi, out of a tarnished and weatherworn heart/of old gold, out of a living dawn gold.   All One People.   Carl Sandburg.   AmFN

Thus I bewaill my faitis repugnant,/Inconstant warld and qwheill contrarious. The Palace of Honor.   Gavin Douglas.   PoEL 1-5

Thus I end my evenings knell.   The Faithful Shepherdess.   John Fletcher. OBS

Thus I have written this poem on a jet seat in mid Heaven.   Kral Majales. Allen Ginsberg.   GP; PoM

Thus I live like a war invalid/with sensations of shot-off fingers.   The Miracle.   Chaim Grade.   VWA

Thus I repay the royal debt I owe,/And cover up the footprints in the snow. Tales of a Wayside Inn.   Henry Wadsworth Longfellow.   AmPP

Thus I revenge me, that as thou/Hast played on them, I've played on you. The Cat and the Lute.   Thomas Master.   PCat

Thus I sleep well.   An Epitaph.   Lady Margaret Sackville.   HBMV

Thus I was saved   Cities and Seas.   Norman Jordan.   PoNe

Thus in a moment to see lost and drown'd/So great riches as like cannot be found!   Visions.   Petrarch.   EnLi 1-2

Thus in my Love Time calls me to relate/My tedious Travells and oft-varying Fate.   Like an Adventurous Sea-Farer Am I.   Michael Drayton.   EtS; MOS

Thus is He here!   Faust: Easter Chorus.   Goethe.   WGRP

Thus it is that the harp in the green window/Day by day is covered deeper with dust.   The Harper of Chao.   Po Chu-i.   UnS

Thus leaving him, I with the consul bode,/Full forty days, or I went thence abroad.   Still This, Still That I Would!   William Lithgow.   OBTV

Thus long to endure/Till that we meet again.   To His Lady.   King of England Henry VIII.   CTC; EBEV; OBSC

Thus making the precursor of his own impious actions.   Epigram on Marcus the Gnostic.   Saint Pothinus.   CAW

Thus making up in usefulness/For what he lacks in taste.   Vulture.   X. J. Kennedy.   GrPl

Thus may our meekness make her great,/Worthy in Freedom's eyes.   My Country, Right!   Thomas Curtis Clark.   PGD

Thus may'st thou ever, evermore rejoice!   Dejection.   Samuel Taylor Coleridge.   AnEnPo; CBEP; EnRP; ERoP 1-2; FiP; ForPo; HBV 1-2; LiTB; LoBV; MasP; MBW 1-2; NAWM 1-2; NOBE; NoP; OAEL 1-2; OAEP; OBNC; OBRV; PoEL 1-5; PPP

Thus men forgot that All deities reside in the human breast.   The Marriage of Heaven and Hell.   William Blake.   LAuP

Thus mirrors heaven's counterpart–your face.   Chameleon.   Gordon LeClaire.   EtS

–Thus much more/Than I loved thee, love, before.   Since We Parted. Edward Robert Bulwer, Earl of Lytton.   HBV 1-2

Thus my lips indite/Great sweetnesses/In the wheat of our morning. Pharaoh and Joseph.   Else Lasker-Schüler.   VWA

Thus Natura works, you see/Sometimes by Antipathy.   If Thou Wouldest Roses Scent.   Francis Daniel Pastorius.   SCAP

Thus nature's refuse, and the dregs of men,/Compose the black militia of the pen.   Epistles to Mr. Pope (excerpt).   Edward Hilton Young.   OBSV

Thus of the whole Sex, all I would desire,/Is to enjoy their Ashes, or their Fire.   Women.   William Cartwright.   ELU; ErPo

Thus on its sounding anvil shaped/Each burning deed and thought.   The Village Blacksmith.   Henry Wadsworth Longfellow.   AA; AmePo; AnNE; BLPL; FaBoBe; FaFP; FaPoR; GoTF; HBV 1-2; HBVY; OBAL; OBCA; PaPo; PoPl; TreF; WBLP

Thus Poets like to Kings (by trust deceiv'd)/Give oftner what is heard of, than receiv'd.   For the Lady Olivia Porter; a Present upon a New-years Day. Sir William Davenant.   JCP; MeLP; MePo; OBS

Thus poor thieves suffer, when the greater 'scape. If He from Heaven That Filched the Living Fire. Michael Drayton. TEP

Thus praise and prayer here beneath the sun/Make lesser mornings, when the great are done. To a Bird after a Storm. Henry Vaughan. TRV

Thus preserving the face from congealing. Limerick: "No matter how grouchy you're feeling." Anthony Euwer. HBMV; LiBL

Thus profit is the guerdon of his pain. The Bee. Charles Fitzgeffrey. EIL

Thus providence did kindness show/When we was so surrounded. The Caesar's Victory. Anonymous. OBSS

Thus reason shows: by my own sword I'm slain. The Scales of Love. Hartmann von Aue. LiTW

Thus Rome and Myra acting many parts,/By often changes lost commanding arts. Caelica, XXX. Fulke, Lord Brooke Greville. FCP

Thus said, and made the slain a martial/grave. Mohammed and Seid. Harrison Smith Morris. AA

Thus sang a king and queen in Babylon. A Duet. Thomas Sturge Moore. OBEV; OBVV

Thus saving the price of a bugle. Limerick: "A bugler named Douglas MacDougal." Ogden Nash. NePA

Thus saying to our Savior; this saw I in my syght. Quid Petis, O Fily? Anonymous. SeCeV

Thus self-love, nursing up the pomp of pride,/Makes beauty wrack against an ebbing tide. Verses under a Peacock Portrayed in Her Left Hand. Robert Greene. PBBP

Thus shall I use me. Pastime. King of England Henry VIII. CTC; EBEV; OBSC

Thus shall my thanks be thanks indeed. Because of Thy Great Bounty. Grace Noll Crowell. TrPWD

Thus shall our wills from hour to hour/Become not ours, but thine. The Thoughts That Move the Heart of Man. Ebenezer S. Oakley. TrPWD

Thus she mourned, and the women wailed in answer. The Iliad. Homer. OBWP

Thus she received from Celia's eye/Funeral flame, tomb, obsequy. A Fly That Flew into My Mistress's Eye. Thomas Carew. CaPo

Thus she said, when she sang last:/"Assay a frend or thou have nede." Assay a Friend. Anonymous. OxBM

–Thus sighed to Jesus the Bethanian fair,/His tear-wet feet still drying with her hair. On Mary Magdalen. William, of Hawthornden Drummond. OAEL 1-2

Thus, sighing, look through the waves of time/For the long-faded glories they cover. Let Erin Remember the Days of Old. Thomas Moore. EnRP

Thus singing, through the air the angels swam,/And cope of stars re-echoed the same. The Angels for the Nativity of Our Lord. William, of Hawthornden Drummond. OxBoCh

Thus speak the slain. Thus Speak the Slain. Carl Holliday. PGD

Thus spent, the joys of new year on earth/can ne'er be told. Forget. Anonymous. STF

Thus still needy dyes/Th' unknowne multitude. Raving Warre, Begot. Thomas Campion. AAS

Thus still the poore man hath the better part. Of True Liberty. Sir John Beaumont. OBS

...Thus subject/to death unknown by heart attack in time. Prayer for Boom. Robert Grenier. APU

Thus the damsel spake and died. The Minstrel's Song. Thomas Chatterton. LoBV

Thus the dark descends/On our means become our ends. A Man-Made World. Stephen Spender. MoRP

Thus the exile lover remembers thee, Makhir Subatu! The Syrian Lover in Exile Remembers Thee, Light of My Land. Ajan Syrian. LiTL

Thus the images/of these four/are engraved/upon me. The Four of Them. Yehuda Karni. VWA

Thus the ride of sin. The Black Riders. Stephen Crane. AA

Thus the shepherd; then throwing his crook away steals/Direct to St. James's and takes up the Seals. The Fire Side. A Pastoral Soliloquy. Isaac Hawkins Browne. NOEC; OBEC

Thus the tale ended. A Skeleton in Armor. Henry Wadsworth Longfellow AA; AmePo; AnNE; AP; AWP; BeLS; BLPL; FaBoBe; HBV 1-2; HBVY; MaC; MCCG; PAH; TreF

...Thus the vast array/Of those fraternal bands were reconciled that day. The Revolt of Islam. Percy Bysshe Shelley. OBWP

Thus the word assumed strange significance. Succumbing. Paul Eaton Reeve. ErPo

Thus think, then drink Tobacco. A Religious Use of Taking Tobacco. Robert Wisdome. EIL; HBV 1-2; OBS

Thus, though we cannot make our Sun/Stand still, yet we will make him run. To His Coy Mistress. Andrew Marvell. AnAnS 1; AtBAP; ATP; AWP; BiP; BoLoP; DiPo; EBEV; ELP; EnLoPo; ExPo; FaBV; FaFP; FF; ForPo; FPL; GBL; GoTF; HAP; HBV 1-2; HeIP; HoPM; InPo; InPS; InvP; JCP; LiTB; LiTL; LoBV; MasP; MAT; MeLP; MePo; NIP; NOBE; NoP; OAEL 1-2; OAEP; OBEV; OBS; PAI; PoEL 1-5; PoLf; PoPl; PoPle; PoRA; PPoe; PPP; PrIm; SCV; SeCePo; SeCeV; SeCP; SeCV 1-2; SoSe; TEP; TreFT; TrGrPo; UnPo; UnTE; ViBoPo; WeW; WHA

Thus thousands to religion are brought o'er,/And made worse devils than they were before. Reformation of Manners. Daniel Defoe. NOEC

Thus, thus the Calf's-Head-Club shall sing,/Leviathan, our god and king. Leviathan. Anonymous. APAS

Thus to sing, and thus to love! Christ the Lord Is Risen Today. Charles Wesley. BePJ

Thus to undergo less torment I agree/to go on living in this martyrdom. If I Could Believe That Death. Gaspara Stampa. PBWP

Thus, truth equals beauty; that's proved. Q.E.D. Ode on a Grecian Urn (parody). E. O. Parrott. BXAP

Thus vicious and thus patient, sits him down/To the black job of burking London Town? London Voluntaries. William Ernest Henley. BrPo; VLP

Thus was Corinth lost and won! The Siege of Corinth. George Gordon, Lord Byron. GoTL

Thus was faith and firme love showne,/As behoves/shepheards loves. Doron's Jigge. Robert Greene. PoEL 1-5

Thus was the hountynge of the Chivyat:/God send vs alle good endyng! The Hunting of the Cheviot (A version). Anonymous. BaBo; ESPB

Thus we both shall have our ends,/And continue special friends. Daphne. Jonathan Swift. NOBL

Thus we drink and dance away,/This glorious INDEPENDENCE DAY! Independence Day. Royall Tyler. PAH

Thus we pass our weary days/And our sleepless nights. Waiting for Death. Mordecai Gebirtig. TrJP

Thus we will all the World excel/In Loving, and in Parting well. Song: "Phillis, let's shun the common Fate." Sir Charles Sedley. SeCV 1-2

Thus without death how sweet it is to die. Come, Gentle Sleep, Death's Image Though Thou Art. Thomas, Marquess of Wharton. OBVE

Thus your fancies fall. The Hour Glass. Edward Quillinan. OBRV

Thutmose, living forever. Hymn of Victory: Thutmose III. Amon-Re. WaaP

Thy arrows quiver, and thy relics shine. Love's Franciscan. Henry Constable. ACP; GoBC

Thy axe shall harm it not. Woodman, Spare That Tree. George Pope Morris. AA; BLPA; BLSo; FaBoBe; FaFP; FPL; FSW; HBV 1-2; OHIP; PaPo; PSoN; TreF; WBLP

"Thy banish'd peace, thy laurels torn." The Tears of Scotland Written in the Year MDCCXLVI. Tobias Smollett. CEP

Thy banners make tyranny tremble,/When borne by the red, white and blue. Columbia the Gem of the Ocean. Thomas a Becket. FSW

Thy beauties glow with full delight. To Amanda. James (1700-48) Thomson. BSV

Thy being's being is contradiction. Human Life: On the Denial of Immortality. Samuel Taylor Coleridge. ChRP

Thy birth has with his blude/Fra fall mortall, originall,/Us raunsound on the rude. Ane Ballat of Our Lady. William Dunbar. EBEV; OxBS

Thy blessed promise, "I am with you always,"/Is ever faithful, O Immanuel! We Long to See Jesus. Anna E. Hamilton. BePJ

Thy blood that streameth for ever and ever/For the sake of us men was shed. Thou Great God. Anonymous. PBA

Thy bloode the Inke, and with compassion/Write thus upon my soule: thy Jesu still. Upon the Ensignes of Christes Crucifyinge. William Alabaster. MePo

Thy blossoms sleeping, tearful sown,/To greet thee in the immortal year! Take Heart. Edna Dean Proctor. HBV 1-2

Thy body and Thy precious blood. Body of Jesus. Arthur Cleveland Coxe. BePJ

Thy bond regard, let sin be veil'd from/Thee. Lo! As the Potter Mouldeth. Anonymous. TrJP

Thy bosom to a thousand cares divide. The Fleece. John Dyer. PoEL 1-5

Thy bottle make my soul, Lord, it to hold. Meditations. Edward Taylor. LiTA

Thy bowels thou dost spin,/I spin my brains. To a Spider. Robert Southey. FM

Thy breasts, thy hands, thy hair upcurled,/and my desire! Crimson Nor Yellow Roses. Theodore Wratislaw. GBL

Thy breathing-space and full translucent air. Paul Veronese. Sir Samuel Ferguson. IrPN

Thy brothr shall rise from his sleep in might. The Lament for Urien. Ernest Rhys. OBMV

Thy brow-garland pushed all aslant/Tells–but I tell not, wanton May! A May Burden. Francis Thompson. HBV 1-2

Thy bursting seed is the act of God. The Psalm of St. Priapus. James Richard Broughton. ErPo

Thy cage shall be made of handbeaten gold,/Thy door of the finest ivory. Pretty Polly (with music). Anonymous. AS

Thy Celia shall receive those charms/With open ears, and with unfolded arms. Boldness in Love. Thomas Carew. AnAnS 2; CaPo; ErPo; MePo; SeCV 1-2; UnTE

Thy chariot drive, winged with ambitious fire,/O'er the dead body of thy mangled sire. The Female Parricide. Anonymous. APAS

Thy circumfused rapture much more then/Must move to love us softer-moulded men. Music. Robert Herrick. CaPo

Thy compassion be on us! The Sea! O the Sea! *Anonymous.* WTO

Thy consort Dear/Mourning, Thee follow'th near,/To bid farewel. A Poem upon the Triumphant Translation of a Mother in Our Israel. John Danford. SCAP

Thy constant flow of love, that knew no fall.... Lines on Receiving His Mother's Picture. William Cowper. CH; OHIP

Thy creature that thou madest/And wilt cast forth no more. For My Funeral. Alfred Edward Housman. CMoP; TrPWD; ViBoPo

Thy creatures bless and grant that we/May feast in paradise with Thee. Be Present at Our Table, Lord. John Cennick. TreFT

Thy cross took up in one,/By way of impress, all my future moan. Affliction. George Herbert. TEP

Thy days still lengthen without least decline. Four Seasons of the Year: Spring. Anne Bradstreet. AnNE

Thy dead beseech thee: to Thy living give/In liberty to live! To the Dead of '98. Lionel Pigot Johnson. HBV 1-2

Thy discontent thou didst bequeath to me. The Passionate Pilgrim. William Shakespeare. EiL

Thy double, and eternity is cupped/In the pale hollow of those ghostly hands. To Man Who Goes Seeking Immortality, Bidding Him Look Nearer Home. Adelaide Crapsey. QFR

Thy dross to consume, thy gold to refine. How Firm a Foundation. George Keith. TreFT

Thy drugs are quick. Thus with a kiss I die. Romeo and Juliet. William Shakespeare. FaFP; FiP; GoTF; LiTL; TreFS; TrGrPo; WHA

Thy duty? What is duty? Fare thee well!' Lucretius. Alfred, Lord Tennyson. OAEL 1-2; VLP

Thy erring children lost and lone. For Every Day. Frances Ridley Havergal. BLRP

Thy eyes are the betrayal/of bells comprehended through incense My Love. Edward Estlin Cummings. ErPo; LiTL; LiTM; VGW

Thy Father's call of love! The Call of the Christian. John Greenleaf Whittier. NOCV

Thy fellowship shall keep me strong. The Fellowship of Prayer. Nancy Byrd Turner. BePJ

Thy firmness makes my circle just,/And makes me end where I begun. A Valediction Forbidding Mourning. John Donne. AnAnS 1; BLPL; CABA; DiPo; EnL; ExPo; FaBoEn; FF; ForPo; HAP; HeIP; HoPM; InPK; InPS; JCP; LiTB; MasP; MBW 1-2; MeLP; MePo; NIP; NOBE; NoP; OAEL 1-2; OAEP; OBS; PAI; PoEL 1-5; PoPle; PPoe; PPP; PrIm; SeCeV; SeCP; SeCV 1-2; SoSe; TEP; TreFT; UnPo

Thy Fledgling calls thee home! The Assumption. John Banister Tabb. ISi

Thy flow'r afloat, goolden zumer clote! The Clote. William Barnes. ELP; PoEL 1-5

...Thy foe/Roves Eden, as did Satan, long ago. A Hare. Walter De la Mare. EBEV

Thy folke shall loke cherely when others loke thin. A Hundreth Good Poyntes of Husbandry. Thomas Tusser. FaBoUs

Thy freedom in her wings! The Bird, Let Loose in Eastern Skies. Thomas Moore. HBV 1-2

Thy friendship is a broken reed/That fails thy friend in greatest need. Madrigal: "Since just disdain." Martin Peerson. EnRePo

Thy garment's hem, which Truth and Good/we name. A Prayer. Edward Rowland Sill. AA

Thy gloom is kindled at the tips,/And passes into gloom again. In Memoriam A.H.H., XXXIX. Alfred, Lord Tennyson. VLP

Thy gloom will soothe my cheerless soul,/When nature all is sad like me! Song: "Again rejoicing Nature sees." Robert Burns. BoNaP; HBV 1-2

Thy Glory then I'le make my fruits and Crop. Meditations. Edward Taylor. AP

Thy God still rules the sea. Why Linger Yet upon the Strand? Louis F. Benson. AH

Thy God, thy life, thy Cure. Silex Scintillans. Henry Vaughan. AnAnS 1

Thy golden censers filled with odours sweet/Shall make thy actions with their ends to meet. Matins, or Morning Prayer. Robert Herrick. CaPo

Thy good embraces ill, and lo, its illness dies! Be with Me, Lord. George Macdonald. TrCP

Thy grace can wash away the stain,/And heaven receive us pardoned. Thou Art, O God, the God of Might. Emily Swan Perkins. AH

Thy gracious balm I need. A Prayer. Paul Laurence Dunbar. TrPWD

Thy great obeisance. Ocean. Robert Pollok. EtS

Thy hand on mine upon the hale. The Everlasting Mercy. John Masefield. AtBAP

Thy Head's in Heaven, and hath a crown for thee. Yee Shall Not Misse of a Few Lines in Remembrance of Thomas Hooker. Edward Johnson. SCAP

Thy heart's transcendence, not my heart's excess,–/Then more a thousandfold thou lov'st than I. Equal Troth. Dante Gabriel Rossetti. MaVP

Thy heart shall know me–I can wait. Then. Rose Terry Cooke. HBV 1-2

Thy Heaven, O Lord, I shall not lose! Heaven, O Lord, I Cannot Lose. Edna Dean Proctor. AA

Thy heinous hours wait on them as their pages. An Outcry upon Opportunity. William Shakespeare. NOBE

Thy hungering ones with manna sweet. For Every Day. Frances Ridley Havergal. BLRP

Thy image should be sung; for thou that goddess art,/Which only we without idolatry adore. Diana. Henry Constable. OBSC

Thy joys and sorrows, with as true a heart/As any thund'rer there. The Task,. William Cowper. FiP

Thy judgement wholly lies/In true sense of sprite/Most wise. Christ to His Spouse. William Baldwin. EiL; NOCV; OxBoCh

Thy kingdom come. Thy Kingdom Come. A.B. Simpson. BePJ

Thy Kingdom shall inherit,/The blessing of the just. Thy Kingdom, Lord, We Long For. Vida Scudder. WGRP

Thy law's abridgment and Thy last command/Is all but love; oh let that last will stand! Holy Sonnets, XVI. John Donne. JCP

Thy life bee written, and not read. An Elegie. Elizabeth T. Corbett. AnAnS 2

Thy lightness can not help or hurt my/fame.' The Writer to His Book. Thomas Campion. OAEP

"Thy line is at end," he said, "but at least I have saved its name." Epitaphs of the War 1914-18. Rudyard Kipling. BrPo; OBWP

Thy little child, left learning at Thy knee. Amor Dei. *Anonymous.* BoC

Thy little world I'll conquer presently. The Gordian Knot. Thomas Tomkis. EiL; UnTE

Thy living temples let us be,/Thine everlasting rest. Jesus, Enthroned and Glorified. Zachary Eddy. AH

Thy locks crowned with eternity? Shall These Early Fragrant Hours. Henry Vaughan. LO

Thy looks are wan, thine eyes are wet. Elegy. George Gordon, Lord Byron. GTBS; GTBS-P

Thy lot, O Man, is good, thy portion, fair! The Pass of Kirkstone. William Wordsworth. HBV 1-2

Thy love and favor, kept to us always. Ancient of Days, Who Sittest Throned in Glory. William Croswell Doane. AA; AH

Thy Love gave me, so thine, not mine. A Song: In the Name of a Lover, to His Mistress... William Wycherley. SeCV 1-2

Thy love I'll sing, complete in thee. Complete in Thee, No Work of Mine. Aaron R. Wolfe. AH

Thy love is sweet and sweeteneth/The very bitterness of death. Love and Death. Caius Valerius Catullus. AWP

Thy love is there advanced to be another Grace. The Faerie Queene. Edmund Spenser. OBSC

Thy love to tell, Thy praise to show. A Teacher's Prayer. Frances Ridley Havergal. BLRP; TRV

Thy loveliness may copy here,/And in the eternal Kingdom see. St. Philip in Himself. John Henry, Cardinal Newman. GoBC

Thy lullyng lessyth my langowr. Modyr Whyt as Lyly Flowr (excerpt). *Anonymous.* AtBAP

Thy mart is thronged today, but few will come to-/morrow. The Roses of Thy Cheeks. Rafi of Merv. LiTW

Thy master's head hath need of sleep and resting. Oh, Sleep, Fond Fancy. *Anonymous.* EiL

Thy memory shall perish only then. In Memory of John Lothrop Motley. William Cullen Bryant. AA

Thy Mercy on Thy People, Lord! Recessional. Rudyard Kipling. AWP; BBV; BLPA; BLPL; BLRP; BoLiVe; BrPo; CABA; EnLi 1-2; EnLit; FaBoPV; FaBV; FaFP; FaPo; FaPoR; GN; GTBS; HBV 1-2; HBVY; InPo; LiTB; MCCG; MoBrPo; NOBE; NOBV; NoP; OAEP; OBEV; OBNC; OBVV; OHFP; TreF; TrGrPo; TRV; UnPo; ViBoPo; VLP; WBLP; WGRP; WHA

Thy mind of neither needs, in both seeing it exceeds. "If Cynthia be a Queen..." Sir Walter Ralegh. FCP; SiPS

Thy music teach the nobler art/To tune the regulated heart. To Miss–. Samuel Johnson. CABA

Thy name, a deathless syllable, remains. Keats. John Banister Tabb. AmP

Thy name be ever praised! O Lord, make us free! Prayer of Thanksgiving. Theodore Baker. BLSo

Thy name, proclaimed by every lip,/The Master of our schools. O Thou Whose Feet Have Climbed Life's Hill. Louis F. Benson. AH

Thy name shall shine, thy fame shall glow. The Centennial Ode: Dear Land of All My Love. Sidney Lanier. GN; PAH; PGD

Thy name, thy fame, thy passions, and/thy throne! Red Jacket. Fitz-Greene Halleck. AA

Thy name unsung, thy grace unknown. Shall Man, O God of Light. Timothy Dwight. AH

Thy Nature, and thy Name is LOVE. Wrestling Jacob. Charles Wesley. CEP; NOBE; NOCV; NOEC; OBEC; OBEV; PoEL 1-5; SeCePo

Thy Nature has cuddled me/That pricks,–to renew its psalm. The Opponent Charm Sustained. Samuel Greenberg. MoPo

Thy nurse will tend thee, as duly as may be. Lullaby. John Phillip. EiL

Thy own Rich Pen (Peace, silly Momus, Peace!)/Hath given them a Lasting Writ of Ease.   To the Learned and Reverend Mr. Cotton Mather... Grindall Rawson.   SCAP

Thy pathway like a distant star.   Love Unsought.   Emma Catharine Embury   AA

Thy peace, O God, send down!   For the Gifts of the Spirit.   Edward Rowland Sill.   TrPWD

Thy pen is full as harmless as thy sword.   The Author's Reply.   Sir Carr Scroope.   APAS

Thy physic a farce is.   David Garrick, the Actor, to Sir John Hill, a Physician...   David Garrick.   TreFT

Thy pile of dust, wherein each crumme/Sayes, Come?   Longing.   George Herbert.   SeCV 1-2

Thy place is changed; thou art the same.   In Memoriam A.H.H, CXXI.   Alfred, Lord Tennyson.   NoP; VLP

Thy power and love, my love and trust/Make one place ev'ry where.   The Temper.   George Herbert.   AnAnS 1; AtBAP; MePo; NOCV; OBS; OxBoCh; PoEL 1-5; WHA

Thy powers of love, or this my amorous flame.   Invites His Nymph to His Cottage.   Philip Ayres.   EnLoPo

...Thy praises flow/From saint and seraph's burning tongue.   O Holy, Holy, Holy Lord.   James Wallis Eastburn.   AH

Thy precious peace sustains.   Thank Thee, Lord.   Georgia B. Adams.   STF

Thy presence is, sweet Solitude.   Ode: Solitude, at an Inn.   Thomas Warton, Jr..   CEP

Thy pure grace blooms as a kiss of Earth/Upheld to the lips of God.   The Cliff Rose.   Ernest Fewster.   CaP

Thy purpose crowning all!   He Hides Within the Lily.   William Channing Gannett.   AH

Thy purpose for thy world we share.   O Son of Man, Thou Madest Known.   Milton S. Littlefield.   AH; TrPWD

Thy realm for ever lasts, thy own Messiah reigns!   Messiah.   Alexander Pope.   OxBoCh

Thy realm shall last, thy own Messiah reigns.   Rise, Crowned with Light.   Alexander Pope.   GoBC

Thy rest, Thy joy, Thy glory share!   For Every Day.   Frances Ridley Havergal.   BLRP

Thy resurrection day will dawn/With deeper meaning now.   O Christ of Calvary, This Lent.   Alice Mortenson.   BePJ

Thy Rich and Sovereign Grace, we will proclaim.   Some Contemplations of the Poor, and Desolate State of the Church...   John Williams.   SCAP

Thy riddle hath been read to me!   Trinitas.   John Greenleaf Whittier.   AmePo

Thy righteous will be done.   Not in Dumb Resignation.   John Milton Hay.   WGRP

Thy righteousness to such men lend.   Thy Mercies, Lord, to Heaven Reach.   William Kethe.   AH

Thy Ritual of Stillness–nothing more!   To Nature.   Mahlon Leonard Fisher.   AnAmPo

Thy rod my guide and comfort, underneath/Thy everlasting arms.   Pere Lalement.   Marjorie Pickthall.   CaP; NOBC; OBCV; PeCV

Thy salt is lodged forever in my blood.   Dreams of the Sea.   William Henry Davies.   EtS

Thy sandals seize, gird on thy clothes,/Or I must leave thee here behind.   The Call.   Jones Very.   MAmP

Thy sea is great, our boats are small.   Voyagers.   Henry Van Dyke.   TRV

...Thy servant/Dadu prayeth for true patience and that he may/be devoted to thee.   Bani.   Dadu.   ILwL

Thy servant's happier farre then I!   I Am So Far from Pitying Thee.   Anonymous.   NCEP

Thy servant's soul in Paradise.   The Death of Grant.   Ambrose Bierce.   AA

Thy shepherds seven/Haste to my salvation!   Rock of My Salvation.   Mordecai Ben Isaac.   TrJP

Thy shrine in Guadalupe's tower/My pilgrim steps shall see.   Song to the Virgin Mary.   Pero Lopez de Ayala.   CAW

Thy silver sounded Lute hang up in silence here.   The Argument of Democritus Platonissans.   Henry More.   SeCV 1-2

Thy smiles are my monopolies.   Of His Lady.   Anonymous.   ElL

Thy Son prepares His flock in recompense.   The Queen of the Angels.   Giovanni Boccaccio.   CAW

Thy soul shall fly to paradise above.   The Maiden's Best Adorning.   Anonymous.   OxBChV

Thy soul the secret hath of good and ill.   Of One Who Seemed to Have Failed.   Silas Weir Mitchell.   AA

Thy sovereign, everlasting love.   Our Fathers' God.   Benjamin Copeland.   AH

Thy sovereign wisdom I adore,/And calmly, sweetly, trust thee still.   Lord, My Weak Thought in Vain Would Climb.   Ray Palmer.   AH

Thy Spirit comes in like a heavenly dove.   O Lord, I Come Pleading.   James Gilchrist Lawson.   BLRP

Thy sting is not so sharp/As friend remember'd not.   As You Like It.   William Shakespeare.   BBV; TreF

Thy straying thoughts henceforth forever rest.   An Hymn of Heavenly Beauty (excerpt).   Edmund Spenser.   WGRP

Thy sweetness stills to rest the winter's pain.   Edith.   William Ellery Channing   AA; HBV 1-2

Thy Sylvia is as chaste as fair.   A Roundelay.   Michael Drayton.   ElL

Thy tablet glimmers to the dawn.   In Memoriam A.H.H., LXVII.   Alfred, Lord Tennyson.   LoBV; OAEL 1-2; OAEP; SeCePo

Thy tea is a'ready an' waiting for thee–/Coo-ee!   Starting Rhymes for Hide-and-Seek: "Green lady, green lady."   Anonymous.   GBP

Thy tears are ended and my pain is stilled.   Night.   Hayim Nahman Bialik.   AWP; LiTW

Thy teeth are crooked, but belong/Inherently to such a tongue.   Portrait.   Walter Savage Landor.   DBV

Thy temple face is chiselled from within.   Everymaid.   John Oxenham.   TrCP

Thy thorn without, my thorn my heart invadeth.   Philomela.   Sir Philip Sidney.   HBV 1-2; NOBE; OBEV

Thy thought is of thy failure; we/List raptured, and thank God for thee.   A Violinist.   Francis William Bourdillon.   OBVV

Thy travel done.   Promise.   George William ("A.E.") Russell.   BoC

Thy truth, be that our firmest stay;/Our only rest to do thy will.   Thou Lord of Hosts, Whose Guiding Hand.   Octavius Brooks Frothingham.   AH

Thy verse created like thy theme sublime,/In number, weight, and measure, needs not/rhime.   On Mr. Milton's Paradise Lost.   Andrew Marvell.   JCP; OAEP; PP

Thy voice along the cloister whispers/"Peace!"   Dante.   Henry Wadsworth Longfellow.   AA; AnNE

Thy voice shall join its world-old notes/divine.   Song and Science.   Millicent Washburn Shinn.   AA

...Thy weak child/Kneels at thy feet, and owns in shame a lie.   To Shelley.   Walter Savage Landor.   ViBoPo

Thy Will is best for me.   God's Will is Best.   Anonymous.   BLRP

Thy wings shall be embalm'd by me,/And all beset with flowers.   To the Western Wind.   Robert Herrick.   CaPo; HBV 1-2; OBEV; SeCV 1-2

Thy wings shall waft me home.   Guardian Angel.   John Henry, Cardinal Newman.   GoBC

Thy Wives pox on thee, and Bess Braughtons too.   An Execration upon Vulcan.   Ben Jonson.   AnAnS 2; SeCP

Thy wooing shall thy winning be.   Wooing Song.   Giles the Younger Fletcher.   ElL; HBV 1-2; OBEV

Thy work it is such men safe in to hem/With kindest care, as with a certain shield.   Psalm V.   Sir Philip Sidney.   FCP

Thy world's unwithered countenance/Is bright as on creation's day.   Faust.   Johann Wolfgang von Goethe.   OBVE

Thy worn-out heart will break at last,/My Mary!   To Mary.   William Cowper.   CBEP; EiCP; EnLoPo; FiP; LAuP; NOEC; OAEP; OBEC

Thy worst effect is banishing for hours/The sex whose presence civilizes ours.   Pernicious Weed.   William Cowper.   InMe

Thy wrath, slay sin, and in they Love mee bench.   Meditations.   Edward Taylor.   AP

Thy wrongs, the world's.   The Banshee.   John Todhunter.   OnYI

Thy yoke and thy light burden, mine.   Be Still.   William Ward Ayer.   BLRP

Thyself removed, thy power to soothe me left.   On the Receipt of My Mother's Picture Out of Norfolk.   William Cowper.   CEP; EnPE; EnRP; FiP; HBV 1-2; NOEC; OAEP; OBEC; WHA

Tick-a-tock-a, tick!   The Big Clock.   Anonymous.   SoPo

Tick, tick, tick, what little iambics/While Homer and Whitman roared in the pines?   Petit, the Poet.   Edgar Lee Masters.   AnFE; APA; CMoP; CoAnAm; InPo; LaNeLa; LoGBV; MoAmPo; MoVE; NoAm; NOBA; OxBA; PPON; TAP

Tickle me, love, in these lonesome ribs.   The Lugubrious Whing-Whang.   James Whitcomb Riley.   NA; YaD

Tickle you under there!   Round and Round the Garden.   Anonymous.   OxNR

Tickling the cittern with his quill.   His Desire.   Robert Herrick.   CABA; OAEP; OBSP

Tiddle-dum-tiddle -dum, faddle whee.   Connecticut Peddler.   Anonymous.   ABF

...The tide goes in and goes out.   The Beach in August.   Weldon Kees.   VGW

The tide run to/fulness.   Gaze North-East.   Anonymous.   BIrV

The tide that from the west/With blood washes Africa/Once washed a wooden cross.   The Tide That from the West Washes Africa to the Bone.   David Rubadiri.   WhB

The tides, the wharves, the dens I contemplate,/Are sweet like wanton loves because I hate.   The White City.   Claude McKay.   BPo; NoAm; TAP; TW

Tidings of peace;/Tidings of Jesus,/Redemption and release.   O Sion, Haste, Thy Mission High Fulfilling.   Mary A. Thomson.   AH

The tie which bound the first endures the last! Epistle to Augusta. George Gordon, Lord Byron. AnEnPo

Tie your notes into one smooth ribbon/and let me hang. Notes from an Analyst's Couch. Anita Endrezze Probst. CDW

The Tiger clawing through eastern azure. Face. Robert Morgan. GeTw

The tiger in his strength his thirst must slake! Tiger. Claude McKay. BPo

The Tiger shouted, "You don't mean peace, but war!" A Legend of Versailles. Melvin B. Tolson. BPo

A tiger-soul on elfin wings. The Wasp. William Sharp. FM

The tiger trembles when a man/Crosses his meridian. The Dignity of Man—Lesson #1. Walter H. Kerr. NePoAm-2

The tigers have found me/and I do not care. For Jane. Charles Bukowski. HoPM

The tigers in the panel that she made/Will go on prancing, proud and unafraid. Aunt Jennifer's Tigers. Adrienne Rich. FaBoWP; HeIP; NIP; NoP; SM

...Tigers/pad soft and restless through the falling flakes. The Lost Carnival. Fred Chappell. GOYP

Tigerspots, taut strings, fearless stars. Violet Twilights. Edith Sodergran. WPOW

Tighter wind the giant coils. Nemesis. Ralph Waldo Emerson. AtBAP; NOBA

'Til a big Yankee guy, with a caste in his eye,/With one wave of his hand laid her low. Blackpool Breezes. *Anonymous.* CoMu

Til Glotoun hadde y-globbed a galoun and a gille. The Vision of Piers Plowman. William Langland. OxBM

Til sound and sight failing me they are lost in the clouds. The Testament of Beauty. Robert Bridges. MoVE

'Til the snowman's just my size. And I'm six today. My Birthday's in Winter. Zhenya Gay. BiCB

Un-til they are so weak, they float/With-out re-sis-tance down his throat. A Penguin. Oliver Herford. FiBHP; PV

'Til you let me spend my life making love to you,/Day and night, night and day. Night and Day. Cole Porter. BLSo

Till a hundred nests gave music,/And the East was gray. A Memory. Frederic Lawrence Knowles. HBV 1-2

Till a weak will began his unlearning. Letter from Paparua. Colin Newbury. AnNZ

Till after-poets only knew/Their first-born brother as a god. The Shepherd of King Admetus. James Russell Lowell. HBVY

Till all be ordered with confusion. The Poet Questions Peace. George Chapman. JCP

Till all be spent, and he his number mist. Orlando Furioso. Lodovico Ariosto. LiTW

Till all I am is lost in Thine. Wash Me Whiter Than Snow. Charles Wesley. BePJ

Till all my days are done!' The Turtle-Dove. *Anonymous.* OxBoLi

Till all my lips open, and you enter/All my dreams. Spring Night. Rana Mukerji. UnTE

Till all of New York was white with pain like snow. I Awoke with the Room Cold. Marge Piercy. NeAC

...Till all the perfumes/of Arabia would not sweeten/this hand. Autobiography. Janet Dube. BrRo

Till all the woods re-echoed loud, "Callooh! Callay!" Jabberwocky. Junius Cooper. InMe

Till all the world is fired/With love that shall not fail. The New Song. Arthur Gordon Field. PGD

Till all the world is harsh and cold and gray. November. Frederick Goddard Tuckerman. NOBA

Till all their sweets are gone, and all again refuse them. Woman's Constancy. Sir John Suckling. CaPo

Till all thy birthdays are come to thee. Written on the Raod. Mary Mapes Dodge. BiCB

Till all thy creatures own thy sway. The Day Thou Gavest. John Lodge Ellerton. FaPoR

Till all thy magick structures rear'd so high,/Were shatter'd into heaps o'er thy false head. Temperance and Virginity. John Milton. OBS

Till all was tranquil as a dreamless sleep. On the Frozen Lake. William Wordsworth. FaBoCh; LoGBV

Till all was tranquil as a summer sea. Influence of Natural Objects. William Wordsworth. AWP; ERoP 1-2; InPo; LoBV; MCCG; OBRV

Till angels wake thee, with a note like thine. An Epitaph upon the Celebrated Claudy Philips, Musician... Samuel Johnson. CBEP; OBEC; UnS

Till as jurymen we sat on/Two deaths by suicide. Call It a Good Marriage. Robert Graves. BoLoP

Till, as one about to die, I linger/Paler than grass is... Ode to Anactoria. Sappho. AWP

Till at last he died with the bitter grief—now they both lie in one tomb. Young Charlottie. William Lorenzo Carter. BeLS; BLPA

Till at length they mate. History. D. H. Lawrence. BrPo

Till at the last he purged away his sin/By loving all the joy he saw within. How Shall a Man Fore-Doomed. Hartley Coleridge. NCEP

...Till Athena/cast sweet sleep upon her eyes. The Odyssey. Homer. NAWM 1-2

Till bacterial cyclones blow./Then let go. Come Unto These Yellow Sands (parody). Paul Dehn. SpRo

Till, beneath the solar fires,/Rankling all, the wretch expires! Song of the Evil Spirit of the Woods. Thomas Moore. OBTV

Till better pleased, "Sweet, sweet' content bewrays. Madrigal: "Sweet Philomel in groves and deserts haunting." *Anonymous.* PBBP

Till both our heads were in his aureole. The House of Life. Dante Gabriel Rossetti. OAEL 1-2

Till bright as blood the peachstone showed. Peachstone. Dannie Abse. OxBC

Till by turning, turning we come round right. 'Tis the Gift To Be Simple. *Anonymous.* AH

Till candles and starlight and moonshine be out. The Merry Wives of Windsor. William Shakespeare. ViBoPo

Till Cecilia turns to a stone. Ode against St. Cecilia's Day. George Barker. PoA

Till change hath broken down/All things save Beauty alone. Hugh Selwyn Mauberley, XIII: Envoi. Ezra Pound. LiTA

Till Cherry ripe themselves do cry. There Is a Garden in Her Face. Thomas Campion. AAS; AtBAP; BiP; CABA; DiPo; EG; EiL; ELP; EnL; ForPo; GoJo; HeIP; InPK; InPo; NIP; NoP; OAEL 1-2; OAEP; PoEL 1-5; PrIm; TrGrPo; ViBoPo; WHA

Till Christ again turn wanderer and child. Christmas Eve under Hooker's Statue. Robert Lowell. AP; CAPP; ConAP; FF; NePA; OxBA

Till Christ be formed in all mankind/And every land be thine. Eternal God, Whose Power Upholds. Henry Hallam Tweedy. AH

Till Christ on high shall rend the sky,/And bid the dead arise. Here Is a Song. John Peck. AH

Till Christ, quhome I àm haldin for to lufe. The Gude and Godlie Ballatis: Till Christ. *Anonymous.* OxBS

Till Christ the Lord descends from High/And takes the Conqu'rors Home. The Whole Armour of God. Charles Wesley. NOCV

Till, clouds and darkness ended,/They see Thee face to face. O Word of God Incarnate. William Walsham How. TRV

Till crushed beneath the furrow's weight/Shall be thy doom! To a Mountain Daisy. Robert Burns. AnEnPo; ATP; EnLi 1-2; EnLit; GN; HBV 1-2; OAEP; PoLf; WBLP

Till Cynthia shine as she hath done before. My Thoughts Are Winged with Hopes. George, Earl of Cumberland Clifford. EIL

Till Cynthia shine as she hath done before. My Thoughts Are Winged with Hopes, My Hopes with Love. Sir Walter Ralegh. GBL

Till Daddy deliberately sneezes. Visitors. Harry Behn. SoPo

Till dawn finds/field is bog, bog lake. Ireland. Richard Ryan. CIP

Till dawn,/till noon,/till night,/were killed year by year. Those Betrayed at Dawn. Stanislaw Wygodski. VWA

Till daylight came/And they went away. As I Lay Quiet. Margaret Widdemer. GoYe

Till de red dawn come. Saturday Night. Langston Hughes. MoAmPo

Till death, and sweeping fire, laid waste the/hostile field. The Assault on the Fortress. Timothy Dwight. PAH

Till death doth close the hapless scene,/And calls its angel home to rest. Verses Written during the War 1756–1763. Thomas Osbert Mordaunt. CBEP; OBEC

Till death drew its grey blind down his face. Father and Son. Frederick Robert Higgins. BoC; OBMV

Till death seizes/and drinks you down. Hummingbird. Marge Piercy. GeTw

Till death thy endless mercies seal,/And make my sacrifice complete. Inextinguishable Blaze. Charles Wesley. NOEC

Till dreadfull death do ease my dolefull state? Imitated from Rime CCLXIX: "The piller pearisht is whearto I Lent. Petrarch (Francesco Petrarca). OBVE

Till dreams of power/entered me again/like magma— Santa Caterina. Myra Glazer Schotz. VWA

Till, dying, all he can resign is breath. Finis. James (1700-48) Thomson. BSV

Till each was both or either, and the soul/Was not afraid. The Land. Victoria Mary (Vita) Sackville-West. AtBAP

Till earth restores her sons to heaven again. I Was Sick and in Prison. Jones Very. NOBA

Till earth's dark night of sin shall turn/To God's own perfect day. The Word of God. J. Harold Gwynne. STF

Till earth's saved and ransomed millions/Join to praise the Savior's name. Glory to the Name of Jesus! A.B. Simpson. BePJ

Till enough footsteps come and go/To make a path for me. Convention. Agnes Lee. HBMV

Till, ere we know it, our weak shrinking feet/Have brought us to the end and all is done. The Road of Life. William Morris. OBNC

Till ev'n His beams sing, and my music shine. Christmas. George Herbert. OxBoCh; SBVL; SeCV 1-2; TrCP

Till everything breaks down. Verigin, Moving in Alone. John Newlove. NeAC

Till evidence of strongest kind/Constrains assent, and clears the mind. Belief and Unbelief. Philip Freneau. AmePo

Till fatigue or error dragged him down,/An ordinary man on ordinary ground. Tightrope Walker. Vernon Scannell. NCSH

Till fley'd awa by Phoebus' light! O Were My Love Yon Lilac Fair. Robert Burns. BSV; GBL; HBV 1-2; OBEV

Till flowers are black mouths/and the stones bleed my song. The Leader. Dorothy Livesay. PeCV

Till for more spite to Myra's heart he flyeth,/Where living to the world, to me he dieth. Caelica, XII. Fulke, Lord Brooke Greville. EnRePo; FCP

Till for the cross my crown I wear. Heavier the Cross. Benjamin Schmolck. BePJ

...Till found by dawn he/reach out to God no trembling hand. Walking the Wilderness. William Stafford. NaP

Till four and twenty broad arrows/Were thrilling in his heart. Young Johnstone (B version). *Anonymous.* ESPB

Till Fowl-death did prevail o'er/Wee, wee tailor. The Oviparous Tailor. Thomas Lovell Beddoes. NBM

Till Freedom cheered and joy-bells rung... Boston. Ralph Waldo Emerson. MC

Till Gabriel blows his trumpet sound/And says the rain's just gone around. Dakota Land. *Anonymous.* CoSo; FSW

An' till Gabriel's horn I will sit an' mourn the ruin of Bobtail Bend. The Ruin of Bobtail Bend. James Barton Adams. PoOW

Till Generation is swallow'd up in Regeneration. Milton. William Blake. EnRP; OAEL 1-2

Till glitter calls to him and he succumbs. "Trade" Rat. Eleanor Glenn. NePoAm

Till glorious from Thy heaven above,/Shall come the City of our God. The City. Frank Mason North. WGRP

Till God's great love, on both, one hopes one Heaven bestow. Sonnets. Sarah Helen Whitman AA

Till God's love set thee at his side again! Idylls of the King. Alfred, Lord Tennyson. CABA; VLP

Till grateful to thy shrine we bring/The tribute of a ransomed land. We Praise Thee, If One Rescued Soul. Lydia Huntley Sigourney. AH

Till growing bold, he laughed and leapt/In the tangles of Love's very hair? Tamerlane. Edgar Allan Poe. AmP; AP; MAmP

...Till gusts arise/More boisterous in their play, then off she flies. The Happy Bird. John Clare. PBBP

Till hands that plighted troth shall re-/unite. A Character. Charlotte Fiske Bates. AA

Till he grow weary with the over-sweet,/And die, or kill. Laurana's Song. Richard Hovey. AA

Till he has won a second soul for glory,/At the point no return. Point of No Return. Robert Graves. BIrV

Till he hears the mighty Tom. Christ Church Bells. Henry Aldrich. CBEP

"Till he larns me that tune called the next market day." The Next Market Day. *Anonymous.* FSW

Till he reaches home. The Dress That My Brother Has Put on Is Thin. Lady Otomo of Sakanoe. AWP

Till he's become the Golden Fool. He Has Observ'd the Golden Rule. William Blake. PV

Till he's lit every lamp in the dark blue sky. The Starlighter. Arthur Guiterman. SiSoSe

Till he sold his barrow/For half a crown. Mr. Tom Narrow. James Reeves. SO

Till he that lingered lost her/Among the leaves of Spring. Ferry Hinksey. Laurence Binyon. HBV 1-2

Till he was ninety-two. The Philosopher. Sara Teasdale. PoToHe

Till her eyes shine I live in darkest night. Sonnet: "Lock up, fair lids, the treasure of my heart. Sir Philip Sidney. EIL

Till her eyes shine, 'tis night within my heart. Oh Yield, Fair Lids. Richard Brinsley Sheridan. OnYI

Till his fingers like snails at last came unstuck/And he fell through the cage of the sun. Death on a Live Wire. Michael Baldwin. MoBS

Till human voices wake us, and we drown. The Love Song of J. Alfred Prufrock. Thomas Stearns Eliot. AP; APA; ATP; AWP; BiP; CMoP; CoBMV; DiPo; EBEV; ExPo; FF; ForPo; HAP; HBMV; HeIP; HoPM; InPK; InPo; InPS; LiTB; LiTM; MAPA; MBW 1-2; MoAB; MoAmPo; MoVE; MP; NAWM 1-2; NePA; NIP; NoAm; NOBA; NOBE; NoP; OAEL 1-2; OAEP; OxBTC; PAI; PoA; PoRA; PPP; PrIm; SeCeV; SoSe; SOTW; TAP; TreFT; TrGrPo; TwCP; ViBoPo

Till I, a shade in heaven, clasp her, a shade. Memory. Erik Johann Stagnelius. AWP

Till I and the bird, the word and the tree, were one. Coppersmith. Richard Murphy. IPY

Till I come to quiet moorings and a watch below,/In the Golden City of St. Mary. The Golden City of St. Mary. John Masefield. GTBS; MCCG

Till I depart, dearest Body, my slave, my queen. Dear Body. Janine Canan. APU

Till I, departing taper, light another. To a Segar. Samuel Low. OBAL

Till I fain would arise and follow, not them, not them,-/but their Lord! The True Apostolate. Ruby T. Weyburn. BLRP

Till I forget my own. Ode to the Evening Star. Mark Akenside. CEP; OBEC

Till I found 'twas to no end/With a Spirit to contend. Her Fair Inflaming Eyes. Thomas Campion. LiTL

Till I go to seek it/Fifty fathom deep. Fisherman's Luck. Wilfred Wilson Gibson. EtS

Till I have found the gates of pearl,/And anchored there. A Rhyme of Life. Charles Warren Stoddard. HBV 1-2

Till I, in robes of white arrayed,/Thy face in glory see. The King in His Beauty. James G. Deck. BePJ

Till I infuse love, hatred, longing, will.-/I do not deprecate. I Will Accept. Christina Georgina Rossetti. OxBoCh

...Till I launch/To thee into eternity/That time which has no end. Great God, Preserver of All Things. Francis Daniel Pastorius. AH

Till I'm sent to bed. Autumn Even. Amelia Andriello. SiSoSe

Till I reach heav'n, and much more thee. Affliction. George Herbert. AnAnS 1; JCP; LoBV; NoP; SeCP

Till I reach heaven's blissful shore. Jesus, Merciful and Mild! Thomas Hastings. AH

Till I saw that slant-legged robin/With autumn on his chest. Late Autumn. Andrew Young. HaMV; MoVE

Till I see the grass/waving on her tomb. Haufi. *Anonymous.* BoWoP

Till I stumble & weave/other richer lives on my own. Goodwill, Inc. Dennis Schmitz. AmPA

Till I too blossom and rejoice and sing. The First Spring Day. Christina Georgina Rossetti. WiR

Till in chains no more to him the lake/yields watery boon. The Loon. Alfred Billings Street. AA

Till in the ocean of thy love/We lose ourselves in heaven above. Evening. John Keble. TrPWD; VLP

Till in thy perfect love I ever live and/move. In Him We Live. Jones Very. AmP; OxBA

Till instead of two cats there weren't any. Limerick: "There once were two cats of Kilkenny." *Anonymous.* CenHV

Till Ireland, a Nation, can build him a tomb. Tone's Grave. Thomas Osborne Davis. OnYI

Till it became the all, the homeless heart. No Faith. Mark Van Doren. AnFE

Till it catches light, makes women/Feel their age, and sigh for liberation. The Seed-Picture. Mebdh McGuckian. FaBoIP

Till it closed and again I resumed my life. The Stockyard. Sir John Collings Squire. OxBTC

Till it find its full fruition/In the brotherhood of man! Not Alone for Mighty Empire. William Pierson Merrill. AH; TrPWD

Till it hath swept those Whigs away/That sign not this address. The Humble Address. *Anonymous.* APAS

Till it have made each green cocoon/Exactly like its brother. Grass. Mary Morison Webster. PeSA

...Till/It's perfect night in you. And then you scream. The Recruits. Ian Hamilton. NoAm

Till Jesus make them comprehend/His ways, his truth and light. Psalms, CXLVII. Christopher Smart. NOCV

Till joy shall overtake/Her perfect peace. Dream-Land. Christina Georgina Rossetti. BrRo; EnLi 1-2; VLP

Till kind earth held him and he spake with/death. Walt Whitman. Harrison Smith Morris. AA

Till Labour has triumphed and Ireland is Free! New Words to the Tune of "O'Donnel Abu." Jim Connell. OnYI

Till lilies in their cheeks be turn'd to roses. Song: "Choose now among this fairest number." William Browne. GBL

Till lost on his aerial rings/In light, and then the fancy sings. The Lark Ascending. George Meredith. CABL; LoBV; OAEP; PBBP; WiR

Till Love construe the cryptic iron faces. Two Men in Armour. John Heath-Stubbs. NeBP

Till love's put off and pain/and wish and death. My Naked Aunt. Archibald MacLeish. NePA

Till love that was, and love too blest to be,/Meet-and the junction be Eternity? To know just how he suffered would be dear. Emily Dickinson. DiPo; InvP

Till, more familiar grown, the table crumbs/Attract his slender feet... The Seasons. James (1700-48) Thomson. PBBP

Till more matter may come.-/By the King's most noble commandment. Skelton Laureate, Defender, against Lusty Garnesche.... John Skelton. TW

Till morning's latest sunlight fades/On the blue tablet of the deep! Daniel Webster. Oliver Wendell Holmes. PAH

Till music be my body. Words Spoken Alone. Dannie Abse. NYBP

Till my feet, cloven too, take hold on hell? The World. Christina Georgina Rossetti. BoWoP

Till my gestures enlarged, wide over the darkening land. Feeding Ducks. Norman MacCaig. OxBS

Till my head rings,/till they tell me. Dime Call. Albert Goldbarth. VWA

Till my raptured soul shall find/Rest beyond the river. Jesus, Keep Me Near the Cross. Fanny J. Crosby. AH

Till my thoughts are worn out/and I no longer hate you On Love. Kyogoku Tamekane. LLLT

Till new grows old, and old grows stale, and all is but/beguiling. Once I Thought to Die for Love. *Anonymous.* EIL

Till now, alas! I know it. Cancion. Juan II of Castile. AWP

Till now, like Icarus mid-ocean-drowned,/Hands, wings, are found. Icarus. Stephen Spender. NoAm; PrIm

Till on a time it betid,/As tellis the writ. The Buke of the Howlat. Sir Richard Holland. OxBS

Till on earth by every creature/Glory to the Lamb be sung. Saviour, Sprinkle Many Nations. Arthur Cleveland Coxe. AH

Till on his last-won wilderness an Empire's outposts stand! The Voortrekker. Rudyard Kipling. HBV 1-2

Till on my country coast our anchor fall. Coming Homeward Out of Spain. Barnabe Googe. EIL; EnRePo

Till on the lucid sky loftier ridges appear. Vestigia Restrorsum: The Vales of the Medway. Arthur Joseph Munby. FaBoPP

Till one knows its being which soon is not. Cars Once Steel and Green, Now Old. Louis Zukofsky. VGW

Till others learn to love thee too/And thus return to God. The Secret of the Cross. M. J. Clarkson. BePJ

Till our banner flaps o'er all/As it crowns Savannah! Sherman's in Savannah. Oliver Wendell Holmes. MC; PAH

Till our hands & eyes/have strength to mould/the concrete beneath our feet For Brother Malcolm. Edward S. Spriggs. CAD

Till our return we must despair to find/Judges so just, so knowing, and so kind. Epilogue Spoken by Mrs. Boutell. John Dryden. SeCV 1-2

Till our skirts shall touch the ground. Red Stockings, Blue Stockings. *Anonymous.* OxNR

Till our souls should rest, in peace, on His breast,/In the heavenly home! The Heart of God. W. E. Littlewood. BePJ

Till—peace on earth! to pardon'd man—good/will!/With tones of heaven the ear of fancy fill. The Omnipresence of the Deity. Robert Montgomery. VLP

Till Phoebus, dipping in the West,/Shall lead the World the way to Rest. Evening Quatrains. Charles Cotton. ExPo; LoBV

Till pigeons settle in/their pigeonholes for good. Possibilities. Peter Kane Dufault. NYBP

'Till reason's morn arise, and light them on their way. The School-Mistress. In Imitation of Spenser. William Shenstone. CEP; LaA; LAuP

Till remembrance has no longer/Care to laugh or weep. The Recessional. Sir Charles G. D. Roberts. HBV 1-2

Till ruddy, like his face, the sun descends. The Shedpherd's Week. John Gay. EiCP

Till, seeming blest, they grow to what they seem. France. Oliver Goldsmith. OBEC

Till she be the reason why/All the world for love may die. A Celebration of Charis. Ben Jonson. AnAnS 2; EnRePo; SeCP; SeCV 1-2

Till she cry "Lover, gold-hatted, high-bouncing lover,/I must have you!" The Great Gatsby: Epitaph. F. Scott Fitzgerald. ELU

Till she do kiss me as she kissed me then. The Kiss. *Anonymous.* OnYI; OxBI

Till she ever, thus defeated,/Yields the sceptre of the main. Song: "O'er the waste of waters cruising." Philip Freneau. PAH

Till she, o'ercome with anguish, shame, and rage,/Danged down to hell her loathsome carriage. Hero and Leander. Christopher Marlowe. AAS; CABA; EBEV; NoP; OBSC; TEP

Till she's as old as brother Jack,/Who now is twice as old as she. A Puzzling Example. Virginia Sarah Benjamin. BiCB

Till she sheds her rough goatskin/and puts on the soft fleece of a lamb Paphnutius (excerpt). Hroswitha von Grandersheim. WPOW

Till shrill larks warn them to their flowery cells.' The Plea of the Midsummer Fairies. Thomas Hood. OBNC; OBRV

Till side by side we lie. The Brothers. Charles Sprague. AA

Till, sleepy, we/And the birds went home. Beach Fire. Frances Frost. TiPo

Till souls, and bodies both, may meet. To My Mistress in Absence. Thomas Carew. AnAnS 2; CaPo

Till spak my wyf. Hyt were plesance I woot. The Eternale Footeman's Tale (parody). George Moor. BXAP

Till such unearthly intercourses shed/A visible halo round his mortal head. The Poet. John Keats. ERoP 1-2

Till suddenly, at Arras, you possessed that hinted land. To Edward Thomas. Alun Lewis. WaP

Till Superstition with unconscious hand/Seat Reason on her throne. The Destiny of Nations. Samuel Taylor Coleridge. EnRP

Till syne ae nicht he jist scales richt/Intil the ocean, fou. The Drunken Dee. Syd Scroggie. PoSH

Till that head from desert sands,/A princess, hot with dancing, carried between her hands. Saint John. Elizabeth Jane Coatsworth. GTBS; MoRP

Till that judge forgive thee. The Judgement. Dora Read Goodale. AA; AnAmPo

'Till that lucky day, you know darned well, Baby,/I can't give you any thing but love. I Can't Give You Anything but Love. Dorothy Fields. BLSo

...Till that predestin'd day/When Erin's self is drowned. The Celtic Cross. Thomas D'Arcy McGee. OnYI

Till that she was close closed under ground. A Poem of a Maid Forsaken. *Anonymous.* PBBP

Till that we both, being toss'd from earth,/Flie hand in hand to heav'n. Sunday. George Herbert. OBS; SeCV 1-2; TrCP

...Till the almond tree flowers/on the mountain, and there is no more sea. Angels. Richard Burns. VWA

Till the best tongue, or heaviest hand prevails. Hope. William Cowper. PoEL 1-5

Till the birds shall fly to the mountains/For one safe bough. Reveille. Lola Ridge. AnAmPo; HBMV

...Till the bitter ocean's tongue/Swells in their cove, and smothers their sweet song. Seals at High Island. Richard Murphy. CIP; IPY

Till the breath becomes natural. Meditation. Carl Rakosi. VWA

Till the church bells are ringing a knellphia. Limerick: "Said a fellow from North Philadelphia." Berton Braley. TDH

Till the continent sinks, and the ocean is dry! Ye Sons of Columbia. Thomas Green Fessenden. PAH

Till the cows come home/That's all. Black and White. Tom Schmidt. NeAC

Till the dawn of endless day. Jesus Comes on Clouds Triumphant. Godfrey Thring. BePJ

Till the dawn-wind, softly, slowly,/Brought to burning eyelids sleep. La Nuit Blanche. Rudyard Kipling. MoBrPo

Till the Day-spring breaks forth again from high. The Bird. Henry Vaughan. AtBAP; FM; LoBV; OBEV; PoEL 1-5; SeCV 1-2

...Till the deep/Dawns with that unimaginable day.' On an Engraving by Casserius. A. D. Hope. CBAP

Till the dew of thy sleep, dear,/Lies soft on thine eyes. Prince Lucifer: Mother-Song. Alfred Austin. HBV 1-2

Till the fear has gone. Fear is the only enemy. Autumn Testament (excerpt). James Keir Baxter. OCNZ

Till the fields where he lived should be known in my/song. The Frightened Ploughman. John Clare. PoEL 1-5

Till the fire is nothing but light!.../Nothing but light! Emily Sparks. Edgar Lee Masters. GLGT

...Till the given/Moment comes to render what we owe. Mirabell, Book 9 (excerpt). James Merrill. HaCAP

Till the gossamer thread you fling catch somewhere, O my soul. Drum-Taps. Walt Whitman. AP

Till the gunpowder ran out at the heels of their boots. The Great Panjandrum. Samuel Foote. FaBoCh; FaBoCo; LoGBV; MoShBr; Par; PoLf

Till the heart-beats of hell shall be/hushed by a hymn from the hunt that/has harried... The Heptalogia. Algernon Charles Swinburne. OAEP

Till the infinite aurora/In the other's eyes. Struck Was I, Nor Yet by Lightning. Emily Dickinson. AnNE

Till the lamp flickers and the memory fails. The Holy Tide. Frederick Tennyson. OBEV; OBVV

Till the last crash of all things low and high/Shall end the spheres? Long Plighted. Thomas Hardy. NOBV

Till the last sun grow pale/Let there be Light! Liberty Enlightening the World. Edmund Clarence Stedman. PAH

Till the loftiest flaming summit died to blue. The Buzzards. Martin Armstrong. HBMV

Till the long night is gone, and the last morn arise. Elegy: In Spring. Michael Bruce. BSV

Till the love of beauty/Fall from me at last. Lesbia Sewing. Harold Vinal. HBMV

Till the Lydian lakes re-echo all the laughter in my home. Return to Sirmio. Caius Valerius Catullus. LiTW

Till the rapture was shut in itself, and the earth sank to rest. Saul. Robert Browning. WGRP

Till the scented voice of the old Jam Fish/Shall melt their scorn to tears. The Jam Fish. Edward Abbott Parry. AmMo; OxBChV

Till the snow comes back, and stays/Here for all our winter plays! The Procession. Margaret Widdemer. YeAr

Till the song, the sorrow,/are lost on the waves. Icarus. Kendrick Smithyman. AnNZ

Till the spring snaps–/And the fun's done! Time of the Mad Atom. Virginia Brasier. QQQ

Till the sun came around. Earth, Sky. Sydney Clouts. PeSA

Till the sweet sun doth die,/Come, come! May (excerpt). John Francis O'Donnell. IrPN

Till the twilight folds and all's/As blue as the bluewashed walls. From Four Lakes' Days. Richard Eberhart. MiAP

Till the unreturning leaves/Imperishably fell. Then when the Ample Season. Richard Wilbur. MiAP

Till the vicar compelled him to Walmisbury. Limerick: "There was a young curate of Salisbury." George Libaire. FaBoCo; LiBL

Till the world goes round and round! Drink that Rot Gut. *Anonymous.* ABF

Till then farewell, and thus I ende my song,/Take it in gree, for else thou doest mee wrong. Councell Given to Master Bartholmew Withipoll... George Gascoigne. AAS

Till then I salute you with a significant look that you do not/forget me. To a Common Prostitute. Walt Whitman. AnAmPo; MoAmPo; ViBoPo

Till then let us sorrow in company. Sympathy. Reginald Heber. BeLS

Till then thou art like starlight on the air,/Or clouds at dawn, unutterably fair. Sonnets. Robert Hillyer. HBMV

Till there isn't as much as the price of a pint to spend. To the Blacksmith with a Spade. Owen Rose O'Sullivan. KiLC

Till there's war no more! The Fourth of July. John Pierpont. AnNE; MC; PAH; PAL

Till they all appear'd on hill and plain/Like living gold. Io! Io! Singing the Reapers Homeward Come. *Anonymous.* OHIP

Till they and I dissolve in one. Summer Interlude. Lionel Stevenson. CaP

Till they be hid o'er with a wood of darts. Good Christians. Robert Herrick. LiTB

Till they cou'd see ye wi' a suit on/O' gude Braid Claith. Braid Claith. Robert Fergusson. BSV; CEP; GoTS; NOEC; OBEC; OxBS

Till they had met great grandpapas/Twit-tittering on the seething coals. Walls. Hervey Allen. HBMV

Till they have had Punishment enough to make them commit/Crimes. Jerusalem. William Blake. OBNC

Till they sink down and feel no more. A Necessitarian's Epitaph. Thomas Hardy. FaBoEE

Till they touch in flood. The Elephant Is Slow to Mate. D. H. Lawrence. LiTM; PPP; TEP

Till Thou hast bound me fast, I am not free. Freedom. *Anonymous.* PGD

Till Thou shalt reign alone,/Great King of Kings. Let War's Tempests Cease. Henry Wadsworth Longfellow. OHIP

Till thou too from the earth thine head shalt thrust. Odes, X. Hafiz. AWP

Till three long years they'd married been,/And then she told the joke to him. Kate and the Cowhide. *Anonymous.* AmFP

Till thro' the lucid Chambers of the South/Look'd out the joyous SPRING, look'd out, and smil'd. Approach of Winter. James (1834-82) Thomson. OBEC

Till thy rapt invocation still/My troubled dreams. To an Obscure Poet Who Lives on My Hearth. Charles Lotin Hildreth. AA

Till thy vague dream im-/print/Its smile/On the unyielding flint. Art. Theophile Gautier. AWP; LiTW

Till Time his glass with Death's last dust shall fill. Humanity. Richard Watson Dixon. OBVV

Till time itself shall be no more. The Temper of Aristippus. John Gilbert Cooper. PBBP

Till time, that buries us, lay bare. Near the Ocean. Robert Lowell. NOBA

Till time too late we make them try/They study false astronomy. Song Set by John Dowland: "What poor astronomers are they." *Anonymous.* OBSC

Till tired he sleeps, and life's poor play is o'er. An Essay on Man. Alexander Pope. FiP; TrGrPo

Till to the home of gladness/With Christ's own Bride they rise. AMEN. Holy Matrimony. John Keble. HBV 1-2; VLP

Till to thy morning brightness I shall wake/As one from happy sleep. Come Slowly, Paradise. James Benjamin Kenyon. AA

Till trouble troubles you. Of All the Sayings in This World. *Anonymous.* OxNR

Till under the dark willows blooms a village. Inscriptions on Chinese Paintings: Lines To Do With Youth. Witter ("Emanuel Morgan") Bynner. PoA

Till under them he, too, shall lie. A Charm for Spring Flowers. Rachel Field. TiPo

Till vernal gales should gently play/To waft us on our homeward way. The Swallow. Lucy Aiken. OxBChV

Till vertue flourish in the light of light. The Shadow of Night. George Chapman. PoEL 1-5

Till very liberty make clean and fair/The nursing earth as sepulchral sea. Cor Cordium. Algernon Charles Swinburne. MaVP; VLP

Till, virgin, thou again delight/To hear a British shell! Ode to Pity. William Collins. CEP; EiCP; EnPE; LAuP

Till we are gathered to Thy home above. Above the Hills of Time. Thomas Tiplady. TRV

Till we from the fiery trail/Pure as purity refine. Hymns and Spiritual Songs. Christopher Smart. EiCP; LAuP

Till we get to the one with the puppy dogs in it. Shop Windows. Rose Fyleman. SoPo; TiPo

Till we git to Buffalo. Ballad of the Erie Canal. *Anonymous.* ABF

Till we have built Jerusalem/In England's green and pleasant land. And Did Those Feet in Ancient Time. William Blake. FaBoCh; FaBV; HAP; LoGBV; MAT; NAWM 1-2; PoRA; PrIm

Till we only hear their whir/In behind a rocky spur,/Just ahead. Morning on the Lievre. Archibald Lampman. SD

Till we reach old Buffalo. Erie Canal. *Anonymous.* ABF

Till we shall meet again. A Lost Love. Henry Francis Lyte. GTBS

Till we sink this murdering system/In the darkest pits of hell! The Kent State Massacre. Barbara and Jack Warshaw Dane. FSW

Till we struck stone at last, to lie/Here on the frozen floor of hell. Micromutations. James Wright. NYBP

Till we up sails with M'riarty Jim/And sail from Beg-Innish. Beg-Innish. John Millington Synge. MoBrPo; OnYI; OxBI

Till we, who smiled at Pyrenees,/Of parishes complain. We miss a kinsman more. Emily Dickinson. OBSP

Till weariness, the spur, or want of food,/Makes gilded curbs of all beasts understood. Caelica, CVII. Fulke, Lord Brooke Greville. FCP

Till Wee Davie Daylicht comes keekin' ower the hill. Auld Daddy Darkness. James Ferguson. HBV 1-2; HBVY; OxBChV

Till when, I leave thee to thy heart's desire–/By him that lives thy virtues to admire. The Earl of Surrey to Geraldine. Michael Drayton. OBSC

Till when, in such assurance live, ye may/Nor feare, or wish your dying day. A Country Life: To His Brother, M. Tho: Herrick. Robert Herrick. CaPo; SeCP; SeCV 1-2

Till which hour, we thy day enlarge, O Valentine. An Epithalamion, or Marriage Song. John Donne. HW

Till who the last rood dareth/Shall find a mother there! Duo. Olive Dargan. HBMV

Till with the refluent dance she reappears. A Country Dance. Turner, Charles Tennyson. NOBV; VLP

Till women waft them over in their tears. Orpheus I Am, Come from the Deeps Below. John Fletcher. GBL

Till wrap'd in flames, in ruin hurl'd,/Sinks the fabric of the world. The Descent of Odin. Thomas Gray. CEP; EiCP; LAuP

Till ye meet it in old Ireland in the dawn–/ing o' the year! The Dawning o' the Year. Mary Elizabeth Blake. AA

"Till you achieve that Female-Male/In which shall culminate the race." As Like the Woman as You Can. William Ernest Henley. HBV 1-2

Till you conquer de lan' an' conquer de ocean! John Henry in Harlem. M. B. Toleson. GoSl

Till you have passed unscathed through fires within. Talk Not of Strength, Till Your Heart Has Know. Ella Wheeler Wilcox. PoToHe

Till younger lives come all their love to prove. The Little Poem of Life. John Oxenham. TRV

Tills for the promise of a later birth/The wilderness of this Elysian earth. True Love. Percy Bysshe Shelley. LoBV

Tilted honeycombs, thunderhead blue. Willowware Cup. James Merrill. NoP

Tilted to sleep, I am biting my lips. Blond. Joseph De Roche. HeIP

Time again subdues her. Wives in the Sere. Thomas Hardy. BrPo; NOBE; NOBV; VLP

Time and again I profit by your angers. To a Teacher of French. Donald Davie. OxBC

Time and disaster and the limping blood. Foliage of Vision. James Merrill. MoPo; VGW

Time and the sea about Tristan da Cunha. Seven South African Poems. David Wright. PeSA

Time (as Korf intended)/neutralizes time. Korf's Clock. Christian Morgenstern. FaBoNo

Time but the servant is of Power Divine. Eternity's Speech against Time. Fulke, Lord Brooke Greville. JCP

Time cannot hold Thy wondrous growth,/No, nor eternity. Jesus, My God and My All. Frederick William Faber. BePJ

Time falls, snow falls, words fall. Geneva. Alastair Reid. NYBP

Time flieth as we sing! Ad Leuconoen. Francis Sylvester ("Father Prout") Mahony. IrPN

Time for springtime is lovetime/and viva sweet love Sweet Spring Is Your. Edward Estlin Cummings. NCSH

Time for the pieces/to move/dumbly back/toward each other. Nightbreak. Adrienne Rich. IHMS

The time goes by, the time goes by. Water Whirligigs. D. J. Opperman. PeSA

Time had no other feature.   The Statue of Shadow.   John Peale Bishop. LiTA

Time hardens. But the bitter Now grows gracious.   Troopship in the Tropics. Alun Lewis.   WaP

The time has come. I am waiting for you.   Epithalamium.   Daniel Halpern. MAYP

The time has come to call a halt.   Songs for a Colored Singer.   Elizabeth Bishop.   MiAP

The time has come to speak.   Mrs. Golightly.   Gertrude Hall.   AA

Time hast'neth fast when it shall be/Tryumphant.   To My Reverend Dear Brother, M. Samuel Stone...   John Cotton.   SCAP

Time hath made free of tears, sighs, and despair./Writing in furrows deep, she once was fair.   Caelica, VIII.   Fulke, Lord Brooke Greville.   AtBAP; FCP

Time having blurred it like that pale/pastel!   Pastel.   Francis Saltus Saltus. AA

Time in the snow is at last,/Is past.   The Snow Fall.   Archibald MacLeish. LOW; PoPl

Time is dying.   Fidelity.   Trumbull Stickney.   AnFE; CoAnAm; LiTA

Time is like the falling snow.   Cressida.   James Keir Baxter.   AnNZ

Time is mountain's promise and sea's contract.   Promises.   Ruth Forbes Sherry.   GoYe

Time is my debtor for my years untold.   Long Time a Child.   Hartley Coleridge.   CBEP; HBV 1-2; NBM; NCEP; PoEL 1-5

Time is the fire in which we burn.   For Rhoda.   Delmore Schwartz. MoAB; MoAmPo; OxBA

Time like a permanent stone, its cold weight judging.   Hoc Est Corpus. Alex Comfort.   LiTB; LiTM

Time, like one wrong/Note in a song,/With their bloom, passes.   Quiet. Marjorie Pickthall.   NOBC; OBCV

Time loses thine eye!   Man.   Samuel Greenberg.   CrMA

The time must be right!/For you both.   The Enchanted Halibut.   Sheila Nickerson.   WOLT

Time must youth and wealth destroy.   The Mouldering Vine.   Anonymous. AmFP

Time, not battle,–that slays.   Epitaphs of the War, 1914-18.   Rudyard Kipling.   BrPo; OAEP; OBWP

The time of creation has come.   The Time of Creation Has Come. Anonymous.   WTO

A time of morning,/a time of night.   A Time of Night.   David Ignatow. FAZ

Time parts the hearts of men.'   Come, Walk with Me.   Emily Bronte. NOBV

The Time passes, this night of Kumulipo/Still it is night   The Kumulipo: Birth of Sea and Land Life.   Anonymous.   WTO

Time passes–yet I lie alone.   Lonely Night.   Sappho.   LiTW

Time rings a snow-change.   The White Hare.   Lilian Bowes Lyon. OxBTC; PoPle

Time rolls his ceaseless/course.   The Lady of the Lake.   Sir Walter Scott. ViBoPo

...Time's/careless nebula of blossom/   Earthly.   Ian Wedde.   OCNZ

Time's noblest offspring is the last.   Verses on the Prospect of Planting Arts and Learning in America.   George Berkeley.   CEP; OBEC; OBTV; SeCePo; ViBoPo

Time's stony palace crumbled down/Before that instant kiss.   A Glimpse of Time.   Laurence Binyon.   AnFE

Time scarce could serve their properties to tell.   The Owle.   Michael Drayton.   FM

Time shall die, and love shall be/Lord as time was over death.   Before Sunset.   Algernon Charles Swinburne.   EG; VLP

Time shall throw a dart at thee.   Epitaph on the Countess Dowager of Pembroke.   William Browne.   CBEP; FaBoEE; LoBV; NOBE; OBS

Time speaks gravely, stroke on stroke.   Song at Summer's End.   A. R. D. Fairburn.   AnNZ

Time still must tick this is, I am, we are.   To Judith Asleep.   John Ciardi. LiTL; LiTM; MiAP; MoLP

...Time takes fresh start again,/On for a thousand years of genius more.   The Adirondacs.   Ralph Waldo Emerson.   GLGT

A time that is not mine/seems to rain inside my eyes.   Time Reminded Me. Julia Uceda.   BoWoP

Time, Thou, Split, Colors, Earth, Sun...and We remain.   Come Unto Us Who Are...Laden.   Harry Roskolenko.   FAZ

...Time thrusts through/the time of no-Time.   There's a Grandfather's Clock in the Hall.   Robert Penn Warren.   NoP

Time-tired souls salute thee from the shore.   Thalatta! Thalatta!   Joseph Brownlee Brown.   AA; HBV 1-2

Time to aim my heels at her seat!   Once upon a Nag.   Michael Beirne McMahon.   PH

The time to give ourselves/to the Revolution.   This Is the Time.   Josina Machel.   WhB

Time to remember and inquire.   The Chase.   J. V. Cunningham.   LiSp; NoAm

Time topples bird and man out of their myth.   Birds All Singing.   Norman MacCaig.   ChMP

Time turns away/a revolution terrifed of the dark.   Why I Like Movies. Patricia Jones.   BlSi

...Time, unchanging blue/and winter frosts: Let the small day be.   Sons. Jack Cope.   PeSA

Time, useless to bones of the dead.   Epitaph: For 2nd Officer James Montgomerie...   William Montgomerie.   PoL

Time/vertical to the horizon   What I Saw Passages 3.   Robert Duncan. NoAm; NOBA

Time waits for moments such as these.   Students.   Florence Wilkinson. HBV 1-2

Time was away and she was here.   Meeting Point.   Louis MacNeice. ChMP; FaBoIP

"Time was, Time is, and Time shall be no more!"   Sonnets on the Sea's Voice.   George Sterling.   EtS

...An Time/Whuds like a flee.   Munestruck.   Hugh" (Christopher Murray Grieve) MacDiarmid.   NeBP

Time will not shift in favor,/Nor circumstance be kind.   Second Night, or What You Will.   Rolfe Humphries.   MoLP

Time will reveal the calyxes of gold.   God's Plans.   May Riley Smith. BLRP

The timeless in time and the regional compass.   Violet Star.   Philip Lamantia.   APU

The timeless life, the fiery star that swings/In an eternal night and there forever sings.   New Year Wishes.   May Sarton.   MoRP

A timeless state of mind.   Riding across John Lee's Finger.   Stanley Crouch. PoBA

Timeless walls/Of time–/Old Abe   Lincoln Monument: Washington. Langston Hughes.   OFD

The times are somehow breeding/A nimbler race of mice.   On a Cat, Ageing. Sir Alexander Gray.   BSV

Timor mortis conturbat me.   Lament for the Makaris.   William Dunbar. ACP; AtBAP; BSV; CBEP; EBEV; GoTS; NoP; OAEL 1-2; OAEP; OBEV; OxBS; PoEL 1-5; PP; ViBoPo

The tinker may do as he's done before,/Kiss the girl behind the door.   The Beverley Maid and the Tinker.   Anonymous.   CoMu

"Tinker to Evers to Chance."   Baseball's Sad Lexicon.   Franklin Pierce ("F.P.A.") Adams.   FaFP; GoTF; InMe; SD; TreFS

Tinkers and shepherds/Have the whole round hill for a road.   Roads. George Mackay Brown.   PoSH

Tinkers, going past, make the sign of the cross.   Unlucky Boat.   George Mackay Brown.   NePoEA-2

The tinkle of the dead leaf by the lone/Sea road, the sad look of the setting star.   The Objects of the Summer Scene.   Thomas Caulfield Irwin.   IrPN; NBM

The tinkling of the bells.   Virgil's Tomb.   Robert Cameron Rogers.   AA

Tinkling/silver/Bell./O/k/i/s/c/e.   The Sharpbreasted Snake (Hokpe Fuske). Louis (LittleCoon) Oliver.   STE

Tinkly, minkly,/Piece of zinc!   A Nonsense Alphabet.   Edward Lear. SoPo; SUS

A tiny brightening den lit the eye/in the blunt cut end of your stick.   A Hazel Stick for Catherine Ann.   Seamus Heaney.   FaBoIP

Tiny buds had sprung up among the weeds.   Seeds.   Thurmond Snyder. NNP

...Tiny crimson jets/poured from it everywhere. Transfused!   A Technical Supplement.   Thomas Kinsella.   IPY

The tiny hand is on the knob   Clean & Clear.   Michael Brownstein. ANYP

A tiny lattice opens on the eternal/glory.   Very Fair My Lot.   Jacob David Kamzon.   TrJP

A tiny little earring in that horrid student's beard.   Riding down from Bangor.   Louis Shreve Osborne.   BLPA

The tiny petals of the mountain-ash.   An Upper Chamber in a Darkened House.   Frederick Goddard Tuckerman.   AnNE; NOBA; TAP

A tiny trembling. Day tatters in the wind.   Recognition.   Georgette Perry. AMV-80

The tiny trickle of my birth/Dwindling back into the earth.   Weir Bridge. Padraic Fallon.   CIP

The tip-end of a swan's wing for your fan/With a handle of porcupine quills. Portrait of a Cree.   Katherine"(Amelia Beers Warnock Garvin) "Hale. CaP

The tip of his small tail may be/A snow-storm in epitome.   The Southern Snow-Bird.   William Hamilton Hayne.   AA

The tipping earth, the swarming stars/Have an eye that sees itself.   The Heart of Herakles.   Kenneth Rexroth.   NU

...Tipping/his hat/in a place like that.   In the Ladies' Room at the Bus Terminal (parody).   William Zaranka.   BXAP

The tips of the lately grated cherry-tree/Are a firm and lacquered black.   11 Rue Daguerre.   John Montague.   FaBoIP

Tipt with a wreath high-curling in the sky.   Winter.   James (1700-48) Thomson.   CoBE

Tired and sad/from praying for the rain.   Waiting for the Rain.   Felix Mnthali.   WhB

Tired of starvin' won't starve no mo'.   Upon de Mountain.   *Anonymous.* TrAS

Tired, to be content with discontent.   Epitaph on Any Man.   Arthur Seymour John Tessimond.   PoL

Tired waiting, tired waiting,/Blackbird, blackbird.   Blackbird's Song. *Anonymous.*   GBP

Tired with all these, from these would I be gone,/Save that to die, I leave my love alone.   Sonnets, LXVI: "Tired with all these, for restful death I cry." William Shakespeare.   AWP; CTC; EBEV; ExPo; FaBoPV; FaFP; GTBS; GTBS-P; HAP; InPo; InPS; LiTB; MBW 1-2; MyFE; NOBE; OAEL 1-2; OBSC; PoEL 1-5; SeCeV; TrGrPo; ViBoPo; WeW; WHA

'Tis a bloody big load to carry.   Responsibility.   *Anonymous.*   FaBoUs; PV

'Tis a foolish fable that the universe is wide./All the world is here.   Gypsy-Heart.   Katharine Lee Bates.   HBMV

'Tis a lie we all do know.   Song: "What think you of this age now." *Anonymous.*   APAS

'Tis a poor world, this, boys,/And Tommy's dead.   Tommy's Dead.   Sydney Thomas Dobell.   HBV 1-2

'Tis a proof that he would rather/Have a turnip than a father.   If the Man Who Turnips Cries.   Samuel Johnson.   HBV 1-2; LBN

'Tis a Sign that he had rather/Have a Turnep than a Father.   Burlesque Translation of Lines from Lope de Vega's "Arcadia'.   Samuel (1612-80) Butler.   EBEV

'Tis all a myth that Autumn grieves!   Autumn's Mirth.   Samuel Minturn Peck.   GN

'Tis all that Heaven allows.   All My Past Life.   John Wilmot, Earl of Rochester.   FF

'Tis all to taverns and to lasses!   Villon's Ballade.   Andrew Lang.   HBV 1-2

'Tis Anguish not a Feather hath/Or too much weight to fly—   Too happy time dissolves itself.   Emily Dickinson.   NOBA

'Tis as if to my free soul for ever/You had shut both Paradise and Hell.   You Are Always New.   Anna Akhmatova.   LiTW

'Tis Bacchus' son who walks below.   Song: "Strew not earth with empty stars."   Thomas Lovell Beddoes.   OBSP; ViBoPo

'Tis bad; nor should it thence too swiftly glide.   Choosing a Wet-Nurse.   M. Saint-Marthe.   FaBoUs

'Tis Beauty sleeping on her bier.   Indian Summer.   Susanna Moodie.   CaP

"'Tis better far the cold to dree/Than give my true love up for thee."   Le Pere Severe.   *Anonymous.*   AWP

'Tis better repenting a sin/Than regretting the loss of a pleasure.   A Logical Song.   *Anonymous.*   ErPo

"'Tis better to have fought and lost,/Than never to have fought at all." Peschiera.   Arthur Hugh Clough.   HBV 1-2

'Tis better to have loved and lost/Than ever to have loved and won. Footnote to Tennyson.   Gerald Bullett.   FiBHP

'Tis better to have loved and lost/Than never to have loved at all.   In Memoriam A.H.H., XXVII.   Alfred, Lord Tennyson.   HBV 1-2; NAWM 1-2; OAEL 1-2; OBNC; TreFS

'Tis but a play to form the youth/By fiction, in the cause of truth.   The Purpose of Fable-Writing.   Phaedrus.   AWP

'Tis but a wanton trick.   'Tis but a Wanton Trick.   *Anonymous.*   UnTE

'Tis but applying worm-seed to the tail.   Farewell to Love.   John Donne. OAEL 1-2

'Tis but newly day.   The Shepherd's Pipe: Dawn of Day.   William Browne. EIL

'Tis but the beginning of life.   A Soul's Soliloquy.   Wenonah Stevens Abbott. BLPA

'Tis but the stopt heart/That Time cannot mend.   Flesh.   Mary Elizabeth ("E") Fullerton.   PoAu 1-2

'Tis but to show how much I grieve.   On One Who Died Discovering Her Kindness.   John, Duke of Buckingham Sheffield.   OBEV

'Tis by succession of delight/That love supports his reign.   On a Bed of Guernsey Lilies.   Christopher Smart.   NOEC; OBEC

'Tis by wanton play and sport/Heedless Virgins you will gain.   When you Love, or speak of it.   Aphra Behn.   BoWoP

'Tis charity here not to love.   The Divorce.   Thomas Stanley.   AnAnS 2; MeLP

'Tis clear the peacock is a fool.   The Loves of the Birds.   *Anonymous.* WTO

'Tis comely young Caroline of Edinboro' Town.   Caroline of Edinboro' Town. *Anonymous.*   AmFP; BFSS

–'Tis conscience makes us sinners, not our sin.   In Answer to a Question. Wilfrid Scawen Blunt.   ViBoPo

'Tis day and we must part.   Parting at Dawn.   *Anonymous.*   WTO

'Tis death, death only, sets a measure.   The Panchatantra: True Friendship. *Anonymous.*   AWP; LiTW

'Tis doubly sweet deceiver to deceive.   The Cock and the Fox.   Jean de La Fontaine.   AWP

'Tis drinking Sally Birkett's ale.   Epigram: "O mortal man, that lives by bread."   Julius Caesar Ibbetson.   FaBoEE

'Tis dust to dust beneath the sod,/But ther, up ther, 'tis heart to heart. Lorena.   *Anonymous.*   BFSS

'Tis Earth, though the air and the water be black/with the blackness of Doom! In the Twilight (excerpt).   John Francis O'Donnell.   IrPN

'Tis far more conquest with one to live/true/Than every hour to triumph lord of/new.   Thou Joy'st, Fond Boy.   Thomas Campion.   OAEP

'Tis folly abounding in a strange surrounding/To be divorced from one's pants. French Lisette: A Ballad of Maida Vale.   William Plomer.   ErPo

'Tis gain to die with Jesus nigh–/The Rock of thy salvation.   Our Rock. Francis Scott Key.   BePJ; STF

'Tis God shall repay: I am safer so.   The Patriot.   Robert Browning. PoRA; TrGrPo

'Tis hard such passion to destroy,/But easy to deceive.   How Hardly I Conceal'd My Tears.   Anne Wharton.   CavP

'Tis hard times, I say.   Cryderville Jail.   *Anonymous.*   ABF

'Tis hard to Root it out.   Most Weeds, Whilst Young.   Francis Daniel Pastorius.   SCAP

...Tis he alone that can/Find out Cursed Policies of Man.   The Heart Is Deep.   Roger Wolcott.   SCAP

'Tis he alone that lives and reigns!   Guilielmus Rex.   Thomas Bailey Aldrich.   AA; AnNE

'Tis he has the blarney/To make a girl Mistress O'Hea.   Barney O'Hea. Samuel Lover.   OnYI

'Tis He that makes men whole.   The Babe of Bethlehem.   Henry Beer. BePJ

'Tis He that still doth keep.   I Was a Wandering Sheep.   Horatius Bonar. BePJ

'Tis his to forge the master-key/That wields the locks of destiny! Guardianship.   Georgia Douglas Johnson.   GoSl

'Tis holier to die/By a Christian gun...   Onward Christian Soldiers!   Frank Marshall Davis.   FB

'Tis in every feature I would make it shine.   The Groves of Blarney. Richard Alfred Millikin.   CBEP; FaBoPP; HBV 1-2; IrPN; OnYI; OxBI; OxBoLi

'Tis in the center of God's will,/May we abide just there.   There Is a Place. Alma Hoellein.   STF

'Tis innocence in the sweet blood/Of Cherry, Apricocks and Plums/To be imbru'd.   An Ode, upon Occasion of His Majesties Proclamation in the Year 1630.   Sir Richard Fanshawe.   MePo; OBS

...'Tis just, that who/did give/So many poets life, by one should live.   To Edward Allen.   Ben Jonson.   OAEP; OBS

'Tis just the same as we had never been.   Against the Fear of Death. Lucretius (Titus Lucretius Carus).   AWP

'Tis just we should adore, 'tis just we should thee sing.   Hymn to Darkness. John Norris.   MePo; OBS; OxBoCh

'Tis last good-night, our Sunne shall never set.   Death.   Henry Vaughan. NCEP

'Tis made by Nothing now againe.   And He Answered Them Nothing. Richard Crashaw.   MePo

'Tis Majesty to rule alone.   Against Them Who Lay Unchastity to the Sex of Women.   William Habington.   AnAnS 2; JCP; MePo; OBS; SeCP

"'Tis man's perdition to be safe,/When for the truth he ought to die." Sacrifice.   Ralph Waldo Emerson.   HBV 1-2; HBVY; TRV

'Tis manna to the hungry soul,/And to the weary rest.   The Name of Jesus. John Newton.   STF

'Tis manners so to do.   Of a Little Take a Little.   *Anonymous.*   OxNR

'Tis merry winnowing.   The Winnowers.   Robert Bridges.   OAEP

'Tis much to dye; 'tis more to fynde/Two of my minde.   A Paradox. Aurelian Townsend.   AnAnS 2; SeCP

'Tis my grief that her ever I knew!   The Stars Stand Up in the Air. *Anonymous.*   AnIV; BIrV

'Tis my loyalty to Her,/To the Girl that once you were.   Time's Revenges. Sir Owen Seaman.   FaBoUs

'Tis night in the Valley of Death.   Death Valley.   Jack H. Lee.   BPAW

'Tis no business of his where it goes.   Song: "When I was a greenhorn and young."   Charles Kingsley.   NBM

...'Tis no mother's breast/Upon the cold lips of thy child thou'st prest!   The Easter Song.   Caelius Sedulius.   OnYI

'Tis nobly done–the day's our own–huzzah, huzzah!   The Song of Braddock's Men.   *Anonymous.*   MC; PAH

'Tis not enough that trees do stand,/If their fruit fall and perish too.   Love Speaks at Last.   Edward, Lord Herbert of Cherbury.   AnAnS 2

'Tis not the guest that will be without it,/But Jesus, Mary's Son.   Hospitality in Ancient Ireland.   *Anonymous.*   OnYI

'Tis not to be improved.   Eros.   Ralph Waldo Emerson.   AnNE; FaBoBe; HBV 1-2

'Tis nothing, Celia, but the losing thee.   Sonnet on Death.   William Walsh. ViBoPo

'Tis of Robin Hood, that archer good,/And how Little John went a begging. Little John a Begging (B version).   *Anonymous.*   BaBo; ESPB

'Tis only God may be had for the asking.   The Vision of Sir Launfal.   James Russell Lowell.   NePA

Tis only she can make you great,/Though place here make you knowne. Pleasure Reconciled to Vertue: A Masque. Ben Jonson. AnAnS 2

'Tis onward, unswerving,/And this is true rest. True Rest. Johann Wolfgang von Goethe. TRV; WBLP

–'Tis past! And here alone I stray/Haunting the Western Moor. A Trampwoman's Tragedy. Thomas Hardy. AtBAP; BeLS; HBMV; MoVE; OBNC; VLP

'Tis pity that they should ever speak word again.' The Seaman's Compass. *Anonymous.* OBSS

'Tis Pope must be ashamed of Craggs. A Dialogue. Alexander Pope. PoL

'Tis pre-engaged and in his room/Townshend's cast page or Walpole's groom. Ireland. Jonathan Swift. FaBoPV

'Tis rais'd upon A.B. the straight, the given line. A Mathematical Problem. Samuel Taylor Coleridge. FaBoUs

'Tis ready polish'd from the mine. An Epistle to Robert Lloyd, Esq. William Cowper. FiP

'Tis seal'd for ever on my heart. Sent to a Lady, with a Seal. Robert Lloyd. FaBoUs

'Tis she who does for pardon cry/That's held the sinner. The Complaisant Swain. Ovid. AWP

'Tis shed upon the tomb of him she loves. Woman's Love. *Anonymous.* WBLP

'Tis silent, and the subterranean dark/ Has crossed the nadir, and begins to climb. Revolution. Alfred Edward Housman. BrPo; ImOP; NoP; OBSP

'Tis snow or sun or rain or shine/If we're together. To F. C. Mortimer Collins. GoTF; HBV 1-2; NOBV; TreFS

'Tis Spring, 'tis summer, still, while thou art mine. The Pine. Augusta Webster. HBV 1-2; OHIP

'Tis still his light they love, less dreadful seen in thee. To the Blessed Virgin Mary. Gerald Griffin. OnYI

'Tis strange that she should thus confess it, though't be true. A Self Accuser. John Donne. FaBoEE

'Tis such a new and gracious miracle. La Vita Nuova. Dante Alighieri. AWP

'Tis summer!'–and it melts away. Snow-Flakes. Mary Mapes Dodge. HBVY

"'Tis sweet, oh, 'tis sweet for our country to die!" The Death of Warren. Epes Sargent. MC; PAH

'Tis sweeter to remember than forget.' On a Thrush Singing in Autumn. Sir Lewis Morris. OBVV

'Tis ten to one but penury/Ends both the spider and the poet. The Spider. Edward Littleton. NOEC

'Tis, that he has both generals in reversion.) At the Gate of Heaven. George Gordon, Lord Byron. OBRV

'Tis the bells of Shandon,/That sound so grand on/The pleasant waters of the river Lee. The Bells of Shandon. Francis Sylvester ("Father Prout") Mahony. ACP; AnIV; CAW; GoBC; HBV 1-2; IrPN; OBRV; OnYI; RoGo; TreFS

'Tis the cur dog of Britain and spaniel of Spain. Epigram: "With favour and fortune fastidiously blest." Jonathan Swift. FaBoEE

'Tis the dawn of the fairy-day. The Culprit Fay. Joseph Rodman Drake. GN

'Tis the fine country/Open below. The Cool, Cool Country. Shaw Neilson. PoAu 1-2

'Tis the folks in the front that I jar. Limerick: "As a beauty I'm not a great star." Anthony Euwer. GoTF; HBMV; HBV 1-2; HBVY; InvP; LiBL; NePA

'Tis the handsome Clara Clark and her true love, brave Monroe. Gerry's Rocks. *Anonymous.* ABF

'Tis the Lord of the World you see. The Lord of the World. G. Anketall "Woodbine Willie" Studdert-Kennedy. PGD

'Tis the Messiah's destined victory. Religious Musings. Samuel Taylor Coleridge. WGRP

'Tis "The old Constitution/And a stern retribution/to the South." The Fight at Sumter. *Anonymous.* PAH

'Tis the old ship of Zion, hallelujah. What Ship Is This? Samuel Hauser. AH

'Tis the one pathway from Despair,/And it is called the Bridge of Prayer. The Unseen Bridge. Gilbert Thomas. HBMV

'Tis the only gospel that some men will/read,/That gospel according to you. The Gospel According to You. *Anonymous.* BLRP; STF

'Tis the only place I know/Have you met Him there? The Hour of Prayer. Georgia B. Adams. STF

'Tis the quare pity o' Brigid MacIlray. Her Sister. Moira O'Neill. OxBTC

'Tis the road to you and the road for me. My Road. Oliver Opdyke. HBV 1-2

'Tis the sole hope of the Rover! The Roving Worker. *Anonymous.* OnYI

'Tis the sword of love, my Son. Which Sword? Jason Noble Pierce. PGD

'Tis the tenderest token of His love so deep. Precious in the Sight of the Lord... *Anonymous.* BLRP

'Tis the time to choose a lover. Time to Choose a Lover. Horace. UnTE

'Tis the tube where descends the celestial breath/Feminine Canaan in the protruding halves. My Mouth Is Often Joined against His Mouth. Arthur Rimbaud. PeHV

'Tis the word that God has spoken,/And it cannot pass away. The Best of All. Fanny J. Crosby. BLRP

'Tis thee (my selfe) that for my selfe I praise,/Painting my age with beauty of thy daies. Sonnets, LXII: "Sinne of selfe-love possesseth al mine eie." William Shakespeare. EBEV; PoEL 1-5

"'Tis then our Hope shall cease to be/With Israel's last son!" Hatikvah–A Song of Hope. Naphtali Imber. TrJP

'Tis there I'd put spells upon Phoebus/To take sunlight forever away. From a Beggarman's Song. *Anonymous.* WTO

'Tis there I would nestle at rest till the quivering moon/Uprose in the golden quiet over the hill. My Sorrow. Seumas (James Starkey) O'Sullivan. HBV 1-2

'Tis there that Albert's gone./How dogs do carry on! Brave Rover. Max Beerbohm. GDP; NLV

'Tis thine to offer with corrupting art/The rotten borough of the human heart. Answer to–'s Professions of Affection. George Gordon, Lord Byron. OBSP

'Tis this, Though man's a fool, yet God is wise. An Essay on Man. Alexander Pope. CEP; EnLit; GoTL; MBW 1-2

Tis thy time to choose a lover. Odes. Horace. OBVE

'Tis time I did things which I could. Limerick: "There was a trim maiden named Wood." William A. Lockwood. LiBL

'Tis time thy prayers were said! Motley. Walter De La Mare. HoPM; MMM

"'Tis time, 'tis time, my dear Marg'ret,/That you were gane awa'." Sweet William and May Marg'ret. Anonymous CH; HBV 1-2

'Tis time to be in hate, to live! The Alarm. Hildebrand Jacob. NOEC

'Tis time to part, but oh! what is to pay? On the Death of an Epicure. Richard Graves. CBEP

Tis to be hop't I may remove/This scorne one day, one day by endless love. To the Tune of, In Fayth I Cannot Keepe my Fathers Sheepe. Sidney Godolphin. OBS

'Tis true that when we trace its source, 'tis beer. Modern Love, XVIII. George Meredith. NBM; PoEL 1-5; VLP

'Tis tyme that the worlde heard the worde about Wynken. Wynken De Worde. Frederick von Ende. PoL

'Tis very sure God walks in mine. My Garden. Thomas Edward Brown. BLPL; EBCP; EnLit; FaBV; GTBS; HBV 1-2; HBVY; InPK; OBEV; OBVV; PeD; PoLf; TreF; TRV; WBLP; WGRP

'Tis very sure my garden's full of snails! My Garden. J. A. Lindon. DBV; InPK; PoL

'Tis want of sense that makes us poor. To the Same Purpose. Thomas Traherne. NoP; SeCV 1-2

'Tis well an old age is out,/And time to begin a new. The Secular Masque. John Dryden. DiPo; ExPo; FaBoRV; HAP; NOBE; OBSP; PoEL 1-5; PrIm; SeCeV; SeCV 1-2; ViBoPo

'Tis what we do, not what we say, that makes us worthy of His/grace. My Creed. Jeanette Gilder. WGRP

'Tis white and lovely like/A wreath of water-lilies... The Dream Queen: Dialogue. Bhasa. LiTW

'Tis wisdom to give much, a gift prevails,/When deep persuading Oratory fails. Hero and Leander. Christopher Marlowe. PeHV

'Tis woman's love. This I believe. Amen. The Lady Jane: A Humorous Novel in Rhyme (excerpt). Nathaniel Parker Willis. OBAL

'Tis you must pay the piper? The Dance. *Anonymous.* PAH

"'Tis your own fault if you don't flourish now." To Mrs. Ann Flaxman. William Blake. OBRV

A-tishoo! A-tishoo!/We all get up again. Ring-a-Ring o' Roses. *Anonymous.* OxNR

Tissues already as withered as their autumn forerunners'. The Very Old. Thomas Galloway. AMV-80

Titania strokes the ass's head/beneath his dark and lucid gaze. Midsummer Night's Dream. Byron Vazakas. NePA

Tnen–suddenly! I swim. The Lesson. Jane W. Krows. SoPo

A:to Q:dwo. Edward Estlin Cummings. OBAL

To a Babe in Bethlehem. The Shepherd Left Behind. Mildred Plew Merryman. ChBR; TrCP

To a continent dark with apples. Apples. Michael Waters. GeTw

To a cosmic tide with the men that man it. Angle of Vision. Robert Rendall. OxBTC

To a dormouse with a paunch and large ears like/leaves or wings. On Hardscrabble Mountain. Galway Kinnell. RFM

To a fine, squaredance grit/Of powdered tooth/And bonemeal. The Best Dance Hall in Iuka, Mississippi. Thomas Johnson. FAZ

To a lad I love beyond all earthly treasures, and he'll soon embrace/his Colleen Rue. Colleen Rue. *Anonymous.* BIrV; OnYI

To a newspaper carelessly left there. Good dog. Dog's Death. John Updike. Psk

To a prize that was won by a slain brother's brand,/I' the brave nights so early.   Earl Brand.   *Anonymous.*   OxBB

To a reservoir of heart safe from harm.   Rural Route.   R. T. Smith.   AMV-81

"To a roast leg of mutton you may go'.   Limerick: "There was a sick man of Tobago."   *Anonymous.*   OxBChV

To a soft, oleaginous mutta.   Limerick: "There was an old man of Calcutta."   Ogden Nash.   NoP

To a thunderous Jullien air?   Reminiscences of a Dancing Man.   Thomas Hardy.   MoVE

To a tongue that licks your lips, a turd's sweet meat.   I Muse Not.   Francis Davison.   TW

To a whiteness older than Time.   Ancient.   George William Russell.   SeCePo

To a woman, a child, a lamp.   Dusk.   Helen Welshimer.   PoToHe

To a world where will be no further throwing/Pearls before swine that can't value them./Amen!   The Flight of the Duchess.   Robert Browning.   VLP

To accept justly what is right.   Life.   *Anonymous.*   PoToHe

To accept such coynes as these;/As my last Remembrances.   Lyrick for Legacies.   Robert Herrick.   FaBoRV; OBS

To accommodate a frien' nex' do'.   The Endless Song.   Ruth McEnery Stuart.   OBAL

To ache/thru his arms.   Seven Poems.   Lorine Niedecker.   VGW

To add to his possessions, attain height and beat the dwarf.   The Dwarf of the Hill Caves.   Lupenga Mphande.   WhB

To admire the skill of the trailing arbutus/in decanting its fragrance.   The Question, Is It?   Alfred Goldsworthy Bailey.   AMV-81

To aggravate the wound it should assuage.   Sonnets to Laura.   Petrarch.   EnLi 1-2

To air the ditty,/And to earth I.   Last Poems.   Alfred Edward Housman.   OAEP

To all appearances.   Magnetized.   Arthur Sze.   BrSi

To all save Undine and her comb...   Fantasia.   Dorothy Livesay.   OBCV

To all temptations is that soul left free/That makes not to itself a curb of me.   Conscience.   Sir Edward Sherburne.   ACP

To all the fat dogs in Kamschatka.   Limerick: "There was an Old Man of Kamschatka."   Edward Lear.   NA; NOBL

To all the lists of clay!   Of All the Souls That Stand Create.   Emily Dickinson.   AA; AmePo; AnNE; APA; DiPo; MAmP; NePA; TrGrPo

...To all who come to her feast/in this faithless time.   Cancer Patient.   Jessica Powers.   AMV-81

To alle unkinde creatures, as Crist Himselve witnesseth:/Amen dico vobis, nescio vos.   The Vision of Piers Plowman.   William Langland.   OxBM

To allow the spider/To seek its pleasure.   Parson's Pleasure.   Barry O. Higgs.   PeSA

To an exercise of Czerny's. It is enough.   August, at an Upstairs Window.   Harold McCurdy.   AMV-80

To an impatient child that hath new robes/And may not wear them.   Romeo and Juliet.   William Shakespeare.   GoTF; HW; LiTL; TreFS

To an isle in the water/With her would I fly.   To an Isle in the Water.   William Butler Yeats.   AWP

To and fro, the blossoms swaying, swaying.   Wind-Song.   *Anonymous.*   SUS

To and to and fro/Fro Niz – nil – imbo.   Metamorphosis.   Wallace Stevens.   InPK; VGW

To announce the Old Woman of Harrow.   Limerick: "There was an Old Woman of Harrow."   *Anonymous.*   FaBoNo

To announce to the sons of man thy/power,/and the honor of the glory of thy/kingdom.   Annul Wars.   Nahman of Bratzlav.   TrJP

To another corner/of the sky.   Four Choctaw Songs.   Jim Barnes.   STE

To another side/of home.   Painted Passages.   Gail N. Harada.   BrSi

To answer for your children's sins as well as for your own.   The Millman's Song.   *Anonymous.*   ShS

To any woman, maid or bride,/Who resolves to go astray.   Written in an Ovid.   Matthew Prior.   FaBoEE; FaBoUs

To arms!   Hear, O Israel.   Andre Spire.   TrJP; VWA

To arms! For peace is here!   Peace.   Harold Trowbridge Pulsifer.   MC

To ashes, like the chestnuts, close together!   The Little Milliner.   Robert Williams Buchanan.   BeLS

To ask why he felt for these strangers/Feelings for which he had no name   The Vowels of Another Language.   Tom Disch.   PoA

To assuage her true distress, her headache, and her exhaustion...   Crepe de Chine.   Tennessee Williams.   NYBP

To attract the attention of passing solutions....   Where Are You Now Superman?   Brian Patten.   FF

To await my Savior's calling/At that great rising day.   Peter Emberley (I).   *Anonymous.*   ShS

To Babylon, my lords; to Babylon!   Tamburlaine the Great.   Christopher Marlowe.   TrGrPo; ViBoPo

To bang the heads of philosophic doubt/Between two rhymes, and knock the feathers out?   A Letter to John Dryden (excerpt).   James Philip McAuley.   CBAP

To banish the less, I find my chief relief.   In Windsor Castle.   Henry Howard, Earl of Surrey.   NOBE; OBSC; SeCePo

To bask in sun,/And see the day.   Seeds.   Walter De la Mare.   TiPo

To bask in the light of your sky!   In the Grass.   Hamlin Garland.   AA

To bask the centuries away/Nor once look up for noon?   A long, long sleep.   Emily Dickinson.   NCEP

To battle for, to die.   Sailors on Leave.   Owen Dodson.   AmNP

To battle, twitching our dust behind him like a gown.   Tan Ta Ra, Cries Mars...   David Wagoner.   NePoAm-2

To be a flower is profound/Responsibility!   Bloom is result.   Emily Dickinson.   PoEL 1-5

To be a simple Trilobite/In the Silurian seas.'   The Lay of the Trilobite.   May Kendall.   CenHV

To be a warning to all men/Who have mamas and pas.   Ballad of the Oedipus Complex.   Lawrence Durrell.   FaBoCo

To be again of a like mind.   Kindness.   Catherine Davis.   NYBP

To be alive, and suffer not, is sleep.   With the Dawn.   Thomas Caulfield Irwin.   BIrV; EnLoPo; IrPN

To be alive in such an age!   Today.   Angela Morgan.   BLPA

To be as forest things are, free,/Lonely, and strange and wild!   Wildness.   Blanche Shoemaker Wagstaff.   HBMV

To be at once together and alone.   The Aged Lover Discourses in the Flat Style.   J. V. Cunningham.   NoAm; SM

To be black/is/to be/very-hot.   But He Was Cool.   Don L. Lee.   BP; BPo; NoAm; PoBA

To be bold as the birds through the air that drive:/Only time!   The Laborer.   Richard Dehmel.   AWP

To be born.   Bedtime.   Hillel Schwartz.   AMV-81

To be broken by the number/Of pennies in a purse.   Hunger.   Mary Carolyn Davies.   AnAmPo

...To be caught/out of the dullness of self by such alien thought?   Down from the Country.   John Blight.   CBAP

To be chewed a second time/Like cows in their kraal.   Biltong.   James Twala.   WhB

To be comforted for ever/Or to look for comfort never....   I have neither plums nor cherries.   Nicholas Breton.   EG

To be dead, and never again behold my city!   My City.   James Weldon Johnson.   BANP; CDC; PoNe

To be deceived in your true heart's desire/Was bitterer than a thousand years of fire!   A Woman's Love.   John Milton Hay.   HBV 1-2

To be decent and clean,/Although they are ever so poor.   Dirty Jim.   Jane Taylor.   HBV 1-2; HBVY

To be drowned in space where all that was/is sound in a deaf ear, fear in a forgotten dream.   The Jungle.   Louis Dudek.   PeCV

To be faithless and faithful together/As we have to be.   Hymn to Priapus.   D. H. Lawrence.   CMoP; CoBMV; MoAB; OBMV

To be filled, like the bucket/at the bottom of the well.   Bucket in the Well.   Connie Wanek.   AMV-80

To be filled with a litter of Sunday newspapers?   The Rock.   Thomas Stearns Eliot.   TRV

To be forgiven is to understand.   Forgiveness.   Elizabeth Sewell.   EaLo

To be fruitful, increase, and multiply, sir.   The Female Husband, Who Had Been Married to Another Female....   *Anonymous.*   CoMu

To be gilded and yet grow old.   Why They Waged War.   John Peale Bishop.   NYBP

To be his lover/or his mother.   Chances.   Brenda S. Stockwell.   AMV-81

To be lean'd and to lean on.   Song of the Broad-Ax (excerpt).   Walt Whitman.   MoAmPo

To be let go.   Running under Street Lights.   Christy White.   AMV-80

To be Long Gone...   Long Gone.   Sterling A. Brown.   BALP; BANP; BPo

To be lost evermore in the main.   A Ballad of the Fleet.   Alfred, Lord Tennyson.   FaPoR

To be made sweet and strong of heart/In Lincoln's brotherhood.   The Man of Peace.   Bliss Carman.   OHIP

To be man/within the totality/of his functioning   Gimel.   Stuart Z. Perkoff.   VWA

To be pilot and stray–witch,/Hansel and Gretel in one.   The Plantation.   Seamus Heaney.   FaBoIP

To be quite sure!   A Shadow of the Night.   Thomas Bailey Aldrich.   AA

To be reading a Japanese lexicon/And to be unable to forget.   The Verb "To Think'.   D. J. Enright.   OxBC

To be reborn,/gaudeamus.   Inside, Outside, and Beyond.   John Ratti.   AMV-80

To be remembered in love, a clear molting sensation.   Rude Awakenings.   Bob Rosenthal.   APU

To be revealed/Next at that great Platonic Year,/And then meet here.   His Winding-Sheet.   Robert Herrick.   AnFE; CaPo; HBV 1-2; OBEV

To be sad and to stay sad.   Being Sad.   Orhan and Halman Veli Kanik.   LLLT

To be so great–so kind, so wise!   On a Picture of Lincoln.   John Vance Cheney.   PGD

To be spiritualized by each new American   Brown River, Smile.   Jean Toomer.   AmNP; PoBA

To be the first name on his Faction's roll.   The Temple of Infamy (excerpt). Charles Harpur.   PoAu 1-2

To be the Horace of our times and his.   To his Friend Ben. Johnson, of his Horace made English.   Edward, Lord Herbert of Cherbury.   AnAnS 2

To be the image each first was.   Primer of Plato.   Jean Garrigue.   MoVE; NOBA

To be the leastest bit afraid of things that couldn't be?   There Are No Wolves in England Now.   Rose Fyleman.   HBMV

To be the things we are.   For My Father on His Birthday.   Greg Kuzma. Str

To be their goddess, serve/The movable feasts of love.   Birth of Venus. Constance Urdang.   PoA

To be their hard sounds/as their bodies leave the water.   The Red Dog. Laura Jensen.   LCAP

To be there,/Oh, to be there.   Spell.   Robert Francis.   GP

To be thrown away   Four Translations from the English of Robert Hershon. Robert Hershon.   NeAC

To be touched/by you   Love Song.   Kosrof Chantikian.   AMV-81

To be ungrateful, cruel, vain, austere!   To a Beautiful but Heartless Coquette. Francisco de Terrazas.   LiTW

To be untangled from these mother's bones.   With Child.   Genevieve Taggard.   AnEnPo; MoAmPo

To be, while winter's horrors last,/The sport of every pelting blast.   Address to Plenty.   John Clare.   OBRV

–To be/within the silver mirror and in her.   Sonnets to Orpheus.   Rainer Maria Rilke.   OBVE

To be young before the heart grows old!   Summer Song.   Edith Nesbit. PoSC

To be your beadsman now that was your knight.   The Old Knight.   George Peele.   OBSC; TrGrPo

To bear the pleasures/as we have borne the pains   Mothers.   Nikki Giovanni.   CNA; UnPo

To beat real iron out, to work the bellows.   The Forge.   Seamus Heaney. FaBoIP

To beat the barking bow-wow.   Hush-a-Bye a Baa Lamb.   Anonymous. OxNR

To beat the leisured snarling drill.   Folk Tune.   Richard Wilbur.   AmFN

To beat with rose and river in one song.,   Beyond Possession.   Elizabeth Jennings.   BoC; NePoEA

To become as quaint as leagues and palms/In an old poem.   Elegy for Yards, Pounds, and Gallons.   David Wagoner.   PoA

To become/other trees   The Underside of Trees.   Charlotte De Clue. TWSS

To become the prey of a shark or whale,/With my drownded shipmates of the Nightingale.   The Nightingale.   Anonymous.   ShS

...To bed go sober,/Falls with the leaf, still in October.   Drink To-day.   John Fletcher.   EnLit; HBV 1-2; OAEP; ViBoPo

To bed with such a bitch!   Grizzel Grimme.   Anonymous.   FaBoEE

To bedrocks out of time, with time to kill.   The Pilot in the Jungle.   John Ciardi.   MiAP

...To begin, to be, to defy.   Beyond the End.   Denise Levertov.   NeAP; VGW

To behold and see/The Trinity. Amen.   The Gift of a Skull.   John Skelton. ACP

To behold the face of Jesus, in/The meeting in the air!   Only One Life. Gladys M. Bowman.   STF

To bend the law to let his mercy out.   Young Lincoln.   Edwin Markham. OHIP

To bid me heed before the approach of winter's sterner day.   October.   Jones Very.   AnNE

To bind the poet's brow, or please the critic's nose.   An Ode: Secundum Artem.   William Cowper.   PP

To bind them to us with the flesh of struggle/and revolt.   They Are Ours. A. B. Magil.   PoNe

To bind us together more: equal in adversity.   That Room.   John Montague. CIP

To birds and me the need to sing!   The Recall.   James Russell Lowell.   AP

To bits that are too little to be heard.   Canonical Hours.   William Dickey. CoAP

To blessed islands and a port of peace.   Invocation and Prelude.   Stefan George.   AWP

To blink behind bars at the zoo.   Famous Poet.   Ted Hughes.   LiTM

To blood beneath, my own blood,/O my sweet wife!   I Think Sometimes... Michael Hartnett.   CIP

To bloom one perfect day, and then to/die.   Gold-of-Ophir Roses.   Grace Atherton Dennen.   AA

To blow a second Crystal Palace.   Epitaph: "A glassblower lies here at rest." J. B. Morton.   FaBoEE

To blow her pipes when I will dance again.   The She Wolf.   Muriel Spark. NYBP

To blow the dust from my family crest, my cup.   Homeward Bound.   Jim Brodey.   ANYP

To blow them out with a breath.   A Birthday Candle.   Donald Justice. NYBP

To blue and green/Is queen   Was Worm.   May Swenson.   BoAnP

To borrow his dog to lead the spheres a-begging.   Invocation.   Thomas Randolph.   MOON

To box the crazy compass of bad dreams.   Plane Geometer.   David McCord. NYBP

To branch and glimmer in the living flood.   Dark Corner.   Graham Hough. NMP

To brave Jack Morrissey and Paddies evermore.   Morrissey and the Russian Sailor (with music).   Anonymous.   AS

To break the axe's edge of time and Fate!   Sonnets.   Frederick Goddard Tuckerman.   AP

To break the wing o' my bonny moorhen.   The Bonny Moorhen. Anonymous.   GBP

To breathe and blossom in the dark!   In the Dark.   Frances Louisa Bushnell. AA

To bring forth tears again.   Is It Because of Some Dear Grace...   Louis Golding.   TrJP

To bring my morning coffee to a boil.   Elegy Written in a Country Coal-Bin. Christopher Morley.   OBAL

To bring our hearts and offer them/Unto our King in Bethlehem!   Star of the East.   Eugene Field.   PGD

To bring the honey to the wind.   Ah Me, If I Grew Sweet to Man.   Michael (Katherine Bradley and Edith Cooper) Field.   EnLoPo

To bring the wonder/To your eyes?   Fifth Birthday Gift.   Marjorie Lederer. BiCB

To Bristol Town then haste ye down,/Your sweethearts to revive all.   A New Song on the Blandford Privateer.   Anonymous.   OBSS

To broaden into boundless day.   In Memoriam A.H.H., XCV.   Alfred, Lord Tennyson.   GTBS-P; LoBV; NAWM 1-2; OAEL 1-2; OAEP; PoEL 1-5

To bryng hys sowlle to the blysse of heven,/For he was a gentyll knyght. The Battle of Otterburn (A vers.).   Anonymous.   BaBo; ESPB

To build a grander future.   Song of the Redwood-Tree.   Walt Whitman. AmPP

To build a kingdom yet to be.   O God, Above the Drifting Years.   John Wright Buckham.   AH

To build a world for the free.   My Name Was Legion.   Hildegarde Hoyt Swift.   AmFN

To bundle time away/That the night come.   That the Night Come.   William Butler Yeats.   CoBMV; PoEL 1-5

To burn forever with a clear flame/and not be taken.   Yahrzeit Candle. Jean Nordhaus.   AMV-81

To burst in twain the galling chain and free our native land.   The Boys of Wexford.   Anonymous.   ELP

To burst into fulfilment's desolate attic.   Deceptions.   Philip Larkin. CABA; CMoP; GTBS-P; NePoEA; NMP

To bury her face in the dust of Puerto Pobre.   Esperanza.   James Scully. LTB; NYP

To bury me, bury me/Deeper, ever so little deeper.   Maud.   Alfred, Lord Tennyson.   AtBAP; OAEP; VLP

To buy a horse to plough.   Richard Dick upon a Stick.   Anonymous. OxNR

To buy a pound o' woo'.   Cripple Dick upon a Stick.   Anonymous.   OxNR

To buy his wife a looking-glass.   Tommy Trot.   Anonymous.   OxNR

To buy sugar plums and honey/For the Terra del Fuegian and the Turcoman and Turk.   Husband and Heathen.   Sam Walter Foss.   OBAL

To buy the bairn a bell.   Dingle Dingle Doosey.   Anonymous.   OxNR

To call each colored weed a flower.   The Unknown Soldier.   Charles A. Wagner.   AnAmPo

To call, in the harsh morning, sleep-stupid faces through the daily gate. Birmingham.   Louis MacNeice.   CMoP; MoAB; MoBrPo

To call your distant soil their own.   The Atlantides.   Henry David Thoreau. ViBoPo

To "Canaan's fair and happy land, where my possessions/lie."   The Old Hymns.   Frank Lebby Stanton.   BLRP

...To career/up the plunge of the hill.   The Way Through.   Denise Levertov. AmC; NeAP; PoM

To carry hope to all the sons of men.   Ad Patriam (excerpt).   William Dudley Foulke.   PGD

To cast the first hard stone.   Black Magdalens.   Countee Cullen.   BANP

To catch a glimpse of April's face?   March.   Robert Loveman.   AA

To catch a sunbeam in her cup.   The Crocus.   Walter Crane.   SoPo

To catch the stars.   Moonbeam.   Hilda Conkling.   BrR

To cause me sing or to rejoice/Within my heart.   Since you will needs that I shall sing.   Sir Thomas Wyatt.   FCP; SiPS

To celebrate the need of comrades.   Calamus.   Walt Whitman.   AP

To celebrate this April, I must be/Younger than ever in my memory. Forsythia Is the Color I Remember.   Joseph Cherwinski.   AMV-80

To celebrate this Holy One,/The GOD of peace and love.   Psalm for Christmas Day.   Thomas Pestel.   OxBoCh

To challenge the child's strength in the hour of fear.   Grandmother and Child.   Ruth Dallas.   AnNZ

To change or alter a love like mine.   Ad Finem.   Ella Wheeler Wilcox.   BLPA; FPL

...To/change/Polis/is this   The Maximus Poems.   Charles Olson.   CAPP; NOBA

To change the green/to gold.   Farmers.   Hortense Roberta Roberts.   AMV-81

To charm our souls, as thou enchant'st our ears.   To Music: A Song.   Robert Herrick.   CaPo

To chase Andromeda, you leave me.   Love–bittersweet, irrepressible–.   Sappho.   BoWoP

To cheat of slumber all her foes/And cheer the wakening nations!   A Ballad of the Boston Tea-Party, December 16, 1773.   Oliver Wendell Holmes.   MC; PAH; PAL

To cheat surprise and prying eyes,/Why, kiss me quick, and go!   Kiss Me Quick and Go.   Silas S. Steele.   BLSo

To cheer God along.   Conscience.   Henry David Thoreau.   AnNE; HBV 1-2

To cheer the plowman with increaseful crops,/And waste huge stones with little water drops.   The Rape of Lucrece.   William Shakespeare.   LiTB; PoEL 1-5

To cherish them and be neglected and not think it inhuman.   Major Macroo.   Stevie Smith.   NLV; SBG

To choose/The Jews.   How Odd.   W. N. Ewer.   FaBoEE

To choose 'twixt love and nausea, heart and belly.   A Channel Passage.   Rupert Brooke.   MOS

...To circumvent/The darkness of the grave with bright intent.   The Cemetery Is.   Audrey McGaffin.   NePoAm-2

To city where the small matter is put down already/To depreciation.   Entry.   Josephine Miles.   AnAmPo

To civilise with graver notes our wits again.   Ode on Leaving the Great Town.   Thomas Randolph.   GoTL

To clarity to power/to the rebirth of real men   Spirits Unchained.   Keorapetse Kgositsile.   PoBA

To clasp in love's captivity,/And keep them one–is mine.   The Lake.   John Banister Tabb.   AmP

To clear away the morning dew.   Come, Let Us Find.   William Henry Davies.   HBMV

To clear her fame, yea, very babes have yearned/Over this saddest story of the isles.   Mary Queen of Scots.   Charles Tennyson Turner.   HBV 1-2

To climb, as now, to Lewesdon's airy top.   Lewesdon Hill.   William Crowe.   NOEC

To climb even higher than Mambo/and put an enduring roof upon this House.   Climbers.   Musaemura Bonus Zimunya.   WhB

To cling about, to strangle, to destroy.   The Sleeper.   Sara Henderson Hay.   DFT

To cling where mostly its infrequent rays/Fall golden on the patience of the dead.   Many Are Called.   Edwin Arlington Robinson.   MAmP; MoVE; OxBA

To cloak my care, but under sport and play.   Caesar, when that the traitor of Egypt.   Sir Thomas Wyatt.   FCP

To close the curtains of her eyes/And bind her golden hair.   The Dying Girl.   Richard D'Alton Williams.   OnYI

To clothe in perdurable pride/Beauty his transient eyes descried.   The Image-Maker.   Oliver St. John Gogarty.   OBEV; OBMV; PoRA

To clutch and hug the rags of yesterday/and sing and dance for the dawn.   The Beauty of Dawn.   Felix Mnthali.   WhB

To coast from Heaven down where the world things are.   Up Silver Stairsteps.   Jesse Stuart.   AmFN; AmFN 005

To coax, where the cry fades, fires which cannot fall.   The Snow Curlew.   Vernon Watkins.   NYBP

To cold quicksilver backing mounted glass.   Chronology.   Turner Cassity.   PoA

To come and ride the starry road/Across the holy circle of the sky.   Thomas Iron-Eyes Born Circa 1840. Died 1919, Rosebud Agency, S.D.   Marnie Walsh.   WPOW

To come and soothe away my bitter pain.   To Our Ladies of Death.   James (1834-82) Thomson.   BSV; GoTS

To come awa a wedded wife,/Gae hame a maid the morn.'   Fair Annie.   *Anonymous.*   ESPB

To come home to.   The Rose.   Robert Creeley.   AP

To come to my house and his shirt'll be done.   The Cambric Shirt.   *Anonymous.*   BaBo; FSW

To come to the aid of their party.   Testing, Testing.   Dan Dillon.   PV

To comfort her who leaves the earth behind.   The Dark Road.   Ethel Clifford.   HBV 1-2

To comfort you and dry the tear/Of penance from your eyes....!   Auf Wiedersehen.   Donald Jeffrey Hayes.   CDC

To comfort you and to lecture me/For trying, she'll say, to be funny.   The Anatomy of Humor.   Morris Bishop.   InMe; NLV

To compass you, and light your souls to death!   Tecumseh.   Charles Mair.   PeCV

To confront night, storms, hunger, ridicule, accidents, rebuffs, as the/trees and animals do.   Me Imperturbe.   Walt Whitman.   NOBA

To conquer the country by trade.   Battle of the King's Mill.   Thomas Dunn English.   MC; PAH

To consecrate the flicker, not the flame.   George Crabbe.   Edwin Arlington Robinson.   AmePo; AP; BLPL; CMoP; CoBMV; LiTA; MAmP; MoAB; MoAmPo; MoVE; NAMP; NePA; NOBA; NoP; OxBA; PoEL 1-5; PP; TAP

To consider Ruin.   Way-Out Morgan.   Gwendolyn Brooks.   BP

To console you for being little/And dead.   Lullaby for My Dead Child.   Denise Jallais.   BoWoP

To continue arrivals of the young   Once and Future.   Diana Chang.   BrSi

To cool her passions, or to fan their flame.   To a Lady, with a Present of a Fan.   Charles Brandling.   FaBoUs; NOEC

To cool in some blue distant place/Till death or dawn should find my face.   Joy o' Living.   Amanda Benjamin Hall.   HBMV

To cool the conflagration in my head.   Wreck.   Noel Polk.   AmC; AMV-81

To country of the dead.   The Coming.   Anthony Delius.   ACV

To court all night and sleep all day.   Rose in the Garden.   *Anonymous.*   AmFP

To court the queen in her high silk pavilion.   The Face in the Mirror.   Robert Graves.   NoP; WeW

To cover it, spilt water on the place.   Amores.   Ovid (Publius Ovidius Naso).   UnTE

To cover up the tired day/In such a cozy sort of way.   The Quilt.   Mary Effie Lee Newsome.   CDC

To covet fetters, though they golden be.   Amoretti, XXXVII.   Edmund Spenser.   AAS; NoP; OBSC; TrGrPo

To cram a lifetime into seven days.   "For Whom the Bell Tolls".   Gavin Ewart.   WaP

To crawl away over the horizon.   These Days.   William Stafford.   NNaP

To create you anew out of my love.   Prayer.   Claire Goll.   TrJP

To creep outside and see the cops were gone.   A Gesture by a Lady with an Assumed Name.   James Wright.   ConAP; LiTM

To crickets' farewell tunes.   Autumn Song.   Elizabeth-Ellen Long.   SiSoSe

To cross it you have to bridge it, and it will not flow uphill.   Lives.   Henry Reed.   BoNaP; LiTB

To cross, spiral, and whirl.   Cincophrenicpoet.   Bob Kaufman.   PoNe

To crown the men who serve me best.   They Pray the Best Who Pray and Watch.   Edward Hopper.   AH

To crown with peace sweet Doneraile.   Blessings on Doneraile.   Patrick O'Kelly.   OnYI

To crush the foe, or sleep with you,/In Flanders Fields.   Another Reply to In Flanders Fields.   J. A. Armstrong.   BLPA; PAL

To crush the low, delicate plants/and dream his weight will never rise.   The Annunciation.   Margot Kriel.   PoDr

To cry, to cry with the violin.   South of the Border.   Virginia Real Nicholas.   AMV-80

To curb the fretful brain and trust the blood.   Wait for the Hour.   William Soutar.   NeBP

To cure the secret sore of ling'ring love.   Concerning the Nature of Love.   Lucretius (Titus Lucretius Carus).   ErPo

To curse–as I have cursed–their birth.   Epigram: "I curse my bearing, childhood, youth."   John Millington Synge.   FaBoEE

To cut his throat before he married.   On an Upright Judge.   Jonathan Swift.   ALV; DBV

To cut loose my roots,/and like the drifting duckweed/Give in to the water's will.   Since I've Felt This Pain.   Ono no Komachi.   WPOW

To cut off a branch of that true-lover's knot,/And buried them both in one grave.   Lord Lovel (A vers.).   *Anonymous.*   BaBo

To cut the throats/Of those old bloats/Who cut the poor miners' wages!   A Curse on Mine-Owners.   *Anonymous.*   TW

To dally by the edge of the stream.   In Between the Curve.   Barbara Bacon.   AMV-80

To dance and sing,/To sing and dance.   Music.   Eleanor Farjeon.   TiPo

To dance & cry,/thank life,/and die./Love,/Andy   Andy-Diana DNA Letter.   Andrew Weiman.   HAP

To dance with a stone wall/would be easy/only listen   A Tribe Searching.   Shlomo Reich.   VWA

To dance with every weekend/to prove that they're alive.   The Gilded Boys.   Felice Picano.   PeHV

To dance with joy on all my legs/and live to lay a thousand eggs.   How and When and Where and Why.   Phyllis Gotlieb.   WHW

...To/darken it more and more toward the color of the human.   Race Riot, Tulsa, 1921.   Sharon Olds.   MAYP

To dat res'less, wretchit fevah evah Sprin'.   Sprin' Fevah.   Ray Garfield Dandridge.   BANP

To Day it self's too late, the Wise liv'd Yesterday. Epigrams. Martial (Marcus Valerius Martialis). OBVE

To-day may then be yesterday–/I may be yours again! A Song of Impossibilities. Winthrop Mackworth Praed. InMe; NA

To-day the garden is gazing/With eyes like anemones. In the Breeze. Boris Pasternak. TrJP

To-day the Kid bears scars, 'tis true,/Brands of the Red God's own. The Wrangler Kid. Anonymous. BPAW

To-day the Roman and his trouble/Are ashes under Uricon. A Shropshire Lad. Alfred Edward Housman. BrPo; GTBS-P; OAEP

To-day! to-day! Glycine's Song. Samuel Taylor Coleridge. CH; OBEV; PoPl

To death the host of all our golden dreams. Saint Germain-en-Laye. Ernest Christopher Dowson. SyP

To deeds of pure self-sacrifice,/And the sweet tasks of love. Beneath the Shadow of the Cross. Samuel Longfellow. BePJ

To delve like a mole or mingle like a nightjar/Into the earth, into the air, into the water. The Battle of Aughrim: Rapparees. Richard Murphy. BIrV; NOBI

To describe ordinary things. On Meeting the Clergy of the Holy Catholic Church in Osaka. Joy Kogawa. BrSi

To desecrate a British workman's grave. They're Shifting Father's Grave. Anonymous. CoMu

To dethe hathe brouth my spouse and me. Alas, That Ever That Speche Was Spoken. Anonymous. EnLoPo

To die again with no heart left to hurt. Four Sonnets to Helen, 2. Pierre de Ronsard. LiTW

To die and know it. This is the Black/Widow, death. Mr. Edwards and the Spider. Robert Lowell. AmP; AP; CAPP; CMoP; CoAP; FaBoMo; HeIP; InPS; LiTA; LiTM; MoAB; MoPo; MoVE; MP; NePoEA; NOBA; NoP; PAI; SeCeV; SoSe; TwCP

To die for home/ - and leant on Heaven/Our hand. New England. James Gates Percival. AA

To die in public/or in the rain. For Cal. James (Olumo) Cunningham. JB

To die!/O my! A Piazza Tragedy. Eugene Field. FiBHP; NLV

To die when he awakes in God! The Moss Supplicateth for the Poet. Richard Henry Dana. AA

To different nations makes their blessings even. Real Happiness. Oliver Goldsmith. OBEC

To dig their own deep grave and lay it there. Short History of Twentieth-Century Scholarship. John Wain. GLGT

To dim the memory of that love outpoured/Upon thee by thy stainless knight and/lord. Lohengrin. William Morton Payne. AA

To Dionysos, god of grapes. The Vine and the Goat. Aesop. AWP

To dip, alas, into some unseemlier world. Old Mansion. John Crowe Ransom. HeIP; NOBA

To discover the world/in its dazzling nakedness Illusion. Jan Rak. LiTW

To dismiss an effigy/Which appears to be singing. America. Bernadette Mayer. ANYP

To disturb that even-tempered summer's repose? Sonnets to Orpheus. Rainer Maria Rilke. OBVE

To dive for Cocles, and to digge for Clamms,/Whereby her lazie husbands guts shee cramms. Kinds of Shel-Fish. William Wood. SCAP

To dive into the eye of the needle. In Quest to Have Not. Edwin Honig. LiTA

To do all which may achieve and cherish a just and/lasting peace among ourselves and with all... America's Task. Abraham Lincoln. PGD

To do without you altogether. Abnegation. Martial (Marcus Valerius Martialis). UnTE

To do good deeds and straight to cloak them, lied. Epigram: "He drank strong waters and his speech was coarse." Rudyard Kipling. PV

To do his will whose glory shines in thame. Sonnet: "The azured vault, the crystal circles bright." King of England James I. ElL; MOON; SeCePo

To do me harm, content to do amiss? When All This All Doth Pass from Age to Age. Fulke, Lord Brooke Greville. EBEV

To do something very common, in my own way. A Valediction Forbidding Mourning. Adrienne Rich. NoAm; NoP

To do the best you can? Suppose. Phoebe Cary. BLPA; BLPL

To do the right deed for the wrong reason. Murder in the Cathedral. Thomas Stearns Eliot. GoTF; TreFT

To do the wrong'd Corinna right for thee. The Imperfect Enjoyment. John Wilmot, Earl of Rochester. BoLoP; ErPo; UnTE

To do what's right/With all your might. Night Blessing. Anonymous. HBVY

To do without eating at all! Limerick: "There was a princess of Bengal." Walter Parke. NA

To do without what blood remained these wounds. A Terre. Wilfred Owen. LiTM; MMM; OxBTC; WaP

To do worthy the writing, and to write/Worthy the reading, and the world's delight? Musophilus. Samuel Daniel. FaBoRV

To doat upon me ever! Love Not Me for Comely Grace. John Wilbye. ALV

To drag my carcass around Cape Horn/A long time ago! Around Cape Horn. Anonymous. AmSS

To draw down the lover's hand/from its lightness to what's/underground. Such Is the Sickness of Many a Good Thing. Robert Duncan. CAPP

To draw water for any stranger. Sudan. Michael Jackson. OCNZ

To draw you these cold winters away. Old May Song. Anonymous. AtBAP

To dream of women whose beauty was folded in dismay,/Even in an old story, is a burden... Under the Moon. William Butler Yeats. EG

To dream on a world of immortality. Kaire. Richard Eberhart. NoAm

To dream sweet, idle dreams of having/strayed/To Arcady, with all its golden lore. The Haunts of the Halcyon. Charles Henry Luders. AA

To dresse and chuse the Corn, take those the Chaffe that will. Emblems. Francis Quarles. AnAnS 1

To drift between the cold forts of the stars. Three Elements. Stephen Vincent Benét. EaLo

To drink a new worlds/Breaking light. Africland. Oliver La Grone. FB

To drink the brack that Ahab spit at heaven. Memories of Aunt Maria-Martha (parody). William Zaranka. BXAP

To drink your wine mixed with sweet drafts of dews. A Song of the Moon. Claude McKay. PoNe

To drive again/bent nail/into old hurt? For Fear. Robert Creeley. NoAm

To drive away the flies, madam. May No Man Sleep in Your Hall. Anonymous. GBP; NCEP

To drive away the thoughts of the darling girl that was so dear to me. The Lone Star Trail. Anonymous. BFSS

To drive us mad. Madhouse. Calvin C. Hernton. IDB; NNP; PoNe

To drop head-foremost in the jaws/Of vacant darkness and to cease. In Memoriam A.H.H., XXXIV. Alfred, Lord Tennyson. OAEL 1-2; SeCePo

To drop in trees, lover by lover. The Stockdoves. Andrew Young. BoAnP

To drown there, stifling in the stiff, cold air. Fisherman. Sacheverell Sitwell. AtBAP

To dry my glazed flesh with/some of your happy brilliance. Little Light. Jim Brodey. APU

To dry those tears, and to blow out those fires? Tears, Flow No More. Edward, Lord Herbert of Cherbury. AnAnS 2; AtBAP; ElL; OBS; SeCP

To dump you dizzied and dreaming in the green grass. Blues for Benny Kid Paret. Dave Smith. LiSp

To Dunvegan hi-o/ro h-oran o a ho-o. A Complaint about Exile. Mairi MacLeod. PBWP

To dwarf the ox he envies for his size. The Georgiad. Roy Campbell. MoBrPo

To dwell a ghost amid the ghosts. Metrum Parhemiacum Tragicum. Pope Eugenius III. WaaP

To dwell with men on earth again. When God Descends with Men to Dwell. Hosea Ballou I. AH

...To each his own/Piss-golden light. To an Alcoholic. Sandra McPherson. MAYP

To each is given what defeat he will. Three Sermons to the Dead. Laura Riding. LiTA

To eat and drink me out of house and home. No Continuing City. Michael Longley. FaBoIP

To eat mutton cold, and cut blocks with a razor. Edmund Burke. Oliver Goldsmith. InvP; OBEC; SeCeV

To eat my rice alone A Sometimes Love Poem. George Leong. BrSi

To eat or forget our real origins. A Letter to Ron Silliman on the Back of a Map of the Solar System. Dennis Schmitz. LCAP

To eavesdrop/On the conversation/Of cooks. The Partial Explanation. Charles Simic. FiCP; NoP

To echo the birdstorms of those early/sunsets, what high river of electron, cell and star? Passenger Pigeons. Robert Morgan. GeTw; MAYP

To end all movements save movements like these. The Glass of Pure Water (excerpt). Hugh" (Christopher Murray Grieve) MacDiarmid. BSV

To end in madness–both in misery. The Dream. George Gordon, Lord Byron. BeLS; CABL; ERoP 1-2; TEP

To end it in the sacred name of man! Peace. Edwin Markham. PGD

To end my life in that I loved best. Would I Were Chang'd into That Golden Shower. Sir Arthur Gorges. GBL

To end, or much the same, to begin. Digging It Out. John Hollander. AmPC

(To end this otherwise would be/Immoral!) Ode to Work in Springtime. Thomas Russell Ybarra. HBMV

To enhance thy dignities. Mot Eran Dous Miei Cossir. Arnaut Daniel. AWP

To enjoy our opportunities they remain. This Is My Carnac, Whose Unmeasured Dome. Henry David Thoreau. EyDe

To enter the ruined monastery of sleep. A Prophecy. Christopher Levenson. ErPo

To err with her/On some other fur? Would You Like to Sin. *Anonymous.* PV

To escape from out the cage/By the edges and the side. The Cage. James Stephens. OxBTC

To every birth its pain/All else is death or life My Name Is Afrika. Keorapetse Kgositsile. PoBA

To every door, O Pain, thou hast a key! My Uninvited Guest. May Riley Smith. AA; WGRP

To every finger's end from rapture deep and still. Sights and Sounds of the Night. Carlos Wilcox. AnAmPo

To every woman a happy ending. Barbie Doll. Marge Piercy. DFF; NIP

To exchange the cock for old Sibylla/Was From Charybdis into Scylla. The Hag and the Slavies. Jean de La Fontaine. AWP; OBVE

To explore lunar dust and Martian clays/For their most distant of cousins. The Supremacy of Bacteria. Robert Frazier. SUW

To face a task with nothing but my skill/and struggle for the mark I must excel. Challenge. Samuel Hazo. SD

To face the still shackling ways of this strange, distant land. Cape Coast Castle Revisited. Jo Ann Hall-Evans. BlSi

To fairies couched on bubbles round the pool. Sonnets, IX: "An isle of trees full foliaged in a meadow." Thomas Caulfield Irwin. IrPN

To faith and hope, and Bethlehem's light! The Forgotten Star. Thomas Curtis Clark. PGD

To fall asleep under the influence/of a different gravity. Waiting. Judith Skillman. SUW

To fall down together, down/down, down, derry down,/down, down, derry dina. The Maid of Tottenham. *Anonymous.* CoMu

To falter would be sin. Right Is Right. F. W. Faber. TRV; WBLP

To Father a Child was none of his/The clean contrary way. The Old Man and Young Wife. *Anonymous.* CoMu

To father and mother we will bid adieu.' New Garden Fields. *Anonymous.* OBET

To father men and poems in your mind. To a Visiting Poet in a College Dormitory. Carolyn Kizer. PoA

To father my bairn on Auld Ingram,/An Lord Wayets beside!' Lord Ingram and Chiel Wyet (C version). *Anonymous.* ESPB

To Father, Son, and Holy Ghost. True Son of God, Eternal Light. P. J. Cormican. AH

To fear himself, and love all human kind. Hymn to Intellectual Beauty. Percy Bysshe Shelley. AnEnPo; BiP; BLPL; BoLiVe; EnL; ERoP 1-2; HAP; HeIP; MBW 1-2; NoP; OAEL 1-2; OAEP; OBNC; OBRV

To feed a bard, and to be praised in verse. To the Immortal Memory of the Halibut on Which I Dined This Day. William Cowper. AnAnS 2; MOS; OBS; PoEL 1-5; SeCePo; SeCP; SeCV 1-2

To feed ez they hev fed me. The Biglow Papers. James Russell Lowell. AnNE

To feed on that which to disused tastes seems tough. His Picture. John Donne. CBEP

To feed such a freak you can't hire us. Limerick: "Of inviting to dine, in Epirus." Carroll Watson Rankin. TDH

To feel if pricking were so good indeed. She sat and sewed... Sir Thomas Wyatt. FCP

To feel once more that fresh, wild thrill/I'd give–but who can live youth over? The Doorstep. Edmund Clarence Stedman. HBV 1-2

To feel that great heart beat,/And recognise my own. The Londoner in the Country. Richard Church. HaMV

To feel the comfort of His soft embrace. The Sacrament of Sleep. John Oxenham. PoLf

To feel the earth as rough/To all my length. To Earthward. Robert Frost. ; APA; BiP; BLPL; BoLiVe; CoBMV; HBMV; InPo; LiTA; MoAB; MoAmPo; MoPo; MoVE; NePA; NoAm; NOBA; NoP; OxBA; PPoe; TAP

To feel the perennial forgetfulness of the sea. Pain. Alfonsina Storni. WPOW

To fell and fiery disaster/Right off the Block Island shore. The Phantom Ship. J. W. De Forest. EtS

To fell kings, guesses/where we go? Coda. Basil Bunting. OAEL 1-2

To fiddle-faddle in a minor key. The Devil's Dictionary: Elegy. Ambrose Bierce. OBAL

To fight and catch the great white butterfly. The Vixen. John Clare. BoAnP

To fight, and to conquer, to conquer or die. Truxton's Victory. *Anonymous.* PAH

To fill my dark with fire, my heart with faith? The Power and the Glory. Siegfried Sassoon. OBMV

To fill my hands with/this poem for you. Batches of New Leaves. Jonathan London. AMV-80

...To fill our days with beauty/from whatever faucet's available. My Sons. Ron Loewinsohn. DFF; NeAP

To fill the catalogue of human woes. Ode: "I hate that drum's discordant sound." John Scott. NOEC

To Fin, Caolte, and Conan, and Bran, Sgeolan, Lomair. The Wanderings of Oisin. William Butler Yeats. BrPo

...To find a jewel/Made of pain in his hands. Folk Wisdom. Thomas Kinsella. TwCP

...To find a new beauty/in some terrible/wind-tortured place. Sheltered Garden. Hilda ("H. D.") Doolittle. PG

To find a permanence in pain, at least. Two Sonnets for a Lost Love. Samuel A. DeWitt. GoYe

To find fault with the rest of us. Charity. *Anonymous.* BLPA

To find himself himself. To stand. To moo. A March Calf. Ted Hughes. NoP

To find in Art no fellow but the wind. The Wind at Penistone. Donald Davie. LiTM; NePoEA-2; NMP

To find it an oblate spheroid. Clerihews. Edmund Clerihew Bentley. FiBHP

To find, like me, by Flames a sudden death? Violets in Thaumantia's Bosome. Sir Edward Sherburne. OBS

To find me now will cost you everything. Whitman. Larry Levis. MAYP

To find milk/sweeter than hummingbird's breath. How Came She to Such Poppy-Breath? Judith Mountain Leaf Volborth. TWSS

To find our suicidal surrogate no longer there. Of a Mouse and Men. A. J. Hovde. AMV-81

To find out how the Ceiling's Feeling. The Ceiling. Theodore Roethke. EyDe

To find set duly on the hollow stone. The Hellenics. Walter Savage Landor. EnRP

To find something worth celebrating/With a good cup of coffee. 40 Acres and a Mule. Dick Gallup. APU

To find that all the sages said/Is in the Book our mothers read. The Book Our Mothers Read. John Greenleaf Whittier. BLRP; TRV

To find that he is not alone. Poem for Easter. Robert Kelly. VGW

To find that the white man wrongs the one/Who never did harm to him. The Indian Hunter. Eliza Cook. BLPA

To find that wisdom in which you shall live. The Swarthmore Phi Beta Kappa Poem. Richmond Lattimore. GLGT

To find the apple, quince, and pear. Little Friend. *Anonymous.* OxNR

To find the invitation/(from the birds of Arles)/was no longer current. The Birds of Arles. David Fisher. NPGG

To find the meaning of the wind/the message of the rain. The Message of the Rain. Norman H. Russell. STE

To find the mystic floodway of the North. The Polar Quest. Richard Burton. AA

To find the people that they knew. Doubting. Louis Simpson. NNaP

To find the right mixture that cures my specialized life. Mixed Media. James Schevill. AMV-81

To find the Walls of Derry/Or the land of the Ever Young. Novelettes III: The Gardener. Louis MacNeice. FaBoIP

To find them kosher/For an owl. Rev Owl. Abraham Moses Klein. TrJP

To find them there in fact, black as intended,/But small enough. Find. Josephine Miles. NoP

To find they have flown away? The Wild Swans at Coole. William Butler Yeats. ACV; BoAnP; CMoP; DiPo; FaBoPP; FaBoRV; FM; HeIP; InPS; MBW 1-2; MoAB; MoBrPo; MoVE; NoAm; NoP; OnYI; PB; PBBP; PPP; SoSe; SOTW; TEP; UnPo; WHA

To find this gripping earth alive with her. The Diver. Leonard Nathan. ErPo

To find 'twas the effort, the essay of love. Too Anxious for Rivers. Robert Frost. CBEP

To find what furies made him man. Goose Pond. Stanley Jasspon Kunitz. PoA

To fire my clay, when I am still. Rumination. Richard Eberhart. LiTA; LiTM

To fire the insurgent freedom of the heart. The Night Loves Us. Louis Adeane. NeBP

To fit a bed for this huge birth. Shepherds Hymn Their Saviour. Richard Crashaw. EG

To fit this slim person of Lynn. Limerick: "There was a gay damsel of Lynn." *Anonymous.* LiBL; NA

To fix a place and choose an early home/With yellow breast and head of solid gold. The Yellowhammer. John Clare. NOBV

To fix in us our frail intent–/A paradox of permanence. August Night, 1953. Elizabeth B. Harrod. NePoEA

To flailing hooves and a hundred sharp suns. My Father Dragged by Horses. T. Alan Broughton. AMV-80

To flare, in the sun-pallor of his rock. The Bird with the Coppery, Keen Claws. Wallace Stevens. AnFE; APA

To flash at last, sparking the mountain falls/of Restigouche–spawning a silver million. Poem on Canada: Cold Colloquy. Patrick Anderson. CaP; NOBC; PeCV

To fle the fendis, than hardely sing/De terra plasmasti me. The Testament of Mr. Andro Kennedy. William Dunbar. OxBS

To flee away, and be at rest. I Would I Were a Careless Child. George Gordon, Lord Byron. ERoP 1-2

To flee the fly who now flew by.　Combinations.　Mary Ann Hoberman. OBCA

To float/off their stems/and go　Loss.　Archie Randolph Ammons. ConAP

...To float on the night-face/Of water, with white stars to drift as a dark world. A Dark World.　E. J. Scovell.　MoVE

To float through/the deluge　An Inhabited Emptiness.　Jiri Gold.　VWA

To flounder where the mountain and the whirlpool meet.　Route 95 North: New Jersey.　P. C. Bowman.　AMV-80

To fly me to the Scilly Islands,/Isles of Scilly, Scilly.　Gaiety of Descendants. Douglas Newton.　NeBP

To follow her superior Road–/Or its advantage–Blue–　I watched the moon around the house.　Emily Dickinson.　MOON

To follow knowledge like a sinking star,/Beyond the utmost bound of human thought.　Ulysses.　Alfred, Lord Tennyson.　TRV

To follow me to the green wood.　Song Set by Robert Jones: "In Sherwood lived stout Robin Hood."　Anonymous.　OBSC

To follow one clear Beacon Light/Across eternity.　Beacon Light.　Leslie Savage Clark.　PGD

To follow the outline/of a city street whose perspective/darkens with the morning light?/Document.　Sexual Privacy of Women on Welfare.　Pinkie Gordon Lane.　BlSi

To follow Thee, to fight for Thee,/Knights of the Holy Ghost.　Victoria. Henry Van Dyke.　TRV

To follow, to seek, to be with her dear dead son.　Come Up from the Fields Father.　Walt Whitman.　AmePo; MCCG; MoAmPo; OBWP; OxBA; PPP; UnPo

To follow you I'll not consent/Because I know which way you went.　A Curt Addendum.　Anonymous.　ShM

To follow you I'm not content,/Until I learn which way you went.　Epitaph: "Remember man, that passeth by."　Anonymous.　GoTF

To follow you is not my intent,/Unless I know which way you went.　An Epitaph and a Reply.　Anonymous.　TreFS

To force a man of the Croydon class/To live, or to love, or to speak! Nervous Prostration.　Anna Wickham.　FaBoWP; TW

To force out each bud to the hungry day.　A Spring Memorandum.　Robert Duncan.　PoA

To forgive an earth that shakes so/with savage important noise?　Nearing Winter.　Ernest Sandeen.　NYBP

To forgive our illusion.　Alonso to Ferdinand.　W. H. Auden.　MoPo

To forgive you once more/your merely human shape?　Old Clothes.　Phil Hey.　GOYP

To form them fair, for them I labor. For them I make.　The Song of Bekotsidi.　Anonymous.　OBVE

To former dust in death we turn,/Till He inspire again.　A Psalm for Sunday Night.　Thomas Pestel.　OxBoCh

To frame her cloudy prison for the soul!　Ode: Autumn.　Thomas Hood. OAEL 1-2; OBNC; OBRV; PoEL 1-5; UnPo; VLP

To free the nigger/in his head?　Watts.　Conrad Kent Rivers.　BOLo; PoBA

To freeze the tongue, and fire the heart.　Upon His Timorous Silence in Her Presence.　Francis Davison.　EG

To freighted ships baffled in wind and blast.　Let Zeus Record.　Hilda ("H. D.") Doolittle.　MoAmPo

To freighted ships, baffled in wind and blast.　Stars Wheel in Purple.　Hilda ("H. D.") Doolittle.　NoAm; NOBA; TAP

To fright the frost out of the grave.　The Sad Shepherd.　Ben Jonson. AtBAP; GoBC

To future age of her this mention may be made.　The Faerie Queene. Edmund Spenser.　OAEL 1-2

To gad my little Being out–/And not begin–again–　It would have starved a gnat.　Emily Dickinson.　MoVE; NAWM 1-2; SBG

To gain a Scepter, oftest better misst.　Paradise Regained.　John Milton. CABL

To gain at harvest an eternal Treasure.　Our Life Is Hid with Christ in God. George Herbert.　OAEL 1-2

To gain Eternity, the goal you sought.　Washington.　John A. Prentice. OHIP

To gain my soul's desire/And see Thy face, O Lord.　The Soul's Desire. Eleanor Hull.　OxBI

To gather my feathers/for quills　Visions of Mexico While at a Writing Symposium in Port Townsend...　Lorna Dee Cervantes.　FIA

To gather the daisies, and drop them, and sleep on the/nursing knees of the Fates.　The Wisdom of Merlyn.　Wilfrid Scawen Blunt.　OBMV; ViBoPo

To gaze, my Lord, on Thee!　I Need Thee.　Frederick Whitfield.　BePJ

To gaze upon the sun with shameless brows.　A Masque Presented at Ludlow Castle (Comus).　John Milton　ViBoPo

To gaze with longing through the grey, mossed rails.　The Pea-Fields.　Sir Charles G. D. Roberts.　NOBC; OBCV; PeCV

To gestures,/and love!　Poem of Holy Madness, IV.　Ray Bremser.　NeAP

To get a man to pity me.　The Milkmaid's Epithalamium.　Thomas Randolph.　BoLoP

To get out of this seaport/You must be a cutter of networks.　Poem. Bernadette Mayer.　ANYP

To get some happiness from life and pass it on to other folk.　An Ancient Prayer.　Thomas H. B. Webb.　BBV; BLPA; FaBoBe

To get the truly-wanted present.　The Christmas Exchange.　Arthur Guiterman.　BrR; ChBR

To get what will be lost as soon as won.　Of the Boy and Butterfly.　John Bunyan.　NIP; OxBChV

To girlhood, boyhood look, the teacher and the school.　An Old Man's Thought of School.　Walt Whitman.　GLGT

To git into a place that sold the "stuff"–when ye had to/be known, old pard! The Tale of the Dixie-Belle.　Frank Chase.　InMe

To give a hint that might suggest the whole.　Dauber.　John Masefield. EtS

To give–and forgive–/Is a good way to live.　Lessons.　Louis Untermeyer. TiPo

To give grace to seek Saint Truth, God grant they/so might!　The Vision of Piers Plowman.　William Langland.　EnLi 1-2

...To give me/in marriage to/I-know-not-who.　To Leave the World Serve God.　Compiuta Donzella.　WPOW

To give our King the victory....　Henry Before Agincourt.　John Lydgate. CH

...To give out/all the temporary ornaments I can to peace.　From Heraclitus. Alan Dugan.　PoA

To give repentance to her lover,/And wring his bosom–is to die.　Song: "When lovely woman stoops to folly."　Oliver Goldsmith.　AWP; BoLoP; LAuP; LiTL; NOBE; NOEC; OBEC; PoPl; SeCePo; TrGrPo; ViBoPo

–To give/thanks, I say, that, distracted, He clap not His/Hands!　October Flies.　Jascha Kessler.　AmPC

To give them seals, never, my soul, consent!　Hamlet.　William Shakespeare. TreFT

To give us honor strong as death/And loyal love as sure.　Young Windebank. Margaret Louisa Woods.　HBV 1-2; HBVY

To give us room to wander was the world/made wide!　The Song of the Sons of Esau.　Bertha Brooks Runkle.　AA

To give us time to make the little more love/We'd dreamed of before the tow truck came.　Warren Phinney.　Bernadette Mayer.　APU

To give us true peace, that mischief may/cease,/And war may give place unto love.　Robin Hood and the Scotchman.　Anonymous.　ESPB

To glad the heart and save from harm.　The Lament of the Flowers.　Jones Very.　MAmP; NOBA; OxBA

To glassed-in children at the window sill.　Questioning Faces.　Robert Frost. ELU; GrPl; NCSH

To glorifie her after death, She'll ne'er/Need Change; She's Angel now, and Heav'n is here.　On Clarastella Singing.　Robert Heath.　OBS

To glorify the earth–and you–and me.　Pennsylvania Station.　Langston Hughes.　AmNP

To glut the worm that never dies–/Hurrah! hurrah! hurrah!　Song of the Three Hundred Thousand Drunkards...(excerpt).　William B. Tappan. PeD

To go hunting I am not good at!　It Is Hard to Catch Trout.　Piuvkaq. WTO

To go on,/To go on!　We Go.　Karl Wolfskehl.　TrJP; VWA

To go three journeys ere your letter came.　Country Letter.　John Clare. CBEP; NCEP

To go unguessed.　Apology.　Amy Lowell.　BoLiVe

To go unto the bride, and use this day/To speak with her while freely speak we may.　Geron and Histor.　Sir Philip Sidney.　SiPS

To go with me/to the darkness/where I go.　Fantasy in Purple.　Langston Hughes.　BANP; CDC

To go with the old grey Widow-maker?　Harp Song of the Dane Women. Rudyard Kipling.　AtBAP; HAP; OAEP; OBNC; PoRA; SeCePo

To go with vestments red on Pentecost.　Tulips.　Padraic Colum.　ImOP

To go without my rib.　"What? Rise Again with All One's Bones."　Samuel Taylor Coleridge.　HBV 1-2

To God alone our praise we give/Who safely brought us there.　The Loss of the Due Dispatch.　Anonymous.　AmFP

To God the Father equal praise/And Holy Ghost through endless days. Ascension Hymn.　Jean-Baptiste de Santeuil.　CAW

To God, to Her, and to the land/Wherein you nursed were.　A Joyful New Ballad.　Thomas Deloney.　ViBoPo

To gods who don't mind being photographed,/who have the aplomb of models. Hold My Hand.　Edmund Pennant.　PoDr

To going straight to where we are?　Our Bias.　W.H. Auden.　AtBAP; ILwL; NoAm; NoP

To gorge the gods and a voracious fire:　The First Olympionique to Hiero of Syracuse.　Pindar.　ATP

To grasp the wind and love inconstancy.　Sicelides: Woman's Inconstancy. Phineas Fletcher.　EIL

To greet a world/Gone mad with mountains.　Cousins.　Paula B. Cullen. AMV-81

To greet the living presence of that old sweetheart of mine.　An Old Sweetheart of Mine.　James Whitcomb Riley.　BeLS; BLPA; FPL; TreFS

To greet us, crying, dancing,/After the long day.　The Cats.　Weldon Kees.　NaP

To grow and gently grow and grow/Is something people should do too.　Lesson.　Harry Behn.　TiPo

To grow more loving every day.　A Prayer.　*Anonymous.*　SoPo

To guard a gleaming pot of gold/For a busy leprechaun.　Could It Have Been a Shadow?　Monica Shannon.　SoPo; TiPo

To guard it so as nothing here shall be/Heavy, to hurt those sacred seeds of thee.　To His Dying Brother, Master William Herrick.　Robert Herrick.　CaPo; OAEP; PoPle; SeCV 1-2

To guard my steps, whatever may betide.　Touch Thou Mine eyes.　Marion Franklin Ham.　AH

To guard the sacred volume of the laws.　The Pleasures of Imagination.　Mark Akenside.　EnPE; EnRP

To guard thee ever gay and free,/Beneath thy green Banana tree!　Christmas in Penang.　John Leyden.　OBTV

To guide men down the years,/Until they cross the last long bridge of sighs.　The Unutterable Beauty.　G. Anketall "Woodbine Willie" Studdert-Kennedy.　TrPWD

To guide us as our footsteps make/The pilgrimage to Paradise.　It Cannot Be.　David Banks Sickels.　HBV 1-2

To hail the King of Glory.　A Christmas Carol.　Christina Georgina Rossetti.　BiCB

To hale a coffined corpse adown the stairs:/For you will die.　Heiress and Architect.　Thomas Hardy.　VLP

To hang all old strange things, let his wife beware.　Antiquary.　John Donne.　EBEV; FF; NIP

To hang his pants on while he slept.　Museum Piece.　Richard Wilbur.　CMoP; ConAP; FaBoMo; MiAP; NePA; NIP; PoPl; PPoe; TAP

To happy worlds, where I/Still in thy love belong.　The Philosopher to His Mistress.　Robert Bridges.　LiTM; OAEP; PoEL 1-5

To harken if the whisper/Of what you knew is dead.　A Pine-Tree Buoy.　Harrison Smith Morris.　AA

To haste me hence, to find my fortune's fold.　Farewell to the Court.　Sir Walter Ralegh.　CBEP; EG; EnRePo; FaBoEn; FCP; OBSC; SiPS

To hate those errors which herself doth give.　O Wearisome Condition.　Fulke Greville, Lord Brooke.　CBEP

To haunt thy sleep.　Never More, Sailor.　Walter De la Mare.　EtS; MOS

To have a little bug all lit/And made to go on wings.　Firefly.　Elizabeth Madox Roberts.　GoJo; NTCP; SUS; TiPo

To have a pair of horns than lose his ears.　The Ear-Maker and the Mould-Mender.　Jean de La Fontaine.　UnTE

To have been quite a sound scheme.　Clerihew.　Edmund Clerihew Bentley.　NOBL

To have free chaise,/And spede as well.　Distant as the Duchess of Savoy.　*Anonymous.*　MeEL

To have her God become her lover.　An Ode Which was Prefixed To a Prayer Booke.　Richard Crashaw.　AnAnS 1

To have his carven agate-stone/On such a bosom rise and fall so!　On an Intaglio Head of Minerva.　Thomas Bailey Aldrich.　HBV 1-2; InMe

To have knowledge of/The way that walk I must.　I Spread Out unto Thee My Hand.　Henry Ainsworth.　AH

To have my part with all the saints,/And with my God.　Paradise.　Christina Georgina Rossetti.　HBV 1-2; OxBoCh; WGRP

To have my stars afford the world their shining.　Resignation.　*Anonymous.*　OBSC

To have one moment of thy dawn,/Than share the city's year forlorn.　Nature.　Henry David Thoreau.　BLPL; FaBoBe; HBV 1-2

To have one's whole life punched by seconds/up to the very end...　The Punching Clock.　Milos Macourek.　LiTW

To have the mastery?　The Sunflower.　Peter Quennell.　AtBAP

To have to go to bed by day?　Bed in Summer.　Robert Louis Stevenson.　GoJo; NLV; OxBChV; PoPl; TreFT

To have,–to hold,–and,–in time,–let go!　The Teak Forest: For This Is Wisdom.　Laurence Hope.　PoLf

To have, when the original is dust,/A name, a wretched picture, and worse bust.　My Days of Love Are Over.　George Gordon, Lord Byron.　OBNC

To have you day and night,/To love me best of all.　If fancy would favor.　Sir Thomas Wyatt.　AAS; FCP; SiPS

To have you with me there below,"–/Said Aucassin to Nicolette.　Provencal Lovers.　Edmund Clarence Stedman.　HBV 1-2

To heal the world with your heart's compassion!　Abraham Lincoln.　Joseph Auslander.　YaD

To heap with many a harvest-dream/The granary of Sleep.　The Reaper.　John Banister Tabb.　ACP

...To hear a boy's heart break.　An Incident in the Early Life of Ebenezer Jones, Poet, 1828.　Sir John Betjeman.　CMoP; NoAm

To hear a cart go jolting down the street!　The Shell.　James Stephens.　BoNaP; CH; CMoP; MoAB; MoBrPo; MOS; MoShBr; MoVE

To hear again her low good-night! good-night!　Good-Night.　Hester A. Benedict.　HBV 1-2

To hear again his living voice.　June.　William Cullen Bryant.　AA; HBV 1-2

To hear bleak winds go moaning down the sand,/By the wild sea.　The Heritage.　Edward Bliss Reed.　EtS

To hear breathing in the still house of the Judge/where I live.　In the House of the Judge.　Dave Smith.　MAYP

To hear first/bear hoots/of spring　Winter, New Hampshire.　David Kherdian.　TAT

To hear his own fury/Wishing his love were dead.　Song: "Make this night loveable."　W. H. Auden.　TW

To hear Lead Belly/spit the Blues out　Lead.　Jayne Cortez.　PoBA

To hear no sound but three times three.　Song: "In his last bin Sir Peter lies."　Thomas Love Peacock.　OBRV; ViBoPo

To hear that seaman tell such wondrous tales...　The Child and the Mariner.　William Henry Davies.　CH

To hear the divine tread fall again and again.　Mr. Brunt.　Robert Siegel.　GeTw

To hear the ecstasy of heaven./Halleluja! Halleluja! Halleluja!　A Christmas Eve Choral.　Bliss Carman.　ISi

To hear the prisoners singing in the sea.　Pick upon Pick...　Alex Comfort.　NeBP

To hear the world applaud the hollow ghost/Which blamed the living man.　Growing Old.　Matthew Arnold.　EnLi 1-2; FaFP; FiP; HBV 1-2; MaVP; NOBV; OAEL 1-2; PoEL 1-5; VLP

To hear them howling/In the hills.　The Monster.　Greg Kuzma.　AmPA

To hear, to feel her tender taken breath,/Half-passionless, and so swoon on to death.　Bright Star (Original version).　John Keats.　NIP

To hear your chorus once again!　John Marr (excerpt).　Herman Melville.　ViBoPo

To hearten up a dowie child,/Fancy's the limmer!　Ille Terrarum.　Robert Louis Stevenson.　OxBS

To Heaven and Earth and men.　Three Hours.　Vachel Lindsay.　ATP

To Heaven her branches and to Hell her roots.　The Progress of Learning: Preface.　Sir John Denham.　OBSP

To Heaven's gate a burden sweet–/The World's low vesper prayer.　At the Edge of the Day.　Clarence Urmy.　HBMV

To heaven's gate upwinging.　Thanksgiving for the Earth.　Elizabeth Goudge.　YeAr

To hell I'd rather run, than I/Would see thy face, and he not by.　No Coming to God without Christ.　Robert Herrick.　EBCP; OBSP; OxBoCh; TRV

To Hell with the King of Siam!　Dynastic Tiff.　Geoffrey Hellman.　ALV

To hell with the man that works!　We Are Four Bums (with music).　*Anonymous.*　AS

"To hell with ye!" says she.　The Brewer's Man.　Leonard Alfred George Strong.　DBV; DTC; ELU; FaBoCo; FiBHP; NLV

To help an ignorant earthling on/to the radiance that he–the bodiless–/is now possessed of!　The Guide.　Arthur Gregor.　GP

To help him with their kind good will.　Riddle: "Promotion lately was bestow'd."　*Anonymous.*　CoBE

–To help me eat up her money.　Song for the Squeeze-Box.　Theodore Roethke.　NePoAm; NLV

To help moon find her feathers in the snowy pools.　Crow's Way.　Duane Niatum.　CDW

To help our cause and break the jaws/Of cruel tyranny.　The Wyoming Massacre.　Uriah Terry.　PAH

To her, a sweeter flower than all the rest.　A Dream of Flowers.　Titus Munson Coan.　AA

To her are echoes sending.　Awake, Mine Eyes!　*Anonymous.*　ElL

To her Dorking Hens she moans,/For the Yonghy-Bonghy-Bo.　The Yonghy-Bonghy-Bo.　Edward Lear.　LBN; NA

To her let us garlands bring.　The Two Gentlemen of Verona.　William Shakespeare.　BLPL; DiPo; ElL; FaFP; GN; HBV 1-2; InPo; LiTB; MCCG; OAEL 1-2; OBEV; SeCeV; TreF; TrGrPo; ViBoPo

To her who gave me all I give these songs.　Offering.　Thomas Macdonagh.　ACV

To herald our perpetual shame/By this perennial bird.)　Cock-Crow: Woodstock.　Henry Morton Robinson.　CAW

To hide a cloud in a frame.　The Ship.　J. F. Hendry.　NeBP

To hide the evidence I am no longer I.　News from a Pacified Area.　James Keir Baxter.　OxBC

To him be glory, power, praise,/From this, unto the last of days.　Easter Hymn.　Henry Vaughan.　EBCP; PoPle

To him belong–/To him, to him, the dead that shall not die!　An Ode: "Not with slow, funereal sound."　Thomas Bailey Aldrich.　PAH

To him belongs nought but the Foul.　To God Alone, the Only Donour.　Francis Daniel Pastorius.　SCAP

To him, in place of men, for he is old, suffice/Melancholy remembrances and vesperal.　The Church of a Dream.　Lionel Pigot Johnson.　OAEL 1-2; OBMV

To him life I gave, on him life I thrust–/Was it–death–too? The Mother. Kathryn White Ryan. CAW

To him shall thanks and praise ascend,/My Saviour and my God. Send Forth, O God, Thy Light and Truth. John Quincy Adams. AH

To him–sums Misery– It Makes No Difference Abroad. Emily Dickinson. DiPo

To Him that heard my wailing voice. As Spring the Winter Doth Succeed. Anne Bradstreet. AH; EBCP

To him that overcometh/The common day is sweet! Christ and the Common Day. Marguerite Wilkinson. BePJ

To Him, through every rescu'd land,/Ten thousand Living trophies stand. An Ode: "Thou Dome, where Edward first enroll'd." Thomas Tickell. OBEC

To him, to whom belongs/All Praise in Prose and Songs. Thy Garden, Orchard, Fields. Francis Daniel Pastorius. SCAP

To Him whose face was covered by a cloud. St. John the Baptist. Arthur William Edgar O'Shaughnessy. HBV 1-2

To his ability to make a deacon's wife the first night. Peg Leg Snelson. Melvin B. Tolson. FAZ

To his extreme annoyance, tempted him. On Lady Poltagrue, a Public Peril. Hilaire Belloc. ALV; FaBoCo; GoTF; PoL; PV; TreFT

To His Father's house and festival/And the right-hand seat. Prodigals. Charles L. O'Donnell. HBMV

To his pale lips lay pressed! The Fifth of May–Napoleon. Alessandro Manzoni. CAW

To his sorrow he finds with his match he has met,/And wishes the devil had Mog the Brunette. Mog the Brunette. *Anonymous.* CoMu

To hiss and spume her orgasm. Our Mother's Body Is the Earth. Mary McAnally. AMV-80

To hold a mountain's heartbeat in his hand No Man, If Men Are Gods. Edward Estlin Cummings. InvP; MoPo; NePA; VGW

To hold her Thermopylae. On Installing an American Kitchen in Lower Austria. W. H. Auden. NYBP

To hold my faith, and to live my life,/Making the most of its shadowy day. In Green Old Gardens. Violet Fane. HBV 1-2

To hold the name of Molly Pitcher. Molly Pitcher. Laura E. Richards. PAH; YaD

...To hold the world together/like hooved up ground/thats what The Hermit Cackleberry Brown, on Human Vanity:. Jonathan Williams. OBAL; PoM

To hold this rampant earth, and fly/My love on the strength of its out-bound stride. Runaway. Kim Kurt. NePoAm-2

To hold you to me, Sweet! To a Lost Sweetheart. Don (Donald Robert Marquis) Marquis. FiBHP; PoL

To home and friends and everything/That gives your mission worth. Soft Landings. Howard Sergeant. OnUR

To honor all their deaths who for her bleed. Astrophel and Stella, XXI. Sir Philip Sidney. CABA

To honour all their deaths who for her bleed. Astrophel and Stella, VII. Sir Philip Sidney. AAS; NIP; SiPS

To hunger, work illegally,/And be anonymous? Our Hunting Fathers. W. H. Auden. FaBoMo; NoAm

To hunt, to hold its mark/–This loved hand. A Hand. Bernard Spencer. NeBP

To hunt, under Springer Mountain,/Deer for the first and last time. Springer Mountain. James Dickey. CAPP

To hurl myself into the changeless grave! Living. William Dean Howells. AmePo

To imagine a language means to imagine a form of life. The Ninth of July. John Hollander. CoAP

To insure courageous chocolate dwells there. The Chocolate Soldiers. Calvin Forbes. MAT; MAYP

To invent, and practise this one way, to annihilate all three. The Will. John Donne. EBEV; LiTB; MePo; OAEP

To Ireland bound–nor message need/From the girl I left behind me. The Girl I Left behind Me. Thomas Osborne Davis. FaFP; OnYI; TreF

To Ireland, on cloud-riven pinions/The Dead and the Fairies go. The Violin Calls. Florence Randal Livesay. CaP

To its work in the morning gay. Dolcino to Margaret. Charles Kingsley. HBV 1-2

To Jesus Christ our Lord, and God,/The hearts and souls of men. Soft Job. William C. Summers. STF

To join quiet hands across the breakfast table. Adversaries. Louis Johnson. ACV

To Jove, dear Theon, be resigned. Plato To Theon. Philip Freneau. AA

To joy, annoy, friends, foes; but 'twill not be. Of the Great and Famous Ever-to-be-Honored Knight, Sir Francis Drake.. Robert Hayman. CH; FaBoCh; NoP

To joyful news divine/Lend us your listening ears. A Carol for Christmas Day. William Byrd. SBVL

To jubilant surprises. Busts and Bosoms Have I Known. *Anonymous.* ErPo; PV

To jump back up into the sky. Starfish. Winifred Welles. SiSoSe

To just such golden ones as these O All Down within the Pretty Meadow. Kenneth Patchen. HAP

To keep a small girl for the tenth of a year. A Thought. James Kenneth Stephen. FiBHP

To keep clearly in mind/That it's probably only your liver! Consolatory! St. John Emile Clavering Hankin. CenHV

To keep from making/a mistake. Counting Sheep. Aileen Fisher. SoPo

To keep grass/Over your grave. Monumentum Aere, Etc. Ezra Pound. NOBA

To keep kids from shitting in the chapel/like they used to do The Grotto. Ray Fraser. NeAC

To keep me free from either ill! Against Women Either Good or Bad. Thomas Norton. EIL; ViBoPo

To keep out the ice and the sleet. The Slushy Snow Splashes and Sploshes. Mary Ann Hoberman. TiPo

To keep the Goddess constant and glad. The Flight of the Goddess. Thomas Bailey Aldrich. HBV 1-2

To keep the tryst, if he come soon or late. Two Paths. Julia Caroline Ripley Dorr. AA

To keep the weather/cool. The Cure All. Don L. Lee CAD

To keep their mother's blondness gay is food. Brothers. Solomon Edwards. NNP

To keep them safe in my own body,/and knew I would again. Amen. The Children. William Heyen. GeTw; GP

To keep to the one furrow,/As I do now? The One Furrow. R. S. Thomas. HoPM; OxBC

...To keep track/of what passes, what preserves. Preserves. Michael Waters. GeTw

To keep what we do/from coming apart at the ends. Saturday Afternoon, when Chores Are Done. Harryette Mullen. AMV-81

To keep white-blowing loveliness in reach. The Newlyweds. Cloyd Mann Criswell. PoLf

To keep, with fairy lanterns,/The world from growing old. Buttercups. Wilfrid Thorley. HBV 1-2; HBVY; OBVV

To keep you from crying, I'll sing for you,/A little evening parting song. Each Day Is Anxious. Anna Akhmatova. AMV-81

To keep your foot out of your food/When mommy says you should. Bad and Good. Alexander Resnikoff. NTCP

To keepe the memory of our Armes alive. To My Friend G. N. from Wrest. Thomas Carew. AnAnS 2; CaPo

To kill all the living/And resurrect the dead. Wang Peng's Recommendation for Improving the People. Paul Eldridge. ShM

To kill us by looking as if she would die. Song: "Methinks the poor town has been troubled too long." Charles, Earl of Dorset Sackville. SeCV 1-2

To kindle, or to slake,/Although in SKELTON's Ryme. To Himselfe and the Harpe. Michael Drayton. OBS

To kiss and clip me till I run away! Venus, with Young Adonis. Bartholomew Griffin. ViBoPo

To kiss and hug in God's insulted view. Sonnets: A Sequence on Profane Love. George Henry Boker. AmePo

To kiss freely: if not, you may go spin. That Beauty I Ador'd Before. Aphra Behn. UnTE

To kiss her sweetest. The Faithful Shepherdess. John Fletcher. ViBoPo

To kiss my body, quivering and cold. The Quiet Woman. Genevieve Taggard. AnEnPo

To kiss the gentle shade, this while that sweetly sleeps. Polyolbion. Michael Drayton. PBBP

To kiss the naked phrase quite unaware. En Monocle. Donald Evans. AnAmPo

To kiss them and how suddenly I say/good luck in cracked Italian as I turn my face. Maratea Porto: Saying Goodbye to the Vitolos. Richard Hugo. MAT

To kiss Thy feet. The Garden of the Holy Souls. Harriet Eleanor Hamilton King. ACP

To kiss upon thy lips a stainless fame. To George Sand: A Desire. Elizabeth Barrett Browning. TEP

To kisse her lippes, and lye next at her hart,/Runne through her vaynes and passe by pleasures part Jove for Europaes Love Tooke Shape of Bull. Barnabe Barnes. AAS

To kneel down, to forget the impossible weight/Of being human, to drink clear water. A Chinese Vase. Edward Hirsch. AMV-80

...To knit/The heart to God, to unbind the sorrow on silent lips. Psalmodist. Leib. VWA

To know and do Thy will. I Do Not Ask Thee, Lord. *Anonymous.* BLRP

To know by the calloused hands steering. If There Is a Perchance. Thomas McAfee. AMV-81

To know he still is warm though I am cold. After Death. Christina Georgina Rossetti. EnLi 1-2; GBL; TEP

To know I'm farther off from heaven/Than when I was a boy. I Remember, I Remember. Thomas Hood. BLPA; CBEP; ELP; EnLit; FaBV; FaFP; FaPoR; FPL; HBV 1-2; LiTB; MyFE; NOBE; OBRV; PoEL 1-5; TreF

To know myself for nought, and Christ for all in all. Dedication. Laurence Housman. TrPWD

To know some word of mine had won/And saved a soul from death? Nothing Better. *Anonymous.* STF

To know, that Love lodg'd in a womans brest,/Is but a guest. A Poem Written by Sir Henry Wotton, in His Youth. Sir Henry Wotton. AnAnS 2

To know/that we're alive/we are alive. Noni Daylight Remembers the Future. Joy Harjo. TWSS

To know this time of completeness gone. Brief Farewell. Anthony Delius. PeSA

To know, too late, the Fairy in disguise. Opportunity. Madison Cawein. AA

To know who I am/why I came there/what and why I am and/made to happen Hotel Transylvanie. Frank O'Hara. NeAP; PoM

To labor and not ask for any reward/save that of knowing that we do Thy will. Amen. Teach Us to Serve Thee, Lord. Saint Ignatius Loyola. TRV

To labor for eternity,/Our wills all Thine. A Prayer for Pentecost. Catherine Bernard Brown. BLRP

To lamp me through inscrutable dusk/And down the catacombs of death. Winter Anemones. Charles Brasch. OCNZ

To lap in sacred sadness, or inspire/Thy strings to Beauty's moods, oh, Summer lyre. Sonnets, II: "The rainbow o'er the sea of afternoon." Thomas Caulfield Irwin. IrPN

To last after touch, taste, sight, hearing. Voice. Stanley Moss. AMV-80

To laugh at pain and trouble and keep up his grit. Hang to Your Grit! Louis E. Taylor. WBLP

To laugh at the rise of the Darling River. Song of the Darling River. Henry Lawson. ACV

To launch off with absolute faith, to sweep through the/ceaseless rings and never be quiet again. Song of the Answerer (excerpt). Walt Whitman. PP

To lay a wounded heart in leafy rest,/And dream of things far off and healing,–Spenser. The Dearest Poets. [James Henry] Leigh Hunt. HBV 1-2

To lay aside their weapons and sleep in each other's arms. Homosexual Sonnets. Kenneth Pitchford. GP

To lay his head upon your fragrant lap/And be surprised. Metamorphoses of M. John Peale Bishop. ErPo

To lay my head in the light's lap'. The Human Fold. Edwin Muir. LiTM

To lay this cold and lovely dust? Ghosts. Ethna MacCarthy. NeIP

To learn that "Later, dear" means never. Grandpa Is Ashamed. Ogden Nash. PV

To learn the angels' song. I Lay My Sines on Jesus. Horatius Bonar. BePJ

To learn the disgrace in which gluttony ends. The Notorious Glutton. Ann Taylor. OxBChV

To learn the rapture of defeat. The Romantic. Colin Ellis. PoL

To learn 'tis not my heart alone/That bears thy sacred name. At Lanier's Grave. John Banister Tabb. AmP

To leave but only the merest possible taint! Suburbs on a Hazy Day. D. H. Lawrence. OBMV

To leave my Boots. Our Photographs. Frederick Locker-Lampson. ALV; DBV

To leave the dead/So alone, so wretched. They Closed Her Eyes. Gustavo Adolfo Becquer. AWP

To leave the wallowing-pool that coats his sides/And back and belly with protective ooze. The Buffalo. Herbert Price. ACV

To leave this life, not loving it, but Thee. To His Ever-Loving God. Robert Herrick. AnAnS 2; TrPWD

To leave Thy own for long in hell–/Have mercy, Lord! Supplication. Edgar Lee Masters. TrCP; TrPWD

To leave with them and thee behind! A Farewell to America. Richard Henry Wilde. AA

To leave your shadow lingering/there? The Shadow Rose. Robert Cameron Rogers. AA

To legalize whoredom and abortion. Greasy Spoon Blues. Len Gasparini. NeAC

To let a thousand such enjoy their quiet. Madrigal: "A sparrow hawk proud did hold in wicked jail." *Anonymous.* PBBP

To let me live, O love and hate me too. The Prohibition. John Donne. EG; EiL; MBW 1-2; MeLP; OBS

To let off steam with the Jews/by the synagogue door. Childhood. Edith Bruck. VWA

To let the doubting see/Resurrected life in me. Voice of the Crocus. Mildred N. Hoyer. AMV-80

To let the old carcase of Mounsey be quiet. On the Physician to Chelsea Hospital by Himself. Messenger Mounsey. FaBoEE

To let the soul march with the quiet stars! No Friend Like Music. Daniel Whitehead Hicky. PoToHe

To let the wide world know I died for love. The Rocky Island. *Anonymous.* AmFP

To let them feel they're not quite as nice as they might be. The English Are So Nice! D. H. Lawrence. NoP

To leven, and leave my leman,/Sweetest of all thing? Alas! How Should I Sing? *Anonymous.* NOBI

To liberate my people from its yoke! Enslaved. Claude McKay. BALP; BPo

To lie down and sleep than to quarrel and fight. Two Little Kittens. *Anonymous.* OBCA; OxBChV

To lie down before it and play dead Poem: "The only response." Bill Knott. InPK

To lie forever in unlovely sleep/Which not a prince on earth has power to break. The True Story of Snow White. Bruce Bennett. SM

To lie, untrodden, in the sun! Crotalus. Bret (Francis Bret Harte) Harte. AA

To lie with me here at mid-stream,/tight in the lap of the rain. Above the Falls at Waimea. Don Johnson. MAYP

To lift a leg and play the baptist. Epigram: "Why should scribblers discompose." Walter Savage Landor. FaBoEE

To lift a stiffened limb, or pluck/The seaming of a shroud. Mole Talk. Leo Kennedy. PeCV

To lift her over the threshold, and let her in/at the door! The Witch. Mary Elizabeth Coleridge. BrRo; NCEP

To lift me up out of the rough/And permit my spirit to soar. I Have Heard. *Anonymous.* FiBHP

To lift one like a lantern in her hands. Winter Apples. Winifred Welles. AnAmPo

...To light a board/Washed on that coast by the grey sea. Cadaver Politic. Tom Paulin. FaBoIP

To light in the mind the violent statue, to unwind the Laocoon. Laocoon. Don Gordon. WaaP

To light me where I soon may see/How to serve you, and you trust me. To Lucasta, from Prison. Richard Lovelace. AnAnS 2; CaPo

To light the first thin taper of the dawn. Moonlight on Lake Sydenham. Wilson MacDonald. CaP

To light the flame of a soldier's fame/On the turf of a soldier's grave. Charade. Winthrop Mackworth Praed. GN

To light there for an instant and everything will crash down/irreparably as the bird flies off. The Gutter. Franco Fortini. VWA

To linger still alive as dead,/What may it avail me? To wish and want and not obtain. Sir Thomas Wyatt. FCP; SiPS

To linger till ninety, like Landor. Obit on Parnassus. F. Scott Fitzgerald. InMe; NLV; NYBP; PrIm

To lisp its secrets to a million reeds/Or tongue its trouble through a waste of weeds. Corn Canon. Patric Stevenson. NeIP

To listen to your singing through its/tears. Little Theocritus. Caroline Wilder (Fellowes) Paradise. AA

To live a life is not to cross a field.' Hamlet in Russia, A Soliloquy. Boris Pasternak. FaBoPV

To live again a butterfly. Caterpillar. Christina Georgina Rossetti. GoJo; OxBChV; SoPo

To live and die/Good news bad news. Good News Bad News. Keith Abbott. APU

To live and lack the thing should rid my pain. A Complaint by Night of the Lover Not Beloved. (Francesco Petrarca) Petrarch. AWP; EiL; FaBoEn; LoBV; TEP

To live as though a pleasant land/Lay just beyond an open door? I Accept. Harold Trowbridge Pulsifer. HBMV

To live at large with liberty,/Birk and green hollin. Hollin, Green Hollin. *Anonymous.* GBP

To live before I sink, deeper than the diver, into the lofty/depth of sleep. Night of Sine. L. Sedar-Senghor. PBA

To live by, in sunlight and moonlight, until they died. Patriotic Tour and Postulate of Joy. Robert Penn Warren. NYBP

To live day by day/Is not to live at all. To Richard Wright. Conrad Kent Rivers. AmNP; IDB; PoBA

To live forever at His side. The Conqueror. Ruth M. Williams. BePJ

To live forgotten, and love forlorn.' Mariana in the South. Alfred, Lord Tennyson. MaVP; VLP

To live, I think of these! Ballade Made in Hot Weather. William Ernest Henley. AnFE

To live in a perpetual spring. The Hours of Sleepy Night. Thomas Campion. EiL

To live in mankind, far, far more than...to live in/a name. The Eagle That Is Forgotten. Vachel Lindsay. AmP; AnFE; APA; ATP; AWP; CMoP; HBV 1-2; LiTA; MoAB; MoAmPo; MoRP; NePA; NOBA; OxBA; ViBoPo; WHA

To live in Paradise alone.... The Garden. Andrew Marvell. CH

To live in this broken world. Fragment of a Pastoral. Barry Schwabsky. AMV-80

To live more nearly as we pray. Help Us to Live. John Keble. TRV

To live on earth, as they in heaven. We Must Not Part. *Anonymous.* DiPo

To live their dreaming. Along South Inlet. Greg Kuzma. WOLT

To live, To die. Moon Deer,/Thee near Beneath this sky. By the Waters of Minnetonka. J. M. Cavanass. BLSo

To live, to love, to be, where now she is. Elegy for Margaret Howard, Lady Buckhurst. Robert Southwell. CoBE

To live upon Tobacco and on hope,/The ones but smoake, the other is but winde. Upone Tabacco. Ayton [(or Aytoun)] Sir Robert. OxBS

To live with him, and sing in endless morn of light. At a Solemn Music. John Milton. ExPo; GTBS; GTBS-P; HBV 1-2; HeIP; LoBV; NOBE; OAEP; SeCeV

To live with more than enough/and everything. February. Larry Moffi. AMV-80

To live with thee and be thy love. Reply. Sir Walter Ralegh. ViBoPo

To live without a friend, and with a wife. Epigram: "There are two miseries in human life." Walter Savage Landor. FaBoEE

To live without him, liked it not, and died. Upon the Death of Sir Albert Morton's Wife. Sir Henry Wootton. AnAnS 2; BoLoP; FaBoEE; NIP; NoP; OBEV; OBS; PoPle; TreFT; ViBoPo; WeW

To live you on afternoons like this. The Double. Irving Feldman. NYBP

To lived unloved, makes us cold; cruel; remote. Search for Love. Henry Johnson. LFAC

To localize her pain with pain. April. John Linthicum. AMV-80

To lofty strains a goodly hand belongs. A Barren Soul. Joseph Ezobi. TrJP

To look again, and link with me in heart. The Looks of a Lover Enamoured. George Gascoigne. ElL; SeCePo

To look for the sunlight hair/That smites like a golden spear! Cressid. Nora Perry. AA

To look into the swarthiest face of things,/For God's sake who has made them. Aurora Leigh. Elizabeth Barrett Browning. OBTV

To lose my wife? A trifle! Last Week I Took a Wife. M. Kelly. BLSo

To love above my poor degree. Alas, Poor Man, What Hap Have I. Sir Thomas Wyatt. FCP; SiPS

To love again, and be again undone. Don Juan. George Gordon, Lord Byron. GoTF; TreF

To Love and Fate an equal Sacrifice. The Exequies. Thomas Stanley. AnAnS 2; MeLP

To love and live with them again! For Andy Goodman–Michael Schwerner– and James Chaney. Margaret Walker. BPo

To love and never seek compassion. You Little Stars That Live in Skies. Fulke, Lord Brooke Greville. ElL; NCEP

To love but him, pardie! Medieval Norman Songs. *Anonymous.* AWP

To love did first apply. What Meanest Thou, My Fortune. *Anonymous.* EnLoPo

To love it is and love alone/That life or luxury is known. The Test. John Banister Tabb. AnAmPo

To love me also in silence with thy soul. Sonnets from the Portuguese, XXI. Elizabeth Barrett Browning. HBV 1-2

To love on, oh yes, to love on. Kissing the Toad. Galway Kinnell. DFT

To love, pacify, or kill. The Friendship. Robert Mezey. NaP

To love so well and live in smart. I Love, Loved, and So Doth She. Sir Thomas Wyatt. EnPo; FCP; SiPS

To love that well which thou must leave ere long. Sonnets, LXXIII: "That time of year thou mayst in me behold." William Shakespeare. AWP; BiP; BoLoP; CTC; DiPo; EBEV; ExPo; FaBoRV; FaBV; FF; FiP; ForPo; GBL; GTBS; GTBS-P; HAP; HBV 1-2; HeIP; HoPM; InPK; InPo; InPS; InvP; LiTB; LoBV; MasP; MBW 1-2; MyFE; NIP; NOBE; NoP; OAEL 1-2; OAEP; OBEV; OBSC; PAI; PoEL 1-5; PoPle; PoRA; PPoe; PPP; PrIm; QFR; SeCeV; SoSe; TEP; TrGrPo; UnPo; ViBoPo; WHA

To love Thee much, to love Thee more and still/More and yet more. Good Friday Evening. Christina Georgina Rossetti. PGD

To love thee still, but goe no more/A begging at a beggars door. I Loved Thee Once. Ayton [(or Aytoun)] Sir Robert. OBS

To love you for your turn and wheel and glide and song. Paradox: The Birds. Karl Shapiro. CrMA

To love you, though I loathe you, so you'll die. All Those I Love Die Young. Bonefonius. DBV

To love your sleep it may not be. Madrigal: "Lady, the birds right fairly." *Anonymous.* PBBP

To low-born arrogance to bend,/Established order spurn, and call each outcast friend. Ode to the German Drama. *Anonymous.* NOEC

To low notes from branches sere. Autumnal Song. Walter Savage Landor. ERoP 1-2; OAEL 1-2

To lull the dog across a bloodless river. Climbing. Jennifer Maiden. CBAP

To lunge up and make monkeys of us all. Oration on the Toes. Edward Brynes. AMV-81

To magnificent pearls they congeal. Limerick: "Said a lachrymose Labrador seal." Oliver Herford. TDH

To maintain thy wife and thy loving family.' The Nobleman and Thresherman. *Anonymous.* OBET

To make a beauty, she. Child and Maiden. Sir Charles Sedley. GTBS; GTBS-P; LiTL

To make a fairer face than heaven,/Of dust and nothing more. The Praise of Dust. Gilbert Keith Chesterton. MoBrPo

To make a poet black and bid him sing! Yet Do I Marvel. Countee Cullen. AmNP; AnAmPo; BANP; BP; BPo; CDC; FF; IDB; MAPA; MOON; NoAm; PoBA; PoNe; TAP; TTY

To make a scolding wife hold her tongue, tongue, tongue. Dumb, Dumb, Dumb. *Anonymous.* OnYI

To make a stone a flower. The Example. William Henry Davies. AnFE; HBMV; MoBrPo; TrGrPo; WHA

To make a Third she joynd the former two. Lines Printed under the Engraved Portrait of Milton. John Dryden. CEP; HeIP; SeCeV; SeCV 1-2

To make a vertue of Necessity. Palamon and Arcite, III: "Parts of the whole are we; but God the whole. John Dryden. NAs

To make a white cake for my Charlie. Over the Water to Charlie. *Anonymous.* OxNR

To make allowance for us all. In Memoriam A.H.H., LI. Alfred, Lord Tennyson. VLP

...To make an end/Of war and want; just this we ask,/We who are Dead. We Who Are Dead. Paul L. Benjamin. PGD

To make dry arroyos run/as singing summer floods In a Double Rainbow. Harold Littlebird. VoR

To make Faith's Countersign/A gray Gull and a Pine! Countersign. Arthur Ketchum. HBMV

To make great summer seem forlorn. Tulip Tree. Sacheverell Sitwell. MoBrPo

To make her a carpet,/To make her a crown. When Mary Goes Walking. Patrick Reginald Chalmers. HBVY

To make his own hole/and one for his wife as well. Johann Gaertner (1793-1887). Gary Gildner. FAZ

To make is such. Let us make. And set the weather fair. A Fanfare for the Makers. Louis MacNeice. NOBE

To make it human good. Morning Prayer. Nissim Ezekiel. ACV

To make me love her and forget her too. Britannia's Pastorals. William Browne. ViBoPo

To make me think of nought but blood and war. Tamburlaine the Great. Christopher Marlowe. TrGrPo

To make me your inheritor. The Division of Parts. Anne Sexton. NePoEA-2

To make men blush there was but one! Washington. George Gordon, Lord Byron. MC; OHIP; PAH; PAL

To make my body full/and moonless light Ghost Poem Five. Mary Norbert Korte. IHMS

To make myself his wench but one half hour. In Francum. Sir John Davies. FaBoEE

To make of night/A forest flowered with light. A Japanese Birthday Wish. Thomas Burnett Swann. GoYe

To make one leaf the next to kiss/That closely by it grew. A Fine Day. Michael Drayton. GN

To make one look only into the centers of their eyes. Saints, and Their Care. Alberto Rios. APU

To make our Christian virtues grow,/And fill our hearts with praise. As Gentle Dews Distill. George Rogers. AH

To make our meanness look like justice in/All histories commissioned by the winners. The Historical Judas. Howard Nemerov. NoP

To make peace with her own monstrous nature. Patience. Elaine Feinstein. BrRo; FaBoWP

To make rocks melt and churches grow. Bard's Chant. James Shirley. ACP

To make sure of not soiling her feet. Limerick: "There was a young lady of Crete." *Anonymous.* OnUR; TDH

To make sure/She couldn't/Hold anything for long. The Lady Pitcher. Cynthia Macdonald. Psk

To make that burning flower. The Maid's Thought. Robinson Jeffers. ErPo

To make the bard, like thee, forget his native sky. To the Canary Bird. Jones Very. AP

To make the coldness visible. Snow-Bound. John Greenleaf Whittier. TrGrPo

To make the harbor glad because she's come. The William P. Frye. Jeanne Robert Foster. MC; PAH

To make the migration of sails/and wings a crying matter. Yachts on the Nile. Bernard Spencer. ChMP

To make the third, she joined the other two. Oyster-Crabs (parody). Carolyn Wells. BXAP

To make thee hear our cries for peace. Faint Falls the Gentle Voice. Henry Timrod. AH

..To make this relation/with the it : to know that I am it. Despisals. Muriel Rukeyser. NMM; Prf

To make up for a lack of meditation. To the Right Person. Robert Frost. GLGT

To make with you my home. Mystic and Cavalier. Lionel Pigot Johnson. MoBrPo; SeCePo; VLP

To make you worthy and lyric and pure. A Kite Is a Victim. Leonard Cohen. NOBC; SD

To make your hope, your health retain,/And me also the most happy. After great storms the calm returns. Sir Thomas Wyatt. FCP; SiPS

To make your one wish come true Armaments Race. Evangeline Paterson. AMV-81

To man's last dust, drain fast towards man's first slime. The Sea and the Skylark. Gerard Manley Hopkins. FM; LiTB; OBMV

To mansions in the skies. Familiar Lines. *Anonymous.* FiBHP

To many a kingdom's rent or tyrant's hoard. The Fleece. John Dyer. NOEC

To many bitter fears/To make a pearl from tears? The Heap of Rags. William Henry Davies. BrPo

To many generations let/His years prolonged be. Give Ear, O God, to My Loud Cry. Thomas Prince. AH

To many, in its beak, no dove brought answer. Memento. Stephen Spender. AtBAP

To mark the periphery/Of what shall be saved from calendars and decay. Three Brown Girls Singing. M. Carl Holman. NIP

To mark those grey untermined seas. Albatross. Charles Burgess. NePoAm-2

To marry a Sailor/Who sails on the sea! Sailor. Eleanor Farjeon. BrR

To marry is to make it ten times worse. Fie on Love. Francis Beaumont. AnEnPo

To marry somebody else's daughter! Song to Be Sung by the Father of Infant Female Children. Ogden Nash. MoAmPo

To mask a king in weeds. Poet. Ralph Waldo Emerson. AnNE; OxBA; PCP

To mastres Anne, that farly swete,/That wonnes at the Key in Temmys strete. Womanhood, Wanton, Ye Want. John Skelton. NCEP

To match the candle with the sun. Give Place, Ye Lovers. Henry Howard, Earl of Surrey. CoBE; FCP; SiPS

To matche the candle with the sonne. Geve Place, Ye Lovers, Here Before. Henry Howard, Earl of Surrey. AAS

To me, a fool, some of your wise brain. Death. Sir Thomas More. EnRePo

To me, at least, your Sherlock give,/'Tis I must learn to die. To a Lady on Reading Sherlock upon Death. Philip Stanhope, Earl of Chesterfield. NOEC

To me Hilo, me Ranzo boy! Huckleberry Hunting. *Anonymous.* ShS

To me it is a pleasant spot--/My husband's tomb. Stranger Call This Not. *Anonymous.* ShM

To me rol, to me rol, to me ride-o. The Ox-Driver. *Anonymous.* FSW

To me sole light he'll e'er remain. Epigram: "Like when the burning sun doth rise." Strato. PeHV

To me they seem no more than weeds or chaff. A Gentle Wind. Fu Hsuan. AWP

To me thy gracious help afford,/Who art the Handmaid of the Lord. The Housewife's Prayer. Blanche Mary Kelly. GoBC

To me tomorrow constantly deny it. Amores. Ovid (Publius Ovidius Naso). UnTE

To me, who tremble so and burn,/Be pitiful! Desideravi. Theodore Maynard. HBMV

To measure Time and Space to mortal Men every morning. Milton. William Blake. OAEL 1-2

To meet hee on the lea rig,/My ain kind dearie, O. My Ain Kind Dearie, O. Robert Burns. GoTS

To meet me in my dreams. When Evening Comes. Yakamochi. AWP

To meet one another again. Home of the Soul. Ellen M. Huntington Gates. BLRP

To meet the healing kisses of the sun. A Storm in the Distance. Paul Hamilton Hayne. AA

To meet thee on the lea-rig,/My ain kind dearie, O! The Lea Rig. Robert Burns. BSV

To meet with friends--where death can play no part. Beyond the Grave. Margaret E. Bruner. PoToHe

To meet with such, pass by nor deign a glance. To Dante. Vittorio Alfieri. AWP

To melt all Ice, but that which walls her heart. To Mr C.B. John Donne. AnAnS 1

To melt the stubborn heart, and teach the eye/To shed the gen'rous tear for other's woe. Ancient and Modern Rome (excerpt). George Keate. OBTV

To memorize how short his span/Upon a thousand clocks! Clocks. Louis Ginsberg. TrJP

...To men/and gods disgusting.--You and I, Cassandra. Cassandra. Robinson Jeffers. HeIP; LiTA; LiTM; NePA; WaP

To mine herte is made a wounde. Jesus to Those Who Pass By. *Anonymous.* MeEL

To mingle in this heavenly harmony. Immortality. Richard Henry Dana. AA; WGRP

To mingle with the common man,/No better or worse than I. The Common Road. Silas H. Perkins. BLPA; FaBoBe

To mingle with thy flock, and never stray. The Life of the Blessed. Luis Ponce de Leon. AWP

To mirror their sweet, humble poverty/In the clear waters of eternal love. Prayer to Go to Paradise with the Asses. Francis Jammes. AWP

To mitigate my sorrows. Love Poem: "Less the dog begged to die in the sky." George Barker. NeBP

To mix the fourth with. Laura Cashdollars. Bernadette Mayer. ANYP

To-morrow for the States--for me,/England and Yesterday. In the States. Robert Louis Stevenson. BrPo

To-morrow Lewti may be kind. Lewti. Samuel Taylor Coleridge. EnRP

To-morrow night 'tis full again,/Golden, and foaming red. What Semiramis Said. Vachel Lindsay. MAPA; MOON

To-morrow's Light/Is always burning 'round the rim of night. I Believe. J. B. Lawrence. BLRP

To-morrow succeeds to-day. Undertones. George R. Sims. NOBV

To-morrow to fresh woods, and pastures new. Lycidas. John Milton. AnEnPo; AnFE; AtBAP; ATP; AWP; BiP; BoLiVe; DiPo; EBEV; ExPo; FaBoRV; FiP; GTBS; GTBS-P; HAP; HBV 1-2; InPK; InPo; InPS; JCP; LiTB; LoBV; MasP; MBW 1-2; MCCG; MyFE; NIP; NOBE; NoP; OAEL 1-2; OAEP; OBEV; OBS; PAI; PoEL 1-5; PPoe; PPP; Prf; PrIm; SeCeV; TrGrPo; UnPo; ViBoPo; WeW; WGRP; WHA

To-morrow, when the headache comes--well, then I'll/satirize ye! Horace I. Eugene Field. ALV

To-morrow--who can say? To Himself. Anacreon. LiTW

"To-morrow will be Monday." As Tommy Snooks and Bessy Brooks. Mother Goose. HBV 1-2; HBVY

To mount the earth in my black people's time! Trellie. Lance Jeffers. CNA; FB

To move from out the darkness You/permit. Degrees of Shade. Helen Pinkerton. NePoAm

To Mr. Punchinello. To Mr. Punchinello. *Anonymous.* OxNR

To Mrs. something Swopes/Dead at 77. La Boheme. Dick Gallup. ANYP

To muck about a British workman's grave. They're Moving Father's Grave. *Anonymous.* FSW

To Muckle-mouth Meg in good earnest! Muckle-Mouth Meg. Robert Browning. HBV 1-2

To mumble your guilty love while your ears die. Some Foreign Letters. Anne Sexton. MoAmPo; PoCh

To muse on Uncle Jim. Uncle Jim. Countee Cullen. BANP

To my aye, aye, aye, aye, Mister Stormalong! Stormalong. *Anonymous.* AmSS; ShS

"To my Beloved." The Lover and the Beloved. Ramon Lull. CAW

To my dear one, the lass wi' the bonny blue een. O, Saw Ye the Lass. Richard Ryan. FaBoBe; HBV 1-2

To my heart, awake. Cradle Song. Josephine Preston Peabody. HBV 1-2

To my inheritance amid/The nation that is not. When Israel out of Egypt Came. Alfred Edward Housman. LiTB

To my mind, to my sight,/must remain a delight. A Face. Marianne Moore. OBSP; PoCh

To my native Belashanny and the winding banks of Erne. Adieu to Belashanny. William Allingham. OxBI

To my own,/my longing/for them. Distance. Robert Creeley. CoPo

To my poore reed. Employment. George Herbert. AtBAP; SeCV 1-2

To my rattle, to my roo-rah-ree! The Rattlesnake. *Anonymous.* BFSS; CoSo

To my right fol diddle dero, to my right fol diddle dee. Hares on the Mountain. *Anonymous.* ErPo

To my tol looral lay. Wonderful Crocodile. *Anonymous.* ABF

To myself/I go,/And tell my woe./Thank God!/Thank God! Thank God. Joseph Rolnik. TrJP

To myself just make it easy/on yourself Poem of Angela Yvonne Davis. Nikki Giovanni. PoBA

To name his actions to the fatal king. Perhaps the Best Time. William Meredith. NePoEA

To name the kneeling animals. When Senses Fled. John Woods. CoPo

To names and doors/my father shut Going Home. Maurice Kenny. STE

To nature's heart, in pain, as I began. Keep in the Heart the Journal. Conrad Aiken. CMoP; NePA

To need to corner all the meat in the world,/Even from your own hunger. Kreutzer Sonata. Ted Hughes. FaBoMo

To neither a word will I say:/But tol de rol. Air XXXV: "How happy could I be with either." John Gay. ViBoPo

To nestle at her heart, and hear/The music she has heard. I Send Our Lady. Sister Mary Therese. ISi

To night and silence sink for evermore! The Pilgrim of a Day. Thomas Campbell. OBRV

To-night I can stay late. To-Night. Edward ("Edward Eastaway") Thomas. PoPle

To-night I'll lay on the damp cold ground,/Along with the Gypsy Daisy. The Gypsy Laddie (C vers.). *Anonymous.* BaBo

To-night it doth inherit/The vasty hall of death. Requiescat. Matthew Arnold. AWP; BoLiVe; ELP; EnLi 1-2; EnLit; FiP; GoTF; GTBS; HBV 1-2; HeIP; InPo; InvP; LiTB; LiTL; MaVP; NOBE; OAEP; OBEV; OBVV; PG; PoRA; TreFS; ViBoPo; WHA

To-night Murad or Ukhbar falls,/Karaman! O Karaman! The Karamanian Exile. James Clarence Mangan. IrPN; OBVV

To night puts on perfection, and a womans name. Epithalamion Made at Lincolnes Inne. John Donne. OBS; SeCP

To-night those soft-fringed eyes shall close/Beneath one roof, my queen! with mine. Calais Sands. Matthew Arnold. OAEP

To-night to lie in the rain. The Rain, It Streams on Stone. Alfred Edward Housman. CMoP

To nod to the mothers of the little girls. Ballroom Dancing Class. Phyllis McGinley. MoShBr

To not ungentle death now forth I run. I Am Like a Slip of Comet. Gerard Manley Hopkins. VLP

To note the part you play/for your sons and daughters/still washed in tears. Is This Africa? Roland Tombekai Dempster. PBA

To nothing, not even Death, not even tears. Lollingdon Downs. John Masefield. ChMP

To Olde Sainte Marke's i' the Bowerie,/Dear Hal,–with thee! Old Flemish Lace. Amelia Walstein Carpenter. AA

To one, the cool and reasoning brain;/To one, the quick, unreasoning heart. Heredity. Thomas Bailey Aldrich. AA; AnAmPo

To one who cannot forget that perfidy. Act of Love. Nicholas Moore. NeBP

To one whose saddled soul to-night/Rides out with Count O'Hanlon. Ballad of Douglas Bridge. Francis Carlin. AnIV; HBMV; OxBI

To open a vault in you, as the one in me. Poem on the Suicide of My Teacher. Joseph Stroud. NPGG

To open himself, to be/the flames? Another Night in the Ruins. Galway Kinnell. CAPP; CoAP

To open its grace and incredible harm/over my life, and I will never die. Passengers. Denis Johnson. MAYP; SM

To open up a simple world of praise! A Last Word. May Sarton. GLGT

To ornament the Gothic of my mind. Gothic. Jean Starr Untermeyer. AnAmPo

To other ghosts–this one, or that, or I. Fragment. Rupert Brooke. BrPo

To other Trulles of tender yeares/Resigne the flagge of Fame. To an Olde Gentlewoman, That Painted Hir Face. George Turberville. EnPo

To others/Only heaven. Luck. Langston Hughes. MoLP

To Our far, vascillating Feet/A first Necessity. Faith–is the Pierless Bridge. Emily Dickinson. AmPP

To our house in the street down town. Samuel Brown. Phoebe Cary. OBAL

...To our journey's end we keep/Along the pathway pointed by its beam. How Easily Men's Cheeks Are Hot. Verner von Heidenstam. LiTW; PoPl

To our uncomprehending children and grandchildren. Parents. William Meredith. FYAP

To overturn the sky. It Is Better to Be Together. Ruth Miller. PeSA

"To own an eland! That's what I call life!" Seele Im Raum. Randall Jarrell. CoBMV; LCAP

To pace about his garden, lost in thought. Altitudes. Richard Wilbur. CMoP

To parachaute on the capitals of gaiety? Weathering the Depths. Al Lee. AmPA

To pardon his life, and seek no more strife."/And so endeth Robin Hood's chase. Robin Hood's Chase. *Anonymous.* BaBo; ESPB

To pardon or to bear it. The Man That Hails You Tom or Jack. William Cowper. PoL

To part her lips, and showed them there/The quarrelets of pearl. Rubies and Pearls. Robert Herrick. HBV 1-2

To pass away the tedious hours, she's fair and Chaste indeed. The Downright Country-Man; or, The Faithful Dairy Maid. *Anonymous.* CoMu

To pass on, (O living! always living!) and leave the corpses behind. O Living Always, Always Dying. Walt Whitman. NOBA

To pay the debt I owe,/My God and Lord. Behold the Man! *Anonymous.* STF

To pay the praises of the thievish groin. Sonnet. Leonard Wolf. ErPo

To pen them for Her! The Dog. William Henry Davies. MoBrPo

To people the suns/of divinities. Brother... Johari (Jewel C. Latimore) Amini. JB

To Peter's soul the spell is bound–/How should it ever pass away? Peter Bell, the Third. Percy Bysshe Shelley. OBSV

To pick up a pin, then he toreham. Limerick: "A thrifty young fellow of Shoreham." *Anonymous.* TDH

To pity a cat like me that/Gallops about doing good. The Galloping Cat. Stevie Smith. BrRo

To places I cannot follow. Follower. Michael Arvey. AMV-80

To plague tomorrow with a testament! Silet. Ezra Pound. MoAB; MoAmPo

To plague us wi' your whining cant. Look up to Pentland's Tow'ring Tap. Allan Ramsay. BSV

To play the school games with the others. The Picnic. John Logan. ConAP; NCSH; NePoEA-2

To play with fools, oh, what a fool was I! If Women Could Be Fair. Edward, Earl of Oxford De Vere. CoBE; EIL; LiTL; OAEP

To play with when this game begins to pall Epiderm. Michael Dransfield. CBAP

To plead his cause, where he by this doth/know/Whether to Caesar he was friend or foe. Bacon's Epitaph, Made by His Man. *Anonymous.* AnAmPo; PAH; SCAP

To please an age more gallant than the last. The Conquest of Granada. John Dryden. FiP; SeCV 1-2

To please the gray-haired boys. The Old Man Dreams. Oliver Wendell Holmes. BLPL; HBV 1-2; PoLf

To pleasure and to health. Ode I Allusion to Horace. Mark Akenside. CEP

To plunge into both at the same moment Some Uses for Poetry. Eve Merriam. PCP

To Pluto's realm, till he shall join me there. In Cnidus Born, the Consort I Became. Heraclides. OBVE

To poke a wistful finger in the ashes. Coach into Pumpkin. Dorothy E. Reid. DFT

To poll the tops that seek such change and gape for joy. The Doubt of Future Foes. Queen of England, Elizabeth I. CTC; PBWP

To Porus and the elephants/and drunkenness in Babylon. On Alexander and Aristotle, on a Black-on-Red Greek Plate. Alan Dugan. PPP

To pour the thick night out upon the earth. London Nightfall. John Gould Fletcher. MoAmPo

To pourchase it by payement and by prayer,/Ye old mule! Ye Old Mule. Sir Thomas Wyatt. AAS

To practise more than heavenly power/permits. Doctor Faustus. Christopher Marlowe. CoBE; PoEL 1-5; ViBoPo; WHA

To praise Eternity contained in Time and coloured glass. Sunday Morning, King's Cambridge. Sir John Betjeman. BoC; EaLo

To praise her, to tell of me, yes; and of you, my King. Pewter. Jack Gilbert. NPGG

To praise you as you are from all I leave. Letter from a Death Bed. John Ciardi. NCSH

To pray for [The] singer of this song,/For he sings to make blithe your/cheer. Rookhope Ryde. *Anonymous.* ESPB

To pray for them. Memo. Hildegarde Flanner. NYBP

...To pray/to the still God, though they call it hurricane. An Antipastoral Memory of One Summer. Dave Smith. MAYP

To prepare/love later. Park Poem. Paul Blackburn. CoPo

To profit so by Eden's blame. The Angel in the House. Coventry Patmore. EBEV

To prove death but a veil to hide/Another life on the other side. One Token. William Henry Davies. BrPo

To prove how stronger you are than my strength. Single Sonnet. Louise Bogan. AnEnPo

To prove that heart, at least, was true. Remorse. Richmond Lattimore. PoA

To prove the reality of endless love? I Am a Book I Neither Wrote Nor Read. Delmore Schwartz. TAP

To prove the Thing within a Thing Without. Sonnet: "How many ways, how many times." John Masefield. WGRP

To prove they still have life with earthly ties? The Hour of Magic. William Henry Davies. MoBrPo

To prove they Daies but Dream and Slumber. Omnia Somnia. Joshua Sylvester. FaBoEE; OBS

"To prove thy love, live thou a nobler life." Thysia. Morton Luce. HBV 1-2

To prove what I meant it to shough. Limerick: "A farmer's boy, starting to plough." D. S. Martin. TDH

To pull yourself up by your own roots; to eat the last meal in your/old neighborhood. Shooting Script (excerpt). Adrienne Rich. FaBoWP; HaCAP

To purchase fame I will go roam. In Praise of Seafaring Men, in Hopes of Good Fortune. Sir Richard Grenville. OBSS; OBTV

To put his pictures on her/with his hands. The Man She Called Honey, and Married. Alberto Rios. MAYP

To put them foully to the flicht. The Battle of Bannockburn. John Barbour. BSV

To quell the rage of literary war! Epitaph. Gabriello Chiabrera. AWP

To question the betraying earth? On the Death of the Evansville University Basketball Team... Robert W. Hamblin. AMV-80

To question this diminishing and feed a minimum/of children their careful slice of suburban cake. Funnel. Anne Sexton. MoAmPo

To question us, "Whence come ye, to what end?" Bleak Season Was It, Turbulent and Wild. William Wordsworth. ERoP 1-2

To quicken space where nothingness has been. Archne. Richard Foerster. AMV-80

To quit the craft that me beguiled. Now all of change. Sir Thomas Wyatt. FCP; SiPS

To race...to homeland...and to/you too. To My Generation. Benyamin Galai. TrJP

To rail at men by nature fools:/But ＊ ＊ ＊ ＊ ＊ ＊ ＊ ＊ ＊ ＊ ＊ ＊ On the Irish Club. Jonathan Swift. OBSV

To rain immortal darkness/On strong eyes. Marching. Isaac Rosenberg. BrPo

To rally 'round the cane-brake/And shoot the buffalo. Shoot the Buffalo. *Anonymous.* ABF; TrAS

To rattle the sycamore tree's dry-shriveled seeds. It Is Winter, I Know. Merrill Moore. MoAmPo

To reach all the sugar and things that I can't/Reach now, when I eat at the table! If. John Kendrick Bangs. OBCA

To reach the cool stream/For which they are yearning. There's a Fire in the Forest. W. W. Eustace Ross. WHW

To reach/with you/timberline. Air Is. John Michael Brennan. MAT

To read her own and trust her down to death. Sense and Spirit. George Meredith. WGRP

To read ice-cream/Upon the bill-of-fare. R is for the Restaurant. Phyllis McGinley. TiPo

To read it well: that is, to understand. To the Reader. Ben Jonson. NoP; OAEP; SeCV 1-2

To read the rage the stallion spent. The White Stallion. Guy Owen. InPK

To realize the purpose which Truth proclaims to be the all-/supreme. Realization. Ananda Acharya. WGRP

To reap the ripen'd fruits the which the earth had/yold. The Faerie Queene. Edmund Spenser. GN

To recognize in me/Its unimpaired ideal of what/An Englishman should be. The Englishman on the French Stage. Sir Owen Seaman. OBTV

...To recognize/my own stern hungers in their fragile cries. The Finches. Thomas W. Shapcott. BoAnP; PoAu 1-2

To reig with thee on high. It is Not Death to Die. George Washington Bethune. AA; BePJ

To remain and realize were the harder task. Salamis. Lawrence Durrell. NYBP

To remain pure, without the stigma of life. Heth. Carlos Montemayor. AMV-81

To remain, somehow, so hungry. Charter Boat. Norman Hindley. WOLT

To remember once it had a great singing family of trees. Improved Farm Land. Carl Sandburg. RFM

To remember with tears! Four Ducks on a Pond. William Allingham. IrPN; NOBI; NOBV; OxBI; PoPle

To remove the blood/that covers me everywhere. Sabbatical. Linda Zisquit. VWA

To render tragic what is merely triste. All Human Things (parody). Peter Schroeder. BXAP

To repent dis side in de tomb./Mone, member, mone. Mone, Member, Mone. *Anonymous.* ABF

To request you won't stay in Dunblane?' Limerick: "There was an old man of Dunblane." Edward Lear. EBEV

To rescue identity from all assemblage/Of night wonders, a way of wishing well. Composition for a Nativity. John Ciardi. MiAP

To rest my weary limbs amid the storms of May. Lines Written on a Very Boisterous Day in May, 1944. John Clare. OBSP

To retrieve the crutches which are essential to them/since they need them to beat us with. Cripples. Nina Cassian. VWA

To return to Jacob who awaits them in their dream. Nine Men out of a Minyan. Haim Guri. VWA

To return to this peace before the nails are hammered El Greco: Espolio. Earle Birney. PeCV

To riddle us with bleeding, gaping questions. The Day before Christmas. Raymond Souster. PeCV

To ride and outlast/the winter's blast. Raisins and Nuts. Charles Reznikoff. VWA

To ris with him fra ded to life. Rise with the Lamb of Innocence. *Anonymous.* MeEL

To rise o'er sin and fear and death,/O love of God, to thee! Thou Grace Divine, Encircling All. Eliza Scudder. AH

To roam all alone on the shore? The Sea Captain. *Anonymous.* ViBoFo

To rock your young baby, hear the nightingales sing! The Nightingale. *Anonymous.* AmFP; BaBo; UnTE

To rock your young baby, hear the nightingales sing! One Morning in May. *Anonymous.* BaBo; FSW

To roll his mare among the trampled lilies. The Zebras. Roy Campbell. AnFE; LiTB; MoBrPo; PoPle; PrIm; ViBoPo

To romp in the falling leaves. October. Judith Goren. AMV-81

To rub on his sore metatarsal. Limerick: "While visiting Arundel Castle." Victor Gray. NOBL

To run like hell, it has been found,/Both feet must be upon the ground. Cave Sedem! Theodore F. MacManus. HBV 1-2

To safe Arcadia beyond the snows. Battles of the Centaurs: Centaurs and Lapithae. Sacheverell Sitwell. AtBAP

To satisfy my mind. Friendship. Ella Wheeler Wilcox. PoToHe

To satisfy your sight until you move Spiral Landscape. Michael Brownstein. ANYP

To save for us one more Spring. Eager Spring. Gordon Bottomley. MoBrPo

To save from adverse winds and waves the gallant British Fleet. The Anchorsmiths. Charles Dibdin. NOEC

To save him from Narcissus' fate. On a Beautiful Youth Struck Blind with Lightning. Oliver Goldsmith. OAEP

To save the Athenian walls from ruin bare. When the Assault Was Intended to the City. John Milton. GTBS; GTBS-P; NoP; RoGo

To save thee from the magic/Of Khristna and his flute. Khristna and His Flute. Laurence Hope. HBV 1-2

To save your life, you'd better heed/The Ethical expansionist! Ballade of Expansion. Hilda Johnson. PAH

To say its message,–"Soul, arise and walk." The Waiting Harp. Gustavo Adolfo Becquer. CAW

To say the closure will be a little, just a little, like this. Poem: "I believe the yellow flowers think with me." Alice Notley. APU

To say things better that were best not said. Adder's Epigrams. Colin Ellis. FaBoEE

To say what he honestly/Thought of Philately. Philatelist Royal. Robert Graves. FaBoCo

To scare myself with my own desert places. Desert Places. Robert Frost. AnFE; AtBAP; BiP; CMoP; CoBMV; DiPo; ForPo; MoAB; MoAmPo; MoVE; NCSH; NoAm; NOBA; OxBA; PPP; TAP; UnPo

To scare the mice away. A Change of Heart. Valine Hobbs. SiSoSe

To scarf our loves in paradisial air. Rise and Shine. Richmond Lattimore. NYBP

To screen from outer darkness/The chaos of the mind. Midnight. Michael Roberts. OBMV

To scrub the floors/with harsh yellow soap. The Great Aunts of My Childhood. Alice Fulton. Str

To sea, to sea, how e'er the wind doth blow. Sailors for My Money. *Anonymous.* OBSS

To sea, to sea, How ere the wind doth blow. Saylors for My Money. Martin Parker. CoMu

To Sea-ward cast their eyes, and pray for happie winds. Polyolbion. Michael Drayton. OBS

To search her eyes/For that quiet look– The Revelation. William Carlos Williams. MoLP

To search in darkness out of limits/The gleam of truth within myself. Loneliness. Franz Werfel. TrJP

To search in the spoils of the furrow,/Where God the Ploughman ploughs. Behind the Plough. James H. Cousins. OxBI

To see all the beautiful flowers/She gets on her birthday from me. Dandelions. Marchette Chute. BiCB

...To see and love thee/Was but one soul's step. Do Not Minute. Thomas Lovell Beddoes. LO

To see fall down, the Column of Gold,/Into the commonest ash. To Be in Love. Gwendolyn Brooks. IHMS; OLR

To see, feel, taste, and love earth's rarest jewel. Her Praises. Anthony Skoloker. EIL

...To see/heaven one/wants a star. Without You. Cid Corman. GP

To see her and a Healer named Placido. Waiting for God. Harry Roskolenko. FAZ

To see her red coats marching from the hill. Gibraltar. Wilfrid Scawen Blunt. ACP; GTBS; HBV 1-2; OBEV; OBVV

To see him laid down in his tomb will be a solemn sight. Lamentation on the Death of the Duke of Wellington. *Anonymous.* OBET

To see if love still burned. Dirge. Louis Johnson. AnNZ

To see my book brought home again. Snatches: "This book is one." *Anonymous.* OxBM

To see my lady joyful in her place. Sonnet: Of His Lady in Heaven. Jacopo da Lentino. AWP

To see Nell Gwynn beckoned/by Charles the Second. When They Found Giotto. Allan M. Laing. FiBHP

To see one sad, ungathered rose/On my ancestral tree. My Aunt. Oliver Wendell Holmes. AnNE; HBV 1-2; MCCG; TAP; TreFS

To see so fair a port, and not to make it! Four Sonnets to Helen, 1. Pierre de Ronsard. LiTW

To see such pleasures gon so suddenly. Visions. Petrarch. EnLi 1-2

To see such silver and gold on things/Makes us all richer than queens and kings. Labor Day. Marnie Pomeroy. PoSC

To see that storm of riches in your sudden gaze. Whispers. Roberta Hill. CDW

To see that the head had turned into the Moon. The Creation of the Moon. *Anonymous.* MOON

To see the abysses of the human heart. The Heart's Abysses. Walter Savage Landor. FaBoEE; OBSV

To see the bunting and the blue balloons. In Memory of the Circus Ship Euzkera, Wrecked in the Caribbean Sea... Walker Gibson. NCSH; NePoAm

To see the cherry hung with snow. Loveliest of Trees. Alfred Edward Housman. AWP; BiP; BLPL; BoLiVe; BoNaP; CMoP; CoBMV; DiPo; ELP; FaBoBe; FaBV; FaFP; FF; GoTF; GTBS; HAP; HeIP; InPK; InPo; InPS; LiTB; LiTM; MasP; MoAB; MoBrPo; NAs; NoAm; NoP; OAEL 1-2; OHIP; OxBTC; PoLf; PrIm; SoSe; TEP; TreFT; TrGrPo; ViBoPo; VLP

To see the green, that old anarchy. Prayer. Stanley Moss. GP; PoL

To see the land I love. Night Journey. Theodore Roethke. AmFN; NYBP; PAI

To see the little Tippler/Leaning against the–Sun– I taste a liquor never brewed. Emily Dickinson. AmePo; CMoP; DiPo; FaBV; FF; GoTF; HeIP; LiTA; LiTM; MAmP; MCCG; MoAmPo; NePA; NOBA; NoP; OxBA; PoEL 1-5; SBG; SeCeV; SoSe; TAP; TreFS

To see the parliament soldiers go by. Parliament Soldiers. *Anonymous.* OxNR

To see the rainbow's wheel ganne, made of flax. A Non Sequitor. Elizabeth T. Corbett. FaBoNo

To see the stars of night hidden behind clouds. A Thing Remembered. *Anonymous.* ErPo

To see the uprising/of the heavenly king.' The Cherry-Tree Carol. *Anonymous.* BaBo; EBEV; ESPB; OBET

To see the water gliding, hear the nightingale sing. One Morning in May. *Anonymous.* AS; BFSS

To see them all a-scampering skip/For nuts across the sand.! The Ship of Rio. Walter De La Mare. CenHV; EtS; MOS; PoPle; TiPo

To see them form and fade before their eyes. Adolescence. P. K. Page. CaP; OBCV

To see them so; fleshed, fair, erected indivisible. The Imaginary Iceberg. Elizabeth Bishop. FaBoWP; LiTM; MoAB; MoAmPo; MoVE

To see these two children sett vpp/In their seats of gold full royallye. The Lord of Lorn and the False Steward. *Anonymous.* ESPB

To see thy love to every one/Hath brought thee to be loved by none. To His Forsaken Mistress. Ayton [(or Aytoun)] Sir Robert. ElL; ErPo; HBV 1-2; OBEV; SeCePo

To see thy shame, and break thy heart. Cupid Ungodded. James Shirley. GoBC

To see thy tow'ring temple shine so fair/Through the night-flaming, elemental air.' Bedlam: A Poem on His Majesty's Happy Escape...(excerpt). *Anonymous.* NOEC

To see us wreck our fellowship/In mad fraternal wars. Housemates. Odell Shepard. MoRP

To see what my black hen doth lay. My Black Hen. *Anonymous.* OxNR

To see what they are, because it's time for lunch! Lunch. Kenneth Koch. SOTW

To see what we have grown. Sun and I. Ken Mammone. AMV-81

To see what you do with your chance in the chamber of days. The Task That Is Given to You. Edwin Markham. WBLP

To see where death was, I look back. And I Am Old to Know. Pauline Hanson. TAP

To see who has the fairest charms. Brigham Young. *Anonymous.* ABF

To see who made those ringing noises in that summer/bay. Glen Lough. Geoffrey Grigson. FaBoPP; OBTV

To see you, is more than food or drink. So Small Are the Flowers of Seamu. *Anonymous.* PBWP

To seek a name in the seas. The Knight Without a Name. *Anonymous.* WiR

To seek for the Happy Isles together. The Flower-Boat. Robert Frost. PoA

To seek new lechery in Death. An Epitaph on M.H. Charles Cotton. EBEV; FaBoEE

To seek the beauteous eye of heaven to garnish,/Is wasteful and ridiculous excess. King John. William Shakespeare. TreFT

To seek the danger out/From among the miserable soldiers Some San Francisco Poems. George Oppen. NNaP

To seek the God that faith hath found. The Lord Our God Alone Is Strong. Caleb T. Winchester. AH

To seem more deep than Robert Frost. The Reader Writes. Carl Crane. PoPl

To sell to exploiters, and the restless rich. For the Market. Jane Mayhall. TAP

To send me forth on a new morning, a/new man. Shadows. D. H. Lawrence. OAEP; OxBTC

To serve, and suffer patiently. Since Love Will Needs That I Shall Love. Sir Thomas Wyatt. FCP; SiPS

To serve him in the thing he does so well–endure. Shore Birds. Vi Gale. GoYe

To serve my gracious Master's ends. One Year to Live. Mary Davis Reed. PoToHe

To serve one master in the night,/Another in the day. Chapter Heading. Ernest Hemingway. PoA

To serve the sun in a life beyond sleep. Ur Burial. Richard Eberhart. NePoAm

To serve thee is to reign. Put Forth, O God, Thy Spirit's Might. Howard Chandler Robbins. AH; TrPWD

To serve to trust to fear. Her Face Her Tongue Her Wit. Sir Arthur Gorges. GBL

To set all women light, but only she. Love, the Delight of All Well-Thinking Minds. Fulke, Lord Brooke Greville. GBL

To set his mouth against a crack/And blow the candle out. Prophecy. Elinor Wylie. AnAmPo; BLPL; BoWoP; FaBoWP; PrIm; VGW

To set the face, and make the heart a stone. The Unpardonable Sin. Vachel Lindsay. BiP; CMoP; NePA

To set the freak flags flying. Celebrating the Freak. Cynthia Macdonald. Psk

To set up a doleful howling/In order to get in! Unsatisfied Yearning. Richard Kendall Munkittrick. GDP; InMe

To set when on what far shore,/Dolphins, dolphins? The Dolphins. Hamish Maclaren. EtS

To shack with history/for the night. Negro Dreams. Doughtry Long. PoBA

To shake the strength of heaven's axletree. The Transformed Metamorphosis: Awake, Oh Heaven. Cyril Tourneur. MOON

...To share the light/of lost long days before midsummer ends. Reports of Midsummer Girls. Richmond Lattimore. PCP

To share this last joy, sweet and desperate. Love Beleagured. Katherine Garrison Chapin. MoLP

To share, unwilling, yet to share at last my passion! No, Never Think. Alexander Pushkin. ErPo

To sharpen others when themselves are blunt. Ad Tusserum. *Anonymous.* FaBoUs

To shed their lurid lustre on the empire that/was Spain. Spain's Last Armada. Wallace Rice. PAH

To shine somewhere like strung beads of coral. After X-Ray. Linda Pastan. PoL

To show a love as prompt as thine/To Him who gives me all. The Dog and the Water-lily. William Cowper. OAEP

...To show/How much I care/For the dear memory of what, you know,/You never were. Among His Books. Edith Nesbit. NOBV

To show in every spot and place/The living glory of His face. The World's Miser. Theodore Maynard. CAW

To show that life has naught to match/Such knighthood as the grave can give. Herndon. Silas Weir Mitchell. PAH

To show the change of winds with his prophetic bill. The Hind and the Panther. John Dryden. SeCV 1-2

To show the sun's fistful of golden darts. The Horn. James Reaney. OBCV; PeCV

To show the world that I died for love. The Butcher Boy. *Anonymous.* AmFP; BaBo; FSW; ViBoFo

To show their forms and hues in the all revealing sun. I Was a Brook. Sara Coleridge. OBRV

To show thy little lamp: go forth, go forth! To the White Fiends. Claude McKay. BANP; PoBA

To show wherein the spirit had food? The Question. Robert Duncan. NeAP

To shroud me from my proper scorn. In Memoriam A.H.H., XXVI. Alfred, Lord Tennyson. VLP

To shun the heaven that leads men to this hell. Sonnets, CXXIX: "Th' expense of spirit in a waste of shame." William Shakespeare. AWP; BiP; DiPo; EBEV; ExPo; FaBoEn; ForPo; GBL; HAP; HeIP; InPo; InPS; LiTB; LiTL; LoBV; MasP; MBW 1-2; NIP; NOBE; NoP; OAEL 1-2; OBEV; OBSC; PAI; PoEL 1-5; PPoe; PPP; QFR; SCV; SeCeV; TEP; TrGrPo; UnPo; ViBoPo; WeW; WHA

To shutter the lock/From the Christmas key? Christmas Amnesty. Edith Lovejoy Pierce. PGD

To signal the falling,/"You're never alone"? To Be Sung. Peter Viereck. FaBV

To simpler's joy and true-love and shoo-fly, shoo! Mountain Medicine. Elizabeth-Ellen Long. AmFN

To sin as before/And more and more,/For evermore. The Sting of Death. Frederick George Scott. OBCV; PeCV

To sing ar we bun,/Let take on loft. The Second Shepherds' Play. *Anonymous.* PoEL 1-5

To sing at our hearths of "Home, sweet Home." The Cricket's Story. Elias Nason. HBV 1-2; HBVY

To sing dirges o'er his stone! The Dead Sparrow. William Cartwright. BoAnP; CH

To sing more pleasing, in the joyful hour, The First Olympionique to Hiero of Syracuse. Pindar. ATP

To sing my faith! To sing my faith/Unto the hearts of men! Poet's Prayer. Adelaide Love. TrPWD

To sing the sweet chorus of "Ha, Ha, He!" Laughing Song. William Blake. BrR; CBEP; DiPo; EnLi 1-2; GoJo; NLV; OxBChV; PoSC; SoPo; SUS; TiPo

To sing throughout eternal years,/He gave Himself for me. He Gave Himself for Me. *Anonymous.* STF

To sing unto the stone/Of which it died. Not with a club. Emily Dickinson. LiTA; WHA

To sing while others sleep. On a Poetess. Gerard Manley Hopkins. PP

To sing with heart and voice,/God save the King! God Save the King. Henry Carey. HBV 1-2; OBEC; PeD; WBLP

To sing with the silver hosannahs of rain. The Palm. Roy Campbell. MoBrPo

To sink in quiet seas. Lethe. Georgia Douglas Johnson. CDC

To sink into the smell of their own farts. Quicksands (parody). William Zaranka. BXAP

To skelp the bairns on Monday. The Schoolmaster. *Anonymous.* GBP; GLGT

To sleep at Comgall's, to visit Canice,/it would be pleasant! Clamour of the Wind Making Music. Saint Columcille. BIrV

To sleep immodestly, a most/Incarnadine and carnal ghost. Epidermal Macabre. Theodore Roethke. NoAm; TW

To sleep inside/the hollow of a bone. Three. Marilyn Kitchell. APU

To sleep on, when his watch was through,–/So he did. Hell's Pavement. John Masefield. BrPo

To sleeping/bag blankets,/warm sheets,/to our mouths. Personal Poem. Ingrid Wendt. NMM

To smile full-faced and yellowly/at a thousand box cameras. The King. Douglas Livingstone. BoAnP

To smolder like a polished block/Of dark Egyptian stone? The Monadnock. John Gould Fletcher. PoA

To soften your fall. Grape Daiquiri. Tina Koyama. BrSi

To some rich desert fly with me. Ballad of Bedlam. *Anonymous.* NA

To something upper wooing us/But not to our Creator–. The Fascinating Chill That Music Leaves. Emily Dickinson. AmePo

To soothe, the in death's transcendent dream,/A sweeter or a nobler soul! I.H.B. William Winter. AA

To soothe the cares, and lift the thoughts of man. Sleep and Poetry. John Keats. OAEL 1-2

To soper thay yede as-swythe,/Wyth dayntes newe innowe. Sir Gawain and the Green Knight: Gawain and the Lady of the Castle. *Anonymous.* OxBM

To span A Fate? Feel Like a Bird. May Swenson. TrGrPo

To spare the child and spoil the rod! Hickory Stick Hierarchy. Len G. Selle. AMV-80

To speak the very truth of thee. Revenge. Robert Nugent, Earl Nugent. PV

To speak what in that tender age became/Your blooming Beauty then your cheifest Fame. To the Rt. Hon. the Lady C. Tufton. Anne Finch, Countess of Winchilsea. SBG

To spill that blood that hath so oft been shed/For Britain's sake, alas, and now is dead! Bonum Est Mihi Quod Humiliasti Me. Henry Howard, Earl of Surrey. SiPS

To spin everlastingly Posterity. Cyril Dabydeen. BrSi

To split my worship too in twain. On Stella's Birthday. Jonathan Swift. InPK; NIP; NOBI; OAEL 1-2

To spoil the first impression. To a Child. Robert Herrick. EG

...To spring/On the first foe whom Lambro's call might bring. Haidee. George Gordon, Lord Byron. OBNC; SeCePo

To sprout in a kinder air. My Autumn Walk. William Cullen Bryant. AA

To stab us with courage and confidence/Daily and nightly. They Live. Randall Swingler. WaP

To stain the stiff dishonoured shroud. Sweeney Among the Nightingales. Thomas Stearns Eliot. AP; APA; BoLiVe; CMoP; CoBMV; DiPo; FaBoMo; HAP; HeIP; InPo; InvP; LiTA; LiTM; MAPA; MBW 1-2; MoVE; NePA; NoAm; NOBA; NOBE; NoP; OAEL; OBMV; OxBA; PPP; SeCeV; UnPo

To stalk their prey from room to haunted room. Miser. Gordon LeClaire. CaP

To stand before their God in Heaven. In Galilee. Jessie MacKay. AnNZ

To stand between two silent floors. The Barren Moors. William Ellery Channing AA

"To stand or move!" If he say true, he lies. A Lame Beggar. John Donne. FF

To stand–to advance–and after all to stand! Autumnal Ode. Aubrey Thomas De Vere. OBNC

To stand upon the new fraternal soil. Architects of Dream. Lucia Trent. PGD

To state at last her brilliant negative/In poems free and helpless and unjust. Cottage Street, 1953. Richard Wilbur. CAPP; FaBoMo; HaCAP

...To stay alive this way, it's hard.... Surviving. James Welch. CDW; STE

To stay at home is best. Home Song. Henry Wadsworth Longfellow. GN

To stay our minds on and be staid. Choose Something Like a Star. Robert Frost. AnNE; MoAB; MoAmPo; PoCh

To stay the violence of the entering Word! The Book of Kells. Padraic Colum. BIrV

To stay with Comgall, to visit Caindech,/it would be sweet. O Son of God, It Would Be Sweet. Colum Cille. NOBI

To steal my Basil-pot away from me!' Isabella, or The Pot of Basil. John Keats. EnRP; ViBoPo

To stiffen through ages of pain/In the rock-rigid realms of death. The Sword of Tethra. William Larminie. OnYI

To sting that heart that would have my place. The Wandering Gadling. Sir Thomas Wyatt. CBEP

To sting these rotted wastes into a flower. To a Pet Cobra. Roy Campbell. AtBAP

To stir his black pots and to bed on straw. The Bards. Robert Graves. DTC; FaBoMo; LiTM; SeCePo; ViBoPo

To stir my fluent blood as never your presence stirred. Absence. Claude McKay. CDC

To stir the wandering urges in searching human hearts. In Memoriam. Dave Gingell. PoSH

To stop the gaps in ourselves, like better halves. Making up for a Soul. David Wagoner. VGW

To strengthen whilst one stands. Goblin Market. Christina Georgina Rossetti. AtBAP; BrRo; DTo; EBEV; GoTL; NOBV; OAEP; OBNV; PeHV; SBG; VLP

To strew the surf-forsaken strand. Inspiration. John Banister Tabb. WGRP

To strike its distant enemy to the heart. Drunken Gunner. Michael Kennedy Joseph. AnNZ

To strive to fix her beams which are/More bright and large than this. An Answer to Another Persuading a Lady to Marriage. Katherine ("Orinda") Philips. CavP; HAP

To strive, to seek, to find, and not to yield. Ulysses. Alfred, Lord Tennyson. ATP; AWP; DiPo; EBEV; EtS; ExPo; FaPoR; FF; FiP; ForPo; FPL; GoTF; HAP; HBV 1-2; HeIP; HoPM; InPK; InPo; InPS; LiTB; LoBV; MaVP; MBW 1-2; MCCG; MOS; MyFE; NAWM 1-2; NIP; NOBE; NOBV; NoP; OAEL 1-2; OAEP; PAI; PoPle; PoRA; PPoe; PPP; PrIm; SCV; SeCePo; SeCeV; SoSe; TEP; TreF; TrGrPo; TRV; UnPo; ViBoPo; VLP; WHA

To strongly, wrongly, vainly love thee still. Love and Death. George Gordon, Lord Byron. EBEV; NOBE

To study all who pass until the lens/Blur or the world run out of specimens. At the Louvre. E. L. Mayo. FAZ

To stumble to that lodging which is You. Prayer of an Unbeliever. Lizette Woodworth Reese. TrPWD

To Stygian Forty-seventh Street below. The West Forties: Morning, Noon, and Night. L. E. Sissman. CoAP; NYBP; NYP

To suck the goatskin oftener than the goat? Silenus in Proteus. Thomas Lovell Beddoes. EnRP

To suffer and give pain. Courage for the Pusillanimous. Paul Roche. GoYe

To suffer no diminution/of its splendor. Poem: "The rose fades." William Carlos Williams. NIP

To sunder it from Heaven! Retrospection. Hubert Church. AnNZ

To Superman,/While the bells ring praises. While the Bells Ring. Lora Dunetz. NePoAm

To supper, Horlicks–bed again/And love that flowers... Busy Old Fool (parody). Ian Kelso. BXAP

To surround dead space with/clues. Macrame. Michael D. Riley. AMV-81

To survive and go on getting worse. Cradle Song. Samuel Hoffenstein. DBV

...To survive the daily/low tide becomes hard work. The Hinge. Sheila Cowing. AMV-81

To swear and damn with a bonne grace. Tom Tiler; or,The Nurse. *Anonymous.* APAS

To sweep, beyond the Stygian lake,/The pavement it has helped to make. The Fate of a Broom–An Anticipation. Thomas Love Peacock. CBEP

To sweeten the dead air. The Garden of God. George William Russell. WGRP

To swing, swing, swing, when the free winds blow. The Trial. Dannie Abse. ACV

To tack again each to its lambkin. Little Bo-Peep. *Anonymous.* OxNR; SpRo

To take a bite from the spacious sky... The Midnight Court. Brian Merriman. BIrV

To take a Part of mine. Polwart on the Green. Allan Ramsay. CEP; NOEC

To take a pleasant walk with him across the fields of barley. Billy Grimes. *Anonymous.* AmFP

To take a scripp and sheapheards grey. Come Not To Me For Scarfs. Aurelian Townsend. AnAnS 2

To take a turn about the garden,/And disappeared forever. Lemon Sherbet. Marvin Solomon. NePoAm

To take away Peace from Earthly Men,/They must Each other kill. The Indians Count of Men as Dogs. Roger Williams. SCAP

To take both life and love away. The Rival Friends: Have Pity, Grief. Peter Hausted. EG

To take her dissolution to my breast! The Colours of Love. Denis Devlin. IPY; OxBI

To take me home/Within Thy Heart to be. Requests. Digby Mackworth Dolben. TrPWD

To take me in/at night Number 5–December. David Henderson. BOLo

To take my troubling, grisly, inner brother! Inner Brother. Stephen Stepanchev. WaP

To take nothing away but his mind's eye. The Water Lily. David Wagoner. PoDr

To take/"the girls"/to/the fairs in. The Intelligent Sheep-Man and the New Cars. William Carlos Williams. NePoAm-2; OBAL

To take the only way to be forgiven. On the Benefactions in the Late Frost, 1740. Alexander Pope. NOEC; OBSP

To take the shapes of life,/Coming and being counted. Tally. Josephine Miles. NoAm

To take the shuddering city in his arms. Brussels in Winter. W. H. Auden. OBTV; OxBTC

To take to whipped syllabub all my life long. Epistle of Condolence. Thomas Moore. OnYI

To take unto itself some olden word: Lilith: The Anguish'd Doubt Broods over Eden. Christopher John Brennan. PoAu 1-2

To take what falls with even mind/Jove wills, and we must be resign'd. Mimnermus Incert. Walter Savage Landor. PoEL 1-5

To take your humble servant lower. A Letter to Sir Robert Walpole. Henry Fielding. CEP

To take your oviform invention from you, for the world. Mrs. Loewinsohn &c. Ron Loewinsohn. NeAP

To talk like Doeg and to write like thee. Absalom and Achitophel. John Dryden. FiP; PoEL 1-5; PPP; SeCV 1-2; TW

To talk of serving God and Mammon. Savonarola. Edmund Clerihew Bentley. OxBoLi

To tame the rudeness of his native land. For a Statue of Chaucer at Woodstock. Mark Akenside. SeCePo

To tame these dead bodies and wet ashes. (Poem) (Chicago) (The Were-Age). Bill Knott. EAS

To Tarquin's everlasting banishment. The Rape of Lucrece. William Shakespeare. BeLS

To taste its own power/at last. My Teeth. Ed Ochester. DFF; GP

...To taste terrain their heirs need not draw near. The Singing Bones. Randolph Stow. CBAP

To taste thy love, be all my choice. Hymn: "Thou hidden love of God, whose height." John Wesley. NOEC

To teach and live thus is the only use/And end of Learning. Learning. George Chapman. SeCePo

To teach me compassion and mercy/For souls He is waiting to bless. How Can You? Maxine Stevens. STF

To teach men how to teach men how to teach. No teacher I of boys or smaller fry. Allen Beville Ramsey. CenHV; PV

To teach the angels avarice/Your kiss first taught to me! Although I put away his life. Emily Dickinson. MoAmPo

To teach the reader what I know about writing in England today. Writing in England Now. Philip O'Connor. OxBTC

To teach vain Wits a science little known,/T' admire superior sense, and doubt their/own. An Essay on Criticism. Alexander Pope. OAEP; PoEL 1-5

To tear out my bowels/and hurl them in the face of this season. Season of Blood. Arnaldo Santos. WhB

To tell a voice that's genuinely good/From one that's base but merely has succeeded. Base Words Are Uttered. W. H. Auden. OBSP; PV

To tell him/who he is. Man Cannot Name Himself. Luci Shaw. TrCP

To tell of great tidings, strange and true. From Far away. William Morris. OHIP

To tell of Him, the Unseen God. The Silent. Jones Very. AmePo

To tell the fate of the cowboy that rode at his right hand. The Texas Cowboys. *Anonymous.* CoSo

To tell the men who tramp the yard/That God's Son died for all. The Ballad of Reading Gaol. Oscar Wilde. OxBI

To tell the old, old story/Of Jesus and his love. I Love to Tell the Story. Katherine Hankey. TreFT

To tell the pretty secret/Of the Butterfly! A fuzzy fellow, without feet. Emily Dickinson. TAP

To tell the sleepy folk on land/All's well at sea. Whistles. Rachel Field. TiPo

To tell this truth, it kills him unforgiven. The People. Tomasso Campanella. AWP; DBV

To tell us She their sweets did give. On Clarastella Walking in Her Garden. Robert Heath. CavP; OBS

To tell us we have found our father-/land? My Fatherland. William Cranston Lawton. AA

To tell your name the livelong day/To an admiring bog! I'm nobody! Who are you? Emily Dickinson. AmePo; AnNE; BoWoP; CBEP; DiPo; GoTF; NCEP; NLV; NOBA; OBCA; OBSP; PoPl; SBG; SO; TAP; TreFS; WHA; YaD

To th'Honor of our Nation, that thy Paynes/Transcends all former, and their glory staines. In the Due Honor of the Author Master Robert Norton. John Smith. SCAP

To thank Thee for the things I miss. The Things I Miss. Thomas Wentworth Higginson. TrPWD

To that blest port of endless rest,/Where storms shall never come. My Father's at the Helm. *Anonymous.* BePJ

To that clobber, and slobber, and scream, between the boxcars? He Was Formidable. Robert Penn Warren. LiSp

To that dark inn, the Grave! The Lord of the Isles (excerpt). Sir Walter Scott. BSV

To that glorious Home, where they shall ever gaze on Thee. The Dream of Gerontius. John Henry, Cardinal Newman. OxBoCh

To that God-forsaken country-o called Michigan I-O. Michigan I-O. *Anonymous.* AmFP

To that God-forsaken gehooley of a place called Colley's Run-i-O! Colley's Run-I-O. *Anonymous.* AmFP

To that loved bowl my spoon by instinct floes. The Hasty Pudding. Joel Barlow. AnNE; AP; LoGBV; NOBA; OBAL; OxBA; TAP

To that new Marriage,/Justified–through Calvaries of Love–. There Came a Day at Summer's Full. Emily Dickinson. AmePo; MAmP; MoAmPo; NoAm; NOBA

To that place day doth unyoke! The Faithful Shepherdess. John Fletcher. EG; OBS

To that small voice that crieth–"Stop her!" Suggestions by Steam. Thomas Hood. NBM

To that strange place where one had first begun. Ball Game. Richard Eberhart. LiSp

To that sweet thief, which sourly robs from me. Sonnets, XXV: "No more be grieved at that which thou hast done." William Shakespeare. CBEP; OBSC; TEP; UnPo

...To the/All-soul's temple of rest. My Faith. Ananda Acharya. WGRP

"To the arms I love the best." As I Roved Out. *Anonymous.* DTC

To the attentive/and obedient mind. Paterson. William Carlos Williams. OxBA

To the bay of Taquamenaw. Hiawatha's Sailing. Henry Wadsworth Longfellow. BBV

To the blushed brim. Grief-In-Idleness. Thomas Lovell Beddoes. AtBAP

To the bone, the careless white bone, the excellence. Gray Weather. Robinson Jeffers. CMoP; NoAm

To the border outlined by tears,/frontier at the country of night. Put Your Word to My Lips. Rachel Korn. VWA

To the burning shores of Africa where the sugarcane does grow. The Flying Cloud (II). *Anonymous.* ShS

To the center all is near. They Made Me Erect and Lone. Henry David Thoreau. OBSP

To the centuries that shall be! Him Evermore I Behold. Henry Wadsworth Longfellow. TRV

To the chamber where/Lies one long sought/With despair? The Witch. William Butler Yeats. ELU

To the cold perfection of unending peace. Theseus: A Trilogy. Yvor Winters. NOBA

To the continuation of their creed/And their lives. Negro Hero. Gwendolyn Brooks. CAPP

To the coronal of my love. A Song of My Heart. Robert Bridges. ACV

To the cross that crowns the spire. Power Station. T. W. Ramsey. HaMV

To the crow's eyes. Let us not Pretend. Ray Mathew. BoAV

To the custom of such a world he offers himself. Waiwera. Kendrick Smithyman. AnNZ

To the dark bed/Of the divine Unknown! Epitaph: "How fair a flower is sown." Coventry Patmore. FaBoEE

To the day-long bitter taste which is one's own? Quatrain. Barend Toerien. PeSA

To the dead and the dying of Bachelor Hall. Bachelor Hall. Eugene Field. BLPA; FPL

To the dead pale prairie grasses? Prairie Wind. Duncan Campbell Scott. ACV

To the death that I shall meet. Ideal. Padraic Pearse. AnIV; AWP; LiTW; OnYI

To the deed that I see/And the death I shall die. Renunciation. P. H. Pearse. NOBI

To the dim brackets of a house,/The dark period of a door. On the Night in Question. Patricia Goedicke. TAP

To the ears that heard, this music was telling the story/of what was to happen to us all. Psalm of the Singing Grave. Alexander Janta. LiTW

To the earth alive with blissful fur. Of Dandelions & Tourists. Joe Rosenblatt. NOBC

To the East or the West I will follow/Till the dusk of my day. Love on the Mountain. Thomas Boyd. AnIV; HBV 1-2; OxBI

To the end of the chapter of Fate. A Ballad of Queensland (Sam Holt). George Herbert Gibson ("Ironbark"). PoAu 1-2

To the end of time trala/trala trala la-le-la Trala Trala Trala La-Le-La. William Carlos Williams. OFD

To the end, to the end, they remain. For the Fallen. Laurence Binyon. AnFE; NOBE; OBEV; OBWP; OxBTC; ViBoPo

To the fancy of Arthur O'Shaughnessy. On the Poet O'Shaughnessy. Dante Gabriel Rossetti. ChTr

To the farm down the long dirt road/by the river. Lost Picture. Ray Fraser. NeAC

To the Father through the features of men's faces. As Kingfishers Catch Fire, Dragonflies Draw Flame. Gerard Manley Hopkins. CMoP; DiPo; EaLo; EBEV; ExPo; FaBoMo; LiTM; MoRP; NOBV; NOCV; NoP; PrIm; VLP

To the featherless, invisible wings/He knows are there. The Owl in the Rabbi's Barn. Dan Jaffe. VWA

To the free skies unpent and glad and strong. Drum-Taps. Walt Whitman. AP

To the frenzy of a people/caught in revolution. Regenesis. Ron Welburn. NBP

To the fullness of the heart...! Pastourelle. Donald Jeffrey Hayes. AmNP

To the glittering Delian king. Song of Apollo. John Lyly. AtBAP; OBSC

To the God-forsaken country they call New Mexico. Boggy Creek. Anonymous. CoSo

To the god of things like they err It Was a Goodly Co. Edward Estlin Cummings. CrMA; LiTA; LiTM; MoVE; WaP

To the Gods belongs Tomorrow. The Epicure. Abraham Cowley. OBS

To the grace of the make-believe bed LV. Ted Berrigan. ANYP

To the grass, to the cows calving in the lot. Spring. James Still. GrPl

To the green leaves and the blue shadows. Interior with Mme. Vuillard and Son. Kathleen Fraser. NPGG

To the green meadows and the blue fjords. In Memoriam. Malcolm Lowry. OBCV

To the green wood now my love is gone. These Words I Write on Crinkled Tin. Lynette Roberts. ChMP

To the heart's weeping, which forgets her not. Ballata: Of His Lady among Other Ladies. Guido Cavalcanti. AWP

To the hearts that are true/And the land where the true hearts dwell. The Song of the Bow. Arthur Conan Doyle. HBV 1-2; MCCG

To the Holy Child who came to stay,/On Christmas Eve. Yet Love Was Born. Charles Hannibal Voss. BePJ

To the honeysuckle at evening now/pouring out its breath. Flowers and Men. D. H. Lawrence. FaBoEE

To the ice-fields: Let here spring thick bright lilies. Warning of Winter. Mary Ursula Bethell. FaBoWP

To the jasper tower of your beautiful flesh. Bitter rain in my courtyard. Wu Tsao. BoWoP

To the jealous his own false terrors. Patrico's Song. Ben Jonson. LoBV

To the land of milk and honey. The Old Testament (excerpt). Anonymous. FaBoUs

To the Land of the Hereafter! The Song of Hiawatha. Henry Wadsworth Longfellow AA

To the light/Of imaginary night. Mingus. Bob Kaufman. PoBA

To the lode of her agony. Suspense. D. H. Lawrence. MoBrPo

To the long parting, and the age to come. Sacramentum Supremum. Sir Henry Newbolt. GTBS

To the loved ones left at home/Throbbing hearts are ever turning. In the Mines. John Swett. BPAW

To the loving turtle-doves who laugh like hell. Sliding Trombone. Ribemont-Dessaignes George. EAS

To the low, slow murmur of the brown round wheel. A Spinning Song. John Francis O'Donnell. IrPN

To the lyrebird's mocking tune. Australia's on the Wallaby. Anonymous. PoAu 1-2

"To the Master of the Workmen, with the tally of/his work!" The Hired Man on Horseback. Eugene Manlove Rhodes. BPAW

To the men who dubbed them "butch-/ers" and have smirched the army's/ fame. The Fight at Dajo. Alfred E. Wood. PAH

To the miller himsel', and his three bonny daughters. Farewell. John Clare. NoP

To the Mistress of the Matchless Mine. Mistress of the Matchless Mine. Clyde Robertson. PoOW

To the moan of the willow water. Balder's Wife. Alice Cary. AA; AnAmPo

To the moaning and the groaning of the bells. The Bells. Edgar Allan Poe AA; BBV; FaFP; FPL; GN; HBV 1-2; LiTA; NePA; OBAL; OBCA; OHFP; PoLf; PoPl; SpRo; TAP; TreF; WBLP

To the mouth of the death for which no one is ready. Pacific Sonnets. George Barker. LiTM

To the Neolithic Mind. Similar Cases. Charlotte Perkins Stetson Gilman. BBV; HBV 1-2; PoLf

To the new row you hoe in fresh greening field. Bridal Song. Clemens Brentano. HW

To the new, strange world that lies/Outstretched to its wondering eyes! Who Knows? Titus Munson Coan. AA

To the nothing/to the sweet nothing All Splendor on Earth. Karin Kiwus. BoWoP

To the old man and the nearsighted hound. The Moments He Remembers. Mark Van Doren. NYBP

To the one worship of a withering face. A Marriage Prospect. William Hurrell Mallock. NOBV

To the open throats of flowers. Butterfly. Peter Armstrong. PCP

To the Paradisial place! Stabat Mater Dolorosa. Pope Innocent III. CAW

To the peace of which my heart can never hold enough. Day's End. Laurence Binyon. OBVV

To the place to which Zapapta/Ordered the famous convention. La Cucaracha (with music). Anonymous. AS

To the pleasant Isle of Aves, to look at it once again. The Last Buccaneer. Charles Kingsley. BeLS; EtS; FaBoBe; HBV 1-2; MCCG

To the poor belongs the treasure/Of the scattered ears behind. Lord of Life, All Praise Excelling. Clement Clarke Moore. AH

To the porcelain edges/of this/Poem. Black Holes. James A. Perkins. SOTS

To the pure almost everything's rotten. Limerick: "Said the Reverend Jabez McCotton." James Montgomery Flagg. LiBL

To the Queen of the Nile/By the green palm tree. The Queen of the Nile. William Jay Smith. GrPl

To the realm of the musical armies. As Yet. W. R. Rodgers. InW

To the river as the sea. As Sun, As Sea. James Sullivan. AMV-81

To the road where my Johnny is. Lost Johnny. Anonymous. AmFP

To the Rose of England I will give free.' Henry the Fifth's Conquest of France. Anonymous. OBET

To the rot of fruit, sweet but invisible, spicing the trails of the /air. Flying Foxes and Others. Kay Boyle. AnAmPo

To the rude, forked, and ever savage root. John Chapman. Richard Wilbur. OxBC

To the running chalk-talk of powder-red/box-cars beyond, while our train waits here. Train Window. Robert Finch. OBCV; PeCV

To the sea, the sea. All That Is Perfection in Woman. William Carlos Williams. BiP

To the sensual song of a woman's hips. A Black Girl Goes By. Emile Roumer. TTY

To the shame and confusion of Perkin Warbeck. A Ballad Called Perkin's Figary. Anonymous. APAS

To the sheep on the hills and the church and the steeple. What Are They Thinking... Bryan Guinness. OxBI

To the singing, to the drums. The Eagle-Feather Fan. N. Scott Momaday. CDW; STE

To the smiling angels it sounds heavy, uncouth. The Word. Gustave Kahn. VWA

To the soul the Abyss. De Profundis. Hugh" (Christopher Murray Grieve) MacDiarmid. SeCePo

To the splendour breaking from you, though you veil it. Notes of an Interview. William Johnson Cory. NBM

To the Spring that comes and kisses his feet. Tears in Spring. William Ellery Channing AA

To the stars and skies above,/To our last longing, to our last love! We Reached Out Far. Peretz Markish. TrJP

To the statistical Sparta of the champs. On Hurricane Jackson. Alan Dugan. CoAP; LiSp; NCSH; PoL; SD

To the stern god of sea. To Pyrrha. Horace. AWP

To the sun unsetting their flag is streaming, answering/flame with flame. The Pageant of Seaman. Mary C. G. Byron. HBV 1-2

To the sunlight of song. A Leave-Taking. Frederick Napier Broome. AnNZ

To the table of the body at which five men and two/women are casually sitting down to eat. Divine Love. Michael Benedikt. AmPA; CoAP; ConAP

To the temple, singing. In the Suburbs. Louis Simpson. CAPP; ELU; MAT

To the Thanksgiving Feast bring Five Ker-/nels of Corn!   Five Kernels of Corn.   Hezekiah Butterworth.   MC; PAH

To the thorn'd brow that makes the heavens pale.   Pain in All Love.   Coventry Patmore.   FaBoEE

To the tinkle of laughter/And crowned with the may.   The Elephant.   Herbert Asquith.   SUS; TiPo

To the trembling daylight/from which it sprang.   Bending the Bow.   Robert Duncan.   CAPP

To the tumultuous throng/Of the sky his cold and passionate song.   Ode: On the Death of William Butler Yeats.   A. J. M. Smith.   OBCV; PeCV

To the uncharted ports of summer dream.   Earthborn.   Peter McArthur.   CaP

To the Valley of the Kings.   Effigy.   Georgia Lee McElhaney.   CoPo

To the warm dashlight of home.   Eagle Squadron.   Vern Rutsala.   AMV-80

To the warp of the world's apocalypse.   The Chronicle of Meola Creek.   Keith Sinclair.   AnNZ

To the white quiet of the churchyar/fold.   Whither.   John Vance Cheney.   AA

To the wind, or to the sign that sways and creaks above the sta-/tioner's door.   Tomorrow.   Kenneth Fearing.   CMoP

To the wind she says, "They have eaten me alive."   In the Park.   Gwen Harwood.   CBAP

To the wisdom and the stillness/Where thy consummations are.   Kinship.   Sir Charles G. D. Roberts.   CaP

To the young dead we consecrate/These lives that now we dedicate.   Cedar Mountain.   Annie Fields.   MC; PAH

To Thee as Lord of little things.   A Business Man's Prayer.   William Ludlum.   BLRP

To thee, dread King,/We homage bring,/And own thy power.   Lord of the Worlds Below!   James Freeman.   AH

To thee for all thy love and grace.   O Jesus Christ, True Light of God.   John F. Ernst.   AH

To thee I consecrate my praise.   Who Here Can Cast His Eyes Abroad.   Abiel Holmes.   AH

To Thee I die; to Thee I only live!   Rise, O My Soul!   *Anonymous.*   OxBoCh

To thee, in faith I can no ferther seye:/His creatures mosten thee obeye.   Lament for Chaucer and Gower.   Thomas Hoccleve.   OxBM

To Thee, my Saviour and my King.   To Thee.   *Anonymous.*   BePJ

To thee my spirit I resign,/Thou maker of my breath.   Great God, How Frail a Thing Is Man.   Mather Byles.   AH

To thee, of thee!   A Song For the Asking.   Francis Orrery [(or Orray)] Ticknor.   AA

To Thee our first fruits give.   We Give Thee but Thine Own.   William Walsham How.   STF

To Thee our praise that we may pay,/To whom our laud is due–for aye.   Hymn for Easter Morn.   *Anonymous.*   TrCP

To thee, queller of sleep,/Looser of the snare of death.   On Waking.   Joseph Campbell.   AnIV

To Thee th' Eternal Fair, the Infinite Unknown.   The Incomprehensible.   Isaac Watts.   CEP; WGRP

To their appointed portion of delight/As queens and kings.   All Things Wait upon Thee.   Christina Georgina Rossetti.   GN

To their house in Great Camomile/Street.   Mr. Ibister.   *Anonymous.*   OxNR

To them Slainthe.   Slainthe!   Patrick MacGill.   AnIV

To them that keep his testament,/The witness of his truth.   I Lift My Heart to Thee.   Thomas Sternhold.   AH

To them, yes, every pane!   On the Asylum Road.   Charlotte Mew.   MoBrPo

To these bare fields, built at today's expense.   Pyrography.   John Ashbery.   PoM

To these the bounteous Godhead gave/These organs but to praise his name!   Thou Art of All Created Things.   Pedro Calderon de la Barca.   WGRP

To think a poor man's bones should lie unbles'd.   The Village.   George Crabbe.   NOEC; OAEL 1-2; PoEL 1-5

To think a soare so deadly/I should so rashly ripp up.   My Muse, What Ails This Ardour?   Sappho.   OBVE

To think how they'll truss up the savior o'th'nation.   The Salamanca Doctor's Farewell.   *Anonymous.*   APAS

To think how to climb from the hole these days are/digging.   Birthday.   P. J. Kavanagh.   NAs

To think how to unthink that thought again.   Confusion (parody).   Christopher Hervey.   BXAP; Par

To think of me while gazing on that little golden ring.   The Little Golden Ring.   *Anonymous.*   ShS

To think on Hers sincerely.   Lines Suggested By the Fourteenth of February.   Charles Stuart Calverley.   ALV; InMe

To think she loved one, and he proved deceitful.   The Blacksmith.   *Anonymous.*   OBET

To think that for your master's good you die?   Ode to a Pig While His Nose Was Being Bored.   Robert Southey.   NOBL

To think the man had printed "not'/When he had written "now.'"   Printer's Error.   P. G. Wodehouse.   FiBHP

...To this day I can/Taste his terror on my hands.   The Trout.   John Montague.   BoAnP; FaBoIP; IPY; NMP

To this dismal row/Of houses where only starved/Antennas grow?   Row of Houses.   John Robert Quinn.   AMV-80

To this long pelt over the back of a chair.   An Otter.   Ted hughes.   CMoP; NePoEA-2; NMP; NoAm

To this new sun.   Turning Fifty.   Judith Wright.   NAs

To this place/of coolness out/of the August sun.   Las Trampas U.S.A.   Charles Tomlinson.   TwCP

To this strange death I vainly yield my life.   Arcadia.   Sir Philip Sidney.   SiPS

To those gallant old times when we fought/'gainst the King.   Macdonald's Raid.   Paul Hamilton Hayne.   PAH

To those that love there are no dead,/Only the long sleepers.   In Memory of a Friend.   George Barker.   OxBTC

To those we love the best....   Those We Love the Best.   Ella Wheeler Wilcox.   PoToHe

To those who Dwell in Realms of day.   Auguries of Innocence.   William Blake.   AtBAP; BiP; BoLiVe; TrGrPo

To those who find on earth their place to stay.   Morning.   Jones Very.   AnNE

To those who have seen from the womb come/Enemies? How not say it?   The Children Look at the Parents.   Arthur Seymour John Tessimond.   ChMP

To thrill with all the sweets of life–is living.   Living.   *Anonymous.*   BLPA; FaBoBe; GoTF; TreFS

To thrive in nature and in man's nature.   The Orb Weaver.   Robert Weaver.   PPON

To throw that faint thin line upon the shore!   Modern Love, L.   George Meredith.   AnFE; EBEV; EnLi 1-2; EnLoPo; GoTF; GTBS; GTBS-P; HAP; HBV; InPo 1-2; NBM; NOBE; NOBV; NoP; OAEL 1-2; OAEP; OBNC; PoEL 1-5; SeCeV; TreFT; TrGrPo; ViBoPo; VLP; WHA

To thump/on the flat red wall.   Treaty-Trip from Shulus Reservation.   Patrick Lane.   NeAC

To thy bright throne as incense rise.   Great Lord of All, Whose Work of Love.   Jacob Duche.   AH

To thy five Joys that have devotion.   To the Virgin.   John Lydgate.   ACP; CAW; GoBC

To Thy great service dedicate.   Expectans Expectavi.   Charles Hamilton Sorley.   FaBoCh; HBMV; LoGBV; WGRP

To thy mercy thow me restore,/salvum me fac, domine.   The Best Song As It Seems to Me.   *Anonymous.*   CoBE

To thy most merciful face of night I kneel.   The Black Virgin.   Gilbert Keith Chesterton.   ISi

To thy renown, I paint what 'longs thereto.)   And Who Has Seen a Fair Alluring Face.   George Peele.   ErPo

To Thy shore, dear Lord, to Thy shore.   Just a Closer Walk with Thee.   *Anonymous.*   FSW

To thy soul as to thy body, O man, 'twould work advantage.   Song of the Forest Trees.   *Anonymous.*   OnYI

To toil for what you here untoiling may obtain.   The Witching Song.   James (1700-48) Thomson.   OBEC

To tolerate such frolics in the shade!   Two Sonnets.   David P. Berenberg.   HBMV

To touch herself.   The Girl in the Willow Tree.   Carolyn Maisel.   IHMS

...To touch the highest degree/Is passing hard; to do the best, sufficing is for thee.   That No Man Should Write But Such as Do Excel.   George Turberville.   EnRePo

To touch the prosperous growth of this tall Wood.   A Masque Presented at Ludlow Castle (Comus).   John Milton.   AtBAP

To touch the red lizard vile, spread on the/damp white bark.   Arcan Sylvarum.   Charles De Kay.   AA

To touch the yellow wonder of her hair.   Of Nicolette.   Edward Estlin Cummings.   HBMV

To tramp on other children's roofs.   Rain Riders.   Clinton Scollard.   SoPo; TiPo

To tread those blest paths which before I writ.   The Pilgrimage.   Sir Walter Ralegh.   EBCP; SiPS

To tribes of gaudy sloth I leave/The vanity of dress.   The Butterfly and the Bee.   William Lisle Bowles.   HBV 1-2; HBVY

To trot with fine disdain/Beside me down the soaked, sweet-smelling lane.   Dogs and Weather.   Winifred Welles.   TiPo

To trust in God and Heaven securely.   Four Things.   Henry Van Dyke.   AA; BBV; GoTF; HBV 1-2; HBVY; PoLf; PoToHe; TreF; TRV

To turn away from my stiff dwindling self/These thirty pair of adolescent eyes.   First Day of Teaching.   Bonaro W. Overstreet.   TrPWD

To turn back to sleep in my dark bed on earth.   Old Moon My Eyes Are New Moon.   Allen Ginsberg.   VGW

To turn off the lights/that burned all night/in the kitchen.   The Widow.   Susan Ludvigson.   MAYP

To turn the frozen pages, blindly bidden. Cleavage. Louise Townsend Nicholl. NePoAm

To tutor two tutors to toot? Limerick: "A tutor who tooted a flute." Carolyn Wells. HBV 1-2; HBVY; LBN; LiBL; SoSe; TiPo; YaD

To twitter amid cold winds and falling leaves! Thomas Trevelyan. Edgar Lee Masters. AnFE; APA; MoPo

To undo the work of the morn. Our Own. Margaret E. Sangster. BLPA; PoToHe

To unmarried and single/chimney pots. The Relationship. Stephen Vincent. NeAC

To uplift their bleeding brothers rescued from the dust. The Way, the Truth, and the Life. Theodore Parker. TRV; WGRP

To us came the Comforter/And the consolation of tongues of flame! Aaron Hatfield. Edgar Lee Masters. LiTA

To us, for all the ills life chose to send. Wedding Anniversary. Margaret E. Bruner. PoToHe

To us, the duller scholars/Of the mysterious bard. To learn the transport by the pain. Emily Dickinson. NOCV

To uses, arts, and charities. Opposition. Sidney Lanier. AnFE; APA; LiTA

To utter love more sweet than praise. In Memoriam A.H.H., LXXVII. Alfred, Lord Tennyson. OAEL 1-2; PP

To utter nothingness? Hast Never Come to Thee an Hour. Walt Whitman. CBEP

To various use their various streams they bring,/The people one, and one supplies the King. The Gardens of Alcinous. Alexander Pope. OAEL 1-2

To view their God they worshipped. To Clelia. Matthew Coppinger. CavP

To virtue, fortune, time, and woman's breast. Advice to the Same. Sir Philip Sidney. SiPS

To voice some subtlety of sylvan grief. An Autumn Breeze. William Hamilton Hayne. AA

To voice the deeper tones, and lead the way/To immortality, through life and death! Poet of Earth. Stephen Henry Thayer. AA

To wait at rich mens' tables, or their door. Worldly Wealth. Rowland Watkyns. FaBoEE

To wait for that great gittin'-up morning–Amen. God's Trombones: Listen, Lord. James Weldon Johnson. BANP

To wait for the lorry to Places Unknown. Tanks. Rhyll McMaster. CBAP

To wait for the next big draw. Like Children of the Summertime Playing at Cards. Julie Herrick White. AMV-80

To wait in Amphitrite's bower. A Masque Presented at Ludlow Castle (Comus). John Milton. AtBAP

To wait till time shall reach its fruitfulness. Mary on Her Way to the Temple. Ruth Schaumann. ISi

To wait until her friends came through/and hug them all with pleasure. The Rime of the Ancient Feminist (excerpt). Stephanie Markman. BrRo

To wake her, when she sleeps. Song for a Child. Helen Bayley Davis. SoPo

To wake, perhaps, in Wonderland. Wonderland. Harry Thurston Peck. AA

To wake to write very real clouds in endlessly sunny days/Does one? The Clouds. Arthur Vogelsang. MAYP

To waken in the sky. Song. Maria White Lowell AA

To walk away and know there's no return. Stabat Mater. Sam Hunt. OCNZ

To walk back/alone toward the rock. The Pass. John Logan. LCAP

..To walk/softly into/that lady's/kitchen. Mrs. Green. David Huddle. PPJ

To walk the dog around the neighborhood. Couple. Mary Swope. AMV-81

To walk the empty plains of hell/forever and ever/more. Lost Moment. Hoyt W. Fuller. PoBA

To walk there would be loss of sense. Lost Acres. Robert Graves. NoAm

To walk with Him whose friendship never palls/May God give strength. May God Give Strength. Peter Van Wynen. BLRP

To walk with the Sons of Morning/Through the glory of Earth the fair. Lord of the Far Horizons. Bliss Carman. TrPWD

To wander unremembered ways/With consciousness undone. Lonely Are the Fields of Sleep. Mary Newton Baldwin. GoYe

To want the higher things, because you care. Because You Care. Frank Crane. PoToHe

To warm men's hearts again and light the land. When They Have Lost. C. Day-Lewis. EnLit; MoAB; MoBrPo

To warm the cold seepage of stone. Welcome to This House. Faye George. AMV-80

To warm the Crow who rode with Custer I had taken sides. What I Did Last Summer. Ron Ikan. AMV-80

To warn thee from the service of the ingrate. The Poet: A Rhapsody. Mark Akenside. PP

To wash her long fingers/In silvery light. Sea Lullaby. Elinor Wylie. BoNaP; MOS

To wash the stain ingrain and to make me clean again. What Would I Give? Christina Georgina Rossetti. OBSP

To watch her beauty move into the earth. Death and the Maiden (excerpt). W. H, Oliver. AnNZ

To watch his head become an explosion/of dream daisies. Peyote Vision. Lew Blockcolski. VoR

To watch me wither and grow old. Lament for Glasgerion. Elinor Wylie. AmLP; PoA

To watch the centuries stream from my foot/And the whole world rock backward into place. Snakebite. Thomas James. SM

To watch the great birds that pass without destination. Words to My Mother. Alfonsina Storni. AMV-80

To watch the October leaves/In the dark Looking for a Home. Bert Stern. FAZ

To watch the tall water close over their heads. Sanctuary. Bruce Boyd. NeAP

To watch their Highnesses without being tempted. Four Lovely Sisters. C. A. Trypanis. ELU

To watching Gunsmoke/And sipping her/Iced lemonade. Six Feet Under. Janet Campbell Hale. VoR

To wear thy favour, and break lance for thee. Regina Confessorum. *Anonymous.* GoBC

To weather him, and his moist wings to dry. The Butterfly. Edmund Spenser. BoC

To weep for words I never said? A Prayer. Mary Dixon Thayer. HBMV; TrPWD

To welcome each and every message/With your hand. For Gabriel. Laya Firestone. VWA

To welcome home friends once more. Little Libbie. Julia A. Moore. ATP; OBAL; PeD

To welcome my true love with ten thousand bright joys. The Rifles. *Anonymous.* OBET

To welcome the new-liveried year. A May Day. Sir Henry Wotton. CH

To west, to east, the God unshrined,/Is still discovering me. New Hymns for Solitude. Edward Dowden. TrPWD

To what far kingdom have they gone/The men whose dust we walk upon? What Far Kingdom. Arthur Stanley Bourinot. CaP

To what God hath so wrought may great souls lend/The fadeless luster of achievements high. Colorado. John D. Dillenback. PoOW

To what I am and I will never be. Prisoner between the Panes of Glass. Silvina Ocampo. AMV-81

To what is already overwhelming. Posthumous Keats. Stanley Plumly. GeTw; SV

To what people in Brooklyn called Joise. Limerick: "There was a young fellow from Boise." John Straley. TDH

To what strange regions, or of bliss or pain,/That subterraneous way? The Home of the Naiads. John Armstrong. OBEC

To-what! To-wit! To-woo! The Canal Bank. James Stephens. GrPl

To what undreamed-of fields and lofty skies! Epochs. Emma Lazarus. SBG

To where a slight breeze broke the mirror/and then its promise, but never the water. Stars Which See, Stars Which Do Not See. Marvin Bell. LCAP

To where beyond these voices there is peace. Idylls of the King. Alfred, Lord Tennyson. EnLit; MaVP

To where my emerald branches call and wave/As to the mystic skies. The City Tree. Isabella Valancy Crawford. CaP

...To where/the lonely green trees and the white graves are. Tropical Towns. Salomon de la Selva. HBV 1-2

To where, vor me, the apple tree/Do lean down low in Linden Lea. My Orcha'd in Linden Lea. William Barnes. NOBV

To which gladnesse, who nede hath, God him bringe! O Blisful Light: Troilus and Criseide. Geoffrey Chaucer. AtBAP

To which I shall, when that thin Skin/Is broken, be admitted in. Shadows in the Water. Thomas Traherne. AtBAP; EnLi 1-2; HAP; LiTB; MePo; NoP; OAEL 1-2; OBS; PoEL 1-5; SeCP

To which our suffering needs/even and all our death must lead. Guerrilla. Cosmo Pieterse. WhB

To which the knuckles of his loose right hand are always returning. Ford Pickup. David Allan Evans. PPJ

To which there's no reply. For here we are. Divine Comedies (excerpt). James Merrill. HaCAP

To whistle and to smile at the johns. As You Leave Me. Etheridge Knight. BP; ConAP; FF; NNaP

To whom a devil–"This is the Lower House. On the Death of Pym. William, of Hawthornden Drummond. ALV

To whom all worship shall be done/In every time and place. Matins–Friday. John Henry, Cardinal Newman. VLP

To whom can I belong? In the Last Flicker of the Sinking Sun. Peretz Markish. VWA

To whom I speak and listen. The Photograph of Myself. Jon Anderson. AmPA

...To whom now shall I fly? Home-Sickness. Charlotte Bronte. GLGT

To whom the four winds of Heaven/Are but a lullaby for sleeping. In the Name of Jesus Christ. Claudia Cranston. HBMV

To whom the punishment belongs/Of Maelgon's crimes and Elphin's wrongs. The Indignation of Taliesin. Thomas Love Peacock. CBEP

To whom these dull dog-days/Between event seem crowned with olive/And golden with self-praise. Under Sirius. W. H. Auden. FaBoMo; NePA

...& To whom/will I complain? Wingwalking in Oregon. Robert Peterson. NeAC

...To whose eternal doom/Must bend the sceptered potentates of earth. Epitaph. Gabriello Chiabrera. AWP

To win a wreath or some cheap figurine/to show the world, if you know what I mean. Between You and Me. Samuel Hazo. GOYP

To win, and not only win but win/Big, win big. The Cancer Match. James Dickey. GP

To win fresh praises from her lover,/And make him offer–is to dye. A Song: "When lovely woman, prone to folly. (parody). Anonymous. FaBoPa

To win one night in her bed A Serious Poem. Ernest Walsh. ErPo

To win the laughter of Thine Easter Day. Good Friday: The Third Nocturn. Peter Abelard. LiTW

To Winton and to Westminster/It ranged, and grew still beautifuller.... The Abbey Mason. Thomas Hardy. PeD

To wipe the dust from my mahogany. The White Dust. W. W. Gibson. MoBrPo

To wit, to join the wild Te Deum/That echoes through the Athenaeum. Bishop Winterbourne. Walter De la Mare. FaBoNo

To witless things, then Love, I hope, since wit/Becomes a clog, will soon ease me of it. Dear, Why Make You More of a Dog than Me? Sir Philip Sidney. PrIm

To witness the bub-bub-beautiful pip-pip-pel-/ican swallow the l-l-ive little fuf-fuf-fish! An Invitation to the Zoological Gardens. Anonymous. BoAnP

To woods and groves, what once she painted, sings. The Third Advice to a Painter. Andrew Marvell. APAS

To work and win–it's simply great! It's Simply Great. Sidney Warren Mase. PoToHe

...To work myself/As a mine, subject to explosions and cave-in. Sailing from the United States. Stanley Moss. VGW

To work upon the railway. Pat Works on the Railway. Anonymous. FSW; TrAS

To worship, in the articulate temple,/The unspeakable god. Aubade: Donna Anna to Juan, Still Asleep. Richard Howard. PoA

...To worship you/on our knees, the common living dirt. The Common Living Dirt. Marge Piercy. GeTw

To wound myself upon the sharp edges of the night? The Taxi. Amy Lowell. BoWoP; MoAmPo; PBWP

To wrap the baby bunting in. Bye, Baby Bunting. Mother Goose. HBV 1-2; OxNR; SoPo; SpRo; TiPo; TrAS

To wrap your bonnie boukie in. Hushie Ba, Burdie Beeton. Anonymous. OxNR

To wrench one banner from the western skies,/And mark it with his name forevermore? Sonnet: "Oh for a poet–for a beacon bright." Edwin Arlington Robinson. PP

To wrestle with the angel–Art. Art. Herman Melville. AP; EyDe; MAmP; NOBA; ViBoPo

To write a mere good-bye. Der Brief, Den Du Geshrieben. Louis Untermeyer. ALV

To write in this red muck/Of things from my heart. Many Red Devils. Stephen Crane. TAP

To write some more about the Don/That dared attack my Chesterton. Lines to a Don. Hilaire Belloc. DBV; FaBoCo; MoBrPo; OBSV; TW

To yet more boastful visions of despair. Recalling War. Robert Graves. CMoP; CoBMV; ForPo; LiTM; MMM; NoAm; OAEL 1-2; OBWP; WaP

To yield what all his sighs could never do. When Damon First Began to Love. Aphra Behn. UnTE

To you each one commits his debt today. Next of Kin. H. B. Mallalieu. WaP

To you gave sense, good-humour, and a poet. Epistle to a Lady: Of the Characters of Women. Alexander Pope. NOEC

To you I pray. Week-Seek. Jim Tollerud. VoR

To you, Mother, I walk, making our poems. Trinity Churchyard. Muriel Rukeyser. NYP

To you, O priceless nails, whose bonds I claim/In rigid union with Him sweet and stern! To Jesus on the Cross. Juan Manuel Garcia Tejada. CAW

To you remembrance naught will bring but grief. Ah Woe Is Me. Sextus Propertius. AWP

To you the truth I reported/Of the lay here unfolded. Goat's-Leaf. Marie de France. PBWP

To you, to us, to our cages. 110 Year Old House. Ed Ochester. Psk

To you, who bear his name, great bounties deal. To Mr. George Herbert, with One of My Seals, of the Anchor and Christ. John Donne. OBVE

To you who sleep where poppies grow/In Flanders Fields. Reply to In Flanders Fields. John Mitchell. BLPA; PAL

"To you, with Love from Me." My Valentine. Kitty Parsons. SoPo

To your brothers' will, your homeland's will, your body's will? Talmudist. Stanley Burnshaw. VWA

To your cream here's strawberries. Fresh Cheese and Cream. Robert Herrick. UnTE

...To your kind hands/that helped me stagger to my feet, and flee. The March 2. Robert Lowell. NoP

To your mistaken shrine, to your false idol Honour. Trail All Your Pikes. Anne Finch, Countess of Winchilsea. ExPo

To your natural shape return! Witches' Spells. Madeleine Edmondson. NTCP

To your own meaning, yourself alone. Poem. Charles Tomlinson. CMoP

To youth and age in common–discontent. Youth's Agitations. Matthew Arnold. CBEP

A toad below a strawberry leaf? On a New Duke. Anonymous. FaBoEE

...The toast/dipped in the yolk of the egg, in the yolk that tells all. It's in the Egg. Joe Rosenblatt. NOBC

Toast me just once in the local anaesthetic. The Poet's Farewell to His Teeth. James Dickey. DFF; GP; PoA

Today–another miracle–the feathered/arrows of my faith may link/God's bow and target. Getting inside the Miracle. Luci Shaw. TrCP

Today as in the past/our hopes are with the blood of Rogh. The Passing of the Poets. Fear Flatha O Gnimh. NOBI

Today belongs to few and tomorrow to no one. Whenever I Go There. William Stanley Merwin. NaP

Today, held firm, is my tomorrow. From a Diary. Frederick Morgan. NYP

Today I must learn to weep in a foreign tongue. Bar Mitzvah. Steve Orlen. GP

Today/I sing yet another song,/A song of exile. Yet Another Song. David Rubadiri. WhB

Today I smelled sawdust and white spirit and dreamed/that I gave up art for the sake of flattery. A Day in the Life... Stef Pixner. BrRo

Today I've got the saddle. Some Day. Shel Silverstein. PH

Today I've killed two true lovers,/And tomorrow I must die! Little Musgrave and Lady Barnard (Little Matthy Groves). Anonymous. AmFP

Today is thine–tomorrow thou art/death's To a Magnolia Flower in the Garden of the Armenian Convent in Venice. Silas Weir Mitchell. AA

Today it is summer,/Tomorrow is fall. September. Edwina H. Fallis. SUS; TiPo; YeAr

Today itself's too late–the wise lived yesterday. Tomorrow You Will Live. Martial (Marcus Valerius Martialis). NIP

Today, O Lord, for your dear sake,/I'll try to keep them when awake. Morning Prayer. Ogden Nash. GrPl; OxBChV

Today ready ripe, tomorrow all too shaken. Brittle Beauty. Henry Howard, Earl of Surrey. AAS; AnFE; EnLoPo; FCP; SiPS; TrGrPo

Today's the day when wise men see/The snowfish frisking in the snow. The Snowfish. Edward Field. GrPl

Today the angels earthward swing/To bless us here below! Christmas Morning. Harry Behn. PCh

"Today the Prince of Peace is born!" A Christmas Carol. James Russell Lowell. PGD

Today they swim with ease in the swift current. The Boats Are Afloat. Chu Hsi. NaP

Today, to all who need Thee most,/In silent ways, return! Jesus Return. Henry Van Dyke. TRV

TODAY, TODAY! Next Year. Nora Perry. PoToHe

Today when the hunters and hounds are running. Blessing the Hounds. Mary Winter. GoYe

"Today will be the day of what we both said." West-Running Brook. Robert Frost. AP; BLPL; DiPo; MoAB; MoAmPo; NOBA; NoP

...Today you know it,/a great rich room, a musical sky. Walking with Your Eyes Shut. William Stafford. GOYP

Together, across the page/we draw toward a name. The Lesson. Beth Bentley. GLGT

Together freed, their gentle spirits fly/To scenes where love and bliss immortal reign. Spring. James (1700-48) Thomson. EiCP; LAuP

Together in guilt and mercy, world without end. A Village Tale. May Sarton. BoAnP; GDP

Together in the twilight of the wood. Man and Dog. Edward ("Edward Eastaway") Thomas. FM

Together on Pali Lookout, father and son. On Pali Lookout. Stephen Shu Ning Liu. BrSi

Together our spirits will make love and give birth/to the seasons Wrap Me in Blankets of Momentary Winds. Harold Littlebird. VoR

Together over the ridge/into the dusk. The Death of an Elephant. Gianfranco Pagnucci. NU

Together, side by side, life's Angelus! At Set of Sun. Mary Ashley Townsend. AA

Together, then/After. Two Are Together. Geoffrey Grigson. GBL

The too fair promise of thy spring. Margaret Love Peacock. Thomas Love Peacock. OBNC; OBRV

Too far away to matter now,/before he hit bottom. Uncle Claude. David Allan Evans. Str

Too far from his half-brothers on the shore,/Hardly conceivable, is left to drown. Lines on Brueghel's Icarus. Michael Hamburger. NIP

Too heavy! The Guarded Wound. Adelaide Crapsey. AnAmPo

....Too late/....alas Point of No Return. Mari E. Evans. NNP

Too late, all the dead in the river are my friends. Supreme Death. Douglas Dunn. FaBoMo

Too late for blaming then. The Journeyman. Ralph Hodgson. AtBAP

Too late for me, the blind does lead the blind. To B. C. Sir John Suckling. CaPo

Too late is a crime. Be Always in Time. Anonymous. OxNR

Too late of tender sighs the poor relief. Sonnets to Laura. Petrarch. EnLi 1-2

Too late shall weep, and curse his thrifty hand,/That would not timely ease the ponderous boughs. Pruning. John Philips. FaBoUs

Too late to question what the tale had meant. The Thousand and Second Night. James Merrill. NYBP

Too late to that young withered beech that keeps/It autumn in the spring. The Beech. Andrew Young. BoNaP

Too late, you fool. The Nightmare. Sorley MacLean. NeBP

Too little wrought. Lessons. Louis Untermeyer. TiPo

Too lonely, to be free. On the Wide Heath. Edna St. Vincent Millay. CMoP

Too long lying in grave-mould, camped with/Death where the dead men lie. Where the Dead Men Lie. Barcroft Henry Boake. BoAV; CBAP; PoAu 1-2

Too long remembered, too long forgotten. Elegy in the Orongorongo Valley. Hubert Witheford. AnNZ

Too long stumbled down a maze/Bewildered. Joy. Clarissa Scott Delany. CDC; PoNe

Too many great-great-great-great aunts to see. Death. L. E. Jones. PoL

Too many nights I have yearned/For one who would not return. Song of Despair. Rangiaho. WTO

Too many waves to mark two more or three. Old Woman. Iain Crichton Smith. BSV; FaBoTw; OxBTC

Too much light. Too much love. The Zodiac, X. James Dickey. TAP

...Too much to build/Respect where none has been, or been owed. Pocket Guide for Servicemen. Hubert Creekmore. WaP

Too much water behind the dam. And the Gas Chamber Drones in the Distance. Greg Forker. LFAC

Too much water, Kin. For the big breakup./On high ground. Some Magic. James Koller. PoM

Too oft, I fear thou wilt remember me. Harden Now Thy Tired Heart. Thomas Campion. AAS; NCEP

Too poor to tax, too numerous to feed. The Modern World. Colin Ellis. FaBoEE

Too proud and high,–good-bye, say I,/To Kate o' Belashanny, O! Kate o' Belashanny. William Allingham. IrPN

Too proud, too proud, too proud, too proud. Quarrel. Jean McDougall. GoBC

Too quiet to hear. The Breathing. Denise Levertov. NaP; RFM

Too-ral li Roo-lal li Lay! Botany Bay. Anonymous. FSW

Too roo dee nay, Too roo dee noo, Too roo dee nay, Too roo dee noo. Springfield Mountain. Anonymous. TrAS

Too save our children/too save yourself Poem for Friends. Quincy Troupe. PoBA

Too shallow now to drown in or to mourn/The courageous and precarious children Some San Francisco Poems. George Oppen. NNaP

Too simple and too sweet for words! The Angel in the House. Coventry Patmore. VLP

Too simple/for he who is tired and has to walk on. Kinaxixi. Agostinho Neto. WhB

Too soon, alas, he will find out/That life is war. Then and Now. Charles Frederick Johnson. AA

Too soon it will be carried away. Teatime Variations. Peter Titheradge. FaBoPa

Too soon its brilliant course is run,/Its beer will soon stop flowing. Election Time (parody). Anonymous. FaBoPa

...Too soon/the unalterable conclusion. The Deceptrices. William Carlos Williams. NYBP

Too soon! too soon! The Pennycandystore beyond the El. Lawrence Ferlinghetti. BiP; CAD; CAPP; CTBA; HeIP; TAP

Too sound for waking and for dreams too deep. Not for That City. Charlotte Mew. MoBrPo

Too tart the fruit it brought! Shut Out That Moon. Thomas Hardy. BrPo; CMoP; MoVE; NoAm; NOBE; ViBoPo

Too tired to cut it off. The Disconnection. Rita Mae Brown. IHMS

Too tired to talk. Hitch Haiku. Gary Snyder. LCAP

Too weary, not to know/Why thou hast all this woe. Tears in My Heart That Weeps. Paul Verlaine. SyP

Too well I know the power to get one down/Exerted by this grey and shuttered town. Afternoons with Baedeker. Osbert Lancaster. FaBoCo; NOBL

Too young/to ever have given Revolutionary. James P. Friel. AMV-81

Took a bite of ice cream/that drove a spike through my head. Ice Cream. Peter Wild. Psk

Took a run, and jumped clean over. Old Farmer Giles. Anonymous. OxNR

Took aim and shot him dead. Plot Improbable, Character Unsympathetic. Elder Olson. NePA

Took freely all the crime upon himself. Epigram. Samuel (1612-80) Butler. FaBoEE

Took his farewell journey to the Promised Land. Casey Jones. Anonymous. BeLS; MaC

Took his lunar honey from the rose of the winds. Moonlight. Guillaume Apollinaire. MOON

Took ole Stackolee to the cemetery/Never to bring him back./Oh poor, poor Stackolee! Stagolee (A vers.). Anonymous. ViBoFo

...Took the bourbon from the shelf/and drank her a tall one, tall. Dream Songs. John Berryman. TAP

Took them in charge while Beelzebub roared for his rum./...None of them come! When Sir Beelzebub. Edith Sitwell. FaBoMo

Took up his Load, and trudg'd into the City. Tom the Porter. John Byrom. CEP; NOEC

Took wife and child with me. Emblems. Allen Tate. VGW

A Tool so singular that it had none. Epigram on the Unknown Inventor of Scissors. L. E. Jones. PoL

Tools of the shaman/Medicine food. Earth. Jim Tollerud. VoR

Toom came the saddle,/But never cam he. Bonnie George Campbell. Anonymous. AmFP; AWP; BoLiVe; CH; ELP; EnLit; EnRP; FaBoBa; GBP; HBV 1-2; InPo; NoP; OxBB

Toora lu, toora lay, oh, it's six miles/from Bangor to Donnahadee. The Old Orange Flute. Anonymous. FSW

Toot, toot, they never came back. Variation. Peter Wild. GP

A tooth,/An udder/Full of milk. The Animals. Charles Simic. GeTw

A tooth, five-cusped: man. In Bed with a River. George Bradley. AMV-80

...A toothless, ancient squaw/Lifted a feeble fist at him and screamed. Red Cloud. John G. Neihardt. BPAW

The top sheet's little tear? Meetings and Absences. Roy Fuller. OnUR

Tophet was made for such Supremacy. Poor Vaunting Earth, Gloss'd with Uncertain Pride. George Alsop. SCAP

The toppled clouds/the squared mountain. The Dark Swimmers. Larry Eigner. PoM

Toppled in that void tossed there, and woke. None. Josephine Miles. VGW

...The Torah is:/suffering begets suffering, that is. A Word about Freedom and Identity in Tel Aviv. Jon Silkin. VWA

The Torch laughs peece-meale to consume. Against the Love of Great Ones. Richard Lovelace. AnAnS 2

The torch my fathers gave in trust,/Thy father gives to thee! The Child's Heritage. John G. Neihardt. HBV 1-2

The torments of confusion. Homunculus et la Belle Etoile. Wallace Stevens. MoAB; MoAmPo

Torn again with that old-fool fervor. Love. Walker Gibson. NePoAm-2

Torn with sharp love of the home left far behind. At the Great Wall of China. Edmund Charles Blunden. GTBS-P; HaMV

Toro, toro! Venga! The Matadors. Josephine Jacobsen. TAP

Toroddle, toroddle, toroll! The Three Jolly Pigeons. Oliver Goldsmith. PoRA

The torpid consciousness, the trance no sound can/shatter. The Sleeping Beauty. Sara De Ford. DFT

...Torrent that gushes,/The tempests that rave. A Dedication. Adam Lindsay Gordon. CBAP

Tortured with longing/As though he had sent me a love letter. Like a Woman. Uri Z. Greenberg. VWA

Toss me the wind of your homeland, the world-old dream/in your eyes. Beggars. Rhys Carpenter. HBMV

Tossed by the waters, at Thy feet I fall. Lord of the Winds. Mary Elizabeth Coleridge. OxBoCh; TrPWD

Tossed everywhere/Like a dead leaf. Autumn Song. Paul Verlaine. LiTW

Tossed to and fro his passions fly/From vanity to vanity. Putney Hymn. Anonymous. TrAS

Tossed with stormes of fortune variable. Visions. Petrarch. EnLi 1-2

The tossing of his mournful waves/Makes sweetest music evermore. The Snow Lies Sprinkled on the Beach. Robert Bridges. NoAm

The total inventory of one wife's general store. One Man's Wife. Philip Booth. NIP; VGW

The total of human shadows bright as glass. When Was It That the Particles Became. Wallace Stevens. PoA

The total past felt nothing when destroyed. Esthetique du Mal. Wallace Stevens. CMoP

Totototo. Song of the Bush-Shrike. *Anonymous.* PeSA

Touch–for there is a spirit in the woods. Nutting. William Wordsworth. CBEP; ERoP 1-2; NU; OAEL 1-2

...Touch it. Touch It. Robert Mezey. NaP

...Touch it without/letting it show the print of your fingers. Poetry. Abraham Sutzkever. VWA

Touch me constantly! The Moment before Conception. Eve Merriam. UnTE

...Touch me. This is the body. I know. What Shines in Winter Burns. T. R. Hummer. MAYP

A touch of wonder/rising in your skull. For the Man Who Stole a Rose. Harley Elliott. FAZ

A touch Sidonian–modern–taking–strange! Orientale. William Ernest Henley. PeD

Touch the jewelry/on my ankles. Jarcha: "I will make love." *Anonymous.* BoWoP

Touch them with gold, they'll turn to what you please. Epigram: "Midas, they say, possessed the art of old." John Wolcot. DBV; ELU

Touch this frozen one. Lupercalia. Ted Hughes. CMoP; NMP

Touch this one thing,/You'll sure feel the other. This Book Is One Thing. *Anonymous.* FaBoUs

The touched thew bearing witness. The Wrestling. Abbie Huston Evans. GP

Touched to immortality/By her finger-tips. The Key-Board. William Watson. HBV 1-2

Touching and melting./Nowhere. The Night Dances. Sylvia Plath. LCAP

Touching in that mighty, empty space. Art in America. Theodore Weiss. AMV-80

Tough in their patience to surpass/The tigress her swift motions. A Summer Night. W. H. Auden. FaBoRV

The tough romance their hands build nothing without. America. Pier Giorgio Di Cicco. CaPN

Tough stalk, and face without a name. The Messenger. Thom Gunn. PoA

...Tour the template, thoroughfare/of noon's atoll. The Harbor of Illusion. Charles Bernstein. APU

Toward Bethlehem–the caravan goes by! Portico. Ruben Dario. CAW

Toward early circle makes return,/The rondure of immensity. The Shape of the Heart. Louise Townsend Nicholl. ImOP

Toward God high taunts I hurled,/With cursing parched my tongue. In Rebellion. John Millington Synge. SyP

...Toward her, each alone,/Glide the dark dreams that seek an English grave. Ypres. Laurence Binyon. MMM

Toward lifting them above their crippling storm. The Elevator Man Adheres to Form. Margaret Danner. PoBA; PoNe

Toward my very first day at school! First Departure. Frances Frost. SiSoSe

Toward some weak, outnumbered, cowering North/That will lay down its arms at Eighty-sixth. Fifth Avenue Parade. Anthony Hecht. NYP

Toward someone. Dreaming with a Friend. Stephen Berg. NaP

Toward that eye of the needle/Love has appointed there/for a joining that is not easy. Sonnet. Robert Duncan. GP

Toward that far country where his wishes/ are? Ariana. Franklin Benjamin Sanborn. AA

Toward that hot neck, for the delicate and final thrust, having/dared trust forth his hand. Say That We Saw Spain Die. Edna St. Vincent Millay. SBG

Toward the exuberant wreckage of August. The Fifth Season. Reg Saner. FYAP

Toward the fires of our Indian world. You Northern Girl. Charles G. Ballard. VoR

Toward the last phase/of our dear West.) The Anathemata. David Jones. NoAm

Toward the river ferry taking sounding after sounding. Lost Letter to James Wright, with Thanks for a Map of Fano. Gibbons Ruark. MAYP

...Toward the unsatable/Inexorable wilderness of feeling. The People at the Party. Lisel Mueller. NePoAm-2

Toward their large, inconsiderate houses. Beached Whales Off Margate. Stephen P. Dunn. LTB

Toward twelve there in the beams of the moon they surrender to us. Song of Myself. Walt Whitman. OnMSP

Toward which all hungers leap, all pleasures pass. A Baroque Wall-Fountain in the Villa Sciarra. Richard Wilbur. AmPP; BiP; CAPP; MP; NePoEA; NoP; NYBP; PoCh; TwCP

Toward which, as to later lives,/Young, later selves of you go futuring. Three Sermons to the Dead. Laura Riding. LiTA

Toward which the moon drags itself like a dog. The Assignation. Juana de Ibarbourou. PBWP

Toward which you lend no part! El Hombre. William Carlos Williams. CABA; CMoP; LiTA

Towards a gate past which being/ceases, let us say, to surprise. Gate. David McAleavey. SUW

Towards the gateposts and the void/(Between them) of his older shape. Death. Roy Fuller. NoAm

Towards the lone northern star and the fair ports of home. D'Avalos' Prayer. John Masefield. MOS; TrPWD

Towards the private/blue tenderness pulsing/there. Cutting Wood on Shell Creek. Gretel Ehrlich. MAYP

Towards the pure insistence/of the bell. Country Nun. Geoff Page. CBAP

Towards the songs' pretended sea. Legacy. LeRoi (Imamu Amiri Baraka) Jones. NoAm; NOBA; PoBA

Towards the subhuman swamp of under-dark? The Butterfly. Margaret Avison. ExPo; OBCV

Towards the uncharted mountain of my shoulder. The Spider. Kenneth Mackenzie. BoAnP

Towards the Wash/and the Lynn Deeps. Oxford. Edward Dorn. NOBA

Towards the whitening dawn. Morning Prayer. Aua. WTO

...A towel/That was neither wove nor spun. Riddle: "I washed my face in water." *Anonymous.* GBP

The tower is on fire./It is today. Watching the Sun Rise over Mount Zion. Ruth Whitman. VWA

"Tower, we're going down. This is PSA." Words. Miller Williams. AMV-81

The tower, your heart. Mad Apples. Diane Keating. CaPN

Towers and steeples rise away/into the towering gulfs of air. Veni Coronaberis. Geoffrey Hill. NoP

...Towers of cloud uplifting/In air their unsubstantial masonry. Venice. Henry Wadsworth Longfellow. EyDe

The towers of their most strategic lies. Sigmund Freud. Howard Nemerov. PoA

Towers to a lily, reddens to a rose. The Poet. William Watson. TrGrPo

The town again, trailing your legs and crying! Wild Swans. Edna St. Vincent Millay. CMoP; PBWP; UnPo

Town and people once again/I commend to God. Amen! The Fortification of New Ross (excerpt). *Anonymous.* NOBI

The town is ruled upon skille. In Praise of Winchester. *Anonymous.* OxBM

A town moored in mud. Galway. Donagh MacDonagh. NeIP

A toy by fitts to play withall at leasure. When I Was Otherwise Than Now I Am. *Anonymous.* NCEP

The toy of time?/and nod my head. A Moment Please. Samuel ("Paul Vesey") Allen. AmNP; IDB; PoBA

Toys of the children wings/of the wasp. The Book of Job and a Draft of a Poem to Praise the Paths... George Oppen. NNaP

Toys with a fair boy on his breast the livelong day! Boys and Sport. Solon. PeHV

Tra la la la la la la la/La/La/La!' Neptune–Polka. Edith Sitwell. NOBE

The trace of all/That I have been. Two Invocations of Death, I. Kathleen Raine. OxBTC

Tracing in crystal the slow way he came. Full Moon: Santa Barbara. Sara Teasdale. BrR; OBCA

Tracing the trite untransferable/Truss-advertisement, truth. Send No Money. Philip Larkin. TW

The track of small feet/like dark fern seed. The Open Door. Elizabeth Jane Coatsworth. DuDa

Trackless and noiseless through the/keen night air. November. Christina Georgina Rossetti. YeAr

...Tracks/smile up ahead–for they/have been here before. The Transandean Railway. Thomas Kretz. AMV-80

Tradition sets the straightest line to sense. Yankee Poet. Robley Wilson, Jr. AMV-81

Traffic flows over the bridge. The Center of Attention. Daniel Gerard Hoffman. FYAP; UnPo

Tragedy as great. The Teacher to Heloise (After Waddell). Daniel Burke. AMV-81

–The tragedy of an unevolved people. The Glen of Silence. Hugh" (Christopher Murray Grieve) MacDiarmid. CMoP; NeBP

The tragickest durn thing I ever heard! Noel Tragique. Ramon Guthrie. ErPo

Trail of my own lost footprints–I go to the plains! The Plains. Maynard Dixon. BPAW

The trail of tears never ends. Red Anger. R. T. Smith. STE

Trailing a Hundred Stars/Over the Night. The Moon. Louise Ayres Garnett. SiSoSe

Trailing my mother/I don't know Elegy. Alan Loney. OCNZ

Trails over the mountain. On the Shore of Nawa. Hioki no Ko-okima. AWP

The train/I'm riding, it don't burn no coal/ Mmmmmmmmmmmmmmmmmmmm. The Panama Limited. Booker White. BluL

Train on Track Four./Aisle Number Two.   Calling Trains.   *Anonymous.*
AmFP

The Train that runs on Time is never late.   Awake! (parody).   Jack Black.
BXAP

The Train will stop and take you in.   The Line to Heaven by Christ Was
Made.   *Anonymous.*   BXAP; PeD

The traitor lurks, the undermining foe.   Pretty Maids Beware!!!   *Anonymous.*
CoMu

A traitor's end, you may depend,/Can be expect'd no better.   Sir James the
Rose.   *Anonymous.*   ESPB

Trak-tak!...I must bury you, Kate my dear;/My bullet has gone through your
head.   The Tryst.   Edward Valpy Knox.   CenHV

The tramp and whistle of the dance, and hear/The drunken babble round.
My Country.   Mikhail Yuryevich Lermontov.   LiTW

Trample and break and charge along the sand!   Sappho.   Bliss Carman.
PeCV

Trampled on the pavement,/impaled on a railing.   The Beginning of the End.
Jon Stallworthy.   OxBC

Trampling the tender bloom of the soft grass.   Full Moon (fragment).
Sappho.   AWP

Tranquil as a fountain in a garden where no/wind blows.   Whale at Twilight.
Elizabeth Jane Coatsworth.   BoAnP

(The tranquil heart may yet outrun/The rocket and the car.)   Window Ledge
in the Atom Age.   E. B. White.   NLV; OBAL

Tranquilly Titicaca–   The Eyeglasses.   William Carlos Williams.   NoAm

Transcendent beyond the barrier of glass.   Come Not Near.   Mary Elizabeth
Osborn.   NePoAm-2

Transcending aught we gaze upon.   The Human Outlook.   John Addington
Symonds.   WGRP

Transeamus!   Rosa Mystica.   *Anonymous.*   CAW; EG; GoBC; ISi

Transferred from man's fowl friend are Bursal Brews/Sought so long by
modern medicine's gurus.   Chicken Soup Therapy: Its Mode of Action.
Caroline Breese Hall.   SUW

Transfigured, bathed in your immortal flame.   Commemoration.   Claude
McKay.   BANP

Transfigured by their purity.   Midwinter.   John Townsend Trowbridge.
AA; AnAmPo; APA; GN; HBV 1-2

Transfixed him then and there with my own stiff prick!   I Have Something
for You to Laugh at, Cato.   Caius Valerius Catullus.   PeHV

Transfixed, in her stone shade.   Casualty.   Diana Witherby.   ChMP

Transform'd to ayre Love entred with my will,/And nowe perforce doth keepe
possession still.   The Authour Still Pursuing His Invention.   Thomas
Watson.   AAS

The transformation in Mary, and seen Jesus tak' root.   Harry Semen.
Hugh" (Christopher Murray Grieve) MacDiarmid.   NoAm

...Transfuse our wandering souls/Out at our lips, and score up sums of
pleasure.   Volpone.   Ben Jonson.   ViBoPo

Transfusing life, health, comfort, and happiness too.   The Song of Hungarrda.
Ngunaitponi.   NOAV

A transient, true, and treasured bliss.   Serenade.   Dorothy Donnelly.
NCSH

Translate thy proud speech of the sunlight–O lory, come down!   To the Red
Lory.   John Shaw Neilson.   NOAV

Translated Daughter, come down and startle/Composing mortals with
immortal fire.   Anthem for St. Cecilia's Day.   W. H. Auden.   TwCP

Transmuted fall in sheafs of rainbows fraught/With storied meaning for
religion's sake.   Fragment.   Amy Lowell.   WGRP

Transmuted into a great golden casket/Entreasuring Pomona's jewelry.   A
Basket of Summer Fruit.   Charles Harpur.   NOAV

Transparent memory, or presage,/of eternity.   Etruscan Notebook.   Elena
Clementelli.   PBWP

Transplanted her clear to Albania.   Something for My Russian Friends.
Edmund Wilson.   OBAL

Transplanting Flow'rs from the green Hill,/To crown her Head, and Bosome
fill.   The Gallery.   Andrew Marvell.   AnAnS 1; MeLP; NoP; OBS

The transport of the bird!   "The wind took up the northern things".   Emily
Dickinson.   AmLP; SOTW

Trapped by water or fire–yet dead?   Dirge for Small Wilddeath.   Judith
Moffett.   LTB

Trapped in my rib-cage something throes and aches!   Sonnet.   John
Berryman.   NoP

;Travel the wholesome road/And give my body to the sun.   June Morning.
Hugh McCrae.   BoAV; PoAu 1-2

Travelling between them/I stay sane.   Ross's Poems.   Geoffrey Lehmann.
CBAP

...Travelling light by mountain roads/To Elsewhere; drank at desert wells;
gained strength.   Mandrakes for Supper.   James Keir Baxter.   OxBC

Travelling on Rapid Sic Transit.   Three Fitts.   Stewart Parker.   CIP

Travelling over the great and luminous Sahara lit by clouds.   Country Roads.
Rolf Jacobsen.   NU

Travelling slowly in the direction of Oxford.   English Train, Summer.
Ralph Pomeroy.   GP

Travellyng men may consydder best/The montanis bair nyxt the southwest.
The Monarche: After the Flood.   Sir David Lindsay.   OxBS

Travels in clouds, seeks manna, where none is.   The Search.   Henry
Vaughan.   SBVL; SeCP

...Tray/Be as dull as his Master, when Phebe's away?   My Dog Tray.   John
Byrom.   SeCePo

The treachery in ears!   Lyric.   Arthur Gregor.   TAP

Tread softly because you tread on my dreams.   He Wishes for the Cloths of
Heaven.   William Butler Yeats.   CMoP; NOBV; OLR; SOTW

Tread sure, keep up with them, and All's your own.   To Be Engraven on a
Dial.   Samuel Sewall.   SCAP

Treading as soft as a tiger cat,/To tell me terrible lies?   The Puritan's Ballad.
Elinor Wylie.   HBMV; LiTL; NMM; PoRA

A treadmill of swallows almost holding their own.   Swallows.   Thomas
Hornsby Ferril.   RFM

The treasure is not thine, but theirs.   Treasure.   Lucilius [(or Lucillius[).
AWP; LiTW

A treasure-ship that journeys/Across its own oblivion?   The Heart
Recalcitrant.   Leonora Speyer.   PG

Treasure the gift/Of spendthrift heaven.   Giving and Taking.   James Kirkup.
EaLo

The treasure within thy fair bosom enclose,/As eggs are enclosed in their
shells.   To Lydia, with a Coloured Egg, on Easter Monday.   John Jones.
FaBoUs

...The treasured/singing, and the little bursts/of flying.   Some Painful
Butterflies Pass Through.   Tess Gallagher.   MAYP

Treat it nicely and it will/Always do just what you want.   A Bestiary.
Kenneth Rexroth.   OBAL

A tree could never/Hold them all.   November Rain.   Maud E. Uschold.
YeAr

A tree is heavy, falling.   The Bushfeller.   Eileen Duggan.   AnNZ

A tree is something in me,/Very still and lonely now.   A Tree Design.   Arna
Bontemps.   CDC

Tree leaves clatter masses/For leaves.   Truth.   Susan Fromberg Schaeffer.
IHMS

Tree-limbs tangle, the bridge/folds like a fan.   Water Picture.   May
Swenson.   BoNaP

A tree outside heavy with snow.   For Years.   Ralph J. Mills, Jr.   AMV-80

...The tree shaken, and under it/ground rooted with our new name.   That
Mulberry Wine.   Janet Sylvester.   MAYP

The tree struggles to exist.   Tree.   Harold LaMont Otey.   LFAC

The tree, the close willow, swayed.   The Visitant.   Theodore Roethke.
CMoP; NMP; PPoe; UnPo

The tree, the peak and all beyond it shiver.   Lady Anne Bathing.   Anthony
Delius.   PeSA

Tree, tree in the darkness/Of air, of water. Still. And alone.   Paradigm.
Babette Deutsch.   TrJP

The tree was bending to the side/And leaning out to look at me.   Strange
Tree.   Elizabeth Madox Roberts.   BoNaP; GrPl; WSC

A tree with tongues will grow.   In Memory of Colonel Charles Young.
Countee Cullen.   PoBA

Trees after the cold snap, bare in the yard.   Biting Through.   Traise
Yamamoto.   BrSi

The trees along our city streets/Are lovely, gallant things.   City Trees.   Vere
Dargan.   PGD

The trees and houses vanishing/in quiet every day.   Quiet Desperation.
Louis Simpson.   SV

Trees are the kindest things I know.   Trees.   Harry Behn.   SiSoSe; SoPo;
TiPo; YeAr

The trees bear fruit.   The Grass Is a Reasonable Colour.   John Newlove.
NeAC

...Trees/Blazing with blackened apples.   Ursula.   David Ray.   VGW

The trees bore skulls as fruit/and we feasted.   Cortes.   Albert Rios.   GP

The trees can't tell the two of them apart.   Field and Forest.   Randall
Jarrell.   LCAP; VGW

The trees darkening/like clusters of frightened wrens.   The Businessman of
Alicante.   Philip Levine.   NaP

Trees gay-leaved with sun, wind fresh and free.   Christmas Dawn.   Fleur
Adcock.   ACV

Trees make a long shadow/And a light sound.   Knowledge.   Louise Bogan.
HBMV

The trees melted in air.   Canto XXIX.   Ezra Pound.   MoPo

The trees/reproduce/more humanely.   Monogram 29.   Martina Werner.
BoWoP

The trees stand. The trees,/sudddenly wait against the moon's face.   Sonnet:
"A wind has blown the rain away."   Edward Estlin Cummings.   MoAB;
MoAmPo

Trees tumble out of twigs and sticks;   Darling! Because My Blood Can Sing.
Edward Estlin Cummings.   InvP; OxBA

Trees? Well, I'm tired/of them and rolled her head away.   The Last Words of
My English Grandmother.   William Carlos Williams.   SOTW

Trees yet in winter bloome, and beare their Summers greene. Polyolbion. Michael Drayton. OBS

Trefoil–hedge sparrow–the stars on the edge at night. The Escape. Ivor Gurney. OBSP

The trefoil of Divinity. Three Persons. Louise Townsend Nicholl. CAW

Treit weill thyself and stand content,/And latt all uthir luvaris be. Fane Wald I Luve. John Clerk. OxBS

Tremble–no bigger than a star! Leaves. William Henry Davies. MoBrPo

Trembles for passion: God was here! Dawn on Mid-Ocean. John Hall Wheelock. EtS

Trembles red-eyed before the claws of death. Okefenokee Swamp. Daniel Whitehead Hicky. AmFN

The trembling beauty/Of an urgent pine. Trees at Night. Helene Johnson. BlSi

Trembling breathlessly at the brink/of realization... Immortality. Frank Horne BANP

Trembling, milk is coming into its own. Milk. James Schuyler. ANYP

Trembling on the pulse of God. Spinster's Lullaby. Vassar Miller. BoWoP; NMM

Trembling the night waves, rocking boat and barge. In Spite of All This Much Needed Thunder. Zack Gilbert. PoNe

Trembling to be rejected/I turn to Thee again. Thoughts of God. *Anonymous.* WTO

Trembling, weeping with anger Bubba Esther, 1888. Ruth Whitman. AMV-81

Trembling with passionate pity/At my blameless life and shaking its flamelike head? The Faithful. Jane Cooper. AmPC; NePoEA-2; SM

...The tremor of that scream/Shattered my being like an empty dream. A Vision. Yvor Winters. AnAnS 2; MoVE; SeCP

...A trench, filled/not with snow only, east of Buchenwald. A Letter from Berlin. Jon Stallworthy. NoAm; OBWP; OxBC

Trenn shall be called a shining town. Eagle of Pengwern. *Anonymous.* PBWP

Tresore full dere, gronded with grace. Most Sovereign Lady. *Anonymous.* MeEL

Trespass and guilt for which He died/Have marked Him with a riven side. Scarred. *Anonymous.* STF

Tri-anti-wonti-/Triantiwontigongolope. The Triantiwontigongolope. C. J. Dennis. AmMo

The trials of abounding wealth. A Little Brother of the Rich. Edward Sandford Martin. AA; HBV 1-2

Tribal elders tell of some/who ran for a mile before/they fell. The Woyi. Lew Blockcolski. VoR

Tribal touchwood at the seams White Earth Reservation 1980. Gerald Vizenor. STE

The tribe of those who neither reap nor sow. Afternoon in a Tree. Sister Maris Stella. GoBC

A tribute to our matriarch/And our digestive juices. You Take the Pilgrims, Just Give Me the Progress. Loyd Rosenfield. QQQ

Trick'd in antique ruff and bonnet,/Ode and elegy and sonnet. Lines in Ridicule of Certain Poems Published in 1777. Samuel Johnson. FaBoCo

The trick of their own bellying walls, which charms/All eyes–themselves it vexes not, nor harms. On a Vase of Gold-Fish. Turner, Charles Tennyson. NOBV

Trifles deleted and the strength recorded. Homestead-Winter Morning. Mary Ballard Duryee. GoYe

Trigger pulled,/now dies. The League of Selves. Alvin Toffler. AMV-80

The triggered poem's no water-pistol toy,/But shoots its cause, and is a source of joy. A Choice of Weapons. Stanley Jasspon Kunitz. LiTM; VGW

A trimmed tree/is no place for song birds. Landeys. *Anonymous.* PBWP

The trip ends, the trip begins. Barnabooth Enters Russia. Paul Hoover. AMV-81

A triple threat that makes me Very,/Very, very apprehensive. Varitalk. Weare Holbrook. NYBP

Trippe a litel with thy foot,/And let thy body gon! A Drunkard. *Anonymous.* OxBM

Tripped me up, and I cracked my head. Andrew's Bedtime Story. Ian Serraillier. DuDa

Tripped the light fantastic/On the sidewalks of New York. The Sidewalks of New York. James W. Blake. BLPA; BLSo; FaBoBe; FSN; FSW; GoTF; TreFS; YaD

Tripping o'er the pearly lawn,/The youthful, charming Chloe. Chloe. Robert Burns. GN; HBV 1-2

Triumph/Is Yours. Need Is Our Name. Luci Shaw. TrCP

Triumphant thou shalt mount the years/Toward thy high goal! Ad Patriam. Clinton Scollard. PAH

Triumphantly he failed the test/and never even knew it. Alexander. Frederick Morgan. AMV-81

Triumphantly to lead us/Along God's holy way. O Young and Fearless Prophet. Samuel Ralph Harlow. AH; TrPWD; TRV

Triumphing over Death, and Chance, and/thee O Time. On Time. John Milton. BLPL; BoC; CABA; DiPo; LiTB; LoBV; MePo; OBEV; OBS; OxBoCh; SeCeV; TRV

Triumphs in gardens full of marigold. Jason. Anthony Hecht. CoPo

The trivial is immortal. Vienna. Peter Porter. OBTV

Trodden under foot today/and here tomorrow morning. Let Other People Come as Streams. Charles Reznikoff. VGW

Trolling an old Moorish song. With Cortez in Mexico. Wilfred (William Wilfred Campbell) Campbell. PAH

...Troopers kneel hunched over/their black Fords, tipped off, waiting. Jurgis Petraskas, the Workers' Angel, Organizes... Anthony Petrosky. FYAP

Troops of the mangroves, uniform, everywhere. Mangrove. John Blight. NOAV

Troopt to these Princes and the Court along th'unmeasur'd/shore... The Iliad. Homer. OBVE

Trophic ambush of the moon. Invocation from a Lawn Chair. Mary Jean Irion. AMV-80

A trophy to bear, as we march, thy band,/South, East, and on to the Pleasant Land! Holy-Cross Day. Robert Browning. VLP

Trotting through the streets/of Santiago. Dogs of Santiago. Eugene McCarthy. BoAnP; GDP

Trouble and grief are not hid from mine/eyes/in the musing of my heart. Blessed Art Thou, O Lord. *Anonymous.* TrJP

Trouble is the answer will be/That Amy'd rather stay in love with me. Once in Love with Amy. Frank Loesser. BLSo

Trouble/Mellows to a golden note. Trumpet Player. Langston Hughes. TTY

Trouble over, choose you a seat 'n' set down. Choose You a Seat 'n' Set Down. *Anonymous.* OuSiCo

"The trouble's with yer liver." The Worried Skipper. Wallace Irwin. BLPA

The trouble with angels is that the world/Has provided no place for them. The Trouble with Angels. Ken Norris. CaPN

A troubled crowd beneath a troubled sky. 14 July 1956. Laurence Lerner. PeSA

The troubled midnight and the noon's repose. La Figlia Che Piange. Thomas Stearns Eliot. APA; BoLiVe; FaBoTw; GBL; HeIP; LiTA; MAT; OxBTC; PoA; TwCV; VGW; ViBoPo

Troubled soul–he understands. Jesus Understands. *Anonymous.* BLRP

The trout will be rising.... When the World Was in Building. Ford Madox Ford. CTC

Troy yet stood, and Priam's towers so high.' The Aeneid. Virgil (Publius Vergilius Maro). OAEL 1-2

The truce was signed, but the attack goes on. Five. Weldon Kees. PPP

A truck backed into a thicket a half-mile downstream. In the Black Camaro. David Bottoms. AmC

...The truck/was what I missed most when I came to the city of light. Open Roads. David Donnell. Str

Trudge, body. Trudge, Body. Robert Graves. MoAB

Trudging the hard gay road/Of the clean-souled sons of men. A Prayer in Time of Blindness. Clement Wood. TrPWD

The true and earthy prayer/of salami. Salami. Philip Levine. NNaP; NOBA; TAP

True, and yet true that I must Stella love. Astrophel and Stella, V. Sir Philip Sidney. AAS; OAEL 1-2; OBSC; SiPS

True comrade and brave foeman/Madonna, intercede. O Mary Pierced with Sorrow. Rudyard Kipling. ISi

The true Correggio then is shown. Epigram: The Man of Taste. William Parsons. OBTV

True father's singing, supposed father's crying,/I think make women laugh that lie a-dying. Caelica, XXIII. Fulke, Lord Brooke Greville. FCP

A true gut-funky blues to make her really dance. The Reception. June Jordan. FaBoWP; NMM

The true heart plays at ease there,/In the music of those mornings. The Rich Interior Life. Richard Eberhart. MoRP

True Hope's a glorious huntress, and her chase/The God of Nature in the field of Grace. On Hope. Richard Crashaw. MePo; NOBE

"True is that vision, Mother." Mary's Vision. *Anonymous.* ISi

...True it is, a wise friend/can take a brother's place in our affection. The Odyssey. Homer. NAWM 1-2

True life, natural breath; not this phantasma. The Pier-Glass. Robert Graves. CMoP; CoBMV; MoAB; NoAm

True love doth pass away! My Silks and Fine Array. William Blake. BoLiVe; CBEP; ELP; GBL; TEP; UnPo

True love lay strangled by Othello. William Wilson. Malcolm Cowley. AnAmPo; MoVE

True lovers even in this. Never Such Love. Robert Graves. BoLoP

True, no one ever thought that you would pay. To Sextus. Pott and Wright. ALV

True Seed! thou shalt prevail! The Patient Church. John Henry, Cardinal Newman. GoBC

True shape of death and power. To a Military Rifle. Yvor Winters. MoAmPo; WaP

A true sign o the Corse for ye. The Gangrel Rymour and the Pairdon of Sanct Anne. Tristan Corbiere. OBVE

& True stories of the empire/the end for instance. The Electric Cop. Victor Hernandez Cruz. PoBA

True Thomas on earth was never seen. Thomas the Rhymer. *Anonymous.* BSV; ELP; EnSB; FaBoCh; GoTS; HBV 1-2; InPS; LiTB; NOBE; OAEL 1-2; OBEV; OnMSP; OxBB; PAI; Prf; SeCeV; ViBoPo

True, though not here as they to themselves elsewhere are. The Still Pool. Kathleen Raine. MoAB

True to our native land. Lift Every Voice and Sing. James Weldon Johnson. FaBV; FSW; GoSl; PoNe

True to the core of you/Barney McGee! Barney McGee. Richard Hovey. HBV 1-2; InMe; OBAL; TreFS

True to the death! Down the Little Big Horn. Francis Brooks. PAH

True to the kindred points of Heaven and home! To a Skylark. William Wordsworth. BoLiVe; HBV 1-2; HBVY; OAEP; PBBP; TrGrPo

True to the kindred points of Heaven and Home! To the Skylark. William Wordsworth. FaFP; GTBS; GTBS-P

...The true/true image of what happened: of the blank world. Handbook of Versification. Gilbert Sorrentino. PoA

True widow maid, still followeth Diana. Fly, Love, That Art So Sprightly. *Anonymous.* NCEP

Truest of friends,/The trees! Trees. Thomas Curtis Clark. PGD

The truest work is learning to be human/definitive texts the poorest can afford. For Angus MacLeod. Iain Crichton Smith. OxBS

Truly, a god did well. Swans. Leonora Speyer. FYAP

Truly I think each woman is a bird. Birds. Seumas (James Starkey) O'Sullivan. OxBI

Truly such a lady/Is a beauty in the land. Companion of Her Lord Till Death. *Anonymous.* HW

Truly, Traubel, aren't you tired? I Like to Sing Also. John Updike. FiBHP

Trumpets tell me yellow. Only ebony is mute. The Blindman. May Swenson. WeW

Trunk and bough,/Naked strength. The Oak. Alfred, Lord Tennyson. PoPl

Trust and let the sunshine of God's love shine through/Every overhanging cloud that darkens over you A Trust-Song. Eben E. Rexford. BLRP

Trust flattering life no more, redeem time past,/And live each day as if it were thy last.' Poems. William, of Hawthornden Drummond. JCP

Trust God, who is all wisdom and doeth all things just. The Ashland Tragedy, I. *Anonymous.* AmFP

Trust him not to breathe a word. Under the Lindens. Walther von der Vogelweide CTC

Trust Him now and enter in. Christ Alone. Shel Helsley. STF

Trust him to God. Dear is the trust. A Generous Creed. Elizabeth Stuart Phelps. WGRP

"Trust in God, Honey. Trust/in God." Sister Rose. Richard Martin. AMV-81

Trust in God, your Saviour, but keep your powder dry. Fare Ye Well, My Darlin'. *Anonymous.* OuSiCo

Trust me, Cloe, this will do. To Cloe. Hildebrand Jacob. NOEC

Trust me; I know these waterways. A Kind Inn. George Dillon. GoYe

Trust, mercy, peace–all those who love him will/Know in their lives his triple blessing still. The Blessing of St. Francis. Sister Maura. CaP

"Trust, my soul, be brave!" A Night in a Village. Ivan Savvich Nikitin. AWP

Trust not, Mother dear,/Hearts ungrateful here! Seguidilla. Jose de Valdivielso. CAW

Trust the Great Artist, He/Who made the earth and sea. Trust the Great Artist. Thomas Curtis Clark. WBLP

Trust thee all my journey through. Happy, Saviour, Would I Be. Edwin H. Nevin. AH

Trust: to lip words/briefs what great (?) discourse well. Peri Poietikes. Louis Zukofsky. CoPo

Trust to thyselfe, and lerne to be wise. Trust Only Yourself. *Anonymous.* MeEL

"Trust us," the Voices said. The Lovely Shall Be Choosers. Robert Frost. AmP; CoBMV; MoAB; MoAmPo; NOBA; OxBA

Trusted the servile womb to breed free men? Advice to Young Ladies. A. D. Hope. NoP

Trusting God and in each other,/We are children of the day. Hast Thou Heard It, O My Brother. Theodore Chickering Williams. AH

...Trusting her/to dream what I have not said. Old Man. Philip Booth. AMV-80

Trusting the wind to blow me home again. Staying in the Mountains in Summer. Yu Hsuan-chi. BoWoP

Trusting Thee with faith sincere. The Two Prayers. Andrew Gillies. BLRP; PoToHe; TRV

Trusting through thee eternal life to inherit. Welcome, Sweet Rest. Michael Wigglesworth. AH

Trusts in God, that as well as he was, he shall be. Epitaph on Himself. Alexander Pope. FaBoEE

Truth? A pebble of quartz? For once, then, something. For Once, Then, Something. Robert Frost. AP; ForPo; NoAm; NOBA

Truth be thy speed, and Truth thy patron be. Vergidemiarum: Prologue: "I first adventure, with foolhardy might." Richard Barnfield. ViBoPo

The truth, he says, flew farther,/But not so high by half. Tall Tale God. Mark Van Doren. CrMA

Truth in their place would watch that star's return. The Appointment. Arthur William Edgar O'Shaughnessy. OxBI

Truth in woman, faith in men! Trust the Form of Airy Things. Henry Harington. LO

Truth is a fixed star,/Eileen aroon! Eileen Aroon. Gerald Griffin. AnIV; GoBC; HBV 1-2; OBEV; OBVV

The truth is great, and shall prevail/When none cares whether it prevail or not. Magna Est Veritas. Coventry Patmore. AnFE; CAW; CoBE; GoBC; GTBS-P; HAP; NOBE; NOBV; OBEV; OBNC; OBSP; OBVV; PG; TreFT

Truth lies between your legs, and so do I. A Lesson in Love. Philip Hobsbaum. OxBTC

"Truth like a bastard comes into the world/Never without ill-fame to him who gives her birth"? Lausanne. Thomas Hardy. FaBoRV; FaBoTw; OBTV

The Truth must dazzle gradually/Or every man be blind– Tell All the Truth but Tell It Slant. Emily Dickinson. DiPo; HeIP; LiTA; LiTM; MAmP; NAWM 1-2; NePA; NoAm; NOBA; NoP; PPP; TAP; UnPo

Truth never dies. Truth Never Dies. *Anonymous.* WBLP

The truth of the positive hour/Composing all of human power. The Goal of Intellectual Man. Richard Eberhart. MoPo

A truth that Grandeur wishes not to know. Resignation: an Ode to the Journeymen Shoemakers (excerpt). John Wolcot. NOEC

...Truths men/thought of years ago without/telling me. Your Absence Has Not Taught Me. Doug Fetherling. NeAC

Truths which the ages for aye repeat,/Unknown to the statesmen at their feet. If I Were a Voice. Charles Mackay. TreF

"Try a smoke, and let's know what you think of it." Ned's Delicate Way. Henry Lawson. CBAP

Try and fail, try and fail and try. Deception. Alfred Corn. PoA

Try before you judge and speak as you find. Saffold's Cures. Thomas Saffold. FaBoUs

Try it on your own big drum. Reilly's Daughter. *Anonymous.* FSW

Try,/just try,/to put fire/in your pocket safely,/young man. Fire Island Poem. Diane Wakoski. BiP

Try not to scream! The Ballad of Sister Anne. Osbert Sitwell. AtBAP

...Try nothing half so daring/As a visit to the Numerella shore. The Numerella Shore. Cockatoo Jack". PoAu 1-2

& Try on everything for size. Museum of Man. Earle Birney. OxBC

Try something else next time. Toys cut no ice. Epigram: "Time was when once upon a time." Glaucus. PeHV

Try that/at Stinson/Beach. Drowning in Spanish. Tom Schmidt. NeAC

Try them and weigh me, whate'er be my due! Equipment. Paul Laurence Dunbar. TrPWD

Try to avoid inhaling the laden air. The Lovers of the Poor. Gwendolyn Brooks. BiP; CAPP; NoAm; NOBA

...Try to call to them/far in the empty face. Glass. William Stanley Merwin. EAS

Try to die–to disappear/And hide. The Sequel. Delmore Schwartz. LiTM

...Try/To keep from happiness. Just try. Gnostics on Trial. Linda Gregg. AMV-80; NPGG

Try to look, but let ourselves be rocked as/In swaying bark on the sea. Ripe, Being Plunged into Fire... Friedrich Holderlin. OBVE

Try to stay awake. Book of the Dead, Prayer 14. Mei-Mei Bersssenbrugge. GP

Try to stay away from the back seat. My Love Wants to Park. Eloise Klein Healy. GP

Try to win there by/candle light. Chick! My Naggie. *Anonymous.* OxNR

Try, try again. Try, Try Again. *Anonymous.* FaFP; GoTF; TreF

Trying hard to remember/the color of light. The Coal Mine Disaster's Last Trapped Man Contemplates Salvation. William Meissner. AMV-80

Trying not to wake up the sun. Ginger Bread Mama. Doughtry Long. BPo; PoBA

Trying to find my way back/to the center of the world/where Grandfather stood/that day. Legacy II. Leroy V. Quintana. GP

Trying to find/the way back. Getting Older Here. Barbara Hauk. AMV-80

Trying to find you/that cricket in the other's closet. Last Night There Was a Cricket in Our Closet. Leroy V. Quintana. GP

Trying to interpose God's perfect details/Between history and his own unready eyes. The Wilderness. Maura Stanton. MAYP

Trying to make me believe/my friends have forgotten me. The Mailman. Victor Contoski. GP

Trying to make/Trouble... The Rebel. Mari E. Evans. AmNP; IDB; IHMS; PoBA

...Trying to read/the white chiselings of the poem/in the white stone. Looking at Your Face. Galway Kinnell. PPJ

Trying to slip in/and pass/for the natural world. Reading Plato. Jorie Graham. MAYP

Tseet, tseet–/then chatter,/all the way home. Sounds. Robert Creeley. GP

Tu n'entends pas mon moulin marcher! Ah! Si Mon Moine Voulait Danser. *Anonymous.* FSW

Tu-whit, tu-whit, tu-whit! The Song of the Owl. Richard Kendall Munkittrick. OBCA

Tuck the earth, fold the sod;/Quiet's here, maybe God. Dirge. William Alexander Percy. HBMV

Tuesday began her heart to ache,/And Thursday night smoked at the stake. The Cruel Sister. *Anonymous.* BaBo

The tufted cavern of an empty grate. Canoe. Patrick Anderson. SD

The tug of laughter and of irony. Mysticism Has Not the Patience to Wait for God's Revelation. Richard Eberhart. MoPo; NoAm

Tugging at my blind mouth. Art Work. Ronald Wallace. PPJ

Tugging at the ropes of fishermen? Did I Ever Think. Ono no Takamura. AWP

...Tugging/The eye of the world open and it saw me. My Grandmother and the Voice of Tolstoy. Steve Orlen. AMV-81

Tugs my divining rod with the habit some call hope. The Buried Stream. James Keir Baxter. OxBC

La tul da rol de day. My Old Beaver Cap. *Anonymous.* BFSS

A tulip like a red badge of courage. Spring Landscape. Melvin Walker La Follette. NePoEA-2

Tum a-tum tum and danky dee-o! Stranger. Elizabeth Madox Roberts. MoAmPo

Tum-te-tum, tum-te-tum, tum-te-tum, into my grave. The Radio under the Bed. Reed Whittemore. NYBP

Tumbala-lai-ka, fraylach zol zain. Tumbalalaika. *Anonymous.* FSW

Tumble in bed, my baby,/My little sleepy head,/To a prairie lullabye. Prairie Lullaby. *Anonymous.* BPAW

Tumble shall heaven, and so down will I. To God. Robert Herrick. TRV; WGRP

Tummy, trouble us,/trouble us. Toe, Trip and Go. *Anonymous.* OxNR

The tumult ceas'd, the colt submitted,/And, like his ancestors, was bitted. The Council of Horses. John Gay. GN

Tuna on toast. The Cost-of-Living Mother Goose. Dow Richardson. QQQ

The tune's image holding in the line. The Lines of This New Song Are Nothing. Louis Zukofsky. VGW

The tune to the reception of your heart. From Prologue, Each to the Other. Christopher La Farge. AnAmPo

The tune was God's making/But I made the words. The Day before April. Mary Carolyn Davies. SUS

Tuned to a prop's pitch on that terrible thinness. V-Letter to Karl Shapiro in Australia. Selden Rodman. WaP

Tuppence a pair an'/they're a' dune. The Man in the Mune Is Making Shune. *Anonymous.* OxNR

Turmoil that is to be our route. Evening in the Country. John Ashbery. CAPP

Turn about Darby's company. Alligoshee. *Anonymous.* OxNR

Turn around & let us meet, me/& me, let us walk on the level. Solid Mountain. George Bowering. NeAC

Turn around!/So I can brush your back, I say! Mama and Daughter. Langston Hughes. UnPo

Turn away your eyes! Supplication. Louis Untermeyer. HBMV

...Turn back to their day, their grieving and staying. Grief. Wendell Berry. GeTw

Turn, beyond knowing,/To what is also his. Angel. Gary Soto. AMV-80

Turn, cheeses, turn. Twirling. *Anonymous.* OxNR

Turn'd into cash, they are laid out again! On the Publication of Diaries and Memoirs. Thomas Hood. FaBoEE

Turn 'em out, knaves all three! Rub-a-Dub-Dub. Mother Goose. HBV 1-2; HBVY

Turn for a moment this way/your abstracted face. To My Father Norman Alone in the Blue Mountains. Jack Lindsay. NOAV

Turn from her, being also pitiful. The Worshiper. Vassar Miller. NePoEA-2

Turn from this/Death/sleep. O.D. Zack Gilbert. CNA

Turn her face to the wall/Till she comes to. Sulky Sue. *Anonymous.* OxNR

...Turn/His labours, for thou canst, to peaceful end. Samson Agonistes. John Milton. SeCeV

Turn hither, mine own, let's drench us with love–/Just for one night! Song: "Misty and dim, a bush in the wilds of Kapa'a." Kaiama. WTO

Turn in the world and bear the day to me. Turn on Your Side and Bear the Day to Me. George Barker. AtBAP; OxBTC

Turn it, turn it,/Brother. Venom. James Dickey. PoA

Turn port and join the singing race/Across the fields to Anne. Across the Fields to Anne. Richard Burton. HBV 1-2

Turn the page. Turn the page. Gloss. Padraic Fiacc. CIP

Turn the poet out of door. To the Thawing Wind. Robert Frost. LOW; OxBA

Turn then again, in the brave hope of harvest,/Singing to heaven. Odes. George Santayana. AmePo; CoAnAm

Turn thro' the iron gate down Sneaking Lane. Mr. Cromek to Mr. Stothard. William Blake. FaBoEE

"Turn to me, sweetheart! Why do you not turn?" A Lost Jewel. Robert Graves. EnLoPo; NYBP

Turn to silver calm. Golden Moonrise. William Stanley Braithwaite. PoBA

Turn to sky. The Blue Church. Peter Balakian. AMV-80

Turn to the east and turn to the west,/And turn to the one that you love best. Little Sally Sand. *Anonymous.* TrAS

Turn to the Lord, forsake all sin,/And he'll forgive the past. Attend, Young Friends, While I Relate. *Anonymous.* AmFP

Turn to the wall. Speak When You're Spoken To. *Anonymous.* OxNR

...Turn to the wall./And remember... On a Summer Day, 1972. Calvin Murry. LFAC

Turn under, plow,/Turn under. Plowman's Song. Raymond Knister. CaP

Turn up your tail and good luck/come to me. To The Magpie. *Anonymous.* OxNR

Turn warnings we see more clearly/On the way back home. The Limits of Departure. Bruce Weigl. AMV-81

Turn your back/On the old submarine. Charlie Chaplin Went to France. Carl Withers. MoShBr

Turnabout/in the thickening room. Moon as Medusa. Vinnie-Marie D'Ambrosio. IHMS

Turned back my cover,/blues all in my bed. My Black Gal Blues. Sleepy John Estes. BluL

Turned blithely up the valley with a song. April. O. C. Auringer. AA

The turned eyes and the opened mouth of love. Baroque Comment. Louise Bogan. CrMA

...Turned in sleep/Away from whatever waited to be endured? About the Phoenix. James Merrill. NoAm

Turned itself into a single/drop of water. Ode to the Watermelon. Pablo Neruda. EAS; NU

Turned my live idol marble and her heart to stone. Epigram: "Because I am idolatrous and have besought." Ernest Christopher Dowson. OBSP

Turning and burning through slow leaves of vague/Urge, shall, until age. He Comes among. George Barker. OBMV

...Turning away/From the ill wind, the sky filthily weeping. Sleet. Norman MacCaig. OBCP

Turning away its face as the ship/takes us away. Leaving Forever. Denise Levertov. InPK

Turning his corner has/overwhelmed the entire city The Poor. William Carlos Williams. MoAB; MoAmPo; NoP; PPP

Turning, I spit in the lock and the knob turns. Meditations in an Emergency. Frank O'Hara. CAPP; TAP

Turning it on either side/Of your path. The Garden. Hilda ("H. D.") Doolittle. AnFE; APA; AtBAP; LiTA; MAPA

Turning/its dark pages. To the Reader. Denise Levertov. AmPP; CoPo; PoM; VGW

Turning like a twig on a spider strand/hung plumb-bob for the web. My Grandfather in Search of Moonshine. George Ella Lyon. GOYP

Turning mortal for thy love. Love's Labour's Lost. William Shakespeare. GTBS; HBV 1-2; ViBoPo

...The turning of her back/Made them all shriek, it looked so ghastly black. The Wedding of Alcmane and Mya. George Chapman. OBSC

...Turning/the black soil again and again in a memory/of love. Marriage. Marea Gordett. AMV-81

Turning the Fenian down once more to be/"bossed by a Dago'" The Modern Romans. Charles Frederick Johnson. AA

Turning the slick, creased page. The Girl/The Girlie Magazine. Pat Gray. AMV-81

Turning to scorn with lips divine/The falsehood of extremes! Of Old Sat Freedom on the Heights. Alfred, Lord Tennyson. HBV 1-2; OAEP

...Turning to you/For comfort in the cold. At the Dark Hour. Paul Dehn. BoLoP; WaP

Turning, turning as the round earth turns. Apple Peeler. Robert Francis. CrMA; LCAP; NePoAm

Turns all the spirits of Man into desire. Caelica, XL. Fulke, Lord Brooke Greville. EnRePo; FCP; JCP

Turns back, and looks again. A Street Scene. Lizette Woodworth Reese. OBCA

Turns flabby and trembles; and–Peace! says War. To Make the People Happy. Victor Hugo. PPON

Turns in her sleep, and murmurs of the Spring. Upon Eckington Bridge, River Avon. Sir Arthur Thomas ("Q") Quiller-Couch. OBVV

Turns in the waking west and goes to sleep. The Harbor Dawn. Hart Crane. AmP; NePA; OxBA

Turns just in time to wave. Postcard from Zamboanga. Barbara J. Esbensen. PoDr

Turns the reft bosom of Nature, his mother,/low sighing,/Greatest, forgive! Pardon. Julia Ward Howe. PAH

...Turns the waste/To shade and fiber, milk and memory. Lost in Translation. James Merrill. FYAP; HaCAP

Turns/with open heart and eyes/in the linked circles of history. Cordoba. Asher Mendelssohn. VWA

Turns with the river's leisure to the trees. The Village of the Presents. James McMichael. AmPA

Turpentine claws, rakes bleeding trail of sexhatred down my/anus-shuddering spine. Allen Ginsberg Blesses a Bride and Groom: A Wedding Night Poem. Robert Peters. GP

Turpentine made it shine,/Sweet, sweet Caroline. Sweet Caroline. *Anonymous.* PoPle

A turquoise monster moving round. Continual Conversation with a Silent Man. Wallace Stevens. LiTM; NePA; NoP

Tush, quoth Baboone, when men do know I come,/For sport, from City, country, they will runne. The Ape, the Monkey and Baboon Did Meet. *Anonymous.* NCEP

Tush, tush! fear boys with bugs. The Taming of the Shrew. William Shakespeare. TreFT

Twa pund emigrant/On a C.P.R. packet. Gin the Goodwife Stint. Basil Bunting. CTC; TW

The twang of a bowstring. Hitch Haiku. Gary Snyder. LCAP

"'Twas a chilly day for Willie/When the mercury went down." Little Willie. *Anonymous.* MoShBr; PoPle; ShM

'Twas a crowing cock as he hailed the morn. The Barn in Winter. Claire Harris MacIntosh. CaP

'Twas a fat Oyster—Live in peace—Adieu. Verbatim from Boileau. Alexander Pope. DBV

'Twas a star-lance in her side! Innocence. Anne Spencer. CDC

'Twas all for fear the knaves should call him fool. The Epistle to Sir Richard Temple (excerpt). Alexander Pope. DBV

'Twas all for fear the knaves should call him Fool. An Essay on Man. Alexander Pope. ViBoPo

'Twas all unlike your great and gracious ways. The Angel in the House. Coventry Patmore. VLP

'Twas better to be dead than poor. The Panchatantra: Poverty. *Anonymous.* AWP

'Twas but the hand of God upon the deep. The Lookout. William Collins. EtS

'Twas but to kiss my hand, dear George, to you! To My Brother George. John Keats. EnRP

'Twas death and death and death/indeed. There Was a Man of Double Deed. *Anonymous.* GBP; OxNR; WeW

'Twas enough to make a man stare. Rub-a-Dub-Dub. *Anonymous.* NOBL; OxNR

'Twas ever yit/Dearest ware of all. To One That Had Little Wit. George Turberville. EnRePo

'Twas him that only died for love/And she that died for sorrow. Barbara Allen. *Anonymous.* CBEP

'Twas human glory, or God's majesty? Rome. Marcelino Menendez y Pelayo. CAW

'Twas I who nailed you naked to the cross. Crucifixion. Madelaine Marie. PeHV

'Twas lately found out by the prudent Addressors. A New Ballad. *Anonymous.* APAS

'Twas laurel'd Martial calling murther. Epigram on Elphinstone's Translation of Martial's Epigrams. Robert Burns. TW

'Twas more significant, she's dead. An Epitaph: "Enough; and leave the rest to Fame." Andrew Marvell. PoPle

"'Twas nothing"/suavely squeaked/The Mountain's Son. Mus Ridiculus Non. Marie De L. Welch. BoAnP

'Twas on a tree they slew Him—last;/When out of the woods He came. The Cross. Sidney Lanier. BePJ

'Twas on a tree they slew him last,/When out of the woods he came. Into the Woods My Master Went. Sidney Lanier. AH

'Twas on the trip to Buffalo from Milwaukee! Bigerlow (with music). *Anonymous.* AS

'Twas once look up, 'tis now look down to/heaven. On the Blessed Virgin's Bashfulness. Richard Crashaw. EnLi 1-2; HAP; ISi; OAEP; OBSP

'Twas over-bought: 'twas sold at second hand. Emblem. Francis Quarles. OAEL 1-2

'Twas roses, roses all the way/Nor any drop to drink. A Vision of Truth. J. C. Squire. NOBL

'Twas so I felt the harlot say/As she knelt proudly down to pray. Sabbath Reflection. Denis Wrafter. NeIP

'Twas so she seemed to saye,/"HERE IS REST!" As I Laye A-Thynkynge. Richard Harris Barham. HBV 1-2

'Twas the bird that sits in the medlar-tree,/Who sang these gardening saws to me. Garden Lore. Juliana Horatia Ewing. OxBChV

..."'Twas the Devil that pulled him through!" How the Fire Queen Crossed the Swamp. Will H. Ogilvie. PoAu 1-2

'Twas the manner of Primitive Man! Double Ballade of Primitive Man. Andrew and Burnett Tylor Edward Lang. CenHV

'Twas the old flute still whistling "The Protestant Boys'. The Old Orange Flute. *Anonymous.* FaBoBa; GBP

'Twas the only way to git rid of 'em all,/'Spacially Jim. 'Spacially Jim. Bessie Morgan. HBV 1-2

'Twas the ould flute still playin' the "Protestant Boys'! The Ould Orange Flute. *Anonymous.* OxBoLi

'Twas there I did hear the charms of the blackbirds and thrushes. A Sweet Country Life. *Anonymous.* OBET

...'Twas thy voice that stilled/The storm within; Thou didst command the calm. Sonnet: "An open wound which has been healed anew." Richard Chenevix Trench. TrPWD

'Twas Thy withholding lightened all my cares/That blessed day. I Thank Thee, Lord. *Anonymous.* BLRP; WBLP

'Twas Victory was slain. The stars are old, that stood for me. Emily Dickinson. PeHV

'Twas well you waked—we've slept too long. The Unfortunate Reminder. William Pattison. UnTE

'Twas when the heavenly house I trod,/And lay upon the breast of God. Morality. Matthew Arnold. GTBS; HBV 1-2

'Tween the gloamin' and the mirk,/When the kye comes hame! When the Kye Comes Hame. James Hogg. HBV 1-2; OxBS

Twelve-foot/pine pole/lightly,/on her head. Eight Sandbars on the Takano River. Gary Snyder. CoPo

Twelve he marries. One I Love. *Anonymous.* OxNR

...Twelve lights go on,/ten don't. They used to blink. A Christmas Package: No. 7 (excerpt). David McCord. PCh

Twelve make our Creed. The Dial's done. The New Dial. *Anonymous.* OBET

Twelve typographical topographers typically translating types. One Old Ox. *Anonymous.* FaBoNo

THE TWENTIETH CENTURY/COMES BUT ONCE/ONLY ONCE, AND STAYS FOR/BUT ONE HUNDRED YEARS. C Stands for Civilization. Kenneth Fearing. TrJP

Twenty early robins/Chuckled at the joke. Twenty Foolish Fairies. Nancy Byrd Turner. SUS

Twenty-four years late. To an Imaginary Father. Wendy Rose. CDW

Twenty, her noble doorway. Pleasant the House. *Anonymous.* BIrV

Twenty-one boys and a great-grandson,/He has a terrible time with that one. Great-Granddad. *Anonymous.* CoSo

Twenty summers roll by. Route Six. Stanley Jasspon Kunitz. AMV-80

Twenty-two minutes/before eight o'clock/nothing ever changes. Twenty-Two Minutes. Lorri Martinez. LFAC

Twenty years/of sweat and bread/and everything to lose Lilith. Donald Finkel. VWA

'Twere better lose the fire, than find the smoke. Such Love Is Like a Smoky Fire. George Chapman. LO

'Twere better then that Man had never been,/Than thus to be perplexed: God save the Queen. As Concerning Man. Alexander Radcliffe. OBSV

'Twere blessed to have seen— I've seen a dying eye. Emily Dickinson. AmPP; BoWoP; FPL; InPo; MAPA; NePA; NOBA; PoEL 1-5; PoLf

'Twere more Significant, She's Dead. An Epitaph Upon–. Andrew Marvell. CavP; LoBV

'Twere perjury to love thee now. Epigram: "I loved thee beautiful and kind." Robert Nugent, Earl Nugent. NOEC

Twice the numbered sands of deserts/and lengths of beaches. Morning Song. Henry Blakely. CNA

A twigfire of icicles burned pale blue. Leaping Falls. Galway Kinnell. NePoAm-2

Twigs, leaves and an infinite black string. Monologue of Two Moons, Nudes with Crests. 1938. Norman Dubie. FiCP

Twikky mikky bikky bee,/Zikky sikky tee.' Mr. and Mrs. Spikky Sparrow. Edward Lear. OxBChV

Twilight and silence and a heart at peace. The Old Woman. John Bunker. CAW

The twilight blackbird flutes, and spring arrives. Cleaning the Candelabrum. Siegfried Sassoon. HaMV

Twilight comes/we light all the lamps. Eveningsong 2. Ramona Wilson. VoR

The twilight hears and darkness hears them call. Partridges. John Masefield. LiSp; OxBTC

'Twill all be forgotten/A hundred years hence. Rye Whisky. *Anonymous.* OxBoLi

'Twill be a lovely sight. The Rain. William Henry Davies. EnLit; OxBTC; TiPo

'Twill be our heaven to find that–he is there!   My Child.   John Pierpont.
AA; HBV 1-2

'Twill be strong enough one day,/wait a little longer.   The Good Time
Coming.   Charles Mackay.   PaPo; VLP

'Twill be Today and Joy again!   Today.   John Kendrick Bangs.   PoToHe

'Twill be well if their godliness turns to their gain.   The Clerical Cabal.
Anonymous.   APAS

Twill haunt your brain like some sweet strain/Forever and a day!   There Is a
Pool on Garda.   Clinton Scollard.   HBV 1-2

'Twill lead you down to hell's dark gate,/And ruin your own soul.   The
Drunkard's Doom.   *Anonymous.*   AS; FSW

'Twill learn of things Divine, and first of Thee to sing.   On the Death of Mr.
Crashaw.   Abraham Cowley.   AnAnS 2; GoBC; MeLP; MePo; OBS;
SeCP; SeCV 1-2; ViBoPo

'Twill not be short, because 'tis all my own.   The Retirement.   John Norris.
CavP; OBS

'Twill please me mair to hear and see't/Than stockit mailins.   The Poet's
Welcome to His Illegitimate Child.   Robert Burns.   BoC

'Twill rise again, they know, when he is laid/With Freedom, in the Capitol, at
rest.   Midnight–September 19, 1881.   John Boyle O'Reilly.   PAH

'Twill serve this race of drunkards, pimps, and fools.   The Last Instructions
to a Painter.   Andrew Marvell.   OBSV

Twin carrion birds/Then o'er the churchyard fly.   Horror.   Peter Baum.
AWP

"Twin champions of the world are we!"   A Flight Shot.   Maurice
Thompson.   AA; AnAmPo

The twin goes exalted to his worms/hail cried "hail'.   The Staircase.   Samuel
(Paul Vesey) Allen.   PoBA

Twin magnets/drawing each other towards sunset.   The Narrows.   Joseph
Bruchac.   FAZ

The twin periods marking/the dead centers of our eyes.   Above It All.
Philip Levine.   NOBA

Twin strengths, with God to friend!   Fair England.   Helen Gray Cone.   AA

Twin voices and shadows swim starward,/and the essence of life is divine.
Indirection.   Richard Realf.   AA; AnAmPo; APA; HBV 1-2

Twine round our dear Lord's knee.   The Morning-Glory.   Maria White
Lowell   AA; HBV 1-2

The twine that untwisteth, untwisteth the twist.   When a Twister, A-Twisting,
Will Twist Him a Twist.   John Wallis.   FaBoNo; OxNR

Twine, wine, and hides, and China teas.   Though All the Fates Should Prove
Unkind.   Henry David Thoreau.   AP; HAP; MAmP

Twined, hidden from sight/With blind-moles under the hill.   A Lover's
Words.   Vernon Watkins.   DTC

Twined in the stalks of the wild salt hay.   This Is the Hay That No Man
Planted.   Elizabeth Jane Coatsworth.   BrR; OBCA

Twining be at amity round about my window now!   Les Belles Roses sans
Mercie.   Arthur Shearly Cripps.   OBVV

Twinkle, twinkle, little star.   The Star.   Jane Taylor.   FaBoBe; FaFP;
GoTF; HBV 1-2; HBVY; OxBChV; SpRo; TreF

Twirling his green moustaches.   Lighthearted William.   William Carlos
Williams.   LOW; SO

Twisting in and out and round about,/As safe as it can be.   The Rabbit.
Georgia Roberts Durston.   SoPo

Twisting this way and that/Yea, haul in the nets.   Fishing Song.
Anonymous.   WTO

Twitch with the stars that shine in thousands there.   Oh, Sweet Content.
William Henry Davies.   CH

Twitching the strings with slow sardonic grin.   The Puppet Player.
Angelina Weld Grimke.   CDC

'Twixt Tweedle-dum and Tweedle-dee!   Epigram on the Feuds between
Handel and Bononcini.   John Byrom.   CEP; NOEC

'Twixt women's love and men's will ever be.   Air and Angels.   John Donne.
BoW; CBEP; EnRePo; JCP; OAEL 1-2

Two and one, they shall be standing/At your door.   The Waiting Watchers.
Henry Treece.   NeBP

Two angels pinned to the wall–again two.   The Shadow Remains.   Lynette
Roberts.   NeBP

The two are now together.   The Leaf-Picking.   Frederic Mistral.   AWP

Two armies, love and certainty,/And love and the reverse.   Dying! To be
afraid of thee.   Emily Dickinson.   MoPo

Two bags of water, it and I/In restless sympathy here lie.   Insomnia the Gem
of the Ocean.   John Updike.   DFF; NLV; QQQ

Two billion particles make up a bird.   The Morning Porches.   Donald Hall.
NePoAm-2

Two birds affronted by my human face.   The Priory of St Saviour,
Glendalough.   Donald Davie.   OxBC

Two black heifers and a red.   Drinking Time.   D. J. O'Sullivan.   OnYI

Two bloated bodies in rotted rags/Stare at the sun from island crags.   War.
Sulamith Ish-Kishor.   GoYe

Two blocks and a half past the Bulletin office.   Spring.   Hugh McCrae.
ACV

Two by two in the ark of/the ache of it.   The Ache of Marriage.   Denise
Levertov.   FF; NoAm; NOBA; PoM; TAP

Two chairs/standing/for the ever-returning/guests.   The Guests.   Louis
Zukofsky.   CoPo

Two children,/bathed in stars   Star.   Joanie Whitebird.   GP

Two children, branches of the same tree of wretched-ness,/are in a doorway,
beneath the torrid night   Two Children.   Nicolas Guillen.   LiTW

...Two children stand/Waiting their turn to work the land.   Generations.
Robert Clark.   PoAu 1-2

Two chrysanthemums/touch in the middle of the lake/and drift apart.   Girl
Powdering Her Neck.   Cathy Song.   MAYP

...Two country mechanics working/fast to beat a spring sunday.   Spring
Sunday on Quaker Street.   Tom Bass.   FAZ

Two crookers,/And a wig-wag.   Riddle: "Four stiff-standers."   *Anonymous.*
GBP; OxNR

Two curried lovers on a rice-white sheet.   Riddle: "Their tongues are knives,
their forks are hands and feet."   Adrian Mitchell.   FaBoEE; GBL

...Two daiquiris/withdrew into a corner of the gorgeous room/and one told the
other a lie.   The Dream Songs.   John Berryman.   NoAm

The two dark eyes go to and fro.   Goldfish on the Writing Desk.   Max
Brod.   LiTW

Two dead sparrows lay in my hollowed hands.   Church of the Holy
Innocents, Dunedin.   Robin Hyde.   ACV

Two dogges and one bone/May never accorde in one.   Snatches: "Two wimen
in one house."   *Anonymous.*   OxBM

Two feet that erase the pattern on the sand.   Silhouette.   Annette M'Baye.
PBWP

Two fingers to hold a fork, a pen, nothing more.   Letters to My Daughters.
Judith Minty.   AMV-81

Two fond hearts were mended.   Little Words.   Benjamin Keech.   PoToHe

Two girls barefoot never coming back   On Growing Old in San Francisco.
Jack Gilbert.   NPGG

Two good "lines'–one you give, one you get.   Limerick: "That the Traylee's
best cigarette."   R. Rhodes.   FaBoUs

...Two green/survivors/Are tangled under the biting rain as I say this.
Working against Time.   David Wagoner.   MAT

...Two/hands in their duty of being just hands,/from beginning to end.
Sphinxes Inclined to Be.   Olga Orozco.   WPOW

Two hearts that Love would blend in one for ever and/for ever!   Ellen Bawn.
James Clarence Mangan.   IrPN

(Two herons still the swift water.)   As I Was Going to Saint Ives.   Daniel
Gerard Hoffman.   NYBP

Two hooks will barely hold him.   Sharks.   Ron Overton.   WOLT

Two hundred wagons, following a Star!   The Oregon Trail.   Arthur
Guiterman.   BPAW

(2) in the grave.   Praise of Women.   Palladas.   LiTW

Two islands that the roaring seas divide/Are not more far apart.   We Never
Said Farewell.   Mary Elizabeth Coleridge.   OBSP

Two laminated toucans pepper meat/as sunlight sheaths behind the sumac
trees.   September.   Marilyn Hacker.   NYP

Two light auras surround their dark bodies.   In the Old City.   Yehuda
Amichai.   VWA

Two, like two ripe shocks of corn.   An Epithalamy to Sir Thomas Southwell
and His Lady.   Robert Herrick.   CaPo

Two lovers that he murdered,/Cut off when in their prime.   Shocking Rape
and Murder of Two Lovers.   *Anonymous.*   CoMu

Two Loves would make all women mad.   Ode to Cupid.   Charles Cotton.
CavP

The two-lugged sacks moved in like great blind rats.   The Barn.   Seamus
Heaney.   HAP

...Two men lying/to the third.   Star Blanket.   Ray A. Young Bear.   CDW

Two met and made a first.   The Windows of Waltham.   John Wieners.
CoPo

Two miles of earth for a marking stone.   Ballad of Springhill.   and MacColl.
Ewan Seeger.   Peggy   FSW

Two miles to Tong.   Wag a Leg, Wag a Leg.   *Anonymous.*   OxNR

...Two/Minds about it–mine. Yours, a third.   Will You, Won't You?   Mark
Van Doren.   NCSH

Two minds shall flow together, the English and the Greek.   An Invocation.
William Johnson Cory.   HBV 1-2; OBVV

Two moons of ice.   The Hills of Cualann.   Joseph Campbell.   AnIV

Two nations which supped full of the same suffering.   Elegy.   Antoni
Slonimski.   VWA

2 o'clock: strong moonlight, few stars.   Track.   Tomas Transtromer.   EAS

Two of the first, like coats in heraldry/Due but to one, and crowned with one
crest.   A Midsummer Night's Dream.   William Shakespeare.   CTC; GN

Two of Thy children all the days of their life will work in Thy/Garden, Lord!
The Garden.   Rose Parkwood.   WGRP

The two of us, at last, together laid.   On the Seventh Anniversary of the
Death of My Father.   Robert Pack.   NePoEA

The two of us laughing together or stepping in silence.   The Widow of
Drynam.   Patrick MacDonogh.   NeIP; OnYI; OxBI

...Two/old players questioning the silence,/carressing the heaven in her. Walking on Water. Mario Petaccia. LFAC

...Two pairs of matching eyes/void of expression. Expression. Thom Gunn. OxBC

...Two parents' torts'/when he was young & gift-strong. The Dream Songs. John Berryman. NoAm

Two people surface and begin to swim. San Francisco Poem. John Logan. NNaP

Two phantom bandits swing and sway. Hangman's Tree. Lillian Zellhoefer White. AmFN

Two potent sexes all their realms supply,/Whence nature hath its just fertility. The Impious Feast. Robert Eyres Landor. OBRV

Two red roses across the moon. Two Red Roses Across the Moon. William Morris. CBEP; PoRA; VLP

Two souns remove, and Thebes towne showde twaine... The Aeneid. Virgil (Publius Vergilius Maro). OBVE

TWO SWANS ASCENDING FROM STILL WATERS/must be a name too hard to remember. Name Giveaway. Phil George. VoR

Two thousand years swirling through my bones at once. I Lie on the Chilled Stones of the Great Wall. Stephen Shu Ning Liu. BrSi

Two tumid surfaces etching/their own postures in space/as they lose themselves. Inside Diameter. Clarence Major. APU

Two turtle doves, and/A partridge in a pear tree. The Twelve Days of Christmas. Anonymous. GoTF; LiTL; OxBoLi; PCh; TreFT

Two vipers tangled into one. Similes for Two Political Characters of 1819. Percy Bysshe Shelley. CBEP; PAI; TW

Two voices ring in the dawn, the morning enters. Woman at the Piano. Marya Zaturenska. MoAmPo

The two will blend:/the flesh, the mind. Two Things. Donald Campbell Babcock. NePoAm

...Two words/turned sightseers into pilgrims. In Canterbury Cathedral. E. W. Oldenburg. EBCP

Two Worlds–like Audiences–disperse–/And leave the Soul–alone– Departed– to the Judgment. Emily Dickinson. CABA

Two years or three, yet God sent him punishment/By his true servant: the Red Rose Redolent! The Ship of Fools. Alexander Barclay. ACP

'Twould crumble with the weight. Could Mortal Lip Divine. Emily Dickinson. DiPo

–'Twould disarm/The spectre Death, had he substantial power to harm. Lake Leman. George Gordon, Lord Byron. OBNC

'Twould learn of yours the winning art,/And quickly steal the rest. The Enchantment. Thomas Otway. HBV 1-2; LiTL; OBEV; ViBoPo

'Twould make such a terrible row. Limerick: There once was a man who said, "How." Anonymous. LiBL; NA

'Twould never reach the nearest star,/Because it is so very far. Facts. Lewis (Charles Lutwidge Dodgson) Carroll. FaBoUs

'Twould thin the land, such numbers to string/Upon Tyburn tree! The Beggar's Opera. John Gay. NOEC

'Twull be best, sir, for you to be fushin'/And me wi' the gaff. Master and Man. Sir Henry Newbolt. OxBTC

Tydynges gode I thyngke to telle. A Christmas Carol. Anonymous. EnLit

Type of all the wealth to be,–/Goldenrod! Goldenrod. Elaine Goodale Eastman. HBV 1-2

The typed and the printed and the spelt all wrong. Night Mail. W. H. Auden. GrPl

Typed on a blue card: LEVELSQUE, A. And: LIFE. The Convict. Anthony Frisch. CaP

Typed on a tag-label tied to his left big toe. Red Indian Corpse. Peter Redgrove. OxBC

The tyrant mind of the present unturned by the many poems... The Man Coming Toward You. Oscar Williams. NePA

Tyrants through fear and malice feed on blood,/Good kings secure at home, seek all men's good. Caelica, XCV. Fulke, Lord Brooke Greville. FCP

U

U-lu-lo, howled the hound. Song for "The Jaquerie". Sidney Lanier. AA

U shers a long, long fate of blood. Poem to Lou. Guillaume Apollinaire. LiTW

U split to becom/one of th wasted ones To a Poet I Knew. Johari (Jewel C. Latimore) Amini. PoBA

U, V, W, X, Y, Z, all had a large/slice and went off to bed. The Alphabet. Kate Greenaway. FaBoUs; HBVY

UBI AMOR IBI OCULUS EST. Canto 90. Ezra Pound. VGW

Ubiquitous, marvellous grass privateer. The Rattlesnake. Alfred W. Purdy. WHW

..."Ugh," he/muttered to his black and white horse. "Get um up, Scout." Tonto. Ronald Koertge. GP

The ugly demon, forest fire,/Is on another tear. The Forest Fire. Arthur W. Monroe. BPAW; PoOW

Ugly with February's drift. Lemons. Ted Walker. NYBP

Uh-huh, in a storm, in a storm. Stewball. Anonymous. ABF

Ultimate bone. Water./The current ours. There Are Oceans. Joy Harjo. TWSS

The ultimate elegance: the imagined land. Mrs. Alfred Uruguay. Wallace Stevens. AP; MoPo; MP; NePA; PAI; TwCP

Ultimate, pitiless, again I ply the knife. Clarence Mangan. Thomas Kinsella. CIP

The ultimate/Stomach. Stomach. Kathleen Norris. OBAL

Ultimately realize the specific beautiful or ugly/innards of/our/selves. Masquerade. Carolyn M. Rodgers. BlSi

Um–m, cain' see nothin' but de stars an' moon. Levee Camp "Holler." Anonymous. ABF

Unable to disguise the space between/what is and what should be. Sundays. Marieve Rugo. AMV-81

...Unable to imagine/The meaning of the flood tide. Jehu. Louis MacNeice. LiTM; MoAB; WaP

Unable to let one more thing/one single blade of grass/die. That Summer. Judith Hemschemeyer. PPJ

Unable to perform, unfit to play. Wasted Night. Anonymous. UnTE

Unaccountably to killing in the spring. Poem: "These grasses, ancient enemies." Keith Douglas. NeBP

Unaging beauty by another name. Wood Witchery. Richard Burton. AnAmPo

Unalphabeted. My, Fellowship, With, God. Jose Garcia Villa. EaLo

Unashamed/shivering deliciously The Bottle of Chianti. Raymond Souster. ELU

The unasked bodily friendship/of her first home. Rebeca in a Mirror. Judith Rodriguez. CBAP

Unasked I'd do it, were it in my power. Letter to Manlius Torquatus. Caius Valerius Catullus. LiTW

Unattained, and things breathe of after, after,/Before even unfolding their wings. Heron Weather. Douglas Crase. NoP

Unawakend, unwilling/to sleep or wake. Tribal Memories. Robert Duncan. CAPP; NOBA

...Unaware/of steaming wound and blood ebbing away. The Triple Dream. Mikhail Yuryevich Lermontov. LiTW

Unbearable memoryless face. Faces Seen Once. James Dickey. UnPo

Unbearable. Unborn. The Unwanted. Mary Gordon. IHMS

The unbecoming dead/sang him to his rest. Evening of the Rose. Anthony Rudolf. VWA

Unbidden, yours; a way to praise. Translation. Rika Lesser. PoA

Unbind those breasts. I Am Long Weaned. Brother Antoninus. NMP

Unbody me–I'm tired–and get me home. The Moor. Ralph Hodgson. MoBrPo

Unborn children in Midnight Market. Poems, IV. Philip O'Connor. EAS

Unborn, that read these words and saw her not. Beauty's Pageant. Dante Gabriel Rossetti. MaVP

Unbound at length, will learn to love no more. Give Me My Work. George Whetstone. EIL

Unbribed, there's/no occasion to. Epigram: "You cannot hope." Humbert Wolfe. FaBoEE

Unbroken march of Mind we sing/From Anselm down (or up) to Inge! Mediaeval Appreciations. William Miller Thomas Gamble. CAW

...Unbroken neck/of an infant now fatherless/in fact. Another Kind of Burning. Ruth Fox. AmC; NYBP

The uncapturable, the indefinable thing, the unlearned. Whenever I Have. Furnley Maurice. NOAV

Uncaptured and unflying, the wings of song. Breath on the Oat. Joseph Russell Taylor. HBV 1-2; PAH

Uncertain how to respond, I whistle. The milk of childhood drains. Issues of the Fall. Sydney Lea. SM

Uncertain which, in ocean or in air. Paradise Lost. John Milton. NIP

The unchained sun, in raging thirst,/Feeds the last day to the first. Transfiguration. Djuna Barnes. EAS

Unchallenged and without affront shall manage/The republic of tall spiders. The Stone Gentleman. James Reeves. OBSP

Unchanged under the ash of Herculaneum. Poetry. Carl Rakosi. GP

The unchanging, hopeless look/Out of which all miracles leap. At Darien Bridge. James Dickey. NoP

Unchanging love swears all's unchanged, and knows/That what it has not, still stays all it has. A Separation. Stephen Spender. MoLP

Unchecked on her way,/Shall Liberty follow/The march of the day. Le Marais du Cygne. John Greenleaf Whittier. PAH

Uncle Devereux would blend to the one color. My Last Afternoon with Uncle Devereux Winslow. Robert Lowell. ForPo; NoP; VGW

Uncle Jim/Clum up beside of him/And squatted down by he. Uncle Simon and Uncle Jim. Artemus Ward. NA

...Uncle Jim's deep-fired, all-fat, real gone/whale steaks. Naughty Boy. Robert Creeley. NoAm

Uncle Sam's boys are coming right along, six hundred thousand/ strong. Hold on, Abraham. *Anonymous.* ABF

Uncle Sam sent out his force/The hungry soon were fed. The Cabin Creek Flood. *Anonymous.* AmFP

Unclouded days, and taste the sweets of life, The First Olympionique to Hiero of Syracuse. Pindar. ATP

Uncomfortably he smiles. Portrait by Alice Neel. Aaron Kramer. EyDe

An uncommon Felicity is due to such uncommon Vir-/tues. The Familiar Colloquies: Sweet Temper and Mutual Affection. Desiderius Erasmus. HW

The uncomplaining stars composed their lucid song. Voltaire at Ferney. W. H. Auden. LiTA; LiTM; NePA; PoA

Unconcerned with the morning star. Poems for My Brother Kenneth. Owen Dodson. IDB; PoBA; PoNe

The unconquerable mind, and Freedom's holy flame. The Progress of Poesy. Thomas Gray. ATP

Unconscious that the oil is out/As that the slave is gone! The lamp burns sure, within. Emily Dickinson. LiTA

Unconsciousness I stare to know. Patrol. Ralph Pomeroy. CoPo

Unconstancy and doubleness depart/When man bends his desires to mend his heart. Caelica, LXVII. Fulke, Lord Brooke Greville. FCP

Uncontrollable joy/of leaving the mind. Behind the Glass Wall. Harold Norse. PeHV

The uncontrollable mystery on the bestial floor. The Magi. William Butler Yeats. BiP; BrPo; CMoP; CoBMV; ELU; FaBoRV; HAP; InPK; MBW 1-2; NoAm; OAEL 1-2; OFD; PAI; PCh; PoA; PPoe; SBVL; TrCP

... Uncovered them, succulent and straight,/immediate with moon-daisies. Photograph of Haymaker, 1890. Molly Holden. OxBTC

Uncut, unique, unknown to Lowndes. The Bibliomaniac's Prayer. Eugene Field. AA

Undaunted, plan/To make the world/A Home for Man. His Task–and Ours. Dorothy Gould. PGD

Undeciphered but surmised. Elegy Just in Case. John Ciardi. AtBAP; MiAP; TwCP

Under a gable: Here lived Francis Jammes. Amsterdam. Francis Jammes. AWP

Under a gray sky ripped apart/By thunder and the changing wind. La Vita Nuova. Weldon Kees. VGW

...Under a leaf sit six daddy longlegs,/Sheltered from the rain. The Origins of Escape. Charles P. R. Tisdale. AMV-81

Under a mountain of masks and dolls–the poem. Letter to My Daughter at the End of Her Second Year. Donald Finkel. CoAP

Under a poplar, shadowed from the sun,/Where merrily to court him she begun. Phoebe on Latmus. Michael Drayton. OBSC

Under a shifting, mostly indifferent sky Meadow Grass. Michael Mott. AMV-80

Under a winter's moon. Song of the Rabbits Outside the Tavern. Elizabeth Jane Coatsworth. AnNE; OBCA

...Under advice to try/the whole of a thought in silence, and to oneself. Of Late. George Starbuck. VGW

Under branches in the zoo or in the subway under/town. The Sloth. Isabella Gardner. BoAnP

Under brand new stars toward home. What She Wished. Marilyn Throne. AMV-81

Under her solemn fillet saw the scorn. Days. Ralph Waldo Emerson. AA; AnNE; AP; APA; ForPo; GoTF; HAP; HeIP; LiTA; MAmP; NOBA; NoP; OBSP; PoEL 1-5; SeCeV; TrGrPo; ViBoPo

Under her summer-green the beautiful lady/Covers it, like a stone cover'd in grass. Sestina: Of the Lady Pietra degli Scrovigni. Dante Alighieri. AWP; OBVE

Under her summer-green the beautiful lady/Covers it, like a stone covered in grass. Sestina (after Dante). Dante Gabriel Rossetti. OAEL 1-2

Under ilk leif ful thik they stik and hing. The Aeneid. Virgil (Publius Vergilius Maro). GoTS

Under it pickets–/To complete the chant for the dead. The Jews. Mieczyslaw Jastrun. VWA

Under its cloak of lies. Summer Oracle. Audre Lorde. BlSi; PoBA

Under its mattresses of vines. Vacancy in the Park. Wallace Stevens. LCAP

Under lamplight in city streets. Snow. Fay Chiang. BrSi

Under my heel... The Piercing Chill I Feel. Buson (Taniguchi Buso). InPK

& Under mysterious orders not to come in. Refusals. Jon Anderson. MAYP

Under stars clustered thick as raisins. Bread. Constance Urdang. GP

Under the antenna, down the long path intended for your feet. Communication on His Thirtieth Birthday. Marvin Bell. CoAP

Under the black coloured, pitch painted roof/Of the well nailed Ark, when there was no need. Genesis (excerpt). *Anonymous.* PBBP

Under the blind man's door, and all is right. Rooming House. Ted Kooser. PoL

Under the blossom that hangs on the bough. The Tempest. William Shakespeare. CTC; GTBS; HBV 1-2; HBVY; NLV; NoP; SeCeV; TreFT; ViBoPo; WHA

Under the blowlamp kisses of the sun. Smelling the End of Green July. Peter Yates. ChMP

Under the blue sky–this serenity! Let Me Speak of Pure Things. Ho Chih-Fang. LiTW

Under the circumstances....What's life for? Rambuncto (parody). Margaret Widdemer. BXAP

Under the Craftsman's sure and knowing hand/Become a life made beautiful! The Mosaic Worker. Arthur Wallace Peach. BLRP

Under the crust of things that die,/Living, unfathomed, here am I. The Soul Speaks. Edward H. Pfeiffer. HBMV

Under the drooping willow tree. Under the Drooping Willow Tree. *Anonymous.* CBEP; OxBoLi

Under the far far harking of the crows. My Wish for My Land. Randolph Stow. NOAV

Under the final green of grass. The Final Green. Leah Bodine Drake. NePoAm

Under the gold hair ornaments/of skyscrapers. Drink. William Carlos Williams. OxBA

Under the grave eyes of women forbidden to age. Picasso's Women. Olga Cabral. PoDr

Under/The green grass/Under the wide grey sky. England Reclaimed (excerpt). Osbert Sitwell. ViBoPo

Under the green hills of the sky. In the Gold Mines. B. W. Vilakazi. TTY

Under the greenwood tree. The Death of Robin Hood. Eugene Field. StPo

...Under the hanging/honeycomb the bees come home and the bees sleep. In Tall Grass. Carl Sandburg. PoA

Under the helmet is friend or fatal face. Poem in Time of War. William Abrahams. WaP

...Under the/influence of star-gazing is the Dream. Moon Watching by Lake Chapala. Al Young. NPGG

Under the lake where the Muse moves. The Illustration–A Footnote. Denise Levertov. PoA

Under the leaves green! Who Shall Have My Fair Lady? *Anonymous.* AtBAP; CBEP; EG; EnLoPo; PoEL 1-5

Under the leaves so green. My Fair Lady. *Anonymous.* UnTE

Under the moongrey nettles, the black mould/And muttering rain. She Weeps over Rahoon. James Joyce. ViBoPo

Under the night's first star I watch you sink,/In the world's twilight fading, fading West. Sails. George Sterling. EtS

Under the night shade/where the shadows fade Clickstone. Rokwaho. STE

Under the olives, in whose night they sleep. Table-Birds. Kenneth Mackenzie. NOAV; PoAu 1-2

...Under the pretence/Of which fair name she cloaketh now her fault. Dido's Hunting. Henry Howard, Earl of Surrey. OBSC

Under the purple thyme and the purple clover/Sleeping at last. Sleeping at Last. Christina Georgina Rossetti. HeIP; TrGrPo

Under the quiet of the evening star. Sketch. Seumas (James Starkey) O'Sullivan. AnIV

Under the receding wave. The Nineteenth Century and After. William Butler Yeats. FaBoEE; MBW 1-2

Under the redbird's wings/Was peace and honeycomb. My Fathers Came from Kentucky. Vachel Lindsay. AmFN; HBMV

...Under the royal action and abstraction/He lived in, he was real. The Room. C. Day-Lewis. PoCh

Under the running tap that are not the hands of a child. Soap Suds. Louis MacNeice. FaBoIP; FaBoMo; NOBI; NoP; SCV

Under the sentence and law of that Medieval light. Exile. Joseph Stroud. NPGG

Under the shadow of that wing. To a Child in Death. Charlotte Mew. MoAB; MoBrPo

Under the shirt, blood rushing/Inside the sleeves and out of the collar. The Clothing's New Emperor. Donald Finkel. NePoEA

Under the silent roof-tree, over the windy floor. The Secret of the Deeps. Sidney Royse Lysaght. EtS

Under the silver, and home again. The Ride-by-Nights. Walter De la Mare. DuDa; SiSoSe; TiPo; WSC

Under the silver moon, sleep, my little one,/sleep my pretty one, sleep. Sweet and Low. Joseph Barnby. FSW

Under-the-Sod, is playing over there by the green tree. The Green Tree. James Reiss. AmPA

Under the tree, for him to wed her now,/as I do thee. The Ring. Robert Pack. FAZ

Under the Trees of Paradise. Vacation Trip. Donald Campbell Babcock. NePoAm

Under the umbrage of the grave remains. Edmund Davie.... Benjamin Tompson. SCAP

Under the vine-trellis laid, O my beloved, with thee!   Amours de Voyage. Arthur Hugh Clough.   FaBoPP; OBNC

Under the walls of Paradise!   Drifting.   Thomas Buchanan Read.   AA; GN

Under the white man's menace, out of time.   Outcast.   Claude McKay.   BALP; BP; PoBA

...Under these signs/I am living.   The Postcards: A Triptych.   Denise Levertov.   PoDr

Under this rock they met together.   The Mountain Tree.   Hugh Connell.   NeIP

Under this the other one has answered. See tomorrow.   Reading the Books Our Children Have Written.   Dave Smith.   HaCAP

Under thy boughs, when I, alas! am dead.   To a Maple Seed.   Lloyd Mifflin.   AA

...Under what wilderness/Of black silent waters weep.   Thrushes.   Ted Hughes.   FaBoMo; GoYe; NePoEA-2

Under which they buried my ancestor alive.   Silence Concerning an Ancient Stone.   Rosario Castellânos.   PBWP

Underdrawers, towels and shirts that weep/slow filthy tears.   Walking Around.   Pablo Neruda.   LiTW

Underlining the moral, explaining doom and truth.   Epilogue to a Human Drama.   Stephen Spender.   CMoP

Underneath wide maples, we fill our nostrils/With a cool abundance of what gives us life?   Oxygen.   Joan Swift.   NYBP

An undersong of terrible holy joy.   The Old Women.   George Mackay Brown.   NePoEA-2; OxBS

Understanding her case, trying to make her understand.   A Primary Ground.   Adrienne Rich.   NNaP

Understood/By those who understand it not.   An Evening.   Robert Mezey.   NaP

The undertaker smiled.   The Death of the Novel.   David Young.   AmPA

Undeveloped, waiting for/immersion.   Seeing in the Dark.   Matthew Brennan.   AMV-81

Undid the world in rituals of fury/and returned to zero.   After the Hurricane.   Samuel Hazo.   GrPl

Undo thin herte, tell me thy thought,/Thy sennes grete and smale.   Undo Your Heart.   *Anonymous.*   MeEL

...Uneasy in the drafty shade, I rock on the veranda,/reminded of Europa...Persephone...Miranda.   At a Summer Hotel.   Isabella Gardner.   GrPl

Uneasy lies the head that wears a crown.   King Henry IV.   William Shakespeare.   FiP; MOS

...Unemployed/with no prospects for work.   Poor Movies.   Will Bennett.   APU

The unencumbered field for cemetery.   Charles Donnelly.   Donagh MacDonagh.   CIP

Unending love unending growth shall be.   After Death.   Charles Francis Richardson.   AA

Unending sweets, imperishable summer.   The Good Humor Man.   Phyllis McGinley.   MoShBr

Unexpected footprints/erased by the sea.   Hieroglyphic.   Myra Sklarew.   SUW

Unexpected, you know!   Jesus the Carpenter.   Catherine C. Liddell.   HBV 1-2

Unexpectedly/his own small widgeon cries.   Widgeon.   Seamus Heaney.   FaBoIP

Unexplored, uncharted, dangerous, and mad.   City.   Raymond Biasotti.   AMV-80

Unfailing sympathy,/Undying Love.   What God Has Promised.   Annie Johnson Flint.   BLRP; STF; TRV; WBLP

Unfalling, trailing white foam, white fire.   Skier.   Robert Francis.   LiSp; NCSH; RFM; SD

An unfathomed oblivion.   The Zodiac: The Valley of Sleep.   Hendrik Marsman.   LiTW

The unfeeling/immovable ones/draw imperceptibly closer   Workday Morning.   Astrid Tollefsen.   PBWP

The unfinished window in Aladdin's tower/Unfinished must remain!   Hawthorne.   Henry Wadsworth Longfellow.   MAmP; NCEP; PoEL 1-5

Unfit for the widow, my laddie.   The Widow.   Allan Ramsay.   HBV 1-2

Unfold a world that I, thy child, might see.   Sonnet: "This infant world has taken long to make."   George Macdonald.   OBVV

Unforeign war/that ever I did see. (Chorus, etc.)   American Heritage.   Robert Sward.   OBAL

Unforgettable Queen.   To Dinah Washington.   Etheridge Knight.   PoBA

The unfortunate mole!   The Unfortunate Mole.   Mary Kennedy.   GoYe

Unfortunately I am/Talked about anyway.   That spring night I spent.   Lady Suwo.   LiTW

Unfortunately,/we don't believe in it.   This world is amazingly flat.   Natalya Gorbanyevskaya.   BoWoP

Unfortunately we're all stuck/with what's between our legs.   World's Fare.   Charles Stetler.   GP

Unhappily we burn, Flaccus and I.   Faithless.   *Anonymous.*   UnTE

Unhappy Hearts Obdurateness.   Biothanatos.   Joseph Beaumont.   OBS

Unhappy woman's but a slave at large.   An Essay on Woman.   Mary Leapor.   NOEC

Unheard by mortals are the strains/That sweetly soothe the Saviour's woe.   Gethsemane.   William B. Tappan.   STF

Unheard, whatever the din of exploding stars.   A Matter of Life and Death.   Anne Ridler.   MoLP

Unhelm ere she dies.   The End of the Duel.   Taylor Rachel Annand.   CAW

Unhindered, unresisted, unwithstood.   So They Went Deeper in the Forest.   Roy Daniells.   WHW

Unhurt, like him, your Charms I'll hear.   A Farewel to Worldly Joyes.   Anne Killigrew.   BoWoP

The Unicorn is not carnivorous!   How to Catch Unicorns.   William Rose Benet.   HBMV

Unimaginable, the frolic of form I lack.   Blind, I Speak to the Cigarette.   Joanne De Longchamps.   GoYe

The unimportant beauty of the moon.   Glimpses.   Roy Helton.   HBMV

The union of bow and waters,/Writes its last lines alone.   At Only That Moment.   Alan Ross.   ErPo

Unite, and swell the song,/To Christ the King!   The Earliest Christian Hymn.   Clement of Alexandria (Titus Flavius Clemens).   BePJ; WGRP

Unite, oh, unite!/Or the billows burst o'er her!   The Downfall of the Gael.   Fearflatha O'Gnive.   AnIV; AWP; OnYI

United all denote the name/Of a large town of Christian fame.   Riddle: "The vase which holds all fat'ning liquor."   *Anonymous.*   CoBE

"United in strength."   Kula...A Homecoming.   Diane Mei Lin Mark.   BrSi

United powers make each the stronger prove.   Astrophel and Stella, LXXXVIII.   Sir Philip Sidney.   AAS; SiPS

United States ahead, by thunder!   In the Catacombs.   Harlan Hoge Ballard.   YaD

The unity of life which can only be forged by love.   Facing the Chair.   Hugh" (Christopher Murray Grieve) MacDiarmid.   FaBoMo

Universal, and the abolition of the poor.   While We Slept.   David Wolff.   AnAmPo; TrJP

The universal blue/And local green suggest.   The Middleness of the Road.   Robert Frost.   CrMA; LiTA; NOBA

The universal law for evermore.   Hymn to Zeus.   Cleanthes.   ILwL; WGRP

The universall song goes smooth and sweet.   The World's a Well Strung Fidle, Mans Tongue the Quill.   Nathaniel Ward.   SCAP

Universally crown'd with highest praises.   Samson Agonistes.   John Milton.   AtBAP; OBS

The universe before God had time to shout.   A Dream of Surreal Science.   Sri Aurobindo Ghose.   ACV

The universe sleeps,/a huge star-infested ear/resting on a paw.   A Cloud in Trousers: Prologue.   Vladimir Mayakovsky.   SOTW

"The universe tottered; I tittered."   Epitaph for a Funny Fellow.   Morris Bishop.   FPL

Unjangled to the end.   Envoy.   William Ernest Henley.   BrPo

The unjust hath the just's umbrella.   The Rain.   *Anonymous.*   FaBoCo; FaFP

The unjust steals the just's umbrella.   The rain it raineth on the just.   Charles, Baron Bowen.   CenHV; FiBHP; NLV; NTCP; PV

Unjustifiable,/Shocking neglect.   No Foundation.   John Hollander.   OBAL

Unkind, I love you not! O me, that eye/Doth make my heart give to my tongue the lie!   What, Have I Thus Betrayed My Liberty?   Sir Philip Sidney.   NIP

...Unkind Starry Mother/Took my poor heart, and gave it to another.   To Etesia Looking from Her Casement at the Full Moon.   Henry Vaughan.   MOON

Unkindly if true love be us'd,/'Twill yield thee little grace.   The Peaceful Western Wind.   Thomas Campion.   EnRePo; LoBV

Unknown are those dwellings, that region and realm.   Fates of the Apostles.   Cynewulf.   AnOE

The unknown is shown/Only by a bend in the known.   The Undiscovered Planet.   Norman Nicholson.   ChMP

The unknown road still marching.   A March in the Ranks Hard-Prest, and the Road Unknown.   Walt Whitman.   AmPP; OxBA

Unknown roads for sleep to walk upon.   In the Footsteps of the Walking Air.   Kenneth Patchen.   EAS

Unknown, scarce seen, whose flickering grace/Faints on the outmost rings of space!   Pre-Existence.   Paul Hamilton Hayne.   HBV 1-2

Unknown the mighty Terrible,/Splendid and tawny-eyed.   Adventure.   Mary Elizabeth ("E") Fullerton.   BoAV

Unknown to me; sure Nature's deck/Was ravished from her snowy neck.   A Question.   *Anonymous.*   CBEP

Unknown to us/but only to their mothers and loafers.   Amagoduka at Glencoe Station.   Mbuyiseni Oswald Mtshali.   WhB

Unknown, unloved–but not alone.   The Room.   Vladimir Nabokov.   NYBP

Unknown, unmarked by others/But to my God laid bare!   Hymn.   Synesius.   CAW

Unknown, unnamed, forgotten, lied/A Georgia Volunteer. A Georgia Volunteer. Mary Ashley Townsend. AA

Unlaurelled, unlamented, vain. What Is That Music High in the Air? A.J.M. Smith. NMP

The unlearned depths of me. Review from Staten Island. Gloria C. Oden. NNP; PoBA; PPP

Unlearnedly and unreasonably poetry is shaped/Awkwardly but alive in the unmeasured womb. Art McCooey. Patrick Kavanagh. FaBoIP

The unleashed tempest shakes the garden walls. The Tempest. Marya Zaturenska. BoLiVe; MoAmPo

Unless by some tin warrant. Lydford Journey. William Browne. CavP

Unless he offer more than she demands. Resolution in Four Sonnets. Charles Cotton. PoEL 1-5

Unless he's drunk all the oil in Venezue.....la. Venezuela. Anonymous. FSW

Unless here tomorrow you'll give me relief. Maria. George Alexander Stevens. UnTE

Unless I choose to let her out. To Julia under Lock and Key (parody). Sir Owen Seaman. BXAP; FaBoPa

Unless I wanted to work in a butcher shop. Butcherboy. Tom Schmidt. NeAC

Unless in bitterness to mock/At having cultivated rock. Plowmen. Robert Frost. SaC

Unless in that damp cell/The dead may have a dream he cannot tell. The Grave. Thomas Gwynn Jones. LiTW

Unless it be, O Father, by your leave. Consolation in July. Rayner Heppenstall. NeBP

Unless it be that men must trade,/And there are men to buy. Retrospection. Dunstan Shaw. NOAV

Unless it trembled with the strings. Romance. Edgar Allan Poe. AP; APA; AtBAP; BoLiVe; NePA; OxBA

Unless like little Agnes/you vanish with early tears. Tear. Thomas Kinsella. IPY; NOBI

Unless, perhaps, white death had kissed me there,/Kissing her hair? Rondel: "Kissing her hair I sat against her feet." Algernon Charles Swinburne. BLPL; FaBoBe; HBV 1-2; ViBoPo

Unless she's sworn to the tax-gatherer? Advice to Julia. Henry Lettrell. OBRV

Unless that he my Vision can unfold. A Vision. Edward, Lord Herbert of Cherbury. AnAnS 2; SeCP

Unless the diamond with its own rich dust/Be cut and polished, it seems little worth. On Reading–. Thomas Bailey Aldrich. AA

Unless they believe that kisses are sweeter/From lips that bear a mustache. A Mustacheless Bard. J. Gordon Coogler. OBAL

Unless, they subject-like, swear to adore/And serve Emaricdulfe for evermore. Emaricdulfe. E. C. EIL

...Unless/this here is a hereafter/death will get her to. The Poetess Ko Ogimi. Helen Chasin. NMM

Unless thou bring Him with thee, thou wilt not find. Pilgrim at Rome. Anonymous. AnIL

Unless, unless–thou dream'st of me. Ben Hur: Song. Lew Wallace. AA

Unless we're as good as can be. The Brown Thrush. Lucy Larcom. HBV 1-2; HBVY; OBCA

Unless with light and tide thou bring my/Donald back to me. Donald. Henry Abbey. AA

Unless you are patient enough/to wait for me piece by sea-/battered piece. Driftwood Dybbuk. Barbara F. Lefcowitz. VWA

Unless you live on oats and hay–/And whinny. Minnie Morse. Kaye Starbird. PH

Unless you love, you please in vain. To a Coquet Beauty. John, of Buckingham Sheffield. CEP

Unless you meet again tomorrow. Phyllis. Thomas Randolph. BoLoP

Unless you're beaten there, you're bound to win. Success. C. C. Cameron. PoToHe

Unless you read love's double mind/Or invent its polar map. The Season's Lovers. Miriam Waddington. OBCV; PeCV

Unlived lives live/mildly for centuries. Children Not Kept at Home. Joyce Carol Oates. DFF

Unloading hell behind him step by step. The Rear-guard. Siegfried Sassoon. ACV; MCCG; MoBrPo; NoAm; OBWP; WaP

Unlock, unlock! Let's feed thy zoo. The Zoo of You. Arthur Freeman. ErPo

Unlucky charms, perhaps. Wild Oats. Philip Larkin. InPS; PAI

Unmake me quite, or give thyself to me! Ode to Beauty. Ralph Waldo Emerson. AP; ForPo; PoEL 1-5

Unmark'd before, like piles of jewels seem! A Brilliant Day. Turner, Charles Tennyson. NOBV

Unmarked on any map or guide. A Mexican Scrapbook. Dave Oliphant. FAZ

Unmask and be the sport of fate. Villanelle. M. D. Feld. SD

Unmasks the character and lays bare the face/Which legend, out of goodness, often hides. Essay on Rime (excerpt). Karl Shapiro. PP

An unmaternal fondness keep/Her alien eyes. Cradle-Song at Twilight. Alice Meynell. NOBV

"Unmelting wedged/Snow in her mouth." Story from Russian Author. Peter Redgrove. NePoEA-2

Unmistakable period. In Despair He Orders a New Typewriter. Elder Olson. AMV-81

...Unmoved by sun or rain,/Within a cold straight house shall lie. The Life and Death of Jason. William Morris. ViBoPo

The unnatural, intolerable day. Vigil. William Ernest Henley. LoBV

Unnecessary to imagine him. Double Mock Sonnet. Charles O. Hartman. SM

The unneighboured and uncomforted cold sea. The Hounds. John Freeman. OBMV; OBSP

Unneth they leave a lock/Of wool among their flock!... Colin Clout. John Skelton. OAEL 1-2

Unnoticeable till/night takes the sun off/the hook. Dial Tone. Felix Pollak. PPJ

...Unnoticed/by her arriving immigrant bees. Blue Horses. Ed Roberson. PoBA

Unpacking parsley, and wet cress, on Second Avenue. Strawberries. Dorothy Hughes. AMV-81

Unpainted, luscious, half-divine/To men who sail in ships. The Sailor. Goodridge MacDonald. CaP

Unpeopled and unfeathered blue and silver,/Before, behind, above. Interruption. Robert Graves. LiTB; LiTM

The unperform'd, more gigantic than ever, advance, advance upon me. Years of the Modern. Walt Whitman. AmePo

Unpitied in its greatness. Starvation Peak Evening. David O'Neil. AnAmPo

Unpleasing to a married ear. Love's Labour's Lost. William Shakespeare. BiP; DiPo; EG; EIL; ExPo; FF; FiP; HAP; HBV; 1-2; HeIP; InPK; InPo; LoBV; NIP; NLV; NOBE; NoP; OAEL 1-2; OBEV; OBSC; PBBP; PoEL 1-5; PoPle; PoRA; PrIm; SeCePo; SeCeV; SoSe; TEP; TreFT; TrGrPo; UnPo; ViBoPo

Unprayed-for,/And final. What Can I Tell My Bones? Theodore Roethke. AmPP; NOBA

The unpredicted voices of our kind. Two Girls Singing. Iain Crichton Smith. BSV

Unquestionable as my sitting up just now. Addressing His Deaf Wife, Kansas, 1916. William Olsen. AMV-81

The unquestionable houseboy's shoulders/that could have been my own. The Badgers. Seamus Heaney. CIP

Unraveling in me like/dark water. The Song. Hemda Roth. VWA

Unravelling deserts behind. Oh, You Wholly Rectangular. E. R. Cole. GoYe

Unreal, as if nothing had been changed at all. As You Leave the Room. Wallace Stevens. AP

Unreconciled into the dark below. The Death of Chiron. James Philip McAuley. BoAV

The unreverberant Profound/That hath no name nor mete! The Inverted Torch. Edith Matilda Thomas. AA

Unripe for revolution or for death. Reflections in Bed. Julian Symons. WaP

Unrival'd reigns, the fairest Lamp of Night. Summer Evening and Night. James (1700-48) Thomson. OBEC

Unrocking on the holy virgin water/Fleckless on every side. Calm Morning at Sea. Sara Teasdale. EtS; MOS

Unroll it inch by inch, to stretch the night. I Cut in Two. Hwang Chin-i. PBWP

Unrolled by the hands/of the waves. Kelp. Nora Dauenhauer. TWSS

Unseals her earth, and lifts love in its shower. The Broken Tower. Hart Crane. AmPP; AP; CMoP; CoBMV; LiTM; MoAB; MoAmPo; MoPo; MoVE; NoAm; NOBA; NoP; OxBA; SyP; TrGrPo

...Unseen in the frozen snow. Night Thoughts over a Sick Child. Philip Levine. NePoEA-2; SM

The unseen jars, the solitary pursuer. Shark's Fin. Eithne Wilkins. NeBP

The unseen, perfect bliss of heaven. Almighty God, Thy Constant Care. Henry Stevenson Washburn. AH

Unseen, undreamt, there still may toil/The patient plough of Hope. The Ploughman. Gilbert Thomas. HBMV

Unseen, unheard, while thought to highest place/Bends all his powers, even unto Stella's grace. Astrophel and Stella, XXVII. Sir Philip Sidney. AAS; SiPS

Unselfish, kind, forgiving/To others every day? Would I Be Called a Christian? Mrs. J. F. Moser. STF

Unsettled yet by deed and free,/That you may leave to her–or me. To Geron. Hildebrand Jacob. NOEC

...Unsheathes her/turpentine claws, rakes bleeding trail of sexhatred down my anus-shuddering/spine. .Blessing a Bride and Groom: A Wedding Night Poem (parody). Robert Peters. BXAP

The unsmiling sons, the sad bewildered daughters. The Children March. Elizabeth Riddell. CBAP

Unspeakable! His Gift! Thanks Be to God. Janie Alford. PGD; PoToHe

...Unspoiled/by insects and waiting/only for the cold. The Hard Listener. William Carlos Williams. OBSP

The unstarched sleeves rolled up for slaughter Lee-ers of Hew... James (Olumo) Cunningham. JB

Unstop her ears, unstitch her eyes/And leave me/To run my life/Alone. Running Blind. Nancy Jones. LiSp

An unsullied country, almost beyond the stars. Remember That Country. Jean Garrigue. VGW

...The unsure/egoist is not/good for himself. The Immoral Proposition. Robert Creeley. LiTM; NeAP; PoM

Unthinking fools, alone despise/The arts, that taught them first to rise. Fables for the Female Sex, V: The Poet and His Patron. Edward Moore. CEP

Until a puffing wind comes by. Outside the Door. Annette Wynne. SoPo; SUS

Until a welcome voice cried—"Next!" The Hospital Waiting-Room. William Henry Davies. BrPo; CBEP

Until all his custom/on the nearby street/is gone. May Evening. Eileen Brennan. NeIP

Until all knowledge be known. The Only Jealousy of Emer. Anonymous. BIrV

Until all things sweet and good/Seem my natural habitude. Andrew Rykman's Prayer (excerpt). John Greenleaf Whittier. TrPWD; TRV

...Until darkness quenched/the vision, the traffic wild and stilled. Surfaces. Jane Mayhall. NYP

Until death it doth us part he shall enjoy my heart, let his riches be great or small. The Shanty-Man's Life (with music). Anonymous. AS

Until everything is continuous again. Exercise. William Stanley Merwin. NOBA

Until for them the very ground/Doth blossom with his fame. He Bringeth Them Unto Their Desired Haven. Lewis Frank Tooker. HBV 1-2

Until for us like morning stars shall rise/The deathless dead. Diffugere Nives, 1917. Maurice Baring. HBMV

Until God loosen over sea and land/The thunder of the trumpets of the night. Laus Veneris. Algernon Charles Swinburne. MaVP; VLP

Until he call my soul away,/Eternal praise to sing! Dear Brethren, Are Your Harps in Tune? Eunice Smith. AH

Until he freed his negroes, lest he be/Too strict with nature and then they less free. The Rooftree. Allen Tate. PoA

Until he hears the call of his midnight. Dream of a Decent Death. Giuseppe Antonio Borgese. NePoAm

"Until he stands like a child/"With surplus of toys." The Ocean Said to Me Once. Stephen Crane. MOS

Until he wins—nervous prostration and death. Making a Man. Nixon Waterman. BLPA

Until her best petticoat's mended/with silk. Pussy Cat Mole. Anonymous. OxNR

Until her dying-bed,/she cursed her circumstances. The Ballad of Sue Ellen Westerfield. Robert Earl Hayden. AmPP; NoAm

Until her fellow sinks to re-appear no more. Incident Characteristic of a Favourite Dog. William Wordsworth. FM

Until His eyes of mercy are turned with love on me. The Eel. Evan Morgan. CAW

Until his mind/could climb into/the open flesh and/mend itself. At Luca Signorelli's Resurrection of the Body. Jorie Graham. HaCAP

Until his smiling murderer comes,/To kill him in the morning light. The Rabbit. William Henry Davies. BoAnP

...Until I am/driven by that density home. On Vacation. Robert Creeley. CAPP

Until I change them for the silent way. Too Late. Philip Bourke Marston. OBNC

Until I dare my fear and call/The lion out to lick my hand. In Waste Places. James Stephens. GTBS; MoAB; MoBrPo; MoVE

Until I drove my harpoon in the beast/And tethered it to/My harpoon line! Hymn to the Air Spirit. Anonymous. WTO

Until I get used to it./HAWHAWHAW When Charlie Bowdre Married Manuela. Michael Ondaatje. PoL

Until I know less. The Relics. Harry Mathews. ANYP

Until I'm covered and there's only one smell,/One word. Burning Shit at An Khe. Bruce Weigl. MAYP

Until I meet/that flickering lantern/at the corner of the street. A God Once Commanded Us. Leah Goldberg. VWA

Until I sank/into darkness. Flying Letters. Zerubavel Gilead. VWA

Until I scale that final peak/And view/The unimagined vistas of eternity. To Alan. Douglas Fraser. PoSH

Until I send my servant now/To bring my coat o mail. The Battle of Harlaw (B version). Anonymous. ESPB

Until I shall have rightly praised/Her standing thus with slight arms upraised. Fiametta. John Peale Bishop. LiTA; LiTL

Until I sleep in the unlaurelled night. Letter to Anne Ridler. G. S. Fraser. OxBS

Until i started/school. Black Sketches, 1. Don L. Lee. NeAC

Until I too begin chasing falcons and start forgetting/about bodies buried shallowly in lakes. The Case. Ken Norris. CaPN

Until I've learned that love, like hate/is always acted out Caledonia. Colleen J. McElroy. BlSi

Until in all the earth thy kingdom come. Lord God of Hosts. Shepherd Knapp. AH

Until, in God's own day,/Mankind be one. My Country, to Thy Shore. Theodore Chickering Williams. AH

Until in our Redeemer's face/We read the meaning of our days. Spirit from Whom Our Lives Proceed. Howard Chandler Robbins. TrPWD

Until it all like incense burns/And unto melting sweetness turns. Noble Love. Richard Flecknoe. ACP

Until it blocked my eyes. The first day's night had come. Emily Dickinson. LiTA; OxBA

Until it ceases to be a problem. Landscapeople. John Ashbery. HaCAP

Until it flashes the sun into my face. Begging on North Main. Dabney Stuart. AMV-81

Until it forms a lightly frozen couch/On which he dreams. Interlude. Maxwell Bodenheim. MAPA

Until it melts. White. Karl Krolow. AMV-81

Until it's almost day! Vive la Canadienne. Anonymous. FSW

Until love turn from us and die/Beneath the drear November trees. Autumnal. Ernest Christopher Dowson. OBNC

Until/my eyes boiled. That Day. John Leax. TrCP

Until my tears will melt/the world of desert stone. Desert Stone. Miriam Waddington. VWA

Until my very soul of souls/Is filled, and overfilled. Flood-Time on the Marshes. Evaleen Stein. AA

Until, one day, he hurt her as he came. The First. Marya Mannes. FAZ

Until our hollow ship was kneeling/Over the longer wave. Pilgrimage. Austin Clarke. CIP; IPY; OxBI

Until our lives are perfected in thee. Lead Us, O Father, in the Paths of Peace. William Henry Burleigh. AH

Until our rent is all spent and then we look for more. The Grimsby Fisherman. Anonymous. OBSS

Until our weary singing ends/In lullabies to-night. Holiday. Horace. AWP

Until someone comes to take me/to the place where I belong. The Working Man. Gregory Donovan. AMV-81

Until that dawn, dear heart, good-night, good-night! A Farewell. George William Russell. OBVV

Until that he came to the yetts of Aboyne,/Where the corpse of his lady was lying. The Earl of Aboyne. Anonymous. BaBo; ESPB

Until that miraculous catfish was still. The Catfish. Michael Waters. WOLT

Until the basket overflows with light. Song for the Sun That Disappeared Behind the Rainclouds. Anonymous. TTY

Until the blessed time that thou art here? Absence. Frances Anne Kemble. PoToHe

Until the bone will break. A Sparrow in the Dust. Ruth Domino. BoWoP

Until the breath of Hampstead touched his/face. Breath of Hampstead Heath. Edith Matilda Thomas. AA

...Until the day flashes and no one lives/to look back and say, a flash, a white flash sparkled. The Fundamental Project of Technology. Galway Kinnell. SM; SUW; SV

Until the day that he/Pronounce the name: Messiah. God's Language. Ruth Fainlight. VWA

Until the days were numbered of that dream. The End which Comes. Mrs. Major Arnold. LoBV

Until the debt I owe for this is paid. Fear. Anna Hajnal. BoWoP

Until the deer come down to die/in pity for my pain. Myths and Texts. Gary Snyder. CAPP

Until the Designated Light/Repudiate the Forge— Dare You See a Soul at the White Heat? Emily Dickinson. MAmP

–Until the entire earth/Is transformed from stones/Into a prayer of flames. A Cathedral. Stanislav Vinaver. VWA

Until the fair-spoken world their lives condemn/Dies in each one's death. They are history. Poland, October. Charles Brasch. AnNZ

Until the first rays of morning. Long Lonely Lover of the Highway. Frederic Will. AMV-81

Until the full-grown wings of human grief/Eclipse thy memory of the kite and dove. Minnie and Her Dove. Charles Tennyson Turner. FM

Until the girl and I are no more. Kearney Park. Gary Soto. NPGG

Until the grief is gone/and you, its messenger,/and I. Let Us Laugh. Zvi Shargel. VWA

Until the last can't be told/from the mermaid's fingernails. Dead Neck. Sue Standing. AMV-81

Until the last word and the last sound/Of this language I am speaking is forgotten. Hearing Steps. Charles Simic. HaCAP

Until the limpid crescent of the moon/Lights the blue east above the evening trees. Spring. Thomas Caulfield Irwin. IrPN

Until the loud cicada shrills/telling the world their names. The Colour of God's Face. Dorothy Livesay. PeCV

Until the moss had reached our lips,/And covered up our names. I Died for Beauty. Emily Dickinson. AmePo; AnFE; AnNE; APA; AWP; BLPL; BoWoP; DiPo; FaFP; InPo; LiTA; LiTM; MAPA; MasP; MoAB; MoAmPo; MoVE; NAWM 1-2; NCEP; NOBA; NoP; SBG; TreFT; WHA

Until the name grow blurred and fade away. Sonnet to My Friend, with an Identity Disc. Wilfred Owen. PeHV

Until the purple blossom is trodden in the ground. One Girl. Sappho. EnLi 1-2

Until the purple blossom is trodden into the ground. Beauty. Dante Gabriel Rossetti. ViBoPo

Until the scarlet life from her lips drawn/Gathers its shattered beauty in the sky. The Princess. Walter James Turner. HBMV

Until the smallest sparrow's song/Is louder than the drums! A White-Throat Sings. Walter Prichard Eaton. HBMV

Until the spirit that here abides,/shall overcome all Amalekites. At Masada. Ernest Neufeld. AMV-81

Until the time we shall be one/and our day over... Bread. Gabriela (Lucila Godoy Alcayaga) Mistral. WPOW

Until the torches deaden at the bedroom door. Speaking of Poetry. John Peale Bishop. LiTA; OxBA; PP

Until the white dawn rises like a dove,/From beneath the wings of a raven/that flees away. The Beauty of the Stars. Moses Ibn Ezra. TrJP

Until the wind roared and softened and died to sleep. Possessions. Ivor Gurney. FaBoPP

Until the wristwatch is taken from the wrist. The Withdrawal. Robert Lowell. NoP

Until the yachat, au reservoir. The Visit. Ogden Nash. FiBHP

Until/their lives burst The Holy Ones, the Young Ones. Chayyim Zeldis. TrJP

...Until there remained in his hands/the skin, the pit, and clinging foam. A Plum. Leib. VWA

Until they are white Hokku: In the Falling Snow. Richard Wright. IDB

...Until they began turning themselves, faster/and faster, as if a destination would arrive. The Kiss. John Yau. APU

Until they come to London Bridge. Upon Paul's Steeple Stands a Tree. *Anonymous.* OxNR

...Until they fade into the blue depth of/space. Hand. Edouard Roditi. EAS

Until they spy land in sweet Botany Bay. The Attractions of a Fashionable Irish Watering-Place. Francis Sylvester ("Father Prout") Mahony. FaBoPP; IrPN; NBM

Until they topple and fall,/And fallen let in the day. The Fathers. Edwin Muir. OxBS

Until they were as sand/Thrown between me and the sky. 'Scaped. Stephen Crane. AA

Until thou bring it to the grave. Had Sorrow Ever Fitter Place. Samuel Daniel. EIL

Until thou wake to light/And love and warmth to-morrow. Holy Innocents. Christina Georgina Rossetti. HBV 1-2; HBVY

Until thy mighty word prevails,/That cries, "All souls are mine." The Prince of Peace His Banner Spreads. Harry Emerson Fosdick. AH; TrPWD

Until tired, wise, content, he halts before/The sign o' The Grave, a cool and quiet inn. The Happy Wanderer. Percy Addleshaw. OBVV

Until trapped at the whirlpool's edge/he plunges to his death. Frankenstein. Edward Field. FF

Until we accept what is written there. What Is There. Marvin Bell. GP

Until we all get settled in some future day. Tittery-Irie-Aye. *Anonymous.* AmFP

Until we are pure spirit at the end. Infirmity. Theodore Roethke. CoAP; NYBP

Until we bask in light, and love,/And perfect peace! The Prince of Peace. Edward Henry, Bishop of Exeter Bickersteth. BePJ

Until we commence a-keepin' house in the/house not made with hands. Out of the Old House, Nancy. Will Carleton. AA

Until we hear in ourselves again/the forgotten song of love. Reading Today's Newspaper. Steve Abbott. AMV-80

Until we join the church above,/And know as we are known. A Parting Hymn We Sing. Aaron R. Wolfe. AH

Until we know even as we are known—/Good-night! Good-night! Good-night! The Christian's "Good-Night". Sarah Doudney. BLPA

Until we make him welcome through the year. December 26. George Edward Hoffman. PGD

Until we meet in Heaven, where all tears have passed away. Face to Face. Frances Cochrane. HBV 1-2

Until we reach the very heart of God. A Woman to Her Lover. Christina Walsh. BrRo

Until we see Him face to face. All Nature Has a Voice to Tell. James Gilchrist Lawson. BLRP

Until we stand upon the height,/And see the perfect day. Patience. G. Anketall "Woodbine Willie" Studdert-Kennedy. TrPWD

Until we've really got the country plann'd. The Town Clerk's Views. Sir John Betjeman. CMoP

Until, with day, another blue be born. Seascape. Francis Brett Young. OxBTC

Until women's tears are reckoned in the budgets of your/wars. An English Mother. Robert Underwood Johnson. HBV 1-2

Until ye start, as if the sea-nymphs quired! Sonnet on the Sea. John Keats. EtS; SeCePo; ViBoPo

Until yesterday I was polite and peaceful... Opinions of the New Student. Regino Pedroso. TTY

Until/you do right. A long while, baby. Riots and Rituals. Richard W. Thomas. PoBA

Until you have learned to play. Porgy, Maria, and Bess. Dubose Heyward. PoNe

Until you resume command/Self is in mutiny. Valediction. Seamus Heaney. PPJ

Until you return. Images. Richard Aldington. MoBrPo; PoA

Until your face falls against Big Brother's boot. Inconsistencies. Michelle Roberts. LFAC

Until your senses, all so aroused/come together, come alive. Erotica. Endre Farkas. CaPN

Untill our painters took their new fashion from France. The Testament of Beauty. Robert Bridges. MoVE

Unto all generations of the faithful heart. Lee in the Mountains. Donald Davidson. MoVE

Unto all love-inscriptions that abide,/Power and dominion over life and death. The Inscription. Elsa Barker. HBMV

Unto an honest faithful grave,/Making our pillows either down or dust. Death. George Herbert. AnAnS 1; JCP

Unto earth's remotest end/Glorified, adored and owned! Thou Art Coming! Frances Ridley Havergal. WGRP

Unto Everyman,/according to his worth, acclaim for his labours. Farmer Goes Berserk. Anne Elder. CBAP

Unto God the One and Three/Through the ages evermore! Laudate for Christmas. Prudentius (Aurelius Clemens Prudentius). CAW

Unto Heven on high my soule I bequeth. A Last Will and Testament. *Anonymous.* MeEL

Unto his ancient and miraculous right. Whitsunday. George Herbert. AtBAP

Unto its name-sake flower. I'll Be As True. Thomas Lovell Beddoes. AtBAP

Unto more beautiful, persistently more/young,/Thy fabulous provinces belong. Philomela. John Crowe Ransom. AmP; CMoP; FaBoPP; MoVE; NoAm; NOBA; OBAL; OBSV; OxBA

Unto morn that it was day. Medieval Mirth. *Anonymous.* ACP

Unto our silent graves mournfully wending. Like Flowers We Spring. *Anonymous.* CBEP; EIL

...:Unto the dark return/Of the world's harmony. The Retreat. Sir Herbert Read. BrPo

Unto the fatherland/Over the starry skies! To Gabriel of the Annunciation. Peter Abelard. CAW

Unto the God-forsaken place called Canada-i-o. Canada-I-O. *Anonymous.* AmFP; BaBo; FSW; ViBoFo

Unto the sad is sadness Heaven's grace,/And to the souls that love is love's embrace. The Magic Mirror. Henry Mills Alden. HBV 1-2

Unto the thinking of the thought divine. O World. George Santayana. FPL; GoTF; HBV 1-2; PoLf; TreFS; TrGrPo; TRV

Unto the which He us bringe/That in heven reigneth eternal Kinge! How the Ploughman Learned His Paternoster. *Anonymous.* OxBM

Unto the world I will the deed proclaim. The Democratic Barber; or, Country Gentleman's Surprise. John Parrish. NOEC

Unto their gentle murmuring noise,/The praise of Neptune's empery. Neptune. Thomas Campion. OBSC

Unto them that bravely fought in the Angel Gabriel. The Honour of Bristol. *Anonymous.* OBSS

Unto thy heart/Shall joy impart. Psalm XXVII. Sir Philip Sidney. FCP

Unto Thy praise, all love and melody,/Tune me, O Lord. Tune Me, O Lord, into One Harmony. Christina Georgina Rossetti. TrPWD

Unto whom the praise and glory. The Annunciation. Saint Nerses. ISi

Unto youth's land no more/Forever goes thy way. Spring Song. Hermann Hesse. AWP

Untold gems and endless nights/of thrashing. There Are in Such Moments. David I. Silverstein. AMV-80

Untouch'd by any yearning feels the peace/That it shall enter when its annals cease! To Sleep. Jan Kochanowski. LiTW

Unused but significant/Of something to come. Peterhead in May. Burns Singer. OxBS

Unvanquished in my atmosphere of devils. The Imperfect Lover. Siegfried Sassoon. BrPo

Unveil our eyes/To recognize/Thyself, for Thy dear sake.   Grace at Evening. Edwin McNeill Poteat.   TrPWD

Unveil the hidden beauty of His Face.   Saint Thomas Aquinas.   Thomas S. Jones.   CAW

Unvexed by July's warm eyes.   Midsummer Frost.   Isaac Rosenberg. MoPo

Unwatched/woman.   Cosmetic.   Gretchen Herbkersman.   AMV-80

Unwearied ever, ever fleet: The First Olympionique to Hiero of Syracuse. Pindar.   ATP

Unwearied, unobnoxious to be pain'd/By wound, though from their place by violence mov'd.   Paradise Lost.   John Milton.   ExPo

Unwept for let the body go.   At Castle Wood.   Emily Bronte.   ViBoPo

Unwept, unhonored, and unsung.   The Lay of the Last Minstrel.   Sir Walter Scott.   BLPA; FPL; GN; OAEP; OHFP; OxBS; TreF; TrGrPo

Unwilling to change their freedom for a god.   Wednesday Night Prayer Meeting.   Jay Wright.   PoBA

Unwilling to retire, though weary.   Written in the Beginning of Mezeray's History of France.   Matthew Prior.   CEP; EiCP; NOBE; OBEC; PoEL 1-5

Unwilling to unlearn/Old Ways.   First Grade.   Phil George.   VoR

Unwind the clock, empty the seasons down/rivers of memory–do not return! Valediction to My Contemporaries.   Horace Gregory.   MoAmPo

Unwinding still the darkening thread?   Rear Vision.   William Jay Smith. NYBP

...Unworded insides of things, the things that are there.   Munch's Scream. Donald Hall.   NePoEA

Unworried and/Warm–secure.   My House.   George Bruce.   OxBS

Up a bit, up a bit,/In a wee house.   Round About, Round About. Anonymous.   OxNR

Up among the rocks where the blueberries grow.   Shepherd's Holiday. Elinor Wylie.   CrMA; HBMV

Up and down they charge and rally!/Ended is my song.   The Monkey's Wedding (with music).   Anonymous.   AS

Up and swallowed Bryan's Bryaness.   The Lion.   Ogden Nash.   CenHV; ShM

Up, brothers, march onward, march/onward to God.   Flowering without End.   Stefan Zweig.   TrJP

Up came a magpie/And bit off her nose.   Song of Sixpence.   Anonymous. OxBoLi

Up, carles, up/And let us dance!   A Drunk Man Looks at the Thistle (excerpt).   Hugh" (Christopher Murray Grieve) MacDiarmid.   EBEV

Up come Bob and Stokes a-walking on their heels.   Hog Rogues on the Harricane.   Anonymous.   OuSiCo

Up, Cursty, up; for God's sake let me gang,/For fear the maister put us in a sang.   Hay-Time; or The Constant Lovers. A Pastoral.   Josiah Relph. NOEC

Up & fell as the deep hidden tides beat/against the rock   Age.   Rae Desmond Jones.   CBAP

Up from our terror, with women: me, you.   Ordinary Women.   Marilyn Hacker.   LTB

Up from the depths of separation,/Float the splinters of my poems.   Prayer. Lev Mak.   VWA

Up goes its tail!   The Whale.   (Taniguchi Buso) Buson.   SoPo

Up half-known roads.   The Send-Off.   Wilfred Owen.   BrPo; LiTB; MoAB; MoBrPo; MoVE; OBWP; OxBTC; PAI

Up he comes, up he comes,/Out at the top.   Putting on Nightgown. Anonymous.   OxNR

"Up here the sun melts all of us/As if we had wings..."   Big City Glissando. Nicholas Christopher.   NYP

Up hill "Too-slow" will need the whip,/Down hill "Too-quick," the chain. Politics.   Alfred, Lord Tennyson.   CoBE

Up in the air and down!   The Swing.   Robert Louis Stevenson.   FaBoBe; FaFP; GoJo; NTCP; SoPo; SUS; TEP; TiPo; TreF

Up in the room where the lockers are and the showers.   After a Game of Squash.   Samuel L. Albert.   GoYe; NePoAm-2

Up, lad: when the journey's over/There'll be time enough to sleep.   A Shropshire Lad.   Alfred Edward Housman.   FPL; OAEP; PoLf

Up our duff, Jack, for spewing up our duff, Jack.   The Kola Run. Anonymous.   OBSS

Up pops a Daddy with a Nikon. Click.   Commencement, Pingree School. John Updike.   Str

Up-rising and down-falling, bares/The last largeness, bold to see.   The Curtains in the House of the Metaphysician.   Wallace Stevens.   PoA

Up, sleepy head!   Getting out of Bed.   Eleanor Farjeon.   SiSoSe

Up tails all!   Duck's Ditty.   Kenneth Grahame.   GoJo; NTCP; SUS

Up the airshaft to where I lie, not quite alone.   In and Out.   L. E. Sissman. NYBP

Up the cave moans the wave,/For ever, ever, ever fled away!   Aeolian Harp. William Allingham.   OnYI

Up the chimbley he did shove her.   Eaper Weaper.   Anonymous.   DBV; FaBoNo; OxBoLi

Up the long sea-curve rides its stately form.   England.   Richard Edwin Day. AA

Up the steep road of life to Heaven's gate.   White Magic: An Ode.   William Stanley Braithwaite.   PoNe

Up there alone, upon the alps of night.   Alexandria.   Lawrence Durrell. MoVE

...Up to her old/tricks I thought.   April Fool.   Sam Hunt.   OCNZ

Up to/it or/all in.   Chasm.   Archie Randolph Ammons.   OBAL

Up to the book of air shut once more/by the Never Again of Masada.   The Never Again.   Charles Dobzynski.   VWA

Up to the empty summit.   Irish Music.   Larry Levis.   MAYP

Up to the heather hills,/Lilian, away!   The Call of the Morning.   George Darley.   OnYI

Up to the kerb she comes; she switches off; she smiles.   On a Scooter.   D. A. Greig.   PeSA

Up! Up and away.   Fatness.   Alan Ansen.   CoAP

Upland country and her suckling child.   The Monaro.   David Campbell. BoAV

Uplifted in adoration to the living Aton,/The maker...   Thy Rising Is Beautiful.   Akhnaton (Amenhotep IV).   ILwL

Upon a background of Eternal Time.   Nox Ignatiana.   James J. Daly. CAW

Upon a hull hit stondez on hee,/Where sent Jamez ferst schalt thou see.   The Way to Jerusalem (excerpt).   Anonymous.   OBTV

Upon a Sabbath day.   Riddle: "Once hairy scenter did transgress." Anonymous.   CoBE

Upon an infant huge tributes of gold/And frankincense and myrrh.   Avarice. Anthony Hecht.   OBSP

Upon her high-heeled Essex smiled/The brave Queen Bess.   Time to Be Wise. Walter Savage Landor.   HBV 1-2; InMe

Upon her perfect lips.   Sir Launcelot and Queen Guinevere (excerpt). Alfred, Lord Tennyson.   ACV

Upon his bed, however, Shakespeare died,/Having endured them all.   To an Artist, to Take Heart.   Louise Bogan.   GrPl; NYBP

Upon it his servant and interlocutor/prayed...   Are We Not the People.   Al-Samua'al Ibn Adiya.   TrJP

Upon my breast place a turtle dove,/To show the world I died for love. London City (B vers. with music).   Anonymous.   AS

Upon my buried body lay lightly, gentle earth.   Aspatia's Song.   Francis Beaumont and John Fletcher.   HAP

Upon my knees, Oh Lord, for Truth I plead.   Truth.   Claude McKay. BPo

Upon my shoulders, God, load Thou/Thy guilt!   Jacob's Destiny.   Richard Beer-Hofmann.   TrJP

Upon my word and honour.   As I Went to Bonner.   Anonymous.   OxBoLi

Upon our haughty foe!   Men of the North.   John Neal.   AA

Upon rows of kisses from all lips.   Rapunzel.   Olga Broumas.   DFT

Upon that ledge we left a pledge/That we shall claim our own!   Haarlem Heights.   Arthur Guiterman.   PAH

Upon the bony scruff of your departing neck.   The Fertile Valley of the Nile. Eve Merriam.   IHMS

Upon the burthen'd stream he floating lies,/Stretches his quivering fins, and gasping dies.   Rural Sports.   John Gay.   FM

Upon the clouds of heaven!   The Clouds.   William Croswell   AA

"Upon the Cross I died for you."   More Than We Ask.   Faith Wells. BLRP

Upon the disc a moving spot/That would be, was, and now was not. Crescent Moon.   William Renton.   NOBV

Upon the earth and elder stands.   A Young Fir-Wood.   Dante Gabriel Rossetti.   GN

Upon the feathers of a bird.   Owls.   John Fuller.   PoL

Upon the forehead, furred/With a light frost, crouched an outrageous bird. Birdwatchers of America.   Anthony Hecht.   CoPo; HoPM; NoAm; NOBA; PPP

Upon the Forehead of a Bust–/That knows–it cannot see–   The difference between despair.   Emily Dickinson.   NoAm; NoP; QFR

Upon the glistening silence of the sands/Whereon no trace of mortal dust was seen.   Pelters of Pyramids.   Richard Henry Horne.   OBTV

Upon the hearse there nods the last.   The Last Fruit off an Old Tree. Walter Savage Landor.   SeCePo

Upon the hill my lover manes/For what has neither blood nor banes.   The House o' the Mirror.   Helen Adam.   MAT; NMM

Upon the hill-top, out of sight/Of me and thee and all the dawning. Dawning.   Richard Watson Dixon.   NOBV

Upon the kindling cliffs of Penmanmawr.   The Beacons.   Henry Hart Milman.   OBRV

Upon the lee my pleasure grows,/Wi' you, my kind deary O!   The Lee Rigg. Robert Fergusson.   BSV

Upon the living stars!   Metropolitan Night.   Jorge Guillen.   NYP

Upon the road to Romany/The birds are calling still!   From Romany to Rome.   William Irwin.   HBV 1-2

Upon the ruthlesse earth his precious teares lets fall.   Polyolbion.   Michael Drayton.   OBS

Upon the shell of night.   Double Ritual.   Dachine Rainer.   CrMA

Upon the sight of lidless eyes in Hell. The House of Life. Dante Gabriel Rossetti. EnLi 1-2

Upon the skiff that flies and seems/To float upon a tide of dreams. En Bateau. Paul Verlaine. AWP

Upon the sweetest flower of all the field. Romeo and Juliet. William Shakespeare. FaBoRV; GN

Upon the thorn-boughs roses stood. Mary Passes. *Anonymous.* ISi

Upon the waters calm/No breath of wind may light. Song of the Three Angels. Gil Vicente. CAW

Upon the wood he used to work–/With the beloved nail! Carpenter of Eternity. E. Merrill Root. PGD

Upon the wooden sides of a boat. The Fisherman's Wife. Amy Lowell. BoWoP

Upon the world. Day and Night. Baldoon Dhingra. ACV

Upon their hillside graves our immortelles! The First Three. Clinton Scollard. MC; PAH

Upon their lips the taunt shall die. America. William Cullen Bryant. AA

Upon this beauty's power shall wreak no/wrong. The House of Life. Dante Gabriel Rossetti. OAEP

Upon thy head be a' this blude,/For mine, I ween, is free.' Johnie Cock (D version). *Anonymous.* ESPB

Upon thy Mount Lycean! Endymion. John Keats. AtBAP; ChRP

Upon what meat doth this our Caesar feed,/That he is grown so great? Julius Caesar. William Shakespeare. GoTF; TreFS

Upon what terms, with how much left unsaid. The Middle-Aged. Adrienne Rich. HaCAP; NePoEA-2

Upon which he relinquished those habits. Limerick: "There was an old Person whose habits." Edward Lear. FaBoNo; LBN; TDH

Upon whose golden rungs we step by step arise. God's Promises. *Anonymous.* BLRP

Upon your knees for mercy cry,/Before, like Archer, bound to die. The Hanging of Sam Archer. *Anonymous.* AmFP

Upon Your sweat, Your thirst,/Your nails, and nakedness I rest/my case. Defense Rests. Vassar Miller. MoAmPo

Upright and pointing about the dining-room table. In Memoriam. Richard Weber. ErPo

Uprising with the breath of all the stars. Sonnet in a Garden. Josephine Preston Peabody. AA

Uproot and bear me in Thy Breast,/And plant me where it please Thee best! The Gardener. Laurence Housman. TrPWD

Uprooted abound in the water and choke in the air. The Voyage. Karl Shapiro. MoLP

Uprose in the golden quiet over the hill. The Starling Lake. Seumas (James Starkey) O'Sullivan. AnIV; AWP

Uprose the Light of man. A Thousand Years Have Come. Thomas Toke Lynch. BLRP

Uprouse ye, then, my merry men!/And use it as ye may. Song of the Outlaws. Joanna Baillie. OBRV

Upside down/And skipping. Windy Wash Day. Dorothy Aldis. TiPo

Upstairs she lies, washed through by the two miracles. In the House of the Dying. Jane Cooper. NMM

An upturned, dented helmet. Hector. Valentin Iremonger. CIP; NeIP; OxBI

Upward for a copper sun. Bridge. S. Foster Damon. AnAmPo

Upward going, upward going! Uru-tu-sendo's Song. *Anonymous.* WTO

Upward in motion with wet wind. Wales Visitation. Allen Ginsberg. CAPP; NNaP; NOBA; NYBP; Prf

Upwards/into the sky. A Day in a Long Hot Summer. Yuri Kageyama. BrSi

Urge no more, and there shall be/Daffodils given up to thee. A Hymn to Bacchus. Robert Herrick. JCP

Urge the vast twilight to immortal bloom. The First Note, Simple; the Second Note, Distinct. Conrad Aiken. LiTA

Urged by despair I throw the burden down. Ad Coelum. William Pattison. OBSP

Urges retreat to that Forgotten Land's/Unthoughtful shores where thou and Silence are! Vers La Vie. Arthur Upson. HBV 1-2

The Urn was little, but the room/More rich than Cleopatra's Tomb. A Trapped Fly. Robert Herrick. WiR

Uru a chim uru a chim b'lev sameach. Hava Nagila. *Anonymous.* FSW

Us, and nowhere but you to be. America. Robert Creeley. MAT

Us light on earth, and here our flight is/stayed. The Chanting Cherubs - A Group by Greenough. Richard Henry Dana. AA

Le us pray: Let us praise. Facing the New Year. Mark Guy Pearse. BLRP

Us raunsound on the Rude. A Hymn to Mary. William Dunbar. MeEL

Us two to all the parish! Jockie, Thine Hornpipe's Dull. *Anonymous.* NCEP

Use all their voices and their instruments/To entertaine divine Zenocrate. Tamburlaine. Christopher Marlowe. BoW

Use all thy powers that blessed power to praise,/Which gives thee power to be, and use the same. An Acclamation. Sir John Davies. OxBoCh

Use arms the Soul–anon there moveth by/A more majestic Angel–and we die! The Glory of Nature. Frederick Tennyson. OBNC

Use it, and live/or cut it off, and die. The Colour of God's Face. Dorothy Livesay. PeCV

Use me, O Lord, use even me. Open My Eyes. Betty Scott Stam. STF

...Use prudence, my lords; not pity. The Case of Thomas More. Sister Mary St. Virginia. GoBC

Use us, our money, talents, time,/In Thy sweet service here. The Perfect Gift. Julia Benson Parker. BePJ

Use what words you wish; they will often be heard/again. The Dog Beneath the Skin. W. H. Auden. NAMP

Used to store muddied pools of rain/to hide the sun from children Freedom. J. Charles Green. LFAC

A useful Lesson to the forward Wife. The Process of Conception. Claude Quillet. FaBoUs

Useless each without the other. The Song of Hiawatha. Henry Wadsworth Longfellow. TRV

Useless, you'll be thrown aside. Sent to Miss Bell H—, with a Pair of Buckles. John Cunningham. FaBoUs

Ushers in a drearier day. Fall, Leaves, Fall. Emily Bronte. CH; ELP; EnLi 1-2; FaBoCh; FaBoRV; FaBV; LoBV; LoGBV; OBSP; PoEL 1-5; TrGrPo

Using black primitive standards. The Black Narrator. Ahmed Legraham Alhamisi. BP

Usually break wind/As they calmly watch you go Their Cone-Like Cabins. Charles G. Ballard. VoR

Usually most people–just shit! To Fez Cobra. Ted Joans. GP

Ut, ah, the walk that afternoon/We saw the water-flags in flower! The Angel in the House. Coventry Patmore. EBEV; EG

Utes are eagles flying high and far.....Hi-yu! Hi-yu! Hi-yu! Hi-ya!!! The Red Ghosts Chant. Lilian White Spencer. PoOW

Utter the clothed or the naked man? Letters. Bernard Spencer. NeBP; WaP

...Uttering a word/That no man living has interpreted. The Word of Water. E. L. Mayo. PoA

Uttering cries that are almost human. American Poetry. Louis Simpson. ELU; NoAm; NOBA; PP; TAP

Utterly secret. I know you, black swan. Music of Colours–White Blossom. Vernon Watkins. LiTM; WaP

V

...The vacant stateliness of claw-footed chairs. Old Roadside Resorts. Molly Peacock. MAYP

Vagabond of Galilee,/Who is every outcast's/Home. Despised and Rejected. Katharine Lee Bates. TrCP

Vagrants, Fugitives and Rogues,/That deserve the Stocks and Strokes. When I Solidly Do Ponder. Francis Daniel Pastorius. SCAP

Vague intimations that made time/A very time of Gold. Reminiscences of a Day: Wicklow. John Francis O'Donnell. IrPN

A vague remembrance/In my head. Forgotten Dreams. Edward S. Silvera. PoNe

A vague sorrow/Crossed my mind. Three Tanka, 2. Yosano Akiko. LiTW

Vain–as it is brief. Turn Me to My Yellow Leaves. William Stanley Braithwaite. BANP

The vain reflection of a helpless smile. For Haroun al Raschid. Abu'l-Atahija. LiTW

The vain things thought when she flourished this? The Sunshade. Thomas Hardy. OxBTC

Vain world, adieu. Vain World Adieu. *Anonymous.* AmFP

Vainly in Hell let Pluto domineer. The Character of Holland. Andrew Marvell. CABL; NOBL; OBSV; OBTV; TW

Vainly–(that sneeze again? Loved one, I'm Off!) Saragossa. Henry Sambrooke Leigh. FaBoCo

...Valery/and Trollope the huntsman are happy to drop out. Last Things, Black Pines at 4 a.m. Robert Lowell. NOBA

Vales, spires, mead'ring streams, and Windsor's tow'ry pride. The Alley. An Imitation of Spenser. Alexander Pope. NOEC

The valiant warrior Kureldei Mirgan/still lives in his own land. Blood Marksman and Kureldei the Marksman. *Anonymous.* WTO

The valley floor appears. Mist. Gill Man. PoSH

Value the intermediate splendor of birds. The Geese. Hyam Plutzik. BiP

Van Gogh was saying, "I am not a tree,/A fish, a serpent, lion, pig, or jay." A Lesson from Van Gogh. Howard Moss. MoAB

Vanish...because it had never been. Time Is a Fox on Quick, Velvet Feet. Louise Leighton. GoYe

Vanish, ye Phantoms! from my idle spright,/Into the clouds, and never more return! Ode on Indolence. John Keats. EnRP; ERoP 1-2; LiTB; OBNC

...Vanishes/Easy and often as each breath.   Blue Moles.   Sylvia Plath.   BiP; NePoEA-2

Vanitas Vanitatum, et omnia Vanitas.   O Wretch, Beware.   William Dunbar. BSV

Vanity is the end/Of all their ways.   Sleep at Sea.   Christina Georgina Rossetti.   MOS; NBM; PoEL 1-5

"Vanity, my little man,/You're nothing of the kind."   Vanity.   James (1834-82) Thomson.   BBV; DBV; FF; NOBV; PV; TreFS

Vanity of vanities,/As the Preacher saith.   Mother Country.   Christina Georgina Rossetti.   OxBoCh

The vanquished die with pleasure.   While on Those Lovely Looks I Gaze. John Wilmot, Earl of Rochester.   CBEP

Var I da love noo tree so well/'S the girt woak tree that's in the dell.   The Oak-Tree.   William Barnes.   OBVV

...Var to chatty and zee vo'ke goo by.   Evening, and Maidens.   William Barnes.   OBEV; OBVV

Varuna, let us be thine own beloved.   Hymn to Varuna, God of Fire and Light.   Anonymous.   LiTW

Varying distance of wind.   Washing between the Buildings.   Larry Eigner. CoPo

Vas dishblayed in dis elegdion py Mishder Hiram Twine.   Breitmann in Politics.   Charles Godfrey Leland.   OBAL

...Vases you endow/with flowers, to disguise this here and now.   Portrait of a Marriage.   Dannie Abse.   NoAm

The vassal world is then thy own.   Love, as a Warrior Lord.   Ovid (Publius Ovidius Naso).   LiTW

The vast and helpless city while it sleeps.   Hymn of the City.   William Cullen Bryant.   AmePo

...The vast black jacket brays in the full forced fell.   Spontaneous Requiem for the American Indian.   Gregory Corso.   MAT; PoM

The vast cold glitter, thin twanging in the spheres/That draws men, crazy, across shadeless tundra.   Back to Base.   Jenny Joseph.   BrRo

Vast, in its fading ratio,/To our penurious eyes!   As by the dead we love to sit.   Emily Dickinson.   NePA

Vayne ys all trust of mans refuge.   Lyve Thowe Gladly, Yff So Thowe May. Sir Thomas Wyatt.   AAS

Veering and wheeling free in the open.   The Harbor.   Carl Sandburg. NCSH; PoPl; TAP

The vegetables are walking.   Onion Bucket.   Lorenzo Thomas.   PoBA

The vegetation still abounds with forms.   Lions in Sweden.   Wallace Stevens. BiP

Veil from our eyes that/Time is in flight.   Love's Language.   Donagh MacDonagh.   NeIP

Veiled by the eelgrass undersea.   Crabbing.   Marky Daniel.   AMV-81

Veiled in her royal darkness,/your crown city of Safed/is waiting for you. Move On, Yiddish Poet.   Jacob Glatstein.   VWA

Veils that hung low o'er the blaze of the truth!   Lost Illusions.   Georgia Douglas Johnson.   BANP

Vein and artery, though ye kill me!   Mithridates.   Ralph Waldo Emerson. AP; NOBA

A vein in the heart of the streams of the sea.   The Triumph of Time. Algernon Charles Swinburne.   BoLiVe; TrGrPo

Velasquez, close those doglike dolorous eyes.   The Unknown Soldier.   Alun Lewis.   MoBrPo

Vell, ve'll git up on der shteeples and ve'll spit down on der peoples,/Mitsch mein ja, ja, ja!   Ja, Ja, Ja!   Anonymous.   ShS

Velvet-green-this landscape perfectly/Moss?   My Friend (parody).   Philip Appleman.   BXAP

Venerated and spared by the ominous hours.   Oxford.   Keith Douglas. NePoEA

Veni, coronaberis.   Veni,Coronaberis.   Anonymous.   AtBAP

Venice, murder, virgins and music, that counts.   Ramble on What in the World Why.   Ralph Gustafson.   AMV-81

Venite adoremus Dominum.   Adeste Fideles.   Anonymous.   PSoN

Ventures, and loseth all in sport/At one most dreadfull throw.   Our English Gamesters Scorne to Stake.   Roger Williams.   SCAP

A Venus kill her bird.   The Sparrow and Diamond.   Matthew Green.   FM; PBBP

Venus, let me ever see.   A Farewell.   Plato.   AWP

Venus, let me never see.   The Lady Who Offers Her Looking Glass. Matthew Prior.   CBEP; FaBoEE; NOEC; OBEV; OBSP; ViBoPo

Venus of the sea, Cupid of the high places.   Polifemo y Galatea: The Love Song of Polyphemus.   Luis de Gongora y Argote.   LiTW

Venus shines bright, night falls at Inishtrahull!   Nightfall in Inishtrahull.   D. J. O'Sullivan.   NeIP

The verb is get.   About Motion Pictures.   Ann Darr.   GrPl

"Verbum caro factum est."   Verbum Caro Factum Est.   Anonymous. SBVL

Verdict-Confined a week in Eldon's larder.   On the Meanness of Lord Eldon. Anonymous.   FaBoEE

Verdict-Ennui, so little work to do.   Inquests Extraordinary, III: On the Same.   Anonymous.   FaBoEE

Verdict-Had tried to wash a shirt marked Wetherell.   On the Uncleanly Habits of Sir Charles Wetherell.   Anonymous.   FaBoEE

Verily yes, ah yes, indeed!   Vista.   Alfred Kreymborg.   MAPA

A vermilioned nothingness, any stick of the mass/Of which we are too distantly a part.   Less and Less Human, O Savage Spirit.   Wallace Stevens. VGW

Vermin are ill to thole.   A Whigmaleerie.   William Soutar.   OxBS

Vermin eaten, fed beastly, in vile ditches meanly.   Canadians.   Ivor Gurney. FaBoTw

Verse, fame, and beauty are intense indeed,/But death intenser-death is life's high meed.   Why Did I Laugh To-night?   John Keats.   CBEP; TEP

Verses a-CRASH! BANG! BLURP!/GLUB"...(end of quote).   Last Words. John Hollander.   OBAL; PV

The verses of that hymn which Seraphs chant above.   Rest.   John Henry, Cardinal Newman.   OBRV; OBVV

The verses written on World War III.   World War III.   Anonymous.   FaFP

A vertical of deliverence.   The Metaphysical Paintings.   John Perreault. ANYP; EAS

Vertue is the roughest way,/But proves at night a Bed of Downe.   Upon the Sudden Restraint of the Earle of Somerset.   Sir Henry Wotton.   AnAnS 2; ELP; JCP; MePo; NOBE; NoP; OBS; SeCP

Vertues braunches wither, Vertue pines.   The Pleasant Comedie of Old Fortunatus.   Thomas Dekker.   AtBAP

The very ant I bruised/My heart held interfused.   The Baying Hounds. Mary Gilmore.   BoAV; PoAu 1-2

Very blessed be/every pilgrimage/under the oak tree.   Song: "Under the oak tree, oak tree."   Anonymous.   BoWoP

The very craziest/of Second Comings.   Christ Climbed Down.   Lawrence Ferlinghetti.   MoRP; SBVL; VGW

Very far from us/And with no knowledge of how to live   Salomon.   Pierre Morhange.   VWA

Very few have a pug.   Fashions in Dogs.   E. B. White.   FiBHP; GDP

The very flame that threaten'd Love/Has lent us light to see him by. Fiorentina.   Ernest Myers.   OBVV

The very ghost of what we were.   Their Party, Our House.   Jon Swan. NYBP

...Very good, I've heard, for tea.   Ode to a Dead Dodge.   David McElroy. AmC; AmPA; DFF

Very little about technique.   Practical Concerns.   William J. Harris.   PoBA

A very little space your heart suffice.   To My Honoured Patron Humphrey Davie...   Benjamin Tompson.   SCAP

The very mice go down upon their knees.   Japanese Beetles.   X.J. Kennedy. HoAn; OBAL

The very next day he....   Gruesome.   Roger McGough.   AmMo

"Very nice, but I still prefer steak."   Limerick: "A careless zookeeper named Blake."   Anonymous.   TDH

A very old messenger/took my seat.   A Boy Who Smells Like Cocoa. Robert Hershon.   NeAC

Very quickly one/of the cashiers/said.   A Sirventes against the Management of the Mammoth Supermarket.   Chuck Wachtel.   APU

...The very sea/moves over mountains man has never known.   Postscript. Mary Mills.   NePoAm

Very small, coming on uphill,/against everything.   The Day the Air Was on Fire.   Reg Saner.   NPAW

The very stocking with the hole/The little mouse gnawed through.   Santa Claus and the Mouse.   Emilie Poulsson.   ChBR

The very thought doth give our blood/A larger circulation!   The Editor's Wooing.   Robert Henry Newell.   OBAL

Very, very specially, heaped/about the roots for nourishment.   A Place (Any Place) to Transcend All Places.   William Carlos Williams.   NYP

Very white sun the intensely white sun.   Poem: "In the corner a violet jug." Pablo Picasso.   EAS

The very world epitomized/In turmoil and delight.   Little Son.   Georgia Douglas Johnson.   CDC

The vesere, the aventaile, his vesturis riche,/With the valiant blode was verrede all over.   Morte Arthur (excerpt).   Anonymous.   PoEL 1-5

Vessels wellformed for grace to fill.   Housewife's Letter: to Mary.   Anne Halley.   NMM

Vestigial virtues, are eaten; we shall survive.   Potato.   Richard Wilbur. TrGrPo

Veteran and novice hold their oath unbroken/Should trolls chumble and the rain strike upward.   To His Coy Mistress (parody).   Peter Scupham. BXAP

Veterans of loving are wary-eyed and scarred/And they see into everything they see.   Veterans.   George Johnston.   NOBC

Vex th'ill-natur'd fools we cannot please.   To Nysus.   Sir Charles Sedley. FaBoEE; OBSV

Vibrate those aging hips again/beneath these trembling hands.   Back from the Word Processing Course, I Say to My Old Typewriter.   Michael C. Blumenthal.   GOYP

Vibration in the summer air.   Midsummer.   James Scully.   MP; TwCP

...The vibrations/Of distant propellers meaning no malice but death. Palermo, Mother's Day, 1943. William Belvin. PoPl

Vicious rope, glaring blade, the gun cocked to kill. Schoolroom on a Wet Afternoon. Vernon Scannell. HaMV

The vict'ry's into Scotland gane,/Tho' sair against their will. McNaughtan (Johnny Scot). *Anonymous.* OxBB

A victim of man's cruelty and greed. Wild Horse Jerry's Story. Sarah Elizabeth Howard. PoOW

The victim soon shall shudder at the stake/And fall in blood: we bring him even now. Six O'Clock. Trumbull Stickney. NCEP; OxBA

Victims/whom are angels/in disguise/questioning/their duties. A Truth... Noah Mitchell. LFAC

The victor is he who can go it alone! The Game of Life. John Godfrey Saxe. BLPA; BLPL

Victor or vanquished, thou the slave of friend or foe. Italy. Vincenzo da Filicaja. AWP

Victory and praise in its own right belong. Hymn of Apollo. Percy Bysshe Shelley. EnL; EnLit; ERoP 1-2; HBV 1-2; MBW 1-2; OAEL 1-2; OAEP; OBRV

Victory! our song shall be,/Like the thunder of the sea! Rise, Ye Children. Justus Falckner. AH

Victory's nearer, perhaps, than/you think it is! Stick to It. Edgar A. Guest. FaFP

A victory should be celebrated with the Funeral Rite. The Tao Teh King (excerpt). *Anonymous.* TRV

A victory worthy to be won,/Nor seek their gain with strife. The Way. Sidney Henry Morse. HBV 1-2

Videlicet, was drunk." Well, where was I?– Tomorrow Is My Birthday: "The thing is sex, Ben." Edgar Lee Masters. NAs

The view from the rocks burrowed by sensitive tunnels. Travellers Turning over Borders (parody). Basil Ransome. BXAP

A view to being recalled as one/of Fashion's tragic figures. Neckwear. Michael Silverton. PV

The vigil of astonishment. Pastoral. Norman Dubie. AmPA

Vigilant among the grasses,/Where a fledgling bobs and passes. The Sandpiper. Witter ("Emanuel Morgan") Bynner. HBMV

Vile belly! take the crust! 'tis nobler food/Than all the capons plucked in servitude. The Gulistan. Muslih-ud-Din Sa'di. AWP

Vile Poverty, and lastly Death with Infamy. The Faerie Queene. Edmund Spenser. PoEL 1-5

The vile snake will always sting you. Anger. Charles and Mary Lamb. FaBoBe; HBV 1-2; HBVY

The village burns us on its tongue,/And all the tale is true. Ivy and Holly. E. H. W. Meyerstein. ELU

The village cryers hang out on the corner. Houston and Bowery, 1981. Diane Burns. TWSS

A village less than Islington will grow,/A solitude almost. Of Solitude. Abraham Cowley. FaBoPP

Villain skips, and all are happy. Curtain! Paul Laurence Dunbar. CenHV

Villon, our sad bad glad mad brother's name. A Ballad of Francois Villon. Algernon Charles Swinburne. EnLi 1-2; PoEL 1-5; PoRA

An' vind that helplessness, wi' right,/Is strong beyond all e'thly might. Withstanders. William Barnes. OxBoCh

...A vine with yellow flowers shading the door. The Buildings. Wendell Berry. EyDe

Viney, go put on de kittle, I got one o'mastah's chickens. Accountability. Paul Laurence Dunbar. AnAmPo; PoLf; YaD

The vintage-chant of nature with the dirging cry of/humankind? Heard on the Mountain. Victor Hugo. AWP

The vintner, and his heavy head/In vineyards overgrown. Love Poem. Janet Lewis. QFR

The vintners that put water in our wine. A Merry Ballad of Vintners. John Payne. ALV

Vinum laetificat/Cor hominis. Temperance. *Anonymous.* CAW

Violent love so slow it cuts/Cage from around the heart Backgammon. Olga Broumas. SUW

...Violent passions/composed for solo insruments. Normal as Two Ships in the Night. Walta Borawski. AMV-81

The violet flashlights and guitars! After I Have Voted. Laura Jensen. AmPA

Violet never woke to know. A Belated Violet. Oliver Herford. AA

...Violets, vernal speedwell, bluebell and/orchis, and commonplace objects. Dewdrops. John Clare. VLP

Violin and sepulcher, the ribbon of the waltz. Little Viennese Waltz. Federico Garcia Lorca. SOTW

The violins begin their proud complaint/In the desert of the world. Symphony: First Movement. John Hall Wheelock. UnS

The violins were no more nor eyes nor arms/hours on hours/following. Sleep. Bravig Imbs. EAS

Vir nulla non donandus lauru.' Every-Day Characters. Winthrop Mackworth Praed. EnRP

Virgil made an austere/Venus Muse of his song. Dedication. Oliver St. John Gogarty. OBMV

A virgin dowered with a heart of gold. To a Cherokee Rose. William Hamilton Hayne. AA

A virgin face–and below–a woman's thighs. You gaze at me teasingly through the window. Praxilla. BoWoP

A virgin/Forest/Is ancient; many-/Breasted,/Stable; at/Climax. Toward Climax. Gary Snyder. SUW

A virgin helpmate Ocean at your knees. Australia. Bernard O'Dowd. PoAu 1-2

The Virgin, long since fled from earth, I see,/T'our times return'd, hath made her heaven in thee. To Thomas Lord Chancellor. Ben Jonson. OBS

A virginal sad tear/For envy of me. The Lass That Died of Love. Richard Middleton. HBV 1-2

The virgins love thee well. Let Him with Kisses of His Mouth. *Anonymous.* AH

...Virro's strained thighs/And those white lips of yours have something in common. Gellius, What Reason Can You Give. Caius Valerius Catullus. PeHV

Virtue dies with too much rest. So Tir'd Are All My Thoughts. Thomas Campion. LoBV

Virtue is that beseems a Man! Chant Royal of High Virtue. Sir Arthur Thomas ("Q") Quiller-Couch. HBV 1-2

Virtue's branches wither, virtue pines. Song: "Virtue's branches wither, virtue pines." Thomas Dekker. ElL; WHA

Virtue to use,/Vice to refuse,/Thus shall I use me. Good Company. King of England Henry VIII. TrGrPo

The virtues of an amulet/and quick surprise. The Warning. Robert Creeley. NeAP; TAP; VGW

Virtues of more sovereign power/Than the garden's gayest pride. What Are Outward Forms. Isaac Bickerstaffe. OnYI

The virtues that a whole world sees,/The by-words of the centuries. Fate. James Fenimore Cooper, Jr.. HBMV

...Virulent summer-/green satisfactions. Dust. Kathleen Spivack. BoWoP

Virus of love, whose counter-dose alone/Is faucet of cut vein or ripsaw bone. Madrigal. John Frederick Nims. MiAP

Viruses when the lens is right/change into a bright bouquet. First Photos of Flu Virus. Harold Witt. SM

The visage of the soul/And not the knees. This dirty little heart. Emily Dickinson. PoEL 1-5

The viscera still shine/with sun, by weed and silver riverflow. A Lament. Margaret Avison. HAP

Visibility very/seriously affected. Wind Force. Bernadette Mayer. ANYP

...A visible/tyrant of light yanks their traces,demanding/they stride apart. Summer Solstice. George Bowering. NOBC

Visibly through His garden walketh God./So fare they. How a Poet's Soul Comes Into Play. Robert Browning. MyFE

The vision of eternity is strange. Sometimes When I Sit Musing All Alone. Agnes Mary Frances (Mme Emile Duclaux) Robinson. WHA

The vision of Our Saviour, face to face... The Lady Venetia Digby. Ben Jonson. GoBC

The vision of that happy child/Will leave my spirits never! Jane Smith (parody). Rudyard Kipling. HBV 1-2; SpRo

The visionary gold/That in my heart I hold/Doth far in worth outshine/All metal from the mine. The Whisperer. Arthur Bullen. HBMV

Visions less fair will sooth my pensive breast,/That asks not happiness, but longs for rest. To Hope. Helen Maria Williams. OBEC

Visions, narcissi, explode from their bulbs. Visions. Kathleen Spivack. AmPA

Visions of an autumn evening. Parting. Shlomo Vinner. VWA

Visions of light and spirit/to wipe terror away Old Indian Trick. Rayna Green. TWSS

Visit my shack! We'll dream we drink/The true Falernian. Horatian Variation. Leonard Bacon. NYBP

...The visiting rain/Lick its tongues in the leaves and pass away. Before Harvest. Robert Fitzgerald. PoPl

The vital, arrogant, fatal, dominant X. The Motive for Metaphor. Wallace Stevens. AP; MoAB; MoAmPo

Viva la muerte! The Opposite House. Robert Lowell. CMoP; NYP

Viva, viva, viva l'Italiane! I Catch-a Da Plenty of Feesh (with music). *Anonymous.* AS; TrAS

Vive l'amour, Vive l'amour, vive la compagnie. Vive la Compagnie. *Anonymous.* FSW; PSoN

The vixen woman/Who came my way. Natural History (excerpt). Harold Monro. OBMV

A vocable, as rath and bullaun. A New Song. Seamus Heaney. FaBoTw

Voi ch'entrate, and your life is in your hands. The Exile's Return. Robert Lowell. AP; MiAP; NePA; OxBA

A voice, a chime, a chant sublime,/Of peace on earth, good-will to men! I Heard the Bells on Christmas Day. Henry Wadsworth Longfellow. AH; NTCP; PoSC

A voice doomed to listen, forever,/to itself.   The Ring.   Diane Wakoski. PoA

A voice fell, life a falling star,/Excelsior!   Excelsior.   Henry Wadsworth Longfellow.   AmePo; FaPoR; GoTF; HBV 1-2; HBVY; OBCA; OnMSP; PaPo; PrIm; SpRo; TreF; WBLP

The voice is yours, whate'er you say.   Upon Lesbia–Arguing.   Alfred Cochrane.   HBV 1-2

...Voice/of a woman singing of a man/who could make her do anything. Reunion.   Carolyn Forche.   MAYP

The voice of her they rue!   Jephthah's Daughter.   Yehoash.   TrJP

The voice of hope and dauntless will,/And breaks the spell of dreams.   The Herald Crane.   Hamlin Garland.   HBV 1-2

The voice of my heart is crying in you.   The Barrel-Organ.   Arthur Symons. NOBV

The voice of Sirens gave us vertigo.   Lamarck Elaborated.   Richard Wilbur. AP; NePoEA

The voice of the bluebird is heard.   Song to Promote Growth.   Anonymous. OBVE

The voice of the dead was a living voice to me.   In the Valley of Cauteretz. Alfred, Lord Tennyson.   BoLoP; NOBE; OBVV; VLP

"The voice of the poet is the voice of God."   Hanukah.   Jakov De Haan. VWA

The voice of the snowman/calls the white-/haired children home.   Winter News.   John Haines.   PPJ

The voice of treason, the voice of love.   Christmas 1944.   Denise Levertov. NeBP

The Voice of Youth/Singing before her throne.   What Is White?   Thomas Macdonagh.   CAW

...A voice proclaiming/The World's mad business–Eternal Absolution.   A Sermon on Swift.   Austin Clarke.   BIrV; IPY

A voice said: "It is no desert."   I Walked in a Desert.   Stephen Crane. AmePo

The voice shriveled and mute/Among the sheer, granite cliffs above Delphi. Sibyl.   Joseph Stroud.   NPGG

The voice that beautifies the land.   The Voice That Beautifies the Land. Anonymous.   AWP

The voice that had called me,/Come, come away!   The Voice.   Walter De la Mare.   WSC

...Voice/That turned a tenderer verse for me.   On a Midsummer Eve. Thomas Hardy.   GTBS

The voiceless Form he chose to feign,/While fluttering in the bushes.   The Green Linnet.   William Wordsworth.   AtBAP; CBEP; GTBS; GTBS-P; HBV 1-2; PBBP

Voices are crying an unknown name in the sky.   Epistle to Be Left in the Earth.   Archibald MacLeish.   BoLiVe; CMoP; ImOP; MoAB; MoAmPo; NOBA; TrGrPo

Voices at night/carried across the blowing water.   In the Soul Hour.   Robert Mezey.   AmPA; NaP

The voices of the summer heat.   The Last Hour.   Ethel Clifford.   HBV 1-2

Voices speaking in the dark.   A Difficult Adjustment.   Lauris Edmond. FaBoWP; OCNZ

Void of wishing and repenting.   Dispraise of a Courtly Life.   Sir Philip Sidney.   FCP; LoBV; OAEP

Voidward from the adoring/Waste of souls.   Night Piece.   James Joyce. NoAm; PoA; SyP

A volley of cold blood/ramrodding the current.   Trout.   Seamus Heaney. CIP

Vomit your essence, Hercules. Be me: Let Heroes Account to Love.   Alan Dugan.   NoAm

Vor I do love noo tree so well/'S the girt woak tree that's in the dell.   The Girt Woak Tree That's in the Dell.   William Barnes.   HBV 1-2

Vor they be now my own, a-bound to me.   To Me.   William Barnes. NBM; PoEL 1-5

Voracious still/for the more unsuspecting/of the feathered young   Afternoon's Angel.   Seymour Mayne.   VWA

Votes for my Lord, and hates the thankless poor.   The Splendid Village. Ebenezer Elliott.   NBM; OBSV

A votive taper between us and God!   The Maid.   Katherine Bregy.   CAW; GoBC

Vous frapperez Falck avec 20 per cent.   A Political Despatch.   George Canning.   FaBoCo

...Vows herself accursed/If hence she dress herself but in his eyes.   Lucasta's Fan, with a Looking-Glass in It.   Richard Lovelace.   CaPo

Vows that pure Seed some harvest, are the snow.   Nam Semen Est Verbum Dei.   Louise Imogen Guiney.   CAW

The voyage, life, is longest made at home.   The Old Man of Verona. Claudian (Claudius Claudianus).   AWP; OBVE

Voyage through death/to life upon these shores.   Middle Passage.   Robert Earl Hayden.   AmNP; BPo; IDB; InPS; NoAm; PoBA

Vrom stwone to stwone the water's bed.   The Lost Little Sister.   William Barnes.   PoEL 1-5

The vulgar herd can never understand.   Epilogue.   Charles Baudelaire. AWP

Vve la Commune!   A Woman's Execution.   Edward King.   AA

...Vying and playing/and gossiping, trying hard to be heard.   Sparrows in College Ivy.   Edgar Wolfe.   AMV-81

W

W'en a feller's itchin' to be spanked.   When a Feller's Itchin' to Be Spanked. Paul Laurence Dunbar.   BALP

W'en dey 'listed colo'ed sojers an' my 'Lias went to wah.   When Dey 'Listed Colored Soldiers.   Paul Laurence Dunbar.   BPo

"W. W./Never more will trouble you, trouble you."   Peter Bell.   John Hamilton Reynolds.   OBNC; OBRV; Par

Wad be my queen, wad be my queen.   Address to a Lady.   Robert Burns. CEP

Wade in de water, children,/God's a-gwineter trouble de water.   God's A-Gwineter Trouble de Water.   Anonymous.   BoAN 1-2

Waft him more swiftly to the Stygian shores.   Epitaph: "See, one physician, like a sculler, plies."   Joseph Jekyll.   FaBoEE

Wafted in all directions O love, for friendship, for you.   Not Heat Flames Up and Consumes.   Walt Whitman.   NePA

Wafting like solace down their length of days.   Birthday.   D. H. Lawrence. NAs

Wafting your Charge to soft Parthenope!   On the Departure of Sir Walter Scott from Abbotsford, for Naples.   William Wordsworth.   EBEV; EnRP

Wag what's left of my tail, and we/roll for a new view.   Shaggy Dog Story. Frank Steele.   Str

...The wages/of dying is love.   Little Sleep's-Head Sprouting Hair in the Moonlight.   Galway Kinnell.   LCAP

Waging war like the lambkins.   It Was Wrong to Do This, Said the Angel. Stephen Crane.   AmP; LiTA; NePA

Wah wah weeeeeeeeeeeeeeee.   Jazz.   Carolyn M. Rodgers.   JB

Wai! springbok child/sleep for me.   Song of the Springbok Does. Anonymous.   PeSA

The waif appeal from lackland hearts/to Sallys name or perhaps anothers New Year's Eve, 1938.   John Frederick Nims.   MiAP

Wail, for the world's wrong!   A Dirge.   Percy Bysshe Shelley.   BoLiVe; DiPo; GTBS; MCCG; NOBE; OAEP; PoRA; SoSe; TEP; TrGrPo; WHA; WiR

A wail of sorrow down the time-washed years.   By Cobequid Bay. Alexander Louis Fraser.   CaP

Wail through the dreary midnight hour/Till waukrife morn.   Elegy on Captain Matthew Henderson.   Robert Burns.   PBBP

Wailed for the golden years.   Worlds on Worlds Are Rolling Ever.   Percy Bysshe Shelley.   TEP

Wailing an old man's fate, as if in pride/And heat of youth he had untimely died.   Madrigal: "Where shall I sorrow great."   Martin Peerson.   EnRePo

Wailing, on wings widespread for sudden flight.   The Owl.   Edward Davison.   PoA

Wailing what you knew–/the love of a stranger/a trapped fox grinning. Gerda, My Husband's Wife.   Eve Triem.   GP

Waillie, Oh Waillie, but love it is bonnie/A little while when it is new. Waillie.   Anonymous.   FSW

Wainwright! The Gloucester!   The Destroyer of Destroyers.   Wallace Rice. PAH

Wait and wait and wait to do/what only the dead find unnecessary.   To the Pay Toilet.   Marge Piercy.   GP

Wait but Death's night, and, lo! the great ball lowers.   A Snail's Derby. Eugene Lee-Hamilton.   FM

Wait for him. Why sweep them now?   Telling My Feelings.   Yu Hsuan-chi. BoWP

Wait for me.   There Are Three Bones in the Human Ear.   Anita Endrezze-Danielson.   STE

Wait for me, dear old days! I'm coming too.   The Grandson.   James Scully. NYBP

Wait for me wait for me   Spinning.   Al Purdy.   NOBC

Wait for the wagon,/And we'll all take a ride.   Wait for the Wagon.   R. Bishop Buckley.   BLSo; FSW; PSoN

Wait for those days, my friend, or get thee fresher flowers.   Sonnet XIV. Frederick Goddard Tuckerman.   QFR

Wait forever/shaken by the rain–/forever!   To an Elder Poet.   William Carlos Williams.   PoA

Wait on his bed and watch me/Till I fall.   End of The Affair.   Geoffrey Grigson.   GBL

Wait, Sir, and see how time will render you,/Who talk of vision but are weak of sight.   A Miltonic Sonnet for Mr. Johnson...   Richard Wilbur.   CAPP; TW

Wait thou within the silence dim/And thou shalt find Him there. The Indwelling God. Frederick Lucian Hosmer. WGRP

Wait 'til I git on my robe,/Oh, yes. Oh, Yes! Oh, Yes! Wait 'Til I Git on My Robe. *Anonymous.* BoAN 1-2

...Wait 'til they learn/I'm dropping out. Marks. Linda Pastan. NIP

Wait, till I come to thee! Ballad. Harriet Prescott Spofford. HBV 1-2

Wait till the Judgment-day. Wait for the Wagon. *Anonymous.* PAH

Wait until we drop down dead. There Are Bad Times Just Around the Corner. Noel Coward. DBV; NOBL

Wait yet awhile! Budding-Time Too Brief. Evaleen Stein. AA

Waited for the hands to move, not round/Her throat, but to her eager breasts? Alternatives. Kingsley Amis. OxBC

Waited with ale and girls for what came next! King Lot's Envoys. Drummond Allison. OBSP

The waiter brought spaghetti; he looked up,/Hemmed, blinked, and fiddled with his coffee-cup. Traumerei at Ostendorff's. William Laird. HBMV

"WAITER!!" "Yessir,' "Wake up, stupid! Biled calves' feet for/Number Two!' The Wail of the Waiter. Marcus Clarke. NOAV

A-waitin' for me–with a knife and fork. The Constant Cannibal Maiden. Wallace Irwin. OBAL

Waitin/to be/defended. Black Jam for Dr. Negro. Mari E. Evans. BPo; PoBA

Waiting around minutely, in baskets,/to be born again. The Roof of the World. Michael Dennis Browne. AmPA

Waiting brief for milkmaid mornstar and worldrise Anglosaxon Street. Earle Birney. HeIP; NOBC

Waiting, deserted, unfinished, as you mourn for this lost/garden. The Deserted Garden. Ann Stanford. AMV-81

Waiting for a fourth cremation. Sanctuary. Dorothy Hewett. CBAP

Waiting for a tropical sky. Poem: "While we were walking under the top." John Ashbery. EAS

Waiting for a wedding, mobbing a bride. Spring. W. R. Rodgers. OnYI

Waiting for carrots, staring, yearning in a row. Five Horses. May Swenson. PH

Waiting for lost travellers to come by. Outside Dunsandle. Sacheverell Sitwell. ChMP

Waiting for nothing to happen. Going to Sleep in the Country. Howard Moss. DFF; PoCh

Waiting for pups. Dame. Susan Astor. AMV-80

Waiting for something immense and unspeakable to uncover its face. Cloud River. Charles Wright. GeTw

Waiting for tea-time, and shadows growing longer. For Posterity. Kathleen Raine. NeBP

Waiting for the chance to run/home free. Roger and Me. Anne Le Dressay. AMV-81

Waiting for the end, boys, waiting for the end. Just a Smack at Auden. William Empson. FaBoCo; LiTM; MoBrPo; UnPo

Waiting for the flesh that dies. The Bull. Ralph Hodgson. AnFE; BrPo; LiTM; MoAB; MoBrPo; MoVE; OBMV; OxBTC

Waiting for the last collection before dark/The pillarbox like an exclamation mark. Eclogue between the Motherless. Louis MacNeice. FaBoIP

Waiting for the life to come.... What Is the Case in Point? Abraham Reisen. VWA

...Waiting/for the shoal he knows will come. Heron. Ted Walker. NYBP

Waiting for the Sleary babies to develop Sleary's fits. The Post That Fitted. Rudyard Kipling. CenHV; HBV 1-2; OnMSP

Waiting for whatever will/be at last the real end of you. Anger. Robert Creeley. CoPo; NaP

Waiting for Willie/To come back to me. Bird in a Cage (with music). *Anonymous.* AS

Waiting, I guess, for me to bring them Barbara. Abstinence. Kenneth Rosen. AmPA

Waiting in my sheath/only for your death. Guerrilla Promise. Mvula Ya Nangolo. WhB

Waiting, in their dark clothes, apart. An Elegy Is Preparing Itself. Donald Justice. HoPM

Waiting the dawn to fly its bird of god. Poem for Easter. Laurie Lee. BoC

Waiting thy advent, as I wait, in vain. Charmides (excerpt). Edmund St. Gascoigne Mackie. PeHV

Waiting till Oudinot enter, to reinstate Pope and Tourist. Amours de Voyage. Arthur Hugh Clough. GTBS-P; OBNC

Waiting till the Scarlet Hunter/Pass upon the endless trail. The Grave-Tree. Bliss Carman. CaP

Waiting to see if your wish comes true! Waiting. Ruth Apprich Jacob. BiCB

Waiting, waiting for rusted/trains in texas grass In Texas Grass. Quincy Troupe. PoBA

Waiting with thy master's wine. Odes. Horace. OBVE

Waitress lips are kissing/our cheeks Hurrah! Route. Joseph Ceravolo. ANYP

Waits but to burn the stem before her idol's throne. Progress of Unbelief. John Henry, Cardinal Newman. GoBC

Waits for crickets/to answer. Goat-Woman Dares. Judith Mountain Leaf Volborth. TWSS

Waits for me to open up the sky. Doorman. Martin Galvin. SUW

Waits jealously till children close their eyes. The Death Room. Robert Graves. NYBP

Waits on a stile. Though He That Ever Kind and True. Robert Louis Stevenson. BBV

Waits the asking;–wants no more. All Needs Met. J.H. Sammis. BLRP

Waits the last wisdom, the merging of the past with whole. Old Men. Nancy Keesing. BoAV

Wak'st Thou, O loving One?– The Virgin Mary to the Child Jesus. Elizabeth Barrett Browning. ISi

Wake, eat, and drink, evacuate, and sleep. Human Life. Matthew Prior. FaBoEE

Wake from sleeping; to the East turn, turn your/eyes! Exhortation: Summer, 1919. Claude McKay. CDC

Wake I, or sleep? The pickle-jar is void. Ode on a Jar of Pickles (parody). Bayard Taylor. BXAP; SpRo

Wake, if thou'rt sleeping still! On the Wall. Immanuel Di Roma. TrJP

Wake, little ladies! The sun is aloft. Minnie and Winnie. Alfred, Lord Tennyson. HBV 1-2; HBVY; NA; OxBChV

Wake up. Rise up. Recognize me. How Did He Get Here? Halper Leivick. VWA

Wake up rusting chain, Speak people of yonderland! The Rusted Chain. Yosef D. Ben Yeshaq. VWA

Wake you with her solemn strain,/And teach pleas'd Echo to complain. Solitude. James Grainger. OBEC

The wakeful bird that to the lighted window sings for dawn. Sonnets. Frederick Goddard Tuckerman. AP

Wakeful–sleepless with heart longing,/With desire–O! The Beloved's Image. *Anonymous.* WTO

Wakeful they lie. Counting the Beats. Robert Graves. DTC; ELP; GBL; GTBS-P; HAP; OxBTC; ViBoPo; WeW

Waken into falling light. Listen. Put on Morning. W. S. Graham. FaBoTw; LiTM; MP; NMP

Wakened to love and music. One Morning. Vassar Miller. AMV-80

The waker, slumber-sooth'd! The Spirit's Odyssey. M. Krishnamurti. PeD

Wakes every child and gladdens every mouse. The Hasty Pudding. Joel Barlow. AmPP

Wakes me, too–sleeping by the hedge–/To morning prayer! Creeds. Karle Wilson Baker. HBMV; WGRP

Wakes to the birth and bloom/Of life and light. The Annunciation. John Banister Tabb. ISi

Waking alive, meet, kiss and understand. Ask No Return. Horace Gregory. MoAmPo; VGW

A waking bugle it might be, a passing bell,/of life, death, life, life telling: it is all one. Spring Snow and Tui. Mary Ursula Bethell. AnNZ

The waking from a dream that Man calls–Life! Death. Florence Earle Coates. HBV 1-2

The waking truth in dying eyes, like frost. Lobotomy. Kenneth Pitchford. PoA

Waking up everybody's children. The Follies. Daniel Mark Epstein. MAYP

Wald slepe thee with/A night under shete. The Pointless Pride of Man. *Anonymous.* MeEL

Wales, full of gentlemen. The Shires. *Anonymous.* OxBM

Walk and talk with Jesus one of these days. Streets of Glory. *Anonymous.* FSW

Walk backward, with averted gaze,/And hide the shame! Ichabod. John Greenleaf Whittier. AA; AnNE; AP; APA; HBV 1-2; LiTA; NOBA; OxBA; PG; PoEL 1-5; TAP

"Walk, damn you, walk!" Walk, Damn You, Walk! William De Vere. PoLf

Walk down fifth avenue,hawkbill/in my hand. Imperial Thumbprint. Tom Weatherly. PoBA

...Walk hand in hand/each long and lovely day, the rutted rue. Poem: "Entombed in my heart." Margery Dodson. AMV-80

Walk in, enjoy my treasures. Gallery of My Heart. King D. Kuka. VoR

Walk, jaw-bone, Jenny come along,/In come Sally wid de bootees on. Walk, Jaw-Bone. Silas S. Steele. TrAS

Walk lean/Together. Today. Langston Hughes. VGW

WALK ON THE MATTRESSES;DON'T WAKE THE BABIES. Poem from Deal. David Shapiro. ANYP

Walk sadly up and down to kill the time. The Georgiad. Roy Campbell. OxBTC

...Walk slowly by/the hacked-out cots of silk/bog children. The Field. Jean Valentine. LCAP

Walk steady, dear, lest all be spilled. Verses. James Russell Lowell. `AP

Walk the moon, but see thy light. This New Day. Vail Read. AH

Walk the resounding way/To the still dwelling. Last Poems. Alfred Edward Housman. OAEP

Walk with everyone. Touch. Thom Gunn. CMoP

Walke, sot,/Rayle not to far. Gup, Scot! John Skelton. OxBoLi

Walked haphazard by starlight straight/Into the kingdom of heaven. BC : AD. U. A. Fanthorpe. OBCP

Walked in his garden in the cool of the evening, waited. Intimate Supper. Peter Redgrove. FaBoMo; OxBC

...Walking across the bridge/for water to be blessed at vespers. Weldon Kees in Mexico, 1965. David Wojahn. MAYP

Walking alone in the valley of the shadow of death. Song: "There is no joy in water apart from the sun." Ralph Nixon Currey. PeSA

Walking amid the mountains of his thought. Dedicatory. Mary Gilmore. BoAV

Walking under the dark pines,/a blue leather bridle in my hand. Poem: "This life like no other." Gregory Orr. AmPA

Walking around in a world which produces plenty. De Rerum Natura. Lucretius (Titus Lucretitus Carus). NAs

Walking around should be its own excuse. Walking Around. David Galler. AMV-81

Walking at night between the two deserts,/Singing. Air. William Stanley Merwin. AmPC; CAPP; CoPo; NaP

Walking backwards/into my life. The Bald Spot. Wesley McNair. AMV-81

Walking down through Laramie with Snagtooth Sal. Snagtooth Sal. Anonymous. ABF

Walking down to the sea &/back again. Round Dance, & Canticle. Robert Kelly. CoPo

Walking home, hunched over, in the rain. The Trip. Carl Dennis. AmC

Walking I come to you. Indian Death. Eda Lou Walton. BPAW

Walking in the speechless night. After Picking Rosehips. Harley Elliott. NeAC

Walking on the crown of the road. Suicide. Louis MacNeice. DTC

Walking on the sea. Miracles. Arna Bontemps. GoSl; PoNe

Walking out in all weathers to these parts. Where I Walk in Nebraska. Nancy G. Westerfield. AMV-80

Walking, shaken, in its sighs and shadows. Villa Sciarra: Rome. Christine Turner Curtis. GoYe

Walking slowly/like the sad Italian peasant/he was— New York City–1935. Gregory Corso. Psk

...Walking the hard straw-strewn beach. High Plains Harvest. Bruce Morton. AMV-81

Walking the moors, keeping apart/And quiet, like. Coroner's Jury. Leonard Alfred George Strong. OxBTC

Walking through the sky. Ts'eekkaayah. Mary Tallmountain. STE; TWSS

Walking to the river. Waiting to Be Fed. Ray A. Young Bear. CDW

Walks or flies but in its living grace. Now Sleeps the Gorge. Alistair Campbell. AnNZ

The wall has pulled them back/into itself,/and covered them over with blackness. At Night. Rachel Boimwall. VWA

The wall of learning has broken. On the Breaking-Up of a School. Tadhg O'g O'Huiginn. AnIL

The wall of the sea replies/with the host of names written on water. Etruscan Notebook. Elena Clementelli. PBWP

Wall, six be da poacher's limit anyway. Antoine and I Go Fishing. David Budbill. WOLT

The wall that stands a long, long time. A Story of How a Wall Stands. Simon J. Ortiz. MAYP

The wall will stand empty,/White as snow. The Shadow. Walter De la Mare. OnUR

Walloping up roads with the milk wagon. An Otter. Ted Hughes. BoC

...Walls ever say, "When we try, we can remember/those shadows"? Wall Shadows. Carl Sandburg. WSC

The walls of sapphire, the towers of burning gold. Burragorang. Nan McDonald. NOAV

Walls of the haunted Memory's arcade. Jardin du Palais Royal. David Gascoyne. MoPo

Walls that still hold the whole prints/Of ancient ferns. Living by the Red River. James Wright. NNaP

Walruses idled in the estuaries. Naked War (parody). Michael Heffernan. BXAP

Walsingham, oh, farewell. The Wreck of Walsingham. Anonymous. ACP

...Walt spat/sweet water and reeled in. Fishing with Buddies. Gary Eddy. WOLT

...Walt, we believe it:/Everywhere, everywhere. Camerados (parody). Bayard Taylor. Par; UnPo

Wan grew her cheeks, she closd her een,/Stretched her soft limbs, and dy'd. Sweet William's Ghost. Anonymous. AWP; BaBo; InPo

Wand'ring around from door to door/have a hard time Motherless Children. Blind Willie Johnson. BluL

Wander our thoughts above the dark abyss. Haunted Houses. Henry Wadsworth Longfellow. AnNE

Wander thou shalt unmarked, flitting forlorn/Among the shadowy, averted dead. Forever Dead. Sappho. AWP; LiTW

The wanderer there a home may find/Within the paradise of God. There Is a Land Mine Eye Hath Seen. Gurdon Robins. AH

Wanderers, chosen of God,/On, through the world! Chosen of God. Stefan Zweig. TrJP

The wanderers to thy fold restore. Dear Saviour, If These Lambs Should Stray. Abby Bradley Hyde. AH

wandering in the mystic rhythm/of jungle drums and the concerto. Piano and Drums. Gabriel Okara. NIP; PBA; TTY

Wandering lost in the night of London,/In the miraculous April weather. April Midnight. Arthur Symons. SyP

Wandering opals keeping tryst/With the rubies of the lime. Les Ballons. Oscar Wilde. NOBV; SyP

Wane, be at rest. Lady Moon. Christina Georgina Rossetti. OxBChV

Want and woe, which torture us,/Thy sleep makes ridiculous. The Humble-Bee. Ralph Waldo Emerson. AA; AmePo; AnNE; FM; GN; HBV 1-2; HBVY; LaNeLa; NOBA; OxBA

Want nothing else, except your wife. To Mr. C, St. James's Place, London, October 22nd. Alexander Pope. OBSP

Want of money makes us sad. Barney Bodkin. Anonymous. OxNR

"Want some tea?" Miss Bitter. N. M. Bodecker. NTCP

Want t' go t'hebb'n in de mo'nin'. O Ride On, Jesus. Anonymous. AH

Want to git your eye knocked out,/Git on the mountain mill. Jinny Git Around. Anonymous. OuSiCo

"Want to have little beds, and tables,/and everything else." As in the Old Days: Passages 8. Robert Duncan. PoM

The wanted collison. Night Driving. Sharyn November. AMV-80

...Wanting a longer unity to go back home to. Things Not of This Union. Linda Gregg. NPGG

Wanting a thousand little things/That time without contentment brings. What Shall I Give? Edward ("Edward Eastaway") Thomas. FaBoCh; LoGBV; OxBChV

Wanting so much to come home. The Mystery of the Caves. Michael Waters. GeTw; MAYP

The wanton laird of young Logie. The Laird o' Logie. Anonymous. CBEP; CH

War! Waste. G. A. Studdert Kennedy. EBCP

The war came down on us here. Galway. Louis MacNeice. OxBI

A war-embrace of wrestling life and death? What is Life? Samuel Taylor Coleridge. ERoP 1-2; FiP

War fails, try peace; put up the useless sword! Disarmament (excerpt). John Greenleaf Whittier. PGD

War has ended? No, the war has just begun. No Armistice in Love's War. Ralph Cheyney. PGD

The war in Spain has ended long ago/Aunt Rose To Aunt Rose. Allen Ginsberg. LiTM; NoP; VGW

War is kind. Do Not Weep, Maiden, for War Is Kind. Stephen Crane. AmePo; BiP; NOBA; OBWP; PAL

War's annals will fade into night/Ere their story die. In Time of "The Breaking of Nations." Thomas Hardy. AnEnPo; BoLoP; CMoP; CoBMV; EBEV; EnLit; ExPo; ForPo; GoTF; GTBS; HAP; LiTB; LiTM; LoBV; MMM; MoAB; MoBrPo; MoRP; NoAm; NOBE; NoP; OAEL 1-2; OAEP; OBEV; OBWP; PoL; PPP; QFR; SeCeV; TreF

War's dust-bin chariot drawing near. Sing, Brothers, Sing! W. R. Rodgers. MoAB; MoBrPo

War's end–/World's end–/Sullen Achilles. Thinking of Tents. Reed Whittemore. TAP

War's glorious art, and gives immortal fame. The Criminality of War. Edward Hilton Young. PGD

"The war will be over before your work is ready." Mendings. Muriel Rukeyser. SaC

War will hit you hard/coming at you like lions raging. Fury against the Moslems at Uhud. Hind bint Utba. WPOW

War with a thousand battles, and shaking a hundred/thrones. Maud. Alfred, Lord Tennyson. FaBoPV

Warbling your native foot-notes mild. I Went to See Irving Babbitt. Richard Eberhart. GLGT; OBAL

Warden, wilt thou softly close the gate/When thou knowest I leave my heart behind? The Lover's Farewell. James Clarence Mangan. IrPN

Ware of the lizard lieth lurking in the grass. Though Ye Suppose. John Skelton. CBEP; OBSP

Warheads of mushrooms round the filter-pond. Idylls of the King. Geoffrey Hill. FaBoPV

Warm as a kiss when love is kind. San Francisco Bay. Joaquin Miller. BPAW

...A warm breath/issues from the nostrils beneath/the mask of death. Summer Rain. Sir Herbert Read. LiTM

A warm full moon will rise/out of the mothering dust, out of the dry corn land. July in Indiana. Robert Fitzgerald. NYBP

Warm harmony along doth suit/Who gladly plays our golden lute.   Das Jahr Der Seele (excerpt).   Stefan George.   AWP

A warm place there for him and love and sleeping.   Old Farmer Alone. Robert P. Tristram Coffin.   MoLP

Warm plates and hot potaters.   Recipe for a Pleasant Dinner-Party. *Anonymous.*   FaBoUs

Warm rooms, soft speech, long years.   Historical Museum, Manitoulin Island. Lisel Mueller.   PoA

The warm rosebuds below.   The World-Soul.   Ralph Waldo Emerson. AmePo

Warm still with the life of forgotten men who made them.   Things Men Have Made–.   D. H. Lawrence.   NoAm; PCP

Warm them worms waitin' undergroun'.   The Yellow Bittern.   Tom MacIntyre.   CIP

Warm up to it. Never take care.   Life Must Burn.   John Hay.   NePoAm

...The warm way/mountains call us citizens in debt.   Turtle Lake.   Richard Hugo.   NPAW

...Warm with popcorn, icy/with strange motives, barbarous splendors!   Triple Feature.   Denise Levertov.   FF; NoP

Warmed again, you wait/while snowflakes swirl in golden double loops.   Quilt Song.   Mark Vinz.   GOYP

The warmest love that can grow old–/This is mother's love.   Mother's Love. F. Montgomery.   PGD

Warming our backs as it reaches west to the wide Barara/country.   The Djanggawul Cycle, 24.   *Anonymous.*   WTO

Warming their speckling bellies/On the turning, star-charged bottom.   Trout. Norman Hindley.   WOLT

Warms what one/can imagine to be its ears.   In Arizona.   Louis Zukofsky. NoAm

A warmth and a blossom/of a feeling, sweetly,/gladly, home.   Let Me Be Held When the Longing Comes.   Stephany.   BPo

A warmth as near as if the Sun/Were shining in your Hand.   To see her is a picture.   Emily Dickinson.   PeHV

Warmth, more warmth, I cry.)   Sketch for a Job Application Blank.   Jim Harrison.   AmPA; NoAm

Warmth of my life.   Alicante.   Jacques Prevert.   BoLoP

Warned by a speaking mare since turned silentiary.   Grotesques.   Robert Graves.   CMoP

Warned by that to give/each figure in the photograph/his living name. Epilogue.   Robert Lowell.   HaCAP

Warning no calm is without pain and death upon the flood?   Night Walkers. Kendrick Smithyman.   AnNZ

Warring in the narrows of this birth.   The Narrows of Birth.   William Everson.   PoM

Warring sighs and groans I'll wage thee!   Ae Fond Kiss.   Robert Burns. AnFE; BSV; ELP; ForPo; HBV 1-2; OAEL 1-2; OAEP; OBEC; OBEV; PoEL 1-5; PPP; SeCeV; TreFT; ViBoPo; WHA

The warrior took that banner proud,/And it was his martial cloak and shroud! Hymn of the Moravian Nuns of Bethlehem.   Henry Wadsworth Longfellow. PAH

Wars cannot change the shapes of continents.   The Geographers.   Karl Shapiro.   OxBA

Wars must right wrongs which Frenchmen have/begun.   The Shoemaker's Holiday.   Thomas Dekker.   EnLi 1-2

Was a butterfly.   Haiku: "The falling flower."   Moritake.   SoSe

Was a dream, but a dream.   The Childless Woman in Heaven.   Katharine Tynan.   BoC

Was a laughing elf-woman/Nobody could see!   Godmother.   Phyllis B. Morden.   BrR; SoPo

Was a mountain of things he intended to/do–Tomorrow.   Do It Now. *Anonymous.*   STF

Was a princely two-an'-six.   Two-An'-Six.   Claude McKay.   BANP; GoSl

Was a small child lost in the bush for ever more.   Australia.   Eve Langley. BoAV

Was a thing some of the people/who live on earth for a while/could believe in. The Man Who Invented Las Vegas.   Gerald Costanzo.   TAT

Was a tipple no stronger than toui.   Limerick: "Once a Frenchman who'd promptly said "oui'."   *Anonymous.*   TDH

Was adored of old the same/Through the Arab darkness then.   Toledo. Jose Zorilla.   CAW

Was afraid in the oft-repeated dream/Of what the tree might do.   The Oft-Repeated Dream.   Robert Frost.   PG

Was, at all hazards, to try to copy the Celt!   The Cult of the Celtic. Anthony C. Deane.   BXAP; NOBL

Was because Dan's mother's cousin's aunt was born in/Cushendall. Cushendall.   *Anonymous.*   WTO

Was born, born, born in Bethlehem.   Children, Go Where I Send Thee. *Anonymous.*   FSW

Was bound towards heaven, but died in the air.   Epitaph: "Sanquhar, whom this earth could scarce contain."   William, of Hawthornden Drummond. FaBoEE

Was but a drop in the world-melting flood.   The Second Brother.   Thomas Lovell Beddoes.   AtBAP

Was but buds or seeds just planted then.   A Child's Thought of Harvest. Susan (Sarah Chauncey Woolsey) Coolidge.   OHIP; PoSC

Was changed by the Flag to a man!   The Kid Has Gone to the Colors.   W. M. Herschell.   PoLf

Was dead and is alive. Amen.   The Task.   Ruth Pitter.   MoBrPo

Was dearer to my soul than its soul-life.   To My Mother.   Edgar Allan Poe. AP; LaNeLa; MAmP; MCCG; NePA; OxBA

Was eaten by the passing ass!   Three Poems.   Basho (Matsuo Basho). LiTW

Was ever a true-hearted man more constant to his love?   Colonel Sharp. *Anonymous.*   BaBo

Was ever lavish.   Genealogical Reflection.   Ogden Nash.   ALV; OBAL

Was ever such, in this wide world, another uncouth knight?   The Uncouth Knight.   Hugh McCrae.   PoAu 1-2

Was faithless, and I am undone.   A Pastoral Ballad in Four Parts.   William Shenstone.   CEP

Was far, far off expelled from this delicious nest.   The Castle of Indolence. James (1700-48) Thomson.   BSV; SeCePo

Was fluent and conspicuously wrong.   Epitaph: "Here lies a poet, briefly known as Hecht."   Anthony Hecht.   PoL

Was heaven sent.   Little Lyric (of Great Importance).   Langston Hughes. NLV; OBAL

Was his most righteous will, and be that will obey'd.   To the Memory of a Lady.   George, Lord Lyttelton.   OBEC

Was I enraged with you?...Well, that is ended...   Count Ten.   Bonaro W. Overstreet.   PoToHe

Was I not bred in Gloucestershire,/One of the Englishmen!   Oak and Olive. James Elroy Flecker.   HBMV

Was I wrong? Was I wrong?   Thought on June 26.   Raymond Mazisi Kunene.   WhB

Was in your cellar, rummaging for beer...   Fate With Devoted...   Arthur Davison Ficke.   AnEnPo

Was in your ears as ever in ours his lyre,/Once, ere the flame received him from the sea.   Dedication: To Edward John Trelawny.   Algernon Charles Swinburne.   VLP

Was innocent in soul compared with me.   The Circuit Judge.   Edgar Lee Masters.   FaBoEE

Was it a thorn that touched the flesh, or did/The pokeberry spit purple on my hand?   Sonnets.   Frederick Goddard Tuckerman.   MAmP

Was it divine?   Egoisme a Deux.   Louisa S. Bevington.   NOBV

Was it for this that Nature lost her wish/To make a man, and made, instead, a fish?   The Aquarium, San Francisco.   Victoria Mary (Vita) Sackville-West. SBG

Was it Goliath was too large,/Or only I too small?   I took my power in my hand.   Emily Dickinson.   NePA

Was it love she believed in?   As in Their Time.   Louis MacNeice.   PoL

Was it someone you thought you knew/Was it me or was it you?   Ballad for the Unknown Soldier.   Allan Taylor.   OBET

Was it truth, or illusion,/Or Adam Hope?   At the Bottom of the Well. Louis Untermeyer.   GoJo

Was just that I was leaving home and my folks were grow-/ing old. Christmas at Sea.   Robert Louis Stevenson.   BBV; BLPL; BrPo; CH; EtS; FaBoBe; FaBV; HBV 1-2; MCCG; MOS; OBTV; OBVV; StPo

Was killed/last night/by the police.   Outlaw.   John Giorno.   ANYP

Was laid in a tomb without a mark,/Ah me!   Song for "The Jaquerie". Sidney Lanier   AA

Was lout, son of lout, by old lout, and was da to a lout.   Blue Blood.   James Stephens.   MoAB; MoBrPo; OBMV; OxBI

Was made for/men   To Bobby Seale.   Lucille Clifton.   CNA; PoBA

Was made the lady of the May.   A Pastoral.   Nicholas Breton.   TrGrPo

Was Mag McGinty's bushtlefast,/That inded Grady's goat.   O'Grady's Goat. Will S. Hays.   PoLf

Was melody delycyus/For to here precyus/Of six menys song.   The Tournament of Tottenham.   *Anonymous.*   OxBoLi

Was Milam, and his death sublime/Linked with undying Liberty!   Ben Milam.   William H. Wharton.   PAH

Was never in this world ought worthy tride,/Without some spark of such self-pleasing pride.   Amoretti, V.   Edmund Spenser.   AAS

Was never said in rhyme.   Happy Insensibility.   John Keats.   GTBS; GTBS-P

Was never scene so sad and fair!   Melrose Abbey.   Sir Walter Scott. SeCePo

Was never wight so starkly made,/But time and years would overthrow.   Old Mortality.   Sir Walter Scott.   EnRP

Was no more than his due who brought good news from Ghent.   How They Brought the Good News From Ghent to Aix.   Robert Browning.   BeLS; BLPL; FaBoBe; FaFP; FaPoR; GN; HBV 1-2; HBVY; HoPM; MCCG; PaPo; RoGo; SpRo; TreF

Was no voice I knew.   Haiku: "into a forest."   Otsuji.   WSC

Was no whit the wiser when he swallowed the/words.   The Riddles.
Anonymous.   EnLit

Was often practically opaque.   Clerihew.   Edmund Clerihew Bentley.   NLV

Was once the old original tough cuss from Bitter Creek.   A Tough Cuss from Bitter Creek.   James Barton Adams.   PoOW

Was once the wisdom of the young.   On Reading Aloud My Early Poems.
John Williams.   WeW

Was one thing more we never did find out.   Loose Woman.   X. J. Kennedy.
WeW

Was permit of return petitioned? No   A Form of Epitaph.   Laurence
Whistler.   GTBS-P

Was pretty Polly Perkins of/Paddington Green.   Polly Perkins.   *Anonymous.*
ELP

Was sharp as a whistle of grass/in my green blood.   Summer.   P. K. Page.
PeCV

Was spent a gedderin bleeberries/Away on Kurkstan fell.   Bleeberrying.
Jonathan Denwood.   MoBS

Was that face by beauty's spell/To the honest soul of Nell.   Nell Gwynne's
Looking-Glass.   Laman Blanchard.   HBV 1-2

Was that human?/Went where?   The Suicide.   Joyce Carol Oates.   Psk

Was that "somebody" you?   Somebody.   *Anonymous.*   FaFP

Was the child that played in the streets of Rome.   Two Pictures.
Anonymous.   BeLS; BLPA; FaBoBe

Was the face of the plodding workman,/From the workshop down the street.
Christ the Carpenter.   Leslie L. Haskin.   BePJ

Was the great God of mercy which proved our redeem.   The Virgin
Unspotted.   *Anonymous.*   OBET

Was the journeyman tailor and the beautiful queen.   The Journeyman Tailor.
Anonymous.   BFSS

Was the one of the three who loved him best.   Three Loves.   Lucy H.
Hooper.   BeLS

Was the same information in Braille.   Limerick: "The breasts of a barmaid of
Crale."   *Anonymous.*   NOBL

Was the size of the Leith police.   The Leith Police Dismisseth Us.
Anonymous.   OxNR

Was the soul of the tailor that came from Mayo.   The Tailor That Came
from Mayo.   Denis A. McCarthy.   OnYI

Was the source of his/undisciplined stamina.   Against Winter.   Elaine
Feinstein.   VWA

Was the thought of duty done and the love/of his fellow-men.   Sherman.
Richard Watson Gilder.   AA

Was the world betrayed and ruined–was by woman's hand/set free.   Irish
Hymn to Mary.   *Anonymous.*   CAW

Was their passion for sex or reason a sharper/Edge to the great gift?–Yes.
Near the Death of Ovid.   Robert Conquest.   NoAm

Was there another Troy for her to burn?   No Second Troy.   William Butler
Yeats.   BrPo; CMoP; EnLoPo; GTBS-P; MBW 1-2; NoAm; NOBE; OAEL
1-2; OxBTC; PoEL 1-5; PPP; SeCePo; WeW

Was there ever any poor young girl/So crossed in love as I?'   Abroad As I
Was Walking.   *Anonymous.*   OBET

Was this coming-full-circle not the question they asked?   Thinking of Iceland.
Tom Paulin.   FaBoIP

Was this the thing Van Horne set out/To conquer?   Towards the Last Spike.
Edwin John Pratt.   OBCV

Was Time, the serpent, with his freezing stare.   The Hunt.   Babette Deutsch.
AnAmPo

Was waking in the glade.   At Common Dawn.   Vivian Locke Ellis.   CH

Was welcome still in the abundant household/of a loving Father.   Deacon
Morgan.   Naomi Long Madgett.   BlSi

Was woven (blessed be his name) by Bach.   The Climbing Rope.   Alice V.
Stuart.   PoSH

Was wringin oot his socks and sark/Wi wry thochts o the dyker!   A Border
Forecast.   William Landles.   PoSH

The wash and whip of brine.   Columbus Goes West.   William Hart-Smith.
BoAV

Wash clear our eyes that we may see/The sky within the blackberry.   The
Blackberry.   Norman Nicholson.   MoBrPo

...The wash of a liquid moon/against lean bows/Is in them, and sea stillness
and sea wonder.   Sea Words.   Mary Sinton Leitch.   EtS

Wash over me, God, with your wind and night,/And leave me clean and cool.
Wind in the Pine.   Lew Sarett.   TrPWD; TRV

Wash over their blood-hot feet with a springing crown of tears.   War.
Joseph Langland.   FF; MP; NePoEA; PoCh

Wash their hands, and drive back to town.   The Ballad of Longwood Glen.
Vladimir Nabokov.   NYBP

Wash themselves several times a day/washing after play   Thumbing Old
Magazines.   Gerald Vizenor.   VoR

Wash, with the crystal coolness of its rills,/Some mouldring abbey's ivy-vested
wall.   Landscape.   William Mason.   OBEC

Wash your hands now.   Warm Hands.   *Anonymous.*   OxNR

Washed blue/bluuuuuuuuuuuuuuu e   Two Tile Beaks.   Maria Amalia Fonte
Boa.   BoWoP

Washed my hair in willows/may also keep my heart.   Keeping Hair.
Ramona Wilson.   VoR

Washed white in the cold moonshine on gray cliffs.   Night Airs.   Walter
Savage Landor.   BoNaP

Washed with a wild and thin/despair of violin.   Always Before Your Voice
My Soul.   Edward Estlin Cummings.   AnFE; CoAnAm; LiTA; MoAmPo;
NePA

Washed with its stains in the blood of the brave!   God Save the Flag.   Oliver
Wendell Holmes.   FaFP; OHFP

An' Washington couldn't tell a lie,/In fourteen ninety-two.   Johnny's Hist'ry
Lesson.   Nixon Waterman.   FPL; PoLf

Wasn't that a pity and a shame?   Poor Little Jesus.   *Anonymous.*   FSW

Wasp bite Nobi on her conch-eye.   A Wasp Bite Nobi on Her Conch-Eye.
Anonymous.   OuSiCo

The waste of poetry, the waste of years.   No Answer.   Laurence Whistler.
MoVE

A waste of time, child. It's in the bone,/like tides and love.   Child with Shell.
Ronald G. Everson.   PeCV

The waste remains, the waste remains and kills.   Missing Dates.   William
Empson.   CMoP; CoBMV; ForPo; HAP; LiTB; LiTM; MoAB; MoBrPo;
MoPo; NoAm; NOBE; NoP; OAEL 1-2; UnPo; ViBoPo

A wastrel who can spend no more.   Heart Specialist.   Elias Lieberman.
ImOP

The wat'ry shore,/Is giv'n thee till the break of day.   Hear the Voice of the
Bard!   William Blake.   CBEP; ELP; EnPE; NOBE; NU; OBEC; OBEV

Watch.   Dream Songs.   John Berryman.   LCAP

Watch a red setter stretch and sink in cloud.   The Broken Home.   James
Merrill.   HaCAP; HAP; NoAm; NOBA; NYBP; PPP

Watch by this bed familiar except/For one strange sleeper. It is time we slept.
The Bed.   James Merrill.   NePoEA

Watch chearfully untill your Lord shall call./By a true...J.S.   An Elegie On
the Deploreable Departure of ...John Hull.   John Saffin.   SCAP

Watch em watching is wholly vain–/Where is your boy tonight?   Where Is
Your Boy Tonight?   *Anonymous.*   PaPo

Watch him stagger through night with the stars/In search of the blue light.
The Blue Light.   Tom Dent.   APU

...Watch it closely.   The Monument.   Elizabeth Bishop.   HaCAP; LiTA;
MoPo; NoAm; NOBA; PP; PPoe

...Watch its tail/flip over and under the rocker.   Titus, Son of Rembrandt:
1665.   Richard J. Lyons.   AMV-81

Watch me rise and go.   Piute Creek.   Gary Snyder.   CAPP; CoAP;
ConAP; NaP; NOBA

Watch my reflection in the water/see an enemy.   Change of Venue.   Jill
Clockadale.   AMV-80

...Watch now, even the night's/a womb that swallows shooting stars.   Those
Guyana Nights.   Richard Foerster.   SOTS

Watch now, or she'll be gone for ever/To the rocks by the brown sandy shore.
Little Fan.   James Reeves.   SO

...Watch out/you sons of bitches who would drive men and women/to the
fields where they can only die   Emergency Haying.   Hayden Carruth.
NNaP

Watch the wall, my darling, while the Gentlemen go by!   A Smuggler's Song.
Rudyard Kipling.   OxBChV; PoPle

Watch the waves/And the beautiful ships.   Shore.   Mary Britton Miller.
SUS

Watch us climb up, run down.   Circumambulation of Mt. Tamalpais.
Andrew Hoyem.   PoA

Watch us... ..join us.   A New Dance.   S. E. Anderson.   NBP

The watch we keep alone–for Love's/dear sake!   A Farewell.   Mary Ainge
De Vere.   AA

Watch where within a slow dawn lightens up another sky.   Immortality.
Susan L. Mitchell.   OnYI

Watch with us thro' dead of night–But expect the morning light.   The Wake
of William Orr.   William Drennan.   OnYI; OxBI

Watched by every human love.   Lay Your Sleeping Head, My Love.   W. H.
Auden.   BoLiVe; BoLoP; ChMP; CoBMV; LiTB; MoAB; MoBrPo; MoPo;
MoVE; SeCePo; TEP

Watched me a moment–and showed no surprise.   Apparition.   John Erskine.
HBMV

...The watched, the unshared–/Awaiting me–I!   The Bottle.   Walter De la
Mare.   MoPo

The watchers smiled in glad surprise.   The Oranges.   Abu Dharr.   TTY

Watches me; and will guerdon me, I trust.   Beatrice Has Gone up into High
Heaven.   Dante Alighieri.   GoBC

Watches the slow, sweet slipping from the unlidded moon.   Templeogue.
Blanaid Salkeld.   NeIP

Watching a tadpole turn into a frog.   A Big Turtle.   *Anonymous.*   SoPo

Watching a unicorn drinking the dew.   The Paint Box.   Emile Victor Rieu.
SO

Watching all the wheels go round.   Engineers.   Jimmy Garthwaite.   SoPo

Watching children at their Christmas mirth.   Winter Portrait.   Robert
Southey.   BoNaP

Watching decor become debris, and sunlight/sanding the floors already. Moving. Frank Steele. GOYP

Watching everything you do. You won last year. Come on. Hometown Piece for Messrs. Alston and Reese. Marianne Moore. OBAL

Watching/For the opening/Of the great, dark gate. Black Flags Are Fluttering. David Vogel. VWA

Watching for two-leaf pine/–spotting that design. Vapor Trails. Gary Snyder. CAPP

Watching from Heaven's window,/Leaning from Heaven's gate. The Watcher. Margaret Widdemer. HBMV; OHIP

Watching me, and judging me. In the Lane. Leonard Alfred George Strong. HaMV

Watching me bag groceries/for hours until my hands sweat. Shoplifters. Maura Stanton. MAYP

Watching me/Watching you/Watching it. To a Man in a Picture Window Watching Television. Mildred Weston. ELU

Watching that white whisper fill his green world. Brindabella. Douglas Stewart. PoAu 1-2

Watching the flushed schoolgirls playing hockey. Osmund Toulmin. Osbert Sitwell. AtBAP

Watching the fun/Of the Victory Ball. A Victory Dance. Alfred Noyes. EnLit; PoLf

Watching the grass that/has grown. Nothing Strange. Tom Kryss. NeAC

Watching the men who calmly watched my death. The Pigs. Geoffrey Lehmann. CBAP

Watching the same rain from our each window. Drought. David Holbrook. OxBTC

Watching the waterdogs/the last truck gone. Hunting. Gary Snyder. NOBA

Watching the whole creation drown/I muse, alone, on Ararat. Lakeshore. F. R. Scott. NOBC; OBCV

Watching the wilderness uproot the doorsill with a weed. Halibut Cove Harvest. Kenneth Leslie. CaP; NOBC

Watching them lurch down the street/Heavy with a funeral. Jane Austen at the Window. Patricia Beer. FaBoWP

Watching your blue day and another year/whisper past unclouded. Finding a Friend Home. Timothy Hamm. AMV-80

Watchman Death–eternal cown–/Crows the hour through Hobart town. Hobart Town, Van Diemen's Land. Hal Porter. NOAV

Watchmen of Zion, ye will not betray. Evening Prayer. Arthur Fitger. AWP

Water and ground in their extremity. The Peninsula. Seamus Heaney. FaBoIP

Water and seed. Puberty. Jon Wallace. AMV-80

Water astonishing and difficult altogether makes a meadow and a/stroke. Tender Buttons: Objects. Gertrude Stein. PBWP

A water bird, a gawky bird, a sing'lar bird, by jingo! The Flamingo. Lewis Gaylord Clark. NA

Water collects and then the writer's name appears on the/saucer: a fine gift. Four Stories. David Shapiro. ANYP

Water comes in from them, coming to us: foaming, spraying and/roaring, out on the sea! The Djanggawul Cycle, 6. *Anonymous.* WTO

Water flow and mirror me. Animal Kingdom. Sydney Clouts. PeSA

The water froze. The Hammam Name. James Elroy Flecker. BrPo; PeHV

Water, here touched by sunshine, here touched by the/eternal.... A Bather in a Painting. Ashton Greene. NePoAm

A water in a golden bowl. Ere the Golden Bowl is Broken. Anna Hempstead Branch. AnAmPo; AnFE; APA

The water in the air without support/Sustained in the serpent's eye. Goodbye to Serpents. James Dickey. NYBP

...Water/Is not to be buried, and the boulders will drift. Bucyrus. John Holmes. CrMA; NePoAm

Water of ancient morning/trembles in my heart. Madrigal to the City of Santiago. Federico Garcia Lorca. CAD

The water of that earlier board/To-night shall turn to wine. The Golden Wedding. David Gray. FaBoBe; HBV 1-2

...Water off a goddamned duck's back. Back. Angela McCabe. AmPA

The water over the rocks/is running clear and cold and pure. Appalachian Front. Robert Lewis Weeks. AmFN; NYBP

...The water/reflects the reeds and the reeds/move on their stalks and rattle drily. To a Friend Concerning Several Ladies. William Carlos Williams. VGW

Water rising and bubbling, splashing and roaring, spreading out/like the tide... The Djanggawul Cycle, 92. *Anonymous.* WTO

Water. Something we choke on. Family Album. Lonny Kaneko. BrSi

The water/spitting rust flecks like blood/on the cellblock floor/finally came back on. Food Strike. Michael Hogan. GP

Water survives its motions. Classic. Archie Randolph Ammons. NOBA

...The water/that Brightens while the sky goes duller. Beginning to Squall. May Swenson. RFM

Water them while our houses wither. Dufferin, Simcoe, Grey. Margaret Atwood. AMV-81

The water was too cold for us. Water. Robert Lowell. CMoP; HeIP; LCAP; NOBA; NoP; SM

A water-watched and river-radiant child. American Child. Paul Engle. AmFN

Water, wide water, greeness and green banks,/And water seen. The Netherlands. Samuel Taylor Coleridge. OBTV

Water will not mix with oil,/Nor vain with careless heart. Vain and Careless. Robert Graves. LOW

...The waters/Advance on the earth as the war tides recede. Just an Old Sweet Song. Donagh MacDonagh. CIP

The waters flow past, older, younger/Than he is, or I am. Youth. James Wright. NaP; NoP

"The waters hurtle through the flooded night..." A Country Walk. Thomas Kinsella. CIP; CMoP; NMP

The waters move & i am alive Hai. Stuart Z. Perkoff. VWA

The waters of the dark mists drop, drop. Incantation for Rain. *Anonymous.* ExPo

The Waterwitch Lurley hath done. Ich Weiss Nicht Was Soll Es Bedeuten. Heinrich Heine. AWP

A wave all white–so white–outside was leaping. The Fair Agnete. Agnes Miegel. CAW

The wave broke fresher, flinging on my lip/Some drops of salt. I shuddered, and turned away. Sonnets. Frederick Goddard Tuckerman. MAmP

Wave-cradled thus and wind-caressed. Song. Celia Thaxter. AA

Wave it, save it, evermore. Our National Banner. Dexter Smith. PAH

The wave may flow, the breeze may blow,/They'll carry me no more! Nanny's Sailor Lad. William Allingham. IrPN

Wave may not foam, nor wild wind sweep,/Where rest not England's dead. England's Dead. Felicia Dorothea Hemans. HBV 1-2

A wave of the great waves of Destiny/Convulsed at a checked impulse of the heart. Modern Love, V. George Meredith. NOBV; VLP

The wave-swept shore, and all the amplitude/Of air and sea, broodeth in starry vastness. The Coming of Night. Thomas Wade. ERoP 1-2

A wave that never finds the shore! Immortal. Sara Teasdale. WGRP

Wave-washed and green and mossy/As green can be! Aloha. William Griffith. HBMV

Wavering back and forth, back and forth/In their depths? A Mona Lisa. Angelina Weld Grimke. BlSi; CDC

A wavering vision entranced to glass and stone. Notre Dame Perfected by Reflection. Harold Witt. HoAn

Waves are circlets of little girls/embracing this world...as they play... Everything Is Round. Gabriela (Lucila Godoy Alcayaga) Mistral. PBWP

The waves carve your hearse and tomb/and toll your voyage out again again Frontispiece. May Swenson. CoAP; NePoEA

The waves laugh, like corn sway slenderly and beckon. Dublin Bay. Ewart Milne. NeIP

Waves, like the cool white hands/of my dreams, lift me, carry me home. Water. Judith McPheron. AMV-81

Waves, oak, earth and oak! The Ancient Briton: The Dance of the Sword. *Anonymous.* WaaP

The waves receded. The Door. Robert Graves. LiTB

Waves spreading out, spraying and splashing, caused by the/fish... The Djanggawul Cycle, 7. *Anonymous.* WTO

The waves, the strides, the feet on which I go? Tristan da Cunha. Roy Campbell. MoBrPo; MoVE; PeSA; RoGo

...Waves/Wash once again on straight and silent ground. It Should Be Easy. Mark Van Doren. CrMA

Waves we've loved in/and cannot claim The Wave. David Phillips. NeAC

The waves which have kept me from reaching you. To the Harbormaster. Frank O'Hara. ANYP; CoAP; MOS; PoM

Waving come back, come back again. Almost Ninety. Ruth Whitman. PCP

...Waving cool, green, shady,/over the (dancing now) African ladies. Sadie's Playhouse. Margaret Danner. PoBA

Waving its little handkerchiefs of steam. Train. Ken Smith. EAS

The way a dream is broken/the moment the sleeper knows he is dreaming. Afterglow. Jorge Luis Borges. NYBP

The way a look or a touch reveals its unexpected magnitudes. Prologues to What Is Possible. Wallace Stevens. LCAP; NePoAm

The Way conforms to its own nature. Tao Teh King. Lao Tse [or Lao Tzu]. ILwL

Way down South in Dixie, oh, boys, ho. Down South on the Rio Grande. *Anonymous.* CoSo

Way down yonder in the paw-paw patch. Paw-Paw Patch. *Anonymous.* FSW

The way eloquence carries hope, faith, and the 4th of July. The Pinta, the Nina and the Santa Maria. John Tagliabue. AmFN

Way, hay, and up she rises, Early in the morning! The Drunken Sailor (Early in the Morning). *Anonymous.* ShS

The way he used to do when he was five. Epitaph on a Madman's Grave. Morris Gilbert. YaD

Way, hey, and up she rises,/Early in the morning. What Shall We Do with a Drunken Sailor? *Anonymous.* FSW

...The way/his eyes beat and grow secret/under this strange love/shaken into me. Passing It On. Reg Saner. GP

The way I watched people/When I was small. People. Orhan and Halman Veli Kanik. LLLT

...The way/Lies open onward to eternal day. Destiny. Sir Edwin Arnold. PoLf

"Way o' the Lord."/"That's right." Vermont Conversation. Patricia Hubbell. CTBA

The way of a man with a maid! Gulls in an Aery Morrice. William Ernest Henley. PBBP

A way of greeting or sally to the world. Old People Working (Garden, Car). Gwendolyn Brooks. SaC

The way of the Sun/as to make them/blacker. A Poem for a Poet. Don L. Lee. PoBA

The way, on windy nights, linoleum lifts. The Old Couple. F. Pratt Green. OxBTC

Way over in the promised land. Where O Where Is Old Elijah? (with music). *Anonymous.* AS

The way swordblades/pierce a magician's box. Morning Song. Gregory Orr. MAYP

The way that I could not afford to go. Plain Fare. Daryl Hine. CoAP

The way the children cluster round/As thick as honeybees. The Ice-Cream Man. Rachel Field. SiSoSe; SoPo

The way the fire cooled to coal. Raven. Duane Niatum. STE

The way the pronoun you will turn dark verses bright. Starlight. William Meredith. NePoEA

The way the three of us walked/was a kind of steady weeping. After a Death. Gregory Orr. GeTw

The way they go shall be their way to perish. Psalm I. Sir Philip Sidney. FCP

The way to go and guide thee with mine eye. Tarry Ye. *Anonymous.* STF

The way to good is never late.' The Palmer's Ode. Robert Greene. CTC; EnRePo; OBSC

'Way up in de middle of de air. Ezek'l Saw de Wheel (excerpt). *Anonymous.* ExPo

"The way was He." Via, Veritas, et Vita. Alice Meynell. WGRP

The way was straight because thou mad'st it so. Washington. Geraldine Meyrich. OHIP

The Way which thou so well hast learn'd below. To the Pious Memory of the Accomplisht Young Lady Mrs. Anne Killigrew. John Dryden. LoBV; OAEL 1-2; PoEL 1-5

Way-worn and spent, another and the same! Another and the Same. Samuel Rogers. OBNC

...The way you/Don't know me, or I know you. Target Practice. Donald Finkel. NePoEA-2

The way you meant to be. Ode to Fidel Castro. Edward Field. CoPo

The wayfarer lost/whom he made to feel at ease. To a Hero Dead at al-Safra. Hind bint Uthatha. WPOW

...The ways/death consummates, like love. The Dying Gaul. Desmond O'Grady. BIrV

The ways of our lord/white as jasmine. Like Treasure Hidden in the Ground. Mahadevi (Mahadeviyakka). WPOW

A wayside hamlet on your twilit field... Your Burnt-Out Body. Peretz Markish. VWA

We a true part did take,/Soggarth aroon! Soggarth Aroon. John Banim. GoBC

We acknowledge each other with a glance. Prisoner Aboard the S.S. Beagle. Calvin Murry. LFAC

We advise you to wait patiently/for your prize/which will either come or not. Ordinance on Winning. Naomi Lazard. GP

We aging downstream faster than a scepter can check. Down the Nile. Robert Lowell. HaCAP

We ain't got no wheres to run to. The Warden Said to Me the Other Day. Etheridge Knight. FF

We all fall down. Ring-a-Ring o' Roses. *Anonymous.* OxNR; SpRo

We all hear his sighs but few hear his whistle. Storm at Sea. Sir William Davenant. RoGo

We all loved our comrade although he'd done wrong. The Cowboy's Lament. *Anonymous.* GBP; MaC

We all must eat our peck of gold. A Peck of Gold. Robert Frost. BPAW; LaNeLa; SO

We all must pay with the current coin/of life/For the honey that we taste. Jonathan. Rachel (Rachel Blumstein). TrJP

We all of us are worshiping/A little Holy Child. Midnight in Bonnie's Stall. Siddie Joe Johnson. PCh

We all scream for ice cream. Ice Cream Chant. *Anonymous.* NTCP

We all shall enter the earth. Ngoni Burial Song. *Anonymous.* PeSA

We all stare incessantly from/darkness to darkness soaring. Circle of Struggle. William Pitt Root. NYBP

We all want to cover our lives in our own hands/and hurl them out among the stars. Coasting toward Midnight at the Southeastern Fair. David Bottoms. AMV-81

We all were happier, if we all/Would copy Jolly Jack. Jolly Jack. William Makepeace Thackeray. HBV 1-2

We all would only drown/If we broke surface more than staying down. The Air in Spring. Basil Dowling. AnNZ

We and our bitterness have left no traces/On Munster grass and Connemara skies. The Dedication to a Book of Stories Selected from the Irish Novelists. William Butler Yeats. NAMP

We and our dolls being but the world were best away. She Turns the Dolls' Faces to the Wall. William Butler Yeats. LiTB

We apologize to Thee/For Thine own duplicity. "Heavenly Father," take to thee. Emily Dickinson. AmePo; ILwL; PoEL 1-5

We/Are/Alive. Prelude to Memorial Song. Phil George. VoR

We are all members of the goatherd Who I Am. Luis Da Gama. TTY

...We are all of us, after all,/seized with vertigo, pine for shade/and find none. Do Not Accompany Me. Shimon Halkin. VWA

We are all old-timers,/each of us holds a locked razor. Waking in the Blue. Robert Lowell. CoAP; HaCAP; MoAmPo; PPP; UnPo

We are all one to-day-/On with the cannon! Sumter. Henry Howard Brownell. MC; PAH

...We are all soiled with this desire, at the last moment,/the last. Drunken Americans. John Ashbery. HaCAP

We are alone, alone with what we are. The Attic. Henri Coulette. NePoEA-2; PoPl

We are Americans looking in the mirror of Africa. Black Trumpeter. Henry Dumas. PoBA

We are among you; we are going to stay. The Pleaders. Peter Davison. NYBP

We are as wind that may not be held. Appearance. Norman H. Russell. STE

We are asleep. Dead Still. Andrei Voznesensky. BoLoP

We are asleep, let us in. Peter. Michael Dennis Browne. NYBP

We are, awhile, like happy, armored men/God's searching whip of anger cannot sting! Jezebel. Scudder Middleton. HBMV

We are beautiful,/Winners. Take Tools Our Strength... Gerald L. Simmons, Jr. NBP

We are betrayed by what is false within. Modern Love: XLIII. George Meredith. AnFE; EnLoPo; HBV 1-2; InPo; NBM; NOBE; OAEP; OBNC; PoEL 1-5; SeCeV; TEP; VLP

We are blind to, a birdhood/to cover the head of the sky. The Ziz. John Hollander. VWA

We are born of everywhere are limitless. Our Movement. Paul Eluard. LiTW

We are both an indifferent ocean and people shouting. Windows in Providence. Aliki Barnstone. BoWoP

We are bound for California! Cape Cod Girls. *Anonymous.* AmSS; FSW

We are "Brothers-in-blood," and "Good/Hunting"/Is America's watchword to-day. Those Rebel Flags. John H. Jewett. PAH

We are busy with our flood. Flood. Irving Feldman. MP

We are called human. C'iao. Dick. Letter to Wagoner from Port Townsend. Richard Hugo. NNaP

We are close; we are clear. Each to Each. Melville Cane. GoYe

We are coming, Father Abraham, three hun-/dred thousand more! Three Hundred Thousand More. James Sloan Gibbons. PAH

We are crazy fellows,"..../Laughingly Love said. I Thought Joy Went by Me. Willard Wattles. HBMV

We are drawn to another light/farther down the road Tyranny of Moths. Gerald Vizenor. VoR

We are dying. When the Vacation Is Over for Good. Mark Strand. NYBP

We are each other's/magnitude and bond. Paul Robeson. Gwendolyn Brooks. CNA; PoBA

We are falling from this life/into the next. Havdolah. Susan Litwack. VWA

We are going to Havana forever! The Skyjacker. Stan Rice. NPGG

We are here by God's help to redress it. To Whom Shall the World Henceforth Belong? John Oxenham. WBLP

We are here, the red earth/passes like light into us/and stays. Red Clay. Linda Hogan. TWSS

We are his, as well as thou. A Christmas Prayer. George Macdonald. PCh; SUS

We are holy, holy, holy. The Salt Pork. Robert Clayton Casto. HeIP

We are just like you, except we got caught. Untitled. Mark Rahschulte. AMV-80

...We are Kay/And Gerda, under a white tent. June. Mebdh McGuckian. FaBoIP

We are laced in dark arms/until morning Auras on the Interstates. Gerald Vizenor. STE

We are learning to make fire   Habitation.   Margaret Atwood.   BoWoP; FaBoWP

We are lost, must/Wizard a track through our own screaming weed.   The Womanhood.   Gwendolyn Brooks.   BALP

We are lucky that we had him for three years.   Thanksgiving, 1963.   Molly Kazan.   TreFT

We are making/back from ireland lake   Ireland Lake.   Robert Hershon.   NeAC

We are many, our bed smells of hay.   Marriage.   Robert Lowell.   NAs

We are marching to Pretoria,/Pretoria, Hurrah.   Marching to Pretoria.   *Anonymous*.   FSW

...We are no more than tiny clusters of/dots, carefully placed together without touching.   Seurat.   Ira Sadoff.   PoDr

We are not afraid of you, we will come out/And gather with you.   Snowfall: A Poem about Spring.   James Wright.   LCAP

We are not/alone   Glenpool.   Annette Arkeketa West.   TWSS

...We are not here.   The Insects.   Nancy Willard.   LCAP

We are not, nor we were not, heard at all.   The Fabulists.   Rudyard Kipling.   ChMP

We are on our knees/everyday to find on the ground/what we'd lost to the sky.   Mile Hill.   Dennis Schmitz.   LCAP

"We are One!"   America to Great Britain.   William Allston.   AA; HBV 1-2

We are one./and are strong.   Upon Your Leaving.   Etheridge Knight.   NeAC; NNaP

We are only the bed, not the source or the giver.'   In October....   Michael Hamburger.   NePoEA

We are our own Deity and Judge and Law.   We.   Vladimir Kirillov.   LiTW

We are paddling fast, we are close to land, to Port Bradshaw.   The Djanggawul Cycle, 12.   *Anonymous*.   WTO

We are perceiving an enemy/to Me, You, Us, and Them.   The K.K.K. Disco... Noah Mitchell.   LFAC

We are precisely like a double nut/Under a single shell.   Sweet Boy, Gentle Boy.   Alexander Pushkin.   PeHV

...We/are ready to follow him to night or death.   Prelude.   Stefan George.   WaaP

We are sailing on skeletal eerie craft over the buoyant ocean.   November Day at McClure's.   Robert Bly.   NU

We are sailing westward, homeward; our/western home is near.   Wild Eden.   George Edward Woodberry.   AA

We are samurai and hustlers/in the rain   Samurai and Hustlers.   Joe Johnson.   CNA

We are satisfied if you are; but why did/I die?   Losses.   Randall Jarrell.   AmP; CoBMV; HaCAP; LCAP; LiTM; MoVE; OxBA; PoA; TAP; UnPo; WaP

We are screaming,/we are flying,/laughing, and won't stop.   Witch.   Jean Tepperman.   NMM

We are Shakespearean, we are strangers.   Dogs are Shakespearean, Children Are Strangers.   Delmore Schwartz.   NoAm

We are so grafted on His wood.   Barnfloor and Winepress.   Gerard Manley Hopkins.   ACP; CAW

We are so prone to these things with our terrible notions/of duty.   Amours de Voyage.   Arthur Hugh Clough.   GTBS-P

We are so weak. O pity our small size.   O Pity Our Small Size.   Benjamin Rosenbaum.   TrJP

We are still sailing under the same flag.   Commentaries on the Song of Songs.   Judith Herzberg.   VWA

We are such friends.   I Have a Friend.   Anne Spencer.   CDC

...We are such stuff/As dreams are made on, and our little life/Is rounded with a sleep.   The Tempest.   William Shakespeare.   DiPo; FaBV; LiTB; PG; TreF; WHA

We/are thankful/for steel.   Five Men Against the Theme "My Name is Red Hot....."   Gwendolyn Brooks.   CNA

We are the children of night   Children of Night.   Richard Shelton.   FiCP

We are the famous Younger brothers and we spare no time to pray.   Cole Younger.   *Anonymous*.   AmFP; BeLS; BFSS; FSW

"We are the ghosts of the blossoms/That died in the early spring."   Ghosts.   Richard Kendall Munkittrick.   AA

We are the holy sunlit wanderers/and we leave gifts behind.   The Ajax Samples.   Laura Jensen.   LCAP

We are the hosts of those who swear:/It shall not be again!   Apparitions.   Thomas Curtis Clark.   PGD; TRV

We are the love that we pursue/Reflected in each other's gaze.   Ascendancy.   Herbert A. Simmons.   NBP

We are the strong women.   A Freedom Song for the Black Woman.   Carole C. Gregory.   BlSi

We are the University.   I Am the Dean of Christ Church, Sir.   Cecil Arthur Spring-Rice.   NOBL

"We are the voice of God," I cried.   The Voice of God.   James Stephens.   WGRP

We are the war-born. What are we to do?   Sonnet: "Where are we to go when this is done?"   Alfred A. Duckett.   PoBA; PoNe

"We are the Witnesses!"   The Witnesses.   Henry Wadsworth Longfellow.   AtBAP

We are there in our hundred thousand pieces!   Fingers in the Door.   David Holbrook.   NePoEA-2

...We are they/whom the gods harm not.   To One Elect.   S. Ichiye Hayakawa.   PoA

We are thine acknowledged people,/thou our acknowledged Lord.   For We Are Thy People.   *Anonymous*.   TrJP

We are thirsty and/have the patience of animals.   Customs.   Juan Gelman.   VWA

... We are/to this child's sun the silent morning star.   Sonnet: "Three silences made him a single word."   Richard P. Blackmur.   PoA

We are together at last, though far apart.   The Ecclesiast.   John Ashbery.   ANYP

We are too poor to get away.   Dakota Land.   *Anonymous*.   AS; BPAW

...We are using our own skins for wallpaper and we/cannot win.   Dream Songs.   John Berryman.   HaCAP; NoP

We are very careful/stop only for gas.   Crossing West Texas (1966).   Kell Robertson.   TAT

We are waiting to fill/all thirteen.   Going through Changes.   Jean Tepperman.   NMM

We are weaving–still weaving.   Weavers.   Heinrich Heine.   TrJP

We are wed to one eternity.   Invitation to Eternity.   John Clare.   NCEP; PoEL 1-5

We are well there is no news./Dad.   A Father in Tennessee.   J. Edgar Simmons.   TAT

We are what we are, and only life surprises.   Foreign Affairs.   Stanley Jasspon Kunitz.   LiTM; NYBP

...We are your brothers and sisters/only a minute away, a second, a song...   A Paragraph.   Hayden Carruth.   FAZ

We are your eager hosts.   News of a Baby.   Elizabeth Riddell.   BoAV

We are your hope.   Neutrality.   Sidney Keyes.   MoAB; MoBrPo

We ask: and wait.   A Harrow Grave in Flanders.   Robert Offley Ashburton.   HBV 1-2

We ask for peace.   Surrender.   Angelina Weld Grimke.   CDC

We asked the cyclone/to go around our barn/but it didn't hear us.   The Man in the Street Is Fed.   Carl Sandburg.   OxBA

We assume/you did not know we loved you.   We Assume: On the Death of Our Son, Reuben Masai Harper.   Michael S. Harper.   AmPA; GeTw; LCAP

We ate our breakfast lying on our backs/Because the shells were screeching overhead.   Breakfast.   Wilfrid Gibson.   OBMV; OxBTC

We await in fear/the new beginning.   No Dawns.   Julianne Perry.   PoBA

We awake among the blest.   In Sorrow.   Thomas Hastings.   AA; HBV 1-2

We awake and are renamed.   Dedication.   Richard Stull.   AMV-81

We backed The Tetrarch and got drunk together.   Sporting Acquaintances.   Siegfried Sassoon.   OxBTC

...We bask in the light/and pass the pipe around.   How Night Falls in the Courtyard.   Christine Rimmer.   AMV-80

We be not brought in tribulation/By the next synod of the nation.   The Dissenters' Thanksgiving for the Late Declaration.   *Anonymous*.   APAS

We begin banking foundations for the long winter.   Autumn.   William Carpenter.   Psk

We begin to hear the noise of the world again.   City Walk-Up, Winter 1969.   Carolyn Forche.   MAYP

We believe without belief, beyond belief.   Flyer's Fall.   Wallace Stevens.   MoAB

We belong now to you.   The Marriage Dance.   Eda Lou Walton.   BPAW

We bend our beer cans like dummies, and sit.   Meeting My Best Friend from the Eighth Grade.   Gary Gildner.   SM

...We bend, we pick up stones.   The Moon Ground.   James Dickey.   MOON

We bent to the paddles.   Drifting.   Kathleen Spivack.   IHMS

We beseech of Thee this help and mercy for Christ's sake.   A Prayer for the Household.   Robert Louis Stevenson.   TRV

"We betrayed me."   Dream Songs.   John Berryman.   CAPP

We better shall by far hold out,/Till the next Year she face about.   The New Year.   Charles Cotton.   GoTL

We bid thee welcome to thine earthly home!   A Welcome to Dr. Benjamin Apthorp Gould.   Oliver Wendell Holmes.   ImOP

We blossom and ask no reason,/The Lord of the Garden knows.   Roadside Flowers.   Bliss Carman.   HBMV

We bomb ourselves back/To the stone age.   More (parody).   Philip Appleman.   BXAP

...We borrowed bit by bit,/until your borrowed life was gone.   Uncle Jack.   David Kherdian.   FAZ

We both know all we can ask/Is to pass God's steady test of endurance.   Poem for John My Brother.   William Aberg.   LFAC

We both together there will dwell?   To My Setter, Scout.   Frank H. Seldon.   BLPA

We both weep at the end of his stories. Christmas Eve. Ted Kooser. GP

...We both were held divine/In Egypt these, man once in Palestine. Man and Cows. Andrew Young. EBEV

We bowed each other entry through the doorway. The Devil and the Angel. Rosemary Dobson. BoAV

We bowed our heads, we closed our eyes/To the mercy of the flies. First Death. Donald Justice. FiCP; SM

We brag upon his chuck and act/Like perfect gentlemen. The Roundup Cook. Robert V. Carr. BPAW; PoOW

...We brain–We heart–We will. We Heart. Laura Chester. NPGG

We brought in no prey to Fionn/but the berries of the tree and two swine./ Swineherd. The Wry Rowan. *Anonymous.* OnYI

We build up nations–this my axe and I! The Axe of the Pioneer. Isabella Valancy Crawford. CaP

We build with Thee, O grant enduring worth/Until the heav'nly Kingdom comes on earth. Builders. Purd E. Deitz. TRV

We buried him down by the river/Where the larks and the whippoorwills sang. Johnny Stiles; or, The Wild Mustard River. *Anonymous.* OuSiCo

We buried him there on the lone prairie. Bury Me Not on the Lone Prairie. *Anonymous.* BPAW; FaBV; FaFP; FSW; TrAS; TreF

We burn this city every day. Coming Home, Detroit, 1968. Philip Levine. TAT

We busse our wantons, but our wives we/kiss. Kissing and Bussing. Robert Herrick. OAEP

We by a quiet graveyard wall,/For love and pity, buried you! A Machine Hand. Thomas Ashe. OBVV

We call for valiant-hearted men. Great Day. *Anonymous.* FSW

"We call not your weak and your lame!" The Waste of War. William L. Stidger. PGD

We call our language Mother Tongue. Father Land and Mother Tongue. Samuel Lover. HBV 1-2

We call the tit's wee lodge a nest. The Difference. Tadhg Dall O'Huiginn. BIrV

We called him wild; but the plover/Watched him, and was tame. The Escape. Mark Van Doren. MoAmPo

We can enjoy the merely/Actual: a good thing for verse. Seal Rocks: San Francisco. Robert Conquest. PP

We can fly to knowledge/Without ever going to college. To Hell with Commonsense. Patrick Kavanagh. CIP; FaBoTw

We can love only the drowned Interview with a Tourist. Margaret Atwood. IHMS

We can manage it for ourselves, thanks/From now on. Progression of the Species. Brian W. Aldiss. FF

We can never hope to be a happy nation. Letter to the Governors, June 8, 1783. George Washington. TRV

"We can supply you with a cradle too." Under the Willow-Shades. Sir William Davenant. BoLoP; ELP

We can't have heaven crammed! We Are God's Chosen Few. Jonathan Swift. TRV

...We can't/say surely what we've undergone,/and need to know, and need to know. Our Strange and Lovable Weather. William Matthews. NPAW

We can't see it, but we feel it all the time. Passage. Richard Eberhart. FAZ

We can weave nothing. Death Bed. Thomas Kinsella. CIP

We cannibals must help these Christians. The Savages. Josephine Miles. LiTM

We cannot all be/Martin Luther King. Look at That Gal. Julian Bond. PoNe; TTY

We cannot be free of each other. My Great-Grandfather's Slaves. Wendell Berry. GeTw

...We cannot/Forget our pride, our faces, our common love. Do They Whisper behind My Back? Delmore Schwartz. LiTA

We cannot hear each other speak. I Wage Not Any Feud with Death. Alfred, Lord Tennyson. PPON

We cannot remember them/Clearly enough. We never will. The Dead. Mark Strand. HeIP

We cannot see what we do. Radar. Alan Ross. DFF; FF

We cannot wish for more. Hymn. John Chadwick. TrPWD

We carry ourselves for candles. How Beautiful You Are: 3. Elaine Edelman. IHMS

We celebrate her feast with our caps on,/whom God has not visited. Dream Songs. John Berryman. NaP

We choose to say goodbye against our will. Departing Words to a Son. Robert Pack. GOYP

We circled home, that last day before snow. Two Lives and Others. Winfield Townley Scott. PoPl

We claim the ordinary Good and in the name of Love love to be cruel. Bottom's Dream. Philip Dow. NPGG

We clang the dull and sodden speech of men. To the Memory of Yale College. Howard Phelps (Phelps Putnam) Putnam. AnAmPo

We clasp upon the stroke, kissing with happy cries. New Year's Eve. John Berryman. LiTM; NMP

We cling to our frosty vapors and/Melt it with hate-heat eyes for warmth. The Languages We Are. F. J. Bryant. NBP

We close wire gates when we leave. Looking at Power. Warren Woessner. AMV-80

We come bearing supper,/our heads on fire. Paper Matches. Paulette Jiles. NOBC

"We concreted the dam," Bert said./Thanks. Requiem for a River. Kim Williams. RFM

We conquer fate and half forget our tears The Mockery of Life. Wilfrid Scawen Blunt. VLP

We conquer only in that sign. Fling Out the Banner! George Washington Doane. AH

"We consecrate ourselves to them, the Con-/secrated!" Lincoln at Gettysburg. Bayard Taylor. PAH

...We continue/talking, growing nervous, drinking/too much coffee. Prayerwheel/2. David Meltzer. NeAP

We continue their life, fearing their style. Family History. Wendy Bishop. AMV-81

...We could be hams/curing in the shade, good to eat. Report from the Correspondent They Fired. David McElroy. AmPA

We could fit/A body into a finger-ring, for a keepsake forever. Counting Small-Boned Bodies. Robert Bly. CAPP; EAS; NaP

We could get there if we didn't have to eat. If We Didn't Have to Eat. Nixon Waterman. FiBHP; OBAL

We could have been desperate lovers met too late. Tableau. Judith Wright. CBAP

We could live on this Earth/without clothes or tools! By Frazier Creek Falls. Gary Snyder. InPS

We could sleep easier in our beds at night. Courtyards in Delft. Derek Mahon. FaBoIP

We couldn't think what to say back. Our Silly Little Sister. Dorothy Aldis. EvOK

We couple in the grace/of that mysterious race. Poem: "At night Chinamen jump." Frank O'Hara. NoAm; NOBA; SM

We crack. We roll away/in waxed limousines, leaving/it all, all, all to the wind. Funeral. Joanna Thompson. AMV-81

We crept in the tall grass and slept till noon. 1916 Seen from 1921. Edmund Charles Blunden. MMM

...We crewed with Arc-/turus, Vega, Polaris,/tacking into the dark. Offshore. Philip Booth. SD

We croon, "yeah." Nigger Song: An Odyssey. Rita Dove. AmPA

We cry, as to the wanderer for a night–/"Good-by." Good-By. Grace Denio Litchfield. PoToHe

We cry (however I whisper) against it (into the westwind). Dana Point. Brewster Ghiselin. AMV-81

We cut the deck, and dealt another hand. Continental Crossing. Dorothy Brown Thompson. AmFN

We cut, to make wit's reputation,/Our total of two friends by half. No Mean City. Patrick MacDonogh. BIrV; OBSP

An' we'd all had a mind to attack–from behind–/That cowardly scoundrel– McGuire. Fighting McGuire. William Percy French. CenHV

"We'd better leave him in the sump," he said. Mending Sump. Kenneth Koch. BXAP; HeIP; InPK; NeAP; NoAm; PV

We'd better leave it up to God,/And save a sad mistake. A Comparison. *Anonymous.* STF

We'd die together shot down by one shot. No More Words! To the Field, to Arms! Veronica Franco. PRWP

We'd make a fairer fairer world of it. Fair and Unfair. Robert Francis. VGW

We'd met, but not as wont we'd met. Not as Wont. Joseph Skipsey. NOBV

We'd not be lying in these vaults. Epitaph: "Here lies I and my three daughters." *Anonymous.* FaBoEE

We'd prospect there for sulphurets–and find 'em, too. Hey,/Prunes? Me and Prunes. Rupe Sherwood. PoOW

We'd the fortune to find them, and homeward to bring/The tidings, a tribute to country and king. The Dolphin's Return. *Anonymous.* OBSS

We dance to many a measure,/That earth never knew. The Others. Seumas (James Starkey) O'Sullivan. AnIV; HBMV; OxBI

We dare not think too long on those who died,/While still so many yet may come to birth. Two Lives. William Ellery Leonard. AnAmPo

We dared not beg you, with one sigh, to stay/Or turn from your discoveries aside. The Scholar. Frances Cornford. BrRo

We dead, in a ship that is dead, becalmed.' Becalmed. John Blight. BoAV; PoAu 1-2

We declare our strength and affirm our might! Rekayi Tangwena. Mudereri Kadhani. WhB

We delighted in the forest. My Sweetheart in the Rippling Hills of Sand. Princess Likelike. WTO

"We Deliver." The Cropdusting (parody). William Zaranka. BXAP

We deviate straight forward to immortal death. Little Ode. Paul Goodman. PoA

We did not look back at the mountains. Crossing. J. Robert Oppenheimer. SUW

We didn't do it–tho'! He Was Weak. Emily Dickinson. PeD

We die of vertigo. Mother Goose's Garland. Archibald MacLeish. OBAL

We died because the shift kept holiday. Epitaphs of the War, 1914-18. Rudyard Kipling. BrPo; OBWP

"We do not know," he said,/"Nor may till we be dead." Wisdom. Ford Madox Ford. HBV 1-2

We do not know them/we never recognize the/36 just men The Lamed-Vov. Rose Auslander. VWA

We do not lack for grace. In a Desert Town. Lionel Stevenson. AmFN

We do not recognize in the brief passing/the dim, distorted image is our own! Image in a Mirror. Mae Winkler Goodman. GoYe

We do not understand, we do not follow. How They Came from the Blue Snows. Arnold Kenseth. PPON

We don't celebrate farts no mo. Rebolushinary x-mas/eastuh julie 4/ etc. etc. etc. etc. Carolyn M. Rodgers. JB

We don't debate./We just give in. The Velvet Hand. Phyllis McGinley. TreFT

We don't know if we remember. Amnesiac. Mark Osaki. BrSi

We don't know/We're asking Land of the Free. Archibald MacLeish. AmFN; MoAB

..We don't really/know them; Coyote, as mentioned before. For Don Allen. Gary Snyder. PoA

We don't: we take things as they are. Lying Awake. W. D. Snodgrass. HoPM; MoAmPo; NYBP

We dream/dreams inside dreams. It Is Finished. Barney Bush. STE

We drew a circle that took him in! Outwitted. Edwin Markham. AnAmPo; BLPA; ELU; FPL; GoTF; MCCG; MoAmPo; TreFT; TRV

We drive past, our speed accelerating./We disappear./We return. Dreaming America. Joyce Carol Oates. GeTw

"We drowned your half-brother. I remember we did." By the Exeter River. Donald Hall. MoBS

We dy'd, thou onely liv'dst that day. Epitaph: On Sir Walter Rawleigh at His Execution. Anonymous. OBS

We each put out an empty hand,/Longing for something to forgive. Father to Son. Elizabeth Jennings. GOYP

We eat it now/Even as we did/in Egypt. The Bread of Our Affliction. Martin Grossman. VWA

We eat the smile/And spit out the teeth. Watermelons. Charles Simic. OBAL; PPJ

We end in joy. The Moment. Theodore Roethke. NYBP

We end our journey 'mong the dead. Welcome, Thou Safe Retreat! William Habington. OxBoCh

We ended by melting away,/hating the air! Poets Hitchhiking on the Highway. Gregory Corso. AmC; NeAP; NoAm; PoM

We endure./We sing. Morning Vigil. Phil George. VoR

We enter the FLOOD For Sergeant Fetta. Ed Sanders. ANYP

...We enter the world of daylight/Blind and unable to find home. World of Darkness. Robert Chatain. PoA

...We escape/Down the cloud ladder, but the problem has not been solved. Our Youth. John Ashbery. CAPP; ConAP; SOTW; VGW

We even flew a little. A Pity. We Were Such a Good Invention. Yehuda Amichai. BoLoP

We ever remove our hats. Old King Cabbage. Richard Kendall Munkittrick. OBCA

We face a glacial distance, who are here/Huddl'd/At your feet. A Christmas Tree. William Burford. NePA; SoSe

We fail the sick, but still may raise the dead. Journal. John Ciardi. PoA

We fan the gold o' the corn,/In the sun's heat. Hymn to the Winds. Joachim Du Bellay. AWP

We fear to change the old, established way. On City Streets. Margaret E. Bruner. PoToHe

We feared a love so like a fear. Chameleon. Paul Engle. CrMA

...We feed/on flesh whose bone we loved too well. Hunger and Thirst. John Peale Bishop. PoA

We feel that we are greater than we know. After-Thought. William Wordsworth. EnL; OAEP; OBNC; OBRV

We feel very sorry for Sally every week, and we don't mean to/dirty our dresses so much any more. The Dolls' Wash. Juliana Horatia Ewing. OxBChV

...We felt the bloom/of veldt and jungle flow through the room. Far from Africa. Margaret Danner. AmNP; PoBA

We felt the South still had some sons/She would not scorn to bury. Mosby at Hamilton. Madison Cawein. PAH

We few will finish the wine/and skulk out on this spring night/together, unsafe on Capitol Hill. At a Private Showing in 1982. Maxine W. Kumin. SV

We figure: why should a dog be different? Arf, Said Sandy. Charles Stetler. PPJ

We /finally contrived to/move/into the chilling,/sad, September night. When All of Tem Ran Off. John Hollander. AmPC

We find; content, content! Content. Dora Greenwell. PoToHe

We find our happiness, or not at all! The French Revolution. William Wordsworth. ERoP 1-2; FiP

We find the crabbed certainty of our true beginnings. Our True Beginnings. Wrey Gardiner. NeBP

We find the thing we call success. Success. Anonymous. FaFP; PoToHe

We find thy name and empty monument. Sopolis. Callimachus. AWP

...We find/you wear a girl's/bonnet behind? Sunflower. John Updike. BoNaP; GrPl

We first endure, then pity, then embrace. Vice. Alexander Pope. ELU; PoPl

We first must sin, before we can Repent. Tho' You May Boast You're Fairer. Anonymous. OBS

We flee, wing-clipped sparrows,/From the thud. The Last Flight of the Great Wallenda. Barbara Helfgott Hyett. AMV-80

We float away on lotuses of sleep. Lotuses. Witter ("Emanuel Morgan") Bynner. MoLP

We float, forgotten by day. Nocturnal Heart. Anne-Marie Kegels. BoWoP

We floating Islands, living Hebrides. On the Memory of Mr. Edward King Drown'd in the Irish Seas. John Cleveland. AnAnS 2; OAEL 1-2; OBS; SeCP

We fly to covert of our Mother's wings. To Mary at Christmas. John Gilland Brunini. ISi

We fold your paper cranes. A Hiroshima Lullaby. Joseph Langland. PPON

We fooled ourselves/with our false smiles. We Are Acrobats. Jozef Habib Gerez. VWA

We forget/about dying here/in this boxed-in today. Birthday on Deathrow. Harold LaMont Otey. LFAC

We forget that never again/Will a god trust in the world. Hedgehog. Paul Muldoon. BIrV

We found her today/wobbling like a wicker basket/in the breeze. Cow. Janet Reed McFatter. GrPl

We found His corpse stretched on the threshold. The Dispossessed. Thomas Kinsella. NOCV

We frolic, while 'tis May. Ode on the Spring. Thomas Gray. CEP; EiCP; GTBS; GTBS-P; HBV 1-2; LAuP; NOEC

We future lights for your sorrow. Chorus of the Unborn. Nelly Sachs. NYBP

We gain by what we give. Alice Ray. Sarah Josepha Hale. AA

We give our thanks/That Thou hast made–/The turmoil of the sea! A Sailor's Prayer. George Hornell Morris. TrPWD

We give Thee praise for all, for all. Thanksgiving. Margaret E. Sangster. TRV

We give to the world every second/as a gift... Poem H. Vicente Rodriguez Nietzche. InW

We go; and "Is he gone?"/Is all our best friends say. Epigram: "Various the roads of life." Walter Savage Landor. FaBoEE

We go/in different directions/down the imperturbable street. Riot. Gwendolyn Brooks. BPo

We go these ways. Free Will. Walter Clark. NCSH

We go together into town and buy wine and yellow candles. We Go out Together. Kenneth Patchen. MoAmPo

We gobble up our child. The Gingerbread House. John Ower. AMV-80; DFT

...We goe to meet/A worthy object, our Lord's FEET. Saint Mary Magdalene. Richard Crashaw. AtBAP; FaBoCo; MeLP; Par; SeCV 1-2

We gon have/mo room! An Inconvenience. John Raven. BPo

We gotta make a nice job. Elmer Ruiz. Peter Oresick. LTB

We grow to one world through/Enlargement of wonder. A Grain of Rice. F. R. Scott. PeCV

We had already entered these mountains an hour ago. The Frontier. John Hewitt. BIrV

We had exchanged our hearts indeed. The Exchange. Samuel Taylor Coleridge. FiBHP; HBV 1-2; OAEP

We had great pleasure outdoors playing hockey. Rink Keeper's Sestina. George Draper. PrIm

We had never been so nearly anonymous. A Small Registry of Births and Deaths: All Night It Bullied You. C. K. Stead. NAs

...We had never learned to distinguish/Between hunger and love? Mundus et Infans. W. H. Auden. LiTB; LiTM; MoAB; MoBrPo; NAs

We had not yet eaten/from the tree in the center of the garden/which taught us/how to know death. Eve's Song in the Garden. Lynn Gottlieb. VWA

We had to let you out. The Refugee. Dabney Stuart. GP

We hae a problem here. Problems. Alexander Scott. FF

We harden like trees, and like rivers grow cold. The Lover: A Ballad. Mary Wortley, Lady Montagu. CEP; NoP; OBEC

We harvested. Us. Anne Sexton. CAPP

We hated more fiercely. Love Longs to Touch. Carol Lee Sanchez. TWSS

We keep our heads down like burrowing animals/that can't see in the daylight. Paradise. Chana Bloch. VWA

We kept the courtesy an internal form/to have the beauty after. As When the Blowfish Perishing. Linda Gregg. NPGG

We kept the Spartan code, and here we lie. On the Army of Spartans Who Died at Thermopylai. *Anonymous.* FaBoEE

We killed him with our feeble fear. The Blue Horse. Melvin Walker La Follette. NePoEA

We kiss'd again with tears. The Princess. Alfred, Lord Tennyson. AtBAP; GoTF; OAEP; OBVV; TreFS

We kiss our destruction. The Dead City. Clinch Calkins. AnAmPo

We kissed again with tears. The Reconciliation. Alfred, Lord Tennyson. HBV 1-2

We knew the wind. Four Choctaw Songs. Jim Barnes. STE

We know for whom we mourn and who is grieving. In Memory of Ernst Toller. W.H. Auden. AtBAP

We know immortal Beauty face to face. Say Not That Beauty. Robin Flower. HBMV; HBVY

...We know/just as they do it's the song birds make good eating. The Girl Who Learned to Sing in Crow. Paul Mariani. GeTw

We know not what to have, nor how to ask. On Change of Weathers. Francis Quarles. OBSP

We know not what we shall be–only this–/That we shall be made like Him–as He is. Seeds. John Oxenham. WGRP

We know not which we most admire,/The dancer, or the dance. On a Female Rope-Dancer. *Anonymous.* NOEC

...We know nothing. Incident. LeRoi (Imamu Amiri Baraka) Jones. NoAm

We know that our master has left us for the day. Waking from Sleep. Robert Bly. CAPP; EAS; NoAm; NOBA; NoP; PAI

We know they are prisons also, the thin walls/Between us and what cowers and shakes inside. Utrillo's World. John Glassco. PeCV

We know those blessings which we must possesse/And judge of future by past happinesse. To His Sacred Majesty, a Panegyrick... John Dryden. OBS

We know we shall not meet him here again. The Bewildered Guest. William Dean Howells. AmePo

We'l begin with a Tallen, a Brimmer to the KING! The Courtier's Health; or, Merry Boys of the Times. *Anonymous.* CoMu

We'l from our owne, adde far more years to his. To the King, Upon his welcome to Hampton-Court. Robert Herrick. AnAnS 2

We laid our hireling in his bed. Datur Hora Quieti. Robert Stephen Hawker. GoBC

We laugh/at my lack/of fish. The Raquette River, Potsdam, New York.... Anthony Piccone. WOLT

We laughed/then went to bed/and kept each other warm. One Time Henry Dreamed the Number. Doughtry Long. BP; BPo; CNA; PoBA

We laughed till we cried. Father. Ted Kooser. Str

We lay it gently on our lap/And dust its little jacket. The Parental Critic. Keith Preston. NLV

...We/lean forward to leap the river/on the way/to May. Moon Light. Freya Manfred. PH

We leap again and again and again. What Could Be. John Gill. NeAC

We leave our arms and some come cleare acrost. Letters from Vicksburg, XII. Gary Gildner. SM

...We leave Santos at once;/we are driving to the interior. Arrival at Santos. Elizabeth Bishop. FaBoWP; OxBC

...We leave them calling/after us, Sorry, Sorry, Sorry, and we don't/look back. Tableau Vivant. Tess Gallagher. GeTw

We leave thy green valley,/Glenaradale. Glenaradale. Walter Chalmers Smith. OBVV

We, left alone, shall seek one bud in vain. Mimma Bella. Eugene Lee-Hamilton. HBV 1-2

We left the island to the mice and birds. The Island. George Woodcock. NeBP

We left them there and went our way. Desire. William Cornish. OBSC; SeCeV

We lie, day creatures, overhearing night. The Sound of Night. Maxine W. Kumin. BoNaP; DFF

We lie down in the fields and leave behind/the corpses of angels. Selective Service. Carolyn Forche. MAYP

We lift our song to Him. The Summer Days Are Come Again. Samuel Longfellow. TRV

We, like dishonored soldiers, ran/The gauntlet of a darkening wood. First Blood. Jon Stallworthy. BoAnP; LiSp

We like the brew Elementary. Jim Tollerud. VoR

We like the little accident/Of fantastic ornament.... Beside a Fall. Jean Garrigue. PoL

We listen. Ride the Turtle's Back. Beth Brant. STE

We listen/to the warm silence. Old Man. Alan J. Carr. AMV-80

We live, and move, and die, through all this earthly glade. Sonnets Written in the Orillia Woods, VII. Charles Sangster. NOBC

We live as best we can. Half Past Four, October. Anna Hajnal. BoWoP

We live in a terrible season. Late at Night. William Stafford. NNaP; PoL; RFM

We live in a time gone black with bravery. Heaven in Ordinarie. Daniel Wolff. SM

We'll all be rooned," said Hanrahan,/"Before the year is out." Said Hanrahan. Patrick Joseph Hartigan. PoAu 1-2

We'll all die defending the Red, White and Red! The Red, White and Red. *Anonymous.* AmFP

"We'll all draw a pension from Casey's death." Mama Have You Heard the News?(B vers. with music). *Anonymous.* AS

We'll all have chicken an' some dumplin's/when she comes. She'll Be Coming 'Round the Mountain. *Anonymous.* FSW

We'll all have tea. Tea-Time. *Anonymous.* OxNR

We'll be married when the iceworms nest again. When the Iceworms Nest Again. Robert W. Service. FSW

We'll be twenty bold sailors all the way from Shanghai. The Dom Pedro. *Anonymous.* AmFP

...We'll be warm,/with blessed sleep as victory. Byron in Greece. Norman Rosten. HoAn

We'll bid adieu to packet-sailing and the Banks of Newfoundland. The Banks of Newfoundland (II). *Anonymous.* GBP; OBSS; ShS

We'll blend our voices with the heavenly throng/And praise our Savior as the years roll on. The Heavenly Aeroplane. *Anonymous.* NOCV

We'll both be friendly and untrue. Love-Songs, At Once Tender and Informative. Samuel Hoffenstein. OBAL

We'll both clasp Hands, in Wedlock Bands,/Marry, and to't again. The Swimming Lady. *Anonymous.* ErPo; UnTE

We'll both go off together/In this delightful weather. The Self-Slaved. Patrick Kavanagh. MoBrPo

We'll both stand in line/counting the coyotes howling in the hills/mountains apart. Turning on Daytime TV. Alex Kuo. APU

We'll bowse her up and be done! Paddy Doyle. *Anonymous.* ShS

"We'll bring them to the surface, or along with them we'll/die." The Donibristle Moss Moran Disaster. *Anonymous.* WTO

We'll build one castle more in Spain,/And dream one more dream there. In a Rose Garden. John Bennett. BLPA; FaBoBe; HBV 1-2

We'll cherish still/Our own beloved bow-wow. For a Good Dog. Arthur Guiterman. GDP

We'll choose him king, and make his mother queen. The Star-Song: A Carol to the King; Sung at White-Hall. Robert Herrick. OxBoCh

We'll dance again the saraband! The Witch's Ballad. William Bell Scott. AnFE; EvOK; NBM; NOBV; OBEV; OBVV; VLP

We'll dance and sing/"Noel Noel" Little tree. Edward Estlin Cummings. LOW; NTCP; OBCP; PCh; RoGo

We'll dance by the light of the moon. Louisiana Girls. *Anonymous.* ABF

"We'll doe ill deeds anew ere night,/Tho it were strucken twall." Sir Aldingar. *Anonymous.* ESPB

We'll drink a cup to Scotland yet,/Wi' a' the honors three. Scotland Yet. Henry Scott Riddell. HBV 1-2

We'll drink to sweet friendship in need and in/deed. The Angler's Invitation. Thomas Tod Stoddart. GN; HBV 1-2

We'll enter, with triumphant song,/The house not made with hands. Jehovah, God, Who Dwelt of Old. Lewis R. Amis. AH

We'll fight and we'll conquer again and again. Heart of Oak. David Garrick. HBV 1-2; NOEC; OBEC; OxBoLi

We'll find ground at the bottom, said Tommy O'Linn. Tommy O'Linn. *Anonymous.* OxNR

We'll find our "Patch of Blue." My "Patch of Blue." Mary Newland Carson. BLPA

We'll find out tomorrow,/And beat him today. Jack. Charles Henry Ross. OxBChV

...We'll find the way/To drench the world with wine. Chorus: "If I drink water while this doth last." Thomas Love Peacock. ViBoPo

We'll fly like brown leaves through/the cold! Winter Feast. Frances Frost. YeAr

We'll follow him with heart and hand,/Wherever he does go. The Gallant Fighting "Joe." James Stevenson. PAH

We'll follow in our own good year. The Exequy. Kildare Dobbs. OBCV

We'll frolic with sweet Dolly. Jog on, Jog on, the Footpath Way. *Anonymous.* GBP

We'll gallop into Toyland! Come, Ride with Me to Toyland. Rowena Bastin Bennett. ChBR; SiSoSe

We'll get wed–behave you villain–Brian Oge. Molly Bawn and Brian Oge. *Anonymous.* OnYI

We'll gladly prie/Fresh noggans o' your reaming graith/Wi' blythsome glee. The Rising of the Session. Robert Fergusson. OxBS

We'll go and find them, we'll go/and ask them for your name again. "Mystery Boy" Looks for Kin in Nashville. Robert Earl Hayden. LCAP; NoAm

"We'll go home by water,' says Brian O'Linn! Brian O'Linn. *Anonymous.* FaBoBa; FaBoNo; NLV; OnYI

We may not work–ah! would we might!–/With slower pen. On the Hurry of This Time. Henry Austin Dobson. HBV 1-2

We may return, but 'twill not be with him!/Hooker's across! Hooker's Across. George Henry Boker. PAH

We may then conclude our love/With a profitable deal. Love-Songs, At Once Tender and Informative. Samuel Hoffenstein. OBAL

We may trust His purpose wholly–/'Tis His children's welfare solely. Security. Lina Sandell. STF

We may, while they strain their Throats,/Wipe our Arses with their Votes... The Legion Club (excerpt). Jonathan Swift. BIrV

We may wish it undone someday. Only a Little Thing. M. P. Handy. PoToHe

We meet again! and meet no more to part. On Visiting the Graves of Hawthorne and Thoreau. Jones Very. AP; TAP

We meet at the white where hill and sky meet,/and black birds gather in and storm. Part Winter. Marilyn Bowering. CaPN

We meet disloyal usage from a friend? True to the Best. Benjamin Keech. PoToHe

"We meet upon the Level and we part upon the Square." The Level and the Square. Robert Morris. BLPA

...We met. We are both worthy. At last love has come. Sulpicia. BoWoP

–We might find a fairy ferry/To that isle where saints make merry! Christmas Island. Katharine Lee Bates. HBMV; HBVY

We might have loved, and you knew this might be! To a Passer-By. Charles Baudelaire. SyP

We might in time become as wise as they. The Three Wise Monkeys. Florence Boyce Davis. WBLP

We might take lessons by the hour/From busy, buzzy Bumblebeaver. The Bumblebeaver. Kenyon Cox. TiPo

We mourn for our country. Take Off Your Hat. Anonymous. WTO

...We move/to ancient Jewish law and strict command. The Survivors. Miriam Waddington. VWA

We muffled up in cloak and plaid,/And trotted home behind the lad. Recreation. Jane Taylor. NBM; OBRV; OxBoLi

We muse on many an ancient tale renown'd. Sonnet: Written at Stonehenge. Thomas Warton, Jr.. CEP

We must accept, as they/The fact of a new day. Children Waking: Indian Hill Station. Ralph Nixon Currey. PeSA

We must achieve what we expect. Essay on Marriage. Anne Finch, Countess of Wilchilsea. FaBoTw

...We must all file on/Through the narrow aisles of pain. Solitude. Ella Wheeler Wilcox. PaPo; PoLf; YaD

We must away, ere break of day,/To win our harps and gold from him! The Hobbit (excerpt). J. R. R. Tolkien. WSC

We must be brave in our dark. Power Failure. Michael Dennis Browne. AmPA

We must be free, we must be free. Freedom Is a Constant Struggle. Anonymous. FSW

We must buy a filter. Aunt Eliza. Harry Graham. FaFP; MaC; NA

We must convince the living/that the dead/cannot sing. A Guerrilla Handbook. LeRoi (Imamu Amiri Baraka) Jones. PoBA

We must/Cover them up/To/The post office. The Couple. Sandra Hochman. CTBA; NYBP

We must create and fashion a new God. How Shall We Rise to Greet the Dawn? Osbert Sitwell. WGRP

We must do the bigger deeds. The Bigger Day. G. E. Bishop. WBLP

We must gather food, and bear/and rear children.' The Two Sisters. Anonymous. NOAV

We must give from our full measure,/To the wanderer without.' The Beggar Boy. Cecil Frances Alexander. OxBChV

We must give gifts to the kings officers;/That gold will serve thee and mee.' Robin Hood and Queen Katherine (B version). Anonymous. BaBo; ESPB

We must go. Alas! the going,/Say "good-bye." Sweet Is Childhood. Jean Ingelow. TreFS

We must go to your house: O my friends, let us re-/joice! Is It True That You Live Where There Is Sorrow. Anonymous. ILwL

We must learn how to read/The letters written/In the stars that circle/Our souls. These Two. Howard Schwartz. VWA

We must live or die by steel. Before Disaster. Yvor Winters. HoPM; QFR

We must/Make it–Now! Urgency. Sarah E. Wright. PoNe

We must move onward to the last frontier. Destiny. Harrison Smith Morris. AA

We must plunge onward; onward, gentlemen.... Salutamus. Sterling A. Brown. CDC

We must shape here a new philosophy. The Refugees. Edwin Muir. NoAm

We must stand this/alone Epitaph: Snake River. Lance Henson. VoR

We must to Virtue for her guide resort,/Or we shall shipwreck in our safest port. The Pilot. George Chapman. EtS

We ne'er saw the fellow of bold Captain Death". Captain Death. Anonymous. CoMu

We ne'er shall see Lord Ronald more! Glenfinlas; or, Lord Ronald's Coronach. Sir Walter Scott. GoTL

We ne'er went more a-Maying/Nor had that sweet fa-laing. Since Bonny-Boots Was Dead. Anonymous. NCEP; PoEL 1-5

We need a child to inherit our belongings. Praise of a Child. Anonymous. WTO

We need a new chauvinism about existence. September 1, 1965. Paris Leary. CoPo

We need a whole lot more of Jesus,/And a lot less rock 'n roll. We Need a Whole Lot More of Jesus. Anonymous. FSW

We need not doubt, for such a wall/Is based in death, and does not fall. The Wall. Henry Reed. LiTB

We need not look for piping mair,/Sen Habbie's dead. The Life and Death of Habbie Simson, the Piper of Kilbarchan. Robert Sempill. OxBS

We need you/and there are so few/left. Eulogy for Alvin Frost. Audre Lorde. CNA

We need you now! On Visiting the Graves of Keats and Marx (excerpt). Anonymous. PeD

We need your help in every place–/Before, behind, beside. Leaders. Anonymous. WBLP

We never did; we had no right to stars. In the First House. Joseph Joel Keith. GoYe

We never enter/Alone. I Cry, Love! Love! Theodore Roethke. LCAP; MoVE

We never heard them go out. Furniture. Chana Bloch. GP

We never laughed like that together Interlude. Welton Smith. PoBA

We never sign the valentines we send in February. Rise and Fall of Valentines. Fairfax Downey. InMe

We never spoke, we simply looked and trembled/And we knew.... The Vestal Virgin. John Plummer Derwent Llwyd. CaP

We never thought about before. Aardvark. Julia Fields. BOLo; CNA

We never yet had lost a man/Or known what death could do. Carentan O Carentan. Louis Simpson. CoAP; MoBS; NMP; NOBA; OBWP; PrIm

We no care–yum poi! Chinatown Chant. Tom MacInnes. CaP

We now debate; who can advise, may speak. Paradise Lost. John Milton. NIP

We nurse our cups, nudge knees, and pick and choose. Elektra on Third Avenue. Marilyn Hacker. MAYP; NYP

We offer ourselves/to the enshrouding/emptiness. NN 616410. Bill Tulloch. PoSH

We on our feet must go/Plodding and walking. Nest Eggs. Robert Louis Stevenson. FM

We only cater to the high-class trade. The Drug Clerk. Eunice Tietjens. AnAmPo; HBMV

...We only have our words. All Friends Together. R. A. Simpson. NOAV

We only know that here it lies. Epitaph on the World. Henry David Thoreau. FF; HeIP

We only know they shall arrive. Oblique. Archibald Rutledge. TRV

–We only want to bring you home. Do Not Think. Carol [(or Carole[) Freeman. CNA

We open our eyes and stare at the coiling darkness,/And enter our dreams again. Multitudes Turn in Darkness. Conrad Aiken. PoA

We ordnance plant and powder sow. The Garden of Appleton House, Laid Out by Lord Fairfax... Andrew Marvell. NOBE

We others too, to sing your praises/Need to hear just such a wonder. The Pariah's Prayer. Johann Wolfgang von Goethe. ILwL

We ought to be together, you and I. You and I. Henry Alford. BLPA; FaBoBe

We ought to die/is the only way we might live. Poem for a Singer. Milton Acorn. NeAC

We out to smash your bourgeois ass/and by we I mean The Community! The Old O. O. Blues. Al Young. NPGG

We owe this world, where vertue must/Frail as our flesh crumble to dust. Epitaph on Maria Wentworth. Thomas Carew. PoEL 1-5

We own the love that calls us back to Thee! A Poem (excerpt). Oliver Wendell Holmes. TrPWD

We ows this world, where vertue must/Frail as our flesh crumble to dust. The Inscription on the Tombe of the Lady Mary Wentworth. Thomas Carew. OBS

We paddle through the shine from the Morning Star, from/Bralgu, slowly along as we see these eggs. The Djanggawul Cycle, 8. Anonymous. WTO

We part and mark you, Peter, by our knowing. Blue Sparks in Dark Closets. Richard Snyder. Psk

We part below to meet on high/Where blissful ages never die. I Die; But When the Grave Shall Press. Emily Bronte. TEP

We pass, but deeds of love endure. Despair and Hope. Israel Zangwill. TrJP

We passed in silence, and the lake/We left without a name. The Unnamed Lake. Frederick George Scott. CaP; NOBC

We passed the Northern Sea! A Ballad of Sir John Franklin. George Henry Baker. AA; HBV 1-2; OnMSP

We sang His birthday song, we did, upon His birthday/morn.   The Waits.
Madeline Nightingale.   SUS

We saved a shitload of that old elegance–   The Old Athens of the West Is
Now a Blue Grass Tour.   James Baker Hall.   TAT

We saw an Indian merchantman/Coming home.   Seascape.   Langston
Hughes.   BrR

We saw how our hands came wrinkled out of that sea.   Out of That Sea.
David Ferry.   NePoAm-2

We saw it, flying down, as the darkness was clearing, "twisting'/its tongue and
whistling.   The Djanggawul Cycle, 22.   Anonymous.   WTO

We saw Our Lady in the candle-light/Her raiment dry, no water on the floor!
Philippine Madonna.   Louise Crenshaw Ray.   ISi

We saw them dance and we heard them sing.   Midsummer Night.   Marion
Edey.   YeAr

We saw them fade within the mist,/And never saw them more.   Glenkindie.
William Scott.   HBV 1-2

We scan the trail of Thought, but all is overcast.   The Red Men.   Charles
Sangster.   CaP

We searcha by camera eye for Gothic things.   Photographing the Facade–San
Miguel de Allende.   Betsy Colquitt.   AMV-80

We see a hand and we call it love.   Photograph.   Quandra Prettyman.
PoBA

We see but what we have the gift/Of seeing; what we bring we find.
Moonlight.   Henry Wadsworth Longfellow.   MOON

We see God clear and high above the town.   Soul's Liberty.   Anna
Wickham.   MoBrPo; OBSP

We see His will and work well done/Yoked with our impotence.   What Is
That in Thine Hand?   Eva Gray.   STF

We see the things we long to see/In fiery iconography?   For the Conjunction
of Two Planets.   Adrienne Rich.   ImOP

We see them floating/down Allegany/call them our deaths   The Others
Hunters in the North The Cree.   Jerome Rothenberg.   PoM

We see them not, but Death/Is palpable–and Love.   The World Is Young
Today.   Digby Mackworth Dolben.   NOBV

We see yellow autumn, a visitor.   The Ragged Robin Opens.   Miklos
Radnoti.   AMV-80

"We see you in your hair,/Air resting around the tips of mountains."   Two
Scenes.   John Ashbery.   ANYP

We seek to see who is god.   Differences.   Ray A. Young Bear.   NU

We send our best apologies to you.   A Wartime Exchange: Letter to an
American Visitor.   Alex Comfort.   OxBTC

We settle, but like feathers on time's flow.   O Dreams, O Destinations.   C.
Day-Lewis   MoPo

We shal haf need thare/Upon Mary to call.   Hail Mary!   Anonymous.
OxBM

We shall all kneel down together.   Five Days Old.   Francis Webb.   PoAu
1-2

We shall awake/And follow Love beyond the unknown west.   Prothalamion
(excerpt).   Robert Hillyer.   MoAmPo

We shall be better friends when he is dead.   Contemporary.   Hortense
Flexner.   PoA

We shall be dust of quite another land/Before the seeds here planted come to
light.   Samos.   James Merrill.   HaCAP

We shall be no older/Than the child and the animals.   The Welcome.   Freda
Laughton.   NeIP

We shall be safe, diddle, diddle,/Out of harm's way.   Love Song.
Anonymous.   OxNR

We shall bloom when the last/screaming shot is stilled in the hills.   But We
Shall Bloom.   Haim Guri.   TrJP

We shall both lie down/At the foot of the hill, and sleep.   Parting.   Alice
Corbin.   BPAW

We shall breathe the air again,/Of the free land in our own beloved home.
Tramp! Tramp! Tramp!   George Frederick Root.   BLSo; PSoN; TreFS

We shall certainly find ourselves in Hell!   We Shall Not Escape Hell.
Marina Tsvetayeva.   BoWoP

We shall come back in the mind's long evening.   Changeless Shore.   Sarah
Leeds Ash.   GoYe

We shall come, rejoicing, bringing in the sheaves.   Bringing in the Sheaves.
Anonymous.   FSW

We shall disparage Providence.   The Cruel Brother: What Is Past.   Sir
William Davenant.   TrGrPo

We shall go forward to the work of another year with steadfastness/and
confidence.   Facing the New Year.   Anonymous.   PGD

We shall go home.   Half Sigh.   Anonymous.   PBA

We shall go mad no doubt and die that way.   The Cool Web.   Robert
Graves.   AWP; ChMP; GTBS-P; NIP; NoAm; NoP; OxBTC; PoA; PrIm;
SCV

We shall have a world of men/treating men only as men,/not as things.
Angry Dusk.   Jack Lindsay.   NOAV

We shall have clarity and hours/Which women shall not take away.   About
Women.   Howard Phelps (Phelps Putnam) Putnam.   AnFE

We shall have fireworks here by this day week.   Autumn Journal.   Louis
MacNeice.   FaBoPV; OxBTC; WaP

We shall have FRIENDS–while God is God!   To Our Friends.   Lucian B.
Watkins.   BANP

We shall have game and sport ynow.   Stag-Hunt.   Anonymous.   OxBM

We shall have the Devil and all/When we come together.   An Evening's
Love.   John Dryden.   CavP

We shall have the sweetest rest.   Going Home with Jesus.   Walter E.
Isenhour.   STF

We shall have to pass through the dewy grass/And waters wide and fleet.
Song: "If thou art sleeping."   Gil Vicente.   AWP; LiTW

We shall have to share also these sufferings,/simpler, more severe, more
unlimited than ours.   Cambrian (excerpt).   Eeva-Liisa Manner.   PBWP

We shall in righteousness behold Thy face.   Unseen.   Fanny J. Crosby.
TrPWD

We shall lie out there.   Ode: To My Pupils.   W. H. Auden.   MoBrPo

We shall look forth from our heaven,/pleased the sweet music to hear.
Elegiac.   James Gates Percival.   AA

We shall meet/and love each other.   Daughters.   Astra.   BrRo

We shall meet our father over there.   We Shall Walk through the Valley.
Anonymous.   FSW

We shall never be able to answer his accusation.   The Dirty Little Accuser.
Norman Cameron.   OxBS

We shall never be older or wiser or dead.   Farewell Voyaging World!
Conrad Aiken.   NYBP

We shall never hear of his death,/Unless the liars lie.   The Lying Muslims.
Anonymous.   WTO

We shall not be moved.   We Shall Not Be Moved.   Anonymous.   FSW

We shall not fear!   The New Year.   Homera Homer-Dixon.   BLRP

We shall not go down, or under,/For He saith, "Thou passest through."
Through the Waters.   Annie Johnson Flint.   STF

We shall not know that all is lost,/So great shall be our bliss.   Lines.
Stopford Augustus Brooke.   IrPN

We shall not miss the Summer's full-blown grace,/Nor hunger for the swift,
exquisite Spring.   Prevision.   Ada Foster Murray.   HBV 1-2

We shall not sleep, though poppies grow/In Flanders fields.   In Flanders
Fields.   John McCrae.   BBV; BLPA; CaP; FaBV; FaFP; FaPo; FaPoR;
FPL; GoTF; GTBS; HBV 1-2; MCCG; NOBC; OBCV; OBWP; OHFP;
PAL; PeCV; PGD; PoPl; SiSoSe; TreF; ViBoPo

We shall not want to use again/Until eternity.   The Bustle in a House.
Emily Dickinson.   APA; ELU; FaBV; FPL; HAP; HeIP; NePA; NoP;
OxBA; PoEL 1-5; PoLf; WGRP

We shall overcome someday.   We Shall Overcome.   Anonymous.   FSW

We shall share, O Lady Fair!   The Wooing of Etain.   Anonymous.   BIrV

We shall share our courage   Fear.   Thomas Love Peacock.   VoR

We shall soon give all our attention to you.   Spring Day.   John Ashbery.
NOBA

..."We shall survive/this way."   Survival This Way.   Simon J. Ortiz.
CDW; STE

We shall wait for you behind an open door/And in your shadow as you walk
the stairs.   Haunted Odysseus: The Last Testament.   Horace Gregory.
MoVE

We shall walk in the snow.   Velvet Shoes.   Elinor Wylie.   CH; FPL; GoJo;
MoAB; MoAmPo; PG; PoPl; SiSoSe; SoPo; TreFS; TrGrPo; WHA

We share the honors without fuss/by frequent alternation.   After You,
Madam.   Alex Comfort.   ErPo; UnTE

We shepherds will adore/Her setting and her rise.   Eclogue.   Michael
Drayton.   OBSC

We should just see God and die?   Is It True?   Sarah Williams.   BLPA

We should like to know how that was done.   The Icosasphere.   Marianne
Moore.   ImOP

We should not be lying here!   Unknown Soldiers.   Edgar Lee Masters.
NoAm; TAP

...We should not wait for the children to/Tell us about our toothless gums or
our showing flies.   On His Royal Blindness Paramount Chief Kwangala.
Jack A. Mapanje.   WhB

We should start an' kick their –ses for 'em/an' tell 'em to–.   Red-Herring.
D. H. Lawrence.   NoAm

We should try to reach the shining shore.   I Kissed Pa Twice after His
Death.   Mattie J. Peterson.   PeD

We sighed for one sweet temperate breeze/To freshen earth with norland cold.
Winter Life and Scenery.   Thomas Caulfield Irwin.   IrPN

We/simply do not know, you know,/we/simply do not know/what/counts.
Zurich, zum Storchen.   Paul Celan.   VWA

We sing, and grieve for what we are/Compared with the intended song.
Stark County Holidays.   Mary Oliver.   Str

We sing to Jesus/in a chain reaction.   Atomic Pantoum.   Peter Meinke.
SM

We singing Jews, we Jews possessed...   Jewboy.   Julian Tuwim.   VWA

We sit in silence, while our thoughts go out–/Like treasure-seeking ships.
This Is My Hour.   Zoë Akins.   HBV 1-2

We sit like drunkards and inhale the swans. Swans. Lawrence Durrell. MoBrPo

We sit on the cold mountain/among the lonely wolves The Cold. Lance Henson. CDW

We smell a rat/close by. The Three Little Kittens. *Anonymous.* OxNR; TreFS

"We smell a rat near by."/"Mee-ow, mee-ow, mee-ow." Three Little Kittens. Eliza Cook. OBCA; SoPo

We smile at the tender Figure and wave goodby. The Allegorical Figure of Brooklyn. Tony Towle. ANYP

We smiled through strands of dripping hair,/Because we felt so dry. The Hut. Hilda Van Stockum. BrR

...We smiled, waited/for the ice truck, buried the dead, called it home. Washington Heights, 1959. Michael C. Blumenthal. HaCAP

We sobbed you our message: ye said, "It/is song, and sweet!" Arraignment. Helen Gray Cone. AA

We soon bid adieu to fair London/And all the flash girls in the town. Ratcliffe Highway. *Anonymous.* OBSS

We sop up with warm white bread. He Fishes with His Father's Ghost. Lewis Nordan. AMV-81

We sow on Burmah's barren plain,/We reap on Zion's hill. In Spite of Sorrow. Adoniram Judson. TRV

We speak in/Now. (The Syl La Ble Speaks En Erg y/Sound). Carol Lee Sanchez. TWSS

We speak/the color/of the/heart Salt Man. Annette Arkeketa West. TWSS

We speak to him and he answers. For One Who Died Young. H. R. Hays. EAS

We spoke/in whispers when/we spoke/at all... The Night-Blooming Cereus. Robert Earl Hayden. FB; NoP

We stand amazed but take the blow, transfigured, idiot. The Beating. T. R. Hummer. MAYP

...We stand/and stare—mindless, diminished—/at their rosy immanence. Lights among Redwood. Thom Gunn. OBTV

...We stare/Across two thousand years, and heaven and hell,/Into each other's gaze. Judas Iscariot. Stephen Spender. MoAB; NIP

We stare and say, "Well, we have come this far." Cirque d'Hiver. Elizabeth Bishop. InPS; LiTA; MiAP

We stare on our dazed trunks at the block kneeling. End of Play. Robert Graves. EBEV

We started through the fields to find the Child. The Shepherd Speaks. John Erskine. TrCP

We steal what we already own. At Summer's End. Saul Hillel Benjamin. AMV-81

We steer'd her toward a crimson cloud/That landlike slept along the deep. In Memoriam A.H.H., CIII. Alfred, Lord Tennyson. OAEP; PoEL 1-5

We still can see our Father's door! The Crooked Footpath. Oliver Wendell Holmes. HBV 1-2; TreF

We still seem to spend an/Eternity in it! A Man about the Kitchen. Rodney Hobson. QQQ

...We still should cry/Not to be born, or, being born, to die? The Life of Man. Francis Bacon. EIL; OBSC; WHA

We still will find a cheerful mind/Around the fire at home! November. C. L. Cleaveland. HBV 1-2

We stipulate—till pitying Snows/Persuade our Feathers Home. 'Tis not that dying hurts us so. Emily Dickinson. BoWoP; DiPo

We stopped for a drink/and stayed a year. Ivesiana. Bill Berkson. ANYP

We sum in port her banquet of degrees. Sea Voyage. William Empson. CMoP; MOS

We surmount our spoilers, sometimes. Gifts. Karen Snow. FYAP

We survive! We Survive! Hirsch Glick. TrJP

We swim the watery years. Fish Story. B. Jo Kinnick. AMV-81

We take our dust and rocks and start back down. The Backward Look. Howard Nemerov. OxBC

We tasted, then chose ours. So What (parody). Philip Appleman. BXAP

We test our lives by thine. Immortal Love, Forever Full. John Greenleaf Whittier. AH

We thank the Keeper of our years. Gratitude. Clyde McGee. BLRP

We thank the Pilgrims, every one! The Pilgrims Came. Annette Wynne. OHIP

We thank Thee for a final golden chance/To rise again and build a nobler world. A Prayer for Thanksgiving. Joseph Auslander. TrPWD

We thank thee for this day. Sunset Song. *Anonymous.* WTO

We, the peoples of the land of Soviets. Meadowland. *Anonymous.* FSW

We–the women–the mothers of our words. As All Things Pass. Diane Bickston. LFAC

...We then commenced/to display our talent,/off into the astonished wild blue yonder. The Truth Made Breakfast. Jeffrey Miller. APU

We then shall see Him face to face–/Oh, glorious day of days! Pray On! *Anonymous.* STF

We think, and thought corrupts love's image of the world. Thought and the Poet. Peter Yates. ChMP

We think of lukewarm water, hope to get in it. Kitchenette Building. Gwendolyn Brooks BALP; BPo; FaBoWP; FF; NoP; PoNe

We think so much about so little/And think so little of so much. The Reason. Leonard Bacon. YaD

We think so then, and we thought so still! The Pelican Chorus. Edward Lear. FaBoNo; PB

We think the world a beetle on its stalk. The Golden Shower. Roy Campbell. OxBTC

We think we can forget/If we sing loud enough. Music and Words. Elizabeth Jennings. UnS

We think we've all heard quite enough of this your/sad disaster!' Alphabet. Edward Lear. FaBoNo

We told the four-wheeler to drive them to town,/And we left them alone in their glory. The Burial of the Bachelor (parody). *Anonymous.* FaBoPa

We too are fools and knaves. Victory. Roger Axford. PGD

We too know it well, We've drunk mead on its shore. Ariosto. Osip Mandelstam. OBVE

We, too, shall be in the rain/A long, long while. Rain. Patrick F. Kirby. GoBC

We too stand and wait. The View from Here. William Stafford. ELU; RFM

We, too, will have children who do not behave! Parenthood. John Farrar. OHIP

We too would hear the bells of cheer/Ring peace and freedom in. The Battle Autumn of 1862. John Greenleaf Whittier. MC; PAH

We took food and drink unstinting/And there we stayed. Birlinn Chlann-Raghnaill. Alexander MacDonald. GoTS

We touch and by that touching farness are alone. The Reconciliation. Archibald MacLeish. MoAmPo

We touch, we hold, we keep/one another free. Degli Sposi. Rika Lesser. FYAP

We tried to make of love/a celebration? Who of Those Coming After. Darcy Gottlieb. AMV-81

We trust they find a happier land,/A brighter sunshine of their own. To the Memory of the Brave Americans. Philip Freneau. AP; PAL; PoLf

...We try to choose our life. Heart's Needle. W.D. Snodgrass. ConAP; NePoEA

We turn and hurry on/Towards Dounreay. The Strath of Kildonan. Betty Morris. PoSH

We turn for strength and comfort to thy creed. Washington. Mae Winkler Goodman. PGD

...We turn/our backs and feel the whiskey burn. Fourth of July in Maine. Robert Lowell. CAPP

We turn the conversation on to men. On Paunch, A Parasite. Hilaire Belloc. PoL

We turn to catch one fading ray/Of joy that's left behind us. The Journey Onwards. Thomas Moore. GTBS; GTBS-P; HBV 1-2; SeCePo

We turn to dust, to sleep, repose. Reflections, Written on Visiting the Grave of a Venerated Friend. Ann Plato. BlSi

We turn to our beginnings. A Still Life. Jascha Kessler. HoAn

We twist away like a released balloon. Moving. William Matthews. PoL

We two are left. They walked through pergolas/And planted well, so that we might do better. Epitaph on a Fir-Tree. Richard Murphy. FaBoTw

We two have listened till he sang/Our hearts and lips together. To A. D. William Ernest Henley. AnFE; HoPM; ViBoPo

We two have made the angels smile! A New Poet. William Canton. HBV 1-2

We two have won. Secret. Cathrine Haydon Jacobs. GoYe

We two pass on–or but one alone. Growing Old. Ella Wheeler Wilcox. BLPA; FPL

We two shall follow through a world remote/The silence whereinto Love's music died. The Silence. Archibald MacLeish. HBMV

We tyrants love, if we can tyrants be;/If not, next wish is we may all be free. On the Prorogation. *Anonymous.* APAS

We've a new race to start. More of a Corpse Than a Woman. Muriel Rukeyser. NMM

We've come too quickly and too far. Shelter. Gene Derwood. NePA

We've done our task together. The Mowers. William Allingham. IrPN

We've found/Shangri-La. The Lost Valley. Gordon J. Gadsby. PoSH

We've got as far as poison gas. Christmas 1924. Thomas Hardy. FaBoEE; OBCP; PV

We've got Franklin D. Roosevelt back again. Franklin D. Roosevelt's Back Again. *Anonymous.* FSW

We've got our harvest in. Harvest. *Anonymous.* OxNR

...We've gotta get/that little critter out. Sidonie. Jack Collom. APU

We've hop'd in thee–let not our hope be vain. The Te Deum. *Anonymous.* AWP

We've learned the lesson that ye taught/In Flanders fields. America's Answer. R. W. Lilliard. BLPA; PAL

We've lost a son,/the music, jazz, comes in. Reuben, Reuben. Michael S. Harper. GeTw

We've really had no fall at all. The Lazy Writer. Bert Leston Taylor. ALV

We vow, in tears: It shall not be again! In the Name of Our Sons. Dorothy Gould. PGD

We wail right on key! The "Duke" and the "Count." Richard Fewell. AMV-81

We wait, thy will to do. Sea and Shore. Harry Lyman Koopman. AA

We wait to be moved. Elsewheres. Donald Justice. LCAP

We walk on, leaves blow past. These Leaves. William Stafford. NNaP

...We walk out/into the darkness and I am cold as I squeeze her buttocks,/her blue, dwarf stars. The Sweet. Ai. GP

...We walk the daytime/world charged with our beauty. Star & Garter Theater. Dennis Schmitz. LCAP; NPGG

We walk with you and we are comforted. For Mary McLeod Bethune. Margaret Walker. PoNe

We walked among the whispering pines. We Walked among the Whispering Pines. John Henry Boner. AA

We walked that ancient thoroughfare,/The Roman Road. He Roman Road. Thomas Hardy. InPo

...We walked/To where it would have wet feet/Had it been water The Forms of Love. George Oppen. NNaP

We want the cake and not the crumb–/We're mad again. Unaccompanied. Harvey Andrews. OBET

...We wanted nothing,/but to be old, do nothing, type and think. Harriet. Robert Lowell. CAPP

We was aided by a poverty of intellect. Talking Nothin'. *Anonymous.* FSW

We was both seventeen. Her Dancing Days. Anna Adams. BrRo

We was very neat about our persons. Crucial Stew. Colette Inez. FAZ

We wash our hands so early in the morning. Sonnet XV: "This is the way we say it in our time." Winfield Townley Scott. ErPo

We watch over his shoulder/as the stubby thumb/stabs out: Calley. Instamatic. Edwin Morgan. FF

We watched a gopher there. Lake Superior. Lorine Niedecker. FaBoWP

We watched the Condors winging towards the Moon. Condors Flying. Padraic Colum. GoJo

We wear the mask. We Wear the Mask. Paul Laurence Dunbar. AmePo; AmNP; CDC; FF; IDB; NoP; PoBA; TTY; UnPo

We weave this love, this light. A Is for Alpha: Alpha Is for A. Conrad Aiken. NePA

We weep, and curse, and smack our lips. Woman. *Anonymous.* UnTE

We weight their stems/with stones, then drive away. Paul Laurence Dunbar. Robert Earl Hayden. NoP

We went back to sleep until we reached home. It was a Special Treat. Luci Tapahonso. STE

We went from house to wood/For change of solitude. Happiness Makes up in Height for What It Lacks in Length. Robert Frost. MoAB; MoAmPo; MoPo

We were a jolly crew. The Schooner Kandahar. *Anonymous.* ShS

We were all under God./Ours were the steps he trod. God. Boris Slutsky. VWA

We were always counting our losses. The Hours. Norman Dubie. GeTw

We were but windfall parties to those falls. Mark Van Doren. James Worley. AMV-81

We were his citizens, and stayed/In a country that his poems made. Lines for a Dead Poet. David Ferry. PP

We were like two fish/darting/in and out of the water/before dawn. Liard Hot Springs. Gordon Massman. CTBA

We were lords of it all.... Conquistador. Archibald MacLeish. AtBAP

We were never together/At table, or/Arm on arm. Dialectique. Hugh Maxton. CIP

We were plighted, I and you! Or Ever God Created Adam. *Anonymous.* WTO

We were rumbling o'er Trumpington stones. The Country Clergyman's Trip to Cambridge. Thomas Babington, Lord Macaulay. NBM; OBSV; OxBoLi

We were sailing after shoals of herring. The Shoals of Herring. *Anonymous.* OBSS

We were simple singing seamen, so of course we could not know! Forty Singing Seamen. Alfred Noyes. AnFE; BBV; OnMSP; StPo

We were taken by a seventy-four. The Wasp's Frolic. *Anonymous.* PAH

We were the best of friends. The Waves Gleam in the Sunshine. Heinrich Heine. TrJP

We were the inheritors, we/couldn't leave fast enough. The Inheritors. Gary Geddes. NOBC

We were there once upon a time. Driving Cross-Country. X. J. Kennedy. TwCP

We were two women of one generation. Twenty-One Love Poems. Adrienne Rich. PeHV

We weren't surprised when the Americans didn't win. R-and-R Centre: An Incident from the Vietnam War. D. J. Enright. OxBC

We what we are. Last Things. Kathleen Raine. NYBP

We whisper in her ear, "You are not true." Epistemology. Richard Wilbur. NePoEA; NoAm; NOBA; OBSP; SUW

We whistle after them, then laugh, for they/stiffen, not knowing what to do or say. Young Girls. Raymond Souster. HeIP

We whites, who can only listen, are blurred with our tears. Baptism. Charles G. Bell. AmFN

We who are only too willing to help Explorers as Seen by the Natives. Doug Fetherling. NOBC

We who are veiled/and without faces. They Say She Is Veiled. Judy Grahn. APU

We who dance hungry and wild/Under a winter's moon. The Rabbits' Song outside the Tavern. Elizabeth Jane Coatsworth. SUS; TiPo

We who dance we find/the/fire/of the fire. Firebowl. Sydney Clouts. VWA

We, who had known their danger, found a swifter/Hunter beside us when the morning was over. The Four Deer. Mary Hoxie Jones. GoYe

We who have looked on the Reapers/Go quietly, all our days. The Reapers. Lauchlan Maclean Watt. PGD

We who have shared so much can still recall! The House. Paula Nelson. GoYe

We who in the beginning/were such an influence/are left to mind the fences. The Survivors. Robert Slater. FAZ

We who like to wander where the waiting vessels/are! Down among the Wharves. Eleanore Myers Jewett. EtS

We who live on charity enjoy the pleasure/of your wealth, the long hours filled/with drunkenness. Bowery. David Ignatow. CTBA

We who must die demand a miracle. For the Time Being. W. H. Auden. OAEP

We, who pray, ourselves are fate. A Prayer of the Peoples. Percy MacKaye. TrPWD; WGRP

We will all be REwritten/whether we like it or not. Conversations with the Nightmare. Carol Lee Sanchez. TWSS

...We will be/aware as never before of the portability of time. The Future. Michael Benedikt. SUW

...We will be buoyed beyond/the dark snags and splinters of what we once were. Tide Pools. Dave Smith. AMV-81

We will be true to thee till death. Faith of Our Fathers. Frederick William Faber. GoTF; TreFS

We will be wed, come Margaret let us go. The Souldiers Farewel to his Love. *Anonymous.* CoMu

We will build it to the glory of the Lord./Hallelujah, I don't know. Timber (with music). *Anonymous.* AS

We will commence our music and the firing of guns. The Wagoner's Lad. *Anonymous.* BaBo

We will cover each other with little attentions I Am Yours & You Are Mine So. Michael Silverton. PoL

We will drink to the health of the little brown bulls. The Little Brown Bulls. *Anonymous.* AmFP; BaBo; OuSiCo

...We will find new ways of being together/among the living. Portoncini dei Morti. Daniel Halpern. MAYP

We will forget how large the world was once. Going Away. Ann Stanford. GP; PH

We will gather up the fragments that remain. Hallelujah! Alfred Edward Housman. FiBHP; NLV; PV; ShM

We will get the bagpipes,/And we'll hae a dance, ladie.' Rob Roy. *Anonymous.* BaBo; ESPB

We will give it to each other. For the Stranger. Carolyn Forche. MAYP

We will go on to the end. Tortoise Gallantry. D. H. Lawrence. CMoP; NoAm

We will have to stamp you out. A Concise History of the World. Ira Sadoff. AmPA

We will have to weave no more. Weaver's Life. *Anonymous.* FSW

We will it so/and so it is/past all accident. The Ivy Crown. William Carlos Williams. NoP; PrIm

We will live together till death us part. Johnny Germany. *Anonymous.* AmFP

We will miss you, tongue, in this room. The Animals. Lewis MacAdams. ANYP

"We will not change our policy,'/Says Harry Fat the Proud. A Rope for Harry Fat. James Keir Baxter. MoBS

We will pass with the sword in the hand and the hand lifted. Reveille. Audrey Alexandra Brown. CaP

We will set it out to grow. The Blue-Flag in the Bog. Edna St. Vincent Millay. AnAmPo

We will store it away gladly/In garner and bin. Song of the Harvest. Henry Stevenson Washburn. OHIP

We will strike if but one 'midst the shifting crowd. At Dawn of the Year. George Klingle. PGD

We will tell our wives of our hard times/And no more a-lumbering go. Once More A-Lumbering Go. *Anonymous.* AmFP

We will tell these dreams over again.' The Brickster. *Anonymous.* OBET

We will turn it in as the public share.   Harvesting Wheat for the Public Share.   Li Chu.   BoWoP; PBWP

We wish'd the Cards had all been burn'd.   Win at First and Lose at Last; or, A New Game at Cards.   Laurence Price.   OxBoLi

We wish they'd come up/and say hello more often.   Americana.   Carl Rakosi.   PAI

We wish to sink. We do not choose to swim.   Fall In.   Lincoln Kirstein.   NoAm

We Wish You a Merry Christmas,/And a Happy New Year!   We Wish You a Merry Christmas.   Anonymous.   FSW

We with the Jews even Christ still crucify,/As not yet come to our impiety.   Caelica, XCVIII.   Fulke, Lord Brooke Greville.   FCP; OxBoCh

We with the sun together/Tomorrow.   Stable-Talk.   Raymond Knister.   CaP

We wither and flourish.   In Stone Settlements When the Moon Is Stone.   Peter Levi.   EBEV

We wither away from the light/without a trace.   We Carry Eggshells.   Hanny Michaelis.   VWA

We won't go home till morning,/Till day light does appear.   We Won't Go Home Till Morning.   Anonymous.   BLSo; PSoN

We work hard/My dad/And I.   Automobile Mechanics.   Dorothy Walter Baruch.   SoPo; TiPo

We would even die.   Among Strangers.   William Stafford.   NNaP

We would/Have killed for you today.   A Flat One.   W.D. Snodgrass.   AmPC; AP; CAPP; LiTM; NePoEA-2; PoCh; SM

We would have no power left to look on that dead face.   A Rebel.   John Gould Fletcher.   MoAmPo

We would have to stop everything to turn it off.   Everything.   James Paul.   HoAn

We would know/the hidden things/of this world   Instructions for the Messiah.   Myra Sklarew.   VWA

We would learn and know!   Night of Spring.   Thomas Westwood.   CBEP; OBVV

We would live merrily, merrily.   The Merman.   Alfred, Lord Tennyson.   GN; WSC

We would no doubt have other rooms then,/Or other names.   Leaving the Motel.   W. D. Snodgrass.   FF; NIP; WeW

We would not dress a flower/Before their naked eyes.   Open Poetry Reading.   Jesus Papoleto Melendez.   AMV-81

We would not long for heaven/If earth held only joy.   Progress.   Anonymous.   STF

We would put the animals back in their cages, and get to/the mainland.   Sudden Things.   Donald Hall.   EAS

We would read the limits of ourselves/in the extravagant migration of light.   February Margins.   Brian Henderson.   CaPN

We would win a wreath immortal/Whose bright flowers ne'er fade and die.   Poem: "In the earnest path of duty."   Charlotte Forten.   BlSi

We wouldn't give in.   My Father.   Rae Dalven.   GoYe

We wouldna' have a coat, neither black nor blue,/If it wasna' for the work of the weavers.   The Work of the Weavers.   Anonymous.   FSW

We write them there forever.   Walt Whitman.   Edwin Arlington Robinson.   AmePo; NePA; OxBA

We yield to his despotic sway,/The only monarch all obey.   Written for My Son...at His First Putting on Breeches.   Mary Barber.   NOEC

We-you? Post-suicides, shall we awaken?   With God Conversing.   Gene Derwood.   LiTA; LiTM; MoRP; NePA

The weak and blind who stand in our light and wreak ourselves such ill.   Breton Afternoon.   Ernest Christopher Dowson.   OBNC

Weak as a photograph emerging in the darkroom pan.   Cedar.   Robert Morgan.   GeTw

The weak remaining shadow of Vala that returns in sorrow/to thee.   Vala; or, The Four Zoas.   William Blake.   ViBoPo

Wealth has a coat of many colours!   Variety: Why Do We Grumble?   Anonymous.   WTO

Wealth I despise in easy competence.   A Pastoral Elegy.   Albius Tibullus.   AWP

Wealth is nothing but lack of people.   Sunday in Glastonbury.   Robert Bly.   ConAP

Wear it on your knots and fans.   Song:"Where shall Celia fly for shelter."   Christopher Smart.   EnLoPo

Wear, like the joys they speak of, the pale cold damp of years!   The Influence of Local Attachment (excerpt).   Richard Polwhele.   NOEC

Wearied, exhausted, dully sleeping.   Spring in New Hampshire.   Claude McKay.   BANP; BPo; GoSl; PoNe

The weariest month of the year, love,/Is shortest, and nearest the spring!   February.   Adeline D. T. Whitney.   YeAr

Wearily the old sun shook/The black birds off of him.   Solar Myth.   Genevieve Taggard.   MoAmPo

Wearing dress and raincoat that I can't see.   Art Gallery.   John Dickson.   AMV-81

Wearing gray flannel suit, knit tie, and Brooks Brothers shirt down the/sunlit street.   Man in the Street.   Robert Penn Warren.   OBAL

Wearing his own last hat, drinking port/and smoking Ideals forever.   An Exchange of Hats.   Stanley Moss.   GP

Wearing its own deep feeling as a crown.   Stanzas.   Edgar Allan Poe.   MAmP

Wearing mittens/Like my hand.   Winter.   Jean Jaszi.   SoPo

Wearing my name and face.   Song for a New Generation.   Gertrude May Lutz.   AMV-80

A-wearing of the linen clothes, a-wearing of the linen clothes.   Hanging Out the Linen Clothes (with music).   Anonymous.   AS

...Wearing/other new dresses, of bloodred velvet.   Sunday Afternoon.   Denise Levertov.   ConAP

Wearing those tight blue jeans.   Out West.   Gary Snyder.   BLPA; BPAW; FaBoBe; FaFP; GoTF; HBV 1-2; NNaP; PoOW; TreF

Wears for a gem the tremulous vesper/star.   Aspects of the Pines.   Paul Hamilton Hayne.   AA; AnAmPo; HBV 1-2

Wears its emblazonry.   Independence.   Henry David Thoreau.   AnNE; TreFS

Weary and famished, fallen and desolate?   The Prodigal Son.   Arthur Symons.   BrPo

"Weary child, come in today."   At the Door of Mercy Sighing.   Thomas Mackellar.   AH

Weary day!–the foul Witch-Bride.   The Witch-Bride.   William Allingham.   NOBV

Weary his woman's face,/The bitter smoke whirls.   The Houses (excerpt).   Robin Hyde.   AnNZ

Weary of joyless life I've grown.   The Soul's Bitter Cry.   Anonymous.   WGRP

...Weary/of the dialogue, tired enough for home.   The Man Who Knew Too Much.   David Wojahn.   MAYP

Weary pilgrim, welcome home!   Life Is Like a Mountain Railroad.   Anonymous.   FSW

A weary world awaits thy reign sublime!   God of the Prophets! Bless the Prophets' Sons.   Denis Wortman.   AH

Weather gathered its forces.   Before the Storm.   Kenneth O. Hanson.   CoAP

...Weather/is far too clear for me to think of/anything but august comedy.   Pity Ascending with the Fog.   James Tate.   NoAm

The weather it will spill.   Wild Geese, Wild Geese, Ganging to the Sea.   Anonymous.   PBBP

Weather-vanes clatter.   Half of Life.   Friedrich Holderlin.   OBVE

A weather-worn, marble triton/Among the streams.   Men Improve with the Years.   William Butler Yeats.   MBW 1-2

Weathercock snowfall starlight cockcrow.   Silent Poem.   Robert Francis.   FiCP; LCAP

...Weathered but not ready/to join the earth/in a last embrace.   Grandmother.   John Paul Minarik.   LFAC

Weave through the pattern every fragment/Of glittered breath that you have known.   Maker of Songs.   Hazel Hall.   HBMV

Weavin' fifty-one weeks of bread/An' one of life.   July Wakes.   Anonymous.   OBET

Weaving a wreath of triumph/For Randolph Bourne.   For Randolph Bourne.   James Oppenheim.   AnAmPo

The weazel, lark and crow.   The Passing of the Shee after Looking at One of A.E.'s Pictures.   John Millington Synge.   BIrV; FaBoEE; OnYI

(The web is wove. The work is done.)   The Curse upon Edward.   Thomas Gray.   OBEV

...The web of routes bunched/To the shapes of beaks or arrowheads at the black dots of the cities.   The Changes.   Robert Pinsky.   NPGG

The web would tangle and cling.   Netted Strawberries.   Gordon Bottomley.   AtBAP

The Websters and the Lincolns and the Roosevelts, you know.   The Modern Baby.   William Croswell Doane.   BLPA; YaD

Wed no man. Remember me.   Death's Warning to Beauty.   Anonymous.   AnIL

The wedding ring/That's bedded forever now/In her clapping hand.   Mother of the Groom.   Seamus Heaney.   OBSP

Wee all (as one) to love her Grace,/That is our Queene, this Marigolde.   A New Ballade of the Marigolde.   Anonymous.   CoMu

Wee chased them to D   Musselburgh Field.   Anonymous.   ESPB

Wee-kee-kee, oriole,/Pattering rain.   Flute-Priest Song for Rain (excerpt).   Amy Lowell.   UnS

A wee naked babe in the cold.   Farewell to the Old Year!   Eleanor Farjeon.   SiSoSe

The Weed not being, I may adore the Wearer.   On the Infancy of Our Saviour.   Francis Quarles.   OBS; OxBoCh; SeCePo

Weed the garden, wind the clock;/Remember the Two.   The Dog beneath the Skin.   W. H. Auden.   OxBTC

Weeds inching up as flowers, unopposed.   To My Sister, from the Twenty-Seventh Floor.   Michael Knoll.   AMV-81

Week-end begins to merge itself in Week.   Week-End.   Harold Munro.   SeCePo

Weel aucht thou be affeirit of the licht. The Golden Targe. William Dunbar. BSV; OxBS; PP

"Weep and mourne, she will not return,–/she cannot return to thee!" Olivia. Edward Pollock. AA

Weep not for me, Loved Woman,/For yourself alone be weeping! Warrior's Song. Mary Austin. BPAW

Weep o'er its ruins, at its follies laugh. A Voyage to Tintern Abbey. Sneyd Davies. NOEC

Weep Shepheard weep, to make mine undersong. Lament for Daphnaida. Edmund Spenser. FiP

Weep thy golden tears! Song: "April, April." William Watson. GoTF; HBV 1-2; HBVY; OBEV; OBVV; PoSC; TreF; TrGrPo

Weep! Weep! Weep! The Thousand and One Nights: Tumadir al-Khansa for Her Brother. Anonymous. PG

Weep, you may weep, for you may touch them not. Greater Love. Wilfred Owen. AtBAP; BrPo; CMoP; EnLoPo; FaBoMo; FaBoRV; FaFP; GTBS-P; LiTM; LiTM; MasP; MoAB; MoBrPo; NAMP; NoAm; OAEP; SeCeV; ViBoPo; WaaP; WaP

Weepe heavens, mourne earth, here Summer ends. Summer's Farewell. Nashe [(or Nash[) Thomas. PoEL 1-5

Weepe then, onely be exprest/Thus much, Hee's Dead, and weepe the rest. Upon the Death of a Gentleman. Richard Crashaw. CavP

Weeping and cheering and crying, "Tamburlaine." Edinburgh Spring. Norman MacCaig. NMP

Weeping bitterly the little child cries: I die one of many. One of Many. Stevie Smith. OxBC

Weeping for lost Babylon. Babylon. Robert Graves. HBMV

Weeping for meagre Ithaca/and plain Penelope. Odysseus' Song to Calypso. Peter Kane Dufault. ErPo

Weeping from their pollen hearts/hunger for your return. Vigil of the Wounded. Phillip Yellowhawk Minthorn. STE

Weeping in the/spring, summer, fall,/and winter of/humiliation. Privation. Hayden Carruth. FAZ

Weeping or smiling pearles to Celia's face. Lips and Eyes. Giambattista Marino. OBVE

Weeping that we can follow naught else. Impressions of Francois-Marie Arouet (de Voltaire) (excerpt). Ezra Pound. MoAB

Weeping, they kiss; to the Squire's lasting shame,/Who broke the heart in both. Kit Logan and Lady Helen. Robert Graves. HBMV

Weeping water maidens/That were once so fair. The Willows. Walter Prichard Eaton. HBMV; OHIP

Weeps at a nude by Michael Angelo. Corporate Entity. Archibald MacLeish. OBAL

Weeps on that placid neck, kisses the God-calmed face. Jacob and the Angel. Brother Antoninus. MoRP

'Weh down Souf. 'Weh Down Souf. Daniel Webster Davis. BANP

Wei la la. After this it gets deep. Limerick: "The Thames runs, bones rattle, rats creep." Wendy Cope. FaBoWP

Weighing a handful of berries,/a handful of stones. Pastoral. Ellen Bryant Voigt. MAYP

Weighs a Pound and a Quarter. A Pint of Water. Anonymous. FaBoUs

Weighs/Two pounds, net. All the Smoke. Eli Siegel. CAD; ELU; FiBHP

A weight more grave than marble on the breast. Caryatid. Léonie Adams. LiTM; MoVE

The weight/of my father's/box Home. Sam Cornish. CNA

...A weight/Of paper, a half-handful of silver speech. Inflation. Charles O. Hartman. PoA

Weightless, it/could fly. Horse. Randy Blasing. PH

The weighty echoes of Bessie's moan. Richard, Richard: American Fuel. Melvin Dixon. LTB

Weill, gin they arena deid, it's time they were. Elegy. Robert (Robert Sutherland) Garioch. OxBS

Weisst nicht wie gut ich dir bin. Du, Du Liegst Mir Im Herzen. Anonymous. FSW

Wel aughte ich hir yerne to wive/Whenne hie bit so for my live.' Floris and Blauncheflour: A Lover's Stratagem. Anonymous. OxBM

Wel may swych a lady/Godes moder be. I Syng of a Mayden. Anonymous. EnPo; OAEP

Welcome Welcome Yule. Anonymous. CAW; CH

Welcome all who lead or follow,/To the Oracle of Apollo. Verses Placed Over the Door at the Entrance into the Apollo Room... Ben Jonson. HBV 1-2

Welcome among my pleasant smart. Farewell the reign of cruelty! Sir Thomas Wyatt. FCP; SiPS

"Welcome be thou Heaven's King,/On Christ's Sunday at morn!" As I Sat under a Sycamaore Tree. Anonymous. ChBR; LiTB; ViBoPo

Welcome celestial mirror and espy! Welcome to the Sun. Gavin Douglas. ACP

Welcome, darling, be blessed three times/for all the hours of our separation. You came. And you did well to come. Sappho. BoWoP

Welcome fair Bethsabe, King David's darling. David and Bethsabe. George Peele. ViBoPo

Welcome home; welcome home. Go Home. Janet Reed McFatter. GrPl

Welcome in the sweet o' the year. The Sweet o' the Year. George Meredith. BoNaP

Welcome love, and welcome gladness!/Hallelujah! Still Thy Sorrow, Magdalena! E. A. Washburn. BePJ

The welcome of thy beckoning hand? Snow-Bound. John Greenleaf Whittier AA

"Welcome, proud lady".' The Heart of Midlothian (excerpt). Sir Walter Scott. AtBAP; BSV; CBEP; CoBE; EnRP; ERoP 1-2; FaBoCh; FF; GoTS; GTBS; HBV 1-2; LoBV; LoGBV; NBM; OAEL 1-2; OAEP; OBEV; OBRV; OxBS; PBBP; PoEL 1-5; SeCePo; SeCeV; TEP; TrGrPo; UnPo

Welcome, sweet Luke, to your life. Firstborn (excerpt). Charles Wright. GP

Welcome the coming of the longed-for May. Spring. Thomas Carew. GN

Welcome, the journey is ended. Song of Welcome. Hermia Fraser. CaP

Welcome then poverty!/flights of strings above the orange trees! Childhood in Jacksonville, Florida. Jane Cooper. TAP

Welcome to mee, my onely joy,/all times be it light or dark. Come Turn to Mee, Thou Pretty Little One. Anonymous. CoMu

"Welcome, welcome, warnin bell,/But the God o Heaven keep me out o hell. The Cruel Mother (B vers.). Anonymous. BaBo; ESPB

Welcomed with Cafe/con Canela. California #2. Victor Hernandez Cruz. TAT

(Welcoming humbly His light and proudly His darkness) I am a little church (no great cathedral). Edward Estlin Cummings. MoRP; NePoAm-2

The welkin flash and thunder to the hoofs/Of Dawn's tremendous team? Horses. Dorothy Wellesley. ChMP; OBMV; OxBTC

Well, and what matters it...while you are too! When Helen First Saw Wrinkles in Her Face. Walter Savage Landor. EnLoPo

"Well! And you?" Heaven. Langston Hughes. GoSl

Well as I might, the parlour I perused... Tales of the Hall. George Crabbe. Par

Well, ask another. Why Do We Live? Israel Zangwill. TrJP

...Well,/at least forget what happens when it thaws. Russians. Keith Douglas. OxBTC

Well, beds are soft,/and I'm no thinner. Songs of Cheng. Confucius. CTC

Well, bliss is in ignorance: what's the harm! At a Watering-Place. Thomas Hardy. BrPo; CMoP

Well–but you mean Lord–? Hush! we mean the same. On a Lord. Samuel Taylor Coleridge. FaBoCo; FiBHP; PV

Well could I wish it would be ever day,/If, when night comes, you bid me go away. Night and Day. Michael Drayton. LiTB

Well, dey lef' po' Bessie dyin'/wid de blood (Lawd) a-streamin' down. Blues for Bessie. Myron O'Higgins. PoNe

Well died, my old cat. My Old Cat. Hal Summers. OxBTC; PCat

Well done, Sir Walter Scott! On a Day's Stint. Sir Walter Scott. NBM

"Well done! you did your best." His Best. Anonymous. STF

Well, endure is all I can do, reduced to.... There's a Man, I Really Believe.... Sappho. WeW

Well, every time I looked, babe,/She'd be on my mind. East St. Louis Blues. Anonymous. AmFP

Well for whatever lonely one/Will find this right place to lay down/His desert in. Midsummer. Thomas Kinsella. IPY

"Well, good-by, Jim:/Take keer of yourse'f!" The Old Man and Jim. James Whitcomb Riley. AA; StPo

..."Well, goodbye now! I'm going!" January. Elizabeth Jane Coatsworth. PoSC

"Well, he don't know Nellie like I do!"/Said the saucy little bird on Nellie's hat. The Bird on Nellie's Hat. Arthur J. Lamb. FSN

Well, he was born in Paris, France. Look, Edwin! Edna St. Vincent Millay. GoJo

Well, here's the man. Thanks for dropping in. Coming of Age in the County Jail. Carter Revard. VoR

Well his wife and his mother naturally cried. O. T.'s Blues. Waring Cuney. MAT

Well I believe I'll marry/Oooooo oooo, lord, and settle down Nothing in Rambling. Memphis Minnie. BluL

Well, I believe it would make me whole. I Am a Pilgrim. Anonymous. FSW

Well I better settle for some other man's milkcow/oooo in this same man's town Milkcow's Calf Blues. Robert Johnson. BluL

Well I'd like to love you, baby/but your good man got me barred Savannah Mama. Blind Willie McTell. BluL

Well, I'd never go to sea/Aboard that handy little bark, the Campanero! The Campanero. Anonymous. ShS

Well, I don't b'lieve I'd 'a' been here, wringin' my hand an' cryin'./Whoa dere! Trouble, Trouble. Anonymous. OuSiCo

Well, I forget the rest. Memorabilia. Robert Browning. ACV; FiP; HBV 1-2; LoBV; MBW 1-2; NOBV; NoP; OAEL 1-2; OAEP; OBNC; PP; SeCePo; TreFT; WHA

Well I hate to hear/that old fireman when he tones his bell/(oh, ring 'em a long time)/Mmmmm..... Flying Crow. Black Ivory King. BluL

Well I just come here/to have a few/words with you Jailhouse Blues. Bessie Smith. BluL

Well I'm gon' leave here On the Wall. Louise Johnson. BluL

Well I'm worried now and I won't be worried long Mind Reader Blues. Bertha Lee. BluL

Well I needs my daddy 'cause my/clock is run down at home. Big Night Blues. Blind Lemon Jefferson. BluL

Well, I never before saw a pig dance a jig! Little Piggy. Thomas Hood. SoPo

Well, I've got the gambler's blues. St. James Infirmary. *Anonymous.* FSW

Well, I will soon enough be twenty-four. Milton's Wife on Her Twenty-Third Birthday. Jane Conant-Bissell. AMV-80

Well, I wish him a thousand harems of a thousand wives apiece,/and a thousand little ones by each.. Piano Tuner, Untune Me That Tune. Ogden Nash. UnS

Well if I had, that wicked way/If I had/Eh Lord/I'd tear this building down If I Had My Way. Blind Willie Johnson. BluL

Well if I/meet my good gal, well I/Won't be back at all Maggie Campbell Blues. Tommy Johnson. BluL

Well is he born that may behold you ever. Amoretti, VIII. Edmund Spenser. AAS; CABA; HBV 1-2; NoP; OAEP; TrGrPo

Well, it hurts me too. When Things Go Wrong with You. *Anonymous.* FSW

Well, it's hey, hey, hey, hey, hey. Easy Rider. *Anonymous.* FSW

Well–it's just a dream house, anyway. Vagabond House. Don Blanding. BLPA

Well–it's Me! Fairies. Rose Fyleman. HBMV; HBVY; OxBChV; SoPo

Well, it's ride, ride, ride. Railroad Bill (with music). *Anonymous.* AS

Well, it's sound sleep and long sleep, and sleep too deep to/wake. Wanderer's Song. Arthur Symons. ViBoPo

Well it's the last chance, shaking in the bed with you Fare Thee Well Blues. Joe Calicott. BluL

Well, it seems like everything/That I do is wrong. Old Hannah. *Anonymous.* FSW

Well, it was, if you like. But we hid it with masterly skill. Back Room Joys. Justin Richardson. FiBHP

–Well, it won't matter so very much, either. Fate and the Younger Generation. D. H. Lawrence. OxBoLi

Well, Jack's avenged; as for the other, gr-r-r-r! The Flight of the Bucket (parody). Rudyard Kipling. BXAP

The well-known faces are all gone,/and the fret is on me. The Old Pensioner. William Butler Yeats. InPK

The well-known secrets of Astolpho's cup/Not to disclose, but with white wax seal up? Caelica, XXXIII. Fulke, Lord Brooke Greville. FCP

Well, make haste home–I've got, I've got no brass.' The Royal Tour. Peter Pindar. NOEC; OxBoLi

Well may I pitie; she must cure thy pain. Piscatorie Eclogues. Phineas Fletcher. SeCV 1-2

Well may she speede and fairely finish her intent. The Faerie Queene. Edmund Spenser. OAEL 1-2; OAEP

Well may such a lady Goddes mother be. I Sing of a Maiden. *Anonymous.* AtBAP; CABA; CBEP; EBEV; EG; ELP; ExPo; FaBoCh; FF; HAP; InPo; InPS; ISi; LiTB; LoGBV; MeEL; MeEV; NOBE; NOCV; NoP; OAEL 1-2; OxBM; PAI; PoEL 1-5; SBVL; SCV; SeCeV; TreFS; TrGrPo; ViBoPo; WeW

Well, maybe–I'm not city-bred. A Pasture. Frederic Lawrence Knowles. AA

Well my wedded Lord loves me. Abenamar, Abenamar. *Anonymous.* AWP

Well named is that bay of the "Hundred/Fires." Cut the Cables. Robert Burns Wilson. PAH

Well, never mind that now. Good night! Good night! Sisters. Amy Lowell. AnNE; NMM; SBG

Well, next time you're passing through/You'll remember what to do. What the Toys Are Thinking. ffrida Wolfe. TiPo

Well, not on our +eotype. Composed in the Composing Room. Franklin Pierce ("F.P.A.") Adams. NIP; OBAL

Well now, away with my wife and welcome,/Then my troubles will have an end. A Poor Man's Work Is Never Done. *Anonymous.* OBET

Well now I love my little woman/I want the whole world to know Remember Way Back. L. C. Green. BluL

Well now you was in the bottom/by the red hot stove Charlie Cherry. Lil' Son Jackson. BluL

Well practis'd in love's schoole, let him within/Weare all his beard, and none uppon his chinn. A Ladies Prayer to Cupid. Giovanni Battista Guarini. OBVE

Well, remember to do it by doing rather than by not doing. Portrait of the Artist as a Prematurely Old Man. Ogden Nash. BLPL; CrMA; FaFP; InPS; LiTA; LiTM; NePA

"Well," said she, "perhaps I may my dear,/When I've nothing else to do." As I'd Nothing Else to Do. Herbert Fry. GoTF; TreFS

Well, since you has come back to me/ooo well well, I hope you have come to stay More Good Whiskey Blues. Peetie Wheatstraw. BluL

"Well, so I came." The Telephone. Robert Frost. AnFE; APA; HBV 1-2; SO; SoSe

"Well, so what–/it was a shot! A shot–/that's all that matters." Soccer. Andrei Voznesensky. LiSp

Well, still I've got my old jack-knife. Luck. Wilfred Wilson Gibson. EtS; MoShBr; OBMV

Well swum swan! Swan Swam over the Sea. *Anonymous.* OxNR

Well taught by that to feel his rights, prepar'd/With this "the blessings he enjoys to guard." The Swiss Peasant. William Wordsworth. OBEC

Well, thank God for rum. Solioquy I. Richard Aldington. BrPo

Well, that's the hobo's lullaby. Hobo's Lullaby. *Anonymous.* FSW

Well,/that's the way it is with me somehow. January Morning. William Carlos Williams. InPS; PAI; SOTW

Well that's the way the ozone goes and goes. Aerosol. Harold Witt. SOTS

Well the cat jumped over and the rat got sober,/Ran back to his hole again. The Intoxicated Rat. *Anonymous.* FSW

Well the row so grassy,/I can hardly go, I can hardly go. If You See My Mother. Mack Maze. WTO

Well, the women oughta carry me, follow me to my grave. The Cowboy's Lament (II). *Anonymous.* CoSo

Well then think of your great great etc. Uncle/Patrick Henry. My Great Great etc. Uncle Patrick Henry. James Tate. GP; OBAL

"Well, then your uncles are–" Lions and Gruel and Uncles. Lewis (Charles Lutwidge Dodgson) Carroll. FaBoNo

Well, there are other Mermaids on the Beach. Myself when Young (parody). Tom Donnelly. BXAP

Well, there's my musing ended. Poets and Linnets (parody). Thomas Hood. CenHV; HBV 1-2

Well they sell your wife skins and/take her away from you Skin Man. Henry Brown. BluL

Well, though the bow's unbent, the wound bleeds on. She Used to Let Her Golden Hair Fly Free. Petrarch (Francesco Petrarca). NAWM 1-2

Well to praise and please her, well to make/this for her sake. For Her Sake. Alastair Reid. PoPl

Well-uddered heifers, bullocks strong and stout. Young Stock. Victoria Mary (Vita) Sackville-West. OxBTC

Well when I leave this time/I'm gonna hang crepe on/Your door The Jinx Blues. Son House. BluL

...–Well, who knows that but God? The Tinkers. Joseph Campbell. OnYI

Well worth the taking, having, and the giving. Firm Belief. *Anonymous.* PoToHe

"Well, yes, your Honour," I said, "that's right." Dooley Is a Traitor. James Michie. NePoEA-2; OxBTC

Well you know I'm a hoochie coochie man/Everybody knows I'm here Hoochie Coochie. Muddy Waters. BluL

Wells in the heart when all thy truth appears,/Lest death should vanquish love. Last Refuge. Buonarroti Michelangelo. LiTW

The wells of his offering,/Pour down. Pour Down. John Holmes. NePoAm

Welsh fish are not fussy. The Moorhen Pond. Tom Earley. BoAnP

Went a-hog hunting as hard as they could stave,/Groundhog. Groundhog. *Anonymous.* FSW

Went–and ne'er returned again! Hope. Emily Bronte. NoP

Went apple-plucking there/In Jaen,/Axa and Fatima and Marien. Song: "Three Moorish girls I loved." *Anonymous.* LiTW

Went down a rope to say/his prayers. A Rat. *Anonymous.* OxNR

Went forth to fight, with murderous faces. A London Fete. Coventry Patmore. HAP; NBM

Went hobble, hobble, hobble. The Girl in the Lane. *Anonymous.* OxNR

Went home, and was cudgel'd again by his wife. Abroad and at Home. Jonathan Swift. DBV

Went home to alabama/to brag about/it. With All Deliberate Speed. Don L. Lee. JB

Went out upon Circumference–/Beyond the Dip of Bell– I saw no way–the heavens were stitched. Emily Dickinson. BoWoP

Went sauntering through the wood. Emerson. Mary Mapes Dodge. AA

...Went to rest/under a hollow rock where swine were sleeping/out of the wind and rain. The Odyssey. Homer. NAWM 1-2

Went under the black sea, and rose with the sun, and am born. Night and the Child. Judith Wright. SeCePo

Were a feste with suche folk, or so fele cockes. The Vision of Piers Plowman. William Langland. OxBM

Were barren as this moorland hill. The Sun upon the Weirdlaw Hill. Sir Walter Scott. BSV

Were defeats with which the Gestapo/continues ceasing and ceasing. The Extermination of the Jews. Marvin Bell. VWA

Were ever able to dispatch, by fear. Epigram. Samuel (1612-80) Butler. FaBoEE

Were fading, and all wars were done. The Dark Hills. Edwin Arlington Robinson. AP; CoBMV; FaFP; GoJo; HAP; LiTA; LiTM; MoAB; MoAmPo; NePA; NoAm; WeW; WHA

Were flooded over with eddying song. The Dying Swan. Alfred, Lord Tennyson. PBBP; WiR

Were gratitude its very best,/Each life would be thanksliving. Thanksliving. Chauncey R. Piety. PGD

Were he divine, how would we have recognized him? Christ. Theodore Holmes. CoPo

Were heard of none beside the mournful/robins. Sonnet Written at the End of "The Floure and the Lefe." John Keats. EnRP

Were I a flea in bed I would not bite you,/But search some other way for to delight you. Lady, the Silly Flea. *Anonymous.* NCEP

Were I come o'er again' cries Chirst "it should be this." The Soldier. Gerard Manley Hopkins. WaaP

Were I not born to be in Dutch. Love-Songs, At Once Tender and Informative. Samuel Hoffenstein. OBAL

Were I open/to any more fullness, I think I'd/turn into a woman. Lines from an Orchard Once Surveyed by Thoreau. Philip Booth. GP

Were it not for making a living, which is rather a nouciance. Introspective Reflection. Ogden Nash. NLV

Were it not for stealing, stealing. Fairies' Song. [James Henry] Leigh Hunt. ALV

Were it not madness to deny/To live because we're sure to die? To a Lady Asking Him How Long He Would Love Her. Sir George Etherege. CEP; HBV 1-2; LiTL; LoBV; OBEV; ViBoPo

Were it undo that is y-do/I wolde be-war. A Forsaken Maiden's Lament. *Anonymous.* SeCePo

Were "John S. Clark as Acres at the Charing Cross tonight." Saved. *Anonymous.* FaBoUs

Were mad to fly forth from their nests in the north,/And follow the trail of the bird. The Trail of the Bird. W. J. Courthope. HBVY

Were models to the universe. Aurora Leigh. Elizabeth Barrett Browning. GLGT

Were more fun to be with. Family Court. Ogden Nash. FiBHP

Were munched by a cow/When mistaken for clover. Third Limick. Ogden Nash. NePA

Were nature's endowments to Val. On the Same. Dante Gabriel Rossetti. FaBoEE

Were never cursed with feeble lungs. Operatic Note. Melville Cane. UnS

Were only kings themselves to fight, there'd be an end to war. Jeannot's Answer. Charles Jeffries. BLPA

Were said to be living together again. Damon & Pythias. Robert Creeley. LCAP

Were selling shrouds my business,/No man would ever die! Out of Luck. Abraham Ibn Ezra. TrJP

Were slily crept into his human powers,/And gave him graceful posture. Coriolanus. William Shakespeare. FaBoPV

Were steps to the great place where trees and torrents go. The Torrent. Edwin Arlington Robinson. NePA

Were't not enclos'd within a pale of gold. On a Seal. Plato. AWP

Were the clothes of a king's son,/Just my size. The Ballad of the Harp-Weaver. Edna St. Vincent Millay. MaC; StPo; WSC

Were the land angels making God a hymn. Sea-Nurtured. Jean Ingelow. EtS

Were the lies killed overnight/Rising from the dead with dawn. The Liar. *Anonymous.* KiLC

Were the only bits of charm/which overcame his folded arms. Uncle Bull-Boy. June Jordan. PoBA

Were thy beauty mine own, or thy lips, or thine eyes. Reproach. Firdausi. LiTW

Were twisted sheets and feather-pillows instead. Undergraduate. Merrill Moore. ErPo

Were we only white birds, my beloved,/buoyed out on the foam of the sea! The White Birds. William Butler Yeats. EnL

Were wrought more bright than brightest skies today. A Wet August. Thomas Hardy. PPP

Were you, indeed? Or did I dream a dream? Kinnereth. Rachel Bluwstein. LiTW; TrJP

Were you spared all this by drowning? Theodosia Burr. Myra Burnham Terrell. GoYe

Were you there or did I only dream? Perhaps. Rachel (Rachel Blumstein). VWA

Were you there when they laid him in the tomb? Were You There. *Anonymous.* AH

Wert thou his wedded bride. Forepledged. John Lancaster Spalding. AA

...Wert thou not blest? The Farewell of Clarimonde (excerpt). Ella Wheeler Wilcox. PeD

The West crowds hard, lustful as sin—/Yet never wholly enters in. Chinatown. Anna Blake Mezquida. BPAW

The west is not awake to where Titanic/Smokes in the morning, huge against the stars. R.M.S. Titanic. Anthony Cronin. BIrV

The West is won again. The Winning of the TV West. John T. Alexander. AmFN

West of the Pecos law was law! The Law West of the Pecos. Squire Omar Barker. BPAW

Westward leading, still proceeding,/Guide us to thy perfect light! We Three Kings of Orient Are. John Henry Hopkins, Jr. AH; OHIP; PCh

Westward, rocks rose through mists with no sense of direction. The Far Side of Introspection. Al Lee. CoAP

Westward the banner rolls/Over my wrong. In Prison. William Morris. AtBAP; NBM

...Wet black/arms there is/no deep enough. The Age of Reason. Jorie Graham. NPGG

The wet centre is bottomless. Bogland. Seamus Heaney. FaBoIP; IPY; NOBI; NoP

A wet dog is the lovingest. The Dog. Ogden Nash. GDP

Wet eyes/earthly sighs/O. Medieval Christ Speaks on a Spanish Sculpture of Himself. Rochelle Owens. CoPo

A wet heat rises up in the/air and touches us. Pot of Tea. Susan Griffin. NPGG

A wet leaf that clings to the threshold. Liu Ch'e. Emperor Wu-Ti. OBVE

Wetting the ground to form our roots Rehearsal. Cyril Dabydeen. BrSi

Wha'd be a king—a petty thing,/When a miller lives so happy? O Merry May the Maid Be. John Clerk. HBV 1-2

Wha e'er he be that winna dance/The Reel o' Tullochgorum. Tullochgorum. John Skinner. BSV; GoTS; OBEC; OxBS

Wha first beside his chair shall fa',/He is the King amang us three! Willie Brew'd a Peck o' Maut. Robert Burns. CEP; InPo; OxBS; ViBoPo

Wha is it hunts my laddie's hounds/Till fa' o' day? My Laddie's Hounds. Marguerite Elizabeth Easter. AA

Wha kens but it may rain? The Plaidie. Charles Sibley. HBV 1-2

Wha'll buy caller herrin',/New drawn frae the Forth? Caller Herrin'. Carolina Oliphant, Lady Nairne. HBV 1-2; MCCG; OBRV; OxBS

Wha my eggs wad tak, tak! Malison of the Stone-chat. *Anonymous.* GBP

Whack de loo-de-dum/Kate, you are my darling. The Shoemaker. *Anonymous.* TrAS

Whack fol de darral lal do. Doran's Ass. *Anonymous.* OnYI

Whacks to the lady to the rum-die-ah. The Frenchman's Ball. *Anonymous.* OuSiCo

Whae ever rides i' the Border side/Will mind the laird o' the Troughend. Parcy Reed. *Anonymous.* OxBB

Whan he of the apple ete and Eve it him betoght. An Adult Lullaby. *Anonymous.* MeEL

Whan ither trades begin to fail,/They can take their bowies and brew. Dugall Quin (B version). *Anonymous.* ESPB

Whan my soule the body parte fro,/Socoure it frome mine enmies' rage. A Short Prayer to Mary. *Anonymous.* MeEL

Whan nicht rov'd through this howe o' space/Afore a world was here. The Star. William Soutar. NeBP

Whan the Hooly Goost the made his habitacle. The Life of Our Lady. John Lydgate. EnPo

Whan the sun an' the moon meet in yon glen,/'Fore I'll return again. Son David. *Anonymous.* OxBB

Whan thow suffredis ded for me. Prayer of the Five Wounds (excerpt). *Anonymous.* AtBAP

Whan ye come hameless here/And ken ye are at hame. Scotland. William Soutar. OxBS

Whar the wicked cease from troublin' an' the weary are at rest. A Veteran Cowboy's Ruminations. John M. Kuykendall. PoOW

Whare'er your sinfu' pintle be. Godly Girzie. Robert Burns. CoMu; ErPo; UnTE

The wharf leans seaward in the ebb-tide chop. Jake's Wharf. Philip Booth. NYBP

What/A. A skull cap Forehead Dead-Ends Half-Way through the Poem (parody). D. C. Berry. BXAP

What a bang-up holiday! In the Motel. X. J. Kennedy. Str

What a bitch!/(and that's meaningful!). They Flee from Me That Sometime Did Me Seek. Gavin Ewart. OxBC

What a brawl until the sun appears/Majestic, like the law. Lobster Cove Shindig. Lillian Morrison. BoNaP

What a charming thing's a battle! The Recruiting Serjeant (excerpt). Isaac Bickerstaffe. NOEC

La, what a climb! The Bean-Stalk. Edna St. Vincent Millay. WSC

What a closed book bound in wrinkled illustration his/father is to him! The Visible Baby. Peter Redgrove. NAs

What a conundrum! The Poultries. Ogden Nash. CenHV

What a different place to-day/Where we live and work and play! Indian Children. Annette Wynne. SoPo; SUS; TiPo

What a fiery/Potentate! King Rufus. Y. Y. Segal. WHW

What a handsome couple they made. Drugs Made Pauline Vague. Stevie Smith. FaBoWP

What a hullabaloo there'd be. The Hen and the Carp. Ian Serraillier. OnUR

What a lad for cutting capers. Any Day Now. David McCord. QQQ; ShM

What a life after death. Vulture. Robinson Jeffers. BoAnP; NOBA; NoP

What a lovely smell, he said, we have here. The Taste of Space. A. J. M. Smith. PV

What a mess they leave. Middle Age. Paula Rankin. MAYP

What a nice fairy tale indeed. A Fairy Tale. Vitomil Zupan. DFT

What a nice smell the new cloth has. Balgu Song. *Anonymous.* CBAP

What a perfect day! What crystal! What paradise! Good Weather. Giuseppe Gioachino Belli. AMV-81

What a place to talk of War. The Closing Album. Louis MacNeice. FaBoIP

What a poky poet! Two Triolets. Harrison Robertson. HBV 1-2

What a pretty sight! Falling Snow. *Anonymous.* SoPo

What a procession of greenery. Girls on Saddleless Horses. R. G. Vliet. PH

What a splish-splash that would be! If All the Seas Were One Sea. *Anonymous.* OnUR; OxNR; SoPo

What a stone you have builded, what bronze/You have moulded, blown out of death! The Skaian Gate (excerpt). Geoffrey Scott. OBMV

"What a time to think of that,"/Said the first, and missed the hat. Rhyme of Rain. John Holmes. GrPl

What a way to go! In Passing. Gerald Jonas. GrPl

What a wonderful life has he! Gull. William Jay Smith. TiPo

What a wonderful piece of work is man. Times Square Parade. Robert Watson. NYP

What a world, what a life, I'm in love. I've Got the World on a String. Ted Koehler. BLSo

What about the flowers? Others. Harry Behn. SoPo; TiPo

What about them? There's always abandoned farms to use. Dialogue–2 Dollmakers. Gregory Corso. NeAP

What absolute nothing But. Edward Estlin Cummings. NoAm

What airs in dress an' gait wad lea'e us,/And ev'n devotion! To a Louse. Robert Burns. BLPA; CEP; FaFP; InvP; LiTB; NOEC; OAEP; OxBS; PrIm; SeCeV; TreF; ViBoPo

What all this new commotion is about. News That Stays News. Paul Mariani. GeTw

What am I and who am I? Should I Be a Rabbi? Hayim Nahman Bialik. TrJP

What an unfathomable world it is! Two Dogs. John Davidson. FM

What, and if, Ourself a bridegroom–/Put Her down–in Italy? Her–"last Poems"–. Emily Dickinson. SBG

What and where they be. Maud. Alfred, Lord Tennyson. AtBAP; EG; OBVV

What angels we should be! Row Gently Here. Thomas Moore. HBV 1-2

What answers we could look for/If on Wednesday you were there. Could You Spare Some Time for Jesus? Lester Knickman. STF

What are all these kissings worth,/If thou kiss not me? Love's Philosophy. Percy Bysshe Shelley. AtBAP; BLPA; BLPL; BoLoP; EnLi 1-2; FaBoBe; FaBV; GoTF; GTBS; GTBS-P; HBV 1-2; HoPM; LiTL; OAEP; OBRV; OLR; PG; TreFT; TrGrPo; UnTE; ViBoPo

What are all those fish that lie gasping on the strand? Three Movements. William Butler Yeats. CMoP; ELU; FaBoEE

What are deep? the ocean and truth. Epigram: "What are heavy? sea-sand and sorrow." Christina Georgina Rossetti. FaBoEE

What are eternal vows!–oh, give me breath/Of one white hour here on the marge of death! April Moment. Arthur Davison Ficke. HBMV

What are left, will hardly be/Better than we spent with thee. Poor Matthias. Matthew Arnold. FM; PoEL 1-5

...What are people doing with their/lives? what are they doing? Bunch Grass #37. Robert Sund. NU

What are slow?/Nursery Rhymes. Ding Dong (parody). Arthur Clement Hilton. BXAP; Par

What are the small final hooks? Distinguishing Ru from Chu. George Hitchcock. OBAL

What are they fear'd on? fools! 'od rot 'em!/Were the last words of Higginbottom. A Tale of Drury Lane. Horace (or Horatio) Smith. FaBoCo

What are we doing here in the dark? George Washington Goes to a Girlie Movie. Aram Boyajian. NeAC

What are we? I know not. The Monk in the Kitchen. Anna Hempstead Branch. AnFE; APA; MAPA; MoAmPo

What are we if not wholly catholic? Night Thoughts. Henri Coulette. FYAP

What are you–banded one? The Pool. Hilda ("H. D.") Doolittle. CMoP; ExPo

What are you better after tonight/Than Ned the beggar or Seaghan the fool? He Meditates on the Life of a Rich Man. Augusta Gregory, Lady Gregory. OBMV

"What are you doing/in this century/if you can't take it?" The Dinner. Gregory Orr. PoL

What are you doing, twinkling there? Twinkle, Twinkle, Little Star (parody). Paul Dehn. SpRo

...What/are you thinking now in the/silence circling up near Buzzard Rock? Reuben's Cabin. Robert Morgan. TAT

What are you waiting for/come home, come home, lost/in the waters, blue and permanent. The Drowned Children. Louise Gluck. HaCAP

What are you waiting for, tardy George? Tardy George. *Anonymous.* PAH

What art thou? His wicked eye/Is cruel to thy cruelty. Limits. Ralph Waldo Emerson. FM; OBSP; PoEL 1-5

What art thou in the scale of universe?/Less, less than nothing! Man's Littleness in Presence of the Stars. Henry Kirke White. WBLP

What Artist laughs? What clever Daemon thinks? Animal, Vegetable and Mineral. Louise Bogan. FM; SBG

What availeth it me though I say nay? The Unhappy Schoolboy. *Anonymous.* OxBChV

What avails it? He who is born must die." Frithiof's Farewell. Esaias Tegner. AWP

What bad thing can be done against us? Dakota: October, 1822. Hunkpapa Warrior. Rod Taylor. WeW

What balance sheet can tot the hideous score/Of this, the least considered crime of war? Time Out. Frances Westgate Butterfield. GoYe

What beards, what bald heads burst now from the bush! The Double Looking Glass. A. D. Hope. CBAP

What beating heart could sink to buy/The copy of the die complete! Construction. Karl Shapiro. PCP

What beauty past believing/Are you remembering? Alien. Archibald MacLeish. EtS

What benefit arises in this sphere/By twisting all one's being towards the sky. The Sloth. George J. Romanes. FM

What better place can Love require,/Than that where grow both shafts and fire? Ladies' Eyes Serve Cupid Both for Darts and Fire. A. W. OBSC

What bitter cups had been your due,/Had He not drank them up for you. His Saviour's Words, Going to the Cross. Robert Herrick. NOCV

What bitter wrongs I bear! Prometheus Bound. Aeschylus. LiTW

What Blood redeemeth you and me! Bethlehem Town. Eugene Field. PGD; WBLP

"What boat, sir, what boat? WHAT BOAT?" Abbreviated Interviews with a Few Disgruntled Literary Celebrities. Reed Whittemore. FiBHP

What bone shall speak for me? Meditation on a Bone. A. D. Hope. TW

What calm catastrophe will yet assuage/This final drouth of penitential tears. John Sutter. Yvor Winters. MoAmPo; MoVE; NoAm; NOBA; PoPl; QFR

What calumnies will feed their word–/To satiate its origin: the animal howl? The Animal Howl. J. M. TrJP

...–What can assuage/That fire or that misfire? The Princess Casamassima. Daniel Gerard Hoffman. GLGT

What can be good to me, since my love is,/To do me harm, content to do amiss? Caelica, LXIX. Fulke, Lord Brooke Greville. EnRePo; FCP

What can be sadder/than water/without sound? Water Without Sound. Malka Tussman. VWA

What can be said between one wave and the next? Seal Rock. Sue Baugh. AMV-81

"What can I do for you to-day?" General Store. Rachel Field. SoPo; SUS

"What can I do? It's my bread and butter." On This Island. W. H. Auden. TRV

What can I do, my cheated heart? The Tortured Heart. Arthur Rimbaud. PeHV

What can I do/To set things right? The Earnest Liberal's Lament. Ernest Hemingway. OBSV

What can it be, good God, good God. O My Belly. *Anonymous.* GBP; PoL

What can it be he does? The Butterfly. Kikaku. SoPo

What can keep his soul away,/From the transports of Mored? An African Song. Thomas Chatterton. LoBV

What can one mortal do against those two! Two Against One. *Anonymous.* UnTE

What can she be/Looking at? In the Mirror. Elizabeth Fleming. OnUR

...What/can't be reconciled is/home and steady at work. Model. Archie Randolph Ammons. FAZ

What can the poet wish his king may doe,/But that he cure the peoples evill too? An Epigram: "Great Charles, among the holy gifts of grace." Ben Jonson. OAEP

What can the road owners do to me, the black centipede,/rushing on, fixed to time? Praises of the Train. Demetrius Segooa. PeSA

What can they teach us, rivers and wars,/endless wars and rivers? December 24, 1979. Roger Weaver. SOTS

What can we do but follow thee. Hither We Come, Our Dearest Lord. Enoch W. Freeman. AH

What can we seek in Heaven, all we blind?   The Blind.   Charles Baudelaire. SyP

...What can you/cover and conceal?   People, male and female.   Mahadevi (Mahadeviyakka).   BoWoP

What can you say?   What Are You Doing for Jesus?   Martha Snell Nicholson.   BePJ

What can you say to me, or I to you?   Sonnets of a Portrait Painter. Arthur Davison Ficke.   AnAmPo

What care can move, what grief can chill?   Country of No Lack.   Jean Starr Untermeyer.   MoAmPo

What care I for howlet's cry,/For boor-tree bank, or warlock craigie?'   O! Are Ye Sleepin, Maggie?   Robert Tannahill.   OBRV; OxBS

What care I for whom she be?   Fidelia: Shall I, Wasting in Despair.   George Wither.   EIL

What care I if good God be/If he be not good to me?   Egocentric.   Stevie Smith.   FaBoNo

What care I what others be?   Answer to Master Wither's Song, "Shall I, Wasting in Despair?"   Ben Jonson.   InMe

What care ye though the world discovers/Your flowers of love, O flower of lovers!   Aucassin and Nicolete.   Francis William Bourdillon.   HBV 1-2

What chance for a squatter like me?   The Broken-Down Squatter. Anonymous.   PoAu 1-2

What clasp, what kiss mine inmost heart/can prove,/O lovely and beloved, O my love?   The House of Life.   Dante Gabriel Rossetti.   OAEP

What clothes he might have left, or other property.   The Sailor's Mother (excerpt).   William Wordsworth.   Par

What comes into your mind when two men fight?   Street Fight.   Harold Monro.   FaBoTw

What complaints have I to register?   Blues #8.   Anonymous.   HW

What confusion would cover the innocent Jesus/To meet so enabled a Man! He preached upon breadth.   Emily Dickinson.   NAWM 1-2; NOCV

What could be subtler/Than the thought of Sam Butler?   English Liberal. Geoffrey Taylor.   FaBoEE

What could offend thee, but my miserie.   De Ponto.   Ovid (Publius Ovidius Naso).   OBVE

What could we tell you/after you dove down into yourself/& were swallowed/ by your poems?   In Sylvia Plath Country.   Erica Jong.   IHMS

What country is this?   Duncan Spoke of a Process.   LeRoi (Imamu Amiri Baraka) Jones.   CAPP

What crown will be yours one day/O Amazon–   Young Girl.   Ricarda Huch.   WPOW

What cry of longing the lips divide?   The Two Burdens.   Philip Bourke Marston.   VLP

What curse, what blessing have you/laid on me/with white bellies which promise/your secret oceans?   Seabirds.   Robert B. Smith.   LFAC

What daily chaff and straw they've spun to gold.   The Name.   Sara Henderson Hay.   DFT

What Death can compare with the jolly Town-Rakes.   The Town-Rakes. Peter Anthony Motteux.   CoMu

What did he think he would become, a God? The devil!   When This Carnival Finally Closes.   Jack A. Mapanje.   WhB

...What did/I care, bobbing off in dark/blue sea, under light blue sky?   When I Was Dying.   William Hathaway.   APU

What did I do to deserve a heart like you?   To a Bad Heart.   Tim Reynolds. TW

What did I know, what did I know/of love's austere and lonely offices? Those Winter Sundays.   Robert Earl Hayden.   BP; CNA; CTBA; DFF; FF; GP; GrPl; HaCAP; HAP; HoAn; IDB; LCAP; NoAm; NoP; PoBA; PPP; SoSe; UnPo

What disregards people does people good.   An Address to the Vacationers at Cape Lookout.   William Stafford.   NYBP

What do a care if my belly be fu'?   John Hielandman.   Anonymous.   GBP

What do I care for dawn!   What Do I Care for Morning.   Helene Johnson. CDC

What do I care for your world of pleasure,/When all I want is a handsome man.   Kind Miss (with music).   Anonymous.   AS

What do I do without my legs?   Ambulance Call.   Lorrie Goldensohn. AMV-81

What do I gain by that I have undone?   What Shall It Profit?   William Dean Howells.   AA

What do they call me? My name is "Peaches."   Four Women.   Nina Simone.   MAT

What do they say as they lean together/In rain or sunshine or windy weather? The Two Old Women of Mumbling Hill.   James Reeves.   ShM

What do we care for their sneers and their hisses so/Long as we run up a goodly amount?   The Kiss-Fest.   Irwin Edman.   InMe

What do we care–we two!   The Turn of the Road.   Alice Rollit Coe.   HBV 1-2

What do we know/beyond the rapture and the dread?   The Abduction. Stanley Jasspon Kunitz.   SV

What do we wait for? Is it all a dream?   The Dance of Dust (parody). Louis Untermeyer.   BXAP

What do you build there./Little baby mine?   The Baby.   James Reaney. NAs

"What do you come for?'/"For YOU!'   The Strange Visitor.   Anonymous. FaBoCh; GBP

What do you do when you're born?   What Do You Do when It's Spring? John Woods.   ConAP

What do you do/with cards like these?   Dream 1971.   Victor Contoski. GP

What do you lack, sir? Come hither to me.   The Great Merchant, Dives Pragmaticus, Cries His Wares.   Thomas Newbery.   OxBChV

What do you seek,/poet, in the sunset?   Poems.   Antonio Machado.   LiTW

(What/do you suppose death will do, then?)   Respondez!   Walt Whitman. AmePo; NoAm; PoEL 1-5

What do you think, Patron Happiness?   Urban Ode.   Sandra McPherson. MAYP

What does it matter, then,/If I die here in a strange land?   Song of a Man about to Die in a Strange Land.   Anonymous.   DL

What does it say over the door of Heaven/But homo fecit?   For the New Railway Station in Rome.   Richard Wilbur.   NePoEA

What does not perish/Lives in thee.   There Is Nothing False in Thee. Kenneth Patchen.   PoPl

What does not reply is the answer to prayer.   The Temple.   C. H. Sisson. OxBTC

What does the second love bring? Only regret for the first.   Distich.   John Milton Hay.   FaBoEE

What doubt, what draining of the spirit's blood,/Were ended where you lay. When All the Young Were Dying.   Edmund Wilson.   AnAmPo

What dreadful tidings to convey unto his family.   Annette Myers; or, A Murder in St. James's Park.   Anonymous.   OxBoLi

What else could we do, for we were in love?   Curfew.   Paul Eluard. BoLoP

What else could we, what else could you, have done?   The Survivors. Adrienne Rich.   NYBP

What else gives light to Eternity?/the Worm, smiling, said to me.   It Was the Worm.   James Richard Broughton.   GP

What else have I to spur me into song?   The Spur.   William Butler Yeats. ELU

What else he does is up to you.   The Centaur.   Theodore Roethke. NePoAm-2

What else is there to sing about?   The One Song.   C. G. Hanzlicek. AMV-80

What else is war for/but to amuse the dead?   Investigation.   Julia Vinograd. IHMS

What else remains of their dark horoscope/But a tall tree and courage and a rope?   The Same Continued.   Wilfrid Scawen Blunt.   VLP

What else she learns,/I am afraid to/name.   White Bear.   Susan Griffin. GP

What envious Time takes from my face,/Bestow upon my mind.   If It Be True.   Esther Johnson.   OBSP

What errors here be found, are in Errataes place.   Upon Mrs. Anne Bradstreet Her Poems, &c.   John Rogers.   SCAP

What eternal hovers in/Him: speak, are you corpse?   The Largess.   Richard Eberhart.   LiTA

"What, everyone's out?/Why, everyone's in!'   Who's In.   Elizabeth Fleming. BrR

What evil, what unspeakable crime/Have you made your life worth?   After Experience Taught Me...   W. D. Snodgrass.   CAPP; CoAP; OBWP; PPP; TAP

What fable should I tell them,/That they should believe me?   When I Came from Colchis.   William Stanley Merwin.   AP; NePoEA; VGW

What farther means can reason now direct,/Or what relief from human wit expect?   Religio Laici.   John Dryden.   OxBoCh

What fearful monsters slouched about the sky?   Mythological Sonnets, VIII: "Suns in a skein."   Roy Fuller.   GTBS-P

What February can do when/She has a mind to!   February Birthday. Nancy Byrd Turner.   BiCB

What fire survive forever/myself is for my time.   Easter Eve 1945.   Muriel Rukeyser.   MiAP; NePA; VGW

What flames felt you who saw her noon of light?   On Archaeanassa.   Plato. AWP

...What flesh would come to/When I ripped off the lid.   Cruelty.   T. R. Hummer.   MAYP

...What fool is not so wise/To lose an oath to win a paradise?   Love's Labour's Lost.   William Shakespeare.   ViBoPo

What fools our fathers were, if this be true!   Vox Populi.   John Dryden. NOBE

What foot through heaven hath worn the milky way!   Poetry and Philosophy. Thomas Randolph.   OBS

What footie will do will be final.   Mips and Ma the Mooly Moo.   Theodore Roethke.   NLV

What footstep moved the fern?   March.   Elizabeth Jane Coatsworth.   YeAr

What fragrance the cool night bore/Along the country lane!   The Shepherd's Star.   Juan Ramon Jimenez.   LiTW

What fun to be a cat!   In Honour of Taffy Topaz.   Christopher Morley.   TiPo

What gain to us would all this bustle bring?   De Rerum Natura.   Lucretius (Titus Lucretius Carus).   CTC

What gaunt, gray thing gallops on o'er/ the world?   Were-Wolf.   Julian Hawthorne.   AA

What ghostly horse shall course the sky?   The Chase.   William Henry Davies.   BrPo

What girl or star sings now/like a swan on the Yellow River?   The Pleiades.   Mary Barnard.   NYBP

What God calls the other/Is not known to me.   At the Cedars.   Duncan Campbell Scott.   CaP; NOBC

What god, man, or hero/Shall I place a tine wreath upon!   Hugh Selwyn Mauberley, III.   Ezra Pound.   CoBMV; NOBA

What good is a star?   On Earth.   Forugh Farrokhzad.   BoWoP

What good is it to know?   Loneliness: An Outburst of Hexasyllables.   Hayden Carruth.   SM

What good is one shoe.   Disintegration.   Richard Shelton.   DFF

What good spirit undulates you still like kites that/Children are guardians of in cold blue?...   The Lighthouse Invites the Storm.   Malcolm Lowry.   NOBC

What grace warms the air like steam.   Motherhood.   Susan Ludvigson.   AMV-81

What grace was in the bleeding Lamb/Who died to make her free.   Hope of Our Hearts.   Sir Edward Denny.   BePJ; STF

What great Effects from slender Causes flow!   Oppian's Halieuticks (parody).   William Diaper.   BXAP; FM; NOEC; PeD

What great PROGRESS that would be!   If All the Thermo-Nuclear Warheads.   Kenneth Burke.   QQQ

What greater power than this has brush or pen:/To bring the thought of God to simple men?   A Flemish Madonna.   Charles Wharton Stork.   HBMV

What ha' years in store for me?   Times o' Year.   William Barnes.   BoNaP

What had 'e had? Had 'e had haddie?   Limerick: "There once was a bonnie Scotch laddie."   *Anonymous.*   LiBL

What hands so urge, what powers compel.   Creatrix.   Anna Wickham.   MoBrPo

What hap, what heaven, what life, were like to love?   Sweet Unsure.   Sir Walter Ralegh.   SiPS

What happened to it in mid-December.   A Backward Spring.   Thomas Hardy.   PPP

What happens and the happening/That will never come to pass.   The Head.   Padraic Fallon.   CIP

What harm is a little brown mouse?   John Watts.   *Anonymous.*   OxNR

What has become of our astonishment/We wonder, now our early gift is spent.   The Way We Wonder.   Robert Pack.   NePoEA

What has the popular report to say/Of us, the Thespians at Thermopylae?   The Thespians at Theermopylae.   Norman Cameron.   ChMP; GTBS-P

What has us listen to what we may not hear?   The Storm.   John Hay.   AMV-81

What hast thou given that I gave not?   Epitaphs of the War, 1914-18.   Rudyard Kipling.   BrPo; OBWP

What hath night to do with sleep?   A Masque Presented at Ludlow Castle (Comus).   John Milton.   EG; WHA

"What have I done, Lord,/Have mercy on me."   Cherry Tree Carol.   *Anonymous.*   AmFP; FSW

What have I done with my life?   The Old Adam.   Denise Levertov.   NaP; UnPo

What have I made.   Poem for a Song.   Heather Cadsby.   AMV-80

What have I not, if I have but her heart!   Her Heart.   Bartholomew Griffin.   TrGrPo

...What have they accomplished, why am I cold?   The Bee Meeting.   Sylvia Plath.   HaCAP; InPS; PAI; PPP

What have they done to the rain?   What Have They Done to the Rain.   Malvina Reynolds.   FSW

What have we bought?/What have we paid for?   Footnote to Enright's "Apocalypse."   Martin Bell.   FaBoMo

What have we given him? Just a/grave!   A Grave in Hollywood Cemetery, Richmond.   Margaret Junkin Preston.   AA

;What have you had anyhow/better than sleep?   Death Snips Proud Men.   Carl Sandburg.   CMoP

What have you not refused?   Stanzas Written on Battersea Bridge during a Southwesterly Gale.   Hilaire Belloc.   GoBC

What havoc, ye gods, shall we have when he wakes?   Sir Dilberry Diddle, Captain of Militia.   *Anonymous.*   NOEC

What he did with every cent.   The Hardship of Accounting.   Robert Frost.   FaBoCh; FaBoCo; FaFP; LoGBV; OBAL

What he had carried home beneath his coat/one afternoon in winter.   Beauty and Sadness.   Cathy Song.   MAYP

What he's to trust to. Boy, give ear!   Cupid's Indictment.   John Lyly.   ElL

What he utters/Will touch/The depths of survival.   Painting.   A. C. Jacobs.   VWA

What height for love could be too high,/Or depth for love too deep?   Deep Waters.   Van Tassel Sutphen.   AA

What hem needeth at here neighebores at non and at/even.   The Vision of Piers Plowman.   William Langland.   PoEL 1-5

...What hides itself/When the skein of Time slowly divides itself?   De Profundis Clamavi.   Charles Baudelaire.   SyP

What hinders but my bosom still might be/Thy heaven to Thee?   Quaerit Jesum suum Maria.   Richard Crashaw.   ACP; CAW

...What his hard Heart denies,/His charitable Vanity supplies.   Timon's Villa.   Alexander Pope.   OBEC

What holds for her Death's garner? And for thee?   Michelangelo's Kiss.   Dante Gabriel Rossetti.   MaVP

What holds my rain so it's hard to overcome?   A Rain of Rites.   Jayanta Mahapatra.   PoA

...What holds you/to what you see of me is/that grasp alone.   Everything That Acts Is Actual.   Denise Levertov.   NoAm

What hope at last can such impes have,/That from the wombe goes to the grave.   Epitaph.   Thomas Morton.   SCAP

What hurts appeased by the sea's handsomeness!   Wreaths.   Geoffrey Hill.   PoA

What I choose/is youse:/baby   Coon Song.   Archie Randolph Ammons.   NoAm; NOBA

What I come to do/is partial, partially kept.   The Innocence.   Robert Creeley.   NeAP; NoAm

What I did, you must have done.'   Damon and Cupid.   John Gay.   EnLoPo

What I do mind is going four to not to.   Epigrams.   Martial (Marcus Valerius Martialis).   OBVE

What I don't know isn't knowledge.   First Come I; My Name Is Jowett.   Henry Charles Beeching.   NOBL

What I feel for the elephants and the miasmas/And the general view.   Lady "Rogue" Singleton.   Stevie Smith.   FaBoWP; OBSP

What I have lost: what I possess forever.   My Dead.   Rachel (Rachel Blumstein).   VWA

What I have written I have written.   What I Have Written I Have Written.   Peter Porter.   NOAV

...What I hear is the murmur/Of underground streams, what I see is a limestone landscape.   In Praise of Limestone.   W. H. Auden.   CMoP; CoBMV; FaBoPV; FYAP; HAP; MoAB; MoVE; NePA; NoAm; NoP; OAEL 1-2; PPP

...What I heard now/was a kind of completion he found/only outside himself.   The Second Violinist's Son.   Debora Greger.   AMV-80

What I keep of you, or you rob from me.   With You a Part of Me.   George Santayana.   TrGrPo

What I left, that I lost.   Epitaph...on the Grave of Thomas Osborne, Died 1749.   *Anonymous.*   TreFS

What I mean by too much metaphor and/simile.   Very Like a Whale.   Ogden Nash.   BLPL; DTC; HAP; InPK; InPS; PoLf; TrGrPo; WeW

What, I pray, is this love in the breast?   Breakers over the Sea.   *Anonymous.*   WTO

What I remember about the tangerine/is how easily the skin came off.   Two Childhood Memories.   Al Zolynas.   LTB

What I sang when Night was on the waters!   Lilium Regis.   Francis Thompson.   HBMV

...What I saw was veil'd/And cover'd; and this Quest was not for me.   Idylls of the King.   Alfred, Lord Tennyson.   GoBC

...What/I took in my hand/grows in weight.   Song: "What I took in my hand."   Robert Creeley.   NoP; PoA

What I will never understand/is the beast who writes this/and claims the centre of life.   Force.   Derek Walcott.   OxBC

What if all you have learn'd but the more endears/Those seven years?   Seven Years.   Robert, Marquess of Crewe.   OBVV

What if he knocked at my empty heart/And said, "Sweet, let me in!"   Doubt.   Elinor Chipp.   HBMV

What if the pawns should give checkmate,/Iscariot?   The Pawns.   Frank Betts.   HBMV

"What, if you please,/Did you mean by The Mill on the Floss?"   T. S. Eliot.   W. H. Auden.   OBAL

What ill, though ask'd, deny.   The Ignorance of Man.   James Merrick.   OxBoCh

What immortal hand or eye,/Dare frame thy fearful symmetry?   The Tiger.   William Blake.   AWP; BBV; EnPE; FaBoBe; FaBoPV; FaFP; FaPoR; FPL; GN; GoTF; HBV 1-2; ILwL; InPS; LiTB; MCCG; MyFE; NIP; NOBE; OBEC; OBEV; PAI; PG; PoLf; PoPl; PoPle; PoRA; PrIm; RoGo; SoSe; SpRo; TEP; TreF; TRV; UnPo; ViBoPo; WGRP; WHA

What, in any case, does it matter what/You want? You're in my way.   Not My Best Side.   U. A. Fanthorpe.   FaBoWP

What in you were words/in them shall be roots.   Message.   Renata Pallottini.   WPOW

What is a pocket but a hole?   Pockets.   Howard Nemerov.   NIP

What is a troubadour?   The Banjo Player.   Fenton Johnson.   AnAmPo; BANP; GoSl; PoNe

What is all our praise to them,/That have one another's eyes?   Deirdre (excerpt).   William Butler Yeats.   ViBoPo

What is history? What you cannot touch.   Mexico.   Robert Lowell.   HaCAP

What is it makes the duck, I wonder, go/Suddenly under?   Regent's Park.   Rose Fyleman.   SoPo

...What is it/makes you take love so hard?   Just.   Judith Johnson Sherwin.   TAP

What is it that you say?   Hospital for Defectives.   Thomas Blackburn.   GTBS-P; OxBTC

What is left?   What Is Left?   Assata Shakur.   AMV-80

What is left is nothing–/Ashes blown along the shore!   Fires of Driftwood.   Isabel Ecclestone MacKay.   CaP

What is left take from seven, and the letter is given.   To Find the Dominical Letter.   *Anonymous.*   FaBoUs

What is left to make us try?   Winter Drive.   James Philip McAuley.   PoA

What is lost shall not be found!   The Bridal Pair.   William Young.   AA

What is Loves Sacrifice but the Broken Heart.   Upon Ford's Two Tragedies...   Richard Crashaw.   OBS

What is my life to me, now you are departed!   Lament of a Man for His Son.   Mary Austin.   AWP; BPAW

...What Is/onto the shrine/of/...What Should Be   Shrine to What Should Be.   Mari E. Evans.   NNP

What is orange? Why, an orange,/Just an orange!   Color.   Christina Georgina Rossetti.   SoPo

What is past is past.   A Harvest to Seduce.   Melville Cane.   NYBP

What is permissively called:/separate and equal amenities!   Pimville Station.   Sipho Sepamla.   WhB

What is promised by one, surely the other/performs.   Steer, Bold Mariner, On!   Friedrich von Schiller.   MC; PAH

What is real? cried the oyster, glob of spit/In a pane of glass.   Terminal Theater.   Robert Sward.   CoPo

What is so be so, what prevails prevail?   A Storm from the East.   Reed Whittemore.   NYBP; PoPl

What is so simple as primitive Monkeydom/Born in the sea with a cold in its head?   Darwinity.   Herman Charles Merivale.   InMe; NA

What is/stopping you?   Underground Poetry.   Pedro Juan Pietri.   NYP

What is't a man sees?–/Fever and ague.   Canzonetta: A Bitter Song to His Lady.   Moronelli da Fiorenza   AWP; OBVE

What is that?/the pigeons?   The Power of Love He Wants Shih (Everything).   Rochelle Owens.   NMM

What is the animal/if not passage out of this life?   Horse.   Louise Gluck.   MAYP

What is the archaic now, in a world all future and space?   Party.   Constance Carrier.   NePoAm-2

What is the good of grieving/if nobody will listen/oh heart!   When I was a good and quick little girl.   *Anonymous.*   BoWoP

What is the key to Everlasting Life?/A blood-stained Cross.   Pennies.   Joyce Kilmer.   CAW

What is the matter with Mary Jane?   Rice Pudding.   A.(lan) A.(lexander) Milne.   BBGG

What is the Virgin Mary now to do?   "Through the Open Door..."   Patrick Kavanagh.   AnIV

What is their pity to me?   Inscription for the Tank.   James Wright.   TwCP

What is there cruel in a sunset sky?   Comfort.   Margaret Widdemer.   GoYe

What is there left for me?/Why, songs of thee.   Inexhaustible.   Israel Zangwill.   TrJP

What is there left to say?   The Curse of Cromwell.   William Butler Yeats.   BIrV; SeCePo

What is this peck,/peck, peck?   Poultry.   Diana Der Hovanessian.   GrPl

What is this thing called/love   Origins.   Keorapetse Kgositsile.   PoBA

What is to befall you, snow-pure one?   You shall be taken up/into Heaven. Vigil of the Assumption.   Gertrude von Le Fort.   ISi

What is water,/That pours silver/And can hold the sky?   Water.   Hilda Conkling.   ExPo; TiPo

What is written on it is that the summer is over....   The Long Picnic.   Russell Edson.   LCAP

What is your pleasure now?   To the Moon.   Yvor Winters.   HeIP

What is your time where so much time is saved?   Rivulose.   Archie Randolph Ammons.   SUW

What it has found out, running,/Is not told to me,/Though I ask.   Navajo.   William Haskel Simpson.   BPAW

What it is to be the guest/dirty unapologetic/of even a minor pinnacle.   Of Only a Single Poem.   G. J. F. Dutton.   PoSH

...What it showed in school.   Still Do I Keep My Look, My Identity...   Gwendolyn Brooks.   PoA

What it was, and it might serve me in a time when jests are few.   Epitaphs of the War, 1914-18.   Rudyard Kipling.   BrPo; FaBoEE; OBWP

What joy I found/Mounting that tiny/Stair of sound.   Late Winter.   James Philip McAuley(PoAu 1-2

What joy to be in flight.   Ode to Joy.   Michael McClure.   GP

What joy to see those diamonds burn/Their own clear space to dance and turn!   When Diamonds, Nibbling in my Ears.   William Henry Davies.   BrPo

What joys! What joys were thine!   To the Man-of-War Bird.   Walt Whitman   AA; AmP; BoAnP; EtS; FaBoBe; FM; HBV 1-2; NePA

What kind of flowers they will be.   April Puddle.   Rowena Bastin Bennett.   TiPo

"What kind of Indian are you?"/"a fuzzy Indian"   48 Words for a Woman's Dance Song.   Jerome Rothenberg.   PoM

What kind of talent have you got?   Rhyme from Grandma Goose.   Annemarie Ewing.   NePoAm

What kindness, sympathy and grace/Lie in the other person's place!   The Other Person's Place.   Donald H. Hover.   STF

What lady would not love a shepherd swain?   The Shepherd's Wife's Song. Robert Greene.   EG; ElL; EnLit; HAP; HBV 1-2; LoBV; OBSC; PG; ViBoPo

What laid her gently upon those sculptured steps?   Deir El Bahari: Temple of Hatshepsut.   D. J. Enright.   OBTV

What lands I was to tread in/Or what death I should dee.'   Mary Hamilton. *Anonymous.*   NOBE; OxBB

What last rite will open our arms/to the anarchy of love?   Beyond the Presidency.   Morgan Gibson.   FF

What lay beyond the western wind.   The Sea-King.   Lewis Frank Tooker.   EtS

What liberty/A loosened spirit brings!   He ate and drank the precious words.   Emily Dickinson.   AA

What lies north of the river/or past those hills that look like beasts   From the North Saskatchewan.   Eli Mandel.   NOBC

What life could not provide/Nor love endure.   Narcissus.   Charles Gullans.   NePoEA

What loads my hands down?   Going.   Philip Larkin.   CMoP

What loneliness.   Dr. Hu.   Norman Mailer.   ELU

...What/love might learn from such a sight.   Something.   Robert Creeley.   NaP

...What magic materialized out of that wind,/and if it rained.   Poem for Pat.   Paula Gunn Allen.   TWSS

What makes life worth the living/Is our giving and forgiving.   Giving and Forgiving.   Thomas Grant Springer.   PoToHe

"What manner of anthology is this/That leaves out Bone, Brook, Potter, Morse, and Bliss!"   Anthologistics.   Arthur Guiterman.   InMe; NLV

What manner of burden was it they proudly bore?   The Rowers.   Laura Benet.   GoYe

What matter if the Congress ignores us?   What Matter?   *Anonymous.*   WTO

...What matter/Who may revel with the rest?   In the Orchard.   Henrik Ibsen.   AWP

What matters now? I know the poem's done,/And wonder what the dickens it all means!   Frangipanni.   *Anonymous.*   NA

...What may be yet/Regaind in Heav'n, or what more lost in Hell?   Paradise Lost.   John Milton.   EBEV

–What may the God not do?   Epitaphs of the War, 1914-18.   Rudyard Kipling.   OBWP

What melodies and/What refrain/Within your song-swept heart!   Motif for Mary's Dolors.   Sister Mary Madeleva.   ISi

What men are kings, what women coil their hair!   The Impatient Poet.   D'Arcy Cresswell.   AnNZ

What men chatter know I not.   Song of Seyd Nimetollah of Kuhistan.   Ralph Waldo Emerson.   NOBA

What menys thys?   What Does This Mean.   Sir Thomas Wyatt.   EnPo; MeEL

What might he not do if he sat down to write   When Klopstock England Defied.   William Blake.   OAEL 1-2

What mind can follow, proving?   Love Wears Roses' Elegance.   Sister Bertken.   LLLT

What mind, what hunger, first saw this as food.   Artichoke.   Henry Taylor.   MAYP

What more do they want? what more can they take?/Unless our eyes, and leaves us blind.   Miners' Wives.   Joe Corrie.   OxBS

What more is needed,/When both forget?   Song.   Alice Duer Miller.   AA

...What more than the self/sometimes needs the self.   Self-Projection.   Archie Randolph Ammons.   FAZ

What more than these I ask'd of Life I am content to have/from Death   An Autobiography.   Ernest Rhys.   ACV; OBEV; OBVV

What mortal hand could put its thumb/So neatly on uranium?   A Leaden Treasury of English Verse.   Paul Dehn.   QQQ

What most we wish, with Ease we fancy near.   Satire.   Edward Hilton Young.   LAuP

What must I love thee, Lord, for then?/For being my king and God. Amen.   O Deus, Ego Amo Te.   Gerard Manley Hopkins.   TrPWD

What my child willed/Is done.   On a Birth.   Geoffrey Grigson.   NAs

What name shall we call our selves now/our mother is gone?   Harriet.   Audre Lorde.   BlSi

...What narrow things/Doors are, that a Soul's wings/Must fold to stoop beneath!   Old Essex Door.   Agnes MacCarthy Hickey.   GoYe

What nature doesn't do to us, will be done by our fellow/man.   The Merry Minuet.   Sheldon Harnick.   DBV; TW

What need lovers wish for more?   Song: "Phillis is my only joy."   Sir Charles Sedley.   EnLoPo; InMe; OBS; SeCV 1-2

What need of bread!   Drink, Friends.   Moses Ibn Ezra.   TrJP

What need–so long as they can climb again?   On Looking at an Old Climbing Photograph.   Douglas Fraser.   PoSH

What need'st thou have more covering than a man?   Going to Bed.   John Donne.   AnAnS 1; GBL; LiTB

What need'st thou put on armes against poore men?   Upon Venus Putting on Mars His Armes.   Richard Crashaw.   SeCP

What need we more, my comrades and my brothers?   Absolution.   Siegfried Sassoon.   MMM

...What news is there to hawk/Of turbulence, water and everlasting air?   Discomfort in High Places.   Sydney Tremayne.   PoSH

What no man learnt yet, in or out of school.   Sedge-Warblers.   Edward ("Edward Eastaway") Thomas.   PoPle

What no one else could wreak/On the room's myth.   The Furnished Room.   James Merrill.   NOBA

What none can ever buy for gold.   The Gifts of God.   Jones Very   AA

What none yet ever knew, or can be known.   The Boat on the Serchio (excerpt).   Percy Bysshe Shelley.   MyFE

What o'erfloweth from her eyes.   Stella.   Charles Henry Crandall.   AA

What of it? Let the dead be dead.   Four Preludes on Playthings of the Wind.   Carl Sandburg.   AmLP; AnAmPo; AnFE; AP; BoLiVe; CMoP; MoAB; MoAmPo; NePA; NOBA; SeCeV

What of man's journey,/Where travels he?   Dark Flows the River.   Arthur Stanley Bourinot.   CaP

What of the Darkness? Is it very fair?   What of the Darkness?   Richard Le Gallienne.   HBV 1-2

What once Europa was Nanet is now.   Cupid a Plowman.   Moschus.   OBVE

What one in the rout/Of the fire-born moods/Has fallen away?   The Moods.   William Butler Yeats.   CTC; VLP

What other men sometimes have thought they've seen.   LXX.   Ted Berrigan.   ANYP; EAS

What other work do I have?   The moon of Id came.   Empress Nur Jahan.   BoWoP

What others are, to feel, and know myself a Man.   Hymn to Adversity.   Thomas Gray.   CEP; GTBS; GTBS-P; OBEC

What otherwise/Defies all other powers of description.   Memo.   Hans Sahl.   VWA

What perilous danger you'd be in,/As she tied her bonnet under her chin.   The Love-Knot.   Titus Munson Coan.   AA; HBV 1-2

What place, I ask her.   The Sky Is Blue.   David Ignatow.   FF; NNaP

What Pleasure like Hunting can cherish the Soul.   Solon's Song.   Thomas D"Urfey.   CEP

What porridge had John Keats?   Popularity.   Robert Browning.   OAEL 1-2; PP

What powerful, but unrecorded, race,/Once dwelt in that annihilated place.   On a Stupendous Leg of Granite, Discovered Standing by Itself...   Horace (or Horatio) Smith.   PrIm

What praise hath been, so be it done/Through all eternity.   Verbum Supernum.   Saint Ambrose of Milan.   CAW

What profit has my whole day won/If now the fair child does not come?   Seasong.   Stefan George.   LiTW

...What raised him/was an unusual lust to break the icon,/joke cruelly, seriously, and be himself.   Stalin.   Robert Lowell.   HaCAP

...What reaches him except disaster?   Self-Portrait, 1969.   Frank Bidart.   HaCAP

What remains but only dying?   Madrigal: "Shall I look."   Robert Jones.   EnRePo

What remains on the other side/is everlasting.   Basketball.   James Lewisohn.   LFAC

What response he may unloose/will offend and thus seduce.   The Voice of Experience.   Johann Wolfgang von Goethe.   ErPo; PV

What rhythm add to stillness/what applause?   The Practice of Magical Evocation.   Diane Di Prima.   PoM

What riddle is it has for answer, Man?   What Riddle Asked the Sphinx.   Archibald MacLeish.   HoPM

...What right now/do I want most in the world!   The Controls.   Harrison Fisher.   APU

...What ritual/It gets is at night, and from his old nurse, a woman poor, nonpolitical.   Two Pieces after Suetonius.   Robert Penn Warren.   NOBA

What room would there be for God to be good?/Said the Devil.   After Reading Certain Books.   Mary Elizabeth Coleridge.   EaLo

What's built upon esteem, can ne'er decay.   To His Book.   William Walsh.   CEP

What's burning is me.   A Dress of Fire.   Dahlia Ravikovich.   VWA

What's death? You'll love me yet!   You'll Love Me Yet!   Robert Browning.   OLR

:What's done by me/Hereafter, shall smell of the Lamp, not thee.   His Farewell to Sack.   Robert Herrick.   AnAnS 2; CaPo; OAEP; SeCP; SeCV 1-2

—What's done is done.   In the End.   Peter Everwine.   NNaP

What's done we partly may compute,/But know not what's resisted.   Address to the Unco Guid, or the Rigidly Righteous.   Robert Burns.   BoLiVe; CEP; EnLit; EnPE; HBV 1-2; LoBV; NOBE; NOCV; NoP; OAEP; OBEC; OxBS; SeCeV; TreFS; TrGrPo; ViBoPo

What's easier done than said.   Lilac Time.   Piet Hein.   PV

What's going on in there?   Jazz.   Frank London Brown.   PoNe

What's heaven? A sea chest with a thousand gold coins.   Beachcomber.   George Mackay Brown.   OxBC

What's holding back my church?   A Dollar I Gave.   *Anonymous.*   STF

What's left?/after gray stones/and green trees/have gone   Leg-acy of a Blue Capricorn.   James (Olumo) Cunningham.   JB

What's left but this to say of any war?   Vale from Carthage.   Peter Viereck.   LiTM; MiAP; MoAmPo

What's left is an inch of silk.   Cocoon.   Ishigaki Rin.   WPOW

What's left of me today will very soon be nothing.   A Useless Burden upon the Earth.   Robert Bridges.   QFR

What's left sleeps in a chair, and when it can/Babbles to strangers, such as you and I.   Under the Casuarina.   Elizabeth Riddell.   PoAu 1-2

What's matter but a hardening of the light?   Hear the Bird of Day.   David Campbell.   GTBS-P; NOAV

What's plural for hysteria?   Singular Singulars, Peculiar Plurals.   Willard R. Espy.   FaBoUs

What's so fine as being a boy?/Ha, Ha!   A Boy's Summer Song.   Paul Laurence Dunbar.   SiSoSe

What's that to I? I lets 'em.   The Candid Physician.   John Coakley Lettsom.   GoTF; TreFT

What's the good of irritatin'?/Let 'im be.   Let Be.   *Anonymous.*   WBLP

What's the reward of all your schemes? You're poor!   A Bad Joke.   Martial (Marcus Valerius Martialis).   UnTE

...What's this relationship–/this one-night stand with the earth?   Relationships.   Pier Giorgio Di Cicco.   CaPN

What's to be next in the world. It's we will be under it!   "Dover Beach"–a Note to That Poem.   Archibald MacLeish.   FF

What's, what's, what's going to happen to the tots?   What's Going to Happen to the Tots?   Noel Coward.   NLV

"What's wrong with two?"   The Same Old Jazz.   Philip Whalen.   NeAP

"What's your age?"/and/"What's your name?"   Mother's Party.   Aileen Fisher.   BiCB

What's your number?/Cucumber.   What's Your Name?   *Anonymous.*   FaBoNo

What sacred drama through her body heaved/When world-transforming Charlemagne was conceived?   Whence Had They Come?   William Butler Yeats.   BoLoP

...What sap/went through that little thread/to make the cherry red!   Nevertheless.   Marianne Moore.   CMoP; ForPo; MoAB; OxBA; SeCeV; SoSe

What save love/can a dove/carol of?/Coo-roo!   Dove.   Norma Farber.   PCh

What saved us? what for?   An Incident Here and There.   Hilda ("H. D.") Doolittle.   CrMA

...What seemed so far away/Is but a child's balloon, forgotten after play.   Above the Dock.   Thomas Ernest Hulme.   FaBoMo; GTBS-P

What sense of importance swelled at the smack/of the stick on the dung-caked dumb flesh.   Blond Hair at the Edge of the Pavement.   Michael Smith.   CIP

What serves for one will serve for t'other.   Epitaphs on Two Piping-Bullfinches of Lady Ossory's.   Horace Walpole.   FaBoEE

What shadow hidden or/Unseen hand in our midst/Ceaselessly touches our faces?   Panic.   Archibald MacLeish.   MoAmPo

"What shall a creature pay Thee in love for the moment of under-/standing?"   Psalm to the Holy Spirit.   A. M. Sullivan.   TrPWD

What shall (Alas!) become of me?   Alexander and Campaspe: Apelles' Song.   John Lyly.   AtBAP; ATP; EnLi 1-2

What shall I answer for?   Letter VI.   W. S. Graham.   ChMP; FaBoMo

What shall I do for pretty girls/Now my old bawd is dead?   John Kinsella's Lament for Mrs. Mary Moore.   William Butler Yeats.   AtBAP; CMoP; DTC; LiTM; MoAB; NoP; OAEL 1-2; OAEP

What shall I do (she cried) my Peace of Mind,/To gain in dying, and to die resign'd?   An Ancient Virgin.   George Crabbe.   OBNC

What shall I do/with these/small/inviolate/knives/that scar the mind.   Modern Kabbalist.   Marcia Falk.   VWA

What shall I hunger for/and not let go   The Light Woman's Song.   Judith Johnson Sherwin.   TAP

What shall I make of this?   What She Said to Her Girl-Friend. Venmanipputi.   PBWP

What shall last is the flavor of you.   Candy Bar.   Tom Veitch.   ANYP

What shall the sleeps of heaven dream but time?   After Sunday Dinner We Uncles Snooze.   John Ciardi.   HoAn

What shall uproot a house and bring this care into his eye?   October 1. Karl Shapiro.   MoAB; MoAmPo; PoA

What shall we do to redeem it?   Game Out of Hand.   Allison Ross.   GoYe

"What shall ye do to redeem it?"   Heavy Heavy Heavy.   John Malcolm Brinnin.   NYBP

What she collects, finally, is pain.   The Collector.   Raymond Souster. ErPo; OBCV

What she would have me, yet not have me know.   Early Love.   Samuel Daniel.   ErPo

What should have been a season of calm weather.   Aristotle to Phyllis. John Hollander.   PoCh

What should I do/with these hands?   The Hand.   Brian Fawcett.   NOBC

What should poking-sticks make there,/When the ruff is set elsewhere? Kisses Loathesome.   Robert Herrick.   CaPo; LiTL; OBSP; UnTE

What should we do for hope and joy,/Fading together?   Hope and Joy. Christina Georgina Rossetti.   OxBChV

What should we have to drink?   If all the world were apple-pie.   Mother Goose.   FaFP; HBV 1-2; OxNR; SoPo

What signifies a mortal man/Whose origin is clay?   Peter Emberley (II). Anonymous.   ShS

What signifies the life of man/When his body it is clay?   Peter Amberley. Anonymous.   AmFP

What slaves you have become now! Who/Shall take you to the King again? Girls from Home.   Abraham Reisen.   VWA

What slides away/Provides.   Give Way, Ye Gates.   Theodore Roethke. CMoP; NMP

What so soon will wake and grow/Utterly unlike the snow.   First Sight. Philip Larkin.   BoNaP; NCSH; NTCP

What songs they sing they always sing again.   Local Places.   Howard Moss. NePoEA-2

What sort of thing men who are masters grow.   He Has Served Eighty Masters.   Lesbia Harford.   PoAu 1-2

What starry horror draws thine abject stare/While jolted jewels goad thy flashing thighs?   "L'Apparition" of Gustave Moreau.   Gordon Bottomley. BrPo

What stays me, my love,/is your hand dripping honey/out of my skinflint heart.   What Changes, My Love.   Edwin Honig.   PPJ

What stranger miracles are there?   Miracles.   Walt Whitman.   BBV; HBVY; LaNeLa; MoRP

What Sunday prisons they recall!/And what miraculous escapes!   Poem: "Time and the weather wear away."   Donald Justice.   PoA

...What Superbard says/Goes. I am going to keep things like this.   Crow Resting (parody).   Edward Pygge.   BXAP; FaBoPa

What surety of life have thou, and I?   An Epitaph on Master Philip Gray. Ben Jonson.   FaBoEE

What surge is this whose question never ceases?   Dr. Sigmund Freud Discovers the Sea Shell.   Archibald MacLeish.   BiP; PPON; SoSe

What suspicion-agonized eyes, what jellies of arrogance and terror/This earth has absorbed.   Iona: The Graves of the Kings.   Robinson Jeffers.   PrIm

What sweetness can match our love?   Flowers for the Brave.   Celia Thaxter. OHIP

What tale shall serve me here among/Mine angry and defrauded young? Epitaphs of the War 1914-18.   Rudyard Kipling.   BrPo; FaBoEE; OAEP; OBWP

What thanks do you get for it? Me don't ask it!   Poems in Praise of Practically Nothing.   Samuel Hoffenstein.   InMe

What thanks do you get? She beats you to it!   Poems in Praise of Practically Nothing.   Samuel Hoffenstein.   InMe

What thanks do you get? The pants get shiny.   Poems in Praise of Practically Nothing.   Samuel Hoffenstein.   InMe

...What the after age/Knows and names a pine, a nation's heritage.   Pan and Luna.   Robert Browning.   VLP

What the deuce do you expect?   A Poem Intended to Incite the Utmost Depression.   Samuel Hoffenstein.   FaBoCo

What the eye loses, let the heart recover.   The Lovers.   Marya Zaturenska. MoAmPo

What the hand of God hath wrought for the Houses and/the Word!   The Battle of Naseby.   Thomas Babington, Lord Macaulay.   HBV 1-2; OBRV

–What the hell is this?   Road's End.   Rolf Jacobsen.   NU

What the hymns say, the first page and the last.   Holy Thursday.   Charles Wright.   GeTw

What the man must do/what the woman must   The Tides.   Paul Blackburn. PoM

What the one promises, the other will surely attain.   Columbus.   Friedrich von Schiller.   OFD

What the river says, that is what I say.   Ask Me.   William Stafford.   FiCP; NPAW

What the snow slackened, the wind felled.   Deadfall.   Martha Keller. GoYe

What the spirit shape to sing.   Permanence in Change.   Johann Wolfgang von Goethe.   HoPM

What the sun burns up of it, the moon puts back.   Plague of Dead Sharks. Alan Dugan.   AP; LiTM; NoAm

What them fellers does is ART!   Art.   Anonymous.   BLPA; NLV

What then?   If I Should Cast Off This Tattered Coat.   Stephen Crane. AmePo

What then can move her? if nor merth nor mone,/She is no woman, but a sencelesse stone.   Amoretti, LIV.   Edmund Spenser.   AAS; NoP; OAEL 1-2

What then remaines but I to ashes burne,/And she to stones at length all frosen turne?   Amoretti, XXXII.   Edmund Spenser.   AAS

–What then remains, but that we still should cry/For being born, or, being born, to die?   The World.   Francis Bacon.   HBV 1-2

What they not feel must not be said to know.   Calling Lucasta from Her Retirement.   Richard Lovelace.   CaPo

What thing has my soul learned/That I shall know soon?   Prescience. Margaret Widdemer.   HBMV

What think you, Sir, of killing Time/With verse address'd to me?   Beau's Reply.   William Cowper.   FaBoCh

What this man speaks is true.   I Think I See Him There.   Waring Cuney. CDC

...What/this means is I love you.   I Think Table and I Say Chair.   Gloria Fuertes.   AMV-81

What though the red leaf fall?   What though the Green Leaf Grow? Maybury Fleming.   AA

What though to-night wrecks you and me,/If so to-morrow saves?   Heaven Overarches Earth and Sea.   Christina Georgina Rossetti.   HBV 1-2

What time the clock slow chimed the hour.   At Lincoln.   Oscar Fay Adams. AA

What 'tis to trust to tombs by thee we easily know.   Poly-Olbion.   Michael Drayton.   FaBoPP

What to say/when you see me.   A Form of Women.   Robert Creeley. AmPC; CAPP; NaP

What triumph did you know, what rose, what thorn?   Etruscan Warrior's Head.   Helen Rowe Henze.   GoYe

What trouble would I make for you, a woman?   Oatmeal Deluxe.   Stephen Dobyns.   AMV-81

What trust to things below, whenas we see,/As men, the heavens have their hypocrisy?   Fair Days; or, Dawns Deceitful.   Robert Herrick.   CaPo

What ultimate insolence would soon be theirs.   The New Tenants.   Edwin Arlington Robinson.   NoAm

What unites us is not our past/but our future.   My People.   Margery Himel. IHMS

What unto themselves was taught.   Stanza from an Early Poem. Christopher Pearse Cranch.   AA; AmLP

What vaileth truth?   What Vaileth Truth?   Sir Thomas Wyatt.   AAS; FCP

What voice/in the warm grass of her belly,/What planet?   Someone Talking. Joy Harjo.   TWSS

What vow shall we vow who love you/For the self that you did not value? To a Comrade in Arms.   Alun Lewis.   FaBoTw; MoBrPo

What was hire bowr?/The rede rose and the lilie-flowr.   The Maid of the Moor.   Anonymous.   NOBE; OAEL 1-2; OxBM

What was it that her mother said?   The Frog Prince.   Robert Pack.   DFT

What was left in the world for me/After the Light was out?   Judas Iscariot. Margaret Nickerson Martin.   PGD

...What was left was ash.   Ash.   George MacBeth.   NMP

What was locked is yours, Michael, as much as mine.   Lines for Michael in the Picture.   John Logan.   CAPP

...What was once so distant/breaks upon me now, while dark water crumbles the moon.   Night along the Mackinac Bridge.   Roberta Hill.   CDW; STE

What was true in flesh, is/Merely beautiful in silver.   An Esthetic of Imitation.   Donald Finkel.   NePoEA

What was water far and wide/Changes with the ebbing tide./Ebbtide.   The Old Woman of Beare Regrets Lost Youth.   Frank O'Connor.   OBMV

"What, waste all our lives raising children/To feed ruddy Lions? Not me!" The Lion and Albert.   Marriott Edgar.   OBNV

"What way is this, God, to make a man stone?"   Arabs.   Alfred Kreymborg. MAPA

What we are is beyond him utterly.   Death Has No Features of His Own. Gwen Harwood.   NOAV

...What we are seeking/Is idle, biologically speaking.   I Shall Forget You Presently, My Dear.   Edna St. Vincent Millay.   TAP

What we become/when we dream   Word Poem   Nikki Giovanni.   BOLo; PoBA

What we below could not see, Winter pass.   Thaw.   Edward ("Edward Eastaway") Thomas.   EBEV; ELU; FaBoTw; FM; GTBS-P; HaMV; MoAB; MoBrPo; OBSP; OxBTC

What we can't find/we'll build but/slowly,/slowly. Builder Kachina: Home-Going. Wendy Rose. TWSS

What we can't seem to manage for man? Sanctuary. John Basil Boothroyd. FiBHP

What we could have done locks to the very core/with what we have. An Artichoke for Montesquieu. Jorie Graham. NPGG

What we do best is breed. A Christening. Donald Davie. OxBC

What we do have/Is Good. So We've Come at Last to Freud. Alice Walker. IHMS

What we don't know/is what you are about to say. Portrait of a Man. Alan Bernheimer. APU

What we hoped for had not come to pass. Interlude. Theodore Roethke. MiAP

What we're gonna do/In the face of/What we remember. Puzzled. Langston Hughes. UnPo

What we then envy'd, now we mourn! On the Death of a Lady's Dog. Wentworth Dillon, Earl of Roscommon. CavP

...What went wrong? Dichterliebe. Robert Klein Engler. AMV-81

What were all else? I dare not risk this loss. Dipsychus. Arthur Hugh Clough. OBNC

What were their threats to her, Bel's daughter and his pride! The Impious Feast. Robert Eyres Landor. OBRV

...What will be done/In the absence of the sun!/Come along! A Bridal Song. Percy Bysshe Shelley. OBRV

...What will be/the sacred words? Ka 'Ba. LeRoi (Imamu Amiri Baraka) Jones. BPo; CAPP; CNA; TAP

What will be yours, ye powerful, wealthy, wise,/By whom the heathen unregarded dies? The Indian's Grave. G. J. Mountain. CaP

What will become of man? Cape Cod. George Santayana. AmePo

What will become of our land? The Leper. Ka-ehu. WTO

What will become of the mice and rats? Hoddley, Poddley, Puddle and Fogs. *Anonymous.* FaBoNo; OxNR

"What will happen?" pleads Eve. In the Beginning. Valerie Sinason. BrRo

What will happen to me/If even wood is stirred? Epigram: "When Graphicus sat by the baths." Strato. PeHV

What will she do when hoary hairs are powdered/in her head! "Wrapt in my careless cloak..." Henry Howard, Earl of Surrey. FCP; SiPS

What will survive of us is love. An Arundel Tomb. Philip Larkin. HeIP; NePoEA-2; PPP

What will that lovely one be like? Fast Bundled Is the Firewood. *Anonymous.* HW

...What will/the dinghies do then? Resort. Kendrick Smithyman. OCNZ

What will they do when soul and body meet? Tombstone Epitaphs. *Anonymous.* PeD

"What will those luckless millions do?" Epigram: "Twelve hundred million men are spread." Rudyard Kipling. PV

What will Thy glory be! Entering by His Door. Richard Baxter. BePJ

What will we do/now? Flutter into butterflies? Suburb Hilltop. Richard Moore. NYBP

What will you do to me, O Book? On Opening a New Book. Abbie Farwell Brown. YeAr

What will you eat at twenty? Maria Jane. Alfred Scott-Gatty. BBGG

What winning's worth this loss of face? Overheard in the Louvre. X. J. Kennedy. ELU

What woeful captives thronged his chariot wheel. The Dray. Laurence Binyon. SyP

What woman is and how to guard her well./Guard her well. A Gentle Echo on Woman. Jonathan Swift. ALV; FaBoCo; FiBHP; LiTL; NLV; NU; OLR; OnYI

What wonder doth in beauty dwell. Against Fulfillment of Desire. *Anonymous.* TrGrPo

What wonder if Sir Launfal now/Remembered the keeping of his vow? The Vision of Sir Launfal. James Russell Lowell. AnNE

What wonder is it, if weak I be slain? The Frailty. Abraham Cowley. CavP

What wool my sheep shall bear, whiles thus they live,/In you it is, you must the judgement give. Arcadia. Sir Philip Sidney. SiPS

What would a little kitchen maid/Be doing with romance? A Song of Diligence. Helen Frazee-Bower. HBMV

"What would I give to hear Wood Jones on this!" The Master. C. G. L.. ImOP

What would my arms do in that girdle's place? The Garland and the Girdle. Buonarroti Michelangelo. AWP

What would they do to you and me/If we should say we knew him? The Poet. Witter ("Emanuel Morgan") Bynner. WGRP

What would you call his feeling for the words/That keep him rich and orphaned and beloved? The Illiterate. William Meredith. NoP

What wounds, what bloody press/Dragged into being/This loveliness? The Only Jealousy of Emer (excerpt). William Butler Yeats. MoAB

...What year will they write/For my poor passage to the stall of Night? On an Anniversary after Reading the Dates in a Book of Lyrics. John Millington Synge. FaBoEE; NOBI; OBMV; PoL

What yo' gwine to do when yo' lamp burn down. What Yo' Gwine to Do When Yo' Lamp Burn Down? *Anonymous.* BoAN 1-2; BPo

...What you Give/Is that which proves your Right to Live. A Poet's Proverbs. Arthur Guiterman. TiPo

What you gonna do/when your trouble get like mine Dry Land Blues. Furry Lewis. BluL

...What you meant/to tell me, out of the body, out of the body travel. For Esther. Stanley Plumly. LCAP

What you please, you parts may call,/'Tis one good part I'ld lie withall. A Celebration of Charis. Ben Jonson. AnAnS 2; SeCP

What you say, it's a great little game! Limerick: "A jug and a book and a dame." Edwin Meade Robinson. HBMV

What you wanted to be among the bastards out there. Death News. Allen Ginsberg. NoAm

What you were like, but only that you were. Fleeting Return. Juan Ramon Jimenez. AMV-80

What your good leddy costs in coal?...I'll burn 'em down to port. McAndrew's Hymn. Rudyard Kipling. CABL; OxBTC

What youth and pleasure prompts us to. Upon Love Fondly Refus'd for Conscience Sake. Thomas Randolph. AnAnS 2; OAEL 1-2

Whate'er betides, Thy love abides,/Our God, for evermore. Auld Lang Syne. John White Chadwick. WGRP

Whate'er thy hands are set to do/Is wrought with tumult of acclaim. In Memoriam A.H.H., LXXV. Alfred, Lord Tennyson. VLP

Whatever flames upon the night/Man's own resinous heart has fed. Two Songs from a Play. William Butler Yeats. CABA; CMoP; ExPo; HAP; MoPo; NOBE; NoP; PPoe; PPP; PrIm; SeCeV

Whatever good I have is what you gave. July. W. Ralph Johnson. AMV-81

Whatever happens, I am ready. Words Most Often Mispronouncd in Poetry. Alex Kuo. APU

Whatever happens, I want to be/Self-respecting and conscience free. Myself. Edgar A. Guest. BLPA; BLPL

Whatever he gained, the loss was ours. Here Huntington's Ashes Long Have Lain. Ambrose Bierce. DBV

Whatever horror nudge her root. To Paint a Water Lily. Ted Hughes. PP

Whatever I forget, you learn. On Mr. Hearne, the Great Antiquary. *Anonymous.* FaBoEE

Whatever I have to do has not yet begun. It Is March. William Stanley Merwin. NaP

Whatever in the world/is she having for lunch? Listen! Lilian Moore. NTCP

Whatever is found or is done/that cannot be lost or changed. An Air by Sammartini. Louis Dudek. OBCV

Whatever is—is best. Whatever Is–Is Best. Ella Wheeler Wilcox. BLPA; GoTF; PoToHe; TreFS

Whatever it is, it bothers me all the time. Laguna Blues. Charles Wright. GeTw

Whatever it is that a wound remembers/After the healing ends. Small Prayer. Weldon Kees. PoA; VGW

Whatever Miss T. eats/Turns into Miss T. Miss T. Walter De La Mare. CenHV; FaBoBe; GoJo; GrPl; MoShBr; NTCP; OnUR; SoPo; SUS; TiPo

Whatever on my heart may fall–remember, I would risk it/all! A Woman's Question. Adelaide Anne Procter. HBV 1-2; LiTL

Whatever sages say and fools,all's well. Being to Timelessness as It's to Time. Edward Estlin Cummings. HAP; NePA

Whatever small flowers/I may have mentioned in summer:/forget them. The Transparence of November. Roo Borson. CaPN; PPJ

Whatever still be love's requests/I would thus still complete them now. Ah Yes, When Love Allows. Hadewijch. PBWP

Whatever their language, they are not speaking to us. Seal Rock. Katha Pollitt. MAYP

Whatever there is to know/That shall we know one day. The Cloud Confines. Dante Gabriel Rossetti. EnLi 1-2

Whatever they fought with on earth/Is removed now: they fight like doves. The Feast of All Saints. Elizabeth Smither. OCNZ

Whatever they raised–/them old Black men. Old Black Men Say. James A. Emanuel. PoBA

Whatever was the best pye going,/In that Ned–trust him–had his finger. Fragment of a Character. Thomas Moore. FaBoCo

Whatever went out from your mind. You Never Can Tell. Ella Wheeler Wilcox. BLPA; BLPL; PoToHe

Whatever wisdom sleep with thee. In Memoriam A.H.H., CVIII. Alfred, Lord Tennyson. SBVL; VLP

Whatever your music, Angela/We embrace. We condone/And we evolve. For Angela. Zack Gilbert. PoBA

Whaur hae they writ them mair sublime/Than on yon gable-ends o' time? The Prows o' Reekie. Lewis Spence. OxBS

The wheat field, the lark wake pleasure in landsmen/only–/Nothing in me. Sea Hunger. John Hanlon Mitchell. EtS

The wheat thou strew'st be souls. Intellect. Ralph Waldo Emerson. GLGT

Whedn she hears of my misfortune she cadn but grieve the more. Charles Gustavus Anderson (I). *Anonymous.* ShS

Whee-oop! Whoop-eee! In Town. *Anonymous.* ABF

A wheel in a wheel, (wheel in a wheel),/Way in the middle of the air. Ezekiel Saw the Wheel. *Anonymous.* FSW

The wheel of Fortune, not the sphere of Love. The Lover Consults with Reason. Thomas Carew. TrGrPo

Wheel, oh, wheel,/Wheel in de middle of a wheel. 'Zekiel Saw de Wheel. *Anonymous.* BoAN 1-2

A wheel slowly spinning... The Flight. John Haines. EAS

Wheeled in the Slavic sun. Tanya. Jay Parini. AMV-80

Wheeling, evening sparrows wail and sob. Sent to Wen T'ing-Yun on a Winter Night. Yu Hsuan-chi. BoWoP

Wheeling the self-same circuit o'er and o'er. A Summer Twilight. Charles Tennyson Turner. OBRV

Wheels from last week's newspaper to the broom. The Limited. Robert Penn Warren. PoA

Wheels jammed, and flaming, on a metal sea. V-J Day. John Ciardi. MiAP; PoPl

The wheels of a mill are going/In every brooklet clear. Whither? Wilhelm Muller. AWP

The wheels roll on and make it all too plain/Who will be there to meet him at the station. Figure of Eight. Louis MacNeice. OBSP

The wheels squealing like the hull/Of a submarine about to burst. Maiden Lane. Al Lee. NYP

Wheesht, wheesht, ye fule! Wheesht, Wheesht. Hugh" (Christopher Murray Grieve) MacDiarmid. BSV; ELU; ErPo; HAP; InPK

When a bombshell set our ship on fire, we were forced to surrender/ then. Flying Cloud. *Anonymous.* ABF

When a hand is on your shoulder in a friendly sort o' way. Fellowship. *Anonymous.* BLPA

When a little Road says, Go. The House and the Road. Josephine Preston Peabody. TreFT

When a maiden moon wakes up in the sky? The New Moon. Sara Teasdale. MOON

When a man gets the blues he catch that train and rides. Big Fat Woman. *Anonymous.* OuSiCo

When a man marries his trouble/begins. Scissors and String, Scissors and String. *Anonymous.* OxNR

When a rich man is ill/to light a lamp/he must wait for a slave. Song of the Poor Man. *Anonymous.* TTY

When a spade is just a spade? A Spade Is Just a Spade. Walter Everette Hawkins. PoBA

When a storm of ghosts shall shake/The dead, until they wake/In the grave. Song from the Waters. Thomas Lovell Beddoes. NOBE

When a stupid old Rest who was voted a dunce,/Came suddenly on them and stopped them at once. First Lessons in Musical Time. *Anonymous.* FaBoUs

When a tyrant's thunder pealed/O'er the trembling seas. The Fourth of July. John Pierpont. YeAr

When a woman is in danger. A Maid's Complaint. Thomas Campion. UnTE

When a woman opens the heart/she is praying for her soul. Inscape. Susan Litwack. VWA

When a yesterday has faded from its page! The Story of Prince Agib. Sir William Schwenck Gilbert. FaBoCo; InMe; LBN; NA

When ah hear me shuttle/Go poverty, poverty knock! Poverty Knock. *Anonymous.* OBET; VLP

When, alas, the fight's within! The Combat. Thomas Stanley. AWP

When all Heaven shall be survey'd/From those Windings and that Shade. The Petition for an Absolute Retreat. Anne Finch, Countess of Winchilsea. OBEC; PoEL 1-5; SBG; TrGrPo

When all I would do/Is to scratch your head/And let you go. To a Squirrel at Kyle-Na-No. William Butler Yeats. FM

When all its kingdoms shall his kingdom be. O God of Youth. Bates G. Burt. AH

When all now dead shall re-appear. Poetry Perpetuates the Poet. Robert Herrick. FaBoEE

When all our yearly tributes/are delivered and set free. In Passing. J. Barrie Shepherd. AMV-81

An' when all the coppertone's gone...? Vive Noir! Mari E. Evans. IHMS

When all the hills are withered up/Nor any waters flow. The Herons. Francis Ledwidge. ACP; OnYI; OxBI

When all the nightmares he most feared/Prosper in daylight and endure. The Note-Book of a European Tramp (excerpt). Michael Hamburger. NePoEA

When all the shadows do increase. A Hymn. James Shirley. GoBC

When all the woods are marching/In triumph of the year? In October. Bliss Carman. YeAr

When all these tyrants rest, and thou/Art warring with the mighty dead? Late Wisdom. George Crabbe. HBV 1-2; OBEV; TrGrPo

When all this will be explained. Good Friday. Arlene De Bevoise. AMV-81

When all thy crying clear/Is but: Lo here! lo there!–ah, me, lo every-/where! Orient Ode. Francis Thompson. CoBE

When all was done, ye hade so evill a grace/Ye stoll awaye and durst no more be seene. Admonition to Montgomerie. King of England James I, OxBS

When all your friends as fossils sleep,/Immortalized in lime! Imitation of Julia A. Moore. Mark (Samuel Langhorne Clemens) Twain. OBAL

When all your world of beauty's gone. To Dianeme. Robert Herrick. CaPo; CBEP; GTBS; GTBS-P; HBV 1-2; JCP; LiTL; NOBE; OBEV; OBS; PoPle; SeCV 1-2; TrGrPo; ViBoPo

When almond buds unclose,/Who doubts of May's red rose? When Almonds Bloom. Millicent Washburn Shinn. AA

When Andrea del Verrocchio was engaged with his bronze/horse...' Tune. Carl Rakosi. GP

When Angelina Johnson comes a-swingin' down de line. Angelina. Paul Laurence Dunbar. HBV 1-2

When Angels dwelt, and GOD himself, with Man! Love of Nature. James (1700-48) Thomson. OBEC

When angels needs must speak, shall man be mute? To the Soul. John Collop. TrGrPo

When April comes a-laughing and a-weeping/Once again/At our hearts? At April. Angelina Weld Grimke. BlSi

When as Cherries come in place? To Cherry-Blossomes. Robert Herrick. SeCV 1-2

When at evening he swims in his rivers here below. Of Swimming in Lakes and Rivers. Bertolt Brecht. SD

When, at His door, denied you'll stand. Christ at the Door. *Anonymous.* BePJ

When at last they opened her/breast, no one dared touch/that red pulsing star Sequence for a Young Widow Passing. Deborah Munro. IHMS

When at the Boot she tugg'd and toil'd,/By WARREN's Blacking brighten'd. The Cat and the Boot. *Anonymous.* FaBoUs

When back to Shiraz' Walls he bent his Way. Persian Eclogues, II. William Collins. CEP

When berdes waggeth all. Snatches: "Jon Jon pike-a-bone." *Anonymous.* OxBM

When Bethlehem and Calvary/Are merged in Paradise. The Litany of the Dark People. Countee Cullen. EaLo; MoRP; TrPWD

When bombs come shrieking down, pray men's minds might be/unfurled. Letter to My Wife. Keidrych Rhys. WaP

When Britain fight the Grand Monarque/Must yield to Britain's King. Louisburg. *Anonymous.* PAH

When Britain took the garrisons away. Intercessors. Austin Clarke. CMoP; NMP

When by the eager wick a spark is set. For Eros II. Audrey Wurdemann. MoLP

When camera clicks with quick, conclusive fact. 3 for 25. William Jay Smith. WaP

When Canaan did with Milk and Honey flow. On Death. Anne Killigrew. BoWoP

When Change it self can give no more,/'Tis easie to be true. A Song to Celia. Sir Charles Sedley. CavP; OBS; SeCePo

When Charlemagne with all his peerage fell/By Fontarabbia. Paradise Lost. John Milton. WHA

When Christ, and Christ alone, shall be/The trembling sinner's stay. The New Testament. Thomas Russell. TreFS

When Christ has come to be our King. The Reign of Peace. Mary Starck. WBLP

When Christ is with us in the ship,/The ship is at the shore. The Ship in the Midst of the Sea. Christopher Wordsworth. BePJ

When civilly addressed. The Bandog. Walter De la Mare. BrPo; EvOK; TiPo

When comes a foe, my wounds with oil and wine to tend. The Good Samaritan. John Henry, Cardinal Newman. OBTV

When conflagration ruins worlds, their God/Regards the heart sincere, sits smiling there. Self-Consciousness Makes All Changes Happy. Jonathan Richardson. NOEC

When Cromwell spake the word Democracy! To Milton. Oscar Wilde. BrPo

When curved toward the full it sharpens. July Dawn. Louise Bogan. NePoAm-2

When Dai touched Gwyneth up with his gloves on. Terrible Beauty. Kingsley Amis. ErPo; NePoEA-2; PV

When damsons I gather,/I will part them all you among. Elisa. Edmund Spenser. OBSC

When darkness sweeps/O'er Calvary's Hill. An Etching. Sister Imelda. CAW

When dawn creeps from afar. Twinkling Gown. Dorothy Vena Johnson. GoSI

When dawn that calls the climber dyes them rose? The Schreckhorn. Thomas Hardy. OAEL 1-2

When dawns that day, that day. To an Ambitious Friend. Horace. AWP

When de golden trumpets sound. Song: "When de golden trumpets sound." *Anonymous.* NAMP

When de good Lord sets you free. When de Good Lord Sets You Free. *Anonymous.* ABF

When de stars begin to fall,/When de stars begin to fall. My Lord, What a Mornin'. *Anonymous.* BoAN 1-2

When death dries out the special planted man. The People Has No Obituary. Eunice Clark. NAMP

..When Death's/nuptial change/leaves us for light the halo of his/hair. The House of Life. Dante Gabriel Rossetti. OAEP

When deeds win meeds, and words love's works/do prove. Song of Coridon and Melampus. George Peele. OBSC

When did my jay all pass me by? Jay A-Pass'd. William Barnes. NOBV

When did you see me naked! When! Indignant Protest. *Anonymous.* UnTE

When distance doth depart us twain. Out of Sight, Out of Mind. Barnabe Googe. EIL; EnRePo; InPS; PAI

When does the melody end/And where does it begin? Church Poem. Joyce Carol Thomas. CNA

When dreaming, with the night, shall pass away. The Dream Called Life. Pedro Calderon de la Barca. AWP

When dreamless rest is mine I shall not need/The tenderness for which I long tonight. If I Should Die Tonight. Arabella Eugenia Smith. BLPA; HBV 1-2; TreF

...When dreams go/Life is a barren field/Frozen with snow. Dreams. Langston Hughes. GoSI

When Dutchy plays th' mouth harp,/In a way to beat th' band. When Dutchy Plays the Mouth Harp. Robert V. Carr. PoOW

When duty fronts death in his Alamo. The Defence of the Alamo. Joaquin Miller. BeLS; BPAW; FaBoBe; HBV 1-2; MC; OnMSP; PAH

When Duty whispers low, Thou must,/The youth replies, I can. Voluntaries. Ralph Waldo Emerson. FPL; PoLf; TRV

When earth's foundation shakes, shall stand,/By providence secured. Lord, Who's the Happy Man. Nicholas and Nahum Tate Brady. AH

When Elate I am Envy'd, When Meek I'm despis'd. O Why Was I Born with a Different Face? William Blake. PoL

When–Enter Taine!–and all is entertaining. On Taine. Alfred Ainger. ALV

When'er they burn, if burn they must,/They'll prove my accusation just. To Stella. Jonathan Swift. EiCP

When ev'ry darker Thought gives way,/Whilst blooming Beauty we survey. The Portrait. Anne Finch, Countess of Winchilsea. OBEC

When even there, where most thou praisest/mee,/For writing better, I must envie thee. To Francis Beaumont. Ben Jonson. OAEP; OBS

When even these suburbs shall give up their dead. Suburban. John Ciardi. NLV

When every one is somebodee,/Then no one's anybody! There Lived a King. Sir William Schwenck Gilbert. FiBHP; PoPle; StPo

"When everything else is gone/the music,/will still be here" Chops Are Flyin. Stanley Crouch. NBP

When, extending its antennae it discovers/not god/but its own miracle. "Let us suppose the mind." Barbara Moraff. IHMS

When faith in God goes, man, the mortal, loses his only hope. Have You Lost Faith? *Anonymous.* WBLP

When fierce winds rock them on the foaming wave. Sonnet: "Go, thou that vainly dost mine eyes invite." Henry, Bishop of Chichester King. OBSP

When first I looked on thee I lost mine eyes. Samson to His Delilah. Richard Crashaw. TrGrPo

When first the ocean spoke unto the sun. In the Beginning. Harriet Monroe. AA

When first we begin/To speak one with another. Introversion. Evelyn Underhill. WGRP

When flame doth meet with flame. Against Platonick Love. *Anonymous.* OBS

When, folded in His loving arms,/The weary are at rest. Our Light Afflictions. *Anonymous.* BLRP

When footsteps are few on the ground? Seasons and Times. William Barnes. NOBV

When forty-nine too, if prime's more than eleven. To Find Easter Limit, or the Day of the Paschal Full Moon... *Anonymous.* FaBoUs

When France shall reign, and laws be all repeal'd! Inscription for the Door of the Cell in Newgate... George Canning. FaBoEE

When Friendship rested in the daytide strong. Trelawny Lies by Shelley. Charles L. O'Donnell. HBMV

When frightened stars hide/In the steely folds of the sea? Die My Shriek. Aaron Kushniroff. TrJP

When from Janiculan heights thundered the cannon of France.' Amours de Voyage. Arthur Hugh Clough. NOBV

When from my labours I shall rest/With Christ above for to be blest. Epitaphium Meum. William Bradford. SCAP

When from your froth we soon shall see/A second Venus rise. On Sight of a Gentlewoman's Face in the Water. Thomas Carew. CaPo; SeCV 1-2

When fruit is ripe the civet's there. Two Young Maids. *Anonymous.* WTO

When fully He the work hath wrought/That caused thy needless fear. Give to the Winds Thy Fears. Paul Gehardt. TRV

When gaunt men lie writhing in the night/Dreaming of their wives. War Swaggers. Emanuel Litvinoff. WaP

When God's will is thy heart's pole,/Then is Christ thy very soul. Approaches. George Macdonald. TRV

When God sent Opportunity/and Benton found the Man! John Charles Fremont. Charles F. Lummis. PAH

When God through thee hath spoken,/Love's message is complete. Incarnate Love. Wilbur Fisk Tillett. BLRP

When God would gi'e woone zunsheen. The Spring. William Barnes. BoNaP; HBV 1-2

When gold or sable turns to grey! Changeful Beauty. Andrew Lang. EnLoPo

When good may have, as well as bad, their prime. Doth Then the World Go Thus, Doth All Thus Move? William, of Hawthornden Drummond. BSV; GTBS; GTBS-P

"When gray goose quills turn to silver pins, oh then, my dear, we'll marry." Trooper and Maid, I. *Anonymous.* AmFP

When grief was on holiday. To Janet. Ralph Pomeroy. NYBP

When half gods go,/The gods arrive. Give All to Love. Ralph Waldo Emerson. AnAmPo; AnEnPo; AnNE; AP; APA; AWP; FaFP; FPL; GoTF; HBV 1-2; InPo; LiTA; LiTL; NePA; NOBA; OBEV; OBVV; OxBA; PoEL 1-5; PoLf; TAP; TreFS; TrGrPo; ViBoPo

When hands are joined and head bows in the dark. Penal Law. Austin Clarke. BoLoP; ELU; GTBS-P; IPY; NoAm; NOBI

When Hawke came swooping from the West. Hawke. Sir Henry Newbolt. BBV

When hawthorn and plum are/Brave with the blossom of Spring. Song: "Heron is harsh with despair." Brenda Chamberlain. NeBP; NeIP

When he assures me he's all mine/and of sweetness make me burst. Marriage Is a Lovely Thing. Christine de Pisan. WPOW

When he breathes in and out/we can cook Gasco; or, The Toad. Gunter Grass. ELU

When he charged through that Rooshian valley with his famous Light Brigade. The Famous Light Brigade. *Anonymous.* ShS

When he'd gather his gear/And go home to Mother. Bucko-Mate. Samuel Schierloh. GoYe

When he died, a swallow seemed to plunge/Into the reflected, the wrong, sky. Didymus. Louis MacNeice. EaLo

When he finishes he will go back/hunting for the lies that are obvious. Burning Hills. Michael Ondaatje. NOBC; NoP

When he found her, O then they fell a-kissing. Fair Phyllis I Saw Sitting All Alone. *Anonymous.* GBL

When he handed me that letter edged in black. The Letter Edged in Black. *Anonymous.* FSW

When he hath passed many years in captivity. A Dispute over Suicide. *Anonymous.* TTY

...When he heard the news/that the place was run by Jews. G. K. Chesterton. Humbert Wolfe. TrJP

When he hears his love is sleeping/Maybe then he'll think of me. Bury Me beneath the Willow. *Anonymous.* FSW

When he his quarry makes upon the grassy plain. Hawking. Michael Drayton. SD

When he lay down at night, in dreams/He tramped from star to star. A Man Called Dante, I Have Heard. Georgiana Goddard King. HBV 1-2

When he lay on the flat spare twigs/And watched the sun in the sky. The Heron. John Lyle Donaghy. NeIP

When he lends any Poets about the Town. A Sessions of the Poets. Sir John Suckling. AnAnS 2; NCEP; SeCV 1-2

When He made the heart of man. The Human Heart. Frank Carleton Nelson. PoToHe

When he notion for anudder tea-party. Siege of Plattsburg. *Anonymous.* ABF

When he of the appel ete and Eve it him betaughte. Lollay, Lollay, Little Child! *Anonymous.* OxBM

When he plucks up your gay Embroider'd Cloaths./With a Fadding, etc. A Ballad of the Courtier and the Country Clown. *Anonymous.* CoMu

When he quite inadvertently slid ag'inst her. Limerick: "There was a young curate of Kidderminster." *Anonymous.* TDH

When he reaches for us in our sleep. The Gossip. Daniel Halpern. SO

When He rounds you up within the Master's fold. Rounded up in Glory. *Anonymous.* CoSo

When he saw her, naked, carrying away his last sheep/Through the Asian rocks. In Memory of Leopardi. James Wright. NaP

When He shall make thy gloom to pass/away,/Thy darkness bright. The Burning of the Law. Meir of Rothenburg. TrJP

When he sit, he sit on what he ain't got almost. The Frog. *Anonymous.* MoShBr; NLV; NTCP; TreFT; YaD

When he slammed the spattered door/on her seventy years/of staying home. When the Ambulance Came. Robert Morgan. Str

When he snores—come kiss your Conqueror! To the Eternal Feminine. Tristan Corbiere. ErPo

When he threads the golden warp of hope/Against the woof of gloom. Warp and Woof. Harry Halbisch. BLRP

When he touched Dilys up with his gloves on. The Evans Country. Kingsley Amis. NOBL

When he tumbled and broke all to bits. Limerick: "There was a young man at St. Kitts." *Anonymous.* LiBL

...When he was a boy,/hilahi', hilahi'yu, long ago. Tsa'lagi Council Tree. Gladys Cardiff. TWSS

When he was young & gift-strong. His Toy, His Dream, His Rest. John Berryman. NOBA

When he will be remembered for/A week, a month, or even more. The Statesman. Hilaire Belloc. NOBE

When he will marry me with a gold/ring. On Saturday Night Shall Be My Care. *Anonymous.* OxNR

When he won and neglected this frail wildwood flower. Wildwood Flower. *Anonymous.* BLSo; FSW

When he wrote Il Penseroso. Clerihew. Edmund Clerihew Bentley. NLV; PV

When hearts are broken, bands will bow;/Sae well's he loved his lady now! Prince Heathen (B version). *Anonymous.* ESPB

When heaven is brimful of starry night. Her Kisses. Thomas Lovell Beddoes. AtBAP; LO

When, helpless, he lay by his fallen bay, but cheered his/comrades on? The Stampede. Arthur I. Caldwell. BPAW

When her Jesus, too, was small. Notre Dame des Petits. Louis Mercier. ISi

...When her nest has once been/plundered,/Ne'er can build another more. Good Counsel. James Clarence Mangan. NOBI

When Hester MacDonagh of Murderkill Creek/haunts the marsh, when the winds are bleak. Hester Macdonagh. Jeannette Slocomb Edwards. GoYe

When high boot-heels were in fashion, and a six-gun was/the law! Back to Arizona. Earl Alonzo Brininstool. BPAW

When high in their murmurous arches/The night breeze ruffles by. Vistas. Odell Shepard. HBMV

When his bride-to-be/Announced "I AM SHE!" Sir Rider Haggard. W. H. Auden. FaBoCo

When his faire forehead with disdain is frowned. Sonnets, I: "Sporting at fancie, setting light by love." Richard Barnfield. PeHV

When His great Godhead peels its stripping strength/In my red earth. The Song of the Body Dreamed in the Spirit's Mad Behest. Brother Antoninus. ErPo

When his heart is light/As the clouds of white/That swim in the summer skies. The Cowboy's Life. *Anonymous.* CoSo

When his language dies and our atom of Earth is finally/split. The Poet's Day. Richard Weber. CIP

When his proud mother took his height/Against the bedroom wall. At Sunrise. Rosa Zagnoni Marinoni. PoToHe

When his soul, a weary lion, cried to God. Moses and Joshua. Else Lasker-Schüler. VWA

When his thin wheyish blood/Is far less comfortable than his tears? The Resolute Courtier. Thomas Shipman. ErPo; GBL

When hope starts staggering. Mortality. Naomi Long Madgett. NNP; PoBA

When howls man's soul, it howls inaudibly. In the Dock. Walter De La Mare. ChMP; LiTM

When humped clouds/crowd low against the ground. Bone Yard. Jim Barnes. CDW

When I alone, who love you most,/Am killed with your Distain. Insulting Beauty. John Wilmot, Earl of Rochester. CavP

When I am a shadow.../I will creep away. A Changeling Grateful. Josephine Preston Peabody. AA

When I am in him, I am in the Kingdom of God/And in the Fatherland of my Soul. The Postern Gate (excerpt). Walter Rauschenbusch. TRV

When/i am in malcolmland/me know me be blacker... Half Black, Half Blacker. Sterling D. Plumpp. PoBA

When I am old,/Say the bells at St. Paul's. The Bells of London. *Anonymous.* PoRA

When I am rotten as a pear,/And mute as any fish. A New Song of New Similes. John Gay. FaBoCo; NOBL

When I am sick and like to die,/He'll row me in his Highland plaidie. As I Came O'er Cairney Mount. *Anonymous.* CoMu

When I am/silent: gather the boundaried vacancies. Unsaid. Archie Randolph Ammons. NOBA

(When I am 28 I will be many) Something Else. Michael Brownstein. ANYP

When I am undone,/When I am no one. Wish for a Young Wife. Theodore Roethke. NoAm; NoP; OBSP; TAP

When I ask a bottle-curled Hassidic boy/the way to Jaffa Gate he lowers his eyes/& does not answer. At the Western Wall. Barbara F. Lefcowitz. VWA

When I at first the forty crowns/For one night's lodging bid. Proffered Love Rejected. Sir John Suckling. CavP; NCEP

When I at last may come to you,/All being well? All Being Well. Wilfrid Gibson. OxBTC

When I awoke, it was noon. Dawn. Arthur Rimbaud. SOTW

When I begin living forever. Armor. James Dickey. CoAP

When I believe and sing, my doubtings cease. Upon the Swallow. John Bunyan. OxBChV

When I broke this crust. Greek Excavations. Bernard Spencer. ChMP

When I came back from Lyonnesse/With magic in my eyes! When I Set out for Lyonnesse. Thomas Hardy. BrPo; InPS; MoBrPo; PAI; SeCePo; VLP

When I can lie/with you,/in our beautiful room. Why Would I Want. William J. Harris. PoBA

...When I dare/disturb the leaf that's wedged against my door. At My Father's Grave. John Ciardi. SM

When I died they washed me out of the turret with a hose. The Death of the Ball Turret Gunner. Randall Jarrell. AP; BiP; CMoP; CoBMV; ELU; ExPo; FF; HAP; HoPM; InPK; LCAP; LiTM; MiAP; MoAmPo; NAs; NIP; NMP; NoAm; NOBA; NoP; OBSP; OBWP; OxBA; PoPl; PrIm; SoSe; TAP; UnPo; VGW; WaaP; WaP

When I drift out on the Silver Sea. The Great Divide. Lew Sarett. HBMV

When I drive a cab/I end the only lit and waitful thing in miles of/darkened houses. Taxi Suite: After Anacreon. Lew Welch. PoM

When I fall asleep on the terrace/On a warm summer night. God Hasn't Made Room. Mririda n'Ait Attik. PBWP

When I fell limp in the grass. Bert Kessler. Edgar Lee Masters. AnFE; APA

When I forget thy thousand ways/Then life and all shall cease. A Child. Mary Ann Lamb. OBEV

When I get there, I hope they forgive me if the knot I tie is/the wrong knot. Hawaii Dantesca. Charles Wright. HaCAP; LCAP

When I get there/I'll pull your hair. From Here to There. *Anonymous.* OxNR

When I give my gold to the golden-rod. The Fallow Field. Julia Caroline Ripley Dorr. AA

When I go I will give you surely/What you will wear if you go with me! Courtship. Alice Corbin. BPAW

When I go to town. Good-By, Pretty Mama. *Anonymous.* ABF

When I go up to London/All the world shall know! Going up to London. Nancy Byrd Turner. HBMV

When I grew up to wither into truth. On Approaching My Birthday. Vassar Miller. IHMS; NMM

When I have added these last words–"The End." Diary (excerpt). Ethel Romig Fuller. PGD

When I have rav'd ten thousand years in fire,/Ten thousand thousand, let me then expire.' The Lament of the Damned in Hell. Edward Hilton Young. OxBoCh

When I hear the trumpet sound in that morning. Oh, When Shall I See Jesus? *Anonymous.* AH

When I hear ye cryin' o'er me, "Arrah! why did ye die?" Molly Brannigan. *Anonymous.* FSW

When I hung my cap and bells upon/Her nutmeg tree. The King of China's Daughter. Edith Sitwell. FaBoMo; MoBrPo

When I landed again with a tithe of my men, on the Isle/of Finn! The Voyage of Maeldune. Alfred, Lord Tennyson. PoEL 1-5

When I last rade down Ettrick. Ettrick. Lady John Scott. BSV

When I laugh a black thing hovers. A Technical Supplement. Thomas Kinsella. CIP

When I lay dis body down. Song: "I know moon-rise. I know star-rise." *Anonymous.* NAMP

When I lay this body down. I Know Moonlight (with music). *Anonymous.* AS; UnPo

When I leave one space/for another/space. In the Planetarium. Siv Cedering Fox. LTB

When I left you alone in the night/to conceal my fire. Darling, I won't be your hot love. Sulpicia. BoWoP

When I lived/I was certainly rotten! Spoon River Anthology. Edwin Meade Robinson. HBMV

When I look way 'cross dat lonesome stream- Dat Lonesome Stream. *Anonymous.* ABF

When I'm a veteran with only one eye/I shall do nothing but look at the sky. Roman Wall Blues. W. H. Auden. DTC

When I'm as big as twenty-five, about? Prattle. John Ciardi. BiCB

When I made history/As Firefrorefiddle, the Fiend of the Fell.' Gus: the Theatre Cat. Thomas Stearns Eliot. CenHV; OBCA; OxBTC

When I might have devoured more pie. Grandmother's Apple Pies. Bruce Weston Munro. PeD

When I mixed up the gas and the brakes. Limerick: "Said a girl from beyond Pompton Lakes." Morris Bishop. LiBL

When I offered you my soul/Heard you what I said? Love and Language. Louisa S. Bevington. NOBV

When I put the cowboy trimmings on that high-toned dance. The Cowboy's Dance Song. *Anonymous.* CoSo

When I reflect, my late fatigues do seem/Only a notion or forgotten Dreem. Thoughts on Pausing at a Cottage near the Paukataug River. Sarah Kemble Knight. SCAP

When I remember that this thing happened!/Men tortured children! Children of Auschwitz. Naum Korzhavin. VWA

When I remember these/Fair sacramental trees! The Temple of the Trees. J. D. C. Pellow. PGD

When I return'd, like a tired child you slept. Deliverance. William James Dawson. OBVV

When I said autumn, autumn broke. Song at the Beginning of Autumn. Elizabeth Jennings. OxBTC

When I saw my sparrow die! The Sparrow's Dirge. John Skelton. FaBoCh; LoGBV; OBSC

When I see Emma smiling/And twirling through the door! The Tryst. Christopher Morley. HBMV

When I see the big view, you see/how it hides its thousand hearts. When I Held You to My Chest, You Fit. Jack Myers. AmPA

When I see them I feel like a hundred men/who know they have slipped out of prison/without a trace. Winter Twilight. Lou Lipsitz. GOYP

When i see them/i understand. Falling down to bed. Nila NorthSun. STE

When I send for thee/Then come thou. Little Maid, Pretty Maid. *Anonymous.* OxNR

When I shall in process destory the world and all. Time. Sir Thomas More. EnRePo

When I shall pass the sundering bar/Our souls must still be wed. A Tryst. Louise Chandler Moulton. HBV 1-2

When I shall sleep with clover clad,/And she beside another lad. Along the Field as We Came By. Alfred Edward Housman. HAP; HBV 1-2; LiTL; MasP; MoAB; MoBrPo; UnTE; WeW

When I should have shouted/her name Errata. Charles Simic. NNaP

When I tell the truth/there is so little to say. Youth. Richard Shelton. DFF

When I think on Bunclody, I'm ready to die. The Streams of Bunclody. *Anonymous.* BIrV

When I took her to the river. The Faithless Wife. Federico Garcia Lorca. BoLoP; ErPo

...When I turned, the house/Had opened its face, gray as a man's. Happening. Edwin Honig. NePA

When I wake before dawn/the room is already light Loving. Shirley Kaufman. VWA

When I wake I will not weep. The Watchers. Muriel Rukeyser. NMP

When I walked alone in a wooded lane/With perfect peace of heart. Youth. Jessie B. Rittenhouse. HBMV

When I was a boy my father told me the mountains/were the earth's sombreros. Habla Usted Espanol? James Reiss. AmPA

When I was a dreamy lad/and the bush was everywhere. The Golden Bird. Rex Ingamells. PoAu 1-2

When I was a King in Babylon/And you were a Virgin Slave. Echoes. William Ernest Henley. BLPA; BLPL; GoTF; TreF

When I was a Purple Polygon,/And you were a Sky-Blue Square. Bygones (parody). Bert Leston Taylor. HBMV

When I was nineteen/I became an Emperor. A Psalm of Onan for Harp, Flue and Tambourine. Alden Nowlan. NeAC

When I was seventeen/I didn't look back either. For Stephen. Christopher Brookhouse. AMV-80

When I was wi' my dearie. Absence. *Anonymous.* GTBS

When i was young/and very colored I used to wrap my white doll up in. Mae Jackson. BOLo; PoBA

When I would love her soul. Any Lover, Any Lass. Richard Middleton. HBV 1-2; OBVV

When I write to you/these notes of myself. All This Everyday (excerpt). Joanne Kyger. APU

When I yelled out something/about waking up tomorrow/and shooting out the sun. Hunting at Dusk. Doug Cockrell. Str

When ich have right good wine/Me liste drinke non ale. I Am Forsaken. *Anonymous.* OxBM

When in all lands, that lie within the sound/Of Sabbath bells, a Witch was burned or/drowned. Giles Corey of the Salem Farms: Prologue. Henry Wadsworth Longfellow. PAH

When in her roundness she burns silver/about the world. The glow and beauty of the stars. Sappho. BoWoP

When in his arms young Ganymede/Snuggles and lifts warm lips to kiss. New Love. Martial (Marcus Valerius Martialis). PeHV

When, in our turn, we show to them a Man. Christ in the Universe. Alice Meynell. ACP; CAW; GoBC; HBMV; MoBrPo; NOBE

When in the night with songs, not cries, I moan,/Lest more should hear what I complain of one. Caelica, LXVIII. Fulke, Lord Brooke Greville. FCP

When in this hush of strings you draw more near/Than any sound of music that I hear. When There Is Music. David Morton. HBMV

When in those gardens of the sea/The lilies of the moon should gleam. The Gardens of the Sea. George Sterling. EtS; EvOK

When in your hate a devil's shape I take. O do not grieve, Dear Heart, nor shed a tear. Margaret Canvendish, Duchess of Newcastle. EnLoPo

When indiscreet—we're call'd TOO GOOD./Never do so again.' Rather Too Good, Little Peggy! Adelaide O'Keeffe. FaBoUs

When it comes my heart breaks forth and sings. Youth and Maidenhood. Sarah Williams. OBVV

When it draws near the witching time of night. The Grave. Robert Blair. ViBoPo

When it flaps on a string/In the top of a tree. The Kite. Harry Behn. TiPo

When it goes, 'tis like the Distance/On the look of Death–. There's a Certain Slant of Light. Emily Dickinson. AmePo; AnFE; AP; APA; AtBAP; BLPL; BoWoP; CMoP; DiPo; ExPo; ForPo; HAP; HeIP; LiTM; LoGBV; MAmP; MasP; MoAB; MoAmPo; MoPo; NAWM 1-2; NePA; NoAm; NOBA; NoP; OxBA; PoEL 1-5; PPP; QFR; SBG; TreFT

When it is over it is all over. Duck-Chasing. Galway Kinnell. MP; NMP; TwCP; VGW

When it is spilled/Is simply water. Haiku: "The dew of the rouge-flower." Kaga no Chiyo. PBWP

When it is–then, now, tomorrow–they're dead. Oystering. Richard Howard. NoAm

When it is time to wake and grow. Waiting. Harry Behn. SiSoSe; TiPo

When it is too late to save the harvest. Views from the High Camp. William Stanley Merwin. ConAP

When it makes a man mad all the days of his life? Bits of Straw. John Clare. WiR

...When it/met the silent current/burst into applause Sunset. David Allan Evans. PPJ

When it's found the people live the small wraths of ease. Th Unifying Principle. Archie Randolph Ammons. NOBA

When it's just past April/and going on May. The Flower-Cart Man. Rachel Field. SiSoSe; SoPo

When it's time he was upstairs in bed? Little Miss Pitt. William Wise. TiPo

When it trembled at Autumn's hue/On our wedding night. Autumn Imagined. Donald Davie. PoA

(When it was full and at the lip) struck down. Poems, XCVIII: "In spring and summer winds may blow." Walter Savage Landor. PG

When it was no longer yours Voice. William Stanley Merwin. NNaP

When Jack had his girl/On Friday night. Music in the Air. Ronald McCuaig. ErPo

When Jeff's men see you comin'/By God, you'll see 'em run! Dan Ellis's Boys. *Anonymous.* AmFP

When Jemmy shall his fame retrieve,/and be in grace again. England's Darling. *Anonymous.* CoMu

When Jerusalem blossomed in the noon-tide bells! The Last Abbot of Gloucester. Wilfred Rowland Childe. CAW

When Jesus groan'd, a trembling fear/Seiz'd all ye guilty world a round. When Jesus Wept. William Billings. TrAS

When Johnnie kneels and kisses me. Dumbarton's Drums. *Anonymous.* FSW

When Johnny comes marching home. When Johnny Comes Marching Home. Patrick Sarsfield (Louis Lambert) Gilmore. BLSo; FSW; PAH; PAL; PoSC; PSoN; TrAS; TreF

When Johnson's ale was new, my boys,/When Johnson's ale was new. Johnson's Ale. *Anonymous.* FSW

When Jove himself added a handful of hail. The Mint Julep. Charles Fenno Hoffman AA; AmePo

When joy comes to our jolly wassail. Thames Head Wassailers' Song. *Anonymous.* OBET

When joys are yours that never cost a sigh. Evening Schoolboys. John Clare. GLGT

When Kings are dust beside forgotten thrones. The Sovereigns. Lloyd Mifflin. AA; AnAmPo; HBV 1-2

When kisses are a shilling each/We should adventure on a few. The Gospel of Mr. Pepys. Christopher Morley. InMe; NLV

When last we camped at Irish Lords, on the road to Ivanhoe. Irish Lords. Charles H. Souter. PoAu 1-2

When leaves fall and cold winds come. The Flight of Love. Percy Bysshe Shelley. FPL; GTBS; GTBS-P; HBV 1-2; PoLf

When leaves fall and cold winds come.　When the Lamp Is Shattered. Percy Bysshe Shelley.　BoLiVe; CBEP; FiP; MCCG; OBRV; PG; PPP; TEP; TreFT; TrGrPo; ViBoPo; WHA

When life falls from us like a withered husk.　Creed.　Mary Ashley Townsend.　BLPA; FaBoBe

When life grows hateful, there's power...　Reference to a Passage in Plutarch's Life of Sulla.　Robinson Jeffers.　CrMA

When life that could not be, comes back!　Once Before.　Mary Mapes Dodge.　AA

When like stars his children crowned,/All in white shall wait around.　Once in Royal David's City.　Cecil Frances Alexander.　OxBChV

When limbs and charm and favour/Are warm but worn away.　When Sadness Fills a Journey.　John Waller.　NeBP

When "Little Blue Ribbons" prefers it so.　Little Blue Ribbons.　Henry Austin Dobson.　BiCB

When little white-tailed rabbits/Make their swift way through.　July Meadow. Louise Driscoll.　YeAr

When living he was able to prevent/and abstain from killing (Isaac),/therefore we preserve life.　Therefore We Preserve Life.　Shen Ch'uan.　TrJP

When, lo! a paler flower than mine/Had blossomed in the gloom!　The White Jessamine.　John Banister Tabb.　HBV 1-2

When lo! more than all the gifts of the world you gave me.　O Tan-Faced Prairie-Boy.　Walt Whitman.　OxBA; PeHV

When, lo! the first star brought me back/thy face!　To Imagination.　Edith Matilda Thomas.　AA

When Love is fled, and I grow old.　Why I Write Not of Love.　Ben Jonson. EnLit; OAEP; OBSP

When lovers, water, and leaves are wholly one.　Three Things.　May Sarton. AMV-80

When Lovewell brave 'gainst Paugus went,/With fifty men from Dunstable. Lovewell's Fight.　Anonymous.　PAH

When, lowering the snake, he sent words to prove the/Fall.　Genesis.　Brian Higgins.　FaBoTw

When lowly, with a broken neck,/The crocus lays her cheek to mire.　The Thrush in February.　George Meredith.　OBNC

When madd'ning rapture goads to vice my throbbing sense.　A Sonnet to Opium; Celebrating Its Virtues.　Orestes".　NOEC

When magic trees their petals shake/Upon each gazing eye.　Fireworks. James Reeve.　OnUR; PoSC

When man and star stood marvelling at His birth.　Holy Night.　Nathaniel A. Benson.　CaP

When man has made the man next door his friend.　The Kindly Neighbor. Edgar A. Guest.　PoToHe

When man in the bush with God may meet?　Good-bye.　Ralph Waldo Emerson.　AnNE; FaFP; GoTF; HBV 1-2; LiTA; MAmP; TAP; TreF

When man with man shall mate/O'er all the world.　My Country Is the World.　Robert Whitaker.　PGD

When May is gone, of all the year the pleasant time is past.　May.　Richard Edwards.　OBSC

When men beeth meriest at her mele/I rede ye thenk on yesterday.　Think on Yesterday.　Anonymous.　OxBM

When men fight for freedom, they must be/victorious.　American Independence.　Francis Hopkinson.　PAH

When men might hope more then they understood.　To Mrs. Diana Cecyll. Edward, Lord Herbert of Cherbury.　AnAnS 2

When mercy seasons justice.　The Merchant of Venice.　William Shakespeare.　BBVV; FaFP; GoTF; LiTB; OHFP; TreF; TrGrPo; TRV; WBLP

When mice with wings can wear a human face.　The Bat.　Theodore Roethke.　OBCA; WSC

When 'mid their light thy light appears.　To Wordsworth.　Walter Savage Landor.　OAEL 1-2

When mop in hand the old world through/The door pressed, dutiful, idiot. In the Last Few Moments Came the Old German Cleaning Woman.　Jane Cooper.　SM

When mortal eyes may glimpse the sight.　Song for Midsummer Night. Elizabeth Jane Coatsworth.　YeAr

When Mother leans to say good night.　Butterfly.　William Jay Smith. GoJo; TiPo

When Mother takes the Fairy Book/And we curl up to hear.　The Fairy Book.　Abbie Farwell Brown.　HBV 1-2; HBVY

When my child's call I hear, I catch her to my heart.　Prayer.　Edward Bliss Reed.　HBMV

When my dear country shall be made/A Nation once again.　A Nation Once Again.　Thomas Davis.　NOBI

When my eye fights my heart with deadly light?　Sonnet XI: "O eyes clear with beauty, O tender gaze."　Louise Labe.　BoWoP

...When my face/comes back I sip more of the wine.　The Night Sits in This Chair.　Alice Notley.　APU

When my father, restless,/is out breaking the cedars of Lebanon.　The Violin Tree.　Joel Rosenberg.　VWA

When my griefs sing to me/from the bright throats of thrushes/I sing back. Old Woman.　Linda Pastan.　FiCP

When my loved lord no longer smiles on me?　A Lyric: "How can I sing light-souled."　Lorenzo de' Medici.　AWP

When my Mide drum/Sounds/For me.　The Sky Clears.　Anonymous. OBVE

When my old cassock (said a Welsh divine)/Is out at elbows, why should I repine?　The Power of Time.　Jonathan Swift.　CBEP; FaBoEE; PV

"When my old cassock," says a Welsh divine,/"Is out at elbows, why should I repine?"　The Bathos.　Richard Porson.　FaBoEE

When my She-sun doth either laugh or lour...　The Marigold So Likes the Lovely Sun.　Thomas Watson.　AtBAP; LO

When my ship comes in.　When My Ship Comes In.　Robert Jones Burdette. FaFP

When my small child did cry for nurse.　The Cry of the Child (parody). William Zaranka.　BXAP

When nature all is sad like me!/And maun I still...　Composed in Spring. Robert Burns.　CBEP

When Nature, whether wild or tame,/Is always pretty much the same!　Ain't Nature Commonplace!　Arthur Guiterman.　FiBHP; InMe

When neither can hinder the other.　Why Should a Foolish Marriage Vow. John Dryden.　HeIP; ViBoPo

When neither overcomes, love's triumph greater is.　Song: "Leave this gaudy gilded stage."　John Wilmot, Earl of Rochester.　OBSP

When neither Time nor Tide can grant/Belief with wishes.　Growing Gray. Henry Austin Dobson.　HBV 1-2

When night comes around you've got to undress yet.　Poems in Praise of Practically Nothing.　Samuel Hoffenstein.　EvOK; FiBHP; InMe

When night had stilled that battle's drum,/They dug his grave at Waterloo. The Drummer Boy of Waterloo.　Anonymous.　BFSS

When no force else can get the masterdom.　Money Gets the Mastery. Robert Herrick.　CaPo

When no one is asleep/even while dreaming.　No One Is Asleep.　Michelle Roberts.　LFAC

When nobody's with me/I'm all alone.　Jumping Joan.　Anonymous. OxNR

When none cares whether it prevail or not.　Truth.　Coventry Patmore. TrGrPo

When not himself, he's mad; when most himself,/he's worse.　Emblem. Francis Quarles.　LoBV

When ol' Sis' Judy pray....　When Ol' Sis' Judy Pray.　James Edwin Campbell.　BANP

When old in dust doe lye, it's best dye too.　Thomas Dudley Ah! Old Must Dye.　Anonymous.　SCAP

When old John Bax drove the coach for Cobb and Co.　Old John Bax. Charles H. Souter.　PoAu 1-2

When on her world-weary pinion,/Flies back my lost love to me.　Take Back the Heart.　Charlotte Allington ("Claribel") Barnard.　TreFT

When on Thy bosom it has leant/And found in Thee its life.　Christ's Bondservant.　George Matheson.　STF; TRV

When once destroyed, can never be supplied.　The Deserted Village.　Oliver Goldsmith.　LiTB; PPON; SeCePo; ViBoPo

When once I am alone and shut the door.　L'Envoi.　Willa Cather.　HBV 1-2

When once I rubbed shoulders with you.　Touching Shoulders.　Anonymous. BLPA

When once they find her flower, her glory, pass.　Sonnet: "But love whilst that thou may'st be loved again."　Samuel Daniel.　EIL

When once they're raised, they're cursed hard to lay.　To My Ingenious and Worthy Friend William Lowndes, Esq.　John Gay.　OBSV

When one was in a passion/The other could forbear.　My Dad and Mam They Did Agree.　Anonymous.　PoL

When one with Thee, my life shall be/Attuned to gladsome Melody.　God's Will.　Edwin H. Nevin.　BLRP

...When our bones rise again/It will be the everlasting springtime.　How to Fly by Standing Still (excerpt).　James Keir Baxter.　OCNZ

When our enemies were in exile.　I have no embroidered headband.　Sappho. BoWoP

When our Lord God boren was/And to the herte stungen.　The Sun of Grace.　Anonymous.　OxBM

When our young days of gathering flowers/Will be an hundred years ago. Love and Age.　Thomas Love Peacock.　HBV 1-2; NOBV; OBEV; OBNC; PoPle; ViBoPo

When out of the woods He came.　A Ballad of Trees and the Master. Sidney Lanier.　AA; AmePo; AP; CAW; EBCP; FPL; GoBC; HBV 1-2; LaNeLa; LiTA; MAmP; NOBA; OxBA; PoEL 1-5; PoLf; TreFT; TRV

When pain and anguish wring the brow,/A ministering angel thou!　O, Woman!　Sir Walter Scott.　GoTF

When Pan, and his Son, and fair Syrinx, return.　The Lady's Song.　John Dryden.　LoBV; SeCeV

When passed been the colde showres,/Right so recovereth he his flowres. Medea's Magic.　John Gower.　OxBM

When peace is prevailing he is spoiling to fight,/The man with a chip on his shoulder. A Chip on His Shoulder. *Anonymous.* BLPA; WBLP

...When peace shall come/With stillness, and long shivers, after death. The Farmer. Fredegond Shove. MMM

When people cramp into their station wagons/and roll up the windows and drive away. At Cove on the Crooked River. William Stafford. ConAP; LiTM; NaP

When people, who have only themselves to give,/offer you their meal. An Invitation to Madison County. Jay Wright. PoBA

When Pop bottles pop-bottles/Pop-bottles pop! Song of the Pop-Bottlers. Morris Bishop. FiBHP

When round as a neep ye come todlen hame. Todlen Butt, and Todlen Ben. *Anonymous.* OBS

When, round as a neep, ye come todlin' hame. Todlin' Hame. *Anonymous.* HBV 1-2

When sampler threads should turn to gray. The Sampler. Rachel Field. BiCB

When Satan still in gaze, as first he stood,/Scarce thus at length failed speech recovered sad. Paradise Lost. John Milton. FaBoPV

When, seeing this gleam,/We saw no time. Time's Bright Sand. Robert Finch. CaP

When selfish greed becomes a social sin/The world's regeneration may begin. Fashion. Ada Cambridge. NOAV

When shall I burn this negative/And hang the receiver up on grief?' Lament for a Cricket Eleven. Kenneth Allott. OxBTC

When shall I hear that voice again? To the Lady with a Book. *Anonymous.* KiLC

When shall I see the wood and plain,/And dream those happy dreams again? The Sleep of Spring. John Clare. ERoP 1-2

When shall men cease to suffer and desire? Benedictio Domini. Ernest Christopher Dowson. CAW

When shall my mind awake/In its own loved scenes again. The Passing of a Dream. John Clare. NOBV

When shall we see thy like again? When Shall We See Thy Like Again? Mary Wingate. PGD

"When shall we three meet again?" Young Training. Lawrence McGaugh. PoBA

When she a Poet to the world doth send. When Heaven Would Strive to Do the Best She Can. Michael Drayton. LO

When she awakes the gate will crumble. Delfica. Gerard de Nerval. NU

When she conversations you/it ain't forever, Gimme! Preference. Langston Hughes. HaCAP; NOBA

When she gets mad, mad, mad,/She would sting me all around when she gets mad. The Dumb Maid. *Anonymous.* BFSS

When she in bed with Mars/By all the gods was seen. A Well-Wishing to a Place of Pleasure. *Anonymous.* GBL

When she is in my arms till night goes by. Dawn. *Anonymous.* UnTE

When she is old/it will be immortality enough. Birthday. Earle Birney. NAs

When she knew her faithful children/Were loving her so much. The Crocuses. Frances E. W. Harper. BlSi

When she see dat yellow boy she almos' faint away. Times Gettin' Hard, Boys (with music). *Anonymous.* AS

When she shall speak, thou'lt learn her tongue/And know she calls it Death. The Card-Dealer. Dante Gabriel Rossetti. MaVP; NBM; VLP

When she stops, stops running,/he gives her a kick. Golden Pheasant. William Hart-Smith. NOAV

When she vanishes your hand is a river you swim in forever. Party at Hydra. Irving Layton. HeIP

When she wakes up, do things for her my way! Prayer for a Very New Angel. Violet Alleyn Storey. BLPA; GoTF; TreFS

When she wakes up she will be completely happy. Woman Asleep on a Banana Leaf. Katha Pollitt. PoDr

When she was a child in Ballybree. Irish Grandmother. Katherine Edelman. AmFN; SiSoSe

When shipwreck's short allowance grows too scanty,/Without being much more horrible than Dante. Don Juan. George Gordon, Lord Byron. FaBoPV

When silence comes, we almost fear/That Earth receives its dead. The Two Stars. William Henry Davies. MoBrPo

When sixpenny loaves but three-pounders appear. The Collier's March. *Anonymous.* OBET

When slavery's galling chains are loosed, and all the oppressed are/free. To the Memory of J. Horace Kimball. Ada Sister Mary. BlSi

When sleep comes down to seal the weary eyes. Ere Sleep Comes down to Soothe the Weary Eyes. Paul Laurence Dunbar. CDC; PoNe

When smoking/i must/weep Old Man Told Me. Lance Henson. VoR

When smoothly go our gondolets/O'er the moonlight sea. Oh, Come to Me when Daylight Sets. Thomas Moore. EnRP

When snow is swirling, the past seems far away. At Times I Feel Like a Quince Tree. John Robert Quinn. AMV-81

When so great prize is had/For the mere asking. Praise of Mary. *Anonymous.* ISi

When, soft as zephyr, his touch shall fall. Within the Veil. Margaret E. Sangster. BLRP

When someone else/is as empty as a shoe. Mothers. Anne Sexton. Str

When someone enters through a door. How Gray the Rain. Elizabeth Jane Coatsworth. SoPo; TiPo

When someone smiled at me today. The day began with dismal doubt. *Anonymous.* PoToHe

When spring/And life are new. In Time of Silver Rain. Langston Hughes. GoSl; SoPo; TiPo

When spring-time cometh with/the summer at her heels. Master Skylark. John Bennett. AA

When Stark and his men went over/The earthworks at Bennington. Bennington. William Henry Babcock. PAH

When stars have set. Fledglings. Thomas Lake Harris. AA

When stars of frost are glowing. Four Seasons. Rowena Bastin Bennett. SiSoSe; TiPo

When "state', not "motion','tis they mean. List of Prepositions. Benjamin Hall Kennedy. FaBoUs

When such depravity is found/It only can live underground. The Rabbit. *Anonymous.* DBV; FaBoCo; FiBHP

When suddenly I am old, and start to wear purple. Warning. Jenny Joseph. FaBoWP; GOYP; OxBTC

When Summer's Everlasting Dower–/Confronts the dazzled Bee. Precious to me–she still shall be. Emily Dickinson. PeHV

When swift-thudding hoofs won the long race with fear. The Pony Express. Dorothy Brown Thompson. AmFN

When teeth do grow unto themselves/as their fathers did before? You and I Will Go to Finegall. *Anonymous.* NOBI

When tha be dead that lov'd it. The Head-Stone. William Barnes. OBVV

When that butt/goes out/the World ends, O.K.? Known. Joel Dailey. APU

When that fierce virgin and her Star/Out of the fabulous darkness called. Two Songs from a Play. William Butler Yeats. CABA; CMoP; ExPo; HAP; MoPo; NoP; PPoe; PPP; PrIm; SeCeV

When that is gone, we'll fill 't again,/Dan diddle dan. The Cobblers' Song. Charles Tilney. OBSC

When that shall fade, my verse distils your truth. Sonnets, LIV: "O, how much more doth beauty beauteous seem." William Shakespeare. AWP; OBEV; OBSC; ViBoPo

When that woman came farming right out of her clothes,/by God,/At the state fair. Adults Only. William Stafford. FF

When the Armstrongs cease from siddling/And the Royces roll no more. The Pedestrian's Plaint. Edward Verrall Lucas. CenHV

When the bell strikes the dog-watch, and the moon is on the/sea. Peg-Leg's Fiddle. Bill Adams. BBV; EtS

When the bells have tinkled,/And the Tale is told. Little Birds. Lewis (Charles Lutwidge Dodgson) Carroll. FaBoNo; OxBoLi

...When the big, enlightening myths/Have sunk beyond the river and we are alone in the dark. Sunday Evenings. John Hollander. NYBP; NYP

When the blasts of winter appear? The Schoolboy. William Blake. BoNaP; CH; FaBoCh; GLGT

When the Blue Bonnets came over the Border. The Monastery: Border Ballad. Sir Walter Scott. BSV; GN; NBM

When the blues overtaken him, he hollered like a newborn child. I Got the Blues. *Anonymous.* TTY

When the bones/speak for themselves. Pond. Fredrick Zydek. AMV-81

When the boom, when the boom, when the boom/of guns punched dark holes in the sky. The Seals in Penobscot Bay. Daniel Gerard Hoffman. MP; TwCP

When the Brazis was risin',/Riley walked the water. Godamighty Drag. *Anonymous.* OuSiCo

When the broken rise and the silent voices speak. Sunday on Hampstead Heath. George Woodcock. NeBP

When the bronze annals of the oak-tree close. Advice to a Prophet. Richard Wilbur. AmPP; CAPP; CoPo; FYAP; MAT; MoAmPo; MoRP; MP; NMP; NYBP; OBWP; OxBC; PPP; SUW; TwCP

When the cause shall call upon us, some to live/and some to die! All for the Cause. William Morris. VLP

When the chase ends. Lone Huntsman. Christie Jeffries. GoYe

When the clapper hits the bell? The Bellman's Song. *Anonymous.* DiPo; EBEV; EIL; SeCePo

When the clock sings no-time night. The Empty House. Russell Hoban. WSC

When the cloudless morning rises cold. Stanzas Concerning Love. Stefan George. AWP

When the cold gray mist brought the ghastly form! St. Swithin's Chair. Sir Walter Scott. WSC

When the cook's on the deck. A Trip on the Erie. *Anonymous.* ABF

When the curse of death is upon your splendid dust. Unseen Flight. Markos Georgeou. AMV-80

When the dancing bear came back with me.   The Dancing Bear.   Albert Bigelow Paine.   OBCA

When the day's pale pinions fold/Where those be that sang of old.   The Bullfinches.   Thomas Hardy.   PB

When the dear love she yielded with a sigh/Was all but thine?   Tutto e Sciolto.   James Joyce.   OBMV; OxBI

When the delight was gone.   Casey Jones.   Edward Vincent Swart.   PeSA

When the devil got well, the devil a monk was he.   Epigram.   *Anonymous.* ALV

When the dew is on the fall.   To an Irish Blackbird.   James MacAlpine. HBMV; HBVY

...When the door closes/and is a door no longer.   The Five Dreams.   John Woods.   FiCP

When the ducks began to lay/Charley Barley flew away.   Charley Barley. *Anonymous.*   OxNR

When the dusk draws/nigh/no/near.   Our Mr. Toad.   David McCord. TiPo

When the dusk is coming down.   W's for Windows.   Phyllis McGinley. TiPo

When the earth shall be filled with the glory of God as the/waters cover the sea.   God Is Working His Purpose Out.   A. C. Ainger.   BLRP; FaPoR

When the earth was void and the deep was/dumb?"/"Quien sabe?"   Quien Sabe?   Madge Morris.   BPAW

When the east brightens, I then would know...   I think of him.   *Anonymous.* BoWoP

When the evening shadows lengthen,/Thou shalt lay thy burden down.   My Grace Is Sufficient for Thee.   *Anonymous.*   BePJ

When the exile ends, and the years are told.   A Night in the Red Sea.   Sir Alfred Comyn Lyall.   OBTV

When the first tomato ripens/to miss me.   In Response to Executive Order 9066: ALL AMERICANS OF JAPANESE...   Dwight Okita.   BrSi

When the flint-hearted Saxons they've chased far away.   O Say, My Brown Drimin.   *Anonymous.*   OnYI

When the flocks are all at rest,/Sleeping on the mountain's breast.   Song for the Spinning Wheel.   William Wordsworth.   OBRV

When the forts of folly fall,/Find thy body by the wall.   The Last Word. Matthew Arnold.   BoLiVe; CABA; EnLi 1-2; FiP; HBV 1-2; NOBE; OAEL 1-2; OBNC; OBVV; PG; PoEL 1-5; TreFT; VLP; WHA

When the frost is on the punkin and the fodder's in the shock!   When the Frost Is on the Punkin.   James Whitcomb Riley.   AmePo; BoNaP; FaBoBe; FaBV; FaFP; FPL; HBV 1-2; HBVY; MCCG; OBAL; PoLf; TreF

When the gloom is soft, and the light is dim.   Too Solemn for Day, Too Sweet for Night.   William Sidney Walker.   OBEV

When the good Lord shall call you home.   Moanish Lady! (with music). *Anonymous.*   AS

When the grass is green again/and bending and half grown.   These Days. Robert Jones.   AMV-81

When the great ships go by.   Messmates.   Sir Henry Newbolt.   CH; HBV 1-2; MCCG

When the grinding shall cease!   The Mother's Song.   Virginia Woodward Cloud.   AA

When the ground glitters white with the fresh fallen snow.   The Holly. Edith King.   ChBR

When the hand of the fiddler surrenders the bow.   The Unicorn.   Emile Victor Rieu.   AmMo

When the heart of the world was young.   Vapour and Blue.   Wilfred (William Wilfred Campbell) Campbell.   CaP

When the Heat is on, you have only to send/For that wonderful one two three four legged/friend.   Macinnes's Mountain Patrol.   Tom Patey.   PoSH

...When the idea of eating/and the idea of pudding/are one.   Little Pudding (parody).   Mary M. Roberts.   BXAP

When the jolly, jolly grog is flowing,/Light falls.   Bold Manning. *Anonymous.*   ShS

When the Jubilee Cup, with John Jones up, was won upon/Wooden Spoon. The Famous Ballad of the Jubilee Cup.   Sir Arthur Thomas ("Q") Quiller-Couch.   InMe; NA

When the Kingdom comes to pass,/Its tents and trumpets will be grass. Sheep.   Samuel Hoffenstein.   AnAmPo; TrJP

When the labor is done and the workers/Before Him, shall stand.   The Vineyard.   *Anonymous.*   STF

When the land lay waiting for her westward people!   Empire Builders. Archibald MacLeish.   OxBA

When the landfolk of Galway converse with a stranger.   Undertone.   W. B. Stanford.   NeIP; OnYI

When the last trumpet rends the air/It shall not be forgiven you.   Ballade d'une Grande Dame.   Gilbert Keith Chesterton.   OxBoLi

When the last warmth is gone/I shall bear in the snow.   Father, the Year Is Fallen.   Audre Lorde.   PoBA

When the leaf decides to fly/Kiss your love goodbye.   Look to the Leaf. *Anonymous.*   UnTE

When the lips and the skin remember...   Return.   Constantine P. Cavafy. ErPo

When the livid Antarctic storm-clouds glow.   The Fortitude of the North. Herman Melville.   AmePo

When the long night is done/Then shall ye sleep.   A Nocturne.   Wilfrid Scawen Blunt.   OBMV

When the Lord, Almighty God, came again to His throne.   A Dream of the Rood.   *Anonymous.*   AnOE; CAW; OAEL 1-2

When the Lord will rise and love them.   Square-Toed Princes.   Robert P. Tristram Coffin.   AmFN

When the maiden hath that she loveth,/She is without longing.   I Have a Young Sister.   *Anonymous.*   CH; EBEV; EnPo; ExPo; MeEL; NoP; OAEL 1-2; OxBM; PoEL 1-5; SeCeV

When the man risen from the dead was trying to get to his feet.   Evil Days. Boris Pasternak.   MoRP

When the manly man goes forth to hold his own on land or sea!   The Manly Man.   *Anonymous.*   BLPA; WBLP

When the morn was shining clear.   Ballad of the Tempest.   James Thomas Fields.   BeLS; BLPL; EtS; FaBoBe; HBV 1-2; PoLf; YaD

When the mune was shinin' clearly.   A Mile an' a Bittock.   Robert Louis Stevenson.   NOBV; OxBS; SeCePo

When the neighborhood chillen gets to slingin' with rocks!   The David Jazz. Edwin Meade Robinson.   HBMV

When the night-processions flit/Through the mind!   The Peace-Offering. Thomas Hardy.   OBSP

When the noisy man comes you remain hidden.   Prayer to the God Thot. *Anonymous.*   TTY

"When the oaken leaves that fall from the trees/Are green and spring up again."   The Unquiet Grave.   *Anonymous.*   FaBoBa; FSW; ViBoFo

When the one that you love,/Baby, is loving someone else?   Mean Mistreater Mama.   Leroy Carr.   BuL

When the Pegasus came sailing from the West.   The Little Commodore (parody).   J. C. Squire.   HBMV

When the people of the city hear my sacred song,/they are ready to die.   A Curse on Uruk.   Enheduanna.   BoWoP

When the phoca has the pica/In the palace of the Queen Chinee!   Trio for Two Cats and a Trombone.   Edith Sitwell.   PBWP

When the Plantagenet saw the avenger Death/Toward him spurring over Bosworth field.   Sonnets to Miranda.   William Watson.   HBV 1-2

When the play was played out so for one man's pleasure.   Stage Love. Algernon Charles Swinburne.   NIP; PoEL 1-5

When the Pleiads were sinking; and he sank with them.   Epitaph of Cleonicus.   Charles Stuart Calverley.   FaBoEE

When the plunging hoofs were gone.   The Listeners.   Walter De la Mare. AWP; BBV; BLPL; BrPo; CMoP; CoBMV; FaFP; GoTF; GTBS; HAP; HBV 1-2; HBVY; HeIP; HoPM; InvP; LiTB; LiTM; MaC; MoAB; MoBrPo; MoPo; MoVE; NAMP; NCSH; NoAm; NOBE; NoP; OAEP; OBEV; OBMV; OBVV; OnMSP; PoPl; PoPle; PoRA; SeCeV; SoSe; TreF; TrGrPo; ViBoPo; WeW; WHA; WSC

When the priest elevates/the Saviour of the world.   Missouri Sequence: Nightfall.   Brian Coffey.   CIP

When the rain smell comes with the wind.   Love Poem.   Leslie Marmon Silko.   UnPo; VoR

When the rain turns into snow/Every beast shall see its track and wonder. Sleep.   Charles Simic.   CoAP

When the renewed for ever of a kiss/Whirls life within the shower of loosened hair!   Modern Love, XIII.   George Meredith.   OBNC; VLP

When the rest have nothing at all to say.   The Storm-Cock's Song.   Hugh" (Christopher Murray Grieve) MacDiarmid.   OxBTC

When the rings of the wind on our upturned wrists/revolve their strange fires. The Phoenix of Mozart.   Claude Vigee.   VWA

When the ripe and bearded barley/Is smiling on the scythe!   The Ripe and Bearded Barley.   *Anonymous.*   BoNaP; GBP

When the rosebud ripened to the rose,/In both I read thy name.   Thine Eyes Still Shined.   Ralph Waldo Emerson.   NOBA

When the Rudyards cease from Kipling/And the Haggards Ride no more? To R. K. (parody).   James Kenneth Stephen.   BXAP; FaBoPa; Par

...When the ruined heart goes forth to/crave/Mercy of the high, austere, unpitying Grave.   Two Days.   William Ernest Henley.   VLP

When the saints come marching in.   When the Saints Come Marching In. Edward C. Redding.   BLSo; EaLo; FSW

...When the salt is put in her mouth she doesn't cry.   Kyran's Christening. Alden Nowlan.   NeAC

When the sandhill crane goes walking.   The Sandhill Crane.   Mary Austin. BPAW; TiPo

When the sculptors get there/they are surprised.   Four Translations from the English of Robert Hershon.   Robert Hershon.   NeAC

When the selfsame nimbus is eerily worn/By a nymph, a child, and a unicorn? About Children.   Phyllis McGinley.   OBAL

When the shrapnel missed the others' head.   The Bus-Stop on the Somme. David Rowbotham.   NOAV

When the shutter/reopened   Profile.   Bronwen Wallace.   AMV-81

When the silver moon is beaming;/Then I'll meet you, Adeline.   Adelina, the Yale Boola Girl.   Charles H. Loomis.   FSN

...When the soul/Hangs poised, with folded wings, 'tween day and night. Saul. Charles Heavysege. CaP

When the spirit comes, sisters,/I want you to jump straight up and down. Preachin' the Blues. Son House. BluL

When the spring comes, and flood, the tassels/rise, as my head. Merce of Egypt. Charles Olson. NoP

When the stars came out in the Christmas sky. Shepherds' Carol. Norman Nicholson. OBCP

When the stars in the elements/Shall tremble with glee. The Cherry-Tree Carol, I. *Anonymous.* AmFP; PCh

...When the stars/of our easy invention have/all but gone away. Driving through the Pima Indian Reservation. Paul H. Cook. AMV-80

When the storm tosses on all sides. Prayer on Making a Canoe. *Anonymous.* WTO

"When the sun and the moon set on yonders green hill,/And I'm sure that never can be." Lizie Wan. *Anonymous.* AmFP; BaBo

When the sun goes down, you'll roll no more. Oh, Roll on, Babe. *Anonymous.* OuSiCo

When the sun is in my eyes and the ladders are shaky and the mortar boards go/wrong, I think of you. Bricklayer Love. Carl Sandburg. AmP

When the sun is out. What to Do. William Wise. TiPo

"When the sun rises never to set,/And you know that'll never be." Edward (C vers.). *Anonymous.* BaBo

When the sun sank down in the west. Changelings. Mary Thacher Higginson. AA

"When the sun shines bright from the northern airt,/And that shall never be." The Dead Brother. *Anonymous.* EnSB

When the Sword came back from sea! The Sailing of the Sword. William Morris. CoBE; OAEP; OBVV; TreFS

When the technician says breathe/I breathe. One More Time. Patricia Goedicke. AMV-80

When the tide falls away from the shore. Give No White Flower. Brenda Chamberlain. NeIP

...When the touched body/Gives forth the divine humors of rain, leaves, and love. Cortege for Colette. Jean Garrigue. NYBP

...When the train stopped and they knew/The end of their journey, I descended too. The Traveller. John Berryman. VGW

When the triumph is reflective/and confusion, retroactive. Old Amusement Park. Marianne Moore. NYBP

When the twenty fled from one ere the rising/of the sun,/In the harbor of Fayal the Azore! The Fight of the Armstrong Privateer. James Jeffrey Roche. PAH

When the two of you are equally beautiful. Hands. Donald Finkel. CoAP; InPK; MAT

When the visitor least expects. The Chimpanzee. Muriel Sly. FiBHP

When the voice has ceased to cry? Ode: The Spirit Wooed. Richard Watson Dixon. OBNC

When the watch went below. One of Wally's Yarns. John Masefield. BrPo

...When the white moon rises/women want to lash out/with a cutting edge? Strawberry Moon. Mary Oliver. InPS

When the wicked rise from heaven and the weary are at rest. The Old-Time Cowboy. *Anonymous.* CoSo

When the Willer so willeth works his wild wonders. My Grandfather's Church Goes Up. Fred Chappell. SM

When the wind blew, you could hear/them rubbing on each other. All That Time. May Swenson. FF

When the wind is in the West,/Then it is at its very best. Proverbial Weather Rhymes. *Anonymous.* FaBoUs

When the wind is out in Erinn/And the sun is in the west. The Wind on the Hills. Dora Sigerson Shorter. HBMV; NOBV

When the winds blow and the seas flow?/Hey nonny no! A Round. *Anonymous.* FaBoCh; LoGBV

When the wool is on the sheep's back, there is no thread. The Lover's Gifts. *Anonymous.* OxNR

...When the word, a supple word,/lived in it, crumbled now to chalk. Paterson. William Carlos Williams. PP

When the word of Enlil rushes forth, eye cannot be-/hold it. Lamentation of Nippur. *Anonymous.* LiTW

When the world is known not to be green forever. The Moment. David Rowbotham. BoAV

When the world turns black and gold,/Then it's Halloween! Black and Gold. Nancy Byrd Turner. SoPo; TiPo; YeAr

When their choirs like birds shall be my only poets/Said the sore-tried woman of the roads. Deirdre and the Poets. Ewart Milne. NeIP

When their men are not looking. Shaman. Esther M. Leiper. AMV-81

When their Muse, as such trollops will truly,/Sails too near the wind.] Poeta Loquitur. Algernon Charles Swinburne. OAEL 1-2

When there's no one about in the Quad.' Limerick: "There once was a man who said, 'God.'." Ronald Arbuthnott Knox. FaBoCo; NLV; NOBL; OxBoLi; PoPle

When there's some urgent duty I dislike. Japanese Beetles. X.J. Kennedy. HoAn; OBAL

When there's trouble on shore, there's peace on the wave,/Afloat in the White Canoe. The White Canoe. Alan Sullivan. CaP

When these people are gone/they will have taken the land/with them. Indian Camp. Janet Reed McFatter. GrPl

...When they are full,/They belch us. Othello. William Shakespeare. DBV

An' when they 'atch, your be cock-sparrers, see? A London Sparrow's If. J. A. Lindon. BoAnP

When they awake on Christmas day. A Christmas Wish. Eugene Field. ChBR

When they bare the iron hand. The Martyr. Herman Melville. AmePo; PoEL 1-5; TAP; TrGrPo

When they be dead that loved it. Readen Ov a Head-Stwone. William Barnes. CH; HBV 1-2

When they came./i had spaced. "In This House, There Shall Be No Idols". Carolyn M. Rodgers. JB

When they can sing no more. Coda. James Tate. AmPA; NYBP

When they decide, it is a bad day. Sayings from the Northern Ice. William Stafford. NU

When they drove to their lodgings in their one horse chay. The One Horse Chay. *Anonymous.* OxBoLi

When they go down to hell they are thrown out again. Killyburn Brae. *Anonymous.* OnYI

...When they had drunk their thirst away/they trailed off homeward drowsily to bed. The Odyssey. Homer. NAWM 1-2

When they have cause to speak of this wild place,/May call it by the name of EMMA'S DELL. It Was an April Morning. William Wordsworth. FaBoPP

& When they have eyes for me it's Heaven. Malest Cornifici Tuo Catullo. Allen Ginsberg. NeAP

When they heard the bell toll/For poor Cock Robin. Who Killed Cock Robin? *Anonymous.* PBBP

When they kiss it is all violence on her part/hard mouth and smouldering glances. Lesbian Play on T.V. Caroline Gilfillan. PeHV

When they learned 'twas a bull–the great Duke of Buccleuch! The Duke of Buccleuch. J. A. Phelp. NOAV

When they love but live no more. Arethusa. Percy Bysshe Shelley. DTo; EnRP; GN; HBV 1-2; OBRV; WiR

When they me pray for help in thy presence. The Child Jesus to Mary the Rose. John Lydgate. CAW; GoBC; ISi

...When they put him to sleep/in a clear glass bed they look in from all sides. The Apron. Stuart Friebert. FiCP

When they quit their laughing and talking and went to walking for a big choc'late cake. At a Georgia Camp Meeting. Kerry Mills. BLSo

When they're done,/they'll want to hire some women. For Hollis Sigler. Elaine Equi. APU

When they say, "It is Roi/who is dead?" I wonder/who will they mean? The Liar. Robert Earl Hayden. AmPP; NOBA

When they see one of them/they know some boat will be lost. Fish. William Carlos Williams. NoAm

When they see the bright, red, beautiful flowers in my window. Tulips and Addresses. Edward Field. NYBP; Psk

When they see the white waves breaking/on the Rock of Avery's Fall! The Swan Song of Parson Avery. John Greenleaf Whittier AA

When they stop/they, suddenly, are/gravel. Ringed Plover by a Water's Edge. Norman MacCaig. OxBC

When they talk about the ilyoustrated press. Take Nothing for Granite. Nate Salsbury. InMe

When they talk to themselves/For company's sake. Down the Rain Falls. Elizabeth Jane Coatsworth. SoPo

When they've saved us with matins and masses. Why, Liquor of Life? Turlough Carolan. OnYI

When they whine, I tell them: climb a hill. Jill, Afterwards. Philip Dacey. SM

When this you see, remember me,/Though I am long forgotten. John Smith Is My Name. *Anonymous.* FaBoUs

When thou, alas, dost in the fancy lie. Beauty. Abraham Cowley. AnFE; TrGrPo

When thou are olde, ther's grief inough for thee! Menaphon. Robert Greene. AtBAP

When thou art more cruel than he,/Then will Love be kind to thee. Four Winds. Sara Teasdale. HBV 1-2

When thou art old there's grief enough for thee. Sephestia's Song to Her Child. Robert Greene. ELP; EnLi 1-2; GTBS; HBV 1-2; LoBV; NOBE; OBEV; OBSC; PoEL 1-5; TrGrPo

When thou art walking, wake me, for my Master's sake! Coleridge. Aubrey Thomas De Vere. GoBC

When thou didst walk in wrath/With thine horses through the sea! A Ballad of the French Fleet. Henry Wadsworth Longfellow. AA; HBV 1-2; MC; PAH

When thou had'st Meat enough, and Orrery?　Lines on Bounce.　Alexander Pope.　FM

"When thou hast thy penance done,/Then thoust come a mayden home."　The Maid and the Palmer.　*Anonymous.*　ACP; BaBo; ESPB

When thou'rt forsaken, and/The shame sits on thy knee.　The Flirt.　William Henry Davies.　EnLoPo

When thou shalt hand, so tremblingly,/Thy empty lamp to Him.　The Lamp.　Sarah Pratt McLean Greene.　AA

When thou shalt spread thy heavenly feast.　Lord Jesus Christ, We Humbly Pray.　Henry Eyster Jacobs.　AH

When thou suffredes ded for me.　Jesu Christ, My Leman Swete.　*Anonymous.*　OxBM

When thousands of students/Cried "All we are in that category!"　On Lady Gregory's Search for Talent.　James Joyce.　FaBoEE

When thy heart enfolds a brother,/God is there.　When Thy Heart with Joy O'erflowing.　Theodore Chickering Williams.　AH

When thy strong hands her veil at last lift up.　Odes, II.　Hafiz.　AWP

When tides are wandering out or in.　The Dead Knight.　John Masefield.　CH; GTBS-P

When Time hath sunder'd shell from pearl.　In Memoriam A.H.H., LII.　Alfred, Lord Tennyson.　VLP

When time said you were dead.　Poem for Vladimir.　G. Ripley.　AMV-81

When time was always within/The purview of my telescopic eye.　Northward.　Dominick J. Lepore.　AMV-80

When Time with us has had his will.　Harry Pearce.　David Campbell.　PoAu 1-2

When to plunge it in the heart-blood of the many-mustered foemen.　Ever Watchful.　Ta' Abbata Sharra.　AWP

When to Thee I have appealed,/Sweet Spirit comfort me!　Holy Numbers Litany to the Holy Spirit (excerpt).　Robert Herrick.　EnLit

When to thy haunts two kindred spirits flee.　Solitude.　John Keats.　EnRP

When trembling voice brings forth that I do Stella love.　Astrophel and Stella, VI.　Sir Philip Sidney.　AAS; SiPS

When 'twas with me alone that you found rest.　Airs of Pei.　Confucius.　CTC

When two clear twilights mingle in the sky/Of glowing June.　Midsummer.　William Allingham.　IrPN

When two strong men stand face to face,/tho' they come from the end of the earth.　The Ballad of East and West.　Rudyard Kipling.　BeLS; BLPL; BrPo; FaBoBe; FaBV; FaPoR; HBV 1-2; MaC; OBNV; TreFT; TRV

When u save me/from myself?　Invitation (To the Night and All Other Things Dark).　Ronda Davis.　JB

When under the shadow of death's shore/We drop its ended dream.　Nights on the Indian Ocean.　Cale Young Rice.　EtS

When up she winds along the brook/To hunt the waterfalls.　Louisa.　William Wordsworth.　EnRP; GBL

When Venus shook her hair/Owre the Soond.　Stars.　George Mackay Brown.　OxBS

When victors' wreaths and monarchs' gems/Shall blend in common dust.　Awake, My Soul!　Philip Doddridge.　WGRP

When wanders each churchyard spirit.　The Window-Glance.　Heinrich Heine.　AWP

When war and strife at last shall cease.　Blow, Bugle!　Thomas Curtis Clark.　PGD

...When was I last/so full of love? So innocent of error?　Lunch with Girl Scouts.　Sharon Bryan.　MAYP

When we all gits to heaven/An' dey meets us at de do'.　I's Gonna Shine.　*Anonymous.*　WTO

When we burned up our Powder, we had to go Home!　The Ballad of Bunker Hill.　Edward Everett Hale.　MC; PAH

When we continue/as if we had portioned our lives exactly.　Beauty.　Paul David Ashley.　LFAC

When we cuddle close together with the happy Fairy-book.　The Fairy Book.　Norman Gale.　HBV 1-2; HBVY; OHIP

...When we do get there, when/that comes about, who shall we do business with?　Those Zionists.　Crescenzo Del Monte.　VWA

When we fall from small hills/Into the common ground.　Tragedy.　Howard Moss.　NePoEA

When we fought here with Harrison,/A long time ago.　Old Fort Meigs.　*Anonymous.*　MC; PAH

When we have learned to bear.　Giving.　*Anonymous.*　PoToHe

When we have not a prayer except ourselves.　Without Ceremony.　Vassar Miller.　CoPo; MoAmPo; SM

When we have wandred all our wayes/Shutts up the story of our dayes.　A Poem of Sir Walter Rawleighs.　Sir Walter Ralegh.　AAS

When we hope, when we hope to be happy again.　Troilus and Cressida.　John Dryden.　NoP

When we laid Maurice down in his grave/Under the snow.　I Never Shall Love the Snow Again.　Robert Bridges.　BrPo; CH; CMoP; FaBV; OAEP

When we learn/we can lose a son.　Dawn and a Woman.　John Logan.　CAPP

When we like being two by two/At night.　Being Twins.　Kathryn Jackson.　BiCB

When we'll have the farmers all under our thumbs.　Pity Poor Labourers.　*Anonymous.*　OBET

When we made friends/With Wind and Rain/On a sunny summer's day.　Beckon Me, Ye Cuillins.　K. G. P. Hendrie.　PoSH

When we meet him on our way/Hand in hand together.　The Newly-Wedded.　Winthrop Mackworth Praed.　HBV 1-2

When we meet to part no more, who have loved.　Our Bondage It Shall End.　Peter Cartwright.　AH

When we're thrown into the hunting of the quark.　Progress.　Felicia Lamport.　QQQ

When we returned to gaze on thee–　To William Shelley.　Percy Bysshe Shelley.　ChRP

When we set down at Seawell it had rained.　Tales of the Islands, X.　Derek Walcott.　OxBTC

When we sleep, or sit, or stand,/Is with us, for He loves us all.　Evening.　Thomas Miller.　OxBChV

When we speak, our words do not match our lips.　Cartoon.　Jim Simmerman.　AMV-81

When we speak to each other our voices are a little gruff.　Beverly Hills, Chicago.　Gwendolyn Brooks.　VGW

When we two tossed up there we never/thought of the deathly adverb "ere."　Definition of the Soul.　Boris Pasternak.　LiTW

When we've shore the last of the jumbucks/On the banks of the Condamine.　The Banks of the Condamaine.　*Anonymous.*　FaBoBa; GBP; NOAV; PoAu 1-2

When we wail with the first knives/of dawn.　Laila Boasting.　Laila Akhyaliyya.　BoWoP

When we wash her down and see the colour freely through the stuff.　Cleaning Up.　Edward Dyson.　PoAu 1-2

When we were sure no sword could sever/Two people born to love forever.　Love-Songs, At Once Tender and Informative.　Samuel Hoffenstein.　OBAL

When we were two east-west trains in the station/Pulling apart, forever, forever.　September: Last Day at the Beach.　Richard Tillinghast.　GOYP

When we will have sung ourselves/gently free of our shells.　Homecoming Celebration.　Rosemary Catacalos.　AMV-80

When, well-a-day, they blew away,/And ne'er were heard of after.　The Dandelions.　Helen Gray Cone.　HBV 1-2

When, when will they bring all I dream of to me?　Day Dreams, or Ten Years Old.　Margaret Johnson.　BLPA

When whichever way it blows it's a cold wind now.　On the Closing of Millom Ironworks.　Norman Nicholson.　FaBoTw

When will I be done/with the force of your magic?　A Voice from the Roses.　Maxine W. Kumin.　NMM

When will I finally become the first president's wife?　Patriotic Poem.　Diane Wakoski.　OFD; VGW

...When will it end?　The Feeling.　William Bronk.　VGW

When will man know what birds know?　Wingtip.　Carl Sandburg.　PCP

When will rain come?　Dafydd Ap Gwilym Resents the Winter.　Rolfe Humphries.　NYBP

When will the God within us/Shatter its shuttle and loom?　The Scarlet Thread.　Daniel Henderson.　HBMV

When will the joy deep in it speak and sing/again and grief of worlds be its own thing?　Protagonist.　Edith Henrich.　MoRP

When will the morning break?　The Night Watch.　William Winter.　AA

When will the unfathomed cave/of a thousand shades stable you?　The Horses of Marini.　Tania Van Zyl.　PeSA

When will tomorrow come?—　A Scene.　Sneyd Davies.　NOEC

When will you whirl your lasso at the sun?/Or bridle it? Or straddle the lightning-flash?　Breakers of Broncos.　Lew Sarett.　BPAW

When wilt thou backwards spin, O faithful twine,/Until no space divides his heart from mine?　Sonnet: "Between my love and me there runs a thread."　Irene Rutherford McLeod.　HBMV

When wilt thou be melody born?　Ilion, Ilion.　Alfred, Lord Tennyson.　LoBV

When Winds take Forests in their Paws-/The Universe-is still-.　He Fumbles at Your Soul.　Emily Dickinson.　AmePo; NOCV

When, winged for heaven, thy soul ascended?　With Wordsworth at Rydal.　James Thomas Fields.　AA

When winter snows upon thy sable hairs.　To Delia.　Samuel Daniel.　EG; NOBE; NoP; OBEV; OBSC; TrGrPo

When with Immanuel we reign,/Forever blest.　Sardis.　*Anonymous.*　AmFP

When with salt rheum and phlegm they powdered are.　Nature's Cook.　Margaret Cavendish, Duchess of Newcastle.　PBWP

When withered in the sun/Or dried in the salt air.　Dialogue.　Howard Nemerov.　NYBP; PoPl

When without these you have not wherewithall.　Ditty in Imitation of the Spanish....　Edward, Lord Herbert of Cherbury.　AnAnS 2; EIL; OBS

When woman hides her virtues, and displays her sins. The Conscience.
Anna Wickham. PoL

When words fail. Strategies. Welton Smith. NBP; PoBA

"When you and I are kings," he says,/"Then we shall meet again." Sons of
the Kings. Joan Agnew. BiCB

When you and I were boys! We Were Boys Together. George Pope Morris.
AA

When you are married, you've all to do. The Single Girl. *Anonymous.*
TrAS

When you are no more young, and I am old. The Last Memory. Arthur
Symons. HBV 1-2

When you are slaughtered for the sacrifice. The Vine to the Goat. Bishop
Euenos. LiTW

When you are the hammer,/strike. Preparedness. Edwin Markham.
FaFP; MoAmPo

When you breathe again/your breath will blow the stone in two. Lapidary.
Bonnie L. Alexander. AMV-80

When you come, Green Eyes, Green Eyes. Encounter in the Cage Country.
James Dickey. CAPP

When you come up behind, to mount? The White Horse. William Henry
Davies. OxBTC

When you cut string/it crawls off/in two directions. The String of My
Ancestors. Nina Nyhart. Str

When you'd me near your heart,/Och hone! Widow Machree! Widow
Machree. Samuel Lover. HBV 1-2

When you die/No heaven issues refunds of life/Only complete blackouts!
Chronique Scandaleuse. Richard Augustine Chima. WhB

When you feel like singin', sing-/Keep a-goin'! Keep A-Goin'. Frank
Lebby Stanton. FaFP; OHFP; WBLP

When you find who the little man is. Santa Claus. *Anonymous.* ChBR;
HBVY

When you fly, I will follow. To a Butterfly. L. Pearl Schuck. AMV-80

When you forget, you return. The Gate. Yasmeen Jamal. LFAC

When you get a lemon/Just make some lemonade. Try This Once.
Anonymous. WBLP

When you get back/to your empty flat... Political Activist Living Alone.
Pat Arrowsmith. BrRo

When you go out, my dear, please buy a rifle;/I want to shoot that thrush.
Inspiration. Edward Valpy Knox. CenHV

When you have grown away and stand at last/at the very centre of the empty
city.' Changes. Seamus Heaney. FaBoIP

When you in anger tried to make us new. You in Anger. James Reeves.
OxBTC

When you lays all night and your Daddy's on benzedrine. Rocks and Gravel.
Anonymous. FSW

When you lies upon the bier. God Made a Trance. *Anonymous.* OBET

When you lose/Your money, learn to lose. Billy Lyons and Stack O'Lee.
Furry Lewis. BluL

When you lost your balance like Li Po/They found unfinished poems in your
sea-chest. Father-in-Law. Derek Mahon. FaBoIP

When you meet a nagging man,/Pitch into him like me. Song Ballet (I Was
Sixteen Years of Age). *Anonymous.* AmFP

When you mistook being here for being there. Here. Marvin Bell. AmPA

When you murder things like that/who comes in and takes over Anaesthesia.
Jean Valentine. TAP

When you need it, and you don't have so much time. The Little Brother
Poem. Naomi Shihab Nye. Str

...When you pass here, traveler,/you too can't keep from making sounds,/like
theirs, that will last Late, Passing Prairie Farm. William Stafford.
GOYP

When you pass the snow falls-all at once-/from my heart, as from a tree in
winter. Death of Rimbaud. David Fisher. NPGG

When you're grown-up, you little blighter,/You'll be a typical first nighter.
To an Unknown Neighbor at the Circus. Rosemary Benet. DBV; InMe

When you read these words/Clasp your ts'ing and come. You Call That a
Ts'ing: A Letter (parody). Jedediah Barrow. BXAP

When you see HIM, you will see ME! There Is a Selfhood in My
Nothingness. Al-Hallaj. ILwL

...When you see/they're gonna throw you, get off. Riding Lesson. Henry
Taylor. NLV; PH

When you should of looked after his fold? Fragment from "Clemo Uti-The
Water Lilies." Ring Lardner. FiBHP

When you stop pirouetting on the gilded lawn,/what then, dancer? What
Then, Dancer? Kay Smith. CaP

When you think I'm sleeping/Snugly in my bed. Moon, So Round and
Yellow. Matthias Barr. HBV 1-2; HBVY

When you tire of pot/Try thought. Problem in Social Geometry-The
Inverted Square! Ray Durem. NBP; PoBA

When you've forgotten how I look in white. The White Dress. Roberta
Spear. MAYP

When you've kissed me/Black and blue! In May. John Millington Synge.
MoBrPo

When you walk around me/Seven times/And I begin to glow. Vessels.
Howard Schwartz. VWA

When you were sweet sixteen. When You Were Sweet Sixteen. James
Cooper and George Thornton. FSW

When you were there, and you, and you. Dining-Room Tea. Rupert
Brooke. BrPo; MoBrPo

When you, wi' me, mid speak to her ear/-in the night. My Love's Guardian
Angel. William Barnes. AtBAP; GBL; NBM; PoEL 1-5

When young eyes look upon it/Through a slender wedding ring. Yes.
Richard Doddridge Blackmore. HBV 1-2

When young "sow wild oats', but when old, grow sage. An Adage. H. J.
Byron. FaBoUs; NLV

When young will end as such. Poem. Robin Blaser. NeAP

When your Daddy comes back home/He'll sing a song for you. Rock, Rock,
Sleep, My Baby. Clyde Watson. NTCP

When your daddy comes home. Dance to Your Daddy. *Anonymous.*
OxNR

When your head lies on his breast. The Splendid Lover. John Richard
Moreland. PGD

When your lined up heart, too,/snaps and lets go. Fishing the Big Hole.
John Holbrook. WOLT

When your one need is me to need you still? Reciprocity. Vassar Miller.
IHMS; NePoEA

When your stones hit my window/I won't care. Minor Key. Teller. J. L.
VWA

Whence his admiring eyes more pleasure took/Than Dis, on heaps of gold
fixing his look. Hero and Leander. Christopher Marlowe. ErPo; OAEL
1-2; TEP

Whence I come sullied out who entered clean. The Diseases of Bath
(excerpt). *Anonymous.* NOEC

Whence is this that I should feed Thee,/Feeding all things from Thy table?
The Christmas Hymn. Saint Ephrem. CAW; ISi

Whence light he draws as from the sun/night's Queen. God and the Soul.
John Lancaster Spalding. AA

Whence love to every crimson petal flows. The Rose and God. Charles
Wharton Stork. HBMV

Whence my hand is weary with writing. Columcille the Scribe. Saint
Columcille. OnYI

Whence perfect wild-flowers leap and shine! A Prelude. Maurice
Thompson. AmePo; HBV 1-2

Whence the trees bloom on forever,/But with the same leaves never.
Autumnal Spring Song. Vassar Miller. NePoEA

Whence the wind doth blow/that comes from behind/a blowing wind. No
End of No-Story. George Macdonald. NOBV

Whence to be born again, helpless and lonely. Ultimate Exile IV. Ralph
Nixon Currey. PeSA

Whence, while men gaze upon this blazing star,/Made slaves, not subjects,
they to tyrants are. Caelica, LXXVIII. Fulke, Lord Brooke Greville.
FCP

Whence you project your naked fantasies. Desires of Men and Women.
John Berryman. LiTM

Whene'er his glorious name shall sound/To shake your sea-girt isle! The
Hero of Bridgewater. Charles L. S. Jones. PAH

Whene'er you lead your well-known way/to death or victory! Zagonyi.
George Henry Boker. PAH

Wheneer they ride i the Border-side,/They'll mind the fate o the laird
Troughend. The Death of Parcy Reed. *Anonymous.* BaBo

Whenever god or nation/Moodily says Tut tut. In a Closed Universe.
James Hayford. NePoAm-2

Whenever I say "America"/So many things I say! Whenever I Say
"America." Nancy Byrd Turner. YeAr

Whenever I wear my new shoes/I always have to sing! New Shoes. Alice
Wilkins. SUS; TiPo

Whenever mortal enters Chartres, he/finds it thronged to its capacity. View
of the Cathedral. Raymond Henri. EyDe

Whenever she caught sight of you/it would start all over again. The Dirty-
Billed Freeze Footy. Judith Hemschemeyer. Str

Whenever we love, we win,/Or else we have never been born. Afterthoughts
of Donna Elvira. Carolyn Kizer. NePoAm-2

Whenever you're right, shut up. A Word to Husbands. Ogden Nash.
PoL

Whenever you sucked off the child. Limerick: "That famous old pederast,
Wilde." *Anonymous.* PeHV

Wher thou art now let me be,/For al my love is laid on thee.' The
Assumption. *Anonymous.* OxBM

Wherby the light of her faire lokes I lost. Complaint That His Ladie after
She Knew of His Love Kept Her Face... Henry Howard, Earl of Surrey.
PoEL 1-5

Where a dozen fat savages ate her. Limerick: "There was a fair maid from
Decatur." *Anonymous.* LiBL

Where a man all day prepared his dying. A Hermit's Song. *Anonymous.*
BIrV

Where a man's on honor to be his best–/Away out West. Away Out West. Sharlot M. Hall. BPAW

...Where a quarrel/of vines crawls into the spilled body of a plane. New Hampshire. Donald Hall. LCAP; NePoEA-2

Where a raven was soaring upside down/under the river, the rocks, the heather... Soaring. Cal Clothier. PoSH

Where a sweet particular girl will say the truth/Over and over until I take it in. Picture of a Castle. William Meredith. NePoEA

Where a thousand ill-kept children/Vie for suck, with one another. South Street. Edward S. Silvera. CDC

Where a young man lands hatless from the air. Death of King George V. Sir John Betjeman. NOBE; OBSP

Where a young man lands hatless from the air. New King Arrives in His Capital by Air... Sir John Betjeman. OxBoLi

Where absolutely anything goes, and there are no shores. First Prelude. Dream in Ohio: The Father. John Logan. LCAP

Where Africa's revolt congealed/its cry pregnant with hope. If You Want to Know Me. Noemia De Sousa. WhB

Where air of curses hung, keel of my calm/Rides our created tide. Fields Where We Slept. Muriel Rukeyser. NNaP

Where all day drives for me/The spoiling sea. On Seeing a Poet of the First World War on the Station at Abbeville. Charles Causley. ChMP; LiTM; NMP

Where all Faiths kneel, as brothers, in one place. Incense. Vachel Lindsay. MoRP

Where all Manhattan that I've seen must disappear. My Sad Self. Allen Ginsberg. NoAm; UnPo

Where all my pipes inspir'de upraise/An heavenly musick, furr'd with praise. Upon a Wasp Chilled with Cold. Edward Taylor. AtBAP; CBEP; NOBA; NOCV; PoEL 1-5

Where all presented to the eye or ear/Oppress'd the soul with misery, grief, and fear. The Borough. George Crabbe. FaBoPP; OBRV

Where all return/spent torch and pilgrim shroud. Puer Aeternus. Kathleen Raine. NYBP

Where all the fathers are crying: My son is mine! August. Adrienne Rich. CAPP; NNaP; PBWP

Where all the love is true love, and/True love goes on for ever. Summer Song I. George Barker. ChMP

Where all the refugee words/are gathered and make shelter Abraham Sutskever. Seymour Mayne. VWA

Where all things go that die/Like flame and sound, and mist and minstrelsy. The Gully. Furnley Maurice. BoAV

Where all tomorrows must be faced alone.... Solitary Travel. Louis MacNeice. OBTV

Where all who know may drown. The Man Against the Sky. Edwin Arlington Robinson. AP; APA; CMoP; CoBMV; LiTA; MAPA; MoVE; NAMP; OxBA

Where all your hot-rugged brothers and sisters are headed./Madam, good-bye! Random Generation of English Sentences; or, The Revenge of the Poets. William Jay Smith. OBAL

Where among stones and roots, the other/Unshattered lovers are. The Room Above the Square. Stephen Spender. ChMP; NOBE

Where anarchy had else sustained alone/The undisputed title to his throne. The Value of Dentistry. Solyman Brown. FaBoUs

Where Angels musicke make,/I may aspire,/When I this life forsake. For a Musician. George Wither. OBS

Where any-angled light/Would congregate endlessly. Water. Philip Larkin. FaBoMo; OBSP

Where/Are my beautiful/Black men? Black Woman. Naomi Long Madgett. BlSi; FB; OLR; PoBA

Where are the dead?/They're gone. Complaint on the Oblivion of the Dead. Jules Laforgue. LiTW

Where are the lion warriors of the Lord? Kindle the Taper. Emma Lazarus. AH

Where are the lords of Ispahan,/O sons of men? The Thousand and One Nights: Inscriptions at the City of Brass. Anonymous. WaaP

...Where are waters,/Mountains and houses, may be also men. Far from the Heart of Culture. W. H. Auden. WaaP

Where are we going, Rubee? Song of Slaves in the Desert. John Greenleaf Whittier. AnAmPo; OxBA

Where are you/and me. Near. Abba Kovner. VWA

Where are you, o liebe breyt? The Lost Language. Irving Feldman. AmPC

Where are you, simple and pure faith of yore? The Pilgrimage to Testour. Ryvel (Raphael Levy). VWA

Where, at his back, a dome of atoms rose. The Progress of Faust. Karl Shapiro. DiPo; MoAB; MP; NYBP

Where Balboa's sea doth mingle/With the waters of thy bay! Discovery of San Francisco Bay. Richard Edward White. PAH

Where Balkh amidst the desert stands. The Blood Horse. Barry (Bryan Waller Procter) Cornwall. GN; HBV 1-2; PH

Where bearded men appear to-day/Just Eton boys grown heavy. Schoolfellows. Winthrop Mackworth Praed. NBM

Where birds escape the fatal gun,/And men alone are shot at. Little Britain. Anonymous. NOEC

Where birds for gladness sing! The Little Beach-Bird. Richard Henry Dana. AA; AnAmPo; AnNE; APA; EtS; HBV 1-2

Where birds sing. Haiku: "Moor:". Basho (Matsuo Basho). FAZ

Where bodies are made whole/as in the woman bodies are made, whole. The Hospital–Retrospections. Kenneth Mackenzie. CBAP

Where breath most breathes,–/even in/the mouths of men. Sonnets, LXXXI: "Or I shall live your epitaph to make." William Shakespeare. OAEP; OBSC

Where breathing is always visible. Sleeping at the Beach. Lucile Burt. AMV-81

Where Bunyan's Statue stands facing where stood his Jail. Ned Bratts. Robert Browning. CABL; VLP

Where, by the way, his family? Cloisters. Anthony Barnett. VWA

...Where Care/In throned state is ever dwelling. Peter Bell, the Third. Percy Bysshe Shelley. OBSV

Where care/None is, slight things do lightly please. His Grange, or Private Wealth. Robert Herrick. AnAnS 2; CaPo; FM; GoJo; OAEP; SeCV 1-2

Where castles stood & grandeur died. The Flitting. John Clare. FaBoPV

Where chance may seem to give/Loves in alternative. Despite and Still. Robert Graves. CBEP

...Where childlike or childish we pursue/Them into worlds where mutual worlds are overcome. All That Summer. Lora Dunetz. NePoAm-2

Where children are unconsoled by wishes,/where tears salt bread. Beginning the Year at Rosebud, S.D. Roberta Hill Whiteman. CDW; TWSS

Where children wait/For the carnival to break up. That There Should Be Laughter. Innocent Banda. WhB

Where children you may get by steam, such pretty little things. My Grandfather's Days. Anonymous. OBET

Where Claribel low-lieth. Claribel. Alfred, Lord Tennyson. AtBAP; PeD

Where close to earth like mice we go/Under the horizontal snow. The Snow Storm. Edna St. Vincent Millay. PoA

Where cold and still, old Heartbreak Hill/Looks down on Ipswich Bar. Ipswich Bar. Esther and Brainard Bates. HBMV

Where cool episcopal bells are calling, calling. Two Bums Walk out of Eden. Robert Francis. PPON

Where cow and horse will eat wall, roof and gable. The Haystack. Andrew Young. PoL

Where Dark doth dwell. Nostalgia. Walter De La Mare. CoBMV; LiTM

Where dawnlight flushes the breathless/verge of the loftiest height! The Hounds of the Soul. Louis Ginsberg. TrJP

Where day and night shall meet/and not be/one. From the House of Yemanja. Audre Lorde. NoP

Where death is waiting, dressed like an admiral. Nothing but Death. Pablo Neruda. EAS

Where Death stands knocking at the gate/To let him in. The Soul. Madison Cawein. AA

Where decoy duck dust/Quacks, clacks, afraid. The Bat. Edith Sitwell. FaBoMo

Where deep in the night I hear a voice. Butcher Shop. Charles Simic. AmPA; LCAP; NNaP

Where did the blood come from? On a Line in Sandburg. R. S. Thomas. NAs

Where do you go? Clouds. Christina Georgina Rossetti. BrR; SoPo

Where do you sing again! Robert Louis Stevenson. Lizette Woodworth Reese. HBV 1-2

Where do you suppose/it stores up all/of the things it knows? The Seed. Aileen Fisher. OnUR

Where down the blind are driven. Eros Turannos. Edwin Arlington Robinson. AnNE; CrMA; PoA

Where dreams come in from the rush and the din/Like sheep from the rains and thunders. I Am Glad Daylong. William Stanley Braithwaite. GoSl

Where dwells her spirit, innocently wise. Deaf. Henry Cuyler Bunner. AA

Where e're they met, or parting place has been. Lovers How They Come and Part. Robert Herrick. AtBAP; GBL; OBSP; OxBoLi; PoEL 1-5

...Where each new hero flings/his careful stone that fades in slow, concentric rings. The Exiled Heart. Maurice Lindsay. OxBS

Where earliest the light/is seen that bids the cock crow The Vineyard. William Stanley Merwin. NNaP

Where Earth unknown bleeds life anew. I Am Alone. V. Bhanot. ACV

Where echoed once Araunah's threshing-floor. Two Sonnets: Harvard. Oliver Wendell Holmes. AP

Where else am I walking even now/Looking for me. Looking for Mushrooms at Sunrise. William Stanley Merwin. NaP; NOBA

...Where/Else could I find my life's illustration? Personal Values. Richard Howard. SM

Where'er I go they shout: "Hello! Where did you get that hat?" Where Did You Get That Hat? Joseph J. Sullivan. FSN; TreF

Where'er I turn, art ever with me there. The Presence. Jones Very. HAP

Where'er the eagle spreads his wings,/From northern pines to southern roses! A Poem for the Meeting of the American Medical Association. Oliver Wendell Holmes. PoEL 1-5

Where'er they go, they make a foe,/Or find a grave. Battle Song. Ebenezer Elliott. OBRV

Where'er we go they dread the name/Of Garryowen in glory. Garryowen. *Anonymous.* OnYI

Where eve has hushed the feathered ways,/And drop a vapoury footfall in the water's/drowsy blaze. The Indian to His Love. William Butler Yeats. VLP

Where every line has three stresses/and only the one word, dark. Voronezh. Anna Akhmatova. FaBoPV

Where every passion wars itself with legions. Caelica, XVI. Fulke, Lord Brooke Greville. EnRePo; FCP; PoEL 1-5

Where every prospect pleases,/Save only that of death. The Devil's Dictionary: Prospect. Ambrose Bierce. OBAL

Where faces redden and the snow is hard. Katherine's Dream. Robert Lowell. ConAP

Where fate is freedom,/Grace and surprise. Runner. W. H. Auden. SD

Where few do hit, whilst thousands miss,/The happy mutual way. To Silvia. Anne Finch, Countess of Wilchilsea. HBV 1-2

Where Finn of the feasts is, they will hail thee with "welcome." The Song of Carroll's Sword. Dallan MacMore. OnYI

Where first the child's glad spirit loves/Its country and its God! The Homes of England. Felicia Dorothea Hemans. FaPoR; PaPo; SBG

Where fish at dawn ignite the powdery lake. To the (Supposed) Patron. Geoffrey Hill. NePoEA-2

Where fishermen set out from pumice isles. The Dirigible. Chris Wallace-Crabbe. CBAP

"Where flies the spindrift? Where went the wind?" Opium Clippers. Daniel Henderson. EtS

Where flowers are pale and few. Ballad of the Londoner. J. E. Flecker. EnLoPo

Where fond Desire as king doth reign. Desire's Government. A. W. ElL

Where force meets force under the sky's shocked arches. To You Who Wait. John Pudney. WaP

Where Frank Sinatra sang only for them. Frank Sinatra. Michael Waters. GeTw

Where, free from duns, they may securely dine. Horse Guards Parade. Thomas (Tom) Brown. FaBoEE

Where freely the truth you may take. Think Not When You Gather to Zion. Eliza R. Snow. AH

Where gaitered gamekeeper with dog and gun/will shout "Turn back'. Who Will Endure. W. H. Auden. FaBoPV

Where genius, wit, and humour sleep with Sterne? Epitaph on Laurence Sterne. David Garrick. FaBoEE

Where George, recover'd, made a scene/Sweet always, doubly sweet. On the Queen's Visit to London. William Cowper. PeD

Where go the birds? Notes: II. Jane Heap. PoA

Where God has written visibly/Brave hintings of her soul. Bodily Beauty. George Rostrevor. HBMV

Where God might write anew the story of the World. Columbus. Edward Everett Hale. MC; PAH

Where "God save the "Queen" to cry are seen/The slaves of the British looms. Song of the Factory Girls. *Anonymous.* SaC

Where God shall sweetening be. God Makes a Path. Roger Williams. PAH; TRV; WGRP

Where God, surprised, blooms/like a white peacock. World Enough. Jeanine Hathaway. AMV-80

Where gold has not been sold and conscience tinned. Key West. Hart Crane. CMoP

Where good cow-boys ride in comfort,/Far beyond the "Great Divide." The Cowboy's Fate. Wallace D. Coburn. PoOW

Where grasses in sleek shallows waver dank,/Or drift in windy ripples greyly by. Sonnets, XIV: "Now, winter's dolorous days are o'er." Thomas Caulfield Irwin. IrPN

Where green grass grows and roses gay,/There in the sun forever. The Shadow-Child. Harriet Monroe. HBV 1-2

Where grief and laughter sleep together. Twenty-One Love Poems. Adrienne Rich. PeHV

Where Grief and Mis'ery can be join'd with Verse. On the Death of Mr. William Hervey. Abraham Cowley. AnAnS 2; CBEP; EBEV; FaBoRV; GTBS; NOBE; OBEV; OBS; SeCP; SeCV 1-2; ViBoPo

Where grieves forth obsolescent landwrack/to infinity. The Biggest Killing. Edward Dorn. CoPo; VGW

Where harmless robin dwells with gentle thrush. Happy Were He. Robert Devereux, Earl of Essex. EIL; OBSP

Where hast thou laid, who comest here,/Thy youth away? Sagesse. Paul Verlaine. EnLi 1-2; SyP

"Where hast thou stayed so long?" Endymion. Henry Wadsworth Longfellow AA; HBV 1-2

Where, having stayed a while, I pay/Her lavish bills, and go my way. On the World. Francis Quarles. HAP

Where He again is visible, tho' in anger. Look You, My Simple Friend. Arthur Hugh Clough. VLP

Where he could lie and, gazing down at the sea,/Recognize his unique and solitary home. The Poem That Took the Place of a Mountain. Wallace Stevens. LCAP

Where he leapt in the final spasm of first love. Adam on His Way Home. Robert Pack. ErPo

Where he may watch the serpents leave, as stars in flight. War Cry: To Mary. Pope Leo XIII. ISi

Where he provides with pastoral strains,/In Lyrics to delight you. The Poets' Paradise. Michael Drayton. WiR

Where he sowed them, the green vine withered, and the smoke/and the armies sprang up. Nightmare, with Angels. Stephen Vincent Benét. MAT

Where He, Whom all declares,/Delights to make be! The South Coast. Brother Antoninus. NeAP

Where healing hands were few. Under the Red Cross. Chauncey Hickox. AA

Where health and purity should ever reign. Tartar. Solyman Brown. FaBoUs

Where heat melts/toward the shadow-side of the rocks. She Rebukes Hippolyta. Hilda ("H. D.") Doolittle. SBG

Where her hand yearns, but not to touch my hand. My Love Is Sleeping. Kenneth Leslie. OBCV

Where Herod bleeds his rage away/And wrings his bloodless hands. The Innocents. Jay Macpherson. OBCV

Where his knocked-off panama hat was in his painfully vanishing hair. The Fiend. James Dickey. PPP

Where his salt dream lies. The Salt Garden. Howard Nemerov. NePoEA

Where Homer's sprite did tremble all for grief,/And cursed th' access of that celestial thief. Of Edmund Spenser's Fairy Queen... Sir Walter Ralegh. FCP

...Where/Honour sits smiling at the sale of truth. Queen Mab. Percy Bysshe Shelley. FF; PPON

Where hope only remains. You wait and see. Waiting Rooms. Howard Nemerov. PoA

Where I, alas dare not approach the cruell/Proud Monument, that doth inclose my Jewell. Sonnet: "They say that shadowes of deceased ghosts." Joshua Sylvester. EIL; OBS

Where I am now, as restless to remain,/Against my will, full pleased with my pain. "The fancy, which that I have served long." Henry Howard, Earl of Surrey. FCP

Where I climbed a ladder of birthdays,/Reading my father's face. My Mother's Table. Hy Sobiloff. NePA

Where I could not escape the rote of the rolling waves. Return to Lane's Island. William H. Matchett. PoPl

Where I defy, and challenge, all thy utmost love. The Author Apologizes to a Lady for His Being a Little Man. Christopher Smart. BoLoP

Where I kneel praying/that my children/will not die politely/either. A Birthday Memorial to Seventh Street. Audre Lorde. CNA

Where I lie in the bed/Of her still eyes. Fox. David Campbell. CBAP

Where I'll get lashings of corned meat, and none of your yellow meal. Yellow Meal. *Anonymous.* ShS

Where I may sit and see/My God and love Thee so. The Lowest Place. Christina Georgina Rossetti. EnLi 1-2; NOBV; TrPWD

Where I may sleep and dream there's Light again. Philosophy. John Kendrick Bangs. PoToHe

Where I may sow and reap those sunny fields of wheat/and barley. He Singeth a Hymn to Osiris, the Lord of Eternity. Book of the Dead. AWP

Where I must try the blind/and final trick of youth. Village of Winter Carols. Laurie Lee. ChMP

Where I pursue, a man who trips and falls/Gets up and seeing me, keeps saying: "No one!" The Street. Octavio Paz. FF

Where I reach out at night/and bat the far air. White Attic. Kenward Elmslie. ANYP

Where I rest but not yet dead/just a flower lad. A Flower. Mvula Ya Nangolo. WhB

...Where I stand/In the hazed gold of her eyes, the world is green. December: Of Aphrodite. William Stanley Merwin. NePoEA

Where I will heal me of my grievous wound. Morte d'Arthur. Alfred, Lord Tennyson. BBV

Where I with friends around me/May lay my burden down. In the Town. *Anonymous.* OBCP; PCh

Where I would be I cannot,/Oh, diddle lilley day,/Oh, de liddle-i-o day. Katy Cruel. *Anonymous.* FSW

Where, if there's any drink, he'll find it out. Epitaph on the Secretary to the Muses. Jane Barker. FaBoCo

...Where ignorance is bliss,/'Tis folly to be wise. Ode on a Distant Prospect of Eton College. Thomas Gray. BLPL; CABA; EiCP; EnPE; ExPo; GTBS; GTBS-P; HeIP; LAuP; LiTB; NOBE; NOEC; NoP; OAEL 1-2; OAEP; OBEC; PoEL 1-5; PrIm; SeCeV; ViBoPo

Where ignorant armies clash by night.　Dover Beach.　Matthew Arnold. AnEnPo; AWP; BiP; BLPA; DiPo; DTC; EaLo; EtS; ExPo; FaBoBe; FaBoPP; FaBoRV; FaBV; FaFP; FF; FiP; ForPo; FPL; GoTF; GTBS; GTBS-P; HAP; HBV 1-2; HeIP; HoPM; InPK; InPo; InPS; InvP; LiTB; LiTL; LoBV; MasP; MAT; MaVP; MCCG; MOS; NIP; NOBE; NOBV; NoP; NU; OAEL 1-2; OAEP; OBNC; OBVV; PAI; PG; PoEL 1-5; PoPl; PoPle; PoRA; PPoe; PPON; PPP; Prf; PrIm; SCV; SeCePo; SeCeV; SoSe; TEP; TreFS; TRV; UnPo; ViBoPo; VLP; WeW; WHA

Where immortal spirits reign,/There may we all meet again.　When Shall We All Meet Again?　*Anonymous.*　AH

Where in despair I beauty curse. Curse love and all fair faces!　Love Is a Secret Feeding Fire.　*Anonymous.*　OBSP

Where, in one long last ray, lingered the yellow sun.　Sigh.　Stephane Mallarme.　AWP; SyP

Where, in sweet vales, the Bride/With Thee, by living fountains,/For ever shall abide. Amen.　The Church's One Foundation.　Samuel John Stone.　VLP

Where in the forest will I find my madman?　My Heart Burns for Him. *Anonymous.*　WTO

Where in their bright result shall rise/Thoughts, virtues, friendships, griefs and joys.　The Mystery of Life.　John Gambold.　NOEC

Where is a weight to lift as welcome?　Now That Your Shoulders Reach My Shoulders.　Robert Francis.　Str

Where is all, there all should be.　The Invitation.　George Herbert.　AnAnS 1

Where is it now, the glory and the dream?　Intimations of Immortality from Recollections of Early Childhood.　William Wordsworth.　ATP

Where is my lover? Where is my lover?　Spinster Song.　Virginia Lyne Tunstall.　HBMV

–Where is my own blue sea?　Where Is the Sea?　Felicia Dorothea Hemans. EtS

Where is my sweetness/going to come from.　Bees Inside Me.　Laura Chester.　NPGG

"Where is my twenty/and why did you run?"　Collect Calls.　Diane Bickston.　LFAC

Where is that child?　To the Wind at Morn.　William Henry Davies.　ELU

Where is that gown I could fashion–alone?　Life.　Nan Terrell Reed. BLPA

Where is that voice coming from?　The Tree.　Joel Sloman.　VGW

Where is the boy?　Where Did He Run To?　Mark Van Doren.　SO

Where is the end for/Solomon Grundy?　The Space Childs' Mother Goose. Frederick Winsor.　QQQ

Where is the fruit/in this land you promised?　Where Is the Fruit.　Innocent Banda.　WhB

Where is the guile enough to comfort me?　The Prince.　Edgar Bowers. ConAP

Where is the man?/Ah, it is so!　Women's Rondo.　*Anonymous.*　NOAV

Where is Their pride, and Their vengeance?　Of a Woman, Dead Young. Dorothy Parker.　SBG

Where is there deeper secret revelation than among/The early morning pandemoniums of the birds?　The Matin Pandemoniums.　Richard Eberhart.　NYBP

Where is thy glory?　I Am Weary of These Times and Their Dull Burden. Lucius Beebe.　RFM

Where is thy mate, and where thy nest?　Sea-Birds.　Elizabeth Akers.　AA; FaBoBe; HBV 1-2

Where is your plump young sister, Snow?　Frost.　William Henry Davies. BoNaP

Where Israel's tents do shine so bright.　Mock On, Mock On, Voltaire, Rousseau.　William Blake.　AtBAP; BiP; HAP; LAuP; NAWM 1-2; NoP; OAEL 1-2; OAEP; OBNC; OBRV; OBSP; OxBoCh; PoEL 1-5; PPoe; PPP; PrIm

Where it for ever shall at anchor lie.　To Her in Absence.　Thomas Carew. CaPo

Where it is nothing, one with its assent.　The People in the Park.　Léonie Adams.　MoVE

Where it is the children go.　White Fields.　James Stephens.　BoNaP; MoShBr; PoSC; SiSoSe; SoPo; SUS

–Where it rises to his wire–and Sergeant T. Quilter takes/over.　In Parenthesis.　David Jones.　OBWP

Where it's never-changing state/Full perfection shall begin.　Ode: "Love thy Country, wish it well."　George Bubb, Baron Melcombe Dodington. OBEC

Where it's too dark to see?　Vegetables.　Rachel Field.　SoPo

Where its own silence goes crazy/and kills itself.　Poem with the Final Tune. Julia de Burgos.　InW

Where its red bead eyes now stare towards the sun.　The Tantanoola Tiger. Max Harris.　MoBS; PoAu 1-2

Where joy has been forgot and hope has fled.　Odes, IX.　Hafiz.　AWP

Where kindly Neptune and this traine abode.　Hero and Leander. Christopher Marlowe.　AtBAP

Where knock is open wide.　The Man of Prayer.　Christopher Smart. BBV; LiTB

Where Kupe and where Cook have trod.　Mercury Bay Eclogue.　Michael Kennedy Joseph.　AnNZ

Where let them wend at will, whilest here I doe respire.　The Faerie Queene. Edmund Spenser.　OAEL 1-2

Where liberty/is the fatherland of men...　Where Are the Men Seized in This Wind of Madness?　Alda Espirito Santo.　TTY; WPOW

Where lidless fishes, broad awake,/Swim staring at a night-mare doom.　Cold-Blooded Creatures.　Elinor Wylie.　ImOP; OBSP; SBG

Where life for sinners death endured,/And life by death for man procured. Hymn to the Holy Cross.　Saint Venantius Fortunatus.　LiTW

Where life is evil now./Nanking. Dachau.　Sonnets from China (excerpt). W. H. Auden.　OBWP

Where life is shrunk to what can be fired from a gun?　Coogan's Wood. Francis Stuart.　NeIP

Where light is the black taste of your body/between my savage teeth　To a Woman Who Wants Darkness and Time.　Gerald William Barrax.　PoBA

Where little was said/and less was known　Motels, Hotels, Other People's Houses.　H. L. Van Brunt.　FAZ

Where living to the world, to me he dieth.　Cupid, Thou Naughty Boy. Fulke, Lord Brooke Greville.　NCEP

Where Lords and Lairds afore did kiss.　Epitaph: "Lo worms enjoy the seat of bliss."　Robert Burns.　FaBoEE

Where love divine is the infinite prize.　God and the Soul.　John Lancaster Spalding.　AA

Where love/is a fly in the net of/a rope ladder to the sun.　Portrait of a Widow.　Avner Strauss.　VWA

Where love is more than lucky in the land.　Communication.　Elizabeth Jennings.　NePoEA

Where love is the leader, grace is never lacking.　The Vision of Piers Plowman.　William Langland.　GoBC

Where love is the scream of anguish/And no curtain drapes the door.　On Diverse Deviations.　Maya Angelou.　BlSi

Where love's lamp gleams along the level.　The Cowboy and His Love. *Anonymous.*　CoSo

Where love will be almost as simple as it looks.　Progression.　Francis Scarfe.　NeBP

Where Martin Luther King could have lived and preached/non-violence.　The Funeral of Martin Luther King, Jr.　Nikki Giovanni.　BOLo; BPo

Where memory folds like calloused hands.　Repetition.　Wyatt Prunty. AMV-81

Where men and women give each other children.　Children, the Sandbar, That Summer.　Muriel Rukeyser.　LCAP

Where men choked Danny's gullet.　Danny.　John Millington Synge. AnEnPo

Where mere belief doth, if not conquer fate,/Surmount, and pass what it doth antedate.　Christian Ethics.　Thomas Traherne.　NOCV; OxBoCh

Where moon-eyed Idiocy, with fallen lip,/Drags the loose knee and intermitting step.　Sonnet: "Ingratitude, how deadly is the smart."　Anna Seward.　NOEC

Where moss upon the roofstwones' edge wer/green.　Green.　William Barnes.　VLP

Where mother sits forever for her photograph.　The Pavilion on the Pier. Byron Vazakas.　NePA

Where motion's once/immobile artifact/had been.　Amphibian.　Amy Clampitt.　SUW

Where music and moonlight and feeling/Are one.　To Jane: The Keen Stars Were Twinkling.　Percy Bysshe Shelley.　NoP

Where music, dance and man's desires/Mingle and burst like sudden fires.　I Enter by the Darkened Door (parody).　Jenny King.　BXAP

Where music is the bough.　Marble Statuette Harpist.　Sara Van Alstyne Allen.　GoYe

Where my bones will shut up, where I'll be good.　Where I'll Be Good. Michael Ryan.　SM

Where, my dear son, you keep/Four better guardians of your sleep.　To My Son (excerpt).　George Barker.　MP; TwCP

Where my head droops to rest,/Leave its bed bare.　Winter Winds Cold and Blea.　John Clare.　GBL; OBNC

Where my images brim and spill/In failures of the full light.　Epigram: Invocation.　Howard Nemerov.　OBAL

Where my mother used to walk/and talk to him.　Clock on Hancock Street. June Jordan.　FaBoWP

Where my Sun-flower wishes to go.　Ah, Sun-Flower.　William Blake. AtBAP; AWP; DiPo; EBEV; ELP; ELU; EnLi 1-2; ExPo; FaBoRV; HAP; InPo; NIP; NOEC; NoP; OBEC; OBNC; PoPle; PPP; PrIm; SeCeV; TEP; UnPo; ViBoPo; WeW

Where my white soul first kissed the mouth of sin.　Taedium Vitae.　Oscar Wilde.　SyP

Where Nature such dilemmas could devise.　Her Dilemma.　Thomas Hardy. BrPo; NOBV

...Where naught else avails, deception's best.　Four Sonnets to Helen, 3. Pierre de Ronsard.　LiTW

Where naught exceeds the shaving, but the beer.   Inscription for the Sign of "The Jolly Barber',...   Jonathan Swift.   FaBoUs

Where neither man nor beast could get near their birds.   Piers the Ploughman.   William Langland.   PBBP

Where no joy dies till love hath gotten more.   Song of the Sirens.   William Browne.   ElL; ViBoPo

Where, no man shall know.   The Frozen Ocean.   Viola Meynell.   CH

Where no one can see us dreaming.   The Blue Room.   Lorenz Hart.   OBAL

Where no one ever came voluntarily before.   Easter.   C. H. Sisson.   OBSP

Where noon is the first few stars they see or the last one.   The Fall of the City: Voice of the Studio Announcer.   Archibald MacLeish.   HoPM

...Where nothing is diminished by perspective.   Equanimity.   Les A. Murray.   NOAV

Where nothing moves except her ghostly spars/That mark the patient watches on the stars.   Ships in Harbour.   David Morton.   EtS

Where now the fowler weaves his subtleties.   A Portrait.   Walter De la Mare.   NoAm

Where? O you the south wind,/Keep soft and strong today.   He's Coming.   Mark Van Doren.   FaBV

Where often clouds shall lean their swan-white neck.   The Pylons.   Stephen Spender.   AWP; EnLi 1-2; NoAm

Where old people stand around/with bluish hands.   Loneliness and July Ninth.   Claribel Alegria.   BoWoP

Where once was life's flood/All is ebb.   The Hag of Beare.   John Montague.   BIrV; CIP; NOBI; OBVE; PBWP

Where once were nine or ten/But two keep house together.   The Doves.   Katharine Tynan.   AnIV; AWP

Where one by one they became/the promises he made us.   When Father Slept.   James Anderson.   AMV-80

Where only a late gull breaks/That deep and populous grave.   Emblems.   Allen Tate.   VGW

Where other Creatures put their eyes–/Incautious–of the Sun–   Before I got my eye put out.   Emily Dickinson.   LiTA; LiTM

Where our blind eyes looked down on him/as dead.   The Travellers.   Mark A. De Wolfe Howe.   AA

Where our white wood caught fire/in the white sand.   An Age.   Laura Jensen.   LCAP

Where peace, where plenty, is for ever found: The First Olympionique to Hiero.   Pindar.   ATP

Where perfect thoughts like bees in amber lie.   Lie on the Sand.   Alistair Campbell.   AnNZ

Where poems like angels like flakes of powder/Quaver above my prickling skin.   Composition in Late Spring.   Irving Layton.   PeCV

Where prophets now and armies greet pale Lyon.   Lyon.   Herman Melville.   PeD

Where purple shadows slanting fall–/In Old Tucson.   In Old Tucson.   Charles Beghtol.   BPAW

Where quiet appears not and quarrels never are ended.   The Epitaph upon Gilbert Glanvill...   Matthew Prior.   FaBoEE

Where red death waits without the gates,/Thy knight, and God's,–I go!   A Good-By.   Ednah Proctor (Clarke) Hayes.   AA

Where rockets rise/to take me home   A Prophecy.   Allen Ginsberg.   TAP

Where rocks of adamant understand/The secrets of the sky.   A Song of Degrees.   W. P. Ker.   PoSH

Where's a poor tortured soul to dwell?   Eutychides.   Lucilius [(or Lucillius)].   UnS

Where's a poor tortured soul to dwell!   Variations of Greek Themes.   Edwin Arlington Robinson.   OBAL

Where's an older friend than fire?   Hearth Song.   Robert Underwood Johnson.   YeAr

...Where's my spade! I've work to do!   Why Tomas Cam Was Grumpy.   James Stephens.   CMoP

Where's no tale, no track,/But a flash, a sigh.   The Look.   Elizabeth Daryush.   PoA

Where's the horse/For a kid that's black?   Merry-Go-Round.   Langston Hughes.   CTBA; PoNe

Where's the peck of pickled peppers Peter Piper picked?   Peter Piper.   Anonymous.   FaBoNo; OxNR; TreFS

Where's the thatching the thatcher of Thatchwood has thatched?   A Thatcher of Thatchwood Went to Thatchet A-Thatching.   Anonymous.   OxNR

"Where's your bloody fan?"   Limeraiku: "There's a vile old man."   Ted Pauker.   NOBL

Where saints and angels draw their bliss/Directly, Lord, from Thee?   Rejoicing in Hope.   Augustus Montague Toplady.   BePJ

Where sea-grass tangles with/shore-grass.   Hermes of the Ways.   Hilda ("H. D.") Doolittle.   LiTA

Where, selfwrung selfstrung, sheathe-and-shelterless thoughts against/thoughts in groans grind.   Spelt from Sibyl's Leaves.   Gerard Manley Hopkins.   BrPo; CMoP; CoBMV; FaBoMo; LiTM; MoPo; NOBV; OAEL 1-2; PrIm

Where seven years is forever/as seven minutes proved it to be   My Atlas Poet.   George Bowering.   NeAC

Where shall he now make war?   War Song.   Anonymous.   WTO

Where shall I be when it soun'. O, Bretheren.   Where Shall I Be when de Firs' Trumpet Soun'?   Anonymous.   BoAN 1-2

Where shall I find the little Blue/Ben?   Little Blue Ben.   Anonymous.   OxNR

Where shall I hide my face and my head?   Breaking.   James Alexander Allan.   PoAu 1-2

Where shall we meet, who knows, who knows?   A Song.   Paul Laurence Dunbar.   AmNP

Where shall you be at–well, say half-past seven/Tomorrow night?   Tonight.   Franklin Pierce ("F.P.A.") Adams.   FiBHP

Where she and her glistening lover race/over a murderous snow.   The Wife of Winter's Tale.   Michael Dennis Browne.   SM

Where she could hardly root,/let alone glorify her wings.   Where She Was Not Born.   Yvonne.   CNA

Where she dare preen and reaffirm/Her womanness.   The Searching.   Alice S. Cobb.   BlSi

Where she did ride, and he for two-and-six mote go.   Ride a Cock Horse (parody).   Barry Pain.   BXAP

Where she is gone there I can never go.   A Broken Song.   Moira O'Neill.   OBVV; PG

Where she lives in the trees till this very day,/Boring and boring for food.   A Legend of the Northland.   Phoebe Cary.   HBV 1-2; HBVY; OBCA; OnMSP

Where she moves by habit, hungering and blind.   The Mother.   S. S. Gardons.   NePoEA-2

Where she stands smiling, we kneel down/to her!   To Hafiz.   Thomas Bailey Aldrich.   AA

Where she wed the simple Ploughboy back from sea.   The Simple Ploughboy.   Anonymous.   FaBoCh; LoGBV

Where shineth thy spirit, there liberty shineth too!   The Irish Peasant to His Mistress.   Thomas Moore.   ACP

Where shiver'd was fair Scotland's spear,/And broken was her shield!   Marmion.   Sir Walter Scott.   ELP; EnRP; PoEL 1-5

Where silent, unrefractive whiteness lies.   Stories of Snow.   P.K. Page.   NOBC; NoP; OBCV; PoA

Where smaller things die early.   The Envies.   George Bowering.   NOBC

Where snow-water leaps–/on wings too bright and bitter/for the hookbilled shrike to swallow.   Advice from Euterpe.   Carter Revard.   VoR

Where stay a firebrand heart/in its nomad blaze.   How Many Fires.   George Reavey.   EAS

Where still those generations, to and fro,/Mysteriously greet.   An Upper Room.   D. L. Kelleher.   NeIP

Where store they found of all, that dainty/was and rare.   The Faerie Queene.   Edmund Spenser.   OAEP

Where storms and stars come from.   Young Sea.   Carl Sandburg.   MOS

Where summer hovered like a falling flare.   Elegy.   William Bell.   NePoEA

Where survival/takes naked and fiery forms.   Blood-Sister.   Adrienne Rich.   NoP

Where swung the lowly benden swing,/On elem boughs, on mossy limbs.   Rings.   William Barnes.   NBM; VLP

Where taste admires and thy still labour thrives.   The Mole.   John Clare.   SeCeV

Where tell/I dwell,/Farewell.   Upon His Departure Hence.   Robert Herrick.   FaBoRV; QFR

Where that one wears the sunlight for a while.   Calypso's Island.   Archibald MacLeish.   MoAB; NoP

Where the air is full of sunlight and the flag is full of stars.   America for Me.   Henry Van Dyke.   BLPA; BLPL; FaFP; HBVY; MC; OHFP; PAL; SoSe; TreFS; WBLP

Where the baths were... It is an admirable thing!   The Ruin.   Anonymous.   EBEV

Where the bitter breath of the naked sky/Might visit thee at will.   Lines: "The cold earth slept below."   Percy Bysshe Shelley.   NCEP

Where the blank field and the still-standing tree/Were bright and fearful presences to me.   Horses.   Edwin Muir.   CMoP; FaBoCh; LoGBV; MoVE; OAEL 1-2; PoPle; SeCePo

...Where the brook's murmuring/Moves the calm spirit, but disturbs it not.   The Ocean.   Moschus.   AWP

Where the buzzards would peck at my bones.   I Wanted to Die in the Desert.   Anonymous.   BPAW; CoSo

Where the caldron mantles and spills/Another dawn on the world!   A Northern Vigil.   Bliss Carman.   OBEV; OBVV; PeCV

Where the city's ashes that we brought with us/flew into the intense sky still burning.   Obsessions.   Denise Levertov.   LiTM; NePoEA-2; SM

Where the corner boys are growing grey,/Dreaming of sunny skies.   Corner Boys.   Bryan MacMahon.   OnYI

...Where the crystals kissed/in cabinets of amethyst and frost.   An Apology for the Revival of Christian Architecture...(excerpt).   Geoffrey Hill.   NoP

Where the dawn has that particular laughter.   You Also, Gaius Valerius Catullus.   Archibald MacLeish.   NoAm; TAP

Where the Dinkey-Bird is singing/In the amfalula tree!   The Dinkey-Bird. Eugene Field.   AA; AmMo; HBVY; LBN; NA; TreFS

...Where the diseased infant writhes and wallows till/death.   Dain Eile (excerpt).   Sorley MacLean.   NeBP

Where the dishevelled seaweed hates the sea.   For the Wine of Circe.   Dante Gabriel Rossetti.   ATP; VLP

Where the drum rolls up the stair, nor tarries.   The Drum: the Narrative of the Drummer of Tedworth.   Edith Sitwell.   BoW

Where the dust of an earthy to-day/Makes the earth of a dusty to-morrow. Quatrain.   *Anonymous.*   NA

Where the empty riders of the horror go.   Ingmar Bergman's Seventh Seal. Robert Duncan.   CAPP; NMP

Where the falling is soft.   Where He Hangs His Hat.   Deborah Lee.   BrSi

Where the first baby/was christened/Melody.   Camp Notes.   Mitsuye Yamada.   WPOW

Where the five tongues of living drink, and are/poem and image.   Image in a Lilac Tree.   Terence Tiller.   NeBP

Where the gelding knife is kept.   Et In Arcadia Ego.   W. H. Auden. CMoP

Where the girls are few and always true,/And my falsehearted love I'll forget I knew.   The Mexico Trail.   *Anonymous.*   BFSS

Where the girls are sweet as sweet can be/And the boys like sugar candy. My Pretty Little Pink (with music).   *Anonymous.*   AS

Where the God of Heaven is hovering/About me everywhere.   God's World. Mildred Keeling.   BLRP

Where the good God sits to spangle through.   Lady, Lady.   Anne Spencer. BlSi; PoBA

Where the good priest them christened/And gave her good kirking.   Hind Etin.   *Anonymous.*   OxBB

Where the great Cyprian mother should receive/Our warm unsullied vows. Daphne.   Bliss Carman.   OBCV

Where the green sod grows upon the grave.   Song from Fragment of an Eccentric Drama.   Henry Kirke White.   OBRV

Where the heart reflects.   Strains of Sight.   Robert Duncan.   CMoP; NMP

Where the heart will know no pain.   The Greenback Dollar.   *Anonymous.* AmFP

Where the hell have you been!   Alley-Walker.   Joan Smith.   AMV-80

Where the hills are blue.   The Hollow Land.   William Morris.   AtBAP; PoEL 1-5

Where the Holy Breath was mixed with the unholy wine.   Dark Rapture. George William Russell.   SeCePo

Where the horrible darkness is impressed with reflections/of desire?   Visions. William Blake.   ErPo

Where the Hudson is getting drunk on its oil.   New York.   Federico Garcia Lorca.   NU; NYP

...Where the inhabitants slay in silence and are silently slain.   Silences. Edwin John Pratt.   OBCV; PoCh

Where the kings and the slaves and the troubadours rest.   Bryan, Bryan, Bryan, Bryan.   Vachel Lindsay.   CMoP; CrMA; LiTA; OxBA; OxBoLi

Where the kite dips, pulling/Its long bright anxious chain.   Shore.   Diana O Hehir.   NPGG

Where the landscape is flattened out thin/and is all/yours   I need only fall asleep.   Ana Blandiana.   BoWoP

Where the last day's dust covers cracks.   Blemishes.   James Hart.   AMV-81

Where the leaping dolphins/celebrate the dawn.   The Dark Lord of Savaiki. Alistair Campbell.   OCNZ

Where the light of her soul fell shining and clean.   The Washer-Woman. Otto Leland Bohanan.   BANP

Where the lions of Judah lie in their fusty lair.   The Library.   Mary Mills. NePoAm

Where the living are silent/in America.   Silent in America.   Philip Levine. NaP

Where the long cloud, the long wood's counterpart,/Sheds doubled darkness up the labouring hill.   Without Her.   Dante Gabriel Rossetti.   CBEP; GBL; MaVP; NCEP

Where the Lord and our loved ones wait.   Easter Beatitudes.   Clarence M. Burkholder.   BLRP

Where the men on white horse   Snow White.   Robert Gillespie.   DFT

Where the moonlit weedy spaces continue.   To My Friends.   Stephen Berg. NaP; NYBP

...Where the most re-/cent traveller/has pitched his blind, enduring tent. Traveller's Guide to Antarctica.   Adrien Stoutenburg.   NYBP

Where the mountain hare has lain.   Memory.   William Butler Yeats.   BIrV

Where the mountains are clouds, lightning, but no rain.   Utah.   Anne Stevenson.   NCSH

Where the music is about to begin.   Marginal Music.   R. K. Meiners. AMV-81

Where the naked hide from day,/And thieves and drunkards meet.   We Live in a Rickety House.   Alexander McLachlan.   NOBC; OBCV

Where the oak is, the woodbird heedless/Hammers at my final house.   The Meaning.   Ralph Gustafson.   OBCV

Where the old cow at her leisure chews her cud.   Bird's Nests.   John Clare. ERoP 1-2; OAEL 1-2

Where the one almighty Father/Reigns in love for evermore.   Through the Night of Doubt and Sorrow.   Sabine Baring-Gould.   FaPoR

Where the one wise word and the strong word/Is the word that the great hush saith.   The Hills and the Sea.   Wilfred (William Wilfred Campbell) Campbell.   CaP

Where the pelican of the silent North/Sits there all silently.   The Northern Seas.   William Howitt.   GN

Where the phantom Tall Men ride!   Tall Men Riding.   Squire Omar Barker. BPAW

Where the place called morning lies!   Will there really be a morning?   Emily Dickinson.   AA; OBCA; SiSoSe; SoPo; WGRP

Where the ploughshares are hot, and your faith is not real.   Matrimony. John Williams.   NOEC

Where the poppy drops its seeds/In the silence and the gloom.   Aftermath. Henry Wadsworth Longfellow.   AP; MAmP; NOBA; TAP

Where the red leaves bleed for ever/And never pale.   Salvation Prospect. LeRoy Smith, Jr.   NePoAm

Where the religious walls have hid the bright reproof.   Legem Tuam Dilexi. Coventry Patmore.   NBM; OxBoCh; PoEL 1-5

Where the road leads along/Through the shine, through the rain.   Twilight Song.   Edwin Arlington Robinson.   HBV 1-2

Where the roads dip and where the roads rise   Landscapes.   Thomas Stearns Eliot.   BiP

Where the royal Queen Mary went weeping away.   The Duke of Grafton. *Anonymous.*   GBP

Where the Sabbath ne'er shall close.   Softly Fades the Twilight Ray.   Samuel Francis Smith.   AH

Where the sad journey home is no journey,/but a reawakening still yet in dream.   Near the Border of Insanities.   Dannie Abse.   PoA

Where the scorpion hungers, carrying his bruise down.   Monsoon.   David Wevill.   NYBP

Where the seaweed gatherer/can come as often as he wants.   Doesn't he realize.   Ono no Komachi.   BoWoP; WPOW

...Where the skier/and the cripple must decide/to recognize each other? Transit.   Adrienne Rich.   NoP

Where the snow ligs baith winter and summer.   Cauld Cornwood. *Anonymous.*   GBP

Where the sombrous red moon sets afar/Past the booming line of the surging bar.   Glints of the Year--from a Window.   Thomas Caulfield Irwin.   IrPN

...Where the/spear of the Roman soldier rammed in between the ribs of/this Jesus of Nazareth.   To a Contemporary Bunkshooter.   Carl Sandburg. WGRP

Where the stint compass of a skylark's wings/Would not put out some tiny golden centre.   How Looks the Night?   Gerard Manley Hopkins.   OBSP

...Where the stranger stood the two/men find a railway ticket to an unknown destination.   Seance.   Edouard Roditi.   EAS

Where the sun was always setting on the play.   The Long Garden.   Patrick Kavanagh.   FaBoIP; IPY

Where the swan drifts upon a darkening flood.   Coole and Ballylee, 1931. William Butler Yeats.   CMoP; GTBS-P; NoAm; NOBI; OBMV; PPP

Where the sweet water meets the salt.   Love Poem.   Maurice James Craig. NeIP

Where the table is set for two.   They Two.   Mrs. Frank A. Breck.   WBLP

Where the tempest now, who feels it? None! the danger's drowned/in wine! Rude Boreas.   *Anonymous.*   OBET

Where the tempest whispers, "Pay him!" and I answer,/"Nevermore!"   The Promissory Note (parody).   Bayard Taylor.   BXAP; HBV 1-2; Par; SpRo

Where the toiler turns to sod/Man beholds the living God.   The Servants. Richard Wightman.   WGRP

Where the trees march firmly/out of rank into the woods.   La Selva.   Cid Corman.   VGW

Where the troubled spirit grows wise/And the heart is comforted.   Spell of Sleep.   Kathleen Raine.   HaMV

...Where the twin still/turns your colors, year after yellow year.   For My Grandfather.   Richard Robbins.   AMV-81

Where the two dear hands I love/Poured the wine, and broke the bread.   The Good Day.   Sir Henry Howarth Bashford.   HBV 1-2

Where the unicorn devoured all buds and traces.   The Beast That Rode the Unicorn.   Conny Hannes Meyer.   VWA

Where the voice of her beloved/soundeth sweeter still/Than fiddles or flutes. Epilogue.   Heinrich Heine.   TrJP

Where the voice of her lover sounds even sweeter/Than fiddles and flutes. The North Sea (excerpt).   Heinrich Heine.   AWP

Where the weary folk are dreaming.   The Faerie's Child.   Thomas Caulfield Irwin.   OnYI

Where the wide waters and their voyager are one.   Death from Cancer. Robert Lowell.   MP; TwCP

Where the wild beasts howls and roars.   The Rocky Mountains. *Anonymous.*   AmFP

Where the wild birds and turtledove can hear my sad cry   I'm Going to Georgia. *Anonymous.* AmFP

Where the wild birds in heaven can hear my sad cry.   On Top of Old Smoky. *Anonymous.* FaFP; TreFT

Where the wild honey bees/Gather honey for their queen!   April (excerpt). Irene Rutherford McLeod.   SUS

Where the wild wind blows on the mountain side.   Stanzas.   Emily Bronte. OBVV

Where the wind breaks, breaks/All day like foam.   Magpie.   Peter Davison. GrPl

Where the winged instruments of celebration?   The Singers.   George Bruce. OxBS

Where their bright glories shone at first.   The Evening Sun.   Emily Bronte. CH

Where their mother, Care, like a drowsy child,/Is laid asleep in flowers.   A Fragment: To Music.   Percy Bysshe Shelley.   BoLiVe

Where their voices rise/as smoke from blue mountain.   Swimmer.   Gladys Cardiff.   CDW

Where then lies my hope of You, and where my/fear?   Sufi Quatrain. Rabi'a bint Isma'il.   WPOW

Where there are Druids/rustling in the leaves.   Green Ice.   Vivienne Finch. BrRo

Where there are no church committees and no fashionable choirs!   Trouble in the "Amen Corner."   Thomas Chalmers Harbaugh.   BLPA

Where there are none to listen or to care.   Vain Gratuities.   Edwin Arlington Robinson.   NePA

Where there could be a mushroom, pale and mysterious,/growing out of the concrete floor.   Rust.   Michael Hogan.   LFAC

Where there is little left to die/And no more Spring.   Where It Is Winter. George O'Neil.   HBMV

Where there is no leaf left/invent one.   Reply to the Question: "How Can You Become a Poet?"   Eve Merriam.   DFF

Where there is reckoning there is sin,/And where there is no reckoning sin is not.   The Righteous Man.   Samuel (1835-1902) Butler.   OBSV

Where there's bread and room for the poor.   No Bread for the Poor (with music). *Anonymous.* AS

Where there was nothing but moving sands and wind!   There Is a Dream Dreaming Us.   Norman Dubie.   GeTw

Where these are not, I despise/Lovely cheeks or lips or eyes.   The Unfading Beauty.   Thomas Carew.   AtBAP; EnLi 1-2; FaBV; LiTL; OBEV

Where they also hold charity raffles/On rainy Monday nights of an eternal November.   Classic Ballroom Dances.   Charles Simic.   LCAP

Where they are, where my lute and drum have fallen?   La Chute.   Charles Olson.   InPK

Where they buried Red Hugh.   Aodhy Ruadh O'Domhnaill.   Thomas MacGreevy.   AnIV; CIP; OBMV; OxBI

Where they have wept without/and I within.   Marvell's Garden.   Phyllis Webb.   OBCV

Where they rattle two pebbles to praise the moon.   Tongue River Psalm. Gary Gildner.   FAZ

Where they sup sour milk in a ram's horn.   Lancashire Born.   *Anonymous.* GBP

Where they wear the tartan, little above the knee?   Were You Ever in Dumbarton?   *Anonymous.* ShS

Where they went to their beds and took the blessing of slumber.   The Iliad. Homer.   NAWM 1-2

Where they who worshipped idol gods have been.   The Eagles.   Jones Very. TAP

Where thine earthly part is lying,/Florence Vane!   Florence Vane.   Philip Pendleton Cooke.   AA; HBV 1-2

Where those curved arms shut in a tranquil sea.   The Lonely Isle.   Claudian (Claudius Claudianus).   AWP

Where thou awaitest the appeal of God.   To the Body.   Alice Meynell. ACP

Where thou ever in heaven's spring/Shalt with saints and angels sing.   To Theodora.   *Anonymous.* OxBChV

Where thou first drew'st thy breath, doest there commence thy reign.   The Golden Age.   *Anonymous.* APAS

Where thou hangs on that pin.   Ane Satire of the Three Estaitis (excerpt). Sir David Lyndsay.   GoTS; OBSV

Where thou were fairest of the fair.   A Song.   Thomas Percy.   CEP

Where, through God's aid, shall ever wave the flag of Washington!   Grand Opening of the People's Theatre.   O. J. Goldrick.   PoOW

Where through my dormer bay/Drizzles the Milky Way.   For the New Year. Norman Nicholson.   NeBP

Where through some sucking pool I will be hurl'd/With rapture to the other side of the world!   He Saw Far in the Concave Green of the Sea.   John Keats.   EtS

Where thy Maker of mightiness most/Is King and thou their Queen is!   To Our Lady.   Robert Henryson.   ACP; CAW

Where thy victory, O Grave?   Easter Hymn.   Charles Wesley.   OHIP; TRV

Where, till the day I die, I will not go.   The Mapmaker on His Art. Howard Nemerov.   NYBP

Where to go/Strapping, apricot.   Detach, Invading.   Ron Padgett.   ANYP

Where, to my bliss, myself may meet/One hastening with pierced feet. Sorrow.   Helen Parry Eden.   CAW

Where to the natives destiny is snow/That is neither to our mind nor of our making.   Sestina d'Inverno.   Anthony Hecht.   NoP

"Where to? what next?"   The People, Yes.   Carl Sandburg.   BoLiVe; MoAB; MoAmPo; NoAm; NOBA; TrGrPo

Where tomorrow he will try and fail his license to live.   Learning Experience. Marge Piercy.   FF

Where trees are actual and take no holiday.   Robinson.   Weldon Kees. NaP; NoAm; NYBP

Where two hearts were united/In love's sweet, happy dream.   California Joe. *Anonymous.* CoSo

Where under tiny spears of jade/The tiny insects pass....   Proud Hollyhock. Marguerite Buller.   BrR

Where undisturbed I may lie,/Sleeping, sleeping.   The Three Seamstresses. Isaac L. Peretz.   TrJP

...Where vertue must/Fraile as our flesh, crumble to dust.   Maria Wentworth, Thomae Comitis Cleveland...   Thomas Carew.   AnAnS 2; ATP; CaPo; JCP; MeLP; MePo; SeCV 1-2

Where virtue's force can cause her to obey.   On Fortune.   Queen of England, Elizabeth I.   PBWP

Where vows grow dim, and men dare do/What once they scorned, help me be true!   A Soldier's Prayer.   Robert Freeman.   TrPWD

Where was it? . . . and why do I still/remember?   The Green Door.   Leah Bodine Drake.   BiCB

Where was it one first heard of the truth? The the.   The Man on the Dump. Wallace Stevens.   HAP; NAWM 1-2

Where was then the pride of man/That now mars his meed?   The Peasants' Song.   *Anonymous.* FaBoPV

Where waters show/as much courtesy/to me as to/a speechless sky.   Tho We All Speak.   Daniel Ort.   AMV-80

Where we cannot/see them.   The Children.   Mark Vinz.   DFF

...Where we'd drive, how we'd survive.   Driving; Driven.   David McAleavey. AMV-80

Where we had our own Adam/And damn near all/The wonders of the world. Wonders.   Lorenzo Thomas.   APU

Where we leave him, froliclavish while he looks about/him, laughs, swims.... Epithalamion.   Gerard Manley Hopkins.   AnEnPo

Where we may sing to thy solace/In excelsis gloria.   When Christ Was Born of Mary Free.   *Anonymous.* MeEV

Where we must stand the shock and must die, &c.   Captain Kid's Farewell to the Seas.   *Anonymous.* OBSS

Where we perish, there is our/grave!   Cargoes of the Radanites.   Harry Alan Potamkin.   TrJP

Where we/run with masks.   Chiaroscuro.   Carol Berge.   ErPo

Where we set blue footprints,/tomorrow, is grass.   Footprints.   Hamish Brown.   PoSH

Where we shall part no more.   The Lord into His Garden Comes. *Anonymous.* AH

Where we suffer to die by the hands of ourselves, and to kill.   Jew.   Karl Shapiro.   VWA

Where we who harvested the grain/Lie buried under weeds.   The Untended Field.   Robert Hillyer.   AnNE

Where we will make our bow-strings twang,/Musick for us most sweet. Robin Hood Rescuing Will Stutly.   *Anonymous.* BaBo; ESPB

Where wealth accumulates, and men decay.   The Deserted Village.   Oliver Goldsmith.   TRV

Where wealth declines and population grows!   On Vital Statistics.   Hilaire Belloc.   PoL

Where well he knows no man to him can come.   Astrophel and Stella, XLIII. Sir Philip Sidney.   AAS; SiPS

Where were you/when I was growing up and needed somebody?   Spring Song.   Rod McKuen.   CAD

Where what comes finds a brim gravity exactly requires.   Lake Chelan. William Stafford.   BiP; NaP

Where wheels have freshly sliced the April mire.   Blue-Butterfly Day. Robert Frost.   RFM

..."Where, where/Does it remind me of?"   Till someone comes.   Grandmother and Grandson.   William Stanley Merwin.   NePoEA-2

Where, where, in what abyss shall I be/groaning.   Hadad: The Demon-Lover. James Abraham Hillhouse.   AA

Where will rest my weary wings? Science turns/away!   Time's Song. Winthrop Mackworth Praed.   EnRP; NBM

Where will the captains run and/to what harbor?   If Something Should Happen.   Lucille Clifton.   MAT

Where/will we ride?   Untitled.   Mah-do-ge Tohee.   STE

Where wilt thou find their like agen?'   Patriotism.   Sir Walter Scott. OBEV

Where wind-sown wildernesses/Keep what is theirs to keep. Belden Hollow. Leslie Nelson Jennings. GoYe

Where with him, with him, all the way,/Went the sad eyes of Guinevere. Lancelot and Guinevere. Gerald Gould. HBV 1-2

Where within the tomb lies buried/All that we shall see no more. The Talmud. Simeon S. Frug. TrJP

Where, wondering at the grace of sleep,/The Guardian Angels stand. The Bog Lands. William A. Byrne. AnIV

Where words throb/hidden in violins. Under the Earth. Abraham Sutzkever. VWA

Where would your lover go to sleep?/Upon your bosom 'tween your breats. O That My Love Were in My Arms. Anonymous. WTO

Where years of long salvation roll,/And glory never dies. The Shortness and Misery of Life. Isaac Watts. NOCV

Where you and I pledged our first love so true. Come Hither, My Dear One. John Clare. ELP

Where you, black moon, warm your hands. Blackwater Mountain. Charles Wright. GeTw

Where you dare not even blink I Would Be a Painter Most of All. Len Chandler. NBP

Where you first/learned to walk/as I watched you. Last Born. Judith Kirkwood. Str

Where you get soft tack every day and none of your yellow meal. Heave away, My Johnny. Anonymous. OBSS

Where you have fallen–is this the/thing that grows? An Irish Wild-Flower. Sarah Piatt. AA

Where you lived Rosa. For Rosa Yen, Who Lived Here. Greg Pape. AmPA

Where you walk lives. The Fugs. Edward Sanders. PoM

Where you, we dream, obtain no right of entry. Dry-Point. Philip Larkin. CMoP; NMP

Where young and old and fair and foul are one. The Incurables. Arthur Upson. AnAmPo

Where your blood is running like a river under its ice. Chicago. Lola Ridge. PoA

Whereafter none may part but be/The rat leaving a sinking ship. Family Evening. Daniel Huws. NYBP

Whereas discomfort sole Y here me dresse/Upon my bed so hard of noyous thought. Ballade: "When fresshe Phebus, day of Seynt Valentyne." Charles, duc d' Orleans. EnPo

Whereas in my house there are only five. Letters from an Irishman to a Rat. Christopher Logue. BoAnP

Whereat he starts, and back his head doth fling. Britannia's Pastorals. William Browne. FaBoPP

...Whereat I/Would raise my voice in song. Agnosto Theo (To an Unknown God). Thomas Hardy. MoPo

Whereat they, while he whimpers, mock the fool. Elegies. Andre Marie de Chenier. AWP

Whereby I pass and may not enter in. The Closed Door. Theodosia Garrison. BLPA; PoToHe

Whereby we come to bury our deserts/In th' obscure grave of singularity. Poet and Critic. Samuel Daniel. OBSC

Wherefore all joy I do refuse,/And cruel will thereof accuse. Heart Oppress'd with Desperate Thought. Sir Thomas Wyatt. SiPS

Wherefore, but this, I do not love the man. Antipathy. Rowland Watkyns. FaBoEE

Wherefore He is called together/Son of God and Son of Man. Romance VIII. Saint John of Damascus. ISi

Wherefore I was among them well I knew. I Dreamed I Moved among the Elysian Fields. Edna St. Vincent Millay. NoP

...Wherefore, let there stir/naught but the softest voices, praising her. Portrait. Ezra Pound. OBVV

Wherefore no time my banning prayers shall pause,/till proud she repent. Menaphon. Robert Greene. OBSC

Wherefore, O summer's day? The Bee Is Not Afraid of Me. Emily Dickinson. LaNeLa

Wherefore, Polly, put the kettle/On at once. Morning. Charles Stuart Calverley. FiBHP; NBM

Wherefore then longer live should I? Being Forsaken of His Friend He Complaineth. E. S. EIL

...Wherefore thus I cross/All lovers pale and starving with their loss. Love's Consolation. Richard Watson Dixon. OBNC

Wherefore to Chinon? Wherefore I"? Joan of Arc: Introduction. Hugh McCrae. PoAu 1-2

Wherefore with tears, my bed, I thee forsake. The restful place, reviver of my smart. Sir Thomas Wyatt. FCP; SiPS

Wherein a little beaten ship/Flew through the spray. The Bead Mat. Walter de la Mare. CBEP

Wherein all pleasures of the world are wove. Upon Julia's Ribband. Robert Herrick. CaPo

Wherein herself she doth declare/Through my lips, and say her prayer. Earth. John Hall Wheelock. AnFE; APA; HBMV; LiTA; MoAmPo; MoRP

Wherein I read/the poem that never ends. True Confessional. Lawrence Ferlinghetti. NAs

...Wherein is/neither day nor night, nor form nor colour, nor ever any/word. Thou Art the Sky. Rabindranath Tagore. OBMV

Wherein my Love had eyes that lighted my delight. To Night. Anonymous. EIL; MOON

Wherein Nature, in a mood ironical,/Has sown a flowering weed? Judge Somers. Edgar Lee Masters. FaBoEE; OBSV

Wherein, self-prisoners, we dwell. Elements. Carolyn Wilson Link. GoYe

Wherein such grain could moulder/and decay! The Talmud Student. Hayim Nahman Bialik. TrJP

Wherein their Noble ashes are, and know yee/ALL END in ALLEN, by a Paragoge. An Elegy upon the Death of That Holy Man...(excerpt). Edward Taylor. PoEL 1-5

Wherein thou liv'st for ever. Dear, farewell. Upon His Sister-in-Law, Mistress Elizabeth Herrick. Robert Herrick. CaPo

Wherein to play your violin with grace. First Fight. Then Fiddle. Gwendolyn Brooks. BP; NIP; PoNe

Wherein to sit and watch the fury pass. Ice. Sir Charles G. D. Roberts. BoNaP; ExPo; OBCV; WHW

Wherein we glory while our eyes are/wet. Vanitas Vanitatum. Israel Zangwill. TrJP

Whereo'er the chariot wheels of life are roll'd/In cloudy circles to eternity. Written in Butler's Sermons. Matthew Arnold. VLP

Whereof each mortal knowing,/Becomes a King. Hail Man! Angela Morgan. WGRP

Whereof his band and he were the most/ holy sign. An Ode in Time of Hesitation: Robert Gould Shaw. William Vaughn Moody. AA

Whereof she dreams and prophesies! Snow-Bound. John Greenleaf Whittier. AA

Whereof she wanders mad, being all unfit/For mortal love, that might not die of it. Oh, Sleep Forever in the Latmian Cave. Edna St. Vincent Millay. ExPo; LiTM; MoAmPo; MoVE; NoAm; NoP; SeCeV; ViBoPo

Whereon no canker lighted, for they bore/The magic stamp of MECHI'S SILVER STEEL. La Mort d'Arthur (parody). William Aytoun. FaBoPa

Whereon the sun hangs motionless, a brassy disc of/flame. Down the Mississippi. John Gould Fletcher. LiTA

Wheresoe'er you are, my heart shall truly love you. Sonnet: "Were I as base as is the lowly plain." Joshua Sylvester. EIL; OBSC; ViBoPo

Whereto two parties once be full content. A Tale for Husbands. Sir Philip Sidney. SiPS

...Whereupon she slapped me again. In Memoriam. Richard Weber. ErPo

Wherever Freedom, pois'd by Toleration, sway'd by/Law,/Stands or is rising thy true monument. Washington's Monument, February, 1885. Walt Whitman. OFD

Wherever he bathes–the rivers become sweet. Song of Praise for an Ox. Abraham Sutzkever. VWA

Wherever he walks/the grass is forbidden to stand up again. The Elephant I. Anonymous. TTY

Wherever hills grow hard, put them to the test. Hills. Robin Munro. PoSH

Wherever I walk now, I wake not here. The Worm in the Whirling Cross. John Malcolm Brinnin. MoPo

...Wherever/It heads for it must get there burning. The Highway. William Stanley Merwin. PoA

Wherever men lay bound he clave. Henry Ward Beecher. Charles Henry Phelps. AA

Wherever strong men truly seek/With character the goal. Where Is Our Holy Church? Edwin H. Wilson. AH

Wherever there is misery,/Wherever there are men. O God, How Many Years Ago. Frederic William Henry Myers. HBMV

Wherever we encounter, there are no categories. Explanation. William Barber. PeHV

Wherever we looked the land would hold us up. One Home. William Stafford. CoAP; NePA; VGW

Wherever you meet Him, He's waiting/there. He Cares. Owen C. Salway. STF

Wherewith in haste half-way return'd, he saw/A smile on Dermid's face relax'd in death. The Death of Dermid. Sir Samuel Ferguson. IrPN

Wherewith they harmless pastime make... Stool Ball. Anonymous. CH

Wherewith this lady speeds it on its way. Sonnet: Of the Eyes of a Certain Mandetta, of Toulouse... Guido Cavalcanti. AWP

Wherfore I was the welcomere algate,/And for a verray gentil man y-holde. La Male Regle de T. Hoccleve. Thomas Hoccleve. EnPo

Whether a husband or a lover,/If he have a feeling is–to cry. When Lovely Woman. Phoebe Cary. ALV; FaBoBe; GoTF; HBV 1-2; TreFS

Whether around a clockface or a world. A Clock in the Square. Adrienne Rich. HeIP; NIP

Whether fools' souls go to heaven or to hell. Upon a Fool. John Hoskyns. FaBoEE

Whether He be Compulsion, or All-Fathering,/Or Fate and blind. Classic Encounter. Christopher (Christopher St. John Sprigg) Caudwell. OxBTC

Whether he be safe or noght/I recke never for he ne roght. An Epitaph. *Anonymous.* MeEL

Whether he die by Musket or Pot. Epitaph to Thomas Thetcher. *Anonymous.* PoPle

Whether he died for England's pride/By battle or by pot. The General Elliott. Robert Graves. DBV

Whether he would or no, with love! Triumph of Love. John Hall Wheelock. MoAmPo

Whether i am there/or not At chadwicks bar and grill. Lance Henson. STE

Whether in God's eye or the eye of a cat. Cat and Mouse. Ted Hughes. EaLo; OBSP

Whether in Mars his field thou bee,/Or Tybers winding streames, I follow thee. Odes. Horace. OBVE

Whether it's frying-pan or fire. Advice to Bachelors. *Anonymous.* UnTE

...Whether/Mrs. Haynes would have hanged herself/early one morning, while/ we passed by to school. Suburban. H. R. Coursen. GOYP

Whether my life shall still decay,/Or when my sorrow end. To His Muse. Nicholas Breton. OBSC

Whether outside, around, or in. Fence Wire. James Dickey. NYBP; VGW

...Whether she/Dreameth in any isle of Lethe dull. Cancelled Stanza of the Ode on Melancholy. John Keats. SyP

Whether the public read her works/Or not! After Horace. Alfred Denis Godley. NOBL

Whether the roses be your lips or your lips the roses. Her Lips. *Anonymous.* EG; LiTL

Whether the third spake verity. Ballad of the Three Spectres. Ivor Gurney. OBWP

–Whether their hearts could break/How can I know? The Sermon. Richard Hughes. BoC; OBMV

Whether there was any meaning in this entire spectacle. A Classic Idyll. Avraham Huss. VWA

Whether thou doest in heaven, or earth appeare,/Be where thou wilt, thou will not harbour here. Ah Sweet Content, where Is Thy Mylde Abode? Barnabe Barnes. AAS

Whether 'tis in us to arise with day/And save ourselves unaided. Storm Fear. Robert Frost. CMoP; HBV 1-2; OxBA; ViBoPo

Whether to wake and weep,/Or wake no more, He knows. We Lay Un Down to Sleep. Louise Chandler Moulton. AA

Whether we will or no. Fire. Dorothy Wellesley. OBMV

Whether within or without me/They were, I cannot say. At Ballyshannon, Co. Donegal. William Allingham. FaBoPP

Whether you are pretty or not, I outlive you,/bend down my strange face to yours and forgive you. All My Pretty Ones. Anne Sexton. CoPo; NoAm

Whether you be the rose, or the rose be you. A Fancy. Thomas Lodge. EIL

Whether you loved or did not love to-day? To One on Her Waste of Time. Wilfrid Scawen Blunt. ViBoPo

Whether you will/offend a mother or father/who has lost a child Remember the Ladies. Lyn Lifshin. LTB

Whether you will or no,/You have accepted him. Essay on Deity. Elder Olson. MoRP

Whether you will warm my aging limbs as a lover For Anna. Irving Layton. NeAC

Whether your kindness,/mother,/Is mother of silences. Seasons of the Soul. Allen Tate. AP; CrMA; MoPo; NePA; OxBA

Whether your servant love or no. How Many New Years Have Grown Old. *Anonymous.* EIL

Whets for the whale-path the heart irresist-/ibly,/O'er tracks of ocean... The Seafarer. *Anonymous.* EnL

Which a well-taught Prince should earn,/With six thousand pounds a year. Royal Education. Winthrop Mackworth Praed. OBSV

Which absorbed that old person of Diss. Limerick: "There was an old person of Diss." Edward Lear. GoJo

Which accounts for the hump on the camel,/And the Sphinx's inscrutable smile. The Sexual Life of the Camel. *Anonymous.* DBV

Which, after a short time, by some mistake Or indiscretion of the Father, died. Vaudracour and Julia (excerpt). William Wordsworth. EvOK

Which ain't revolutionary, you/dig? Down Wind against the Highest Peaks. Clarence Major. NBP

Which, alas! ask me not to explain. Odes, XI. Hafiz. AWP

Which all her composition proves/–Glory be! Pat Young. Kenneth Mackenzie. PoAu 1-2

Which almost burst to belch it in the sea. Richard III. William Shakespeare. MOS

Which, alone and immaculate and white,/Blossoms beyond the temporal hour. The Quiet Flower. Josephine Winslow Johnson. MoRP

Which an empty dream discovers. Mab the Mistress-Fairy. Ben Jonson. EIL; WiR

Which Anguish was the utterest–then–/To perish, or to live? 'Twas Like a Maelstrom, with a Notch. Emily Dickinson. AmePo; CMoP; ExPo; LiTA; LiTM; NePA; SeCeV

Which answers to all doubts so eloquently well. Childe Harold's Pilgrimage: Canto III. George Gordon, Lord Byron. OBRV

Which are harrowed, and beaten, and scared away. Epilogue. Stephen Spender. MoBrPo

Which are never entirely accidents. Not when one sings. No White Bird Sings. John Ciardi. AMV-80

Which are strangely bound by magic/Of their autonomous cohesion. Ars Poetica. Victor van Vriesland. TrJP

Which, as a map, her regency discovers/In camps, in courts, and in the way of lovers. Fame and Fortune. Michael Drayton. OBSC

Which as a warme, and moistned spring,/Gave them their ever flourishing. Upon Roses. Robert Herrick. SeCP

Which, as the years pass by me,/All soundlessly unfold. The Book of Pilgrimage. Rainer Maria Rilke. ILwL

Which astonished that girl from Majorca. Limerick: "There was a young girl of Majorca." Edward Lear. LiBL

Which bears eternity/To the last command. The Reply. Philip Levine. PoA

Which, because of radiation/Will be cared for by the nation.) A Leaden Treasury of English Verse. Paul Dehn. DBV

Which being restrained, a heart is broken. Dearest, Do Not You Delay Me. John Fletcher. ViBoPo

Which bends to fashion, and obeys the rules,/Imposed at first, and since observed by fools. The Prophecy of Famine. Charles Churchill. NOEC

Which bewept to the grave did go/With true-love showers. Hamlet. William Shakespeare. AnFE; EBEV; EnLoPo; GBL; GoBC; InPo; LiTB; LiTL; OBSC; PoRA; QFR; TrGrPo; ViBoPo

Which bind the strengths of Nature wild/To the conscience of a child. Wealth. Ralph Waldo Emerson. ImOP

Which breeds all wrath and right, and shall not die/In earth, and finds some hope upon the sky. Sonnets, II: "Our doom is in our being." James Agee. MoAmPo

Which brother, you or I, shall swiftly go. The Rooftree. Allen Tate. PoA

Which brought the God of Freedom's battles/down/To place on patriot brows the victor's crown! The Mecklenburg Declaration. William C. Elam. PAH

Which burns for me alone with friendly light. Epigram: "Lo! Beauty flashed forth sweetly." Meleager. PeHV

Which but expressions be of inward evils. Caelica, C. Fulke, Lord Brooke Greville. EnRePo; FCP; HAP; OAEL 1-2

Which, but for me, had still been empty visions. Columbus in Chains. Philip Freneau. MC; PAH

Which by the houres he measured, besought/Them go to rest. So all unto their bowres were brought. The Faerie Queene. Edmund Spenser. NoP

Which can do nothing, and is doing that. The Sweeper of Ways. Howard Nemerov. HaCAP

Which can make me thus to leave you,/And from louts to run away. Voices at the Window. Sir Philip Sidney. NOBE

Which can never be undone/Until the destruction of language. Permanently. Kenneth Koch. CAPP; CoAP; NoP; PoA; PoM; PPP

Which can thy glorious praises sing out best. Meditations. Edward Taylor. AP

Which Claus of Innsbruck cast in bronze for me! My Last Duchess. Robert Browning. AWP; BeLS; BiP; DiPo; ExPo; FaBoPV; FaFP; FF; FiP; ForPo; FPL; GoTF; GTBS-P; HAP; HBV 1-2; HeIP; HoPM; InPK; InPo; InPS; LiTB; MasP; MAT; MaVP; MBW 1-2; MCCG; NIP; NOBE; NOBV; NoP; OAEL 1-2; OAEP; OBNC; PAI; PoEL 1-5; PoLf; PoPle; PPP; PrIm; SCV; SeCeV; SoSe; TEP; TreFS; TrGrPo; VLP; WeW; WHA

Which concluded that person of Cromer. Limerick: "There was an old person of Cromer." Edward Lear. TDH

Which concludes this very interesting song. Roy Bean. *Anonymous.* BeLS; BPAW; OBAL

Which consist of just settin' and lookin'. Limerick: "This bird is the Keel-billed Toucan." Howard Ketcham. LiBL

Which cover lightly, gentle earth. On My First Daughter. Ben Jonson. AnAnS 2; EBEV; FaBoEE; HoPM; InPS; JCP; LoBV; NOBE; NoP; OBS; SeCP; SeCV 1-2; TEP

Which crowns my heart when ere it dyes,/In that it falls her sacrifice. Sonnet: "Tell me no more how fair she is." Henry, Bishop of Chichester King. EnLoPo; MeLP; MePo; SeCP; ViBoPo

Which dawns into a perfect star. To a Child. George Edgar Montgomery. AA

Which distracted that virulent Bull. Limerick: "There was a young lady of Hull." Edward Lear. MoShBr

Which distressed all the people of Brussels.   Limerick: "There was an old person of Brussels."   Edward Lear.   FaBoNo

Which distressed all the people of Chertsey.   Limerick: "There was an old lady of Chertsey."   Edward Lear.   OxBChV

Which do you think was broken?   Vases.   Nan Terrell Reed.   BLPA

Which done, he bravely marches on,/And then cuts off his head.   David and Goliath.   Nathaniel Crouch.   OxBChV

Which drew down God with such attractive love?   Sonnet LVI.   William Alabaster.   SBVL

Which drones no windier than you/Or duller, nor expects an answer.   To a Talkative Hairdresser.   Phyllis McGinley.   DBV

Which drove me on trying to memorize/The Encyclopedia Britannica!   Frank Drummer.   Edgar Lee Masters.   NoAm

Which e'en the Angels, high in Heaven,/Might lean to earth to hear.   Lines.   Ada Sister Mary.   BlSi

Which eagles cleave upmounting from their nest.   Hyperion.   John Keats.   ATP

Which eats into itself, and rusts ingloriously.   Childe Harold's Pilgrimage: Canto III.   George Gordon, Lord Byron.   OBRV

Which eats up nights and days and all our life.   The Specter.   Ernst Hardt.   AWP

Which ended in a sepia November/Four years before my birth.   The Great War.   Vernon Scannell.   OBWP

Which equally rid you of all your sorrow.   Hangover Cure.   Nicochares.   FaBoUs

Which erring made mankind arise,/To deeds of sin, to blood and wars.   Ode to Peace.   *Anonymous.*   PAH

Which Eve has left her daughters since her fall.   Don Juan.   George Gordon, Lord Byron.   OBRV

Which even a butterfly must bear/to be a worm again!   After Wings.   Sarah Piatt.   AA; HBV 1-2

Which even then washed him away past pardon.   The Remorse for Time.   Howard Nemerov.   NCSH

Which even to us were lost when we looked back.   Two.   Winfield Townley Scott.   NYBP

Which everyone has sat except a man.   A Politician.   Edward Estlin Cummings.   DBV; InPK; NLV; OBAL; TW

Which failure cannot cast down/Nor success make proud.   Rock and Hawk.   Robinson Jeffers.   MoVE; NoAm; NOBA; OxBA

Which false apostates never knew.   Broad Is the Road.   Isaac Watts.   AH

Which feels in thee a Comrade strong,/In every soul a friend of thine.   Wanderers.   Thomas Curtis Clark.   TrPWD

Which fills the enormity of the sky.   For Avi Killed in Lebanon.   Mark Osaki.   BrSi

Which flowered, but shall not wither, at his will.   Love in Time's Despite.   Edwin Muir.   LiTL

Which flows not every day, but ever!   When, Dearest, I but Think of Thee.   Sir John Suckling.   HBV 1-2; JCP; OBEV

Which fools us young, and beggars us when old.   Aureng-Zebe.   John Dryden.   FiP

Which, for my Muse her self now tired has/Unto another Canto I will overpass.   The Faerie Queene.   Edmund Spenser.   HW

Which frightened both the heroes so/They quite forgot their quarrel.   Tweedle-Dum and Tweedle-Dee.   *Anonymous.*   NA; NOBL

Which frightened Miss Muffet to bits.   Rhymes for a Modern Nursery.   Paul Dehn.   FiBHP; ShM

Which from a distance looked like/a field of wild buttercups.   Pastoral.   Ron Loewinsohn.   NeAP

Which, from the Universal Church receiv'd,/Is try'd, and after for its self believed.   Religio Laici.   John Dryden.   OBS

Which 'gainst all adverse winds may serve for fort.   Contemplations.   Anne Bradstreet.   WPOW

Which gathers such sense out of envy's beams,/As still casts imputations on supremes.   Caelica, LXXIX.   Fulke, Lord Brooke Greville.   FCP

Which God, my east, my sun, reveals.   Resignation.   Thomas Chatterton.   TrCP

Which goes on gaily/quite unchecked/until everyone is dead   "The killers that run...'.   Leonard Cohen.   NOBC

(Which goes with Bridge, and Women and Champagne).   On a General Election.   Hilaire Belloc.   FaBoCo; FaBoEE; MoVE; NOBE; NOBL; OBSV; OxBTC

Which goes with earth and is itself the light.   Time in the Sun.   Louise Townsend Nicholl.   NePoAm-2

Which golden love doth unto med rehearse.   Elegies.   Ovid (Publius Ovidius Naso).   OBVE

Which grieved that Old Man of the Dee.   Limerick: "There was an Old Man of the Dee."   Edward Lear.   FaBoNo

Which grows near the full circle/of this/world   Warrior Nation Trilogy.   Lance Henson.   VoR

Which, had it been alive,he would have killed.   Campaign Promise.   Henry Taylor.   TW

Which hand will you have,/High or low?   Handy Dandy.   *Anonymous.*   OxNR

Which has no human gesture and no word.   The Diver.   E. L. Mayo.   CoAP

Which has no stage.   Guest Lecturer.   Darwin T. Turner.   BALP

The which hath sent,/By good assent,/To us his only Son.   Welcome! Our Messiah.   *Anonymous.*   MeEL

The which hath whool my service and mine hert.   A Mistress without Compare.   Charles, duc d' Orleans.   MeEL

Which having heard, I'll do the like for thee.   Madrigal: "Come, doleful owl, the messenger of woe."   *Anonymous.*   PBBP

Which he certainly knew you knew, U Nu.   Just Dropped In.   William Cole.   FiBHP; GoJo; PoL; PoPl

Which he keeps in an underground aviary.   Limerick: "A vice most obscene and unsavoury."   *Anonymous.*   NOBL

Which, hearing them, would call their brothers fools.   The Merchant of Venice.   William Shakespeare.   TrGrPo

Which heart to heart, and mind to mind,/In body and in soul can bind.   The Lay of the Last Minstrel.   Sir Walter Scott.   OBRV

Which heaves but with the heaving deep.   In Memoriam A.H.H., XI.   Alfred, Lord Tennyson.   NOBE; OAEP; PoEL 1-5

Which helped that Old Man in a Barge.   Limerick: "There was an old man in a Barge."   Edward Lear.   EBEV

Which hopes from thee, and thee alone, a cure!   Time and Grief.   William Lisle Bowles.   HBV 1-2; OBEV

Which how Dexterously I doe,/Heare and make Example too.   A Celebration of Charis.   Ben Jonson.   AnAnS 2; SeCP

Which howled and lugged its entrails, trailing wet/With blood back to its doorstep, almost dead.   Tales of the Islands, IX.   Derek Walcott.   OxBTC

Which I believe (though fatall) will afford/An Endless name unto their ruin'd Lord.   Tristium.   Ovid (Publius Ovidius Naso).   OBVE

Which I gather in a song.   The Apology.   Ralph Waldo Emerson.   AmePo; AP

Which I guess just goes to show/how good you know English/don't count for everything   To Bert Campaneris.   Tom Clark.   LiSp

Which I have loved long since, and lost/awhile.   Lead, Kindly Light.   John Henry, Cardinal Newman.   BLPL; FaBoBe; FaPoR; GoTF; MyFE; TreF

...Which I mean to do/One day, as I said before. .   By the Fire-Side.   Robert Browning.   MBW 1-2; OAEL 1-2; VLP

...Which I shall forget on the/day of my death for the long sleep/within my tomb?   What Profit?   Immanuel Di Roma.   TrJP

Which I want to give you on this day in vain.   A Hymn About a Spoonful of Soup.   Jozef Wittlin.   VWA

Which I will use now to draw my line under this present story.   The End of Fall.   Francis Ponge.   NU

Which if it last woe to all simple hearts.   Psalm XII.   Sir Philip Sidney.   FCP

Which if she graunt, then live, and my love cherish,/If not, die soone, and I with thee will perish   Amoretti, II.   Edmund Spenser.   AAS

Which if you pluck not from the stalk, will fall within/this hour.   The Lover Exhorteth His Lady to Take Time, While Time Is.   George Turberville.   EnRePo

Which in an instant winds do scatter.   Fuimus Fumus.   Joshua Sylvester.   FaBoEE

Which, in mazes of the breast,/Wanders in the night.   To the Moon.   Johann Wolfgang von Goethe.   MOON

Which in the world is upside down,/The fish hook or the question mark?   Casting.   Howard Nemerov.   OBSP

Which in your bosom seeks his only shrouding?   My Only Star.   Francis Davison.   EIL

Which is all mystery or nothing.   Thoughts during an Air Raid.   Stephen Spender.   MoBrPo; ViBoPo

Which is all we poets/wrapped in our loneliness/are trying to say.   Poetry.   Nikki Giovanni.   NIP

Which is as white and hair-less as an egge.   Her Legs.   Robert Herrick.   SpRo

Which is in me/like a hill.   The Hill.   Robert Creeley.   ConAP; NoAm

Which is like to our head; let us protect it worthily.   The Serpent's Nature.   *Anonymous.*   MeEV

Which is my heart and for himself alone.   A Sonnet.   Amelie Troubetzkoy.   AA

Which is only to say/That a poet needs to get under/His own light.   Viewpoint.   George Scarbrough.   AMV-81

Which is played upon the shingles/By the pattern of the rain.   Rain on the Roof.   Coates Kinney.   HBV 1-2

Which is proud, and yet a wretched thing.   Man.   Sir John Davies.   EIL; OBEV

Which is the gate of death, the gate of birth.   Credo.   Arthur Symons.   OBVV

Which is the old back yard   To.   William Carlos Williams.   OBAL

Which is the only music I know how to play.   From the Commonwealth.
Sandra Maria Esteves.   LTB

Which is the sun bound/In the arms of the sea.   Response to Rimbaud's
Latter Manner.   Thomas Sturge Moore.   OBMV; SyP

Which is to be a place of perpetual undulation.   The Place of the Solitaires.
Wallace Stevens.   SyP

Which is unruly like the clouds/and as homeless as the wind.   Under Restless
Clouds.   Hanny Michaelis.   VWA

Which is variable as you drink forever.   George Towle.   Tony Towle.
ANYP

Which is why I have got to keep being/So damned objective with you.   To
My Friends.   Peter De Vries.   FiBHP

Which is why I reckon I does/have to work after all.   Necessity.   Langston
Hughes.   NOBA

Which is your luck.)   The Ballad of Billie Potts.   Robert Penn Warren.
NOBA; OxBA

Which isn't how the story should have ended.   The Tale of Jorkyns and
Gertie; or, Vice Rewarded.   R. P. Lister.   NYBP

Which Joshua could command but for an hour.   The Body Is Like Roots
Stretching.   Charles Reznikoff.   VWA

Which keeps the river of the song/A beauty out of sight.   Orara.   Henry
Clarence Kendall.   CBAP; PoAu 1-2

Which knew our happy, graceful/unending bouts of love.   The Wanton
(excerpt).   Vidya.   PBWP

Which labors and loves and suffers and sings/Under the sun!   Rutherford
McDowell.   Edgar Lee Masters.   EyDe; LiTA; OxBA

Which lacketh will to change his place.   For Want I Will in Woe I Plain.
Sir Thomas Wyatt.   SiPS

Which, laden with motes, strikes across the floor.   The Barn.   Stephen
Spender.   HaMV

Which life God sent me to mine ending day.   Childhood.   Sir Thomas More.
EnRePo

...Which long/remembers nothing, neither wind nor wake.   Writing.
Howard Nemerov.   NYBP

Which, mad to be born for no one/Neither can flow nor be still.   Another
Fan Belonging to Mademoiselle Mallarme.   Stephane Mallarme.   SyP

Which made hell shake and devils tremble.   Our Saviour's Love.
Anonymous.   OBET

Which made him a person of note.   Limerick: "There was an old stupid who
wrote."   Walter Parke.   LiBL; NA; TDH

Which made him considerably dephyr.   Limerick: "A farmer once called his
cow "Zephyr'."   Anonymous.   TDH

Which made poor Charley hop.   Charley.   Anonymous.   OxNR

Which made the men so fond of her,/Hey nonny nonny noe.   She Smiled
Like a Holiday.   Anonymous.   OxBoLi

Which made the old woman go Hipertihop,/He Hi, Hipertihop.   Old Roger.
Anonymous.   OxBoLi

Which mak'st each place a heaven wherein thou art.   To My Most Gracious
Dread Sovereign.   Sir John Davies.   SiPS

Which make me mad in the stark, raving moonlight?   The Storm.   Robert
David Cohen.   NYBP

Which make the patents of true worldly bliss,/Hath no misfortune but that
Rich she is.   Astrophel and Stella, XXXVII.   Sir Philip Sidney.   AAS;
SiPS

Which makes exhausted nature trip and fall/Just at the point where it becomes
divine.   Sonnets: A Sequence on Profane Love.   George Henry Boker.
AmePo

Which makes it stand up.   Crab Tree.   Oliver St.John Gogarty.   AnIL;
OxBI

Which makes me wish you'd change your lakes for ocean.   Don Juan.
George Gordon, Lord Byron.   OAEP

Which makes the high transcendent bliss/Of knowing thee, so rarely known.
The Queer.   Henry Vaughan.   PoEL 1-5

Which makes the world his apple, and forces him to eat.   Life Cycle of
Common Man.   Howard Nemerov.   NIP; NLV

Which makes thee wealthy to thine heir,/a beggar to thy self.   Of a Rich
Miser.   George Turberville.   EnRePo

Which maketh each place a heaven wherein thou art.   To Queen Elizabeth.
Sir John Davies.   OBSC

Which may a second laugh provoke,/And leave the biter bit.   The Bald
Cavalier.   Anonymous.   OxBChV

Which may explain why he remains obscure.   Ameinias.   John Simon.
ELU

Which may not flood the earth but only steal in/Through rifts in your souls.
Jehovah.   Israel Zangwill.   WGRP

Which may serve as armament for the next expedition.   Voyage to the Moon.
William Dickey.   MOON

Which may soften the heart of that cow.'   Limerick: "There was an Old Man
who said: "How."   Edward Lear.   EvOK; OxBChV

Which means I can just be me.   A Poem for Positive Thinkers.   Barbara
Mahone.   PoBA

Which means Until the end.   The End Is Near the Beginning.   David
Gascoyne.   EAS

Which meant suffering for others,/subdued rejoicing.   The Homeless.   Joan
Joffe Hall.   AMV-81

Which men can neither want, nor well endure.   Epigram.   Samuel (1612-80)
Butler.   FaBoEE

Which might be fair to tell but which I hide.   Of England, and of Its
Marvels.   Petrarch.   AWP

Which minstrels, servants of the Muses, tell.   Hymn to Selene.   Anonymous.
AWP

Which mirrors quietly the light/Of the snow, and the new year.   New Year's
Poem.   Margaret Avison.   LiTM; NOBC; OBCV

Which moved the suckers when they'd seen enough. Get out of town.   A
Valedictory to Standard Oil of Indiana.   David Wagoner.   NYBP

Which music never fails to give is being given.   Apocalypse.   D. J. Enright.
NMP; OBSV

Which must soon come–as I cannot forget.   A 14-Year-Old Convalescent Cat
in the Winter.   Gavin Ewart.   OBSP

Which my unflinching watch hath sealed/For harvest once again.   The
Scarecrow.   Walter De la Mare.   MoBrPo; OxBTC

Which name my Muse to highest heaven shall raise/By chaste desire, true love,
and virtue's praise.   Idea's Mirrour.   Michael Drayton.   OBSC

Which need not break.   The Judge.   Kenneth A. McClane.   AMV-81

Which neither can surprise/In any other pair of eyes.   Change.   Robert
Graves.   OxBTC

Which never more, oh youth! believe,/Shall either earth or heaven unweave.
Rhododaphne.   Thomas Love Peacock.   OBRV

Which never so blossomed since Jesus was born.   Down in the Forest.
Anonymous.   OBET

Which never there was seen before,/And it never will again.   Lady Alice (B
version).   Anonymous.   ESPB

Which Night and Day, I wou'd with Tears repeat.   The Iliad.   Homer.
OBVE

Which No-body can deny, &c.   Contentment: or, The Happy Workman's
Song.   John Byrom.   CEP

Which no kangaroo, 'possum or guppy'll.   Limerick: "An unusual thing called
a Troupial."   Milton Bracker.   TDH

Which nobody can deny.   For He's a Jolly Good Fellow.   Anonymous.
BLSo

Which nobody can deny.   Sweet Meat Has Sour Sauce.   William Cowper.
NOEC; OBSV

Which nobody can deny, deny,/Which nobody can deny.   The Mother
Country.   Benjamin Franklin.   PAH

Which none the less cry out in grief/Beneath the mocking, loving tones.   The
Family Cat.   Roy Fuller.   OxBC; TEP

Which nothing can intimidate but danger.   The ordinary valour only works.
Christopher Anstey.   CenHV

Which now and forever hold communion over/you.   On the Death of William
Edward Burghardt Du Bois...   Conrad Kent Rivers.   NBP; PoBA

Which now and then she changes/For moccasins of snow.   Footwear.   May
Justus.   SoPo; YeAr

Which now of grief grew dead, and sprung no more.   A Vision of the World's
Instability.   Richard Verstegan.   EIL

...Which now/Stands empty till his ashes fall in it.   The Vase of Life.   Dante
Gabriel Rossetti.   MaVP; SyP

Which now the angels sing.   The Angels' Song.   Edmund Hamilton Sears
AA; AmePo

Which Nymphs with Scorn repay,/More deaf, more hard, than they.   The
Eccho.   Richard Leigh.   MePo

Which, of all paths his feet knew well,/Were steeper found than Heaven or
Hell.   Dante at Verona.   Dante Gabriel Rossetti.   MaVP

Which of them really loved her best?   Which Loved Best?   Joy (Mary A.
Cragin) Allison.   OHIP; WBLP

Which of us will die?/which of us?/which of us?   Song of Agony.   Gouveia
De Lemos.   WhB

Which of us will survive the other   The accident has occurred.   Margaret
Atwood.   NMM

Which of us would first bite our tongues/asking forgiveness of the other?
Isolation Cell Poem.   J. Charles Green.   LFAC

Which offers only/the cold.   Blackbird Winter.   Annette Arkeketa West.
TWSS

Which oft our stage hath shown; and for their sake/In you fair minds let this
acceptance take.   King Henry V.   William Shakespeare.   CTC

...Which on a steeple/stands for hope.   The Steeple-Jack.   Marianne Moore.
BoWoP; CMoP

Which once was grand, but now to naught, to nothing-naught returns.   Burial
of the Spirit.   Richard Hughes.   MoBrPo

Which one like a city of white/stands in the sky at the end of its light...   The
Grief.   Rainer Maria Rilke.   AMV-81

Which one new year makes soft her marriage-bed.   A Dark Day.   Dante
Gabriel Rossetti.   MaVP

Which one's the mockingbird? which one's the world? The Mockingbird.
Randall Jarrell. DuDa; NYBP; RFM

Which one will soon be wearing/the darkly woven patterns/of her dress?
Woman through the Window. Marcia Falk. VWA

Which only goes to show you/That it pays to advertise. It Pays to Advertise.
Anonymous. GoTF; TreFT

Which only makes him bawl the more–/"Excelsior!" Excelsior (parody).
Anonymous. BXAP

Which ought I to be? Dilemma. Patricia Beer. OxBC

Which out of sight and sound is passing, passing? Ships That Pass in the
Night. Paul Laurence Dunbar. BANP; CDC; MOS

Which part wrote Scott, and which part wrote Liddell? Tow men wrote a
lexicon. *Anonymous.* CenHV

Which partly assuaged his despair. Limerick: "There was an old man whose
despair." Edward Lear. FaBoNo; VLP

Which passes, shivering the denim, back/into the stream. Dressing Game.
Dennis Schmitz. NPGG

Which peace men shuld enserch with bisinesse/And knit it sadly, holding in
holynesse. Keep the Sea. *Anonymous.* OxBM

Which penetrates and stirs my own heart. Nocturne II. Ruben Dario.
AMV-81

Which, perchance, shall set me free/From the damned with Sycorax. Ariel in
the Cloven Pine. Bayard Taylor. AA

Which perplexed that Old Person of Cassel. Limerick: "There was an old
person of Cassel." Edward Lear. EBEV

Which, please God, shall never die! Independence Bell–July 4, 1776.
Anonymous. BLPA; FaBoBe; FPL; MC; PAL

Which pleased all the people of Shoreham. Limerick: "There was an Old
Person of Shoreham." Edward Lear. NBM

Which points a scream, a face–a face–alone. Shoplifter. Solomon Edwards.
NNP

Which Pope must bear as well as I. On the Death of Doctor Swift.
Jonathan Swift. ViBoPo

Which ratifies the deed that you have done/With plain approval. Other plea
seek none. Troilus and Cressida. Aubrey Thomas De Vere. IrPN

Which refreshed that old man of Ewell. Limerick: "There was an old person
of Ewell." Edward Lear. TDH

Which, rejecting the thirties, gives th' epact you sought. A General Rule for
the Epact. *Anonymous.* FaBoUs

Which relieved that Old Man and his nose. There Was an Old Man, on
Whose Nose. Edward Lear. SoPo

Which relieved that old man of Three Bridges. Limerick: "There was an old
man of Three Bridges." Edward Lear. FaBoNo

Which rise from the forgotten past and the fading future. The Room and the
Windows. Feng Chih. LiTW

Which sadly annoyed Mistress Towl. Limerick: "There was an Old Woman
named Towl." *Anonymous.* FaBoNo; OxBChV

Which sails for the islands of balm/Luxuriant and warm. Kindness.
Thomas Sturge Moore. OBMV

Which seems to keep/Something inviolate. A living something. Einstein.
Archibald MacLeish. AnFE; APA; MoPo

Which, shaken out, take wing and breed/new altercations, the old silences.
Moving in Winter. Adrienne Rich. DFF

Which shakes which unflowers unleafs/the bush and the forest rose. Veneris
Venefica Agrestis. Lucio Piccolo. OBVE

Which shall confound with its loud whistling noise/Her pleasing shrieks, and
fan thy panting joys. On the Marriage of T. K. and C. C. the Morning
Stormy. Thomas Carew. BoLoP

Which shall keep me safe till I wake/And rise, and fall away. After the
Night Hunt. James Dickey. PoA

Which she may reward with half a gentle smile. Women Don't Travel in
Clubcars. George Jonas. NeAC

Which shocked all the pure and fastidious. Limerick: "There once was a
sculptor called Phidias." Oliver Herford. LiBL

Which show, through gaps and tatters, red stains half-/hidden away. Down
the Mississippi. John Gould Fletcher. LaNeLa

Which shows that gambling's not a sin/Provided that you always win. Snow
White and the Seven Dwarfs. Roald Dahl. DFT

Which side are you on? Which Side Are You On? Florence Reese. FSW

Which side is the mirror on? A Game of Glass. Alastair Reid. NePoEA;
PoCh

Which side?/This side. The Most Beautiful Girl in the World. Lorenz
Hart. OBAL

Which Simus here hath set/His buried child to mourn. The Fountain at the
Tomb. Nicias. AWP

...Which sinks at length/Prone, and the aerial ice clings over it. Prometheus
Unbound. Percy Bysshe Shelley. PBBP

Which, sir, are you, and which am I,/Upon an August day? In lands I never
saw, they say. Emily Dickinson. NePA

Which slashed the Ideal/and himself to bits. Die Neuen Heiligen (excerpt).
John Updike. DBV

Which smiled upon them, once, in Paradise. Butterflies. Alfred Noyes.
BoC

Which some strong tide had roll'd upon the place. The Borough. George
Crabbe. OBRV

Which spares the lazy, Proud, yet Bashful Wit,/The Trouble, Pains, or Shame
of asking it. To a Witty Man of Wealth and Quality... William
Wycherley. SeCV 1-2

Which spent, one death bring to ye both one grave. The Entertainment, or
Porch-Verse, at the Marriage.... Robert Herrick. CaPo

Which star he sees since Hesper set. Night-Piece. Léonie Adams. MoAB;
MoAmPo

Which still must bear the title of my wrong,/Caused by those cruel beams tht
were so strong. To Delia. Samuel Daniel. OBSC

Which storms lay low in kindly doom,/And kill them in their flush of bloom.
On the Slain Collegians. Herman Melville. MAmP

Which streams upon her stream, and glass'd within it glows. Childe Harold's
Pilgrimage: Canto IV, XXVIII. George Gordon, Lord Byron. AnFE

(Which stroll hither and thither through the/evening in bruised narrow
questioning faces). Two X "16 heures l'Etoile." Edward Estlin
Cummings. FaBoMo

...Which take light/never so well as under the deep mourning of the night?
Evening Twilight. Charles Baudelaire. SyP

...Which the/click of the powerful but well-oiled spring pleasantly confirms.
The Delights of the Door. Francis Ponge. NU

Which the coming day will ask. Prime. W. H. Auden. CMoP

Which the keen evening star is shining through. Evening. Percy Bysshe
Shelley. SyP

Which the men who uncover our graves/will find in a thousand years/shining
and whole. Gold. Donald Hall. ConAP; PAI

Which the same I am free to maintain. The Heathen Pass-ee. Arthur
Clement Hilton. CenHV; FaBoCo; NOBL

Which the same I am free to maintain. Plain Language from Truthful James.
Bret (Francis Bret Harte) Harte. BeLS; BLPA; BPAW; CTC; FaBoBe;
FaBoCo; HBV 1-2; InMe; NOBL; OBAL; TreF; YaD

Which thing was done with good intent,/And thus I left them feasting.
Nymphidia. Michael Drayton. OAEP

Which think ye looked the more fair? Hope and Despair. Lascelles
Abercrombie. HBV 1-2; OBMV

Which through the deep dark night in the olden time/Came sounding o'er the
lone Ionian. The Deep Dark Night. Alfred, Lord Tennyson. SeCePo

Which thus breath'd out with earthquake of his heart. Arcadia. Sir Philip
Sidney. SiPS

Which till their eyes ache, let iron men envy! O Sweet Delight. Thomas
Campion. EG

The which to heare vouchsafe, O dearest/dread, a-while! The Faerie Queene.
Edmund Spenser. EnLit; FiP; OAEP

Which to that shining muster/Yields in a sweet surrender. The Dispraise of
Absalom. *Anonymous.* BIrV

Which to the poor and the oppressed,/Gives its best time and thought.
Christ, the Man. William Henry Davies. WGRP

Which true lovers always admire. Lord Lovel. *Anonymous.* AmFP; FSW

Which tugged at the tree roots below the river. In the Deep Channel.
William Stafford. NaP

Which us in Him, and Him in us,/United keeps for ever. The Knot. Henry
Vaughan. ISi

Which used to lead something into somewhere) Ponder, Darling, These
Busted Statues. Edward Estlin Cummings. CMoP; NIP; NoAm

Which vexed all the folks on the Border. Limerick: "There was an Old Man
on the Border." Edward Lear. CenHV; EBEV

Which vexed the fat man of Bombay. Limerick: "As a little fat man of
Bombay." *Anonymous.* OxBChV

The which vouchsafe O goddesse to accept,/Amongst thy deerest relicks to be
kept. Amoretti, XXII. Edmund Spenser. AAS

Which walk upon the sea, and chant melodiously! Prometheus Unbound.
Percy Bysshe Shelley. NOBE; PBBP; ViBoPo

Which wanting, I must die,/Or having, I shall live? The Crazy World.
William Gay. BoAV; PoAu 1-2

Which was a cater-piller. So t'will dye. On Court-Worme. Ben Jonson.
SeCP

...Which was all/your life, Mother, and/all of mine. Childhood. Sherod
Santos. AMV-81

Which was best?/The heart knows. Adam's Dying. Ridgely Torrence.
FYAP

Which was it? Vague Lyric by G.M. Max Beerbohm. FaBoEE

Which was lucky since the house fell in right after,/Like a ton of brick. The
Fall of the House of Usher. Reed Whittemore. GP

The which was never defiled./Terly terlow. Terly Terlow. *Anonymous.*
AtBAP; CBEP

...Which was once/From thy mild manners quietly exalted. Epitaph.
Gabriello Chiabrera. AWP

Which was our star this night? This Night. William Heyen. MAYP

Which was your image), ride more slowly on.　The Statue.　Hilaire Belloc. MoVE; PoL

Which wasn't exacaly fair.　March Hares.　Walter De la Mare.　FaBoNo

Which way the little white doves　The Sea Shroud.　Jack Kerouac.　PoM

"Which way to the post office, boy?"/"I don't know. You don't know/much, do you?"...　The People, Yes.　Carl Sandburg.　OBAL

Which way, which way, with hope hard as a boulder?　Tired of Eating Kisses.　Edward Vincent Swart.　PeSA

Which we are and shall be forever.　Fellow-Citizens.　Verner von Heidenstam.　PoPl

Which we both thought was yours/A comparatively short time ago. Temporal.　George Jonas.　NOBC

Which we dutifully offer to our mother-land!　Anglicized Utopia.　Sir William Schwenck Gilbert.　OBSV

Which we have reared in asceticism/and chastity/And the yoke of the Ten/ Commandments.　This Be Our Revenge.　Saul Tchernichovsky.　TrJP

Which we held in idea, a little handful.　The Horse Chestnut Tree.　Richard Eberhart.　AtBAP; CMoP; CrMA; LiTM; MoAB; MoAmPo; NePA; NePoAm; PoPl

Which we painted out. Which we painted out.　The Empire Clock.　Bernard Spencer.　OBTV

Which were covered with doglime,/angel hair and bad news.　A Box for Tom.　James Tate.　FiCP

Which were our enemies, which were our friends!　To a President.　Witter ("Emanuel Morgan") Bynner.　OBAL

Which when as fame in her shrill trump shal thunder/Let the world chose to envy or to wonder.　Amoretti, LXXXV.　Edmund Spenser.　AAS

"Which, when in happy contrast join'd,/Delights th'inform'd, well-judging mind."　The Tour of Dr. Syntax: In Search of the Picturesque.　William Combe.　OBRV

Which when Sol's rays were once display'd/Sunk in their sockets and decay'd. On His Mistress.　William Strode.　PoEL 1-5

Which, when they fall, then look for a confusion.　Rare News.　Nicholas Breton.　NIP

Which, while they also fall, tell time like clocks.　The River God. Sacheverell Sitwell.　MoBrPo

Which who in death would live to see/Must learn in life to die like thee.'　A Hymn to the Name and Honour of the Admirable Saint Teresa.　Richard Crashaw.　HAP; JCP; LoBV; NOBE; NoP; OAEP; OBEV; OBS; PoEL 1-5; SeCV 1-2

Which, whosoe'er first stamps it, brings in trouble/All that receive it.　An Execration against Whores.　John Webster.　TW

Which will close again behind it.　The Kings of the World...　Rainer Maria Rilke.　NU

Which will shine like stars/on some Lady's neck in some City's night. Magaica.　Noemia De Sousa.　WhB

Which willfully parades in/its room, refusing to move.　Poem: "I watched an armory combing its bronze bricks."　Frank O'Hara.　NoP

Which wine itself enough can do.　The Cup.　John Oldham.　AWP

Which wins–Earth's poet or the Heavenly Muse.'　Thamuris Marching. Robert Browning.　OAEL 1-2

Which with the Morn for Lustre strive,/That I may look on her, and live. Song. Set by Mr. Coleman.　Charles Cotton.　OBS

Which with unnumbered cares this caitiff crew shall rive.　A Burlesque Ode, on the Author's Clearing a New House...(excerpt).　George Keate.　NOEC

Which wore a Star for God's own Son!　Discarded Christmas Tree. Elizabeth-Ellen Long.　ChBR

Which would a gone into the seas and brought proud Ward to me.'　Captain Ward and the Rainbow.　Anonymous.　BaBo; ESPB; OBET; ViBoFo

Which would be inconvenient/but final.　I Can Change Myself.　Margaret Atwood.　NeAC

Which would not be our way/if we truly thought we were gods.　These Green-Going-to-Yellow.　Marvin Bell.　FYAP; LCAP

Which you had never seen, or could not taste.　Hogarth.　Charles Churchill. DBV

Which you in breast, hair, heart, and face, may see.　Laura.　Robert Tofte. EIL

Which you won't let me see.　We Are Standing Facing Each Other. Margaret Atwood.　NeAC

Whiche lyfe god sende me to myne endyng day.　I Am Called Childhood. Sir Thomas More.　NCEP

Whichever way I chanced to blow.　A Kite.　Anonymous.　SoPo; TiPo

Whil'st I do talk with my Creator thus.　A Sinner's Lament.　Edward, Lord Herbert of Cherbury.　SeCP

Whil'st still the more he kick'd and/spurr'd,/The less the sullen jade has stirr'd.　Hudibras.　Samuel (1612-80) Butler.　SeCV 1-2

While a bird jigs and ol' Bunk/Johnson blows his horn.　A History of Love. William Carlos Williams.　VGW

While a blue tomb/lurks icily in/the dark.　Love.　Tom Dent.　NNP

While a bolder note than this might swell/From my lyre within the sky. Israfel.　Edgar Allan Poe.　AmePo; AP; APA; AWP; BLPL; HBV 1-2; InPo; LiTA; MAmP; NePA; NOBA; OxBA; PoEL 1-5; TAP; TreFS; WHA

While a cloud that floats o'er is reflected within it.　A Fable for Critics. James Russell Lowell.　AnNE; OxBA; TAP

While a coarse English tongue will itch/For whore and rogue; and dog and bitch.　An Epigram on Scolding.　Jonathan Swift.　FaBoEE

While a shaggy-haired man/Climbed up after a broomstick leaning against the wall.　The Air Vision.　Jakov van Hoddis.　VWA

While a tubular hunger/Slowly consumes him.　Stages.　Roy Macnab. ACV

While a white picket fence/Goes racing through the yard.　After Midnight. D.G. Jones.　WHW

While above, a meteor, luminous and brief,/is accepting and releasing our piece of light.　At Camino.　Timothy Sheehan.　SUW

While, above them, that harp assumes their sighs.　Seascape.　Stephen Spender.　AtBAP; CoBMV; MOS; NoP

While age and youth in chorus join/And praise the majesty divine.　Almighty Sovereign of the Skies!　Nathan Strong.　AH

While Albert Pierce could but respond, "Hey,/Shoo!" and had him till next Monday.　The Virus.　Christian Morgenstern.　PV

While all about us peal the loud, sweet, Te Deums of the/Canterbury bells. Madonna of the Evening Flowers.　Amy Lowell.　AmLP; PeHV; TreFT

While all around me the walleyes/are pop-eyed at my feet.　Stockton Lake; Stockton, Missouri.　Mark Sanders.　WOLT

...While all around the bags/crank up slack as widow's dugs in rain.　Hard Times, But Carrying On.　Dave Smith.　TAT

While all heaven is beaming o'er us,/Safe in the promised land.　Where Now Are the Hebrew Children?　Anonymous.　AH

While all my children leaped/Out of the glowing wood.　The Scourge. Stanley Jasspon Kunitz.　CrMA

While all night I lie awake and listen/In a damned and ghostly house in Houndsditch!　The Vindictive Staircase or The Reward of Industry. Wilfred Wilson Gibson.　AnFE

While all the little brown birds sing upon the spray.　Ditty to an Air from Bach.　Robert Louis Stevenson.　TrGrPo

While all the rivers of her red veins move into the sea.　Keine Lazarovitch. Irving Layton.　ACV

While all their duty is to shine for love.　Titian's "Bacchanal" in the Prado at Madrid (excerpt).　Thomas Sturge Moore.　QFR

While all who honour Virtue, gently mourn/LLANGOLLEN's vanish'd Pair, and wreath their sacred urn.　Llangollen Vale (excerpt).　Anna Seward. PeHV

While all your Neighbor Princes unto you/Like Joseph's Sheaves pay reverence and bow.　A Panegyrick to My Lord Protector.　Edmund Waller.　OBS

While america wanders/dumb with her wet bowels.　Poem: "Look at Me 8th Grade."　Sonia Sanchez.　PoBA

While Ampersy-and he licked the dish.　A Curious Discourse That Passed between the Twenty-Five Letters...　Anonymous.　FaBoUs

While an avalanche whispers our names.　In a Museum in the Capital. William Stafford.　LCAP

While an elephant raised his hat.　Look at All Those Monkeys.　Spike Milligan.　OnUR

While any dog living/Outroars a dead lion.　Koheleth.　Louis Untermeyer. TrJP

While, as my strength, my rock, my all,/Saviour! I cling to Thee?　My Soul Shall Cling to Thee.　Charlotte Elliot.　BePJ

While at a window someone stood and cried.　The Adepts.　Lawrence Durrell.　ErPo

A while at labour not too heavy; it would be/delightful!　St. Columcille's Island Hermitage.　Anonymous.　AnIL

While beauties reddest inke Venus for him doth sturre.　Astrophel and Stella, CII.　Sir Philip Sidney.　AAS; SiPS

While below herds crop the well-kept fields by night.　The Dysynni Valley (Wales).　Theodore Holmes.　CoPo

While billows endless round the beaches die.　The Enviable Isles.　Herman Melville　AA; AnAmPo; FaBoBe

While black hands dip/Lumps of their constitution/In the same soup bowl. The Change.　Samuel Chimsoro.　WhB

While blowing kisses through my hoary hair.　It's True I'm No Miss America.　Stephanie Slowinsky.　AMV-80

While boys and tides maraud about her bows.　Freighter.　Bruce Ruddick. CaP

While broken tea-cups, wisely kept for show,/Rang'd o'er the chimney, glisten'd in a row.　The Deserted Village.　Oliver Goldsmith.　AnFE

While bugs and diamonds agonize my roots.　You All Are Static; I Alone Am Moving.　Peter Viereck.　LiTA

While bushes weep loud tears to see it go.　Snow Harvest.　Andrew Young. BoNaP

While Captain Slocum's riding lights/Danced a jig between the poles.　Sailing, Sailing.　Gray Burr.　CoPo; NYBP

While cars and buses grunted by him on both sides.　Uptown.　Paul Zweig. NYP

While cheeks burn, arms open, eyes shut and lips meet!　Now.　Robert Browning.　CBEP; VLP

While Christ rode on ahead.   Captain of the Years.   Arthur R., Jr. Macdougall.   TRV

While clothed in soft, white light, the dark wolf digs.   Nightwood.   William Jay Smith.   PoA

While comrade flags flame forth on wall and towers!   My Love for Thee. Richard Watson Gilder.   HBV 1-2

While countless generations pass away.   On the Building of Springfield. Vachel Lindsay.   MoRP; NAMP; OHFP; WHA

While David held the head/For those who stood by.   Killing.   Samuel Greenberg.   LiTA

While de wind blows down de chimney we will shake with fright.   Jesse James. (Version B).   *Anonymous.*   ABF

While Death and Winter closed the autumn scene.   The Closing Scene. Thomas Buchanan Read.   AA; HBV 1-2

While death waits on either side,–before/and behind us, Death!   When the Most Is Said.   Mary Ainge De Vere.   AA; HBV 1-2

While deep within our souls it glows/From all His starry studios!   In God's Eternal Studios.   Paul Shivell.   HBV 1-2

While Dolly's afraid she shall die an old maid,/Mumpaty, mumpaty, mump. Roger and Dolly.   Henry Carey.   CoMu; NOEC

While dust turns back to dust.   Ash Wednesday.   Daniel Burke.   AMV-80

While Earth's splendor and renown/Mounted light as thistle-down.   St. Michael the Weigher.   James Russell Lowell.   AnFE; AnNE; APA; CAW

While either transporting a star or letting go of a street.   2nd Dance–Seeing Lines–6 February 1964.   Jackson MacLow.   CoPo

While elsewhere the profane crowds would walk/Unthinking their free and many ways to death.   Praising the Poets of That Country.   Howard Nemerov.   PP

While ever to her young Eulalie upturns her violet eye.   Eulalie. A Song. Edgar Allan Poe.   EvOK; LaNeLa; Par

While every man swore he was poisoned/By eating Miss Fogerty's cake. Miss Fogerty's Cake.   *Anonymous.*   BLPA; NLV

While every upright shining hair/On its short ruffle of a mane,/Dances with joy.   The Newborn Colt.   Mary Kennedy.   PH

While everyone else shouts helpfully to the gears to shift.   Human Relations. Emmett Jarrett.   NeAC

While fades the song of what but seems.   Noon's Dream-Song.   Eugene Lee-Hamilton.   NOBV

While fairies ride the silver ferry/Between the rose-bud and the cherry.   Of a Spider.   Wilfrid Thorley.   BrR

While fairy zephyrs deck each brow!   Uprising See the Fitful Lark. *Anonymous.*   NA

While faithful love the watch should keep,/To banish danger from thy sleep. Winter Song.   Elizabeth Tollet.   NOEC

While folks less confident than they/Stare, in mute wonder,–and give way. Advice to Julia.   Henry Luttrell.   OBRV

While for the princess? She went back to play!/Tra-rill-a-la-lo!   The Yak. Virna Sheard.   CaP; PeCV; WHW

While freed Religion, like primeval light/Bursting from chaos, spreads her warmth/divine.   Ode Written at Vale-Royal Abbey in Cheshire.   Thomas Warton, Jr..   CoBE

While friends, heartbroken, search for Paul/MacGregor James D. Cuthbert Hall.   The Revolving Door.   Newman Levy.   ShM

While from below all Grub Street rings.   The Progress of Poetry.   Jonathan Swift.   CABA; CBEP; EiCP; InvP; NOBI; OnYI

While from former valleys/mountains now are made.   The Calendar of Oengus: Prologue (excerpt).   *Anonymous.*   NOBI

...While from quivering leaves/Streams down deep slumber.   Orchard Song. Sappho.   LiTW

While from the glade a worthier maid looked on with longing eyes.   It Always Happens.   Horace.   UnTE

While girlish in a corner/a dream sobs tenderly.   Abishag Writes a Letter Home.   Itzik Manger.   VWA

While God is marching on.   The Battle Hymn of the American Republic. Julia Ward Howe.   AA; AH; AmLP; AnAmPo; APA; BLPA; BLSo; EaLo; FaBoBe; FaFP; FaPo; FaPoR; FSW; GN; GoTF; HBV 1-2; HBVY; MC; NePA; NOBA; NOCV; OBVV; OBWP; OHIP; PAH; PAL; PSoN; SCV; TAP; TrAS; TreF; TRV; WBLP; WGRP; YaD

While God's hand in secrecy/Builds thy bright eternity.   O Land Beloved. George Edward Woodberry.   PAH

While grass and stars and flowers spell out His name.   Life's Common Duties.   Minot Judson Savage.   WBLP

While greasy Joan doth keel the pot.   Love's Labour's Lost.   William Shakespeare.   AWP; BiP; BoNaP; DiPo; EiL; ExPo; FaBoCh; FaBoEn; FF; FiP; GN; GoJo; GTBS; GTBS-P; HAP; HBV 1-2; HeIP; InPK; InPo; LiTB; LoGBV; MCCG; NIP; NOBE; NoP; OAEL 1-2; OBEV; OBSC; PAI; PBBP; PoEL 1-5; PoRA; PoSC; PrIm; RoGo; SeCePo; SeCeV; SoSe; TEP; TreFS; TrGrPo; UnPo; ViBoPo; WeW; WHA; WiR

While he had strength, and you/Know that all that love can do.   A Juggle of Myrtle Twigs.   Edward Codish.   VWA

While he is away.   The Absence.   Sylvia Townsend Warner.   MoBrPo

While he joined the wheel again/for another/crack at all.   DOA in Dulse. Diane Burns.   STE

...While he lives, let him alone.   An Artist.   Robinson Jeffers.   VGW

While he remains king upon the dry land/I'll remain king of the sea.   Sir Andrew Barton (Andrew Batann).   *Anonymous.*   AmFP

While he swings on a temple bell filched from/Lahore.   Deprecating Parrots. Beulah May.   EtS

:While he was passed/by even the worst of men at least sour wine.   Ecce Homunculus.   R. A. K. Mason.   AnNZ

While he who carved you burns with fiery blood.   The Venus of Bolsover Castle.   Sacheverell Sitwell.   HBMV

While Heaven gave him his cherry-/stones and file!   An Art Master.   John Boyle O'Reilly.   AA

While Heaven seems just within our reach/At timber line.   At Timber Line. Frank H. Mayer.   PoOW

While her pillow stilled her screaming,/she dissected her own heart.   Emily Dickinson.   Inger Hagerup.   AMV-81

While her tired husband and her children sleep.   The Nymphs (excerpt). [James Henry] Leigh Hunt.   OBRV

While here by Eden's gate I linger/Love's tryst to keep, with truant Eve. The Lover and the Syringa Bush.   Herman Melville.   OBAL

While here, half-mad, half-fed, half-sarkit,/Is a' th' amount.   The Vision. Robert Burns.   BSV

While here I cling, in life's short agony,/To God, and to your deathless memory.   Thysia.   Morton Luce.   HBV 1-2

While, here the Nap, oh sad mishap,/Is taken by the Lilliputians!   To Sir Hudson Lowe.   Thomas Moore.   OBSV

While here their name and race shall last.   In Pleasant Lands Have Fallen the Lines.   James Flint.   AH

While high above, the restless children dance/Across the tightrope of their unconcern.   The Circus.   Milton Kaplan.   GoYe

While his bow'd head seem'd list'ning to the Earth,/His ancient mother, for some comfort yet...   Hyperion.   John Keats.   ExPo

While His patience holds out for you!   Will God's Patience Hold Out for You?   Edythe Johnson.   STF

While History on her ample page/The virtues shall enroll/Of that Paternal Soul.   Abraham Lincoln.   Richard Henry Stoddard.   AA; FaBoBe; PAH

While I am at my own work/To bring difficulty to clearness.   The Monk and His Pet Cat.   *Anonymous.*   CH; OnYI

While I am carried by the wind/Across the sky.   Song of the Thunders. *Anonymous.*   OBVE

While I am doom'd–by life's long storm opprest,/To gaze with envy on their gloomy rest.   Press'd by the Moon, Mute Arbitress of Tides.   Charlotte Smith.   SBG

While I, at whom their grim lips curled, live on/And will be young when their last dust is gone!   The Poet.   Anita Grannis.   HBMV

While I can either sing, or whistle,/Your friend and servant.   Holy Willie's Prayer.   Robert Burns.   EnRP

While I can have the woods and fields.   I Fear No Power a Woman Wields. Ernest McGaffey.   AA; HBV 1-2

While I despair my sun's sight to enjoy.   Astrophel and Stella, XCVII.   Sir Philip Sidney.   AAS; SiPS

While I droop here.   I Am a Parcel of Vain Strivings Tied.   Henry David Thoreau.   AnNE; AP; LiTA; MAmP; NOBA; NoP; PoEL 1-5; TAP

While I endure her Chains.   Love's Slavery.   John, of Buckingham Sheffield. CEP

While I every moment am reborn.'   Reborn.   Kingsley Amis.   OxBC

While I examine my hands.   The Leap.   James Dickey.   NIP

While I have such a lovely brain/And you have such a lively body.   Equals. Louis Untermeyer.   UnTE

While I...I suffer wordlessly,/Because he left the sea for me.   A Sailor's Wife. Clara Bernhardt.   CaP

While I in wonder sing this sacrifice,/To beauty sacred, and those Angell-eyes. Song: "O faire sweet face, O eyes celestiall bright."   Francis Beaumont and John Fletcher.   PoEL 1-5

While I'm out hunting tigers–/not for dinner, just for tigers.   In the Field. Phyllis Janik.   IHMS

While I–oh, ask not what I do with mine!/Would I were such!   To a Swallow Building under Our Eaves.   Jane Welsh Carlyle.   HBV 1-2; OBRV

While I rust here.   The Black Knight.   John Todhunter.   OBVV

While I shall sleep, while I–while I–forget!   Rispetto.   Agnes Mary Frances (Mme Emile Duclaux) Robinson.   HBMV

While I shall strive to rouse her sons once/more.   The British Lyon Roused. Stephen Tilden.   PAH

While I speak out–a broken-record warning:/Kyrie eleison, forsaken. Censorship.   Philip Brasfield.   LFAC

While I stay under the cedar, fixed here?   Sitting in the Woods: A Contemplation.   W. R. Moses.   NCSH

While I tickle round your knee.   An Old Maid, an Old Maid.   *Anonymous.* OxNR

While I, upon an unknown, well-known shore,/Keep vigil.   Vigil.   Marjorie Freeman Campbell.   CaP

"The while ich thrille me a thred,/Nu ich have ned." Snatches: "So longe ich have, lavedy." *Anonymous.* OxBM

While in God's patient hands his arrows rust! Sonnets: A Sequence on Profane Love. George Henry Boker. AmePo

While in Grandma's lap, with a broken thread,/The finished stocking lies. Sermon in a Stocking. Ellen A. Jewett. BLPA

While in his ears the eternal bugles blow. The Storm-Child. Mary C. G. Byron. HBV 1-2

While in his inner chamber Alkinoos/retired to rest where his dear consort lay. The Odyssey, VII. Virgil (Publius Vergilius Maro). NAWM 1-2

While, in its secret valley,/Withers the herb of joy. The Lingam and the Yoni. A. D. Hope. MAT; NoAm; WeW

While in my Dream's despite/The minutes run to hours. To Music. William Kean Seymour. HBMV

While in other circles move the frail/Inquirers, trailing printed liberty. Scholar II. Seamus Deane. CIP; NOBI

While in the corner a hound/& bitch are quarreling/over the hero's bone. Hero's Portion. John Montague. NOBI

While in this Coach these sweetly sing,/As they to Glory ride therein. The Joy of Church Fellowship Rightly Attended. Edward Taylor. AmP; CBEP; MAmP; OxBA; SCAP

While it breaks, breaks, breaks on the sheltering bars. The Heart of a Woman. Georgia Douglas Johnson. BANP; BlSi; CDC; PoLf; PoNe

While it condemns a less delinquent for 't. The Law. Samuel (1612-80) Butler. NLV

While it consumes the substance of my own. Five Birds Rise. William Hayward. NYBP

While it lives its breath is Summer's glow! Autumn Song. Johann Ludwig Tieck. AWP

While it supplants Hell. Song of a Rat. Ted Hughes. CMoP; NoP

While jocund we follow our Hounds in full cry. A Hunting Song. Paul Whitehead. OBEC

The while John Gilbert spoke–The/Epilogue. An Epilogue at Wallack's. John Elton Wayland. AA

While Jove's planet rises yonder, silent over Africa. Home-Thoughts, from the Sea. Robert Browning. AWP; CBEP; FaBoCh; FaPoR; FiP; GTBS; InPo; MaVP; MBW 1-2; MOS; NOBE; OAEP; OBEV; OBSP; OBVV

While Knavery, laughing, rung her passing bell. Plain Dealing's Downfall. *Anonymous.* OBSV

While lasting joys the man attend/Who has a polish'd female friend! The Female Friend. Cornelius Whur. FaBoCo

While Law, that still should help the weak,/Gave spurs to aid the strong. Ye Simple Men. John Stuart Blackie. PoSH

While like a knife a scarlet bird/sings deserts in the lemon-trees. The Last Summer. Vivian Smith. PoAu 1-2

While like a seamless garment overhead/Stretched endlessly the blue, unclouded skies. To One Who Died in Autumn. Virginia McCormick. HBMV

While, like a skylark, sings his last glad sculpture/Its flame salute. At the Salon. Florence Wilkinson. HBV 1-2

While, like wise English, unconcern'd, you sit,/And see us play the Tragedy of Wit. Aureng-Zebe. John Dryden. FiP; SeCV 1-2

While lingers in the heart one line/The nameless poet hath a shrine. The Unknown Grave. Letitia Elizabeth Landon. VLP

While London, queen of cities! proudly vies,/And often grasps the well-disputed prize. Cricket. An Heroic Poem. James Dance. NOEC

A while longer,/Still here. Before the Stuff Comes down. Gary Snyder. HeIP

While lost and empty lies Eternity. Variations on a Time Theme. Edwin Muir. NoAm

While louts who never learned their letters/Are perched in Heaven above their betters? Scholars. *Anonymous.* DBV; KiLC

While Love still spends itself in Motherhood. Motherhood. Karl M. Chworowsky. PGD

While Lucifer is left, condemn'd and/unforgiven. The Dream of Gerontius. John Henry, Cardinal Newman. VLP

While man–his hill is hardly crowned/Before another hill is found! Three Green Trees. Angela Morgan. HBMV

While Maritza/tunes the two chords of her guitar. The Road Is Wider Than Long (excerpt). Roland Penrose. EAS

While master fiddles his fiddle-stick/For dame and doodle doo. Cock a Doodle Doo. *Anonymous.* HBVY; OxNR

While me tender mother her hair she ture. As I Was Walkin' Down Wexford Street (with music). *Anonymous.* AS

While men and angels, stars and suns,/Unite to praise Thee evermore! Reconciliation. Elizabeth Doten. TrPWD

While men were meditating war with which the world still bleeds. Uneasy Peace. Edmund Charles Blunden. BrPo

While Morning buckles on his red,/And on the Dachshunds go. Dachshunds. William Jay Smith. OBAL

While Mother coolly bakes beside/Her little jugged apocalypse. Bendix. John Updike. NYBP

While mother-naked after/A laurel branch I bore. The Herd Boy. Haniel Long. HBMV

While mourns one ardent heart, one poet-brain,/For vanished Hellas and Hebraic pain. Venus of the Louvre. Emma Lazarus. AA; AnAmPo; SBG

While my battered conscience tussles/With my thought-resistant brain. Summer Song. W. W. Watt. FiBHP; QQQ

While my face of yellow horn plunges in the wind. The Fathers. Benjamin Saltman. VWA

While my hard-laboured poem pines/Unsold upon the printer's lines. To Dr. Delany (excerpt). Jonathan Swift. PP

While my jolly little farmer goes whistling to his plow. The Jolly Farmer. *Anonymous.* BFSS

While my lady sleeps in the shade below. The Siesta. *Anonymous.* AWP

While my mother doggedly straightened the mirrors. Cleaning Day. Jose Kozer. VWA

While Nancy earns the praise to Shakespeare due,/For glorious puddings and immortal pies. William Shakespeare to Mrs. Anne,... Thomas Gray. CEP

While nine lions topple for every lion that roars. Dog Alive. Harold Witt. BoAnP

While o'er my soul God spreads his mantle–peace. Life's Evening. Dudley Foulke. WGRP

While o'er our cabinets Confucius nods,/Midst porcelain elephants and china gods. Of Taste; An Essay. James Cawthorn. NOEC

While o'er thy myrtled lawns I stray/Beneath, O maiden Moon! thy ray. Moon. Henry Rowe. OBEV

While on his face a death's head sat/And waved a bit of crape. For a Pessimist. Countee Cullen. ShM

While on this fluent globe my glasse shall role,/And run the rest of my remaining dust. Tears at the Grave of Sir Albertus Morton. Sir Henry Wotton. SeCP

While one dove on a branch mourns/or birds fly. Lamenting Tauaba. Laila Akhyaliyya. BoWoP

While our hearts remember Bethlehem,/And a cross on a far green hill. We Have Seen His Star in the East. Molly Anderson Haley. PGD

While our hosannahs all along the passage/Shout the Redeemer. The Day of Judgement. Isaac Watts. CEP; HAP; LoBV; NOBE; NOEC; NoP; OBEC; OBEV; SeCePo

While our joyes so multiply,/As shall mocke the envious eye. Counting Kisses. Caius Valerius Catullus. LiTW

While our joyes so multiply,/As shall mocke the envious eye. Out of Catullus. Richard Crashaw. CavP

While our spurs Clink! Clink! up the Esplanade and down? Budmouth Dears. Thomas Hardy. CH; MoVE; PoPle

While over her tan impassivity/Shot silk is shining. A Street in Bronzeville: Southeast Corner. Gwendolyn Brooks. VGW

While over the animal sea my first-drawn sob/Straightened to share your dawn. For Thomas Hardy. Jane Cooper. AmPC

While over us the elaborate night/Mysteriously gleams and glares. Cat. Lytton Strachey. PCat

While overhead, ignored in the walk,/are the leaves touching each other and/the sun. Promenade. David Ignatow. TrJP

While overhead the far, uncaring stars wheel by. Desert Shipwreck. Barbara Leslie Jordan. GoYe

While pain sits ever closer to my heart. Tears. Khansa. AWP

While, patient in the eaves, the shadows wait. A Room in the Villa. William Jay Smith. NYBP

While Patty Sweet Patty Sat Locked In My/Arms. Child Harold: Ballad. John Clare. FaBoPP; OBNC; VLP

While pitiless the tempest wild/Sore on you beats. A Winter Night. Robert Burns. BSV; MCCG

While poets sing in tripping rime/That Spring's a simply ripping time! Twist-Rime on Spring. Arthur Guiterman. PoSC

While poor black cherubs rise at seven/To do celestial chores. For a Lady I Know. Countee Cullen. CDC; GoSl; HeIP; IDB; InPK; NIP; OBAL; PoNe; ShM; TAP

While poor Leigh's one vaunted stunt/Was with Jenny. Osculation. Henry Sydnor Harrison. InMe

While promises were made by all/To come enmasse to our next ball. The Fight at Nevadaville. *Anonymous.* PoOW

While proud, cold England sinks with shame. The Dying Sergeant. *Anonymous.* AmFP

While pulse and leaf rustle and grow climatic. Summer Resort. P. K. Page. CaP

While Rabelais pipes you a wished-for death/On a kazoo quaint and silvered. Letter to a Librarian. Irving Layton. MAT; TW

While rain depends, the pensive cat gives o'er/Her frolics, and pursues her tail no more. The Cat and the Rain. Jonathan Swift. PCat

While Rameses and Romeo/And little Ariadne sleep. Birthright. John Drinkwater. HBV 1-2; OxBTC; WHA

While richer boys are keeping/The girls that do not fade.   With Rue My Heart Is Laden (parody).   Samuel Hoffenstein.   UnPo

While rival beaux and jealous belles exist,/So long, White Conduit House, shall be thy fame.'   White Conduit House.   William Woty.   NOEC

While round bright Troy Achilles whirls/A corpse with streaming hair.   Ballad of Hector in Hades.   Edwin Muir.   NoAm; NOBE

While round these hallowed walls the storm/Of earthborn passion dies.   Dedication.   William Cullen Bryant.   BLRP

While sadly I lay powerless, less.   Personal Poem.   Kendrick Smithyman.   AnNZ

While Sally shall attend to the bar.   Blooming Sally.   *Anonymous.*   OBET

While self-dependent power can time defy,/As rocks resist the billows and the sky.   Farewell to Poetry.   Oliver Goldsmith.   OBEC

While she lies sleeping/Softly, now softly lies/Sleeping.   Tears.   *Anonymous.*   NOBE; OBEV

While sitting still, as still, as still/As anyone ever sat!   Narcissa.   Gwendolyn Brooks.   GrPl; NTCP

While sixteen chorus men sang Over There.   Victory in the Cabarets.   Louis Untermeyer.   HBMV

While small birds nestle in the hedge below.   Autumn Birds.   John Clare.   PBBP

While Solomon's towers crashed between,/The gird of Babylon's mirth.   The Destruction of Jerusalem by the Babylonian Hordes.   Isaac Rosenberg.   VWA

While some faint gleamings we can see/Of Freedom's coming morn?   We Will Speak Out.   James Russell Lowell.   GoTF; TreFT

While some glad girl beyond the hill/Dreamt of a new-born king.   Christmas Eve.   John Drinkwater.   HBMV

While some were homeward bound,/Sixteen hundred had to drown.   The Titanic (A vers.).   *Anonymous.*   ViBoFo

While someone from afar off/blows birthday candles for the world.   The Birth of Tragedy.   Irving Layton.   NoP; OBCV; PeCV

While song yet speaks an English tongue/By Charles' or Thamis' wave!   Henry Austin Dobson.   Henry Wadsworth Longfellow.   HBV 1-2

While Spenser is alive, it is no question.   Upon Master Edmund Spenser, the Famous Poet.   Francis Beaumont.   FaBoEE

While Stella holds her station still.   To Dr. Swift on His Birthday, 30th November 1721.   Esther Johnson.   EnLoPo

While steps to the door deliver us/From disappearing things, from things to begin from.   Moving Day.   Lewis B. Horne.   HoAn

While still so many yet must come to birth.   Indian Summer.   William Ellery Leonard.   HBMV; PG

While strength and hours run/checkless downhill.   Night-Music: Time Exposures.   Muriel Rukeyser.   PoA

...While struggling/for the words to write.   It is her cousin's death...   Gail Fox.   NOBC

While summer day to summer evening passes.   Summer Afternoon.   Basil Dowling.   AnNZ

While summer is hurrying its way in and out,/over and over,/in their room.   In the Beach House.   Anne Sexton.   PPP

While surgeons rinsed their bitter gloves.   Ulster.   Hans Adler.   AMV-81

While tears fell and wetted my clothes.   Return.   *Anonymous.*   LiTW

While that fine soil, which all these joys did yield,/By broken fence is proved a common field.   Caelica, CCCVIII.   Fulke, Lord Brooke Greville.   JCP

While that fine soyle, which all these joyes did yeeld,/By broken fence is prov'd a common field.   Caelica. I.   Fulke, Lord Brooke Greville.   AAS; FCP

While that futile Old Gentleman dozed.   Limerick: "There was an Old Man who supposed."   Edward Lear.   LBN; LiBL; NA; NOBV; NoP

While that Goose says, "Eat no more."   The Goblin Goose (parody).   *Anonymous.*   FaBoPa

While the arm of his friend rested upon him also.   Recorders Ages Hence.   Walt Whitman.   MoAmPo; NePA

While the band of music/Shall be sounding through the air.   You Will See Your Lord A-Coming.   *Anonymous.*   AH

While the bare rafters tick under the moon.   Bat Angels.   Larry Levis.   AmPA

(While the birds change from green to blue to brown).   To a Daughter with Artistic Talent.   Peter Meinke.   Psk

While the bitter bile/Overflows in my breast.   In the Sky, Clearest Blue.   Rosalia de Castro.   PBWP

While the blood-red target-sun, over our hill,/Topples to death.   Landscape, Deer Season.   Barbara Howes.   GoJo; LiSp; PoL

While the bluebird stole the carrot/And returned the glue to me.   The Monkey's Glue.   Goldwin Goldsmith.   NA

While the bold harpooneer is a-striking of the whale!   Captain Bunker.   *Anonymous.*   AmFP

While the bone moon/watches from a windless sky   Poem for Carroll Descendant of Chiefs.   Lance Henson.   VoR

...While the city/For which all long has never yet been built.   Peace in the Welsh Hills.   Vernon Watkins.   ChMP; GTBS-P; OxBTC

While the corn grows ripe and the apples mellow.   August.   Celia Thaxter.   YeAr

While the crack o' a laugh came back to me.   The Mountainy Childer.   Elizabeth Shane.   HBMV

While the crowd cowered/In sheer terror beneath them.   One Night away from Day.   John Digby.   EAS

While the dark houses harden into sleep.   Christmas Eve in Whitneyville, 1955.   Donald Hall.   UnPo

While the deft hand is sweeter than the eye.   The Shadowgraphs.   Richmond Lattimore.   NYBP

...While the distant goal/Of whispering horizons lures your sighs.   City Girl.   Maxwell Bodenheim.   HBMV

While the dog in the road/Dragging his injured hindquarters/To the curb/Teaches.   The Accident.   Raymond Richard Patterson.   CAD

While the earth bears a plant, or the sea rolls its waves.   Adams and Liberty.   Robert Treat Paine.   MC; PAH

While the equinoctials blow.   Autumn's Processional.   Dinah Maria Mulock.   GN

While the eternal ages watch and wait.   Three Sonnets on the Divina Commedia.   Henry Wadsworth Longfellow.   SeCeV

While the fields of his century move far,/& then farther away.   My Grandfather Always Promised Us.   Liam Rector.   AMV-80

While the fire went on quietly burning!   The House Remembers.   Robert Francis.   DFF

While the foaming sea-horses/Toss and turn over.   The Horses of the Sea.   Christina Georgina Rossetti.   GoJo; NTCP; SUS

While the fool may well be jolly/Though why he cannot say.   Though a Fool.   Robert Francis.   GP

While the goat calls hush-/a-bye.   Lullaby.   Anne Sexton.   NoAm

While the good wind blew out the lamp.   Cherry Blossoms.   Michael Lewis.   UnTE

An' while the gossamer's light netten/Sparkled to the zun a-zetten.   Zun-Zet.   William Barnes.   PoEL 1-5

While the Hand is writing on the wall?   The Handwriting on the Wall.   Knowles Shaw.   AmFP; BLPA

While the hands of the rude, insatiate clock/Go tick, tock, tick, tock.   Time Passes.   R. P. Lister.   NYBP

While the hollow oak our palace is,/Our heritage the sea.   A Wet Sheet.   Allan Cunningham.   BSV; EG; EtS; GoTF; GoTS; GTBS; GTBS-P; HBV 1-2; HBVY; MCCG; OBRV; PaPo; RoGo; TiPo; TreFS

While the judgments of God sweep the wicked away.   Echo Canyon.   *Anonymous.*   AmFP

While the lank sails clacked idly by/High on the windy hill.   Crazed.   Walter De la Mare.   OBSP

While the lifeblood/Runs in Gao-haida-gai!   The Copper Song.   Hermia Fraser.   CaP

...While the liquor flows like lava/In the parlour of the Marchioness of Dufferin and Ava.   Notes for a Revised Sonnet (parody).   Edward Pygge.   BXAP

While the long way behind is prophecy/Of those perfections which are yet to be.   The Rise of Man.   John White Chadwick.   AA

While the Lord holds his soul in command.   The Wild Mustard River.   *Anonymous.*   AmFP

While the lord of their desire/Sleeps below the crimson thorn.   Morning Glory.   Siegfried Sassoon.   TrCP

While the Loves all in a ring/Softly stroke the stiffened wing.   The Death of the Starling.   Samuel Taylor Coleridge.   PBBP

While the Loves all in a ring/Softly stroked the stiffened wing.   The Death of Lesbia's Bird.   Caius Valerius Catullus.   AWP

While the man I married twice/dressed and left for work.   Reject Jell-O.   Lucille Day.   AMV-81

While the masculine weenies were grabbin' er!   Limerick: "Our ambassador to Venus, Mz Abner."   *Anonymous.*   PeHV

The while the masons slowly closed the arch.   The Bridge.   Albert Verwey.   LiTW

While the mayor sits with his head in his hands.   The Great Society.   Robert Bly.   CAD; NoAm; NYP

While the men go to lecture with the wind in their gowns.   Autumn Morning at Cambridge.   Frances Cornford.   HBMV; MoVE; OBVV

While the menopause strikes at puberty.   Limerick: "Though the music of love is Schubery."   *Anonymous.*   PeHV

While the moaning of a tree/Will be all my elegy...   Soon at Last My Sighs and Moans.   Louis Ginsberg.   TrJP

While the morning sun flickered in the hollow sockets of my/eyes.   Algonkian Burial.   Alfred Goldsworthy Bailey.   OBCV

...While the mortal pair/Lie drowned in dreaming weariness.   The Small Man Orders His Wedding.   Clive Staples Lewis.   HW

While the musing sheep proceed/Fasting and mourning in sleep.   Complaint.   Joseph Bennett.   LiTA

While the old man unto Our Lady prays.   Autumn.   Detlev Freiherr von Liliencron.   AWP

While the one eludes, must the other pursue. Love's Pursuit. Robert Browning. TreFT

While the one who is saying goodbye/Lets go the hand of the one left standing. Goodbye. Sherod Santos. MAYP

While the other imaginatively rifles your drawers. Human Relations. C. H. Sisson. PoL; TW

While the other three will demons be, confined in Hell to stay. The Ashland Tragedy, II. *Anonymous.* AmFP

While the other was reading small print. Limerick: "There was a young lady of Flint." *Anonymous.* CenHV

While the prayerfulling miracle is given: Starry skies, arise! Bow Down, Mountain. Norma Farber. AH

While the Queen of the Wunks drifted over the tide/With a long piece of crape to her tail. Craqueodoom. James Whitcomb Riley. OBAL

...While the red evening/Climbs the fence and is gone. August at the Lake. David Young. AmPA

While the rest of us are beaten/into pebbles, plowshares, and fossils. The Law. Albert Haynes. NBP

While the rooster stretches/To the day not there yet. At the Cantina. Gary Soto. MAYP

While the sad waters of separation/Bear us on to the ultimate night. Exile. Ernest Christopher Dowson. BoLoP; BrPo

While the sands of night have run? On Waking from a Dreamless Sleep. Annie Fields. AA

While the scale with the soul in't so mightily fell/That it jerked the philosopher out of his cell. The Philosopher's Scales. Jane Taylor. HBV 1-2

While the slow mosses weave an end of my forgotten name. Who Were before Me. John Drinkwater. OBMV

While the Stars in their courses/Do fight on our side? An Astrologer's Song. Rudyard Kipling. MoBrPo

...While the Stock-dove breathes/A melancholy Murmur thro' the whole. Birds in Spring. James (1700-48) Thomson. OBEC

While the sun a good post-horse is found,/So merrily we'll run round. Fool's Song. Thomas Holcroft. NOEC

While the sun rides up the sky/in the cool morning./in the cool morning! An Old Woman's Song. Akjartoq. WPOW

While the sun slowly went his way/Across the sky. Remembering. Akjartoq. WTO

While the sun squats upon the waveless seas. More Sonnets at Christmas. Allen Tate. LiTA; LiTM; NePA; WaP

While the sun-warmed beaches and the sea/thunder their slow, eternal wars. Nocturne. Frances Frost. BoNaP

While the sunny beauty of blushing water/Came over the cheeks of MacSorley's daughter. Virgins. Francis Carlin. HBMV

...While the talk ran/Noisily by them, glib with prose. Poetry for Supper. R. S. Thomas. OxBC

While the talkers wear themselves out and/sit in corners alone, and glower. The Dancers Inherit the Party. Ian Hamilton Finlay. FF

While the tax gatherer spiders for his prey. Literary Zodiac. R. A. Piddington. PV

While the tropic sun on a grand deed done/Looks with his piercing eye! The Charge at Santiago. William Hamilton Hayne. MC; PAH

While the True Church remains below/Wrapt in the old miasmal mist. The Hippopotamus. Thomas Stearns Eliot. AnAmPo; AWP; HoPM; LiTB; NAMP; OBMV; PoPl; VGW

While the wild beast corpses, grouped like great bulbs/up-torn, cumbered the hollow places,... The Mu'allaqat: Ode. Imr el Kais. AWP

While the wind like a nightingale/sang with its whirling war axe. When he sailed into the harbor. Korinna. BoWoP

"While the woman I am/And the man you are/Are as far apart/As star and star." Idol. Louise Driscoll. HBMV

While their Breasts and their Bellies went Pintle a Pantle. A Ballad of Andrew and Maudlin. *Anonymous.* CoMu

While their uplifted souls rejoice. The Cedars of Lebanon. Alphonse Marie Louis de Lamartine. AWP

...While there is light in them. The Death of a Cat (excerpt). Louis MacNeice. PCat

While there wept underground the eyes/Of stone. Orphic Interior. Leonardo Sinisgalli. LiTW

While these again have greater still, and greater still, and so/on. Great Fleas. *Anonymous.* ALV; BXAP

While these cold nights freeze me dead. Shall I Come, Sweet Love, to Thee. Thomas Campion. AAS; EBEV; EG; EIL; EnRePo; GBL; HAP; LoBV; OAEP; OxBoLi; PoEL 1-5; ViBoPo

The while they cool themselves, they freshness/give,/And moisture, that the bowery green may live. Minnows. John Keats. GN

While they drift farther away in the invisible morning In the Winter of My Thirty-Eighth Year. William Stanley Merwin. NOBA

While they gossiped around/A tea-caddy. The Gossips. *Anonymous.* OxNR

While they repeated his prayer, and said, "O Father, forgive/them!" Evangeline. Henry Wadsworth Longfellow. TreF

While they were quarreling, ate it all. A Party. Laura E. Richards. BiCB; SiSoSe; SoPo

While thine forgot lie closed in a tomb. Sonnet: "Sweet Spring, thou turn'st with all thy goodly train." William, of Hawthornden Drummond. EIL

While thine unfeigning lids gloriously upward flew. Eyeing the Eyes of One's Mistress. Ebenezer Jones. NOBV

While this heart, once so gay,/Shall be cold in Clonmala. The Convict of Clonmala. *Anonymous.* AnIL; AnIV; IrPN; NBM; OnYI; OxBi; SD

While those again have greater still, and greater still, and so on. On Fleas. Augustus De Morgan. TreFS

...While those/Who sped them stand to wave a last farewell. Morning Express. Siegfried Sassoon. HaMV

While through the bluebells and the fern/Sister and brother made their way. The Sphere of Glass. John Lehmann. ChMP

While through the vestry doorway come the cries/From out the barnyard and the gallant crowing. The Parish Church. Julio Herrera Reissig. CAW

While thy word, and thy love, and thy promise are mine. I Am Weary of Straying. Sarah E. York. AH

While time endures, First Citizen of earth. Washington. James Jeffrey Roche. MC; PAH

While Time ticked silent on, men drew/A deeper breath than passion knew. Armistice Day. John Freeman. MMM

...While tired/Savage eyed whores paraded the street. Fish Peddler and Cobbler. Kenneth Rexroth. NNaP

While to the west off our own shores the mackerel/Are fat–on the flesh of your kin. Neutrality. Louis MacNeice. CoBMV

While twirling candles/On his nose? A Circus Garland. Rachel Field. OBCA; SoPo

While under its storm-beaten breast/Cried out the hollows of the sea. On a Political Prisoner. William Butler Yeats. FaBoPV; OAEL 1-2; OBMV

While unsuspecting Cycles/Wheel solemnly away! Papa above. Emily Dickinson. AmPP; FM

While Victory lay weeping by his side. On Gustavus Adolphus, King of Sweden. Sir Thomas Roe. FaBoEE

While waking I recalled my wandering brain. The Washers of the Shroud. James Russell Lowell. AP; HBV 1-2; PAH

While warmly round me cluster lives/More dear to me than mine. Contented at Forty. Sarah N. Cleghorn. HBMV

While warmth of wood/and the sun follow. The Fox. Marjorie Somers Scheuer. GoYe

While we all walk the/shadows of greatness. Mwilu/ or Poem for the Living. Don L. Lee. JB

While we are far over/The treacherous sea. Fife Tune. John Streeter Manifold. BoAV; CBAP; ExPo; FaFP; GoJo; InPS; LiTB; LiTL; LiTM; LoGBV; NLV; NOAV; WaaP; WaP

While we are in the calm and proud possession of eternal/things. Babylon. George William Russell. HBMV

While we are waiting.../let us love And While We Are Waiting. Carolyn M. Rodgers. JB

While we at home, brother, sister, sucked the bloody air. Genitori. David Ray. TW

While we–by collie!–take life easy. The Collies. Edward Anthony. GDP

While we erect in your old places/Something considerably worse. The Revolutionaries. R. P. Lister. NOBL

...While we gaze and gaze/at the low valleys, and the meandering rivers. The Mountains. Louis Dudek. CaP

While we lie loving, passionate and mute. Flower of Love. Claude McKay. BALP

While we live Here, we must Provision make. A Dooms-Day Thought Anno 1659. Thomas Flatman. CEP

While we, released/from that pale paradise,/ponder the darkness in another place. The Woods. Derek Mahon. NOBI

...A while we rest/From the unending, endless quest. Ultima Thule. Henry Wadsworth Longfellow. MOS; ViBoPo

While we shall be merry and sing.' The Gaberlunzie Man. *Anonymous.* BSV; EnSB; GoTS; OxBB

...While we stand by/And shake the killer by the hand. Grey October. "The Critics." OBET

While we stand insolent, as poets stand. To a Scottish Poet. G. S. Fraser. BSV

While we the noblest Passions do extend/The Love to Hermes, Aphrodite the Friend. To the Fair Clarinda, Who Made Love to Me, Imagin'd More than Woman. Aphra Behn. SBG

While we think of all that was/In the long ago. An End. Christina Georgina Rossetti. FaBoRV; GBL

While we wept idly o'er thy little bier! Sonnet: Oft o'er My Brain. Samuel Taylor Coleridge. ChRP

While we were marching through Georgia. Marching through Georgia. Henry Clay Work. FaPoR; FSW; PAH; PSoN

While we young maidens walk out and in.   Queen Anne.   *Anonymous.*
OxNR

While weeping Diogenes hurled his flame/to the barren soil.   Watts.   Alvin
Saxon.   PoBA

While whispering: "Await, await/Your golden, perfect hour."   I Closed My
Shutters Fast Last Night.   Georgia Douglas Johnson.   PoNe

While Willing's willing shot went right/Through Schott's anatomy.   The
Duel.   *Anonymous.*   ShM

While wind and man woo in the glade/Another tree, another maid.   A
Woman Is a Branchy Tree.   James Stephens.   ErPo

While, with a feeling skill, I paint my hell.   Astrophel and Stella, II.   Sir
Philip Sidney.   AAS; OAEL 1-2; SiPS

While with a widening soul on me she/stared.   Modern Love, XLVI.
George Meredith.   OAEP; VLP

While, with my mouth, I begin again to cover your cooling/hair.   After Love.
Vicente Aleixandre.   AMV-80

While wooly white sheep jump over the fence/To nibble the moonbeam clover.
Shop of Dreams.   Mary Jane Carr.   BrR

While worms are turning handsprings in the sod.   Couplets for WCW.
Martha Christina.   AMV-80

...While years/Obliterate the rolls of human fame.   Mimma Bella.   Eugene
Lee-Hamilton.   HBV 1-2

While yet the flames have not gone out.   May It Be.   Boris Pasternak.
TrJP

While you and I, diddle diddle, keep the bed warm.   The Lady's Song in
Leap Year.   *Anonymous.*   GBP

While you await me, always young.   February 11, 1977.   Frederick Morgan.
AMV-80

While you're down, down, down.   Down, Down, Down.   *Anonymous.*
OuSiCo

While you're ridin' on the old bed-ground.   I'm Ridin' Tonight round the
Dam Bed-Ground.   *Anonymous.*   CoSo

While you talk about your own.   The greatest bore is boredom.   *Anonymous.*
CenHV

While you, you have champagne.   A Rhemish Carol.   Robert Finch.   NAs

While youth has hope, and love is yet divine.   At the Mermaid Inn.   Charles
Lotin Hildreth.   AA

While youth is ours, turn to me for a space/The marvel of your rapture-lighted
face!   View from Heights.   Arthur Davison Ficke.   HBMV

While Zeus breathes friendly on your sails.   O Gentle Ships.   Meleager.
AWP

The whiles the maskers marched forth in trim array.   The Faerie Queene.
Edmund Spenser.   FiP

Whilest loving thou mayst loved be with equall crime.   Gerusalemme Liberata
(excerpt).   Torquato Tasso.   OBVE

Whilest one might trace, with half an eye,/The still triumphant carrot through.
Tema con Variazioni.   Lewis (Charles Lutwidge Dodgson) Carroll.
FaBoNo; SpRo

Whilst all his hopes do faint, and life is failing.   Madrigal: "Come, sable
night."   John Ward.   EnRePo

Whilst all the Nymphs on solemn instruments/Sound dainty music to their
sweet laments.   Endymion's Convoy.   Michael Drayton.   OBSC

Whilst bishops may be damn'd the nearest way.   The Vicar.   George Crabbe.
AnFE

Whilst both contribute to your own undoing.   On His Mistresse Going to Sea.
Thomas Cary.   OBS

Whilst by self-ended knaves deluded kings/Make England's interest, and their
own, two things.   On Squire Neale's Projects.   *Anonymous.*   APAS

Whilst each glad parent told and blessed/The secrets of each other's breast.
Hymn for St. John's Eve.   *Anonymous.*   AWP

Whilst Echo cries, "What shall become of me?"   Diana.   Henry Constable.
OBSC

Whilst England and Columbia, quitting fear,/Kissed–and let in the eager
waters there.   Darien.   Sir Edwin Arnold.   MC; PAH

Whilst every house does seem a swarm.   Evening Quatrains.   Charles
Cotton.   EG

Whilst he who lacks that which the world commends/Must pace a stranger,
e'en in his own lands.   The Gulistan.   Muslih-ud-Din Sa'di.   AWP

Whilst I am singing and mowing/my corn.   My Maid Mary.   *Anonymous.*
OxNR

Whilst I in wonder sing this sacrifice,/To beauty sacred, and those Angel-eyes.
Women Pleased.   John Fletcher.   OBS

Whilst I the whining Fools despise,/That pay their Homage to my Eyes.
Song in the Same Play, by the Wavering Nymph.   Aphra Behn.   SBG

Whilst 'neath our pines thou feignest/deathlike sleep?   Hawthorne.   Amos
Bronson Alcott.   AA

Whilst others beds are downe, his pillowes stone.   The Malcontent.   John
Marston.   PoEL 1-5

Whilst our hands, hearts, and swords are all true to the crown.   The Western
Rebel.   *Anonymous.*   APAS

The whilst poor mortals startle at the sound/Of unseen footsteps on the
haunted ground.   Fairies.   Thomas Tickell.   OBEC

Whilst rancor's frost nips merit in her bud.   Madrigal: "Vain Hope, adieu."
John Attey.   EnRePo

Whilst that in Heav'n, this light on earth must shine.   First Three Verses of
an Ode to Cary and Morison.   Ben Jonson.   AnFE

Whilst the rodent in the foundations/Lies curled in a tangle of respiration
But There Was Once a Time When the Bones.   Eleni Vakalo.   WPOW

Whilst the scorched shiv'ring world new-born/Now feels it all the day one
rising morn.   Night.   Richard Lovelace.   CaPo

Whilst thine the victor is, and free.   Love in Fantastic Triumph.   Aphra
Behn.   CBEP; OAEP

Whilst thou under a bush shalt sit and smile.   The Affectionate Shepherd
(excerpt).   Richard Barnfield.   PBBP

Whilst thus I sing, I am a king,/Although a poor blind boy.   The Blind Boy.
Colley Cibber.   CEP; GTBS; GTBS-P; HBV 1-2; NOEC; OBEC; OxBChV;
RoGo; TreFS

Whilst upper life the slender rill/Of human sense doth overfill.   Art.   Ralph
Waldo Emerson.   AmePo; MAmP

Whilst virtue starves unpitied, unregarded.   Sonnet: "I fear to me such
fortune be assign'd."   William, of Hawthornden Drummond.   NCEP

Whilst we glad songs of praise prepare/For thine almighty name.   Our States,
O Lord.   John Mycall.   AH

Whilst weary creatures sleep.   The Setting Sun.   George Moses Horton.
BALP

Whilst you, great sir, at Notre Dame,/Te Deum sing in quiet!'   A Paraphrase
from the French.   Matthew Prior.   OxBoLi

Whimpers and speaks in the throat/of the Indian Princess.   Florida.
Elizabeth Bishop.   AmP; MP; TwCP

Whip 'em up and down the sides/And hit the shortest trail.   Dogie Song.
Anonymous.   CoSo

Whip little David's bum.   Ut, Re, Mi, Fa, Mi, Re, Ut.   *Anonymous.*
FaBoNo

The whippoorwill is surer of her name/than we are sure of anything.
Watching My Daughter Sew.   Katharine Privett.   AMV-81

The whippoorwills complain beside/The lonely Kankakee.   Mark.   Ernest
McGaffey.   AA

Whips to the Quaker's hide/And made him spring!   My Country 'Tis of Thee.
Ambrose Bierce.   YaD

Whirl the spurned chaff adown the void of Time!   The Harvest Waits.
Lloyd Mifflin.   HBV 1-2

The whirl will be marred. This I know.   Tomorrow Is a Birthday.
Gwendolen Haste.   GoYe

...Whirling/around in the yard,/making her long dress swirl.   Dancer.   Roy
Scheele.   GOYP

Whirling, extinguishing the last red wisp of light.   Rain in the Desert.   John
Gould Fletcher.   BPAW; NCSH

Whirls up and sinks,/a green stone.   Storm.   Hilda ("H.D.") Doolittle.
TiPo

Whisky, whisky, Nancy, O.   The Calton Weaver.   *Anonymous.*   FSW

A whisper between the night and the day.   Expectant Mother.   Penelope
Shuttle.   BrRo

A whisper cometh, which shall rend/What thunder hath not riven.   The Tree
of Rivelin.   Ebenezer Elliott.   VLP

Whisper in odorous heights of even.   Milton.   Alfred, Lord Tennyson.
EnLi 1-2; OAEP

...The whisper/Of time to space.   Systole and Diastole.   Conrad Aiken.
CrMA

Whisper to him that I will/Wait...beyond the farthest hill.   To Atalanta.
Dorothy Dow.   HBMV

...Whispered Mary His Mother,/Her tears falling down on His hands.   The
Spinner.   Charles L. O'Donnell.   GoBC; ISi

Whispered their dying messages to me...   The Messages.   Wilfred Wilson
Gibson.   MCCG; OHIP

Whispering, a big fish without eyes,/The most profound unhappiness.
Emblems.   Douglas Dunn.   FaBoMo

Whispering Bells or Filaree, come,/come home!   A Farewell.   Hildegarde
Flanner.   AMV-81

...Whispering children/riding to burial on their father's sled.   Blue Bog
Children.   Roger Weingarten.   AmPA

Whispering, consoling, promising: I am Love.   The Museum.   William
Abrahams.   WaP

Whispering Dear Warlock-Williams: Why, of course–   Vers de Societe.
Philip Larkin.   InPK

A:whispering drunkard passes   (One!).   Edward Estlin Cummings.   CAD

Whispering each other's name to the impossible windows.   The Flirtation.
Michael C. Blumenthal.   AMV-81

Whispering her own poems/In her ear as she sleeps beside me.   I Can Give
Myself to Her.   Yosano Akiko.   WPOW

Whispering in the dark: 'for ever and ever"?   The Survivor.   Robert Graves.
CMoP; MoVE

Whispering like a garden of secrets.   Sloops in the Bay.   James Tate.
MAYP

The whispering of wind through wire/carries scant legend, no hint of history. The Captive Stone. Jim Barnes. CDW

Whispering they give back/Young feet to the lame. Flowers in the Ward. Shaw Neilson. CBAP

Whispering to fool the wind/which always carries a secret farther. Sundays Visiting. Alberto Rios. Str

Whispering weirdly in the grey/Of the dumb cold evening air. December. Thomas Caulfield Irwin. IrPN; NBM

Whispering worshipping Mice in the Hay. Leslie Norris. OBCP; PCh

Whispering/you fool/you fool/you fool. Boxer Shorts Named Champion. Melvin Douglass Brown. LFAC

Whispers antiphonal in azure swing. Atlantis. Hart Crane. AtBAP; LiTM; NePA

Whispers his heart dimly guesses,/secrets he never may know. Yosemite. Millicent Washburn Shinn. AA

Whispers its pink flowers. Violets for Mother. Lonny Kaneko. BrSi

The whispers of the Desert-wind; the Tinkling of the camel's-bell. The Kasidah. Sir Richard Francis Burton. HBV 1-2

The whispers of the most flung shores/from Gloucester out From Gloucester Out. Edward Dorn. CoPo; NoAm; NOBA; PoM

Whispers to/me Dawn in January. Lance Henson. CDW

A whistle blew shrilly. Idaho. John Ashbery. ANYP

The whistle fades,dragging freight cars,day coaches and/the caboose. Landscape as Metal and Flowers. Winfield Townley Scott. AmFN; GoJo; MiAP

Whistle o'er the lave o't. Whistle O'er the Lave o't. Robert Burns. BSV; CEP; GBP

...–The whistle of the birds/Fails on her breast. Statue and Birds. Louise Bogan. EyDe; MoAB; MoAmPo

Whistle through the dark. To Laddie. Anne Robinson. SUS

Whit's this I hae upon my back; the Warld?' Sanct Christopher II. Giuseppe Belli. OBVE

A whit the wiser when the word had been swallowed. Riddle. Bookworm: "A moth ate a word." Anonymous. EnLi 1-2

A Whit-too-who–A whit-too-who-o-o-o. The Owl and the Fox. Anonymous. BLPA

White against a ruddy cliff you stand, chalcedony on sard. The Cameo. Edna St. Vincent Millay. FYAP; LiTA; MoAmPo; UnPo

A white and cankered rose. The Window Sill. Robert Graves. AtBAP; EnLoPo

The white and moving sand that will not bear a print. The Flight into Egypt. Peter Quennell. LiTB; LiTM

A white and shapeless mass. The Waning Moon. Percy Bysshe Shelley. CH; MOON; OBSP; PoPle; TrGrPo

The white angel, the one/who always cries/"Please don't lay a hand"/is on leave. The Akedah. Aliza Shenhar. VWA

White, Anglo-Saxon, one-half Protestant? Birth Report. X. J. Kennedy. NAs

White Antelope is my name Sand Creek. Charles G. Ballard. UnPo; VoR

White ants, white ants and the little ribs. Snow. Charles Wright. LCAP

White are the April beds Ann's House. Dick Lourie. DFF

The white-arm'd girls in dark blue bathing-gowns,/Among the snowy gulls and summer spray.' The Artist on Penmaenmawr. Charles Tennyson Turner. FaBoPP; OBNC

White as allyblaster. Snow. Anonymous. GBP

White as bones, white as petals in the grass. The Orchard. Michael Spence. AMV-80

White as forked lightning/Rending the sleet?) Simaetha. Hilda ("H. D.") Doolittle. MAPA

White as his teeth would seem to be. But Since I Know Thy Falsehood and Thy Pride. Abraham Cowley. LO

White as the celluloid about his throat. Halo. Ralph Nixon Currey. PeSA

The white blossoms of the apple trees/wet to knee high. When Both My Fathers Die. Robert Gillespie. FAZ

...White bottoms–a hundred of them–/Shock the Burmese lasses. Namkwin Pul. Bernard Gutteridge. WaP

The white chrysanthemums. Haiku: "No one spoke." Ryota. LiTW

The white-cloud-vision of Mont Blanc, and up/beyond Les Contamines, the seven shrines. St. Gervais. Michael Roberts. FaBoCh; LoGBV

...White clouds moved in silent lines/Across the untroubled blue. Bombardment. Richard Aldington. MMM

The white cluster of tombs. View of Louisiana. Cleopatra Mathis. TAT

The white cup shrivels round the golden heart. The House of Life. Dante Gabriel Rossetti. PoEL 1-5

White delivery van/Loaded with watermelons. Around the World. Gary Lenhart. APU

A white enormous/silent owl nesting on. The Boat. Robert Kelly. CoPo

The white face and thigh of the thief. Spring of the Thief. John Logan. BiP; CAPP; NNaP

A white figure steps through/and leaps into the dark. Sleep. Dana Naone. CDW

The white flake of snow/That has just fallen in the horse's mane! Watering the Horse. Robert Bly. CAPP; NaP; NCSH

White flowers their mourners are, nature their passing–/bell. Graves of Infants. John Clare. ERoP 1-2; OBVV

White garments from Thy stainless life/Oh, give me, Lord, to wear! His Garments. Esther Lloyd Hagg. PGD

A white hair fallen from my father's beard. Heirloom. Abraham Moses Klein. NIP; NOBC; OBCV; PeCV; TrJP

White hair tossed, a black cape flecked with snow. Casement's Funeral. Richard Murphy. NOBI

...A white handkerchief/that kept becoming a pigeon. The Magician. Bin Ramke. MAYP

White herons would be/But a line of snow. Herons. Anonymous. SUS

White Horsemen with Christ their Captain: for ever He! Te Martyrum Candidatus. Lionel Pigot Johnson. ACP; BoC; CAW; HBV 1-2; OBMV; OxBoCh

White in a face of stone. Sister, cold lover, come. Gipsy Queen. John Alexander Chapman. OBEV

White in the moon the long road lies/That leads me from my love. White in the Moon. Alfred Edward housman. AWP; CMoP; ELP; LiTB

The white iris beautifies me. In the Carolinas. Wallace Stevens. VGW

...The white/lie already forming/like a blister on his lips. Whitley at Three O'Clock. Jeff Worley. GOYP

White lilies in a row! Lilies. Shiko. SUS; TiPo

White...Locked.../John Status Symbol. Mari E. Evans. IDB

...A white look/in the bottom of a pail. Greeting Descendants. A. G. Sobin. FAZ

White men, I leave you all curse-free/In my broken heart's disdain! The Runaway Slave at Pilgrim's Point. Elizabeth Barrett Browning. BrRo; PoNe; SBG

White men's children in black men's skin. The Riddle. Georgia Douglas Johnson. PoBA

A white moth flew. Why am I grown/So cold? Cinquain: A Warning. Adelaide Crapsey. MCCG; WeW

The white owl in the belfry sits. Song: The Owl. Alfred, Lord Tennyson. GoJo; HBV 1-2; HBVY; MyFE; OBRV; SUS

The white owl in the belfry sits. When Cats Run Home. Alfred, Lord Tennyson. CH

The white pine sword gleaming between my teeth. Halcyon Days. Jim Barnes. CDW

The white plumed Asphodel. She Sits upon Her Bulbul. Edward Lear. FaBoNo

White purity is only negative. Five Epigrams. Donald Hall. NePoAm-2

White ribbons one was binding/About a flowery wreath. The Unknown Beloved. John Hall Wheelock. HBMV

The white room swallowing what was passed. The Room. Gregory Orr. GeTw

The white rose meant surrender. The White Flag. John Milton Hay. HBV 1-2

The white Sabbath of her arm. All Last Night... Lascelles Abercrombie. FaBoTw; HBV 1-2

White sails on a green sea. Ben Alder 1963-1977. Des Hannigan. PoSH

The white she wore was like a windless cold. The Exile. Larry Rubin. GoYe

White sheep, white sheep,/Where do you go? Clouds. Anonymous. BrR; SoPo

The white skin shaken like a white snowflake. Winter Love. Elizabeth Jennings. BoLoP; NePoEA; PPJ

The white slim body my senses fed upon/And all the secret shadows shot with fire? Loss. Richard Aldington. BrPo

...A white snail/eating holes in a leaf. Driving Home after a Funeral. Gregory Orr. GeTw

The white, strange road thro' Bogac Ban. Bogac Ban. Darrell Figgis. AnIV

White/sweet/May/again The Locust Tree in Flower. William Carlos Williams. SOTW

White, the pallor of the dead. Grandmother Poems. Marilyn Chin. BrSi

White thorn too much! Spring Ecstasy. Lizette Woodworth Reese. MoAmPo

White throats that could only last the night. Corner Lot. Sharon Bryan. MAYP

White trees, black sand, waves, sun. Voice from Danang. Thomas Dillon Redshaw. MAT

A white unicorn? Black Poet, White Critic. Dudley Randall. BPo; ConAP

White, warm, and soft to lie with me. More White Than Whitest Lilies. Robert Herrick. UnTE

White weeds on fire/at the fingertips of each hand shoot/and she's got at least fifty of them A Gentle Heart: Two. Judith Johnson Sherwin. BoWoP

White white on white. Twinings Orange Pekoe. Judith Moffett. PoA; SM

White, white," sang she! Daft Jean. Sydney Thomas Dobell. VLP

The white wings of the Holy Ghost/Stoop, seen or unseen, o'er the heads of all. The Shadow and the Light (excerpt). John Greenleaf Whittier. TrPWD

The whitened planking of the mill/Is now in shade and now in sun. The Upper Skies Are Palest Blue. Robert Bridges. VLP

The whiteness of the rebel Rose? To Miss Eleanor Ambrose... Philip Stanhope, Earl of Chesterfield. EnLoPo

Whiter than milk on the grass, so white is he. Once Upon a Great Holiday. Anne Wilkinson. WHW

The whitest soul of my chivalry,/For Little Giffen of Tennessee. Little Giffen. Francis Orrery [(or Orray(] Ticknor. AA; HBV 1-2; MaC; MC; PAH; TreFS

Whither away? The Flight of the Birds. Edmund Clarence Stedman. GN

"Whither has he crossed over?" Hymn to Tammuz. Anonymous. LiTW

Whither the fearless footsteps go. The Changing Road. Katharine Lee Bates. HBV 1-2

Whither the yesterdays have fled, or if they were. I Cry to You as I Pass Your Windows. Christopher John Brennan. PoAu 1-2

Whithersoever his footsteps turn in his farings,/Save a few tombs? In Front of the Landscape. Thomas Hardy. OBNC

Whitman's walk unchanged after its fashion. Whitman in Black. Ted Berrigan. APU

(Whitmanic morning task: waking the country to itself). On Walt Whitman's Birthday. Anne Waldman. APU

The whiz, the slime–and the sky is whole. I Break the Sky. Owen Dodson. PoBA

Who, against pikes and burning brands,/built the future with bare hands. Lancashire Winter. Tony Connor. OxBTC

Who, alas! departed from us/In that noisy way. Little Thomas. F. Gwynne Evans. BBGG

Who All Things finds convey'd to him alone,/Must needs adore the Holy One. The Vision. Thomas Traherne. ILwL

Who almost am too tired, too weak, to pray. Sonnet VII. William Sharp. SyP

Who always are ready, steady, boys, steady,/To fight for their freedom again and again. The Virginia Song. Anonymous. PAH

Who always float down to us/with alarmed and startled eyes. After the Anonymous Swedish. Jim Harrison. VGW

Who always on earth's little ones hath/smiled. Lincoln. Silas Weir Mitchell. PAH

...Who am I, oh God,/and in what time have you placed your servant? Psalm. Eugene Heimler. VWA

Who am I the heavens assume? an/All am I, and I am one. Assumpta Maria. Francis Thompson. ISi

Who am not nothing worth/If worthy to be thine. Canzonetta: Of His Lady, and of His Making Her Likeness. Jacopo da Lentino. AWP

Who am self-complete as a flower or a stone? The Solitary. Sara Teasdale. MoAmPo; WHA

Who am the first-born of night's pain. Solomon and Morolph, Their Last Encounter. Oscar Levertin. VWA

Who are a little wise the best fools be. The Triple Fool. John Donne. CoBE; DiPo; OAEP; PP

Who are also a part/of him, & your & he/& I make trio of/kind congruity. Number Song. Anne Waldman. APU

Who are as beautiful as me. Easter Parade. Marchette Chute. BrR; SiSoSe

Who are come to make our shattered faces/whole. Outside. Audre Lorde. NIP

Who are not sallow, sick, and spare! The Aesthete to the Rose (parody). Anonymous. BXAP

Who are standing in the way of the thing called/Civilization. Printed Words. Liz Sohappy Bahe. CDW

Who are the air itself, the breath ashake/Among the leaves–the bird no longer there. The Quarry. Vassar Miller. NePoEA-2

Who are the brilliance of that day/the glory of this night To the Muse. Philip Whalen. PoM

Who are these below? What inn is this. Emily Dickinson. MasP; NePA

Who are those kings? Why do the oxen kneel? The Witnesses. X.J. Kennedy. PCh

Who are too old in any case to go to the War. Private Means is Dead. Stevie Smith. OxBC

Who are too valuable at seventy-four/to throw away. A Proposal for Recycling Wastes. Marge Piercy. GP

Who are, with the Indians,/the first Americans. When Something Happens. James A. Randall, Jr. BPo

Who are you? and with whom do you sleep here? Doctor Drink. J. V. Cunningham. QFR

Who art the love of love, the eternal light/of light! After-Song. Richard Watson Gilder. AA; TrPWD

Who, as they walk abroad, make tinkling with their feet. A Portrait (parody). John Keats. BXAP

Who-ay hay-ay-hay, for yonder comes my beau. The Sun Shines over the Mountain. Anonymous. AmFP

Who bears no useless burden from the past/Will find the miles ahead are always best. Thought for a New Year. Gail Brook Burket. PGD

Who bears our night and morning drinks/So noisily through town! The Milk-Cart Pony. Eleanor Farjeon. SUS

Who begs, a thousand times he dies. The Price of Begging. Emmanuel Frances. TrJP

Who bicker till his gavel calls a halt. The Rebel General. Chris Wallace-Crabbe. CBAP

Who blocked the Seine with battle-ships/Round Paris on the Isle. The Ballad of the White Horse. Gilbert Keith Chesterton. ACP

Who boasts that in his spotless strain/Mingles the blood of Betty Zane. Betty Zane. Thomas Dunn English. PAH; PAL

Who born of silence has burned back to silence. Elegy for an Unknown Soldier. James Keir Baxter. AnNZ

Who bought me with his precious blood,/From endless misery. Sweet Rivers of Redeeming Love. John A. Granade. AH

Who bravely wore on Boyne's red shore/The royal loyal Lily O. The Orange Lily. Anonymous. FaBoPV

...Who breathes/Comes to nothing: absence, a world. God Poem. Stanley Moss. VGW; VWA

Who brings us equal, if not greater, bliss. His Petition to Queen Anne of Denmark (1618). Sir Walter Ralegh. SiPS

Who broke the laws of God, and man, and metre. Epitaph on Peter Robinson. Francis, Lord Jeffrey Jeffrey. OxBoLi

...Who/brought the revolution/uncramping their lives. Teaching the Penguins to Fly. Barry Spacks. GP

Who brought us salvation–his praises we'll sing. Rejoice and Be Merry. Anonymous. EBCP

Who builds him a house of a rhyme or two/Must look for the rain on his head! Builders. Hortense Flexner. HBMV

Who bury the dead/to rise again. The Heavenly Tree Grows Downward. Gerrit Lansing. CoPo

...Who but I/Coil there and squat, and pay your fee? Interview with Doctor Drink. J. V. Cunningham. NMP; OBSP; TW; VGW

Who but the extremest skirts of glory sees,/And hears celestial echoes with delight.' Sonnet: True Ambition. Benjamin Stillingfleet. OBEC

Who, by low creatures, leads to heights of love. Flush or Faunus. Elizabeth Barrett Browning. BoC; FM; NBM

Who, by the might of thy majestic scene,/Bringest down that age and minglest it with this. Paul Veronese. Sir Samuel Ferguson. IrPN

Who Caelica's chaste heart then seeks to move/Must joy to suffer all the woes of love. Caelica, LIX. Fulke, Lord Brooke Greville. FCP

Who calls his love his own? The Lover's Song. Alfred Austin. OBVV

Who came but for Friendship, and took away Love! A Temple to Friendship. Thomas Moore. BeLS; HBV 1-2

Who can break down Wall Street with a poem? That Poem. Juan Saez Burgos. InW

Who can claim the strange harvest of this/incessant wintry assault on ourselves? High Summer. Jascha Kessler. AmPC

Who can express what 'tis he likes. To Cloris. Sir Charles Sedley. BoLoP; CEP

Who can feel his children through all distance and time! Water under the Earth. Robert Bly. NNaP

Who can hold its heartiness/fermented to a man's delight,/if he is held in love. Joyful Prophecy. Vassar Miller. CoPo

Who can keep us caged? Poem for the Creative Writing Class, Spring 1982. Merle Woo. BrSi

Who can make soft, simple speeches/Pleases Myra full as well. Sent to Him, as He Whisper'd. Sir Hildebrand Jacob. FaBoEE

Who can say what may not happen to-day? Higgledy, Piggledy! See How They Run! Kate Greenway. TiPo

Who can shew all his love, doth love but lightly. To Delia. Samuel Daniel. LoBV; OAEP; OBSC

Who can take the multitude and lock it in a cage? The Poem of Joao. Noemia De Sousa. WhB

Who can understand you? Inanna and An. Enheduanna. BoWoP

Who cannot guess God's presence out of/sight. Sonnets from the Portuguese, XX. Elizabeth Barrett Browning. CoBE

Who cannot live content in thee,/Or wants for anything (but cash). Hail South Australia. Anonymous. NOAV

Who cares for caring, has caress. Caring. F. R. Scott. PeCV

Who carry the brunt of the strife! We Are the Burden-Bearers (excerpt). William L. Stidger. PGD

Who cartwheel out of sight, end over end. Closing Time. David Wagoner. NYBP

Who climb, a desperate lover,/With hand and knee. The Paps of Jura. Andrew Young. PoSH

Who climbed these stairs, who died within this room. The New House. Joseph Easton McDougall. CaP

Who climbs with toil, wheresoe'er,/Shall find wings waiting there. Bicycling Song. Henry Charles Beeching. GN

Who climbs with toil, wheresoe'er,/Shall find wings waiting there. Going Down Hill on a Bicycle. Henry Charles Beeching. BBV; HBV 1-2; HBVY; OBEV; OBVV

Who collapse the cloud to steal from it/our secret. To Modigliani to Prove to Him That I Am a Poet. Max Jacob. TrJP

Who come at last from drought and fast/To sit in God's Green Inn. The Green Inn. Theodosia Garrison. HBMV

Who come out of the silence? Listening. Alice Corbin. BPAW

Who comes into the world with naught/Can scarce go out with more. Epitaph. Alfred Edgar Coppard. OBMV

Who comes when he pleases, and keeps/the secrets of the tribe. Deer in the Bush. Chana Bloch. MAYP

Who comforts like raisins,/Who kisses like snow. Dunce Song 6. Mark Van Doren. DuDa

Who command his robes, expose/His moving likeness on the page. Lens. Anne Wilkinson. NOBC; OBCV; PeCV

Who composed our quarrel early and in good season/Buried the hatchet in our father's brain. The Entailed Farm. John Glassco. NOBC

Who, content, to-night are sleeping–/Painless, dreamless, there! Requiem for a Young Soldier. Florence Earle Coates. OHIP

Who could be so heartless as to hate you/for trying to find freedom, and failing? Apology to My Lady. Edward Falco. AMV-80

"Who could believe it? Who could believe it?" Paper Mill. Joseph Kalar. AnAmPo

Who could have foretold/I would live to write at fifty? Praise. Jane Cooper. TAP

Who could love utterly/Beyond the meaning of these words and tears. The Clock. Francis Scarfe. NeBP

Who could not, at one time,/Have saved them from the gas. "It Out-Herods Herod, Pray You Avoid It." Anthony Hecht. CoAP; NCSH; NIP; NoAm; NOBA; OxBC

...Who could tell you now of flittings,/night-vigils, let-downs, women's cried-out eyes. The Wanderer. Seamus Heaney. CIP

Who could wish evil to the state of France! Ballad against the Enemies of France. Francois Villon. AWP

Who covers their retreat, dies at his gun. Behold the Manly Mesomorph. W. H. Auden. OBSP

Who cracked his throat with crowing. The Little Black Dog Ran Round the House. Anonymous. OxNR

Who crossed cold Lethe, thought it Rubicon. Fording the River. Seamus Deane. CIP

Who crouches in the bulbs with his shears/And hasn't got the hots for anyone. Central Park West. Jack Spicer. PeHV

Who crowd the press with hourly trash. Critics. Jonathan Swift. OBEC; SeCePo

Who crushed/The grapes of joy/And dripped their juice/On you? Midnight Dancer. Langston Hughes. FF

Who cry "O Daughter!" Sunglasses. Tom Clark. ANYP

"Who cut the gentle jugulars of sheep!" The Peasant. Leonard Wolf. NYBP

Who'd burn the papers and correct the leaves. Epigram: Absent-Minded Professor. Howard Nemerov. OBAL

Who'd not die such a death? To Clarastella on St. Valentines Day Morning. Robert Heath. OBS

Who dare trust upon to-morrow,/When nor time nor life sojourns not? Old Damon's Pastoral. Thomas Lodge. OBSC

Who dared to be traitor to Union when/Union was traitor to Right! Wendell Phillips (excerpt). John Boyle O'Reilly. AA

Who dares have virtue in a vicious age. Verses Written in the Chiosk at Pera, Overlooking Constantinople. Mary Wortley, Lady Montagu. OBTV

Who dares not worship you? Inanna and the City of Uruk. Enheduanna. BoWoP

Who dares to call Himself a man. Jehovah Buried, Satan Dead. Edward Estlin Cummings. NePA

Who dares to say that love is like the war? This Loneliness for You Is Like the Wound. Dunstan Thompson. WaaP; WaP

Who deems obedience better praise/Than sacrifice of erring awe. Preludes. Coventry Patmore. HBV 1-2

Who degrades or defiles the body of the dead is not more cursed. The Bodies of Men and Women Engirth Me. Walt Whitman. AmePo

Who devoured that Old Man of Leghorn. Limerick: "There was an Old Man of Leghorn." Edward Lear. NA

Who did from death deliver us,/When we were left forlorn. The Singers in the Snow. Anonymous. OHIP

"Who did not, now can not, assist the community, YE DIE!" Epistle II: To a Socialist in London. Robert Bridges. FM

Who did not see in his own house the knave that kissed/his wife? The Gulistan. Muslih-ud-Din Sa'di. AWP

Who did see this awful murder/and watch poor Johnson die? Johnson. Anonymous. FSW

Who did so bravely play their parts at the taking of Porto Bello. English Courage Displayed. Anonymous. OBSS

Who die without a candle, or remain/To citizen the natural state of man. Every Earthly Creature. John Malcolm Brinnin. LiTA

Who died, as firm as Sparta's king,/Because his soul was great. The Private of the Buffs. Sir Francis Hastings Doyle. HBV 1-2; OBEV; OBTV; OBVV; PaPo; VLP

Who died in the pass, and will not die again? Thermopylae. Michael Thwaites. PoAu 1-2

Who died so young although they lived so long. Christenings. Peter Porter. NAs

Who died upon a Tree. Mater Dolorosa. John Banister Tabb. AnAmPo

Who dies for you can do no more. Ode: "Good night, my Love, may gentle rest." Charles Cotton. ViBoPo

Who dies if England live? For All We Have and Are. Rudyard Kipling. FaPoR

Who dies in sinnes unpaid, that soule/His light's eternall night. I Have Heard Ingenuous Indians Say. Roger Williams. SCAP

Who dies now anywhere in the world,/without cause dies in the world,/looks at me. Solemn Hour. Rainer Maria Rilke. PoPl; TrJP

Who dies today, and will as long be so,/As he who died a thousand years ago. De Rerum Natura. Lucretius (Titus Lucretius Carus). OAEL 1-2

Who dissect away the wings and the haggard heart/from the dove. Letter to Alex Comfort. Dannie Abse. FaBoTw; MP; TwCP

Who do not fear the melancholy of the stair. The Location of Things. Barbara Guest. NYP

Who do you think would want/Such an ugly face? A Jealous Man. Anonymous. KiLC

Who does God's work will get God's pay. God's Pay. Anonymous. STF

Who does his better part recall/And of his fault make funeral. Fame and Friendship. Henry Austin Dobson. OBEV

Who does what, and with which, and to whom?' Limerick: "A lesbian girl of Khartoum." Anonymous. NOBL

Who don't know what to make of what, who tremble and obey. Rainer Maria Rilke Returns from the Dead... John Engman. LTB

Who don't really think at all/being rudely rusty inside. There's Nothing Polite about a Tank. John Paul Minarik. LFAC

Who doth for ever to his Thoughts bequeath/The Legacy of your lamented Death. An Elegy Upon My Best Friend. Henry, Bishop of Chichester King. AnAnS 2

Who doth his better part recall/And of his fault make funeral. Fame Is a Food That Dead Men Eat. Henry Austin Dobson. GTBS; HBV 1-2

Who doth the world so gloriously behold,/That cedar-tops and hills seem burnished gold. Venus Abandoned. William Shakespeare. OBSC

...Who dream of nothing/But a pad on Eighth Street and your approbation. Application for a Grant. Anthony Hecht. SaC

Who dreamed of a village/cool among the stars. From Jerusalem: A First Poem. Gabriel Preil. VWA

"Who dreams my fountain's laughter/Shall feed my wells with tears." Santa Barbara Beach. Ridgely Torrence. HBMV

Who drinketh shall not drink in vain./I drink and love! The Same Forever. Horatius Bonar. BePJ

Who drinks the deepest? Here's to him. A Song of Sack. Anonymous. OBS

Who drove the sea in swollen tempest/in Egypt once, on chariots and riders/and whelmed all. The Defeat of the Norsemen (excerpt). Sedulius Scottus. NOBI

Who drove the train to Glasgow. The Train to Glasgow. Wilma Horsburgh. OnUR

Who durst defy th' Omnipotent to arms. Paradise Lost. John Milton. NIP

Who dyes to-day, and will as long be so,/As he who dy'd a thousand years ago. The Latter Part of the Third Book of Lucretius... John Dryden. FaBoRV

Who e'er would marry that could be/Blest with such Opportunity,/Never me. To Chuse a Friend, but Never Marry. John Wilmot, Earl of Rochester. CoMu

Who, early in the alphabet, recited/More than I could learn until tonight? Student. Josephine Miles. NoP

Who eat up a fat goose, but could not digest her. Epitaph on Dr. Keene. Thomas Gray. FaBoEE

Who else do I want for drinking companions? Moon, Flowers, Man. Su Tung-P'o. NaP

Who else? Under the earth the blossoms hide. Who Bids Us Sing? Rhys Carpenter. WGRP

Who, ere the first down bloomed on the chin,/Had sow'd these fruits, and got the harvest in. A Part of an Ode. Ben Jonson. OBEV

Who, ere the first down bloomed on the chin,/Had sowed these fruits, and got the harvest in. To the Immortal Memory and Friendship of That Noble Pair... Ben Jonson. NOBE; NoP; OAEL 1-2

Who erstwhile worked his will on worms. Fisherman. Robert Francis. PPJ

Who ever loved, that loved not at first sight?   Hero and Leander.
  Christopher Marlowe.   BLPL; BoLiVe; NOBE; TrGrPo; ViBoPo; WHA
Who ever would love or be tied to a wife/When it makes a man mad all the
  days of his/life?   Song.   John Clare.   VLP
Who ever yet saw a pig in a wig?   Where Are You Going.   Eliza Lee
  Follen.   SoPo
Who exalt not the Father/Shall tunelessly sing!   A Song to the Wind.
  Taliesin.   FaBoCh
Who "faced a firing squad, received 8 bullets/through the body and head, yet
  LIVED!"   Hubert's Museum.   Louis Simpson.   OxBC
Who failed to break a son into a friend.   Lines to My Father.   Leslie
  Daiken.   NeIP; OxBI
Who hain would have to be new, tender, quick.   Love Unknown.   George
  Herbert.   JCP; Prf
Who falls for love of God, shall rise a star.   An Epistle to a Friend, to
  Persuade Him to the Wars.   Ben Jonson.   TEP
Who falters now shames God, and dies.   The Goal and the Way.   John
  Oxenham.   PGD
Who fawn'd like man, but ne'er like man betray'd.   On His Dog.   John Gay.
  ALV
Who fawned like man, but ne'er like man betrayed.   An Elegy on a Lap Dog.
  John Gay.   DiPo; HBV 1-2
Who ferries no one to a happy shore.   Lost.   W. H. Auden.   FaBoEE
Who fill'd half of this churchyard.   On Dr. Chard.   Anonymous.   FaBoEE
Who fillest from thy fullness/Time and eternity.   O Day of Light and
  Gladness.   Frederick Lucian Hosmer.   AH
Who finds himself, loses his misery!   Self-Dependence.   Matthew Arnold.
  BBV; HBV 1-2; MaVP; MCCG; OAEP; TreFS; VLP; WGRP
Who finds no reason to be proud at all.   Swordy Well.   John Clare.   WHA
Who fired France for Mary without spot.   Duns Scotus's Oxford.   Gerard
  Manley Hopkins.   CoBE; EBEV; EyDe; FaBoPP; GTBS-P; NAMP; NoAm;
  OBMV; PoEL 1-5; VLP
Who fired the shot, the blue or the grey?   The Virgin Sturgeon.   Anonymous.
  FSW
Who firm'd his name on such a Pyramid.   To My Honoured Friend Mr.
  George Sandys.   Henry, Bishop of Chichester King.   AnAnS 2
Who flung a pot of paint in the public's eyes/and opened mine.   Nocturne:
  Homage to Whistler.   Ruth Feldman.   AMV-81
Who fold over and over the fragile white rounds/Of your demanding country.
  The Return.   Jon Silkin.   NePoEA-2
Who for a long time/Waved a tanned hand after me.   Walking Along the Sea
  of Galilee.   Dovid Knut.   VWA
Who, for a single glance, gave up her life.   Lot's Wife.   Anna Akhmatova.
  BoWoP; PBWP
Who for one time loved in them the truth concealed:/And now must leave
  them in the truth revealed.   Sonnets, XIX: "Those former loves wherein our
  lives have run."   James Agee.   MoAmPo
Who 'fore they'd strike, will nobly sink/Our brave Yankee boys.   The United
  States and Macedonian.   Anonymous.   PAH
Who fought their way from night to day and struggled/up to God.   The
  Unsung Heroes.   Paul Laurence Dunbar.   BPo
Who fought to save his country, and whose/lot/It was to die unknown and
  rest forgot?   May 30, 1893.   John Kendrick Bangs.   AA
Who from death eternal frees us,/Yea, Who life eternal gives.   Unchanging
  Jesus.   Karl J.P. Spitta.   BLRP
Who from eating dust will end up/With a fate just like mine.   Drill Man
  Blues.   George Sizemore.   WTO
Who from his cross of pain/Cried to the dying comrade,/"Lad, we shall meet
  again."   Comrades of the Cross.   Willard Wattles.   HBMV
Who from my mouth-grate, and eye-window bawl.   To His Mistress for Her
  True Picture.   Edward, Lord Herbert of Cherbury.   AnAnS 2; SeCP
...Who/From the bridging of Lamrach shall gain, or rue?   Song of the Fairies.
  Anonymous.   OnYI
...Who gambled nothing,/gave nothing, and could never receive enough.   In
  Place of a Curse.   John Ciardi.   HoAn
Who gathered their ragged classes behind a friendly hedge.   The Hedge
  Schoolmasters.   Seumas MacManus.   CAW
Who gave that strength to Samson, can not/Break the cords of Man.   Prayer.
  Thomas Washbourne.   WGRP
Who gives his hoot for joy as he flies./Alights.   An Owl Is an Only Bird of
  Poetry.   Robert Duncan.   NeAP; PoM
Who gives no other affirmation/Than love's retractless forfeiture?
  Deprivation.   Helen Pinkerton.   NePoAm
Who gives these stars their names/More bright ten thousand fold.   When Sun
  Doth Rise.   Roger Williams.   AH
Who glue their vile unsatiated maws/& freedoms birthright from the weak
  devours.   The Fallen Elm.   John Clare.   FaBoPV
Who gobbles the milk o' the Queen's ain breast.   Mad Marjory.   Hugh
  McCrae.   PoAu 1-2
Who goes on strange adventurous ways/Through tortured days and dangerous
  nights.   I Think of Him as One Who Fights.   Anna Hempstead Branch.
  HBMV

Who goes to join the men of Agincourt.   The Volunteer.   Herbert Asquith.
  MMM; OBWP; OxBTC
...Who greeted them with open hands/that had been changed into flowers.
  The Drunken Stones of Prague.   David Scheinert.   VWA
Who grinds his own bones and his child's for bread?/Tally hi-o, the grinder!
  The Grinders, or the Saddle on the Right Horse.   Anonymous.   GBP
Who grows the roses/Of Paradise.   Old Woman's Song.   Thomas Cole.
  NePoAm-2
Who guards the conqueror with his conquering hands.   A Captive of Love.
  Ovid (Publius Ovidius Naso).   AWP
Who—h'm—will hardly thank you for your pains.   There Is a Tide.   Rudyard
  Kipling.   OBSP
Who had always been so careful while her mistress lived.   Aunt Helen.
  Thomas Stearns Eliot.   OBAL; PoA
Who had pity on a poor Parley-voo!   The Darned Mounseer.   Sir William
  Schwenck Gilbert.   NOBL
Who had sighed moon-sick then./I have you!   Baby.   Florence Kiper Frank.
  HBMV
Who had the power and virtue to remove/Such monsters from the labyrinth of
  love.   Love's Triumph.   Ben Jonson.   EnRePo
Who had your God for Father, Spouse and Son!   To Our Blessed Lady.
  Henry Constable.   ACP; CAW; GoBC; ISi; OBSC
Who hanged himself one morning for a change.   Epitaph: "Here lies Sir John
  Plumpudding of the Grange."   Anonymous.   FaBoEE
Who hanker for/a book to read.   Books Fall Open.   David McCord.
  OBCA
Who harried the Welshmen and held the land.   The Battle of Brunanburh.
  Anonymous.   AnOE
Who has been born this evening in the house.   After Midnight.   Charles
  Vildrac.   AWP
Who has buried them both in a cardboard box.   The Drawer.   George
  MacBeth.   NePoEA-2
Who has done with all his enemies before he entered.   No Uneasy Refuge.
  Blanaid Salkeld.   AnIV
Who has ever denied you homage,/lady, supreme over the land?   Inanna and
  the Anunna.   Enheduanna.   BoWoP
Who/has had a hand in it.   The Knot.   Tom Clark.   HoAn
Who has lost youth's peace!   The Babiaantje.   Frank Templeton Prince.
  ACV; MoBrPo
Who has my love and prayers!   My Little Girl.   Samuel Minturn Peck.
  AA
Who has not grieved to return to the world downstairs?   Burr Oaks: The
  Attic.   Richard Eberhart.   MoAB
Who has taught me what it is to love.   Sonnet Sequence.   Darwin T. Turner.
  BALP
Who has the hills as a lover,/Will find them wondrous kind.   I Leave Tonight
  from Euston.   Anonymous.   PoSH
Who has won for once over the world's/weight.   Juggler.   Richard Wilbur.
  AmP; CMoP; LiTM; MoAB; NCSH; NePA; NePoEA; NYBP; TAP
Who hast the red pavilion of my heart?   Arab Love-Song.   Francis
  Thompson.   AWP; EG; MoAB; MoBrPo
Who hast the starlight on thy marble breast.   The Final Faith.   George
  Sterling.   CAW
Who hath my heart truly,/Be sure, and ever shall!   The Holly.   King of
  England Henry VIII.   CTC; OBSC
Who hath no chippe muste rowe in bote or barge.   The Dance of Death.
  John Lydgate.   EnPo
Who have ambrosia eaten and yet live.   The Ambrosia of Dionysus and
  Semele.   Robert Graves.   NYBP
Who have broken down through/the surface.   Stone.   Juliet Chayat.
  AMV-80
Who have brought forth the urchin grief.   It Is the Sinners' Dust-Tongued
  Bell Claps Me to Churches.   Dylan Thomas.   OxBTC
Who have brought glory and posterity/Unto this widow land and people
  hopeless?   "My days' delight, my springtime joys fordone."   Sir Walter
  Ralegh.   FCP
Who have escaped the dispersion,/And have got rid of the damned/Yiddish.
  Where the Cedars.   Jacob Glatstein.   TrJP
Who have known the forgetting of dying to a life one lonely pain.   Blanid's
  Song.   Gordon Bottomley.   BrPo
Who have left their loves to fame,/And their earth to earth again.   Epitaph of
  Pyramus and Thisbe.   Abraham Cowley.   FaBoEE
Who have lived in joy and laughed into the face of/Death.   Her Courage.
  William Butler Yeats.   LiTB
Who have no child to die.   Bereaved.   James Whitcomb Riley.   AA
Who have no wedding ring or mutual bed?   The Lucky Marriage.   Thomas
  Blackburn.   GTBS-P
Who have nothing to sign it with but a blunt mark.   May Day
  Demonstrators.   Maurice Lindsay.   ACV
Who having two or three,/Will be content with one?   The Poet Loves a
  Mistress, But Not to Marry.   Robert Herrick.   ALV; CaPo; ErPo

Who heals the whole world's pain.   Elegy on an Australian Schoolboy.   Zora Cross.   PoAu 1-2

Who hear not for the beating of their hearts.   Al Aaraaf.   Edgar Allan Poe.   AP

Who hear the breakin' bar an' think/O' Jerry home an'–me.   Jerry an' Me.   Hiram Rich.   HBV 1-2

Who heard a great friend's death without a change of voice.   The Mummy.   Vernon Watkins.   MoPo; NeBP

Who heard the silly sailor-folk and gave them back their/sea!   The Last Chantey.   Rudyard Kipling.   BoLiVe; EtS; FaBoCh; LoGBV; MoBrPo; MOS; OBVV

...Who hears your voices in their mountains/Shall be ripped like mandrakes shrieking out.   Oracle.   E. L. Mayo.   MiAP

Who hobbles after you a little way/Fierce and ridiculous.   To the Girls of My Graduating Class.   Irving Layton.   ErPo

Who humbly sips her learning from Reviews,/Or flutters in the Magazines.   To Mr. Gray.   David Garrick.   OBEC

Who hung like a Hero and never would flinch.   Clever Tom Clinch Going to be Hanged.   Jonathan Swift.   CEP; CoMu; FaBoBa; NOBI; SeCeV

Who imagine the silence of a guest/to be mysterious, or wrong.   The Parachutist.   Jon Anderson.   AmPA; LiSp

Who in a bearded coat does gayly go.   Summer Rain.   Henry David Thoreau.   AnNE

Who, in His longanimity and love for our/Small dignities, enfeebles, for a time, His power.   Sonnet: "The Bible says Sennacherib's campaign was spoiled."   Clive Staples Lewis.   TrCP

Who, in his own time, resumed the dark, the straw.   The Outlaw.   Seamus Heaney.   NoAm; OxBC

Who in his poor beheld their Lord.   Father, Who Mak'st Thy Suff'ring Sons.   Arthur Cleveland Coxe.   AH

Who in more fiendish war-paint shine?   Poets in Africa.   Roy Campbell.   ACV

Who, in my youth, loved, as thou must, in vain.   Sweeter Far Than the Harp, More Gold Than Gold.   Michael (Katherine Bradley and Edith Cooper) Field.   OBMV

Who in the morning, noon, and evening did decree/As reminders to the wise, of duty's call?   Zoroaster Devoutly Questions Ormazd.   Zoroaster.   AWP; WGRP

Who in the world I do my business with/Said it ain't nobody's business but mine   'Tain't Nobody's Business.   Frank Stokes.   BluL

Who is already translating me/Into other men's throats.   Destiny of the Poet.   Claude Vigee.   VWA

Who is as happy as Catullus is?   Veranius, My Dear Friend.   Caius Valerius Catullus.   PeHV

...Who is better in arithmetic,/you or your mother?   Arithmetic.   Carl Sandburg.   ImOP

...Who is coming to kill us once again.   Clap Your Hands for Herod.   Josef Hanzlik.   OBCP

Who is companion blue-hued well-marked   Image-Nation (the Poésis).   Robin Blaser.   PoM

Who is divine? This bird.   The Blinded Bird.   Thomas Hardy.   AnFE; BiP; CMoP; EaLo; LiTM; NoAm

"Who is ever the guardian of peace"   Man As He Shall Be.   Rochelle Owens.   CoPo

...Who is/Frank Moore?   The Librarian.   Charles Olson.   CAPP; CoPo

Who is he? I do not know....   The Brother.   Semion Y. Nadson.   TrJP

Who is his master? Is he too a slave?   Who Reigns?   Percy Bysshe Shelley.   SeCePo

Who is honorable?/He who treats all men honorably.   The Good Man.   Talmud.   TrJP

...Who is it/on his way now moves/and plays havoc with my footsteps?   On the Way.   Mordechai Husid.   VWA

Who is it that behind and beneath sings/ever through us, now whispering, /now thundering, "I am"?   Choir Practice.   Ernest Crosby.   AA

Who is it, then, that love deceives?   Juan's Song.   Louise Bogan.   NYBP

Who is listening to your name.   Mahalia.   Michael S. Harper.   FAZ

Who is more secret than any words can show.   La Vita Nuova.   Dante Alighieri.   AWP

Who is more welcome to my dish/Than to my angle was my fish.   The Angler's Song.   Izaak Walton.   LiSp; SD

Who is most trew, and pleasing to thee, then/When she'is embrac'd and open to most men.   Holy Sonnets, XVIII.   John Donne.   MasP; MeLP; OAEP; OBS

Who is so proud of being Rational.   Were I, Who to My Cost Already Am.   John Wilmot, Earl of Rochester.   SCV

Who is that capers on the sand?   Ballad of No Proper Man.   Daniel Gerard Hoffman.   MAT

...Who is the maniac, and why everywhere at the same time....   Das Kapital.   LeRoi (Imamu Amiri Baraka) Jones.   PoM

Who is the Master of our spring/And all the bloom we owe.   Piping Peace.   James Shirley.   ACP; LoBV; NOBE; OBEV

Who is the source of soul?/ADONAI Who?   Dan Jaffe.   FAZ

"Who is there as small as you?"   Yang-Se-Fu.   Yehoash.   TrJP

Who is this glorious King? The Lord of armies guiding,/Even He the King of glory hight.   Pslam XXIV.   Sir Philip Sidney.   FCP

Who is this man running with me,/The shadow of whose hands I see?   Foot Race Song.   Anonymous.   NU; OBVE

Who is to tell the stories he saw/flashing in the dust?   The Idiot.   Keith Wilson.   Psk

Who is trying to speak to us?   A Handful of Dust.   James Oppenheim.   TrJP

Who is waiting and waiting for you to come down/Out of the heaven into her arms.   Young Men You Are So Beautiful up There.   Patricia Goedicke.   GP

Who is walking a small, white dog/through the plum-brown, silvery trees.   Not Seeing Is Believing.   Paul Petrie.   TAP

Who it is stays me when again I'm still.   Wind.   Anonymous.   AnOE

Who join'd with Norman-French compound the Breed/From whence your True-Born Englishmen proceed.   The English Race.   Daniel Defoe.   OBEC

Who jumped out with meat–/my meat!   Chops.   Alan Dixon.   BoAnP

Who keep a frog (and, by the way,/They are extremely rare).   The Frog.   Hilaire Belloc.   FaBoBe; FaBV; FiBHP; GoJo; HBV 1-2; InMe; MoShBr; NA; NTCP; OxBChV

Who keeps her secret in the leaves Who is You Her dark Her/green outspreading Zohara.   Jack Hirschman.   VWA

"Who keeps the tongue doth keep his soul."   The Tongue.   Phillips Burrows Strong.   PoToHe; TreFT; WBLP

Who killed all the birds that died/last summer.   One-Eyed Gunner.   Anonymous.   OxNR

"Who kissed you through the dark, dear guesser?"   A Child's Thought of God.   Elizabeth Barrett Browning.   TRV

Who knew when the war was going to end.   Rumors.   Reginald Arkell.   GoTF; TreFT

Who know not any sorrow yet,/Call it the dew.   Sympathy.   Althea Gyles.   HBV 1-2

Who know not whence I am sped, nor to what port I sail.   The Hope of the World.   William Watson.   WGRP

Who know them best despise them most.   On Seeing the Royal Palace at Stirling in Ruins.   Robert Burns.   DBV

Who, knowing stars, was fearless of the night.   Ad Matrem in Coelis.   Linda Lyon Van Voorhis.   GoBC

Who, known to all, unknown to himself dies.   Happy He.   Anonymous.   EIL

Who knows but all is for the best?   Song: "Indeed, my Caelia, 'tis in vain."   Sir John Henry Moore.   OBEC

Who knows but the rest will be nicer than these?   Ambition.   Aline Kilmer.   HBMV

Who knows how wide its realm may be?/Its depths, how deep?   A Grave.   John Richard Moreland.   HBMV

(Who knows? the best yet unexpress'd and lacking.)   The Unexpress'd.   Walt Whitman.   NePA; PP

Who knows what themes,/What lunar senses,/Compel his dreams?   Meditation on a Memoir.   J. V. Cunningham.   QFR

Who knows what there yet may be?   Our Flag.   Frances Crosby Hamlet.   PGD

Who knows what vagrant dreams may ride/On this frail ship forevermore?   Thoughts upon a Walk with Natalie, My Niece, at Houghton Farm.   Harold Trowbridge Pulsifer.   HBMV

Who knows where!   Who Knows Where.   Detlev Freiherr von Liliencron.   AWP

...Who knows where that/man and that feeling are now.   My Past.   Dennis Cooper.   APU

Who knows without these guarded doors,/What wind across the desert roars?   Allah's Tent.   Arthur Colton.   HBV 1-2

Who lacks the imagination to be cautious/lacks the ignorance to be afraid   Einstein's Father.   Daniel L. Klauck.   LTB

Who lay in the dark thinking Roses, Roses, Roses.   The Sleeping.   Lynn Emanuel.   MAYP

Who lead through forests of darkness to the dawn?   Need of an Angel.   Raymond Souster.   CaP

...Who learn of happiness/from the report of their own actions.   Europe.   Louis Dudek.   OBCV; PeCV

Who learns my carol and carries it away?   The Yule Days.   Anonymous.   GBP

Who least hath some, who most hath never all.   Tymes Goe by Turnes.   Robert Southwell.   FaBoEn

Who left England for Virginia/in sixteen seventeen/and died off Gravesend.   The Ambassadors.   Paul Lawson.   GP

Who, let me say, is this stranger regards me,/With the gray eyes, and the lovely brown hair?   Separation.   Matthew Arnold.   HBV 1-2

Who lets me quickly go will surest gain.   Riddle: "I have no wings, but yet I fly."   Mary Austin.   SoPo; TiPo

Who lied in the Chapel/Now lies in the Abbey.   Epitaph for William Pitt. George Gordon, Lord Byron.   FaBoEE

Who lies deeper in the drifting dark than life.   Now That My Father Lies down Beside Me.   Stanley Plumly.   GeTw

Who lies with dogs, shall rise with fleas.   Bad Company.   Rowland Watkyns.   FaBoEE

Who like an alien sadly dwells/Within your chime, sweet Sunday Bells!   Sunday Bells.   William Allingham.   IrPN

Who, like us, has yet to know,/if ever,/the losers from the winners.   Winslow Homer, Prisoners from the Front.   Roger Blakely.   PoDr

Who lingers in the purlieus of the towns/With unexplored grace and savage frowns.   To the Mountains.   Henry David Thoreau.   PoEL 1-5

Who list to know, this abstract will declare.   New English Canaan, the Authors Prologue.   Thomas Morton.   SCAP

Who live by killing you and me.   A Sword in a Cloud of Light.   Kenneth Rexroth.   NMP

Who lived as a man among men his days,/And belongs to the ages now!   Abraham Lincoln.   Samuel Valentine Cole.   OHIP

Who lives on hills robed with the jungle.   To Krishna Haunting the Hills.   Andal.   BoWoP

Who liveth and is young for ever and ever.   Hymn to the Sun.   Akhnaton (Amenhotep IV).   LiTW; TTY

Who living, loved, in death were not divided.   The Slide at the Empire Mine.   Harriet L. Wason.   PoOW

Who'll buy my daffydillies?   Who'll Buy My Valley Lilies?   Eleanor Farjeon.   BrR

Who'll buy my white sand?   White Sand and Grey Sand.   *Anonymous.*   CBEP

"Who'll come a-waltzing Matilda with me?"   Waltzing Matilda.   *Anonymous.*   GBP

Who'll come and join me in a spree?   Champagne Charlie.   George Leybourne.   BLSo; PSoN

"Who'll come on ops in a Wimpey with me?"   Ops in a Wimpey.   *Anonymous.*   CoMu

Who'll feed on them living, and foul them when dead.   The Living Dog and the Dead Lion.   Thomas Moore.   OBRV

Who'll laugh loudest?/Let us try.   School Is over.   Kate Greenaway.   TiPo

Who'll lay down under my darkened thigh?   The Shrouded Stranger.   Allen Ginsberg.   NeAP

Who'll let me out some gala day,/With implements to fly away,/Passing pomposity?   Bring me the sunset in a cup.   Emily Dickinson.   MoAmPo

Who'll take care of the cats?   Dear Girl.   Gregory Corso.   NoAm

Who long have paved hell with their good intentions.'   At the Gate of Heaven.   George Gordon, Lord Byron.   OBRV

Who longing, longing, longing am to Match her/Whose my Dear Sheaf, and I her only/Thatcher.   A Love Letter to Elizabeth Thatcher.   Thomas Thatcher.   SCAP

Who look for death, and fear it ev'ry day.   Epigram.   *Anonymous.*   EnLi 1-2

Who (look). ,startled.   Four III "here's a little mouse."   Edward Estlin Cummings.   FaBoMo

Who, looking on our grief, hath often grieved.'   La Vita Nuova.   Dante Alighieri.   AWP

Who love, better than the earth,/Wild plum at night.   Wild Plum.   Orrick Johns.   HBMV; PG

Who Love can temper thus,/Good Lord, deliver us!   A Litany.   Sir Philip Sidney.   OBSC; UnPo

Who love others, they love Him.   Christ Is Here.   Robert Lowell.   BePJ

Who loved blood as an alderman loves marrow.   Don Juan.   George Gordon, Lord Byron.   OAEL 1-2

Who loved to play cars/with empty cartons of milk.   Javier.   Jose Y., Jr. Teran.   LFAC

Who loves himself loves me who love myself.   Sather Gate Illumination.   Allen Ginsberg.   NeAP

"Who loves not wine, woman, and song,/He is a fool his whole life long!"   A Credo.   William Makepeace Thackeray.   HBV 1-2

...Who loves or works here assumes/For better or worse, the ground rules. A fate.   Fifty-Seventh Street and Fifth.   Alfred Corn.   NYP

Who made his bed for years beneath the stars.   The Earth Will Stay the Same.   Frank Ernest Hill.   AnAmPo

Who made me known must make me/live unseen.   The Complaint of Rosamond.   Samuel Daniel.   OAEP

Who made that advance–/After Johnson's dance?   After Johnson's Dance.   Charles H. Souter.   PoAu 1-2

Who made the back-band? Whoa, goddam!   Whoa Back, Buck.   *Anonymous.*   FSW

Who made the world's best one hand snatch   Meet Mr. Universe.   Edward Estlin Cummings.   OBAL

"Who make up a heaven of our misery."   The Chimney Sweeper.   William Blake.   AtBAP; BoW; EnPE; NAWM 1-2; PPP; SaC; TEP

Who makes from each storm-wracked harvest/The bread of brotherhood.   Bread of Brotherhood.   Lucia Trent.   PGD

Who makes our thrall and bondage cease.   Behold with Joy.   Elhanan Winchester.   AH

Who makes the one, so it be first, makes both.   An Epitaph on Master Vincent Corbett.   Ben Jonson.   JCP

Who makes the whole world fair.   Chanson of the Bells of Oseney.   Cale Young Rice.   AnFE; APA; HBV 1-2

Who might, but never does, arrive on the next train.   Where the Single Men Go in Summer.   Nina Bourne.   FiBHP

Who might have meetly used it.   A Placid Man's Epitaph.   Thomas Hardy.   MoBrPo

–Who might have wished for something lasting,/Like a wooden box.   The Monuments of Hiroshima.   D. J. Enright.   OBSP

Who, minus you, am nothing but a nought.   Love Song out of Nothing.   Vassar Miller.   NePoEA

Who mourn the death of beauty and the death of grace.   The Age of a Dream.   Lionel Pigot Johnson.   OBMV

Who moved their muscles to another's mind.   A Green and Pleasant Land.   John Peale Bishop.   PoPl

Who murdered little Omie down by the mill dam.   Omie Wise.   *Anonymous.*   FSW

Who must about our necks the millstone bear.   Lachesis.   Kathleen Raine.   NYBP

Who must be slaughtered backward into time.   The Man from the Top of the Mind.   David Wagoner.   NePoEA-2

Who mute upon her tomb doth pray,/Till the resurrection day.   The Poetry of a Root Crop.   Charles Kingsley.   LoBV

Who ne'er in those encounters fight/To die–but get their living by't.   A Survey of the Amphitheatre.   Moses Browne.   NOEC

Who need no moon/to dream by.   Dervish.   Georgia Lee McElhaney.   CoPo

Who needed to touch, touched, still/touches these pages of the chestnut rain.   Auction.   William Heyen.   MAYP

...Who needs/them? Wills. Lovers. You.   For an Obligate Parasite.   Alan Dugan.   TW

Who never by any chance hurt one of them.   On Apis the Prizefighter.   Lucilius [(or Lucillius)].   WeW

Who never held up anybody.   The Shooting of John Dillinger Outside the Biograph Theater...   David Wagoner.   CoAP; FYAP; SM

Who never in his life forgave a friend.   Epigram: "To forgive enemies Hayley does pretend."   William Blake.   FaBoEE

Who never inherited song/From the twittering birds of the sky.   The Song of the Trout Fisher.   Ikinilik.   WTO

Who never made, or saw, a joke.   The Old Songs.   Sir Owen Seaman.   InMe

Who never more will trouble you, trouble you.   On William Wilson, Tailor.   *Anonymous.*   FaBoEE

Who never, never goes!   My Familiar.   John Godfrey Saxe.   AnNE; GoTF

Who now, deposed, surveys my plain abode/And his late kingdom, only from the road.   My House, I Say. But Hark to the Sunny Doves.   Robert Louis Stevenson.   FM; NOBV

Who now flares here the contriver/manifest.../and indifferent.   Women of Trachis: Choruses.   Sophocles.   CTC; OBVE

Who now goes drunkenly out/And leaves her too much alone.   The Beautiful Toilet.   *Anonymous.*   OBVE

Who now hover above his track/and at night light upon his back.   For Freckle-Faced Gerald.   Etheridge Knight.   BPo; LFAC; NeAC

Who now is venturing their lives in North America.   On the Late Engagement in Charles Town River.   *Anonymous.*   OBSS

Who now triumphs, and in th'excess of joy/Sole reigning holdst the Tyranny of Heav'n.   Paradise Lost.   John Milton.   SCV

Who, of all saints, the Lord and Savior was.   The Song of Mary the Mother of Christ.   Henry Walpole.   ISi

...Who of all the poets are kind to one another?   Cliques and Critics.   Sa'ib of Isfahan.   LiTW

Who of little Love–know how to starve–   Victory comes late.   Emily Dickinson.   InPK

Who offered life, instead of lonely days.   Elegy.   G. S. Fraser.   NeBP

Who oft doth think, must needsd die well.   The Pilgrimage.   Sir Walter Ralegh.   CAW

Who oft fore-judge my after-following race,/By only those two starres in Stellas face.   Astrophel and Stella, XXVI.   Sir Philip Sidney.   AAS; OAEL 1-2; SiPS

Who on earth no comfort own/Save Thy death and Cross alone!   The Tree of the Cross.   Angelus Selesius (Johannes Scheffler).   CAW

Who on her skimming-dish carves her name.   Song: "Oh the charming month of May!"   Joseph Addison.   NOEC

Who, on the other side of the brook/Blows a surging flute?   Multitudinous Stars.   Ping Hsin (Hsieh Wang-ying).   PBWP

Who once desired you, but desire no more!   Keats to Fanny Brawne.   Edgar Lee Masters.   PoA

...Who once had caught/A wink, a glimpse, of Paradise.   The Raising of the Dead.   Rosemary Dobson.   PoAu 1-2

Who once has trodden stars seeks peace no more.   Who Has Known Heights. Mary Brent Whiteside.   BLPA

Who once lives, never dies!'   The Night-Wind.   Emily Bronte.   OAEP

Who once said all his say, when he was young!   Egan O Rahilly.   James Stephens.   CBEP; EBEV; NoAm; OBMV; SeCePo

Who, one way or another, were made ghosts/in all their country's wars.   A Letter for Allhallows.   Peter Kane Dufault.   NYBP

Who only come for love.   The Wayside.   James Herbert Morse.   AA

Who only spend the night alone/And strike my fist upon the stone.   The Mill-stream, Now that Noises Cease.   Alfred Edward Housman.   GBL

Who? oooh/The wind.   The Wind.   Betty Miller.   BrR

Who or which or why or what Is the Akond of Swat?   The Akond of Swat.   Edward Lear.   ALV; CenHV; FaBoCh; FaBoCo; FaBoNo; FiBHP

...Who otherwise shall dine,/Are like a troop marauding for their prey.   Gastrology (excerpt).   Archestratus.   FaBoUs

...Who, over the subway station,/steals in, with Sandals gray, but no elation.   Nuit Blanche: North End.   Conrad Aiken.   OxBA

Who pay no praise or wages/Nor heed my craft or art.   In My Craft or Sullen Art.   Dylan Thomas.   BoLoP; ChMP; CMoP; DiPo; GTBS-P; HAP; HeIP; InvP; LiTM; MAT; NeBP; NIP; NoAm; NoP; OAEP; PP; SeCeV; WeW

Who peaceful lived with poverty content.   Abdolonymus the Sidonian. Jones Very.   AP

Who perished in the cause of Right.   The Death of Lincoln.   William Cullen Bryant.   AmePo; AmP; AP; ForPo; TAP

Who plays the hand that plays the instrument?   Bard.   Theodore Black. AMV-81

Who ploughs foaming billows in search of adventure!   The India Guide.... Sir George Dallas.   NOEC

Who praise not grandly/But wish they could   The Everlasting Contenders. Kenneth Patchen.   CrMA; NaP

Who prefers to live/Glissandissimo,/Pianissimo.   Eine Kleine Snailmusik. May Sarton.   NLV

Who press their fortunes to the hilt,/Respond to duty's call.   Great Churches. *Anonymous.*   STF

...Who prostrate lies,/Without the power to drink or rise.   Not Drunk Is He. Thomas Love Peacock.   ViBoPo

Who rais'd? Who mine/Did make the same? What hand divine?   The Rapture.   Thomas Traherne.   OBS

...Who ran/The race we run, when Heaven recalls him hence.   On the Death of Southey.   Walter Savage Landor.   OBVV

Who read to doubt, or read to scorn.   Sir Walter Scott's Tribute.   Sir Walter Scott.   WBLP

Who reads the most, is most refin'd,/And polish'd by the Master's hand. Hymns for the Amusement of Children.   Christopher Smart.   NOCV

Who really lives there?   At the Tourist Center in Boston.   Margaret Atwood.   NoP

Who reigns, and shall forever reign.   Come, Let Us Tune Our Loftiest Song. Robert A. West.   AH

Who rests on this old grey wall/Lays a hand on the shoulder of God!   The Old Grey Wall.   Bliss Carman.   CaP

Who ride Thy realms on Birds of Steel.   Prayer for a Pilot.   Cecil Roberts. BBV

Who rides through gold to murder,/To quicklime and to clay.   The Man from Strathbogie.   Robert D. FitzGerald.   NOAV

Who roared and reached and caught and held her there.   In a Railway Compartment.   John Fuller.   NePoEA-2

Who Rodantha driv'st away/From my dreams by break of day.   The Swallow.   Thomas Stanley.   AWP

Who roots their vice out, must pierce deeper in.   Caelica, CVI.   Fulke, Lord Brooke Greville.   FCP

"Who's a pretty boy then?" Budgie cried.   Budgie Finds His Voice (parody). Wendy Cope.   FaBoPa

Who's coming out with me?   Growing Up.   A.(lan) A.(lexander) Milne. BiCB

Who's doing better, then? What about you?   The Evans Country.   Kingsley Amis.   NOBL

Who's getting it today? We freeze and listen,/then all but one of us knows it isn't him...   Iambes VIII.   Andre Marie de Chenier.   FaBoPV

Who's ill?/Me? A pill?   Thin Ice.   David McCord.   TiPo

Who's that fallen—me or him?   A Serenade.   Thomas Hood.   NLV

Who's the fool now?   Martin Said to His Man.   *Anonymous.*   FaBoNo; NA

Who's to say/what follows after?   Judas, Joyous Little Son.   Norma Farber. AMV-80

Who's within there?   Tamburlaine the Great.   Christopher Marlowe. EBEV; PoEL 1-5

Who said it had horns, but was not a beast.   Riddle: "Itum Paradisum all clothed in green."   *Anonymous.*   GBP

Who said Let there be light?   Ward Two.   Francis Webb.   CBAP

Who sat upon the pulpit stair and prayed.'   A Legend.   Adelaide Anne Procter.   GoBC

Who saw her stand beside the hearth,/The firelight garbing her in gold?   The Beatific Vision.   Gilbert Keith Chesterton.   MoRP

Who says that butterflies,/Are brief?   Butterflies.   Haniel Long.   HBMV

Who says, There is neither Transgression nor Sin;/A Doctrine that brings many Customers in.   Letter Containing a Panegyric on Bath.   Christopher Anstey.   OBEC

Who says two sexes aren't enough?   Love-Songs, At Once Tender and Informative.   Samuel Hoffenstein.   OBAL

Who/Says/We shall not survive among the turbines?   Cornfields in Accra. Christine Ama Ata Aidoo.   WPOW

Who says, with "SOUTHERN DARING,"/"I'LL FIND A WAY, OR MAKE IT!"   On Fort Sumter.   *Anonymous.*   MC; PAH

Who scorn'd any Fence but a jolly Abdomen?   Extempore Verses upon a Trial of Skill....   John Byrom.   OBEC

Who see by faith the cloudy hem/Of Judgment fringed with Mercy's light! Astraea at the Capitol.   John Greenleaf Whittier.   PAH

Who see the world's great anguish and its wrong/And dare not speak! Mourn Not the Dead.   Ralph Chaplin.   HBMV; ViBoPo

Who seeks alway thine honour to preserve.   The Golden Gift That Nature Did Thee Give.   Henry Howard, Earl of Surrey.   AAS; FCP; SiPS

Who seeks their kin, left naked now,/To dig in Gwanas' graves may go.   The Song of the Graves.   Ernest Rhys.   OBMV

Who sees her must love and who loves her must die.   Silvia.   Sir George Etherege.   CavP

Who sees their glories on the earth must pry;/Who seeks true glory must look to the sky.   Caelica, LXII.   Fulke, Lord Brooke Greville.   FCP

Who sees, will spew; who smells, be poison'd.   A Beautiful Young Nymph Going to Bed.   Jonathan Swift.   DBV; EiCP; NIP; NOEC; UnTE

Who sent us—so be pardoned all her faults—/A dozen dukes, some kings, a queen—and Waltz.   The Waltz: Hail, Spirit-Stirring Waltz.   George Gordon, Lord Byron.   OBSV

Who serves her truly, sometimes serves the State.   Serve in Thy Post. Arthur Hugh Clough.   PGD

Who shakes the fire on the snowy pave.   The Jew at Christmas Eve.   Karl Shapiro.   VGW

Who shall abide its noon-tide hour?   To a Very Young Lady.   Edmund Waller.   EG

Who shall explain the majesty of women/To us? to us? Exaltation, softness, pleasure.   Green Grass Growing.   Patrick Evans.   NeBP

Who shall his corpse in the best dish present.   Of Death.   Samuel Harding. CBEP

...Who shall his fame impair/When thou art dead, and all thy wretched crew? Sonnet: Written on the Day that Mr. Leigh Hunt Left Prison.   John Keats. ChRP

Who shall put forth on thee,/Unfathomable Sea?   Time.   Percy Bysshe Shelley.   EnLi 1-2; FaBoRV; FPL; MOS; Par; PoLf

Who shall say I am not/the happy genius of my household?   Danse Russe. William Carlos Williams.   CMoP; ForPo; InPS; NOBA; NoP; PAI; PPP; TAP

Who shivers the taut shrouds, and singeth there.   Five Degrees South. Francis Brett Young.   EtS

Who should be saved by them and joined with them.   Paracelsus.   Robert Browning.   WGRP

Who should have arrived/for a visit days ago.   Days Ago.   Dianne Hai-Jew. BrSi

Who showed themselves to me down in Ragwort Meadow.   Midsummer Magic.   Ivy O. Eastwick.   BrR; TiPo

Who side by side will stand or fall.   The Pines.   Julie Mathilde Lippmann. AA

...Who sings/and sings in the deepending well/of your sleep.   Keeping You Alive.   Tess Gallagher.   GP

Who sings thy praise? onely a scarf or glove/Doth warm our hands, and make them write of love.   Love.   George Herbert.   AnAnS 1

Who sins, ye rich, if He stands starving here?   For a Blind Beggar's Sign. Clemente Biondi.   CAW

...Who sipped Love in their prime/Must gulp it down at Closing Time.   To His Not-So-Coy Mistress.   Wynford Vaughan-Thomas.   BXAP; NOBL

Who sleeps in Paradise.   To a Happy Warrior.   Wilfrid Scawen Blunt. AnEnPo

Who sleeps in the zoo   Five Songs.   David Shapiro.   ANYP

Who slowly ford the Mystery/Which thou hast leaped across!   Pass to thy Rendezvous of Light.   Emily Dickinson.   NAWM 1-2

Who snatcheth it—lost we not Phaedrus so?   On Alexis.   Plato.   AWP

Who-so festeth hope on him,/He shal him folwen to helle dim.   The Bestiary: The Whale.   *Anonymous.*   OxBM

Who-so may nought do his dede, he shall to parke,/Barefoot withouten shone, and go with Lyarde.   Lyarde Is an Old Horse.   *Anonymous.*   OxBM

Who spares the first and keeps the last unspent,/Shall find that sparing yields a goodly rent.   Gascoigne's Memories.   George Gascoigne.   EnRePo

Who speaks of the Belov'd's woe as not his/Speaks infidelity, true Lovers know!   The Bustan.   Muslih-ud-Din Sa'di.   AWP

Who spoke out for the dumb and the down-trodden then! A Fable for Critics. James Russell Lowell. AP; OxBA

Who spurned me for seeing what he could not see. The Nettles. Thomas Hardy. OBSP

Who squandered here life's mystery. Breughel's Winter. Walter De la Mare. SeCePo

Who stands erect in self-respect,/And acts the man for a that. For A' That and A' That (parody). *Anonymous.* BXAP

Who stares, sips water, and remembers/Everything we say. Antipater of Thessalonica. Kenneth Rexroth. CrMA

"Who started the Great War?'/I did, I did, I did. Question Time. Jack Lindsay. NOAV

Who stealeth thise boke/Ye divel shall cooke. Who Folds a Leafe Downe. *Anonymous.* FaBoUs

Who steals the common from the goose. Epigram: On Inclosures. *Anonymous.* FaBoCo; OxBoLi

Who still, 'mid War's embattled lines,/Gave this one touch of Nature. Music in Camp. John Reuben Thompson. AA; BLPA; HBV 1-2

Who still must ask why it all began. A Primer for Schoolchildren. Richard Weber. CIP

Who still tends to titles as if all of us/Are reading a new book called THE NEW LIFE. The Complete Introductory Lectures on Poetry. Bernadette Mayer. APU

Who still would fear, who judge? Without More Weight. Giuseppe Ungaretti. PoPl

Who stirs the clutter in her little room Out of Chaos Out of Order Out. Michele Roberts. BrRo

Who stole my Cadillac, my coupe de ville,/and who got away with my girl. Don't Anybody Move. Daniel Mark Epstein. AmC

Who straight, "Your suit is granted," said, and died. Redemption. George Herbert. AnAnS 1; CABA; EaLo; EBCP; ExPo; FF; HAP; InPK; InPS; JCP; LiTB; MeLP; MePo; NOBE; NOCV; NoP; OBS; PAI; SCV; SeCeV; SeCP; SeCV 1-2; SoSe; TEP; TrCP

Who studies this,/Travels in Clouds, seekes Manna, where none is. Silex Scintillans. Henry Vaughan. AnAnS 1

Who suffer here on earth. Rebirth. Margaret E. Bruner. PoToHe

Who suffers, I fear, by comparison. Limerick: "There's a vaporish maiden in Harrison." Morris Bishop. LiBL; TDH

Who summons him forth, and now/Pulls wide the great, thoughtful arrow. The Summons. James Dickey. LiSp

...Who sums his years/(Like me) with no arithmetic, but tears The Anniverse: An Elegy. Henry, Bishop of Chichester King. JCP

Who sure intended him to stretch a rope. The Boss. James Russell Lowell. OBAL; SaC

Who swam ten miles out–and nine back. On Being Much Better Than Most and Yet Not Quite Good Enough. John Ciardi. GOYP

Who swim about the pond with her/And do as they are told. The Duck. Edith King. HBVY

Who takes my place when I'm gone. Here Is a Toast That I Want to Drink. Walter Lathrop. PoLf

Who takes off his clothes/And holds out his hands to the stove. Warmth. Barton Sutter. GOYP

Who taught me betimes to love Working and Reading. The Sluggard. Isaac Watts. CEP; CH; HAP; HBV 1-2; HBVY; MoShBr; NOEC; OBEC; OxBChV; PaPo; PoEL; 1-5; SpRo

Who taught me the serpent's word, but yet the word. The Dark and the Fair. Stanley Jasspon Kunitz. PoCh

Who taught you your deft poise? Chapel Deacon. R. S. Thomas. ACV

Who teaches the place where couches the sun?/(If not I) The Mystery. Douglas Hyde. OnYI; OxBI

Who teaches us how to faint? After he stripped off my clothes. Vallana. BoWoP

Who teacheth; nor who doth, from wise in heart. A Counsel of Moderation. Francis Thompson. MoBrPo

"Who telleth one of my meanings/Is master of all I am." The Sphinx. Ralph Waldo Emerson. AP; DiPo; MAmP; NOBA; OxBA

Who that's human would refuse it,/When a little water does it? Cleanliness. Charles and Mary Lamb. OxBChV

Who the celestial C.O.? Star Drill. T. Inglis Moore. PoAu 1-2

Who then, when thou art gone, will fire all bosoms/most! Solvitur Acris Hiems. Francis Sylvester ("Father Prout") Mahony. IrPN

Who therefore censures God with fleshly sprite,/As well in time may wrap up infinite. Caelica, CIII. Fulke, Lord Brooke Greville. FCP

Who thinks he's a poet San Francisco County Jail Cell B-6. Conyus. PoBA

Who thinks he will croon his way/out of this? A Photo of Miners. Brendan Galvin. LTB

Who thinks most–feels the noblest–acts the best. The Aim of Life: A Country Town. Philip James Bailey. PoToHe

Who this snowy night/rubs her small hands/wishing them lined with earth. This Poem Is for Nadine. Paul B. Janeczko. GOYP

Who, though he ulcers have in ev'ry part,/Is nowhere so corrupt as in his heart. The Hypocrite. John Caryll. APAS

Who thought on failure of our church to perpetrate a joke. How We Built a Church at Ashcroft. Jack Leahy. PoOW

Who thought on three men dead. Flannan Isle. Wilfred Wilson Gibson. CH; MoVE; OBVV; PoRA; StPo

Who through the billows/Did make a road and to dry land did lead you. Oh, Sing to God. Jacob Steendam. AH

Who thus inflames them with heroick Fires. The Iliad. Homer. OBVE

Who thus proceeds, for aye, in sacred mount/shall reign. Psalm XV. Sir Philip Sidney. FCP

Who to have had it, would have been/Contenteder–to die– My portion is defeat–today. Emily Dickinson. OBWP

Who to the wretched creature's caudal part/Its foolish empty-jingling "burden' ties." After Dilettante Concetti (parody). Henry Duff Traill. BXAP; CenHV; FaBoCo; HBV 1-2; Par

Who to wedlock, his wonder wedlock,/Deals triumph and immortal years. At the Wedding March. Gerard Manley Hopkins. HW

Who took my flesh and bone for armour/And doublecrossed my mother's womb. Before I Knocked and Flesh Let Enter. Dylan Thomas. FaBoTw

Whos toss and sigh and cannot rest. The Moon at the Fortified Pass. Li Po. LiTW; WaaP

Who touch my body with a silence/more beautiful than poetry Kiss. Al Young. PoBA

Who touch quick fingers fluttering like a bird/Whose songs shall never be heard. Spectral Lovers. John Crowe Ransom. GBL; HeIP

Who tread the crooked path and hollow way. Hope. Theognis. AWP

Who tread the mossy track to dip their pails/Into the lonely Spring– Fragment: "Near where the riotous Atlantic surge." William Allingham. IrPN

Who turn her meads to graves. Spring. Henry Timrod. AP

Who turns the veriest sullen unto laughter. Song of Breath. Peire Vidal. AWP

Who understands him. The Wise Woman. Louis Untermeyer. ALV; HBMV

Who undertakes this subject to commend/Shall nothing find so hard as how to end. A Funeral Elogy... John Norton II. SCAP

Who undiscovered, yet will us betray,/And sell their country in a closer way. Advice to a Painter. *Anonymous.* APAS

Who use the language of thieves/are thieves Why I Never Went into Politics. Richard Shelton. Str

Who used to stroll over the fields through the whole divine/night. Bread and Wine, Part 7. Friedrich Holderlin. NU

Who vowed if ere he lived for to be a man,/O' the treacherous Scots revengd hee'd be. Johnie Armstrong (A vers.). *Anonymous.* ViBoFo

Who waiteth for thy fruits in vain,/Should also take the rod? Symbols. Christina Georgina Rossetti. VLP

Who waits, at the terrible door, but I? The Terrible Door. Harold Monro. BoLoP; EnLoPo; FaBoTw

Who walk by right/On the naked hills. We Who Were Born. Eiluned Lewis. BiCB; TiPo

Who walk the wilds this night. Christmas Eve. Liam P. Clancy. ISi

Who walked with Adam once in the green shade. To My Father. James Keir Baxter. AnNZ

Who walking makes no footprint and/no shadow on soft-fallen snow. Hospital Evening. Gwen Harwood. FaBoWP

Who walks thy garden eve on eve, and bows his head, and calls thee Friend. Gates of Damascus. James Elroy Flecker. AnFE; BrPo; HBMV

Who was a man. Malcolm X. Gwendolyn Brooks. BALP; BP; CNA; OFD; PoBA; TTY

Who was a Saint of course! (Genuflecton.) Parliament of Cats. D. J. Enright. NMP

Who was alive and is dead,/There's no more to be said. Epigram on Prince Frederick. *Anonymous.* FaBoCo

Who was all this and ours, and all men's,–/WASHINGTON. Under the Old Elm. James Russell Lowell. GN; PAL; PGD

Who was always beginning things and never ended 'em. Epitaph upon Himself. Hilaire Belloc. FaBoEE

Who was neither ingenious, sober, nor kind. Epitaph. Francis, Lord Jeffrey Jeffrey. OxBoLi

Who was, nor this, nor that, but all we find,/And all we can imagine in mankind. Upon Ben. Johnson. Edmund Waller. SeCV 1-2

Who was not even an Academician. On Himself. *Anonymous.* FaBoEE

Who was not even, not ever,/Taken from your side. Ark Overwhelmed. Jay Macpherson. NOBC

Who was she? For that matter, who was I? Memoir. Robert Guy Howarth. PV

Who was She to withold from me/Penury and Home? Frigid and sweet her parting face. Emily Dickinson. PeHV

Who was so fine once, whose hands were so soft. Tales of the Islands, III. Derek Walcott. OxBTC

Who was so proud, so witty, and so wise. Homo Sapiens. John Wilmot, Earl of Rochester. NOBE

Who was St. Vincent St. Vincent's. William Stanley Merwin. NYP

Who was the Beautiful. The Beautiful. John Aylmer Dorgan. AA

Who was the beginning of all light. A Brave-Hearted Maid. *Anonymous.* ISi

Who was then a gentleman? When Adam Delved. *Anonymous.* SaC

"Who was this old stone man beneath our toes?" The Children and Sir Nameless. Thomas Hardy. NoP

"Who was this Romney?" The Romney. Harriet Monroe. HBMV

Who was tho a gentleman? Snatches: "When Adam dalf and Eve span." *Anonymous.* OxBM

Who watch your image/flaming in the sun For Malcolm Who Walks in the Eyes of Our Children. Quincy Troupe. CNA; PoBA

Who wear our bones inside. Lower Forms of Life. Mary Winter. GoYe

Who wears the scent of violets/on her young breasts. If my nipples were to drip milk. Sappho. BoWoP

Who wears the uniform of death? Lan Nguyen: The Uniform of Death 1971. David Mura. BrSi

Who weeps over fallen trees? Place-of-Many-Swans. Charlotte DeClue. STE; TWSS

Who went at dawn to that high star/Where Washington and Lincoln are. Grover Cleveland. Joel Benton. PAH

Who wert and art and evermore shalt be! Who Wert and Art and Evermore Shalt Be. William Channing Gannett. TrPWD

Who, when asked for a remedy, sent down a rope. An Ode to the Framers of the Frame Bill. George Gordon, Lord Byron. CoMu; SaC

Who, when he had won all, renounced all, and sought in the/bosom of his family and of nature... Inscription at Mount Vernon. *Anonymous.* PGD

WHO? WHO? WHO? O WHO? Thirteen O'Clock. Kenneth Fearing. ExPo

WHO? WHOOOOOO? in aching heat. A Simple Story. Gwen Harwood. FaBoWP; NOAV

Who will be brave enough/To wait for them? Python. *Anonymous.* WTO

Who will be wounded most? Romantic. George Garrett. HoPM

Who will deal alone with God? The Mythos of Samuel Huntsman. Hyam Plutzik. LiTM

Who will die first? Catechisms: Talking with a Four-Year-Old. George Ella Lyon. Str

Who will guide me to the dwelling of Abla? Abla. Antar [(or Antana)]. LiTW

Who will kneel them gently down/before the Lord, new-born? Words from an Old Spanish Carol. Ruth Sawyer. BrR; ChBR; PCh

Who will not hear and make his word their friend. Life. Jones Very. AP

Who will not leave her/Till her hair is white. Song of Snow-White Heads. Cho Wen-chun. BoWoP

Who will not save a penny/Shall never have many. Penny and Penny. *Anonymous.* OxNR

Who will not stop to hear it/On any April day. The Concert. Phyllis McGinley. YeAr

Who will remain the ash-monuments/Witnessing the explosions of our revenge. Vengeance. Raymond Mazisi Kunene. WhB

...Who will remember/This lady of the West Country? An Epitaph. Walter De la Mare. LiTM

Who will remember this music/if the reeds forget when the wind stops? Museum with Chinese Landscapes. Walter Cybulski. AMV-81

...Who will save us/after my mother's son is buried? Rain to the Tribe. Al-Khansa. BoWoP

Who will sew your buttons on?/My, my, my! Old Ben Golliday. Mark Van Doren. SO

Who will speak these days,/if not I,/if not you? The Speed of Darkness. Muriel Rukeyser. LCAP

Who will start another fire? Before Chilembwe Tree. Jack A. Mapanje. WhB

Who will study war until they are free! Sing Me a New Song. John Henrik Clarke. PoBA

Who will to them more kind protection lend/Than He which did protect me in distress? To the Right Noble, Valourous, and Learned Prince Henry... Sir John Davies. SiPS

Who will walk when he can dance? Sings a Bird. John Nist. AMV-80

Who willed us greater tasks, when set his sun. Abraham Lincoln, the Master. Thomas Curtis Clark. OHIP

Who wilt, by killing, finally release. Sonnet: "Leave me, all sweet refrains my lip hath made." Luîs de Camoens. AWP

Who with each heartbeat fight the fear of change. Need. Babette Deutsch. MoLP; PCP

Who, with heart in breast, could deny you love? Ceann Dubh Deelish. Sir Samuel Ferguson. IrPN; SeCePo

Who with intemperate crepitation sue/To keep sweet crooning sounds from me to you. Static. Rolfe Humphries. UnS

...Who, with our spleens,/Would all themselves laugh mortal. Measure for Measure. William Shakespeare. GoBC; TreFT; WHA

Who with salt tears this last farewell did take. Before the Birth of One of Her Children. Anne Bradstreet. BoWoP; MAmP; MAT; NAs; NOBA; SBG; WPOW

Who, with their floodgates sundered, drowned when they/were stormed. In the Interstices. Ruth Stone. ErPo

Who with their lives have banished hence the serpent and the/faceless insect. The Cultural Presuppostion. W.H. Auden. CABA

...Who with/Thy Tent/Of Peace dost shelter us that pray, and/all/Thy folk of Israel, and Jerusalem. Evening Prayer. *Anonymous.* TrJP

Who witnessed Havre's smoking plains,/And Hampton's female cries. Sea and Land Victories. *Anonymous.* PAH

Who witnesses, believes. Her face was in a bed of hair. Emily Dickinson. NU

Who won or lost their game and died. A Song about Great Men. Michael Hamburger. NePoEA

Who work in the Pentagon Building. Pentagonia (parody). G. E. Bates. NYBP; SpRo

Who worships thee till music fails/Is greater than thy nightingales. The Moon. William Henry Davies. BrPo; MoBrPo; MoVE

Who wot now that is here/Where he shall be another year? Another Year. *Anonymous.* HAP

Who would buy cycles, failing to try cycles first. Bicycles! Tricycles! John Banister Tabb. OBAL

...Who would expect such/throbbing/from one gland left on earth–my leaden heart? Psychology Today. Judson Jerome. AMV-81

Who would fain his strength renew,/Were it but to pleasure you. To His Mistresses. Robert Herrick. CaPo; ErPo; UnTE

..."Who would fly/From such a fortune sure were scant of wit." Of Three Damsels in a Meadow. John Payne. OBVV

Who would follow in their footsteps/At the risin' of the moon! The Rising of the Moon A.D. 1798. John Keegan Casey. IrPN; OnYI

Who would follow the wind must go/The wind's way. The Wind's Way. Grace Hazard Conkling. HBV 1-2

Who would have a shoemakker? The Shoemakker. *Anonymous.* OBET

Who would have abandoned so young a child this deeply in the/woods? A Natural History of Southwestern Ontario, III. Christopher Dewdney. CaPN

...Who would have dreamed this/infinitely little too much? Science. Robinson Jeffers. NU; OxBA

Who would have gone unto the sea/And brought proud Ward to me.' The Famous Sea Fight between Captain Ward and the Rainbow. *Anonymous.* OBSS

Who would have thought she'd end that way? Mourning Poem for the Queen of Sunday. Robert Earl Hayden. HaCAP; HoAn; NoP; PoBA

Who would have thought so full of change? Who Would Have Thought. Thomas Howell. EIL; PoL

Who would have thought that a guy like that/Had the radio under his hat? Mr. Vachel Lindsay Discovers Radio (parody). Samuel Hoffenstein. BXAP

Who would hold perpetual lease/Of an isle in seas of peace. Patmos. Edith Matilda Thomas. HBV 1-2

Who would I show it to. Elegy. William Stanley Merwin. HaCAP

Who would not cut the Body from the Head. Friend, on This Scaffold Thomas More Lies Dead. J. V. Cunningham. InPK

Who would not die upon the spot. To the State of Love. John Cleveland. MePo; PeD

Who would not follow to the fray,/Their glorious struggle proudly sharing? The Women's Marseillaise. F. E. M. Macaulay. BrRo

Who would not have it so? Tender, Slow. Wallace Rice. ErPo

Who would not pay away his dearest sin/To let such service in? Barter. Margaret Widdemer. HBMV; WGRP

Who would not weep, if Atticus were he? An Epistle from Mr. Pope to Dr. Arbuthnot. Alexander Pope. TW

Who would not write verses with such an assistant? A Ballad to the Tune of "The Cut-Purse." Jonathan Swift. PP

Who would roast my bird/and eat it. The First of May. Barbara Guest. AmPC

Who would saddle me/Had better walk instead/In his quiet garden. The Stallion. Boynton Merrill, Jr. PH

Who would the music be. Each More Melodious Note I Hear. Henry David Thoreau. OBSP

Who would want to steal from us? Who? Being Refused Local Credit. Paula Rankin. MAYP

Who would win, on land or wave,/Must be wise as well as brave. Dewey at Manila. Robert Underwood Johnson. HBV 1-2; MC; PAH

Who would work if he had it to do. An Appeal by Unemployed Ex-Service Men. *Anonymous.* OBET

Who wouldn't be a mountaineer! From Garden to Garden, Ridge to Ridge. John Muir. RFM

Who wouldn't even hear you if you asked her. Sing Song. Robert Creeley. NMP

Who wouldn't lead the life of a jolly wagoner? The Jolly Wagoner. *Anonymous.* TrAS

Who wrestled with the ages/To give the world a bride. The Bride. Ralph Hodgson. HBMV

Who writes him well shall well deserve the Bayes. Britannia's Pastorals. William Browne. OBS

Who wrote like an angel, but talk'd like poor Poll. On Oliver Goldsmith. David Garrick. FaBoEE

Who wrote the world–then heard no more. Emily Dickinson Postage Stamp. Lynn Strongin. NMM

"Who, you?" To praise the Lord, His gracious ways. Elegy for a Bad Poet, Taken from Us Not Long Since. John Frederick Nims. TW

"Whoa! Har! Come 'ere!" The Corn Song. John Wesley Holloway. BANP

Whoa! skew, till I saddle you, whoa! The Skew-Ball Black. *Anonymous.* CoSo

Whoa! Whoa! Whoa! Pinto, whoa! Pinto. *Anonymous.* CoSo

Whoe'er it be I am not now within. The Melancholy Knight: The Poetaster. Samuel Rowlands. ElL

Whoe'er sighs most is cruellest, and hastes the other's/death. A Valediction: of Weeping. John Donne. AtBAP; ATP; CBEP; EG; HAP; HeIP; InPS; MBW 1-2; MeLP; MePo; NoP; OAEL 1-2; OBS; SeCP

Whoever accepts me he or she shall be blessed and shall bless me. Song of the Open Road (excerpt). Walt Whitman. AtBAP

Whoever he be, cannot resist a rhyme. Bathymeter. William Hart-Smith. BoAV

Whoever he was, is now all finished being. Manet: The Execution of Emperor Maximilian. W.D. Snodgrass. AmPC

Whoever holds the/string/will not let go. The Face. Lucien Stryk. GP

Whoever looks round sees Eternity there. Autumn. John Clare. BoNaP; HAP; NBM; NU; PoEL 1-5

Whoever named it, named it well. The Bar. *Anonymous.* STF

...Whoever passes shivers/In the sun and hurries on. The Curse. Robert Francis. TW

Whoever saw a Cinnamon Yak/In the middle of Washington Square. I Took a Bow and Arrow. John Ciardi. EvOK

...Whoever wants to give/only one meaning to that, has untutored taste. Canzone. Marilyn Hacker. SM

Whoever you are, we too lie in drifts at your feet. As I Ebb'd with the Ocean of Life. Walt Whitman. AmPP; LoBV; MAmP; NOBA; PrIm; TAP

The whole air whitens with a boundless tide/Of silver radiance, trembling round the world. The Autumnal Moon. James (1700-48) Thomson. NOBE

The Whole are called Nine Parts of Speech,/Which reading, writing, speaking teach. Grammar in a Nutshell. *Anonymous.* GoTF; HBVY; TreFS

Whole as an apple,/Kind as a friend. A Wasted Day. Frances Cornford. HBMV; MoBrPo

Whole crowds have miscarried/At sight of this dreary Duke. The Duke Is the Lad. Thomas Moore. OnYI; TW

...The whole/earthen bowl churned into foam. A Sound from the Earth. William Stafford. NNaP; RFM

The whole family's weeping/Because the mama's dead. Go Tell Aunt Rhody. *Anonymous.* AmFP

The whole/house shakes. Blueline. Ken Belford. NeAC

The whole land bound in closer amity! The Men of the Maine. Clinton Scollard. MC; PAH

The whole landscape flushes on a sudden at a sound. Fragment. Gerard Manley Hopkins. ELU

The whole massed weight of the night! Cuvier Light. Pat Wilson. AnNZ

Whole name they'll see page fifty-three. Whoe'er This Book, if Lost, Doth Find. *Anonymous.* FaBoUs

Whole nations grew old/In the dust of the fields! Return of a Reaper. Alan Creighton. CaP

The whole of darkness rose in me and is. Voice in the Dark. Avner Strauss. VWA

The whole of heaven wake/And wander in a flower. I Need No Sky. Witter ("Emanuel Morgan") Bynner. EaLo

The whole of the whole the/whole other whole Oscar. Bill Berkson. ANYP

The whole place trembled with lust. You Must Have Been a Sensational Baby (excerpt). Harold Norse. GP

The whole race is a poet that writes down/The eccentric propositions of its fate. Men Made out of Words. Wallace Stevens. MoAB; NOBA; OBSP; TAP; VGW

The whole race sunk beneath the oppressor's/rod,/And left a blank among the works of God. The Lust of Gold. James Montgomery. PAH

The whole/room will/bloom. A Late Spring: Eastport. Philip Booth. Psk

A whole sea of spinach-heads leaned to my hand. Memoirs of a Spinach-Picker. Sylvia Plath. GrPl

The whole swelling difficulty. The Song. Edward Dorn. CoPo; VGW

The whole thing a star/breathing. The Aelf-Scin. Michael McClure. CoPo; PoM

The whole thing only a touch of the hand. Song of the Bride. Susan Mernit. VWA

The whole time/Death was working. Clandestine Work. Yvan Goll. VWA

...The whole to have/Harmony like a bell. His Request. Owen Roe O'Sullivan. BIrV

...The whole world holds its breath/To hear the crimson Gallic rooster crow! To France. Ralph Chaplin. HBMV

The whole world knows you've never yet given up the secret of/where you've hidden your nests. A Flock of Guinea Hens Seen from a Car. Eudora Welty. GrPl; NYBP; PrIm

The whole world's Consolation is my woe! Our Lady of the Passion. John Mauropus. ISi

The whole world stalls. Tourist Guide: How You Can Tell for Sure When You're in South Dakota. Jim Heynen. GP

The whole world/turning in wet/and silence, a/damp mill wheel. Mad Sweeny. John Montague. FaBoIP

Wholly evident: the rain in the white basin, and I/vigilant. May You Always Be the Darling of Fortune. Jane Miller. AMV-80

Wholly unworthy the head or the heart of Your Own Correspondent? Amours de Voyage. Arthur Hugh Clough. EBEV; OBSV

Whom during her life I thought nothing of. Satires of Circumstance. Thomas Hardy. BrPo

Whom God deigns not to overthrow/Hath need of triple mail. Ballad for Gloom. Ezra Pound. LiTM; MoAmPo; NePA; OBVV

Whom God deludes is well deluded. Reply to Dipsychus. Arthur Hugh Clough. FaBoCo

Whom God grant long to reign! The Chronicle. Abraham Cowley. CEP; GoTL; SeCV 1-2

Whom God hath joined together/to have and not to hold. Walking against the Wind. Jon Stallworthy. OxBC

Whom he reckons up by dozens, and his aunts. I Am the Monarch of the Sea. Sir William Schwenck Gilbert. TreFT

Whom I have known, but you were not of them. The Ghost. Hilary Corke. NYBP

Whom I may whisper, Solitude is sweet. Retirement. William Cowper. BLPA

:Whom must we get to know/To die, so you live and we know? The Grapevine. John Ashbery. ANYP

Whom Nature's charms inspire, and love of humankind. The Minstrel. James Beattie. CEP; EnPE; NOEC

Whom no man living could pin down for keeps. Last Lines. X.J. Kennedy. OBAL

Whom none but Thy essential Word/And Spirit comprehend. Hymn to God the Father. Samuel Wesley. OxBoCh

Whom other tyrants with the lash shall awe. Of Narrow Streets. John Gay. EnLi 1-2

Whom patience finally must crown. Samson Agonistes. John Milton. NOBE; NOCV; SeCeV

Whom Phyllida unjustly thus/Hath murdered with disdain. Harpalus' Complaint. *Anonymous.* OBSC; ViBoPo

Whom sadder can I say? she said. The Mask. Elizabeth Barrett Browning. CBEP; OBNC; OBVV

Whom she crooned to sleep and rocked upon/her knees. Mater Amabilis. Emma Lazarus. OHIP

Whom should I seek but Thee, my path, my way? Emblem. Francis Quarles. TrPWD

Whom should my Muse then flye to, but/the best/Of kings for grace; of poets, for my test? To King James. Ben Jonson. OAEP

Whom the land shall bless/In joy and distress/Forever and a day! From Potomac to Merrimac. Edward Everett Hale. PAH

Whom the shy fox from the hill/Arouses... Paracelsus. Robert Browning. OBRV

Whom these frail, broken/Hands hold fast. His Hands. John Richard Moreland. TRV

Whom they empoisoned arrows cause complain?' Cupid in a Bed of Roses. *Anonymous.* EIL

Whon thou soffredest deth for me. Jesus, My Sweet Lover. *Anonymous.* MeEL

Whoop, 'tis but a Wanton Trick. The Wanton Trick. *Anonymous.* CoMu

The whore to come out, or the lecher come in. No Lock Against Lechery. Robert Herrick. CaPo

...The whores of death/Whom we have found in our beds today, today? To Any Member of My Generation. George Barker. LiTM; ViBoPo; WaP

Whos passing skill lo Hobbies pen displaise/To Brittain folk, a work of worthy praise. Commendatory Sonnet to Hoby's Courtier. Thomas, Earl of Dorset Sackville. AAS

Whose accent no farewell can know. Voyages. Hart Crane. AnFE; HAP; MoAB; MoAmPo; SeCeV; UnPo

Whose action is no stronger than a flower.   Variations on a Line from Shakespeare's Fifty-Sixth Sonnet.   E. L. Mayo.   PoCh

Whose apteryx rhymed with apteryx!   Limerick: "O limerick, Learest of lyrics."   David McCord.   InMe

Whose arms to clasp us on the cross were spread.   On the Brink of Death. Buonarroti Michelangelo.   AWP

Whose basalt and sandstone have gone/like Napoleon into Egypt.   Politik. Tom Paulin.   FaBoIP

Whose beauty was my vision!   To —.   Winthrop Mackworth Praed.   HBV 1-2

Whose blazing forth extinguishes the stars.   Epigram: "The boys of Tyre are beautiful."   Meleager.   PeHV

Whose blood is that efficient lackey-tom motherfuckers?   Orishas.   Larry Neal.   NBP

Whose bloody hands grope about the lion's mouth searching for/success.   The Beast with Chrome Teeth.   Thurmond Snyder.   NNP

Whose body, stabbed and bleeding, was plunged into the Low Lands Low. Young Edmondale.   *Anonymous.*   BFSS

Whose bones I guard, bestriding this his grave.   The Lion over the Tomb of Leonidas.   *Anonymous.*   AWP

Whose brains are made of gingerbread.   Portrait.   Edward Estlin Cummings. AnAmPo

...Whose breasts/are "so moist and tender, you can eat them like candy." The Guest.   Pentti Saarikoski.   PV

Whose brightness dies to image. And the snow.   Twelfth Night.   Peter Scupham.   OBCP

...Whose calm concealed/The tutelary of that upland field.   The Hand at Callow Hill Farm.   Charles Tomlinson.   NePoEA-2

Whose capped and sterile teeth/Whisper the great lie, "Love."   Fire Island. Rita Mae Brown.   IHMS

Whose care is how they fall, not why.   The Net and the Sword.   Douglas LePan.   NOBC

Whose ceremonial art/Is dying into light.   When the Light Falls.   Stanley Jasspon Kunitz.   MoAmPo

Whose changing reveries they seem.   Pomegranates.   Roy Campbell. AtBAP

Whose children will be colder killers/than the words of this or any other song. Envoi.   Eli Mandel.   NOBC

Whose cinders yet with envy they do eat.   Another Tribute to Wyatt. Henry Howard, Earl of Surrey.   SiPS

...Whose/combustious face and eyes are bright/with apoplexy, bulk, and booze. On a Portrait by Copley.   Arthur Freeman.   DBV

Whose course in often stayd, yet never is astray.   The Faerie Queene. Edmund Spenser.   MOS

Whose crafty course no cunning can find out.   The Royal Palace of the Highest Heaven.   Alexander Montgomerie.   GoTS

Whose dark green oaks his noontide leisure shield.   Solitude.   John Clare. OBSP

Whose deathless eyes once fixed on mine/Would draw me downward through the brine!   A Shadow Boat.   Arlo Bates.   HBV 1-2

Whose disappointment broke into a rainbow of tears.   These Lacustrine Cities.   John Ashbery.   ANYP; CAPP; HaCAP; PoM; UnPo

Whose dread commands o'er awe-struck lands are borne on/eagle's wings. The Islands of the Sea.   George Edward Woodberry.   MC; PAH

Whose dull knife beats the inside of your chest.   Nine Charms against the Hunter.   David Wagoner.   TW

Whose earthquake-shaken leaves bore graves for nests.   Lines: "I followed once a fleet and mighty serpent."   Thomas Lovell Beddoes.   NBM

Whose face would greet me in hell's fiery way.   To—.   Robert Nichols. HBMV

Whose faces form a gravely mocking sentence.   Soldiers.   Maxwell Bodenheim.   MAPA

Whose fair fulfilment all the earth shall be,/And all the Future tell.   The Dead President.   Edward Rowland Sill.   PAH

Whose father had met with a coal miner's doom.   The Miner's Doom. *Anonymous.*   AmFP

Whose fathers made both myth and progeny.   November, 1941.   Roy Fuller. MoPo

Whose feet are so deep in the sand.   Yves Tanguy.   David Gascoyne.   EAS

Whose feet he has on loan from the tracks left in the snow outside/ Ferlinghetti's Walk-up.   Leaps over the Aisle of Syllogism (parody).   D. C. Berry.   BXAP

Whose fire from which I came, has now grown cold?   One Flesh.   Elizabeth Jennings.   FaBoWP; OxBTC; PBWP

Whose fire's so oft extinguished by a match?   'Tis Highly Rational, We Can't Dispute.   Richard Garnett.   HBV 1-2

Whose fish, fish.   Nature's Lineaments.   Robert Graves.   FaBoTw

Whose foolish fault to death himself hath done.'   Here Lieth Love.   Thomas Watson.   EiL

Whose footfall is my beating heart.   The Secret Muse.   Roy Campbell. BoC; PeSA

Whose friend was God, but God swore not to aid me!   Lines Written on a Window-Shutter at Weston.   William Cowper.   EiCP; LAuP

Whose fruit so sov'reign is/That all who taste it are from death restored. Seek the Lord.   Thomas Campion.   OxBoCh; TrCP

Whose fruitless work is broken with least wind.   Penelope, for Her Ulysses' Sake.   Edmund Spenser.   NIP

Whose full-Possession (to it's utmost Line)/By an Eternal Gift, is firmly Thine. In Consort to Wednesday, Jan. 1st. 1701...   Richard Henchman.   SCAP

Whose future specifies its past, whose past/Precedes it, and whose history is its being.   Agnosco Veteris Vestigia Flammae.   J. V. Cunningham.   QFR; VGW

Whose gifts are greater than his own.   Himself.   Daniel Gerard Hoffman. AMV-80

Whose glory fills the earth.   Morning Hymn.   Saint Gregory the Great. CAW; WGRP

Whose good and evil no man can foresee.   Hillside.   Alexander Craig. PoAu 1-2

Whose grass-grown surface overlies/The victims of that sacrifice.   Pentucket. John Greenleaf Whittier.   MC; PAH

Whose green adventure is to run to seed.   Remembering the Thirties. Donald Davie.   FaBoPV; NePoEA; OxBTC; PP

Whose hands rise up from feet and knees,/Encircle head and rub the eyes. Tir-Nan-Og.   J. F. Hendry.   NeBP

Whose hanging heads did seeme his carefull case to weepe.   January Eclogue. Edmund Spenser.   FiP

Whose happiness/Even here/Is being sacrificed?   Like a Beach.   Harvey Shapiro.   VWA

...Whose harmonies are sweeter/than those of Paradise.   Hunger.   Gaspara Stampa.   WPOW

Whose heart in this four-footed thing lies.   On the Collar of Mrs. Dingley's Lap-Dog.   Jonathan Swift.   FaBoEE; FM

Whose heart is snares and nets,/And whose hands are bands.'   Ecclesiastes. Morris Bishop.   HBMV

Whose heart on heaven is set.   Earth and Fire.   Vernon Watkins.   NYBP

Whose heart with fear doth freeze, with love doth fry.   Thule, the Period of Cosmography.   *Anonymous.*   HAP; NCEP; OBSP

Whose heart with fear doth freeze, with love doth fry.   Wonders. *Anonymous.*   EiL; FaBoCh

Whose hearts alway on Christ do stay/And do him ever mind.   If Thou Wilt Hear.   John Grave.   AH

Whose hearts are on fire in the snow.   The Cubical Domes.   David Gascoyne.   EAS

Whose hearts are true and right.   Such as in God the Lord Do Trust. William Kethe.   AH

Whose hearts have lain a moment/On that eternal breast.   Over the Wintry Threshold.   Bliss Carman.   HBV 1-2

Whose heaven/is like ours, a detritus of lights.   The Car Cemetery.   Ciaran Carson.   CIP

Whose hidden fountains but few may guess.   Beautiful Things.   Ellen Palmer Allerton.   WBLP

Whose honour and whose glory you defend.   A Farewell to Sir John Norris and Sir Francis Drake.   George Peele.   OBSC

Whose humble and sweet poverty will appear/Clear in the clearness of your eternal love.   Francis Jammes: A Prayer to Go to Paradise with the Donkeys.   Richard Wilbur.   EaLo

Whose image the fleet waters break but cannot bear away.   Images. Kathleen Raine.   NYBP

Whose islands on its bosom float,/Like emeralds chas'd in gold.   Marmion. Sir Walter Scott.   FaBoPP

...Whose knowledge hath a touch/Of God's divine simplicity.   Implicit Faith. Aubrey Thomas De Vere.   GoBC

Whose language he would live, upon the way.   Required Course.   Frances Stoakley Lankford.   GoYe

Whose last letter flew like a prayer.   Dream Songs.   John Berryman.   NoP

Whose laughter plays like summer lightning there.   Cattle Show.   Hugh" (Christopher Murray Grieve) MacDiarmid.   BSV; FaBoMo; GoTS; HAP; MoBrPo; OBMV; OxBTC

Whose life is in midwinter, and must soon/Come to the shortest day of all my year!   Frost-Morning.   William Alexander.   IrPN

Whose lives although decayed, yet loves decayed never.   The Faerie Queene. Edmund Spenser.   OBSC

Whose lofty argument uplifting me,/Shall lift you up unto an high degree. Amoretti, LXXXII.   Edmund Spenser.   AAS; HeIP

Whose love comes laden with the scent of youth,/Through twenty years of death.   Forever.   John Boyle O'Reilly.   HBV 1-2; OnYI

Whose love did ne'er/Forsake thee.   Flow, O My Tears!   *Anonymous.*   EiL

Whose love home to our Father's house shall win us.   Easter Hymn. Michael Thwaites.   MoRP

Whose love imperial is, whose power sublime.   Is This the Time To Sound Retreat?   Charles Sumner Hoyt.   BLRP

Whose loves/Were just as kind as his, whose lives/Were precious, being irreplaceable.   The Dead.   A.J.M. Smith.   NOBC

Whose many fortunes are followed/by the many who have not one.   Things We Dreamt We Died For.   Marvin Bell.   CoAP

Whose maudlin plumes and pommels/Urge the adventure past return.)   Auspice of Jewels.   Laura Riding.   LiTA; NoAm

Whose meaning, charlatan history, tells!   Ironic:LL.D.   William Stanley Braithwaite.   BANP

Whose modest tresses were bound up for thee.   To Spring.   William Blake.   ATP; BLPL; BoC; BoNaP; ERoP 1-2; HBV 1-2; LAuP; NOEC; OAEL 1-2; OBEC; OBEV; PoEL 1-5; PoLf; PPP; WiR

Whose mother still must weep o'er him the tears I weep o'er/thee!   The Irish Mother in the Penal Days.   John Banim.   AnIV

Whose muffled motions blindly drown/The bases of my life in tears.   In Memoriam A.H.H., XLIX.   Alfred, Lord Tennyson.   VLP

Whose music is the gladness of the world.   O May I Join the Choir Invisible.   George Eliot.   GTBS; OBNC; TreFS; TRV

Whose name is love & which only of all light love can eat   The Alchemist.   Robert Kelly.   CoPo

Whose name/passes/for/a city.   A State of Nature.   John Hollander.   NIP

Whose name supplies the long-sought rhyme/for "orange'.   Local Note.   Arthur Guiterman.   NLV

Whose names are on monthly cheques, who have/succeeded.   Names.   D. J. Enright.   FaBoCo

Whose new flowers black green and gold/Are a worker's song of fidelity/To the land that mothered you   New Age.   Keorapetse Kgositsile.   WhB

Whose nights are clearer than the days.   Upon Visiting His Lady by Moonlight.   A. W.   CTC; MOON; OBSC

Whose nostrils bleed, whose life runs out from eye and ear.   The Slaughter-House.   Alfred Hayes.   LiTA

Whose note full many a man doth mark,/And dares not answer nay.   A Midsummer-Night's Dream.   William Shakespeare.   CTC; ViBoPo

"Whose number do you suppose this is?"   Moving Again.   William Matthews.   NPAW

Whose outward splendour is but folly's dress,/Exposing most, when most it gilds distress.   Truth in Poetry.   George Crabbe.   OBEC; SeCePo

Whose page is blanker than the raining skies.   On the Edge.   Philip Levine.   CoAP; TAP

Whose pages turn without me.   The Plants.   Michael Dennis Browne.   GP

Whose passion in one stormy moment spent/Bore giant sons of iron and cement.   Madison Square.   Glanz-Leyeles. A.   VWA

Whose passion thrills her in the pain/Of the loud languorous nightingale.   Fantoches.   Paul Verlaine.   AWP; OBMV

Whose past is parting: strangers side by side.   Ever Since.   Archibald MacLeish.   NePA

Whose peace abides in the dark avenue/Amid the bitterness of things occult.   For Our Lady of the Rocks by Leonardo da Vinci.   Dante Gabriel Rossetti.   VLP

Whose perplexed heart did evil, foolishly,/A long while since, and by some other sea.   Waikiki.   Rupert Brooke.   OBTV

Whose poison doubles after one has spent it.   An Angry Word.   Margaret E. Bruner.   PoToHe

Whose praises be through earth's most distant regions/Ever resounding.   Behold, the Shade of Night Is Now Receding.   Saint Gregory the Great.   AH

Whose precise nature never will be known.   The Hittites.   Roy Fuller.   OBSP

...Whose pride/Will leave no trace in the quenching tide.   Icarus.   Ronald Bottrall.   GTBS-P

Whose prize for unremitting care/Is only not to be disgraced.   A Northern Suburb.   John Davidson.   NBM; NOBV; OBNC

Whose purse, men know it, was exceeding light.   On a Poet.   Henry Parrot.   FaBoEE

Whose ravening monsters mighty men shall/slay,/Not the poor singer of an empty day.   The Earthly Paradise.   William Morris.   CoBE; LiTB; LoBV; NoP; OAEL 1-2; ViBoPo; VLP

Whose reek of pleasure/hangs in the morning air?   Three Songs from the Temple.   Don Domanski.   NOBC

Whose restless heart must rove for rest.   The Sliprails and the Spur.   Henry Lawson.   PoAu 1-2

Whose reverence for reverence grows bigger each day/and less fastidious.   A Tale Told by a Head.   Lois Moyles.   NYBP

Whose ribs the laths are, and whose flesh the loam.   The Body.   Robert Herrick.   CaPo

Whose ring is that upon your finger?   Jealousy.   *Anonymous*.   WTO

Whose roots are said to dispel pain   The Judgment of Paris.   William Stanley Merwin.   NNaP

...(Whose roots settle/for earth, old earth, with a blackboy endurance.)   At the Nature-Strip.   Judith Rodriguez.   CBAP

Whose rough agglomerate smashes the sea.   Aspects of the World Like Coral Reefs.   William Bronk.   VGW

Whose sad head/looms over any choice you make?   For My Husband.   Ellen Bryant Voigt.   NoP

Whose scales turn aside the sun's sword with their polish.   An Egyptian Pulled Glass Bottle in the Shape of a Fish.   Marianne Moore.   PBWP

Whose shadow is less given to change than he.   Upon His Picture.   Thomas Randolph.   CBEP; MePo; NOBE

Whose shoulder bears the heavier load,–/Is it not Mine?   The Priest's Lament.   Robert Hugh Benson.   ACP

Whose silence shrieks so soon?   Moon.   Derek Walcott.   NoAm

Whose silence was not golden, but just yellow.   Here Lies Sir Tact.   Timothy Steele.   NLV; TW

Whose sinew conspired from our sperm   Greed.   Douglas Blazek.   LTB

Whose slender finger wears the sky for a ring.   The Temple by the Sea.   Geoffrey Dutton.   ACV

Whose soft bewitching Influence/Had Damn'd him to the Hell of Impotence.   The Disappointment.   Aphra Behn.   SBG

Whose songs are marble/and whose marble sings.   A Poet Speaks from the Visitors' Gallery.   Archibald MacLeish.   NYBP

Whose soul is carrion now,–too mean to yield/Some Starveling's ninth allotment of a ghost.   On the Site of a Mulberry-Tree.   Dante Gabriel Rossetti.   CBEP; NCEP; TW

Whose spittle only could restore the blind.   Silex Scintillans.   Henry Vaughan.   AnAnS 1

Whose spurious birth once caused no small dispute.   Dialogue with a Door.   Caius Valerius Catullus.   UnTE

Whose steadfast faith yet never mov'd./Forget not this!   The Lover Beseecheth His Mistress Not to Forget...   Sir Thomas Wyatt.   ViBoPo

Whose steadfast faith yet never moved;/Forget not this!   Steadfastness.   Sir Thomas Wyatt.   NOBE; OBSC

Whose strength but waits to fold thee home.   Come Back.   Henry William Herbert.   AA

Whose suit he shuns, and doth aspire/Hero's fair tower, and his desire.   Hero and Leander.   Christopher Marlowe.   OAEP

Whose sword is laid and his armor hung in the House of/Ashtoreth.   Saul.   George Sterling.   HBMV

Whose teeth I know/I cannot trust.   Bridgework.   Annette Lynch.   FF

Whose thorns are in his hands.   Written in the Visitors' Book at the Birthplace of Robert Burns.   George Washington Cable.   AA

Whose thoughts are all the mysteries?   Beauty.   Kenneth Slade Alling.   HBMV

...Whose tone/Is most offensive to the nation.   To Disraeli.   Shirley Brooks.   NOBL

Whose touch is soft as fur.   Night.   Lois Weakley McKay.   SiSoSe

Whose tranquil presence shames our dis-/content.   Tellus.   William Reed Huntington.   AA

Whose treachery had filled that house with pain.   The Odyssey.   Homer.   NAWM 1-2

Whose unclaimed Hat and Jacket/Sum the History–   How the waters closed above him.   Emily Dickinson.   DL; PoEL 1-5

Whose understanding is/In trying no more to understand.   Estuary.   William Montgomerie.   OxBS

Whose unobtrusive excellence awed back/delusion's tide!   Mistress Hale of Beverly.   Lucy Larcom.   PAH

Whose very map and compass are/the mortal hour?   We Shall Have Far to Go.   James Wreford Watson.   CaP

Whose victims bled by thousands, alas, alas, what for?   A Soldier from Missouri.   *Anonymous*.   BFSS

Whose waters are the crystal tides of sleep.   The Enduring Music.   Harold Vinal.   EtS

Whose white head is lost for this province?   South-Folk in Cold Country.   *Anonymous*.   CrMA; OBVE

Whose white waterfall could bless/Travellers in their last distress.   Now the Leaves Are Falling Fast.   W. H. Auden.   CoBMV

Whose wild bad father loves you well.   A Sympathy, a Welcome.   John Berryman.   GrPl; NYBP

Whose will the water's will!   Epitaph for a Sailor Buried Ashore.   Sir Charles G. D. Roberts.   EtS

Whose wind blows louder than their speech.   I Love a Flower.   Robert Nichols.   ChMP

Whose wing eludes the lifted wave.   Elemental.   George Dillon.   AnAmPo

Whose woods drop honey, and her rivers skip with wine.   Christ's Victory and Triumph.   Giles the Younger Fletcher.   JCP

Whose words are as mixed with comfort and terror/as rain on the sea.   Analyst.   David Fisher.   NPGG

Whose worth they rev'rendly forbear to rate.   Gondibert.   Sir William Davenant.   CEP

Whoso deserves not Heaven/May never hope to have her company.   Death, Always Cruel.   Dante Alighieri.   LiTW

Whoso doth the will of the King.   The Holy Man.   *Anonymous*.   OnYI

Whoso fasteneth hope on him/Shall follow him to hell so dim.   The Whale's Nature.   *Anonymous*.   MeEV

Whoso wol seche true love/In her it shall be found.   The Virgin.   *Anonymous*.   GBP

Whosoever hem shomes he will be shent,/I say algate.   Be True to Your
  Condition in Life.   John Audelay.   MeEL
Why a little curtain of flesh on the bed of our desire?'   The Secrets of the
  Earth.   William Blake.   NOBE
...Why add my barrel to her notch?   A Teen-Ager.   W. D. Snodgrass.   TW
Why am I crying after love?   Spring Night.   Sara Teasdale.   BLPL;
  FaBoBe; HBMV; LiTA; LiTL; MoAmPo; PG
...Why am I grown/So cold?   The Warning.   Adelaide Crapsey.   AnAmPo;
  WSC
Why am I in love/with him?   Song to a Lover.   *Anonymous.*   BoWoP
Why am I in love with such a man as he?   Trousers of Wind.   *Anonymous.*
  PBA; TTY
"Why am I so intensely plain?"   Not Quite Fair.   Henry Sambrooke Leigh.
  InMe
Why am I watching the wheel change/With impatience?   The Wheel Change.
  Bertolt Brecht.   ELU
Why, Amoret, why should not wee.   To Amoret Gone from Him.   Henry
  Vaughan.   CBEP; MeLP; OBS
...Why are the beautiful sick and divided/like myself?   Cold Term.   LeRoi
  (Imamu Amiri Baraka) Jones.   BPo; CNA; SOTW
Why are we in this life.   Pilgrims.   Jean Valentine.   LCAP; TAP
Why are we life-taught men, why poor ephemerals they?   The Burden of
  Egypt (excerpt).   Richard Monckton, Lord Houghton Milnes.   OBTV
Why are ye then so cruel foe,/Unto your own that loveth you so?   Ye know
  my heart...   Sir Thomas Wyatt.   FCP; LoBV; SiPS
Why are you not here to overpower me with/your tense and urgent love?
  Vernal Equinox.   Amy Lowell.   MAPA
...Why are/you part of the world that/we seek?   The Hooded Crow.   Rennie
  McOwan.   PoSH
Why aren't we all like that wise old/bird?   A Wise Old Owl Sat in an Oak.
  Anonymous.   OxNR
Why birds must fly, seeing the flight of birds.   No Question.   George Dillon.
  AmLP
Why bother with the boy next door?   For a Neighbor Girl.   Yu Hsuan-chi.
  BoWoP
Why can't he wait till I've gone up to bed?   "He Didn't Oughter..."   Sir
  Alan Patrick Herbert.   ALV; FiBHP
Why can't we all be like that bird?   A Wise Old Owl.   Edward Hersey
  Richards.   BLPA; FaBoBe; FaFP; GoTF; TreF; YaD
Why can't you play on that?'   Little Raindrops.   Jane Euphemia Browne
  (Aunt Effie).   HBV 1-2; HBVY; OxBChV
Why cannot all of us together--why?--/Achieve the one simplicity: to die?
  London Despair.   Frances Cornford.   OBMV
Why children on the buffaloes/watch the/sky.   Containing Communism.
  Charlie Cobb.   PoBA
Why could I think of nothing/But--"What darling eyes he has!"   Wet or Fine.
  Amory Hare.   HBMV
Why could'st thou not remain at school?   Of One Self-Slain.   Charles
  Hanson Towne.   WGRP
Why couldn't I have stayed a poet/Thus naive!   In My Old Verses.   Charles
  Guerin.   CAW
Why Democracy means/Everybody but me.   The Black Man Speaks.
  Langston Hughes.   TreFT
"Why did the children/pour molasses on the cat/when the one thing we told
  the children/they must...   The People, Yes.   Carl Sandburg.   OBAL
Why did the maid weep?   Behold, the Grave.   Stephen Crane.   TAP
Why did they dig Ma's grave so deep?   Why Did They Dig Ma's Grave So
  Deep?   George Cooper.   TreFS
Why did you eat the dumplings?   Pussy Cat.   *Anonymous.*   OxNR
Why did you keep me waiting?   After the Last Dynasty.   Stanley Jasspon
  Kunitz.   NMP; TAP
Why did you put her falsely in prison?   To the Noble Woman of Llanarth
  Hall.   Evan Thomas.   PV; TW
Why dies one sweetness when another blows?   The Violet and the Rose.
  Augusta Webster.   HBV 1-2
Why do I always wish I was Tu Fu?   On the Road to Paradise.   Garrett
  Kaoru Hongo.   HoAn
Why do I contradict/Myself? Do not inquire.   Inconsistent.   Mark Van
  Doren.   ELU
Why do I sit in the moonshade, while the eye-star mocks me/while I ask what
  I am?/Why? Why? Alone.   *Anonymous.*   NA
Why do I still long/for the floating world?   I, who cut off my sorrows.
  Akazome Emon.   BoWoP; WPOW
Why do I watch your face?   The Natural History of Pliny.   Vincent
  McHugh.   NePoAm-2
...Why do people lie to one another?   Mummy of a Lady Named
  Jemutesonekh XXI Dynasty.   Thomas James.   AmPA; SM
WHY DO Third World animals/have to pay...such heavy/lifetime dues?   Zoo
  You Too!   Ted Joans.   GP
Why do you always fly away?   The Lonely Scarecrow.   James Kirkup.
  GrPl

Why do you ask? Someone/caught in the thorn.   Absalom.   Zerubavel
  Gilead.   VWA
Why do you conceal Your face,/my Lord?   Seal of Fire.   Mordecai Temkin.
  VWA
Why do you remain outdoors?   The Bones of Incontention.   Robert David
  Cohen.   NYBP
Why do you wipe your face away?   Autumn Evening.   George Anthony.
  EAS
Why do your eyes pity me?   The Old Men.   Alexander Javitz.   TrJP
Why do your fingers try/To kill the little love?/Soon it would die.
  Frightened Face.   Marion Strobel.   HBMV
Why does God Almighty or anybody else care whether I take a/new name to
  go by?   Blacklisted.   Carl Sandburg.   SaC
Why does he want so much to be/Here in my little room with me?   The
  Wind.   Elizabeth Rendall.   HBVY
Why does no light come through as those doors close?   El Greco.   E. L.
  Mayo.   HoPM; MiAP
Why does she come, when she knows what I have to tell?   A Winter's Tale.
  D. H. Lawrence.   MoAB; MoBrPo
Why doesn't that fly stop buzzing--stop buzzing up there!   Country Burying
  (1919).   Robert Penn Warren.   LiTM
...Why don't I/reflect some therapeutically?/You tell me.   Letters to Live
  Poets.   Bruce Beaver.   CBAP
Why don't the pawties compwamise?   Swell's Soliloquy.   *Anonymous.*
  FiBHP
..."Why don't you get out of the rain?"   I wrung my hands under my dark
  veil...   Anna Akhmatova.   BoLoP
Why don't you love her now?'   Friendship.   Katherine Mansfield.   PeHV
Why don't you save us/with a poem, sweet Diane?   Sweet Diane.   George
  Barlow.   CNA
Why, don't you see, my friend, the fellow's talking.   Mendax.   Gotthold
  Lessing.   PV
Why don't you try writing something?   Teaching the Ape to Write Poems.
  James Tate.   GP
Why dost thou tread down Death? It is that I/Am Death's own slayer, who
  can never die.   Religion.   Jean Vauquelin de la Fres   CAW
Why, drive a phaeton and four.   On Tom Onslow, Earl of Onslow.
  Anonymous.   FaBoEE
Why, even their meanings now are obsolete.   Antiques.   Walter De la Mare.
  PoA
Why, for an amulet, I fain would beg/The turquoise of some robin's egg.
  The Robin's Egg.   Annie Charlotte Dalton.   CaP
Why?/For it's ay ay, ay ay.   The Window (excerpt).   Alfred, Lord
  Tennyson.   PBBP
Why, grandma herself would have died an old maid!   Grandma's Advice.
  Anonymous.   OBET
Why have they changed that way to wood?   Sestina.   Donald Justice.
  NePoEA
Why have they wakened me?   Men's Voices.   Inger Christensen.   BoWoP
Why, he'll live till men weary of Collins and Gray.   A Fable for Critics.
  James Russell Lowell.   PP
Why he turned them inside outside.   The Modern Hiawatha (parody).
  George A. Strong.   FaBoPa; FiBHP; HBV 1-2; InMe; MoShBr; SpRo; YaD
Why heaven did not break away/And tumble blue on me.   It troubled me as
  once I was.   Emily Dickinson.   ImOP
Why, hoity-toity!--he is fain,/So I'll be cold and haughty!   Gwendoline
  (parody).   Bayard Taylor.   BXAP
"Why, house-leek," said the Bishop. "That's all."   Hyssop.   Walter De La
  Mare.   BoC
Why hurry to tell Belshazzar/What soon enough he would know?   The
  Bearer of Evil Tidings.   Robert Frost.   CBEP; NoAm
Why I had to wring/his inadequate neck.   Dead Bird (parody).   David R.
  Slavitt.   BXAP
Why? I saw deep in our woodland lot/A seagull sitting on a little hill.   Storm
  Warning.   Alice Bardsley.   AMV-80
Why in His wisdom He hath led me so.   He Leadeth Me.   H. H. Barry.
  BLRP
"Why is a hall? is a hall? is a hall?"   Room 000.   William Stafford.   GLGT
Why is fragrance in the hair?   Doubts.   Rupert Brooke.   CH
Why is she angry?   Questions ¼.   Donald Hall.   FF
Why is the sea-gull flying?   A Visit from the Sea.   Robert Louis Stevenson.
  FM; GN; MOS
Why is there nothing/I have ever done with anybody/that seems to me so
  obviously right?   Gracious Goodness.   Marge Piercy.   BoAnP; HoAn;
  Psk
Why is this air so sacred and so still?   In the Backs.   Frances Cornford.
  BrRo
"Why is this night so different from..."   Seder, 1944.   Friedrich Torberg.
  VWA
"Why it's Miss Nancy! Come along, you rat!"   Going Back to School.
  Stephen Vincent Benét.   LaNeLa
Why?/Just because.   Just Because.   Moishe Leib Halpern.   VWA

Why, let them who make the quarrel be the only men to fight. Jeannette and Jeannot. Charles Jeffries. BLPA

Why linger? I must haste,/or lose the Delphick bays. Pericles and Aspasia. Walter Savage Landor. OBRV

Why look already how far off she has flown, she is no fool. To School! Stevie Smith. FaBoEE

Why, man of morals, tell me why? Drinking. Abraham Cowley. BLPL; CABA; FF; LoBV; MePo; NOBE; PG; PoPle; SeCP; SeCV 1-2; TrGrPo; WeW

Why marvel at the hectic blood/That flushes this wild fruit? Fruit of the Flower. Countee Cullen. PoLf

Why may not I, as well as these,/Grow lovely, growing old? Let Me Grow Lovely. Karle Wilson Baker. BLPA; FaBoBe; HBMV; TrPWD

Why, Mors, need we tell you, m o r s, MORS. The Search. Michael Hamburger. VWA

Why must I die when I had hoped to fall? On This My Sick-Bed Beats the World. Jiri Wolker. WaaP

Why must I still remember her/From whom I parted after? The Circus. E. B. White. InMe

Why must I this short life share with/Randal Groveling? Song from a Two-Desk Office. Byron Buck. NYBP

Why n'adde he stonde, vile gorel? Snatches: "At the wrastlinge my lemman I ches." Anonymous. OxBM

Why, never mix your liquors, lads,/But always take them neat. Ben Backstay. Anonymous. AmSS

Why not, as well as doctor Swift? A True and Faithful Inventory of the Goods Belonging to Dr Swift... Jonathan Swift. FaBoUs

Why not live sweetly, as in the green trees? I Had a Dove. John Keats. CH; FM

Why not me/O let me/get in. Skeleton Key. John Hollander. AmC; NoP

Why not...Oh, come in, Spring. Snowfall. Hone Tuwhare. OCNZ

Why nothing now, but lonely sit,/And over-read what I have writ. The Departure of the Good Daemon. Robert Herrick. FaBoRV

Why now the word "Kalahari"? Kalahari. Luis Palés Matos. InW

Why, O why should I despair? Song: "Only tell her that I love." John, Lord Cutts. HBV 1-2

Why our eyes come shaped like footballs from God's passing/hand. New Year's 1978. Howard Nemerov. SOTS

Why part the silk curtains by my bed? In Spring. Li Po. LiTW

Why, rain's my choice. Rain. James Whitcomb Riley. BoNaP

Why remember more than that? At a Time. Ray Mathew. PoAu 1-2

Why shou'd I hope to shun? Song: The Hopeless Comfort. Robert Gould. CEP

Why should he do me any harm?' Queer Things. James Reeves. WSC

Why should I be bound to thee,/O, my lovely mirtle tree? To My Mirtle. William Blake. HW

Why should I frighten sea-gulls, even with a thought? My Lodge at Wang-Ch'uan after a Long Rain. Wang Wei. LiTW

Why should I labor for naught, seeing how naked the/end? Vanity of Vanities. Palladas. AWP; TRV

Why should I not sing them, the dead, the innocent? First Elegy for the Dead in Cyrenaica. Hamish Henderson. OxBS

Why should I question this or that?/I have not doubted love. Belief. Ruth Fitch Bartlett. InMe

Why should I sign/my name? The Weather of Six Mornings. Jane Cooper. IHMS; NYBP

Why should I wake or weep? Epicedium. Horace L. Traubel. AA

Why should mortals wonder if God hears prayer? Proof. Ethel Romig Fuller. TRV

Why should not I love my love,/Gallant hound sedelee? Came You Not from Newcastle. Anonymous. GBP

Why should not she/Still joy to reign in me? Song Set by John Daniel: "Let not Chloris think, because." Anonymous. OBSC

Why should that horrify me so? The Basilisk. Philip Child. CaP

Why should the wild child/weep for the scientists/why. Meditations for a Savage Child. Adrienne Rich. LCAP

Why should they make what all/their lives/The gentle dames have had? Woman's Will. John Godfrey Saxe. FaFP; GoTF; HBV 1-2; TreFT

Why should they miss their yearly due/Before their time? They too will die. In Memoriam A.H.H., XXIX. Alfred, Lord Tennyson. VLP

Why should this guest go wrinkling up his nose? Man Is a Spirit. Stevie Smith. OxBC

Why should we honor the gods, or join the sacred dance? King Oedipus. Sophocles. LiTW

Why should we only toil, the roof and crown of things? The Lotos-Eaters. Alfred, Lord Tennyson. HeIP

Why should we then with wrinkl'd care,/Deface what Nature made so fair? Song. Matthew Stevenson. CavP

Why should we, why should we be kept in the dark? A Ballad on the Taxes. Edward Ward. OxBoLi; PPON

Why should we, why should we, be kept in the dark? A Ballad on the Times. Henry Hall. APAS

Why should you not marry me for a change? A Remonstrance. James Kenneth Stephen. NOBV

"Why sir, it was–he died one day!" On Seeing a Pompous Funeral for a Bad Husband. Anonymous. ShM

"Why, so it is, father–whose wife shall I take?" Epigram. Thomas Moore. ALV

Why so worried, sisters, why?/Sing the silver bells of Wye. Gwalia Deserta. Idris Davies. DTC

Why speak not they of comrades that went under? Spring Offensive. Wilfred Owen. BrPo; GTBS-P; LiTB; MoVE

Why stay'st thou then my soul; o fly, fly, thither haste thee. On the Crucifixion. Giles the Younger Fletcher. EBCP; OxBoCh

"Why, sunlight and worms!' said the little blue wren. The growth of Sym. C. J. Dennis. ACV

Why take it?/To remake it. Question and Answer. Langston Hughes. BPo

Why tarry here? The Pine at Timber-Line. Harriet Monroe. PoA

...Why tempt/The stone, which is incapable? Epigram: "You recline that magnificant pair of buttocks." Strato. PeHV

Why, that's the very Thing I mean. Epigram on Miltonicks. Samuel Wesley. OBEC; PoL

Why, that's two tree boughs rubbing in the wind. Mapooram. Anonymous. NOAV

"Why,/the bees." Socratic. Hilda ("H. D.") Doolittle. AnEnPo; HoPM

Why, the next time I'll visit your trees. In a Cell I Am Bunked. Martial (Marcus Valerius Martialis). DBV

Why the white, a-meade feairest on you. Black an' White. William Barnes. VLP

Why the wound could not heal itself/Once we had awakened. Adam's Dream. Howard Schwartz. VWA

Why, then be rebels for the right/By Aguinaldo's side! Rebels. Ernest Crosby. PAH

Why then despaire, goe packe thee hence away,/I live in hope to have a golden daie. This Passion Is All Framed in Manner of a Dialogue. Thomas Watson. AAS

Why then for hell the match is somewhat even. Carmen Elegiacum. Thomas Morton. SCAP

Why, then, let the soldier drink. Limerick: "And let the canakin clink." William Shakespeare. LiBL

...Why then my name/would have been mother... A Castaway (excerpt). Augusta Webster. BrRo

Why then should I accoumpt of little paine,/That endlesse pleasure shall unto me gaine. Amoretti, XXVI. Edmund Spenser. AAS

...Why, then, should I find/a child's face bright with tears haunting my mind? The Oak and the Olive. George Barker. FaBoMo; OBTV

Why then should man, teazing the world for grace,/Spoil his salvation for a fierce miscreed? On Fame. John Keats. CABA

Why then should that poor shell-less Slug/provoke but one reaction: ug? A Bestiary of the Garden for Children Who Should Know Better. Phyllis Gotlieb. WHW

Why then should they carry history/Like an ark, and the remembering/Already begun? Exodus. Harvey Shapiro. VWA

Why, then, the devil take/Both her and him; and love; and her; and me. She who is always in my thoughts prefers. Bhartrihari. BoLoP

Why then we must ship some sailors like the handsome cabin boy. The Female Cabin Boy. Anonymous. OBSS

Why then we sartainly must starve. Good night! Eclogue. William Barnes. NBM

Why, there's no more to be said. Epitaph on Prince Frederick. Anonymous. OxBoLi

Why, there was that pumpkin entire on his stalk! The Pumpkin. Robert Graves. WSC

Why think it will/After tonight? After Tonight. Gary Soto. GP

Why this injustice in your Universe? A Fine Thing. Tom Veitch. ANYP

"Why this is hell, nor are you out of it." At the Spa. James H. Bowden. AMV-81

Why toil I, then, in vain distress,/Seeing the end is nakedness? Naked I Came. Palladas. NIP

Why tread you death? "I only cannot die." Virtue. Nicholas Grimald. OBSC

...Why twhen/you run out of a body for miles/is there any more? Jogging. Gary Stein. AMV-81

Why we must leave off kissing/and think of the foggy dew.' The Foggy Dew. Anonymous. OBET

Why, what a most particularly pure man/this pure young man must be! Patience: Bunthorne's Recitative and Song. Sir William Schwenck Gilbert. CoBE

Why, what care I, I lets 'em. On Dr. Lettsom. Anonymous. FaBoEE

Why, what the hell's the matter–have I lost my nerve? Wild Bronc Peeler. Anonymous. CoSo

Why, when it prospers, none dare call it treason. Of Treason. Sir John (1561-1612) Harington. ALV; ExPo; FaBoEE; FF; InPK; NLV; OxBoLi

Why, why, what is this why/But virtus verbi Domini? What Is This Why? *Anonymous.* OxBM

Why will you at the Saviour spurn,/Who offers you his grace? Turn, Turn, Unhappy Souls, Return. Henry Alline. AH

Why woman is a wow, or should I say a wowess. Oh, Please Don't Get Up! Ogden Nash. NePA

Whyle Johnie livd on the border-syde,/Nane of them durst cum neir his hald. Johnie Armstrong (B vers.). *Anonymous.* ViBoFo

Wi' ae lock o' his yellow hair/I'll chain my heart for evermair. The Lament of the Border Widow. *Anonymous.* CH; GBP; HBV 1-2; OxBB

Wi' ilka neebor doo/On the lums of Balgedie. Gin I Were a Doo. *Anonymous.* GBP

Wi October's wind and rain. The Rooks. *Anonymous.* GBP; HBMV; MoBrPo

Wi' you, my fancy's ev'ry pleace/Wer ever fay, vor you wer there. The Zun A-Lighten Eyes A-Shut. William Barnes. VLP

Wi' your head lyin' soft in the sand. The Rambling Sailor. Charlotte Mew. HBMV; PoRA

Wich deceased of thier emocion on a past excursion day. Wellcome, to the Caves of Arta! Robert Graves. NLV; NOBL; NYBP

The wick flares up/should a glance light it. The Firstborn Land. Ingeborg Bachmann. BoWoP

A wicked man in the bathroom cupboard. Miss Twye. Gavin Ewart. ErPo; FiBHP; NeBP; NOBL; PV

"Wicked Uncle Crocodile,/To gobble up our brother!" The Monkeys and the Crocodile. Laura E. Richards. ShM; SoPo; SUS; TiPo

The wicket is the harbour and the garden is the shore. Pirate Story. Robert Louis Stevenson. BeLS; TiPo

Wid yer too-ri-aa, fol-the-did-dle-aa./Too-ri-oo-ri-oo-ri-aa. Mrs. McGrath. *Anonymous.* FaBoBa; FSW

Wide as o'er land and sea/Floats the fair emblem her heroes have won! Lexington. Oliver Wendell Holmes. MC; PAH

Wide as the realms of air or planet's curving sweep. Love's Trinity. Alfred Austin. OBVV

Wide awake. The Being. James Dickey. NMP

Wide cloud with hands extended, and black girdle. Yellow Cloud. Liagarang. WTO

The wide earth darkened so. Evening. James Wright. NOBA; NYBP; PrIm

...Wide empty grin/that never lost a vote (O Adlai mine). Dream Songs. John Berryman. LCAP

The wide-eyed stranger sky-line look at me? Thomas Gray in Patterdale. Norman Nicholson. ACV

The wide mouth'd bowl will surely catch them all! The Hasty Pudding. Joel Barlow. AmPP; AnNE; AP

Wide wind, and wild stars, and hunger of the/quest! Lone Dog. Irene Rutherford McLeod. CoSo; GDP; MCCG; TiPo

A widening of experience, for him it marked no end. Various Ends. Ruthven Todd. NeBP; SeCePo

The widest arc of its elliptical turn. Achieving Perspective. Pattiann Rogers. MAYP

A widow on a front porch puckers her lips/And whispers. In Ohio. James Wright. NNaP

The widow puts no obol, nor the son,/To pay the ferry in the world beneath. Idle Charon. Eugene Lee-Hamilton. NOBV; OBVV

A width, a shining peace, under the night. The Dead. Rupert Brooke. MCCG

Wielder of the stateliest measure ever molded by the lips/of man. To Vergil. Alfred, Lord Tennyson. AWP; InPo

Wielders of power and welders of a new world. You That Love England. C. Day-Lewis. FaBoMo

Wielding a mighty hammer/Today. Summer Storm. Richard B. Kent. AMV-80

The wife'll drop 'un mighty soon. When Fog Come Creepin' over Beccles (parody). Molly Fitton. BXAP

"A wife?" quoth he. "I never was so mad." A Mad Answer of a Madman. Robert Hayman. FF

The wife rubbed herself with bear grease & waited. The Farmer. Terry Stokes. PoL

...Wife,/the poems are time's wings. Spread them darkly. Milos Radnoti. Willis Barnstone. VWA

Wiggle waggle went his tail. Niddle Noddle. *Anonymous.* OxNR

Wil soone conceive, and learne to construe well. Amoretti, XLIII. Edmund Spenser. AAS

Wild animal of the blue ocean. Praises of Henry Francis Fynn. *Anonymous.* WTO

Wild arms which did not hold this way before. Alba after Six Years. Christopher Middleton. NePoEA-2

Wild as a dingo, fresh as a brumby? A Country Song. Douglas Stewart. NOAV

The wild-beast mark of panther's fangs. At a Month's End. Algernon Charles Swinburne. VLP

The wild bird with its hardware in its claws. Local Politics. Robert Pinsky. MAYP

Wild birds are flying south. Indian Summer. Wilfred (William Wilfred Campbell) Campbell. CaP; NOBC; OBCV; PoPl; WHW

Wild born be wild still, though by force made tame. Thus I Resolve. Thomas Campion. OBSP

The wild cry of your blossoming? Alternatives. Peter Cooley. AmPA

Wild feet that go where none save Beauty's go! Epitaph for the Poet V. Arthur Davison Ficke. HBMV

The wild from above was as wild below. The Trees in the Road. James Still. GrPl

The wild geese rose, and the storm winds blew over. Barnacle Geese. Charles Higham. PoAu 1-2

Wild Hamlet with the features of Horatio. Coureurs de Bois. Douglas LePan. CaP; NOBC

–The wild hide-out, Morgan would/have accepted. Morgan. John Blight. CBAP

Wild horses won't tear them apart. Waving a Bough. Boris Pasternak. TrJP

Wild lilac/chokes the garden. The Idea of Trust. Thom Gunn. Psk

Wild pageant of the accumulated past/That clangs and flashes for a drowning man. The Soul's Sphere. Dante Gabriel Rossetti. MaVP

Wild pigeon of the leaves,/You are/Brother of lovers. The Thousand and One Nights: Birds. *Anonymous.* AWP; LiTW

Wild provoke of the endurance sky! Wild Provoke of the Endurance Sky. Joseph Ceravolo. ANYP

The wild swan's, chanting her death melody. Ione. Aubrey Thomas De Vere. IrPN

Wild to be wreckage forever. Cherrylog Road. James Dickey. AmC; BiP; CoAP; HaCAP; HAP; InPS; NIP; NYBP; PAI; PrIm; TwCP

Wild warbling Nature all, above the reach of Art! The Castle of Indolence. James (1700-1748) Thomson. ViBoPo

Wild Weeds of Song–not all ungracious/things! To the Milkweed. Lloyd Mifflin. AA

Wild with rushing dreams and deep with the sadness,/That dwells at the core of all things. Rapids at Night. Duncan Campbell Scott. CaP

Wild woodland music on the pipes of Pan. Enchantment. Madison Cawein. HBV 1-2

Wildered and dark, and gave me to possess/Peace, and this Cot, and thee, heart-honored Maid! The Aeolian Harp. Samuel Taylor Coleridge. NoP

The wilderness it comprehends/It can explain, like summer snow. The Track into the Swamp. Samuel French Morse. CrMA

The wilderness of this Elysian earth. Epipsychidion. Percy Bysshe Shelley. OBNC

A wilderness of water. Long Trip. Langston Hughes. MOS

The wildest bee in black and yellow. Hist, oh hist. Thomas Lovell Beddoes. EG

Wildly then shake hands all four/(Hum and Ho, the end is Hi). The Noble Tuck-Man. Jean Ingelow. NA

Wilhelmj, I think it would killmj. Limerick: "Oh, King of the fiddle, Wilhelmj." Robert Jones Burdette. TDH

Will always be/a tenant and hold/as much as I can. The Story of My Life. Carroll Arnett. VoR

Will anyone wake up today? Sunday. Vern Rutsala. DFF

Will anything sadden the flower-like face? Somebody's Child. Louise Chandler Moulton. HBV 1-2

Will average out. Meditation on Statistical Method. J. V. Cunningham. CoAP; ForPo; QFR; VGW

The will awaits its gradual end. Modes of Pleasure. Thom Gunn. PeHV; PPP

Will be buried with secrets/This scares me. Eulogy for Populations. Ron Welburn. PoBA

Will be changed by the love into sunshine again. Sweet Peril. George Macdonald. BLPA; FaBoBe; TreFS

Will be easily as large/and as ambiguous as the rest. Horn, Mouth, Pit, Fire. William Dickey. AMV-81

Will be ground by the grinders of Gambart. Limerick: "There is an old he-wolf named Gambart." Dante Gabriel Rossetti. CenHV

Will be his own man soon, without ecstasy. Odysseus. Padraic Fallon. CIP

Will be sure to tell you, jeering/What it means to yearn for home. Ahasuerus. Joseph Roth. VWA

...Will be torn down like Babel/By that last decree. The Defiant One. Alice Morrey Bailey. AMV-80

Will bear the fruit of many an after-thought,/Bright in the dubious track of after-years. The Ionian Islands (excerpt). Richard Monckton, Lord Houghton Milnes. OBTV

Will begin in the year of that Lightning Eternal Paradise Epiphany/Apocalyse! Amurrika! (parody). Philip Appleman. BXAP

Will bend in one live length/Closer than side by side. Beasts. Paul Engle. PoCh

Will blossom from the ashes of my kitchen! Dedication of the Cook. Anna Wickham. MoBrPo

Will blow us to the kingdom of shared graves. Sterkfontein. Ruth Miller. PeSA

Will boost my grip in holding onto dreams/I must remember. Matrix III. Ed Lipman. LFAC

Will break anon: Lo! where the gray is white! Sonnets. Frederick Goddard Tuckerman. AP

Will bring no comfort home to me. The Ocean Wood. John Byrne Leicester Warren, Lord De Tabley. CBEP

Will bring them to an early grave/On the shores of Pensacola. On the British Invasion. Philip Freneau. PAH

Will bring to them more gladness than/they brought to us of yore. Man in Nature. William Roscoe Thayer. AA

Will bury only me/and my sorrow. Sometimes I Want to Go Up. Rachel Korn. VWA

Will ca' me and draw me/Until the day I dee. The Spell o' the Hills. Douglas Fraser. PoSH

Will chase all our vapours away. The Huntsman's Rouse. Henry Carey. SeCePo

Will come over the water to me. Viking Terror. Anonymous. AnIL; OnYI

Will come the Gardener in white,/and gather'd flowers are dead, Yasmin! Hassan's Serenade. James Elroy Flecker. OBEV

Will contest the last will of the Sperms. An Armada of Thirty Whales. Daniel Gerard Hoffman. NePA

Will descend to cutting throats. Epigrams. Martial (Marcus Valerius Martialis). OBVE

Will drum me up to London and proclaim my pedigree? Nessie. Ted Hughes. AmMo

Will ever after handsome be. The Maid Who, On the First of May. Anonymous. HBVY

Will ever be the constant wish/of/Jockie Mein. Hallowe'en. John Mayne. HBV 1-2

Will fall into a stillness/That remains within/Its shores. Pause a Moment. Asya (Asya Gray). VWA

Will fall on Yell'ham; but not then/On that sweet form of thine. The Comet at Yalbury or Yell'ham. Thomas Hardy. CMoP; ExPo; GBL; VLP

Will fall one day to flood this tower. The Red-Gold Rain. Sacheverell Sitwell. AtBAP; MoBrPo

Will feed on geese both noon and night. Fable VII: The Lion, the Fox, and the Geese. John Gay. EiCP

Will fill thee with surprise. And Canst Thou, Sinner, Slight. Abby Bradley Hyde. AH

Will find his attitude his occupation. Epigram: "The man who goes for Christian resignation." J. V. Cunningham. PV

Will find them both an air that doth devour. The Test of Manhood (excerpt). George Meredith. WGRP

Will fire rockets to destroy the world/he came that Christmas Day to save? Christmas Story (1980). Pat Arrowsmith. BrRo

Will get up and leave the circle,/return to his bunk. The County Jail. Jimmy Santiago Baca. LFAC

Will give old Time his silken wings. A Love Song. W. F. Hawley. OBCV

Will give us crumb for crust,/Over here, over here. The Praties. Anonymous. FSW

Will glitter for your eyes. Fiend's Weather. Louise Bogan. MoVE

Will go/To tea/With the children/Again? Extremely Naughty Children. Elizabeth Godley. BBGG

Will guady flies adventure in the air,/Nor any lizard sun his spotted skin. Spring Hath Her Own Bright Days of Calm and Peace. Robert Bridges. VLP

Will have made off with my blessings and my daughter. The Father. Donald Finkel. CoPo

Will have our skins at last. 5:30 A.M. Adrienne Rich. NMM; NOBA

Will have your answer. Spring. William Stanley Merwin. NaP

Will He His children bless. Contentment. Benjamin Schlipf. BLRP

Will He—Should He,/Have time for you? No Time For God. Norman L. Trott. BLRP

...Will he/Think me the happier, or I him? Without and Within. James Russell Lowell. HBV 1-2

Will he touch my cheek as he used to, and laugh and be/kind? The Little Sister of the Prophet. Marjorie Pickthall. HBV 1-2

...Will he wake? Scenes from the Life of the Peppertrees. Denise Levertov. LiTM; NeAP; NoP; PoM

Will hear and heed the noble words they say. Decorating the Soldiers' Graves. Minot Judson Savage. OHIP

Will hear no music but the song of death. End of the Flower-World (A.D. 2300). Stanley Burnshaw. AnAmPo

Will hear the wind sigh through the leaves of a tree. The Farmer of Tilsbury Vale. William Wordsworth. EBEV

Will heave one tuneful sigh, and sooth my hov'ring Shade. Ode to a Friend. William Mason. OBEC

Will henceforth be em-/ployed to make statues/of the brass. A Petite Histoire of Red Fascism. Andrei Codrescu. APU

Will hide his head under his wing,/Poor thing! The North Wind Doth Blow. Mother Goose. HBV 1-2

...Will I cry/to be buried or gratefully begin/to nurse at the world I thirsted for? Queen of Heaven Mausoleum. Dennis Schmitz. LCAP

Will I ever find your like, you who have been shown to me only/once? A Woman Sings of Her Love. Anonymous. WTO

Will I ever get it? Zizi's Lament. Gregory Corso. NeAP; VGW

Will I find myself tomorrow? Sire. William Stanley Merwin. CoAP; NaP; VGW

Will I recognize the woman who stands/at the grave? Professional Prisoner. Jessica Scarbrough. LFAC

Will it be summer when we meet,/Or autumn ere you come? When Will Love Come? Pakenham Beatty. HBV 1-2

Will it seem the song you sung/When we were together young. Egyptian Serenade. George William Curtis. HBV 1-2

Will it still be possible to reopen it, and explore? The Reservoir. Edward Field. GP

Will it yield its soul unto the Heavenly Vision,/Or sink despairing into its own hell? The Valley of Decision. John Oxenham. PGD

Will join to ours, make light our lightless stones. Between Seasons. Anne Welsh. PeSA

Will keep revolving in its orbit/Till heat and motion reabsorb it. The Sun. J. Davis. NA

Will keep the promise too. Ecce in Deserto. Henry Augustin Beers. AA; AnFE; APA

Will keep you dizzy most of your life. Age and Youth. Anonymous. UnTE

Will know, will know, will know. Night Music. Chester Kallman. PoPl

Will learn, in school of tribulation,/The folly of his expectation. The Retired Cat. William Cowper. FM; PCat

...Will leave us/no shadows except our own. Thinning out the Grove. Judith Neeld. SOTS

Will lie between me and my troubled lord. Fatal Interview. Edna St. Vincent Millay. VGW

Will linger, though enjoyed, like joy in memory yet. Stanzas Written in Dejection, Near Naples. Percy Bysshe Shelley. CABA; ERoP 1-2; FaBV; FiP; GTBS; GTBS-P; MCCG; NAWM 1-2; NoP; OAEP; OBRV; PoRA; TEP; ViBoPo; WHA

Will lose the cot and keep the sot. Proverbial Advice on Marriage. Anonymous. NLV

Will make a man successful, if he has a little Luck. Ballad of the Faithful Clerk. Albert Stillman. DBV; InMe

Will make its summer in the heart again. Now Blue October. Robert Nathan. FYAP

Will make my flesh stand sooner than my hair. On Meeting a Gentlewoman in the Dark. Anonymous. FaBoEE

Will make the whole read human and exact. The Devil's Advice to Story-Tellers. Robert Graves. CBEP; LiTM; NoAm

Will make them old before their years. Tommy's Tears, and Mary's Fears. Anonymous. HBV 1-2; HBVY

Will make your glistering gold but more to shine. The Prologue. Anne Bradstreet. AP; BoWoP; NOBA; OxBA; SBG; SCAP; TAP

Will meet no spirit but some sprite. Who Sleeps by Day and Walks by Night. Henry David Thoreau. PoEL 1-5

...Will never be willing to tell/us what she knows, and what we do not know. After the Flood. Arthur Rimbaud. SOTW

Will never get a blessing from sermons or from prayers. What the Choir Sang about the New Bonnet. M.T. Morrison. BLPA

Will never hear a syllable/From out the lips of any tree. Be Deferent to Trees. Mary Carolyn Davies. HBMV; HBVY; OHIP

Will never pull, for example, apart/from where we are going. The Bicycle. Stan Rice. NPGG

Will never rise to fight again. He That Fights and Runs Away. Anonymous. TreF

Will no' drive Willie Wastle doon. Scottish Castle. Anonymous. OxNR

...Will no God do right? The Leper. Algernon Charles Swinburne. GBL; NOBV

Will none?–Then let my memory die/In after days! In After Days. Henry Austin Dobson. EnLit; HBV 1-2; OBEV; OBVV; TreFS

Will not cry with joy, "Pompeii!"/To the hills return! I have never seen volcanoes. Emily Dickinson. PoEL 1-5

...Will not eat this month/One little mess of whelks, so he may 'scape!] Caliban upon Setebos. Robert Browning. AWP; EBEV; MaVP; NOBV; NoP; OAEL 1-2; OAEP; VLP; WGRP

Will not forget His foes. John Brown's Body. Stephen Vincent Benét. AtBAP; PoNe

Will not in cold and useless ruin fade. Alma Venus (excerpt). Bernard O'Dowd. PoAu 1-2

Will not, in his prayer, recall/That he is chastised at all. Rabia. James Freeman Clarke. HBV 1-2

Will not linger broken but pass/suddenly with great pain into the Indian night. Lynx. R. A. D. Ford. CaP

...Will not praise Homer/Because Helen's conduct is "unsuitable'. Homage to Sextus Propertius, Part V. Ezra Pound. CrMA

Will now be yours in your last loneliness. Unknown Man in the Morgue. Merrill Moore. MoAmPo

Will nurse the sad afflicted till health may be restored. The Sherman Cyclone. *Anonymous.* BFSS

The will of the wind for my pilot only, the stardrift/my compass and guide. Wind of the Prairie. Grace Clementine Howes. GoYe

Will one day find her bosom ready,–/That never thought to be forgiven. The Changed Woman. Louise Bogan. HBMV

Will our wild errors be forgiven! Chamber Scene. Nathaniel Parker Willis. HBV 1-2

Will pay compensation/Of seventeen dollars a week. Help Wanted. Franklin Waldheim. BLPA

Will perfume the perfume. Perfume. *Anonymous.* UnTE

Will pillow your bright head/By the incurious dead. A Girl. Babette Deutsch. HBMV

Will purge good manners and religion out. The True-Born Englishman. Daniel Defoe. OBSV

Will read on hist'ry's pages of the great McCloskey fight. Throw Him Down, McCloskey. J. W. Kelly. FSN; TreF

Will rear no blossom from the sand. Epigram: "I dug and dug amongst the snow." Christina Georgina Rossetti. FaBoEE

Will remain when there is no heart to break for it. Credo. Robinson Jeffers. AnEnPo; MoAB; MoAmPo; PoPl

Will repossess this ground. Summer Noon: 1941. Yvor Winters. CrMA

Will ring even-on i' my ear/Till the close o my mortal times. Lintie in a Cage. Alice V. Stuart. OxBS

Will rise from their ashes in ten million years? Pre-History Repeats. Robert J., Jr. McKent. QQQ

Will rive his linty locks awa/And lave him bell and bare. (a dandelion.) A Riddle. William Soutar. OxBS

Will save the dandelion from hell War with the Weeds. Keith Sinclair. AnNZ

Will scatter grace and sweetness everywhere. Inscription on an Ancient Bell. *Anonymous.* ISi

Will send you bounding to your hills again. Summer. James (1700-48) Thomson. EnLi 1-2

Will shape our lives to richer states/And heap our measures fuller. The Bobolinks. Christopher Pearse Cranch. AA; GN

Will she kiss me to-morrow? A Kiss. Henry Austin Dobson. ALV; CenHV; HBV 1-2

...Will she not rot/Without us and die/In childbed leaving/Monstrous issue– The People, the People. George Oppen. GP

Will shoulder through with joy Cut Lilac. Tony Beyer. OCNZ

Will shout "Turn back." No Change of Place. W. H. Auden. OxBTC

Will sing for us, for us forever,/In our eternity. By Sandy Waters. Jesse Stuart. AmFN

Will sleep secure, right free from injury/Of cankered hate or rankest villainy. To Everlasting Oblivion. John Marston. CBEP; LoBV; OBSC

Will smack their lips and cry "Delicious!" Egoism. W. Craddle. FiBHP

Will speed its freight/dismal time/to its sodden grave. The last one. Nelly Sachs. BoWoP

Will square the circle one bright day. Reliques. Edmund Charles Blunden. ImOP

Will stand all night/so tall/the sun will rise. Giraffe. Stanley Plumly. AmPA

Will still be thought a pretty gem/When all your world of beauty's dim. To Vanity. Darwin T. Turner. PoNe

Will still break through. My heart, thinking. Lady Otomo of Sakanoe. AWP; LiTW

Will still flow on in strain sublime/When stones, and even men, are mute. Written on the Plain of Thebes. John William Burgon. OBTV

Will still remain till I have reached my rest. The Ghost's Promenade. Thomas Caulfield Irwin. IrPN

Will strive for to spell. The Good Boy. *Anonymous.* OxNR

Will sweeter taste than these red berries be. The Barberry-Bush. Jones Very. AP

Will take her to itself again. Babylon. Ralph Hodgson. BrPo; HBMV

Will take the sun out of the skies/Ere freedom out of man. Ode: "O tenderly the haughty day." Ralph Waldo Emerson. PAL

Will take you down the easiest way to Hades. The Easiest Way. *Anonymous.* UnTE

Will tell each little world its character. Sleep Will Come Singly. W.H. Oliver. AnNZ

Will tell you how he wrote, and talk'd, and spit. Doctor Johnson. Soame Jenyns. FaBoEE

Will tell you why I think that I/can get across it if I try. I May, I Might, I Must. Marianne Moore. ELU; FaBoWP; FF; OBAL; OBSP

Will that awful thing seem plain. The Thought. William Brighty ("Matthew Browne") Rands. OBEV; OBVV

The Will that makes the Wheel go round? New York. George William Russell. OBMV

Will the champak think to blossom? Substantiations (excerpt). Vidya. PBWP

Will the earth's womb not be filled,/will the grave have never done! Lament for a Warrior. *Anonymous.* PeSA

Will the fire of the heart and the fire of the mind be one Heart and Mind. Edith Sitwell. AtBAP; ChMP; MoPo; MP; OAEP; OxBTC; SiPS; TwCP

Will the machinegunners please step forward? A Poem Some People Will Have to Understand. LeRoi (Imamu Amiri Baraka) Jones. BPo; NOBA

Will the real President Nixon please pick up the Cross? Nixons at Calvary. Howard Nemerov. SOTS

Will the roses grow wild over me? The Popular Wobbly. T-Bone Slim. FSW

Will the sound of the clock ever fade, or the voice of the vendor some-/time stop? Pay-Off. Kenneth Fearing. CMoP

Will there be a spring/for the downtrodden Jews? Song: "On the side of the road." Edmond Jabes. VWA

Will there not be a tomb for me?/For me, no. How Placidly Shine. Rosalia de Castro. PBWP

Will they be as bright again?/Not if kissed by other men. Song: "Often I have heard it said." Walter Savage Landor. HBV 1-2

Will they rise up, their resurrection day. The Airman. W. R. Rodgers. WaP

Will they shatter the moment's quiet perfection? Renoir's Confidences. J. Michael Pilz. AMV-81

The will to win it makes us free. Creation's Lord, We Give Thee Thanks. William deWitt Hyde. AH

Will travel much faster than/planes. Genius. R. J. P. Hewison. FaFP

Will twenty eagles pay homage to him? Six Eagles. Thomas Love Peacock. VoR

Will wait for us till we can climb up/as it heads for the blue west. The Blue West. Dahlia Ravikovich. PBWP

Will wake from sleep and perhaps bark back. Cemetery Nights. Stephen Dobyns. SV

Will wake up in the dark night screaming/as his hideous body grabs them. The Bride of Frankenstein. Edward Field. CoAP; HeIP

& Will want to be remembered/as realpeople. We Walk the Way of the New World. Don L. Lee. BPo; NeAC; PoBA

...Will we grant them/sleep? Memorial Day. William E. Brooks. PAL; PGD

Will wear in your hearts forever/The glory of long ago! No More the Thunder of Cannon. Julia Caroline Ripley Dorr. OHIP

Will whisper, "That's it," and "That's it." There. William Harmon. AMV-80

Will, with my willow-wreath also,/Come forth and sweetly dye. The Willow Garland. Robert Herrick. OAEP

Will Ye No Come Back Again? Will Ye No Come Back Again? Lady Nairn. BSV

Will you always stand there shivering? The Poplar. Richard Aldington. HBMV

"Will you be my Valentine?" February. Frank Dempster Sherman. YeAr

Will you, because you might not/particularly care to see it so? The Map. Gloria C. Oden. AmNP; NNP; PoNe

Will you come back now/Or will you hesitate? The Hesitating Blues. W. C. Handy. GoSl

WILL YOU COME OUT NOW? Will You Come Out Now? Valerie Sinason. BrRo

Will you come to me at midnight. Can You Change a Shilling? Toni Del Renzio. EAS

Will you find your lost dead among them? Coda. Ezra Pound. NOBA

Will you go, lassie, go? Will You Go, Lassie, Go? *Anonymous.* FSW

Will you grow on mine? Simon and the Tarantula. James Wright. NNaP

Will you have us your slaves to lie to you, flatter and–leave/you? Amours de Voyage. Arthur Hugh Clough. OBNC

Will you help him learn to use it/In your home and Sunday school? A Sunday School Teacher Speaks. *Anonymous.* STF

Will you make it clear I'm not that sort of boy? They Answer Back: To His Ever-Worshipped Will from W. H. Francis. FiBHP

Will you marry it, marry it, marry it. The Applicant. Sylvia Plath. MAT; NaP; NMM; NOBA; SBG; TwCP

Will you maybe succeed in keeping your good name/clear. Good Repute Is Water Carried in a Sieve. Lalleswari. WPOW

Will you never let us go? Song of the Galley-Slaves. Rudyard Kipling. GTBS-P; HAP; PoEL 1-5

...Will you stay looking/straight at me/awhile longer Gabriel. Adrienne Rich. VGW

Will you swallow, will you deny them, will you lie your way/home? Rape. Adrienne Rich. GP

Will you then my heart decline?"/"No, Sir! no, Sir! no, oh, no, no!" The Scottish Merchant's Daughter. *Anonymous.* BFSS

Will you, won't you, will you, won't you, won't you join the/dance? The Lobster Quadrille. Lewis (Charles Lutwidge Dodgson) Carroll. MoShBr; OxBChV; Par; PoPle

William was then aged sixty-four/And Samuel sixty-two. The Bards. Walter De La Mare. DTC; FaBoNo; NOBL; PV

Willie's slain! My Luve's in Germany. *Anonymous.* CH

...Willie says again/and again, "Gimme the goddamn ball." Charge. Christopher Gilbert. MAYP

Willing a little at the very last? Chryseis. Walter Conrad Arensberg. AnAmPo

Willing it, my ailment. No Road. Philip Larkin. EBEV; MoBrPo

The willing Muses were debauch'd at Court. The Court of Charles II. Alexander Pope. OBEC

...Willows/Now and again dipping their long oval leaves in the water. Betrothed. Louise Bogan. LLLT

Willy, and John, whose life and art, if any,/I never knew. Willy Lyons. James Wright. HaCAP; NNaP

Willy-nilly born it was, divinely formed and fair. The Unwanted. C. Day-Lewis. PoPl

Wilt flee, or wilt thou stay? Fickle Hope. Harrison Smith Morris. AA

Wilt Thou receive them, Lord of grace,/And give to me a crown? My Heart's Desire. *Anonymous.* STF

Wilted like foam or daisies from their thirst. Sailor. P. K. Page. ACV

Win all your winnings and leave naught,/But sorrow and repentance. Gambling. Royall Tyler. TAP

Win and wear thee he that may. Philarete to His Mistress (excerpt). George Wither. PeD

De win' gwine rise, baby, an' blow my blues away. Woman Blue. *Anonymous.* ABF

De win' sing sperrichals/Through deir dus'. Memphis Blues. Sterling A. Brown. BANP

Win them, I'll be at your Devotion. Katy's Answer. Allan Ramsay. CEP

...Wincing rubber/tires: I am home. Night: Landing at Newark. Jonathan Holden. PPJ

A wind among the grass and, sighing,/Carries my spirit to hers. Waking. Patrick MacDonogh. NeIP

The wind, an Indian paintbrush, sweeps the sky. Independence Day. William Jay Smith. MP; TwCP

...Wind and steam and speed/And clamour and the night. We are in Ghent. A Trip to Paris and Belgium (excerpt). Dante Gabriel Rossetti. OBTV

The wind arrives/With the flutter of something really happening. Summer. Douglas Crase. NoP

The wind begins to sound along the bar. A May Sunday. Thomas Caulfield Irwin. IrPN

The wind blew away his name. When at Night. Mark M. Perlberg. AMV-80

"The wind-blown clamour of the barnacle-geese." Beggar to Beggar Cried. William Butler Yeats. CMoP; NoAm

A wind blown room. The Truth Is Quite Messy. William J. Harris. BOLo

...The wind/blows through/The window beside me, fresh and cool. Hospital Observation. Julian Symons. WaP

The wind blows with the sound of eggshells/the day you are born. The Day You Are Born. Cathy Song. BrSi

Wind broke its longest bough. The Willow. Tu Fu. NaP

The wind brushes adobe walls away/grain by grain. Old Women beside a Church. Keith Wilson. Psk

Wind cries in roses gone wild. Roses Gone Wild. John Taylor. AMV-80; FAZ

The wind did blow and it ain't no wonder/And they (?) blew them both into their graves. In Brunton Town. *Anonymous.* BaBo

Wind dries the blood on the moving sand. Merthymawr. George Woodcock. NeBP

Wind far away that poplar-skirted stream. Recollections of Burgos. Richard Chenevix Trench. OBRV

...The wind feathering my hair/at pier's end, might hold us aloft this night. The Berkeley Pier. John Addiego. AMV-81

The wind finally bearing away/the darkness that is/a flock of small birds. My Grandfather Burning Cornfields. Roger Sauls. Str

A wind from the pine-tree trickles on my bare head. In the Mountains on a Summer Day. Li Po. AWP; SD

Wind from the west, bite the best. How They Bite. *Anonymous.* SD

The wind has blown them all away. Ballade of the Heresiarchs. Hilaire Belloc. MoVE

Wind has never sung song of Nation/in my black face. To Vietnam. Charlie Cobb. PoBA

Wind in the briar is you, you are here/on the grass in this lucid ferment. Gothic Notebook (excerpts). Mario Luzi. LiTW

Wind in the reeds:/it is not words that speak of death. Words That Speak of Death. Anadad Eldan. VWA

The wind is an old beggar/rattling our bones in his cup. November Song. Mark Vinz. Psk

The wind is carrying me round the sky. Alice Corbin Is Gone. Carl Sandburg. PoA

The wind is carrying me round the sky. The Wind. Alice Corbin. BPAW

The wind is everything to them. The Marriage. Mark Strand. BIrV; EAS; GTBS-P; NoAm

...The wind is going over/everything tonight, proofing for error. A Theory of Wind. Albert Goldbarth. MAYP

Wind is lord and change is sovereign of the/strand. A Midsummer Holiday, VI: The Cliffside Path. Algernon Charles Swinburne. VLP

The wind is passing by. Who Has Seen the Wind? Christina Georgina Rossetti. BrR; GoJo; HBVY; NTCP; SUS

...A wind is rising,/and the rivers flow. You Can't Go Home Again (excerpt). Thomas Wolfe. TRV

The wind is watching over it. Ballad of Luna, Luna. Federico Garcia Lorca. SOTW

The wind it blows, the ship it goes,/Though where and whither, no one knows. All Is Well. Arthur Hugh Clough. EnLi 1-2

The wind it blows, the ship it goes,/Though where and whither, no one/knows. Whate'er You Dream with Doubt Possest. Arthur Hugh Clough. OAEP

The wind makes desolate sounds in the night curtains. Written on Seeing the Flowers, and Remembering My Daughter. Kao Ch'i. DL

The wind-moved tamarisk/trees as beautiful/as graygreen chinchilla fur. Baja–Outside Mexicali. Michael McClure. GP

The wind never missed them. There were still the clouds. The Broken. William Stanley Merwin. LCAP

The wind of Death's imperishable wing? The House of Life. Dante Gabriel Rossetti. GTBS-P

Wind, overturn the goblet, spill/On me the everlasting skies! The Wind. Harold Monro. OBVV

The wind perceives and orders. Before the Pacific. Blanca Varela. BoWoP

The wind pours down. Ploughing on Sunday. Wallace Stevens. AmLP; GoJo; NCSH; PoPl; SOTW

Wind rattles the moon. December. Maurice Kenny. STE

Wind rising out of the alleys/Carrying stuff of flame. Wind in the Alleys. Lola Ridge. OnYI

...The wind's blue fingers laid/A migrant on the rock. Dream of Winter. George Mackay Brown. FaBoTw

...The wind's not come quiet/though the harper's gone who lied through it. Lament for Turlough O'Carolan. David Hopes. SM

Wind's stability,/Is mortality. Mortality. *Anonymous.* CBEP

Wind's word, apple-heart, haven of grasses. Apology. Richard Wilbur. NePoAm; Psk

The wind shall be thy changeful loom,/Thy web, the shifting sand! Featherstone's Doom. Robert Stephen Hawker. OBNC

The wind shall blow my topknot off. Tom, He Was a Piper's Son. *Anonymous.* GBP

The wind shall not blow my plaid away. The Elfin-knight. *Anonymous.* BuBa

The wind shifting south. Song: "From whence cometh song?–". Theodore Roethke. NCSH

...Wind that blends/Bluegum and cordite with the southern sea. Heureux Qui Comme Ulysse... John Streeter Manifold. WaaP; WaP

The wind that blows, that wind is best. Whichever Way the Wind Doth Blow. Caroline Atherton Briggs Mason. GoTF; TreFS

Wind that levels all before it. Wind. *Anonymous.* WTO

The wind that whistles through his empty bag. The Friar. Julian del Casal. CAW

Wind the clock and hear it chime! Gallop, Gallop to a Rhyme. Monica Shannon. SiSoSe

The wind, the wind, the wind, the wind,/May blow her home again. The Piper on the Hill. Dora Sigerson Shorter. HBV 1-2; HBVY; OnYI

...The wind/travelling from where it began. The Stethoscope. Dannie Abse. SUW

...The wind walks on the sea,/printing the water's face with charity. At the Sea's Edge. Gwen Harwood. CBAP

...The wind was rattling/The dry husks of corn. The Wreck of the Great Northern. Robert Hedin. AMV-81

The wind was telegraphing, hundreds/Of miles. All Ireland raced. A Strong Wind. Austin Clarke. BoNaP

Wind whispers in: and the yacht again/Asserts direction on the trackless tide. Off Banks Peninsula. Denis Glover. AnNZ

The wind will blow, the dawn will glow,/Ere thou hast sailed them through. A Myth. Charles Kingsley. GN

Windfall Water and Jamison. Mountain Meadows. Martha Keller. BoNaP

A winding glass around we'll pass, and to hell with blubber whaling. Blow Ye Winds. *Anonymous.* OBSS

Winding his sinuous way in the dark to the/depths of the forest.   The War-Token.   Henry Wadsworth Longfellow.   PAH

Winding the trail regret?   What Need Have I for Memory?   Georgia Douglas Johnson.   CDC

...Winding ways/Of hoar Antiquity, but strown with flowers.   Sonnet: "Deem not, devoid of elegance, the sage."   Thomas Warton, Jr..   SeCePo

...Windmill of ankles/and wrists, she had to turn/thirteen.   Meantime.   Heather McHugh.   GeTw

The windmill still turns/but someone pulled up the pipe/and shot the cistern full of holes.   Driving to Sauk City.   Warren Woessner.   TAT

A window an orange a shadow of an/odor.   The Passengers.   David Antin.   NYBP

A window flies across a pasture.   Tornado Watch.   Paul Shuttleworth.   AMV-80

The window is dark and the night is cold,/And the story forever told.   Lost Light.   Elizabeth Akers.   HBV 1-2

Window lit into darkness–/under the light of the family circle.   Just a While.   Frantisek Gottlieb.   VWA

A window–not a looking-glass.   Letter to a Friend.   Jon Stallworthy.   NoAm

The windowpanes were crying.   Three Floors.   Stanley Jasspon Kunitz.   SM

The windows are glass, &/behind that the house is not empty.   The House.   George Bowering.   NOBC

The windows blurred by the same warm, slow, still rain?   Memo.   Kenneth Fearing.   CMoP

...Windows faintly holding/The feathery filigree of frost.   A December Day.   Sara Teasdale.   YeAr

Windows look out on mountains and the walls are kind.   The Work of Happiness.   May Sarton.   MoRP

Windows, rapturous windows!   Dead Color.   Charles Wright.   HaCAP; LCAP

Windows the now elegiac light pours through.   Dead Wasp.   Kenneth Slade Alling.   NePoAm

Winds are cold when it is gone.   Fame.   Eleanor Hollister Cantus.   GoYe

The winds around on pointed/rocks/Settled like bats innumerable, ready to fly abroad.   The Four Zoas.   William Blake.   BoW

Winds blow for the dead.   Dirge.   Gavin Bantock.   OxBTC

Winds bring a fine and bitter snow.   The Coming of the Cold.   Theodore Roethke.   OBCP

The winds of difference freezing us to stone.   Chilled by Different Winds.   Alice Mackenzie Swaim.   AMV-80

The winds of heaven would sing the praise of him...   The Vow of Washington.   John Greenleaf Whittier.   MC

Winds' stability,/Is mortality.   An Inscription.   *Anonymous.*   EiL

Winds that bite with/teeth of winter ice.   Blood.   Barney Bush.   STE

Windseed is barren takes no truehold/in heart tendrilled tight with existence of you   This Page My Pigeon.   Earle Birney.   PeCV

Windy fire.   Burning the Small Dead.   Gary Snyder.   CAPP; NNaP

The wine and bread protect our ecstasy.   Harvest and Consecration.   Elizabeth Jennings.   NePoEA-2

Wine for old Adam, digging in the briars!   Cana.   Thomas Merton.   TrCP

Wine for our drinking.   Come to Me from Crete to This Holy Temple.   Sappho.   WPOW

The wine of Beauty and the bread he breaks.   Who Walks with Beauty.   David Morton.   BLPA; FaBoBe; GoTF; HBMV; TreFT

The wine of the Immortals/Forbids me to die!   The Visit of the Gods.   Friedrich von Schiller.   OBVE

The wine-press holds the unbidden Christ.   In Portugal, 1912.   Alice Meynell.   NOCV; OxBoCh

Wine vintage–long diluted.   Thirst of the Dragon.   Dianne Hai-Jew.   BrSi

The wine we drank, the man we knew.   A Decanter of Madeira, Aged 86, to George Bancroft, Aged 86.   Silas Weir Mitchell.   AA; ViBoPo

Wine will do the work alone.   Would You Be a Man of Fashion?   *Anonymous.*   ALV

A wing brushes my left hand,/but it's not my wing.   Dog Day Vespers.   Charles Wright.   LCAP

The wing feather of a sea-bird fiercely wild.   The Old Boat.   Lenore Pratt.   CaP

A wing was open'd at me everywhere!   Gout and Wings.   Turner, Charles Tennyson.   NOBV

The winged skulls shriek: None shall escape the wrath/Of the King of Terrors.   Letters for the New England Dead.   Mary Baron.   HoAn

The winged Victory of Samothrace.   Survival.   Florence Earle Coates.   AA

Wings of strange birds that are burning/Themselves alive.   A Mad Fight Song for William S. Carpenter, 1966.   James Wright.   LiSp

Wings/zippe zappe/and crow   Calypso.   William Carlos Williams.   NePoAm-2

Winifred will come back cured,/Let us hope, of crying.   Winifred Waters.   William Brighty ("Matthew Browne") Rands.   OxBChV

Wink as they will. Wink most when widows wince.   A High-Toned Old Christian Woman.   Wallace Stevens.   AP; CMoP; CoBMV; MoVE; NoAm; NOBA; TAP

Winks his nose and sits all sunny.   And Timid, Funny, Brisk Little Bunny.   Christina Georgina Rossetti.   TiPo

Winnow'd away and purified/By the vibrations of my heart.   Going to Church.   Coventry Patmore.   LoBV

The winnowing years/will prove it chaff or wheat.   Sifting.   Victor E. Beck.   GoYe

Winter and earth to ashes with its love.   In Defense of Felons.   Robert Mezey.   NePoEA

Winter-burning in the fields.   The Crows.   Louise Bogan.   FaBoWP; NMM

Winter came.   The Last Flower.   John Travers Moore.   PoSC

...Winter frown/And the storms of sleet come down?   February, Tall and Trim.   Anna Neil Gilmore.   YeAr

Winter goes,/Crowned with daffodils!   March.   Arthur Guiterman.   YeAr

Winter has a place/No season can erase.   Winter on Black Mingo (excerpt).   *Anonymous.*   FiBHP

Winter is all my year.   Idle Verse.   Henry Vaughan.   AtBAP; OAEP

Winter is almost summer where they grow.   Firwood.   John Clare.   EG; TrGrPo

"Winter is in the wood!" the winds/In the warm chimney cry.   Cold Winter Now Is in the Wood.   Elizabeth Jane Coatsworth.   TiPo

Winter makes haste, and summer's quickly gone.   To Certain Maidens Playing with Snow.   Edward May.   FaBoEE

Winter of the blue snow.../mavericks/loners/free men.   Letter to an Imaginary Friend.   Thomas McGrath.   GP

Winter, post-coital triste.   Spring Is Hard on Us.   *Anonymous.*   ErPo; PV

Winter's frost a forgotten/land, and time a revolving/flame/   Migration.   Pinkie Gordon Lane.   BlSi

Winter shall pass, fair weather return,/The sun-hot summer, the restless sea.   Gnomic Lines.   *Anonymous.*   LiTW

Winter: slippy, drippy, nippy.   Spring Is Showery, Flowery, Bowery.   Mother Goose.   TiPo

Winter, Spring, Summer times!   A Song for the Seasons.   Bryan Waller Procter.   HBV 1-2

The winter-storm the serpent breathes/Has never withered.   O Crimson Blood.   Hildegard von Bingen.   WPOW

A winter-struck bush for his/foreground to/complete the picture...   Pictures from Brueghel.   William Carlos Williams.   LCAP

Winter, whom Spring shall kill.   You Are Like the Snow Only.   Edward Estlin Cummings.   AtBAP

...Winter/with a cold red nose!   November.   Aileen Fisher.   SiSoSe; TiPo

The wintry Earth fulfil/With Peace and Plight!   Christmas 1898 (excerpt).   Sir Lewis Morris.   TrPWD

The wintry winds hae dung it doon,/Now hid 'mang weeds and grass.   The Auld House.   Carolina Oliphant, Lady Nairne.   HBV 1-2

Wipe out poverty everywhere in the world/in its most obvious form, the poor.   Manifest Destiny.   Anselm Hollo.   APU

Wipe Thou the widow's tears that fall!   The Dead Coach.   Katharine Tynan Hinkson.   HBV 1-2

Wiped Buddha clean with toilet paper/and threw it to the wind.   A Mountain-Toilet Thief.   Al Robles.   BrSi

Wiping out in a blue flash and curlicue of smoke/600 million Chinese without a trace...   The Not-So-Good Earth.   Bruce Dawe.   CBAP

Wiping out the stains and gloom/With the power of Love once more!   Chant of the Ninth Order of Seraphim.   Inigo de Mendoza.   CAW

Wiping the scythe blade with fresh cut grass;/Then, mowing again.   At the Place of the Roman Baths.   Richard Scrace.   CaP

Wiping wet palms/on our green thighs.   Butter.   Tom Schmidt.   NeAC

Wire in the gapped hedge saved the uncaptured hare...   Escape to Love.   Patrick MacDonogh.   BIrV

...A wiry soul/That must escape the knife.   Autobiography of a Lungworm.   Roy Fuller.   NoAm; NoP; OxBC

Wisdom and Wit are little seen,/But Folly at full length.   On Mr. Nash's Present of His Own Picture at Full Length...   Philip Stanhope, Earl of Chesterfield.   NOEC

Wisdom has a hard mouth.   Pedigree.   Mary Mills.   NePoAm

Wisdom is knowing when you can't be wise.   You Can't Be Wise.   Paul Engle.   PoPl

WISDOM IS VAIN, AND PROPHESY.   The Conflict of Convictions.   Herman Melville.   AP; MAmP; NOBA

Wisdom of age is not facade!!!   Soul.   Austin Black.   NBP

The wisdom of the gazelle/Remains in my head.   Wisdom of the Gazelle.   George P. Solomos.   GoYe

The wisdom of the wise, and prancings of the great.   The Complaint, or Night Thoughts on Life, Death and Immortality.   Edward Hilton Young.   NOEC

The wisdom of woman to the distaff is bound.   Woe Is Me, My Soul Says, How Bitter Is My Fate.   Rahel Morpurgo.   PBWP

Wise and simple, rich and poor,/Thou hast known them all before!   To My Old Schoolmaster.   John Greenleaf Whittier.   NOBA

Wise and thoughtless joy.   Out of Your Hands.   Theodore Weiss.   CoPo

Wise Heaven's too just to let them thrive in spite.   The Diet of Poland, a Satire.   Daniel Defoe.   OBTV

Wise men shun the tongues that rattle.   Tongues.   Thomas Sturge Moore.   HBMV

Wise messenger of the gods, their child.   I Remember the Room Was Filled with Light.   Judith Hemschemeyer.   SM

Wise once, and wise thence evermore.   Lone Founts.   Herman Melville.   AnFE; LiTA; ViBoPo

Wise silence is best music unto bliss.   Astrophel and Stella, LXX.   Sir Philip Sidney.   AAS; SiPS

The wise who, having known, can never/die.   Commemoration Ode.   Harriet Monroe.   AA

Wisecracks and wonderment/spring up like dandelions.   Spring Storm.   Jim Wayne Miller.   GOYP

Wiser than all men's knowing.   O Simplicitas.   Madeleine L'Engle.   EBCP; OBCP; PCh

Wiser than any we know if the solving's a matter/For life, not death.   Garden Puzzle.   Gray Burr.   CoPo

Wiser than the living, they have shown/How true Nobility is bred in The Bone.   Only the Dead.   Reed Whittemore.   NYBP

Wiser were the lovers/In the days of old.   In the Days of Old.   Thomas Love Peacock.   HBV 1-2

A wish, and half believe it will come true.   Autumn.   Frances Winwar.   GoYe

The wish and power to act, forgive, and bless.   Their Last Will and Testament.   Louis MacNeice.   NAMP

A wish for ease and leisure, and ere/long/Found here that leisure and that ease I/wish'd.   The Task.   William Cowper.   OAEP

Wish for the good,/And the best do.   Love the Beautiful.   Moses Mendelssohn.   GoTF; TreFT

Wish I may, wish I might,/Have this wish I wish tonight.   Wishing Poem.   Anonymous.   NTCP

Wish not for death, and fear it not.   What Makes a Happy Life.   Martial (Marcus Valerius Martialis).   AWP

Wish on the ninth horse, your wish will come true.   White Horses.   Eleanor Farjeon.   PH

The wish that sticks in your heart/and will not let you be/until it is made art.   IT.   Richmond Lattimore.   PP

Wish/they was/white/i say/they is   Honky.   Charles Cooper.   PoBA

Wish to God that I could be,/In Abilene, my Abilene.   Abilene.   Anonymous.   FSW

Wish you were here./Love, Carolyn.   Postcards from Rotterdam.   Carolyn Kizer.   GP

Wished that I too could turn to stone.   Girl.   Dom Moraes.   NePoEA-2

Wished we were going/nowhere at all.   The Drive.   Janet Reed McFatter.   GrPl

Wishes so simple they laugh at a vow.   Birthday Poem, November 4th.   John Thompson, Jr.   WaP

Wishing each moment for to see/Come sailing in the Victory.   Disconsolate Judy's Lamentation.   Anonymous.   OBSS

Wishing happiness to all Seamen, old or young,/in their sailing in the Low-lands.   Sir Walter Raleigh Sailing in the Low-Lands.   Anonymous.   OBSS; OxBoLi

Wishing him luck on The Lost Range down yonder against/the sky.   The Lost Range.   Henry Herbert Knibbs.   BPAW

Wishing me luck in placing myself/elsewhere.   After Grave Deliberation...   Elizabeth Flynn.   AMV-80; NLV

Wishing myself the good voyage.   Departure's Girl-Friend.   William Stanley Merwin.   ConAP; LCAP

Wishing to see that face and finding this.   Lais.   Hilda ("H. D.") Doolittle.   MoAmPo

Wissing all luvaris leill to haif sic chance,/That thay may haif us in remembrance.   Up, Helsum Hairt.   Alexander Scott.   OxBS

Wistfully, silently–vanished too soon.   The Curtain (Old Tabor Grand Opera House.).   Jean Milne Gower.   PoOW

Wit's a Disease consumes men in few yeares.   On Mr. Francis Beaumont (then newly dead).   Richard Corbet.   OBS

Wit's forge and fire-blast, meaning's press and screw.   On Donne's Poetry.   Samuel Taylor Coleridge.   CBEP; ERoP 1-2; InvP; NoP; OAEL 1-2; OAEP; PP

Wit that can creep, and pride that licks the dust.   An Epistle from Mr. Pope to Dr. Arbuthnot.   Alexander Pope.   OBSV; TW

A witch makes her broom from a sassafras stick.   Witchwood.   May Justus.   SiSoSe

Witches' broom and the dwarf mistletoe.   Tamarack.   Eugene McCarthy.   GrPl

With a beautiful thing that shall never grow wise.   The Cherry-Blossom Wand.   Anna Wickham.   MoBrPo

With a bed and a shroud of the beautiful snow.   The Beautiful Snow.   John Whittaker Watson.   TreF; WBLP

With a blessing/From the dark sun/Of their source.   The Prayers.   Howard Schwartz.   VWA

With a bottle of good brandy, and on my knee a girl!   The Green Bed.   Anonymous.   AmFP

With a bum like a jelly on springs.   Limerick: "There was a young Fellow of King's."   Anonymous.   NOBL

With a chaff-bag under his Sunday pants,/On the Field of the Cloth of Gold.   The Field of the Cloth of Gold.   Patrick Joseph Hartigan.   NOAV

With a child's pleasure/All her life's round.   Rain on a Grave.   Thomas Hardy.   CoBMV; HBV 1-2; OAEP

With a child's trust leans on a Father's breast.   The Riddle of the World.   John Greenleaf Whittier.   TRV

...With a clink and glitter of keen bronze/stood by his chair, in the forefront near his father.   The Odyssey.   Homer.   NAWM 1-2

With a clover in her hand.   The Question.   Frederick Goddard Tuckerman.   AP

With a cool breeze/To sooth an aching back.   On Passing Two Negroes on a Dark Country Road Somewhere in Georgia.   Conrad Kent Rivers.   IDB; NNP

With a crack that from my chisel blow/runs to the furthest star.   The Little Chisel.   N. P. Van Wyk Louw.   PeSA

With a deep yearning I think of the Sages of Antiquity.   Shady, Shady.   T'ao Ch'ien.   AWP

With a dildo he kept in his purse.   Limerick: "A young fairy with habits perverse."   Anonymous.   PeHV

With a face of golden pleasure/Elegantly destroy.   Water.   Ralph Waldo Emerson.   AmPP; OBSP; PoEL 1-5

With a face too white/And a cheek too red.   The Goldsmith's Wife.   Anonymous.   KiLC

With a fearful shriek, he leaped and fell across the picture–dead.   The Face Upon the Floor.   Hugh Antoine D'Arcy.   BeLS; BLPA; FaBoBe; FPL; HBV 1-2; PaPo; YaD

...With a feeling of delay and retarding–/rather than out of nervousness.   A Sequence.   Leslie Scalapino.   NPGG

With a film of stale gossip coating his tongue.   Autumn Sequence.   Adrienne Rich.   VGW

–With a flower/Of the world, notwithstanding all still dear?   The Man Closes the Shutters.   Lionello Fiumi.   LiTW

With-a-fountain's shining-shot furls.   Harry Ploughman.   Gerard Manley Hopkins.   FaBoMo

With a four-horse team, we'll soon be seen/Way out in Idaho.   Way Out in Idaho.   Anonymous.   BPAW; CoSo; FSW; OuSiCo

With a full but soft emotion,/Like the swell of Summer's ocean.   Stanzas for Music.   George Gordon, Lord Byron.   AWP; ChRP; DTC; EnLi 1-2; FiP; HBV 1-2; MBW 1-2; MCCG; NoP; OAEL 1-2; OAEP; OBRV; PoRA; TrGrPo

With a garland on her brow.   She Wore a Wreath of Roses.   Thomas Haynes Bayly.   BeLS

With a gasp we/realize that the temperature stands at 18 degrees.   Homer.   Dick Gallup.   ANYP

With a glad, sad–I still don't know.   So Long Folks, Off to the War.   Anthony Ostroff.   NePoAm-2; PoPl

With a good push–/Over the bowling green.   Swinging.   Anonymous.   OxNR

With a good stiff breeze an' a wake o' shining foam.   Cleaning Ship.   Charles Augustus Keeler.   EtS

With a green flag either side of her/And a gold flag overhead.   May Janet.   Algernon Charles Swinburne.   VLP

With a groan, like those gods on the roof/that Samson pulled down.   Celebration.   Leonard Cohen.   ErPo

With a gude claymor in every hand,/And O but they shin'd bonie.   The Rantin Laddie (A vers.).   Anonymous.   BaBo

...With a/halflike like that the action/will last one lifetime   Eat 'Em Up Smith Tells All in South Africa.   Judith Johnson Sherwin.   NoAm

With a hallelujah hello from a nest of fur.   Sleighride.   Patrick Anderson.   CaP; OBCV

With a handsome lover/you can stand pain.   Love Songs.   Anonymous.   BoWoP

With a haul-ey hi-ho/Haul 'em away.   Little Sally Racket.   Anonymous.   FSW

With a hauley high, and a hauley low,/Alabama, John Cherokee.   John Cherokee.   Anonymous.   GBP

With a headstone for his bride.   Now We've Met.   Anonymous.   OBET

With a health to each jovial and true-hearted soul.   Spanish Ladies.   Anonymous.   OBSS

With a health to our dead, since we've no/living friends.   The Old Man's Carousal.   James Kirke Paulding.   AA

With a heart He may always see.   Reflection.   Anonymous.   STF

With a Heigho, maybe Begorrah, and certainly Fiddlededee.   Irish Song: Rosie O'Grady.   Noel Coward.   NLV

With a hey and a heigh and a ho!   The Light-Hearted Fairy.   Anonymous.   SUS

With a hey-nonny-nonny and I don't mean maybe.   The Witch's Work Song.
T. H. White.   FaBoNo

With a joy untold my kin would rally/To dower with gifts the Lamb of God.
A Gaelic Christmas.   Liam P. Clancy.   ISi

With a jug of liquor in her arm/And a .45 across her knee.   Darling Cory.
Anonymous.   AmFP

With a kind of light like the knife that you used/while it was in your hand.
The Knife.   Juan Gelman.   VWA

With a knotted promise/To come back home.   To Come Back Home.
Samuel Chimsoro.   WhB

"A" with a "komets" spells "O!"   Oyfn Pripetshuk.   Mark Warshawsky.
FSW

With a large heart, with a weary heart,/Today you go away.   Slowly, Slowly.
Anonymous.   WeW

With a leap and a bound the swift Anapests throng.   Metrical Feet.   Samuel
Taylor Coleridge.   SoSe

With a leg at every corner.   The Hen It Is a Noble Beast.   William
McGonagall.   NLV

With a lengthened loud halloo,/Tu whoo, tu whit, tu whit, tu whoo-o-o.
Second Song–To the Same.   Alfred, Lord Tennyson.   PBBP

With a like sadness would consume my heart.   The Evening of the Feast-Day.
Giacomo Leopardi.   LiTW

With a little bit of bloomin' luck!   With a Little Bit of Luck.   Alan Jay
Lerner.   FaFP

With a little gift of sand.'   Softly the Evening (parody).   William Hurrell
Mallock.   BXAP

With a little help, was able/to make/his father one.   Grandfathers.   Michael
Castro.   VWA

With a long cry it clasps the djuda, watching the water at/Wagulwagul, rising
against the mat.   The Djanggawul Cycle, 67.   *Anonymous.*   WTO

With a long piece of crape to her tail.   The Spirk Troll-Derisive.   James
Whitcomb Riley.   LBN; NA

With a louder note.   The Beloved Person Must I Think.   Ki-no-Akimine.
AWP

(With a Mene Tekel and otototoi).   'Twixt Cup and Lip.   Mark Hollis.
FiBHP; NLV

With a merry ding-dong, happy let us be!   Merry Are the Bells.
Anonymous.   HBV 1-2; HBVY; MoShBr; TiPo

With a merry, merry haw, haw, haw.   Crows in the Garden.   *Anonymous.*
ABF

With a misery in her head.   Go Tell Old Nancy.   *Anonymous.*   LaNeLa

With a muff and a cloak and a tippet–poor Anne.   On Lady Anne Hamilton.
Richard Brinsley Sheridan.   FaBoEE

With a nice resarved sate, says the Shan Van Vocht.   Lord Waterford.
Anonymous.   ChTr; GBP

With a paper-muslin ghost.   The Japanese Lovers.   *Anonymous.*   BeLS;
BLPA

With a parched/pitcher and piece/of bread.   The Story of Abraham and
Hagar.   Edna Aphek.   VWA

With a patient hand removing/All the briars from the way.   If We Knew.
May Riley Smith.   BLPA

With a peacock's feather in its cap.   Don't Sleep.   Ingrid Jonker.   WPOW

With a place for you in my heart.   There Is Always a Place for You.   Anne
Campbell.   PoToHe

With a prayer to Him who my soul will save.   The Dying Cowboy.
Anonymous.   CoSo

With a rainbow of silence branching from his lips.   Full Fathom Five.   A.
R. D. Fairburn.   AnNZ

With a ramble, scramble, chittery tit,/And lost the name of Growly.   The
Bear and the Squirrels.   Christopher Pearse Cranch.   OBCA

With a rod, a net,/And a pickle-jar.   Roger Francis.   Wilfrid Thorley.   BrR

With a rope so short it seems fit/only for a hanging.   Contentment.   Mark
Osaki.   BrSi

With a shy pity pouting in the mouth.   A La Promenade.   Paul Verlaine.
AWP; OBVE

With a sigh, a smile?   April Love.   Ernest Christopher Dowson.   PG

With a single heart to the narrow verge where/craft and statecraft join.
Arizona.   Sharlot M. Hall.   PAH

With a slow judicious hand!   Footnote to History.   Elizabeth Jane
Coatsworth.   SiSoSe

With a slow sound the ferries pace/A milky way of light.   San Francisco.
Mary Austin.   BPAW

With a soft-footed child skipping jump on the quay at the/Mill.   Poor Old
Horse.   David Holbrook.   NePoEA-2

With a speed which even thou didst not discover!   The Wheel.   Rene Sully-
Prudhomme.   ImOP

With a stein on the table in the fellowship of spring.   A Stein Song.
Richard Hovey.   AnAmPo; HBV 1-2

With a stump of scraggy fang/Bared for a hunter's boot.   The Return.
Theodore Roethke.   PoA

With a thousand clear answers/to everything.   Among His Effects We Found
a Photograph.   Ed Ochester.   Str

With a three- or four-chambered heart/that still sighs with your ear held close.
Fossils.   Arthur Stewart.   SUW

With a throaty swan song.   It Must Be Summer.   Sandor Csoori.   AMV-81

With a tongue that is empty and heavy/as a cairn.   Telephone Ghosts.
Robert Frazier.   SUW

With a twisted cue,/And elliptical billiard balls!   My Object All Sublime.
Sir William Schwenck Gilbert.   TreFT

With a volume of notes on its knee/Is the spectre of Andrew M"Crie.
Andrew M'Crie.   Robert Fuller Murray.   CenHV; FaBoCo

With a whisper that holds the smile you cannot/shape.   Hill-Side Tree.
Maxwell Bodenheim.   MAPA

With a wife and two babies at home?   Soldier, Soldier, Won't You Marry
Me?   *Anonymous.*   FSW

With a woman foolish and light.   Th Church Bell at Night.   *Anonymous.*
OnYI

With a woman's shift and apron you will have to go to sea.   A Great
Favourite Song, Entitled The Sailor's Hornpipe.   *Anonymous.*   OBSS

With a world of pain so near I cannot share.   Sonnet for a Loved One.
Dorothy Joslin.   AMV-80

With a yeo, yeo, yeo!   I Am a Brisk and Sprightly Lad.   *Anonymous.*
AmSS

With Acme's and Septimius's life.   Ode: Acme and Septimius.   Caius
Valerius Catullus.   OBVE

With ale and beer and brandy I'll drink about galore.   The Sea-Captain.
Anonymous.   BaBo

With all around the ache of space, the glare/Of heat, and at my feet the stone,
the stone.   Glitter of Pebbles.   Dom Moraes.   ACV

With all desirous souls/I cry, Amen.   Amen.   Arthur Christopher Benson.
OBVV

With all he left her then/to lay open/bitten.   His Lunch Bucket.   Doug
Cockrell.   Psk

With all her royal nymphs in train/Could so lead on the Spring.   Song: "You
wear the morning like your dress."   Hilaire Belloc.   OBEV; OBVV

With all its waters, all its warring waves.   Bonac.   John Hall Wheelock.
MoVE

With all manner of rubbish and all manner of lies.   Flycatchers.   Robert
Bridges.   MoVE

With all my heart.   Crimes of Passion.   Terry Stokes.   AmPA

With all my memories that could not sleep.   Spleen.   Ernest Christopher
Dowson.   BrPo; CBEP; MoBrPo; NCEP; NOBV; SyP

With all of us there, our anonymities.   Mossbawn: Two Poems in Dedication.
Seamus Heaney.   CIP; FaBoIP

With all our powers to praise and love/Our Saviour, God, and King.
Proclaim the Lofty Praise.   Sarah Judson.   AH

With all such glories in their bloom,/As I in vision view'd!   The Steam-
Engine (parody) (excerpt).   T. Baker.   BXAP

With all the joy of spring/And morning in her eyes.   February.   Francis
Brett Young.   HBMV; HBVY

With all the prettiness of feign'd alarm/And anger insignificantly fierce.
Squirrel in Sunshine.   William Cowper.   BoAnP

With all the quiet of a thought/And all the passion of a dream/Link'd in a
golden spell together.   Mater Desiderata.   Winthrop Mackworth Praed.
OBVV

With all these stains upon me I'll/Arrive in heaven's promised land.   I'm Not
Rich.   Joseph Rolnik.   VWA

With all your faults I'd live and die with you,/You old deceiver!   The Teasing
Lovers.   Horace.   UnTE

With an apple in his pocket/Which he gave to Birkett's wife.   Birkett's Eagle.
Dorothy S. Howard.   MoBS

With an arrow from his sheath.   At the Door.   Lillie Fuller Merriam.
PoToHe

With an honest heart and a childlike trust/That God will do the rest.   Face
to Face with Trouble (excerpt).   Margaret E. Sangster.   PoToHe

...With an unidentified glow/on a person's posteerier.   The Firefly.   Ogden
Nash.   FPL

With Andre-sparing mercy, still more dear/Had been his name–if that, indeed,
could be!   Andre.   Charlotte Fiske Bates.   MC; PAH

With angel words that pierce the sky/All earth with joy is ringing.   Today in
Bethlehem Hear I.   St John Damascene.   BePJ

With antique sinew and with modern art.   Corn.   Sidney Lanier.   AP;
MAmP

With arched fastidious wrists to be so gentle.   The Statue and the Perturbed
Burghers.   Denis Devlin.   OnYI

With arrogant eyes, and narrow hands/Miraculously shaped.   Castilian.
Elinor Wylie.   AnAmPo; HBMV; NAMP

With arts unknown before, to reconcile/The willing Graces to the Gothic pile.
Verses on Sir Joshua Reynold's Painted Window at New College, Oxford.
Thomas Warton, Jr..   CEP; NOEC; OBEC; PoEL 1-5

With balls of shining red/Decking a leafy head;/Oh fair to see!   Cherry Tree.
Christina Georgina Rossetti.   YeAr

With bending Sails each vessel of our Fleet: Panegyrick upon O. Cromwell.
Edmund Waller.   SeCV 1-2

With berries burning through! The Holly. Walter De la Mare. CMoP

With big brother's chisel and hammer! Limerick: "A mother in old Alabama." William Jay Smith. TDH

With/black/people. The New Integrationist. Don L. Lee. BOLo

With blackberries large/And ripe and sweet. Mickleham Way. Ivy O. Eastwick. BrR

With blind and witless confidence men cling/To well-known forms and give them pleasing breath. Metaphysical Poem. Maxwell Bodenheim. AnAmPo

With bloody plumes, the Irish stand—the field is fought and/won! Fontenoy. Thomas Osborne Davis. HBV 1-2; OnYI

With blossoms in our hands. Haiku: "After a long winter, giving." Chiyo. BoWoP

With bonnets and hats, old dresses and brats,/Made up into bundles as you have seen Pat's. Railroad to Hell. Anonymous. VLP

With book in hand to have thy dying day. To Doctor Bale. Barnabe Googe. EnRePo

With both of us looking the other way. Palindrome. Lisel Mueller. IHMS

With bread and cheese for supper I could dream it all again! The Dream of a Boy Who Lived at Nine Elms. William Brighty ("Matthew Browne") Rands. OxBChV

With bread and jam for supper I could dream it all again! The Dream of a Girl Who Lived at Sevenoaks. William Brighty ("Matthew Browne") Rands. OxBChV

With breast as marble cold, as marble pure. On His Lady's Waking. Pierre Ronsard. AWP

With bridles in the evening come. At Grass. Philip Larkin. HaMV; HAP; NePoEA; OxBTC; SD

With bruise of lash or stone. Simon the Cyrenian Speaks. Countee Cullen. BBV; BPo; HAP; MoAmPo; TrCP; TTY

With buds of roses in her hair and kisses on her mouth. Out There Somewhere. Henry Herbert Knibbs. BLPA

With but a single/Thought! Hat Bar. Mildred Weston. FiBHP

With but foure words, my words, Thy will be done. The Crosse. George Herbert. AnAnS 1

With ceaseless whispers of eternity. As Happy Dwellers by the Seaside Hear. Celia Thaxter. EtS

With cedar paddle, scented, red,/He pushed out from the lily bed. The Lily Bed. Isabella Valancy Crawford. PeCV

With chastened and holy delight. Limerick: "W's a well-informed wight." Oliver Herford. TDH

With cheerful hearts and smiling faces. Common Sense. James Thomas Fields AA

With Chinamen but not with me. Birds in Their Little Nests Agree. Hilaire Belloc. PoL

With Circes lct thcm dwcll that think not so. The Shepherd's Praise of Diana. Sir Walter Ralegh. SiPS

With circular roads/going nowhere-- Circular Roads. Kizito Z. Muchemwa. WhB

With clanging chains and tinware/All sounding eerily. Ballad of the Drover. Henry Lawson. PoAu 1-2

With cloud for shift/how will I hide? Question. May Swenson. HeIP; LiTM; NePoEA; PrIm; SM; VGW

With Colman's glorious heritage I'd part/To bear thee company! The Lay of Prince Marvan. Anonymous. AnIV

With courage to live, courage to try again. Courage to Live. Grace Noll Crowell. PoToHe

With cruel Skill the backward Reed/He sent; and as He fled, He slew. To a Lady: She Refusing to Continue a Dispute with Me... Matthew Prior. CEP; NoP; WHA

With curators on every corner and a red light. Old World, New World. Harry Roskolenko. AMV-81

With Damned Hipocrites the world Delude/As men on Indians Glass, for gems obtrude. Consideratus Considerandus. John Saffin. SCAP

With deadly intent of love. The Beholders. James Dickey. AP

With death heroic, this Passover night! Pesach Has Come to the Ghetto Again. Binem Heller. TrJP

With death undying due/To soothe the pang of life. The Conviction. John Millington Synge. SyP

With diet and correction, men distraught/(Not too far past) may to their wits be brought. Idea. Michael Drayton. JCP

With difficulty persist here and there on earth. Another Epitaph on an Army of Mercenaries. Hugh" (Christopher Murray Grieve) MacDiarmid. DBV; NoAm; OBWP

With ditties and with dirges infinite. The House of Life. Dante Gabriel Rossetti. OAEL 1-2

With/dream/-S. Sunset. Edward Estlin Cummings. MoAmPo

With dreams of loving bliss. The Seasons. Kalidasa. AWP

With drede we dwellen,/With drede we wenden. The Life of This World. Anonymous. OxBM

With drede we wenden. This Life. Anonymous. FaBoRV

With drowning Peter: "Lord delivere me"/by this White Host. Immolation. Robert Farren. OnYI

With dull, sea-spent eyes. Meeting-House Hill. Amy Lowell. LoGBV; MoAmPo; OxBA; SBG

With dust at her feet/And dust in her eyes. Dust. Sydney King Russell. ShM

With dust behind my ears,/& nearer godlessness. A Delicate Impasse. Kenneth John Atchity. AMV-80

...With each deep/probing cough, they are mining. Mine. Andrew Hudgins. AMV-80

...With eagerly, utterly offering heart/All things whatsoever I do. Whatsoever I Do. Mary Louise Hector. GoBC

With eagle wings outspread for flight. Dawn. Frederick George Scott. CaP; PoPl

With ear of faith, His footfall drawing near! Look Up. Martha Snell Nicholson. BePJ

With earth once more. To Drift Down. Janet Carncross Chandler. AMV-81

With earthworms creeping through my hair. Tombstone Epitaphs. Anonymous. PeD

With ease they bear the loss of Delf. To a Lady. John Gay. OBEV

With either sex at either end. Five Epigrams. J.V. Cunningham. UnTE

With empty palms/Held out shaking/To every passer-by. Our Childhood Spilled into Our Hearts. David Vogel. VWA

With energy and light on each leaf of the stacked flesh-pages. To the Postmaster General. Peter Redgrove. AMV-81

With envy these, and those with love! On Snow-Flakes Melting on His Lady's Breast. William Martin Johnson. AA; AmLP

With envy, what the Old Man hardly feels. Animal Tranquillity and Decay. William Wordsworth. ERoP 1-2

With equal measures, weights and coins,/And just and righteous laws. The World Hymn. James Gilchrist Lawson. WBLP

With equal mind/We thank Thee, Lord! We Thank Thee. John Oxenham. PGD

With everlasting Concord hand in hand. The Flood of Years. William Cullen Bryant. AA

With every light gone out, the door blown open. Suppose This Moment Some Stupendous Question. Alden Nowlan. NOBC

With ewer and basin, with clothing and with food? Sinfonia Domestica. Jean Starr Untermeyer. HBMV; MoAmPo

With exactness grinds he all. Retribution. Henry Wadsworth Longfellow. GoTF; TreF

With eyes like a lizard. Humanities Lecture. William Stafford. GLGT; NNaP

With eyes of soft humility and wonder, love, and awe. The Lark's Song. William Blake. WiR

With eyes that see two things instead of one. Big Sheep Knocks You About. Sharon Bryan. MAYP

With fake gray fur/and satin ribbons. The Life of the Wolf. Gary Gildner. AmPA

...With falling flakes/Shall nurse the soil for next year's scythes and rakes. From Harvest to January. Turner, Charles Tennyson. NOBV

With falling Oars they kept the time. Bermudas. Andrew Marvell. AnAnS 1; AtBAP; AWP; ExPo; FaBoCh; GN; HBV 1-2; InPo; JCP; LoBV; LoGBV; MePo; MOS; NOBE; NOCV; NoP; OAEP; OBEV; OBS; OBTV; PAH; SeCeV; SeCP; SeCV 1-2; ViBoPo

With fantasies/of Ethiopia spreading her gorgeous wings. Summertime and the Living.... Robert Earl Hayden. BPo; NCSH; PoBA; PPP; TwCP

With fatal, fatal Love, a girlhood goes. Of Joan's Youth. Louise Imogen Guiney. AA; HBV 1-2

With fear/of being/uneaten Self. Norman Henry Pritchard II. PoBA

...With features/Resolute and unchangeably your own. At the Savoy Chapel. Robert Graves. HW

With feet nailed to the cross, Thou'rt waiting still for me! The Good Shepherd. Felix Lope de Vega Carpio. BePJ; CAW

With fellow-angels you enjoy it now. On the Death of Mrs. Bowes. Mary Wortley, Lady Montagu. BoWoP

With fervent prayers the boy might soon be mine. Epigram: "Passing the flower-stalls." Strato. PeHV

With few associates, and not wishing more. In His Mental Illness, William Cowper Finds He Is Not Alone. William Cowper. BoC

With few will be ever content. Come, Chloe, and Give Me Sweet Kisses. Charles Hanbury Williams. HBV 1-2; UnTE

With fifteen spitting tommy-guns/To keep a jungle back. Men in Green. David Campbell. BoAV; PoAu 1-2

With fingers through her lovely hair/one of them is studying you. A Glance. Anonymous. NOBI

With five pups to give me/A surprise. Familiar Friends. James S. Tippett. SoPo; SUS

With flesh the imminent two converts one. Love Redeemed. William Baylebridge. PoAu 1-2

With flint in the bosom and guts in the head.   The Stars Have Not Dealt Me the Worst They Could Do.   Alfred Edward Housman.   EBEV; ELU; EnLi 1-2; GTBS-P; OxBoLi; SeCeV

With flower-like faces glowing.   Through the Blowing Leaves.   Glenn Ward Dresbach.   BoC

With folded wings.   An Australian Symphony.   George Essex Evans.   ACV

...With fortitude/The ceremony she withstood.   Long Live Our Dear and Noble Queen.   Edward Edwin Foot.   FaBoCo

With freshened winds for warning,/Came water–everywhere!   First Rain.   Zoë Akins.   HBMV

With friendly Stars my safety seek/Within some little winding Creek;/And see the storm a shore.   Horat. Ode 29. Book 3. Paraphras'd in Pindarique Verse.   John Dryden.   SeCV 1-2

With friends, who make his tomb their loving care.   Echoes from Theocritus.   Edward Cracroft Lefroy.   OBVV

With frost-fringed flanks, and nostrils jetting steam.   A January Morning.   Archibald Lampman.   ACV; OBCV

With frowzy pores, that taint the ambient air.   On Jacob Tonson, His Publisher.   John Dryden.   FaBoEE; OBSV

With fruits of thy good spirit filled,/More than a hundred-fold.   When the Seed of Thy Word Is Cast.   Cotton Mather.   AH

With frustration how beautiful!   Spray.   D.H. Lawrence.   BoNaP

With furrowed bole and black the Poplar stands.   Poplar Tree.   Padraic Colum.   NePoAm

With general love our voices rise/In one great general peal.   General Wonder in Our Land.   Anonymous.   NOBI

With giant sails of yellow, strangely/shaped.   A Vision.   Hugo von Hofmannsthal.   TrJP

With glancing light.   Chirstographia 35.   Eugene Warren.   AMV-80

With glimpses of creeks and a vision of mosses.   Bell-Birds.   Henry Clarence Kendall.   NOAV; PoAu 1-2

With God the Holy Paraclete/Through endless ages, as is meet.   Deus Immensa Trinitas.   Anonymous.   CAW

With Gorgon's gear and barebill, thongs and fangs.   Andromeda.   Gerard Manley Hopkins.   EBEV; LiTB; VLP

With great bounding leaps like the mind of God.   Deer at the Roadside.   Iain Crichton Smith.   PoSH

With green pomegranates, and no end of Bass.   After Tennyson: "Spoonmeat at Bill Porter's in the Hall."   Edward Lear.   FaBoNo

With guilty hope at every change of moon!   Marriage.   Austin Clarke.   BIrV; GTBS-P

With hapless hand no man hath wraught/Such hap as I.   Such Hap as I Am Happed in.   Sir Thomas Wyatt.   FCP; SiPS

With hayseed in my hair.   Ante-Natal Dream.   Patrick Kavanagh.   NAs

With hazel woods in his two eyes.   Glenarm.   John Lyle Donaghy.   NeIP

With heart and hand, with mind, and all/Which we from Thee possess.   Hymn.   Philip Howard   ACP; CAW

With heart and with hand, like our fathers before.   Football Song.   Sir Walter Scott.   SD

With heartfelt fervency, which I should deem/It far less rash to praise than to reprove.   To Bulow–2.   August von Platen.   PeHV

With heaven's own patience are calm and/sweet.   Extras.   Richard Burton.   AA

With Heaven's tidings shod/About their brave, unwearied feet.   Fleet Street.   Shane Leslie.   OnYI

With her alike concludes th' advent'rous flight.   The Paper Kite (excerpt).   Samuel Bowden.   NOEC

With her dead brother's valour/For an example still?   Her Race.   William Butler Yeats.   LiTB

With her foot hanging out,/testing the world.   Breech Birth.   Nora Dauenhauer.   TWSS

With her hair unbound, and he his own skiffsman!   Poem by the Bridge at Ten-Shin.   Li Po.   OBVE

With her moist mouth through half the year.   In December.   Andrew Young.   SeCePo

With her odours of bergamot and/Plasma, and her soft rind filled with tripes?   Metamorphoses.   Roy Fuller.   OxBTC

With her reproach and her bony children/Before rain.   Watchers.   William Stanley Merwin.   NaP

With her so I may live and die, my weal cannot be told.   A Truelove.   Nicholas Grimald.   OBSC

With her toys and her joys/Jill came from the Fair.   Jill Came from the Fair.   Eleanor Farjeon.   TiPo

With her we may be summoned too/To heaven's bright, happy home!   The Dead Sister.   Caroline Gilman.   OBCA

With herons blowing like smoke/Across the sky.   Chinoiseries.   Amy Lowell.   AnAmPo

With "Hey, trim' and "Trixy' too/Their banners they display.   Haltersick's Song.   John Pikeryng.   OBSC

With hey trim and trixy too/Their banners they display.   Song: "Farewell, adieu, that court-like life!"   John Pickering.   ElL

With hill-clay always victor in the game.   Grubber's Day.   Jay G. Sigmund.   AnAmPo

With him as minstrel, ardent, young, and trim,/Bowing "New Sabbath' or "Mount Ephraim'.   A Church Romance.   Thomas Hardy.   FaBoTw; NOBE; OxBTC; VLP

...With Him divinity/swept into the flesh/and made it real.   Christmas Eve.   Archie Randolph Ammons.   NAs

With him I'd sit and drink and play,/And save the world this worthless lay.   The Dumb World.   William Henry Davies.   BoAnP

With Him we trust thee, beautiful child!   To Laura W—, Two Years Old.   Nathaniel Parker Willis.   HBV 1-2

With his coat worn bare, and his straggling hair,/And his green umbrella-case.   The Cure's Progress.   Henry Austin Dobson.   HBV 1-2

With his demand "Lend me your ears."   Transplantitis.   Lester A. Sobel.   QQQ

With His hammer of wind,/And His graver of frost.   To a Snowflake.   Francis Thompson.   BoLiVe; BoNaP; EBCP; FaBV; HBV 1-2; ImOP; LoBV; MoAB; MoBrPo; PoPl; SeCePo; TrGrPo

With his head like a wig, and the tuft on his knee,/His hide....   The Song Called "His Hide Is Covered with Hair.'.   Hilaire Belloc.   FaBoNo; FM

With his heart completed/And his words in his arms.   Generalities.   Robert Conquest.   OxBC

With his kinde mother, who partakes thy woe.   Nativitie.   John Donne.   AnAnS 1; OBS

With his knapsack for a pillow/And his musket on his breast.   The Wisconsin Soldier Boy.   Anonymous.   BFSS

With his long-legged heart in his hand.   Ballad of the Long-Legged Bait.   Dylan Thomas.   CoBMV; SeCeV

With his old shoes on and his leggin's.   Old Shoes and Leggin's.   Anonymous.   OuSiCo

With his or any/Father's son.   Birthday Gift.   Ethel Barnett De Vito.   BiCB

With his own intricate/Simplicities of horn.   Horn.   James Hayford.   NePoAm-2

With his pick-axe, sexton, coffin, funeral, skeleton,/and bone-house.   A Maiden There Lived.   Anonymous.   NOBL

With his pinks and red roses and fine garden fruit.   Willie Leonard.   Anonymous.   AmFP; BaBo

With his prod, prod, prod,/And jerk.   The Woodpecker.   Richard Church.   HaMV

With his right he summons me to sport with him./Oh, the joy!   Wedding Song.   Anonymous.   LiTW

With his ring ting tinny,/And his ring ting ho.   If He'd Be a Buckaroo.   Anonymous.   OuSiCo

With his saddle for a pillow and his rifle across his breast.   The Dying Ranger.   Anonymous.   CoSo

With his shirttails, in style Oriental,/Outside of his pants.   Those Flapjacks of Brown's.   Bert Leston Taylor.   OBAL

With his soul (his own) at peace, soothed by Walter Lippmann, and sustained by/Haig & Haig.   Portrait.   Kenneth Fearing.   MoAmPo

...With his soviet/Grammar and tickle too?   Building Society Blues.   Roger Roughton.   EAS

With his stern golden eye over the entire length of your quilt.   For Stephen Drawing Birds.   Pattiann Rogers.   MAYP

With his taring scythe in order to mow the meadows down.   The Mower.   Anonymous.   OBET

With hissing stir, among the dusty beams.   Haying.   John Frederic Herbin.   CaP; PeCV

With "Ho! for Harry and red Agincourt!"   On a Boy's First Reading of "King Henry V".   Silas Weir Mitchell.   AA

With Holy Ghost in One. Amen.   Through Warmth and Light of Summer Skies.   Austin Faricy.   AH

With Homer chanting down the street.   Tradition.   Arthur Guiterman.   DBV

With hues more rubicund than Cibber's nose...   If Pope Had Written 'Break, Break, Break'.   Sir John Collings Squire.   CenHV; FaBoPa

With implements to fly away,/Passing pomposity?   Bring me the sunset in a cup.   Emily Dickinson.   NOCV

...With infant Screams/She yields her Breath, and there reluctant dies.   Hare-Hunting.   William Somervile.   OBEC

...With infinite care/you waltz, twirl, and twinkle/all night!   All Night !   Leon Baker.   LFAC

With innocence, the wale of sense,/At wauking of the fauld.   Peggy.   Allan Ramsay.   OBEV; ViBoPo

With instantaneous Kodak-shots/Secured by ushers on the spots!   The Schoolmaster Abroad.   Sir Owen Seaman.   OBTV

With its angelus of birds/and its covenant of blue.   Poem: "To be sad in the morning."   [(or Pillin)] William Pillen.   VWA

With its dark nipple in a cloud.   The Mind's Liberty.   William Henry Davies.   MoBrPo

With its fry still live in its mouth.   It's Not Bad Once the Water Goes Down.   Thomas Reiter.   WOLT

With no one can they talk about/this great/at-birth-ordained/event.　The Old Folk.　Tove Ditlevsen.　PBWP

With no other worlds to conquer.　The Condor.　Michael Hogan.　LFAC

With north/over/the barn　Wherelings Whenlings.　Edward Estlin Cummings.　HAP; WeW

With "Not at Home" to anyone/Excepting Alfred Tennyson.　The Menu.　Thomas Bailey Aldrich.　HBV 1-2

With not the least demurring word/Ought we to interfere?　John Gilbert Was a Bushranger.　*Anonymous.*　NOAV

With notes as of one who brass is filing　The Spruce and Limber Yellow-Hammer.　Samuel Taylor Coleridge.　FM; PBBP

With notes that seem but the protracted/sounds/Of glassy runnels bubbling over rocks.　The Dead Eagle.　Thomas Campbell.　EnRP; OBTV

With nothing but Black Jack Davey.　Black Jack Davey.　*Anonymous.*　MAT

With occasional thumps on the gong.　Limerick: "There was a composer named Bong."　*Anonymous.*　TDH

With October's wind and rain.　On the First of March.　*Anonymous.*　OxNR

With old and not too gentle/Colorless apartheid?　Where? When? Which?　Langston Hughes.　BPo; NePoAm-2

With old faith, with bold faith to find a wider dawn.　Pioneers.　Badger Clark.　FaBoBe

With one brief hour of madness and joy.　One Hour of Madness and Joy.　Walt Whitman.　AnAmPo

With one faithful friend but to witness thy dying,/In the arms of Hellvellyn and Catchedicam.　Hellvellyn.　Sir Walter Scott.　FM; TEP

With one gray glimpse of sea.　Prologue to General Hamley.　Alfred, Lord Tennyson.　FaBoPP

With one green sparkle ever and anon/Dipt by itself, and we were glad at heart.　Audley Court.　Alfred, Lord Tennyson.　NOBV

With one lick of his vermilion tongue.　Night Clouds.　Amy Lowell.　MoAmPo; PoPl; WHA

With one pure deed restores the natural night.　After Reading St. John the Divine.　Gene Derwood.　LiTM; NePA

With one united voice!　Now Help Us, Lord.　*Anonymous.*　AH

With one wet match and all man's desolation.　Welcome the Wrath.　Stanley Jasspon Kunitz.　VGW

With only wind blowing in the mirror.　Mirror.　Tada Chimako.　BoWoP

...With only your foolish/heart for a witness you begin to long bitterly for home.　Home.　Steve Kowit.　AMV-81

With Orange flags flying and on God relying,such music will lead us to conquer or die.　William of Orange.　*Anonymous.*　BFSS

With orthography not so injiouxrious.　Prevalent Poetry.　Charles Follen Adams.　CenHV

With others hast thou no will to make company.　Canzone: Donna Mi Priegha.　Guido Cavalcanti.　CTC

With our arms around each other's waists,/in support.　Waiting Inside.　David Ignatow.　CAPP

With our Cross in each place to please thy majesty.　A Song of Four Priests who Suffered Death at Lancaster.　*Anonymous.*　ACP

With our day-old Henholme chickens peeping in their box.　The Smell of Coal Smoke.　Les A. Murray.　NOAV

With-outen he fynde hit mylke and pap/a long while-ey./Byuan hys my name iet.　The Last Time I the Well Woke.　*Anonymous.*　NCEP

With pain/Immortal bow'd, these mortals weak/Gentle and unsubdued remain.　The Statues.　Laurence Binyon.　OBEV; OBVV

With pain in that amputated arm/that is no longer his.　Why Has This Ache.　Gevorg Emin.　AMV-81

With paper and paste and trains and toys.　Windy Morning.　Harry Behn.　TiPo

With patience lows thee quiet and delight.　Barmenissa's Song.　Robert Greene.　FaBoRV

With peace, let tares and acorns be my food.　The Country Mouse.　Abraham Cowley.　SeCP

With Peace, let Tares and Acorns be my food.　Satires.　Horace.　OBVE

With peace on earth, good-will to men!　Christmas Bells.　Henry Wadsworth Longfellow.　AmePo; BLRP; EBCP; FaFP; HBV 1-2; HBVY; OBCP; PCh; PGD; TreFT; TRV; WBLP

With peace, which lends me strength and fortitude.　For One Who Is Serene.　Margaret E. Bruner.　PoToHe

With penicillin, needles, gut.　Birth.　Craig Raine.　NAs

With perilous stairs/Between.　The Treehouse.　James A. Emanuel.　AmNP; BPo; NNP; PoBA

With pitiful complaint and scalding fire,/That from my breast deceivably doth start.　The Lover Sendeth Sighs to Move His Suit.　Sir Thomas Wyatt.　LiTL

With Pitt on his knees at my dirty feet.　George II.　William Makepeace Thackeray.　FaBoEE

With ploughs and furrows left behind!　Untrodden Ways.　Agnes Maule Machar.　CaP

With poison in his beak, and hatred in his wings...　The Bird.　Robert Greacen.　NeIP

With pox o' Chancellour, villanous Chancellour,/Damnable Chancellour, oh.　The Lord Chancellours Villainies Discovered.　*Anonymous.*　CoMu

With proclamation that the first of May,/At Ma-re Mount shall be kept hollyday.　The Poem: "Rise Oedipeus, and if thou canst unfould."　Thomas Morton.　SCAP

With proper young men and tall.　The Jilted Nymph.　Thomas Campbell.　EnLoPo

With proud and tilted chin...!　Haven.　Donald Jeffrey Hayes.　AmNP; PoNe

With quick indifferent nods/And rare understanding.　The Sparrows at the Airport.　Anthony Ostroff.　NePoAm-2

With quickened hearts,/That find Thee everywhere,/We thank Thee, Lord.　We Thank Thee.　John Oxenham.　BLRP

With quiet dreams and poppy-flowers,/Down in the pixies' hollow.　Dream Song.　Richard Middleton.　HBV 1-2

With rapture, with power, with ease!　Your World.　Georgia Douglas Johnson.　AmNP

With reasons for your choice.　To the Cuckoo.　F. H. Townsend.　FaBoNo

With red/Proof of virginity, emblem of victory.　The Bed.　Giambattista Marino.　HW

With respect to the understanding of what is symbolized.　Money.　Howard Nemerov.　OxBC; WeW

With rhythm that now is fallen utterly into rout.　Song for Peace.　W. R. Rodgers.　NeBP

With rising reluctance he would begin a motion again.　If My Hands Were Mute.　Manfred Winkler.　VWA

With Robin at their head, and Marian.　Sonnet to—.　John Hamilton Reynolds.　OBRV

With room for one, and an empty place, if love should come.　The Deviator.　Bertram Warr.　OBCV

With Saint and Angel, ox and ass,/To hail the King of Glory.　Before the Paling of the Stars.　Christina Georgina Rossetti.　HBVY; TrCP

With saints and angels say Amen.　The Maid of Honour.　Philip Massinger.　ACP; GoBC

With saints and angels, there to dwell in joy and peace and love.　The Blind Man's Regret.　*Anonymous.*　BFSS

With saints' and sinners' lies and laws/For a new everlasting reign.　In the Beginning Was a Word.　Robert Graves.　PoA

With salt dried like bloom on them.　Estuary.　Ted Walker.　NYBP

With satyrs dancing sarabands.　Vacation Exercise.　Michael Kennedy Joseph.　AnNZ

With savage joy, and efforts wild,/To smash his rocks with a dead child.　The Sea.　William Henry Davies.　FaBoTw

With shapeless ruin spread around!　Inscribed upon a Rock.　William Wordsworth.　SyP

With sharp observance of law divine.　White-Capped Waves.　James Freeman Clarke.　EtS

With shining tears expel my black despair./A different wind.　Footsteps of Spring.　Hayim Nahman Bialik.　VWA

With shooting stars, slip loose, let go!　Saddle.　William Haskel Simpson.　BPAW

With sightless unquenched grief to walk alive　Dew.　Jennifer Maiden.　CBAP

With Sisyphus thus do I roll the stone,/And turn the wheel with damned Ixion.　Idea.　Michael Drayton.　HBV 1-2

With slaves succumbing to his rod and kiss,/Has a beginning in my blood.　The Battle of Aughrim.　Richard Murphy.　CIP; IPY

With so much pity/was he moved/towards it.　Love.　Jorie Graham.　NPGG

With soldiers for dung./With poets for a song.　Pilgrims.　Joseph Brodsky.　VWA

With something finished, something unfulfilled.　Still Life.　Vivian Smith.　AMV-80; AMV-81

With song far too profound for words.　Three City Cantos.　Charles A. Wagner.　GoYe

With songs I sent her in love's day and live with my loved friends forever.　My Buried Friends.　*Anonymous.*　AmFP

With songs in execrable German.　Limerick: "An anal erotic named Herman."　*Anonymous.*　PeHV

With songs that must shatter/on stone.　Love Song for a Tyrant.　Marion Brimm Rewey.　AMV-81

With sons he's sent to fatal slumber!　Unknown Soldier.　Alta Booth Dunn.　PGD

With sorrow of the meanest thing that feels.　Hart-Leap Well.　William Wordsworth.　BeLS; MyFE

With sorrows from the Seven Seas.　Cape Coloured Batman.　Guy Butler.　PeSA

,With sounding voice/Put foemen to flight. Now ask what I'm called.　Horn.　*Anonymous.*　AnOE

With splendid salutations of white smoke.   Shunting.   Basil Dowling.
AnNZ

With spring, their green tongues speaking from the mud.   Sweeney to Mrs.
Porter in the Spring.   L. E. Sissman.   NYBP

With stark naked, unsacred,/Motorcycle Irene.   Motorcycle Irene.   Skip
Spence.   MAT

With stones like white sheep in its pastures/by a silver-circletted sea.   Piano
Practice.   Derek Walcott.   NYP

With strangely fashioned giant yellow sails.   Experience.   Hugo von
Hofmannsthal.   AMV-81

With such a beautiful stranger.   Singles.   Michael Waters.   GeTw; MAYP

With such a drought/that the land ate the lakes/and the men ate the land.
Many Years Ago.   Arlindo Barbeitos.   WhB

With such a lot of nice fresh air/All sandwiched in between.   I'm Glad.
Anonymous.   HBVY

With such a lot of nice fresh air/All sandwiched in between.   I'm Glad the
Sky Is Painted Blue.   *Anonymous.*   SoPo

With such a sound of gently pitying laughter.   My Grandmother's Love
Letters.   Hart Crane.   BLPL; CMoP; FaBoBe; MoAB; NoAm; NOBA;
NoP

With such as see I serve and suffer woe.   Of purpose love chose first for to be
blind.   Sir Thomas Wyatt.   FCP

With such faint brightnesses.   With the Face.   Laura Riding.   NoAm

With such feeling as cast-iron gratitude.   Humphrey Hardfeature's
Descriptions of Cast-Iron Inventions.   *Anonymous.*   OBET

With such fond hopes, for you have not come back.   Her Absent Lord
(excerpt).   Ugga Byan.   LiTW

With summer's best of weather,/And autumn's best of cheer.   September
Days Are Here.   Helen Hunt Jackson.   GoJo; OBCA; TiPo; YeAr

With summer toil will find rest in the west wind.   Lounge in the shade of the
luxuriant laurel's/beautiful foliage.   Anyte.   BoWoP

With sunken head/In dropping leaves.   Static Autumn.   Yvor Winters.
PoA

With survival's bare wings/beating at the windows.   There Isn't Enough
Bread.   Charles Culhane.   LFAC

With swans upon the moorlands.   Swansong on the Moorlands.   Steingrimur
Thorsteinsson.   LiTW

With sweet-briar/And bon-fire/And strawberry wire/And columbine.   Lily,
Germander, and Sops-in-Wine.   *Anonymous.*   AnFE

With switch her horse, and hearts with ev'ry look.   Cynthia on Horseback.
Philip Ayres.   EnLoPo

With sword unbroken, and with broken heart.   Enfant Perdu.   Heinrich
Heine.   AWP

With tallants prowling, theire face wan withred in hunger,/With famin
upsoaken.   The Aeneid.   Virgil (Publius Vergilius Maro).   OBVE

With tears–a friend at hand to close their eyes!   Ode–Imitated from the
Psalms.   Nicolas Joseph Florent Gilbert.   CAW

With tears of recognition never dry.   A Farewell.   Coventry Patmore. ;
AnFE; EnLoPo; NOBE; PoEL 1-5; TrGrPo

With teeth of obsidian and hair like kelp/Flashing and glimmering at the edge
of the horizon.   East Coast Journey.   James Keir Baxter.   NoP

With tender heart, lo, thus to God he sings: Penitential Psalms: Introduction.
Sir Thomas Wyatt.   FCP

...With thanks/for our congratulations/sent on his hundreth birthday.'
Dubrovnik Poem (Emilio Tolentino).   Anthony Rudolf.   VWA

With that awful change in his face?   Love's Change.   Anne Reeve Aldrich.
AA

With that clear sterile skull to take/your pleasure or that soft pulsing slime.
The Balance.   Judith Johnson Sherwin.   GP

With that fat-faced man/Who comes, my age himself.   Birthdays.   C. J.
Driver.   PeSA

With that he let the whole pack loose.   The Wolf in the Kennels.   Ivan
Andreyevich Krylov.   LiTW

With that love wounded my loves hart,/But Diane beasts with Cupids dart.
Four Anacreontic Poems, 2.   Edmund Spenser.   AAS

With that maid that is so bright,/Redemptoris Mater.   My Thought Was on a
Maid So Bright.   *Anonymous.*   ISi

With that misformed spright he backe re-/turned againe.   The Faerie Queene.
Edmund Spenser.   CoBE

With that more learn'd professor–Ruhncken.   Epigram on an Academic Visit
to the Continent.   Richard Porson.   OxBoLi

With that old silver heart I gave,/My first gift–and my last.   Maritae Suae.
William Philpot.   OBVV

With that other, unseen world,/our spirit's home.   We Men Are of Two
Worlds.   Mary Elizabeth Colman.   CaP

With that the Wretched Child expires.   Henry King.   Hilaire Belloc.
BBGG; CenHV; DTC; FaBoUs; HBMV; NLV

With that wave of her white-gloved hand,/And that chestnut hair.   The
Rejected Member's Wife.   Thomas Hardy.   VLP

With the accuracy of a Chinese Zen master answering a student/has painted a
fly   Geo-Politics.   Alvaro Cardona-Hine.   PoDr

With the actual weight/of each hooded victim,/slashed and dumped.   The
Grauballe Man.   Seamus Heaney.   CIP

With the adorable gentle Matilda/On the green mossy banks of the Lee.   The
Green Mossy Banks of the Lee.   *Anonymous.*   OBET

With the All-Highest's Son, inseparable from Him...   Patmos.   Friedrich
Holderlin.   OBVE

With the best of good Subjects be reckon'd.   The Angler's Ballad.   Charles
Cotton.   CEP

With the Blest Spirit, He who filleth all things,/Unity Trinal!   Sancte
Confessor.   Rhabanus Maurus.   CAW

With the blood toward my hands, through/me to retain possession.   Loot.
Thom Gunn.   ErPo; NePoEA-2

With the Blue Birds buccaneering/On his British sky–   We like March–his
shoes are purple.   Emily Dickinson.   SOTW

With the breath of God about us on the King's Highway.   The King's
Highway.   John S. McGroarty.   BLRP; BPAW; HBV 1-2; TRV

With the breeze and the comfortable shore.   The Diver.   W. W. Eustace
Ross.   NOBC; OBCV; PeCV; WHW

With the broadcloth under his arm.   In Good Old Colony Times.
Anonymous.   BFSS

With the broken statues standing on the shore.   High Poetry and Low.
Wallace Stevens.   PoA

With the bulge and nuzzle of the sea   When God Lets My Body Be.
Edward Estlin Cummings.   MoAB; MoAmPo; NOBA

With the bursting roar and uprush of song!   Birds Waking.   William Stanley
Merwin.   NOBA

With the clean water of my plaintive voice.   I Korinna am here to sing the
courage.   Korinna.   BoWoP

...With the/common sky & sun,–or at night the moon & stars.   Beauty.
Walt Whitman.   WeW

With the cool, calm shadow at the wheel.   To Beachey, 1912.   Carl
Sandburg.   TiPo

With the Cross of Jesus/Going on before.   Onward, Christian Soldiers.
Sabine Baring-Gould.   FaBoBe; FaFP; FaPoR; FSW; GoTF; HBV 1-2;
TreF; VLP; WGRP

With the dark shapes of men ascending still.   The Common Street.   Helen
Gray Cone.   AnAmPo; HBV 1-2

With the dark so deep I dare not sleep/All night on Halloween.   Halloween.
Marnie Pomeroy.   PoSC

...With the dark, strange/water of the moon.   Crystal.   Faye Kicknosway.
IHMS

With the dew of the lower boughs!   For My Sister's Sake.   Hitomaro.
AWP

With the dirge, and the sound of lamenting and voices of/women who weep?
Meditations of a Hindu Prince.   Sir Alfred Comyn Lyall.   WGRP

With the droppings of last year's chickens/blazing into magazines under my
feet.   Walking through a Cornfield in the Middle of Winter... (parody).
Barbara Harr.   BXAP

With the dust of thousands of game-bird bones.   The Pheasant Hunter and
the Arrowhead.   Julian Gitzen.   AMV-80

With the faint, otherworld song of monks/Chanting in the Dragon Temple at
dawn.   The Room above the White Rose.   Joseph Stroud.   NPGG

With the fierce gaze and implacable small smile.   On Being Asked for a Peace
Poem.   Howard Nemerov.   OxBC

With the first light breaks the first thought–my Friend.   To My Friend.
Francis Thompson.   PoA

With the friar of Rubygill.   Song: "It was a friar of orders free."   Thomas
Love Peacock.   ViBoPo

With the glowing diamond in its center.   Full Consciousness.   Juan Ramon
Jimenez.   NU

With the golden feelers of their light.   Motor Cars.   Rowena Bastin Bennett.
SoPo; TiPo

With the grave's narrowness, though not its peace.   Sick Love.   Robert
Graves.   BoLoP; CMoP; EBEV; GTBS-P; HAP; NoAm; NOBE; OAEL 1-2

With the Great Overdog/That romps through the dark.   A Sky Pair.
Robert Frost.   MoAB; MoAmPo

With the great sun in your hands/Till evening.   Psalm.   A. Ben-Yitzhak.
VWA

With the gum of lips you stealing stormed to starve.   To a Faithless Lover.
Robert Greacen.   OnYI

With the gypsies dancing round me.   Johnny Faa, the Gypsy Laddie.
Anonymous.   AtBAP

With the hard-fighting arm of the West!   The Springfield Calibre Fifty.
Joseph Mills Hanson.   PoOW

With the head of a fool and the heart of a bard.   Ballad.   Henry Treece.
WaP

With the janitor's red-haired boy.   The Janitor's Boy.   Nathalia Crane.
PoLf

With the juice, with which it joyously fills!   Sonnets to Orpheus.   Rainer
Maria Rilke.   SOTW

With the knowledge ahead of us, to wrap our throats.   Aspects of Some
Forsythia Branches.   Ralph Gustafson.   PeCV

With the light of two worlds,/this one and this one. The Porpoise. Greg Pape. MAYP

With the lilt of sunlight in their bones. Hymn to the Sun. Michael Roberts. FaBoCh; LoGBV

With the little figure without hands in the brown-tree clothes. Homage to Hieronymus Bosch. Thomas MacGreevy. BIrV; EAS; OnYI

...With the lives, burned-off,/Of young men and boys. A Thousand Killed. Bernard Spencer. OBWP

With the lost flush of last year's autumn leaves. En Route. Duncan Campbell Scott. NOBC; OBCV

With the low piping of their discontent. The Barricades. Denise Levertov. NeBP

With the mad wings and the day moon. Tor House. Robinson Jeffers. AnAmPo; LoBV

With the merry gay coral, ding, ding, a-ding, ding. The Baby's Dance. Ann Taylor. OxBChV

With the mist, long ages past begotten,/Of the Sun. Homes of the Cliff Dwellers. Stanley Wood. PoOW

With the nice caution of a Sword between. The Antiplatonick. John Cleveland. AnAnS 2; MePo; SeCP

With the noises they make. Snoring. Aileen Fisher. SoPo

With the old hunger, born of his kind. Affinity. R. S. Thomas. HaMV

With the one I'd say, "How are you?"/With the other, "Good bye to you." Mananitas (with music). Anonymous. AS

With the pain/of loving you, beloved man. I'm Soaked through with You. Rachel Korn. VWA

With the paper on my knee! Early Bacon. Archibald Stodart-Walker. CenHV

With the Pawnees, lying low,/Lying low. The Flower-Fed Buffaloes. Vachel Lindsay. AmFN; ATP; BPAW; CMoP; ExPo; GoJo; LoBV; LoGBV; MoAmPo; NOBA; OBCA; PPON; RFM; VGW

With the Peoples of the World.../We advance! Dark Symphony. Melvin B. Tolson. BALP; PoNe

With the quarest smile on his wizened face! Tim, the Fairy. Florence Randal Livesay. CaP

With the red wounds of fear/Of Muirtach Og/Our O'Sullivan Beare! The Lament for O'Sullivan Beare. Anonymous. AnIV

With the relish/of a gypsy. And This Is My Father. Marcus J. Grapes. AMV-80

With the resisting mass. Ars Victrix. Theophile Gautier. CTC; HBV 1-2; HBVY; SyP; VLP

With the rigor mortis of military design. The Martyr and the Army. Jock Henderson. AMV-81

With the salesman lying beside her,/will cry out/our unfamiliar name. Everything We Do. Peter Meinke. GOYP

With the scent of a freshly dug mine Sleep. M. R. Doty. AMV-80

With the sea-dirge they mix not: they clamour to me! Dirge. Aubrey Thomas De Vere. IrPN

With the secret on his brow. Sandy Star. William Stanley Braithwaite. BANP; HBMV

With the sharp sword of mockery/Stab one's heart. Alone. Elsie Laurence. CaP

With the slow motion of my prow/And dripping oar. Loch Luichart. Andrew Young. PoSH

With the slow smokeless burning of decay. The Wood-Pile. Robert Frost. AmP; CABA; CoBMV; LiTA; MAmP; MAPA; NoAm; NoP; SeCeV; VGW

With the smile of your own face. On the House of a Friend. John Logan. DFF

With the song of the lake/Beneath her feet. Skating. Herbert Asquith. BrR; SoPo; SUS; TiPo

With the sound/of a thousand insects. Learning to Understand Darkness. Wendy Rose. TWSS

With the soundness of the backward/Where the sense can be heard. The Ethnic Life. Daniel Halpern. AmPA

With the spilt-out blood of the rose-red wine. In the Gold Room. Oscar Wilde. SyP

With the stern impartiality of age/And age's impotence. The Discriminator. Vernon Scannell. OxBC

With the strain of trying to be/Funny every week. The Seamy Side of Motley. Sir Owen Seaman. InMe

With the sun in my eyes, sir. I ran for a catch. Coulson Kernahan. CenHV

With the sun of peace never setting. Comrade, Remember. Raymond Kresensky. PGD

With the swallows flees/The final harrowing. Quiet. Giuseppe Ungaretti. PoPl

With the swing of his demon's tail. The Tom-Cat. Don (Donald Robert Marquis) Marquis. BoAnP; PoRA

With the swinging rainbow on his shoulder. Legend. Judith Wright. BoAV; NOAV; SO

With the thought of the light/Of the eyes of my Annie. For Annie. Edgar Allan Poe. AmP; AP; APA; BLPL; HBV 1-2; LiTA; NePA; NOBA; OBEV; OBVV; OxBA; TreFS

With the torch of freedom, March on! March on!/March on and on! Chee Lai! (Arise!). Anonymous. FSW

...With the traffic/-gongs ringing like glory. On the "Sievering" Tram. Bernard Spencer. NAs

With the trees before long dripping in sunlight/all in a sweat about nothing. Sophistication. Vassar Miller. NCSH

The, with the vision in thy heart,/Turn strong to meet thy day. Begin the Day with God. Anonymous. TRV

With the water singing koto strings in her ears. My Mother Takes a Bath. Yuri Kageyama. BrSi

With the white frost, and leaf the brown trees tall. The Earth-Spirit. William Ellery Channing, II. AnNE

With the white world creaming over the rim.... The Twinkling Earn. John Davidson. PoSH

With the whole of their Christmas shopping done. Annar-Mariar's Christmas Shopping. Eleanor Farjeon. ChBR

With the will of God and the aid of the glorious Virgin. I Lie Down with God. Anonymous. AnIV

With the wind over/and over to be as/it was before. The Term. William Carlos Williams. InvP; LiTA

With thee each day is Pentecost,/Each night Nativity. I Worship Thee, O Holy Ghost. William F. Warren. AH

With thee I cannot live,/And turn from thee–in vain. Prayer of the Young Stoic. Stephen P. Dunn. TrPWD

With thee, my adored one! my own attar-gul! Eastern Serenade. Sir Theodore and Aytoun, William E. Martin. Theodore InMe

With thee, O Master, let me live. O Master, Let Me Walk with Thee. Washington Gladden. AH; WGRP

With their ballet dancer's/Legs. Frogs. Norman MacCaig. BoAnP

With their daggers towards the foe! The Call to the Colors. Arthur Guiterman. PAH

With their native customs, and Lundres they named it. The Brut. Layamon. MeEV

With their riddle cum dinky dee. Why Does It Snow? Laura E. Richards. BrR; OBCA; SiSoSe

With their sharp and broken stalks,/which may scratch my breasts. Please keep an eye on my house for a few moments. Vidya. BoWoP

With their sweet lives, as pure from sin and stain,/As his when Eden held his virgin heart. Forest Leaves in Autumn (excerpt). John Keble. OBNC

With Their swift Spirit winged with love for Both,/Three-always-One! Hymn for Second Vespers;Feast of the Apparition of Our Lady of Lourdes. Anonymous. ISi

With their weak charms, moving here and there among the/lamps? Ill. Bernard Spencer. NeBP

With their wires they have bound the whole world together for/themselves. The Ever-Touring Englishmen... Anonymous. WTO

With them shalt reign in never-ending NOW. The Final Mystery. Sir Henry Newbolt. WGRP

With these celestial wisdom calms the mind,/And makes the happiness she does not find. The Vanity of Human Wishes. Samuel Johnson. ATP; CEP; EBEV; EiCP; EnPE; HeIP; LaA; LAuP; LoBV; MasP; NOEC; NoP; OAEL 1-2; PoEL 1-5; PrIm; TEP

...With these/Our very souls pass overseas. This Night Sees Ireland Desolate. Aindrais MacMarcuis. BIrV

With these, she steals men's hearts for her relief,/Yet happy he that's robbed of such a thief. Idea. Michael Drayton. EnRePo

With these things of no note. Song for Music. G. S. Fraser. ChMP

With these we choose our lot and part,/Till liberty is safe on sea and shore. Mare Liberum. Henry Van Dyke. PAH

With these words carved, "I hoped, but was not sure." Afterwards. Violet Fane. HBV 1-2; OBVV

With thinking of that youth I love. On My Sweet Mother. Sappho. PoPl

With this bereavement troubling me. A Broken Gull. John Moore. NCSH

With this dream which obsesses me. Three Tanka, 1. Yosano Akiko. LiTW

With this prophetic blessing–Be thou dull... Thomas Shadwell the Poet. John Dryden. ChTr

With this regard from Dodsley turn away,/And lose the name of authors. Hamlet's Soliloquy Imitated (parody). Richard Jago. FaBoPa

With this regard their currents turn Hamlet. William Shakespeare. BiP; DiPo; FaFP; HoPM; LiTB; MasP; OHFP; PoPl; TreF; WBLP; WHA

With this regard their currents turn awry/And lose the name of Wedlock. Shakespearean Soliloquy in Progress: "To wed or not to wed?" (parody). Anonymous. BXAP

...With this secret method of defying birth controls I popu-/late the world with poets. De Rerum Natura. Andrei Codrescu. APU

...With this thought/Content myself, although my chance be nought. A Vow to Love Faithfully, Howsoever He Be Rewarded. Henry Howard, Earl of Surrey. ViBoPo

With this thread from out the tomb my dead hand shall/tether thee! Sister Songs (excerpt). Francis Thompson. OBMV

With this you light the dust/That clouds my road. Her Way. William Rose Benet. HBMV

With this, your semblance to a sculptured tomb/That clasps a rosary of nothingness. To an Old Lady Dead. Siegfried Sassoon. PoPle

With those to study, and with these to dine. Philosopher, Whom Dost Thou Most Affect." Richard Garnett. HBV 1-2

With thoughtful heart and tearful eye/I sadly watched that solemn sky. It's Over Now; I've Known It All. Emily Bronte. NOBV

With throbbing heart, tip-toe I stole away. The Music of a Tree. Walter James Turner. MoBrPo

With thund'ring hammers made the air resound. Ramble of the Gods through Birmingham (excerpt). James Bisset. NOEC

With thy green darkness overshadowing me. To the Ivy. John Clare. CBEP

With Thy large glance Thou readest all our state,/And wilt be patient of our empty years. Omniscience. Blanche Mary Kelly. TrPWD

With thy last dim journey taken/Home through the night. All through the Night. Anonymous. TreFS

...With thy love/Water and cheer this sorrowing heart of mine! Easter Song. Leo Alishan. CAW

With thy Saviour thou shalt rest,/Crowned, and glorified, and blest. Brother, Though from Yonder Sky. James Henry Bancroft. AH

With thy soft, ravishing, vocal music ever to compare! A Pindaric on the Grunting of a Hog. Samuel Wesley. NOBL

With thy voices for ever! September in Australia. Henry Clarence Kendall. OBVV; PoAu 1-2

With thyself upraise me to the skies. Easter Hymn. Saint John of Damascus. BePJ

With topsy turvy signs of screamy play. After Tennyson: "To watch the tipsy cripples on the beach." Edward Lear. FaBoNo

With torturing voice and with hid face return/Faintly, as even now, to bid us mourn. Sonnets to Aurelia. Robert Nichols. OBMV

–With tranquil heart/Upon the loved and lost I think. Elegy. Richard Chenevix Trench. IrPN

With trembling wings sobbed forth, I love, I love. Sonnet: "Dear quirister, who from those shadows sends." William, of Hawthornden Drummond. ViBoPo

With trenchours and with broken mete/They sayd that noble knight. Ipomadon: Ipomadon Plays the Fool at Court. Anonymous. OxBM

With trew love a thousandfold. The One I Love Is Gone Away. Anonymous. MeEL

With triumph shall smile on the spots where they fell. The Song of the MicMac. Joseph Howe. CaP

With true adoration shall lisp to Thy praise. The Majesty and Mercy of God. Sir Robert Grant. OHIP; WGRP

With truth a silver trumpet at his lips. Mazeppa. Roy Campbell. AnFE

With tuppence change till Doomsday on his eyes. Henry Turnbull. Wilfrid Gibson. ELU; FaBoTw

With two small shadows following after it. The Water-Ousel. Mary Webb. CH

With us, her passing image: but herself/Far over the dark hills and the long sea. A Stranger. Lionel Pigot Johnson. NOBV; VLP

With vanished light like dead men's eyes. The Day of Judgment. Dugald Buchanan. GoTS

With violent achings heaving to burst the/sleep that is now not long. The North Country. D. H. Lawrence. OAEP

With virus ta'en from the best-bred cow/Of Lord Althorpe's–now Earl Spencer. Miss Kilmansegg and Her Precious Leg. Thomas Hood. NAs

With wanting more of it. Tant' Amare. Anonymous. ErPo

With warm tears for healing. Knife and Sap. Kenneth Leslie. PoL

With water moving over their legs/More like living cover than it is. Bums, on Waking. James Dickey. NYBP

With water on the brain. Instruction sore long time I bore. Charles Kingsley. CenHV

With waves and angels, balanced on a shell. In a Cafe. Rosemary Dobson. CBAP

With weary feet, to toil and plod/Through nature, back to nature's God... To an Indian Skull (excerpt). Alexander McLachlan. CaP

With weeds, mould, dung, and stale, a compost form,/Of force to fertilize the poorest soil. How to Fertilize Soil. James Grainger. FaBoUs

With what a rich precision he would draw/The endless ladder, and the booming wheel! The Steam Threshing-Machine. Charles Tennyson Turner. OBNC; VLP

With what a swift astonished tenderness. It Scarcely Seems Worth While. Vladislav Khodasevich. LiTW

With what she had done and spoken,/That therewith my song is broken. The Eighth Sonnet. Sir Philip Sidney. OAEP

With which he often wept the vast/and hopeless/Incurable affliction of his brothers. The New Jewish Hospital at Hamburg. Heinrich Heine. TrJP

With which I seemed to have/Nothing at all to do. Burning. Gary Snyder. NOBA

With which I sing to sleep my restless love for thee! And So Men Say, I Love Thee! Derwent Coleridge. CBEP

With which the changing world outside peeped in. Slepynge Long in Greet Quiete Is Eek a Greet Norice to Leccherie. John Hollander. AmPC; ErPo

With which the clouds and mountains pave/A lake's blue chasm. The Isle. Percy Bysshe Shelley. SyP

With which we all might sing for the children. After the Speech to the Librarians. David Wagoner. NPAW

With which we have nothing, we like to hope, in common. In Praise of Limestone. W.H. Auden. CABA

With white faces like town children. Autumn. Thomas Ernest Hulme. FaBoMo; LOW; MOON; SeCePo

With white-hot darkness in his eyes. The Expanding Universe. Norman Nicholson. SeCePo

With whom cold hearts are counted castaway. The House of Life. Dante Gabriel Rossetti. VLP

With whom cold hearts are counted castaway. Youth's Spring-Tribute. Dante Gabriel Rossetti. MaVP

With whom shall we live then? Condemnation. Thich Nhat Hanh. PPON

With whom we had been buried nine long years! "As Eponina Brought, to Move the King." Frederick Goddard Tuckerman. AmePo

With whom the Angels deigned to measure swords! The Knight Fallen on Evil Days. Elinor Wylie. MoAmPo

With whose dun beams inwoven darkness seemed/To mingle. Alastor. Percy Bysshe Shelley. ChRP

With wild and elemental meanings/from our living sun. Fires. William Heyen. MAYP

With wind-blown blushes that never bring tears. Riding. Harry Amoss. CaP

With wind-delighting clamour of glad voice. Prayer for the Royal Marriage. John Masefield. HW

With windlessness, empty heat, or the taste of grapes. Sun Moon Kelp Flower or Goat. Linda Gregg. NPGG

With wine at my elbow,/And sword beneath the pillow,/I shall perfect all. The Young Cordwainer. Robert Graves. MoBS

With Wine I wash away my Cares,/And then to Love again. Upon Drinking in a Bowl. John Wilmot, Earl of Rochester. CEP; OBS; OxBoLi; SeCV 1-2

With wine, with poetry, or with virtue, as you will. Be Drunken. Charles Baudelaire. SyP

With wings outspread forever greets/Death in fire. Sacco-Vanzetti. Moishe Leib Halpern. VWA

With woe and pain my life is spent. The Knight of Curtesy: The Eaten Heart. Anonymous. TrGrPo

With womanhood endued,/With virtue well renewed. To Mistress Gertrude Statham. John Skelton. OAEP

With women and men,/A middle ground. A Problem in Morals. Howard Moss. ErPo

With words too sad and strange to syllable. Two in August. John Crowe Ransom. AWP; InPo; MoPo; NePA; OxBA; PPP

With X, and Y, and charming little Z. Ultimate Anthology. Martin Bell. PoL

With yellow beaks/And red tails... Poem of the Conscripted Warrior. Rui Nogar. TTY

With yellow robe and begging bowl. A Word to Peter Olds. Charles Brasch. OCNZ

With yo' swo'd in yo' han'/You fight on. You Fight On (with music). Anonymous. AS

With you and your people./Hau! Hau! Hau! For Tom Numkena, Hopi/Spokane. Harold Littlebird. VoR

With you at night, about you at sunrise. Of Women. Anonymous. ErPo; PV

With you I'll toy, and kiss and play,/But hang me if I marry! The Philanderer. Moses Mendes. TrJP

With you Marvin X/poet with you please? For Some Poets. Mae Jackson. BOLo; PoBA

With you, O sweetest friend,/My night shall never end. The Blinded Soldier to His Love. Alfred Noyes. PoPl

With young archers driving by his side. What Her Girl-Friend Said to Her. Okkur Macatti. BoWoP; PBWP

With young offsunder'd from the young in/sleep. Shellbrook. William Barnes. OBNC; VLP

With your arms around me/I feel as if I belong to the Pharoah. With You Here at Mertu. Anonymous. PBWP

With your Death full of Flowers Kaddish. Allen Ginsberg. NeAP

With your depreciating luggage laden. Maiden Name. Philip Larkin. GTBS-P

With your enemies, the swift-devouring years. Elegy. Sidney Keyes. WaP

With your kiss on my cold lips, and never rise more. A Drunkard to His Bottle. Joseph Sheridan Lefanu. OnYI

With your mouth wide open to drink in lead. The Marginal Field. Stephen Spender. PoA

With your mute patience, forming/The only true likeness of myself. My Shoes. Charles Simic. CoAP; HaCAP

With your one-stringed instrument, our desperate glory. Face on the Daguerreotype. Norman Rosten. HoAn

With your own child in your bosom. The Child of Peace. Selma Lagerlof. PoPl

With your own smile/abandoned the world. Time of Waiting in Amsterdam. Ingrid Jonker. BoWoP

With your presence, drifting/toward her like smoke Sailing in Crosslight. Anita Skeen. IHMS

With your roaring rams and your pretty little lambs/And your five and forty wives. Brigham Young. *Anonymous*. CoSo; FSW

...With your skysail set/For ports beyond the margin of the stars. To-Day I Saw Bright Ships. Eloise Robinson. HBMV

With your song of Caty-did. To a Caty-Did. Philip Freneau. AA; TAP

With your tiny, timorous toes. Grass Fingers. Angelina Weld Grimke. CDC

With your two notes of innocence. Autumn Song. Noel Harry Brettell. ACV

With your vast pity, wash it smooth again. At Night. Frances Cornford. MoBrPo

Withdraws–and leaves the dazzled Soul/In her unfurnished Rooms– Did our best moment last. Emily Dickinson. NOBA

Wither beneath the palate, and the heart/Faints, faded by its heat. A Dream of Fair Women. Alfred, Lord Tennyson. OBRV

Withered leaves you shall find/And shall lose after finding. O Sower of Sorrow. Joseph Mary Plunkett. CAW

Withered my hand, and palsy-struck my tongue. To His Friend, on the Untunable Times. Robert Herrick. CaPo

Withers benumbed in a world his joy might have helped/to illume. On a Forsaken Lark's Nest. Mathilde Blind. FM

Withhold him...... Duino Eleges. Rainer Maria Rilke. LiTW

Withholding Faith that opes the doors of/heaven. A Prayer for Faith. Buonarroti Michelangelo. ILwL

Within a spacious ring, by the beholders made,/According to law. Wrestlers. Michael Drayton. SD

Within a world. World within a World. Debra Woolard Bender. AMV-80

Within are nought but mortar, flint and lead. Bussy d'Ambois. George Chapman. ViBoPo

Within each crack/a story You Lovely People. Virginia Cerenio. BrSi

"Within her heart she rocks a dead child, crying/"My son, my little son.'" The Only Son. Sir Henry Newbolt. HBV 1-2

Within it, featured even in death divine,/Is lying a dead infant, slain by thee. Modern Love, XI. George Meredith. VLP

Within its arms of lumber and of stone. For a New Home. Rosa Zagnoni Marinoni. PoToHe

Within low doors the boozy boors/Cat-naps take in pipe-bowl light. The Bench of Boors. Herman Melville. OBAL

Within my father's house. Within my/mother's arms./High in years–! My Death. Carl Zuckmayer. TrJP

Within my heart, that it may be/A quiet chamber kept for Thee. All Hail, Thou Noble Guest. Martin Luther. TrPWD

Within my thatched retreat I find/(What these ne'er feel) true peace of mind. Fable II: The Vulture, the Sparrow, and Other Birds. John Gay. EiCP

...Within our/Bodies' compass there is no need to fight gravity. Apartments on First Avenue. Cynthia MacDonald. NYP

Within the grinning shell/he's sworn by secret law to wear. Marriage Contract. Vern Rutsala. DFF

Within the passing of a night. Infallibility. Thomas Stephen Collier. AA

Within the rock the undiscovered suns/release their light. Baha'u'llah in the Garden of Ridwan. Robert Earl Hayden. PoBA

Within the Scope of whose Great Mind,/We all in their true Nature find. Consummation. Thomas Traherne. SeCV 1-2

Within the spendors of love's power. Epilogue. Lascelles Abercrombie. MoBrPo

Within the windless deeps of memory? Bells. Duncan Campbell Scott. CaP

Within, there is the peace of God. Minot's Ledge. Fitz-James O'Brien. OnYI

Within these armes for ever swim. To My Mistris Sitting by a Rivers Side. An Eddy. Thomas Carew. AnAnS 2

Within this oak-shade one more minute even,/Hearing the winds their Maker magnify. Faint Yet Pursuing. Coventry Patmore. OxBoCh

Within this place/Lives Doctor Case. Over Case's Door. John Case. FaBoUs

Within to antedate/Heaven's Age of fearless rest. The Trance of Time. John Henry, Cardinal Newman. OxBoCh

Within where the wrapt machines/are praying... The Semblables. William Carlos Williams. AP; FaBoMo; NOBA

Within, without, the vassal heart–its reasoning who/knows? Recessional. Georgia Douglas Johnson. CDC; PoNe

Within, your bones are clear flutes/from which I can conjure notes/to enthrall even death... Songs in Flight (excerpt). Ingeborg Bachmann. WPOW

Within your magic web of hair lies furled/The fire and splendor of the ancient world. The Web of Eros. Edith Sitwell. HBMV

Within your shadow I am bound. The Mirabeau Bridge. Guillaume Apollinaire. BoLoP

Without a balance stick to guide. I'll Walk the Tightrope. Margaret Danner. BP

Without a blessed thing to do/Until he comes in sight. The Ostrich Is a Silly Bird. Mary E. Wilkins Freeman. LBN; OBCA; SoPo; TiPo

Without a cordial interview/With God. Spring is the Period. Emily Dickinson. TAP

...Without a cry/upraised to win us–suddenly–a day. The Rain's Already With Us. Salvator Quasimodo. PoPl

...Without a heart/to suffer and forgive. The Doll. Robert Friend. GP

Without a hope, he died. The Four Calls. Lydia Hadley. STF

Without a king, to see the end of time. To a Republican. Philip Freneau. AmPP

Without a little of Barleycorn. John Barleycorn. *Anonymous*. OBET

...Without/a man awake to taste its profits. The Sleepers. William Aberg. LFAC

Without a script and fretting for directions. God and Man. Samuel Hazo. ELU

Without a simultaneous plop. Modern Love. J. V. Cunningham. PoL

Without/a/sound. Before Good-Bye. P. Wolny. PPJ

Without a sprain or twist. Harper. *Anonymous*. AnIL; KiLC

Without a word/like the rain. A Burial, Green. Marcia Southwick. MAYP

Without all hope of day! Samson Agonistes. John Milton. AnFE

Without any exceptions, you'll be turned out-of-doors. Young Johnny. *Anonymous*. BFSS

Without any feet, these two little men/Climb Blanket Hill and slide down again. Blanket Street. Inez Hogan. BiCB

Without any necks. Haiku: "A bitter morning:". J. W. Hackett. BoAnP

Without being able to sleep. Hoping All the Time. *Anonymous*. AWP

Without being prosecuted as a felon,/Spy, or disturber of the public peace. Out of the Frying Pan into the Fire. James Henry. NOBV

Without breaking anything. Spring Is Like a Perhaps Hand. Edward Estlin Cummings. NePA; NoP; SOTW; TAP; VGW

Without breath, and their blood humming on the/ground! Ireland Weeping. William Livingston. GoTS

Without clairvoyance, close to her. Woman Looking at a Vase of Flowers. Wallace Stevens. CrMA

Without contributing ten dollars and costs/To the school fund of Spoon river! Daisy Fraser. Edgar Lee Masters. CMoP; HAP; MoVE

Without dark, how could we sleep? Rhyme for Night. Joan Aiken. DuDa

Without even saying, "Good-baii!" Limerick: "There was an old man of Hawaii." *Anonymous*. TDH

Without ever a penny of money. The Three Travelers. *Anonymous*. UnTE

Without ever discharging a gun. Limerick: "There was a young man who said, "Run." *Anonymous*. LiBL

Without ever having felt sorry for itself. Self-Pity. D. H. Lawrence. BoAnP; OxBTC

Without ever knowing the head or the tail of it. P Is for Paleontology. Milton Bracker. FiBHP; InMe

Without her I am sad as an old mother/Hearing of the death of her many sons. The Mu'allaqat: Pour Us Wine. Ibn Kolthum. AWP

Without his love it cannot last. Gain without Gladness. Liadan. WPOW

Without it could not find his way. The Torch of Love Dispels the Gloom. Walter Savage Landor. GBL

Without it/how shall I live? Plants Don't Talk, People Say. Rosalia de Castro. WPOW

Without it no people, no life, no art. The Point. Evan Jones. NOAV

Without its genius, each exploit falls short. Tercets. Llywarch Hen. LiTW

Without knowing a page/Of it/Themselves. In These Dissenting Times. Alice Walker. PoBA

–Without love, without hope, but/without renunciation. Breakfast. Thom Gunn. OxBC

Without oil, hasp or uranium. In the Longhouse, Oneida Museum. Roberta Hill Whiteman. STE

Without one chastening fire made to start/From altars built around its polar heart. The Sea Cathedral. Edwin John Pratt. CaP

Without poetry,/without seemliness,/without love. The Mutes. Denise Levertov. IHMS; NaP; NOBA

Without question,/without kiss. Lethe. Hilda ("H. D.") Doolittle. AmLP; CMoP; FaBoWP; LiTM; MoAmPo; PG; PoRA; TrGrPo; VGW; ViBoPo; WHA

Without relief seeking lost love. Lost Love. Robert Graves. AWP; CH; FaBoCh; LoGBV; MoAB; MoBrPo; NoP

Without respect, or tact, or taste, or anything. "Oxford is a Stage." Edward Nolan. CenHV

Without salutation, without close. The Skein. Carolyn Kizer. PrIm; VGW

Without sleep at my side/on this slope of all. Never. George Reavey. BIrV

Without smile,/sadness,/or tears. From Here to There. Rachel Korn. VWA

Without Succession, and without a Sunne. Silex Scintillans. Henry Vaughan. AnAnS 1

Without the assuring skull beneath the lip. Love and Death. John Frederick Nims. HoPM; SM

Without the date, like Consciousness or Immortality– Lest any doubt that we are glad that they were born Today. Emily Dickinson. NAs

Without the Gate of Los, among the dark Satanic wheels. Jerusalem. William Blake. OBRV

Without the passion of exceeding love. La Vita Nuova. Dante Alighieri. AWP

Without the woman in the wagon,/Would you have won the West? The Woman in the Wagon. Clyde Robertson. PoOW

Without thee, love, I travel not, but stray. To His Mistress. John Wilmot, Earl of Rochester. LiTL

Without this just gradation could they be/Subjected, these to those, or all to thee? An Essay on Man. Alexander Pope. HeIP

Without this/what is/worth doing. Land. Carroll Arnett. VoR

Without to-morrow, without yesterday. Let Us Forget. Agnes Mary Frances (Mme Emile Duclaux) Robinson. WHA

Without waiting the attack/Of their youngest daughter's frown? The Conquest. Oliver St. John Gogarty. OBMV

Without watching for daylight. The Wanderer. Claude Vigee. VWA

Without you all the grains will fall through. Knowing. Mary Coghill. BrRo

Without you I'll never know joy again. Song of the Ill-Married. Anonymous. BoWoP

Withouten he find it milk and pap/A long while-ey. The Wake at the Well. Anonymous. GBP

Withouten repentyng, myn herte swete! The Legend of Good Women. Geoffrey Chaucer. AtBAP

Withouten these no water could be good. Description of a New England Spring. John Josselyn. SCAP

Witness Burgoyne, and two famous Bro-/thers! A New Song: "Has the Marquis La Fayette." Joseph Stansbury. PAH

Witness her lying/–in other arms. Love's night & a lamp. Meleager. BoLoP

Witness/Of so much majesty. Stars. Sara Teasdale. HBMV; MoRP; TiPo

A witness, standing/alone/in a prison/courtyard/in Korea. Solitary. Sharon Olds. SOTS

Witness/the drawing out of colour. The Drawing out of Colour. Christopher Dewdney. CaPN

Wits and black eyes, the skittles and the king! A House and Grounds. [James Henry] Leigh Hunt. CBEP; OBRV

Wits are game-cocks to one another. Fable X: The Elephant and the Bookseller. John Gay. EiCP

A witty man, or one that's out of's wits. The Poet. Thomas Randolph. PoL

Wo, Eadie, go way. Eadie. Anonymous. OuSiCo

"Wo ho ho! I crie; "I come," then saie,/Make me as glad as hee! The Lover Compareth Himself to the Painful Falconer. Anonymous. EnPo; PBBP

Wo–Lawdy, well, next pay day. Po' Laz'us. Anonymous. OuSiCo

Wo worth marriage for evermair! The Wife Who Would a Wanton Be. Anonymous. FaBoCo

"Woe for Cytherea, for Adonis' beauty dead!" Lament for Adonis. Bion. LiTW

Woe for the fall of the glorious tree. The Brereton Omen (excerpt). Felicia Dorothea Hemans. CTC

Woe is me! Dove's Song in Winter. Anonymous. WTO

Woe is me, my stolen daughters! The Farewell. John Greenleaf Whittier. AA; AWP; InPo; PoNe

Woe is me, perhaps she's gone/For ever and for ever! The Banks of Banna. George Ogle. IrPN

Woe is me, that e'er my sight/Dwelt on charms so deadly bright! The Fair-Haired Girl. Anonymous. OnYI

Woe should I turn traitor to/Wine and love and lyre! Wine and Love and Lyre. Anonymous. UnTE

The woe that tell-tale tears confess. Within My Heart. Judah Al-Harizi. TrJP

Woe to him that deserts his mighty Lord! The Life of St. Cellach: He Who Forsakes the Clerkly Life. Anonymous. OnYI

Woe to him who slanders women! Woe to Him Who Slanders Women. Gearoid Iarla Mac Gearailt. NOBI

Woe to the conqueror! Peace to the Slumberers. Thomas Moore. HBV 1-2; OnYI

Woe to Ulster!/Hail men of Ireland!' The Tain: Before the Last Battle. Anonymous. NOBI

Woe unto him who has no home this night. The Solitary. Friedrich Wilhelm Nietzsche. AWP

...Woe,/Which only breeds your beauty's overthrow. In Lacrimas. Anonymous. GTBS

Woe worth such choosing! Of Disdainful Daphne. M. H. Nowell. ElL

The woeful from dread, as He oft has done. Christ 1: Advent Lyrics, I. Anonymous. AnOE

Woeful his fate whose doom is to wait/With longing heart for an absent love. The Wife's Lament. Anonymous. AnOE; LiTW

...Woefully worried/about his diabetes-glaucoma The Day of the Pancreas. David McFadden. NeAC

A woful disaster, he says Pater-Noster,/but has neither Money nor Cloaths. The Crafty Miss of London; or, The Fryar Well Fitted. Anonymous. CoMu; OxBB

Woke from the nap, forgetting him; and ate him. The Wedding. Conrad Aiken. AnAmPo; CMoP; TAP

Wolf and lamb lie down together. Love Song for the Future. Vassar Miller. NCSH

"Wolf and wether, leon and ox,/Sal comen samen, and lamb and fox." Cursor Mundi: The Flight into Egypt. Anonymous. CoBE

Wolf said we are human. Recollection. Donald D. Govan. NBP

The wolf that follows, the fawn that flies. Atalanta in Calydon. Algernon Charles Swinburne. AWP; BoLiVe; CTC; EvOK; ExPo; GoTF; GTBS; GTBS-P; HAP; HBV 1-2; HeIP; InPo; MasP; NOBE; NoP; OBEV; PoEL 1-5; PoPle; SeCeV; TEP; TrGrPo; ViBoPo; WHA

The wolf treading its circuits towards sleep. Christopher at Birth. Michael Longley. CIP

The wolf winds blow/and we shall have snow. Are You There, Mrs. Goose? John V. Hicks. AMV-80

The wolfish blood in their veins. The Train Dogs. [(Emily[) Pauline Johnson. GDP; WHW

The wolves of evening will be much abroad. Runes for an Old Believer. Rolfe Humphries. NYBP

Wolves sharp-eyed at the/heels of spirit. The Riven Quarry. Gloria C. Oden. PoBA

A woman among them, painting. Painters. Muriel Rukeyser. EyDe

The woman as witness, the clamor of crickets. Pelvic Meditation. Bruce Smith. AMV-80

Woman bore me, I will rise. A Shropshire Lad. Alfred Edward Housman. OAEP

A woman desolate and forlorn. The Death of Cleopatra. Horace. EnLi 1-2

A woman everywhere is only cunt. Epigram: "My better half, why turn a peevish scold." Martial (Marcus Valerius Martialis). PeHV

A woman/fishes in the water/for a stone. Rock Tumbler. Monty Reid. CaPN

A woman fit to be reproduced. Misogynist. Richard Conniff. DBV

Woman full of wile/I would give you all! Autumn. Frank O'Connor. OBMV

,The woman gone/Into the house, from which the wailing starts? Le Livre Est sur la Table. John Ashbery. ANYP

...Woman half so sweet,/Or death so bitter, or at such dear feet? He Has Fallen from the Height of His Love. Wilfrid Scawen Blunt. ViBoPo

The woman I have always tried/to keep subdued/under lock/and ink. The Woman in My Notebook. Lorna Dee Cervantes. WPOW

Woman in man, and man in womb. On Looking into Henry Moore. Dorothy Livesay. OBCV

...A woman/is answering sleep. Elms bend against the night. Midnight on Front Street. Roberta Hill Whiteman. CDW; TWSS

A woman is her mother./That's the main thing. Housewife. Anne Sexton. NMM

Woman is mortal woman. She abides. In Her Praise. Robert Graves. BIrV

A woman laughs; the stalking light leaps. Private. Baron Wormser. SM

A woman lay with golden skin. Night Songs. Thomas Kinsella. ACV

Woman, let me learn of you. Triumph of Sensibility. Sylvia Townsend Warner. MoAB; MoBrPo

A woman like me once had hands/Like these. Amaze. Adelaide Crapsey. AnAmPo; QFR

A woman living soft and idly/Sees misfortune bring the bill. Epigram: "A woman working hard and wisely." Kassia. WPOW

Woman of that girl. Boys of These Men Full Speed. Muriel Rukeyser. NNaP

Woman quit me, throwed my trunk outdoors I Wilp Turn Your Money Green. Furry Lewis. BluL

–The woman/reels/And drops without a moan: Dixon is/dead. A Savage. John Boyle O'Reilly. AA

The Woman's deaf, and does not hear. On a Certain Lady at Court. Alexander Pope. ALV; BoLiVe; HBV 1-2; NOBE; NOEC; OAEP; OBEC; OBEV; OBSP; PoPle; TrGrPo

A woman's dream for her/daughter is much stronger/than your death. The Place of O. Ray A. Young Bear. VoR

The woman's laughter holds the lilt/Of the wench she used to be.) Nostalgia. Gertrude Millard. BPAW

The woman's mouth makes a sound like the word Mama. Hmmmm, 8. Leslie Scalapino. NPGG

The woman's question every time/absorbs the murder's relevance. The Brockton Murder: A Page out of William James. Knute Skinner. TW

A woman's voice/warping the afternoon/with its one choice. Components. Roger McDonald. CBAP

A woman said: "Farewell, my son!" The Little House in Lithuania. Samuel Marshak. VWA

Woman, tear out thy voice. Nudities. Andre Spire. AWP; ErPo; TrJP; VWA

The woman, tearless, lets him go. The Great Farewells. Amanda Benjamin Hall. GoYe

Woman, tell me, when love dies/Do you know where then it lies? Three Rimas, 2. Gustavo Adolfo Becquer. LiTW

The woman that I love leaps forth to me,/Naked and bold! Twins. Edward Bulwer-Lytton. ErPo

The woman that kissed him and–pinched his poke–was the lady that's/known as Lou. The Shooting of Dan McGrew. Robert W. Service. FaBoBe; FaFP; FPL; GoTF; MaC; PoLf; PoRA; TreF; WHW

Woman, thou art dust–remember! This Mad Carnival of Loving. Heinrich Heine. TrJP

"Woman, thy vows are traced in sand." To Woman. George Gordon, Lord Byron. HBV 1-2; ViBoPo

A woman was the cause of it all. St. James Infirmary. Anonymous. AmFP

The woman washing dishes/in a pan of stars. Campfire Extinguished. Raymond F. Roseliep. SM

A woman who could bend to grief/But would not bend to shame. Vashti. Frances E. W. Harper. BlSi

The Woman Who Understands! The Woman Who Understands. Everard Jack Appleton. PoLf

Woman whom we call Twilight, when night's pall/You lift across our Earth to cover it. Twilight. Olive Custance. CAW; HBV 1-2

The Woman with the Serpent's Tongue. The Woman with the Serpent's Tongue. William Watson. HBV 1-2

Woman you put into the world a body always the same/Yours/You are resemblance. You Rise Up. Paul Eluard. PoPl

Women and care, and care and women, and women and care/and trouble. Epigram: The World Is Full of Care." Nathaniel Ward. PoL

Women and elephants never forget. Ballade of Unfortunate Mammals. Dorothy Parker. ALV; InMe

Women are noe longer Chast/Then untempted; they would tast/Men, with Equall Heat, and Hast. Anti-Platonicke. George Daniel. CavP

The women are running out of it, into a summer lake of air Professional Amnesia. Erin Moure. CaPN

Women faint from sweet scents/and hot fear. In the Dry Riverbed. Zelda. VWA

Women felt it was no longer any use being a linger-longer-Lucy. Energetic Women. D. H. Lawrence. InPS

The women go wailing/To pick up the dead. Where the Fight Was. Alice Corbin. BPAW

The women hear her in the new moon's madness. On a Celtic Mask by Henry Moore. Horace Gregory. PoA

Women like some other Fruit/Lose their relish when too Mellow. Song. Anonymous. ErPo

...Women like you who had/Ever lived, had stepped across my grave. Maximian Elegy V. Kenneth Rexroth. CrMA

Women listen/all along the line. Counry-Western Music. Ted Kooser. TAT

Women may pretend, yet they always dismiss/Everything but mere being just like this. The Two Parents. Hugh" (Christopher Murray Grieve) MacDiarmid. FaBoTw; OxBTC

Women monogamous. Hogamus, Higamus. Anonymous. ELU

Women/should be/pedestals/to men Women. May Swenson. BoWoP; NMM; Prf

...Women should be/silently riding their zebras. An Apology. Diane Wakoski. TAP

Women together/Little Better. Observation. Richard Weber. PoL

...Women will relent/When as they find such moving blandishment. The Metamorphosis of Pygmalion's Image (excerpt). John Marston. OAEL 1-2

De womens in Jackson, all dressed in black,/Said, in fact, he was a cracker-jack. Casey Jones (D vers.). Anonymous. ViBoFo

Won't even notice when we choose to go. The Roc. Edward Lowbury. AmMo

Won't it be nice? Plans. Dorothy Brown Thompson. BiCB

Won't last half an hour. A Sunshiny Shower. Anonymous. FaBoBe; HBV 1-2; OxNR

Won't some good man/tell me some woman's name Stocking Feet Blues. Blind Lemon Jefferson. BluL

Won't you do the baby cake-walk/For me? Do the Baby Cake-Walk. Clyde Watson. NTCP

Won't you get on board./Oh, get on board. Union Train. Millard and Lee Hays Lampell. FSW

Won't you give me some gentle reminder? Limerick: "Cleopatra, who thought they maligned her." Newton Mackintosh. LiBL; NA

Won't you let me go with you?–yes, my love, yes. The Cruel War Is Raging. Anonymous. FSW

Won't you move over.../just a little closer? Meeting Halfway. R. Wayne Hardy. LFAC

Won't you ring, old hammer?/Hammer, ring. Hammer, Ring. Anonymous. AmFP

Won with an egg, and lost again with shell. Why Then (Quod I) Old Proverbs Never Fail. George Gascoigne. LO

The wonder and the awe of God. The Wonderer. Robert W. Service. BBV

The Wonder flooding at his heart,/The apple in his hand. Inspiration. Mary Elizabeth ("E") Fullerton. AA; AmPP; AnFE; AP; BLPL; PoAu 1-2

Wonder is shorter liv'd than Love. To Amoret. Edmund Waller. SeCV 1-2

Wonder is that I livie! Snatches: "I may come to my lef bute by the watere." Anonymous. OxBM

Wonder just what sort of people/Could have had this house before... Wraith. Edna St. Vincent Millay. WSC

...The wonder of the brain that/hears that music and of our/skill sometimes to record it. The Desert Music (excerpt). William Carlos Williams. UnS

The wonder of winter/And new white snow! New Snow. Catharine Bryant Rowles. YeAr

Wonder outwaiting pain/as in a wintry tree. Desire Is Dead. D. H. Lawrence. FaBoEE

Wonder to heaven with somewhat shaken trust. A Development of Idiotcy. Ebenezer Jones. OBNC

Wonder what fate you have in store for me. The Hunter. Raymond Souster. NOBC

...Wonder/what got into me? The Dead Seal. A. W. Purdy. NoAm

Wonderful in the silvery shine/Of the round, lovely, thoughtful moon. It Was the Lovely Moon. John Freeman. BoNaP

Wonderful name of our wonderful Lord! And His Name Shall Be Called Wonderful. Martha Snell Nicholson. BePJ

The wonderful tart flavor that was waiting for me/Under the stubby fingers of the leaves. The Girl in the Foreign Movie. Patricia Goedicke. FAZ

Wonderfully God endows/Poet-hearts that give Him pleasure. Poet-Hearts. Baron Joseph von Eichendorff. CAW

Wonderin' whose dream/it'll be to commence/the next pogrom so as/to preserve their/independence day Red White & Another Ism. Harold LaMont Otey. LFAC

Wondering/at the bar's/delay Ostriches & Grandmothers! LeRoi (Imamu Amiri Baraka) Jones. NeAP

Wondering how belly-hunger with this quill of spray and storm/Could forge such a dazzling signature Writing on the Wall. Padraic Fallon. NeIP

Wondering, how did we survive? Mixed Sketches. Don L. Lee. BPo

Wondering/how far the fat-cheeked/boy's hands/have plowed/by now. On the Poet's Leer. David Ray. NePoEA-2

...Wondering how to sleep/in this lie of memory, unless it be made clean. Housework. William Matthews. NPAW

Wondering if hers is among them. Or perhaps not. A Long Way Outside Yellowstone. Thomas McGrath. VGW

...Wondering if/I was just another loss/he'd divided his days into. April Fools' Day. Yusef Komunyakaa. MAYP

Wondering/stillnesses I Flung up My Arm Half from Sleep. Tram Combs. MP

Wondering where he shall journey, O where? The Sign-Post. Edward ("Edward Eastaway") Thomas. ViBoPo

...Wondering which steps/to take across the snows/of this first long winter/in the new world. My Feet. Louis Jenkins. GP

The wonders that I dreamed that night. The Book of the Duchess. Geoffrey Chaucer. WHA

Wondring to drink of Waters not her own. Metamorphoses. Ovid (Publius Ovidius Naso). OBVE

Wondrous and fair and wise! It must be so.   Morning in the Hills.   Bliss Carman.   NOBC

The wondrous boon will gain for me,/God's face to see.   One Gift I Ask. Virginia Bioren Harrison.   HBV 1-2

"Wondrous life!" cried Marvell at Appleton House.   Round.   Weldon Kees. CoAP; NaP; NoAm

A wondrous softness on her grey old face.   At Quebec.   Jean Blewett.   CaP

The wood-path strews its milky way.   Spring.   Aubrey Thomas De Vere. OBNC

The wood resounds: he wheels, he drops, he dies.   Rural Sports.   John Gay. PBBP

The wood shall ring, and the old wife sing,/Of Robin Hood, Arthur, and John. Robin Hood and the Tanner.   Anonymous.   BaBo; ESPB; MaC

The wooden-headed lunatic still thinks that he's a/saint.   The Figure-Head. Crosbie Garstin.   EtS; StPo

Wooden Lady Eleanora von Alleyne!   The Ride Round the Parapet. Friedrich Rueckert.   AWP

Wooden you give up also? I would.   Limerick: "A woodchuck who'd chucked lots of wood."   J. F. Wilson.   TDH

A woodland rivulet–a Poet's death.   Sonnet: After Dark Vapors.   John Keats.   AtBAP; OBNC

Woods, and Hills, and every thing,/Beare witnesse we are merry.   A Christmas Carroll.   George Wither.   OBS

The woods are waving, "Farewell, Summer."   Harvest Home.   Arthur Guiterman.   YeAr

Woods devoid of beasts, roads that please the foot.   Against Romanticism. Kingsley Amis.   NePoEA; NoAm

Woods harmlesse Shades have only true Delights.   A Solitary Life.   William, of Hawthornden Drummond.   OBS

...The woods lock us up/In the secret crimes of our intent.   Forest.   Jean Garrigue.   LiTM; NOBA

The woods no more us answer, nor our eccho ring.   Epithalamion.   Edmund Spenser.   FiP; NAs

Woods' silent shades have only true delights.   Thrice Happy He.   William, of Hawthornden Drummond.   BoNaP; HBV 1-2

The woodspurge has a cup of three.   The Woodspurge.   Dante Gabriel Rossetti.   AtBAP; EBEV; ELP; GTBS-P; HAP; HeIP; LoBV; NBM; NOBE; NOBV; NoP; OAEL 1-2; OAEP; OBEV; OBNC; PoEL 1-5; PrIm; TreFT; UnPo; VLP; WeW; WHA

Wooed a host of mermaids after dusk.   Prometheus, with Wings:.   Michael Ondaatje.   PeCV

The Wooers' appetites in blood of one,/The most select our choise can fall upon.'   The Odyssey.   Homer.   CTC

Wooing the boulders with his Song of Love.   Big Thompson Canon.   Jean Milne Gower.   PoOW

Woolly clouds come creeping.   A Little Song of Spring.   Mary Austin. YeAr

Wor aud cage sent his notice in,/Just to vex the maisters.   The Row between the Cages.   Thomas Armstrong.   VLP

A word and a jest.   When Helen Lived.   William Butler Yeats.   CMoP; ViBoPo

The word for all coming/Turned into one.   Advent: A Carol.   Patric Dickinson.   OBCP

The word has power, the chant is going up.   Revolutionary Letters.   Diane Di Prima.   GP

Word I had no one left but God.   Bereft.   Robert Frost.   AtBAP; LiTM; MoAB; MoAmPo; OxBA; SoSe

A word in season, as from Thee,/To weary ones in needful hour.   For Every Day.   Frances Ridley Havergal.   BLRP

The word in the word wakes me.   Rune.   Muriel Rukeyser.   SM

The word is the web we take from the womb.   The Journal of Albion Moonlight (excerpt).   Kenneth Patchen.   NaP

"The Word made Flesh has dwelt among us,'/Is still our ever-new delight. Ave-Maria Bells.   Charles Warren Stoddard.   ISi

A word of inscrutable meanin'.   Limerick: "There once was a person of Benin."   Cosmo Monkhouse.   LiBL; NA

The word outleaps the world, and light is all.   Four for Sir John Davies. Theodore Roethke.   AP; CoBMV; MoAmPo; NoAm; NOBA

The word was whispered through the ranks, Advance.   At Midnight's Hour. Henry David Thoreau.   LiTA; PoEL 1-5

Wording me even to the spring of doom   In the Cemetery of the Sun. Wilfred Watson.   PeCV

...Wordless,/as real things always are.   This Decoration.   Hayden Carruth. NNaP

Words alwone vrom her a-vallen,/Would be jay vor all the night.   Light or Sheade.   William Barnes.   NOBV

...Words/Are flocks of singing birds?   To a Poet.   Sister Mary Angelita. GoBC

Words are for those with promises to keep.   Their Lonely Betters.   W. H. Auden.   GoJo; LOW

The words are very like: the name is new.   Modern Love, XV.   George Meredith.   VLP

Words at once true and kind,/Or not untrue and not unkind.   Talking in Bed.   Philip Larkin.   BoLoP; NoP

Words from our poems/Menace the night.   The Meadow.   John Wieners. CoPo

Words grew in the heart and clanged, the color of noon.   Spring Morning– Santa Fe.   Lynn Riggs.   BPAW

The words he spoke were with her till she/died.   The Contrast.   Helen Gray Cone.   AA

Words mean whatever one wants   Words.   Ulalume Gonzales De Leon. AMV-81

Words melt away/Like hills in fog.   Mocking Song against Qaqortingneq. Piuvkaq.   WTO

The words: "My darling, my beloved one."   The Letter.   John Hall Wheelock.   AnEnPo; LiTL

Words of a night, she said, to bring the day.   An Escape.   Abu Nuwas. ErPo

The words of life from Christ the Lamb.   A King Shall Reign in Righteousness.   Sebastian Streeter.   AH

Words off Indian tongue/–from mind shell.   Wagon Full of Thunder.   Louis (LittleCoon) Oliver.   STE

...Words ought to have their weight.   Prayers Must Have Poise.   Robert Herrick.   LiTB

Words sweet words,/learn wings instead.   Kissing the Dancer.   Robert Sward.   CoPo

...Words that are left unsaid/And the undetectable words used in their stead. Words.   Robert Finch.   PoA

The words that are not heard again.   In Memoriam A.H.H., XVIII.   Alfred, Lord Tennyson.   VLP

The words that made her love the loveliest.   The Love-Letter.   Dante Gabriel Rossetti.   MaVP

The words they speak are nothing more than spoken words.   Chekhov Comes to Mind at Harvard.   William T. Freeman.   AMV-81

Words/3poets   Yellow.   De Leon Harrison.   PoBA

The words were hard to understand.   In Memoriam A.H.H., LXIX.   Alfred, Lord Tennyson.   VLP

Words were meant/To catch meanings in.   Poet's Protest.   Doris Hedges. CaP

The words you gathered here will be/alive still in a foreign tongue.   Homage to John Millington Synge.   Mairtin O Direain.   NOBI

Work and wait unwearying,–/Keep a-pluggin' away.   Keep A-Pluggin' Away. Paul Laurence Dunbar.   MCCG

The work begun by great Judas/Maccabeus/and his four brothers, all men of/ renown....   Alexander Jannai.   Constantine P. Cavafy.   TrJP

Work beside me, O my brother,/All for one and one for all!   Hymn for Nations.   Anonymous.   FSW

Work done, betrayals yet to come.   The Liberator.   Lucien Stryk.   GP

Work & fear be the basis for his terrible cry/not to forget his name.   Dream Songs.   John Berryman.   CAPP

Work for many hands he does alone.   A Call to Action.   Callinus.   WaaP

...The work is/all done for the day.   Take down the Fiddle, Karl!   Shaw Neilson.   CBAP

Work mischief, Lord, let be thy will/To keep me free from either ill!   A Man May Live Thrice Nestor's Life.   Thomas Norton.   InvP

Work, my friend, and so farewell.   Toil Away.   John Jay Chapman. HBMV

The work of death was done!   The Execution of Montrose.   William Aytoun. HBV 1-2; OnMSP

The work of our Lord's hand.   May Day.   Anonymous.   OxNR

Work that to life, and let me ever dwell/In thy remembrance (Julia). So farewell.   His Sailing from Julia.   Robert Herrick.   PoEL 1-5

Work, while the night is dark'ning,/When man's work is o'er.   Work, for the Night Is Coming.   Annie L. Walker.   SaC

Work wrought through Love!   The Lincoln-Child.   James Oppenheim. HBMV

Worke we despise which bringeth advauntage.   Egloge V (excerpt). Alexander Barclay.   EnPo

Worked his tongue, like a thought, behind the bait.   Bobber.   Raymond Carver.   GeTw

Workers and peasants/Stop displaying your ribs;/Eat cakes.   Why?   Richard Augustine Chima.   WhB

Workers of the south.   We Are Building a Strong Union.   Anonymous. FSW

Working and waiting to prove His Word.   Somebody Prayed.   Anonymous. STF

Working, working near.   The Hinds of Kerry.   William S. Wabnitz.   GoYe

Works hard, my knife, till all are served.   On the Gift of a Knife. Muireadhach Albanach O Dalaigh.   NOBI

The works of ages start to view,/And ancient Wit elicits new.   Conversation. Hannah More.   OBEC

Works of William Shakespeare?/Probably.   Easier.   James Harrison. AMV-80

The World a Monarch, and that Monarch You. Astraea Redux. John Dryden. CEP; OBS

The world a swaying reed. Morning Fancy. Mary McNeil Fenollosa. AA

The world as black/lightning. Black Lightning. Arthur Sze. BrSi

The world as it might be? Reading the Brothers Grimm to Jenny. Lisel Mueller. DFT; NYBP

The world as witnessed by Miss Lee. Cornelia's Window. Julie Kane. AMV-81

The world being/everywhere equally foreign. Cedar Needles. Chase Twichell. MAYP

The world believes nor one, nor/t'other. To an Acquaintance. *Anonymous.* FaFP

World-besotted traveler; he/Served human liberty. Swift's Epitaph. William Butler Yeats. CMoP; NAMP; OBVE

The world broken open, spilling life. More Than. Susan Fitzpatrick. AMV-80

World broods with warm breast and with ah! bright wings. God's Grandeur. Gerard Manley Hopkins. AnFE; AWP; BBV; BiP; BLPL; BoC; BrPo; CMoP; DiPo; EBCP; ExPo; FaFP; FF; ForPo; HAP; ILwL; InPK; InPo; InvP; LiTB; LiTM; LoBV; MoAB; MoBrPo; MoPo; MoRP; MoVE; NoAm; NOBE; NOBV; NoP; OAEL 1-2; OBNC; OxBoCh; PPP; PrIm; SeCeV; SoSe; SOTW; TEP; TrCP; TreFT; TrGrPo; UnPo; VLP

The world demands/New proof in deeds. The Challenge. Grenville Kleiser. BLRP

The world does what it pleases. It Pleases. Gary Snyder. TAT

The world doesn't oblige, and old pipes stink. The Walk Home. Reed Whittemore. ConAP

The world fell into a blood-bath tub! The Saturday Tub. Mary Gilmore. NOAV

A world found dying of the death you died. Sonnets for a Dying Man. Burns Singer. NePoEA-2

The world had quite forgotten it must die. The Earthly Paradise. William Morris. EG; VLP

...The world has grown so wide,/That we don't know which one of us has died. Sonnets for a Dying Man. Burns Singer. NePoEA-2

The world has much to give. Take Time to Live. Thomas Curtis Clark. PoToHe

The world has set all its soul bare/Before God in the storm. I Didn't Know My Soul. A. Ben-Yitzhak. VWA

The world has surrendered to me. Spring. Moishe Kulbak. VWA

The world his country, and his God his guide. At Dover Cliffs, July 20, 1787. William Lisle Bowles. EnRP; ViBoPo

The world illuminated and myself awake. First Dream (Excerpt). Sister Juana Ines de la Cruz. BoWoP

The world, in its turn, will not take/ Pleasure in contemplating. A Caution to Poets. Matthew Arnold. CBEP; FaBoUs; PV

The world in two I have divided fit,/Myself to you, and all the rest to it. Caelica, LX. Fulke, Lord Brooke Greville. FCP

The world inherits wormliness. Reversionary. Stevie Smith. FaBoEE

"The world is better that I lived today." A Morning Prayer. Ella Wheeler Wilcox. PoToHe

The world is capable of, the infinite/Pattern of truth the poet rearranges. Of the Mathematician. Alice Clear Matthews. GoYe

The world is dying now for the want of/someone/to tell them of the Saviour's matchless/love. Have I Done My Best for Jesus? Edwin Young. STF

The world is full of cherries. Cherries. Zalman Schneour. TrJP

The world is full of folks, it's true,/But there was only one of you. Miss You. *Anonymous.* PoToHe

...The world/is holding us up/very well, today. To Ben, at the Lake. Cilla McQueen. OCNZ

The world is not hers, she has to win it. To Our Daughter. Jennifer Armitage. BrRo

The world is safe because it floats in Thee. The Great River. Henry Van Dyke. TrPWD

The world is so new you could talk with God,/In the Yucca land. In the Yucca Land. Madge Morris. BPAW

The world is something I must try. Tragedy. Mark Van Doren. NePoAm-2

The world is taking off her clothes. Rondel. X. J. Kennedy. SM

The world is too much for us, wait and see! Magnificat in Transit from the Toledo Airport. George Starbuck. SUW

The world is ugly,/And the people are sad. Gubbinal. Wallace Stevens. SOTW

The world is wearier, grown dark to grieve/Her child that was a pilgrim and a king. To My Father. Iris Tree. HBMV

The world is weary of the past,/Oh, might it die or rest at last! Final Chorus. Percy Bysshe Shelley. OBRV

World is wind and bloom and billow. Beauty of This Earth. Martin Opitz. LiTW

The world may pardon us to hold thee dear. Farther. John James Piatt. AA

The world men made were man's no more. Winter Night. Roy Fuller. NeBP

...The world must be its own/witness, we judge ourselves, raise your hands. Giovanni da Fiesole on the Sublime or Fra Angelico's "Last Judgment." Richard Howard. Prf

A world of love shut in. Home. Dora Greenwell. HBV 1-2

World of make-believe, live as children–the/Parade. The Parade. Ashton Greene. NePoAm

A world of money, promise and disease. The Man from Washington. James Welch. CDW; GP

A world of shouts and grunts and groans/Has vanished with the megaphones. Crew Cut. David McCord. SD

The world on the first of May/Shining after the rain? May Day. Sara Teasdale. BoNaP; PoSC

The world rocks/like a carriage with a baby in it. Wedding. Ewa Lipska. VWA

The world's a wood in which all lose their way,/Though by a diff'rent path each goes astray. In Defense of Satire. Sir Carr Scroope. APAS

The World's and his Hyperion. A Hymne for the Epiphanie. Sung as by the Three Kings. Richard Crashaw. AnAnS 1

The world's but theirs; but my Beloved's mine. A Divine Rapture. Francis Quarles. HBV 1-2; OBEV

The world's denied. The Two Fires. Judith Wright. MoBrPo

...The world's work await/Such boys when they grow to be men. The Boy We Want. *Anonymous.* WBLP

...The world's your oyster. Open wide, now. Read. Can Zone; or, The Good Food Guide. Rika Lesser. MAYP

The world shall never say I love in vain. Of a Mistress. Sir Aston Cokayne. CavP

The world should listen then–as I am listening now. To a Skylark. Percy Bysshe Shelley. AtBAP; BoAnP; BoLiVe; DiPo; ERoP 1-2; FaBoBe; FaBV; FaFP; FPL; GN; GTBS; GTBS-P; HAP; HBV 1-2; HBVY; InPS; InvP; LiTB; LoBV; MCCG; MyFE; NoP; OAEL 1-2; OAEP; OBEV; OBNC; OBRV; OHFP; PAI; PB; PBBP; PoLf; RoGo; TEP; TreFS; TrGrPo; WHA

The world takes rare and little note/Of any plucky deed. The Panchatantra: The Penalty of Virtue. *Anonymous.* AWP

"The world that you inhabit has not yet been created." Shells. Kathleen Raine. ImOP

A world the color of salt with no young music in it. Places and Ways to Live. Richard Hugo. GP

The world, the same wide den–of thieves,/or what ye will. Childe Harold's Pilgrimage: Canto IV. George Gordon, Lord Byron. CoBE

The world then to an end shall come/In Eighteen Hundred and Eighty-one. Mother Shipton's Prophecies. Charles Hindley. BLPA

The world to her, and both at her blest feet,/In whom the circles of all Empire meet. De Guiana, Carmen Epicum. George Chapman. OBSC

The World Turned Upside Down! The Ride of Tench Tilghman. Clinton Scollard. MC

The world wakens up to the children's sweet laughter. Christmas Legend. Edna Randolph Worrell. ChBR

The world/Walking off/into space. Concert. Robert Sward. VGW

The world was always yours: you will not take it. Speech to a Crowd. Archibald MacLeish. MoAB; MoAmPo; NePA

The world was His word, the realm of His radiant mouth. Today I Have Touched the Earth. William Jay Smith. WaP

The world was wide and life was fair. Troia Fuit. Reginald Wright Kauffman. HBV 1-2

The world, when waste, he peopled with increase,/And warring nations reconcil'd in peace. Apology for Love. Giovanni Boccaccio. LiTW

The world whispers: Hier bin i'. A Game at Salzburg. Randall Jarrell. MiAP; NoAm

The world will not be understood. Comedy. Mark Van Doren. NePoAm-2

The world will see thy picture there. Secrecy Protested. Thomas Carew. AnAnS 2; CaPo; OAEP; SeCP

The world will soon break up into small colonies of the saved Those Being Eaten by America. Robert Bly. CoAP; NaP

A world withered, graves in number. An Evil World. *Anonymous.* OnYI

World without end–and not in vain–/Are rowing this world along! The Strong Swimmer. William Rose Benet. PoNe

World without end, let still His blessing flow;/O so! O be it so! Psalm XLI. Sir Philip Sidney. FCP

World without end, providing man,/Favored above all creatures, with food. Kashrut. Edouard Roditi. VWA

The world would die that thou shouldst be no more. "What tears, dear prince, can serve to water all." Sir Walter Raleigh. FCP

The world would have its end before its time. Lutea Allison. Sir John Suckling. ErPo

The world would listen then–as I am listening/now. Ode to a Skylark. Percy Bysshe Shelley. BoLiVe; MBW 1-2; NOBE

World you are good for me. A Round Song. Rhyll McMaster. CBAP

The worlds revolve like ancient women/Gathering fuel in vacant lots. Preludes. Thomas Stearns Eliot. DiPo; HeIP; LiTA; MoVE; MP; NoP; OBMV; PAI; PoPl; PPP; SeCePo; SOTW; TwCP; UnPo; VGW; WeW

Worlds we love and which are little/Harbour the most glorious things. Entoptic Colours. Johann Wolfgang von Goethe. SUW

The worm and butterfly–it is not long! The Term of Death. Sarah Piatt. AA

The worm climbs wind and we the range/Of all our focus. The Butterfly. Gray Burr. CoPo

A worm rehearsing perpetually the life of a butterfly/but a worm to the end Lame Angel. Donald Finkel. VWA

The worm was punished, sir, for early rising! Early Rising. John Godfrey Saxe. AnNE; BLPL; HBV 1-2; InMe; PoLf

The worm which devours itself with the beak of a dead bird. The Earth Asks and Receives Rain. Phyllis Haring. PeSA

Worm, with small-talk from hell. The Silent Room. Kingsley Amis. OxBC

The worms and creeping things are my waiting maids,/To wait on me whilst I am asleep. The Grey Cock (A vers.). Anonymous. BaBo

The worms eat only death away. I Danced Before I Had Two Feet. Max Dunn. BoAV; PoAu 1-2

The worms of Conscience that within me swarm,/Prove that my plaints are less than is my harm. Stanzas from Saint Peter's Complaint. Robert Southwell. ACP; CAW

Worn out with coaxing, sleep. Long Pursuit. Anonymous. UnTE

Worn with life's cares, love yet was love. A Marriage Ring. George Crabbe. BoLoP; EnLoPo; OBEV

Worried thoughts/slow/my/every movement. Chile. Susan Griffin. NPGG

...Worry/from rejection slips/and final notices from the Finance company. Arthur Ridgewood, M.D. Frank Marshall Davis. BPo

The worrying old woman of Surrey. Limerick: "There was an old woman in Surrey." Anonymous. OxBChV

Worrying the carcase of an old song. Welsh Landscape. R. S. Thomas. FaBoMo

Worse than their sires, of wider range,/And much more durable. Science Fiction. Kingsley Amis. NePoEA-2

...Worse to waken/from that harsh sobbing to the bed's shudder. Again. Jon Stallworthy. OxBC

Worship Christ the new-born King. Nativity. James Montgomery. NOCV; OBRV

The worship of thy mother's eyes. To a New-Born Baby Girl. Grace Hazard Conkling. HBV 1-2

Worshipped eternally,/Lord of Infinity! Highest Divinity. Anonymous. TrJP

Worshipped such stones until/the coming of good Patrick to Armagh. The Plain of Adoration. Anonymous. BIrV

The worst a coat upon a coat-hanger. The Apparitions. William Butler Yeats. CMoP; LiTM

...The worst/stories we/war-bonneted braves ever had/heard. A Second Molting. Ralph Salisbury. STE

The worst that I could write would be no more/Than what thy very friends have said before. On Poet Ninny. John Wilmot, Earl of Rochester. APAS

Worth finishing with a stigma C. A Little Something for William Whipple. Dave Oliphant. FAZ

The worth of all it so despised. Only the Polished Skeleton. Countee Cullen. PrIm; VGW

The worth of that is that which it contains,/And that is this, and this with thee remains. Sonnets, LXXIV: "But be contented: when that fell arrest." William Shakespeare. OBSC

Worthwhile the struggle, sure the prize,/Since Easter, aye, is true! If Easter Be Not True. Henry H. Barstow. BLRP; PGD; TRV

A worthy daughter, or a noble son... What Does It Mean to Be American? Roselle Mercier Montgomery. MC

A worthy fool! Botley's the odly wear–attishu! A Cold Rendering (parody). Anonymous. BXAP

A worthy object; Our Lords Feet. The Weeper. Richard Crashaw. AnAnS 1; MePo; OAEL 1-2; OBEV; SeCP; ViBoPo

A worthy pair, who helped advance/Sound parish views. The Conformers. Thomas Hardy. EnLi 1-2; ViBoPo

Would all did so as well as I! My Mind to Me a Kingdom Is. Sir Edward Dyer. BLPL; CoBE; EIL; EnLi 1-2; FaBoBe; GoTF; HBV 1-2; LiTB; MCCG; NIP; NOBE; PG; TreFS; TrGrPo; ViBoPo; WGRP

Would any of them ever miss the Sleepytown Express! The Sleepytown Express. James J. Montague. HBMV

Would anybody call him great/For such a wicked thing? How Big Was Alexander? Elijah Jones. BLPA

Would bark outside the gates of Heaven,/To open them for Her! The Dog. William Henry Davies. GDP

Would be more so by praising Him often. The burning–at first–would be probably worst. James Kenneth Stephen. CenHV

Would be nicer to be/Fed intravenously? Observations in a Cornish Teashop. Kenneth Rexroth. OBAL

Would be transformd into a rose as thou. On a Damaske Rose Sticking upon a Ladies Breast. Thomas Carew. AnAnS 2

Would beat anew a little while, and then no more. And Then No More. James Clarence Mangan. AnIV; BIrV; BLPA; IrPN

Would bite the back in the kingdom of dead God. The Death of God. Howard Nemerov. OBSP; OxBC

Would boast the merit of a friend. The Man and the Weasel. Phaedrus. AWP

Would brood like a ghost, and as still as a post,/Old Nicholas Nye. Nicholas Nye. Walter De La Mare. HBMV; HBVY

Would copy John Tomkins, the hedger and ditcher. Contented John. Jane Taylor. HBV 1-2; HBVY

Would die a destin'd sacrifice/Than live at home and free. Love Restored (excerpt). Ben Jonson. UnS

Would dream such softness, like a picture hung,/Is wrought of human thunder, iron, blood? Brooklyn Bridge at Dawn. Richard Le Gallienne. HBMV

Would drink her down, and turn her into a sow. Satire upon the Licentious Age of Charles II. Samuel (1602-80) Butler. NOBL

Would gaze at each other with a wild surmise. Footnotes to "The Autobiography of Bertrand Russell." Mona Van Duyn. HAP

Would God be wasting a dog like Tim? Tim, an Irish Terrier. W.M. Letts. BoC; GDP

"Would God,' cried Francis, on his knees,/"I had a forest of such trees!' Brother Juniper. Blanche Mary Kelly. GoBC

Would God my woes were at an end,/Thy joys that I might see. The New Jerusalem. Anonymous. HBV 1-2; OBEV; OxBoCh; ViBoPo

Would God that I shall seem/So beautiful in death. The Last Quarter Moon of the Dying Year. Jonathan Henderson Brooks. CDC

...Would have been as true/As the sun declining in the West. Legend. Jules Laforgue. Prf

Would he begin to doubt his purpose here/before that light touch binds him to those eyes? Michelangelo: "The Creation of Adam." Gregory Djanikian. AMV-81

...Would he/Die if it were forbidden him to write? Questions for the Candidate. John Holmes. PP

Would he had stayed! After He Had Gone. Sylvia Townsend Warner. MoBrPo

...Would he leave me so much on my own/to cry and get scared? The House of Desire. Sherley Anne Williams. BlSi

Would he tell us: Odes and Documents must live to win/men? The Book-Burning Pit. Lo Yin. GLGT

Would I could wish my wishes all away,/And learn to wish the wishes that I ought. Would That I Were. Arthur Hugh Clough. TrPWD

Would I had loved him more! The First Grief. Felicia Dorothea Hemans. CH

Would I might, with your ecstatic buoyance,/Fare forth singing! Cricket. Clinton Scollard. HBV 1-2

Would I were a yellow stork/And could fly to my old home! Lament of Hsi-Chun. Hsi-chun. BoWoP

Would I were heaven! I would behold/Thee then with all mine eyes. The Lover to His Lady. George Turberville. CTC; FaBoEE; FF; OBSC

Would I were where my people are! The Lost Tribe. Ruth Pitter. WPOW

Would I were with the leaves that thread by thread/Soften to soil, I would that I were one. Now in the Palace Gardens. Trumbull Stickney. AnFE; CoAnAm; LiTA; NCEP

Would it not be the most/prized gift that ever was! Saint Nicholas,. Marianne Moore. NYBP

Would look when perched in a barber chair! Yak. William Jay Smith. TiPo

Would make a weeping willow laugh. The Laughing Willow. Oliver Herford. HBV 1-2

Would make an end of poverty. Market Day. Mary Webb. CH

Would make you swallow these Atlantic words. A Time of Change. Egan O'Rahilly. BIrV; FaBoPV

–Would my soul forget Madrid? Segovia and Madrid. Rose T. Cooke. AA

Would never see her more. Song. Ambrose Philips. CEP

Would not be far wrong/if I took you for the gardener. An Easter Garland. Carol Rumens. FaBoWP

Would not be going/To let it happen yet. The Current. James Merrill. NYBP

Would not the jest–/Have crawled too far! I Know That He Exists. Emily Dickinson. AmePo; AnFE; APA; MAmP

Would one think that my Chloe ne'er thought it was she. Chloe. Charles, Earl of Peterborough Mordaunt. CEP; OBEC

Would pulse with all the life there was within. The Battle. Louis Simpson. InPS; OBWP

Would read the secret in your simple ways.   An Open Secret.   Caroline Atherton Briggs Mason.   AA

Would remind us of/what we experienced/together.   The sweat.   Nila NorthSun.   STE

Would ride through the air/On a very find gander.   Old Mother Goose. *Anonymous.*   PBBP

Would rise to parch my throat–and I would flee.   Repeated Pilgrimage. John Gilland Brunini.   GoBC

Would see the smoke and know that ships still fought the war at/sea.   The Inspection.   Frederick B. Watt.   CaP

Would seem cast in gentler mould, would seem full of love and spring.   Lady of Castlenoire.   Thomas Bailey Aldrich.   BeLS

Would she could make of me a saint,/Or I of her a sinner.   Song: "Pious Selinda goes to prayers."   William Congreve.   BoLoP; FaBoCo; InMe; NIP; NLV; NOEC; OBSP

"Would she could pass this way/again."   I Shall Not Pass This Way Again. Eva Rose York.   FaFP; OHFP; WBLP

Would she not come?   If She but Knew?   Arthur William Edgar O'Shaughnessy.   HBV 1-2

Would sink, like her, in chilly arms of earth.   Aged Ninety Years.   Wilbert Snow.   AnAmPo

Would starve the horse to death and prize his turds.   Japanese Beetles.   X.J. Kennedy.   HoAn; OBAL

Would still go on/Farther than any wandering star has gone.   On Middleton Edge.   Andrew Young.   ELU; SD

Would stroke that sheep's black nose.   A Child's Pet.   William Henry Davies.   CH

Would tell me who I was before I died.   After Music.   Josephine Preston Peabody.   AA

Would that I could see/Her whose graceful beauty/Lost is now to me!   The Field-Path.   Charles Swain.   OBVV

Would that I had wings like a bird/To fly over those farther away.   Absent Lover.   *Anonymous.*   PBA

Would that I were as clear and/transparent as the water streaming/down a mountain-slope...   Like Water Down a Slope.   Zalman Schneour.   TrJP

Would that my heart could still/Its bitter weeping!   David's Lament for Jonathan.   Peter Abelard.   LiTW; PeHV

Would that one of us were dead!   The Snoring Bedmate.   *Anonymous.* BIrV

Would that then make us free?   Everything Is Possible.   Robert Pack.   PPP

Would that your lot were mine.   Aoibhinn, a leabhrain, do thriall. *Anonymous.*   AnIV; BIrV; OxBI

Would the Eden be an Eden,/Or the earl an earl?   Did the Harebell.   Emily Dickinson.   FaBV

Would the olive leaf once more?   Chorus from a Tragedy.   Leonard Bacon. ViBoPo

Would they could find us both in bed together!   To a Lady That Forbad to Love before Company.   Sir John Suckling.   CaPo

Would this man, could he see you now, ask why?   Epitaph for the Unknown Soldier.   W. H. Auden.   FaBoCo

Would to God I had died for thee, O Absalom, my son, my son.   David's Lamentation.   William Billings.   TrAS

"Would to God that all the Lord's people were/Prophets."   Milton. William Blake.   EnRP

Would turn and call him Cousin–for the likeness.   Polonius.   Walter De La Mare.   AtBAP

Would you be calm and placid/If you were full of formic acid?   The Ant. Ogden Nash.   FaBV; OBAL

Would you buy these woids?   Ode to New York.   Reed Whittemore.   NYP

Would you come back if I said the earth/was at the tip of my fingers?   Would you come back if I said the earth.   Nadia Tueni.   BoWoP

Would you ever believe the size of his you-know-what!   For Every Last Batch When the Next One Comes Along.   James Dickey.   GP

...Would you go go to sleep, go to sleep?   Lullaby.   Frederick Eckman.   FAZ

Would you have called me a nobody?   Epigram: "Somebody being a nobody." Alfred, Lord Tennyson.   FaBoEE

Would you have known delight/If it had knocked you down?   Reunion. William Stanley Merwin.   AmPC

Would you if Death were Flesh?   Flesh.   Stan Rice.   NPGG

Would you insist I'm lazy/Because I am an African?   The African Trader's Complaint.   Dennis C. Osadebay.   PBA

Would you kindly direct me to hell?   Coda.   Dorothy Parker.   DBV; GoTF; InMe; SBG; TreFS

Would you lay well? Don't watch.   Ars Poetica.   X. J. Kennedy.   ErPo; NIP; PP; PV

Would you love me, dearest, as fondly in return,/Could you but learn?   If You But Knew.   *Anonymous.*   BLPA; FaBoBe

..."Would you mind if I changed my name to/Tangerine?"   The Romance of Citrus.   Christy Sheffield Sanford.   APU

Would you still, unchanged as I,/Choose the lover you have chosen?   Intermezzo.   Robert Silliman Hillyer.   NePoAm

Would you think Mrs. Howard ne'er thought it was she?'   I Said to My Heart.   Charles, Earl of Peterborough Mordaunt.   NOEC

Would you turn her treat/into surprise observing/happy birthday   If You Saw a Negro Lady.   June Jordan.   IHMS; NMM

Wouldn't be no captain keep me out on this line.   Ain't No More Cane on This Brazos.   *Anonymous.*   FSW

Wouldn't even go my bail.   Roll in My Sweet Baby's Arms.   *Anonymous.* FSW

Wouldn't it be dreadful if you'd no nose to tell/Of every wonderful, wonderful smell?   The World Is Full of Wonderful Smells.   Zhenya Gay.   TiPo

Wouldn't it be glorious? Wouldn't it be fun?   Very Lovely.   Rose Fyleman. SoPo; TiPo

Wouldn't no good fellow/Be your man.   To Midnight Nan at Leroy's. Langston Hughes.   AnAmPo

Wouldn't you like to know?   Wouldn't You Like to Know.   John Godfrey Saxe.   HBV 1-2

Wouldst thou have me the bright lot forego?/Oh! no! no!   The Dying Enthusiast.   James Clarence Mangan.   IrPN

Wound in mind's wandering/As mummies in the mummy-cloth are wound. All Souls' Night.   William Butler Yeats.   MoVE

Wound me, that I, through endless sleep,/May bear the scar of you.   Blue Squills.   Sara Teasdale.   HBMV

A wound that never will heal.   The Shadow.   Richard Henry Stoddard. AA

Wounded and dedd my dere sone, dere.   Mary Complains to Other Mothers. *Anonymous.*   MeEL

A wounded beast upon the marriage bed/from which Love ran.   At Christmas.   Robert Duncan.   NoAm

The wounded hands, the weary human face.   E Tenebris.   Oscar Wilde. BrPo; CABA; CAW; MoBrPo; TreFT; TrPWD

Wounderis of the sownd and ferly at he hes sene.   The Aeneid.   Virgil (Publius Vergilius Maro).   OBVE

Wounding one soul, you wound the soul of all,/The unity of Life, the soul of God.   Crucifixion.   Eva Gore Booth.   WGRP

Wounding their patrons whom they ought to love.   Ingratitude.   Francis Thynne.   PBBP

The wounds/perfectly/cut   Words.   David Phillips.   NeAC

Wow! Wow! Wow!   Speak Roughly to Your Little Boy.   Lewis (Charles Lutwidge Dodgson) Carroll.   FaBoCh; FaBoCo; LoGBV; NLV; Par

A wowl is the ultimate substance.   When It Burns before the Harps and Freezes behind the Easels.   Hans Arp.   FaBoNo

The wrack may drift ashore.   Sea Wrack.   Moira O'Neill.   OnYI

Wracks triumphs be which Love high-set doth breed.   Astrophel and Stella, XLII.   Sir Philip Sidney.   AAS; SiPS

Wrap it round me when I die!   The Battle-Flag of Sigurd.   Dora Greenwell. OBVV

Wrap their old limbs with sombre ivy twine.   November.   Hartley Coleridge. LoBV; OBRV

Wrap up in flannel for the night that started/thousands of miles before, hundreds of times away.   Living in the Moment.   Marilyn Hacker.   NYP

Wrapped in a cloak of unremembrance,/Forever remaining without speech. Blessed Are Those Who Sow and Do Not Reap.   A. Ben-Yitzhak.   VWA

Wrapped in a veil of yellow gauze.   Impressions.   Oscar Wilde.   SyP

Wrapped one by one/in the terrible headlines.   The Mummies.   Maxine W. Kumin.   Psk

Wrapped up in blankets.   Poem for a Suicide.   George Economou.   DFF

Wrapped up, O Lord, in man's degeneration.   Caelica XCVII.   Fluke, Lord Brooke Greville

The wrath of stone.   A Holy Hill.   George William Russell.   AWP

Wreath and enlap and anoint them/Behind separate doors.   Sunday Afternoon in Italy.   D. H. Lawrence.   BrPo

A wreath of/green-green melodies.   Poem for Thel–the Very Tops of Trees. John Major.   NBP

A wreath to lay upon his bier.   Atonement.   Margaret E. Bruner.   PoToHe

Wreathed shall with incense be/Thy sharp-thorned may.   The Hawthorn Hath a Deathly Smell.   Walter De la Mare.   AtBAP; BrPo

The wreaths of Pere-la-Chaise!   La Grisette.   Oliver Wendell Holmes   AA; HBV 1-2

The wreck and ruin of what once was great.   To My Native Land.   James Clarence Mangan.   AnIL; IrPN

The wreck of matter and the crash of worlds.   Cato's Soliloquy.   Joseph Addison.   GoTF; TreFS; WBLP

A wreck upon the shores of Paradise.   An Epitaph.   J. C. Squire.   HBMV

The wren had ate the porridge down.   Greed.   *Anonymous.*   OxNR

...Wren on a cattail-stalk,/Chortling what he meant to sing!   Counting-Out Rhyme for March.   Frances Frost.   YeAr

Wrestling the Devil seemed to be/Quite a relief to Anthony.   The Temptations of Saint Anthony.   Phyllis McGinley.   OBSP

...Wrestling/with strangers on the couch.   Piccante.   Mary Di Michele. AMV-81

A wretch but lean relief on earth can find.   Antonio and Mellida (excerpt). John Marston.   ViBoPo

The wretch that dares not die! Macpherson's Farewell. Robert Burns. BSV

Wretched in this alone, that thou mayst take/All this away, and me most wretched make. Sonnets, XCI. "Some glory in their birth, some in their skill." William Shakespeare. CBEP

Wretches, alas! that know not where we go. Song: "We'll, placed in Love's triumphant chariot high." William Cavendish, Duke of Newcastle. OBSP

Wriggling, giggling, noise, and tattling. Polly, Dolly, Kate and Molly. *Anonymous.* BBGG

Wringing her hands and gnashing her teeth,/And no redemption for relief. Wicked Polly. *Anonymous.* BFSS

Wrinkled acknowledgement of the moon's clarity. Memory of Hills (excerpt). Rex Ingamells. CBAP

...Wrist watches over the pulses of/airmen eager to go to France... Clocks. Carl Sandburg. CrMA

Writ in a language no man living reads. Etruscan Tombs. Agnes Mary Frances (Mme Emile Duclaux) Robinson. WHA

Write: about the stillness here./Yes. Starvation Camp near Jaslo. Wislawa Szymborska. WPOW

Write, and I'll come. Me to You. Alastair Reid. NYBP

Write, do write. Write, Do Write. Marilyn Chin. BrSi

"Write me a poem!" Simplicity. Louis Simpson. PAI; Prf

Write nothing more; say that he loved old ships. Say That He Loved Old Ships. Daniel Whitehead Hicky. EtS

Write on a fairer, whiter page,/The record of thy happier reign. Centennial Hymn. William Cullen Bryant. PAH

Write on the wind, write on the rushing waves. My Woman. Caius Valerius Catullus. PoPl

Write/or come back, before I forget/what we both look like. Lines for a Friend Who Left. John Logan. DFF

...Write, then, on thy womb,/Of the not born, yet buried, here's the tomb. To Fine Lady Would-Be. Ben Jonson. FaBoEE; JCP; NoP; OBSP

Write this on my tomb, that in love I was true. The Green Willow. *Anonymous.* OBSC

Write when you can. Love,/Sharon. Empty at the Heart of Things. Frank Polite. APU

The writer and the named are gone. Thesis, Antithesis, and Nostalgia. Alan Dugan. CAD; PCP

Writes different, more helpful messages/in the high skies of the old country. If You Don't Stay Bitter for Too Long. Charles Mungoshi. WhB

Writhed into a stiff pool. Pool. Carl Sandburg. AP

Writing a last word. Driftwood. Daniel Smythe. RFM

...Writing/details of agony carefully into the Night Report. The Malice of Innocence. Denise Levertov. NNaP

Writing out love like this. Russian Asylum. Marilyn Bowering. CaPN; NOBC

Writing red in the spaces where it said red,/yellow where it said yellow. The Fashionable Heart. Jack Gilbert. NPGG

Writing these poems!/Imagine!' Autobiographia Literaria. Frank O'Hara. NNaP; NOBA

The writings are my only wings away. Without That Once Clear Aim. Stephen Spender. CMoP

The wrong angel takes over the lesson. Two Fishermen. Stanley Moss. CoAP; VWA

Wrong rules the land and waiting Justice sleeps. God, Give Us Men! Josiah Gilbert Holland. BLPA; GoTF; PAL; TreF; WBLP

Wrong's own darkness comes the welcome strength of/Right. Life's Lesson. Ella Wheeler Wilcox. PoToHe

Wrong since genesis. Grandmother. Henry Carlile. DFF; GP

Wrong sways the sceptre and Justice must yield. The Death of Justice. Walter Everette Hawkins. PoBA

The wrong with power by right and not by wrong suppressing. On Mercenary and Unjust Bailiffs. Henricus Selyns. SCAP

Wrongs fade beyond the shore and time invites/an easy confabulation. The Grand Duke of New York. Dan Pagis. VWA

Wrote it, and erased again. Anthony. Jane Shore. DFF

Wrote personal poems read by everyone,/naming no one. To My Friends. Peter Levi. NePoEA-2

Wrote, Shall not perish from the earth... and stopped. They Will Look for a Few Words. Nancy Byrd Turner. AmFN

Wrought by this pendulum that swings/Sedately to and fro. The Eight-Day Clock. Alfred Cochrane. HBV 1-2

Wrought of high laughter, loveliness and ease? Upon a House Shaken by the Land Agitation. William Butler Yeats. CMoP

Wrung with despair, profound/Audiences of the dead. Strangers. R. S. Thomas. NMP

Wumman's beauty gies man true content. Flooer o the Gean. George Campbell Hay. OxBS

Wy, I'm a kind o' peri-Wig. The Biglow Papers. James Russell Lowell AA

Wynken/Blynken,/And Nod. Wynken, Blynken, and Nod. Eugene Field. BeLS; FaFP; HBVY; MOON

Wyoming/ from the train/yesterday. Snow Country. Dave Etter. AmFN

X

X,Y,Z is the name on our stern. The Sailor's Alphabet. *Anonymous.* AmFP; OBSS

XYZ and &/All wished for/a piece in hand The Tragical Death of A, Apple Pie. *Anonymous.* OxNR

Y

Y'are left here to lament/Your poor estates, alone. To Meadows. Robert Herrick. AWP; CaPo; CBEP; HBV 1-2; InPo; JCP; LoBV; NOBE; OBEV; QFR; ViBoPo

Y-dight in stew ful swithe wel,/Powdred with gilofre and canel. The Land of Cockayne. *Anonymous.* OxBM

Y-e-a-h! Dream Boogie. Langston Hughes. AmPP

Y Franco se va paseo. Venga Jaleo. *Anonymous.* FSW

Y vaith wooll wee, that wee wooll y vaith lo! Coame, Malkyn, Hurle Thine Oyz at Hodge Trillindle. *Anonymous.* NCEP

Ya gotta give it to me/if ya really want it/i'm/the only one/can handle it Somebody Almost Walked Off Wid Alla My Stuff. Ntozake Shange. WPOW

...Ya/Know what I mean? Tact. Paul Pascal. PV; WeW

Yah! Yah! I want to go home to my ma! Life in a Half-breed Shack. *Anonymous.* CoSo

Yammering fearfully at the sound of drums. Jungle. Phyllis Haring. PeSA

The Yankee tars for fighting are the dandy, O! The Constitution and Guerriere. *Anonymous.* ABF; AmFP; AmSS; FSW; PAH; ViBoFo

A yard of Holland for an ell of Cotton. On Tom Holland and Nell Cotton. *Anonymous.* FaBoEE

...The yardman's/Flung brick perfected his laugh. Medallion. Sylvia Plath. HeIP; SM

The yards are so much higher. The Sun's over the Foreyard. Christopher Morley. EtS

Yasumiko have I got! I have got her. Fujiwara no Kamatari. LiTW

Yawning, and content to fall/Into any bed at all. Bridal Couch. Donald J. Lloyd. NIP

Yawning like a cobweb/stretched across/the bay. September Butterfly. Mollie Boring. AMV-80

Yawns & passes out/muttering...agnes...agnes Agnes. Mah-do-ge Tohee. STE

Yawns sobbingly, his head falls back, he sleeps. Pilots, Man Your Planes. Randall Jarrell. MoAB; MoAmPo

"Ye, and continue', quod Consience; and to the kirke I/wente. The Vision of Piers Plowman. William Langland. OxBM

Ye are many—they are few.' The Mask of Anarchy. Percy Bysshe Shelley. CABL; LoBV; OBSV; SCV

Ye aye sall be my dearie!' Ca' the Yowes to the Knowes. Isobel Pagan. OBEV

Ye be my friends, and so be but few else. Luckes, my fair falcon, and your fellows all. Sir Thomas Wyatt. AAS; FCP

Ye beir the name of landis of lenth and breid,/The well of vertew and flour of womanheid. The Well of Vertew and Flour of Womanheid. *Anonymous.* OxBS

Ye call me by the ear and eye! O to Be Up and Doing. Robert Louis Stevenson. GoTF; TreFT; TRV

Ye cannot stifle her sincere lament. Wine and Grief. Solomon Ibn Gabirol. LiTW; TrJP

Ye cry aloud, and then are still, O Bells of/Lynn! The Bells of Lynn. Henry Wadsworth Longfellow. AA

Ye do lie,/Poor girls, neglected. To Violets. Robert Herrick. CaPo; EG; FaBoMo; HBV 1-2; JCP; MBW 1-2; NoP; OBEV; OBS; SeCP; TrGrPo; ViBoPo

Ye dogs of Rome must die! Song of Hannibal: Rome. Marcus B. Christian. GoSl

Ye Fish! A Warryer's not for pece that soone Sonnet: "My Duchess was the werst she laffed she bitte." Ernest Walsh. ErPo

Ye gods! he leaves me and my babe to be! Theseus and Ariadne. Lloyd Mifflin. AA

An ye had a mind to save my life,/Ye should na shamed me here.' Mary Hamilton (B version). *Anonymous.* CBEP; ESPB

"Ye have done it unto Me." Little Things. *Anonymous.* STF

Ye have souls in heaven too,/Double-lived in regions new! To the Poets. John Keats. HBV 1-2; ViBoPo

Ye have the future grand and great,/The safe appeal of Truth to Time! For Righteousness' Sake. John Greenleaf Whittier. AmePo; PoEL 1-5

Ye hinna traivelled far'er than the Hielan' Hills o' Mar.' Dolomites. J. C. Milne. PoSH

Ye living men, come, view the ground/Where you must shortly lie. Plenary. Anonymous. AmFP

An' ye'll get a cakie/When the baker comes in. Hush-a-Baa, Baby. Anonymous. OxNR

Ye'll get a whippie/And a supple Tam! In Scotland. Anonymous. OxNR

Ye'll happy be and ye'll happy be,/For they are frank and free. The Rantin Laddie. Anonymous. AmFP

Ye'll keep none when death's come, say I! Song: "Old Farmer Oats and his son Ned." John Jay Chapman. PoEL 1-5

Ye'll know it's under rue an' rose that I would like to be,/That I would like to be. Grandmither, Think Not I Forget. Willa Sibert Cather. HBV 1-2

Ye'll no gather your nieves fou. Riddle: "Banks fou, braes fou." Anonymous. GBP

Ye'll think na mair o your bonny/hyn/Beneath the hollin tree.' The Bonny Hind. Anonymous. ESPB; OxBB; ViBoFo

Ye love me, though, since mine is not/The mystery of wrath! Song of the Mariner's Needle. C. R. Clarke. EtS

Ye love that God which bought you deare. Of Gods Omnipotencie. Alexander Hume. NOCV

An ye may boast in southin lans/Your sister's playd you scorn.' The Gay Goshawk (A version). Anonymous. ESPB

Ye may harowe their troth in St. Madron's/well. The Doom-Well of St. Madron. Robert Stephen Hawker. VLP

Ye may my life save or expel/Even as ye list. As power and wit will me assist. Sir Thomas Wyatt. FCP; SiPS

Ye may not see, for peeping flowers, the grass. Not Iris in Her Pride. George Peele. ViBoPo

Ye may tak' ten–before folk. Behave Yoursel' before Folk. Alexander Rodger. HBV 1-2

Ye may tell their wives and bairnies/They're sleepin at Harlaw. The Battle of Harlaw (A version). Anonymous. ESPB

Ye Men of Kent, 'tis victory or death! To the Men of Kent. William Wordsworth. OBWP

Ye Mice, ye Mice, my great Avengers rise! The Battle of the Frogs and Mice. Homer. OBVE

Ye mith slain Clerk Saunders in open/field,/And no in bed wi me.' Clerk Saunders. Anonymous. ESPB

Ye must delve and I shall spin/In care to ledyn our life. Miracle Play: The Lament of Eve. Anonymous. ACP

Ye rains arise, ye winds arise,/Arise! Arise! Invocation for a Storm. Anonymous. WTO

Ye're welcomer to tak me, than to let me be. A Dainty Song. Allan Ramsay. OBEC

Ye's get as mieckle o my free lan/As he'll ride about in a summer's/day.' Lady Elspat. Anonymous. BuBa; ESPB

Ye saints, ascend the skies. Why Do We Mourn Departing Friends? Isaac Watts. AH

Ye shall another man obtain,/And I mine own and yours no more. Madam, withouten many words. Sir Thomas Wyatt. CBEP; FCP; NoP; OBSP

Ye shall find the embers burning,/Still, upon the ruined hearth! The Jewish May. Morris Rosenfeld. TrJP

Ye sir: helpe me to it now I beseche yow. Art Thou Heywood. John Heywood. NCEP

Ye that have bullied and bribed, tyrants, hypocrites, liars! The Rebel. Padraic Pearse. OnYI

Ye that have passions for a tear,/Give nature vent, and drop it here! The Power of Innocence. C. G. H. NOEC

"Ye, that is good," quod he; "now shul we here/Som deyntee thing, me thinketh by his chere." The Canterbury Tales: Prologue to Sir Thopas. Geoffrey Chaucer. Par

Ye that through your hearts to-day/Feel the gladness of the May! The Gladness of May. William Wordsworth. YeAr

Ye think you buy your face, and hire your muse. Epigram: "All praise your face, your verses none abuse." Horace Walpole. FaBoEE

Ye three Elizabeths for ever live,/That three such graces did unto me give. Amoretti, LXXIV. Edmund Spenser. AAS

Ye were but little at the first,/But mighty at the last. Little and Great. Charles Mackay. HBV 1-2; HBVY; PoLf

Ye who now will bless the poor,/Shall yourselves find blessing. Good King Wenceslas. John Mason Neale. FSW; HBV 1-2; HBVY; OHIP; OnMSP; TreFS

Ye who pass by, listen to my prayer: harm/me not. To the Wayfarer. Anonymous. SiSoSe

Ye will me thole to anchor in your heaven. Ship-Broken Men Whom Stormy Seas Sore Toss. William Fowler. BSV; GoTS

Ye write such words–as these of those who were! The Future. George Frederick Cameron. OBCV

Yea, all her peoples shout to thy name. God of Our Fathers. Melancthon W. Stryker. AH

Yea, all this world can give thee of delight,/And then eternity. To Colman Returning. Saint Colman. BIrV

Yea, and his own soul did he save/From burning in hell-fire. Canonicus and Roger Williams. Anonymous. PAH

Yea, and in quiet sleep/When all is done. A Man's Bread. Josephine Preston Peabody. YeAr

Yea, and with more abiding memories fraught. Night. Henri de Regnier. AWP

Yea, beds for all who come. Up-Hill. Christina Georgina Rossetti. BLPA; FaBoBe; FaBoRV; FPL; GoTF; HAP; HBV 1-2; LoBV; MCCG; NoP; OAEL 1-2; OAEP; OBNC; PoRA; TrCP; TreFS; ViBoPo; VLP; WHA; WiR

Yea, Dinah, whar 'ould you be now, exceptin' fur dat pra'r? The Power of Prayer. Sidney and Clifford Lanier. HBV 1-2

Yea, ere we knew, Sir Philip's sword was drawn/With valiant cut and thrust, and he was gone. The Knight in Disguise. Vachel Lindsay. HBV 1-2

...Yea, even that Noon/When darkness filled the earth till the ninth hour. Zermatt. Thomas Hardy. OBNC

Yea, even the bitterness of love/Is bitter-sweet. Winter Love Song. Anonymous. LiTW

Yea, flesh itself is bursting into song! Love Redeemed. William Baylebridge. PoAu 1-2

Yea, forehead to chin burn–/That I ensconce Swinburne! A Refusal. Thomas Hardy. FaBoCo; LiTB

Yea, from Delos up to Limerick and back! The Song of the Banjo. Rudyard Kipling. FaBoCh; PrIm; VLP

Yea from his own mouth he will freely unfold,/The sum and the substance of what I have told. Man's Amazement. Anonymous. CoMu

"Yea he; and he brought such; and you'll know him/anon." Who's in the Next Room? Thomas Hardy. PoEL 1-5; PoPle; QFR; WSC

Yea I'll fall upon the rock. I Will Bow and Be Simple. Anonymous. EaLo

"Yea, in good fayth. Then am I yours/alsoo." Love Dialogue. Anonymous. CoBE

Yea, Jesus be Himself to thee the Same/As that He is declared by His Name. A Wish. Anonymous. CAW

Yea, Jesus, Son of God, has not a stone/Whereon to lay His head! Jesus. Ramon Pimentel Coronel. CAW

Yea Lett the Lord confound them, who with spight/Against his Truth maliciously Fight. Claudius Gilbert Anagram. Tis Braul I Cudgel. John Wilson. SCAP

Yea, love through heart it dies–it dies. O Softly Singing Lute. Francis Pilkington. OAEP

Yea. Millions-of-Years, O my Mother, my Heart! He Approacheth the Hall of Judgment. Book of the Dead. AWP

Yea, Mother of Living,/Thou dost not permit!... Pursuit. Julian Tuwim. TrJP

Yea, O my Saviour, for ever and ever. Communion Hymn of the Ancient Irish Church. Anonymous. CAW

Yea, right gladly/Will I come. After Work. John Oxenham. TRV

Yea, strange things and spectral may men have beheld in Jezreel! Jezreel. Thomas Hardy. NoP

Yea! sun and moon are sent by her,/And every wistful waiting star. Song: "She's somewhere in the sunlight strong." Richard Le Gallienne. HBV 1-2; OBEV; OBVV

Yea, thankfully,/For joy. Upon a Spider Catching a Fly. Edward Taylor. AmP; AmPP; AP; CBEP; MAmP; NePA; NOBA; NoP; OxBA; PoEL 1-5; SCAP; TAP

Yea, they shall sing for love when Christ shall come. If Only. Christina Georgina Rossetti. EBCP; OxBoCh; TrCP

Yea, though I'm sorry for thee. A Youth Mowing. D. H. Lawrence. InPK; MoAB; MoBrPo; NoAm; TrGrPo

Yea, turn back awhile to thy travail when the/Gods stood aloof to behold? Iceland First Seen. William Morris. OBTV; PoEL 1-5; VLP

Yea unto thee beldams drink metheglin,/And anises, and caraway, and gin. Where Didst Thou Find, Young Bard. John Keats. CBEP

Yea, we twain shall sleep together in an equal bed. Next of Kin. Christina Georgina Rossetti. HBV 1-2

Yeah, damn near drunk and dancing in the streets. Dark Prophesy: I Sing of Shine. Etheridge Knight. GP

Yeah, I'll find you baby/'cause you rode that old YM & V Y M & V Blues. Lost John Hunter. BluL

"Yeah i'm in here"/"ok." Inside a Prison Cell at Count Time. Daniel L. Klauck. LFAC

Yeah if i were/a poet i'd kid/nap you Kidnap Poem. Nikki Giovanni. BPo; GOYP; NoAm; TAP

Yeah, poor me's down so low, baby/ooo lord gal, Big Bill is looking up to down Looking Up at Down. Big Bill Broonzy. BluL

Yeah, stranger! You bet he did! The Wickedest Man in Memphis. Alex J. Brown. BeLS

Yeah, they gonna be gathering all round my throne Alley Blues. Wright Holmes. BluL

Yeah, they helped me. Did They Help Me at the State Hospital for the Criminally Insane? Mbembe Milton Smith. FAZ

...Yeah watermelon is what I'm talking/about Watermelon. Watermelon. Ted Joans. GP

Yeah, Winter's coming/darkness–God!–I hate to see it come. Chickens. Geof Hewitt. FAZ

Year after year of them must pass/Till I go to his home. Widow's Lament. *Anonymous.* BoWoP

Year by year on his way to the South Sea. The South. Wang Chien. AWP

Year follows year,/And life goes on. The Hermit. Hsu Pen. RFM

A year for every yard. Art and Reality. James Simmons. CIP

A year from today; together/With all whom we like. More Power. Egan O'Rahilly. BIrV; OnYI

The year his winter cloak lets fall. Rondeau. Charles, Duc d' Orleans. LiTW

The year lays down his mantle cold. Spring. Charles d'Orleans. AWP; CTC

The year/the century this day/makes complete. The Newest Banana Plant Leaf. Ingrid Wendt. NMM

A year to welcome gain or loss,/and humbly all Thy blessings claim. Another Year. Oswald J. Smith. STF

Yearn'd to be free from time, and felt that this life is a thraldom. A Vision of Judgement. Robert Southey. FaBoPP

Yearned outward toward the rocky land. The Migrations of People. Dorothy Leiser. AMV-80

Yearning for a patch of grass. The Drivers of Boston. June Gross. AMV-80

Yearning for that far home that might have been. To N. V. de. G. S. Robert Louis Stevenson. BrPo

Yearning toward Heaven until its wish was heard,/Desire unspeakably to be a bird? To an Oriole. Edgar Fawcett. HBV 1-2

A yearning, upward burning/spirit-fire. Within Us, Too. R. H. Grenville. AMV-80

...The years/a forest of giant stones, of fossil stumps,/blocking the altar. The Poem Unwritten. Denise Levertov. CAPP

The years are smoke. "Luckies". Reginald Gibbons. MAYP

Years from now, wanting to be remembered. Tonight when You Leave... Gayle Elen Harvey. AMV-81

The years have taken from me. Softly I go now, pad pad. Pad, Pad. Stevie Smith. ELU

Years I have loved in, lived in, and been glad! Birthday. Elaine V. Emans. BiCB

The years their disappointments waste/On a memory so chaste. Love-Songs, At Once Tender and Informative. Samuel Hoffenstein. OBAL

...Years whose casual ignorant lovers/We were for a season. The Repeated Journey. Thomas McGrath. NePoEA

Yeeld to Samela. Menaphon. Robert Greene. AtBAP

(Yeh/Play it a long time now boy) Stamp Blues. Tony Hollins. BluL

Yelled theyre leathalle knelle, sonke ynn the waves, and dyde. Elinoure and Juga. Thomas Chatterton. LAuP

A yellow angel pedals about the world. Sun Filters through My Window. Artie Gold. CaPN

The yellow ash, so close. Elegy. Olga Broumas. LTB

A yellow candle flame/no wind or weather dare extinguish. Myrtle. Ted Kooser. GOYP

Yellow chicken lying broken but/efficient on its shelf. Shopping. Jane Chance Nitzche. AMV-80

Yellow clay on dust! The Poet and His Book. Edna St. Vincent Millay. AmLP; MoAmPo; NePA

A yellow night/in another kingdom. It Was Gentle. Hedva Harkavi. VWA

The yellow of sulfur, the finger, the road home. Yellow. Charles Wright. AmPA

Yellow space. The blackness, blank. Too Many Miles of Sunlight between Us. Jack Myers. AMV-80

An' yer should o' 'eard 'im larf. The Little Nipper an' 'Is Ma. George Fauvel Gouraud. AA

"Yes, Amigo"–hand on shoulder–/"It was I." The Use of Fiction. Naomi Shihab Nye. MAYP

Yes, and chilled with fear and despair. Judith of Bethulia. John Crowe Ransom. CrMA; DTC; FaBoMo; FYAP; LiTA; LiTM; MoPo; NePA; NoAm; NOBA

Yes, and in hell would whisper, I have known. The Inner Light. Frederic William Henry Myers. HBV 1-2; WGRP

Yes, and my heart going like mad and yes saying yes/I will yes! Emily Dickinson's Sestina for Molly Bloom. Barbara F. Lefcowitz. SM

Yes, and the field flowers, these deceptive blossoms,/Break from the furnace. The Furnace of Colors. Vernon Watkins. NYBP

Yes, be so col'! My Old Hammah (with music). *Anonymous.* AS

Yes, boss/I will be your coal! Black Cry. Jose Craveirinha. WhB

Yes! but not his–'tis Death itself that dies. My Baptismal Birthday. Samuel Taylor Coleridge. NOCV

"Yes, but the stars are now his dwelling-place." The Tomb of Diogenes. *Anonymous.* AWP

Yes, by golly, when the tide comes in. Nursery Rhyme: "Yellow-belly, yellow-belly, come and take a swim." *Anonymous.* OxBoLi

"Yes, dear! they are all at home." Are the Children at Home? Margaret Sangster. HBV 1-2

Yes. Devoting myself entirely to that boy. Some Litanies. Michael Benedikt. CoAP; TwCP

Yes; drive a phaeton and four. On Thomas, Second Earl of Onslow. *Anonymous.* FaBoCo

Yes, God and man might now approve me/If thou hadst lived, and lived to love me! To a Lock of Hair. Sir Walter Scott. GTBS-P

...Yes he's death's, he's/eternity's, one-tenth. The Tip. Albert Goldbarth. HaCAP

Yes he says/what is it? Responses. Robert Hershon. PoL

Yes; here it was! The Mound. Thomas Hardy. OxBTC

Yes:–his pointless perpetual ditty/Perplexes pyramidal piles! Ravings (parody). Tom (Thomas Hood, Jr.) Hood. BXAP; Par

Yes. I am looking. I wish I could be like them. Behold the Lilies of the Field. Anthony Hecht. CoPo; NePoEA-2

Yes, I have discovered yes... Of Reason and Discovery. Don Mattera. WhB

Yes, I have heard the nightingale. Hast Thou Heard the Nightingale? Richard Watson Gilder. AA

Yes, I hear it; 'tis somebody that's callin' out for help. Johnny Rich. Will Carleton. PeD

Yes, I hear your faint voice: "This is/rest, and like sleeping!" The Unillumined Verge. Robert Bridges. AA

Yes I hope that things will work out somehow. The Return of the Proconsul. Zbigniew Herbert. FaBoPV

Yes, I'm always true to you, darlin', in my way. Always True to You in My Fashion (excerpt). Cole Porter. NLV

Yes I'm goin' to fishin'/I'm a-goin' to fishin' too. Fishing Blues. Henry Thomas. BluL

Yes, I must love some one, really/And it might as well be you! Tell Me Pretty Maiden. Owen Hall. FSN

Yes, I think you can count on that, old boy–tonight'll be a thick/night. Officers' Mess. Gavin Ewart. OxBTC

Yes, I want God's heab'n to be mine,/Save me, Lord, save me. I Want God's Heab'n to Be Mine. *Anonymous.* BoAN 1-2

Yes, I want to go to heab'n when I die,/To see God's bleedin' Lam'. To See God's Bleeding Lam'. *Anonymous.* BoAN 1-2

Yes, I was dancing-mad, and how/That came to be the bears and Yeats would know. Four for Sir John Davies. Theodore Roethke. NOBA; UnS

Yes, if I don't see you tomorrow/I hope I'll meet you early the next day Katie May. Lightning Hopkins. BluL

Yes. In the echo of my deaths/there is still fear. Fear. Alejandra Pizarnik. AMV-80

Yes, indeed.... Slim Greer. Sterling A. Brown. BALP; BANP

Yes, it was a hard death. Resurrection–An Easter Sequence (excerpt). W. R. Rodgers. ACV

Yes, Jesus loves me,/The Bible tells me so. Jesus Loves Me, This I Know. Anna B. Warner. AH

Yes, Lizbie Browne! To Lizbie Browne. Thomas Hardy. DTC; ELP; EnLit; NOBV

"Yes, love," said he, "by marriage." Repartee. *Anonymous.* GoTF; TreFT

Yes masked balls./Poor Augustine. Ladies' Voices. Gertrude Stein. SOTW

Yes more than naked, dressed in not even skin. The Waltz. Hilary Corke. NYBP

Yes, mother, I will get up,/I will get up today. Lazy Mary. *Anonymous.* AmFP

Yes, mourner, you shall be free,/When the good Lord sets you free. Old Marse John. *Anonymous.* TTY

"Yes, my darling, by and by." BOO! Old Woman All Skin and Bone. *Anonymous.* TrAS

Yes, my Neaera! yes, 'tis thee! Neaera's Kisses. Johannes Secundus. UnTE

Yes, not quite/the same. The Tower. Philip Booth. NePoEA-2

Yes, old Rattler was a-barkin' at the moon. John Henry (variant). *Anonymous.* ABF

Yes, one in a graven silence no bird breaks. Father and Son. Frederick Robert Higgins. ACV; BIrV; OxBI

Yes, or else go alive to heaven. No, I Am Not as Others Are. Francois Villon. AWP

"Yes," said Uncle Alfred, "This is Raven Brook,/and here is Jake waiting for us."   Novembers or Straight Life.   Maureen Owen.   APU

"Yes"–sh! sh! sh!   Sing-Song Rhyme.   Anonymous.   SiSoSe

Yes, she'a a rare and fair land–/This native land of mine.   My Land. Thomas Osborne Davis.   HBV 1-2; PAL

Yes, she's a good little girl/but she just won't be true   You Never Miss the Water.   L. C. Williams.   BluL

Yes sir/that was/a specialist   To the Heart.   Tadeusz Rozewicz.   PoL

Yes, ten years of smouldering in jail,/about to erupt in death...   Ordinary People on Sunday.   Tom Veitch.   ANYP

Yes, then, up there, we'll understand.   Some Time We'll Understand. Maxwell N. Cornelius.   BLRP; WBLP

Yes, they/are blue and/now gone–/amazing.   Aves.   Ted Morison. AMV-81

Yes, this is where the People take tea.   In a Chain-Store Cafeteria.   Paul L. Grano.   NOAV

"Yes. This one. This time. This is the place."   Crossing with the Light. Dwight Okita.   BrSi

"Yes, Tim, you would."   Journey Back to Christmas.   Gwen Dunn.   OBCP

Yes! Washington would be the place for me.   Shakespearean Soliloquy in Progress: "Tubby or not tubby–" (parody).   Sir Francis Cowley Burnand. BXAP

Yes, we are still here.   Dawn Walk.   Edward Hirsch.   MAYP

Yes we did!/Yes we did!   Martin's Blues.   Michael S. Harper.   CNA; HaCAP; PoBA

Yes, we'll trust in the Lord,/And he will provide.   In Some Way or Other the Lord Will Provide.   Mrs. M. A. W. Cook.   AH

Yes, we're all dodging out a way through the world.   The Dodger. Anonymous.   AmFP; FSW; OuSiCo

Yes, we were looking at each other   Looking at Each Other.   Muriel Rukeyser.   NNaP

"Yes. Well, I'll be going. Kiss me..." "Good/night"..."Good night."   In the Orchard.   Muriel Stuart.   ErPo; FF; OxBTC

Yes, yes, I will forever sit/There, where thy Side was split.   We Greet Each Other in the Side (parody) (excerpt).   Anonymous.   BXAP; PeD

Yes, you can be friendly.   Be Friendly.   Walter E. Isenhour.   STF

Yes, you know this life I'm living I been living/Oh lord, for a great many years.   Death Bells.   Lightning Hopkins.   BluL

Yes, you mus' be lovin' at God's comman'.   Gimme Yo' Han'.   Anonymous. BoAN 1-2

Yes, you must go.   Bootie Black and the Seven Giants All Sipping Chili... Mike Cook.   JB

Yes, you're the one/Will have the blues.   The Backlash Blues.   Langston Hughes.   BPo

Yes,/you've got something here.   Brooklyn Bridge.   Vladimir Mayakovsky. NYP

Yesterday a Mountain he–/But a shade today!   Cuchullain's Lament over Fardiad.   Anonymous.   AnIV

Yesterday i thot id die loving u/or (be loving u when i die)?   Sex Play in Four Acts.   Doug Fetherling.   NeAC

Yesterday, today, forever,/Jesus Christ, the same.   Saints in Glory, We Together.   Nehemiah Adams.   AH

Yesterday we had a world to lose.   The Last Picnic.   Stanley Jasspon Kunitz.   NoAm

Yet a druidic difference/Enhances nature now.   Farther in summer than the birds.   Emily Dickinson.   PoEL 1-5; QFR

Yet a Druidic Difference/Enhances Nature now.   Further in Summer Than the Birds.   Emily Dickinson.   ForPo; LiTA; MAmP; NOBA; NoP

, Yet a face the beach wears between sunset and/dusk.   Sandhill People. Carl Sandburg.   CMoP

Yet a feeling's ever present/That the Old Times were the best.   The Old Times Were the Best.   James Whitcomb Riley.   FaFP

Yet a little clay/Will fill it by and by.   Three Proverbs.   James Clarence Mangan.   IrPN

Yet a the beds is na sae saft/As the bellies of the lasses O.   Green Grows the Rashes.   Anonymous.   GBP

Yet aching almost as promptly as a boy.   Versions of Love.   Roy Fuller. LiTM

Yet, after all, I think I've gleaned my/modicum of Laughing-Stuff.   The House of a Hundred Lights.   Ridgely Torrence.   AA

Yet ah! how much must that poor heart endure,/Which hopes from thee, and thee alone, a cure!   Sonnet: "O Time! who know'st a lenient hand to lay." William Lisle Bowles.   OBEC

Yet, ah, my maiden Muse doth blush to tell the best.   Astrophel and Stella, LXXVII.   Sir Philip Sidney.   AAS; SiPS

Yet, alas! the sooner turning/Into hopeless, endless mourning...   Sleep Not, Dream Not.   Emily Bronte.   LoBV

Yet, alexandra's night shadow is soaked and drips with my tears.   A Poem in Black and White.   Mongane Wally Serote.   WhB

Yet all are in one body, and as one appeare.   The Faerie Queene.   Edmund Spenser.   FaBoEn

Yet all in order sweet and lovely. Men are sick with love.   The Vision of Beulah.   William Blake.   NOBE

Yet all like Fox can game–like Pitt can drink.   On Imitation.   Samuel Taylor Coleridge.   OBSP

Yet all men henceforth be afraid to write.   To Fletcher Reviv'd.   Richard Lovelace.   OBS

Yet all of a piece and clever/And at some level, true.   On Falling Asleep to Birdsong.   William Meredith.   PoCh

Yet all of these drink blood.   Glory.   D. H. Lawrence.   OBSP

Yet all other music is poor and thin/By the side of this which thou never shalt win!   The Boy and the Flute.   Bjornstjerne Bjornson.   AWP; PoPl

Yet all the day I glowed before the fire.   Two at a Fireside.   Edwin Markham.   TRV

Yet all the winters cannot blow its sweetness quite away.   A Spring Journey. Alice Freeman Palmer.   HBV 1-2

Yet all the world may see/Phillida flouts me.   The Disdainful Shepherdess. Anonymous.   OBSC

Yet all these fences and their whole array/One cunning bosom-sin blows quite away.   Sin.   George Herbert.   NoP; ViBoPo

Yet always I keep coming back.   Forest.   Harriet Gray Blackwell.   GoYe

...Yet/another preferred to baas this dragon's land.   Era.   Jaki Seroke. WhB

...Yet any wild bird would envy you/This aviary, whenever you free all the birds in me.   Aviary.   Mebdh McGuckian.   FaBoIP

Yet are always saved/by judgment of good men.   Someone, I tell you. Sappho.   BoWoP

Yet are the bleak graves lonely in the rain.   The Last Furrow.   Edwin Markham.   AA

"Yet at least with the rose/Went a kiss that I'm wearing."   A Rose.   Arlo Bates.   HBV 1-2

:Yet at length quietness/Will cover those wistful eyes.   Joy.   Robinson Jeffers.   CMoP

Yet be fastidious, and have such friends/That when I think of them my soul ascends!   Shine on Me, Secret Splendor.   Edwin Markham.   TrPWD

Yet best, oh! best of all doth he/Who helps a fallen enemy.   Best of All. Anonymous.   WBLP

Yet between us the Atlantic.   Sundered.   Israel Zangwill.   TrJP

Yet blithe was she wi' Rab to cleek,/In marriage, wi' the care o't.   Marriage and the Care O't.   Robert Lochore.   HBV 1-2

Yet both of us will find it...   Love Play.   William Cavendish, Duke of Newcastle.   ErPo

Yet both stand idle, till God's call/Set them to worke for God.   How Busie Are the Sonnes of Men?   Roger Williams.   SCAP

Yet, brothers, pray for but one thing–/The marvelous peace of God.   They Cast Their Nets in Galilee.   William Alexander Percy.   AH

Yet burnished by its passage, and still warm.   The Harvest Bow.   Seamus Heaney.   FaBoIP

Yet by God's death the stars shall stand/And the small apples grow.'   King Alfred Answers the Danes.   Gilbert Keith Chesterton.   OxBoCh

Yet by thy weapon liv'st! Thou hast one good part.   To Pertinax Cob.   Ben Jonson.   JCP

Yet cannot blink and cannot bless/God's manifest ungraciousness. Reflections in a Little Park.   Babette Deutsch.   ELU; NePoAm

Yet cannot they, while thou art present, weep.   La Vita Nuova.   Dante Alighieri.   AWP

Yet certain am I of the spot/As if the chart were given.   I never saw a moor. Emily Dickinson.   AA; AnNE; DiPo; EBCP; EvOK; FaFP; FPL; GN; GoTF; HBV 1-2; HeIP; LiTA; LiTM; MoAB; MoAmPo; NePA; PoLf; PoPl; TAP; TreF; TrGrPo; TRV; WGRP

Yet Christ is with me all the day.   The Second Crucifixion.   Richard Le Gallienne.   HBV 1-2; OBVV; WGRP

Yet Christ to Crowne will thee to heaven soone fet.   Mr. Eliot, Pastor of the Church of Christ at Roxbury...   Edward Johnson.   SCAP

Yet come I as I came of old,/From out the heart of Summer's joy.   Pomona. William Morris.   NOBV; WiR

Yet come it will when wisdom may control,/And one sound policy conduct the whole.   The Emigrant.   Standish O'Grady.   NOBC

Yet come no better off, for my quick ear.   Fatal Interview.   Edna St. Vincent Millay.   VGW

Yet cry, when tortured, where is Providence?   Inebriety (parody).   George Crabbe.   BXAP

...Yet despair/Touches me not, though pensive as a bird/Whose vernal coverts winter hath laid bare.   Composed near Calais, on the Road Leading to Ardres, August 7, 1802.   William Wordsworth.   FaBoPV

Yet did love at last relieve him.   Tityrus to His Fair Phyllis.   John Dickenson.   EIL

Yet do I know I run into the glede.   Some fowls there be...   Sir Thomas Wyatt.   FCP

Yet do I know Thy Love: have mercy, Lord...   The Scribe's Prayer.   Robert W. Service.   TrPWD

Yet do you know I shall carry always/that blemish on my breast?   Sadness. Barbara Guest.   AmPC

Yet do you up and leave me–then/I scream to have you back again? On Being a Woman. Dorothy Parker. FPL; PoLf

Yet docile, childlike, full of Life and Love! A Tombless Epitaph. Samuel Taylor Coleridge. OBRV

Yet envies none, none are unenviable. Musketaquid. Ralph Waldo Emerson. AP

Yet even these ne'er change their love. Song: "'Tis affection but dissembled." Sidney Godolphin. JCP

Yet every time I am caught,/every time waved down,/and taken for questioning. Living with You. Angela Langfield. FF

Yet, fair unkind, too good to be disgraced. Sonnet: "If chaste and pure devotion of my youth." Michael Drayton. ViBoPo

Yet far from us their influence is shown/In outward circles ever widening. The Trinity. Marian Osborne. CaP

Yet few there are that found them; Sin and Love. Philosophers Have Measured Mountains. George Herbert. TRV

Yet, for all your pomp and train,/Securer lives the silly swain. Jack and Joan. Thomas Campion EG; EnL; FaBoCh; FaPoR; HBV 1-2; OAEP

Yet for my sake make ye good chere;/Now have good day! I Am Christmas. Anonymous. OxBM

Yet for old sakes' sake she is still, dears,/The prettiest doll in the world. The Little Doll. Charles Kingsley. OxBChV

Yet from thee, Lord, all mercy flowes,/And each manns work is paid by thee. Psalm 62. Donne Deo. Mary Herbert, Countess of Pembroke. PBWP

Yet fundamentally/diamond-backed. For Windows. Robert Grenier. APU

Yet, girl, we hold love's possibility. Girl in Front of the Bank. Robert Wallace. DFF

Yet god all whole that may enjoy/Thy body as it is. Blest, Blest and Happy He. Anonymous. BSV; GBL; GoTS

Yet grant with me that Gascoignes passions past./Ever or Never. Gascoigne's Passion. George Gascoigne. NCEP

Yet grasse is greene, when flowers doe fade away. Where Wards Are Weak. Robert Southwell. NCEP

Yet growest more wretched than thy nature bears/By being placed in such a wretch as I. Astrophel and Stella, XCIV. Sir Philip Sidney. AAS; SiPS

Yet Gulielma was by far more fair. Elegy in Six Sonnets. Frederick Goddard Tuckerman. QFR

Yet had I rather thus for to remain/Than laugh, and live, not feeling lover's pain. Except I Love. Robert Parry. EIL

Yet, hang me, but I love her dearly. Lesbia Railing. Caius Valerius Catullus. AWP; LiTW

Yet harken Heaven's hymns to our combin'd:/Assumpta est Maria. Assumpta est Maria. Liam Brophy. ISi

Yet have I seen despised/Dainty white lilies, and sad flowers well prized. Song Set by Nicholas Yonge. Anonymous. CTC; OBSC

Yet he lived happily/I tell you. If Ever You Go to Dublin Town. Patrick Kavanagh. AnIL; CIP; CMoP; InPS; IPY; NMP

Yet he n'er falters–so, petrel, spring/Once more o'er the waves on thy stormy wing! The Stormy Petrel. Barry (Bryan Waller Procter) Cornwall. EtS; HBV 1-2

Yet he treated them all to the show! The Humours of Donnybrook Fair. Charles O'Flaherty. OnYI

...Yet here I am/More truly now this abstract act become. The Constructed Space. W. S. Graham. PoA

Yet here it weeps–long blind, long blind–/And cannot understand. Little Gray Songs from St. Joseph's, XLVII. Grace Fallow Norton. HBV 1-2

Yet Hiram Hopper needs no inspiration/But water on the brain. On a Prohibitionist Poem. Gilbert Keith Chesterton. ViBoPo

Yet his soul within is sweet. Pain. George William Russell. MoBrPo

Yet his was of amber only. Amber. Holger Drachmann. LiTW

Yet I am sure, wherever you have gone,/your martyrdom is hard as my black dawn. Sonnet XXIII: "What good is it to me if long ago." Louise Labe. BoWoP

Yet I am wounded for thee unto death. An Unbeliever. Anna Hempstead Branch. WGRP

Yet I am yourn, and you are mine! Palabras Grandiosas. Bayard Taylor. OBAL

Yet I await what hope the turning yields/And beg with empty hand. The Lonely Road. Kenneth Rand. HBV 1-2

Yet I cannot help but wonder why/a pigeon struts when he can fly. Pigeons. Robert F. Whisler. AMV-80

Yet I could lug him by the ears/For beating honest Cherry. Young Master's Account of a Puppet Show. John Marchant. OxBChV

...Yet I'd swear/That his cloak's much less worn than the hole in his rump. On Hedylus. Martial (Marcus Valerius Martialis). PeHV

...,Yet I draw courage to front the/way. O Desolate Eves. Christopher John Brennan. CoBE; PoAu 1-2

Yet I felt curiously healed/as if life were about to begin. Breathing the Strong Smell. Harold Norse. PeHV

Yet I have hope, by thy great power,/to spring; though now a wither'd flower. To God, on His Sickness. Robert Herrick. OxBoCh

Yet I have known no loneliness like this,/Locked in your arms and bent beneath your kiss. Solitude. Babette Deutsch. HBMV

Yet I have recklessly/Slept in strange places and strange ways. From That First Night. Izumi Shikibu. PBWP

Yet I keep the way of my will to the sea, when ye and your/race are not! The Song of the Colorado. Sharlot M. Hall. HBV 1-2

Yet I know not where to find her. The Wavering Planet. Anonymous. MOON

Yet I love refinement, and beauty and light/are for me the same as desire for the sun. Here are fine gifts, children. Sappho. BoWoP

Yet I preferred you so/My flower Yesterday Evening I Saw Your Corpse. Joyce Mansour. WPOW

Yet I shudder'd and thought like a fool of the sleep of death. The Sleeping House. Alfred, Lord Tennyson. OBNC

...Yet I/Still cannot fathom how they danced,/Or why. The Psalter of Avram Haktani. Abraham Moses Klein. PeCV

Yet I with them may share/The King's "well done!" This I Can Do. H. T. Lefevre. STF

Yet I write so much like me. So That's Who I Remind Me Of. Ogden Nash. BLPL; PoLf

Yet if thy love will not end,/Love thyself and friend. The Counsel. Alexander Brome. CavP

Yet in her eyes the doom of all change carries. Change. Fulke, Lord Brooke Greville. OBSC

Yet in my hart I then both speake and write,/The wonder that my wit cannot endite. Amoretti, III. Edmund Spenser. AAS; HBV 1-2; OAEP; PoEL 1-5

Yet, in something I was first–first to lose all five. First in the Pentathlon. Lucilius [(or Lucillius)]. LiSp

Yet in the morning may be seen/Where we the night before have been. The Fairy Queen. Anonymous. PoPle

Yet in the thought of Thee I will be strong! Be Thou My Guide. Florence Earle Coates. TrPWD

Yet in them all thy name dost write. Pastoral Hymn. John Hall. OxBoCh; TrPWD

Yet interpose no barrier between them,/that she may move in both. Lisa. Constance Carrier. SoSe

Yet is a secret lute/Awake in my heart. Independence. Mary Elizabeth ("E") Fullerton. BoAV

Yet is day over long. Villanelle of the Poet's Road. Ernest Christopher Dowson. OBMV; TrGrPo; UnPo

Yet is the fancy grosser than your lusts were gross? The Succubus. Robert Graves. OAEL 1-2

Yet it is but one mask of many worn/By the Great Face behind. The Last Chrysanthemum. Thomas Hardy. CMoP; LiTB

Yet it proves by demonstration/Newton's law of gravitation. Science for the Young. Wallace Irwin. BBGG; DBV; QQQ

Yet it was hers. And time's result/Is love's most fair, most speechless fable. Winter Tryst. Mark Van Doren. LiTA

Yet Joseph Moodey's name continue must. Tombstone Epitaphs. Anonymous. PeD

Yet leave no lustre on our page of death. On Finding a Small Fly Crushed in a Book. Charles Tennyson Turner. FM

Yet leaves him happy as a child at play. The Cottager. John Clare. OBRV

Yet leaves me nourished by so many roots/That I shall never cease ceasing to be. Silverthorn Bush. Robert Finch. NOBC

Yet leaving here a name, I trust,/That will not perish in the dust. My Days among the Dead Are Past. Robert Southey. EnRP; HBV 1-2; OBRV; TEP

Yet left Content, a Genuine Stoick He,/Great without Patron, rich without South-Sea! A Reply to an Imitation of the Second Ode....of Horace. Richard Bentley. OBEC

Yet let me with the shadow play. To Avisa. Henry Willoby. EIL

Yet let none despayre/But to finde as fayre as you. Dear If I with Guile. Thomas Campion. NCEP

Yet life is often queer like that. A Memory. Leonard Alfred George Strong. FaBoCo; NOBL; PoPl

...Yet like stones they make/His blood's sweet current much more loud to be. Church Lock and Key. George Herbert. AnAnS 1; OBSP

Yet lingered not the day, but morning scard me. Elegies. Ovid (Publius Ovidius Naso). OBVE

Yet live for ever, though against her will,/And speake her good, though she requite it ill. Amoretti, XLVIII. Edmund Spenser. AAS

Yet long must I lament thy hapless doom,/Thy lavish'd life and early hasten'd tomb. To the Departing Spirit of an Alienated Friend. Anna Seward. PeHV

Yet, Lord, I wait Thy will. In Harbor. Lizette Woodworth Reese. TrPWD

Yet love I best of any creature!' The Complaint of Troilus. Geoffrey Chaucer. NOBE

Yet lowly still vouchsafe to looke on me,/Such lowlinesse shall make you lofty be. Amoretti, XIII. Edmund Spenser. AAS

Yet man is for the woman made/And the woman made for man. Man Is for Woman Made. Peter Anthony Motteux. UnTE

Yet man persisted: she will bring forth. Adam. Rainer Maria Rilke. MoRP

Yet may the lily and the rose/Bloom on my grassy bed. On the Death of Dermody, the Poet. Henry Kirke White. PeD

Yet meet my flames and thou shalt see/That equal love knows no disparity. To Celia Pleading Want of Merit. Thomas Stanley. MeLP

Yet men and boys came all safe home again,/Though they had gone through such dangers. The Golden Voyage. *Anonymous.* OBSS

Yet men have called thy swift return a bore! Serio-Comic History of Bridgwater. E. H. Burrington. FaBoPP

Yet merry it is, and quiet. The Quiet Life. William Byrd. ElL; GoBC; HBV 1-2

Yet mine the steps and portal!' Evening Melody. Aubrey Thomas De Vere. GoBC; HBV 1-2

Yet must I love thee, dear, and as thou art. As to His Choice of Her. Wilfrid Scawen Blunt. ViBoPo

Yet must it still forever pose him/To match—what Celia never shows him. Hint from Voiture. William Shenstone. EnLoPo

Yet my open eyes can see all night/That lifelong trouble of your brow. An Elegy. Yuan Chen. LiTW

Yet nathelesse it could not doe him die,/Till he should die his last, that is eternally. The Faerie Queene. Edmund Spenser. OAEP

Yet needed no reminder to give theirs/to others. Oh, Would That I Knew. Al-Samua'al Ibn Adiya. TrJP

Yet neither life nor death should end/The being of a faithful friend. A Widow's Hymn. George Wither. OBEV

Yet never doubt that Sisyphus/Achieved at last the mountain top. The Journey. Scudder Middleton. HBMV

Yet, never, in Extremity,/It asked a crumb—of Me. Hope Is the Thing with Feathers. Emily Dickinson. AmP; BLPL; CBEP; DiPo; MoAB; MoAmPo; MoShBr; NOBA; OxBA; PG; SBG; TAP; WeW

Yet never none other/Like our God's Mother. Carol Naive. John McClure. HBMV

Yet never, through the ages, commonplace. I Have Found Such Joy. Grace Noll Crowell. PoToHe

Yet never will be saved from the majestic brute/I drew myself. The Painter in the Lion Cage. Betti Alver. BoWoP

Yet nevertheless, the truth to express,/Still Little John they did him call. Robin Hood and Little John. *Anonymous.* BaBo

Yet newest, and sweet to learn. A Song. Hildegarde Hawthorne. AA; FaBoBe; HBV 1-2

Yet no god loved as loves this poor frail dust. Prelude. Richard Aldington. BrPo

Yet no one weeps for me. Another Song of the Same Woman, to Some Partridges... Florencia del Pinar. BoWoP

Yet none but names him the finest man of them all. The Song of Lo-Fu. *Anonymous.* AWP

Yet none here knows her history–/Has heard her name. The Marble-Streeted Town. Thomas Hardy. FaBoPP

Yet, not all hopeless, eye His boundless grace. Angelic Guidance. John Henry, Cardinal Newman. GoBC

Yet not find so much brain as in Oliver's porter. Vox Clero, Lilliburlero. *Anonymous.* APAS

Yet not forget this flooded spring/And scarce-saved lambs of Westmoreland. The Lambs of Grasmere, 1860. Christina Georgina Rossetti. FM

Yet not stay heedless when I heard/The tip-tap nothings of a tiny bird. The Tomtit. Walter De la Mare. FM

Yet not still secure. Just Beguiler. Thomas Campion. AtBAP

Yet not surprised should the river suddenly/Yield a hundredfold, every hunger appeased. Men Fishing in the Arno. Elizabeth Jennings. OBTV

Yet nothing did he dread, but ever was ydrad. The Faerie Queene. Edmund Spenser. GoBC

Yet now and then your men of wit/Will condescend to take a bit. Flattery. Jonathan Swift. GoTF; TreFT

Yet O! to see him once again. Edith and Harold. Arthur Gray Butler. OBVV

Yet of this greater gift no word was spoken. The Greater Gift. Margaret E. Bruner. PoToHe

Yet oft we hear, in height of stupid pride,/Some senseless idiot curse a lettered bride. Hypatia (excerpt). Elizabeth Tollet. NOEC

Yet one exempts, and one of these redeems. Twin. Phyllis Haring. PeSA

Yet one floating forever free. The Beach Homos. Forrest Anderson. PeHV

Yet one poor word so fiercely angers me,/That I must strive to pardon it in vain! Of Impatience Which Brings All Our Gains to Nothing. Jacopone da Todi. CAW

Yet out of that I have written these songs.) Sometimes With One I Love. Walt Whitman. CBEP; GBL; OBSP

Yet-perfect intricacies/Of lichens, seeds and crystals. A Quilled Quilt, a Needle Bed. Brad Leithauser. MAYP; SM

...Yet perhaps the best/Of all we do and dream of lives unguessed. Magnets. Laurence Binyon. HBMV

Yet plucked not any more of them. The Honeysuckle. Dante Gabriel Rossetti. CBEP; SyP

...Yet, plucking nervously/The pregnant twigs, I stay. Good morning, comrades. The Ides of March. Roy Fuller. PoCh

(Yet praying) When this cruel war is over,/Praying that we meet again. Weeping Sad and Lonely. Henry and Charles C. Sawyer Ucker. FSW; TrAS

Yet real somewhere. A Lost God (excerpt). Francis William Bourdillon. WGRP

Yet reluctant we go. The Old Men. Walter De la Mare. MoAB; MoBrPo

Yet remain an outlaw still! Grizzly. Bret (Francis Bret Harte) Harte. AA; AnAmPo; BPAW

Yet scarce more a corpse than ere/His last breath was drawn. Siberia. James Clarence Mangan. BIrV; IrPN; NOBI; NOBV; RoGo

Yet scarecrow-like I'll walk, as one/Neglecting thy derision. To Fortune. Robert Herrick. OBSP; SeCV 1-2

Yet scorn the Jews. But Not So Odd. Cecil Browne. DBV

Yet seemed it winter still, and, you away,/As with your shadow I with these did play. Sonnets, XCVIII: "From you have I been absent in the spring." William Shakespeare. AWP; DiPo; EBEV; InPo; LiTB; NOBE; OBEV; OBSC; PoPle; TEP; ViBoPo

Yet Servants, knowing Minikin nor Base,/Are still allow'd to fiddle with the Case. Elinda's Glove. Richard Lovelace. OBS

Yet shall I burn bright through a long day. The Cicada. H. M. Green. PoAu 1-2

Yet she challenged Pindar. Although I was her pupil. Korinna. BoWoP

Yet she has steeds of fire/And men of gold! The Reaper. Leslie Holdsworth Allen. PoAu 1-2

Yet she's a good-for-nothing cat,/As all the world may see. The Lazy Pussy. Palmer Cox. OBCA

Yet she/Will be/False ere I come, to two or three. Go and Catch a Falling Star. John Donne. BiP; FaBV; FF; LiTB; LiTL; NAWM 1-2; PoRA; TEP

Yet since your light hath once enlumind me,/With my reflex yours shall encreased be. Amoretti, LXVI. Edmund Spenser. AAS

Yet sings/Knowing he hath wings. Be Like the Bird. Victor Hugo. SoPo; SUS; TiPo

...Yet slowly/through seventy years Pause. Dorothy Livesay. AMV-81

Yet so they mourn, becoming of their woe,/That every tongue says beauty should look so. Sonnets, CXXVII: "In the ole age black was nor counted fair." William Shakespeare. CBEP; DiPo

Yet some blazing hand will remake the chaos/of earth, people, and death. The Titans. Betti Alver. BoWoP

Yet somewhere/resurrected nazis/are still burning Mendelssohn. Cubist Blues in Poltergeist Major. Allan F. Kipp. AMV-81

Yet sovereign of thyself, whate'er may speed. Wellington. Benjamin Disraeli. OBVV

...Yet still/Enjoy his lust, eat well and play the flute? Soliloquy at Potsdam. Peter Porter. NOAV

Yet still feasts on the gall/of his gastronomical past. Black Man's Feast. Sarah Webster Fabio. PoBA; PoNe

Yet still I heard his joyous hymn come faintly down the wind. The Shepherd Boy. Edward J. O'Brien. HBMV

–Yet still I shudder with distress/To find detested tracks of his old way. The Fear. Lascelles Abercrombie. OBMV

Yet still I stand by tilth and filth and praise. Tilth. Robert Graves. FaBoEE; OBSV

Yet still she twisted, sleeked and tossed/Her beauteous hair about. Lovelocks. Walter De la Mare. MoVE

...Yet still surrounded & pierced through with night. Starship. David McAleavey. AMV-81

Yet still their love comes home to me. After Aughrim. Emily Lawless. OBEV; OxBI

–Yet still they march rejoicing on. The Seekers. Charles Hamilton Sorley. WGRP

Yet still thou wanderest the lily-seed to find. The Wind. William Morris. NBM

Yet still, throughout the world, there stands/His house, that is not made with hands. Subversive. William Rose Benet. MoRP

Yet still we praise that crocus head,/April! For City Spring. Stephen Vincent Benét. BXAP; NLV; PoPl

...Yet still we press/Westward, in search, to death, to nothingness. The Lemmings. John Masefield. CMoP; NIP; NoAm

Yet stood the fair maid nigh me and told me all/her love. Where She Told Her Love. John Clare. VLP

Yet that faith in men doth dwell,/Who travels constancy can tell. Caelica, LXXV. Fulke, Lord Brooke Greville. FCP

Yet that purpose survives–/and is/love   Vanzetti.   Charles Buckmaster. CBAP

Yet that's how I preferred you/my flower.   Last night I saw your corpse. Joyce Mansour.   BoWoP

Yet that things go round and again go round/Has rather a classical sound. The Pleasures of Merely Circulating.   Wallace Stevens.   LiTA; LOW; MAT; OBAL

Yet the afternoon sun falls upon faces/Less tame than tigers.   Over the Wall: Berlin, May 1975.   C. H. Sisson.   OBTV; OxBC

Yet the artist's kindly craft shall not retain/The filming eye, and beak that gasp'd with pain.   The Vacant Cage.   Charles Tennyson Turner.   FM

Yet the devil may hold all your blue and your gold/Were I only once back there!   In Spain.   Emily Lawless.   AnIV

Yet the fruit were scarce worth peeling,/Were it not for stealing, stealing. Song of Fairies Robbing an Orchard (excerpt).   [James Henry] Leigh Hunt. OBRV

Yet the General was rubbish in the end.   The Great Statue of the General Du Puy.   Wallace Stevens.   LiTA

Yet the language so lovely! like the dyes from gas-tar.   When I Read Shakespeare–.   D. H. Lawrence.   NoAm

Yet the light of a whole life dies/When love is done.   The night has a thousand eyes.   Francis William Bourdillon.   BoLoP; FaFP; GoTF; GTBS; HBV 1-2; LiTL; MCCG; OBEV; OBSP; OBVV; OHFP; PoToHe; TreF; WBLP

Yet the Lord of both worlds will enter there.   In the Secret Rose Garden. Sa'd ud-din Mahmud Shabistari.   LiTW

Yet the Maiden on her throne, boys, shall be a maiden still.   The Maiden City.   Charlotte Elizabeth Tonna.   HBV 1-2

Yet the sign is on her   The Once-Over.   Paul Blackburn.   ErPo; NeAP; PoM

Yet the sorrow of parting is still unsubdued.   To Li Chien.   Po Chu-i. LiTW

Yet the staying is a death that is never soften'd with sleep.   Come Out, Come Out, Ye Souls That Serve.   Christopher John Brennan.   PoAu 1-2

...Yet the thief/Was no wiser for the words he gorged.   Riddle: The Book-Worm: "A moth ate a word."   *Anonymous.*   CoBE

Yet the turf that I'm clad with is strange to me quite.   Ortho's Epitaph. Charles Stuart Calverley.   FaBoEE

Yet their Three praises praise but One; that's Lawes.   To Master Henry Lawes, the Excellent Composr of Lyrics.   Robert Herrick.   CaPo

Yet there are spirits here that to the strain/Would send a still small voice responsive back/again.   On the Death of Commodore Oliver H. Perry. John Gardiner Calkins Brainard.   PAH

Yet there are witless folk will say/they don't exist.   Suppose You Met a Witch (excerpt).   Ian Serraillier.   WSC

Yet there delight blooms in remorseless cold.   Memory.   Babette Deutsch. PoA

Yet there is no joy.   Fill and Illumined.   Joseph Ceravolo.   ANYP

Yet there is one who holds us as we/fall/eternally in his hands' tenderness. Autumn.   Rainer Maria Rilke.   TrJP

Yet there isn't a train I wouldn't take,/No matter where it's going.   Travel. Edna St. Vincent Millay.   InMe; LaNeLa; MoShBr; OBCA; TiPo

Yet they escaped. For I stayed.   Epitaphs of the War, 1914-18.   Rudyard Kipling.   BrPo

Yet they promised me fair and lovingly.   Everyman: The Desertion of Beauty and Strength.   *Anonymous.*   ACP

Yet they shall crumble to the dust before/The battering thistle-down. Beleaguered Cities.   F. L. Lucas.   HaMV

Yet they sit up/and show vast bellies to the children.   Elephants in the Circus.   D. H. Lawrence.   BoAnP

Yet they will scatter the red hordes of Hell,/Who went to battle forth and always fell.   They Went Forth to Battle, but They Always Fell.   Shaemas O'Sheel.   AnAmPo; APA; HBV 1-2; WaaP; WGRP

Yet thieves break in and steal the gold.   Riddle: "In marble halls as white as milk."   *Anonymous.*   GBP; HBV 1-2; HBVY; OxNR; PoPle

Yet thine, too, this solacing music, as we earthfolk stumble along.'   Thomas Hardy.   Walter De la Mare.   NoAm

Yet think not prayer and fast were given/To make one step 'twixt earth and Heaven.   Weakness of Nature.   Richard Hurrell Froude.   OBRV

Yet thinke, that Death shall spoyle your godly features.   Visions.   Petrarch. AWP

Yet, this is the thing our souls must ask,/What have we done today?   What Have We Done Today?   Nixon Waterman.   WBLP

Yet this is you.   Portrait d'une Femme.   Ezra Pound.   AP; APA; CMoP; FF; ForPo; HBMV; InPS; MoAB; MoAmPo; MoVE; MP; NoAm; NOBA; NoP; PPP; TAP; TwCP

...Yet/this passing has the shape/of farewell.   The Goodbye.   Myra Sklarew. GOYP

Yet this plaguey old woman would never keep quiet.   There was an old woman, and what do you think.   Mother Goose.   FaBoCh

...Yet this savory mess/Scarce brings humility to thy high crest.   Proud Resignation.   Mordecai Marcus.   SOTS

Yet this shall I ne'er know, but live in doubt,/Till my bad angel fire my good one out.   Sonnets, CXLIV: "Two loves I have of comfort and despair." William Shakespeare.   CBEP; EBEV; InvP; LoBV; NIP; OAEL 1-2; OAEP; PeHV; PoEL 1-5

Yet this was but a simple bird,/Alone, among dead trees.   Overtones. William Alexander Percy.   HBMV; HBVY

–Yet thou say'st I do not love thee!   Canzonet.   *Anonymous.*   EG

Yet thus unhappy must I serve,/And other have that I deserve.   I see that chance hath chosen me.   Sir Thomas Wyatt.   FCP; SiPS

Yet thy thoughts doth not half know her.'   Fain I Would.   *Anonymous.* EIl

Yet, till it is burned out, you must remain.   Genius.   Edward Lucas White. AA; WGRP

The yet-to-be-dismantled elms, the geese.   Poem: "About the size of an old-style dollar bill."   Elizabeth Bishop.   FYAP; HaCAP

Yet to break forth/out of His Word.   More Truth and Light.   John Robinson.   TRV

Yet, to my grief, you let al-mustari beguile you!   Angry at Zaidun's Interest in Her Maid...   Wallada.   PBWP

Yet, to the last, a rugged wrinkled thing/To which young sweetness may delight to cling!   Hast Thou Not Seen an Aged Rifted Tower.   Hartley Coleridge.   EnRP

Yet to this shape all must be brought.   On the Tombs in Westminster Abbey. Francis Beaumont.   LoBV; NOBE

Yet to you this little village is dear as the moon.   Dear as the Moon. *Anonymous.*   WTO

Yet trembles forth a word of prayer and/praise.   An Unpraised Picture. Richard Burton.   AA

Yet trembling on the verge of speech.   The Yule Log.   William Hamilton Hayne.   AA

Yet trusting not in mine, but in His strength alone!   First-Day Thoughts. John Greenleaf Whittier.   AmPP; TrCP

Yet understand the exact/and tribal, intimate revenge.   Punishment.   Seamus Heaney.   FaBoPV; NoP

Yet, uneasy is his life/Who is married to a wife.   The Joys of Marriage. Charles Cotton.   InMe

Yet use I not my foes as I use Thee.   Unkindness.   George Herbert.   HBV 1-2

Yet virtue makes the truest kings and queens.   An Invective Against the Wicked of the World.   Nicholas Breton.   ViBoPo

Yet, was I un-vanquished. Had I not happiness, I at/their hands in Daret, Daret of Juljuli?   Weep Love's Losing.   Imr el Kais.   LiTW

Yet was not courage wanting in the child...'   Masar.   Walter Savage Landor. LoBV

Yet we are the most beautiful world of the world   A Text for These Distracted Times.   Rodney Hall.   CBAP

Yet we deny the brotherhood/The human heart demands.   There Is So Much of Loneliness.   *Anonymous.*   PoToHe

Yet we'll go no more a roving/By the light of the moon.   So, We'll Go No More a Roving.   George Gordon, Lord Byron.   AnFE; AtBAP; AWP; BLPL; BoLoP; ELP; ERoP 1-2; ExPo; FaFP; FF; FiP; HAP; HeIP; InPo; LiTB; LoBV; MBW 1-2; MyFE; NOBE; NoP; OAEL 1-2; OAEP; OBNC; OBRV; OBSP; OLR; OxBS; PoEL 1-5; PoPle; PoRA; PrIm; SeCeV; TreFS; ViBoPo; WeW; WHA

Yet we must all/Down fall,/And perish at the last.   Upon the Troublesome Times.   Robert Herrick.   CaPo

Yet we were looking away!   The Self-Unseeing.   Thomas Hardy.   EBEV; HAP; MoBrPo; NOBE; NOBV; OBNC; PrIm; VLP

Yet what I can I give Him,/Give my heart.   A Christmas Carol.   Christina Georgina Rossetti.   BiCB; InPS; NOBV; OHIP; PCh; SBVL

Yet when his fame is to the highest borne,/We know enough to laugh his praise to scorn.   Caelica, XCIII.   Fulke, Lord Brooke Greville.   FCP

Yet, when they have it, they abuse it,/For they know not how to use it. Women's Longing.   John Fletcher.   HBV 1-2

Yet when we would express it, words suddenly fail us.   I Built My Hut. T'ao Chi'en.   AWP

Yet while I live, you cannot wholly die.   Sonnet for My Father.   Donald Justice.   DFF

Yet while 'tis dark, one shuts one's lids,/And still dreams on.   If I Had but Two Little Wings.   Samuel Taylor Coleridge.   OHIP

Yet who this language to the people speaks,/Opinion's empire, sense's idol breaks.   Caelica, LV.   Fulke, Lord Brooke Greville.   FCP

Yet why the moon to-night's a daffodil/When it is March–Do you remember, still?   To Butterfly.   William Alexander Percy.   HBMV

Yet will arise   A Phoenix at Fifty.   Lawrence Ferlinghetti.   NAs

Yet will I be mer-r-r-r-r-r-y.   Hey, Ho, Nobody Home.   *Anonymous.* FSW

Yet will I love her till I die.   "There Is a Lady Sweet and Kind." *Anonymous.*   CH; EBEV; EIl; FaFP; GBL; GoTF; HBV 1-2; HeIP; LiTB; NoP; OAEP; OBEV; TreFS; TrGrPo

Yet will I serve, although I die therefore.   I Serve a Mistress.   Anthony Munday.   EIl; HAP

Yet will she wear the sweet woodbine,/The primrose and the violet. Henceforth I Will Not Set My Love. Sir Arthur Gorges. GBL

"Yet, will this pass, and pass shall I?" A Popular Personage at Home. Thomas Hardy. FM

Yet wilt undo me more should'st thou not come at night. Dialogue after Enjoyment. Abraham Cowley. BoLoP

Yet with an equal joy let me behold/Thy chariot o'er that way by others rolled.' A Prayer. Sir William Rowan Hamilton. IrPN

Yet with what words I'd welcome thee–/Couldst thou return, dear mystery! Love Once Was Like an April Dawn. Robert Underwood Johnson. HBV 1-2

Yet without love nought worth to me. Of His Cynthia. Fulke, Lord Brooke Greville. EIL; ELP; NoP

Yet without sin he suffered more/Than ever sinners did before. The Stranger. John Clare. OxBoCh

Yet would I kneel and kiss thy gentle hand! Sonnet to a Young Lady Who Sent Me a Laurel Crown. John Keats. EnRP

Yet would I warn thee, World: treat well/Whom thou call'st fool. Angels. Gertrude Hall. AA

Yet you cannot catch a bowl full. Riddle: "A hill full, a hole full." Mother Goose. SoPo; TiPo

Yet you might think you saw at twilight/A little, crafty face. The Toadstool Wood. James Reeves. DuDa; WSC

"Yet you would laugh as heartily, as I." Merlin, They Say. Fulke, Lord Brooke Greville. NCEP

Yet you would mourn for evermore. Mourn for Yourself. Geoffrey Keating. BIrV

Yeve us ones drinken er we gon henne. A Last Drink. Anonymous. OxBM

Yeven as the Center in each perfait rounde. The Last Booke of the Ocean to Scinthia (excerpt). Sir Walter Ralegh. FaBoEn

The Yew alone burns lamps of peace/For them that lie forlorn. Trees. Walter De la Mare. OHIP

Yews, I am a rainbow/Being night nor day. Day and Night. Lewis Alexander. CDC

Yi Yi, the cowboy's eyes/are blue. The top of the sky/is too. Vaquero. Edward Dorn. NeAP; PoM

Yield up, O love, thy crown and hearted throne/To tyrannous hate! Othello. William Shakespeare. TW

Yielding to dark:/the carolla. Parallel Texts. Robert Kelly. CoPo

Yields to his fate–so ends my tale. The Three Warnings. Hester Thrale Piozzio. BeLS; HBV 1-2

Yif I may, it shal him rewe,By this day. Now Sprinkes the Spray. Anonymous. ABF; AtBAP; PoEL 1-5

Yif ic of luve can. I Ought to Weep. Anonymous. MeEL

Yif thou be nyd night or day,/Say, "Passio Christi conforta me." In His Utter Wretchedness. John Audelay. MeEL

Yiif I may, it shall him rewe/By this day!' The Singing Maid. Anonymous. MeEL

Yippy-I-O-Ki-Ay, Yippy-I-O-Ki-Ay. I'm an Old Cowhand. Johnny Mercer. OBAL

"Yis, dame,' quod he, "tel forth, and I wol here.' The Canterbury Tales: The Wife of Bath Prologue. Geoffrey Chaucer. EnL; EnLi 1-2; FiP; OAEL 1-2; PoEL 1-5

Yit mony in a grit rout/For lak of rowme stud about. Colkelbie Sow (excerpt). Anonymous. OxBS

Ynne heav'n Godd's mercie synge! Bristowe Tragedie. Thomas Chatterton. CEP; OBEC; OxBB

Yo' body no carcass fo' barbecuin' on a spree! Sistern and Brethren. Anonymous. TrAS

Yo ha! Yo ho! Come down with a will/And bring the main-sheet aft. The Main-Sheet Song. Thomas Fleming Day. EtS

Yo-ho-ho and a bottle of rum! Derelict. Young Ewing Allison. BBV; BLPA; EtS; FaBoBe; FaFP; HBMV; MCCG; OnMSP; TreFS

Yo soy chicana/pero no soy Tribal Chant. Carol Lee Sanchez. TWSS

Yolp, yolp, yolp, yolp. Yolp, Yolp, Yolp, Yolp. Anonymous. EIL

Yon is the Howe, an' this the Hill! Bennachie. Charles Murray. PoSH

Yon's the road the wicked gae,/An that's the road to hell.' The Queen of Elfan's Nourice. Anonymous. ESPB

Yonder. The Leaden Echo and the Golden Echo. Gerard Manley Hopkins. BrPo; CMoP; CoBMV; DTC; EnLi 1-2; FaFP; GTBS-P; LiTB; LiTM; LoBV; MasP; MoAB; MoBrPo; MoVE; NOBV; OAEP; OBMV; OBNC; SOTW

"Yonder comes the ugliest thing/That ever lived or died." Blue-Eyed Girl. Anonymous. AmFP

Yonder! Yonder/Points our direction; father, let us wander. Mignon. Johann Wolfgang von Goethe. LiTW

Yoo-hoo, Gerald's here, yoo-hoo... A Voice in the Garden. Selima Hill. FaBoWP

You a shadow until the day of days. Privilege. Alejandra Pizarnik. VWA

You abandon your intent. A Jellyfish. Marianne Moore. OBSP; PCP

You act like you were kind of disappoint-/Ed god doesn't broadcast. There isn't any point–. Sonnet on a Somewhat Inferior Radio Outfit. Cary Ross. AnAmPo

You ain't gonna worry my life anymore. Worried Life Blues. Anonymous. AmFP

You ain't no friend to you. Gonna Lay My Head down on Some Railroad Line. Anonymous. AmFP

...You ain't ruined,' said she. The Ruined Maid. Thomas Hardy. BoLoP; BrPo; CABA; CMoP; FiBHP; HeIP; LiTB; NIP; NLV; NOBL; NoP; OxBTC; PPoe; SCV; SeCeV; TEP; WeW

You'all better leave God's moon alone,/Else he ain't gonna turn it on, no more! Moon Poem. Saundra Sharp. QQQ

...'You alone can do it,/Come immediately." The Call. Jules Supervielle. NU

You alone can lose yourself/Within a sky, and rob it of its blue! Advice to a Blue-Bird. Maxwell Bodenheim. HBMV

...You alone,/Saints, will dare to fix it with your gaze. All Saint's Day (excerpt). Margherita Guidacci. PBWP

You also are laid aside. Fan-Piece, for Her Imperial Lord. Ezra Pound. MoAB

You also think of you. To J.S. Robert J. Misch. ALV

You also will cease to be,/my Lord. Your Presence. Mordecai Temkin. VWA

You always see me not at all. Love-Songs, At Once Tender and Informative. Samuel Hoffenstein. OBAL

You and Blue Mountain will reach the sea. Blue Mountain. Roberta Hill. VoR

You and I are six today! Our Birthday. Marion Edey. BiCB; SiSoSe

...You and I/Follow but feebly where our words aspire. Late Tutorial. Vincent Buckley. PoAu 1-2

You and I keep choosing not to lose. Patty Hearst Hoists the Carbine. Sibyl James. SOTS

You and I must gather under elms. Falling Moon. Roberta Hill. CDW

You and I must wait for God,/My Ishmael,/Must wait for God. Hagar to Ishmael. Deborah Eibel. VWA

You and I, my lyf, and Amyas Latet Anguis. Anonymous. OBEV

You and I plucking rushes/Had not plucked a handful when night came! Plucking the Rushes. Anonymous. BoLoP; OBVE; OLR

You and I will go there when Kenneth is dead. A Poem of the Forty-Eight States. Kenneth Koch. NNaP; OBAL

You and I will never meet again,/Till we meet at the bonny town o Torry. Earl Rothes. Anonymous. BaBo; ESPB

You and I will walk alone. The Power of Fancy. Philip Freneau. AP

You and the tender lambies,/now you know! Sudden Assertion. Kenneth Leslie. BoAnP; GDP; PoL

You are. Poem. Helene Johnson. AmNP; BANP

You are a bird denied, the blood/Of earth in flying attitude. Bound. Theodore Roethke. PoA

...You are a fraud/and friend, a haunting light and lonely lord. Borges. Willis Barnstone. AMV-80

You are a great deal bigger than you are. Sonnet to the Sea Serpent. John Gardiner Calkins Brainard. EtS

You are a line and yet another line. A Latter Purification. Haim Guri. VWA

You are a mist/of snow: white, little flowers. The Walls Do Not Fall. Hilda ("H. D.") Doolittle. PBWP

You are a mountain Thoughts for You (when She Came back from the Mountains). Ranice Henderson Crosby. NMM

You are an Alfred-seeable sky. Alfred-Seeable Philadelphia Sky. Eli Siegel. CAD

You are an episode of life under constant scrutiny. Cosmic Eye. A. K. Redwing. VoR

You are beyond my last night, my first dawn. In the Year of Two Thousand. Menke Katz. AMV-81

You are blessed out of measure. An Assurance. Nicholas Breton. OBSC

You are brave. But you need to be touched. What You Need. Kathleen Fraser. AmPA

You are but dust and even Caesar died. Human Greatness. Edwin Barclay. PBA

You are coming very slowly, why do you delay/O my black cobra? My Cobra Girl. Anonymous. WTO

You are dead. Gangrene. Philip Levine. AmPC; VGW

You are desolate, fort of kings.' You Are Desolate, Fort of Kings. Anonymous. NOBI

"You are fairer than I,' said the rose. Morning Compliments. Sydney Dayre. OxBChV

You are flying home. Bone Poem. Nancy Willard. HoAn

You are gone. Never More Will the Wind. Hilda ("H. D.") Doolittle. CTC

You are her shadow, she is where you are.   Eagle Sonnets.   Clement Wood.
HBMV

You are him, and think yourself yourself.   Tattoos.   Charles Wright.
HaCAP

You are, I sense, the dearer.   A Delicate Balance.   Laura Schreiber.
AMV-80

You are in heaven now.   Remembrance.   George Parsons Lathrop.   AA

You are, in truth, one in a million,/At once mammalian and reptilian.   For
an Amorous Lady.   Theodore Roethke.   NLV

You are jesting with my pain.   Make Believe.   Alice Cary.   HBV 1-2

You are like our poets, O my swallows!   O My Swallows.   Ernst Toller.
TrJP

You are lost in light.   On a Picture of Your House.   D. G. Jones.   NOBC

You are lovelier than ever, I do believe.   The Mother in the House.
Hermann Hagedorn.   HBMV; OHIP

You are mighty cute–and here is one of your bargains.   A Boston Ballad.
Walt Whitman.   OBAL

(You are Mine said she)   May I Feel Said He.   Edward Estlin Cummings.
BoLoP; ErPo; FF; HeIP; NLV; NOBA

You are most loved, most lost, most beautiful.   Sea-Change.   Genevieve
Taggard.   EtS

You are much uglier...and so am I.   Reunion.   Paul Dehn.   PV

You are my eternal guests.   What Is Lived.   Carmen Valle.   InW

You are Nancy, that old Nancy;/Nancy Dawson.   Nancy Dawson.   Herbert
P. Horne.   HBV 1-2

You are no longer alone.   Talking Designs.   Liz Sohappy Bahe.   CDW

"You are not a dead bird."   The Dead Bird.   Andrew Young.   FM

You are not called when journey's/done.   Journey's End.   Humbert Wolfe.
TrJP

You - are - not - it.   Dips or Counting Out Rhymes: "Dip, dip, dip."
Anonymous.   GBP

You are not old.   How Old Are You?   H. S. Fritsch.   PoLf; PoToHe

"You are on U.S. 40 Headed West."   You Are on U.S. 40 Headed West.
Vera White.   AmFN

You are only a troubled guest/on the dark earth.   The Holy Longing.
Johann Wolfgang von Goethe.   NU

You are our feldspar, definite as deeds.   Peasantry.   Eileen Duggan.   CoBE

...You are out of rhyme/With the busy, hustling throng.   Hustle and Grin.
Anonymous.   WBLP

You are past love, praise, indifference, blame.   Your Last Drive.   Thomas
Hardy.   OBNC

You are sad. It is the same with me.   Nocturne at Bethesda.   Arna
Bontemps.   BALP; BANP; CDC; PoNe

You are silent,/only the days/count the milestones/of our meeting.   Between
Life and Death.   Frantisek Gottlieb.   VWA

& You are singing. What song/is that The words/are beautiful.   The
Clearing.   LeRoi (Imamu Amiri Baraka) Jones.   CoPo

You are, sir, magni-oral, semi-anal,/A model for a prophylactic firm.   A
Periphrastic Insult, Not a Banal.   J. V. Cunningham.   TW

You are stained, stained/to perfection.   Field Work.   Seamus Heaney.
FaBoIP

You are still there. And I know who is here.   Toussaint l'Ouverture.   Edwin
Arlington Robinson.   PoNe

You are sure of that.   Laying By.   Randall Williams.   AMV-80

You are that image which had never died/in me, Eve, of my primavera,
personified.   The Creek.   Roland Robinson.   NOAV

You are the baby in the barn.   Nick and the Candlestick.   Sylvia Plath.
CAPP; CoAP; LCAP; PBWP

You are the best.   Four Stories.   David Shapiro.   ANYP

You are the heroes without name/Or origin.   Scenes of Childhood.   James
Merrill.   CoAP

–You are the landscape that you would admire.   Sonnet: "You waken slowly.
In your dream you're straying."   William Bell.   NePoEA

You are the lark-song/Calling me home!   All Paths Lead to You.   Blanche
Shoemaker Wagstaff.   BLPA; FaBoBe

...You are the messenger who opens/mysteries that unfold forever, but avoids
words.   The Second Hymn to the Night.   Novalis (George Friedrich
Philipp von Hardenerg).   NU

You are the most golden of all.   Child.   E. N. Sargent.   NYBP

You are the night interpreted/you are/you   The Anti-Semanticist.   Everett
Hoagland.   BPo

You are the palace of a fairy.   Bubbles.   George H. Shorey.   PoPl

You are the priest tonight.   To Mary: At the Thirteenth Station.   Raymond
F. Roseliep.   ISi

"You are the smartest man that walks/On the deck of the Baltimore!"   The
City of Baltimore.   Anonymous.   ShS

...You are the stranger/who gets stranger by the hour.   Consumed.   James
Tate.   MAT

You are the surge of deep music,/I–but a cry!   I Am the Wind.   Zoë Akins.
HBV 1-2

You are the tidings that they bring!   The Smallest Angel.   Elsie Binns.
ChBR

You are the white-hot steel, taking your shape/Under the hammer blows of
Time....   Between Two Furious Oceans.   Dick Diespecker.   CaP

...You are too new/To want the world in a glass hat.   New Year on
Dartmoor.   Sylvia Plath.   FaBoWP

You are too splendid for this city street.   Sonnet to A Negro in Harlem.
Helene Johnson.   BANP; CDC; NIP

You are turning in the wind   Second Skins–A Peyote Song.   Joseph
Bruchac.   CDW

You are welcome in the secret club they have formed.   What Thou Lovest
Well, Remains American.   Richard Hugo.   GP; NIP; NPAW

You are went!   Mellow Groove Grave Elegy.   Michael C. Ford.   SOTS

You are white's evening nature of my thought.   White.   George Woodcock.
NeBP

You are Zechariah. You are Zoroaster. You are Zebedee.   Direction from
Zulu.   Daniel Halpern.   FAZ

You ask me to believe You and/I only see decay.   On a Portrait of a Deaf
Man.   Sir John Betjeman.   NoAm

"You bad old man to sit and tell/Such gibberybosh about a Bell!"   The
Philosopher and Her Father.   Shirley Brooks.   CenHV

"You bade me speak the truth."   The Poets at Tea.   Barry Pain.   Par

...You bade the soul drink deep/Of infinite things, saying: "The rest is naught."
Villiers de L'Isle-Adam.   Aldous Huxley.   HBMV

...You, Bangalawi, you, her husband, you indeed,/all by yourself, you can help
her in childbirth!   The Blowflies Buzz.   Djalparmiwi.   NOAV; WTO

You banished me, before I fled from you.   Truth's Complaint over England.
Thomas Lodge.   ACP

You bear no wool, and loss is all my gain.   Arcadia.   Sir Philip Sidney.
FCP

You become one with Him.   Inscription on the Pyramid of Unas.
Anonymous.   LiTW

You been a long, long time 'bout makin' it up, Lawd, in yo' min'.   Pauline.
Anonymous.   OuSiCo

...You/been home been home   When Thy King Is a Boy (excerpt).   Ed
Roberson.   PoBA

You believe me that I did?   Detail from an Annunciation by Crivelli.
Rosemary Dobson.   PoAu 1-2

You bet I would!   The Rich Man.   Franklin Pierce ("F.P.A.") Adams.
FiBHP; InMe; NLV; OBAL

An' you better believe it.   When I Heard Dat White Man Say.   Zack
Gilbert.   PoBA

You better come on/in my kitchen/'cause it's going to be raining outdoors
Come On in My Kitchen.   Robert Johnson.   BluL

You better get back to the city cause you one of them/technical niggers and
you'll have problems h   Conversation.   Nikki Giovanni.   CTBA

You better learn how to treat that drunkard/For you got to go down.   You
Got to Go Down.   Blind Gary Davis.   BluL

You big black boundin' beggar–for/you bruk a British square.   Fuzzy-Wuzzy.
Rudyard Kipling.   BrPo; EnLit; HBV 1-2; MCCG; MoBrPo; TrGrPo

You bird, you dream, you wife.   Songs to a Lady Moonwalker.   Abraham
Sutzkever.   VWA

You both will feel better by breakfast time.   City without Walls.   W. H.
Auden.   NYBP; NYP

You breathe me I inscribe you/circular memory   Memory Air.   Charles
Dobzynski.   VWA

You bring me closer/to home....   Poem for the Conguero in D-yard.
Raymond Ringo Fernandez.   LFAC

"You brought up something to die"   I Met This Guy Who Died.   Gregory
Corso.   NAs; Psk

You burdened heart/of my heart.   Grandma Shorba and the Pure in Heart.
Freya Manfred.   FAZ

You burn into the yellow grass of winter,/into one reed, trembling on the
plain.   Winter Burn.   Roberta Hill.   VoR

You but do with a sword what your pills did before.   Though a Soldier at
Present.   Thomas Moore.   DBV

You but unlock, so we each other bless.   To a Lady That Desired I Would
Love Her.   Thomas Carew.   AnAnS 2; CaPo; LiTL; LoBV; MeLP; MePo;
OBS; SeCV 1-2

"You Callow Coyote, don't dance with no/Star!   Coyote and the Star.
Arthur Guiterman.   BPAW

You came into the world too late,/And I depart so soon.   Florine.   Thomas
Campbell.   BSV

You can always sing to a copper pan.   Spanish Song.   Charles Divine.
HBMV

You can always tell your pal,/If you've ever navigated on the Erie Canal.
The Erie Canal.   William S. Allen.   AmFN; TrAS

You can be short, but never sweet.   At the Nadir.   Gerta Kennedy.   PoPl

You can boast yourself somebody,/But you can't fool God!   You Can't Fool
God.   Grenville Kleiser.   STF

"You can cut yourself on a sheet of paper/and your skin's about as thin."
Rhymes.   Frank Steele.   PPJ

You can force the world to cheer you.   This Is Your Hour.   Herbert
Kaufman.   PoToHe

You can forget: ah then, forgive! Lines. Aubrey Thomas De Vere. IrPN

You can go as far as you like with me,/In my merry Oldsmobile. In My Merry Oldsmobile. Vincent Bryan. FSN

You can guess where she gives me a pain./'Way down in Cuba! 'Way Down in Cuba. Anonymous. AmSS

You can hang or drown at last. A Short Song of Congratulation. Samuel Johnson. CABA; EBEV; EiCP; ELP; HAP; InPK; InPS; InvP; LAuP; LoBV; NOBE; NOEC; NoP; OBEC; OBSV; PAI; PoEL 1-5; TEP

You can have what you ask for, ask for/everything Revolutionary Letter #19. Diane Di Prima. IHMS

You can hear the far deep rumour of sea on stone. Back Road Farm. Charles Bruce. CaP

You can hear their golden laughter/All the garden through! Sunflowers. Clinton Scollard. HBMV

You can hope to stand by the Devil's side,/And yell, "They can't do that!" They Can't Do That. Anonymous. WTO

You can leave it with Him, for you are His care-/You, you know. Leave It with Him. Anonymous. BLRP

...You can like it or not,/but I'll be just what I am. The Melting Pot. Dudley Randall. BALP; BPo

You can love and think, and the Earth cannot! The Wonderful World. William Brighty ("Matthew Browne") Rands. HBV 1-2; HBVY; TiPo

You can make blossom in me/Flowers of fire. To the Tune "Soaring Clouds'. Huang O. PBWP; WPOW

You can make it the heir of all your land/And she your gaily dee. Johnny Scot. Anonymous. BaBo

You can make no more of me, only destroy. Time Eating. Keith Douglas. NeBP

You can never get enough. Cuba, 1962. Florence Anthony ("Ai"). AmPA

You can never teach either oak or beech/To be aught but a greenwood tree. Song: "For the tender beech and the sapling oak." Thomas Love Peacock. OHIP

You can never wipe off the tears of woe. If You Trap the Moment. William Blake. DiPo

You can say that again, he'd say it again. What Kind of a Guy Was He? Howard Nemerov. PCP

You can see his moonlit hair/From the next far hill. The Toll-Gate Man. Wilson MacDonald. CaP

...You can see it on the sixth of May. It will eat you. The Altarpiece Finished. John Hollander. NoAm

You can see that I've given up. Hide and Seek. Dan Pagis. AMV-81

You can see the tiger blaze/In her tiger eyes, her tiger face. Here She Is. Mary Britton Miller. TiPo

You can see your own sweet face/In the bright tin. At Grandfather's. Clara Doty Bates. OBCA

You can steal my best woman/but you sure can't make her stay Someday Baby. Big Joe Williams. BluL

You can stop crying now. Do the Dead Know What Time It Is? Kenneth Patchen. HoPM; MoAmPo

You can't catch a spoonful. Riddle: "House full, yard full." Anonymous. NTCP

"You can't get something for nothing" daydreams. A Lost Mohican Visits Hell's Kitchen. A. K. Redwing. VoR

You can't just die and take yourself away. The Immigration Act of 1924. Laureen Mar. BrSi

You can't leave a house of air. The Hermit. Daniel Halpern. AMV-80

You can't lift your hands, you stand there, leaving. Don't Forget. Stephen Berg. PoA

You can't look in the mirror/my son! Momma's Not Gods Image... Noah Mitchell. LFAC

You can't make a livin' at a cotton mill. Cotton-Mill Colic. Anonymous. OuSiCo

...You can't tell a shotgun/or a man what to do. Almost Grown. Ai. MAYP

You can tear up his shirt for his minin's all done. The Collier's Rant. Anonymous. OBET

You can tell them you was robbed by Dick Turpin. Dick Turpin and the Lawyer. Anonymous. ViBoFo

You can wake up the world with YOUR row-de-dow. The Diakka. Gerald Massey. NOBV

You cannot bend to the shores of the world/Or strive with the great dark sea. Ballad of the Two Tapsters. Vernon Watkins. MoBS

You cannot comprehend its price/Nor its infrequency. Your Thoughts Don't Have Words Every Day. Emily Dickinson. DiPo; MAmP

You cannot dream/Things lovelier. Things Lovelier. Humbert Wolfe. TrJP

You cannot drive that deer away. Riddle: "On yonder hill there is a red deer." Anonymous. GBP

You cannot fancy what a fool/Poor rich uneducated Brown is. The Folly of Brown. Sir William Schwenck Gilbert. InMe

You cannot know how I, your mother,/Think of you and weep. Cradle Song. Anonymous. TrJP

-You cannot light a match on a crumbling wall. British Leftish Poetry, 1930-40. Hugh" (Christopher Murray Grieve) MacDiarmid. CMoP; FaBoTw; NMP; NoAm

You cannot miss it, though you shut your eyes. The Last Journey. of Tarentum Leonidas. AWP

You cannot rise, and we the living must. Views of Boston Common and Nearby. Richard P. Blackmur. MoVE

You cannot sleep till man has understood/That peace is Universal Brotherhood! Your Glory, Lincoln. Mae Winkler Goodman. PGD

You cannot smile at me and make an end.' A Mirror for Poets. Thom Gunn. LiTM; NePoEA

You cannot touch his body now/or burn his poems. On the Death of Ho Chi Minh. Eli Mandel. NIP

You cannot travel where they are. A Letter Is a Gypsy Elf. Annette Wynne. SUS

You cannot untouch that touch. Permanence. Francis Meynell. HBMV

You cant see me/see you Woman. Elouise Loftin. PoBA

You carry Caesar and his fortunes-steady! In Hospital. William Ernest Henley. VLP

You cat you/Cat. Cat Ballerina Assoluta. Emilie Glen. GoYe

You caused me to walk and talk with you,/Like I ne'er done before. Look Down That Lonesome Road. Anonymous. BLSo

You charm and entangle, merrily captivate. The Enemy. John Waller. NeBP

...You children prepared for,/And you stalwart loins. Pent-Up Aching Rivers (excerpt). Walt Whitman. ViBoPo

You choke the pretty harmless chickens. The Shrimp. Moses Browne. NOEC

You choose by the Master with whom you ally. Is It Nothing to You? L. James Kindig. BePJ

...You chose/What each must reckon with. Rembrandt's Late Self-Portraits. Elizabeth Jennings. EyDe

You closing around me/like a cat. Reconcilable Differences. Roger Sauls. AMV-81

You come-a stranger from your eyes/Looks out-and, meeting, first we part. Meeting After Long Absence. Lilla Cabot Perry. AA

...You come to/Paguate sometimes and visit us... Prologue. Carol Lee Sanchez. TWSS

You come too. Do You Know, I Would Quietly. Rainer Maria Rilke. OLR

You come too. The Pasture. Robert Frost. SUS

You comprehend your loneliness, I ween. The Disdainful Mistress. Anonymous. WTO

You copper-sulphate blue bird! The Blue Jay. D. H. Lawrence. FM

You could always hear me sing. Young Hunting. Anonymous. FaBoBa

...You/could die out there. You/could live for ever. Instructions to the Double. Tess Gallagher. FaBoWP

You could go on...But won't. Salute. Oliver Pitcher. PoBA

& You could hardly bear/how much you wanted in The End. Sharon Thesen. CaPN

You could have learned to live. Spider Reeves. Henry Carlile. Psk

You could hear the cracking of bones/from the seventh row. Rites of the Eastern Star. Janine Pommy-Vega. APU

You could lie down where you were and listen to the dead. The Iron Lung. Stanley Plumly. AmPA; GeTw; LCAP

You could not, could not tell/my heart from my hand. Innocence. James Scully. LTB

You could not have kept her a week on a penny. An Old Woman. Charles Henry Ross. OxBChV

"You could not reach us if you did not/die." Faith's Vista. Henry Abbey. AA

You could swear the voice you hear is kind,/calling you home, little Jewboy in alarm. Getting Lost in Nazi Germany. Marvin Bell. VWA

You couldn't hit a bear in the ass/with a handful of rice! Hunting. Gary Snyder. NOBA

You coward...this baby that I bleed. The Abortion. Anne Sexton. CAPP; IHMS; MAT; NMM; SM; VGW

...You cross all the rivers/as if they were only one. Animal Songs: Zebra. Anonymous. PeSA

You'd almost think it was despair. The Combat. Edwin Muir. CMoP; LiTB; MoBrPo; NOBE

You'd be better in the silver cage of a merchant. The Keeper of the Midnight Gate. George Mackay Brown. OxBC

You'd be colder than I and not half as cute! Canine Amenities. Anonymous. GDP

You'd be surprised/what she does/with the roses. Lecture Noir. Sharon Thesen. CaPN

...You'd/Best leave these blood-soaked notions/To those who find them useful. A Bestiary. Kenneth Rexroth. OBAL

You gonna follow poor Crudup/down to his burying ground. Death Valley Blues. Arthur ("Big Boy") Crudup. BluL

You got a right, I got a right,/We all got a right to de tree of life. You Got a Right. *Anonymous.* BoAN 1-2

You got another papa on the Salt Lake Line! Casey Jones. *Anonymous.* ATP; TrGrPo

You got it! Unemployment/Monologue. June Jordan. WPOW

You got the blues and still ain't satisfied Got the Blues, Can't Be Satisfied. Mississippi John Hurt. BluL

You got to take me/Like I am. Me and the Mule. Langston Hughes. IDB

You got your mouth wide open–/You don't know what to say. Good Morning Blues. *Anonymous.* FSW

You gotta have your tips on fire/Carnal. You Gotta Have Your Tips on Fire. Victor Hernandez Cruz. InW

You grow too warm. I must be moving on. At Knaresborough. Donald Davie. NePoEA

You had a father: let your son say so. Sonnets, XIII: "O! that you were yourself; but, love, you/are." William Shakespeare. OAEP; TEP

You had always been pointing to/with such insistence/in the undistinguishable distance. Sylvia. Giacomo Leopardi. NaP

You had better not think of Skye. A Warning. Alexander Nicolson. PoSH

You had gone mad like me. The Mistress (excerpt). John Wilmot, Earl of Rochester. AtBAP

You had to be there. God,/it was a lovely thing! Formations. William Freedman. VWA

You half expect them to spill. Poppies. Roy Scheele. PPJ

You hand me two children, two roses. Kindness. Sylvia Plath. BoC; FaBoWP

You hate the flow, and yet it flows. Memory of the Present. David Shapiro. APU

...You have a costume,/you have meaning. Notes for a Lecture. David Ignatow. NNaP

You have brought the dead/To a grove of suns. The Archaeology of Love. Richard Murphy. EnLoPo

"You have crossed the water to visit me." Second Sight. Michael Longley. FaBoIP

You have dropped your handkerchief. Life. Artie Gold. NOBC

You have failed to comfort Me. Unawares. Emma A. Lent. PoLf

You have forgot to tread the ancient way. Eli the Thatcher. William and Max Beerbohm Rothenstein. FaBoNo

You have forgotten me well. When You Have Forgotten Sunday: The Love Story. Gwendolyn Brooks. BPo; FF; WPOW

You have forgotten that the election is near. Election Songs. *Anonymous.* WTO

You have found the one-armed man/and found him certain kin. Poem for David Janssen. R. T. Smith. AMV-81

You have gathered the holy essences and worn them/tightly on your breasts. Inanna and the Divine Essences. Enheduanna. BoWoP

You have him living to Eternity. On John Donne's Book of Poems. John Marriot. CH

You have inherited. New Year's. Charles Reznikoff. VGW

You have kept up with the times and I am glad! LII. Ted Berrigan. ANYP

You have kill'd three Niggers in the first degree,/No bail. You've Been a Good Old Wagon, But You've Done Broke Down. Ben Harney. OBAL

You have killed the bravest butcher boy/In North Amerikee! The Three Butchers. *Anonymous.* BFSS

You have kissed/the final crescent of my heart/& made it full. Dearest Man-in-the-Moon. Erica Jong. MOON

You have lost Egypt though you saved your ships. The Old Saint. Muriel Stuart. HBMV

...You have...made/a record in my heart./Goodbye. Phone Call to Rutherford. Paul Blackburn. CTBA; PoM

You have mistook the jest. The Defiance. Aphra Behn. EnLoPo

You have my thanks, let me your comfort have. Arcadia. Sir Philip Sidney. FCP

You have no one to bludgeon but each other! Farewell to Europe. [(or Pillin)] William Pillen. VWA

You have nothing on me today. While Dissecting Frogs in Biology Class Scrut Discovers... George Roberts. GOYP

You have nothing to fear/from the poet/but the truth Voice in the Crowd. Ted Joans. AmNP

You have only to begin/again To Begin. Fran Winant. BrRo

...You have seen it, when obstacles happened/to bar/the path, rise automatically. Sojourn in the Whale. Marianne Moore. SBG

You have sent me only your handmaids. To Kaaon. Ezra Pound. PoA

"You have sinned: Such/Furies as we know shall/be set upon thee." Vivisection (excerpt). Gene Fowler. LFAC

You have started your count./I cannot. Downtown-Boy Uptown. David Henderson. NNP; PoNe

...You have tasted your own blood. Siegfried. Randall Jarrell. MiAP

You have the reply The Question Is Proof. Elizabeth Bartlett. NePoAm-2

You have to close your mind and go on living! Aunt Gladys's Home Movie No. 31, Albert's Funeral. Jim Wayne Miller. Str

You have to improve the blank page. Young Poets. Nicanor Parra. PoL

...You have to/like it better than being loved. For the Young Who Want To. Marge Piercy. Psk

You have to lose to prove you've got it. Good Sportsmanship. Richard Armour. LiSp

You have to plant your table under its leaves and begin eating. The Power of Maples. Gerald Stern. NU

You have translation's statutes best fulfilled,/That, handling, neither sully nor would gild. To His Worthy Friend Doctor Witty.... Andrew Marvell. GLGT; PP

You have twenty or thirty children waiting for me./Whom I shall bear! Obatala, the Creator. *Anonymous.* WTO

You have used our skulls/for ashtrays. A Poet Recognizing the Echo of the Voice. Diane Wakoski. NIP

You have white pearls/And blue stones Five Songs. David Shapiro. ANYP

You have won your vengeance, brave! The Gold Seekers. Marion Muir Richardson. PoOW

You have your own telephone Lily Flower. Michael Brownstein. ANYP

You haven't even got a window/and his is full of houses. Wellington. Bill Manhire. OCNZ

You haven't?–I wonder–What of God? If You Had a Friend. Robert Lewis. PoToHe

You, having discovered fire,/hastily trade your liver. Prometheus. Jenny Mastoraki. BoWoP

You, having once made such a lovely fuss/on Love's behalf, betrayed her, worse than us. John Donne. James Simmons. CIP

You hear me speak. But do you hear me feel? The Woman Poet. Gertrud Kolmar. VWA

You hear that contrapuntal pawnshop beat. North Infinity Street. Conrad Aiken. AP

You hearken to the melody of my steam-callipe/Yawp! Home, Sweet Home. Henry Cuyler Bunner. BXAP; InMe

You hit up a faster gait–/Do it now! Do It Now! *Anonymous.* BLPA; WBLP

You hold him no Philosopher at all. Moral Essays. Alexander Pope. LiTB

You hold it to/a clock-shadow's ear/at dusk. Over Three Nipple-Stones. Paul Celan. VWA

"You! hypocrite lecteur!–mon semblable,–mon frere!" The Waste Land. Thomas Stearns Eliot. CMoP; CoBMV; HAP; LiTA; LiTM; MasP; MoAB; MoAmPo; MoPo; MoVE; NAWM 1-2; NePA; NoAm; NOBE; NoP; OAEL 1-2; OxBA; OxBTC; TAP; UnPo

You & I, Wulf, the one/with the other/& singing Wulf. Bill Manhire. OCNZ

You imagine a rich man, maybe,/with his money. Spring. Linda McCarriston. AMV-81

You in his spotted garments/Shall yourself lie wrapped. To Bring the Dead to Life. Robert Graves. MoBrPo

You include yourself in the latter class. From a Lavatory Wall. *Anonymous.* FaBoEE

You incongruous old woman of Smyrna! Limerick: "There was a young person of Smyrna." Edward Lear. NBM; OxBoLi; TEP

You interest me. Note Delivered by Female Impersonator. Heather McHugh. AmPA

You jealous/Bridegroom of blood Zippora Returns to Moses at Rephidim. Rose Drachler. VWA

You jest a little bit o' woman but you/Sound like a great big crowd. Morning After. Langston Hughes. NLV; NoAm

...You jot/it down, jump up, look/at me and giggle. Miss Cho Composes in the Cafeteria. James Tate. SM; WeW

You just come right back here,/Lucille. At the Airport in Dallas. Stephen Mooney. TAT

You just cross Jefferson, Texas. Naomi Shihab. TAT

You just getting ready/honey, for the cypress grove Cypress Grove Blues. Skip James. BluL

You just invent your own games and teach us old ones/how to play Poem for Black Boys. Nikki Giovanni. BPo

You just punch a hole in the son of a bitch. The Virtues of Carnation Milk. *Anonymous.* OBAL

You killed my poor pappy,/Now, dang you, try me. Rye Whiskey (Clinch Mountain). *Anonymous.* TrAS

You kiss me hard/& go to her. Another. Ellen Marie Bissert. PeHV

You knew, delicately, through amber, that August day. Remembering Althea. William Stafford. NYBP

...You knew more than any of us/That such is the Signature of all things. Signature. Joseph Stroud. NPGG

...You knew that. Everyman's Library. John Ashbery. NoP

You know again you have to wait. This Is the Place to Wait. Horace Gregory. MoAmPo

You know as much about that face as I do. Faces. John Ciardi. BiP

You know, birds! Wings and Wheels. Nancy Byrd Turner. SoPo; SUS; TiPo

You know, he said/two birds with one stone Vietnam #4. Clarence Major. BOLo; FF; PoBA

You know I ain't got no true religion, baby/mmmm well, I don't want to be baptized Homeless Blues. Lil' Son Jackson. BluL

You know I always loved you. Attack of the Crab Monsters. Lawrence Raab. AmPA; NoP

"You know I'm D E F!" Repartee. Charles Follen Adams. OBAL

You know, I'm sorry today/That I ever knowed your name. Special Rider Blues. Anonymous. AmFP

You know I'm still your master. Ghoul Care. Ralph Hodgson. AnEnPo; MoBrPo

You know it don't belong to you. Take Your Fingers off It. Anonymous. FSW

You know it–you are welcome to it. I close, and go in peace. The Page of Illustrations. Peter Schjeldahl. ANYP

You know the children can go in the daytime/oooo boy, and the old folks have it at night Working Man Blues. Sleepy John Estes. BluL

You know the deep love of the heart. The Well: Two Songs. Anonymous. WTO

You know/the way he can travel/is a low down/old dirty shame The Pony Blues. Son House. BluL

You know the way to Heaven's door. Church Music. George Herbert. AnAnS 1; OBSP; SeCV 1-2; UnS

You know they think their work was done/In partnership with Him. Farmers. William Alexander Percy. WGRP

You know this well/You that have been there too. All Things Confine. Hadewijch. PBWP

You know 'twas in the dark you taught me! The Kiss. Thomas Moore. EnLoPo

You know what to do with your diesel and shale. Diesel and Shale. Anonymous. OBSS

You know whose naked breast supports his brow/Where he lies now. All-Knowing Lamp. Anonymous. UnTE

You know why, and for whom, and for what. A Reply from the Akond of Swat. Ethel Talbot Scheffauer. FiBHP

You know you have died. Paranoia. Michael Dennis Browne. AmPA

You know. You're inside us. Hustlers. Dennis Cooper. APU

You know your friends; you know your bill of fare. The Invitation. Leonard Welsted. NOEC

You lack charm. Poem. James Schuyler. ANYP

You, Lady, are the Tree. Annunciation. Rainer Maria Rilke. OBVE

You,/landlord/of my heart. Greed, Part 4. The Turtle. Diane Wakoski. NoAm

You leave us with more/Than you touch with decay. To Death. Oliver St. John Gogarty. FaBoEE; OBMV

...You leave/your shape on the lawn in the wet blades. Singing yet. Singing Death. Stan Rice. FYAP

You left behind immortal lines/for other happy singers. On Learning to Play the Guitar. Ray Fraser. NeAC

You left me at the parting of the way/And sacrificed the world and all its ken. A Faded Letter. William J. Fischer. CAW

You let yourself be harnessed–nag! The Horse and the Whip. Eliezer Steinbarg. VWA

"You lie." Early Morning. Morris Bishop. PV

You lie! Nocturne. Naomi Long Madgett. BALP

...You lie/Attended by cold worms and hedgerow priests/More hungry and less merciful than I. Bagman O'Reilly's Curse. Les A. Murray. TW

"You lie," he cried,/And ran on. I Saw a Man Pursuing the Horizon. Stephen Crane. AmePo; LiTA; LiTM; LoGBV; MAT; NePA; NOBA

You lie in my arms,/I wrestle with the angel. Apocrypha. Stanley Moss. VWA

You lie there/thinking of nothing/watching the sky... Late Abed. Archibald MacLeish. NCSH

You lift those eyes that praise the sea,/Freezing my corpse. Now Is Farewell. Blanaid Salkeld. NeIP

You light my page, but no light leaps its rim. Mailed to G. B. Gene Derwood. NePA

You, lion in nakedness,/As citizen must pose. In Nakedness. Marnie Pomeroy. ErPo

You'll learn it/Prig,/You/ARE! When We Were Very Silly. J.B. Morton. FaBoPa

You live forever at Your mother's side! Prayer That an Infant May Not Die. Francis Jammes. CAW

You live in this, and dwell in lovers' eyes. Not Marble. William Shakespeare. AnEnPo

You'll all be beef-stew in the sweet by and by. Git Along Little Dogies. Anonymous. BPAW

You'll all the better please/Grandpapa. To My Grandmother. Frederick Locker-Lampson ALV; HBV 1-2; InMe; OBVV

You'll always go to sleep/more times than you'll wake Letter for Duncan. Larry Eigner. PoM

You'll be longing for Oklahoma and your good old feather bed. Arizona. Anonymous. AmFP

You'll be our cow! Our Little Calf. Dorothy Aldis. TiPo

You'll be safely in the fashion/If you blame things on the church. Some Who Do Not Go to Church. Anonymous. WBLP

You'll be the sweetest girl in town. Hush, Li'l Baby. Anonymous. BLSo; FSW; OuSiCo

You'll be "truly great'. Fiction and the Reading Public. Philip Larkin. NOBL; OBSV

You'll break a leg ere close of day. The Shropshire Lad's Cousin (parody). Samuel Hoffenstein. BXAP

You'll break me you'll break me you'll break me. Between God's Eyelashes. Jose Garcia Villa. CrMA

You'll easy draw a lang-kent face,/But no sae weel a stranger. To an Artist. Robert Burns. EyDe

You'll ever give/Or get. For a Far-Out Friend. Gary Snyder. NeAP; PoM

You'll feel my hand in blessing on your brow. Eternal. Agnes Foley Macdonald. CaP

You'll find her somewhere in the litany/With pride, vainglory, and hypocrisy. A Madame, Madame B. Beaute Sexagenaire. Charles, Earl of Dorset Sackville. APAS

You'll find him if you go to Trenton Falls. Fitz Adam's Story. James Russell Lowell. AmePo

You'll find once more the dreams you thought were dead. The Spring Will Come. Henry Dawson Lowry. BoNaP

"You'll find the people here the same,"/The wise man said. The Right Kind of People. Edwin Markham. BLPA; FPL; PoToHe

You'll forget the little plough-boy that whistled o'er the lea. Air: "A flaxen-headed cow-boy, as simple as may be." John O'Keefe. NOEC

You'll gain at least a knighthood, or the bays. The First Satire of the Second Book of Horace Imitated (excerpt). Alexander Pope. OBSV

You'll get spanked, Miss Betwixt-and-betweeny!' Limerick: "A young lady of fair Mytilene." Anonymous. CenHV

You'll get the best of the whole show–/That's pep! Pep. Grace G. Bostwick. WBLP

You'll get what you want. You'll get your oblivion. Night Song. Louise Gluck. MAYP; SV

You'll hang like me, a murderer,/All on the gallows high. The Wexford Girl. Anonymous. AmFP; ShS; ViBoFo

You'll have time to grow wise in their company. Marcus Argentarius. Kenneth Rexroth. CrMA

You'll have to make the boy, I fear,/An architect or auctioneer. How to Raise a Son. Martial (Marcus Valerius Martialis). LiTW

You'll have to ride alone tonight. Reasons to Go Home. Greg Forker. LFAC

You'll hear an instant click, a tear will start/Imprinted with an abstract of his case. Nothing in Heaven Functions As It Ought. X. J. Kennedy. SM

...You'll hear in high limbs/voices of dry leaves. A Little Song. Charles O. Hartman. SM

You'll hear me call your name. Should You Go First. Albert K. Rowswell. BLPL; PoLf; PoToHe

..."You'll hear more/about it soon!"–and hung up– Cuento. Carlos Cumpian. FIA

You'll hear Patch-Shaneen cry. Patch-Shaneen. John Millington Synge. LoBV

You'll hear the roses speak to the moon. Roses. J. Corson Miller. CAW

You'll keep a wind, as long as he did fight. A Long Prologue to a Short Play... Sir Henry Sheers. APAS

You'll know it by the three gold ones over the door. Objets d'Art. Cynthia MacDonald. NMM

You'll know it's nothin' but the Devil himself,/raisin' hell about the knots in his tail. Tyin' a Knot in the Devil's Tail. Gail Gardner. ABF; FSW

You'll know me easy, because/I'm wearing a black tie, love.' The Evans Country. Kingsley Amis. NOBL

You'll know the Puk-Wudjies are somewhere around! Puk-Wudjies. Patrick Reginald Chalmers. HBVY

You'll know you slept too long. Newsreel. C. Day-Lewis. MoAB; MoBrPo

You'll learn it by lookin' at Moggy an' me. Moggy and Me. James Hogg. HBV 1-2

You'll leave such tyrants far behind! A Convict's Lament on the Death of Captain Logan. Anonymous. PoAu 1-2

"You'll look that way when you are dead," hm,hm, hm. There Was an Old Woman. Anonymous. BFSS

You'll lose sleep but not food or dreams if kept/tight as shark or ship at either end. Handlining Tockers & Gizmos. Allen Planz. WOLT

You'll love me–won't you? Do You Remember. Thomas Haynes Bayly. HBV 1-2

You'll meet without fail on the Midnight Mail/The Cat of the Railway Train.' Skimbleshanks: the Railway Cat. Thomas Stearns Eliot. FaBoCh; FaBoCo; LoGBV; NOBL

You'll need to wait a long, long while. Reunion. Cyril Tawney. OBET

You'll neither laugh nor smile/At the tickling of your knee. If You Are a Gentleman. *Anonymous.* OxNR

You'll never be mentally sober. On Rachmaninoff's Birthday. Frank O'Hara. CAPP; PoM

You'll never feel like touching anything or anyone/Again/And then you do. Dispersion and Convergence. Tom Clark. APU

You'll never get a chance to put your big legs on me no more/(Yeah). Big Woman. Washboard Sam. BluL

You'll never get rich/On the salary which/You get in the Army now. You're in the Army Now. *Anonymous.* BLSo

You'll never know. My God, they were beautiful, the old books. The Old Books. Vernon Scannell. OxBC

You'll never miss your ham till a–/nother mule be in your stall. Don't Fish in My Sea. Ma Rainey. BluL

You'll never thrive again. Warning. *Anonymous.* OxNR

You'll nEverest if you're Tensing."; Poem, Neither Hillaryous Norgay. Gardner E. Lewis. FiBHP

You'll not forget me–ever, ever, ever? Dialogue on the Headland. Robert Graves. ACV

You'll notice the library's books are all blank on the inside. View from an Institution. Franz Wright. AMV-81

You'll only double trouble, and trouble others too. Don't Trouble Trouble. Mark Guy Pearse. WBLP

You'll permit me, I hope, to die in my/shoes. Epigram. *Anonymous.* PAH

You'll say, no doubt, 'tis both of these; and still/Give other reasons, too. And yet ask why? On Walking Back to the Bus. Alan Gardner. PoSH

You'll see a real valentine–/my heart in formaldehyde! Valentine. Len Gasparini. NeAC

You'll see–we'll meet. No Escape. Harriet L. Delafield. GoYe

You'll show a hat that's white, or a feather. John Burns of Gettysburg. Bret (Francis Bret Harte) Harte. HBV 1-2; MC; OHIP; PAL

You'll sit there till you rot! Turn on the Footlights: The Perils of Pedagogy. John Marshall Carter. AMV-80

You'll still be the sweetest little/Baby in town. The Mocking Bird. *Anonymous.* AmFP

You'll wade out deep for the big one. Feeling for Fish. Leonard Trawick. AMV-81

You'll win–what I mean take it easy–but take it. Talking Union. Millard and Lee Hays Lampell. FSW

You, long years; and your father, health! To Mistress Anne Cecil. William Cecil, Lord Burleigh. ElL; OBSC

You look over, stretching your sad neck/toward the far hill. Deer. No Ch'on-myong. PBWP

You look upon the air. Late. Louise Bogan. PBWP; VGW

You looking into flames wondering/what it would have really/been like. Another Old Song. Barney Bush. STE

You lose yourself/Where the tall buildings meet. The Elevated Train. James S. Tippett. SUS

You love His church and righteous cause/And give with no unjust reserve. If You're the Man You Ought to Be. Walter E. Isenhour. STF

"You love...?love...?love...?' all on an indrawn breath. Modern Love, XLII. George Meredith. NOBV; ViBoPo; VLP

You love me for a frailer Part. The Fall. John Wilmot, Earl of Rochester. EnLoPo; UnTE

You love not me? A Broken Appointment. Thomas Hardy. BiP; CBEP; DTC; GBL; NoAm; NOBV; NoP; OAEP

You made your calm patrol. A Nocturne for October 31st. Yvor Winters. PoA

"You make everything/So dizzy." And he did. How Einstein Started It Up Again. R. H. W. Dillard. SUW

You may also look most absurd with a miserable face. Dear Female Heart. Stevie Smith. FaBoEE

–You may be Dirty Dinky. Dinky. Theodore Roethke. OBAL; OBCA; SM

You may believe when it tells you the French are at Civita/Vecchia. Amours de Voyage. Arthur Hugh Clough. FaBoPV

You may–but they'll be mine! The Nun. [James Henry] Leigh Hunt. OBRV

You may call her a vision, but you must not call her a sight. What One May and May Not Call a Woman. *Anonymous.* GoTF; TreF

You may catch all the others, but you wo–– The Slithergadee Has Crawled out of the Sea. Shel Silverstein. AmMo; NLV; OnUR; WSC

You may eat a bit of the pie. The Derby Ram. *Anonymous.* OxNR

You may find this advertisement: "Wanted–A girl to/cook." A Paradox. *Anonymous.* ShM

You may follow her by the smell. Old Pudding-Pie Woman. *Anonymous.* OxNR

You may forget the singer,/But don't forget the song. Young Companions. *Anonymous.* CoSo

You may get there by candle-light. How Many Miles to Babylon? Mother Goose. ExPo; GBP; OBSP; OxNR

You may get to like them. A Reunion. James Schuyler. ANYP

You may go round the world/By the Old Marlborough Road. The Old Marlborough Road. Henry David Thoreau. PoEL 1-5

You may have forgot, you was drunk when you died. Epigram: "When Bibo thought fit from the world to retreat." Matthew Prior. FaBoEE

You may love no man as you have loved me,/Who have loved you as I may not love again. Retractions. James Branch Cabell. HBMV

You may make a Mistake–and think slightly of This. The Haunch of Venison, A Poetical Epistle to Lord Clare. Oliver Goldsmith. CEP

...You may need help. Help Is on the Way. Herbert Scott. GP

You may pass close by their encampments and never/know. The Navajo. Elizabeth Jane Coatsworth. AmFN

You may put the blame on the stars and the sun and the/white road and the sky! Wander-Thirst. Gerald Gould. HBV 1-2; TiPo

You may say what you will, they are the nicest people in the/world. I Like Americans. Nancy Boyd. YaD

You may take from it now their fragrant souvenir. The Roses of Sa'adi. Marceline Desbordes-Valmore. BoWoP; LiTW; WPOW

You may than live in joy perdurably. Epitaph of La Graunde Amoure. Stephen Hawes. FaBoRV

You may think what you please–but they both were content. The Pleasing Constraint. Richard Brinsley Sheridan. ALV

"You mean," he said, "a crocodile." The Purist. Ogden Nash. DBV; FiBHP; GoJo; InPS; MoAmPo; MoShBr; NLV; OBCA; PV; ShM; TreFT

You merit more; nor cou'd my Love do less. To My Dear Friend Mr. Congreve, on His Comedy... John Dryden. CEP; EBEV; FiP; OBS; PoEL 1-5; SeCV 1-2

You met a Lion unaware,/And felled him flying through the air. Of Baiting the Lion. Sir Owen Seaman. NA

"You might as well answer the door, my child,/the truth is furiously knocking." The Light That Came. Lucille Clifton. GeTw

You might as well live. Resume. Dorothy Parker. ALV; DBV; DL; HeIP; InMe; InPK; NLV; NoP; OBAL; PoPl; ShM; TrJP

You might as well take that. Refugee. Naomi Long Madgett. PoNe

You might be surprised right out the window, whistling dixie on the/way Poem for Half-White College Students. LeRoi (Imamu Amiri Baraka) Jones. BPo; CAPP; TAP; UnPo

You might catch her a small bird or two. Two Maids Went A-Milking One Day. *Anonymous.* FSW

You more then any may be dignify'd. The Brown Beauty. Edward, Lord Herbert of Cherbury. AnAnS 2

You morsel left half-cold on Caesar's plate. Lesbia. Richard Aldington. PoLf

You most of all, are weak. To a Severe Nun. Thomas Merton. CoPo

You motherfucking SAVAGE! The Boy; or, Son of Rip-Off (parody). Malcolm Glass. BXAP

You move on,/muttering old benedictions/as you go. Cinema Verite. Dorothy Walters. IHMS

You must be mad beyond redress,/If my next wish you cannot guess! A Hinted Wish. Martial (Marcus Valerius Martialis). AWP; LiTW

You must be proud, if you'll be wise. To the Ladies. Mary Lee, Lady Chudleigh. NOEC; WPOW

You must bear all the venom of his tooth! Modern Love, XXVI. George Meredith. HBV 1-2; VLP

You must carry your mother and your father at your breasts. The Messenger. Jean Valentine. LCAP

You must change your life. Archaic Torso of Apollo. Rainer Maria Rilke. LiTW; NAWM 1-2; NU

You must change your words. An Ordinary Day beyond Kaitaia. Kendrick Smithyman. OCNZ

You must do in two. Hoo, Suffolk. *Anonymous.* GBP

You must either prevent all these whims,/Or a way, love, to humour them find. Whimper of Awakening Passion. Ebenezer Jones. NOBV

You must fight, sink, or swim, or die by the sword. The Female Warrior. *Anonymous.* ShS

You must find out, for I don't know. Three Wise Old Women. Elizabeth T. Corbett. BLPA; OBCA; OxBChV

You must forget the warmth of beauty/Even in your dreams. Epigram: "Love brought me quietly." Meleager. PeHV

You must have a soul to clutch. Neighbors. Anne Spencer. CDC

You must have been great/alive. Benediction. Bob Kaufman. PoNe

"You must have given me up." Kidnaper. Tess Gallagher. AmPA

You must I carve to tell the world of him. To Luigi del Riccio, after the Death of Cecchino Bracci. Buonarroti Michelangelo. PeHV

You must keep their memory green. May Thirtieth. *Anonymous.* PoSC

You must live, get on with your life. A Farewell. A. R. D. Fairburn. AnNZ

You must love me, dilly dilly,/'Cause I love you. Lavender Blue. *Anonymous.* CH; FSW; LiTL

"You-must-never-go-down-to-the-end-of-town/-if-you -don't-go-down-with ME!" a f N w . Disobedience. A.(lan) A.(lexander) Milne. NTCP

You must not go to the wood at night! The Magic Wood. Henry Treece. DuDa; EAS

You must not hope to arrive. The Tourist from Syracuse. Donald Justice. TwCP

You must not think that you alone are blessed of God. On a Sunday. Charles Reznikoff. DFF

You must obey my every need. Lately I've felt a grave concern. Countess Beatriz de Die. BoWoP

You must reach inside and pull me/like a silver bullet/from your arm. Inside Out. Diane Wakoski. CoAP; NYBP

You must remain silent. To Boris Pasternak. Alexander Kushner. VWA

You must seek Him in the morning/If you want Him through the day. The Secret. Ralph Spaulding Cushman. STF; TRV

You must slosh it on here with a squeegee.' Limerick: "When Gauguin was visiting Fiji." Victor Gray. NOBL

You must stay awake until this ends. View from an Apartment. Michael Palmer. APU

You must stay there/forever. I am yours. Frau Ava. BoWoP

–You must think/On the true nature of Hope, whose eye is round and/does not wink. End of Season. Robert Penn Warren. LiTA

You must travel back/to the cold bud of water/In the hard rock. Welcome. R. S. Thomas. NMP

You must try it, if not now/very soon. The Beast Section. Welton Smith. PoBA

You must wear them until you are dead.' Limerick: "There was an Archdeacon who said." *Anonymous.* OxBoLi

You, my comrade, had to go,/I to stay. Sentence. Witter ("Emanuel Morgan") Bynner. HBV 1-2

You, my oldest son Peter, age 10,/going on 11. This Is a Poem to My Son Peter. Peter Meinke. DFF; GP

You ne'er saw a girl like my sweet Robinette. Sweet Robinette. *Anonymous.* CoMu

You ne'er saw the like. King Pippin. *Anonymous.* OxNR

You need not be an atom of a poet. Villanelle. Walter William Skeat. FaBoCo; FiBHP

–You need not look just the way I want. Homeward Bound. Ezekiel Mphahlele. WhB

...You need/Their answers in the fundamental act. Satyr. Charles Gullans. PoA

You never can contrive to make/Old Hecuba young Helen. Artificial Beauty. Lucian [or Lucianus]. AWP

You never can falter/With Gustav/And Walter/And Franz. Alma. Tom Lehrer. NLV

You never can teach either oak or beech/To be aught but a greenwood tree. Beech and Oak. Thomas Love Peacock. CBEP

You never can tell. Those Two Boys. Franklin Pierce ("F.P.A.") Adams. ALV; FiBHP; TrJP

You never can tell till you try. Limerick: "There was a young maid who said, "Why." *Anonymous.* LiBL; NA; SoSe

You never can tell/What will sell. Alfred Lord Tennyson. Reed Whittemore. PP

You never know when you hear one ring/Who may be waiting there! Doorbells. Rachel Field. TiPo

You not there. Away. Walter De la Mare. NoP

You, now so shaken and so powerless–/High priestess of your home. Autumn. Jean Starr Untermeyer. HBMV; MCCG

You, O Xgoro/son of the Thundercloud. Song of the Thunder. *Anonymous.* PeSA

You, of course, are a rose–/But were always a rose. The Rose Family. Robert Frost. NIP; OBAL; OBCA; SoSe

You, oh our dearest, have no place. Visit to a Hospital. Jean Valentine Chace. GoYe

You, oh, you, because I wanted you. The Needle's Eye. *Anonymous.* AmFP

You only came to wrestle, and I lost. Vetus Flamma. Robert Mezey. PoA

You or I must be he. Hinx, Minx. *Anonymous.* OxNR

You ought to be four. Joan's Door. Eleanor Farjeon. BiCB

You ought to seen John Hardy getting away. John Hardy. *Anonymous.* FSW

You, our maker/you, O Tsui-Xgoa. Hymn to Tsui-Xgoa. *Anonymous.* PeSA

You paint me a ship as is like a ship...an' that'll do/for me!' Pictures. C. Fox Smith. EtS

You pass my door and you don't come in. Careless Love. *Anonymous.* FSW

You passed by me like a she nanny goat. Don't You Like It? *Anonymous.* OuSiCo

You people of Dingaan. The Springtime of the Earth. Isaiah Shembe. WTO

(You pig) Apres le Bain. William Carlos Williams. OBAL

You plant in your son the soul of the desert. Song for Dov Shamir. Dannie Abse. VWA

You play the sun all day/like a ukulele Begin Summer. Ingrid Jonker. PeSA

You possess me, I am blest! Altar Prayers. *Anonymous.* WTO

You pray in vain for Carrousel. The Ballad of a Barber. Aubrey Beardsley. NOBV; SyP

You press a hidden nerve in your wrist/and completely disappear. Tonsilectomy. James W. Rivers. AMV-81

–You probably contain a germ. The Germ. Ogden Nash. CenHV; MoShBr

You proceed with caution, as though you were an endless night/scarcely touching the earth. No Such Thing. Marcia Southwick. AMV-81

You put me down; God knows I don't see why! C.C. Rider (with music). *Anonymous.* AS

You raise me now in song. Silence. Bella Akhmadulina. BoWoP

You're a better man than I am, Gunga Din! Gunga Din. Rudyard Kipling. BBV; BrPo; FaFP; FPL; GoTF; HBV 1-2; LiTB; MCCG; MoBrPo; OBTV; OnMSP; PoPl; TreF; VLP

You're a monkey, too! So Many Monkeys. Dorothy and Marion Edey Grider. SoPo; TiPo

You're a pip/They say/If you can breathe. On the Meatwheel. Dick Gallup. APU

You're a sport so they say, and imagine Broadway only forty-five minutes from here. Forty-Five Minutes from Broadway. George M. Cohan. FSN

You're a wonderful fellow! Spider. Padraic Colum. RoGo

...You're/All right with me,/You are. Poem: "Little brown boy." Helene Johnson. PoBA

You're all that I can call my own. Woman Work. Maya Angelou. SaC

You're all the hurt geography I own. Geography Lesson. Carol Rumens. FaBoWP

You're all too black and dirty/with a Ransi-tansi-tay! Ransi-Tansi-Tay. *Anonymous.* PoPle

You're asked to blow each light, each year,/out with your own breath. A Birthday Poem: for Rachel. James Simmons. OBSP

You're black in the mornin'/beige in the sun,/candy black all night long. Black Blues. Bloke Modisane. PBA

You're blind to, ten miles from your eyes, stark misery. To White South Africa. Cosmo Pieterse. WhB

You're blue/and going for mold. RIP. Jean Balderston. SOTS

You're bound to have a hard time wherever you go. George Britton. *Anonymous.* CoSo

You're dead, and dead, and dead indeed. A Man of Words. *Anonymous.* CBEP; FaBoBe; FaBoCh; FaFP; FF; GoTF; HBV 1-2; LoGBV; OxBoLi; TreFS

...You're desired to dispense/With the want of true grammar, good English, or sense. An Excellent New Ballad Giving a True Account of the Birth... Charles, Earl of Dorset Sackville. APAS

You're determined to float on your back/until you can stand on your feet. To Be in Love While in Prison. John Paul Minarik. LFAC

You're divine!said he/(you are Mine said she) No Thanks. Edward Estlin Cummings. UnTE

You're encased in vinyl. Perdido, Duke? Robert McGovern. SOTS

You're fair and I am dark. The Barrier. Claude McKay. BANP

You're fast asleep, you're fast asleep. Lady Bates. Randall Jarrell. MiAP

You're going forever, Vince. For the Death of Vince Lombardi. James Dickey. LiSp

You're going to be sorry, dear. Waking. Annie Higgins. ELU

You're going to reap just what you sow. You're Going to Reap Just What You Sow. *Anonymous.* AmFP

You're happy as a bug in a rug. Money (with music). *Anonymous.* AS

You're killing me. Raise the Shade. Edward Estlin Cummings. VGW

"You're looking good for your age today, old man." Idiot Boy. Rowland M. Hill. AMV-81

..."You're mine,"/she said, fiercely to the large/angelic flesh beside her. She lay wrapped... Gail Fox. NOBC

You're my fate./My blessing. Loyal Sins. Jacob Glatstein. VWA

You're not the survivor. Lobo. Charles Lillard. NOBC

"You're right!"/says Rooster Two. Roosters. Elizabeth Jane Coatsworth. SO

You're suffering martyrdom as much as I. Elegy XXIII. Louise Labé. WPOW

You're the flower of my heart,/Sweet Adeline. Sweet Adeline. Richard H. Gerard. FSW; GoTF; TreFT

You're the one I'd live for, die for–/And I'll be your Valentine. February 14, 22 B. C. Franklin Pierce ("F.P.A.") Adams. InMe

You're too dam heartsick fer to scold,/And too dam weak to pick up gold! Californy Stage. *Anonymous.* BPAW

You're vanquished by the might of Venus. In the Balance. *Anonymous.* OLR

..."You're welcome, lovely William, from the plains of/Waterloo." The Plains of Waterloo. *Anonymous.* OBET

You're welcome, lovelye Nancy, to my arms once more. The Mantle So Green (Lovely Nancy). *Anonymous.* AmFP

You're welcome, Sir, to this and more,/To quench your raging fire. The Very Pretty Maid of This Town... *Anonymous.* CoMu

...You read/a lot of books. Of All Things for You to Go Away Mad. Joanne Kyger. PoM

You read and doze, too real for me, too deep. Mother. Sharon Mayer Libera. IHMS

...You remain/As once, a creature singularly plain. To a Jilt. Martin Armstrong. FaBoEE

You remind me of some flower/Where love and beauty grows. Johnny German. *Anonymous.* BFSS

You replace your heart in your breast and go on your way Superballs. Tom Clark. ANYP; EAS

You retained an undivided silence. A "Case of Assault." Lydia Stephanou. BoWoP

You risk the danger of plunging into nothingness. Faust. Johann Wolfgang von Goethe. LiTW

You roam forlorn along the streets of gold. The Investiture. Siegfried Sassoon. NoAm

You roared across at me,/Chorus-leading, splashing out the wine. A Postcard from North Antrim. Seamus Heaney. FaBoIP; IPY

You rob my poor pockets, Of silver and gold. A Way Up on Clinch Mountain (A vers. with music). *Anonymous.* AS

You roll away. This Night. Dianne Hai-Jew. BrSi

You roll like cattle never rolled before. Diamond Joe. *Anonymous.* CoSo; OuSiCo

"You said a mawfl,/Pop'epetl!" The Axolotl. David McCord. FiBHP; OBAL

You said I know that/day Landscape with Leaves and Figure. Olga Broumas. BoWoP

"You said it, brother," said Mr. McNally. I Wonder What Became of Rand, McNally... Newman Levy. InMe

You said, Yes, I do too, we are smooth and smell/so good. Friday Night after Bathing. Stephen Levy. VWA

You sang a race from wood and stone to Christ. O Black and Unknown Bards. James Weldon Johnson. BANP; BPo; HeIP; PoBA; PoNe; TTY; UnPo; UnS

..You sang/and the shadow was terrified, gone like a bird. The Seven-League Boots. Ilarie Voronca. VWA

You say they squeak, but they will swear they sing. First Satire: Prologue.. Persius (Aulus Persius Flaccus). AWP

You'se a leetle too dumb,/Fo' to stay up here... Slim in Hell. Sterling A. Brown. BPo; FB

You see; dat's de way de Hoosiers feeds way out in Arkansaw. The Old Section Boss. *Anonymous.* BPo

You see his figure, slanted like a pen,/Writing his own and winter's signature. River Skater. Winifred Welles. SD

You see how it stiffens, fires to a beautiful red. Rodin to Rilke. Emily Grosholz. AMV-80

You see, I am alive, I am alive. The Delight Song of Tsoai-Talee. N. Scott Momaday. CDW; GrPl; STE

You see, I want to slip you/A verse or two myself. To Natalie. Morrie Ryskind. HBMV

You see, it is my heart. The Letter. Beatrice M. Murphy. PoNe

...You see it so well/On the faces of the self-reliant dead. Stoic. Lawrence Durrell. NYBP

You see now what I mean about the saint. Old Man in the Park. Mary Elizabeth Osborn. NePoAm-2

You see the jewels you brought gleam/On the dead as they go on talking. Hansel and Gretel Return. David Ray. DFT

You see the sky. How to Write a Poem about the Sky. Leslie Marmon Silko. NoP

You see what I am: change me, change me! The Woman at the Washington Zoo. Randall Jarrell. AP; CoAP; HaCAP; HAP; InPK; LiTM; MP; NMP; OxBC; TAP; TwCP; UnPo

You see what rambling and drinking rum/And a sporting life has done. Dupree (A vers.). *Anonymous.* ViBoFo

...You seem to have just fallen/into my heart at its dusk. Sketch. Robert Farnsworth. GOYP

You send me to Museums; I smile up Madison's/bright miles, among crowds changingly beautiful. New York Sonnet. Judith Rodriguez. NOAV

You shall be attended,/Now, now, now. I Am the Duke of Norfolk. *Anonymous.* GBP

You shall be ever pleas'd, and young maids long. Come Hither, You That Love. John Fletcher. EG; ELP

You shall be happy when you grow old. Old Maids. *Anonymous.* AmFP

You shall be punished with a deathless crown/For your dark head, resist it how you may. The Wreath. Robert Graves. BoLoP

You shall be sweetly help'd and warn'd. The Angel in the House. Coventry Patmore. VLP

You shall be true to them, who'are false to you. The Indifferent. John Donne. AnAnS 1; BiP; BoLoP; CABA; DiPo; EnL; NAWM 1-2; OAEP; SeCV 1-2; TEP; UnTE

You shall Confesse, and fame shall tell you, I/At Ister dare as well as Tyber dye. De Ponto. Ovid (Publius Ovidius Naso). OBVE

You shall get a coatie when the boat comes in! Dance to Your Daddie. *Anonymous.* PoPle

You shall get a fishy, when the boat comes home. Dance to Your Daddie. Mother Goose. TiPo

You shall give it me every night Sir Missy Sick. *Anonymous.* CoMu

You shall have for your share."/It's down, down, derry derry down. Johnny and the Highwayman. *Anonymous.* BFSS

You shall have her lying down/Upon the smoking mountains. To Frighten a Storm. Gladys Cardiff. CDW; STE

You shall know the Cornishmen. Cornishmen. *Anonymous.* FaBoUs

You shall lick the dust for meat;...' The Everlasting Gospel. William Blake. OxBoCh

You shall lie happily, smiling in your sleep. The Dark Cavalier. Margaret Widdemer. HBMV

"You shall neuer gett more from/mee." Thomas Cromwell. *Anonymous.* ESPB

You shall never remain in Thermopylae.' Limerick: "There was an Old Man of Thermopylae." Edward Lear. CenHV; EBEV; EvOK; FaBoNo; LBN; LiBL; NA; NBM; NOBL

You shall not be a myth, I promise you. The Myth of Arthur. Gilbert Keith Chesterton. HBMV

You shall not deny the Stranger. Chorus from the Rock—III. Thomas Stearns Eliot. LiTB

You shall not even hear me breathe your name. To W.J.M. G. G. PeHV

You shall not kiss me. Open the Door, Who's There Within? *Anonymous.* EG; ElL; GBL

You shall not rumple my Commode. The Coy Lass Dress's Up in Her Best. *Anonymous.* ErPo

You shall not see me now (quoth he), good night. Epigram: "A fool much bit by fleas put out the light." Richard Lovelace. FaBoEE

...You shall not stay alone/Till holy church incorporate two in one. Romeo and Juliet. William Shakespeare. GoBC

You shall not when you will, sir."/Down, derry, down. There Was a Knight. *Anonymous.* UnTE

You shall perish in the nether furnace. The Worthless Heart. Immanuel Di Roma. TrJP

You shall sit at home with me, my love, and go to sea no more.' The Dockyard Gate. *Anonymous.* OBSS

You shan't have none at all. Manners in the Dining-Room. *Anonymous.* OxNR

You should be praised for taking them away. Success. William Empson. OxBTC

You should carry it, and walk along with me. Courtesy. Mary Mapes Dodge. BrR

You should have come/before the wind. Spring. Princess Shikishi. PBWP

You should have iced them jazzy bees. One More Time. Alvin Aubert. GP

You should have stuck to spewing beer, not ink. A Poet's Epitaph. Kingsley Amis. DBV

You should not be. I cannot wish you dead. Last Child. X. J. Kennedy. OBSP

You should not have been Knight of the Bath,/But have bowed to the order of Garter. St. Kevin. Samuel Lover. OnYI; WTO

You should see me in my new straw hat! An Intermezzo for the Fourth Act. William Allen White. InMe

You should see them—Eb and Flo. The Tides of Love. Thomas Augustin Daly. InMe; PoPl; YaD

You should stand at my shoulder an outcast from Eden too. By the Weir. Wilfrid Gibson. MoVE

You shoved the gun in your mouth/& took off. Cuba. Lawrence Kearney. AMV-81

You showed me, how under snow and darkness,/the grasses breathe for miles. E Uni Que A The Hi A Tho, Father. Roberta Hill. VoR

You sigh for love as well as I. To Sycamores. Robert Herrick. CaPo

You silenced it/and in Maidanek woods/finished it off with a few shots. I'll find My Self-Belief. Jacob Glatstein. VWA

You silent lovers, wander hand in hand. Spring. Andre Spire. AWP

You silly, bloody fool! The Optimist. *Anonymous.* PV

You sister/You heart of grey snow. Painting of a White Gate and Sky. Louise Erdrich. TWSS

You sit drinking the tulip-colored wine/In the midst of this green earth/With all her waters.   The Thousand and One Nights: To Lighten My Darkness.   *Anonymous*.   AWP

You sit still and I'll go and find it.   Grandma's Lost Balance.   Sydney Dayre.   OBCA

You sleep with your head upwind/of both your boots and your butt.   Conestoga.   George E. Murphy, Jr.   AMV-81

You, small worm, worm-mouth, worm-hate, master/of death and/life. You can't go in. They say.   Nobody will open the door for you.   Blanca Varela.   BoWoP

You smile and cross over me like a welcome storm.   At Midsummer.   Norman Dubie.   MAYP

You soar...Is death so bad?...I wish you'd say.   To a Very Wise Man.   Siegfried Sassoon.   BrPo

You some ugly chile.   Ugly Chile.   Clarence Williams.   TW

You–someone?–waded, holding up a skirt.   Out of the Past.   Robert Wallace.   PoL

"You son of a bitch!" sits bolt upright in bed,/as if he'd been scalded.)   New York Bird.   Andrei Voznesensky.   NYP

You soon will touch the skies.   The Name.   Eileen Duggan.   ISi

You speak   The Clearing.   Peter Everwine.   NNaP

You, spread here like butter,/Like doubloons, like flowers.   Luxury.   Donald Justice.   HeIP

You stand in a long tradition; and we who are left salute you.   In Memory of George Whitby, Architect.   Sir John Betjeman.   EyDe

You stare through centrifugal bones/Of the revolving and dissolving world.   To a Spanish Poet.   Stephen Spender.   OAEP

You start to want to crazy.   Letter from an Institution, III.   Michael Ryan.   AmPA

You still are the stranger,/And I'm Donahue.   Brave Donahue.   Jack Donahue.   PoAu 1-2

You still-or so thou tellest me?-mean?   Love Song.   Reed Whittemore.   AmFN

You still the unseen light/Guiding my way.   Take Back the Virgin Page.   Thomas Moore.   HBV 1-2; OBNC

You stir and listen in your dreamless sleep.   Fallen Leaves.   Kathryn Munro Tupper.   CaP

You stood with women in a row.   Love-Songs, At Once Tender and Informative.   Samuel Hoffenstein.   OBAL

You stranger do not know.   Prelude.   Christine Ama Ata Aidoo.   PBWP

You strike fire in me, wake me to madness.   I Heard the Old Song.   B. W. Vilakazi.   PeSA

You strikes me as ornery.   Dream Songs.   John Berryman.   CAPP

You struggle. I spank you with foam. And we both/are equal in our dance.   Song for a Dance.   Abraham Sutzkever.   VWA

You stump toward Moscow on a wooden leg.   L'Aigle a Deux Jambes.   Turner Cassity.   GP

You stupid Old Man of Melrose.   Limerick: "There was an Old Man of Melrose."   Edward Lear.   LBN

You sure get bit on Meesh-e-gan.   On Meesh-e-gan.   *Anonymous*.   ABF; TrAS

You sure won't miss your jelly/till your jelly roller's gone   You'll Never Miss Your Jelly.   Lil Johnson.   BluL

You sure you aint just feeling sorry for yourself?   Margaret Are You Drug.   George Starbuck.   MAT

You surely would have turned to gladsome-/ness from pain.   The Final Struggle.   Louis James Block.   PAH

You sweat in the winter in the north,/and you are afraid,/sweetheart.   What Music.   Joy Harjo.   TWSS

You swell my emptiness, materialize my fate.   Apology for E. H.   William Hathaway.   FAZ

You take and hold my dead fingers/Declaring summer.   In the Cathedral.   Patricia Beer.   OxBC

You take the rest.   The Crossed Apple.   Louise Bogan.   BiP; HeIP

You take trips to contain the mystery.   One West Coast.   Al Young.   NPGG

You talk too much. Go'n wash up.   Me, Colored.   Peter Abrahams.   PBA

You taught me here docility–and how to save my soul.   To a Little Girl.   Helen Parry Eden.   HBV 1-2

You teach, by vehement revision,/that labor is a way to love.   Snapshot.   George Garrett.   NePoAm-2

You tell me.   Ross's Poems.   Geoffrey Lehmann.   CBAP

You tell me that the voice is still/That should have welcomed me.   Twilight on Tweed.   Andrew Lang.   BSV; OBVV

You tell me your dream,/I'll tell you mine.   You Tell Me Your Dream, I'll Tell You Mine.   Rice. Seymour Brown. Albert H.   FSN

You that alone I cared to keep.   Song of a Second April.   Edna St. Vincent Millay.   CMoP; OxBA

You the days from St. David's to Easter obtain.   To Find Easter Day.   *Anonymous*.   FaBoUs

You the divinity of it have proved,/"Whom Jesus loved."   Whom Jesus Loved.   John Barford.   PeHV

You, the ghost, or I, the living man?   The Hosts.   George M. Brady.   NeIP

You the hunter, or I the prey?   Man and Beast.   Clifford Dyment.   BoAnP

You then might see what Clancy saw/And know what Clancy knew.   Old Australian Ways.   Andrew Barton ("Banjo") Paterson.   NOAV

You think about the first thing you ever stole, or lied about, or killed   Visiting Day.   Al Young.   NPGG

You think I'm happy? Well–Perhaps you're right!   The Beautiful.   F. S. Woodley.   PeHV

You think they are.   Long Distance.   William Stafford.   ELU; SO; WSC

You think your life is over?/It's just begun.   To a Child Trapped in a Barber Shop.   Philip Levine.   InPK; NoAm; NOBA; TAP; VGW

You thorns are the best part of you.   Roses Only.   Marianne Moore.   AnFE; CoAnAm; LiTM

You thought it was a falling leaf we heard.   Rondel for September.   Karle Wilson Baker.   HBMV

You throw off the weeds/Of the fled and the dead/For the now living creeds.   To the Laggards.   Joseph Bovshover.   TrJP

You thrust the spear within His side.   Christ Is Crucified Anew.   John Richard Moreland.   PGD

You, to whose care so oft I owe,/That I'm alive to tell you so.   Stella's Birthday.   Jonathan Swift.   LoBV; NoP; OAEL 1-2; OBEC

You told me once/But I forgot.   Do You Love Me.   *Anonymous*.   PoSC

You told us too that when we died/we should return again.   Re-Birth.   *Anonymous*.   PeSA

You too dreaming the same.   Housing Shortage.   Naomi Replansky.   NMM

...You too rehearse your/constituent parts, your intervals/of utter jubilee   Poke-Pole Fishing.   Dennis Schmitz.   AmPA

You too were schooled in love!   Rain, Night, and Wine.   Asclepiades.   LiTW

You too will be silent.   The Second Poem the Night-Walker Wrote.   Johann Wolfgang von Goethe.   NU

You too. You too. You too.   In a Parlor Containing a Table.   Galway Kinnell.   ELU; NLV; OBSP

You treat me like a liar! I order you:/Burn me!   The Burning of Books.   Bertolt Brecht.   PoPl

You treat me like my trouble has just begun   Wartime Blues.   Blind Lemon Jefferson.   BluL

You turn, I turn.   You Turn for Sugar an' Tea.   *Anonymous*.   OuSiCo

You turn your back to quit me: woman, and you don't know how   Easy Rider Blues.   Blind Lemon Jefferson.   BluL

You turned my true-love from my door,/Who died for love of me!'   Annie of Lochroyan.   *Anonymous*.   BuBa

You understand me? I have said/enough?   Faith.   Robert Browning.   TreFT

You undressed first and went to bed.   Passing the Graveyard.   Andrew Young.   DTC

You, unsuspecting, feel for me/Almost a loneliness.   With a Flower.   Emily Dickinson.   LiTL

You've all eternity in which to read it.   Letter to Lord Byron.   W. H. Auden.   FaBoPV; NOBL; OBSV

You've always had a queer imagination, she is told.   Night.   Joyce Carol Oates.   GeTw

You've brought me/the tranquillity of a snail/contemplating its snout...   In Praise of Blur.   G. S. Sharat Chandra.   FAZ

You've come back/to count bodies again/in your own backyard.   Come Back Blues.   Michael S. Harper.   PoBA

You've cursed the only civil hour we've had.   Epigram.   *Anonymous*.   ALV

You've finished with the Flesh, my lord!   Heriot's Ford.   Rudyard Kipling.   PoRA

You've got to be carefully taught!   You've Got to be Carefully Taught.   Oscar, II Hammerstein.   AmFN

...You've got to go back down/before the crows laugh you straight to hell.   Sweating It Out on Winding Stair Mountain.   Jim Barnes.   CDW

You've got to quit your quittin'.   The Quitter.   *Anonymous*.   BLPA; WBLP

You've got to speculate/To accumulate.   Financial Wisdom.   *Anonymous*.   FaBoUs

You've had your orange/now lie in it.   Trader.   Jim Harrison.   NoAm

You've killed the dawn for me!   Dawn.   Constance Ortmayer.   SaC

You've left, with all the songs I'd sung.   Quatrain: "Gone are the games we played all night."   Mahsati.   WPOW

You've lettn your bride be stown frae/you,/For a' your armed men.'   Bonny Baby Livingston (A version).   *Anonymous*.   BaBo; ESPB

You've robbed my poor pockets of silver and gold.   Rye Whiskey.   *Anonymous*.   FSW

You've tore my hood, you shall make it good/If it cost me forty pound!   A Song: "Good neighbour, why do you look awry?"   *Anonymous*.   TW

You wake in billingsgate, haggling for a drab/dead slice of Dreamfish on a beryl slab.   Uncertain Sonnets.   Martin Johnston.   CBAP

You walk around one/As if he were the City Hall/After that.   Catalogue (excerpt).   Rosalie Moore.   NTCP

"You want a girl, maybe?"   Habana.   Julian Bond.   NNP

You want help. you are sorry you are born with ears. John Coltrane an Impartial Review. A. B. Spellman. CNA; NNP; PoBA

You want her Much: seek her in Christ/And you will find her there. Profit and Loss: An Elegy upon the Decease of Mrs. Mary Gerrish... John Danforth. SCAP

...You watch for New Orleans,/the white cluster of tombs. Aerial View of Louisiana. Cleopatra Mathis. MAYP

...You watch/for the one too slow to stop your leap, your/teeth in time. Catching One Clear Thought Alive. Paula Gunn Allen. WPOW

You watch us, eat your egg, and laugh aloud. The Egg Boiler. Gwendolyn Brooks. PoBA

You water-drinker! Song of the Lioness for Her Cub. *Anonymous.* BoWoP

You wear the gold calypso Alice wore. This Alice. Herbert Morris. PoRA

You welcome your man from his long mowing/Of the harsh, unmannerly, mountain hay? Ire. R. S. Thomas. OBSP

You WERE a charming girl! Elizabeth Ann Peabody. Ivy O. Eastwick. BrR

You were a kind man and you died in want. Ford Madox Ford. Robert Lowell. MP; OxBC; PoCh; TwCP

You were advised to leave me well alone. Protestation. Bertrand. LiTW

You were all huff and puff, a bolt of plaid/woven out of dropped names. Sporting the Plaid. Chris Wallace-Crabbe. NOAV

You were cast for a common or casual pig,/But you play the invincible bore. To a Boy-Poet of the Decadence. Sir Owen Seaman. CenHV; FiBHP

You were his true-blue pal. Obituary. Kenneth Fearing. VGW

You were in her heart, and kept it beating/by pacing back and forth. Elegy for My Father. Robert Louthan. AMV-80

You were lit to terror by God's image/reflected in his worlds of pallid stone. Poem About Your Face. Nathan Alterman. VWA

...You were never/wanted and she always said come in. Drums in Scotland. Richard Hugo. LCAP

You were not keyed or pitched like these true-blue ones/Though all of you consort now underground. In Memoriam Francis Ledwidge. Seamus Heaney. FaBoIP

You were not like that, Corinna,/in the old days. Fragments. Corinna. PBWP

You were not wilful and you made no slaves. December 1970. John Tagliabue. GP

You were once a caterpillar,/Wriggly, wiggly fellow. Fuzzy Wuzzy, Creepy Crawly. Lillian Schulz Vanada. SoPo; SUS; TiPo

You were put in the hole for good reason. A Memory. Marvin Bell. GP

You were running, running, with a flower for me. The Flower. John Holmes. LiTL

...You were the girl in the dress/Red as a house burning down. Of Your Father's Indiscretions and the Train to California. Lynn Emanuel. MAYP

You were the hailstorm of that bitter season. Pedagogue Arraigned. John Wain. GLGT

You were to put the pink and blue/on the beachball on the next page. High Heels. Ron Padgett. APU

You were told where to go, but not how/or when to leave the room. New Jersey. Will Bennett. APU

You were: you were alone. At a Solemn Musick. Delmore Schwartz. EG; MoRP; OBEV; OBS; PoEL 1-5; UnS

...You were young/Then/You/Died. Fall Down. Calvin C. Hernton. CNA; PoBA

You weren't even a/revolutionary but/i loved you. To L. Julianne Perry. PoBA

You what I am, I what you were before. To the Unconstant Cynthia. Sir Robert Howard. CavP

You whisper, at last I've found you! A Slight Confusion. James Reiss. AmPA

You White Folks ain't ready for integration!' Harlem Gallery (excerpt). Melvin B. Tolson. TTY

You who are difficult and dear-/excuse me. Beauty, Sleeping. Arthur Freeman. DFT

You who are free,/rescue the dead. Rescue the Dead. David Ignatow. CAPP; ConAP; PrIm; VGW

...You/who are never there The Owl. William Stanley Merwin. PPP

...You/who are now my enemy, leave me. Love Making. James Tate. EAS

You who, being younger,/Will probably forget. A Childhood. Stephen Spender. NeBP

You, who gave your Precious Gift. Immaculate Palm. Joseph Joel Keith. ISi

You, who have let my people die without a name. Many Die Here. Gayl Jones. BlSi

You who have taken with you/All I once possessed? Autumn. Amy Lowell. NMM

You who maddened my heart with love, my Dion! Epigram: "For Hekabe." Plato. PeHV

You who made me see have gone from sight. Malcolm. Kattie M. Cumbo. BOLo

You who never even learned to queue? Father in the Railway Buffet. U. A. Fanthorpe. FaBoWP

You who perceive this thing, you shall return to spring. Return to Spring. Florence Ripley Mastin. GoYe

You, whom he chose in love-/no one will thrust away. In Praise of Virginity. Hroswitha von Grandersheim. PBWP

You, whom no darkened island waits. Crossing the Straits. Charles Brasch. AnNZ

You whom no one told her of. To the Sistine Madonna. Cornelia Otis Skinner. ISi

...You whom of all women/I most desire. O Gongyla, my darling rose. Sappho. BoWoP

You wife of the Copper-bodied man. Dance-Song of the Lightning. *Anonymous.* PeSA

You will answer for your fool. Juniper. Eileen Duggan. CAW

You will as learned, wise,/And–happy be!' The Dunce. Walter De la Mare. ImOP

You will bark forth brightness into the depths of the/night. On a Puppy. Feng Chih. LiTW

You will be a sorry guest/On the sombre earth. Trance and Transformation. Johann Wolfgang von Goethe. LiTW

You will be a tale of wonder for ever, Deirdre. The Foretelling of Cathbad the Druid at Deirdre's Birth. *Anonymous.* LiTW

You will be known as Lump Skull Buddha! Technicalities for Jack Spicer. Philip Whalen. PoM

You will be ready! The Boy Washington. Dorothy Brown Thompson. SiSoSe

You will be whole at last. Karl Marx. Al Lee. AmPA

You will believe me/a rose/to the end of time. To Be Recited to Flossie on Her Birthday. William Carlos Williams. VGW

You will break the lie of men's thoughts/and cherish and shelter us. Sea Gods. Hilda ("H. D.") Doolittle. AtBAP; LiTA; MOS

You will come back; I care not what the time,/Be it the green of Spring or Winter's rime. Certainty. Evelyn Hardy. HBMV

You will drown with open eyes in light,/if behind you the seagull dives and cries. The Great Freight. Ingeborg Bachmann. PBWP

You will find a joy in service/That will bless the world and you! You Will Find a Joy in Service. Dorothy Conant Stroud. STF

You will find us burning in the night. Burning in the Night. Thomas Wolfe. AmFN

You will gather the spit of your chest/and plant it in their faces. Notes for My Son. Alex Comfort. LiTM; MoBrPo; NeBP; SeCePo

You will get the dark all over you. June Fugue. Thomas W. Shapcott. NOAV

You will go back directly to Bow!' Limerick: "There was an old person of Bow." Edward Lear. EBEV; VLP

You will go down, dandy horse and all,/And bruise your latter end. The Dandy Horse. *Anonymous.* OBET

You will have smiled, I shall have tossed your hair. A Quoi Bon Dire. Charlotte Mew. HBMV; OxBTC

You will have the wrong key in your hand. Foreign Summer. William Stanley Merwin. AmPC

You will hear the drumming hooves Earth and I Gave You Turquoise. N. Scott Momaday. CDW; PoPl; UnPo

You will kneel in very rapture,/When you read the Bible through! Read the Bible Through. Amos R. Wells. STF

You will know I love you,/And fear I do not know. Lo Que Digo (with music). *Anonymous.* AS

You will know I'm trying/With my Granite lip! If I shouldn't be alive. Emily Dickinson. FM; MAPA; PG

You will know not to answer it. Commanding a Telephone to Ring. Jack Anderson. AMV-81

...You/will like me less than you expected to. Estimable Mable. Gwendolyn Brooks. FB

You will look so when you are dead. The Skin-and-Bone Lady. *Anonymous.* AmFP

You will never get another. A Bestiary. Kenneth Rexroth. OBAL

You will never have known me. The Other. Peter Cooley. AMV-80; MAYP

You will never know when a cold may strike. Improved 4-Way. Tom Veitch. ANYP

You will never meet another grizzly bear. Grizzly Bear. Mary Austin. BPAW; GoJo; OnUR; SoPo; TiPo

You will never run dry. Pisces Child. Sandra McPherson. NMM

You will not again/Love over much. Finis. Waring Cuney. AmNP; BANP

You will not allow me to refuse/My daily bread. Cycle. Ruth Miller. PeSA

You will not grasp the meaning, you will be in it. Out of Sleep. Allen Curnow. AnNZ

You will not have a home. The New Ahasuerus. Jozsef Kiss. VWA

You will not hear it. Sleep, my darling. Lullaby. Dom Moraes. NePoEA-2

You will not lack your reward. Reflection and Advice. Ezra Pound. OBSV

You will not live in vain. Humble Service. Lillian G. Heard. STF

You will not see the sorrow of no time. No Time. Terence Tiller. NeBP

You will not stay when summer goes. Passing Love. Langston Hughes. BiP

You will not store it away amongst old gifts/And forget it, long before it is worn out. A Present from the Emperor's New Concubine. Pan Chieh-yu. BoWoP

You will not trouble me again/In the great peace where I attain. The Flying Wheel. Katharine Tynan Hinkson. WGRP

You will not understand me, brother! The Words Will Resurrect. Jorge De Lima. TTY

You will pass all your life in that box.' Limerick: "There was an Old Man on some rocks." Edward Lear. NOBV

You will remember that the/road runs east as well as west. If All the Voices of Men. Horace L. Traubel. AA

You will say, "That is how we lived, you and I." The Young Price and the Young Princess. John Ashbery. ConAP

You will see the young couples/Leaving again in rags Some San Francisco Poems. George Oppen. NNaP

...You will see when your true love comes/And when she goes away.' The Broomfield Wager. Anonymous. OBET

You will see your woman with another, and your children at/my table! The Lowly Peasant. Anonymous. PBWP

You will sing out for yams,/the food of the living. Lament for a Husband. Anonymous. BoWoP

You will soon discover what we One-ways lack! One-Way Song. Percy Wyndham Lewis. CTC

You will spin and turn/and women will bleed. Lunar Eclipse. Jessica Scarbrough. LFAC

You will still be just a scar/On a little, lonesome star. To Chicago at Night. Mildred Plew Merryman. HBMV

You will strike fire,/that new thing! Little Girl, My Stringbean, My Lovely Woman. Anne Sexton. NYBP

You will taste sweetly, served with green peas. I Had a Duck. Archibald Stodart-Walker. FM

You will the bird let build her nest in it. Alone. Francis Jammes. CAW

You will wake, and remember, and understand. Evelyn Hope. Robert Browning. BoLiVe; HBV 1-2; TrGrPo; VLP

You will wake,/if it comes,/near morning. If It Comes. Philip Booth. NCSH

You will wake up/to a much deeper sleep. Forms, LXXVII. Theodore Enslin. CoPo

You will? You'll go to Gladys 'cross the way?/Stay. Broken Monologue. Michael Lewis. UnTE

"You win," she called,/but Lou didn't hear. One-Upmanship. Miriam Chaikin. NTCP

You with the flowers and pigeons. Spring Poem. Julian Symons. NeBP

You with your back to the wall. Orion. Adrienne Rich. NIP; NoAm; NoP

You with your regular,/Meaningless circles are!' Switchback. Edith Sitwell. PBWP

You won't be well paid./Aetat. 6 Invocation to the Muse. Richard Hughes. MoBrPo

You won't find satisfaction/even if you climb to the morning star. The House of Madam Juju. Kanai Mieko. BoWoP

You won't find the bones,/the blood, but the bullets. Talking to the Townsfolk in Ideal, Georgia. Isaac J. Black. CNA

You won't get sunburned walking bare. Some Sound Advice from Singapore. John Ciardi. GrPl

You won't remember any of this. Joe Gillon Hypnotizes His Son. Albert Goldbarth. SM

You wonder how long this can go on. Your Dog Dies. Raymond Carver. GeTw

You wonder/who is/it/now. Freeze Tag. Gordon Henry. STE

You wonder why my feet/move in dance to a distant drum Coming Back. Joseph Bruchac. CDW

You wont touch me. but you will, my friend, you/will I Wake, My Friend, I. Faye Kicknosway. IHMS

...You worthy be,/Yet without love naught worth to me. Song to His Cynthia. Fulke, Lord Brooke Greville. ViBoPo

You would be hurt so night and day,/Yet love me. A Soldier. Sir John Suckling. SeCV 1-2

You would hardly find/it possible to live without/my joke and me. Sphinx. Robert Earl Hayden. HaCAP

...You would have known/if I am/the one for you. Swahili Love Song. Anonymous. LLLT

You would have named the monster destroying the vessel/And you. Storm and Quiet. Richard Eberhart. AMV-81

You would know why. Refugee in America. Langston Hughes. AmFN

...You would not from its whole ridge/See a man who so loves you as your fond S. T. COLERIDGE. Metrical Feet. Samuel Taylor Coleridge. NIP

You would not have me roar, or crow. After Galen. Oliver St. John Gogarty. FaBoEE; OBMV; PoRA

You would not know/I wept. I Weep. Angelina Weld Grimke. CDC

You would say it was dying it is immortal. The Room. William Stanley Merwin. NaP; NOBA

You would sink into Perdition. The Zealous Puritan. Anonymous. OBS

You would soon certainly kill me? O Hymen! O Hymenee! Walt Whitman. ErPo

You wouldn't have Me Up at Does. Edward Estlin Cummings. NYBP; OBSP; WeW

You, wretched man,/are already on your way into the earth. A Lamentation. Carl Rakosi. VWA

You yield to history nothing. Kinnaird Head. George Bruce. BSV; NeBP

You young men of Shaka/Before the uMsindisi. Let Zulu Be Heard. Isaiah Shembe. WTO

You yourself are all the Nine. The Mutual Congratulations of the Poet's Anna Seward and Hayley. Richard Porson. FaBoEE; OBSV

Youle find that all compulsion, is nought but that Nim-rod. A Lover of Peace..... Samuel Gorton. SCAP

Young Al the old lamp-rubber. Mingled Yarns. X. J. Kennedy. OBCA

The young brown-throated reapers pass,/Like silhouettes against the sky. Impressions. Oscar Wilde. SyP

Young Corydon without a rival reigns. Eclogues. Virgil (Publius Vergilius Maro). AWP

The young dead weeping! Armistice Day. Roselle Mercier Montgomery. MC

Young eyes opening to take the cold. From Garvey's Farm: Seneca, Wisconsin. Ed Hoeppner. AMV-80

--Young feet that fretted so to roam/Have missed the road returning home. The Road to Babylon. Margaret Adelaide Wilson. HBMV

Young Jack perhaps, and now a Wiltshireman/As he has oft been since his days began. Lob. Edward ("Edward Eastaway") Thomas. MoVE

Young ladies all, of beauty bright,/Take warning by her last good-night. The Cruel Mother (P version). Anonymous. ESPB

Young ladies, marry, marry while you may! The Advice. Thomas Flatman. CavP

Young lambs must find de way. De Old Sheep Dey Know de Road. Anonymous. BPo

Young love, the strong love, burning in the rain. Rainy Song. Max Eastman. FaBoBe; HBMV

Young maids, beware of vanity! The Spring Beauties. Helen Gray Cone. AA

Young maids must marry. Sing Heigh-Ho! Charles Kingsley. ALV; HBV 1-2

A young man. Green Apples. Dudley Randall. FB

The young man feels his pockets/And wonders what's to pay. The Fairies Break Their Dances. Alfred Edward Housman. MoVE; NoAm; OBSP

A young man he come scampering home/Saying, "Kiss me, my dear wife." I Have Always Heard of These Old Men. Anonymous. AmFP

Young Mary cried, in sorrow died/For the constant farmer's son. The Constant Farmer's Son. Anonymous. OBET

Young men now all beware/Lest you are drawn into a snare. Van Dieman's Land (A vers.). Anonymous. OBET

...Young men who have come to nothing. Now and Then. Ian Hamilton. NoAm

Young men would turn drakes and soon follow after. Hares on the Mountain. Anonymous. OBET

A young moon on his breast. Li Po. Ruth Gilbert. AnNZ

The young Phyllis and William all from the greenwood tree. William and Phyllis. Anonymous. OBET

The young Republic like a sun/Rise from these crimson seas of war. Ave Imperatrix! Oscar Wilde. HBV 1-2

Young Samuel Allen, oh! lack-a-day,/Was taken and carried to Canada. Bars Fight, August 28, 1746. Lucy Terry. BlSi; PoNe

The young soldier's tawdry song/Told us that she would never die. Women Are Not Gentlemen. Harley Matthews. NOAV

The young summer's wind/blows against my dark windowpane. Candle. Jacob Isaac Segal. VWA

Young Tamlane to the seas he's gane,/And a' women's curse in his company's/gane. Burd Ellen and Young Tamlane. Anonymous. ESPB

Young virgins, plucked suddenly,/on a spring night, when the ice breaks up on the rivers-- Young Virgins Plucked Suddenly. Berl Pomerantz. VWA

The Younger melts in fondness in his arms. Passage to India. Walt Whitman. ILwL

The youngest am I. Comparison. Mary Ann Hoberman. BiCB

The youngest sorrows till death. The Elected Knight. *Anonymous.* AWP

The younkers hear the boatswains say/How Captain Giles that awful day/ Preserved the sinking yawl. The Shipwreck. E. H. Palmer. NA

Your absence haunts the landscape of my sleep. Sleeping Alone. Kurt J. Fickert. AMV-80

Your ancient years are but a withered grass. Respice Finem. Thomas Proctor. OBSC

Your anklebone/And your anklebone/Lie big in the bed. Christmas Card. Ted Hughes. OBCP

Your arm in a tee shirt/out the window. Jimmy Bruder on Quincey Street. Carol Artman Montgomery. AMV-81

Your articulation is a silent, Amen. Malcolm, a Thousandth Poem. Conrad Kent Rivers. CNA

Your ashen hair Shulamith Fugue of Death. Paul Celan. OBVE; PPoe

Your baby smell could almost make me sleep. To a Friend's Child. Aliki Barnstone. BoWoP

Your basic igneous boulder with a hole for music/drilled into her heart. Patience on a Monument. Mary di Michele. CaPN

Your beauteous shape compels me still/To sing, but short or long just as you will. Fealty. Eschenbach, Sir Wolfram von LiTW

...Your beautiful eyes,/Full of the tears of the ages, said everything dies. In Memory of V. R. Lang. Mac Hammond. PoA

Your beauty shall be turn'd to earth. E'en as the Flowers Do Wither. *Anonymous.* EG

Your beauty waits this ending. Woman, believe–and/fear! Revenge to Come. Sextus Propertius. AWP; LiTW

...Your body/Is my wild apple-tree, my poor man's treasure. The Apple Tree. James Keir Baxter. OxBC

Your breast shall be to-morrow/The cradle of a King. Gates and Doors. Joyce Kilmer. HBV 1-2; HBVY

Your breast will not lie by the breast/Of your beloved in sleep. He Hears the Cry of the Sedge. William Butler Yeats. OxBTC

...Your breath is on this air,/And you are theirs and of their mystery. The Tourist and the Town. Adrienne Rich. NePoEA-2

Your breathing, and the secrets of the room. Elegy. Robert. Layzer. NePoEA; PoPl

Your breathing is the blast, the bullet,/and the final sky. A Moment of War. Laurie Lee. OBWP

Your brother Abel guards you from all evil. Brothers. Dan Pagis. VWA

Your brown and butter hair/drenching my face like/summer rain. Waking Up. Tom Schmidt. GP

Your bum is a gorgeous basket brimming with fruits and/meat. The Peasant Declares His Love. Emile Roumer. ErPo; LiTW; TTY

Your cage will be made of the glittering gold,/And hung on yon willow tree. Lady Isabel and the Elf Knight. *Anonymous.* FSW

Your cake is dough, for I by sifting well/Have quite reduced your dust to Bacon-powder. At Shakespeare's Grave. Irving Browne. AA

Your capped teeth flash and tear flesh. Killing Rabbits. Ed Ochester. LTB

"Your careless praise for it was my first despair." Speak This Kindly to Her. Robert Bagg. NePoAm-2

Your cause shall be protected. I Am the Lord. Alexander Mack. AH

Your children, George. They thought that you/Would understand. (Most fathers do–) Conversation with Washington. Myra Cohn Livingston. OFD

Your/children's graves. Re-Act for Action. Don L. Lee. BPo; NBP

Your city/spilled among the Judean hills./Jerusalem. Dan, the Dust of Masada Is Still in My Nostrils. Ruth Whitman. VWA

Your client keeps by slipping through the yard. Epistles. Horace. OBVE

Your cloud sleds to the moon Poem, to Jane Wilson on Television. Jim Broley. ANYP

...Your cold Medusa stare/Has turned a heart to stone. Valediction. John Hall Wheelock. NePoAm

Your connoisseur in Liquors/Consults the Bumble Bee– A drunkard cannot meet a cork. Emily Dickinson. InPS; PAI

...Your conscience is/What we come back to in the armistice. The Conscientious Objector. Karl Shapiro. OxBA

Your cowboy is never complete/Without a cigarette in his hand. The Cowboy Up to Date. *Anonymous.* CoSo

Your cows will take a railing, and/The farmer take offense. The Harmonious Heedlessness of Little Boy Blue. Guy Wetmore Carryl. BoAnP

Your crabsticks are the best physicians.' The Citizen and the Red Lion of Brentford. Christopher Smart. NCEP

Your cries give my escape another draw-plate/From the last known escape. To Children. Lawrence McGaugh. PoBA

Your cuckoo sings by kind. All's Well That Ends Well, I, iii: "For I the ballad will repeat." William Shakespeare. BiP; ViBoPo

Your dancing girl is dead. Dark Girl. Arna Bontemps. GoSl

Your dancing/Rolls my staring skull slowly away into outer space. Gnat-Psalm. Ted Hughes. NoAm

Your daughters' love, tgive them their way,/For force oft breeds their lives' decay. The Suffolk Miracle (A vers.). *Anonymous.* BaBo; ESPB

Your death is his survival/your dust is pure. Toward Tenses Two Moons. George Rachow. LFAC

Your death is moving towards you,/travelling at the speed of light. The Astrologer Argues Your Death. Charles deGravelles. AMV-81

Your death my passion. Requiem. Kathleen Raine. NeBP

Your destination waits where you left it. You Drive in a Circle. Ted Hughes. NYBP

Your destiny waddling before you down the road? Girl Walking. Charles G. Bell. ErPo; NePoAm-2

Your Donkey is better behaved, I trust. The Donkey. Theodore Roethke. GrPl; OBCA

Your drawers match your tie. I wanted to see you. Leila Miccolis. BoWoP

Your dreams are not enough/to keep me warm. Parting from My Son. Evangeline Paterson. AMV-80

...Your dreams/Moving through Belgium now, full of your trip. Pretending Not to Sleep. Ian Hamilton. NoAm

Your drums and your dolled-up Virgins and your ignorant/dead. Valediction. Louis MacNeice. AnIL; FaBoIP; MoVE

Your dutiful Klabauterfrau. Klabauterwife's Letter. Christian Morgenstern. WSC

...Your duty is not to the/Sick but to the unborn. Perform it. Mother Superior. George MacBeth. NMP

Your dying is our breath! The Ram. Robert P. Tristram Coffin. AnAmPo

–Your ears are made only to hear lamentations that rise from/the four corners of the earth. The Ancient Law. Andre Spire. VWA

Your embryo knight has never questioned how. Father of the Man. Elizabeth Mabel Bryan. GoYe

Your emotions?/Are those of a maitre-de-cafe. Epilogue. Ezra Pound. OxBA

Your epitaph shall travellers undeceive/Who in few letters many years shall see.' The First Solitude. Luis de Gongora y Argote. OBVE

Your evening is here. The End of the Street. John Haines. LCAP

Your Ever loveing friend whilest Hee/Desolved is: or Cease to bee. Sweetly (My Dearest) I Left Thee Asleep. John Saffin. SCAP

Your eyes/are not stars/are not hummingbirds. O Night Flower. Arlindo Barbeitos. WhB

Your eyes are/the sound of morning becoming the wind Your Eyes. Kosrof Chantikian. AMV-81

Your eyes belie/your talking mouth. Encounter. Dorothy Livesay. AMV-81

Your eyes burn to see/a dove turn blue/or seem to. Wife of Kohelet. Shlomit Cohen. VWA

Your eyes can only teach us love,/But cannot take it in. Song: "Where did you borrow that last sigh." Sir William Berkeley. OBSP

Your eyes gleam strange and dark above the half door,/Your hand's white grace. The Half Door. Seumas (James Starkey) O'Sullivan. AnIV

Your eyes I do believe in–/And in your wicked heart. Religion. Heinrich Heine. LiTW

Your eyes of a promise in thc land? John Otto. William Stanley Merwin. AP

Your eyes/sing/empty psalms To the Man Who Sidled Up to Me and Asked: "How Long You in fer, Buddy?" Etheridge Knight. NeAC

...Your eyes were/a dark lake bruised by the winter trees. Going to Moscow. Lauris Edmond. OCNZ

Your face a virgin's, all beneath a bride. Fragments. Praxilla. PBWP

Your face against its velvet set,/And blue stars overhead. Peace by Night. Sister Mary Madeleva. GoBC

"Your face, as you tell/Of all the horriblest things you've seen." Horrible Things. Roy Fuller. OnUR

Your face is hurt/all the same. A Reason. Robert Creeley. NaP

Your face is virgin; lower down you are a married/woman. Girl of the Lovely Face. Praxilla. WPOW

Your face possesses my despair. Like a Pearl Dropped. Trumbull Stickney. NCEP

Your face/so close to mine/it chilled me For a Friend. Lyn Lifshin. NeAC

Your face, that I shall never see/Again, though I search every place. The Accusation. James Wright. AmPC

YOur face too looks like a ridge of stone. Baboon. *Anonymous.* WTO

"Your fader was a rich merchant in Stambouli." A Draft of XXX Cantos, XII: "Said Jim X..." Ezra Pound. NAs

Your faith as deathless as the outcry of the ruled sun. In Country Sleep. Dylan Thomas. LiTB

Your faithful friend, and will be to my last. The Promise of a Constant Lover. *Anonymous.* EIL

Your father's hands sweeping off dust. Stonecarver. Carole Oles. Str

Your fatigue/is an elegy etched/for a moment/on disappearing flesh Yehuda Amichai. Seymour Mayne. VWA

Your favour will give crutches to our faults.   Prologue to Antonio's Revenge.
John Marston.   LoBV

Your feet remembered/By the blades of grass...!   Benediction.   Donald
Jeffrey Hayes.   AmNP; PoNe

Your final destiny, 'scape for life!   Remember, Sinful Youth.   *Anonymous.*
AH

Your fingerprints still clear on the base.   Uncle Robert.   Robert Morgan.
GeTw

Your first word.   Spelling.   Margaret Atwood.   NoP

Your firy heate lets not her glory passe,/But (Phoenix-like) shall make her live
anew.   I Once May See when Yeares Shall Wreck My Wrong.   Samuel
Daniel.   AAS

Your flesh, breathed in a muted sentence,/instructed me in mine.   Encounter.
Vassar Miller.   GP

...Your floor, I/notice, is a roof of clouds.   Vertigo.   Brian Henderson.
CaPN

Your flute and his/regret their beginnings/in the songs of both your sorrows.
Flute Players.   Jean Rabearivelo.   PBA

Your foot is bruised against my head.   Spring Song.   Donald Finkel.
NYBP

Your footfall was my own heart's beat.   The Footsteps.   Paul Valery.
LiTW

Your freedom too/Was no better than a fool's story   Living Together.
Tomioka Taeko.   WPOW

Your friend!!!   A Friend.   Marguerite Power.   FaBoCo; FaFP

Your gaze enkindles me somehow.   Madonna's Lullaby.   Saint Alphonsus
Liguori.   ISi

Your glory is eternal and fixed in space,/while mine can pass by in a few days.
Holy angels, in envy I cast no sigh.   Gaspara Stampa.   BoWoP

Your goalie/in his frightening mask/dreams perhaps/of gentleness.   To a Sad
Daughter.   Michael Ondaatje.   GOYP

Your grandchildren's children/will hold to their noses.   Nosegay.   Elizabeth
Jane Coatsworth.   OBCA

Your grandfather sings for us/beyond the dry rustling cornstalks.   Once
Again.   Liz Sohappy Bahe.   CDW

Your grandfather watched trains as a young man./I waited.   The Chosen–
Kalgoorlie, 1894.   Fay Zwicky.   VWA

Your hair grey, your legs weakened/from long standing.   For One Moment.
David Ignatow.   NNaP

Your hair is black, for that's the way you buy it.   To Chloe.   *Anonymous.*
UnTE

Your hand in mine keeps us straight ahead.   Father.   Myra Cohn
Livingston.   NTCP

Your hand is on the door. This is where you came in.   The Door.   Mark
Strand.   NoAm

Your hand on the softness/of the world, will make/of nakedness/also a prayer.
The Ancestors.   Anita Barrows.   VWA

Your hands are cold.   Song: "Stop! Don't touch me."   *Anonymous.*
BoWoP

Your hands are cold, feeling me in the dark.   To the Contemporary Muse.
Edgar Bowers.   ELU

Your hands are filled with treasure.   The Journey nears the Road-End.
Rabindranath Tagore.   DL

& Your hands/are still/in your pockets   Sooner or Later.   Sam Cornish.
CNA

Your happy, happy, orphan boy!   The Orphan Boy's Tale.   Amelia Opie.
PaPo

Your head-down, tail-up hunt in a bottom drawer/For the black plunge-line
nightdress.   The Skunk.   Seamus Heaney.   FaBoIP; OxBC

Your head so much concerned with outer,/Mine with inner, weather.   Tree at
My Window.   Robert Frost.   AnNE; BLPL; BoLiVe; BoNaP; FaBoBe;
MoAB; MoAmPo; MoVE; NePA; NoAm; OxBA; TAP; TrGrPo

Your head will not lie on the breast/Of your beloved in sleep.   Aedh Hears
the Cry of the Sedge.   William Butler Yeats.   VLP

Your heads heavy with promises for another season.   Relics.   David
Wagoner.   FAZ

Your heart is going to find its spring.   Song for a Jewess.   Yvan Goll.
TrJP

Your heart of anger.   High Country Weather.   James Keir Baxter.   AnNZ

Your heart offered in sacrifice.   In Memory of My Arab Grandmother.
Evelyn Arcad Zerbe.   WPOW

Your heart, raised high in your hand,/flowers over the wall.)   In Jail.   Juan
Antonio Corretjer.   InW

Your heart will thump away from you.   Kangaroo by Nightfall.   Noel
Macainsh.   PoAu 1-2

Your heel will measure a worm's girth.   Warning.   Harold Lewis Cook.
AnAmPo

Your heir, Gerald, may he never inherit!   The Widow's Curse.   *Anonymous.*
NOBI

Your hobby is you.   Ego Sum.   Gelett Burgess.   InMe

...Your iron keels/are stronger/Than ghostly ships that sailed from Tyre a
thousand/years ago.'   The Dhows.   Francis Brett. Young.   EtS

Your irreversible/witness.   Etched away From.   Paul Celan.   OBVE

Your jelly-mouth and, crushed, your polyp eyes.   Prophecy on Lethe.
Stanley Jasspon Kunitz.   PoA

Your Jew! Your Jew! Your hated Jew!   To Russia.   Joaquin Miller.   AA;
AnAmPo

Your joys on earth will soon be/gone,/Your flesh in dust be laid.   Liverpool.
Anonymous.   AmFP

Your kind, dear eyes shine in your dear, dear face.   The Sanctuary.   Ford
Madox Hueffer.   PoA

Your kiss incurious as the windless air.   Recitative.   Ronald McCuaig.
PoAu 1-2

Your knees, or hands, or voice.   The Limits of Equitation.   Barbara Winder.
AMV-81

Your knock smiting the silence like a gong.   After the Blitz, 1941.   J. R.
Ackerley.   PeHV

Your labour which has exceeded that of St Mary.   Madrid.   Pai Wei.
PBWP

Your Land's the Wildernesse.   Adulteries, Murthers, Robberies, Thefts.
Roger Williams.   SCAP

Your leaves will teach me, also.   Oh Tannenbaum.   *Anonymous.*   FSW

Your letter came!   A Winter-Piece to a Friend Away.   John Berryman.
NOBA

Your life continues in those who continue the Revolution.   Josina, You Are
Not Dead.   Samora M. Machel.   WhB

Your life depends on it/if you want to be happy/at 40.   Happy at 40.   Peter
Meinke.   GP

Your life is pushing us to our feet, O leaf!   Life on Earth (excerpt).   Frank
O'Hara.   UnPo

Your life shall never lack a friend.   If You Have a Friend.   *Anonymous.*
FaFP

Your light steps or the sighs they cost?   Popular Songs of Tuscany.
Anonymous.   AWP

Your little, faithful, barking ghost/May leap to lick my phantom hand.   The
Curate Thinks You Have No Soul.   St. John Lucas.   BLPA

Your little flivver still/works so well.   Auto Mobile.   Archie Randolph
Ammons.   FF; OBAL

Your little hands were never made/To tear each other's eyes.   Quarrelling, or
Let Dogs Delight.   Isaac Watts.   BLPA

Your little mind!   Love-Songs, At Once Tender and Informative.   Samuel
Hoffenstein.   NLV; OBAL

Your lookes nice ye let them run too wide.   Well, Wanton Eye.   Charles,
duc d' Orleans.   HAP

Your losses to profit, your wayward onwardness.   Sailboat, Your Secret.
Robert Francis.   SD

Your love's great realm, my separation measures.   Written in Exile.
Kathleen Raine.   TrCP

Your love still close and watching through the years.   Mother.   *Anonymous.*
PoToHe

Your lown I'll never be, Sir.   O My Bonny, Bonny May.   *Anonymous.*
GBP

Your meekness who taught you?–"The Willow."   Scene in a Madhouse.
Aubrey Thomas De Vere.   OnYI

Your mill grinds rats and mice.   Grinding.   *Anonymous.*   OxNR

Your mind is light, soon lost for new love.   Philon the Shepherd–His Song.
Anonymous.   ALV; NOBE; OBSC

Your most natural clear/Child's laugh that charms the air.   Album Leaf.
Stephane Mallarme.   OBVE

Your mother swallows/what she has lost.   Sing with Your Body.   Janice
Mirikitani.   WPOW

Your mother weeps Yiddish/your father sneezes/ashes & gold.   The
Unveiling.   Suzanne Bernhardt.   VWA

Your mother will dress/Her head with flowers.   Jo Jo, My Child.
Anonymous.   TrJP

Your mou's fou o' draff, quo' Harpkin.   Harpkin.   *Anonymous.*   GBP

Your mountains build their monument,/Though ye destroy their dust.   Indian
Names.   Lydia Huntley Sigourney.   AmFN; HBV 1-2; MC; OBCA; PAH;
PoLf

Your mouth, and your hand running over me/Deft as a lizard, like a sinew of
water?   A Song from Armenia.   Geoffrey Hill.   FaBoMo

Your mouth, dear child, is envied of the bees.   The Thousand and One
Nights: Haroun's Favorite Song.   *Anonymous.*   AWP

Your mouth shows a faint bone-white scar.   Black Rocks.   Laureen Mar.
BrSi

Your moving mouth,lips pyrex-cool,/sizzles like ice cubes in hot spray.   I
Can't Figure You Out.   Elliot Fried.   AMV-81

Your murmuring waters and turf-scented air.   The Small Towns of Ireland.
Sir John Betjeman.   OBTV

Your muscle is hard from your head to your toe!   The Red Light Saloon.
Anonymous.   ShS

Your muse is a gipsy, e'en tho' she were tipsy/She cou'd ca' us nae waur than
we are.   The Kirk's Alarm.   Robert Burns.   OxBoLi

Your mute voice on the crystal embers flinging. The Phoenix. J. V. Cunningham. NoAm; QFR

"Your name, child?'/A thousand birds cry 'Venus.!" Earth-Visitors. Kenneth Slessor. BoAV

...Your name, like mine,/is a song. Write soon,/Caroline. Letter from Caroline Herschel (1750-1848). Siv Cedering Fox. SUW

Your name's the name which half the world divided/Henceforth shall bear. Europa. William Johnson Cory. NBM

Your name will glow, your praise shall/flow,/Through all the coming years. Lecompton's Black Brigade. Charles Graham Halpine. PAH

Your name will live/In this place/And perhaps in this poor house of proverbs here. Lament. Matangi Hauroa. WTO

Your named and nameless who are mixed with fate. Canal Street. John Wheelwright. PoA

Your neck seems long, long/To the covetous eyes of the hunter. Kob Antelope. *Anonymous.* WTO

Your nerves the nerves of a midwife/learning her trade The Mirror in Which Two Are Seen as One. Adrienne Rich. NNaP

Your ode to death is in the lifting/of a single eyelash. Lift it and see. Preludes to Definition: Time in the Rock (excerpt). Conrad Aiken. MoVE

Your offspring avert their faces from you. Shema. Primo Levi. VWA

Your only way is, in your arms to catch me. Sorrow seldom killeth any. Francis Davison. EG

Your ordinariness was renewed there. Night Drive. Seamus Heaney. FaBoIP

Your other half, mesdames, the man within. The Man Within. Annemarie Ewing. NePoAm-2

...Your own expanding galaxies/wash down now Coalface universe. Kristjana Gunnars. CaPN

Your own hands are lying. Taking Off My Clothes. Carolyn Forche. AmPA

Your own love cold on your cairn in Aghadoe. Aghadoe. John Todhunter. AnIL; AnIV; OBVV; OxBI

Your own! What would ye more of me? "Since fortune's wrath envieth the wealth." Henry Howard, Earl of Surrey. FCP; SiPS

Your palm/against/my cheek,/light as/a snowflake. Love Letters, Unmailed. Eve Merriam. DFF

Your pals of the Yankee team. To Lou Gehrig. John Kieran. SD

Your particular fate and experience, poor leaf. Thoughts of Thomas Hardy. Edmund Charles Blunden. PoCh

Your path shall be the empty streets of air. Blue Juniata: The Streets of Air. Malcolm Cowley. PoA

Your person, your place. Places, Loved Ones. Philip Larkin. CMoP; NePoEA

Your phoenix-red simplicity, enshrined/In that not extinguished fire. A Fire-Truck. Richard Wilbur. NCSH

Your pity dries the morning's tears/And fills the world with joy again! A Dream of Artemis. Francis Ledwidge. TrPWD

Your "poor moralist" betake me,/In my "solitary fly." Hic Vir, Hic Est. Charles Stuart Calverley. NBM; OxBoLi

Your poor old friend, what, will you leave him there? Epistle in Form of a Ballad to His Friends. Francois Villon. AWP; LiTW

Your portion of worry and labor and care? Two Kinds of People. Ella Wheeler Wilcox. PoToHe

Your presence a blessing, your friendship a truth,/Ben Bolt of the salt-sea gale. Ben Bolt. Thomas Dunn English. AA; FaBoBe; HBV 1-2; TreF

Your private holding pattern over hell. Best Friends. Judith Hemschemeyer. AMV-81

Your're downright rogues, they only knaves and fools. To the Respective Judges. *Anonymous.* APAS

...Your reluctant beauty sways/In the old weary rhythms of unwearied love! Vaudeville Dancer. John Hall Wheelock. UnS

...Your rich friend, Dick. Letter to Levertov from Butte. Richard Hugo. NNaP

Your rosy wrist peeps out between/And sends it home–and speeds it home. The Serving Maid. Arthur Joseph Munby. NOBV

Your's sweet in mee, and mine in you. To One Admiring Her Selfe in a Looking-Glasse. Thomas Randolph. AnAnS 2; LiTL; ViBoPo

Your sad tires in a mile-a. A Winter's Tale. William Shakespeare. TrGrPo

...Your salt tears/Must still fall, dropping from their spheres. Flow Not So Fast. *Anonymous.* ViBoPo

Your servant Jana pours out her prayer/before the saints. She was my staff and I am blind. Jana Bai. BoWoP

Your shade falls over on the floor To Lindsay. Allen Ginsberg. ConAP

Your sheepe, and you they will deceave. Masques. Ben Jonson. AnAnS 2

"Your shooting star is dead." Has Been. Alice F. Worsley. AMV-80

Your skin wild, chanting my name at the fat moon. Bent Tree. Peter Serchuk. AMV-80

...Your/small, damp hand in mine,/no heavier than a leaf. Walking Late. John Montague. CIP

Your small hand warm in my big brown glove! A Skater's Valentine. Arthur Guiterman. SiSoSe

Your smile/eyes knees and of your Etcetera) My sweet old etcetera. Edward Estlin Cummings. AmPP; CMoP; FF; HeIP; InPS; NAMP; NePA; OBAL; OBWP; OxBA; PAI; PPP; SOTW; WaaP; WaP

Your sons to struggle for this grim, new heaven. Spain. Dorothy Livesay. NOBC

Your soul through faithless hours. Hath Any Loved You Well, Down There. Arthur William Edgar O'Shaughnessy. EnLoPo

Your souls, that must be passionate,/Shining and swift, as mine? Souls. Fannie Stearns Gifford. HBMV

Your spear-thrust left great wounds/gushing hot blood. At the Badr Trench. Safiya bint Musafir. WPOW

Your spears/have begun to flower, too! Autobiography: Hollywood. Charles Reznikoff. VWA

Your sport in summer as the spring runs an-/grily. Hold Hard, These Ancient Minutes. Dylan Thomas. CoBE

Your star is steady over Oxford Town. V.D.F. *Anonymous* HBV 1-2

Your starved and ancient Presence O Lord I wait in my room at/your Mercy. The Lion for Real. Allen Ginsberg. HaCAP

Your striff and your strength shall be stroyed. Miracle Play: Satan and Pilate's Wife. *Anonymous.* ACP

Your tabu is gone! your holy of holies invaded!/Broke down by a stranger! The Kona Sea. *Anonymous.* WTO

...Your tears/Are as nice as the sea, as icy and salt as it is. Seymour and Chantelle or Un Peu de Vice. Stevie Smith. SBG

Your tears: You are not worth their merriment. Apologia Pro Poemate Meo. Wilfred Owen. ChMP; CoBE; CoBMV; FaBoRV; LiTM; MoAB; MoBrPo

Your thoughts are sharp/as day/enters night/as song. Donna. Paula Gunn Allen. TWSS

Your thoughts as thick as fireflies/All shiny in your mind! Some People. Rachel Field. NTCP

Your throat so ringed about/it is in chains for certain... Lady of Shrouding Hair. *Anonymous.* NOBI

Your time about my wrist. The Rite. Peter Dale. NAs

Your time is up. Thou art a little/soul bearing about a corpse. Fire and Ice. Michael Pettit. MAYP

Your tired white face, still trembling, all in tears... Elegy: "Child, your white face is chanting memories." Karel van de Woestijne. LiTW

Your travelling days will soon be over. Freeborn Man. Ewan MacColl. OBET

Your triumph is not commensurate with stone. Letter to a Friend. Robert Penn Warren. MoAmPo

Your true and faithful friend. Dan Taylor. *Anonymous.* CoSo

Your true arid husband. The Arid Husband. E. L. T. Mesens. EAS

Your unhappy becomes in need of rest in 5,280 feet-a. Autolycus' Song (parody). Richard Leighton Greene. SpRo

Your unknown in the debris of time. Poem for My Thirty-Second Birthday. John Ciardi. MiAP

Your velvety glances,/the glances of blind steel. Somewhere You Exist. Manfred Winkler. VWA

Your voice gentle as my father's For My Brother Jesus. Irving Layton. NoP

Your voice was an omen, an echo. Tak for Sidst. Babette Deutsch. PoA

Your voyage be happy, my sailor of seven! My Sailor of Seven. Gerald Brenan. BiCB

–Your wage is a social affront!' Limerick: "One morning old Wilfrid Scawen Blunt." Victor Gray. NOBL

Your white bones drifting like herons across the moon. The Hill Above the Mine. Malcolm Cowley. NAMP; PoPl; SaC

Your wife's the only thing, I guess,/That all of us have shared with you. Concerning Mme. Robert. Deems Taylor. UnTE

Your wild heart beats with the rhythm of spray-flung/hours! Flying Fish. J. Corson Miller. EtS

Your wings/Are red/Up there–in the coolness. The Gull. Nakasuk. WTO

Your winter gnaws at my bones with the strength/of your unceasing melancholy... Winter Day. Susannah Fried. VWA

Your wisdom has done this, sages of Harvard. Address to the Scholars of New England. John Crowe Ransom. LiTM; NePA

Your women don't know how to rob;/they're too doggone scared to steal Robbing and Stealing Blues. Gene Campbell. BluL

Your wood, your nymph, your kiss, your rhyme,/And all your godlike summer-time! A Note from the Pipes. Leonora Speyer. HBMV

Your wool is rich, no tongue can tell my gain. Arcadia. Sir Philip Sidney. FCP

...Your words,/every one of them, are volunteers. After Jericho. R. S. Thomas. OxBC

Your words lost in the labyrinth of my ear. Uncertain Sonnets. Martin Johnston. CBAP

Your words to me, your words! At Night. Alice Meynell. CH; HBV 1-2; LiTL; OBVV

Your younger brothers shall confirm in joy/This that I swear.　The Vow. Anthony Hecht.　ConAP; InPK; NePoEA; PoCh; Prf

Your youth is like a water-wetted stone,/Bright with a beauty that is not its own.　Susan to Diana.　Frances Cornford.　MoVE

Youre swete love with blody nailes,/Whiche fedeth mo lice than quailes.　A Grotesque Love-Letter.　*Anonymous.*　MeEL

Yours be the advantage all; for we/Claim naught but th' honour of the victory.　Masque of the Virtues against Love. From Guarini.　Mary Monck.　NOEC

Yours for terror and symbolism,/ole Fred.　Rimbaud Fire Letter to Jim Applewhite.　Fred Chappell.　SM

Yours has been the startling flash.　The Radiance of Extinct Stars.　Allan Kolski Horvitz.　VWA

Yours is a lower, and a happier star!　Modern Love, XXII.　George Meredith.　VLP

Yours is much the better part,/For it lies above my heart.　Turn to the Left.　Deems Taylor.　UnTE

Yours is the face, my dear.　When the Green Lies over the Earth.　Angelina Weld Grimke.　CDC; PoNe

Yours is the fault and mine the great annoy.　If amour's faith...　Sir Thomas Wyatt.　FCP

Yours is the heaven that lies in the common dust,/and you are there for me, you are there for all.　Yours.　Rabindranath Tagore.　MoRP

Yours is the only death I cannot bear.　Requiem for Sonora.　Richard Shelton.　Psk

Yours to absolve of ruin, or make an end.　Christ Walks in This Infernal District Too.　Malcolm Lowry.　NOBC

Yours truly, in friendship still strong.　The Death of Custer.　John Wallace (Jack) Crawford.　PoOW

Yours was yesterday's nonsense; and ours is today's!　Epigrams: "Need from excess—excess from folly growing."　Samuel Bishop.　NOEC

Yours will be filed accordingly,/answered in its turn.　In Answer to Your Query.　Naomi Lazard.　GP; NLV

Yours will I be, and with this only thought/Comfort myself when that my hope is nought.　Set Me whereas the Sun Doth Parch the Green.　Henry Howard, Earl of Surrey.　AAS; CBEP; FCP; ForPo; HAP; SiPS; TEP

Yourself making and remaking until it is perfect.　The Dress.　Mark Strand.　GeTw

Yourself to love, still haggling at the price.　Reproach to Julia.　Robert Graves.　ELU; FaBoEE

&)Youth goes/right on/gr/owing old　Old Age Sticks.　Edward Estlin Cummings.　InPS; PAI

Youth has her perfect crown, and age her old desire.　Athletic Ode.　George Santayana.　AmePo

Youth hurts. And then/It's gone.　The Young Ones, Flip Side.　James A. Emanuel.　PCP

Youth, I am in love with you!　Love Song to King Shu-Suen.　Kubatum.　WPOW

Youth is the day, the precious day,/When mercy may be found.　Remember Thy Creator Now.　Peter Long.　AH

Youth of all youth, ancient of days,/Follow us.　The 151st Psalm.　Karl Shapiro.　EaLo; VWA

The youth replies, I can.　Duty.　Ralph Waldo Emerson.　AnNE; FaFP; GN; GoTF; HBV 1-2; TreF; YaD

The youth replies, "I must."　Duty.　– Cook.　YaD

Youth's a stuff will not endure.　Twelfth Night.　William Shakespeare.　AWP; BiP; BoLoP; CTC; EiL; ELP; ExPo; FaBV; FaFP; FiP; GBL; GTBS; GTBS-P; HAP; HBV 1-2; HeIP; InMe; InPo; InPS; LiTB; LiTL; MCCG; NLV; NOBE; OAEL 1-2; OAEP; OBEV; OBSC; OBSP; OLR; PAI; PoRA; SeCeV; ViBoPo; WHA

Youth's stubborn, immature, unburied dead.　Depression.　Michael (Katherine Bradley and Edith Cooper) Field.　SyP

Youth's ta'en, and beauty's fled,/O then deplore her!　Dirge: "Wail! wail ye o'er the dead!"　George Darley.　OBRV

Youth's years how few, age how sure!　The Autumn Wind.　Emperor Wu Ti.　FaBoCh; LoGBV

Youth shows but half; trust God, see all nor be afraid.　Rabbi Ben Ezra.　Robert Browning.　BiCB; PoPl; PoToHe; TRV

Youth to whom my love is given, see, I watch beside thy/bed.　The Sleep-Song of Grainne Over Dermuid.　*Anonymous.*　AnIV

Youth undying for hearts that treasure/Imogen dancing, dancing still.　Imogen.　Sir Henry Newbolt.　HBMV

Youths and maidens: let us pray　Annie died the other day.　Edward Estlin Cummings.　ErPo

Yu don't remember/The other verses/Anyway....　To Those Who Sing America.　Frank Marshall Davis.　FB

Yupi tas yi chauntra/sticks/oa　Mswaki.　Jim Brodey.　ANYP

Ywis, pole hatchet, she bleared thine eye.　My Darling Dear, My Daisy Flower.　John Skelton.　NoP

Ywis, poule-hachet, she blerid thine i.　Lullay, Lullay.　John Skelton.　EnPo; PoEL 1-5

Z

Z is for Zero–close the book!　The ABC Bunny.　Wanda Gag.　TiPo

Z is the Zuyder Zee, dwelt in by coots.　A Single-Rhyme Alphabet.　*Anonymous.*　FaBoUs

Z stands for Zero, or nothing at all.　The Alphabet.　Charles Stuart Calverley.　HBV 1-2

Z was a Zany, a poor harmless fool.　Tom Thumb's Alphabet.　*Anonymous.*　HBV 1-2; HBVY; OxNR

Z was a zany, a silly old fool.　A Was an Archer.　*Anonymous.*　FaBoUs; OxBChV

Zaccheus he/Did climb the tree/His Lord to see.　An ABC.　*Anonymous.*　GBP

Zealot without a face　Zealot Without a Face.　Charles Dobzynski.　VWA

Zed is for Zero, in the cold winter time,/And now I have brought all these letters in rhyme.　The Lumberman's Alphabet.　*Anonymous.*　ShS

A zephyr light its secret would disclose.　My Love Sways, Dancing.　Moses Ibn Ezra.　LiTW

Zephyr's breezy foot beneath.　Chorus of Spirits.　George Darley.　OnYI

Zeugmas, and rhymes he de-/Plored in his prose.　Vice.　Anthony Hecht.　OBAL

Zion's folk, free of yoke, O assure/"Forgiven!"　Ay, 'Tis Thus.　*Anonymous.*　TrJP

Zion, shout, the Lord is here.　We Are Watching, We Are Waiting.　William O. Cushing.　AH

Zip a duden duden duden zip a duden day.　Zip Coon.　*Anonymous.*　PSoN

Zip it up, and zip it down,/And hurry out to play.　My Zipper Suit.　Marie Louise Allen.　BrR; SUS; TiPo

Zobo bird–so/who are you?　Monster Alphabet.　Robert Fisher.　AmMo

The Zodiac is changed into a sphere.　Chosen.　William Butler Yeats.　BoLoP; CMoP

Zoo, iff 'twer mine, I'd let aluone/The girt wold house o' mossy stuone.　The Old House.　William Barnes.　OBVV

Zoo in the dusk ov evenen, zome/Went back to drink, an' zome went hwome.　Whitsuntide an' Club Walken.　William Barnes.　VLP

Zoo let it vlee, if God do gi'e/Sweet Jessie vor a gift to me.　The Bean Vield.　William Barnes.　VLP

Zoo ridden house is such a caddle,/That I would rather keep my staddle.　Leady-Day, an' Ridden House.　William Barnes.　VLP

An' zoo there's noo pleace lik' the drong,/Where I do hear the blackbird's zong.　The Blackbird.　William Barnes.　HBV 1-2

Zorba the Bomb　Dear Mister Congressman.　Bob Dylan.　MAT

ZOT!!!!!!　Voodoo on the Un-Assing of Janis Joplin:Warning:To Ole Tom.　Carolyn M. Rodgers.　JB

ZS zs zs z.　Concrete poem: Siesta of a Hungarian Snake.　Edwin Morgan.　InPK

The zwell o' thy bosom, thy eyes' sparklen light.　A Zong.　William Barnes.　BoLoP

ZZZZZZZZ.'　Two Old Crows.　Vachel Lindsay.　FaBoNo; LOW; OBAL

TITLE INDEX

1

1,000 Illustrations & a Complete Concordance.   Michael André.   I never resent a communication.   APU

1,2, Buckle My Shoe.   *Anonymous*.   My plate's empty.   OxNR

1 September 1939.   John Berryman.   The animals ran, the Eagle soared and dropt.   NIP

10:X:57, 45 Years Since the Fall of the Ch'ing Dynasty.   Philip Whalen.   Out of the Empress's bedroom furniture on the Phoenix-Viewing/Terrace roasting their wienies.   PoM

100 Year Old Woman at Christmas Dinner.   Colin Style.   Bending in the green rain.   AMV-80

104 Boulevard Saint-Germain.   Kenneth Pitchford.   that you long for but deny, in your chaste North.   NYBP

108 Tales of a Po'Buckra, No. 106.   Will Inman.   "I told my wife/that besides marriage/and the mystery of children,/I have one friend."   GP

10th Dance–Coming on As a Horn–20 February 1964.   Jackson MacLow.   albeit thine ending be one wherein thou reactest to orange/hair.   CoPo

11 Rue Daguerre.   John Montague.   The tips of the lately grated cherry-tree/Are a firm and lacquered black.   FaBoIP

110 Year Old House.   Ed Ochester.   to you, to us, to our cages.   Psk

112 at Presidio.   Virginia Long.   of an age we had long believed/outgrown.   AMV-80

12 Gates to the City.   Nikki Giovanni.   aquarius died when/they buried atlantis this/is the age of pisces/check it out   IHMS; PoBA

12 O'Clock News.   Elizabeth Bishop.   ...or of the sad/corruption of their leaders.   GP; OxBC; WeW

12 Oct.   Allen Planz.   finding fish before the birds.   WOLT

12 October.   Myra Cohn Livingston.   Columbus found/that far beyond the flat on flat/the world was round?   NTCP

12 Photographs of Yellowstone.   Ronald Koertge.   These are the homosexual elk cruising each other in/Angel's Meadow.   GP

12th Dance–Getting Leather by Language–21 February 1964.   Jackson MacLow.   this ends by going over things.   CoPo

13 Ways of Eradicating Blackbirds (parody).   Mark DeFoe.   Pound them to soup. Win! Win! Win! Die! Die! Die!   BXAP

13th Dance–Matching Parcels–21 February 1964.   Jackson MacLow.   At the end, those are all saying things about making gardens.   CoPo

14 July 1956.   Laurence Lerner.   A troubled crowd beneath a troubled sky.   PeSA

A 14-Year-Old Convalescent Cat in the Winter.   Gavin Ewart.   which must soon come–as I cannot forget.   OBSP

14th St./new york.   Patricia Jones.   like a medieval bazaar   NYP

The 151st Psalm.   Karl Shapiro.   Youth of all youth, ancient of days,/Follow us.   EaLo; VWA

16. ix. 65.   James Merrill.   Return with honey on our drunken feet.   NAs

1614 Boren.   Richard Hugo.   that was the place he was really moving from.   LCAP

17. IV. 71.   Paul Blackburn.   carrying anything I want downstairs to take it for/a ride on the bicycle .   PoM

18,000 FEET.   Ed Roberson.   i/learned.   PoNe

18 West 11th Street.   James Merrill.   O deepening spring.   NYP

1867: Last Sounds.   Gerry O'Egan.   howling of dogs at the empty homes...   PoL

1886 A.D.   George Lynde Richardson.   So on (ad infinitum). Such is fame!   AA

1894 in London.   Charles Spear.   Prayer-Book revision time down Lambeth way.   AnNZ

1912-1952, Full Cycle.   Peter Viereck.   By God, who'll start a brandnew Nineteen Twelve?   OBAL

The 1913 Massacre.   Woody Guthrie.   "See what your greed for money has done."   FSW

1916 Seen from 1921.   Edmund Charles Blunden.   We crept in the tall grass and slept till noon.   MMM

1930's.   Robert Lowell.   gone like the summer in their yellow bus.   NoP

1937 Ford Convertible.   Tom McKeown.   ...pointing/toward the factory/far down the hill.   PPJ

1939 Mercury.   Albert Drake.   ...smoke drifting/past neon like dreams/into the night.   AmC

1944–On the Invasion Coast.   Jack Beeching.   ...No life without our dying.   WaP

1948 Plymouth Abandoned on the Ice.   Bill Meissner.   a loyal eye that stares/for years at the speedometer/waiting for it to turn over.   AmC

The 1st.   Lucille Clifton.   nothing about the emptied family.   InPS; PAI

1st Dance–Making Things New–6 February 1964.   Jackson MacLow.   & finally either rewards someone for something or goes up/under something.   CoPo

2

2 Little Whos.   Edward Estlin Cummings.   aflame with dreams/incredible is)   OLR

2 Poems for Black Relocation Centers.   Etheridge Knight.   A faggot in steel boots.   NNaP; NoAm

2001: The Tennyson/Hardy Poem.   Gavin Ewart.   The literati will raise the cry:/Ewart's a genius!   FaBoCo

209 Canal.   Richard Howard.   Like a mouth to open wider After Hours.   NYP; TAP

The 20th Century.   Darrell Gray.   exposed to the polished strangeness,/asleep or awake.   APU

22 Miles.   Jose Angel Gutierrez.   Damn./Damn./Damn.   FIA

224 Stoop.   Victor Hernandez Cruz.   TOLD ME HE WAS PROUD.   BOLo

25 December 1960.   Ingrid Jonker.   the praying mantis in unending prayer.   PeSA

25 Spontaneous Lines Greeting the World.   Jim Tyack.   the Grateful Dead & Amelia Earhart hello to you from me   AMV-80

28 VIII 69.   Laura Chester.   ...opening like a morning glory/then wrapping us together   IHMS

29 (A Dream in Two Parts).   Ai.   She never looks back.   MAYP

29th Dance–Having an Instrument–22 March 1964.   Jackson MacLow.   –in short, whichever has an instrument.   CoPo

The 29th Month.   Stan Rice.   is to have another baby/while the real one dies.   NPGG

2nd Air Force.   Randall Jarrell.   But for them the bombers answer everything.   CMoP; WaP

2nd Dance–Seeing Lines–6 February 1964.   Jackson MacLow.   while either transporting a star or letting go of a street.   CoPo

2nd Light Poem: For Diane Wakoski.   Jackson MacLow.   In just such a manner might this being be illuminated during a time gambol.   PoM

3

3:16 and One Half...   Charles Bukowski.   I'm going where the summer flies have gone,/try to catch me.   GP

3 A. M.   Lauris Edmond.   It is not pain we fear, but triviality.   OCNZ

3 a.m. in New York.   Jean Valentine.   the shut out of his eye.   NYP

3 for 25.   William Jay Smith.   when camera clicks with quick, conclusive fact.   WaP

3 More Things.   Elinor Nauen.   Instead her hand lands on the tiny car. He gets in & hits the road.   APU

3 Stanzas about a Tree.   Marvin Bell.   Have I (think!) wanted to be the tree, or/one, two or three stanzas about a tree?   Prf

34 Blues.   Charlie Patton.   Oh Lord, oh Lord/let me see a brand new year.   BluL; FaBoPV

37th Dance–Banding–22 March 1964.   Jackson MacLow.   No it's when still others are boiling delicate things,/keeping up that process till the end.   CoPo

3rd Dance–Making a Structure with a Roof or under a Roof...   Jackson MacLow.   They smoke awhile,/& then they make structure with a roof or under a roof.   CoPo

3rd Migration, Third Series.   Brian Henderson.   that a word you don't sound could send awry.   CaPN

Abdullah Bulbul Amir. *Anonymous.* And the name that she murmurs so oft as she weeps/Is Ivan Petrofsky Skovar. AS; BLPA; FPL; FSW; StPo; TreF

Abel. Demetrios Capetanakis. "I am my brother opening the gate!" AtBAP; GTBS-P; WaaP

Abel. Else Lasker-Schüler. Have you slain the sweet birds/In your brother's face? VWA

Abel's Bride. Denise Levertov. ...there are bones at the hearth. FaBoWP; VGW

Abelard at Cluny. Grover, III Rees. Retire to my penitential madness. AMV-80

Abenamar, Abenamar. *Anonymous.* Well my wedded Lord loves me. AWP

Aberdeen, Mississippi Blues. Booker White. They even has the poor boy/ all/hobbled down BluL

Aberdeen Train. Edwin Morgan. a Chinese moment in the Mearns. BSV

Abide, Good Men. *Anonymous.* And in my mercy have affiance,/And thou shall get my grace.' OxBM

Abide in Me, O Lord, and I in Thee. Harriet Beecher Stowe. Come, and abide in me, and I in thee. AH

Abide Not in the Realm of Dreams. William Henry Burleigh. And, duty done, that rest shall be/Full of beatitudes to thee. AH

Abide with Me; Fast Falls the Eventide. Henry Francis Lyte. In life, in death, O Lord, abide with me. Amen. VLP

Abide with Us. Horatius Bonar. Thou wilt abide with me,/And I with Thee! BePJ

Abiding. A. B. Simpson. Glorious Lord, and coming King! STF

The Abiding Love. John White Chadwick. Our God, forever more. BLPBe; FaBoBe

Abigail's Lamentation for the Loss of Mr. Harley... William Walsh. And Cardiff cliffs obscured Ramillia's field. APAS

Abiku. Wole Soyinka. In the silence of webs Abiku moans/Shaping mounds from the yolk. PBA

Abilene. *Anonymous.* Wish to God that I could be,/In Abilene, my Abilene. FSW

Abishag. Jacob Fichman. his heart makes music of the tears of/my Spring. TrJP; VWA

Abishag. Rainer Maria Rilke. And sought himself in his remaining blood. AWP

Abishag. Andre Spire. Only my beard, only my wrinkles/near thee! TrJP

Abishag Writes a Letter Home. Itzik Manger. while girlish in a corner/a dream sobs tenderly. VWA

Abla. Antar [(or Antana)]. Who will guide me to the dwelling of Abla? LiTW

Abnegation. Martial (Marcus Valerius Martialis). To do do without you altogether. UnTE

Abner Silver's "Pu-leeze! Mr. Hemingway!" Ring Lardner. Pu-leeze! Mister Hemingway! OBAL

The Abnormal Is Not Courage. Jack Gilbert. It is the normal excellence, of long accomplishment. CoAP; NPGG

Aboard at a Ship's Helm. Walt Whitman. Ship of the body, ship of the soul, voyaging, voyaging, voyaging. NePA; NOBA; OxBA

Abolitionist Hymn. *Anonymous.* Be, like the wind that fans it, free. TrAS

The Abominable Baseball Bat. X. J. Kennedy. Now ever since, my bat and I/Walk every time we bat. WSC

An Aboriginal Mother's Lament. Charles Harpur. For but a single palmful/Of water now for thee. ACV

Aboriginal Sin. John Hay. –the dove/An ancient turtle egging love. NePoAm-2

Aborigine. Hugo Williams. Beautiful in the manner of his country. OBTV

Abortion. Florence Anthony ("Ai"). and there is room only for one man in this house. BoWoP

An Abortion. Frank O'Hara. ...From our tree/dropped, that she not wither,/autumn in our terrible breath. TAP

The Abortion. Anne Sexton. you coward...this baby that I bleed. CAPP; IHMS; MAT; NMM; SM; VGW

Abou Ben Adhem. [James Henry] Leigh Hunt. And lo! Ben Adhem's name led all the rest. BeLS; BLPA; FaBoBe; FaBoRV; FaBV; FaFP; FaPoR; FPL; GN; GoTF; HBV 1-2; HBVY; MCCG; NOBE; OBEV; OBVV; OHFP; TreF; TRV; WBLP; WGRP

About a Year after He Got Married He Would Sit Alone... James Whitehead. ...Bring their play to ruin. GP

About an Allegory. Walter Conrad Arensberg. That warms the hands of a cold God. AnAmPo

About an Excavation. Charles Reznikoff. a flock of bright red lanterns/has settled. NTCP; PCP; PrIm; VGW; WeW

About Children. Phyllis McGinley. When the selfsame nimbus is eerily worn/By a nymph, a child, and a unicorn? OBAL

About Marriage. Denise Levertov. in a green/airy space, not/locked in NMM

About Motion Pictures. Ann Darr. The verb is get. GrPl

About My Poems. Donald Justice. –Now the long silence. Now the beginning again. PoA

About Savannah. *Anonymous.* Huzza for the King and Prevost, sir. PAH

About the Cool Water. Kenneth Rexroth. And it is as though I held/In my arms the bird filled/Evening sky of summer. ErPo

...About the Cool Water. Sappho. slumber pours down... OBVE

About the Cows. Roger Pfingston. as they crowd each other toward the woods/where Stoutes Creek flows past the quarry. FAZ

About the Heavenly Life. Luis Ponce de Leon. There would it live/Close to your flock, nor ever errant wander. ILwL

About the Phoenix. James Merrill. ...turned in sleep/Away from whatever waited to be endured? NoAm

About the Teeth of Sharks. John Ciardi. I'll never know now! Well, goodbye. OBCA

About This Course. David Shapiro. The fountain is slowed down, as if controlled/by your calm hands. PoA

About to Die. *Anonymous.* So do not look at me with your crooked eyes. WTO

About Women. Howard Phelps (Phelps Putnam) Putnam. We shall have clarity and hours/Which women shall not take away. AnFE

About Women's Liberation. Maria Saucedo. And began making tortillas and Revolution. FIA

Above Ben Loyal. Arthur Ball. The cloud, the sky, can see. We are the blind. PoSH

Above in Inverkirkaig. Norman MacCaig. a litter of tiny Suilvens, each one/the dead spit of his father. PoSH

Above It All. Philip Levine. the twin periods marking/the dead centers of our eyes. NOBA

Above Machu Picchu, 129 Baker Street, San Francisco. Joseph Stroud. As I do now/that distant morning/In that long ago room. NPGG

Above Pate Valley. Gary Snyder. Ten thousand years. CoAP; ConAP; LCAP; NaP; NoP

Above Salerno. Ada Foster Murray. This world of beauty, color, and perfume;/Hoary with age, yet of unaging bloom. HBV 1-2

Above the Arno. May Swenson. –pink/as the breasts of Botticelli's Venus– foretinting dawn. NYBP

Above the Bright Blue Sky. Albert Midlane. And everyone is happy,/Nor could be happier there. OxBChV

Above the Dock. Thomas Ernest Hulme. ...What seemed so far away/Is but a child's balloon, forgotten after play. FaBoMo; GTBS-P

Above the Falls at Waimea. Don Johnson. to lie with me here at mid-stream,/tight in the lap of the rain. MAYP

Above the High. Geoffrey Grigson. This selfsame cold abstract/So ancient town. EnLoPo

Above the Hills of Time. Thomas Tiplady. Till we are gathered to Thy home above. TRV

Above the Pool. John Montague. ...in this/my last summer of loneliness. NOBI

Above the Rocking Heads of the Mothers. Nelly Sachs. fresh branches of the trees surviving winter. PBWP

Above the Stable. Nona Keen Duffy. Lies a Sovereign/High and Holy! BrR; ChBR

Above the Wall. Susannah P. Malarkey. Still should I surely/Hear you call. AMV-80

Above These Cares. Edna St. Vincent Millay. Kicking in frenzy, a swimmer enmeshed in weeds. NoP

Abracadabra. Dorothy Livesay. Little boy blue/Blows a blue tune/On a wicked afternoon. WHW

Abraham. George Bogin. Everyone is dead who would know/the little there is to know/about Abraham. GOYP

Abraham. Stephen Mitchell. ...grope/In the alien light, toward a goal/He could be sure of never reaching. VWA

Abraham. Edwin Muir. Far from his father's house, in alien Canaan. EBCP; MoRP

Abraham:. Delmore Schwartz. The angel of death comes to make the alienated and indestructible/One a part of his famous society. VWA

Abraham. Eisig Silberschlag. I shall not return to Ur. VWA

Abraham and Isaac. Else Lasker-Schüler. But He did love His servant. BoWoP; VWA

Abraham and Sarah. Itzik Manger. Even a deaf mute can hear. VWA

Abraham Davenport. John Greenleaf Whittier. That simple duty hath no place for fear. AnNE; NoP

Abraham in Egypt. Howard Schwartz. And followed it as far as I could/ Knowing it would lead me/Out of Egypt. VWA

Abraham Lincoln. A. S. Ames. His work goes on increasing through all time. OHIP

Abraham Lincoln. Joseph Auslander. To heal the world with your heart's compassion! YaD

Abraham Lincoln. Rosemary and Stephen Vincent Benét. Lincoln kept on growing. NAMP; PoSC; TiPo; YeAr

Abraham Lincoln. Henry Howard Brownell. Then slept, with their swords, and died. GN

Ad Infinitum. Joan Aronsten. They turn to tread the impetus/that moves about their feet. NOAV

Ad Johannuelem Leporem, Lepidissimum, Carmen Heroicum. *Anonymous.* Feathers lopped off, spurs everywhere did lie. FaBoNo

Ad Lesbiam. Niall Sheridan. The frenzied kisses that you gave and got. OxBI

Ad Leuconoen. Horace. The longest life is brevity. AWP

Ad Leuconoen. Francis Sylvester ("Father Prout") Mahony. Time flieth as we sing! IrPN

Ad Librum. Samuel Danforth II. This Sheet that brought thee in shall lay thee out. SCAP

Ad Limina. Joseph Campbell. Come to my haggard gate, my very doorstep. BIrV

Ad Matrem. Julian Fane. So shall I live with Thee, and thy dear fame/ Shall link my love unto thine honored name. HBV 1-2

Ad Matrem in Coelis. Linda Lyon Van Voorhis. Who, knowing stars, was fearless of the night. GoBC

Ad Ministram. William Makepeace Thackeray. And tipple my ale in the shade. HBV 1-2

Ad Patriam. Clinton Scollard. Triumphant thou shalt mount the years/ Toward thy high goal! PAH

Ad Patriam (excerpt). William Dudley Foulke. To carry hope to all the sons of men. PGD

Ad Persephonen. Franklin Pierce ("F.P.A.") Adams. My darling daughter, pretty Puff,/And you'll be mine. InMe

Ad Tusserum. *Anonymous.* To sharpen others when themselves are blunt. FaBoUs

Ad Xanthiam Phoceum. Horace. Besides, the number of my years/Is over forty. AWP

An Adage. H. J. Byron. When young "sow wild oats', but when old, grow sage. FaBoUs; NLV

Adam. Philip Booth. say all the sea's grave names, and build/with words this beach that is the world. MoLP

Adam. Anthony Hecht. It shall reach you yet. CoPo

Adam. Rainer Maria Rilke. Yet man persisted: she will bring forth. MoRP

Adam and Eve. Itzik Manger. And H-U-S-H spells–hush! TrJP

Adam and Eve. Karl Shapiro. And it was autumn, and the present/world. AmP

Adam and Eve. C. H. Sisson. For the second the process was reversed/ And that one was without pride. FaBoTw

Adam and Eve at the Garden Gate. Marsha Pomerantz. ...Eat, then watch/the core brown in your hand. VWA

Adam and Eve: The Recognition of Eve. Karl Shapiro. She was already turning beautiful. MoAB

Adam and Eve: The Sickness of Adam. Karl Shapiro. On earth. Sadly the angel watched them go. AP; CoBMV; MoAB

Adam Bel, Clym of the Cloughe, and Wyllyam of Cloudesle. *Anonymous.* And all that with hande-bowe shoteth,/That of heuen they may neuer mysse! BuBa; ESPB; OxBB

Adam Driven from Eden. *Anonymous.* Ther was Adam sore aferd,/For labour coude he werken non. OxBM

Adam, Eve and the Big Apple. Edward Watkins. Once was champagne and laughter, Lunt and Fontanne! AMV-81

Adam in Love. Stephen Mitchell. His hands behind his back, a tiny smile/ Flickering from the distance like a glowworm. VWA

Adam in the Garden Pinning Leaves. *Anonymous.* Adam in the garden pinning leaves. FSW; NoP; OuSiCo

Adam Lay I-Bowndyn. *Anonymous.* Ther fore we mown syngyn/Deo Gracias. AtBAP; BoW; CBEP; CTC; EG; EnPo; GoBC; HAP; InPS; MeEL; NOBE; NOCV; OAEL 1-2; OAEP; OxBM; OxBoCh; OxBoLi; PAI; PoEL 1-5; PPoe; SeCeV

Adam, Lilith, and Eve. Robert Browning. "I saw through the joke!" the man replied/They re-seated themselves beside. HBV 1-2

Adam on His Way Home. Robert Pack. Where he leapt in the final spasm of first love. ErPo

Adam's Apple. Coleman Barks. he just nodded. PPJ

Adam's Complaint. Denise Levertov. still it's not deep enough/to drink the moon from. BoWoP; NNaP; PP; SOTW; TEP

Adam's Curse. William Butler Yeats. As weary-hearted as that hollow moon. BIrV; CMoP; CoBMV; DiPo; NoAm; NoP; OAEL 1-2; VLP

Adam's Death. Gabriel Levin. Tomorrow I'll swallow my words,/Closing my eyes on each letter. VWA

Adam's Dream. Howard Schwartz. Why the wound could not heal itself/ Once we had awakened. VWA

Adam's Dying. Ridgely Torrence. Which was best?/The heart knows. FYAP

Adam's Footprint. Vassar Miller. The foot of Adam leaves the mark/Of some child scrabbling in the dark. NePoEA; NIP

Adam's Hymn in Paradise. Joost van den Vondel. Gavst immortality, free will,/And language not involved in dark! WGRP

Adam's Race. Muslih-ud-Din Sa'di. A son of Adam is no name for thee. LiTW

Adam's Song of the Visible World. Ridgely Torrence. And my blind ways in darkness be no more. TrPWD

Adam's Song to Heaven. Edgar Bowers. And knowledge in your sombre depth/Embraces your perfection and your sleep. ConAP; QFR

Adam's Task. John Hollander. Naming's over. Day is done. NIP; NoP; PPP

Adam Smith. Edmund Clerihew Bentley. But he was backed through thick and thin/By all his kin. FaBoCo

Adam–The First Kiss. Hal Porter. and through the Garden hurls the voice· of God. ACV

Adams and Liberty. Robert Treat Paine. While the earth bears a plant, or the sea rolls its waves. MC; PAH

Adapt Thyself. Shem-Tob Palquera. But if an ass thou meetest, simply/ bray! TrJP

Adare (excerpt). John Francis O'Donnell. And I am, with the sun, alone. IrPN

Addendum to the Ten Commandments. *Anonymous.* But thank the Lord you're not forbidden/To covet your neighbour's daughter. DBV

Adder's Epigrams. Colin Ellis. To say things better that were best not said. FaBoEE

Addict. Jack Montgomery. "Since you're up, try Channel Four." QQQ

The Addict. Larry Rubin. ...I saw my father's eyes were warm. GoYe

The Addict. Anne Sexton. Now I'm borrowed./Now I'm numb. CTBA

Addio a la Mamma. Noe Jitrik. someone is in charge of telling mother that she'll never see us again. VWA

Addition to Kipling's "The Dead King (Edward VII), 1910." Max Beerbohm. For we know that in Heaven above at this moment he's saving/God. FaBoEE

An Additional Poem. John Ashbery. ...we/Rise with the night let out of the box of wind. FaBoMo

Additional Verses to Hail Columbia. Oliver Wendell Holmes. Ever shall the circling sun/Find the Many still are One! PAH

Address Not Known. John Heath-Stubbs. Finds the frost in the day's air, and the nights which appear too/long. ChMP

Address to a Child during a Boisterous Winter Evening. Dorothy Wordsworth. Here's a cosy warm house for Edward and me. OxBChV

Address to a Haggis. Robert Burns. But, if ye wish her gratefu' prayer,/ Gie her a haggis! ViBoPo

Address to a Lady. Robert Burns. Wad be my queen, wad be my queen. CEP

Address to a Mummy. Horace (or Horatio) Smith. Although corruption may our frame consume,/The immortal spirit in the skies may bloom! HBV 1-2; RoGo

Address to an Absolute. Roy McFadden. Lost in a wound, not even questioning. NeIP

Address to Certain Gold Fishes. Hartley Coleridge. Deck'd in Oriental pride,/By homely British fire-side. VLP

Address to Children. *Anonymous.* But time or tide won't wait for you, if you are tied for/time. FaBoUs

An Address to His Elbow-Chair, New Cloath'd. William Somervile. On his great voyage, to the world unknown. CEP; OBEC

An Address to Miss Phillis Wheatley (excerpt). Jupiter Hammon. Among the heathen live no more,/Come magnify thy God. AmPP

Address to Mr. Cross, of Exeter 'Change on the Death of the Elephant. Thomas Hood. Or turn about their literary den–/Shoot me! FM

Address to My Infant Daughter. William Wordsworth. The second glory of the Heavens?–Thou hast. EvOK; Par

Address to My Malay Krees. John Leyden. And many a life-blood owe thee still. OBTV

Address to My Soul. Elinor Wylie. Accept the stricter mould/That makes you singular. APA; AWP; LiTM; MoRP; OxBA

Address to Plenty. John Clare. To be, while winter's horrors last,/The sport of every pelting blast. OBRV

Address to the Crown. Charles L. O'Donnell. And went to His death in their diadem. GoBC

Address to the Deil. Robert Burns. I'm wae to think upo' yon den,/Ev'n for your sake! CEP; EiCP; EnPE; GoTS; LAuP; NOEC; OAEL 1-2; OAEP; OxBS; PoEL 1-5

An Address to the New Tay Bridge. William McGonagall. Near by Dundee and the bonnie Magdalen Green. PeD

An Address to the Plebeians. John Learmont. Mak ay true honesty your law/An' safest shield. FaBoPV; NOEC

Address to the Scholars of New England. John Crowe Ransom. Your wisdom has done this, sages of Harvard. LiTM; NePA

An Address to the Soul Occasioned by a Rain. Edward Taylor. Such fireballs dropping in the Temple Flame/Burns up the building: Lord, forbid the same. AP; OxBA; PoEL 1-5

Address to the Unco Guid, or the Rigidly Righteous. Robert Burns. What's done we partly may compute,/But know not what's resisted.

BoLiVe; CEP; EnLit; EnPE; HBV 1-2; LoBV; NOBE; NOCV; NoP; OAEP; OBEC; OxBS; SeCeV; TreFS; TrGrPo; ViBoPo

An Address to the Vacationers at Cape Lookout.   William Stafford.   What disregards people does people good.   NYBP

Address to Venus.   Lucretius (Titus Lucretitus Carus).   O graunt that of my love at last I may not misse!   AnEnPO; AWP

Addressed to a Gentleman at Table Who Kept Boasting...   Robert Burns.   Though it crawl on the locks of a queen.   DBV; PV

Addressed to a Young Lady.   William Cowper.   And heav'n reflected in her face.   EnRP

Addressed to Haydon.   John Keats.   Listen awhile ye nations, and be dumb.   CBEP; EnRP

Addressed to Lady ****, Who Asked What the Passion of Love Was?   Charles Morris.   And to hear it I'd always be willing and mute.   NOEC

Addressing His Deaf Wife, Kansas, 1916.   William Olsen.   unquestionable as my sitting up just now.   AMV-81

Adelaide Crapsey.   Carl Sandburg.   And the sea shouldered its salt in long gray combers hauling/new shapes on the beach sand.   HBMV

Adelaide Neilson.   William Winter.   Nor any grief so black as this!   AA

Adelina, the Yale Boola Girl.   Charles H. Loomis.   When the silver moon is beaming;/Then I'll meet you, Adeline.   FSN

Adelita.   Anonymous.   And on land in a military train.   AS; FSW

The Adepts.   Lawrence Durrell.   While at a window someone stood and cried.   ErPo

Adequacy.   Elizabeth Barrett Browning.   I ask thee not my joys to multiply,–/Only to make me worthier of the least.   SBG

Adeste Fideles.   Anonymous.   Venite adoremus Dominum.   PSoN

Adeste Fideles.   Saint Bonaventure.   O come, let us adore Him, Christ the Lord.   CAW; WGRP

The Adhesive Autopsy of Walt Whitman.   Jonathan Williams.   "that he was a Kosmos is a piece of news we were/hardly prepared for..."   PoM

Adieu.   Thomas Carlyle.   Adieu for ever now.   HBV 1-2; OBRV

Adieu My Lovely Nancy.   Anonymous.   And when our money is all gone we'll boldly go to sea.   OBET

Adieu, the Years Are a Broken Song.   Anonymous.   And the old days never will come again.   NOAV

Adieu to Belashanny.   William Allingham.   To my native Belashanny and the winding banks of Erne.   OxBI

Adieu to Bon County.   Anonymous.   And play on the fiddle to pass away time!   ABF

Adieu to His Mistress.   Alexander Montgomerie.   Sic blissing in kissing/I quit till we twa meet.   BSV

An Adieu to My Landlady.   George Farewell.   I can't forbear to flog the wicked witch.   NOEC

Adieu to Old England.   Anonymous.   ...I am glad of a drop of cold water/That runs from town to town.   OBET

Adieu to the Stone Walls.   Anonymous.   My song is now ended, I'll bid you farewell,/To enjoy a heaven instead of a cell.   OuSiCo

Adina.   Harold Milton Telemaque.   ...Adina in the breezes/Blazing effulgent in the Caribbean.   TTY

Adios.   Donald Campbell Babcock.   God abide the coming day!   NePoAm-2

The Adirondacs.   Ralph Waldo Emerson.   ...Time takes fresh start again,/On for a thousand years of genius more.   GLGT

Adjectives.   Moishe Nadir.   Juicy cherries tremble and fall on my lips.   TrJP

Adjuration.   Charles Enoch Wheeler.   Speak for the comfort of the weary/Who weep to know.   AmNP; PoNe

Adjustment.   John Greenleaf Whittier.   And the new gospel verifes the old.   WGRP

Adlestrop.   Edward ("Edward Eastaway") Thomas.   Farther and farther, all the birds/Of Oxfordshire and Gloucestershire.   BrPo; CH; FaBoPP; GoJo; HAP; LiTB; NOBE; OBEV; OxBTC

Adman into Toad.   Frank Polite.   ...content to be/my own incredible imagery.   APU

An Adminsitrator.   Geoffrey Grigson.   The merely nasty alters into vile.   FaBoEE

Admiral.   John Alexander Allen.   ...though each oblivious night/Shoulders aloft your golden epaulets.   NYBP

Admiral Benbow.   Anonymous.   And with a fury still he faced/England's foe, England's foe.   CBEP; EnSB

Admiral Byng.   Anonymous.   Because it is their doom, so maun I.   OBSS

Admiral Byrd.   Ogden Nash.   And another Huzza for the U. S. A./Which produces so many heroes like they.   InMe; YaD

Admiral Death.   Sir Henry Newbolt.   And they sleep with Admiral Death.   VLP

Admiral Hosier's Ghost.   Richard Glover.   Think on vengeance for my ruin,/And for England–shamed in me.   HBV 1-2; NOEC; ViBoPo

The Admiral's Daughter.   E. G. Burrows.   never able to come alongside.   HoAn

The Admiral's Ghost.   Alfred Noyes.   If your soul's like a North Sea storm?   BBV

Admirals All.   Sir Henry Newbolt.   And honour, as long as waves shall break,/To Nelson's peerless name!   FaPoR; MOS

Admire Cranmer!   Stevie Smith.   And made the flames burn crueller.   Admire Cranmer!   NoAm

Admonition.   Philip Stack.   Nothing you have to give can equal these!   BLPA

Admonition for Spring.   L. A. Mackay.   The heavy hyacinth remembering death.   CaP; OBCV; PeCV

Admonition to a Traveller.   William Wordsworth.   ...from the day/On which it should be touch'd, would melt away!   GTBS; GTBS-P

Admonition to Montgomerie.   King of England James I,   When all was done, ye hade so evill a grace/Ye stoll awaye and durst no more be seene.   OxBS

Admonition to the Muse.   Geoffrey Taylor.   So run along now to your chamber Miss and rhyme with bliss.   FaBoEE

An Admonition to Young Lassies.   Alexander Montgomerie.   Flee whilom love, and it will follow thee.   BSV

Admonitions.   Lucille Clifton.   she is a poet/she don't have no sense   BPo; NMM; PAI

An Adobe House.   Witter ("Emanuel Morgan") Bynner.   And the other heard only the summons of the/wind/And wondered where it was calling.   BPAW

Adolescence.   Gregory Orr.   ...Hands/on skin; how good it feels.   Psk

Adolescence.   P. K. Page.   to see them form and fade before their eyes.   CaP; OBCV

Adolescence.   Dennis Schmitz.   forcing boy & girl to lie/down together untaught/in the adjacent dark.   FAZ

Adolescence–II.   Rita Dove.   Night rests like a ball of fur on my tongue.   AmPA; HaCAP

Adolf Hitler Meditates on the Jewish Problem.   Oscar Hahn.   Take this flyswatter and exterminate the angels.   AMV-81

Adolphus Elfinstone.   Gelett Burgess.   But soon it grows quite big and furious.   BBGG

Adon 'Olam.   Anonymous.   The Lord doth guard, I have no fear!   EaLo

Adonais.   William Wallace Harney.   In the happy harvest-fields as the sun/sinks low.   AA; HBV 1-2

Adonais.   Percy Bysshe Shelley.   The soul of Adonais, like a star,/Beacons from the abode where the Eternal are.   AtBAP; EBEV; ERoP 1-2; FaBoPP; FiP; GoTF; GoTL; HBV 1-2; HoPM; LoBV; MasP; MCCG; NoP; OAEL 1-2; OAEP; OBNC; OBRV; PoEL 1-5; SCV; TreFS; TrGrPo; ViBoPo; WGRP; WHA

Adonis.   Hilda ("H. D.") Doolittle.   each of us like you/stands apart, like you/fit to be worshiped.   AP; AWP; BoC; InPo; LiTA; PoPl

The Adorable Paratroopess.   Michael Silverton.   all things come to him who waits   PoL

Adoramus Te, Christe.   David O Bruadair.   Pure like her never grew in womb/nor will till the end of time.   NOBI

Adoration.   Jeanne Marie Guyon.   Our source, our center and our dwelling-place!   STF; WGRP

Adoration of the Disk by King Akhn-Aten and Princess Nefer Neferiu..   Book of the Dead.   In the great dawn, then lift up me, thy son.   AWP

The Adoration of the Magi.   Christopher Pilling.   at one with an astonished soldier.   OBCP

The Adoration of the Wise Men.   Cecil Frances Alexander.   Love, and Faith, and true devotion,/For our Saviour, God, and King.   HBVY

Adore We the Lord.   Anonymous.   Earth's sea white with waves.   NOBI

Adoro Te Devote.   Saint Thomas Aquinas.   And may be blest Thy glory in beholding!   CAW

Adrian and Bardus.   John Gower.   Ayain the which reson debateth,/And every creature it hateth.   OxBM

Adrian Block's Song.   Edward Everett Hale.   And I name it Roses Island.   PAH

Adriani Morientis ad Animam Suam.   Matthew Prior.   Thou dread'st and hop'st Thou know'st not what.   CEP; OBSP; OBVE

Adriatic.   Robert Conquest.   The clear Promethean spirit/Through a broken tragic age.   PP

Adrift.   Elizabeth Dickinson Dowden.   Come safe to land and Love be left behind.   WGRP

Adsum.   Richard Henry Stoddard.   He answered, "I am here."   AA

Adulescentia.   Robert Fitzgerald.   That dun, worn, airy to-be-bounced/Treasurable and humble dweller in closets.   SD

An Adult Lullaby.   Anonymous.   Whan he of the apple ete and Eve it him betoght.   MeEL

Adulteries, Murthers, Robberies, Thefts.   Roger Williams.   Your Land's the Wildernesse.   SCAP

Adultery.   James Dickey.   God bless you. Guilt is magical.   TAP; WeW

Adultery.   Alan Dugan.   They pray the insignificance/of most private behavior.   CAPP

Adultery at a Las Vegas Bookstore.   Stephen Shu Ning Liu.   cold terrace, "Swear! O Hamlet, swear!"   BrSi

Adultery at the Plaza.   John Thompson.   The skaters are gone home. All is dark. I leave you these hours.   WeW

African Poems: We're an Africanpeople. Don L. Lee. burning blacker softly, softer. CNA

An African Song. Thomas Chatterton. What can keep his soul away,/From the transports of Mored? LoBV

African Sunday. Maureen Owen. he huffed "Of Course she flew!" APU

African Things. Victor Hernandez Cruz. dance & tell me black african things/i know you know InW

The African Trader's Complaint. Dennis C. Osadebay. Would you insist I'm lazy/Because I am an African? PBA

The African Tramp. Geoffrey Haresnape. The sun, the big flower, looked at him through the leaves. PeSA

Africland. Oliver La Grone. To drink a new worlds/Breaking light. FB

After. Robert Browning. Cover the face. BoLiVe; EG; TrGrPo

After. Caroline Grayson. After the prayer and the praise/Cometh His blessing again. BLRP

After. Ralph Hodgson. "On the wings of the cinnamon bee." MoBrPo

After. Philip Levine. the fingers hidden, home/to a name written in water. VWA

After. Philip Bourke Marston. And eternity to sleep in. HBV 1-2; NOBV

After. Lizette Woodworth Reese. Oh, the scent of mint was plain! HBV 1-2

After. Michael Ryan. The sun goes down. He sees nothing./It's calm. MAYP

After a Death. Gregory Orr. The way the three of us walked/was a kind of steady weeping. GeTw

After a Game of Squash. Samuel L. Albert. Up in the room where the lockers are and the showers. GoYe; NePoAm-2

After a Hundred Years. Emily Dickinson. Instinct picking up the key/Dropped by memory. AWP; InPo; MoPo; OxBA

After a Journey. Thomas Hardy. Our days were a joy, and our paths through flowers. AtBAP; CMoP; DTC; EBEV; ELP; EnLoPo; FaBoPP; GBL; GTBS-P; MoVE; OBNC; OxBTC; PoEL 1-5

After a Lecture on Keats. Oliver Wendell Holmes. The hyacinth my garden gave/Shall lie upon that Roman grave! AA; ViBoPo

After a Little While. James Ryder Randall. I fain would rest,/After a little while. CAW

After a Parting. Alice Meynell. They draw my life, my life, out of my heart. NOBV

After a Passage in Baudelaire. Robert Duncan. complique, mais eurythmique. CMoP; PoA

After a Time. Catherine Davis. And we go stripped at last the way we came. NePoEA

After Alcman. Dick Gallup. the swarms of extended wings. ANYP

After All. Donald Jeffrey Hayes. And thus know the all of each. CDC

After All These Years. May Sarton. After all these years/Let sleeping beauty wake. AMV-81

After an All-Night Cackle with Sloth & Co. I Enter the Mansion... Gary Gildner. & drop my chalky crap, my gnats & flies,/in the gutter with such distinction. GP

After an Eclipse of the Sun. Eugene Heimler. and slowly now, their strength renewed, the words/set off along the road, renewed. VWA

After an Interval. Walt Whitman And the duo of Saturn and Mars! AA

After Annunciation. Anna Wickham. That you, dear Plant, have birth. MoBrPo

After Apple-Picking. Robert Frost. Or just some human sleep. AnNE; CMoP; CoBMV; DiPo; ForPo; FPL; InPS; LiTA; MoAB; MoAmPo; MoPo; MoVE; NoAm; NOBA; NU; OxBA; PPP; PrIm; RoGo; TAP; UnPo; ViBoPo

After Aughrim. Arthur Gerald Geoghegan. Than live a slave without a blow/For the Green! OnYI

After Aughrim. Emily Lawless. Yet still their love comes home to me. OBEV; OxBI

After Bombardment. John Pudney. After the guns, when men smile in a street. WaP

After Chagall. Rene Wenger. I'm not asking for kisses,/just a roof under my feet. PoDr

After Christmas. Michael Richards. and look for snowdrops. OBCP

After-Christmas Poem. Elizabeth-Ellen Long. Something of His love to last/Until next Christmas Eve! ChBR

The After-Comers. Robert and Spence Traill Lowell. In canvas, stone, or written pages. AA

After Commencement. Howard Nemerov. Have made the silence deeper by degrees. GLGT

After Dark. Adrienne Rich. At the last, your hand feels steady. LCAP; LiTM; VGW

After Death. R. A. K. Mason. but not for me. AnNZ

After Death. Fanny Parnell. Now mine eyes have seen her glory! AnIV; OBVV; OnYI; OxBI

After Death. Charles Francis Richardson. Unending love unending growth shall be. AA

After Death. Christina Georgina Rossetti. To know he still is warm though I am cold. EnLi 1-2; GBL; TEP

After Death. Algernon Charles Swinburne. "Flesh to feed hell's worm upon." NOBV

After Death in Arabia. Sir Edwin Arnold. He that died at Azan gave/This to those who made his grave. HBV 1-2; WGRP

After Dilettante Concetti (parody). Henry Duff Traill. Who to the wretched creature's caudal part/Its foolish empty-jingling "burden' ties." BXAP; CenHV; FaBoCo; HBV 1-2; Par

After Dinner We Take a Drive into the Night. Tony Towle. dropping to the ground and rolling down the bowling alley of/the sky. ANYP

After Drinking All Night with a Friend... Robert Bly. No longer caring if we drift or go straight. NaP

After Elegies. Jean Valentine. earth your face fern coal LCAP

After Emerson. Anonymous. Letters that we ought to burn. NOBL

After Ever Happily. Ian Serraillier. ...Now, to finish my rhyme,/I'll start it properly: Once upon a time– SO

After Experience Taught Me... W. D. Snodgrass. What evil, what unspeakable crime/Have you made your life worth? CAPP; CoAP; OBWP; PPP; TAP

After Five Years. Augustus Young. ...He was offspring of the generation in between. BIrV

After Frost. Brian Patten. It's rest enough for anyone. EBEV

After Galen. Oliver St. John Gogarty. You would not have me roar, or crow. FaBoEE; OBMV; PoRA

The After-Glow. Mathilde Blind. And lend to loss itself a joy divine? OBNC

After Goliath. Kingsley Amis. That the right man lay in the dust. NePoEA-2; NOBL; OxBTC; PoCh

After Grave Deliberation... Elizabeth Flynn. wishing me luck in placing myself/elsewhere. AMV-80; NLV

After great pain, a formal feeling comes. Emily Dickinson. First–Chill–then Stupor–then the letting go– BoWoP; CABA; ForPo; HAP; InPo; InPS; LiTA; MAmP; MoAB; MoAmPo; MoPo; MoVE; NAWM 1-2; NePA; NIP; NOBA; NoP; PAI; PPoe; PrIm; SBG; TAP; UnPo; WeW

After great storms the calm returns. Sir Thomas Wyatt. To make your hope, your health retain,/And me also the most happy. FCP; SiPS

After Greece. James Merrill. ...May I/Also survive its meanings, and my own. ConAP; NOBA; NYBP

After Grey Vigils. George Santayana. Engulf the planets. I have seen the best. WHA

After Grief. Stanley Plumly. And you, my anonymous father,/be with me when I wake. AmPA; LCAP

After He Had Gone. Sylvia Townsend Warner. Would he had stayed! MoBrPo

After he stripped off my clothes. Vallana. who teaches us how to faint? BoWoP

After Her Death. Anne Stevenson. absorbed in its one story. HoAn

After Hilary, Age 5. Faye Kicknosway. and your mother will be gooseflesh/and your father will die. APU

After Horace. Alfred Denis Godley. Whether the public read her works/Or not! NOBL

After Hours. Robert Mezey. ...and I see/the coming time loose and dark/above me, with new strength AmPC; NaP

After I Had Worked All Day. Charles Reznikoff. Surely, the tide comes in twice a day. PrIm; VGW

After I Have Voted. Laura Jensen. the violet flashlights and guitars! AmPA

After Illness. Vi Gale. "thirty Rattvik fiddlers in skinpants!" GP

After Jericho. R. S. Thomas. ...your words,/every one of them, are volunteers. OxBC

After Johnson's Dance. Charles H. Souter. Who made that advance–/After Johnson's dance? PoAu 1-2

After kicking on the swing. Anonymous. And lean flirtatiously against the door,/Tasting a green plum. BoWoP

After Laughter. Grace Buchanan Sherwood. Faith's mountain spreads its roots beyond this ground. GoYe

After Li Ch'ing-Chao. Anne Waldman. but I long to clutch my lover's body/& he sink into me. APU

After Long Busyness. Robert Bly. Every day I did not spend in solitude was wasted. CAPP; PoA

After Long Silence. William Butler Yeats. We loved each other and were ignorant. BoLoP; CMoP; DiPo; ELU; EnLoPo; HeIP; HoPM; LiTL; LiTM; MBW 1-2; OAEL 1-2; OBMV; PoPl; PPP; PrIm; UnPo

After Lorca. Robert Creeley. And the poor love it/and think its crazy. ConAP; LCAP; NaP; PAI; PoL

After Lorca. Ted Hughes. A song with a man's face/That God holds up in his fingers. PoA

After Love. Vicente Aleixandre. while, with my mouth, I begin again to cover your cooling/hair. AMV-80

After Love. Maxine W. Kumin. lay lightly down, and slept. NMM; TAP

After Making Love We Hear Footsteps. Galway Kinnell. this blessing love gives again into our arms. InPS

After Mardi Gras. Sister Mary Honora. Ash trays and ashes, ashen Sybarite. NePoAm-2

After Midnight. D.G. Jones. While a white picket fence/Goes racing through the yard. WHW

After Midnight. Louis Simpson. Counting the singles carefully. CAPP; NoAm

After Midnight. Charles Vildrac. Who has been born this evening in the house. AWP

After Midsummer. E. J. Scovell. And the sky have changed, and the further dales come up. OxBTC

After Music. Josephine Preston Peabody. Would tell me who I was before I died. AA

After My Death. Hayim Nahman Bialik. He had one more poem/And that poem is lost,/For ever. VWA

After Nightfall. William Renton. And selfless self-approval of the hills. NOBV

After Our War. John Balaban. After our war, how will love speak? FAZ

After Passing the Examination. Meng Chiao. In a single day I have seen all the flowers of Ch'ang-an. GLGT

After Peckinpah. Barry Dempster. ...landslides of/bodies, all bigger than any one of us. CaPN

After Picking Rosehips. Harley Elliott. walking in the speechless night. NeAC

After Plotinus. William Stafford. mortality. And it makes our world stone. PoA

After Rain. P.K. Page. clear of the myriad images that still–/do what I will–encumber its pure line. NOBC

After Rain. Edward ("Edward Eastaway") Thomas. Crystals both dark and bright of the rain/That begins again. NCSH

After Reading a Book on Abnormal Psychology. Ernest G. Moll. Or only more intelligently mad? ELU

After Reading a Child's Guide to Modern Physics. W. H. Auden. Is something we shall learn. NYBP

After Reading Certain Books. Mary Elizabeth Coleridge. What room would there be for God to be good?/Said the Devil. EaLo

After Reading Homer. Digby Mackworth Dolben. O dear divine old Giant, at thy feet. GoBC

After Reading Nelly Sachs. Linda Pastan. ...bright teeth/that surely time will cut through/like a rough knife kerneling corn. VWA

After Reading Saint Teresa, Luis De Leon and Ramon Lull. Muna Lee. Afar within its depths I too have seen/The star that glitters on the lilies there. CAW

After Reading St. John the Divine. Gene Derwood. With one pure deed restores the natural night. LiTM; NePA

After Reading Sylvia Plath:. Alta. i cry, bursting free... IHMS

After Reading the Life of Mrs Catherine Stubbs... Isaac Hann. And no good thing will he from them withhold. NOCV

After Reading Twenty Years of Grantland Rice. Don Skene. The stalwart smash as putter meets ash/Where April holds the way. InMe

After Sex. Greg Kuzma. fictions of will and need. GP

After Shakespeare. Alex Comfort. That first act of our own/is still the best act left. Let's go to bed. ErPo

After Shiki. Larry Eigner. the man from the country FAZ

After Six Thousand Years. Victor Hugo. And the lark sings. WaaP

After Snow. Walter Clark. And now she has gone. NCSH

After Some Day of Decision. Reed Whittemore. He dreams of being tried and pronounced–"Dead." NePoEA

After-Song. Richard Watson Gilder. Who art the love of love, the eternal light/of light! AA; TrPWD

After Speaking of One Dead a Long Time. Padraic Colum. "The simple things that we will always have." GoYe

After Spending All Day at the National Museum of Art. Alan Britt. An awkward word,/like a tiny white parachute/follows me everywhere I go. FAZ

After St. Augustine. Mary Elizabeth Coleridge. Thee thyself we could not lose. TrPWD; TRV

After Storm. David Morton. "Nothing of this is beautiful as you." HBMV

After Summer. Philip Bourke Marston. And below the poppy flowers/Steals no dream. HBV 1-2

After Sunday Dinner We Uncles Snooze. John Ciardi. what shall the sleeps of heaven dream but time? HoAn

After Sunset. William Allingham. These few are sacred moments. One More Day/Drops in the shadowy gulf of bygone things. IrPN

After Sunset. Grace Hazard Conkling. And terror shall be past, and grief, and war. AnAmPo; HBMV; MoRP

After Tempest. Percy MacKaye. Reaching toward eternity/All-unavailing antennae! FYAP

After Tennyson: "Spoonmeat at Bill Porter's in the Hall." Edward Lear. With green pomegranates, and no end of Bass. FaBoNo

After Tennyson: "To watch the tipsy cripples on the beach." Edward Lear. With topsy turvy signs of screamy play. FaBoNo

After the Agony in the Garden. Daryl Hine. resplendent upon us who sleep. PeCV

After the Agony in the Guest Bedroom. Margaret Atwood. ...and you/are sick in the bathtub. NeAC

After the Annunciation. Eileen Duggan. Ripen within me, O vine of the world! ISi

After the Anonymous Swedish. Jim Harrison. who always float down to us/with alarmed and startled eyes. VGW

After the Ball. Charles K. Harris. Many's the hopes that have vanished, after the ball. BLSo; FSN; FSW; GoTF; TreF

After the Battle (1930). George Sylvester Viereck. And nothing matters in the end. GoYe

After the Blitz, 1941. J. R. Ackerley. Your knock smiting the silence like a gong. PeHV

After the Broken Arm. Ron Padgett. Dispatch this note to our hero at once ANYP; ConAP; EAS

After the Burial. James Russell Lowell And argues your wisdom down. AA; UnPo

After the Centennial. Christopher Pearse Cranch. Can feed the fire as in its youth–/Can hold the runners lest they fall! PAH

After the Comanches. Anonymous. Bring her home on the crupper,/A scalp on either side. PAH

After the Cries of the Birds. Lawrence Ferlinghetti. Agape we are & agape we'll be CAPP

After the Dark. Enola Chamberlain. And show that God is still/Holding the reins of life. STF

After the Dazzle of Day. Walt Whitman. Silent, athwart my soul, moves the symphony true. NePA

After the Death of an Elder Klallam. Duane Niatum. In the dream songs of my Great Uncle,/Joseph, elder to hawk and sparrow. CDW

After the Death of Her Daughter in Childbirth... Izumi Shikibu. Her child it must have been. PBWP

After the Deformed Woman Is Made Correct. Robert Lietz. I will pardon them/my mars. AMV-80

After the Dentist. May Swenson. surprised when one/side smiles. DFF; GP

After the Fair. Thomas Hardy. At their meeting-times here, just as these! CMoP; HAP; VLP

After the Festival. Stefan George. And let us lose our way in woods of sombre Fate. LiTW

After the fiercest pangs of hot desire. Richard Duke. She hugs the dart that wounded her, and dies. BoLoP

After the Fire. Oliver Wendell Holmes. The cloudless azure whence they came! MC; PAH

After the First Frost. Lew Blockcolski. and I have/never worried about those things. VoR

After the Flight of the Earls. Fear Flatha O Gnimh. –and I pray God rest her soul. NOBI

After the Flood. Arthur Rimbaud. ...will never be willing to tell/us what she knows, and what we do not know. SOTW

After the Funeral. Dylan Thomas. And the strutting fern lay seeds on the black sill. CMoP; CoBMV; DiPo; FaBoMo; MoAB; MoVE; NoP; OAEL 1-2; OAEP

After the Gentle Poet Kobayashi Issa. Robert Hass. pond snails crying/in the saucepan. GeTw

After the Hunt. Detlev Freiherr von Liliencron. The guests' departure leaves us soon alone. AWP

After the Hurricane. Samuel Hazo. undid the world in rituals of fury/and returned to zero. GrPl

After the Industrial Revolution, All Things Happen at Once. Robert Bly. And the Whiskey Boys are drunk outside Philadelphia. CoAP; ConAP

After the Killing. Dudley Randall. And after the killing/there will be peace. CNA; SoSe

After the Last Breath. Thomas Hardy. In view of which our momentary bereavement/Outshapes but small. VLP

After the Last Bulletins. Richard Wilbur. The songbirds in the public boughs. CoAP; ConAP; MoAB; MoAmPo; NePoAm; NYBP; TrGrPo; ViBoPo

After the Last Dynasty. Stanley Jasspon Kunitz. why did you keep me waiting? NMP; TAP

After the Martyrdom. Scharmel Iris. And for the stone I threw at him/My heart must bear a stone. HBV 1-2

After the Movement. Peter Oresick. Moonlight: lead me over. LTB

After the Murder of Jimmy Walsh. Joan Murray. and never hear each other's truth. LTB

After the Night Hunt. James Dickey. Which shall keep me safe till I wake/And rise, and fall away. PoA

After the Party. Frances Cornford. The rank, primeval innocent smell of night! ELU

After the Persian. Louise Bogan. Let the crystal clasp them/When you drink your wine, in autumn. NePoAm; NYBP; PoA

After the Plague. *Anonymous.* Ah, woeful lordship alone to lead, no friend, no peer! LiTW

After the Pleasure Party. Herman Melville. O pray! Example take too, and have care. AP; MAmP; PoEL 1-5

After the Pow-Wow (excerpt). Harold Littlebird. but I will remember to sing for him also. STE

After the Publication of Under the Volcano. Malcolm Lowry. And had been left in darkness forever to founder and/fail. FaBoTw

After the Quarrel. Paul Laurence Dunbar. We'll go our ways, the world is wide. CDC

After the Quarrel. Barbara Gibson. and then oh baby we loved FF

After the Quarrel. Adam Lindsay Gordon. In a thousand years we shall all forget/The things that trouble us now. OBVV

After the Rain. Edward A. Collier. Beyond what I have asked or thought. BLRP

After the Rain. Stanley Crouch. And we, like all oceans,/would know/and love each other./Salaam. CNA

After the Rain. Paul B. Janeczko. laugh and wish I were/the sky. PCP

After the Release of Ezra Pound. Dannie Abse. And Thomas Jefferson would have cursed. NMP

After the Revolution. Marilyn Hacker. ...Not/as one might have wished. AmPA

After the Sea-Ship. Walt Whitman. Following the stately and rapid ship, in the wake/following. CBEP; MOS; NePA

After the Seance. David Clewell. ...And who/will be the spirit guide tonight? AMV-81

After the Second Operation. Patricia Goedicke. Glancing off you like the light/That hovers but will not stay. TAP

After the Show. Sam Harrison. cheated of all the summer should have brought. NeIP

After the Shower. Archibald Lampman. The heart of all the perfumes of the wood. CaP

After the Spanish Chroniclers. William Bronk. But we're extensible; we don't leave room. GP

After the Speech to the Librarians. David Wagoner. With which we all might sing for the children. NPAW

After the Storm. Elizabeth Bartlett. ...and she walked quietly/Into the house to help with the next meal. GoYe

After the Storm. Henry Vaughan. Make lesser mornings, when the great are done. BoC

After the Supper and Talk. Walt Whitman. Garrulous to the very last. MoAmPo

After the Surprising Conversions. Robert Lowell. The small-mouth bass breaks water gorged/with spawn. AmPP; AP; CoBMV; ConAP; HAP; NePoEA; NoAm; NoP; PPP; SeCeV

After the Swimmer. Robert Wallace. from which he climbed. LiSp

After the Visit. Thomas Hardy. And why we were here, and by whose strange laws/That which mattered most could not be. NOBE; OBNC

After the War. Douglas Dunn. He went inside just as the convoy passed. OxBC

After the War. Richard Le Gallienne. Seeking a loveliness she scarcely knows,/Whose meaning is beyond the reach of Time. MC; PAH

After the War. Hayim Naggid. Like the sweet sleep of the butterfly/In thin silk. VWA

After the Winter. Claude McKay. And ferns that never fade. BANP; GoSl; IDB; PoBA

After They Have Tired of the Brilliance of Cities. Stephen Spender. Around us, dazing us with its light like snow. AtBAP; FaBoMo; LiTM

After They Put Down Their Overalls. Lenrie Peters. So they can carry their dark glasses in their hand. TTY

The After-Thought. Stevie Smith. That's odd. I can hear you quite distinctly. OxBC

After-Thought. William Wordsworth. We feel that we are greater than we know. EnL; OAEP; OBNC; OBRV

After Tonight. Gary Soto. Why think it will/After tonight? GP

After Trinity. John Meade Falkner. They are singing Emmanuel's birth. OxBTC

After Tsang Chih. Alice Notley. On their way through town, on the way to my World. APU

After Tschaikowsky. Wallace Gould. I shall wait. But I shall not weep. I shall not care. AnAmPo

After Twenty Years. Fadwa Tuquan. Give her then the glass rings/And the blue bracelets. PBWP

After Two Thousand Years. Hugh" (Christopher Murray Grieve) MacDiarmid. ...lip-serve the Cross, and keep/The working-classes carrying it. DBV

After Two Years. Richard Aldington. God has done well to me. GTBS; HBV 1-2; MoBrPo; PG; PoPl; WHA

After Vacation. Katherine Hanley. Our Eden-glances follow us as well. AMV-81

After Verlaine. Anselm Hollo. that is what love is all about FAZ

After Visiting a Home for Disturbed Children. Lou Lipsitz. like the eyes of a girl who is buried alive. LTB

After War. Ivor Gurney. Sweet to the chilled frame, nerves soothed were so sore shaken. OBSP

After Wings. Sarah Piatt. Which even a butterfly must bear/to be a worm again! AA; HBV 1-2

After Winter. Sterling A. Brown. An' fo' de little feller/Runnin' space... GoSl; PoBA; PoNe

The After Woman. Francis Thompson. This song is sung and sung not, and its words are sealed. ISi

After Work. John Oxenham. Yea, right gladly/Will I come. TRV

After Work. Gary Snyder. as it grows dark/drinking wine. HoPM; NNaP

After Working. Robert Bly. The road goes on ahead, it is all clear. NaP

After X-Ray. Linda Pastan. to shine somewhere like strung beads of coral. PoL

After You, Madam. Alex Comfort. We share the honors without fuss/by frequent alternation. ErPo; UnTE

After Your Death. David James. again/inside/this small body. AMV-80

Afterbirth. Beryle Williams. such flesh such bones allow/the heart and hands to repeat. PoDr

Afterglow. Jorge Luis Borges. the way a dream is broken/the moment the sleeper knows he is dreaming. NYBP

Afterlives. Derek Mahon. I might have grown up at last/And learnt what is meant by home. CIP

An Aftermath. Thomas Blackburn. Moments of clarity we also share. NMP

Aftermath. Henry Wadsworth Longfellow. Where the poppy drops its seeds/In the silence and the gloom. AP; MAmP; NOBA; TAP

Aftermath. Margaret McCulloch. This city razed,/This my son dead. PGD

Aftermath. Sylvia Plath. The crowd sucks her last tear and turns away. SBG

Aftermath. Siegfried Sassoon. Look up, and swear by the green of the Spring that you'll never forget! AnFE; AP; BrPo; MCCG; MoBrPo; TrJP; ViBoPo; WaP

The Aftermath. William Carlos Williams. Good! the air of the/uplands is stimulating. FAZ

Afternoon. Louisa S. Bevington. In the "line of least resistance',/Flows the life of Afternoon. NOBV

Afternoon. Donald Hall. And we will walk together, for a while. Str

Afternoon. Lucien Stryk. I'm off to Asia Minor. FAZ

Afternoon 3. Saburoh Kuroda. A crab puts its face into the pit. EAS

Afternoon: Amagansett Beach. John Hall Wheelock. His footprint is his image fallen from heaven. BoNaP; MoVE; NePA

Afternoon at Cannes. Paul Davis. ...more sensuous than broiling flesh spread dumb. AMV-81

Afternoon in a Tree. Sister Maris Stella. The tribe of those who neither reap nor sow. GoBC

Afternoon in Anglo-Ireland. Bruce Williamson. Fold up the deck-chairs, dear. There will be some/Not needed next year, no matter how warm the sun. NeIP

An Afternoon in Artillery Walk. Leonard Bacon. Satan exalted sate. AnAmPo

Afternoon in the Garden. Ethel Anderson. Do again what lordly Joshua did. NOAV

An Afternoon in the Garden. Murray Edmond. A prayer for you, a poem for you, a time together. OCNZ

Afternoon in the Tropics. Ruben Dario. or roaring of a fierce/lion given to/the wind. LiTW

The Afternoon of a Faun: Eclogue. Stephane Mallarme. Adieu, both! I shall see the shade you became. SyP

Afternoon on a Hill. Edna St. Vincent Millay. I will mark which must be mine,/And then start down! GrPl; NTCP; OBCA; OxBA; SoPo

Afternoon's Angel. Seymour Mayne. voracious still/for the more unsuspecting/of the feathered young VWA

Afternoon Sleep. Robert Bly. And instructions to Norwegian immigrants. NaP

Afternoon with Grandmother. Barbara A. Huff. And I say, "YES, WE DID!!!" GeTw

Afternoon, with Just Enough of a Breeze. Robert Sund. he nearly/touches his shadow. BoAnP

Afternoons with Baedeker. Osbert Lancaster.
Heard on this coast, the music of the spheres/Would sound like something from The Gondoliers. FaBoCo; NOBL
If only History were wired for sound. NOBL
The prison scene from Trovatore/Dies on a dozen radios. FaBoCo
Shouting stale slogans on the Liffey quays. NOBL
Too well I know the power to get one down/Exerted by this grey and shuttered town. FaBoCo; NOBL

Afterthought. Elizabeth Jennings. And peace on earth for men. OBCP

Afterthought. Justin Richardson. She murmured "Homo"...and then added "Sap!" PV

Afterthoughts of Donna Elvira. Carolyn Kizer. Whenever we love, we win,/Or else we have never been born. NePoAm-2

The Afterwake. Adrienne Rich. slowly, till scissors of cockcrow snip the air. NOBA; Prf

Afterward. Mary Matheson. And said it was the wind that stirred. CaP

Afterward. Elizabeth Stuart Phelps Ward. Because we love, he is. Then trust awhile. HBV 1-2

Afterwards. Violet Fane. With these words carved, "I hoped, but was not sure." HBV 1-2; OBVV

Afterwards. Thomas Hardy. "He hears it not now, but used to notice such things"? AnFE; BoNaP; CBEP; CH; CMoP; EBEV; FaBoRV; ForPo; GTBS-P; InPS; LiTB; LiTM; MoAB; MoBrPo; MoVE; NAMP; NOBE; NoP; OAEL 1-2; OAEP; OBNC; PAI; PoEL 1-5; PoPle; QFR; SeCeV; TreFT; TrGrPo; ViBoPo

Afterwards. Frances Ridley Havergal. Right was the pathway leading to this. BLRP

Afterwards (excerpt). Gertrude Stein. And there is no worry in a hurry. LOW

Afterwards, They Shall Dance. Bob Kaufman. And open little sensuous parasols, singing the nail-/in-the-foot song, drinking cool beatitudes. PoNe; TwCP; VGW

Afterword. Anonymous. ...and what is left/of your traces/Is so goddamned beautiful. ILwL

An Afterword: For Gwen Brooks. Don L. Lee. poets. minor poets ruined by/minor fame. JB

Afterword: Song of Song. James Richard Broughton. It/is the song you have been singing/all your life. GP

Afton Water. Robert Burns. Flow gently, sweet Afton, disturb not her dream. BiP; BoNaP; FaBoPP; HeIP; LAuP; OAEP; PG

The Aga Khan. Steve Orlen. And when would he ever stop? Psk

Again. Frantisek Halas. And our enemy, he who keeps still! WaaP

Again. Charlotte Mew. So we shall meet! MoAB; MoBrPo

Again. Jon Stallworthy. ...worse to waken/from that harsh sobbing to the bed's shudder. OxBC

Again as Evening's Shadow Falls. Samuel Longfellow. But in the Spirit's secret cell/May hymn and prayer forever dwell. AH

Again for Hephaistos, the Last Time. Richard Howard. ...After you, because of you,/all songs are possible. GP

Again My Fond Circle of Doves. Baxter Hathaway. And light is on their wings/As they come to my shoulders. HoAn

Againe. Robert Herrick. Die, and be turn'd into a Lute. SeCP

Against a Second Coming: The Walking Woman. Sidney Keyes. Cries the still passionate, the walking woman. AtBAP

Against Absence. Sir John Suckling. For surfeits sooner kill than fasts. CaPo

Against an Old Lecher. Sir John (1561-1612) Harington. Some smile, I sigh, to see thy madness such/That that which stands not, stands thee in so much. FaBoEE

Against Blame of Woman. Gerald, Earl of Desmond. Speak not ill of woman kind. AnIL; BIrV

Against Borders. Yevgeny Yevtushenko. and I want an art/that is something/else, is an exciting sound–/like myself! CAD

Against Botticelli. Robert Hass. the one with sad eyes who represents pleasure,/had a canvas to herself, entirely to herself. AmPA; NPGG

Against Broccoli. Roy, Jr. Blount. Loccoli. NLV; OBAL

Against Constancy. John Wilmot, Earl of Rochester. I'll change a mistress till I'me dead–/And fate change me to worms. GBL

Against Dark's Harm. Anne Halley. despair, distress,/and all self-sickness. NMM

Against Death. Peter Redgrove. As the hot bodies of the sparrows increase each summer. NMP

Against Education. Charles Churchill. And chancellors, who nothing know at all. TW

Against Friars. Anonymous. Let never man after me have will/For to make him frere! OxBM

Against Fruition. Sir John Suckling. In keeping us in hopes strange things to see/That never were, nor are, nor e'er shall be. ErPo

Against Fulfillment of Desire. Anonymous. What wonder doth in beauty dwell. TrGrPo

Against Garnesche (excerpt). John Skelton. Challenge yourself for a fool, call me no more knave! ViBoPo

Against Gaudy-Bragging-Undoughty Daccus. John, of Hereford Davies. A leaden rapier in a golden sheath. FaBoEE

Against Gravity. Edith E. Cutting. Each one/With earth foundation/Reaches up. AMV-80

Against Hope. Abraham Cowley. And th'other chases woman, whilst she goes/More ways and turns than hunted nature knows. LiTB; LoBV; MeLP; OBS; SeCV 1-2

Against Indifference. Charles Webbe. More love or more disdain I crave. HBV 1-2; OBEV

Against Love. Sir John Denham. His prince, his country and his friends. CBEP

Against Love. Katherine ("Orinda") Philips. And is not much transported, but still pleased. BoWoP; SBG

Against Marriage. Anonymous. And now his Blessing is, he can't be Curst. DBV

Against Marriage to His Mistress. William Walsh. And why the devil should we stay,/When once that love is past? FaBoUs

Against Meaning. Andrei Codrescu. But through a little hole in the boring report/God watches us faking it. APU

Against Modesty in Love. Matthew Prior. And Cynthia gave what she for years/Had foolishly denied. ErPo

Against Mosquitoes. Meleager. Or you shall smart from the strength of my jealous/hands! LiTW

Against Negritude. Emanuel Corgo. and that we struggle/once twice or a thousand times/until there is built a better world. WhB

Against Parting. Natan Zach. ...He's/most definitely/(my father's died)/against parting. VWA

Against Platonick Love. Anonymous. When flame doth meet with flame. OBS

Against Proud Poor Phryna. John, of Hereford Davies. Sith that is rich, and all her rareness shows? FaBoEE

Against Quarrelling and Fighting. Isaac Watts. He sees what Children dwell in Love,/And marks them for his own. OBEC; OxBChV; SeCePo

Against Romanticism. Kingsley Amis. Woods devoid of beasts, roads that please the foot. NePoEA; NoAm

Against Seasons. Robert Mezey. Change is illusion–yet I hate/The silence and the changeless dark. AmPC; NYBP

Against Still Life. Margaret Atwood. tell me/everything/just as it was/from the beginning. NMM

Against Surrealism. James Wright. ...It's just a matter of common sense. LCAP

Against the Age. Louis Simpson. That wind is carrying the world away. NePoEA-2

Against the Barons' Enemies. Anonymous. Edward, thou dudest ase a shreward,/Forsoke thine eme's lore. MeEL

Against the Court of Rome. Petrarch (Francesco Petrarca). That it dothe stincke before the face of God. LiTW

Against the Evidence. David Ignatow. Against the evidence, I live by choice. NNaP

Against the False Magicians. Thomas McGrath. The rituals of our humanity. NePoEA; PP

Against the Fear of Death. Lucretius (Titus Lucretitus Carus). 'Tis just the same as we had never been. AWP

Against the Friars. Anonymous. Flattering both more and less. OxBM

Against the Grain. Michael Brownstein. Most of the people were eating already. ANYP

Against the Love of Great Ones. Richard Lovelace. The Torch laughs peece-meale to consume. AnAnS 2

Against the Magpie. Anonymous. T'devil tak t' pynot an' God save me. GBP

Against the Silences to Come. Ron Loewinsohn. ...further harmonies/are implied in the harmonies we state PoM

Against the Thieves of Liddesdale. Sir Richard Maitland. Hing on a tree till they be deid. BSV

Against Them Who Lay Unchastity to the Sex of Women. William Habington. 'Tis Majesty to rule alone. AnAnS 2; JCP; MePo; OBS; SeCP

Against Unworthy Praise. William Butler Yeats. Half lion, half child, is at peace. AnFE

Against Winter. Elaine Feinstein. was the source of his/undisciplined stamina. VWA

Against Witches. Anonymous. Put the witches to their speed. GBP

Against Women. Anonymous. Beware! therfore: the blind eteth many a fly. MeEL

Against Women. Juvenal (Decimas Junius Juvenalis). But hadst thou seen her plaster'd up before,/'Twas so unlike a face, it seem'd a sore.... LiTW

Against Women Either Good or Bad. Thomas Norton. To keep me free from either ill! EIL; ViBoPo

Against Women's Fashions. John Lydgate. By example of her your horns cast away. ACP

Against Women Unconstant. Geoffrey Chaucer. In stede of blew, thus may ye were al greene. NoP

Agamemnon. Aeschylus.
Above the eternal tide of tears? AWP; LiTW; PPON; WaaP
Devouring a poor pregnant rabbit. CTC
...I may close up these eyes, and rest. LiTW
Resistless, toward the eternal shore. WGRP

Agamemnon's Tomb. Sacheverell Sitwell. They neither care, nor care not, they are only dead. LiTB; MoBrPo; OBMV

Agatha. Alfred Austin. And, with her forehead 'gainst the pane,/Envies the dying year. HBV 1-2

Agatha. Nadine Major. of other husbands, lovers, wives. PoL

Agathon: Song of Eros. George Edward Woodberry. Are like thee, young Desire. AA

Agbor Dancer. John Pepper Clark. Lose myself in her warm caress/ Intervolving earth, sky and flesh. PBA

Age. Abraham Cowley. And manage wisely the last stake. AWP; CavP

Age? H. R. Hays. As if tearing the bandage/From an incurable wound. PoL

An Age. Laura Jensen. where our white wood caught fire/in the white sand. LCAP

Age. Rae Desmond Jones. up & fell as the deep hidden tides beat/against the rock CBAP

Age. Walter Savage Landor.
Ah! he strikes all things, all alike,/But bargains: those he will not strike. ELU; PoEL 1-5
But bargains: those he will not strike. ELU; FaBoEE; NBM; NOBV

Age. Philip Larkin. Or spoor of pads, or a bird's adept splay. CMoP

Age. Marya Mannes. and lets her arms sustain him in their sphere. FAZ

Age. Sir Thomas More. Chargeable matters shall of love oppress/The childish game and idle business. EnRePo

Age. William Winter. Life and I are old! HBV 1-2

Age and Youth. Anonymous. Will keep you dizzy most of your life. UnTE

The Age Demanded. Ezra Pound. Here drifted/An hedonist. InPo; NoP

Age in Prospect. Robinson Jeffers. ...a creature progressively/Thirsty for life will be for death too. MoAB; MoAmPo

Age in Youth. Trumbull Stickney. This is a scar upon the year. NCEP

The Age Is Great and Strong. Victor Hugo. The echo of Thy voice still feebler grows! WGRP

Age Not to Be Rejected. Anonymous. It will be told/That you are old/By those true tears y'are weeping. OBS

The Age of a Dream. Lionel Pigot Johnson. Who mourn the death of beauty and the death of grace. OBMV

The Age of Animals. Anonymous. Thrice the age of a deer is that of an eagle. FaBoUs

The Age of Bronze: Rent, Rent, Rent! George Gordon, Lord Byron. Their good, ill, health, wealth, joy, or discontent,/Being, end, aim, religion–rent, rent, rent! OBSV

Age of Gold. Pietro Metastasio. Candour still thy substance is. CTC

The Age of Reason. Jorie Graham. ...wet black/arms there is/no deep enough. NPGG

The Age of Sheen. Dorothy Hughes. ...having no thought/Of the river, and the irony underneath. NYBP

The Age of the Butcher. Stuart Friebert. They sleep from midnight till eight in/a little bed a mile behind their meat. AMV-80

The Age of Wisdom. William Makepeace Thackeray. Alone and merry at Forty Year,/Dipping my nose in the Gascon wine. ALV; HBV 1-2

The Aged Aged Man (parody). Lewis (Charles Lutwidge Dodgson) Carroll. That summer evening long ago,/A-sitting on a gate. BXAP; FaBoPa; OxBChV; SpRo

Aged Fisherman. Witter ("Emanuel Morgan") Bynner. Fishing for people/ And hooking the sun. GoYe

The Aged Lover Discourses in the Flat Style. J. V. Cunningham. To be at once together and alone. NoAm; SM

The Aged Lover Renounceth Love. Thomas, Lord Vaux. So shall ye waste to dust. EiL; EnPo; EnRePo; OAEL 1-2; OAEP; PoEL 1-5

Aged Ninety Years. Wilbert Snow. Would sink, like her, in chilly arms of earth. AnAmPo

The Aged Pilot Man. Mark (Samuel Langhorne Clemens) Twain. A moment stood. Then wondering turned,/And speechless walked ashore. OBAL

The Aged Stranger. Bret (Francis Bret Harte) Harte. Some three years before the war. AA; AmFN; MaC; TreFS

The Aged Wino's Counsel to a Young Man on the Brink of Marriage. X. J. Kennedy. I say: son, wed you half as well. FF

The Aged Woman to Her Sons. Babette Deutsch. There is grey in your hair. AMV-81

An Aged Writer. Roy McFadden. Now let them be your elegy. NeIP

The Ageing Hunter. Avane. Saw the great beast fall and lie/With muzzle deep in mire. WTO

Ageless. Anonymous. She'll do, my friend, whatever you desire. UnTE

The Ageless Christ. B. L. Byer. He's my Christ forever more! BePJ

Agent of Love. A. K. Redwing. over lovers fornicating breathlessly in the fields VoR

Agent Orange. Rita Brady Kiefer. but go on shedding blood/to sign our doors. SOTS

The Agents. Robert Conquest. It is to this that everybody listens. EAS

Ages and Ages Returning at Intervals. Walt Whitman. Offspring of my loins. AP

The Ages of Man. Abraham Ibn Ezra. As at his birth he was,/So shall he be.) TrJP

Aghadoe. John Todhunter. Your own love cold on your cairn in Aghadoe. AnIL; AnIV; OBVV; OxBI

Agincourt. Michael Drayton. Or England breed again/Such a King Harry? BeLS; EIL; FaBoBe; FaBoCh; FaPoR; GoTL; HBV 1-2; LoGBV; MCCG; OBEV; WHA

The Agincourt Carol. Anonymous. That we with merth mowe savely sing/ "Deo gracias." OAEL 1-2; OBET; OxBM

Aging. Randall Jarrell. Not time but–/but, alas! eternity. PoA

Aging. Diane Wakoski. This winter/is so beautiful to me. AMV-81

The Aging Athlete. Neil Weiss. and you smashed the tape with your chest/and sank into the arms of many lovers. LiSp

The Aging Poet, on a Reading Trip to Dayton... Richard Snyder. It was primitive, I its proselyte. Psk

Agitato Ma Non Troppo. John Crowe Ransom. And I am shaken; but not as a leaf. OxBA

Aglaia. Nicholas Breton. Never strike a pleasing strain/Till she come abroad again! OBSC

Agnes. Henry Francis Lyte. She was fairest of all! GTBS

Agnes. Mah-do-ge Tohee. yawns & passes out/muttering...agnes...agnes STE

Agnosco Veteris Vestigia Flammae. J. V. Cunningham. Whose future specifies its past, whose past/Precedes it, and whose history is its being. QFR; VGW

The Agnostic's Creed. William Malone. If a God decrees my downfall, I shall stand it like a man. HBV 1-2

Agnosto Theo (To an Unknown God). Thomas Hardy. ...whereat I/Would raise my voice in song. MoPo

Agnus Dei. Victor Kinon. Drop from Thy lips Thy syllables of quiet! CAW

Ago. Elizabeth Jennings. I do without all and face the winter regretting./ The child in me who can play no longer. GOYP

The Agonie. George Herbert. Love is that liquour sweet and most divine,/ Which my God feels as bloud; but I, as wine. AnAnS 1; MePo

The Agonizing Memory. Pierre Louys. ...and what/she asks and what she gives. PeHV

An Agony. As Now. LeRoi (Imamu Amiri Baraka) Jones. It burns the thing/inside it. And that thing/screams. AmPP; BALP; BPo; LiTM; PPP

The Agony in the Garden. Felicia Dorothea Hemans. Save, or we perish, Son of God! TrCP

Agreeable Monsters. Amy Clampitt. such/agreeable monsters go/up and down Third Avenue. AmC

The Agricultural Irish Girl. Anonymous. It's "The full of the house" of Irish love is Mary Ann Malone. OnYI

The Agricultural Show, Flemington, Victoria. Furnley Maurice. Quiet lakes and milking sheds; "Fares please, fares please." CBAP

Aguinaldo. Bertrand Shadwell. And cry against thee unto God. PAH

Ah, Are You Digging on My Grave? Thomas Hardy. I am sorry, but I quite forgot/It was your resting-place. BoAnP; BrPo; DL; MoAB; MoBrPo; PAI; TEP

Ah, Be Not False. Richard Watson Gilder. Take love sublimely. AA; HBV 1-2; HBVY

Ah Blackbird, Giving Thanks. Anonymous. from the otherworld, your whistle! NOBI

Ah Cloris! That I Now Could Sit. Sir Charles Sedley. Since none alive can truly tell/What Fortune they must see. CavP; OAEP; OBS

Ah Cupid, I mistook thee. Francis Davison. So thou, with fencing art,/ Feigning to wound mine eyes, hast hit my heart. EG

Ah Dearest Love, for How Long. Mechtild of Magdeburg. And God, your glorious grave, your home. ILwL

Ah Fading Joy. John Dryden. Dash, dash, upon the ground,/To gentle slumbers call. GoTF; LoBV; OAEP; TreFT; ViBoPo

Ah! Give Me, LORD, the Single Eye. Augustus Montague Toplady. His light shall in my darkness shine,/And guide me to His throne. OxBoCh

Ah! Leave My Harp and Me Alone. Anonymous. God grant, that in the mills, a day/May be blest, "Ten hours" long. SaC

Ah! Lovely Appearance of Death! Charles Wesley. My flesh be consigned to the tomb. AH

Ah'm Broke an' Hungry. Lawrence Gellert. Ah'm here in this unfriendly world/Don' know what to do. TrAS

Ah Me! Am I the Swaine. George Wither. And therefore, bid I you,/And every one,/Adieu. OBS

Ah Me, Do You Remember Still. Agnes Mary Frances (Mme Emile Duclaux) Robinson. Resolved, abandoned by us two! WHA

Ah Me, If I Grew Sweet to Man. Michael (Katherine Bradley and Edith Cooper) Field. To bring the honey to the wind. EnLoPo

Ah Me! The Mighty Love. George Frederick Cameron. Feel each and all the inhumanities. CaP

Ah My Dere. Anonymous. Naylit full sore/Upon a tree. AtBAP; BoW

Ah, necromancy sweet! Emily Dickinson. Nor Herb of all the plain/Can heal! NOBA

Ah, Now I Know What Day This Is.   Statius Publius Papinius.   The day on which the nuptials/Of Stella and Violentilla/Are to the world proclaimed. HW

Ah, Poor Bird.   *Anonymous.*   Far above the sorrows of/This sad night. FSW

Ah, Poverties, Wincings, and Sulky Retreats.   Walt Whitman.   It shall yet stand up the soldier of ultimate victory.   CBEP; OBSP

Ah, Ra, Chickera.   *Anonymous.*   Ickerman, chickerman, chinee-choo. OxNR

Ah! Si Mon Moine Voulait Danser.   *Anonymous.*   Tu n'entends pas mon moulin marcher!   FSW

Ah, Sun-Flower.   William Blake.   Where my Sun-flower wishes to go. AtBAP; AWP; DiPo; EBEV; ELP; ELU; EnLi 1-2; ExPo; FaBoRV; HAP; InPo; NIP; NOEC; NoP; OBEC; OBNC; PoPle; PPP; PrIm; SeCeV; TEP; UnPo; ViBoPo; WeW

Ah Sweet Content, where Is Thy Mylde Abode?   Barnabe Barnes.   Whether thou doest in heaven, or earth appeare,/Be where thou wilt, thou will not harbour here.   AAS

Ah, Sweet Is Tipperary.   Denis Aloysius McCarthy.   Ah, sweet is Tipperary in the spring!   HBV 1-2

Ah, Teneriffe!   Emily Dickinson.   I'm kneeling–still–   InPS; PAI

Ah Were She Pitiful.   Robert Greene.   She would be gathered, though she grew on thorn.   TrGrPo; ViBoPo

Ah! What Woes Are Mine.   Edmond O'Ryan.   And its last sighs shall breathe to bless thee!   OnYI

Ah! Why, Because the Dazzling Sun.   Emily Bronte.   Let me sleep through his blinding reign,/And only wake with you!   BrRo

Ah Woe Is Me.   Sextus Propertius.   To you remembrance naught will bring but grief.   AWP

Ah, Yes, I Wrote "The Purple Cow."   Gelett Burgess.   I'll kill you if you quote it!   DBV; FiBHP; PoPl

Ah Yes, When Love Allows.   Hadewijch.   Whatever still be love's requests/I would thus still complete them now.   PBWP

Ah (You Say), This Is Holy Wisdom.   Hilda ("H. D.") Doolittle.   different yet the same as before.   CrMA

Ahab Mohammed.   James Matthew Legare.   His deeds are more to God, yea more than/finest gold.   AA

Ahasuerus.   Joseph Roth.   Will be sure to tell you, jeering/What it means to yearn for home.   VWA

Ahmad.   James Berry Bensel.   Ahmed was dead, and justice done.   AA

Aideen.   *Anonymous.*   All Aideen herself will own/Is that she will not sleep alone.   KiLC

Aideen's Grave.   Sir Samuel Ferguson.   ...The Fenians sped/Three mighty shouts to heaven; and left/Ben Edar to the dead.   NOBI

Aidenn.   Katrina Trask.   And I a woman clinging close to thee?   AA

Aids for Latin.   Gordon Perry.   Like horses use ne for the negative sound. FaBoUs

Aids to Composition.   Robert Conquest.   And the problems of the universe seemed solved.   PP

L'Aigle a Deux Jambes.   Turner Cassity.   You stump toward Moscow on a wooden leg.   GP

Aiken Drum.   *Anonymous.*   And he played upon a razor,/and his name was Willy Wood.   FaBoCh; LoGBV

The Ailing Parent.   Lora Dunetz.   He lives forever, while his children perish.   NePoAm-2

The Aim.   Sir Charles G. D. Roberts.   I bless Thy goad of discontent. PeCV

The Aim of Life: A Country Town.   Philip James Bailey.   Who thinks most–feels the noblest–acts the best.   PoToHe

The Aim Was Song.   Robert Frost.   The aim was song–the wind could see. NoP; PP; SoSe

Aimee McPherson.   *Anonymous.*   'Cause there's still a lot of cottages/down at Carmel-by-the-sea.   FSW

Aimless.   Louis Palagyi.   Ordain'd my path a pathless maze.   TrJP

Ain' Go'n' to Study War No Mo'(with music).   *Anonymous.*   Down by de ribber-side, down by de ribber-side, I'm go'n' to ride with my King Jesus. AS

Ain' No Mo' Cane on de Brazis.   *Anonymous.*   Done groun' it all in molazzis, O–O–O.   ABF

Ain't Gonna Grieve My Lord No More.   *Anonymous.*   Ain't a-gonna grieve my Lord no more.   FSW

Ain't Gonna Let Nobody Turn Me Round.   *Anonymous.*   Lord, marching up to freedom land.   FSW

Ain't Gonna Rain (with music).   *Anonymous.*   Swing yo' ladies round and round/Ain't gonna rain no mo'.   AS

Ain't I a Woman?   Sojourner Truth.   together women ought to be able to turn it/rightside up again.   BlSi

Ain't It a Shame.   *Anonymous.*   Ain't it a shame.   FSW

Ain't It Fine Today!   Douglas Malloch.   It may rain–but, say,/Ain't it fine today!–   WBLP

Ain't It Hard to Be a Right Black Nigger?   *Anonymous.*   Po' nigger ain' got no show.   OuSiCo

Ain't Nature Commonplace!   Arthur Guiterman.   When Nature, whether wild or tame,/Is always pretty much the same!   FiBHP; InMe

Ain't No Grave Can Hold My Body Down.   *Anonymous.*   Ain't no grave can hold my body down.   AmFP

Ain't No More Cane on This Brazos.   *Anonymous.*   Wouldn't be no captain keep me out on this line.   FSW

Ain't No Tellin.   Mississippi John Hurt.   Ain't no telling/what she might do BluL

Ain't Workin' Song.   *Anonymous.*   Because I never liked to work-a nohow. OuSiCo

Air.   Edwin Denby.   The airless secret I strangle not to share/With all the others as others share the air.   CrMA

Air.   LeRoi (Imamu Amiri Baraka) Jones.   I wd do anything/to be loved/& this/is a stupid/mistake.   SOTW

Air.   William Stanley Merwin.   Walking at night between the two deserts,/ Singing.   AmPC; CAPP; CoPo; NaP

Air.   Kathleen Raine.
   The bird of god descends between two moments/Like silence into music, opening a way through time.   MoAB; MoBrPo
   Like silence into music, opening a way through time. MoAB; MoBrPo

Air.   Tomaz Salamun.   burns with terrible flames and smells.   VWA

Air: "A flaxen-headed cow-boy, as simple as may be."   John O'Keefe.   You'll forget the little plough-boy that whistled o'er the lea.   NOEC

Air an' Light.   William Barnes.   But I, though fair he still mid glow,/Do miss a zight he cannot show.   VLP

Air and Angels.   John Donne.   'Twixt women's love and men's will ever be. BoW; CBEP; EnRePo; JCP; OAEL 1-2

An Air by Sammartini.   Louis Dudek.   Whatever is found or is done/that cannot be lost or changed.   OBCV

Air: Cat Bird Singing.   Robert Creeley.   O lady hear me. I have no/other/ voice left.   Prf

The Air in Spring.   Basil Dowling.   We all would only drown/If we broke surface more than staying down.   AnNZ

Air Is.   John Michael Brennan.   to reach/with you/timberline.   MAT

The Air of June Sings.   Edward Dorn.   Oh, the stones not yet cut.   NeAP; PoM

Air (parody).   Philip Dow.   galloping deception, giving us visions/hysteric BXAP

The Air Plant.   Hart Crane.   Its apotheosis, at last–the hurricane!   MoAB; MoAmPo; NoP

Air Raid.   Peter Wild.   ...I saw/him looking up, say to us "All clear. All clear."   Psk

Air: Sentir Avec Ardeur.   Marie Beauveau.   Long, frilly/Palaver is silly. CTC; WPOW

The Air Sentry.   Patrick Barrington.   And thus I guard my native land still. CenHV

Air: "So full of courtly reverence."   Dudley, Lord North.   Oblige me in a more obliging way,/Or know such over-acting spoils the play.   OBSP

Air: "The Love of a Woman."   Robert Creeley.   ...it was the/song he made which made her/happy, so she lived.   VGW

Air Travel in Arabia.   Sir Charles Johnston.   It looked like Eaton Square– but pink.   OBTV

The Air Vision.   Jakov van Hoddis.   While a shaggy-haired man/Climbed up after a broomstick leaning against the wall.   VWA

Air XXIII: "Sleep, O sleep."   John Gay.   Our utmost wish possessing;/So may I always keep.   ViBoPo

Air XXXV: "How happy could I be with either."   John Gay.   To neither a word will I say:/But tol de rol.   ViBoPo

Aircraft, Landing.   Colin Thiele.   rising gently to receive our thrusting feet. ACV

Airey-Force Valley.   William Wordsworth.   Powerful almost as vocal harmony,/To stay the wanderer's steps and soothe his/thoughts.   VLP

An Airline Breakfast.   William Matthews.   ...dragging/a shadow-plane, an anchor/that will not grab.   AMV-80; MAYP

Airliner.   Francis Webb.   ...lest I drunkenly sing/Of wattles, wars, childhoods, being at last home.   CBAP; NOAV

Airly Beacon.   Charles Kingsley.   All alone on Airly Beacon,/With his baby on my knee!   GTBS; HBV 1-2; OBEV

The Airman.   W. R. Rodgers.   Will they rise up, their resurrection day. WaP

The Airman's Alphabet.   W. H. Auden.   and time of attack.   NAMP

The Airman Who Flew over Shakespeare's England.   Hyam Plutzik.   And on the bridge, faces upturned to a roaring/Falcon.   PoPl

Airs of Pei.   Confucius.   when 'twas with me alone that you found rest. CTC

Airship.   Hy Sobiloff.   And I heard the trumpets blowing earthly sounds NePA

An Airstrip in Essex, 1960.   Donald Hall.   Smoke rises from the stones; no, it is mist.   LCAP; LiTM; PAI; PoCh

Airwaves.   Warren Woessner.   Three cyclists, like a school of delicate fish,/ sway in your lights, darting home.   TAT

The Airy Christ. Stevie Smith. ...he only wishes they would hear him sing. NOCV

A Is for Alpha: Alpha Is for A. Conrad Aiken. we weave this love, this light. NePA

Aishah-Schechinah. Robert Stephen Hawker. Her God upon her lap: the Virgin-Bride,/Her awful Child: her Son! GoBC; ISi; OBNC; OxBoCh

Aisling. Austin Clarke. My women dance to bright steel that is wed,/Starlike, upon the anvil with one stroke. AnIV

Aix-la-Chappelle, 1945. Edgar Bowers. And his malignant growth shall be/Monstered by lucid violence. NePoEA

Aja's Lament over His Dead Wife. Kalidasa. For all my passions centered, dear, in you. LiTW

Ajanta. Muriel Rukeyser. The journey, and the struggles of the moon. LiTA; LiTM; MiAP; MoAB; MoAmPo; NNaP

Ajax. Sophocles.
The deepest, bitterest curse thine ancient house hath/borne! AWP
Few be they/Who, reaching Friendship's port, have there found rest. LiTW
Henceforth he talks in Hades with the dead. LiTW

Ajax and Ulysses: The Glories of Our Blood and State. James Shirley. Only the actions of the just/Smell sweet, and blossom in their dust. TrGrPo; WaaP

The Ajax Samples. Laura Jensen. We are the holy sunlit wanderers/and we leave gifts behind. LCAP

Aka. Frederick Eckman. do I really want to go in drag on such a hot day? FAZ

The Akathistos Hymn. Anonymous. ...keep all from every hurt, and deliver from/all wrath to come those who cry to thee:/ALLELUIA. ISi

Akawense. Phyllis Wolf. Grandfather smooths out/footprints. STE

The Akedah. Matti Megged. Only from time to time I hear the voice/Of an old liar/Laughing at my/Extinction. VWA

The Akedah. Aliza Shenhar. The white angel, the one/who always cries/"Please don't lay a hand"/is on leave. VWA

Akhnaton. Thomas S. Jones, Jr. Call on my name and it shall never fail. AnAmPo

Akiba. Muriel Rukeyser. The signs, the journeys of the night, survive. VWA

The Akond of Swat. Edward Lear. Who or which or why or what Is the Akond of Swat! ALV; CenHV; FaBoCh; FaBoCo; FaBoNo; FiBHP

Akriel's Consolation. [(or Pillin)] William Pillen. flickers of dust in a lighted window. AMV-80

Al Aaraaf. Edgar Allan Poe. Who hear not for the beating of their hearts. AP

Al Capone in Alaska. Ishmael Reed. They gallantly sail out &/shoot them as if the Pacific/were a Chicago garage on/St. Valentine's day TW

Al Fitnah Muhajir. Nazzam Al Sudan. A soulful tune/Salaam, salaam. NBP

Al Nist by the Rose. Anonymous. Ant yet ich bar the flour away. AtBAP

Al the Meryere. Anonymous. And to the herte stongyn. AtBAP; BoW

Ala, Mala, Mink, Monk. Anonymous. Ah, vah, vack. OxNR

Alabado. Anonymous. Amen, Jesus and Mary:/Jesus, Mary and Joseph. TrAS

The Alabama. Anonymous. Oh, ROLL, Alabama, ROLL! ShS

The Alabama. Maurice Bell. And the brave ship that bore him to glory! PAH

Alabama. Julia Fields. For singing/Whatever beauty there is. PoBA; PoNe

Alabama. Judy Dothard Simmons. ...leaving red trails/for a hearse CNA

Alabama-Bound. Anonymous.
Ef de train don' run, I got a mule to ride. ABF
I'm Alabama bound. FSW

Alabama Bound. Mance Lipscomb. Leave a dime for beer BluL

Alabama Bus. Brother Will Hairston. Lord an Alabama boy but I don't wanna ride BluL; FaBoPV

Alabama Centennial. Naomi Long Madgett. A hundred years past due./Now! BALP; BPo

Alabama Earth. Langston Hughes. Love–and chains are broken. AmFN; GoSl

Alabaster Boxes. Anonymous. Flowers cast no/fragrance backward over the weary way. PoToHe

Aladdin. James Russell Lowell. For I own no more castles in Spain! AnNE; HBV 1-2; RoGo; TreFT

Aladdin and the Jinn. Vachel Lindsay. "I am your slave," said the Jinn. AnAmPo; AnFE; APA; CoAnAm; MAPA

Alajire. Anonymous. But every wrong way I take,/Can become the right way towards your wisdom. WTO

Alamance. Seymour W. Whiting. Thou first-fought field of freedom–/Alamance. PAH

The Alarm. Hildebrand Jacob. 'Tis time to be in hate, to live! NOEC

The Alarm Clock. Mari E. Evans. It don't do/to wake up/quick... BOLo

The Alarmed Skipper. James Thomas Fields. "Nantucket's sunk, and here we are/Right over old Marm Hackett's garden!" EtS; HBV 1-2; NLV; YaD

Alarum. Urszula Koziol. in death till now there is nothing but grief. WPOW

The Alarum. Sylvia Townsend Warner. Appointments must be kept. MoBrPo

Alas, Alack. Walter De La Mare. Then turned to his sizzling,/And sank him back. EvOK; FaPON; OxBChV; TiPo

Alas! Carolina! J. Gordon Coogler. And learn to be physically and mentally strong,/By the solemn proceeds of thy "innocent" rum. OBAL

Alas! for the South! J. Gordon Coogler. She never was much given to literature. HBV 1-2; OBAL

Alas for Youth. Firdausi. Alas for youth, for youth gone by! AWP; LiTW

Alas How Long. Anonymous. And when found, 'tis lost even then. ErPo

Alas! How Should I Sing? Anonymous. To leven, and leave my leman,/Sweetest of all thing? NOBI

Alas, Kind Element. Léonie Adams. Alas, kind element! which comes to go. MoVE

Alas! madam, for stealing of a kiss. Sir Thomas Wyatt. The next shall clean out of my breast it pluck. BoLoP; FCP; OAEP

Alas, My God. Thomas Shepherd. I count each moment for a day,/Each minute for a year. OxBoCh

Alas, Poor Man, What Hap Have I. Sir Thomas Wyatt. To love above my poor degree. FCP; SiPS

Alas! Poor Queen. Marion Angus. And the pigeon with the blue ruff/She had from Monsieur d'Elboeuf. ACV; BSV; GoTS; OxBS

Alas, That Ever That Speche Was Spoken. Anonymous. To dethe hathe brouth my spouse and me. EnLoPo

Alas the grief and deadly woeful smart! Sir Thomas Wyatt. I quit th' enterprise of that that I have lost,/To whomsoever lust for to proffer most. FCP; SiPS

Alas! 'Tis Very Sad to Hear. Walter Savage Landor. The grave is cold enough for me/Without you and your poetry. GTBS-P; TW; WeW

Alaska. Joaquin Miller. Of yon ice mountain hurled/Down this unfinished world. PAH

Alaskan Mountain Poem #1. Leslie Marmon Silko. And the mountain/was gone. VoR

Alastor. Percy Bysshe Shelley.
...and woven hymns/Of night and day, and the deep heart of man. FiP; WHA
Birth and the grave, that are not as they were. CABL; OAEL 1-2; OAEP
With whose dun beams inwoven darkness seemed/To mingle. ChRP

Alba. Samuel Beckett. only I and then the sheet/and bulk dead BIrV

Alba. Ezra Pound. She lay beside me in the dawn. GBL; HAP; SOTW; WeW

Alba. Derek Walcott. Dawn is not one of them. GoJo; PCP

Alba after Six Years. Christopher Middleton. wild arms which did not hold this way before. NePoEA-2

Alba Innominata. Anonymous. Ah God! Ah God! That dawn should come so soon! AWP; LiTW

Alba: March. Marilyn Hacker. I'll draw the coleus again, its leaves/a curvilinear trap for light. GP

Albany Schmalbany. George Starbuck. Beckoned, and so did the/Harriman firm. PV

The Albatross. Charles Baudelaire. He cannot walk, borne down by his giant wings. EnLi 1-2; SyP

Albatross. Charles Burgess. To mark those grey untermined seas. NcPoAm-2

Albatross. Lele-io-Hoku. Sweet clever acts/Like Wai-"ale"ale. WTO

The Albatross. William Pember Reeves. And rushing with the tempest finds the night. AnNZ

Albatross. Charles Warren Stoddard. Defiant to the last! AA; EtS

Albemarle Cushing. James Jeffrey Roche. Joyful mother of the bravest of the/brave! PAH

Albert Ayler: Eulogy for a Decomposed Saxophone Player. Stanley Crouch. now a slimy brown harpsichord slapped ashore/November 25, 1970. PoBA

Albert Sidney Johnson. Kate Brownlee Sherwood. One heart, one hope, one destiny, one flag/from sea to sea. MC; PAH

Albert Sidney Johnston. Francis Orrery [(or Orray)] Ticknor. Passed in light from the house of dust/To the Home of the Glorified! PAH

Alberta. Anonymous. Alberta, don't you treat me unkind. FSW

Albi, Ne Doreas. Horace. Love mocks us all! AWP

Albinovanus. Anonymous. Though art, and care, and cost/Do promise nature's help in vain. FCP

The Albion Battleship Calamity. William McGonagall. ...the stronger we our houses do build,/The less chance we have of being killed. BXAP; PeD

Albuera. Thomas Hardy. Better than waking is to sleep! Albuera! WaaP

The Album. Cecil Day Lewis. ..."all that you missed/there/Has grown to be yours." ChMP; EnLoPo; OxBI; OxBTC

Album. Josephine Miles. Past the energy of survival/In its sadness/The hard life of the young. FaBoWP

Album. Carol Papenhausen. in their ageless, safe oblivion. AMV-81

Album Leaf. Stephane Mallarme. Your most natural clear/Child's laugh that charms the air. OBVE

Alcaics: to H. F. B. Robert Louis Stevenson. Dear to me here in my Alpine exile. EG; NBM; OBEV; OBVV

Alceste in the Wilderness. Anthony Hecht. Peruked and stately for the final act. ConAP; PoA

Alcestis. Euripides.
And bravery is set upon the mind/That man may act what truth he has divined. LiTW
Hail, lady, be gracious to usward; that alway her honor/abide. AWP

Alcestis. Isabel Williams Verry. Nor wish nor will/can strike a fingerling of fire from one/who died for your too acquiescent sake. GoYe

Alcestis in Ely. Nicholas Moore. ...and the wind blows in the chestnuts,/ Gently discerning. NeBP

Alcestis on the Poetry Circuit. Erica Jong. & after she dies, we will cry/& make her a saint. AmPA

The Alchemical Cupboard. Asa Benveniste. and finally to voices/in the gates/of home. VWA

The Alchemist. Louise Bogan. Passionate beyond the will. AWP; LLLT; MoAmPo

The Alchemist. Richard Church. Saw him cool from fire to bronze,/to aluminium,/To water,/And vanish. OxBTC

The Alchemist. Robert Kelly. whose name is love & which only of all light love can eat CoPo

The Alchemist. Ezra Pound. Elain, Tireis, Allodetta/Quiet this metal. LiTA; NePA; WSC

The Alchemist, 1610. Ben Jonson. ...perfumed/With gums of paradise and eastern air. EBEV; ViBoPo

The Alchemist in the City. Gerard Manley Hopkins. And pierce the yellow waxen light/With free long looking, ere I die. NoP

Alchemy. Adelaide Love. Each gift is gold and frankincense and myrrh. PGD

The Alchemy of Day. Anne Hebert. ...day rises in words like huge poppies/exploding on their stems. BoWoP

Alcibiades to a Jealous Girl. Arthur Davison Ficke. Oh the wine-cup/ Elevates me to be one/Of the company of all the gods! HBMV

Alcide Pavageau. Miller Williams. and honkie plunk/in Preservation/Hall. TAT

Alciphron and Leucippe. Walter Savage Landor. Alas! and not play too? OBEV; VLP

Alcohol. Louis MacNeice. The last way out that leads not out but in. LiTM

Alcoholic. John Berryman. I pray that my will may be attuned to/Your will for & with me. NOCV

Alcoholic. F. D. Reeve. lying/by chance/on the kitchen floor. NYBP

Alcyone. Frances Laughton Mace. I follow, follow to Alcyone! AA

Aldfrid's Itinerary Through Ireland. Flann Fionn. I found them all–I have written sooth. OnYI

Alec Yeaton's Son. Thomas Bailey Aldrich. Then let the stalwart skipper drown/And the little child go free! EtS; MOS

Alehouse Sonnets: The Dressing Station. Norman Dubie. and our Pope's most recent encyclical on contraception. AmPA

Aleph. Stuart Z. Perkoff. the power of the single/thrust, the pure/gesture of/self VWA

The Aleph Bet. Fay Lipshitz. And yet burn so high,/and fly so bright? VWA

Alexander. Frederick Morgan. Triumphantly he failed the test/and never even knew it. AMV-81

Alexander and Campaspe: Apelles' Song. John Lyly. What shall (Alas!) become of me? AtBAP; ATP; EnLi 1-2

Alexander and the Gymnosophists. Anonymous. For-thy I chase to cheve as chaunce is me demed.' OxBM

Alexander Graham Bell Did Not Invent the Telephone. Robert P. Tristram Coffin. Helped him make the whole world neighbor. TiPo

Alexander Jannai. Constantine P. Cavafy. the work begun by great Judas/ Maccabeus/and his four brothers, all men of/renown.... TrJP

Alexander's Feast. John Dryden.
He raised a mortal to the skies/She drew an angel down. ATP; CEP; CoBE; FiP; GoBC; GTBS; GTBS-P; HBV 1-2; LoBV; NOBE; OAEP; OBS; SeCeV; SeCV 1-2; TrGrPo; WHA
None but the brave deserves the fair! ATP
She drew an angel down! ATP; BoLiVe; CEP
Sweet is pleasure after pain. ATP
Think, O think, it worth Enjoying. GoTF; TreFS

Alexander the Great. Anonymous. It was not foolish women's talk/What those four sang. CH

Alexander to His Horse. Eleanor Farjeon. But men, my horse, with men! PH

Alexandria. Lawrence Durrell. Up there alone, upon the alps of night. MoVE

An Alexandrine Magazine. Howard Nemerov. An avenue of demonstrators and police/Contained between tall buildings where the money is. SOTS

The Alexandrite Ring. Margaret Ryan. I have it still, the alexandrite ring, this heart of stone. AMV-81

Alfonso Churchill. Edgar Lee Masters. Nor any the less a part of the question/Of what the drama means. GLGT

Alfred Corning Clark. Robert Lowell. motionless/as a lizard in the sun. NoAm

Alfred Lord Tennyson. Reed Whittemore. You never can tell/What will sell. PP

Alfred-Seeable Philadelphia Sky. Eli Siegel. You are an Alfred-seeable sky. CAD

Alfred the Harper. John Sterling. And slew ten thousand foes. BeLS

Algernon Sidney's Farewell. Anonymous. One plunge at once t' his death, his grave, his Hell. APAS

Algonkian Burial. Alfred Goldsworthy Bailey. while the morning sun flickered in the hollow sockets of my/eyes. OBCV

Algy. Anonymous. The bulge was Algy. MoShBr; PoPle; ShM

Ali. Djangatolum. Ali/Is our prince BOLo; CNA; PoBA

Ali Ben Shufti. Anthony Thwaite. And for fifty piastres I give you a past to belong to. OxBTC

Alibazan. Laura E. Richards. A May Day in the morning. OBCA

Alibi. Zoe A. Tilghman. "That was young owl. He don't know!" BPAW

Alibi (parody). Arthur Guiterman. How could I love thee, Dear, the most,/Loved I not others, some? BXAP

Alicante. Jacques Prevert. Warmth of my life. BoLoP

Alice. Herbert Bashford. Nay, nay! She is my baby girl. HBV 1-2

Alice B. (with music). Anonymous. Singin' fare-thee, O my honey, fare-thee-well! AS

Alice Corbin Is Gone. Carl Sandburg. The wind is carrying me round the sky. PoA

Alice Fell; or, Poverty. William Wordsworth. Proud creature was she the next day,/The little orphan, Alice Fell! BeLS; OBNV; SpRo

Alice Ray. Sarah Josepha Hale. We gain by what we give. AA

Alice's Recitation. Lewis (Charles Lutwidge Dodgson) Carroll. So, when he lost his temper, the Owl lost its life. FaBoNo; SpRo

Alice, Where Art Thou? Wellington Guernsey. Alice, I know art thou! VLP

Alicia's Bonnet. Elisabeth Cavazza Pullen. And many humming-bids were fastened on/it. AA

Alien. Helen Frazee-Bower. How near they are at last to finding me. HBMV

Alien. Donald Jeffrey Hayes. In the scent of the sea...! AmNP

Alien. Archibald MacLeish. What beauty past believing/Are you remembering? EtS

Alien. William Price Turner. I hope he dies before/they teach him a new tongue. OxBS

Alienation. Harry Kemp. But the ghosts of our old madness/Will rise and walk again. HBMV

Alimentary. Clifton Fadiman. And walk over to the Emersons' for a/ chicken dinner. PV

The Aliscamp. Frederic Mistral. And, kneeling under the willow-trees,/ Piously prayed for their souls' peace. CAW

Alison. Anonymous.
All other women?–forgotten! I've/discovered Alison! HAP
And lyht on Alysoun. AtBAP; CTC; EnLi 1-2; FaBoCh; MeBV; OAEL 1-2; OBEV; OxBB; PoEL 1-5
Herkne to my roun! MeEL; NoP

Alison. Artie Gold. so I leave a note on your doorstep; alison, wake up–/ the clouds can be beautiful! CaPN

Alison and Willie. Anonymous. She was buried an bemoaned,/But the birds waur Willie's companaie. BaBo; ESPB

Alison Gross. Anonymous. And no more I toddle about the tree. BuBa; WSC

Alive or Not. Al Purdy. and there is a certain amount of horror NOBC

Alive, this man was Manes, a common slave. Anyte. Dead, even great Darius is not his peer. BoWoP

Alive Together. Lisel Mueller. and knowledge and tears and chance. IHMS

All. Leona Gom. and we are a family again,/young and laughing/on the front porch. Str

All. Antoni Slonimski. It's so little, and yet it's all. TrJP

All a Green Willow Is My Garland. John Heywood. For all a green willow is your garland. EIL

All Aboard for Bombay. Leroy F. Jackson. All aboard for Bombay/On a floating cedar log! BrR

All, All A-lonely. Anonymous. All, all a-lonely,/Down in the green wood shady. OxBoLi

All Alone in My Little Cell. Anonymous. and I there all alone. NOBI

All Animals Like Me. Raymond Souster. makes the four-poster of a dream. WHW

All Around Man. Bo Carter. And I can do most anything that come my hand BluL

All Being Well. Wilfrid Gibson. When I at last may come to you,/All being well? OxBTC

All but Blind. Walter De la Mare. So, blind to Some-one/I must be. FaPON; HBMV; MoAB; MoBrPo

All Day and All October. Laurence Lerner. I and my wordy lust/Long since away. PeSA

All Day It Has Rained. Alun Lewis. On death and beauty till a bullet stopped his song. GTBS-P; OBWP; OxBTC

All Day We've Longed for Night. Sarah Webster Fabio. ...all that we/may hope to be, locked in/our day-long longing for night. BlSi

The All-Embracing. Frederick William Faber. And our lives would be all sunshine/In the sweetness of our Lord. BLRP; TRV

All Fellows (excerpt). Laurence Housman. And listen to man's great desire/Holding a Heart to burst? WGRP

All Flesh. Francis Thompson. Inestimably naught! BrPo

All Fools' Day. Anonymous. On purpose for pure merriment. SiSoSe; SoPo

All for Love. Anonymous. That, after all, concerns no one. UnTE

All for Love. John Dryden.
:a peal of groans/Cry'd Egypt is no more... BoW
'T is more than one man's work to please you all. DiPo
Take in good part, from our poor poet's board,/Such riveled fruits as winter can afford. DiPo

All for the Cause. William Morris. When the cause shall call upon us, some to live/and some to die! VLP

All Friends Together. R. A. Simpson. ...We only have our words. NOAV

All Goats. Elizabeth Jane Coatsworth. they gaze upon him with a/most/satiric eye. BoAnP

All God's Children Got Shoes. Anonymous. Gonna fly all over God's heaven. FSW

All God's Chillun Got Wings. Anonymous. I'm goin' to walk all ovah, goin' to talk all ovah God's Heab'n. BoAN 1-2; TreFS

All Gold. Anonymous. Mingling in one glow her ringlets/And her rings. KiLC

All Hail the Power of Jesus' Name. Edward Perronet. Now shout in universal song/The crowned Lord of all. NOCV

All Hail, Thou Noble Guest. Martin Luther. Within my heart, that it may be/A quiet chamber kept for Thee. TrPWD

All Hallows. Louise Gluck. And the soul creeps out of the tree. AmPA; HaCAP; NU

All Hands Unmoor! William Falconer. And far abroad the canvas wings extend. EtS

All heavy minds. Sir Thomas Wyatt. For else all other suit/Is clean in vain. EG; FCP; SiPS

All Human Things (parody). Peter Schroeder. To render tragic what is merely triste. BXAP

All Hungers Pass Away. Arthur Nortje. Pathetic, this, the dark posture. WhB

All Hushed and Still Within the House. Emily Bronte. Memory has power as real as thine. FaBoCh; NOBV; VLP

All I Ask–. D. H. Lawrence. ...insisting/on being loved, when there is no love in them. PoL

All I Do, De Church Keep A-Grumblin'. Anonymous. I do, I do, I do,/Yes, all I do, Lord, all I do. BoAN 1-2

All Ignorance Toboggans into Know. Edward Estlin Cummings. we'll move away still further:into now NOBA; OxBA; WaP

All in a Garden Green. William Ernest Henley. "Nay, Sweet, now nay, now nay!/I am not ready." OBMV

All in Due Time. J. V. Cunningham. They will not need them: in due time one dies. NIP

"All in green went my love riding". Edward Estlin Cummings. my heart fell dead before. AmLP; CMoP; FaBV; GoJo; HeIP; InPo; LiTA; LiTM; NePA; NoAm; NoP; OxBA; PoRA; SD

All in June. William Henry Davies. Sit on their soft, fat, velvet bums,/To wriggle out of hollow flowers. OBSP

All in the Downs. Thomas Hood. One can't always be stirring the fire. ALV; CenHV

All in the Downs (Susan and William). Anonymous. For thou art with me, for thou art with me wheresoe'er I go. AmFP

All in the Morning. Anonymous. And sweet Jesus we'll call him by name. BiCB

All Intents. Larry Eigner. but here we are, we are. VGW

All Is God's. Jakov De Haan. I praise God's one name. VWA

All Is Vanity, Saith the Preacher. George Gordon, Lord Byron. But then it stings for evermore/The soul that must endure it. TrCP

All Is Well. Arthur Hugh Clough. The wind it blows, the ship it goes,/Though where and whither, no one knows. EnLi 1-2

All Jolly Fellows That Follow the Plow. Anonymous. And I'll give you a jug of the best of brown ale.' OBET

All-Knowing God, 'Tis Thine to Know. Anonymous. And charity our language prove/Derived from thee, O God of love? AH

All-Knowing Lamp. Anonymous. You know whose naked breast supports his brow/Where he lies now. UnTE

All Last Night... Lascelles Abercrombie. The white Sabbath of her arm. FaBoTw; HBV 1-2

All Legendary Obstacles. John Montague. Kissing, still unable to speak. BIrV; CIP; FaBoIP; IPY; NOBI

All Lovely Things. Conrad Aiken. They pass, they pass, and know not whither. PoRA

All Morning. Theodore Roethke. All morning! All morning! NaP

All Morning. Terry Stokes. my friend, oh, my friend. AmPA

All My Love, Leave Me Not. Anonymous. Then sall they savit be/Through Thy mercy alone. BSV; GoTS

All My Past Life. John Wilmot, Earl of Rochester. 'Tis all that Heaven allows. FF

All My Pretty Ones. Anne Sexton. Whether you are pretty or not, I outlive you,/bend down my strange face to yours and forgive you. CoPo; NoAm

All My Trials. Anonymous. All my trials, Lord, soon be over. FSW

All Nature Has a Voice to Tell. James Gilchrist Lawson. Until we see Him face to face. BLRP

All Needs Met. J.H. Sammis. Waits the asking;–wants no more. BLRP

All Night ! Leon Baker. ...with infinite care/you waltz, twirl, and twinkle/all night! LFAC

All Night by the Rose. Anonymous. And yet I bore the flower away. CBEP; GBL; HeIP

All Night I Heard. Gertrude MacGregor Moffat. And flowers that opened in a song. CaP

All Night Long. Anonymous. All night long, from midnight on. FSW

All Night Long. Nina Cassian. I had slept too deeply/to enjoy that beautiful scene. VWA

All Night Long Fooling Me. Anonymous. Better quit fooling, fooling me. AmFP

All Night Long (with music). Anonymous. Do, Lawd, delibbah po' me! AS

The All-Night Waitress. Maura Stanton. ...recording passage/on a brain so small how could it hurt? AmPA

All-Nite Donuts. Albert Goldbarth. ...like plastic spoons/being worked in a hardening cheese dip. GeTw; MAYP

All of a Row. Anonymous. Shot at a pigeon,/And killed a crow. PBBP

All of a Sudden. Teresa de Jesus. and they swallow the boy,/the girl,/for 15 days,/for a month,/for ever WPOW

All of Her. Samuel L. Albert. For I was all of her, and she was all of me. NePoAm-2

All of Us Always Turning away for Solace. Delmore Schwartz. The bouncing ball you turned from for solace. OxBA

All on a Summer's Day. Anonymous. Rise up and choose another love,/All on this summer's day. PoPle

All One. Millen Brand. found her forgetting/which was her or which was him. GP

All One People. Carl Sandburg. Thus Hiamovi, out of a tarnished and weatherworn heart/of old gold, out of a living dawn gold. AmFN

All or Nothing (parody). Bayard Taylor. Or anything else remarkable,/Thou must follow me! BXAP

All Other Love Is Like the Moon. Anonymous. "In Marie mild and free/I shall be found, ac more in Crist." OxBM

All Our Griefs to Tell. John Newton. He sees, He hears, and from on high/Will make our cause His care. BePJ

All Our Joy Is Enough. Geoffrey Scott. Forget. OBMV

All Out and Down. Leadbelly. A jet black woman make a rabbit hug a hound/Won't he, baby? BluL

All-Over Love. Abraham Cowley. For thy love, like a mark, is stamped on all. LiTL

All Over the World. Geoffrey Johnson. Of bearing rearing the troublesome sons of men. HaMV

All Paths Lead to You. Blanche Shoemaker Wagstaff. You are the lark-song/Calling me home! BLPA; FaBoBe

All Praise to Thee. F. Bland Tucker. And God the Father be by all adored./Alleluia! AH

All Quiet. David Ignatow. running my whole family off a cliff. BeLS; CAPP; ConAP; FaBoBe; FaFP; TreFS

All Quiet along the Potomac. Ethel Lynn Beers. The picket's off duty forever! AA; PaPo; PSoN; TrAS

All Revelation. Robert Frost. All revelation has been ours. CABA; MoPo; NePA

All Ruin Is the Same. Emanuel Litvinoff. All ruin is the same. WaP

All's Vast. Francis Thompson. The grandeurs of his Babylonian heart. MoAB; MoBrPo

All's Well! William Allen Butler. "All's well! All's well!" HBV 1-2

All's Well. Harriet McEwen Kimball. All's well, whichever side the grave for/me/The morning light may break. AA

All's Well. John Greenleaf Whittier.
The glaring sunshine never knew! CBEP; OBSP

On gleams of star and depths of blue/The glaring sunshine never knew! CBEP; OBSP; OBVV

All's Well That Ends Well.   *Anonymous.*   My scolding wife has gone among the rest.   FaFP

All's Well That Ends Well, I, iii: "For I the ballad will repeat."   William Shakespeare.   Your cuckoo sings by kind.   BiP; ViBoPo

All Saint's Day (excerpt).   Margherita Guidacci.   ...You alone,/Saints, will dare to fix it with your gaze.   PBWP

All Saints'.   Edmund Yates.   "Oh, where is All Sinners' if this is All Saints'?"   HBV 1-2

All Saints' Day, Nov. 1.   Christopher Wordsworth.   God the Father, God the Son, and God the/Holy Ghost adore.   VLP

All Service Ranks the Same with God.   Robert Browning.   ...God's puppets, best and worst,/Are we; there is no last or first.   TreFT

All Shams.   *Anonymous.*   And leave both your honors' estates and your wives,/On condition that you may depart with your lives   APAS

All Songs.   B. Sanford Page.   Some are written in green rain and stone.   AMV-81

All Souls.   D. H. Lawrence.   I am a naked candle burning on your grave.   FaBoRV

All-Souls' Day.   Siegfried Sassoon.   In Thee, O ultimate power, who art/Our victory and our vision.   MoRP

All Souls' Eve.   Mary E. Mannix.   Cleaving the clouds, and quivering to the sky—/"Orate pro nobis!"   GoBC

All Souls' Night.   Frances Cornford.   He did not think me strange or older,/Nor I, him.   EnLoPo; OBSP; OxBTC

All Souls' Night.   William Butler Yeats.   Wound in mind's wandering/As mummies in the mummy-cloth are wound.   MoVE

All Splendor on Earth.   Karin Kiwus.   to the nothing/to the sweet nothing   BoWoP

All Still.   William Barnes.   Agean, the pleace is ever dumb.   NOBV

The All-Sufficient Christ.   Bernice W. Lubke.   He'll plead for me.   BLRP

All Sung.   Richard Le Gallienne.   Only the dead men know the tunes/The live world dances to.   OBVV

All That Glitters Is Not Gold.   *Anonymous.*   But all through your life, remember child/All that glitters is not gold.   TreFT

All That I Am.   Verna Arvey.   All I ever can be:/This I surrender, Oh, my Lord, to thee.   AH

All That Is, and Can Delight.   Robert Farren.   Make all that is, and can delight,/from every atom run.   OxBI

All That Is Left.   Michael Hartnett.   and hollow fragile strands in twos/rayed like tendrils/out about a root.   NOBI

All That Is Lovely in Men.   Robert Creeley.   for all/that is lovely in women.   NaP

All That Is Perfection in Woman.   William Carlos Williams.   to the sea, the sea.   BiP

All That Jazz.   Yasmeen Jamal.   Ask Art Tatum,/He watches me.   LFAC

All That Matters.   Edgar A. Guest.   And all that matters is to live it well.   ATP

All That Matters...   Waltler Sorell.   and her hands held on to herself.   GoYe

All That's Bright Must Fade.   Thomas Moore.   All that's sweet was made/But to be lost when sweetest.   OxBI

All That's Past.   Walter De La Mare.   Silence and sleep like fields/Of amaranth lie.   AnFE; GoJo; MoAB; NOBE; OAEL 1-2; OAEP; OBMV; OxBTC; SeCeV; TreFT; TrGrPo; ViBoPo; WHA

All That Summer.   Lora Dunetz.   ...where childlike or childish we pursue/Them into worlds where mutual worlds are overcome.   NePoAm-2

All That Time.   May Swenson.   When the wind blew, you could hear/them rubbing on each other.   FF

All That Was Mortal.   Sara Teasdale.   Footprints of birds record a brief alighting/In flight begun and ended in the air.   MoRP

All That You Have Given Me, Africa.   Anoma Kanie.   So that your heaven-given task/May be safe forever.   PBWP

All the Bells Were Ringing.   Christina Georgina Rossetti.   And all the birds are singing.   TiPo

All the Dead Dears.   Sylvia Plath.   Deadlocked with them, taking root as/cradles rock.   IHMS

All the Death-Room Needs...   Michael Hartnett.   and the ritual/of prayer: and cries:/and Christ's chrism.   CIP

All the Farewells.   Byron Vazakas.   ...find/interdependence in the flux of things.   MoPo

All the Fruit...   Friedrich Holderlin.   ...Let us learn to live swaying/As in a rocking boat on the sea.   NU

All the Hills and Vales Along.   Charles Hamilton Sorley.   So be merry, so be dead.   EBEV; EnLit; FaBoCh; HBMV; MMM; MoBrPo; OBWP

All the Hosts of Heaven.   Simeon Ben Abun.   The Lord shall reign for evermore.   TrJP

All the Past We Leave Behind.   Walt Whitman.   Moving yet and never stopping,/Pioneers! O Pioneers!   AH

All the Pretty Little Horses.   *Anonymous.*   Go to sleepy, little baby.   ABF; AmFP; FSW; OxBoLi

All the Roary Night.   Kenneth Patchen.   And in which we don't figure at all.   LiTM

All the Scenes of Nature Quicken.   Christopher Smart.   Lasting life and long enjoyment/Are not here, and are not yet.   ELP

All the Slaves.   Thomas Lux.   They're slaves with slaves' morals,/all these slaves within me.   SM

All the Smoke.   Eli Siegel.   Weighs/Two pounds, net.   CAD; ELU; FiBHP

All the Spirit Powers Went to Their Dancing Place.   Gary Snyder.   Earth is our dancing place now.   UnPo

All the Things You Are.   Oscar, II Hammerstein.   I'll know that moment divine,/When all the things you are, are mine.   BLSo

All the Way from There to Here.   Jack Gilbert.   the beauty as the marriage steadily failed.   NPGG

All the Way My Savior Leads Me.   Robert and Fanny J. Crosby Lowry.   Jesus led me all the way.   FSW; STF

All the while, believe me, I prayed.   Sappho.   our night would last twice as long.   BoWoP

All the World.   *Anonymous.*   That the uttermost peoples, hearing,/Shall hail Thee crowned King.   TrJP

All the World Moved.   June Jordan.   I survived His innocence/without my own.   NBP; PoBA

All the World's a Stage.   Sir Walter Ralegh;   Only we die in earnest, that's no jest.   NLV; NOBE; OBSC

All These Birds.   Richard Wilbur.   Put on the reins of love.   NOBA; Prf

All Things Are Current Found.   Henry David Thoreau.   Take me to your clime.   AnNE; ViBoPo

All Things Be Dear but Poor Mens Labour.   *Anonymous.*   For all do know, unto their woe/all things be dear but poor mens labour.   CoMu

All Things Being Equal.   J. Lee Humphrey.   Me and a couple a sonsabitches we done got equal yestiddy.   AMV-81

All Things Bright and Beautiful.   Cecil Frances Alexander.   How great is God Almighty,/Who has made all things well.   FaPoR; OHIP; OxBChV

All Things Can Tempt Me.   William Butler Yeats.   Colder and dumber and deafer than a fish.   CMoP; OBSP

All Things Confine.   Hadewijch.   You know this well/You that have been there too.   PBWP

All Things Decay and Die.   Robert Herrick.   Droops, dies, and falls without the cleaver's stroke.   CaPo

All Things Drink.   Thomas Stanley.   Is it reason then, d'ye think,/I should thirst when all else drink?   AWP

All Things Have Savour.   *Anonymous.*   Nay, a box on the eare hath no smell at all.   FaBoCo

"All Things Must Have an End; the World Itself."   Henry Wadsworth Longfellow.   Into the dark abyss, with her dead crew.   AmePo

All Things Wait upon Thee.   Christina Georgina Rossetti.   To their appointed portion of delight/As queens and kings.   GN

All This Everyday (excerpt).   Joanne Kyger.   when I write to you/these notes of myself.   APU

All This Sunday Long.   B. S. Johnson.   thus do I wilfully increase my load.   ELU

All This World's Riches.   Edmund Spenser.   Her mind, adorned with virtues manifold.   LiTL

All Those Hymnings Up to God.   Abbie Huston Evans.   I trust them more than the foot rule. Bach may yet have been right.   MoRP

All Those I Love Die Young.   Bonefonius.   To love you, though I loathe you, so you'll die.   DBV

All Thro' the Year.   *Anonymous.*   May with God's love shine bright/All thro' the year.   BLRP

All through the Night.   *Anonymous.*   With thy last dim journey taken/Home through the night.   TreFS

All through the Night.   Harold Boulton.   Breathes a pure and holy feeling,/All through the night.   FSW

All through the Rains.   Gary Snyder.   In the shade of the down/Eucalyptus on the hill.   ConAP

All through the Stranger's Wood.   Isaac L. Peretz.   Oh, how it stabbed, the stranger's/rose!   TrJP

All Thumbs.   David Giber.   because your eyes have ruled this a mismatch already.   AMV-81

All to Myself.   Wilbur D. Nesbit.   But I keep each olden, golden while/All to myself.   BLPA

All Too Late.   *Anonymous.*   Of al this world ne give ich a pese!   OAEL 1-2; OxBM

All Too Little on Pictures.   Charles Black.   And the real presence is you.   AMV-80

All Tropic Places Smell of Mold.   Karl Shapiro.   ...Rome, the armpit of the universe.   VGW

All Turns into Yesterday.   *Anonymous.*   And ever among thou thee en-nuye/Into this world and yesterday.   MeEL

All Up and Down the Lines.   Robert Cooperman.   and beautiful young men died/all up and down the lines.   AMV-80

All Watched over by Machines of Loving Grace.   Richard Brautigan.   and all watched over/by machines of loving grace.   MAT

Alone. Elsie Laurence. With the sharp sword of mockery/Stab one's heart. CaP

Alone. Itzik Manger. But where to go late at night?/All alone? VWA

Alone. Edgar Allan Poe. And the cloud that took the form/(When the rest of Heaven was blue)/Of a demon in my view. LaNeLa; MAmP

Alone. Siegfried Sassoon. And all but inmost faith is overthrown. BoLiVe; MoBrPo

Alone. E. J. Scovell. Even in this being alone I meet with you. GBL

Alone. Richard Shelton. the fireflies are naked and cold/in the rags of their light NYBP

Alone. Carolyn Wells. The other meaning we're alone–apart. PoToHe

Alone. Hubert Witheford. I yield before the silence and I know/Your servants who are waiting at my side. AnNZ

Alone am I, and alone I wish to be. Christine de Pisan. Alone am I, my love no longer living. BoWoP

Alone by the Hearth. George Arnold. And, as I gaze in the coals, I remember/Days long agone! HBV 1-2

Alone by the Road's Edge. Diana O Hehir. Its harsh dance, its grave eccentric song. NPGG

Alone (fragment). Sappho. And still I'm lying in my bed alone. AWP

Alone in an Inn at Southampton, April the 25th, 1737. Aaron Hill. Smile at discharge from care, and shut out light. NOEC

Alone in April. James Branch Cabell. Lifting your red lips up to me,/Ettarre, and kiss, with no man to see! HBMV

Alone in the House. George Bogin. I ran down the stairs/out the door/into his arms. AMV-80

Alone Is the Hunter. Harold Littlebird. and accept fully/all that was given VoR

Alone up Here on the Mountain. Anonymous. let me not dread pale death,/though the horror come when I am alone. NOBI

Alone with the Dawn. Matthew Sweeney. And tonight I had no need of sleep/beside you. AMV-80

Along History. Muriel Rukeyser. his penis erect with/fantasy NNaP

Along Shore. Herbert Bashford. They rocked the infant Time! AA

Along South Inlet. Greg Kuzma. to live their dreaming. WOLT

Along the Banks. Joel Barlow. And raise her children to eternal day. AH

Along the Field as We Came By. Alfred Edward Housman. When I shall sleep with clover clad,/And she beside another lad. HAP; HBV 1-2; LiTL; MasP; MoAB; MoBrPo; UnTE; WeW

Along the River. D. J. Enright. How can the young do such a/thing? DFF

Along the Road. Robert Browning Hamilton. But oh, the things I learned from her/When Sorrow walked with me! BLPA; BLPL; GoTF; TreFS

Along the Strand. Alfred Mombert. Golden gleamed the woman's hair. TrJP

Along Walking. Anonymous. And thus an end. CBEP

Alons au Bois le May Cueillir. Charles d'Orléans. We'll to the woods and gather may. AWP

Alonso to Ferdinand. W. H. Auden. To forgive our illusion. MoPo

Alonzo the Brave and Fair Imogine. Matthew Gregory Lewis. And his consort, the False Imogine!' OBEC

Aloof. Christina Georgina Rossetti. And hope felt strong and life itself not weak. BoLiVe; OBEV; OBVV; TrGrPo

Alouette. Anonymous. Les pattes/Le cou FSW

Alpha November Golf Sierra Tango. Tom Clark. Come in, come in, they call. APU

The Alphabet. Anonymous. I'd buy me a johnny to fill up my trunk,/I'd go for a soldier the bounty to jump. BFSS

The Alphabet. Charles Stuart Calverley. Z stands for Zero, or nothing at all. HBV 1-2

An Alphabet. Charles Edward Carryl. Are Zebras full of zeal? LBN

The Alphabet. Kate Greenaway. U, V, W, X, Y, Z, all had a large/slice and went off to bed. FaBoUs; HBVY

An Alphabet. Edward Lear.
We think we've all heard quite enough of this your/sad disaster!' FaBoNo

The Alphabet. James Reaney. N O P Q R S T U V W X Y Z. ACV

The Alphabet. Karl Shapiro. And all is rolled back in the book of days. MoRP; NoAm; PoA; VWA

The Alphabet Came to Me. Jerome Rothenberg. the distances to every side of us/as in a poem VWA

The Alphabet of Aristotle. Mayster Benet. A mesurabulle meane Way is best for us alle. FaBoUs

An Alphabet of Christmas. Anonymous. A merry merry Christmas, and many may you see! ChBR

An Alphabet of Famous Goops. Gelett Burgess. And Yet, he Drove his Mother Crazy-he was so Slow, he was so/Lazy! BBGG

Alphabetical Song on the Corn Law Bill. Anonymous. They must be muzzled in the dog days for fear they might/go mad. OxBoLi

Alpheus and Arethusa. Eugene Howell Daly. They turned them into water! AA

Alphonso of Castile. Ralph Waldo Emerson. So shall ye have a man of the sphere,/Fit to grace the solar year. AP; NOBA

Alpine. R.S. Thomas. The mind has its own level to find. BoNaP; LiSp; PoL; RFM

The Alpine Flowers. Lydia Huntley Sigourney. And freer dreams of heaven. AnAmPo

Alpine Spirit's Song. Thomas Lovell Beddoes. Lonely like a spectre's love,/Earth beneath, and stars above. OBNC; OBTV

Alpine View. Melville Cane. The higher up the altitude,/The swifter down the plummet. PoPl

Alps. Rosanna Warren. ...speak/of those un-mountainous matters, in few words, without fraud. MAYP

Also Watches (parody). D. C. Berry. and while you are/watching, I too,/slowly. BXAP

The Altar. George Herbert. And sanctify this Altar to be Thine! AnAnS 1; ATP; HoPM; InPS; JCP; OAEL 1-2; PAI; SeCP; SeCV 1-2; TrCP; TrGrPo

The Altar. Jean Starr Untermeyer. Proud of love's pain and humble to its healing. HBMV

Altar Prayers. Anonymous. You possess me, I am blest! WTO

The Altarpiece Finished. John Hollander. ...you can see it on the sixth of May. It will eat you. NoAm

Altars and Sacrifice. Jay Wright. and the rhythm of the smith. FB

The Altars in the Street. Denise Levertov. fragile, insolent, absolute. CAPP

Altarwise by Owl-Light. Dylan Thomas.
And hemleock-headed in the wood of weathers. CMoP; NoAm
And rivers of the dead around my neck. CMoP; NoAm
And share my bed with Capricorn and Cancer. CMoP; NoAm
And sirens singing from our lady's sea-straw. NoAm
Arc-lamped thrown back upon the cutting flood. CMoP
My nest of mercies in the rude, red tree. CMoP; CoBMV; FaBoMo; LiTM; MasP; NoAm
Said the antipodes, and twice spring chimed. CMoP
Suffer the heaven's children through my heartbeat. CMoP; NoAm

Alter? When the Hills Do. Emily Dickinson. I will of you! AA; AmPP; AnNE

An altered look about the hills. Emily Dickinson. And Nicodemus' mystery/Receives its annual reply. OxBA; PPP

Alternative Endings to an Unwritten Ballad. Paul Dehn. Immense on the marshes, stood...MRS. RAVOON! FiBHP

Alternatives. Kingsley Amis. Waited for the hands to move, not round/Her throat, but to her eager breasts? OxBC

Alternatives. Peter Cooley. the wild cry of your blossoming? AmPA

Although he has no form. Mukta Bai. Mukta says: Words cannot contain him,/yet in him all words are. BoWoP

Although I Do Not Know. Saigyo Hoshi. My tears well forth. AWP

Although I Had a Check. Henry Howard, Earl of Surrey. For sure I will assay/If I can give thee mate. SiPS

Although I put away his life. Emily Dickinson. To teach the angels avarice/Your kiss first taught to me! MoAmPo

Although I Remember the Sound. Robert Huff. The sweet, new smell which rose after the fall. SM

Although I was her pupil. Korinna. yet she challenged Pindar. BoWoP

Although in a Crystal. Anselm Parlatore. Or under a flat rock/slowly lifted/sucks air/from the bog. SUW

Although It Is Not Plainly Visible to the Eye. Fujiwara-No- Toshiyuki. By the noise of the wind! AWP

Although Tormented. Kalonymos Ben Judah. They who, in life were wedded,/Through hallowed death are reunited. TrJP

Altitudes. Richard Wilbur. To pace about his garden, lost in thought. CMoP

Alulvan. Walter De la Mare. The doom of lone Alulvan! MoVE

Alumnus Football. Grantland Rice. He writes–not that you won or lost–but/how you played the Game. FPL; GoTF; PoLf; TreFS

Always. Pablo Neruda. alone upon the earth/to begin life. OLR

Always Battling. Thomas O'Brien. "I don't believe that all of it is true!" NeIP

Always Before Your Voice My Soul. Edward Estlin Cummings. washed with a wild and thin/despair of violin. AnFE; CoAnAm; LiTA; MoAmPo; NePA

Always Begin Where You Are. Thomas Hornsby Ferril. Then mount and ride away/To any dream deserving the sensible world. PrIm; VGW

Always Finish. Anonymous. Do it well or not at all. BLPA; FaBoBe; WBLP

Always, from My First Boyhood. John Peale Bishop. Cracks its light on the fissile planes of the mirror. VGW

Always in the Parting Year. Else Lasker-Schüler. Drop heavy on my heart. TrJP

Always Modern Times. Bradford Stark. It is always modern times. LTB

Always the Following Wind. W. H. Auden. The out-of-sight, buried too deep for shafts. MoBrPo

Always the Melting Moon Comes. Margot Osborn. "Always the melting moon comes." CaP

Always True to You in My Fashion (excerpt). Cole Porter. Yes, I'm always true to you, darlin', in my way. NLV

Always We Watch Them. Paul Mariah. ...He is engaged/To marry/The Electric Holding Company. LFAC

Am Driven Mad. Allen Polite. A high rushing tide of dark hair NNP

Am I Failing? George Meredith. But, as you will! we'll sit contentedly,/ And eat our pot of honey on the grave. CABA; GBL

Am I to Lose You? Louisa S. Bevington. "I greatly need your friendship: leave it me." NOBV

Amagansett Beach Revisited. John Hall Wheelock. On the now vanished past. NYBP

Amagoduka at Glencoe Station. Mbuyiseni Oswald Mtshali. unknown to us/but only to their mothers and loafers. WhB

Amalek. Friedrich Torberg. him, said the Lord, him you shall hate. VWA

Amanda. Anonymous. And all he asked was kindness and food/From the parents of Amanda to the chief of the wood. BFSS

Amanda Barker. Edgar Lee Masters. But I proclaim from the dust/That he slew me to gratify his hatred. NoAm

Amanda Dreams She Has Died and Gone to the Elysian Fields. Maxine W. Kumin. For an hour/we are incorruptible. GP

Amanda Is Shod. Maxine W. Kumin. lest anyone cast a spell on Amanda. PH

Amanda, Playing. C. W. Truesdale. at the very tip her arched tongue/his name Ben. PoDr

Amanda's Complaint. Philip Freneau. Bermudian damsels are not fair! AP

Amantium Irae. Ernest Christopher Dowson. Doff sorry pride for pardon,/ Or ever love go by. HBV 1-2; OBEV

Amantium Irae. Richard Edwards. The falling out of faithful friends, renewing is of love. ElL; HBV 1-2; LoBV; OBSC

The Amaranth. Coventry Patmore. And more to-day than yesterday. LoBV

Amaryllis I did woo. George Wither. 'Cause to be of one possest/Barr'd the hope of all the rest. EG

Amasis. Laurence Binyon. The Satrap smiles, and on his finger turns/The all-envied emerald. OBVV

The Amateur Flute (parody). Anonymous. And the tootle, tootle, tooting of its toot. BXAP; Par; SpRo

Amaturus. William Johnson-Cory. Too dearly, dearly bought thee/To part with thee in vain. HBV 1-2

Amaze. Adelaide Crapsey. A woman like me once had hands/Like these. AnAmPo; QFR

Amazing Grace. Anonymous. The hour I first believed. ABF

Amazing Grace. Anselm Hollo. indianola, iowa PoM

Amazing Grace. John Newton. And there's a cross for me. BLSo; FSW

Amazing Sight! The Saviour Stands. Henry Alline. And bar yourselves from heaven? AH

Ambarvalia. Arthur Hugh Clough. And find thee changeless, Pont-y-wern. FaBoPP

The Ambassadors. Paul Lawson. who left England for Virginia/in sixteen seventeen/and died off Gravesend. GP

Amber. Holger Drachmann. Yet his was of amber only. LiTW

The Amber Bead. Robert Herrick. More rich than Cleopatra's tomb. CaPo

Amber Beads. Audrey Alexandra Brown. And eat the earth and drink the sea? CaP

Amber the Sky. Rokwaho. of ferns & flowers & butterflies STE

The Ambience of Love. Isidor Schneider. new shadow to let rinse/my hot hair in the wind. PG

The Ambiguous Dog. Arthur Guiterman. His bite is at the growly end. GDP

Ambition. Edith Agnew. But now I have to go and feed the pig. TiPo

Ambition. Morris Bishop. And I swung in ahead of him and landed fine/ Behind 9W-7679. AmFN

Ambition. William Henry Davies. Let my descent and fall, O Lord,/Be into Paradise. MoBrPo; TrGrPo

Ambition. Robert Herrick. Each one, by nature, loves to be a king. CaPo

Ambition. Aline Kilmer. Who knows but the rest will be nicer than these? HBMV

Ambition. Alexander Pope. If not, by any means get wealth and place. DBV

Ambition. Nathaniel Parker Willis. He sends us, stripped and naked, to the grave. OBCA

The Ambition of Ghosts. Rosemarie Waldrop. and every fraction/must be solved. APU

Ambitious. Jim Gustafson. At the time it seems/like a good idea. APU

The Ambitious Ant. Amos R. Wells. "How glad I am that I crossed the sea!" OBCA

Amboyna; or, The Cruelties of the Dutch.... John Dryden. And least hope wit; in Dutchmen that would be/As much improper as would honesty. OBSV

The Ambrosia of Dionysus and Semele. Robert Graves. Who have ambrosia eaten and yet live. NYBP

Ambulance Call. Lorrie Goldensohn. What do I do without my legs? AMV-81

Ambulances. Philip Larkin. And dulls to distance all we are. FaBoTw; OxBC

Ambuscade. Hugh McCrae. Of angry nostrils webbed with leaping veins,/ The stallions come. BoAV; PoAu 1-2

Ambushed by Angels. Gustav Davidson. Is any less real than that in which I move. GoYe

Ameinias. John Simon. Which may explain why he remains obscure. ELU

Amelia Mixed the Mustard. Alfred Edward Housman. "Observe," she said, "the action/Of mustard on Mamma." DBV; FaBoNo

Amelia Street. Frank Ormsby. Some taint by proxy prickles on my skin. CIP

Amen. Arthur Christopher Benson. With all desirous souls/I cry, Amen. OBVV

Amen. Frederick G. Browning. And try to still/Each rising murmur, and to God's sweet will/Respond–AMEN. BLRP

Amen. Alvaro Mutis. like a hunter who in his return/recognizes his wasted shells in the woods. AMV-81

Amen. Jaime Sabines. for I have reached that stage of life when youth/can be contracted solely by contagion. AMV-81

Amen. Richard W. Thomas. Through the funnel of graves PoBA

Amend Me. Anonymous. In heven ther to see His face,/Wher we shall mend and pair nought. OxBM

The Amendis to the Telyouris and Sowtaris... William Dunbar. Telyouris and Sowtaris, blist be ye. OBSV

Amendment. Thomas Traherne. He made our Souls to make his Creatures/Higher. SeCV 1-2

Amends to Nature. Arthur Symons. And suddenly the world becomes/A part of me and I of it. GTBS; HBMV

Amends to the Tailors and Soutars. John Skelton. Tailors and soutars, blest be ye. BSV; CBEP

Amergin's Songs. Anonymous. "A flood of fish/fish-teeming sea!"' NOBI

America. Donald Campbell Babcock. A famine of the heart, and bitter cold. AA; FaBoBe; NePoAm

America. William Cullen Bryant. Upon their lips the taunt shall die. AA

America. Arthur Cleveland Coxe. He gave them the spirit his own to defy. MC; PAH

America. Robert Creeley. us, and nowhere but you to be. MAT

America. Pier Giorgio Di Cicco. the tough romance their hands build nothing without. CaPN

America. Sydney Thomas Dobell. ...Shall we fight? OBVV

America. Henry Dumas. but the eagle will never fly. BOLo; PoBA

America. Allen Ginsberg. America I'm putting my queer shoulder to the wheel. CAPP; CoAP; HaCAP; InPS; NaP; NMP; NoAm; PoM; PPoe; PPP

America. Bobb Hamilton. My black self. BOLo

America. Bernadette Mayer. To dismiss an effigy/Which appears to be singing. ANYP

America. Claude McKay. Like priceless treasures sinking in the sand. AnAmPo; BALP; CDC; NIP; NoAm; PoBA; PoNe; TAP; TTY

America. Herman Melville. And left her on the crag. MAmP

America. John Newlove. ...If they live/in the Empire, it matters what they say. NOBC

America. Wendy Rose. and give them back/their eyelessness. CDW

America. Samuel Francis Smith. Protect us by Thy might,/Great God, our King. AA; BLSo; FaBoBe; FaFP; GoTF; HBV 1-2; HBVY; PAL; PoLf; PSoN; TreF; WBLP; YaD

America. Bayard Taylor. She makes it glory, now, to be a man. AA; PAL

America A Prophecy. William Blake.
And the fierce flames burnt round the heavens & round the abodes of men OAEL 1-2
His knees and thighs like silver, & his breast and/head like gold.' EnRP

America, America! Delmore Schwartz. ...It is the city consciousness/Which sees and says: more: more and more: always more. NYP

America Bleeds. Angelo Lewis. down, down, be finished at/last. PoBA

America (excerpt). James M. Whitfield. Bound to a petty tyrant's nod,/ Because he wears a paler face. BPo

America First! G. Ashton Oldham. ...I say with all my/heart and soul, "AMERICA FIRST!" PGD

America for Me. Henry Van Dyke. Where the air is full of sunlight and the flag is full of stars. BLPA; BLPL; FaFP; HBVY; MC; OHFP; PAL; SoSe; TreFS; WBLP

America, I Love You. Harry and Bert Kalmar Ruby. Don't bite the hand that's feeding you. FiBHP; InMe

America Is Great Because... de Tocqueville. and if America ever ceases to be good,/America will cease to be great. TreFT

"America, My Country..." Ralph Waldo Emerson. Land of the forest. AmePo

America Prays. Arthur Gordon Field. Through all the days Thy name we raise/Who made our nation great. PGD

America Remembers (excerpt). Paul Engle. A newer breed of men?) NAMP

America Resurgent. Wendell Phillips Stafford. And a helmet full of Stars! MC

America's Answer. R. W. Lilliard. We've learned the lesson that ye taught/In Flanders fields. BLPA; PAL

America's Gospel. James Russell Lowell. And the soul's fealty to none but God. PGD

America's Prosperity. Henry Van Dyke. These are prosperity and vital wealth! PGD

America's Task. Abraham Lincoln. To do all which may achieve and cherish a just and/lasting peace among ourselves and with all... PGD

America's Wounded Knee. Phil George. One more remains–just one per cent left. VoR

America the Beautiful. Katharine Lee Bates. And crown thy good with brotherhood/From sea to shining sea! BLPA; EaLo; FaBoBe; FaBV; FaFP; FSW; GoTF; HBMV; HBVY; MC; MCCG; PAL; TAP; TreF; WBLP; WGRP; YaD

America the Beautiful. Stan Rice. nerves and follicles and arteries/ablaze in the suaveness of night. NPGG

America to England. George Edward Woodberry. Justice we love, and next to justice peace. AA

America to Great Britain. William Allston. "We are One!" AA; HBV 1-2

America Was Promises. Archibald MacLeish. O believe this! AmFN; PAL

America Was Schoolmasters. Robert P. Tristram Coffin. They shaped our minds and morals/With switches on the seat! PAL

American against Solitude. Alan Dugan. ...full/of life, death, insanity, and grace! CAPP

American Ash. Stanley Plumly. branch, green, the sudden burden of the leaves. GeTw

American Bandstand. Michael Waters. forever awkward,/each partner dreaming of grace. MAYP

The American Book of the Dead: Six Selections. John Giorno. rewarding a crowd of 200 persons/standing vigil for the event. ANYP

An American Boyhood. Jonathan Holden. ...how/in this world we were going/to be necessary. Psk

American Change. Allen Ginsberg. Men to prevent foul conterfeit. CABL; HaCAP

American Child. Paul Engle. A water-watched and river-radiant child. AmFN

American Classic. Louis Simpson. That's why I say, an American classic. AmC

American Commencement. Aram Boyajian. one hundred will go/to school and IndoChina NeAC

The American Dream. Johnie Scott. bluebloods blue books as in dogs and sex-freaks NBP

American Dreams. Louis Simpson. It is strange to me/and strange, I think, even to themselves. CAPP; GP

The American Eagle. D. H. Lawrence. Laying that golden egg,/That addled golden egg? OAEL 1-2

American Falls. Greg Keeler. no forebay, just water in a hard, thin line. SM; WOLT

American Farm, 1934. Genevieve Taggard. Economy, economy! Who'll till this land? VGW

The American Flag. Joseph Rodman Drake. And Freedom's banner streaming o'er/us? AA; AmLP; FaBoBe; FaFP; GN; HBV 1-2; HBVY; MC; PAH; PAL; PaPo; PGD; TreF; WBLP

The American Flag. Charles Constantine Pise. My native land forever! CAW

An American Girl. Brander Matthews. A free and frank young Yankee maiden. AA

American Gothic. Samuel ("Paul Vesey") Allen. How about that! IDB

American Heartbreak. Langston Hughes. The great mistake/That Jamestown/Made long ago. AmPP; BPo; LiTM

American Heritage. Robert Sward. Unforeign war/that ever I did see. (Chorus, etc.) OBAL

The American Hero. Nathaniel Niles. Life is redoubled. WaaP

American History. Michael S. Harper. Can't find what you can't see/can you? BPo; HaCAP

American History. W. R. Moses. They long for the easy diversion, but that is gone. LiTA

American Independence. Francis Hopkinson. When men fight for freedom, they must be/victorious. PAH

The American Indian. *Anonymous.* Oh! no, they just sold them for bioux. FaBoCo; FiBHP; NLV

Un-American Investigators. Langston Hughes. The committee shivers/With delight in/Its manure. BPo

American Jump. *Anonymous.* Or, Round the world? OxNR

American Landscape with Clouds & a Zoo. Jon Anderson. ...I'm all there is/Forever, chum, just see it my way, & I do. MAYP

American Laughter. Kenneth Allan Robinson. –They crossed hard times to the Comstock Lode! AmFN; TreFS

American Letter. Archibald MacLeish. I think of the masts at Cette and the sweet rain. AmFN; AmPP; OxBA

American Lights, Seen from Off Abroad. John Berryman. Here comes a cropper'. That's what I said. LCAP; OBAL

An American Love-Ode. Thomas Warton, Sr.. Stay, lovely, fearful Adder stay. CEP

American Muse. Stephen Vincent Benét. And none is false, and none is wholly true. PAL

American Names. Stephen Vincent Benét. Bury my heart at Wounded Knee. AmFN; LaNeLa; LoGBV; OBAL; OxBA; PG; TreFT; YaD

The American Patriot's Prayer. *Anonymous.* Single to serve th' erron'ous throng,/Spite of themselves, be mine. PAH

The American Poet–"But Since It Came to Good..." William Hathaway. I see those mice skittering back/night after night in the dusty plate. APU

American Poetry. Louis Simpson. Uttering cries that are almost human. ELU; NoAm; NOBA; PP; TAP

American Portrait: Old Style. Robert Penn Warren. And love is a hard thing to outgrow. FYAP

American Primitive. William Jay Smith. And I love my Daddy like he loves his Dollar. FF; InPK; MoAmPo; MP; NePoAm; NePoEA; OBSP; PoPl; PPON; TwCP

American Rhapsody. Kenneth Fearing. Is this, baby, what you were born to feel, and do, and be? MoAmPo

The American Soldier. Philip Freneau. She leaves her soldier–famine and a name! TAP

The American Soldier's Hymn. *Anonymous.* And nations, strangers to His name,/Shall thus be taught to sing His praise. PAH

An American Takes a Walk. Reed Whittemore. How in that Eden could Adam/Be really, wholly lost? MoVE

An American to France. Alice Duer Miller. And who loves beauty must be stern of soul. HBMV

The American Traveller. Robert Henry Newell. And now is making nutmegs at/Moosehicmagunticook. FaBoCo; OBAL

American Twilights, 1957. James Wright. God, God have pity on man apart. CoAP

American Vineyard. Mildred Cousens. A many tendrilled vine. GoYe

Americana. Carl Rakosi.
and makes them instant/democrats. InPS; PAI
I know I am in your honest presence. PAI
I picked them/all/only yesterday. PAI
We wish they'd come up/and say hello more often. PAI

Americanized. Bruce Dawe. She loves him...and the frightening fact sinks in. CBAP

Americans Are Afraid of Lizards. Karl Shapiro. Or playing at making designs. AmFN

Americans in an Orange Grove. Arthur Vogelsang. "It won't be all right in the end, it just won't." MAYP

Ametas and Thestylis Making Hay-Ropes. Andrew Marvell. And go and kiss within the hay. ALV; CavP; InvP; SeCP

Amid the Din of Earthly Strife. Henry Warburton Hawkes. And lay my heavy burden down/With Him of Galilee. TRV

Amid the Myrtles. Judah Halevi But the spicery of their savor entrances his scent. HW

Aminta: Chorus I. Torquato Tasso. But unto us the light/Dies once for all; and sleep brings on eternal night. AWP; OBVE

Amintas and Claudia. *Anonymous.* And laught out with a ha, ha, ha, ha, ha, ha, ha,/ha, ha, ha, ha, ha, ha. CoMu

The Amish. William Doreski. and puzzle on the grief of the land. SOTS

The Amish. John Updike. The licensed fools who travel far/To gaze upon these simple folk. OBAL

Amnesiac. Mark Osaki. We don't know if we remember. BrSi

Amnesiac. Sylvia Plath. I am never, never, never coming home! NYBP

Amo, Amas. John O'Keefe. Hic hoc horum genitivo. GBL

Among All Lovely Things My Love Had Been. William Wordsworth. Oh! joy it was for her, and joy for me! GBL; MyFE

Among Blackberries. Michael Waters. the blackberries sweating in their bucket. GeTw

Among Commuters. Jon Swan. reluctantly, as if it had too often/reached its destination. NYP

Among Friends. Greg Kuzma. For they, too, have been on the heights,/ and have come down. AMV-80

Among Hawks. Lance Henson. the reasons/for our being/among them VoR

Among High Hills. William Soutar. ...from them I learn/A living faith– From them alone. PoSH

Among IIis Books. Edith Nesbit. ...to show/How much I care/For the dear memory of what, you know,/You never were. NOBV

Among His Effects We Found a Photograph. Ed Ochester. with a thousand clear answers/to everything. Str

Among Iron Fragments. Tuvia Ruebner. I found you/my wounded face in the wind and my arms open wide. VWA

Among School Children. William Butler Yeats. How can we know the dancer from the dance. AnIL; BLPL; CMoP; CoBMV; DiPo; ForPo; GTBS-P; HAP; InPS; LiTB; LiTM; MBW 1-2; MoAB; MoBrPo; MoVE; NAWM 1-2; NIP; NoAm; NOBE; NoP; OAEL 1-2; OAEP; OxBTC; PPoe; PPP; PrIm; SeCeV; TrGrPo; WeW

Among Sharks. Al Lee. Opens her prehistoric jaw and lunges. AmPA

Among Strangers. William Stafford. We would even die. NNaP

Among the Anthropophagi. Ogden Nash. One's friends are one's sarcophagi. CenHV

Among the Beautiful Pictures. Alice Cary. The one of the old forest/Seemeth the best of all. BLPA

Among the Coffee Cups and Soup Toureens Walked Beauty. Jack Spicer. Counting with kingly eye the subjects of his power/Who sleep with beauty and are unappeased. PeHV

Among the Daffadillies. Giles Farnaby. And loosing, lost both labour, shaft, and/shooting. OAEP

Among the Ferns. Edward Carpenter. Death shall change as the light 'twixt moonset and dawn. WGRP

Among the Finger Lakes. Robert Wallace. shaggy at evening, to drink among the shadowy lakes. GrPl

Among the Firs. Eugene Lee-Hamilton. And slowly up the tree trunk climbs the sun. NOBV

Among the Heather. William Allingham. Love'll warm me as I go through the snow, among the/heather. IrPN

Among the Hills: Prelude. John Greenleaf Whittier. ...Love,/The sole necessity of Earth and Heaven! OxBA; PoEL 1-5

Among the Millet. Archibald Lampman. For ever shepherd you across/The shining field of heaven. CaP; WHW

Among the Narcissi. Sylvia Plath. The narcissi look up like children, quickly and whitely. FaBoMo; FaBoWP; SCV

Among the Orchards. Archibald Lampman. Or cling half-drunken to the rotting peach. PeCV

Among the Pine Trees. Moshe Dor. over pine-tree tops and can no longer/be heard. Although we listen sadly. VWA

"Among the Savages..." Ralph Salisbury. ...thanks/for the gift of corn. STE

Among the Worst of Men. Henry David Thoreau. And we went on to heaven the long way round. LiTA; PoEL 1-5

Among These Turf-Stacks. Louis MacNeice. Or turn blind wantons like the gulls who scream/And rip the edge off any ideal or dream. LiTB; SeCePo; WaP

Among Those Killed in the Dawn Raid Was a Man Aged One Hundred. Dylan Thomas. And a hundred storks perch on the sun's right hand. InPo; MoPo

Amor Dei. *Anonymous.* Thy little child, left learning at Thy knee. BoC

Amor Loci. W. H. Auden. shrugged at, abandoned/by a frivolous worldling,/does not abandon? NOCV

Amor Mundi. Christina Georgina Rossetti. This downhill path is easy, but there's no turning/back. NBM; NoP; PoEL 1-5

Amor Mysticus. Sister Marcela de Carpio. Oh! sweet is the anguish/Of death to me! AWP; CAW; LiTW

Amor Triumphans. Arthur Symons. And will not knock again. BrPo

De Amore. Ernest Christopher Dowson. And let me not blaspheme. OBNC; TrPWD

Amores. Ovid (Publius Ovidius Naso).
But my ambitious ranging mind approves? UnTE
The cause acquits you not, but I that wink. UnTE
I add, "Corinna, don't do this again!" NAs
To cover it, spilt water on the place. UnTE
To me tomorrow constantly deny it. UnTE

Amores. Jay Parini. These afternoons are rare. MAYP

Amoret. Mark Akenside. Sweet Amoret in all her prime. HBV 1-2; OBEV

Amoret. William Congreve. She is the thing that she despises. ViBoPo

Amoretti, I. Edmund Spenser. Leaves, lines, and rymes, seeke her to please alone,/whom if ye please, I care for other none. AAS; ATP; EBEV; OAEL 1-2

Amoretti, II. Edmund Spenser. Which if she graunt, then live, and my love cherish,/If not, die soone, and I with thee will perish AAS

Amoretti, III. Edmund Spenser. Yet in my hart I then both speake and write,/The wonder that my wit cannot endite. AAS; HBV 1-2; OAEP; PoEL 1-5

Amoretti, IV. Edmund Spenser. Prepare your selfe new love to entertaine. AAS

Amoretti, V. Edmund Spenser. Was never in this world ought worthy tride,/Without some spark of such self-pleasing pride. AAS

Amoretti, VI. Edmund Spenser. Then thinke not long in taking litle paine,/To knit the knot, that ever shall remaine. AAS

Amoretti, VII. Edmund Spenser. Such life should be the honor of your light,/Such death the sad ensample of your might. AAS

Amoretti, VIII. Edmund Spenser. Well is he born that may behold you ever. AAS; CABA; HBV 1-2; NoP; OAEP; TrGrPo

Amoretti, IX. Edmund Spenser. Then to the Maker selfe they likest be,/Whose light doth lighten all that here we see. AAS

Amoretti, X. Edmund Spenser. That I may laugh at her in equall sort,/As she doth laugh at me and makes my pain her sport. AAS; NoP

Amoretti, XI. Edmund Spenser. All paine hath end and every war hath peace,/But mine no price nor prayer may surcease. AAS

Amoretti, XII. Edmund Spenser. So Ladie, now to you I doo complaine,/Against your eies that justice I may gaine. AAS

Amoretti, XIII. Edmund Spenser. Yet lowly still vouchsafe to looke on me,/Such lowlinesse shall make you lofty be. AAS

Amoretti, XIV. Edmund Spenser. And if those fayle, fall downe and dy before her,/So dying live, and living do adore her. AAS

Amoretti, XV. Edmund Spenser. But that which fairest is, but few behold,/Her mind adornd with vertues manifold. AAS; HeIP; OAEL 1-2; TrGrPo

Amoretti, XVI. Edmund Spenser. Had she not so doon, sure I had bene slayne,/Yet as it was, I hardly scap't with paine. AAS; OAEL 1-2

Amoretti, XVII. Edmund Spenser. A greater craftsmans hand thereto doth neede,/That can expresse the life of things indeed. AAS

Amoretti, XVIII. Edmund Spenser. So doe I weepe, and wayle, and pleade in vaine,/Whiles she as steele and flint doth still remayne. AAS

Amoretti, XIX. Edmund Spenser. Therefore O love, unless she turn to thee/Ere cuckoo end, let her a rebel be. AAS; OBSC

Amoretti, XX. Edmund Spenser. Fayrer then fayrest, let none ever say,/That ye were blooded in a yeelded pray. AAS

Amoretti, XXI. Edmund Spenser. Thus doth she traine and teach me with her lookes,/Such art of eyes I never read in bookes. AAS

Amoretti, XXII. Edmund Spenser. The which vouchsafe O goddesse to accept,/Amongst thy deerest relicks to be kept. AAS

Amoretti, XXIII. Edmund Spenser. Such labour like the Spyders web I fynd,/Whose fruitlesse worke is broken with least wynd. AAS; CoBE 060

Amoretti, XXIV. Edmund Spenser. But since ye are my scourge, I will entreat/That for my faults ye will me gently beat. AAS; HBV 1-2

Amoretti, XXV. Edmund Spenser. That greater meed at last may turn to me. AAS; EnRePo

Amoretti, XXVI. Edmund Spenser. Why then should I accoumpt of little paine,/That endlesse pleasure shall unto me gaine. AAS

Amoretti, XXVII. Edmund Spenser. Faire be no lenger proud of that shall perish,/But that which shal you make immortall, cherish. AAS

Amoretti, XXVIII. Edmund Spenser. But in your breast his leaf and love embrace. AAS; CABA

Amoretti, XXIX. Edmund Spenser. Then would I decke her head with glorious bayes,/And fill the world with her victorious prayse. AAS

Amoretti, XXX. Edmund Spenser. Such is the power of love in gentle mind,/That it can alter all the course of kind. AAS; FF; TrGrPo

Amoretti, XXXI. Edmund Spenser. But did she know how ill these two accord,/Such cruelty she would have soone abhord. AAS

Amoretti, XXXII. Edmund Spenser. What then remaines but I to ashes burne,/And she to stones at length all frosen turne? AAS

Amoretti, XXXIII. Edmund Spenser. Ceasse then, till she vouchsafe to grawnt me rest,/Or lend you me another living brest. AAS

Amoretti, XXXIV. Edmund Spenser. In secret sorrow and sad pensiveness. AAS; AnFE; CoBE; DiPo; EnLi 1-2; HBV 1-2; OBSC

Amoretti, XXXVI. Edmund Spenser. But by his death which some perhaps will mone,/Ye shall condemned be of many a one. AAS

Amoretti, XXXVII. Edmund Spenser. To covet fetters, though they golden be. AAS; NoP; OBSC; TrGrPo

Amoretti, XXXVIII. Edmund Spenser. Chose rather to be praysed for dooing good,/Then to be blam'd for spilling guiltlesse blood. AAS

Amoretti, XXXIX. Edmund Spenser. More sweet than Nectar or Ambrosiall meat,/Seemd every bit, which thenceforth I did eat. AAS

Amoretti, XL. Edmund Spenser. So my storm-beaten heart likewise is cheered,/With that sunshine when cloudy looks are cleared. AAS; OBSC

Amoretti, XLI. Edmund Spenser. O fayrest fayre let never it be named,/That so fayre beauty was so fowly shamed. AAS; OAEP

Amoretti, XLII. Edmund Spenser. Onely let her abstaine from cruelty,/And doe me not before my time to dy. AAS

Amoretti, XLIII. Edmund Spenser. Wil soone conceive, and learne to construe well. AAS

Amoretti, XLIV. Edmund Spenser. 'Mongst whom the more I seek to settle peace,/The more I find their malice to increase. AAS

Amoretti, XLV. Edmund Spenser. But if your selfe in me ye playne will see,/Remove the cause by which your fayre beames darkned be. AAS

Amoretti, XLVI. Edmund Spenser. Enough it is for one man to sustaine,/The stormes, which she alone on me doth raine. AAS

Amoretti, XLVII. Edmund Spenser. And think they die with pleasure, live with pain. AAS; TrGrPo

Amoretti, XLVIII. Edmund Spenser. Yet live for ever, though against her will,/And speake her good, though she requite it ill. AAS

Amoretti, XLIX. Edmund Spenser. Such mercy shal you make admyred to be,/So shall you live by giving life to me. AAS

Amoretti, L. Edmund Spenser. Then my lyfes Leach doe you your skill reveale,/And with one salve both hart and body heale. AAS

Amoretti, LI. Edmund Spenser. Onely my paines wil be the more to get her,/But having her, my joy wil be the greater. AAS

Amoretti, LII. Edmund Spenser. So I her absens will my penaunce make,/That of her presens I my meed may take. AAS

Amoretti, LIII. Edmund Spenser. As in their Maker ye them best may see. AAS; EnRePo

Amoretti, LIV. Edmund Spenser. What then can move her? if nor merth nor mone,/She is no woman, but a senceless stone. AAS; NoP; OAEL 1-2

Amoretti, LV. Edmund Spenser. Then, since to heaven ye likened are the best,/Be like in mercy as in all the rest. AAS; HBV 1-2; TrGrPo

Amoretti, LVI. Edmund Spenser. That ship, that tree, and that same beast am I,/Whom ye doe wreck, doe ruine, and destroy. AAS

Amoretti, LVII. Edmund Spenser. Make peace therefore, and graunt me timely grace./That al my wounds wil heale in little space. AAS

Amoretti, LVIII. Edmund Spenser. That to yourself ye most assured are? AAS; EnRePo

Amoretti, LIX. Edmund Spenser. Most happy she that most assured doth rest,/But he most happy who such one loves best. AAS

Amoretti, LX. Edmund Spenser. But let my loves fayre Planet short her wayes/This year ensuing, or else short my dayes. AAS

Amoretti, LXI. Edmund Spenser. Such heavenly formes ought rather worship be,/Then dare be lov'd by men of meane degree. AAS

Amoretti, LXII. Edmund Spenser. So likewise love cheare you your heavy spright,/And chaunge old yeares annoy to new delight. AAS; OBSC

Amoretti, LXIII. Edmund Spenser. All paines are nothing in respect of this,/All sorrowes short that gaine eternall blisse. AAS; EBEV; FaBoEn; OAEL 1-2; OAEP; OBSC

Amoretti, LXIV. Edmund Spenser. Such fragrant flowres doe give most odorous smell,/But her sweet odour did them all excell. AAS; OAEL 1-2

Amoretti, LXV. Edmund Spenser. There fayth doth fearlesse dwell in brasen towre,/And spotlesse pleasure builds her sacred bowre. AAS

Amoretti, LXVI. Edmund Spenser. Yet since your light hath once enlumind me,/With my reflex yours shall encreased be. AAS

Amoretti, LXVII. Edmund Spenser. Strange thing me seemd to see a beast so wyld,/So goodly wonne with her owne will beguyld. AAS; EnRePo; HeIP; NoP; OAEP; PoEL 1-5; TrGrPo

Amoretti, LXVIII. Edmund Spenser. Love is the lesson which the Lord us taught. AAS; HAP; HBV 1-2; InPS; NOCV; NoP; OxBoCh; SeCeV; TrPWD

Amoretti, LXIX. Edmund Spenser. Gotten at last with labour and long toil AAS; CoBE

Amoretti, LXX. Edmund Spenser. For none can call again the passed time. AAS; AWP; CABA; FaBoEn; HAP; HBV 1-2; InPS; NoP; OBSC; SeCeV

Amoretti, LXXI. Edmund Spenser. And all thensforth eternall peace shall see,/Betweene the Spyder and the gentle Bee. AAS

Amoretti, LXXII. Edmund Spenser. But here on earth to have such heaven's bliss. AAS; EG; EnLi 1-2; OAEP; OBSC

Amoretti, LXXIII. Edmund Spenser. Him lodging in your bosom to have lent. AAS; CoBE

Amoretti, LXXIV. Edmund Spenser. Ye three Elizabeths for ever live,/That three such graces did unto me give. AAS

Amoretti, LXXV. Edmund Spenser. Our love shall live, and later life renew. AAS; AnFE; AWP; EBEV; HAP; HBV 1-2; HeIP; InPS; NoP; OAEL 1-2; OAEP; SeCeV

Amoretti, LXXVI. Edmund Spenser. Sweet thoughts I envy your so happy rest,/Which oft I wisht, yet never was so blest. AAS

Amoretti, LXXVII. Edmund Spenser. Her brest that table was so richly spredd,/My thoughts the guests, which would thereon have fedd. AAS

Amoretti, LXXVIII. Edmund Spenser. Ceasse then myne eyes, to seeke her selfe to see,/And let my thoughts behold her selfe in mee. AAS

Amoretti, LXXIX. Edmund Spenser. All other fayre lyke flowres untymely fade. AAS; AWP; EnLi 1-2; HBV 1-2; NoP

Amoretti, LXXX. Edmund Spenser. But let her prayses yet be low and meane,/Fit for the handmayd of the Faery Queene. AAS

Amoretti, LXXXI. Edmund Spenser. But this the worke of harts astonishment. AAS; NoP

Amoretti, LXXXII. Edmund Spenser. Whose lofty argument uplifting me,/Shall lift you up unto an high degree. AAS; HeIP

Amoretti, LXXXIII. Edmund Spenser. All this worlds glory seemeth vayne to me,/And all theyr shewes but shadowes saving she. AAS

Amoretti, LXXXIV. Edmund Spenser. Onely behold her rare perfection,/And blesse your fortunes fayre election. AAS

Amoretti, LXXXV. Edmund Spenser. Which when as fame in her shrill trump shal thunder/Let the world chose to envy or to wonder. AAS

Amoretti, LXXXVI. Edmund Spenser. But joyous hours do fly away too fast. AAS; EG

Amoretti, LXXXVII. Edmund Spenser. So sorrow still doth seeme too long to last,/But joyous houres doo fly away too fast. AAS

Amoretti, LXXXVIII. Edmund Spenser. But with such brightnesse whylest I fill my mind,/I starve my body and mine eyes doe blynd. AAS

Amoretti, LXXXIX. Edmund Spenser. And dead my life, that wants such lively bliss. AAS; EG

Amoris Exsul. Arthur Symons. And I would that my ship went down within sight of/the shore! OBNC; PBBP; VLP

The Amorist. *Anonymous.* I'd turn your snow to flame. UnTE

An Amorous Dialogue between John and His Mistress. *Anonymous.* I know when I'me well, I was never so mad,/To forsake a good thing when 'tis to be had. CoMu; UnTE

The Amorous War: Time. Jasper Mayne. Let the harmonious spheres in music roll! EG

The Amorous Worms' Meat. Petrarch (Francesco Petrarca). My gray-haired style would have broken a stone/With words, and made it weep from tenderness. LiTW

Les Amours. Charles Cotton. I'll be content to take them both. HBV 1-2

Amours de Voyage. Arthur Hugh Clough.

     Ah, good Heaven, but I would I were out far away from the/pother! FaBoPV

     All have been seized everywhere for the use of this dreadful/Mazzini. FaBoPV

     Am I to turn for this unto thee, great Chapel of Sixtus? OBNC

     Brings him with gold to the shrine, brings him in arms to the/gate? OBNC

     Dreamt of a sword at my side and a battle-horse underneath/me. FaBoPV

     O happy England, and oh great glory of self-laudation. OBSV

     On the whole, we conclude the Romans won't do it, and I/shan't. FaBoPV

     Under the vine-trellis laid, O my beloved, with thee! FaBoPP; OBNC

     Waiting till Oudinot enter, to reinstate Pope and Tourist. FaBoPP; GTBS-P; OBNC

     We are so prone to these things with our terrible notions/of duty. GTBS-P

     When from Janiculan heights thundered the cannon of France.' NOBV

     Wholly unworthy the head or the heart of Your Own Correspondent? EBEV; OBSV

     Will you have us your slaves to lie to you, flatter and–leave/you? OBNC

     You may believe when it tells you the French FaBoPV

Amphibian. Amy Clampitt. where motion's once/immobile artifact/had been. SUW

Amphibious Crocodile. John Crowe Ransom. And quite invisible but for the end of his nose. AnAmPo; OBAL

Amphimachos the Dandy. Vincent McHugh. confused the drama with the true NePoAm-2

Amphitrion. John Dryden. Love that's true, is Love for ever. CavP

The Amphora. Fyodor Sologub. A careless touch should pour unbidden/Its bitterness upon my breast. AWP

Ample make this bed. Emily Dickinson. Let no sunrise' yellow noise/Interrupt this ground. AtBAP; MoAB; MoAmPo; OxBA; PoEL 1-5

The Ampler Circumscription. William Baylebridge. The All-wise no offering takes till man hath writ/The goal, the road, the yea and nay, on it. BoAV

The Amputation. Helen Sorrells. And not to think of it any more. DFF

The Amputee Soldier. Philip Dacey. I will make signs/In the air. Even I/shall not understand them. GOYP

Amsterdam. Jean Garrigue. Intervals then, only intervals when the clair of the pane looked through, not ever ascendant... TAP

Amsterdam. Francis Jammes. Under a gable: Here lived Francis Jammes. AWP

Amsterdam Letter. Jean Garrigue. Horse, sky, cow, tree, thank you, I mean,/Beauty, and love. NYBP

Amsterdam Street Scene, 1972. Raphael Rudnik. he gets behind, driving off–into the city's secret heart. AMV-81

Amtrak. Elliot Fried. ...All night I'm rocked beneath cold stars/to a destination too well known to fear. PPJ

Amurrika! (parody). Philip Appleman. will begin in the year of that Lightning Eternal Paradise Epiphany/Apocalyse! BXAP

Amusing Our Daughters. Carolyn Kizer. Sending our messages over the mountains and waters. VGW

Amy. James Matthew Legare. My Amy is the only leaf/In all that forest sear. AA

Amy Margaret. William Allingham. Dearer twenty-thousand-fold/Than gold, is Amy Margaret. BiCB

Amy Wentworth. John Greenleaf Whittier. Beyond its own sweet will! BeLS

Amynta. Gilbert Elliot. The moments neglected return not again. HBV 1-2

Amyntas Led Me to a Grove. Aphra Behn. Oh! who can guess the rest? ErPo

L'an Trentiesme de Mon Eage. Archibald MacLeish. And by what way shall I go back?   AmLP; APA; LiTM; MoVE; NePA; NoAm; NOBA

Ana(Mary-Army)gram. George Herbert. In whom the Lord of Hosts did pitch his tent!   CABA; OAEL 1-2

Anabasis. Rodney Nelson. A solo clarinet in western wind.   AMV-81

Anabasis. St.-John (Alexis Saint-Léger Léger) Perse.
...And some there are who have knowl/edge thereof...   LiTW
the most rapt god-drunken,/drawing to our dockyards eternal keels. AtBAP
(The shadow of a great bird falls on my face.) AtBAP

Anabasis. Eithne Wilkins. confess, laconically:/"Hard."   NeBP

Anabasis, IV. Saint-John Perse.   -profession/of his father: dealer in scent-bottles.   AtBAP; OBVE

Anachronism. Oliver St. John Gogarty. The great dark beggar roared again.   FYAP

Anacreon's Dove. Samuel Johnson. I have chatter'd like a pye.   AWP

Anacreon to the Sophist. B. H. Then go rolling home to Hades,/Roses round each lovely brow.   InMe

Anacreontea: Love. Anonymous. Love tunes my Heart just to my strings. OBVE

Anacreontea: The Cheat of Cupid. Anonymous. Adieu, mine Host, Adieu,/Ile leave thy heart a dying.   OBVE

Anacreontea: The Grasshopper. Anonymous. Oh how near thy happy state/Comes the Gods to imitate!   OBVE

Anacreontea: Young Men Dancing. Anonymous. For his Heart belies his Haires.   OBVE

Anacreontic. Austin Clarke. And unpetalled the rose-bud from Paestum. NOBI

Anacreontic. Robert Herrick.
For I know, in the tombs/There's no carousing.   CaPo; OAEP; OxBoLi
Next day/We may/See erected. CaPo

Anacreontic, On Parting with a little Child. Samuel Wesley. Age in woe and wisdom grey/Vainly mourns for them that play.   NOEC

Anacreontic to Flip. Royall Tyler. It's due on swop, for pie-bald mare. OBAL

Anacreontics. Abraham Cowley. Tho' men say thou bring'st the Spring. OBEV

Anactoria (excerpt). Algernon Charles Swinburne. Thick darkness and the insuperable sea.   AtBAP; ViBoPo

Anadarko John. Carroll Arnett. "Nom. But she/taught me not to/piss on my fingers."   VoR

Anaesthesia. Jean Valentine. when you murder things like that/who comes in and takes over   TAP

Analogue of Unity in Multeity. Richard Eberhart. A point of agate reference.   NoAm

Analogy. Brian Higgins. How can they know that I long to leave? FaBoTw

Analysands. Dudley Randall. they drop asleep on sofa, chair or floor. BPo

Analyst. David Fisher. whose words are as mixed with comfort and terror/as rain on the sea.   NPGG

Anarchist. Anthony Cronin. And proudly and carelessly ride for a fall. CIP

Anarchist. Norman Dugdale. ...You dredge/The darkness still that irrigates my/day.   BoAnP

An Anarchist's Letter. Harald Wyndham. Mabel–when is the bomb set to PoL

Anasazi at Mesa Verde. Reg Saner. our singing, our hands, our stream. NPAW

Anastasia McLaughlin. Tom Paulin. He watches the mills prosper and grow derelict,/As he starts his journey to the Finland Station.   FaBoIP

Anastasis. Albert E. S. Smythe. The man you may be tonight/If you turn to the Valley of Light.   CaP

Anath. Haim Guri. I pass and gather your bones into my pack,/into the tomb of my memory.   VWA

Anathema of Cats. John Skelton. That slew so cruelly,/My lytell pretty sparowe.   PCat

The Anathemata. David Jones.
He would berth us/to schedule.   FaBoTw
I am your Bread? AtBAP
They come–and they go, captain. EBEV
toward the last phase/of our dear West.) NoAm

Anatole France at Eighty. Gladys Oaks. A generation laughs...and lights again.   AnAmPo

Anatomy. Gilbert Sorrentino. ...sit with them/once in a while.   PoL

The Anatomy of Angels. Alden Nowlan. marking the bed they'd shared, with a great stone.   PeCV

The Anatomy of Baseness: To The Detracted. John Andrews. And of heaven's joys itself did disinherit.   EiL

The Anatomy of Happiness. Ogden Nash. A condition which I could face with equanimity.   LiTA; TAP

The Anatomy of Humor. Morris Bishop. To comfort you and to lecture me/For trying, she'll say, to be funny.   InMe; NLV

Anatomy of Monotony. Wallace Stevens. And this the spirit sees and is aggrieved.   BiP

An Anatomy of the World. The First Anniversary. John Donne. And all the world would be one dying swan,/To sing her funeral praise, and vanish then.   JCP

Ancestor. Jimmy Santiago Baca. out of the long felt nights and days of yesterday.   LFAC

Ancestor. Thomas Kinsella. ...through the red hangings/to the scullery, and down to the back room.   BIrV; FaBoIP; NOBI

The Ancestor. Dave Smith. but cold Buck's merciless, locked to the Eagles. SM

The Ancestors. Anita Barrows. your hand on the softness/of the world, will make/of nakedness/also a prayer.   VWA

The Ancestors. John Peale Bishop. Of passions rivalling the sculptured tomb!   PoA

The Ancestors. Christopher Middleton. they march us out with, from one/to the next lost place.   NMP

Ancestors. Dudley Randall. dreamed up in fantasies/of bygone glory. BPo; CNA

Ancestors. Harold Schimmel. and convenience such as ten poor Jewish mammas/could not hope to give him.   VWA

The Ancestors. Judith Wright. that feeds the living, thousand-lighted stream/up which we toiled into this timeless dream.   BoAV

Ancestors' Graves in Kurakawa. Joy Kogawa. Accepting the pebbles that melt through my eyes.   BrSi

Ancestral Faces. Kwesi Brew. They have not changed!   PBA

Ancestral Weight. Alfonsina Storni. ...and my/soul just can't bear/all that weight.   WPOW

Ancestry. Louis Daniel Brodsky. Asking me for my body to inhabit again. AMV-81

Ancestry. Stephen Crane. At least, for the little man/Who stood against the mountains.   AA

Anchises. Blanaid Salkeld. Sometimes, in my sad breast,/I wish him dead, best.   OxBI

Anchor. Anonymous. Strength in the struggle. Ask me my name!   AnOE

The Anchor's Aweigh. Anonymous. Farewell, fare you well, my own true love.   ShS

Anchorage. Joy Harjo. those who were never meant/to survive?   STE; TWSS

Anchorage. Pat Wilson. Down twenty, thirty feet below.   AnNZ

The Anchorsmiths. Charles Dibdin. To save from adverse winds and waves the gallant British Fleet.   NOEC

Ancient. George William Russell. To a whiteness older than Time. SeCePo

Ancient and Modern Rome (excerpt). George Keate. To melt the stubborn heart, and teach the eye/To shed the gen'rous tear for other's woe.   OBTV

The Ancient Briton: The Dance of the Sword. Anonymous. Waves, oak, earth and oak!   WaaP

An Ancient Castle. William Morris. Many dames with footfall light.... SeCePo

The Ancient Couple on Lu Mountain. Mark Van Doren. ...How deep this pool is/Only the dark cranes know that never come.   VGW

An Ancient Custom. Anatoly Steiger. And all this together is called love. VWA

An Ancient Degree. Bernadette Mayer. An allusion of degree to the wife of sudden passion.   ANYP

The Ancient Doctrine. Robert Browning. Give earth yourself, go up for gain above!   OBVV

An Ancient Gesture. Edna St. Vincent Millay. He learned it from Penelope.../Penelope, who really cried.   NMM

Ancient Historian. Chris Wallace-Crabbe. And the lean Goths encroaching silently.   PoAu 1-2

Ancient History. Arthur Guiterman. They started the fuss/And left it to us!   OBCA

The Ancient Law. Andre Spire. –Your ears are made only to hear lamentations that rise from/the four corners of the earth.   VWA

Ancient Lights. Austin Clarke. Take half our heavens with a roar.   BIrV; CMoP; IPY; NMP; OxBI

Ancient Lullaby. Gerald Griffin. Sullen sounds and gloomy seeming/Soon shall mingle in thy dreaming.   IrPN

The Ancient Mansion. George Crabbe. And every changing season of the year/Stamps on the scene its English character.   FaBoPP

Ancient Murderess Night. Anna Margolin. and sing and sing and sing to life/my praise of death.   VWA

Ancient Music. Ezra Pound. Sing goddamm, sing goddamm, DAMM. BXAP; DBV; FaBoCo; FaBoPa; FF; HeIP; LiTM; NePA; NLV; OBAL; OxBA; PPON; SpRo; TW

Ancient of Days. Anthony Rudolf. remains but one oak/broader/than six/men in a ring.   VWA

Ancient of Days, Who Sittest Throned in Glory. William Croswell Doane. Thy love and favor, kept to us always.   AA; AH

The Ancient One. Charles Culhane. for I saw it more than once/and a city of light many times. LFAC

An Ancient Prayer. Thomas H. B. Webb. To get some happiness from life and pass it on to other folk. BBV; BLPA; FaBoBe

An Ancient Prophecy. Philip Freneau. And your Lion shall growl, but hardly bite/more.– PAH

Ancient Quatrain. *Anonymous.* Their love makes them forget all time. HW

The Ancient Sacrifice. Mahlon Leonard Fisher. About the blood-stained shrine of bygone wars! AnAmPo

The Ancient Sage. Alfred, Lord Tennyson. She finds the fountain where they wailed "Mirage!" WGRP

Ancient Songs of the Women of Fez. *Anonymous.* I will paint my eyes with tears instead of khol. BoWoP

The Ancient Speech. Kathleen Raine. Our words keep no faith with the soul of the world. PoSH

The Ancient Thought. Watson Kerr. Surely God is nigh. TRV; WGRP

An Ancient to Ancients. Thomas Hardy. Nay, rush not: time serves: we are going,/Gentlemen. CMoP; CoBMV; GTBS-P; LiTM; MoPo; MoVE; OxBTC

An Ancient Virgin. George Crabbe. What shall I do (she cried) my Peace of Mind,/To gain in dying, and to die resign'd?' OBNC

Ancient Wisdom, Rather Cosmic. Ezra Pound. Hence his contentment. NOBA

And. Robert Creeley. They are all dead now. LCAP

And. Ricardo Gonsalves. (but remember to pay the bill). FIA

And Again (parody). Humphrey Evans. I'll wake up by and by/And play squash for an hour. BXAP

And All the While the Sky Is Falling... Lora Dunetz. It might as well be smoke and ashes–it isn't worth a/farthing. NePoAm

And Already the Minutes. Conrad Aiken. And know you still the best. InPo

And Angling, Too. George Gordon, Lord Byron. The quaint, old, cruel coxcomb, in his gullet/Should have a hook, and a small trout to pull it. SD

And Art Thou Come, Blest Babe? *Anonymous.* The more it needs Thee, and the more I love. OxBoCh

And As For Me. Geoffrey Chaucer. For fere of nyght, so hateth she derknesse!..... CH

A and B. C. H. Sisson. Perhaps all will be well. OxBC

And Backwards. *Anonymous.* And C, B, A. OxNR

And Can the Physician Make Sick Men Well. *Anonymous.* And columbine. AtBAP; ELP

And Canst Thou, Sinner, Slight. Abby Bradley Hyde. Will fill thee with surprise. AH

And Death Shall Have No Dominion. Dylan Thomas. And death shall have no dominion. ACV; CMoP; EaLo; ExPo; LiTM; MoAB; MoBrPo; MoRP; MoVE; NeBP; NoAm; OAEP; PPoe; SeCePo

And Did the Animals? Mark Van Doren. Or did they even dream, those specimen souls? VGW

And Did Those Feet in Ancient Time. William Blake. Till we have built Jerusalem/In England's green and pleasant land. FaBoCh; FaBV; HAP; LoGBV; MAT; NAWM 1-2; PoRA; PrIm

And Don't Bother Telling Me Anything. Cesar Vallejo. or sitting drunk in my coffin... EAS

And Dust to Dust. Charles David Webb. He always had a shrewd head for business. NePoAm-2

And Fall Shall Sit in Judgment. Audre Lorde. that love in all seasons/is false, but the same. NNP

And Forgetful of Europe. Geoffrey Grigson. And forgetful of Europe, walked to bed/In the warm wind from the mountain. OBTV

And Forgive Us Our Trespasses. Aphra Behn. Forgive, O Lord, forgive our Trespasses. EBEV

And Grow. John Hay. and grow like birds, from ugliness to wings. WaP

And Happy Am I. Syd Scroggie. And happy am I. PoSH

And Have the Bright Immensities. Howard Chandler Robbins. There heavenly splendors shine. AH

And He Answered Them Nothing. Richard Crashaw. 'Tis made by Nothing now againe. MePo

And His Name Shall Be Called Wonderful. Martha Snell Nicholson. Wonderful name of our wonderful Lord! BePJ

And I Am Old to Know. Pauline Hanson. to see where death was, I look back. TAP

And "I Know Why the Caged Bird Sings": A Villanelle. George, Jr Mosby. it whips us whips us whips us dazed. LFAC

And if an eye may save or slay. Sir Thomas Wyatt. Then fears not the eye to show the heart. FCP; SiPS

And If at Last. Louise Labe. Knowing in life no lovelier thing than death. LiTW

And If I Turn. Marilyn Bowering. Remember what else there was,/and warm your lightened body in it. CaPN

And in Her Morning. Jessica Powers. And in her morning I can see Thy face. ISi

And in That Drowning Instant. Abraham Moses Klein. For the third time my body rises/and finds the good, the lasting shore! VWA

And in the Hanging Gardens. Conrad Aiken. One drop of wine, wherewith wild rain has/mixed. MAPA; MoAB; MoAmPo

And Is It Night? *Anonymous.* O dearest life! joy's sweet! O sweetest love! EIL; GBL

And It Came to Pass at Midnight. Yannai. And to midday change the/midnight. TrJP

And Jesus Don't Have Much Use for His Old Suitcase Anymore. Tom Kryss. like empty parachutes/these ballads/without men. NeAC

And Jesus Wept. Sir Samuel Egerton Brydges. That we, obedient to Thy word,/May weep with those that weep. BePJ

And Lightly, Like the Flowers. Pierre Ronsard. And lightly, like the flowers. AWP

And Lo, the Star! Molly Anderson Haley. This Holy Night and make His rule your own. PGD

...And Mr. Ferritt. Judith Wright. Nothing will cure it. MoBrPo

And Now... John Basil Boothroyd. Can't someone have the rumba banned?/(Shicker-shick) FiBHP

And Now a Fig for the Lower House. Patrick Cary. For spent is his last groat. JCP

And Now Farley Is Going to Sing While I Drink a Glass of Water! Albert Goldbarth. saying something for us. GeTw

And Now, Kind Friends, What I Have Wrote. Julia A. Moore. And not criticize as some have done/Hitherto herebefore. FaBoCo; FiBHP

And of Columbus. Horace Gregory. And in Havana under the Southern Cross, all that is his/is where his bones lie. OFD

And of Laughter That Was a Changeling. Elizabeth Rendall. But at dusk when I lifted her, laughing, laughing,/Over the brook–I knew. HBMV

And on My Eyes Dark Sleep by Night. Michael (Katherine Bradley and Edith Cooper) Field. Put me on Phaon's lips to rest,/And cheat the cruel day! OBMV

And on My Return. Haim Guri. But I am not an angel nor have I come in a dream. VWA

And on This Shore. M. Carl Holman. On what does this shadow feed/And shall it not fade? AmNP; PoBA

And One Shall Live in Two. Jonathan Henderson Brooks. And one shall live in two each year. PoNe

And Only Our Shadow Walks with Us. Eithne Wilkins. big love or angler's luck. NeBP

And She Washed His Feet with Her Tears,... Sir Edward Sherburne. Pearl in her tears, and in her hair/Offers thee gold. CBEP; MeLP; OBS; OxBoCh

And So Men Say, I Love Thee! Derwent Coleridge. With which I sing to sleep my restless love for thee! CBEP

And So Should You. *Anonymous.* Then rises up anew, to take/The desert road... STF

And So the Day Drops By. Frederick Goddard Tuckerman. Hears the dry thunder roll, and knows no rain. AnNE

And That's All. *Anonymous.* And put him on the wall,/And that's all. OxNR

And That Will Be Heaven. Evangeline Paterson. never turning away/again EBCP

And the Bitter Storm Augments; the Wild Winds Wage. John Josselyn. Art stood amaz'd in Ambiguity. SCAP

And the Cock Begins to Crow. Richard K. Avery. ...oh-h-h/Yes, the cock begins to crow. AH

And the Days Are Not Full Enough. Ezra Pound. And life slips by like a field mouse/Not shaking the grass. PCP

And the Dead. Sean Jennett. perfection in the final negative. NeBP

And the Earth Rebelled. Yuri Suhl. The thunder of a Jewish Fighter's/gun! TrJP

And the Gas Chamber Drones in the Distance. Greg Forker. too much water behind the dam. LFAC

And the Old Folks Said. Diane Mei Lin Mark. floating/down/stream. BrSi

...And the Old Women Gathered. Mari E. Evans. the sound of it/stayed in our ears... BlSi; NNP; PoBA

And the Same Words. David Ignatow. ...the same words/that began love/end it/with changed emphasis. NNaP

And the Seventh Dream in the Dream of Isis. David Gascoyne. and glass were the faces in the last looking-glass. EAS

And the Silver Turns into Night. Nathan Yonathan. And the next final flowering/Into a night-bird's last flight. VWA

And the Winner Is. Greg Forker. and my stepfather dropped dead during a/photo-finish at Santa Anita. LFAC

And the World's Face. Julian Symons. They tell me we shall win the bloody war. WaP

And Then It Rained. Mark Van Doren. And the waterfall, thinning,/Was bright as glass. BoNaP

And Then No More. James Clarence Mangan. Would beat anew a little while, and then no more. AnIV; BlrV; BLPA; IrPN

And Then the Sun. Pradip Sen. Ran down the hill. ACV

And Then There. Frantisek Halas. Inalienable. LiTW

And Then What? Dave Kelly. "Coors," I said, that being/what I seemed to be/drinking. PoL

And there is nothing at all–neither fear. Natalya Gorbanyevskaya. –my lover's shoulder/still smells to me of pine shavings. BoWoP

And There shall Be No More Death (excerpt). Ruth Gilbert. And know you dead, yet cannot take death in. AnNZ

And There Was a Great Calm. Thomas Hardy. And again the Spirit of Pity whispered, Why? CMoP; FaBoRV; LiTM; MoRP; OAEL 1-2

And There Will I Be Buried. Thomas Davidson. And around and over me/Winds and clouds for ever going. BSV

And This Is Love. Paula Reingold. And everything we do is love. IHMS

And This Is My Father. Marcus J. Grapes. with the relish/of a gypsy. AMV-80

And This of All My Hopes. Emily Dickinson. Never a Worm so confident/Bored at so brave a Root ForPo

And Thou, Dalhousie, the Great God of War. *Anonymous.* Lieutenant-Colonel to the Earl of Mar. FaBoCo

And Three Hundred and Sixty-Six in Leap Year. Ogden Nash. ...and then I will die either of laughing or of a/clean cut throat. NePA

And Through the Caribbean Sea. Margaret Danner. or any style of any age or any place or name. BPo

And Thus in Nineveh. Ezra Pound. As lesser men drink wine. PP; VGW

And Timid, Funny, Brisk Little Bunny. Christina Georgina Rossetti. Winks his nose and sits all sunny. TiPo

And to the Young Man. Merrill Moore. Over which nymphs and under which naiads dream. MoAmPo

And Tomorrow Wend Our Ways. *Anonymous.* For tonight together billet,/ And tomorrow wend our ways. WTO

And Truly It Is a Most Glorious Thing. William Bradford. And marvellous to them his works have been. AH

And Ut Pictura Poesis Is Her Name. John Ashbery. ...so that understanding/May begin, and in doing so be undone. InPS

And Was Not Improved. Lerone Jr. Bennett. and wondered again/why anyone bothered. CNA; PoBA

And We Conquered. Rob Penny. our children turned to us & said/"umph! dig it!" PoBA

And What About the Children. Audre Lorde. nor give a damn/whose wife/I am. PoBA

And What Is Love? Misunderstanding, Pain. J. V. Cunningham. Distinguished, and familiar, and aloof. HoPM

And What of Me? Liz Sohappy Bahe. but what of me? CDW

And What Shall You Say? Joseph Seamon, Jr. Cotter. And, brother,what shall you say? BANP; CDC; PoBA; PoNe

And What Sordello Would See There. Robert Browning. Having that once drunk sweetness to the dregs. MyFE

And What with the Blunders... Kenneth Patchen. there are so many little dyings that it doesn't matter which of/them is death. NaP

And When I Am Entombed. Ralph Waldo Emerson. For fear of human eyes swerved from his plan. ViBoPo

And When I Lamented. Heinrich Heine. You flourish my trumpet all the time. TrJP

And When the Green Man Comes. John Haines. exalted in/the streaming rain. ConAP; NCSH

And When the Prince Came. Robert Silliman Hillyer. Sleep, Beloved, safe for ever/From the one who loved too much. DFT

And When the Revolution Came. Carolyn M. Rodgers. and while we're on our knees, at that. GP

And When They Fall. James J. Montague. She's mandatory of a cow beside the Golden Horn! HBMV

And Where Do You Stand on the National Question? Tom Paulin. he's a bit thick–not a high-flyer–/but he'll do the trick. FaBoIP

And While We Are Waiting. Carolyn M. Rodgers. while we are waiting.../ let us love JB

And Who Has Seen a Fair Alluring Face. George Peele. To thy renown, I paint what 'longs thereto.) ErPo

And with March a Decade in Bolinas. Joanne Kyger. Great Breath, I give you, Great Breath! APU

And Would You See My Mistress' Face? Thomas Campion. And this is what my soul pursueth. OAEP

And Yet. (or Molodovski) Kadya, (or Kadia) Molodovsky. that aims me/ where I will go/and will arrive,/my dears. VWA

And Yet–. Arthur B. Rhinow. And yet He loves me,/Tenderly and true. BLRP

And Yet–. Errol B. Sloan. And yet–He of the pierced palm/Will point the way. BLRP

And Yet We Are Here! Karl Wolfskehl. Then, when the trumpet's holy Yes/rings clear,/We shall be here! TrJP

And You Are There. Tom Clark. Maybe they're Wally Pipp's LiSp

And You As Well Must Die, Beloved Dust. Edna St. Vincent Millay. Or how beloved above all else that dies. FPL; PoLf; PoRA; TAP

And You, Helen. Edward ("Edward Eastaway") Thomas. And myself, too, if I could find/Where it lay hidden and it proved kind. BoLoP

The Andalusian Sereno. Francis Saltus Saltus. And the Sereno knows that he has seen/The spectre of the Past,the ghost of Spain. AA

Andante, Ma Non Assai. Rufinus Domesticus. Just then the dearest of wives is a joyless problem. ErPo; LiTW

The Andante of Snakes. Arthur Symons. Then these fat, foul, unbreathing, moving/things/Droop back to stagnant immobility. VLP

Andonis, My Daughter. Thomas Love Peacock. Andonis is the spring song, me-na-wah– VoR

Andraitx–Pomegranate Flowers. D. H. Lawrence. red flamelets here and there reveal/a man, a woman there. NoAm; NoP

Andre. Charlotte Fiske Bates. With Andre-sparing mercy, still more dear/ Had been his name–if that, indeed, could be! MC; PAH

Andre. Gwendolyn Brooks. They were the one I always had! TiPo

Andre Chenier. Marina Tsvetayeva. And no one living looks quite human. FaBoPV

Andre's Request to Washington. Nathaniel Parker Willis. I ask that I may perish/By a soldier's death! MC; PAH

Andre's Ride. A. H. Beesly. Ay, would to God that day were back/When Andre rode to Pont-du-lac! HBV 1-2

Andrea Del Sarto. Robert Browning. Again the Cousin's whistle! Go, my Love. ATP; CTC; DiPo; EnL; HBV 1-2; MaVP; NOBV; NoP; OAEL 1-2; OAEP; PoEL 1-5; VLP; WHA

Andrew. Thomas William Parsons He was our peacemaker, who mid the storm/Of the great conflict, served the Prince/of Peace. AA

Andrew Bardeen. *Anonymous.* If he can reign king over all dry land,/I can reign king o'er the sea. BFSS

Andrew Jackson. Stephen Vincent Benét. Old Hickory,/The pride of the frontier. InMe

Andrew Jackson. Martha Keller. Andrew Jackson–hickory wood! AmFN; MaC

Andrew Jackson's Speech. Robert Bly. His voice rose in the noisy streets of Detroit. ConAP

Andrew Lammie. *Anonymous.* For the love o thee now I maun die;/I come, my bonny Annie!' ESPB

Andrew M'Crie. Robert Fuller Murray. With a volume of notes on its knee/Is the spectre of Andrew M"Crie. CenHV; FaBoCo

Andrew Magrath's Reply to John O'Tuomy. Andrew Magrath. But your thoughts are all guileful and gloomy! OnYI

Andrew Rose. *Anonymous.* Never treat a British sailor/Like they did young Andrew Rose. OBSS

Andrew Rykman's Prayer (excerpt). John Greenleaf Whittier. Until all things sweet and good/Seem my natural habitude. TrPWD; TRV

Andrew's Bedtime Story. Ian Serraillier. Tripped me up, and I cracked my head. DuDa

Andromache. Euripides. Crossed over a storm, and rained down murder. WaaP

Andromache's Wedding. Sappho. and sang of Hektor and Andromache like gods. BoWoP

Andromeda. Thomas Bailey Aldrich. A legend's shadow shall not move you so! AA

Andromeda. Robert Browning. ...secure that God/Will come in thunder from the stars to save her. OBRV

Andromeda. Gerard Manley Hopkins. With Gorgon's gear and barebill, thongs and fangs. EBEV; LiTB; VLP

Andromeda. James Jeffrey Roche. O Ireland! O my country! he comes to/ break thy chain! AA; HBV 1-2

Andromeda forgot. Sappho. Even in Hades/I am with you. BoWoP

Andy-Diana DNA Letter. Andrew Weiman. to dance & cry,/thank life,/ and die./Love,/Andy HAP

Andy's Gone with Cattle. Henry Lawson. God grant 'twill bring us Andy. PoAu 1-2

Ane Ballat of Our Lady. William Dunbar. Thy birth has with his blude/ Fra fall mortall, originall,/Us raunsound on the rude. EBEV; OxBS

Ane Sang of the Birth of Christ, with the Tune of Baw Lula Low. *Anonymous.* The gracious gift of this New Year. BSV

Ane Satire of the Three Estaitis (excerpt). Sir David Lyndsay. Where thou hangs on that pin. GoTS; OBSV

Ane Supplication in Contemptioun of Syde Taillis. Sir David Lyndsay. Nane suld fra that exemptit be/Except the Queenis Majesty. GoTS

Ane to Anither. Duncan Glen. ayont ony dout/–in my mind! PoSH

Anecdote for Fathers. William Wordsworth. Could I but teach the hundredth part/Of what from thee I learn. EnRP

Anecdote from William IV Street. D. J. Enright. "An image of Jesus Christ approximately this high." OxBC

Anecdote of 2 A.M. John Wain. She dreamed her question and we lay alone. NMP

An Anecdote of Love. John Clare. Those wild flowers stand the bl NOBV

Anecdote of the Jar. Wallace Stevens. Like nothing else in Tennessee. AP; CMoP; CoBMV; ExPo; HaCAP; HeIP; HoPM; InPK; LiTA; MoAB; MoVE; NAWM 1-2; NePA; NIP; NoAm; NOBA; NoP; OBSP; OxBA; PoA; PPP; PrIm; SOTW; TAP; UnPo

Anecdote of the Prince of Peacocks. Wallace Stevens. As sleep falls/In the innocent air. SOTW

Anecdote of the Sparrow. Robert Pack. Or in the glass come see your face. NePA

Anemones for Miss Austen. Bernard Bergonzi. how they managed with breakfast or bed. HaMV

The Angel. William Blake.
And grey hairs were on my head. CH
And 'twixt earnest and joke/Enjoy'd the Lady. LiTB

The Angel. Alfred Hayes. he watches the angelic mouth stain/with the sweet wine. FYAP; MAYP; TrJP]

Angel. James Merrill. He does not want even these few lines written. ConAP; PoA

Angel. Robin Skelton. And the woman removed the tight curlers/once she lay small in death. NMP

Angel. Gary Soto. Turn, beyond knowing,/To what is also his. AMV-80

Angel and Stone. Howard Nemerov. And mirrored to the lord of everything that is by one and one and one. NYBP

The Angel and the Anchorite. Richard Shelton. some of the stones are broken/but they are my friends NPAW

An Angel Describes Truth. Ben Jonson. And see! descended from her chariot now,/In this related pompe shee visits you. OBS

Angel Eye of Memory. John Malcolm Brinnin. Rifle the air to make farewell forever. PoA

The Angel in the House. Coventry Patmore.
And eats its dead-dog off a golden dish. VLP
And Love in tears too noble is/For pity, save of Love in smiles. LO
And some one in the Study play'd/The Wedding-march of Mendelssohn. FaBoPP
..."Be dumb,/Or speak but of forgotten things to far-off times/to come." VLP
The children of the sod, and this/Rose in the sun, and flew for hours. VLP
Gave to love's feast its choicest gust,/A vague, faint augury of despair. VLP
Its odour quickens all my brain. VLP
Live greatly; so shalt thou acquire/Unknown capacities of joy. VLP
Me you shall not mock. I can wait. VLP
More form and more fair stateliness/Than heretofore between us two. FaBoPP
Quick, tender, virginal, and unprofaned! VLP
Rewards me with variety/Which men who change can never know. VLP
She's not and never can be mine. EG; VLP
Swathed by the red breath of the sun. VLP
Sweet moon between her lighted clouds! PeD; ViBoPo
That and the Child's unheeded dream/Is all the light of all their day. EG; GTBS-P; LO
That those conditions must endure,/Which, wanting, I myself should miss. VLP
They go so clad with lovely awe/None but the noble dares desire. EG
To profit so by Eden's blame. EBEV
Too simple and too sweet for words! VLP
'Twas all unlike your great and gracious ways. VLP
ut, ah, the walk that afternoon/We saw the water-flags in flower! EBEV; EG
You shall be sweetly help'd and warn'd. VLP

The Angel Michael. Anath Bental. And only his voice/Still echoes/Inside me. VWA

The Angel of Death. Anonymous. There's a man going 'round taking names. AmFP

The Angel of Patience. John Greenleaf Whittier. He kindly trains us to endure. WGRP

Angel of Peace, Thou Hast Wandered Too Long. Oliver Wendell Holmes. Angels of Bethlehem, echo the strain! AH

De Angel Roll de Stone Away. Anonymous. De angel roll de stone away. BoAN 1-2

The Angel's Whisper. Samuel Lover. Said, "I knew that the angels were whispering with thee." OnYI

Angel Spirits of Sleep. Robert Bridges. Threading dances light? CH

Angel Surrounded by Paysans. Wallace Stevens. ...quickly, too quickly, I am gone? HaCAP; LCAP; PPP

An Angel Unawares. Anonymous. Be you our angel unawares. BLRP; TRV

Angela Davis. Alice S. Cobb. The battle is yet to be won. BlSi

Angelic Guidance. John Henry, Cardinal Newman. Yet, not all hopeless, eye His boundless grace. GoBC

The Angelic Vilancete. Gil Vicente. Archangels' voices ring,/"Holy, Holy," ceaselessly. CAW

Angelica and the Ork. Sir John (1561-1612) Harington. But by the way be sure he did not miss/To give her many a sweet and friendly kiss. OBSC

Angelina. Paul Laurence Dunbar. When Angelina Johnson comes a-swingin' down de line. HBV 1-2

L'Angelo. Thomas Caulfield Irwin. The stars look on the glory of my grief. IrPN

Angelo Orders His Dinner (parody). Bayard Taylor. ...Stay, now! a seat/Is bare: I, Angelo, will sit and eat. BXAP; Par

Angels. Dannie Abse. slowly open their gorgeous, Carnaby wings. PoA

Angels. Richard Burns. ...till the almond tree flowers/on the mountain, and there is no more sea. VWA

Angels. Gertrude Hall. Yet would I warn thee, World: treat well/Whom thou call'st fool. AA

Angels. Anne Szumigalski. blessing her and the air/as they back away into the mist. NOBC

The Angels at Hamburg. Randall Jarrell. He looks from his grave for life,and/judgment/Rides over his city like a star. AmP

The Angels Came A-Mustering. Israel Zangwill. Through all the circles seven come,/To fetch the Torah down! EaLo

The Angels for the Nativity of Our Lord. William, of Hawthornden Drummond. Thus singing, through the air the angels swam,/And cope of stars re-echoed the same. OxBoCh

De Angels in Heab'n Gwineter Write My Name. Anonymous. O, write my name,/De Angels in de heab'n gwineter write my name. BoAN 1-2

Angels in the House. Jerred Metz. as it writes it sings of each room in turn/praising each room's name. VWA

Angels in Winter. Nancy Willard. so tame and defenseless/even the air could kill us. FiCP; LCAP

The Angels of Buena Vista. John Greenleaf Whittier. And still thy white-winged angels hover dimly/in our air! BeLS; PAH

Angels, Roll the Rock Away! Tom Scott. Christ the Lord is risen today. BePJ

Angels' Song. Charles Causley. And his gifts of love and peace/To his people never cease. BePJ; FaPo; OBCP

The Angels' Song. Edmund Hamilton Sears Which now the angels sing. AA; AmePo

The Angels Sung a Carol. Edward Taylor. Bur'ing thy grave in thy sepulchre's reach. AH

Angels We Have Heard on High. Anonymous.
Gloria in excelsis Deo. FSW
Mary, Joseph, lend your aid,/While our hearts in love we raise. TreFS

Angelus. Solomon Blumgarten (Yehoash) Ding-dong....Ding-dong....Unwillingly I drink/the wine/Of consolation of a God that is not mine. LiTW

The Angelus. Florence Earle Coates. At home with Nature, and at one with God! HBV 1-2

Angelus-Time near Dublin. W. B. Stanford. At twelve bell answers bell,/as Mary to Gabriel. NeIP

Anger. Robert Creeley. waiting for whatever will/be at last the real end of you. CoPo; NaP

Anger. Charles and Mary Lamb. The vile snake will always sting you. FaBoBe; HBV 1-2; HBVY

Anger's Freeing Power. Stevie Smith. Often my tears fall in a shower/Because of Anger's freeing power. OxBC

The Anger That Breaks a Man Down into Boys. Cesar Vallejo. the anger of the poor/owns one deep fire against two craters. EAS

Angina Pectoris. W. R. Moses. That he slept with plenty of quilts to keep him warm. LiTA; NCSH

Anglais Mort a Florence. Wallace Stevens. Before the colors deepened and grew small. AP

Angle of Geese. N. Scott Momaday. On the dark distant flurry. CDW; QFR

Angle of Vision. Martha Bosworth. He said it like goodbye. AMV-80

Angle of Vision. Robert Rendall. To a cosmic tide with the men that man it. OxBTC

The Angler. Bhartrihari. And then, alack! to end the cruel game/Are broiled on love's quick flame. LiTW

The Angler. John Chalkhill. Other joys/Are but toys,/And to be lamented. HBV 1-2

Angler. Mark Vinz. are circling near the bottom/in the deepest water of the lake. WOLT

The Angler's Ballad. Charles Cotton. With the best of good Subjects be reckon'd. CEP

The Angler's Invitation. Thomas Tod Stoddart. We'll drink to sweet friendship in need and in/deed. GN; HBV 1-2

The Angler's Reveille. Henry Van Dyke. Steady, be ready,/Good luck! GN

The Angler's Song. Izaak Walton. Who is more welcome to my dish/Than to my angle was my fish. LiSp; SD

An Angler's Vade Mecum. John Engels. But I think/careful copies might/be made, which will be/just as good. WOLT

An Angler's Wish. Henry Van Dyke. And just a day on Nature's heart. AA

The Angler's Wish. Izaak Walton. A quiet passage to a welcome grave. HBV 1-2

The Anglers Song. William Basse. I therefore strive to follow those/Whom he to follow him hath chose. OBS

Anglicized Utopia. Sir William Schwenck Gilbert. Which we dutifully offer to our mother-land! OBSV

Angling, a Day. Galway Kinnell. ...but fishermen know/there are days when you don't catch anything. WOLT

Anglo-Eire Vignette. Patric Stevenson. And that most distressful dire land/ He'd rechristen, merely..."Ireland'.' NeIP

Anglo-Irishman's Complaint. Anonymous. Have mickly holp thereto. AnIL

Anglo-Saxon. E. L. Mayo. And scattered vowels of Jerusalem. MiAP

The Anglo-Saxon Race. Martin Farquhar Tupper. That the world may be blest in the Saxon Race! PeD

Anglosaxon Street. Earle Birney. waiting brief for milkmaid mornstar and worldrise HeIP; NOBC

Angola Question Mark. Langston Hughes. For you and me/There's/Woe. BPo; TTY

The Angora. Jim Gerard. That the home in which we dwell is hers. AMV-80

Angry at Zaidun's Interest in Her Maid... Wallada. Yet, to my grief, you let al-mustari beguile you! PBWP

Angry Dusk. Jack Lindsay. we shall have a world of men/treating men only as men,/not as things. NOAV

The Angry Poet. Frank O'Connor. Her nose in the tail of the hound. CIP

An Angry Word. Margaret E. Bruner. Whose poison doubles after one has spent it. PoToHe

Anguish. Stephane Mallarme. Fearing to die if I but sleep alone. AWP; SyP

Anima. Diana O Hehir. Hiding, water-polished, under our sleep's blue shelf. NPGG

Animal. Max Eastman. ...fill my faltering human/Heart's hunger with a more celestial love. FYAP

Animal Acts. Charles Simic. Marking the cards in the new deck. LCAP

Animal Crackers. Christopher Morley. Having cocoa and animals once more for tea! SoPo; SUS; TiPo

Animal Fair. Anonymous. And that was the end of the monk. AS; BLPA; FaBoBe; FPL; MoShBr; NTCP; PoPle; SoPo; YaD

Animal Fair. Philip Booth. they leave so green, so jungle green. NePoAm-2

The Animal Howl. J. M. What calumnies will feed their word–/To satiate its origin: the animal howl? TrJP

The Animal I Wanted. Kenneth Patchen. I can hear it crying/When I sit like this away from life. VGW

Animal Kingdom. Sydney Clouts. water flow and mirror me. PeSA

Animal Magnetism. Laurence Hynes Halloran. He from her presence sneaked, completely humbled! NOEC

Animal Pictures. Lawrence Locke. Like a clutch of startled/Debutantes, the flamingos/Lift a foot and stare. GrPl

The Animal Runs, It Passes, It Dies. Anonymous. The man has passed, the shade has vanished, the prisoner/is free!.... WeW

Animal Song. Heather McHugh. how animal is soul, and not its opposite. MAYP

Animal Songs. Anonymous. Ebony-tree with the big spreading leaves. PeSA

Animal Songs: Baboon. Anonymous. hill over that far-off hill. PeSA

Animal Songs: Baboon 2. Anonymous. and your face too looks like a ridge of stone. PeSA

Animal Songs: Giraffe. Anonymous. full of people sitting together. PeSA

Animal Songs: Hyena. Anonymous. Big-toothed one. PeSA

Animal Songs: Hyena's Song to Her Children. Anonymous. Do I get anything so easily? PeSA

Animal Songs: Lion. Anonymous. you, drinker at the water-hole. PeSA

Animal Songs: Springbok. Anonymous. rolling himself together like a blanket. PeSA

Animal Songs: Zebra. Anonymous. ...you cross all the rivers/as if they were only one. PeSA

Animal Songs: Zebra Stallion. Anonymous. O you who like a woman/are so full of jealousy. PeSA

The Animal Store. Rachel Field. If I had a hundred dollars to spend,/Or maybe a little more. SoPo; TiPo

The Animal That Drank Up Sound. William Stafford. It listens now, and practices at night. VGW

Animal Tranquillity and Decay. William Wordsworth. With envy, what the Old Man hardly feels. ERoP 1-2

Animal, Vegetable and Mineral. Louise Bogan. What Artist laughs? What clever Daemon thinks? FM; SBG

The Animalcule, A Tale. Richard Savage. Nor equal, nor encrease his own. PeD

The Animals. Stephen Berg. The spine, the tail, the mercy/of dark clothing and work. NaP

The Animals. Josephine Jacobsen. Flying with green in her beak; the dove also had come. GoYe

Animals. Robinson Jeffers. Besides the slow oxidation of carbohydrates and amino-acids. NU

The Animals. Lewis MacAdams. We will miss you, tongue, in this room. ANYP

The Animals. Edwin Muir. On the sixth day we came. CMoP; EBCP; EBEV; HeIP; MoBrPo; NoP

The Animals. Charles Simic. A tooth,/An udder/Full of milk. GeTw

Animals Are Passing from Our Lives. Philip Levine. ...No. Not this pig. CoAP; NoAm; NOBA; SM; TAP; TW

The Animals' Arrival. Elizabeth Jennings. They slept for the waiting day. PBWP

The Animals' Carol. Charles Causley. Man is God, and God is Man. NAs

The Animals' Christmas. Philip Dacey. From their nostrils/they breathe good news. GP

The Animals in That Country. Margaret Atwood. They have the faces of/ no-one. NoP

The Animals in the Ark. Anonymous. And each fowl that ledden makes/In this ship men may find. GBP

The Animals Sick of the Plague. Marianne Moore. The court says white is black or that black crimes are white. InPS

Animals That Stand in Dreams: The Panda. Harley Elliott. both comic/ and full of unspeakable grief. NeAC

Animation and Ego. Jody Swilky. leaving a handful of kisses/on their billboard smiles. AMV-80

Animula. Thomas Stearns Eliot. Pray for us now and at the hour of our birth. LiTB; MoVE; NAs

Animula. William Stanley Merwin. and the nights are not separate/ remember CAPP

Animula Vagula. A. Y. Campbell. But thou art playing with it absently/ And dreaming, like a girl. HBMV

Animula Vagula, Blandula. Emperor (Publius Aelius Hadrianus) Hadrian. Nor Jests wilt thou afford me more. FaBoRV

Anishinabe Grandmothers. Gerald Vizenor. tasting the rain/singing/the world will change VoR

Ank'hor Vat. Denis Devlin. His look will flow like oil over us. BIrV; CIP; IPY; NOBI

Anke von Tharau. Anonymous. Now and forever, our hearts become one. HW

Anklet Song. Anonymous. But that I'd pluck and wear in my wreath,/If thou wert but a flower! WTO

Ankotarinya. Anonymous. Red, too, is the hollow in which I am resting. CBAP

Ann and the Fairy Song. Walter De La Mare. And wash your grubby hands, my dear,/For dinner's on the table! FaBV

Ann Grenville, Countess Temple, Appointed Poet Laureate... Horace Walpole. A silver penny shall be found/Within the compass of her shoe–/ And so we bid you all adieu! OBEC

Ann's House. Dick Lourie. white are the April beds DFF

Anna. Robert Burns. And I'll gae to my Anna. TrGrPo; UnTE

Anna. Joe Johnson. anna anna anna anna CNA

Anna Elise. Anonymous. And ever since then/she's been turning around. OxNR

Anna-Marie, Love, Up Is the Sun. Sir Walter Scott. But think not I dream of thee, Tybalt, my love. ViBoPo

Anna Playing in a Graveyard. Caroline Gilman. Oh bitter drops will start– /O'er graves, when friends depart–/In life's maturer years. OBCA

Annabel Lee. Edgar Allan Poe. In her tomb by the side of the sea. AA; AP; AWP; BeLS; BLPA; DiPo; DL; EtS; FaFP; FPL; GoTF; HBV 1-2; HBVY; HeIP; InPo; LiTA; LiTL; LoGBV; MaC; MAmP; MCCG; NePA; NOBA; NoP; OBCA; OBVV; OnMSP; OxBA; PG; PoPl; PrIm; RoGo; SeCeV; SpRo; StPo; TAP; TreF; TrGrPo; ViBoPo; WBLP

Annabel Lee (parody). Stanley Huntley. But I should have had my Annabel Lee. SpRo

Annales: "Like a shower of rain." Ennius. He labors greatly/He cannot breathe. WaaP

Annan Water. Anonymous
And he never saw his bonny lady! CH; HBV 1-2
For over thee I'll build a bridge,/That ye never more true love may sever. BaBo

Annar-Mariar's Christmas Shopping. Eleanor Farjeon. With the whole of their Christmas shopping done. ChBR

Anne. Lizette Woodworth Reese. I wonder how my forty years/Look by her sweet sixteen! AA

Anne and the Peacock. Noel Welch. dead leaves pile round her feet. FF

Anne Hutchinson's Exile. Edward Everett Hale. Home, home, here's my baby's home! PAH

Anne Rutledge. Edgar Lee Masters. From the dust of my bosom!
AmFN; AmLP; CMoP; FaFP; FaPo; HAP; InPo; LiTA; LiTM; MCCG;
MoAmPo; MoVE; NePA; NoAm; NOBA; OFD; OxBA; PoPl; PoSC

Anne Sexton. Hans Juergensen. Anne,/have you made/peace with peace?
AMV-81

Annette Myers; or, A Murder in St. James's Park. *Anonymous.* What
dreadful tidings to convey unto his family. OxBoLi

The Anniad. Gwendolyn Brooks. Kissing in her kitchenette/The minuets
of memory. BlSi

Annie and Willie's Prayer. Sophia P. Snow. And made you His agent to
answer their prayers. BeLS; BLPA

Annie Breen. *Anonymous.* His finger pressed the trigger and he shot him
through the heart. CoSo

Annie died the other day. Edward Estlin Cummings. youths and maidens:
let us pray ErPo

Annie Laurie. William Douglas. And for bonnie Annie Laurie,/I'd lay me
doun and dee. FaBoBe; FaBV; FaFP; FSW; GN; HBV 1-2; LiTL; MCCG;
PoPle; TreF; WBLP

Annie of Lochroyan. *Anonymous.* You turned my true-love from my
door,/Who died for love of me!' BuBa

Annie Shore and Johnnie Doon. Patrick Orr. As if they'd sinned, he knew
not how. HBV 1-2

Annihilation. Conrad Aiken. All that we know in love is bitter./And it is
not much. CrMA; GBL; MoAB; MoAmPo

The Annihilation of Nothing. Thom Gunn. Purposeless matter hovers in
the dark. NePoEA-2; NoAm

The Anniversary. Ai. and we can blast another hole in ourselves without
a/sound. GP

The Anniversary. William Dickey. I cannot tell your voice from my own
voice. GOYP

An Anniversary. Thomas Hardy. And the man's eyes then were not so
sunk that you saw the socket-/bones. OxBTC

Anniversary. Ted Kooser. ...Through the wall/you flush your toilet like a
lonely call. SM

Anniversary. Richmond Lattimore. and twenty years gone in an afternoon.
NYBP; PoCh

The Anniversary. Roberta Spear. saying as the earth says after rain/this
one is on me. MAYP

Anniversary. John Wain. And like bricks fearsome in their everyday
squareness. MP; NePoEA-2

Anniversary. Daniel Weissbort. The rock sunders. VWA

Anniversary in September. Beatrice Curtis Brown. Daisies grasped in
Phoebe's fist/Would be charming, I insist. BiCB

An Anniversary of Death. John Wieners. sun shines and larks break forth
from winter branches. PoM

An Anniversary on the Hymeneals of My Noble Kinsman, Thomas Stanley...
Richard Lovelace. Thousands of new-born loves with your chaste eyes.
CaPo

Anniversary Poem for the Cheyennes Who Fell at Sand Creek. Lance
Henson. our voices the color of watching VoR

The Anniverse: An Elegy. Henry, Bishop of Chichester King. ...who sums
his years/(Like me) with no arithmetic, but tears JCP

Anno 1829. Heinrich Heine. For when they see this town they fly,/And
anxiously increase their speed. AWP; LiTW

Anno Domini. E. M. Walker. An empty lap, an hour to tea, a knit, a nod,
a nap, ennui. PoL

Annot and John. *Anonymous.* In annote is hire name–nempneth it non!/
Whoso right redeth roune to Johon. OxBM

Annotations of Auschwitz. Peter Porter. And all poultry eaters are
psychopaths. NMP; OxBTC

Announced by All the Trumpets of the Sky. Ralph Waldo Emerson. In a
tumultuous privacy of storm. TiPo

The Announcement. George Ellenbogen. and the grass stayed green that
year/right through August. AMV-80

Annual Gaiety. Wallace Stevens. And joy of snow and snow. MoAB;
MoAmPo

Annual Legend. Winfield Townley Scott. Spread like a field of death; gold
on the sea. CoAP; LiTM; WaP

The Annual Solution. Edwin Meade Robinson. Spend it, and render our
mutual Christmastide/Happy! InMe

The Annuity. George Outram. I'm charged for her annuity! HBV 1-2

Annul Wars. Nahman of Bratzlav. To announce to the sons of man thy/
power,/and the honor of the glory of thy/kingdom. TrJP

The Annunciation. *Anonymous.*
Him so her for to serven/That he us to him take. MeEL; OxBM
She carried Him till Christmas morn/When Jesus Christ the Lord was born.
ISi

The Annunciation. Margaret Devereaux Conway. By thy dear Son are we
all saved–/Gramercy, lady free. ISi

Annunciation. John Donne. Immensity cloistered in thy dear womb.
AnAnS 1; ISi; OBS; TrCP

The Annunciation. John Duffy. The silhouetted pitcher waiting to be filled.
ISi

Annunciation. D. G. Jones. The air is not just air, it is an arctic/
Confidence of flowers. PeCV

The Annunciation. Margot Kriel. to crush the low, delicate plants/and
dream his weight will never rise. PoDr

Annunciation. Sister Maura. a small man/with a broken nose/angel of the
annunciation. TAT

The Annunciation. William Stanley Merwin. And make the word with my
breath. AP

The Annunciation. Edwin Muir. As if their gaze would never break.
CMoP; NOCV

The Annunciation. Saint Nerses. Unto whom the praise and glory. ISi

The Annunciation. Amrita Pritam. ...old Mother Earth/Is come upon me.
I am ready to give birth. WPOW

Annunciation. Rainer Maria Rilke. You, Lady, are the Tree. OBVE

The Annunciation. John Banister Tabb. Wakes to the birth and bloom/Of
life and light. ISi

Annunciation Night. Katherine Eleanor Conway. The Hope of the Worlds
hidden under her heart! CAW

Annunciation Night. Abby Maria ("Maria Josephine") Hemenway. Leaves
her to her radiant rest/Guarded by an angel-guest. ISi

Annunciation over the Shepherds (excerpt). Rainer Maria Rilke. ...Now
shall a new thing be,/by which the world shall spread in wider circles.
PCh

Annunciations. Geoffrey Hill. ...be vigilant, strive/To recognise the damned
among your friends. NePoEA-2

Annus Mirabilis. John Donne. And on the Lunar world securely pry.
MOS

Annus Mirabilis. John Dryden.
And hoods the flames that to their quarry strove. FiP
For all the glories which the Fight did yield. OBS
She, trembling, creeps upon the ground away,/And looks back to him with
beseeching eyes. FiP

Annus Mirabilis. Philip Larkin. Between the end of the Chatterley ban/
And the Beatles' first L.P. NIP; NLV; NOBL

An Anodyne. Thomas Ken. Short pains can never grievous be,/Which
work a blest eternity. OxBoCh

Anonymous. Victor Hernandez Cruz. All admire my taste/Within thou
mambo of much more haste. APU

Anonymous. John Banister Tabb. But name upon the canvas, none. AA

Anonymous Drawing. Donald Justice. Simply to leave him out of the scene
forever. CoAP; EyDe; HeIP; NePoEA-2

Anonymous Gravestone. Erich Kastner. Because for all the things he left
undone/There is no possible excuse. ELU

Anonymous Reply to the Above. *Anonymous.* And Chesterfield the Elder.
FaBoEE

Another. Ellen Marie Bissert. you kiss me hard/& go to her. PeHV

Another. Anne Bradstreet. Then while we live, in love let's so persevere/
That when we live no more, we may live ever. SBG

Another. Thomas Carew.
The flames, the arrows, all lie here. CaPo; OBEV

Another. Robert Herrick.
Perplexe him in his hinder parts. AnAnS 2
Pray be silent and not stir/Th' easy earth that covers her. OBEV

Another. Richard Lovelace.
He wanders with his Country too. AtBAP; CaPo; PoEL 1-5
Only a cloud or two hangs here and there. SeCP

Another. J. E. Thorold Rogers. Drop anything except a tear. FaBoEE

Another Academy. Charles Bukowski. I thought that was/rather good.
TAT

Another and Another and Another. James Henry. Sunrising and sunsetting
evermore. NOBV

Another and the Same. Samuel Rogers. Way-worn and spent, another and
the same! OBNC

Another Birthday. Ben Jonson. ...Then/The Birthday shines, when logs not
burn, but/men. WiR

Another Canto (parody). J. B. Morton. Quelque chose tres deep, ma foi!
FaBoPa

Another Charme for Stables. Robert Herrick. This observ'd, the Manes
shall be/Of your horses, all knot-free. WSC

Another Coast. David Wojahn. call me when you get up. MAYP

Another Color. Frank Stewart. in this mirror, the world itself is another
color. AMV-81

Another Cross. Stephen Gardner. O wildest of untouched dreams.
AMV-80

Another Cynical Variation. Helen". Say I'm young and strong, but Lord/
Gerald kissed me! InMe

Another Day. Isabella Maria Brown. A DIME WIL OPEN THE DOOR.
PoNe

Another Death. D. E. Borrell. She looked like a stranger when she died.
FF

Another Dying Chieftain. Rayna Green. there's no good day to die/in these wars. TWSS

Another Easter. John Ridland. At which some needy sage/Taps out his needed fable/Across a trackless page. SM

Another Epitaph on an Army of Mercenaries. Hugh" (Christopher Murray Grieve) MacDiarmid. With difficulty persist here and there on earth. DBV; NoAm; OBWP

Another Face. Ray A. Young Bear. keeping close to the rock. CDW

Another Fan Belonging to Mademoiselle Mallarme. Stephane Mallarme. Which, mad to be born for no one/Neither can flow nor be still. SyP

Another for the Briar Rose. William Morris. Thine eyes were light; thy lips were life. NOBV

Another Full Moon. Ruth Fainlight. Marked forever as her creature and her fool. BrRo

Another Generation. J. C. Squire. One only comprehending pair,/Unique, since first the world began. HBMV

Another Given: The Last Day of the Year. William Dickey. tell Michael the truth, if we know what the truth is. AMV-80

Another. In Defence of Their Inconstancie. Ben Jonson. For were the worthiest woman curst/To love one man, he'd leave her first. SeCP

Another Island Groupage. Kenward Elmslie a black rock avalanche repaints/the persiflage of the victim's "Greece". ANYP

Another Kind of Burning. Ruth Fox. ...unbroken neck/of an infant now fatherless/in fact. AmC; NYBP

Another Late Edition (excerpt). Olga Cabral. But not one hair of the head of the/seven-year-old boy/in a village that went up in napalm. PPON

Another Letter to Her Husband, Absent upon Publick Employment. Anne Bradstreet. Let's still remain but one, till death divide. SCAP

Another Letter to Joseph Bruchac. Jack Anderson. rather than hurting/openly/for still another/Hour. LFAC

Another Letter to Lord Byron. David R. Slavitt. It is, as I am, sir, yours, very truly. SM

Another Life. Frank Bidart. ...on each side, the unreadable/fresco of my life... HaCAP

Another Little Drink. *Anonymous.* And another little drink wouldn't do us any harm. TrAS

Another Man Done Gone. *Anonymous.* Another man done gone. FSW

Another Meeting. Lawrence A. Lucas. As another meeting/Is about to begin. AMV-80

Another Mother and Child. Joe-Anne McLaughlin. ...so that not even an artist, a Renoir,/could have told the difference. FAZ

Another Night in the Ruins. Galway Kinnell. to open himself, to be/the flames? CAPP; CoAP

Another Night on the Porch Swing. Cathleen Quirk. ...and probably a baby/or two; someone strange, respectable. NMM

Another Night with Telescope. Leonard Cohen. from sky to sky they rake/our lives with pins of light PeCV

Another November. Stanley Plumly. someone's face at the window. LCAP

Another of Seafarers, Describing Evil Fortune. *Anonymous.* And leave the seas with their annoy,/At home at ease to live in joy. OBSS

Another of the Same. Sir Walter Ralegh. Of all which speak our English tongue, but those/of thy device. FCP

Another Old Song. Barney Bush. you looking into flames wondering/what it would have really/been like. STE

Another on Her. Robert Herrick. The Storax, Spiknard, Myrrhe, and Ladanum. SpRo

Another on the Same. Hilaire Belloc. But Death's what even Politicians fail/To bribe or swindle, bully or blackmail. OBSV

Another One for the Devil. David C. Childers. they were gone. AMV-80

Another Poem about the Madness of Women. Tom Wayman. She knows there is a woman in each one. NOBC

Another Poem for Me. Etheridge Knight. now that death has fled these quiet corridors NNaP

Another Poem on Absalom. Nathan Yonathan. I wanted, my little fool, only you, Absalom. VWA

Another Prince Is Born. Adrian Mitchell. Brings a six-foot teddy bear/From the Birmingham Toy Fair. NAs

Another Reply to In Flanders Fields. J. A. Armstrong. To crush the foe, or sleep with you,/In Flanders Fields. BLPA; PAL

Another Return. Winfield Townley Scott. Lie down again beside me. ELU

Another September. Thomas Kinsella. Moving like women: Justice, Truth, such figures. BIrV; CIP; FaBoIP; PoCh

Another Sin I Had Forgot. *Anonymous.* I killed him there and threw him out, PeD

Another Song. Donald Justice. And Jack from Joan, and they shall never marry. ConAP; NePoEA-2; VGW

Another Song. William Ross. ...but I shall depart to sleep forever in the/hall of the dead bards. GoTS

Another Song. Marion Strobel. Oh, if I say I love you, can you know/It better, for my having told you so? MoLP

Another Song of the Same Woman, to Some Partridges... Florencia del Pinar. yet no one weeps for me. BoWoP

Another Spirit Advances. Jules Romains. Space in communion binds us in one thought. AWP

Another Stone Poem. Philip Dacey. Lasts the better part of a day. AMV-81

Another Sunday Morning. Carter Revard. as the dew vanished away. VoR

Another Sunset. John Minczeski. like a peacock throne/or the sigh of peaches. PoDr

Another Time. W. H. Auden. Another time has other lives to live. OxBA

Another to the Maids. Robert Herrick. Dead the fire, though we blow. OHIP

Another to Urania. Benjamin Colman. If more from Earth and Sense refin'd/W' are patient, pray'rful, meek, resign'd. SCAP

Another Tribute to Wyatt. Henry Howard, Earl of Surrey. Whose cinders yet with envy they do eat. SiPS

Another True Maid. Matthew Prior. That maids make not half such a tumult, as wives. FaBoEE

Another Villon-ous Variation. Don (Donald Robert Marquis) Marquis. But where are the Crooks of Yesteryear? HBMV

Another Way. Ambrose Bierce. I had more pleasure in the other dream. AA

Another Weeping Woman. Wallace Stevens. And you are pierced by a death. MoVE

Another While. Morris Rosenfeld. Another while–and I shall drag no/more... TrJP

Another Year. *Anonymous.* Who wot now that is here/Where he shall be another year? HAP

Another Year. Oswald J. Smith. A year to welcome gain or loss,/and humbly all Thy blessings claim. STF

Another Year Come. William Stanley Merwin. And the hands of the clock still knock without entering. NYBP; OFD; PCP

Another Year Is Dawning. Frances Ridley Havergal. Another year for Thee! WBLP

Anseo. Paul Muldoon. And raise their hands/As their names occurred. FaBoPV

Answer. Leah Goldberg. and the huge stones/of our Jerusalem hills? VWA

The Answer. George Herbert. Show me, and set me, I have one reply,/Which they that know the rest, know more than I. TEP

The Answer. Robinson Jeffers. drown in despair when his days darken. MoRP
...,or/drown in despair when his days darken. CMoP; GoYe; MoRP

Answer. Leonora Speyer. And in the stillness after song,/There is a Sound! PG

The Answer. Sara Teasdale. I found more joy in sorrow/Than you could find in joy. PoA

The Answer. Chuck Wachtel. that when you cut it/in the box you never press/as hard. APU; FaBoRV

The Answer of Mr. Waller's Painter to His Many New Advisers. *Anonymous.* And, lastly, that done, three large dashes by/I doubt would serve to paint your destiny. APAS

The Answer that Ye Made to Me, My Dear. Sir Thomas Wyatt. Late, or too soon, let it not rule the gain/Wherewith free will doth true desert retain. FCP; SiPS

Answer to a Child's Question. Samuel Taylor Coleridge. "I love my Love, and my Love loves me!" EnRP; FaBoBe; HBV 1-2; HBVY; OxBChV; PoPle

An Answer to a Lady Advising Me to Retirement. Mary Wortley, Lady Montagu. And unconcerned my future fate I trust/To that sole Being, merciful and just. TEP

An Answer to Another Persuading a Lady to Marriage. Katherine ("Orinda") Philips. To strive to fix her beams which are/More bright and large than this. CavP; HAP

Answer to Master Wither's Song, "Shall I, Wasting in Despair?" Ben Jonson. What care I what others be? InMe

Answer to Pauper. Thomas Hood. If such as you don't like this world–/We'll pass you to the next. NBM

Answer to–'s Professions of Affection. George Gordon, Lord Byron. 'Tis thine to offer with corrupting art/The rotten borough of the human heart. OBSP

An Answer to Some Verses Made in His Praise. Sir John Suckling. I must admire aloof, and for my part/Be well contented, since you do't with art. PP

An Answer to the Parson. William Blake. "Because I don't want you to shear my fleece." FaBoEE; NLV

Answer to Voznesensky & Evtushenko. Frank O'Hara. Mayakovsky's hat worn by a horse HoAn; NNaP; PoM

–Answer to Yo/Question of Am I Not Yo/Woman... Sonia Sanchez. and nites that/multiply by twos. BPo

The Apple-Tree. Brian Vrepont. Oh, spring,/To maid of the flowering apple-breath/Clinging! PoAu 1-2

The Apple Trees. Louise Gluck. the dead fields, women rooted to the river. HaCAP

The Apple Trees at Olema. Robert Hass. and then he wanders among strangers all he wants. NPGG

Apple Wassail. *Anonymous.* Hatful, capful, pocketful, lapful,/Holla, boys, holla, hip hip hurrah! OBET

Apples. Donald Hall. in the round/hill of the peacock, in the resounding hill. LCAP

Apples. Shirley Kaufman. ...swallowing/apples, swallowing her life. NMM

Apples. Lisel Mueller. ...its orange and yellow grasp/on the reality of the idea of apples. NePoAm-2

Apples. Michael Waters. to a continent dark with apples. GeTw

Apples Be Ripe. *Anonymous.* Petticoats up/And trousers down. GBP

Apples in New Hampshire. Marie Gilchrist. Next year the trees will rest and apples will be few. BoNaP

Appleton House (excerpt). Andrew Marvell These massacre the grass along... AtBAP

The Applicant. Sylvia Plath. Will you marry it, marry it, marry it. MAT; NaP; NMM; NOBA; SBG; TwCP

Application for a Grant. Anthony Hecht. ...who dream of nothing/But a pad on Eighth Street and your approbation. SaC

Appoggiatura. Donald Jeffrey Hayes. "Sea-Woman–slim-fingered-water-thing..." AmNP; PoBA; PoNe

The Appointment. Maxine W. Kumin. After that,/he puts his red eyes out/under the extra blanket. NMM

The Appointment. Arthur William Edgar O'Shaughnessy. Truth in their place would watch that star's return. OxBI

The Appointment. Leonard Alfred George Strong. ...cried/Mortally, like a bird the cat has caught. OxBTC

An Appointment. William Butler Yeats. No government appointed him. AnEnPo

The Appology. Anne Finch, Countess of Winchilsea. Ther's lesse to be Applauded then forgiven. SBG

Appomattox. Mackinlay Kantor. And struck his hands together. AnAmPo

Appraisal. Sara Teasdale. And a tenderness too deep/To be gathered in a word. MoAmPo

Appreciation. Thomas Bailey Aldrich. As much beauty as they sing. AA

Appreciation. George Meredith. That change in thee, if not thyself, I claim. ViBoPo

Apprehension. Douglas Ainslie. He is so beguiling,/That dearest of dears. OBVV

The Apprentice Painter. Jack Myers. from the last job on earth/to the moon's jumbled houses. AmPA

Apprenticed. Jean Ingelow. And parson stood within the rails, a-marrying me and/thee, O! LiTL; OBVV

Apprentices. Robin Munro. Not that long to go/And testing. PoSH

The Approach. Thomas Traherne. Instructed then even by the Deity. OxBoCh; TrPWD

Approach of Evening. George Croly. Brightening with every shade that on its surge doth/ride. IrPN

The Approach of the Storm. *Anonymous.* That which lives there/Is coming, and makes a noise. OBVE

Approach of Winter. James (1834-82) Thomson. Till thro' the lucid Chambers of the South/Look'd out the joyous SPRING, look'd out, and smil'd. OBEC

Approach to a City. William Carlos Williams. always for there is small holiness/to be found in braver things. CAD

The Approach to Thebes. Stanley Jasspon Kunitz. And the story's this: I made the monster me. PoA

Approaches. George Macdonald. When God's will is thy heart's pole,/Then is Christ thy very soul. TRV

The Approaches. William Stanley Merwin. Canaan/where the fight is NOBA; Prf

Approaching America. J. C. Squire. In random rivalry they climb/The oddest pinnacles of Time. HBMV

Approaching Washington Heights. James Reiss. ...though his face is also a map/of Israel, his eyes are tiny/dead seas. NYP

Apres le Bain. William Carlos Williams. (You pig) OBAL

L'Apres Midi d'une Fille aux Cheveux de Lin. Ronald McCuaig. A lover of Renoirs who has forgotten her name? PoAu 1-2

Apricot Tree. Magda Isanos. Then I saw him,/the childhood friend I loved. BoWoP

April. O. C. Auringer. Turned blithely up the valley with a song. AA

April. Remy Belleau. Sudden light on earth and air. AWP

April. Vidame de Chartres. And evil-speaking shall part. AWP

April. Ralph Waldo Emerson. The masters quite omitted/The lore we care to know. ViBoPo

April. Theodosia Garrison. And here was April come back again. HBMV

April. John Linthicum. to localize her pain with pain. AMV-80

April. John Francis O'Donnell. And, merged in vapour, the half-risen moon/Leans on the trunked forests, vague and dim. IrPN

April. Linda Pastan. How many leaves/open their green shutters now/to let April through. Psk

April. Ezra Pound. Pale carnage beneath bright mist. CMoP

April. Dora Sigerson Shorter. Their rill-like voices called and cried/Until the dawn began. HBMV; HBVY

April. Sara Teasdale. I could not be so sure of Spring/Save that it sings in me. PoSC; SoPo; TiPo; YeAr

April. Samuel Thompson. And thinks he hears the cuckoo's song. BIrV

April. Eunice Tietjens. Spring laughing with a windy sound. SoPo; YeAr

April. Jean Valentine. Let's speak/as the bees do. TAP

April. Yvor Winters. solid in the/spring and serious/he walks away. ELU; RFM

April 1885. Robert Bridges. ...and banks of cloud uptower/In bulging heads that crowd for miles the dazzling south. NBM; OBSP; OxBTC

April 1940. Patrick Maybin. the quick whip of the wind, and the sting of rain. NeIP

April, 1942. Mark Van Doren. And takes this bitterest bite out of our time. WaP

April 1962. Paul Goodman. ...or trudge to and fro/gloomily in front of the public school? NMP; VGW

April 5, 1974. Richard Wilbur. Flowers, I said, will come of it. GP; HaCAP

April 68. Sam Cornish. there is something/being said CNA

An April Adoration. Sir Charles G. D. Roberts. God in all the concord of their mirth/Heard the adoration-song of Earth. HBV 1-2

April–And Dying. Anne Reeve Aldrich. For me is death. AA

April and May. Anne Robinson. And ties their little bonnets/On the buttercup and clover. SUS

An April Day. Joseph Seamon, Jr. Cotter. Sufficient is it just to live/On such a day as this. CDC

The April Earth. Max Eastman. A sky-thrown torch has kindled me to flame. AnEnPo

April (excerpt). Irene Rutherford McLeod. Where the wild honey bees/Gather honey for their queen! SUS

April Fantasie. Mackay Ellen Hutchinson Cortissoz. April hath a fickle mind. AA

April Fool. Elizabeth Jane Coatsworth. Didn't you feel them there at the hem?/APRIL FOOL! YeAr

April Fool. Eleanor Hammond. And smiled a rainbow/Overhead! SoPo

April Fool. Sam Hunt. ...Up to her old/tricks I thought. OCNZ

April Fool's Day. Marnie Pomeroy. It's only you, you April fool! PoSC

April Fools' Day. Yusef Komunyakaa. ...wondering if/I was just another loss/he'd divided his days into. MAYP

April Fourth. Robert Mezey. All that/Wrinkles like heat and disappears into thin air. NaP

April, Glengarry. Philip Coxon. ...the scattering/of Curlew-calls like raindrops from the source of Spring. PoSH

April Inventory. W.D. Snodgrass. Preserves us, not for specialists. AP; BiP; CABA; CAPP; CoAP; HAP; LiTM; MP; NePoEA; NoAm; NoP; PoPl; PPoe; TAP; TwCP

April Is in My Mistress' Face. *Anonymous.* But in her heart a cold December. GBL; HeIP

April Love. Ernest Christopher Dowson. With a sigh, a smile? PG

April Midnight. Arthur Symons. Wandering lost in the night of London,/In the miraculous April weather. SyP

April Moment. Arthur Davison Ficke. What are eternal vows!–oh, give me breath/Of one white hour here on the marge of death! HBMV

An April Morning. Bliss Carman. The golden daffodillies/Are blowing in the sun. HBMV; HBVY

April Mortality. Léonie Adams. Blew delicately down to death. AnAmPo; MoAB; MoAmPo

The April of the Ages. Digby Mackworth Dolben. Now stored away our thirst to stay/In ever-dewy pages. GoBC

April Puddle. Rowena Bastin Bennett. What kind of flowers they will be. TiPo

April Rain. Mathilde Blind. The rain-clouds flash with April mirth,/Like Life on earth. HBV 1-2

April Rain. Robert Loveman. It's raining violets. HBV 1-2; HBVY; SUS; TrJP

April Rain Song. Langston Hughes. And I love the rain. NTCP; OBCA; SUS; TiPo

April Rise. Laurie Lee. If ever world were blessed, now it is. BoC

"April's amazing meaning". George Dillon. Their lips together. AmLP

April Showers. James Stephens. It is a happy thing, I say,/To be alive on such a day. TiPo

The April Snow. Jones Very. This snowy mantle for her robe of bloom. AP

Arctic Tern in a Museum. Mary Effie Lee Newsome. One single symbol–/ Flight. PoNe

An Arctic Vision. Bret (Francis Bret Harte) Harte. See the real magician's hammer. MC; PAH

Arcturus Is His Other Name. Emily Dickinson. Over the stile of pearl! FaBV; NOBA; SUW

Ardan Mor. Francis Ledwidge. Nor any waters flow. AnIV; AWP

Ardor. Gamaliel Bradford. But my songs must tickle and bite/And burn with the ardor of living. HBMV

Are All the Children In? *Anonymous.* "Are all the children in?" STF

Are the Children at Home? Margaret Sangster. "Yes, dear! they are all at home." HBV 1-2

Are the Sick in Their Beds as They Should Be? Joan McIntosh. Ah, we are each at our station./Nothing is amiss. AMV-80

Are They Dancing. Edward Dorn. And are they dancing; or gazing at the earth? NeAP; PoM

Are They Not All Ministering Spirits? Robert Stephen Hawker. That which an Angel's touch hath blest/Is meet, my love, for thee! CoBE; GoBC; HBV 1-2

Are They Shadows That We See? Samuel Daniel. Thought must length it in the heart. ATP; EiL; ExPo; InvP; LoBV; NoP; SeCeV

Are We Not the People. Al-Samua'al Ibn Adiya. Upon is His servant and interlocutor/prayed... TrJP

Are We Thankful? *Anonymous.* That we cannot pause to thank Him/For the blessings of today. STF

Are Women Fair? Francis Davison. Or so kind-hearted, any may procure them. HBV 1-2

Are Ye Right There, Michael? Percy French. "And it might now, Michael, so it might!" WTO

Are You Born? Muriel Rukeyser. The starry form of love. MoRP

Are You Glad. *Anonymous.* Are you glad you've sold us? WTO

Are You Just Back for a Visit or Are You Going to Stay? Francis Coleman Rosenberger. Hey, are you just back for a visit or are you going to/stay? AMV-81

Are You the New Person Drawn toward Me? Walt Whitman. Have you no thought O dreamer that it may be all maya, illusion? NePA; NoAm; OBSP; PPP

Are You There? Strickland Gillilan. Our Father calls, and all my fret is done! PoToHe

Are You There, Mrs. Goose? John V. Hicks. The wolf winds blow/and we shall have snow. AMV-80

Are You What Your Faire Lookes Expresse? Thomas Campion. Let our loving mindes then meete,/For pure meetings are most sweet. AAS

Areas. Leslie Scalapino. Coming to that level and spoiled. NPGG

Ares. Albert Ehrenstein. In me there howls a lust/To finish you finally. TrJP

The Arethusa. Prince Hoare. And all that belong to the jovial crew/On board of the Arethusa. FaPoR

Arethusa. Percy Bysshe Shelley. When they love but live no more. DTo; EnRP; GN; HBV 1-2; OBRV; WiR

Arf, Said Sandy. Charles Stetler. we figure: why should a dog be different? PPJ

Argent Solipsism. Howard Blake. Needing no self beyond a self I know. PoA

The Argument. Jane P. Moreland. ...Do you need to sit/beside the buried rotting peel of a banana/to recall its fruit? AMV-80

The Argument Begins with A. Sharon Thesen. ...A heart-shaped/wing. A beating stillness. A/motionless weight. CaPN

The Argument of Democritus Platonissans. Henry More. Thy silver sounded Lute hang up in silence here. SeCV 1-2

The Argument of His Book. Robert Herrick.
I write of Hell; I sing (and ever shall)/Of Heaven, and hope to have it after all. AnAnS 2; AtBAP; AWP; CaPo; CoBE; EBEV; EnL; EnLi 1-2; EnLi; ForPo; HAP; HBV 1-2; InPo; InvP; JCP; NoP; OAEL 1-2; OAEP; OBS; PoEL 1-5; PoPle; PoRA; SeCeV; SeCP; SeCV 1-2; TrGrPo; ViBoPo; WHA
Of Heaven, and hope to have it after all. AnAnS 2; AtBAP; SeCePo

An Argument–Of the Passion of Christ. Thomas Merton. They still will clamour for a sign! CrMA

An Argument: To Any Phillis or Chloe. Thomas Moore. Come, then, at least we may enjoy/Some pleasure for our punishment! NIP; OBSP

Aria. Rolfe Humphries. No shade on the golden ground. NYBP

Aria. Delmore Schwartz. Suspend their dread and civil war. ErPo

Aria for Flute and Oboe. Joseph Langland. And stars wash over his limbs in the mothering night? NePoEA

Ariana. Franklin Benjamin Sanborn. Toward that far country where his wishes/ are? AA

The Arid Husband. E. L. T. Mesens. Your true arid husband. EAS

The Arid Lands. Herbert Bashford. The home of Silence and of Heat! AA

Aridity. Michael (Katherine Bradley and Edith Cooper) Field. That quiet waiteth for His Voice. BoC; OBMV; OxBoCh; TRV

Aridity. Clive Staples Lewis. Still turning round the earth. BoC

Ariel. David Campbell. And glaciers move through the great beast's heart. CBAP; PoAu 1-2

Ariel. Sylvia Plath. Eye, the cauldron of morning. CMoP; HaCAP; HeIP; LCAP; NMP; NoAm; NOBA; NoP; PBWP

Ariel in the Cloven Pine. Bayard Taylor. Which, perchance, shall set me free/From the damned with Sycorax. AA

Arignota Remembers. Sappho. high her call to us rings: Come to me... LiTW

Ariosto. Osip Mandelstam. We too know it well, We've drunk mead on its shore. OBVE

Arise and Pick a Posy. *Anonymous.* But there's none so sweet a flower/As the lad that I adore. OBET

Arise and See the Glorious Sun. Francis Hopkinson. And kindly gives the nights still shades/For wearied man to rest. AH

Arise, Arise. *Anonymous.* If you cross the briny ocean/Without your fortune you must go.' OBET

Arise, My Soul! With Rapture Rise! Samuel J. Smith. And all thy paths are paths of peace. AH

Arise, O Glorious Zion. William G. Mills. Each ordinance appointed/To save us, will reveal. AH

Arise, Ye Saints of Latter Days. *Anonymous.* And seraphs shout, Amen! AH

Aristeides. Antipater of Sidon. And near his cabin, where the sound/No more was heard of lowing, died. AWP

An Aristocratic Trio. Judson France. King Domcome, Lord Howlong, and Baron Fig-tree. PV

Aristocrats. Keith Douglas. It is not gunfire I hear but a hunting horn. FaBoMo; NePoEA; OBWP

Aristocrats of Labor. W. Stewart. Their peerage is from God! PGD

Aristophanes' Symposium. Rita Mae Brown. And one day you will call me, "Woman." IHMS

Aristotle to Phyllis. John Hollander. What should have been a season of calm weather. PoCh

Arithmetic. Carl Sandburg. ...who is better in arithmetic,/you or your mother? ImOP

Arithmetic on the Frontier. Rudyard Kipling. Are cheap, alas! as we are dear. OBWP; VLP

Arizona. *Anonymous.*
And vanished from earth in a blaze of blue. ABF
You'll be longing for Oklahoma and your good old feather bed. AmFP

Arizona. Sharlot M. Hall. With a single heart to the narrow verge where/ craft and statecraft join. PAH

The Arizona Boys and Girls. *Anonymous.*
And they're down, down, and they're down. CoSo
Let him go to the devil and seek his offense./Let 'em rip! Fa-lo, fa-larie, fa-la. BFSS

Arizona Highways. James Welch. ...distant/as the cloud I came in on. CDW

Arizona Nature Myth. James Michie. Moon's left town. Moon's clean gone. NOBL

Arizona Village. Robert Stiles Davieau. The pack rats scurry home–and suddenly/Comes desert peace. AmFN

The Ark. Irving Feldman. Crow lost in a world of wrack. AmPC

The Ark. John Milton. All left in one small bottom swum imbark'd. EtS

Ark Anatomical. Jay Macpherson. Hangs deep in the dark body/A divining heart. NOBC

The Ark and the Dove. Daniel Sargent. This little song of foam which silver rang/Through worlds a-drowse. EtS

Ark Apprehensive. Jay Macpherson. May not gape sheer under you/As he does for me. NOBC

Ark Artefact. Jay Macpherson. From the grief of the always wounded,/ Always closing sea? NOBC

Ark Articulate. Jay Macpherson. How shall I rock my pain/In the arms of a tree? NOBC

Ark Astonished. Jay Macpherson. Man, I know your need,/But not your mind. NOBC; PoA

Ark of the Covenant. Louise Townsend Nicholl. Ocean and light the proof, the pact. ImOP

Ark Overwhelmed. Jay Macpherson. Who was not even, not ever,/Taken from your side. NOBC

Ark Parting. Jay Macpherson. Fare well, From your dream/I only shall not rise. NOBC

Ark to Noah. Jay Macpherson. Inward as all the creatures/Drawn through my bone. NOBC

Arkansas. Jackman Young. Beat out the rhythm of life/on the back of a kitchen chair. TAT

The Arkansas Traveler. *Anonymous.* My cabin never leaks when it doesn't rain! FSW

The Arkansas Traveller. *Anonymous.* Tolerable, thank you, how do you do sir? PSoN

The Arkansaw Traveler. *Anonymous.* It'll be by means of a telescope from here to Arkansaw! ViBoFo

Arlington. David McKee Wright. He falls–and yet old Arlington will never rise again! AnNZ

Arlington Cemetery Looking toward the Capitol. Winthrop Palmer. Not man, not God, only Rome. GoYe

Arlo Will. Edgar Lee Masters. And through unnumbered heavens/To the final flame. LiTA

Arm, Arm, Arm, Arm! John Fletcher. That many a life hath cost. EiL

Arm Wrestling with My Father. Jack Driscoll. and have turned slowly away to watch the stars/without counting losses. GOYP

The Armada, 1588. John Wilson. It was the Lord that saved us. OxBChV

The Armada: A Fragment. Thomas Babington, Lord Macaulay. And the red glare on Skiddaw roused the burgh-/ers of Carlisle. BeLS; FaBoCh; FaPoR; GN; HBV 1-2; LoGBV; OBNC; OBRV; WBLP

An Armada of Thirty Whales. Daniel Gerard Hoffman. will contest the last will of the Sperms. NePA

The Armadillo. Elizabeth Bishop. ...and a weak mailed fist/clenched ignorant against the sky! HaCAP; NoAm; NOBA; NoP; NYBP; SM; TAP; VGW

Armageddon. John Crowe Ransom. "These Armageddons weary me much," he said. LiTA

Armageddon, Armageddon (excerpt). Paul Muldoon. And I know something of how he felt. CIP

Armagh. W. R. Rodgers. ...garrulous kings/Who at last can agree. NoAm

Armaments Race. Evangeline Paterson. to make your one wish come true AMV-81

Armed Vision. N. P. Van Wyk Louw. thing which looks down into/the ashpit: and arms itself. PeSA

The Armful. Robert Frost. And try to stack them in a better load. CMoP; OBSP

Armida, the Sorceress. Tasso. So doth thy virtue, so thy power persuade. EnLi 1-2

Armistice. Elizabeth Daryush. Airships, reconnoitering,/All day, in the silent sky. AMV-81

Armistice. Paul Dehn. Gangrene was corn, and monuments went mad. OxBTC

Armistice. Charles Buxton Going. ...And then it all/Is blurred by the insistent tears! HBMV

Armistice. Sophie Jewett. Arrayed and strong, the battle wait. AA

Armistice. Eunice Mitchell Lehmer. In open comradeship to all the world? PGD

Armistice Day. Charles Causley. A cold bugle calls, and the city moves on. OBWP

Armistice Day. John Freeman. While Time ticked silent on, men drew/A deeper breath than passion knew. MMM

Armistice Day. Roselle Mercier Montgomery. The young dead weeping! MC

Armistice Day. Lucia Trent. Dare to have pity and forgive. PGD

Armistice Day Vow. Dorothy Gould. For truth and justice, and God's valiant right! PGD

The Armless. Don Welch. I too came to know the right side/of the world. AMV-81

Armor. James Dickey. When I begin living forever. CoAP

The Armorer's Daughter. Debora Greger. ...This world shines,/rings and shines, like his dream of heaven. MAYP

The Armorer's Song. Harry Bache Smith. The armorer–that is I! AA; OHIP

Armorial. Ralph Gustafson. My love wept. ACV; PeCV

Armour's Undermining Modesty. Marianne Moore. There is the tarnish; and there, the imperishable wish. AP; CoBMV

An Armoury. Alcaeus. These are things we must remember now our duty shall begin. WaaP

Arms and the Boy. Wilfred Owen. Nor antlers through the thickness of his curls. AnEnPo; BrPo; CMoP; FaFP; HAP; LiTB; LiTM; MoAB; MoBrPo; NAMP; OAEL 1-2; OAEP; OBSP; WaP; WeW

Arms and the Woman. Dorothea Mackellar. God be thanked, I carry a knife. NOAV

The Armstrong at Fayal. Wallace Rice. For the fighting Captain and the men/Of the Yankee Privateer. PAH

Armstrong Spring Creek. Lloyd Davis. It's a fine day. AMV-81

Army Bugle Calls: Fatigue Call. *Anonymous.* Down in the ditch you go! TreF

Army Bugle Calls: Mess Call. *Anonymous.* coffee, coffee, coffee, without any cream. TreF

Army Bugle Calls: Reveille. *Anonymous.* An' the captain's worst of all! TreF

Army Bugle Calls: Sick Call. *Anonymous.* And cure, and cure, all your ills, and cure your ills. TreF

Army Bugle Calls: Stable Call. *Anonymous.* And then you will rue it, as sure as you're born. TreF

Army Bugle Calls: Taps. *Anonymous.* Peaceful dreams! TreF

An Army Corps on the March. Walt Whitman. As the army corps advances. InPS; PAI; PAL; PoLf; PPoe

Army, Navy... *Anonymous.* Law. OxNR

Arnold. *Anonymous.* Arnold shall stink to latest times. PAH

Arnold at Stillwater. Thomas Dunn English. Fell from the patriot's heaven down to the/loyalist's hell! PAH

Arnold, Master of the Scud. Bliss Carman. Arnold, Master of the Scud. EtS

Around Cape Horn. *Anonymous.* To drag my carcass around Cape Horn/A long time ago! AmSS

Around Thanksgiving. Rolfe Humphries. Of warmth and love abounding. OFD

Around the Block. Keith Waldrop. the differences between shadows. AMV-80

Around the Child. Walter Savage Landor. Pride, Envy, Malice, are his Graces. HBV 1-2

Around the Corner. *Anonymous.* "I feel I'd like to go:/"Around the corner..." FSW

Around the Corner. Charles Hanson Towne. Around the corner, a vanished friend. PoLf; PoToHe

Around the Fish: After Paul Klee. Howard Moss. The spawnless salmon strike to kill! MoPo

Around the Kitchen Table. Gary Gildner. blushing as the young blond Polish priest/bites into his chicken next to her. Str

Around the Rough and Rugged Rocks the Ragged Rascal Rudely Ran. John Ashbery. It has begun to snow. InPS

Around the World. Gary Lenhart. White delivery van/Loaded with watermelons. APU

Around You, Your House. William Stafford. The last piece flames up the draft and out/into the night, and I give you the rain. NPAW

Arraignment. Helen Gray Cone. We sobbed you our message: ye said, "It/is song, and sweet!" AA

The Arraignment of a Lover. George Gascoigne. Thus am I Beauties bounden thrall,/At hir commaunde when shee doth call./Ever or never AAS

Arran. *Anonymous.* Delightful at all times is Arran! FaBoCh; FaBoPP; LoGBV

Arrangements with Earth for Three Dead Friends. James Wright. She does not beg for anything, who knew/The change of tone, the human hope gone gray. NIP

Arras. P. K. Page. another bird assumes its furled disguise. OBCV

The Arrest of Oscar Wilde at the Cadogan Hotel. Sir John Betjeman. And was helped to a hansom outside. CMoP; DTC; EBEV; InvP; MoBrPo; NoAm; NoP; OxBTC

Arrival. John Wain. caressed by light, I lay/small, in the human day. EBEV

Arrival and Departure. Charles Eglington. Rocks on the tide, tugs at the anchor chain. PeSA

Arrival at Santos. Elizabeth Bishop. ...We leave Santos at once;/we are driving to the interior. FaBoWP; OxBC

Arrival at the Waldorf. Wallace Stevens. After that alien, point-blank, green and actual Guatemala. HaCAP; NYP; PP

Arrival in Hell. Ricarda Huch. the stone of Sisyphus rushes/down. PBWP

The Arrival of My Mother. Keith Wilson. ...drums, drums should have beaten/for the arrival of my mother. DFF; GP

The Arrival of the Bee Box. Sylvia Plath. The box is only temporary. FaBoMo; FaBoWP; HaCAP; NaP

Arrival: The Capital. Desmond O'Grady. Home to my provincial town/having spoken to no one. NMP

Arrivals and Departures. Melvin Walker La Follette. God knows, I sing! CoPo

Arrivals at a Watering-Place. Winthrop Mackworth Praed. I'm not at home if people call. NOBL

Arrivals, Departures. Philip Larkin. Or if, this night, happiness too is going. MoBrPo

Arriving. Daniel Halpern. The cabin is a bed and desk–a shroud/Of moth wings on the screen, starving for light. HoPM

Arriving. Gabriel Preil. ...is the structure of the suggestive,/the space flowing between the lines. VWA

Arrogance. Walter De la Mare. And sawdust trickled from his wounded side. OBSP

Arrogance Repressed. Sir John Betjeman. Do please tell me all about it, what you do and who you are. FiBHP

The Arrogant Frog and the Superior Bull. Guy Wetmore Carryl. THE MORAL: Everybody knows/How ill a wind it is that blows. StPo

The Arrow. Clarence Urmy. "They fail, and they alone, who have not striven." HBMV

The Arrow. William Butler Yeats. This beauty's kinder, yet for a reason/I could weep that the old is out of season. EG

The Arrow and the Song. Henry Wadsworth Longfellow I found again in the heart of a friend. AA; AnNE; FaFP; GoTF; HBV 1-2; HBVY; PoPl; TreF

The Arrow of Desire. *Anonymous.* His arrow has become the pillar of my house. WTO

Arrowhead Christian Center and No-Smoking Luncheonette. Janet Sylvester. ...pretending/I would never go near the luncheonette again. MAYP

Arrowheads. Leona Gom. and all of us harvesting still/that history. AMV-81

Arrows. William Heyen. ...the last chamber/of wolf- or bear-heart, where/all arrows wait, rot, and fly. SM

Arrowtown. Denis Glover. And the silt of the river is grey/In the golden sun. AnNZ

Arroyo. Tom Weatherly. jane in the morning.me tarzan. PoBA

Ars. Marina Tsvetayeva. lyre, my lyre, are your swanlike curve and hiss. BoWoP

Ars Amoris. J. V. Cunningham. Love's wilful potion/Veils the ensuing,/And brief, commotion. QFR

Ars Poetica. Horace. ...at whose disposing will/The power, and rule of speaking resteth still. OBVE

Ars Poetica. X. J. Kennedy. Would you lay well? Don't watch. ErPo; NIP; PP; PV

Ars Poetica. Archibald MacLeish. A poem should not mean/But be. AP; AWP; BiP; CMoP; CoBMV; DiPo; ExPo; FPL; HAP; HeIP; HoPM; InPK; InPo; LiTA; LiTM; MoAB; MoAmPo; NIP; NOBA; NoP; OxBA; PoPl; PP; SoSe; TAP

Ars Poetica. Arturo Trias. and let us sleep easy,/deeply and long. InW

Ars Poetica. Victor van Vriesland. Which are strangely bound by magic/Of their autonomous cohesion. TrJP

Ars Poetica. Adam Wazyk. I know what it is not but I don't know what it is VWA

Ars Poetica About Ultimates. Tram Combs. ship with Him! MP; TwCP

Ars Victrix. Theophile Gautier. With the resisting mass. CTC; HBV 1-2; HBVY; SyP; VLP

The Arsenal at Springfield. Henry Wadsworth Longfellow. The holy melodies of love arise. AmPP; AnNE; AP; HBV 1-2; MCCG; PGD; WaaP

Arsenic. Howard Moss. Frantic with their reasons to live? CoAP; NYBP

Arson and Cold Lace (or How I Yearn to Burn Baby Burn). Worth Long. We have found you out/False faced America/We have found you out NBP

Art. *Anonymous.* What them fellers does is ART! BLPA; NLV

Art. Ralph Waldo Emerson. Whilst upper life the slender rill/Of human sense doth overfill. AmePo; MAmP

L'Art. Frederick Feirstein. Matisse preferred to paint this scene, not I. SM

Art. Hjalmar Flax. Eat it/and find a pearl in my mouth. InW

Art. Theophile Gautier. Till thy vague dream im-/print/Its smile/On the unyielding flint. AWP; LiTW

Art. Herman Melville. To wrestle with the angel—Art. AP; EyDe; MAmP; NOBA; ViBoPo

Art. Alfred Noyes. Recall the gods that die/To rule/In Parian o'er the sky. OBEV

Art. Lilla Cabot Perry. This happy failure, this is Art. AA

Art. Jose Asuncion Silva. A simple drop alone. CAW

Art. James (1834-82) Thomson.
And shrivels all the lines. EnLi 1-2; OBVV
But they are not the Life for which they stand. NOBV
For ever its fire breaks out at last,/And shrivels all the lines. OBVV

L'Art, 1910. Ezra Pound. ...Come, let us feast our eyes. HeIP; OxBA

Art above Nature, to Julia. Robert Herrick. I must confess, mine eye and heart/Dotes less on Nature, then on Art. AnAnS 2

Art and Civilization. Robert Conquest. And clarity is but an edge/To the great weighted blade. NoAm

Art and Life. Lola Ridge. Then like a new Jill/Toiling up a hill/Life scrambles after. HBMV

Art and Reality. James Simmons. A year for every yard. CIP

Art for Art's Sake. Marc Blitzstein. All the art for Art's sake! TrJP

Art Gallery. John Dickson. wearing dress and raincoat that I can't see. AMV-81

Art in America. Theodore Weiss. touching in that mighty, empty space. AMV-80

An Art Master. John Boyle O'Reilly. While Heaven gave him his cherry-/stones and file! AA

Art McCooey. Patrick Kavanagh. Unlearnedly and unreasonably poetry is shaped/Awkwardly but alive in the unmeasured womb. FaBoIP

The Art of Cookery. William King. Crowd not your table: let your number be/Not more than seven, and never less than three. FaBoUs

The Art of Dancing. Soame Jenyns. And oft th'approaching petticoat offend. FaBoUs

The Art of Enforced Deprivation. Alta. i still dont know. GP

The Art of Eyes. Edmund Spenser. Such art of eyes I never read in books! LiTL

The Art of Happiness. Edward Hilton Young. ...but (how unlike All else/We seek on Earth?) 'tis never sought in vain. PoL

The Art of Holding On. Dwight Okita. Heads. BrSi

The Art of Love. Richard Grossman. And when we combine, it is matter/doing and doing and doing and doing. AMV-81

The Art of Love. Ovid (Publius Ovidius Naso).
Another's is as harsh as if she bray'd. FaBoUs
But here 'tis time to rest myself and you. FaBoUs; UnTE
Thank with their Tongues, but curse you with their Heart. ErPo

The Art of Love: Happy the Man Who Has Two Breasts to Crush. Kenneth Koch. Of Living, attention, please pay attention, greeniness and/mountains, oh this is the art of love! GP; NNaP

The Art of Love: Life Is Full of Horrors and Hormones. Kenneth Koch. Nor the eyes wear out, and the streets are filled with/beautiful breasts and words. GP

The Art of Making Puddings. William King.
For the receipt is learned Dr Harmer's. FaBoUs
Nutmeg, the glory of the British toast. FaBoUs
A silver soil bedeck'd with streams of gold! FaBoUs

The Art of Picasso. Salvador Dali. if I have the time/and the inclination. EAS

The Art of Poetry. John Dryden. Neglected heaps we in bye-corners lay,/Where they become to worms and moths a prey. PP

The Art of Poetry. Horace. And never leave till they have read men dead. EnLi 1-2

An Art of Poetry. James Philip McAuley. By which the spirit gains. ACV; NOCV

The Art of Poetry. Paul Verlaine. And all the rest is literature. SyP

The Art of Politics. James Bramston. Can there be any trusting to our words? NOEC

The Art of Preserving Health (excerpt). John Armstrong. And all the horrors that the guilty feel/With anxious flutterings wake the guiltless breast. NOEC

Art of the Sonnet: LVI. Gil Orlovitz. ...We haven't thought of ourselves/enough as shelters, and I am practicing. PoA

The Art of War (excerpt). Joseph Fawcett. Light-footed trip,–the feast, the feast of blood! NOEC

The Art of Wenching (excerpt). *Anonymous.* For who can say "Misfortunes know not me"? NOEC

L'Art poetique. Nicholas Boileau-Despreaux.
And in all times a forward scribbling fop/Has found some greater fool to cry him up. EnLi 1-2
Makes David Logan crown his head with bays. EnLi 1-2

Art's Variety. David McFadden. deep in the centre of her brain. NeAC

Art Thou Afraid the Adorer's Prayer. Walter Savage Landor. It leaves no stain upon the shrine. GBL

Art Thou Heywood. John Heywood. Ye sir: helpe me to it now I beseche yow. NCEP

Art Thou Lonely? John Oxenham. And thy loneliness is ended. PoToHe

Art Thou Poor, Yet Hast Thou Golden Slumbers? Thomas Dekker. Honest labour bears a lovely face,/Then hey noney, noney, hey noney, noney. CBEP; HAP; InPS; OAEP; PAI; UnPo; ViBoPo

Art Thou That She? *Anonymous.* My wit doth teach me shun/Such foolish, foolish men.' OBSP; ViBoPo

Art Thou the Same. Frances Dorr Tatnall. And ye unchanged, the same–the same? AA

Art Thou Weary? John Mason Neale. "Angels, Martyrs, Prophets, Virgins,/Answer, Yes!" CAW

Art Work. Ronald Wallace. tugging at my blind mouth. PPJ

D'Artagnan's Ride. Gouverneur Morris. And I ride and I rede/To Callice. AA

Artemis. Peter Davidson. "Die," she screams, riding. ErPo

Artemis. Dulcie Deamer. God-like you have grasped the Whole! PoAu 1-2

Artemis. Gerard de Nerval. The Saint of the Pit is holier in my eyes! LiTW

Artemis Prologizes. Robert Browning. Await, in fitting silence, the event. AnEnPo

Arthur. Tom Paulin. I'd want you away. FaBoIP

Arthur. William Winter. And know once more the name of rest. AA

Arthur McBride. *Anonymous.* For delaying our walk this fine morning. GBP; OBET

Arthur Mitchell. Marianne Moore. reveal/and veil/a peacock-tail. PoNe

Arthur Ridgewood, M.D. Frank Marshall Davis. ...worry/from rejection slips/and final notices from the Finance company. BPo

Arthur's Seat (excerpt). Thomas Mercer. Debas'd, debas'd the nation lyes/In gloom fanatic, cant, and lies! OxBS

Artichoke. Henry Taylor. what mind, what hunger, first saw this as food. MAYP

As I Walked Out One Morning. *Anonymous.* I'll have my girl I love the best, in spite of her darned old mammy. AmFP

As I Walked through the Meadows. *Anonymous.* And I plucked her a handful of may. OBET

As I was coming down the stair. *Anonymous.* I wish that man would go away! CenHV

As I was going by Charing Cross. *Anonymous.* Oh dear, my heart was ready to burst! CH; FaBoCh; LoGBV

As I Was Going to Saint Ives. Daniel Gerard Hoffman. (Two herons still the swift water.) NYBP

As I Was Going up Pippen Hill. *Anonymous.* I'd spend it all upon you. OxNR

As I Was Going up the Hill. *Anonymous.* And all the song that he could sing/Was, "Carry me safe to Dover'. OxNR

As I Was Laying on the Green. *Anonymous.* So I left it laying in the same position. FiBHP

As I Was Standing in the Street. *Anonymous.* A great big ugly man came up/And tied his horse to me. NTCP

As I Was Walkin' Down Wexford Street (with music). *Anonymous.* While me tender mother her hair she ture. AS

As I Went A-Walking down Ratcliffe Highway. *Anonymous.* Sing tu-re-lye laddie, I tu-re-lye-lay. ShS

As I Went A-Walking One Fine Summer's Evening. *Anonymous.* And pleasing the baby and the child not his own. OuSiCo

As I Went Down to David's Town. George Craig Stewart. Shine upon you all the way/Till Christmas comes again! AH

As I Went out for a Ramble. *Anonymous.* But if she ever proves true to me/I'll marry and settle down. OuSiCo

As I Went out on Christmas Day. *Anonymous.* Alas, I go with child./Kyrie eleison. CBEP

As I Went over the Water. *Anonymous.* I took up my little black stick,/And kocked out all their teeth. PBBP

As I Went Singing over the Earth. Mary Elizabeth Coleridge. A song that was of little worth,/And the song of a bird. UnS

As I Went to Bonner. *Anonymous.* Upon my word and honour. OxBoLi

As I Went up the Brandy Hill. *Anonymous.* Blow the bellows old man. OxNR

As I Went up the Humber Jumber. *Anonymous.* I'd never have let Sir Hoker Poker/Carry away campeenio. FaBoNo

As If a Phantom Caress'd Me. Walt Whitman. And those appear that are hateful to me and mock me. GBL

As If from Her Nest. *Anonymous.* Oh, how I never want to part from him! HW

As If You Had Never Been. Richard Eberhart. It is as if you had never been. EyDe

As imperceptibly as grief. Emily Dickinson. Our Summer made her light escape/Into the Beautiful. CMoP; DiPo; ExPo; ForPo; LiTA; LiTM; NOBA; NoP; PBWP; PoEL 1-5; QFR

As in a Dusky and Tempestuous Night. William, of Hawthornden Drummond. And made all eyes with wonder thee behold. LO

As in a Rose-Jar. Thomas S. Jones, Jr. The haunting fragrance that still lingers here/As in a rose-jar, so within my heart. PoLf

As in Smooth Oil the Razor Best Is Whet. *Anonymous.* Both pain the heart when exquisitely keen. HBV 1-2

As in the Land of Darkness. Robert Miklitsch. I stop to wonder at our/stubborn appetite for joy. AMV-80

As in the Midst of Battle There Is Room. George Santayana. Despair before us, vanity behind. AnFE; APA; AWP; NePA

As in the Old Days: Passages 8. Robert Duncan. "want to have little beds, and tables,/and everything else." PoM

As in Their Time. Louis MacNeice.
...For all that the cannibals/Ate her one day they had nothing else to do. PoL
It broke about even, made no sense. PoL
Was it love she believed in? PoL

As into the Garden Elizabeth Ran. Alfred Edward Housman. She will tread on a toad if she possibly can. NLV

As Is the Sea Marvelous. Edward Estlin Cummings. of your/soul/upon/my lips. MOS

As It Looked Then. Edwin Arlington Robinson. Arching a world where nothing had occurred. CMoP; NePA; NoAm

As Joe Gould Says In. Edward Estlin Cummings. if i/'d/OH/n/lygawntueco/llege. FiBHP

As Joseph Was A-Walking. *Anonymous.* But with fair spring water/With which we were christened. OHIP; ViBoPo

As Kingfishers Catch Fire, Dragonflies Draw Flame. Gerard Manley Hopkins. To the Father through the features of men's faces. CMoP; DiPo; EaLo; EBEV; ExPo; FaBoMo; LiTM; MoRP; NOBV; NOCV; NoP; PrIm; VLP

As Lambs into the Pen. Dorothy Wellesley. Love to Death is gathered in. FaBoTw

As Life What Is So Sweet? *Anonymous.* He would not reave them of their happy breath. OBSP

As Like the Woman as You Can. William Ernest Henley. "Till you achieve that Female-Male/In which shall culminate the race." HBV 1-2

As Long as the Heart Beats. Christine Zawadiwsky. Someone knows that time can't fly. AMV-81

As Love and I, Late Harbour'd in One Inn. Michael Drayton. Fools as we met, so fools again we parted. GBL

As Night Comes On. Cecil Cobb Wesley. And not a twig and not a thought/Remember where they used to be. GoYe

As Ocean's Stream. Fyodor Tyutchev. And we sail onward, and our wake is fire. AWP

As Oft as I Behold and See. Henry Howard, Earl of Surrey. The thing that breedeth his unrest. SiPS

As Often as Some Where before My Feet. Francis Daniel Pastorius. Pure, Bright, and Glorious be/Whose wondrous works I see. SCAP

As on Serena's Panting Breast. *Anonymous.* Then, buzzing 'round her snowy breast,/He crept into the hive. UnTE

As on the Heather. Reinmar von Hagenau. That love is ripening while they surmise/Escapes their eyes! AWP

As One Put Drunk into the Packet-Boat. John Ashbery. But night, the reserved, the reticent, gives more than it takes. HaCAP; HAP

As One Who Bears beneath His Neighbor's Roof. Robert Hillyer. His jest eternal, and our lives so short. MoAmPo

As One Who Wanders Into Old Workings. C. Day-Lewis. Lovely the leap, explosion into light. FaBoMo; LiTM

As Oyster Nan Stood by Her Tub. *Anonymous.* She daily ventures at the same,/And shuts and opens like an Oyster. CoMu

As power and wit will me assist. Sir Thomas Wyatt. Ye may my life save or expel/Even as ye list. FCP; SiPS

As Proper Mode of Quenching Legal Lust. Gerald Massey. She must show black and blue, or no divorce/Is granted by the Law of Physical Force. NOBV

As Rivers of Water in a Dry Place. Anna Bunston de Bary. Fresh as God's latest word! HBMV

As Rocks Rooted. Howard G. Hanson. and touching, and within call. AMV-80

As Sand. Natan Zach. But this is heaven's way,/and possibly, nature's. VWA

As Some Mysterious Wanderer of the Skies. Henry Jerome Stockard. Thou knowest, eternal God, and thou alone! AA

As Soon as Ever Twilight Comes. Walter De la Mare. Stars peep into the room. SiSoSe

As Spring the Winter Doth Succeed. Anne Bradstreet. To Him that heard my wailing voice. AH; EBCP

As Sun, As Sea. James Sullivan. To the river as the sea. AMV-81

As the Day Breaks. Ernest McGaffey. The night is gone. AA

As the Dead Prey upon Us. Charles Olson. ...The automobile/has been hauled away. NeAP

As the Holly Groweth Green. King of England Henry VIII. Be sure, and ever shall! ViBoPo

As the Mist Leaves No Scar. Leonard Cohen. So will we endure/When one is gone and far. NoP

As the Rains of Spring. Izumi Shikibu. And green spreads everywhere. PBWP

As the Team's Head-Brass. Edward ("Edward Eastaway") Thomas. After the ploughshare and the stumbling team. ExPo; GTBS-P; MMM; OBWP; OxBTC; PoPle

As the Window Darkens. Laura Jensen. The ocean is a dish of water carried by a woman,/where the worry of our lives lies down. LCAP

As the World Turns. Larry Mollin. like the hoola hoop dream dance/for singles only NeAC

As Thro' the Land at Eve We Went. Alfred, Lord Tennyson. O there above the little grave,/We kiss'd again with tears. LiTB; LiTL

As Thy Days. Grant Colfax Tullar. For as Thy days, Thy strength shall be. BLRP

As Thy Days So Shall Thy Strength Be. Georgiana Holmes. But we can go, if by God's power/We only bear the burden of the hour. TRV

As to Being Alone. James Oppenheim. Have the life-surging heavens no/business but this? TrJP

As to His Choice of Her. Wilfrid Scawen Blunt. Yet must I love thee, dear, and as thou art. ViBoPo

As Toilsome I Wander'd Virginia's Woods. Walt Whitman. Bold, cautious, true, and my loving comrade. AmePo; HBV 1-2; SeCeV; ViBoPo

As Tommy Snooks and Bessy Brooks. Mother Goose. "To-morrow will be Monday." HBV 1-2; HBVY

As Tranquil Streams. Marion Franklin Ham. Proclaim the truth that makes men free. AH

As Vesta Was from Latmos Hill Descending. *Anonymous.* Long live fair Oriana. OAEP

As We Are So Wonderfully Done with Each Other. Kenneth Patchen. Don't let anyone in to wake us ErPo

Asleep. Wilfred Owen. ...He sleeps less tremulous, less cold/Than we who must awake, and waking, say Alas! MMM

Asleep. William Winter. And he said,"My love was weary–God/bless her! she's asleep." AA

Asleep at the.Switch. *Anonymous.* I'd been taking a nap in my bed and had not been asleep at the switch. PaPo

Asleep at the Switch. George Hoey. And had not been asleep at the switch. BeLS

Asleep in Jesus. Margaret Mackprang MacKay. Securely shall my ashes lie,/And wait the summons from on high. BePJ

Asleep in the Bosom of Youth. Judah Halevi. Pursue after thy King in the intimate company/Of souls that flow unto the goodness of the Lord. LiTW

Asleep in the Deep. Arthur J. Lamb. So beware! beware! FSN; TreFT

Asmodai. Geoffrey Hill. Closing the doors of the house and the head also! NePoEA

Asolando. Robert Browning.
God is it who transcends. OAEL 1-2; VLP
"Strive and thrive!" cry "Speed,–fight on, fare ever/There as here!" EnLit; FaBV; FiP; GTBS; HBV 1-2; HBVY; OAEP; TEP; TreFT; TrGrPo; VLP

Asparagus. Jonathan Swift. O, 'tis pretty Picking/With a tender Chicken. NCEP

Aspatia's Song. Francis Beaumont and John Fletcher. Upon my buried body lay lightly, gentle earth. AWP; HBV 1-2; NOBE; OBEV; PoPle

An Aspect of Love, Alive in the Ice and Fire. Gwendolyn Brooks. in different directions/down the imperturbable street. CAPP; TAP

Aspecta Medusa. Dante Gabriel Rossetti. ...but be/Its shadow upon life enough for thee. OBSP; VLP

Aspects. Norman MacCaig. In such clean qualities as time and space. BSV; OxBS

Aspects of Robinson. Weldon Kees. ...all covering/His sad and usual heart, dry as a winter leaf. CoAP; NaP; NYBP; NYP

Aspects of Some Forsythia Branches. Ralph Gustafson. With the knowledge ahead of us, to wrap our throats. PeCV

Aspects of Spring in Greater Boston. George Starbuck. ...brings mosaic/to dusty windshields, to the waking, music. NYBP

Aspects of the Pines. Paul Hamilton Hayne. Wears for a gem the tremulous vesper/star. AA; AnAmPo; HBV 1-2

Aspects of the World Like Coral Reefs. William Bronk. whose rough agglomerate smashes the sea. VGW

The Aspen and the Stream. Richard Wilbur. Even if that blind groping but achieves/A darker head, a few more aspen leaves. NYBP

The Aspen's Song. Yvor Winters. The summer holds me here. PoL

Aspens. Edward ("Edward Eastaway") Thomas. Or so men think who like a different tree. ChMP; InPS; PAI

Asphodel. David Malouf. ...Earth holds firm under my heel. CBAP

Asphodel, That Greeny Flower. William Carlos Williams. and every man/who wants to die in peace in his bed/besides. CMoP; PP and so/it brought us together. FaBoMo

Aspiration. Mario De Andrade. And I feel larger, equalizing myself to the equal men!... TTY

Aspiration. William Drennan. And half illume the long departed dead. IrPN

Aspiration. Charles Lamb. A Catholic, Madonna fair, to worship thee. CAW

The Aspiration. John Norris. She'd for no angels' conduct stay,/But fly, and love-on, all the way. LoBV; OxBoCh

Aspiration. Edward William Thomson. And whisper'd Christ, as if the soul had heard/Tidings of some exceeding sweet design. OBVV

The Ass. Edwin Allan. that only a halter/can alter/the middlecrass assitude. PoPl

The Ass. Moses Mendes. For he who his pleasures puts off for/a day,/Deserves to be reckon'd an Ass. TrJP

Ass-Face. Edith Sitwell. Expelled from the golden bars! OBMV

The Ass in the Lion's Skin. Aesop. That's just the way with asses, just the way. AWP; LiTW

Assailant. John Raven. I'm talkin' 'bout a rat! BPo

The Assassin's Fatal Error. Lawrence Raab. Nothing but this. AmPA

The Assassination. Robert Hillyer. "How funny, Hope." AnNE; MoAmPo; OFD

Assassination. Don L. Lee. in the/wrong/direction. BOLo; BP; FF; NeAC; OFD; PoBA

The Assassination of President McKinley. Paul Blackburn. ...gone/under the final two strokes of Trinity's bell. NYP

Assassination Poems. John Ridland. and we do as He says MAT; OFD

The Assault. Robert Nichols. Cool madness. MCCG

The Assault on the Fortress. Timothy Dwight. Till death, and sweeping fire, laid waste the/hostile field. PAH

Assay a Friend. *Anonymous.* Thus she said, when she sang last:/"Assay a frend or thou have nede." OxBM

Assembly. William Stanley Merwin. others sing clapping their hands. GP

Assembly: Harlem School. Eugene T. Maleska. Oh, let it ring! GoYe

Assembly Line. Adrien Stoutenburg. Beneath, the earth is six feet deep;/the grass is optional and spare. AmC

Asses. Padraic Colum. For a ragged man/With a pound or two. LOW

The Assignation. Juana de Ibarbourou. toward which the moon drags itself like a dog. PBWP

The Assignation. Imr el Kais. The ripening clusters hang) rivaled the deep mid-/night.... LiTW

The Assignation. James Wright. I saw the picnic vanish down the hill,/And waved the moon awake, with empty hands. NePoEA

Assignation with a Somnambulist. John Streeter Manifold. Shaping our burrows in the sand. CBAP

Assignment: Descriptive Essay. Gary Willis. the irresolvable mystery/of the human heart. AMV-81

Assimilation. Irving Feldman. And I wake up kicking and screaming, Lemme go!/Lemme go! AmPC

Assisi. Alfred Noyes. Assisi grew into the light, as flowers and children grow. GoBC

The Assistance. Paul Blackburn. that gave me courage/lo que me dio valor. NeAP; PoM

Assuming the Name of Any Next Child. John Tagliabue. He came into the world with Absolute Continuity. AMV-80

Assumpta est Maria. Liam Brophy. Yet harken Heaven's hymns to our combin'd:/Assumpta est Maria. ISi

Assumpta Maria. Francis. Thompson. Who am I the heavens assume? an/All am I, and I am one. ISi

The Assumption. *Anonymous.* Wher thou art now let me be,/For al my love is laid on thee.' OxBM

The Assumption. Sir John Beaumont.
Flames with flames t'unite. GoBC
Now she sits with the Sun. ACP; CAW

The Assumption. John Gilland Brunini. The Mother of Fair Love has come to dwell/In God–O, angels, praise the glory of her face! ISi

Assumption. Padraic Fallon. ...Foreign tongues/Commune above her in a drift of wings. BIrV; NOBI

The Assumption. Saint Nerses. Daniel, the mount whence the great stone was taken! CAW

The Assumption. John Banister Tabb. Thy Fledgling calls thee home! ISi

Assunpink and Princeton. Thomas Dunn English. And ebb-tide for ever and ever had passed. MC; PAH

An Assurance. Nicholas Breton. You are blessed out of measure. OBSC

Assurance. George Herbert. Now Love and Truth will end in man. OxBoCh

Assurance. Ida Norton Munson. I, too, know "Christ is risen, as he said." PGD

Assynt. Alan Gilchrist. life, sweet savage life, goes on. PoSH

Aster. Plato. Now, having died, thou art as Hesperus, giving/New splendor to the dead. LiTW

The Asteroid Light. *Anonymous.* Oh, for the life at the speed of c! FSW

Astraea. Ralph Waldo Emerson. Daily stoops to harbour there. AnNE

Astraea. John Greenleaf Whittier. As now in heaven! AA

Astraea at the Capitol. John Greenleaf Whittier. Who see by faith the cloudy hem/Of Judgment fringed with Mercy's light! PAH

Astraea Redux. John Dryden. The World a Monarch, and that Monarch You. CEP; OBS

The Astrologer Argues Your Death. Charles deGravelles. Your death is moving towards you,/travelling at the speed of light. AMV-81

An Astrologer's Song. Rudyard Kipling. While the Stars in their courses/Do fight on our side? MoBrPo

Astrology. Tom Marshall. give me the whole fire of your heart. PeCV

Astronaut's Choice. M. M. Darcy. Their astronaut may choose to settle/Down upon the farthest star. QQQ

An Astronomer's Journal. Jane Shore. "Actually, the universe is introspective." PoA

The Astronomers of Mont Blanc. Edgar Bowers. The perfect order trusted to the dead. PoA; QFR

Astronomy. Alfred Edward Housman. Is buried with the pole. OBWP

Astrophel and Stella, I. Sir Philip Sidney. "Fool," said my Muse to me, "look in thy heart, and/write." AAS; AWP; CABA; EBEV; EG; EnLi 1-2; GBL; HAP; HBV 1-2; InPS; NoP; OAEL 1-2; OAEP; OBSC; SiPS; TEP; TreFT; TrGrPo; ViBoPo

Astrophel and Stella, II. Sir Philip Sidney. While, with a feeling skill, I paint my hell. AAS; OAEL 1-2; SiPS

Astrophel and Stella, III. Sir Philip Sidney. But copying is, what, in her, Nature writes. AAS; OAEL 1-2; OBSC; SiPS

Astrophel and Stella, IV. Sir Philip Sidney. That, Virtue, thou thyself shalt be in love. AAS; SiPS

Astrophel and Stella, V. Sir Philip Sidney. True, and yet true that I must Stella love. AAS; OAEL 1-2; OBSC; SiPS

Astrophel and Stella, VI. Sir Philip Sidney. When trembling voice brings forth that I do Stella love. AAS; SiPS

Astrophel and Stella, VII. Sir Philip Sidney. To honour all their deaths who for her bleed. AAS; NIP; SiPS

Astrophel and Stella, LXXXIII. Sir Philip Sidney. Leave that sir Phip, least off your necke be wroong. AAS; SiPS

Astrophel and Stella, LXXXIV. Sir Philip Sidney. Hundreds of yeares you Stellas feet may kisse. AAS; OAEP; OBSC; SiPS

Astrophel and Stella, LXXXV. Sir Philip Sidney. Thou but of all the kingly Tribute take. AAS; SiPS

Astrophel and Stella, LXXXVI. Sir Philip Sidney. No doom should make man's heaven become his hell. AAS; SiPS

Astrophel and Stella, LXXXVII. Sir Philip Sidney. I had been vext, if vext I had not been. AAS; SiPS

Astrophel and Stella, LXXXVIII. Sir Philip Sidney. United powers make each the stronger prove. AAS; SiPS

Astrophel and Stella, LXXXIX. Sir Philip Sidney. I feel the flames of hottest summer day. AAS; SiPS

Astrophel and Stella, XC. Sir Philip Sidney. And love doth hold my hand, and makes me write. AAS; OBSC; SiPS

Astrophel and Stella, XCI. Sir Philip Sidney. If you hear that they seem my heart to move:/Not them, O no, but you in them I love. AAS; SiPS

Astrophel and Stella, XCII. Sir Philip Sidney. Say all, and all, well sayd, still say the same. AAS; SiPS

Astrophel and Stella, XCIII. Sir Philip Sidney. I cry thy sighs, my dear, thy tears I bleed. AAS; SiPS

Astrophel and Stella, XCIV. Sir Philip Sidney. Yet growest more wretched than thy nature bears/By being placed in such a wretch as I. AAS; SiPS

Astrophel and Stella, XCV. Sir Philip Sidney. Thank-worthiest yet when you shall break my heart. AAS; SiPS

Astrophel and Stella, XCVI. Sir Philip Sidney. For that at length yet doth invite some rest,/Thou though still tired, yet still doost it detest. AAS; SiPS

Astrophel and Stella, XCVII. Sir Philip Sidney. While I despair my sun's sight to enjoy. AAS; SiPS

Astrophel and Stella, XCVIII. Sir Philip Sidney. That worms should have their sun and I want mine. EnLoPo; SiPS

Astrophel and Stella, XCIX. Sir Philip Sidney. Forced by their lord, who is asham'd to find/Such light in sense with such a darkened mind. SiPS

Astrophel and Stella, C. Sir Philip Sidney. All mirth farewell, let me in sorrow live. AAS; SiPS

Astrophel and Stella, CI. Sir Philip Sidney. Knowing worlds pass ere she enough can find/Of such heaven-stuff to clothe so heavenly a mind. AAS; SiPS

Astrophel and Stella, CII. Sir Philip Sidney. While beauties reddest inke Venus for him doth sturre. AAS; SiPS

Astrophel and Stella, CIII. Sir Philip Sidney. Let Honor's self to thee grant highest place! AAS; HBV 1-2; SiPS

Astrophel and Stella, CIV. Sir Philip Sidney. ...and puffing proves that I/Do Stella love: fools, who doth it deny? AAS; SiPS

Astrophel and Stella, CV. Sir Philip Sidney. Curst be the coachman that did drive so fast,/With no less curse than absence makes me taste. AAS; SiPS; SiPS 10]

Astrophel and Stella, CVII. Sir Philip Sidney. And scorning say, "See what it is to love." AAS; HBV 1-2; NoP; SiPS

Astrophel and Stella, CVIII. Sir Philip Sidney. That in my woes for thee thou art my joy,/And in my joyes for thee my only annoy. AAS; SiPS

Astrophel and Stella, CX. Sir Philip Sidney. Eternal Love, maintain thy life in me. NIP; TEP

Aswelay. Norman Henry Pritchard II. the bird who watched/what would be called/a dream PoBA

Asylum. David R. Clark. Poetry, insanely sweet. PPON

Asylum. John Freeman. ...and wise men here should find/Asylum from the thought and fear of Death. OBMV

The Asylum, II. Hayden Carruth. But we, with rifles poised, kept on our search. SM

At 21. Eugene L. Belisle. Create me well, or I shall be self-born. AMV-81

At 79th and Park. Barbara Howes. All have been vacuumed up. NYP

At 85. Richard Ardinger. ...and lean against/another autumn wind. AMV-81

At a Bach Concert. Adrienne Rich. Only such proud restraining purity/Restores the else-betrayed, too-human heart. NePoEA; NIP; SM

At a Calvary Near the Ancre. Wilfred Owen. But they who love the greater love/Lay down their life; they do not hate. MoRP

At a Child's Baptism. Vassar Miller. Softly, too, by this most gentle/Rein of all, this drop of water. GoJo

At a Chinaman's Grave. Wing Tek Lum. these tombstones,/by the rest. BrSi

At a Concert of Music. Conrad Aiken. And all I can grasp is an earlier, more haunted moment,/And a happier place. MoAB; MoAmPo; UnS

At a Country Dance in Provence. Harold Monro. Suddenly am quite alone/With the beating of my heart. OBVV

At a Country Fair. John Holmes. On the merry-go-round. MoShBr

At a Cowboy Dance. James Barton Adams. Keno! Promenade to seats! BPAW; HBV 1-2; PoOW

At a Georgia Camp Meeting. Kerry Mills. When they quit their laughing and talking and went to walking for a big choc'late cake. BLSo ·

At a Hasty Wedding. Thomas Hardy. For now they solace swift desire. InPK; VLP

At a Loss. James L. Weil. Almost an impertinence/To him embracing her. GoYe

At a Low Mass for Two Hot-Rodders. X. J. Kennedy. But, inches from it, felt, and turned aside. Psk

At a March against the Vietnam War. Robert Bly. We make war/Like a man anointing himself. EAS

At a Month's End. Algernon Charles Swinburne. The wild-beast mark of panther's fangs. VLP

At a Parade. Frank Templeton Prince. And all the gilded tissues lost, unloosed. NeBP; WaP

At a Potato Digging. Seamus Heaney. Then, stretched on the faithless ground, spill/Libations of cold tea, scatter crusts. IPY

At a Private Showing in 1982. Maxine W. Kumin. we few will finish the wine/and skulk out on this spring night/together, unsafe on Capitol Hill. SV

At a Reading. Thomas Bailey Aldrich. A high complexion without fleck/Or flaw, and curls about her neck. OBAL

At a Ruined Croft. John Manson. And at the east gable/A corroded pipe—one in a hill of 500 acres–/Works PoSH

At a Solemn Music. John Milton. To live with him, and sing in endless morn of light. ExPo; GTBS; GTBS-P; HBV 1-2; HeIP; LoBV; NOBE; OAEP; SeCeV

At a Solemn Musick. Delmore Schwartz. You were: you were alone. EG; MoRP; OBEV; OBS; PoEL 1-5; UnS

At a Summer Hotel. Isabella Gardner. ...Uneasy in the drafty shade, I rock on the veranda,/reminded of Europa...Persephone...Miranda. GrPl

At a Time. Ray Mathew. Why remember more than that? PoAu 1-2

At a Vacation Exercise. John Milton. Are held with his melodious harmonie/In willing chains and sweet captivitie. JCP; OBS; PP

At a Watering-Place. Thomas Hardy. Well, bliss is in ignorance: what's the harm! BrPo; CMoP

At a Welsh Waterfall. Gerard Manley Hopkins. It was a hard thing to undo this knot. FaBoPP

At a Window. Carl Sandburg. And wait and know the coming/Of a little love. FaBoBe; HBMV; MoLP; PoToHe; TrPWD

At an Exhibition of Historical Paintings, Hobart. Vivian Smith. the pathos of the past, the human creature. CBAP; NOAV

At an Inn. Thomas Hardy. Ere death, once let us stand/As we stood then! NOBV

At Annika's Place. Siv Widerberg. I wish it was like Annika's place/at our place. NTCP

At April. Angelina Weld Grimke. When April comes a-laughing and a-weeping/Once again/At our hearts? BlSi

At Arley. Andrew Young. I see the solid hill/Flow backward for a moment and stand still. FaBoPP

At Arm's Length. Shirley Bossert. and I would let him in. FAZ

At Baia. Hilda ("H. D.") Doolittle. Lover to lover, no kiss,/no touch, but forever and ever this. AnFE; APA; LiTA; MAPA; NOBA

At Ballyshannon, Co. Donegal. William Allingham. Whether within or without me/They were, I cannot say. FaBoPP

At Barstow. Charles Tomlinson. ...that execrable conjunction/of gasoline and desert air. NoAm; TwCP

At Bedtime. Mariana Griswold Van Rensselaer. But when he sang his song for me, 'twas Darling that I heard. HBMV

At Belle Isle. Anonymous. At the siege of Belle Isle. OxNR

At Best. John Boyle O'Reilly. The ship that holds the straightest course/Still sails the convex sea. AA

At Bickford's. Gerald Stern. I will lose half my hatred/at the round tables. NYP

At Birth. Anthony Thwaite. And echoed with your crying/Your living paradox. NePoEA-2

At Boot Hill in Tombstone, Arizona. Anonymous. No Les/No More. ShM

At Brill on the Hill. Anonymous. I know no more than this. GBP; OxNR

At Bungendore. James Philip McAuley. Irised by the gleam/Of tears, as it does now. PoAu 1-2

At Cambridge. Audrey McGaffin. ...the mind/that directed the pride that the/hand killed. NePoAm

At Camino. Timothy Sheehan. while above, a meteor, luminous and brief,/is accepting and releasing our piece of light. SUW

At Candlemas. Charles Causley. But still within the elder tree/The strong sap rose, though none could see. OBCP

At Carbis Bay. Arthur Symons. The peace of the sky. FaBoPP

At Carmel. Mary Austin. And the contented blether of the Mission sheep. AmFN

At Carmel Highlands. Janet Lewis. An ancient speech, hushed in tremendous ease. PoA

At Last. Katrina Trask. "The Lord of Life be praised! I, too,/have died." AA

At Last. John Greenleaf Whittier.
And find at last, beneath Thy trees of healing,/The life for which I long. TreFS; TrPWD
I find myself by hands familiar beckoned/Unto my fitting place. WGRP
The life for which I long. AP; TreFS

At last love has come. Sulpicia. ...We met. We are both worthy. BoWoP

At Last the Secret Is Out. W.H. Auden. There is always a wicked secret, a private reason for this. InPS; SeCePo

At last, to be identified! Emily Dickinson. ...Ah! what leagues there are/Between our feet and day! WGRP

At Last We Killed the Roaches. Lucille Clifton. my hands were blades and it was murder murder/all over the place. GP; NIP

At last withdraw your cruelty. Sir Thomas Wyatt. No man alive nor I/Of double death can die. FCP; SiPS

At Least. Don Mattera. let me unclench my being/to stroke the yellow flowers1 WhB

At Least–To Pray–Is Left–Is Left. Emily Dickinson. Say, Jesus Christ of Nazareth–/Hast thou no Arm for me? AmePo

At Length the Busy Day Is Done. Francis Hopkinson. Nought but religion is sincere. AH

At Length There Dawns the Glorious Day. Ozora S. Davis. Of our great Lord and King. AH

At Liberty. Anne S. Perlman. They melt. SUW

At Lincoln. Oscar Fay Adams. What time the clock slow chimed the hour. AA

At Little Virgil's Window. Edwin Markham. And our God be glad and our world be sweeter! TRV

At Long Last. Lindsay Patterson. ...corduroy/Gayla that makes you stand out/Even in a festive crowd. CNA

At Lord's. Francis Thompson. O my Hornby and my Barlow long ago! LiSp; OBSP

At Luca Signorelli's Resurrection of the Body. Jorie Graham. until his mind/could climb into/the open flesh and/mend itself. HaCAP

At Lucky Moments We Seem on the Brink. W. H. Auden. But, even then, an honest eye should wink. PV

At Lulworth Cove a Century Back. Thomas Hardy. And bend with reverence where his ashes lie. ChMP

At Majority. Adrienne Rich. And gather in your brow and air/The stillness of antiquity. NePoEA-2

At Masada. Ernest Neufeld. until the spirit that here abides,/shall overcome all Amalekites. AMV-81

At Mass. Robin Flower. I looked at you once, and the half of my soul was lost. OxBI

At Mass. Vachel Lindsay. Once in a thousand days your voice/Has laid temptation low. VGW

At Max Gate. Siegfried Sassoon. Someone had taken Mr. Hardy's place. NoAm

At Melville's Tomb. Hart Crane. This fabulous shadow only the sea keeps. AP; CoBMV; HAP; InPo; MoAmPo; MOS; NePA; NoAm; NoP; PoA; TAP; UnPo; VGW

At Mexican Springs. Laura Tohe. and I will live to tell my children these things. STE

At Mid-Ocean. Robert Bly. ...sunlight/sliding over ocean water a thousand miles from land. LLLT

At Midnight. Ted Kooser. a rich cape/woven of many loves/swept recklessly/about his shoulders. GOYP

At Midnight. Frank Dempster Sherman. And out of this flower of Time/Twelve petals are wafted down. AA

At Midnight's Hour. Henry David Thoreau. The word was whispered through the ranks, Advance. LiTA; PoEL 1-5

At Midsummer. Norman Dubie. You smile and cross over me like a welcome storm. MAYP

At Morning an Iris. Patrick Evans. Combs her electrical head. NeBP

At most mischief. Sir Thomas Wyatt. My lute and I/Continually/Shall us apply/To sigh and moan. FCP; SiPS

At Mount Vernon. Thomas Curtis Clark. One name shall shine with splendor–WASHINGTON. PAL; PGD

At Mrs. Appleby's. Elizabeth Upham McWebb. It's spring at Mrs. Appleby's! BrR; SiSoSe; TiPo

At My Father's Grave. John Ciardi. ...when I dare/disturb the leaf that's wedged against my door. SM

At My Father's Grave. Hugh" (Christopher Murray Grieve) MacDiarmid. And ony sma'er thocht's impossible. ELU; GTBS-P

At My Grandmother's. David Malouf. and watched the old grey hands wind out his blood. PoAu 1-2

At My Mother's Knee. *Anonymous.* And keep me a pilgrim forever/To the shrine at my mother's knee. STF

At My Whisper. John Lyle Donaghy. endow the fallow plain. AnIV

At Newmarket. Samuel Bishop. Like groom, like peer! like peer, like groom! PV

At Night. Bella Akhmadulina. through the dry leaves of last autumn. BoWoP

At Night. Rachel Boimwall. The wall has pulled them back/into itself,/and covered them over with blackness. VWA

At Night. Frances Cornford. With your vast pity, wash it smooth again. MoBrPo

At Night. Richard Eberhart. My father's hands, my mother's eyes. Str

At Night. Margherita Guidacci. and listen to subterranean voices. WPOW

At Night. Alice Meynell. Your words to me, your words! CH; HBV 1-2; LiTL; OBVV

At Night. George Edgar Montgomery. The stars grow real to me like deathless/Rome. AA

At Night. Alan Proctor. I am thinking about the cannisters of nerve gas/honeycombed outside Salt Lake City. FAZ

At Nightfall. Charles Hanson Towne. After the day's great sun. BLPA; FaBoBe

At Nine O'Clock in the Spring. Elissa Bishop. and you, in that landscape,/are as small as a snowflake. AMV-80

At North Farm. John Ashbery. That we think of him sometimes,/Sometimes and always, with mixed feelings? HaCAP

At One Glance. Mihri Hatun. Let me burn in the hellfire/Of that sin PBWP

At One O'Clock in the Morning. Charles Baudelaire. ...that I am not/inferior to those I despise. SyP

At Only That Moment. Alan Ross. The union of bow and waters,/Writes its last lines alone. ErPo

At Parting. Algernon Charles Swinburne. Love can but last in us here at his height/For a day and a night. HBV 1-2; ViBoPo

At Penshurst. Edmund Waller. But from those gifts which Heav'n has heap'd on her. AnAnS 2; OAEP; OEAL 1-2; SeCV 1-2

At Piccadilly Circus. Vivian de Sola Pinto. Blown through the stifling streets of slums. OBMV

At Pont-Aven, Gauguin's Last Home in France. Andrew Grossbardt. ...for distant islands/so remote we can never know their names. AMV-81

At Port Royal: Song of the Negro Boatman. John Greenleaf Whittier. O nebber you fear, if nebber you hear/De driver blow his horn! GN

At Quebec. Jean Blewett. A wondrous softness on her grey old face. CaP

At Queensferry. William Ernest Henley. The still, strange land, unvexed of sun or stars,/Where Lancelot rides clanking thro' the haze. VLP

At Rest in the Blast. Marianne Moore. At rest in the blast. MoAB; MoAmPo

At Roblin Lake. Alfred W. Purdy. For this bit of green costume jewellery/A nescient, obscure love. PeCV

At Rochdale. Ian Young. "Man, everything is so profound..." NeAC

At Saint Patrick's Purgatory. Donnchadh mor O'Dala. And I with a heart not softer than a stone! AnIL; LiTW; OnYI

At Sainte-Marguerite. Trumbull Stickney. Thou askest nothing, evermore at home/In thy own self's perennial masterdom. LiTA; MoVE; NCEP; OxBA

At Sea. James Whitcomb Riley. And waft us home again! MOS

At Sea. D.H. Rogers. In the blinding drift from the angry sea. AnNZ

At Sea. Jean Toomer. Felt the pang of transcience. BALP

At Sea. John Townsend Trowbridge. I heard the soothing summer-rain. AmePo; EtS

At Set of Sun. George Eliot. Than count that day as worse than lost. PoPl; PoToHe; TRV

At Set of Sun. Mary Ashley Townsend. Together, side by side, life's Angelus! AA

At Shagger's Funeral. Bruce Dawe. ...caught with his britches down/By death, whom he'd imagined out of town? NOAV

At Shakespeare's Grave. Irving Browne. Your cake is dough, for I by sifting well/Have quite reduced your dust to Bacon-powder. AA

At Slim's River. John Haines. and I went down. NPAW

At St. Jerome. Frances Harrison. Among the hills of St. Jerome/I would not fear to make my home. WHW

At Staufen. Michael Hamburger. Or the sand alone,/For the blank sand. VWA

At Such a Time, in Such a Spot. Emily Bronte. My love–and nothing more! VLP

At Summer's End. Saul Hillel Benjamin. we steal what we already own. AMV-81

At Sunrise. Rosa Zagnoni Marinoni. When his proud mother took his height/Against the bedroom wall. PoToHe

At Sunset. Louis V. Ledoux. Clasp her and hold and love. HBV 1-2

At Swindon. Reginald, Viscount Esher Brett. Make light of love, and check the trembling tears. PeHV

At Tea. Thomas Hardy. And he throws her a stray glance yearningly. BrPo

At That Moment. Raymond Richard Patterson. ...But the police were too late./It had already happened. PoBA

At the Airport. John Malcolm Brinnin. Their coming down again. MoAB

At the Airport in Dallas. Stephen Mooney. You just come right back here,/Lucille. TAT

At the Algonquin. Howard Moss. And, getting up, he said, "Ah, there you are!" Psk

At the Altar-Rail. Thomas Hardy. I had eaten the apple ere you were weaned.' BrPo

At the Appointed Hour They Came. Michael Smith. In the evening the air sank with the weight of darkness. CIP

At the Aquarium. Max Eastman. Sometimes a pale and cold surprise. AnAmPo; HBMV; WGRP

At the Ascension. Luis Ponce de Leon. How beggared wilt thou leave us, how obscure!– CAW

At the Badr Trench. Safiya bint Musafir. Your spear-thrust left great wounds/gushing hot blood. WPOW

At the Ball! Charles Henry ("John Paul") Webb. Do you wish to go home from the ball? OBAL

At the Ball Game. Roswell Martin Field. I'll proudly strike the stars, and so be out of sight. InMe

At the Ball Game. William Carlos Williams. permanently, seriously/ without thought. CMoP; ExPo; LiSp; NoAm; NOBA

At the Band Concert. John Malcolm Brinnin. ...schemes the peace/Of days potential, like discovered seas. PoA

At the Battery Sea-Wall. Clifford James Laube. I am a stranger in an alien port. GoYe

At the beginning of winter a cold spirit comes. Anonymous. I fear that you will never know or guess. BoWoP

At the Beginnings of the Andes. Barbara Ras. let the cane fields bloom into white wands. AMV-81

At the Bomb Testing Site. William Stafford. The hands gripped hard on the desert. CAPP; CoAP; LiTM; NoP; OBWP

At the Bottom of the Well. Louis Untermeyer. Was it truth, or illusion,/ Or Adam Hope? GoJo

At the British Museum. Richard Aldington. About the cleft battlements of Can Grande's/castle... MoBrPo

At the British War Cemetery, Bayeux. Charles Causley. ...All we ask/Is the one gift you cannot give. OBWP; OxBC

At the Cannon's Mouth. Herman Melville. The star ascended in his nativity. PAH

At the Cantina. Gary Soto. While the rooster stretches/To the day not there yet. MAYP

At the Carnival. Anne Spencer. I implore Neptune to claim his child to-day! BANP; BlSi; CDC; NoAm; PoNe

At the Cavour. Arthur Symons. A look half miserably wise,/Half heedlessly ironical. NOBV; OBSP

At the Cedars. Duncan Campbell Scott. What God calls the other/Is not known to me. CaP; NOBC

At the Cenotaph. Hugh" (Christopher Murray Grieve) MacDiarmid. I'm the civilization you're fighting for. NAMP

At the Center of Everything Which Is Dying. Patricia Goedicke. There's a stagnant pool that wants to be fed/New bodies, every day. FAZ

At the Church Gate. William Makepeace Thackeray. And see, through heaven's gate,/Angels within it. HBV 1-2

At the Closed Gate of Justice. James David Corrothers. "Merely a Negro"–in a day like this! BANP

At the Comedy. Arthur Stringer. But you and I knew–Oh, too well!–/Life went another way!) HBV 1-2

At the Corner of Muck and Myer. Paul Violi. casual interrogations, short/ walks with attendant... APU

At the Crossroads. Richard Hovey. In the teeth of all winds blowing. BBV; HBV 1-2

At the Crucifixion. Anonymous. So rewful ded was nevere non.'... OxBM

At the Dark Hour. Paul Dehn. ...turning to you/For comfort in the cold. BoLoP; WaP

At the Discharge of Cannon Rise the Drowned. Hubert Witheford. Back from mortality the huge sails slide. AnNZ

At the Dog Show. Christopher Morley. Such were the judger and the judged MoShBr

At the Door. Lillie Fuller Merriam. With an arrow from his sheath. PoToHe

At the Door of Mercy Sighing. Thomas Mackellar. "Weary child, come in today." AH

At the Doors. Der Nistor. Birds go flying by. TrJP

At the Drapers. Thomas Hardy. I left you to your adorning. BrPo

At the Edge of the Bay. Thomas Caldecot Chubb. Black against the same moon in an unsame sky. EtS

At the Edge of the Day. Clarence Urmy. To Heaven's gate a burden sweet–/The World's low vesper prayer. HBMV

At the Edge of the Jungle. Patrick Lane. the bird as it beats its blunt head/again and again into the earth. NOBC

At the Edge of Town. William Stafford. Some days, yes. We look up and follow. NNaP

At the End of Spring. Yu Hsuan-chi. I am a loosed boat floating a thousand miles. BoWoP

At the End of the Affair. Maxine W. Kumin. ...tangle in the same old snare/saying the little lies again. TAP

At the End of the Day. Richard Hovey. Here's in the teeth of to-morrow/ To the glory of to-day! HBVY

At the End of Things. Arthur Edward Waite. Since the voice of death must be His true voice. WGRP

At the Entrance. Douglas Stewart. And on into the distance and the mist. CBAP

At the Executed Murderer's Grave. James Wright. Dirt of my flesh, defeated, underground. AmPC; HaCAP

At the Ferry. U. A. Fanthorpe. Claiming me, Charon, for life. FaBoWP

At the Fillmore. Philip Levine. and whatever else was theirs. NNaP

At the Firth of Lorne. Iain Crichton Smith. I no great Adam and you no bright Eve. BSV

At the Fishhouses. Elizabeth Bishop. our knowledge is historical, flowing, and flown. CoAP; FaBoWP; HaCAP; HAP; LCAP; LiTM; MoVE; NoP; NYBP

At the Fishing Settlement. Alistair Campbell. That dog, and that bare bitter place. AnNZ

At the Fountain. Marcabrun. But heaven is very far away. AWP

At the Front. John Erskine. Peace in themselves, which is their sole applause. HBMV

At the Funeral of Great-Aunt Mary. Robert Bly. The frail body must wait till dusk/To be lowered/In the hot and sandy earth. Str

At the Gate of Heaven. George Gordon, Lord Byron.
And certes often like Sir Philip Francis. OBRV
'Tis, that he hath both generals in reversion.) OBRV
Who long have paved hell with their good intentions.' OBRV

At the Grave of a Land-Shark. Ernest G. Moll. ...I wonder how/He'll turn the lot he's stuck with now! DBV

At the Grave of Burns. William Wordsworth. Chanted in love that casts out fear/By Seraphim. EnLi 1-2; EnRP

At the Grave of Champernowne. John Albee. And sailless seas beat the untrodden shore. HBV 1-2

At the Grave of Henry James. W. H. Auden. And giver of all good things. LiTA; MoPo; NoP

At the Grave of Henry Vaughan. Siegfried Sassoon. And here stand I, a suppliant at the door. CMoP; EaLo; GTBS-P; PoPle

At the Grave of My Brother. William Stafford. Brother: Good-bye. Str

At the Grave of Walker. Joaquin Miller. And se a sad face to the sea. AA; AnAmPo; AnFE; APA

At the Great Wall of China. Edmund Charles Blunden. Torn with sharp love of the home left far behind. GTBS-P; HaMV

At the Hacienda. Bret (Francis Bret Harte) Harte. Old when these old walls were young,/"Manuela of La Torre." AA

At the Hammersmith Palais... Alan Riddell. the sustained violence of her terpsichorean expertise. NOAV

At the Holi festival of color. Mira Bai [(or Mirabai)]. Mira belongs to Girdhar Nagar,/a slave at his feet. BoWoP

At the Indian Killer's Grave. Robert Lowell. As through the trellis peers the sudden Bridegroom. NOBA; VGW

At the Jewish Cemetery in Prague. Oscar Levertin. Do not bring flowers here as homage/Of love, nor twigs of green! Bring stone! VWA

At the Jewish Museum. Olga Cabral. and nets to catch the whispers/of the stars. PoDr

At the Jewish Museum. Linda Pastan. in a coal cellar, on Ludlow Street/in Nineteen hundred. VWA

At the Keyhole. Walter De La Mare. Grill me some bones!' DTC; MoAB; MoBrPo

At the Klamath Berry Festival. William Stafford. he took two steps, he took two steps,/past the sociologist. InPK

At the Last. Vincent David Engels. And stars shall watch another race toil on. CAW

At the Last. Philip Bourke Marston. Take thou the heart with the heart's Paradise. HBV 1-2

At the Lavender Lantern. Charles Divine. As long as there are art and girls, and onions in the stew. HBMV

At the Lincoln Tomb. John H. Bryant. ...and save the State/From selfish greed. For this we wait. PGD

At the Long Island Jewish Geriatric Home. Jorie Graham. or mind nothing can slit her/free of. NPGG

At the Loom. Robert Duncan. the heroic Hektor who raised/that reflection of the heroic/in his shield... VGW

At the Louvre. E. L. Mayo. To study all who pass until the lens/Blur or the world run out of specimens. FAZ

At the Manger. W. H. Auden. Dream while you may. EBCP; ILwL

At the Mermaid Inn. Charles Lotin Hildreth. While youth has hope, and love is yet divine. AA

At the Mid Hour of Night. Thomas Moore. Faintly answering still the notes that once were so dear. AnIV; GoBC; GTBS; GTBS-P; HBV 1-2; NBM; NOBE; OAEP; OBEV; OBNC; OBRV; OxBI; PoEL 1-5; TreFS; ViBoPo

At the Millinery Shop. Daniel Mark Epstein. ...bonnet crowned with flowers/that casually tries itself on her. MAYP

At the Museum. John Malcolm Brinnin. That men are gods, the blessed and the unblessed. EyDe

At the Museum of Modern Art. May Swenson. elongations of the coils of light itself/(engine of color) and motion (motor of form). NYP

At the Nadir. Gerta Kennedy. you can be short, but never sweet. PoPl

At the National Black Assembly. LeRoi (Imamu Amiri Baraka) Jones. & caught a plane/to/petit bourgeois/negro/heaven. GP

At the Natural History Museum. William Meredith. Perhaps nothing dies but husks. NYP

At the Nature-Strip. Judith Rodriguez. ...(Whose roots settle/for earth, old earth, with a blackboy endurance.) CBAP

At the New Year. Kenneth Patchen. Other bells that we would ring. AnFE; LiTM

At the News from Fal's High Plain I Cannot Sleep. Seathrun Ceitinn. and sail them out wandering safe on the waves of Cliona. NOBI

At the Nursing Home. John Cain. ...And the joy of packing/the present is enough. Almost, enough FAZ

At the Ocean's Verge. Ralph Gustafson. Crashing foams and ravels once/Was muted marble Athens owned. OBCV

At the Pantomime. Oliver Wendell Holmes. Peace be upon thee, Israel! AnNE

At the Party. W. H. Auden. ...but each ear/Is listening to its hearing, so none hear. OBSP

At the Party. Patricia Goedicke. Come on up, come on up. FAZ

At the Party. Freda Laughton. And I alone/Hear candle-voices waver as they burn. NeIP

At the Piano. Algernon Charles Swinburne. Love me and save me, take me or waive me; death/takes one so soon! FaBoNo

At the Place of the Roman Baths. Richard Scrace. Wiping the scythe blade with fresh cut grass;/Then, mowing again. CaP

At the Place of the Sea. Annie Johnson Flint. In his place that His hand hath made. BLPA; STF

At the Playground. William Stafford. away up high, away down deep. LCAP

At the Polo-Ground. Sir Samuel Ferguson. For no one must suppose I've anything/To hide–and show myself in Grafton Street. NOBI

At the President's Grave. Richard Watson Gilder. That even his hopes became a part/Of earth's eternal heritage. PAH

At the Roadside. John Knoepfle. this is the end of the world FAZ

At the Roman Baths, Bath. Edward Lucie-Smith. This sign of a god's ownership/Can make me feel uneasy still. NePoEA-2

At the Round Earth's Imagin'd Corners, Blow. John Donne. As thou hadst seal'd my pardon, with thy blood. BLPL; CBEP; EaLo; FaBoRV; LiTB; PoPle

At the Salon. Florence Wilkinson. While, like a skylark, sings his last glad sculpture/Its flame salute. HBV 1-2

At the San Francisco Airport. Yvor Winters. And I remain in light and stare–/In light, and nothing else, awake. ForPo; HeIP; InPK; NIP; NOBA; QFR

At the Saturday Club. Oliver Wendell Holmes. blest is he who dreams! AmePo

At the Savoy Chapel. Robert Graves. ...with features/Resolute and unchangeably your own. HW

At the Scenic Drive-In. David McAleavey. through which clusters, constellations,/galaxies–if nothing else–/somehow pass. SUW

At the Sea's Edge. Gwen Harwood. ...The wind walks on the sea,/printing the water's face with charity. CBAP

At the Sea-Side. Robert Louis Stevenson. In every hole the sea came up,/Till it could come no more. NTCP; OxBChV; SUS; TiPo

At the Setting of the Sun. *Anonymous.* I meet my true love at the rising of the sun. CBEP

At the Shelter-Stone. Brenda G. Macrow. outside, the vast/calm of the hills beneath a vestal moon. PoSH

At the Ship. R. P. Lister. Draw me another pint of old and mild. FiBHP

At the Shrine. Richard Kendall Munkittrick. Are sold on Barclay Street. AA

At the Sign-Painter's. Jared Carter. Forming out of all that darkness, that huge disorder. FYAP

At the Slackening of the Tide. James Wright. ...and heard the sea far off/Washing its hands. AmPC; MOS; UnPo; VGW

At the Smithsonian. Vanessa Haley. ...searching/in stillness for jewels of sight. AMV-81

At the Spa. James H. Bowden. "Why this is hell, nor are you out of it." AMV-81

At the St. Louis Institute of Music. Ronald Wallace. I miss the crazy bastard,/and wish him back to abuse me/into song. GOYP

At the Symphony. Robert Nathan. Low over clarinet and flute/Hung heaven upon a single note. HBMV

At the Tavern. *Anonymous.* O drank ones, I wold drink yet. OxBM

At the Telephone Club. Henri Coulette. How cold the stars are, how clear! CoAP

At the Tennis Clinic. I. L. Martin. For if someone returned it/It made him impossibly nervous. SD

At the Theater. Sir Alan Patrick Herbert. Don't brathe upon my neck so much. FiBHP

At the Tomb of Rachel. Yehoash. A beacon in the night, to light my way. TrJP

At the Tomb of Washington. Clinton Scollard. Fame never, never may/His laurels dim! MC; OHIP

At the Tombs of the House of Savoy. William Jay Smith. As fishbone-fine his steps through vaults resound. NePoAm-2

At the Top of My Voice (excerpt). Vladimir Mayakovsky. Socialism/built/in battle. LiTW

At the Top of the Road. Charles Buxton Going. "Lord of the Land! but men have named me Death." HBV 1-2

At the Tourist Center in Boston. Margaret Atwood. Who really lives there? NoP

At the Treatment Center. Jerome Sala. This therapy works with amazing success. APU

At the Trough. Arthur Gregor. no different then from them. FAZ

At the Un-National Monument along the Canadian Border. William Stafford. hallowed by neglect and an air so tame/that people celebrate it by forgetting its name. HAP; HeIP

At the Water Zoo. Edward Valpy Knox. Tomorrow I should like to come/And see four thousand fish again. BoAnP

At the Wedding March. Gerard Manley Hopkins. Who to wedlock, his wonder wedlock,/Deals triumph and immortal years. HW

At the Well. Malka Tussman. I taste tomorrow's/tears. VWA

At the Western Shore. Sarah Youngblood. ...Even the moss grows old/Upon the shallowest rocks. IHMS

At the Western Wall. Barbara F. Lefcowitz. When I ask a bottle-curled Hassidic boy/the way to Jaffa Gate he lowers his eyes/& does not answer. VWA

At the Woodpile. Raymond Henri. The bleeding wedge had not once split true/before I bashed the sledge askew/and smashed its shaft. SaC

At the Worst. Israel Zangwill. And Death awaits us? Rest is but our due. TRV; WGRP

At the "Ye that do truly." Charles Williams. But now the solitudes are here. NOCV; OxBoCh

At the Zoo. Walter De La Mare. There showed small semblance of a missing link! BoAnP

At the Zoo. A.(lan) A.(lexander) Milne. But I give buns to the elephant when I go down to the Zoo! TiPo

At the Zoo. William Makepeace Thackeray. Mercy, how unpleasantly they–Smelt! NTCP; OxBChV

At the Zoo. Israel Zangwill. My heart is with you, and I understand/The lion turning in his living grave. TrJP

At Their Place. Paul Mariah. ...He is not in third/Grade,/Will he ever be in fourth? LFAC

At Thomas Hardy's Birthplace, 1953. James Wright. Having been nursed beyond the sopping rain,/Back down the stair. ConAP

At Tide Water. Sir Charles G. D. Roberts. And in their mastery teach me to be wise. PeCV

At Timber Line. Frank H. Mayer. While Heaven seems just within our reach/At timber line. PoOW

At Times I Feel Like a Quince Tree. John Robert Quinn. When snow is swirling, the past seems far away. AMV-81

At Toledo. Arthur Symons. God is in league with their forgetfulness. BrPo

At Torrey Pines State Park. Jerome Mazzaro. ...Though trees, you/write, have not had much to say to your work,/the happiness is pure. FiCP

At Twilight. Peyton Van Rensselaer. And one that I love is dead. AA

At Veronica's. Robert Peterson. I hum a mortal tune/and/am all and none of those. NeAC

At Vshchizh. Fyodor Tyutchev. Into that peace all history must feed. OBWP

At War. Russell Atkins. Listen a moment–! Sh! Listen–!/that hurrying as of a shore of/fugitives! AmNP

At War. Charles Madge. And fire will presently split the air. FaBoMo

At White River. John Haines. she had found a rock to keep,/and I went down. FiCP

At Wonder Donut. Laureen Mar. their newborn eyes pale and soft. BrSi

At Woodward's Gardens. Robert Frost. It's knowing what to do with things that counts. ImOP; PoA

At Year's End. Richard Wilbur. New New-year bells are wrangling with the snow. MiAP; NePA; NYBP

Atalanta. Ovid (Publius Ovidius Naso). ...as the race/Was run, the girl was beaten, and the winner/Led off his prize. LiSp

Atalanta in Calydon. Algernon Charles Swinburne.
  Filled full of the foam of the river. EnLi 1-2; MaVP
  His life is a watch or a vision/Between a sleep and a sleep. ACV; BoLiVe;
    FaFP; HeIP; MasP; NoP; OBEV; OBVV; TrGrPo; ViBoPo; WHA
  The wolf that follows, the fawn that flies. AWP; BoLiVe; CTC; EvOK;
    ExPo; GoTF; GTBS; GTBS-P; HAP; HBV 1-2; HeIP; InPo; MasP;
    NOBE; NoP; OBEV; PoEL 1-5; PoPle; SeCeV; TEP; TrGrPo; ViBoPo;
    WHA
Atalanta's Race. William Morris. Shall give to Venus offerings rich enow,/
  Her maiden zone, her arrows, and her bow. DTo
Atameros. John Beevers. Through them he gazed/And saw the beatings of
  her heart. EAS
Ataraxia. Bert Leston Taylor. The new one, if not better, can't be worse.
  HBMV; InMe
Atavism. Richard Lake. And the deep night, and sleep, and the pines
  dripping. NCSH
Atavism. Elinor Wylie. Tall plumes surmount a painted mask of death.
  AnEnPo; HBMV; PoA; SBG
Athalie: Chorus (excerpt). Jean Baptiste Racine. But of almighty love a
  brighter sign,/Shines forth thy law, pure, perfect and divine. WGRP
Athanasia. Oscar Wilde. It is the child of all eternity. BrPo
Atheist. E. Y. Harburg. But only fools like me, you see,/Can make a God,
  who makes a tree. PV
The Atheist Buries His Son. Abu'l-Atahija. But now, my little boy, you
  preach to me. LiTW
The Atheist's Prayer. Miguel de Unamuno. ...God, since if it were that
  you/Were to exist, then I would really too. ILwL
The Atheist's Tragedy. Cyril Tourneur.
  And hide itself for shame of such a deed. ViBoPo; WaaP
  He died in war, and yet he died in peace. EIL
Atheling Grange: or, The Apotheosis of Lotte Nussbaum. William Plomer.
  ...Tomorrow Mrs Clunch/Will have no drudge to cook her blasted lunch.
  OBNV
Athene's Song. Eavan Boland. Holds its peace and holds its own. CIP
An Athenian Garden. Trumbull Stickney. ...I/Looked after him thro'
  happy tears. NCEP
Athlete. Don Maynard. ...say to him drawn back/like an arrow on a bow
  PoAu 1-2
Athletes. Walker Gibson. Nor death like any shower room. LiSp; SD
Athletic Employment. Anonymous. And vigour attends it by which life is
  lengthened. SD
Athletic Ode. George Santayana. Youth has her perfect crown, and age her
  old desire. AmePo
Athol Brose. Thomas Hood. How goot dere Athol Boetry must be!'
  FaBoCo
Atlantic Charter: 1942. Francis Brett Young. And who shall say us Nay?
  AmFN; PAL
The Atlantides. Henry David Thoreau. To call your distant soil their own.
  ViBoPo
Atlantis. W. H. Auden. Lifting up, dear, upon you/The light of His
  countenance. PoPl
Atlantis. Hart Crane. Whispers antiphonal in azure swing. AtBAP;
  LiTM; NePA
The Atlas. Kenneth Slessor.
  And somewhere, for the hand that seeks,/Perhaps a Sultan's pearl! PoAu
    1-2
  Measuring mileposts of eternity. PoAu 1-2
  They are GONE like the cracking of a bubble. PoAu 1-2
  Those other countries of the mind,/So tousled, dark and undefined! PoAu
    1-2
The Atoll in the Mind. Alex Comfort. one dark as water, its root among
  the bones. LiTB; LiTM; SeCePo
Atom from Atom. Ralph Waldo Emerson. As moon from earth, or star
  from star. ImOP; TiPo
Atomic Courtesy. Ethel Jacobson. The atom may/Return the compliment.
  FaFP; QQQ
Atomic Pantoum. Peter Meinke. we sing to Jesus/in a chain reaction.
  SM
Atonement. Margaret E. Bruner. A wreath to lay upon his bier. PoToHe
Atropos. John Myers O'Hara. Endless and no/Whisper of death.
  AnAmPo
The Attack. Thomas Buchanan Read. She sank, thank God! unsoiled by
  foot of/traitor! PAH
Attack. Siegfried Sassoon. Flounders in mud. O Jesu, make it stop!
  MCCG; MoBrPo; NOBE; OxBTC
Attack of the Crab Monsters. Lawrence Raab. You know I always loved
  you. AmPA; NoP
Attack of the Squash People. Marge Piercy. as we salt and freeze and
  pickle/for the too little to come. NLV
Attainment. Madison Cawein. And no soul attains who fears. WGRP
Attainment. Algernon Tassin. And yet was never there a rose but died in/
  blooming. AA

Attainment. Ella Wheeler Wilcox. Material things must answer and obey.
  WGRP
An Attempt at Jealousy. Marina Tsvetayeva. How is it, my love? Worse
  than for me/With another man? WPOW
Attend, Young Friends, While I Relate. Anonymous. Turn to the Lord,
  forsake all sin,/And he'll forgive the past. AmFP
Attending Church. Anonymous. For we always go to church/When we've
  nothing else to do. STF
Attention. Adrienne Rich. ...my lips/half-parted, steady as the mouths/of
  antique statues. TAP
The Attic. Henri Coulette. We are alone, alone with what we are.
  NePoEA-2; PoPl
The Attic Landscape. Herman Melville.
  The All-in-All seems here a Greek. NOBA
  Respond, and share their sculptural grace. OBAL
Attica Is. Stewart Brisby. only a/dull/whining/ache/in the minds/of those
  who live. LFAC; SOTS
Attis. Caius Valerius Catullus. others trap in the snarl of frenzy.' OBVE
Attitudes of a New Zealand Poet. Allen Curnow. Not I, some child, born
  in a marvellous year,/Will learn the trick of standing upright here. AnNZ
An Attorney General. Ambrose Bierce. But sleeps upon it, and for action–
  snores. DBV
Attraction. Anonymous. In Himself by grace we enter,/Where there is the
  mercy seat! STF
Attraction. Ella Wheeler Wilcox. ...the meadow leaped, and took/The
  leaning mountain in a close embrace. PeD
The Attractions of a Fashionable Irish Watering-Place. Francis Sylvester
  ("Father Prout") Mahony. Until they spy land in sweet Botany Bay.
  FaBoPP; IrPN; NBM
Au Bout du Temps. Andrei Codrescu. so late in the century/in the 20th
  Century. APU
Au Clair de la Lune. J. B. and Charles Fonteyn Manney Lully. All behind
  her door is carefully concealed. FSW
Au Jardin des Plantes. John Wain. They cup their heads in prodigal
  idleness. NePoEA-2; OxBTC
Au Tombeau de Mon Pere. Ronald McCuaig. "This the wine, and this the
  bread." NOAV; PoAu 1-2
Aubade. William Empson. The heart of standing is we cannot fly.
  FaBoMo; FaBoTw; LiTB; OxBTC
Aubade. Anselm Hollo. here i come, dear shoes. APU
Aubade. Dilys Bennett Laing. The great light of morning/shines and
  shakes/in my eyes NMP
Aubade. Philip Larkin. Postmen like doctors go from house to house.
  SoSe
Aubade. Ruth Lechlitner. I was far too young to know/the white flame, or
  the cold whisper of snow. AMV-80
Aubade. Louis MacNeice.
  ...dawn/Of sallow and grey bricks, and newsboys crying war. ViBoPo
  Not the twilight of the gods but a precise dawn/Of sallow and grey bricks,
  and newsboys crying war. NIP
Aubade. Mekeel McBride. ...the first deep whisper of the rising sun.
  MAYP
Aubade. Frank O'Hara. ...breathes/upon these vessels by the sea,/to be
  wrought in the frothing waves. SM
Aubade. Karl Shapiro. Et c'est la fin pour quoy sommes ensemble. GP;
  VGW
Aubade. Edith Sitwell. The morning light creaks down. CMoP; ExPo;
  MoAB; MoBrPo; NoAm; PoRA
Aubade after the Party. Tom O'Grady. Dancing before last night's dishes/
  Like a thief. FAZ
Aubade: Dick, the Donkey-Boy. Osbert Sitwell. Amid the jostled cries and
  laughter. HaMV
Aubade: Donna Anna to Juan, Still Asleep. Richard Howard. To worship,
  in the articulate temple,/The unspeakable god. PoA
Aubade for Hope. Robert Penn Warren. Above the ash and spittle croaks
  and leans. MoAmPo
Aubade: Lake Erie. Thomas Merton. And grope, in the green wheat,/
  Toward the woodwinds of the Western freight. NYBP
Aubade: N.Y.C. Robert Wallace. still oh and the roaches are sleeping
  HoPM
Aubade: The Desert. Frederick Bock. ...on sweetness through these
  kitchen/Odors and the stink backway? PoA
Aubade Triste. Agnes Mary Frances (Mme Emile Duclaux) Robinson. The
  day has come for all. NOBV
Aube Provencale. Marilyn Hacker. and crow, it's already/morning.
  AmPA
Auburn. Paul Verlaine. Oh how real to me you are! ErPo
Aucassin and Nicolete. Francis William Bourdillon. What care ye though
  the world discovers/Your flowers of love, O flower of lovers! HBV 1-2
Aucassin and Nicolette: Who Would List. Anonymous. But is healed, but is
  glad,/'Tis so sweet. CTC

The Authour Still Pursuing His Invention. Thomas Watson. Transform'd to ayre Love entred with my will,/And nowe perforce doth keepe possession still. AAS

Auto Mobile. Archie Randolph Ammons. your little flivver still/works so well. FF; OBAL

Auto Wreck. Karl Shapiro. Across the expedient and wicked stones. AmC; AmLP; BiP; CMoP; FF; LiTM; MiAP; MoVE; NIP; PoPl; VGW

Autobiographia Literaria. Frank O'Hara. writing these poems!/Imagine!' NNaP; NOBA

Autobiographical Fragment. Kingsley Amis. The old bore stopped calling. NePoEA-2

Autobiographies. Derek Mahon. Like the nymphs dancing together/In the "Allegory of Spring'. FaBoIP

Autobiography. Sonja Akesson. and crushed by feet in the yellow grass. BoWoP

An Autobiography. Bairam at Tunisie. the first o the second o the third o LiTW

Autobiography. Charles Causley. And I turn from the tactful friend to the candid sky. LiTM

Autobiography. Mbella Sonne Dipoko. Our thoughts dusting the past. TTY

Autobiography. Janet Dube. ...till all the perfumes/of Arabia would not sweeten/this hand. BrRo

Autobiography. Gloria Fuertes. Now I've got two minor convictions/and a kiss from time to time. PBWP

Autobiography. Louis MacNeice. Come back early or never come. FaBoIP; NOBI

Autobiography. Dan Pagis. And even this is only half a revenge. VWA

An Autobiography. Ernest Rhys. What more than these I ask'd of Life I am content to have/from Death ACV; OBEV; OBVV

Autobiography, Chapter XII. Jim Barnes. other voices are also somehow dimly you. AMV-81

Autobiography, Chapter XVII. Jim Barnes. ...and the small/knowledge that the river takes you over all. STE

Autobiography: Hollywood. Charles Reznikoff. your spears/have begun to flower, too! VWA

Autobiography: Last Chapter. Jim Barnes. ...she knows you are running back into/yourself. CDW

Autobiography of a Lungworm. Roy Fuller. ...a wiry soul/That must escape the knife. NoAm; NoP; OxBC

Autochthon. Sir Charles G. D. Roberts. The foreknowledge veiled in our face. CaP

The Autocrat of the Breakfast Table. Oliver Wendell Holmes. Not bad, my bargain! Price one dime! AA

An Autograph. James Russell Lowell Shall 'scape Oblivion's broom so long. AA

An Autograph. John Greenleaf Whittier May God forgive him wholly. AA

Autograph Book/Prophecy. Anne Halley. There's a joke there somewhere./Get it? NMM

Autolycus' Song (parody). Richard Leighton Greene. Your unhappy becomes in need of rest in 5,280 feet-a. SpRo

The Automobile. Russell Edson. Father and mother watch an automobile with a just married sign on it grow-/ing smaller in a road. LCAP

The Automobile. James Lewisohn. they ride against the mothering earth. AmC

The Automobile. Percy MacKaye. The shrill, primeval hawk gazed down—and screamed. AnAmPo

Automobile Mechanics. Dorothy Walter Baruch. We work hard/My dad/And I. SoPo; TiPo

Autonomous. Mark Van Doren. And thinks that he was present in the dark/When skin was chosen over root and bark. LiTA

Autosonic Door. Dorothy Brown Thompson. ...Man must have his wonder. GoYe

Autres Betes, Autres Moeurs. Ogden Nash. In such a fix to be so fertile. GoTF; NAMP; TreFS

Autumn. Bella Akhmadulina. suddenly will look up/with a pale, clear sadness. BoWoP

Autumn. Anonymous.
Hazel nuts thud in the forest/From the wearied boughs. KiLC
Then, not despised, I'll not complain,/But cherish Autumn in her stead. NOEC

Autumn. Douglas Ridley Beeton. Think that he is right, young and right. PeSA

Autumn. Roy Campbell.
The grape will redden on your fingers/Through the lit crystal of the cup. GTBS-P; MoBrPo; OBMV; OxBTC
Through the lit crystal of the cup. GTBS-P; MoBrPo

Autumn. William Carpenter. we begin banking foundations for the long winter. Psk

Autumn. John Clare.

All these have passed, and silence at her ease/Dreams autumn's melancholy life away. SaC

The grunting pigs, that wait for all,/Scramble and hurry where they fall. EG

Whoever looks round sees Eternity there. BoNaP; HAP; NBM; NU; PoEL 1-5

Autumn. Edwin Curran. And am not sad, but feel her marvelous charm/ `As splendidly she plunges in the fight. HBMV

Autumn. Walter De la Mare. Silence where hope was. OxBTC

Autumn. Thomas Hood.
Enough of fear and shadowy despair,/To frame her cloudy prison for the soul! LiTB

Autumn. Thomas Ernest Hulme.
And round about were the wistful stars/With white faces like town children. FaBoMo; LoBV
...stars/With white faces like town children. ViBoPo
With white faces like town children. FaBoMo; LOW; MOON; SeCePo

Autumn. Thomas Caulfield Irwin. And naught is heard, save on the wind afar/The sultry whisper of the dry-eared corn. IrPN

Autumn. Philip Levine. we have snow on your eyelids,/on your hair. NNaP

Autumn. Detlev Freiherr von Liliencron. While the old man unto Our Lady prays. AWP

Autumn. Henry Wadsworth Longfellow. And, following thee, in thy ovation splendid,/Thine almoner, the wind, scatters the golden leaves! OBVV

Autumn. Amy Lowell. You who have taken with you/All I once possessed? NMM

Autumn. Itzik Manger.
And Itzik Manger sleeps on the hard ground,/stripped of all his dreams. VWA
It will be the loveliest song we know. TrJP

Autumn. Nashe [(or Nash)] Thomas. From winter, plague and pestilence, good Lord, deliver us! EIL; LoBV; OAEL 1-2; OBSC; TrGrPo

Autumn. Frank O'Connor.
Hazel nuts thud in the forest/From the wearied boughs. PoSC
Woman full of wile/I would give you all! OBMV

Autumn. Alexander Pushkin. And nourishing the long thoughts in my soul.... AnEnPo; AWP

Autumn. Rainer Maria Rilke. Yet there is one who holds us as we/fall/eternally in his hands' tenderness. TrJP

Autumn. Elizabeth Madox Roberts. And shook his fist in a cornstalk's face. AnAmPo; YaD

Autumn. W. R. Rodgers. Leaving the rough hedge-cheeks long-strawed and streaked/with their weeping. NeBP

Autumn. Christina Georgina Rossetti. And lonesome, very lonesome, is my strand. BrRo

Autumn. Vernon Scannell. Makes mirrors vague. It is the mist that I most favour. OxBTC

Autumn. Thomas W. Shapcott. I make a bone with you a bone I must make/into magic or a flute. CBAP

Autumn. Percy Bysshe Shelley. And make her grave green with tear on tear. CH

Autumn. Princess Shikishi. I am as disturbed as before. PBWP

Autumn. William Jay Smith. And turkey-red the leaves come down. NePoAm

Autumn. Rabindranath Tagore. ...the myriad/murmuring waves of Rhythm surrounding Thy throne. WGRP

Autumn. James (1700-48) Thomson. In mingled murder fluttering on the ground. LoBV

Autumn! Nancy Byrd Turner. Rabbits and chipmunks, clear the track! YeAr

Autumn. Jean Starr Untermeyer.
High priestess of your home. MCCG; MoAmPo
You, now so shaken and so powerless—/High priestess of your home. HBMV; MCCG

Autumn. William Watson. And soul of all regret! OBVV

Autumn. Frances Winwar. A wish, and half believe it will come true. GoYe

Autumn. Humbert Wolfe. love, youth, and the sound of wings. PoLf

Autumn 1940. W. H. Auden. ...and the shining/Light be comprehended by the darkness. LiTA

Autumn Along the Beaches. John Hall Wheelock. A myriad waves all moving the one way. AnAmPo

Autumn: An Ode. Charles Gullans. This progress to completion moves like death. NePoEA

Autumn Apples. Laurie Lee. the hollow and the whole. BoC

Autumn Begins in Martins Ferry, Ohio. James Wright. And gallop terribly against each other's bodies. CAPP; HaCAP; InPK; InPS; NaP; PAI; PoL

Autumn Birds. John Clare. While small birds nestle in the hedge below. PBBP

An Autumn Breeze. William Hamilton Hayne. To voice some subtlety of sylvan grief. AA

Autumn Burial: A Meditation. Charles Gullans. Through all the years,/ Immutable stands this event. QFR

Autumn Change. John Clare. Season of sudden storms and brilliant suns. VLP

Autumn Chapter in a Novel. Thom Gunn. And leaves thrust violently upon the pane. FaBoMo; OxBTC

Autumn Color. Tom Robinson. I'd color every tree and bush/And spill paint on the ground. YeAr

Autumn, Crystal Eye. Margot Ruddock. longing for the white/Frozen bough. OBMV

Autumn, Dark Wanderer. Elizabeth Daryush. Now seated by your tattered tent she broods/On timeless heights, eternal solitudes. QFR

Autumn Dawn. Antonio Machado. His eager gun at rest, a hunter stalking game. PoPl

An Autumn Day. Sorley MacLean. Six men dead at my shoulder/on an Autumn day. AMV-81

Autumn Day. Rainer Maria Rilke. restlessly wander when dead leaves are/ blown. TrJP

The Autumn Day Its Course Has Run. Charlotte Bronte. Sit silent Nun–sit there and be/Comrade and Confidant to me. NOBV

Autumn Daybreak. Edna St. Vincent Millay. The hill all summer hid from me. LaNeLa

Autumn Even. Amelia Andriello. Till I'm sent to bed. SiSoSe

Autumn Evening. George Anthony. Why do you wipe your face away? EAS

Autumn Fashions. Edith Matilda Thomas. ...–indeed,/they look like huge bouquets! YeAr

Autumn Fields. Elizabeth Madox Roberts. And the land where he had been. BrR

Autumn Fires. Robert Louis Stevenson. Fires in the fall! BrR; SUS; TiPo; YeAr

Autumn Flowers. Jones Very. Along thy path the autumn flowers shall smile,/And to its close life's pilgrimage beguile. MAmP

An Autumn Garden. Bliss Carman. And up from the loveliest garden/ Must climb for a glimpse of sea. HBV 1-2

Autumn Healing. Jean Ward. In a birth of forgetting your tears must die. LaNeLa

The Autumn House. George M. Brady. And down the draughty/Passage- way nobody walks. OnYI

Autumn Imagined. Donald Davie. When it trembled at Autumn's hue/On our wedding night. PoA

Autumn in the West. William Davis Gallagher. And golden-sphered persimmons spread o'er all. AA; AnAmPo

Autumn Journal. Louis MacNeice.
And a faggot of useless memories. AnIL; BIrV; FaBoIP
And in the end–with time and luck–to dance. CMoP
Its body in a rag-tag army. OBWP
We'll rape the angels off the golden reredos/Before we're done. NOBL
We shall have fireworks here by this day week. FaBoPV; OxBTC; WaP

Autumn Journey. Denise Levertov. over the hill, among the burning worlds. NeBP

The Autumn Leaves. *Anonymous.* They're falling through the atmosphere/ And also through the air. NA

Autumn Leaves. Janie Screven Heyward. A little crumpled, but lovely still. HBMV

Autumn Leaves. Charles Henry ("John Paul") Webb. These leaves that autumn branches bear/Are an autumnal bore. OBAL

Autumn Love. Ibycus. goes reluctantly on to the race with the hurrying wheels. LiTW

The autumn made colors burn. Venus Khoury-Gata. I sketch you with quivering leaves BoWoP

Autumn Melancholy. Janet Hamill. beneath the folds of drapery suggested the languor of a convales-/cent. APU

Autumn Morning at Cambridge. Frances Cornford. While the men go to lecture with the wind in their gowns. HBMV; MoVE; OBVV

Autumn Mushrooms. Kenneth Mackenzie. and in each microscopic spore to see/the enormous pattern of eternity. CBAP

Autumn Music. Gabriel Preil. but I am sure the spellbound king/drawing out his reign/a little longer VWA

Autumn Night. Evelyn Scott. She is Death enjoying Life,/Innocently,/ Lasciviously. AnAmPo

Autumn on the Upper Thames. William Morris. And all is a tale for thee and me. FaBoPP

Autumn Orchard. Catherine Haydon Jacobs. I should be told that there is, after all,/An essence and an irony in fall. AMV-80

An Autumn Park. David Gascoyne. And imminent glory breaking through Man's circumstance. MoPo

Autumn Poem. Anthony Cronin. We pawn to pay for sleeping space this winter/Out of the fog and traffic of the brain. CIP

Autumn Rain. D. H. Lawrence. falling as rain. BrPo

Autumn Rain. Kenneth Rexroth. Steep rocks through the soaking ferns. NU

Autumn Refrain. Wallace Stevens. The stillness is all in the key of that desolate sound. LiTA; WeW

An Autumn Road. Glenn Ward Dresbach. There were arms that, clinging,/Would not let me go. HBMV

Autumn's Fete. Alice Sutton McGeorge. Everybody looks his best/At this annual ball. YeAr

Autumn's Mirth. Samuel Minturn Peck. 'Tis all a myth that Autumn grieves! GN

Autumn's Processional. Dinah Maria Mulock. While the equinoctials blow. GN

Autumn Scene. Basil Dowling. The sound floats upward like a bird to me. BoNaP

Autumn Sequel, IV. Louis MacNeice. I stayed. On my peacetime feet. There was little alternative. FaBoIP

Autumn Sequence. Adrienne Rich. with a film of stale gossip coating his tongue. VGW

Autumn Song. Noel Harry Brettell. With your two notes of innocence. ACV

An Autumn Song. Edward Dowden. Drinking great ardours; and the rapturous birth/Of winged things. ACV; OnYI

Autumn Song. Elizabeth-Ellen Long. To crickets' farewell tunes. SiSoSe

Autumn Song. Dante Gabriel Rossetti. ...death seems a comely thing/In Autumn at the fall of the leaf? ViBoPo

Autumn Song. Stephen Stepanchev. Thousands of new selves/Rose joyously out of those deaths. FAZ

Autumn Song. Johann Ludwig Tieck. While it lives its breath is Summer's glow! AWP

Autumn Song. Paul Verlaine. Tossed everywhere/Like a dead leaf. LiTW

Autumn Song on Perry Street. Lloyd Frankenberg. If her voice didn't carry, he might. GrPl

Autumn Squall–Lake Erie. Lola Ingres Russo. These autumn nights I think that he/Imagines he's the ocean. AmFN

Autumn Testament (excerpt). James Keir Baxter. Till the fear has gone. Fear is the only enemy. OCNZ

Autumn Twilight. Henri de Regnier. Drop by drop Time fades, and rose by rose! LiTW

An Autumn Walk. Witter ("Emanuel Morgan") Bynner. And I remain alive instead/Along the year. GoYe

The Autumn Wind. John Clare. In solitude the musing mind/Must ever love the autumn wind. BoNaP

The Autumn Wind. Emperor Wu Ti. Youth's years how few, age how sure! FaBoCh; LoGBV

Autumn Woods. William Cullen Bryant. And waste its little hour. AnNE

Autumn Woods. James S. Tippett. That have fallen/From the bare trees/ Overhead. SUS; TiPo

The Autumnal. John Donne. I shall ebb out with them, who homeward go. TEP; ViBoPo

Autumnal. Ernest Christopher Dowson. Until love turn from us and die/ Beneath the drear November trees. OBNC

Autumnal. Rolfe Humphries. Face it. You must. You can. MoRP

Autumnal Consummation. Patric Stevenson. ...there lies/Upon its head of thorns a crown of beads. NeIP

An Autumnal Evening. William Sharp. Great dusky moths go flitting by. PoSC; SyP

The Autumnal Moon. James (1700-48) Thomson. The whole air whitens with a boundless tide/Of silver radiance, trembling round the world. NOBE

Autumnal Ode. Aubrey Thomas De Vere. To stand–to advance–and after all to stand! OBNC

Autumnal Song. Walter Savage Landor. To low notes from branches sere. ERoP 1-2; OAEL 1-2

Autumnal Spring Song. Vassar Miller. Whence the trees bloom on forever,/But with the same leaves never. NePoEA

Autumnall. Joseph Bennett. The leaves, the quenching leaves that drown upon the flesh. NePA

Autumnus. Joshua Sylvester. Leaving, worldling, of thine own/Neither fruit nor leaf behind thee. EiL; OBS; SoSe

Aux Carmelites. Katharine Tynan Hinkson. The dancers dance while the dawn is grey. OnYI

Aux Italiens. Owen Meredith. Non ti scordar di me! TreFS

Avalanche. Adrien Stoutenburg. pile up, and fill my seedless eyes. NYBP

Avalon. Thomas Holley Chivers. Oh! Avalon! my son! my son! APA

Avalon. Audrey McGaffin. And this, her priestess and her daughter. NePoAm

D'Avalos' Prayer. John Masefield. Towards the lone northern star and the fair ports of home. MOS; TrPWD

Avarice. Anthony Hecht. Upon an infant huge tributes of gold/And frankincense and myrrh. OBSP

Avarice. George Herbert. And while he digs out thee, falls in the ditch. FaBoRV; LiTB

Ave.   Dante Gabriel Rossetti.   O Mary Virgin, full of grace!   GoBC; ISi; OxBoCh

Ave Atque Vale.   *Anonymous.*   Await me in heaven, ah stand at the door. WTO

Ave Atque Vale.   Thomas S. Jones, Jr.   Giving you back her deathless love of you!   HBV 1-2

Ave Atque Vale.   Algernon Charles Swinburne.   All waters as the shore. EnLi 1-2; MaVP; NOBE; OAEL 1-2; OAEP; OBNC; SyP; ViBoPo; VLP

Ave Atque Vale.   Rosamund Marriott Watson.   Dream of the golden splendors of your smile,/Dream you remember yet.   HBV 1-2

Ave Caesar.   Robinson Jeffers.   ...we love our/luxuries.   FaBoPV; MoVE; NoAm; NOBA; OBSP; OxBA

Ave Eva.   John Wheelwright.   ...tearing roses. and trampling the gooseberries and the strawberries.   MoPo

Ave Imperatrix!   Oscar Wilde.   The young Republic like a sun/Rise from these crimson seas of war.   HBV 1-2

Ave Maria.   Henriette Charasson.   And blessed is the fruit of thy womb, Jesus.   CAW; ISi

Ave Maria.   Hart Crane.   Te Deum laudamus O Thou Hand of Fire NePA

Ave Maria.   Frank O'Hara.   movies you wouldn't let them see when they were young   ANYP; HaCAP; NNaP; NoP; PoM

Ave-Maria Bells.   Charles Warren Stoddard.   "The Word made Flesh has dwelt among us,'/Is still our ever-new delight.   ISi

Ave Maria Gratia Plena.   Oscar Wilde.   And over both the white wings of a Dove.   CAW; ISi

Ave Maris Stella.   *Anonymous.*
Forty days of pardon God grant him.   CTC
Three in One confess thee.   ISi

Ave! Nero Imperator.   Duffield Osborne.   May plead for they poor shade in days/to come.   AA

Ave Regina Coelorum.   *Anonymous.*   Intercede for us always to Jesus.   ISi

Ave, Vita Nostra!   Clifford J. Laure.   Mourning and weeping in this valley of tears.   ISi

The Avengers.   Robert Graves.   Monsters of thought through earth we stray/And how remission comes, God knows.   HBMV

The Avengers.   Edwin Markham.   They come on wool-soft sandals/But they strike with iron hands.   MoAmPo

The Avenging Daughters.   *Anonymous.*   All the penance they got for Sir Erlend's slaughter/Was Fridays three on bread and water.   LiTW

L'Avenir.   Sydney Thomas Dobell.   And thro' the dusty tumult God arose. VLP

The Avenue Bearing the Initial of Christ into the New World.   Galway Kinnell.
And the Chinese laundry closes on Saturday.   ConAP; NePoEA-2; NMP
And the leeks, and the onions, and the garlic.   NePoEA-2
The babybirds pipe down. It is day. CAD; NePoEA-2
Bury me not Bunko damned Catholic I pray in Egypt. LiTM; NMP
In Kugler's glass headdown dangling by yellow legs. NMP
Nobody knows for sure what is left of him. NePoEA-2; NMP
Our little lane, what a kingdom it was!/oi weih, oi weih. CoPo; NaP; NePoEA-2

Avenue Y.   Anita Barrows.   So he touched pearblossom, appleblossom VWA

The Avenues.   David St. John.   —looking for breakfast or a little peace. AMV-80; MAYP

The Average Man.   Margaret E. Sangster.   The commonplace, average man. WBLP

Aves.   Ted Morison.   Yes, they/are blue and/now gone–/amazing. AMV-81

Aviary.   Mebdh McGuckian.   ...yet any wild bird would envy you/This aviary, whenever you free all the birds in me.   FaBoIP

Aviemore.   Janet Waller.   Makes a break, too (for us/Not Sisyphus). PoSH

The Avocado Pit.   Carl Rakosi.   or we were looking/at the rivers/from a satellite.   FAZ

Avoidances.   Ron Welburn.   ...the heart beats away wishes/before they fester on the drum.   PoBA

Avoiding News by the River.   William Stanley Merwin.   If I were not human I would not be ashamed of anything.   NaP

The Avon.   Henry Jacobs.   Heaven-pointing spires shall beautify thy plain AnNZ

The Avondale Mine Disaster.   *Anonymous.*   And oft-rent cries may rend the skies all around through/Avondale.   AmFP; BaBo; ViBoFo

Avran.   James Clarence Mangan.   In ashes warms the hero's heart! SeCePo

Awake.   Mary Elizabeth Coleridge.   Hath not enough of sadness, and my heart/Is stifled for a cry.   OBNC

Awake!   W. R. Rodgers.   ...Awake! before it is too late.   LiTM; WaP

Awake!   Walther von der Vogelweide.   Arise! we slept, nor of the peril recked.   AWP

Awake, Arise, You Drowsy Sleeper.   *Anonymous.*   And I'll forsake both father, mother,/And with you I'll run away.   AmFP

Awake, Awake!   Thomas Campion.   Then watch and labour while time is. ELP

Awake! Awake!   John Ruskin.   And the Wolf is dead in Arcady and the Dragon in the sea!   HBV 1-2

Awake, Awake to Love and Work.   G. Anketall "Woodbine Willie" Studdert-Kennedy.   The God who gave all worlds that are,/And all that are to be. TRV

Awake, Mine Eyes!   *Anonymous.*   To her are echoes sending.   EIL

Awake, My Fair.   Judah Halevi.   Lo, I myself then of thy dream/The interpreter will be.   TrJP

Awake, My Heart.   Robert Bridges.   And awake, my heart, to be loved, awake, awake!   GTBS-P; HBV 1-2; MoAB; MoBrPo; NOBE; OBEV; OBVV

Awake, My Lute.   Clive Staples Lewis.   And the bed of that sea was my bed.   CenHV; FaBoNo

Awake, My Soul!   Philip Doddridge.   When victors' wreaths and monarchs' gems/Shall blend in common dust.   WGRP

Awake, My Soul.   Moses Ibn Ezra.   And in my heart make straight the/crooked way.   TrJP

Awake My Soul, Betimes Awake.   Isaac Chanler.   Grant me thy presence, Lord, I pray,/And keep me from all sin.   AH

Awake, My Soul! In Grateful Songs.   Andrew Fowler.   And bring us wanderers home.   AH

Awake! (parody).   Jack Black.   The Train that runs on Time is never late. BXAP

Awake Yee Westerne Nymphs, Arise and Sing.   Samuel Danforth.   How Heathen shrubs kisse Jesus for their King.   SCAP

The Awakened War God.   Margaret Widdemer.   And scourged the crouching lands again.   WGRP

Awakening.   Robert Bly.   ...the living/awakened at last like the dead. ConAP; NaP

The Awakening.   Robert Creeley.   moving at all as all men, because you must.   NeAP

Awakening.   John Haines.   shifts in his soiled flesh/and remembers...   EAS

The Awakening.   Don (Donald Robert Marquis) Marquis.   And he is wrought of the anguish of them that have greatly/needed him.   HBMV

The Awakening.   Angela Morgan.   O faith of mine, be big! be big!   OHIP

Awakening.   David Robinson.   Impatiently casting glimpses of itself/Back toward time.   AMV-81

Awakening–.   Nelly Sachs.   rooting/backwards/in their eyes.   PBWP

Awakening.   Margaret E. Sangster.   The song! the green and the gold!   AA

Awakening.   Lucien Stryk.   At this hour I am always happy,/ready to be taken myself,/fully aware.   SV

Awaking.   Stephen Spender.   And my aware awaking loves/The day–until I start to care.   NYBP

Award.   Ray Durem.
And before it's all through,/I may be following you!   IDB; PoBA; PPON
but she was my daughter, only three,/who had to pee. BP; BPo; NNP; SoSe; TTY

Aware.   D.H. Lawrence.   I follow her down the night, begging her not to depart.   BoNaP; MoBrPo

Awareness.   Don L. Lee.   THINK BLACK.   BOLo; PoBA

Away.   Walter De la Mare.   You not there.   NoP

Away.   Max Ehrmann.   Come, Love, let us away from here.   PoToHe

Away!   Robert Frost.   And I may return/If disssatisfied/With what I learn/From having died.   NOBA

Away.   Josephine Miles.   I give over/And they take it away.   GP

Away.   James Whitcomb Riley.   He is not dead–he is just away.   BLRP; TreFT; TRV; WGRP

Away.   Lucien Stryk.   I bow to Master Takayama/who smiles all the way from Japan.   GP

Away Above a Harborful.   Lawrence Ferlinghetti.   stand out the bright steamers/to kingdom come   BoLoP; ErPo; NMP

Away, Delight.   Francis Beaumont and John Fletcher.   ...Men cannot mock us in the clay.'   EIL; NOBE; OBEV; ViBoPo

Away from You.   Cecilia Meireles.   oblivious of its transparent silence. AMV-81

Away in a Manger.   *Anonymous.*   And stay by my side/Until morning is nigh.   AH

Away in a Manger.   Martin Luther.   And fit us for heaven to live with Thee there.   GoTF; TreFS

Away, Melancholy.   Stevie Smith.   Away with it, let it go.   OxBTC; PBWP

Away Out West.   Sharlot M. Hall.   Where a man's on honor to be his best–/Away out West.   BPAW

Away out Yonder in Arizony.   *Anonymous.*   A-a-all pewtrified, ladies and gentlemen,/Completely pewtrified.   OuSiCo

Away to Twiver, Away, Away!   *Anonymous.*   I'll say no more but so give o'er.   EIL

Away Vane World.   Alexander Montgomerie.   Chryst is my love alone–I feir not.   NOCV

Away We Go.   Aileen Fisher.   away we go, away we go.   TiPo

Away with Bloodshed.   Alfred Edward Housman.   And Jane Eliza, she still snores on.   ShM

Away with Funeral Music.   Robert Louis Stevenson.   The cup of life's for him that drinks/And not for him that sips.   GoTF; TreFT

Away with Rum.   *Anonymous.*   Away, away with rum by gum;/The song of the Salvation Army.   FSW

Aweary Am I.   Abu-l-Ala al-Maarri.   Even thus do the favors flow of disgustful Fortune.   AWP; LiTW

Awee'.   Nia Francisco.   no, they do not forget me so   STE

Awful Fix.   Buddy Boy Hawkins.   Now your little daddy's gone/Now who you gonna get to chop your wood?   BluL

The Awful Mother.   Susan Griffin.   Only the awful mother stirs stricken/with grief.   NPGG

An Awful Responsibility.   Keith Preston.   And yet I think I had more fun,/When I was a cabin boy.   PoPl

Awkward Goodbyes.   Vassar Miller.   since whatever pig-/latin we talked, none called it love.   FAZ

Ax.   Charles Simic.   Lacking itself, in its essence, a future.   GP

The Axe-Helve.   Robert Frost.   'See how she's cock her head!'   CABL; OxBA

The Axe in the Wood.   Clifford Dyment.   In that tall lovely legacy of wood.   ACV

The Axe of the Pioneer.   Isabella Valancy Crawford.   We build up nations– this my axe and I!   CaP

Axioms.   Gad Hollander.   ...three syllables/rose from the corners of my skull.   VWA

Axle Song.   Mark Van Doren.   So growled the earth's revolving heap;/And will forever.   MoPo

The Axolotl.   David McCord.   "You said a mawfl,/Pop'epetl!"   FiBHP; OBAL

Ay, Ay, This Is the Day.   *Anonymous.*   Ay, ay, so that we may/Wend with Him at domesday.   OxBM

Ay or Nay?   Ralph Schomberg.   I've no time to throw away.   TrJP

Ay, 'Tis Thus.   *Anonymous.*   Zion's folk, free of yoke, O assure/"Forgiven!"   TrJP

Ay Waukin O.   Robert Burns.   Sleep I can get nane,/For thinking on my dearie...   NOEC

Aye, There's Hills.   Hamish Brown.   I'll hae ma piece at hame, mun.   PoSH

Aye Waukin' O!   *Anonymous.*   Sleep can I get nane,/For thinkin' o' my dearie.   BSV; GoTS

Ayii, Ayii. I Walked on the Ice of the Sea.   *Anonymous.*   Brings health/To the place of feasting.   RFM

Ayii, Ayii. The Great Sea Has Set Me in Motion.   *Anonymous.*   And I am left/Trembling with joy.   RFM

Aylmer's Field.   Alfred, Lord Tennyson.
   All at one mark, all hitting: make-believes/For Edith and himself.   GN
   Follows the mouse, and all is open field.   VLP

Ayohu Kanogisdi Death Song.   Carroll Arnett.   hello death   STE

The Azalea.   Coventry Patmore.   Sweet to myself that am so sweet to you!   ELP; GBL; GoBC

The Aziola.   Percy Bysshe Shelley.   Sad Aziola! from that moment I/Loved thee and thy sad cry.   CBEP; EBEV; PBBP

Azouou.   Mririda n'Ait Attik.   And our two hearts will be together.   WPOW

The Azra.   Heinrich Heine.   Men who perish if they love.   AWP

Azrael.   Henry Wadsworth Longfellow.   I was upon my way to seek him there.   AnAmPo

Azrael.   Robert Gilbert Welsh.   Look up beneath those folded wings,/And find them lined with gold.   HBV 1-2

The Aztec City.   Eugene Fitch Ware.   No one that visited this fiery hive/Ever alive/Came out but me–I, I alone, survive.   AA; HBV 1-2

Aztec Figurine.   John Beecher.   ...Our Lady/of Guadalupe and by her side Fidel.   GP

B

B.   Larry Eigner.   I know/the waving sun/the/constant ephemerals   NeAP

B-52s.   Arnold Kenseth.   They lean over and touch the rose dead.   PPON

B Negative.   X. J. Kennedy.   I pick up after them in Central Park.   ConAP; NePoEA-2; WeW

B's the Bus.   Phyllis McGinley.   It has to stop obligingly/If you but raise your hand.   SoPo; TiPo

B Stands for Bear.   Hilaire Belloc.   Decisive action in the hour of need/Denotes the Hero, but does not succeed.   ShM

Ba Cottage.   Andrew Young.   That slowly made me dry again.   OBSP

Baa, Baa, Black Sheep.   Mother Goose.   And one for the little boy that lives in the lane.   AmFP; FaBoBe; FaFP; HBV 1-2; HBVY; OxNR; SoPo; TiPo

Baal Shem Tov.   Abraham Moses Klein.   Like moss upon a stone at a brook's edge.   CaP; TrJP

Bab-Lock-Hythe.   Laurence Binyon.   Our hearts sang together.   MoVE; SD

The Babe.   Monk Gibbon.   Most rich endowed whose infant mind/Guesses not yet there is the rose.   OxBI

The Babe of Bethlehem.   Henry Beer.   'Tis He that makes men whole.   BePJ

Babel.   Gary Pacernick.   talin glaring from that rising sickle moon.   AMV-81

The Babes in the Wood.   *Anonymous.*
   Lest God with such like misery/Your wicked minds requite.   HBV 1-2; HBVY; OBNV
   Oh the sad fate of/The babes in the wood!'   OxBChV

Babi Yar.   Lev Ozerov.   Don't forget!/Do not forgive!   VWA

The Babiaantje.   Frank Templeton Prince.   Who has lost youth's peace!   ACV; MoBrPo

The Babie.   Jeremiah Eames Rankin.   Our babie straight frae Heaven.   AA; HBV 1-2

The Babies.   Mark Strand.   Let us try to save the babies.   GeTw; NYBP

Babies Haven't Any Hair.   Samuel Hoffenstein.   Between the cradle and the grave/Lies a haircut and a shave.   NLV

Babies of the Pioneers.   Eunice W. Luckey.   The laughing babies of the pioneers.   BPAW

Baboon.   *Anonymous.*   YOur face too looks like a ridge of stone.   WTO

Babushka.   Edith Matilda Thomas.   "Nay, farther must I go."   OnMSP

Baby.   Elaine Goodale Eastman.   Through sin, at least, thine Eden is not lost.   AA

Baby.   Florence Kiper Frank.   Who had sighed moon-sick then./I have you!   HBMV

The Baby.   Sir William Jones.   Thou then mayst smile while all around thee weep.   GoTF

Baby.   George Macdonald.   God thought about you, and so I am here.   BiCB; GoTF; HBV 1-2; HBVY; TreF; TRV

Baby.   Joyce Carol Oates.   The baby grows.   GeTw

The Baby.   James Reaney.   What do you build there./Little baby mine?   NAs

The Baby.   Ann Taylor.   His mother's kindness is a debt,/He never, never will forget.   OHIP

Baby and I.   *Anonymous.*   And so we crept out of the pot.   OxNR

Baby and Mary.   *Anonymous.*   And mother held up her forefinger at Mary.   NA

Baby Bell.   Thomas Bailey Aldrich.   And thus went dainty Baby Bell/Out of this world of ours.   HBV 1-2

Baby Cobina.   Gladys May Casely Hayford.   "Bells, guard our Baby Cobina from all devils and all/harm."   CDC

The Baby Goes to Boston.   Laura E. Richards.   Loky moky poky stoky/Smoky choky chee!   TiPo

The Baby Hilary, Sir Edmund.   Kathleen Leland Baker.   just because it's there.   NLV

Baby-Land.   George Cooper.   And her love,/Born above,/Guides the little feet.   HBV 1-2; HBVY

Baby Lon; or, The Bonnie Banks o' Fordie.   *Anonymous.*   And he's twyn'd himself o' his ain sweet life/On the bonnie banks o' Fordie.   SeCePo

Baby May.   William C. Bennett.   That's May Bennett, that's my baby.   HBV 1-2

Baby Mine.   *Anonymous.*   'Cause I'm goin' round the world, baby mine.   FSW

Baby Mine.   Charles Mackey.   He is coming back to thee! Baby mine!   BLSo

Baby, Please Don't Go.   *Anonymous.*   Baby, please don't go.   FSW

Baby Running Barefoot.   D. H. Lawrence.   Or firm and silken as young peony flowers.   NoP

Baby's Awake Now.   Bill Berkson.   And breath comes faster than the hounds/To sanction what remembered, what stuck.   APU

Baby's Breakfast.   Emilie Poulsson.   That was all the "Thank you"/He knew how to say.   HBV 1-2; HBVY

The Baby's Dance.   Ann Taylor.   With the merry gay coral, ding, ding, a-ding, ding.   OxBChV

The Baby's Debut (Parody on Wordsworth).   Horace and James Smith.   I'll blow a kiss to you.   ALV; OBRV; Par

Baby's Drinking Song.   James Kirkup.   Drop a little/On the table/Top a little.   NTCP

Baby's in Jail; the Animal Day Plays Alone.   Charles Henri Ford.   Baby will come to love and grief.   MoVE

The Baby's Name.   Tudor Jenks.   And we called the baby John.   BiCB

A Baby Sardine.   Spike Milligan.   "It's only a tin full of people."   OnUR

Baby Seed Song.   Edith Nesbit.   Little brown brother, good-bye.   HBV 1-2; HBVY

A Baby-Sermon.   George Macdonald.   But the stars and the stillness/Are always at home.   OxBChV

Baby-Sitting.   Gillian Clarke.   It will not come. It will not come.   FaBoWP

Baby Sleeps. Samuel Hinds. From present griefs, and future unknown harms,/And baby sleeps. HBV 1-2

Baby Song. Thom Gunn. But all time roars outside this room. NAs

Baby Taffy. *Anonymous.* His heels upright. OxNR

A Baby Ten Months Old Looks at the Public Domain. William Stafford. Northwest in the direction/Of his cosmic section. NYBP

Baby Toes. Carl Sandburg. Shall we ride/To the blue star/Or the white star? LaNeLa; SUS

Baby Toodles. Joseph S. Newman. At the very next word out of you! BBGG

Baby Tortoise. D. H. Lawrence. Invincible fore-runner. BoAnP; CMoP

Baby Villon. Philip Levine. Myself made otherwise by all his pain. CoAP; NaP

Babyhood. Josiah Gilbert Holland See! He is hushed in sweet repose! AA

Babylon. *Anonymous.*

Babylon. Robert Graves. Weeping for lost Babylon. HBMV

Babylon. Ralph Hodgson. Will take her to itself again. BrPo; HBMV

Babylon. George William Russell. While we are in the calm and proud possession of eternal/things. HBMV

Babylon. Siegfried Sassoon. Auguries of self-annihilation loom. MoRP

Babylon. Viola Taylor. The happy streets in Babylon, when once the dream was/truth. HBV 1-2

Babylon and Sion (Goa and Lisbon). Luîs de Camoens. Sion, had I not memory of thee! AWP

Babylon Revisited. LeRoi (Imamu Amiri Baraka) Jones. and your eyes peel to red mud BPo; NoAm; TW

Babysitter's Song. *Anonymous.* But I must wash the baby's panties! FSW

The Babysitters. Sylvia Plath. Everything has happened. NoP

Baccalaureate. David McCord. Sing cuccu, Phye Betta Cappe, nu! BXAP; NLV; OBAL; SpRo

The Bacchai: The Home of Aphrodite. Euripides. And peace to adore thee, thou spirit of Guiding Fire! AWP

Bacchanal. Irving Layton. May we, as he spins us in the cool gloom,/Be forever in his keeping. OBCV

Bacchanalia (excerpt). Matthew Arnold. The evening comes, the fields are still. FaBoRV; OAEL 1-2

The Bacchante to Her Babe. Eunice Tietjens. Look out with those round wondering eyes,/and squirm, and gurgle–and grow wise! HBMV

Bacchus. Ralph Waldo Emerson. The dancing Pleiads and eternal men. AmePo; AnNE; AP; APA; AWP; HBV 1-2; LiTA; MAmP; NOBA; OBEV; OxBP; PoEL 1-5; ViBoPo

Bacchus. William Empson.
And rang like bells the vaults and the dark arches. NoAm; PoCh
Leper scales fall always from his eyes. PoA
Pasturing the stallions in the standing corn. PoA

Bacchus in Tuscany (excerpt). Francesco Redi. That sparkles warm in Sansovine. AWP; OBVE

Bacchus on Beverages. Francesco Redi. And drink of the wine of the the vine benign/That sparkles warm in Sansovine. LiTW

Bacchylides. George Mason Whicher. "Of that far land where bide the dead/heroic race." AA

Bachelor. William Meredith. A man of action dials the telephone. NoAm

Bachelor Bold and Young. *Anonymous.* My brandy bottle's my best friend. AmFP

Bachelor Farmer. Roger McDonald. but close by, unchanging, incomplete. CBAP

Bachelor Hall. Eugene Field. To the dead and the dying of Bachelor Hall. BLPA; FPL

The Bachelor's Ballade. David Fisher Parry. So you take Virginia and I'll take vanilla. InMe

The Bachelor's Complaint. *Anonymous.* And still be a-trying to get him a wife. AmFP

Bachelor's Hall. John Finley. Bad luck to the pictur of Bachelor's Hall! HBV 1-2

The Bachelor's Lament. *Anonymous.* Farewell wheelbarrow,/Little wife and all. OxNR

The Bachelor's Lay. *Anonymous.* For this is the way the old bachelor done. OuSiCo

A Bachelor's Life. *Anonymous.* Thou berest thy love behind thy back',/In every place whereso he go. OxBM

Back. Wilfred Wilson Gibson. Though I must bear the blame/Because he bore my name. GTBS; TreFT

Back. Weldon Kees. I have come back/As empty-handed as I went. NaP; PrIm

Back. Angela McCabe. ...Water off a goddamned duck's back. AmPA

Back. Robert Mezey. nothing but mine, persisting one more night. AmPA

Back Again from Yucca Flats. Reeve Spencer Kelley. Across that fused Goliath's ring. AmFN

Back Again, Home. Don L. Lee. "Back Again,/BLACK AGAIN,/Home." BALP; BPo

Back Aways. Clark Coolidge. recalling the nothing from the nothing gate. APU

Back Country. Joyce Carol Oates. dogs get in the way. Psk

Back from the Paved Way. Robert D. FitzGerald. and the tune steps out light-footed upon the air. PoAu 1-2

Back from the Word Processing Course, I Say to My Old Typewriter. Michael C. Blumenthal. vibrate those aging hips again/beneath these trembling hands. GOYP

Back Gnawing Blues. Ramblin' (Willard) Thomas. If you allow me a chance/I will gnaw your backbone half in two BluL

Back in the States. Louis Simpson. Already becoming like the rest of us. AMV-81

Back into the Garden. Sarah Webster Fabio. But making it/the shiny seed's/your prize and/genesis. BlSi

Back Lane. R. D. Murphy. And on this compost, like a rose,/Fragrance of children's laughter blows. PoAu 1-2

Back Road. Bruce Guernsey. the snowball/packed with rock/aimed at my face. AMV-81

Back Road Farm. Charles Bruce. You can hear the far deep rumour of sea on stone. CaP

Back Room Joys. Justin Richardson. Well, it was, if you like. But we hid it with masterly skill. FiBHP

Back through the Looking Glass to This Side. John Ciardi. a good guy coming home, the long day done. NLV

Back to Arizona. Earl Alonzo Brininstool. When high boot-heels were in fashion, and a six-gun was/the law! BPAW

Back to Base. Jenny Joseph. The vast cold glitter, thin twanging in the spheres/That draws men, crazy, across shadeless tundra. BrRo

Back to Dublin. R. A. D. Ford. That was my ticket to come in. CaP

Back to Griggsby's Station. James Whitcomb Riley. Back where we ust to be so happy and so pore! BLPA; BLPL

Back to Life. Thom Gunn. As if each leaf were, so, better prepared/For falling sooner or later separate. NoP

Back to the Angels. William Walter De Bolt. maybe it would be better/to go back to the angels. AMV-81

Back to the Ghetto. Jacob Glatstein. I weep with the joy of coming back to/you. TrJP

Back Water Blues. *Anonymous.* There were thousands of poor people/didn't have no place to go. FSW

Back Yard, July Night. William Cole. How I wonder which you are. BoNaP

Backgammon. Olga Broumas. Violent love so slow it cuts/Cage from around the heart SUW

Backing into the Fan Mail (Unreceived). Dick Gallup. That was my first disappointment with the US Mails. APU

The Backlash Blues. Langston Hughes. Yes, you're the one/Will have the blues. BPo

Backward–Forward. *Anonymous.* Because of nobler work and sweeter rest. BLRP

The Backward Look. Howard Nemerov. We take our dust and rocks and start back down. OxBC

A Backward Spring. Thomas Hardy. What happened to it in mid-December. PPP

A Backwards Journey. P.K. Page. ...that tiny image/could smash the atom of space and time. WHW

Backwater Pond: The Canoeists. William Stanley Merwin. All afternoon, they cannot say why. PoPl

A Backwoods Hero (excerpt). Alexander McLachlan. And may the turf upon him laid,/Lie lightly on his breast! CaP

Backyard. Alice Notley. ...If you love me, all/of nature, let the wind blow. APU

Backyard Swing. Janet Campbell Hale. Groaning when the/Wind moves it. STE

Bacon's Epitaph, Made by His Man. *Anonymous.* To plead his cause, where he by this doth/know/Whether to Caesar he was friend or foe. AnAmPo; PAH; SCAP

Bad and Good. Alexander Resnikoff. To keep your foot out of your food/When mommy says you should. NTCP

The Bad Apple. Bruce Bennett. He began to speak. LTB

Bad Bishop Jegon. *Anonymous.* And bring thy poor/commonwealth into decay. GBP

The Bad Boy. *Anonymous.* So they sent me down to Huntsville to wear my life away. CoSo

A Bad Break. W. T. Goodge. "How toothless than a serpent's child/It is to have a sharper's thanks!" NOAV

Bad Company. Rowland Watkyns. Who lies with dogs, shall rise with fleas. FaBoEE

Bad Day on the Boulder. Lloyd Davis. There's whiskey in the car. WOLT

Bad Dream. Louis MacNeice. One shriek. The arm was gone. FaBoIP; NoAm

Bad Dreams. Robert Browning.

My heart break, I loved on the same.' OAEP; OBSP
Oh, Nature–good! Oh, Art–no whit/Less worthy! Both in one–accurst!
OAEL 1–2; VLP

Bad Example. Isabella Fey. In short, of behaving like men. BoAnP

Bad Girl Blues. Memphis Willie Borum. They ain't playing for no secret/
they playing it a wide open hand BluL

The Bad Girl's Lament; or, St. James Hospital. *Anonymous.* I'm a young
maiden. I know I've done wrong. ViBoFo

The Bad Habit. Charles Henri Ford. Rider on the bat-winged horse.
EAS

Bad I am, but yet they child. Gerard Manley Hopkins. Help me, Sir, and
so I will. BoC

A Bad Joke. Martial (Marcus Valerius Martialis). What's the reward of all
your schemes? You're poor! UnTE

The Bad Kittens. Elizabeth Jane Coatsworth. And out of the darkness they
peer/With a goblin light in their eyes. OBCA

Bad Luck Blues. Blind Lemon Jefferson. I mean Santy–singing about Fee–/
be on my my way to what you call/loving Tennessee BluL

Bad Luck Blues. Sonny Boy Williamson. Now, but tell 'em if they be good
they'll come to see me/People, on the Resur-rection Day BluL

Bad Luck to This Marching. Charles James Lever. And think twice ere I'd
leave it to be a dragoon! OnYI

Bad Man Ballad. *Anonymous.*
An' all I ever done is kill my wife. ABF
I'm loading the coal out every day. AmFP

The Bad Man from the Brazos. *Anonymous.* I'm a fighter, I am fly, and I
am flip. CoSo

Bad Morning. Langston Hughes. I's frustrated! OBAL

The Bad Mother. Susan Griffin. she drives with all her magic down a/
different route to darkness where/all life begins. NPGG

The Bad Old Days. Kenneth Rexroth. And the misery, and the/Anger,
and the vow are the same. NNaP; NoAm

The Bad Season Makes the Poet Sad. Robert Herrick. Knock at a star
with my exalted head. AnAnS 2; CABA; CaPo; LiTB; OAEP; PrIm;
SeCeV

A Bad Sleeper. Paul Verlaine. Am I happy? Totus in benigno positus!
PeHV

The Bad-Tempered Wife. *Anonymous.* She's not fit for heaven and she's too
mean for hell. MaC

The Badger Grunting on His Woodland Track. John Clare. Burnt by the
boys to get a swarm of bees FM; InPS; PAI

The Badgers. Seamus Heaney. The unquestionable houseboy's shoulders/
that could have been my own. CIP

Badman of the Guest Professor. Ishmael Reed. dey want me to help score
d ambush BPo

Baedeker for Metaphysicians. Brian Higgins. See, when you have stopped,
that the journey is/completed. FaBoTw

The Baffled Knight. *Anonymous.*
If you will not when you may,/You shall not when you will, sir. ViBoFo
Spare not for her gay clothing,/But lay her body flat on the ground. BaBo;
ESPB

The Bag. George Herbert. ...Sighs will convey/Any thing to me. Harke,
despair away. AnAnS 1; SeCP

The Bag of the Bee. Robert Herrick. She kist, and wip'd their dove-like
eyes;/And gave the bag between them. OAEP

A Bag of Tools. R. L. Sharpe. A stumbling block/Or a steppingstone.
BLPA; GoTF; PoToHe; TreFT; YaD

La Bagarede. Galway Kinnell. at having loved one who dies–is shin-/ing.
NYBP

A Bagatelle. James Reeves. Moving and childish as an ancient rhyme.
PoL

The Bagel. David Ignatow. and strangely happy with myself. CAPP;
ConAP; FF; TwCP

Baggot Street Deserta. Thomas Kinsella. My quarter-inch of cigarette/
Goes flaring down to Baggot Street. CIP; CMoP; FaBoIP; IPY; NMP

Bagley Wood. Lionel Pigot Johnson. These stars, these nightingales, these
scents: then shame would cease. AnFE; VLP

Bagman O'Reilly's Curse. Les A. Murray. ...you lie/Attended by cold
worms and hedgerow priests/More hungry and less merciful than I. TW

The Bagpipe Man. Nancy Byrd Turner. The funny old bagpipe man!
TiPo

Bagpipe Music. Hugh" (Christopher Murray Grieve) MacDiarmid. And
does...while we human beings lie cramped and fearful. OAEL 1–2

Bagpipe Music. Louis MacNeice. But if you break the bloody glass you
won't hold up the weather. CMoP; ExPo; GTBS-P; LiTB; LiTM; NLV;
NoAm; NOBE; NOBL; NoP; OAEL 1–2; OAEP; OBSV; OnYI; OxBTC;
SeCePo; SeCeV; ViBoPo

Bagpipes. *Anonymous.* We'll have a wedding at our good house. OxNR

Bags of Meat. Thomas Hardy. One can fancy a tear runs down his face/
When the butcher wins, and he's driven from the place. BoAnP; FM

Bags Packed and We Expected This. Ramona Wilson. in the end we do
but sleep. VoR

Bah! Walter De La Mare. And I don't think they ought to say "Bah!"
BoAnP

Baha'u'llah in the Garden of Ridwan. Robert Earl Hayden. Within the
rock the undiscovered suns/release their light. PoBA

Bahamas. George Oppen. ...across the miles/Of the Atlantic, and the
blinding/glitter/Of the sea. NYBP

Bahnhofstrasse. James Joyce. Nor old heart's wisdom yet to know/The
signs that mock me as I go. NoAm

Baiamai's Never-failing Stream. William Hart-Smith. dabbling among those
cold stones. BoAV

The Bailey Beareth the Bell Away. *Anonymous.* After their life grant
them/a place eternally to sing/Amen. SeCePo

The Bailiff's Daughter of Islington. *Anonymous.* For now I have found mine
own true-love,/Whom I thought I should never see more. AmFP; BaBo;
ESPB; FaBoBa; FSW; GN; HBV 1–2; OAEP; OBET; OxBB; OxBoLi;
ViBoFo

The Bait. John Donne. Alas, is wiser far than I. AnEnPo; CABA; DiPo;
ErPo; HoPM; InPK; InPS; LiTL; NIP; OAEL 1–2; OAEP; PAI; PoRA; SD;
TEP

Bait Shop. Thomas Reiter. then clean us to the bone. WOLT

Baith Gud and Fair and Womanlie. *Anonymous.* And luf hir best attour all
thing,/Baith gud and fair and womanlie. GoTS; OxBS

Baits for Various Fish. Thomas Barker. Follow Barker's advice to cook the
fish. FaBoUs

Baja. Gerald Stern. a little kindness for insects, a little pity for the dead.
SV

Baja–Outside Mexicali. Michael McClure. The wind-moved tamarisk/trees
as beautiful/as graygreen chinchilla fur. GP

The Baker's Boy. Mary Effie Lee Newsome. At least I have no doubt.
CDC; GoSl

A Baker's Dozen of Wild Beasts. Carolyn Wells.
And he answered, "I'm very well-buttered." OBCA
But he cares not a penny for that. OBCA
If you sprinke me thickly with mustard. OBCA
Or felt awfully cut up, at least. OBCA

A Baker's Duzzen Uv Wize Sawz. Edward Rowland Sill. Them ez will,
kin. FaBoBe; FaFP; GoTF; HBV 1–2; HBVY; InMe; TreFS

Baking Day. Rosemary Joseph. All bent toward nourishing her children.
Str

Balaam. John Keble. O teach our love to grow/Up to thy heavenly light,
and reap what Thou hast sown. OBNC; OBVV

Balaclava. *Anonymous.* For the England they had fought for on that wild
October day. OBET

Balade Simple: "Fairest of stars." John Lydgate. Fortuned have his lady
for to win. GBL

Balalaika. Norman Dubie. There is the sound of the balalaika waking in
heaven. AmPA

Balance. Philip Schultz. Lord of Mercy, the dead still need bus fare &
salvation! MAYP

The Balance. Judith Johnson Sherwin. with that clear sterile skull to take/
your pleasure or that soft pulsing slime. GP

The Balance of Europe. Alexander Pope. For nothing's left in either of the
Scales. SeCeV

A Balanced Bait in Handy Pellet Form. Allen Curnow. 30 g/kg (3%)
Metaldehyde, in the form of a pellet. OCNZ

Balboa. Nora Perry. ...this gallant soul,/Divinely guided, reached the goal.
PAH

Balboa, the Entertainer. LeRoi (Imamu Amiri Baraka) Jones. music trails,
or your fingers/slip/from my arm NoAm

The Balcony. Charles Baudelaire. These vows, these perfumes, and those
countless kisses? AWP; NAWM 1–2

The Balcony Poems. Douglas Smith. these axioms of light/repeat their
lessons to a failing world. AMV-81

A Balcony with Birds. Howard Moss. The mind downed in the dark may
dream them on. NePoEA

Bald. Bill Zavatsky. And even its teeth fall out. APU

The Bald Cavalier. *Anonymous.* Which may a second laugh provoke,/And
leave the biter bit. OxBChV

The Bald Spot. Wesley McNair. walking backwards/into my life.
AMV-81

Balder. Sydney Thomas Dobell. A Paramount Supreme. PeD

Balder's Wife. Alice Cary. To the moan of the willow water. AA;
AnAmPo

Baldpate Pond. E. F. Weisslitz. It will be enough. NYBP

Baldy Bane. W. S. Graham. Get up and clean the grate. NePoEA

Baldy Green. *Anonymous.* But Baldy saved the gold. PoOW

Balearic Idyll. Frederick Packard. Then see them home in a baruig.
FiBHP

The Balena. *Anonymous.* Not another ship could make that trip but the
Balena, I declare. OBSS

Balgu Song. *Anonymous.* what a nice smell the new cloth has. CBAP

Balinda's Dance. Louise Erdrich. ...like piers/rocking and trembling in my current. TWSS

Balkis. Lascelles Abercrombie. She said, "I will go to Solomon." HBV 1-2

The Ball and the Club. Forbes Lindsay. And the club–with a couple of nicks and a bend,/I found again in the bag of a friend. SD

Ball Game. Richard Eberhart. To that strange place where one had first begun. LiSp

The Ball Poem. John Berryman. ...I am not a little boy. CoAP; FF; LiSp; MoAmPo; NoAm; NOBA; NoP

Ball's Bluff. Herman Melville. Far footfalls died away till none were left. OBWP

Ballad. Archie Randolph Ammons. and see if he will be moved. GP

Ballad. Maurice Baring. But they were died with crimson/Before the day was done. HBV 1-2

Ballad. May Kendall. Into the sunless land they went,/Into the starless land. HBV 1-2

Ballad. Charles Kingsley. Sail Westward ho, and away! GN

A Ballad. Sir Charles Sedley. Justice has bid the World adieu,/And dead Men have no Friends. CoMu

Ballad. Marjorie Allen Seiffert. In your eyes my sorrow. HBMV

Ballad. Charles Simic. Little girl skipping the owl's hushed way. LCAP

Ballad. William Soutar. And found your ain true love. NeBP

Ballad. Harriet Prescott Spofford. Wait, till I come to thee! HBV 1-2

Ballad. Henry Treece. With the head of a fool and the heart of a bard. WaP

Ballad against the Enemies of France. Francois Villon. Who could wish evil to the state of France! AWP

Ballad by Hans Breitmann. Charles Godfrey Leland. De maiden mit nodings on. BXAP; CenHV; NOBL; PaPo

A Ballad Called Perkin's Figary. Anonymous. To the shame and confusion of Perkin Warbeck. APAS

A Ballad Called the Haymarket Hectors. Anonymous. How the bullets would whistle, the cannon would roar! APAS

Ballad: "Father, through the dark that parts us." Roy Fuller. I shall never leave you, darling,/Do not fear. ELU

Ballad for Gloom. Ezra Pound. Whom God deigns not to overthrow/Hath need of triple mail. LiTM; MoAmPo; NePA; OBVV

A Ballad for Katharine of Aragon. Charles Causley. And I lie here alone. FaBoTw; NePoEA

Ballad for the Unknown Soldier. Allan Taylor. Was it someone you thought you knew/Was it me or was it you? OBET

A Ballad from the Seven Dials Press... Anonymous. So pray attend to what you hear./And a warning take I pray. CoMu; VLP

Ballad: "He passed by with another." Gabriela (Lucila Godoy Alcayaga) Mistral. And he will go with another/through eternity. OLR

Ballad: "I put my hat upon my head." Samuel Johnson. And there I met another man/Whose hat was in his hand. NOBL

A Ballad in Blank Verse of the Making of a Poet. John Davidson. And here are men to know, women to love. BSV

Ballad in Blonde Hair Foretold. Robert Bagg. Now he is only sound. NePoAm-2

A Ballad in "G". Eugene Fitch Ware. A song of the swag and the swig. PoLf

Ballad: "Mother mine, Mother mine, what do you see?" Annemarie Ewing. That sees things and not people. Dear Mother,/good-bye... NePoAm

Ballad: "My lady was found mutilated." Leonard Cohen. and we danced upon her grave. OBCV

A Ballad, November 1680. Anonymous. But to throw out the bishops who threw out the bill. APAS

Ballad: "O what is that sound which so thrills the ear." W. H. Auden. And their eyes are burning. MoAB; ViBoPo

The Ballad of a Barber. Aubrey Beardsley. You pray in vain for Carrousel. NOBV; SyP

A Ballad of a Bun. Sir Owen Seaman. And second-cousin to the worm!' CenHV

A Ballad of a Mine. Robin Skelton. Goodbye the day. Good luck to me. MoBS

A Ballad of a Nun. John Davidson. Dawn lightly laid her rosy hand. BeLS; HBMV; MoBrPo; OnMSP

Ballad of a Strange Thing. Howard Phelps (Phelps Putnam) Putnam. But no more Jack, and we were more/Dull and baffled than before. MoVE; OxBA

A Ballad of Abbreviations. Gilbert Keith Chesterton. He may tell you quite succinctly it is Hell. NOBL

The Ballad of Adam's First. Leland Davis. Her beads and her beauty/Were raiment rare! HBMV

Ballad: "Of all the Girls that e'er were seen." John Gay. As does that Part that lies between/Her Left Toe, and her Right Toe. CoMu

A Ballad of All the Trades. Anonymous. But his Trull, but his Trull, but his Trull/holds up the Kettle. CoMu; ErPo; UnTE

Ballad of an Empty Table. Tom Kryss. rifles and tables explode/pretty much the same. NeAC

A Ballad of Andrew and Maudlin. Anonymous. While their Breasts and their Bellies went Pintle a Pantle. CoMu

Ballad of Another Ophelia. D. H. Lawrence. Did you see the wicked sun that winked? CoBMV; MoVE

Ballad of Badmen. Owen Dodson. My God, my God, my God for more. FB

The Ballad of Ballymote. Tess Gallagher. Cabbage and bones, said she. Cabbage/and bones. GP

The Ballad of Banners. John Lehmann. Though the alternate stars were there/To watch all history? MoBS

The Ballad of Barnaby. W. H. Auden. And Barnaby's soul they bore aloft,/Singing with voices sweet and soft. OBNV

Ballad of Bedlam. Anonymous. To some rich desert fly with me. NA

The Ballad of Billie Potts. Robert Penn Warren. Which is your luck.) NOBA; OxBA

The Ballad of Billy Rose. Leslie Norris. Poor Billy Rose. God, he could fight/Before my three sharp coins knocked out his sight. MoBS

The Ballad of Billy the Kid. Henry Herbert Knibbs. And so ends the true story of Billy the Kid. BPAW

Ballad of Birmingham. Dudley Randall. But, baby, where are you? BPo; HeIP; InPK; NIP; NoAm

The Ballad of Blossom. Mona Van Duyn. Eros wings down to a fir to sit/and hoot like a Long-eared Owl. SM

The Ballad of Bouillabaisse. William Makepeace Thackeray. –Here comes the smoking Bouillabaisse! FaBoUs; HBV 1-2; InMe; OBEV; OBTV; OBVV; ViBoPo

The Ballad of Bunker Hill. Edward Everett Hale. When we burned up our Powder, we had to go Home! MC; PAH

A Ballad of Burdens. Algernon Charles Swinburne. This is the end of every man's desire. EnLi 1-2

The Ballad of Camden Town. James Elroy Flecker. I have so little to forgive;/So much, I can't forget. EnLit; HBV 1-2

The Ballad of Charity. Charles Godfrey Leland. Oh, how hard is life for many! oh, how sweet it is for some! InMe

The Ballad of Chickamauga. Maurice Thompson. As one old soldier's ballad borne on breath of battle-song. MC; PAH

The Ballad of Chicken Bill. F. E. Vaughn. But over there is Fryer hill/Quietly producing millions still. PoOW

A Ballad of Christmas. Walter De la Mare. Herod and Pilate riding by,/And Judas, one of three. OBCP

Ballad of Culinary Frustration. Phyllis McGinley. We're having a chop. FiBHP

Ballad of Davy Crockett. Anonymous. They make the world light when the moon is out of sight. ABF

The Ballad of Dead Ladies. Francois Villon. But where are the snows of yester-year? AWP; CTC; ExPo; GoBC; HBV 1-2; OBVE

The Ballad of Dead Men's Bay. Algernon Charles Swinburne. And the sand quakes ever; and ill fare they/That look upon that light. MOS

The Ballad of Dead Yankees. Donald Petersen. For all of these, the early dead,/Who've gone where no ovations are. HeIP; LiSp

A Ballad of Death. Algernon Charles Swinburne. Death shall come in with thee. MaVP

Ballad of Don Juan Tenorio and the Statue of the Comendador. Roy Campbell. The statue would not speak one word. PeSA

Ballad of Douglas Bridge. Francis Carlin. To one whose saddled soul to-night/Rides out with Count O'Hanlon. AnIV; HBMV; OxBI

The Ballad of Downal Baun. Padraic Colum. Silently rocking and rocking,/The moon-cradle out in the sky. SUS

The Ballad of Dreamland. Algernon Charles Swinburne. Only the song of a secret bird. HBV 1-2

The Ballad of East and West. Rudyard Kipling. When two strong men stand face to face,/tho' they come from the end of the earth. BeLS; BLPL; BrPo; FaBoBe; FaBV; FaPoR; HBV 1-2; MaC; OBNV; TreFT; TRV

Ballad of Faith. William Carlos Williams. (the horn sounds hoarsely) OBAL

The Ballad of Father Gilligan. William Butler Yeats. Had pity on the least of things/Asleep upon a chair. AnIV; EaLo; HBV 1-2; InPo; MoBrPo; OnYI; PoRA

The Ballad of Fisher's Boardinghouse. Rudyard Kipling. The little silver crucifix/That keeps a man from harm. PoRA

A Ballad of Francois Villon. Algernon Charles Swinburne. Villon, our sad bad glad mad brother's name. EnLi 1-2; PoEL 1-5; PoRA

The Ballad of Halfmoon Bay (excerpt). Keith Sinclair. Fair or weather or a two-reef gale. AnNZ

The Ballad of Hampstead Heath. James Elroy Flecker. And fell asleep again. MoBrPo

A Ballad of Heaven. John Davidson. The music that you made below/Is now the music of the spheres. BeLS; EnLit

Ballad of Hector in Hades. Edwin Muir. While round bright Troy Achilles whirls/A corpse with streaming hair. NoAm; NOBE

A Ballad of Hell. John Davidson. Hell raised a hoarse, half-human cheer. AnEnPo; HBMV; HoPM; MoBrPo; WHA

The Ballad of Helmut Franze. Jerome Sala. And there the traitor Helmut lives/A communist today. APU

A Ballad of Heroes. Henry Austin Dobson. The deeds you wrought are not in vain! HBV 1-2; HBVY; OHIP

A Ballad of High Endeavor. Anonymous. Low love fulfilled of low success?/(Ah me! ah me!/Hey diddle dee!) NA

The Ballad of Hiram Hover. Bayard Taylor. Draw, from every beast they snare,/Comfort for a wedded pair! BXAP; FaBoCo; OBAL

Ballad of Ho Chi Minh. Ewan MacColl. Peace and freedom and Ho Chi Minh. FSW

Ballad of Human Life. Thomas Lovell Beddoes. We're boy and girl, and lass and lad, and man and wife together. BeLS

The Ballad of Imitation. Henry Austin Dobson. And the man who plants cabbages imitates, too! HBV 1-2

Ballad of Ira Hayes. Peter La Farge. And his ghost is a-lyin' thirsty in the ditch where Ira died. MAT

The Ballad of Ishmael Day. Anonymous. Honor be to old Ishmael Day! PAH

Ballad of John Cable and Three Gentlemen. William Stanley Merwin. Flags of white water/Are his company. CoAP; NePoEA; NOBA

A Ballad of John Silver. John Masefield. A little south the sunset in the Islands of the Blest. EvOK

A Ballad of Johnny Appleseed. Helmer O. Oleson. Only happy for the winesaps/In tomorrow's applesauce! SiSoSe; TiPo

The Ballad of Keith of Ravelston. Sydney Thomas Dobell. O Keith of Ravelston,/The sorrows of thy line! HBV 1-2; OBEV; OBVV

The Ballad of Kynd Kittok. William Dunbar. Drink with my Guddame, as ye ga by,/Anys for my saik. BSV; GoTS

Ballad of Ladies' Love, Number Two. Francois Villon. Not all can nick it that will, heigho! ErPo

The Ballad of Lager Bier. Edmund Clarence Stedman. Come back! come back! and help me pay for/The bread and cheese and Lager Bier. OBAL

Ballad of Lieutenant Miles. Clinton Scollard. Gallant young Lieutenant Miles/And his valiant volunteers! MC

A Ballad of Life. Algernon Charles Swinburne. And kiss thee with soft laughter on thine eyes,/Ballad, and on thy mouth. HBV 1-2; MaVP

A Ballad of London. Richard Le Gallienne.
And no man sails to Babylon. HBMV
He shall most utterly abase,/And set a desert in their place. FaBoPP

The Ballad of Longwood Glen. Vladimir Nabokov. Wash their hands, and drive back to town. NYBP

Ballad of Low-Lie-Down. Madison Cawein. ...Forth they wandered,/John-a-dreams and Low-lie-down. HBV 1-2

Ballad of Luna, Luna. Federico Garcia Lorca. The wind is watching over it. SOTW

A Ballad of Manila Bay. Sir Charles G. D. Roberts. It is Dewey's glory to-day, as Nelson's/A hundred years ago! PAH

The Ballad of Mary Baldwin. Stephen Sandy. Go do the dishes. Go to bed. MAT

A Ballad of Master McGrath. Anonymous. "Three cheers for old Ireland,' says Master McGrath. FaBoBa

The Ballad of Minepit Shaw. Rudyard Kipling. And more things true than are told. PoPle

Ballad of Mistress Death. Denis Devlin. Oh, there will need no porters/When all those doors open! NMP

The Ballad of Mrs. Noah. Robert Duncan. Ah! the Rainbow's awake/and we will not fail! NoAm; NOBA

The Ballad of Nat Turner. Robert Earl Hayden. And bided my time. BALP; BPo; SM; VGW

The Ballad of New Orleans. George Henry Broker. And under its shade, like a lion,/Were resting the will and the power. PAH

Ballad of No Proper Man. Daniel Gerard Hoffman. Who is that capers on the sand? MAT

The Ballad of O'Bruadir. Frederick Robert Higgins. Ghosting glory from the water! EtS; OBMV

Ballad of Old Women & of How They Are Constrained to Stimulate... Norman Talbot. but a charmer has to know. NOAV

The Ballad of Oriskany. O. C. Auringer. At last, far from Oriskany AA

A Ballad of Orleans. Agnes Mary Frances (Mme Emile Duclaux) Robinson. Sixty forts at our gates last night–To-day there is not one! HBV 1-2

The Ballad of Paco Town. Clinton Scollard. Down through the years to us shall be/Ever and ever the victory! PAH

A Ballad of Past Meridian. George Meredith. Of Death, of Life, those inwound notes are mine. OAEL 1-2; VLP

The Ballad of Persse O'Reilly. James Joyce. For there's no true spell in Connacht or hell/(Bis) That's able to raise a Cain. FaBoBa; LiTB

The Ballad of Private Chadd. A.(lan) A.(lexander) Milne. And bellowed, with his best salute,/"A happy birthday, Father!" CenHV

A Ballad of Queensland (Sam Holt). George Herbert Gibson ("Ironbark"). To the end of the chapter of Fate. PoAu 1-2

The Ballad of Reading Gaol. Oscar Wilde.
And the iron gin that waits for Sin/Had caught us in its snare. MoBrPo; TrGrPo
And the red rose would but blow more red,/The white rose whiter blow. OAEL 1-2; OBMV
The brave man with a sword! AnFE; BeLS; BrPo; DTo; GoTF; HBV 1-2; LiTB; OnYI; PoPl; TreF
For he who lives more lives than one/More deaths than one must die. NOBV; ViBoPo
Nor drop feet foremost through the floor/Into an empty space. NOBE
Nor the kiss of Caiaphas. NOBV; OBNC; TEP; WHA
To tell the men who tramp the yard/That God's Son died for all. OxBI

The Ballad of Red Fox. Melvin Walker LaFollette. And blood upon his red red brush/Shall red fox die. BoAnP; LOW; NePoEA

A Ballad of Redhead's Day. Richard Butler Glaenzer. An elder was he in the Church of Christ,/Immortal at thirty; his faith sufficed. MC; PAH

A Ballad of Remembrance. Robert Earl Hayden. a poem of remembrance, a gift, a souvenir for you AmNP; BPo; IDB; PoBA; PoNe

The Ballad of Sally in our Alley. Henry Carey. O then we'll wed and then we'll bed,/But not in our Alley. CEP; NOEC; OBEC

Ballad of Sam Hall. Anonymous. God damn their eyes! FSW; VLP

A Ballad of Sarsfield. Aubrey Thomas De Vere. A century after, Sarsfield's laughter/Was echoed from Dungannon. GoBC

The Ballad of Sir Brian and the Three Wishes. Newman Levy. But the jewels were never found. FiBHP

A Ballad of Sir John Franklin. George Henry Baker. We passed the Northern Sea! AA; HBV 1-2; OnMSP

The Ballad of Sir Patrick Spens. Anonymous. And there lies gude Sir Patrick Spens/Wi' the Scots lords at his feet! EtS; RoGo

The Ballad of Sister Anne. Osbert Sitwell. Try not to scream! AtBAP

Ballad of Springhill. and MacColl. Ewan Seeger. Peggy Two miles of earth for a marking stone. FSW

The Ballad of Sue Ellen Westerfield. Robert Earl Hayden. Until her dying-bed,/she cursed her circumstances. AmPP; NoAm

The Ballad of Sweet P. Virginia Woodward Cloud. Mistress Penelope Penwick, she,/Called by her father, "My Sweet P." PAH

The Ballad of the Angel. Theodosia Garrison. And 'tis my touch shall swing the gates/Of Heaven when you die! HBV 1-2

The Ballad of the Billycock. Anthony C. Deane. I mean to take to writing it myself! ALV

The Ballad of the Boat. Richard Garnett. O stream, is this thy bar of sand? O boat, is this the bay? HBV 1-2

Ballad of the Boll Weevil. Anonymous. Ain't got no home. FSW; TrAS

A Ballad of the Boston Tea-Party, December 16, 1773. Oliver Wendell Holmes. To cheat of slumber all her foes/And cheer the wakening nations! MC; PAH; PAL

Ballad of the Bushman. Eileen Duggan. But God, if one of them could farm! CoBE

A Ballad of the Captains. Edwin James Brady. And they hear no more the calling/Of the watches, or the falling/Of the sea rain in the night. EtS

The Ballad of the Children of the Czar. Delmore Schwartz. Thinking of my father's fathers/And of my own will. MiAP

Ballad of the Common Man. Alfred Kreymborg. Keep on building Men! PAL

A Ballad of the Conemaugh Flood. Hardwick Drummond Rawnsley. Did they hear Heaven's great "Well done"? PAH

Ballad of the Cool Fountain. Anonymous. I'll never marry you! BoWoP

A Ballad of the Courtier and the Country Clown. Anonymous. When he plucks up your gay Embroider'd Cloaths./With a Fadding, etc. CoMu

The Ballad of the Cross. Theodosia Garrison. And in His hold the cross lay cold/Between her heart and His! HBMV; HBVY

Ballad of the D-Day Dodgers. Anonymous. Those are the D-Day Dodgers who'll stay in Italy. WTO

The Ballad of the Dark Ladie. Samuel Taylor Coleridge. Between my comely bachelors/And blushing bridal maids. EnRP

Ballad of the Days of the Messiah. Abraham Moses Klein. O Messiah, he stands grimy in his/tank! TrJP

Ballad of the Despairing Husband. Robert Creeley. Oh, lady, grant me time,/please, to finish my rhyme. AmPC; NeAP; NoP; OBAL; SM

Ballad of the Double Bed. Eve Merriam. So marrily to life's house I sped:/And herein shape our double bed. UnTE

Ballad of the Drinker in His Pub. N. P. Van Wyk Louw. how all bright things decay. PeSA

Ballad of the Drover. Henry Lawson. With clanging chains and tinware/All sounding eerily. PoAu 1-2

The Ballad of the Emeu. Bret (Francis Bret Harte) Harte. All through/The voracity of that Emeu! NLV

Ballad of the Epiphany. Charles Dalmon. And, in its gentle mother's arm,/The Baby fast asleep. HBMV; OnMSP

Ballad of the Erie Canal. Anonymous. Till we git to Buffalo. ABF

Ballad of the Faded Field. Robert Burns Wilson. But beauty's soul abideth still. AA

Ballad of the Faithful Clerk. Albert Stillman. Will make a man successful, if he has a little Luck. DBV; InMe

A Ballad of the Fleet. Alfred, Lord Tennyson. To be lost evermore in the main. FaPoR

Ballad of the Flood. Edwin Muir. He's lighted down at Ararat,/And there he's made his hame. MoBS

The Ballad of the Foxhunter. William Butler Yeats. The hounds wail for the dead. EnLit

A Ballad of the French Fleet. Henry Wadsworth Longfellow. When thou didst walk in wrath/With thine horses through the sea! AA; HBV 1-2; MC; PAH

A Ballad of the Gold Country. Helen Hunt Jackson. He did not know us then; he might/Upon another day! BPAW

Ballad of the Golden Bowl. Sara Henderson Hay. It is sad—it is all we have/To remember him by... OnMSP

A Ballad of the Good Lord Nelson. Lawrence Durrell. Aboard the Victory, Victory O. ErPo; LiTM

Ballad of the Goodly Fere. Ezra Pound. Sin' they nailed him to the tree. CAW; CMoP; HBV 1-2; LiTA; LiTM; MoAB; MoAmPo; MoBS; NePA; NoAm; OFD; PoRA; TrCP; TrGrPo

The Ballad of the Harp-Weaver. Edna St. Vincent Millay. Were the clothes of a king's son,/Just my size. MaC; StPo; WSC

Ballad of the Hidden Dragon. Anonymous. From the beginning to the end/ And with absolutely nothing left untold. WTO

Ballad of the Hoppy-Toad. Margaret Walker. "O hoppy-toad," he cried. BlSi; FB; HoPM

Ballad of the Hyde Street Grip. Gelett Burgess. And the hush of midnight falls upon the Hyde Street Grip! BPAW

Ballad of the Icondic. John Ciardi. (Now sleep, and may you dream just what/the GAWNOSE WATT was doing.) OBAL

The Ballad of the Ivanhoe. Bill Adams. And half her crew, slow stealing through the Golden Gate. BBV

Ballad of the Landlord. Langston Hughes. JUDGE GIVES NEGRO 90 DAYS IN COUNTY JAIL. HaCAP; NOBA

Ballad of the Lincoln Penny. Alfred Kreymborg. Abe will lead you through! YaD

Ballad of the Little Black Hound. Dora Sigerson Shorter. The laugh of a little child. OnYI; StPo

Ballad of the Londoner. J. E. Flecker. Where flowers are pale and few. EnLoPo

Ballad of the Long-Legged Bait. Dylan Thomas. With his long-legged heart in his hand. CoBMV; SeCeV

Ballad of the Lords of Old Time. Francois Villon. Even with the good knight Charlemain. AWP

Ballad of the Morning Streets. LeRoi (Imamu Amiri Baraka) Jones. ...let me live with you/and dig your blazing. CNA; SOTW

Ballad of the Mouse. Robert Wallace. tall, foolish, furious; alone. NYBP

A Ballad of the Mulberry Road. Ezra Pound. They stand and twirl their moustaches. LOW

Ballad of the Oedipus Complex. Lawrence Durrell. To be a warning to all men/Who have mamas and pas. FaBoCo

Ballad of the Outer Life. Hugo von Hofmannsthal. Like heavy honey out of hollow combs. AWP; LiTW; TrJP

The Ballad of the Oysterman. Oliver Wendell Holmes. And now they keep an oyster-shop for mermaids down below. AnNE; AP; EtS; FaFP; HBV 1-2; HBVY; MCCG; MOS; MoShBr; TreFS

A Ballad of the Rising in the North. Anonymous. Sir Thomas Plumtre is hanged on a tree. ACP

Ballad of the Spanish Civil Guard. Federico Garcia Lorca. O city of gypsies, game of moon and of sand. LiTW

A Ballad of the Strange and Wonderful Storm of Hail. Anonymous. Into the Pit of Darkness they must go. CoMu

Ballad of the Tempest. James Thomas Fields. When the morn was shining clear. BeLS; BLPL; EtS; FaBoBe; HBV 1-2; PoLf; YaD

Ballad of the Ten Casino Dancers. Cecilia Meireles. Ten mothers would weep at the sight/of those dancers hand in hand. BoWoP

Ballad of the Three Coins. Vernon Watkins. The sun and the moon know nothing,/And between them I know less. NoAm

Ballad of the Three Spectres. Ivor Gurney. Whether the third spake verity. OBWP

Ballad of the Trial of Sodom. Vernon Watkins. And he lost his case. MoRP

Ballad of the Two Tapsters. Vernon Watkins. You cannot bend to the shores of the world/Or strive with the great dark sea. MoBS

The Ballad of the White Horse. Gilbert Keith Chesterton.
He saw heaven fall and the world end,/O God, how long ago! ACP
That you have left to darken and fail,/Was cut out of the grass. ACP; MoVE
Who blocked the Seine with battle-ships/Round Paris on the Isle. ACP

Ballad of the Women of Paris. Francois Villon. But no good girl's lip out of Paris. AWP

The Ballad of Tonopah Bill. Anonymous. But I'm off to join the others, for the rumor might be true. BPAW

A Ballad of Trees and the Master. Sidney Lanier. When out of the woods He came. AA; AmePo; AP; CAW; EBCP; FPL; GoBC; HBV 1-2; LaNeLa; LiTA; MAmP; NOBA; OxBA; PoEL 1-5; PoLf; TreFT; TRV

The Ballad of William Bloat. Anonymous. But the sheet was Belfast linen. DBV; NOBL

The Ballad of William Sycamore. Stephen Vincent Benét. And my buffalo have found me. AnAmPo; HBMV; MoAmPo; PoRA; TreFT

The Ballad of Yukon Jake. Edward E., Jr. Paramore. But the wickedest born from the Pole to the Horn/Was the Hermit of Shark-Tooth Shoal! BeLS; BLPA

A Ballad on the Taxes. Edward Ward. Why should we, why should we be kept in the dark? OxBoLi; PPON

A Ballad on the Times. Henry Hall. Why should we, why should we, be kept in the dark? APAS

A Ballad (parody). Guy Wetmore Carryl. 'E's crowdin' us out!-'er majesty's poet-soldier an' sailor too! BXAP; Par

Ballad to a Traditional Refrain. Maurice James Craig. May the Lord in His mercy be kind to Belfast. SeCePo

A Ballad to Queen Elizabeth. Henry Austin Dobson. And where are the galleons of Spain? ALV; OBVV

A Ballad to the Tune of "The Cut-Purse." Jonathan Swift. Who would not write verses with such an assistant? PP

A Ballad upon a Wedding. Sir John Suckling.
And did not mean to stay behind/Above an hour or so. HBV 1-2
But I believe it was no more/Than thou and I have done before/With Bridget, and with Nell. AtBAP; CABA; CABL; CaPo; EBEV; InvP; JCP; LoBV; NoP; OBS; Par; SeCeV; UnTE; ViBoPo

A Ballad upon a Wedding: The Bride. Sir John Suckling. They came as good as ours, or better,/And are not spent a whit... TrGrPo

A Ballad upon the Popish Plot. John Gadbury. But with their false Plots I hope they will end,/At Tyburn where th' Rabble will surely attend. CoMu

Ballad with an Ancient Refrain. Anonymous. And the birk and the broom blooms bonny. NA

Ballad Written for a Bridegroom. Francois Villon. This is the end for which we twain are met. AWP

Ballade. Paul Fort. And they went off a-field to work, as they do every day. AWP

A Ballade-Catalogue of Lovely Things. Richard Le Gallienne. So runs my catalogue of lovely things. HBMV

Ballade d'une Grande Dame. Gilbert Keith Chesterton. When the last trumpet rends the air/It shall not be forgiven you. OxBoLi

Ballade de Marguerite. Anonymous. O mother, hath one grave room for two? AWP

Ballade des Belles Milatraisses. Rosalie Jonas. On their knees at the last? "C'est pas zaffaire a tou!" BlSi

Ballade Made in Hot Weather. William Ernest Henley. To live, I think of these! AnFE

Ballade of a Friar. Andrew Lang. La Frere Lubin is not the man! HBV 1-2

Ballade of a Talked-Off Ear. Dorothy Parker. Poets alone should kiss and tell. DBV

Ballade of Andrew Lange. Dugal Sutherland MacColl. Of Mods, of Greats, of Weekly Dues,/And yet he is an Andrew Lang. CenHV

Ballade of Big Plans. Dorothy Parker. And love is a game that two can play at. InMe

Ballade of Boys Bathing. Frederick William Rolfe. I'll fix on my canvas if so I may dare/The boys who bathe in Saint Andrew's Bay. PeHV

Ballade of Dead Actors. William Ernest Henley. As dust that drives, as straws that blow,/Into the night go one and all. ALV; OBMV

Ballade of Dead Friends. Edwin Arlington Robinson. Death will end our crying/For friends that come and go. AA

Ballade of England. Louis MacNeice. We looked to see our fortunes made,/But there is nowhere left to look. NYBP

Ballade of Expansion. Hilda Johnson. To save your life, you'd better heed/ The Ethical expansionist! PAH

Ballade of Faith. Tom MacInnes. But I would that I knew where my Lord is gone! CaP

Ballade of Good Counsel (modern version). Geoffrey Chaucer. And Truth shall make thee free, there is no fear! TrGrPo

Ballade of Hell and of Mrs. Roebeck. Hilaire Belloc. And Mrs. Roebeck will be there. MoVE

Ballade of Illegal Ornaments. Hilaire Belloc. Through blurred and glazing eyes to see/A Female Figure with a Child. ACP

A Ballade of Islands. Lucy Robinson. Napoleon, thou wast island-born! AA

Ballade of Ladies' Names. William Ernest Henley. Anna's the name of names for me! HBV 1-2

A Ballade of Lawn Tennis. Franklin Pierce ("F.P.A.") Adams. I like the Game of Tennis best. SD

Ballade of Liquid Refreshment. Edmund Clerihew Bentley. Excuse me while I go and have a drink. FaBoCo

Ballade of Lost Objects. Phyllis McGinley. But where in the world did the children vanish? NLV; PoCh

Ballade of Middle Age. Andrew Lang. Life's more amusing than we thought! HBV 1-2

Ballade of Muhammad Din Tilai. *Anonymous.* And your hair is a panther's shadow. PG

Ballade of My Lady's Beauty. Joyce Kilmer. No lady is so fair as mine. HBV 1-2

Ballade of Sayings. William Stanley Merwin. the air is clear as though we should live forever NNaP

Ballade of Schopenhauer's Philosophy. Franklin Pierce ("F.P.A.") Adams. The best you get is an even break. HBMV

Ballade of Soporific Absorption. J. C. Squire. But I'm not so think as you drunk I am. InMe

A Ballade of Suicide. Gilbert Keith Chesterton. I think I will not hang myself to-day. ALV; FiBHP; HBV 1-2; InMe; NLV

Ballade of the Back Road. Ron Block. ..."No problem. Everything touches everything." SM

Ballade of the Dreamland Rose. Brian Hooker. A petal falls from the Dreamland Rose. HBMV

Ballade of the Fair Helm-Maker. Francois Villon. No more than money that's called in. UnTE

Ballade of the Grindstones. Judith Johnson Sherwin. that night which makes us all lie down the same? SM

Ballade of the Hanged Men. Francois Villon. But pray God's mercy upon all of us. LiTW

Ballade of the Harrowing of Hell. Dominic Bevin Wyndham Lewis. The soul of Lady Barbeque. CoBE

Ballade of the Heresiarchs. Hilaire Belloc. The wind has blown them all away. MoVE

The Ballade of the Incompetent Ballade-Monger. James Kenneth Stephen. My verses are only so so,/But I hope I have kept to the rules. VLP

A Ballade of the Nurserie. John Twig. Hush thee, hush thee, dear little soul. NA

Ballade of the Old-Time Engine. Eda H. Vines. Now speed alone is king, romance is dead. QQQ

Ballade of the Poetic Life. Sir John Collings Squire. For this the poets lived–and died. OBMV

Ballade of the Primitive Jest. Andrew Lang. I am a Merry Jest! HBV 1-2

A Ballade of the Scottyshe Kynge. John Skelton. And god save noble/Kynge/Henry/the VIII. CoMu; FaBoBa

Ballade of the Session after Camarillo. David Galler. ...I laughed and you were gone. NMP

Ballade of the under Side. Don (Donald Robert Marquis) Marquis. i see things from/the under side InvP

Ballade of Unfortunate Mammals. Dorothy Parker. Women and elephants never forget. ALV; InMe

Ballade of Villon and Fat Margot. Francois Villon. In this the brothel where we ply our trade. UnTE

Ballade of Youth and Age. William Ernest Henley. These are a type of the world of Age. VLP

Ballade on Eschatology. Sister Mary Madeleva. God, I shall not forget the four last things. GoYe

Ballade: To a Fish of the Brooke. John Wolcot. God give thee strength, O gentel trout,/To pull the raskall in!! CBEP

Ballade to His Mistress. Francois Villon. Should help a man, not drag him in the mire. WeW

Ballade to My Psychoanalyst. Kenneth Lillington. I go about in guilt and shame. FiBHP

Ballade to Our Lady of Czestochowa. Hilaire Belloc. And publish that in which I mean to die. ACP; ISi

Ballade to Rosamund. Geoffrey Chaucer. Do what you list, I will your thrall be founde,/Thogh ye to me ne do no daliance. MeEL

Ballade Tragique a Double Refrain. Max Beerbohm. The King–is–duller than–the Queen. OBSV

Ballade: "When fresshe Phebus, day of Seynt Valentyne." Charles, duc d' Orleans. Whereas discomfort sole Y here me dresse/Upon my bed so hard of noyous thought. EnPo

The Ballant o' the Laird's Bath. Douglas Young. ...the lave/nae to get tint in a wuid. BSV

Ballat O the Hingit. Francois Villon. But pray the Lord shaws mercy til us aa. OBVE

Ballat O the Leddies O Langsyne. Francois Villon. Ay, whaur are the snaws of langsyne? OBVE

Ballata: Concerning a Shepherd-Maid. Guido Cavalcanti. There Love in very presence seemed to be. AWP

Ballata: He Reveals, in a Dialogue, His Increasing Love for Mandetta. Guido Cavalcanti. My heart is dead in me.' AWP

Ballata: He Will Gaze upon Beatrice. Dante Alighieri. Albeit felt of none/Save of him who, desiring, honors her. AWP

Ballata: His Talk with Certain Peasant-Girls. Franco Sacchetti. And I would be for ever where they were. AWP

Ballata: In Exile at Sarzana. Guido Cavalcanti. And thou, Soul, worship her/Still in her purity. AWP

Ballata: Of a Continual Death in Love. Guido Cavalcanti. That I say: "Lady, I am wholly thine." AWP

Ballata: Of His Lady among Other Ladies. Guido Cavalcanti. To the heart's weeping, which forgets her not. AWP

Ballata of Love's Power. Guido Cavalcanti. That my proud life should be/Acceptable, delightful, to his ways. LiTW

Ballata: Of True and False Singing. *Anonymous.* There is no room for pupils any more. AWP; UnS

Ballata: One Speaks of the Beginning of His Love. *Anonymous.* With lilies underfoot and overhead. AWP

Ballata V: "Light do I see within my Lady's eyes." Guido Cavalcanti. Then shalt thou see her virtue risen in heaven. CTC

Ballatetta. Ezra Pound. Lest they should parch too swiftly, where she passes. VGW

Ballet. Brenda Hillman. ...Father/Mispronounced the French. But he had grace. AMV-81

Ballet. Milton Kaplan. I really believed/it might all/be possible. SOTS

Ballet Blanc. Katha Pollitt. Tomorrow you will wake up ordinary. SM

De Ballet of De Boll Weevil (with music). *Anonymous.* I'd have a home, I'd have a home. AS

The Ballet of the Boll Weevil (A vers.). *Anonymous.* And it's full of holes, it's full of holes. ViBoFo

The Ballet of the Boll Weevil (B vers.). *Anonymous.* I'll have a home, I'll have a home. ViBoFo

The Ballet of the Fifth Year. Delmore Schwartz. Such grace, so self-contained, was the best escape to know. MoAB; MP; OxBA; TwCP

Ballet under the Stars. Robert Stewart. ...every bug that can fly/is down at the spotlight. FAZ

Ballinderry. *Anonymous.* "Oh, Philemy Hyland, come back to me:/Och anee! Och anee!" WTO

Balliol Rhymes, I. *Anonymous.* What I don't know isn't knowledge. FaBoCo

Balliol Rhymes, II. *Anonymous.* I dine at Blenheim twice a week. FaBoCo

Ballit of De Boll Weevil. *Anonymous.* Jes a-lookin' for a home. ABF; NOBA

Les Ballons. Oscar Wilde. Wandering opals keeping tryst/With the rubies of the lime. NOBV; SyP

The Balloon. Alfred, Lord Tennyson. ...Memory,/Sowed my deep-furrowed thought with many a name,/Whose glory will not die. RoGo

Balloon. Colleen Thibaudeau. H O L D M E T I G H T L Y. WHW

Balloon Faces. Carl Sandburg. , this will be about all. CMoP

The Balloon Man. Dorothy Aldis. He turns around, and waves his hand,/And blows his horn again. TiPo

The Balloon Man. Rose Fyleman. They would look pretty in the sky! SoPo; SUS

Balloon Man. Jessica Nelson North. Peddling joy/On the end of a string. SoPo

The Balloon of the Mind. William Butler Yeats. That bellies and drags in the wind/Into its narrow shed. PoL

Balloons. Sylvia Plath. A red/Shred in his little fist. FaBoWP; NCSH

The Ballot. John Pierpont. As lightning does the will of God. AA

Ballroom Dancing Class. Phyllis McGinley. To nod to the mothers of the little girls. MoShBr

Ballstown. *Anonymous.* Exceeds a thousand days of mirth. AmFP

Ballydavid Pier. Thomas Kinsella. The misbirth touches the surface/And glistens like quicksilver. BIrV; FaBoIP

Ballyhoo for a Mendicant. Carlton Talbott. Come on, men,/Give it a trial! AnAmPo

Ballykinlar: May 1940. Patrick Maybin. ...but from the deep/recesses of the heart before the darkness falls. NeIP

Ballymurphy. *Anonymous.* If you hate the R.U.C., clap your hands. FSW

Ballynahinch. George Canning. They would all have been Loyal–like Ballynahinch. FaBoCo

Ballywaire. Tom Paulin. My heart is stone. I will not budge. FaBoIP

Balm in Gilead. *Anonymous.* There is a balm in Gilead, to heal the sin-sick soul. FSW

Balme. Edmund Spenser. Into that same he fell: which did from death him save..... CH

Balow. *Anonymous.* They'll use us then they care not how–/Balow, la-low! OBEV

Balsham Bells. Kenrick Prescot. Expiring notes–they and these lines are done. NOEC

Balulalow. James, John, Robert Wedderburn. And sing that richt Balulalow! LoBV; OxBoCh

Bamboo. William Plomer. Bamboo, bamboo, bamboo! PeSA

Bamboo. Eric Rolls. But I sing of the quality of bamboo. NOAV

Banalbufar, A Brazier, Relativity, Cloud Formations... Paul Blackburn. even when sun is not. CoPo

Banana. Charles G. Bell. The shocking abandon of fertile and phallic bloom. ErPo; NePoAm-2

Banana. Adrian Mitchell. a phallus going around a corner/carefully PV

Banbury Fair. *Anonymous.* I sold them all—then home to dine,/From famous Banbury fair. OxNR

The Band. Carl Dennis. That something left behind in their rooms/Won't look the same when they return. AMV-80

The Band in the Pines. John Esten Cooke. And the voices of old years. AA

Band Music. John Fuller. Grow out in lines like cabbages while men/In gold braid blow among the hollyhocks. NePoEA-2

De Band o' Gideon. *Anonymous.* How I long to see dat day./Gwine to see dat day,/To see dat day. BoAN 1-2

The Band of Gideon. Joseph Seamon, Jr Cotter. "The sword of the Lord and Gideon." BANP; CDC

The Band Played On. John E. Palmer. He'd ne'er leave the girl with the strawberry curls,/And the Band played on. FSN; OBAL; TreF

The Band Played Waltzing Matilda. Eric Bogle. Someday no-one will march there at all. OBET

The Banded Cobra. C. Louis Leipoldt. It's living blood at the bushes' roots/That feeds them in its flood.' PeSA

Bandit. Abraham Moses Klein. And snatch his broken snuff-box, and sneeze himself away. WHW

The Bandit Peter Mancino's Death. *Anonymous.* And weeping with his priest, in penance died. CAW

La Banditaccia, 1979. Rika Lesser. ...Broken/ground, uninhabited, pure space. MAYP

The Bandog. Walter De la Mare. When civilly addressed. BrPo; EvOK; TiPo

The Bands and the Beautiful Children. P. K. Page. their lips stiff from an imaginary trumpet. PeCV

Bang Street. Livingston Welch. Out dog!...And let me into/Sputnik Number Two. FaFP

Bangkok. F. R. Scott. And forced me to turn back. OBCV

Bani. Dadu. ...Thy servant/Dadu prayeth for true patience and that he may/be devoted to thee. ILwL

The Banished Duke of Grantham. *Anonymous.* And the Royal Queen of England/Goes weeping away. EnSB

The Banished Gods. Derek Mahon. And wisdom a five-minute silence at moonrise. OxBC

Banishment from Ur. Enheduanna. My beautiful face is dust. BoWoP

The Banjo. Robert Winner. It's hard to know which life is sleep/Or where the door is with my real name on it. FF

The Banjo of the Past. Howard Weeden. De banjo disappears! AA

The Banjo Player. Fenton Johnson. What is a troubadour? AnAmPo; BANP; GoSl; PoNe

The Bank of the Arkansaw. *Anonymous.* Hadn't a-been for Cotton-eyed Joe,/I'd a-been married a long time ago. OuSiCo

The Bank Thief. J. R. Farrell. And God alone will know his sin upon the judgment day. BeLS; BLPA

Bankers Are Just Like Anybody Else, Except Richer. Ogden Nash. good old money, which is nothing short of providential. ATP; LiTA

Banking Coal. Jean Toomer. All money ever saved by banking coal. PoNe

The Bankis of Helicon: "Declair, ye banks of Helicon." *Anonymous.* For bewtie,/Of dewtie/Sould yeild and give hir place. OxBS

The Bankis of Helicon: Fairweill. *Anonymous.* I tak my leif aganis my will. OxBS

The Bankis of Helicon: Remeidis of Luve. *Anonymous.* Content yow. This ye get no moir. OxBS

The Bankis of Helicon: Thair Is Nocht Ane Winche. *Anonymous.* Scho sall nocht begyle me, be God,/For ocht that scho can. OxBS

Bankrupt. Cortlandt W. Sayres. How—how in God's name—I could pay! PoLf; PoToHe

The Banks o' Doon. Robert Burns.
   And my fause luver staw the rose,/But left the thorn wi' me. CEP; EG; LoBV; MCCG; NOBE; NOEC; OBEC; OBEV; TrGrPo; ViBoPo; WBLP; WHA
   And sae I flourish'd on the morn,/And sae was pu'd on noon. BoLoP; GoTF; PrIm; TreFS

The Banks of a River. Abraham Sutzkever. Broadcast it all over the world./Amen. VWA

The Banks of Banna. George Ogle. Woe is me, perhaps she's gone/For ever and for ever! IrPN

The Banks of Champlain. *Anonymous.* By the feat he performed on the banks of Champlain. AmFP

The Banks of Claudy. *Anonymous.* And once we've met on Claudy banks/We'll never part again.' AmFP; OBET

The Banks of Dee. *Anonymous.* "Sweet Mary, weep no more for me." AmFP

The Banks of Dundee. *Anonymous.* And her uncle she slew/On the banks of a-Dundee. BaBo

The Banks of Gaspereaux. *Anonymous.* Likewise those kind old people we left in Gaspereaux. BaBo

Banks of Marble. Les Rice. And the vaults are stuffed with silver/That the farmer sweated for. FSW

The Banks of Newfoundland (I). *Anonymous.* The mountain waves run o'er their graves on the banks of/Newfoundland.] OBSS

The Banks of Newfoundland (II). *Anonymous.* We'll bid adieu to packet-sailing and the Banks of Newfoundland. GBP; OBSS; ShS

The Banks of Sacramento (with music). *Anonymous.* There's plenty of bones, so I've been told,/On the banks of the Sacramento. AS

The Banks of Sweet Dundee. *Anonymous.* Then he closed his eyes, no more to rise on the banks of the Sweet and Dee. AmFP

The Banks of Sweet Primroses. *Anonymous.* And every moment blows blustrous wind. ELP

The Banks of the Condamaine. *Anonymous.* When we've shore the last of the jumbucks/On the banks of the Condamine. FaBoBa; GBP; NOAV; PoAu 1-2

The Banks of thc Gaspereaux. *Anonymous.* But he thinks upon the dear old folks he left in Gaspereaux. AmFP; ShS

The Banks of the Nile. *Anonymous.* No more we'll go a-roving on the banks of the Nile.' OBET

Banks of the Ohio. *Anonymous.* On the banks of the Ohio. FSW

Banks of the Pamanaw. *Anonymous.* On the banks of the Pamanaw. ABF

The Banks of the Roses. *Anonymous.*
   And I can go and court some other! ShS
   By the lovely, sweet banks of the roses. FSW

The Banks of the Sacramento. *Anonymous.* For there's plenty of gold,/So I've been told,/On the banks of the Sacramento. AmSS

The Banner of the Jew. Emma Lazarus. Strike! for the brave revere the brave! AA; TrJP

The Banquet. George Herbert. Strive in this, and love the strife. AnAnS 1

A Banquet. Sotades. ...This sir is what I do,/Not learning from recipes or books of cookery. FaBoUs

The Banquet of the Century in Persepolis. Alamgir Hashmi. God, there were Men like Spiro Agnew. SOTS

The Banshee. John Todhunter. Thy wrongs, the world's. OnYI

The Bantam Husband. *Anonymous.* Oh, my Lord, a manikin, not a man. OuSiCo

Bantams in Pine-Woods. Wallace Stevens. And fears not portly Azcan nor his hoos. AtBAP; CMoP; InPo; InPS; MoVE; NOBA; OxBA; PAI; SeCeV; UnPo

Bantry Bay. James Lyman Molloy. All peacefully from Bantry Bay. OnYI

Baptism. Charles G. Bell. We whites, who can only listen, are blurred with our tears. AmFN

Baptism. Claude McKay. A stronger soul within a finer frame. AnEnPo; PoNe

Baptism. Alden Nowlan. each time with gently disapproving hands. PoL

Baptism. Dale Zieroth. ...our own/mid-river laughter as the warmth begins again. NOBC

The Baptist. William, of Hawthornden Drummond. Rung from their flinty caves, "Repent! Repent!" TrGrPo

The Bar. *Anonymous.* Whoever named it, named it well. STF

A Bar at Night. Sakutaro Hagiwara. In the wall of a bar at night. LiTW

Bar Harbor. Marita Garin. by which cach of us moves/toward the other/in a series of subtractions. AMV-81

Bar Kochba. Emma Lazarus. Nobler the conquered than the/conqueror's end! TrJP

Bar Mitzvah. Isaac Goldemberg. my old, gray father celebrating this rite curled up like a fetus. VWA

Bar Mitzvah. Steve Orlen. Today I must learn to weep in a foreign tongue. GP

Bar Not the Door. Thomas Campion. Here's the way, bar not the door. UnTE

A Bar on the Piccola Marina. Noel Coward. In a bar on the Piccola Marina.' NLV

Bar-Room Matins. Louis MacNeice. Give us this day our daily news. EaLo

Barbara. Alexander Smith. There is no rest upon the earth, peace is with/Death and thee—/Barbara! BSV; GoTS; HBV 1-2; OBVV

Barbara Allen. *Anonymous.*
   And at the top twined in a lovers' knot/The red rose and the briar. AS; FaBoBa; FSW; PrIm
   And there they locked in a true-lover's knot,/For true lovers to admire.] OBET; ViBoFo
   My love has died for me to-day,/I'll die for him to-morrow. FaBoBe; ViBoFo
   'Twas him that only died for love/And she that died for sorrow. CBEP

Barbara Allen's Cruelty.　*Anonymous.*　Henceforth take warning by the fall/ Of cruel Barbara Allen.　HBV 1-2; OBEV; ViBoPo

Barbara Frietchie.　John Greenleaf Whittier.
　And ever the stars above look down/On the stars below in Frederick town.
　AmePo; AnNE; AP; BeLS; CTC; FaBoBe; FaBV; FaFP; FaPo; FaPoR; FPL; GN; GoTF; HBV 1-2; HBVY; MaC; MC; NOBA; OBAL; PAH; PAL; PoLf; PoSC; TreF; TrGrPo; WBLP; YaD
　Flag of Freedom and Union, wave! OBCA
　Shone over it with a warm good-night. PaPo

Barbara's Land Revisited–August 1978.　Geary Hobson.　Claude, I'm not writing anymore poems about you.　STE

Barbarian.　Arthur Rimbaud.　the pennant....　LiTW

Barbarians.　John Fowles.　Do not think they lack/Precisely the same intentions.　PoL

Barbarossa.　Friedrich Rueckert.　So must I sleep enchanted another hundred year.　AWP; WSC

Barbecue Blues.　Barbecue Bob Hicks.　Some brown skin woman/gon' be the death of you　BluL

Barbed Wire.　Eithne Wilkins.　and the day's unheard-of cry.　NeBP

A Barbed Wire Fence Meditates upon the Goldfinch.　Don McKay.　no one is above the law.　NOBC

The Barber.　Roy Fuller.　There is just time enough for that.'　NoAm

The Barber.　John Gray.　That maddened me, until I laughed and wept.　NOBV; SyP

Barber, Barber, Shave a Pig.　Mother Goose.　Give the barber a pinch of snuff.　HBV 1-2; HBVY

The Barber's.　Walter De la Mare.　Then out a-shin-shan-shining/In the bright, blue day.　GoJo; SoPo; SUS

Barber's Clippers.　Dorothy Walter Baruch.　Straight up the middle/Of my neck.　SoPo

Barber, Spare Those Hairs.　John, Jr. Love.　And ne'er this story tell,/But keep it to yourself.　YaD

Barberries.　Mary Aldis.　Do you love barberries?　HBMV

The Barberry-Bush.　Jones Very.　Will sweeter taste than these red berries be.　AP

Barbie Doll.　Marge Piercy.　To every woman a happy ending.　DFF; NIP

Barbie-Doll Goes to College.　Ronald Gross.　Folds/neatly/away.　WeW

The Barcarole of James Smith.　Herbert Sherman Gorman.　So willingly I row and row/And let you wonder while I know.　HBMV

Barcarolle.　Arthur William Edgar O'Shaughnessy.　Sink sail! for such a dream as Love is lost before the/waking.　NBM

Bard.　Gavin Bantock.　And sound is a long journey.　FaBoTw

Bard.　Theodore Black.　Who plays the hand that plays the instrument?　AMV-81

The Bard.　William Blake.　That walked among the ancient trees.　TRV; WGRP

The Bard.　James Shirley.　Oh she mist her maiden-head.　ErPo

The Bard. A Pindaric Ode.　Thomas Gray.　Deep in the roaring tide he plunged to endless night.　CEP; EiCP; EnL; EnPE; GTBS; GTBS-P; LAuP; NOBE; NOEC; OAEL 1-2; OAEP; OBEC; SeCePo; TW

The Bard of Armagh.　*Anonymous.*　And forget Phelim Brady, the Bard of Armagh.　FSW

Bard's Chant.　James Shirley.　To make rocks melt and churches grow.　ACP

The Bard's Song.　Sir Robert Stapylton.　And the swallow flies high.　SeCePo

The Bards.　Walter De La Mare.　William was then aged sixty-four/And Samuel sixty-two.　DTC; FaBoNo; NOBL; PV

The Bards.　Robert Graves.　To stir his black pots and to bed on straw.　DTC; FaBoMo; LiTM; SeCePo; ViBoPo

The Bards We Quote.　Bert Leston Taylor.　I find the habit hard to break,/Don't you?　HBMV

Bare Almond-Trees.　D. H. Lawrence.　...climbing the slopes/Of uneatable soft green!　FaBoPP; OBTV

The Bare Arms of Trees.　John Tagliabue.　As I pass these things in the evening, as I walk.　Psk

The Bare Branches Tremble.　Tzu Yeh.　My lover loves me,/And I am proud of my young beauty.　WPOW

The Bare Tree/Alternate.　Larry Eigner.　and then the individual/identity/ clearing　PoM

A Barefoot Boy.　James Whitcomb Riley.　Like unto the clasp of an old pocketbook.　FaFP

The Barefoot Boy.　John Greenleaf Whittier.　Ah! that thou couldst know thy joy,/Ere it passes, barefoot boy!　AA; AmePo; AnNE; FaBoBe; FPL; GN; GoTF; HBV 1-2; HBVY; LaNeLa; LiTA; OBAL; OBCA; OBVV; OHFP; PoLf; PoPl; TreF; WBLP

Barefoot Days.　Rachel Field.　Such a summer morning!　YeAr

Bargain.　Louise Driscoll.　But when they came away/They had all bought age.　HBMV

The Bargain.　Reuental Neidhart von　Merry heart, go buy thy portion of the treasure!　LiTW

Bargain.　Ruth Stone.　"I will," said poverty.　GP

A Bargain Sale.　S. E. Kiser.　The rubbish must be cleared away!　PoToHe

The Barge.　Rose Fyleman.　Oh, think what a joy/To look after a barge.　BrR

The Barge Horse.　Sean Jennett.　their barges built from fear you never know.　PH

The Bargeman's ABC.　*Anonymous.*　And X Y and Z is the name on our stern.　OBSS

Barine, the Incorrigible.　Horace.　Light-hearted Circe!　UnTE

Bark.　Don Welch.　Bark just trunk-chuckles, and occasionally/cuts off their sap.　GP

A Barley-Break.　Sir John Suckling.　So Love and Folly were in hell.　CaPo; SeCV 1-2

Barley-Break; or, Last in Hell.　Robert Herrick.　We'll wish in hell we had been last and first!　CaPo

Barmenissa's Song.　Robert Greene.　With patience lows thee quiet and delight.　FaBoRV

The Barn.　Wendell Berry.　And we rest, having done what men are best at.　EyDe

The Barn.　Edmund Charles Blunden.　The barn is old, not strange.　MoBrPo; SeCePo

The Barn.　Elizabeth Jane Coatsworth.　By the bright strange light of a star!　AnNE; ChBR; OBCP; SoPo

The Barn.　Seamus Heaney.　The two-lugged sacks moved in like great blind rats.　HAP

The Barn.　Stephen Spender.
　Laden with motes, on the boards of a floor.　CMoP
　Which, laden with motes, strikes across the floor. HaMV

The Barn.　Edward ("Edward Eastaway") Thomas.　Once I fancied 'twas starlings they built it for.　EyDe

Barn Fire.　Thomas Lux.　the horses run back into the barn.　LCAP

The Barn in Winter.　Claire Harris MacIntosh.　'Twas a crowing cock as he hailed the morn.　CaP

Barnabooth Enters Russia.　Paul Hoover.　the trip ends, the trip begins.　AMV-81

Barnacle Geese.　Charles Higham.　The wild geese rose, and the storm winds blew over.　PoAu 1-2

Barney Bodkin.　*Anonymous.*　Want of money makes us sad.　OxNR

Barney Google.　Billy Rose.　Barney Google with his goo-goo-googly eyes.　OBAL

Barney McGee.　Richard Hovey.　True to the core of you/Barney McGee!　HBV 1-2; InMe; OBAL; TreFS

Barney O'Hea.　Samuel Lover.　'Tis he has the blarney/To make a girl Mistress O'Hea.　OnYI

Barney's Invitation.　Philip Freneau.　A fearful heart betrays the knave–/Success to the Hyder Ali.　PAH

Barnfire during Church.　Robert Bly.　They churn the ancient wall-stones to a dust.　NePoEA

Barnfloor and Winepress.　Gerard Manley Hopkins.　We are so grafted on His wood.　ACP; CAW

Barnsley and District.　Donald Davie.　...felt as deeply/As any of these, with as much or as little reason.　OxBC

The Barnyard.　*Anonymous.*　And the bird went (whistle).　AmFP

The Barnyard.　Maud Burnham.　Thanks his animals, ev'ry one,/For the work that has been done.　TiPo

Barnyard Melodies.　Fred Emerson Brooks.　By whistling the only tune he knows:–/"Yankee Doodle!"　OBAL

Barnyards of Delgaty.　*Anonymous.*　Linten, lowrin, lowrin, lowrin,/The barnyards of Delgaty.　FSW

The Baron o Leys.　*Anonymous.*　An I'll sell a', to my silk gowns,/An get hame my rantin laddie.'　ESPB

The Baron of Brackley (A version).　*Anonymous.*　Ther's dool i the kitchin, and mirth i/the ha,/The baronne o Braikley is dead and/awa.　BaBo; ESPB; OxBB

The Baron of Brackley (B version).　*Anonymous.*　There is dule in the kitchen, and mirth/i the ha,/But the Baron o B　ESPB

Baron Renfrew's Ball.　Charles Graham Halpine.　The beautiful slipper deposited there/By his highness, the Prince of Wales.　PAH

The Baron's Last Banquet.　Albert Gorton Greene.　Old Rudiger sat, dead.　AA; BeLS

Baroque Comment.　Louise Bogan.　The turned eyes and the opened mouth of love.　CrMA

A Baroque Gravure.　Thomas Merton.　And (as if it had a meaning)/Views her sorrow.　CoPo

A Baroque Wall-Fountain in the Villa Sciarra.　Richard Wilbur.　Toward which all hungers leap, all pleasures pass.　AmPP; BiP; CAPP; MP; NePoEA; NoP; NYBP; PoCh; TwCP

Barracks Apt. 14.　Theodore Weiss.　the music will confound you.　CoAP; NePoAm-2; TAP

Barrage.　Richard Aldington.　Leaping, full-mouthed, in murderous pursuit!　BrPo

Barred Islands.　Philip Booth.　how the islands were one.　NePoEA

The Barrel-Organ. Alfred Noyes. Come down to Kew in lilac-time (it isn't far/from London!) BLPL; EnLit; FaBV; HBV 1-2; MCCG; MoBrPo; PoRA; TreF

The Barrel-Organ. Arthur Symons. The voice of my heart is crying in you. NOBV

Barren. Rachel (Rachel Blumstein). And yet I wait/For him. TrJP

The Barren Moors. William Ellery Channing To stand between two silent floors. AA

Barren Poem. Michael Ryan. Breathless, I pretend to enter her with knives. AmPA

The Barren Shore. Coventry Patmore. And well it were to know no more/The burthen of the barren shore! GBL

A Barren Soul. Joseph Ezobi. To lofty strains a goodly hand belongs. TrJP

Barren Woman. Sylvia Plath. The moon lays a hand on my forehead,/Blank-faced and mum as a nurse. OBSP

Barricades. Michael S. Harper. in the halls of ivy:/the barricades come down– PoBA

The Barricades. Denise Levertov. with the low piping of their discontent. NeBP

The Barrier. Louis Lavater. Is like a barrier round about us,/A barrier we may neither branch nor overpass. NOAV

The Barrier. Claude McKay. You're fair and I am dark. BANP

Barriers Burned. Charles K. Field. They're gettin' together and layin' a plan/For buildin' the city again! BPAW

Bars Fight, August 28, 1746. Lucy Terry. Young Samuel Allen, oh! lack-a-day,/Was taken and carried to Canada. BlSi; PoNe

Du Bartas: His Divine Weeks...Fifth Day of the First Week (excerpt). Joshua Sylvester. Thereby to make frail mortal man immortal. PBBP

Barter. Marie Blake. For one far summit, blue against the sky. PoPl; PoToHe

Barter. Sara Teasdale. And for a breath of ecstasy/Give all you have been, or could be. FaBV; GoTF; MCCG; SoSe; TreFS

Barter. Margaret Widdemer. Who would not pay away his dearest sin/To let such service in? HBMV; WGRP

Barthelemon at Vauxhall. Thomas Hardy. It spread to galleried naves and mighty quires. UnS

The Bartholdi Statue. John Greenleaf Whittier. A lightning-flash the wretch to smite/Who shields his license with thy name! PAH

Bartholomew. Norman Gale. No mother has a sweeter one! BiCB; HBV 1-2; HBVY

Barthram's Dirge. Anonymous. And a friar shall sing for Barthram's soul,/While the Headless Cross shall bide. FaBoRV

Bartleme Fair. George Alexander Stevens. And thus ends the ballad of Bartleme Fair-o. ELP; NOEC

Bartol. Amos Bronson Alcott. I glory in thy genius, and take hope! AA

Bas-Relief. Carl Sandburg. Five geese deploy mysteriously. CrMA

Base Chapel, Lejeune 4/79. Archie Hobson. relax, and wander off to pass the holy day. AMV-81

Base Details. Siegfried Sassoon. I'd toddle safely home and die–in bed. DBV; FF; HeIP; MMM; MoBrPo; NIP; OBSP; SoSe

The Base of All Metaphysics. Walt Whitman. Of city for city and land for land. NePA

The Base Stealer. Robert Francis. Delicate, delicate, delicate, delicate–now! GoJo; LiSp; NCSH; NTCP; SD

Base Words Are Uttered. W. H. Auden. To tell a voice that's genuinely good/From one that's base but merely has succeeded. OBSP; PV

Baseball. Tom Clark. There is no ball. ANYP; LiSp

Baseball. Frank Dempster Sherman. And keeps our sturdy boys to-day/The rivals of the ancient Greeks. OBCA

Baseball and Writing. Marianne Moore. O flashing Orion,/your stars are muscled like the lion. BoWoP; LiSp

Baseball Note. Franklin Pierce ("F.P.A.") Adams. He gets his uniform out. SD

Baseball Pitcher. Mabel M. Kuykendall. My eye is fixed on you. LiSp

Baseball's Sad Lexicon. Franklin Pierce ("F.P.A.") Adams. "Tinker to Evers to Chance." FaFP; GoTF; InMe; SD; TreFS

The Basement Watch. Thomas Tolnay. ...breathless above/your overpowering grasp of reality. AMV-80

Basia. Thomas Campion. Then what we sow/With our lips let's reap, love's gains dividing. GTBS

Basia, VIII. Johannes Secundus. That thou again the same severe/Revenge for the same Crime would'st prove. OBVE

Basic. Ray Durem. Because what keeps me/From my honey/Is money. PoNe

Basic Communication. Thomas Hornsby Ferril. No victory, no grace, no sprig of laurel. NePoAm-2

Basic Writing 702. John Paul Minarik. my grade book is ashamed/and my soul is/a sentence fragment. LFAC

The Basilisk. Philip Child. Why should that horrify me so? CaP

A Basket of Summer Fruit. Charles Harpur. Transmuted into a great golden casket/Entreasuring Pomona's jewelry. NOAV

Basketball. James Lewisohn. what remains on the other side/is everlasting. LFAC

Basketball. Stephen Vincent. ...This time/I am going to win. LiSp; NeAC

Basking Shark. Norman MacCaig. The tall fin slid away and then the tail. BoANP

Bast. William Rose Benet. But empresses came back as cats! HBMV

The Bastard. Richard Savage.
His heart unbiassed, and his mind his own. NOEC; OBSV
The raptures languish, and the numbers groan. CBEP; OBEC

The Bastard from the Bush. Anonymous. may you slip back through your arsehole and break your fucking/neck!' NOAV

The Bastard King of England. Anonymous. God bless the Bastard king of England. FSW

Bat. D. H. Lawrence. Not for me! BrPo; GTBS-P; HAP; OAEL 1-2; OBTV

The Bat. Ogden Nash. A fact of which men spend their lives/Attempting to convince their wives. PV

The Bat. Ruth Pitter. Go hunt the hurtful fly, and bear/My blessing to your kind in air. FM

The Bat. Theodore Roethke.
For something is amiss or out of place/When mice with wings can wear a human face. GoJo
When mice with wings can wear a human face. OBCA; WSC

The Bat. Edith Sitwell. Where decoy duck dust/Quacks, clacks, afraid. FaBoMo

The Bat. Roberta Spear.
and the wind, in one word,/offered itself to the earth. MAYP
of a gust that kept insisting/and swept toward you. AmPA

The Bat. Ellen Bryant Voigt. ...the cat/who shuttles easily between two worlds. MAYP

The Bat and the Scientist. J. S. Bigelow. Let go of a bat if he bites your ear. QQQ

Bat Angels. Larry Levis. while the bare rafters tick under the moon. AmPA

The bat is dun, with wrinkled wings. Emily Dickinson. Beneficent, believe me,/His Eccentricities– FM

Batches of New Leaves. Jonathan London. to fill my hands with/this poem for you. AMV-80

The Bath. Harry Graham. He lost, at one fell swoop (or plunge)/His aunt, his honour, and his sponge! CenHV; ShM

Bath. Lincoln Kirstein. Strait-jacket us quick into stinky shorts, dead shoes, sodden shirt. NoAm

The Bath. Rudolph Chambers Lehmann. And in one glorious minute needs/More soapsuds and another bath. GDP

The Bath. Joel Oppenheimer. in his tub. in his water. wife. NeAP

The Bath. Gary Snyder. Come out from the bath. CAPP; GP; NNaP; TAP

Bathed Is My Blood. Oliver La Grone. In argosies to shores of dawn. NNP

A Bather in a Painting. Ashton Greene. Water, here touched by sunshine, here touched by the/eternal.... NePoAm

The Bathers. Hart Crane. She came in such still water, and so nursed/In Silence, beauty blessed and beauty cursed. SyP

Bathers. Terence Tiller. in the fast pale of boisterous thighs. ChMP; NeBP

A Bathing Girl. Johannes V. Jensen. That is my soul, my darling! PoPl

Bathing Song. Anne Ridler. And, floating, follow the lazy yachts of the sky. NYBP

Bathing the Aged. Paul Monette. this halt and blasted gang? Yes, you would. AmPA

Bathing with Father. Doug Fetherling. grow more distant from the others on/the beach. NeAC

The Bathos. Richard Porson. "When my old cassock," says a Welsh divine,/"Is out at elbows, why should I repine?" FaBoEE

The Bathtub. Ezra Pound. O my much praised but-not-altogether-satisfactory lady. NIP

Bathtubs. Richmond Lattimore. through slippery space, and past the floating stars. NYBP

Bathymeter. William Hart-Smith. Whoever he be, cannot resist a rhyme. BoAV

The Bats. Robert Hillyer. The bats headdown from roots that are its bough. GoYe

Bats. Randall Jarrell. She folds her wings about her sleeping child. BiP; GrPl; NTCP; NU; OBCA; RFM

Bats. George Macbeth. Man, you can't even/hear them; bats,/are they? NoAm

Bats. Mary Effie Lee Newsome. All upside-down, and try to doze. GoSl

Batson. Anonymous. And I believe he's dead and gone. OuSiCo

Batte's Song. Michael Drayton. From it ne'er let me remove/Nor let it remove from me. LoBV

The Battel of the Summer-Islands. Edmund Waller.

Hearts sure of brass they had, who tempted first/Rude Seas that spare not what themselves have nurs   SeCV 1-2

Much blood the Monsters lost, and they their Arms. AnAnS 2; SeCV 1-2

Battery Moving Up to a New Position from Rest Camp: Dawn.   Robert Nichols.   Death, honour, and fierce battle wait.   MMM

Battery Park, High Noon.   Ben Belitt.   In some astonished dream of sailing....   NYP

The Battle.   Chu Yuan.   Captains among the ghosts, heroes among the dead.   WaaP

A Battle.   Isabella Valancy Crawford.   ...for the strength/That is not of the Heavens is of Hell.   NOBC

The Battle.   William Henry Davies.   But when I come that red Rose leaps/To battle for my sake.   BrPo

The Battle.   Louis Simpson.   Would pulse with all the life there was within.   InPS; OBWP

The Battle Autumn of 1862.   John Greenleaf Whittier.
Ring peace and freedom in.   MC; PAH
We too would hear the bells of cheer/Ring peace and freedom in. MC; PAH

A Battle Ballad.   Francis Orrery [(or Orray)] Ticknor.   We pledge to thee, O Liberty!/The life-blood of the brave.   PAH

Battle Cry.   John G. Neihardt.   Grant that the woman who bore me/Suffered to suckle a Man!   HBMV

Battle Cry.   William Henry Venable.   Granada and Leon and haughty Navarre/Shall lower their banner to Cuba's lone star!   PAH

The Battle-Cry of Freedom.   George Frederick Root.   And we'll hurl the rebel crew from the land/we love the best,/Shouting the battle-cry of freedom.   FaBoBe; FSW; PAH; PSoN; TreFS; YaD

The Battle Eve of the Brigade.   Thomas Osborne Davis.   Lie the soldiers and chiefs of The Irish Brigade.   AnIV; OnYI

The Battle-Field.   William Cullen Bryant.   The blast of triumph o'er thy grave.   AA; FPL; PoLf; TRV

The Battle-Field.   Lloyd Mifflin.   And War's gaunt Vultures that were lean,/have grown/Gorged in the darkness in a single night!   PAH

The Battle-Flag.   Mary Evelyn Moore Davis.   Shine out, O splendid stars, and light/Our thinning columns through the night!   BPAW

The Battle-Flag of Sigurd.   Dora Greenwell.   Wrap it round me when I die!   OBVV

Battle: Hit.   Wilfred Wilson Gibson.   Among the dead men in the trench.   MCCG

Battle Hymn.   Gustavus Adolphus.   A mighty chorus to thy praise/World without end! Amen.   WGRP

The Battle Hymn of the American Republic.   Julia Ward Howe.   While God is marching on.   AA; AH; AmLP; AnAmPo; APA; BLPA; BLSo; EaLo; FaBoBe; FaFP; FaPo; FaPoR; FSW; GN; GoTF; HBV 1-2; HBVY; MC; NePA; NOBA; NOCV; OBVV; OBWP; OHIP; PAH; PAL; PSoN; SCV; TAP; TrAS; TreF; TRV; WBLP; WGRP; YaD

Battle Hymn of the Spanish Rebellion.   L. A. Mackey.   The bombing-planes of Jove.   OBCV

The Battle in the Clouds.   William Dean Howells.   Chanting solemn music for the souls that/passed below.   PAH

The Battle of Antietam Creek.   Anonymous.   And there he sleeps beneath the sod by Antietam's rippling wave.   AmFP

The Battle of Aughrim.   Richard Murphy.   With slaves succumbing to his rod and kiss,/Has a beginning in my blood.   CIP; IPY

The Battle of Aughrim: Rapparees.   Richard Murphy.
Into the earth, into the air, into the water.   BIrV
To delve like a mole or mingle like a nightjar/Into the earth, into the air, into the water.   BIrV; NOBI

The Battle of Baltimore.   Anonymous.   That America may always boast/That we are brave Virginians.   PAH

The Battle of Bannockburn.   John Barbour.   To put them foully to the flicht.   BSV

The Battle of Bennington.   Thomas P. Rodman.   For ever where the bravest fall/The best beloved die.   MC; PAH

The Battle of Blenheim.   Robert Southey.   "But 'twas a famous victory."   BeLS; EnRP; FaBoPV; FaBV; FaPoR; FPL; GN; HBV 1-2; HBVY; InMe; MCCG; OBNC; OBRV; OBWP; PaPo; PoLf; TreF; TrGrPo; WBLP

The Battle of Bothwell Bridge.   Anonymous.   But lang we'll mind and sair we'll rue/The bloody battle of Bothwell Hill.   OxBB

The Battle of Boyne.   Anonymous.   Orange flags flying and on God relying, such music will lead us to conquer or die.   BFSS

The Battle of Bridgewater.   Anonymous.   Such dismal night, such heaps of slain,/Foe mix'd with foe promiscuously.   PAH

The Battle of Brunanburh.   Anonymous.
Hunger of glory gat/Hold of the land.   CoBE; EnLit; OBVE; OBWP; TrGrPo; WaaP
Who harried the Welshmen and held the land.   AnOE

The Battle of Brunanburh (excerpt).   Anonymous.   The greedy war-hawk and that grey beast,/The wolf in the wood...   PBBP

The Battle of Bull Run.   Anonymous.   Stripped to the pants, we did advance at the Battle of Bull Run!   AmFP

The Battle of Bunker Hill.   Anonymous.   Their heads for signs shall hang up high,/Upon that hill call'd Beacon.   PAH

The Battle of Charleston Harbor.   Paul Hamilton Hayne.   And thou in clear-eyed faith hast seen God's/angels near the guns!   PAH

The Battle of Charlestown.   Henry Howard Brownell.   There's an end of old John Brown!   PAH

The Battle of Dunbar.   Anonymous.   Them drow to Dumbar!   OxBM

The Battle of Erie.   Anonymous.   Though they're lords of the sea, we'll be/lords of the lakes.   PAH

The Battle of Eutaw.   William Gilmore Simms.   And the oak-tree for many a season/Bears fruit for the vultures of fate!   PAH

The Battle of Finnsburg.   Anonymous.   Asked how the warriors survived their wounds,/Or which of the young men...   AnOE

The Battle of Glentilt (1847).   Sir Douglas Maclagan.   An' let Balfour/Gang through your Hielan' hills, man.   PoSH

The Battle of Harlaw (A version).   Anonymous.   Ye may tell their wives and bairnies/They're sleepin at Harlaw.   ESPB

The Battle of Harlaw (B version).   Anonymous.   Until I send my servant now/To bring my coat o mail.   ESPB

The Battle of Ivry.   Thomas Babington, Lord Macaulay.   And glory to our Sovereign Lord, King Henry of Navarre.   WBLP

The Battle of King's Mountain.   Anonymous.   And may our good country/Have quietude and wealth.   PAH

The Battle of La Prairie.   William Douw Schuylr-Lighthall.   Like old Valrennes, be ready with/"I'm here to answer you!"   MC; PAH

The Battle of Lake Champlain.   Philip Freneau.   And she may want, and very soon,/Her armies for her own defence.   PAH

The Battle of Lookout Mountain.   George Henry Boker.   Standing, like demigods, in light and triumph upon their own/Lookout!   MC; PAH

The Battle of Lovell's Pond.   Henry Wadsworth Longfellow.   And their names are engraven on honor's/bright crest.   PAH

The Battle of Maldon.   Anonymous.
He humbled and hewed down until at last he fell himself....   OBWP
He was not the Godric who fled from the fight. AnOE; OAEL 1-2

The Battle of Manila.   Richard Hovey.   For England and America/Will keep and hold the sea!   PAH

The Battle of Monmouth.   Anonymous.   Death for this is ne'er the nigher,/Welcome mirth, and fear farewell.   PAH

The Battle of Monmouth.   Thomas Dunn English.   the country grand they wrought for,/Is their monument to-day, and for aye.   PAH

The Battle of Morris' Island.   Anonymous.   Look out for the battle that's yet to come/Down there on Morris' Island!   PAH

The Battle of Murfreesboro.   Kinahan Cornwallis.   Hail! to the courage of the Boys in Blue,/Who fought so grandly, to their Country true.   PAH

The Battle of Muskingum.   William Harrison Safford.   Captain O'Flan dismissed each man/To breakfast on cold porridge.   PAH

The Battle of Naseby.   Thomas Babington, Lord Macaulay.   What the hand of God hath wrought for the Houses and/the Word!   HBV 1-2; OBRV

The Battle of Navarino.   Anonymous.   And the tyrant that treads on her laws,/May the first honest man knock him down, Sir.   CoMu

The Battle of New Orleans.   Anonymous.   That out of thirty thousand men but few of you returned.   AmFP

The Battle of New Orleans.   Thomas Dunn English.   The soul of Andrew Jackson/Shone forth in glory there.   MC; PAH

The Battle of Oriskany.   Charles D. Helmer.   Sink reddening through the sullied shades–/From lost Oriskany.   PAH

The Battle of Otterburn (A vers.).   Anonymous.   To bryng hys sowlle to the blysse of heven,/For he was a gentyll knyght.   BaBo; PAH

The Battle of Otterburn (B vers.).   Anonymous.   Earl Douglas was buried at the braken-bush/And the Percy led captive away.   BaBo; BSV; ESPB; FaBoCh; GoTS; HBV 1-2; OnMSP; OxBB

The Battle of Otterburn (C vers.).   Anonymous.   That he hadna either killd or taen/Ere his heart's blood was cauld.   ESPB

The Battle of Philiphaugh.   Anonymous.   For they hae vanquishd great Montrose,/Our cruel enemy.   ESPB

The Battle of Plattsburg.   Anonymous.   He'll fight, they say, another day,/Who saves himself by running!   PAH

The Battle of Plattsburg Bay.   Clinton Scollard.   And humbled her pride who is queen of the main!   MC; PAH

The Battle of Queenstown.   William, Jr Banker.   But few, I fear, will tell their wives/The doleful tale of wo.   PAH

The Battle of Shiloh.   Anonymous.   His body lies at Shiloh.   AmFP

A Battle of Similes.   Anonymous.   But like a flowered cloth you show,/That when 'tis washed will sweeter smell.   WTO

The Battle of Sole Bay.   Anonymous.   And here's the house of Stuart.   GBP

Battle of Somerset.   Cornelius C. Cullen.   Oh, would they'd fight their friends no more,/And cease this bloody strife.   PAH

The Battle of Stonington on the Seaboard of Connecticut.   Philip Freneau.   It cost the king ten thousand pounds/to have a dash at Stonington.   PAH

The Battle of the Baltic.   Thomas Campbell.
By thy wild and stormy steep,/Elsinore!   FaPoR; OBEV

Singing glory to the souls/Of the brave!– CBEP; GN; GTBS; GTBS-P; HBV 1-2; NBM; RoGo

Battle of the Bonhomme Richard and the Serapis.   Walt Whitman.   These so, these irretrievable.   UnPo

The Battle of the Cowpens.   Thomas Dunn English.   Ha! no music like that crushing through/the skull-bone to the brain.   PAH

The Battle of the Frogs and Mice.   Homer.   Ye Mice, ye Mice, my great Avengers rise!   OBVE

The Battle of the Jarama.   Pablo Neruda.   Keep vigil on your shores.   WaaP

The Battle of the Kegs.   Francis Hopkinson.   They'll make their boasts and brag, Sir.   OBAL

Battle of the King's Mill.   Thomas Dunn English.   To conquer the country by trade.   MC; PAH

The Battle of Tippecanoe.   Anonymous.   Come Gaul or Briton; if array'd/For fight–he'll feel a freeman's blade.   PAH

The Battle of Trenton.   Anonymous.   Let's touch the tankard while we can,/In memory of that day.   MC; PAH

The Battle of Valparaiso.   Anonymous.   Crying, "Sweetly may they sleep/'Neath the wave."   PAH

The Battle of Waterloo.   George Gordon, Lord Byron.   Showing no visible sign, for such things are untold.   FaFP

Battle Pledge.   Anonymous.   Then the warrior son of my father has become a witless fool.   WTO

Battle Problem.   William Meredith.   In not the usual sense of company.   NoAm; NYBP

Battle Report.   Bob Kaufman.   Attack: The sound of jazz./The city falls.   CAD; TTY

Battle Royal.   Anonymous.   And drummed them out of town.   OxNR

The Battle Royal between Dr. Sherlock, Dr. South, and Dr. Burnet.   William Pittis.   Religion took her flight, sir,/And ne'er was heard of since.   APAS

Battle Song.   Ebenezer Elliott.   Where'er they go, they make a foe,/Or find a grave.   OBRV

Battle Song.   Macuilxochitl.   he grows drunk with them,/he who is at our side.   WPOW

Battle Song.   Robert Burns Wilson.   Remember, remember the Maine!"   MC; PAH

Battle-Song of Failure.   Amelia Josephine Burr.   Forth, and make firm a highway for the King!   HBMV

Battle-Song of the Oregon.   Wallace Rice.   From stoker's flame to gunner's aim/The race that rules the wave!   PAH

Battle Songs of the King Tshaka.   Anonymous.   He scattered the enemy/he struck the nations.   PeSA

The Battle Within.   Christina Georgina Rossetti.   Break off the yoke and set me free.   TRV

Battle Won Is Lost.   Phil George.   They said, "To die is glorious."/They lied.   GrPl

Battledore.   John Gray.   Peace, croaks the mother, Peace, the angelus!   NOBV

Battlefield.   Richard Aldington.   Priez pour lui.'   MMM; OBWP

Battles of the Centaurs: Centaurs and Lapithae.   Sacheverell Sitwell.   To safe Arcadia beyond the snows.   AtBAP

Battleship of Maine.   Anonymous.   It was all about that Battleship of Maine.   FSW

Batyushkov.   Osip Mandelstam.   eternal dreams, blood samples/pouring from one glass to the next.   OBVE

Baucis.   Erinna.   Erinna, handmaid of the Muses, penned.   AWP

Baucis and Philemon.   Katherine Hoskins.   ...shadows long and straight and spare/As of young trees, new-leaved.   PoA

Baucis and Philemon.   Jonathan Swift.

In short they both were turned to yews.   GN; StPo

So, the next Parson stubb'd and burnt it.   CEP; EiCP; GoTL; NOEC; OAEL 1-2; OBEC

Baudelaire.   Delmore Schwartz.   Please send me money enough for at least three weeks.   MP; TwCP; VGW

Baudelaire in Brussels.   Anthony Cronin.   God punishes in the person of his mother/One who endured before he chose his fate.   BIrV

Baudelaire Series (excerpt).   Michael Palmer.   ...It is/a head from another century, the last one or the next.   APU

Bavarian Gentians.   D. H. Lawrence.

among the splendor of torches of darkness, shedding darkness/on the lost bride and her groom.   AtBAP; DiPo; FaBoCh; FaBoMo; GoJo; GTBS-P; HAP; InPK; InPS; LiTB; LoGBV; NoAm; NOBE; NoP; OAEL 1-2; OAELP; PAI; SeCeV; SOTW; ViBoPo

For I will go to the wedding, and be wedding-guest/At the marriage of the living dark.   CMoP; OAEL 1-2; PPoe

Bay Bank.   Archie Randolph Ammons.   sends a song up/reed and wind rise to.   DFF

The Bay Fight.   Henry Howard Brownell.   The green were one wide grave.   PAH

The Bay of Biscay.   Anonymous.   Here's a long, fare you well to the bay of Biscay-o.   AmFP

Bay Poem.   Lance Henson.   on the edge/of/rain   VoR

Bay Violets.   Sister Maris Stella.   The children never forget them. They can never forget.   GoBC

The Bayadere.   Francis Saltus Saltus.   Lulls the grim, drowsy cobra on her arm.   AA

Bayard Taylor.   John Greenleaf Whittier.   ...softening the surprise/Of his rapt gaze on unfamiliar skies!   HBV 1-2

The Baying Hounds.   Mary Gilmore.   The very ant I bruised/My heart held interfused.   BoAV; PoAu 1-2

The Bayonet and the Needle.   Eliezer Steinbarg.   But people you can pierce forever,/What will you create from them?   VWA

Bayonne Turnpike to Tuscarora.   Allen Ginsberg.   Crash of machineguns, ring of locusts, airplane roar,/calliope yell, bzzzs.   NNaP

BC : AD.   U. A. Fanthorpe.   Walked haphazard by starlight straight/Into the kingdom of heaven.   OBCP

Be a Monster.   Roy Fuller.   Or it may be she's tricked by me/Wearing her grandpa's hat.   AmMo

Be Always in Time.   Anonymous.   Too late is a crime.   OxNR

Be Beautiful.   Jose Garcia Villa.   Essential but secret like a rose.   AnFE; CrMA

Be-Bop Boys.   Langston Hughes.   Pop-a-da!   OBAL

Be Careful.   Anonymous.   I never know from day to day/Which ones I'll have to eat.   NLV

Be Careful What You Say.   Joseph Kronthal.   Don't speak of others' faults until/We have none of our own.   STF

Be Daedalus.   Nanina Alba.   Be Daedalus; make wings,/Make even feathered wings...   PoBA; PoNe

Be Deferent to Trees.   Mary Carolyn Davies.   Will never hear a syllable/From out the lips of any tree.   HBMV; HBVY; OHIP

Be Drunken.   Charles Baudelaire.   With wine, with poetry, or with virtue, as you will.   SyP

Be Friendly.   Walter E. Isenhour.   Yes, you can be friendly.   STF

Be Frugal.   Richard Church.   God help you on that fatal day.   OBSP; OxBTC

Be Gone Ye Blockheads.   Diogenes Laertius.   I scorn the multitude, alive and dead.   GLGT

Be Hopeful.   Strickland Gillilan.   Press on, for victory's ahead. Be hopeful, friend, and win it.   PoToHe

Be Just (Domestick Monarchs) unto Them.   George Alsop.   They may serve Eight, instead of serving Four.   SCAP

Be Kind.   Margaret Courtney.   More precious than wealth or renown.   PoToHe

Be Kind to Me.   Sappho.   I pray that you will/come soon.   PeHV

Be Like the Bird.   Victor Hugo.   Yet sings/Knowing he hath wings.   SoPo; SUS; TiPo

Be Not Proud of Your Sweet Body.   Anonymous.   Be not proud of your fair body.   WTO

Be Not Silent.   Anonymous.   They cried: Depart! let us be/murdered!   TrJP

Be off!   Stevie Smith.   I'll stay with the girls who are happy and fat.'   OxBC

Be Patient.   George Klingle.   There's such a little way to go.   PoToHe

Be Present at Our Table, Lord.   John Cennick.   Thy creatures bless and grant that we/May feast in paradise with Thee.   TreFT

Be Sad, My Heart.   Francis Quarles.   But, most of all, my heart, beware thyself.   NIP

Be Still.   William Ward Ayer.   Thy yoke and thy light burden, mine.   BLRP

Be Still.   Betsy W. Kline.   And let time roll till I fill my soul/With the light from the Master's face.   STF

Be Still As You Are Beautiful.   Patrick MacDonogh.   Be silent as the rose.   AnIV; NeIP; OxBI

Be Still, My Heart.   Anonymous.   Then hold thee still, my heart,/For I shall wait His lead.   STF

Be Still, My Soul.   Katharina von Schlegel.   Be still, my soul: the waves and winds still know/His voice who ruled them while he dwelt below.   TRV

Be Still. The Hanging Gardens Were a Dream.   Trumbull Stickney.   And Error loves and nourishes thy soul.   AmePo; AmLP; APA; LiTA; NCEP; NePA

Be Strong.   Maltbie Davenport Babcock.   Faint not–fight on! To-morrow/comes the song.   AH; BLPA; FaBoBe; FaFP; OHFP; WBLP

Be Swift O Sun.   R. A. K. Mason.   make haste and run/to light up the dark fields of France.   AnNZ

Be Thankful.   Mark Bullock.   And the Lord will doubly bless you/For the joy you brought His heart.   STF

Be the Best of Whatever You Are.   Douglas Malloch.   Be the best of whatever you are!   BLPA; YaD

Be Thou My Guide.   Florence Earle Coates.   Yet in the thought of Thee I will be strong!   TrPWD

Be Thou Then by Beauty Named.   Thomas Campion.   Ile love thee, serve thee, and adore.   AAS

Be True.   Horatius Bonar.   Live truly, and thy life shall be/A great and noble creed.   FaBoBe; GN; HBV 1-2; TRV

Be True to Your Condition in Life. John Audelay. Whosoever hem shomes he will be shent,/I say algate. MeEL

Be Useful. George Herbert. ...All worldly joys go less/To the one joy of doing kindnesses. GN

Be Wise, and Fly Not. Thomas Campion. This place shall I remember. UnTE

Be with Me, Lord. George Macdonald. Thy good embraces ill, and lo, its illness dies! TrCP

Be Ye in Love with April-Tide? Clinton Scollard. I' faith, in love am I! AA; HBV 1-2

The Beach. Robert Graves. That every ocean smells alike of tar. OBSP

The Beach. Robert Peters. ...it/grows extinct,/is not. GP

The Beach at Veracruz. George Bowering. thighs move two & two toward me. NeAC

Beach Burial. Kenneth Slessor. Enlisted on the other front. BoAV; CBAP; PoAu 1-2

Beach Fire. Frances Frost. Till, sleepy, we/And the birds went home. TiPo

Beach Glass. Amy Clampitt. redefinition of structures/no one has yet looked at. FaBoWP

The Beach Homos. Forrest Anderson. yet one floating forever free. PeHV

Beach House. Mary Rita Hurley. Long dead reminders/That the sea/Can wait. PoPl

The Beach in August. Weldon Kees. ...The tide goes in and goes out. VGW

Beach Queen. David Campbell. An aircraft scribbles slogans on the sky. BoAV

Beach Talk. Norman MacCaig. ...Do not cry/Because its light fails to be obvious. PoA

Beachcomber. George Mackay Brown. What's heaven? A sea chest with a thousand gold coins. OxBC

Beachcomber. W.H. Oliver. Of roses hammered from gold and dyed with his own blood. AnNZ

Beached Whales Off Margate. Stephen P. Dunn. toward their large, inconsiderate houses. LTB

The Beaches (excerpt). Robin Hyde. I hoped you'd see the sandgrains on my coat. AnNZ; FaBoWP

Beachhead Preachment. Ahmos Zu-Bolton. in the sails of their wings. AMV-81

Beachy Head (excerpt). Charlotte Smith. His spirit, from its earthly bondage freed,/Had to some better region fled for ever. SBG

The Beacon. Arthur Gregor. characteristic of only the spirits/attributed only to gods. GP

Beacon Light. Leslie Savage Clark. To follow one clear Beacon Light/Across eternity. PGD

The Beacons. Henry Hart Milman. Upon the kindling cliffs of Penmanmawr. OBRV

The Bead Mat. Walter de la Mare. Wherein a little beaten ship/Flew through the spray. CBEP

The Beadle's Testimony. Jerome Rothenberg. He will bless his mother too. NNaP

The Beads. Jaime Jacinto. forever mourning themselves/into dust. BrSi

Beads from Blackpool. Anne Ridler. Speaks of sequence, denies the absolute death. NMP

The Beagle's Cry. Anonymous. nevertheless the cry is musical to me./A beagle's cry. OnYI

Beagles. W. R. Rodgers. A tether that held me to the hare/Here, there and everywhere. FaBoTw; GDP; OnYI; SD

The Beak. Elizabeth Smither. ...not eating/Himself, or speaking, just taking the air. OCNZ

The Beaks of Eagles. Robinson Jeffers. ...no more changed in fact in ten/thousand years than the beaks of eagles. NOBA

Beale Street. Langston Hughes. The loss/Of the dream/Leaves nothing/The same. PPP

Beale Street, Memphis. Thurmond Snyder. The naked eye of truth/Bears the stain of a lonely tear. NNP

A Beam of Light. John Jerome Rooney. And the soul of the man walked free in the/fields of the universe! AA

The Bean Eaters. Gwendolyn Brooks. and receipts and dolls and clothes, tobacco crumbs, vases and fringes. BlSi; GrPl; HAP; HeIP; MAT; NoP; PoA; PoBA; PrIm; TAP; TTY

Bean Spasms. Ted Berrigan.
  born again/thinking of you ANYP
  Don't you? like when you ask to leave the room/& go to the moon. EAS

The Bean-Stalk. Edna St. Vincent Millay. La, what a climb! WSC

The Bean Vield. William Barnes. Zoo let it vlee, if God do gi'e/Sweet Jessie vor a gift to me. VLP

Beans, Bacon and Gravy. Anonymous. I know I'll have another mess of beans. FSW

Beans in Blossom. John Clare. Strong scented with the summer's warm delight. VLP

The Bear. Robert Frost. A baggy figure, equally pathetic/When sedentary and when peripatetic. AmP; MoAB; MoAmPo; NoAm

The Bear. Ted Hughes. His price is everything. FaBoMo

The Bear. Galway Kinnell. ...that/poetry, by which I lived? CAPP; CoAP; InPS; NNaP; RFM; TAP; VGW

The Bear. N. Scott Momaday. as buzzards control,/imperceptibly, their flight. CDW

The Bear. Ann Stanford. Some day we meet the dwarf and force the answer. WSC

Bear a Horn and Blow It Not. Anonymous. Beware to whom thou tellest thy tale,/But bere a horn and blow it naught. OxBM

The Bear and the Squirrels. Christopher Pearse Cranch. With a ramble, scramble, chittery tit,/And lost the name of Growly. OBCA

Bear, Cat and Dove. Eliezer Greenberg. ...and the price/Is what the dove must pay. BoAnP

Bear Dance. Ron Rogers. We have danced in the shadow of the Stone Man. STE

Bear Hunting. Aua. So I thrust my spear into its side. WTO

Bear in Mind, O Ye Recording Angels. Norman Cameron. Are children gazing in a sweetshop window. ELU

Bear in the Hill. Anonymous. The priest was a painter (panther), I've heard people say. ABF

The Bear on the Delhi Road. Earle Birney. in the tranced dancing of men. BoAnP; HeIP; NOBC; NoP; NYBP; PoCh; PrIm

Bear's blood. Ileana Malancioiu. the bear's blood unable to heal them BoWoP

The Bear's Song. Anonymous. For her I made this song and for her I sing it. AWP

Bear Song. John R. Swanton. I do not know the place./Chief, chief, chief. BPAW

The Bear That Came to the Wedding. Howard McCord. ...thinking it might mean/Love. GP

Bear the News, Mary. Anonymous. I'm a-hunting a home to go to. ABF

The Bear Went over the Mountain. Anonymous. the other side of the mountain,/Was all that he could see! BLSo

The Bear Who Came to Dinner. Adrien Stoutenburg. but he'll lug the whole dark/across your door sill. SO

Bearded Oaks. Robert Penn Warren. That we may spare this hour's term/To practice for eternity. AmP; LiTM; MoAmPo; MoVE; MP; NoAm; NOBA; PoA; TAP; TwCP

The Bearer of Evil Tidings. Robert Frost. Why hurry to tell Belshazzar/What soon enough he would know? CBEP; NoAm

Bearhug. Michael Ondaatje. How long was he standing there/like that, before I came? PPJ

Bears. Arthur Guiterman. Sure that what is voted for is just as good as done. PoRA

Bears. Adrienne Rich. My bears, who keeps you now, in pride and fear? NCSH; NePoEA; NYBP

Bears and Waterfalls. May Sarton. As they were once designed/In Eden for us all. GP

The Beast. Brian Patten. ...this creature/at last come home to me. AmMo

The Beast. Theodore Roethke. And I wept there, alone. AmLP; SO

Beast Enough. Robert Billings. ...By/Summerhill, I have a lust/for words in my mouth. AMV-81

The Beast in the Space. W.S. Graham. ...Give him your love. FaBoTw; PoA

The Beast Section. Welton Smith. you must try it, if not now/very soon. PoBA

The Beast That Rode the Unicorn. Conny Hannes Meyer. where the unicorn devoured all buds and traces. VWA

The Beast with Chrome Teeth. Thurmond Snyder. Whose bloody hands grope about the lion's mouth searching for/success. NNP

Beasts. Paul Engle. Will bend in one live length/Closer than side by side. PoCh

Beasts. Richard Wilbur. Navies fed to the fish in the dark/Unbridled waters. CrMA; LCAP; MP; NePoAm; NU; PPoe; PPP; TwCP

Beasts and Birds. Adelaide O'Keeffe. And who so proud as he? OxBChV

The Beasts Are Very Wise. Rudyard Kipling. "Nay, 'twas the whip that spoke." BoAnP

The Beasts' Confession. Jonathan Swift. Beasts may degenerate into men. CEP

The Beasts of Boston. Betty Lowry. they stalk on Newbury Street. AMV-80

Beata L'Alma. Sir Herbert Read. ...In the sky the unsullied sun lake. FaBoMo

The Beaten Path. Anne Goodwin Winslow. Alike led lovers down the track/That knows no turning back. HBMV

The Beatific Sea. Thomas Campbell. ...,bard after bard/Shall sing thy glory, beatific Sea! EtS

The Beatific Vision. Gilbert Keith Chesterton. Who saw her stand beside the hearth,/The firelight garbing her in gold? MoRP

The Beating. T. R. Hummer. We stand amazed but take the blow, transfigured, idiot. MAYP

The Beating Heart. Heinrich Heine. "It beats–God knows for whom!" UnTE

Beatrice Has Gone up into High Heaven. Dante Alighieri. Watches me; and will guerdon me, I trust. GoBC

Beatrix Is Three. Adrian Mitchell. As I wish silently/That the stairs were endless. NAs

Beatus Vir. Richard Le Gallienne. Happy the man. HBMV; OHIP

The Beau's Receipt for a Lady's Dress. *Anonymous.* A la-mode de francois, you're a bit for his grace. CoMu

Beau's Reply. William Cowper. What think you, Sir, of killing Time/With verse address'd to me? FaBoCh

Beaucourt Revisited. Sir Alan Patrick Herbert. "The new men know not Beaucourt, but we are here–we/know." MMM

Beauregard. Catherine Ann Warfield. Like its leader, free and grand,/Beauregard! MC; PAH

La Beaute. Charles Baudelaire. Are crystal mirrors of eternity. AWP

Beauties, Have Ye Seen This Toy. Ben Jonson. Since yee heare his falser play;/And that he is Venus' run-away. OAEP

The Beauties of Santa Cruz. Philip Freneau. And paint with rapture, her inspiring shades. AmPP; MAmP

Beautiful. *Anonymous.* Ain't it fierce to be so brainy! ABF

Beautiful. W. A. Bixler. Beautiful winter, with snowflakes again. WBLP

The Beautiful. William Henry Davies. Showing her child before it is born. ELU

The Beautiful. John Aylmer Dorgan. Who was the Beautiful. AA

The Beautiful. F. S. Woodley. You think I'm happy? Well–Perhaps you're right! PeHV

The Beautiful American Word, Sure. Delmore Schwartz. In dark accidents the mind's sufficient grace. CrMA; LiTA; VGW

Beautiful Black Men. Nikki Giovanni. ...beautiful beautiful/black men with outsight afros BPo; NMM

Beautiful Black Women... LeRoi (Imamu Amiri Baraka) Jones. let me help you, daughter, wife/lover, will you BPo; PoM

Beautiful Brown Eyes. *Anonymous.* I'll never see blue eyes again. FSW

The Beautiful Changes. Richard Wilbur. For a moment all that it touches back to wonder. CMoP; CoAP; HaCAP; InPS; NIP; PAI

Beautiful Dreamer. Stephen Collins Foster. Beautiful dreamer, awake unto me. BiP; BLSo; FSW

Beautiful Hands. Ellen M. Huntington Gates. And where the old are young again,/I'll clasp my mother's hands. TreF

The Beautiful Horses. Donald Hall. Beautiful winners, collared with pink roses. NePoAm-2

Beautiful Isle of Somewhere. Jessie B. Pounds. Land of the true, where we live a-new/Beautiful Isle of Somewhere! FSN; TreFT

The Beautiful Lawn Sprinkler. Howard Nemerov. The rainbow in its scattering grains of spray. PCP

Beautiful Lily. Alice Mortenson. Perfect at last/In the image of Him! BePJ

The Beautiful Negress. Ruth Pitter. Night, tragedy, the veiled, the end prefer? MoVE

A Beautiful Night. Thomas Lovell Beddoes.
And lent his senses unto death himself. ChRP
For sleep is fair and warm– LoBV

The Beautiful Ruined Orchard. Daniel Berrigan. ...only/a bony ghost the contemptuous wind makes light of. FYAP

Beautiful Savior. Charlotte M. Kruger. Beautiful Savior! I'm Thine evermore. BePJ

The Beautiful Snow. John Whittaker Watson. With a bed and a shroud of the beautiful snow. TreF; WBLP

Beautiful Sunday. Jake Falstaff. So they just stood still and looked wise. BoNaP

The Beautiful Swimmer. Walt Whitman. Swiftly and out of sight is borne the brave corpse. PeHV

Beautiful Things. Ellen Palmer Allerton.
Over worn-out hands–oh! beautiful sleep! BLPA
Whose hidden fountains but few may guess. WBLP

The Beautiful Toilet. *Anonymous.* Who now goes drunkenly out/And leaves her too much alone. OBVE

The Beautiful Train. William Empson. So firm, so burdened, on such light gay feet. MoVE

Beautiful Woman. Dale Zieroth. caught and held in the light that spills/off the floor and stains the bed/like wine. NOBC

The Beautiful Woman Who Sings. Paula Gunn Allen. making the children laugh./making butterflies sing. TWSS

The Beautiful World. W. L. Childress. Here's a song of praise for a beautiful world. OHIP

A Beautiful Young Nymph Going to Bed. Jonathan Swift.
But must, before she goes to bed,/Rub off the daubs of white and red. PPON

Who sees, will spew; who smells, be poison'd. DBV; EiCP; NIP; NOEC; UnTE

Beautiful Youth. Gottfried Benn. Oh, how the little muzzles squeaked. PoL

A Beautifull Mistress. Thomas Carew. So as alike thou driv'st away/Both light and darkness, night and day. EG; OBS

Beauty. Kenneth Slade Alling. Whose thoughts are all the mysteries? HBMV

Beauty. *Anonymous.* So beauty blemished once for ever lost,/In spite of physic, painting, pain, and cost. OBSC

Beauty. Paul David Ashley. when we continue/as if we had portioned our lives exactly. LFAC

Beauty. Basho (Matsuo Basho). on the snow! SoPo

Beauty. Laurence Binyon. And her steps were lost in the dew. MoBrPo

Beauty. Abraham Cowley.
Thou murth'rer which hast kill'd, and devil which/wouldst damn me. LiTB; PoEL 1-5
When thou, alas, dost in the fancy lie. AnFE; TrGrPo

Beauty. E.-Yeh.-Shure (Louise Abeita). In your work,/And even in your rest. TiPo

The Beauty. Thomas Hardy ...none cares whether, alas,/Its wearer live or die! LO

Beauty. Peter Hille. That sets the soul on fire AWP

Beauty. Isaac Rosenberg. Purged of the flames that loved the/wind/Is the pure glow that has not sinned. TrJP

Beauty. Dante Gabriel Rossetti. Until the purple blossom is trodden into the ground. ViBoPo

Beauty. Edmund Spenser. For soul is form, and doth the body make. OBSC

Beauty. Joel Elias Spingarn. All, all, and only, in my heart of hearts. HBMV

Beauty. Thomas Stanley.
Fire and sword with ease subdues. AWP
She, that can this weapon use,/Fire and sword with ease subdues. AWP; PG

Beauty. Walt Whitman. ...with the/common sky & sun,–or at night the moon & stars. WeW

Beauty. Elinor Wylie. Enshrine her and she dies, who had/The hard heart of a child. OxBA

Beauty, a Silver Dew. *Anonymous.* Beauty decays, love dies, desire doth fly. CBEP

Beauty, Alas, Where Wast Thou Born. Lodge, Thomas Greene, Robert. Heigh-ho! and yet he eyes me not. EiL

Beauty and Duty. Ellen Hooper. And thou shalt find thy dream to be/A noonday light and truth to thee. HBV 1-2

Beauty and Love. Andrew Young. Making a wind among the flowers. GBL

Beauty and Sadness. Cathy Song. what he had carried home beneath his coat/one afternoon in winter. MAYP

Beauty and Terror. Lesbia Harford. Brighter than the brightness they destroy. CBAP; PoAu 1-2

Beauty and the Bird. Dante Gabriel Rossetti. ...I heard the throng/Of inner voices praise her golden head. FM

Beauty as a Shield. Elsie Robinson. And if there's something, I can still hope on. BLPA; PoToHe

Beauty Bathing. Anthony Munday. As when I fell a-sleeping./Hey nonny, nonny, etc. NOBE; OBEV

Beauty–be not caused–it is. Emily Dickinson. Deity will see to it/That You never do it– TAP

Beauty Clear and Fair. John Fletcher. I am your servant and your thrall. CBEP; OAEP; OBEV; ViBoPo

Beauty Eternal: To-Day I Saw a Butterfly. Teresa Hooley. And these will still be beautiful/When all the wars are done. TiPo

Beauty I Would Suffer for. Marge Piercy. Even at intervals during the day I would/suffer an occasional eclair/for the sake of appearance. NIP

Beauty Imposes. Shaw Neilson. Grave as the birds in last solemnities/Assembling to depart. PoAu 1-2

Beauty in Trouble. Robert Graves. But would you to the marriage of true minds/Admit impediment? NYBP

Beauty Is But A Painted Hell. Thomas Campion. Is the excesse of sadnesse. AtBAP; BiP

Beauty Is Ever to the Lonely Mind. Robert Nathan. There beauty walks, wherever it may be,/And paints the sunset on the quiet sea. HBMV

Beauty Is Most at Twilight's Close. Par Lagerkvist. I shall fare alone–/Nor track nor trace. LiTW; PoPl

The Beauty of Dawn. Felix Mnthali. to clutch and hug the rags of yesterday/and sing and dance for the dawn. WhB

The Beauty of Job's Daughters. Jay Macpherson. In all the land no women found so fair. ACV; NOBC; PoCh

The Beauty of My Land Peers Warily. Dennis Brutus. But all of these my unwearying ardor mocks/when sunfire ignites the miles of rippling corn. WhB

The Beauty of the Friend It Was That Taught Me.   Makhfi.   I soar, a Huma, to the source of day.   WPOW

The Beauty of the Ship.   Walt Whitman.   I only saw, at last, the beauty of the Ship.   MOS

The Beauty of the Stars.   Moses Ibn Ezra.   Until the white dawn rises like a dove,/From beneath the wings of a raven/that flees away.   TrJP

The Beauty of Things.   Robinson Jeffers.   The love, lust, longing: reasons, but not the reason.   PoA

Beauty of This Earth.   Martin Opitz.   World is wind and bloom and billow.   LiTW

Beauty Rohtraut.   Eduard Moricke.   Hush! hush! wild heart.   AWP; OBVE

Beauty's Hands Are Cool.   Karle Wilson Baker.   She will not dim her lucid peace/With bitterness.   GoYe

Beauty's Pageant.   Dante Gabriel Rossetti.   Unborn, that read these words and saw her not.   MaVP

Beauty's Queen.   Kisa'i of Merv.   Lip and eye are bale and bliss.   LiTW

Beauty, Since You So Much Desire.   Thomas Campion.   There, there, O there lies Cupid's fire.   ErPo; OAEL 1-2

Beauty, Sleeping.   Arthur Freeman.   You who are difficult and dear–/excuse me.   DFT

A Beauty That All Night Long.   Julal ed-Din Rumi.   If the water of life should come to thee, it would not/stir thee from the flame.   AWP; LiTW

The Beaver Island Boys.   Anonymous.   For we'll sleep in Lake Michigan where the stormy winds blow.   OuSiCo

Beaver Moon–The Suicide of a Friend.   Mary Oliver.   ...life/is becoming moment by moment/unbearable.   GOYP

Beaver Pond.   Anne Marriott.   for sticks or stones or softest coaxing words.   ACV; NOBC

The Beaver's Story.   Vernon Watkins.   I do not sprawl. I saw to the level of need.   NYBP

Beaver Sign.   Kenneth Porter.   I saw the rendezvous.   NePoAm

Becalmed.   John Blight.   We dead, in a ship that is dead, becalmed.'   BoAV; PoAu 1-2

Becalmed.   John Banister Tabb.   As when upon the treacherous shoals of/sleep.   AA

Because.   Edward Fitzgerald.   And a chaise-and-four to Dover.   HBV 1-2

Because.   Paul Johnson.   and no walls could hold him!   AMV-81

Because.   James Philip McAuley.   Older than any hope I ever knew.   CBAP; NOAV

Because.   Edward Teschemacher.   Because God made thee mine.   BLSo; FSN; TreFT

Because.   B. W. Vilakazi.   And run over the pure hands/Of the souls who see all.   PeSA

Because Going Nowhere Takes a Long Time.   Kenneth Patchen.   No, I admit–not necessarily of heaven...   NaP

Because He Is Young.   Okura.   That on his shoulders he might carry him!   AWP; LiTW

Because He Liked to Be at Home.   Kenneth Patchen.   In that room he could never, never enter again.   NaP

Because He Lives.   Adele Lathrop.   And failure, fear, disease, and death,/Love crowns with victory.   BLRP

Because He Was Tempted.   Anonymous.   We have such a loving High Priest/A refuge to whom we flee.   STF

Because I Could Not Dump (parody).   Andrea Paterson.   And hoped Joe'd come my Way–   BXAP

Because I Could Not Stop for Death.   Emily Dickinson.   I first surmised the Horses Heads/Were toward Eternity–.   AmePo; AmP; AnNE; APA; AWP; BoWoP; CMoP; DiPo; DL; EBCP; ExPo; FF; ForPo; FPL; GoTF; HAP; HeIP; InPK; InPo; LiTA; LiTM; MAmP; MAPA; MasP; MoAB; MoAmPo; MoPo; MoRP; MoVE; NAWM 1-2; NePA; NIP; NoAm; NOBA; NoP; OxBA; PBWP; PoEL 1-5; SBG; SCV; SeCeV; SoSe; SOTW; TAP; TreFS; TRV; WGRP

Because I Liked You Better.   Alfred Edward Housman.   And say the lad that loved you/Was one that kept his word.   EnLit; GBL; NOBV; OxBTC; PeHV

Because I Live.   Evelyn Ames.   And all but break under orchard bloom.   GoYe

Because I Paced My Thought.   John Hewitt.   and the picture carried with singing into the temple.   CIP

Because I Were Shy.   Anonymous.   So I think I were lucky because I were shy.   StPo

Because in This Sorrowing Statue of Flesh.   Kenneth Patchen.   For it seems a fact still of some importance, that I am dying.   NaP

Because My Faltering Feet.   Hilaire Belloc.   Swear that's true now, and I'll believe it then.   OxBoCh

Because of Clothes.   Laura Riding.   We pause between sense and foolishness,/And live.   LiTA; NoAm

Because of Her Who Flowered So Fair.   Leonard Feeney.   Beelzebub, will butt at blue!   ISi

Because of Thy Great Bounty.   Grace Noll Crowell.   Thus shall my thanks be thanks indeed.   TrPWD

Because of You.   Sophia Almon Hensley.   Life will be sweeter and more worth the living,/Because of you.   HBV 1-2

Because One Is Always Forgotten.   Carolyn Forche.   Tenderness is in the hands.   MAYP

Because Our Past Lives Every Day.   Ed Lipman.   ...they grip and flex/like small animals, restless/at the ends of his arms, waiting.)   LFAC

Because river-fog.   Kiyowara Fukuyabu.   As though it were hanging in the sky.   AWP; LiTW

Because San Quentin Killed Two More Today.   Ed Lipman.   and soon those myths are silent,/placed with respect/in books nobody knows.   LFAC

Because She Would Ask Me Why I Loved Her.   Christopher John Brennan.   And life in me is what you give.   CBAP

Because Sometimes You Can't Always Be So.   Kenneth Patchen.   There are a lot better ways to have a ball/Than scraping the hair off your own head.   NaP

Because that you are going.   Emily Dickinson.   He will refund us finally/Our confiscated Gods.   MoAmPo

Because the Three Moirai Have Become the Three Maries...   Constance Urdang.   Beautiful motherly monster, watch over me still.   MOON

Because They Were Very Poor That Winter.   Kenneth Patchen.   ...and only the thinking of clouds/Keeps the world on its untroubled course.   NaP

Because We Do Not See.   Anonymous.   Some one unknown perhaps, and far away,/On bended knee.   BLRP

Because we suspected.   Lady Ise.   Nevertheless my name/is being bandied like dust.   BoWoP

Because You Care.   Frank Crane.   To want the higher things, because you care.   PoToHe

Because You Prayed.   C. B. B.   Has brought them life at last./Because you prayed.   STF

Because You're You.   Henry Blossom.   So I know I love you, dear,/Because you're you!   BLSo

Becket's Diadem.   Anonymous.   And all around where abouten it lay wharof men token/great game.   ACP

The Beckett Kit.   Linda Gregg.   how can you go on saying you're happy?   AmPA

Beckon Me, Ye Cuillins.   K. G. P. Hendrie.   When we made friends/With Wind and Rain/On a sunny summer's day.   PoSH

Becky Deem.   Leadbelly.   I spent it all on/This big ugly man of mine   BluL

Becoming a Dad.   Edgar A. Guest.   "It's no cinch to become a dad."   BLPL; PoLf

Becoming a Frog.   Paul R. Jones.   i will go up there and continuously breathe.   DFT

Becoming a Nun.   Erica Jong.   The sky is clearer when I'm not in heat,/& the poems/are colder.   MAYP

Becoming Is Perfection.   Tom Johnson.   The secret of flight is hidden from those who fly.   AMV-81

Becoming Real.   Barry Goldensohn.   and we are hammered into one another's dreams/of comfort in the pure imagined past.   AMV-81

The Bed.   A. D. Hope.   Soon brings another patient/Who loves her just as much.   NoAm; OBSP; OxBC

The Bed.   Giambattista Marino.   With red/Proof of virginity, emblem of victory.   HW

The Bed.   James Merrill.   Watch by this bed familiar except/For one strange sleeper. It is time we slept.   NePoEA

The Bed.   Dennis Saleh.   but what makes the city what it is.   NeAC

The Bed.   Karl Shapiro.   And let your prothalamium be sweet.   NYBP

Bed Charm.   Anonymous.   And two to guard my soul asleep.   HBVY

Bed in Summer.   Robert Louis Stevenson.   To have to go to bed by day?   GoJo; NLV; OxBChV; PoPl; TreFT

A Bed of Campanula.   John (Norman Gregor Guthrie) Crichton.   Be for a while a little bit/Of landscape borrowed from the sky.   CaP

Bed Time.   Anonymous.   We'll sup before we go.   OxNR

Bed Time.   Peter Davison.   In bed we depend on nothing but bed.   UnPo

Bed-Time.   Ralph M. Jones.   How gaily would I put my work away/And go with you.   HBMV

Bed-Time Song.   Emilie Poulsson.   Baby now must go to sleep.   HBV 1-2; HBVY

A Bed with a Woman.   Raymond Souster.   ...And you may join her there/In those hours between sleeping and dawn.   ELU; ErPo

Bedbug.   Anonymous.   Good-by, Miss Liza Jane!   GoSl

The Bedbug.   Tony Harrison.   A mere performance for your microphone.   PV

Bedelia.   William Jerome.   I've made up my mind to steal ye, steal ye, steal ye, Bedelia dear.   FSN

Bedlam: A Poem on His Majesty's Happy Escape...(excerpt).   Anonymous.   To see thy tow'ring temple shine so fair/Through the night-flaming, elemental air.'   NOEC

Bedlam Hills.   Vivian Smith.   and emptiness where no life moves/beneath a stone.   PoAu 1-2

The Bedlamite.   Thomas Mozeen.   An angel, now in heaven.   NOEC

Bedouin Love Song. Bayard Taylor. And the leaves of the Judgment Book unfold. AA; AnAmPo; BBV; FaBoBe; HBV 1-2; MCCG; PaPo; TreFT

The Bedouins of the Skies. James Benjamin Kenyon. Ere Ishmael's spirit drives them forth/again. AA

The Bedpost. Robert Graves. And Abel wanes with the spent candle–/"Sweetheart, good-night!" SO

The Beds of Fleur-De-Lys. Charlotte Perkins Stetson Gilman. The beds of fleur-de-lys. AA

Bedtime. Francis Robert St. Clair Erskine. Paid me my precious wages–"Baby's Kiss." HBV 1-2; HBVY

Bedtime. Eleanor Farjeon. Can't I stay one minute more? SoPo; TiPo

Bedtime. Ian Hamilton Finlay. My love, I love, I love. BSV

Bedtime. Denise Levertov. by day we are singular and often lonely. IHMS; NaP; SM; TwCP

Bedtime. Hillel Schwartz. to be born. AMV-81

Bedtime Stories. Lilian Moore. Something nice/To make me sleepy. NTCP

Bedtime Story. Lou Lipsitz. Goodnight. VGW

Bedtime Story. George MacBeth. ...blown by the/Wind, like the dodo's. NePoEA-2; NoAm; SoSe

A Bedtime Story. Robert Mezey. Come, love, come close, and murder me with a kiss. NePoEA

Bedtime Story for My Son. Peter Redgrove. It need not spend itself on fancy and the empty air. NePoEA-2

The Bee. *Anonymous.* Think what those feel who'r' stung by thee. TrAS

The Bee. James Dickey. .."Coach Norton, I am your boy." LiSp; SoSe

The Bee. John Fandel. I saw a million flowers for the bee. GoYe

The Bee. Charles Fitzgeffrey. Thus profit is the guerdon of his pain. EIL

The Bee. Henry Hawkins. She was the Bee, the hive her sacred womb. ACP

The Bee and the Petunia. Katherine Hoskins. Nor ever drunken falls. ErPo

A bee his burnished carriage. Emily Dickinson. Remained for her–of rapture/But the humility. NOBA

Bee! I'm Expecting You! Emily Dickinson. Or better, be with me,/Yours, Fly. BoAnP; SO; SOTW

The Bee Is Not Afraid of Me. Emily Dickinson. Wherefore, O summer's day? LaNeLa

Bee-Master. Victoria Mary (Vita) Sackville-West. Let gardeners too remember sowing-time. HaMV

The Bee Meeting. Sylvia Plath. ...what have they accomplished, why am I cold? HaCAP; InPS; PAI; PPP

The Bee, the Ant, and the Sparrow. Nathaniel Cotton. She bore the vicious bird away. OxBChV

Bee Wassail. *Anonymous.* And God made the little boy/To holla off the crow./Holla, boys, holla, hip hip hurrah! OBET

The Bee-Wisp. Charles Tennyson Turner. So man, the insect, stands on his defence/Against the very hand of Providence. FM

The Beech. Andrew Young. Too late to that young withered beech that keeps/It autumn in the spring. BoNaP

Beech and Oak. Thomas Love Peacock. You never can teach either oak or beech/To be aught but a greenwood tree. CBEP

Beech Leaves. James Reeves. Down to the shining, pebbly sea/And kick the frothing waves aside. OnUR

The Beech Tree's Petition. Thomas Campbell. Spare, woodman, spare the beechen tree! GTBS; HBV 1-2

Beech Trees. Sister Mary Madeleva. Beeches in May, beeches in February. BBV

Beecher Island. Arthur Chapman. All's peace to-day at Beecher Isle. PoOW

Beef. Leon Stokesbury. ...He/wolfed down dark red catsup with his french fries. GP

Beehive. Jean Toomer. And curl forever in some far-off farmyard flower. IDB; PoBA; TTY

The Beekeeper's Daughter. Sylvia Plath. The queen bee marries the winter of your year. IHMS

The Beekeeper's Dream. Katharine Auchincloss Lorr. the sun directs the angle of their flight. SUW

Been in the Pen So Long (with music). *Anonymous.* Been in the pen so long,/O honey, I'll be long gone. AS

Beeny Cliff. Thomas Hardy. And nor knows nor cares for Beeny, and will laugh there never-more. OBNC

Beer. George Arnold. Then do I wear the crown/Without a cross! AA; OBAL

Beer. Charles Stuart Calverley. "Fate cannot touch me: I have dined to-day." BXAP; CenHV; FaBoCo; FiBHP

Beer Bottle. Ted Kooser. sort of a/miracle. SM

Beer Drops. Melba Joyce Boyd. crushing a dandelion/skull. BlSi

The Bees. Monk Gibbon. "And from the yellow sod/The bees return to God." OnYI

Bees Inside Me. Laura Chester. Where is my sweetness/going to come from. NPGG

The Bees of Middleton Manor. May Probyn. Middleton luck it's done and dead. GoBC

Beethoven. John Hall Wheelock. And beat back homeward in a shower of song! PoA

Beethoven's Death Mask. Stephen Spender. ...Then splitting skull and dream, there come/Blotting our lights, the Trumpeter, the sun. OxBTC; UnS

Beetle Bemused. R. P. Lister. I roll upon my side and break my glasses;/Time passes. PV

Beetle on the Shasta Daylight. Shirley Kaufman. ...the shape of it tilting/at me crushed under the sun. PeCV

Beets. Alden Nowlan. her eyes unfocused, mouth half-open. PeCV

Before. Albert Goldbarth. –Maybe the water itself,/the message its salt. MAYP

Before. Ann Stanford. Like the sea in which I floated. GP

Before a Fall. Geoffrey Grigson. With little hope, and slowly. EAS

Before a Saint's Picture. Walter Savage Landor. And woos the arts with such pure sighs. OxBChV

Before a Statue of Achilles. George Santayana. The perfect body is itself the soul. HBV 1-2

Before Action. Leon Gellert. ...I ran into the night/Wondering why I smiled. BoAV; CBAP

Before Action. William Noel Hodgson. Help me to die, O Lord! WGRP

Before an Old Painting of the Crucifixion. N. Scott Momaday. ...The hours advance/Like flecks of foam borne landward and destroyed. QFR

Before/and After... Johari (Jewel C. Latimore) Amini. that i am yr soil, come/& build here JB

Before and After Marriage. Anne Campbell. Strange, is it not, that I love you more? PoToHe

Before Breakup on the Chena outside Fairbanks. David McElroy. ...I explained/the blood each month and blood the first time. Psk

Before Chilembwe Tree. Jack A. Mapanje. Who will start another fire? WhB

Before Dawn. Elinor Chipp. But I lay awake; and my heart was heavy with pain. HBMV

Before Dawn. Horace Hamilton. Over and over again. NYBP

Before Dawn in the Woods. Marguerite Wilkinson. And knowing, can we love and let them pass? HBMV

Before Day. Siegfried Sassoon. Hungered for what my heart shall never say. WGRP

Before Disaster. Yvor Winters. We must live or die by steel. HoPM; QFR

Before Good-Bye. P. Wolny. without/a/sound. PPJ

Before Harvest. Robert Fitzgerald. ...the visiting rain/Lick its tongues in the leaves and pass away. PoPl

Before I got my eye put out. Emily Dickinson. Where other Creatures put their eyes–/Incautious–of the Sun– LiTA; LiTM

Before I Knocked and Flesh Let Enter. Dylan Thomas. Who took my flesh and bone for armour/And doublecrossed my mother's womb. FaBoTw

Before I Stumbled. Francis Carlin. That all the jealous little birds/Went off from me completely. HBMV

Before Invasion, 1940. Sir John Betjeman. Plant of an age of railways, for flowering into today! MoVE

Before It Is Too Late. Frank Herbert Sweet. Before it is too late. PoToHe

Before Life and After. Thomas Hardy. Ere nescience shall be reaffirmed/How long, how long? FaBoRV

Before Olympus. John Gould Fletcher. But who will reap them when our scythes are falling? MoAmPo

Before Parting. Algernon Charles Swinburne. And love, kissed out by pleasure, seems not yet/Worth patience to regret. NOBV

Before Passover. Seymour Mayne. bartering in the bazaars of genes and death. NOBC

Before Rereading Shakespeare's Sonnets. Thomas Sturge Moore. Once, forest leaves, they murmured round his soul. BrPo

Before Salamis. W. B. Stanford. and clasped their children in the shadowy rooms. NeIP

Before Sedan. Henry Austin Dobson. Death will not have it so. GoTF; TreFS

Before Sentence Is Passed. Richard P. Blackmur. It is my right: I stand here in your stead. LiTA

Before Sleep. Prudentius (Aurelius Clemens Prudentius). The heart shall still remember/Christ in its very sleep. LiTW

Before Sleep. Anne Ridler. Into this being, half yours, I creep. NeBP

Before Sleeping. *Anonymous.* And if I die before I wake,/I pray that Christ my soul will take. CAW; GoTF; TreF

Before Sunrise in Winter. Edward Rowland Sill. And through the sea of space we slip,/That flows all round the world. AA

Before Sunset. Algernon Charles Swinburne. Time shall die, and love shall be/Lord as time was over death. EG; VLP

Before the Actual Cold. Ray A. Young Bear. ...they have left/the snow falling inside/the earth. VoR

Before the Anaesthetic; or, A Real Fright. Sir John Betjeman. Say all the bells about the Throne. EBCP; SeCePo

Before the Beginning. Christina Georgina Rossetti. O Lord All-Merciful, be merciful to me. OxBoCh

Before the Big Storm. William Stafford. "Are you warm?" NaP

Before the Birth of One of Her Children. Anne Bradstreet. Who with salt tears this last farewell did take. BoWoP; MAmP; MAT; NAs; NOBA; SBG; WPOW

Before the Breaking. Lee Pennington. above where my father lay. AMV-81

Before the Carnival. Thom Gunn. Robes of bright scarlet, horns that were never blown. NePoEA

Before the Cashier's Window in a Department Store. James Wright. It will be Spring. So: this/Is what it feels like. CoAP; NYBP; NYP

Before the Dive. Elizabeth Kempf. flukes flashing/silver/before the dive. AMV-81

Before the Feast of Shushan. Anne Spencer. Love is but desire and thy purpose fulfillment;/I, thy King, so say! BANP; BlSi

Before the Flowers of Friendship Faded Faded, XXI. Gertrude Stein. and then and how and all around we think and found that it is time to/cry she and I. NMM; PeHV

Before the Ikon of the Mother of God. Constantine of Rhodes. By our poor brush thy beauty/Is here outlined and writ. ISi

Before the Mirror. Algernon Charles Swinburne. The flowing of all men's tears beneath the sky. OBEV; OBVV

Before the Mountain. Elizabeth Libbey. In your photograph of no survivors, I'm smiling. AmPA

Before the Pacific. Blanca Varela. The wind perceives and orders. BoWoP

Before the Paling of the Stars. Christina Georgina Rossetti. With Saint and Angel, ox and ass,/To hail the King of Glory. HBVY; TrCP

Before the Poetry Reading. Louis Simpson. This has been the poetry reading. OxBC

Before the Rain. Thomas Bailey Aldrich. ...and the lightening now/Is tangled in tremulous skeins of rain! GN

Before the Rain. Amelie Troubetzkoy. The nimble-footed rain doth rush! AA

Before the Statue of a Laughing Man. William C. Bowie. ...how it is these selves,/recently, are coming more quickly. AMV-81

Before the Statue of Apollo. Saul Tchernichovsky. But they bound him up in straps–/phylacteries. TrJP

Before the Storm. Richard Dehmel. Then first the lightning broke. AWP

Before the Storm. Kenneth O. Hanson. weather gathered its forces. CoAP

Before the Stuff Comes down. Gary Snyder. A while longer,/Still here. HeIP

Before the sun goes down. Astrid Hjertenaes Andersen. and my kisses will live like birds on your shoulder BoWoP

Before the Thaw. John Gill. and are waiting like me for the thaw. NeAC

Before the War. Marilyn Hacker. Tell me what that eruption on the sun/is. AmPA

Before the War. James Pendergast. All questions answered. AMV-81

Before the World Was Made. William Butler Yeats. I'd have him love the thing that was/Before the world was made. GTBS-P

Before This Loved One. W. H. Auden. A backward love. OBMV

Before Thy Throne. William Boyd Carpenter. More pure, more true, more nobly wise. TRV

Before Vicksburg. George Henry Boker. More cartridges, sir,–calibre fifty-four! PAH

Before Your Waking. Anna Greki. ...and he/Who holds me today will in the end/Love me in another's body. WPOW

Beforehand. Witter ("Emanuel Morgan") Bynner. For we shall know, too late to know/Or care. HBMV

Beg-Innish. John Millington Synge. Till we up sails with M'riarty Jim/And sail from Beg-Innish. MoBrPo; OnYI; OxBI

Bega. Marjorie Pickthall. God to guard me, God to love me. CaP

Begetting. Dorothea Spears. And gods are not begot from devils' sperm. PeSA

The Begetting of Cain. Hyam Plutzik. The beasts, the birds in the nest, the fireflies in the air. VWA

The Beggar. Anonymous. Some were lame and some were blind/And some they could not hear. OBET

The Beggar. Margaret E. Bruner. My spirit had been fed? PoToHe

The Beggar. H. L. Doak. The beggar is happy to lie on his back in the dirt. HBMV

The Beggar. Adrian Mitchell. But who, bar me, hawks in this town/A dead branch and an evil eye? FaBoTw

The Beggar. Thomas Moss. Oh! give relief–and heaven will bless your store. NOEC

Beggar. Nicanor Parra. And/toss/me/down/a/coin. CAD

The Beggar Boy. Cecil Frances Alexander. We must give from our full measure,/To the wanderer without.' OxBChV

The Beggar-Laddie. Anonymous. She came to gued by grait misgiding,/By the follouing of her laddie. ESPB

The Beggar Maid. Alfred, Lord Tennyson. "This beggar maid shall be my queen!" BeLS; HBV 1-2; OnMSP

The Beggar Man. Lucy Aiken. More glad than they had done before. OxBChV

The Beggar on the Beach. Horace Gregory. ...Now you may drop/Your money in my hat. NMP

The Beggar's Opera. John Gay.
  And How do you do again. ErPo; PoEL 1-5
  And the Statesman, because he's so great,/Thinks his Trade as honest as mine. CEP
  And turns all their Lead to Gold. CEP
  And we cry, There dies an Adonis! AtBAP; NOEC; PoEL 1-5; SeCeV
  Her kisses/Dissolve us in pleasure, and soft repose. CEP; EnLoPo; TEP
  If lawyer's hand is feed, sir,/He steals your whole estate. CEP; NOEC; TEP
  If with me you'd fondly stray/Over the Hills and far away. PoEL 1-5
  Life never knows the return of Spring. CEP
  Rots, stinks, and dies, and is trod under feet. TEP
  She heeds them not (poor Bird) her soul's with him. PoEL 1-5
  'Twould thin the land, such numbers to string/Upon Tyburn tree! NOEC

Beggar's Serenade. John Heath-Stubbs. And are you sure where you will lie tonight, woman? BoLoP; ErPo; NeBP

Beggar's Song. Gregory Orr. screaming for more. LTB

Beggar to Beggar Cried. William Butler Yeats. "The wind-blown clamour of the barnacle-geese." CMoP; NoAm

Beggar to Burgher. A. R. D. Fairburn. learn that the man of straw has had his hour. AnNZ

The Beggar to Mab, the Fairie Queen. Robert Herrick. I return your Almes agen. CaPo; WSC

The Beggar Wind. Mary Austin. So takes their dole and leaves behind/The ice on lakes and rivers. BoNaP

The Beggar Woman. William King. But, ere you get another, 'ti'n't amiss/To try a year or two how you'll keep this.' NOEC

Beggars. Rhys Carpenter. Toss me the wind of your homeland, the world-old dream/in your eyes. HBMV

Beggars. Ella Higginson. And I, alas! for peace. AA

Begging A.I.D. David Rubadiri. for Tips/that will bring home/Toys of death. WhB

A-Begging Buttermilk I Will Go. Anonymous. "Thou'st reckoned thy chickens before they were hatched." OBET

Begging on North Main. Dabney Stuart. Until it flashes the sun into my face. AMV-81

Begin Summer. Ingrid Jonker. You play the sun all day/like a ukulele PeSA

Begin the Day with God. Anonymous. The, with the vision in thy heart,/Turn strong to meet thy day. TRV

Beginners. Walt Whitman And how the same inexorable price must still be paid for the same great purchase. AA

Beginning. Alden Nowlan. followed by darker shame. Thus I was made. NeAC; NOBC

Beginning. Marcos Rodriguez Frese. I believe the heart/overflows its beats.... InW

Beginning. David Rokeah. and a dream sprouting like grass/between roof tiles. VWA

The Beginning. Wallace Stevens. Now the first tutoyers of tragedy/Speak softly, to begin with, in the eaves. VGW

A Beginning and an End. Edouard Roditi. Nor did they know it, knowing as yet no shame. VWA

Beginning by Example. Christopher Gilbert. ...there is no sound but a window/opened wide to show more air. FYAP

Beginning My Studies. Walt Whitman. But stop and loiter all the time to sing it in ecstatic songs. CBEP; OxBA

The Beginning of a Long Poem on Why I Burned the City. Lawrence Benford. And I went off to college/With a Gasoline can. NBP; TTY

Beginning of an Undergraduate Poem. Anonymous. Cry, Damn it, how hot we shall be! FaBoCo

The Beginning of the End. Gerard Manley Hopkins. A boy feels when the poet he pores upon/Grows less and less sweet to him, and knows/no cause. VLP

The Beginning of the End. Jon Stallworthy. trampled on the pavement,/impaled on a railing. OxBC

Beginning the Year at Rosebud, S.D. Roberta Hill Whiteman. where children are unconsoled by wishes,/where tears salt bread. CDW; TWSS

Beginning to Live. Ruth Stone. I'll go in and build a fire. GP

Beginning to Squall. May Swenson. ...the water/that Brightens while the sky goes duller. RFM

Beginnings. Erez Biton. Short hymns of Bach/In Jewish/Moroccan. VWA

The Beginnings (1914-1918). Rudyard Kipling. With long arrears to make good,/When the English began to hate. TW

Beginnings (excerpt). Robert Earl Hayden. She was more than six feet tall. At ninety could/still chop and tote·firewood. CNA

The Beginnings of Faith. Sir Lewis Morris. Thoughts which, at last, shall lead/To some clear, firm assurance of a satisfying creed. WGRP

Begotten of the Spleen. Charles Simic. The floodlights/in the guard towers. LCAP

Behave Yoursel' before Folk. Alexander Rodger. Ye may tak' ten–before folk. HBV 1-2

Behaviorally. Anselm Hollo. that poets are not/sensible. APU

Behaviour of Fish in an Egyptian Tea Garden. Keith Douglas. .and she sits alone at the table, a white stone/useless except to a collector, a rich man. FaBoMo; OBTV

Behaviour of Money. Bernard Spencer. Or die? Or dance in the street the day that the world/goes crack? LiTB

Behind me–dips eternity–. Emily Dickinson. And Maelstrom–in the Sky– PBWP

Behind That Wall My Roommate Fucks His Girl. Geof Hewitt. and easy, quiet in the night, disturbing no one. NeAC; PoL

Behind the Closed Eye. Francis Ledwidge. I'll go and close the mountains' door/On the city's strife and din. MCCG

Behind the Falls. William Stafford. ...how far/mere honesty or justice is from all they need. RFM

Behind the Glass Wall. Harold Norse. uncontrollable joy/of leaving the mind. PeHV

Behind the Line. Edmund Charles Blunden. And still you wander muttering on/Over the shades of shadows gone. ChMP

Behind the Plough. James H. Cousins. To search in the spoils of the furrow,/Where God the Ploughman ploughs. OxBI

Behind the Stove. James Hearst. glad to find a spark among the ashes/and make the time seem warm. TAT

Behind the Waterfall. Winifred Welles. And I saw the crystal city/That's behind the waterfall. TiPo

Behind the Wheel. Michael Brownstein. the girl parachutes onto the plain. ANYP

Behold. Mary Kawena Pukui. Behold this lovely world. WTO

Behold a Wonder Here! *Anonymous.* In giving Love his sight/And striking Folly blind. ALV; TrGrPo

Behold, Love, Thy Power How She Despiseth! Sir Thomas Wyatt. And, as his lord, the lowly entreateth./Behold, love. FCP; GBL

Behold, My Cross Was Gone! Alice Mortenson. Behold: my cross was gone! BePJ

Behold, O Man. Edmund Spenser. Refuse such fruitless toil, and present pleasures choose. EIL

Behold, One of Several Little Christs... Kenneth Patchen. Over the gambler and the bitch followed by the whole human pack. NaP

Behold the Deeds! Henry Cuyler Bunner. Behold the deeds that are done of Mrs. Jones! ALV; HBV 1-2; InMe; NLV

Behold, the Grave. Stephen Crane. Why did the maid weep? TAP

Behold the Lilies of the Field. Anthony Hecht. Yes. I am looking. I wish I could be like them. CoPo; NePoEA-2

Behold the Man! *Anonymous.* To pay the debt I owe,/My God and Lord. STF

Behold the Manly Mesomorph. W. H. Auden. Who covers their retreat, dies at his gun. OBSP

Behold the Meads. Guillaume de Poitiers. Their hearts are high, their might is great,/Who will endure. AWP

Behold the Sea. Aaron Kurtz. ...singing/to our brother, singing to/our might. PPON

Behold, the Shade of Night Is Now Receding. Saint Gregory the Great. Whose praises be through earth's most distant regions/Ever resounding. AH

Behold This Dreamer. Elizabeth Bartlett. They burn a path through timeless sleep. NePoAm-2

Behold This Little Bane. Emily Dickinson. Not elsewhere–if in Paradise/Its Tantamount be found–. AmePo

Behold with Joy. Elhanan Winchester. Who makes our thrall and bondage cease. AH

Behold Your King! Frances Ridley Havergal. Oh, think of His sorrow, that we may know/His wondrous love in His wondrous woe! BePJ

The Beholders. James Dickey. With deadly intent of love. AP

Bei Hennef. D. H. Lawrence. Strange, how we suffer in spite of this! BrPo

The Being. James Dickey. Wide awake. NMP

Being a Christian. *Anonymous.* Being a Christian is seeking/The many lost souls to win. STF

Being a Giant. Robert Mezey. flashing the commandments of the sun/to the empty hills. GrPl

Being Adult. Bill Zavatsky. A smaller role for peanut butter. PoL

Being Aware. Dennis Cooper. take me back before everything. APU

Being Born Is Important. Carl Sandburg. It must be older than the moon, older than salt. NAs

Being Called For. Rosemary Dobson. Nevertheless I have put in a basket/The coins for the ferry. CBAP

Being Forsaken of His Friend He Complaineth. E. S. Wherefore then longer live should I? EIL

Being Gypsy. Barbara Young. And then I'd hie me home! SoPo

Being Her Friend. John Masefield. The hymn to beauty written on her face. GTBS

Being Herded Past the Prison's Honor Farm. David Wagoner. ...tells me/Exactly where I can go, steering me, cutting me out of the herd. SoSe·

Being Natural. Carl Rakosi. The character is gone. GP

Being Refused Local Credit. Paula Rankin. Who would want to steal from us? Who? MAYP

Being Sad. Orhan and Halman Veli Kanik. To be sad and to stay sad. LLLT

Being Sick. Jimmy Garthwaite. And other things at school. BrR

Being Somebody. Edwin Honig. but what if he was/completely somebody else? TAP

Being to Timelessness as It's to Time. Edward Estlin Cummings. Whatever sages say and fools,all's well. HAP; NePA

Being Twins. Kathryn Jackson. When we like being two by two/At night. BiCB

Being with Men. Linda Gregg. It might look like he is guilty of something. NPGG

Beinn a' Ghlo. Bill Tulloch. among the resting deer, who/splash up away and vanish. PoSH

Beinn Naomh, IV: The Summit. Kathleen Raine. Brushes a grain of quartz from the unmoved hill. OxBS

The Beirut–Hell Express. Etel Adnan. I announce your resurrections/and your death. WPOW

Bel M'es Quan Lo Vens M'Alena. Arnaut Daniel. Following so fair a prize/I could nevermore go wrong. AWP; LiTW

A Belated Violet. Oliver Herford. Violet never woke to know. AA

Belden Hollow. Leslie Nelson Jennings. Where wind-sown wildernesses/Keep what is theirs to keep. GoYe

Beleaguered Cities. F. L. Lucas. Yet they shall crumble to the dust before/The battering thistle-down. HaMV

Belfast. Donald Revell. ...Tonight, the ruined counties prepare. SM

Belfast: High Street. Padraic Colum. Their mingled strokes tell over again. NePoAm

Belfast Linen. *Anonymous.* For the razor blade was German made,/But the sheet was Belfast linen. WTO

Belfast Lough. *Anonymous.* Over the loch/upon a golden/whin, a blackbird/stirred. BIrV

The Belfry. Laurence Binyon. Bowed heads look up, and lo, the day is done... CH

The Belfry of Bruges. Henry Wadsworth Longfellow. Lo! the shadow of the belfry crossed the sun-illumined/square. HBV 1-2

Belgravia. Barbara Guest. I am in love with him/Who only among the invited hastens my speech. AmPC

Belief. Ruth Fitch Bartlett. Why should I question this or that?/I have not doubted love. InMe

Belief. Josephine Miles. ...the ancient slogan/Noblesse oblige. FaBoWP; NoAm; TAP

Belief and Unbelief. Philip Freneau. Till evidence of strongest kind/Constrains assent, and clears the mind. AmePo

Belief in Plan of Thee. Walt Whitman. And all the world a dream. TRV

Believe and Take Heart. John Lancaster Spalding. Doubt is disease. AA

Believe It. John Logan. ...And I will invite you in as my first guest. LCAP

Believe Me, If All Those Endearing Young Charms. Thomas Moore. The same look which she turned when he rose. AnFE; BLPA; CBEP; ELP; EnRP; FaBoBe; FaBV; FaFP; FPL; FSW; GoTF; HBV 1-2; LiTB; LiTL; MCCG; OBNC; OBRV; OnYI; PoEL 1-5; PoPl; TEP; TreF; WBLP

Believe Not. Isaac L. Peretz. Oh, think not there is no judgment or/judge! TrJP

Believe the Bible. A. B. Simpson. If we always would remember/That He means just what He says. STF

Belisarius. Henry Wadsworth Longfellow. –I still/Am Belisarius! PoEL 1-5; WiR

Belita. Alberto Rios. covered now by that handkerchief, kissed by the children. LTB

A Bell. Clinton Scollard. There should be Joy! AA

Bell-Birds. Henry Clarence Kendall. With glimpses of creeks and a vision of mosses. NOAV; PoAu 1-2

Bell-Bottomed Trousers. *Anonymous.* Let him climb the rigging like his daddy used to do. AmSS; FSW; UnTE

Bell Horses, Bell Horses, What Time of Day? Mother Goose. One o'clock, two o'clock, three and away. OxNR; TiPo

A Bell in the Orthodox Steeple. Thomas Waltner. In the Russian Orthodox steeple/a bell sings, "Goodnight, goodnight." LFAC

The Bell of the Hermitage. *Anonymous.* I had liefer go to a tryst with thee/Than to a tryst with a foolish woman. CAW

Bell Speech. Richard Wilbur. Still gather to a language without flaw/Our loves, and all the hours of our death. AP; CABA; MoAB; MoAmPo; MoVE

Bell Too Heavy to Ring. Tom Kryss. and melted them down into a bell/too heavy to ring. NeAC

Bell Tower. Léonie Adams. It fill the sky to beat on an airy shell. AmLP; MoAB; MoAmPo; PoPl

Bell Weather. Lewis Turco. near the blue spruce whose needles/knit and ravel darkness. AMV-80

Bella and the Golem. Rossana Ombres. Bella has gone back to her cape of nettles. VWA

La Bella Bona-Roba. Richard Lovelace. Pass rascal deer, strike me the largest doe. AtBAP; CaPo; CavP; EBEV; OAEL 1-2; PoEL 1-5; SeCP

Bella Ciao. Anonymous. This is the most beautiful flower/Of the Partisans who died for freedom. FSW

La Bella Donna Della Mia Mente. Oscar Wilde. O House of love! O desolate/Pale flower beaten by the rain! UnTE

Belle. Anonymous. But to forget is slow, Babe. OuSiCo

La Belle Confidente. Thomas Stanley. But this pursues us to the urn,/And marries either's dust. JCP; MeLP; MePo; OBS

La Belle Dame sans Merci. A. R. D. Fairburn. Oh Mr Tennyson, your dream of fair women,/how it echoes remotely, at this late date, a lemon! AnNZ

La Belle Dame Sans Merci. John Keats. And no birds sing. AtBAP; ATP; AWP; BeLS; BLPA; DTo; ELP; ERoP 1-2; ExPo; FaBoBe; FaBoCh; FaFP; FiP; FPL; GoTF; GTBS; HAP; HBV 1-2; InPK; InPo; InPS; InvP; LiTB; LoBV; LoGBV; MaC; MBW 1-2; MCCG; MyFE; NAWM 1-2; NIP; NOBE; NoP; OAEL 1-2; OAEP; OBEV; OBNC; OBRV; OLR; PAI; PG; PoEL 1-5; PoPle; PoRA; PPoe; Prf; PrIm; SCV; SeCeV; SoSe; StPo; TEP; TreFT; TrGrPo; UnPo; ViBoPo; WeW; WHA; WSC

La Belle Dame sans Merci (parody). T. Griffiths. Looking twice my age. BXAP

Belle de Jour (parody). George Melly. But for nine-till-fiver Linda, a thrifty working girl. FaBoPa

La Belle Ennemie. Thomas Stanley. Though got by Beauty, kept by Love. CavP

The Belle of the Balkans. Newman Levy. Mr. Gilbert does a handspring in his grave. ALV; FiBHP

La Belle Saison. Jacques Prevert. Place de la Concorde/At noon August Fifteenth. CAD

La Belle Sauvage. John Hunter Duvar. And lead us to the happier hunting woods. OBCV

Belle Starr. Anonymous. "Come in, I care not who you are,/I'm Belle Starr." BPAW

Bellerophon: There Are No Gods. Euripides. ...All Divinity/Is built up from our good and evil luck. EaLo

Les Belles Roses sans Mercie. Arthur Shearly Cripps. Twining be at amity round about my window now! OBVV

The Bellman. Robert Herrick. My masters all, Good day to you. CaPo; CBEP

The Bellman's Song. Anonymous. When the clapper hits the bell? DiPo; EBEV; EiL; SeCePo

Bellower with the Antlers. Suibne Geilt. is the leafy oak sapling/moving and restless! NOBI

The Bellows Maker of Oxford. John Hoskyns. He that made bellows, could not make breath. FaBoEE

The Bells. Anonymous. But sing-a-ling-a-ling for me. FiBHP

The Bells. Antonio Fogazzaro. Peace. CAW

The Bells. Edgar Allan Poe To the moaning and the groaning of the bells. AA; BBV; FaFP; FPL; GN; HBV 1-2; LiTA; NePA; OBAL; OBCA; OHFP; PoLf; PoPl; SpRo; TAP; TreF; WBLP

Bells. Duncan Campbell Scott. Within the windless deeps of memory? CaP

The Bells Are Ringing for Me and Chagall. Terence Winch. Or it is enough when what is wanted, unfortunately or not,/is more than enough. APU

The Bells at Midnight. Thomas Bailey Aldrich. Surely, some chieftain's soul! PAH

Bells for John Whiteside's Daughter. John Crowe Ransom. Lying so primly propped. AmP; AP; CMoP; CoBMV; CrMA; DTC; FF; HAP; HeIP; HoPM; InPo; InPS; LiTA; LiTM; MoAB; MoAmPo; MoVE; NePA; NIP; NoAm; NOBA; NoP; OxBA; PAI; PPON; PPP; PrIm; SoSe; TAP; TreFT; UnPo; VGW; WeW

Bells in the Country. Robert Nathan. And maybe nearer God. BrR; HBMV

Bells of Grey Crystal. Edith Sitwell. The clouds, grey Chinese geese,/Sleek through the sky. OBSP

The Bells of Heaven. Ralph Hodgson. And little hunted hares. BrPo; EaLo; GoJo; LiTM; MoAB; MoBrPo; NOBE; OBEV; OBSP; PPON; SiSoSe; TreFT

The Bells of London. Anonymous.

Gay go up and gay go down/To ring the bells of London town. BrR; EvOK

I am sure I don't know,/Says the great bell at Bow. HBV 1-2; HBVY

When I am old,/Say the bells at St. Paul's. PoRA

The Bells of Lynn. Henry Wadsworth Longfellow. Ye cry aloud, and then are still, O Bells of/Lynn! AA

Bells of New Year. Arthur Gordon Field. A bright new world of peace. PGD

The Bells of Peace. Aileen Fisher. and through the earth a glad rebirth/of brotherhood is spreading! SiSoSe

The Bells of San Blas. Henry Wadsworth Longfellow. It is daybreak everywhere. AmP; OxBA

The Bells of San Gabriel. Charles Warren Stoddard. In the tower that is left the tale to tell/Of Gabriel, the Archangel. ACP; CAW; HBV 1-2; OBEV; OBVV

The Bells of Shandon. Francis Sylvester ("Father Prout") Mahony. 'Tis the bells of Shandon,/That sound so grand on/The pleasant waters of the river Lee. ACP; AnIV; CAW; GoBC; HBV 1-2; IrPN; OBRV; OnYI; RoGo; TreFS

The Bells of Ste. Anne des Monts. Leo Cox. And time move only in the stars and tide... CaP

Belly Dancer. Diane Wakoski. or how I dance for their frightened,/unawakened, sweet/women. NIP

The Belly Dancer in the Nursing Home. Ronald Wallace. with just enough breath left to whisper/And sing. And dance. And swear. GOYP

The belly of the land. Luci Tapahonso. and even into the belly of the land. STE

The Belongings. Theodore Enslin. but to me they bring a promise/which should be in you–not them–high, in your room. CoPo

The Beloved. Katharine Tynan Hinkson. For one who forsook for my garden/His Paradise! HBV 1-2

The Beloved. May Probyn. And His Right Hand doth embrace me.' GoBC

Beloved, from the Hour That You Were Born. Corinne Roosevelt Robinson. And welcome Pain, that is Love's counterpart! HBMV

Beloved, It Is Morn. Emily Henrietta Hickey. Faithful to God and thee. CAW; OnYI

Beloved, Let Us Once More Praise the Rain. Conrad Aiken. Orion in a cobweb, and the World. LiTA; UnPo

The Beloved Person Must I Think. Ki-no-Akimine. With a louder note. AWP

The Beloved's Image. Anonymous. Wakeful–sleepless with heart longing,/With desire–O! WTO

Below Bald Mountain. Janice Townley Moore. In it he finds his own words. AMV-80

Below Hekla. Selima Hill. give our love to the Beatles, good-bye. FaBoWP

Below Mount T'ui K'oy, Home of the Gods.... Joseph Stroud. Keening a music like distant surf breaking/Within the very heart of the mountain. NPGG

Below the Surface-Stream, Shallow and Light. Matthew Arnold. The central stream of what we feel indeed. InPK; NOBV; OBSP

Belshazzar. Emily Dickinson. Can read without its glasses/On revelation's wall. AmePo; CBEP; MoRP

Belsnickel. Arthur Guiterman. So act in the way that will tickle/Belsnickel. BBGG

Beltway. Laura McLaughlin. diamonds one way,/rubies the other. AmC

Ben. Thomas Wolfe. His hair shines like that of a young boy–/It is crinkled and crisp as lettuce. NCSH

Ben Alder 1963-1977. Des Hannigan. white sails on a green sea. PoSH

Ben Allah Achmet. Sir William Schwenck Gilbert. In proud Stamboul they sleep their slumber. VLP

Ben Backstay. Anonymous. Why, never mix your liquors, lads,/But always take them neat. AmSS

Ben Bolt. Anonymous. See, the old rustic porch, with its roses so sweet,/Lies scatter'd and fallen to the ground. PSoN

Ben Bolt. Thomas Dunn English. Your presence a blessing, your friendship a truth,/Ben Bolt of the salt-sea gale. AA; FaBoBe; HBV 1-2; TreF

Ben Hur: Song. Lew Wallace. Unless, unless–thou dream'st of me. AA

Ben. Johnsons Sociable Rules for the Apollo. Ben Jonson. And while we stay, let us be always warm. SeCV 1-2

Ben Jonson Entertains a Man from Stratford. Edwin Arlington Robinson. Perhaps he does...O Lord, that House in Stratford! APA; ATP; CoAnAm; MAPA; MoAB; MoAmPo; MoPo

Ben Milam. William H. Wharton. Was Milam, and his death sublime/Linked with undying Liberty! PAH

Ben Plays Hide & Seek in the Deep Woods. Geof Hewitt. Or I'll have to find you all over the place FAZ

The Bench of Boors. Herman Melville. Within low doors the boozy boors/Cat-naps take in pipe-bowl light. OBAL

Bend as the Bow Bends. Conrad Aiken. by continents of snow to find a home. CMoP

Bessy and Mary. *Anonymous.* Bessy always had to wait,/While Mary lived in plenty. OxNR

Bessy Bell and Mary Gray. *Anonymous.* They bigget a bower on yon burn brae/And theekit it o'er wi' rashes. BSV; ESPB; OxBB; ViBoFo

The Best. Elizabeth Barrett Browning. –Something out of it, I think. OBSP; OBVV

Best? Siv Widerberg. It's best to be best/right? NTCP

The Best and the Worst. *Anonymous.* It is the worst world that ever was known. TreFT

The Best Choice. *Anonymous.* He gives the very best to those/Who leave the choice with Him. STF

The Best Dance. *Anonymous.* The dareemo grass is the best hay,/Of this I have always been sure. WTO

The Best Dance Hall in Iuka, Mississippi. Thomas Johnson. To a fine, squaredance grit/Of powdered tooth/And bonemeal. FAZ

The Best Firm. Walter G. Doty. But the best is probably "Grinn & Barrett." HBV 1-2; HBVY

The Best for Me. *Anonymous.* Still I can trust His love to give/What is best for me. STF

The Best for Us. Olive H. Burnett. For He has planned the best for us/And will lead us all the way! STF

The Best Friend. William Henry Davies. Pleasure laughed sweet,/But Joy kissed me. OBMV

Best Friends. Judith Hemschemeyer. your private holding pattern over hell. AMV-81

The Best Game the Fairies Play. Rose Fyleman. But steeple-sliding's best! SoPo

The Best Line Yet. Edward Allen. But yield to me my darling, Stamford's finest Susan Kitchell. PoL

Best Loved of Africa. Margaret Danner. Huge and beautifully black as he ever was.../But dead. PoBA; PoNe

The Best Memory Course. *Anonymous.* And you will find, through age and youth,/That many hearts will love you. STF

Best of All. *Anonymous.* Yet best, oh! best of all doth he/Who helps a fallen enemy. WBLP

The Best of All. Fanny J. Crosby. 'Tis the word that God has spoken,/And it cannot pass away. BLRP

Best of Show. Barbara Howes. Best of show! GDP

Best of Two Worlds. John Basil Boothroyd. Besides, it's not my tree at all,/But overhanging from next door. BoAnP

The Best Old Fellow in the World. *Anonymous.* "Then I'd cry my eyes out, my kind old husband,/The best old fellow in the world." AmFP

The Best Religion. Heinrich Heine. Goose-giblets, too, are good. TrJP

The Best Road of All. Charles Hanson Towne. But, best of all, I love a road that leads to God knows where. HBMV

The Best Song As It Seems to Me. *Anonymous.* To thy mercy thow me restore,/salvum me fac, domine. CoBE

The Best Time for Conception. Claude Quillet. Tho hard, yet proper for a vig'rous Strain. FaBoUs

The Best Treasure. John J. Moment. The best we shall find is a friend. TRV

Bestiary. Abraham Moses Klein. The beast Nebuchadnezzar. OBCV

A Bestiary. Kenneth Rexroth.
And do their best to kill you. OBAL
And frightens all the people. OBAL
...and will/stick you with it if they can. OBAL
As they surely will, say "No." OBAL
But especially Englishmen. OBAL
But one of the nicer gods. OBAL
...But when the state/Plays with death, it really dies. OBAL
...but zoo tricks are cut/And make everybody laugh. OBAL
Control your environment. OBAL
...for he/Combines domestication,/Venery, and independence. OBAL
...From there it/Had sneaked off to Africa. OBAL
Here a false face won't help you. OBAL
I can't think of one, can you? OBAL
If offered a crown, refuse. OBAL
...keep your/Mouth shut and don't volunteer. OBAL
Lambs who got their just deserts. OBAL
...Let Y stand for yes. OBAL
Lions terrify most men/Who buy meat at the butcher's. OBAL
Men have invented several/Thousand ways of killing them. OBAL
NEVER MAKE FUN OF BABIES!). OBAL
Or a thief's colors at Ascot. OBAL
Papist intellectuals/Can be very misleading. OBAL
The reason is under "N." OBAL
See if you can apply this/To your history lessons. OBAL
There are better things to do/With it than make a home of it. OBAL
There are not many better/Things than a unicorn horn. OBAL
There is another kind of/Eagle on flags and money. OBAL
...There is/Much more of it than something. OBAL
...These characteristics he shares/With the body politic. OBAL

They throw coconuts at us. OBAL
Treat it nicely and it will/Always do just what you want. OBAL
...you'd/Best leave these blood-soaked notions/To those who find them useful. OBAL
You will never get another. OBAL

Bestiary for the Fingers of My Right Hand. Charles Simic. It takes the mote out of the eye. AmPA; LCAP

A Bestiary of the Garden for Children Who Should Know Better. Phyllis Gotlieb.
alive under the wing of evening. WHW
i think they need some tranquillizers. WHW
the Rabbit with a sudden leap/is gone. WHW
they're all the same to your behind. WHW
why then should that poor shell-less Slug/provoke but one reaction: ug? WHW

The Bestiary: The Whale. *Anonymous.* Who-so festeth hope on him,/He shal him folwen to helle dim. OxBM

La Bete Humaine. James Kirkup. They show them to you sometimes at a terminus. NeBP

Bete Humaine. Francis Brett Young. Must slay to live, but what excuse had I? CH; HBMV

Beth Appleyard's Verses. Peter DeVries.
And Cinderella sleeps content beside/The kind and well-adjusted cobbler. OBAL
And that's what comes of reading/Pessimistic verse. OBAL
She brews and bottles, unfermented,/The stupid and abiding jelly. OBAL

Beth Gelert. William Robert Spencer. The consecrated spot shall hold/The name of "Gelert's Grave." BeLS; BLPA; GDP; OBNV; TreFS

Bethel. A. J. H. Duganne. "Column! Forward!" PAH

Bethinking Hymself of His Ende. Thomas, Lord Vaux. "Rise up out of your grave, for now the Judge is come."' EnPo

Bethlehem of Judea. *Anonymous.* The Hope of all/The world was born. BiCB; ChBR

The Bethlehem Star Shines On! Alice Mortenson. So remember, dear heart, whatever may come,/The Bethlehem Star shines on! BePJ 033

Bethlehem Town. Eugene Field. What Blood redeemeth you and me! PGD; WBLP

Bethou Me, Said Sparrow. Wallace Stevens. A sound like any other. It will end. CrMA; NePA

Betjeman, 1984. Charles Causley. Lord, but how much beauty was there/Back in 1955!' FaBoCo; NOBL; OxBTC

Betjeman at the Post Office (parody). Stanley J. Sharpless. Half-forgotten lust runs through me–/Senex becomes seventeen. FaBoPa

Betrayal. Hester H. Cholmondeley. For thirty pieces Judas sold/Himself, not Christ. TRV

The Betrayal. Alice Furlong. The lips that falsely kissed, shall kiss but Death. AnIV

The Betrayal. Josephine Winslow Johnson. –And broke the useless knife across my knee. MoRP

Betrayal. John Banister Tabb. He kissed the Dawn-Star pale. ACP

Betrayal. Sir Thomas Wyatt. How should I/Be so pleasant/In my semblant,/As my fellows be? OBSC

The Betrayal of the Rose. Edith Matilda Thomas. In the red rose's way! AA

The Betrayed Maiden. *Anonymous.* Saying, "Would our son but rise again,/We would send for Betsy over the main." OBET

The Betrothal. Edna St. Vincent Millay. There's few enough as it is. PG

A Betrothal. E. J. Scovell. And I will hold you, roots and fruit and fallen leaf. GBL

Betrothed. Louise Bogan.
And the sound of willows/Now and again dipping their long oval leaves in the water. NMM
...Willows/Now and again dipping their long oval leaves in the water. LLLT

The Betrothed. Rudyard Kipling. If Maggie will have no rival, I'll have no Maggie for spouse! HBV 1-2

Betsey and I Are Out. Will Carleton. If we loved each other the better because we quarreled here. PaPo

Betsy Baker. *Anonymous.* Take her up and shake her. OxNR

Betsy from Pike. *Anonymous.* "Goodby, you big lummix, I'm glad you backed out." BaBo

Betsy Jane's Sixth Birthday. Alfred Noyes. And the happiest eyes in the world that day were the eyes of Betsy/Jane. BiCB; SiSoSe

Betsy's Battle-Flag. Minna Irving. For Betsy's battle-flag! MC; PAH

A Better Answer (to Cloe Jealous). Matthew Prior. For thou art a girl as much brighter than her,/As he was a poet sublimer than me. AWP; ELP; ExPo; InPo; NOEC; PoEL 1-5; SeCeV

The Better Bargain. William Congreve. I'll take her body, you her mind:/Who has the better bargain? UnTE

The Better Part. Matthew Arnold. If we then, too, can be such men as he! MCCG

A Better Resurrection. Christina Georgina Rossetti. O Jesus, drink of me. EBCP; HBV 1-2; NOBV; OxBoCh; TrPWD; VLP

Better Than Gold. Abram Joseph Ryan. And center there, are better than gold. FaFP; PoToHe

Better to Spit on the Whip than Stutter Your Love Like a Worm. Colette Inez. old men cloaked in wisdom/stuttering their love. TW

The Better Way. Walter Leaf. Send him to Blank the oculist. FaBoCo

Better, Wiser and Happier. Ella Wheeler Wilcox. As the hand that plants an acorn/Shelters armies from the sun. WBLP

Betty and Dupree. Anonymous. You don't mind sailing, you'll be gone so doggone long. FSW

Betty at the Party. Anonymous. "I didn't laugh," said Betty,/"'Cause it was I that fell." BiCB; OnUR

Betty Blue. Anonymous. And then she may walk out in two. OxNR

Betty Botter Bought Some Butter. Anonymous. So t'was better Betty Botter/Bought a bit of better butter. OxNR

Betty by the Sea. Ronald McCuaig. Like still seas, to vacant skies. BoAV; NOAV

Betty Pringle's Pig. Anonymous. Johnny Pringle he, Betty Pringle she,/and Piggy Wiggy. OxNR

Betty Zane. Thomas Dunn English. Who boasts that in his spotless strain/Mingles the blood of Betty Zane. PAH; PAL

Between a Good Hat & Good Boots. Kell Robertson. drank three quick beers/& left in a hurry. TAT

Between Birthdays. Ogden Nash. The songs I've heard, the things I've done,/Make my unbirthdays not so un– OnUR

Between Brielle and Manasquan. Oliver St. John Gogarty. So gaily flew the flagstaff's bunting. OnYI

Between God's Eyelashes. Jose Garcia Villa. You'll break me you'll break me you'll break me. CrMA

Between Here and Illinois. Ralph Pomeroy. over all the graves that lie between here and Illinois. Psk

Between Leaps. Brad Leithauser. ...the place's spell/is lifted: the trunk bare, the frog elsewhere. MAYP

Between Life and Death. Frantisek Gottlieb. You are silent,/only the days/count the milestones/of our meeting. VWA

Between Me and Anyone Who Can Understand–. Sharon Scott. it must be because of a/certain/strait jacket/i feel. JB

Between Namur and Liege. William Wordsworth. From the smooth meadow-ground, serene and still! MCCG

Between Our Folding Lips. Thomas Edward Brown. I know not–He is fond of flowers. PeD

Between Ourselves. Audre Lorde. I do not believe/our wants/have made our lies/holy. WPOW

Between Rivers and Seas. Lance Henson. the song of the child/rings in the heart/of ancient men. VoR

Between Seasons. Anne Welsh. Will join to ours, make light our lightless stones. PeSA

Between the Acts. Stanley Jasspon Kunitz. It is that knave who answers in my heart. ELU

Between the Karim Shahir. Rochelle Owens. between the Karim Shahir/M'lefaat-Zawi/record says/in the/kurdish hills. CoPo

Between the Lines. Wilfred Wilson Gibson. He rose, and crawled away into the night. MCCG

Between the Porch and the Altar. Robert Lowell. He watches me for Mother, and will turn/The bier and baby-carriage where I burn. MiAP; NePoEA; PAI

Between the Sunken Sun and the New Moon. Paul Hamilton Hayne. A shining Jacob's ladder of the mind. AA

Between the Tides. Emily Sargent Councilman. beyond all measure/of time. AMV-80

Between the Traveller and the Setting Sun. Henry David Thoreau. A hound stands o'er the carcass of a man. PoEL 1-5

Between the Walls of the Valley. Elisabeth Peck. "Not room enough to pull his thread out/Between the walls of the valley." AmFN

Between the World and Me. Richard Wright. ...my face a stony skull staring in/yellow surprise at the sun.... AmNP; IDB; LiTM; NoAm; PoBA

Between Two Furious Oceans. Dick Diespecker. You are the white-hot steel, taking your shape/Under the hammer blows of Time.... CaP

Between Two Prisoners. James Dickey. In the end, at the end of a war. AP

Between Two Worlds. Rosemary Thomas. and in that lambent medium/tomorrows bite off yesterday. NYBP

Between Us. Stephen Berg. plunging into itself without me. NaP

Between Walls. William Carlos Williams. pieces of a green/bottle HoPM; SOTW; TAP; VGW

Between You and Me. Samuel Hazo. to win a wreath or some cheap figurine/to show the world, if you know what I mean. GOYP

Betweens. Norman MacCaig. Shielding the truth and giving birth to it. EAS

Betwixt and Between. Hugh Lofting. They've been alike as a pair of pins/Since they could scarcely toddle. BiCB

Beulah Land. John R. and Page. Edgar Sweeney. My heav'n, my home forevermore. FSW

The Beverley Maid and the Tinker. Anonymous. The tinker may do as he's done before,/Kiss the girl behind the door. CoMu

Beverly Hills, Chicago. Gwendolyn Brooks. When we speak to each other our voices are a little gruff. VGW

Beware. Dora Sigerson Shorter. I found a dying human soul. GTBS

Beware : Do Not Read This Poem. Ishmael Reed. a space in the lives of their friends BPo; CNA; NCSH; NIP; NoP; PoBA; WeW; WSC

Beware Fair Maide. Anonymous. From Lord to Lackey, and at last to all. OBS

Beware of Dogmas. Ebenezer Elliott. And keeps, abjuring rum and gin,/A Temperance inn. FaBoEE

Beware of Doubleness. John Lydgate. A myghty shelde of doublenesse. EnPo

Beware of Figs. Nicophon. And falling on him brings up much black bile. FaBoUs

Beware of Larry Gorman. Anonymous. But little she knew I was Gorman,/The man who made the songs! ShS

Beware, Oh, Take Care. Anonymous. Beware, oh, take care. FSW

Beware the Cuckoo. Ernest G. Moll. Keep a wing over your heart. BoAV; NOAV

Beware the Months of Fire They Are Twelve and Contain a Year. Patrick Lane. and mice to find wrapped around their bones. NeAC

Bewick and Graham. Anonymous. But 't will be talk'd in Carlisle town/That these two BaBo; ESPB

The Bewick and the Graeme. Anonymous. I durst hae ridden the world around/Had Christie Graeme been at my back. OxBB

Bewick Finzer. Edwin Arlington Robinson. Familiar as an old mistake,/And futile as regret. AnNE; CMoP; CoBMV; ForPo; MoAB; MoAmPo; PPP

The Bewildered Guest. William Dean Howells. We know we shall not meet him here again. AmePo

A Bewilderment at the Entrance of the Fat Boy into Eden. Daryl Hine. Interbound the bitter with the sweet. NOBC; OBCV

The Bewteis of the Fute-Ball. Anonymous. Thir are the bewteis of the fute-ball. BSV; FaBoCo; GoTS

Beyond. Lionel Pigot Johnson. I near me to your sleeping city. BrPo

Beyond. Hannah Parker Kimball. But O the wind, the sun, the light! AA

Beyond Belief. Tom Luhrmann. only one. AMV-81

Beyond Biology. Robert Francis. ...but the empress/(How like an empress) was implacably shocked. NePoAm

Beyond Feith Buidhe. Hamish Brown. Like spindrift flinging, in great joy or pain/Pass on and come no more. PoSH

Beyond Kerguelen. Henry Clarence Kendall. Moans in the South by the ghost of a sea. NOAV; PoAu 1-2

Beyond Labelling Me. Pier Giorgio Di Cicco. ...like a lonely hunger/for the hours when you love me. CaPN

Beyond Memory. Monny De Boully. The sentence without appeal, the sentence without appeal remains a/dead letter! VWA

Beyond Possession. Elizabeth Jennings. To beat with rose and river in one song., BoC; NePoEA

Beyond Rathkelly. Francis Carlin. And if a star were falling now/I'd wish for her again. HBMV

Beyond Recall. Mary Emily Bradley. As Life–and you–have proved to/me! AA

Beyond Religion. Lucretius (Titus Lucretius Carus). Each in the end when each is overthrown. AWP

Beyond the Alps. Robert Lowell. Now Paris, our black classic, breaking up/like killer kings on an Etruscan cup. NOBA

Beyond the Chagres. James Stanley Gilbert. That beyond the Chagres River/All paths lead straight to hell! PoLf

Beyond the End. Denise Levertov. ...to begin, to be, to defy. NeAP; VGW

Beyond the Firehouse. Patrick Worth Gray. I rescue them again and again. AMV-80

Beyond the Grave. Margaret E. Bruner. To meet with friends–where death can play no part. PoToHe

Beyond the Hunting Woods. Donald Justice. Nor home from the hunting woods/Ever, ever come? ConAP; NCSH; NePoEA; NYBP; PoPl

Beyond the Last Lamp. Thomas Hardy. And will, while such a lane remain. MoVE; NOBE; OBNC

Beyond the Nigger. Sterling D. Plumpp. the black soul cracks the universe./free. PoBA

Beyond the Potomac. Paul Hamilton Hayne. Hath his grave not been hollowed, and woven/his pall,/Since they passed o'er the river? PAH

Beyond the Presidency. Morgan Gibson. What last rite will open our arms/to the anarchy of love? FF

Beyond the Profit of Today. Anonymous. The name of Business Man;/Amen! PoToHe

Beyond the Smiling and the Weeping. Horatius Bonar. Lord, tarry not, but come. HBV 1-2

Beyond the Tapestries. Norma Farber. and pheasants preen on the moist verge. GoYe

Beyond the Wall. J. J. Maloney. Or feel some presence staring, glaring out at you/It's only me. LFAC

Beyond Wars. David Morrow. And a man ploughs, a woman sews and/sings. PAH

Beyond Words. Robert Frost. And you, you...you, you utter.../You wait! TW

The Bhagavad-Gita: Considerations of Murder. *Anonymous.* Now let them kill me,/That will be better. LiTW

Bhagavad-Gita: Debate Between Arjuna and Sri Krishna. Prabhavananda, Isherwood, tr *Anonymous.* Changeless, eternal,/For ever and ever. WaaP

Bhagavad Gita (excerpt). *Anonymous.* Therefore, the thing being unavoidable,/Thou shouldst not mourn. DL

Bhagavad Gita: Never the Spirit Was Born. *Anonymous.* And passeth to inherit/a residence afresh. GoTF; TreFT

Bhagavadgita: The One. *Anonymous.* that, you may know, is only a fragment/of my own splendor. ILwL

Bi-focal. Hal Porter. Striae of Grief by Grief by Grief. BoAV

Biafra. L. V. Mack. Biafra. O mother, hear the growl, the night/is cold, cold, cold. PoBA

Bianca. Arthur Symons. And, hot against my finger-tips,/The pulses leaping in her throat. UnTE; VLP

Bianca among the Nightingales. Elizabeth Barrett Browning. The nightingales, the nightingales! BrRo; GTBS-P

The Bible. David Levi. Peacefully round him circling,/Pursued their Heavenly way. TrJP

The Bible. Dorothy Conant Stroud. And our Saviour paid its cost! STF

The Bible. Thomas Traherne. And shall be sated with celestial mirth. LoBV

The Bible is an antique volume. Emily Dickinson. It did not condemn– NoP

Orpheus' Sermon captivated–/It did not condemn–. AmePo; MAmP; NoP

Bible Stories. Lizette Woodworth Reese. The little Jesus supped with me. BrR

Bibliographer. Josephine Miles. I will take them up/And gently gent-/Ly love them, tell them/What they have probably meant. FaBoWP

Bibliolaters: God Is Not Dumb. James Russell Lowell. Still at the prophets' feet the nations sit. WGRP

The Bibliomaniac's Prayer. Eugene Field. Uncut, unique, unknown to Lowndes. AA

Bibliotheca Bodleiana. Geoffrey Grigson. O Illuminatio mea, I wait/For your entering smile. GBL

Bicycalamity. Edmund W. Peters. The six-day riders/Want a five-day week! SD

The Bicycle. Stan Rice. will never pull, for example, apart/from where we are going. NPGG

The Bicycle Rider. Thomas W. Shapcott. The sweat creeps out on his forehead, it scatters in the sun. CBAP

The Bicycle Rider. David Shapiro. like the bicycle rider/irrationally dropping his books. ANYP

Bicycles! Tricycles! John Banister Tabb. Who would buy cycles, failing to try cycles first. OBAL

Bicycling Song. Henry Charles Beeching. Who climbs with toil, wheresoe'er,/Shall find wings waiting there. GN

Bid Adieu to Maidenhood. James Joyce. And softly to undo the snood/That is the sign of maidenhood. HBV 1-2; LiTL; OBEV; OnYI

Bid Me Sin No More. Charles Wesley. Love me freely, seal my peace,/And bid me sin no more. BePJ

A Bidding Prayer. *Anonymous.* And for alle that on erthe us feden and foster,/Saye we nu alle the haly Pater Noster. OxBM

Biddy, Biddy. *Anonymous.* John saw the island. OuSiCo

Bide a Wee! John Oxenham. –"Bide a wee, and dinna weary!"/Is a heartsome song. TRV

Bidean Nam Bian. Henry Austin Dobson. And the day complete that we shall remember. PoSH

Biftek aux Champignons. Henry Augustin Beers. That blue September day. AA; AmLP; HBV 1-2

Big Apple Blues. Sonny Boy Williamson. I just deswear we won't be here long BluL

The Big Baboon. Hilaire Belloc. How like this Big Baboon would be/to Mister So-and-so! MoShBr

The Big Bell in Zion. Theodore Henry Shackleford. Ding, Dong, Ding! BANP

Big Cars. Wesley McNair. ...are riding/on soft shocks, under a sun roof,/toward the great plenty of the New World. AmC

Big Chief Blues. Furry Lewis. I say, when I marry gonna marry a Indian squaw/So the Big Chief can be my daddy-in-law. BluL

Big City. Michael Brownstein. And keep looking, until big letters appear on one side. ANYP

Big City Glissando. Nicholas Christopher. "Up here the sun melts all of us/As if we had wings..." NYP

The Big Clock. *Anonymous.* Tick-a-tock-a, tick! SoPo

Big Crash out West. Peter Viereck. Never hot with doubt nor faith nor reverence for tears? AmC; PoPl

Big Dam. W. R. Moses. And lose the arid prairie in a lake. AmFN

Big Dog. Philip Booth. may all your stolen bones be sweet. BoAnP; GDP

Big Dog. Anselm Hollo. i'll get up and/be a man again. APU

Big Dream, Little Dream. Louis Simpson. and before you know there is war. PoL

Big, Fat Summer–and the Lean and Hard. Frederick Bock. Or shipped on commodious sands whatever pleasure/Of the moment as august as sorrow burned. NYBP

Big Fat Woman. *Anonymous.* When a man gets the blues he catch that train and rides. OuSiCo

The Big Five-Gallon Jar. *Anonymous.* In the old Virginia lowlands, lowlands low,/In the old Virginia lowlands low! ShS

Big Friend of the Stones. Steve Orlen. I sneezed again and it was winter. Psk

Big Fun. Diane Burns. We're gonna sing all night/bring your blanket/or/be that way then! STE; TWSS

Big Grave Creek. Cid Corman. And slowly lose them. HoAn

Big Jim. *Anonymous.* Long, long, long are de years! ABF

Big Man. Mason Jordan Mason. sharp on the hard ground/in the hard cold PoNe

Big Momma. Don L. Lee. eats joyously with her own/real teeth. BPo; CNA

The Big Nasturtiums. Robert Beverly Hale. "I never expected the big nasturtiums/To come in my lifetime!" Grandpa said. BoNaP; NYBP

Big Night Blues. Blind Lemon Jefferson. Well I needs my daddy 'cause my/clock is run down at home. BluL

The Big One. Luis Cabalquinto. struck by bass!/in the brain. BrSi

The Big One. Edward Morin. ...aluminum canoe/or weedless spoon–or whatever it is. WOLT

Big Road Blues. Tommy Johnson. And the wind goin'/Blow my/Blues away BluL

The Big Rock Candy Mountain. *Anonymous.* By the lemonade springs where the bluebird sings,/In the Big Rock Candy Mountain. AmFP; FSW; GBP; MaC; NOBA; OBAL; TreFT

Big Rock Jail. Barefoot Bill. I don't get nothing but the/mean old high sheriff. BluL

Big Sheep Knocks You About. Sharon Bryan. With eyes that see two things instead of one. MAYP

A Big Ship Sailing. *Anonymous.* Heigh-ho, back again. FSW

Big Steamers. Rudyard Kipling. And if any one hinders our coming you'll starve! Par

The Big Sunflower. Bobby Newcomb. And my heart is as light as the wind that blows/The leaves from off the trees. BLSo

The Big Swing-Tree Is Green Again. Mary Jane Carr. All the children waiting turns/Standing in a row. BrR; SiSoSe

Big Thompson Canon. Jean Milne Gower. Wooing the boulders with his Song of Love. PoOW

The big trimmer. Ronald P. Tanaka. and i sneeze. BrSi

A Big Turtle. *Anonymous.* Watching a tadpole turn into a frog. SoPo

Big Wind. Theodore Roethke. Carrying her full cargo of roses. AmPP; CMoP; GoJo; InvP; NCSH; NoP; PPoe; VGW; ViBoPo

Big Woman. Washboard Sam. You'll never get a chance to put your big legs on me no more/(Yeah). BluL

Bigerlow (with music). *Anonymous.* 'Twas on the trip to Buffalo from Milwaukee! AS

The Bigger Day. G. E. Bishop. We must do the bigger deeds. WBLP

The Biggest Killing. Edward Dorn. where grieves forth obsolescent landwrack/to infinity. CoPo; VGW

The Bight. Elizabeth Bishop. All the untidy activity continues,/awful but cheerful. FaBoWP; HaCAP; NYBP

The Bigler. *Anonymous.* On our down trip to Buffalo from Milwaukee. AmSS; OuSiCo

The Biglow Papers. James Russell Lowell.
An' all I know is they was cried/In meetin' come nex' Sunday. AA; AnNE; NOBA; OBAL

Ef there's thousands o' my mind. AnNE

I'm safe enlisted fer the war,/Yourn,/BIRDOFREDUM SAWIN. OxBA

An' I shouldn't gretly wonder/Ef there's thousands o' my mind. OxBA

Runs down, a brook o' laughter, thru the air. FaBV

Sez the world'll go right, ef he hollers/out Gee! AA; AnNE

To feed ez they hev fed me. AnNE

Wy, I'm a kind o' peri-Wig. AA

Bijou. Vern Rutsala. ...odorless horses/spring onto the screen below waving flags. DFF

Bile Them Cabbage Down. *Anonymous.* The only song that I can sing/Is bile them cabbage down. AmFP; FSW

Bill. Peter Kocan. Let your very bloodbeat drag/The lush world to the bars! CBAP

Bill. J.L. Salzburg. I only know I'm Billy Brown,/Four years old. BiCB

The Bird, Let Loose in Eastern Skies. Thomas Moore. Thy freedom in her wings! HBV 1-2

Bird Nest Bound. Charlie Patton. You don't need no telling, mama/Take you in my car BluL

The Bird of Night. Randall Jarrell. And the night holds its breath. DuDa; NCSH; RFM

The Bird of Paradise. William Henry Davies. Don't touch that bird of paradise,/Perched on the bedpost there!' AtBAP; BrPo; MoVE

Bird of Power. Jim Tollerud. The last pound of the drum. VoR

Bird on Briar. Anonymous. Joye and blisse were ere, were ere me newe. OxBM

The Bird on Nellie's Hat. Arthur J. Lamb. "Well, he don't know Nellie like I do!"/Said the saucy little bird on Nellie's hat. FSN

Bird Riddle: "As I went out, so I came in." Anonymous. Tell me the riddle and then hang me. GBP

Bird Riddle: "One day I went down in the golden harvest field." Anonymous. In three weeks it stood alone. GBP

Bird Riddle: "What is it more eyes doth wear." Anonymous. Against the sun, when they do stand? GBP

A Bird's Nest. Erez Biton. Good fortune for us, our living here/At a station/Along the way. VWA

The Bird's Nest. John Drinkwater. The sound of me watching, if I had been a bird. EvOK; SoPo

The Bird's Nest. Elizabeth Turner. ...though she left them behind/To seek for them suitable food. OHIP

Bird's Nests. John Clare. Where the old cow at her leisure chews her cud. ERoP 1-2; OAEL 1-2

Bird Scarer's Song. Anonymous. Shua-O! Shua-O! OxNR

A Bird-Scene at a Rural Dwelling. Thomas Hardy. Just such enactments, just such daybreaks seen. FM

Bird Shadows Mounting. Larry Eigner. ...not any of the/stars hide and seek. CoPo

A Bird Sings to Establish Frontiers. Jack Gilbert. ...All those gentlemen. NPGG

Bird Song. John Hay. The air! and careless, far, far...fly it. Fly. NePoAm-2

Bird Song. Laura E. Richards. But the oriole, the oriole,/Sings "Joy! joy! joy!" HBV 1-2

Bird Song. Betsy Rosenberg. But it's true about the bird, believe me. VWA

Bird-Song. Mary Dixon Thayer. My love a shadow that passes... CAW

A Bird Was Singing. Sir Dietmar von Aist. Short has my pleasure, long has my sorrow been. AWP; LiTW

Bird Watcher. Ronald Wallace. every finger a bird. PPJ

The Bird with a Broken Wing. Hezekiah Butterworth. But the bird with a broken pinion/Never soars as high again. WBLP

The Bird with the Coppery, Keen Claws. Wallace Stevens. To flare, in the sun-pallor of his rock. AnFE; APA

Bird-Witted. Marianne Moore. intellectual cautious-/ly creeping cat. CMoP; FM

The Birdcatcher. Ralph Hodgson. They fly into my Head. MoBrPo

The Birde's Marriage-Cake. Anonymous. That glory of glories–the Bride's Marriage-Cake. HW

Birdie McReynolds. Samuel Hoffenstein. That's one thing I never got enough of/In my business,/Or I wouldn't be here. BXAP; NLV

The Birds. Anonymous. My beauty do I give to you–/Tsucroo, Tsucroo, Tsucroo. PCh

The Birds. Aristophanes.
O highest of the gods! HW
That we are to you all as the manifest Godhead that/speaks in prophetic Apollo? AWP

The Birds. William Blake. Among green leaves and blossoms sweet. CH; OBRV

The Birds. Blossius Aemilius Dracontius. They seem worthy of His Hand. CAW

Birds. Robinson Jeffers. Rock-shores of the world and the secret waters. AP; CoBMV; VGW

Birds. D. H. Lawrence. ...And all birds/have their voices, each means a different thing. BoAnP

Birds. Llywelyn. ...like theirs arise/On callous earth and careless skies. PoAu 1-2

Birds. Ruth Miller. His beggarman bones with the charity of their wings. PeSA

Birds. Moira O'Neill. Ay, thon's the wee bird for me. HBV 1-2

Birds. Seumas (James Starkey) O'Sullivan. Truly I think each woman is a bird. OxBI

The Birds. David Posner. and the bones of sparrows. NYBP

The Birds. J. C. Squire. These are unchanging: man must still explore. HBMV

Birds. Richard Henry Stoddard. In the little cage of Song! AA; HBV 1-2

Birds All Singing. Norman MacCaig. Time topples bird and man out of their myth. ChMP

Birds and Bees. Anonymous. Girls believe and men deceive the whole world over. UnTE

Birds and Fishes. Robinson Jeffers. That is their quality: not mind, not goodness, but the beauty of/God. NoP

Birds and Roses Are Birds and Roses. William Heyen. their bush cast a shadow like a bell. GeTw

Birds Are Drowsing on the Branches. Leah Rudnitsky. Over fields and over valleys/Flew his orphaned cry. VWA

Birds at Winter Nightfall. Thomas Hardy. And all the berries now are gone! ELU; MoBrPo

The Birds' Ball. C. W. Bardeen. Flew to their nests from the birdies' ball. BLPA

The Birds' Courting Song. Anonymous. I'd have a new string to tie to my bow."/Towdy owdy, dil-do dum/tol-lol-li-do dil-do day. TrAS

The Birds Do Thus. Robert Lee Frost. I choose to sleep. AmePo

Birds in Snow. Hilda ("H. D.") Doolittle. proclaims what's left unsaid/in Egypt of her dead. PoA

Birds in Spring. James (1700-48) Thomson. ...while the Stock-dove breathes/A melancholy Murmur thro' the whole. OBEC

Birds in the Flax. Stanley Snaith. Save for a quiet unbroken as we stood/Each in his solitude. HaMV

Birds in the Night. Luis Cernuda. better if it were a cockroach, simply to squash it. PeHV

Birds in the Wood. Anonymous. All the grief I've had/For best of flesh and blood! HAP

Birds in Their Little Nests Agree. Hilaire Belloc. With Chinamen but not with me. PoL

Birds' Lament. John Clare. But after her I'll whoop and hollo. PoEL 1-5

Birds' Nests. Edward ("Edward Eastaway") Thomas. And grass and goose-grass seeds found soil and grew. HeIP

The Birds of America. James Richard Broughton. coo ahh, choo eee, coo coo! AmFN; BoAnP

The Birds of Arles. David Fisher. to find the invitation/(from the birds of Arles)/was no longer current. NPGG

The Birds of Bethlehem. Richard Watson Gilder. And smile upon his mother's breast. AA

The Birds of Killingworth. Henry Wadsworth Longfellow. Amid the sunny farms of Killingworth. OnMSP; OxBA; WBLP

The Birds of Paradise. John Peale Bishop. And this is grief to me. GoJo

The Birds of Scotland (excerpt). James Grahame. She, sole of all the innumerous feathered tribes,/Passes a stranger's life, without a home. PBBP

The Birds of the Air. Hollis Freeman. And are we not better than they? STF

The Birds of Tin. Charles Madge. In vain we call to them/Or entreat them to open their wings. EAS; NeBP

The Birds' Rondel (modern version). Geoffrey Chaucer. And drive away the nights so long and black! TrGrPo

Birds Waking. William Stanley Merwin. With the bursting roar and uprush of song! NOBA

Birdsong. James Burns Singer. Or these sharp spangles trammelling the wind's beak. FaBoTw

The Birdsville Track. Douglas Stewart.
All strikes like iron in the mind. CBAP
Harsh as the loose sheet of iron that bangs in the wind. CBAP

Birdwatcher. Henry Treece. ...a man in red/Will blood his boy and carry home the brush. WaP

Birdwatchers of America. Anthony Hecht. Upon the forehead, furred/With a light frost, crouched an outrageous bird. CoPo; HoPM; NoAm; NOBA; PPP

Birkett's Eagle. Dorothy S. Howard. With an apple in his pocket/Which he gave to Birkett's wife. MoBS

The Birks of Aberfeldy. Robert Burns. Bonie lassie, will ye go/To the birks of Aberfeldy! CTC; ViBoPo

The Birks of Endermay. David Mallet. Adieu the Birks of Endermay. OBEC

Birlinn Chlann-Raghnaill. Alexander MacDonald. We took food and drink unstinting/And there we stayed. GoTS

Birmingham. Julia Fields. In their effervescent youth/And for indifferent seasons. PoNe

Birmingham. Louis MacNeice. To call, in the harsh morning, sleep-stupid faces through the daily gate. CMoP; MoAB; MoBrPo

Birmingham. Margaret Walker. The forge of bitter hate. PoBA

Birmingham 1963. Raymond Richard Patterson. Alone amid the rubble, amid the people/Who perish, being innocent. CNA; GP; PoBA

Birmingham Sunday. Langston Hughes. As yet unfelt among/Magnolia trees. PoNe

Birth. Edith Bruck. or North America of yesterday today and tomorrow... BoWoP

Birth. James Dickey. Change, to include a new horse. NOBA

The Birth. Rosemary Dobson. I speak as of a mystery. PoAu 1-2

Birth. Amir Gilboa. O God, how embraced we have been! OFD; VWA

Birth. Langston Hughes. Some'word/To tell. NAs

Birth. George Ella Lyon. like a root pulled from the water/like a heartroot torn free. Str

Birth. Gabriela Melinescu. They hold up my temples with their tusks. BoWoP

Birth. Craig Raine. with penicillin, needles, gut. NAs

Birth. Annie R. Stillman. Peace laid upon her breast a child. AA

Birth. Constance Urdang. She thinks nothing was/Before she came. VWA

Birth and Death. Algernon Charles Swinburne. Joy nor sorrow knows not from each other/Birth and death. MaVP

Birth by Anesthesia. George Scarbrough. The Lady Anne came home. GoYe

Birth-Dues. Robinson Jeffers. Have paid my birth-dues; am quits with the people. MoAB; MoAmPo

The Birth in a Narrow Room. Gwendolyn Brooks. Across old peach cans and old jelly jars. BlSi; NAs; PoNe

Birth of a Country. Agnes Gergely. I'll dream of it tonight. VWA

Birth of a Great Man. Robert Graves. But evade the sesquipedalian school inspector/With his muzzle and his bag! NYBP

The Birth of a Shark. David Wevill. He learned his place among the weeds. TwCP

Birth of Christ. Rainer Maria Rilke. But (thou wilt see): He brings joy. MoRP

The Birth of Galahad: Ylen's Song. Richard Hovey. Like the peace of summer noons/Beside the sea. AA

The Birth of John Henry. Melvin B. Tolson. "Lousyana was my home. so scram!" BPo

Birth of Love. Robert Penn Warren. I do not know what promise it makes to him. UnPo

The Birth of Moshesh. David Granmer T. Bereng. Stronghold given by God to Thesele. PeSA; TTY

The Birth of My Father. Barry Dempster. ...I worry/when he phones taxis, offer to drive him myself. CaPN

Birth of Rainbow. Ted Hughes. Left to God the calf and his mother. NAs

The Birth of Robin Hood. Anonymous. But it was in the good green-wood,/Among the lily-flower. BuBa; OAEL 1-2; OxBB; ViBoPo

The Birth of Shaka. Mbuyiseni Oswald Mtshali. "Lo! you can kill me/but you'll never rule this land!" WhB

The Birth of St. Patrick. Samuel Lover. And we keep up the practice from that day to this. HBV 1-2

Birth of the Foal. Ferenc Juhasz. Like golden flowers/envy withered the last stars. BoAnP; PH

The Birth of the Poet. Quandra Prettyman. life/he/tries/to/tell. BOLo

The Birth of the Squire. John Gay. In copious gulps of potent ale expires. EiCP; NOEC; PoEL 1-5

The Birth of Tragedy. Irving Layton. while someone from afar off/blows birthday candles for the world. NoP; OBCV; PeCV

The Birth of Venus. Anonymous. The Beautiful is born, and sea and earth/May well revere the hour of that mysterious birth. EtS

Birth of Venus. Constance Urdang. To be their goddess, serve/The movable feasts of love. PoA

Birth Report. X. J. Kennedy. White, Anglo-Saxon, one-half Protestant? NAs

The Birth Song of Christ. Edward Hamilton Sears. And bright on Bethlehem's joyous plains/Breaks the first Christmas morn. BePJ

Birthday. Earle Birney. when she is old/it will be immortality enough. NAs

Birthday. John Ciardi. "Don't shrug away," he said, "There's nowhere to go." NAs

The Birthday. Philip Dacey. I wish I could tell you. AmPA

Birthday. Elaine V. Emans. Years I have loved in, lived in, and been glad! BiCB

A Birthday. Rachel Field. And candles for a birthday's sake? BiCB; SiSoSe; TiPo

Birthday. P. J. Kavanagh. To think how to climb from the hole these days are/digging. NAs

Birthday. D. H. Lawrence. Wafting like solace down their length of days. NAs

Birthday. James Merrill. Tell me I will live another year. NAs

A Birthday. Edwin Muir. And stand where first they stood. BSV; NAs

A Birthday. Christina Georgina Rossetti. Because the birthday of my life/Is come, my love is come to me. AWP; BLPL; BoLiVe; FaFP; GoTF; GTBS; InvP; LiTB; LiTL; LoBV; NAs; NOBE; NOBV; OAEL 1-2; OAEP; OBEV; OBVV; OLR; TreFS; TrGrPo; ViBoPo; VLP; WHA; WiR

Birthday. William Stafford. and we watch the clear sky bend. NAs

Birthday. Yevgeny Yevtushenko. give him a drink of milk and watch him go. NAs

The Birthday Bus. Mary Ann Hoberman. I'd accept it at once without making a fuss. BiCB

The Birthday Cake. Victoria Chase. That's what goes into a birthday cake! BiCB

Birthday Cake. Ivy O. Eastwick. Oh! Birthday Cake/Is VERY nice! BiCB

Birthday Cake. Aileen Fisher. I bet a birthday CHEESE cake/would please them most of all. BiCB it didn't have CANDLES on top of it! BiCB

The Birthday-Cake Glockenspiel. Elizabeth Henley. Three cheers for John,/Eating his bread and butter! BiCB

A Birthday Candle. Donald Justice. To blow them out with a breath. NYBP

Birthday Candles. Louise Binder Scott. As one by one we blow. BiCB

Birthday Card for a Psychiatrist. Mona Van Duyn. ...we're glad that forty years ago you came/to join us in this neurotic enterprise. IHMS

The Birthday Child. Rose Fyleman. Isn't it delicious/To be a birthday child? BiCB; SiSoSe

The Birthday Crown. William Alexander. Give her the unfading crown!' OBVV

The Birthday Dream. James Dickey. ...I was/forty. NAs

Birthday Garden. Ivy O. Eastwick. I've the prettiest birthday-garden/and I'm six years old today. BiCB

Birthday Gift. Ethel Barnett De Vito. With his or any/Father's son. BiCB

Birthday Gifts. Herbert Asquith. But the lady had floated into the leaves/With the blue mist of the fire. BiCB; OFD; SiSoSe

A Birthday in Hospital. Elizabeth Jennings. I've heard of "gift of tears" but did not know,/Until this moment, what the words could mean. NAs

A Birthday Memorial to Seventh Street. Audre Lorde. where I kneel praying/that my children/will not die politely/either. CNA

A Birthday Ode to Mr. Alfred Austin. Sir Owen Seaman. If memory serve us, we propose to keep/His natal day. NOBL

Birthday of but a single pang. Emily Dickinson. Afflictive is the Adjective/But affluent the doom– NAs; OFD

The Birthday of the Lord. Mary Jane Carr. And keep the birthday of the Lord/With merriment and singing. BiCB; ChBR

Birthday on Deathrow. Harold LaMont Otey. we forget/about dying here/in this boxed-in today. LFAC

Birthday Party. Patti Patton. the lights are cruel. AMV-80

Birthday Poem. Al Young. But of course you already know about that/from your own random suffering/& sudden inexplicable bliss. NPGG

A Birthday Poem: for Rachel. James Simmons. you're asked to blow each light, each year,/out with your own breath. OBSP

Birthday Poem for Thomas Hardy. C. Day-Lewis. And in us, warmer-hearted and brisker-eyed/Since you have been. CoBMV

Birthday Poem from Venice. Patricia Beer. A cat, five minutes created, sits with a pigeon./Happy birthday. OxBC

Birthday Poem, November 4th. John Thompson, Jr. Wishes so simple they laugh at a vow. WaP

A Birthday Prayer. John Finley. In His name, who blessed the children,/This I humbly ask. TrPWD

Birthday Sonnet. Elinor Wylie. Into the dust, defend Thy prodigal. BoLiVe; MoAB; MoAmPo

Birthday: Tara Regina. George, Jr Mosby. but a daughter shouldn't be a picture/on a prison bunk/on her birthday. AMV-81

Birthday Verses Written in a Child's Album. James Russell Lowell. And drops, ere he suspect the ill,/Into the inexorable sea. OxBChV

A Birthday Wish. Dorothy Nell Mcdonald. And God's sweet peace when every day is done. PoToHe

Birthdays. Marchette Chute. Take all of our family of rabbits/To bed with us just for tonight. BiCB; SiSoSe

Birthdays. Hilde Domin. they get up/at once/and go. BoWoP

Birthdays. C. J. Driver. With that fat-faced man/Who comes, my age himself. PeSA

Birthing: 2000. Pancho Aguila. Get thee away/with a rose/in your heart. LFAC

The Birthnight: To F. Walter De la Mare. Thou, lovely thing. NAs

Birthplace. Duane Big Eagle. in the eyes of the woman/I'm about to love. STE

The Birthplace. Robert Frost. And now her lap is full of trees. EyDe; LoGBV; OFD

The Birthplace. Seamus Heaney. ...and I heard/roosters and dogs, the very same/as if he had written them. FaBoIP

Birthplace. Tahereh Saffarzadeh. Male supremacy/never fattened me at its table. WPOW

Birthplace Revisited. Gregory Corso. I pump him full of lost watches. CAD; NeAP; PoM; VGW

Birthright. John Drinkwater. And little Adriadne sleep. CH While Rameses and Romeo/And little Ariadne sleep. HBV 1-2; OxBTC; WHA

Birthright. Geraldine Kudaka. blood & spit... BrSi

Birthsong. Jessica Scarbrough. again the wombs live. LFAC

Black Is a Soul. Joseph Blanco White. I'm black. I'm black/& I'm from Look Back. IDB; PoBA

Black is Best. Larry Thompson. But I keep saying:/Black is best. BOLo; PoBA

Black Is the Color. *Anonymous.*
Black, black, black is the color of my true love's hair. FF
But still I hope the time will come/When you and I will be as one. FSW

Black Is the Colour. *Anonymous.* I love the ground whereon she stands. GBP

Black Jack Davey. *Anonymous.* With nothing but Black Jack Davey. MAT

Black Jack Davie. *Anonymous.* She said farewell forever. BaBo

Black Jack Davy. *Anonymous.* By the side of the Black Jack boy. OuSiCo

Black Jackets. Thom Gunn. And on the right the slogan Born To Lose. HeIP; MP; TwCP

Black Jam for Dr. Negro. Mari E. Evans. waitin/to be/defended. BPo; PoBA

Black Jess. Peter Kane Dufault. a dot on Long Island Sound. NYBP

A Black Job. Thomas Hood. But still their nigritude offends the sight,/We mean to gild 'em! VLP

The Black Knight. John Todhunter. While I rust here. OBVV

Black Lightning. Arthur Sze. the world as black/lightning. BrSi

Black Lotus/a Prayer. Alicia Loy Johnson. then make/our move./a-men. NBP

The Black Madonna. Albert Rice. Pity them, Mother,/the untaught/of earth. CDC

Black Magdalens. Countee Cullen. To cast the first hard stone. BANP

Black Magic. Sonia Sanchez. black/magic is your/touch/making/me breathe. BPo

Black Mail. Alice Walker. burning righteous,/but burning blind. AmPA

Black Majesty. Countee Cullen. "And we were black," three shades reply, "but kings." PoBA; VGW

Black Mammies. John Wesley Holloway. Peace on eart' amids' huh sorrows, an' up yonder heavenly/res'! BANP

A Black Man. Sam Cornish. the new man in the ovens. CNA; PoBA

Black Man's Feast. Sarah Webster Fabio. yet still feasts on the gall/of his gastronomical past. PoBA; PoNe

The Black Man's Son. Oswald Durand. The Black Man's son held a terror, you see. TTY

The Black Man Speaks. Langston Hughes. Why Democracy means/Everybody but me. TreFT

A Black Man Talks of Reaping. Arna Bontemps. They have not sown, and feed on bitter fruit. BANP; BPo; CDC; FB; IDB; PoBA; PoNe

Black Maps. Mark Strand. and the black grass/is holding up the black stars. PoA

Black Marble. Arthur William Edgar O'Shaughnessy. The lion and the serpent and the man/Watched her the while with each his own desire. SyP

Black Marigolds. Bilhana. The heavy knife. As to a gala day. AWP; ErPo; LiTW

The Black Mesa. James Merrill. Dust of my dust, when will it all be plain? PoA

Black Mesa. Ron Rogers. Rocks mesas cactus blood. STE

Black Money. Tess Gallagher. some black star climbing/the deep globe of his eye. GeTw; LTB

Black Mother. Viriato Da Cruz. THE DAY OF HUMANITY. WhB

Black Mountain Blues. Bessie Smith. I'm out here for trouble/and I've got the Black Mountain Blues. BluL

Black Muslim Boy in a Hospital. James A. Emanuel. So captive in a starched embrace?) PoNe

Black Narcissus. Gerald William Barrax. I will laugh when I see that I am still black. PoBA

The Black Narrator. Ahmed Legraham Alhamisi. using black primitive standards. BP

A Black November Turkey. Richard Wilbur. Dawn after mortal dawn, with vulgar joy/Acclaim the sun. AmLP; BoAnP; LCAP; MoAB; NCSH

Black-Out. Robinson Jeffers. Darkness and silence, the two eyes that see God. Great/staring eyes. LiTA; LiTM; NePA; WaP

The Black Panther. John Hall Wheelock. And I lie silent–but my body shakes. FF; HBMV; LiTM

A Black Patch on Lucasta's Face. Richard Lovelace. But the sweet little Bees large Monument. AnAnS 2; CaPo; SeCP

Black People! LeRoi (Imamu Amiri Baraka) Jones. ...look in your/face and curse you by/pitying your tomish ways. BPo

Black People: This Is Our Destiny. LeRoi (Imamu Amiri Baraka) Jones. the primitives the first men who evolve again to civilize the/world. CAPP; CNA

A Black Pierrot. Langston Hughes. I went forth in the morning/To seek a new brown love. OLR

The Black Plateau. William Stanley Merwin. the bird moves apart from his cry. NNaP

Black Poet, White Critic. Dudley Randall. A white unicorn? BPo; ConAP

A Black Poetry Day. Alicia Loy Johnson. I am waiting for/a BLACK POETRY DAY. BOLo

Black Pony Eating Grass. Robert Bly. the Great Bear is seven old men walking. FAZ

Black Poplar-Boughs. John Freeman. Than boughs that comb swift heavens and shake/Rain upon rainy lakes. HBMV

Black Power. Alvin Saxon. the day held no insurmountable fears/for me. PoBA

Black Power Poem. Ishmael Reed. may the best church win . shake hands now and come/out conjuring. BPo

Black Pride. Margaret Goss Burroughs. Like Moses, you will lead our people over/And through. BlSi

The Black Regiment. George Henry Boker. Never, in field or tent,/Scorn the black regiment! GN; HBV 1-2; PAH

The Black Riders. Stephen Crane.
But the sage was a sage. YaD
Thus the ride of sin. AA

The Black Rock of Kiltearn. Andrew Young. And trumpet of your resurrection. FaBoTw

Black Rocks. Laureen Mar. Your mouth shows a faint bone-white scar. BrSi

Black Rook in Rainy Weather. Sylvia Plath. The long wait for the angel,/For that rare, random descent. LiTM; NePoEA-2; NIP; NoP; SM

Black Sailor's Chanty. Charles Augustus Keeler. But d'aint no smokin' possum while de cook am lyin'/sick. EtS

Black Sheep. Richard Burton. And maybe they hear, and wonder why,/And marvel, out in the cold. AA; HBV 1-2

Black Silk. Tess Gallagher. ...I thought, with that/other mind, and stood still. FaBoWP; MAYP

Black Sister. Kattie M. Cumbo. ...So, brother,/proclaim the beauty that you see, in your black/sister. BlSi

Black Sketches, 1. Don L. Lee. until i started/school. NeAC

Black Sketches, 2. Don L. Lee. & didn't have a/dime. NeAC

Black Sketches, 3. Don L. Lee. peace corps to/europe. NeAC

Black Sketches, 4. Don L. Lee. insufficient funds. NeAC

Black Sketches, 5. Don L. Lee. everything/was/all right. NeAC

Black Sketches, 6. Don L. Lee. his momma too. NeAC

Black Sketches, 7. Don L. Lee. because somebody/called him/black. NeAC

Black Sketches, 8. Don L. Lee. he lost/there too. NeAC

Black Sketches, 9. Don L. Lee. no even/me. NeAC

Black Sketches, 10. Don L. Lee. even me. NeAC

Black Sketches, 11. Don L. Lee. & roy wilkins on/the mod squad. NeAC

Black Snake. John Lee Hooker. That mean mean black snake/He won't bother/me no more/Mmmmmmmmmmmmmmmmm. BluL

A Black Soldier Remembers. Horace Coalman. I have nothing she needs but the/sad smile she already has. FAZ

Black Soldier's Civil War Chant. *Anonymous.* An' de slave'll be free/In dese hard times. TAP

Black Soul of the Land. Lance Jeffers. and America shall cease to be its name. FB

Black Spring. Annensky. ...there is nothing/sorrier than the marriage of two deaths. NaP

Black Star Line. Henry Dumas. Dip into this river with your ebony cups. CNA; PoBA

Black Students. Julia Fields. The body a roving, singing automation. NBP

The Black Swan. Randall Jarrell. And stroked all night, with a black wing, my wings. CMoP; NMP

The Black Swan. James Merrill. Forever to cry aloud/In anguish: I love the black swan. MoPo

Black Taffy. Peggy Susberry Kenner. singing/"we/shall/over/come". JB

The Black Tail Range. *Anonymous.* He'll hear a sample of my mind, the chief of the Black Tail/Range. CoSo

Black Tambourine. Hart Crane. And, in Africa, a carcass quick with flies. AP; CoBMV; InPS; NAMP; NoAm; OBSP; OxBA; PPP; TAP

Black Tarn. Victoria Mary (Vita) Sackville-West. And the dwellings of men, the safety, and the ease. SBG

Black Thing. *Anonymous.* And draged out the brains with my little black thing. CoMu

The Black Tower. William Butler Yeats. Old bones upon the mountain shake. CMoP

Black Trumpeter. Henry Dumas. we are Americans looking in the mirror of Africa. PoBA

The Black Virgin. Gilbert Keith Chesterton. To thy most merciful face of night I kneel. ISi

The Black Vulture. George Sterling. Their hearts, contemptuous of death, shall dare/His roads between the thunder and the sun. AmLP; BPAW; HBV 1-2; PB

Black Warrior. Norman Jordan. I hurl a brick through/a store front window/and disappear. PoBA

Black Water and Bright Air. Constance Carrier. back into summer light,/ back into lucid air. SD

A Black Wedding Song. Gwendolyn Brooks. Come to your Wedding Song. CNA

Black Woman. Georgia Douglas Johnson. I must not give you birth! BALP

Black Woman. Naomi Long Madgett. Where/Are my beautiful/Black men? BlSi; FB; OLR; PoBA

Black Woman. Leopold Sedar Senghor. Before jealous destiny burns you to ashes to nourish the roots of life. TTY

Black Your Honour's Shoes? Anonymous. And charge but a penny. OxNR

The Blackberry. Norman Nicholson. Wash clear our eyes that we may see/ The sky within the blackberry. MoBrPo

Blackberry Fold. Anonymous. For he's made her his lady instead of his whore. OBET

Blackberry-Picking. Seamus Heaney. Each year I hoped they'd keep, knew they would not. BoNaP

Blackberry Sweet. Dudley Randall. jump stop shake. BOLo; HAP; InPS; NBP; NCSH; PAI; WeW

Blackberry Winter. Peter Huggins. The same, that mocks the memory/ With sweet, not sour. AMV-81

Blackberry Winter. John Crowe Ransom. And hoping a little, a little, that either may be. OxBA; PoRA

Blackberrying. Sylvia Plath. Beating and beating at an intractable metal. HaCAP; HAP; NoAm; NOBA; NYBP

The Blackbird. Anonymous.
And laurel shall crown/My Blackbird with honor wherever he be. NOBI; OnYI
Sweet, soft, peaceful is thy note. AnIL; OnYI
The sweetest bird that ever was,/In friendly sort, farewell. EIL

A Blackbird. Marcus Argentarius. But vines bear grapes–and Bacchus loves a song. LiTW

The Blackbird. William Barnes. An' zoo there's noo pleace lik' the drong,/ Where I do hear the blackbird's zong. HBV 1-2

The Blackbird. Henry Charles Beeching. Thou pin'st, to hear by wood or lawn/Apollo's nightingale. OBVV

The Blackbird. William Ernest Henley. Our hearts and lips together. HBV 1-2; MoBrPo; TrGrPo

Blackbird. Christopher Leach. ...the news/Of another cosmonaut. BoAnP

The Blackbird. Alfred, Lord Tennyson. Caught in the frozen palms of Spring. FM; HBV 1-2; PB; PBBP

The Blackbird. Humbert Wolfe. sings for us two/especially. GoJo; GrPl; HBMV; HBVY; SUS; TiPo

The Blackbird by Belfast Lough. Anonymous. A blackbird on/His leafy throne/Tossed it alone/Across the bay. KiLC

The Blackbird Calls in Grief. Anonymous. Hence the grief that is in my heart. NOBI

The Blackbird of Derrycairn. Anonymous. Listen! That song that shakes my feathers/Will thong the leather of your satchels. BIrV

The Blackbird of Derrycairn. Austin Clarke. Stop, stop and listen for the bough top/Is whistling... NeIP

Blackbird's Song. Anonymous. Tired waiting, tired waiting,/Blackbird, blackbird. GBP

Blackbird Sestina. Candice Warne. The stars fall down to become blackbirds. SM

A Blackbird Singing. R. S. Thomas. But fresh always with new tears. BoAnP; BoC

A Blackbird Suddenly. Joseph Auslander. Like you–a bird! TiPo

Blackbird Winter. Annette Arkeketa West. which offers only/the cold. TWSS

Blackbirds and Thrushes. Anonymous. The divil a man would eat fish of a Friday. GBP

The Blackcock. Joanna Baillie. Thou art already on the wing! PBBP

Blackfish Poem. Milton Acorn. just a knife-edge/this side of the horizon. NeAC

Blackfoot Sin-ka-ha. William S. Lewis. Thou powerful one, help me to bring also a scalp of my foe, that/my people may rejoice at my coming. BPAW

Blackfriars. Eleanor Farjeon. And the seventh one caught an old cart-wheel. OxBChV

Blackheads. Knute Skinner. secret imperfections/kept virginal for a lover? GP

Blackie Thinks of His Brothers. Stanley Crouch. "Don't give yo/right name no/No NO" PoBA

The Blackleg Miners. Anonymous. For that may not be far away,/Ye dorty blackleg miners! GBP; OBET; VLP

Blacklisted. Carl Sandburg. Why does God Almighty or anybody else care whether I take a/new name to go by? SaC

Blackmen: Who Make Morning. Angela Jackson. because we have promised tomorrow to ourselves. CNA

Blackmwore Maidens. William Barnes. O' beauty, then is still in bud/In Blackmwore by the Stour. HBV 1-2

Blackpool Breezes. Anonymous. 'Til a big Yankee guy, with a caste in his eye,/With one wave of his hand laid her low. CoMu

The Blacksmith. Anonymous. To think she loved one, and he proved deceitful. OBET

Blacksmith Pain. Otto Julius Bierbaum. No rust corrodes,/What Pain has forged. AWP

The Blacksmith's Serenade. Vachel Lindsay. And though the town went crazy, she is his wife today. StPo

The Blacksmith's Song. Anonymous. Here's to old Cole, and to young Cole, and the old Cole of all. GBP

Blacksmiths. Anonymous. May no man for bren-wateres on night han his rest. CABA; OxBM; WiR

The Blackstone Rangers. Gwendolyn Brooks.
The rhymes of Leaning. BALP; NoAm; PoBA
Sores in the city/that do not want to heal. CAD

Blackwater Mountain. Charles Wright. Where you, black moon, warm your hands. GeTw

The Blade of Grass Sings to the River. Leah Goldberg. the silent soul declares/the glory of the world. TrJP

Blades. C. K. Williams. I still can't. GeTw

The Blades of Grass. Stephen Crane. "Oh, best little blade of grass!" he said. AmP; GoTF; MoAmPo; PoPl; TreFT

Blah, Blah, Blah. Ira Gershwin. Blah, blah, blah, blah, blah, darling, with you! OBAL

Blake Leads a Walk on the Milky Way. Nancy Willard. but a handful of dirt to the rat. OBCA

The Blake Mistake. Sandie Castle. The next time I go lookin for some uh company I'mma bring/home a plumber or somthin. APU

Blame Not My Cheeks. Thomas Campion. Poor Cupid sits and blows his nails for cold. AAS; EG; UnPo

Blame Not My Lute, for He Must Sound. Sir Thomas Wyatt. And if perchance this sely rhyme/Do make thee blush at any time,/Blame not my lute. AAS; FCP; SiPS

Blanaid's Song. Joseph Campbell. –So her song closes! OxBI

Blancheflour and Jellyflorice. Anonymous. For ere this-day-month come and gang/My wedded wife ye'se be.' ESPB

Blanid's Song. Gordon Bottomley. Who have known the forgetting of dying to a life one lonely pain. BrPo

The Blank Book Letter. Samuel Greenberg. The earth no gain. LiTA

Blank Verse for a Fat Demanding Wife. Jim Lindsey. I don't come/every fifteen seconds. TW

The Blanket around Her. Joy Harjo. it is the whole earth TWSS

The Blanket Injun. Arthur Chapman. Dash me, partner, if I don't! BPAW

Blanket Street. Inez Hogan. Without any feet, these two little men/Climb Blanket Hill and slide down again. BiCB

The Blantyre Explosion. Anonymous. Shed a tear for the victims who're laid to their rest. OBET

A Blason. A. D. Hope. Harvester, harbinger, harrow my heaven. NOAV

The Blasphemies. Louis MacNeice. ...The sin/Against the Holy Ghost– What is it? FaBoIP

The Blasted Herb. Mesech Weare. Though thou art coveted by some,/ Who're destined to be poor. PAH

Blasting from Heaven. Philip Levine. and with no morning the day is sold. CoAP

Blaydon Races. Anonymous. Gannin alang the Scotswood Road te see the Blaydon Races. ELP

The Blazing Heart. Alice Williams Brotherton. Than stand in cool shadows by him forgot! AA

Bleak Season Was It, Turbulent and Wild. William Wordsworth. To question us, "Whence come ye, to what end?" ERoP 1-2

Bleat of Protest. Mildred Weston. Let us find/A new location. FiBHP

Bleeberrying. Jonathan Denwood. Was spent a gedderin bleeberries/Away on Kurkstan fell. MoBS

Bleecker Street. Jean Garrigue. And night comes round the corner after you... NYP; TAP

Blemishes. James Hart. where the last day's dust covers cracks. AMV-81

Blenheim. Joseph Addison. And, fill'd with England's Glory, smiles in Death. OBEC

Blenheim (excerpt). John Philips. ...and solemn sound/Of drums, o'er came their groans. NOEC

Blennerhassett's Island. Thomas Buchanan Read. Proclaims how Ruin rules with full content-/ment here. PAH

Bless, Dear Saviour, This Child. Beck. A sharer in Thy dying love,/A follower of thine. BePJ

Bless Him. Anonymous. "None like Jehovah is holy." TrJP

Bless the Blessed Morn. Horatius Bonar. Praise ye the King that comes to reign. BePJ

Bless This House. Helen Taylor. Bless this door, that it may prove/Ever open to joy and love. TreFT; TRV

Bless You, Bless You, Burnie-Bee. Anonymous. Fly to him I love the best. OxNR

Blessed... Soné. and their portion–the wordless/permanence. TrJP

Blessed and Resting Uncle. Harley Elliott. like some hawk caught/in fingers of a foreign tree. NeAC

Blessed Are They. Wilhelmina Stitch. Pleasant to live with and blessed are they. PoToHe

Blessed Are Those Who Sow and Do Not Reap. A. Ben-Yitzhak. Wrapped in a cloak of unremembrance,/Forever remaining without speech. VWA

Blessed Art Thou, O Lord. Anonymous. trouble and grief are not hid from mine/eyes/in the musing of my heart. TrJP

Blessed Assurance, Jesus Is Mine. Fanny J. Crosby. Praising my Saviour all the day long. AH

Blessed Be the Holy Will of God. Anonymous. And God's high praise sung to us,/For ever and for aye. OnYI

Blessed Comforter Divine. Lydia Sigourney. The blessings of thy grace. AH

The Blessed Damozel. Dante Gabriel Rossetti. And wept. (I heard her tears.) AnFE; AWP; BLPL; BoLiVe; DiPo; GoTL; GTBS; HBV 1-2; LiTB; LoBV; MasP; MaVP; NOBE; NOBV; NoP; OAEL 1-2; OAEP; OBEV; OBNC; OBVV; OHFP; PoEL 1-5; SeCeV; SpRo; TEP; TrGrPo; VLP; WHA

Blessed Is Everyone. Anonymous. Peace on Israel. AH

Blessed Is God. Anonymous. And the blessed shall bless the name/That is holy forever and ever. TrJP

Blessed Lord, What It Is to Be Young. David McCord. The singer, the song, and the sung. NTCP

Blessed Mary. Anonymous. Succour it from mine enemies' rage. OBSP

The Blessed Match. Hannah Senesh. Blessed the match that was burned and/ignited flames. TrJP

The Blessed Name. George Washington Bethune. We love to sing of Christ our King/And hail Him, blessed Jesus. BLRP

Blessed Nearness. Mary Bullock. And lingers like sweet fragrance in my/soul. STF

The Blessed Task. Harriet McEwen Kimball. No other service would I ask/Than this my blessed, blessed task. BePJ

The Blessed Virgin compared to the Air we Breathe. Gerard Manley Hopkins. Fold home, fast fold thy child. BrPo; ISi; MoPo; NOBV; OxBoCh; VLP

The Blessed Virgin Mary Compared to a Window. Thomas Merton. My light–the Lamb of their Apocalypse. ISi

The Blessed Virgin's Expostulation. Nahum Tate. I trust the God–but oh! I fear the child! ISi

The Blessing. Ruth Berman. Cleanliness is godliness/Said the sphinx. AMV-81

A Blessing. Mekeel McBride. and blessed in the silver lake of a coffee spoon. MAYP; SM

Blessing. Melvin Wilk. Then, before he is immersed,/he calls me by my Jewish name. VWA

The Blessing. James Wright. ...if I stepped out of my body I would break/Into blossom. AmPC; ConAP; GrPl; HeIP; InPK; InPS; LLLT; NaP; NoAm; NOBA; NoP; PPP; TwCP

Blessing a Bride and Groom: A Wedding Night Poem (parody). Robert Peters. ...unsheathes her/turpentine claws, rakes bleeding trail of sexhatred down my anus-shuddering/spine. BXAP

Blessing, and Honor. Horatius Bonar. Dying in weakness, but rising to reign. TRV

Blessing at Kellenberger Road. Maxine Kent Valian. Kellenberger Road announces itself. AMV-80

A Blessing in Disguise. John Ashbery. And then I start getting this feeling of exaltation. ANYP; PoM

Blessing Mrs. Larkin. Margery Mansfield. And see them branching, turning into trees! GoYe

The Blessing of St. Francis. Sister Maura. Trust, mercy, peace–all those who love him will/Know in their lives his triple blessing still. CaP

Blessing of the Firstborn. Howard Schwartz. Before the circle they inscribe/Becomes a full moon/At rest. VWA

Blessing of the Priests. Anonymous. The Lord incline his countenance unto/thee and give thee peace: Amen./Selah. TrJP

A Blessing on the Cows. Seumas (James Starkey) O'Sullivan. My blessing on the patient cows. BoAnP

Blessing over Food. Hayim Nahman Bialik. Blessed be He/And blest His name! YeAr

Blessing the Dance. Irwin Russell. O Mahsr! call yo' chillen soon, an' take 'em home! Amen. AnAmPo

Blessing the Hounds. Mary Winter. Today when the hunters and hounds are running. GoYe

Blessing without Company. Anonymous. Dey eats mos' all our victuals from us. BPo; PoL

Blessings. Linda Hogan. Blessed/are those who listen/when no one is left to speak. TWSS

Blessings Are. Cid Corman. Empty/receives most. GP

The Blessings of Surrender. Mary J. Helphingtine. Of my grief Thou makest glory,/Of my labor greatest gain. STF

Blessings on Doneraile. Patrick O'Kelly. To crown with peace sweet Doneraile. OnYI

The Blessings That Remain. Annie Johnson Flint. For the blessings that remain. BLRP

Blest Be the Day. Petrarch (Francesco Petrarca). And blest that thought of thoughts which is her own,/Of her, her only, of herself alone! NAWM 1-2

Blest Be the Tie That Binds. John Fawcett. And perfect love and friendship reign/Throughout eternity. HBV 1-2

Blest Be the Wondrous Grace. George Barrell Cheever. Behold thy glorious face/And count all other things but loss. AH

Blest, Blest and Happy He. Anonymous. Yet god all whole that may enjoy/Thy body as it is. BSV; GBL; GoTS

Blest Is the Man Whose Tender Breast. Abijah Davis. Or bear his willing soul aloft. AH

Blest Leaf! Whose Aromatic Gales Dispense (parody). Isaac Hawkins Browne. And let me taste thee unexcis'd by kings. BXAP; Par

Blest Retirement. Oliver Goldsmith. His Heaven commences ere the world be past! OBEC

Blest Statesman He, Whose Mind's Unselfish Will. William Wordsworth. Perilous is sweeping change, all chance unsound. VLP

Blest Winter Nights. John Armstrong. And at my table find himself at home. OBEC

Bleue Maison. Edmund Charles Blunden. And in the rifts of blue above the trees/Pass the full sails of natural Odysseys. BrPo

Blight. Arna Bontemps. But I hear the beating of dead boughs. BANP; CDC

Blight. Ralph Waldo Emerson. Chilled with a miserly comparison/Of the toy's purchase with the length of life. AmePo; AP; NOBA; NoP

Blighters. Siegfried Sassoon. And there'd be no more jokes in Music-halls/To mock the riddled corpses round Bapaume. CMoP; FaBoTw; MMM; MoVE; NoAm; OBSP

De Blin' Man Stood on de Road an' Cried. Anonymous. O, my Lord, Save-a me/De blin' man stood on de road an' cried. BoAN 1-2

Blind. John Kendrick Bangs. Is blind of soul, and cannot see! PoToHe

The Blind. Charles Baudelaire. What can we seek in Heaven, all we blind? SyP

Blind. Harry Kemp. Amid such unguessed glories–/That I am worse than blind. HBMV

Blind. Norman V. Pearce. And thank my God and do not ask for more. PoToHe

Blind Adolphus. Angela McCabe. ...Mother said, "Well, he had thirty-four good/years..." AmPA

The Blind Beggar. Anonymous. And then the blind beggar dropped five thousand more. AmFP

The Blind Beggar of Bednall (Bethnal) Green. Anonymous. The most beautiful creature that ever was seen/Was the Blind Beggar's daughter of Bethlem Green. BaBo

The Blind Boy. Colley Cibber. Whilst thus I sing, I am a king,/Although a poor blind boy. CEP; GTBS; GTBS-P; HBV 1-2; NOEC; OBEC; OxBChV; RoGo; TreFS

The Blind Boy's Pranks. William Thom. An' herds o' common men! OBEV

Blind but Happy. Fanny J. Crosby. I cannot, and I won't. TRV

Blind Date. Conrad Aiken. and we shall keep it with the keeper of the golden gates. DL; MoVE; ViBoPo

The Blind Fiddler. Anonymous. I am a blind fiddler and far from my home. FSW

Blind Geronimo. Bill Berkson. as if you had always known it would turn out that way. ANYP

The Blind Girl. Nathalia Crane. If the odor of the roses and the better things were there. MCCG

Blind Girl. William Stanley Merwin. ...and instantly her repose/Be silent and final. NePoEA-2

Blind, I Speak to the Cigarette. Joanne De Longchamps. unimaginable, the frolic of form I lack. GoYe

The Blind Leading the Blind. Lisel Mueller. There are two of us here. Touch me. IHMS

The Blind Linnet. Robert Williams Buchanan. She murmurs an old air/That she used to know! FM

Blind Louise. George Washington Dewet And morn upon her face! AA

Blind Man. Anonymous. Blin' man stood on de road an' cried. TrAS

Blind Man. Michael Hamburger. The apple that hangs unplucked, grown fabulous. NePoEA-2

The Blind Man. James Lewisohn. it finds him walking in his sleep again/balanced on his supplicating hands. LFAC

The Blind Man. Margaret E. Sangster. A hand will find us in the dark/And guide us on our way. PoToHe

The Blind Man at the Fair.   Joseph Campbell.   And darkness everywhere I go.   AnIV; AWP

The Blind Man (excerpt).   Judith Wright.   I am the voice of music and the ended dance.   CBAP

Blind Man Lay Beside the Way (with music).   *Anonymous.*   O Lord, won't you help-a me!   AS

Blind Man's Buff.   *Anonymous.*   Did you think you'd caught me?/Blind, blind man!   OxNR

Blind-Man's Buff.   William Blake.   Then laws are made to keep fair play.   WiR

The Blind Man's Regret.   *Anonymous.*   With saints and angels, there to dwell in joy and peace and love.   BFSS

The Blind Men and the Elephant.   John Godfrey Saxe.   And prate about an Elephant/Not one of them has seen!   AmePo; AnNE; BLPA; FaBoBe; FPL; GoTF; HBV 1-2; HBVY; MaC; OBCA; OnMSP; OnUR; PoToHe; StPo; TreF; WBLP

Blind Old Woman.   Clarence Major.   as she shuffles into street sounds.   PoBA

Blind Panorama of New York.   Federico Garcia Lorca.   that give on the flush of its fruits.   NYP

The Blind Psalmist.   Elizabeth Clementine Kinney   and in thy songs, find speech.   AA

Blind Samson.   William Plomer.   And stopped their grinning eyes.   PeSA

The Blind Sheep.   Randall Jarrell.   I am a Sheep, and not an Ass.   NYBP; OBAL

The Blind Singer.   Friedrich Hoelderlin.   Take from my heart this divine existence!   LiTW

Blind Steersmen.   Francis Ernest Kobina Parkes.   The salvation of the world lies in a deserted garden–/in a blind worm's crawl.   PBA

The Blinded Bird.   Thomas Hardy.   Who is divine? This bird.   AnFE; BiP; CMoP; EaLo; LiTM; NoAm

The Blinded Soldier to His Love.   Alfred Noyes.   With you, O sweetest friend,/My night shall never end.   PoPl

The Blindman.   May Swenson.   Trumpets tell me yellow. Only ebony is mute.   WeW

Blindman's Buff.   Peter Viereck.   (The lovers think of death.)   LiTM; MiAP; MoAmPo

Blindness.   Delmira Agustini.   Give me your light and hide the world from me!   PBWP

The Blindness of Samson.   John Milton.   Myself, my sepulcher, a moving grave.   LiTB

Bliss.   George Johnston.   And hear them wheeze would make a fellow wise.   NOBC

A Blith and Bonny Country Lass.   Thomas Lodge.   And thus my Roundelay is past.   ALV

The Blithe Mask.   Dollett Fuguet.   He whistled that he might not weep.   TRV

Blizzard.   Patricia Garfinkel.   ...Our voices join the birds who wait for/our eyes to freeze like berries in the face of winter.   AmC

The Blizzard Ape.   Kenneth Pitchford.   and April was german with his mating call.   CoPo

The Bloated Biggaboon.   Henry Cholmondeley-Pennell.   So he puff'd himself out in his shirt,/Like a b'loon.   NA

Block City.   Robert Louis Stevenson.   I'll always remember my town by the sea.   EyDe; NTCP; SoPo; TiPo

Blockhouse.   Olga Kirsch.   And to read the wall-script dares not turn his head.   PeSA

Blocking the Pass.   Charles Madge.   And alone, on a tall stone, stood Grant.   FaBoMo

Blocks.   Frank O'Hara.   And thus they grew like giggling fir trees.   ANYP; EAS; HaCAP

Blok Let Me Learn the Poem.   Aram Boyajian.   poems that stick like blood/closing wounds   NeAC

Blond.   Joseph De Roche.   Tilted to sleep, I am biting my lips.   HeIP

Blond Hair at the Edge of the Pavement.   Michael Smith.   What sense of importance swelled at the smack/of the stick on the dung-caked dumb flesh.   CIP

Blondel.   Clarence Urmy.   And link thy name by deathless art/With Richard of the Lion Heart!   AA; HBMV

Blood.   Ray Bremser.   gone suddenly straight beyond this blood/of our deaths.   NeAP

Blood.   Barney Bush.   winds that bite with/teeth of winter ice.   STE

The Blood.   Nina Cassian.   the lights were out and the blood/had been wiped off the table.   VWA; WPOW

Blood and the Moon.   William Butler Yeats.   Everything that is not God consumed with intel-/lectual fire.   MBW 1-2

The Blood Horse.   Barry (Bryan Waller Procter) Cornwall.   Where Balkh amidst the desert stands.   GN; HBV 1-2; PH

Blood Hound Blues.   Victoria Spivey.   But if the blood hounds ever catch me/in the 'lectric chair I'll die.   BluL

Blood Is Thicker Than Water.   Wallace Rice.   Blood is thicker, sir, than water, now as then.   PAH

The Blood-Letting.   Joy Harjo.   It does not scatter the heart,/but gathers the branches tenderly/into a slender, dark woman.   TWSS

Blood Marksman and Kureldei the Marksman.   *Anonymous.*   The valiant warrior Kureldei Mirgan/still lives in his own land.   WTO

Blood on the Saddle.   *Anonymous.*   For his bronco fell on him/And mashed in his head.   FSW

Blood on the Sails.   Phil and June Colclough.   May the blood on the sails all be fishermen's tales.   OBET

Blood Red Roses.   *Anonymous.*   Go down you blood red roses, go down.   FSW

Blood River Day.   Dennis Brutus.   the good smell of the dust/that is the same/everywhere around the earth.   WhB

Blood-Sister.   Adrienne Rich.   where survival/takes naked and fiery forms.   NoP

The Blood-Strained Banders.   *Anonymous.*   O good Shepherd, feed my sheep.   AmFP; OuSiCo

The Blood Supply in New York City Is Low.   Terry Stokes.   ...Snails are licking/the moon's full body, all the parts/we will never see.   NYP

Blood to Blood.   Alvin Aubert.   ...close to his private/parts. blood to blood.   GP

The Bloodhound.   Edward Anthony.   Folks either must avoid temptation/Or face my nasal accusation.   GDP

Bloody Bill.   D. M. Ross.   And paid for Bloody Bill.   AnNZ

The Bloody Conquests of Mighty Tamburlaine (excerpt).   Christopher Marlowe.   That this my life may be as short to me/As are the days of sweet Zenocrate.   WHA

Bloody Cranesbill on the Dunes.   E. J. Scovell.   As if they had been always known, yet could not be.   ChMP

The Bloody Injians.   *Anonymous.*   Than to fight the bloody In-ji-ans.   CoSo

Bloody Pause.   Astra.   so i shall offer up this bloody piece to her/and pause a while   BrRo

The Bloody Sire.   Robinson Jeffers.   Old violence is not too old to beget new values.   CMoP; LiTM; NePA; PoA

Bloom.   Alfred Kreymborg.   need any man be told what flowers are,/that hold a star?   HBMV

Bloom is result.   Emily Dickinson.   To be a flower is profound/Responsibility!   PoEL 1-5

Bloom Street.   Angela McCabe.   I will not remember the sound of your voice/in my hand.   AmPA

Blooming Nelly.   Robert Burns.   He vowed, he prayed, he found the maid/Forgiving all and good.   UnTE

Blooming Sally.   *Anonymous.*   While Sally shall attend to the bar.   OBET

The Blossom.   William Blake.   Pretty, pretty Robin,/Near my bosom.   CBEP; GoJo; PB; PBBP

The Blossom.   John Donne.   There to another friend, whom we shall find/As glad to have my body as my mind.   AWP; InPo; LiTB; UnPo

Blossom.   Stanley Plumly.   He spits his apple out and shoots himself in the mouth with his/finger.   GeTw

The Blossom of the Branches (excerpt).   Ruth Gilbert.   I have no richer gift/Than this, no warmer manger.   ACV

The Blossom of the Soul.   Robert Underwood Johnson.   Its sunshine, or its dew?   AA

Blossom Time.   Wilbur Larremore.   Our hearts close knit shall feel no chilling/change.   AA

Blossoms.   Frank Dempster Sherman.   They thought it best to disappear.   OBCA

The blossoms have fallen.   Princess Shikishi.   In the wide vacant sky/The spring rains are falling.   BoWoP

Blou Northerne Wynd (excerpt).   *Anonymous.*   Blou! blou! blou!   AtBAP

Blouzelinda's Funeral.   John Gay.   In ale and kisses they forget their cares,/And Susan Blouzelinda's loss repairs.   OBEC

Blow away the Morning Dew.   *Anonymous.*
Blow away the morning dew,/how sweet the winds do blow.   FSW
Oh never mind her squalling/Or the rumpling of her gown.   OBET

Blow, Boys, Blow.   *Anonymous.*   Blow, boys, blow!/Blow, my bully boys, blow!   ShS; TrAS

Blow, Bugle!   Thomas Curtis Clark.   When war and strife at last shall cease.   PGD

Blow, Bugles, Blow.   John S. McGroarty.   Sigh, breezes, sigh.   HBV 1-2

Blow, Bullies, Blow.   *Anonymous.*   Blow, my bully boys, blow!   AmSS

Blow Gabriel.   Blind Gary Davis.   Gonna meet my father   BluL

Blow High! Blow Low!   Charles Dibdin.   Blow high, blow low! let tempest tear....   HBV 1-2

Blow Me Eyes!   Wallace Irwin.   I didn't think she'd treat me so–/But, blow me eyes, she did!   HBMV; InMe; StPo

Blow, Northern Wind.   *Anonymous.*   Blow, northerne wind,/Blow, blow, blow!   GBL; OBEV; OxBM

Blow Softly, Thrush.   Joseph Russell Taylor.   Breathe it, veery thrush!   HBV 1-2

Blow the Candle Out.   *Anonymous.*   Then I will prove my indebtedness/By blowing the candle out.   FaBoBa; FSW

Blow the Candle Out (The Jolly Boatsman). *Anonymous.* They are seeking out a way/For to blow the candle out. AmFP

Blow the Fire, Blacksmith. *Anonymous.* And ne'er a smock to wear. OxNR

Blow the Man Down. *Anonymous.* Give me some time to blow the man down. ABF; AmFP; BLSo; FSW; TrAS

Blow the Winds, I-Ho. *Anonymous.* And if ever I meet another maid,/I rede that maid beware.' GBP; OxBoLi

Blow, Wind, Blow! and Go, Mill, Go. Mother Goose. And send us some hot in the morn. BrR; HBV 1-2; TiPo

Blow, Ye Winds. *Anonymous.*
     Clear away your running gear, and blow, ye winds, high-o! AmFP; AmSS; FSW
     A winding glass around we'll pass, and to hell with blubber whaling. OBSS

Blow Ye Winds Westerly. *Anonymous.* We're bound to the southward, so steady we go. FSW

The Blowflies Buzz. Djalparmiwi. ...You, Bangalawi, you, her husband, you indeed,/all by yourself, you can help her in childbirth! NOAV; WTO

Blowing Bubbles. William Allingham. Leaving but a sprinkle,/As of tears. GN

The Bludy Serk. Robert Henryson. And for his lufe that bocht us deir/Think on the BLUDY SERK! OxBoCh

Blue Alert. Eve Merriam. box it/back in? PCP

The Blue and the Gray. Francis Miles Finch. Love and tears for the Blue,/Tears and love for the Gray. AA; BLPA; BLPL; FaBoBe; GoTF; HBV 1-2; MC; PAH; PAL; PaPo; TreF; WBLP

Blue and White. Mary Elizabeth Coleridge. And both for him, so tender-true,/Him that doth love me! OBEV; OBVV

The Blue Animals. John Anderson. I saw there was no harm/at all, though you were gone. AmPA; SM

Blue Bell. *Anonymous.* He came up again and said there was/none there. OxNR

The Blue Bells of Scotland. Dorothy and Annie McVicar Jordan. But it's oh! in my heart that/I do wish he may not die. FSW; HBV 1-2; TreFS

The Blue-Bird. Herman Melville. The Bird's transfigured in the Flower. BLPL; NOBA

The Blue-Bird. Alexander Wilson. He comes to remind us of sunshine and/pleasure. AA

Blue Black. Bloke Modisane. the one, no-one/that is us all. PBA

Blue Blood. James Stephens. Was lout, son of lout, by old lout, and was da to a lout. MoAB; MoBrPo; OBMV; OxBI

Blue Bog Children. Roger Weingarten. ...whispering children/riding to burial on their father's sled. AmPA

The Blue Booby. James Tate. like the eyes of a mild savior. AmPA; EAS; NoAm; NoP

Blue Bottle. *Anonymous.* How happy we were in all those days! OuSiCo

Blue Bottle. Patricia Hampl. blue night was exposed. AMV-81

The Blue Bowl. Blanche Bane Kuder. "It's good to be at home," you said. BLPA; FaBoBe

Blue-Butterfly Day. Robert Frost. Where wheels have freshly sliced the April mire. RFM

Blue Calf. *Anonymous.* Stay a night until/Our enemy the cock shall crow. WTO

The Blue Church. Peter Balakian. turn to sky. AMV-80

The Blue Closet. William Morris. For their song ceased, and they were dead. NBM; VLP

Blue Ey'd Mary. *Anonymous.* Abnd lo! her blue eyes are now sealed in death. CoMu

Blue-Eyed Girl. *Anonymous.* "Yonder comes the ugliest thing/That ever lived or died." AmFP

Blue-Eyed Mary. Mary E. Wilkins Freeman. Blue-eyed Mary is a flower. OBCA

A blue-eyed phantom far before. Christina Georgina Rossetti. I hope I shall lie down some day,/Lie down and sleep. EG

The Blue-Eyed Precinct Worker. Henri Coulette. we have chosen the short straw. MAT

Blue Flag. Dorothy Donnelly. jewel-winged, a weld of blue fire and air. NYBP

The Blue-Flag in the Bog. Edna St. Vincent Millay. We will set it out to grow. AnAmPo

The Blue Flag (parody). Chris Miller. Let's sing and dance down Brighton Pier/And fly the skull and crossbones here. FaBoPa

Blue Fly. Joaquim M. De Assis. ...he does not know/How it was he lost his bright blue fly. TTY

The Blue-Fly. Robert Graves. Nor did the peach complain. CMoP; MoVE; NoAm

Blue Funk. Joel Oppenheimer. I wish eastern standard/time, etc. rang their changes in our hearts. NeAP

Blue Ghosts. Stanley Snaith. A smudge of blue dust on my hand. ChMP

The Blue Gift. David Perkins. The seed within the husk. NCSH

Blue Girls. John Crowe Ransom. Since she was lovelier than any of you. AmP; AnFE; APA; CMoP; GBL; GoTF; LiTA; LiTL; MoAB; MoAmPo; MoVE; NoAm; PrIm; TAP; TreFT; VGW; WeW

Blue Glass. Fleur Adcock. She turns the necklace/kindly in her fingers, and soothes the beads. FaBoWP

The Blue Heron. Theodore Goodridge Roberts. Death-still–and sudden as death. CaP; NOBC; OBCV; PeCV

Blue Heron. Don Welch. ...and his neck comes back/in indented satisfaction. GP

The Blue Hill Is My Desire. Hwang Chin-i. Never forgetting the hill, I wonder,/does the stream cry as it leaves? PBWP

Blue Hills Beneath the Haze. Charles Goodrich Whiting. But that which has no birth/Or breath within the ken/Of transitory men. AA

The Blue-Hole. Charles G. Bell. And recessive evening drowned in the ocean of stars. GrPl

Blue Homespun. Frank Oliver Call. ...then turned and looked once more/Upon her sky-blue cloth, and closed the door. CaP

The Blue Horse. Melvin Walker La Follette. We killed him with our feeble fear. NePoEA

The Blue Horses. James Philip McAuley. A sudden movement shakes the crowd/Stampeded on the hooves of fate. BoAV

Blue Horses. Ed Roberson. ...unnoticed/by her arriving immigrant bees. PoBA

Blue Horses: West Winds. Anita Endrezze-Danielson. their blue tails as whip-sharp as a March wind. STE

"Blue Is the Hero... Bill Berkson. ...the fuel/streaming down the sides, like fun in the sun, air in the air. ANYP

Blue Island Intersection. Carl Sandburg. The owl car blutters along in a sleep-walk. MoAmPo

Blue Jay. Robert Francis. Still, still the wild blue feather/brings my mild father. ELU; PCP

The Blue Jay. D. H. Lawrence. You copper-sulphate blue bird! FM

A Blue Jeaned Rock Queen in Search of Happiness... A. K. Redwing. like an unemployed idea/pretending it's a drop of rain. VoR

Blue Juniata: The Streets of Air. Malcolm Cowley. Your path shall be the empty streets of air. PoA

Blue Lantern. Cathy Song. leaving our bodies beached/but unbruised,/white and firm like shells. MAYP

The Blue Light. Tom Dent. Watch him stagger through night with the stars/In search of the blue light. APU

Blue Like Death. James Welch. the snow and you, your stalking home. CDW

Blue Mason Jars. Keith Abbott. spattered/with red rose petals. APU

Blue Max. Harvey Shapiro. Or if he hadn't just stepped out. GP

The Blue Meridian. Jean Toomer. And above our waking limbs unfurl/Spirit-torsos of exquisite strength! BALP; PoNe

Blue Moles. Sylvia Plath. ...vanishes/Easy and often as each breath. BiP; NePoEA-2

Blue Monday. *Anonymous.* "Operator, your work we don't need." AmFP

Blue Moonshine. Francis G. Stokes. Teach despairing crags to number/Blue infinities of bliss. NA

Blue Mountain. Roberta Hill. You and Blue Mountain will reach the sea. VoR

Blue Owl Song. Alfred Kittner. that lies behind night/and draws you into its silence. VWA

Blue Peter. Stanislaus Lynch. But you and I know better...'Tis good-bye to Horn and Hound. OnYI

A Blue Ribbon at Amesbury. Robert Frost. And warrant prudence in a man. NePA

Blue Ridge. Elizabeth Hodges. ...Another/shadow that will pass. AMV-81

The Blue Ridge. Harriet Monroe. Hush me, O slumbering mountains–/Send me dreams. HBMV

Blue Ridge. Ellen Bryant Voigt. like the fireflies dragging among the trees/their separate, discontinuous lanterns. MAYP

The Blue Room. Lorenz Hart. Where no one can see us dreaming. OBAL

Blue Ruth: America. Michael S. Harper. I am telling you this:/history is your own heartbeat. PoBA

Blue Sleigh. Winfield Townley Scott. ...across/The hills to time's malignant sun. MP; NePoAm

Blue Smoke. Frances Frost. The peaks will be white and the leaves be gone. SiSoSe

Blue Sparks in Dark Closets. Richard Snyder. We part and mark you, Peter, by our knowing. Psk

Blue Springs, Georgia. Ree Young. ...and/watch the snowflakes fall in her eyes. GOYP

Blue Squills. Sara Teasdale. Wound me, that I, through endless sleep,/May bear the scar of you. HBMV

The Blue Swallows. Howard Nemerov. Because the mind's eye lit the sun. BiP; NoP

Body Fished from the Seine. Gregory Corso. –A Break of camera calm. GP; SM

The Body Is Like Roots Stretching. Charles Reznikoff. which Joshua could command but for an hour. VWA

The Body Is the Victory and the Defeat of Dreams. Katrina Anghelaki-Rooke. its earth bursts like a watermelon/and it's finished. WPOW

Body of Jesus. Arthur Cleveland Coxe. Thy body and Thy precious blood. BePJ

Body of John. R. A. K. Mason. but his bones lie stark hereunder. AnNZ

The Body of Summer. Odysseus Elytis. And amid your naked vigor by the sky. LiTW

Body of the Queen. Donald Evans. Still I have you–so I am not afraid! AnAmPo

The Body Politic. Donald Hall. Man lives by love, and not by metaphor. MP; NePoEA; TwCP

Body's Freedom. Helen Neville. the body flies/within the bone. NePA

Body's Head: Head Itself. Laura Riding Gottschalk. And civilize it as well as they can. PoA

The Body's Speech. Donal, Earl of Clancarty, MacCarthy. Speak in that speech beyond reproach/The body's speech. KiLC

The Bofors A.A. Gun. Gavin Ewart. The pheasant-shooter be himself the pheasant! WaP

Bog. Leen Volwerk. and rise/up/to engulf/you. PoSH

Bog and Candle. Robert D. Fitzgerald. the putting-out of the candle in the blind man's room. CBAP

The Bog Lands. William A. Byrne. Where, wondering at the grace of sleep,/The Guardian Angels stand. AnIV

Bogac Ban. Darrell Figgis. The white, strange road thro' Bogac Ban. AnIV

Bogey. Lee L. Berkson. "here's looking at you, kid." AMV-81

Boggy Creek. Anonymous. To the God-forsaken country they call New Mexico. CoSo

Bogland. Seamus Heaney. The wet centre is bottomless. FaBoIP; IPY; NOBI; NoP

The Bogus-Boo. James Reeves. He has no bite/And very little bark. AmMo

La Boheme. Dick Gallup. To Mrs. something Swopes/Dead at 77. ANYP

Bohemia. Dorothy Parker. God, for a man that solicits insurance! CrMA; NAMP; NLV

The Bohemian Hymn. Ralph Waldo Emerson. Nor hymn, nor prayer, nor church. WGRP

The Bohemians. Ivor Gurney. In Artois or Picardy they lie–free of useless fashions. MMM

Bohernabreena. Leslie Daiken. but a last wildrose tells a beautiful lie/to the frost-bitten earth and funereal sky. OnYI

A Boisterous Poem about Poetry (excerpt). John Wain. So, no more talk of funerals. Begin! PP

Bold Adventures of Captain Ross. Anonymous. And they gave him three cheers in a bumper,/Drank to trade and to commerce in wine. OBSS

A Bold Dragoon. Anonymous.
And devil a cat for Monday./Oh Monday, oh Monday.' OBET
So send it to Victoria that wears the British crown. OBET

The Bold Fenian Men. Anonymous. Must out and make way for the bold Fenian Men! FSW

The Bold Fisherman. Anonymous. And now she's got her fisherman/To row her down the sea. BaBo

Bold General Wolfe. Anonymous. And they will fight for evermore.' OBET

Bold Jack Donahue. Anonymous. And scorn to live in slavery bound down by iron chains. AmFP; FSW

Bold Manning. Anonymous. When the jolly, jolly grog is flowing,/Light falls. ShS

The Bold Pedlar and Robin Hood. Anonymous. They went to a tavern, and there they/dined,/And bottles cracked most merrilie. AmFP; BaBo; ESPB

Bold Phelim Brady, the Bard of Armagh. Anonymous. Then forget Phelim Brady, the Bard of Armagh. OnYI

The Bold Princess Royal. Anonymous.
For the bold Princess Royal from the pirate sailed away! ShS
For while we've got sea room, bold lads, never fear.' OBSS

Bold Rangers. Anonymous. Just through the woods we'll run, brave boys,/Just through the woods we'll run. BFSS

Bold Reynard the Fox. Anonymous. And drink my lord's health in good wine. OBET

Bold Robert Emmet. Tom Maguire. I'll lay down my life for the Emerald Isle. OnYI

The Bold Soldier. Anonymous. Not because he loved them, but only through fear. FSW

Bold Troubleshooters. Peter Veale. For 'er Majesty's bold troubleshooters is flyin' to sort out the mess. NOBL

Boldness in Love. Thomas Carew. Thy Celia shall receive those charms/With open ears, and with unfolded arms. AnAnS 2; CaPo; ErPo; MePo; SeCV 1-2; UnTE

The Boll Weevil Song. Anonymous. A-lookin'for a home, a-lookin'for a home. AS; BLSo

Bologna, and Byron. Samuel Rogers. All was enjoyment. Not a cloud obscured/Present or future. OBRV

Bolsum Brown (with music). Anonymous. There's a red light on the track for Bolsum Brown. AS

The Bomb Disposal. Ciaran Carson. ...noting the boarded windows,/the drawn blinds. CIP

Bombardment. Richard Aldington. ...white clouds moved in silent lines/Across the untroubled blue. MMM

Bombardment. D. H. Lawrence. It curves in a rush to the heart of the vast/Flower: the day has begun. MMM

The Bombardment of Bristol. Anonymous. And all their firing and their racket/Shot off the topmast of a packet. PAH

The Bomber. Robert Lowell. And Christ gave up the Ghost? WaaP

The Bomber. Brian Vrepont. The bomber roared over their dream. BoAV; NOAV

Bombers. C. Day-Lewis. And haunt the houses you never built? CMoP; MoAB

Bombing Casualties: Spain. Sir Herbert Read. extinct in the dry morning air. PPON

A Bon Mot. Anonymous. "Tho' shortest the day is–the night, sir, is longest." PoL

Bona de Mortuis. Thomas Lovell Beddoes. ...and speckled hatreds hide/Like toads among them. ELU; TW

Bonac. John Hall Wheelock. With all its waters, all its warring waves. MoVE

Bone China. R. P. Lister. Or drink rice wine by moonlight with my former. NYBP

Bone Poem. Nancy Willard. You are flying home. HoAn

The Bone That Has No Marrow. Emily Dickinson. Old Nicodemus' Phantom/Confronting us again! AmePo; TAP

Bone Thoughts on a Dry Day. George Starbuck. Here, a dark sea speaks with white hands. GoYe; MP; TwCP

Bone Yard. Jim Barnes. when humped clouds/crowd low against the ground. CDW

Bones. Walter De La Mare. And with his parcel 'neath his arm/He slowly moved away. FiBHP; ShM

The Bones. William Stanley Merwin. They extend farther than a man can see. ConAP; LiTM; NePoEA-2

Bones. Frederick Morgan. another meaning is coming, wait and see. FAZ

Bones. Carl Sandburg. Sling me...under the sea. MOS

Bones in the Desert. Ned White. For the desert keeps her secrets,/When she has claimed her own. BPAW

Bones of a French Lady in a Museum. Richard Gillman. Now are not her, but especially hers. NePoAm

The Bones of Chuang Tzu. Chang Heng. Poured my hot tears upon the margin of the road. AtBAP; AWP

The Bones of Incontention. Robert David Cohen. Why do you remain outdoors? NYBP

Boney Was a Warrior. Anonymous. Boney broke his heart and died./John Franswah! FSW

The Bonfire. Robert Frost. The best way is to come up hill with me/And have our fire and laugh and be afraid.' InvP

Bonfire of Kings. Donald Evans. All men are equal. Dupes of democracy! AnAmPo

The Bongaloo. Spike Milligan. Do you think that I'd tell you a lie? AmMo

The Bonhomme Richard and Serapis. Philip Freneau. They trembled and ador'd. PAH

Bonnard: A Novel. Richard Howard. Once home, we shall have a little supper of Lucie's fresh-/picked morels. CoAP; NYBP

Bonne Entente. F. R. Scott. DEEP APPLE PIE/TARTE AUX POMMES PROFONDES. FiBHP; OBCV; PeCV

Bonner's Ferry. Peter Schjeldahl. But there is always at least one germ around/O mortals. ANYP

Bonner's Ferry Beggar. Duane Clark. No,/says the closing door. AMV-81

Bonnets So Blue. Anonymous. For dearly do I love his sweet bonnet so blue. OBET

Bonnie Annie (A version). Anonymous. He made his love a coffin of the gowd/sae yellow,/And buried his bonnie love doun in a/sea valley. ESPB

Bonnie Annie (B version). Anonymous. They made her a coffin o the gowd sae/yellow,/And buried her deep on the high banks/o Yarrow. ESPB

Bonnie Annie Livieston. Anonymous. And a' that ere the same did see/Knew they had true lovers been. OxBB

The Bonnie Banks O Fordie (A vers.). Anonymous. He's taken out his wee pen-knife,/And he's twyned himsel o his ain sweet life. BaBo; BuBa

The Bonnie Banks O Fordie (B vers.). *Anonymous.* So she took his life and laid it by,/To keep her sisters compan-eye. BaBo; BuBa

Bonnie Barbara Allen (C vers.). *Anonymous.* They were buried on Easter Monday. BaBo

Bonnie Black Bess. *Anonymous.* Now, farewell forever,/My Bonnie Black Bess. BFSS; BPAW; CoSo

The Bonnie Blue Flag. Annie Chambers Ketchum. The gazing world afar/ Shall greet with shouts the Bonnie Blue/Flag/That bears the cross and star! PAH

The Bonnie Blue Flag. Harry Macarthy. Hurrah! for the Bonnie Blue Flag that bears a Single Star! BLSo; PSoN

The Bonnie Broukit Bairn. Hugh (Christopher Murray Grieve) MacDiarmid. The haill clanjamfrie! FaBoCh; GoTS; HAP; InPS; PAI

The Bonnie Cravat. Mother Goose. I've tied it so often, I'll tie it no more. BrR

The Bonnie Earl of Moray. *Anonymous.* Ere she see the Earl of Moray/ Come sounding thro' the toun. AnFE; ESPB; FaBoCh; FSW; LoGBV; OBS

Bonnie George Campbell. *Anonymous.* Toom hame cam the saddle,/But never cam he. AmFP; AWP; BoLiVe; CH; ELP; EnLit; EnRP; FaBoBa; GBP; HBV 1-2; InPo; NoP; OxBB

The Bonnie House of Airlie. *Anonymous.* But though I had an hundred mair,/I'd gie them a' to King Charlie. BaBo; ESPB; OBEV; OxBB; OxBS

Bonnie James Campbell. *Anonymous.*
My barn is to build,/and my babe is unborn.' ESPB
My corn's unshorn,/my meadow grows green.' ESPB
Oh, hame cam his guid horse,/but never cam he! ESPB

The Bonnie Laddie's Lang a-Growin'. *Anonymous.* And that pit an end tae his grouwin'. OxBS

Bonnie Lesley. Robert Burns. There's nane again sae bonnie! AtBAP; CTC; GTBS; GTBS-P; NOBE; OBEC; OBEV

The Bonnie Ship the Diamond. *Anonymous.* For the bonnie ship the Diamond,/Goes a-fishing for the whale. FSW

Bonnie Wee Thing. Robert Burns. I wad wear thee in my bosom,/Lest my jewel I should tine. HBV 1-2

The Bonniest Bairn in a' the Warl'. Robert Ford. Bonniest bairn in a' the warl'. GN

Bonny at Morn. *Anonymous.* (Thou's ower lang in thy bed),/Bonny at morn. GBP

Bonny Baby Livingston (A version). *Anonymous.* You've lettn your bride be stown frae/you,/For a' your armed men.' BaBo; ESPB

Bonny Barbara Allan. *Anonymous.* Since my love died for me today,/I'll die for him tomorrow. BiP; BoLiVe; EnLit; InPK; LiTL; TrGrPo

Bonny Barbara Allen (B vers.). *Anonymous.* There they twined in a true-lover's knot,/For all true lovers to admire. BaBo

Bonny Bee Hom. *Anonymous.* So their twa souls flew up to heaven,/And there shall ever remain. BaBo; ESPB

The Bonny Birdy. *Anonymous.* An I hope ilk ane sal sae be servd/That treats ane honest man sae. ESPB

The Bonny Bunch of Roses. *Anonymous.* The name of young Napoleon will enshrine the Bonny Bunch of/Roses, O.' OxBoLi

The Bonny Earl of Livingston. *Anonymous.* For ye will be married ere this day week/Tho' the same death you should die. OxBB

The Bonny Earl of Murray (A vers.). *Anonymous.* Eer she see the Earl of Murray/Come sounding thro the town! BaBo

The Bonny Earl of Murray (B vers.). *Anonymous.* Ere you in Dinnybristle town/Will daurna to be seen. BaBo

Bonny Eloise. J.R. and Elliot. C. W. Thomas. The belle of the Mohawk Vale. FSW

Bonny George Campbell. *Anonymous.* O hame cam' his gude horse,/But never cam' he! BSV; GoTS; OxBoLi; PoPle; ViBoPo

The Bonny Grey. *Anonymous.* And away we went with our bonny grey. GBP

The Bonny Harvest Moon. John Barr. May grateful hearts rejoice to see/ The bonny harvest moon. AnNZ

The Bonny Hind. *Anonymous.* Ye'll think na mair o your bonny/hyn/ Beneath the hollin tree.' ESPB; OxBB; ViBoFo

Bonny John Seton. *Anonymous.* There's not a man in Highland dress/Can face the cannon's fire. BaBo; ESPB

The Bonny Keel Laddie. *Anonymous.* And brings the white money to me O. GBP

Bonny Kilmeny Gaed up the Glen. James Hogg. Late, late in a gloamin' Kilmeny came hame! BSV; GoTS

The Bonny Lass of Anglesey. *Anonymous.*
But before 't was ten o'clock at night/He gaed it oer as shamefully. ESPB
He danc'd full fast, but tired at last,/And gae it up as shamefullie. ESPB

Bonny Lassie O! John Clare. Bonny lassie O! CH

Bonny Lizie Baillie. *Anonymous.* O fare you well, my mother dear,/I leave you all compleatly. BaBo; ESPB

The Bonny Moorhen. *Anonymous.* To break the wing o' my bonny moorhen. GBP

Bonum Est Mihi Quod Humiliasti Me. Henry Howard, Earl of Surrey. To spill that blood that hath so oft been shed/For Britain's sake, alas, and now is dead! SiPS

Bonus. Archie Randolph Ammons. the hemlocks, muffled,/deepen to the grim/taking of a further beauty on. HaCAP

Bony. Simon J. Ortiz. We loved it without question,/its history and ours. CDW

Boogie with O. O. Gabugah. Al Young. ...he chooses to dictate his poems/ through me rather than write them down himself. NPGG

Boogie-Woogie Ballads. St. Clair McKelway. And let's dig a place in de col', col' groun'/For Mr. and Mrs. Massa! PoNe

The Book. William Carson Fagg. They have not forgotten/even if I did. LFAC

The Book. Winfred Ernest Garrison. I shall work better all my other days. TRV

A Book. Hannah More. And no monarch alive has so many pages. PoSC

A Book. Lizette Woodworth Reese. A book/May be a staff, a crook. YeAr

The Book. Henry Vaughan. Give him amongst thy works a place,/Who in them lov'd and sought thy face! JCP; SeCV 1-2

The Book-Burning Pit. Lo Yin. Would he tell us: Odes and Documents must live to win/men? GLGT

The Book I Held Grew Cold. Ernst Toller. And over all/My pair of swallows. TrJP

Book-Lender's Lament. *Anonymous.* For as they have not found me Gay,/ They have not left me Sterne. FaBoUs

Book-Moth. *Anonymous.* ;and the thieving guest/Was no whit the wiser for the words it ate. AnOE

The Book of Books. Sir Walter Scott. But better had they ne'er been born/ That read to doubt or read to scorn. GoTF; TreFT

The Book of Day-Dreams. Charles Leonard Moore.
Fear now no thing but immortality. AA
Nor immortality immortal is. AA
One still at heart, that so thyself beguilest. AA
Speak, O dim traveller, speak: thy host/believes! AA
Thou mayst control her limbs, but not begin/To know what planet rules the tides within. AA

The Book of God's Madness. Ralph Chubb. And he made answer on high, "Is any here/Of fuller being than I? I'll bow to him!" PeHV

The Book of Hours (excerpt). Rainer Maria Rilke. So does Thy Realm, my God, around me rise. CAW

The Book of Hours of Sister Clotilde. Amy Lowell. And treasured therein/ A dried snake-skin. APA

The Book of How. Merrill Moore. Eternally distant and luminous in the air. MoAmPo

The Book of Job and a Draft of a Poem to Praise the Paths... George Oppen. toys of the children wings/of the wasp. NNaP

The Book of Juniper. Tom Paulin. the bandaged elm,/and the jolly jolly chestnut. FaBoIP

The Book of Kells. Padraic Colum. To stay the violence of the entering Word! BIrV

The Book of Kells. Howard Nemerov. Out of the living word/Come flower, serpent and bird. EaLo

The Book of Lies. James Tate. ...Can you believe/that? I give you my word. SM

The Book of Merlin. Jack Spicer. I say there will be no fruit in Britain for seven years unless/something happens. CoPo

A Book of Music. Jack Spicer. Poetry ends like a rope. PoM

The Book of Mysteries. Anthony Barnett. I formed you, the anger and the nothing that would/hold you; I, on you, hold. VWA

The Book of Nightmares. Galway Kinnell.
...even if it is the book of nightmares. NNaP
even these feathers freed from their wings forever/are afraid. NNaP
in all the windows/of stone. NNaP
...se if you can find/the one flea which is laughing. NNaP

The Book of Percival. Jack Spicer. "Fool," they sang in voices more like angels watching/"Fool." CoPo

The Book of Persephone. Robert Kelly. comfort in the steady sun, time beating down. PoM

The Book of Pilgrimage. Rainer Maria Rilke. Which, as the years pass by me,/All soundlessly unfold. ILwL

Book of the Dead, Prayer 14. Mei-Mei Berssenbrugge. Try to stay awake. GP

The Book of the Duchess. Geoffrey Chaucer. The wonders that I dreamed that night. WHA

The Book of the Duchesse. Geoffrey Chaucer. Ne in al the welkin was a cloude. FiP

The Book of the People. Robert de Lamennais. ...as thick mists gathered upon the horizon/vanish at the rising of the sun. PGD

The Book of the World. William, of Hawthornden Drummond. It is some picture on the margin wrought. HBV 1-2

The Book of Thel. William Blake. Fled back unhinder'd till she came into the vales of Har. CEP; ERoP 1-2; LAuP; NoP; OAEL 1-2; OBNC; PoEL 1-5; TEP

The Book of True Love (excerpt). Juan, Archpriest of Hita, Ruiz. Take from the lady what you yearn for every time you/can.... ErPo

The Book of Two Married Women and the Widow. William Dunbar. This is the legeand of my lif, thought Latine it be/nane. PoEL 1-5

A Book of Verses. Mordecai Marcus. that widens to meet an opening world? AMV-80

The Book of Wild Flowers. Joseph Ceravolo. against the knoll. ANYP

The Book of Wisdom. Stephen Crane. Strange that I should have grown so sud-/denly blind. HoPM; MoAmPo

The Book Our Mothers Read. John Greenleaf Whittier. To find that all the sages said/Is in the Book our mothers read. BLRP; TRV

Book Review. Russell Davies. Not all the cream is clotted. FaBoEE

The Book Rises Out of the Fire. Edmond Jabes. But the order of summits,/the order of ruins,/is wedding gladness. VWA

Booker T. and W. E. B. Dudley Randall. "I don't agree,"/Said W. E. B. BP; NoAm

Bookra. Charles Dudley Warner. Panic and war postponed another day. AA; HBV 1-2

Books. William Baer. from so many different and interesting/points of view AMV-81

Books. George Crabbe. And half our Judges are our Rivals too. OBEC

Books. Eleanor Farjeon. Books hold all things for their lovers. YeAr

Books Are Keys. Emilie Poulsson. Books are friends. Come let us read. SiSoSe

Books Fall Open. David McCord. who hanker for/a book to read. OBCA

A Bookshop Idyll. Kingsley Amis. And couldn't write. NePoEA

The Bookworm. Walter De la Mare. I'm tried of books," said Jack. TiPo

The Bookworms. Robert Burns. And spare his golden bindings! ELU; FiBHP

Boolee, the Bringer of Life. Mary Gilmore. Out of the whirlwind I came. BoAV

Boom! Howard Nemerov. Miss Universe, for Thy Name's Sake, Amen. LiTM; MP; NIP; NLV

Boom. Julian Lee Rayford. speaking when you touch me. AMV-80

Boomer Johnson. Henry Herbert Knibbs. It's where they ain't no matches and they don't need kerosene. BPAW

Boomerang. William Hart-Smith. and, afraid of the gift of sudden blood,/beats back to his hand and melts once more to wood. NOAV

The Boomerang. Carrie May Nichols. And the sun will shine through the whole glad day. PoToHe

Boomerang. John Perreault. I throw away my life/and my life comes back. ANYP; EAS

A Boon. William Meredith. The risk itself cries out to be possessed. NePoEA

Boosting the Booster. Anonymous. If you'd make your city better/Boost it to the final letter. WBLP

Booth Killed Lincoln. Anonymous. "Of all the actors in this town, I loved Wilkes Booth the best." AmFP; OFD

The Boothbay Whale. Anonymous. Now step right up and take a little swig/and you'll soon see a Boothbay whale. FSW

Bootie Black and the Seven Giants All Sipping Chili... Mike Cook. Yes, you must go. JB

Boots. Rudyard Kipling. An' there's no discharge in the war! BLPA; FaPoR; FPL; MoBrPo; WHA

Boots and Saddles. Nicolas Saboly. Boots and saddles, mount and ride. OHIP

Booze Turns Men into Women. Bernadette Mayer. A glass of Schaeffer'll/Make your kid a general. APU

Bop Lyrics. Allen Ginsberg. I'm so lucky to be nutty. OBAL

Bordello. Lewis Turco.
...and I find/in the flesh a little peace of mind. SM
In this dark place I am still with God. SM

Bordello, Revisited. Eve Triem. the children need Prang paints, tablets,/spelling books. GP

A Border Ballad (parody). Thomas Love Peacock. And the true meed of conquest our minstrels shall fix/On the promise to pay of our Willimondswicks. BXAP

A Border Burn. J.B. Selkirk. The picter's deed, and this is leevin'. PoSH

A Border Forecast. William Landles. Was wringin oot his socks and sark/Wi wry thochts o the dyker! PoSH

Border Line. Langston Hughes. I think the distance/Is nowhere. PoCh

Border River. Alfred Goldsworthy Bailey. that hands could seize and quicken together and hold forever. CaP

Bordering Manuscript. James Applewhite. ...she waits in her surface, her name my speech's/mistress. PoA

Borderline Ballad. Richard Weber. And tell me then if you'll not find/The whole lot's back in quantity. PPON

The Bore. Horace. A mob collects: thank Phoebus, I am freed. ATP; EnLi 1-2

Bored. Horatio Brown. I liked their footman, John, the best. PeHV

The Bored Mirror. Syuichi Nagayasu. I guess I'll sleep now. LiTW

Borges. Willis Barnstone. ...You are a fraud/and friend, a haunting light and lonely lord. AMV-80

Born Again. Forugh Farrokhzad. dying at night of a kiss/and by a kiss reborn each day PBWP

Born Was the Island. Anonymous. Hawaii appeared an island. WTO

Born Without a Chance. Edmund Vance Cooke. "Poor little devil! born without a chance!" BLPA

Born Yesterday. Philip Larkin. Catching of happiness is called. HaMV; NAs

The Borough. George Crabbe.
And give a sadness to serenity. OBRV
And, sparing Criminals, attack the Crime. CTC
Pearl-shells and rubied star-fish they admire,/And will arrange above the parlour-fire. FaBoPP
Where all presented to the eye or ear/Oppress'd the soul with misery, grief, and fear. FaBoPP; OBRV
Which some strong tide had roll'd upon the place. OBRV

Borrowed. Anonymous. They rightly were mine–instead. BLRP

The Borrowed Child. Howard Weeden. It teches 'em so light–one's still/A gal at forty year! AA

The Borrowing Days. Anonymous. The silly poor hoggs came hirpling hame. GBP

Bos'n Hill. John Albee. There's one amongst them shall not fail/To join the Bos'n's Crew. AA

The Bosky Steer. Henry Herbert Knibbs. "Back, hell, nothin'! There's a bear in here!" BPAW

The Boss. James Russell Lowell. Who sure intended him to stretch a rope. OBAL; SaC

The Boss Machine-Tender after Losing a Son. Paul Corrigan. lies the night he shut down/machine number nine/to pull out his boy. AMV-81

The Boss's Wife. Anonymous. She dropped the light and she fainted quite,/'Twas Chin-ti, the Chinese cook! CBAP

Boston. John Collins Bossidy. And the Lowells speak only to God. AmFN; FaBoCo; NLV; OBAL; OxBoLi

Boston. Ralph Waldo Emerson. Till Freedom cheered and joy-bells rung... MC

Boston. John Boyle O'Reilly. Let us show that twice-sent desolation/On every true heart in the nation/Has conquest achieved. PAH

A Boston Ballad. Walt Whitman. You are mighty cute–and here is one of your bargains. OBAL

The Boston Burglar. Anonymous.
Adieu to all bad company! adieu to all bad rum! AmFP; ViBoFo
A-serving out my twenty-one years in the penitentiary. CoSo; FSW

Boston Charlie. Walt Kelly. Boola boola Pensacoola hullabaloo! FiBHP; GoJo

The Boston Evening Transcript. Thomas Stearns Eliot. And I say, "Cousin Harriet, here is the Boston Evening Transcript." InPK; NePA

Boston Hymn. Ralph Waldo Emerson. My thunderbolt has eyes to see/His way home to the mark. AnNE; LaNeLa; MC; PAH; PAL; TRV; WGRP

Boston in Distress. Anonymous. Nor be one brother by the other slain. NOEC

Boston, Lincolnshire. Anonymous. And a coast as souls are lost on. FaBoPP; GBP

A Boston Toast. John Collins Bossidy. And the Cabots talk only to God. BLPA; YaD

Bosworth Field: Richard III's Speech. Sir John Beaumont. But most with murmur sigh "God save the King'. JCP

The Botanic Garden. Erasmus Darwin. And armies shrink beneath the shadowy cloud. NOEC

The Botanist's Vision. Sydney Thomas Dobell. And all the living world and all the dead/Began a march which did not end at morn. VLP

Botany Bay. Anonymous.
I'll shun all evil company,/Bid adieu to Botany Bay. ViBoFo
Or you'll meet us in Botany Bay. PoAu 1-2
Too-ral li Roo-lal li Lay! FSW

Botany Bay. John Freeth. Be sent to the bottom of Botany Bay. NOEC

Botany Lesson. F. D. Reeve. the rest bend low in the wind–the slaves. AMV-80

Both Less and More. Richard Watson Dixon. And not far off was the churchyard gate. LoBV

Both My Child. Teitoku. Stood on their feet/This very morning. OFD

Both My Grandmothers. Edward Field. I won't ever forget you again. Str

The Bothie of Tober-na-Vuolich. Arthur Hugh Clough.
And the Antipodes too have a Bothie of/Tober-na-vuolich. VLP
Here into pure green depth drop down from lofty ledges. BoNaP
Holding it, not for enjoyment, but simply because we are in/it. FaBoPV
I who had never once thought a thing,–/in my ignorant Highlands. VLP

See by the loch-side ye come to the Bothie of Tober-na-/vuolich. FaBoPV

Bothwell Bridge. *Anonymous.* But lang we'll mind, and sair we'll rue,/The bloody battle of Bothwell Hill. BaBo; ESPB

The Botticellian Trees. William Carlos Williams. above the muffled words– AmP; AmPP; LiTA

The Bottle. Walter De la Mare. ...the watched, the unshared–/Awaiting me–I! MoPo

The Bottle. Al Levine. And it stings on the way down. GrPl

The Bottle of Chianti. Raymond Souster. unashamed/shivering deliciously ELU

Bottle Should Be Plainly Labeled Poison. Sara Henderson Hay. The man who takes it to forget/Must know how little will suffice. GoYe

Bottle Up and Go. *Anonymous.* All you high power women, all got to bottle up and go. FSW

Bottled. Helene Johnson. But inside–/Gee, that poor shine! BlSi; CDC; GoSl; PoBA

Bottom's Dream. Philip Dow. We claim the ordinary Good and in the name of Love love to be cruel. NPGG

Boudoir Lament. Yu Hsuan-chi. Only the sound of washboards through silk curtains. BoWoP

Bought. Francis Douglas Davison. in thoughts' weave rest unrest. NeBP

A Bought Embrace. G. S. Fraser. ...I/Lightly with dry lips brush your placid neck. WaP

Bought Locks. Martial (Marcus Valerius Martialis). For I know where she bought it. AWP; LiTW

Boulder Dam. May Sarton. And when we are all dead, this dam will stand and give. SaC

Bounce Buckram. *Anonymous.* But when it's gone it's never near. OxNR

Bouncing Ball. Sara Ruth Watson. And empty all its store of rain/On me, our house, and you. SoPo

Bound. Theodore Roethke. You are a bird denied, the blood/Of earth in flying attitude. PoA

Bound down to Newfoundland. *Anonymous.* Bound down to Newfoundland. ShS

Bound No'th Blues. Langston Hughes. These Mississippi towns ain't/Fit fer a hoppin' toad. AmNP; BiP

Boundaries. Carrol B. Fleming. Inheriting not only ocean/Blood, but also bone. SUW

Boundaries. Roberta Spear. a bud in the shadows/kissing its way/into this world. MAYP

Bounty. Josephine Miles. And Purcell is the man whose shore it is. NoAm

The Bounty of Jehovah Praise. George Sandys. For from the King of Kings/Eternal mercy springs. AH

The Bounty of Our Age. Henry Farley. But unto any pious motion/There's little coin and less devotion. FaBoCh

A Bouquet for Jerry Ford. Mordecai Marcus. Jimmy doesn't understand much of it either. SOTS

Bouquet in Dog Time. Hayden Carruth. ...all so true/like a bit of yarrow and of rue. GrPl

Bouquet of Belle Scavoir. Wallace Stevens. Someone before him to see and to know. MoAB; MoAmPo

Bouquets. Robert Francis. ...I want/to hear what it is saying. DFF; GP

Bourbons. Walter Savage Landor. Though I may but trail a verse/Languider than Lamartine's. OBSV

The Bourgeois Poet–67. Karl Shapiro. ...Parents like the word "aver"/though they don't use it. PP

The Bourgeois Poet–7. Karl Shapiro. ...neat as a child's football lying under the/tree, waiting for whose hands to pick it up. PP

The Bourne. Christina Georgina Rossetti. There a very little girth/Can hold round what once the earth/Seemed too narrow to contain. ELP; HBV 1-2; LoBV; NOBV; OBNC

Bout with Burning. Vassar Miller. Have waked marooned upon the coast of morning. LiTM; MoAmPo; NePoEA

Bouzouki. Kenneth O. Hanson. Every day a new landscape/and the heart, peeled like an onion. GP

Bow Down, Mountain. Norma Farber. While the prayerfulling miracle is given: Starry skies, arise! AH

Bow Down Your Head and Cry. *Anonymous.* Stop thinking of the girl you love,/Bow down your head and cry. CoSo; WTO

Bow-Wow, Says the Dog. *Anonymous.* And what cuckoos say you know. OxNR

Bow, Wow, Wow! Mother Goose. Little Tommy Tinker's dog./Bow, wow, wow! TiPo

The Bower of Bliss. Edmund Spenser. The gentle warbling wind low answered to all. CH; LoBV; UnS

The Bower of Peace. Robert Southey. Rest in the bower of Peace. MC; PAH

The Bowery. Charles Hale Hoyt. The Bowery! The Bowery! I'll never go there anymore! FSN; GoTF; TreF

Bowery. David Ignatow. We who live on charity enjoy the pleasure/of your wealth, the long hours filled/with drunkenness. CTBA

The Bowge of Courte. John Skelton. Now constrewe ye what is the resydewe. AAS

A Bowl of Roses. William Ernest Henley. O, was it you? EnLi 1-2; MoBrPo

Bowling Green. *Anonymous.* Hey, good old Bowling Green. FSW

The Bowling-Green (excerpt). William Somervile. In thick mundungus clouds he hides his head. NOEC

A Box for Tom. James Tate. which were covered with doglime,/angel hair and bad news. FiCP

The Boxcar Poem. David Young. ...a crow/on either shoulder. AmPA

Boxcars. Diane Keating. Boxes of fallen stars/shunt along the track/that shines before us. CaPN

Boxer. Joseph P. Clancy. And leave, a tired workman going home,/Who carved a marble image on the air. SD

Boxer Loses Face and Fortune. Lucilius [(or Lucillius)]. and swore he belonged to somebody else. LiSp

Boxer Shorts Named Champion. Melvin Douglass Brown. whispering/you fool/you fool/you fool. LFAC

The Boxer Turned Bartender. Gary Allan Kizer. Both of us hearing/The roar of our dreams. LFAC

A Boy. John Ashbery. The observer, the mincing flag. An unendurable age. NeAP

The Boy. Eugene Field. His rubber boots are full of feet/and his tippet full of ears. NA

The Boy Actor. Noel Coward. I never learned to bat or bowl/But I heard the curtain going up. OxBTC

The Boy and the Flute. Bjornstjerne Bjornson. Yet all other music is poor and thin/By the side of this which thou never shalt win! AWP; PoPl

The Boy and the Geese. Padraic Fiacc. I would rather have geese for their mystery. NeIP

The Boy and the Lantern (excerpt). Evaristo Ribera Chevremont. his miraculous lantern will shine,/effulgent forever. InW

The Boy and the Mantle. *Anonymous.* Euerye such a louely ladye,/God send her well to speede! BaBo; ESPB; OxBB; UnTE

The Boy and the Parrot. John Hookham Frere. That is the thing that I should do/If I had little hands like you.' OxBChV

The Boy and the Snake. Charles and Mary Lamb. Then lightly tripping, ran away. OxBChV

Boy and the Wandering Recluse. Al Robles. The snow is still thick around/Your bamboo flute. BrSi

The Boy and the Wolf. Aesop. Liars are not believed, forsooth,/Even when liars tell the truth. MaC

The Boy and the Wolf. John Hookham Frere. But you yourself would be to blame. HBV 1-2; HBVY

Boy at a Certain Age. Robert Francis. From chin to toe smooth as a pebble. DFF

Boy at Target Practice: A Contemplation. W. R. Moses. Not you or I or the wisest man of us/Can live with them. But aren't they marvellous? NYBP

Boy at the Window. Richard Wilbur. Such warmth, such light, such love, and so much fear. NoP

Boy Blue. *Anonymous.* For if I do,/He's sure to cry. OxNR

Boy Breaking Glass. Gwendolyn Brooks. A hymn, a snare, and an exceeding sun. NoAm; NoP

Boy! Bring an Ounce of Freeman's Best (parody). Isaac Hawkins Browne. Britons, if undone, can go,/Where tobacco loves to grow. BXAP; Par

Boy Brittan. Forceythe Willson. My darling, thou shalt rest! MC; PAH

The Boy Fishing. E. J. Scovell. Safe in my jar. I shall have ten more yet. FaBoWP; HaMV

A Boy He Had an Auger (with music). *Anonymous.* (And the G is silent as in "Fish.") AS

Boy in Ice. Laurie Lee. Thus frozen shall we ever stay/Locked in this paradise. NYBP

Boy in the Lamont Poetry Room, Harvard. D. G. Jones. Like so many cows, Chagall's, in a shaken world? PeCV

Boy in the Roman Zoo. Archibald MacLeish. ...he'll run/toward the flamingos in the sun. NCSH

Boy-Man. Karl Shapiro. Establish them, that values may go on. NYBP; SoSe

The Boy; or, Son of Rip-Off (parody). Malcolm Glass. you motherfucking SAVAGE! BXAP

Boy Playing an Organ. Francis Sweeney. Builds his battlements of music up/Amid a falling world. GoBC

Boy Remembers in the Field. Raymond Knister. Soil glistens, the furrow rolls, sleet shifts, brightens. CaP; NOBC

Boy Riding Forward Backward. Robert Francis. The last trees take them. LCAP; NePoAm-2

Boy's Day. Ruth Evelyn Henderson. On phantom feet/He rushed into slumber. BiCB

A Boy's Mother. James Whitcomb Riley. An' I hug her, an' hug my Pa/An' love him purt'nigh much as Ma. HBVY; OHIP

A Boy's Need. Herbert Clark Johnson. And dream of being men–and boys should dream. PoNe

A Boy's Prayer. Henry Charles Beeching. Take the thanks of a boy. GN

A Boy's Song. James Hogg. That"s the way for Billy and me. BSV; CH; FaPoR; HBV 1-2; HBVY; MoShBr; OBEV; OnUR; OxBChV; PoPle; WiR

A Boy's Summer Song. Paul Laurence Dunbar. What's so fine as being a boy?/Ha, Ha! SiSoSe

Boy's Will, Joyful Labor without Pay, and Harvest Home (excerpt). Robert Penn Warren. And grins, then wipes the sweat from his hair. SaC

The Boy Serving at Table. John Lydgate. Before thy sovereign scratch nor rub thee nought. OxBChV

The boy stood in the supper-room. Anonymous. The bread-crumbs and the tea. CenHV

A Boy Thirteen. Jerry Irish. I don't understand. DL

Boy Trash Picker. Jim Howard. I'd hop all the way down the next long block. FAZ

Boy Wandering in Simms' Valley. Robert Penn Warren. And stood wondering what life is, and love,/and what they may be. DFF; SoSe

The Boy Washington. Dorothy Brown Thompson. You will be ready! SiSoSe

The Boy We Want. Anonymous. ...the world's work await/Such boys when they grow to be men. WBLP

The Boy Who Dreamed the Country Night. C. J. Koch. ...Grandma's hair, secret, let down only here.' NOAV

The Boy Who Laughed at Santa Claus. Ogden Nash. Donder and Blitzen licked off his paint. BBGG; CenHV; MaC; StPo

A Boy Who Smells Like Cocoa. Robert Hershon. A very old messenger/took my seat. NeAC

The Boy with a Cart (excerpt). Christopher Fry. In root and sky we can discern the hand. LiTB

Boy with a Hammer. Russell Hoban. It was his fort, he said, and he would make it strong. PCP

Boy with His Hair Cut Short. Muriel Rukeyser. the blue vein, bright on her temple, pitifully beating. ExPo; LiTM; MoAB; MP; NAMP; PoPl; RoGo; TwCP; VGW

The Boyhood of Christ. Anonymous. and overhead they all could hear/the singing of the birds. NOBI

The Boyne Walk. Frederick Robert Higgins. So here, will you take it–hall-marked by a day/Over the hills and far away? OxBI

The Boyne Water. Anonymous. It was not in their power to stop what the rabble they designed. AnIV; FaPoR; NOBI; OnYI

The Boys. Oliver Wendell Holmes. Dear Father, take care of thy children, THE BOYS! HBV 1-2; WBLP

Boys. Winifred M. Letts. Heartscalds and torments–but sorra a mother/Has got one to spare. HBMV

Boys and Sport. Solon. Toys with a fair boy on his breast the livelong day! PeHV

Boys. Black. Gwendolyn Brooks. Make of my Faith/a Black Star. I am Beckoning. CNA

The Boys Brushed By. Catherine Gonick. Never would be man enough for me. AMV-80

Boys, By Girls Held in Their Thighs. John Peale Bishop. The brute approach of ecstasy. ErPo

Boys in October. Irving Layton. ...they'll not use/The gold but hold it as a memorial/To Chance and their own abstinence. OBCV

Boys' Names. Eleanor Farjeon. And there's John, like John. BiCB; SUS; TiPo

The Boys of Mullabaun. Anonymous. And sent for transportation with the Boys of Mullabaun. BIrV; GBP

The Boys of Sanpete County. Anonymous. But we soon again shall meet them in that better land above. AmFP

The Boys of the Island. Anonymous. They go out when they like and come in when they please. ShS

Boys of These Men Full Speed. Muriel Rukeyser. woman of that girl. NNaP

The Boys of Wexford. Anonymous. To burst in twain the galling chain and free our native land. ELP

Bozzy and Piozzi (excerpt). Peter Pindar. Nor ev'n the greatest difficulties chafe at,/Whilst such an animal is near, to laugh at. PoEL 1-5

Br'er Sterling and the Rocker. Michael S. Harper. ...Br'er Sterling's rocker glows. LCAP

The Bracelet. Thomas Stanley. Secur'd from Conquest by Captivity. AnAnS 2

The Bracelet of Grass. William Vaughn Moody. O the sweeping past of the ruined sky! AP

The Bracelet: To Julia. Robert Herrick. If I could, I would not so. EG; HBV 1-2; OBEV; TrGrPo

Bracken Hills in Autumn. Hugh" (Christopher Murray Grieve) MacDiarmid. And will also be dead/When its rude cover is shed. NoP

Braddan Vicarage. Thomas Edward Brown. And stand outside these nations and their noise. FaBoPP

Braddock's Defeat. Anonymous. And the streams of that river ran red down with blood. ABF

Braddock's Fate, with an Incitement to Revenge. Stephen Tilden. Get home unto thy plow. PAH

Brady's Bend. Martha Keller. Chief Bald Eagle was/The tomahawk of hell. StPo

Brady (with music). Anonymous. Brady, where you at?/Struttin' in hell with his Stetson hat! AS

Braemar. Galway Kinnell. Pale bodies the sea's farness from their shore. PoA

The Braes o' Gleniffer. Robert Tannahill. The dark days o' winter were simmer to me! OBRV

The Braes o Yarrow (A version). Anonymous. She tied it round "her white hause-bane,/"And tint her life on Yarrow.' CEP; ESPB; OBEC; ViBoFo

The Braes of Yarrow. John Logan. And now with him she sleeps in Yarrow. BSV; GTBS; GTBS-P; HBV 1-2; OBEC

Braggart! Denis Wrafter. My arms around you to-night would banish/That stripling out of your delicate head. OnYI

Braggin' Bill's Fortytude. C. Wiles Hallock. No saddle yaps, I know, could fill/The noble boots of Braggin' Bill. BPAW

Bragging Song. Anonymous. ...and if he dies, why, that was my Purpose. LiTW

Brahma. Ralph Waldo Emerson. Find me, and turn thy back on heaven. AA; AnNE; AP; APA; AWP; BiP; DiPo; EaLo; GoTF; HAP; HBV; 1-2; ILwL; InPo; LiTA; MAmP; NePA; NOBA; NoP; OBEV; OBVV; OxBA; PoRA; SeCeV; TAP; TreF; TrGrPo; UnPo; ViBoPo; WGRP; WHA

Brahma (parody). Andrew Lang. The roller, pitch, and stumps, and all. BXAP; CenHV; FaBoCo; NOBL

Brahma, the World Idea. Anonymous. He who watches over it in the highest heaven/Knows indeed–or haply knows not. WGRP

The Brahms. Herbert Morris. ...prolong/the whiteness of your body in the song. NePoAm-2

Braid Claith. Robert Fergusson. Till they cou'd see ye wi' a suit on/O' gude Braid Claith. BSV; CEP; GoTS; NOEC; OBEC; OxBS

Braille. Gerald Costanzo. by tapping it gently/with a stick. AMV-81

Brain. Coleman Barks. looking through the empty/limbs. PPJ

The Brain Cells. Donald Hall. ...and watch/the replays, in black and white, over and over. TAP

Brain Coral. Lois Bassen. and I hold in my hand a hemisphere/of limestone silence. SUW

The Brain–Is Wider than the Sky. Emily Dickinson. And they will differ–if they do–/As Syllable from Sound– AmP; AnNE; MAmP; MoAB; MoAmPo; NAWM 1-2; NIP; NoAm; OxBA

The Brain, Within It's Groove. Emily Dickinson. And trodden out the Mills– DiPo; NoAm; NOBA

Brainstorm. Howard Nemerov. Inside his head he heard the stormy crows. HAP; NCSH; NoAm; SM

Brainwashing Dramatized. Don Johnson. Gone-With-The-Grin Lip Remover. PoNe

The Bramble Briar. Anonymous. The sea ship sinking and the waves were dashing,/They were both drowned in the deep. BFSS

Branch of the Sweet and Early Rose. William Drennan. And who inhale thy breath divine? IrPN

Branches Back Into. Ken Belford. too afraid/to tell him. NeAC

Brand Fire New Whaling Song Right from the Pacific Ocean. Anonymous. His breath, long spent, now finds a vent,/Like steam from boiler gushing. EtS

Brand Speaks. Henrik Ibsen. His heir, the Adam that he wrought! WGRP

The Branding Iron Herd. Ralph Rigby. And, you bet, the boss pair of branding irons. PoOW

The Brandy Glass. Louis MacNeice. "Only let it form within my hands once more." FaBoIP

Brandy Leave Me Alone. Anonymous. Remember I must go home. FSW

Braque. Michael Kennedy Joseph. all the patterned dark of their shadows. AnNZ

Brasilia. Sylvia Plath. The glory/The power, the glory. CAPP

The Brass Horse. Drummond Allison. He writhes his motionless metallic reins. FaBoTw

Brass Spittoons. Langston Hughes. Com'mere, boy! BANP; MoAmPo; NoAm

Brass Tacks. Denise Levertov. and found himself/smiling. InPS

Brats. X. J. Kennedy. Phil's not one of them there highbrows. NLV

The Bratzlav Rabbi to His Scribe. Jacob Glatstein. Nathan,/Take this down! TrJP

The Brave at Home. Thomas Buchanan Read. Sheds holy blood as e'er the sod/Received on Freedom's field of honor! HBV 1-2

Brave Collier Lads. Anonymous. There is none in this world like a pitboy for me. OBET

Brave Donahue. Jack Donahue. You still are the stranger,/And I'm Donahue. PoAu 1-2

A Brave-Hearted Maid. *Anonymous.* who was the beginning of all light. ISi

Brave Lord Willoughby. *Anonymous.* And thus I end the bloody bout/Of brave Lord Willoughby. FaPoR

The Brave Man. Wallace Stevens. That brave man. SOTW

Brave New World. Archibald MacLeish. The old stale bitter world plays new–/And the new world old. AmP; NOBA; OFD; OxBA

The Brave Old Duke of York. *Anonymous.* They were neither up nor down. OxNR

The Brave Old Oak. Henry Fothergill Chorley. But he never shall send our ancient friend/To be tossed on the stormy sea. FaBoBe; HBV 1-2

The Brave Old Ship, the Orient. Robert and Spence Traill Lowell. Such a ship as nevermore will be. AA; FaBoBe

Brave Old World. Elisabeth Lambert. I plan to freeze my neighbors to the marrow/By being the inventor of the bow and arrow. FaFP

Brave Paulding and the Spy. *Anonymous.* Success to North America,/Ye sons of liberty! BFSS; MC; PAH

Brave Rover. Max Beerbohm. 'Tis there that Albert's gone./How dogs do carry on! GDP; NLV

Brave Wolfe. *Anonymous.*
At last, said brave Wolfe,/I die with pleasure. BaBo
So then replies brave Wolfe, "I die with pleasure." BaBo

The Bravest Battle. Joaquin Miller. Are fought in these silent ways! WBLP

Braving the Wilds All Unexplored. Robert Freeman. God of the Christlike, grant that we/Do follow, follow worthily! AH

Brazen Tongue. William Rose Benet. And, white with ashes, wonder why/In the devil I am I. MoAmPo

Brazil, January 1, 1502. Elizabeth Bishop. and retreating, always retreating, behind it. FaBoWP; NoAm

Brazilian Fazenda. P. K. Page. so I can stare/at the sugar white pillars/and black lace grills/of this pink house. FaBoWP

The Brazos River. *Anonymous.* There's a-many a river that waters the land. PrIm

Bread. Stanley Burnshaw. For birds, and fields, and for bread. TrJP

Bread. James Dickey. I ate the food I ne'er had eat. LCAP

Bread. Nancy Keesing. The child swelling the womb. PoAu 1-2

Bread. Abraham Moses Klein. Bind me forever in your ritual, your/Worship and prayer, me, and all mankind! PeCV

Bread. William Stanley Merwin. raising its radiance to the moon. EAS

Bread. Gabriela (Lucila Godoy Alcayaga) Mistral. until the time we shall be one/and our day over... WPOW

Bread. R.S. Thomas. The live bread for the starved folk. BoC

Bread. Constance Urdang. under stars clustered thick as raisins. GP

Bread and Milk. Christina Georgina Rossetti. And a crumb for robin redbreast/On the cold days of the year. CBEP

Bread and Wine, Part 7. Friedrich Holderlin. Who used to stroll over the fields through the whole divine/night. NU

The Bread Hot from the Oven. John Thompson. a moment held/in our empty hands. NOBC

Bread Is Born. Anne Hebert. ..And daylight straddles the world. BoWoP

Bread Loaf to Omaha, Twenty-Eight Hours. Patrick Worth Gray. Another old man, lost/In America, trying to get home. TAT

Bread of Brotherhood. Lucia Trent. Who makes from each storm-wracked harvest/The bread of brotherhood. PGD

Bread of Heaven, on Thee We Feed. Josiah Conder. JESU! may we ever be/Grafted, rooted, built in Thee. Amen. TrCP; VLP

The Bread of Our Affliction. Martin Grossman. We eat it now/Even as we did/in Egypt. VWA

Bread the Holy. Elizabeth Jane Coatsworth. Silently, slowly, the great clouds are piled/In pale straw-colored mows against the blue. MoRP

Breadth. Circle. Desert. Monarch. Month. Wisdom. John Hollander. Claims its huge dominions not by kinship, nor bond/Of common ending. PoA

The Break. E. N. Sargent. breathe; burn; and change. NYBP

Break, Break, Break. Alfred, Lord Tennyson. But the tender grace of a day that is dead/Will never come back to me. ATP; AWP; BiP; BoLiVe; DiPo; DL; EtS; FaBoBe; FaBV; FaPoR; FF; FiP; GoJo; GoTF; GTBS; GTBS-P; HAP; HBV 1-2; HeIP; InPo; LiTB; MaVP; MBW 1-2; MCCG; MOS; NIP; NOBE; NOBV; NoP; OAEP; OBNC; PoEL 1-5; PoPl; PoRA; PPoe; PrIm; TEP; TreF; TrGrPo; WBLP; WeW; WHA

Break, Break, Break (parody). J. C. Squire. (After which the poet gets into his proper stride.) BXAP

Break My Heart of Stone. Charles Wesley. And break my heart of stone. BePJ

Break of Day. John Clare. At the pleasant time of morning/When the shepherd goes to fold. CBEP

Break of Day. John Donne. He which hath business and makes love doth do/Such wrong as when a married man doth woo. CABA; EG; EIL; EnRePo; LiTB; LiTL; TrGrPo

Break of Day. John Shaw Neilson. Again, as someone lost in a quaint parable,/Comes up the Sun. BoAV; PoAu 1-2

Break of Day in the Trenches. Isaac Rosenberg. Just a little white with the dust. BrPo; FaBoMo; GTBS-P; MMM; MoBrPo; NIP; NOBE; NoP; OAEL 1-2; OBWP; PoA; SeCePo; ViBoPo; VWA; WaaP; WaP

Break the News to Mother. Charles K. Harris. Then kiss her dear, sweet lips for me,/And break the news to her. FSN; TreFS

Break Thou the Bread of Life. Mary Artemisia ("Aunt Mary") Lathbury. And I shall find my peace,/My All in All. AH; TRV

The Break-Up. Abraham Moses Klein. and last year's blue and bloated suicides. NOBC

The Breakdown. Sherod Santos. ...but the hand/did not loosen, in the darkness, its grip. MAYP; SM

Breake Now My Heart and Dye! Thomas Campion. The Grecian, inchanted all parts but the heele,/At last a shaft daunted, which his hart did feele. AAS

Breakers of Broncos. Lew Sarett. When will you whirl your lasso at the sun?/Or bridle it? Or straddle the lightning-flash? BPAW

Breakers over the Sea. *Anonymous.* What, I pray, is this love in the breast? WTO

Breakfast. Wilfrid Gibson. We ate our breakfast lying on our backs/Because the shells were screeching overhead. OBMV; OxBTC

Breakfast. Thom Gunn. –without love, without hope, but/without renunciation. OxBC

Breakfast. Robin Shectman. The taste of you will be/the first thing/to pass my lips. AMV-80

A Breakfast for Barbarians. Gwendolyn MacEwen. by God that was a meal NOBC

Breakfast in a Bowling Alley in Utica, New York. Adrienne Rich. in the softened bitterness/of his heart. CoPo

The Breakfast Song. Emilie Poulsson. So you can guess the rest. HBVY

Breakfast Song in Time of Diet. Stoddard King. Doctor's orders. Pass the bran. OBAL

Breakfast Time. James Stephens. ...I think its mother wakens it. SUS

Breakfast with Gerard Manley Hopkins. Anthony Brode. Come fresh-from-the-oven flakes direct from the heart of the corn. BXAP; FaBoPa; FiBHP; NOBL; Par

Breaking. James Alexander Allan. Where shall I hide my face and my head? PoAu 1-2

The Breaking. Margaret Steele Anderson. Though I am God–to see thee so submit!) HBV 1-2

Breaking Green. Michael Ondaatje. and tossed it like a river into the grass. NOBC

Breaking Ground in Me. Tom Kryss. out through the end of a log/and into the sky. NeAC

The Breaking of the Day. Peter Davison. And, half believing, only half deny. CoPo

Breaking Off from Waiting. Clarisse Nicoidski. and none of us knows what can stop/the blood VWA

Breaking Point. Sylvia Auxier. Small wonder that the tree had cracked/Under their weight. GoYe

Breaking Silence. Janice Mirikitani. Our language is beautiful. BrSi

Breaking Tradition. Janice Mirikitani. She is breaking tradition. BrSi

Breakings. Henry Taylor. ...and think of the kinds of breakings/there are, and the kinds of restraining forces. GrPl

Breakthrough. Carolyn M. Rodgers. at this lopsided crystal sweet moment... BPo

Breakthrough. John Sinclair. lovely human selves. NBP

Breakwaters. Ted Walker. Dour, malignant to the core,/they will try to outlive him. NYBP

The Breastplate of Saint Patrick. *Anonymous.* Alone, and in a multitude. BBV

The Breastplate of St. Patrick. Frances Alexander. Salvation is of Christ the Lord. OxBI

Breasts. Maxine Chernoff. Bogart is staring at Lauren Bacall's breasts/as if they might start speaking. APU

Breasts. Tess Gallagher. it was your blundering mercies kept me alive/when heaven was a luckless dream. AmPA

Breasts. Donald Hall. There is something between us. OBAL

Breasts. Charles Simic. Into the hive/Of my drowsy mouth. NNaP

Breasts. Barbara Unger. Like a tree that fissures/Out of the center of all things. DFT

The Breasts of Mnasidice. Pierre Louys. ...Since I shall never have/children and since they are so far from my/mouth, kiss them for me.' PeHV

A Breath. Mary Ainge De Vere. The selfsame breath can blow it out. AA

Breath. James Dickey. Then come to us slowly, out of nowhere and anywhere/risen,/Breathlessly bright. SM

Breath. Reginald Gibbons. there is no waking, not anywhere. MAYP

Breath. Heather McHugh. his ghost and only song. GeTw

Breath. Mark Strand. that breath is what I give them when I send my love. HaCAP

Breath in My Nostrils. Lance Jeffers. and forgot that he was a slave! CNA

A Breath of Air. James Wright. And things were as they were. NOBA; PoPl

Breath of Hampstead Heath. Edith Matilda Thomas. Until the breath of Hampstead touched his/face. AA

The Breath of Night. Randall Jarrell. By the Strife that moves the stars. CrMA

Breath on the Oat. Joseph Russell Taylor. Uncaptured and unflying, the wings of song. HBV 1-2; PAH

Breathe dust... Fred Wah. and flailed the messsage without air. NOBC

Breathe on the Glass. Raymond Stineford. Over faces/carried in the/darkened stream. AMV-81

The Breathers. James Reiss. breathing, robbing the air. AmPA

The Breathing. Denise Levertov. too quiet to hear. NaP; RFM

Breathing the Strong Smell. Harold Norse. yet I felt curiously healed/as if life were about to begin. PeHV

Breathless. Wilfred Noyce. Heart aches,/lungs pant/dry air/sorry, scant. OBTV

Breaths. Birago Diop. Hear in the wind/The bush sob:/It is the ancestors' breath. TTY

Brebeuf and His Brethren. Edwin John Pratt.
As the shepherd-priest with Chaumonot led back/the remnant of a nation to Quebec. NOBC
He faced the arrows and died in front of his church. ACV; OBCV; PeCV

Brebeuf and His Brethren. F. R. Scott. Then is priest savage, or Red Indian priest? NOBC

The Breech. Michael McClure. Rosy, rust-red, Orange, white! NeAP

Breech Birth. Nora Dauenhauer. with her foot hanging out,/testing the world. TWSS

The Breed of Athletes. Euripides. ...Prowess of such sort/is to all the city a boon, to all Hellenes. SD

Breeze and Billow. Albert Durrant Watson. And the breeze o'er the billows blowing. CaP

The Breeze Is Blowing. Anonymous. I am left behind here/Living with my love for you. WTO

Breitmann in Politics. Charles Godfrey Leland. Vas dishblayed in dis elegdion py Mishder Hiram Twine. OBAL

Brendan Gone. Padraic Fiacc. A corpse once young and sweet. CIP

Brennan on the Moor. Anonymous.
Bold, brave and undaunted/Was young Brennan on the Moor. AmFP; FSW; GBP; OnYI; OuSiCo
Saying "I wish, Willie Brennan, in your cradle you had died." BaBo; FaBoBa; ViBoFo

Brent: A Poem to Thomas Palmer Esq. William Diaper.
For though the world be burned, this never will be Brent. OBSV
...here in one common sty/Men and their fellow-brutes with equal honor lie. FaBoPP; NOEC; OBSV

The Brereton Omen (excerpt). Felicia Dorothea Hemans. Woe for the fall of the glorious tree. CTC

Brest Left behind. John Chipman Farrar. "I don't see very many tears," he says. PAH

Breton Afternoon. Ernest Christopher Dowson. The weak and blind who stand in our light and wreak ourselves such ill. OBNC

Breughel's Winter. Walter De la Mare. Who squandered here life's mystery. SeCePo

Brevard Fault. Robert Morgan. and builds the grudge of kinship/under quiet blue slopes. SUW

Brevities. Siegfried Sassoon. Looks once on life and goes his wordless way. PoLf

The Brewer's Man. Leonard Alfred George Strong. "To hell with ye!" says she. DBV; DTC; ELU; FaBoCo; FiBHP; NLV

The Brewing of Soma. John Greenleaf Whittier. O still, small voice of calm! AmePo; NOCV; PoEL 1-5; TrPWD

Brian O'Linn. Anonymous. "We'll go home by water,' says Brian O'Linn! FaBoBa; FaBoNo; NLV; OnYI

The Brick. Paul Roche. And millions of atoms/are its children. NYBP

A Brick Not Used in Building. Naomi Replansky. A brick not used in building/Can smash a window pane. PoL

Bricking the Church. Robert Morgan. puts on a hard shell/for weathering this world. MAYP

Bricklayer Love. Carl Sandburg. When the sun is in my eyes and the ladders are shaky and the mortar boards go/wrong, I think of you. AmP

The Bricklayer's Labours. Robert Tatersal. And all the joyous scene revolves again. NOEC

The Brickster. Anonymous. We will tell these dreams over again.' OBET

The Bridal Bed. Jenny Mastoraki. The City/was taken exactly forty-eight hours later/when we were washing away the blood. PBWP

Bridal Couch. Donald J. Lloyd. Yawning, and content to fall/Into any bed at all. NIP

The Bridal Pair. William Young.
That hath been which shall not/be! AA; NOBE
What is lost shall not be found! AA

Bridal Piece. Louise Gluck. ...He reaches for me in his sleep. SM

Bridal Song. Clemens Brentano. To the new row you hoe in fresh greening field. HW

Bridal Song. Thomas Dekker. Of wedlock, love, and youth is Hymen king. OBSC; TrGrPo

A Bridal Song. Percy Bysshe Shelley.
As the fruit is to the tree/May their children ever be! HW
...what will be done/In the absence of the sun!/Come along! OBRV

The Bride. Bella Akhmadulina. My love, what more can happen/To you and to me? BoWoP; PBWP

The Bride. Ambrose Bierce. "I my-/self/Am Reason. and the Other was a Dream." AA

The Bride. Ralph Hodgson. Who wrestled with the ages/To give the world a bride. HBMV

The Bride. Laurence Hope. Art thou not ever, though slave of his daytime,/Choti Tinchaurya, queen of his night? HBV 1-2

The Bride. D. H. Lawrence. And her dead mouth sings/By its shape, like thrushes in clear evening. NoAm; OxBTC

The Bride. Ruth Comfort Mitchell. Then they'll see me and the darling day/Footing it over the Hill together! HBMV

The Bride of Abydos. George Gordon, Lord Byron. As weeping Beauty's cheek at Sorrow's/tale! OAEP; OBRV

The Bride of Frankenstein. Edward Field. will wake up in the dark night screaming/as his hideous body grabs them. CoAP; HeIP

The Bride of Lammermoor (excerpt). Sir Walter Scott. Easy live and quiet die. BSV

The Bride's Farewell: Two Songs. Anonymous. The calf has gone to a stranger's land. WTO

A Bride's Hours. Jean Valentine. Our honeymoon lake, ignoring the lit-up land,/Shows blank Orion where to dip his hand. FaBoWP

Bride's Lament. Sappho. I have gone forever,/Forever. HW

The Bride's Prelude. Dante Gabriel Rossetti. And kept in silence the same place. SeCePo

The Bride's Song. William Johnson Cory. For this, this, 'twas worth my while/To flit across the sea. OBTV

The Bride's Toilette. Ellen Mackay Hutchinson Cortissoz. The bridal is over! AA

The Bride's Tragedy: Poor Old Pilgrim Misery. Thomas Lovell Beddoes. Alack, and woe is me! EnRP

Bride Song. Christina Georgina Rossetti. Eager saints and angels ask in Heaven's zone,/Who is this? OBVV

Bridegroom Dick (excerpt). Herman Melville. Dick drinks from your eyes and he finds no lack! PoEL 1-5

The Bridegroom Is So Tall. Sappho. He surpasses all, as the poets of Lesbos/Surpass the poets of other lands. HW

The Bridegroom of Cana. Marjorie Pickthall. For the winds of the dawn say, "Follow, follow/Jesus Bar-Joseph, the carpenter's son." CaP; TrCP

The Brides. A. D. Hope. Concatenation of the poppet heads. HAP

Bridesmaid. Robley Wilson, Jr. they shoulder one another to be taken first. AMV-80

Bridge. Archie Randolph Ammons. into the natural light, come, sweat, bloodblessings,/and thinning sheaf of days. CoAP

Bridge. S. Foster Damon. Upward for a copper sun. AnAmPo

The Bridge. Willibald Kohler. And streamward every traveler fares. CAW

The Bridge. Henry Wadsworth Longfellow. As the symbol of love in heaven,/And its wavering image here. GoTF; HBV 1-2; TreF

The Bridge. Frederick Peterson. With kindly thoughts to hearten/The children of their race. HBV 1-2

The Bridge. James (1834-82) Thomson. —And here it comes dancing over the bridge! OBVV

The Bridge. Albert Verwey. The while the masons slowly closed the arch. LiTW

The Bridge. Derek Walcott. and the man/feel in his muscles the river's startled flowing. NYP

The Bridge Builder. Will Allen Dromgoole. Good friend, I am building the bridge for him. BLPA; GoTF; PoToHe; TreFS; TRV

The Bridge from Brooklyn (excerpt). Raymond Henri. the bridge is everlasting monument. EyDe

Bridge-Guard in the Karroo. Rudyard Kipling. Details guarding the line! OBWP

The Bridge: Indiana. Hart Crane. stranger,/son,/–my friend– CoAnAm

A Bridge Instead of a Wall. Anonymous. There never will be room for walls to rise! PoToHe

The Bridge of Death. Anonymous. And the marriage bell was tolled in hell/For the souls of him and her. AWP

The Bridge of Heraclitus. George Reavey. His goal half-won, but Dulcinea still his talisman. BIrV

The Bridge of Sighs. Thomas Hood. And leaving, with meekness,/Her sins to her Saviour! BeLS; EBEV; EnLi 1-2; EnRP; FaPoR; FPL; GoTF; GTBS; GTBS-P; HBV 1-2; OBEV; OBVV; PeD; PG; TreF; WBLP; WHA

Bridge of the Carousel. Rainer Maria Rilke. amid a blindly passing breed of men. AMV-80

The gutteral sorrow of the refugees. LiTM; MoAB; MoBrPo; NOBE; SeCePo; WaP

The British Prison Ship: Canto III. The Hospital Prison Ship. Philip Freneau. And his last triumphs more than damn the first. AmPP

The British Tar. Sir William Schwenck Gilbert. And this should be his customary attitude! ALV

British Valor Displayed. Francis Hopkinson. That years to come, if they get home,/They'll make their boasts and brags, Sir. PAH

Brittan's Remembrancer (excerpt). George Wither. ...And always praised be/for that abundant Love, which is in thee? SeCV 1-2

Brittle Beauty. Henry Howard, Earl of Surrey. Today ready ripe, tomorrow all too shaken. AAS; AnFE; EnLoPo; FCP; SiPS; TrGrPo

Broad Gold. Anna Akhmatova. Forgive me those whom I mistook/For you—alas, they were too many. LiTW

Broad Is the Road. Isaac Watts. Which false apostates never knew. AH

Broads (parody). David R. Slavitt. ...poems like these/you'll never understand. BXAP

Broadway. Walt Whitman. Thou visor'd, vast, unspeakable show and lesson! NYP

A Broadway Pageant. Walt Whitman. They shall now also march obediently eastward for your sake/Libertad. NYP

Brobdingnag. Adrien Stoutenburg. hot and intent with a strange love/for what they can light upon and keep. NYBP

Broccoli. Tom Schmidt. My budding heart swells,/ready to burst clusters/of yellow flame against/the clear sky. GP

The Brockton Murder: A Page out of William James. Knute Skinner. the woman's question every time/absorbs the murder's relevance. TW

Broke and Hungry. Blind Lemon Jefferson. For I can leave at once and hunt/me somewhere to go BluL

The Broken. William Stanley Merwin. The wind never missed them. There were still the clouds. LCAP

A Broken Appointment. Thomas Hardy. You love not me? BiP; CBEP; DTC; GBL; NoAm; NOBV; NoP; OAEP

Broken Bodies. Louis Golding. Not for the broken bodies,/Dear Lord–the broken hearts! HBMV

The Broken Bowl. James Merrill. Love's monuments like tombstones on our lives. PoA

The Broken Bowl. Jones Very. Come, every one who thirsts, to me. AP

The Broken-Down Digger. Anonymous. I'm a broken-down digger on Kiandra plain. PoAu 1-2

The Broken-Down Squatter. Anonymous. What chance for a squatter like me? PoAu 1-2

Broken-Face Gargoyles. Carl Sandburg. I shall yet be footloose. AmPP; MoAmPo; OxBA

The Broken Girth. Robert Graves. Old age, not Fairyland, was his delusion. BIrV

A Broken Gull. John Moore. With this bereavement troubling me. NCSH

The Broken Heart. Thomas Beedome. Hearts may breake, that be in love. OBS

The Broken Heart. John Donne. But after one such love, can love no more. AtBAP; DiPo; EBEV; LiTL

The Broken Heart. John Ford.
Doe, shall, and must obey. AtBAP
Loves Martyrs must be ever, ever/dying. AtBAP
No tempests of commotion shall disquiet/The calmes of my composure. PoEL 1-5

Broken Heart, Broken Machine. Richard E. Grant. ...pulls shabby tricks in the/guillotine hour/(don't worry baby) PoBA

The Broken-Hearted Gardener. Anonymous. And honour my death with a double encore. GBP

The Broken Home. James Merrill. Watch a red setter stretch and sink in cloud. HaCAP; HAP; NoAm; NOBA; NYBP; PPP

Broken Home. William Stafford. that never really led to tomorrow. NNaP

Broken Monologue. Michael Lewis. You will? You'll go to Gladys 'cross the way?/Stay. UnTE

Broken Music. Dante Gabriel Rossetti. O bitterly beloved! and all her gain/Is but the pang of unpermitted prayer. MaVP

The Broken Oar. Henry Wadsworth Longfellow. And flung his useless pen into the sea. AmePo

The Broken One. John Holmes. Saw, and carried the big bird off, a pardon/For no crime, for which there is no name. MiAP

The Broken Pitcher. Ayton [(or Aytoun)] Sir Robert. How he met the Moorish maiden beside the lonely well. InMe

Broken Sky. Carl Sandburg. It is an army blanket and the sleeper/slept too near the fire. PCP

A Broken Song. Moira O'Neill. Where she is gone there I can never go. OBVV; PG

The Broken String. Anonymous. and the old places are not sweet any more/for what they did. PeSA

The Broken Token. Anonymous. I have just returned for to marry thee. AmFP

The Broken Tower. Hart Crane. Unseals her earth, and lifts love in its shower. AmPP; AP; CMoP; CoBMV; LiTM; MoAB; MoAmPo; MoPo; MoVE; NoAm; NOBA; NoP; OxBA; SyP; TrGrPo

Broken Treaties: Teeth. Victor Contoski. reminding what is soft/of what is hard. GP

The Brome Abraham and Isaac. Anonymous. Now Jesu, that wore the crown of thorn,/Bring us all to heaven's bliss! EnLi 1-2

Bronc Peeler's Song. Anonymous. Good-by, Liza, poor gal,/She died on the plain. CoSo

The Broncho That Would Not Be Broken. Vachel Lindsay. O broncho that would not be broken of dancing. BBV; BPAW; LaNeLa; NePA; PH; RoGo

Broncho Versus Bicycle. John Wallace (Jack) Crawford. That's nothin', I'm thinkin', kin foller them things/In the way of surprisin' inventions but wings. BPAW

Bronco Busting, Event #1. May Swenson. ...From the dust gets up a buster named Tucson. LiSp; PH

A Bronze Head. William Butler Yeats. And wondered what was left for massacre to save. LiTB; MBW 1-2

A Bronze Statuette of Kwan-Yin. Charles Wharton Stork. Can you ever be less than kind? GoYe

Bronzes. Carl Sandburg. And mention the dynasties/And pass them along. EyDe

Bronzeville Man with a Belt in the Back. Gwendolyn Brooks. In such an armor he cannot be slain. IDB; PoBA

Brooding Grief. D. H. Lawrence. Of leaves and lamps and traffic mingled before me. CMoP; LoBV

Brooding Likeness. Louise Gluck. like grit caught on a wheel, like shining freight. MAYP

The Brooding of Sigurd. William Morris. Ere Sigurd came to the Niblungs and faced their gathered foes. SeCePo

The Brook. William Wilberforce Lord. "It is the stream! it is the stream!" AA

The Brook. Alfred, Lord Tennyson. For men may come and men may go/But I go on for ever. BoNaP; FaBV; GN; GoJo; MCCG; PoPle

The Brook. Edward ("Edward Eastaway") Thomas. ...found/A word for, while I gathered sight and sound. MoVE; SeCeV

The Brook (excerpt). William Bull Wright. And those soft flashings of their silver/feet. AA

The Brook in February. Sir Charles G. D. Roberts. A babbling whisper you shall hear/Of birds and blossoms, leaves and light. BoNaP; OBCV; WHW

A Brook in the City. Robert Frost. The thoughts may not have risen that so keep/This new-built city from both work and sleep. OxBA

Brook Song. James Herbert Morse. And the wind in the willow tree. AA

Brookfield (excerpt). William E. Marshall. And prove the settler's worth, beyond the body's wants... CaP

The Brooklyn at Santiago. Wallace Rice. Send such a chief, with men like these,/On such a ship! PAH

Brooklyn Bridge. Vladimir Mayakovsky. Yes,/you've got something here. NYP

The Brooklyn Bridge. Edna Dean Proctor. And winds the sea-clouds bear! MC; PAH

Brooklyn Bridge. Sir Charles G. D. Roberts. The rock respects your stable towers. PAH

Brooklyn Bridge at Dawn. Richard Le Gallienne. Would dream such softness, like a picture hung,/Is wrought of human thunder, iron, blood? HBMV

Brooklyn Heights. John Wain. Be the citizens of the true survival! LiTM; NYP; OBTV; OxBTC

Brooklyn Summer. Lou Lipsitz. hanging over the edge/like a root. LTB

The Brooklyn Theater Fire. Anonymous. The lives of our dear friends to take. AmFP

The Brookside. Richard Monckton, Lord Houghton Milnes. For the beating of our own hearts/Was all the sound we heard. GoTF; HBV 1-2; TreFS

The Broom. Giacomo Leopardi. Made so by destiny or by ourself. LiTW

Broom at Twilight. Robyn Sarah. banking on where I thought the road must be. CaPN

The Broom Flower. Mary Howitt. And dear it is on summer days/To lie at rest among it. HBV 1-2

Broom, Green Broom. Anonymous. This is better than cutting of broom.' LiTB; OxBoLi

The Broom of Cowdenknows (A version). Anonymous. I've gotten now the bonniest lass/That is in the hale country.' ESPB

The Broom of Cowdenknows (B version). Anonymous. And I have gotten the bonniest lass/That is in this countrie.' ESPB

The Broom Squire's Song. Anonymous. Come buy o' me a broom. OxNR

The Broomfield Hill. Anonymous. For a doe never ran through the street so fast/As the maid ran through the town. AmFP

The Broomfield Wager. *Anonymous.* ...you will see when your true love comes/And when she goes away.' OBET

Brooms. Dorothy Aldis. And swash and sweep it/Blue again. SoPo

Brooms. Charles Simic. Already sacked by robbers,/Once, long ago. AmPA; LCAP; NNaP

The Broomstick Train. Oliver Wendell Holmes. On the rattling rail by the broomstick train! MCCG

Brother... Johari (Jewel C. Latimore) Amini. to people the suns/of divinities. JB

The Brother. Peter Everwine. and no bread in his pocket. FYAP; NNaP

The Brother. Semion Y. Nadson. Who is he? I do not know.... TrJP

Brother. Richard Shelton. but what were you searching for/in such dark places/where I was searching for love. Str

Brother and Sister. Lewis (Charles Lutwidge Dodgson) Carroll. Moral: Never stew your sister. BBGG; FaBoNo; ShM

Brother and Sister. George Eliot.
And so I learned, luck was with glory wed. NOBV
Bearing me onward through the vast unknown. NOBV
His years with others must the sweeter be/For those brief days he spent in loving me. GN
My present Past, my root of piety. NOBV

Brother and Sisters. Judith Wright. There is nothing to be afraid of. Nothing at all.' FaBoWP

Brother Ass. Eric Irvin. Seeing the world outside with eyes that shun/The greater glasshouse round his smaller one. BoAV

Brother Ass and St. Francis. John Banister Tabb. And bless thee, Brother Ass. AnAmPo

Brother Astolfo Sated Appetite. Pietro Aretino. Alberto would have earned a hero's praise. PeHV

Brother Baptis' on Woman Suffrage. Rosalie Jonas. Ain't shame all de debbil yit, outen de Boss! BlSi

Brother, Can You Spare a Dime? E. Y. Harburg. Buddy, can you spare a dime? SaC

Brother Dog. Luis Anibal Sanchez. Before the white body of the poor dog slain by chance bullets,/the divine Francis wept. CAW

The Brother Eagles. *Anonymous.* His trail let him lay! NOAV

Brother Fire. Louis MacNeice. Echo your thought in ours? "Destroy! Destroy!" AtBAP; MoAB; NoAm; NOBE; OAEP; WaaP

Brother Green. *Anonymous.*
Farewell, farewell, temptation. BFSS
For this, dear wife, I've lost my life, to put down this rebellion. AmFP

Brother, Hast Thou Wandered Far. James Freeman Clarke. Call upon him; He is near. AH

The Brother-in-Law. Larry Rubin. Haunt him in his massive hour–/child, I call. GP; TW

Brother Jonathan, Brother Kafka (excerpt). Vincent O'Sullivan. and the child himself standing, irreducible grain. OCNZ

Brother Jonathan's Lament for Sister Caroline. Oliver Wendell Holmes. Remember the pathway that leads to our door! HBV 1-2; MC; PAH

Brother Juniper. Blanche Mary Kelly. "Would God,' cried Francis, on his knees,/"I had a forest of such trees!' GoBC

Brother, Lift Your Flag with Mine. Josephine Dodge Daskam Bacon. All for one and one for all! PoSC

Brother Malcolm: Waste Limit. Clarence Major. the pettiness got him with metal. BP

Brother Noah. *Anonymous.* Halleloo, halleloo, halleloo, hallelujah! AmSS

Brother of My Heart. Galway Kinnell. in this emptiness only the singing sometimes almost fills. FAZ

Brother, Though from Yonder Sky. James Henry Bancroft. With thy Saviour thou shalt rest,/Crowned, and glorified, and blest. AH

Brotherhood. Edwin Markham. Make way for Brotherhood–make way for Man! BBV; PGD

Brotherhood. Jose Luis Vega. I can only be whatever you are. InW

Brotherhood. J.J. W. And we are brothers, you and I,/I and you. PeHV

Brotherhood (excerpt). Sir Lewis Morris. Be as Christ would have him–brother unto brother. PGD

Brothers. Robert Currie. the circle of Young Jacob's cries/tightening like a noose. Psk

Brothers. Solomon Edwards. To keep their mother's blondness gay is food. NNP

The Brothers. John Holloway. Gazed at each other. Turned their backs. NMP

Brothers. Gerard Manley Hopkins. I'll cry thou canst be kind. OAEP

Brothers. James Weldon Johnson. "Brothers in spirit, brothers in deed are we?' BANP

The Brothers. Edwin Muir. And in a vision I have seen/My brothers playing on the green. GTBS-P; HeIP; NoP; PrIm

Brothers. Dan Pagis. Your brother Abel guards you from all evil. VWA

The Brothers. Charles Sprague. Till side by side we lie. AA

Brothers (I). James Reiss. the perfect razor of my rage. AMV-81

Brothers Together in Winter. Harley Elliott. and our faces are like mirrors. NeAC

Broughty Wa's. *Anonymous.* That if water were my prison strong/I would swim for libertie.' ESPB

Brow Bender. *Anonymous.* Lift up the latch–walk in. HBV 1-2; HBVY

Brow, Brow, Brenty. *Anonymous.* Catch a flea, catch a flea. OxNR

Brow of Nephin. *Anonymous.* Each day rises barren and bare. AnIL

Brown Adam (A version). *Anonymous.* He's gard him leave a better pledge,/Four fingers o his right han. ESPB

Brown Adam (B version). *Anonymous.* That he wald gae to see his luve,/By the le licht of the mune. ESPB

The Brown Bear. Mary Austin. Old Honey-Paw sleeps in the wood. PoSC

The Brown Beauty. Edward, Lord Herbert of Cherbury. You more then any may be dignify'd. AnAnS 2

Brown Boy to Brown Girl. Countee Cullen. And felt my heart forbear, my pulse grow still. PoBA

Brown-Eyed Lee. *Anonymous.* For the girl I loved so well with dark brown eyes and hair. CoSo

The Brown Family. Colleen Thibaudeau. Something we can take up in our hands and bear away. NOBC

The Brown Girl. *Anonymous.* Here three young lovers all died to-day,/God send them all to rest! BaBo

The Brown Girl (A version). *Anonymous.* I'll dance and sing on my love's grave/A whole twelvemonth and a day.' ESPB

The Brown Girl (B version). *Anonymous.* I'll dance above your green, green grave/Where you do lie beneath.' ESPB

A Brown Girl Dead. Countee Cullen. She'd be so proud she'd dance and sing/To see herself tonight. BP; TAP

Brown Is My Love. *Anonymous.* Dainty white lilies and sad flowers well prized. AtBAP; CBEP; EG; EiL; GBL

The Brown Jug. Francis Fawkes. So here's to my lovely sweet Nan of the Vale. CBEP; ViBoPo

Brown Like Us. Gary Soto. Creased and bundled with a rubber band,/In which she is the first one. NPGG

Brown of Ossawatomie. John Greenleaf Whittier. And every gate she bars to Hate shall open wide to Love! AmePo; HBV 1-2; MC; PAH

Brown Penny. William Butler Yeats. One cannot begin it too soon. BoLoP; CMoP; ELP; ExPo; FaBoCh; LLLT; LoGBV; OLR

Brown River, Smile. Jean Toomer. To be spiritualized by each new American AmNP; PoBA

Brown Robin (A version). *Anonymous.* But she came never back again,/Her auld father to see. ESPB; OxBB

Brown Robin (B version). *Anonymous.* Tomorrow ere I eat or drink/High hanged shall he be.' ESPB

Brown Robyn's Confession. *Anonymous.* But a' is for your fair confession/You've made upon the sea.' ACP; CH; ESPB; GBP

Brown's Descent; or, The Willy-Nilly Slide. Robert Frost. ...and took the long way home/By road, a matter of several miles. EvOK; MoAmPo; PoRA; StPo

Brown's Ferry Blues. *Anonymous.* Lord, Lord, got those Brown's Ferry Blues. FSW

Brown Skin Girl. Tommy McClennan. Just a little bit of loving,/And then you can be gone BluL

The Brown Thrush. Lucy Larcom. Unless we're as good as can be. HBV 1-2; HBVY; OBCA

The Brownies' Celebration. Palmer Cox. In forest shade they disappeared. OBCA

Browning. Robert Louis Stevenson. I wasn't pleased with Browning/Nor he with my review. NOBV

Browning at Asolo. Robert Underwood Johnson. But the love of the warm heart lingers/here. AA

Brownsville Blues. Sleepy John Estes. Because I'm 'quainted with John Law/and they won't let me down BluL

Bruadar and Smith and Glinn. *Anonymous.* Amen, dear God, I pray!/Amen! AnIV

The Bruce. John Barbour.
And relief thaim with his baneir. OxBS
Bot othir wayis all yheid the gle. OxBS
...fredome mar to pryss/Than all the gold in warld that is. ViBoPo
Schortly to say, is nane can tell/The halle condicioun off a threll. OxBS
Tharfor is neidfull that yhe be/Worthy and wicht, but abaysyng. OxBS

Bruce Addresses His Army. John Barbour. That your honour aye savit be. GoTS

Bruce and the Spider. Bernard Barton. And Patience wins the race. BeLS

Bruce Consults His Men. John Barbour. Na nane pain sall refusit be/Till we have made our country free. GoTS

Bruce Meets Three Men with a Wethe. John Barbour. His foster brother thar was dede. OxBM

Bruckner. James Camp. "Please don't let them make fun of my music." MAT

Bruises. Coleman Barks. paint samples. PPJ

Brumana. James Elroy Flecker. And dream and dream that I am home again! BrPo

Brummell at Calais. John Glassco. ...the solemn report of those/Who have done nothing and will never die. PeCV

Brush Up Your Shakespeare. Cole Porter. Brush up your Shakespeare/And they'll all kowtow. NLV; OBAL

Brussels in Winter. W. H. Auden.
And fifty francs will earn a stranger right/To take the shuddering city in his arms. OBTV
To take the shuddering city in his arms. OBTV; OxBTC

The Brut. Layamon.
All of my enemies shall make a doomed journey. MeEV
And for his own soul, that it be the better for them. Amen. MeEV
And here shall your bones lie beside Bath. MeEV
Of wondrous things about Arthur the kind. MeEV
That an Arthur shulde yete com Anglen to fulste. OxBM
That was an evil thought that her death she wrought. MeEV
This the fays gave him, and thus the child thrived. MeEV
Throughout the world be exalted; and thou be hale and sound. MeEV
With their native customs, and Lundres they named it. MeEV

Bruton Town. Anonymous. She drew a kerchief from her pocket/And wiped his eyes, though they were blind. EnSB

Bryan, Bryan, Bryan, Bryan. Vachel Lindsay. Where the kings and the slaves and the troubadours rest. CMoP; CrMA; LiTA; OxBA; OxBoLi

Bryan O'Lin Had No Breeches to Wear. Mother Goose. "Ah ha, that is warm!" said Bryan O'Lin. BrR

Bryan O'Lynn. Anonymous. Oh, we'll go home by boat, says Bryan O'Lynn. GBP

Bryan's Last Battle (The Scopes Trial). Anonymous. And leads me to the Rock of Ages, my Saviour's love is a starlit way. AmFP

Buachaille Etive Mor and Buachaille Etive Beag. Naomi Mitchison. The frayed rope and the boot tht slips on the rocks. PoSH

Bubba Esther, 1888. Ruth Whitman. trembling, weeping with anger AMV-81

The Bubble. John Banister Tabb. A life–complete in death–complete to/die. AA

The Bubble: A Song. Robert Herrick. And break thyself in shivers on her eye. CaPo

Bubbles. Bill Berkson. "You go to bed with everyone else–why not me?" APU

Bubbles. George H. Shorey. You are the palace of a fairy. PoPl

Bubbling Wine. Abu Zakariya. Dancing hailstones spin,/The wine's own kin. TTY

The Bubbul. Sir Owen Seaman. At me and you./Kuchi!/Kuchoo! NA

The Buccaneer. Nancy Byrd Turner. He merely barked: "A lady doll/I found out in the garden!" TiPo

The Buccaneer: The Island. Richard Henry Dana. Pirate and wrecker kept their revels then. AnNE

Buchlyvie. Anonymous. Nor a chair to sit doon. GBP; TW

The Buck in the Snow. Edna St. Vincent Millay. Life, looking out attentive from the eyes of the doe. AmLP; BoAnP; CrMA

The Buck's Elegy. Anonymous. Let them fire over me when I lay low. OBET

Buckaroo Sandman. Anonymous. In your little corral/Asleep with mother again. BPAW

Buckdancer's Choice. James Dickey. On the wings of the buck and wing. NoAm; NOBA; NoP; NYBP; PoNe

Buckee Bene. Anonymous Shall I come away? CH

Bucket in the Well. Connie Wanek. to be filled, like the bucket/at the bottom of the well. AMV-80

Bucket of Sea-Serpents. Howard Ant. "Not snakes," he called. "Serpents. And they eat ships." GoYe

Buckeye Jim. Anonymous. Go weave and spin, you can't go,/Buckeye Jim. FSW

Bucking Bronco. Anonymous. In the spring up the trail on his bucking bronco. ABF; AmFP; BPAW; CoSo; FSW

Buckingham Palace. A.(lan) A.(lexander) Milne. "Sure to, dear, but it's time for tea.'/Says Alice. OxBChV

Buckinghamshire. Anonymous. If you beat a bush, you'll start a thief. GBP

The Buckle. Walter De la Mare. Only the ivy and the wind/May tell of it at all. BrR

Bucko-Mate. Samuel Schierloh. When he'd gather his gear/And go home to Mother. GoYe

Buckskin Joe. Anonymous. And I'm a meek little child and as harmless as a lamb. CoSo

Bucolic. William Stanley Merwin. Nodding, whether in agreement or sleep. NMP

Bucolic Eclogues: Waking, Child, While You Slept. Ethel Anderson. The knight, his grandson, and the judge, his son. PoAu 1-2

Bucyrus. John Holmes.
Is not to be buried, and the boulders will drift. NePoAm
...water/Is not to be buried, and the boulders will drift. CrMA; NePoAm

Buddha. Theodore Holmes. He offers us nothing but the vision of the illumination that/he is. CoPo

Buddha. Arno Holz. It is a blood red ruby/in a naked belly of gold. AWP

Buddha. Herman Melville. Nirvana! absorb us in your skies,/Annul us into thee. HeIP

The Buddha at Kamakura. Rudyard Kipling. Is God in human image made/No nearer than Kamakura? LoBV; OBTV

The Buddha in the Womb. Erica Jong. Flesh is merely a lesson./We learn it/& pass on. MAYP

A Buddhist Priest. Ho Xuan Huong. Pray hard: you too can be a Superior/And squat, proud, on a lotus. PBWP

Budding Spring. Jack Lindsay. ...Not in any days/This journey shall be done. PoAu 1-2

Budding-Time Too Brief. Evaleen Stein. Wait yet awhile! AA

Budgie Finds His Voice (parody). Wendy Cope. "Who's a pretty boy then?" Budgie cried. FaBoPa

Budmouth Dears. Thomas Hardy. While our spurs Clink! Clink! up the Esplanade and down? CH; MoVE; PoPle

Buen Matina. Sir John Salusbury. Dear, for thy love I would not wear the willow.' EIL

Buena Vista. Albert Pike. AND EVERLASTING GLORY UNTO BUENA/VISTA'S DEAD! PAH

Buff. Anonymous. And that was all/My penny's worth. OxNR

Buffalo. Louis Daniel Brodsky. From being trampled to death by stampeding beasts. AMV-80

Buffalo. Florence Earle Coates. And swallow up that radiance in night? PAH

Buffalo. Roy Daniells. Strong to obstruct, tenacious to delay. CaP

Buffalo. Henry Dumas. ...if I ever/caught the American bull/I would die. PoBA

Buffalo. Charles Eglington. The Bull of Heaven charging down/To graze the pastures, tame and lourd. PeSA

The Buffalo. Herbert Price. To leave the wallowing-pool that coats his sides/And back and belly with protective ooze. ACV

Buffalo Bill's. Edward Estlin Cummings. how do you like your blueeyed boy/Mister Death. AmFN; CMoP; HeIP; InPK; LiTA; NePA; NOBA; OBSP; TAP; VGW

Buffalo Boy. Anonymous. Not even if the weather be good. AmFP; FSW

Buffalo Creek. John Le Gay Brereton. Has never drowned the silent sound/Within my happy heart. PoAu 1-2

Buffalo Dance. Alice Corbin. Strike ye our land/With curved horns! BPAW

Buffalo Dusk. Carl Sandburg. And the buffaloes are gone. BPAW; OBCA; RFM; TiPo

Buffalo Gals. Anonymous. Buffalo gals won't you come out tonight,/And dance by the light of the moon? BLSo; FSW

The Buffalo Hunters. Anonymous. And such a peculiar way they have of raising hunters' hair. CoSo

Buffalo–Isle of Wight Power Cable. Anselm Hollo. slowly he drove up to the starting line PoM

Buffalo marrow on black. Lance Henson. buffalo woman/this is all/this is all. STE

Buffalo Skinners. Anonymous. For God's forsaken the buffalo range and the damned old buffalo. ABF; AmFP; AS; BaBo; BFSS; BPAW; CoSo; FSW; GBP; ViBoFo

Buffalo Trace. Robert Morgan. then ebbed back into the horizon/and back of the stars. GeTw

Buffel's Kop. Roy Campbell. That from its wings let fall a silver plume. ChMP; PeSA

Bufo. Alexander Pope. Of all thy blameless Life the sole return/My Verse, and QUEENSB'RY weeping o'er thy Urn! OBEC

Bugger Burns. Anonymous. If Bugger Burns was a brother of mine,/I'd kill that bastard and serve my time. OuSiCo

Bugle Song of Peace. Thomas Curtis Clarke. The day has dawned at last. WBLP; WGRP

The Bugler's First Communion. Gerard Manley Hopkins. Forward-like, but however, and like favourable heaven heard these. NoAm; OAEP; PeHV

Bugs. Will Stokes. An' the bigger bugs have other bugs/An' so–ad infinitum. MoShBr

Buick. Karl Shapiro. And I touch you again as you tick in the silence and settle in sleep. AmC; BiP; CMoP; DFF; HoPM; MiAP; MoAB; TrGrPo; ViBoPo

The Builder. Caroline Giltinan. But I must build and build and build/Until a temple stands. HBMV

The Builder. Francis Sherman. Come, and claim thy part thereof,–/I have fashioned it for thee! CaP

The Builder. Willard Wattles.
And what buildest thou?"/"Heaven," he said. HBMV
"Heaven," he said. AnAmPo; HBMV

Builder Kachina: Home-Going. Wendy Rose. What we can't find/we'll build but/slowly,/slowly. TWSS

The Builder of Houses. Jane Cooper. And sovereign childhood with its unrelenting hand. AmPC

A Builder's Lesson. John Boyle O'Reilly. And habit builds the bridge at last! PoLf; PoToHe

Builders. Purd E. Deitz. We build with Thee, O grant enduring worth/Until the heav'nly Kingdom comes on earth. TRV

Builders. Hortense Flexner. Who builds him a house of a rhyme or two/Must look for the rain on his head! HBMV

The Builders. Henry Wadsworth Longfellow. And one boundless reach of sky. FaFP; OHFP; TreFS

The Builders. Judith Wright. Seed falls there now, birds build, and life takes over. SeCePo

The Builders (excerpt). Henry Van Dyke. Reveal thyself in every law,/And gild the towers of truth with holy awe. TrPWD

Building a House. Dick Gallup. For the Swift passing of our visiting guests. ANYP

Building a Person. Stephen P. Dunn. And, as always, the same folks/will go home emptyhanded. FAZ

Building a Skyscraper. James S. Tippett. The tall towers rise/Like Jacob's ladder/Into the skies. OnUR

Building Bridges. Solomon Mahaka. He shook his head/And shook his fist. WhB

Building for Eternity. N.B. Sargent. A temple the Father will own/In the city of light above? BLPA

Building in Nova Scotia. Stephen P. Dunn. and the small imperialist in my body/gathered in the stars. GP

Building in Stone. Sylvia Townsend Warner. –Man, so soon hushed–the silence which endures/To bear in mind, and bless. MoBrPo

The Building of a New Church. Anonymous. They made the back part shabby. EyDe

The Building of the Long Serpent. Henry Wadsworth Longfellow. They who to the Saga listened/Heard the name of Thorberg Skafting/For a hundred year! EtS

The Building of the Nest. Margaret Sangster. And sing to our hearts as we watch again/Your fairy building grow. HBV 1-2; HBVY

The Building of the Ship. Henry Wadsworth Longfellow. Are all with thee,–are all with thee! AA; AnNE; EtS; MOS; OHFP; PGD; TreF; YaD

Building Society Blues. Roger Roughton. ...with his soviet/Grammar and tickle too? EAS

The Buildings. Wendell Berry. ...a vine with yellow flowers shading the door. EyDe

Buildings. Daniela Gioseffi. I am thrilled by my own loneliness. FAZ

The Buke of the Howlat. Sir Richard Holland. Till on a time it betid,/As tellis the writ. OxBS

A Bulb. Richard Kendall Munkittrick. Imperious, dainty lily for a soul. AA; PoL

The Bulge. George Johnston. Multiple sweet Bridget, what will she drop? PV

A Bull. Babette Deutsch. Clustering flies mate round his red-rimmed eyes. BoAnP; LiSp

The Bull. Ralph Hodgson. Waiting for the flesh that dies. AnFE; BrPo; LiTM; MoAB; MoBrPo; MoVE; OBMV; OxBTC; WHA

The Bull. Freda Laughton. That ripens on the branches of my horns.' NeIP

The Bull. William Carlos Williams. and eyes matted/with hyacinthine curls LiTM; MoVE; MP; NoP; TwCP

The Bull. Judith Wright. runs the great bull, the dogs upon his heels. GrPl; PoAu 1-2

The Bull Calf. Irving Layton. I turned away and wept. InPK; OBCV; PeCV

The Bull Moose. Alden Nowlan. ...All the young men/learned on their automobile horns as he toppled. NOBC

The Bull Moses. Ted Hughes. I kept the door wide,/Closed it after him and pushed the bolt. NoP

Bull-Whacker. Anonymous. Root hog or die. ABF

The Bullard's Song. Anonymous. Come stump away to Stamford. OBET

The Bulldog on the Bank. Anonymous. She fished him out with a ten-foot pole/and sent him off to school./Singing tra la la la la la la.. FSW

The Bulldozer. Robert Francis. No, not the bulldozer. PPJ

The Bulldozer. Donald A. Stauffer. I promise this machine will not be lost/For want of this one nail. WaP

Bulldozers. Frederick Dec. All never yielding/To a bulldozer approaching. PCP

The Bullfinches. Thomas Hardy. When the day's pale pinions fold/Where those be that sang of old. PB

Bullfrog. Ted Hughes. No bigger than a rat, with all dumb silence/In your little old woman hands. NYBP; RFM

Bullfrog Blues. William J. Harris. Hey, the sun gonna shine in/my back door some day BluL

Bullfrogs. David Allan Evans. ...looking up at us,/asking for their legs. Psk

Bullocky. Judith Wright. The prophet Moses feeds the grape,/ and fruitful is the Promised Land. BoAV; CBAP; PoAu 1-2; SeCePo

Bullocky Bill. Anonymous. Then the dog sat on the tucker-box/Five miles from Gundagai. PoAu 1-2

The Bullwhacker. Anonymous. I'll make her my little wife–/Root hog or die. CoSo

A Bully. Anonymous. He finds that private business asserts a prior claim. WTO

The Bully. John Wilmot, Earl of Rochester. And there's an end of bully. CBEP; InvP

The Bully Song. Charles E. Trevathan. I'm a lookin' for that bully and he must be found. BLSo

The Bulwark of Liberty. Abraham Lincoln. Destroy this spirit, and we have planted the seeds of despotism/at our own doors. PGD

Bum. W. Dayton Wedgefarth. For the good Lord knows I can buy more clothes, but never a friend/like that! BLPA

Bum's Rush. Michael Dransfield. out across the bay to where the ice is thinnest and let yourself vanish. CBAP

The Bumblebeaver. Kenyon Cox. We might take lessons by the hour/From busy, buzzy Bumblebeaver. TiPo

Bumi. LeRoi (Imamu Amiri Baraka) Jones. don't say I can heal/or bring back/the dead. PoBA

The Bumper Sticker on His Pickup Said, "I'm a Lover, I'm a Fighter..." Eldon Ray Fox. it's hard to keep it up, he said) LiSp

Bums, on Waking. James Dickey. With water moving over their legs/More like living cover than it is. NYBP

Bunch Grass #37. Robert Sund. ...What are people doing with their/lives? what are they doing? NU

The Bunch of Grapes. George Herbert. Ev'n God himself, being pressed for my sake. AnAnS 1

A Bunch of Roses. John Banister Tabb. Half-way with rosy fingers meet,/To kiss and play together. HBVY

Bunches of Grapes. Walter De la mare. "A bumpity ride in a wagon of hay/For me," says Jane. GoJo; GrPl; HBV 1-2; HBVY; MoShBr; OxBChV; SUS; TiPo

Bundaberg Rum. W. N. Scott. as they toast the archangels in Bundaberg rum. NOAV

Bundles. John Farrar. Now wouldn't it be much more fun/If shoppers carried things undone? BrR; ChBR; TiPo

Bundles. Carl Sandburg. I have asked to be left a few tears/And some laughter. MoAmPo

Bung Yer Eye. Anonymous. And sent the mossbacks prancing. ABF

Bungaloid Growth. Colin Ellis. And set to work to spoil the countryside. FaBoEE

The Bungalows. John Ashbery. Moving on towards death. But sometimes standing still is also/life. CoAP

Bunhill's Fields. Anne Ridler. part for ever in the gape of hell. NeBP

Bunker Hill. George Henry Calvert. His steed he spurred, in haste to lead such noble men. BeLS; FaBoBe; MC; PAH

Bunker's Hill; or, the Soldier's Lamentation. John Freeth. And knaves of high and low degree/Be destined to the cord. NOEC

Bunky Boy Boy Who's My Little Bunky Boy. Larry Mollin. and smile so proudly/to the camera. NeAC

Bunny. Christopher Fahy. I saw it where your mother hung it/hopelessly/above her kitchen stove. TAT

A Bunny Romance. Oliver Herford. And gains the glorious title of/"Most Timid in the Land." OBCA

The Bunyip. Douglas Stewart. For I'll catch the moon by her silver hair and dance her around/the sky. AmMo

The Bunyip and the Whistling Kettle. John Streeter Manifold. And loud it screamed, the lifeless metal,/Far into the malicious night. LiTB; PoAu 1-2; WaP

The Buoy-Bell. Charles Tennyson Turner. And strike the key-note of each grateful prayer,/Breathed in their distant homes by wife or child! EtS

Burbank with a Baedeker: Bleistein with a Cigar. Thomas Stearns Eliot. Thought Burbank, meditating on/Time's ruins, and the seven laws. HBMV

Burd Ellen and Young Tamlane. Anonymous. Young Tamlane to the seas he's gane,/And a' women's curse in his company's/gane. ESPB

Burd Isabel and Earl Patrick. Anonymous. The hundred evils enterd him,/And he fell oure the brim. BaBo; ESPB

The Burden. Francesca Yetunde Pereira. But make not a mute of me. PBA

The Burden of Decision. Peter Everwine. He knows me by the little song I start to sing,/shifting from foot to foot. NNaP

The Burden of Egypt (excerpt). Richard Monckton, Lord Houghton Milnes. Why are we life-taught men, why poor ephemerals they? OBTV

The Burden of Everyday. Buddhadeva Bose. That ponderous, murderous burden of everyday. LiTW

The Burden of Junk. John Glassco. Leaves at last on a hillside to rot away with the seasons. OBCV

Burning Shit at An Khe. Bruce Weigl. Until I'm covered and there's only one smell,/One word. MAYP

Burning the Cat. William Stanley Merwin. Death, however reckoned, is hard to dispose of. NIP

Burning the Christmas Greens. William Carlos Williams. the shining fauna of that fire. CoBMV; LiTM; MoPo; NePA; NoAm; NOBA

Burning the Letters. Gwendolyn Grew. And nurse it she will through one more acted night. HoPM

Burning the Letters. Randall Jarrell. And accepted life whose fragments I cast here. MiAP; MoAB; MoAmPo

Burning the Root. Margaret Gibson. ...smoke of a cigarette/held to a bound woman's nipple. MAYP

Burning the Small Dead. Gary Snyder. windy fire. CAPP; NNaP

Burning the Tomato Worms. Carolyn Forche. Kept it from me/Whatever she saw. AmPA

Burns. Fitz-Greene Halleck. The name of Robert Burns? AA

Burns and His Highland Mary. Anonymous. For the sake of your Burns, you loved, oh, so dear. ShS

Burns at Tea. Barry Pain. And gin the next, I'm dull as you:/Mix a' thegither. HBV 1-2

Burns's Log Camp. Anonymous. And thus I was greeted at Burns's log camp. ShS

Burnt. Boris Slutsky. And quietly repeating:/burnt. VWA

The Burnt Bush. Jack R. Clemo. ...now in God's ken/I stand unsoiled again. FaBoTw

A Burnt Offering to Your Greenstone Eyes, Tangaroa. Hone Tuwhare. Ah, then watch him froth and gag, Earth./Watch him heave! OCNZ

A Burnt Ship. John Donne. They in the sea being burnt, they in the burnt ship drowned. EBEV; InPK; OBWP; WaaP

Burr Oaks: The Attic. Richard Eberhart. Who has not grieved to return to the world downstairs? MoAB

Burragorang. Nan McDonald. The walls of sapphire, the towers of burning gold. NOAV

The Burro. J. J. Gibbons. Most useful is the modest ass. PoOW

Bury Her at Even. Michael (Katherine Bradley and Edith Cooper) Field. Bury her at even,/And then leave her! CAW; OBMV

Bury Me beneath the Willow. Anonymous. When he hears his love is sleeping/Maybe then he'll think of me. FSW

Bury Me In a Free Land. Frances E. W. Harper. ...my yearning spirit craves,/Is bury me not in a land of slaves. BPo

Bury Me in America. Arno Karlen. ...I want/to be buried at home. FAZ

Bury Me Not on the Chickamauga. Anonymous. From the blood-stained lips of a youth who lay/On the battlefield of Chickamauga. BFSS

Bury Me Not on the Lone Prairie. Anonymous. We buried him there on the lone prairie. BPAW; FaBV; FaFP; FSW; TrAS; TreF

Bury Me Out on the Prairie. Anonymous. Recalls some similar woman,/And thinks of his mouldering bones. BPAW; CoSo

Bury Our Faces. Bob Millard. and how closely looms our destination. AMV-80

Bury Them. Henry Howard Brownell. Lest, haply, we be found/(Ah, dread no brave hath drowned!)/Fighting against Great God. PAH

Burying Blues for Janis. Marge Piercy. deadly as the icy sleet of skag that froze your blood. GeTw; NeAC

Burying Ground by the Ties. Archibald MacLeish. And the trains going over us here in the dry hollows... NAMP

The Bus. Leonard Cohen. metallic, painted, solitary,/with New York plates. CAD; HeIP

Bus Ride. Lenore Kandel. leaping from the bus to scurry home, intact/one time again NMM

Bus Stop. Donald Justice.
...lights/In quiet rooms/Left on for hours,/Burning, burning. FYAP
Or like the lights/In quiet rooms/Left on for hours,/Burning, burning. LCAP

Bus Stop. Vincent O'Sullivan. As close as one brushes with truth/in half an hour. OCNZ

The Bus-Stop on the Somme. David Rowbotham. When the shrapnel missed the others' head. NOAV

The Bus Trip. Joel Oppenheimer. assail him. constantly. what shall he do. NeAP

Busby, Whose Verse No Piercing Beams, No Rays. Richard Moore. they trot the field, lofty as horses' asses. TW

The Bush Aboon Traquair. John Campbell Shairp. And the luve that ance was there, aye fresh and green. OBVV

A Bush Christening. Andrew Barton ("Banjo") Paterson. How he came to be christened Maginnis! PoAu 1-2

The Bush (excerpt). Bernard O'Dowd. And dewed with dream, her silence flower in song. CBAP; PoAu 1-2

The Bush-Fiddle. Judith Green. so full so still/I cannot mend it. PoAu 1-2

Bush Justice. Charles Harpur. And for Justice! what has she to do with the Bush? CBAP

The Bush on Mount Venus. Donald Finkel. the labyrinth, as a kind of school/for heroes, artificers, and mice. CoPo

The Bush Speaks. Ernest G. Moll. And the crows will finish/What I have begun. NOAV

Bushed. Earle Birney. And now he could only/bar himself in and wait/for the great flint to come singing into his heart NOBC; NoP; OBCV; PeCV

Bushed. Charles Lillard. from nowhere to nowhere across/our faces that lonely stunned look. NOBC

Bushed. Barry McKinnon. ...& if you could sing, the song/is all that wld go/anywhere. NOBC

Bushes and Briars. Anonymous. So the green grave shall ease me if I cannot have that man.' OBET

The Bushfeller. Eileen Duggan. A tree is heavy, falling. AnNZ

A Bushman's Song. Andrew Barton ("Banjo") Paterson. So I makes for up the country at the old jig-jog. PoAu 1-2

A Bushranger. Kenneth Slessor. They would run barefoot through Patrick's Plains. CBAP; NOAV

The Bushrangers. Edward Harrington. The ghosts of the Kellys still ride from the range. PoAu 1-2

The Business. Robert Creeley. There are records. CAPP

Business as Usual. Mark Vinz. in the last lovely light/of the moon, the moon, the moon. Str

Business as Usual 1946. A.J.M. Smith. ...the spears/That clank–but gently clank–but clank again! NMP

Business Is Business. Berton Braley. "And that Business is to serve!" WBLP

The Business Life. David Ignatow. ...familiar/to your ear, your senses and your dignity. NNaP; TW

A Business Man's Prayer. William Ludlum. To Thee as Lord of little things. BLRP

Business Trips. Laurie Taylor. other wives. AMV-80

The Businessman of Alicante. Philip Levine. the trees darkening/like clusters of frightened wrens. NaP

Bussy d'Ambois. George Chapman.
And cast my selfe off, as I ne're had beene. PoEL 1-5
And rise Thou with it in thy greater light. ViBoPo
Within are nought but mortar, flint and lead. ViBoPo

The Bustan. Muslih-ud-Din Sa'di.
Take what the Friend gives as a bliss and joy. AWP
Who speaks of the Belov'd's woe as not his/Speaks infidelity, true Lovers know! AWP

Buster Keaton. Michael McFee. the god of light, poetry, and movies/still laughs at that one, Buster. AMV-81

Buster Keaton & the Cops. George Keithley. and goodbye to the fragrant world. NPGG

The Bustle in a House. Emily Dickinson. We shall not want to use again/Until eternity. APA; ELU; FaBV; FPL; HAP; HeIP; NePA; NoP; OxBA; PoEL 1-5; PoLf; WGRP

Busts and Bosoms Have I Known. Anonymous. To jubilant surprises. ErPo; PV

The Busy Body. Rachel Field. For who pretends to ticking clocks,/Or wooden chair and stool? InMe

Busy Carpenters. James S. Tippett. As we drive the nails/In the wood. SoPo

The Busy Heart. Rupert Brooke. I have need to busy my heart with quietude. HBV 1-2; MoBrPo

A Busy Man Speaks. Robert Bly. The stones of cheerfulness, the steel of money, the father of/rocks. ConAP

Busy Old Fool (parody). Ian Kelso. To supper, Horlicks–bed again/And love that flowers... BXAP

Busy with love, the bumble bee. Meleager. Such news to me was never new/whose honey's long been mixed with rue. BoLoP

A Busy Yellow Bee. Anonymous. flies contented across the great plain/home to his welcome in the honeycomb. NOBI

But. Edward Estlin Cummings. what absolute nothing NoAm

But Art Thou Come, Dear Saviour? Anonymous. But here's the cure; Thy presence, Lord, alone/Will make a stall a court, a cratch a throne. OxBoCh

But Can See Better There, and Laughing There. Gwendolyn Brooks. Reached no Alps: or, knows no Alps to reach. PoNe

But Choose. John Holmes. Die as you are, or living speak like them. But choose. MiAP

But for Lust. Ruth Pitter. Somewhere, somewhere it is so. FaBoTw; OxBTC

But Give Me Holly, Bold and Jolly. Christina Georgina Rossetti. For the day when I make merry,. BrR; ChBR; TiPo

But God's Own Decent. Robert Frost. Of the soul's ethereal/Into the material. EaLo; MoRP

But He Was Cool. Don L. Lee. to be black/is/to be/very-hot. BP; BPo; NoAm; PoBA

But How It Came from Earth. Conrad Aiken. stammered in a dark dream of men and birds. MoAB; MoAmPo

But I am Growing Old and Indolent. Robinson Jeffers. A man grows old and indolent. AP; NoAm; NOBA; TAP

But I Do Not Need Kindness. Gregory Corso. Can I say people, sitting in parks, are kinder? CoPo; NeAP

But I Shall Weep. Beatrice Redpath. But I shall weep...I shall weep. CaP

But Not So Odd. Cecil Browne. Yet scorn the Jews. DBV

But now the dentist cannot die. Andrew Lang. Begins the vast biography. CenHV

But Once. Theodore Winthrop. Then sudden heart to heart was wildly/ pressed. AA

But, Our Winter Come, in Vain. Sir Richard Fanshawe. Love may return, but never lover. LO

But Perhaps. Nelly Sachs. for the sucking mouths/of light. BoWoP

But Since I Know Thy Falsehood and Thy Pride. Abraham Cowley. White as his teeth would seem to be. LO

But, Still, He. Henry N. Lucas. he screams the silent screams. AMV-81

But Still in Israel's Paths They Shine. Carter Revard. they change, and pass,/and are the same. VoR

But That Is Another Story. Donald Justice. And peering through the windows where they sleep. CoAP; NePoEA-2

But That Was Yesterday. Aileen Fisher. And so I guess I'll go and borrow/Johnny's boat until tomorrow. SoPo

But Then and There the Sun Bore Down. N. Scott Momaday. And gone to ashes, cold and gray. CDW

But There Was Once a Time When the Bones. Eleni Vakalo. Whilst the rodent in the foundations/Lies curled in a tangle of respiration WPOW

But Thou My Deere Sweet-Sounding Lute Be Still. Richard Lynche. But I must love her (Tigresse) too too much,/Forc'd must I love, because I finde none such. AAS

But Two There Are... C. Day-Lewis. And buy our liberty with our last breath. OxBI

But We by a Love, So Much Refined. John Donne. Care less, eyes, lips, and hands to miss. LO

But We Shall Bloom. Haim Guri. We shall bloom when the last/screaming shot is stilled in the hills. TrJP

But Whan the Cok: Troilus and Criseide. Geoffrey Chaucer. Er Troilus out of Criseides herte. AtBAP

But What Is the Reader to Make of This? John Ashbery. ...Make it sweet again! InPS

But You, My Darling, Should Have Married the Prince. Kathleen Spivack. and we who screamed to know it/know it, and grow old. AmPA; NMM

Butch Is Back. Earl Gene Box. and came back/to your senses/like a recharged/robot LFAC

"Butch" Weldy. Edgar Lee Masters. "I didn't know him at all." NePA; SaC

The Butcher. Hugo Williams. ...His smile/Is the official seal on my marriage. OxBTC

The Butcher Boy. Anonymous. To show the world that I died for love. AmFP; BaBo; FSW; ViBoFo

Butcher's Wife. Herbert Scott. a big center slice/of fried ham. GP

Butcher Shop. Charles Simic. Where deep in the night I hear a voice. AmPA; LCAP; NNaP

Butcherboy. Tom Schmidt. unless I wanted to work in a butcher shop. NeAC

Butchery. Sandra McPherson. I have scrubbed knowing the smell will stay on my hands/A few more hours, like perfume or gloves. LCAP

Buthaina. Jamil. My love remains immortal though, as mortal, I must die. LiTW

Butler's Proclamation. Paul Hamilton Hayne. Naught left to mark the mother's name,/Save—immortality of shame! PAH

Butter. Tom Schmidt. wiping wet palms/on our green thighs. NeAC

Butter's Etymological Spelling Book, &c. Hartley Coleridge. They'd rather eat than study butter. GLGT

The Butterbean Tent. Elizabeth Madox Roberts. A long, long while in the butterbean tent. GoJo; SUS

Buttercups. Louis Ginsberg. O buttercups, buttercups,–/Rooted birds! HBVY

Buttercups. Wilfrid Thorley. To keep, with fairy lanterns,/The world from growing old. HBV 1-2; HBVY; OBVV

Buttercups and Daisies. Mary Howitt. Gave them likewise hardy strength/ And patient hearts to bear. HBV 1-2; HBVY; OHIP; OxBChV

Butterflies. John Davidson. There only came to her forlorn/Butterflies all black. HBV 1-2

Butterflies. Haniel Long. Who says that butterflies,/Are brief? HBMV

Butterflies. Alfred Noyes. Which smiled upon them, once, in Paradise. BoC

Butterflies. Clive Sansom. Down the polished floors of space. BoAnP

Butterfly. Anonymous. Died in half an hour. OxNR

Butterfly. Peter Armstrong. to the open throats of flowers. PCP

The Butterfly. Margaret Avison. towards the subhuman swamp of under-dark? ExPo; OBCV

The Butterfly. Gray Burr. The worm climbs wind and we the range/Of all our focus. CoPo

Butterfly. Hilda Conkling. "I have to go the opposite way." TiPo

The Butterfly. Pavel Friedmann. There are no butterflies, here, in the ghetto. VWA

The Butterfly. Alice Archer (Sewall) James. O Earth, O Sky, you use is done,/Take care of me. AA

The Butterfly. Kikaku. what can it be he does? SoPo

The Butterfly. D. H. Lawrence. ...I saw you vanish into air. SOTW

The Butterfly. Adelaide O'Keeffe. My stock of wisdom I'll improve,/Nor be a butterfly. HBV 1-2; HBVY

The Butterfly. Alice Freeman Palmer. I can break my chrysalis too! HBV 1-2

Butterfly. William Jay Smith. When Mother leans to say good night. GoJo; TiPo

The Butterfly. Edmund Spenser. To weather him, and his moist wings to dry. BoC

The Butterfly and the Bee. William Lisle Bowles. To tribes of gaudy sloth I leave/The vanity of dress. HBV 1-2; HBVY

The Butterfly and the Caterpillar. Joseph Lauren. ...the gaudy moths and millers,/Are only dressed-up caterpillars. OnMSP

Butterfly Bones; or, Sonnet against Sonnets. Margaret Avison. ...blind/like Adam's lexicon locked in the mind? LiTM

A Butterfly in Church. George Marion McClellan. Confessionals and agonies of prayer. BANP

Butterfly in the Fields. Joseph Campbell. I am blind, and do not play–/ Dallan De! Dallan De! BoAnP

Butterfly Maidens. Lahpu. How they frolic 'mid the corn,/Singing, singing, thus:/O-o, o-ho,/O-he, e-lo! WTO

Butterfly on Rock. Irving Layton. And felt the rock move beneath my hand. NOBC

The Butterfly's Ball. William Caldwell Roscoe. For no watchman is waiting for you and for me. OnUR; OxBChV

Butterfly Song. Anonymous. The clouds sprinkle down the rain. OBVE

Buttermilk Hill. Anonymous. Johnny has gone for a soldier. FSW

Button to Chin. Anonymous. Cast not a clout/Till May be out. OxNR

Buttons. Walter De La Mare. Anthropophagy reigns in the kitchen. DTC; FaBoNo

Buxom Lass. Anonymous. It's watered by a spring, that makes it grow so fast. ErPo

The Buxom Young Dairy Maid. Anonymous. I'll warrant I'll make him quickly give out. OBET

Buy Any Buttons? Anonymous. Buttons, a farthing a pair. OxNR

Buy Me an Ounce and I'll Sell You a Pound. Edward Estlin Cummings. here we come NCSH; OxBA

Buy One Now. D. J. Enright. And can be found in practically any magazine/You care to mention. NOBL

Buy Tobacco. Anonymous. I'll pay a'! PBBP

Buy Us a Little Grain. Christine Lavant. nor ever again with vinegar will I accustom/my cursing throat to prayer. WPOW

Buying a Record (parody). Robert Peters. ...I/may sell it to you, and/I may not. BXAP

Buying a Shop on Dizengoff. Erez Biton. For the journey back to a separate life/And to a very different Hebrew. VWA

Buying the Dog. Michael Ondaatje. he won't be coming back– Str

Buzz. Jim Tollerud. This makes no sense? VoR

The Buzz Plane. Robert Francis. Fie, fie, fie on you! And the word has power! TW

"Buzz," Quoth the Blue Fly. Ben Jonson. He ate the dormouse,/Else it was he. TEP

Buzzard. Michael Daugherty. one among God alone knows/how many roads beneath my feet. PoSH

The Buzzards. Martin Armstrong. Till the loftiest flaming summit died to blue. HBMV

The Buzzing Doubt. Donald L. Hill. Nor honey an adequate theme? NCSH

Bwagamoyo. Lebert Bethune. Bwagamoyo–lay down your heart here on the coast of your/homeland. PoBA

The Bwoat. William Barnes. Aye, all but my own ruffled mind. VLP

By a Bank of Pinks and Lilies. Anonymous. I would; I would–Ah! would you? ErPo

By a Chapel. Anonymous. And by a chapel as I com. GBP; OxBM

By a Lake in Minnesota. James Wright. I stand, waiting/For dark. AmFN

By a Rich Fast Moving Stream. John Tagliabue. reader in fast pursuit/of summer transformations. ELU

By Achmelvich Bridge. Norman MacCaig. His small soft foghorn quavering through the air. OxBS

By an' By. Anonymous. O, by an' by, by an' by,/I'm gwinter lay down my heavy load. BoAN 1-2

By an Evolutionist. Alfred, Lord Tennyson. As he stands on the heights of his life with a/glimpse of a height that is higher. EnLi 1-2

By and By. *Anonymous.* Good Lord, by and by. FSW

By Babel's Streams. Philip Freneau. For thou shalt reign unrivalled there. AH

By Blue Ontario's Shore (excerpt). Walt Whitman. How dare you place any thing before a man? FaBoPV

By Candlelight. Sylvia Plath. Five balls! Five bright brass balls!/To juggle with, my love, when the sky falls. SBG

By Canoe through the Fir Forest. James Dickey. Here, in the dark, it is being. NYBP

By Cobequid Bay. Alexander Louis Fraser. A wail of sorrow down the time-washed years. CaP

By Coelia's Arbor. Richard Brinsley Sheridan. But tears of sorrow shed by me. OnYI

By Cool Siloam's Shady Rill. Reginald Heber. In childhood, manhood, age, and death,/To keep us still Thine own! ELP; NOCV; OxBoCh

By Day and by Night. William Stanley Merwin. And his death/is your freedom. AmPC

By Deputy. Arthur St. John Adcock. Perhaps had someone written mine/I might have been as great as they are. CenHV

By-Election Idyll. Peter Dickinson. CANDIDATE; So, Echo, you will vote for me I know./ECHO; No. FiBHP

By Fiat of Adoration. Oscar Williams. The ease with which beauty is beauty LiTL; LiTM; NePA

By Frazier Creek Falls. Gary Snyder. We could live on this Earth/without clothes or tools! InPS

By Gentle Love. *Anonymous.* And for thy Truth the world endure. TRV

By Hallucination Visited. Robert Horan. ...rain would confuse him,/or he would be reminded thereof. EAS

By Her Aunt's Grave. Thomas Hardy. She passively nods. And they go that way. BrPo

By Loe Pool. Arthur Symons. It is noontide, and the fishes leap in the pool. VLP

By-Low, My Babe. *Anonymous.* My heart shall not forsake him; so/By-low, lie low. TrGrPo

By'm By (with music). *Anonymous.* Good Lawd, by'm by. AS

By Memory Inspired. *Anonymous.* Here's the memory of the friends that are gone! AnIV

By Moonlight. *Anonymous.* This alone is certain:/Not a light was lit. UnTE

By Moonlight. May Sarton. The lovely changing moon! MoLP

By Mrs. Hopley, on Seeing Her Children Say Goodnight to Their Father. Gerard Manley Hopkins. They kiss the Rod with filial submission. FaBoEE

By Night. Philip Jerome Cleveland. Dark hours of grief and pain reveal/The undreamed constancy of love. TRV

By Night. Robert Francis. I never heard that sound by day. PoL; VGW

By Now. Ralph Salisbury. icicle roots/I know, by now, must melt. STE

By Plain Analogy We're Told. Ambrose Bierce. There guarded from the wolf and-sheared. DBV

By-Products. Baron Wormser. ...because there's a difference between being hurt and being afraid. MAYP

By Rail through Istria. Robert Conquest. I learn to seek the fruitful thing or act. NoAm

By Rail through the Earthly Paradise, Perhaps Bedfordshire. Denise Levertov. lost in the sedge to watch the centuries. NNaP

By Return Mail. Richard Aldridge. I send this verse along to make you see. NePoAm-2

By Sandy Waters. Jesse Stuart. Will sing for us, for us forever,/In our eternity. AmFN

By the Babe Unborn. Gilbert Keith Chesterton. If only I were born. NAs

By the Beautiful Ohio. Joan LaBombard. And never dreamed the river flowed away. SM

By the Beautiful Sea. Thomas Cole. ...Lady no parasol. Be gay! NePoAm-2

By the Boat House, Oxford. Anne Stevenson. ...or disdain the loving/that living alone, or else lonely in pairs, impairs? FaBoWP

By the Bridge. Ted Walker. ...The dance/of the multiple suns is done. NYBP

By the Conemaugh. Florence Earle Coates. But I cannot hide them away from Him! PAH

By the Deep Sea. George Gordon, Lord Byron. Such as the creation's dawn beheld, thou rollest now. OBNC

By the Dominical Letter, to Find on What Day of the Week... *Anonymous.* Good Christopher Finch, and David Frier. FaBoUs

By the Exeter River. Donald Hall. "We drowned your half-brother. I remember we did." MoBS

By the Fire. *Anonymous.* I'm very well just now. OxNR

By the Fire-Side. Robert Browning. ...which I mean to do/One day, as I said before. MBW 1-2; OAEL 1-2; VLP

By the Ford. Edward ("Edward Eastaway") Thomas. And many cases of stuffed fish, vermin, and/kingfishers. OBSP

By the Hoof of the Wild Goat. Rudyard Kipling. As She sinks in the mire of the Tarn,/Even now-even now-even now! OBNC

By the Klondike River. Alan Coren. Oh, I'd much rather have my mummy/Than all the gold in the world! OnUR

By the Margin of the Great Deep. George William Russell. Growing one with its silent stream. HBMV; OBEV; OBVV

By the Moon. Thomas Ravenscroft. And about go we, and about go wee. CH

By the North Sea. Algernon Charles Swinburne.
Here, where Time brings pasture to the sea. FaBoPP
My dreams to the wind everliving,/My song to the sea. PoEL 1-5; VLP
Once, now calm as earth whose only change is/Wind, and light, and wind, and cloud, and wind. FaBoPP

By the Pacific. Herbert Bashford. The darkness pushing down upon the land. AA

By the Pacific Ocean. Joaquin Miller. Their ghosts illume my lurid West. AA; AnAmPo

By the Pool. Allen Grossman. The night has come. AMV-80

By the Pool at the Third Rosses. Arthur Symons. That some old peace I had forgotten/Is crying to come back again? FaBoPP

By the Potomac. Thomas Bailey Aldrich. And all our heavy heritage of grief. PAH

By the River Eden. Kathleen Raine. But over my gray head/The plover's unageing cry. NYBP

By the Road. Geoffrey Grigson. "Go away,' I said, "Go away.' OxBTC

By the Road to the Air-Base. Yvor Winters. I hear my neighbour's bees. CrMA

By the Salt Margin. Abbie Huston Evans. Jehovah's final name is deep I AM. NePoAm

By the Saltings. Ted Walker. ...alone/as you are and as fearful/as some crab beneath some stone. NYBP

By the Sea. Richard Watson Dixon. ...So of the soul. OBNC

By the Sea. John Hollander. Between us and the scene before us, fading/Softly to darkness. AmPC

By the Sea. Christina Georgina Rossetti. Are born without a pang, and die/Without a pang, and so pass by. BoNaP; MOS; NOBV

By the Sea. William Wordsworth. And doth with his eternal motion make/A sound like thunder-everlastingly. EtS

By the Statue of King Charles at Charing Cross. Lionel Pigot Johnson. The stars and heavenly deeps/Work out a perfect will. BoC; BrPo; FaBoRV; HBV 1-2; MoBrPo; NBM; NOBE; OBEV; OBMV; OBNC; OBVV; PoEL 1-5; RoGo; VLP

By the Turnstile. John Francis O'Donnell. Sure you wouldn't come hither if you didn't love me? IrPN; NBM

By the Waterfall. Friedrich Adler. Because it only lives, doubly alive. TrJP

By the Waters of Babylon. Benjamin Fondane. Simply a human face and no more! VWA

By the Waters of Babylon. Heinrich Heine. And his dying head he rested/On Jerusalem's fair knees. TrJP

By the Waters of Minnetonka. J. M. Cavaness. To live, To die. Moon Deer,/Thee near Beneath this sky. BLSo

By the Weir. Wilfrid Gibson. You should stand at my shoulder an outcast from Eden too. MoVE

By the Wood. Robert Nichols. Be worthy of our deaths and your delight. ChMP 059; HBMV; MMM

By Vows of Love Together Bound. Eleazar Thompson Fitch. Lead them-a happy household band-/Forever near to thee. AH

By Wauchopeside. Hugh" (Christopher Murray Grieve) MacDiarmid. Like a louch look in a lass's een. EBEV

By Way of Pretext. Yakamochi. But it was really to see you! AWP

By Winter Seas. George Brandon Saul. Of that mortality/Which is its mystery? AMV-80

By Yon Burn Side. Robert Tannahill. There we'll meet, my ain dear Jean, down by yon burn/side. HBV 1-2

Bye Baby Bother. Stevie Smith. Oh would the day had died first when you were born. TW

Bye, Baby Bunting. Mother Goose. To wrap the baby bunting in. HBV 1-2; OxNR; SoPo; SpRo; TiPo; TrAS

Bye Bye. Sean O'Huigin. GLUMP. WHW

Bye Bye Baby Blues. Blind Boy Fuller. there's one in my bosom,/t'other one in my heart. BluL

The Byfield Rabbit. Katherine Hoskins. Emporcelained, became/A term for excellence. SaC

Bygones (parody). Bert Leston Taylor. When I was a Purple Polygon,/And you were a Sky-Blue Square. HBMV

Byre. Norman MacCaig. And kittens miaow in circles, stalking/With tail and hindleg one straight line. BoAnP; BSV

The Byrnies. Thom Gunn. A little group above the foreign wood. NePoEA-2; NoAm; OxBTC

Byron. J. Gordon Coogler. All that was evil-to thy mother. OBAL

C

Caelica, XXXIV. Fulke, Lord Brooke Greville. Therefore, if thou wilt prove thyself a god,/In thy sweet fires, let me burn this fair rod. FCP

Caelica, XXXV. Fulke, Lord Brooke Greville. May not make merry, when they heare me cry. AtBAP; FCP

Caelica, XXXVI. Fulke, Lord Brooke Greville. But which are worse, kings ill or easily led,/Schools of this truth are yet not brought a-bed. FCP

Caelica, XXXVII. Fulke, Lord Brooke Greville. Love is not his that raves; hope is untrue. FCP

Caelica, XXXVIII. Fulke, Lord Brooke Greville. By broken fence is proved a common field. EnRePo; FCP

Caelica, XXXIX. Fulke, Lord Brooke Greville. But when I thought myself of herself free,/All's changed, she understands all men but me. FCP

Caelica, XL. Fulke, Lord Brooke Greville. Turns all the spirits of Man into desire. EnRePo; FCP; JCP

Caelica, XLI. Fulke, Lord Brooke Greville. Therefore the doom is, wherein thou must rest,/Myra that scorns thee shall love many best. FCP

Caelica, XLII. Fulke, Lord Brooke Greville. I'll hold no more, false Caelica, live free,/Seem fair to all the world, and foul to me. FCP

Caelica, XLIII. Fulke, Lord Brooke Greville. I, like the child, whom nurse hath overthrown,/Not crying, yet am whipped, if you be known. FCP

Caelica, XLIV. Fulke, Lord Brooke Greville. Since in the gilt-age Saturn ruled alone,/And in this painted, planets every one. FCP; OAEL 1-2

Caelica, XLV. Fulke, Lord Brooke Greville. Absence is pain. EnRePo; FCP; PoEL 1-5

Caelica, XLVI. Fulke, Lord Brooke Greville. Since not to feel what wrong I bear in this,/A senseless state, and no true patience is. FCP

Caelica, XLVII. Fulke, Lord Brooke Greville. Atlas bare heaven, such burdens be of grace;/Caelica, in heaven, is the angel's place. FCP

Caelica, XLVIII. Fulke, Lord Brooke Greville. If on the next day Cynthia change and leave,/Would you trust your eyes, since her eyes deceive? FCP

Caelica, XLIX. Fulke, Lord Brooke Greville. Then, Myra give me leave for Cupid's sake/To kiss thee oft that I may court'sy make. FCP

Caelica, L. Fulke, Lord Brooke Greville. If husbands now should only deck their own,/Silk would make many by their backs be known. FCP

Caelica, LI. Fulke, Lord Brooke Greville. If I have spoken to the common sense,/It envy kills, and is a wise offense. FCP

Caelica, LII. Fulke, Lord Brooke Greville. Sweet saint 'tis true, you worthy be,/Yet without love nought worth to me. AtBAP; FCP

Caelica, LIII. Fulke, Lord Brooke Greville. And who entreats, you know entreats in vain,/That love be constant, or come back again. FCP

Caelica, LIV. Fulke, Lord Brooke Greville. Then teach desire, hope, not rage, fear, grief,/Powers as unapt to take, as give relief. FCP

Caelica, LV. Fulke, Lord Brooke Greville. Yet who this language to the people speaks,/Opinion's empire, sense's idol breaks. FCP

Caelica, LVI. Fulke, Lord Brooke Greville. None can well behold with eyes/But what underneath him lies. EnRePo; FCP; PoEL 1-5

Caelica, LVII. Fulke, Lord Brooke Greville. I, like the fish bequeathed to Neptune's bed,/No sooner taste of air but I am dead. FCP

Caelica, LVIII. Fulke, Lord Brooke Greville. And now again, her own black hair puts on/To mourn for thoughts by her worths overthrown. FCP

Caelica, LIX. Fulke, Lord Brooke Greville. Who Caelica's chaste heart then seeks to move/Must joy to suffer all the woes of love. FCP

Caelica, LX. Fulke, Lord Brooke Greville. The world in two I have divided fit,/Myself to you, and all the rest to it. FCP

Caelica, LXI. Fulke, Lord Brooke Greville. For constant faith is made a drudge/But when requiting love is judge. FCP

Caelica, LXII. Fulke, Lord Brooke Greville. Who sees their glories on the earth must pry;/Who seeks true glory must look to the sky. FCP

Caelica, LXIII. Fulke, Lord Brooke Greville. And let him know that thinks with faith to move,/They once had eyes, that are made blind by love. FCP

Caelica, LXIV. Fulke, Lord Brooke Greville. For what before was filled by me alone,/I now discern hath room for everyone. FCP

Caelica, LXV. Fulke, Lord Brooke Greville. Caelica, you say you love me, but you fear,/Then hide me in your heart, and keep me there. FCP

Caelica, LXVI. Fulke, Lord Brooke Greville. Since outward wisdom springs from truth within,/Which all men feel, or hear before they sin. FCP

Caelica, LXVII. Fulke, Lord Brooke Greville. Unconstancy and doubleness depart/When man bends his desires to mend his heart. FCP

Caelica, LXVIII. Fulke, Lord Brooke Greville. When in the night with songs, not cries, I moan,/Lest more should hear what I complain of one. FCP

Caelica, LXIX. Fulke, Lord Brooke Greville. What can be good to me, since my love is,/To do me harm, content to do amiss? EnRePo; FCP

Caelica, LXX. Fulke, Lord Brooke Greville. The boy hath stol'n your thoughts some other way,/Where wantonlike they do with many play. FCP

Caelica, LXXI. Fulke, Lord Brooke Greville. And I no more will stir this earthly dust/Wherein I lose my name to take on lust. FCP

Caelica, LXXII. Fulke, Lord Brooke Greville. Since love no doomsday hath, where bodies change,/Why should new be delight not being strange? FCP

Caelica, LXXIII. Fulke, Lord Brooke Greville. I found desert, and to desert am true,/Still dealing by it, as I dealt by you. FCP

Caelica, LXXIV. Fulke, Lord Brooke Greville. Myra leaves him and knows best/What shall become of all the rest. FCP

Caelica, LXXV. Fulke, Lord Brooke Greville. Yet that faith in men doth dwell,/Who travels constancy can tell. FCP

Caelica, LXXVI. Fulke, Lord Brooke Greville. I smile to see desire is never wise,/But wars with change, which is her paradise. FCP

Caelica, LXXVII. Fulke, Lord Brooke Greville. Faith, truth, worth, law, all popular protections. FCP

Caelica, LXXVIII. Fulke, Lord Brooke Greville. Whence, while men gaze upon this blazing star,/Made slaves, not subjects, they to tyrants are. FCP

Caelica, LXXIX. Fulke, Lord Brooke Greville. Which gathers such sense out of envy's beams,/As still casts imputations on supremes. FCP

Caelica, LXXX. Fulke, Lord Brooke Greville. Can place, or stamp make current aught but worth? FCP

Caelica, LXXXI. Fulke, Lord Brooke Greville. Fortune can here claim nothing truly great,/But that this princely creature is her seat. FCP

Caelica, LXXXII. Fulke, Lord Brooke Greville. Reader! then make time, while you be/But steps to your eternity. FCP

Caelica, LXXXIII. Fulke, Lord Brooke Greville. For Greiv-Ill, pain, forlorn estate do best decipher me. FCP; PoEL 1-5

Caelica, LXXXIV. Fulke, Lord Brooke Greville. But, Cupid, now farewell, I will go play me/With thoughts that please me less, and less betray me. FCP

Caelica, LXXXV. Fulke, Lord Brooke Greville. For glory's of eternity a frame,/That by all bodies else obscures her name. FCP; JCP

Caelica, LXXXVI. Fulke, Lord Brooke Greville. Or, man, forsake thyself, to heaven turn thee,/Her flames enlighten nature, never burn thee. FCP; JCP

Caelica, LXXXVII. Fulke, Lord Brooke Greville. Then living men ask how he left his breath,/That while he lived never thought of death. FCP; PoEL 1-5

Caelica, LXXXVIII. Fulke, Lord Brooke Greville. For goodness only doth God comprehend,/Knows what was first, and what shall be the end. FCP; JCP; OxBoCh

Caelica, LXXXIX. Fulke, Lord Brooke Greville. The earth must burn, ere we for Christ can look. FCP; NOCV

Caelica, XC. Fulke, Lord Brooke Greville. Opinion bodies may to shadows give,/But no burnt zone it is where people live. FCP

Caelica, XCI. Fulke, Lord Brooke Greville. And in our flesh, the vanities' false glass,/We thus deceived, adore these calves of brass. FCP

Caelica, XCII. Fulke, Lord Brooke Greville. For place a coronet on him you will,/You straight see all great in him, but his ill. FCP

Caelica, XCIII. Fulke, Lord Brooke Greville. Yet when his fame is to the highest borne,/We know enough to laugh his praise to scorn. FCP

Caelica, XCIV. Fulke, Lord Brooke Greville. For lest man should think flesh a seat of bliss,/God works that his joy mixed with sorrow is. FCP

Caelica, XCV. Fulke, Lord Brooke Greville. Tyrants through fear and malice feed on blood,/Good kings secure at home, seek all men's good. FCP

Caelica, XCVI. Fulke, Lord Brooke Greville. A boat, to which the world itself is sea,/Wherein the mind sails on her fatal way. FCP; NOCV

Caelica, XCVII. Fulke, Lord Brooke Greville. We with the Jews even Christ still crucify,/As not yet come to our impiety. EnRePo; FCP

Caelica, XCVIII. Fulke, Lord Brooke Greville. Wrapped up, O Lord, in man's degeneration. FCP; OxBoCh

Caelica, XCIX. Fulke, Lord Brooke Greville. Deprived of human graces, not divine,/Thus hath his death raised up this soul of mine. EnRePo; FCP; OxBoCh; PPoe

Caelica, C. Fulke, Lord Brooke Greville. Which but expressions be of inward evils. EnRePo; FCP; HAP; OAEL 1-2

Caelica, CI. Fulke, Lord Brooke Greville. Then, though kings, player-like, act glory's part,/Yet all within them is but fear and art. FCP

Caelica, CII. Fulke, Lord Brooke Greville. Sin, then we knew thee not, and could not hate,/And now we know thee, now it is too late. FCP

Caelica, CIII. Fulke, Lord Brooke Greville. Who therefore censures God with fleshly sprite,/As well in time may wrap up infinite. FCP

Caelica, CIV. Fulke, Lord Brooke Greville. Now if of God both these have but the name,/What mortal idol then can equal fame? FCP; OxBoCh

Caelica, CV. Fulke, Lord Brooke Greville. Devils, there many be, and Gods but one. FCP; NOCV; PoEL 1-5

Caelica, CVI. Fulke, Lord Brooke Greville. Who roots their vice out, must pierce deeper in. FCP

Caelica, CVII. Fulke, Lord Brooke Greville. Till weariness, the spur, or want of food,/Makes gilded curbs of all beasts understood. FCP

Caelica, CVIII. Fulke, Lord Brooke Greville. Ask them that from the ashes of this fire/With new lives still to such new flames aspire. FCP

Caelica, CIX. Fulke, Lord Brooke Greville. Rather sweet Jesus, fill up time, and come/To yield the sin her everlasting doom. EnRePo; FCP; PoEL 1-5

Caenlochan. Helen B. Cruickshank. And beauty glimpsed was swift withdrawn/As startled stag and soft-eyed fawn. PoSH

Caesar. William Stanley Merwin. Hoping he's dead. LCAP; NaP

Caesar. Paul Valery. Not knowing what thunder collects in the center of Caesar. WaaP

Caesar and Pompey. George Chapman. Sustained but for an hour. ViBoPo

Caesar Remembers. William Kean Seymour. Caesar, shivering,/Heard repeat/Spades on the hillside,/Sentries' feet. HBMV

Caesar's Lost Transport Ships. Robert Lee Frost. And overhead the petrel wafted wide. AmePo

The Caesar's Victory. Anonymous. Thus providence did kindness show/When we was so surrounded. OBSS

Caesar, when that the traitor of Egypt. Sir Thomas Wyatt. To cloak my care, but under sport and play. FCP

Caesura. Kenneth MacKenzie. and suddenly hears again the endless steps. BoAV; CBAP; NOAV

Cafe: 3 A.M. Langston Hughes. Police lady or Lesbian/over there?/Where? HaCAP

Cafe in Warsaw. Allen Ginsberg. or lean together laughing to notice this wild haired madman who sits/weeping among you a stranger. HAP

Cafe Tableau. May Swenson. he wades into the pool of her/stagnant desire. ErPo

Cafes. Robert B. Smith. as behind a cage of glass it slowly/pumps and stops, pumps and stops. LFAC

The Caffer Commando (excerpt). Thomas Pringle. And the edict is written in African blood! ACV

The Cage. Elizabeth Bartlett. How this false spring tree/Clings that I perch on NePoAm-2

The Cage. John Berryman. And the great cage suffers nothing whatever no PoA

The Cage. David Gascoyne. And I shall have gone away. EAS

The Cage. John Montague. the mark of an old car/accident beating on his/ghostly forehead. CIP; FaBoIP

The Cage. James Stephens. To escape from out the cage/By the edges and the side. OxBTC

The Cage. Avner and Levenston. E. A. Treinin. Quiet, my bride, till morning comes/and your voice shall sound in the caves of my heart. VWA

The Caged Bird. Arthur Symons. It does not even hate me with its eyes. BrPo

Caged Rats. Ebenezer Elliott. And death shall have no funeral/From shipless sea to sea. EBEV; VLP

The Caged Skylark. Gerard Manley Hopkins. For a rainbow footing it nor he for his bones risen. CMoP; FM; LiTM; MoAB; MoBrPo; MoPo; OBMV; PBBP; SoSe

Cages. Marvin Solomon. The little boy would get to see, in time. NYBP

Cain. Irving Layton. Or perhaps a joke we didn't quite hear. PeCV

Cain's Song. Donald Finkel. it is a sound/Cain will remember/till he dies VWA

Cain Shall Not Slay Abel Today on Our Good Ground. Malcolm Lowry. For at dawn is the reckoning and the last night is long. OBCV; PeCV

Cairngorm, November 1971. Martyn Berry. Others will come. We make it so. PoSH

Cairo Jag. Keith Douglas. ...a man with no head/has a packet of chocolate and a souvenir of Tripoli. NePoEA

The Caisson Song. Edmund L. Gruber. Then in peace I'll abide when I take my final ride/On a caisson that's rolling along. BLSo; PAL; TreF

Cake. Miriam Clark Potter. I wait and think,/Then wish—and blow! BiCB

Cakewalkman. Sam Abrams. scott joplin/university. APU

Calais, August 15, 1802. William Wordsworth. Consul, or King, can sound himself to know/The destiny of Man, and live in hope. NAs

Calais Sands. Matthew Arnold. To-night those soft-fringed eyes shall close/Beneath one roof, my queen! with mine. OAEP

Calamiterror, VI. George Barker. I felt it crack my abdomen, the world. EAS

Calamity. F. R. Scott. The starch came raining down. PeCV

Calamity Jane Greets Her Dreams. Kathleen Lignell. She pictures her face and breasts/lit by that tin badge/flashing in the sun. AMV-80

Calamus. Walt Whitman.
But you will last very long. AP
To celebrate the need of comrades. AP

Calculating Female. Jill Hellyer. Before his arms encompass/The sweet comptometress. PoL

The Calculation. David Wagoner. On top of my head, I walked the rest of the night. NYBP

A Calder. Karl Shapiro. And iron is blooded. EyDe

Caldwell of Springfield. Bret (Francis Bret Harte) Harte. But not always a hero like this—and that's all. MC; PAH

Caledonia. Colleen J. McElroy. until I've learned that love, like hate/is always acted out BlSi

Caledonia. Anthony Powell. By this one Scotchman, pacing in the Square. NOBL

The Caledonian Market. William Plomer. Let us hope that they'll make your grandchildren smile. ChMP; HaMV

Calendar. Cecil Bodker. Next year it will be flies. BoWoP

The Calendar of Oengus: Prologue (excerpt). Anonymous. while from former valleys/mountains now are made. NOBI

Calenture. Alastair Reid. I walked toward her on the flowering water. NYBP; PrIm

The Calf-Path. Sam Walter Foss. But I am not ordained to preach. HBV 1-2; HBVY; PoLf

The Calf, the Goat, the Little Lamb. Samuel Hoffenstein. And so did I, my little lamb,/And so will you. DBV

Caliban in the Coal Mines. Louis Untermeyer. Fling us a handful of stars! HBV 1-2; MoAmPo; PoPl; TreFS; TrJP; TRV

Caliban upon Setebos. Robert Browning. ...will not eat this month/One little mess of whelks, so he may 'scape!] AWP; EBEV; MaVP; NOBV; NoP; OAEL 1-2; OAEP; VLP; WGRP

Calico Pie. Edward Lear. They never came back to me. CBEP; FaBoCh; LoGBV; SoPo; TrGrPo

California. Thomas Lake Harris Made young by joys that live from ours. AA

California. J. P. Robson. Farewell to splint, choke damp/and blast!/Hurrah, for Californy! VLP

California. Lydia Huntley Sigourney. Like the mother of the Gracchi,/Folds her jewels to her heart. MC; PAH

California #2. Victor Hernandez Cruz. Welcomed with Cafe/con Canela. TAT

California Dead. G. E. Murray. ...one Indian guide/who returned them to this wild territory. MAYP

A California Idyl. Ernest McGaffey. And dashed his beak through the rattlesnake. BPAW

California Joe. Anonymous. Where two hearts were united/In love's sweet, happy dream. CoSo

The California Phrasebook. Dennis Schmitz. houses sway at the slightest/tremor. AmPA; NPGG

California Quail in January. Will C. Jumper. And dry leaves churn in whirlwinds from their wings. GrPl

The California Stage Company. Anonymous. So the people must root hog or die. CoSo

California, This Is Minnesota Speaking. Stephen P. Dunn. and you say hello and see if you can survive. GP

California Winter (excerpt). Karl Shapiro. And yet one feels the sumptuousness of this dirt. AmFN

California (with music). Anonymous. There's plenty of gold in the world, I'm told,/On the banks of the Sacramento shore. AS

The Californian. Jesse Hutchinson. Peradventure they foresaw the day/Now dawning in Californi-a. AmFP

The Californians. Theodore Spencer. And a hateful wish to be empty and tall like you. NYBP; TW

Californy Stage. Anonymous. You're too dam heartsick fer to scold,/And too dam weak to pick up gold! BPAW

Caligula. Robert Lowell. my namesake, and the last Caligula. CoPo

The Call. Anonymous. Come home again, come home again! OBEV

The Call. Thomas Curtis Clark. O God of Freedom, stir us in our night/That we set forth, for justice, truth and right! PGD

The Call. Daniel Corkery. The fierce old Irish dead! OnYI

The Call. James Dickey. And touching every tree upon the hill. NePoEA-2

The Call. John Hall. Nay, thou maist prove/That mans most Noble Passion is to Love. MeLP; MePo; OBS; ViBoPo

The Call. Reginald Wright Kauffman. Love comes laughing up the valleys,/Hand in hand with hoyden Spring. HBV 1-2

The Call. Charlotte Mew. Though yet we do not know/Who called, or what marks we shall leave upon the snow. ChMP

The Call. Jules Supervielle. ..."You alone can do it,/Come immediately." NU

The Call. Jones Very. Thy sandals seize, gird on thy clothes,/Or I must leave thee here behind. MAmP

The Call across the Valley of Not Knowing. Galway Kinnell. as the creation/touches him a last time all over his body? GP

Call All. Anonymous. A common triumph or a single grave. PAH

A Call for a Song. Anonymous. For ye have been famed/The worst in this contray! OxBM

Call from the Afterworld. Jozef Habib Gerez. Come my friends come/I am waiting for you. VWA

Call It a Good Marriage. Robert Graves. Till as jurymen we sat on/Two deaths by suicide. BoLoP

Came You Not from Newcastle. *Anonymous.* Why should not I love my love,/Gallant hound sedelee? GBP

Camel. Laila Akhyaliyya. but day already smells of autumn. BoWoP

Camel. Gene Derwood. Thump against loud whiteness foreseeing no night. NePA

Camel. William Stanley Merwin. Even from far off smell the true water. NePA

Camel. Mary Britton Miller. But kneel no more upon the sands/To mount the kings of Eastern lands. TiPo

The Camel. Ogden Nash. I'm never sure. Are you? CenHV; SoPo

Camel. Jon Stallworthy. A glint of snows above Baluchistan. BoAnP

The Camel-Rider. *Anonymous.* Other than this, my song of love to thee. AWP

The Camel's Hump. Rudyard Kipling. Kiddies and grown-ups too! EvOK

The Camelopard. Hilaire Belloc. And I will slay this fearful brute/With stones and sticks and guns and slings. FaBoNo

The Camels Have Come. *Anonymous.* Go early, go quick, and get a good view. PoOW

Camels in Persia. Dorothy Wellesley. I was Cyrus the Great.' OBTV

Camels of the Kings. Leslie Norris. How is it that we know the world is changed? OBCP; PCh

The Cameo. Edna St. Vincent Millay. White against a ruddy cliff you stand, chalcedony on sard. FYAP; LiTA; MoAmPo; UnPo

Cameo No. II. June Jordan. great great proto-/typical BPo

Camera. Ted Kooser. this little battery without a spark. Psk

The Camera Obscura. John Addington Symonds. Then pass into the shadowy night,/Where formless shades blindfold the light. NOBV

Camerados (parody). Bayard Taylor. ...Walt, we believe it:/Everywhere, everywhere. Par; UnPo

Camilla. Charles Augustus Keeler. Ah, sweet Camilla, thy songs for Felipe,/the fearless, are vain! AA

Camoens. Herman Melville. Flame to the height of epic song. ViBoPo

Camoens in the Hospital. Herman Melville. Serving high God with useful good. ViBoPo

Camoes and the Debt. Sophia de Mello Breyner Andresen. This country kills you slowly BoWoP

Camouflage. Amy Clampitt. And that much grief, for a day,/bankrupted our economy. SUW

Camouflage. John Streeter Manifold. ...teach this hate of mine/The patience and integrity of the steel. WaP

Camp. Patrick Anderson. and never spoke a word. OBCV

Camp Fire. Beatrice Marion Bromley. Over the veld broods Night. ACV

The Camp Hymn. Mary S. Edgar. Keep me ever, by Thy Spirit,/Pure and strong and true. TRV

A Camp in the Prussian Forest. Randall Jarrell. The star laughs from its rotting shroud/Of flesh. O star of men! AP; MiAP; MoAmPo; NMP; OBWP; OxBC; SM

Camp Notes. Mitsuye Yamada.
I am drowning. WPOW
where the first baby/was christened/Melody. WPOW

The Camp of Souls. Isabella Valancy Crawford. Come the dusky plumes of red "Singing Leaves'. NOBC

The Camp Within the West. Roderic Quinn. Perhaps large stars will burn above/Their camp within the West. PoAu 1-2

The Campaign. Joseph Addison.
And those who paint 'em truest praise 'em most. CEP
Rides in the whirlwind, and directs the storm. OBWP

Campaign Promise. Henry Taylor. which, had it been alive,he would have killed. TW

The Campanero. *Anonymous.* Well, I'd never go to sea/Aboard that handy little bark, the Campanero! ShS

The Campbells Are Comin'. *Anonymous.* The Campbells are comin',/O-ho, O-ho! FSW

Camper's Night Song. Robert Louis Stevenson. At God's green caravanserai. BBV

Campfire Extinguished. Raymond F. Roseliep. the woman washing dishes/in a pan of stars. SM

Campi Flegrei. Barend Toerien. ...the goatherd blows his flute/and calls the cattle up the slope. PeSA

Campidoglio. Giuseppe Belli. because it shaws we're gey near Judgment-day. OBVE

Camping at Thunder Bay. David Fedo. steadfastly maintains the illusion. AMV-81

Camping Out. William Empson. See where they blur, and die, and are outsoared. CMoP; FaBoMo; MoVE; OxBTC

Camping Out on Rainy Mountain. Jim Barnes. His shadow has missed you by a mile. Too high. CDW

Camptown. John Ciardi. And we're late and lost unless we run. WaP

De Camptown Races. Stephen Collins Foster.
De hoss I fancy am de bobtail nag,/He'll walk away from de bay. TrAS
Somebody bet on de bay. FSW; PSoN

The Campus. David Posner. A question bangs in our heads like an old door/That will not stay closed, for all our knowledge. NYBP

A Campus in Summer. Reed Whittemore. Cheerily they may arrive, three months behind. GLGT

The Campus on the Hill. W.D. Snodgrass. The clock just now has nothing more to say. AP; LiTM; MP; NIP; NoAm; TAP; TwCP

Can Doleful Notes to Mesur'd Accents Set. John Danyel. Bring back the same, then dye and dying last. UnS

Can. Hist. Earle Birney. (except for the French/who still want to be Mensch) OxBC

Can I Believe. Lodovico Ariosto. Against their will Thou only hast the might! CAW

Can I Forget? Sidney Goodsir Smith. Sun an mune an the warld, ma dear? NeBP; SeCePo

Can I Not Sing. *Anonymous.* For in his pipe he made so much joy. ViBoPo

Can I Say. Dolly Bird. ...see him raise his/arms to the sun, hear him say/ "Thank you father"/...again WPOW

Can I Tempt You to a Pond Walk? James Schuyler. I have nothing to say, but, well, yes. PoA

Can. Lit. Earle Birney. it's only by our lack of ghosts/we're haunted NOBC

Can-Opener. David McAleavey. squirrel, rain, grass, tree–which now the cat runs up. AMV-81

Can't. Harriet Prescott Spofford. The steadfast man whose name was Grant. MC; PAH

Can't They Dance the Polka! *Anonymous.* Oh, you New York gals, can't they dance the polka! FSW; ShS

Can't You Live Humble? *Anonymous.* Can't you live humble/To de dyin' Lam'? BoAN 1-2

Can the Circle Be Unbroken? *Anonymous.* There's a better home a-waiting/In the sky, Lord, in the sky. FSW

Can the Mole Take. Cecil Day-Lewis. I see the constellations,/But by their gaps. OBMV

Can Ye Sew Cushions? *Anonymous.* But your daddie's a-rockin'/Upon the saut sea. FaBoCh; LoGBV

Can You Change a Shilling? Toni Del Renzio. Will you come to me at midnight. EAS

Can Zone; or, The Good Food Guide. Rika Lesser. ...The world's your oyster. Open wide, now. Read. MAYP

Cana. Thomas Merton. Wine for old Adam, digging in the briars! TrCP

Cana Revisited. Seamus Heaney. The consecration wondrous (being their own)/As when the water reddened at the feast. FaBoMo

Canaan. Muriel Spark. Since she is plighted to me, a wilderness, and I to/ The silver country of Canaan. NYBP

Canada. Sir Charles G. D. Roberts. How on thy breast, and o'er thy brow,/Bursts the uprising sun! PeCV

Canada-I-O. *Anonymous.* Unto the God-forsaken place called Canada-i-o. AmFP; BaBo; FSW; ViBoFo

The Canadian Authors Meet. F. R. Scott. More ways to set the selfsame welkin ringing! ACV; NOBC; OBCV

Canadian Boat Song. *Anonymous.* Beat heavily beyond the Atlantic roar. BSV; GoTS; OxBS

Canadian Boat Song. John Galt. But we are exiles from our fathers' land. BLPA; CaP; CBEP; FaBoCh; FaPoR; LoGBV; OBEV; OBNC; OBRV

A Canadian Boat Song. Thomas Moore. The Rapids are near and the daylight's past. GoBC; HBV 1-2; OBRV

The Canadian Exile. Antoine Gerin-Lajoie. Fondly shall my last look wander/To thee, beloved, far away. CaP

Canadian Farmer. Genevieve Bartole. And on the wrinkled earth a snipe has landed. CaP

The Canadian Herd-Boy. Susanna Moodie. Quick jingling comes the cattle-bell. OBCV

The Canadian Prairies View of Literature. David Donnell. the corn under my shirt awkward a little rough light brown dry/and making me itch at times NOBC

The Canadian Rossignol. Edward William Thomson. ...Then awakes once more/His song, ecstatic with the May. CaP

Canadians. Ivor Gurney. Vermin eaten, fed beastly, in vile ditches meanly. FaBoTw

Canadice Lake. Bob Mondy. Between us are many fish. WOLT

Un Canadien Errant. *Anonymous.* And till the day I die, my thoughts/will be of thee. FSW

The Canal. Aldous Huxley. Creates within that barren water-way/New life, new loveliness, and passes on. HBMV

The Canal Bank. James Stephens. To-what! To-wit! To-woo! GrPl

Canal Bank Walk. Patrick Kavanagh. From green and blue things and arguments that cannot be/proven. CIP; CMoP; FaBoTw; IPY; MoBrPo; NoAm; NOBI

Canal Street. John Wheelwright. your named and nameless who are mixed with fate. PoA

Car Episode. Coco Gordon. This is the room, hands oarlocked,/in which you will work. AmC

Car swerves,/injures 11; driver held. Aram Saroyan. driver held ANYP

Car Wash. Myra Cohn Livingston. how good to see you again/shining, gleaming. NTCP

Caravaggio Dying, Porto Ercole, July 1610, Aged 36. Edward Lucie-Smith. ...Now this keyhole shows him/My conquest of Amore Vincitore. PeHV

The Caravan. Hovhannes Blouz. "Dost think with such unwieldy bundle/The mart of Paradise to gain?" CAW

Caravan. Michael Longley. ...my history/Stiffening with the tea towels/Hung outside the door to dry. FaBoIP

A Caravan from China Comes. Richard Le Gallienne. The little moon my cargo is. BrR

Caravans. Josephine Preston Peabody. I would have had the winged Mirage of/yonder desert. AA

Caravatt's Junkyard. Elizabeth Morgan. ...opening/on goldenrod,/hinging on air. GrPl

Carcassonne. Gustave Nadaud. He never gazed on Carcassonne. BLPA; FaBoBe; HBV 1-2

The Card-Dealer. Dante Gabriel Rossetti. When she shall speak, thou'lt learn her tongue/And know she calls it Death. MaVP; NBM; VLP

A Card Game: Kinjiro Sawada. Patricia Y. Ikeda. characters only a priest can read. BrSi

A Card of Invitation to Mr. Gibbon, at Brighthelmstone. William Hayley. That he may boast around his grove/A visit from the BIRD OF JOVE. OBEC

The Card-Players. Philip Larkin. Rain, wind, and fire! The secret, bestial peace! OxBC

The Card-Players. David Ray. ...and/see that their wives have been loyal/in their absence. VGW

Cardinal. Barbara Howes. The cardinal's red cursive/Line, written on winter, writing to spring... DFF

A Cardinal. W. D. Snodgrass. replenishing the verses/of nobody else's world. PP

The Cardinal and the Dog. Robert Browning. Heaven keep us Protestants from harm: the/rest...no ill betide! VLP

Cardinal Bembo's Epitaph on Raphael. Thomas Hardy. Eclipse while he lived, and decease at his dying. EyDe; FaBoEE

The Cardinal Bird. William Davis Gallagher The cardinal bird. AA

Cardinal Fisher. John Heywood. That by that time the Hat/came he had no head. ACP

Cardinal Ideograms. May Swenson. Open? Open. Shut? Shut. OBCA

Cardrona Valley. Ian Wedde. Mouth of dark spaces/the valley waits for the mountain. OCNZ

Care. Virginia Woodward Cloud. And while the whole world slept. AA; HBV 1-2

Care. Josephine Miles. Help me. NYBP

Care. Richard Murphy. The children came to tell me when she died. IPY

Care Away! Anonymous. Of his penans God do him mede!/Careful is my hart therfore. OxBM; OxBoLi

Care-Charmer, Sleep. Samuel Daniel. And never wake to feel the day's disdain. ForPo; InPS; LiTB; LoBV; OAEL 1-2

Care-Charmer Sleep. Bartholomew Griffin. I fear at night he will not come again. AAS; NIP

Care Is Heavy. Conal O'Riordan. And thrust my brother in the sea. CAW

Careers. Marjorie Welish. ...there is a fire/"raging" throughout a house, and a company-No. 7-/pulling a hose toward it. APU

The Careful Angler. Robert Louis Stevenson. And, breathing forth a pious wish,/Will cram his belly full of fish. LiSp; SD; SoSe

The Careful Husband. Anonymous. But she's got such a start that I doubt if you'll find her. OnYI; OxBI

Careless Content. John Byrom. I am Content, I do not care. CEP; HBV 1-2; NOEC; OBEC

The Careless Gallant. Thomas Jordan. All comes to nothing a hundred years hence. CoMu; HAP; OxBoLi

The Careless Good Fellow Written March 9, 1680. John Oldham. This is the Profession, that never will alter. APAS; CEP; SeCV 1-2

Careless Love. Anonymous.
All for the love of a railroad man. TrAS
And take me back where I come from. BLSo
I'd leave them both for lovin' you. UnTE
Love, oh love, oh careless love/Has broke this heart of mine. BFSS
See what careless love has done. UnPo
You pass my door and you don't come in. FSW

Careless Love. Lonnie Johnson. And shoot you four or five times/And stand over you until you finish dying BluL

Careless Love. Stanley Jasspon Kunitz. This nymphomaniac enjoys/Inexhaustibly is boys. WaP

Careless Love (with music). Anonymous. And it'll break that heart of yours some time. AS

The Careless Lover. Sir John Suckling. Ere I'll die for love, I'll fairly forego it. CavP

Careless Seems the Great Avenger. James Russell Lowell. Standeth God within the shadow, keeping watch above his own. TreFT

Careless Talk. Mark Hollis. Known/As Joan. FiBHP; NLV

Careless Willie. Anonymous. Now, Willie dear, don't scratch the paint. BBGG

The Carelesse Nurse Mayd. Thomas Hood. O! foolishe Mayd to be soe sadde/The Momente that her Care was drownd! FaBoNo; VLP

Carentan O Carentan. Louis Simpson. We never yet had lost a man/Or known what death could do. CoAP; MoBS; NMP; NOBA; OBWP; PrIm

Caresses. Elsa Barker. The pollen-chambers of the infinite/Flower, and its petals only half uncurled. HBMV

Cargoes. John Masefield. Firewood, iron-ware, and cheap tin trays. AnEnPo; BLPL; CMoP; DiPo; ExPo; FaBV; FaPo; FaPoR; GoTF; GTBS; InPK; LiTM; MCCG; MoAB; MoBrPo; MOS; NOBE; OBEV; OBMV; OBVV; PoRA; RoGo; SeCeV; TEP; TreF

Cargoes of the Radanites. Harry Alan Potamkin. Where we perish, there is our/grave! TrJP

The Cariboo Horses. Al Purdy. in the gasoline smell of the/dust and waiting 15 minutes/at the grocer's HeIP; NOBC

Caries. Solyman Brown. Most justly damned to everlasting fame! FaBoUs

The Carillon. Rosalia Castro de Murguia. And the dead-how strangely bare! CAW

Caring. F. R. Scott. Who cares for caring, has caress. PeCV

Carious Exposure. Gladys Cardiff. covering my probings, as you do,/With quiet conversation. CDW

Carl Hamblin. Edgar Lee Masters. But the multitude saw why she wore the/bandage. AmP; CMoP; LiTA; LiTM; OBSV

The Carle He Came O'er the Croft. Allan Ramsay. Sae Lawty says I shou'd na hae him. OxBS

Carlyle and Emerson. Montgomery Schuyler. The star that beams above the seas. AA

Carmarthen Bar. John Malcolm Brinnin. Together then we smiled, and walked inland. HoAn

Carmel Point. Robinson Jeffers. ...and become confident/As the rock and ocean that we were made from. NoP

Carmen. Victor Hernandez Cruz. SHE GOES REAL SMOOTH CAD; PoBA

Carmen. Newman Levy. ...So ring/down the curtain, poor Carmen's at rest. ALV; FiBHP

Carmen Bellicosum. Guy Humphreys McMaster. And rounder, rounder, rounder, roared the/iron six-pounder,/Hurling death! AA; GN; HBV 1-2; MC; PAH; PAL

Carmen Elegiacum. Thomas Morton. Why then for hell the match is somewhat even. SCAP

Carmen Genesis. Francis Thompson. And named, while Nature to its height/Quailed, the enormous Name. CoBE

Carmen Miranda. Frank Polite. I split the sky with cherry pits. GP

Carmen Possum. Anonymous. Since ista possum is a goner! BLPA; NLV

Carmen Saeculare. Horace. Are not these drifting figures the chorus? OBVE

Carmina. Caius Valerius Catullus.
And art, mine own unrivalled Fair! OBVE
And seizing with precipitation/The slight neglects of conversation.' OBVE
...but what women say to kind/Lovers, we write in rapid streams and wind. OBVE
But you, Catullus, your destiny's obdurate. OBVE
I know not, but I burn and feel it so. OBVE
...I must confess/I love thee more, but I esteem thee less. OBVE
I see 'tis folly, but I feel 'tis woe. OBVE
If I don't strangely love her. OBVE
It beats me. I feel it done to me, and ache. OBVE
Lesbia! I must love you still. OBVE
My good Egnatius! for what's half/So silly as a silly laugh? OBVE
Of which once smelt, the gods thou wilt implore/Fabullus that they'd make thee nose all ore. OBVE
Or cease to wonder why they fly you thus. OBVE
Quickly we others Errors find,/But see not our own Load behind. OBVE
...squandering in my love's amorous/vice longer than you wished it, marred but poignant. OBVE
This Sculker I shall never find. OBVE

Carmina Amico. Edward James.
I am the bugle for the mouth of love. PeHV
Still past their lashes-still, the treasure slips? PeHV

Carmina Burana (excerpt). Anonymous. I cry/for myself. BoWoP

Carmina, II, 28. Sextus Propertius. Then tell, O tell, how thou didst murther me. OBVE

The Carnal and the Crane. Anonymous.
Even the blessed Virgin/She's now brought forth a son. ESPB
The provender the asses left/So sweetly he slept on.' OBET

Carrowmore. George William Russell. And the old enchantment lingers in the honey-heart of/earth. HBMV

Carry Her over the Water. W. H. Auden. And the horses drawing your carriage/Sing agreeably, agreeably, agreeably of love. FaBoTw

Carry Me Back. John Holmes. ...Old boy next door, and old me. AmFN; NePoAm-2

Carry Me Back to Old Virginny. James A. Bland. There's where the old darkey's heart am longed to go. BLSo; FaBoBe; FaFP; GoSl; PSoN; TreF

Carry On! Robert W. Service. Carry on, my soul! Carry on! HBV 1-2

Cars Once Steel and Green, Now Old. Louis Zukofsky. Till one knows its being which soon is not. VGW

Carta Canadensis. Ralph Gustafson. Lean, provincial, burning/In their plot. PeCV

La Carte. Justin Richardson. For less than they quote/For the table d'hote. ELU; FiBHP

The Carter. Anonymous. And as I did sing it you must learn it along. OBET

Carthusians. Ernest Christopher Dowson. Though the world fall apart, surely ye shall/prevail. VLP

A Cartload of Shoes. Abraham Sutzkever. From our old Vilna streets/They drive us to Berlin. VWA

Cartography. Louise Bogan. Beyond our fate/And distant from our eyes. PoPl

Cartography. Joel Oppenheimer. this is the first action. CoPo

Cartoon. Jim Simmerman. When we speak, our words do not match our lips. AMV-81

Carved by Obadiah Verity. Don Welch. and I left that place full of/breed, and brood, and cross-hatching. PoDr

Carved on an Areca Nut... Ho Xuan Huong. If we come together let it turn red,/Not leaf-flat, lime-insipid. PBWP

Caryatid. Léonie Adams. A weight more grave than marble on the breast. LiTM; MoVE

Casa d'Amunt. Alastair Reid. The garden is not ours. NePoEA

Casa de Pollos. Kathleen Fraser. "for death to flap in on. But I carry the knife." AmPA

Casabianca. Elizabeth Bishop. ...And love's the burning boy. FaBoWP; OBSP

Casabianca. Felicia Dorothea Hemans. But the noblest thing that perished there/Was that young, faithful heart. BeLS; BLPA; EtS; FaBoBe; FaFP; FPL; GoTF; HBV 1-2; HBVY; PaPo; TreF; WBLP

Casanova. Richard Usborne. The skirts of young girls on their way to church. PoL

The Cascade. Edgell Rickword. in whose dim glades each hunter finds/his own torn spirit in his mesh. ChMP; FaBoTw

Cascadilla Falls. Archie Randolph Ammons. that I can live my life/by this single creek. NIP; NOBA

Cascando. Samuel Beckett. I and all the others that will love you/if they love you/3/unless they love you. NOBI

A Case. Anonymous. I wish to God he'd go away! FaBoCo

The Case. H. R. Hays. Skeletons of birds/Fell like snowflakes./Fell continually. EAS

Case. Phyllis Janowitz. ...the smell of food raking/through its middle like a red hot fingernail. AMV-81

The Case. Ken Norris. until I too begin chasing falcons and start forgetting/about bodies buried shallowly in lakes. CaPN

A Case at Sessions. Walter Savage Landor. He quotes the Scripture and eats hares.' OBSV

The Case for Miners. Siegfried Sassoon. And that's the reason why I'd almost like/To see them hawking matches in the gutter. SaC

A "Case of Assault." Lydia Stephanou. You retained an undivided silence. BoWoP

The Case of Thomas More. Sister Mary St. Virginia. ...Use prudence, my lords; not pity. GoBC

A Case to the Civilians. Anonymous. Civilian, is the child he then begot/To be allow'd legitimate, or not? FaBoEE

Casement's Funeral. Richard Murphy. White hair tossed, a black cape flecked with snow. NOBI

Casey at the Bat. Ernest Lawrence Thayer. But there is no joy in Mudville: Mighty Casey has struck out. AmePo; BBV; BeLS; BLPA; FaBoBe; FaFP; FPL; GoTF; HBV 1-2; InMe; LiSp; MaC; OBAL; OBCA; PaPo; PoPl; PoRA; SD; StPo; TreF; YaD

Casey Jones. Anonymous.
And now he's mining in the promised land. AmFP
Got anothr papa on the Salt Lake Line! ATP; OxBoLi
Kase he's been on de cholly so long. ABF
Tales that are earnest, noble and gran'/Belong to the life of a railroad man. AS; GoTF; TreF; ViBoFo
Took his farewell journey to the Promised Land. BeLS; MaC
You got another papa on the Salt Lake Line! ATP; FaBV; TrGrPo

Casey Jones (A vers.). Anonymous. Kase dose two locomotives is boun' to bump. ViBoFo

Casey Jones (B vers.). Anonymous. "Hush your mouth, don't draw a breath;/We'll draw a pension from Casey's death!" ViBoFo

Casey Jones (C vers.). Anonymous. Said, "I'm going to ride the scoundrel to Niagra Fall." ViBoFo

Casey Jones (D vers.). Anonymous. De womens in Jackson, all dressed in black,/Said, in fact, he was a cracker-jack. ViBoFo

Casey Jones (E vers.). Anonymous. Good engineer but he's dead and gone./Dead and gone.//On the road again... ViBoFo

Casey Jones (Union). Joe Hill. "That's what you get for scabbing on the S.P. Line." FSW

Casey Jones. Edward Vincent Swart. When the delight was gone. PeSA

Casey's Daughter at the Bat. Al Graham. But there's still no joy in Mudville–Casey's daughter/has struck out. InMe

Casey's Revenge. James Wilson. But Mudville hearts are happy now–for Casey hit the ball! BLPA; GoTF; OnMSP; TreFS

Casey's Table d'Hote. Eugene Field. I lay it all to thinkin' of Casey's tabble dote. PoOW

Casey–Twenty Years Later. S. P. McDonald. "I'm mighty Casey who struck out just twenty years ago." BLPA

Cash In. Sharlot M. Hall. And the Dealer will understand. BPAW

Cash Only, No Refund, No Return. Daniel Mark Epstein. He just stood there behind the display case. MAYP

Cashel of Munster. Anonymous.
And, O, may no other maiden know such reproach as I! AnIV; BIrV; GBL; IrPN; OBEV; OBVV; OnYI; OxBI

Casida of the Rose. Federico Garcia Lorca. it was searching for something else. NU

Casino. W. H. Auden. And what was godlike in this generation/Was never to be born.' MoPo

Casino Beach. Thomas Rabbit. ...pries/Open finger after finger for the small change inside. MAYP

Cassamen and Dowsabell. Michael Drayton. Quoth he, "There's never shepherd's boy/That ever was so blest." OBSC

Cassandra. Louise Bogan. Not the dumb earth, wherein they set their graves. AnAmPo; HAP; MoAmPo; MoVE; PBWP; SBG; VGW

Cassandra. Robinson Jeffers. ...to men/and gods disgusting.–You and I, Cassandra. HeIP; LiTA; LiTM; NePA; WaP

Cassandra. Edwin Arlington Robinson. ...None heeded, and few heard. CMoP; ExPo; LiTA; LiTM; NePA; NoAm; OxBA; PPON; SeCeV

Cassandra Southwick. John Greenleaf Whittier. And tamed the Chaldean lions, is mighty/still to save! PAH

Cassie O'Lang. Anonymous. She tried to kill her husband with a boomerang. ShM

Cassinus and Peter. Jonathan Swift. Oh! Celia, Celia, Celia shits!' OAEL 1-2; PPP

Cassius Hueffer. Edgar Lee Masters. Now that I am dead I must submit to an epitaph/Graven by a fool! NoAm; OxBA

Cast Down, but Not Destroyed. Anonymous. And, fearless, trust our cause to God! PAH

Cast Our Caps and Cares Away. John Fletcher. All which happiness, he brags,/He doth owe unto his rags. ViBoPo

Cast Thy Bread upon the Waters. Phoebe A. Hanaford. If thou sowest with liberal hand. AH

Castara. William Habington. All her vows religious be,/And she vows her love to me. HBV 1-2; LiTL

The Castaway. William Cowper. And whelm'd in deeper gulfs than/he. AtBAP; CABA; CEP; CoBE; EiCP; ELP; EnPE; FiP; GTBS; HeIP; InPo; MOS; NOBE; NOEC; NoP; OAEL 1-2; OAEP; OBEC; PoEL 1-5; PPoe; PPP

Castaway. John Nerber. He too, at last, became no more than goat. PoA

A Castaway (excerpt). Augusta Webster. ...why then my name/would have been mother... BrRo

Castile. Miguel de Unamuno. if worthy of you to the world they'll come/down from the uplands. PoPl

Castilian. Elinor Wylie. With arrogant eyes, and narrow hands/Miraculously shaped. AnAmPo; HBMV; NAMP

Casting. Howard Nemerov. Which in the world is upside down,/The fish hook or the question mark? OBSP

Casting All Your Care upon God, for He Careth for You. Thomas Washbourne. He that so much for you did do,/Will do yet more, and care for you. OxBoCh

Casting All Your Care Upon Him. Anonymous. His grace accepts and now sustains/our load. STF

Casting at Night. Allen Hoey. night behind me with the dim/vocabulary of rocks and stream ahead. AMV-80; WOLT

The Castle. Sidney Alexander. the grown-up white man and the grown-up black. PoNe

The Castle. Edwin Muir. Our only enemy was gold,/And we had no arms to fight it with. LiTB

The Castle by the Sea. Ludwig Uhland. No maiden was by her side! AWP

Catching One Clear Thought Alive. Paula Gunn Allen. ...you watch/for the one too slow to stop your leap, your/teeth in time. WPOW

Catching Soft Craws. William J. Vernon. tails like vibrators/used to shock as a joke/when shaking hands. WOLT

Catching Up. David Walker. the steps I must stumble almost/fail me in his stride. FAZ

Catechism, 1958. W. M. Ransom. Both of us kept on going. CDW

Catechism Elegy. Margaret Gibson. the only answer no one questioned,/a radiance that ripened. MAYP

Catechisms: Talking with a Four-Year-Old. George Ella Lyon. Who will die first? Str

The Caterpillar. Anselm Hollo. surely it is so. FAZ

Caterpillar. R. E. Rashley. The real longing is for the irrecoverable,/Barely-forgotten, child's world. CaP

Caterpillar. Christina Georgina Rossetti. To live again a butterfly. GoJo; OxBChV; SoPo

The Caterpillar and the Ant. Allan Ramsay. ...I spread my wing/In air, while you're a creeping Thing. SeCePo

Caterpillars. John Freeman. In a heaving ring returning the same regrets. ChMP

The Catfish. Michael Waters. until that miraculous catfish was still. WOLT

The Cathedral. James Russell Lowell. Missed in the commonplace of miracle. AmePo; MAmP

A Cathedral. Stanislav Vinaver. –Until the entire earth/Is transformed from stones/Into a prayer of flames. VWA

The Cathedral of Rheims. Edmond Rostand. The blundering German cannon wuld provide/Their shame forever and our Parthenon. CAW

The Cathedral of Rheims. Emile Verhaeren. The old cathedral, to the years to be/Showing, with wounded arms, their own disgrace. CAW

Cathedrals. W. S. Doxey. and other monuments. AMV-80

Cathemerinon: O Noble Virgin. Prudentius (Aurelius Clemens Prudentius). And golden light, and Golden Light! ISi

Catherine. Karla Kuskin. I thanked her but I wouldn't dream/Of eating cake without ice cream. NTCP

Catherine Kinrade. Thomas Edward Brown. And for a space again there was no voice in Heaven. OBVV

Catherine Ogg. Edgar Lee Masters. And starved a little, and brooded much/To the end of the farce! GLGT

Cathexis. F. J. Bryant, Jr., ...Mike called me,/nigger,/hurt. PoBA

Cathleen. Anonymous. Of course it shows. BIrV

Cathleen Sweeping. George Johnston. I give it up. Why should I doubt delight? NOBC

The Catholic Bells. William Carlos Williams. ring ring ring ring ring!/·Catholic bells–! CMoP; NOBA; OxBA

The Catholic Faith. Kenelm H. Digby. And to serene and constant thoughts gives birth. CAW

Catkin. Anonymous. Now what do you think of that! TiPo

Cato. C. H. Sisson. I wait here and hope it may be morning. NOCV

Cato's Address to His Troops in Lybia. Nicholas Rowe. And his great Head be hid, within an humble Tomb. OBEC

Cato's Soliloquy. Joseph Addison. The wreck of matter and the crash of worlds. GoTF; TreFS; WBLP

Cats. Marchette Chute. It often likes to be alone. SoPo

The Cats. Samuel Exler. ...that is what they were like/Before we agreed to be friends. GOYP

Cats. Eleanor Farjeon. Cats sleep/Anywhere. PCat

Cats. Robert Francis. Cats walk neatly. DFF

The Cats. Weldon Kees. To greet us, crying, dancing,/After the long day. NaP

Cats. Francis Scarfe.
And stroke their ears and smooth their breast, and hold/Their paws, and gaze into their eyes of gold. PCat
Not knowing who she was, or what she meant. BoAnP; NeBP

Cats. Arthur Seymour John Tessimond. Cats, no less liquid than their shadows,/Offer no angles to the wind. BoAnP; HaMV; PCat

Cats and Dogs. Howard Moss. "In Pusseyville, it's raining cats and dogs!" OBAL

Cats and Egypt. Andrew Hughes. ...he seems content/to warm himself on my cold thighs. AMV-81

Cats Climb Trees. Tom Veitch. My sister wrote that. ANYP

Cats Is Wheels. Faye Kicknosway. the cats claws/lie sleepun. APU

The Cats of Campagnatico. Peter Porter. ...there are only/Cypress moments lingering and the long tray of the sky. OBTV

The Cats' Tea-Party. Frederic Edward Weatherly. Then knocked their tea-cups over, and scampered through the door. TiPo

Cattle. Anonymous. Knee-deep within the stream. SoPo

Cattle. Berta Hart Nance. Texas grew from hide and horn. BPAW

Cattle. Peter Skrzynecki. That man will decipher/As an omen of his final hunger. CBAP

The Cattle of His Hand. Wilbur Underwood. Onward we strain with a mighty resound-/ing of hoof-beats. AA; WGRP

Cattle Show. Hugh" (Christopher Murray Grieve) MacDiarmid. Whose laughter plays like summer lightning there. BSV; FaBoMo; GoTS; HAP; MoBrPo; OBMV; OxBTC

The Cattle Thief. Tekahionwake. And blame, if you dare, the hunger that drove him to be/a thief. WPOW

Catullus Talks to Himself. Caius Valerius Catullus. But let her go, man, let her go. UnTE

Catullus to Lesbia. James Reeves. Should bring down curses on our heads/To think what he has missed. ErPo

Catullus viii. Louis Zukofsky. Come on Catullus, you can/take it. NoAm

Catwalk. Daniel L. Klauck. green and sticky/gushes everywhere/and he cries. LFAC

Catwise. Philip Booth. the dumbshow out of which/(humanly) you have come. NePoAm-2

The Caucasus. Boris Pasternak. My poems then I would really live! PoPl

The Caughnawaga Beadwork Seller. William Douw Lighthall. Thine own child to thee returns. CaP

Caught by Chance. T. W. Ramsey. I found you, and with you/My own defeat. HaMV

Caught in the Pocket. William D. Barney. Five words of scripture tell, alas,/His tale of woe: And it came to pass. LiSp

Cauld Cornwood. Anonymous. Where the snow ligs baith winter and summer. GBP

The Cauliflower. John Haines. dreaming only on the yellow/and green magnificence/that is hardening within them. GP

The Caulker. M. A. Lewis. I gave the brute fresh water, when of course he wanted salt. StPo

Cause and Effect. Anonymous. And all for the want of a horseshoe nail. GoTF; TreFT

Cause and Effect. Matthew Prior. Poor Lubin fears that he may die;/His wife, that he may live. NLV

A Cause for Wonder. Anonymous. The Lord that bought free and thrall/Is found in an ass's stall/By his moder Mary. MeEL

Cause of Our Joy. Sister Maris Stella. on that first Christmas night through Christ, our Brother. ISi

The Cause of This I Know Not. Haniel Long. And hearts are made to be broken/And love is always woe. HBMV

Causes. Mona Van Duyn. as the earth rolls over, inverting billions of houses. SM

The Causes of Color. Ann Rae Jonas. She loved it before it was understood. SUW

Causeway. Allan Block. Ancestral green and the bright chromium. TAT

Caution. Anonymous.
And don't go near the water. OxNR
Keep your head. Remain a virgin. UnTE

A Caution to Everybody. Ogden Nash. ...he forgot how to walk and learned how to fly before/he thought. NePA

A Caution to Poets. Matthew Arnold. The world, in its turn, will not take/ Pleasure in contemplating. CBEP; FaBoUs; PV

A Cautionary Tale. Anne Wilkinson. Lord have mercy upon/Her sweet white bones. Amen. OBCV; PeCV

Cautionary Verses to Youth of Both Sexes. Theodore Hook. But parents ne'er should let you go unpunished for a pun. HBV 1-2; OxBChV

The Cautious Struggle. Anonymous. But–are you sure you shut the door? UnTE

Cavalier. Richard Bruce. My new mistress, My Lady Death. CDC

Cavalier Lyric. James Simmons. I could not love you half so well/without my practice shots. PoL

The Cavalier's Escape. Walter Thornbury. Safe from the canting band. FaBoBe; GN; HBV 1-2

The Cavalier's Song. William Motherwell. Our business is like men to fight,/And hero-like to die! GN; HBV 1-2

Cavalier Tunes. Robert Browning.
Boot, saddle, to horse, and away! HBV 1-2; MCCG
Give a rouse: here's, in hell's de-/spite now,/King Charles! BoLiVe; EnLit; HBV 1-2
Great-hearted gentlemen, singing/this song! EnLit; HBV 1-2

The Cave. Glenn Ward Dresbach. And we are lucky if we keep them still. RFM

Cave. Jose Emilio Pacheco. or in a cave which only the dead inhabit. AMV-81

The Cave-Drawing. Vernon Watkins. And again like a vein behind the iris leaping. LiTB

The Cave of Night. John Montague.
cave of night blooms/with fresh explosions. CIP
David's brethren/in the Land of Goliath. CIP
a solitary being begins/its slow dance... CIP

Cave of Staffa, I. William Wordsworth. ...the sovereign Architect,/Has deigned to work as if with human Art! VLP

Cave Sedem! Theodore F. MacManus. To run like hell, it has been found,/Both feet must be upon the ground. HBV 1-2

The Cavern. Charles Tomlinson. the self's unnameable and shaping home. CMoP; NMP

The Caverns of the Grave I've Seen. William Blake. In my Golden House on high,/There they Shine Eternally. NCEP

Caves. David Baker. falling, no less, yet surely no more, than I. MAYP

The Caves. Michael Roberts. These were our footprints, seven lives ago. ChMP

Cawsand Bay. *Anonymous.* All chips of the old block from the stem to the starn. PoPle

The CCC. Thomas Whitbread. And make forgotten the works of the CCC. NYBP

Cean-Salla. James Clarence Mangan. But I mourn for Cean-Salla! OnYI

Ceann Dubh Deelish. Sir Samuel Ferguson. Who, with heart in breast, could deny you love? IrPN; SeCePo

Cease, Then, My Tongue! Edmund Spenser. His glorious Face! which glistereth else so bright/That the angels' selves cannot endure His sight. ILwL

Cecil County. Ron Welburn. our Jesus all these years/keeps them burning out their lives. PoBA

Cecilia. *Anonymous.* Sautez, mignonne Cecilia,/Ah! Ah! Cecilia! WHW

Cedar. Robert Morgan. weak as a photograph emerging in the darkroom pan. GeTw

Cedar Mountain. Annie Fields. To the young dead we consecrate/These lives that now we dedicate. MC; PAH

Cedar Needles. Chase Twichell. the world being/everywhere equally foreign. MAYP

The Cedar River. Reginald Gibbons. ...the rod/that nods like an innocent stalk of wild rice. MAYP

Cedar Waxwing. William H. Matchett. In a scathing, scolding lecture he's too happy to resent. ELU

The Cedars of Lebanon. Alphonse Marie Louis de Lamartine. While their uplifted souls rejoice. AWP

The Ceiling. Theodore Roethke. To find out how the Ceiling's Feeling. EyDe

Ceiling Unlimited. Muriel Rukeyser. Ceiling unlimited. Visibility unlimited. MoAmPo

Ceix and Alceone. John Gower. Hir bridges yet, as it is seene,/Of Alceoun the name bere. OxBM

Celan. Asya (Asya Gray). See how the East flames up,/An eternal candle. VWA

Celan. Anthony Barnett. Executor,/estranged, prayerless,/by a followed memory. VWA

Celandine. Edward ("Edward Eastaway") Thomas. Gone like a never perfectly recalled air. OxBTC

Celanta at the Well of Life. George Peele. And every hair a sheaf shall be,/And every sheaf a golden tree. LoBV

Celebrant. David Mitchell. only hooves. OCNZ

Celebrated Return. Clarence Major. Gloria Patri. AmNP

Celebrating the Freak. Cynthia Macdonald. To set the freak flags flying. Psk

Celebrating the Mass of Christian Burial. Cleopatra Mathis. rising past the boundaries we know, past the season/of our own deaths. LTB

Celebration. Leonard Cohen. with a groan, like those gods on the roof/that Samson pulled down. ErPo

The Celebration. James Dickey. A mortal, a dutiful son. VGW

The Celebration. Robert Mezey. In the seventh year a blossom. FAZ

Celebration. Elizabeth Newton Sachs. their circle is complete. AMV-81

A Celebration. May Sarton. His light was there. I miss the light. NePoAm-2

Celebration. Ray A. Young Bear. leaving her eyes/to the east. CDW

Celebration 1982. Terri Meyette Wilkins. They won't look/they will just say/no one died. LFAC

Celebration for My Mother. Wendy Rose. please believe in me. CDW

The Celebration in the Plaza. Adrienne Rich. All we have left, their pedagogues reply. NePoEA

A Celebration of Charis. Ben Jonson.

And if such a verse as this,/May not claime another kisse. AnAnS 2; SeCP

(And that quickly) speake your Man. AnAnS 2; SeCP

Bit shee's Juno, when she walkes,/And Minerva, when she talks. AnAnS 2; SeCP

But of one, if short he came,/I can rest me where I am. SeCP

Let who will thinke us dead, or wish our death. AtBAP; OAEP; SeCP

Or else one that plaid his ape,/In a Hercules-his shape. AnAnS 2; EnRePo; OAEP; SeCV 1-2

Till she be the reason why/All the world for love may die. AnAnS 2; EnRePo; SeCP; SeCV 1-2

What you please, you parts may call,/'Tis one good part I'ld lie withall. AnAnS 2; SeCP

Which how Dexterously I doe,/Heare and make Example too. AnAnS 2; SeCP

Celebrations. Austin Clarke. And looters braved the street. IPY; OxBI

Celery. Ogden Nash. But celery, stewed,/Is more quickly chewed. FaBoUs; NePoAm

The Celestial City. Giles the Younger Fletcher. And things unseen do see, and things unheard do hear. NOBE; OBS

The Celestial City (Excerpt). Humbert Wolfe. interpreted her heart and spoke for her. BoC

The Celestial Country. John Mason Neale. Thou shalt be, and thou art! GoBC

Celestial Evening, October 1967. Charles Olson. ...the new moon new in all/the ancient sky PoM

Celestial Love. Buonarroti Michelangelo. ...our love makes still more fair/Our friends on earth, fairer in death on high. AWP

The Celestial Passion. Richard Watson Gilder. So shall my days be full of heavenly light! AA; AnAmPo

The Celestial Pilot. Dante Alighieri. And he departed swiftly as he came. WGRP

Celestial Queen. Jacopo Sannazaro. Guide thou my efforts and inspire my song. ISi

The Celestial Surgeon. Robert Louis Stevenson. And to my dead heart run them in! BBV; BrPo; EBCP; GoTF; HBV 1-2; HBVY; MoBrPo; TreFS; TrGrPo; TrPWD; TRV; ViBoPo; WGRP

Celestial Wisdom. Juvenal (Decimas Junius Juvenalis). And makes the happiness she does not find. AWP

Celestine. Robert Fitzgerald. ...the last/Marches of that giant Past/Faint upon the intense invisible. MoVE

Celia. Ellen Bass. the throb of cilia with cilia. NMM

Celia Bleeding, to the Surgeon. Thomas Carew.

Shed all the blood, felt all the smart. AnAnS 2; PeD

Thou struckst her arme, but 'twas my heart/Shed all the blood, felt all the smart. AnAnS 2; PeD; SeCP

Celia Celia. Adrian Mitchell. I think of you with nothing on. FaBoEE

Celia's Home-Coming. Agnes Mary Frances (Mme Emile Duclaux) Robinson. By the hearth a holier Lar! OBEV; OBVV

Celia Singing. Thomas Carew.

Awake and see the rising sun. EG; EnLit

Such matchless beauty with disdain,/Are all turn'd into stones again. OAEP

Celia Singing. Thomas Stanley. Kill those that live, and dead things animate. AnAnS 2

The Cell. George Rostrevor. In that green solitude I'll dwell,/And praise Thee all day long. TrPWD

Cell. Dennis Shady. reflected/in a macrocosmic I. LFAC

Cell-Mates. Louis Untermeyer. Let's go to sleep...good-night...an' see ye/Frid'y. HBMV

The Cell of Himself. Arthur Freeman. My cry caught in my throat, while the thin walls/thicken like distance, I am most alone. TwCP

Cell-Rap #27. Raymond Ringo Fernandez. out of/the unguarded/window/for the boys/upstate.... LFAC

Cell Song. Etheridge Knight. can there anything/good come out of/prison. NNaP; PoBA

A Celebration of Charis. Ben Jonson. I can rest me where I am. AtBAP

The Cello. Richard Watson Gilder. No face of all can ever seem the same. AA

Cello Entry. Paul Celan. all is less than/it is,/all is more. VWA

Cells Breathe in the Emptiness. Galway Kinnell. How many inert molecules are ready to break into life? NaP; VGW

The Celt in Me. Keith Wilson. ...dim men with old robes/walk gravely through the Danube mists/their arms outstretched for me. GP

Celtic Cross. Norman MacCaig. Such understanding that it seems like love. OxBS

The Celtic Cross. Thomas D'Arcy McGee. ...till that predestin'd day/When Erin's self is drowned. OnYI

The Celtic Fringe. Stevie Smith. Eh, Kathleen, the cat is gone. FaBoNo

The Celtic Lyric (parody). J. C. Squire. Of lost stars and suns forlorn/And moons bereft. BXAP

The Celts. Thomas D'Arcy McGee. They of your song sublime! OnYI; OxBI

The Celts. Stevie Smith. All the same she is not so beautiful as she was. NoP

The Cemetery at Academy, California. Philip Levine. ...that in time one comes/to be a stranger to nothing. NaP; NYBP

The Cemetery by the Sea. Paul Valery. This tranquil roof where jib-sails hunt in flocks. LiTW

A Cemetery in New Mexico. Alfred Alvarez. They are waiting for me. Why won't they call my name? VWA

The Cemetery Is. Audrey McGaffin. ...to circumvent/The darkness of the grave with bright intent. NePoAm-2

Cemetery Nights. Stephen Dobyns. will wake from sleep and perhaps bark back. SV

The Cenci. Percy Bysshe Shelley.

My heart is beating with an expectation/Of horrid joy. TW

My Lord,/we are quite ready. Well, 'tis very well. EnRP; FiP

The Cenotaph. Charlotte Mew. ...and some young, piteous, murdered face. MMM

Cenotaph of Lincoln. James T. McKay. ...anywhere/Save in the tomb. Not there–he is not there. OHIP

Censorship. Philip Brasfield. while I speak out–a broken-record warning:/ Kyrie eleison, forsaken. LFAC

Censorship. John Ciardi. and the plumbing would howl from Hell, "We're watching/you!" NLV; TW

Censorship. Arthur Waley. On the sightless horse, riding into the bottomless abyss. OxBTC; WaP

The Centaur. Theodore Roethke. What else he does is up to you. NePoAm-2

The Centaur. May Swenson. Rob Roy, he pulled some clover/as we crossed the field, I told her. FaBoWP; GrPl; MP; NePoAm-2; NMM; PH; SO; TwCP

The Centaur Overheard. Edgar Bowers. But I do not look, move, or make a noise. ConAP

Centaur Song. Hilda ("H. D.") Doolittle. bid the stars shine forever. VGW

The Centaurs. James Stephens. They raced into the wood! AmMo; AnEnPo

The Centenarian's Story. Walt Whitman. Stands forever the camp of that dead brigade. CTC

Centennial Hymn. William Cullen Bryant. Write on a fairer, whiter page,/ The record of thy happier reign. PAH

Centennial Hymn. John Pierpont. On these our hills. AnNE; PAL

Centennial Hymn. John Greenleaf Whittier Let the new cycle shame the old. AA; MC; PAH; PAL

The Centennial Ode: Dear Land of All My Love. Sidney Lanier. Thy name shall shine, thy fame shall glow. GN; PAH; PGD

The Center of America. Robert Siegel. revolving across Kansas. AMV-81

The Center of Attention. Daniel Gerard Hoffman. Traffic flows over the bridge. FYAP; UnPo

The Center of the Garden. Ann Stanford. but a warm wall in winter, an old coat thrown around you. AMV-80

Centerfold Reflected in a Jet Window. Sandra McPherson. because she loved, because she had always loved. GeTw; MAYP

The Centipede. Samuel Hopkins Adams. But I would rather, could I choose,/Feed him than buy his boots and shoes. InMe

The Centipede. Sir Alan Patrick Herbert. In either case it's dead. CenHV

A Centipede Was Happy Quite. Anonymous. Considering how to run. ALV; OnUR; SoPo; TiPo

Central. Ted Kooser. Hello? Is there anyone there? Psk

Central Heating System. Stephen Spender. They bark at the ice-fanged killer/Who leaves no footstep in the night. GrPl

Central Park. Robert Lowell. ...each flowering shrub,/hides a policeman with a club. LiTM; NYP

Central Park. Howard Nemerov. And see the shadow children home again. NYP

Central Park, 1916. Pamela Stewart. A new guardian of the Park's pond, sad/And giant swan! NYP

Central Park Some People (3 P.M.). Nancy Morejo. and forfeit his whole life/rabidly/companeros. PBWP

Central Park South. Donald Revell. ...Now it is a street beside the park. NYP

Central Park Tourney. Mildred Weston. Another two/Try. AmFN

Central Park West. Stanley Moss. And fly into battle with broken aeriels. PCP

Central Park West. Jack Spicer. Who crouches in the bulbs with his shears/And hasn't got the hots for anyone. PeHV

The Centuries Are His. Georgia Moore Ebeling. His Kingdom shall yet rule though stars be dust. TRV

A Century of Couplets (excerpt). Richard Chenevix Trench. Large fire from smallest spark has many times been brought. OBRV

A Century Piece for Poor Heine. John Logan. And one with the mended, broken arm of Art. NNaP

Cerberus. H. L. Van Brunt. and ask yourself if you care/about his cold or chain FAZ

The Ceremonial Band. James Reeves. Oh! the fiddles and the flutes were the finest in the land. OnUR

Ceremonial Ode Intended for a University. Lascelles Abercrombie. And trade with his Eternity. OBVV

Ceremonies. Ann Stanford. I am a gray frog/Out there in the chorus. HW

The Ceremonies for Candlemas Day. Robert Herrick. And where 'tis safely kept, the fiend/Can do no mischief there. EnLit; OAEP

Ceremonies for Candlemas Eve. Robert Herrick. New things succeed, as former things grow old. CaPo; JCP; OAEP; OBS

Ceremonies for Christmas. Robert Herrick. And the plums stand by/To fill the paste that's a-kneading. AnAnS 2; GN; HBV 1-2; OHIP; PCh; TEP

Ceremony. Kattie M. Cumbo. I wait for the new year. BlSi

Ceremony. Johari M. Kunjufu. the Mothers of the Generations of Life/we the/libation. BlSi

Ceremony. Vassar Miller. Has clothed my nakedness in ceremony. NePoEA

Ceremony. Howard Nemerov. Between Orion and the Pleiades. AMV-80

Ceremony. William Stafford. In that river my blood flowed on. LCAP

Ceremony. Richard Wilbur. I think there are most tigers in the wood. CoAP; MiAP; NoAm; PP

Ceremony after a Fire Raid. Dylan Thomas. The sundering ultimate kingdom of genesis' thunder. CMoP; CoBMV; ExPo; MoPo; WaP

Ceremony for Birth and Naming. Ridgely Torrence. In the three names of Love, Light, and your/Divine Humanity I name you– MoRP

Ceremony upon Candlemas Eve. Robert Herrick. So many goblins you shall see. OBCP

Cerne Abbas. Hal Summers. ...And the air's/Sweet with silence and vegetable smoke. HaMV

Cernunnos. Hugh Maxton. And your feet turned in, your ears/reddened with obituaries. CIP

A Certain Age. Phyllis McGinley. Heels to the shoes and lipstick on the mouth. NePoAm-2

Certain Artists Bring Her Dolls and Drawings. William Butler Yeats. We have naught for death but toys. LiTB

Certain Choices. Richard Shelton. ...That's the way it is/with friends. We make certain choices. Psk

Certain Dead. John Haines. they lie there now,/feeding your country's dwindling soil. LCAP

A Certain Lady. Dorothy Parker. And what goes on, my love, while you're away,/You'll never know. NIP

Certain Maxims of Archy. Don (Donald Robert Marquis) Marquis. the notion of using/cockroaches for bait InMe; OBAL seriously debating/the intention of the gods/towards their civilization. NLV

Certain Maxims of Hafiz. Rudyard Kipling. Are the links of thy fetters so light that thou cravest an-/other man's chain? HBV 1-2

Certain Mercies. Robert Graves. Pampering the spirit/With obscure, proud merit? CoBMV; GTBS-P

A Certain Peace. Nikki Giovanni. and i had a day of mine/that made me as happy/as yours did you CNA

Certain True Woords Spoken Concerning One Benet Corbett. Elizabeth T. Corbett. Ask who they were, and thou hast done. AnAnS 2; SeCP

A Certain Young Lady. Washington Irving. And you know very well whom I mean. FaBoBe; HBV 1-2

Certainties. Margaret Widdemer. Comes the one scar that your heart shall hide/Till the day you die! HBMV

Certainty. Evelyn Hardy. You will come back; I care not what the time,/ Be it the green of Spring or Winter's rime. HBMV

Certainty before Lunch. John Berryman. I know You are there. The sweat is, I am here. LCAP; OxBC

Certainty Enough. Amelia Josephine Burr. But I have certainty enough/ For I am sure of you. HBMV

Certified Copy. Ann Deacon. only the skin remembers, swirling to clench/ the archetypal wound: the center holds. NIP

Cervera. Bertrand Shadwell. Spain, in her pride, has set/Honor above them. PAH

Cesar Franck. Joseph Auslander. Even for a while, hear an exalted speech/ And know Death by his smile. HBMV

Ceylon. A. Hugh Fisher. Dream! and be one with these. HBV 1-2

Cezanne. Gertrude Stein. There where the grass can grow nearly/four times yearly. TAP

Ch'in Chia's Wife's Reply. Anonymous. The tears fall down and wet my skirt. BoWoP

The Chaff. William Stanley Merwin. calling with voices of young birds/to its wheat. PPP

Chagrin. Isaac Rosenberg. And hang from implacable boughs. ChMP; MoBrPo; VWA

Chahcoal Man (with music). Anonymous. Hyeh come de chahcoal man-n-n-n./Chahcoal! AS

Chain. Audre Lorde. how do I learn to love her/as you have loved me? BlSi

Chain Gang Blues. Anonymous.
If you won't work, I'll kill you dead. OuSiCo
Ninety days on the county road, and the judge didn't even smile. WTO

Chain Gang Trouble. Charlie Lincoln (Hicks). nothing I/can't get/but bad news. BluL

Chain Letters. Alice Fulton. Copy this ten times and pass it on. LTB

Chair, Dog, and Clock. Hilary Corke. ONE TWO THREE you're dead. NYBP

Chairs. Henry Petroski. ...And the chairs applaud their one/Creator and mirror their mother chair. PoDr

Chairs. Valerie Worth. Some even stretch out their arms/To/Rest. NTCP

Chairs to Mend. Anonymous. I never would cry, Old chairs to mend. OxNR

The Chalk Angel. Dennis Schmitz. ...a measurement/of astral bodies. NPGG

Chalk from Eden. Howard Moss. And write of love on wall and sidewalk. NePA

The Chalk-Pit. Edward ("Edward Eastaway") Thomas. Between us still we breed a mystery. BrPo

The Challenge. *Anonymous.* Blushing from the field of battle. UnTE

Challenge. Sterling A. Brown. And that was foolish, wasn't it, my dear? CDC

Challenge. Thomas Curtis Clark. As brothers all, we build a Friendly World. PGD

Challenge. Samuel Hazo. to face a task with nothing but my skill/and struggle for the mark I must excel. SD

A Challenge. James Benjamin Kenyon. Be the proud captain still of thine own/fate! AA

The Challenge. Grenville Kleiser. The world demands/New proof in deeds. BLRP

The Challenge. Henry Wadsworth Longfellow. Christ, the great Lord of the army,/Lies dead upon the plain! AP

Challenge. Kenton Foster Murray. Do you know more? HBV 1-2

The Challenge. Calvin Murry. eyes livid invitations,/as you challenged me one-on-one. LFAC

The Challenge. Alexander Pope. And take off Ladies Limitations./With a fal, la, la. PoEL 1-5

Challengers. Alfred Dorn. And know the earth is smaller than a man. GoYe

Chamber Music. John Ditsky. ...Her makeup left/upon the second face, she smiles. AMV-81

Chamber Music. James Joyce.
All day, all night, I hear them flowing/To and fro. FaBoCh
And fingers straying/Upon an instrument. LOW
He is a stranger to me now/Who was my friend. OLR
Lean out of the window,/Goldenhair. LOW
Love is aweary now. MoLP; OLR
My love goes lightly, holding up/Her dress with dainty hand. LOW
O cool and pleasant is the valley/And there, love, will we stay. HW

The Chamber Over the Gate. Henry Wadsworth Longfellow. O Absalom, my son! AP; MAmP

Chamber-Pot Rhyme. *Anonymous.* And what I see/I'll never tell. GBP

Chamber Scene. Nathaniel Parker Willis. Will our wild errors be forgiven! HBV 1-2

The Chambered Nautilus. Oliver Wendell Holmes Leaving thine outgrown shell by life's unresting sea. AA; AnNE; AP; DiPo; EtS; FaBoBe; FaFP; FPL; GN; HBV 1-2; HBVY; HoPM; LiTA; MCCG; MOS; NePA; NOBA; NoP; OBVV; OHFP; PoEL 1-5; PoLf; PrIm; TreF; TRV; WGRP

The Chambermaid's Second Song. William Butler Yeats. His spirit that has fled/Blind as a worm. ErPo

Chambers of Jerusalem. Yehuda Karni. he would have the visage/of a prophet/or a priest. VWA

Chameleon. Paul Engle. We feared a love so like a fear. CrMA

Chameleon. Gordon LeClaire. Thus mirrors heaven's counterpart–your face. EtS

The Chameleon. James Merrick. Nor wonder, if you find that none/Prefers your eyesight to his own. HBV 1-2

The Chameleon. Matthew Prior. Is in the chair; prescribes the law;/And lies with those he never saw. OBSV

Chamonix. George Hookham. Through life I have heard you, in death I shall hear. OBVV

Champ de Manoeuvres. Sir Herbert Read. Gathering to its shell my startled soul. BrPo

Champagne. Rita Dove. ...The hurt we feel is delicate–/all for ourselves and all for nothing. MAYP

Champagne. Mebdh McGuckian. ...such ivory/As elephants hold lofty, like champagne. FaBoIP

Champagne Charlie. George Leybourne. Who'll come and join me in a spree? BLSo; PSoN

Champagne Rosee. John Kenyon. Hear unconcern'd the oar/That dips itself in wine! OBEV; OBRV; OBVV

The Chance. John Holmes. ...One is not bored/In a world where everything happens at least once. NePoAm-2

The Chance. Arthur Sze. even if the darkness precedes and follows/us, we have a chance, briefly, to shine. BrSi

Chance Meeting. Susan Griffin. I fed this child/through the night/whom now/I run from. NPGG

The Chancellor's Nightmare. Sir William Schwenck Gilbert. ...thank goodness/they're both of them over! FaBoNo

A Chancery Suit. Sir George Rose. And the Chancellor said, I doubt. FaBoCo

The Chances. Wilfred Owen. The bloody lot all rolled in one. Jim's mad. MMM; OxBTC

Chances. Brenda S. Stockwell. to be his lover/or his mother. AMV-81

The Chances of Rhyme. Charles Tomlinson. Let rhyme be my conclusion. FaBoMo; PoA

Chances "R". Allen Ginsberg. along a Wichita tree avenue/traversed with streetlights on the plain. HaCAP

The Chandelier as Protagonist. William Virgil Davis. breathing in the glow of herself. AMV-80

Chandler Nicholas. Edgar Lee Masters. My liver scorned by the vultures./And self-devoured! NAMP

The Chandler's Wife. *Anonymous.* And give her so much of that/she doesn't need any more. FSW

Chang'd, Yet Constant. Thomas Stanley. Of lovers they are onely true/Who pay their Hearts where they are due. AnAnS 2

The Change. Samuel Chimsoro. While black hands dip/Lumps of their constitution/In the same soup bowl. WhB

Change. Mary Elizabeth Coleridge. And the blue sea turns emerald as he goes. MoVE

The Change. Abraham Cowley. My outside Woman, and your inside Man. AnAnS 2; CoBE; MeLP; MePo; OBS; SeCP; SeCV 1-2

Change. John Donne. ...Change is the nursery/Of music, joy, life and eternity. ViBoPo

Change. Robert Graves. Which neither can surprise/In any other pair of eyes. OxBTC

Change. Fulke, Lord Brooke Greville. Yet in her eyes the doom of all change carries. OBSC

Change. William Dean Howells. The, in the deathless days before she died. AA

Change. Raymond Knister. I shall not wonder more, then,/But I shall know. CaP; OBCV; PeCV

The Change. David O'Bruadair. I'll do better with English than a poem. BIrV

Change and Immutability. Syd Scroggie. The May month oystercatcher flights/Were madly piping still. PoSH

A Change in Style. Eochaidh O Heoghusa. Give thanks for this turn for the better. NOBI

Change Is Not Always Progress. Haki R. Madhubuti. arrogantly/scrape/the/sky. TAP

Change of Address. Kathleen Fraser. ...And then, would you recognize me? NYBP

A Change of Heart. Valine Hobbs. To scare the mice away. SiSoSe

Change of Life. Constance Urdang. her voice comes to you through the lips of a crone. VWA

Change of School. Elizabeth Smither. Three days later he is transferred to another class. OCNZ

Change of Venue. Jill Clockadale. watch my reflection in the water/see an enemy. AMV-80

Change Should Breed Change. William, of Hawthornden Drummond. Deck thee with flowers which fear not rage of days! OBEV; OxBoCh

Change the Can Cheerily. *Anonymous.* "Disdaining to strike while a stick is left standing." AmSS

Change Thy Mind Since She Doth Change. Robert Devereux, Earl of Essex. She was best, but yet untrue. EIL

Change-Up. Don L. Lee. and yr/children will look at u differently/ than we looked at our parents. CNA; PoBA

Changed. Charles Stuart Calverley. I'll drink my arrowroot, and go/To bed. ALV; FiBHP; NOBV

The Changed Woman. Louise Bogan. Will one day find her bosom ready,–/That never thought to be forgiven. HBMV

Changeful Beauty. Andrew Lang. When gold or sable turns to grey! EnLoPo

Changeless Shore. Sarah Leeds Ash. We shall come back in the mind's long evening. GoYe

The Changeling. Charlotte Mew. I shall never come back again! CH

A Changeling Grateful. Josephine Preston Peabody. When I am a shadow.../I will creep away. AA

Changeling VIII. Kristjana Gunnars. name me broadleaved woods. CaPN; NOBC

Changelings. Mary Thacher Higginson. When the sun sank down in the west. AA

Changes. Seamus Heaney. when you have grown away and stand at last/at the very centre of the empty city.' FaBoIP

The Changes. Robert Pinsky. ...the web of routes bunched/To the shapes of beaks or arrowheads at the black dots of the cities. NPGG

Changes around the Bay. Michael Palmer. It's also greater/than before/we came/It's also later. NPGG

The Changes to Corinna. Robert Herrick. But you must die/As well as I. JCP

The Changing Road. Katharine Lee Bates. Whither the fearless footsteps go. HBV 1-2

The Changing Wind. Julian Orde. There is no being alone again. NeBP

Changsha Shoe Factory. Willis Barnstone. our tubs of hot water, the glue, and please,/remember me. Or we are lost. SaC

Channel Crossing. George Barker. The answer with a silent face. ACV; ChMP; GTBS-P

Channel Firing. Thomas Hardy. And Camelot, and starlit Stonehenge. BiP; BrPo; CABA; CMoP; CoBMV; EBEV; ExPo; ForPo; HAP; HeIP; InPK; LiTB; MoPo; NIP; NoAm; NoP; OAEL 1-2; OAEP; OxBTC; PoEL 1-5; PoRA; PPON; PrIm; SeCeV; SoSe; UnPo; WaaP

A Channel Passage. Rupert Brooke. To choose 'twixt love and nausea, heart and belly. MOS

A Channel Passage. Algernon Charles Swinburne. And the sense that a rapture so royal may come/not again in the passage of life. VLP

Channel U.S.A.–Live. Adrien Stoutenburg. and left the image that we keep. AmFN

Channel Water. Virginia Scott Miner. guard him well whose child I bear! AMV-80

Channing. Amos Bronson Alcott. O realize his Pentecostal dream! AA

Chanson d'Or. Ann Hamilton. I will have him kill you/With a gold sword. HBMV

Chanson de Chateaulaire. Herbert Sherman Gorman. The era with a testament. AnAmPo

Chanson de Rosemonde. Richard Hovey. Thou art so long away! HBV 1-2

Chanson: "If they say my furred cloak." Pernette Du Guillet. hits me cleanly in the heart,/never winging honour:/this I do know! PBWP

Chanson Innocent. Edward Estlin Cummings. far/and/wee. AmLP; CAD; MoAB; MoAmPo; MoShBr; NIP; WeW

Chanson Mystique. Anonymous. My heart toward heaven flies. CAW

Chanson Naive. John McClure. Creep-mouse, creep-mouse,/In the twilight! HBMV

Chanson of the Bells of Oseney. Cale Young Rice. Who makes the whole world fair. AnFE; APA; HBV 1-2

Chanson un Peu Naive. Louise Bogan. Cry, song, cry,/And hear your crying lost. HBMV

Chant. Oscar Williams. Rejoicing is where we are from. MoRP

Chant for Dark Hours. Dorothy Parker. (All your life you wait around for some damn man!) SBG

Chant for Reapers. Wilfrid Thorley. Smile again on your children. OBEV; OBVV

Chant for Skippers. Katharine Gallagher. This is the fall o' the year! SiSoSe

A Chant for Young / Brothas & Sistuhs. Sonia Sanchez. c'mon down from yo / wite / highs/and live. BPo

Chant of Departure. Alfred Joseph Barrett. Stand by my side beneath the Southern Cross. GoBC; ISi

A Chant of Hate against England. Ernst Lissauer. We have one foe and one alone:/England! HBV 1-2

Chant of the Ninth Order of Seraphim. Inigo de Mendoza. Wiping out the stains and gloom/With the power of Love once more! CAW

A Chant out of Doors. Marguerite Wilkinson. God of silent noon,/Hear my salutation! TrPWD

Chant-Pagan. Rudyard Kipling. So I think I will go there an' see./Me! FaBoPV; OAEP; VLP

Chant Royal. Robert Morgan. adequate for survival, withstanding all knocks. SM

Chant Royal From a Copydesk. Rufus Terral. I would atone for headlines I have done. InMe

Chant Royal of High Virtue. Sir Arthur Thomas ("Q") Quiller-Couch. Virtue is that beseems a Man! HBV 1-2

Chant Royal of the Dejected Dipsomaniac. Don (Donald Robert Marquis) Marquis. My way of life can end in nothing good! HBMV

Chant to Io. Tiwai Paraone. And at once the moving earth lay stretched abroad. WTO

A Chanted Calendar. Sydney Thomas Dobell. And rubies in her hair. HBV 1-2; HBVY; OBEV

Chantey of Notorious Bibbers. Henry Morton Robinson. For history is a record of good men wrong on licker. InMe

Chanticleer. William Austin. Hail, O Sun of Righteousness! EBCP; OxBoCh

Chanticleer. John Farrar. Or if he's only guessing. SoPo; TiPo

Chanticleer. Margaret Irvin. ...from each impassive dream,/Repentantly the PoAu 1-2

Chanticleer. Katharine Tynan. He summons back the light! HBV 1-2; HBVY; TiPo

The Chanting Cherubs - A Group by Greenough. Richard Henry Dana. Us light on earth, and here our flight is/stayed. AA

Chanting the Square Deific. Walt Whitman. Breathe my breath also through these songs. AmePo

Chanuke, O Chanuke. Anonymous. Thank God and dance merrily! FSW

Chapel Deacon. R. S. Thomas. Who taught you your deft poise? ACV

The Chaperon. Henry Cuyler Bunner. Ah, me! I wish that I were quite/As young–as young as she! AA; HBV 1-2

A Chaplet of Southernwood (excerpt). John Gambril Nicholson. I love him, love him, love him past belief! PeHV

Chaplin's Sad Speech. Rafael Alberti. evaporates a naked corpse inside the pharmacy. LiTW

Chaplinesque. Hart Crane. Have heard a kitten in the wilderness. AP; CMoP; CrMA; LiTM; NoAm; NOBA; OxBA; VGW

Chapter Heading. Ernest Hemingway. To serve one master in the night,/Another in the day. PoA

The Chapter of Kings. John Collins. All come to be Kings in their turn. FaBoUs

A Character. Charlotte Fiske Bates. Till hands that plighted troth shall re-/unite. AA

Character. Ralph Waldo Emerson. His action won such reverence sweet/As hid all measure of the feat. AA; AnFE; AnNE; APA; LiTA; OBSP

The Character of a Certain Whig. William Shippen. A monster whom no vice can bigger swell,/Abhorred by Heaven and long since due to Hell. APAS

The Character of a Good Person. John Dryden. He needs no foil, but shines by his own proper light. NOCV

The Character of a Happy Life. Sir Henry Wotton. And having nothing: yet hath all. AnAnS 2; EiL; FaPoR; GTBS; GTBS-P; HBV 1-2; HBVY; LiTB; MCCG; NOBE; OBEV; OBS; TreF; TrGrPo; ViBoPo

The Character of a Roundhead. Anonymous. And there they got a Roundhead. FaBoPV

The Character of a Trimmer. Anonymous. Like a state Janus or a church spread-eagle. APAS

The Character of Holland. Andrew Marvell. Vainly in Hell let Pluto domineer. CABL; NOBL; OBSV; OBTV; TW

The Character of Love Seen as a Search for the Lost. Kenneth Patchen. ...and there are/Many desperate arms about us and the things we know. NaP; VGW

Character of the Happy Warrior. William Wordsworth.
  He labors good on good to fix, and owes/To virtue every triumph that he knows. BoLiVe
  This is the happy warrior; this is he/That every man in arms should wish to be. EnLit; EnRP; FaBoBe; FaFP; HBV 1-2; HBVY; LiTB; LoBV; OBRV; TreF

Characteristics of a Child Three Years Old. William Wordsworth. The many-coloured images imprest/Upon the bosom of a placid lake. ERoP 1-2; OBRV

Characters of Women. Alexander Pope. Then never break your heart when Cloe dies. NOBE; OBEC

Characters of Women. Edward Hilton Young. Nor conquer art, and nature, to be rude. OBEC

Charade. Winthrop Mackworth Praed. To light the flame of a soldier's fame/On the turf of a soldier's grave. GN

The Charcoal-Burner. Sir Edmund Gosse. Be all that's left to love him. OBVV

Charcoal Man. Anonymous. I sells mah chah-coal two bits a sack/Chah-coal, chah-coal. TrAS

Chard Whitlow. Henry Reed. And pray for Kharma under the holy mountain. BXAP; DTC; FaBoCo; FaBoNo; FiBHP; LiTM; NLV; NOBL; NoP; OxBTC; Par; UnPo

Charge. Christopher Gilbert. ...Willie says again/and again, "Gimme the goddamn ball." MAYP

The Charge. Denise Levertov. ...Let be/what is gone. NePoEA-2

A Charge. Herbert Trench. And one must perish–let it not be he/Whom thou art sworn to obey. HBV 1-2; OBEV; OBVV

The Charge. Jay Wright. no savior,/rises still to fill/our vacant eyes. FB

The Charge at Santiago. William Hamilton Hayne. While the tropic sun on a grand deed done/Looks with his piercing eye! MC; PAH

The Charge by the Ford. Thomas Dunn English. Give them the roll of the drum! PAH

The Charge of the Light Brigade. Alfred, Lord Tennyson. Noble six hundred! BeLS; BLPA; FaBoBe; FaBV; FaFP; FaPo; FaPoR; FPL; GN; GoTF; HBV 1-2; HBVY; HoPM; MaC; MaVP; MCCG; NIP; NOBV; OBWP; OHFP; PaPo; PoPl; PrIm; TEP; TreF; WBLP

A Charge to Keep I Have. Charles Wesley. Assured, if I my trust betray,/I shall forever die. HBV 1-2

A Charge to the Poets (excerpt). William Whitehead. And many a dirty street, on Thames's side,/Is yet by stool and brush unoccupied. OBSV

Charing Cross. Cecil Roberts. That Science should skilfully mend what it skilfully shatters. HBMV

Le Chariot. John Wieners. This is the card that reads as seven. VGW

Charioteer. Witter ("Emanuel Morgan") Bynner. She runs ahead, beyond the fallen horse. AnFE

Chariots. Witter ("Emanuel Morgan") Bynner. Day holding one and moving solemnly–/Night holding two. HBMV

Charitas Nimia, or the Deare Bargain. Richard Crashaw. As then in Death, so now in Love. AnAnS 1; JCP; MePo; NOCV; OxBoCh

Charite Esperance et Foi. Earle Birney. or if they ever found their Faith again. OxBC

Charity. Anonymous. To find fault with the rest of us. BLPA

The Chauffeur of Lilacs. George Hitchcock. ...They all,/passengers and crew, the dream/and the artist alike, dissolve/into sepia fractions. GP

The Chaunt of the Brazen Head (excerpt). Winthrop Mackworth Praed. That there are fifty roads to Town,/And rather more to Heaven. OBSV

Chavez. Mildred McNeal Sweeney. His spirit heed, still winged with golden prophecies. HBV 1-2

Che Guevara Is Dead. Peter Schjeldahl. Death, that great/Underliner, has made me notice this today. ANYP

Che Sara Sara. Vicor Plarr. Seeing that thou, beloved, art so sweet! HBV 1-2

The Cheat of Cupid: or, The Ungentle Guest. Robert Herrick. I'll leave thy heart a-dying. AWP; PG; SeCeV

Check. James Stephens And she/Stared back solemnly at me! AnIL; GTBS; HBMV; LOW; OnUR; SiSoSe; SUS; TiPo

Checking the Firing. R. T. Smith. I see it etched in fire. AMV-80

Cheddar Pinks. Robert Bridges. On a May morning. ChMP; MoVE; SeCePo

Chee Lai! (Arise!). Anonymous. With the torch of freedom, March on! March on!/March on and on! FSW

Cheer for the Consumer. Nixon Waterman. I'm only a consumer, and it really doesn't matter. OBAL

Cheer'ly, Man. Anonymous. And stretch her luff, hio! AmSS

The Cheer of the Trenton. Walter Mitchell. And the tale he told in fo'c's'le song/Of the flagship Trenton's parting cheer. EtS

The Cheerful Chilterns (parody). Frank Sidgwick. Nettles, docks, thistles;/Praeterea nihil. BXAP

The Cheerful Horn. Anonymous And I'll zing Tally ho! CH

A Cheerful Welcome. Anonymous. And with gud hert he doth to you say,/"What cher?" MeEL

Cheerfulness. Anonymous. And such a lot of nice fresh air/All sandwiched in between. GoTF; TreFT

Cheerio My Deario. Don (Donald Robert Marquis) Marquis. i admire her spirit. FaBoCo

Cheers. Eve Merriam. How do you spell Success?/With an S-S-S! LiSp

Cheetie-Poussie-Cattie, O. Anonymous. O' Cheetie-Poussie-Cattie, O.' FaBoCh

Chekhov Comes to Mind at Harvard. William T. Freeman. the words they speak are nothing more than spoken words. AMV-81

Chelmsfords Fate. Benjamin Tompson. Out of her ashes let a Phoenix rise/That may outshine the first and be more wise. SCAP

The Chelsea. Derek Walcott. ...Happier lives,/settled in ruts, and great for wanting less. NYP

Chelsea Churchyard. Ralph J. Mills, Jr. ...nothing/but to be/where their shadows meet. FAZ

The Chemist to His Love. Anonymous. Agree to form a Johnsonate of Briggs? InMe; QQQ

The Chemistry of Character. Elizabeth Dorney. God in His wisdom created them all. BLPA

Chenille. James Dickey. As rain began greatly to fall,/And closed the door of the Ark. NoAm

The Cherokee Dean. Norman H. Russell. the deer have formed their snow circle/two hills beyond. STE

Cherries. Zalman Schneour. The world is full of cherries. TrJP

The Cherries. A Parable. Thomas Moore. Curse the corm'rants! stone 'em, shoot 'em,/Any thing–to save our cherries. OBSV

Cherries: "So when the hammers of the witnesses of heaven.." Edward Kamau Brathwaite. man, manwart, manimal. NAs

Cherry. Gene Baro. flesh of the cherry, dark and sweet. ErPo

The Cherry and the Slae (excerpt). Alexander Montgomerie. Or Muses that uses/At fountain Helicon. GoTS

Cherry Beggar. Gerard Manley Hopkins. Those goldnails and their gaylinks that hang along a lime FaBoPP

The Cherry-Blossom Wand. Anna Wickham. With a beautiful thing that shall never grow wise. MoBrPo

Cherry Blossoms. Michael Lewis.
And when I take it I both live and die. UnTE
So farewell–until tonight. UnTE
So we can snuff the candle out together. UnTE
Tears at my flimsy dress. UnTE
While the good wind blew out the lamp. UnTE

The Cherry Boy (excerpt). Royston Ellis. The cherry boy, once the sweetest prize,/was growing gnarled before my eyes. PeHV

The Cherry Fair. Anonymous. That shede His blode for my redempcion! FaBoRV

Cherry-Pit. Robert Herrick. I got the pit, and she the stone. OAEP

Cherry-Ripe. Robert Herrick. All the year where cherries grow. CaPo; CH; CoBE; ELP; LiTL; OBEV; TEP

Cherry Robbers. D. H. Lawrence. If she has any tears. MoAB; MoBrPo

The Cherry Tree. Thom Gunn. She knows nothing about babies. Psk

Cherry Tree. Christina Georgina Rossetti. With balls of shining red/Decking a leafy head;/Oh fair to see! YeAr

Cherry Tree. Sacheverell Sitwell. Ripe cherries and a honeycomb must make my bread and wine. AtBAP

The Cherry-Tree Carol. Anonymous.
O the sun and the moon, mother,/shall both rise with me. BaBo; BoLiVe; CBEP; DiPo; ELP; EnSB; ESPB; FaBoBa; GBP; HeIP; LoBV; OAEL 1-2; OAEP; OFD; OnMSP; OxBB; OxBoCh; OxBoLi; SBVL; SeCeV; ViBoFo
Then Mary went home/with her heavy load. AnEnPo; TrGrPo
To see the uprising/of the heavenly king.' BaBo; EBEV; ESPB; OBET
"What have I done, Lord,/Have mercy on me." AmFP; FSW

The Cherry-Tree Carol, I. Anonymous. When the stars in the elements/Shall tremble with glee. AmFP; PCh

The Cherry-Tree Carol, III. Anonymous. And loud they cried to all. AmFP

The Cherry-Tree Carol, IV. Anonymous. But within a stall. AmFP

The Cherry Trees. Edward ("Edward Eastaway") Thomas. This early May morn when there is none to wed. OBWP; PoPle

A Cherry Year. Anonymous. A dumb year. OxNR

Cherrylog Road. James Dickey. Wild to be wreckage forever. AmC; BiP; CoAP; HaCAP; HAP; InPS; NIP; NYBP; PAI; PrIm; TwCP

The Cherub-Folk. Enid Dinnis. And tells the Cherub-folk in heaven/The wonder tale of Bethlehem. CAW

The Cherubic Pilgrim. (Johannes Scheffler) "Angelus Selesius". And thou, my soul, wilt still/On thine old earth-clod lie! WGRP

The Cherubim (excerpt). Thomas Heywood. My God is, and there's none but HE. WGRP

The Cherwell Water Lily. Frederick William Faber. And died in little swells. CAW; GoBC

Chesapeake. Gerta Kennedy. It's moving that counts. NYBP

Chesapeake and Shannon. Anonymous. That in fighting as in love/The true British tar is the dandy O! PAH; ViBoFo

Cheshire Cat. Kenneth Allott. On a damned continent without a name. NeBP

The Chess-Board. Edward Robert Bulwer, Earl of Lytton. Play chess, as then we played together! HBV 1-2

Chesspieces. Joseph Campbell. Are tame, indeed, beside your angry Dogs!' OxBI

Chester. William Billings. Their ships were shatter'd in our sight/Or swiftly driven from our coast. TrAS

The Chestnut Avenue at Alton House. Charles Tomlinson. Their green indifference barbarous at its panes. FaBoTw

Chestnut Stands. Rachel Field. If chestnut men forgot to come/To cities in the fall. SiSoSe

The Chestnut Vendor. Karl Szelki. must shout to be heard above/the October wind PCP

Le Chevalier Malheur. Paul Verlaine. "Once only can the miracle avail.–Be wise!" SyP

Chevaliers de la Table Ronde. Anonymous. Now the moral of this long story,/Is to drink while you're still alive. FSW

Chevy-Chace. Anonymous. And grant, henceforth, that foul debate/'Twixt noblemen may cease! EnLi 1-2; FaBoBa; GN; HBV 1-2; OBET; ViBoFo

Chevy Chase. Anonymous. God send us all good ending! BuBa; EnRP; EnSB; OxBB; ViBoPo; WHA

Chew Mail Pouch. Daniel L. Klauck. and big gray barns leaning/slightly to the wind AMV-81

Chewing Chawing Gum. Anonymous. Chawing chewing gum, chewing chawing gum. AmFP; FSW

Cheyenne. Anonymous. Cheyenne-a, Cheyenne, I'm a-leaving Cheyenne. CoSo

Cheyenne Mountain. Helen Hunt Jackson. And ere thou change all human song shall die! BPAW; PoOW

Chez Brebant. Francis Alexander Durivage. Ma foi! Chez Brebant ces choses sont rares! AA

Chez Jane. Frank O'Hara. in the air to aggravate the truly menacing. CoAP; NeAP; NoAm; NOBA; PoA

Chez Madame. Sam Harrison. the sombre city that will never cease/its lost unhappy crying in the night. NeIP

Chez-Nous. A. G. Austin. Old Rat/And Flea/And Bird/And Me. PoAu 1-2

Chiaroscuro. Carol Berge. where we/run with masks. ErPo

Chiaroscuro: Rose. Conrad Aiken. But leave my thoughts to me. MAPA

Chic Freedom's Reflection. Alice Walker. powdered her nose/tip-/toe/in a badge. NMM

Chicago. Bret (Francis Bret Harte) Harte. The gifts her kinship and our loves reveal. PAH

Chicago. Galway Kinnell. Revive the embrace in that melted glow. NePoAm

Chicago. John Boyle O'Reilly. Answering her "Miserere!" PAH

Chicago. Lola Ridge. Where your blood is running like a river under its ice. PoA

Chicago. Carl Sandburg. Laughing the stormy, husky, brawling laughter of Youth,/half-naked, sweating, proud... BiP; BLPL; HBMV; NoAm; OxBA; VGW
Player with Railroads and Freight Handler to the Nation. AP; AmPP; CMoP; FaBV; GoTF; LiTM; LoGBV; MoAB; MoAmPo; MoVE; NePA; NOBA; NoP; PoA; PoPl; TAP; TreF; UnPo; ViBoPo; YaD

Chicago. John Greenleaf Whittier. And love is still miraculous! MC; PAH

Chicago Allegory. Stewart Parker. The black belt scarcely buckles, maw. CIP

Chicago Analogue. Keith Preston. So long as I can have my beer,/I'll glady miss the skittles. NLV

Chicago Boy Baby. Carl Sandburg. ...surely a big man/now, votes this year for Smith or Hoover. NAs

The Chicago Defender Sends a Man to Little Rock, Fall, 1957. Gwendolyn Brooks. The loveliest lynchee was our Lord. AmNP; PoBA

Chicago Idyll. E. Merrill Root. And then the hogs moved on once more/Upon their screaming way. AnAmPo

Chicago: Near West-Side Renewal. Dennis Schmitz. the lover who was a guest leaves. AmPA

Chicago Poem. Lew Welch. A small part of it will die if I'm not around/feeding it anymore. NeAP; PoM

Chicago, Summer Past. Richard Snyder. ...feel/a soft, inward squeeze like a rubber ball. Psk

Chick! My Naggie. Anonymous. Try to win there by/candle light. OxNR

Chickadee. Hilda Conkling. Drop into water.../Chick-a-dee-dee-dee... TiPo

The Chickadees. John Hay. should he look up and laugh? NePoAm-2

Chicken. Walter De la Mare. They came at Bessie's call. TiPo

Chicken. Dave Etter. A chief is no bigger than his blanket,/I said, waving her away. MAT

Chicken. Dennis Kelly. I oughtta/be a foot long/when I'm 17. PeHV

Chicken-Licken. Maya Angelou. Autopsy: read/dead of acute peoplelessness. FF

Chicken Soup Therapy: Its Mode of Action. Caroline Breese Hall. Transferred from man's fowl friend are Bursal Brews/Sought so long by modern medicine's gurus. SUW

The Chickens. Anonymous. "If you want any breakfast,/Just come here and scratch." MoShBr

Chickens. Geof Hewitt. Yeah, Winter's coming/darkness–God!–I hate to see it come. FAZ

The Chickens Are A-Crowing. Anonymous. The chickens they are crowing, for it is almost daylight. TrAS

Chickens the Weasel Killed. William Stafford. and then appeal to the ground with their wings. NaP

Chickitten Gitten! Ted Joans. AND JUMP HAPPY ALL OVER PUSSY LOVING ME!! GP

Chickory. Zerubavel Gal'ed. Like wine,/Aged and tart. TrJP

Chief Leschi of the Nisqually. Duane Niatum. ...he will eat little/And speak less before he hangs. CDW; STE

Chief Petty Officer. Charles Causley. His narrow forehead ruffled by the Jutland wind. OxBTC

Chiefly to Mind Appears. C. Day-Lewis. Itself the more intact. MoAB; MoBrPo

Chiffons! William Johnson. Death drones the answer, far away, HBV 1-2

A Child. Richard Watson Gilder. The music faded from the air,/The color from the day. AA

The Child. Donald Hall. he stops suddenly/to hear the black water. NCSH; NePoEA-2

The Child. George Keithley. ..."Be anyone at all"/but not that child. NPGG

A Child. Mary Ann Lamb. When I forget thy thousand ways/Then life and all shall cease. OBEV

Child. Tom MacIntyre. my breath,/my clay,/my open hand. CIP

The Child. Reginald Massey. Let us wait for the morrow. ACV

The Child. William Stanley Merwin. The child that will lead you. NoAm

The Child. Frank Ormsby. And no voice calls, "Come in." AMV-81

Child. Sylvia Plath. ...this dark/Ceiling without a star. HaCAP; PBWP

The Child. Ivor Popham. knowing the ways of Wisdom well/and in all names, the Name. EaLo

Child. Carl Sandburg. For the young child, Christ, straight and wise. TRV

Child. E. N. Sargent. you are the most golden of all. NYBP

The Child. John Banister Tabb. Became as white as snow. AA

A Child Accepts. Michael Hamburger. Those hidden rocks that wrecked him into song. NMP

The Child an' the Mowers. William Barnes. Aye! the zwath-flow'r's a-killed by the zun. VLP

Child and Boatman (excerpt). Jean Ingelow. Martin, you'll ask your wife about the songs/When you go in at dinner-time?"/"Not I." FM

Child and Maiden. Sir Charles Sedley. To make a beauty, she. GTBS; GTBS-P; LiTL

Child and Poet. Algernon Charles Swinburne. Come back to us, child, if you love us,/And bring us your love. EnLit

The Child and the Mariner. William Henry Davies. To hear that seaman tell such wondrous tales... CH

The Child and the Shadow. Elizabeth Jennings. It is our shadow that slides in between. NePoEA-2

A Child Asleep. Elizabeth Madox Roberts. But I came down the stair. AnAmPo

The Child at Winter Sunset. Mark Van Doren. Mourned too, for more to come. NCSH

The Child Bearers. Anne Sexton. lest our children/go so fast/they go. BoWoP

Child Bearing. Charles Ghigna. spinning in silence. AMV-81

Child Beater. Florence Anthony ("Ai"). O daughter, so far, you've only had a taste of icing,/are you eady now for some cake? BoWoP

The Child-Bride. Joyce Carol Oates. The bridal gown used as a shroud, an old custom. GeTw

Child, Child. Sara Teasdale. Only through love will you enter heaven. HBV 1-2

The Child Compassion. Margot Ruddock. Do suckle thee/Upon my breast. OBMV

Child Crying. Anthony Thwaite. And in her language share/Her blind and trivial cries. NePoEA-2

The Child Dying. Edwin Muir. I did not know death was so strange. ChMP; FaBoTw; GTBS-P

Child Harold: Ballad. John Clare. While Patty Sweet Patty Sat Locked In My/Arms. FaBoPP; OBNC; VLP

A Child Ill. Sir John Betjeman. Oh, little body, do not die. DTC

A Child in Prison. Gofraidh Fionn O Dalaigh. an earthly mansion is only grief,/prisoners all the living. NOBI

The Child in the Garden. Henry Van Dyke. I am the little child you used to be. HBV 1-2

The Child in the Rug. John Haines. threads of the flowerprints/coming loose from her sky of wool. DFF; GP

A Child Is Born. Anonymous. A King has come today. STF

The Child Is Father to the Man. Gerard Manley Hopkins. How can he be? The words are wild. FaBoCo; NOBV

The Child Jesus to Mary the Rose. John Lydgate. When they me pray for help in thy presence. CAW; GoBC; ISi

The Child-King. Morris Wintchevsky. And the woods with happy laughter/Echo all the day. TrJP

Child Maurice. Anonymous. Soe haue I done one of the fairest ladyes/That euer ware womans weede! BaBo; ESPB

Child Maurice (B version). Anonymous. For if you had told me he was your son,/He should neer have been slain by me.' ESPB

Child Maurice (D version). Anonymous. And or the mornin bells was rung/The threesome were a' gane. ESPB

The Child-Musician. Henry Austin Dobson. "Kind God!" was the last he said. GN

A Child My Choice. Robert Southwell. Correct my faults, protect my life, direct me when I die! CAW; GoBC; HBV 1-2; OxBoCh

Child Naming Flowers. Robert Hass. A moment ago I felt so sick/and so cold/I could hardly move. MAYP; NPGG

Child of Blue. Michael Hogan. And bless this day which pulled you from the sea/gasping and hungry for life. LFAC

Child of God. Anonymous. Tell him I'm a child of God. FSW

A Child of Hers. T. Walking Eagle Marietta. Her child stops and mumbles... LFAC

Child of Loneliness. Norman Gale. God's love, God's wisdom, Child of loneliness. WGRP

Child of My Winter. W.D. Snodgrass. Increase the deepening harvest here before/It snows again. MoAmPo

Child of Our Time. Eavan Boland. Sleep in a world your final sleep has woken. CIP

The Child of Peace. Selma Lagerlof. With your own child in your bosom. PoPl

Child of silence and shadow. Yvonne Caroutch. You don't see the sun shining/like the first morning on earth. BoWoP

Child of the Romans. Carl Sandburg. Standing slender on the tables in the dining-cars. LaNeLa

Child of the World. Edna L. S. Baker. I am your child. GoYe

A Child of To-Day. James Buckham. How strange!–perhaps death's conqueror/sits smiling on my knee! AA

The Child on the Judgment Seat. Elizabeth Rundle Charles. In a look of his own for thee. BLPA

Child on Top of a Greenhouse. Theodore Roethke. And everyone, everyone pointing up and shouting. AtBAP; ELU; LCAP; LOW; MiAP; NCSH; PoPl

Child Owlet. Anonymous. But drappit o Childe Owlet's blude/and pieces o his flesh. ESPB

Child Poem. Annette Arkeketa West. making it good/to feel you/among us. TWSS

The Child Reads an Almanac. Francis Jammes. They weigh salt, coffee and the souls of men. AWP

A Child's Christmas Day. *Anonymous.* And Nurse too is cross as she bears him away. OBCP

A Child's Christmas Song. Thomas Augustin Daly. Let Your angels waken me/On Your birthday morn. BiCB

A Child's Christmas without Jean Cocteau. David Fisher. that one has children in order/to be forgiven! NPGG

The Child's Dream. Susan Ludvigson. over and over, like a song. AMV-80; MAYP

A Child's Evening Prayer. Samuel Taylor Coleridge. That after my great sleep I may/Awake to thy eternal day! Amen. OxBChV; TrPWD

The Child's First Grief. Felicia Dorothea Hemans. Oh, while my brother with me played,/Would I have loved him more. BLPA

A Child's Future. Algernon Charles Swinburne. Fear not at all; for a slave, if he fears not, is free. EnLi 1-2

Child's Game. Judson Jerome. night night sleep tight. DuDa

A Child's Grace. Robert Burns. And sae the Lord be thankit. BrR; MoShBr

A Child's Grave Marker. Ted Kooser. ...On this hill,/overlooking a river in Iowa,/it melts in its own sweet time. GOYP

The Child's Heritage. John G. Neihardt. The torch my fathers gave in trust,/Thy father gives to thee! HBV 1-2

A Child's Laughter. Algernon Charles Swinburne. Laughs a child of seven. BiCB; BLPL; HBV 1-2; PoLf

A Child's Nativity. John N. Morris. Enormous thin sheep/Intent as wolves/Surround Him. GP

Child's Natural History. Oliver Herford.
And, for that mat-ter, nor does he. HBV 1-2
And so there would be no ex-cuse/For MILTON, but for you–Mon-goos! HBV 1-2
For chil-dren to de-ride and scorn? HBV 1-2
He runs Fur-bear-ance in the ground. HBV 1-2

A Child's Pet. William Henry Davies. Would stroke that sheep's black nose. CH

The Child's Power of Wonder. P. K. Saha. An old bit of china with worn-off design. ACV

A Child's Prayer. *Anonymous.* Evermore Thy child to be. BLRP

The Child's Prayer. Robert de Montesquiou-Fezensac. Chaplet of perfumes on the Rosary of Love. CAW

A Child's Prayer. John Banister Tabb. And may I ask you how you find/Yourself, dear Lord, today? GoTF; TreF; YaD

A Child's Question. Elias Nason. My soul this day hath tasted death! AA

The Child's Sight. Hy Sobiloff. They have given me back the bliss of my senses VGW

Child's Song. Robert Lowell. Sometimes the little muddler/can't stand itself! NMP

Child's Song. Thomas Moore. And feel his little silvery feet. GoBC; OxBI; SUS; ViBoPo

Child's Song. Algernon Charles Swinburne. Love's worth love. GTBS; OBVV

Child's Song in Spring. Edith Nesbit. I love him best of all! HBV 1-2; OHIP; OxBChV

A Child's Song of Christmas. Marjorie Pickthall. O, heaven was in His sight, I know,/That little Child of long ago. HBV 1-2; HBVY; YeAr

A Child's Song to Her Mother. Winifred Welles. I long, when we shall meet again,/To be as tall as you. HBMV

Child's Talk in April. Christina Georgina Rossetti. Love-time would bring me back to you/And build our happy nest again. GN

A Child's Thought. Bertha Moore. It's bery difficult to try/To be like God, up in the sky! PaPo

A Child's Thought of God. Elizabeth Barrett Browning. "Who kissed you through the dark, dear guesser?" TRV

A Child's Thought of Harvest. Susan (Sarah Chauncey Woolsey) Coolidge. Was but buds or seeds just planted then. OHIP; PoSC

A Child's Visit to the Biology Lab. Kathleen Spivack. oh alter ego, fluttered at the glass. AmPA

A Child's Winter Evening. Gwen John. And dusk with fire, and flames with shadows race. CH

A Child's Wish. Abram Joseph Ryan. A home all holy for each Host/That comes in love to me. AA; CAW

The Child's Wish Granted. George Parsons Lathrop. Another Father now, more than I,/Has borne you voiceless to your dear blue sky. AA; HBV 1-2

A Child Screening a Dove from a Hawk. Letitia Elizabeth Landon. A hawk for every dove! VLP

A Child That Has a Cold We May Suppose. Thomas Dibdin. Like wintry weather–Why?–It blows its nose. FaBoNo; PV

A Child to His Sick Grandfather. Joanna Baillie. You do not hear me, dad. NOEC

Child Waters. *Anonymous.*

And the bridal and the churching both,/They shall be upon one day.' BaBo; ESPB; FaBoBa; OAEP; OBET; OxBB; ViBoFo

For your marriage an your kirkin too/Sal baith be in ae day.' ESPB

The Child Who Walks Backwards. Lorna Crozier. breaks his leg/while she lies/sleeping. CaPN

The Child Who Was Shot Dead by Soldiers at Nyanga. Ingrid Jonker. the child grown into a giant journeys over the whole world/Without a pass. PeSA

Child with a Cockatoo. Rosemary Dobson. So one might find a meteor from the sun/Or sound one trumpet ere the play's begun. CBAP

Child with Shell. Ronald G. Everson. A waste of time, child. It's in the bone,/like tides and love. PeCV

Child with Six Fingers. Carol Muske. Instead I watch birds fly/Thinking of wings. AmPA

Childbirth. Ted Hughes. Righted the stagger of the earth. NAs

Childe Harold's Pilgrimage: Canto I. George Gordon, Lord Byron.
For some slight cause of wrath, whence life's warm stream must flow. LiSp
Smile on–nor venture to unmask/man's heart, and view the Hell that's there. MBW 1-2

Childe Harold's Pilgrimage: Canto II. George Gordon, Lord Byron. The dust thy courser's hoof, rude stranger! spurns around. OBRV

Childe Harold's Pilgrimage: Canto III. George Gordon, Lord Byron.
And burning with high hope, shall moulder cold and low. AnFE
And Evan's, Donald's fame rings in each clansman's ears! AnFE
And feed on bitter fruits without accusing Fate. FiP
Arm! Arm! it is–it is–the cannon's opening roar! AnFE
As if they did rejoice o'er a young earthquake's birth. LiTB
As, with a sigh, I deem thou might'st have/been to me. CoBE; OAEP
But hush! hark! a deep sound strikes like a rising knell! AnFE
Gazing upon the ground, with thoughts which dare not/glow? PoEL 1-5
He rush'd into the field, and, foremost fighting, fell. AnFE
I turn'd from all she brought to those she could not bring. FiP; MCCG; OBRV
If such there were–with you, the moral of his/strain. EnRP
Of his impeded soul would through his bosom eat. OBRV
Or whispering, with white lips–"The foe! they come! they come!" AnFE
Since upon night so sweet such awful morn could rise! AnFE
Which answers to all doubts so eloquently well. OBRV
Which eats into itself, and rusts ingloriously. OBRV

Childe Harold's Pilgrimage: Canto IV. George Gordon, Lord Byron.
And laid my hand upon thy mane–as I do here. FaBV; FiP; GN; HBV 1-2; LiTB; PoEL 1-5; TrGrPo; WGRP
Behold the Imperial Mount! 'tis thus the mighty falls. EBEV; FaBoPP; FaBV; GN; MBW 1-2; MOS; OAEL 1-2; OAEP; OBRV; TrGrPo; WaaP; WHA
Floats through the azure air–an island of the blest! AnFE
In hearts all rocky now the late remorse of love. FiP
The last still loveliest,–till–'t is gone–and all is gray. AnFE
The world, the same wide den–of thieves,/or what ye will. CoBE
Which streams upon her stream, and glass'd within it glows. AnFE

Childe Maurice. *Anonymous.* But could they not have holden me/When I was in all that wrath? TrGrPo

Childe Roland, etc. Elder Olson. Nowadays, I observe, poetry is chiefly lyrical. OBAL

Childe Roland to the Dark Tower Came. Robert Browning. And blew. "Childe Roland to the Dark Tower came." ATP; DTo; MaVP; MBW 1-2; NOBV; NoP; OAEL 1-2; OAEP; OBNV; PPP; ScCcV; VLP

Childe Rolandine. Stevie Smith. Childe Rolandine bowed her head and in the evening/Drew the picture of the spirit from heaven. BrRo

Childhood. Johari (Jewel C. Latimore) Amini. owned/bi/esther feldman JB

Childhood. Jens Baggesen. God! may I never, never lose that too! AWP

Childhood. William Barnes. A-screen'd vrom the cwold blowen storm/That the timber avore em must rue. NOBV

Childhood. Anne Bradstreet. I've done; unto my elders I give way,/for 'tis but little that a child can say. SBG

Childhood. Edith Bruck. to let off steam with the Jews/by the synagogue door. VWA

Childhood. Frances Cornford. As I was helplessly young. FaBoWP; OBSP; OxBTC

Childhood. Donald Justice. Forlorn suburbs, but with golden names! LCAP

Childhood. Donagh MacDonagh. Holding the lily and the Child. NeIP

Childhood. Sir Thomas More. Which life God sent me to mine ending day. EnRePo

Childhood. Edwin Muir. And from the house his mother called his name. CMoP; HeIP; NoP; SeCePo

Childhood. Ned O'Gorman. and lift his arms and cry aloud like Man. PoPl

Childhood. Sir Herbert Read. Their red coats and the swift whimpering hounds. BrPo

Childhood. Rainer Maria Rilke. O childhood, o images slipping from us/ Whither? Whither? SOTW

Childhood. Sherod Santos. ...which was all/your life, Mother, and/all of mine. AMV-81

A Childhood. Stephen Spender. You who, being younger,/Will probably forget. NeBP

Childhood. Maura Stanton. The floor so far away I can't determine/Which room I'm in, which year, which life. MAYP; SM

Childhood. John Banister Tabb. Thine old companion, on the rack/Of Age, should sadden even thee. HBV 1-2

Childhood. Thomas Traherne. Shall still revive and flourish in the dust. TrGrPo

Childhood. Henry Vaughan. For sure that is the narrow way. OxBoCh

Childhood. Margaret Walker. and only bitter land was washed away. BOLo; IHMS; PBWP; PoBA; WPOW

Childhood Church. Pat Wilson. Though church-bells must have been its symbol then. AnNZ

Childhood Fled. Charles Lamb. That I may seek thee, the wide world around? EnRP

Childhood in Jacksonville, Florida. Jane Cooper. Welcome then poverty!/ flights of strings above the orange trees! TAP

Childhood Is the Kingdom Where Nobody Dies. Edna St Vincent Millay. You drink it standing up,/And leave the house. FaBoWP

Childhood, IV. Arthur Rimbaud. ...It can only be the end/of the world ahead. PoPl

The Childhood of an Equestrian. Russell Edson. that seemed like a soft moon entrapped in the branches of/the forest. AmPA

A Childish Game. Reinmar von Hagenau. Love, a childish game thou art! AWP

A Childish Prank. Ted Hughes. Crow went on laughing. OAEL 1-2; OxBC

Childless. Giollabhrighde MacConmidhe. Let no poet empty-handed/Leave the dwelling of his lord. BIrV; KiLC

The Childless Father. William Wordsworth. And he went to the chase with a tear on his cheek. CH

A Childless Witch. Raquel Chalfi. First, though,/let me consume all/with a craving like this,/a craving like this. VWA

The Childless Woman in Heaven. Katharine Tynan. Was a dream, but a dream. BoC

Childlessness. James Merrill. Has fallen onto the shoulders of my parents/ Whom it is eating to the bone. ConAP

Childlike Heart. Ellen Weston Catlin. That God and man are kin. PGD

The Children. Charles Monroe Dickinson. May the little ones gather around me,/To bid me good night and be kissed! AA; HBV 1-2

The Children. Clifford Dyment. My grown uncertain way from life to death. ChMP

Children. Russell Edson. ...a rat with its tail down the body's back. AmPA

The Children. William Heyen. to keep them safe in my own body,/and knew I would again. Amen. GeTw; GP

The Children. Susan MacDonald. I love them,/wanting them gone. IHMS

Children. Sandra McPherson. or go out of our single mind/to have another child. FaBoWP

The Children. Constance Urdang. made/love made/children. CoAP; IHMS

The Children. Mark Vinz. where we cannot/see them. DFF; GP

The Children. William Carlos Williams. and place one/on each headstone. NePoAm-2

Children among the Hills. Linda Gregg. ...But inside everything/was moving, shivering with wind. We knew that much. NPGG

The Children and Sir Nameless. Thomas Hardy. "Who was this old stone man beneath our toes?" NoP

The Children Band. Sir Aubrey De Vere. In sands, in fens, they died—no mother near! OBEV

Children, Go Where I Send Thee. Anonymous. Was born, born, born in Bethlehem. FSW

The Children Grown. Haywood Jackson. a late-thirties couple in a roadside motel/on a second, desperate, honeymoon. SOTS

Children, It's Time. Michael Brownstein. Take your pick/While I take mine. ANYP

The Children Look at the Parents. Arthur Seymour John Tessimond. To those who have seen from the womb come/Enemies? How not say it? ChMP

The Children March. Elizabeth Riddell. The unsmiling sons, the sad bewildered daughters. CBAP

Children Not Kept at Home. Joyce Carol Oates. unlived lives live/mildly for centuries. DFF

Children of a Future Age. William Blake. That shakes the blossoms of my hoary hair!' CBEP

Children of Adam. Walt Whitman. And you stalwart loins. AP

Or in front, and I followed her just the same. AP

Children of Auschwitz. Naum Korzhavin. When I remember that this thing happened!/Men tortured children! VWA

Children of Darkness. Robert Graves. We loathe to gaze upon the sun? NoAm

The Children of Greenock. W. S. Graham. Striking two towns, and fed its flocks. FaBoTw

Children of Light. Robert Lowell. ...the ancient blood of Cain/Is burning, burning the unburied grain. AP; CMoP; MoAB; OxBA; PoPl

Children of Love. Harold Monro. But Jesus went weeping away, and left him there wondering why. MoBrPo

Children of Night. Richard Shelton. we are the children of night FiCP

The Children of Stare. Walter De la Mare. By the awful breath of God. BrPo

Children of the Heavenly King. John Cennick. Only Thou our leader be,/ And we still will follow Thee. WGRP

The Children of the Night. Edwin Arlington Robinson. Let us be Children of the Light,/And tell the ages what we are! NePA; OxBA

The Children of the Owl and the Pussy-Cat. Edward Lear. Because we take no interest in poltix of the day.) FaBoNo

The Children of the Poor. Gwendolyn Brooks. Holding the bandage ready for your eyes. PoA; PoCh

The Children of the Poor. Victor Hugo. He sends us clothed about with wings,/And finds them ragged babes that weep! LiTW

The Children of the State. James Lewisohn. The Children of the State/ forever countable/forever indispensable. LFAC

Children of the Sun. Fenton Johnson. Liberty! Fraternity! BANP

The Children's Bells. Eleanor Farjeon. The fathers will hear you. CH

The Children's Carol. Eleanor Farjeon. Give a single penny that we may not sing in vain. PCh

The Children's Crusade. Philip Levine. ...Never/to wait! Now they were free. NaP

Children's Crusade, 1939. Bertolt Brecht. The dog, who was starving, is dead. MoBS

A Children's Don't. Harry Graham. That is a game that two can play. BBGG

Children's Elegy. Muriel Rukeyser. I want to grow up. To come back to love.... LCAP

The Children's Ghosts. Winifred M. Letts. Make haste! Before it is too late!/For Death stands knocking at the gate! HBMV

The Children's Hour. Henry Wadsworth Longfellow. And molder in dust away. AA; AmePo; AmP; AnNE; FaBoBe; FaBV; FaFP; FPL; GoTF; HBV 1-2; HBVY; LaNeLa; OBAL; OBCA; OHFP; PoEL 1-5; PoLf; PoPl; TreF; WBLP

Children's Lenten Wisdom. James A. Houck. Ashes, ashes, all fall down. AMV-80

The Children's Letters. Dorothy Livesay. they leap on shafts of sunlight/ through the mind's/shutters. NOBC

Children's Prayers. Eugene Henry Pullen. I pray the Lord my soul to take. BLRP

Children's Rhymes. Langston Hughes. Liberty And Justice–/Huh!–For All? BOLo; BPo Salt'peanuts!/De-dop! InPS; PAI

Children's Runes and Omens. Anonymous. "May your wish and my wish never be broke." MAT

Children's Song. Ford Madox Ford. Goodness, how we'd like to know/If things will always alter so. HBV 1-2

Children's Song. Arye Sivan. and the glass breaks/the sun into fragments. VWA

Children's Song. R.S. Thomas. That mock the faded blue/Of your remoter heaven. BoC

Children, the Sandbar, That Summer. Muriel Rukeyser. Where men and women give each other children. LCAP

Children Waking: Indian Hill Station. Ralph Nixon Currey. We must accept, as they/The fact of a new day. PeSA

Children When They're Very Sweet. John Ciardi. Get a stick and make them mind. BBGG

Childs Memory. Terri Meyette Wilkins. ...I fall a/sleep in sweaty hay and dream my hair is made of feathers. LFAC

Chile. Susan Griffin. worried thoughts/slow/my/every movement. NPGG

The Chilean Elegies: 5. The Interior. Tom Wayman. And there is not a government in the world that wants to abolish/the factory. NOBC

Chiliasm. Richard Eberhart. I am Love and I am Wrath. EaLo

Chill of the Eve. James Stephens. And the grey, chill day/Slips away with a frown. OnYI

Chilled by Different Winds. Alice Mackenzie Swaim. The winds of difference freezing us to stone. AMV-80

Chilled by the Blasts of Adverse Fate. Jacob Duche. O then let every orphan breast/With grateful transport beat. AH

Chilly Water. Anonymous. Chilly water, Chilly water,/Hallelujah to dat Lam'. BoAN 1-2

Chilly Winds. *Anonymous.* An' I'm goin' to my dark lonesome home. OuSiCo; TrAS

The Chilterns. Rupert Brooke. And I daresay she will do. MoBrPo

Chimera. Barbara Howes. phantom or real,/I have looked on a noble animal. MP; TwCP

The Chimera. Alfred Mombert. of the terrible chimera with the murderous eyes. VWA

Chimes. Alice Meynell. And flies with the cloud. AnFE; CH

Chimes. Dante Gabriel Rossetti. And the heavy rain to follow. OBNC

Chimney Swallows. Horatio Nelson Powers. I sank in arms that folded me from fears,/And like an infant, slept. HBV 1-2

The Chimney Sweeper. *Anonymous.* Join your right hands, this broom step over,/And kiss the lips of your own true lover. AmFP

The Chimney Sweeper. William Blake.
So if all do their duty they need not fear harm. AtBAP; DiPo; EnPE; FaBoPV; FF; HeIP; InPK; NAWM 1-2; OAEL 1-2; OxBChV; PPP; SaC; SoSe; TEP
"Who make up a heaven of our misery." AtBAP; BoW; EnPE; NAWM 1-2; PPP; SaC; TEP

The Chimney-Sweeper's Complaint. Mary Alcock. Oh, could I hide me under ground,/How thankful should I be! NOEC

The Chimpanzee. Oliver Herford. Be horrid Chimpanzees today. FaBV; FiBHP; LBN; NA

The Chimpanzee. Muriel Sly. When the visitor least expects. FiBHP

China. William Empson. Most wrecked and longest of all histories. OBTV

The China Policy. Carl Rakosi. by simply looking at a heron crossing a stream. FAZ

A Chinaman's Chance. Marilyn Chin. Pulled down from the source, a cardboard bolt. BrSi

A Chinaman's Chance. Alex Kuo. ...In a sense we have all survived/Our words depend on it, with each chance. APU

Chinatown. Anna Blake Mezquida. The West crowds hard, lustful as sin–/Yet never wholly enters in. BPAW

Chinatown Chant. Tom MacInnes. We no care–yum poi! CaP

Chinatown Games. Wing Tek Lum. hands to waist clinging on/for dear life. BrSi

Chinatown Talking Story. Kitty Tsui. into the armor of warriors. BrSi

Chinese Baby Asleep. Dorothy Donnelly. ...her breath as it/flows in and out like light through opals. NCSH

The Chinese Banyan. William Meredith. ...a fear/That runs by analogy/On your page, in your house, for your dear. NePoEA

The Chinese Book of Rites (excerpt). *Anonymous.* Evil king is known by his imposts. OBVE

Chinese Camp, Kamloops (circa 1883). Andrew Suknaski. across angular bodies seeming thinner/and solid/as anvils. NOBC

The Chinese Graves in Beechworth Cemetery. Philip Mead. silence has passed to speech/and back again to silence. AMV-81

A Chinese Mural. Carlos Baker. The river contains no map. All's over with me. EyDe

The Chinese Nightingale. Vachel Lindsay. Spring came on forever,"/Said the Chinese nightingale. HBMV; MAPA; MoAmPo; NePA

Chinese Poems: Arthur Waley. C. A. Fair. And go, though our paths separate for good. PeSA

Chinese Serenade for the Ut-Kam and Tong-Koo. Thomas Holley Chivers. And the stars shine bright.... PeD

A Chinese Vase. Edward Hirsch. To kneel down, to forget the impossible weight/Of being human, to drink clear water. AMV-80

Chinese Winter. Frederick Robert Higgins. Footprints of fiery moments/Flash out memorials in silent ice. BIrV

Ching a Ring. James Robinson Planché. China must be broken in pieces. NOBL

Chinoiserie. Charles Wright. Outside the body, all things are encumbrances. AmPA

Chinoiseries. Amy Lowell.
Stained her rain-blue dress like tears. AnAmPo
They will be covered and gone. AnAmPo
With herons blowing like smoke/Across the sky. AnAmPo

Chip. George Starbuck. Generalissimo:/Able to cope. OBAL

A Chip on His Shoulder. *Anonymous.* When peace is prevailing he is spoiling to fight,/The man with a chip on his shoulder. BLPA; WBLP

Chipeta. Eugene Field. And write on the whitest of God's white clouds/Chipeta's name in eternal blue. PoOW

Chipeta's Ride. John W. Taylor. I tell this tale, as she told it to me,/In the year of eighteen ninety three. PoOW

The Chipmunk's Day. Randall Jarrell. ...the chipmunk/Dives to his rest. NCSH; OBCA

Chippewa Lake Park. Warren Woessner. and walk home across the empty/giant parking lot. TAT

Chippewa Love Song. *Anonymous.* Darling, I've been waiting/long/for you to come. BoWoP

Chiqui and Terra Nova. Jessica Hagedorn. ...strolling down the/streets arm-in-arm / like tropical apparitions / only visible to a/few. APU

Chiquita. Bret (Francis Bret Harte) Harte. And then, y know, boys will be boys, and/hosses–well, hosses is hosses! AA; BPAW

Chirstographia 35. Eugene Warren. with glancing light. AMV-80

The Chisizas I. Guy C. Z. Mhone. It behooves us/Yah, to do/What Yatu, Du/Craved for. WhB

The Chivalrous Shark. *Anonymous.* He's the man-eating shark/Who will eat neither woman nor child. FSW

Chivalry. George William Russell. And I was weeping in the Iron Age. MoRP; ViBoPo

Chivalry at a Discount. Edward Fitzgerald. Instead of breaking Priscian's head,/I had been breaking lances! HBV 1-2

Chloe. Robert Burns. Tripping o'er the pearly lawn,/The youthful, charming Chloe. GN; HBV 1-2

Chloe. Charles, Earl of Peterborough Mordaunt. Would one think that my Chloe ne'er thought it was she. CEP; OBEC

Chloe Divine. Thomas D'Urfey. And yet 'tis flesh and blood alone/That makes her so divine. HBV 1-2; OBEV

Chloride of Lime and Charcoal. Louis Zukofsky. at the thought of touching your knees. CoPo

Chloris and Hilas. Made to a Saraban. Edmund Waller. The Oak now resembles which lightning hath blasted. SeCV 1-2

Chloris Farewell. *Anonymous.* But make my constant meales at home. OBS

Chloris, 'Tis Not in Your Power. Sir George Etherege. Chloris, at worst, you'll in the end/But change your Lover for a Friend. HBV 1-2

Chock House Blues. Blind Lemon Jefferson. She's a fine looking fair brown/but she ain't never learned Lemon's rule. BluL

The Chocolate Soldiers. Calvin Forbes. To insure courageous chocolate dwells there. MAT; MAYP

Chocolates. Louis Simpson. they agreed that it had been a most/unusual conversation. InPS; LCAP; OxBC

A Choctaw Chief Helps Plan a Festival... Jim Barnes. So look dumb, play poor, form car pools or walk. TAT

The Choice. Hilary Corke. And what shall I choose, if I am free to choose? MP; NYBP

Choice. J. V. Cunningham. Rejecting vain delights/For quiet nights. VGW

Choice. Emily Dickinson. Behold the atom I preferred/To all the lists of clay! AA

Choice. John Farrar. And the sweetness of a lollypop/Is something that will last. BrR; SiSoSe

The Choice. John Masefield. Escape from prison. MoAB; MoBrPo

Choice. Angela Morgan. Alone I'd rather go my way/Throughout eternity. PoLf

The Choice. Frederick Morgan. as he sits in his studious chair all night/reading the breathing book. AMV-81

The Choice. John Norris. And dies a stranger to himself alone. CavP

The Choice. John Pomfret. All Men wou'd wish to Live, and Dye like me. CEP; NOEC; OBEC

The Choice. Nahum Tate. From silent life I'd steal into my grave. OBSP

The Choice. George Wither. For I know the hand of Nature/Will not make a fairer creature. OBEV

The Choice. William Butler Yeats. Or the day's vanity, the night's remorse. CMoP; NoAm; OBSP; OxBTC

The Choice of the Cross. Dorothy L. Sayers. That cross, that thorn, and those five wounds bear witness. TrCP

A Choice of Weapons. Stanley Jasspon Kunitz. The triggered poem's no water-pistol toy,/But shoots its cause, and is a source of joy. LiTM; VGW

The Choir Boys. Heinrich Heine. And all the ladies swim through tears/Toward such a work of art. LiTW

Choir Practice. Ernest Crosby. Who is it that behind and beneath sings/ever through us, now whispering, /now thundering, "I am"? AA

The Choirmaster's Burial. Thomas Hardy. Such the tenor man told/When he had grown old. DTC

"Cholly" Blues. *Anonymous.* I'll fin' me a woman, babe, an' roam no' mo'. ABF

Chomei at Toyama. Basil Bunting. My tongue/clacked a few prayers. OxBTC

Choose. Verna Bishop. Much is lost each hour you delay! STF

Choose Something Like a Star. Robert Frost. To stay our minds on and be staid. AnNE; MoAB; MoAmPo; PoCh

Choose You a Seat 'n' Set Down. *Anonymous.* Trouble over, choose you a seat 'n' set down. OuSiCo

Choosing. Eleanor Farjeon. There! have them all! TiPo

Choosing a Death. Alberta Turner. "Choose then". LCAP

Choosing a Mast. Roy Campbell. Shall fly, the feathered arrow of the foam. BoC; FaBoTw; PeSA

Choosing a Name. Charles and Mary Lamb. I will leave papa to name her. HBV 1-2; OxBChV

Choosing a Name. Anne Ridler. A home not mine, dear outcast. NOBE

Christmas Bells. Henry Wadsworth Longfellow. With peace on earth, good-will to men! AmePo; BLRP; EBCP; FaFP; HBV 1-2; HBVY; OBCP; PCh; PGD; TreFT; TRV; WBLP

Christmas Bells. Alice Mortenson. Saying, "Give your heart to Jesus,/For He's comming, coming soon!" BePJ

Christmas Bills. Joseph Hatton. That the time is bringing in with the bills. OBCP

Christmas Birthday. Grace Ellen Glaubitz. I've never been nine till now, you know! BiCB; SiSoSe

Christmas Brownie. Rowena Bastin Bennett. Because he gave himself. ChBR

The Christmas Candle. Kate Louise Brown. Glad shall ring, "A Christ is born!" SoPo

Christmas Card. Ted Hughes. Your anklebone/And your anklebone/Lie big in the bed. OBCP

A Christmas Carol. *Anonymous.*
And I shall syng:/"By-by, baby, lullay!" TrGrPo
Earth has become a smiling Paradise. OHIP
For His star it shineth clear. GN
I wish you a Merry Christmas/And a Happy New Year. BrR; ChBR; OHIP; SiSoSe; TiPo
Tydynges gode I thyngke to telle. EnLit

A Christmas Carol. Harry Behn. Rules all of God's creatures/In peace and love! BiCB; PCh

A Christmas Carol. Phillips Brooks. Everywhere, everywhere, Christmas to-night! OHIP; SoPo

A Christmas Carol. Gilbert Keith Chesterton. And all the stars looked down. ChBR; FaFP; GoBC; HBV 1-2; HBVY; OBCP; OHIP; SUS

A Christmas Carol. Fred Cogswell. Shadows of Calvary. ACV

A Christmas Carol. Samuel Taylor Coleridge. Peace, Peace on Earth! The Prince of Peace is born! ISi; OxBoCh

Christmas Carol. Sister Francisca Josefa del Castillo. See Fire itself in ice beshrouded,/And Ice in joy ablaze! CAW

Christmas Carol. Thomas Helmore. As 'twas foretold,/In the days of old,/By Gabriel. OHIP

A Christmas Carol. Robert Herrick. Heart, Ear, and Eye, and everything/Awake! PCh

A Christmas Carol. James Russell Lowell. "Today the Prince of Peace is born!" PGD

Christmas Carol. J. R. Newell. "Peace on earth, good will to men!" BLRP

Christmas Carol. D. J. Opperman. a bantam clucks with a suspicious stare. PeSA

Christmas Carol. May Probyn.
Small cheek against her cheek, He/Sleepeth, three hours old. GoBC; HBMV; OBVV
There Mary hath kissed her Child. ACP; CAW; ISi

A Christmas Carol. Christina Georgina Rossetti.
Thank God, thank God, for Christ was born/Ages ago, as on this morn. PCh
To hail the King of Glory. BiCB
Yet what I can I give Him,/Give my heart. BiCB; InPS; NOBV; OHIP; PCh; SBVL

A Christmas Carol. Algernon Charles Swinburne. Mary that is most wise,/Bring us to thy Son's eyes. Amen. SBVL

A Christmas Carol. Gilbert Thomas. Guide them with their sacrifice of frankincense and myrrh. MoRP

A Christmas Carol: "There's a song in the air!" Josiah Gilbert Holland. And we greet in his cradle our Saviour and King! HBVY

A Christmas Caroll, Sung to the King in the Presence at White-Hall. Robert Herrick. And Lord of all this Revelling. GoJo

Christmas Carols. Patricia Beer. David's city after dark./Honor tibi, Domine. OxBC

A Christmas Carroll. George Wither. Woods, and Hills, and every thing,/Beare witnesse we are merry. OBS

Christmas Chant. Isabel Shaw. That he may share/Our Christmas cheer. ChBR; SiSoSe

A Christmas Childhood. Patrick Kavanagh.
And I had a prayer like a white rose pinned/On the Virgin Mary's blouse. AnIL; DTC; FaBoIP; IPY; OxBI
I looked and three whin bushes rode across/The Horizon–the Three Wise Kings. PCh

Christmas Comes... Earle Birney. could be any day every day now and forever! ACV

Christmas Comes but Once a Year. *Anonymous.* A pocket full of money, and a cellar/full of beer. OxNR

Christmas Comes to Moccasin Flat. James Welch. Blackbird builds his fire. Outside, a quick thirty below. CDW; GP; MAT

A Christmas Cradlesong. Félix Lope de Vega Carpio. Hold these branches at rest,–/My babe is asleep. PoPl

Christmas Creek. Henry Clarence Kendall. And they named the stream that saved them–named it fitly–/"Christmas Creek'. CBAP

Christmas Dawn. Fleur Adcock. Trees gay-leaved with sun, wind fresh and free. ACV

A Christmas Dawn at Sea. Eva Morgan. A Child stretched out His arms that we might pray! EtS

Christmas Day. John Meade Falkner. I may go up to Jerusalem/Out of Galilee. NOCV

Christmas Day. Roy Fuller. Just for the birth long ago of a boy. OBCP

Christmas Day. Andrew Young. I sang praise to the Father,/The Son and Holy Ghost. OBCP

Christmas Day in the Workhouse. George R. Sims. Say what you did for me, too, only last Christmas Day. BeLS; BLPA; TreF

Christmas Day Is Come. Luke Wadding. Is there not sumptuous palace nor any inn at all/To lodge His heav'nly mother but in a filthy stall? OxBI

Christmas Dinner. Michael Rosen. Much nicer place to be–/for a worm. OBCP

Christmas Eve. Archie Randolph Ammons. ...with Him divinity/swept into the flesh/and made it real. NAs

Christmas Eve. *Anonymous.*
I would not bar a single door/Where love might enter in. TRV
The pot began to play with the ladle. OxNR

Christmas Eve. Patricia Beer. Charming as a yacht. OBCP

Christmas Eve. Bill Berkson. ...Is there someone/you would like to invite no one. ANYP

Christmas Eve. Liam P. Clancy. Who walk the wilds this night. ISi

Christmas Eve. John Davidson. Of magic music wild and sweet,/Anemones and clarigolds. OHIP

Christmas Eve. C. Day Lewis. If through centuries, clouded and dingy, this Day/can keep/Expectation alive. EaLo

Christmas Eve. John Drinkwater. While some glad girl beyond the hill/Dreamt of a new-born king. HBMV

Christmas Eve. Marion Edey. "Peace on earth, goodwill to men." YeAr

Christmas Eve. Eugene Field. Thou shalt hear the Master calling. OHIP

Christmas Eve. Ted Kooser. we both weep at the end of his stories. GP

Christmas Eve. Catherine Parmenter. I share Thy dream tonight! PGD

Christmas Eve. Karl Shapiro. Curse lightly and pronounce Your serious name. NYBP

Christmas Eve–Another Ceremony. Robert Herrick. And a deal of nightly fear/To watch it. OHIP

A Christmas Eve Choral. Bliss Carman. To hear the ecstasy of heaven./Halleluja! Halleluja! Halleluja! ISi

Christmas Eve (excerpt). Robert Browning. "I died, and live forevermore!" TrCP

Christmas Eve in France. Jessie Redmond Fauset. Shall live for evermore. BANP

Christmas Eve in Whitneyville, 1955. Donald Hall. While the dark houses harden into sleep. UnPo

Christmas Eve Legend. Frances Frost. All creatures knelt to worship the Child. BiCB

Christmas Eve Service at Midnight at St. Michael's. Robert Bly. A large man living and dead is flying over the water with wings/spread, a wound on his chest. NNaP

Christmas Eve under Hooker's Statue. Robert Lowell. Till Christ again turn wanderer and child. AP; CAPP; ConAP; FF; NePA; OxBA

Christmas Everywhere. Phillips Brooks. No palace too great, no cottage too small. BLRP; FaFP; OHFP; WBLP

The Christmas Exchange. Arthur Guiterman. To get the truly-wanted present. BrR; ChBR

Christmas Family Reunion. Peter De Vries. I long for time to pass, so I/Can think of all this with nostalgia. NLV; NOBL

A Christmas Fold-Song. Lizette Woodworth Reese. For that they housed Him from the cold! ChBR; HBMV; HBVY; OBCA; OHIP; OnMSP; SUS; TrCP

A Christmas Ghost-Story. Thomas Hardy. But tarries yet the Cause for which He died. EnLi 1-2; OBWP

A Christmas Hymn. Cecil Frances Alexander. All in white shall wait around. OHIP

A Christmas Hymn. Alfred Domett. In the solemn midnight/Centuries ago. GN; HBV 1-2; OBVV; PGD; WGRP

The Christmas Hymn. Saint Ephrem. Whence is this that I should feed Thee,/Feeding all things from Thy table? CAW; ISi

A Christmas Hymn. Richard Wilbur. By whose descent among us/The worlds are reconciled. CoPo; MoRP; OBCP; OFD; PCh; TrCP

Christmas in Freelands. James Stephens. –That all we love is born again. TrCP

Christmas in Penang. John Leyden. To guard thee ever gay and free,/Beneath thy green Banana tree! OBTV

Christmas in the Heart. *Anonymous.* But the dearest, truest Christmas/Is the Christmas in the heart. ChBR; OHIP; SiSoSe

Christmas in the Olden Time. Sir Walter Scott. A Christmas gambol oft could cheer/The poor man's heart through half the year. GoBC

Christmas in the Wood. Frances Frost. The shy hearts of the wilderness. BrR; ChBR; TrCP

Christmas Is Coming. *Anonymous.* If you haven't got a ha'penny,/God bless you! NTCP; OxNR; PCh; SoPo

Christmas Is Really for the Children. Steve Turner. or whether there's any connection. EBCP; OBCP

Christmas Is Remembering. Elsie Binns. And all the world caroling/Songs of joy. BiCB; ChBR; SiSoSe

Christmas Island. Katharine Lee Bates. –We might find a fairy ferry/To that isle where saints make merry! HBMV; HBVY

Christmas Landscape. Laurie Lee. in the cry of anguish/the child's first breath is born. OBCP

A Christmas Legend. Frank Sidgwick. ...Christmas Babe who smiled/In the eyes of great god Pan. OHIP

Christmas Legend. Edna Randolph Worrell. The world wakens up to the children's sweet laughter. ChBR

Christmas Legends. Denis Aloysius McCarthy. Even the wildest beast afar/Knows the light of the Saviour's star. ChBR

Christmas Letter Home. G. S. Fraser. And so, good-night, this Christmas, and God bless! OxBTC

Christmas Lights. Valerie Worth. Full of deep blue/Mysterious stars. PCh

Christmas Lullaby. Ulrich Troubetzkoy. And Mary hums a lullaby. YeAr

Christmas Lullaby for a New-Born Child. Yvonne Gregory. So close your eyes, while I pray, dear child,/That the star may shine in you. AmNP

Christmas Mass for a Little Atheist Jesus. Claude Maillard. I answer you/amen. BoWoP

A Christmas Message. Gavin Ewart. ...Those he loves, he deceives. FaBoMo

Christmas Morn. Ruth Sawyer. And many children–God give them grace,/bringing tall candles to light Mary's face. OBCP

Christmas Morning. Harry Behn. Today the angels earthward swing/To bless us here below! PCh

Christmas Morning. Elsie Melchert Fowler. Christmas Dream come true! ChBR

Christmas Morning. Steven Lautermilch. and the sharpness of the straw. AMV-80

Christmas Morning. Elizabeth Madox Roberts. And when I'd tiptoe softly out/I'd meet the wise men coming in. ChBR; MoAmPo; PCh; PoSC; SUS

Christmas Morning I. Carol [or Carole] Freeman. sewing a new/button my last year/ragdoll. PCh; PoBA; TTY

Christmas Mourning. Vassar Miller. May wound the Man no more. CoPo; MoAmPo

Christmas Myth, 1973. Robert McGovern. Angels singing/To silly shepherds/Of a child born for death/To save us from our fantasy. SOTS

Christmas Night. Hugh MacCawell. O Mary, if you let me I/Will wrap him warmly in my own. KiLC

Christmas Night. Lawrence Sail. gazing in safety at/a star solid as flesh. OBCP

Christmas Night of '62. William Gordon McCabe. My home is in the bivouac. AA

Christmas Now Is Drawing Near. *Anonymous.* And crown my soul with the higher Trinity. OBET

Christmas Ornaments. Valerie Worth. Nightingales with/Pearly tails. PCh

A Christmas Package: No. 7 (excerpt). David McCord. ...Twelve lights go on,/ten don't. They used to blink. PCh

A Christmas Package: No. 8 (excerpt). David McCord. So far, so good. PCh

Christmas Pageant. Margaret Fishback. And wise men, from the upper classes/Look very wise, in horn-rimmed glasses. PoSC

A Christmas Prayer. Molly Anderson Haley. And make us brave to live the angels' song! PGD

A Christmas Prayer. Herbert H. Hines. Accept the gift and all the life we bring. PGD

A Christmas Prayer. George Macdonald. We are his, as well as thou. PCh; SUS

Christmas Prayer. Madeline Morse. And help the age of peace to come/From a Dreamer's martyrdom. PGD

A Christmas Prayer. Robert Louis Stevenson. Evening bring us to our beds with/Grateful thoughts, forgiving, and/Forgiven, for Jesus' sake. Amen TrCP

Christmas Rede. Jane Barlow. Shall burn rose-red while stars be sped; tho' stars dropt/dead would burn. OBVV

A Christmas Sermon: To Be Honest, To Be Kind. Robert Louis Stevenson. here is a task for all that a man has of fortitude and delicacy. PoLf

Christmas Shoppers. Aileen Fisher. for there's Christmas, merry Christmas in the air. ChBR

Christmas Shopping. Louis MacNeice. Moves its arms like a giant Swedish drill whose/Mind is a vacuum. OBCP

The Christmas Silence. Margaret Deland. In burst of music, love, and light! OHIP

Christmas Singing. Elsie Williams Chandler. The latch-string's hanging at the door/For you! For you! ChBR; SiSoSe

Christmas Song. Bliss Carman. They all are dancing in the morn/Because a little child is born. PeCV; PoSC

Christmas Song. Eugene Field. Therefore little children sing. YeAr

Christmas Song. Elizabeth-Ellen Long. For they were first to look with love/Upon the Christmas Child! ChBR; SiSoSe

Christmas Song. Lydia Avery Coonley Ward. So the little children sing. OHIP

Christmas Songs. Gerta Kennedy. come again to the earth/for all men to remember. PoPl

A Christmas Sonnet. Edwin Arlington Robinson. Something is here that was not here before,/And strangely has not yet been crucified. EaLo

Christmas Still Lives. Clarence Hawkes. Then will Christ and Christmas be/The hope of all humanity. BePJ

Christmas Story (1980). Pat Arrowsmith. will fire rockets to destroy the world/he came that Christmas Day to save? BrRo

Christmas Thank You's. Mick Gowar. and just sent me/a fiver/to spend. OBCP

Christmas, the Year One, A. D. Sara Henderson Hay. And little Jesus safe among/The holier gifts of love. PoRA

A Christmas Thought. Mrs. Frank A. Breck. That we might have riches eternal,/And with Him forever abide. BePJ

Christmas Thoughts, by a Modern Thinker. William Hurrell Mallock. And go and get my portrait done. NOBV

Christmas-Tide. *Anonymous.* And save young Bobby some. OxNR

Christmas-Time. Rose Fyleman. And isn't it a sweet to-do? ChBR

The Christmas Tree. Patricia Beer. Perhaps it will look down on the thatch yet. OBCP

A Christmas Tree. William Burford. We face a glacial distance, who are here/Huddl'd/At your feet. NePA; SoSe

Christmas Tree. Stanley Cook. Isn't there the child, beneath the presents/We heap upon him, that we are fond of? OBCP

The Christmas Tree. Peter Cornelius. The children gathered, the candles alight–That music to hear, to see that sight. PCh

Christmas Tree. Aileen Fisher. the Christmas carols/of the chickadees. ChBR

Christmas Tree. Laurence Smith. Spangled with fire/Warm over cold. OBCP

The Christmas Tree in the Nursery. Richard Watson Gilder. And before you can wink/The tree stands bare! HBVY; OHIP

The Christmas Trees. Mary Frances Butts. Now in completeness/We wait. OHIP

Christmas Trees. Robert Frost. In wishing you herewith a Merry Christmas. BiP

Christmas Trees. Geoffrey Hill. We hear too late or not too late. NOCV

A Christmas Wish. Eugene Field. When they awake on Christmas day. ChBR

Christofo Columbo. *Anonymous.* Son-of-a-gun, Columbo! AmSS

Christophe. Russell Atkins. Highly th' imperial sign/shone in his glory! PoNe

Christopher at Birth. Michael Longley. The wolf treading its circuits towards sleep. CIP

Christopher Columbus. Franklin Pierce ("F.P.A.") Adams. I refer to the United States of America,/Goes marching on. InMe

Christopher Columbus (excerpt). William Hart-Smith. "Christ be with us!" he said, as the ship sped west. PoAu 1-2

Christopher Marlowe. Michael Drayton. For than fine madness still he did retain/Which rightly should possess a poet's brain... ChTr

Christopher Marlowe. Algernon Charles Swinburne. Not yet might'st thou be praised enough of men. TrGrPo

A Christopher of the Shenandoah. Edith Matilda Thomas. Come life or come death I couldn't do less/than follow his guide. PAH

Christopher Street Liberation Day, June 28, 1970. Fran Winant. sisters and sisters/brothers and brothers/together. PeHV

Christopher White. *Anonymous.* Looke that you love your old loves best,/For infaith they are best companye.' ESPB

Christs Sleeping Friends. Robert Southwell. No Joan ivy, no Zacheus tree,/Were to the world so great a losse as he. AnAnS 1

Christus Matthaeum et Discipulos Alloquitur. Sir Edward Sherburne. I shall be more (alas!) than one be sold. ACP

Christus Triumphans. Conde B. Pallen. Thou art but shadow with a broken glaive,/Within thy futile hands His winding-sheet. CAW

Chrome Babies Eating Chocolate Snowmen in the Moonlight. A. K. Redwing. the feathers land selectively in living rooms/from Maine to Seattle... VoR

Chromis. Phineas Fletcher. So on thy shore the fisher-boys shall sing/Sweet songs of peace to our sweet peace's King. LoBV

Chromo. Sarah Webster Fabio. chromo.../chromo.../chromo... CNA

A Chronicle. *Anonymous.* But what it ought to be/Has quite escaped my mind! BLPL; NA

The City Child. Alfred, Lord Tennyson. Daisies and kingcups and honeysuckle-flowers.' OxBChV

The City Church. E. H. K. And still they stab their souls and slink away. WGRP

The City Clerk. Thomas Ashe. A simple farmer's lad, among the girls in the hay. OBVV

The City Dead-House. Walt Whitman. Months, years, an echoing, garnish'd house–but dead, dead, dead. AmePo

A City Eclogue. W." J. Our headstrong spouses still will have their way! NOEC

A City Flower. Henry Austin Dobson. Some flake of the dust is brushed away/That had settled over my heart. TEP

City Girl. Maxwell Bodenheim. ...while the distant goal/Of whispering horizons lures your sighs. HBMV

A City Graveyard. Joyce Carol Oates. our small tireless names/murmured in their voices. DFF

The City in the Sea. Edgar Allan Poe. Hell, rising from a thousand thrones,/Shall do it reverence. AA; AnAmPo; APA; ForPo; HBV 1-2; LiTA; MAmP; MAT; MOS; NePA; NOBA; NoP; OxBA; PoEL 1-5; TAP; ViBoPo; WHA

The City in the Throes of Despair. Tony Towle. or relaxing on the train back to New York, the parachute as a/souvenir. ANYP

City Jail. J. J. Maloney. blushing quietly beneath the skin/of a face lit up in the black light/of paranoia. LFAC

City Johannesburg. Mongane Wally Serote. Jo'burg City, you are dry like death,/Jo'burg City, Johannesburg, Jo'burg City. WhB

City Life. D. H. Lawrence. hooked fishes of the factory world. CAD; OAEP

The City Limits. Archie Randolph Ammons. and fear lit by the breadth of such calmly turns to praise. HaCAP; NoAm; NOBA; NoP; NYP

The City, Lord, Where Thy Dear Life. William E. Dudley. God, make thy people live. AH

The City: Midnight. Bruce Dawe. And all their playthings crumble into light. PoAu 1-2

The City Mouse and the Garden Mouse. Christina Georgina Rossetti. Pedigreed bitches pregnant with bloodhounds. FaPON
Poor little timid furry man. FaBoBe; HBV 1-2; HBVY; NTCP; SUS; TiPo

City Nights, I: In the Train. Arthur Symons. Out into the night, and down/The dazzling vista of streets! VLP

The City of Baltimore. Anonymous.
"You are the smartest man that walks/On the deck of the Baltimore!" ShS
You fought your way right fore and aft on The City of Baltimore. OBSS

The City of Beggars. Alfred Hayes. The garibaldian cape shot full of bullet holes. WaP

The City of Dreadful Night. James (1834-82) Thomson.
...all, renewed assurance/And confirmation of the old despair. GTBS-P; OAEP
Although proclaimed aloud for evermore. GoTS; OAEP
As brooding on that"End it when you/will." EBEV; OAEP
But I, what do I here? WiR
The empyrean is a void abyss. GTBS
I pondered long that cold majestic face/Whose vision seemed of infinite void space. OAEP

The City of Falling Leaves. Amy Lowell.
All Venice is a falling of autumn leaves,/Brown, and yellow streaked with brown. SUS; TiPo
They fall,/Flutter,/Fall. MAPA

The City of God. Samuel Johnson. The Eternal City stands. AA; FaPoR; TRV; WGRP

The City of God. Francis Turner Palgrave. Be in the midst of them,/God's own Jerusalem! WGRP

The City of Golf. Robert Fuller Murray. I will yield to fate and be a golfer too! SD

City of Light. Nahum Bomze. Oh, lead me, lead me/with your pale hands/to the dark side/of the light. VWA

City of Monuments. Muriel Rukeyser. stone cedes to blossom everywhere. NAMP

City of Orgies. Walt Whitman. Lovers, continual lovers, only repay me. NYP

The City of Prague. William Jeffery Prowse. The beautiful City of Prague! CenHV

The City of Satisfaction. Daniel Gerard Hoffman. If I could only make this broken top/Fit snug back on this casket CoPo; Prf

The City of Slaughter. Hayim Nahman Bialik. And send thy bitter cry into the storm! TrJP

The City of the Dead. Richard Burton. For they lie at ease and know that life is done. HBV 1-2

The City of the End of Things. Archibald Lampman. For the grim Idiot at the gate/Is deathless and eternal there. NOBC; OBCV

The City of the Moon (excerpt). Kenneth Rexroth. ...Besides/These there are many/Thousands of other truths, more/Than can ever be numbered. GP

The City of the Soul. Lord Alfred Bruce Douglas. Like a lean knife between the ribs of Time. HBMV

City Pigeons. Helen Chasin. ...supplicants/in lime-specked groves/to dirty mysteries. WeW

City Rain. Rachel Field. And the rain like a rumbling tune that sings/Through everything I do. SoPo; TiPo

The City Rat and the Country Rat. Jean de La Fontaine. And would not swap for pleasure/So mix'd with fear and trembling. OBVE

The City Rises. James (Olumo) Cunningham. rises/as only stunted structures can. JB

City Roofs. Charles Hanson Towne. The driftwood of the town who have no roof-tops, and no home! BLPA

The City's Crown. Dudley Foulke. So may the city that I love be great/'Till every stone shall be articulate. HBMV; WGRP

City: San Francisco. Langston Hughes. Hanging lights/About its head. AmFN; GoSl

A City Song. John Hanlon Mitchell. Paddle weary feet. CaP

City Songs. Mark Van Doren. That was a child; and he was/Change. NYBP

City Sparrow. Jane Mayhall. As people try to deny their hidden joys. TAP

City-Storm. Harold Monro. All people weep. MoBrPo

City Streets and Country Roads. Eleanor Farjeon. Oh, take me away/To the country again! BrR; SoPo; TiPo

The City Tree. Isabella Valancy Crawford. To where my emerald branches call and wave/As to the mystic skies. CaP

City Trees. Vere Dargan. The trees along our city streets/Are lovely, gallant things. PGD

City Trees. Edna St. Vincent Millay. I know what sound is there. LaNeLa

City Walk-Up, Winter 1969. Carolyn Forche. we begin to hear the noise of the world again. MAYP

City without Smoke. Edwin Denby. Except that each looks at it with his mortal face. NYP

City without Walls. W. H. Auden. You both will feel better by breakfast time. NYBP; NYP

Civil Defense. Kenneth Burke. Can reek and retch and rot in perfect safety. OBAL

Civil Elegies (excerpt). Dennis Lee. they crowd in a dense baffled throng and the sun does not shine/through. NOBC

Civil Irish and Wild Irish. Laoiseach Mac an Bhaird O man who follow English ways. AnIL

Civil Riot. G. D. H. Cole. Oh I don't suppose it mattered;/But I happened to be there. OxBTC

Civil War. Austin Clarke. But we remember how they shot/Rory O'Connor. NOBI

Civil War. Charles Dawson Shanly. Load again, rifleman, keep our hand in! HBV 1-2; PAH

Civil War. Mark Van Doren. But the dark wind is earless, and the day/Is endless, and the grasses hiss and hiss. MoVE

The Civil Wars between the Two Houses of Lancaster and York. Samuel Daniel. And with what store of blood kings are undone. OBWP

Civilisation and Its Discontents. John Ashbery. Performing once again, for you and for me. CAPP; LCAP; TwCP

Civilities. Thomas Whitbread. ...and make/Your opponent yours by a nicety of name. SD

Civilities of Lamplight. Charles Tomlinson. Hollows the hedge-bound track, a sealed/Furrow on dark, closing behind him. OxBC

Civility a Bogey; or, Two Centuries of Canadian Cities. Margaret Avison. It's all one. NOBC

Civilization. Tom Schmidt. as he dips/his brown head/to drink. NeAC

Civilization. Yuan Chen. I find myself standing and wondering, perplexed,/Whether Saints and Sages have really done us good. LiTW

Civilizing the Child. Lisel Mueller. I go scot-free, acquitted/by her happiness-tinged cheeks,/my judges, my blind jury. CTBA

De Civitate Hominum. Thomas MacGreevy. Holy God makes no reply/Yet. CIP

Clabe Mott. James Still. The oaks go down with thunder in the singing air. GrPl

Clad All in White. Abraham Cowley. Of Peace and yielding who would doubt,/When the white Flag he sees hung out? SeCV 1-2

The Claim. Edith Nesbit. Admit that I have better taste. NOBV

The Claim That Has the Canker on the Rose. Joseph Mary Plunkett. That all the glories formerly I knew/Shone from the cloudy splendour of your name. OxBI

Claim to Love. Giovanni Battista Guarini. Fire where it burns more truly dwells/Than where it scatters light. AWP

Claiming the Promise. Charles Wesley. And bid our inmost souls rejoice,/In hope of perfect love. BePJ

Clair de Lune. Anthony Hecht. And the stone god of morning will restore/The rose to the vast processions of its ground. NYBP

Clair de Lune. Arthur Symons. And I fade into a dream. SyP

The Clamdigger. Dionis Coffin Riggs. And the upland plover whistling beyond/The wild-rose edges of the pond. TAT

Clamming. Reed Whittemore. ...Son, when you clam,/Clam. NYBP; TAP

Clamour of the Wind Making Music. Saint Columcille. to sleep at Comgall's, to visit Canice,/it would be pleasant! BIrV

Clams. Ishigaki Rin. I could only sleep through the night,/my mouth slightly open. PBWP

Clams. Stanley Moss. a salt foot, too humble to have a voice,/thumps for representation, joy. GP

Clancy. David Wagoner. Of her mind and his, digesting this wild good fortune. PH

Clancy of the Overflow. Andrew Barton ("Banjo") Paterson. But I doubt he'd suit the office, Clancy, of The Overflow. PoAu 1-2

Clandestine Work. Yvan Goll. The whole time/Death was working. VWA

Clap Hands, Clap Hands. Anonymous. For father's got money,/But mother's got none. OxNR

Clap Hands, Daddy Comes. Anonymous. And a cake for Johnny. OxNR

Clap Hands, Daddy's Coming. Anonymous. And his hands full of clay. OxNR

Clap Your Hands for Herod. Josef Hanzlik. who is coming to kill us once again. OBCP

Clara. Ezra Pound. She will neither stay in, nor come out. DTC

Clare Coast. Emily Lawless. Hearts like lead in our breasts. OxBI

Clare De Kitchen. Anonymous. Old Virginny never tire. BLPA

Clare's Dragoons. Thomas Osborne Davis. And the Shamrock shine forever new! OnYI

Clarel. Herman Melville.
Amid the dragon's staring crew. AmPP
And prove that death but routs life into victory. AP; MAmP
As bride and suite let pass a bier–/So pass the coming canto here. AmPP
...Come, in stream we'll cool/The wine ere quaffing.–Muleteer! OxBA
No New World to mankind remains!' OxBA

Claremont. Robert Peters. ...At home/Ann sat beside the fire/unable to eat her dinner. GP

Clarence. Shel Silverstein. And you'll be as happy as little Clarence. OBCA

Clarence Mangan. Thomas Kinsella. Ultimate, pitiless, again I ply the knife. CIP

Claribel. Alfred, Lord Tennyson. Where Claribel low-lieth. AtBAP; PeD

Clarimonde. Theophile Gautier. Hast thou returned to pay the debt of kisses/Thou owest to me? AWP

Clarinda's Indifference at Parting with Her Beauty. Anne Finch, Countess of Winchilsea. But unconcern'd, can lett thy glories passe. SBG

The Clarion-Call. Anonymous. O Church of God, awake! BLRP

Claritas. Denise Levertov. Light/light light light. VGW

Clarity. Archie Randolph Ammons. scores of knowledge/now obvious and quiet. HaCAP; TAP

The Clarity of Apples. Terry M. Perlin. The repentance of laughter/Haste and chance. AMV-80

Clark Sanders. Anonymous. The dew it falls na sooner down/Then ay it is full weet. OxBB

A Clash with Cliches. Vassar Miller. take flesh of my tired bones. AMV-80; FAZ

Clasping of Hands. George Herbert. Or rather make no Thine and Mine. ILwL; PoEL 1-5

The Class. Josephine Jacobsen. and in glazed brightness the sun says, Live... GP

Class Dismissed. Anonymous. Good-by to dull old Hesiod. UnTE

Class Incident from Graves. Alan Brownjohn. "Mitchell's still in there, hob-nobbing with the officers." OxBTC

Class of 19–. Frederick Dec. Smiling now from a/Yellowed/Yearbook page. PCP

Classic. Archie Randolph Ammons. water survives its motions. NOBA

Classic Ballroom Dances. Charles Simic. Where they also hold charity raffles/On rainy Monday nights of an eternal November. LCAP

A Classic Case. Gilbert Sorrentino. lovely Major Hoople. NeAP

Classic Encounter. Christopher (Christopher St. John Sprigg) Caudwell. Whether he be Compulsion, or All-Fathering,/Or Fate and blind. OxBTC

A Classic Idyll. Avraham Huss. Whether there was any meaning in this entire spectacle. VWA

A Classic Ode. Charles Battell Loomis. Long as the spear of Arnon, twice as long,/What time he hurled it at King Pharaoh's feet. NA

Classic Scene. William Carlos Williams. the other remains/passive today– AmP; OxBA

A Classic Waits for Me. E. B. White. By the manly love of classics BXAP; InPK; NYBP; Par; SpRo

Classical Autumn. Robert Clayton Casto. ...finely, slenderly made. AMV-81

Classical Criticism. George Lynde Richardson. Jupiter! What's the difference? Let/them go! AA

A Classical Quatrain. Paul Goodman. the homicidal hurry in his soul/embarrassed into an uncertain smile. VGW

The Classical Style. Michael Palmer. ...a possible extension bridge/extending from the more recent past/into the less/renamed the presen NPGG

Classroom in October. Elias Lieberman. No ablative is ever absolute. GoYe

Claud Halcro's Invocation. Sir Walter Scott. Hence pass till Hallow-mass!–my spell is spoken. NBM

Claude Allen. Anonymous. Or you may be like poor Claude Allen/And have this awful debt to pay. AmFP

Claudius Gilbert Anagram. Tis Braul I Cudgel. John Wilson. Yea Lett the Lord confound them, who with spight/Against his Truth maliciously Fight. SCAP

Claus Von Stauffenberg. Thom Gunn. –Falling toward history, and under snow. OBWP

Clausa Germanis Gallia. Millen Brand. and some read the letters now coming back from/"Amerika." GP

Claustrophobia. Sean O Riordain. ...I will be/a republic of light/till the day comes. NOBI

Clavering. Edwin Arlington Robinson. I say no more for Clavering. CrMA; HBMV; OxBA

The Clavichord. May Sarton. She wreathes the air with green/And weaves the stillness in. UnS

Clay. Edward Verrall Lucas. Bid him renounce his wish and kneel/In thanks for this same kindly clay. HBV 1-2

Clay and Water. Sandra Hochman. Standing like an old man/Cemented in the strong window. Str

Clay Hills. Jean Starr Untermeyer. And set it in a high, clean place,/To recall the granite strength of my desire. HBMV

The Clay Jug. Anonymous. Friend, listen: the God whom I love is inside. NU

Clean Clara. William Brighty ("Matthew Browne") Rands. She brings out her broom at six o'clock. HBVY

Clean & Clear. Michael Brownstein. The tiny hand is on the knob ANYP

Clean Hands. Henry Austin Dobson. Make this thing plain! TrPWD

Cleaning Day. Jose Kozer. while my mother doggedly straightened the mirrors. VWA

Cleaning Fish. Richard Behm. ...Bass merely circles,/mouth larger and larger. WOLT

Cleaning Ship. Charles Augustus Keeler. With a good stiff breeze an' a wake o' shining foam. EtS

Cleaning the Candelabrum. Siegfried Sassoon. The twilight blackbird flutes, and spring arrives. HaMV

Cleaning the Fish. Robert Pack. ...And Sam, well we'll find out/whether he has an appetite for fish! SM

Cleaning the Well. Paul Ruffin. ...It's just/one more secret you got to live with. Str

Cleaning Up. Edward Dyson. When we wash her down and see the colour freely through the stuff. PoAu 1-2

Cleaning Up, Clearing Out. Daniel Ross Bronson. Grown men, so sad, in coats too big too fit. AMV-80

Cleanliness. Charles and Mary Lamb. Who that's human would refuse it,/When a little water does it? OxBChV

Cleanness (excerpt). Anonymous. So abhorrent of evil is the ever-righteous. NOCV

Cleansing. Heinrich Suso Waldeck. They also, then, shall hear the Sabbath's cry. CAW

Cleansing Fires. Adelaide Anne Procter. And the furnace of living pain! WGRP

Clear. Angelo Lewis. & on into/Streets... PoBA

Clear After Rain. Tu Fu. A single wild goose climbs into the void. PoPl

The Clear Air of October. Robert Bly. ...pheasants/Are waiting at the head of the stairs with robbers' eyes. NaP; NoAm

Clear Bright. Li Ch'ing-chao. There'll be no second helpings/When you get to the Nine Springs. BoWoP

Clear Eyes. Walter De la Mare. It loves not, nor grieves. MoVE; ViBoPo

A Clear Midnight. Walt Whitman. Night, sleep, death and the stars. HAP; OBSP

Clear Night. Charles Wright. And the gears notch and the engines wheel. GeTw

Clear Night, Small Fire, No Wind. Reg Saner. A moment, amazed at its size. NPAW

Clear or Cloudy, Sweet as April Showering. Anonymous. And let your weeds lack dew, and duly sterve. ElL

A Clear Shell. Frances Bellerby. ...shows Death/Smilingly over the place,/Trusting this new face. FaBoWP

Clear the Way. John Montague. Condemned, like all his family, to Clear the Way! FaBoIP

The clear water of the imperial pond. Ise Tayu. Just so, I am grateful to be singled out though I am of low birth. BoWoP

The Clearing. Peter Everwine. You speak NNaP

The Clearing. Robert Graves. Though the twigs crackling under a light foot/Declare her immanence. NYBP

The Clearing. LeRoi (Imamu Amiri Baraka) Jones. & you are singing. What song/is that The words/are beautiful. CoPo

Clearing at Dawn. Li Po. Blown by the wind slowly scatters away. AWP

Clearing for the Plough. Ernest G. Moll. Half loth, for sorrow, to awaken/ The lesser music of the grass. NOAV

Cleator Moor. Norman Nicholson. And feels the iron in his soul. FaBoTw; NeBP

Cleavage. Archie Randolph Ammons. getting off/the ground OBAL

Cleavage. Louise Townsend Nicholl. To turn the frozen pages, blindly bidden. NePoAm

Cleitagoras. of Tarentum Leonidas. So shall you honor well the shades, from whom/Are thanks–and from the dead is gratitude. AWP

Clement Attlee. Michael Benedikt. ...Cautiously, a frayed/black monocle cord starts to make its way back across my/cheek... PAI

Clementine. Anonymous. Though in life I used to kiss her, now she's dead, I draw the line. AmFP

Clementine. Percy Montrose. Thou art lost and gone forever,/Dreadful sorry, Clementine. BLSo; FSW; OBAL

Cleobulus' Epitaph. Simonides (of Ceos). I shall tell those who pass that Midas here lies buried. PoPl

Cleon. Robert Browning. Their doctrine could be held by no sane man. MaVP; MBW 1-2; OAEL 1-2; OAEP; VLP

Cleopatra. William Wetmore Story. And love as you loved me then! AA

Cleopatra. Algernon Charles Swinburne. Goddess by god, with Antony. BeLS

Cleopatra and Antony. John Dryden. Lie still and peaceful there. I'll think no more on't. FiP

Cleopatra: Chorus. Samuel Daniel. Doth Order order so/Disorder's overthrow? OBSC

Cleopatra Dying. Thomas Stephen Collier. Egypt, Antony, farewell. BLPA; BLPL; FaBoBe; TreFT

Cleopatra to the Asp. Ted Hughes. Swim like a fish toward Rome. EBEV

Clepsydra. Charles Cotton. Sobriety's no charm, I dubt,/Against a Cannon-Bullet. CavP

A Cleric Courts His Lady. Anonymous. That I nam thine and thou art mine,/To don all they wille.' MeEL

The Clerical Cabal. Anonymous. 'Twill be well if their godliness turns to their gain. APAS

Clerical Oppressors. John Greenleaf Whittier. And Truth and Right throughout the earth be/known/As in their home above. PAH; PPON

Clerihew: "Albert Durer." W. Leslie Nicholls. But that doesn't really matter. PV

Clerihew: "Edmund Clerihew Bentley." William Jay Smith. Found that it contained that very new/Verse form, the clerihew. PV

Clerihew: "Instead of blushing cherry hue." Allan M. Laing. Mr. E. C. Bentley/just smiles gently. PV

Clerihew: "Spinoza." Anonymous. Bawdy belles-lettres,/Etc. NOBL

Clerihew: "The Empress Poppaea." Anonymous. Only no one could stop her/From being improper. PV

Clerihew: "The Saturday Review." William Cole. Or with anything very much. PV

Clerihew: "William Penn." William Jay Smith. He had only one mania–/ Pennsylvania. PV

Clerihews. Edmund Clerihew Bentley.
All of you seem to make. NOBL
An opinion resented most bitterly/By the people of Italy. FiBHP
And wrote Principles of Political Economy. FiBHP
At so grotesque a blunder. FiBHP; NOBL; PV
Atishoo! Atishoo! PV
But Biography is about Chaps. NOBL; PV
"But I do know how to paint." NLV
But I sees their point of view.' NOBL
Dropped by the Black Prince. PV
L'Etat C'est Moi and Ich Dien. PV
He is really perfectly serious/About the universe being mysterious. NLV
He lived in the odium/Of having discovered sodium. NLV
He wrote the Inferno/On a bottle of Pernod. NLV
"It smells as if a town/"Was being burnt down.' NLV
It smells as if a town/Was being burnt down. FiBHP
Kick outer the Litany. NOBL
None of you ases/Can condense gases. NLV
"Say I am designing St. Paul's." FiBHP; NLV; PV
There is a great deal to be said/For being dead. NOBL
To find it an oblate spheroid. FiBHP
To have been quite a sound scheme. NOBL
Was often practically opaque. NLV
When he wrote Il Penseroso. NLV; PV

Clerimont's Song. Ben Jonson. That strike mine eyes, but not my heart. BoLiVe; LoBV; OAEL 1-2; PAI; PPP; SeCP; SeCV 1-2

Clerk Colvill (A version). Anonymous. His brither he has unbent his bow,/ 'T was never bent by him again. BuBa; EnSB; ESPB

Clerk Colvill (B version). Anonymous. O brother, take my sword and spear,/For I have seen the false mermaid.' BaBo; ESPB; FaBoBa; GBP; OxBB; ViBoFo

The Clerk's Twa Sons o Owensford. Anonymous. For I'll neither eat nor drink,/Nor set a fit on ground.' BaBo; ESPB

Clerk Saunders. Anonymous.
For it was neither lord nor loune/That was in bower last night wi mee.' ESPB
Her lover vanish'd in the air/And she gaed weeping away. OxBS
Ne'er love him as ye did me. AnFE; OBEV; SeCeV
'T was Clerk Saunders, that good earl's/son,/That pledgd his faith to marry me.' ESPB
There'll never coal nor candle-light/Shine in my bower nae mair.' FaBoBa; ViBoFo
Ye mith slain Clerk Saunders in open/field,/And no in bed wi me.' ESPB

A Clerk Ther was of Cauntebrigge Also (parody). Walter William Skeat. Swich maner study was to him but game. BXAP

The Clerks. Edwin Arlington Robinson. Clipping the same sad alnage of the years. AA; AnNE; MAmP; MoAB; MoAmPo; MoVE; PoEL 1-5

Clevedon Church. Andrew Lang. Far, far below I hear the Channel sweep/ And all his waves complain. BSV; GoTS

Clever Peter and the Ogress. Katharine Pyle. And never, never play again/ At truant from the school. OBCA

The Clever Skipper. Anonymous. And this is the last of the tailor we do hear./Tum a rally tolly dolly, tum a rolly tolly day. AmFP

Clever Tom Clinch Going to be Hanged. Jonathan Swift. Who hung like a Hero and never would flinch. CEP; CoMu; FaBoBa; NOBI; SeCeV

A Clever Woman. Mary Elizabeth Coleridge. O evil Angel, set me free! BrRo

Click Go the Shears. Anonymous. He works hard, he drinks hard, and goes to hell at last! NOAV

Click Go the Shears, Boys. Anonymous. And curses the old snagger with the blue-bellied "joe". PoAu 1-2

Click o' the Latch. Nancy Byrd Turner. Hurry, my heart, be swift, my heart,–/How did we wait so long! HBMV

Clickety-Clack. Paul Blackburn. clickety-clack/Horseman, pass by. NoAm

Clickstone. Rokwaho. under the night shade/where the shadows fade STE

The Cliff. David Rowbotham. And stared without a word of thanks,/Into the gutter. NOAV

The Cliff Dwelling. Arthur W. Monroe. But ever sleep in your mystery,/ And in your silence rejoice. PoOW

Cliff Klingenhagen. Edwin Arlington Robinson. As happy as Cliff Klingenhagen is. AmP; AP; CoBMV; HBMV; MoAB; MoAmPo; TreFS

The Cliff Rose. Ernest Fewster. Thy pure grace blooms as a kiss of Earth/ Upheld to the lips of God. CaP

The Cliff-Top. Robert Bridges. The sea beneath my feet. BoNaP

Clifton Chapel. Sir Henry Newbolt. Sed miles, sed pro patria.' OBEV; OBVV

Clifton Grove (excerpt). Henry Kirke White. In shades like these to live, is to be blest. OBNC

The Climate. Edwin Denby. In our record climate I look pleased or glum. ANYP

The Climate of Paradise. Louis Simpson. O even in Paradise/the mind would make its own winter. NOBA

The Climate of Thought. Robert Graves. The moon, grand, not fanciful with clouds. MoAB; ViBoPo

Climb. Winifred Welles. For by the evening I shall be a star. BiCB

Climb in Torridon. Brenda G. Macrow. And free us all the wandering winds that blow/across the ruined rooftops of the world. PoSH

The Climber Surveys His Mountain. Hugh Ouston. Reward and release,/ Of Rannoch, Schiehallion and Mamore. PoSH

The Climbers. Elizabeth Jennings. And, not arriving, dream in no resentment. NePoEA

Climbers. Musaemura Bonus Zimunya. to climb even higher than Mambo/ and put an enduring roof upon this House. WhB

Climbing. Tom Clark. Picking us up in one state and putting/Us down in a different one every time. APU

Climbing. Daniel Mark Epstein. Sadly he rides the elevator down/and starts again at the foot of the blind wall. AMV-80

Climbing. Gloria Fuertes. I've got Death really thinking/because she couldn't make me mad. PBWP

Climbing. Jennifer Maiden. To lull the dog across a bloodless river. CBAP

Climbing in Glencoe. Andrew Young. Balanced I rode it like a circus horse. LiSp; SD

The Climbing Rope. Alice V. Stuart. Was woven (blessed be his name) by Bach. PoSH

Climbing You. Erica Jong. but you'll wait years maybe/for the next doomed expedition. PoA

Climbing Zero Gully. David J. Morley. stand, chin in hand,/suddenly vigilant. PoSH

Cling to Me. John Le Gay Brereton. —Perchance upon that desolate quest again. PeHV

Clinic Day. Jo Barnes. in a defiant gesture, that's my girl! BrRo

Clinic: Examination. Audrey Conard. from whom she picks and chews,/absorbed, the viral nits. AMV-80

The Clink of the Ice. Eugene Field. Of the clink of the ice in the pitcher the boy brings up the/hall. InMe

Clinton South of Polk. Carl Sandburg. And I could sleep to their musical threats and accusations. AmFN

Clio's Protest. Richard Brinsley Sheridan. But easy writing's vile hard reading. FaBoEE

The Clipper. Thomas Fleming Day. Then pushing out her shapely bow she braves/The next tall sea, and, leaping, onward goes. EtS

Clipper Ships. John Anderson. The hollow-roaring Forties echo, "Where?" EtS

Clippety Cloppity. George Starbuck. He was no dope. PV

Clipping. Tom Veitch. Remember me to Pa-/ulette when you see/her, will you please? ANYP

Cliques and Critics. Sa'ib of Isfahan. ...who of all the poets are kind to one another? LiTW

The Cloak. Violet Anderson. and a tidy empty chair. CaP

Cloak of Laughter. Abigail Cresson. And sees the grief within. PoToHe

The Clock. Jovan Ducic. A dreadful tremor, a panic in all the frame of things. LiTW

The Clock. Felice Holman. I've fixed it somehow/so the clock is/resting. GrPl

The Clock. Jean Jaszi. It's a cozy sound at night. SoPo

Clock. Harold Monro. Of the great roaring waves that break and fall. BrPo

The Clock. Francis Scarfe. Who could love utterly/Beyond the meaning of these words and tears. NeBP

Clock-a-clay. John Clare. Here I live, lone clock-a-clay,/Watching for the time of day. CBEP; ERoP 1-2; LiTB; LoBV; NBM; OAEL 1-2; OBNC; PoEL 1-5; SeCeV; TrGrPo; VLP; WHA

A Clock in the Square. Adrienne Rich.
And all the rings in which we're spun and swirled,/Whether around a clockface or a world. HeIP; NIP
Whether around a clockface or a world. HeIP; NIP

Clock on Hancock Street. June Jordan. where my mother used to walk/and talk to him. FaBoWP

The Clock's Song. Rose Hawthorne Lathrop. Eileen! Eileen!... AA

A Clock Stopped. Emily Dickinson. Decades of arrogance between/The dial life and him. AnFE; APA; CoAnAm; MAmP; MAPA; NCEP; NoP; PoEL 1-5

Clock Symphony. John Frederick Nims. And through a tinsel gear of watch motors the heavy sky. MiAP

The Clock Tower. Colleen Thibaudeau. And we all move and love/To the grace of her sweet face. WHW

Clock without Hands. John Frederick Nims. Only like heaven's own logic: hard to read. PoA

The Clock Works. Lewis MacAdams. and the gleaming suitcases that are filling up this room. ANYP

The Clocking Hen. Anonymous. "Hallo!" said the barn-yard cock,/"Cock-a-doodle-doo." HBVY

Clocks. Louis Ginsberg. To memorize how short his span/Upon a thousand clocks! TrJP

Clocks. Malka Locker. they stubbornly show the hour/it occurred. VWA

Clocks. Carl Sandburg. ...wrist watches over the pulses of/airmen eager to go to France... CrMA

The Clod. Edwin Curran. "I have been a man," the clod said. HBMV

The Clod and the Pebble. William Blake. And builds a Hell in Heaven's despite. AWP; BoLiVe; CABA; EBCP; EnLoPo; FaBV; InPS; LoBV; NOBE; NoP; OBEC; OBNC; OBSP; PAI; PrIm; SCV; TEP; TrGrPo; ViBoPo

Cloe. [or Grenville], George, Baron Lansdowne Granville. Such Cloe is, and common as the air. FaBoCo; FaBoEE; NIP

Cloister. Conrad Aiken. ...And they are you. MoAB; MoAmPo

Cloister. Charles L. O'Donnell. For these vast hearts it was a narrow room. CAW

Cloistered. Alice Brown. My heart of love, that heart Thou gavest/me,/Shall beat on in the dark. AA

Cloisters. Anthony Barnett. Where, by the way, his family? VWA

The Cloisters. Samuel Yellen. A smile denotes the cheerless captive become the cheer-/ful guest. NePoAm

Clonakilty. Anonymous. But of the towns which I have seen/Worst luck to Clonakilty. FaBoEE

Clonard. Thomas S. Jones, Jr. Just as they did a thousand years ago/In morning meadows when the world was young. HBMV

Clonfeacle. Paul Muldoon. ...their sermons/Ending in the air. CIP

Clonmacnoise. Thomas William Rolleston. Many a blue eye of Clan Colman the turf covers,/Many a swan-white breast. AnIV; OBMV

Clonmel Jail. Anonymous. That's the end of O'Donnell and forever say a prayer for him. BIrV

Clorinda and Damon. Andrew Marvell. For all the World is our Pan's Quire. AnAnS 1; SeCP

Cloris and Mertilla. Michael Drayton. Those yet unborn shall offer up their Vows. LoBV

The Clorox Kid. Kirk Robertson. as i dipped my mop/in/& started scrubbing. GP

The Close Clan. Mark Van Doren. And carry it all day, and sweeten it. GoYe

Close, Mortal Eyes. Ruth Pitter. No syllable that may be said or sung./Close, mortal eyes. BoC

The Close of Day. Wesley Curtwright. Return to peaceful dreaming dearly bought. CDC

Close Quarters. John Banister Tabb. Nor so little room for the crew. OBAL

Close Season for Marriage. Anonymous. But Trinity sets thee free again. FaBoUs

Close Shave. Anonymous. Cut off his nose,/And popped it in a basin. OxNR

Close to Me. Gabriela (Lucila Godoy Alcayaga) Mistral. Do not slip from my arms:/sleep close to me! PoPl

Close-Up. Archie Randolph Ammons. it couldn't help/itself. PoA

Close-Ups of Summer. Norman MacCaig. ..invisible judges/sit, wrapped in their knowledge,/taking terrible notes. OxBC

Close Your Eyes! Arna Bontemps. Close your eyes; walk bravely through. AmNP; CDC; FB; PoBA; PoNe

The Closed Door. Theodosia Garrison. Whereby I pass and may not enter in. BLPA; PoToHe

The Closed System. Larry Eigner. in all proportion/the outsized Men. VWA

The Closed World. Denise Levertov. the dry indifferent glare in my mind's eye/wavered but burned on. NoP

Closer First to Earth. Anne Hazlewood-Brady. ...instruction/from a woman juggler, closer first/to earth, might have saved your life. IHMS

The Closing Album. Louis MacNeice.
Grey stone, grey water,/And brick upon grey brick. OBTV
What a place to talk of War. FaBoIP

Closing Cadence. John Moffit. Attend me out of time. MoRP

The Closing of the Rodeo. William Jay Smith. Dark drum the vanishing horses' hooves. MP; NePoEA; SaC; SD; TwCP

Closing Piece. Rainer Maria Rilke. he dares to weep/in the midst of us. PCP

Closing Prayer. Johnstone G. Patrick. That moment when my soul/And body part! TrPWD

The Closing Scene. Thomas Buchanan Read. While Death and Winter closed the autumn scene. AA; HBV 1-2

Closing Time. James Michie. The rain returns into their lives. NePoEA-2

Closing Time. David Wagoner. Who cartwheel out of sight, end over end. NYBP

The Clote. William Barnes. Thy flow'r afloat, goolden zumer clote! ELP; PoEL 1-5

The Cloth of Gold (excerpt). M. Krishnamurti. That dreaded word of gloom!) PeD

The Clothes. Rayzel Zychlinska. my blue dress is dreaming of you. VWA

Clothes Do But Cheat and Cozen Us. Robert Herrick. Is won with flesh, not drapery. ALV; CaPo

Clothes Make the Man. Jack Conway. and then we all just naked again. NLV

Clothes Make the Man. Theodore Weiss. So let's go home to bed,/Renee, and dress and dress and dress. NoAm

The Clothes Pit. Douglas Dunn. The litter of pop rhetoric blows down Terry Street,/Bounces past their feet, into their lives. OxBTC

The Clothing's New Emperor. Donald Finkel. Under the shirt, blood rushing/Inside the sleeves and out of the collar. NePoEA

Cloud. Samuel Hoffenstein. Goes up in steam, comes down in less! AnAmPo

The Cloud. Sidney Lanier. Sure of the Father, Self, and Love, alone. AmePo

The Cloud. Edwin Muir. Beloved, world-without-end lamented face;/And not a blindfold mask on a pillar of dust. OBTV

Cloud and Flame. John Berryman. At Hastings, by the Bloody Lake. AP

Cloud and Wind. Dante Gabriel Rossetti. And that Hope sows what Love shall never reap? MaVP

The Cloud Chamber. Arthur Sze. it leaves on a film/is immortal. BrSi

The Cloud Confines. Dante Gabriel Rossetti. Whatever there is to know/That shall we know one day. EnLi 1-2

The Cobbler in Willow Street. George O'Neil. A song of us and Willow Street,/Tapping a heel all out of time... HBMV

The Cobblers' Song. Charles Tilney. When that is gone, we'll fill 't again,/ Dan diddle dan. OBSC

The Coble o Cargill. *Anonymous.* There is mony a man and mother's son/ That was at my love's burial.' ESPB

Cobweb. Winifred Welles. And cries that Love is lovely–isn't it? AnAmPo

Cocaine Bill and Morphine Sue. *Anonymous.* Oh, honey, won't you have a little sniff on me,/Have a sniff on me. FSW

Cocaine Blues. *Anonymous.* Cocaine all around my brain. FSW

Cocaine Lil and Morphine Sue. *Anonymous.* "She died as she lived, sniffing cocaine." AS; GBP; MAT; OxBoLi; TrAS

Cock. Aharon Amir. but without the crow/–of the cock. AMV-81

The Cock. Ewa Lipska. But in the wilderness of my brain/the cock of the future crows. VWA

Cock-a-Bandy. *Anonymous.* And oh! but he is handsome. OxNR

Cock a Doodle Doo. *Anonymous.* While master fiddles his fiddle-stick/For dame and doodle doo. HBVY; OxNR

The Cock Again. *Anonymous.* see his mane! SoPo

Cock and Hen. *Anonymous.* If I'd crow my hea-rt out. OxNR

The Cock and the Bull. Charles Stuart Calverley. And might, odds-bob, sir! in judicious hands,/Extend from here to Mesopotamy. ALV; BXAP; FaBoCo; FaBoNo; FaBoPa; InMe; NA; Par; VLP

The Cock and the Fox. Jean de La Fontaine. 'Tis doubly sweet deceiver to deceive. AWP

The Cock and the Hen. John Heywood. Then will I surely overcackle thee.' PBBP

Cock before Dawn. Norman MacCaig. It's time I crowed. The sun will be waiting. OxBC

Cock-Crow. *Anonymous.* The ducks in the river/Are swimming away. OxNR

Cock-Crow. Ralph Nixon Currey. Making the heart of God rejoice. PeSA

Cock-Crow. Robert Herrick. A sin, then fall to weeping when 'tis done. PBBP

Cock-Crow. Edward ("Edward Eastaway") Thomas. The milkers lace their boots up at the farms. GTBS-P; MoAB; MoBrPo; OBSP

Cock-Crow Song. *Anonymous.* Round the Palace and up over the walls crows and/magpies are flying. LiTW

Cock-Crow: Woodstock. Henry Morton Robinson. To herald our perpetual shame/By this perennial bird.) CAW

Cock-Crowing. Henry Vaughan. Though with no Lilie, stay with me! AtBAP; MePo; OAEL 1-2; PBBP; SeCV 1-2

A Cock Crowing in a Poulterer's Shop. John Ferguson. The night that Peter said, "I know Him not." BoAnP

The Cock Crows in the Morn. *Anonymous.* Makes a man healthy/And wealthy and wise. HBVY; OxNR; PBBP

The Cock Gaed to Rome. *Anonymous.* And yet I aye gang barefit, barefit! PBBP

The Cock of the Game. *Anonymous.* For they're looking for lads like the cock of the game. OBET

Cock Robin Got up Early. *Anonymous.* And when he got unto the end,/ Then he began again. OxNR; PBBP

Cock-Throwing! Martin Lluellyn. Oh, the bears and the bulls/Are but corpulent gulls/To the valiant Shrove-tide martyr. PBBP

Cockayne Country. Agnes Mary Frances (Mme Emile Duclaux) Robinson. (But it is far away.) OBVV

Cockcrow. Eithne Wilkins. into a mere at daybreak, and the drowned cockerels crow. NeBP

A Cocker of Snooks. Phyllis Gotlieb. owed us nothing but the grace of God. NOBC

Cockies of Bungaree. *Anonymous.* So if you will believe me now, it's the truth I did unfold. PoAu 1-2

Cockle-Shell and Sandal-Shoon. Herbert T. J. Coleman. Life is a pilgrimage, they say. CaP

Cockles and Mussels. *Anonymous.* Crying, "Cockles and mussels: alive, alive O!" ELP; OnYI

Cockley Moor, Dockray, Penrith. Norman Nicholson. Ouside, a stone forgets that it was born. NeBP

The Cockney of the North. Harry Graham. And over tarred macadam and pavements parched and white/I've walked till my feet are sore! CenHV

Cockpit in the Clouds. Dick Dorrance. Down there, we're just another noise. TiPo

Cockroach. Mary Ann Hoberman. Is there nothing to be said about the cockroach which is good? OBCA

The Cocks. Boris Pasternak. in rain, in earth, in love, in all, in all. LiTW

Cocky Doodle Doodle Doo. *Anonymous.* Then do it like this, cocky doodle doodle doo. OuSiCo

The Cocoa-Tree. Charles Warren Stoddard. Beck'ning the tardy ships, the ships that never come! AA; AmePo; CAW

The Coconut. Angela Milne. O buy it, pray, for me! FiBHP

Coconut. Mario Satz. And there the palm tree grows in its mirror, high/in the sky's center. VWA

A Coconut for Katerina. Sandra McPherson. for more empty and hopeful boats and their sails. FiCP; LCAP

Cocoon. Ishigaki Rin. What's left is an inch of silk. WPOW

Cocoon. David McCord. And that's the end of three good tries. OBCA

The Cocooning. Frederic Mistral. Dance to the tinkling tambourine. AWP; PoPl

Cocteau's Opium: 1. Donald Finkel. begins to wonder if it is possible he has been forsaken. CoPo

Cocteau's Opium: 2. Donald Finkel. every morning, rising, rising, rising, ask yourself. CoPo

The Cod-Fisher. Joseph C. Lincoln. Dear Lord, be kind to those who wait. EtS

Cod Liver Ile. *Anonymous.* If me wife don't quit drinking your cod liver ile. FSW; OuSiCo

Coda. Basil Bunting. to fell kings, guesses/where we go? OAEL 1-2

Coda. Fred Johnson. and pushes shaking itself loose from/the sigh. CNA

Coda. Louis MacNeice. Maybe we shall know each other better/When the tunnels meet beneath the mountain. FaBoIP

Coda. Dorothy Parker. Would you kindly direct me to hell? DBV; GoTF; InMe; SBG; TreFS

Coda. Ezra Pound. Will you find your lost dead among them? NOBA

Coda. James Tate. when they can sing no more. AmPA; NYBP

Coda. William Carlos Williams. and begun again to penetrate/into all crevices/of my world. NOBA

Coda: Revising History. Paul Mariani. Here! Take a toke of this. MAYP

The Code. Robert Frost. "Discharge me? No! He knew I did just right." MaC; OBNV; PAI; PoA; UnPo

A Code of Morals. Rudyard Kipling. They know the worthy General as "that most immoral/man'. FaBoCo

Code of the Cow Country. Squire Omar Barker. These few is all it takes to be/A cowboy an'...a man! PoOW

Codes. Diana Chang. mountains/women/fish BrSi

Codes. Lois Seyster Montross. Or wander naked with the wind,/They clothe in worsted still. HBMV

Codex. Stephen Rodefer. ...I like your voice./Look where it's come from. APU

The Codfish Shanty. *Anonymous.* And we're bound for South Australia. GBP

Codicil. Mabel MacDonald Carver. knowing a part of me is with you still. GoYe

Codicil. Ruth Stone. I think about them when I think of you. BoWoP

Codicil. Derek Walcott. All its indifference is a different rage. NoAm

Coedmon's Hymn. *Anonymous.* the Lord everlasting,/almighty God. EBEV

Coelacanth. Christopher Dewdney. A map/with/no/corresponding/ geographical/landmarks CaPN

De Coenatione Micae. Martial (Marcus Valerius Martialis). Bid you be merry and remember death. FaBoCh; LoGBV

Coeur de Lion to Berengaria. Theodore Tilton. Come back to me! Come back to me! AA

Coffee. J.V. Cunningham. I waste it for the waste. MoAmPo; PrIm; VGW

A Coffee-House Lecture. Robert Mezey. And they are living still. CABA

The Coffin. Heinrich Heine. And my too heavy care. AWP

The Coffin-Worm. Ruth Pitter. Love in his heart, his empty hands, his eyes. MoBrPo

Cogitabo Pro Peccato Meo. William Habington. Pale cowards there must stand. CoBE

The Coin. Sara Teasdale. Is the safe-kept memory/Of a lovely thing. HBMV; TiPo

Coin in the Fist. Florence Kerr Brownell. A bright butterfly for our slow perusal? GoYe

Coins and Coffins under My Bed. Diane Wakoski. and the sun catching it, as he swings. CoPo

Cois na Teineadh. T. W. Rolleston. The soul of Ireland seems to bend/ Above her children there. AnIV

Cokaygne. *Anonymous.* Amen, pour saint charite. AnIL

Cokboy, Part Two. Jerome Rothenberg. guess I got nothing left to say NNaP

Cokkils. Sydney Goodsir Smith. The thocht o my true-luve/Continuallie. OxBS; PoA

Cold. Robert Francis. I huddle, hoard, hold out, hold on, hold on. LCAP; NePoAm-2; PoA

The Cold. Lance Henson. we sit on the cold mountain/among the lonely wolves CDW

Cold. Dorothy Roberts. In the burning bush of antiquity/With starry flowers. NOBC

The Cold. Charles Simic. A flicker of a light or two/Far above and beyond the large cage. HaCAP

Cold and Heat.   *Anonymous.*   The heat compels me to go,/I must go.
WTO

Cold-Blooded Creatures.   Elinor Wylie.   Where lidless fishes, broad awake,/
Swim staring at a night-mare doom.   ImOP; OBSP; SBG

Cold Blows the Wind.   John Hamilton.   Than rise in the morning early.
CH

Cold! Cold!   *Anonymous.*   Is it any wonder I say: "Cold!"   NOBI

Cold, cold the year draws to its end.   *Anonymous.*   My falling tears wet the
double gates.   BoWoP

The Cold Divinities.   James Wright.   Her cold divinities of death and
change.   AmPC

Cold Fact.   Dick Emmons.   The snow has melted.   PoPl

Cold Feet in Columbus.   William Heath.   look out the dusty window/and
make love to death   TAT

Cold Fire.   George Starbuck.   ...do I flicker there like coal?   NYBP

Cold Front.   Peter Sharpe.   the air full of bones.   AMV-80

A Cold Front.   William Carlos Williams.   quick action is the main thing.
NAs

Cold Glow: Icehouses.   David Wojahn.   ...there through a tangent of ice,/his
face and hands ashimmer.   AMV-81; MAYP

The Cold Green Element.   Irving Layton.   a breathless swimmer in that cold
green element.   NOBC; NoP; OBCV

The Cold Heaven.   William Butler Yeats.   By the injustice of the skies for
punish-/ment?   AWP; CTC; GTBS-P; HAP; InPo; MoVE; NAMP; NoAm;
OAEL 1-2; OAEP; OBSP; TEP; WeW

The Cold Irish Earth.   Knute Skinner.   the Killaspuglonane graveyard/is
wet to the bone.   InPK

Cold Iron.   Rudyard Kipling.   Iron out of Calvary is master of men all!'
OnMSP

Cold Is the Winter.   *Anonymous.*   I could bring great silence on armies/–
though tonight I am freezing cold.'   NOBI

Cold Logic.   Barney Hutchinson.   He dives, I suppose,/For divers reasons.
SD

A Cold Night.   Bernard Spencer.   ...everything is/done against Time.   WaP

A Cold Rendering (parody).   *Anonymous.*   A worthy fool! Botley's the odly
wear–attishu!   BXAP

Cold's the Wind.   Thomas Dekker.   Ill is the weather that bringeth no
gain,/Nor helps good hearts in need.   ViBoPo

Cold, Sharp Lamentation.   Augusta Gregory, Lady Gregory.   Oh! there was
loneliness in all of them together.   OBMV

Cold Snap.   Kathy Mangan.   I don't want that fistful/of glazed tulips you
will bring.   AMV-80

A Cold Spring.   Elizabeth Bishop.   every evening now throughout the
summer.   MP; TwCP

Cold Term.   LeRoi (Imamu Amiri Baraka) Jones.   ...Why are the beautiful
sick and divided/like myself?   BPo; CNA; SOTW

Cold Water.   Donald Hall.   over the speechless needles/of pines which are
dead or born again.   NCSH

Cold Water Flat.   Philip Booth.   in the city that a murderer designed?
NePoAm

Cold Wave Blues.   Barbecue Bob Hicks.   Cold wave, cold wave/don't be so
hard on me   BluL

Cold Winter Now Is in the Wood.   Elizabeth Jane Coatsworth.   "Winter is
in the wood!" the winds/In the warm chimney cry.   TiPo

The Colder the Air.   Elizabeth Bishop.   (It is this clock that later falls/in
wheels and chimes of leaf and cloud).   MiAP

The Coldness.   Jon Silkin.   All Europe is touched/With some of frigid
York,/As York is now by Europe.   VWA

Cole's Island.   Charles Olson.   ...That is the fullest possible/account I can
give, of the encounter.   PoM

Cole Younger.   *Anonymous.*   We are the famous Younger brothers and we
spare no time to pray.   AmFP; BeLS; BFSS; FSW

Colebrook Dale (excerpt).   Anna Seward.   And to a gloomy Erebus
transform/The destined rival of Tempean vales.   NOEC

Colenso Rhymes for Orthodox Children.   Bret (Francis Bret Harte) Harte.
And never since then has this Bishop been quiet.   OBAL

Coleridge.   Aubrey Thomas De Vere.   When thou art walking, wake me, for
my Master's sake!   GoBC

Coleridge.   George Sidney Hellman.   And burst in music, and are seen no
more.   AA

Coleridge.   Theodore Watts-Dunton.   But lets the poet see how heav'n can
shine.   HBV 1-2; OBVV

Coleridge Crossing the Plain of Jars: 1833.   Norman Dubie.   I knew the
chipped fire of pond ice/Was in her eyes like a widow's soul.   LCAP

Colin.   Anthony Munday.   Hey nonny ronny!   GTBS; GTBS-P

Colin and Lucy.   Thomas Tickell.   And fear to join him there.   CEP;
OBEC

Colin Clout.   John Skelton.
Nor how far Temple Bar is/From the Seven Starres.   OBSV
That is their whole devotion! TrGrPo
Unneth they leave a lock/Of wool among their flock!... OAEL 1-2

Colin Clout at Court.   Edmund Spenser.   Their plain attire such glorious
gallantry/Disdains so much, that none them in doth call.   OBSC

Colin Clout's Come Home Again.   Edmund Spenser.   All loth to part, but
that the glooming skies/Warnd them to draw their bleating flocks to rest.
CABL; OAEL 1-2

Colin's Complaint.   Nicholas Rowe.   His Ghost shall glide over the Green.
OBEC

The Coliseum.   George Gordon, Lord Byron.   Even at the moment when
they should array/Themselves in pensive order.   MCCG

The Coliseum.   Edgar Allan Poe.   Clothing us in a robe of more than glory.
AP; NOBA

Colkelbie Sow (excerpt).   *Anonymous.*   Yit mony in a grit rout/For lak of
rowme stud about.   OxBS

Collaboration.   Tony Towle.   It is not safe to walk on the sand or through
the trees.   ANYP

A Collage for Richard Davis–Two Short Forms.   De Leon Harrison.
(silence)   PoBA

Collages and Compositions.   Richmond Lattimore.   this is art.   PP

Collapsars.   Sandra McPherson.   ninety-eight point six?   LCAP

Collapsible.   Tom Raworth.   her breath always only half an inch from the
corner of my eye.   EAS

The Collar.   George Herbert.   Me thought I heard one calling, "Child";/
And I replied, "My Lord."   AtBAP; ATP; AWP; BiP; BLPL; CBEP;
CoBE; EaLo; EBEV; EnLi 1-2; ExPo; ForPo; HAP; HBV 1-2; HeIP; InPo;
InPS; JCP; LiTB; LoBV; MasP; MeLP; MePo; NIP; NOBE; NOCV; NoP;
OAEL 1-2; OAEP; OBS; OxBoCh; PAI; PoEL 1-5; PoPle; PoRA; PPoe;
PPP; SCV; SeCePo; SeCeV; SeCP; SeCV 1-2; TEP; TrGrPo; ViBoPo; WHA

The Collar-Bone of a Hare.   William Butler Yeats.   Through the white thin
bone of a hare.   AtBAP; OxBTC

Collect Calls.   Diane Bickston.   "Where is my twenty/and why did you
run?"   LFAC

The Collection.   Bill Manhire.   The music. The music of water.   OCNZ

A Collection of Emblemes, Ancient and Moderne (excerpt).   George Wither.
New Life, with endlesse Glorie, God will give thee.   SeCV 1-2

A Collection of Hymns...of the Moravian Brethern (excerpt).   *Anonymous.*
There is my bed, table and dish,/And all things.   NOEC

The Collector.   Richard Behm.   and collect the strange runes/that fall from
their dreaming mouths.   AMV-81

The Collector.   Desiree Flynn.   Hear again the spirit sound of silence.
BrRo

The Collector.   Raymond Souster.   What she collects, finally, is pain.
ErPo; OBCV

The Collector.   Robert F. Whisler.   feeling's magnification and the work in
our words.   AMV-81

The Collector of the Sun.   Dave Smith.   sees dark birds pass, then us,/and is
himself again, staring, blessed.   SM

Colleen Oge Asthore.   *Anonymous.*   Duty dearest, love sincerest,/Colleen,
Colleen Oge, asthore.   OnYI

Colleen Rue.   *Anonymous.*   To a lad I love beyond all earthly treasures, and
he'll soon embrace/his Colleen Rue.   BIrV; OnYI

The College Cat.   Alfred Denis Godley.   That calm tranquillity of soul/Is
thine?   CenHV

The College Colonel.   Herman Melville.   Ah heaven!–what truth to him.
AA; AmePo; OBWP

College Formal: Renaissance Casino.   Langston Hughes.   gold and brown.
BALP

College of Flunkeys, and a Few Gentlemen.   John Berryman.   ...for your
incurable sins some salve.   GLGT

College of Surgeons.   James Stephens.   Poor dusty leaf,/Whistled into a hall!
AnIL; LOW

College Song.   Edward Anthony.   For it takes the Texas Aggies/To produce
real fighting men!   InMe

College Yell.   *Anonymous.*   Right in the neck–THERE!   ExPo

Colley's Run-I-O.   *Anonymous.*   To that God-forsaken gehooley of a place
called Colley's Run-i-O!   AmFP

The Collier.   Vernon Watkins.   And gold on my neck the sun.   DTC;
FaBoTw; MoVE

The Collier Lad's Lament.   *Anonymous.*   "Let these poor colliers have their
rights, and give them better pay."   OBET

The Collier Lass.   Frankie Armstrong.   And I'll be no longer a poor collier/
lass.   BrRo

The Collier's March.   *Anonymous.*   When sixpenny loaves but three-
pounders appear.   OBET

The Collier's Rant.   *Anonymous.*   You can tear up his shirt for his minin's
all done.   OBET

The Collier's Wedding.   Edward Chicken.   So, curtseying, mumbled up his
kiss.   NOEC

The Collier's Wife.   D. H. Lawrence.   I sh'd think 'e'll get right again.
HaMV; OxBTC

The Collies.   Edward Anthony.   While we–by collie!–take life easy.   GDP

Collige Rosas.   William Ernest Henley.   The dream that comes, the wish
that goes,/The memories that follow!   OBVV; PG

Collin My Deere and Most Entire Beloved.   William Smith.   They wich have tasted of the muses spring,/I hope will smile upon the tunes they sing.   AAS

Colloquial.   Rupert Brooke.   Heart of my heart.   BrPo

Colloquy.   Weldon Kees.   I had his answer, wise as yours.   NaP; NYBP

Colloquy at Peniel.   William Stanley Merwin.   It will be your body that will fall.   NePoEA

Colloquy in Black Rock.   Robert Lowell.   The blue kingfisher dives on you in fire.   AnNE; CAPP; CoBMV; MiAP; MoAB; MoAmPo; NoAm

A Colloquy of Silences.   Michael Heffernan.   beyond the gray spaces around tree branches/where the silences of birds are the answer.   SM

Colloquy of the Ancients (excerpt).   *Anonymous.*   In battle his shield never cried out.   OnYI

Colloquy with a King-Crab.   John Peale Bishop.   Though I consent like him to go on claws.   LiTA; MoPo

A Colloquy with God.   Sir Thomas Browne.   O come that hour, when I shall never/Sleep again, but wake for ever.   OBS

A Colloquy with Gregory on the Balcony.   Howard Moss.   Be reasonable! Stop! For God's sake! Greg!...   FAZ

Collusion between a Alegaiter and a Water-Snaik.   J. W. Morris.   He slowly went off for to cool.   NA

Colly, My Cow.   *Anonymous.*   For Colly will give me/no more milk now!   EvOK

Cologne.   John Bate.   the interacting sorrow of their foes.   NeBP

Cologne.   Samuel Taylor Coleridge.   But tell me, Nymphs, what power divine/Shall henceforth wash the river Rhine?   DBV; FaBoEE; HBV 1-2; InMe; NLV; OBTV; PV; TW

Cologne.   Hilde Domin.   The dead and I/we swim/through the new doors/of our old houses.   VWA

Colombine.   Hugh McCrae.   Softly the 'cellos sing:/"Colombine".../ "Colombine"...   BoAV; PoAu 1-2

Colonel B.   Constance Carrier.   ..."On that subject I/am coy," said Aaron Burr.   NePoAm-2

Colonel Chartres.   John Arbuthnot.   ...by bestowing it on the/most UNWORTHY of ALL MORTALS.   OBSV

Colonel Ellsworth.   Richard Henry Stoddard.   And should we pause; the thought of Ells-/worth slain/Will steel our aching hearts to strike again!   PAH

Colonel Fantock.   Edith Sitwell.   Cold Death had taken his first citadel.   AnFE; MoAB; MoBrPo; MoVE; OBMV

Colonel Fazackerley.   Charles Causley.   Colonel Fazackerley went in to dine.   OnUR

The Colonel's Soliloquy.   Thomas Hardy.   Things may not be as then.'   OBWP

Colonel Sharp.   *Anonymous.*   Was ever a true-hearted man more constant to his love?   BaBo

Colonial Nomenclature.   John Dunmore Lang.   The future slave may lisp the patriot's name/And his breast kindle with a kindred flame!   NOAV

Colonial Set.   Alfred Goldsworthy Bailey.   The rampikes of the forest/attain a brittle silence.   OBCV

Colonialism.   Cabdullaahi Qarshe.   The birds which are flying/And gliding about above/Will some day tire/And descend to earth.   WTO

A Colonist in His Garden.   William Pember Reeves.   A sweeter English rose?   ACV; AnNZ

Colophon.   Oliver St. John Gogarty.   Off, before the Fool comes on!   OBMV

Colophon for Lan-t'ing Hsiu-Hsi.   John Peck.   Therefore my notes on this feast,/These poems/I, Wang Hsi-chih.   AmPA

The Color.   John Haines.   They all drew back/into themselves,/and immediately/began building walls.   GP

Color.   Langston Hughes.   Not moan or cry.   BOLo

Color.   Christina Georgina Rossetti.   What is orange? Why, an orange,/Just an orange!   SoPo

Color Alone Can Speak.   Louise Townsend Nicholl.   Into a legend nevermore believed.   NePoAm

Color Blind.   Carol Paine.   That has made us afraid of the shade of the flesh?   PV

Color–Caste–Denomination.   Emily Dickinson.   Our minuter intuitions–/Deem unplausible–   EaLo; TAP

Color in the Wheat.   Hamlin Garland.   A glory of olive and amber and wine,/Runs the color in the wheat.   BPAW

The Color of Many Deer Running.   Linda Gregg.   But I think it will be hard to be with me.   NPGG

The color of the flowers.   Ono no Komachi.   as my body/passed through the world.   BoWoP

Colorado.   John D. Dillenback.   To what God hath so wrought may great souls lend/The fadeless luster of achievements high.   PoOW

Colorado.   Robert Fitzgerald.   ...my miniscule/Part in the swaying and tranquil grandeur here.   MoPo

A Colorado Sand Storm.   Eugene Field.   Oh, the dust!/How it's cuss'd.   PoOW

The Colorado Trail.   *Anonymous.*   All along, along, along/The Colorado Trail.   AS; CoSo; FSW

Coloratura.   Geoff Page.   So much, so little space/between two faces/of a wall.   AMV-81

Coloring Margarine.   William Hathaway.   I wor-ry and won-der/you're close to me/now/but whe-re is your he-art?   AMV-81

Colors.   Yevgeny Yevtushenko.   and that the colors in my eyes will vanish/when your face sets.   LLLT

Colors for Mama.   Barbara Mahone.   ...sanity/is colorblind.   CNA; PoBA

The Colors of Night.   N. Scott Momaday.   ...And always, just there, is a shadow which the/firelight cannot cleave.   STE

Colosseum.   Harold Norse.   The broken word, the broken arch.   TrJP

The Colossus.   Sylvia Plath.   No longer do I listen for the scrape of a keel/On the blank stones of the landing.   CAPP; FaBoWP; HaCAP; LiTM; MP; NePoEA-2; NoAm; NOBA; NoP; TAP

The Colour of God's Face.   Dorothy Livesay.   until the loud cicada shrills/telling the world their names.   PeCV Use it, and live/or cut it off, and die.   PeCV

The Colours of Love.   Denis Devlin.   To take her dissolution to my breast!   IPY; OxBI

Colts.   *Anonymous.*   Rustling, zoro-zoro, like a lady's/train.   SUS

Colum-Cille's Farewell to Ireland.   *Anonymous.*   And all but thy government, Eire, have pleased me,/Thou waterful land.   AnIV

Columbia.   *Anonymous.*   Hush anarchy's sway, and give peace to the world.   AmFP

Columbia.   Timothy Dwight.   The queen of the world, and the child of the skies.   HBV 1-2; MC; PAH

Columbia College, 1796.   Joseph Shippey.   Placed number four, with twenty-eight below.   PeD

Columbia's Agony.   Robert Henry Newell.   And we must wait for day to see the sun.   OBAL

Columbia's Emblem.   Edna Dean Proctor.   But the wide Republic's emblem/Is the bounteous, golden Corn!   GN

Columbia the Gem of the Ocean.   Thomas a Becket.   Thy banners make tyranny tremble,/When borne by the red, white and blue.   FSW

Columbia, Trust the Lord.   *Anonymous.*   Columbia, bless the God who built the skies.   AH

The Columbiad: One Centred System.   Joel Barlow.   Have waved at last in union o'er the world.   AP

The Columbine.   Jones Very.   My weary eyes shall close like folding flowers in sleep.   AP; NOBA

Columbus.   Arthur Hugh Clough.   Is a pure wonder, I must say, to me.   AmFN

Columbus.   Florence Earle Coates.   Found justice, truth, and human liberty!   MC

Columbus.   Edward Everett Hale.   Where God might write anew the story of the World.   MC; PAH

Columbus.   Percy Adams Hutchison.   My bait of pearls and gold was well devised!   EtS

Columbus.   Leroy F. Jackson.   How he crossed the seas, a sailor bold,/In fourteen-ninety-two.   SiSoSe

Columbus.   James Russell Lowell.   ...One day, with life and heart,/Is more than time enough to find a world.   PGD

Columbus.   Joaquin Miller.   ...he gave that world/Its grandest lesson: "On! sail on!"   AA; AmePo; BeLS; EtS; FaBoBe; FaFP; GN; GoTF; HBV 1-2; HBVY; MC; MCCG; MOS; OHFP; PAH; PAL; PaPo; PGD; TreF; YaD; YeAr

Columbus.   Ogden Nash.   Because it has a very important moral, which is, Don't be a discoverer, be a/promoter.   NoP; OFD

Columbus.   Friedrich von Schiller.   What the one promises, the other will surely attain.   OFD

Columbus.   Lydia Huntley Sigourney.   All glorious, – yet forlorn.   AA; MC; PAH

Columbus.   Annette Wynne.   And the wisest know he was more than wise.   TiPo

Columbus and the Mayflower.   Richard Monckton, Lord Houghton Milnes.   Safe on the perilous heights of power and wealth,/As in the straitness of the ancient ways.   MC; PAH

Columbus at the Convent.   John Townsend Trowbridge.   And helped him on his way, what praise/And gratitude are due!   MC; PAH

Columbus Dying.   Edna Dean Proctor.   Into Thy hands I give my soul!   MC; PAH

Columbus (excerpt).   Alfred, Lord Tennyson.   I am but an alien and a Genovese.   OFD

Columbus Goes West.   William Hart-Smith.   The wash and whip of brine.   BoAV

Columbus in Chains.   Philip Freneau.   Which, but for me, had still been empty visions.   MC; PAH

Columbus Never Knew.   Gail Brook Burket.   Acclaim for reaching greater goals/Than any he had sought.   PGD

Columbus Reaches Juana, 1492. Ralph Gustafson. Jesus be with you. NOBC

Columbus Stockade Blues. *Anonymous.* Leave, little darlin', I don't mind. FSW

Columbus the World-Giver. Maurice Francis Egan. Is one clear trumpet call to Faith and Will. PGD

Columbus to Ferdinand. Philip Freneau. Reason shall steer, and skill disarm the gale. OBCA; PAH

Columcille's Greeting to Ireland. Saint Columcille. It is quiet and it is delightful./Delightful. OnYI

Columcille the Scribe. Saint Columcille. Whence my hand is weary with writing. OnYI

Column A. Michael Silverton. It made me feel like letting off some air for decoration. PV

Coma. Dennis Schmitz. they pinch for it as it rolls/out of the therapist's hands, very small. NPGG

Comanche. Tom Clark. Everything good is from the Indian. ANYP

Comanche. Gary Gildner. and then they shot me full of nothing. PH

Comanche Ghost Dance. Lance Henson. in all that grows while the winter reaps/we will live again. VoR

Comatas. Harry Mathews. Comatas sang this as dusk came. ANYP

The Comb. Walter De la Mare. She kissed me through her tears, and set/On high this spangling comb. FaBoRV

The Combat. Edwin Muir. You'd almost think it was despair. CMoP; LiTB; MoBrPo; NOBE

The Combat. Thomas Stanley. When, alas, the fight's within! AWP

The Combat of Ferdiad and Cuchulain. *Anonymous.* Let them not arise!' OnYI

The Combe. Edward ("Edward Eastaway") Thomas. That most ancient Briton of English beasts. FM; GTBS-P

Combe Florey. Paul Durcan. And so saying, she gave tiny feet back to my boulder and/pain. FaBoIP

Combinations. Mary Ann Hoberman. To flee the fly who now flew by. OBCA

Combing. Gladys Cardiff. Plaiting the generations. CDW; STE

Comcomly's Skull. Jim Barnes. The eyes stay empty. The sky grows full. STE

Come! David Ignatow. But let us wipe out a few hundred million. CAPP

Come All Ye Fair and Tender Ladies. *Anonymous.* Says: "Let this be a faithful warning/for those who keep true-lovers apart." AmFP

Come All Ye Fair and Tender Maidens. *Anonymous.* I'll sit right down in my grief and sorrow,/And let my troubles pass me by. TreFT

Come All Ye Mourning Pilgrims. John A. Granade. Nor earth, nor all her empty joys/Shall long detain me here. AH

Come, All Ye People. George R. Seltzer. From age to age, the only Lord. AH

Come, All Ye Youths. Thomas Otway. Think of my fate, and shun her snares. OAEP

Come All You Bold Canadians. *Anonymous.* And to our bold commander, brave General Brock by name! ShS

Come All You Fair and Tender Ladies. *Anonymous.* That the sun rose in the west. FSW

Come All You Young Ladies and Gentlemen. *Anonymous.* For if I were single again, I'd be cussed if I ever got married. OBET

Come an' Meet Me wi' the Childern on the Road. William Barnes. Come an' meet me, wi' the childern, on the/road. VLP

Come and Go with Me to That Land. *Anonymous.* Go with me to that land where I'm bound. FSW

Come and Welcome. Thomas Haweis. Come and welcome, sinner, come. BePJ

Come away, Come Sweet Love. *Anonymous.* Hast then sweet Love our wished flight. OAEP; PoEL 1-5

Come away, Death. Edwin John Pratt. Etched by a foreign stylus never used/On the outmoded page of the Apocalypse. PeCV

Come away, Sweet Love. John Dowland. Haste then, sweet love, our wished flight! LoBV

Come Back. Arthur Hugh Clough. Rather than not for heavenly light/Wait on to show the truly right. NCEP

Come Back. Henry William Herbert. Whose strength but waits to fold thee home. AA

Come Back. William Stanley Merwin. It is the same way there. NaP

Come Back Blues. Michael S. Harper. you've come back/to count bodies again/in your own backyard. PoBA

Come Back, Lincoln. Chauncey R. Piety. And set your people free. PGD

Come Back to Erin. Charlotte Allington ("Claribel") Barnard. And it's Killarney shall ring with our mirth. TreFS

Come, Blessed Bird. *Anonymous.* Long live fair Oriana. NCEP

Come, Break with Time. Louise Bogan. Come, cruel ease. ATP; MoAmPo

Come, Captain Age. Sarah N. Cleghorn. I shall be rich and splendid/With the spoils of the Indies of Age. HBMV

Come, Chearfull Day, Part of My Life, to Mee. Thomas Campion. So ev'ry day we live, a day wee dye. AAS; EG; EIL

Come, Chloe, and Give Me Sweet Kisses. Charles Hanbury Williams. With few will be ever content. HBV 1-2; UnTE

Come Christmas. David McCord. All stars are hung so every Christmas tree/has one above it. Let's go out and see. PCh

Come, Come Away, to the Tavern I say. *Anonymous.* Anon, anon, anon, Sir, what is't you say? OBS

Come, Come, What Doe I Here? Henry Vaughan. A bed, and sleep/To wake in thee. MePo; SeCV 1-2

Come Dance a Jig. *Anonymous.* And pussy cat shall crowdy. OxNR

Come Dance with Kitty Stobling. Patrick Kavanagh. ...thank you sincerely/For giving me my madness back, or nearly. FaBoIP; NoAm

Come, Death—My Lady Is Dead. Charles, duc d' Orleans. O! woful wretche! O! wretche, lesse ones thy speche! MeEL

Come Down. George Macdonald. And there, O my Father,/Be what thou art? TrPWD

Come down, You Bunch of Roses, Come down. *Anonymous.* Oh, you pinks and poses,/Come down, you bunch of roses, come down. ShS

Come, Every Soul. John H. Stockton. He will save you now. AH

Come, Follow Me. Thomas Campion. Grace can make our foes our friends. EnRePo

Come Forth, Come Forth! John Wilson. I am too glad to be alone,/come forth with me to-day! OBRV

Come, Friends and Neighbors, Come. Lewis Hartsough. Heed Mercy's call. AH

Come from Thy Palace. Thomas Randolph. And then, amazed with grief, laugh out thine eyes. OBSP

Come, Gaze with Me upon This Dome. Edward Estlin Cummings. the son of man gaze on war/with trumpets clap and syphilis. NoAm; OxBA

Come, Gentle Death! Thomas Watson. That, brought from cold, it never will desire/To rest with me, which am more hot than fire. EIL

Come, Gentle Sleep, Death's Image Though Thou Art. Thomas, Marquess of Wharton. Thus without death how sweet it is to die. OBVE

Come Green Again. Winfield Townley Scott. O all come green again. PoPl

Come, Happy Children. *Anonymous.* O, then give me cold water. AH

Come Harken unto Me. *Anonymous.* Nor yet his own benignity/Turned away from me. AH

Come Here Lord! *Anonymous.* Come here, Lord!/Sinner cryin' come here, Lord. BoAN 1-2

Come Hither, My Dear One. John Clare. Where you and I pledged our first love so true. ELP

Come Hither, You That Love. John Fletcher. You shall be ever pleas'd, and young maids long. EG; ELP

Come, Holy Babe! Mary Dickerson Bangham. Make my dull spirit glow/This Silent Night! PGD

Come Holy Spirit, Dove Divine. Adoniram Judson. The sealing unction from above/The breath of life, the fire of love. AH

Come, holy tortoise shell. Sappho. ...and become a poem. BoWoP

Come Home. *Anonymous.* Come, come home. PeSA

Come Home, Come Home! Arthur Hugh Clough. Is there indeed, or is there not a shore/That is our home? HAP

Come In. Robert Frost. And I hadn't been. AnNE; BoNaP; DiPo; FaBVo; ForPo; LiTA; LiTM; MoAB; MoAmPo; NOBA; NoP; TrGrPo

Come In. Isaiah Shembe. Descendants of Dingana/And of Senzangakhona. WTO

Come into Animal Presence. Denise Levertov. And old joy returns in holy presence. AP; HeIP; NaP; NU

Come into the Garden, Maud. Alfred, Lord Tennyson. And blossom in purple and red. CBEP; ExPo; HBV 1-2; LiTL; NOBE; TreF

Come into the Orchard, Anne. Algernon Charles Swinburne. And the pimpernel muddles his head. FaBoNo

Come, Landlord, Fill the Flowing Bowl. *Anonymous.* Ought to have his lips cut off,/And never kiss another. OxBoLi

Come Laugh with Me. *Anonymous.* Come, talk with me. My body is alone. WTO

Come, Let's to Bed. *Anonymous.* Says Greedy-gut,/Let's sup before we go. GBP; OxBoLi

Come, Let Us Find. William Henry Davies. To clear away the morning dew. HBMV

Come Let Us Make Love Deathless. Herbert Trench. And nobler for the fading of those eyes/The world seen once for all. EG; HBMV; OBVV

Come, Let Us Sing. *Anonymous.* Oh, one's the one that's left alone,/A-mourning to be alone. BFSS

Come, Let Us Sound with Melody, the Praises. Thomas Campion. Author of number, that hath all the world in Harmony framed. UnS

Come, Let Us Tune Our Loftiest Song. Robert A. West. Who reigns, and shall forever reign. AH

Come Live with Me (parody). Naomi Marks. The case continues. BXAP

Come, Lord Jesus. Charles Wesley. O that our hearts were all a heaven,/Forever fill'd with God. BePJ

Come, Love, Let's Walk. *Anonymous.* Fair beauty mixed with chastity. EIL

Come Love or Death. Will Henry Thompson. And I had power to kill! AA

Come Michaelmas. A. Newberry Choyce. And then, belike, your dad will hear/An ash-stick tapping on his door. HBMV

Come, My Celia. Ben Jonson. These have crimes accounted been. CABA; EIL; FaBV; FF; HeIP; NIP; NLV; NoP; TEP; TrGrPo; WHA

Come, my sweet, whiles every strain. William Cartwright. May not know in whom they be. EG

Come Not Near. Mary Elizabeth Osborn. transcendent beyond the barrier of glass. NePoAm-2

Come Not near My Songs. *Anonymous.* Lest from out my singing/Leaps my heart upon you! AWP; PG

Come Not the Seasons Here. Edwin John Pratt. Or the hoot of a horned owl/On a glacial stone. NoP; PeCV

Come Not To Me For Scarfs. Aurelian Townsend. To take a scripp and sheapheards grey. AnAnS 2

Come Not When I Am Dead. Alfred, Lord Tennyson. Go by, go by. FaBoRV; GBL

Come, O Come. Thomas Campion. As swift to me as heav'nly light. AtBAP; EG; EIL; InvP

Come, O Friend, to Greet the Bride. Solomon H Alkabez. Come, O Bride. TrJP

Come, O Lord, Like Morning Sunlight. Milton S. Littlefield. At the radiant close of labor/May our souls find rest in Thee. TrPWD

Come, O Sabbath Day. Gustav Gottheil. Thou shalt rest, thou shalt rest. AH

Come on Home. Sharon Scott. But– leave/the/dead/noisemakers/alone. JB

Come on In. *Anonymous.* Guess I'll have to/Count to ten. SD

Come On in My Kitchen. Robert Johnson. You better come on/in my kitchen/'cause it's going to be raining outdoors BluL

Come Out, Come Out, Ye Souls That Serve. Christopher John Brennan. yet the staying is a death that is never soften'd with sleep. PoAu 1-2

Come Out into the Sun. Robert Francis. Into the sun, come out, come in. NYBP

Come Out, Lazarus! *Anonymous.* "Com out' hath felld it al with fight. OxBM

Come Out of Crete. Sappho. And mix it deftly with/Our dancing and mortal wine. OBVE

Come, Precious Soul. *Anonymous.* And he'll help thee climb up Calvary. AH

Come Ride and Ride to the Garden. Gregory Lady. There's barley there, and water there,/And stabling to your mind. SUS

Come, Ride with Me to Toyland. Rowena Bastin Bennett. We'll gallop into Toyland! ChBR; SiSoSe

Come, Said My Soul. Walt Whitman. Signing for Soul and Body, set to them my name... NOBA

Come, Says Jesus' Voice. Anna Laetitia Barbauld. Rest, eternal, sacred, sure. BePJ

Come, Sirrah Jack, Ho! *Anonymous.* The sweet of Trinidado. NCEP; OAEP

Come Slowly–Eden. Emily Dickinson. Enters–and is lost in Balms. CMoP; UnTE

Come Slowly, Paradise. James Benjamin Kenyon. Till to thy morning brightness I shall wake/As one from happy sleep. AA

Come, the wind may never again. Emily Bronte. And you must crush the love in your heart, and I the love/in mine! EnLoPo

Come, Thou Almighty King. Charles Wesley. And ne'er from us depart,/ Spirit of power. WGRP

Come to Birth. Abbie Huston Evans. And what shall happen I no longer know. NePoAm

Come to Calvary's Holy Mountain. James Montgomery. Signed when our Redeemer died,/Sealed when He was glorified. BePJ

Come to Me. *Anonymous.* Only jump over the wall and all delight shall be yours. WTO

Come to Me, Beloved. Digby Mackworth Dolben. Thou, the Man Christ JESUS,/Strength in flesh made weak. OxBoCh

Come to Me, Dearest. Joseph Brenan. Come to the heart which is throbbing to press thee! HBV 1-2

Come to Me from Crete to This Holy Temple. Sappho. wine for our drinking. WPOW

Come to Me Soon. Sir Walter Ralegh. "Forego me now; come to me soon." UnTE

Come to the Stone. Randall Jarrell. Come to the stone and tell me why I died. VGW

Come to your Heaven, You Heavenly Choirs! Robert Southwell. Then flit not from this heavenly Boy. EG; OxBoCh

Come Turn to Mee, Thou Pretty Little One. *Anonymous.* Welcome to mee, my onely joy,/all times be it light or dark. CoMu

Come unto Me. Flora L. Osgood. Come, and in coming to Me you find/A sweet and perfect rest. STF

Come unto Me. John Stuart. And they who faithful serve below/Shall rule with Me on high. STF

Come unto Me, When Shadows Darkly Gather. Catharine H. Watterman. Come unto me, and I will give you rest. AH

Come Unto These Yellow Sands (parody). Paul Dehn. Till bacterial cyclones blow./Then let go. SpRo

Come Unto Us Who Are...Laden. Harry Roskolenko. Time, Thou, Split, Colors, Earth, Sun...and We remain. FAZ

Come Up from the Fields Father. Walt Whitman. To follow, to seek, to be with her dear dead son. AmePo; MCCG; MoAmPo; OBWP; OxBA; PPP; UnPo

Come Up, Methuselah. Cecil Day-Lewis. This spark that crackles in the void/As between fate and fate. OBMV

Come up, My Horse, to Budleigh Fair. *Anonymous.* Home again, home again,master/and dame. OxNR

Come Visit My Garden. Tom Dent. clean/brick walls. NNP

Come, Walk with Me. Emily Bronte. Time parts the hearts of men.' NOBV

Come Wary One. Ruth Manning-Sanders. That cage of wizardry. CH

Come When You're Called. *Anonymous.* Never be chid. HBVY; OxNR

Come Where My Love Lies Dreaming. Stephen Collins Foster. Come where my love lies dreaming,/Dreaming the happy hours away. GoTF; TreFS

Come with Me. Robert Bly. And those roads in South Dakota that feel around in the darkness... AmC; NoAm; NOBA

Come with Me into Winter's Disheveled Grass. Karen Swenson. now that death is gone. GrPl

Come, Ye Disconsolate. Thomas Moore. "Earth has no sorrow that God cannot heal." CAW; WGRP

Come, Ye Lads, Who Wish to Shine. *Anonymous.* Danger face, maintain your ground/And see your country righted. PAH

Come Ye Sons of Art (excerpt). Henry Purcell. Sing our patroness's praise/In cheerful and harmonious lays. UnS

Come, You Pretty False-Eyed Wanton. Thomas Campion. So trustless is love's treasure. ELP

Comedian. Louis Johnson. his grin must drag his breeches out of Hell. AnNZ

The Comedian. Irving Layton. each time men touch you and you freeze in hell AMV-81

The Comedian as the Letter C. Wallace Stevens. So may the relation of each man be clipped. NePA; OxBA

The Comedian Said It. Duff Bigger. and having the knob come off/in your hand. FAZ

Comedy. Mark Van Doren. The world will not be understood. NePoAm-2

The Comedy of Billy and Betty. *Anonymous.* I think that the girl is gone mad. OxNR

Comes Fall. Robert Nathan. I go my way, and God knows best. HBMV

Comes Winter, the Sea Hunting. Norman Dubie. ...This was the very first wall/that you had to have passed through. MAYP

The Comet. Emil Makai. And there is no goal to reach. VWA

The Comet. Michael Palmer. as forecast long ago by the prophets/in a circus farce NPGG

The Comet at Yalbury or Yell'ham. Thomas Hardy. Will fall on Yell'ham; but not then/On that sweet form of thine. CMoP; ExPo; GBL; VLP

Comets and Princes. Samuel Johnson. Comets! come every day–and stay a year. FaBoEE

Comfort. Elizabeth Barrett Browning. He sleeps the faster that he wept before. HBV 1-2; TRV

Comfort. May Doney. Our hearts were thwarted by so frail a fence,/And could not break the weak wall that divides. HBMV

Comfort. Margaret Widdemer. What is there cruel in a sunset sky? GoYe

Comfort and Tidings of Joy. *Anonymous.* And we wish them a happy, a happy New Year! FSW

Comfort for the Sleepless. H. C. Bradby. And let me know Thee right. BoC

Comfort in Affliction. Ayton [(or Aytoun)] Sir Robert. Give me thy flannel petticoat/To wrap around my head! InMe

Comfort in Extremity. Christopher Harvey. "As I have made thee now, I take thee." OxBoCh

Comfort in Puirtith. Helen B. Cruickshank. A routh o' donnert feckless fules/Wha dinna coont a dang! OxBS

Comfort of the Fields. Archibald Lampman. Drink, and be filled, and ye shall understand! CaP

The Comfort of the Stars. Richard Burton. My trouble merged in wonder and in love. AnAmPo

The Comfort of the Trees. Richard Watson Gilder. Found comfort in the moving green of trees. PAH

A Comfort Stop. Tony Beyer. ...their/dark sorority/exempts them from. OCNZ

Comfort thyself, my woeful heart. Sir Thomas Wyatt. Sigh there thy last, and therewith break! FCP; SiPS

Comfort to a Youth That Had Lost His Love. Robert Herrick. And lull asleep/Thy woes, and weep/No more. NOBE; OBEV

Comfortable Strangers. Terence Winch. My legs ache & I feel lonely. APU

Comforted. Amy Carmichael. My heart is comforted in Thee. TRV

The Comforters. Dora Sigerson Shorter. The kind little feet of the rain ran by my side. CH; HBMV

Comforting Lines. *Anonymous*. Eyes, from whose beauty God has/banished weeping/And wiped away the tear. STF

The Comic Adventures of Old Mother Hubbard and Her Dog. Sarah Catherine Martin. The dog said "Bow-wow". OxBChV

The Comin' o' the Spring. Lady John Scott. And there's nought but joy in my ain land at the comin' o' the Spring! BSV

Comin' Thro' the Rye. Robert Burns. But whaur his hame, or what his/name,/I dinna care to tell. ExPo; FaFP; FSW; HBV 1-2; LiTB; LiTL; OxBS; SpRo; TreF; UnTE; WBLP

Comin' to Town. Robert V. Carr. Fer she knows a thing or two. BPAW

The Coming. Anthony Delius. to country of the dead. ACV

Coming. Philip Larkin. And starts to be happy. MoBrPo; OxBTC

Coming across. Mehri. Too bad it's all for so brief a space. WPOW

The Coming American. Sam Walter Foss. Bring me Men. AmFN; BBV; BLPA; FaBoBe

Coming and Going. Mitchell Goodman. Please omit/flowers. VGW

Coming and Going. Louis Johnson. ...Its colour/glows in the room where I have closed the door. OCNZ

The Coming and the Appearing. *Anonymous*. Lamb of God for sinners slain. STF

Coming Around the Horn. *Anonymous*. Had sold the ship and cargo, sent the money to the States. ABF; AmFP

Coming Awake. D. H. Lawrence. And the airy primulas, oblivious/Of the impending bee–they were fair enough sights. BrPo

Coming Back. Joseph Bruchac. you wonder why my feet/move in dance to a distant drum CDW

Coming Back. Linda Gregg. I who looked at the drying leaves with my heart/have learned to come back. NPGG

Coming Back Home. Ray A. Young Bear. before it left, barking down the road. CDW

Coming Back to America. James Dickey. ...the thing that/sustains us forever/In other places! NYBP; NYP

The Coming Child. Richard Crashaw. Great little one! whose all-embracing birth/Lifts earth to heaven, stoops heav'n to earth! TRV

Coming Down to It (parody). Malcolm Glass. ...Though dressed in metaphor,/abstract celebration's still a bore. BXAP

Coming Events. John Montague. perspective leads us to admire is the brown calfskin of the/principal executioner's boots. FaBoIP

The Coming Forth by Day of Osiris Jones: The Nursery. Conrad Aiken. and footsteps pause behind the door– LOW

Coming Home. Rolfe Humphries. The self is never lost. MoRP

Coming Home. John Stone. close to the only motor/in the world. NIP

Coming Home, Detroit, 1968. Philip Levine. We burn this city every day. TAT

Coming Home from Abroad. David Holbrook. ...and so we sail/Steering irrevocably into the Felixstowe fog. OBTV

Coming Home from Camp. Lonny Kaneko. we're scattered across the floor and forced to make/ourselves at home, wherever we happen to be. BrSi

Coming Home in March. Harold Littlebird. lump in my throat growing harder. STE; VoR

Coming Homeward Out of Spain. Barnabe Googe. Till on my country coast our anchor fall. EIL; EnRePo

The Coming K–. *Anonymous*. And ices pass around, and beauty smiles/Upon the pigeonry of Guelpho's Knights. VLP

Coming of Age in the County Jail. Carter Revard. Well, here's the man. Thanks for dropping in. VoR

The Coming of Arthur: Merlin's Riddling. Alfred, Lord Tennyson. From the great deep to the great deep he goes. FaBoRV

The Coming of Christ. *Anonymous*. I come from an uncouth land as a sely pilgrim/That far hath sought. ACP

The Coming of Dusk upon a Village in Haiti. Henry Rago. ...so the heart, that last/Bloom of conspiracy, would not be lost! HoPM

The Coming of Good Luck. Robert Herrick. ...as the trees/Are, by the sunbeams, tickled by degrees. CBEP; ELU; FaBoEE; JCP; OBSP

The Coming of His Feet. Lyman Whitney Allen. I listen for the coming of His feet. BLPA

The Coming of Light. Mark Strand. and tomorrow's dust flares into breath. HaCAP; PPJ

The Coming of Night. Thomas Wade. The wave-swept shore, and all the amplitude/Of air and sea, broodeth in starry vastness. ERoP 1-2

The Coming of Pharaoh. Caedmon. Howl along the hostile trail–hideous slaughter of the host. CAW

The Coming of Spring. Nora Perry. That winter's had its day. HBVY; SoPo; YcAr

The Coming of the Cold. Theodore Roethke. Winds bring a fine and bitter snow. OBCP

The Coming of the Lord. Jones Very. Thou wilt to us Thy word of promise keep. BePJ; MAmP

The Coming of the Plague. Weldon Kees. And heard the sound of rushing wind. NaP; VGW

The Coming of War: Actaeon. Ezra Pound. The silent cortege. CMoP; PoA

The Coming of Wisdom with Time. William Butler Yeats. Now I may wither into the truth. DiPo; FaBoEE; PoL; SoSe

Coming Out. Jacqueline Lapidus. and I am upstream among my sisters/spawning. IHMS

Coming out of. Robert Duncan. coming out again and again. EAS

Coming Suddenly to the Sea. Louis Dudek. ending my long blind years, a fistful of blood-red weed in my/hand. NOBC

Coming to This. Mark Strand. no place to go, no reason to remain. HaCAP

Coming Up & Falling Down. Stephen Vincent. Come on. Let's go. I want an answer. NeAC

Cominus, You Reprobate Old Goat. Caius Valerius Catullus. Give dogs the guts, and leave the wolves the rest. DBV

The Comman Man. A.J.M. Smith. ...The ignorant policeman walks the yard. NOBC

Commander Lowell. Robert Lowell. he was "the old man" of a gunboat on the Yangtze. VGW

Commanders of the Faithful. William Makepeace Thackeray. And would be neither Turk nor Pope. ALV

Commanding a Telephone to Ring. Jack Anderson. you will know not to answer it. AMV-81

Commanding Elephants. Philip Levine. ...smelling/of soap, they lay at his sides/as though they were listening. NaP

Commemoration. Claude McKay. Transfigured, bathed in your immortal flame. BANP

Commemoration. Sir Henry Newbolt. Lightly as drifted leaves on an endless plain. FaBoTw; OBVV

The Commemoration Ode. James Russell Lowell. New birth of our new soil, the first American. PGD

Commemoration Ode. Harriet Monroe.
  Shall lead man up through happy realms of/light/Unto his goal sublime. AA
  The strong who, having wrought, can never/die. AA
  The wise who, having known, can never/die. AA

Commemorative of a Naval Victory. Herman Melville. The shark/Glides white through the phosphorus sea. AP; HAP; MOS; UnPo

Commencement, Pingree School. John Updike. Up pops a Daddy with a Nikon. Click. Str

The Commendations of Mistress Jane Scrope. John Skelton. She is worthy to be enrolled/With letters of gold./Car elle vault. OBSC

Commendatory Sonnet to Hoby's Courtier. Thomas, Earl of Dorset Sackville. Whos passing skill lo Hobbies pen displaise/To Brittain folk, a work of worthy praise. AAS

Comment. Dorothy Parker. And I am Marie of Roumania. ALV; InMe; NIP; NLV; OBAL

Commentaries on the Song of Songs. Judith Herzberg. we are still sailing under the same flag. VWA

Comments. Peggy Susberry Kenner. any knowledge/of/illegitimacy. JB

Commercial Traveller. Lauris Edmond. Let him suck his thumb. OCNZ

Commination. Walter Savage Landor. And I too had a mind to let her. ALV

Commissary Report. Stoddard King. They're sick. ALV; ShM

Commission. Ezra Pound. Be against all sorts of mortmain. BoLoP; MP; NIP; TwCP

The Commission Man. Robert V. Carr. And, by Jup', you do–that's all. BPAW

Commitment in a City. Margaret Tsuda. a piece would be missing/from my jigsaw-puzzle day. CTBA

The Committee. C. Day-Lewis. And all the committee, all the one-man committee. BiP; CMoP

Common Bill. *Anonymous*. So I thought the matter over/And I rather think I will. AmFP; AS; FSW

Common Blessings. Thomas Curtis Clark. Lord of my days, how thankful I/For a thankful heart, as life goes by! TrPWD

The Common Cormorant. Christopher Isherwood. And steal the bags to hold the crumbs. FaBoCh; FaBoCo; FaBoNo; FiBHP; LoGBV; NLV

Common Dawn. Guy Butler. The sunlight everywhere. PeSA

Common Dust. Georgia Douglas Johnson. The same as from the start? AmNP; PoBA; TTY

The Common Grave. James Dickey. At just the wrong time to be heard,/ Others, others. CoAP

A Common Ground. Denise Levertov. ...mountains/sing to each other across the cold valleys. PoM; PP

A Common Inference. Charlotte Perkins Stetson Gilman. They shriek beneath the sod,/"There is no God!" AA; AnAmPo; WGRP

A Common Light. Steve Orlen. I slice an apple for us. Str

The Common Living Dirt. Marge Piercy. ...to worship you/on our knees, the common living dirt. GeTw

The Common Lot. Adelbert Sumpter Coats. ...a symphony/Of highest joy and deepest agony! TrPWD

A Common Poem. Carolyn M. Rodgers. the things of this earth/are the things that give us pleasure. CNA

The Common Road. Silas H. Perkins. To mingle with the common man,/ No better or worse than I. BLPA; FaBoBe

The Common's Petition to King Charles II. Anonymous. We'll make him, for the time to come,/The greatest Prince in Christendom. FaBoCo

The Common Sailor. Anonymous. With lords and dukes and all the highest folks must share our/common lot. OBSS

Common Sense. James Thomas Fields With cheerful hearts and smiling faces. AA

Common Sense and Genius. Thomas Moore. Genius, left to shiver/On the bank, 'tis said,/Died of that cold river. NBM

The Common Street. Helen Gray Cone. With the dark shapes of men ascending still. AnAmPo; HBV 1-2

The Common Tasks. Grace Noll Crowell. That at our given work we do our best. PoToHe

The Common Woman. Judy Grahn.
The common woman is as solemn as a monkey/or a new moon. GP
I swear it to you on my common/woman's/head. GP

Commonplace. Susan (Sarah Chauncey Woolsey) Coolidge. Out of commonplace lives makes His beautiful whole. GoTF; TreFT

The Commonplace. Walt Whitman. The democratic wisdom underneath, like solid ground for all. MoAmPo; TrGrPo

A Commonplace Day. Thomas Hardy. And undervoicings of this loss to man's futurity/May wake regret in me. NOBV; PoPle

Commonplaces (parody). Rudyard Kipling. And....this is the end of my lay. HBV 1-2

Commonwealth. Ambrose Bierce. Avenging the friend whom I couldn't work in. DBV

The Commonwealth of Birds. James Shirley. There the Larks are, and we shall/See them, when the sky doth fall. GoBC

The Commonwealth of Toil. Ralph Chaplin. And there's joy and peace for all,/In the Commonwealth of Toil that is to be. FSW

Communal. Mary Elizabeth ("E") Fullerton. And gained sufficient power/ For ten evangelists. PoAu 1-2

Communication. Elizabeth Jennings. Where love is more than lucky in the land. NePoEA

Communication in Whi-te. Don L. Lee. the paris peace talks, 1968. BPo

Communication on His Thirtieth Birthday. Marvin Bell. under the antenna, down the long path intended for your feet. CoAP

A Communication to Nancy Cunard. Kay Boyle. It don't seem to me like we're getting anywheres at all. NMM; PoNe

Communication to the City Fathers of Boston. George Starbuck. Strange how not one prepared a dirge for Boston. NYBP

Communion. Edward Dowden. At last my heart found voice,–"Take me, O Lord,/And do with me according to thy word." TrPWD

Communion. Caroline Giltinan. Bring thy Baby back to me! CAW

Communion. Wallace Gould. I am glad that they whom I have loved are as far off as the/stars. AnAmPo

Communion. David Ignatow. not a friend to bury. CAPP

Communion. P. M. Snider. No longer I,/But, We! PoToHe

Communion. J.L. Spicer. And we with God Himself commune. BLRP

Communion. John Banister Tabb. Life's everwidening circles run/Revealing God to man. WGRP

A Communion Hymn. Alice Freeman Palmer. And let me make my earth a Heaven/Till next Communion Day. TrPWD

Communion Hymn of the Ancient Irish Church. Anonymous. Yea, O my Saviour, for ever and ever. CAW

Communion of Saints: The Poor Bastard under the Bridge. Marie Ponsot. And welcome welcome welcome him. VGW

Communism. Ella Wheeler Wilcox. That is raging in my soul? PeD

Commuter. E. B. White. And then rides back to shave again. FaBoCo; NLV; PV; TreFT

Commuter's Entry in a Connecticut Diary. Robert Penn Warren. ...like the city dump, at night/Outside Norwalk, Conn. AMV-81

The Companion. Edwin Arlington Robinson. Doubt will have a dwelling there. NoAm

Companion of Her Lord Till Death. Anonymous. Truly such a lady/Is a beauty in the land. HW

The Companions. Howard Nemerov. Nor read the glowworms' constellations when they glisten. NYBP

Companions, a Tale of a Grandfather... Charles Stuart Calverley. And what this is all about. FaBoCo; HBV 1-2; NA; NOBL

Companionship. Maltbie Davenport Babcock. I shall forever be·with Thee/ Because Thou art with me. STF

Companionship. Mary Elizabeth Coleridge. These be thy verities, to have, to hold! NBM

Company. William Dean Howells. Then, "Why, no,"/I thought, "Why should I, if the rest are so?" AmePo

Company Cook. Anonymous. And his household crockery. ABF

Company in Loneliness. Anonymous. and embrace this orphan over all/ who never leaves me lonely. NOBI

The Company of Lovers. Judith Wright. Death draws his cordons in. BoAV

The Company of Scholars. Helen Bevington. Puts on his glasses, and resumes his reading GLGT

The Company One Keeps. Aimor R. Dickson. At which the pig got up and slowly walked away. GoTF; TreFT

Comparatives. N. Scott Momaday. mute and mean,/perceptible–/that is all. SM

Compared with Christ. Augustus Montague Toplady. I'm rich to all the intents of bliss,/If Thou, O God! art mine. BePJ

A Comparison. Anonymous. We'd better leave it up to God,/And save a sad mistake. STF

The Comparison. Thomas Carew. So be within as faire, as good, as true. AnAnS 2

A Comparison. William Cowper. Neglected, leaves a dreary waste behind.. OBSP

The Comparison. John Donne. She, and comparisons are odious. ErPo; TEP

A Comparison. John Farrar. Filled with dreams. BrR

Comparison. Mary Ann Hoberman. The youngest am I. BiCB

The Comparison and Complaint. Isaac Watts. Nor travel swifter through the sky,/Nor with a zeal so warm. TrPWD

The Comparison (excerpt). Anonymous. Ere smoky towns shall vie with rural plains,/And city cockneys rival country swains. NOEC

Comparison of Love to a Streame Falling from the Alpes. Sir Thomas Wyatt. The first eschue is remedy alone. FaBoEn

A Comparison of the Life of Man. Richard Barnfield. Comes Death, and takes the table clean away. OBSC; OBSP

Comparisons. Christina Georgina Rossetti. But the rose with all its thorns excels them both. OxBChV

The Compasses. George MacBeth. Ready shield and swords/Beside his crumbling hand. NePoEA-2

Compassion. Thomas Hardy. And "Blessed are the merciful!"/Calls a yet mightier one. FM

Compassion So Divine. Anne Steele. Glad captives of Thy matchless grace,/Thy righteous rule obey. BePJ

The Compassionate Fool. Norman Cameron. I pitied him for his small strategy. CBEP; GTBS-P; OBSP; OxBTC

Compel Them to Come In. Leonard Dodd. Let Love Divine through human hearts/Compel them to the fold. BLRP

Compelled to Love. Walter Stone. From that fierce marriage falling, gently going. ErPo

Compensation. E. M. Brainard. The sweetness and the peace of real content. PoToHe

Compensation. James Edwin Campbell. Ride on, young lord, ride on! BANP

Compensation. Thomas Stephen Collier. And hunger cannot make its home with/death. AA

Compensation. Paul Laurence Dunbar. Offers the boon of death. AmNP; BPo; HBV 1-2; PoNe

Compensation. Ralph Waldo Emerson.
And, like thy shadow, follow thee. AP; ForPo; NOBA
And now their hour is come. AnNE; APA; FPL; LiTA; TAP

Compensation. Gerald Gould. But the gulls fly over. HBMV

Compensation. Robinson Jeffers. ...beauty and good/Show from the mountainside of solitude. MoAB; MoAmPo

Compensation. Virginia Maughan Kammeyer. But, oh, the loaves of bread I've made. AMV-80

Compensation. Lizette Woodworth Reese. A dream can bring me to your arms once more. HBMV

Compensation. Celia Thaxter. And little birds break out in rippling song. HBV 1-2

The Complacent Cliff-Dweller. Margaret Fishback. And autumn leaves are selling at fifty cents a bunch. PoLf

The Complaint. Mark Akenside. Or placed thy friends above her stern decrees? OBEV

Complaint. Joseph Bennett. While the musing sheep proceed/Fasting and mourning in sleep. LiTA

Complaint. Ian Hamilton. I know how to behave. NoAm

Complaint. William Carlos Williams. I pick the hair from her eyes/and watch her misery/with compassion. QFR

Comrades. Felix McGlennon. But my comrade sprang to save me,/And receiv'd it in his heart! FSN

Comrades. George Edward Woodberry. Through the reach of the desert my soul leaps pursuing/My star where it rises a Star of the Dead. HBV 1-2

Comrades As We Rest Within. Ronald Hambleton. And finds it a little strange/Beginning with a miniature hell. CaP

Comrades in Arms: Conversation Piece. *Anonymous.* "Oui, oui–/ Combien?" ErPo

Comrades of the Cross. Willard Wattles. Who from his cross of pain/Cried to the dying comrade,/"Lad, we shall meet again." HBMV

The Concealment: Ishi, the Last Wild Indian. William Stafford. And sometimes whisper his name–/"Ishi." NaP

Conceit upon the Feet (parody). William Zaranka. A foot in mouth gives safisfaction rare/As two left feet belied with false compare. BXAP

A Conceited Man. *Anonymous.* God Himself will humble you. WTO

Conceits. Arlo Bates.
Lest, too, thou have his wings. AA
Limned in excuse your face. AA

The Concept of Force. Robert Sargent. Though of course you may think what you wish. SUW

Conception. Waring Cuney. "Mary, chile, kiss ma'han'." BANP

Conception. Josephine Miles. He can go among strangers/To save lives. FaBoWP; GP

Concepts and Their Bodies (The Boy in the Field Alone). Pattiann Rogers. And it will be so hereafter. MAYP

Concerning Mme. Robert. Deems Taylor. Your wife's the only thing, I guess,/That all of us have shared with you. UnTE

Concerning One Responsible Negro with Too Much Power. Nikki Giovanni. and i've got to negotiate/for my people's freedom. BPo

Concerning the Awakening of My Soul. H. Roland-Holst. ...it is the long-awaited. WPOW

Concerning the Dead. Mark Halperin. ...They stare,/fouling our acts of love. FAZ

Concerning the Dead Women: The Munitions Plant Explosion: June, 1918. Elizabeth Libbey. only the ribbons. AmPA

Concerning the Nature of Love. Lucretius (Titus Lucretius Carus). To cure the secret sore of ling'ring love. ErPo

Concerning Them That Are Asleep. Rossiter Worthington Raymond. He smiled: "Abide in me." STF

Concerning Unnatural Nature: An Inverted Form. Hollis Summers. ...Indeed it is to be lamented. ErPo

Concert. Michael Arvey. sweetened by the orchards of the earth. AMV-81

The Concert. Phyllis McGinley. Who will not stop to hear it/On any April day. YeAr

Concert. Helen Quigless. and sweetness comes to him. NBP

Concert. Robert Sward. The world/Walking off/into space. VGW

Concert at Sea. Hubert Creekmore. Our course is secret; it is a time of war. WaP

Concert at the Station. Osip Mandelstam. for the last time, we seem to be hearing the music. AMV-81; VWA

Concert-Interpretations (Le Sacre du Printemps). Siegfried Sassoon. And the delighted Audience is clapping. CBEP

A Concert Party. Siegfried Sassoon. Silent, they drift away, over the glimmering/sand. EnLit; MMM

Concert Scene. John Logan. ...Suddenly the color/Is intense. And he finds no defense. NePoEA-2

Concertmaster. Richard Burgin. Fathers are Time/And sons are thyme. AMV-81

A Concise History of the World. Ira Sadoff. We will have to stamp you out. AmPA

Conclusion. John Frederick Nims. ...The Almighty will/Aeons late stumble on it with surprise. PoA

The Conclusion. Sir Walter Ralegh. My God shall raise me up, I trust. EG; EvOK; HBV 1-2; OBEV; WGRP

Conclusion. Siegfried Sassoon. Inheritance of doom. MoBrPo

The Conclusive Voyage. Juan Ramon Jimenez. And the birds will still be there, singing. PoPl

Concord Hymn. Ralph Waldo Emerson.
And Time the ruined bridge has swept/Down the dark stream which seaward creeps. ViBoPo
The shaft we raise to them and thee. AA; AmFN; AmP; AP; AWP; BLPA; BLPL; ExPo; FaBoBe; FaFP; FaPo; FaPoR; GN; GoTF; HAP; HBV 1-2; HBVY; HeIP; InPo; LiTA; MC; MCCG; NePA; NOBA; NoP; OBWP; OHFP; OxBA; PAH; PAL; SeCeV; TAP; TreF; TrGrPo; WaaP; YaD

Concordance. Paul Violi. At this the shadow wept, melting away. AMV-81

Concrete poem: Apfel. Reinhard Dohl. Apfel. InPK

Concrete poem: Concrete Cat. Dorthi Charles. litterbox. InPK

Concrete Poem: Moon. Raymond Federman. Moon. MOON

Concrete poem: Siesta of a Hungarian Snake. Edwin Morgan. ZS zs zs z. InPK

Concrete poem: The Horizon of Holland. Ian Hamilton Finlay. thehorizonofholland. InPK

Condemnation. Thich Nhat Hanh. With whom shall we live then? PPON

The Condemned. Edward Howland. Believing as I always have believed/ That God is just. AA

The Condemned. Edmond Jabes. on a cut braid/on a cut/on a broken/ neck. VWA

Condemned Women. Charles Baudelaire. Mix with the foam of pleasure tears of pain. SyP

Condemning the Moongod Nanna. Enheduanna. They are made for you. BoWoP

The Condition. T Carmi. Later, perhaps, we'll speak. VWA

La Condition Botanique. Anthony Hecht. His daily and all-nourishing bread. MP; NePoEA; NoAm

Conditions. Jose Luis Vega. Emit small propitious birds. InW

Condo Girl. Elaine Equi. She moves like a she-tortoise/head tilted over/1983's Guide to Real Estate. APU

Condone. Ambrose Bierce. So man to his revenge supplies/The added terrors of surprise. DBV

The Condor. Michael Hogan. With no other worlds to conquer. LFAC

Condors Flying. Padraic Colum. We watched the Condors winging towards the Moon. GoJo

Conduct. Samuel Greenberg. The beach-tide summer of people desired. CrMA; LiTA

Conductor Bradley. John Greenleaf Whittier. God give us grace to live as Bradley died! PaPo

Conemaugh. Elizabeth Stuart Phelps Ward. "Teach us, altho' we die, to stand." PAH

Conestoga. George E. Murphy, Jr. you sleep with your head upwind/of both your boots and your butt. AMV-81

A Coney Island Life. James L. Weil. before the game is up. AmFN

A Coney Island of the Mind. Lawrence Ferlinghetti.
the also imaginary/wafers of grace PPP
her fair eternal form/spreadeagled in the empty air/of existence. LiTM; NeAP; PoM

Confab. Kenneth Rosen. ...in my prison men assert their/innocence, their significance as men. AmPA

Confess Jehovah. *Anonymous.* ...His benigne-mercie/continueth forever. TrAS

Confess, Marpessa. Robert Graves. Confess, Marpessa, who is your new lover? TEP

Confess We All, Before the Lord. John Wilson. (For all the danger thou wert in)/Of the infectious dart. AH

Confessio Amantis. John Gower.
And beads in hand, I homeward/turned,/My thoughts all filled with wisdom/learned. AtBAP; MeEV
And in this wise, soth to sein,/Homward a softe pas I wente. PoEL 1-5
Strawht ther he was into the Bot. AtBAP

Confessio Fidei. John Dryden. I need no revelation to believe. NOBE

The Confession. Richard Harris Barham. It's that confounded cucumber/I ate, and can't digest. FiBHP

Confession. Elsa Barker. And full of understanding as the stars/That shone in wonder over Galilee. HBMV

Confession. Lucille Clifton. the angels stream before me/like a torch. GeTw

The Confession. Peter Cooley. I nod. Sure, the kids went to sleep easily. AmPA

Confession. Donald Jeffrey Hayes. (Ivory was her breast!) CDC

Confession. George Herbert. They shall be thick and cloudie to my breast. AnAnS 1; JCP

Confession. Kenneth MacKenzie. Such as to better men was never given. BoAV

A Confession. Robert Mezey. and bend and touch you on the cheek. AmPA; NaP

Confession. Ralph Pomeroy. down the stairs. CoPo

Confession. D. S. Savage. Ink in the vein. NeBP

A Confession. Paul Verlaine. And what I have, my God, I give to Thee. CAW; WGRP

The Confession. Wen Yi-tuo. His imagination is a gnat's and he crawls through muck. ChTr; LiTW

Confession in Holy Week. Christopher Morley. And that, Father Daly, explains why I lied/To tell how the milk soured on Mrs. McBride. HBMV

Confession of a Glutton. Don (Donald Robert Marquis) Marquis. but the boss said never mind old scout/time wears disgraces out. GDP

Confession of a Stolen Kiss. Charles, duc d' Orleans. My ghostly fader, I me confesse,/First to God and then to you. MeEL

Confession of Faith. Elinor Wylie. I dream no ill of Death. AnAmPo; APA; MoAmPo; SBG

The Confession of Golias (abridged). Archpoet of Cologne. Tasting bitters when they want/Sweets will make men grumble. LiTW

Confession Overheard in a Subway.   Kenneth Fearing.   I have done my duty, as a public spirited citizen, in any/case.   LiTA; LiTM; WaP

The Confession Stone.   Owen Dodson.   Oh my boy Jesus: rest./Shushhh, you need the rest.   TTY

Confession to J. Edgar Hoover.   James Wright.   Father, forgive me./I did not know what I was doing.   CAPP; ConAP

Confession to Settle a Curse.   Rosemarie Waldrop.   I'm not/in turn locking/ a child/in my arms.   TW

The Confessional.   Anonymous.   Hurry! Let her in!   UnTE

The Confessional.   Robert Browning.   Lies–lies, again–and still, they lie!   ViBoPo

Confessions.   Elizabeth Barrett Browning.   And no gentler than these.'   OBVV

Confessions.   Robert Browning.   But then, how it was sweet!   ELP; GTBS-P; MBW 1-2; NOBE; NOBV; PoPle; ViBoPo

Confessions of a Born Spectator.   Ogden Nash.   And reassure myself anew/ That you're not me and I'm not you.   LiSp

Confessions of the Life Artist.   Thom Gunn.   For the loss, as for the life,/ there will be no excuse, there/is no justification.   CMoP

The Confessor.   Giuseppe Gioachino Belli.   Tomorrow, at my own house, around midnight.   ErPo

Confide in a Friend.   Anonymous.   But to get quick relief, just confide in a friend.   PoToHe

Confidence.   Anonymous.   The Old we leave without a tear,/The New we hail without a fear.   BLRP

Confidence.   Marsden. Hartley.   even sea gulls love the shape of roses/ere day closes.   AnFE

Confidential.   Winfield Townley Scott.   ...He hides them/To be published in his seventies.   ELU

Confined Love.   John Donne.   But doth waste with greediness.   AnEnPo

Confirmation.   Art Lange.   ...riddled/with rationale,/like vaudeville.   APU

The Confirmation.   Edwin Muir.   Not beautiful or rare in every part,/But like yourself, as they were meant to be.   OxBS

The Confirmation.   Karl Shapiro.   And woke the hidden boy.   ErPo

The Confirmers.   Archie Randolph Ammons.   earnest of mind and of motion lithe.   TAP

Confiteor.   Anonymous.   And gyve me grace and forgyvenes/Of my mys-dede.   CoBE

Conflict.   Caroline Clive.   Oft won, oft lost, and O! too dear to lose!   OBVV

The Conflict.   C. Day Lewis.   Between two fires.   AnEnPo; LiTB; LiTM; MoAB; MoBrPo; NoP

Conflict.   Lincoln Fitzell.   More thundering than that of worms.   AnAmPo

Conflict.   F. R. Scott.   Find the central human urge/To make a thousand roads converge?   CaP; PeCV

The Conflict of Convictions.   Herman Melville.   WISDOM IS VAIN, AND PROPHESY.   AP; MAmP; NOBA

The Conformers.   Thomas Hardy.   A worthy pair, who helped advance/ Sound parish views.   EnLi 1-2; ViBoPo

Confounded Nonsense.   Tom (Thomas Hood, Jr.) Hood.   And blatant wildernesses close around.   FaBoNo

Confrontation.   John Hart.   the simple and the chambered eye.   PoL

Confrontions of March.   H. C. Dillow.   ...dislodging a single cone/Which drops away without a sound.   AMV-80

Confusion.   Victor Hernandez Cruz.   that it had/4,269 specks/of dust on/its wings.   APU

Confusion (parody).   Christopher Hervey.   To think how to unthink that thought again.   BXAP; Par

Congal: Simile.   Sir Samuel Ferguson.   "I am not good enough, oh God, nor pure enough/for this!'–   IrPN

Congal: The Land Is Ours.   Sir Samuel Ferguson.   It and its increase, and the crown and dignity thereof!'   IrPN

The Conger Eel.   Patrick MacGill.   That vampire Conger eel.   OnYI

The Congo.   Vachel Lindsay.   Mumbo...Jumbo...will...hoo-doo...you.   AmP; CMoP; FaFP; LiTA; MCCG; MoAB; MoAmPo; NoAm; NOBA; OxBA; PoNe; PoRA; TAP; TreF; WHA

Congratulations: Two Versions.   Sappho.   Love has been good to you.   HW

A Congratulatory Poem to the Honoured Edmund Morris, Esq....   Elkanah Settle.   And make the STOCK Immortal whence they grew.   HW

A Conjecture.   Charles Francis Richardson.   Seen love make bright our yearning faces.   AA

Conjectured to Be upon the Death of Sir Walter Ralegh.   Henry, Bishop of Chichester King.   Thou died'st an envious wonder, whose high fate/The world must still admire, scarce imitate.   EG

Conjugation of the Verb, "To Hope."   Lou Lipsitz.   One day,/I will risk everything.   FiCP

Conjuration.   Agnes Gergely.   But with this I haven't said much.   VWA

A Conjuration, to Electra.   Robert Herrick.   In love with none, but me.   AtBAP; GBL; PoEL 1-5

Conjuring Roethke.   James Tate.   Let's tango together/down to the clear/ glad river.   OBAL

The Conjuror.   Edward Verrall Lucas.   The life I shall ever adore.   BiCB

A Connacht Caoine.   Anonymous.   And his offspring–och, och–hidden within me!   AnIV

Connais-Tu le Pays?   Richard Shelton.   Outside, the water is moving/past in search of some/low place to lie down.   NYBP

The Connaught Rangers.   Winifred M. Letts.   And the green flags on their bayonets will flutter in the wind.   HBMV

The Connecticut Elm.   Emma Swan.   and what will be left/of magnificence in/Connecticut then?   PoP1

Connecticut Peddler.   Anonymous.   Tiddle-dum-tiddle -dum, faddle whee.   ABF

Connoisseur of Chaos.   Wallace Stevens.   For which the intricate Alps are a single nest.   CABA; LiTM; MoPo; SUW

Connolly.   Liam MacGowan.   –And I was picked to kill/A man like that.   OnYI

Connubii Flores, or the Well-Wishes at Weddings.   Robert Herrick.   Live in the love of doves, and, having told/The raven's years, go hence more ripe than old.   HW

Conon in Alexandria.   Lawrence Durrell.   ..."Music is only love, looking for words."   MoPo

Conquered.   Zoë Akins.   O love! O wonder!   HBMV

The Conquered Banner.   Abram Joseph Ryan.   For its people's hopes are fled!   AA; GoTF; HBV 1-2; PAH; TreF

The Conquering Love of Jesus.   Charles Wesley.   And set my soul at liberty/By Thy victorious love.   BePJ

The Conqueror.   Ruth M. Williams.   To live forever at His side.   BePJ

The Conqueror's Grave.   William Cullen Bryant.   That ministered to thee, is open still.   AA

The Conqueror Worm.   Edgar Allan Poe   And its hero, the Conqueror Worm.   AA; ÀnAmPo; AP; APA; AWP; BLPL; HBV 1-2; InPo; LiTA; MAmP; NOBA

The Conquerors.   Paul Laurence Dunbar.   Afterward thanks, that the present yet knows/Not to ply!   AmePo

The Conquerors.   Harry Kemp.   Came Christ, the Swordless, on an ass!   AnAmPo; HBV 1-2

The Conquerors.   Phyllis McGinley.   But ah! how wondrously they slew/ With what they had to go on.   DBV

Conquerors.   Henry Treece.   There was not one who did not think of home.   GOYP

Conquest.   Elizabeth Jane Coatsworth.   the rivers bridged, and new towns named.   AmFN

Conquest.   Philippe Desportes.   Such eyes, such hair, such wit, and such a hand?   AWP

The Conquest.   Oliver St. John Gogarty.   Without waiting the attack/Of their youngest daughter's frown?   OBMV

Conquest.   Georgia Douglas Johnson.   As I go fighting down the years.   AmNP

A Conquest.   Walter Herries Pollock.   He swore by the rood that he had not lied.   OBVV

The Conquest of Granada.   John Dryden.
I had rather love Phillis both false and unkind,/Than ever be freed from her power.   DiPo
Restores those pains which that sweet folly lost.   FiP
To please an age more gallant than the last.   FiP; SeCV 1-2

Conquistador.   Archibald MacLeish.
"And nevertheless we had the choice to take them!..."   AtBAP
As the light in America comes: without leaves....   NoAm
Delight like the sun's mouth and the water's weight....   AtBAP
"That which I have myself seen and the fighting'...   NAMP
We were lords of it all....   AtBAP

Conquistador.   Georgia Lee McElhaney.   build a nest of bone feather and leaf/on treebranch/just below the sun.   CoPo

Conquistador: The Argument.   Wallace Stevens.   Of that world's conquest and the fortunate wars...   AtBAP

Conrad.   Antoni Slonimski.   I too heard, like Lord Jim,/A voice which tempted: "Jump!"   VWA

Conrad in Twilight.   John Crowe Ransom.   A man's face as weathered as straw/By the summer's flare and winter's flaw.   OxBA

Conscience.   Charles Churchill.   And hates that form She knows to be her own.   OBEC

Conscience.   George Herbert.   The bloudie crosse of my deare Lord/Is both my physick and my sword.   AnAnS 1

Conscience.   Melech Ravitch.   I cower in silence/And in anguish/Lick the boots of my burning conscience.   VWA

Conscience.   Sir Edward Sherburne.   To all temptations is that soul left free/ That makes not to itself a curb of me.   ACP

Conscience.   Charles William Stubbs.   That to sit alone with my conscience/ Will be judgment enough for me.   BLPA

Conscience.   Henry David Thoreau.   To cheer God along.   AnNE; HBV 1-2

The Conscience.   Anna Wickham.   When woman hides her virtues, and displays her sins.   PoL

Conscientious Objector. Edna St. Vincent Millay. ...never through me/Shall you be overcome. WPOW

The Conscientious Objector. Karl Shapiro. ...Your conscience is/What we come back to in the armistice. OxBA

Conscious. Wilfred Owen. There is no time to ask–he knows not what. MMM

Conscripts of the Dream (excerpt). Edwin Markham. And lit the ages as they ran. PGD

Consecration. *Anonymous.* ...But now impart/That sterner grace–to offer Thee my head. TRV

Consecration. Anna Hoppe. O my Belov'd, a smile of Thine/Is heav'n enough for me. BePJ

Consecration. Patrick F. Kirby. Lifting a deathless Christ, the cross stands/At Calvary! GoBC

A Consecration. John Masefield. Of these shall my songs be fashioned, my tales/be told. EnLit; HBMV; MCCG; MoAB; MoBrPo; NoAm; WHA

Consecration of the House. W. S. Fairbridge. Be powerful above us all. Be sure. PoAu 1-2

Consequences. William Meredith. By our code it is fair. We play fair. The world is fair. NoAm

Conservancies. Josephine Miles. Gives everybody on his plate of malathion/A rich spoonful of air. GP

A Conservative. Charlotte Perkins Stetson Gilman. The creature madly climbing back/Into his chrysalis. AA; HBV 1-2

Conservative. Harold Witt. deeper and deeper down, before the dark. AMV-80

The Conservative Shepherd to His Love. Jack D'Arcy. I'll buy you a farewell dinner/And take you home to meet the wife. InMe

Conserving the Magnitude of Uselessness. Archie Randolph Ammons. dry wind only is still talking among the oldest stones. NoAm

Consider. Giovanni Pico della Mirandola. Let Him not lose what He so dear hath bought. CAW

Consider. Christina Georgina Rossetti. Much more our Father seeks/To do us good. GN; TRV

Consider a Move. Michael Ryan. Then what is? I ask. What is? MAYP; SM

Consider the Auk. Ogden Nash. Because he forgot how to walk and learned how to fly/before he thinked. QQQ

Consider the Lilies. Dorothy Donnelly. counter dark clouds like the seven-tiered arch of the rainbow! HoAn

Consider the Lilies. William Channing Gannett. See how the lily grows! WGRP

Consider These, For We Have Condemned Them. C. Day Lewis. The break with the past, the major operation. LiTB; LiTM; NAMP; SeCePo

Consider This and in Our Time. W. H. Auden. Or lapse for ever into a classic fatigue. FaBoMo; LiTB

Consider Well. Sir Thomas More. Nor be that lost which he so dearly bought. ACP; CAW; GoBC

A Considerable Speck. Robert Frost. On any sheet the least display of mind. AmP; MoAB; MoAmPo; OBAL; PPP

The Considerate Crocodile. Amos R. Wells. Of the dear little fish that I just now ate! OBCA

Considerations. David Helwig. a place to start. NOBC

Considerations of Norfolk Island (excerpt). Kenrick Smithyman. and stab our history to the heart. AnNZ

Considerations on Certain Music of J.S. Bach (excerpt). J. C. Beaglehole. ;then to our fifth French Suite. AnNZ

Consideratio Considerandus. John Saffin. With Damned Hipocrites the world Delude/As men on Indians Glass, for gems obtrude. SCAP

A Considered Reply to a Child. Jonathan Price. Someone beside you (rather like "crying') weeping. BoLoP

Considering the Bleakness. Moishe Leib Halpern. Dragging from behind only/A skull on a rope/Tied to his belt. VWA

Considering the Death of John Wayne. Louis Phillips. Hey, Duke, why do you go ride/On a terrible old nag like that? SOTS

Considering the Snail. Thom Gunn. ...imagined the slow passion/to that deliberate progress. GrPl; LiTM; MP; NePoEA-2; TwCP

Consolation. *Anonymous.* And leave at the foot of the cross. STF

Consolation. George Darley. And so was soothed my sorrow for the dead. ERoP 1-2

Consolation. Henry Howard, Earl of Surrey. Joyful at length may be my fate. NOBE; OBSC

Consolation. William Butler Yeats. But where the crime's committed/The crime can be forgot. OBSP

Consolation in July. Rayner Heppenstall. Unless it be, O Father, by your leave. NeBP

Consolation in War. Lewis Mumford. If we do well,/Their death is justified. NYBP

The Consolation of Philosophy. Boethius.
  For none are rich without content. OBVE
  Path, motive, guide, original, and end. OBVE
  She faints and quits her hold. OBVE

That sought our Pearles, and div'd to find/Such pretious perils for mankind! OBVE

Consolation (parody). Arthur Guiterman. All are gone, those damsels fair,/But you're here, so I don't care! BXAP

Consolations of Art. Roy Fuller. Despairing of the State, Euripides/Became a quietist. Thus creators end. OxBC

Consolations of Philosophy. Derek Mahon. Like daisies from a clover field in summer. BIrV; CIP

Consolatory! St. John Emile Clavering Hankin. To keep clearly in mind/That it's probably only your liver! CenHV

A Consolatory Poem. Nicholas Noyes. Heav'n, Heav'n will make amends for all! SCAP

Consorting with Angels. Anne Sexton. I'm no more a woman/than Christ was a man. NMM

The Conspiracy. Robert Creeley. I will send a picture too/if you will send me one of you. PPJ

The Conspiracy of Charles, Duke of Byron. George Chapman. Dark earth would ope and hide us in our graves. MOON; ViBoPo

The Conspirators. Frederic Prokosch. The birds, the birds, sob for the time of man. LiTM; NAMP; NePA; PrIm; WaP

A Constable Calls. Seamus Heaney. And the bicycle ticked, ticked, ticked. FaBoPV; IPY; NOBI

Constance Kent. *Anonymous.* Then will be cleared up all mystery. OBET

Constancies. *Anonymous.* Are constant–as the fall of dice. UnTE

Constancy. Samuel Daniel. Sound out aloud so rare a thing,/That all the hills and vales may ring. OBSC

Constancy. John Boyle O'Reilly. And last night–I changed the lock! OnYI

Constancy. Minor Watson. Perchance it is of them the poet saith/"Dear as remembered kisses after death." HBV 1-2

Constancy: A Song. John Wilmot, Earl of Rochester. For such a faithful tender Heart/Can never break, can never break in vain. CavP; OBS

The Constancy of a Lover. George Gascoigne. And when I change, let vengeance on me fall. EnRePo; QFR

Constancy to an Ideal Object. Samuel Taylor Coleridge. The enamoured rustic worships its fair hues,/Nor knows he makes the shadow, he pursues! ERoP 1-2

Constancye. Sidney Godolphin. Though not a Pallace, it will prove/the most wisht monument. MePo

The Constant. Archie Randolph Ammons. miracle, this massive, drab constant of experience. HAP

Constant. Emily Dickinson. Even as herself, O friend!/I will of you! AA; FaBoBe

The Constant Bridegrooms. Kenneth Patchen. Their names are spoken/Somewhere at world's end. CrMA; LiTM; NaP

The Constant Cannibal Maiden. Wallace Irwin. A-waitin' for me–with a knife and fork. OBAL

Constant Defender. James Tate. I was alone when it hit me. MAYP

The Constant Farmer's Son. *Anonymous.* Young Mary cried, in sorrow died/For the constant farmer's son. OBET

A Constant Labor. James W. Thompson. the fertile midnight, straining/in the lavish bed of morning. BPo

The Constant Lover. Louis Simpson. But she is changeless/And seems more beautiful as time/passes. NYBP

The Constant Lover. Sir John Suckling. A dozen dozen in her place. AWP; CaPo; FaBV; FaFP; FPL; HBV 1-2; HeIP; InPo; JCP; LiTB; LiTL; MCCG; NOBE; OBEV; OLR; SeCePo; TreFS; TrGrPo

The Constant Lover. Aurelian Townsend. Thou shalt have no displeasure/By knocking at my breast. OxBoLi

The Constant North. J. F. Hendry. As a restless needle held by the constant north/we always have in mind. NeBP; OxBS

The Constant One. George Dillon. Or if all else has vanished into air,/Take me. AmLP

Constant Penelope Sends to Thee, Careless Ulysses. Ovid. Nor used this complaint, nor have thought the day to be so long. GBL

The Constant Swain and Virtuous Maid. *Anonymous.* ...let us be named/The constant swain, the virtuous maid. HBV 1-2

Constantly Risking Absurdity. Lawrence Ferlinghetti. spreadeagled in the empty air/of existence CAPP; SoSe; TAP

The Constellation. Henry Vaughan. And so repair these Rents, that men may see/And say, Where God is, all agree. SeCV 1-2

The Constellation and the Insurgente. *Anonymous.* And now "the girl we love the most!"/My brave Yankee boys. PAH

The Constitution and Guerriere. *Anonymous.* The Yankee tars for fighting are the dandy, O! ABF; AmFP; AmSS; FSW; PAH; ViBoFo

Constitution for a League of Nations. Arthur Guiterman. And Tuesday, Wednesday, Thursday, Friday,/Saturday and Sunday.) InMe

The Constitution's Last Fight. James Jeffrey Roche. "Old Ironsides" means victory,/Acrost the Western ocean. MC; PAH

The Constructed Space. W. S. Graham. ...Yet here I am/More truly now this abstract act become. PoA

Contributions: For Instance. Robert McAlmon. too easily attain a cool supremacy of being/for our fumbling competition. PoA

The Contrite Heart. William Cowper. And if it be not broken, break,/And heal it, if it be. EiCP; PoEL 1-5; TrPWD

Controlling the Tongue. Geoffrey Chaucer. A tongue cutteth friendship all a-two. OxBChV

The Controls. Harrison Fisher. ...What right now/do I want most in the world! APU

Conundrum. Carl Clark. I am inside myself. JB

The Conundrum of the Workshops. Rudyard Kipling. By the favor of God we might know as much–as our/father Adam knew. HBV 1-2; MoBrPo

Convalescence. James Philip McAuley. I drown in silence and endure/The thought of never getting better. CBAP

The Convent. Gilbert Keith Chesterton. Because my name is Lazarus and I live. GoBC

The Convent. Jeanne D'Orge. Nice to be God... AnAmPo

The Convent. Seumas (James Starkey) O'Sullivan. By praying on your bended knees/Within a darkened room. PoL

Convent Cemetery: Mount Carmel. Sister Mary St. Virginia. Night will be good; and Morning will be better. GoBC

The Convent Threshold. Christina Georgina Rossetti.
And love with old familiar love. MasP; NoP; PoEL 1-5
Save love, for love is all in all... LO

Conventicle. Gerrit Lansing. we ride in every day/or drown. CoPo

Convention. Alfred Kreymborg. The sails that are blown by the strength of/your will. MAPA

Convention. Agnes Lee. Till enough footsteps come and go/To make a path for me. HBMV

Convention Song. Anonymous. And commerce fill our purses. PAH

The Convergence of the Twain. Thomas Hardy. And consummation comes, and jars two hemispheres. BiP; BrPo; CoBMV; FaBoTw; HeIP; InPK; InPo; InPS; LiTB; LiTM; MoAB; MoBrPo; MoPo; MOS; MoVE; NoAm; NoP; OAEL 1-2; OAEP; OxBTC; PeD; PrIm; SeCeV; TEP

Conversation. Florence Anthony ("Ai"). Could anyone alive survive it? LTB

Conversation. John Berryman. The guns and enemies that face/Into this delicate and dangerous place. LiTA; LiTM; NePA; WaP

Conversation. (Taniguchi Buso) Buson. Are walking and talking together. NTCP

Conversation. Berenice C. Dewey. A sudden madness seized him, and he tore/His hair and dashed the tea-cup to the floor. InMe

Conversation. Nikki Giovanni. you better get back to the city cause you one of them/technical niggers and you'll have problems h CTBA

A Conversation. Barbara Howes. a molten gong–whose full/Resonance an artist/Brocades upon the soul. IHMS

Conversation. Louis MacNeice. Intimacy but by mistake interpolate/Swear-words like roses in their talk. TEP

Conversation. K. Malley. I think we've played this one before. AMV-80

Conversation. David McCord. ("–all right.")/"Good night!" GrPl; SO

Conversation. Hannah More. The works of ages start to view,/And ancient Wit elicits new. OBEC

Conversation. Gyorgy Raba. as I spin off beyond the front gardens/like a fresh galaxy in outer space. VWA

Conversation. Anne Robinson. And barked his "Yap...yap!"... SUS

A Conversation. Percy Bysshe Shelley. And those who suffer with their suffering kind/Yet feel their faith, religion.' ERoP 1-2

A Conversation. Dylan Thomas. Seas gliding with swans/In the seal-barking moon. RFM

Conversation between Mr. and Mrs. Santa Claus. Rowena Bastin Bennett. And tomorrow I'll start filling it,/For next year's girls and boys. ChBR; SiSoSe; TiPo

Conversation between the Chevalier de Chamilly and Mariana Alcoforado. The Three (Maria Isabel Barreno and Maria Teresa Horta and Maria Velho da Costa) Marias. —Sap in your mouth/terror/in your member BoWoP

Conversation Galante. Thomas Stearns Eliot. And–"Are we then so serious?" HBMV

Conversation in Avila. Phyllis McGinley. There is no perfect record standing by/Of God's reply. EaLo

Conversation in Black and White. May Sarton. Than the one world-embraceing look we shared. GoYe

The Conversation in the Drawingroom. Weldon Kees. Everything is blissfully quiet now. I am ready for sleep. EAS

The Conversation of Prayer. Dylan Thomas. Dragging him up the stairs to one who lies dead. EBEV; GTBS-P; NoP

Conversation Piece. Arthur Freeman. Glancing, I go by–dry-eyed–/(I've swung.) ErPo

Conversation Piece. Robert Graves. And how the moon trembles on the crag's brink. GrPl

Conversation with a Countryman. Antoni Slonimski. "But listen, Warsaw is there!" so he doesn't understand. VWA

Conversation with an April Fool. Rowena Bastin Bennett. Led not into stupid old Farmerville/But straight into Fairyland. SiSoSe

Conversation with God. Jeanine Hathaway. ...It blesses/as it moves toward your own. AMV-80

Conversation with Rain. Louise D. Gunn. For the time being, for the time being,/Peace. GoYe

Conversation with Three Women of New England. Wallace Stevens. That talk shifts the cycle of the scenes of kings? NePA

Conversation with Washington. Myra Cohn Livingston. Your children, George. They thought that you/Would understand. (Most fathers do–) OFD

Conversational. Anonymous. Came the climax, "How's your parents?" ALV; FiBHP

The Conversational Reformer. Harry Graham. Meanwhile I seek with some avid:/The fav: of your polite consid:. InMe; YaD

Conversations between Here and Home. Joy Harjo. they are grinding the mortar/between straw-thin teeth/and broken families. TWSS

Conversations from Childhood: The Victrola. Joseph Langland. I am singing, still. of the world's goodwill. SM

Conversations in Courtship (excerpt). Anonymous. Seven days and/she has abandoned me. CTC

Conversations with the Nightmare. Carol Lee Sanchez. we will all be REwritten/whether we like it or not. TWSS

Conversing with Paradise. Howard Nemerov. Able to do these mortal miracles/In silence and solitude, without a word. PoDr

Conversion. Frances Angermayer. Strange–since I met You–I'm not afraid to die. PGD; PoLf; TreFS

Conversion. Geof Hewitt. And caressing church tight breasts. NeAC

Conversion. Thomas Ernest Hulme. As any peeping Turk to the Bosphorus. FaBoMo; LoBV; OBSP; ViBoPo

The Conversion of the Magdalene. Pedro Malon de Chaide. Thou lightest the peaks with Thine eternal beam. CAW

The Convert. Margaret Danner. ...blazing forms ascending the centuries/in their muted sheens, matter to me. BPo

The Converts. Chana Bloch. ...I covet/what they think we've got. AMV-81

The Convict. Anonymous. Ah, don't you hear the clinking of my chain? CoSo

The Convict. Anthony Frisch. Typed on a blue card: LEVELSQUE, A. And: LIFE. CaP

The Convict of Clonmala. Anonymous. While this heart, once so gay,/Shall be cold in Clonmala. AnIL; AnIV; IrPN; NBM; OnYI; OxBI; SD

A Convict's Lament on the Death of Captain Logan. Anonymous. You'll leave such tyrants far behind! PoAu 1-2

A Convict's Tour to Hell. Francis MacNamara. I woke and found 'twas but a dream. NOAV

Convicted (excerpt). Harry Edward Mills. Of him whose grief was fatally sincere. PeD

The Conviction. John Millington Synge. With death undying due/To soothe the pang of life. SyP

The Convicts' Ball. Ambrose Bierce. And Hubert Howe Bancroft sent his regrets. BPAW

The Convicts' Rum Song. Anonymous. If ye'll only gimme RUM! NOAV

Convinced by Sorrow. Elizabeth Barrett Browning. Be pitiful, O God! BLRP; WBLP

The Convoy. Juan Antonio Corretjer. This is a pause/for love. It is only/a brief pause. InW

Convoy. William Jay Smith. Ask the man struck dead by the life raft somewhere aft. WaP

Coo-Pe-Coo. Anonymous. And it will do, do, do. PBBP

Coogan's Wood. Francis Stuart. Where life is shrunk to what can be fired from a gun? NeIP

The Cook. Ray A. Young Bear. ...three dwarves in search/of tobacco. CDW

Cook County. Archibald MacLeish. And snow on the sand where in summer the water was... CrMA

The Cooky-Nut Trees (A Tale of the Pilliwinks). Albert Bigelow Paine. Enticing the gingerbread goodies that grew/At the top of the cooky-nut tree. OBCA

The Cool, Cool Country. Shaw Neilson. 'Tis the fine country/Open below. PoAu 1-2

The Cool Gold Wines of Paradise. Robert Farren. joyful and gathering thirst for joy/throughout Unending Day. AnIV; SeCePo

The Cool, Grey City of Love. George Sterling. O cool, grey city of love! BPAW

Cool Tombs. Carl Sandburg. get more than the lovers...in the dust...in the cool/tombs. AmP; AmPP; AnFE; AP; AtBAP; BLPL; BoLiVe; CMoP; CoAnAm; HAP; HBMV; HeIP; MoAB; MoAmPo; MoVE; NoAm; NOBA; OBSP; PAL; PoLf; TAP; TrGrPo; ViBoPo; WHA

The Cool Web. Robert Graves. We shall go mad no doubt and die that way. AWP; ChMP; GTBS-P; NIP; NoAm; NoP; OxBTC; PoA; PrIm; SCV

Coole and Ballylee, 1931. William Butler Yeats. Where the swan drifts upon a darkening flood. CMoP; GTBS-P; NoAm; NOBI; OBMV; PPP

Corner Boys. Bryan MacMahon. Where the corner boys are growing grey,/ Dreaming of sunny skies. OnYI

The Corner Knot. Robert Graves. "Ay, a remembrancer, but nothing more." NYBP

Corner Lot. Sharon Bryan. white throats that could only last the night. MAYP

Corner Meeting. Langston Hughes. His words jump down/to stand/in their/places. CAD

The Corner of the Field. Frances Cornford. Then calmly smiled at him before they kissed. ELU

Corner Seat. Louis MacNeice. Then why does your reflection seem/So lonely in the moving night? MoVE

The Corner Stone. Walter De la Mare. And even of man not a shadow remain/Of all he has done? BrPo

The Cornet. Henry Howard, Earl of Surrey. In summer's sun, in winter breath of frost,/Of your fair eyes whereby the light is lost. OBSC

Cornfield. Leo Cox. A sweet surmise of grief of harassed corn? CaP

The Cornfield. Elizabeth Madox Roberts. It comes together like a fan. GoJo; SUS

Cornfield Holler. Anonymous. Den sometimes I think she ought to be buried alive. ABF

Cornfield Myth. Mary Goose. Long, long ago one hot summer day. STE

Cornfields in Accra. Christine Ama Ata Aidoo. Who/Says/We shall not survive among the turbines? WPOW

A Cornish Litany (excerpt). Anonymous. ...Things that go bump in the Night,/Good Lord deliver us. WSC

Cornishmen. Anonymous. You shall know the Cornishmen. FaBoUs

Cornwallis. Tony Beyer. decoy/for sharks in the night OCNZ

Cornwallis's Surrender. Anonymous. And may Great Britain rue the day/ Her hostile bands came hither. PAH

The Coromandel Fishers. Sarojini Naidu. Row, brothers, row, to the blue of the verge, where the low/sky mates with the sea. BBV; EtS; MCCG

Corona. Paul Celan. It is time it were time./It is time. VWA

La Corona. John Donne. Salvation to all that will is nigh. OBS

Coronach. Alexander Scott. I hear their wae/Greetan greetan dark and daw,/Their dregy ere I dae. OxBS

Coronary Thrombosis. William Price Turner. the doomed only trade that he knows. OxBS

Coronation. Helen Fiske Jackson. And made his eldest son one day/Slave in his father's stead. AA; BeLS; GN; HBV 1-2

Coronation. Edward Perronet. And crown Him Lord of all! BLSo; HBV 1-2; TreFS; WGRP

Coronation Day at Melrose. Peter Bladen. Coronation Day was over in the little town of Melrose. PoAu 1-2

Coronemus Nos Rosis Antequam Marcescant. Thomas Jordan. Must all come to nothing a hundred years hence. HBV 1-2; OBEV

Coroner's Jury. Leonard Alfred George Strong. Walking the moors, keeping apart/And quiet, like. OxBTC

The Coronet. Andrew Marvell. May crown thy Feet, that could not crown thy Head. AnAnS 1; LoBV; MeLP; MePo; NCEP; NOCV; NoP; OBS; OxBoCh; PoPle; PP; SeCV 1-2

A Coronet for His Mistress Philosophy. George Chapman. But dwell in darkness; for your god is blind. CoBE

Corporal Pym. Walter De la Mare. He had no fear of death;/Nor Death of him. FaBoEE

Corporal Stare. Robert Graves. A fag-end dropped on the silent road. BrPo

Corporate Entity. Archibald MacLeish. Weeps at a nude by Michael Angelo. OBAL

Corposant. Peter Redgrove. Spoiling the market value of the house. NePoEA-2; OxBTC

Corps d'Esprit. Heather McHugh. the body of your life goes under. AmPA

The Corpse. George Moore. I read, and, bending, kiss her reverently. SyP

Corpse-Bearing. Thomas Ashe. Never to carry a corpse/Again, to my dying day. NOBV

The Corpse-Keeper. Anonymous. It will not be long/Before I come and visit you. BoWoP

The Corpse-Plant. Adrienne Rich. Only death's insect whiteness/crooks its neck in a tumbler/where I placed its sign by choice. CoPo

Corpses in the Wood. Ernst Toller. O! Violated.../O! Murdered... TrJP

Corpus Christi (B vers.). Anonymous. At that bed's head there grows a thorn,/Which was never so blossomed since Christ was born. BaBo; GBP

The Corpus Christi Carol (from Scotland). Anonymous. Stemming the wounds when they did bleed. GBP

Corpus Christie (A vers.). Anonymous. And by that bede side there standeth a stone,/Corpus Christi wreten there on. BaBo; EnPo; FaBoBa; GBP; MeEL; NOBE; NoP; OAEL 1-2; OxBM; SCV

The Corral. Earle Thompson. Head arched, eyes glancing/toward the passing school bus. STE

A Correct Compassion. James Kirkup. ...a correct compassion, that performs its love, and makes it live. ChMP; FaBoTw; ImOP; OxBTC; SeCePo

Correspondence. Laura Chester. ...And let the paper/fall, just as I make (imaginary) love to you–Real in the mail. APU

Correspondence:. Lady Ise. embroidered on my sleeve/is wet with tears. BoWoP

Correspondence between Mr. Harrison in Newcastle and ... Stevie Smith. Than go to church with oily Sue and afterwards to bed. FaBoNo; NLV; OxBC

The Correspondence School Instructor Says Goodbye... Galway Kinnell. their loneliness/given away in poems, only their solitude kept. NOBA; NoP; TAP

Correspondences. Charles Baudelaire.
Amber and myrrh, benzoin and musk condense/To transports of the spirit and the sense! AWP; LiTW
Like myrrh, or musk, or amber, that excite/The ecstasies of sense, the soul's delight. NAWM 1-2
That seize the spirit and the senses exquisite. SyP

Correspondences. Robert Duncan. ...cause areas of torment in the unreal like stones in an open/field. PoM

Correspondent. Witter ("Emanuel Morgan") Bynner. Out of a dead man's grave, whom no one knows. AnFE

Corrib. An Emblem. Donald Davie. A nymph took root, and here and there a laurel. PoCh

The Corridor. Thom Gunn. And go, one hand held out, to meet a friend? NePoEA; PPP

Corries. Janet M. Smith. Springs, streams and water, the hills' own life. PoSH

The Corrs. Tom MacIntyre. But burrow seed, you're root and rind. CIP

The Corrupt Man in the French Pub. Brian Higgins. He said he was drinking too much. OxBTC

Corruption. Patu Simoko. and my spear is bent on more struggle! WhB

Corruption. Henry Vaughan.
And he was sure to view them. CAW
"Arise! Thrust in thy sickle"? JCP; NOCV; OAEL 1-2; OBS; OxBoCh; Prf; SeCP; SeCV 1-2

Corrymeela. Moira O'Neill. Sweet Corrymeela, an' the same soft rain. AnIV; AWP; HBV 1-2

A Corsage Bouquet. Charles Henry Luders. Myrtilla, to-night/Wears Jacqueminot roses. HBV 1-2

Corsons Inlet. Archie Randolph Ammons. that tomorrow a new walk is a new walk. CoAP; NoAm; NOBA; NoP; PPP

Cortege. Paul Verlaine. Of her familiar animals/Indifferent or unaware. AWP; OBVE

Cortege for Colette. Jean Garrigue. ...when the touched body/Gives forth the divine humors of rain, leaves, and love. NYBP

Cortes. Albert Rios. The trees bore skulls as fruit/and we feasted. GP

Coruisk. Walter Chalmers Smith. And Bidein's turret struck with sunset fire. PoSH

Corydon and Tityrus. Anonymous. The neighbors all to this thrice blessed stall. CAW

Corydon's Complaint. Samuel Pordage. I'le yield to destiny. CavP

Corydon's Farewell, on Sailing in the Late Expedition Fleet. Anonymous. The homefelt joys, beyond expression dear,/Deserve an elegy, a parting tear. NOEC

Corydon to His Phyllis. Sir Edward Dyer. She cannot love, and therefore thou must die! EIL

Cosher Bailey's Engine. Anonymous. Did you ever see/Such a funny thing before? FSW

Cosmetic. Gretchen Herbkersman. unwatched/woman. AMV-80

Cosmic Eye. A. K. Redwing. you are an episode of life under constant scrutiny. VoR

The Cosmic Fabric. Yakov Polonsky. Smooth and fine, with beauty stored,/Shines the garment of the Lord! EaLo

Cosmogony. Edgell Rickword. splashes, and half recalls a waking dream. FaBoTw

Cosmogony (parody). D. C. Berry. The chin is where you fall off/When I look at my shoes. BXAP

Cossimbazar. Henry Sambrooke Leigh. Join in the chorus, my hookabadar. NA

The Cost. Anthony Hecht. Or remember that that fifteen-year campaign/ Won seven years of peace? OxBC

The Cost. Flora L. Osgood. If you put Jesus first and His glory/All things will be added to thee. STF

The Cost-of-Living Mother Goose. Dow Richardson. Tuna on toast. QQQ

The Cost of Pretending. Peter Davison. ...One who survives everything/ Will shortly survive even himself. TW

The Cot. Grover Amen. adrift in true night with the stars, the river winds and the abstract/faiths of October. NYBP; NYP

The Country Clergyman's Trip to Cambridge. Thomas Babington, Lord Macaulay. We were rumbling o'er Trumpington stones. NBM; OBSV; OxBoLi

The Country Clown. John Trumbull. And every voice shall echo thine. AnAmPo

A Country Club Romance. Derek Walcott. And the blondes pray God to "teach us/To profit from her mistake." OxBC

Country Club Sunday. Phyllis McGinley. Moans, shuns the light, and gulps tomato juice. CrMA

The Country Curate. Henry Taylor. And falls, alas! unpitied, as he lived before. NOEC

Country Dance. Edith Sitwell. He runs like the rough satyr Sun./Come away! NoAm

A Country Dance. Turner, Charles Tennyson. Till with the refluent dance she reappears. NOBV; VLP

The Country Doctor. Will Carleton. And the weak old country doctor/Is entitled to a furlough for his brain and for his heart. BLPA

Country Drive-In. Josephine Jacobsen. How can I fit her mammoth grief/into the dark below my matchstick ribs? AmC

The Country Faith. Norman Gale. This is the country faith/And best of all! HBV 1-2; OBEV; OBVV; WGRP

The Country Fiddler. John Montague. So succession passes, through strangest hands. FaBoIP

The Country Girl's Policy; or, The Cockney Outwitted. *Anonymous.* If she has but Wit to take care of her T–, she may pass for a/Maid again. CoMu

A Country God. Edmund Charles Blunden. And summer not to come again. MoBrPo

Country Gods. Cometas. Somewhere in this sunny plain/Echo waits upon her lover. FaBoCh; LoGBV

Country Greeting. Frank Steele. and waggles his graves at me. Psk

Country Hirings. *Anonymous.* ...all sorts of weather/Both cold, wet and snow. OBET

The Country House. Louis Simpson. and I can't think or write. NOBA

The Country Inn: Song: "Though richer swains thy love pursue." Joanna Baillie. But how will Nan prefer my boon,/In tatter'd hose and clouted shoon! OBRV

The Country Justice. John Langhorne.
Here, then, O JUSTICE thy own Power forbear;–/The sole Protector of th' unpitied Fair! LaA
His creeping soul in Sternhold's creeping lays! NOEC

Country Landscape. Sherod Santos. They have never forgotten. AMV-80

Country Letter. John Clare. To go three journeys ere your letter came. CBEP; NCEP

A Country Life. Randall Jarrell. The angel kneeling with the wreath/Sees, in the moonlight, graves. MiAP; MoAmPo

A Country Life: To His Brother, M. Tho: Herrick. Robert Herrick. Till when, in such assurance live, ye may/Nor feare, or wish your dying day. CaPo; SeCP; SeCV 1-2

The Country Lovers. *Anonymous.* Let me be king, diddle diddle,/You be the queen. UnTE

The Country Lovers. George Smith. They'll meet us ere we leave the narrow way. NOEC

The Country Man (excerpt). George Farewell. Here limited shall stand my wildest wish. NOEC

The Country Mouse. Abraham Cowley. With peace, let tares and acorns be my food. SeCP

The Country Mouse and the City Mouse. Richard Scrafton Sharpe. And I feast on fat bacon and charming grey peas.' OxBChV

Country Music. Plato. And lull thy dreamy eyelids to sweet forgetful bliss. LiTW

The Country North of Belleville. Al Purdy. and we must enquire the way/of strangers– NOBC

Country Nun. Geoff Page. towards the pure insistence/of the bell. CBAP

The Country of a Thousand Years of Peace. James Merrill. ...its finish and sharp weight/Flashing in his own hand. PoCh

Country of No Lack. Jean Starr Untermeyer. What care can move, what grief can chill? MoAmPo

Country Pastor. Mitsuko Inoue. Though she sometimes gets angry like a nail. LiTW

Country Pleasures. Martial (Marcus Valerius Martialis). And still in Rome a pale-faced client be! AWP

Country Press. Rosemary Dobson. I shall go homewards in the Western Star. FaBoWP; NOAV

Country Reverie. Carol Coates. stand tiptoe to touch the stars. CaP

Country Roads. Rolf Jacobsen. travelling over the great and luminous Sahara lit by clouds. NU

Country School. Allen Curnow. And the things you drew on the wall. AnNZ

Country Singer. Jean Nordhaus. carrying ahead of us/our twin bouquets of light. AmC

A Country Song. Sir Philip Sidney. More envied Phoebus for his western flying. OBSC; SiPS

A Country Song. Douglas Stewart. Wild as a dingo, fresh as a brumby? NOAV

Country Stars. William Meredith. the bright watchers are still there. GrPl

Country Statutes. *Anonymous.* With love and honour spend the night at statutes, fairs and races. OBET

The Country Store. *Anonymous.* Are found in heaps and stacks and piles within the country store. BLPA

Country Summer. Léonie Adams. Morning and evening in the corn. AnEnPo; GoJo; LiTM; MoAB; MoAmPo; MoPo; MoVE; TrGrPo; ViBoPo

Country Thought. Sylvia Townsend Warner. And One at Idbury. MoBrPo

Country Towns. Kenneth Slessor. I'll think it's noon at half-past four! CBAP; PoAu 1-2

Country Trucks. Monica Shannon. They know more trucks are coming/As surely as the moon. BrR; TiPo

Country Tune. Elizabeth Riddell. The cowboy's eyes of bitter blue/Or the brave black fellow. BoAV

Country Villa. Jean Garrigue. The children had put small Siennese banners in its prickly/sides and the colors drooped... TAP

A Country Walk. Thomas Kinsella. "The waters hurtle through the flooded night..." CIP; CMoP; NMP

Country Walk. Geoffrey Taylor. And then not Truth as seen–but as seen from. OxBI

A Country Wedding. *Anonymous.* Now when shall we see such a wedding in town? HBV 1-2

The Country Wedding. Thomas Hardy. And carried 'em there in an after year. UnPo

A Country without a Mythology. Douglas LePan. ...daubed/With war-paint, teeters some lust-red manitou? NOBC

Country Wooing (parody) (excerpt). J. C. Squire. Some good old hermit of a horse that fed/With loud bite in his dark and tranquil field. BXAP

The Countryman's Return. Dylan Thomas. And O to cut the green field, leaving/One rich street with hunger in it. OxBTC

A Countryman's Wooing. Theocritus. She went to tend her flock; while Daphnis ran/Back to his herded bulls, a happy man. ErPo

A Countrywoman of Mine. Elaine Goodale Eastman. She's but to please herself the world to/please. AA

The County Ball (excerpt). Winthrop Mackworth Praed. Let youth take fire!–Sir Paul takes snuff. OBNC

County Guy. Sir Walter Scott. But where is County Guy? OBRV

The County Jail. Jimmy Santiago Baca. will get up and leave the circle,/return to his bunk. LFAC

County Mayo. Anthony Raftery. For age itself would leave me there and I'd be young again. AnIL

The County of Mayo. *Anonymous.* And I be sailing, sailing from the County of Mao. AnIV; BIrV

The County of Mayo. George Fox. And I sailing, sailing swiftly from the county of Mayo. IrPN; OBEV; OnYI; OxBI

County Roads. Thomas Rabbit. Can't be traffic. There's no one here but you. MAYP

County Sligo. Louis MacNeice. Like the tombs of nameless kings. OnYI

Coup de Grace. A. D. Hope. O, what a round of applause! DFT; PPP

The Coup de Grace. Edward Rowland Sill. I am a phantom, and all mortals seem/But phantoms, and my life fades as a dream. AA

The Couple. Ana Blandiana. He'll see only the back from which he broke,/Bleeding, chilling,/Of the other. WPOW

The Couple. Sandra Hochman. We must/Cover them up/To/The post office. CTBA; NYBP

The Couple. Joel Oppenheimer. how else to be fecund if not/to put up with a man. CoPo

Couple. Walter Stone. Some compromise is possible with life. NYBP

Couple. Mary Swope. to walk the dog around the neighborhood. AMV-81

The Couple Overhead. William Meredith. After a while it dies. HoPM; NoAm; TW

The Couple Upstairs. Hugo Williams. And talk excitedly about ourselves, like guests. PoL

Couplets for WCW. Martha Christina. while worms are turning handsprings in the sod. AMV-80

Couplets, XX. Robert Mezey. Be joined to the small grains of the brotherhood. FYAP

Courage. Matthew Arnold. Joined to its clearness, of their force! OAEL 1-2

Courage. Stopford Augustus Brooke. Sweet hallelujahs shall be sung/To welcome us to God. WGRP

Courage. Helen Frazee-Bower. But I shall smile with less than joy,/And laugh with more than pain. HBMV

Courage. Paul Gerhardt. And publish with our latest breath,/The love and guardian care. WGRP

Courage, All. Edwin Markham. And the Great Word is waiting to be spoken! HBMV

Cowboy Jack. *Anonymous.* Out·on the lonely prairie, where skies are always blue. CoSo

The Cowboy's Ball. Henry Herbert Knibbs. But this beats dancin' at the Cowboys' Ball. PoOW

The Cowboy's Dance Song. *Anonymous.* When I put the cowboy trimmings on that high-toned dance. CoSo

The Cowboy's Dream. *Anonymous.* Have your name in his big Tally Book! MaC

The Cowboy's Dream. Charles J. Finger. Roll on, little dogies, roll on. BPAW

The Cowboy's Fate. Wallace D. Coburn. Where good cow-boys ride in comfort,/Far beyond the "Great Divide." PoOW

Cowboy's Gettin'-Up Holler. *Anonymous.* Git up now and get it while it's hot. CoSo; TrAS

The Cowboy's Lament. *Anonymous.*
All wrapped in white linen as cold as the clay. BLSo
For I'm a poor cowboy and I know I've done wrong. BFSS
We all loved our comrade although he'd done wrong. GBP; MaC

The Cowboy's Lament (I). *Anonymous.* "This Jasper was slow with a gun." CoSo; FaFP; TreFS

The Cowboy's Lament (II). *Anonymous.* Well, the women oughta carry me, follow me to my grave. CoSo

The Cowboy's Lament (III). *Anonymous.* Got shot though the bowels, and you see where I lay. CoSo

The Cowboy's Lament; or, The Streets of Laredo (A vers.). *Anonymous.* For I'm a young cowboy and dying alone. ViBoFo

The Cowboy's Lament; or, The Streets of Laredo (B vers.). *Anonymous.* For I'm a wild lumberjack, and I know I've done wrong. ViBoFo

The Cowboy's Life. James Barton Adams. As the clouds of white/That swim in the summer skies. BPAW

The Cowboy's Life. *Anonymous.*
His saddle his kingly throne. AmFN; SoPo; TiPo
When his heart is light/As the clouds of white/That swim in the summer skies. CoSo

The Cowboy's Life Is a Very Dreary Life. *Anonymous.* But you better stay at home with your kind and loving little wife. AmFP

The Cowboy's Meditation. *Anonymous.* And off round the herd I go dashing,/A reckless cowboy of the plains. CoSo

The Cowboy's Return. *Anonymous.* Saying, "See, I am your own true cowboy,/Who has seven long years been gone from thee." BFSS

Cowboy's Salvation Song. Robert V. Carr. So it's move along, you dogies, 'fore th' devil brands you sure. PoOW

Cowboy Song. Charles Causley. And my suit is made of wood. NePoEA

Cowboy Song. Tom Veitch. Burning down Fear Village/And last week's jokes. ANYP

Cowboy to Pitching Bronco. *Anonymous.* Flamdoozleledum! ABF

The Cowboy Up to Date. *Anonymous.* Your cowboy is never complete/Without a cigarette in his hand. CoSo

The Cowboys' Christmas Ball. William Lawrence Chittenden. ...and I'll oftentimes recall/That lively gaited sworray–"The Cowboys' Christmas/Ball." BPAW; CoSo

The Coweta County Courthouse. James Miller Robinson. I knelt and cried and almost prayed. AMV-80

The Cowman's Prayer. *Anonymous.* But I've had my say, and now, Amen. CoSo

Cowper at Tea. Barry Pain. Pray, Mary, fill the teapot up,/And do not make it strong. HBV 1-2

Cowper's Grave. Elizabeth Barrett Browning. And I, on Cowper's grave, should see his rapture in a vision. HBV 1-2; OBVV

Cowper's Three Hares. Charles Tennyson Turner. And mix your woodland breath with Cowper's sighs. FM

Cows. James Reeves. A-chewing,/A-mooing,/To pass the hours away. NTCP; PoSC

Cows Are Coming Home in Maine. Robert P. Tristram Coffin. The cows are coming home in Maine. DuDa

The Cows at Night. Hayden Carruth. ...And then/very gently it began to rain. SV

Cows Grazing at Sunrise. William Matthews. now that we call the little/we remember of it "the past"? AMV-81; NPAW

The Cows near the Graveyard. Howard Nelson. like two hands about to touch. NU

The Coy Lass Dress's Up in Her Best. *Anonymous.* You shall not rumple my Commode. ErPo

The Coy Shepherdess; or, Phillis and Amintas. *Anonymous.* But night being come they hasted home,/and kindly kist and parted. CoMu

Coyote. Bret (Francis Bret Harte) Harte. A four-footed friar in orders of gray! BPAW

The Coyote. Carter Revard. The storm made music, when it changed my world. VoR

The Coyote and the Locust. *Anonymous.* Playing a flute! AWP

Coyote and the Star. Arthur Guiterman. "You Callow Coyote, don't dance with no/Star! BPAW

Coyote Brother Song. Annette Arkeketa West. far from the fist/of your mother's/flesh TWSS

Coyote, Coyote, Please Tell Me. Peter Blue Cloud. Coyote,/he belongs to none. STE

Coyote's Daylight Trip. Paula Gunn Allen. I bury my dead. I mourn/for four full days. TWSS

Cozzo Grillo. H. B. Mallalieu. Throbbing, beneath the wound, the whole world's pain. WaP

The Crab. Conrad Aiken. a single crusty/or crustacean/word. BoAnP·

Crab. John Blight. But such creatures; much of this wild-shaped chance! BoAV

Crab-Apple. Ethel Talbot. "Crab-apple red!"/Said they, and I woke up in bed. BiCB; TiPo

Crab Orchard Sanctuary: Late October. Thomas Kinsella. A slow hot glare out on the lake/spreading over the water. IPY

The Crab Tree. Oliver St. John Gogarty.
Is sweet or is bitter/Which makes it stand up. OxBI
Which makes it stand up. AnIL; OxBI

Crabbing. Marky Daniel. veiled by the eelgrass undersea. AMV-81

Crabbing. Norman Levine. The earth made windows. Who watched our homecoming. CaP; OBCV

Crabe dans Calalou. *Anonymous.* Sleep, baby mine,/Crabs are in the pot. OuSiCo

Crabs. Marge Piercy. like love or any other stubborn itch. NLV

The Crack. Michael Goldman. ...but had begun/serious work on staring at a face/his hammer had laid bare by luck alone. NYBP

The Crack. J. C. Hall. The garden reverberate with the voice/I hid from once, now run to find. HaMV

Crack in the Wall Holds Flowers. Adam David Miller. Is not soothed by the prospect of flowers. PoBA

The Crackling Twig. James Stephens. In three great jumps, he bounded to the shade,/And disappeared among the greenery! ELU

The Cracks. Robert Creeley. ...be left/with a memory/or an insinuation or two/of cracks in a pavement. ConAP

The Cradle. Roland Robinson. cradles you in the trees, as the arm/of the mountain holds the light of the farm. NOAV

The Cradle and the Cross. Albert Simpson Reitz. Our deepest devotion and homage we/bring. STF

Cradle and Throne. *Anonymous.* Shall give Thee a scepter, a crown, and/a throne. STF

Cradle Hymn. Martin Luther. And stay by my cradle/Till morning is nigh. BiCB; ChBR; OHIP; SUS

Cradle Hymn. Isaac Watts.
Here's no oxen near thy bed. SoPo; SUS
Not a mother's fondest wishes/Can to greater joys aspire. CEP; LoBV; OBEC; OxBoCh; PoEL 1-5; SBVL
See His face, and sing His praise! HBV 1-2; OBEV; OxBChV; TreFS

Cradle Song. *Anonymous.* You cannot know how I, your mother,/Think of you and weep. EaLo; TrJP

A Cradle Song. William Blake.
Heaven and earth to peace beguiles. EnRP; OBCP; OBEC; SBVL; ViBoPo
Then the dreadful night shall break. FPL; GTBS; HBV 1-2; HBVY; OBEV; PoLf; PoPl

A Cradle Song. Nicholas Breton. God bless my babe, and lullaby/From this my father's quality. HBV 1-2; NOBE; OBEV

A Cradle Song. Padraic Colum. Mary puts round him/Her mantle of blue. CAW; GoBC; ISi; OnYI; OxBI

Cradle-Song. Adelaide Crapsey. My baby, my dear son. HBMV; ISi

Cradle Song. James L. Duff. This little while, oh, Thou art mine,/Jesukin. ISi

Cradle Song. Lawrence Durrell. mimic your mother's lovely face. NAs

Cradle Song. Samuel Hoffenstein. To survive and go on getting worse. DBV

Cradle Song. Louis MacNeice.
And wind us up for ever and ever. MoAB; MoBrPo; OxBI
Awake all night who know/The pity of it all. PoPl

Cradle Song. Sarojini Naidu. A little lovely dream. BrR

Cradle Song. Josephine Preston Peabody. To my heart, awake. HBV 1-2

Cradle Song. Yona Wallach. that's not/what/will calm me/no/that's not it. VWA

A Cradle Song. William Butler Yeats. Ah, how I shall miss you/When you have grown. NOBV; PoPl

Cradle-Song at Twilight. Alice Meynell. An unmaternal fondness keep/Her alien eyes. NOBV

Cradle Song for Miriam. Louis MacNeice. No one remembers us. NAs

Cradle Song of the Virgin. *Anonymous.* But lay Thy feet to my breast/And keep Thee from the cold. ISi

The Craftsman. Marcus B. Christian. "He who creates true beauty ever lives." PoNe

Craftsman. Luci Shaw. Carpenter's son, carpenter's son,/was it a job well done? TrCP

Craftsmen. Victoria Mary (Vita) Sackville-West. But holds them all beneath his hands at last. OxBTC

The Crafty Farmer. *Anonymous.* Saying, "If ever our daughter gets wed,/It will help to enlarge her portion." BaBo; ESPB

The Crafty Farmer (The Oxford Merchant). *Anonymous.* Laddy tell I day, tell I do, laddy laddy tell I day. AmFP

The Crafty Miss of London; or, The Fryar Well Fitted. *Anonymous.* A woful disaster, he says Pater-Noster,/but has neither Money nor Cloaths. CoMu; OxBB

Crag Jack's Apostasy. Ted Hughes. Keep more than the memory/Of a wolf's head, of eagles' feet. EaLo

Craigbilly Fair. *Anonymous.* And away went the beggar-men all in a row. GBP

Cranach. Sir Herbert Read. sly naked damsels nodding their downy plumes. BrPo; FaBoMo

The Cranberry Song. Barney Reynolds. And wish the cranberries would never play out. AmFP

Crane. Joseph Langland. And flipped, past sparkling regions, underground. NYBP

The Crane. Charles Tomlinson. For lifting intangible weights/Into real walls. MoBrPo

The Crane Is My Neighbour. Shaw Neilson. And the ripples are thoughts coming out to the edge of a dream. CBAP; PoAu 1-2

The Crane's Ascent. Nick Bozanic. above everything, and the sun/rising. AMV-81

Cranes. J. R. S. Davies. Getting used to themselves having been numb too long. PoL

The Cranes. Po Chu-i. The garden-boy is leading the cranes home. OBVE

The Cranes of Ibycus. Emma Lazarus. Bore him the greetings of the deathless/dead! AA

The Cranial Nerves. *Anonymous.* A Finn And German Vault And Hop. FaBoUs

Cranmer. C. H. Sisson. And saw in the smithy his own fire burning. FaBoTw

Cranston near the City Line. Ted Berrigan. ...it was his happy song, happy with me, it was 1942 or 4,/and he was 53. APU

Crapshooters. Carl Sandburg. This too was in the savvy of the Chaldeans. VGW

Craqueodoom. James Whitcomb Riley. While the Queen of the Wunks drifted over the tide/With a long piece of crape to her tail. OBAL

Crash at Leithfield. Allen Curnow. Like foul birds over the dead, and none to drive them away. AnNZ

Crass Times Redeemed by Dignity of Souls. Peter Viereck. In every soul the soul of all our souls. HoPM; MiAP

Craven. Sir Henry Newbolt. Princes of courtesy, merciful, proud, and strong. HBV 1-2; HBVY; PAH

Cravings during Pregnancy. M. Saint-Marthe. And Putid Clotts defil'd her Breasts obscene. FaBoUs

The Craw's Killed the Poussie, O! *Anonymous.* But waur than a', the mickle craw/Has ta'en and killed our poussie, O! BoAnP

Crawdad. *Anonymous.* Honey, sugar baby mine. FSW

Crawl Blues. Vincent McHugh. Got my hooks on the ladder an I'm climbin up the wall ErPo

Crawl into Bed. Quandra Prettyman. Pretend very dead. BOLo

Crawl, Laugh. Issa. For you are two years old/This morning. OFD

Crayon House. Muriel Rukeyser. and the beginning was real. The drawing of a child. EyDe

Crazed. Walter De la Mare. While the lank sails clacked idly by/High on the windy hill. OBSP

A Crazed Girl. William Butler Yeats. But sang, "O sea-starved, hungry sea." PAI

Crazed Man in Concentration Camp. Agnes Gergely. and it meant nothing to him to be shot dead. BoWoP

The Crazed Moon. William Butler Yeats. They are spread wide that each/May rend what comes in reach. MOON

Crazy Arithmetic. D'Arcy Wentworth Thompson. But how can 2 and 3 make four,/If 3 and 2 make faces? FaBoCo

Crazy Bill to the Bishop (parody). Robert Peters. Gyres run on, and we poor souls/Hurry after. BXAP

Crazy Dogholkoda. Mary Tallmountain. "Crazy dogholkoda, hah?" he growled,/looking over his shoulder. TWSS

Crazy Horse. Lance Henson. in/the/hollow/wind VoR

Crazy Horse Returns to South Dakota. Harley Elliott. they stare into their coffee cups. NeAC

Crazy Jane and Jack the Journeyman. William Butler Yeats. Mine must walk when dead. CMoP

Crazy Jane on the Mountain. William Butler Yeats. And I cried tears down. CMoP

Crazy Movie. Gregorio Barrios. the road was invisible in the dark. FIA

Crazy Song to the Air of "Dixie. (with music). *Anonymous.* I do. I don't. She was bred in old Kentucky. AS

Crazy to Be Alive in Such a Strange World. Lawrence Ferlinghetti. Are you by any chance a registered/DEMOCRAT? CTBA

The Crazy World. William Gay. Which wanting, I must die,/Or having, I shall live? BoAV; PoAu 1-2

The Created. Jones Very. He saw the lord of all His creatures/stand. AmP; MAmP; NOCV; QFR

The Creation. *Anonymous.* That death may not cleave to us. WTO

Creation. V. N. Bhushan. And play at precedence over each other's might! ACV

Creation. Ambrose Bierce. He woke–His smile alone illumined/space. AA

Creation. Robin Gurr. Nor does the Father do, for/already He has done. NOAV

The Creation. James Weldon Johnson. And man became a living soul./Amen. Amen. BALP; BANP; CDC; FaBV; GoSl; MoAmPo; PoBA; PoPl; TrCP; YaD

Creation. Louise Townsend Nicholl. And it will sound like mourning when he cries/And waits for no reply. GoYe

Creation. Alfred Noyes. And taste of Love and Death.' GoBC; OBVV

The Creation: According to Coyote. Simon J. Ortiz. And you know, I believe him. CDW

Creation Myths. Burton Raffel. ...I greet/My finished cosmology, I smile as a theory vanishes. AMV-80

The Creation of Man. *Anonymous.* Then rested in/Bliss of calm and quiet. WTO

The Creation of My Lady. Francesco Redi. And fashioned in the looms of Paradise. AWP

Creation of the Child. Susan Litwack. ...I awake/at the unforgettable instant/he dies. VWA

The Creation of the Moon. *Anonymous.* to see that the head had turned into the Moon. MOON

Creation's Lord, We Give Thee Thanks. William deWitt Hyde. The will to win it makes us free. AH

Creative Force. Maude Miner Hadden. Nature, instinct, creative force,/Fanned to a living flame. GoYe

Creator of Infinities. Chadwick Hansen. In gladness may thy will be done. AH

Creatrix. Anna Wickham. What hands so urge, what powers compel. MoBrPo

Creatures. Maxine W. Kumin. and all, all except the black horseleech/let pass my entering pale enormous flesh. BoAnP

Crecy. Francis Turner Palgrave. So let him have the spurs, and the glory! BeLS; HBV 1-2

Credences of Summer. Wallace Stevens. Complete in a completed scene, speaking/Their parts as in a youthful happiness. AP; CoBMV

Credit. *Anonymous.* Help me, Lord, in stress and struggle/Just to keep my eyes on Thee. STF

The Creditor. Louis MacNeice. Over and under and all ways/All days and always. EaLo

Credo. Leonard Cohen. the feet of fierce or humble priests/trample out the green. PeCV

Credo. Zona Gale. Only to feel this touching at my sleeve. TrPWD

Credo. Brewster Ghiselin. And sleep, the undivided sphere. PoA

Credo. Robinson Jeffers. Will remain when there is no heart to break for it. AnEnPo; MoAB; MoAmPo; PoPl

Credo. Georgia Douglas Johnson. ...conscience within/Is guidance enough for the conduct of men. PoBA

Credo. Alfred Kreymborg. He who can make the most of transient skies,/It seems to me deserves the only prize. AnAmPo

Credo. Seumas (James Starkey) O'Sullivan. The Lord of life has died. OnYI

Credo. John Oxenham. Not what, but Whom! BLRP

Credo. Edwin Arlington Robinson. I feel the coming glory of the Light! AnNE; CMoP; MoAmPo; NePA; OxBA; TAP; TrCP; TreFT; WGRP

Credo. Arthur Symons. Which is the gate of death, the gate of birth. OBVV

Credo. Saul Tchernichovsky. And the wreath to crown the singer/Shall be gathered from my grave. LiTW

A Credo. William Makepeace Thackeray. "Who loves not wine, woman, and song,/He is a fool his whole life long!" HBV 1-2

Credo (excerpt). Richard Watson Gilder. Eternal Good that rules the summer flower/And all the worlds that people starry space! TrPWD

A Creed. *Anonymous.* Let me face the summons calmly/When Death beckons me away. STF

Creed. Walter Lowenfels. Beat on my tomb, rain-gods. PoNe

A Creed. Edwin Markham. The soul of man is cast. BLPA; PoPl

A Creed. John Masefield. Be smithied all to kingly gold. MoRP

A Creed. Norman McLeod. In the large and full assurance/Of its triumph,–I believe. WGRP

Creed. Anne Spencer. And He dare not be silent or send me away. CDC

Creed. Mary Ashley Townsend. When life falls from us like a withered husk. BLPA; FaBoBe

Creed of Mr. Nicholas Culpeper.   Patricia Beer.   And turned me into some concoction of his own.   OxBC

Creede.   Cy Warman.   And there is no night in Creede.   BPAW; PoOW

Creeds.   Karle Wilson Baker.   Wakes me, too–sleeping by the hedge–/To morning prayer!   HBMV; WGRP

Creeds.   Willard Wattles.   They look at stars, and think they are/Denominational.   HBMV

The Creek.   Roland Robinson.   You are that image which had never died/in me, Eve, of my primavera, personified.   NOAV

The Creek.   W. W. Eustace Ross.

The Creek of the Four Graves (excerpt).   Charles Harpur.   Thrilled to the roots for very happiness.   PoAu 1-2

The Creek-Road.   Madison Cawein.   And now a barefoot truant and his dog.   AA

Creep Afore Ye Gang.   James Ballantine.   Creep awa', my bairnie, creep afore ye gang.   HBV 1-2

The Creeper.   Tom Schmidt.   ...I rake the mess/the vines I rake/the vines.   NeAC

Creide's Lament for Cael.   Anonymous.   Many leaders fell at his hand/but his shield on the day of need was silent.'   NOBI

Cremation.   Robinson Jeffers.   Scatter the ashes.   ELU

The Cremation of Sam McGee.   Robert W. Service.   I cremated Sam McGee.   BLPL; FaFP; GoTF; MaC; NOBC; OBNV; PoLf; ShM; StPo; TreF

Crematorium.   Sir John Betjeman.   Strong, sly, and painful, doubt inserts its knife.   PoA

Cremona.   Arthur Conan Doyle.   For the evening air is chilly in Cremona.   HBV 1-2

Creole Girl.   Leslie Morgan Collins.   Blue nights and casual canzonets,/Creole Girl?   PoNe

A Creole Slave-Song.   Maurice Thompson.   I cannot cut the cane today.   AA

Crepe de Chine.   Tennessee Williams.   to assuage her true distress, her headache, and her exhaustion...   NYBP

Crepes Flambeau.   Tess Gallagher.   ...rough boards,/spotted horses in the frame.   AMV-81; MAYP

Crepuscular.   Richard Howard.   Max and I know this too: it will be night.   TwCP

Crescent Moon.   William Renton.   Upon the disc a moving spot/That would be, was, and now was not.   NOBV

Crescent Moon.   Elizabeth Madox Roberts.   It made us jump and laugh to see/The little new moon above the tree.   SUS

Cresophontes: Prayer to Peace.   Euripides.   and bitter strife whose pleasure is the sharp sword.   PoPl

Cresseid's Complaint against Fortune.   Robert Henryson.   Fortoun is fikkill, quhen scho beginnis and steiris.   MeEL

Cressid.   Nora Perry.   To look for the sunlight hair/That smites like a golden spear!   AA

Cressida.   James Keir Baxter.
–The amber necklace then, and the grey dress.   AnNZ
And rubbed it off again.   AnNZ
Is flawed by our inconstant waking dream.   AnNZ
O my dear and only.   AnNZ
–Their voices drown in the hiss of steam.   AnNZ
Time is like the falling snow.   AnNZ

Crest Jewel.   James Stephens.   In Him who dreams in me and you.   AnIL; MoAB; MoBrPo

Crethis.   Callimachus.   Sleeps here the sleep that must be slept by all.   AWP

Crew Cut.   David McCord.   A world of shouts and grunts and groans/Has vanished with the megaphones.   SD

Crew-Cuts.   Donald Hall.   and as merciless/as women.   MAT

A Crew Poem.   Edward Augustus, Jr. Blount.   The cock-swain almost crew.   AA

Crew Practice on Lake Bled, in Jugoslavia.   James Scully.   and wish you better than I do.   NYBP

The Crib.   Robert Finch.   Strange they should trouble to give the creche a crib.   OBCP

The Crib.   Christopher Morley.   That there was my/Immortality!   BiCB

The Cricket.   Vincent Bourne.   Lives not, aged though he be,/Half a span, compared with thee.   HBVY; PoLf

Cricket.   No Ch'on-myong.   retain the sorrow of my night again/there behind the stone steps.   PBWP

Cricket.   Clinton Scollard.   Would I might, with your ecstatic buoyance,/Fare forth singing!   HBV 1-2

The Cricket.   Frederick Goddard Tuckerman.   Rejoice or mourn, and let the world swing on/Unmoved by cricket song of thee or me.   FM; MAmP; NOBA; QFR

Cricket. An Heroic Poem.   James Dance.   While London, queen of cities! proudly vies,/And often grasps the well-disputed prize.   NOEC

The Cricket and the Greshope Wenten Hem to Fight.   Anonymous.   I may not shake my bagge for you.'   EBEV

The Cricket and the Star.   Mary Effie Lee Newsome.   If the cricket were that far away/I'd never hear it night or day.   GoSl

A Cricket Bowler.   Edward Cracroft Lefroy.   And the mid-stump three somersaults in air.   OBVV

The Cricket Kept the House.   Edith Matilda Thomas.   And sung from dawn to dark, from dark to dawn.   OBCA

The Cricket's Story.   Elias Nason.   To sing at our hearths of "Home, sweet Home."   HBV 1-2; HBVY

The Cricket Sang.   Emily Dickinson.   And so the night became.   MAPA

Crickets.   David McCord.   Alas, alas, in ever acre,/every one a ticket-taker.   NTCP

Crickets.   Aram Saroyan.   crickets   ANYP; MAT

Crickets and Locusts, Cicadas.   Rosalia de Castro.   I don't know whether it's pain.   PBWP

The Crier.   Michael Drayton.   Either impound it for a stray,/Or send it back to me!   EIL; InvP; OAEP

Cries Out of Blindness.   Tristan Corbiere.   I hear the knelling horn.   LiTW

Crime.   Robert Penn Warren.   Names over your name, and mourns/under the dry rafter.   AmP

Crime at Its Best.   Stoddard King.   So in spite of our virtue, it's hard to suppress/A sneaking affection for Frank and for Jess.   NLV

Crime Club.   Weldon Kees.   Screaming all day of war, screaming that nothing can be solved.   NaP

The Crimean Heroes.   Walter Savage Landor.   Despite of all your generals, ye prevail.   ALV

The Crimes of Lizzie Borden.   Anonymous.   She hit her mother forty-one.   FaBoCo; FaFP

Crimes of Lugalanne.   Enheduanna.   throw this man out of the city/and capture him!   BoWoP

Crimes of Passion.   Terry Stokes.
...that is all/anyone can ever ask.   AmPA
with all my heart.   AmPA

The Criminality of War.   Edward Hilton Young.   War's glorious art, and gives immortal fame.   PGD

The Crimson Cherry Tree.   Henry Treece.   Forgetting the black seasons of a race.   WaP

Crimson Nor Yellow Roses.   Theodore Wratislaw.   Thy breasts, thy hands, thy hair upcurled,/and my desire!   GBL

Crimson Tent.   John Dos Passos.   Nodding in her robes/On a roaring dromedary.   PoA

Criole Candjo.   Anonymous.   Oui, Miche, mo'oule rire.   ABF

Cripple Creek.   Anonymous.   Goin' down Cripple Creek/To 'ave some fun.   AmFP; FSW

Cripple Dick upon a Stick.   Anonymous.   To buy a pound o' woo'.   OxNR

The Cripple for Life.   Anonymous.   God bless you, dear Maggie, you've given new life to a poor volunteer.   AmFP

Crippled Child at the Window.   Melissa Cannon.   Earthlings! If you are my equals,/prove it and fly! Fly!   AMV-80

The Crippler.   Danny Siegel.   and promise my own children/that there are other ways/better ways/to be chosen.   VWA

Cripples.   Nina Cassian.   to retrieve the crutches which are essential to them/since they need them to beat us with.   VWA

Cripples.   J. D. Reed.   o hairlips pooping speech. O men and women.   NeAC

Crisis.   W.H. Auden.   Have to express our need of forgiveness.   AtBAP

The Crisis.   Robert Creeley.   Laughter releases rancor, the quality of mercy is not/strained.   FF; PPP

Crisis.   G. S. Fraser.   ..."there is something/Far wrong, certainly, somewhere. But with me or the world?"   NeBP

The Crisis.   John Greenleaf Whittier.   And mountain unto mountain call, Praise/God, for we are free!   PAH

Crispus Attucks.   Robert Earl Hayden.   ...propped up/by bayonets, forever falling.   CNA

Crispus Attucks.   John Boyle O'Reilly.   And so great a boon, by a brave man's death,/is never dearly bought!   PAH

Crispus Attucks McCoy.   Sterling A. Brown.   the soul of our hero goes marching on.   BPo

Cristina.   Robert Browning.   This world's use will have been ended.   MaVP; MBW 1-2; OAEP

The Critic.   John Farrar.   But poems are far, far better/For putting boys to sleep!   SoPo

A Critic.   Walter Savage Landor.   Have proved by every line you write.   ChTr; DBV; FaBoEE

Critic.   E. B. White.   He scarcely saw the play at all/For watching his reaction to it.   NLV

Critic and Poet.   Robert Fuller Murray.   Is himself a minor poet.   DBV

The Critic on the Hearth.   L. E. Sissman.   Thank God the silly bastard is extinct.   TW

The Critic's Rules.   Robert Lloyd.   Present you with a perfect piece,/Form'd on the model of old Greece.   OBEC

A Critical Fribble.   Charles Churchill.   And disappointed pedants stalk'd away.   OBEC

Critical Observations.   Archibald MacLeish.   Let us await the late American novel!   OBAL

Critics.   Martial (Marcus Valerius Martialis).   I would my guests should praise it, not the cooks.   AWP

The Critics.   Theodore Spencer.   And then the barnacles fastened on.   NYBP

Critics.   Jonathan Swift.   Who crowd the press with hourly trash.   OBEC; SeCePo

Critics and Connoisseurs.   Marianne Moore.   in proving that one has had the experience/of carrying a stick?   AnAmPo; AnEnPo; CMoP; FaBoWP; NePA; NoAm; NOBA; OxBA

Critics and Poets.   Geoffrey Grigson.   Sit down, with Shakespeare, to a P.E.N. Club supper.   FaBoEE

Critter.   W. M. Ransom.   Saw white.   CDW

Crochet Castle.   Thomas Love Peacock.   Has a grain of common sense in it, except my own.   ALV

Crockery.   Julia Budenz.   Each from a blue-veined pot.   AMV-80

The Crocodile.   *Anonymous.*   It's ten to one you'll find the shell of the wonderful crocodile.   CBEP

The Crocodile.   Oliver Herford.   I suppose if I must starve, I must!   OBCA

Crocodile.   William Jay Smith.   Came proudly down the steps to greet/The happy Crocodile!   OBCA

Crocodiles.   Mira Teru Kurka.   methodically tearing small holes/with her fingernails, sharp/as crocodile teeth.   APU

The Crocus.   Walter Crane.   To catch a sunbeam in her cup.   SoPo

Crocus.   Alfred Kreymborg.   and then lead on again the universe?   HBMV

Crocus.   Joan Murray.   Each year they are the first to rise.   AMV-80

Crocus Night.   James Schuyler.   Then the moon goes crocus.   PoM

The Crocuses.   Frances E. W. Harper.   When she knew her faithful children/Were loving her so much.   BlSi

Crocuses.   Josa.   And I must pick a few.   TiPo

Crocuses in the Grass.   John Gray.   And stir not–with their yellow eyes.   CAW

Croesus in Autumn.   Robert Penn Warren.   Now green is blown and every gold gone sallow.   AnAmPo

Cromek.   William Blake.   O Mr Cromek, how do ye do?   FiBHP; PV

Cromwell.   Robert Francis.   And just outside the door/The swords.   GP

Cromwell, Our Chief of Men.   John Milton.   Of hireling wolves, whose Gospel is their maw.   CABA

The Croodin Doo.   *Anonymous.*   Make my bed, mammie, now!   OxNR

Crooked Carol.   Norma Farber.   Mary had a baby:/Sing Whose, Whose!   PoL

The Crooked Footpath.   Oliver Wendell Holmes.   We still can see our Father's door!   HBV 1-2; TreF

The Crooked Gun.   *Anonymous.*   Now don't you think that I can live a noble gentleman?   OuSiCo

The Crooked Trail to Holbrook.   *Anonymous.*   Here's luck to every puncher that follows the bronco steer.   CoSo

A Croon on Hennacliff.   Robert Stephen Hawker.   O what a savoury supper/For my old dame and me.'   NOBV

The Cropdusting (parody).   William Zaranka.   "We Deliver."   BXAP

The Cropper Lads.   *Anonymous.*   Press forward evry gallant man/With hatchet, pike and gun.   OBET

The Croppy Boy.   *Anonymous.*   And you good Christians that do pass by/Just drop a tear for the Croppy Boy.   AmFP; AnIL; AnIV; CBEP; FaBoBa; FSW; NOBI; OxBoLi

The Croppy Boy.   William B. McBurney.   Breathe a prayer and a tear for the Croppy boy.   OnYI

Croquet.   David Huddle.   "Keep your manners but play for keeps."   Str

The Cross.   Pedro Calderon de la Barca.   Since alone for sinners' sake/God on thee endured to die.   CAW

Cross.   Langston Hughes.   Being neither white nor black?   BANP; IDB; LiTM; PoBA; PoLf; SoSe; TAP

The Cross.   Sidney Lanier.   'Twas on a tree they slew Him–last;/When out of the woods He came.   BePJ

The Cross.   Charles Nelson Pace.   It is a beacon ever lit/By One identified with it.   BePJ; BLRP

The Cross.   Allen Tate.   Instructed by the fiery dead.   AP; AWP

The Cross and the Tomb.   Annie Johnson Flint.   For the Lord is risen; He dies no/more.   STF

The Cross and the Tree.   William L. Stidger.   As if each stalwart oak had roots/That reached to Calvary!   PGD

Cross and Throne.   Horatius Bonar.   Hellelujah!/Throne and Cross forever.   BePJ

The Cross-Eyed Lover.   Donald Finkel.   Only a brassiere salesman in his blue suede/shoes/could look on her face, long,/and not go blind.   Prf

The Cross of Gold.   David Gray.   Knowing she went to rest/This cross upon her breast.'   AA

The Cross of Snow.   Henry Wadsworth Longfellow.   And seasons, changeless since the day she died.   AP; HeIP; MAmP; NOBA; OxBA; TAP

A Cross on a Hill.   Carl S. Weist.   That is all the world has:/A Cross on a Hill.   BePJ

Cross Patch.   Mother Goose.   Then call your neighbors in.   BrR; EvOK

The Cross Spider.   May Swenson.   ...Experiment frittered.   SUW

Cross Ties.   X. J. Kennedy.   I let them sprinkle water on my child.   CoPo; HoPM

The Cross Was His Own.   *Anonymous.*   The Cross was His own.   BePJ; BLPA

The Crosse.   George Herbert.   With but foure words, my words, Thy will be done.   AnAnS 1

La Crosse at Ninety Miles an Hour.   Richard Eberhart.   Small division between the world and the spirit.   AmFN

The Crossed Apple.   Louise Bogan.   You take the rest.   BiP; HeIP

The Crossed Swords.   Nathaniel Langdon Frothingham.   Hail this eet cross at last.   AA

Crossroads.   Martin Staples Shockley.   This only true:/E = mc2   FF

Crosses.   Robert Herrick.   Crosses do still bring forth the best events.   CaPo

Crossing.   Anthony Barnett.   ...but you remain/with your Jewishness.   VWA

The Crossing.   Paul Blackburn.   by all those migrations/of thousands and thousands of birds.   NYBP

Crossing.   Philip Booth.   CABOOSE!   AmFN

Crossing.   Archibald MacLeish.   Pressed between two pages in this place?   PoL

Crossing.   J. Robert Oppenheimer.   We did not look back at the mountains.   SUW

Crossing a Creek.   Herbert Clark Johnson.   By bridge or log, he'll always feel its beat/Against his body, even in his dreams.   PoNe

Crossing Alone the Nighted Ferry.   Alfred Edward Housman.   And free land of the grave.   ChMP; FaBoRV; GTBS-P; NOBE; NoP; OBSP

The Crossing at Fredericksburg.   George Henry Boker.   One more cheer for Massachusetts,/And one more for Michigan!   PAH

Crossing Brooklyn Ferry.   Walt Whitman.   Great or small, you furnish your parts toward the soul.   AA; AP; DiPo; InPS; LiTA; MAmP; NoAm; NOBA; NoP; NYP; TAP

Crossing Kansas by Train.   Donald Justice.   sons asleep/in their workclothes.   NYBP

Crossing Portsmouth Bridge.   Alan Chong Lau.   that we were never/here   BrSi

Crossing Raquette Lake at Night.   Greg Kuzma.   in some place darker than ours.   WOLT

Crossing the Atlantic.   Anne Sexton.   This dead street never stops!   MOS; NoAm

Crossing the Bar.   Alfred, Lord Tennyson.   I hope to see my Pilot face to face/When I have crost the bar.   BiP; BLRP; BoLiVe; DiPo; DL; EnL; EtS; FaBoRV; FaBV; FaFP; FaPoR; FF; FiP; FPL; GoTF; GTBS; HBV 1-2; HBVY; HeIP; LiTB; MaVP; MBW 1-2; MCCG; MOS; NOBE; NOBV; NoP; OAEL 1-2; OAEP; OBEV; OBNC; OBVV; OHFP; PoLf; SoSe; TEP; TrCP; TreF; TrGrPo; TRV; ViBoPo; VLP; WBLP; WGRP; WHA

Crossing the Border into Canada.   Joy Harjo.   ...Following us/into the north.   STE

Crossing the Colorado River into Yuma.   Simon J. Ortiz.   Sing a bit, be patient./Wait.   TAT

Crossing the County Line.   Elizabeth Randall-Mills.   And at this starting point of truth/Await a widening of the known.   GoYe

Crossing the Park.   Howard Moss.   Those parks, those paintings in which I live.   NYBP

Crossing the Plains.   Joaquin Miller.   Kings even in captivity.   AA; AmePo; AmLP; BPAW; GN

Crossing the Straits.   Charles Brasch.   You, whom no darkened island waits.   AnNZ

Crossing the Tropics.   Herman Melville   Love, love, it is as death were past!   AA

Crossing the Water.   Sylvia Plath.   This is the silence of astounded souls.   HaCAP

Crossing West Texas (1966).   Kell Robertson.   we are very careful/stop only for gas.   TAT

Crossing with the Light.   Dwight Okita.   "Yes. This one. This time. This is the place."   BrSi

Crosspatch.   *Anonymous.*   And call your neighbours in.   GBP

Crotalus.   Bret (Francis Bret Harte) Harte.   To lie, untrodden, in the sun!   AA

Crotalus Rex.   Brewster Ghiselin.   Rings in his darkness that we cannot heed?   MoVE

Crotchet Castle.   Thomas Love Peacock.   And we'll sit till day, but we'll find the way/To drench the world with wine.   NLV

The Crow.   Rita Boumi-Pappas.   I shall shout for help!   PBWP

The Crow.   William Canton.   And on its topmost twig the Crow/Takes the glad morning's sun and air.   HBV 1-2

The Crow.   Robert Creeley.   Sickness is the hatred of a repentance/knowing there is nothing he wants.   TW

The Crow.   P. K. Page.   ...in the mist/stands/the crow.   WHW

Crow and Pie.   *Anonymous.*   I trust to recouer my harte agayne,/And Crystes curse goo wythe yow!'   ESPB

The Crow and the Crane.   *Anonymous.*   And farther he pursued them not/Into Egypt's land.'   BuBa

The Crow and the Fox.   Jean de La Fontaine.   Swore, but too late, he shouldn't catch him twice.   AWP; MaC

The Crow and the Nighthawk.   Watson Kirkconnell.   Successive broods of little Hanks/Rise up to give their father thanks.   CaP

Crow Blacker Than Ever.   Ted Hughes.   Flying the black flag of himself.   TEP

The Crow-Children Walk My Circles in the Snow.   Ray A. Young Bear.   suddenly leap out at the thought of white wings.   CDW

Crow Country.   Kenneth Slessor.   Stabbed by the needles of the mind.   BoAV

Crow, Crow, Get out of My Sight.   *Anonymous.*   Or I'll kill your father and mother tonight.   PBBP

Crow Jane.   LeRoi (Imamu Amiri Baraka) Jones.   ...And Damballah, kind father,/sew up/her bleeding hole.   PoM

The Crow-Marble Whores of Paris.   James Schevill.   Statues of their carved embraces.   NMP

Crow on the Fence.   *Anonymous.*   Rain will come down.   PBBP

Crow Resting (parody).   Edward Pygge.   ...What Superbard says/Goes. I am going to keep things like this.   BXAP; FaBoPa

Crow's Ditty.   *Anonymous.*   Gloor! Gloor! Gloor!   GBP

Crow's First Lesson.   Ted Hughes.   Crow flew guiltily off.   NoAm; PAI

Crow's Last Stand.   Ted Hughes.   Crow's eye-pupil, in the tower of its scorched fort.   PAI

Crow's Nest.   Richard F. Armknecht.   ...known only/To lookouts watching high and lonely.   GoYe

Crow's Way.   Duane Niatum.   to help moon find her feathers in the snowy pools.   CDW

The Crow Sat on the Willow.   John Clare.   His milking-maid the ploughman sung/Till all the fields around him rung.   VLP

Crow, Straight Flier, but Dark.   Laya Firestone.   A chain of souls connected by/Names.   VWA

Crow Voices.   Gail Tremblay.   he was so clever he could take the sun.   AMV-81

The Crowd.   John Masefield.   These twenty threadbare men with frost-bit ears/And canvas bags and little chests of gears.   OxBTC

Crowded Out.   Florence White Willett.   And days are doubly full and rich/Since He's not crowded out.   STF

Crowded Ways of Life.   Walter S. Gresham.   And my heart sings its praise to the Master of all,/Who is helping me serve in the road.   BLPA

Crowdieknowe.   Hugh" (Christopher Murray Grieve) MacDiarmid.   –Fegs, God's no blate gin he stirs up/The men o' Crowdieknowe!   InPS; NoAm; NoP; OxBS; PAI

Crowds.   Charles Baudelaire.   those who pity them for their chaste lives and troubled/fortunes.   SyP

Crowds of Men and Women.   Walt Whitman.   And you that cross from shore to shore years hence are/more to me, and more in my meditations...   CTBA

The Crowing of the Red Cock.   Emma Lazarus.   His nobler task is–to forget.   AA; HBV 1-2

Crown of Days.   *Anonymous.*   The Rock of Ages chose thee for His/rest.   TrJP

Crown of Happiness.   Anne Hebert.   The poem on the summit of a high head/Crown of happiness   BoWoP

A Crown of Wildflowers.   Christina Georgina Rossetti.   I twist them in a crown today,/And tonight they die.'   OxBChV

Crowned.   Amy Lowell.   A diadem woven with rue.   HBV 1-2

The Crowned Heart.   *Anonymous.*   And send it in a worse estate/Than when it came to thee.   PoPle

A Crowned Poet.   Anne Reeve Aldrich.   He, too, is a king/To whom God giveth song.   AA

Crowned with flowers, I saw fair Amarillis.   *Anonymous.*   Blew all her faith and sand away together.   EnLoPo

The Crowning Gift.   Gladys Cromwell.   I would have courage now to love,/And lay aside the strength I knew.   HBMV

The Crowning of Dreaming John.   John Drinkwater.   He held before a shouting throng,/A crowning of his own.   HBMV

The Crowns.   John Freeman.   The radiant blossom of English earth–is dead!   CH

The Crows.   Louise Bogan.   Winter-burning in the fields.   FaBoWP; NMM

Crows.   Philip Booth.   The crows in possession.   DFF

Crows.   Tom Clark.   Out of a continuous process of succession   DFF

The Crows.   John Engels.   ...back like the joyous alarm/of the sun-greeting voice of the crow.   AMV-81

The Crows.   Zulfikar Ghose.   ...they appear more/like intensely dedicated politicians.   BoAnP

Crows.   David McCord.   I like the sight/Of crows for my good night.   RFM; TiPo

The Crows.   Maria Valli.   And melted away in their cries.   CBAP

Crows.   William Witherup.   and the wit of his sharp eye.   PCP; PoL

Crows in Spring.   John Clare.   And there a new nest nearly made/Proclaims the winter by.   EnRP

Crows in the Garden.   *Anonymous.*   With a merry, merry haw, haw, haw.   ABF

Crucial Stew.   Colette Inez.   We was very neat about our persons.   FAZ

The Crucible of Life (excerpt).   Edgar A. Guest.   From the crucible of life when you've poured off the/scum.   PeD

Crucified to the World.   *Anonymous.*   Then yef I little of kith or kin,/For ther is alle gode./Amen.   MeEL

The Crucifix.   Alphonse Marie Louis de Lamartine.   Summons the dead who sleep beneath thy shadow/Around the Crucified!   CAW

Crucifix.   Elder Olson.   The agony we comprehend; of the rest, know nothing.   MoRP

The Crucifix.   Alexander Pushkin.   The common man, perhaps, is Not Allowed?   LiTW

The Crucifix.   Sir Herbert Read.   We have smashed you!   BrPo

A Crucifix.   Paul Verlaine.   I write these verses in acknowledgment.   SyP

The Crucifixion.   *Anonymous.*
...the grief/Which for His sake/Came upon His mother.   OnYI
He bring us to winne,/That hath us dere boght!   MeEL
Not a word, not a word, not a word.   BoAN 1-2; BPo; TAP; TrGrPo

Crucifixion.   Eva Gore Booth.   Wounding one soul, you wound the soul of all,/The unity of Life, the soul of God.   WGRP

Crucifixion.   Waring Cuney.   Think, think...Oh, think...   BANP; GoSl

Crucifixion.   Hugh O. Isbell.   He bears the insult–Love his only crime.   PGD

Crucifixion.   Madelaine Marie.   'Twas I who nailed you naked to the cross.   PeHV

The Crucifixion.   Kuno Meyer.   Sorer to Him was the grief/That was upon her for His sake.   OxBI

The Crucifixion.   Alice Meynell.   Forsaken He went down, and was afraid.   OxBoCh

The Crucifixion.   Henry Hart Milman.   Son of God! 'tis Thou! 'tis Thou!   BePJ

Crucifixion.   Mrs. Roy L. Peifer.   So blind are we, and selfish, too,/We crucify Him every day!   STF

The Crucifixion of Noel.   Marsden Hartley.   The cymbals now have whitened.   AnAmPo

Crucifixion to the World by the Cross of Christ.   Isaac Watts.   Love so amazing, so divine,/Demands my soul, my life, my all.   NOCV; NOEC; OBEC

Cruciform.   Winifred Welles.   ...could lie down and fit/Our desolate arms and bodies into it.   NYBP

Crucifying.   John Donne.   Moyst, with one drop of thy blood, my dry soule.   AnAnS 1; OBS

Crude Foyer.   Wallace Stevens.   At last, there, when it turns out to be here.   LiTM; NePA

Cruel Boys.   Gary Soto.   And shouts, "You ain't nothing but a hound dog,"/As the spitballs begin to fly.   NPGG

The Cruel Brother.   *Anonymous.*   "A rope and a gallows for to hang him on."   AmFP

The Cruel Brother (A version).   *Anonymous.*   But it would have made your heart/right sair,/To see the bridegroom rive his haire.   BaBo; EnLit; ESPB; OxBB; ViBoFo

The Cruel Brother (B vers.).   *Anonymous.*   "And what will you leave to your brother John's wife?"/"Grief and misfortune all her life."   BaBo; ESPB

The Cruel Brother: What Is Past.   Sir William Davenant.   We shall disparage Providence.   TrGrPo

Cruel Clever Cat.   Geoffrey Taylor.   Nice mice to an untimely death.   FaBoEE

The Cruel Falcon.   Robinson Jeffers.   And dig under the straws for a stone/To bruise himself on.   BiP

The Cruel Maid.   Robert Herrick.   Love killed this man. No more but so.   CaPo

The Cruel Mother.   *Anonymous.*
And the green leaves they grow rarely.   InPK; OxBB
And there you'll burn both early and late.'   OBET
Mother, oh, mother, it's Hell for you.   FSW
"O cursed mother! hell is deep,/And there thou'll enter step by step."   ViBoFo

The Cruel Mother (A vers.).   *Anonymous.*   "O mother dear, when I was thine,/You did no prove to me sae kind."   BaBo; ESPB; FaBoBa

The Cruel Mother (B vers.).   *Anonymous.*   "Welcome, welcome, warnin bell,/But the God o Heaven keep me out o hell.   BaBo; ESPB

The Cruel Mother (C vers.).   *Anonymous.*   "I'll dress you up in satin so fine,"/Al down by the greenwood si-de.   BaBo; ESPB

The Cruel Mother (Down by the Greenwood Side).   *Anonymous.*   "Now we are up in heaven to dwell,/And you are doomed to hell."   AmFP

The Cruel Mother (P version). *Anonymous.* Young ladies all, of beauty bright,/Take warning by her last good-night. ESPB

The Cruel Naughty Boy. *Anonymous.* The cruel little naughty boy,/Was never heard of more. BBGG

The Cruel Sister. *Anonymous.*
By the bonny milldams of Binnorie. OxBB
Tuesday began her heart to ache,/And Thursday night smoked at the stake. BaBo

The Cruel War Is Raging. *Anonymous.* Won't you let me go with you?—yes, my love, yes. FSW

Cruel You Be. George Puttenham. But ye to blame, thus to refuse/My service, and to let me die. EIL

A Cruell Mistris. Thomas Carew. That burnt the temple where she was ador'd. AnAnS 2

Cruelty. T. R. Hummer. ...what flesh would come to/When I ripped off the lid. MAYP

The Cruise of the Fair American. *Anonymous.* Success to fair America/And our good privateer. PAH

The Cruise of the Monitor. George Henry Boker. Hurrah for the Monitor's famous cruise! MC; PAH

The Cruise of the Mystery. Celia Thaxter. And she will sail for evermore. OBCA

The Cruise of the P.C. *Anonymous.* He squoffled once, he squirled, and then/He wrote what's writ above. NA

A-Cruising We Will Go. *Anonymous.* And a-cruising we will go! AmSS

The Cruiskeen Lawn. *Anonymous.* Gra machree a coolin bawn. HBV 1-2; OnYI

Crumbling is not an instant's act. Emily Dickinson. Slipping—is Crashe's law. AmPP; DiPo; NOBA; PPP

Crumbs. Walter De la Mare. And every pool lies still as stone. SoPo

Crumbs or the Loaf. Robinson Jeffers. For it seems compassion sticks longer than the other colors, in this/bleaching cloth. CMoP

Crusade. Hilaire Belloc. And young Lord Raymond stormed Jerusalem. GoBC

The Crusade. Rinaldo d'Aquino. The grief my heart is bearing/Will waste away my life. CAW

The Crusader. Dorothy Parker. About that noisy nuisance, Gabriel. ShM

Crusader's Song. *Anonymous.* That in loving you I've almost/Oft forgot my God of yore! CAW

The Crusaders Behold Jerusalem. Torquato Tasso. Catch the glad sounds, and shout, "Jerusalem, all hail!" CAW

The Crusaders knew the Holy Places. Jenny Mastoraki. The papers of the period/spoke of bloodless operations. BoWoP

The Cruse. Louise Townsend Nicholl. And love's the only oil that flows in both. NYBP

Crusoe in England. Elizabeth Bishop. –And Friday, my dear Friday, died of measles/seventeen years ago come March. HaCAP

Crusoe's Island. Derek Walcott. Can bless them as the bell's/Transfixing tongue can bless. NoAm

The Crust of Bread. *Anonymous.* Oh! how I wish I had the bread/That once I threw away! HBV 1-2; HBVY

Crustaceans. Roy Fuller. Regard with such pity, disgust, absorption, crabs? NeBP; NoAm

Crusty Critics. George Crabbe. And, spite of Truth, let Mercy guide your Pen. OBEC

Crutches. Robert Herrick. ...and to pour down/Upon thee many a benison. CaPo

The Cry-Bird Journey. Stan Rice. So we all fled on. NPGG

Cry Faugh! Robert Graves. Proud remnants of a visionary race. CoBMV; MoBrPo

Cry for a Disused Synagogue in Booysens. Mannie Hirsch. And his voice lies buried in the amber glass. VWA

A Cry for Light. *Anonymous.* That they our light may share. BLRP

Cry from the Battlefield. Robert Menth. Mother of men, this bleeding face/Awaits the wonder of your love's embrace. ISi

A Cry from the Canadian Hills. Lilian Leveridge. Over the hills of God, laddie, the beautiful hills of Home. BLPA

A Cry from the Ghetto. Morris Rosenfeld. They fight, they fall, they sink into/the night. TrJP

A Cry from the Shore. Ellen Mackay Hutchinson Cortissoz. Take up thy life and go! AA

The Cry of a Dreamer. John Boyle O'Reilly. And a toiler dies in a day. BLPA; GoTF; TreFS

The Cry of an Aged One. Ray Fraser. all he wants/is for someone/to hold his hand NeAC

The Cry of Generations. Mordechai Husid. how can I stop to unload this burden/when the cry of generations drives me on. VWA

The Cry of the Age. Hamlin Garland. My heart is aflame to be right. WGRP

The Cry of the Child (parody). William Zaranka. When my small child did cry for nurse. BXAP

The Cry of the Children. Elizabeth Barrett Browning. But the child's sob in the silence curses deeper/Than the strong man in his wrath. EnLi 1-2; HBV 1-2; OAEP; ViBoPo; VLP

The Cry of the Lovelorn. Sir Theodore and Aytoun, William E. Martin. Rest thee with thy yellow nabob, spider-hearted Cousin Amy! CenHV

The Cry of the Peoples. Alter Brody. This is the cry of the peoples/That rang in the empty sky! TrJP

A Cry to Arms. Henry Timrod. And for the lily's sake! PAH

A Cry to Mary. Saint Godric. Bring me to winne with the self God. MeEL

Cryderville Jail. *Anonymous.* 'Tis hard times, I say. ABF

Crying. Galway Kinnell. I wept it! Ha ha! NTCP

Crying in Early Infancy: Sonnet. John Tranter. and the countryside is well advised to be empty. CBAP

The Crying of Water. Arthur Symons. As the water all night is crying to me. AnEnPo

The Cryptic Streets. Abu-l-Ala al-Maarri. He makes a mess of me to nourish you,/Then makes a mess of you to nourish me. LiTW

The Crystal. George Barker. Or remove the eyelid/To see the end. LiTM; OBMV

The Crystal. Titus Munson Coan. And leaps to life beneath a kindred spell. AA

Crystal. Faye Kicknosway. ...with the dark, strange/water of the moon. IHMS

The Crystal. Sidney Lanier. Jesus, good Paragon, thou Crystal Christ? AmePo; AmP; TrPWD; TRV

The Crystal Cabinet. William Blake. I fill'd with woes the passing Wind. CH; DiPo; ERoP 1-2; FaBoCh; LoGBV; NCEP; OAEL 1-2; OBNC; OBRV; PoEL 1-5

The Crystal Gazer. Sara Teasdale. And the little shifting pictures of people rushing/In tiny self-importance to and fro. MoAmPo

The Crystal Lithium. James Schuyler. "Look," the ocean said (it was tumbled, like our sheets), "look in my/eyes" PoM

The Crystal Palace. William Makepeace Thackeray. That takes his ayse/As he surveys/This Cristial Exhibition. InMe

The Crystal Skull. Kathleen Raine. All that will remain/Is the love/That burns away the sun. NeBP

Crystals Like Blood. Hugh" (Christopher Murray Grieve) MacDiarmid. My treadmill memory draws from you yet. HAP; NoP; PAI

Cuba. Lawrence Kearney. you shoved the gun in your mouth/& took off. AMV-81

Cuba. Harvey Rice. Confided to her trust,/The key to lands of gold! PAH

Cuba. Edmund Clarence Stedman. And her sure revenge shall be that of/Tamar!"/Speak at last! PAH

Cuba, 1962. Florence Anthony ("Ai"). you can never get enough. AmPA

Cuba Libre. Joaquin Miller. Love and Liberty allied. MC; PAH

Cuba to Columbia. Will Carleton. If out of the starry Western land,/Should come my Lafayette! MC; PAH

Cuban Refugees on Key Biscayne. Barbara Winder. Gulls circle Veradero/with cries. TAT

Cubes. Mary Elizabeth ("E") Fullerton. There's the Bodleian! PoAu 1-2

A Cubic Triolet. *Anonymous.* ISLITTLEFUN. PV

The Cubical Domes. David Gascoyne. Whose hearts are on fire in the snow. EAS

Cubist Blues in Poltergeist Major. Allan F. Kipp. Yet somewhere/resurrected nazis/are still burning Mendelssohn. AMV-81

Cubist Portrait. Marjorie Allen Seiffert. From here to yonder, to become silent emptiness at last. PoA

The Cubistic Lovers. Charles Edward Eaton. Their bodies scatter type as if block letters make/the news. AMV-81

La Cucaracha (The Cockroach). *Anonymous.* oh no she hasn't marihuana for to smoke. TrAS

La Cucaracha (with music). *Anonymous.* To the place to which Zapapta/Ordered the famous convention. AS

Cuchillo. Joy Harjo. that calls itself/knife/(cuchillo). TWSS

Cuchulain Comforted. William Butler Yeats. They had changed their throats and had the throats of birds. CMoP; LiTM; OAEL 1-2

Cuchulains's Fight with the Sea. William Butler Yeats. And fought with the invulnerable tide. AnIL

Cuchullain's Lament over Fardiad. *Anonymous.* Yesterday a Mountain he—/But a shade today! AnIV

The Cuckoo. *Anonymous.*
And I'll walk as proud by him as he walks by me. FSW
And when he sings Cuckoo, the summer draweth near. CBEP; GBP; OxNR
And when their back's to me,/I will love whom I please. AmFP
I would bid them remember/The flower as it dies. PoPle
In June she beats upon the drum,/And then she'll fly away. OBET
She had the fewer for what she did. AnOE

Cuckoo! Hilaire Belloc. In woods so long time bare. MoVE

The Cuckoo. Patrick Reginald Chalmers. And make a song unique as his/And shirk responsibilities. BoAnP; CenHV

Cuckoo. R. P. Lister. One loses patience with a bird like that. BoAnP

The Cuckoo. Frederick Locker-Lampson. For me it never sings in vain. HBV 1-2

The Cuckoo. Edward ("Edward Eastaway") Thomas. The cuckoo's note would be drowned by the voice of my dead. BrPo

The Cuckoo (A vers.). Anonymous. And if I am forsaken/I know not for why. OBET

The Cuckoo and the Nightingale. Thomas Clanvowe.
I pray to God that evil fire him brenne!' PBBP
Since of all good you are the best alive. MeEV

The Cuckoo (B vers.). Anonymous. For he's madly mistaken/If he thinks that I mourn. OBET

Cuckoo, Cherry Tree. Anonymous.
Give it my brother. PBBP
Let it hail or rain or snow. OxNR

The Cuckoo Comes in April. Anonymous. And then he flies away. OxNR

Cuckoo, Cuckoo. Anonymous. In August,/Go I must. PBBP

The Cuckoo Is a Merry Bird. Anonymous. That she may sing Cuckoo!/Three months in the year. PBBP

Cuckoo, noisy among the Shenbaka flowers. Andal. Sing,/but not too loudly, so he will come. BoWoP

Cuckoo, Scabbed Gowk. Anonymous. Mickle said, little wrought. PBBP

Cuckoo Song. Anonymous. Ne swik thu naver nu! EnLit; NoP

Cuckoo Song. Katharine Tynan Hinkson. Cold is August, cold is August! OnYI

Cuckoo Waltz (with music). Anonymous. Fare thee well, my charming girl,/With golden slippers on. AS

Cuddle Doon. Alexander ("Surface man") Anderson. "O, bairnies, cuddle doon." GN; HBV 1-2; OHFP

The Cudgelled but Contented Cuckold. Jean de La Fontaine. And heartily thereto I pledged will be. UnTE

Cudworth's Undergraduate Ode to a Bare Behind. John Ower. Soft putty to their strong demands. AMV-81

Cuento. Carlos Cumpian. ..."You'll hear more/about it soon!"–and hung up– FIA

Cui Bono? Thomas Carlyle. One small grave is all he gets. HBV 1-2; OBRV; WGRP

Cuisine Bourgeoise. Wallace Stevens. Are they men eating reflections of themselves? LiTA

Culbin Sands. Andrew Young. And tombstones rewrite names on dead men's graves. GTBS-P; OxBS; OxBTC

Cullen. P. K. Page. He knew there was reason, but couldn't find it/and marched to battle half an inch behind it. CaP

Culloden and After. Iain Crichton Smith. and from his Minch of sherries mumble laws. OxBS

The Culprit Fay. Joseph Rodman Drake.
And the beach of sand is reached at last. GN
Bitter had been thy punishment. GN
But his voice in a softened accent broke: GN
Hence! to the water-side, away! GN
In the tricksy pomp of fairy pride. GN
Round the wild witch-hazel tree. AA; GN
'Tis the dawn of the fairy-day. GN

The Cult of the Celtic. Anthony C. Deane. Was, at all hazards, to try to copy the Celt! BXAP; NOBL

The Cultivation of Christmas Trees. Thomas Stearns Eliot. Because the beginning shall remind us of the end/And the first coming of the second coming. OFD

Cultural Exchange. Langston Hughes. Hurry up!/Make haste! BPo; PoBA; PoNe

Cultural Notes. Kenneth Fearing. "Shut your trap, you. The question is, what about Karl Marx?" CMoP

The Cultural Presuppostion. W.H. Auden. Who with their lives have banished hence the serpent and the/faceless insect. CABA

Culture. Ralph Waldo Emerson. And the world's flowing fates in his own mould recast. AmePo

Culture in the Slums. William Ernest Henley. In fact, my form's the Bloomin' Utter! CenHV; HBV 1-2; InMe

The Cultured Girl Again. Ben King. For she yelled, "How shall I fix the 'taters,/Fried, lionized, baked, biled, or mashed?" FiBHP; OBAL

The Cumberbunce. Paul West. "I thought all people understood/The difference 'twixt "might" and "could"!" NA

The Cumberland. Henry Wadsworth Longfellow And without a seam! AA; AnNE; EtS; MC; PAH

The Cumberland. Herman Melville. Long they'll roll it on the tongue–/Cumberland! Cumberland! PAH

The Cumberland and the Merrimac. Anonymous. The Stars and Stripes still floated from the maintop's highest peak! AmFP

Cumberland Gap. Anonymous. Fourteen miles to the Cumberland Gap. AmFN; FSW

The Cumberland's Crew. Anonymous. And never forgotten," sang the Cumberland's crew. AmFP; ShS

Cumberland Station. Dave Smith. ...I wish I had the guts/to tell you this is a place I hope/I never have to go through again. HaCAP; MAYP

The Cummerbund. Edward Lear. Lest horrid Cummerbunds should come,/And swallow you outright. CenHV; OBTV

Cumnor Hall. William Julius Mickle. The haunted tow'rs of Cumnor Halle. BeLS; CEP; OBEC; OxBB; ViBoPo

De Cunjah Man. James Edwin Campbell. O chillen, run, de Cunjah man! BANP

The Cunning Clerk. Anonymous. And three ribs o' the auld wife's side/Gaed knip knap ower in twa. OxBB

The Cunning Cobbler Done Over. Anonymous. He said you brute, I'll never go out mending any more. CoMu

The Cup. John Oldham. Which wine itself enough can do. AWP

The Cup. John Townsend Trowbridge. And the fire that maddens the poet's brain/With wild sweet ardor and heavenly pain. HBV 1-2

The Cup. Judith Wright. Then I shan't be dead,/but waiting for something to come in. FaBoWP

The Cup of Blessing. Charles Wesley. The broken bread Thy body be,/To cheer each languid heart. BePJ

The Cup of Happiness. Gilbert Thomas. And dost Thou not of pain a mingling pour,/To make the cup but overflow the more? TrPWD

The Cup of O'Hara. Turlough O'Carolan. In another health to Kian. AnIV; OnYI

The Cupboard. Walter De la Mare. There's Banbury Cakes, and Lollipops/For me, me, me. BrR; FaPON; NTCP; SoPo; TiPo

Cupid. Anonymous. For if you hit me, slave, I'll call thee, beggar. EIL

Cupid. Bernard O'Dowd. It matters not to me/If sheep or tiger, man or worm/Earth's victor-captain be. NOAV

Cupid a Plowman. Moschus. What once Europa was Nanet is now. OBVE

Cupid and Death: Victorious Men of Earth. James Shirley. Shall have the cunning skill to break a heart. TrGrPo

Cupid Drowned. [James Henry] Leigh Hunt. I feel him tickling my heart-strings. HBV 1-2

Cupid Far Gone. Richard Lovelace. And triple Cerberus from below/Must leashed t' himself with him a hunting go. CaPo

Cupid in a Bed of Roses. Anonymous. Whom they empoisoned arrows cause complain?' EIL

Cupid Mistaken. Matthew Prior. I took you for your likeness, Cloe. EiCP; InMe

Cupid's Darts. Sir Alan Patrick Herbert. Than be spitted by the many pins that bristle from your hat. CenHV

Cupid's Indictment. John Lyly. What he's to trust to. Boy, give ear! EIL

Cupid's Pastime. Francis Davison. And laughed that pleasant sight to see. UnTE

Cupid's Revenge. Francis Beaumont and John Fletcher. Love hates the too-ripe fruit that falls alone. EIL; FaBoEn

Cupid Stung. Thomas Moore. How must the heart, ah, Cupid! be,/The hapless heart that's stung by thee! HBV 1-2

Cupid the Ploughboy. Anonymous. Oh Cupid was that ploughing boy/Who caused me all my pain. OBET

Cupid, Thou Naughty Boy. Fulke, Lord Brooke Greville. Where living to the world, to me he dieth. NCEP

Cupid Ungodded. James Shirley. To see thy shame, and break thy heart. GoBC

Cupidon. William Jay Smith. And the wind crept up his accordion stair,/And under his iron door. NePoEA

Cupids Call. James Shirley. Nature no med'cine can impart/When age once snows upon your heart. ErPo

Cups of Illusion. Henry Bellamann. As unremembered,/As bird shadows on the grass. HBMV

The Curate's Kindness. Thomas Hardy. Let me jump out o' waggon and go back and drown me/At Pummery or Ten-Hatches Weir. CoBMV

The Curate Thinks You Have No Soul. St. John Lucas. Your little, faithful, barking ghost/May leap to lick my phantom hand. BLPA

The Cure. Mebdh McGuckian. In the diocese of Derry it's a reserved sin. FaBoIP

The Cure All. Don L. Lee to keep the weather/cool. CAD

A Cure for Poetry. Anonymous. Thro' which the living Homer begg'd his bread. FaBoEE

A Cure for the Spleen. Matthew Green. Perhaps to blossom soon again. OBEC

The Cure's Progress. Henry Austin Dobson. With his coat worn bare, and his straggling hair,/And his green umbrella-case. HBV 1-2

Curfew. Paul Eluard. What else could we do, for we were in love? BoLoP

Curfew. Henry Wadsworth Longfellow Reign over all. AA; MCCG; OxBA

The Curfew Breakers. Samuel Chimsoro. and die in the evening/as a curfew breaker/is also for the love of life. WhB

A Curfew: December 13, 1981. Amy Clampitt. a raging mimic of the universe's grand indifference. SUW

Curfew Must Not Ring To-Night. Rose Hartwick Thorpe. Curfew will not ring to-night! BeLS; BLPA; BLPL; FaBoBe; HBV 1-2; PaPo; TreF; WBLP

Curiosity. Harry Behn. Tell me! or don't even grown-ups know? SoPo

Curiosity. Alastair Reid. and that dead dogs are those who do not know/ that dying is what, to live, each has to do. SoSe

Curiosity: Fiction. Charles Sprague. Puts out her light, and turns away to sleep. AA

The Curiosity-Shop. Peter Redgrove. With my one love's grief, and my appetite for curiosity. OxBC

Curiosity: The News. Charles Sprague. Insulted virtue's hiss – thou canst not fly. AA

A Curious Discourse That Passed between the Twenty-Five Letters... *Anonymous.* While Ampersy-and he licked the dish. FaBoUs

Curious Something. Winifred Welles. Or something curious in its place? TiPo

Curly Joe. *Anonymous.* For I tried it and changed ranges to a far and better land. BPAW

Curly Locks. Mother Goose. And feed upon strawberries/Sugar and cream. HBV 1-2; HBVY; OxNR; SoPo

The Current. James Merrill. Would not be going/To let it happen yet. NYBP

Currente Calamo. Arthur Hugh Clough. The pictures come, the pictures go,/Quick, quick, currente calamo. LoBV

Curriculum Vitae. Ingeborg Bachmann. and dream the next caress/of its devouring arms. BoWoP

The Curse. John Donne. Nature before hand hath out-cursed mee. CBEP; OAEP; TW

A Curse. Irving Feldman. May slugs jam every turnstile slot/If I forget thee not. TW

The Curse. Robert Francis. ...Whoever passes shivers/In the sun and hurries on. TW

Curse. Robert Greacen. You goddam bloody genius, John Logie Baird! TW

The Curse. John Hollander. Their bright, unhollowed eyes. UnPo

A Curse. Daughter of Ka'b, Rabi'a. In loneliness, and know my worth too late. LiTW

The Curse. John Millington Synge. And I'm your servant, J. M. Synge. ChTr; DBV; FaBoCo; FaBoEE; GoTF; NOBI; PV; TreFT; TW

The Curse: A Song. Robert Herrick. Know, I have prayed to Fury that some wind/May blow my ashes up and strike thee blind. CaPo

A Curse against the Owner. Barton Sutter. May he have more than he bargained for. TW

A Curse for a Nation. Elizabeth Barrett Browning. THIS is the curse. Write. SBG; WPOW

Curse of a Fisherman's Wife. Lila Chalpin. May huge holes hex his hull. AMV-80

The Curse of Cromwell. William Butler Yeats. What is there left to say? BIrV; SeCePo

The Curse of Doneraile. Patrick O'Kelly.
And may Grim Pluto's inner jail,/For ever groan with Doneraile. DBV; OnYI
May ev'ry hour new woes reveal/That Hell reserves for Doneraile. TW

The Curse of Faint Praise. Irwin Edman. "He's a clever versifier." InMe

The Curse of Kehama. Robert Southey. And the Curse shall be on thee/ For ever and ever. LoBV; OBRV

Curse of the Cat Woman. Edward Field. love had won, and heaven pardoned her. WeW

A Curse on a Closed Gate. James H. Cousins. And turn back the stone of his fate. AnIV

A Curse on Mine-Owners. *Anonymous.* To cut the throats/Of those old bloats/Who cut the poor miners' wages! TW

A Curse on the Cat. John Skelton. The manticors of mountains/Might feed upon thy brains! EvOK

A Curse on Uruk. Enheduanna. When the people of the city hear my sacred song,/they are ready to die. BoWoP

The Curse upon Edward. Thomas Gray. (The web is wove. The work is done.) OBEV

Curses. Joseph Duemer. a little thumb of flame. AMV-80

Cursor Mundi: The Flight into Egypt. *Anonymous.* "Wolf and wether, leon and ox,/Sal comen samen, and lamb and fox." CoBE

Cursor Mundi: The Pound of Flesh. *Anonymous.* If thou will do as we thee bid,/To shew us quar that cros is hid.' OxBM

A Curt Addendum. *Anonymous.* To follow you I'll not consent/Because I know which way you went. ShM

Curtain! Paul Laurence Dunbar. Villain skips, and all are happy. CenHV

Curtain. Lance Henson. the/same/first/dust VoR

The Curtain (Old Tabor Grand Opera House.). Jean Milne Gower. Wistfully, silently–vanished too soon. PoOW

The Curtain Poem. Edwin Brock. And, singing, seize the cloth across again. NMP

Curtain Speech. Michael Braude. Limbo! Limbo! Now and forever! AMV-81

Curtains for a Spinster. Walter H. Kerr. like a trace of a vanished breath. NePoAm-2

The Curtains in the House of the Metaphysician. Wallace Stevens. Uprising and down-falling, bares/The last largeness, bold to see. PoA

The Curtains Now Are Drawn. Thomas Hardy. And death may come, but loving is divine. CMoP

Cushendall. *Anonymous.* Was because Dan's mother's cousin's aunt was born in/Cushendall. WTO

Cushie Butterfield. George Ridley. An' they caal hor Cushie Butterfield,/ An' aa wish she wes heor. VLP

Cushla Ma Chree. John Philpot Curran. May heaven defend its own cushla ma chree! HBV 1-2

Cushy Cow, Bonny. *Anonymous.* If thou wilt let down thy milk to me. GBP

Custer. Edmund Clarence Stedman. And from it blazes down/The light of thy renown! BPAW; PAH

Custer (1). Alison Baker. ...charring darker/bodies with your/caucasian flames FAZ

Custer (2). Alison Baker. I think I'm the hot tuna. FAZ

Custer Lives in Humboldt County. Janet Campbell Hale. The past is best forgotten. STE; VoR

Custer Must Have Learned to Dance. Elizabeth Woody. birthing aboriginal psychosis. STE

Custer's Last Charge. Frederick Whittaker. ...the cup of his glory/Needed but that death to render it full. BPAW; HBV 1-2; MC; OnMSP; PAH; PoLf

Custer's Last Fierce Charge. *Anonymous.* And the mother waiting at home for her boy/Will learn that he is dead. BFSS

The Custom of the World. Louis Simpson. The custom of the world is wearing clothes. BoLoP

Customs. Juan Gelman. we are thirsty and/have the patience of animals. VWA

Customs Change. *Anonymous.* And after this shall things uprise/That men set now but at little price. OxBChV

Cut. David J. Feela. filming that one wheel still spinning/in the motionless air. AMV-81

Cut. Sylvia Plath. Dirty girl,/Thumb stump. CAPP; TAP

A Cut Flower. Karl Shapiro. Must I die now? Is this a part of life? BoNaP; HAP; WeW

Cut Grass. Philip Larkin. Moving at summer's pace. OxBC; PrIm

Cut It Down. Mary Elizabeth Coleridge. The summer air those wrinkled leaves forsook/Nor ever played in them. MoVE

Cut Lilac. Tony Beyer. will shoulder through with joy OCNZ

Cut the Cables. Robert Burns Wilson. Well named is that bay of the "Hundred/Fires." PAH

Cut the Grass. Archie Randolph Ammons. less than total is a bucketful of radiant toys. HAP; PPP; TAP

Cut Thistles in May. *Anonymous.* Cut them in July,/Then they will die. OxNR

The Cutting Edge. Philip Levine. a conversation of stone. NYBP

Cutting Redbud: An Accidental Death. Sarah Cotterill. I gather up the leaves and give them back. AmC

Cutting the Jewish Bride's Hair. Ruth Whitman. but this little amputation/ will shift the balance of the universe. HW

Cutting Wood on Shell Creek. Gretel Ehrlich. towards the private/blue tenderness pulsing/there. MAYP

Cuttings. Theodore Roethke. Pokes through a musty sheath/Its pale tendrilous horn. HaCAP; LCAP; NoAm; NOBA; TAP

Cuttings, later. Theodore Roethke. I quail, lean to beginnings, sheath-wet. AP; HaCAP; LCAP; NoAm; NOBA; PPoe; TAP

Cutty Sark. Hart Crane. Taeping?/Ariel? FaBoMo

The Cutty Wren. *Anonymous.* In brass pans and cauldrons, said John the Red Nose. CBEP; FSW; GBP; NCEP; OxBoLi; WiR

Cuvier Light. Pat Wilson. The whole massed weight of the night! AnNZ

Cwmrhydyceirw Elegiacs. Vernon Watkins. Let our tears for the dead earn the forgiveness of dust. PoA

The Cyclamen. Arlo Bates. If she but live, what are the dead! AA; HBV 1-2

Cyclamens. Michael (Katherine Bradley and Edith Cooper) Field. Am struck to the heart by the chiselled white/Of this handful of cyclamen. NOBV

Cycle. Langston Hughes. But the newly budding blossoms/Are equally gay. GoSl

Cycle. Sean Jennett.
and to the child conceived in the unborn womb/War. WaP
I am a brittle bone projecting from the sand. OnYI

Cycle. Frank Lonergan. Through your ghost steps...to be forgiven. AMV-81

Cycle. Ruth Miller. You will not allow me to refuse/My daily bread. PeSA

Cycles, Cycles. Suzanne Berger Rioff. our guts in love NMM

Cycling to Dublin. Robert Greacen. Gallop the miles, the straight-backed miles without number. OnYI

The Cyclists. Lawrence Kearney. the feet & the pedals a single blur. AMV-80

The Cyclone. Stewart Brisby. the loss of toy balloons. LFAC

A Cyclone at Sea. William Hamilton Hayne. Dark Bedouin of the waves. AA

Cyclone Blues. Anonymous. A-payin' fer the chattels/What the cyclone blowed away. CoSo

Cyclops. Euripides. Soon pied flowers, sweet-breathing,/shall thy head be wreathing. AWP

Cyder, I: How to Catch Wasps. John Philips. ...such doom/Waits luxury, and lawless love of gain! FaBoUs

Cymbeline. William Shakespeare.
And renowned be thy grave! AWP; CAW; CTC; DiPo; EBEV; EG; EiL; ELP; ExPo; FaBoCh; FaFP; FF; FiP; ForPo; GBL; GTBS; GTBS-P; HAP; HBV 1-2; HeIP; InPo; InPS; LiTB; LoBV; LoGBV; MCCG; NOBE; NoP; OAEL 1-2; OAEP; OBEV; OBSC; PAI; PoEL 1-5; PoPle; PoRA; PPoe; PrIm; QFR; RoGo; SCV; SeCeV; SoSe; TreF; TrGrPo; ViBoPo; WHA
My lady sweet, arise:/Arise, arise! ATP; AWP; BoLiVe; DiPo; EiL; EnL; ExPo; FaBoCh; FaBV; FaFP; FiP; GN; HBV 1-2; HeIP; InPo; LiTB; LoBV; LoGBV; NIP; NoP; OBEV; OBSC; PrIm; SeCeV; TreF; TrGrPo; ViBoPo; WHA

Cymon and Iphigenia. John Dryden. And happy each at home enjoys his love. OBNV

Cynddylan on a Tractor in Spring. R.S. Thomas. As Cynddylan passes proudly up the land. BoC

The Cynic. Theodosia Garrison. Nay, rather I laugh that I thought to own it/For more than a day. HBMV

The Cynic. St. George Tucker. Our cynic cries—"How damned absurd/To take such pains to make a—!" NLV; OBAL

Cynical Ode to an Ultra-Cynical Public. Charles Mackay. Detestable, stupid, degraded/Pig of a public! DBV

Cynical Portraits. Louis Paul. He died years ago. InMe; NLV

Cynicus to W. Shakspere. James Kenneth Stephen. And only all the women players. CenHV

Cynisca. Anonymous. The only woman in all of Greece to win. LiSp

The Cynneddf. Rolfe Humphries. They would see from the mound/A wonder go by. CrMA

The Cynotaph. Richard Harris Barham. And that put him out of his pain! FM

Cynthia. Sir Edward Dyer. "O! Cynthia, thou hast angel's eyes,/But yet a woman's heart." OBSC

Cynthia, Cynthia. Sextus Propertius. Love will return with all its olden fire. LiTW

Cynthia in the Snow. Gwendolyn Brooks. So beautiful it hurts. TiPo

Cynthia on Horseback. Philip Ayres. With switch her horse, and hearts with ev'ry look. EnLoPo

Cynthia's Revels. Ben Jonson.
Goddess, excellently bright. AtBAP; GN; MOON; TrGrPo
Since Nature's pride is now a withered daffodil. AtBAP; EG; TrGrPo

The Cypress Curtain of the Night. Thomas Campion. But all do not afford such food to thee/As this poor one, the worser part of me. LoBV

Cypress Grove. Austin Clarke. Elegant past blown out like a torchere. IPY

Cypress Grove Blues. Skip James. You just getting ready/honey, for the cypress grove. BluL

Cypresses. Robert Francis. How many years they have been teaching birds/In little schools, by little skills,/How to be shadows LCAP

Cypresses. D. H. Lawrence. And mechanical America Montezuma still. FaBoPP

A Cyprian Woman. Margaret Widdemer. All that life can tell. AnAmPo; HBV 1-2

Cyrano de Bergerac, III: "Love, I love beyond Breath." Edmond Rostand. ...and you/Have made me thus! OLR

Cythera. Paul Verlaine. The folly of Love's sacrifices. AWP; SyP

D

The D-Day Dodgers. Hamish Henderson. They are the D-Day Dodgers who stay in Italy. FSW

The D.L. and W.'s Phoebe Snow. Anonymous. The season's right/The distance slight/Upon the Road of Anthracite. TreF

The D Minor. E. L. Mayo. Mutters in sleep: "Bridegroom, behold your bride." MiAP

Da Capo. Henry Cuyler Bunner. But one thing is left us now; that is—/Begin it again. HBV 1-2

Da Leetla Boy. Thomas Augustin Daly. He was so cold, me leetla boy,/He no could wait. HBV 1-2

Da's All Right, Baby. Anonymous. Da's all righ'. baby. ABF

Da Silva Gives the Cue. Walter Hart Blumenthal. Hail, Jew Antonio, methinks you sit/With mien ironic in the prompter's pit. TrJP

A Dab of Color. Theodore Weiss. that a little dab/of color, aptly mixed,/makes all the difference. VGW

Dabbling in the Dew. Anonymous. But it's dabbling in the dew makes the milkmaids fair! CH; UnTE

Dachau. John Malcolm Brinnin. bunkers, barracks, crematoria.... GP

The Dachshund. Edward Anthony. No, do not underrate the dachsie! GDP

Dachshunds. William Jay Smith. While Morning buckles on his red,/And on the Dachshunds go. OBAL

Dad. Elaine Feinstein. Rest in peace, Yisroel ben Menachem Mendel! VWA

Dad and the Cat and the Tree. Kit Wright. Stuck/Up/The/Tree! OnUR

Dad's Greatest Job. Anonymous. For I'll know I've been successful as a/little fellow's dad. STF

Daddy. Lucille Clifton. I comfort my son with the hope/the life in the confident man. NIP

Daddy. Rose Fyleman. Like funny people in a pantomime. SiSoSe

Daddy. Sylvia Plath. Daddy, daddy, you bastard, I'm through. BiP; BoWoP; CAPP; CMoP; CoAP; HaCAP; InPK; InPS; LiTM; NaP; NIP; NMM; NMP; NoAm; NOBA; NoP; PAI; PrIm; TW; TwCP; UnPo

Daddy Shot a Bear. Anonymous. Shot him through the keyhole/An' never touch a hair... OuSiCo

Daedalus. Alastair Reid. My son has birds in his head. NCSH; NYBP

The Daemon. Louise Bogan. It said "Once more." NYBP

The Daemon. Mikhail Yuryevich Lermontov. And indifferent as they. AWP

Daffadowndilly. Mother Goose. In a yellow petticoat/And a green gown. NTCP; SoPo; TiPo

Daffodil's Return. Bliss Carman. For Daffodil comes home today. CaP

Daffodils. Ruth Guthrie Harding. There flames the first gay daffodil/Where winter-long the snows have lain! HBMV

Daffodils. Michael Heffernan. and someone outside them, watching. AMV-80; SM

Daffodils. Kikurio. We have the daffodils. TiPo

Daffodils. Lizette Woodworth Reese. Gone like a snatch of song upon the stair. AA

Daffodils. William Wordsworth. And dances with the daffodils. AnFE; BLPA; FaBoBe; FaBV; FaFP; FiP; FPL; GN; GoJo; GoTF; GTBS; GTBS-P; LiTB; MCCG; NOBE; OBEV; OBNC; OHFP; PPoe; SCV; SeCeV; TreF; TrGrPo; WBLP

The Daft-Days. Robert Fergusson. Be thou prepared/To hedge us frae that black banditti,/The City-Guard. BSV; CEP; NOEC

Daft Jean. Sydney Thomas Dobell. White, white," sang she! VLP

Dafydd Ap Gwilym Resents the Winter. Rolfe Humphries. When will rain come? NYBP

The Dagger. Jorge Luis Borges. ...and the/years slip by, unheeding. NYBP

Dagger. Mikhail Yuryevich Lermontov. Like you, my iron-hearted friend! AWP

Dagonet's Canzonet. Ernest Rhys. O soul, was she not fair! HBV 1-2

The Daguerreotype. William Vaughn Moody. Strong eyes and brave,/Inexorable to save! AnAmPo

Daguerreotype of a Grandmother. Celeste Turner Wright. Burdened with love she cannot give away. Str

Daguerreotype Taken in Old Age. Margaret Atwood. I am being/eaten away by light BoWoP

Dahlias. Padraic Colum. Above bright Ophir and dark Gades sees. GoJo; NePoAm

Daily Bread. Anonymous. Glowing yet with gratitude! BePJ

Daily Courage Doesnt Count. Alta. but i tell you, i came out of those marriages/one smart bitch. GP

The Daily Grind. Fenton Johnson. God has blest you. AmNP

Daily Growing. Anonymous. And death put an end to his growing. FSW

Daily I Fall in Love with Waitresses. Elliot Fried. but they never stand still long enough/as they serve serve serve. GP

The Daily Manna. Sara Henderson Hay. The short way home... GoYe

Daily News. Tom Clark. As I return to my newspaper. ANYP; EAS

Daily Paradox. Sara Henderson Hay. And drags her husband out to dinner. InMe

The Daily Round. Ronald McCuaig. The evening kicks him on his homing tangent. BoAV

Daily the Drum. Anne Wilkinson. These are the sounds that murder. NOBC

Daily the Ocean between Us. Patricia Goedicke. Daily the ocean between us/Grows deeper but not wider. TAP

Daily Trials. Oliver Wendell Holmes. ...men never can be still/But in their graves. PoEL 1-5

Daily Wages. Amrita Pritam. And leave no grain for tomorrow. PBWP

Daily with You. Annie Johnson Flint. Christ, still interceding–stay with us to-day! BLRP

Dain do Eimhir (excerpt). Sorley MacLean. ...and the marvel of a beautiful face. NeBP

Dain Eile (excerpt). Sorley MacLean. ...where the diseased infant writhes and wallows till/death. NeBP

A Dainty Song. Allan Ramsay. Ye're welcomer to tak me, than to let me be. OBEC

The Dainty Young Heiress of Lincoln's Inn Fields. Charles, Earl of Dorset Sackville. May wound her heart deeper than any. PoL

The Daisies. Bliss Carman. And all of their dancing was, "Life, thou art good!" BoNaP; HBV 1-2

Daisies. Alden Nowlan. and her body burst like a fountain of flowers. NeAC

The Daisies. James Stephens. And she and I went hand in hand/In the field where the daisies are. AnIV; AWP

Daisies. Valerie Worth. As if earth were glad/To see us passing here. PCP

Daisies. Andrew Young. Through the long night in which I lie/Stars will be shining in my sky. GoJo

Daisies of Florence. Kathleen Raine. Ripening the transient under her veil. NYBP

The Daisy. Robert Burns. And low thou lies! BoNaP

The Daisy. Alfred, Lord Tennyson. My fancy fled to the South again. EnLoPo; NOBV; OBNC; OBVV; PoEL 1-5

Daisy. Francis Thompson. And perish in our own. BeLS; BrPo

Daisy. William Carlos Williams. blades of limpid seashell. MoAB; MoAmPo

The Daisy. Marya Zaturenska. And in a flower white-frocked like my small daughter. GrPl; MoAmPo

Daisy Bell (A Bicycle Built for Two). Harry Dacre. But you'll look sweet/On the seat of a bicycle built for two! BLSo; FSN; GoTF; TreF

Daisy Fraser. Edgar Lee Masters. Without contributing ten dollars and costs/To the school fund of Spoon river! CMoP; HAP; MoVE

Daisy's Song. John Keats. Lambs bleat my lullaby. BoNaP

Dakota Badlands. Elizabeth Landeweer. And heals the land with one quick lover's kiss. AmFN

Dakota: Five Times Six. Joseph Hansen. But Mrs. Aherne sold taste rainbows at/Two for one cent, and from her shelves rained sugar. NYBP

Dakota Land. Anonymous.
Till Gabriel blows his trumpet sound/And says the rain's just gone around. CoSo; FSW
We are too poor to get away. AS; BPAW

Dakota: October, 1822. Hunkpapa Warrior. Rod Taylor. What bad thing can be done against us? WeW

A Dakota Wheat-Field. Hamlin Garland. Before the wind's feet/In the wheat! OBCA

The Dalesman's Litany. Anonymous. From Hull and Halifax and Hell,/Good Lord, deliver me. OBET

Daley's Dorg Wattle. W. T. Goodge. That there dorg had got that inseck in the bottle. GDP; PoAu 1-2

The Dalliance of Eagles. Walt Whitman. She hers, he his, pursuing. AA; AmPP; BiP; BoAnP; FM; HAP; HeIP; NoP; PoL; PPoe; PPP; PrIm; TAP

Dalmatian Nocturne. Aleksa Santic. O'er blackened ridges crawls. LiTW

Dalyaunce. Anonymous. And this seven yere I have ben his page/And kept his commaundement... AtBAP; CH

The Dam, Glen Garry. Robert Symmons. Better to leave it so–and to escape/Whatever in the landscape may be strange. PoSH

Dam Neck, Virginia. Richard Eberhart. But of the beautiful disrelation of the spiritual. LiTA; MoAB; WaP

The Damage You Have Done. Ellis Ayitey Komey. ...I'll set to work/If the land is to recover/From the damage you have done. PBA

Damages, Two Hundred Pounds. William Makepeace Thackeray. And if after this you lose her–why you're paid two hundred/pound. OBSV

Dame. Susan Astor. Waiting for pups. AMV-80

Dame Liberty Reports from Travel. Dorothy Cowles Pinkney. She knows it's there, it's there. GoYe

The Dame of Dundee. Anonymous. And she sold them/Three farthings a pint. OxNR

Dame Trot. Anonymous. Purr, says the cat. OxNR

Dame Wiggins of Lee. Anonymous. All welcome once more,"/Cried Dame Wiggins of Lee. FaBoBe; OxBChV

Damelias' Song to His Diaphenia. Henry Constable. Then in requite, sweet virgin, love me! ELP; HBV 1-2; OBSC; PoEL 1-5; ViBoPo

Damis, an Author Cold and Weak. Anonymous. Good vinegar of sorry wine. HBV 1-2

Damn the Filipinos. Anonymous. And return us to our own beloved homes. ABF

Damnation of Vancouver: Speech of the Salish Chief. Earle Birney. I walked down to the home of the Seal Brother.... OBCV

Damned Women. Charles Baudelaire. Fulfil your doom, disordered minds, and fly/The infinite you carry in your soul. BoLoP

Damocles. Robert Graves. And swords of Damocles. NYBP

Damon and Cupid. John Gay.
But readily resort/To Bellenden's or Lepell's. SeCeV
What I did, you must have done.' EnLoPo

Damon & Pythias. Robert Creeley. were said to be living together again. LCAP

Damon the Mower. Andrew Marvell. For Death thou art a Mower too. AnAnS 1; JCP; OAEL 1-2

The Dampe. John Donne. Naked you'have odds enough of any man. SeCP

The Damsel. Omar B. Abi Rabi'a. He who the morn may awake from her kisses/Drinks from the cup of the blessed in heaven! AWP; LiTW

Dan Bartholmew's Dolorous Discourses. George Gascoigne. Bear with my Muse, it is not as it was. EnRePo

Dan Dunder. John Ciardi. And get a job with it–as thunder! BBGG

Dan Ellis's Boys. Anonymous. When Jeff's men see you comin'/By God, you'll see 'em run! AmFP

Dan Taylor. Anonymous. Your true and faithful friend. CoSo

Dan, the Dust of Masada Is Still in My Nostrils. Ruth Whitman. your city/spilled among the Judean hills./Jerusalem. VWA

Dana Point. Brewster Ghiselin. we cry (however I whisper) against it (into the westwind). AMV-81

Danae. Simonides (of Ceos). Oh, forgive my hardihood/If I speak offending. LiTW

The Dance. Anonymous. 'Tis you must pay the piper? PAH

The Dance. Thomas Campion. And like lovers hand in hand/March around and make a stand. EiL; FaBoCh; LoGBV

The Dance. Hart Crane. The serpent with the eagle in the boughs. AnAmPo; LiTM; OxBA

The Dance. Robert Duncan. I'll slip away before they're up/and see the dew shining. NeAP

The Dance. Jim Gustafson. but mostly/we just danced. APU

The Dance. Daniel Halpern. No one's dancing here tonight–wouldn't you know it. MAYP

The Dance. LeRoi (Imamu Amiri Baraka) Jones. create a self of your own. One/that will love me. CoPo

The Dance. Rudolph Chambers Lehmann. Leaving never a trace of their gay little selves/Or the winter-night dance of the fairies and elves. HBMV

The Dance. Mark Strand. And who isn't borne again and again into heaven? GeTw

Dance. Lula Lowe Weeden. They are too big for toys. CDC

The Dance. William Carlos Williams. in Breughel's great picture, The Kermess. AmP; AmPP; CMoP; ExPo; GoJo; GrPl; HAP; HeIP; InPK; LiTM; LoGBV; NCSH; NIP; NoAm; NOBA; NoP; OxBA; PoL; PrIm; SoSe; TAP; WeW

Dance a Baby Diddy. Anonymous. So dance, my baby deary. OxNR

The Dance Called David. Theodore Weiss. ...these scarred years that are/journeying and pity, of myself. CoPo

A Dance Chant. Anonymous.
May I be able to take horses! WGRP
Preserver of all things visible and invisible! WGRP

Dance & Eye Me (Wicked)ly My Breath a Fixed Sphere. Rochelle Owens. purest light brilliant & ruddy/so/favorable! NMM

Dance Figure. Ezra Pound. None with swift feet. AnAmPo; AnFE; HeIP; HW; MoAB; MoAmPo

A Dance for Ma Rainey. Al Young. or play the veins of their strong tender arms/with needles/to prove how proud we are. NBP

A Dance for Militant Dilettantes. Al Young. & shake the shit out of them. PoBA

A Dance for Rain. Witter ("Emanuel Morgan") Bynner. Rain, rain in Cochiti! BPAW

Dance Hymn. Isaiah Shembe. I do not fear anything,/Because I am perfect. WTO

Dance Instructions for a Young Girl. Kimiko Hahn. belong to you, a woman. BrSi

The Dance of Death. Henry Austin Dobson. There is no King more terrible than Death. HBV 1-2

Dance of Death. Aulus Persius Flaccus. The pines dance on, the quick and dead together. AnAmPo

The Dance of Death. John Lydgate.
But many a man, yif I shal not tarye,/Ofte daunceth, but no thinge of herte. PoEL 1-5
Who hath no chippe muste rowe in bote or barge. EnPo

The Dance of Despair. Hayim Nahman Bialik. And be ye of good cheer–and go to the/devil! TrJP

The Dance of Dust (parody). Louis Untermeyer. What do we wait for? Is it all a dream? BXAP

The Dance of Gray Raccoon. Arthur Guiterman. And the snow wraiths whirl to the eldritch/tune/Of the medicine dance of Gray Raccoon. BPAW

The Dance of Love. Sir John Davies. That Love, this art in every part might show. EIL; SeCePo

The Dance of Saul with the Prophets. Saul Tchernichovsky. And all that night...naked.../naked...naked. TrJP

Dance of the Abakweta. Margaret Danner. Quick as Aladdin rubbing his lamp, she would. PoNe

The Dance of the Daughters of Herodias. Arthur Symons. May hear your dancing fainter than the drift/Of the last petals falling from the rose. BrPo

The Dance of the Elephants. Michael S. Harper. and what love as the elephant chimes. LCAP

Dance of the Infidels. Al Young. hold onto the heart & the hearts of others./I love you PoBA

Dance of the Macabre Mice. Wallace Stevens. The arm of bronze outstretched against all evil! CMoP; NePA; NOBA; OxBA; SeCeV

The Dance of the Rain. Eugene Marais. Oh, the dance of our sister! PeSA

The Dance of the Seven Deadly Sins. William Dunbar. That in the deepest pit of Hell/He smoorit them with smuke. BSV; GoTS; OxBS

Dance on Pushback. James Still. Night will be fading and moonlight dying. GrPl

Dance Song. *Anonymous.* Alas for the unicorn! FaBoCh; LoGBV

A Dance Song. Burkhard von Hohenfels. My girl advances and glances: my chance is to fall in/the trap! LiTW

Dance-Song. Jaroslav Seifert. And now that one does not exist either. AMV-81

Dance-Song of the Lightning. *Anonymous.* you wife of the Copper-bodied man. PeSA

Dance to Your Daddie. *Anonymous.* You shall get a coatie when the boat comes in! PoPle

Dance to Your Daddie. Mother Goose. You shall get a fishy, when the boat comes home. TiPo

Dance to Your Daddy. *Anonymous.*
Dance to your daddy, my little lamb. FSW
When your daddy comes home. OxNR

Dance with Banderillas. Richard Duerden. in common with the building, the monkey, land etcetera. NeAP

The Dancer. Joseph Campbell. Clay in his thoughts,/And lightning in his tread! OBMV; OxBI

The Dancer. Ednah Proctor (Clarke) Hayes. The music dies in whispered ecstacies. AA

Dancer. Roy Scheele. ...whirling/around in the yard,/making her long dress swirl. GOYP

The Dancer. Walter James Turner. As though upon the face of Night/Lay the bright wreck of day. NOAV; OBMV

The Dancer. Edmund Waller. Moves with the numbers which she hears. TrGrPo

The Dancer. Al Young. as I dig my spoon into the belly of a melon. PoBA

The Dancer at Cruachan and Cro-Patrick. William Butler Yeats. Acclaiming, proclaiming, declaiming Him. UnS

Dancer: Four Poems. Paul Engle. ...The dancer falls/Then rises like an oriole over walls. AMV-80

...The Dancer from the Dance. Suzanne Juhasz. the finale is always the same. IHMS

A Dancer's Life. Donald Justice. Her life–she feels it closing about her now/Like a small theater, empty, without lights. LCAP

The Dancers. Babette Deutsch. And love triumphant treads among the stars. HBMV

The Dancers. Wilfred Wilson Gibson. And dainty dancing demoiselles/Above the dreamless dead. MMM

The Dancers. Roland Robinson. above the plains, mountains and trees of earth. ACV

Dancers at the Moy. Paul Muldoon. Give their earthen floors/The ease of trampolines. BIrV

The Dancers Inherit the Party. Ian Hamilton Finlay. While the talkers wear themselves out and/sit in corners alone, and glower. FF

The Dancers of Colbek. [(or Manning)] Robert Mannyng. "The nere the cherche, the firther from God." OxBM

Dances of Death. Alexander Blok. a chemist's shop, a street, a lamp. OBVE

Dancing at Whitsun. Austin John Marshall. And the ladies go dancing at Whitsun. OBET

The Dancing Bear. Rachel Field. More like a child's lost in woods at night/Than the eyes of a big brown bear. NTCP

The Dancing Bear. Albert Bigelow Paine. When the dancing bear came back with me. OBCA

The Dancing Bear. Robert Southey. For seven long years, this precious syllogism/Hath baffled justice and humanity! FM

The Dancing Cabman. J. B. Morton. In square black boots/The cabman dances. MoShBr; NOBL

The Dancing Faun. Robert Cameron Rogers. How canst thou dream Pan dead when/still/Thou seem'st to hear him sing! AA

Dancing Gal. Frank Marshall Davis. I see a long lean god/Standing in painted splendor. FB

A Dancing Girl. Frances Sargent Osgood She had been talking all the while. AA

Dancing-Girl's Song. Kshetrayya. Leaving me in a daze of shameless desire. BoWoP

Dancing Partners. Philip Child. ..."If I were dead, were dead/What would you do?" CaP

The Dancing Ploughmen. Michael Kennedy Joseph. Stare upwards at the starry wheel. ACV

Dancing School. Jonathan Holden. ...but Liddy/outdid me: she'd pretend/to be grateful. Psk

The Dancing Seal. Wilfrid Gibson. On that moonshiny, Island-strand,/For ever and for evermore. HBMV; OnMSP

The Dancing Sunshine Lounge. Thomas Rabbit. She can't care. She loves us each like a friend. MAYP

Dancing the Shout to the True Gospel. Rita Mae Brown. A luxury diminishing death. NMM; PeHV

Dandelion. Annie Rankin Annan. The fields once blossomy we scour/Where the old poets plucked the flower. HBV 1-2

Dandelion. Hilda Conkling. There is only the grass to fight! TiPo

The Dandelion. Vachel Lindsay. By noon you raise a sea of stars/More golden than before. BrR

The Dandelion Gatherer. Robert Francis. The gleaming wineglass and the golden wine. PPJ

Dandelions. John Albee. A spirit form, till on the sight it dies. AA

Dandelions. Marchette Chute. To see all the beautiful flowers/She gets on her birthday from me. BiCB

The Dandelions. Helen Gray Cone. When, well-a-day, they blew away,/And ne'er were heard of after. HBV 1-2

Dandelions. Frances Frost. These are the small gold buttons/On earth's green, windy coat. TiPo

Dandelions. Gerda Mayer. Such brazen slatterns; but later, white-haired, genteel. PoL

Dandelions. Howard Nemerov. And the liberation from the lion's mouth. DFF; NePA

Dandelions for Chains. Sarah Kirsch. extends across the seventeenth parallel where head-/sized jungle flowers bloom. WPOW

Dandoo. *Anonymous.*
How the old man tans his mutton skin."/Ramyam gilliam dandoo, ah! TrAS
Hurry me, burry me, hickey ho,/To wag dum mingo. BFSS

The Dandy Horse. *Anonymous.* You will go down, dandy horse and all,/And bruise your latter end. OBET

The Dandy O. *Anonymous.* The ladies all are dying for the Dandy O. CoMu

Dane-Geld. Rudyard Kipling. And the nation that plays it is lost!' OxBTC

Danebury. *Anonymous.* Recalls the scenes of Childhood to her view,/And lives those pleasing moments o'er anew. PeHV

Danger. Helen Hunt Jackson. Lies hid the pebble for the fatal sling. AnFE; APA

Danger. Theodora L. Paine. House of the Future, built upon the sand. PGD

The Danger of Writing Defiant Verse. Dorothy Parker. Oh, Lord! I see on reading this,/He is an awful sap! InMe

Dangerous Condition: Sign on Inner-City House. Russell Atkins. seek out the lives/with a rifle,/for a bulldozer?/to the death? CNA

A Dangerous Music. Michael Knoll. her voice lifting us into trees. LFAC

The Dangers of Foot-Ball. John Gay. And gingling sashes on the pent-house sound. EnLi 1-2; SD

The Dangers of Sexual Excess. John Armstrong. And coy perdition every hour pursue. FaBoUs

Dangers of the Journey to the Happy Land. Joseph Ceravolo. Mayan sub-flowers in/the shade. ANYP

Daniel at Breakfast. Phyllis McGinley. And, kissing his wife abruptly at the door,/Stamps fiercely off to catch the 8:04. OBSV

Daniel Boone. Arthur Guiterman. "Elbow room!" laughs Daniel Boone. MaC; MoShBr

Daniel Boone, 1735-1820. Rosemary and Stephen Vincent Benét. And all lost, wild America/Is burning in their eyes. AmFN; NAMP

Daniel Defoe. Walter Savage Landor. A Rodney and a Nelson may/Without him not have won the day. NCEP

Daniel Gray. Josiah Gilbert Holland. I shall be sure to find old Daniel Gray. AA; HBV 1-2

The Daniel Jazz. Vachel Lindsay. And gave him his job again. CBEP; TrGrPo

Daniel Saul. *Anonymous* Spitalfields weaver, and that's all. FaBoEE

Daniel Saw de Stone. *Anonymous.* Daniel saw de stone,/Cut out de mountain widout hands. BoAN 1-2

Daniel Webster. Oliver Wendell Holmes. Till morning's latest sunlight fades/On the blue tablet of the deep! PAH

Daniel Webster's Horses. Elizabeth Jane Coatsworth. They were fine horses–/See their shoes fit. AmFN; AnNE; MoAmPo; OBCA; PH

Danish Wit. John Hollander. "Something is Groton in/Denmark, at least!" NLV; PV

Danny. Malcolm Cowley. Or mumble petulant inanities? PoA

Danny. John Millington Synge. Where men choked Danny's gullet. AnEnPo

Danny Boy. Anonymous. Then I simply sleep in peace, until you come to me. FSW

Danny Deever. Rudyard Kipling. After hangin' Danny Deever in the mornin'. AnFE; BrPo; DiPo; ExPo; FaBoBa; FaPoR; FPL; GoTF; GTBS; GTBS-P; HBV 1-2; InPS; LiTB; MaC; MCCG; MoBrPo; NOBE; NOBV; OAEP; OxBoLi; OxBTC; PAI; PoLf; SCV; SeCePo; TEP; TreFS; TrGrPo; UnPo; VLP; WaaP

Danny Murphy. James Stephens. –But when he laughed, then you could see/He was as young as young could be! OnUR; RoGo

Danny's Wooing. David McKee Wright. "Now, Danny, we'll tell/A small word to the priest." PoAu 1-2

Dans l'Allee. Paul Verlaine. The slightly simpering sparkle of the eye. AWP

Danse Russe. William Carlos Williams. Who shall say I am not/the happy genius of my household? CMoP; ForPo; InPS; NOBA; NoP; PAI; PPP; TAP

Dante. William Cullen Bryant. The richest harvest reaped on earth/Crowns the last century's closing year. ViBoPo

Dante. Robert Duncan. He wakes from deepest sleep/upon a distant signal and waits/as if crouching, springs/to life. PoM

Dante. Henry Wadsworth Longfellow. Thy voice along the cloister whispers/"Peace!" AA; AnNE; OBEV

Dante. Buonarroti Michelangelo. Ne'er walked the earth a greater man than he. AWP

Dante at Verona. Dante Gabriel Rossetti. Which, of all paths his feet knew well,/Were steeper found than Heaven or Hell. MaVP

Dante's Angel. Dante Alighieri.
Bearing our fleshly burden willed to go.' BoC
As every sense is vanquished by excess. BoC

Danville Girl. Anonymous. Never did look back. FSW

Daphnaida (excerpt). Edmund Spenser. And with the same fill every hill and dale. PoPle

Daphne. Bliss Carman. Where the great Cyprian mother should receive/Our warm unsullied vows. OBCV

Daphne. Hildegarde Flanner. Beneath a tree that had no name,/Silence turned and slept. HBMV

Daphne. Thomas S. Jones, Jr. ...half maid/Half tree? OHIP

Daphne. Selden Rodman. And our hair that the god had breathed upon turned laurel. PoNe

Daphne. Edith Sitwell. And now I seek through the sere summer/Where no trees are shady. HBMV

Daphne. Jonathan Swift. Thus we both shall have our ends,/And continue special friends. NOBL

Daphne and Apollo. George Macy. There is no prize for loving, but there's laurel in a rhyme! InMe

Daphne and Apollo. Matthew Prior. May thy good-will be equal to thy pow'r! NOEC

Daphne Stillorgan. Denis Devlin. Birds (O unreal whitewashed station!)/Compose no more that invisible architecture. CIP

Daphnis Came on a Summer's Day. Anonymous. Her lily breast doth stain/All flowers and lilies far. ViBoPo

Daphnis to Ganymede. Richard Barnfield. And, last of all, I'll give thee a little lamb/To play withal, new-weaned from her dam. EiL

Dappled Grey. Anonymous. Through the old town of Windsor. OxNR

Darby and Joan. St. John Honeywood. Forgive the past, and strive to mend. AA

The Darby Ram. Anonymous. But the man who told this story, sir,/Was a lyin' son of a —. FSW

Dare Quam Accipere. Mathilde Blind. For still I hold it that to give/Is sweeter than to take. OBVV

Dare You? Edward Rowland Sill. If you dare come with us, be/Lost in love's great unity. AnNE

Dare You See a Soul at the White Heat? Emily Dickinson. Until the Designated Light/Repudiate the Forge– MAmP

Daredevil. Kirby Congdon. behind the coffin lid/closing like an office door. PeHV

Darest Thou Now O Soul. Walt Whitman. Equal, equipped at last, (O joy! O fruit of all!) them to fulfil, O soul! AA; AmLP; HBV 1-2; NePA; TrGrPo; TRV; ViBoPo; WGRP

Darien. Sir Edwin Arnold. Whilst England and Columbia, quitting fear,/Kissed–and let in the eager waters there. MC; PAH

Daring. Carol Konek. bring you down/to me. IHMS

Darius Green and his Flying-Machine. John Townsend Trowbridge. The moral is–Take care how you light. BeLS; BLPL; FaBoBe; HBV 1-2; HBVY; InMe; MoShBr; OBAL; OBCA; OxBChV; PoLf; YaD

The Dark. Roy Fuller. I dread it still at sixty-two. DuDa

Dark. Eloise Klein Healy. I've taken to hiding a piece of flint in my shoe. AMV-80

The Dark. William Heyen. The dark has many doors. EyDe

The Dark and Falling Summer. Delmore Schwartz. Everywhere was full of the pulsing of the loud and fallen dusk. NYBP

The Dark and the Fair. Stanley Jasspon Kunitz. Who taught me the serpent's word, but yet the word. PoCh

Dark Angel. Elizabeth Bartlett. Swung in its orbit, bringing you, dark angel, down. NePoAm-2

The Dark Angel. Lionel Pigot Johnson. Divine, to the Divinity. ACP; CAW; GTBS-P; LiTB; MoBrPo; NOBE; NOBV; OAEL 1-2; OBMV; VLP; WHA

Dark Area. Russell Atkins. somewhere near/the volumed/dun? FB

Dark Aspect and Prospect. Anonymous. An eclipse of the sun for days and weeks/Forebodes disaster in Constantinople! PeD

The Dark Birds. Bert Meyers. and sunlight warmed the stones,/fire undressed my bones. VWA

The Dark Brother. Lewis Alexander. And you through love my blackness shall endure! CDC

The Dark Cat. Audrey Alexandra Brown. –The last laugh's mine!–and so escape forever. CaP

The Dark Cavalier. Margaret Widdemer. You shall lie happily, smiling in your sleep. HBMV

The Dark Chamber. Louis Untermeyer. The music, the silence....These will remain. MoAmPo; MoLP; WHA

The Dark Chateau. Walter De la Mare. My dark chateau. BrPo

Dark Conclusions. Ruth Stone. And find the center rustating, malevolent. BoWoP

Dark Corner. Graham Hough. To branch and glimmer in the living flood. NMP

A Dark Country. Derek Mahon. Or enough to suffer the relief and the pity. BIrV

Dark Danny. Ivy O. Eastwick. Dark Danny knows all/These lovely things. BrR; TiPo

A Dark Day. Dante Gabriel Rossetti. Which one new year makes soft her marriage-bed. MaVP

The Dark Dialogues, II. W. S. Graham. May hear the lonely leagues/Of the kittiwake and the fulmar. OxBS

Dark Earth and Summer. Edgar Bowers. Caught in the wide, implacable,/Clear gaze of the basilisk. QFR

The Dark-Eyed Gentleman. Thomas Hardy. That his daddy once tied up my garter for me! MoAB; MoBrPo; NLV; UnPo; VLP

Dark-Eyed Lad Columbus. Nancy Byrd Turner. Dark-eyed lad of long ago! SiSoSe

The Dark-Eyed Sailor. Anonymous. For a cloudy morning, a cloudy morning/Oft brings a pleasant day. FSW; ShS

Dark Eyes at Forest Hills. I. L. Martin. For she was the nearest linesman/And he didn't like the call. SD

Dark Flows the River. Arthur Stanley Bourinot. What of man's journey,/Where travels he? CaP

Dark Girl. Arna Bontemps. Your dancing girl is dead. GoSl

The Dark Girl Dressed in Blue. Anonymous. Especially a dark girl dressed in blue. BeLS

The Dark Girl's Rhyme. Dorothy Parker. Living for a hating,/Dying of a love? InMe

A Dark Hand. Itzik Manger. I know that soon I will stand before you/And spit at your face with my blood. VWA

The Dark Hills. Edwin Arlington Robinson. Were fading, and all wars were done. AP; CoBMV; FaFP; GoJo; HAP; LiTA; LiTM; MoAB; MoAmPo; NePA; NoAm; WeW; WHA

The Dark House. Anonymous. And in that dark, dark box, there was a GHOST! NTCP

Dark in the Reich of the Blond. William Heyen. as we wait here with our papers. Lie here quiet. MAYP

The Dark Lady. Anonymous. God kepe hem, bothe in feeld and towne,/And thenne shal I be kept ful wel. OxBM

The Dark Lord of Savaiki. Alistair Campbell. where the leaping dolphins/celebrate the dawn. OCNZ

The Dark Man. Nora Hopper. But my fiddle knows–and I talk to her. HBV 1-2

The Dark Memory. John Hall Wheelock. Shed for my sake–and how you wept alone. LiTL

The Dark Morning. Thomas Merton. Through all the coiling passages of/(Curled ear) my prison! PoA

Dark Mountains. Milton Lockyer. There sure was a lot of noisy conversation at Pawirra Pool. CBAP

The Dark Night of the Soul. Saint John of Damascus. Amid the lilies drowning all my care. ErPo; LiTW; WeW

The Dark Palace.　Alice Milligan.　'Gainst the Saxon stranger on the day of danger/Out of Aileach Neid.　AnIV

Dark People.　Kattie M. Cumbo.　dark people do.　BOLo

Dark Phrases.　Ntozake Shange.　lady in purple/you're it.　BlSi

Dark Pines under Water.　Gwendolyn MacEwen.　There is something down there and you want it told.　NOBC

The Dark Planet.　John Heath-Stubbs.　Implacable, that sky-wanderer. Its name is Love.　OAEL 1-2

Dark Prophesy: I Sing of Shine.　Etheridge Knight.　Yeah, damn near drunk and dancing in the streets.　GP

Dark Rapture.　George William Russell.　Where the Holy Breath was mixed with the unholy wine.　SeCePo

The Dark-Red Shadow-Spots.　Yumei Kanbara.　My thought is disordered.　LiTW

The Dark Road.　Ethel Clifford.　To comfort her who leaves the earth behind.　HBV 1-2

Dark Road Blues.　Willie Lofton.　Cryin' I was standin' right there/po-lice had me barred　BluL

Dark Romance.　Lucha Corpi.　A scent of vanilla drifts/on the evening air.　WPOW

Dark Room.　Fredrick Zydek.　It was the hour of inquisition, when darkness/wasn't strange to those who dwelled there.　AMV-80

Dark Rosaleen.　Owen Roe MacWard.　Ere you can fade, ere you can die,/My Dark Rosaleen!　BIrV; OnYI

Dark Rosaleen.　James Clarence Mangan.　My dark Rosaleen!　ACP; CH; EnRP; GTBS; HBV 1-2; IrPN; NOBI; OBEV; OBVV; OxBI; ViBoPo

Dark Rosaleen.　Hugh O'Donnell.　Ere you can fade, ere you can die,/My Dark Rosaleen!　AWP; LiTW

Dark Rosaleen, IX.　David McKee Wright.　If daylight and night-shine/Were not in your kiss.　PoAu 1-2

The Dark Scent of Prayer.　Rose Drachler.　The striped wasp/Confused by the Book/Can thrive on/The dark scent of prayer.　VWA

Dark Shadows.　John Hall.　evidence of/chaotic times.　NBP

Dark Song.　Archie Randolph Ammons.　old, departing,/can confer/nothing.　MAT

Dark Song.　Edith Sitwell.　The dark earth, furry as a bear,/Grumbled too!　CMoP; FaBoTw; PBWP

The Dark Stag.　Isabella Valancy Crawford.　The brown earth crimsons as he dies,/The strong and dusky stag.　NOBC; PeCV

The Dark Swimmers.　Larry Eigner.　the toppled clouds/the squared mountain.　PoM

Dark Symphony.　Melvin B. Tolson.　With the Peoples of the World.../We advance!　BALP; PoNe

Dark Testament.　Pauli Murray.　Friend and brother to every other man.　AmNP; BlSi

Dark Thoughts Are My Companions.　J. V. Cunningham.　Though I come to it with a broken head/In the cat-house of the dishevelled dead.　TW

Dark Was the Night.　Anonymous.　My head upon His breast.　AmFP

The Dark Way Home: Survivors.　Michael S. Harper.　lovely, like this.　CNA

Dark Wings.　James Stephens.　Sing while you may.　PoA

Dark Wood.　Ian Wedde.　a breath/of what the dark/wood took.　OCNZ

A Dark World.　E. J. Scovell.　...to float on the night-face/Of water, with white stars to drift as a dark world.　MoVE

Darkened in the Soul.　Napa.　A great terrible blackness,/Dreadful.　WTO

The Darkened Mind.　James Russell Lowell.　Not so much of thee is left among us/As the hum outliving the hushed bell.　MAmP

Darkened Windows.　Ronald Bottrall.　For the hazardous cliff-face and the promised land.　PoA

Darkening Hotel Room.　Alfred Corn.　Indifferent to, unaware of us.　MAYP

The Darkling Chicken (parody).　Robert Peters.　Some chicken-bliss whereof he knows/And I am unaware.　BXAP

The Darkling Thrush.　Thomas Hardy.　And I was unaware.　AnFE; ATP; BoLiVe; BrPo; CMoP; CoBMV; DiPo; EvOK; ExPo; FaFP; ForPo; FPL; GTBS; HAP; HBMV; InPS; LiTB; LiTM; MasP; MoAB; MoBrPo; MoPo; NIP; NoAm; NOBE; NOBV; NoP; OAEL 1-2; OAEP; OBEV; OBNC; OBVV; PAI; PBBP; PPP; RoGo; SeCeV; SoSe; TEP; TreFT; TrGrPo; UnPo; VLP; WaP

Darkmotherscream.　Andrei Voznesensky.　Rome fell/not having grasped the phrase: darkmotherscream.　NU

Darkness.　Peggy Bacon.　his meal the whole world.　BrR

Darkness.　George Gordon, Lord Byron.　And the clouds perish'd; Darkness had no need/Of aid from them–She was the Universe.　EnRP; ERoP 1-2; LiTB; MBW 1-2; OAEL 1-2; OAEP; PoEL 1-5; TEP

Darkness.　Joseph Campbell.　I look at it, and pass on.　BIrV

Darkness.　Arthur Hugh Clough.　For this, O human beings, mourn we may.　OBSP

The Darkness.　Lionel Pigot Johnson.　Have mercy, and give light, and stablish me!　BrPo

Darkness.　Greg Kuzma.　and know what the fish know.　WOLT

Darkness.　James Naumberg Rosenberg.　Is it for this that Thou hast shut mine/eyes?　AA

Darkness Music.　Muriel Rukeyser.　And my wild bed turns slowly among the stars.　BoWoP

Darky Sunday School.　Anonymous.
And hear such Bible stories as you never heard before.　ABF
If this ain't a proper ending, then you can go to Hell.　OxBoLi

Darlin'.　Anonymous.
I'd be home in mama's bed, darlin', darlin'.　FSW
O darlin', you can't love five.　ABF

Darlin' Corey.　Anonymous.　They're preachin' Corey's funeral,/In the lonesome graveyard ground.　FSW

Darling! Because My Blood Can Sing.　Edward Estlin Cummings.　trees tumble out of twigs and sticks;　InvP; OxBA

Darling Cora.　Anonymous.　Pretty woman has killed me stone dead.　TrAS

Darling Corey.　Anonymous.　She was drinking down her troubles/With a low-down, sorry man.　OuSiCo

Darling Cory.　Anonymous.　With a jug of liquor in her arm/And a .45 across her knee.　AmFP

Darling, I won't be your hot love.　Sulpicia.　when I left you alone in the night/to conceal my fire.　BoWoP

Darling, If You Only Knew.　Edward Newman Horn.　Fresh and fragrant little nightful.　ErPo

Darling Nellie Gray.　Benjamin Russel Hanby.　Farewell to the old Kentucky shore.　BLSo; FSW; PSoN; TrAS; TreFS

Darling of Gods and Men, beneath the Gliding Stars.　Basil Bunting.　give peace to write and read and think.　NoAm

Darling, Tell Me Yes.　John Godfrey Saxe.　The day you answered yes!　HBV 1-2

The Darned Mounseer.　Sir William Schwenck Gilbert.　Who had pity on a poor Parley-voo!　NOBL

The Dart.　Anonymous.　Every year thou claimest a heart.　GBP

Dartmoor.　Coventry Patmore.　Clung thick as bees, when brazen chimes/Call down the hiveless swarms.　NBM

Dartmoor: Sunset at Chagford.　Thomas Edward Brown.　But please remember that I am not dead,/Nor even dying.　NOBV

Dartmouth Winter-Song.　Richard Hovey.　In the pledge of fellowship./Skoal!　AA

Darwin in 1881.　Gjertrud Schnackenberg.　He lies down in his boots and overcoat,/And shuts his eyes.　SM

Darwin on Species.　Anonymous.　And black bears dabbling in the sea for play,/Lapsed into whales, and grandly swam away.　FaBoUs

Darwinism in the Kitchen.　Anonymous.　Have developed from a flea!　FiBHP; NLV

Darwinity.　Herman Charles Merivale.　What is so simple as primitive Monkeydom/Born in the sea with a cold in its head?　InMe; NA

Das Jahr Der Seele (excerpt).　Stefan George.　Warm harmony along doth suit/Who gladly plays our golden lute.　AWP

Das Kapital.　LeRoi (Imamu Amiri Baraka) Jones.　...Who is the maniac, and why everywhere at the same time....　PoM

Das Liebesleben.　Thom Gunn.　such as washing the dishes.　ErPo

Das Schloss.　Lincoln Kirstein.　The Grafin's greed, her son's need, mine, nor how to supply them.　NoAm

The Dash for the Colors.　Frederick G. Webb.　Our dark disgrace atoned for by a glorious victory.　BeLS

Dat Lonesome Stream.　Anonymous.　When I look way 'cross dat lonesome stream-　ABF

Datur Hora Quieti.　Robert Stephen Hawker.　We laid our hireling in his bed.　GoBC

Datur Hora Quieti.　Sir Walter Scott.　But Leonard tarries long!　GTBS; GTBS-P

Dauber.　John Masefield.
But after thirty days a ghostly sun/Gave sickly promise that the storms were done.　CMoP
He had got manhood at the testing-place.　BBV
Knew nothing but the wind, the cold, the pain.　AnFE; EtS; MoAB; MoBrPo; WHA
To give a hint that might suggest the whole.　EtS

Daufuskie.　Mari E. Evans.　Janis in d'new house/she' glad/she' glad.　BlSi

Daughter.　Kimiko Hahn.　than waking with a stranger.　BrSi

Daughter.　Ellen Bryant Voigt.　that leaves me stunned/by your survival.　AMV-80

The Daughter at Evening.　Robert Nathan.　And–now I laymen down ee beep.　HBMV

A Daughter of Admetus.　Thomas Sturge Moore.　Head for, and nest with her adored!　FaBoTw

The Daughter of Jairus.　Marina Tsvetayeva
For the last time?　BoWoP
In this most Christian of worlds/all poets are Jews.　BoWoP

The Daughter of Mendoza.　Mirabeau Buonaparte Lamar.　Sweet daughter of Mendoza!　AA; BPAW; HBV 1-2

The Daughter of the Regiment.   Clinton Scollard.   Just one more cheer for her, Kady Brownell!   PAH

A Daughter's House.   Norma Hope Richman.   My crazy green kitchen gets a cloud of white dust./Hello.   GOYP

The Daughter's Rebellion.   Francis Hopkinson.   In which the purse she would deposit,/As safely as in nurse's closet.   PAH

Daughters.   Astra.   we shall meet/and love each other.   BrRo

The Daughters of Blum.   Charles Wright.   Gloves waiting for hands. CoAP; SM

The Daughters of the Horseleech.   Stanley Jasspon Kunitz.   And who will keep his five charming daughters?   CrMA; TW

Daughters of War.   Isaac Rosenberg.   They are my sisters' lovers in other days and years.   BrPo

Daughters Will You Marry?   *Anonymous.*   Singing and dancing all of my life,/Yea, father, yea.   FSW

Davening.   Rochelle Ratner.   there are always new words/new books he can turn to/till the breath becomes natural.   VWA

The Daventry Wonder.   Agricola.   Let learned Macclesfield say what he will,/Spite of New Style, we'll keep old Christmas still.'   NOEC

David.   Earle Birney.   That day, the last of my youth, on the last of our mountains.   CaP; NOBC

David.   Mary Carolyn Davies.   She who heard the songs first, was her pride like mine?   HBMV

David.   Walker Gibson.   Of course, we tell him what we can.   CrMA; NePoAm

David.   Eli Mandel.   my forehead aching with stars.   PeCV

David and Bethsabe.   George Peele.
   And on thy wings bring delicate perfumes/To play the wanton with us through the leaves.   ViBoPo
   That wand'reth lightly. AtBAP; ATP; ExPo
   Then fight, brave captains, that these joys may fly/Into your bosoms with sweet victory. ViBoPo
   Welcome fair Bethsabe, King David's darling. ViBoPo

David and Goliath.   Nathaniel Crouch.   Which done, he bravely marches on,/And then cuts off his head.   OxBChV

David Ap Gwillam's Mass of the Birds.   Padraic Colum.   It was the thrush who, as the sun appeared,/Held up the Monstrance, a dew-circled leaf. CAW

David Garrick.   Oliver Goldsmith.   And Beaumonts and Bens be his Kellys above.   CBEP; OBEC; SeCeV

David Garrick, the Actor, to Sir John Hill, a Physician...   David Garrick. Thy physic a farce is.   TreFT

David Homindae.   Marjorie Stamm Rosenfeld.   The manly droop of marble./And its vein.   AMV-80

David in April.   Betty Booker.   no more than a nod/or a leaning away. PPJ

The David Jazz.   Edwin Meade Robinson.   When the neighborhood chillen gets to slingin' with rocks!   HBMV

David's Lament for Jonathan.   Peter Abelard.   Would that my heart could still/Its bitter weeping!   LiTW; PeHV

David's Lamentation.   *Anonymous.*   O my son! O my son!   AmFP

David's Lamentation.   William Billings.   Would to God I had died for thee, O Absalom, my son, my son.   TrAS

David's Song.   Robert Browning.   I have lived, seen God's hand through a lifetime, and all was/for best"?   FaBV

Davideis.   Abraham Cowley.
   And pity this base world where Friendship's made/A bait for sin, or else at best a Trade.   PeHV
   And tun'd the harsh disorders of his Soul. OBS
   In him he all things with strange order hurl'd;/In him, that full Abridgment of the World. OBS
   She low obeisance made, and disappear'd. OxBoCh
   Since when the dismal solace of their woe,/Has only been weak mankind to undo. OxBoCh
   Sleep, sleep again, my Lyre, and let thy Master dy. SeCV 1-2
   Straight into shapeless air unseen he fell. SeCV 1-2

Davis Matlock.   Edgar Lee Masters.   Or sleep is the golden goal.   LiTA; LiTM

Davy Dumpling.   *Anonymous.*   And eat him while he's hot.   OxNR

Davy, the Dicer.   Sir Thomas More.   For lending me now some leisure to make rhymes.   DiPo

Daw's Dinner.   Joyce Kilmer.   ...And the very best songs that ever are sung/Are sung while the heart is bleeding.   CAW

Dawlish Fair.   John Keats.   And ginger-bread nuts are smallish.   PoPle

The Dawn.   *Anonymous.*
   At dawn the sun will bring good cheer to me.   PoToHe
   Come dyry, come dyry, come dawn, hey ho! OBSC
   Heralds all of day's approaching. WTO
   When she is in my arms till night goes by. UnTE

Dawn.   Gordon Bottomley.   Because an owl goes home.   MoBrPo

Dawn.   Louis Dudek.   and it stood still, so beautiful it left me crazed. PeCV

Dawn.   Paul Laurence Dunbar.   Men saw the blush and called it Dawn. AmNP; GoSl; PoLf; PoNe

Dawn.   John Ford.   Fly hence, shadows, that do keep/Watchful sorrows charm'd in sleep!   OBEV

Dawn.   George B. Logan, Jr.   And the beginning hath no end.   HBV 1-2

Dawn.   John Masefield.   Though the feet halt and the heart ache.   BrPo

D-Dawn.   Margaret McGarvey.   This is Invasion Morning!   GoYe

Dawn.   Eileen Myles.   I see me I see me again.   APU

Dawn.   Constance Ortmayer.   You've killed the dawn for me!   SaC

Dawn.   P.S.M".   A lark arose....   MCCG

Dawn.   Alejandra Pizarnik.   like a fire, like a poem/written on a wall. VWA

Dawn.   Rachel (Rachel Blumstein).   Dust of thy road, my land, and thy/Grain waving golden in the sun!   TrJP

Dawn.   Arthur Rimbaud.   When I awoke, it was noon.   SOTW

Dawn.   Frederick George Scott.
   My dauntless spirit mutely stands/With eagle wings outspread for flight. CaP; PoPl
   With eagle wings outspread for flight. CaP; PoPl

Dawn.   Frank Dempster Sherman.   And lo–the dawn!   TRV

Dawn.   David Shevin.   if this is not the true/tomb of David, surely/that was one/of his sons.   VWA

Dawn.   William Carlos Williams.   glorified in full release upward–/songs cease.   MoAB; MoAmPo; PoPl

The Dawn.   William Butler Yeats.   Ignorant and wanton as the dawn. MoVE

Dawn Amid Scotch Firs.   William Sharp.   For one brief moment dazzlingly. SyP

Dawn and a Woman.   John Logan.   when we learn/we can lose a son. CAPP

Dawn and Dark.   Norman Gale.   Looked at our world; and the dark/Grew dawn.   HBV 1-2

Dawn-Angels.   Agnes Mary Frances (Mme Emile Duclaux) Robinson. From East to West ran one white shiver,/And waxen strong their song was Day.   HBV 1-2

Dawn Boy's Song.   *Anonymous.*   On the beautiful trail am I, with it I wander.   FaBV

Dawn: God.   Harold Monro.   I sing forever though I sing in vain.   WGRP

Dawn Has Yet to Ripple in.   Melville Cane.   Rat within or bird without. MoAmPo

Dawn Hippo.   Sydney Clouts.   Thunder and lightning jostle on his bones. PeSA

A Dawn Horse.   William Harmon.   Lowering his head for a moment/He starts to step.   FYAP

The Dawn in Britain.   Charles M. Doughty.   For gladness, shedding piteous tears between.   PoEL 1-5

Dawn in Inishtrahull.   D. J. O'Sullivan.   Flings out its arms, day breaks on Inishtrahull!   OnYI

Dawn in January.   Lance Henson.   whispers to/me   CDW

Dawn in the Heart of Africa.   Patrice Emery Lumumba.   A free and gallant Congo–black blossom from black seed!   PBA; TTY

A Dawn of Jaffa Pigeons.   Eli Bachar.   rise black angels in white robes/ riding bicycles.   VWA

The Dawn of Love.   Henrietta Cordelia Ray.   Speak! fairy Moon, interpret this!   BlSi

Dawn of the Space Age.   John Ciardi.   Just the way the world began. OBAL

Dawn of Womanhood.   Harold Monro.   Thus have I made the woman of my dream.   HBV 1-2

Dawn on Mid-Ocean.   John Hall Wheelock.   Trembles for passion: God was here!   EtS

Dawn on the East Coast.   Alun Lewis.   The living come back slowly from the dead.   OBWP

Dawn on the Headland.   William Watson.   Mid the sound of the speed of the worlds, the rushing/worlds, and the peal/Of the thunder of Life.   HBV 1-2

The Dawn on the Lievre.   Archibald Lampman.   Still threaded with the mountain mist, the morn/Sat like some glowing conqueror satisfied.   CaP

Dawn on the Night-Journey.   Dante Gabriel Rossetti.   The day whose end shall give this hour as sheer/As chaos to the irrevocable Past.   NCEP

Dawn Patrol: Chicago.   Richard V. Durham.   Night slowly staggers away/ And then the day.   GoSl

The Dawn's Awake!   Otto Leland Bohanan.   Has come, has come!   BANP

Dawn Song–St. Patrick's Day.   Violet Alleyn Storey.   For everywhere the Irish are,/Much gayety's aborning.   YeAr

Dawn-Song to Waken the Lovers.   *Anonymous.*   She leans across the hilltop: see, the light!   LiTW

Dawn Wail for the Dead.   Kath Walker.   Fires lit, laughter now,/And a new day calling.   CBAP

Dawn Walk.   Edward Hirsch.   Yes, we are still here.   MAYP

Dawning.   Richard Watson Dixon.   Upon the hill-top, out of sight/Of me and thee and all the dawning.   NOBV

The Dead Brother. *Anonymous.* "When the sun shines bright from the northern airt,/And that shall never be." EnSB

The Dead Butterfly. Denise Levertov. ...only those/that lie dead revealing/their rockgreen color and the bold/cut of the wings. NoP

The Dead by the Side of the Road. Gary Snyder. The dead by the side of the road. HAP; InPS

A Dead Calm and Mist. William Sharp. Save just a dream of amethyst. SyP

Dead Center. Chester Kallman. Between. Between. Between. Between. Between. Between. PoA

Dead Center. Ruth Whitman. I'll beat my poem into a trap/for the stingy fox, to prove/that you were here. NYBP

The Dead Child. George Barlow. She will not smile to-day, for she is dead. OBVV

The Dead Child. Ernest Christopher Dowson. And share thy rest. BrPo

A Dead Child. Lucian [[or Lucianus]]. So were his troubles small. EnLi 1-2; LiTW

The Dead Cities Speak to the Living Cities. Edmond Fleg. Here's a land of snow and blue furs. VWA

The Dead City. Clinch Calkins. We kiss our destruction. AnAmPo

The Dead Coach. Katharine Tynan Hinkson. Wipe Thou the widow's tears that fall! HBV 1-2

Dead Color. Charles Wright. Windows, rapturous windows! HaCAP; LCAP

Dead Cow Farm. Robert Graves. And the Cow's dead, the old Cow's dead. BrPo

The Dead Crab. Andrew Young. Or does it make for death to be/Oneself a living armoury? BSV; FaBoTw; FM; LoBV

Dead Dog. Vernon Scannell. I have no recollection of the school/Where I was taught my terror of the dead. OxBC

Dead Drunk Blues. Lillian Miller. 'Cause when I'm drunk, nothing don't worry my mind BluL

The Dead Eagle. Thomas Campbell. With notes that seem but the protracted/sounds/Of glassy runnels bubbling over rocks. EnRP; OBTV

Dead Embryos. Judit Toth. flung on the sands of a sunless eternity. WPOW

The Dead Faith. Fanny Heaslip Lea. But through long nights she stared into the dark,/And knew she lied. HBV 1-2; WGRP

The Dead Feast of the Kol-Folk. John Greenleaf Whittier. O dead, to the dying/Come home! PoEL 1-5

The Dead Fiddle. Humbert Wolfe. This was a fiddle, and thus it spoke,/and now it speaks no longer. TrJP

Dead Fires. Jessie Redmond Fauset. Better the choking sigh, the sobbing breath/Than passion's death! BANP; PoNe

Dead Fly. Eilean Ni Chuilleanain. As David, his kingdom sure, could not forget Saul. CIP

Dead Girl. Anna Hajnal. a moon drifting, light, alive. VWA

Dead Hand. William Stanley Merwin. Hang it up till the rings fall. CAPP

A Dead Harvest. Alice Meynell. Bosom nor barn is filled with these. MoVE

Dead Heroes. Karoniaktatie. we lovingly call/hero) STE

The Dead Heroes. Isaac Rosenberg. And claim God's kiss. MoBrPo

The Dead Horse. *Anonymous.* Oh, poor old horse! AmSS; AS

The Dead Horse. Cecilia Meireles. O heavy breast of the dead horse! PBWP

Dead in Bloody Snow. Meridel Le Sueur. A people's dream that died in bloody snow. GP

The Dead in Europe. Robert Lowell. Our sacred earth in our day is our curse. CMoP; DTC; LiTM; NePA; NePoEA; OxBA; OxBC

The Dead in Melanesia. Randall Jarrell. And the isles confuse him with their own black dead. MiAP

Dead in the Sierras. Joaquin Miller. And iron is rust. AA; BPAW

Dead in Wars and in Revolutions. Mary Devenport O'Neill. Are whitening in the savage glare of truth. NeIP

A Dead King. Algernon Charles Swinburne. Here is no room for thee; go down to hell. VLP

The Dead Knight. John Masefield. When tides are wandering out or in. CH; GTBS-P

The Dead Lady Canonized. LeRoi (Imamu Amiri Baraka) Jones. sew up/her bleeding hole. CAPP

A Dead Leaf. Howard Moss. The first snow. NYBP; NYP

A Dead Letter. Henry Austin Dobson. And what of John? The less that's said/Of John, I think, the better. HBMV

The Dead Liebknecht. Hugh" (Christopher Murray Grieve) MacDiarmid. And wi' his white teeth shinin' yet/The corpse lies smilin' underfit. FaBoPV; OBVE

Dead Love. Mary Mathews Adams. And not within a living heart. AA

Dead Love. Elizabeth Siddal. And this is only earth, my dear,/Where true love is not given. NOBV

The Dead Make Rules. Mary Carolyn Davies. I pray you, for my own pain's sake,/Break the rules that I shall make! HBMV

The Dead Man Ariseth and Singeth a Hymn to the Sun. Book of the Dead. Millions of years shall come. Thou art above the years! AWP

The Dead Man Dragged from the Sea. Carl Gardner. They were never sad enough/In burying the dead man dragged from the sea. PoBA

Dead Man's Dump. Isaac Rosenberg. And our wheels grazed his dead face. BrPo; CABL; FaBoMo; GTBS-P; LiTM; MMM; MoPo; NoP; OBWP; TrJP; VWA; WaP

Dead Man's Song, Dreamed by One Who Is Alive. *Anonymous.* For every time the sun goes up/Over the heavens,/ayi, yai, ya. WTO

A Dead March. Cosmo Monkhouse. Ah, for the face–the face of flowers–that blossoms on/earth no more. HBV 1-2; OBVV

Dead Marine. Louis O. Coxe. For good to sound the coral at the hearts of men. WaP

The Dead Marten. Walter Savage Landor. Nor grief, nor reason to repine,/As there is now in this of mine. FM

The Dead Men. Sophia de Mello Breyner Andresen. For they already know to where we are going. PBWP

Dead Men Tell No Tales. Haniel Long. Old tales of life, of love and hate,/Of time and space, and will and fate. HBMV; MCCG

A Dead Mole. Andrew Young. Buried within the blue vault of the air? FM; GTBS-P; OBSP

The Dead Moon. Danske Dandridge. By this white, awful Mystery,/Haggard and dead. AA

The Dead Musician. Charles L. O'Donnell. Homesick for harpings of eternity. CAW

Dead Musicians. Siegfried Sassoon. They're dead...for God's sake stop that gramophone. BrPo

Dead Neck. Sue Standing. until the last can't be told/from the mermaid's fingernails. AMV-81

The Dead of the Wilderness. Chaim Nachman Bialik. Stillness returns as of old. Desolate stretches the desert. AWP

The Dead of the World. Jeanne Finley. thinking they are gone. AMV-81

Dead of Winter. Anthony Towne. Astonishment of sky, and I, I think of you, I think that you know why. NYBP

Dead on the Desert. Harrison Conrard. And starved coyotes answered shriek on shriek. BPAW

Dead on the War Path. *Anonymous.* Three times! four times! Then leave us now! WTO

The Dead Pan. Elizabeth Barrett Browning. Pan, Pan is dead. VLP

A Dead Past. C. C. Munson. Hence alive the Past must be. BLRP; WBLP

The Dead Pig. *Anonymous.* As good a pair o' bed-flops as iver flopped bugs. FaBoNo

The Dead Player. Robert Burns Wilson. But, like a noble Phidian marble, stands/The memory of him. AA

The Dead Poet. Lord Alfred Bruce Douglas. And so I woke and knew that he was dead. HBMV; PeHV; ViBoPo

The Dead Poet. Al Purdy. and know where the words came from. NOBC

Dead Ponies. Brenda Chamberlain. soft entrails have gone to make the hawk arrogant. NeBP

The Dead President. Edward Rowland Sill. Whose fair fulfilment all the earth shall be,/And all the Future tell. PAH

The Dead Prospector. Arthur Chapman. Enough for him Fall's golden glows,/And colors in the sunset wrought. BPAW

The Dead Quire. Thomas Hardy. From Moaning Hill towards the mead–/The Mead of Memories. OAEP

The Dead Ride Fast. Richard P. Blackmur. in my own glass I trim my snakey locks. MoPo

The Dead Sea. Henryk Grynberg. but will start childbearing again/through potash and bromide. VWA

The Dead Seal. A. W. Purdy. ...wonder/what got into me? NoAm

The Dead Seal near McClure's Beach. Robert Bly. ...I climb the cliff and go home the other way. NNaP; NU

The Dead Shall Be Raised Incorruptible. Galway Kinnell.
of my iron will, my fear of love, my itch for money, and/my madness. GP
This corpse will not stop burning! NOBA

The Dead Sheep. Andrew Young. The eye-pits darted a dark ray/That searched me to my shadowy skeleton. FM

The Dead Ship of Harpswell. John Greenleaf Whittier. Nor see the Angel at the helm/Who steers the Ship of Death! EtS

The Dead Singer. Mary Ashley Townsend. The shining stars pass silently from sight! AA

The Dead Sister. Caroline Gilman. With her we may be summoned too/To heaven's bright, happy home! OBCA

Dead Snake. William Jay Smith. And inconclusive the triumph of Good. NePoAm-2

Dead Soldier. Nicolas Guillen. THERE'RE PLENTY OF SOLDIERS. TTY

A Dead Soldier. George Edgar Montgomery. And fought his battles with anointed spears. AA

Dead Soldiers. James Fenton. Either the lunches or the dead soldiers. OBTV; OBWP

The Dead Solomon. John Aylmer Dorgan. And King Solomon was dead! AA

The Dead Sparrow. William Cartwright. To sing dirges o'er his stone! BoAnP; CH

The Dead Sparrow. Caius Valerius Catullus. Receptacle of life's decay. EnLi 1-2

Dead Still. Andrei Voznesensky. We are asleep. BoLoP

The Dead Tribune. Denis Florence McCarthy. One new world would seek, and one/Would save the old! ACP

A Dead Warrior. Laurence Housman. But in that safe and secret dust/Which shall not rise again. HBMV

Dead Wasp. Kenneth Slade Alling. Windows the now elegiac light pours through. NePoAm

The Dead Water. Wen I-to. See from it what a world may still be wrought! LiTW

A Dead Weasel. David Helwig. ...I must pity/even the destruction of such small life. NOBC

Dead "Wessex" the Dog to the Household. Thomas Hardy. I shall not listen to you,/Shall not come. FM

The Dead Wingman. Randall Jarrell. The lives' long war, lost war–the pilot sleeps. MiAP

The Dead Words. Vernon Watkins. Cinders are priestlike in their tale of fire. LiTM

Deadfall. Martha Keller. What the snow slackened, the wind felled. GoYe

Deadly Kisses. Pierre Ronsard. If thou wilt kiss me in such wise. AWP

Deadsong. Don Domanski. my tongue's none the wiser/for death's uninteresting taste. NOBC

Deaf. Henry Cuyler Bunner. Where dwells her spirit, innocently wise. AA

Deaf. Barry O. Higgs. doesn't the wild wind/whistle. PeSA

Deaf-and-Dumb School. Anthony Delius. Only the white statue and the darkness realize. PeSA

Deaf Girl Playing. James Tate. ...I knelt in a corner and tried to/imagine what I would say to her, the girl in the field. AmPA

Deaf School. Ted Hughes. A face that was simply the front skin of the self concealed and separate. NoP

The Deaf Woman's Courtship. Anonymous. "I thank you very kindly, Sir, I hear you quite clearly." BFSS

Deafness. Richard Ryan. ...not the mere being/without, but the not knowing,/at all.... BIrV

The Dean. Alan Porter. Those who have killed the dream and left me poor. AnAmPo

Dean-Bourn, a Rude River in Devon, by Which Sometimes He Lived. Robert Herrick. Rockes turn to Rivers, Rivers turn to Men. SeCV 1-2

Dean Inge. Humbert Wolfe. bored with immortality. FaBoEE

The Dean's Lady. George Crabbe. And flies the glory that would not pursue/To yon small cot, a poorly jointured Blue. LoBV

Dear America. Robert Peterson. go bomb a canoe. PPON

Dear as the Moon. Anonymous. Yet to you this little village is dear as the moon. WTO

Dear, Beauzteous Death! Henry Vaughan. Could man outlook that mark! LO

Dear Body. Janine Canan. till I depart, dearest Body, my slave, my queen. APU

Dear Brethren, Are Your Harps in Tune? Eunice Smith. Until he call my soul away,/Eternal praise to sing! AH

Dear Child Whom I Begot. J. V. Cunningham. But in yourself your own. NAs

Dear Companion. Anonymous. It makes me think of your disgrace. FSW

Dear Country Cousin. E. G. Burrows. After the dirigible comes the cow. HoAn

Dear, Do Not Your Fair Beauty Wrong. Thomas May. ...love hath wings,/And flies away from aged things. ViBoPo

Dear Fanny. Thomas Moore. Love reasons much better than Reason. HBV 1-2; InMe

Dear Father Christmas (parody). Russell Davies. For who can bear to feel himself/At Christmas?/Yours documentarily,/W. H. AUDEN (master). FaBoPa

Dear Father, Look up. Robert Henry Newell. I did it with my little hatchet. OBAL

Dear Female Heart. Stevie Smith. You may also look most absurd with a miserable face. FaBoEE

Dear Folks. Patrick Kavanagh. Detached in love where pygmies cannot pin you/To the ground like Gulliver. So good luck and cheers. FaBoTw

Dear Friend, Whose Presence in the House. James Freeman Clarke. The miracle again is wrought,/And water changed to wine. AH

Dear Friends. Edwin Arlington Robinson. The gold I miss for dreaming is all yours. AmePo

Dear gentle soul, who went so soon away. Luîs de Camoens. As from my own he swept you far away. BoLoP

Dear Girl. Gregory Corso. Who'll take care of the cats? NoAm

Dear Happy Souls. Eunice Smith. And never stop your joyful song/To everlasting days. AH

Dear Harp of My Country. Thomas Moore. And all the wild sweetness I wak'd was thy own. AnIL; EnRP; NOBI; OAEP

Dear If I with Guile. Thomas Campion. Yet let none despayre/But to finde as fayre as you. NCEP

Dear John, Dear Coltrane. Michael S. Harper. a love supreme, a love supreme– AmPA; GeTw; NIP

Dear John Wayne. Louise Erdrich. ...inside of everything/we see, burning, doubling, splitting out of its skin. TWSS

The Dear Ladies of Cincinnati. Anne Stevenson. And the river grows ugly in their perpetual service. HoAn

Dear Lady, When Thou Frownest. Robert Bridges. The sum of my love for thee/Seems poor, scant, and unworthy. LiTL

Dear Lord, Behold Thy Servants. Hosea Ballou I. May we fulfil the works of love. AH

Dear Maiden. Heinrich Heine. They also speak my own. AWP

Dear March, come in! Emily Dickinson. That blame is just as dear as praise/And praise as mere as blame. YeAr

Dear Master, in Whose Life I See. John Hunter. O thou whose deeds and dreams were one. TRV

Dear Men and Women. John Hall Wheelock. Lost, and all mine, all mine, forever. NYBP; Prf

Dear Mister Congressman. Bob Dylan. Zorba the Bomb MAT

Dear Mother. Emmett Jarrett. ...he's just like his father NeAC

Dear Mrs. McKinney of the Sixth Grade:. David Kherdian. ...only time and loss, not/you and I, are the subject to be held. GLGT

Dear Old Dad. Eva Gilbert Shaver. Start pinning laurels on your Dad, He's/done a lot for you. STF

Dear Old Girl. Richard Henry Buck. And my broken heart is calling, calling for you,/Dear old girl. FSN

Dear Old Mothers. Charles Sarsfield Ross. Sweet mothers!–as they pass, one sees again/Old garden-walks, old roses, and old loves. PGD

Dear Old Stockholm. Al Young. & at the music & the men, wishing it would never end NPGG

Dear Patty Dear Tania. Richard Mathews. holding myself hostage and there's no way out GP

Dear Possible. Laura Riding. That fate, that dear fate. LiTA

The Dear President. John James Piatt. Abraham Lincoln, the Dear President. MC; PAH

Dear Reader. Peter Meinke. let's go to the movies/just the 2 of us/love/peter. Psk

Dear Reader. James Tate. half hating you,/half eaten by the moon. EAS

Dear Saviour, If These Lambs Should Stray. Abby Bradley Hyde. The wanderers to thy fold restore. AH

Dear, though the night is gone. W. H. Auden. And I, submissive, felt/Unwanted and went out. BoLoP; InvP

Dear Uncle Stranger. Conrad Aiken. good men and women gone too soon to bed. NoAm; NOBA

Dear, Why Make You More of a Dog than Me? Sir Philip Sidney. To witless things, then Love, I hope, since wit/Becomes a clog, will soon ease me of it. PrIm

Dear Wordsworth. William Hathaway. Mrs. Curtis says she smoked cigars! APU

Deare, If You Change. Anonymous. E're I prove false to faith, or strange to you. AtBAP; PoEL 1-5

Dearest, Do Not You Delay Me. John Fletcher. Which being restrained, a heart is broken. ViBoPo

Dearest Friend, Thou Art in Love. Heinrich Heine. I can see thy flaming heart/Burn already through thy vest. TrJP

Dearest Man-in-the-Moon. Erica Jong. You have kissed/the final crescent of my heart/& made it full. MOON

The Dearest Poets. [James Henry] Leigh Hunt. To lay a wounded heart in leafy rest,/And dream of things far off and healing,–Spenser. HBV 1-2

Dearest Reader. Michael Palmer. and grackles by the shadow of a fountain. NPGG

The Dearest Spot on Earth. W. T. Wrighton. All the world beside I've slighted/For home, sweet home. FaBoBe

Death. Maltbie Davenport Babcock. And work, nor care to rest, and find the last the best. WGRP

Death. Maxwell Bodenheim. Between the cold waves of his hair, as he tip-/toes off. AnAmPo; MAPA; TrJP

Death. Emily Bronte. Thus, at least, its mouldering corpse will nourish/That from which it sprung–Eternity. OBNC; VLP

Death. Howard Byatt. I found him sitting there/Dead eyes gaping at a dead television. FF

Death. Madison Cawein. Death's towering ruin from the past/Makes black the land that round me/lies. AA

Death. John Clare. And the grave whereon the bright snowdrops grow/ Shall be the same soil as the beauty below. ERoP 1-2; GTBS-P

Death. Florence Earle Coates. The waking from a dream that Man calls– Life! HBV 1-2

Death. Mary Elizabeth Coleridge. Bid me, O Lord, in that most dreadful hour,/Not fall, but fly away! TrPWD

Death. Roy Fuller. Towards the gateposts and the void/(Between them) of his older shape. NoAm

Death. Patty L. Harjo. An invisible spirit/Watching. VoR

Death. George Herbert. Making our pillows either down, or dust. AnAnS 1; JCP; MePo; NoP; OBS; SeCP; SeCV 1-2

Death. Thomas Hood. No resurrection in the minds of men. EG; OBEV

Death. Mildred Jeffrey. That's all. AMV-80

A Death. Elizabeth Jennings. Rather to please us were the flowers she gave. NMP

Death. L. E. Jones. Too many great-great-great-great aunts to see. PoL

Death. Bill Knott. It will look as though I am flying into myself. EAS

Death. Jeffrey Miller. o yikes/o yikes. APU

Death. Sir Thomas More. To me, a fool, some of your wise brain. EnRePo

Death. James Oppenheim. This will be true a hundred million years from now,/As it is now, at this moment. WGRP

Death. Sean O Riordain. though I am/no woman. NOBI

Death. George Pellew. They are divine, all-comprehending Death. AA

Death. William Bell Scott. And the hair from thy crown/Be blown like thistle-down. NOBV

Death. Percy Bysshe Shelley. Love itself would, did they not. DiPo

Death. Darwin T. Turner. into the manet of indifferent Night. BALP

Death. Henry Vaughan. 'Tis last good-night, our Sunne shall never set. NCEP

Death. William Carlos Williams. just bury it/and hide its face–/for shame. OxBA; VGW

Death. Charles Wright. Darkness, black moth the light burns up in. FiCP

Death. William Butler Yeats. Man has created death. ChMP; OBSP

Death Again (parody). T. Hope. Or is it mere sophistry, John "Doctor' Donne? BXAP

Death, Always Cruel. Dante Alighieri. Whoso deserves not Heaven/May never hope to have her company. LiTW

Death and Birth. Algernon Charles Swinburne. Ill met still are warm and wintry weather,/Death and birth. MaVP

Death and Doctor Hornbook. Robert Burns. I took the way that pleas'd mysel,/And sae did Death. OxBS

Death and Love. Ben Jonson. Except Love's fires the virtue have/To fright the frost out of the grave. NOBE

Death and Night. James Benjamin Kenyon. That weariness which makes us love the/night? AA

Death and Resurrection. George Croly. "Earth to earth, and dust to dust!" WGRP

Death and the Arkansas River. Frank Stanford. ...so quiet/Not a soul is wakened. FiCP

Death and the Bridge. Robert Lowell. "God's ways are dark and very seldom pleasant." HaCAP

Death and the Cobbler. Anonymous. The squire will out-poll us and 'peach you again. APAS

Death and the Fairies. Patrick MacGill. And it's Death and not the Fairies/Who is holding carnival. HBMV

Death and the Lady. Léonie Adams. Death said to the Lady. MoAB; MoAmPo

Death and the Maiden. Anonymous. My girl, I say be on your guard. KiLC

Death and the Maiden. Dick Gallup. Like a baked glistening afternoon/ But only for a minute. ANYP

Death and the Maiden (excerpt). W. H, Oliver. To watch her beauty move into the earth. AnNZ

Death and the Plowman. Sidney Keyes. But cold security, the one and only/Right of a workless man without a home. OxBV

Death and the Three Revellers. Geoffrey Chaucer. Thus endeth been these homicides two,/And eek the false empoisoner also. OBNV

Death as a Lotus Flower. Anonymous. I am the pure lotus,/that blossomed in the field. TTY

Death As History. Jay Wright. they charge us with the improbable. PoBA

Death at Daybreak. Anne Reeve Aldrich. And how is a soul to see? AA

The Death Balloon. Patricia Goedicke. Escaped bubbles of gas crawl/Like maggots everywhere. FAZ

A Death-Bed. James Aldrich And walked in Paradise! AA

The Death Bed. Waring Cuney. And all the time he wondered/What it was they could be saying. CDC

The Death Bed. Thomas Hood. ...–she had/Another morn than ours. EnRP; GTBS; GTBS-P; HBV 1-2; MCCG; NOBE; OBEV; OBNC; OBRV; OBVV; PG; TreFS

Death Bed. Thomas Kinsella. We can weave nothing. CIP

The Death-Bed. Siegfried Sassoon. Then, far away, the thudding of the guns. LiTM; MMM; MoVE; PoPle

Death-Bed Hymn of Saint Anthony of Padua. Saint Anthony of Padua. Father and Holy Spirit, Three–/Through ages without end! CAW

Death-Bed Reflections of Michel-Angelo. Hartley Coleridge. For that vast love, that hangs upon the Cross. EyDe

Death-Bed Song. Anonymous. And changed in a moment go shouting away/To mansions of love in the skies. AmFP

Death Bells. Lightning Hopkins. Yes, you know this life I'm living I been living/Oh lord, for a great many years. BluL

Death by Drowning. Elizabeth Brewster. And must be forced, and forced again, to die. NOBC

Death by Rarity. Marguerite Young. Sleet in the golden vein. LiTA

Death by Water. Thomas Stearns Eliot. Consider Phlebas, who was once handsome and tall as you. OBVE

Death Chant. Peter Blue Cloud. O, bear/O, turtle/I sing. VoR

The Death Circus. John Tranter. the salamander circus/followed like a hungry dog CBAP

Death & Co. Sylvia Plath. Somebody's done for. CMoP; ConAP; FF; LCAP; PrIm

Death Come to My House He Didn't Stay Long. Anonymous. O, my Lord, I'm gwinter see my mother again,/Hallelu. BoAN 1-2

Death Comes for the Old Cowboy. Kevin Clark. ...circling/on the endless curve/of that sweet pedal steel. AMV-81

Death Comes to the Salesman. Louis Daniel Brodsky. On this perfectly normal Saturday morning. AMV-81

Death Deposed. William Allingham. Or stay!–because thou art/Only Myself. OnYI

Death, Don't Be Boring (parody). Roy Kelly. Death, be a chum and make it soon. BXAP

Death-Doomed. Will Carleton. For the murderous gallows, black and grim, is cheated of its dead! PaPo

Death & Empedocles 444 B.C. Horace Gregory. Each waiting for a comet in the sky. PoA

Death for the Dark Stranger. Thomas McGrath. So again the miraculous thunder of discovering wings is/heard. VGW

Death from Cancer. Robert Lowell. Where the wide waters and their voyager are one. MP; TwCP

Death Has No Features of His Own. Gwen Harwood. What we are is beyond him utterly. NOAV

A Death in Hospital. John Lehmann. His friends, who stayed and wept. AtBAP

Death in Leamington. Sir John Betjeman. And tiptoeing gently over the stairs/Turned down the gas in the hall. ACV; NoP; PoPl

Death in Life. Thomas, Lord Vaux. Is this a life? Nay, death you may it call,/That feels each pain and knows no joy at all. OBSC

Death in the Corn. Detlev Freiherr von Liliencron. and the head sinks and he is gone. WaaP

A Death in the Desert. Robert Browning.
And, having gained truth, keep truth: that is all. TRV
But 'twas Cerinthus that is lost. GoTL; OxBoCh

A Death in the Desert. Charles Tomlinson. receded as speechless and as wide as death. FF

Death in the Home. Thomas Sturge Moore. Gay with fond glances/Good with long talks. BrPo

A Death in the Streets. Mario Petaccia. the dead rises from his grave/in the clothes of a magician,/shedding his miracles. LFAC

Death in Yorkville. Langston Hughes. Death ain't/No jive. PoBA

Death Invited. May Swenson. Here comes trotting, snorting death/let loose again. BoAnP; LiSp

Death Invoked. Philip Massinger. In one short hour's delay, is tyranny. ACP

Death is a dialogue. Emily Dickinson. Just laying off, for evidence,/An overcoat of clay. WGRP

Death Is a Door. Nancy Byrd Turner. Death is only a quiet door/In an old wall. BLPA

Death Is a Second Cousin Dining with Us Tonight. Geraldine Kudaka. In a calm voice, I ask you if you want some bread. BrSi

Death Is Awful. Reed, Doc Hall, Vera. Just spare me over/another year. BluL

Death Is but Death. Will Dyson. Tears are but Tears! BoAV

Death Killed the Rich. Anonymous. That a man who has many children/ Shall never die without a trace. WTO

Death-Lace. David Ray. Charley with the motor running and that girl goosed. MAT

Death Looks Down. Linda Gregg. Lying still, always facing the constant motion. NPGG

Death May Be Very Gentle. Oliver St. John Gogarty. And beautiful; and many a little child. PoRA

Death May Leap on a Sunny Day. Raymond Thompson. DEATH JUST MAKES IT SEEM REAL/ LFAC

Death News. Allen Ginsberg. What you wanted to be among the bastards out there. NoAm

Death of a Bird. Jon Silkin. From my mind a space is taken away. BoAnP; NePoEA

Death of a Cat. James Schevill. Like sparks snapping through the foam of a fire. NMP

The Death of a Cat (excerpt). Louis MacNeice. ...While there is light in them. PCat

Death of a Fair Girl. Alpheus Butler. One wonders at her fate. PeD

Death of a Friend. Pauli Murray. And songs of dead poets haunted me all day? PoBA

Death of a Hind. Alasdair MacLean. It unclenches its fist inside her heart. PoSH

Death of a Jazz Musician. William Jay Smith. And forward still the boatman moved, and made no sound. NePoAm-2

Death of a Naturalist. Seamus Heaney. That if I dipped my hand the spawn would clutch it. HAP; NCSH; OxBC

The Death of a Negro Poet. Conrad Kent Rivers. or return the scolding promise/to wish me safe love again. BPo

Death of a Poet. Charles Causley. I went across the road to a pub; wrote this. OxBTC

Death of a Ram. Sedulius Scottus. And your brothers too, I shall ever love. Farewell. NOBI

The Death of a Snake. William Plomer. These, that the wind removed, in memory remain. ELU

The Death of a Soldier. Wallace Stevens. The clouds go, nevertheless,/In their direction. ForPo; OBSP; OBWP; OFD; QFR

Death of a Son. Jon Silkin. And out of his eyes two great tears rolled, like stones, and/he died. FF; GTBS-P; NePoEA; NoAm; OxBTC; TwCP; VWA

The Death of a Toad. Richard Wilbur. The haggard daylight steer. AmP; AP; BiP; CMoP; ForPo; LiTM; MiAP; MoVE; NMP; NoAm; NoP; PoA

Death of a Vermont Farm Woman. Barbara Howes. Is it time now? MoAmPo; SM

The Death of a Warrior. Jenny Mastoraki. and a traffic sign/that forbids/the passing of parades. BoWoP

Death of a Whale. John Blight. but at the immolation of a race who cries? CBAP; PoAu 1-2

Death of a Young Son by Drowning. Margaret Atwood. I planted him in this country/like a flag. BoWoP; NOBC

The Death of Admiral Benbow. Anonymous.
And a third in remembrance of Admiral Benbow. OBSS
As our fathers did before/Long ago. GBP
I value not half a score,/Nor their noise, nor their noise. CoMu

The Death of Adonis. Theocritus. His Am'rous Tusks sing'd in the Flame. OBVE

The Death of Ailill. Francis Ledwidge. And knew by the cold touch that he was dead. OnYI

Death of an Aircraft. Charles Causley. And, armed like an archangel, returned. MoBS

The Death of an Angel. Russell Edson. Ah, that's better! cried one of the doctors. LCAP

The Death of an Elephant. Gianfranco Pagnucci. together over the ridge/into the dusk. NU

Death of an Irishwoman. Michael Hartnett. She was a child's purse, full of useless things. CIP

The Death of an Old Man. Michael Hamburger. ...the silences that grew/within him for a life-time, intertwined? NePoEA

The Death of Azron. Alice Wellington Rollins. The chisel fell. AA

The Death of Ben Hall. Will H. Ogilvie. ...sleep with the dead Ben Hall/Than go where that traitor went. PoAu 1-2

The Death of Carmen Miranda. Stephen E. Smith. but with fruit in its hair. AMV-81

The Death of Chiron. James Philip McAuley. Unreconciled into the dark below. BoAV

The Death of Cleopatra. Horace. A woman desolate and forlorn. EnLi 1-2

The Death of Colman. Thomas Frost. For—God of Waves!—none could repress/One choking thought–the loneliness! PAH

The Death of the Crazy Horse. John G. Neihardt. These many grasses and these many snows. BPAW

The Death of Cuchulain. William Butler Yeats. And the waves flowed above him, and he died. GoTL

The Death of Custer. John Wallace (Jack) Crawford. Yours truly, in friendship still strong. PoOW

The Death of David. Hayim Nahman Bialik. "David, King of Israel, yet liveth and/endureth!" TrJP

The Death of Dermid. Sir Samuel Ferguson. Wherewith in haste half-way return'd, he saw/A smile on Dermid's face relax'd in death. IrPN

The Death of Digenes Akritas. John Heath-Stubbs. Lay me decent, light a candle,/Keep the ritual orthodox. NePoEA

The Death of Don Pedro. Anonymous. Fled the fiercest soul that ever/In a Christian bosom dwelled. AWP

Death of Dr. King. Sam Cornish. the city boils/black men/jump out of trees. CNA; OFD; PoBA

The Death of Europe. Charles Olson. Let us who live/try. NeAP

The Death of Fathers. Theodore Weiss. the lesson never learned. SV

The Death of Friends. Adele Levi. Now the dead bury us/with their final falling. GoYe

Death of Gaudentis. Harriet Annie". Beneath heaven's cloudless dome. WBLP

The Death of General Pike. Laughton Osborn. And, thus pillowed, Pike expired. PAH

The Death of General Uncebunke: A Biography in Little. Lawrence Durrell. Presently will come the two welcome angels/Noise in the hall, the last supper served. FaBoMo

The Death of God. Howard Nemerov. Would bite the back in the kingdom of dead God. OBSP; OxBC

The Death of Goody Nurse. Rose Terry Clarke. "Father forgive," He said. PAH

The Death of Grant. Ambrose Bierce. Thy servant's soul in Paradise. AA

The Death of Harrison. Nathaniel Parker Willis. From the round at the top he has stepp'd to/the sky! PAH

The Death of Janis Joplin. Robert Phillips. Part of something at last. SOTS

The Death of Jefferson. Hezekiah Butterworth. Gone his soul into all nations, gone to live and/not to die. PAH

The Death of Justice. Walter Everette Hawkins. Wrong sways the sceptre and Justice must yield. PoBA

The Death of King Edward I. Anonymous. Bidde we God and oure Ledy/To thilke blisse Jesus us sende./Amen. MeEL

The Death of King Edward VII. Anonymous. Has saved the country more than one billion. OxBoLi

Death of King George V. Sir John Betjeman. Where a young man lands hatless from the air. NOBE; OBSP

The Death of Leonidas. George Croly. Bring forth the self-same men? BeLS

The Death of Lesbia's Bird. Caius Valerius Catullus. While the Loves all in a ring/Softly stroked the stiffened wing. AWP

The Death of Lester Brown, House Painter. Rod Taylor. and it will be hard to keep on living. WeW

The Death of Lincoln. William Cullen Bryant. Who perished in the cause of Right. AmePo; AmP; AP; ForPo; TAP

Death of Little Boys. Allen Tate. There is a calm for you when men and women/Unroll the chill precision of moving feet. LiTA; MoAB; MP; TwCP

The Death of Lyon. Henry Peterson. And grave thy name immortal. PAH

The Death of Marilyn Monroe. Sharon Olds. ...listening to a/woman breathing, just an ordinary/woman/breathing. MAYP

The Death of Meleager. Algernon Charles Swinburne. That law may fulfil herself wholly, to darken man's face/before God. OBVV

The Death of Morgan. Anonymous. Remember this, how true it is, bushranging hath no charms! FaBoBa

The Death of Moses. Anonymous. Thou, our shepherd, go in peace. TrJP

Death of My Aunt. Anonymous. A baccy box without a lid,/And half a farthing candle. OxBoLi

The Death of Myth-Making. Sylvia Plath. And turned the farmboy's temper wolfish,/The housewife's, desultory. PoA

The Death of Nelson. Anonymous. May rest in the fleet with you, Lord Collingwood. OxBoLi

The Death of Nick Charles. LeRoi (Imamu Amiri Baraka) Jones. I am sleeping/& you will not be able/to wake me. CoPo

The Death of Old Joe Yazzie. Ron Rogers. And the winds the crying winds/Were full of butterflies, many colored. STE

The Death of Parcy Reed. Anonymous. Wheneer they ride i the Border-side,/They'lll mind the fate o the laird Troughend. BaBo

The Death of Parcy Reed (A vers.). Anonymous. And the three false Halls of Girsonsfield,/They'll never be trusted nor trowed again. BaBo; ESPB

The Death of Peter Esson. George Mackay Brown. There came a wave and stood above your mast. NePoEA-2

The Death of Prince Leopold. William McGonagall. Britain had nothing else to fear, as far as you could/think... EvOK

The Death of Professor Backwards. X. J. Kennedy. How every watcher in whole spellbound crowds/Would light the wrong end of a cigarette. SOTS

The Death of Puck. Eugene Lee-Hamilton. And all we velvet-jackets mourn his loss. HBMV; OBVV

The Death of Queen Jane. Anonymous.
And its mother's poor body/Lying mouldering away. AmFP
And the best flower in England will flourish no more. AmFP; BaBo; ESPB; ViBoFo
And the pikes and the muskets did trail on the ground. BaBo; ESPB

But poor Queen Jane beloved lay cold as a stone. OBET
The flower of England/Shall never be no more. BaBo

The Death of Richard Wagner. Algernon Charles Swinburne. Speech as of powers whose uttered word laid bare/The world's great heart. LoBV

Death of Rimbaud. David Fisher. When you pass the snow falls–all at once–/from my heart, as from a tree in winter. NPGG

The Death of Robin Hood. *Anonymous.*
But Little John his grave hath digged–/It was hard by Kirkeslie. EnSB
Hey! down-a-down, a-down. BuBa

The Death of Robin Hood. Eugene Field. Under the greenwood tree. StPo

The Death of Robin Hood (excerpt). *Anonymous.* Here lies bold Robin Hood! ViBoPo

Death of Saint Guthlac. Cynewulf. All its Field-floor shook. ACP

The Death of Samuel Adams. *Anonymous.* And judge he read the verdict:/ A life in the Frankfort pen. AmFP

The Death of Slavery. William Cullen Bryant. Dwell thou, a warning to the coming times. AA

The Death of Sohrab. Matthew Arnold. ...from whose floor the new-bathed stars/Emerge, and shine upon the Aral Sea. FiP

The Death of Tammuz. Saul Tchernichovsky. For Tammuz, the beautiful Tammuz is/dead. TrJP; VWA

The Death of the Ball Turret Gunner. Randall Jarrell. When I died they washed me out of the turret with a hose. AP; BiP; CMoP; CoBMV; ELU; ExPo; FF; HAP; HoPM; InPK; LCAP; LiTM; MiAP; MoAmPo; NAs; NIP; NMP; NoAm; NOBA; NoP; OBSP; OBWP; OxBA; PoPl; PrIm; SoSe; TAP; UnPo; VGW; WaaP; WaP

The Death of the Bird. A. D. Hope. Receives the tiny burden of her death. PoAu 1-2

The Death of the Bronx. Chana Bloch. and we eat/the last of the honeycake/behind the drapes. MAYP

Death of the Cat. Ian Serraillier. Hooray!/The cat/is/dead! SO

The Death of the Craneman. Alfred Hayes. A stiff, naked, without a name. LiTA; NAMP; NCSH; WaP

Death of the Day. Walter Savage Landor. The fairest form, the sweetest breath,/Away he bore. NoP

The Death of the Epileptic Poet Yesenin. Aram Boyajian. He laughingly kisses them/with his gashed tongue/of poems. NeAC

The Death of the First Man. Nancy Sullivan. Even as it happens. NIP

The Death of the Flowers. William Cullen Bryant.
And sighs to find them in the wood and by the/stream no more. GN
So gentle and so beautiful, should perish/with the flowers. AA; AnNE; BLPL; BoNaP; GoTF; HBV 1-2; OBCA; PoLf; TreF; WBLP

The Death of the Gods. An Ode. L. Ker. Their power is gone, and my life is the token. NOEC

The Death of the Hired Man. Robert Frost. "Dead," was all he answered. AnNE; CMoP; HoPM; MaC; MoAB; MoAmPo; NoP; OxBA; SeCeV; SoSe; TrGrPo

Death of the Lincoln Despotism. *Anonymous.* Shall own our independence of "Yankee-Doodledom." PAH

The Death of the Moon. David Wagoner. Then her white knife,/Her closing eyelid./Her darkness. PoA

The Death of the Novel. David Young. The undertaker smiled. AmPA

The Death of the Old Year. Alfred, Lord Tennyson. And a new face at the door, my friend,/A new face at the door. HBV 1-2; PoSC

The Death of the Sailor's Wife. Fred Barton. over the darkening waters. AMV-80

The Death of the Sheriff. Robert Lowell. The thirsty Dipper on the arc of night. MoAB; MoAmPo

The Death of the Starling. Samuel Taylor Coleridge. While the Loves all in a ring/Softly stroke the stiffened wing. PBBP

The Death of Venus. Robert Creeley. there I saw her. AmPC; NOBA

The Death of Vitellozzo Vitelli. Irving Feldman. But his shadow hurries from his feet to his face. MP; TwCP

The Death of Warren. Epes Sargent. "'Tis sweet, oh, 'tis sweet for our country to die!" MC; PAH

The Death of Will. Charles Tomlinson. Someone should trace all those who/knew Will, to interview them. OxBC

The Death of Wolfe. *Anonymous.* For those prepared who merit just applause/By bravely dying in their country's cause. PAH

The Death of Yeats. George Barker. And remember that the great harp-breasted eagle/Is now a grave. LiTB

Death on a Crossing. Evangeline Paterson. and no sweet chariot swung, to carry him home. EBCP

Death on a Live Wire. Michael Baldwin. Till his fingers like snails at last came unstuck/And he fell through the cage of the sun. MoBS

Death on the Farm. Cary Waterman. filling with water the dark space/that goes between us/when we are not even looking. GP

Death Rites II. *Anonymous.* Khvum, Khvum, come in answer to our call! TTY

Death Rode a Pinto Pony. Whitney Montgomery. Then slowly turned his pinto horse/And rode away again. BPAW

The Death Room. Robert Graves. Waits jealously till children close their eyes. NYBP

Death Row. Charles Culhane. "My token expression for the day,"/I-said. With dignity. LFAC

Death's Apology. Francisco Manuel de Mello. How greater care of me can you demand? CAW

Death's Blue-Eyed Girl. Linda Pastan. The magician waved and bowed, showed us his/empty sleeves and she was gone. PPJ

Death's Gwineter Lay His Cold Icy Hands on Me. *Anonymous.* Death is gwineter lay his cold icy hands on me, Lord! BoAN 1-2

Death's Head. Phyllis Gotlieb. and yet I seem to get to sleep NOBC

Death's Jest-Book. Thomas Lovell Beddoes.
And he, who shall embrace thee,/Is at hand, and so farewell. NOBV
And the drowned and the shipwrecked have happy graves. NOBV
...ghosts shall shake/The dead, until they wake/In the grave. OBRV
It's only two devils, that blow/Through a murderer's bones, to and fro,/In the ghosts' moonshine. EnRP
The new Dodo is finished. O! come to my nest.' NOBV
Of love's stars, thou'lt meet her/In eastern sky. OBRV
The sails swell full. To sea, to sea! OBRV
Sate like a beggar upon Heaven's threshold,/Muttering its wrongs. CTC

Death's Lecture at the Funeral of a Young Gentleman. Richard Crashaw. ...only you/Of all interpreters read Nature True. SeCP

Death's Songsters. Dante Gabriel Rossetti. Say, soul,–are songs of Death no heaven to thee,/Nor shames her lip the cheek of Victory? MaVP

Death's the Classic Look. John Ciardi. and death looks like no look at all. PoA

Death's Transfiguration. Israel Zangwill. And touches vulgar life with silver/light. TrJP

Death's Vision (excerpt). John Reynolds. Commenced a more than Newton in abstruse philosophy. NOEC

Death's Warning to Beauty. *Anonymous.* Wed no man. Remember me. AnIL

Death Seed. Ricarda Huch. Behold, it was Death I had met. PBWP

The Death Sentence. Stevie Smith. The Law allows it/And the Court awards. NoP

Death; She Was Always Here. Yona Wallach. she was always here, an obverse view in my land, in her land. VWA

Death Snips Proud Men. Carl Sandburg. ;what have you had anyhow/ better than sleep? CMoP

A Death Song. Paul Laurence Dunbar. Ef I's layin' 'mong de t'ings I's allus/knowed. AA; BANP; CDC; PoLf; PoNe

Death Song. Robert Stephen Hawker. I cannot leave the unburied bones,/ And I fain would go my way. OBNC; OBRV; OBVV

Death Song. Alonzo Lewis. And tell to his tribe that his murderer sleeps. PAH

Death Songs. *Anonymous.*
How can they bury in a grave/Someone who died from love? BoWoP
I'll keep you as my guest. BoWoP
I'm young. I won't rot. BoWoP

Death Songs. L.V. Mack.
chasing into nothing. PoBA
i have forgotten you. PoBA
shatter the night with fear. PoBA
that you have forgotten that/you will forget. PoBA
...there is nothing/for you. PoBA

Death Sonnet I. Gabriela (Lucila Godoy Alcayaga) Mistral. No hand will reach into the obscure depth/to argue with me over your handful of bones. BoWoP

Death Stands above Me. Walter Savage Landor. Of his strange language all I know/Is, there is not a word of fear. LiTB; NOBE; NoP; OAEL 1-2; OAEP; OBNC; OBSP; PoEL 1-5; SoSe

Death Sting Me Blues. Sara Martin. Oh death please sting me,/and take me out of my misery. BluL

Death Sweet. Thomas Lovell Beddoes. In love and the enamelled flowers of song? NOBV

Death Swoops. Kenneth Pitchford. no joy-dazzled shepherds crowd. CoPo

Death, the Conqueror. James Shirley. Shall have the cunning skill to break a heart. GoBC

Death the Great. Elis Wyn o Lasynys. The gulf of Fear, 'twixt Heaven and Hell. LiTW

Death, Thou Hast Seized Me. Isaac Luzzatto. So see I Life within Death's shadowy/place. TrJP

A Death to Us. Jon Silkin. So I must carry his death about me/Like a large fly, like a large frail purpose. NePoEA

Death to Van Gogh's Ear. Allen Ginsberg. ...and eternity's strong mills grind out/vast paper of illusion! NaP; VGW

Death Valley. Jack H. Lee. 'Tis night in the Valley of Death. BPAW

Death Valley Blues. Arthur ("Big Boy") Crudup. You gonna follow poor Crudup/down to his burying ground. BluL

Death Walks through the Mind's Dark Woods. Henry Treece. And grave is never far away. NeBP

Death Warnings. Francisco Gomez de Quevedo y Villegas. And not a single thing my eyes behold/But speaks the word of Death's impending fate. CAW

Death Was a Woman. Sydney King Russell. And when he saw the beauty of her face/It took his breath away. GoYe

The Death Watchers. Alice Ryerson. and comfort us like the fingers of rain. AMV-80

The Death-Wish. Louis MacNeice. As a man in spring desires to die in woman. AnFE

Death with a Coda. Giuseppe Gioachino Belli. The bitch eternity is going to be eternal. AMV-81

The Deathless. Ednah Proctor (Clarke) Hayes. Still, down the glades of Arden, dance/The feet of Rosalind. AA

The Deathless Ones. Eleanor Glenn Wallis. As great tears fell from the eyes of these immortals/For the dead. NePoAm

Deathless Principle, Arise. Augustus Montague Toplady. Such the glorious vista Faith/Opens through the shades of death. OxBoCh

The Deaths. Solveig von Schoultz. The future creeps like a shadow across the meadow/And while I lose I love unspeakably. LiTW

The Deaths at Paragon, Indiana. John Woods. And cry for love, and hear no answer. CoPo

Deathward. John Lyle Donaghy. dying into death-- BIrV

Deathwatch. Michael S. Harper. Survivors will be human. AmPA; PoBA

The Debate in the Sennit. James Russell Lowell. "It perfectly true is/Thet slavery's airth's grettest boon," sez he. HBV 1-2; PAH

The Debate of the Body and the Soul. Anonymous. No sin so great, but Christ's dear love shall more prevail. MeEV

The Debate of the Body and the Soul (excerpt). Anonymous. And thou shalt come, with flesh and fell,/On doomes-day to be with me. CoBE

A Debate on Marriage versus Virginity. Caius Valerius Catullus. Hymen oh Hymenaeus, come, Hymen oh Hymenaeus. HW

Debate: Question, Quarry, Dream. Robert Penn Warren. And lift up my eyes to consider more strictly the ap-/palling logic of joy. VGW

Debate with the Rabbi. Howard Nemerov. We Jews are that way, I replied. PoPl

Debora Sleeping. William Logan. Sleep by other means continues dialogue. MAYP

Deborah as Scion. James Dickey.
In the one depth/Without levels, deepening for us. SV
With my dead full-time and work-singing. SV

Deborah Lee. Yvonne. I am not stealing from anybody. CNA

Debout (excerpt). Tchicaya U Tam'si. night will come my soul is ready PBA

Debridement: Operation Harvest Moon: On Repose. Michael S. Harper. insert large chest tube; catch blood drain bottle... GeTw

Debt. Anonymous. The sun is in eclipse. WTO

The Debt. Paul Laurence Dunbar. God! but the interest! BANP; CDC; SoSe; TRV

Debts. Jessie B. Rittenhouse. Of one who makes you sing again/When all the songs were mute? HBMV

Debussy and Proust. John Tagliabue. murmur prayers and the reverence/of things past. FAZ

Debutantrum. William Rose Benet. Farewell! Some day you'll merely be/"Among the patronesses"! InMe

A Decade. Amy Lowell. But I am completely nourished. MoAmPo; PoPl

A Decanter of Madeira, Aged 86, to George Bancroft, Aged 86. Silas Weir Mitchell. The wine we drank, the man we knew. AA; ViBoPo

Decay. George Herbert. And calling Justice, all things burn. AnAnS 1; SeCP; SeCV 1-2

The Decay of a People. William Gilmore Simms If that we waste, in vain walled town and/lofty tower! AA

Decay of Piety. William Wordsworth. That, struggling through the western sky, have won/Their pensive light from a departed sun! TrCP

A Decayed Monastery. Thomas Dermody. And lend a venerable dread/To the lone abbey's rocking head. OnYI

Decayed Time. Jean Wahl. An old hope shivers far in the cold air. VWA

Deceased. Cid Corman. now there is nothing/to say. PCP; VGW

The Deceased. Keith Douglas. He had an excellence which you miss. FaBoTw

Deceitful Brownskin Blues. Blind Lemon Jefferson. Every time it shakes/it's a sign my baby's home BluL

Deceiver. Anonymous. Ah, old man, do you serve me so? OxNR

December. John Clare. The shadow still of what hath been,/Which fashion yearly fades away. OBCP

December. Aileen Fisher. but you feel all warm.../with Christmas coming! SiSoSe

December. Robert Francis. By cold intent or accident but always/My death? LCAP

December. John Heath-Stubbs. ...it's less than/Three weeks' shopping time to Christmas. OBCP

December. Thomas Caulfield Irwin. Whispering weirdly in the grey/Of the dumb cold evening air. IrPN; NBM

December. John Keats. Nor numbed sense to steal it,/Was never said in rhyme. GN

December. Maurice Kenny. Wind rattles the moon. STE

December. Ron Padgett. in my little cup. EAS

December. Christina Georgina Rossetti. For I've a carol which some shepherds heard/Once in a wintry field. YeAr

December. James Schuyler. ...cheek/grow warm next to your own in hushed dark familial December. ANYP; NoAm

December 18, 1975. Michael Hogan. you do not awaken. FAZ

December 18th. Anne Sexton. ...that/will be that. CAPP

December 1970. John Tagliabue. You were not wilful and you made no slaves. GP

December 21st. Jean Valentine. and the infant's red-brown mouth a star/at the star of the girl's nipple... LCAP

December 24, 1979. Roger Weaver. What can they teach us, rivers and wars,/endless wars and rivers? SOTS

December 24 and George McBride is Dead. Richard Hugo. ...I'm in the kitchen,/fat and writing, drinking beer and shaking. HoPM

December 26. George Edward Hoffman. Until we make him welcome through the year. PGD

December 27, 1966. L. E. Sissman. So far above the feverish, shivering/Nightwatchman pressed against the falling glass. SM

December among the Vanished. William Stanley Merwin. In one of them I sit with a dead shepherd/And watch his lambs. NaP

December Blues. Robert Pinsky. ...Oh Little Town, enveloped in unease. MAYP

A December Day. Sara Teasdale. ...windows faintly holding/The feathery filigree of frost. YeAr

December Day, Hoy Sound. George Mackay Brown. Or howl like Lear, or laugh like a green child. OxBS

December Eclipse. Margo Lockwood. ...participate in the cosmos/like a peeping tom. Psk

December Fragments. Richmond Lattimore. angels in curling pins, with paper wings,/bells of spun glass, and drifts of mineral snow. PCh

A December Frost. Vesna Krmpotic. and our fruit gravitates toward the earth,/our fruit, indigent before its flowering. WPOW

December Night. William Stanley Merwin. I find a single prayer and it is not for men. CAPP

December: Of Aphrodite. William Stanley Merwin. ...where I stand/In the hazed gold of her eyes, the world is green. NePoEA

December Stillness. Siegfried Sassoon. Teach me to travel far and bear my loads. CMoP; MoRP

December Storm. John Hay. Having been whipped across the eyes/Like penitents, to make us see. NePoAm

December Sunset. Jonathan Holden. ...And less. And/less. And less... FAZ

Decent Burial. Lois Seyster Montross. The grave is neatly kept by you and me. HBMV

Deception. Alfred Corn. Try and fail, try and fail and try. PoA

Deceptions. Philip Larkin. To burst into fulfilment's desolate attic. CABA; CMoP; GTBS-P; NePoEA; NMP

The Deceptive Grin of the Gravel Porters. Gavin Ewart. and all we have are bruised and bleeding hands. FaBoMo

The Deceptive Present, The Phoenix Year. Delmore Schwartz. In the green warm opulence of summer, and the/inexhaustible vitality and immortality of the earth? BoNaP

The Deceptrices. William Carlos Williams. ...too soon/the unalterable conclusion. NYBP

Decision. Anonymous. How poor if you should turn him from the door. PoToHe

The Decision. Owen Dodson. Longing for each homesick heart/To make a pilgrimage among all men? PoNe

The Decision. Theodore Roethke. As a man turns to face on-coming snow. VGW

A Decision. Edith Sodergran. not a poem, but the marks of talons. PBWP

Deck the Halls. Anonymous. Heedless of the wind and weather./Fa la la la la, la la la la. FSW

Decks. Robert Phillips. ...They harbor/no hostilities Some have great gifts. GeTw; NYP

Decks Awash. Archilochus. Now of the wave's blade. OBVE

The Declaimer. Sir Henry William Baker. But in less than half an hour/Kneeled and whined at Celia's feet. NOEC

The Declaration. Nathaniel Parker Willis. –She had been asleep! OBAL

Declaration at Forty. Judson Crews. That for one moment she at least/was not utterly alone. UnTE

Declaration of Independence. Michael Brownstein. Hours eating from this planet's tasty/Dwindling peace of mind. APU

Declension. Stephen Sandy. ...All this is what is not/For you, and the words rise outward toward your smile. PoA

Decline and Fall of a Roman Umpire. Ogden Nash. And he is happy now because the spectators only call him a/little bum. SD

The Declining of a Gallant. *Anonymous.* Ablativo ab his, thus a gallant declined is. FaBoUs

Decorating the Soldiers' Graves. Minot Judson Savage. Will hear and heed the noble words they say. OHIP

Decoration. Louise Bogan. A crystal tree lets fall a crystal leaf. MoAB; MoAmPo

Decoration. Thomas Wentworth Higginson. I strew lilies on the grave/Of the bravest of the brave. AA; OHIP

Decoration Day. George Hurlbut Barbour. Such deeds of valor, swelled their hearts with pride. OHIP

Decoration Day. Julia Ward Howe. A pledge of blessing to the world. OHIP

Decoration Day. Henry Wadsworth Longfellow. The memory shall be ours. MC; OHIP; PoSC

Decoration Day. Bennie Lee Sinclair. ...this knelling/for green bones as well as brittle. TAT

Decoy. John Ashbery. Husband and wife/Man and wife. PoM

The Decoys. W. H. Auden. Its love from living. CMoP; SyP

A Decrepit Old Gasman. *Anonymous.* And, as everyone who knows/anything about/poetry can tell you, he also/ruined the meter. FaFP

The Decress of God. Chao Ying-Tou. ...we rever-/ently prepare for the majestic de-/scent of the fragrant flame. TrJP

The Dedicated. Philip Larkin. The quenching of candles. OxBC

Dedication. Drummond Allison. I had not learned I could dispense with love/Like a blind man unhindered by the gloom. FaBoTw

A Dedication. Karin Boye. My hungry pulse beats to the rhythm of your rhythm,/to the tempo of your gait. PBWP

Dedication. William Cullen Bryant. While round these hallowed walls the storm/Of earthborn passion dies. BLRP

Dedication. Sir James Chamberlayne. Lord, 'tis my All, and due to Thee. CavP

A Dedication. Gilbert Keith Chesterton. One standing at each end. FiBHP

A Dedication. Mary Elizabeth Coleridge. That which his eyes alone to thee unfold! TrPWD

Dedication. Pope Eugenius III. Keep sinners in thy maiden mantle gently furled. ISi

Dedication. Oliver St. John Gogarty. Virgil made an austere/Venus Muse of his song. OBMV

A Dedication. Adam Lindsay Gordon.
Such songs have been mine. PoAu 1-2
... torrent that gushes,/The tempests that rave. CBAP

Dedication. Ralph Gustafson. And died, a silent writing down. CaP

Dedication. Laurence Housman. To know myself for nought, and Christ for all in all. TrPWD

Dedication. Victoria Saffelle Johnson. I will rise from death to Thee. GoBC; TrPWD

A Dedication. Rudyard Kipling. Help me to need no aid from men,/That I may help such men as need! GTBS; HBV 1-2; OBVV

Dedication. Richard Stull. We awake and are renamed. AMV-81

Dedication. Francis Thompson. I give your own giving. CoBE

Dedication for a Book of Criticism. Yvor Winters. Then, in justice, take my book. GLGT

Dedication for a Building. Alan Dugan. and not mis-treat the desperate. CAD; NYP

Dedication of a Mirror. Plato. And can not see myself as once I was. LiTW

Dedication of the Chronicles of England and France. Robert Fabyan. That by thine aid this work may have good speed. ISi

Dedication of the Cook. Anna Wickham. Will blossom from the ashes of my kitchen! MoBrPo

Dedication on the Gift of a Book to a Child. Hilaire Belloc. ...pray/For men that lose their fairylands. EBEV; HBVY

The Dedication to a Book of Stories Selected from the Irish Novelists. William Butler Yeats. We and our bitterness have left no traces/On Munster grass and Connemara skies. NAMP

Dedication: To Edward John Trelawny. Algernon Charles Swinburne. Was in your ears as ever in ours his lyre,/Once, ere the flame received him from the sea. VLP

A Dedication to G**** H******* Esq. Robert Burns. A steady, sturdy, staunch believer. OBSV

Dedication to Hunger. Louise Gluck. ...like a god/for whose deed/there is no parallel in the natural world. FaBoWP

Dedication, to Leigh Hunt, Esq. John Keats. ...I could please/With these poor offerings, a man like thee. ViBoPo

A Dedication to My Wife. Thomas Stearns Eliot. These are private words addressed to you in public. BoLoP; FF

Dedication to the Final Confrontation. Djangatolum. man-kind/white/kind/of man PoBA

Dedication to the Generation Knocking at the Door. John Davidson. The miracle and magic of the deed. BrPo

The Dedication to the Sermons. Charles Churchill. How low, how mean, and full as poor as I./Cetera desunt. QFR

Dedicatory. Mary Gilmore. Walking amid the mountains of his thought. BoAV

Dedicatory Ode: They Say That in the Unchanging Place. Hilaire Belloc. There's nothing worth the wear of winning,/But laughter and the love of friends. PoLf

Dedicatory Sonnet to S. T. Coleridge. Hartley Coleridge. That good, my sire, I dedicate to thee. ERoP 1-2; OAEL 1-2

The Deean Tractorman, Clear. Edith Anne Robertson. It wiz for me ye grat! OxBS

The Deean Tractorman, Deleerit. Edith Anne Robertson. For her and me, I'll drive her there afore she skids awa. OxBS

Deedle, Deedle, Dumpling, My Son John. Mother Goose. Deedle, deedle, dumpling, my son John. BrR

Deeds of Kindness. Epes Sargent. How many things a child may do/For others by its love. HBV 1-2; HBVY

Deeds of Valor at Santiago. Clinton Scollard. A song, we say, for the men of to-day, who have proved/themselves their peers. HBV 1-2; MC; PAH

Deem Not. George Santayana. From so much sorrow–of whom I am one. AnEnPo; TrGrPo

The Deep. John Gardiner Calkins Brainard. There's quiet in the deep. AA; EtS

Deep Blue Sea. *Anonymous.* It was Willie what got drowned in the deep blue sea. FSW

The Deep Calling. John Rothfork. rising up from deep waters. WOLT

The Deep Dark Night. Alfred, Lord Tennyson. Which through the deep dark night in the olden time/Came sounding o'er the lone Ionian. SeCePo

Deep Dark River. Lloyd Roberts. The gleam of one more broken dream, O Ottawa! CaP

Deep Down the Blackman's Mind. R. E. G. Armattoe. Fit him to breed aught but a servile race. ACV

Deep in Love. Bhavabhuti. still talking when/the night had gone. LLLT

Deep Night. Juan Ramon Jimenez. The echo of the crippled Negro, king of the city, makes a/turn around the night in the sky... NYP

Deep River. *Anonymous.* Deep river, Lord; I want to cross over into camp ground. ABF; BoAN 1-2; BPo; FSW; TAP; TrAS

The Deep-Sea Cables. Rudyard Kipling. "Let us be one!" VLP

Deep-Sea Fishing. Hugh" (Christopher Murray Grieve) MacDiarmid. Omnipotence o' God than a fribble like me. SeCePo

Deep Sea Soundings. Sarah Williams. He who knows all, fears not. Great Death shall die. EtS; WGRP

Deep Sea Tug. *Anonymous.* Oh your tired mind starts to dream/Of the comforts at the trawler wharf/In the port of Aberdeen. OBSS

Deep Spring. *Anonymous.* Burst through the gloomy shades of death,/And shine above the skies. AmFP

A Deep-Sworn Vow. William Butler Yeats. Suddenly I meet your face. CMoP; ELU; OAEL 1-2; PCP; UnPo

Deep Water. *Anonymous.* And throw him in the deep water/that flows through the land. FSW

Deep Waters. Van Tassel Sutphen. What height for love could be too high,/Or depth for love too deep? AA

Deep Well. Roland Robinson. holding the restless finches and a single star. CBAP; NOAV

Deeper in the Tank–The Last Middle East Crisis, 1972. Eugene Ruggles. not to be extinguished,/but for gas. SOTS

Deeper into the Forest. Roy Daniells. Good-bye to playwrights, and good-bye to you! PeCV

The Deeper Seas. Henry Bellamann. Go boldly on with no land-looking doubt/Through the increasing seas to yet more sea. EtS

The Deepest Bow. Marie Takvan. The deepest bow of all–/and the most painful. AMV-81

The Deepest Sensuality. D. H. Lawrence. and the next deepest sensual experience/is the sense of justice. NoAm

Deeply Repentant of My Sinful Ways. Gaspara Stampa. o gentle Saviour, leave me not to die. WPOW

The Deer. Asya (Asya Gray). His horns dip into the sun. VWA

Deer. John Drinkwater. Beautiful flocks of the mind. CH

Deer. No Ch'on-myong. You look over, stretching your sad neck/toward the far hill. PBWP

The Deer. Laurie Shceck. as if it were this easy. AMV-80

The Deer and the Snake. Kenneth Patchen. Thinking that many Christs could hang there, crying. MoAmPo

Deer at the Roadside. Iain Crichton Smith. with great bounding leaps like the mind of God. PoSH

Deer Hunt. Judson Jerome. since I, to be a man, had taken one. RFM

Deer Hunt, Salt Lake Valley. Helen Handley. down to the edge, down to the hard, final edge. GrPl

Deer in Aspens. Kay DeBard Hall. And we see their eyes,/Innocent as Christ's. GoYe

Deer in the Bush. Chana Bloch. who comes when he pleases, and keeps/ the secrets of the tribe. MAYP

Deer Isle. Philip Booth. If I didn't go now, I never would. BiP; VGW

The deer on pine mountain. Onakatomi Yoshinobu. Only by the sound of his own voice. LiTW

Deer on the Mountain. Grace Fallow Norton. I have never seen them, but now–at last–I know.... HBMV

Deer's Cry. *Anonymous*. Of the Creator of Creation. AnIL; CAW

Deer's Cry. Saint Patrick.
Salus tua, Domine, sit semper nobiscum./Amen. OnYI
Through a confession of the Oneness/Of the Creator of creation. AnIL; CAW; WGRP

Deer Song. Confucius. probe to the utmost plan,/here the sincerity to rest a man. CTC

Deer Song. Leslie Marmon Silko. I will go with you/because you love me/ while I die. VoR

The Deer Which Lives. Onakatomi Yoshinobu. Only by its own cry. AWP

The Deevil's Waltz. Sydney Goodsir Smith. Black as auld widdie-fruit, Mahoun/Bestrides a redeless mapamound. FaBoTw

Defeat. Witter ("Emanuel Morgan") Bynner. It is again ourselves that we defeat. PoNe

A Defeat. Denise Levertov. my shadow,/in your dark boat. PBWP

Defeat and Victory. Wallace Rice. Don't give up the ship! MC; PAH

Defeat O' the Hert. Sydney Goodsir Smith. And wi oblivion's kiss/Ye win. AtBAP

The Defeat of the Armada. Thomas Dekker. As they did, you know when- a. CoBE

The Defeat of the Norsemen (excerpt). Sedulius Scottus. Who drove the sea in swollen tempest/in Egypt once, on chariots and riders/and whelmed all. NOBI

Defeat of the Rebels. Robert Graves. ...that never had been robbed/But for our sloth and hesitancy. WaP

The Defeated. William Stanley Merwin. It has woven its simple nest among my bones. AmPC

Defeated Farmer. Mark Van Doren. The greener wood has private ways/ That posted death may not remark. AnAmPo

The Defence of Guenevere. William Morris. The knight who came was Launcelot at/good need. OAEP; TEP; VLP

The Defence of Lawrence. Richard Realf. As though a seraph's voice had stirred/The pulses of the grass. PAH

The Defence of Night. Buonarroti Michelangelo. Purging the spirits of the pure from grief. CAW

A Defence of Poetry. Giollabrighde Macconmidhe. the Gael will lose respect/and freemen turn to clowns. NOBI

The Defence of the Alamo. Joaquin Miller. When duty fronts death in his Alamo. BeLS; BPAW; FaBoBe; HBV 1-2; MC; OnMSP; PAH

Defenceless Children, Your Great Enemy. Kendrick Smithyman. And ruefully you testify his power. AnNZ

Defend Us, Lord, from Every Ill. John Hay. The path which leads to heaven and thee! AH

The Defender. Arthuir M. Sampley. But stoutly at the outer brink/Defends the fort he overthrows. GoYe

The Defense of Lucknow. Alfred, Lord Tennyson. And ever aloft on the palace roof the old banner of England blew. BeLS

Defense Rests. Vassar Miller. upon your sweat, Your thirst,/Your nails, and nakedness I rest/my case. MoAmPo

Defensive Position. John Streeter Manifold. The gunner twitches, and unreprimanded/Eases two tensions, running home the bolt. MoBrPo

The Defiance. Aphra Behn. You have mistook the jest. EnLoPo

The Defiance. Thomas Flatman. Th' Usurper Death will make thee lay it down. OBS

Defiance. Solomon Ibn Gabirol. This heart of mine, that, albeit young/in years,/Is none the less rich in deep, keen-eyed experience TrJP

Defiance. Walter Savage Landor. Like a slim brook the gamesome maid/ Sparkled, and ran into the shade. HBV 1-2; VLP

The Defiant One. Alice Morrey Bailey. ...will be torn down like Babel/By that last decree. AMV-80

Definition. Grace Noll Crowell. I search for words for her–and there are none. PoToHe

Definition. Edwin Rolfe. is worth enough to soil this word or mar this world. NAMP

Definition. May Sarton. This huge passion, this small breath. MoLP

Definition. Lauren Shakely. ...the eye of flesh/that saw love couldn't last. FYAP

Definition for Blk/Children. Sonia Sanchez. the policeman/is a pig./(oink/ oink). PoBA

The Definition of Beauty. Robert Herrick. Flashed out between the middle and extreme. CaPo

The Definition of Love. Andrew Marvell. And opposition of the Stars. AnAnS 1; BLPL; BoLiVe; BoLoP; CBEP; DiPo; EBEV; ForPo; GBL; HoPM; InPS; JCP; LiTB; LiTL; LoBV; MeLP; MePo; NOBE; NoP; OAEL

1-2; OAEP; OBEV; OBS; PAI; PoEL 1-5; SeCePo; SeCeV; SeCP; SeCV 1-2; TEP; TreFT; TrGrPo; UnPo; WHA

Definition of My Brother. W. S. Graham. Away to best the morning at its gates! NeBP

Definition of Nature. Eugene B. Redmond. And any bush becomes/our Bantu wonderland. PoBA

Definition of the Soul. Boris Pasternak.
...The throb/Of concrescence could give it no/thought. TrJP
When we two tossed up there we never/thought of the deathly adverb "ere." LiTW

Definitions. Joseph Joel Keith. and never telling yourself/a lie. PoToHe

Definitions of the Word Gout. Tina Koyama. he breathes out the last of the wind/as if it were a word. BrSi

The Deformed Mistress. Sir John Suckling. Judge whether I am happy, yea or no. BXAP; ErPo

Degas. Paul Monette. for now, I am the first to know. AmPA

A Degenerate Age. Solomon Ibn Gabirol. They know and hate it–for it is lofty. TrJP

Degli Sposi. Rika Lesser. We touch, we hold, we keep/one another free. FYAP

Degrees of Gray in Philipsburg. Richard Hugo. and the girl who serves you food/is slender and her red hair lights the wall. CoAP; NoP; NPAW

Degrees of Shade. Helen Pinkerton. To move from out the darkness You/ permit. NePoAm

Dei Genitrix. Aubrey Thomas De Vere. Not Him. Thine Infant dies to save. IrPN

Deid Sall Ye Ligg, and Ne'er a Memorie. Sappho. amang derk ghaists stravaigan sichtlesslie. OBVE

Deidre's Lament for the Sons of Usnach. Sir Samuel Ferguson. Lay me on my true Love's body. SeCePo

The Deil o' Bogie. Sir Alexander Gray. My auld calamitie!' BSV

Deir El Bahari: Temple of Hatshepsut. D. J. Enright. What laid her gently upon those sculptured steps? OBTV

Deirdre. James Stephens. ...No man can ever be/The friend of that poor queen. AWP; CMoP; GTBS; HBMV; NoAm; OBMV; PG; PoRA; ViBoPo

Deirdre and the Poets. Ewart Milne. When their choirs like birds shall be my only poets/Said the sore-tried woman of the roads. NeIP

Deirdre (excerpt). William Butler Yeats. What is all our praise to them,/ That have one another's eyes? ViBoPo

Deirdre's Farewell to Alba. *Anonymous*. And tarry I may not when love cries away. OnYI

Deirdre's Farewell to Scotland. *Anonymous*. Had I not come with my beloved. OnYI

Deirdre's Lament. *Anonymous*. I shall be beside the noble ones. LiTW; OnYI

Deirdre's Song at Sunrise. Sister Maura. Lord of the days new and olden,/ Shine on and gladden the earth. CaP

Deities and Beasts. John Updike. ...and the Sparrow, whose fall/Is never mentioned in the press at all. ELU

Deja Vu. Shirley Kaufman. ...She/climbs the dusty path home. LCAP

Deja Vu. J. B. Mulligan. The echo groping for the sound. AMV-80

Dejection. Robert Bridges. I praise my days for all they bring,/Yet are they only not enough. QFR

Dejection. Samuel Taylor Coleridge.
Might startle this dull pain, and make it move and live! SeCePo
Thus may'st thou ever, evermore rejoice! AnEnPo; CBEP; EnRP; ERoP 1-2; FiP; ForPo; HBV 1-2; LiTB; LoBV; MasP; MBW 1-2; NAWM 1-2; NOBE; NoP; OAEL 1-2; OAEP; OBNC; OBRV; PoEL 1-5; PPP

Del Cascar. William Stanley Braithwaite. Hot the tears Del Cascar wept. BANP; CDC

Delay. Charlotte Fiske Bates. Averted graciously by kind Delay! AA

Delay. Elizabeth Jennings. And love arrived may find us somewhere else. NePoEA; OxBTC

Delay Has Danger. George Crabbe. ...he ponder'd for a while,/Then met his Fanny with a borrow'd smile. FaBoPP

Delayed till she had ceased to know. Emily Dickinson. Doubtful if it be crowned! AA

Delaying Tactics. Christopher Wiseman. the slow suburban cars outside. AMV-81

Delfica. Gerard de Nerval. When she awakes the gate will crumble. NU

Delia Holmes. *Anonymous*. Good-bye, mother, friends and all;/All I had done gone. AmFP

Delia's Gone. *Anonymous*. Delia's gone, one more round. FSW

Delia Very Angry. *Anonymous*. Do you think one has nothing to do but forgive? NOEC

A Delicate Balance. Laura Schreiber. you are, I sense, the dearer. AMV-80

A Delicate Impasse. Kenneth John Atchity. with dust behind my ears,/& nearer godlessness. AMV-80

Delicate Mother Kangaroo. D. H. Lawrence. But all was silent save for parrots occasionally,/in the haunted blue bush. GrPl

The Delicate, Plummeting Bodies.   Stephen Dobyns.   like a net to catch the delicate and plummeting bodies.   FYAP

Delicate the Toad.   Robert Francis.   But have you/Caught, among small/ Stars, his flute?   DuDa

Deliciae Sapientiae de Amore.   Coventry Patmore.   And inly clad/With the bridal robes of ardour virginal.   OxBoCh

Delight in Books from Evening.   Francis Daniel Pastorius.   On waspish men (who taking wing/Surround us) that they can not sting.   SCAP

Delight in Disorder.   Robert Herrick.   Do more bewitch me than when art/ Is too precise in every part.   ALV; AnAnS 2; AnFE; BiP; BoLiVe; CaPo; EnLoPo; FaBV; FF; GTBS; HAP; HBV 1-2; HeIP; InMe; InPK; InPS; JCP; LiTB; LiTL; LoBV; NIP; NOBE; NoP; OAEL 1-2; OAEP; OBEV; OBS; PAI; PoPle; PoRA; PP; PPoe; PPP; PrIm; SeCePo; SeCeV; SeCP; SeCV; TreFS; TrGrPo; ViBoPo; WHA 1-2

The Delight Song of Tsoai-Talee.   N. Scott Momaday.   You see, I am alive, I am alive.   CDW; GrPl; STE

The Delights of the Door.   Francis Ponge.   ...which the/click of the powerful but well-oiled spring pleasantly confirms.   NU

Delilah.   Rudyard Kipling.   Of, Delilah Aberyswith and most mean Ulysses Gunne!   BrPo

The Delinquent Travellers.   Samuel Taylor Coleridge.   And merriest, too, believe me, Sirs!/Are your Delinquent Travellers!   OBTV

Delirium in Vera Cruz.   Malcolm Lowry.   He smashed all the glass in the room. (Bill: $50.)   FaBoTw; OxBTC

Deliver Me.   Amy Carmichael.   Make me Thy fuel, Flame of God.   STF

Deliver Me, O Lord, from My Daily Bread.   Jeanne Murray Walker.   Deliver me once more from my daily bread.   AMV-80

Deliverance.   William James Dawson.   When I return'd, like a tired child you slept.   OBVV

Deliverance.   Frances E. W. Harper.   had not we women radicals/Just got right in the way....   WPOW

Deliverance from a Fit of Fainting.   Anne Bradstreet.   O Lord, no longer be my days/Than I may fruitful be.   TAP

Delivering Children.   David Holbrook.   How the dead grass dances on under the passing lamps,/under the large star Way!   NePoEA-2

The Dell.   Gavin Ewart.   the dell an excuse for one more delay/on our homeward way.   OxBC

The Della Cruscans.   William Gifford.   Begotten without thought, born without pains,/The ropy drivel of rheumatic brains.   OBEC

Delos.   Lawrence Durrell.   Aimed across Delos at a star.   NeBP

Delphic Hymn to Apollo.   Algernon Charles Swinburne.   All, aswarm as bees, give ear,/Who by birth hold Athens dear.   VLP

Delphine.   Teresa Anderson.   and wishing he would remove/the pins from her heavy, dark hair.   LTB

The Delta.   Michael Dennis Browne.   And will let no lovers in tonight.   NYBP

Delta Farmer in a Wet Summer.   James Whitehead.   And stench, contains the element of/chance a Christian needs.   TAT

Delta Traveller.   Charles Wright.   Rising and falling back and rising.   AmPA; LCAP

Deluge.   John Clare.   E'een the olf stone pit, deep as house is high,/Was brimming o'er and floated o'er the top.   BoNaP

Delusions VI.   Charles Madge.   ...streams ever repeat/Their senseless noise to perfect solitude.   NeBP

Dem Bones.   *Anonymous.*   My Lawd, down in the valley one day.   OuSiCo

The Demagogue.   Phyllis McGinley.   How sweet the noise of silence is.   FaBoEE

Demands of the Muse.   Vernon Watkins.   And serves me in my way and not another.   PoA

Deme As Ye List uppon Goode Cause.   Sir Thomas Wyatt.   And if yt be not as I think,/Lyke wyse to think yt is not.   PoEL 1-5

Demeanour.   *Anonymous.*   And at bed, soft and sad.   OxBChV

Dementia Praecox.   Morris Bishop.   Bellows of joy into the sodden air.   PoA

Demeter and Persephone.   Alfred, Lord Tennyson.   Along the silent field of Asphodel.   MBW 1-2; VLP

The Demiurge's Laugh.   Robert Frost.   Thereafter I sat me against a tree.   OxBA

The Democratic Barber; or, Country Gentleman's Surprise.   John Parrish.   Unto the world I will the deed proclaim.   NOEC

Democritus and Heraclitus.   Matthew Prior.   Hurt, can I laugh? and honest, need I cry?   OBSP

Les Demoiselles de Sauve.   John Gray.   ...and springtime/grass/Tangles a snare to catch the tapering toe.   NOBV; VLP

Demolition.   Philip Raisor.   ...as dead bricks leap/to souvenirs like old women/remembering birth.   AMV-81

The Demolition.   Anne Stevenson.   She cries on his stairs.   OBSP

The Demon Lover.   *Anonymous.*
And sank her in the sea.   EnSB
For while they are robbing the House-Carpenter,/And coaxing away their wives.   BaBo

The Demon Lover.   Adrienne Rich.   Seasick, I drop into the sea.   IHMS

The Demon of the Mirror.   Bayard Taylor.   And they sign the cross in saying: "God in mercy keep her soul!"   BeLS

The Demon Speaks.   Pedro Calderon de la Barca.   ...and I have wandered over/The expanse of these wide wildernesses/In this great ship--   CAW

Demonstration.   Margaret Finefrock.   perform the dance/of my own being.   AMV-80

Demophilus.   Henry Wellesley.   Demophilus strikes up; the screech-owl dies.   ALV

Demos.   Edwin Arlington Robinson.   Still to be wrangling in a noisy grave.   AP

A Denial.   Elizabeth Barrett Browning.   "Look in my face and see."   GBL; OBNC

Denial.   George Herbert.   They and my mind may chime,/And mend my rhyme.   AnAnS 1; EnL; InPo; JCP; LoBV; MePo; NOBE; NoP; OAEL 1-2; PoEL 1-5

Denials 1.   Jane Somerville.   She was a ringing tree of fragile glass,/ shivering in a leaf storm.   AMV-80

Denise.   Robert Beverly Hale.   Denise of the delicate crossed paws.   GDP; GrPl

Denmark.   Humbert Wolfe.   ...the evening star, the pale/cool-throated star, that rises with the Danish nightingale.   OBTV

Denouement.   Ruth Stone.   Murderer, I whispered, you tricked me.   BoWoP

The Dentist.   Rose Fyleman.   I should go riding up and down upon the velvet chair.   SoPo; TiPo

A Dentist's Window.   James Keir Baxter.   I fear the stab, the graunch, the touch of metal.   OxBC

Dentyne.   Annie Lurie.   days when I got the front seat to myself/to chew with my father/singing with the radio.   AmC

A Denunciation.   Mahammed A. Hassan.   Those who have driven me into the dusty sands of the desert...   WTO

Denunciation; or, Unfrock'd Again.   Philip Whalen.   I sat down in my house and ate a carrot.   NeAP

Deny Yourself.   Christopher Morley.   Many of the nicest people do.   YaD

Deo Gracias.   *Anonymous.*   In the name of God, whatever be wrought,/I shal say "Deo Gracias'...   OxBM

Deo Opt. Max.   George Sandys.   And now my Vowes have at thy Altar paid.   OBS

Deo Optimo Maximo.   Louise Imogen Guiney.   Oh, close my hand on Beatitude!/Not on her toys.   TrPWD

Deor's Lament.   *Anonymous.*   That evil ended. So also may this!   AnOE; EBEV; EnLi 1-2; EnLit; OAEL 1-2; TEP

Depart from Me.   Mary Elizabeth Coleridge.   I know Thee not. Abide with me!   TrPWD

The Departed.   John Banister Tabb.   Like lifted clouds, reach on.   AA

A Departed Friend.   Julia A. Moore.   Let him slumber, sweetly slumber,/ Till God calls him from the tomb.   FiBHP

Departed--to the Judgment.   Emily Dickinson.   Two Worlds--like Audiences-- disperse--/And leave the Soul--alone--   CABA

Departing Words to a Son.   Robert Pack.   We choose to say goodbye against our will.   GOYP

Departmental.   Robert Frost.   But how thoroughly departmental.   AnNE; DiPo; GoYe; HeIP; HoPM; MoAB; MoAmPo; NIP; NOBA; NOBL; OBAL; SoSe

Departmental Ditties: Prelude.   Rudyard Kipling.   And ye know what the jest is worth.   VLP

Departure.   Kingsley Amis.   Not a bland refraction of sweet mirrors.   NePoEA

Departure.   Edmund Charles Blunden.   And carter-like comes whistling along/Our casual Anglian train.   OBSP

Departure.   Carolyn Forche.   ...like the smallest/of cities we slipped through.   AMV-80

Departure.   J. Charles Green.   and a black parachute/carried my brain to an alien place.   LFAC

Departure.   George Hitchcock.   kneel and gather those bits of/thread which dropped from your hand/to the bare, bare floor.   GP

The Departure.   Henry, Bishop of Chichester King.   And he with saddest circumstance doth part,/Who seals his farewell with a bleeding heart.   SeCP

Departure.   Genny Lim.   I won't flinch/I won't cry.   BrSi

A Departure.   Derek Mahon.   It merges into the funeral/Cloud-continent of night/As if it belongs there.   CIP

Departure.   Edna St. Vincent Millay.   There goes the kettle, I'll make the tea.   MoAmPo

The Departure.   Robert Pack.   And wakening, you'll be expecting dreams again.   NePoEA

The Departure.   Jeremy Robson.   And the dust settled again/On the pavements of prayer.   VWA

Departure.   May Riley Smith.   I ever liked thy wine, though salt with/tears.   AA

The Departure.   Frank Steele.   ...curtains/blowing at the window/speaking to me.   GOYP; PPJ

Departure. Leonard Alfred George Strong. Lost in a sundering throb and a shower of spray. HaMV

The Departure. Reed Whittemore. Art in its arty way keeps saying: goodbye. TAP

The Departure from Hydra. Kenneth Koch. I smiled, and closed the door. AmPC

Departure in the Dark. C. Day Lewis. And will be, even to the last of his dark departures. ChMP; CoBMV; MoPo; MP; TwCP

The Departure of the Good Daemon. Robert Herrick. Why nothing now, but lonely sit,/And over-read what I have writ. FaBoRV

Departure Platform. Kenneth Allott. Now there is nothing new. NeBP

Departure's Girl-Friend. William Stanley Merwin. Wishing myself the good voyage. ConAP; LCAP

Deportation. A. Glanz-Leyeles. clench your heart into your fists and/your mouth–seal it firmly. TrJP

A Deposition by John Wilmot. Vincent McHugh. go in one ear/and out the other ErPo

A Deposition from Beauty. Thomas Stanley. And thy despis'd disdain too late shall find/That none are fair but who are kind. EG; HBV 1-2

A Deposition from Love. Thomas Carew. But he that is cast down/From enjoy'd beauty, feels a woe,/Only deposed Kings can know. AnAnS 2; CaPo; CavP; MeLP; OAEP; OBS

The Depot. Lewis Turco. There may be smoke and a thin sound. GrPl

Depot Blues. Anonymous. I can't get no sassin', baby, on the tele– telephone. AmFP

Depot Blues. Charlie Lincoln (Hicks). Rather drink muddy water/go sleep in a hollow tree/Than to hear my kid gal/say she don't want me. BluL

Depot in Rapid City. Roberta Hill. ...Clear as tracks,/are callings and cold signals on the wind. BoWoP

Deprecating Parrots. Beulah May. While he swings on a temple bell filched from/Lahore. EtS

Depreciating Her Beauty. Wilfrid Scawen Blunt. And that thy bosom in my bosom lay. OBMV

Depressed by a Book of Bad Poetry, I Walk toward an Unused Pasture... James Wright. ...a dark cricket begins/In the castles of maple. ConAP

Depressed by the Death of the Horse... (parody). Henry Taylor. Minnesota is what I mant to say,/And they may never know. BXAP

Depression. Robert Bly. I want to go down and rest in the black earth of silence. NaP

Depression. Rex Burwell. ...I feel the ease/of whiskey and the gallows and I rest. AMV-80

Depression. Wendy Cope. I can no more cross this room/Than Zeno's arrow. FaBoWP

Depression. Michael (Katherine Bradley and Edith Cooper) Field. Youth's stubborn, immature, unburied dead. SyP

Depression before Spring. Wallace Stevens. But no queen comes/In slipper green. OBAL; SOTW

Depression (excerpt). Charles Reznikoff. and, seeing only faces turned away,/did not even go down the aisle as beggars do. CTBA

Deprivation. Helen Pinkerton. Who gives no other affirmation/Than love's retractless forfeiture? NePoAm

The Depths. Denise Levertov. ...may the taste of salt/recall to us the great depths about us. NaP; NU

The Depths of Sorrow. Anonymous. For the deep limits of sorrow's tears are not yet found. WTO

Der Blinde Junge. Mina Loy. How this expressionless "thing"/blows out damnation and concussive dark/Upon a mouth-organ. QFR

Der Brief, Den Du Geshrieben. Louis Untermeyer. To write a mere good-bye. ALV

Der Deitcher's Dog. Septimus Winner. Dey makes um mit dog und dey makes em mit horse,/I guess de makes em mit he.... PSoN

Der Heilige Mantel Von Aachen. Benjamin Francis Musser. ...Our Lady takes/Her cloak and, questing souls, goes out from Aix. ISi

Der Mond Ist Aufgegangen. Heinrich Heine. The singing of my sisters/Whom the sea hath drowned so long. AWP

Deranged. Padraic Fiacc. Liefer would I turn and love/The ox in the by-path, the barn-yard dove! NeIP

The Derby Ram. Anonymous.
And what was left, I'm told, sir,/Was served out to the fleet. ViBoFo
That's the tid i fa la truth. FaBoNo; GBP
You may eat a bit of the pie. OxNR

The Derby Ram, I. Anonymous. Just you go down to Derby,/And you'll see the same as I! AmFP

The Derby Ram, II. Anonymous. And the boy who wrote this song, sir,/Was a lying son of a bitch. AmFP

Derbyshire Bluebells. Sacheverell Sitwell. Nor find our bluebells honeyless. ChMP

Dere's a Han'writin' on de Wall. Anonymous. Oh, won't you come an' read it,/See what it say,/Dere's a han' writin' on de wall. BoAN 1-2

Dere's No Hidin' Place down Dere. Anonymous. Dere's no hidin' place down dere. BoAN 1-2; BPo

Derelict. Young Ewing Allison. Yo-ho-ho and a bottle of rum! BBV; BLPA; EtS; FaBoBe; FaFP; HBMV; MCCG; OnMSP; TreFS

The Derelict. Lucius Harwood Foote. Her battered hulk is heaving to and fro. AA

Derelict. Henry Johnson. and his staccato snores,/pounding against the walls/like jack-hammers. LFAC

The Derelict. Rudyard Kipling. Falling afraid lest any keel come near! BrPo

Derelict. Elisabeth Cavazza Pullen. A ship condemned, like a lost soul. AA

Derry. Seamus Deane. It might be so forever, someone fears,/Or for days. CIP

Derry Morning. Derek Mahon. A Russian freighter bound for home/Mourns to the city in its gloom. NOBI

Dervish. Georgia Lee McElhaney. who need no moon/to dream by. CoPo

Derwent: An Ode. John Carr. Not a lake in the land like the Sneep. NOEC

Descartes and the Stove. Charles Tomlinson. And the moist reciprocation of his palms. FaBoMo

Descend, Fair Sun! George Chapman. And on him endless youth attends. EIL

Descendancy. Tom Paulin. has pulled up at a roadblock/a shade far from Garrison? FaBoIP

Descending. Valentin Iremonger. Of the wind in her hair will be stopped much too soon. EnLoPo

Descending. Robert Pack. ...gates–/Closing behind the hill of the road/That narrows behind me–beckon me back. NePoEA-2

Descending Figure. Louise Gluck. her head covered with black feathers... FaBoWP; GeTw

Descent for the Lost. Philip Child. Green, green grows the grass/Behind our tired feet. CaP

The Descent of Odin. Thomas Gray. Till wrap'd in flames, in ruin hurl'd,/Sinks the fabric of the world. CEP; EiCP; LAuP

The Descent of Winter (Section 10/30). William Carlos Williams. and disappeared/in silence/to the left. InPK

The Descent on Middlesex. Peter St. John. I hail'd the place where months before,/The Tories took me from the shore. PAH

Descent to Bohannon Lake. Jim Barnes. ...on this a hot summer's day. FAZ

Describes the Place Where Cynthia Is Sporting Herself. Philip Ayres. And those are streams of tears which thence distil. EnLoPo

A Description. Edward, Lord Herbert of Cherbury. I sing her Worth and Praises hy,/Of whom a Poet cannot ly. AnAnS 2; SeCP

Description and Praise of His Love Geraldine. Henry Howard, Earl of Surrey. Happy is he that can obtain her love. AAS; OAEP

A Description of a City Shower. Jonathan Swift. Dead Cats and Turnip-Tops come tumbling down the Flood. CABL; CBEP; CEP; EiCP; EnLi 1-2; ExPo; HeIP; LoBV; MAT; NOEC; NoP; OAEL 1-2; OBSV; OnYI; PPP; SeCePo; SeCeV; TEP; ViBoPo

The Description of a Good Boy. Henry Dixon. He smiles and looks gay. OxBChV

Description of a New England Spring. John Josselyn. Withouten these no water could be good. SCAP

Description of a Ninety Gun Ship. William Falconer. And with triumphant navies rule the main. PeD

A Description of a Strange (and Miraculous) Fish. Martin Parker. O rare/beyond compare/in England nere the like. CoMu

Description of a Summer's Eve. Henry Kirke White. Then both to bed together creep,/And join the general troop of sleep. OBRV

Description of a View. William Empson. A dome compact of all but visible stars. ACV

A Description of an Author's Bedchamber. Oliver Goldsmith. A cap by night–a stocking all the day! BIrV

The Description of an Irish Feast, or O'Rourk's Frolic. Hugh MacGowran. A blow on the weam,/Or a kick on the arse. OBVE; OnYI

A Description of Beauty, Translated out of Marino. Samuel Daniel. Pluck, pluck betime thy flower,/That springs, and perisheth in one short hour. OBSC

The Description of Castara. William Habington. And her love she vowes to me. AnAnS 2

Description of Elysium. James Agee. Through hornleaved holly. CrMA

A Description of His Ugly Lady. Thomas Hoccleve. And she singeth full like a papejay. MeEL

Description of Holland. Samuel (1612-80) Butler. A land that rides at anchor, and is moored/In which they do not live, but go aboard. OBTV

A Description of London. John Bancks. This is London! How d'ye like it? NOEC

A Description of Love. Sir Walter Ralegh. And shepherd, this is Love, I trow. ALV; EIL; ELP; LiTL; OAEL 1-2; OBSC; UnTE

A Description of Maidenhead. Anonymous. Cracks, and rejoices in the flame. NOBL

The Description of Sir Geoffrey Chaucer. Robert Greene. Thus did this ancient poet look. AnFE; CTC; OBSC

Description of Spring. Henry Howard. Each care decays, and yet my sorrow springs. AnEnPo; AtBAP; ElL; LiTB; LoBV; OAEP; OBEV; SeCePo; SeCeV

A Description of the Morning. Jonathan Swift. And school-boys lag with satchels in their hands. CABA; CEP; EBEV; EiCP; ExPo; FF; HAP; InPS; NIP; NOBE; NOEC; NoP; OAEL 1-2; Prf; SeCeV; TEP; ViBoPo; WeW

A Description of the Spring in London. *Anonymous.* In gay Vauxhall now saunter beaux and belles,/And happier cits resort to Sadler's Wells. NOEC

A Description of Tyme. Alexander Montgomerie. Tak tyme in tyme, or tyme will not be tane. OxBS

A Descriptive Poem, Addressed to Two Ladies.... John Dalton. Creative Commerce, these are thine! NOEC

Dese Bones Gwine to Rise Again. *Anonymous.* Dese bones gwine to rise again. ABF; AS; OxBoLi

Desert. Agnes Gergely. and as a sign of his respect/said to the Great Shade: "same thing." VWA

The Desert. Henry Herbert Knibbs. Just a rain-washed track and an empty gun–/and the old home trail ahead. BPAW

The Desert. Charles Erskine Scott Wood. And braids her hair with the constellations. AnAmPo

Desert Bloom. Gertrude Thomas Arnold. That is the message of "Desert Bloom." BPAW

Desert Claypan. Frederick T. Macartney. endurance asks no recompense. PoAu 1-2

Desert Flowers. Keith Douglas. Lay the coin on my tongue and I will sing/of what the others never set eyes on. FaBoTw

Desert Gulls. Dan Gillespie. in a blizzard of doves. TAT

Desert Holy Man. John Beecher. Old Charley spit on his hands/and stood the drinks around. TAT

Desert in the Sea. Brian Swann. The oars we spent years to learn/Push air by us in tight bundles. AmPA

The Desert Lark. Eugene Marais. My little grey sister, Gampta,/I see you! PeSA

Desert March. Gerda Norvig. grounded,/I return home. VWA

The Desert Music (excerpt). William Carlos Williams. ...the wonder of the brain that/hears that music and of our/skill sometimes to record it. UnS

The Desert of Love. Janos Pilinszky. ...And hope/is like a tin-cup toppled into the straw. OBVE

Desert Places. Robert Frost. To scare myself with my own desert places. AnFE; AtBAP; BiP; CMoP; CoBMV; DiPo; ForPo; MoAB; MoAmPo; MoVE; NCSH; NoAm; NOBA; OxBA; PPP; TAP; UnPo

Desert River. Patricia Benton. Salt without tears. GoYe

Desert Shipwreck. Barbara Leslie Jordan. While overhead the far, uncaring stars wheel by. GoYe

Desert Song. Glenn Ward Dresbach. But if you come with dreams for baggage/Sit with us by the cedar fire! BPAW

Desert Song. John Galsworthy. The scent of rain, the scent of rain! BPAW

Desert Stone. Miriam Waddington. until my tears will melt/the world of desert stone. VWA

Desert Warfare. Michael Longley. She might be a mirage, and my long/Soliloquies part of the action. CIP

Deserted. Madison Cawein. The moon comes misty white. MCCG

A Deserted Barn. Larry Woiwode. Reflections, at night, from the reflected light of the moon. WeW

Deserted Buildings under Shefford Mountain. John Glassco. Dull meadows that have gone to seed? OBCV

Deserted Farms. Richard Burton. Or toward the peopled cities set your face. AnAmPo

The Deserted Garden. Elizabeth Barrett Browning. That I who was, would shrink to be/That happy child again. HBV 1-2

The Deserted Garden. Ann Stanford. waiting, deserted, unfinished, as you mourn for this lost/garden. AMV-81

A Deserted Home. Sidney Royse Lysaght. Once sped the dance when the corn was on the floor. CH

The Deserted Home. Kuno Meyer. And therefore is my heart so sad. OxBI

The Deserted Homestead. Loren C. Eiseley. Deride the hackneyed misery–/Earth's only yield. PoA

The Deserted House. Mary Elizabeth Coleridge. Nor any bird of the air. CH; MoVE

The Deserted Kingdom. Edward John, Lord Dunsany. I bow not to the monkey bands. AnIV

The Deserted Mountain. *Anonymous.* I lived in pleasant times. BIrV

The Deserted Pasture. Bliss Carman. The snowy hosts of heaven arrive/To pitch their tents therein. HBV 1-2

Deserted Shrine. Avner Treinin. And the priest still unrevealed. VWA

The Deserted Village. Oliver Goldsmith.
And filled each pause the nightingale had made. TreFS

And rural mirth and manners are no more. OBSV

As rocks resist the billows and the sky. BeLS; BIrV; EBEV; EnPE; FaFP; GoTL; HBV 1-2; LaA; LAuP; MasP; MCCG; NOBI; NOEC; NoP; OAEL 1-2; OAEP; OnYI; OxBI; PoEL 1-5; TEP

The country blooms–a garden and a grave. OBSV

Eternal sunshine settles on its head. TrGrPo; TRV; WGRP

The heart distrusting asks, if this be joy? EBEV; LoBV

That one small head could carry all he knew. GLGT; TrGrPo

These were thy charms–but all these charms are fled. TrGrPo

When once destroyed, can never be supplied. LiTB; PPON; SeCePo; ViBoPo

Where wealth accumulates, and men decay. TRV

While broken tea-cups, wisely kept for show,/Rang'd o'er the chimney, glisten'd in a row. AnFE

The Deserter. Joseph Seamon, Jr Cotter. Caring no more to dwell within/The house where faith is dead. CDC

The Deserter. Alfred Edward Housman. And lie there with your leaden lover/For ever and a day.' OBMV; SeCeV

The Deserter. John Streeter Manifold. And say, "I know. But then what can I do?" CBAP

The Deserter. Stevie Smith. I shall quite simply never speak to the fellow again. FaBoWP

The Deserter. Bayard Taylor. "It was love–sweetest love–led that soldier away." PaPo

The Deserter's Lamentation. John Philpot Curran. Let us be merry/Before we go! FaBoRV; IrPN; SeCePo

The Desertion of the Women and Seals. George Mackay Brown. Round Howie's impotence drew in the night. OxBC

Desertmartin. Tom Paulin. I see a culture of twigs and bird-shit/Waving a gaudy flag it loves and curses. FaBoIP

Deserts. Leigh Hanes. In streaks of light across the desert's heart. GoYe

Deservings. *Anonymous* A little is the sum of all. HBV 1-2

Desideravi. Theodore Maynard. To me, who tremble so and burn,/Be pitiful! HBMV

Desideria. William Wordsworth. That neither present time, nor years unborn/Could to my sight that heavenly face/restore. BLPL; GTBS; GTBS-P; OBEV

Desiderium. Phineas Fletcher. So shall I first begin, so last shall end thy will. OBS

Design. Robert Frost. If design govern in a thing so small. AP; BLPL; CMoP; CoBMV; CrMA; ForPo; HeIP; InPS; NIP; NoAm; NOBA; NoP; PAI; PPP; PrIm; SeCeV; SoSe; TAP

The Design. Clarence Major. No matter what I might say/she is not bored. PoBA

Design. Peter Redgrove. And pipeclay features with blacking sockets, General. OxBC

Design for a Bowl. Anacreon. I tremble for the rosy boys. UnTE

Design for a Stream-Lined Sunrise. Sister Mary Madeleva. Beyond potential beauty, beautiful. GoBC

Design for Mediaeval Tapestry. Abraham Moses Klein. And like a bloodhound swoops across the sky. CaP

Design for Peace. Janet Norris Bangs. The battleline is drawn in every heart! PGD

Desire. Matthew Arnold. From the cradle to the grave,–/Save, O Save! WGRP

Desire. William Cornish. We left them there and went our way. OBSC; SeCeV

Desire. Isaac De Botton. ...and my eyes,/shut, will not see/gorgeous flowers any more. VWA

The Desire. Katharine Tynan Hinkson. As Mary once her Paradise,/Just four years old. HBV 1-2

Desire. Kathleen Raine. and forest burn in their own funeral. MoPo

Desire. George William Russell. Ah, with what longing once again I turn! ILwL; OBMV; TrPWD

Desire. Thomas Traherne. All which are founded in desire,/As light in flame and heat in fire. OxBoCh

Desire, alas, my master and my foe. Sir Thomas Wyatt. Even now by hate again I dread the same. FCP

Desire for Hermitage. *Anonymous.* And as I shall go from it. AnIL

Desire Is a Witch. C. Day-Lewis. Needs no other proof/Than its own fire. CMoP

Desire Is Dead. D. H. Lawrence. wonder outwaiting pain/as in a wintry tree. FaBoEE

Desire Knows. Asclepiades. flower/of Love and of Persuasion. LiTW

The Desire of Water. Mark Jarman. rise toward the dam's lip too much for flood gates. PoA

Desire's Government. A. W. Where fond Desire as king doth reign. ElL

The Desired Swan-Song. Samuel Taylor Coleridge. Should certain persons die before they sing. UnS

Desires. Connie Bensley. Hoping you'll turn and snap at me/To pick my feet up, and not to slouch. FaBoWP

Desires of Men and Women. John Berryman. Whence you project your naked fantasies. LiTM

The Devil's Dictionary: Orthography. Ambrose Bierce. And his sepulchre shall not be whicted. OBAL

The Devil's Dictionary: Prospect. Ambrose Bierce. Where every prospect pleases,/Save only that of death. OBAL

The Devil's Dictionary: Safety-Clutch. Ambrose Bierce. Moral of this woful poem:/Frequent oil your safety-clutch. OBAL

The Devil's Nine Questions. Anonymous. And you are the weaver's bonny. AmFP; WSC

The Devil's Thoughts. Samuel Taylor Coleridge. It was general conflagration. FaBoCo; OBSV; OxBoLi

The Devil's Thoughts (excerpt). Richard Porson. For I sat myself like a cormorant once/Hard by the tree of knowledge. DBV

The Devil's Walk. Robert Southey. As a gentleman swishes his cane. PV

Devilish Mary. Anonymous.
   Come a dairy, come a dairy. FSW
   Come a fa la ling, come a derry. OuSiCo
   Prettiest little girl in all this world,/Her name was Devilish Mary. AmFP

Devils. Norman Mailer. nostrils/like/devil's feet OBAL

Devoide of Reason, Thrale to Foolish Ire. Thomas Lodge. And full of furie on their maister feede,/To hasten on my haplesse death with speede. AAS

Devon to Me. John Galsworthy. Feel o' the red earth!/Devon to me! HBMV

A Devonshire Rhyme. Anonymous. Sit by the fire and spare shoe leather. BrR; SiSoSe

A Devonshire Song. Anonymous. Ich thither Hie, for this place I/Do take it in great dudgeon. OBS

Devotion. Anonymous. I serve thee with my heart,/And fall before thee. LiTB; OBEV

Devotion. Thomas Campion. It shall suffice that they were breathed and died for her delight. NOBE; OBEV

Devotional Incitements. William Wordsworth. So shall the seventh be truly blest,/From morn to eve, with hallowed rest. OxBoCh

Devotions. John Donne. ...never send to know/for whom the bell tolls; it tolls for thee. PoPl

Devotions of the Fowls. John Lydgate. This melodious hymn with great solace,/O lux beata Trinitas. PBBP

Devout Fits. John Donne. Those are my best days, when I shake with fear. SeCePo

A Devout Lover. Thomas Randolph. And come unto my courtship as my prayer. EG; HBV 1-2; HoPM; LiTL; OBEV

The Devout Man Prays to His Relations. William Herebert. Sathan shall nout spede,/With wrenches ne with crok. Amen. MeEL

A Devout Prayer of the Passion. Anonymous. As thou rose up on Estre Day,/In joy and blisse to live aye./Amen. MeEL

Dew. Jennifer Maiden. With sightless unquenched grief to walk alive CBAP

Dew. Charles Reznikoff. the tellers will be Jews and their speech Hebrew. VWA

The Dew Each Trembling Leaf Inwreath'd. Mary Balfour. But, oh! the smile that gave the charm/No longer beams for me! IrPN

Dew on a Dusty Heart. Jean Starr Untermeyer. The dewy rest they dream of and call heaven. MoAmPo

Dew Sat on Julia's Hair. Robert Herrick. Have their reflected light/Danc'd by the streams. ELP

Dewdrop, Wind and Sun. Joseph Skipsey. And with her pride did into Lethe pass. OBVV

Dewdrops. John Clare. ...violets, vernal speedwell, bluebell and/orchis, and commonplacc objccts. VLP

Dewey and His Men. Wallace Rice. And the wildfire lights as Dewey fights on the/broad Manila Bay. PAH

Dewey at Manila. Robert Underwood Johnson. Who would win, on land or wave,/Must be wise as well as brave. HBV 1-2; MC; PAH

Dewey in Manila Bay. R. V. Risley. For fighting's part of what a Yankee knows! MC; PAH

Dexter. Joan Byers Grayston. And like Black Beauty neighs his lonesomeness/For the child to come and ride. PH

Dey Got Each and de Udder's Man. Anonymous. Bet yo' life dey got/Each and de udder's man. WTO

The Dhows. Francis Brett Young. ...Your iron keels/are stronger/Than ghostly ships that sailed from Tyre a thousand/years ago.' EtS

Di Great Insohreckshan. Linton Kwesi Johnson. nevah mine Scarman/will bring a blam-blam. FaBoPV

Diaduminius. Pierre Benoit. In the old house to which one will return. CAW

Diagnosis. Janine Canan. ...She/opened all the drawers and doors and windows—and a cool bay/breeze shot through. APU

The Diakka. Gerald Massey. You can wake up the world with YOUR row-de-dow. NOBV

Dial Call. Christopher Morley. And gets more prompt reply. NLV

The Dial Tone. Howard Nemerov. After you left that it was before you came. NYBP

Dial Tone. Felix Pollak. unnoticeable till/night takes the sun off/the hook. PPJ

Dialect Quatrain. Marcus B. Christian. "Makeum-Tell-It Squad." AmNP

Dialectics of Flight. John Hall Wheelock. ...landing gear/Needed for the interval between flight and flight. NePoAm-2

Dialectique. Hugh Maxton. We were never together/At table, or/Arm on arm. CIP

Dialog outside the Lakeside Grocery. Ishmael Reed. "They keep me out of the bars". APU

Dialogue. Agathias. The heart struck silly by Love's shaft/Forgets its arithmetic! OLR

Dialogue. John Erskine. Reason to hate me–none at all/For loving you. HBMV

Dialogue. George Herbert. Ah! no more: thou break'st my heart. MePo; OBEV; OBS; SeCV 1-2

A Dialogue. David Ignatow. ...I will go/and die there/in sorrow. NNaP

Dialogue. Sister Mary Madeleva. And say, "This is my Flesh and Blood"; Thy Word is my reply. CAW

Dialogue. Howard Nemerov. When withered in the sun/Or dried in the salt air. NYBP; PoPl

A Dialogue. Alexander Pope. 'Tis Pope must be ashamed of Craggs. PoL

Dialogue. Adrienne Rich. or whether I knew, even then/that there was doubt about these things. TAP

A Dialogue. Algernon Charles Swinburne. Then shall we know full surely, quick or dead,/Death, if thou be. PoEL 1-5

Dialogue–2 Dollmakers. Gregory Corso. What about them? There's always abandoned farms to use. NeAP

Dialogue 4 1 Voice Only. Doug Fetherling. Dont breathe heavy less u really mean it. NeAC

Dialogue after Enjoyment. Abraham Cowley. Yet wilt undo me more should'st thou not come at night. BoLoP

Dialogue at the Cross. Frederick Spee. I yield Thee to the cruel cross! CAW

Dialogue between a Squeamish Cotting Mechanic and his Sluttish Wife... Edward Ward. He thinks, poor cuckold, that he bears the rule,/When heaven knows I do but gull the fool. NOEC

Dialogue, between Crab and Gillian. Thomas D'Urfey. And so you may ring the bells. NOEC

A Dialogue between King William and the Late King James... Charles Blount. For subjects are the surest guard of kings. APAS

Dialogue between Mary and Gabriel. W. H. Auden. ...child, it lies/Within your power of choosing to/Conceive the Child who chooses you. ISi

A Dialogue between the Lovelorn Sir Hugh and Certain Ladies.... Thomas Deloney. O that fair Winifred would once say so. UnTE

A Dialogue between the Resolved Soul and Created Pleasure. Andrew Marvell. The rest does lie beyond the Pole,/And is thine everlasting Store. MeLP; MePo; OAEL 1-2; OBS; SeCV 1-2

A Dialogue between the Soul and Body. Andrew Marvell. Green trees that in the forest grew. AnAnS 1; HAP; InPS; JCP; MeLP; MePo; NoP; OAEL 1-2; OBS; OxBoCh; PoEL 1-5; PPP; SeCP; TEP

A Dialogue between Thyrsis and Dorinda. Andrew Marvell. So shall we smoothly pass away in sleep. SeCP

A Dialogue betweene Araphill and Castara. William Habington. Noble hearts Love onely joynes. AnAnS 2

A Dialogue betwixt GOD and the Soul. Sir Henry Wotton. A foolish Toy, yet once more I/Would with Thee live, and for thee die. MeLP; OBS; OxBoCh

A Dialoguc betwixt Time and a Pilgrim. Aurelian Townsend. Together twists their threads, and yet draws hers the longer. AnAnS 2; MePo; NOBE; OAEL 1-2; OBS; PoEL 1-5; SeCP

A Dialogue from Plato. Henry Austin Dobson. Nay, more than this, I hold it still/Profoundly confidential. HBV 1-2

Dialogue: Lover and Lady. Ciullo d'Alcamo. It is best so, sith so it was to be. AWP

A Dialogue of Self and Soul. William Butler Yeats. Everything we look upon is blest. CABA; CMoP; DTC; ExPo; FaBoMo; LiTB; LiTM; MasP; MoBrPo; NoAm; OAEP

Dialogue of the Way. Harold Stewart. Faint but distinct, uttered by drinking ground. BoAV

Dialogue on the Headland. Robert Graves. You'll not forget me–ever, ever, ever? ACV

Dialogue with a Door. Caius Valerius Catullus. Whose spurious birth once caused no small dispute. UnTE

A Diamond. Robert Loveman. Held in eternal bondage there. AA

Diamond Cut Diamond. Ewart Milne. And one cat under/A witch elm/Tree. FaBoCh; LoGBV; NeIP; PCat

Diamond Joe. Anonymous. You roll like cattle never rolled before. CoSo; OuSiCo

Diana. Henry Constable.
   And he in ruth of my distressed cry/Plants me a weeping star within mine eye. OBSC

For by the wind which from my sighs doth come,/Your praises round about the world are blown. OBSC

For lo! mine heart, resolved to moistening air,/Feedeth mine eyes which double tear for tear. OBSC

Her beauty's wonder lives again in me. OBSC

I feel my sun's heat, though his light I miss. OBSC

My heart is love, for these in it are grounded. HBV 1-2; OBSC

Of greater wonders heard we never tell,/Than for the dumb to speak, the dead to live. OBSC

On earth but love there is no other pleasure. OBSC

Or by his grace I never more may love. OBSC

Or help me soon, or cast me off for ever! OBSC

The rain, wherewith she watereth the flowers,/Falls from mine eyes, which she dissolves in showers. HBV 1-2; OBSC

So beauty thou, beauty is not in thee. OBSC

Thy image should be sung; for thou that goddess art,/Which only we without idolatry adore. OBSC

Whilst Echo cries, "What shall become of me?" OBSC

Diana. Ernest Rhys. Ah, dear Diana! OBVV

Diana Enamorada: Ring Forth, Fair Nymphs, Your Joyful Songs. Gaspar Gil Polo. End nymphs, your songs, that in the clouds are/ringing. HW

Diana's Hunting-Song. John Dryden. And Echo turns hunter and doubles the cry. SeCePo

Dianae Sumus in Fide. Caius Valerius Catullus. ...now and forever, sing Diana! MOON

Diary. David Wagoner. And love in a coil. On Sunday, I wrote this. CoAP

Diary. Black Bear's Moon. Charlotte De Clue. they shove your anger in your face. TWSS

Diary (excerpt). Ethel Romig Fuller. When I have added these last words– "The End." PGD

Diary. Moon of the Hiding Doe. Charlotte De Clue. i reek with sorrow. TWSS

Diary of a Church Mouse. Sir John Betjeman. Except at Harvest Festival. BoC; OxBTC

Diary of a Raccoon. Gertrude Ryder Bennett. His page concluded with the dawn. GoYe

The Diary of Amanda McFadden. Linda Hogan. blue rivers running their course,/a gesture of calm. TWSS

The Diary of Izumi Shikibu (excerpt). Izumi Shikibu. and say I love you? BoWoP

A Diary of the Sailors of the North. David Shulman. be bound up in our spring of blood. VWA

The Diary of the Waning Moon (excerpt). Abutsu. Even the waves rise in the image of flowers. PBWP

Diary. Solitary Moon. Charlotte De Clue. this morning i wept. TWSS

Diary. The Deer Break Their Horns. Charlotte De Clue. (it is not the stuff of poetry.) TWSS

The Diaspora. W. H. Auden. And all they had to strike now was the human face. LiTA

Diaspora Jews. Rachel Boimwall. Alas, when Jews get together/they sigh. VWA

Dibdin's Ghost. Eugene Field. Says I to Dibdin's ghost. AA

Dicamus Bona Verba. Albius Tibullus. bless him with many children to tumble and romp at his/feet. NAs

The Dice Were Loaded. Mary Gilmore. The loaded dice were thrown for me/Upon the night that I was born. BoAV

Dichterliebe. Robert Klein Engler. ...What went wrong? AMV-81

Dick, a Maggot. Jonathan Swift. Like a fresh turd just dropped on snow. NLV; TW

Dick and Will. Elizabeth Madox Roberts. And watching ants go in a row. BiCB

Dick Briggs from Australia. Charles R. Thatcher. Cried Dick, as he surveyed them o'er,/"You wouldn't do for Australia." NOAV

Dick & Jane. Judith Kroll. She can leave him alone. AmPA

The Dick Johnson Reel. Jake Falstaff. I, Dick Johnson,/Killed Tecumseh! EvOK

Dick O the Cow. Anonymous. And Buragh under Stanemiur there dwels Dickie. BaBo; ESPB; OxBB

Dick Turpin and Black Bess. Anonymous. Fare-thee-well now forever, my bonnie black Bess. AmFP

Dick Turpin and the Lawyer. Anonymous. You can tell them you was robbed by Dick Turpin. ViBoFo

Dick Turpin's Ride. Anonymous. For Dick Turpin she lived and she died. OBET

Dickens in Camp. Bret (Francis Bret Harte) Harte. This spray of Western pine! BPAW; HBV 1-2

Dicky Dilver. Anonymous. So he threw her in the river. OxNR

The Dictionary Is an Historian. Judith McCombs. 9. Bringer of woe; by whimsical etymological deriva-/tion from woe + man. Obs. IHMS

Dictum: For a Masque of Deluge. William Stanley Merwin. Heavy, the wind a low portent of rain. AP; NoAm

Dictum Sapienti. Charles Henry ("John Paul") Webb. Before they are off with the old? ALV

Did any bird come flying. Christina Georgina Rossetti. The lamb and the dove/Were preachers sent from God. EG

Did I Ever Think. Ono no Takamura. Tugging at the ropes of fishermen? AWP

Did Not. Thomas Moore. And yet, who did not. ALV; BoLoP; ErPo; NBM

Did our best moment last. Emily Dickinson. Withdraws–and leaves the dazzled Soul/In her unfurnished Rooms– NOBA

Did the Harebell. Emily Dickinson. Would the Eden be an Eden,/Or the earl an earl? FaBV

Did They Help Me at the State Hospital for the Criminally Insane? Mbembe Milton Smith. Yeah, they helped me. FAZ

Did We Laugh or Did We Cry? Patu Simoko. nothing has changed! WhB

Did Ya Hear? Yasmeen Jamal. Lil' Johnny Castro was two years old when/they collected. LFAC

Did You Ever, Ever, Ever. Anonymous. Kiss his weef, wife, woaf. AS; FaBoNo

Did You Ever Hear an English Sparrow Sing? Bertha Johnston. I'm sure I'll hear that English sparrow sing. BLPA

Did You Feed My Cow? Anonymous. "Flop! Flop! Flop!" GoSl

Did You Not See. Alex Kuo. this incomprehensible blue. BrSi

Did You See My Wife? Anonymous. And dimity petticoats over her knee. OxNR

Didactic Sonnet. Melvin Walker La Follette. For he shall eat your sweetbreads, like a dog. NePoEA; PoA

Diddie Wa Diddie. Blind Blake. I wish somebody would tell me what diddie wa diddie means. BluL

Diddle, Diddle, Dumpling, My Son John. Anonymous. Diddle, diddle, dumpling, my son John. OxNR

Didn' My Lord Deliver Daniel? Anonymous. An' de Hebrew chillum from de fiery furnace,/An' why not every man? TrAS

Didn' Ol' John Cross the Water on His Knees? Anonymous. Didn' ol' John wade the water, water on his knees? OuSiCo

Didn't He Ramble. Will Handy. Oh! didn't he ramble, ramble,/He rambled 'til the butchers cut him down. FSW

Didn't My Lord Deliver Daniel? Anonymous.
Didn't my Lord deliver Daniel/An' why not-a every man. BoAN 1-2; FSW
It landed me over on Canaan's shore,/And I'll never come back any more. AH

Didn't Old Pharaoh Get Los'? Anonymous. Didn't old Pharaoh get los'./In de Red Sea True believer, O. BoAN 1-2

Dido. Thomas Campion. And let twenty Didos burn/So you get daily new. CBEP

Dido's Farewell. Linda Pastan. my own heart knocking/at my ribs, demanding/to be let out. GOYP

Dido's Hunting. Henry Howard, Earl of Surrey. ...under the pretence/Of which fair name she cloaketh now her fault. OBSC

Dido: Swarming. Kathleen Spivack. I harden like a scab. PoA

Dido to Aeneas. Richard Stanihurst. I shall hear, I doubt not, thy pangs in Limbo related. AnIV

Didyma. Anonymous. But what gives greater heat than coal on fire? UnTE

Didymus. Louis MacNeice. When he died, a swallow seemed to plunge/Into the reflected, the wrong, sky. EaLo

Die Blauen Veilchen Der Augelein. Heinrich Heine. And only the heart is withered and sere. AWP

Die Heimkehr (excerpt). Heinrich Heine. All good things go vanishing. AWP

Die in de Fiel'. Anonymous. I'm on my journey home. BoAN 1-2

Die Lotosblume Angstigt. Heinrich Heine. Exhaling, weeping, trembling/With ever-yearning love. AWP

An die Musik. David Malouf. ...Beethoven's Tenth is what it breathes. CBAP

Die My Shriek. Aaron Kushniroff. When frightened stars hide/In the steely folds of the sea? TrJP

Die Neuen Heiligen (excerpt). John Updike. which slashed the Ideal/and himself to bits. DBV

Die Not, Fond Man. Anonymous. Shall conclude a happy peace. EIL

Die Pelzaffen. Charles Spear. Entwine like harp notes on time's weltering curve. AnNZ

Die Rose, Die Lilie, Die Taube. Heinrich Heine. And rose is, and lily, and moon and dove. AWP

Die Welt Ist Dumm, Die Welt Ist Blind. Heinrich Heine. And how they burn with passion. AWP

Died. Elizabeth Barrett Browning. Then slowly lift so frail a fame,/Or softly drop so poor a shame. NOBV

Died of Love. Anonymous.
And she will come like me at last. CBEP

Dinosaur Spring. Marilyn Waniek. its fathomless love, like the salt mill/at the bottom of the sea. MAYP

Dinosaur Tracks in Beit Zayit. Shirley Kaufman. at night when everyone's sleeping/she hears the silence of the world. FiCP

Dinosaurs. Carolyn Stoloff. they are our steady progress and the lack of it. NYBP

Dinosaurs. Valerie Worth. But they/Still walk/About heavily/In everybody's/Head. NTCP

Diodorus Siculus. Anonymous. He thought a thimble/Was the phallic symbol. ErPo

Diogenes. Morris Bishop. And there is the trouble with pub-/licity! NLV

Diogenes. Max Eastman. I'll ask no thing,/Of God or king,/But to clear away his shadow. HBV 1-2

Dion of Tarsus. Anonymous. I was not ever wed, and would my father had not been! AWP

Dionysus. Sophia de Mello Breyner Andresen. That serene ardent glory/Which distinguishes the gods from mortals. PBWP

Dionysus. Irving Layton. bringing peace to their humid limbs. ErPo

The Dipper. Phoebe Hesketh. And from his rocky rostrum the dipper bows, and blesses/Every river sound and sight. PoSH

Dips or Counting Out Rhymes: "Dip, dip, allebadar." Anonymous. Duck shee shantamar. GBP

Dips or Counting Out Rhymes: "Dip, dip, dip." Anonymous. You - are - not - it. GBP

Dips or Counting Out Rhymes: "Eachie, peachie, pearie, plum." Anonymous. Eachie, peachie, pearie, plum. GBP

Dips or Counting Out Rhymes: "Ex and squary." Anonymous. O–U–T, etc. GBP

Dips or Counting Out Rhymes: "Hickety pickety i sillickety." Anonymous. Out - goes - he. GBP

Dips or Counting Out Rhymes: "I saw a doo flee our the dam." Anonymous. Black trout,/Ye're oot. GBP

Dips or Counting Out Rhymes: "Zeenty, peenty, heathery, mithery." Anonymous. Eerie, oorie, you're oot. GBP

Dipsychus. Arthur Hugh Clough.
In the stones, bread, and life in the blank mind. OBVV
Peace, peace! I come. VLP
So pleasant it is to have money. FaBoPV; OAEL 1-2
What were all else? I dare not risk this loss. OBNC

Diptych. Velma West Sykes. Even a queen must not defy a king. IHMS

Direct Address. Amy Gerstler. ...so she went/upstairs, to have herself one last look. APU

Direct Song. Eve Merriam. The more I give you gives me the more pleasure. UnTE

Direction. Roberta Hill. this thunder, growing. CDW

Direction from Zulu. Daniel Halpern. You are Zechariah. You are Zoroaster. You are Zebedee. FAZ

Directions. William Matthews. ...the next one/eats along the glow/of your extinguished hunger and turns/to the living. AmPA

Directions. Onitsura. Spring flowers! SoPo

Directions for Making a Birth-Day Song: "To form a just..." Jonathan Swift. Like atoms, are exempt from blows. NAs

Directions to a Rebel. W. R. Rodgers. That blind and deafen you to compromise. LiTM

Directions to the Nomad. James Welch. then get the hell out, fast. CDW

Directive. Robert Frost.
Drink and be whole again beyond confusion. AP; BLPL; CMoP; CoBMV; CrMA; DiPo; ForPo; HAP; InPS; LiTA; LiTM; MasP; MAT; MoAB; NePA; NoAm; NOBA; NoP; PPP; PrIm; SeCeV
This was no playhouse but a house in earnest. MoAmPo

Diretro al Sol. Charles G. Bell. Of night stirred with light and the rush of wings. NePoAm

Dirge. Anonymous. ...I didn't know you/from the flowers. BoWoP

Dirge. Louis Aragon. ...profiles loomed high/Thrown by anger against a white sky. WaaP

Dirge. Gavin Bantock. Winds blow for the dead. OxBTC

Dirge. Madison Cawein. These be the watchers still/Over her stone. AA

Dirge. Austin Clarke. Cardinal Spellman/Lies in state. CIP

Dirge. Adelaide Crapsey. Thou wilt not hear at all,/My dear, my dear. HBV 1-2

A Dirge. William Augustus Croffut. Shade of Leigh Hunt! Oh, guide this laggard pen/To write of one who loved his fellow men! InMe

Dirge. Aubrey Thomas De Vere. With the sea-dirge they mix not: they clamour to me! IrPN

Dirge. Charles Gamage Eastman She to heaven has passed. AA

Dirge. Kenneth Fearing.
Blue across the country and away across/the sea. AmP
bong, Mr., bong, Mr., bong, Mr., bong. AmP; FF; HeIP; HoPM; NAMP; NIP; PoRA; TrJP

Dirge. John Ford. Love only reigns in death; though art/Can find no comfort for a broken heart. LoBV

Dirge. Felicia Dorothea Hemans.

But oh! a brighter home than ours/In heaven, is now thine own. HBV 1-2
They that have seen thy look in death/No more may fear to die. OBEV

Dirge. Louis Johnson. To see if love still burned. AnNZ

Dirge. Sarojini Naidu. And flowering springs that mock her empty years? ACV

Dirge. Thomas William Parsons. Long as the stars do gleam upon it,/Shall memory come to dream upon it. GN; HBV 1-2; PAH

Dirge. William Alexander Percy. Tuck the earth, fold the sod;/Quiet's here, maybe God. HBMV

A Dirge. Christina Georgina Rossetti. And all winds go sighing/For sweet things dying. LoBV; NOBV; SBG; VLP

A Dirge. Percy Bysshe Shelley. Wail, for the world's wrong! BoLiVe; DiPo; GTBS; MCCG; NOBE; OAEP; PoRA; SoSe; TEP; TrGrPo; WHA; WiR

Dirge. James Shirley. Onely the actions of the just/Smell sweet, and blossom in their dust. ACP; AWP; InPo; OAEL 1-2; PoEL 1-5; TreFT

Dirge. Hazel Townson. It makes one wonder if they really care. PV

Dirge. Quincy Troupe. of the soundless that speaks too us/of the ruin of our heritage PoBA

Dirge for a Bad Boy. Emile Victor Rieu. For a poor sinner in his bed. BBGG

Dirge for a Righteous Kitten. Vachel Lindsay. Ding-dong, ding-dong, ding-dong. SUS

Dirge for a Soldier. George Henry Boker. Lay him low! AA; APA; HBV 1-2; MC; OBVV; PAH; PeD; WaaP

Dirge for Ashby. Margaret Junkin Preston. Ashby is dead! PAH

Dirge for Fajuyi. Arowa. Omobayode So it is the soldier goes away! WTO

A Dirge for McPherson. Herman Melville. Sarpedon of the mighty war. AP; PAH; PoEL 1-5

Dirge: For One Who Fell in Battle. Thomas William Parsons Shall memory come to dream upon us. AA

Dirge for Small Wilddeath. Judith Moffett. trapped by water or fire–yet dead? LTB

Dirge for the Ninth of Ab. Anonymous. Lift up thine hands to Him,/to Him implored. TrJP

Dirge for the Year. Percy Bysshe Shelley.
And April weeps–but, O, ye Hours,/Follow with May's fairest flowers. HBV 1-2; HBVY
See, it smiles as it is sleeping/Mocking your untimely weeping. GN

Dirge for Two Clavichords and Bowler Hat. Kendrick Smithyman. The hounds of doorways think this is no great matter. AnNZ

Dirge for Two Veterans. Walt Whitman. My heart gives you love. BoLiVe; MoAmPo; PoEL 1-5

Dirge: "If thou wilt ease thy heart." Thomas Lovell Beddoes. And then alone, amid the beaming/Of love's stars, thou'lt meet her/In eastern sky. EG

Dirge in the Woods. George Meredith. And we drop like the fruits of the tree,/Even we,/Even so. BoLiVe; EG; FF; LoBV; OAEP; OBEV; OBNC; OBVV; SeCeV; VLP; WHA; WiR

Dirge of Alaric the Visigoth. Edward Everett. Before the name of Attila. BeLS

The Dirge of Kildare. Aubrey Thomas De Vere. The mother sees nought: the bride shall see/The Herald and Death-flag far off–not thee. IrPN

Dirge of O'Sullivan Bear. Jeremiah Joseph Callanan. Our O'SULLIVAN Bear. IrPN; NBM

Dirge of Rory O'More. Aubrey Thomas De Vere. Rolls the dirge of thy last and thy bravest–O'More! IrPN

Dirge of the Lone Woman. Mary M. Colum. And I alone with no other one–/With no other one! AnIV

Dirge of the Moolla of Kotal. George Thomas Lanigan. If any one knows it,/Let him disclose it! NA

Dirge of the Munster Forest 1581. Emily Lawless. Lay bare my dead, who died, and died for me. OBVV; OnYI

Dirge on the Death of Art O'Leary. Anonymous. It is I who am the lonely one/In Inse Carriganane. AnIV

Dirge Sung at Death. Anonymous. But yet with me still/Shall ever rest my own beloved. WTO

A Dirge upon the Death of the Right Valiant Lord, Bernard Stuart. Robert Herrick. And times to come shall, weeping, read/thy glory,/Lesse in these Marble stones, then in thy/story. SeCV 1-2

Dirge: "Wail! wail ye o'er the dead!" George Darley. Youth's ta'en, and beauty's fled,/O then deplore her! OBRV

Dirge without Music. Edna St. Vincent Millay. ...And I am not resigned. AnNE; CMoP; DL; LiTA; MoRP; NePA; NoAm; PG; PPON; SBG; TrGrPo

Dirge Written for a Drama. Thomas Lovell Beddoes. Then we weep for ourselves, and wish thee good-/bye. EnRP

The Dirigible. Ralph W. Bergengren. And we little fishes/Were staring at him. SoPo

The Dirigible. Chris Wallace-Crabbe. Where fishermen set out from pumice isles. CBAP

The Dirt Doctor. Melvin Douglass Brown. he died close to the dirt. LFAC

The Dirtiest Man in the World. Shel Silverstein. And who's almost as dirty as me. OBCA

The Dirty-Billed Freeze Footy. Judith Hemschemeyer. whenever she caught sight of you/it would start all over again. Str

The Dirty Dozens. Speckled Red. Now your poppy is your cousin/And your mama do's the lawdy lawd. BluL

Dirty Jim. Jane Taylor. To be decent and clean,/Although they are ever so poor. HBV 1-2; HBVY

Dirty Joke. Daniel L. Klauck. but jackson/thanks two gods for that/every sunday LTB

The Dirty Little Accuser. Norman Cameron. We shall never be able to answer his accusation. OxBS

Dirty Mistreatin' Women. Anonymous. Have another man an' play sick on you. ABF

The Dirty Word. Karl Shapiro. ...and I have murdered it in my early manhood.) CoAP; InPK; MiAP; PoA; PoCh

A Dis, a Dis, a Green Grass. Anonymous. And she shall have a young prince,/For her own fair sake. PoPle

Dis Alitr Visum; or, le Byron de nos Jours. Robert Browning. Here comes my husband from his whist. VLP

Dis Mornin', Dis Evenin', So Soon (with music). Anonymous. Dey brought Bill home wid his toes a-dragging',/Dis mornin' dis evenin', so soon. AS

Disabled. Wilfred Owen. And put him into bed? Why don't they come? BiP; BrPo; CMoP; FF; InPS; LiTM; MMM; NAMP; NIP; NoAm; OxBTC; PAI; WaP

The Disabled Debauchee. John Wilmot, Earl of Rochester. And being good for nothing else, be wise. BoLoP; HAP; NOBL; OBSV; PPP; WeW

A Disagreeable Feature. Edwin Meade Robinson. Is plain as is the nose on your/Face. HBMV

The Disagreeable Man. Sir William Schwenck Gilbert. And I can't think why! ALV; FiBHP

A Disappearance in West Cedar Street. L. E. Sissman. Did Shriner die or make it to New York? TwCP

The Disappointed Sailor. Anonymous. If the fault be great, love, 'tis none of mine,/So don't speak so harshly of womankind.' OBSS

Disappointment. Anonymous. Let me answer, unrepining–/Father, "Not my will, but Thine." TRV; WBLP

A Disappointment. Joanna Baillie. And Tray responsive joins with long and piteous yell. NOEC

The Disappointment. Aphra Behn. Whose soft bewitching Influence/Had Damn'd him to the Hell of Impotence. SBG

Disappointment. Thomas Stephen Collier. And on the cold hearth break the empty/glass. AA

Disappointment. John Boyle O'Reilly. That her heart was a cinder instead of a coal? ACP; OnYI

The Disappointment. John Wilmot, Earl of Rochester. Had damn'd him to the depths of impoetence. UnTE

The Disappointment. Jane Taylor. Real pleasure and peace in her paths you may gain,/Nor will disappointment ensue.' FaBoUs

Disappointment. Edith Lillian Young. Father, "Not my Will, but Thine." TRV

Disarm the Hearts. Ethel Blair Jordan. Disarm the hearts, for that is peace. PGD

Disarmament (excerpt). John Greenleaf Whittier. War fails, try peace; put up the useless sword! PGD

Disarmed. Laura Redden Searing. Go! I forgive thee all/In weeping over this! AA

Disaster. James Clarence Mangan. And the heart's recollections/May hallow their shrine to the last! IrPN

Disaster (parody). Charles Stuart Calverley. If some big dog should swallow Tiny. HBV 1-2; SpRo

Discarded Christmas Tree. Elizabeth-Ellen Long. Which wore a Star for God's own Son! ChBR

Discerning the Lord's Body. Carrie Judd Montgomery. My body shall be glorified/And shall be made like His. STF

Discipleship. C. O. Bales. Then gladly will I leave my all/To follow Christ my Lord. STF

Discipline. George Herbert. Throw away Thy wrath. BoLiVe; EG; ExPo; FPL; HBV 1-2; LiTB; LoBV; MeLP; MePo; NOBE; NOCV; NoP; OBEV; OBS; OxBoCh; PG; PoLf; SeCePo; SeCeV; TrGrPo; ViBoPo

Disclaimer of Prejudice. Eli Siegel. It's the city. PV

Disco Chinatown. Yuri Kageyama. poor ChinaMAN-child. BrSi

Discomfort in High Places. Sydney Tremayne. ...What news is there to hawk/Of turbulence, water and everlasting air? PoSH

The Disconnection. Rita Mae Brown. Too tired to cut it off. IHMS

The Disconnections. John Engels. ...gravid/with bodies, trembling/to give birth. WOLT

Disconsolate Judy's Lamentation. Anonymous. Wishing each moment for to see/Come sailing in the Victory. OBSS

The Discontented Student. St. George Tucker. "G–d– your books!" the testy father said,/"I'd not give–for all you've read." OBAL

Discontents in Devon. Robert Herrick. Than where I loathed so much. AnAnS 2; CaPo; OAEP; OBSP; PoL; SeCV 1-2

Discord in Childhood. D. H. Lawrence. The other voice in a silence of blood, 'neath the noise of/the ash. CBEP; ELU

Discordants. Conrad Aiken. They knew you once, O beautiful and wise. LiTM; NOBA; PG; PoA

Discouraged. Lucille Stanaback. The thing that's best will come, if we in/God will put our trust. STF

Discourse. Sharon Thesen. The small vocabulary/of love needs its own/thin blue dictionary. CaPN

Discourse Heard One Day. Donald Campbell Babcock. And, gravely acquiescent, bows his head. NePoAm-2

Discourse on the Real. Samuel Yellen. ...beguiled/By which of this is fiction which is real. NePoAm

Discovered in Mid-Ocean. Stephen Spender. Hands, wings, are found.... MoBrPo

The Discoverer. Arthur Gordon Field. ...He sought a shorter path/To distant Ind, and here he found–a world. PGD

The Discoverer. Edmund Clarence Stedman. And his eyes behold/Things that shall never, never be to mortal/hearers told. AA; HBV 1-2

The Discoverer of the North Cape. Henry Wadsworth Longfellow. "Behold this walrus-tooth!" AnNE; AtBAP

Discoveries. Vernon Watkins. By loss; the moment known to Kierkegaard. LiTM; WaP

Discoveries in America. James Wright. Maybe she's never seen you either. NoP

Discoveries of Bones and Stone. Geoffrey Grigson. ...Or, bones in/live flesh are better than scattered dry bones. Or/of course, all bones are bones. OBTV

Discovering–. Sharon Scott. and meetin' julia.* JB

Discovering God Is Waking One Morning. John L'Heureux. my whole world sings a hymn, awaking. BoNaP

Discovering My Daughter. Dabney Stuart. ...a singular island where people may come/Together, as we have, making a singular place. SM

Discovery. Hilaire Belloc. That those who loved you best despised you most. DBV; OBSP; ViBoPo

The Discovery. Charles Brasch. And drifted towards them and was land. AnNZ

Discovery. Hildegarde Flanner. They never told me that I was/White-armed and amber-eyed. HBMV

The Discovery. Monk Gibbon. Only the cry, "Abel, awake, awake!" OnYI

Discovery. Benjamin Keech. Since there is play in pleasant work? PoToHe

The Discovery. Gwendolyn MacEwen. I mean the moment when it seems most plain/is the moment when you must begin again. NOBC

The Discovery. John Henry, Cardinal Newman. A Saint–a Saint was there! OBRV

The Discovery. Sir John Collings Squire. Columbus' doom-burdened caravels/Slant to the shore, and all their seamen land. OFD; PoSC

The Discovery of America. James Logie Robertson. It was the great Columbus/Dragging his prize to land. NOBV

The Discovery of LSD a True Story. Anselm Hollo. "phew! wow! pow! zat voss somsink!" PoM

Discovery of San Francisco Bay. Richard Edward White. Where Balboa's sea doth mingle/With the waters of thy bay! PAH

Discovery of the New World. Carter Revard. Then we will be safe, and rich, and happy here forever. VoR

The Discovery of the Pacific. Thom Gunn. The full caught pause of their embrace. HeIP

Discovery of This Time. Archibald MacLeish. There were all of us–all together–and we came. LiTA; WaP

The Discovery of Tradition. Lawson Fusao Inada. (the rhythm of tradition.) goodbye. LTB

Discretion. Anonymous. But bear a horn and blow it not. CBEP

Discretions of Alcibiades. Robert Pinsky. Market for salt; and dance to tinkly music. NPGG

The Discriminations: Virtuous Amusements and Wicked Demons. Jim Bogan. Kuan-yin/Deliver us. PoDr

The Discriminator. Vernon Scannell. With the stern impartiality of age/And age's impotence. OxBC

A Discussion of the Vicissitudes of History under a Pine Tree. Katha Pollitt. sky neither blue nor gray. MAYP

Disdain Me Not without Desert. Sir Thomas Wyatt. Disdain me not. FCP; SiPS

Disdain Me Still. William Herbert, Earl of Pembroke. Love surfeits with rewards, his nurse is scorn. EIL

Disdain Returned. Thomas Carew. Some power in my revenge convey/That love to her I cast away. AWP; CaPo; CavP; EnLit; HBV 1-2; InPo; OBS; SeCV 1-2; TEP; TrGrPo; ViBoPo

Distrust. Robert Herrick. Hear all men speak, but credit few or none. CaPo

Disturb Me Not. *Anonymous.* And let me gaze on what ye soon must be. WTO

Disturbing the Sallies Forth. Clark Coolidge. And wonder is a twine of wands lodged/to spine of nothing I know at least to hold. APU

A Disused Shed in Co. Wexford. Derek Mahon. Let not our naive labours have been in vain! CIP; FaBoIP; FaBoPV; NOBI; OxBC

The Disused Temple. Norman Cameron. Abandon the whole township, and migrate. ChMP; OxBS; OxBTC

Dithyramb in Retrospect. Peter Hopegood. By the Wind that walks the Night/I am baptized into sight. BoAV; PoAu 1-2

Ditty. Sir Robert Chester. Love is a holy, holy, holy thing. EIL

A Ditty. John Day. Ha' done, ha' done, ha' done, for I ha' done my ditty. EIL

A Ditty. Bertha Jacobs. His love has given me so great a worth,/That I care no more for things of this earth. WPOW

A Ditty. Edmund Spenser. I will part them all you among. FaBoCh

Ditty in Imitation of the Spanish.... Edward, Lord Herbert of Cherbury. When without these you have not wherewithall. AnAnS 2; EIL; OBS

The Ditty of the Six Virgins. Thomas Watson. O beauteous Queen of second Troy,/Accept of our unfeigned joy! OBSC

Ditty to an Air from Bach. Robert Louis Stevenson. While all the little brown birds sing upon the spray. TrGrPo

The Divan. Richard Henry Stoddard. And on those little cheeks of thine. AA

Dive. Langston Hughes. after dark. CAD; NYP

Dive for Dreams. Edward Estlin Cummings. (for god likes girls/and tomorrow and the earth). OLR

Diver. Robert Francis. Make us see. LiSp

The Diver. Robert Earl Hayden. somehow began the/measured rise. AmPP; BPo; LiSp; MOS

The Diver. John Frederic Herbin. And bears him as a courser bears a king. CaP

The Diver. Ben Howard. A self outside himself, and again a man,/Spent and cleansed in a chaos not his own. SM

The Diver. E. L. Mayo. Which has no human gesture and no word. CoAP

The Diver. Leonard Nathan. To find this gripping earth alive with her. ErPo

The Diver. Nikos Phocas. Terror of his terror, nightmare of his nightmare. AMV-81

The Diver. W. W. Eustace Ross. With the breeze and the comfortable shore. NOBC; OBCV; PeCV; WHW

Diver. R. A. Simpson. Then arms pine up and up/Like worship. CBAP

The Divers. Peter Quennell. Momentary, soon quenched, like a strangled flame. MoBrPo; MoVE

Divers Thy Death. Henry Howard, Earl of Surrey. As Pyramus did on Thisbes brest bewayle. FCP; NCEP

Diversions for an Unhappy Princess. *Anonymous.* "Gramercy, father, so mote I thee,/For all these thinges liketh not me." OxBM

Diversions of the Re-Echo Club. Carolyn Wells. But I think I'd rather see one/Than to be one, anyhow. OBAL

Diversity. Evarard V. Thompson. How else could He have saved a world/Filled with such diverse souls? BePJ

Diversity of Doctors. *Anonymous.* And one the care without the cure. ALV

The Diverting History of John Gilpin. William Cowper. And, when he next doth ride abroad,/May I be there to see! BeLS; EiCP; FaBoBe; FiP; GN; HBV 1-2; HBVY; InMe; LAuP; OBEC; OBNV; PoPle; RoGo; TreFS

Diverus and Lazarus. *Anonymous.* For to sit upon a serpent's knee. ATP; OBET

Dives and Laz'us. *Anonymous.* Ring-a dat big bell,/In Ab'ham's breas' at last. TTY

Dives and Lazarus. *Anonymous.*
And your other five brothers will end in hell/If they have not repented. AmFP
Then the devil should have no power. BaBo; ELP; ESPB; FaBoBa; OxBB

Divided. David Gray. And dieth towards thee with the dying day! AA

Divided. Jean Ingelow. I say "Thy breadth and thy depth for ever/Are bridged by his thoughts that cross to/me." HBV 1-2; OBNC; SpRo; VLP

The Divided Heart. George Wither. And now I care for neither. TrGrPo

Dividends. Hubert Creekmore. These loans are canceled forever. WaP

Dividing the Field. William Aberg. His sister's bedroom lights/Blink off, on, then off again. LFAC

Dividing the House. James Richardson. ...I wonder/how they will do without us. AMV-80

Divina Commedia. Henry Wadsworth Longfellow.
O'er all the house-tops and through heaven above/Proclaim the elevation of the Host! AmPP; OxBA
That perfect pardon which is perfect peace. AmPP; OxBA

Divina Commedia. Dante Alighieri.

And ever fresh fire from its gazing caught. ExPo; ILwL; ISi; LiTW; NAWM 1-2

And I fell, like a body falling dead. EnLi 1-2; ExPo; NAWM 1-2; TreFT "Manibus o date lilia plenis!" CAW

The serpent fled, and round the Angels wheeled,/Up to their stations flying back alike. CAW

Divination. Jerred Metz. hidden springs wine/and shoulder blades. VWA

Divination by a Cat. Anthony Hecht. And the collected tails of all your lives/Shall drive the moral home. LiTA

Divination by a Daffodil. Robert Herrick. Lastly, safely buryed. CaPo; CavP; OBS; SeCV 1-2

Divine Abundance. *Anonymous.* Then leave it with Him; He has everywhere/Ample store. BLRP

The Divine Blacksmith. Matthew Prior. Burn'd Him to th'Pot, and sour'd his curdled Blood. FaBoNo

Divine Comedies (excerpt). James Merrill. To which there's no reply. For here we are. HaCAP

Divine Compassion. John Greenleaf Whittier. A heart that still can feel, and eyes that still can weep. MAmP

The Divine Hand. William Williams. Feed me till I want no more. BLRP

A Divine Image. William Blake.
The human face a furnace sealed,/The human heart its hungry gorge. AtBAP; ChTr; NoP; OBNC; TEP
There God is dwelling too. CEP; EBCP; EnL; EnPE; EnRP; NOBE; NoP; OAEL 1-2; OBEC; OBNC; OxBoCh; PPP; TEP; TRV; ViBoPo; WGRP

The Divine Insect. John Hall Wheelock. Deeper and deeper now, and more and more. GoYe; NYBP

Divine Love. Michael Benedikt. To the table of the body at which five men and two/women are casually sitting down to eat. AmPA; CoAP; ConAP

The Divine Lover. Charles Wesley. Rise to all eternity. BLRP

A Divine Mistris. Thomas Carew. You Gods teach her some more humanitie. AnAnS 2

The Divine Narcissus. Sister Juana Ines de la Cruz. Through Time turned centuries, and worlds a grove! CAW

The Divine Office of the Kitchen. Cecily Hallack. "Can any good thing come to God out of poor Nazareth?" BLRP; GoTF; PoLf; TreFT

The Divine Paradox. *Anonymous.* Believe, and leave to wonder. MeEV

The Divine Passion. Hortensio Felis Paravicino y Arteaga. With malice that against its God it bore. CAW

Divine Poems. Jose Garcia Villa.
And doom this First, pioneering Genius. MoRP
From Life, the gem/He died for. So Death–I live! MoRP

The Divine Presence. Aubrey Thomas De Vere. From Thee, O God, we fly–to Thee. GoBC

A Divine Rapture. Francis Quarles. The world's but theirs; but my Beloved's mine. HBV 1-2; OBEV

Divine Songs to Ahura Mazda. Zoroaster. I shall hear distinct the sweet echo of my prayers from/Thy Abode of Songs. LiTW

The Divine Tragedy: The Fate of the Prophets. Henry Wadsworth Longfellow. Nor the sublime/Fore-running of their time! WGRP

The Divine Wooer. Phineas Fletcher. I would but cannot hope: such wondrous love amazes. TrPWD

Divinely Superfluous Beauty. Robinson Jeffers. Divinely superfluous beauty. HeIP; LiTL; MoLP; PoPl

The Diviner. Seamus Heaney. It lay dead in their grasp till nonchalantly/He gripped expectant wrists. The hazel stirred. FaBoIP

Diving for Pearls. Traise Yamamoto. the sea; its pearls, seeds, children. BrSi

Diving into the Wreck. Adrienne Rich. a book of myths/in which/our names do not appear. CAPP; HaCAP; HeIP; InPK; InPS; MOS; NIP; NoAm; NOBA; NoP

Divinities. William Stanley Merwin. Even the dead sing them an unending hymn. PoA

Division. John Ratti. see the lean tree of their arms/spread/out and could hear each color they/said. NYBP

The Division of Parts. Anne Sexton. to make me your inheritor. NePoEA-2

Divorce. Kate Jennings. and on each floor and in/each room no/one. AMV-80

Divorce. Erica Jong. Another egg is boiling in the pot. GP

Divorce. Bink Noll. spent your childhoods in this house left almost/as she left it and kept for you. And her. MAT

The Divorce. Thomas Stanley. 'Tis charity here not to love. AnAnS 2; MeLP

Divorce. Anna Wickham. Let me out in the dark, let me go, let me go! MoBrPo

Divorce. Siv Widerberg. And their son/newborn/was the apple of his eye. CTBA

The Divorce Dress. Jeanne Finley. ...At night/it wakes women up for miles. AMV-80

The Divorce of a Lover.　George Gascoigne.　That I may leave both love and life, & thereby purchase/rest./Haud ictus sapio.　AAS

Dixie.　Daniel Decatur Emmett.　Away, away, away down south in Dixie! BLSo; FaFP; FSW; TrAS; TreF; YaD

Dixie.　Albert Pike　And conquer peace for Dixie!　ΛΛ; MC

Dixie's Green Shore.　Anonymous.　She sighed for the ruins of her country/ As she strolled along Dixie's green shore.　BFSS

Djalbarmiwi's Song.　Anonymous.　all by yourself, you can help her in childbirth!　CBAP

The Djanggawul Cycle, 1.　Anonymous　Sound, as the sacred poles are moved about with the rolling of/the canoe!　WTO

The Djanggawul Cycle, 4.　Anonymous　Sound of the sea from the Djanggawul's paddling!　WTO

The Djanggawul Cycle, 6.　Anonymous.　Water comes in from them, coming to us: foaming, spraying and/roaring, out on the sea!　WTO

The Djanggawul Cycle, 7.　Anonymous.　Waves spreading out, spraying and splashing, caused by the/fish...　WTO

The Djanggawul Cycle, 8.　Anonymous.　We paddle through the shine from the Morning Star, from/Bralgu, slowly along as we see these eggs.　WTO

The Djanggawul Cycle, 10.　Anonymous.　It e wood is a stranger from Bralgu, from the source of the/Star's shine.　WTO

The Djanggawul Cycle, 11.　Anonymous.　...It cries/as it circles, away out from Port Bradshaw.　WTO

The Djanggawul Cycle, 12.　Anonymous.　We are paddling fast, we are close to land, to Port Bradshaw.　WTO

The Djanggawul Cycle, 18.　Anonymous.　Our heads are grey from the foam...we are tired from/paddling.　WTO

The Djanggawul Cycle, 21.　Anonymous.　Our paddles! We drag them along, the flat and the narrow/paddles...　WTO

The Djanggawul Cycle, 22.　Anonymous.　We saw it, flying down, as the darkness was clearing, "twisting'/its tongue and whistling.　WTO

The Djanggawul Cycle, 24.　Anonymous.　Warming our backs as it reaches west to the wide Barara/country.　WTO

The Djanggawul Cycle, 27.　Anonymous.　We have arrived, oh waridj! WTO

The Djanggawul Cycle, 30.　Anonymous.　Clouds we saw, making us feel good as we walk, swaying our/hips, oh waridj Djanggawul.　WTO

The Djanggawul Cycle, 33.　Anonymous.　..."I am drying myself, my red/ breast feathers, my rangga feathers–my children!"　WTO

The Djanggawul Cycle, 51.　Anonymous.　We reach Bulibuli. We are tired, waridj, but we sing as we go/along!　WTO

The Djanggawul Cycle, 57.　Anonymous.　Ducks, crying out! We look at them, and leave them to go their/way.　WTO

The Djanggawul Cycle, 67.　Anonymous.　With a long cry it clasps the djuda, watching the water at/Wagulwagul, rising against the mat.　WTO

The Djanggawul Cycle, 84.　Anonymous.　Crying, as the rays disappear from the inner peak of the mat,/from its transverse fibre.　WTO

The Djanggawul Cycle, 92.　Anonymous.　Water rising and bubbling, splashing and roaring, spreading out/like the tide...　WTO

The Djanggawul Cycle, 135.　Anonymous.　From the sound of the Baijini talking, the smell of the sea...　WTO

The Djanggawul Cycle, 144.　Anonymous.　The sacred pendants, the feathered strings...　WTO

The Djanggawul Cycle, 166.　Anonymous.　Quietly they shine, covered up, for they are sacred...　WTO

The Djanggawul Cycle, 172.　Anonymous.　..covered/up like younger siblings, so no one may see, in sacred/taboo-ness...　WTO

The Djanggawul Cycle, 174.　Anonymous.　It is done: they are asleep. WTO

The Djanggawul Cycle, 182.　Anonymous　Splashed with foam from far away on the wide sea, near the/Spirit Country.　WTO

DNA Lab.　Michael Spence.　...or born/Out of a strange and glorious darkness.　SOTS

Do Come Back Again.　Anonymous.　Oh, will soon fade away.　OuSiCo

Do Don't Touch-A My Garment, Good Lord, I'm Gwine Home.　Anonymous.　Good Lord, good Lord, I'm gwine home.　BoAN 1-2

Do I Love Thee?　John Godfrey Saxe.　Darling! take my answer so.　HBV 1-2

Do I Really Pray?　John Burton.　And help me when I seek Thy grace/To mean the words I say.　STF

Do It Now!　Anonymous.
Do it now!　BLPA; FaFP; WBLP
Was a mountain of things he intended to/do–Tomorrow.　STF

Do It Now.　Berton Braley.　For he cannot read his tombstone when he's dead.　BLPA; FaFP; WBLP

Do It Right.　Samuel O. Buckner.　Strive for an honored name–/Do it Right;　WBLP

Do It Yrself.　Larry Eigner.　–they are taller than their cars.　NeAP; PoM

Do Li A.　Anonymous.　Do li th' dil len dol,/Do lia a.　GBP

Do, Lord, Remember Me.　Anonymous.　Oh, do Lord, remember me. AmFP

Do Not Accompany Me.　Shimon Halkin.　...We are all of us, after all,/ seized with vertigo, pine for shade/and find none.　VWA

Do Not Ask.　Christine Lavant.　for that bud is only mine/on the back of my own stone/and reserved for my next night.　WPOW

Do Not Die.　William Stanley Merwin.　as this world is made I might/live forever.　CAPP

Do Not Embrace Your Mind's New Negro Friend.　William Meredith.　But island by island we must go across.　WaP

Do Not Expect Again a Phoenix Hour.　C. Day-Lewis.　Leafy the boughs– they also hide big fruit.　CMoP; FaBoMo; LiTB; LiTM; MoAB; MoBrPo; NoAm; OxBI; OxBTC; PoRA

Do Not Go Gentle Into That Good Night.　Dylan Thomas.　Rage, rage against the dying of the light.　ACV; BiP; CoBMV; DiPo; DL; FaFP; FF; GoTF; HAP; HeIP; HoPM; InPK; InPS; LiTM; MoAB; MoBrPo; MoVE; MP; NIP; NoAm; NOBE; NoP; OAEL 1-2; OxBTC; PAI; PPON; PrIm; SCV; SeCeV; SoSe; TEP; TreFT; TW; TwCP; UnPo; ViBoPo; WeW

Do Not Go Gentle (parody).　Tim Hopkins.　e.g. your rage when I switched off the light!　BXAP

Do Not Minute.　Thomas Lovell Beddoes.　...To see and love thee/Was but one soul's step.　LO

Do Not Open Until Christmas.　James S. Tippett.　Shaking will not tell. ChBR

Do Not Think.　Carol [(or Carole)] Freeman.　–we only want to bring you home.　CNA

Do Not Torment Me, Lady.　Anonymous.　So it is just that you should give/ your love in the same measure.　NOBI

Do Not Torment Me, Woman.　Anonymous.　O woman, love of my soul, do not pursue me of/all men.　AnIL

Do Not Weep, Maiden, for War Is Kind.　Stephen Crane.　War is kind. AmePo; BiP; NOBA; OBWP; PAL

Do Nothing Till You Hear from Me.　David Henderson.
day of the vernal winds/1967.　PoBA
the last time blues/with no hesitations...　CNA

Do Something.　Anonymous.　There's nothing on earth can help you/So much as a kindly deed!　STF

Do the Baby Cake-Walk.　Clyde Watson.　Won't you do the baby cake-walk/For me?　NTCP

Do the Dead Know What Time It Is?　Kenneth Patchen.　You can stop crying now.　HoPM; MoAmPo

Do They Miss Me at Home?　S. M. Grannis.　Because I am with them no more?　TreFS

Do They Think of Me at Home.　Joseph Edward Carpenter.　"Do they think of me at home?"　FaBoBe; TreFS

Do They Whisper behind My Back?　Delmore Schwartz.　...we cannot/ Forget our pride, our faces, our common love.　LiTA

Do We Not Hear Thy Footfall?　Amy Carmichael.　In hush of adoration see Thee there.　TRV

Do What Thy Manhood Bids Thee Do.　Richard Burton.　A breath, a wind, a sound, a voice, a tinkling of the camel-bell.　GoTF; TreFS

Do What You Will.　Dorothy Hobson.　...ether-shod,/Ran straight for comfort up to God.　GoBC

Do You Fear the Wind?　Hamlin Garland.　But you'll walk like a man! AA; GoTF; HBV 1-2; HBVY; MCCG; PoPl; TreFT; YaD

Do you have a sweet thought, Cerinthus.　Sulpicia.　if when I am sick, your heart/is calm?　BoWoP

Do You Just Belong?　Anonymous.　Or do you just belong?　STF

Do You Know, I Would Quietly.　Rainer Maria Rilke.　You come too. OLR

Do You Love Me.　Anonymous.　You told me once/But I forgot.　PoSC

Do You Love Me?　Robert Watson.　Animals have it over man.　PoL

Do You Not Hear?　James Picot.　These things were made beautiful by sleep.　BoAV

Do You Plan to Speak Bantu?　Ogden Nash.　In a suit with two pr. pantsk. FiBHP

Do You Remember.　Thomas Haynes Bayly.　You'll love me–won't you? HBV 1-2

Do You Remember Me?　Walter Savage Landor.　And at your voice Pride from his throne must/rise.'　EnRP; OBNC; ViBoPo

Do You Remember That Night?　Anonymous.　I am ready to go with you. AnIV; BIrV; OnYI

DOA in Dulse.　Diane Burns.　while he joined the wheel again/for another/ crack at all.　STE

Doan't You Be What You Ain't.　Edwin Milton Royle.　He's gwyne to git his.　BLPA

Dob and Mob.　Anonymous.　Bob was Dob's dog,/Chitterabob Mob's cat. OxNR

Dobbin.　George Bowering.　...that rope/may now hang from some rotted fence.　NOBC

Dobbin Dead.　William Barnes.　That you woon't vind the fellow to thik there/wold yew.　VLP

Dock-Leaves.　William Barnes.　Do bring to mind what we did do/Among the dock-leaves years agoo.　VLP

Dock Rats. Marianne Moore. shipping/is the/most interesting thing in the world. AnAmPo

Docker. Seamus Heaney. ...quiet/At slammed door and smoker's cough in the hall. NoAm; NOBI; TW

Dockery and Son. Philip Larkin. And age, and then the only end of age. NoAm

The Dockyard Gate. Anonymous. You shall sit at home with me, my love, and go to sea no more.' OBSS

Docteur Foster. Anonymous. He sat in a chair,/And gave all the people a nod. OxNR

Doctor Bill Williams. Ernest Walsh. ...besides the taxes are due on the/Thirty-first and the mirrors forget everything they see. InvP

Doctor Blenn. Ambrose Bierce. Our physicians all are men. DBV

Doctor Drink. J. V. Cunningham. Who are you? and with whom do you sleep here? OBAL; QFR

Doctor Emmanuel. James Reeves. That Doctor Emmanuel's head contains. PV

Doctor Faustus. Anonymous. And then he whipped them back again. GLGT

Doctor Faustus. Geoffrey Hill.
By the torn waters. NMP
...no loud/Voice (though innocently loud). NMP

Doctor Faustus. Christopher Marlowe.
I'll burn my books!–Ah, Mephistophilis! AtBAP; HeIP
Terminat hora diem; terminat auctor opus. BoLiVe; TrGrPo
To practise more than heavenly power/permits. CoBE; PoEL 1-5; ViBoPo; WHA

Doctor Faustus: Another Part of the Fable. Geoffrey Hill. A blinded god believes/That he is not blind. NePoEA-2; NMP

A Doctor Fell in a Deep Well. Anonymous. Doctor, mind the sick/And leave the well alone. ShM

Doctor Foster. Anonymous. And never went there again. OxBoLi; OxNR

Doctor Freud. David Lazar. Of the followers of Doctor Sigmund Freud. FSW

Doctor Major. Lionel Pigot Johnson. No, Sir! we'll to the Mitre: Frank! my wig. BrPo

The Doctor Rebuilds a Hand. Gary Young. and be delivered, unafraid, from whatever I touched. AMV-80; SUW

The Doctor's Story. Will Carleton. I'll give her medicine made by men. BLPA

The Doctor Who Sits at the Bedside of a Rat. Josephine Miles. So rat and doctor may converse together. VGW

Doctors' Row. Conrad Aiken. for an audience of gods, and superwords. AP; HAP; NYP; PoPl

Doctrinal Point. William Empson. They rise above a vault into the air. AtBAP

Document. Tuvia Ruebner. out of fear of my voice to say yes/in the empty space. VWA

Documentary. Joseph Stroud. ...The quiet glow on the water. NPGG

A Documentary on Airplane Glue. David Henderson. & then suddenly wonderfully/soaring/ultimately away/ MAT

The Documentary on Brazil. Alfred Corn. Self's the long exile we appear to choose. MAYP

Documentation. Michael Palmer. The sky moves that quickly through the frame. NPGG

The Dodger. Anonymous.
But look out, girls, he's telling you a lie. GBP
Yes, we're all dodging out a way through the world. AmFP; FSW; OuSiCo

Dodo. Henry Carlile. an entity in name only/and that taken in vain. GP; Psk

The Dodo. Edward Lucie-Smith. Immortalized by his extinction. PoL

Dodona's Oaks Were Still. Patrick MacDonogh. Dodona's oaks were still. NeIP

Doe. Philip Dow. and toward everything I fear in my dark/mind lost to my suddenly brilliant throat. NPGG

A Doe at Evening. D. H. Lawrence. Does not my fear cover her fear? BrPo

Doe-Face. Erin Moure. Bringing in our arms, like game wardens,/a warm shot for her CaPN

Does Daddy Go? Anonymous. Bible school would have helped/But Daddy wouldn't go. STF

Does It Matter? Siegfried Sassoon. And no one will worry a bit. MoBrPo; PPON; WaP

Does the Pearl Know? Helen Hay. Does the heart know? AA

Does the Spearmint Lose Its Flavor on the Bedpost Overnight? Billy Rose. Does the Spearmint lose its flavor on the bedpost overnight? OBAL

Doesn't he realize. Ono no Komachi. where the seaweed gatherer/can come as often as he wants. BoWoP; WPOW

Doesn't It Seem to You. Gevorg Emin. And write poems, or,/Maybe...make a wish? AMV-81

The Dog. Anonymous. No dog, however mean or rude,/Is guilty of ingratitude. WBLP

The Dog. William Henry Davies.
To pen them for Her! MoBrPo
Would bark outside the gates of Heaven,/To open them for Her! GDP

The Dog. Frederick William Faber. Of the old times was dearer to the creature/Than the new friend of one bright afternoon. FM

Dog. Lawrence Ferlinghetti. some Victorious answer/to everything. HoPM

The Dog. Oliver Herford. I'd choose his bark, however bad. FaBV'

The Dog. Valentin Iremonger. Breaking the night's maidenhead. BIrV; NeIP

Dog. Ingrid Jonker. from my kennel white moon, white master/in the night. PBWP

Dog. Harold Monro. Into the bed-delicious hours of night. MoBrPo

The Dog. Ogden Nash. A wet dog is the lovingest. GDP

Dog. John Crowe Ransom. Blaze two red eyes as hot as cooking-coals. InPS; LiTA; OBAL; PAI

Dog. William Jay Smith. People you've seen somewhere? Bowwow! GoJo

A Dog. Charlotte Zolotow. Suddenly a wet cold nose/nuzzles/my empty hand. GDP

Dog Alive. Harold Witt. while nine lions topple for every lion that roars. BoAnP

The Dog and the Water-lily. William Cowper. To show a love as prompt as thine/To Him who gives me all. OAEP

Dog and Tiger. Eliezer Greenberg. He would rather be stinking dead. BoAnP

Dog around the Block. E. B. White. Dog around the block, sniff. GDP

The Dog beneath the Skin. W.H. Auden.
And Life lurks, evil, out of its epoch. OxBTC
Use what words you wish; they will often be heard/again. NAMP
Weed the garden, wind the clock;/Remember the Two. OxBTC

Dog Body and Cat Mind. Jenny Joseph. And then the cat got up and started walking. BrRo

Dog Creek Mainline. Charles Wright. The tongue is a white water.). AmPA; LCAP

A Dog Day. Rachel Field. I'll always love the dog days best. SiSoSe

Dog Day Vespers. Charles Wright. A wing brushes my left hand,/but it's not my wing. LCAP

Dog, Dog in My Manger. George Barker. O dog my god, how can I cease to praise? LiTM

Dog Fight. Eric Rolls. A morse signal sounds the end of transmission. NOAV

The Dog from Malta. Tymnes. Along those roads we cannot hear him bark. GDP

Dog Hospital. Peter Wild. and the shadows around them that they/seeing now bark at. AmPA; GP

A Dog in San Francisco. Michael Ondaatje. Now I want to be a dog. GOYP

Dog in the Fountain. Raymond Souster. lets itself be born over again. GDP

A Dog in the Quarry. Miroslav Holub. an immense fanfare/of the dog's yapping... BoAnP; GDP

The Dog in the River. Phaedrus. Both shade and substance, beef and bone. AWP

The Dog in Us. John Barnie. ...deny/The dog is us, the everyman. AMV-81

Dog Lake with Paula. Richard Hugo. ...a new Tasmanian/method of love, howl of the arctic whale. WOLT

Dog, Midwinter. Raymond Souster. bark your crazy head off. GDP

A Dog Named Ego, the Snowflakes as Kisses. Delmore Schwartz. And left me no recourse, far from my home. LiTA; LiTM; MiAP

The Dog of Art. Denise Levertov. ...the Dog/of Art turns to the world/the quietness of his eyes. NoAm

The Dog Parade. Arthur Guiterman. They lead their charges down the street, and some-/times to the curb. BoAnP; GDP

Dog (parody). D. C. Berry. Throw them platter and all to the licking dog. BXAP

Dog Prospectus. Peter Redgrove. Piss on this university. OxBC

A Dog's Best Friend Is His Illiteracy. Ogden Nash. And if I ended up with raccoons every guest would/turn out to be a raccoonteur. BoAnP

The Dog's Cold Nose. Arthur Guiterman. The nose of a healthy dog always is cold! GDP; StPo; TiPo

A Dog's Death. J. C. Squire. Nor trouble what we do when we do it; nor would have/it otherwise. FM

Dog's Death. John Updike. To a newspaper carelessly left there. Good dog. Psk

A Dog's Vigil. Margaret E. Bruner. Had seen a lonely dog pass by that night. PoToHe

Dog Sacrifice at Lake Ronkonkoma. William Heyen. and the sun rises, clothed in the dogs' blood. AmPA

A Dog Sleeping on My Feet. James Dickey. Assembling the self I must wake to,/Sleeping to grow back my legs. PP

And lower the price of rouge–at least some winters. PoEL 1-5

And mean, next winter, to be quite reclaimed. NoP

...and night was on the ridge/Of twilight, as the party crossed the bridge. PAI

And read your Bible, sir,`and mind your purse.' SCV

And so–for God's sake–hock and soda-water! CTC

And that's the reason why you do–or do not. OBRV

And the sad truth which hovers o'er my desk/Turns what was once romantic to burlesque. FiP

And they were happy, for to their young eyes/Each was an angel, and earth paradise. EnRP

Behold the world! and curse your victories! FiP; OBRV

...the bubbling cry/Of some strong swimmer in his agony. LiTB; MCCG; OBRV; ViBoPo; WHA

But if you don't, I'll lay it on, by G–d! OBRV

But in such matters Russia's mighty empress/Behaved no better than a common sempstess. OAEL 1-2

But let us to the story as before. OAEL 1-2

...but not being great in mind/Have left undone the greatest–and mankind. OBSV

...but poets still,/And duly seated on the Immortal Hill. PPoe

By the sea-shore, whereon she loved to dwell. EnLit

Can sneer at him who drew "Achitophel!" OAEL 1-2; SeCeV

Dash down yon cup of Samian wine! AnFE; OBTV; SeCeV

The death-cry drowning in the battle's roar. OBWP

Each was an angel, and earth paradise. CoBE; HAP

Exposed to lose his life as well as breeches. OBSV

The fact:–I've heard it,–once perhaps too much. OBRV

Flock o'er their carrion, just like men below. EBEV

For David lived, but Juan nearly died. UnTE

For God's sake, reader! take them not for mine! EnL; MBW 1-2; OAEL 1-2; OAEP

For soon or late Love is his own avenger. EnRP; OAEP; WHA

Further, old Baba rather briskly enter'd. PoEL 1-5

The grand Napoleon of the realms of rhyme. OAEP

...he from his welling throat untied/A kerchief, crying "Give Sal that!'–and died. FiP

He was so great a loss to good society. OBRV

I chose a modern subject as more meet. OAEL 1-2

I learned the title that I know by this. ViBoPo

I'll prove that such an opinion of the critic is/From Aristotle passim.– See... EnLi 1-2; MBW 1-2

Is it not so, my Tory, Ultra-Julian? BoLiVe; CTC; EnRP; OAEL 1-2; OBSV

Let spendthrifts' heirs inquire of yours–who's wiser? UnPo

Like garden gods–and not so decent either. WHA

A loving languor, which is not repose. MOON

Men have all these resources, we but one,/To love again, and be again undone. GoTF; TreF

Men love in haste, but they detest at leisure. TW

Mourns o'er the beauty of the Cyclades. CoBE; FiP

...night was on the ridge/Of twilight, as the party crossed the bridge. InPS

No doubt in fable, as the unforgiven/Fire which Prometheus filch'd for us from heaven. OBRV; PoEL 1-5; PPP; ViBoPo

Not finding that the additions much encumber. ErPo

Not what you seem, but always what you see. FaBoPV; OxBoLi

Pillage to soldiers, prize-money to seamen. MCCG

Rider and horse, friend, foe, in one red burial blent. FaBoBe

Should let itself be snuff'd out by an article. OBRV

So nobody arrived on shore but him. MOS

The sun's true sun, no vapour, but a ray. OAEL 1-2

That painting is no idol, 'tis too like. ISi

Think you, if Laura had been Petrarch's wife,/He would have written sonnets all his life? UnTE

This paradise of pleasure and ennui. NOBL

Thou shalt not steal from Samuel Rogers, nor/Commit–flirtation with the muse of Moore. FiP

To love again, and be again undone. GoTF; TreF

When shipwreck's short allowance grows too scanty,/Without being much more horrible than Dante. FaBoPV

Which Eve has left her daughters since her fall. OBRV

Which makes me wish you'd change your lakes for ocean. OAEP

Who loved blood as an alderman loves marrow. OAEL 1-2

Don Juan. Lucius Harwood Foote. Is all that is left of his wide domain. AA

Don Juan. D. H. Lawrence. It is Isis the mystery/Must be in love with me. PoA

Don Juan. Canto XVII. Isaac Clason. And the gaunt earthquake rocks herself to sleep. PeD

Don Juan in Hell. Charles Baudelaire. Gazed back, and would not offer one look round. AWP; SyP

Don Juan's Address to the Sunset. Robert Nichols. Evening's first star and golden as a bee/In the sun's hair–for happiness is here! OBMV

Don Larsen's Perfect Game. Paul Goodman. ...But that was yesterday LiSp

Don Leon (excerpt). Anonymous. Then brought him gently to the beach,/And wiped the briny moisture from his breach. PeHV

Don' Let Yo' Watch Run Down (with music). Anonymous. Hnag down yo' heads an' cry. AS

Don Quixote. Craven Langstroth Betts. Dear, foiled enthusiast, teach our hearts to/feel! AA

Don Quixote. Henry Austin Dobson. Ah! would but one might lay his lance in rest,/And charge in earnest–were it but a mill. HBV 1-2; HBVY

Don Quixote. Arthur Davison Ficke. And died of the unworthiness of the world. HBMV

Don's Holiday. George Rostrevor Hamilton. As one would hardly credit from a lesser/Person than a history professor. FaBoCo

Don't. Anonymous. Earth's dearest treasure is the few/True friends who love and prize you. STF

Don't. James Jeffrey Roche. Forget what I've been proving,/Sweet Phyllis, and love me! HBV 1-2

Don't Answer the Phone for Me the Same. Gerald Locklin. please, therefore, cut that shit out. GP

Don't Anybody Move. Daniel Mark Epstein. who stole my Cadillac, my coupe de ville,/and who got away with my girl. AmC

Don't Ask Me What to Wear. Sappho. a girl/whose hair is yellower than/torchlight should wear no/headdress but fresh flowers. PBWP

Don't Ask Me Who I Am. James A. Randall, Jr. the only open door/is the door to man BPo

Don't Be Foolish Pray. Anonymous. And so dear Hodge, to church let's go,/And don't be foolish pray. CoMu

Don't Be Sorrowful, Darling. Rembrandt Peale. The gate that leads out of life, good wife,/Is the gate that leads to Him. HBV 1-2

Don't Break It. Joseph Ceravolo. Going back we looked at the few/plastic clouds into the dark moony/trees. ANYP

Don't Care. Anonymous. Don't Care was put in a pot/And boiled till he was done. GBP

"Don't Care" and "Never Mind." John Kendrick Bangs. If some other gets "Don't Care"–/I'll take "Never Mind!" FaFP

Don't Copy Cat. Mark (Samuel Langhorne Clemens) Twain. Nor upon a cold stove lid. GoTF; TreFT

Don't Fish in My Sea. Ma Rainey. You'll never miss your ham till a-/nother mule be in your stall. BluL

Don't Forget. Stephen Berg. you can't lift your hands, you stand there, leaving. PoA

Don't Give Up. Anonymous. "There is no failure save in giving up!" FaFP; PoToHe

Don't Go. Larry Eigner. stars shone/on deadly fish. PoM

Don't Grow Weary, Boys. Anonymous. Don't grow weary, boys,/For we're going to the ball. CoSo

Don't Hope to Gain by What Has Preceded. Joanne Kyger. ...happiness/dreamed for, brain spinner,/garbage maker. PoM

Don't Let Your Deal Go Down. Anonymous. For my last old dollar's gone. FSW

Don't Quit. Anonymous. It's when things seem worst that you mustn't quit. BLPA; FPL; STF

Don't Say. Moshe Yungman. Don't wake me up. VWA

Don't Say You Like Tchaikowsky. Paul Rosner. At least until the hostess has undressed. FiBHP

Don't Show Me. Ruth Beker. Don't tell me anymore./Don't. VWA

Don't Sing Love Songs. Anonymous. 'Cause I've been warned and I've decided/To sleep alone all of my life. FSW

Don't Sit under the Apple Tree with Anyone Else but Me! Robert Pack. Asking, as I do, to be loved? CoPo; FF

Don't Sleep. Ingrid Jonker. with a peacock's feather in its cap. WPOW

Don't Steal. Ambrose Bierce. Successfully in business. Cheat. NLV; PoL

Don't Talk about It. Anonymous. Don't crowd aroun' me, (hanh!)/'Roun me, if you do I'll die. (hanh!) OuSiCo

Don't Tell Me. Anonymous. Don't say what you hope to be,/But tell me what you are. STF

"Don't Touch Me!" I Scream at Passers-By. Natalya Gorbanyevskaya. I am roasting over a slow fire. LLLT

Don't Trouble Trouble. Mark Guy Pearse. You'll only double trouble, and trouble others too. WBLP

Don't Wanna Be. Sonia Sanchez. it gots to beeeEEE, yeah. yeah. yeah. CNA

Don't Want No Hungry Woman. Floyd Council. Hey boy, if you think we gon' help you/swear you better change your mind. BluL

Don't You Be Like the Foolish Virgin. Anonymous. O Zion, When the bridgroom come. AH

Don't You Hurry Worry with Me. Anonymous. I'm gonna pack up your eyes with sand. OuSiCo

Don't You Like It? Anonymous. You passed by me like a she nanny goat. OuSiCo

Don't You Weep after Me. *Anonymous.* Oh, I don't want you to weep after me. FSW

Don'ts. D. H. Lawrence. That the risen Christ should be risen. LiTB; LiTM; NoAm; OxBoLi

Donal Ogue. *Anonymous.* And God as well, or I'm much mistaken. KiLC

Donald. Henry Abbey. Unless with light and tide thou bring my/Donald back to me. AA

Donald Caird. Sir Walter Scott. Donald Caird's come again. BSV

Done For. Rose T. Cooke. It's twice dead not to see! AA

Done Foun' My Los' Sheep. *Anonymous.* Done foun' my los' sheep,/Done foun' my los' sheep. BoAN 1-2

Done Is a Battell on the Dragon Blak. William Dunbar. Surrexi Dominus de sepulchro. BSV; HAP; NoP

Donec Eris Felix Multos Numerabis Amicos. *Anonymous.* They packe them thence, to place of ritcher haunt. EnPo

Doney Gal. *Anonymous.*
And we'll laugh at the storms, the sleet and snow,/When we reach the little town of San Antonio. OuSiCo
Got to drive these dogies down the trail. FSW
Me and my Doney-gal a-bound to go. BPAW; CoSo

The Dong with a Luminous Nose. Edward Lear. "The Dong with a luminous Nose!" AmMo; CBEP; CenHV; FaBoCo; FaBoNo; FaBV; LBN; NBM; NOBV; PoEL 1-5; VLP; WiR

The Donibristle Moss Moran Disaster. *Anonymous.* "We'll bring them to the surface, or along with them we'll/die." WTO

The Donkey. *Anonymous.* I prayed the world/Might be good to him. BiCB

The Donkey. Gilbert Keith Chesterton. There was a shout about my ears,/And palms before my feet. BoC; EBCP; FaBV; FaPoR; FPL; GoBC; HBVY; InPK; MoBrPo; OBEV; PoLf; TreFT; WGRP

The Donkey. P. R. Kaikini. He curses, curses all the way. ACV

The Donkey. Theodore Roethke. Your Donkey is better behaved, I trust. GrPl; OBCA

Donkey. Mark Van Doren. Stubborn of heart/And stiffened of hair/Even then, even there. EaLo

The Donkey and the Lapdog. Jean de La Fontaine. And that ended the comedy. OBVE

Donkey, Donkey, Do Not Bray. *Anonymous.* My butter's melting in the sun. OxNR

Donkey Riding. *Anonymous.* Hey, ho! Away we go!/Riding on a donkey. WHW

A Donkey Will Carry You. Jakov Steinberg. Only death will taste bitter/In the shameful ointment. VWA

Donkeys. Edward Field. And their masters who are equally convinced of being/right/Beat them and hear nothing. BoAnP

Donna. Paula Gunn Allen. your thoughts are sharp/as day/enters night/as song. TWSS

La Donna E Mobile. A. K.. So hail to Mira, the Inconstant Star! FiBHP; InMe

La Donna Perpetuum Mobile. Irwin Edman. I mean—well, really, that's just what I mean. FiBHP; NYBP

Donne Redone. Joseph Paul Tierney. Relax; they're not for you. ShM

The Donner Party (excerpt). George Keithley. I propped my rifle toward heaven/and fired a shot in the air/for the others to hear. NPGG

Donought Would Have Everything. Ebenezer Elliott. Hey, for cattle cook'd and cut! NOBV

Dont Tell Bad Dreams Says Tita's Mother. John Oliver Simon. thru the waisthigh yellow/grass when i was looking/in the mirror NeAC

Dont Worry Yr Hair. Bill Bissett. opens like a flowr all around yu,/to th light NOBC

The Donzella and the Ceylon. *Anonymous.* We safely got in our life boat and reached St. Peter's Lock. ShS

Doodledy, Doodledy, Doodledy, Dan. *Anonymous.* Doodleldy, doodledy, doodledy, dan. OxNR

Dooley Is a Traitor. James Michie. "Well, yes, your Honour," I said, "that's right." NePoEA-2; OxBTC

Doom. Arthur William Edgar O'Shaughnessy. None shall undo what God hath done. OBVV

Doom-Devoted. Louis Golding. The strangled songs, the dreams defiled. HBMV

The Doom of Beauty. Buonarroti Michelangelo. That death should spare perfection so complete? AWP; LiTW

The Doom of Devorgoil, II, ii: Bonny Dundee. Sir Walter Scott. For it's up with the bonnets of Bonny Dundee! EnRP

The Doom-Well of St. Madron. Robert Stephen Hawker. Ye may harowe their troth in St. Madron's/well. VLP

The Doomed City. E. L. Mayo. The city that will not die. FAZ

The Doomed City. Edgar Allan Poe. And Death to some more happy clime/Shall give his undivided time. OBRV

The Doomed Man. Joseph Addison Alexander. the hidden boundary between/God's patience and His wrath. TRV

Dooms-Day. George Herbert. And the musick shall be praise. JCP; SeCP; SeCV 1-2

A Dooms-Day Thought Anno 1659. Thomas Flatman. While we live Here, we must Provision make. CEP

Doomsday. Elinor Wylie. Loud as the ultimate loud clarion/Or the first murther. CrMA

Doomsday Morning. Genevieve Taggard. And God may call...and call...and/call. MoAmPo

The Door. Robert Creeley. ...as the Lady's skirt/moves small beyond it. NaP; NeAP; NoAm; PoM; VGW

The Door. Mary Carolyn Davies. I kept the little fortress fast./–Be good to me. HBMV

The Door. Robert Graves. The waves receded. LiTB

A Door. William Stanley Merwin.
and no door anywhere. LCAP
and there in front of me a life/would open. CAPP

The Door. Mark Strand. Your hand is on the door. This is where you came in. NoAm

The Door. Leonard Alfred George Strong. Such desperate beauty they never had seen/before. MoBrPo

The Door. Charles Tomlinson. ...little/has been said/of our coming through and leaving by them. PoA

The Door and the Window. Henry Reed. The dearest look nor the longest kiss assuages? NeBP

Door and Window Bolted Fast. Mani Leib. Sleep, my darling son. TrJP

The Door-Bell. Charlotte Becker. I never her it ring without/That funny little thrill. PoToHe

The Door-Keeper Has Big Feet. Sappho. And ten shoemakers to make/A pair of sandals to fit him. HW

Door-Mats. Mary Carolyn Davies. They keep their men from going in/With muddy feet to God. HBMV; YaD

The Door to the Future. Dick Gallup. After that/I didn't see you anymore. ANYP

Doorbells. Rachel Field. You never know when you hear one ring/Who may be waiting there! TiPo

Doorman. Martin Galvin. waits for me to open up the sky. SUW

Doors. Tom Clark. She replaces the packages under her arms/And walks through the door. ConAP

Doors. Hermann Hagedorn. The quiet shutting, one by one, of doors. AnAmPo

The Doors. Lloyd Mifflin. And then a Voice,–"Who next that enter-/eth?" AA

Doors. Therese Plantier. a circular house/punctuated by innumerable incinerations. BoWoP

Doors. Carl Sandburg. Doors forget but only doors know what it is/doors forget. LOW

Doors of the Temple. Aldous Huxley. Revealing, not God's radiant throne,/But the fires of wrath and agony. HBMV

The Doorstep. Edmund Clarence Stedman. To feel once more that fresh, wild thrill/I'd give–but who can live youth over? HBV 1-2

Doorway to Time in Three Voices. Luis Palés Matos. faithful, fugitive, abolished Fili-Mele. InW

Dopefiends Trip. Hector Angulo. This here prison stew...... FIA

The Doppelganger. Daryl Hine. The complex reason of your simple doubt. OBCV

Dora versus Rose. Henry Austin Dobson. ...But no matter, the sequel/Is easily guessed. ALV; NOBL

Dora Williams. Edgar Lee Masters. See what they chiseled: "Contessa Navigato/Implora eterna quiete." HAP

Doralicia's Song. Robert Graves. In time I loath'd that now I love,/In both content and pleas'd. LoBV; OBSC

Doran's Ass. *Anonymous.* Whack fol de darral lal do. OnYI

Dorcas. George Macdonald. She died–they wept about the room,/And showed the coats she made. OBVV

The Dorchester Giant. Oliver Wendell Holmes. And pay for the punch beside. OnMSP

Doria. Ezra Pound. Remember thee. MoAB; MoAmPo; MoVE; ViBoPo

Doric. Anghelos Sikelianos. might lock their limbs, and in the sweat embrace!... ErPo

Doricha. Edwin Arlington Robinson. Again to Naucratis and to the Nile. AWP; FaBoEE; OBVE

Doris. William Congreve. And she, like Sol, alone retires/To shine elsewhere of course. NOEC

Doris: A Pastoral. Arthur Joseph Munby. No more a servant, nor yet a child. HBV 1-2

Doris and Philemon (parody) (excerpt). J. C. Squire. But only scornful Echo made reply. BXAP

Dornroschen. Hayden Carruth. That you will know/the instant you are really kissed. DFT

Doron's Description of Samela. Robert Greene. For beautie, wit, and matchlesse dignitie/yeeld to Samela. LoBV; PoEL 1-5

Doron's Jigge.   Robert Greene.   Thus was faith and firme love showne,/As behoves/shepheards loves.   PoEL 1-5

Dorothea.   Sarah N. Cleghorn.   All in magic murmurs she/Laps and lulls the wee one lying,/Pearl of twilight, on her knee.   HBMV

Dorothy.   Alfred Kreymborg.
bronze of a sea,/under the flame.   AnAmPo
I'd then sound the noise.   AnAmPo
or is it a whirlpool/twitching with memory?   AnAmPo
Paying coin/to gypsies/maybe-.   AnAmPo

Dorothy.   Rose Hawthorne Lathrop.   Are more lost than my heart, which died/not when it broke!   AA

Dorothy Q.   Oliver Wendell Holmes   Through a second youth of a hundred years.   AA; AnNE; AP; HBV 1-2; InMe; NOBA; TreFS

Dorus's Song.   Sir Philip Sidney.   And think not she doth hurt our solitariness,/For such company decks such solitariness.   LoBV

Dory Miller.   Sam Cornish.   his medal somewhere in the pages/of a book.   CNA

The Dosser in Springtime.   Douglas Stewart.   Says the white old dosser in the cave.   ErPo

Dostoievsky's Daughters.   Michael Hamburger.   Of a love that could not redeem/But maimed her, Aimee.   NAs

Doth Then the World Go Thus, Doth All Thus Move?   William, of Hawthornden Drummond.   When good may have, as well as bad, their prime.   BSV; GTBS; GTBS-P

The dots of de dondi.   Kristjana Gunnars.   how our lifespan has become/an American crayon drawing   CaPN

The Double.   Irving Feldman.   To live you on afternoons like this.   NYBP

The Double Autumn.   James Reeves.   Then practise dumbly staring at your plight.   OBSP

The Double Axe.   Anne Hazlewood-Brady.   The double axe will fall like boulders of thunder.   IHMS

A Double Ballad of Good Counsel.   Francois Villon.   Good luck has he that deals with none!   AWP

Double Ballade of Primitive Man.   Andrew and Burnett Tylor Edward Lang. 'Twas the manner of Primitive Man!   CenHV

Double Duty.   W. E. Farbstein.   By applying the book/As well as applying the text.   PoPl

Double Exposure.   Ian Young.   as I took pictures of Jimmy/with an imaginary camera.   NeAC; PeHV

Double Feature.   Theodore Roethke.   And remember there was something else I was hoping/for.   DFF

The Double Fortress.   Alfred Noyes.   The last wall down, look heavenward. We have wings.   GoBC

Double Gift.   Anonymous.   Enjoy them both in bloom before they wither. UnTE

The Double-Headed Snake of Newbury.   John Greenleaf Whittier.   The Amphisbaena is living still!   AmePo

Double-Header.   John Stone.   marked by bases I must run all night/for everything I should/by now/be worth.   TAT

The Double Looking Glass.   A. D. Hope.   What beards, what bald heads burst now from the bush!   CBAP

Double Mock Sonnet.   Charles O. Hartman.   Unnecessary to imagine him. SM

Double Monologue.   Adrienne Rich.   Both serve, and still/our need mocks our gear.   NePoEA-2

Double Ode.   Muriel Rukeyser.   Do I move toward form, do I use all my fears?   LCAP

The Double Play.   Robert Wallace.   (the pitcher walks), casual/in the space where the poem has happened.   SD

Double Ritual.   Dachine Rainer.   Upon the shell of night.   CrMA

Double Semi-Sestina.   George Starbuck.   ...the county/womenfolk are in Iowa City Iowa/asking for you and for the St. Patrick's Hospital.   SM

The Double Shame.   Stephen Spender.   And you have only yourself to blame.   LiTB; LiTL; LiTM

Double Sonnet.   Anthony Hecht.   Speechless, inept, and totally unmanned. SM

The Double Standard.   Franklin Pierce ("F.P.A.") Adams.   Says Advertising Mr. Hyde.   OBAL

A Double Standard.   Frances E. W. Harper.   And what is wrong in woman's life/In man's cannot be right.   BlSi

Double Take at Relais de l'Espadon.   Thadious M. Davis.   Is he the son who shackled my father and me.   BlSi

The Double Transformation.   Oliver Goldsmith.   Serenely gay, and strict in duty,/Jack finds his wife a perfect beauty.   OBNV

The Double Tree.   Winfield Townley Scott.   For this little while in the sun's season.   PoPl

The Double Vision.   Lewis, Cecil Day.   Answer my rays and cluster to a theme!   AtBAP; NoAm

The Double Vision of Manannan.   Anonymous.   Exempt from mortal sin. BIrV

Doubt.   Elinor Chipp.   What if he knocked at my empty heart/And said, "Sweet, let me in!"   HBMV

Doubt.   Margaret Deland.   O Lord! speak soon to me-"Lo, here am I!" TrPWD

Doubt.   Fernand Gregh.   Here is life's holy amplitude/Thee who perhaps art not at all!   WGRP

Doubt.   Helen Hunt Jackson.   Hid in the husks which on that day/My instinct would not throw away!   WGRP

Doubt.   Pat Nolan.   I should have written/"doubt"/when I had it.   APU

Doubt.   Robert Cameron Rogers.   Thou comest with tired limbs to sink be-/side/The ashes of his fire and find them cold.   AA

Doubt me, my dim companion!   Emily Dickinson.   Dwell timidly with thee! ViBoPo

The Doubt of Future Foes.   Queen of England, Elizabeth I.   To poll the tops that seek such change and gape for joy.   CTC; PBWP

The Doubter.   Richard Watson Gilder.   I know not what I think; I know/ Only that thou art what I need.   TrPWD

The Doubter's Prayer.   Anne Bronte.
Forsake it not, it is Thine own,/Though weak, yet longing to believe. WGRP
A shield of safety o'er my head,/A spring of comfort in my heart.   TrPWD

Doubting.   Louis Simpson.   to find the people that they knew.   NNaP

A Doubting Heart.   Adelaide Anne Procter.   And angels' silver voices stir the air.   HBV 1-2

Doubts.   Rupert Brooke.   Why is fragrance in the hair?   CH

Dough Roller Blues.   Garfield Akers.   I said "That's all right sweet mama/ our troubles gon' come some day"   BluL

The Douglas Tragedy.   Anonymous.
And a' the warld might ken right weel/They were twa lovers dear. TrGrPo
And all true lovers that go thegither,/May they have mair luck than they. OxBB
And so they grew ever closer together,/As all true lovers desire.   MaC
For he pu'ed up the bonny brier,/And flang't in St. Mary's Lough.   BoLiVe; HBV 1-2; NoP

The Dove.   Anonymous.   The dove in the heavens/Is the one I choose. GBP

The Dove.   Victor J. Daley.   He took a ruler in his hand,/And struck the white dove dead.   NOAV

The Dove.   Thomas Stearns Eliot.   Consumed by either fire or fire.   BoC

Dove.   Norma Farber.   What save love/can a dove/carol of?/Coo-roo! PCh

The Dove.   Judah Halevi.   Ah! would my tribe should chance/On such deliverance!   TrJP

A Dove.   Ted Hughes.   Bubbling molten, wobbling top-heavy/Into one and many.   OxBC

The Dove.   Ewan MacColl.   And if you don't harm her she'll tell you no lies.   OBET

The Dove Apologizes to His God for Being Caught by a Cat.   Anthony Eaton.   that with my life you gave me no apology,/and hear them whence they come.   PeSA

The Dove of Dacca.   Rudyard Kipling.   Dacca is lost from the roll of the kings!   GN

The Dove of New Snow.   Vachel Lindsay.   The glittering, angelic meadow. MoAmPo

The Dove's Loneliness.   George Darley.   And leave me to my loneliness again!   OBNC

Dove's Nest.   Joseph Russell Taylor.   "Birdie!" Sylvia cried, "come back!" HBV 1-2

Dove's Song in Winter.   Anonymous.   Woe is me!   WTO

The Dove Says.   Anonymous.   Love me, and I'll love you.   OxNR

The Dove Says, Coo, Coo.   Anonymous.   I have got ten,/And keep them all like gentlemen.   PBBP

Dover Beach.   Matthew Arnold.
Ah, love, let us be true/To one another!   ATP
Where ignorant armies clash by night.   AnEnPo; AWP; BiP; BLPA; DiPo; DTC; EaLo; EtS; ExPo; FaBoBe; FaBoPP; FaBoRV; FaBV; FaFP; FF; FiP; ForPo; FPL; GoTF; GTBS; GTBS-P; HAP; HBV 1-2; HeIP; HoPM; InPK; InPo; InPS; InvP; LiTB; LiTL; LoBV; MasP; MAT; MaVP; MCCG; MOS; NIP; NOBE; NOBV; NoP; NU; OAEL 1-2; OAEP; OBNC; OBVV; PAI; PG; PoEL 1-5; PoPl; PoPle; PoRA; PPoe; PPON; PPP; Prf; PrIm; SCV; SeCePo; SeCeV; SoSe; TEP; TreFS; TRV; UnPo; ViBoPo; VLP; WeW; WHA

"Dover Beach"-a Note to That Poem.   Archibald MacLeish.   What's to be next in the world. It's we will be under it!   FF

The Dover Bitch.   Anthony Hecht.   And sometimes I bring her a bottle of Nuit d'Amour.   BXAP; MAT; NePoEA-2; NIP; NLV; NOBA; NOBL; OBAL; PP; PPP; UnPo; VGW

Dover to Munich.   Charles Stuart Calverley.
And now, the saints deliver/Us from fleas.   NOBL
Layer on layer, the night came on.   OBTV

Doves.   Joachim Neugroschel.   like a fading allegory,/like doves,/like our own far-blood on forgotten altars.   VWA

The Doves. Katharine Tynan. Where once were nine or ten/But two keep house together. AnIV; AWP

The Doves of Venice. Laurence Hutton. Are nothing but a roosing-place/For German turtle-doves! AA

Dow's Flat. Bret (Francis Bret Harte) Harte. No? Well, then the next time you're passin'; and ask after/Dow–and thet's me. FaBoBe; HBV 1-2

Dowager. John Montague. An old bitch, with a warm mouthful of game. IPY

The Dowie Dens of Yarrow. Anonymous. She lay deid in her lover's airms,/Between that day and morrow. FSW

The Dowie Houms o' Yarrow. Anonymous.
A fairer rose did never bloom/Than now lies cropp'd on Yarrow. OBS
I wiss that they had a' gane mad,/Whan they cam' first to Yarrow.' BSV; GoTS; OBEV; OxBS

Down a Sunny Easter Meadow. Nancy Byrd Turner. Easter's coming!"/And they hurried. SiSoSe; SoPo

Down a Woodland Way. Mildred Howells. Save three wild violets among the grass. AA

Down among the Wharves. Eleanore Myers Jewett. We who like to wander where the waiting vessels/are! EtS

Down and Out. Clarence Leonard Hay. The claws of the tropics will gather your pile and the dealer gets it all. BeLS; BLPA

Down at the Docks. Kenneth Koch. For you and that big dark blue. PrIm; VGW

Down Below. Joan Aiken. He believes there's stowaways down there–but, good/lord, what kind? WSC

Down by the Glenside. Peadar Kearney. Glory O! Glory O! to the Bold Fenian Men. AnIV

Down by the Old Mill Stream. John Read. We passed the time away,/Down by the old mill stream. TreFS

Down by the River. Anonymous. He bought her a ring/And a damascene gown. OxNR

Down by the Salley Gardens. William Butler Yeats. But I was young and foolish, and now am full of tears. CMoP; CTC; EnLoPo; FSW; HBV 1-2; NoAm; OBEV; OBVV; OnYI; OxBI; PG; PoEL 1-5; PrIm; SoSe

Down by the Station, Early in the Morning. John Ashbery. ...the light/From the lighthouse that protects as it pushes us away. HaCAP

Down Dip the Branches. Mark Van Doren. Shut, shut, shut your eyes. DuDa

Down! Down! Eleanor Farjeon. The leaves are falling over the town. NTCP; SoPo; SUS; TiPo

Down, Down Derry Down (with music). Anonymous. As for the highwayman, he's lost all his store, let him go a-robbing until he gets more. AS

Down, Down, Down. Anonymous. While you're down, down, down. OuSiCo

Down, Down, Down. Heather McHugh. ...He won't come back. SUW

Down from the Country. John Blight. ...to be caught/out of the dullness of self by such alien thought? CBAP

Down Hall. Matthew Prior.
She has lain in the church-yard full many a year. MyFE
Thus ends the First part of the Ballad of DOWN./Derry down, down, hey derry down. CEP

Down Home. Randolph Outlaw. and long to return/down home down home. LFAC

Down in a Coal Mine. Anonymous. For what would America be without the lads that look for coals? AmFP

Down in Alabam'. J. Warner. Aint I glad I got out de wilderness,/Down in Alabam'. PSoN

Down in Dallas. X. J. Kennedy. He stood and they bound him foot and hand/To the cross of a rifle sight. CoPo; FF; OFD

Down in Lehigh Valley. Anonymous. And I'll hunt the runt that stole my girl,/If it takes 'til judgment day. TreF

Down in the Forest. Anonymous. Which never so blossomed since Jesus was born. OBET

Down in the Hollow. Aileen Fisher. I wonder if the ladybug/knew that I was there. SoPo; SUS

Down in the Jungle. Anonymous. Better than a pre-fab–/No rent! WTO

Down in the Land of the Center-Fire Saddle. Anonymous. For we're bound for the Rio Grandy. CoSo

Down in the Lonesome Garden. Anonymous. Nor down in my lonesome gyardin. BPo

Down in the Meadows. Anonymous. As it grows older, it grows colder/And fades away like morning dew. CBEP

Down in the Valley. Anonymous.
And back it is in care of/The Barbourville jail. ABF; FaFP; FSW; WTO
Angels in heaven know I love you. AS; TreFT
Hang your head over, hear the wind blow. BLSo

Down in the Willow Garden. Anonymous. For I have murdered my own true love,/Whose name was Rose Connelly. FSW

Down in Yon Forest. Anonymous. And I love my Lord Jesus above anything. FSW

Down in Yonder Meadow. Anonymous. Hear her singing Handy Dandy up and down the stair. PoPle

Down on My Luck. A. R. D. Fairburn. close to the end of my tether. AnNZ

The Down-Pullers. Walter E. Isenhour. For by such plans you'll never gain/The height of one who should be tall. STF

Down South on the Rio Grande. Anonymous. Way down South in Dixie, oh, boys, ho. CoSo

Down the Bayou. Mary Ashley Townsend. And through the gloom the wild deer shyly/gaze. AA; AnAmPo

Down the Field. Rolfe Humphries. "Christ! get that dirty player, Death!" AnAmPo

Down the Little Big Horn. Francis Brooks. True to the death! PAH

Down the M4. Dannie Abse. ...I whistle/no hymn but an old Yiddish tune my mother knows. It won't keep. OxBC

Down the Mississippi. John Gould Fletcher.
Above the pink explosion of the calyx of the dawn. AmFN; LiTA
A blue-black negro with gleaming teeth waits for his/chance to leap. LiTA
Far southward where a single chimney stands out aloof/in the sky. LiTA
I will curl up in it at last and sleep an endless sleep. LiTA
Over white lakes of cotton, like moonfields on every side. LiTA
Whereon the sun hangs motionless, a brassy disc of/flame. LiTA
Which show, through gaps and tatters, red stains half-/hidden away. LaNeLa

Down the Nile. Robert Lowell. we aging downstream faster than a scepter can check. HaCAP

Down the Rain Falls. Elizabeth Jane Coatsworth. When they talk to themselves/For company's sake. SoPo

Down to Sleep. Helen Hunt Jackson. The mother will not fail to keep/Where we can "lay us down to sleep." GN

Down to the Sacred Wave. Samuel Francis Smith. Let glory o'er these scenes be shed,/And smile on us today. AH

Down, Wanton, Down! Robert Graves. Be gone, have done! Down, wanton, down! BoLoP; CMoP; FaBoTw; HeIP; InPK; LiTM; NoAm; NoP; OAEL 1-2; TEP

Down Went McGinty. Joseph Flynn. Dress'd in his best suit of clothes. FSN; TreF; YaD

Down Wind against the Highest Peaks. Clarence Major. Which ain't revolutionary, you/dig? NBP

Down with the Lambs. Anonymous. Run to bed children/Before it gets dark. OxNR

The Downfall of Charing Cross. Anonymous. For fear the king should rule again,/I'd pull down Tiburn too. FaBoCo

The Downfall of Heathendom. Anonymous. All the quiet valleys/Tossed up to the sky. KiLC

The Downfall of Piracy. Benjamin Franklin. How they kill'd the Pirates many,/They'd Applause from young and old. PAH

The Downfall of the Chancellor. Anonymous. I've said enough of linsey-woolsey Hyde–/His sacrilege, ambition, lust, and pride. APAS

The Downfall of the Gael. Fearflatha O'Gnive. Unite, oh, unite!/Or the billows burst o'er her! AnIV; AWP; OnYI

The Downright Country-Man; or, The Faithful Dairy Maid. Anonymous. To pass away the tedious hours, she's fair and Chaste indeed. CoMu

Downstream. Thomas Kinsella. Searching the darkness for a landing place. FaBoIP

Downtown-Boy Uptown. David Henderson. You have started your count./I cannot. NNP; PoNe

Downwards. C. K. Williams. It stands still on the water, rocking, blinking. GeTw

Downy Hair. Lucien Stryk. ...downy/hair fragrant with leafsmoke. FAZ

Downy Hair in the Shape of a Flame Moving up the Stomach... Coleman Barks. should have/a name: PV

Doxology. Bert Leston Taylor. And who remains, for all our debt,/A modest sweet white violet. OBAL

The Doze. James Reeves. The damp, despised, and aimless Doze. AmMo

Dr. Birch and His Young Friends: The End of the Play. William Makepeace Thackeray. Be peace on earth, be peace on earth,/To men of gentle will. GN

Dr. Coppelius. Wrey Gardiner. Shimmering on the quiet floor of our private world. NeBP

Dr. Dimity Is Forced to Complain. Cynthia Macdonald. "A flood of painful memories," says Dr. Doctor. SUW

Dr. Dimity Lectures on Unusual Cases. Cynthia Macdonald. Next week I will discuss:/Life and the Liver in Sibling Kidney Transplant. SUW

Dr. Donne. Kenneth Slade Alling. The social debt to death was satisfied. NePoAm

Dr. Hu. Norman Mailer. What loneliness. ELU

Dr. Joseph Goebbels. W. D. Snodgrass. Soon, once more, all things shall be equal. TW

Dr. Potatohead Talks to Mothers. Judith Johnson Sherwin. and the teeth/there the mouth/open NoAm

A Dream. Charles Tomlinson. the reader's rest and editor's colophon. OxBC

A Dream. Charles Williams. ..."It draws more near/Daily; and here shall it be in the end–or here?" OBEV

Dream. Harold Witt. Jack making a touchdown for the winning team. SM

Dream 1971. Victor Contoski. what do you do/with cards like these? GP

Dream 2: Brian the Still-Hunter. Margaret Atwood. ...he has been gone/twenty years and not heard from. BoWoP

A Dream about an Aged Humorist. Aaron Zeitlin. and when I thought of his new joke in my sleep,/I shuddered. VWA

The Dream about Junior High School in America. Dick Lourie. ...Smith and/Wesson pistols and Winchester rifles". NeAC

Dream about Sunsets. Annabelle Hebert. She was most exuberant. GrPl

Dream after Touring the Tokyo Tokei. Joy Kogawa. And beyond this another resurrection. BrSi

Dream and Image. Sir. Heinrich von Morungen. And loves it until death releases him. LiTW

The Dream and the Blood. Louis Untermeyer. Give me myself but for an hour. Go back, dark blood. UnTE

Dream and the Song. James David Corrothers. The dream is lovelier than the song. BANP

A Dream as Reported. Virginia Earle. and I took your hand, and we smiled. GoYe

Dream Barker. Jean Valentine. Bone dry, old, in a dry land, Jim, my Jim. PrIm; VGW

Dream Boogie. Langston Hughes. Y-e-a-h! AmPP

The Dream Called Life. Pedro Calderon de la Barca. When dreaming, with the night, shall pass away. AWP

Dream Data. Robert Duncan. ...These, the Prince said,/when I was in love/were always with me where I was. NeAP

Dream, Dump-Heap, and Civilization. Robert Penn Warren. Is civilization possible without it? NoP

Dream Fantasy. Fiona Macleod. O, is this sleep, or waking where/Lie hush'd the Valleys of Dream? WGRP

Dream Farmer. Jill Witherspoon Boyer. and labor with the faith/of desert blooms. CNA

The Dream Feast. Anita Endrezze-Probst. At her smile, the feast begins. VoR

Dream Fishing. Jim Thomas. the purest fishing remained a dream. WOLT

The Dream-Follower. Thomas Hardy. And my dream was scared, and expired on a/moan,/And I whitely hastened away. VLP

Dream Girl. Carl Sandburg. A film of hope and a memoried day. MoLP

Dream Girl. Karen Snow. sweetened and re-dressed. HoAn

A Dream: "Guid-mornin to your majesty." Robert Burns. The laggen they hae clautet/Fu' clean that day. NAs

Dream House. Catherine Parmenter Newell. All of life and love my house shall know! PoToHe

The Dream House. Marjorie Allen Seiffert. The maple-leaves lie deep. HBMV

A Dream in Early Spring. Fredegond Shove. Long after this and many another dream. MoVE

Dream Land. Frances Anne Kemble. It is no fault of mine! OBVV

Dream-Land. Edgar Allan Poe. I have wandered home but newly/From this ultimate dim Thule. AmP; AP; APA; LiTA; NePA; NOBA; OxBA

Dream-Land. Christina Georgina Rossetti. Till joy shall overtake/Her perfect peace. BrRo; EnLi 1-2; VLP

Dream-Love. Christina Georgina Rossetti. And a dove, may be,/Return to nestle here. CH; GTBS; HAP; NBM; PoEL 1-5

The Dream Motorcycle. Pete Winslow. I wasn't invited back. PV

A Dream Observed. Anne Ridler. Blessings that outdo all distress/Implicit in his sleeping head. NeBP

Dream of a Baseball Star. Gregory Corso. Hosannah the home run! NoAm; SD; VGW

The Dream of a Boy Who Lived at Nine Elms. William Brighty ("Matthew Browne") Rands. With bread and cheese for supper I could dream it all again! OxBChV

Dream of a Decent Death. Giuseppe Antonio Borgese. until he hears the call of his midnight. NePoAm

Dream of a Father. Shirley G. Cochrane. I awoke before you got in. AmC

The Dream of a Girl Who Lived at Sevenoaks. William Brighty ("Matthew Browne") Rands. With bread and jam for supper I could dream it all again! OxBChV

The Dream of Aengus Og. Eleanor Rogers Cox. That face of the Sun and Mist begotten,/Its singing lips and death-cold eyes. HBMV

A Dream of Artemis. Francis Ledwidge. Your pity dries the morning's tears/And fills the world with joy again! TrPWD

A Dream of Burial. James Wright. ...the horse/Stood saddled, browsing in grass,/Waiting for me. NaP

The Dream of Dakiki. Firdausi. He made ablaze with light my soul of shade! WGRP

A Dream of Death. Lucy White Jennison. Arise, and love me, Helena! AA

A Dream of Death. William Butler Yeats. She was more beautiful than thy first love,/But now lies under boards. GBL

The Dream of Eugene Aram. Thomas Hood. And Eugene Aram walked between,/With gyves upon his wrist. BeLS; EnRP; HBV 1-2; StPo

A Dream of Fair Women. Kingsley Amis. The night after tonight. FF; MP; NMP; NoAm; OAEL 1-2

A Dream of Fair Women. Alfred, Lord Tennyson. Wither beneath the palate, and the heart/Faints, faded by its heat. OBRV

A Dream of Flowers. Titus Munson Coan. To her, a sweeter flower than all the rest. AA

The Dream of Flying Comes of Age. Howard Nemerov. It's not the joystick now, but the control column. BiP

The Dream of Gerontius. John Henry, Cardinal Newman.
And I will come and wake thee on the morrow. CoBE; OxBoCh; VLP
And see Him in the truth of everlasting day. OxBoCh
In all his words most wonderful,/Most sure in all his ways. NOCV
Should teach His brethren and inspire/To suffer and to die. NOBV; PoEL 1-5
So pray for me, my friends, who have not strength to pray. ACP
To that glorious Home, where they shall ever gaze on Thee. OxBoCh
While Lucifer is left, condemn'd and/unforgiven. VLP

A Dream of Governors. Louis Simpson. And spreads the dragon's wing. NYBP

A Dream of Horses. Ted Hughes. The forever itself a circling of the hooves of horses. NePoEA-2

A Dream of Jealousy. Seamus Heaney. ...O neither these verses/Nor my prudence, love, can heal your wounded stare. CIP; FaBoIP

A Dream of Judgement. Douglas Dunn. There is singing of morals in Latin and Greek. OxBC

A Dream of November. Sir Edmund Gosse. Dark bronze, bright leaves, pure silken threads, in triple/flower. SyP

Dream of Rebirth. Roberta Hill Whiteman. Some will rise that clear morning like the swallows. CDW; TWSS

A Dream of Suffocation. Robert Bly. Old warships drowning in the raindrop. NaP

A Dream of Surreal Science. Sri Aurobindo Ghose. The universe before God had time to shout. ACV

Dream of the Black Mother. Marcelin Dos Santos. She dreams of marvelous worlds/Marvelous worlds/Where her son will be able to live. WhB

The Dream of the Cabal. Anonymous. And if Cabal thus serve us Englishmen,/'Tis ten to one but I shall dream again. APAS

The Dream of the Cross. Anonymous. Almighty God suffered/Died and Rose/through the cross,/Of glory.' EBEV

Dream of the Forgotten Lover. Lucia Fox. The feeling/is a little like when the Tarot cards by chance/turn up the Hanged Man. BoWoP

Dream of the Lynx. John Haines. and the ever-deepening track/of the unseen, feeding host. NU

The Dream of the Romaunt of the Rose. Geoffrey Chaucer. Ful cler was than the morowtyde,/And ful attempre, out of drede. LoBV

The Dream of the Rood. Anonymous.
All wan beneath the welkin. All creation wept. ACP
it was they who girt me with gold and silver...' NOCV
When the Lord, Almighty God, came again to His throne. AnOE; CAW; OAEL 1-2

The Dream of the Rood. Cynewulf. The Lord Most High, at his home at last. EnLi 1-2

A Dream of Venus. Bion. But what he taught me I learnt all by heart. AWP

Dream of Winter. George Mackay Brown. ...The wind's blue fingers laid/A migrant on the rock. FaBoTw

A Dream of Women. Carolyn Maisel. the empty shacks/home IHMS

A Dream, or the Type of the Rising Sun. Jean Adams. Its worth was less than anything I saw,/But I observed it keeped most in awe. NOEC

Dream-Pedlary. Thomas Lovell Beddoes.
This would I buy. AtBAP; FaBoBe; GoTF; OBEV; OBVV; TreFS
Thus are old dreams made true/Ever to last! AnFE; EnRP; HAP; LiTB; LoBV; NOBE; OBNC; OBRV; PoEL 1-5; TrGrPo; ViBoPo; WiR

The Dream Queen: Dialogue. Bhasa. 'Tis white and lovely like/A wreath of water-lilies... LiTW

Dream Record: June 8, 1955. Allen Ginsberg. of an unvisited garden in Mexico. ConAP; NOBA

Dream Sequence, Part 9. Naomi Long Madgett. ...thought I knew I built it/And led you there./Was it you? BPo

Dream Song. Lewis Alexander. Then call the lost dream back. PoBA; PoNe

Dream Song. Anonymous. The thunder, it is good. OBVE

Dream-Song. Walter De la Mare. In a world of wonders far away. PoPle

The Dreary Change. Sir Walter Scott. And Araby's or Eden's bowers/ Were barren as this moorland hill. ERoP 1-2; FaBoPP; OAEL 1-2; OBNC

Dregs. Ernest Christopher Dowson. This is the end of all the songs man sings. HBV 1-2; NCEP; OBMV; SeCePo

The Dreme: Of the Realme of Scotland. Sir David Lindsay. Justice may nocht have Dominatioun,/Bot quhare Peace makis habitatioun. OxBS

The Dreme: The Compleynt of the Comoun Weill of Scotland. Sir David Lindsay. Bot I beseik God for to send the grace/To rewle thy realme in unitie and peace. OxBS

The Drenching Night Drags On. Aogan O Rathaille. I'd wedge your ugly howling down your throat! NOBI

The Dress. Christopher Middleton. Have my hand under/Her blue dress when she is there. NMP

The Dress. Mark Strand. yourself making and remaking until it is perfect. GeTw

Dress Me, Dear Mother. Avraham Shlonsky. And at the break of dawn, lead me/To work. VWA

A Dress of Fire. Dahlia Ravikovich. what's burning is me. VWA

The Dress of Spring. May Justus. And stitched with a rainbow seam. YeAr

The Dress That My Brother Has Put on Is Thin. Lady Otomo of Sakanoe. Till he reaches home. AWP

A Dresscessional. Carolyn Wells. Have mercy on us, Future Girl! WBLP

A Dressed Man and a Naked Man. George Orwell. A dressed man and a naked man/Stood by the kip-house fire. EBEV

Dressed to Kill. Clarence Major. They turn slowly/especially in public/ when one must be polite. APU

Dressed Up. Langston Hughes. But I ain't got nobody/For to call me sweet. GoSl

Dresses. Kathleen Fraser. Mrs. Brown's dresses still button to my chin. NMM

Dressing Game. Dennis Schmitz. which passes, shivering the denim, back/ into the stream. NPGG

The Dressmaker's Dummy as Scarecrow. Barbara Howes. The spring may find her still, and grow towards her. DFF

Dried Apple Pies. Anonymous. But don't pass me dried-apple pies. BLPA

Dried Fruit (parody). Philip Dow. I will make it shrivel. BXAP

Drift. Denis Glover. Castaways of wind and weather/Drifting aimlessly together. AnNZ

The Drifter. Anonymous. For I am a rusty cowboy/And Pumpkin Creek's my home. CoSo

Drifters. Bruce Dawe. "Make a wish, Tom, make a wish." CBAP

Drifting. D. Maitland Bushby. Drifting to the desert gleaming/Underneath a jewelled sky. BPAW

Drifting. John Francis O'Donnell. Around the oaks the brown bats go. IrPN

Drifting. Thomas Buchanan Read. Under the walls of Paradise! AA; GN

Drifting. Kathleen Spivack. We bent to the paddles. IHMS

Drifting away. Charles Kingsley. Ah, God! My God! Thou wilt not drift away. OxBoCh

A Drifting Petal. Mary McNeil Fenollosa. A thought had blossomed, and shaken/free/One sheath of its innermost soul for me. AA

Drifting Sands and a Caravan. Yolande Langworthy. Lustrous eyes 'neath Eastern skies, and a woman's veiled face. BLPA

Driftwood. Witter ("Emanuel Morgan") Bynner. There's a fire under the moon. FYAP

Driftwood. Daniel Smythe. Writing a last word. RFM

Driftwood. Trumbull Stickney. Spell, "Come back." HBV 1-2

Driftwood Dybbuk. Barbara F. Lefcowitz. unless you are patient enough/ to wait for me piece by sea-/battered piece. VWA

The Drill. Harry Brown. And the voices of our approaching generations. WaaP

Drill Man Blues. George Sizemore. Who from eating dust will end up/ With a fate just like mine. WTO

Drill Ye Tarriers, Drill. Thomas F. Casey. And drill ye tarriers drill,/And blast and fire. FSW

Drilling in Russell Square. Edward Shanks. And still the brown leaves drift in Russell Square. OBMV

Drilling Missed Holes. Don Cameron. As unanimous verdicts/Of drilling missed holes. PoOW

Drink. William Carlos Williams. under the gold hair ornaments/of skyscrapers. OxBA

Drink, Friends. Moses Ibn Ezra. What need of bread! TrJP

Drink from My Empty Cup. Zindzi Mandela. that you are so oppressed/ you even laugh at yourself. WhB

A Drink of Milk. John Montague. he puts the mug to his head,/grunts, and drains it clean. FaBoIP

A Drink of Water. Seamus Heaney. Remember the Giver fading off the lip. FaBoIP; OxBC

Drink that Rot Gut. Anonymous. Till the world goes round and round! ABF

Drink To-day. John Fletcher. ...to bed go sober,/Falls with the leaf, still in October. EnLit; HBV 1-2; OAEP; ViBoPo

A Drink with Something in It. Ogden Nash. I'm forced to conclude it's the liquor. PoPl

Drinker. Patrick Anderson. and in his sandy mouth there bursts its melting flower. PeCV

Drinking. Abraham Cowley. Why, man of morals, tell me why? BLPL; CABA; FF; HBV 1-2; LoBV; MePo; NOBE; PG; PoPle; SeCP; SeCV 1-2; TrGrPo; WeW

Drinking. Hsin Ch'i-chi. Pushing against it, I said: "Go away!" LiTW

Drinking. Virginia R. Terris. our roots knotting themselves/in that dark world/that allows us our drunkenness. FAZ

Drinking Alone in the Moonlight. Li T'ai-po. I do not proclaim them to the sober. AWP

Drinking Alone with the Moon. Li Po. I watch the long road of the River of Stars. LiTW

Drinking Cold Water. Peter Everwine. like a hard, white root. NNaP

Drinking Fountain. Marchette Chute. And don't get any/Drink at all. TiPo

Drinking Song. Anonymous.
And let the cupp go rounde!' EnLit; OxBM
If I can tell you more of Pyretic/Saline manufactured by Lamplough. FaBoUs
Let her go to the devil!–there's no more to be said. NOBL

Drinking Song. Alexander Brome. Then I'll fall to my loving and drinking amain. PoPle

A Drinking-Song. Henry Carey. And let that Wine be all for me! OBEV

Drinking Song. Thomas Dekker. Ring compass, gentle joy! TrGrPo

Drinking Song. John Fletcher. Falls with the leaf still in October. EIL

Drinking Song. Jim Harrison. ...she was in NY forever and I, fishing and/ drinking. WOLT

Drinking Song. Anthony Hecht. This measuring hand. We are beholden all. NMP

Drinking Song. James Kenneth Stephen. And you'd better get someone who can. NOBL

A Drinking-Song... William Wycherley. For as the Head is made more weak,/Man is more busie, bold, and free. SeCV 1-2

A Drinking Song. William Butler Yeats. I look at you, and I sigh. BoLoP; OAEL 1-2; PoL

Drinking Song: "Drink that rotgut, drink that rotgut". Anonymous. Drink it straight and swig it mighty,/Till the world goes round and round! CoSo

Drinking Song for Present-Day Gatherings. Morris Bishop. And the toastmaster's having convulsions.) ALV

Drinking the Wind. Tan Ying. She flies into the night, and with one draught drinks/All the sighs of a thousand miles. WPOW

Drinking Time. D. J. O'Sullivan. Two black heifers and a red. OnYI

The Drive. Janet Reed McFatter. wished we were going/nowhere at all. GrPl

Drive a Tractor. Anonymous. Drive a tractor. NLV

Drive Away Blues. Blind Willie McTell. (But I won't be back no more, mama) BluL

Drive Imagining. Arthur Vogelsang. My twisted mouth around your fear. MAYP

Drive It On. Anonymous. Oh, Captain, that's been here and gone, oh, Lawd,/Oh, Lawdy, Lawd. OuSiCo

Driven by desire I did this deed. Sir Thomas Wyatt. That who so trusteth ere he know/Doth hurt himself and please his foe. FCP

The Driver. James Dickey. For thousands of miles on the water. VGW

The Driver in Italy. Nicholas Christopher. The back of his own head. MAYP

A Driver's Prayer. Anonymous. And that its purpose is to serve/Mankind, but not destroy. STF

The Drivers of Boston. June Gross. yearning for a patch of grass. AMV-80

Drivin' Steel (with music). Anonymous. This old hammer weighs forty pounds, sah,/Can't kill me, Baby, can't kill me. AS

Driving. Myra Cohn Livingston. over and over and ever and along. InPK

Driving at Dawn. William Heyen. burns again for the steelman/who burned like hell for their women. SaC

Driving By. Robert Wallace. lichen of the blue American nights/from which we come. LiSp

Driving Carl's '56 Chevy. Warren Woessner. and that's my ring around her neck/on the strongest chain in the world. AmC

Driving Cattle to Casas Buenas. Roy Campbell. And rice and rabbit for the stranger./Thank you very much! PeSA

Driving Cross-Country. X. J. Kennedy. We were there once upon a time. TwCP

Driving; Driven. David McAleavey. ...where we'd drive, how we'd survive. AMV-80

Driving Home. Jonathan London. this is the last curve/in the last curve home AMV-81

Driving Home after a Funeral. Gregory Orr. a white snail/eating holes in a leaf. GeTw

Driving Home the Cows. Kate Putnam Osgood. Together they followed the cattle home. AA; BeLS; HBV 1-2; PAH; TreFS

Driving in Oklahoma. Carter Revard. he flies so easy, when he sings. VoR

Driving in the Park. Anonymous. No one ever know–/Riding in the Park. OxBoLi

Driving into Enid. Michael Van Walleghen. ...her chewed fingers/are tatooed SUE on one hand DAVE on the other. FYAP

Driving North from Kingsville, Texas. Naomi Shihab. making ourselves at home. TAT

Driving North from Savannah on My Birthday. Paul Zimmer. Driving my car hard north/Against their fragile yearnings. AmC; AMV-81

Driving Saw-Logs on the Plover (with music). Anonymous. Than to drive saw-longs on the Plover,/And you'll never get your pay. AS

Driving the Mule. Anonymous. I chew and I spit/All over my sweetheart's behind. GBP

Driving through Belgium. Michael Brownstein. Gentlefolk fall away in crumble sadness/past the shifting potholes of our day. ANYP

Driving through Coal Country in Pennsylvania. Jonathan Holden. just dump trucks in the distance/raising dust. GOYP

Driving through Minnesota during the Hanoi Bombings. Robert Bly. Shot in the chest, taken back to be questioned. NoP

Driving through the Pima Indian Reservation. Paul H. Cook. ...when the stars of our easy invention have/all but gone away. AMV-80

Driving to Sauk City. Warren Woessner. The windmill still turns/but someone pulled up the pipe/and shot the cistern full of holes. TAT

Driving to Town Late to Mail a Letter. Robert Bly. Driving around, I will waste more time. BoNaP; CAPP; ELU; HeIP; InPK; NaP; VGW

Driving toward the Lac Qui Parle River. Robert Bly. A few people are talking low in a boat. ConAP; LCAP; NaP; NCSH; NoP

Driving Wheel. Sherley Anne Williams. History is them; it is also theirs to make. BlSi

Driving While under the Influence. Michael Casey. fifty million dumb cops in the world/and this one has to be a genius. AmC

A Drizzling Easter Morning. Thomas Hardy. For endless rest–though risen is he. CMoP

The Dromedary. A. Y. Campbell. There was not any yearning in his eye,/But on his lips and nostril infinite scorn. HBMV

Dromedary. Francois Dodat. that dull assignment/of being the world's/most sober animal BoAnP

Drone v. Worker. Ebenezer Elliott. At Famine's Feast, ye ken, man. FaBoPV; NBM; OBSV

Drop a Pebble in the Water. James W. Foley. Over miles and miles of water just by dropping one kind word. BLPA; PoToHe

Drop, Drop, Slow Tears. Phineas Fletcher. Nor let his eye/see sin, but through my tears. NOBE

A drop fell on the apple tree. Emily Dickinson. The East put out a single flag,/And signed the fete away. BoNaP

Drop Me the Seed. John Masefield. Through dusty Time its beauty shall make plain/Man, and, Without, a spirit scattering grain. MoRP

A Drop of Dew. Shimon Halkin. Filled with itself and yet transparent. TrJP

A Drop of Ink. Joseph Ernest Whitney. Dropped–mockery of life's a quick-wasted lot–Dropped on a virgin sheet 't is but a blot! AA

Drop the Wires. Hugh Seidman. I can hear my father saying/you had to let it go AmPA

Drop Thy Still Dews. John Greenleaf Whittier. And let our ordered lives confess/The beauty of Thy peace. ILwL

Dropping Your Aitches. Joseph Warren Beach. As a true confession, an istorical. NYBP

Drops of Gall. Gabriela (Lucila Godoy Alcayaga) Mistral. and the voracious worm upbraiding you. BoWoP

Drought. David Holbrook. Watching the same rain from our each window. OxBTC

Drought. Geoffrey Johnson. Blazing with noon and dripping with its pomp. HaMV

Drought. Oumar Ba. The natural fatality of existence. PBWP

Drought (excerpt). Francis Carey Slater. Implacable Drought. ACV

The Drove-Road. Wilfred Wilson Gibson. Even the best rum tasted better, shared. EnLit; OxBTC

A Drover. Padraic Colum. ...scant croppings/Harsh with salt of the sea. AnIV; AWP; HBV 1-2; MoBrPo; OBMV; OxBI; ViBoPo

Droving Man. Thea Astley. ...his eye/Would find in hers a startled twin of wonder. PoAu 1-2

The Drowned. Norman MacCaig. drifts in the song, complete/as an archangel. OxBC

The Drowned. Stephen Spender. And forget these bones all day. MOS

The Drowned Children. Louise Gluck. What are you waiting for/come home, come home, lost/in the waters, blue and permanent. HaCAP

The Drowned Mariner. Elizabeth Oakes Smith. Away from decay, and away from the storm. AA

Drowned Sailor. Neufville Shaw. And the careful trace turned fluid. CaP

The Drowned Seaman. Maude Goldring. "Sailor, what is your will of me?" HBMV

Drowning in Spanish. Tom Schmidt. Try that/at Stinson/Beach. NeAC

Drowning is Not so Pitiful. Emily Dickinson. Is shunned, we must admit it,/Like an adversity. CMoP; ExPo; OBSP

Drowning of Conaing. Anonymous. On all the gods who guard his home. AnIL

The Drowning Poet. James Merrill. ...a compliment/To all accomplishment. PP

Drowning with Others. James Dickey. And me laid out and alive/For nothing at all, in his arms. CoPo

The Drowsy Sleeper (A vers.). Anonymous. And I'll forsake, I'll forsake father and mother,/Forsake them all and go with you. BaBo

The Drowsy Sleeper (B vers.). Anonymous. And we'll be wed, my own sweet lover,/And let them talk when we are gone. BaBo

The Drug Clerk. Eunice Tietjens. We only cater to the high-class trade. AnAmPo; HBMV

Drug Store. Karl Shapiro. They slump in booths like rags, not even drunk. CMoP; MoVE; MP; OxBA; TwCP

Drug Store. John V. A. Weaver. That's a man's business!.../If I ever get it.... HBMV; YaD

Drugged. Walter De la Mare. Than dream more meagre and awful,/Reality. BrPo

Drugs Made Pauline Vague. Stevie Smith. What a handsome couple they made. FaBoWP

The Druid. John Banister Tabb. As in their fate foreshadowing his own. AA

The Drum. John Farrar. And beat him soundly for the band. BrR

Drum. Langston Hughes. Calling all life/to Come! Come!/Come! MoAmPo

A Drum for Ben Boyd. Francis Webb.
And finding a thousand faces round your boots. ACV
The old fighting and the old peace. PoAu 1-2

De Drum Majah. Ray Garfield Dandridge. So am de ban'. BANP

Drum-Taps. Walt Whitman.
And over all the sky-the sky! far, far out of reach,/ studded, breaking out, the eternal stars. AP
Are the things so strange and marvelous you see or have seen? PoNe
But the hot sun of the South is to fully ripen my songs. AP
By the bivouac's fitful flame. AP
Dead and divine and brother of all, and here again he lies. AP
Good-bye–and hail! my Fancy. AP
The guidon flags flutter gayly in the wind. AP
Many a soldier's kiss dwells on these bearded lips. AP
So strong you thump O terrible drums-so loud you bugles blow. AP
There in the fragrant pines and the cedars dusk and dim. AP
Till the gossamer thread you fling catch somewhere, O my soul. AP
To the free skies unpent and glad and strong. AP

The Drum: the Narrative of the Drummer of Tedworth. Edith Sitwell. Where the drum rolls up the stair, nor tarries. BoW

Drumdelgie. Anonymous. I leave ye as I got ye–/A maist unceevil crew. GBP

A Drumlin Woodchuck. Robert Frost. I have been so instinctively thorough/About my crevice and burrow. GoYe; NoAm; NOBA

The Drummer. Anne Robinson. Rabbit, the drummer,/Straightens his ears/And marches with summer. SUS

Drummer Boy. William Stafford. All that I did has turned into this song. FAZ

The Drummer-Boy and the Shepherdess. William Brighty ("Matthew Browne") Rands. And a drum and a drummer boy under a tree. MoShBr

The Drummer Boy of Shiloh. Anonymous. How many loved the drummer boy/Who prayed before he died! AmFP

The Drummer Boy of Waterloo. Anonymous. When night had stilled that battle's drum,/They dug his grave at Waterloo. BFSS

Drummer Hodge. Thomas Hardy. And strange-eyed constellations reign/His stars eternally. AWP; BrPo; CoBMV; EBEV; GTBS-P; HAP; InPo; InPS; NoAm; NOBV; NoP; OBWP; PAI; SeCeV; VLP

Drumochter. Anne B. Murray. Here where the wind skins Drumochter/Only the storm moves fast. PoSH

Drums in Scotland. Richard Hugo. ...You were never/wanted and she always said come in. LCAP

Drums of Haiti. Marcus B. Christian. Beat–beat–beat–drums–beat. GoSl

Drunk. Carroll Arnett. or a wall to lie by/myself there being/nowhere else to go. VoR

Drunk as drunk on turpentine. Pablo Neruda. And lay like fish/Under the net of our kisses. BoLoP

The Drunk in the Furnace. William Stanley Merwin. Stand in a row and learn. CAPP; LiTM; MAT; MP; NePoEA-2; NoAm; SM; TwCP

Drunk Last Night.   *Anonymous.*   For one of us could drink it all alone.   FSW

Drunk Last Night with Friends, I Go to Work Anyway.   Philip Dow.   A snail/dreaming in the throat of an old wine bottle.   NPGG

The Drunk Man.   *Anonymous.*   Drunken/Stricken with fists.   NOAV

A Drunk Man Looks at the Thistle (excerpt).   Hugh (Christopher Murray Grieve) MacDiarmid.   Up, carles, up/And let us dance!   EBEV

A Drunkard.   *Anonymous.*   Trippe a litel with thy foot,/And let thy body gon!   OxBM

The Drunkard.   Fenton Johnson.   I will be true to my new wife. You can have the other.   AnAmPo

The Drunkard.   Philip Levine.   "Life was a dream, Oh, may this death be sleep."   NePoEA-2

A drunkard cannot meet a cork.   Emily Dickinson.   Your connoisseur in Liquors/Consults the Bumble Bee–   InPS; PAI

The Drunkard's Doom.   *Anonymous.*   'Twill lead you down to hell's dark gate,/And ruin your own soul.   AS; FSW

A Drunkard to His Bottle.   Joseph Sheridan Lefanu.   With your kiss on my cold lips, and never rise more.   OnYI

The Drunkards.   *Anonymous.*   It must be that they are coming from the garden to the garden.   NU

The Drunkards.   Malcolm Lowry.   And the spider of life sits, sleep.   NYBP

Drunken Americans.   John Ashbery.   ...We are all soiled with this desire, at the last moment,/the last.   HaCAP

The Drunken Boat.   Arthur Rimbaud.   Nor swim beneath the convict-hulks' appalling eyes!   LiTW; SyP

The Drunken Dee.   Syd Scroggie.   Till syne ae nicht he jist scales richt/Intil the ocean, fou.   PoSH

The Drunken Fisherman.   Robert Lowell.   On water the Man-Fisher walks.   AP; CMoP; CrMA; LiTA; LiTM; MoPo; MoVE; NOBA; OxBA; SeCeV; VGW

The Drunken Fool.   *Anonymous.*   But I never saw a mustache/On a baby's face before.   BFSS

Drunken Gunner.   Michael Kennedy Joseph.   To strike its distant enemy to the heart.   AnNZ

Drunken Heracles.   Wallace Gould.   Beware of it,–/for long ago you strangled two great snakes.   AnAmPo

Drunken Lover.   Owen Dodson.   Open all the windows to the north/For the wind to cool my head.   AmNP

The Drunken Man.   Steve Orlen.   Go home. Go home to my noisy wife.   MAYP

Drunken Poem.   David Helwig.   There is no conclusion to this poem. Ever.   NOBC

The Drunken Sailor (Early in the Morning).   *Anonymous.*   Way, hay, and up she rises, Early in the morning!   ShS

The Drunken Stones of Prague.   David Scheinert.   ...who greeted them with open hands/that had been changed into flowers.   VWA

Drunken Streets.   Malka Locker.   petrified like skeletons.   VWA

Drunken Winter.   Joseph Ceravolo.   Oak sky.   ANYP

The Drunkeness of Pain.   Aliza Shenhar.   The Foundation Stone/did not make its own back tremble/nor did it falter.   VWA

Dry Be That Tear.   Richard Brinsley Sheridan.   Nor let us lose our heaven here–/Dry be that tear.   OnYI

Dry July.   Arnold Adoff.   legs dust shoes and/we keep still.   CAD

Dry Land Blues.   Furry Lewis.   What you gonna do/when your trouble get like mine   BluL

The Dry-Landers.   *Anonymous.*   But hit to your toil in the mornin' or you'll soon be driftin' away.   CoSo

Dry Loaf.   Wallace Stevens.   And that drums had to be rolling, rolling, rolling.   AtBAP; CrMA; NOBA; OxBA; PoRA

Dry (parody).   Samuel Hoffenstein.   Cripes! but I'm agin it!   BXAP

Dry-Point.   Philip Larkin.   Where you, we dream, obtain no right of entry.   CMoP; NMP

Dry Your Tears, Africa!   Bernard Dadie.   They return to clothe you/in their dreams and their hopes.   TTY

Dryad Song.   Margaret Fuller.   Gathering strength, gaining breath,–/naught can sever/Me from the Spirit of Life!   AA; WGRP

The Drynaun Dhun.   *Anonymous.*   And welcome home the blossom of the Drynaun Dhun.   GBP

Du, Du Liegst Mir Im Herzen.   *Anonymous.*   Weisst nicht wie gut ich dir bin.   FSW

The Dual Site.   Michael Hamburger.   Still may meet again and together build/One house before we die.   MP; NePoEA-2

Duality.   Dannie Abse.   lest four tears from two eyes fall.   NoAm

Duality.   Kenneth Slade Alling.   Needs likewise its duality.   AnAmPo; CAW

Duality.   Arthur Sherburne Hardy.   Those wondrous secrets which it knows–/and keeps.   AA

Duality.   Katherine Thayer Hobson.   The roots of life are deep and dearly won.   GoYe

A Dubious Night.   Richard Wilbur.   I weary of the confidence of God.   CAPP

Dublin.   Louis MacNeice.   And brick upon grey brick.   ACV; CIP; FaBoPP; OxBI; OxBTC

A Dublin Ballad - 1916.   Dermot (Sir Arnold Bax) O'Byrne.   We're free to sentimentalize/By corners where the martyrs fell.   AnIV; OxBI

Dublin Bay.   *Anonymous.*   And the ship went down with the fair young bride/Who sailed from Dublin Bay.   BFSS

Dublin Bay.   Ewart Milne.   The waves laugh, like corn sway slenderly and beckon.   NeIP

Dublin Doggerel.   Richard Conniff.   Christ, what a pity.   DBV

Dublin Made Me.   Donagh MacDonagh.   Stirs proudly and secretly in my blood.   AnIV; NeIP; OxBI; OxBTC

Dublin: The Old Squares.   Padraic Colum.   And take her for a midnight stroll!   NePoAm

Dublinesque.   Philip Larkin.   As if the name meant once/All love, all beauty.   OxBC

Dubrovnik Poem (Emilio Tolentino).   Anthony Rudolf.   ...with thanks/for our congratulations/sent on his hundreth birthday.'   VWA

Duchess.   Lilian Bowes Lyon.   She conjures the snow softly into bloom.   HaMV

The Duchess of Malfi.   John Webster.
   Cover her face: mine eyes dazzle: she died young.   AnFE
   End your groan, and come away.   FaBoEn; HAP; HW; NoP; OBEV; OBS; PAI; QFR; SeCePo; ViBoPo

The Duchess of York's Ghost.   *Anonymous.*   Thus having said, the vision disappears,/Leaving the trembling princess drowned in tears.   APAS

The Duchess's Lullaby.   Lewis (Charles Lutwidge Dodgson) Carroll.   For he can thoroughly enjoy/The pepper when he pleases!/Wow! wow! wow!   FaBoNo; SpRo

Duchesses.   David Campbell.   And the tears of the women fall on the doilies.   NOAV

Duck.   John Lyle Donaghy.   Both quiet on the old brown dresser.   BIrV; OxBI

The Duck.   Edith King.   Who swim about the pond with her/And do as they are told.   HBVY

The Duck.   Ogden Nash.   It bottoms ups.   MoShBr

Duck.   Valerie Worth.   ...take/Him home with us, put him/Away, on a shelf, to keep.   NTCP

The Duck and the Kangaroo.   Edward Lear.   And who so happy–O who,/As the Duck and the Kangaroo?   OxBChV

Duck-Chasing.   Galway Kinnell.   When it is over it is all over.   MP; NMP; TwCP; VGW

Duck in Central Park.   Frances Higginson Savage.   Maintaining, both in sun and shade,/The semblance of a smile!   GoYe

The Duck Pond at Mini's Pasture, a Dozen Years Later.   Philip Dow.   On set wings, down/slowly, into the last light–   AmPA; NPGG

Duck's Ditty.   Kenneth Grahame.   Up tails all!   GoJo; NTCP; SUS

Duckle, Duckle, Daisy.   Leroy F. Jackson.   Duckle, duckle, daisy.   ChBR

Ducks.   Robert Bly.   They are needed somewhere!   PV

Ducks.   Frederick William Harvey.
   And he's probably laughing still at the sound that came out of its/bill.   BoC; EBCP
   And slime they gobble and peer/Saying "Quack! Quack!"... OnUR

Ducks.   Phoebe Hesketh.   And cattle stand and stare.   BoAnP

The Ducks.   Alice Wilkins.   They glide most gracefully.   TiPo

Ducks and Drakes.   *Anonymous.*   Slitherum, slatherum, take her.   OxNR

Ducks at Dawn.   James S. Tippett.   And slept to tunes/Of "Quack! Quack! Quack!"   SiSoSe; SoPo; TiPo

Ducks down in the Meadow.   William Stafford.   ...seen/dawn arrive in gold, there along the crest,/the way it does for us.   NPAW

Ducks in the Millpond.   *Anonymous.*   Lord, Lord, gonna get on a rinktum.   OuSiCo

Due Date.   Seymour Cain.   And our fabled double kingdom/Of life and of death.   AMV-80

Due North.   Benjamin R. C. Low.   Oh, eager, clear-like love in eyes–/The soul of you.   EtS; HBMV

The Due of the Dead.   William Makepeace Thackeray.   Knowing those cared for whom they love.   OBWP

The Duel.   *Anonymous.*   While Willing's willing shot went right/Through Schott's anatomy.   ShM

The Duel.   Abraham Cowley.   For from the Body can they fly?   AnAnS 2

The Duel.   Eugene Field.   ...And that is how I came to know.)   BeLS; CenHV; FaBoBe; FaFP; FPL; GoTF; HBV 1-2; HBVY; MoShBr; OBAL; OBCA; OHFP; OnMSP; PoLf; PoPl; PoRA; SoPo; TiPo; TreF

The Duel.   Richard Lovelace.   The only way t' undo this enemy/Is to laugh at the Boy, and he will cry.   CaPo

The Duel.   Theodore Maynard.   This is a duel to the death, and when/We part as friends we meet as foes again.   CAW

The Duel.   Harold Trowbridge Pulsifer.   Nor how that wounded spirit/Left blood on my sword hand.   HBMV

Duel in the Park. Lisa Grenelle. Are these the same men/who played here last year? GoYe

Duel with Verses over a Great Man. *Anonymous.* Their tongue was directed to heaven,/Now it lies in the dust. TrJP

The Duellist. Charles Churchill. Behold him, full and perfect quite,/A false saint, and true hypocrite. OBSV

The Duenna (excerpt). Richard Brinsley Sheridan.
I will do so when I see/That heaving bosom sigh for me. NOEC
Oh, what a plague is an obstinate daughter! DBV

Duermete, Nino Lindo. *Anonymous.* So rest in the arms of your mother/Who sings you a la ru. FSW

A Duet. Thomas Sturge Moore. Thus sang a king and queen in Babylon. OBEV; OBVV

Duet. Leonora Speyer. But not on my back,/Because of my wings! HBMV

Duet. Alfred, Lord Tennyson. Love that is born of the deep coming/up with the sun from the sea. GBL

The Duff. David McKee Wright. It's all that cursed duff!' "I'm sinking too,' says he,/"And fast enough.' AnNZ

Dufferin, Simcoe, Grey. Margaret Atwood. water them while our houses wither. AMV-81

Duffy's Hotel. *Anonymous.* Bid adieu to the kind friends and boarders/That hang 'round at Duffy's Hotel! ShS

The Dug-Out. Siegfried Sassoon. And when you sleep you remind me of the dead. AtBAP; MCCG; MoBrPo; MoVE; OHIP; WaaP; WaP

Dugall Quin (A version). *Anonymous.* An she has marred Dugall Quin,/An lives belou Strathbogy. ESPB

Dugall Quin (B version). *Anonymous.* Whan ither trades begin to fail,/They can take their bowies and brew. ESPB

Duino Elegies. Rainer Maria Rilke.
Superabundant being/wells up in my heart. NAWM 1-2
that harmony which now enraptures and comforts and helps us. NAWM 1-2
Withhold him...... LiTW

The "Duke" and the "Count." Richard Fewell. we wail right on key! AMV-81

The Duke Is the Lad. Thomas Moore. Whole crowds have miscarried/At sight of this dreary Duke. OnYI; TW

The Duke o' Athole's Nurse. *Anonymous.* But for a' that they ca'd, and for a' that they socht,/They left the young squire busy bakin'. OxBB

The Duke of Athole's Nurse. *Anonymous.* And for a' that they did search and ca,/For a kiss o the knight they were striving. BaBo

The Duke of Atholl's Nurse (A version). *Anonymous.* She promised to come hersel,/But she sent three men to slay me.' ESPB

The Duke of Atholl's Nurse (B version). *Anonymous.* And twenty times they passd/The squire at his baking. ESPB

The Duke of Benevento. Sir John Henry Moore. Inspire my raptur'd heart, and make it virtuous as your own.' CEP; OBEC

The Duke of Buccleuch. J. A. Phelp. When they learned 'twas a bull–the great Duke of Buccleuch! NOAV

The Duke of Buckingham. Alexander Pope. There, Victor of his health, of fortune, friends,/And fame, this lord of useless thousands ends. NOBE; OBEC

The Duke of Gordon's Daughter. *Anonymous.* Mount and go to Northumberland,/There a countess thou shall be.' BuBa; ESPB

The Duke of Grafton. *Anonymous.* Where the royal Queen Mary went weeping away. GBP

The Duke of Marlborough. *Anonymous.* And ne'er was bribed by gold. OBET

Duke of Parma's Ear. Eli Siegel. For the Duke of Parma's ear. ELU

The Duke of Plaza-Toro. Sir William Schwenck Gilbert. The Duke of Plaza-Toro! ALV; FiBHP

The Duke of York's Statue. Walter Savage Landor. And raised thee up to where thou art. FaBoEE

Duke William. *Anonymous.* ..."Blessed be that glorious day on which was born Duke/William." OBSS

Dulce et Decorum. T. P. Cameron Wilson. So sweet to live? Magnificent to die! HBMV

Dulce et Decorum Est. Wilfred Owen. The old Lie: Dulce et decorum est/Pro patria mori. AnFE; CMoP; CoBMV; DL; FaBoPV; FaBoTw; FaBV; FF; HeIP; HoPM; InPK; InvP; LiTB; LiTM; MMM; MoAB; MoBrPo; NIP; NoAm; NoP; OAEL 1-2; OAEP; OBWP; PPON; PPP; PrIm; SoSe; TW; UnPo; WaP

Dulce Ridentem. Stephen Vincent Benét. The moth-wing soul of Jane. LOW

Dulcimer Maker. Carolyn Forche. It will not be as far away,/as unfamiliar. SaC

Dulcina. Sir Walter Ralegh. Forgo me now, come to me soon. ALV

The Dule's i' This Bonnet o' Mine. Edwin Waugh. He wants noan o' th' bonnet, thae foo! HBV 1-2

Dull Is My Verse. Walter Savage Landor. "The bird upon its lonely bough/Sings sweetest at the close of day." PoEL 1-5

Dulnesse. George Herbert. Look onely; for to love thee, who can be,/What angel fit? AnAnS 1

Dum and Dee. *Anonymous.* They quite forgot their quarrel. OxNR

Dum Vivimus Vigilemus. Charles Henry ("John Paul") Webb. That I've been borne away to bed. AA

Dumb Dick. Leslie A. Fiedler. I will not lie dead. ErPo

Dumb, Dumb, Dumb. *Anonymous.* To make a scolding wife hold her tongue, tongue, tongue. OnYI

The Dumb Maid. *Anonymous.*
So perhaps you may charm/her tongue, tongue, tongue. CoBE
When she gets mad, mad, mad,/She would sting me all around when she gets mad. BFSS

The Dumb Soldier. Robert Louis Stevenson. I must lay him on the shelf,/And make up the tale myself. OxBChV

The Dumb Wife Cured. *Anonymous.* For to make a scolding woman hold her/Tongue, tongue, tongue. MaC

The Dumb World. William Henry Davies.
And rather see a battle than/A dumb thing near a drunken man. OxBTC
With him I'd sit and drink and play,/And save the world this worthless lay. BoAnP

Dumbarton's Drums. *Anonymous.* When Johnnie kneels and kisses me. FSW

The Dumbfounding. Margaret Avison. sound dark's uttermost, stangely light-brimming, until/time be full. NOBC

The Dump. Greg Kuzma. the chaff of life, the most of it,/its miscellaneous debris. PoA

Dumpy Ducky. Lucy Larcom. And my plump little sisters cry/"We want a drink!" Good-by! OBCA

Dun Colour. Ruth Pitter. O that I too were attired in such dun colours! FM; MoVE

Duna. Marjorie Pickthall. And the little stars of Duna/Call me home. HBV 1-2; MCCG

Dunbar. Anne Spencer. Ah, how poets sing and die! BANP; CDC

Duncan and Brady. *Anonymous.* In their big Mother Hubbards and their stockin' feet. OuSiCo

Duncan Gray. Robert Burns. Ha, ha, the wooing o't. ALV; BSV; CoMu; EnLit; ErPo; GoTS; GTBS; GTBS-P; LiTL; MCCG; OBEC

Duncan Spoke of a Process. LeRoi (Imamu Amiri Baraka) Jones. what country is this? CAPP

The Dunce. *Anonymous.* And he piped his eye like a fool, oh! OxNR

The Dunce. Walter De la Mare. You will as learned, wise,/And–happy be!' ImOP

Dunce Song 6. Mark Van Doren. Who comforts like raisins,/Who kisses like snow. DuDa

The Dunciad. Alexander Pope.
And the hoarse nation croak'd, God save King Log. CEP
And universal darkness buries all. AtBAP; CoBE; EBEV; EnLi 1-2; FaBoPV; FiP; NOEC; NoP; OAEL 1-2; OBSV; PoEL 1-5; SCV; ViBoPo
And with her own fool's colours gilds them all. OBSV
Fruits of dull Heat, and Sooterkins of Wit. AtBAP
Sound forth, my Brayers, and the welkin rend. AtBAP

Dunciad Minor. A. D. Hope. Stand up and catch his mantle as it falls!' BXAP

Duncton Hill. Hilaire Belloc. A boy that sings on Duncton Hill. GoBC

Dunderbeck. *Anonymous.* And Dunderbeck was meat! Bang! FSW

Dundonnel Mountains. Andrew Young. A false step would suffice/To make me both its priest and sacrifice. PoSH

Dunedin Revisited. Denis Glover. And the manuka hills/Know the slow smoke of burning. AnNZ

The Dungeon. Samuel Taylor Coleridge. By the benignant touch of love and beauty. MCCG

Dunkirk. Robert Nathan. And held him true and steered him home. MaC

Dunlavin Green. *Anonymous.* For his loyal brothers, who were shot on Dunlavin Green. FaBoBa

The Dunmow Flitch of Bacon. *Anonymous.* Marked with a flitch of bacon! OBET

Duns Scotus. Thomas Merton. And sings like the African sun. CoPo

Duns Scotus's Oxford. Gerard Manley Hopkins. Who fired France for Mary without spot. CoBE; EBEV; EyDe; FaBoPP; GTBS-P; NAMP; NoAm; OBMV; PoEL 1-5; VLP

Duo. Olive Dargan. Till who the last rood dareth/Shall find a mother there! HBMV

Duo-tang. Kenward Elmslie. The sheet had dried. ANYP

The Duplicity of Women. John Lydgate. Sette on youre brest, yourself t'assure,/A mighty shelde of doublenesse. MeEL

Dupree. *Anonymous.* Don't mind you sailin', but you'll be gone so dog-gone long. OuSiCo

Dupree (A vers.). *Anonymous.* You see what rambling and drinking rum/And a sporting life has done. ViBoFo

Dupree (B vers.). *Anonymous.* The judge tol' Dupree, "I believe you quit too late,/Because it is already your fate." ViBoFo

The Durable Bon Mot. Keith Preston. The smart tale dogs the wag. HBMV

Durand of Blonden. Ludwig Uhland. Ever calling, "Blanca! Blanca!" through the desert halls/of Heaven. AWP

Durer: Innsbruck, 1495. Ern Malley. ..I am still/The black swan of trespass on alien waters. CBAP

Durer's Piece of Turf. Norbert Krapf. and the bells of St. Sebald's Church. PoDr

Durham Field. *Anonymous.* Now save and keepe our noble king,/And maintaine good yeomanry! ESPB

The Durham Lock-Out. *Anonymous.* For every man who hears this song will know we're not to blame. CoMu

Durham Old Women. *Anonymous.* For the joyful days are coming./Fal la la. GBP

Duriesdyke. *Anonymous.* There was never bairn born of a woman/That was born mair bitterly. OxBB

During a Bombardment by V-Weapons. Roy Fuller. Now all the permanent and real/Furies are settling in upstairs. OBSP

During a Chorale by Cesar Franck. Witter ("Emanuel Morgan") Bynner. And where you come, an exquisite/Image of death and lover of it,/Life sings a serenade. AnAmPo; HBMV

During December's Death. Delmore Schwartz. astonishment, its endlessness. NYBP

During His Courtship. Charles Wesley. Thou shalt be/Mine Eternal heaven. NOCV

During Music. Arthur Symons. All that her eyes could read in mine/Or mine in hers had read. NOBV

During the Eichmann Trial (excerpt). Denise Levertov. each a mirror/for man's eyes. NMP

During the Pageant at Medicine Lodge. Charles G. Ballard. ...but the Indians,/whoever they were, did not arrive. VoR

During Thoughts after Ofay-Watching. Mongane Wally Serote. But the river shall flow like the song of birds. WhB

During Wind and Rain. Thomas Hardy. Down their carved names the rain-drop ploughs. CMoP; ELP; ExPo; ForPo; GTBS-P; HAP; NIP; OAEL 1-2; OxBTC; PoPle; PPoe; PPP; QFR; SeCeV; TEP

Dusk. Ken Belford. Cutting brush every day/And folding his clothes carefully. NeAC

Dusk. Angelina Weld Grimke. And the dusk. CDC

Dusk. DuBose Heyward. And these my songs, my all, belong to her. HBMV

Dusk. Abraham Lopez-Penha. As with a rampant lion's hungry/claw/Grips at the lapiz-lazuli of heaven. TrJP

Dusk. Archibald MacLeish. And heart in heart we weep Love's body laid. HBMV

Dusk. Gabriela (Lucila Godoy Alcayaga) Mistral. and I feel my life fleeing/hushed and gentle like the gazelle. BoWoP

Dusk. Marcia Southwick. I can be touched/and not feel like a passing shadow. MAYP

Dusk. Helen Welshimer. To a woman, a child, a lamp. PoToHe

Dusk Chant. Judith Mountain Leaf Volborth. "Save me from what,/a flock of sheep?" TWSS

Dusk in the Domain. Dorothea Mackellar. Seven slum children from/Wooloomooloo! PoAu 1-2

Dusk in Winter. William Stanley Merwin. It has brought its flute it is a long way. NaP

The Dusk of Horses. James Dickey.
Quiet, fragrant, and relieved. AP; LiTM
The stalls are put up around them. NYBP

Dusk of the Gods (excerpt). S. Funaroff. My joy, it rose,/a new-found land. NAMP

Dusk of the Revolutionaries. John Haines. as the great cloud-utopias/burn out in the west. NPAW

Dusk Song. William H. A. Moore. Dear heart, pale and long. BANP

Dust. Rupert Brooke. One moment, what it is to love. ALV; HBV 1-2; MoBrPo; OBVV; OxBTC

Dust. Waring Cuney. Civilization continually shifts/Upon the places of the earth. CDC

The Dust. Gertrude Hall. That kissed in some forgotten May... AA

The Dust. Lizette Woodworth Reese. Clerks, bishops, kings go by–/To-morrow so shall I! HBMV

Dust. George William Russell. And haunted by all mystery. WGRP

Dust. Sydney King Russell. With dust at her feet/And dust in her eyes. ShM

Dust. Andre Spire. Duster, dust away, my friend,/Never will your dusting end. TrJP

Dust. Kathleen Spivack. ...virulent summer-/green satisfactions. BoWoP

Dust. Randolph Stow. But the neighbours slept behind sealed doors, with feather/dusters beside their beds. CBAP; PoAu 1-2

Dust Bowl. Robert A. Davis. In our dreams. GoSl; IDB

Dust Bowl. Langston Hughes. The land wants me to come back. PoA

Dust of Snow. Robert Frost. And saved some part/Of a day I had rued. CMoP; MoShBr; OBSP; OxBA; PrIm; SoSe; TAP; TiPo; UnPo; WeW

The Dust of the Overland Trail. James Barton Adams. And their lips fashioned jests as they beat from their breasts/The dust of the Overland Trail. PoOW

The Dust of Time (fragment). Sappho. They cut them off with sharpened shears. AWP

Dust on Spring Street. Louis Grudin. And seize his fiery hand. NoP

Dust to Dust. Walter De La Mare. Heavenly Archer, loose thy string. TrPWD

The Dust Will Settle. Luci Tapahonso. this will change. STE

The Dustbowl. Kenward Elmslie. and headed on mules for the mountains, that autumn of the glut. ANYP

Dusting. Rita Dove. Long before the shadow and/sun's accomplice, the tree./Maurice. HaCAP; MAYP

The Dusting of the Books. Dorothy Hughes. The mannerly word hiding its wilderness root. GoYe

The Dustman. Frederic Edward Weatherly. Leads them through the sweet green shadows,/Far away in slumberland. HBV 1-2

The Dutch. George Canning.
Is offering too little and asking too much. DBV; OxBoLi
So we clap on Dutch bottoms just 20 per cent. OBTV

Dutch April. Daniel Halpern. Its load of ripe Edam upon the quay. GrPl

Dutch Interior. May Sarton. Remaking chaos into an intimate order/Where sometimes light flows through a windowpane. SM

A Dutch Picture. Henry Wadsworth Longfellow. And capture another Dean of Jaen/And sell him in Algiers. EtS; ExPo; HBVY; MoShBr

A Dutch Proverb. Matthew Prior. And great Thy Wisdom, VANDER BRUIN. CEP; FaBoEE; NOEC; PoL

The Dutch Seamen and New Holland. William Pember Reeves. And long, wild cries seemed shouts of fear and war. AnNZ

The Dutchess of Monmouth's Lamentation for the Loss of her Duke. *Anonymous.* Then from her Eyes, with fresh supplies, down trickles many a/brinish Tear. CoMu; FaBoBa

The Dutchman. Don Welch. our hands leaving little glittering pieces of feeling/behind us. WOLT

Duty. – Cook. The youth replies, "I must." YaD

Duty. Ralph Waldo Emerson. The youth replies, I can. AnNE; FaFP; GN; GoTF; HBV 1-2; TreF; YaD

Duty. Ellen S. Hooper. A noonday light and truth to thee. BLPA; GoTF; TreFS

Duty. Edwin Markham. And bring seven other duties to your door. HBMV; HBVY

Duty to Death, LD. Dick Roberts. Like the ground I might at any moment/Choose to lie down upon. WaP

Dvonya. Louis Simpson. on a summer night in Odessa. NNaP; NOBA

Dwainie. James Whitcomb Riley. And answers not at all. AA

The Dwarf. Gerald Locklin. either of them know the human thing/is not to be snow-white but to be ugly. DFT; GP

Dwarf of Disintegration. Oscar Williams. There's nothing here to salvage, and yours is another problem. LiTM; MoPo; NePA; PoCh

The Dwarf of the Hill Caves. Lupenga Mphande. to add to his possessions, attain height and beat the dwarf. WhB

Dwell with Me, Lovely Images. Theodore Maynard. A candle in my darkest need,/Twin to a star. GoBC

The Dwelling. Moshe Dor. its cries a sea/of darkness I do not know my name VWA

The Dwelling-Place. Henry Vaughan. My God, I mean my sinful heart. MeLP; OBS; OxBoCh; TrPWD; WGRP

Dying. Alfred Alvarez. Death/like homesickness/like homecoming after captivity. VWA

Dying. Emily Dickinson. And then the windows failed, and then/I could not see to see. MAPA

Dying. Jessie Holt. Something he meant, who stumbled with a cross! PGD

Dying. Robert Pinsky. Bored and impatient in the monster's mouth. AMV-81; HaCAP; MAYP

The Dying Airman. *Anonymous.* And assemble the engine again. FaBoNo; FaFP; OxBoLi

Dying: An Introduction. L. E. Sissman. But as green/As anything:/As spring. NYBP

The Dying Californian. *Anonymous.* Brother, hear my last farewell. AmFP; BFSS; BPAW; TrAS

The Dying Child. John Clare. He died so quietly. CBEP; EnRP; NCEP; TrGrPo

The Dying Child's Request. Hannah Flagg Gould. The soul that made that form so bright,/To Heaven had passed away. OBCA

The Dying Christian to His Soul. Alexander Pope. O Death! where is thy sting? CAW; GoBC; GoTF; HBV 1-2; OBEV; TreF

The Dying Cowboy. *Anonymous.*
In a narrow grave, just six by three,/We buried him there on the lone prairie. BFSS; FaBoBe

With a prayer to Him who my soul will save. CoSo

The Dying Cowboy of Rim Rock Ranch. *Anonymous.* For I'm riding away on my Brown Girl,/Where the sun is sinking low. CoSo

The Dying Desperado. *Anonymous.* For when he shoots he shoots for keeps and piles his victims up in/heaps. CoSo

The Dying Eagle. Edwin John Pratt. Over the lost empire of the peaks. ACV

The Dying Enthusiast. James Clarence Mangan. Wouldst thou have me the bright lot forego?/Oh! no! no! IrPN

The Dying Father's Farewell. *Anonymous.* For you will shortly come to me,/Where we shall never part. AmFP

The Dying Fisherman's Song. *Anonymous.* Now his head resembles heaven,/For there is no parting there. TreFT

The Dying Garden. Howard Nemerov. Somber November in amber and umber embering out. Psk

The Dying Gaul. Desmond O'Grady. ...the ways/death consummates, like love. BIrV

The Dying Girl. Richard D'Alton Williams. To close the curtains of her eyes/And bind her golden hair. OnYI

The Dying Gladiator. George Gordon, Lord Byron. ...–Arise! ye Goths, and glut your ire! NOBE

The Dying Hobo. *Anonymous.* His comrade stole his coat and hat and kept on headin' West. AmFP

The Dying Hogger (with music). *Anonymous.* And put within my cold, still hand/A monkey-wrench and the old oil can. AS

Dying Hymn. Alice Cary. O death, where is thy sting! HBV 1-2

The Dying Indian. Joseph Warton. I go! great Copac beckons me! farewell! NOEC

The Dying Lover. Richard Henry Stoddard. They will be no more to me then/Than mine are now to you! HBV 1-2

The Dying Man in His Garden. George Sewell. Nor one of all thy plants that grow/But Rosemary will with thee go. GTBS-P

The Dying Mine Brakeman. Orville J. Jenks. Just to meet me over yonder/On that bright and golden shore. AmFP

The Dying Patriot. James Elroy Flecker. ...fleet of stars is anchored and the young Star-captains glow. HBMV; ViBoPo

The Dying Prostitute, An Elegy. Thomas Holcroft. Or bloom thy laurels o'er my winding-sheet? NOEC

The Dying Ranger. *Anonymous.* With his saddle for a pillow and his rifle across his breast. CoSo

The Dying Reservist. Maurice Baring. O brother Death,–I knew you when you smiled. HBV 1-2

The Dying Sergeant. *Anonymous.* While proud, cold England sinks with shame. AmFP

The Dying Stockman. *Anonymous.*
In the shade where the coolibahs grow. PoAu 1-2
Sometimes think of the stockman below. ViBoFo

The Dying Swan. Thomas Sturge Moore. ...Pain, teach thou/The god to love, let him learn how. OBMV; SeCePo; SyP

The Dying Swan. Alfred, Lord Tennyson. Were flooded over with eddying song. PBBP; WiR

Dying That I Might Live. Charles Wesley. And where Thou art is heaven. BePJ

Dying Thief. Itzik Manger. And singing still the nightingales die. VWA

A Dying Tiger–Moaned for Drink. Emily Dickinson. But 'twas–the fact that He was dead–. PeD

Dying! To be afraid of thee. Emily Dickinson. Two armies, love and certainty,/And love and the reverse. MoPo

Dying under a Fall of Stars. Mark Elliott Shapiro. The news/Like a final stab of darkness. VWA

A Dying Viper. Michael (Katherine Bradley and Edith Cooper) Field. Mocking the charm of death. O God, it knows! FM

A Dying Wife to Her Husband. Moses Ibn Ezra. And knock at the door of my grave/With a loving hand. TrJP

The Dying Words of Stonewall Jackson. Sidney Lanier. Solace hast thou for pain! PAH

The Dyke-Builder. Henry Treece. Cruel fingers setting the ocean's curls. LiTB; WaP

The Dykes. Rudyard Kipling. That our own houses show as strange when we come back in the dawn! OBWP; VLP

Dykes in the Garden. Sharon Barba. strolling arm in arm, perhaps with cigars/through our own American Beauties. PeHV

Dylan, Who Is Dead. Samuel ("Paul Vesey") Allen. Hail oracle, shine/in that dark night! PoBA

Dynamic Tension. Steve Sanfield. Just a word from you and my dime/will be flying through the mails. SOTS

Dynamite Song. *Anonymous.* And we live on powder/AND DYNAMITE! AmFP

Dynastic Tiff. Geoffrey Hellman. To Hell with the King of Siam! ALV

The Dynasts. Thomas Hardy.
And flowers in the bud that will never bloom. CMoP; WaaP
And their great Confederacy dissolves like the diorama of a dream. WaaP

From to-morrow's mist-fall till Time be sped! MoAB; OBWP

Opposed, opposers, in a common plight/Are scorched together on the dusk champaign. CMoP

save for the soft hiss of the rain that falls impartially on/both the sleeping armies. OAEL 1-2

That night at Trafalgar! MOS; WaaP

You'd treat, if met where any bar is,/Or help to half-a-crown. WHA

The Dysynni Valley (Wales). Theodore Holmes. While below herds crop the well-kept fields by night. CoPo

Dyvers Dothe Use as I Have Hard and Kno. Sir Thomas Wyatt. But let it passe and think it is of kinde/That often chaunge doth plese a womans minde. AAS

Dyvers Thy Death Doo Dyverslye Bemone. Henry Howard, Earl of Surrey. ...from whence suche streames avayle/As Pyramus did on Thisbes brest bewayle. AAS

E

E. B. B. James (1834-82) Thomson. Fairest land while land of slaves/Yields their free souls no fit graves. HBV 1-2

E'en as the Flowers Do Wither. *Anonymous.* Your beauty shall be turn'd to earth. EG

E Questo Il Nido in Che la Mia Fenice? A. D. Hope. That in my glowing embers he might see/The burning bird and tree. OxBC

The E-RI-E. *Anonymous.* And I scarcely think/We'll get a drink/Till we get to Buffalo,/Till we get to Buffalo. AS; FSW

E Tenebris. Oscar Wilde. The wounded hands, the weary human face. BrPo; CABA; CAW; MoBrPo; TreFT; TrPWD

E, the Feasting Florentines. Daniel Gerard Hoffman. and ate them thick with butter. VGW

E Uni Que A The Hi A Tho, Father. Roberta Hill. You showed me, how under snow and darkness,/the grasses breathe for miles. VoR

Each a Part of All. Augustus Wright Bamberger. Sends a little of His heaven/To every living thing. WBLP

Each and All. Ralph Waldo Emerson I yielded myself to the perfect whole. AA; AnNE; AP; AWP; BLPL; HBV 1-2; MAmP; MCCG; NePA; NOBA; OHFP; OxBA; TAP; WGRP

Each Bird Walking. Tess Gallagher. I said, "That's good, that's enough." FaBoWP; MAYP; SV

Each Day. David Ignatow. I too wanted love pure and simple. NNaP

Each Day Is Anxious. Anna Akhmatova. To keep you from crying, I'll sing for you,/A little evening parting song. AMV-81

Each Found Himself at the End of... Ebbe Borregaard. rigid with it NeAP

Each in His Own Tongue. William Herbert Carruth. Some call it Consecration,/And others call it God. AmePo; BBV; BLPA; HBV 1-2; OHFP; TRV; WBLP; WGRP

Each More Melodious Note I Hear. Henry David Thoreau. Who would the music be. OBSP

Each Morning. LeRoi (Imamu Amiri Baraka) Jones. This is known/as genealogy. IDB; PoBA

Each to Each. Melville Cane. We are close; we are clear. GoYe

Eadie. *Anonymous.* Wo, Eadie, go way. OuSiCo

Eadwacer. *Anonymous.* It takes little to loose a link never made,/our gladness together. PBWP

Eager Spring. Gordon Bottomley. To save for us one more Spring. MoBrPo

The Eagle. Richard Blessing. I am never remembering, we lie always, Love, in one another. AMV-80

Eagle. Tom Bowker. But etched on our minds/Forever. PoSH

The Eagle. James Daly. And drown all lesser cries/Your ears have known. AnAmPo

The Eagle. William Sharp. The eagle scans his vast domain. FM

Eagle. Robin Skelton. I am the final judgement and the rock. NOBC

The Eagle. Alfred, Lord Tennyson. And like a thunderbolt he falls. BoLiVe; DiPo; ExPo; FaBoCh; FF; FiP; FM; GN; GoJo; GTBS; GTBS-P; HBV 1-2; HeIP; InPK; LoGBV; MyFE; NOBV; NoP; NTCP; OAEL 1-2; OAEP; OBSP; PB; PBBP; PoPle; PPoe; PrIm; SeCePo; SeCeV; SoSe; SUS; SyP; TreFT; TrGrPo; UnPo; WiR

The Eagle. Andrew Young. He looks as though from his own wings/He hung down crucified. ELU; PoSH

The Eagle and the Beetle. Jean de La Fontaine. Conceal'd and dormant under ground. OBVE

The Eagle and the Mole. Elinor Wylie. And disembodied bones. AnFE; APA; AWP; BoLiVe; BoWoP; HBMV; LiTA; LiTM; MoAB; MoAmPo; PG; TreFT; UnPo; ViBoPo; WHA

The Eagle and Vulture. Thomas Buchanan Read. And for heroes like Winslow is shouting,/"Thank God!" PAH

The Eagle-Feather Fan.   N. Scott Momaday.   To the singing, to the drums. CDW; STE

The Eagle of Corinth.   Henry Howard Brownell.   And his thunderous wings be furled,/In the gaze of a gladdened world,/On the nation's loftiest dome PAH

Eagle of Pengwern.   *Anonymous.*   Trenn shall be called a shining town. PBWP

The Eagle of the Blue.   Herman Melville   The Eagle of the Blue.   AA

Eagle Plain.   Robert Francis.   Perhaps we do not altogether either/who cannot touch him.   AmFN

The Eagle's Fall.   Charles Goodrich Whiting.   Gathered exulting to insult your/Great eagle in his fall?   AA

The Eagle's Nature.   *Anonymous.*   Take to him thus the soul's food,/Through our Lord's own might.   MeEV

The Eagle's Song.   Richard Mansfield.   Now that the two are one again! HBV 1-2; HBVY; MC; PAH

Eagle Sonnets.   Clement Wood.
And the gulls tumble; and the homing ships/Peer for the harbor; and the sand drips.   HBMV
The heavens at last will end, as all things must–/To let new heavens ripple out of dust.   HBMV
Its silence sings a dusty song of dust.   HBMV
Know, man is sure of three, and never more.   HBMV
You are her shadow, she is where you are.   HBMV
You dread to learn you are remote from worth,–/And find you are her shadow on the earth.   HBMV

Eagle Squadron.   Vern Rutsala.   to the warm dashlight of home.   AMV-80

The Eagle Swift.   Adam of St. Victor.   God and His ark are onward rolled,/High above earth in heaven.   BePJ

The Eagle That Is Forgotten.   Vachel Lindsay.   To live in mankind, far, far more than...to live in/a name.   AmP; AnFE; APA; ATP; AWP; CMoP; HBV 1-2; LiTA; MoAB; MoAmPo; MoRP; NePA; NOBA; OxBA; ViBoPo; WHA

Eagle Valor, Chicken Mind.   Robinson Jeffers.   ...the bloody and/shabby/Pathos of the result.   ELU; LiTA; OBSP; OxBA; WaP

The Eagles.   Jones Very.   Where they who worshipped idol gods have been. TAP

Eagles.   Elizabeth Woody.   The eagle waves away/turning the earth/as an edge in the sky.   STE

Eagles and Isles.   Wilfrid Gibson.   My soul withdraws into itself, and seeks/The peaks and isles and eagles of the mind.   PoSH

Eagles on a Half.   Geechie Wiley.   I love you daddy/what you done it for BluL

Eagles Over the Lambing Paddock.   Ernest G. Moll.   And coolly then would flow through heart and brain/Respect for life again.   PoAu 1-2

Eaper Weaper.   *Anonymous.*   Up the chimbley he did shove her.   DBV; FaBoNo; OxBoLi

The Ear.   Louis MacNeice.   Follow the terrible drone of a cockchafer, or the bleak/Oracle of a barking dog.   OBSP

Ear Is Not Deaf.   Irene Dayton.   ...The ear/hear's time's cadence, her ontoward flight.   GoYe

The Ear-Maker and the Mould-Mender.   Jean de La Fontaine.   To have a pair of horns than lose his ears.   UnTE

Earl Bothwell.   *Anonymous.*   And through the Queene of Englands/good grace/Now in England shee doth remaine.   ESPB

Earl Brand.   *Anonymous.*
And I hope every couple that ever do love/May see more pleasure than they.   FSW
To a prize that was won by a slain brother's brand,/I' the brave nights so early. OxBB

Earl Brand (A vers.).   *Anonymous.*   Sae ald Carl Hood was not the dead o ane,/But he was the dead o hale seeventeen.   BaBo; ESPB

Earl Brand (B vers.).   *Anonymous.*   And there they tied a true lover's knot,/And the rose ran round the briar.   BaBo

Earl Brand; or, The Douglas Tragedy (A vers.).   *Anonymous.*   And when they could na farther gae,/They coost the lovers' knot.   FaBoBa; ViBoFo

Earl Brand; or, The Douglas Tragedy (B vers.) (excerpt).   *Anonymous.*   I wish myself in old Ireland/And you in the middle of the sea.   ViBoFo

Earl Brand (Sweet William).   *Anonymous.*   Sweet William died from the wounds that he received,/Fair Ellen died for sorrow.   AmFP

Earl Crawford.   *Anonymous.*   "An it be true that Lillie's dead,/The sun shall nae mair shine on me."   BaBo; ESPB

Earl Mar's Daughter.   *Anonymous.*   But they saw a flock o' pretty birds/That took their bride away.   BuBa; GN; HBV 1-2

Earl Mertoun's Song.   Robert Browning.   And by noontide as by midnight make her mine, as hers she/makes me!   HBV 1-2; OBEV; PoPle

The Earl O' Quarterdeck.   George MacDonald.   Into the heaven wi' pride? BeLS; EtS

The Earl of Aboyne.   *Anonymous.*   Until that he came to the yetts of Aboyne,/Where the corpse of his lady was lying.   BaBo; ESPB

The Earl of Errol.   *Anonymous.*   And the thing we ca the ranting o't,/The lady lies her lane.   ESPB

The Earl of Mar's Daughter.   *Anonymous*
As ye said, it shall be sae...   CH
He signd a bond o unity,/And visits now they pay. BaBo; ESPB

The Earl of Surrey to Geraldine.   Michael Drayton.   Till when, I leave thee to thy heart's desire–/By him that lives thy virtues to admire.   OBSC

The Earl of Westmoreland.   *Anonymous.*   If euer your Grace doe stand in neede,/Champion to your Highnesse again/I'le bee.'   ESPB

Earl Rothes.   *Anonymous.*   You and I will never meet again,/Till we meet at the bonny town o Torry.   BaBo; ESPB

The Earliest Christian Hymn.   Clement of Alexandria (Titus Flavius Clemens).   Unite, and swell the song,/To Christ the King!   BePJ; WGRP

Earliest Spring.   Denise Levertov.   ...Each pause/brings us to bells or flames. LCAP

Earliness at the Cape.   Babette Deutsch.   ...bladed/Like a shell, and as it opens, cuts.   FYAP; NePoAm-2; NYBP

Early.   Bruce Bennett.   spawned in a different sea.   WOLT

Early April.   Robert Frost.   And you're two months back in the middle of March.   YeAr

Early Arrival: Sydney.   Vivian Smith.   But here the huge hotels still sway in space/with the exactness of a foreign place.   NOAV

Early Bacon.   Archibald Stodart-Walker.   With the paper on my knee! CenHV

An Early Bluebird.   Maurice Thompson.   The hope that floods thy throat! AA

An Early Christian.   Robert Barnabas Brough.   Showing such weakness to a fallen foe?'   OBVV

Early Chronology.   Siegfried Sassoon.   I thought she had a pre-dynastic look.   GLGT

Early Copper.   Carl Sandburg.   In her eyes copper men living next to the earth for her sake.   HeIP

The Early Days.   Basil Dowling.   And their passionate hearts are quiet and cold/In the early, early days.   AnNZ

Early Death.   Hartley Coleridge.   But holy death is kinder?   GoTF; HBV 1-2; OBEV; TreFS

Early Discoveries.   David Malouf.   ...That night I eat them, boiled, with oil and vinegar.   CBAP

Early Dutch.   Jennie M. Palen.   Here I will drift through time like a lazy swimmer/and cities may pass me by.   GoYe

Early, Early Easter Day.   Aileen Fisher.   Early, early Easter Day.   SiSoSe

Early, Early in the Spring.   *Anonymous.*   Than be in a false woman's company.   OBET

Early Evening Quarrel.   Langston Hughes.   I wonder is there anywhere a/Do-right man?   HoPM; UnPo

Early Fall: The Adirondacks.   Carolyne Wright.   ...a light comign steadily/through an interstellar mist?   AMV-81

The Early Frogs.   Harry Edward Mills.   And love's channel way unclogs/In the croaking of the frogs.   PeD

An Early Illinois Winter.   Alex Kuo.   I repeat asking to myself/the question whose answer I know.   BrSi

Early in One Spring.   *Anonymous.*   Also the girls who break promises,/To marry a man for all his riches.   BFSS

Early in the Morning.   *Anonymous.*   Early in the morning!   AmSS

Early in the Morning.   Louis Simpson.   On the cold morning/Of a cold day. ConAP; LCAP; PPoe

Early in the Spring.   *Anonymous.*   And remember, love, I died for thee. AmFP

Early in the Springtime.   *Anonymous.*   As the stars shine bright in the sky. OBET

Early Influences.   Mark Akenside.   ...and fix'd the color of my mind/For every future year.   OBEC

Early January.   William Stanley Merwin.   A stranger to nothing/In our hiding places.   VGW

Early June.   R. P. Dickey.   a bit too much/because the car was hot.   TAT

Early Losses: A Requiem.   Alice Walker.   Her only treasure,/and never spent.   BlSi

Early Love.   Samuel Daniel.   What she would have me, yet not have me know.   ErPo

Early Lynching.   Carl Sandburg.   The slum man they killed, the mountain man lives on.   MoAmPo

Early Meadow-Rue.   Stanley Plumly.   going to work.   LCAP

Early Moon.   Carl Sandburg.   a silver papoose, in the Indian West? BPAW; LaNeLa; PG

Early Morn.   William Henry Davies.   As they would vanish for a dream. CH

The Early Morning.   Hilaire Belloc.   My brother, good morning: my sister, good night.   BoNaP; HBMV; HBVY; OBSP

Early Morning.   Morris Bishop.   "You lie."   PV

Early Morning.   Philip Dow.   ...lacking even/the body of a shadow/to share. DFF

Early Morning at Bargis.   Hermann Hagedorn.   O man, what fools are we/In prison-walls to dwell!   HBV 1-2

Early Morning Feed.   Peter Redgrove.   For the hunter, death, disaster.
  BoC

Early Morning Meadow Song.   Charles Dalmon.   And St. Mary's rings for
  mass!   ALV; HBMV

Early Morning of Another World.   Tom McKeown.   she will not know.
  AMV-80

Early Morning Woman.   Joy Harjo.   beginning with the woman/in the early
  morning   TWSS

Early News.   Anna Maria Pratt.   The news that dawn had come again.
  AA

Early Nightingale.   John Clare.   And soon the village brings the woodman's
  tale/Of having heard the new-come nightingale.   PBBP

Early One Morning.   *Anonymous.*   Always seeking for a girl that is new.
  FSW

Early One Morning.   Edward ("Edward Eastaway") Thomas.   I'm bound
  away for ever,/Away somewhere, away for ever.   MoVE

Early Pregnancy.   Penelope Shuttle.   Stormfree runner soon to rise/out of
  the ancient climate of the womb   BrRo

The Early Purges.   Seamus Heaney.   But on well-run farms pests have to be
  kept down.   NCSH

Early Rising.   John Godfrey Saxe.   The worm was punished, sir, for early
  rising!   AnNE; BLPL; HBV 1-2; InMe; PoLf

Early Spring.   Sidney Keyes.   And pain like a cat will come home to share
  your room.   MoBrPo

Early Spring.   Alfred, Lord Tennyson.   The blackbirds have their wills,/The
  poets too.   HBV 1-2; HBVY

An Early Start in Mid-Winter.   Robyn Sarah.   ...And zero floats you into
  morning.   CaPN

Early Summer Night.   Wen I-to.   Are you not shuddering, O most
  benevolent God in the/skies?   LiTW

Early Summer Sea-Tryst.   Frederick T. Macartney.   This exultation when I
  consummate/The passion of my body for the sea.   CBAP

Early Supper.   Barbara Howes.   And night is a dark tower.   DuDa; GoJo;
  GrPl; NCSH; PoPl; SM

Early Thoughts.   William Edward Hartpole Lecky.   The thoughts that we
  thought when young.   OnYI

Early Thoughts of Marriage.   Nathaniel Cotton.   If few those faults, you
  must not flout him.   OxBChV

Early Unfinished Sketch.   Austin Clarke.   "In the line she draws?"   ErPo

Early Waking.   Léonie Adams.   And fetterless high morning dip/Her two
  cold sandals in the stream.   LiTM; MoVE

Early Warning.   Shirley Marks.   And if it's by missile,/Forget about three.
  QQQ

Early Winter.   Weldon Kees.   I watch the snow, feel for the heartbeat that
  is not there.   NaP

Earlye, Earlye, in the Spring.   *Anonymous.*   For I'd rather be on the raging
  sea/As to be in a false love's company.   AmFP

The Earnest Liberal's Lament.   Ernest Hemingway.   What can I do/To set
  things right?   OBSV

Earning a Dinner.   Matthew Prior.   Full hardly earneth Mat. his dinner.
  NLV

Ears.   Sonja Akesson.   My god, what are ears for?   WPOW

Ears in the Turrets Hear.   Dylan Thomas.   Hold you poison or grapes?
  FaBoTw

Earth.   William Cullen Bryant.
  And Envy, watch the issue, while the lines,/By which thou shalt be judged,
    are written down.   AmePo; AP
  By which thou shalt be judged, are written down.   AmePo; AP

The Earth.   Ralph Waldo Emerson   Strikes never moon or star.   AA

The Earth.   Leonard Mann.   Food of the spirit, the soul's hive,/Home and
  haven of Holy Ghost?   BoAV

Earth.   Jim Tollerud.   Tools of the shaman/Medicine food.   VoR

The Earth.   Jones Very.   And from my bosom find a surer rest.   AmP;
  OxBA

Earth.   John Hall Wheelock.
  Intelligent beings must have been living there.   LiTM; PV; SoSe
  Wherein herself she doth declare/Through my lips, and say her prayer.
    AnFE; APA; HBMV; LiTA; MoAmPo; MoRP

Earth and Fire.   Wendell Berry.   ...I have risen up from her,/time and
  again, a new man.   FF; GP

Earth and Fire.   Vernon Watkins.   Whose heart on heaven is set.   NYBP

Earth and I Gave You Turquoise.   N. Scott Momaday.   You will hear the
  drumming hooves   CDW; PoPl; UnPo

The Earth and Man.   Stopford Augustus Brooke.   Have left it younger than
  a boy.   HBV 1-2; OnYI

Earth and Sky.   Euripides.   Old things are changed, and new revealed.
  EaLo

Earth and Sky.   Eleanor Farjeon.   How green your Tree grows there.
  PoSC; SUS

The Earth Asks and Receives Rain.   Phyllis Haring.   The worm which
  devours itself with the beak of a dead bird.   PeSA

Earth Buried.   Kenneth Mackenzie.   ...There's little nourishment in ashes.
  CBAP

Earth-Canonized.   Henry Morton Robinson.   Then striking boldly seaward,
  reach/The smooth-stoned slope of heaven's beach.   CAW

Earth Changes.   Kent Shire.   I took his face in my hands.   AMV-80

The Earth Cycle Dream.   Phillip Yellowhawk Minthorn.   he will let go
  STE

Earth Dweller.   William Stafford.   It is our only friend.   LCAP

Earth Felicities, Heavens Allowances. A Blank Poem.   Richard Steere.
  From Heav'n on Earth, to Heav'n in Heav'n ascend,/Where our felicities
  can know no/End.   SCAP

Earth Has Shrunk in the Wash.   William Empson.   And pump the valley
  with the tunnel dry.   CMoP

The Earth in Spring.   Judah Halevi.   Methinks sometimes she pales the/
  stars/That have in heaven their dwelling.   TrJP

Earth Is Enough.   Edwin Markham.   ...Ours the stuff sublime/To build
  Eternity in time!   GoTF; TreFS; TRV

The Earth, Late Choked with Showers.   Thomas Lodge.   I sad and pensive
  wholly.   EIl; ViBoPo

Earth Listens.   Katharine Lee Bates.   At last, at last Earth listens:/Peace!
  Good will!   PGD

Earth, My Likeness.   Walt Whitman.   I dare not tell it in words, not even in
  these songs.   NePA; OxBA

Earth out of Earth.   *Anomymous*   Thane shall erthe of erthe have a foulle
  stinke./Mors solvit omnia.   CBEP; MeEL

Earth Psalm.   Denise Levertov.   standing on end at echo even.   PPP

Earth's Answer.   William Blake.   That free Love with bondage bound.'
  CBEP; EnPE; InPS; NAWM 1-2; OAEL 1-2; PAI

Earth's Bondman.   Betty Page Dabney.   He wears Earth's livery still.
  GoYe

"Earth's Holocaust."   James Schuyler.   Starfish/have no sense of time, at all.
  ANYP

Earth's Night.   William Allingham.   And even thus the Soul's/Dark hours
  are made.   IrPN; TRV

Earth, Sky.   Sydney Clouts.   Till the sun came around.   PeSA

Earth Song.   Thomas Love Peacock.   our invisible tongues of silence/
  understand   VoR

The Earth-Spirit.   William Ellery Channing, II.   With the white frost, and
  leaf the brown trees tall.   AnNE

Earth Took of Earth.   *Anonymous.*   Then earth in earth had of earth its fill.
  HAP

Earth Trembles Waiting.   Blanche Shoemaker Wagstaff.   Earth trembles
  waiting/For the sun again...   PoLf

Earth Tremor in Lugano.   James Kirkup.   And staring up at the house
  that/wears/Telephone wires like a shawl.   NYBP

Earth-Visitors.   Kenneth Slessor.   "Your name, child?'/A thousand birds
  cry 'Venus.!"   BoAV

Earth Walk.   William Meredith.   I'll meet a trooper with a soft, wide hat/
  who will take away my Earth-rocks and debrief me.   MAT

The Earth Will Stay the Same.   Frank Ernest Hill.   Who made his bed for
  years beneath the stars.   AnAmPo

The Earth Worm.   Denise Levertov.   ...aerates/the ground of his living.
  NOBA

Earthborn.   Peter McArthur.   To the uncharted ports of summer dream.
  CaP

Earthly.   Ian Wedde.
  ...hello'ing/them & howling them & hallowing them.   OCNZ
  My fumbling voices clap their hands & shout.   OCNZ
  ...time's/careless nebula of blossom/   OCNZ

Earthly Love.   Joseph Bennett.   Frangible, a honeycomb of pores.   NePA

The Earthly Paradise.   William Morris.
  And all thy thousand peaceful happy words.   ViBoPo
  That through the hall bemocked the lost year's/wrong!   VLP
  ...they made a little mirth/Until the great moon rose upon the earth.   VLP
  Whose ravening monsters mighty men shall/slay,/Not the poor singer of an
    empty day.   CoBE; LiTB; LoBV; NoP; OAEL 1-2; ViBoPo; VLP
  The world had quite forgotten it must die.   EG; VLP

The Earthquake.   *Anonymous.*   Destroy thy children:/Thy valuable
  children,/Thy valuable children.   WTO

Earthquake.   R.A.D. Ford.   The blast with her too late warning/And
  testimony of love.   NOBC

Earthy Anecdote.   Wallace Stevens.   Later, the firecat closed his bright eyes/
  And slept.   CMoP; GoJo; RFM

Ease It to Me Blues.   Barbecue Bob Hicks.   I'm gonna kill every body/ever
  treat me mean   BluL

Easier.   James Harrison.   works of William Shakespeare?/Probably.
  AMV-80

The Easiest Way.   *Anonymous.*   Will take you down the easiest way to
  Hades.   UnTE

Easily onward, thorough flowers and weed...   John Keats.   Easily onward,
  thorough flowers and weed....   CoBE

East Anglian Bathe.   Sir John Betjeman.   And your warm freshwater ripples, Horsey Mere.   NoP; SD

East Bronx.   David Ignatow.   always alone and always/the sun shining.   ConAP

East Coast–Canada.   Elizabeth Brewster.   There is the sea. Space. The wind blowing.   CaP

East Coast Journey.   James Keir Baxter.   With teeth of obsidian and hair like kelp/Flashing and glimmering at the edge of the horizon.   NoP

East Coast Lullaby.   Lady Anne Lindsay.   Lullaby and lullaloo; sleep, lammie, noo.   EtS

East Coker.   Thomas Stearns Eliot.   ...In my end is my beginning.   ChMP; MoVE; NePA; PPP; VGW

East Hampton: The Structure of Sound.   Philip Appleman.   as the dawn comes up like thunder/out of Brooklyn, the shaper of sunrise.   NYP

East London.   Matthew Arnold.   Thou mak'st the heaven thou hop'st indeed/thy home.   OAEP; WGRP

East River (New York).   Rosemary Thomas.   Stagger for stagger,/Star for star.   AmFN

East St. Louis Blues.   Anonymous.   Well, every time I looked, babe,/She'd be on my mind.   AmFP

East Texas.   Leon Stokesbury.   ...She shook/Me saying I was talking in my sleep.   SM

East Virginia.   Anonymous.
All in gold, sir, all in gold.   OuSiCo
And to know you'll never be mine.   FSW

The East Wind.   George Cabot Lodge.   The passion of mine own infinity.   AmePo

Easter.   Elizabeth Jane Coatsworth.   Be still and listen/To your heart,/And hear it beating merrily!   YeAr

Easter.   Mary Carolyn Davies.   As brave as you and as gay!   OHIP

Easter.   George Herbert.
And make up our defects with His sweet art.   TrCP
And then this day my life shall date.   BoC; OBEV; TRV
There is but one, and that one ever.   AtBAP; FaBoCh; LoGBV; NOBE; OBS; OHIP; SeCV 1-2; TrGrPo

Easter.   Joyce Kilmer.   The happy earth looks at the sky/And sings.   SoPo; TiPo

Easter.   Howard Nemerov.   ...as the long war/Begins again, not by our doing or desiring.   NoP

Easter.   Frank O'Hara.   ...pelted by the shit of the stars at last in flood/like a breath.   EAS

Easter.   Edwin L. Sabin.   Behold, how God each April gives/The miracle of Spring.   OHIP; PoSC

Easter.   C. H. Sisson.   Where no one ever came voluntarily before.   OBSP

Easter.   Robert Whitaker.   In the full sun-burst of Eternity!   PGD

Easter, 1916.   William Butler Yeats.   A terrible beauty is born.   BrPo; CABA; CMoP; CoBMV; DiPo; FaBoMo; FaBoPV; FaPoR; HAP; InPS; LiTM; MBW 1-2; MoAB; NAWM 1-2; NIP; NoAm; NOBE; NOBI; NoP; OAEL 1-2; OBWP; OxBI; OxBTC; PAI; PPoe; PPP; SeCeV

Easter,1923.   John G. Neihardt.   And only men forget!   AnAmPo; HBMV

Easter Beatitudes.   Clarence M. Burkholder.   Where the Lord and our loved ones wait.   BLRP

The Easter Bunny Blues; or, All I Want for Xmas Is the Loop.   Ebon.   and placed/above the sun.   PoBA

An Easter Canticle.   Charles Hanson Towne.   Green April is Thy very soul,/Thou great Lord God.   OHIP; TrPWD

Easter Carol.   George Newell Lovejoy.   And Christ is risen to-day!   OHIP; PGD

An Easter Carol.   Christina Georgina Rossetti.   ...this is the time of loves.   OHIP

Easter Communion.   Gerard Manley Hopkins.   Lo, God shall strengthen all the feeble knees.   BrPo; OFD

Easter Day I.   Arthur Hugh Clough.   Christ is not risen.   OAEP; VLP

Easter Day II.   Arthur Hugh Clough.   Christ is yet risen.   OAEP; PGD; VLP

Easter, Day of Christ Eternal.   Maurice Moore.   Matchless Christ, Oh, wondrous story.   STF

Easter Egg.   Alan Kieffaber.   Then hatched/And lives!   AMV-80

Easter Eve.   James Branch Cabell.   "Forgive them, for they know not what they do."   HBMV

Easter Eve 1945.   Muriel Rukeyser.   What fire survive forever/myself is for my time.   MiAP; NePA; VGW

Easter Flood.   Brenda S. Stockwell.   astonished/at the implications of the stone.   AMV-81

An Easter Garland.   Carol Rumens.   would not be far wrong/if I took you for the gardener.   FaBoWP

Easter Hymn.   Alfred Edward Housman.   Bow hither out of heaven and see and save.   CABA; EaLo; EBEV; MoAB; OAEP; OFD; SeCeV

Easter Hymn.   Saint John of Damascus.
Hail, with His triumphant band.   CAW
With thyself upraise me to the skies. BePJ

An Easter Hymn.   Richard Le Gallienne.   Teach us to say: "I will arise."   OHIP

Easter Hymn.   Michael Thwaites.   Whose love home to our Father's house shall win us.   MoRP

Easter Hymn.   Henry Vaughan.   To him be glory, power, praise,/From this, unto the last of days.   EBCP; PoPle

Easter Hymn.   Charles Wesley.   Where thy victory, O Grave?   OHIP; TRV

Easter in the Woods.   Frances Frost.   and gaze on earth with shy glad eyes.   BrR; SiSoSe

Easter Island.   Frederick George Scott.   Looking towards heaven, yet seeing no more than they.   OBCV

Easter Joy.   Nancy Byrd Turner.   Easter is back in the beautiful world–/Sing, everyone, sing!   YeAr

Easter Monday.   Michael McFee.   carnation: my Lord and my God.   AMV-80

Easter Monday.   Christina Georgina Rossetti.   Let us wax on and wane.   NOCV

Easter Morn.   Giles the Younger Fletcher.   There would ye all await, and humble homage do.   EIL; NOCV

Easter Morning.   Archie Randolph Ammons.   ...fresh as this particular/flood of burn breaking across us now/from the sun.   HaCAP; NoP

Easter Night.   Alice Meynell.   He rose again behind the stone.   BrRo; OHIP

Easter Parade.   Marchette Chute.   Who are as beautiful as me.   BrR; SiSoSe

Easter Poem.   Kathleen Raine.   But man, oh Lord, how thin you've grown.   LiTB

Easter Snowfall.   Harry Behn.   And sparkly egg the bunnies bring/At Easter with the world inside!   TiPo

Easter Song.   Leo Alishan.   ...With thy love/Water and cheer this sorrowing heart of mine!   CAW

An Easter Song.   Anonymous.   Grante us, Crist,/With thyn uprist/To gone.   OxBM

An Easter Song.   Susan (Sarah Chauncey Woolsey) Coolidge.   Earth's saddest day and gladdest day,/Were just three days apart!   TRV

Easter Song.   Mary Artemisia ("Aunt Mary") Lathbury.   How He rose, the Lord of glory.   OHIP

Easter Song.   Kenneth Leslie.   Softly ring, He comes to rest/In the quiet of my breast.   MoRP

The Easter Song.   Caelius Sedulius.
And all the sands where all the oceans flow!   OnYI
He orders that we keep immaculate. OnYI
...the Tempest springs/In joy away on softly wafting wings. OnYI
...'tis no mother's breast/Upon the cold lips of thy child thou'st prest! OnYI

Easter Sunday, 1945.   Giuseppe Antonio Borgese.   So let me step westward; my shadow/is long.   NePoAm

Easter Thought.   Leo Cox.   But the hedgerows renew their green breath/When taken each winter by death.   CaP

Easter Week.   Anonymous.   In Pearse and Plunkett's graves./GOD SAVE IRELAND.   OnYI

Easter Week.   Charles Kingsley.   Like the birds who build and sing.   OHIP

Easter Wings.   George Herbert.   Affliction shall advance the flight in me.   ATP; ExPo; HAP; HeIP; InPK; InPS; LiTB; MeLP; MePo; NIP; NoP; OAEL 1-2; OAEP; OBS; PAI; PoEL 1-5; PP; PPP; SeCP; TEP; TrCP

Easter Zunday.   William Barnes.   He meade the maidens squeal an' run,/Because 'twer Easter Zunday.   VLP

Eastern Serenade.   Sir Theodore and Aytoun, William E. Martin. Theodore   With thee, my adored one! my own attar-gul!   InMe

Eastern Tempest.   Edmund Charles Blunden.   Of wisdom infinitely calm.   MoBrPo

Eastertide.   Anonymous.   And we'll come no more pace-egging/Until the next year.   OxNR

Eastside Chick with Drive.   Albert Spector.   Last I heard, she went to a college upstate.   CTBA

Eastside Incidents.   Gregory Corso.   I see them now/but they aren't there.   GP; NYP

Eastward I Stand, Mercies I Beg.   Anonymous.   that they may upset the words which have been spoken.   EaLo

Eastward to Eden.   Edgar Bogardus.   Cut square and thin in a bowl of ice water.   PoL

Easy as a Bat.   Anonymous.   Take her in a ditch/Easy as a bat.   WTO

An Easy Decision.   Kenneth Patchen.   I invited them home   CTBA; LOW

Easy Does It.   Henry Chapin.   I slowed me down.   FAZ

An Easy Poem.   Terry Kennedy.   so help me God!   AMV-80

Easy Rider.   Anonymous.   Well, it's hey, hey, hey, hey, hey.   FSW

Easy Rider Blues.   Blind Lemon Jefferson.   You turn your back to quit me: woman, and you don't know how   BluL

Easy to Grow.   John Giorno.   Easy to grow.   ANYP

Eat and Walk.   James Norman Hall.   The rule of the place is Eat and Walk.   BLPA

Eat 'Em Up Smith Tells All in South Africa.   Judith Johnson Sherwin.   ...with a/halflike like that the action/will last one lifetime   NoAm

Eat with Care. *Anonymous.* Fish-bones choke us. FaBoUs

The 'Eathen. Rudyard Kipling. Mind you keep your rifle an' yourself jus' so! OxBTC

Eating. Reginald Gibbons. and sleeping, all night long, they were hungry. MAYP

Eating Bamboo-Shoots. Po Chu-i. For each breath of the south-wind makes a new bamboo! OBVE

Eating Fish. George Johnston. Choose the squirming sea. WHW

Eating Lechon, with my Brothers and Sisters. Luis Cabalquinto. I feel at peace: tonight at least, content. BrSi

Eating Poetry. Mark Strand. I romp with joy in the bookish dark. GrPl; MAT; NoAm; PPP; TAP

L'Eau Dormante. Thomas Bailey Aldrich. For Lydia will be seventeen. HBV 1-2

Eau-Forte. Frank Stewart Flint. Their clattering feet-/their clattering feet!/ to the slaughterhouse. OxBTC

Ebb. John Lyle Donaghy. but the dust sinks/like loosened pearl/in a tide softly. NeIP

Ebb and Flow. George William Curtis. It said-"Dream on!" and "Dream no/more!" AA; HBV 1-2

The Ebb and Flow. Edward Taylor. Away mine ashes, then Thy fire doth/ glow. AmP; AmPP; AnNE; AP; SCAP

Ebb Tide. Marjorie Pickthall. Borne from the fight and the full endeavour/ On an ebb tide. CaP

The Ebb Tide. Robert Southey. Alas! how hurryingly the ebbing years/ Then hasten to old age! OBNC

Ebbe Skammelson. *Anonymous.* Sour is the wine, and harsh the mead,/ Where such sad news is told. BaBo

Ebbtide at Sundown. Michael (Katherine Bradley and Edith Cooper) Field. Closed in beating heart we could not be/To the sunk sun, the far, surrendered sea. CAW

The Ebenezer. *Anonymous.* Oh, git along, boys, git along, do,/Be handy, boys, be handy! ShS

Ecce Homo. Witter ("Emanuel Morgan") Bynner. But the god who climbs, is I. WGRP

Ecce Homo. David Gascoyne. That man's long journey through the night/ May not have been in vain. ChMP; LiTM; NeBP; OBWP

Ecce Homunculus. R. A. K. Mason. :while he was passed/by even the worst of men at least sour wine. AnNZ

Ecce in Deserto. Henry Augustin Beers. Will keep the promise too. AA; AnFE; APA

Ecce Puer. James Joyce. Forgive your son! BIrV; EBEV; NAs; NoAm; PoPl; TrCP

Ecce Quomodo Moritur Justus. Diogenes Laertius. And, with that observation, died. LiTW

The Eccho. Richard Leigh. Which Nymphs with Scorn repay,/More deaf, more hard, than they. MePo

The Ecclesiast. John Ashbery. We are together at last, though far apart. ANYP

Ecclesiastes. Morris Bishop. Whose heart is snares and nets,/And whose hands are bands.' HBMV

Ecclesiastes. Gilbert Keith Chesterton. The rest is vanity of vanities. MoBrPo; OBSP

Ecclesiastes. Joseph Langland. It was not love but fear that made him tame. NePoEA; PoPl

Ecclesiastes. Derek Mahon. ...stand on a corner stiff/with rhetoric, promising nothing under the sun. BIrV; CIP

An Ecclesiastical Chronicle (excerpt). John Heath-Stubbs. From our contemporary Dr.—, of —. NOBL

Ech, Sic a Pairish. *Anonymous.* They Pu'd down the steeple, and drunkit the bell. FaBoCo; FiBHP

Eche Man Me Telleth I Chaunge Moost My Devise. Sir Thomas Wyatt. But alwaies oon, your owne boeth ferme and stable. AAS

Echo. Walter De la Mare. In the silence, "Who cares/ Who cares?"/ Wailed to and fro. MoVE; OBMV; SeCeV

Echo. Pamela Grey, Viscountess Grey of Falloden. "Air..." CH

Echo. Elizabeth Stanton Hardy. The echo waits, the years close in. GoYe

Echo. Thomas Moore. Is by that one, that only dear,/Breath'd back again. ELP; GoBC; OxBI

Echo. Christina Georgina Rossetti. As long ago, my love, how long ago. BoLoP; CH; ELP; GBL; LiTL; LoBV; NIP; NOBE; NOBV; NoP; OAEL 1-2; OBNC; PoEL 1-5; SeCeV; ViBoPo

Echo. John Godfrey Saxe. Quoth Echo (sotto voce),-"Take her!" AnNE

Echo. Mildred Weston. As good as most. BoNaP

Echo Canyon. *Anonymous.* While the judgments of God sweep the wicked away. AmFP

Echo in a Church. Edward, Lord Herbert of Cherbury. Echo I am. AnAnS 2

Echo of Mandela. Zindzi Mandela. the people are calling/South Africa, are you listening? WhB

Echo Poem. M. Allan. It's guilt! FiBHP

Echo to a Rock. Edward, Lord Herbert of Cherbury. Thou art my Monument, and this my last farewell./Echo Well. AtBAP; PoEL 1-5

Echoes. William Ernest Henley. When I was a King in Babylon/And you were a Virgin Slave. BLPA; BLPL; GoTF; LoBV; TreF

Echoes. Emma Lazarus. Misprize thou not these echoes that belong/To one in love with solitude and song. SBG

Echoes from the Sabine Farm. Eugene Field. The cooling brooks that from thy nooks/Singing and dancing go. AA

Echoes from Theocritus. Edward Cracroft Lefroy.
And leap, and dive, and see the tunnies swim. OBVV
Peace by the way, and port of noble fame! OBVV
With friends, who make his tomb their loving care. OBVV

Echoes of Childhood. Alice Corbin. Of the banjo and the fiddle/And the plaintive Negro croon.) PoNe

Echoes of Love's House. William Morris. "And is my praise nought worth for all my life undone?" GTBS

Echoes of Wheels. Furnley Maurice. Swallowed along the hidden road/ Turning among the trees! NOAV

The Echoing Cliff. Andrew Young. Are filled with sea-birds and their cries. PoSH

The Echoing Green. William Blake. And sport no more seen/On the darkening Green. CBEP; OBEC; UnPo; WiR

Eclipse. William Carson Fagg. It hurts to explain the reason/Grandma didn't snore. LFAC

Eclipse. Anita Endrezze Probst. Once you said it was in my eyes. CDW

Eclipse. Amir Rashidd. I touched her hand and she/disintegrated. NBP

Eclipse. Ed Roberson. and brilliant obscuring of the hole. PoNe

Eclipse. Tomaz Salamun. Every drawer I will paint a different color. VWA

Eclipse. F.R. Scott. He put on dark glasses. WHW

Eclipse. Timothy Sheehan. and the invisible stars. SUW

The Eclipse. Henry Vaughan. But O Thy grief, Thy grief, doth kill! HBV 1-2; OBSP

The Eclipse of Faith. Theodore Dwight Woolsey. And faith forbid to burn. AA

Eclipses. Nancy Sullivan. that old movie, your lives, while/mumbling here in the sun? TAP

The Ecliptic: Cancer, or, The Crab (excerpt). Joseph Gordon ("Adam Drinan") Macleod. Is there nothing more soluble, more gaseous, more imper-/ceptible?/Nothing. NeBP

Eclogue. William Barnes.
Or I must goo to workhouse, I do fear. VLP
Why then we sartainly must starve. Good night! NBM

Eclogue. David Bergman. splashing about in the blue exhaust? AMV-80

Eclogue. John Davidson. He is an artist, not an artisan. BrPo

Eclogue. William Diaper. And all lies wrapt in silence, and unactive ease. SeCePo

Eclogue. Michael Drayton. We shepherds will adore/Her setting and her rise. OBSC

Eclogue. Edward Lear. And time restores a world of happier hours. FaBoNo

Eclogue. Frederic Prokosch. A cry; a living sleep. ViBoPo

Eclogue. Virgil (Publius Vergilius Maro). Hard old oaks drip honey. PoPl

Eclogue between the Motherless. Louis MacNeice. Waiting for the last collection before dark/The pillarbox like an exclamation mark. FaBoIP

An Eclogue for Christmas. Louis MacNeice. They say, interpret it your own way, Christ is born. FaBoMo; MoPo; MoVE; NoAm; OBMV

Eclogue IV. The Poet (excerpt). Charles Jenner. I'll stray no more to seek the vagrant muse/But ev'n go write at home, and save my shoes. NOEC

Eclogues. Dennis Schmitz. the fire rubs/itself for warmth & the windows/ go white with frost. NPGG

Eclogues. Virgil (Publius Vergilius Maro).
And deeper grow the shadows of the hills. AWP
And find a friend at court, I'll find a voice. AWP
The God with meate hath not Thy hunger fed,/Nor goddesse laid thee in a little bed. OBVE
He comes, he runs, he leaps to my desiring arms. EiCP
No god shall crown the board, nor goddess bless the bed. AWP
Young Corydon without a rival reigns. AWP

Eco Right. Walt Gavenda. 'Cause wormy apples are organic. QQQ

Ecole St. Luc. Ray Fraser. and that's still a distressing sight NeAC

Ecological Lecture. Burton Raffel. And next, the cow. AMV-81

Economics. Mona Van Duyn. Christ, what are poems for? SM

The Ecstasy. Al-Hallaj. Thou art these tears-wilt flow from my lids away/ from me? ILwL

Ecstasy. *Anonymous.* And I'd praise God in his bright abode. AmFP

The Ecstasy. John Donne. Small change when we are to bodies gone. ATP; BoLoP; CABA; DiPo; EnRePo; ExPo; FPL; HAP; InPS; JCP; LiTB; LoBV; NOBE; NoP; OAEL 1-2; OBEV; PAI; PPoe; PrIm; TEP; TrGrPo; UnTE; ViBoPo

Ecstasy. Duncan Campbell Scott. Sing there! Sing there! CaP

Eerily Sweet. Elizabeth Jane Coatsworth. The proud cocks crow. ChBR

The Effect of Example. John Keble. Lest in that world their cry/Of woe thou hear. HBV 1-2; HBVY

The Effect of Snow. Robert Finch. Eluding every word I would fit it to. ACV

Effectively coming through slaughter. Judith Fitzgerald. because I was flesh/I was my worst fear CaPN

Effendi. Michael S. Harper. and is pure, new, even lovely/and is you. CNA; PoBA

Effervescence and Evanescence. Keith Preston. And flop to something flipper. OBAL

Efficiency Apartment. Gerald William Barrax. Dennis Jerry Josh PoBA

Effie. Sterling A. Brown. And that is the Paradise crowning her days. BANP

The Effigy. Guido Cavalcanti. And draw away with me your every thought. LiTW

Effigy. Georgia Lee McElhaney. to the Valley of the Kings. CoPo

Effort at Speech. William Meredith. Hatred and guilt have left us without language/who might have held discourse. NYP; Prf; SM; WeW

Effort at Speech between Two People. Muriel Rukeyser. Everyone silent, moving....Take my hand. Speak to me. FYAP; MoAB; MoAmPo; MP; TrGrPo; TrJP; TwCP; WeW

Effortlessly Democratic Santa Fe Trail. Martha Baird. And sunflowers grew up on both sides of it:/Blessing it. PoPl

Egan O Rahilly. James Stephens. Who once said all his say, when he was young! CBEP; EBEV; NoAm; OBMV; SeCePo

The Egg. George Bowering. ...as if I had brought/those tender stinking wings to earth. NeAC

The Egg. Clarence Day. Oh, join me gentlemen, I beg,/In honoring our friend, the egg. NLV

Egg. Jay MacPherson. Let be, or else consume me quite. WHW

Egg-and-Dart. Robert Finch. Then the droll recommencement of the search. OBCV

The Egg and the Machine. Robert Frost. The next machine that has the power to pass/Will get this plasm in its goggle glass. CABA; MoAmPo

The Egg Boiler. Gwendolyn Brooks. You watch us, eat your egg, and laugh aloud. PoBA

The Egg of Nothing. John Taylor. A fall, no flight. AMV-81

Eggomania. Felicia Lamport. It's also the only reliable/Device for producing a chicken. NLV

The Eggplants Have Pins and Needles. Novella Matveyeva. And the rooster's faint shadow/Smells distinctly of the cold. WPOW

Eggs. Herbert Asquith. If those eggs began to sing! BrR

The Eggs. Peter Redgrove. High up in the clear butter of her mother floated). NAs

Eggs and Marrowbone. *Anonymous.* So if you want to do him in,/You must sneak up behind. FSW

Egloge V (excerpt). Alexander Barclay. Worke we despise which bringeth advauntage. EnPo

Egnatius, Because His Teeth Are White. Caius Valerius Catullus. ...Those white teeth only show/How much you've swallowed from your chamber pot. DBV

Ego. Philip Booth. I used to get all revved up. MP; TwCP

Ego. Norman MacCaig. Destroy the evidence to keep them secret still. GTBS-P

Ego. Robert Siegel. ...glistening snout/ready to shove up the privates of the world. PoA

Ego Dominus Tuus. William Butler Yeats. Their momentary cries before it is dawn/Would carry it away to blasphemous men. CMoP

Ego's Dream. Alfred Kreymborg. That little brown ball, the earth? MAPA

Ego Sum. Gelett Burgess. Your hobby is you. InMe

Ego Tripping. Nikki Giovanni. I mean...I...can fly/like a bird in the sky... NoAm; Psk

Egocentric. Stevie Smith. What care I if good God be/If he be not good to me? FaBoNo

Egoism. W. Craddle. Will smack their lips and cry "Delicious!" FiBHP

Egoisme a Deux. Louisa S. Bevington. Was it divine? NOBV

The Egoist Dead. Elizabeth Brewster. Finds a neat and compact space/In the hollow of his hand. CaP

Egotism. Edward Sandford Martin. For I am he, and he is I. AA

The Egotist. H. A. C. Evans. Into a vast, reverberating void. PoL

Egrets. Max Eastman. But give the wild will never. AnEnPo

Egrets. Judith Wright. and, whiter yet, those egrets wading. GoJo; NCSH

Egypt. Hilda ("H. D.") Doolittle. Hellas re-born from death. HBMV

Egypt's Might is Tumbled Down. Mary Elizabeth Coleridge. These remain. CH

Egyptian Dancer. Terence Tiller. a last groan of the drum, panting she drops/into the darkness of past love. OBTV

Egyptian Hieroglyphics. *Anonymous.*
And my heart grieves no longer. BoWoP

I offer him the magic of my thighs/He is caught in the spell. BoWoP

If they roam towards me/I enter into life. BoWoP

Let us go up and embrace him/And keep him here all day long. BoWoP

Like this, to the end of eternity. BoWoP

Since I have lain with you/you have lifted my heart high. BoWoP

The Egyptian Lotus. Arthur Wentworth Hamilton Eaton. The old world worshipped thee, O Lotus/flower/Then carved its sphinx and reared its pyramid. AA

An Egyptian Passage. Theodore Weiss. ...fumbled/for her coat and bag, and lurched out. CoPo; TAP

An Egyptian Pulled Glass Bottle in the Shape of a Fish. Marianne Moore. Whose scales turn aside the sun's sword with their polish. PBWP

Egyptian Serenade. George William Curtis. Will it seem the song you sung/When we were together young. HBV 1-2

An Egyptian Tomb. William Lisle Bowles. And the streets ringing to the stir of life. OBTV

Eheu Fugaces. Richard Harris Barham. Sighing I murmur, "O mihi praeteritos!" FaBoEE; NBM; OxBoLi

Eichmann. Douglas Blazek. stare at him as if/he were the universe. LTB

Eidolons. Walt Whitman. A round full-orb'd eidolon. AmePo

Eight Aspects of Melissa. Lawrence Durrell. And yet not envying them their childhood/Since he endured his own? NeBP

The Eight-Day Clock. Alfred Cochrane. Wrought by this pendulum that swings/Sedately to and fro. HBV 1-2

Eight Lines for a Script Girl. George Jonas. I'll know you even less. NeAC

Eight Miles South of Grand Haven. Dave Kelly. that this is an ocean because there isn't any land on any/other side. AMV-80

Eight O'Clock. Alfred Edward Housman. And then the clock collected in the tower/Its strength, and struck. BrPo; CABA; CMoP; ExPo; InPK; InPo; LoBV; MoAB; MoBrPo; NoAm; NoP; OBSP; SoSe; TrGrPo

Eight O'Clock. Christina Georgina Rossetti. And three for dear Mamma. TiPo

Eight O'Clock Bells. *Anonymous.* Then he gave me sixpence/To kiss him on the stairs. PoPle

Eight Oars and a Coxswain. Arthur Guiterman. Steady! Pull it thro-o-o-ough! SD

Eight Sandbars on the Takano River. Gary Snyder. twelve-foot/pine pole/lightly,/on her head. CoPo

Eight Volunteers. Lansing C. Bailey. Eight men! Who speaks? PAH

Eighteen. Maria Banus. I am eighteen. BoWoP; VWA

Eighteen. Sister Mary Honora. ...this joy/between our daughter and the neighbor boy. NePoAm-2

Eighteen-Forty-Three. *Anonymous.* The Kirk without the people. FaBoCo

Eighteen-Ninety. E. Richard Shipp. "Think I'll roll in,/good-night, boys, and.../well...Damn the Sheep!" PoOW

Eighteen-Seventy. Arthur Rimbaud.
He sleeps. In his right side are two red holes. OBWP

her great sou knotted in a handkerchief. OBWP

men of the Second Empire, I mean you! FaBoPV; OBWP

presents a blue and scarlet ass–to what? OBWP

soirees at Saint Cloud...a bluish vapour. FaBoPV; OBWP

Eighteen Verse Sung to a Tatar Reed Whistle. Ts'ai Yen. How I hate to live this way! BoWoP; WPOW

Eighteen Verses Sing to a Tatar Reed Whistle. Ts'ai Yen. But no onle knows my agony and grief. BoWoP; PBWP; WPOW

Eighteen Verses Sung to a Tartar Reed Whistle. Ts'ai Yen. Ill broken, heart broken, I sing to myself. BoWoP; PBWP; WPOW

Eighteen Verses Sung to a Tatar Reed Whistle. Ts'ai Yen.
I try to strangle my sobs/But my tears stream down my face. WPOW
...sorrow for my sons/At the first notes pierces my heart's core. WPOW

The Eighteenth Song. Hadewijch. How my heart would never yield/To me the joy I long to feel. LiTW

Eighth Air Force. Randall Jarrell. I find no fault in this just man. FF; MiAP; MoVE; NoAm; NOBA; NoP; OBWP; PoCh; SM

The Eighth Sonnet. Sir Philip Sidney. With what she had done and spoken,/That therewith my song is broken. OAEP

Eighth Street West. Rachel Field. Smelling each Christmas smell. ChBR; SiSoSe

The Eighties Becoming. Bob Rosenthal. just for the right to crawl after my children. APU

Eileen Aroon. Gerald Griffin. Truth is a fixed star,/Eileen aroon! AnIV; GoBC; HBV 1-2; OBEV; OBVV

Eileen Aroon. Carrol O'Daly. O welcomes forever here!/Eivlin a ruin! OnYI

Eine Kleine Snailmusik. May Sarton. Who prefers to live/Glissandissimo,/Pianissimo. NLV

Einstein. Archibald MacLeish. Which seems to keep/Something inviolate. A living something. AnFE; APA; MoPo

Einstein (1929). Archibald MacLeish. Solve them to unity. ImOP

Einstein's Father. Daniel L. Klauck. who lacks the imagination to be cautious/lacks the ignorance to be afraid LTB

Eire. William Drennan. Rise–Arch of the Ocean, and Queen of the West! OnYI

Eire. David O'Bruadair. Her placket no longer open to the Saxon. BIrV

Eisenhower's Visit to Franco, 1959. James Wright.
Clean new bombers from America muffle their engines/and glide down now. NMP
Of bare fields,/In Spain. CAPP; NaP

The Ejected Wife. Anonymous. Present pain never come to an end. OBVE

El-A-Noy. Anonymous. And rise to wealth and honor,/In the State of El-a-noy. TrAS

El-A-Noy (with music). Anonymous. And cross at Shawnee ferry/To the State of El-a-noy. AS

El Alamein Revisited. Roy MacNab. ...only the sand and wind forget to die. PeSA

El Blot Til Lyst. William Morton Payne. That mark thee now but pander to the/crowd! AA

El Camino Verde. Paul Blackburn. the/reaches/of Africa where an actual/measure/exists. CoPo

El Capitan-General. Charles Godfrey Leland. Even two like Don Alonzo Estaban San/Salvador. AA; HBV 1-2; YaD

El Dorado. Richard Ryan. drift slowly away. BIrV

El Emplazado. William Henry Venable. Heaven reechoes the auto-da-fe. PAH

El Greco. E. L. Mayo. Why does no light come through as those doors close? HoPM; MiAP

El Greco: Espolio. Earle Birney. to return to this peace before the nails are hammered PeCV

El Gusano. Irving Layton. Carry its political news/to Castile and to Aragon. PeCV

El-Hajj Malik El-Shabazz (Malcolm X). Robert Earl Hayden. ...became/much more than there was time for him to be. CNA; PoBA

El Hombre. William Carlos Williams. toward which you lend no part! CABA; CMoP; LiTA

El Ropero. Antonio de Montoro. Now thou, too, mayst persecute/Those poor wretches, like a brute. TrJP

El Sueno de la Razon. Jane Cooper. Poor furious girl, our voices sound/alike (your nurse told me), discreet and gentle. FaBoWP

El Vaquero. Lucius Harwood Foote. Greek of the Greeks he must remain. AA

The Elaboration. Bill Manhire. and I shall not come to it OCNZ

The Elder Edda: Part of the Lay of Sigrdrifa. Anonymous. Strong trouble ariseth now already. OBVE

The Elder Edda: The Beginning and the End (abridged). Anonymous. The bodies of men on his wings he bears,/The serpent bright: but now must I sink. LiTW

The Elder Edda: The First Lay of Gudrun. Anonymous. Amid wind-swept wood/Now when dead he lieth.' OBVE

The Elder Edda: The Short Lay of Sigurd (excerpt). Anonymous. Naught but truth have I told–/–And now make I ending.' OBVE

The Elder, or Bourtree. Anonymous. Since our Lord was nail'd t' ye. GBP

An Elder's Reproof to His Wife. Abdillaahi Muuse. On one of these three I am resolved: make your choice! TTY; WTO

Elder Tree. Conrad Aiken. Come back again from blood; and they are strong.' AP

Elderberry Flute Song. Peter Blue Cloud. and thus were born/the vast multitudes/from the song/of a flute. STE

The Elderly Gentleman. George Canning. And in plumped this son of a woman to follow his wig, cane,/and hat. NA

Eldorado. Edgar Allan Poe. "If you seek for Eldorado!" AP; APA; AWP; FaBoBe; FaBoCh; FPL; HBV 1-2; InPo; LaNeLa; LoGBV; NePA; NOBA; NoP; OxBA; TAP; WiR

Eleanor Rigby. The Beatles. All the lonely people, where do they all belong? InPK; PAI; PPoe; PrIm; WTO

Eleazar Wheelock. Richard Hovey. Eleazar was the faculty and the whole curriculum/Was five hundred gallons of New England rum. OBAL

The Elected Knight. Anonymous. The youngest sorrows till death. AWP

Elected Silence. Siegfried Sassoon. O earth and heaven not made with hands! MoBrPo

An Election. Mordecai Marcus. Like us he is holy and sinful. SOTS

The Election. Robert Pack. I had not expected this. The kids/Are screaming and tearing at my eyes. CoPo

An Election Address. James Kenneth Stephen. Profundity I cannot claim;/Respectability I can. NBM

Election Reflection. M. Keel Jones. And keep the public memory short. NLV; PV

Election Songs. Anonymous. You have forgotten that the election is near. WTO

Election Time (parody). Anonymous. Too soon its brilliant course is run,/Its beer will soon stop flowing. FaBoPa

Electra. Francis Howard Williams. And weaves delight through all the griev-/ing years. AA

The Electric Cop. Victor Hernandez Cruz. & true stories of the empire/the end for instance. PoBA

An Electric Sign Goes Dark. Carl Sandburg. Say to their pals and wives now: I see by the papers Anna/Held is dead. HBMV

The Electric Telegraph. Thomas Baker. And guards with arm of superhuman might/This favour'd land of liberty and light. FaBoUs

Electricity Is Funny! John Currier. Electricity's a riot!/The End. GrPl

Electrocution Script. P. L. Jacobs. not really quiet/sizzling electricity. LFAC

Elegiac. Mimnermus. and no man/Lives, but to whom God gives bountiful measure of ill. LiTW

Elegiac. James Gates Percival. We shall look forth from our heaven,/pleased the sweet music to hear. AA

Elegiac Stanzas Suggested by a Picture of Peele Castle... William Wordsworth. Not without hope we suffer and we mourn. FaBoPP

An Elegiack Verse On the Death of the Pious and Profound... Nehemiah Walter. Elijah's Chariot born on Seraph's wings,/Mounts with this Treasure to the port of Bliss. SCAP

An Elegie. Elizabeth T. Corbett. Thy life bee written, and not read. AnAnS 2

Elegie. William Habington. :from which to be/Exempted, is in death to follow thee. AnAnS 2

An Elegie. Thomas Randolph. All other Love is to your sexe, not You. MePo

An Elegie Made by Mr. Aurelian Townshend in Remembrance of the Ladie.. Aurelian Townshend. And walke her Mourner, in this Black and Whight. SeCP

An Elegie On the Deploreable Departure of ...John Hull. John Saffin. Watch chearfully untill your Lord shall call./By a true...J.S. SCAP

An Elegie on the Lady Jane Pawlet, Marchion: of Winton. Ben Jonson. And, sure of Heaven, rides triumphing in. SeCP

An Elegie upon the Death of the Reverend Mr. Thomas Shepard (excerpt). Urian Oakes. Lest it be said, "With him New England fell!" NOCV

Elegies. Andre Marie de Chenier.
Kneel down, and take her pardon at her feet. AWP
They have but changed one for another woe. AWP
Whereat they, while he whimpers, mock the fool. AWP

Elegies. Ovid (Publius Ovidius Naso).
I'll live, and as he pulls me down, mount higher... ChTr
Jove send me more such after-noones as this. OBVE
Which golden love doth unto med rehearse. OBVE
Yet lingered not the day, but morning scard me. OBVE

Elegies for the Hot Season. Sandra McPherson. ...like the search-beam/Of my father's flashlight, at every swing discovering/Death. AmPA

Elegy. Joseph Auslander. And the geese honk north again and/the heron's going. TrJP

Elegy. Baruch of Worms. Not Jew, nor Jewess was there found,/Who would commit a traitor's crime. TrJP

Elegy. William Bell.
and the moon dips and drowns, but no man heeds. FaBoTw
o silent choirs, what can prevent your song? NePoEA
where summer hovered like a falling flare. NePoEA

Elegy. Duane Big Eagle. on a warm evening/in childhood. STE

Elegy. Olga Broumas. the yellow ash, so close. LTB

Elegy. George Gordon, Lord Byron. Thy looks are wan, thine eyes are wet. GTBS; GTBS-P

Elegy. Leonard Cohen. And build their secret nests/In his fluttering winding-sheet. HeIP

Elegy. Immanuel Di Roma. And now no more my trust in Him/I show. TrJP

Elegy. Philip Dow. nears its nest/over the porch door. NPGG

Elegy. Robert Fitzgerald. In the slow autumn air, the still fountains. AnAmPo

Elegy. G. S. Fraser. Who offered life, instead of lonely days. NeBP

Elegy. Robert (Robert Sutherland) Garioch. Weill, gin they arena deid, it's time they were. OxBS

An Elegy. David Gascoyne.
Astride his crippled mastiff's back was borne/Slowly away into the utmost dark. FaBoTw; TwCP
Slowly away into the utmost dark. FaBoTw; MP

Elegy. Sandra M. Gilbert. invisible insects dwelling uncomfortably/in the margins, in the white spaces around words. PoA

Elegy. Arthur Guiterman. Think what a lovely time they had! InMe

Elegy. Robert Hillyer. Only a fable like all our strange and beautiful dreams. EtS

The Elegy. A. D. Hope. Drink to his resurrection later on. ErPo; NoP

Elegy. Moses Ibn Ezra. And showed my own place waiting by/their side. TrJP

Elegy. David Ignatow. ...if in fact I have not been good to my friends/I will be so now to a stranger. NNaP

Elegy. Louis Johnson. Breathes a new myth into the elegy. AnNZ

Elegy. Karoniaktatie. people; let us nourish & protect each other STE

Elegy. Sidney Keyes. With your enemies, the swift-devouring years. WaP

Elegy. Robert. Layzer. Your breathing, and the secrets of the room. NePoEA; PoPl

Elegy. Alan Loney.
...Grains of dirt/strewn thru my body OCNZ
That poor stutterer will disappoint/who gave him birth OCNZ
trailing my mother/I don't know OCNZ

Elegy. John, Lord Dreghorn Maclaurin. A country-wedding shall thy hopes deprive. NOEC

Elegy. Roy McFadden. And the red clay drawing his body home. NeIP

Elegy. William Stanley Merwin. Who would I show it to. HaCAP

Elegy. Howard Nemerov. If Death should stroke thee, Thompson, scratch Him for me. PPJ

Elegy. Aleksandr Pushkin. Even love will drop around to smile goodbye. AMV-81

Elegy. Theodore Roethke. Bearing down with two steady eyes,/On the quaking butcher. CTBA; DFF; NCSH

Elegy. Pinhas Sadeh. The deep gold of the flames/of death. VWA

Elegy. David St. John. Once. I will walk out into the day. LCAP

An Elegy. E. J. Scovell. The child's walk in the darkening afternoon. ChMP

Elegy. Antoni Slonimski. Two nations which supped full of the same suffering. VWA

Elegy. William Jay Smith. I say, dear friend, good morning and good night. NePoEA

Elegy. Tony Towle. The moon turns them to chalk and they collapse. ANYP

Elegy. Richard Chenevix Trench. —with tranquil heart/Upon the loved and lost I think. IrPN

Elegy. John Hall Wheelock. No, not even in death. NYBP

An Elegy. Yvor Winters. Through the last stone age, for the pastoral kings. VGW

An Elegy. Yuan Chen. Yet my open eyes can see all night/That lifelong trouble of your brow. LiTW

Elegy V. George Barker. Perfect. Beast, brute, bastared. O dog my God! FaBoTw

Elegy XI. William Shenstone. Then sinks untimely, and defrauds the chase. NOEC

Elegy XIII. Sydney Goodsir Smith. And maybe tae the pox–/Ach,weill! BSV

Elegy XXIII. Louise Labé. You're suffering martyrdom as much as I. WPOW

Elegy Against a Latter Day. Kendrick Smithyman. by terms of grief which her example holds, and pardons. AnNZ

Elegy and Flame. Horace Gregory. I have come a long way/after Death. FYAP

Elegy and Kaddish. D. Rosenmann-Taub. And my poem will have no meaning. VWA

Elegy Before Death. Edna St. Vincent Millay. Only the grace from simple stone. AnFE; APA; CMoP; LiTA; LiTM

Elegy: "Child, your white face is chanting memories." Karel van de Woestijne. Your tired white face, still trembling, all in tears... LiTW

Elegy: E. W. L. E. Sissman. As grave and serious at heart as you. NYBP

Elegy (excerpt). Frank Bidart. I want to be buried in a mausoleum at eye-level. HaCAP

Elegy for 41 Whales Beached in Florence, Ore., June, 1979. Linda Bierds. And here is fire. AMV-81

Elegy for a Bad Poet, Taken from Us Not Long Since. John Frederick Nims. "Who, you?" To praise the Lord, His gracious ways. TW

Elegy for a Countryman. Padraic Fallon. And stare at me till I speak and speak/Lest my heart break. NeIP

Elegy for a Cricket. J. V. Cunningham. That I gave you my last, I have none other. NoAm

Elegy for a Dead Confederate. Robert McGovern. Refreshing us to face our lost world's pain. SOTS

Elegy for a Dead Soldier. Karl Shapiro. Know that one soldier has not died in vain. AP; CoBMV; HAP; LiTM; MiAP; OBWP; OFD; OxBA; WaP

Elegy for a Diver. Philip Booth. ...this son/with sculpin, coin, and bone,/become the dark he must explore. LiSp

Elegy for a Diver. Peter Meinke. now & forever I praise your skill. Psk

Elegy for a Nature Poet. Howard Nemerov. At last, he goes to her without a word. BoNaP; HoPM; PP

Elegy for a Puritan Conscience. Alan Dugan. and fell in love with sin. NoAm; SM

Elegy for a School-Friend. Augustus Young. ...his bas-relief/name chisels to dust. BIrV

Elegy for a Woman Who Remembered Everything. David Wagoner. Nothing will escape her. DFF

Elegy for Alfred Hubbard. Tony Connor. and sticks at a job until it's done. SoSe

Elegy for an Estrangement. John Holloway. Streets of an endless town. Night falls in rain. NePoEA

Elegy for an Unknown Soldier. James Keir Baxter. Who born of silence has burned back to silence. AnNZ

An Elegy for Bob Marley. William Matthews. ...our lives and bodies/and all that we hope survives them. MAYP

Elegy for Chief Sealth (1786–1866). Duane Niatum. The reed's lost shadow. CDW

An Elegy for D. H. Lawrence. William Carlos Williams. now the crinkled spice-bush/in flower. NoAm

Elegy for Doctor Dunn. Edward, Lord Herbert of Cherbury. Such vice avail more then their vertues can. AnAnS 2

Elegy for Drowned Children. Bruce Dawe. Over thresholds of welcome dream with wet and moonlit skin. NOAV

Elegy for Dylan Thomas. Edith Sitwell. Old men that tap their way through worlds of dust/To find Man's path near the Sun. PoA

Elegy for Ezra. Raymond F. Roseliep. Bless Thou our sweet goddam. SOTS

Elegy for Former Students. Virginia Scott Miner. Come visit. I shall welcome you. AMV-81

Elegy for Helen Trent. Paris Leary. along The Lincoln Highway of the dead. CoPo

Elegy for Her Brother Sakhr. Al-Khansa. as a wind of dust blew under a freezing cloud. BoWoP

Elegy for Her Brother, Sakhr. Khansa. Camel-slaughterer/rebel's refuge/healer of broken bones. WPOW

Elegy (For Himself). Moses Rimos. The end of the matter! The Justice of/God I acknowledge. TrJP

Elegy for Jack Bowman. Joseph Bruchac. Old Man, the last of my old men. CDW

Elegy for Jane. Theodore Roethke. Neither father nor lover. AP; CAPP; FF; NoP; PAI; TwCP

Elegy for Lucy Lloyd. Llewelyn Goch. Sad lingerer, that gave to thee/His heart, his hope, his melody. LiTW

Elegy for Margaret Howard, Lady Buckhurst. Robert Southwell. To live, to love, to be, where now she is. CoBE

Elegy for Minor Poets. Louis MacNeice. Did we not underwrite them when we were born? FaBoIP; HaMV; PP

Elegy for Mr. Goodbeare. Osbert Sitwell. Could remember/No more? AnFE; MoBrPo

Elegy for My Father. Robert Louthan. You were in her heart, and kept it beating/by pacing back and forth. AMV-80

Elegy for My Father. Howard Moss. ...How I would take you from,/Now, if I could, its whirling vacuum. NePoEA; VWA

Elegy for My Father. Mark Strand.
Because it is winter and the new year. GeTw; HaCAP; LCAP; UnPo
I have carried it with me too long. I give it back. Prf

Elegy for My Mother. Richard Katrovas. I strike a match and watch it burn, finding/in its one act of mercy what we are. SM

Elegy for N. N. Czeslaw Milosz. I understood it as you did: indifference. SV

Elegy for Our Dead. Edwin Rolfe. ...Deeds were their last words. WaP

Elegy for the Duke of Marmalade. Luis Palés Matos. Oh my fine, my honey-colored Duke of Marmalade!? InW

Elegy for the Forgotten Oldsmobile. Adrian C. Louis. I could have had some/good times in high school... STE

Elegy for the Giant Tortoises. Margaret Atwood. our holy and obsolete symbols. BoWoP

Elegy for the Monastery Barn. Thomas Merton. Thinking upon this barn His gentle doom! CoPo; VGW

Elegy for the Silent Voices and the Joiners of Everything. Kenneth Patchen. Our houses need holes for new air and we will get them through/our heads. NaP

Elegy for the Wife of a Friend. Yu Hsuan-chi. From mourning, there is no relief. BoWoP

Elegy for Two Banjos. Karl Shapiro. The devil's had the final say. AtBAP; LiTA; TrJP; WaP

Elegy for William Soutar. William Montgomerie. Sunken fourteen years in that aquarium. NeBP; OxBS

Elegy for Yards, Pounds, and Gallons. David Wagoner. To become as quaint as leagues and palms/In an old poem. PoA

Elegy in a Country Churchyard. Gilbert Keith Chesterton. They have no graves as yet. DBV; GoTF; MMM; MoBrPo; OBSP

Elegy in a Presbyterian Burying-Ground. R. N. D. Wilson. –I would be proud to be the stoneyard mason/Who had incised his name. BIrV

Elegy in a Theatrical Warehouse. Kenneth Fearing. Everything that never held a single thing at all. NYBP

An Elegy in Memory of the Worshipful Major Thomas Leonard Esq....
Samuel Danforth II. He joy'd in Hope, that now were laid Foundations/
Of Piety for many Generations./Maestus Composuit. SCAP

Elegy in Six Sonnets. Frederick Goddard Tuckerman.
And yet I know the splendor of the light/Will break anon. Look! where the
gray is white!/ QFR
The glass falls from the window, part by part,/And ringeth faintly in the
grassy stones. QFR
Here in the forest-heart, hung blackening/The wolfbait on the bush beside
the spring. QFR
The Shay's man with the green branch in his hat,/Or silent sagamore, Shaug
or Wassahoale. QFR
With lips that work, with eyes that overwell. QFR
Yet Gulielma was by far more fair. QFR

Elegy: In Spring. Michael Bruce. Till the long night is gone, and the last
morn arise. BSV

Elegy in the Cemetery of Spoon River...(parody). J. C. Squire. "There is an
end to even the worst career!" BXAP

Elegy in the Orongorongo Valley. Hubert Witheford. Too long
remembered, too long forgotten. AnNZ

An Elegy Is Preparing Itself. Donald Justice. Waiting, in their dark
clothes, apart. HoPM

Elegy: Ise Lamenting the Death of Empress Onshi. Lady Ise. cry out as
they fly off,/indifferent to us. BoWoP

Elegy Just in Case. John Ciardi. Undeciphered but surmised. AtBAP;
MiAP; TwCP

Elegy, Montreal Morgue. Goodridge MacDonald. There is white quiet at
the end. CaP

Elegy of Fortinbras. Zbigniew Herbert. and that water these words what
can they do what can they do/prince. FaBoPV; OBVE

Elegy: On a Lady, Whom Grief for the Death of Her Betrothed Killed.
Robert Bridges. Rejoice, for thou art near to thy possession. OBEV;
OBVV

An Elegy on a Lap Dog. John Gay. Who fawned like man, but ne'er like
man betrayed. DiPo; HBV 1-2

Elegy on a Nordic White Protestant. John Gould Fletcher. Rising, forever,
rising! PoNe

Elegy on Albert Edward the Peacemaker. *Anonymous.* A symphony of
praises loud we sing/In faithful memory of our Peaceful King. CoMu

Elegy on an Australian Schoolboy. Zora Cross. Who heals the whole
world's pain. PoAu 1-2

Elegy on Any Lady by George Moore. Max Beerbohm. Dead women tell
no tales. FaBoEE

An Elegy on Ben Jonson. John Cleveland. In that one word alone I had
paid more,/Than can be now, when plentie makes me poore. MeLP; OBS

Elegy on Captain Matthew Henderson. Robert Burns. Wail through the
dreary midnight hour/Till waukrife morn. PBBP

Elegy on Coleman. *Anonymous.* Then all are pleased, for Coleman's in his
grave. ALV

Elegy: On Delia's Being in the Country. James Hammond. I'll do,--I'll
plough or dig as DELIA's slave. CEP

Elegy on Gordon Barber. Gene Derwood. And all our mourning should be
to rejoice. FaFP; NePA

Elegy on Herakleitos. Callimachus. Shall not touch them with his blind all-
canceling fingers. LiTW

Elegy on Mistress Boulstred. John Donne. Because the chain is broke,
though no link lost. JCP

Elegy on My Father. Allen Curnow. That the salt winds which scattered
us blow softer. AnNZ

Elegy on Shakespeare. William Basse. That unto us and others it may be/
Honour hereafter to be laid by thee. CBEP; FaBoRV; OBS

Elegy on the Death of a Mad Dog. Oliver Goldsmith. The dog it was that
died! BeLS; BLPA; CBEP; FaBoBe; FPL; GDP; GoTF; HBV 1-2; HBVY;
LBN; MCCG; NA; NLV; NOBI; OAEP; PoPle; RoGo; ShM; TEP; TreF

An Elegy on the Death of Dobbin, the Butterwoman's Horse. Francis
Fawkes. Dame Jolt's brown horse, old Dobbin, is no more. NOEC

An Elegy on the Death of Furuhi. Yamanoue Okura. Be true and lead him
up/Straight along the road to heaven! DL

Elegy on the Death of Mme. Anna Pavlova (excerpt). E. H. W. Meyerstein.
Less in the flutes than in those feet we heard/The pride that lifts men far
above their fate. UnS

Elegy on the Dust. Thom Gunn. In endless hurry round the world.
NoAm

Elegy on the Eve. George Barker. I am the dead, the only happy one.'
WaaP

An Elegy on the Glory of Her Sex, Mrs. Mary Blaize. Oliver Goldsmith.
She had not died today. OnYI

Elegy on the L.C. John Donne. He, and about him his, are turned to
stone. ATP

An Elegy on the Late King of Patagonia. St. John Emile Clavering Hankin.
As much regretted by mankind/As Patagonia's ACHILLES! CenHV

Elegy on Thomas Hood (parody). Martin Fagg. And charged this very
vital spark/To jump his mortal coil. FaBoPa

Elegy on Thyrza. George Gordon, Lord Byron. Than aught except its
living years. GTBS; GTBS-P

An Elegy, or Friend's Passion, for His Astrophel (excerpt). *Anonymous.* So
was the friend that made this moan. PBBP

Elegy over a Tomb. Edward, Lord Herbert of Cherbury. Tell us alas, that
cannot tell our grief,/Or hope relief. AnAnS 2; AtBAP; EiL; OBS

Elegy: Three. Seamus Deane. Is hurled like a flaw/Into his numbed palate.
CIP

An Elegy, to an Old Beauty. Thomas Parnell. He wrapped in wisdom, and
they whirled by whim. CEP; NOEC

Elegy: to Delia. James Hammond. She knows my Wrongs, and will regard
my Pray'r. CEP

Elegy to Sports. David Shapiro. And the women, the pedestrians, and the
detective/Desert the champ. ANYP

Elegy to the Memory of an Unfortunate Lady. Alexander Pope. The Muse
forgot, and thou beloved no more! ACP; FiP; HBV 1-2; NOBE; NOEC;
OAEL 1-2; OBEC; OBEV; SeCeV; TEP

Elegy to the Sioux. Norman Dubie. Out of the big sky into Montana...
MAYP

An Elegy Upon My Best Friend. Henry, Bishop of Chichester King. Who
doth for ever to his Thoughts bequeath/The Legacy of your lamented Death.
AnAnS 2

An Elegy upon the Death of That Holy Man...(excerpt). Edward Taylor.
Wherein their Noble ashes are, and know yee/ALL END in ALLEN, by a
Paragoge. PoEL 1-5

An Elegy upon the Death of the Dean of St. Paul's, Dr. John Donne.
Thomas Carew. Apollo's first, at last the true God's priest. CABA

Elegy while Pruning Roses. David Wagoner. And love, in memory of the
flourishing dead. AMV-80

Elegy Written at the Sea-Side, and Addressed to Miss Honoria Sneyd. Anna
Seward. They yield to no inevitable hour,/But will on lasting tablets write
thy name. PeHV

Elegy Written in a Country Churchyard. Thomas Gray. The bosom of his
Father and his God. BiP; BoLiVe; DL; EiCP; EnPE; ExPo; FaBoBe;
FaBoPP; FaBoPV; FaBoRV; FaFP; FaPoR; FPL; GN; GoTF; GoTL;
GTBS; GTBS-P; HAP; HBV 1-2; HBVY; HeIP; HoPM; InPK; InPo; InPS;
LaA; LiTB; LoBV; MasP; MCCG; MyFE; NOBE; NOEC; NoP; OAEL 1-2;
OBEC; OBEV; OHFP; PAI; PoEL 1-5; PoLf; PPoe; PPP; PrIm; SCV;
SeCeV; TEP; TreF; TrGrPo; UnPo; ViBoPo; WBLP; WHA

Elegy Written in a Country Coal-Bin. Christopher Morley. To bring my
morning coffee to a boil. OBAL

Elegy Written on a Frontporch. Karl Shapiro. She turned her back upon
the day/But will not lie at night alone. MoPo

Elegy Wrote in the Tower, 1554. John (fl. 1550) Harington. Even so
likewise by death was freedom wrought. EiL

An Elegye. Thomas Campion. If grac't, firme he stands, if not, easely falls.
AAS

Elektra on Third Avenue. Marilyn Hacker. We nurse our cups, nudge
knees, and pick and choose. MAYP; NYP

Element. P. K. Page. as dime flipped or gull on fire or fish/silently hurt–its
mouth alive with metal. PeCV

Elemental. George Dillon. Whose wing eludes the lifted wave. AnAmPo

Elemental. D. H. Lawrence. Somehow they are a lie. NoP

Elementary. Jim Tollerud. We like the brew VoR

Elementary Cosmogony. Charles Simic. The submission to chance. NNaP

The Elementary Scene. Randall Jarrell. I, I, The future that mends
everything. CMoP; LCAP

An Elementary School Class Room in a Slum. Stephen Spender. The
history theirs whose language is the sun. MoPo; MP; OAEP; PPON;
TwCP

The Elements. William Henry Davies. I am a bird. MoBrPo; OBVV

The Elements. Tom Lehrer. And there may be many others, but they
haven't been/discarvard. FaBoUs

Elements. Carolyn Wilson Link. Wherein, self-prisoners, we dwell. GoYe

The Elements. John Henry, Cardinal Newman. ...Keys of either home,/
Earth and the world to come. GoBC

The Elements. Oscar Williams. Man blows the golden horn of mind/And
hunts beside his elements. NAMP

Elements of Grammar. Calvin C. Hernton. by the silver of the stars.
NBP

The Elements of San Joaquin. Gary Soto. And nothing will heal/Under the
rain's broken fingers. NPGG

Elena's Song. Sir Henry Taylor. And feel like flowers that fade. OBRV;
OBVV

Elene. Cynewulf. Fortune in battle, glory and fame/And an earthly
kingdom, through the Holy Cross. AnOE

Eleonora Duse as Magda. Laurence Binyon. At last, it is I, it is I! SyP

The Elephant. *Anonymous.* But he takes it wherever he goes. OnUR

The Elephant. Herbert Asquith.
Of what is he thinking/Between those wide ears? SoPo

To the tinkle of laughter/And crowned with the may. SUS; TiPo

The Elephant. Hilaire Belloc. So LARGE a trunk before. SoPo; TiPo

Elephant. Alan Brownjohn. dance to show how very little a/thing happiness can be really. OnUR

The Elephant. Sandra Hochman. Each night/I prepare our departures. BoAnP

Elephant. David McFadden. Stars shine on his back. WHW

The Elephant and the Flea. *Anonymous.* Boom, boom, ain't it great to be crazy? TrAS

The Elephant I. *Anonymous.* Wherever he walks/the grass is forbidden to stand up again. TTY

The Elephant II. *Anonymous.* Elephant hunter, take your bow! TTY

The Elephant Is Slow to Mate. D. H. Lawrence. till they touch in flood. LiTM; PPP; TEP

The Elephant, or The Force of Habit. Alfred Edward Housman. The force of habit is so strong. NOBL; PV

Elephant Rock. Primus St. John. I could never understand–/JESUS SAVES PoBA

The Elephant's Trunk. Alice Wilkins. It's part of his head–it's grown! SoPo; TiPo

The Elephant to the Girl in Bertram Mills' Circus. Anthony Cronin. I am the loser for my tenderness. CIP

Elephants. Patrick Lane. buried under the grade of the new/highway. NeAC

Elephants Are Different to Different People. Carl Sandburg. "Sunday comes only once a week," they told each other. MoAmPo

Elephants from the Sea. Ian Young. in a world of gigantic cushioncovers,/ and enormous bamboo fans. NeAC

Elephants in the Circus. D. H. Lawrence. Yet they sit up/and show vast bellies to the children. BoAnP

Elephants May Parade Before Your House. *Anonymous.* But you will have to go and knock at the House of the Dead. WTO

Eletelephony. Laura E. Richards. (I fear I'd better drop the song/Of elephop and telephong!) GoJo; NLV; NTCP; OBCA; OnUR; OxBChV; SoPo; TiPo; YaD

The Elevated Train. James S. Tippett. You lose yourself/Where the tall buildings meet. SUS

Elevation. Charles Baudelaire. Knows the flowers' speech and the speech of silent things! AWP

Elevator Landscapes. Stephen Vincent.
and nods us/back in thru/those open doors. NeAC
...My lips/are sealed/like sour artichokes. NeAC

The Elevator Man Adheres to Form. Margaret Danner. toward lifting them above their crippling storm. PoBA; PoNe

Eleven. Archibald MacLeish. Like a root growing– HAP; NCSH; WeW

Eleven Addresses to the Lord. John Berryman.
I even feel sure you will assist me again, Master of insight & beauty. CAPP; OxBC; WeW
I identify with everybody, even the heresiarchs. CAPP; OxBC
I leave her in wise Hands. OxBC
I pray I may be ready with my witness. CAPP
Let me lie down exhausted, content with that. OxBC
One sudden Coming? Many so believe./So not, without knowing anything, do I. OxBC
Shield & fresh fountain! Manifester! Even mine. OxBC
sole watchman of the wide & single stars. OxBC; UnPo

The Eleventh and Last Book of the Ocean to Cynthia. Sir Walter Ralegh. Her love hath end; my woe must ever last. NCEP

The Eleventh Commandment (excerpt). John Holmes. He lifted the tablets up before them saying/The word that gave them all words: Listen. MoRP

Eleventh Song. Sir Philip Sidney. And from louts to run away! EG; EnLi 1-2; TEP

Eleventh Sunday after Trinity. John Keble. This was no world of rest for thee! VLP

The Elf and the Dormouse. Oliver Herford. –And that's how umbrellas/ First were invented. AA; FaBoBe; HBV 1-2; HBVY; OnMSP; SoPo; TiPo

The Elf Child. James Whitcomb Riley. Er the gobble-uns'll git you/Ef you/Don't/Watch/Out! AmePo

Elf Night. Ron Rogers. Making off with the flour and beans. STE

Elf Owl. Mary Austin. And get me back to my burrow. BPAW

Elfer Hill. *Anonymous.* Nor sleep upon its side. AWP

The Elfin Knight. *Anonymous*
And ore the hill and far awa'. CH
The wind shall not blow my plaid away. BaBo; BuBa; ESPB; FaBoBa; GBP

Elfin Skates. Eugene Lee-Hamilton. And tell thee when the skaters are about.' OBVV

Elfin Town. Rachel Field. ...come back to Elfin Town/For it's here that you were born! WSC

The Elfin Wife. Jake Falstaff. Doing the duties of her grave delight? BoC

Eli, Eli. Judith Wright. and all the while, he knew there was no river. CBAP

Eli the Thatcher. William and Max Beerbohm Rothenstein. You have forgot to tread the ancient way. FaBoNo

Elijah Speaking. Doug Fetherling. for as a child I knew I was no child/as now I know I am not old NOBC

Elinda's Glove. Richard Lovelace. Yet Servants, knowing Minikin nor Base,/Are still allow'd to fiddle with the Case. OBS

Elinor Rumming (excerpt). John Skelton. And. thus beginneth the game. ViBoPo

Elinoure and Juga. Thomas Chatterton. Yelled theyre leathalle knelle, sonke ynn the waves, and dyde. LAuP

Eliot's Oak. Henry Wadsworth Longfellow. And is forgotten, save by thee alone. AmePo

Elisa. Edmund Spenser. When damsons I gather,/I will part them all you among. OBSC

Elisa, or an Elegy upon the Unripe Decease... Phineas Fletcher. Still live I in thy thoughts, but as in heaven I live. ViBoPo

L'Elisir d'Amore. Dallas E. Wiebe. And a glass/of warm and oily/ Cincinnati water. MAT

The Elixir. George Herbert. For that which God doth touch and own/ Cannot for less be told. FaBoCh; GN; LoGBV; NoP; OHIP; TrGrPo; WGRP

Eliza. Erasmus Darwin. And clasp'd them sobbing, to his aching breast. PaPo

Eliza Telefair. Jocelyn Macy Sloan. Nothing, yet all, she went down the pier,/wrapped in her glittering shroud of air. GoYe

Elizabeth. George Brandon Saul. A sense of flowers drifting down the wind. HBMV

Elizabeth. Sylvia Townsend Warner. If it be not of Death. MoAB; MoBrPo

Elizabeth Ann Peabody. Ivy O. Eastwick. You WERE a charming girl! BrR

Elizabeth at the Piano. Horace Gregory. ...it is snowing everywhere. UnS

Elizabeth's War with the Christmas Bear: 1601. Norman Dubie. Every inch of you, a terrible vision, not bear, but virgin! LCAP; MAYP

Elizabethan Days. Thomas Caulfield Irwin. And slanting o'er an ebon cloud/Falls night's last moon-beam like a sword! IrPN

Elizabethan Tragedy: A Footnote. Howard Moss. Although the Prince is on the angels' side,/What got him there is wholesale homicide. NePoEA

The Elizabethans Called It Dying. James Schuyler. it must've been lousy NeAP

Elk Ghosts: A Birth Memory. Dave Smith. Composed, they suffer your coming. GeTw

The Elk. The Whelk. Robert Williams Wood. It indicates the Whelk is out. NLV

Ella, in a Square Apron, along Highway 80. Judy Grahn. The common woman is as common/as a rattlesnake. NMM

Ella of the Cinders. Mary Blake French. I shall use the shivered glass for my own collage. DFT

Ella Speed. *Anonymous.* So I won't have so long to lay? AmFP

Ellas and the Statues. Guften Akin. Breathing knowledge into them PBWP

Ellen Bawn. James Clarence Mangan. Two hearts that Love would blend in one for ever and/for ever! IrPN

Ellen Flannery. *Anonymous.* The crime he had committed/Will send his soul to hell. AmFP

Ellen Irwin; or, The Braes of Kirtle. William Wordsworth. And its forlorn Hic jacet! PeD

Ellen M'Jones Aberdeen. Sir William Schwenck Gilbert. Especially Ellen M'Jones Aberdeen. HBV 1-2; InMe

Ellen Taylor. *Anonymous.* For she's gone to Manchester the summer months to stay. OBET

Ellie Mae Leaves in a Hurry. Peter Klappert. it's just the sort of news that gets around. SM

Elliott Hawkins. Edgar Lee Masters. How do you like my silence from mouths stopped/With the dust of my triumphant care? OxBA

Ellis Park. Helen Hoyt. Do you hear this praise of you,/Little park that I pass through? HBMV

Ellora. Leonard Nathan. It is cruel and hard to be real. GP

Ellsworth. *Anonymous.* Such a sacred offering/God will not despise. PAH

Elm. Sylvia Plath. ...the isolate, slow faults/That kill, that kill, that kill. NoAm

The Elm. Odell Shepard. The midnight never tells. HBMV

The Elm Beetle. Andrew Young. Roller-striped fields, and smooth cow-shadowed pond. LoBV

Elm Fuck Poem. Ed Sanders. & the elm branch is the dryad's breast. ANYP

The Elm's Home. William Heyen. my lightning lord,/my home. MAYP

Elmer Ruiz. Peter Oresick. We gotta make a nice job. LTB

The Elms Dispatch. Ron Padgett. The close call packed away and sniffing at the edge ANYP

Empedocles. Thomas S. Jones, Jr. Older than night, the silent stars, or death. AnAmPo

Empedocles. George Meredith. And him reads Reason at his heels,/If heels in air the last of him! VLP

Empedocles on Etna. Matthew Arnold.
...and stray/For ever through the glens, placid and dumb. GTBS-P
Harsh Gods and hostile Fates/Are dreams! this only is– TW
The stars in their calm. FaBoRV; MaVP; OAEL 1-2; OAEP; VLP

Empedocles on Etna. H. B. Mallalieu. My death has become a necessary myth. PoA

The Emperor. Tu Fu. ...and leaves his/grave Mandarins to look at each other in silence. AWP

The Emperor of Ice Cream. Wallace Stevens. The only emperor is the emperor of ice-cream. AP; BiP; CMoP; CoBMV; FaBoMo; FF; HaCAP; HAP; InPK; LiTA; MoPo; MoVE; NAWM 1-2; NePA; NIP; NoAm; NOBA; NoP; OxBA; TAP; ViBoPo; WeW

Empire Builders. Archibald MacLeish. When the land lay waiting for her westward people! AmP; OxBA

The Empire Clock. Bernard Spencer. Which we painted out. Which we painted out. OBTV

Empire of Dreams. Charles Simic. I have a kind of halloween mask/Which I am afraid to put on. LCAP

Empires. Francis Burdett Money-Coutts. But the axles of their wheels were hot/With the same frenzies as our own. OBVV

The Employee. Rudi Holzapfel. I'll burn away such sickness from the Earth. DBV

Employment. George Herbert.
So we freeze on,/Until the grave increase our cold. JCP; OBS; OxBoCh; SeCP; TEP
To my poore reed. AtBAP; SeCV 1-2

The Empress. Diane Wakoski. Commotion for/every syllable. CoPo

The Empress Brand Trim: Ruby Reminisces. Sherley Anne Williams.
...Tonight you/pay homage to the/pussy Blues made."/And they always did. BlSi

Empties Coming Back. Angelo De Ponciano. –just empties coming back. BLPA

The Empty Apartment. Aaron Zeitlin. a begetter/who abandons his offspring. VWA

Empty at the Heart of Things. Frank Polite. Write when you can. Love,/Sharon. APU

Empty Bed Blues. Bessie Smith. They'll double-cross you and leave you with them empty bed blues. UnPo

The Empty Cradle. Jose Selgas y Carrasco. They flew away. CAW

Empty Dwelling Places. Kenneth Patchen. I swear to you I knew it once. PoA

The Empty Glen. R. Crombie Saunders. And wondered, Are they ever coming back? OxBS

Empty Holds a Question. Pat Folk. how I could be at twenty-two/as old as all mankind. GOYP

The Empty House. Walter De la Mare. ...How black it is/Beneath these thick-boughed trees! BrPo

The Empty House. Russell Hoban. When the clock sings no-time night. WSC

The Empty House. William Dean Howells. And haunted with the ghost of home. AmePo

The Empty House. Harold Monro. And the forgotten people who since then/Were born in it, or lived and died in it. BrPo

The Empty House. Stephen Spender. And everything he'd touched, an exposed nerve. NYBP; PCP

The Empty House. Max Williams. and demolition workers putting back the sky. CBAP

The Empty Jar. William Stenhouse. And keep frae us when we are auld/An empty jar. AnNZ

Empty Kettle. Louis (LittleCoon) Oliver. I sing. STE

The Empty Pain-Killer Bottles. Tom Raworth. annabella, such a ridiculous name for a breakfast cereal. EAS

Empty Saddles. *Anonymous.* Empty saddles in the old corral. BPAW

An Empty Threat. Robert Frost. That need endless talk-talk/To make them out.' RFM

Empty Vessel. Hugh (Christopher Murray Grieve) MacDiarmid.
The licht that bends owre a' thing/Is less ta'en up wi't. BSV; FaBoTw; OxBS

The Empty Woman. Gwendolyn Brooks. And bouffants that bustle, and rustle. IHMS

The Emulation. Sarah Fyge Egerton. No, we'll be wits, and then men must be fools. NOEC

Emus. Mary Elizabeth ("E") Fullerton. The Bush, the hills, the range,/And the dark flats under. BoANP; PoAu 1-2

En Bateau. Paul Verlaine. Upon the skiff that flies and seems/To float upon a tide of dreams. AWP

En Garde, Messieurs. William Lindsey. I am a whit impatient, and 'tis ill/To cross a hungry dog, Messieurs, en garde. AA

En Las Internas Entranas. Saint Theresa of Avila. And goodly were the deeds it wrought. WPOW

En Monocle. Donald Evans. To kiss the naked phrase quite unaware. AnAmPo

En Passant. Andrei Codrescu. I praise the lava holes/whence issued my first passport. APU

En Route. E. L. Mayo. Hunched above us, waiting what earth means. MiAP

En Route. Duncan Campbell Scott. With the lost flush of last year's autumn leaves. NOBC; OBCV

The Enamel Girl. Genevieve Taggard. Now terror touches me when I/Dream I am touching a butterfly. HBMV; MoAmPo

Enamored Architect of Airy Rhyme. Thomas Bailey Aldrich. They fail, and they alone, who have not striven. AnNE; APA; HBV 1-2; MCCG

Enamoured of the Miniscule. Michael Hartnett. making unwearable golden shoes. BIrV

The Enchanted Castle. Jeanne D'Orge. "You don't mean to say/you believe that faery story?" AnAmPo

The Enchanted Halibut. Sheila Nickerson. The time must be right/For you both. WOLT

The Enchanted Heart. Edward Davison. Long ago..in a dream...O never again! HBMV

The Enchanted Island. Luke Aylmer Conolly. The fairy isle is seen no more. OBRV

The Enchanted Knight. Edwin Muir. ...Now he tries to lift/The insulting weight that stays and breaks his heart. MoVE

The Enchanted Region: or, Mistaken Pleasures. Walter Harte. Christian joys are joys for ever! EBEV

The Enchanted Shirt. John Milton Hay. And the king was well and gay. BBV; BLPA; GN; MaC; PaPo

The Enchanted Spring. George Darley. Come! sip it freshly as it flows. BoNaP; NBM

Enchantment. Lewis Alexander. Terror reigns like a new crowned king. PoBA

Enchantment. Madison Cawein. Wild woodland music on the pipes of Pan. HBV 1-2

The Enchantment. Thomas Otway. 'Twould learn of yours the winning art,/And quickly steal the rest. HBV 1-2; LiTL; OBEV; ViBoPo

Encirclement. Mieczyslaw Jastrun. ...I cannot budge. AMV-81

An Encomium upon a Parliament. Daniel Defoe. Go home and look after your wives. APAS

The Encounter. Paul Blackburn. and crawled all the way back to El Paso NeAP

Encounter. Denis Devlin. Along the boulevard laid with yellow evening. BIrV; OnYI

Encounter. Geraldine Hammond. Am I freed or bound now/by a cry that dives/back into silence?/Both. IHMS

Encounter. Uys Krige. I walk in your light! PeSA

Encounter. Dorothy Livesay. your eyes belie/your talking mouth. AMV-81

Encounter. Vassar Miller. your flesh, breathed in a muted sentence,/instructed me in mine. GP

The Encounter. Edgell Rickword. and left my Twittingpan to lie it out. OxBTC

Encounter in Jerusalem. Fay Lipshitz. The body but a wisp of smoke, that lightly wove/Through the shadows of the waiting City. VWA

Encounter in Safed. Yungman. And she stretches out a half-dried bread:/"Take." VWA

Encounter in the Cage Country. James Dickey. When you come, Green Eyes, Green Eyes. CAPP

Encounter with Hunger. Brian Vanderlip. these children/eating/themselves. AMV-81

Encouraged. Paul laurence Dunbar. I could not disappoint you and so prevailed. TRV

Encouragement to Exile. Arbiter (Caius Petronius Arbiter) Petronius.
...Greatly be thou as one/Who disembarks, fearless, on alien sands. AWP

The End. Walter De La Mare. And a Sea whose menace leaves the quick/Colder than churchyard stone? OAEP

The End. Allen Ginsberg. come Poet shut up eat my word, and taste my mouth in your/ear. ConAP

The End. A.(lan) A.(lexander) Milne. So I think I'll be six now for ever and ever. BiCB; SiSoSe

The End. Wilfred Owen. Nor my titanic tears, the seas, be dried. CH; FaBoRV; HBMV; MMM

The End. Wallace Rice. A little folding of the hands to sleep. AA

An End. Christina Georgina Rossetti. While we think of all that was/In the long ago. FaBoRV; GBL

The End. Sharon Thesen. & you could hardly bear/how much you wanted in CaPN

The End. Mark Van Doren. Add gossip girls and western-throated boys. ViBoPo

The End. Marguerite Wilkinson. "Even the sunbeams falter, flicker and bend–/I am the end." HBMV

The End Bit. Jim Burns. and counts it/as part of the/pattern of things. FF

The End Is Near the Beginning. David Gascoyne. Which means Until the end. EAS

The End Is Now. Madelaine Marie. The end is now! PeHV

The End of a Day in the Provinces. Jules Laforgue. And the moon is the same here as in Paris, as over the/Mississippi, as in Bombay. SyP

The End of a Dynasty. Zbigniew Herbert. As for the valet, he stood against a partition and tried to/imitate the tapestry. FaBoPV

The End of a Leave. Roy Fuller. Against a whole world's pull. NeBP

The End of a Meaningful Relationship. Kurt J. Fickert. ...in place/of two is one who hurries down the stairs. AMV-81

The End of a War. Sir Herbert Read. eternal/bright OBMV

End of a Year. Robert Lowell. bright sky, bright sky, carbon scarred with ciphers. HaCAP

End of Another Home Holiday. D. H. Lawrence. Asking something more of me,/Yet more of me. DTC; EBEV; FaBoMo; MoVE

The End of April. Robert Fuller Murray. And James is going in for his degree. CenHV

End of August. Gregory Orr. ...my books piled/beside me, wiping blue mold from the spines. MAYP

The End of Being. (Lucius Annaeus Seneca) Seneca. His pleasure lies, but in the piety/Of consecrated hearts and lives devout. WGRP

The End of Clonmacnois. Anonymous. "Gnawing the guts of men." KiLC

The End of Clonmacnois. Frank O'Connor. Foxes round churchyards bare/Gnawing the guts of men. CIP

The End of Day. William Butler Yeats. "Come in and leave the play." LiTB

The End of Desire. Hugh McCrae. Lo!–Nothing but some sarcenet/Deep-buried in a pile of dust. BoAV

The End of Exploring. David Campbell. With love to dog-bark, gate and sweet cockcrow. SeCePo

The End of Fall. Francis Ponge. which I will use now to draw my line under this present story. NU

The End of His Work. Robert Herrick. and here my ship rides, having anchor cast. CaPo

The End of It. Francis Thompson. Her own self-will made void her own self's will. NOBV; OBSP

The End of Man Is Death. Moses Ibn Ezra. The bits of chalk and the precious/stones. TrJP

The End of Man Is His Beauty. LeRoi (Imamu Amiri Baraka) Jones. are not unlike/night's. BALP

The End of May. William Morris. More love in woe's despite,/More hope to perish soon. NOBV

The End of My Sister's Guggenheim. John Malcolm Brinnin. The gorgeous cabbages of Ghent! GLGT

End of Play. Robert Graves. We stare on our dazed trunks at the block kneeling. EBEV

End of Season. Robert Penn Warren. –you must think/On the true nature of Hope, whose eye is round and/does not wink. LiTA

The End of Sorrow. Edmond Fleg. the nightfall a step on the path to/Thee. TrJP

End of Steel. Thomas Saunders. But he had squatted at the end of steel. CaP

End of Summer. Stanley Jasspon Kunitz. And a cruel wind blows. AmLP; CrMA; MoAmPo; Psk; VGW

The End of Summer. Edna St. Vincent Millay. I know that summer, scarcely here,/Is gone until another year. BoNaP

The End of Summer. Judith Minty. ...I want him/to fly now before October and guns. FiCP; GeTw

End of Summer. Berl Pomerantz. Goats lolled at the doorways,/innocently spreading a smell of peace. VWA

(End) of Summer (1966). Bill Knott. I have work to dream. EAS

End-of-Summer Poem. Rowena Bastin Bennett. They've all disappeared with the passing of the summer. SiSoSe

End of Term. Anonymous. And trip the teachers on the stairs! PoPle

End of the Affair. Curtis W. Casewit. one last time? AMV-80

End of The Affair. Geoffrey Grigson. Wait on his bed and watch me/Till I fall. GBL

End of the Comedy. Louis Untermeyer. The moonlight is laid/Like a drawn sword. PoA

The End of the Day. Robert Creeley. night, good, good/night, has come. AmPC

The End of the Duel. Taylor Rachel Annand. Unhelm ere she dies. CAW

End of the Flower-World (A.D. 2300). Stanley Burnshaw. Will hear no music but the song of death. AnAmPo

End of the Line. John Taylor. ...keep moving till then. FAZ

The End of the Parade. William Carlos Williams. full of sweet breath. NYBP

End of the Picnic. Francis Webb. Standing in ribbons, over our heads, for an hour. NOAV

End of the Season on a Stormy Day–Oban. Iain Crichton Smith. ...drives through cold/towards his roped stone quay, his dead fish fold. NePoEA-2

End of the Seers' Convention. Kenneth Fearing. Or a handful of cinders fell on the small, black umbrellas/they raised against the sky. LiTA

The End of the Story. Terence Tiller. and fresh your garlands. ChMP; NeBP

The End of the Street. John Haines. Your evening is here. LCAP

End of the War in Merida. Anthony Ostroff. This holiday, personal,/exotic, paid, is our last one. FAZ

The End of the Way. Harriet Cole. "The toils of the road will seem nothing/When I get to the end of the way." BLRP

The End of the Weekend. Anthony Hecht. Some small grey fur is pulsing in its grip. ConAP; FaBoMo; HAP; LiTM; NePoEA-2; SM; WeW

The End of the World. Gordon Bottomley. He can stay with me while I do not lift them. BrPo; CH; MoBrPo; MoVE

End of the World. Jakov van Hoddis. And from the bridges dangle trains and trams. VWA

End of the World. Else Lasker-Schüler. A longing throbs against the planet/On which we must die. BoWoP

The End of the World. Archibald MacLeish. Of nothing, nothing, nothing–nothing at all. AP; BLPL; CMoP; LiTM; MAT; MoAB; MoAmPo; NCSH; NePA; NoAm; NOBA; OBAL; OxBA; TAP; TrGrPo; VGW

The End of the World. Thomas McGrath. Postpones the end of the world: in which we live forever. SM

The End of the Year. Su Tung-P'o. And we grow older and less strong. PoPl

The End of World War One. Sharon Olds. the soldiers of World War Two. AMV-81

End Song. Ruth Krauss. ...a dream/bends when the night in it dissolves LLLT

The End which Comes. Mrs. Major Arnold. Until the days were numbered of that dream. LoBV

Endimion Porter and Olivia. Sir William Davenant. For I shall know Olivia by her Voice. MePo; NOBE

Ending. Anonymous. Of up-rearing billows that come hither from Kahiki. WTO

The Ending. Paul Engle. still burning from their final touch of you. NYBP

Ending. Gavin Ewart. Romance, expected once to stay,/has left a note saying GONE AWAY. NLV; OBSP

Ending. Norman Jordan. For we both have been blessed. PoNe

Endless. Muriel Rukeyser. the broken and their children born and unborn/of the endless war. NYBP

An Endless Chain. Abraham Reisen. Any ship that sails goes/To a brother's land! VWA

The Endless Song. Ruth McEnery Stuart. To accommodate a frien' nex' do'. OBAL

Endpiece. Anonymous. And Christ be with me on the Judgment Day. KiLC

Endurance. Elizabeth Akers Allen. Lo, all things can be borne! PoToHe

Endurance. Carolyn Forche. I am trying to tell you something. SV

Endurance Test. Dacre Balsdon. from a tray marked IN to another marked OUT. DBV; FiBHP

Endure Hardness. Christina Georgina Rossetti. Somewhere or other doubtless/These make the blackthorn blow. NOBV

The Enduring Music. Harold Vinal. Whose waters are the crystal tides of sleep. EtS

Endymion. John Keats.
And I have told thee all thou mayest hear. ViBoPo
Are things to brood on with more ardency/Than the death-day of empires. ViBoPo
Easily onward, through flowers and weed. ATP; EnLit; TRV
Her playmate, and her wooer in the shade. OAEP; OBEV; OBRV
Hide in deep herbage.... CTC
If human souls did never kiss and greet? OBRV; ViBoPo
In starlight, by the three Hesperides. OBRV
My soul to keep in its resolved course.' SeCePo
Pouring unto us from the heaven's brink. MCCG; OBRV; TrGrPo
Rained violets upon his sleeping eyes. SeCePo
They always must be with us, or we die. BLPL; BoC; GoTF; LiTB; PG; TreF; ViBoPo
Upon thy Mount Lycean! AtBAP; ChRP

Endymion. Henry Wadsworth Longfellow. "Where hast thou stayed so long?" AA; HBV 1-2

Endymion. Edna St. Vincent Millay. For mortal love, that might not die of it. AnEnPo

Endymion. Oscar Wilde. Thou hast the lips that should be kissed! HBV 1-2

Endymion, I.   John Keats.   They stept into the boat, and launch'd from land.   EnRP

Endymion, II.   John Keats.   He saw the giant sea above his head.   EnRP

Endymion, II (excerpt).   John Keats.   Love's standard on the battlements of song.   OBNC

Endymion, III.   John Keats.   That I can think away from thee and live!'   EnRP

Endymion, III (excerpt).   John Keats.   And Tellus feels his forehead's cumbrous load.   MOON

Endymion, IV.   John Keats.   Home through the gloomy wood in wonderment.   EnRP

Endymion's Convoy.   Michael Drayton.   Whilst all the Nymphs on solemn instruments/Sound dainty music to their sweet laments.   OBSC

The Enemy.   Randolph Stow.   and wring your blood out on Hiroshima.   NOAV

The Enemy.   John Waller.   You charm and entangle, merrily captivate.   NeBP

Enemy, Enemy.   Cecil J. Mullins.   The civil words I have to say. And yet...   AMV-80

The Enemy's Portrait.   Thomas Hardy.   "I thought they were the bitterest enemies?"   EyDe; TW

Energetic Women.   D. H. Lawrence.   women felt it was no longer any use being a linger-longer-Lucy.   InPS; PAI

Energy.   Victor Hernandez Cruz.   playing with/bleeding/blue lips   PoBA

Energy.   Judith Fitzgerald.   ...allows dispersion/to gather each molecule/in its vast uniting storm   CaPN

Energy for a New Thang.   Ernie Mkalimoto.   from andrew hill's steel fingers/guaran/teed to set us back on our souls again   NBP

The Energy of Light.   John Hay.   It swoops, and fires the sky wall.   NePoAm-2

L'Enfant Glace.   Harry Graham.   Our darling's now completely frappe!'   FaBoCo; NLV

Enfant Perdu.   Heinrich Heine.   With sword unbroken, and with broken heart.   AWP

Enfidaville.   Keith Douglas.   I seem again to meet/the blue eyes of the images in the church.   HaMV

The Engagement.   Arthur Hugh Clough.   All that needs to be done, said he, shall be done, and/quickly.   NBM

Engine.   James S. Tippett.   I guess it knows the switchman/Will keep the tracks clear.   SoPo; SUS

Engine 143.   Anonymous.   And the very last words poor Georgie said/Was "Nearer my God to Thee."   FSW

The Engine: A Manual.   Michael Dobberstein.   ...now you can tell/Exactly what's wrong.   AMV-81

The Engine Driver's Story.   William Wilkins.   We're going out with the express.   BeLS

Engine Failure.   Timothy Corsellis.   No sights of despair for to-day.   WaP

The Engineer's Story.   Anonymous.   Blesses me ever more.   BeLS

The Engineer's Story.   Eugene J. Hall.   She's my wife. Ther' ain't none better than ole Filkin's daughter Nell.   PaPo

Engineers.   Jimmy Garthwaite.   Watching all the wheels go round.   SoPo

England.   Grace Ellery Channing-Stetson   He is not of the Island race!   AA

England.   William Cowper.   Or all that we have left is empty talk/Of old achievements, and despair of new.   OBEC

England.   Richard Edwin Day.   Up the long sea-curve rides its stately form.   AA

England.   Gerald Massey.   For there's life in the Old Land yet.   HBV 1-2

England.   George Edgar Montgomery.   And with defiant courage she has taught/Red Tyranny to cringe before the Eight.   AA

England.   Marianne Moore.   ...It has never been confined to one locality.   CrMA; FaBoWP; LiTA; MoAB; MoAmPo

England.   John Henry, Cardinal Newman.   So gives He them by turn, to suffer or be blest.   ACP; CAW; GoBC

England.   Mary Jo Salter.   Through miles of glass and cloud, I thought of you.   AMV-80

England, 1802.   William Wordsworth.
And pure religion breathing household laws.   OBEV; PPON
But equally a want of books and men!   OBEV
Felt for thee as a lover or a child!   OBEV
The lowliest duties on herself did lay.   OBEV
Of Earth's first blood, have titles manifold.   OBEV

England and America.   James Kenneth Stephen.
Of very little use,/And execrably plain.   InMe
Or anything, in fact,/That people ought to be.   OBTV

England and America in 1782.   Alfred, Lord Tennyson.   From that deep chord which Hampden smote/Will vibrate to the doom.   MC; PAH

England Expects.   Ogden Nash.   ...they always land on their own or somebody/else's feet.   DBV

England Expects?   Sir Owen Seaman.   Nothing just now would seem to be/So certain as the unexpected.   NOBL

England, My England.   William Ernest Henley.   Out of heaven on your bugles blown!   BLPL; EnLi 1-2; HBV 1-2; MoBrPo; OBEV; QBVV; PoLf; TreF

England Reclaimed (excerpt).   Osbert Sitwell.   Under/The green grass/Under the wide grey sky.   ViBoPo

England's Darling.   Anonymous.   When Jemmy shall his fame retrieve,/and be in grace again.   CoMu

England's Dead.   Felicia Dorothea Hemans.   Wave may not foam, nor wild wind sweep,/Where rest not England's dead.   HBV 1-2

England's Difficulty.   Seamus Heaney.   ...manned every speech with check-/points and reported back to nobody.   CIP

England's Great Loss by a Storm of Wind.   Anonymous.   And to old England it may be more/Than nine sail of ships on shore.   OBSS

England's Heart.   Martin Farquhar Tupper.   A man's a bit of English stuff,/True from head to heel!   PaPo

England's Prayer.   William Blundell of Crosby.   That we, all children of the Spouse,/May live as brethren in Thy house.   GoBC

England's Sovereigns in Verse.   Anonymous.   And "God Save the King!" all his subjects' hearts say.   BLPA

England's Triumph.   Anonymous.   His Joys I wish may ne'r have end,/but gain his subjects' love and praise.   CoMu

England, Unprepared for War.   Mark Akenside.   And equal prowess still shall equal palms obtain.   OBEC

The English.   Anonymous.   Gay cotes graceles,/maketh Englande thriftles.   GBP

The English Are So Nice!   D. H. Lawrence.   To let them feel they're not quite as nice as they might be.   NoP

An English Ballad, on the Taking of Namur by the King...   Matthew Prior.   That He may lose Dinant next Year,/And so be Constable of France.   PoEL 1-5

English Bards and Scotch Reviewers.   George Gordon, Lord Byron.
He brays, the laureate of the long-eared kind.   AtBAP; ERoP 1-2; OAEL 1-2; OBRV; PP
He had not sung of Wales, nor I of him.   EiCP
Nor any dare to take thy name in vain.'   EnRP
Or any other thing that's false, before/You trust in critics.   DBV
The petrifactions of a plodding brain,/That, ere they reach the top, fall lumbering back again.   OBSV
Reforms each error, and refines the whole.   OBRV; OBSV

English Beach Memory: Mr. Thuddock.   Osbert Sitwell.   On the cold granite slab that covers his bones.   NYBP

English Counties.   Anonymous.   And Middlesex for sin.   PoL

English Courage Displayed.   Anonymous.   Who did so bravely play their parts at the taking of Porto Bello.   OBSS

An English Elegy.   Daryl Hine.   ...not only the wise and the well-bred have ten/thousand a year.   NoAm

The English Garden (excerpt).   William Mason.   And rein with Reason's curb fantastic Taste.'   NOEC

English Girl.   Edward Powys Mathers.   They never regarded your warm feet,/But I regarded.   OBMV

English History in Rhyme...(excerpt).   Edward B. Goodwin.   The Manchester Railway great progress denoted.   FaBoUs

The English Labourer.   Anonymous.   But now he laughs their threats to scorn with the Union at his back.   OBET

The English Language.   William Wetmore Story.   Grandly the thought rides the words, as a good/horseman his steed.   GN

English Liberal.   Geoffrey Taylor.   What could be subtler/Than the thought of Sam Butler?   FaBoEE

An English Mother.   Robert Underwood Johnson.   Until women's tears are reckoned in the budgets of your/wars.   HBV 1-2

An English Padlock.   Matthew Prior.   And clap your PADLOCK–on her Mind.   CEP; OBEC

English Poetry.   Samuel Daniel.   Show weakness speaks in prose, but power in verse.   OBSC

The English Queen.   Henry Lawson.   That selfish, callous woman whom the English call "the Queen'.   NOAV

The English Race.   Daniel Defoe.   Who join'd with Norman-French compound the Breed/From whence your True-Born Englishmen proceed.   OBEC

The English Retort.   Anonymous.   They tumbed in Twede/That woned by the see.   OxBM

The English Rider.   Robin Hyde.   God save the King! God, somehow, free the free.   AnNZ

The English Succession.   Anonymous.   Late may the second pass from earth to heaven!   OxBChV

English Thornton.   Edgar Lee Masters.   My avenging ghost will wipe out/Your city and state.   OxBA

English Train, Summer.   Ralph Pomeroy.   Travelling slowly in the direction of Oxford.   GP

An English Wood.   Robert Graves.   Small pathways idly tend/Towards no certain end.   BrPo

The Englishman. Eliza Cook. Is breathed in the words, "I'm an Englishman." PaPo

The Englishman. Sir William Schwenck Gilbert. Hurrah!/For the true-born Englishman! NOBL

The Englishman in Italy. Robert Browning.
...brittle great fig-trees/Snap off, figs and all.... SeCePo
He heard and he knew this life's secret/I hear and I know. FaBoPP
–If 'twere proper, Scirocco should vanish/In black from the skies! ExPo; OBTV; PoEL 1-5

The Englishman on the French Stage. Sir Owen Seaman. To recognize in me/Its unimpaired ideal of what/An Englishman should be. OBTV

The Enigma. Richard Eberhart. His would survive, though never to him cleave. NYBP

Enigma. Jessie Redmond Fauset. There is no peace with you/Nor ever any rest! PoNe

Enigma. Hugh McCrae. The child's first vision of the insatiate sea. BoAV; PoAu 1-2

Enigma. Richard Murphy. Her future is an apple tree, his past a dark old yew/Growing together in this orchard now. CIP

Enigma. R. S. Thomas. Or would the cracked lips, parted at last, disclose/The embryonic thought that never grows? ChMP

Enigma for Christmas Shoppers. Phyllis McGinley. How what goes up so frequently/So seldom cometh down. PoPl

The Enigma Variations. Paul Petrie. though time is the heart of music. NYBP

Enigmas. Pablo Neruda. the only thing caught, a fish trapped inside the wind. NU

The Enigmatic Traveler. Byron Vazakas. Not Notre Dame as intricate design. AMV-80

Enjoy Thy April Now. Samuel Daniel. That springs and parcheth in one short hour! ElL; ELP

The Enjoyment. *Anonymous.* Down, at once, we sunk to heaven. ErPo

Enjoyment. Theognis. A load of wine will lighten your despair. AWP

The Enkindled Spring. D. H. Lawrence. Less than the wind that runs to the flamy call! NoAm

Enlightenment. Robert V. Carr. Old Spot's respectable and he/Won't stand fer no profanity. BPAW

The Enlightenment. Patricia Sheppard. Make of it what you will. AMV-81

Ennui. Langston Hughes. Being always/poor. OBAL; OBCA

Ennui. Peter Viereck. Sometimes I almost wish I were alive. NYBP

Enoch. Jones Very. And left unfinished and in ruins still/The only temple He delights to fill. HAP

Enoch Arden. Alfred, Lord Tennyson.
And the low moan of leaden-colour'd seas. FaBoPP
Had seldom seen a costlier funeral. BeLS
The sea is His; He made it. TRV

The Enormous Aquarium. Sherod Santos. Like some ancient and magnificent tribe. MAYP

Enough. Arthur Gregor. the far-off lines that feed and feed. TAP

Enough. Tom (Thomas Lansing Masson) Masson. And now I do not greatly care/To shoot more rockets in the air. OBAL

Enough. Marianne Moore. ...it is enough/if present faith mend partial proof. NOBA

Enough! James Scully. It is more/than enough. LTB

Enough Not One. Benjamin Franklin. The rich too much,/Enough not one. TRV

Enough of Thought, Philosopher. Emily Bronte. And vanquished Good, victorious Ill/Be lost in one repose. NCEP

The Enquiry. John Dyer. And made my self quiet, and happy again. OBEC

Enraptured I Gaze. Francis Hopkinson. And the charms of her mind are a heav'n to me. BLSo

Enrica, 1865. Christina Georgina Rossetti. Deep at our deepest, strong and free. TEP

Ensamples of Our Saviour. Robert Southwell. So prayer revives/The soule, by prayer it lives. PoEL 1-5

Enslaved. Claude McKay. To liberate my people from its yoke! BALP; BPo

The Entailed Farm. John Glassco. Who composed our quarrel early and in good season/Buried the hatchet in our father's brain. NOBC

Enter No (Silence is the Blood Whose Flesh. Edward Estlin Cummings. never imaginable mystery)/descend. AP

Entering by His Door. Richard Baxter. What will Thy glory be! BePJ

Entering the Body: The Survivor. Stephen Berg. my fists hardened many days/in the last ovens. NaP

Entering the Desert: Big Circles Running. Wendy Rose. carried into the sky/on the backs of bees/pollinating with poems. TWSS

Entering the Room. Roger Pfingston. and something new will begin/though nothing like what you are thinking. PoDr

Enterprise. Nissim Ezekiel. Home is where we have to gather grace. ACV

Enterprise and Boxer. *Anonymous.* And more, much more can be obtain'd/Upon the same condition. PAH

The Entertainer. Bruce Beaver. ...the brief and everlasting/human story written on the lapsing sands. NOAV

The Entertainment of War. Roy Fisher. Have realized a little what they meant, and for the first time/been afraid. FaBoMo

The Entertainment, or Porch-Verse, at the Marriage.... Robert Herrick. Which spent, one death bring to ye both one grave. CaPo

Enthusiasm. James Clarence Mangan. Beauty, ever let thy magic presence/Shed its glory round my clouded lot. IrPN

The Enthusiast. Herman Melville. Though light forsake thee, never fall/From fealty to light. MAmP

The Enthusiast: an Ode. William Whitehead. And see them all uniting show/That man was made for man.' OBEC

The Enthusiast: or, The Lover of Nature. Joseph Warton. Grace the soft Warbles of her honied Voice. CEP; EnPE; LAuP

Entirely. Louis MacNeice. Road that is right entirely. CMoP; LiTB

Entoptic Colours. Johann Wolfgang von Goethe. Worlds we love and which are little/Harbour the most glorious things. SUW

Entrance Exams. Cuthbert (Edward Bradley) Bede.
7. Name the prima donnas who have appeared in the operas of/Virgil and Horace since... FaBoNo
6. Reduce two academical years to their lowest terms. FaBoNo

Entreaty. Robert Fitzgerald. about the lean hindquarters of my yelping, unpleasant guest. OBSP

The Entrepreneur Chicken Shed His Tail Feathers, Surplus. Josephine Miles. And why he crossed the road. NoAm

Entropy. Theodore Spencer. (The God of order is called Love.) ImOP

Entry. Josephine Miles. To city where the small matter is put down already/To depreciation. AnAmPo

Entwined. *Anonymous.* My mistress, mind you, was not born. WTO

Enueg. Samuel Beckett.
doch doch I assure thee NoAm
...meat bleeding/on th silk of the seas and the arctic flowers/that do not exist. CIP

The Enviable Isles. Herman Melville. While billows endless round the beaches die. AA; AmLP; AnAmPo; FaBoBe

The Envies. George Bowering. where smaller things die early. NOBC

The Envious Critick. William Wycherley. Acting like Demons, that would All deprive/Of heav'n, to which themselves can ne'er arrive. PV

Environ S. Larry Eigner. ...a space/on this side, hut for clouds. NeAP

Environment. Lionel Kearns. So you won't be too surprised when it happens NOBC

L'Envoi. Thomas Lovell Beddoes. Love only on the cheek, which is to me most fair. OBNC

L'Envoi. Willa Cather. When once I am alone and shut the door. HBV 1-2

Envoi. Charles Causley. My name is love. FF

Envoi. J. V. Cunningham. Anger, my ode is written. VGW

L'Envoi. Rudyard Kipling.
Shall draw the Thing as he sees It/for the God of the Things as They are! FaFP; HBV 1-2; OHFP; PoPl; TRV; WGRP
We're down, hull down on the Long Trail–the trail that/is always new. OBEV; OBVV

L'Envoi. Frederic Lawrence Knowles. My life is lifeless till it live in Thee! TrPWD; TRV

Envoi. Dominic Bevin Wyndham Lewis. Should I have warmed my poor old feet as well? FiBHP

Envoi. Eli Mandel. whose children will be colder killers/than the words of this or any other song. NOBC

Envoi. E. L. Mayo. Rumbling on stone that will run us out tomorrow. FAZ

L'Envoi. William Morris. The idle singer of an empty day. EnLi 1-2

Envoi. John G. Neihardt. And Oh, the luring thought of it/Is prayer! HBV 1-2; WGRP

Envoi. Kathleen Raine. oh gladly, love, for you I bear! NeBP; NOBE

L'Envoi. Edwin Arlington Robinson. God's touch will keep the one chord quivering. TrCP

Envoi. Algernon Charles Swinburne. All to the haven where each would be,/Fly. GoJo; SUS; VLP

Envoi. Arthur Symons. And to have done with love/For ever, for your sake. UnTE

Envoi. Anna Wickham. Give me one perfect thing. MoBrPo

L'Envoi: The Return of the Sire de Nesle A.D. 16–. Herman Melville. But blest to fold but thee. APA

Envoy. Bliss Carman. And I drank who now am here/Where my dust with dust confers. HBV 1-2

Envoy. Robert Duncan. Day's lord erases. VGW

Envoy. William Ernest Henley. Unjangled to the end. BrPo

L'Envoy. George Herbert. And then bargain with the winde/To discharge what is behinde. AnAnS 1

Envoy. Richard Hovey.

Epigram: "Exhausted now her sighs, and dry her tears." Walter Savage Landor. God ought to bow profoundly for the favour. FaBoEE

Epigram: "Fair Ursly, in a merry mood." *Anonymous.* My constant physic make it. FaBoEE

Epigram: Fatum Supremum. *Anonymous.* All that we have is but deaths livery. OBS

Epigram: "First in his pride the orient sun's display." Hilaire Belloc. Juliet appears, and changes earth to heaven. FaBoEE

Epigram: "For Hekabe." Plato. You who maddened my heart with love, my Dion! PeHV

Epigram for the Dead at Tegea. *Anonymous.* ...and themselves to go down in the first wave. WaaP

Epigram: "Gathering the bloom of all the fairest boys that be." Strato. Since, like a fragrant grove, these boys all flower in thee. PeHV

Epigram: "Give me a boy whose tender skin." Martial (Marcus Valerius Martialis). And for his sake may no girl win/A corner in my heart. PeHV

Epigram: "Give pensions to the Learned Pig." William Blake. But in the journeyman's labour. FaBoEE

Epigram: "Glad youth had come thy sixteenth year to crown." Decimus Magnus Ausonius. Rather with blithe Adonis shall thou rove/And play the Ganymede to highest Jove. PeHV

Epigram: "God scatters beauty as he scatters flowers." Walter Savage Landor. And at each shrine I bend my knee in turn. FaBoEE

Epigram: "Gold priests, wooden chalices." *Anonymous.* Golden chalices, wooden priests,/as the wretched world stands now. NOBI

Epigram: "Good Fortune, when I hailed her recently." J. V. Cunningham. And could no longer recollect my name. PV

An Epigram: "Great Charles, among the holy gifts of grace." Ben Jonson. What can the poet wish his king may doe,/But that he cure the peoples evill too? OAEP

Epigram: "Great woe, fire & woe." Skythinos. So I lie awake & let my hands fight unfilled love. PeHV

Epigram: "Grown old in love from seven till seven times seven". William Blake. I oft have wished for Hell for Ease from Heaven FaBoEE; OAEL 1-2

Epigram: "Had we two met, blythe-hearted Burns." Walter Savage Landor. Is there a hand-rail to the stairs? FaBoEE

Epigram: "Hail, blissfulest maiden." *Anonymous.* God's Embryo within thy womb. ISi

Epigram: "He drank strong waters and his speech was coarse." Rudyard Kipling. To do good deeds and straight to cloak them, lied. PV

Epigram: "He is my love." *Anonymous.* a boy he is–/for him a kiss. BIrV

Epigram: "Heat goes deep as cold." *Anonymous.* But envy strikes to the marrow/and sticks there for ever. NOBI

Epigram: "Hetero-sex is best." Marcus Argentarius. And it's easy to pretend you're screwing her brother. PeHV

Epigram: "How often, when life's summer day." Walter Savage Landor. And lovers shrivel into friends! FaBoEE

Epigram: "How shall I know if my love lose his youth." Strato. And if I love today, tomorrow's light/Against our love will e'en forbear to fight. PeHV

Epigram: "I am provoked." Strato. Green grapes may be touched, but his ripe/chastity will be guarded. PeHV

Epigram: "I celebrate Rhegion." *Anonymous.* ...piled high/with/thick ivy and a bed of white reed. NOBI

Epigram: "I curse my bearing, childhood, youth." John Millington Synge. To curse–as I have cursed–their birth. FaBoEE

Epigram: "I delight in the prime of a boy of twelve." Strato. If you want the older ones, you don't play/any more, but seek & answer back. PeHV

Epigram: "I dined with Demetrios." Automedon. "Do you teach these boys at night as well?" PeHV

Epigram: "I don't care for women." *Anonymous.* So are the loves they inflame. PeHV

Epigram: "I dreamt that I was God Himself." Ezra Pound. And all the angels sat about/And praised my verses. FaBoEE

Epigram: "I dug and dug amongst the snow." Christina Georgina Rossetti. Will rear no blossom from the sand. FaBoEE

Epigram: "I know him." *Anonymous.* He'll give you what his kind allows,/Cows. BIrV

Epigram: "I like them pale." Strato. But when a glance is sparkling black/It drives me wild. PeHV

Epigram: "I loved thee beautiful and kind." Robert Nugent, Earl Nugent. 'Twere perjury to love thee now. NOEC

Epigram: "I ran upon life unknowing, without or science or art." Alfred, Lord Tennyson. "Here is the first pretty snowdrop"–and it was the dung of a/crow! FaBoEE

Epigram: "I read about the Blaskets and Dunquin." John Millington Synge. And I'd a filthy job–to waste and die. FaBoEE

Epigram: "I was thirsty." Meleager. Antiochus/pours now for me! PeHV

Epigram: "If thou seekest the dread throne of God." *Anonymous.* and straightway bent their unbending necks. ISi

Epigram: "If true that notion, which but few contest." *Anonymous.* For 'tis their glory to be short, and sweet. FaBoEE

Epigram: "If you see someone beautiful." Adaios. shame will bar the only way/to all you want to do. PeHV

Epigram, in a Maid of Honour's Prayer-Book. Alexander Pope. As decent to repent in, as to sin in. FaBoEE

Epigram: "In all those who got". Edward Estlin Cummings. on&off bandwagons/(MEMORIAM. FaBoEE

Epigram: Invocation. Howard Nemerov. Where my images brim and spill/In failures of the full light. OBAL

Epigram: "Ireland never was contented." Walter Savage Landor. Emeralds big as half the county. FaBoEE

Epigram: "It is true that I held Thero fair." Meleager. The delights of hirsute sex/let us leave to Welsh shepherds. PeHV

Epigram: "Just as he is growing a beard." Aulus Persius Flaccus. Fate is quick to revenge. PeHV

Epigram: "Kissing Hippomenes." Paulus Silentiarius. lie cursed between the stale sheets of/paupered monogamy. PeHV

Epigram: "Lasses, like nuts at bottom brown." Allan Ramsay. And syn prove good for nought. FaBoEE

Epigram: "Lately our poets loiter'd in green lanes." Walter Savage Landor. I find the laurel also bears a thorn. FaBoEE

Epigram: "Like when the burning sun doth rise." Strato. To me sole light he'll e'er remain. PeHV

Epigram: "Listen, you who know the pains of love." Meleager. The home of beautiful boys. PeHV

Epigram: "Lo! Beauty flashed forth sweetly." Meleager. Which burns for me alone with friendly light. PeHV

Epigram: "Long hair, endless curls." Strato. Laid on by your merchants of the romantic. PeHV

Epigram: "Loss of our learning brought darkness, weakenss and woe." *Anonymous.* Oaks have entered the places of the poets/and taken the light of the schools from everyone. NOBI

Epigram: "Love brought me quietly." Meleager. You must forget the warmth of beauty/Even in your dreams. PeHV

Epigram: Lucilius. Howard Nemerov. May he continue making love to the mother. OBAL

Epigram: "Me Polytimus vexes and provokes." Martial (Marcus Valerius Martialis). Rather than lead a sumpuous tinselled life/With twenty million dollars and a wife. PeHV

Epigram: "Midas, they say, possessed the art of old." John Wolcot. Touch them with gold, they'll turn to what you please. DBV; ELU

Epigram: "Milo's from home; and, Milo being gone." Martial (Marcus Valerius Martialis). The lands lay fallow, but the wife was till'd. OBVE

Epigram: "Most inexplicable the wiles of boys I deem." Rhianus. The bloom of youth from all, and fair curls turn to grey. PeHV

Epigram: "My better half, why turn a peevish scold." Martial (Marcus Valerius Martialis). A woman everywhere is only cunt. PeHV

Epigram: "My heart still hovering round about you." Robert Nugent, Earl Nugent. How I lived with you is the wonder. NOEC

Epigram: "My soul, sit thou a patient looker-on." Francis Quarles. ...every day/Speaks a new scene; the last act crown the play. PoPle

Epigram: "My soul, what's lighter than a feather? Wind." Francis Quarles. This bubble world. What than this bubble? Nought. FaBoEE

Epigram: Mythological Beast. Howard Nemerov. Blind rider whom it will pluck down and eat. OBAL

Epigram: "Neither in idleness consume thy days." Walter Savage Landor. Nor bend thy back to mow the weeds of praise. FaBoEE

Epigram: "Nicander, ooh..." Alcaeus. How the lovers flee you, and years go. PeHV

Epigram: "No charm can stay, no medicine can assuage." Walter Savage Landor. Makes soft the couch and calms the final rest. FaBoEE

Epigram: "No more of your titled acquaintances boast." Robert Burns. Tho' stack to the cunt of a Queen. FaBoEE

Epigram: "Now art thou fair, Diodorus." Strato. E'en should'st thou wed a woman,/From thee we'll not depart. PeHV

Epigram: "O death, thy certainty is such." Henry Luttrell. How men were ever cheerful. FaBoEE

Epigram: "O Diodorus." *Anonymous.* So in which sea I swim my heart may know. PeHV

Epigram: "O King of the Friday." *Anonymous.* May some fruit from the tree of thy passion/Fall on us this night! BIrV

Epigram: "O mortal man, that lives by bread." Julius Caesar Ibbetson. 'Tis drinking Sally Birkett's ale. FaBoEE

An Epigram of Martial, Imitated. Sir Charles Hanbury Williams. But the wretch that can number his kisses/With few will be ever content. OBEC

Epigram: Of Treason. Sir John (1561-1612) Harington. For if it prosper, none dare call it treason. NIP

Epigram: "Of virtues I most warmly bless." Gerard Manley Hopkins. I own a preference for Pride. FaBoEE

Epilogue to Rhymes and Rhythms. William Ernest Henley. Mama, how long–how long! ViBoPo

Epilogue to the Outrider. Dorothy Livesay. This struggle is our miracle new found. CaP

Epilogue to the Satires. Alexander Pope.
And opes the Temple of Eternity. CoBE
And write next winter more Essays on Man. OAEL 1-2
Like the last Gazette, or the last Address. OBSV
"Nothing is sacred now but Villany." OBSV
Show there was one who held it in disdain. OAEL 1-2
Speak out, and bid me blame no rogues at all. OBSV

Epiphany. Eileen Duggan. King of Europe, King of Asia! ISi

Epiphany. Eileen Shanahan. The Kings kneel to the trinity/And Christ is come again. NeIP

The Epiphany. George Strong. I saw again the common face/And heard the ordinary speech. GoYe

Epiphany: For the Artist. Elizabeth Sewell. ...conceive it how you please/ But paint me these. EyDe

Epipsychidion. Percy Bysshe Shelley.
And come and be my guest,–for I am Love's. EnRP; ERoP 1-2
I pant, I sink, I tremble, I expire! OBRV
I wept, and though it be a dream, I weep. EnLi 1-2
One Heaven, one Hell, one immortality,/And one annihilation... OAEL 1-2
A sepulchre for its eternity. ChRP
Then smile on it, so that it may not die. ISi
The wilderness of this Elysian earth. OBNC

Episode. Cassiano Nunes. I found in it a mark/of consideration and even a touch/of class. PeHV

Episode of the Cherry Tree. Mildred Weston. A patriot/Who would not lie. PV

The Epistemological Rag. Gray Burr. Man a fancy, earth a coral,/Dualism double zero. CoPo

The Epistemologist, over a Brandy, Opining. Robert Sargent. The message unclear. AMV-80

Epistemology. Richard Wilbur. We whisper in her ear, "You are not true." NePoEA; NoAm; NOBA; OBSP; SUW

An Epistle. Robert Browning. The madman saith He said so: it is strange. CABL; VLP

An Epistle. A. D. Hope. ...and through/That dance she moves, and dances too. PoAu 1-2

An Epistle Answering to One That Asked to be Sealed of the Tribe... Ben Jonson. Sir, you are sealed of the tribe of Ben. SeCV 1-2

The Epistle Dedicatory to Chapman's Translation of the Iliad. George Chapman. (Best Prince) then use best; which is Poesies worth. OBS

Epistle for Spring. R. Ellsworth Larsson. ice-clear fire of your name CAW

An Epistle from a Half-Pay Officer in the Country. Richardson Pack. O cursed effects of Honourable Peace! NOEC

Epistle, from Algiers, to Horace Smith. Thomas Campbell. I will palm no more puns upon you. OBTV

An Epistle from Mr. Pope to Dr. Arbuthnot. Alexander Pope.
He helped to bury whom he helped to starve. OBSV
Thus far was right, the rest belongs to heav'n. NOEC
Who would not weep, if Atticus were he? TW
Wit that can creep, and pride that licks the dust. OBSV; TW

Epistle from Mrs. Yonge to Her Husband. Mary Wortley, Lady Montagu.
And you the father of a glorious race/Endowed with Ch–l's strength and Low–r's face. NoP

Epistle II: To a Socialist in London. Robert Bridges. "Who did not, now can not, assist the community, YE DIE!" FM

Epistle in Form of a Ballad to His Friends. Francois Villon. Your poor old friend, what, will you leave him there? AWP; LiTW

Epistle of Condolence. Thomas Moore. To take to whipped syllabub all my life long. OnYI

The Epistle of Othea to Hector (excerpt). Christine de Pisan. And yet is it feeble hold on a slipper eel. PBWP

The Epistle of Rosamond to King Henry the Second. Michael Drayton. In this shew Mercie, as I ever lov'd thee. AnAnS 2

Epistle to a Desponding Sea-Man. Philip Freneau. I would clew up my topsails, and bid him farewell. MOS

An Epistle to a Friend, to Persuade Him to the Wars. Ben Jonson. Who falls for love of God, shall rise a star. TEP

An Epistle to a Lady. Mary Leapor. Thousands may enter through the gates of death. NOEC

Epistle to a Lady: Of the Characters of Women. Alexander Pope.
Then break your heart when Cloe dies. OBSV
To you gave sense, good-humour, and a poet. NOEC

Epistle to a Young Friend. Robert Burns. And may ye better reck the rede,/Than ever did th' adviser! EBEV; MCCG

Epistle to Augusta. George Gordon, Lord Byron. The tie which bound the first endures the last! AnEnPo

Epistle to Augustus (excerpt). Alexander Pope. The silly bard grows fat, or falls away. EBEV

Epistle to Be Left in the Earth. Archibald MacLeish. Voices are crying an unknown name in the sky. BoLiVe; CMoP; ImOP; MoAB; MoAmPo; NOBA; TrGrPo

Epistle to Davie, a Brother Poet. Robert Burns. The heart ay's the part ay,/That makes us right or wrang. OBEC

Epistle to Dr. Blacklock. Robert Burns. That's the true pathos and sublime/Of human life. OBEC

Epistle to Elizabeth, Countess of Rutland. Ben Jonson. And such, or my hopes fail, shall make you shine. JCP

Epistle to George Keats (excerpt). John Keats. Like a sweet nun in holy-day attire? ChRP

Epistle to Henry Wriothesley, Earl of Southhampton. Samuel Daniel. Only the best composed and worthiest hearts/God sets to act the hard'st and constant'st parts. EnRePo

Epistle to James Smith. Robert Burns. Content wi' you to mak a pair,/ Whare'er I gang. BSV; CABL; MCCG; OBEC

Epistle to John Guthrie. Sydney Goodsir Smith. Jeez! wha'ld use ale for Athol Brose? OxBS

Epistle to John Hamilton Reynolds. John Keats.
It spoils the singing of the Nightingale. ERoP 1-2
Than with these horrid moods be left i' the lurch. OBNC
Take refuge–Of bad lines a centiane dose/Is sure enough–and so "here follows prose." OAEL 1-2

Epistle to Miss Teresa Blount, on Her Leaving the Town... Alexander Pope. Look sour, and hum a Tune, as you may now. EBEV

Epistle to Mr. Murray. George Gordon, Lord Byron. But please, sir, to mention your pay. FaBoUs

An Epistle to My Friend J. B. Robert Dodsley. Dire rocks! near which whoever came,/Was sure to split, and sink and damn. NOEC

An Epistle to R. William Dunkin. Is but a shell without the gem. NOEC

An Epistle to Richard Boyle, Earl of Burlington (excerpt). Alexander Pope.
And laughing Ceres reassume the land. NOEC
And swear no day was ever passed so ill. OBSV

An Epistle to Robert Lloyd, Esq. William Cowper. 'Tis ready polish'd from the mine. FiP

An Epistle to Sir Edward Sackville, Now Earl of Dorset. Ben Jonson. Donnor's or Donnee's to their practise shall/Find you to reckon nothing, me owe all. NCEP

The Epistle to Sir Richard Temple (excerpt). Alexander Pope. 'Twas all for fear the knaves should call him fool. DBV

Epistle to the Gentiles. Alfred Hayes. Of course they kill. Why did I ever/ delude myself they do not kill? TrJP

Epistle to the President, Vice-President, and Members...(excerpt). Alexander Geddes. I'll pledge my pen, you'll judgment pass/In favor of the Scottis lass. OxBS

Epistle to the Reader. Walker Gibson. ...I say it's funny/That life is dearest when it costs us money. PP

An Epistle to the Right Hon. Charles James Fox (excerpt). Thomas Maurice. And show mankind a righteous ruler reigns. NOEC

Epistle to the Right Honourable William Pulteney, Esq. John Gay. All Frenchmen are of petit-maitre kind. OBTV

An Epistle Written in the Country to.... Soame Jenyns. We home return, a wondrous token/Of Heaven's kind care, with limbs unbroken. OBSV

Epistles. Horace.
And each should mete himself by his own measure. OBVE
No; do the work you know, and tarry where you are. OBVE
That angry mood engendered rooted hate,/War to the knife, and an untimely fate. OBVE
Your client keeps by slipping through the yard. OBVE

Epistles to Mr. Pope (excerpt). Edward Hilton Young. Thus nature's refuse, and the dregs of men,/Compose the black militia of the pen. OBSV

Epistolary Briefs to Proclus. Jose I. de Diego Padro. Nothing, nothing, nothing happens here. InW

An Epistolary Essay from M.G. to O.B. upon Their Mutual Poems. John Wilmot, Earl of Rochester. These things considered make me, in despite/Of idle rumor, keep at home and write. APAS

Epistrophe. LeRoi (Imamu Amiri Baraka) Jones. I wish some weird looking animal/would come along. CAD; NNP; PoNe

Epitahlamium for Cavorting Ghosts. Dachine Rainer. I have all sensuous hell to love you in. NePoAm-2

Epitaph. Lascelles Abercrombie. ...I am;/Perfection: I am nothing, I am dead. MoBrPo; ViBoPo

Epitaph. Sholom Aleichem. He suffered–God alone knows it–/In secret– revealed it no none. TrJP

An Epitaph. *Anonymous.*
And am amazed that Death, that tyrant grim,/Should think of me, who never thought of him. ExPo
And his soul is bound up in the bundle/of life. TrJP
And set its crown of glory upon your/head. TrJP
He will see, in its stead, with his/spiritual eye. TrJP

An Epitaph of the Death of Nicholas Grimald. Barnabe Googe. But fortune favors fools, as old men say,/And lets them live, and takes the wise away. EnRePo

Epitaph on a Bombing Victim. Roy Fuller. Do not ask his nation; that/ Was History's confederate. NeBP

Epitaph on a Career Woman. William Cole. In hopes that they'd be detected. PV

Epitaph on a Child Killed by Procured Abortion. *Anonymous.* Honour, in spite of love, pronounced thy death. NOEC

Epitaph on a Dentist. *Anonymous.* John Brown is filling his last cavity. FaBoEE; GoTF; OxBoLi; TreFS

Epitaph on a Dormouse, Which Some Children Were to Bury. *Anonymous.* Repent of yours in time. OxBChV

Epitaph on a Fir-Tree. Richard Murphy. We two are left. They walked through pergolas/And planted well, so that we might do better. FaBoTw

Epitaph on a Free but Tame Redbreast. William Cowper. Nor was, like theirs, his bosom cold,/But always in a flame. PBBP

Epitaph on a Great Sleeper. Sir Aston Cokayne. Had the Devil a bed, he would pray him to take him. FaBoEE

Epitaph on a Hare. William Cowper. And, partner once of Tiney's box,/ Must soon partake his grave. FiP; FM; HAP; HBV 1-2; HBVY; HeIP; NOEC; NoP; PoEL 1-5; PoPle; SeCeV

Epitaph on a Madman's Grave. Morris Gilbert. The way he used to do when he was five. YaD

Epitaph on a Marf. *Anonymous.* 'E'd 'a' split 'is fice in 'arf. PV

Epitaph on a Party Girl. Richard Usborne. Goes to bed beneath this stone/Early, sober, and alone. FaBoEE

Epitaph on a Pessimist. Thomas Hardy. My dad had done the same. FaBoEE; FF

Epitaph on a Quack. *Anonymous.* Go to my son, by whom my medicine's sold. FaBoUs

An Epitaph on a Robin-Redbreast. Samuel Rogers. But Love, and Joy, and smiling Spring/Inspire their little souls to sing! FaBoEE; FM; PBBP

Epitaph on a Schoolmaster. Robert Burns. For clever deils he'll mak them! FaBoCo

Epitaph on a Tuft-Hunter. Thomas Moore. Genteelly damn'd beside a Duke,/Than sav'd in vulgar company. FaBoCo; FaBoEE

Epitaph on a Tyrant. W. H. Auden. And when he cried the little children died in the streets. ELU; HeIP; OBSP

Epitaph on a Vagabond. Alexander Gray. Though in my life I never thought of death,/Death thought of me. HBMV

Epitaph on a Waiter. David McCord. God caught his eye. NIP; NLV; OBAL; PPJ

Epitaph on a Warthog. J. B. Morton. Delights us yet, as Lady A–. PV

Epitaph on a Well-Known Poet. Thomas Moore. Peace to his manes; and may he sleep/As soundly as his readers did! DBV

Epitaph on a Willing Girl. Thomas Rowlandson. The scabbard of ten/ Thousand pricks. FaBoEE

Epitaph on a Worthy Clergyman. Benjamin Franklin. And learn each grace his pulpit taught before. TRV

Epitaph on a Young Child. Ivor Gurney. Or girl's beauty–a Western spirit in a loved coloured dress of/flesh. FaBoEE

Epitaph on a Young Poet Who Died before Having Achieved Success. Amy Lowell. Of one who died of growing pains. OBAL

Epitaph on Achilles. *Anonymous.* Sea Thetis bore may hear its dirge of the sea. AWP

Epitaph on an Army of Mercenaries. Alfred Edward Housman. And saved the sum of things for pay. BrPo; CMoP; CoBMV; ForPo; MMM; MoAB; MoVE; NIP; NoAm; NOBE; OBEV; OBWP; OxBTC; PPP; PrIm; SaC; UnPo; ViBoPo; WaaP

Epitaph on an Engraver. Henry David Thoreau. He ne'er will get translated to the skies. EyDe

Epitaph on an Infant. Crinagoras. And, earth, lie lightly on his little grave. AWP

Epitaph on an Irish Priest. *Anonymous.* I hope I still may play the lyre. FaBoEE

Epitaph on an Unfortunate Artist. Robert Graves. This formula for drawing comic rabbits made. FaBoEE; NOBL

Epitaph on Any Man. Arthur Seymour John Tessimond. Tired, to be content with discontent. PoL

Epitaph on Charles II. John Wilmot, Earl of Rochester. Nor ever did a wise one. DBV; FaBoCo; FiBHP; GoTF; HBV 1-2; TreFS; TrGrPo

Epitaph on Colonel Francis Chartres. John Arbuthnot. ...by his bestowing it on the/most UNWORTHY of ALL MORTALS. FaBoEE

An Epitaph on Doctor Donne, Deane of Pauls. Elizabeth T. Corbett. He must be dead first, let' it alone for mee. AnAnS 2

Epitaph on Dr. Johnson. Soame Jenyns. A Christian and a scholar–but a brute. ELU

Epitaph on Dr. Keene. Thomas Gray. Who eat up a fat goose, but could not digest her. FaBoEE

Epitaph on Dr. Keene's Wife. Thomas Gray. She had a bad face, which did always molest her. FaBoEE

An Epitaph: On Elizabeth Chute. Ben Jonson. And till the coming of the soul/To fetch the flesh, we keep the roll. EnRePo

Epitaph on Elizabeth, L. H. Ben Jonson. Fitter, where it died to tell,/Than that it lived at all. Farewell. BiP; CABA; EIL; ELP; EnL; ForPo; HAP; HBV 1-2; HeIP; InPo; NIP; NoP; OBEV; ViBoPo; WHA 1-2

Epitaph on Erotion. [James Henry] Leigh Hunt. But this tomb here be alone,/The only melancholy stone. OBRV

Epitaph on Floyd. *Anonymous.* And steal your linen from your mould'ring clay. PoL

Epitaph on Francis Atterbury, Bishop of Rochester. Matthew Prior. On a single surmise that the owner is dead. FaBoEE

Epitaph on Himself. Samuel Taylor Coleridge.
All alone and unknown, at Edinbro' in an inn. FaBoEE
He ask'd, and hoped, through Christ. Do thou the same! OxBoCh

Epitaph on Himself. Alexander Pope. Trusts in God, that as well as he was, he shall be. FaBoEE

Epitaph on Himself. Mathurin Regnier. That Death should turn her thoughts on me,/Who never thought of her at all. LiTW

An Epitaph on His Grandfather. Thomas Shipman. Being born in good days, but deceased in bad. CBEP

Epitaph on James Grieve, Laird of Boghead. Robert Burns. Then welcome–hail! damnation. TW

Epitaph on James Moore Smythe. Alexander Pope. For how can no-thing be annihilated?/Ex nihilo nihil fit. FaBoEE

Epitaph on John Dove. Robert Burns. And port was celestial glory. FaBoCo

Epitaph on John Knott. *Anonymous.* And here he lies and still is Knott. FaBoEE; ShM

Epitaph on Johnson. William Cowper. By fame on earth–by glory in the skies! EiCP

Epitaph on Laurence Sterne. David Garrick. Where genius, wit, and humour sleep with Sterne? FaBoEE

An Epitaph on M.H. Charles Cotton. To seek new lechery in Death. EBEV; FaBoEE

Epitaph on Maria Wentworth. Thomas Carew. We owe this world, where vertue must/Frail as our flesh crumble to dust. PoEL 1-5

An Epitaph on Master Philip Gray. Ben Jonson. What surety of life have thou, and I? FaBoEE

An Epitaph on Master Vincent Corbett. Ben Jonson. Who makes the one, so it be first, makes both. JCP

Epitaph on Mistress Mary Draper. Charles Cotton. They must strive to be as good/Alive; or 'tis impossible. CavP

Epitaph on Mr. Robert Port. Charles Cotton. And here with him entomb'd do lye/Honour, and Hospitalitie. CavP

Epitaph on One Lockyer, Inventor of a Patent Medicine. *Anonymous.* This Verse is lost, his PILL embalmes him safe/To future Times without an Epitaph. FaBoUs

Epitaph on Pegasus, a Limping Gay. Antonio Beccadelli. So, like the ancients, I advise/You too should make this sacrifice. PeHV

Epitaph on Peter Robinson. Francis, Lord Jeffrey Jeffrey. Who broke the laws of God, and man, and metre. OxBoLi

Epitaph on Prince Frederick. *Anonymous.* Why, there's no more to be said. OxBoLi

Epitaph on Prince Henry. Hugh Holland. So fair a star as Harry. FaBoEE

Epitaph on Queen Elizabeth, Wife of Henry VII. *Anonymous.* And owr kyn Harry long lyff and pease. AtBAP

Epitaph on Robert Southey. Thomas Moore. Oh! may the earth on him lie lighter/Than did his quartos upon us! FaBoCo; FaBoEE; PP

Epitaph on S.P. a Child of Q. El. Chappel. Ben Jonson.
But, being so much too good for earth,/Heaven vowes to keepe him. SeCP; SeCV 1-2
Heaven vowes to keepe him. AnAnS 2; SeCP

Epitaph on Sir Edward Giles and His Wife. Robert Herrick. And so to bed: pray wish us all good rest. PoPle

Epitaph on Sir Walter Pye, Attorney of the Wards... John Hoskyns. The Devil, long since, had had this dish. FaBoEE

Epitaph: On Sir Walter Rawleigh at His Execution. *Anonymous.* We dy'd, thou onely liv'dst that day. OBS

An Epitaph on the Admirable Dramatic Poet, W. Shakespeare. John Milton. That kings for such a tomb would wish to die. FaBoEE; HBV 1-2

Epitaph on the Countess Dowager of Pembroke. William Browne. Time shall throw a dart at thee. CBEP; FaBoEE; LoBV; NOBE; OBS

Epitaph on the Duke of Grafton. Sir Fleetwood Shepherd. But here lies Henry, Duke of Grafton. FaBoEE

Epitaph on the Earl of Leicester. Sir Walter Ralegh. Here lies the Lord of Leicester that all the world did hate. EnRePo; SiPS

Epitaph on the Earl of Strafford. John Cleveland.
Here lies blood, and let it lie/Speechless still, and never cry. CavP; FaBoEE; FaBoPV; NOBE; SeCePo

Epitaph on the Earl of Stratford. John Cleveland. Here lies blood. And let it lie/Speechless still, and never cry. JCP

Erosion. Edwin John Pratt. The sculpture of these granite seams/Upon a woman's face. CaP; CoBE

Erotic Suite (excerpt). Jose Luis Vega.
I come you go/like the waves/of loving. InW
My love, like the vast majority,/lives touching poetry. InW

Erotica. Endre Farkas. until your senses, all so aroused/come together, come alive. CaPN

Erotion. Algernon Charles Swinburne. Lull thee or lure, more fond thou wilt not find. PoEL 1-5

The Errand Imperious. Edwin Markham. The splendors of the sunrise in your heart. PAL; PGD

Errant. John Godfrey. ...I make sure that last/taxi docks at the red light, and then there's my key. APU

Errantry. Robert Fitzgerald. Green-eyed, bedizened, at the dappled center. NYBP

Errata. Charles Simic. when I should have shouted/her name NNaP

Erris Coast, 1943. Hugh Connell. The sound of Brendan's bell, and the sloughed-off pelt of a wild/swan. NeIP

Error Pursued. Helen Pinkerton. ...offending will would still deny/Dependence, know denial too must/end. NePoAm

Errore. Pier Giorgio Di Cicco. ...it is all right, you can come/out now, god is sorry about the wrong wrapper. NOBC

Errors of Ecstasie. George Darley. Hence come thy misery. Answer, if you can. OnYI

Es Fallt Ein Stern Herunter. Heinrich Heine. The swan has sung his dying lay. AWP

Es Stehen Unbeweglich. Heinrich Heine. My heart's own darling's face. AWP; TrJP

Esau. Leib Kwitko. Lay your hand upon them,/Your old, hairy hand. VWA

Escalade. Arthur Symons. I yield, I'll love you, lest it be/I die of you ere you of me! UnTE

The Escalator. Alex Glasgow. Floating slowly down the escalator,/Slowly, lonely, to another train. OBET

The Escapade. David Ignatow. they sink to their deaths,/the haul beside them still theirs. PP

Escapade. Kenneth Leslie. This she'll remember, when off the foggy banks/The clammy cod lie quivering on her planks. EtS

An Escape. Abu Nuwas. Words of a night, she said, to bring the day. ErPo

Escape. Robert Graves. O Life! O Sun! BrPo; MoBrPo

The Escape. Ivor Gurney. Trefoil–hedge sparrow–the stars on the edge at night. OBSP

Escape. Georgia Douglas Johnson. Hug me round/In your solitude/Profound. PoBA

Escape. Andrew McCord Jones. These fools of time/Who know no distance. LFAC

The Escape. Edwin Muir. I'll see the enemy's face. WaP

Escape. Ilya Rubin. I ran until gallows tripped over/remembering the skill of love. VWA

The Escape. William Stafford. down the page and on out like this over the edge. NNaP

The Escape. Mark Van Doren. We called him wild; but the plover/Watched him, and was tame. MoAmPo

Escape. Elinor Wylie. The silver wasp-nests hang like fruit. AnFE; APA; LiTA; MoAmPo

Escape and Return. Elizabeth Jennings. ...the landscape drained/Of everything but its own light NePoEA

Escape at Bedtime. Robert Louis Stevenson. And the stars going round in my head. BrR; HBVY; TiPo; TreFS; TrGrPo

Escape to Love. Patrick MacDonogh.
But no friend to the breed that threw them out. BIrV
Wire in the gapped hedge saved the uncaptured hare... BIrV

Escapist's Song. Theodore Spencer. Her skin was satin and gold. PoL

Eshu, the God of Fate. Anonymous. And kills a bird yesterday. WTO

Eskimo Chant. Anonymous. Follow its old footprints/In the winter night. RFM; WHW

Eskimo Occasion. Judith Rodriquez. Mummy is singing at breakfast and dancing!/So big! CBAP; FaBoWP; NOAV

Eskimoes Again. Dick Gallup. A fine yellow film follows where they go/The ancient rugged Eskimoes. ANYP

ESP. Carter Revard. of empty blowing prairie/on the coldest winter day. VoR

Especially When the October Wind. Dylan Thomas. By the sea's side hear the dark-vowelled birds. CABA; DiPo; LiTB; MoAB; MoBrPo; NeBP; OAEP; OxBTC

Esperanza. James Scully. to bury her face in the dust of Puerto Pobre. LTB; NYP

Essay. Bernadette Mayer. Tenants of a vision we rent out endlessly. APU

Essay in Defense of the Movies. Walker Gibson. Of all that's sacred, first comes motherhood. NePoAm

An Essay on Criticism. Alexander Pope.
And bid alternate passions fall and rise! UnPo
As all looks yellow to the jaundiced eye. OAEP; PoEL 1-5; PPoe
Flies o'er the unbending corn, and skims along the main. BoLiVe
Hills peep o'er hills, and Alps on Alps arise!... ChTr Make use of ev'ry friend–and ev'ry foe. TreFT
Make use of ev'ry friend–and ev'ry foe. TreFT
Nature, like liberty, is but restrain'd/By the same laws which first herself ordain'd. TreFT
Not free from faults, nor yet too vain to mend. ATP; MBW 1-2; PoEL 1-5
Or one vain wit's, that might a hundred tire. OBSV
To teach vain Wits a science little known,/T' admire superior sense, and doubt their/own. OAEP; PoEL 1-5

Essay on Deity. Elder Olson. Whether you will or no,/You have accepted him. MoRP

Essay on Lunch. Walker Gibson. And let the hasty hustle, if they will. NYBP

Essay on Man. Anonymous. And then hangs curtains up to shut it out. PoToHe

An Essay on Man. Alexander Pope.
All partial evil, universal good. WGRP
And all of God, that bless Mankind or mend. ViBoPo
And all our Knowledge, is OURSELVES TO KNOW. ATP; CEP; MBW 1-2
Behind the cloud-topped hill, an humbler heaven. TrGrPo
From thee to nothing. ImOP
The glory, jest, and riddle of the world! DiPo; GoBC; GoTF; NOEC; PrIm; TreFS; TrGrPo; TRV; ViBoPo
His faithful dog shall bear him company. GoTF; NU; OBEC; TreFS
An honest man's the noblest work of God. AnFE; GoTF
Is not thy reason all these pow'rs in one? NU
One truth is clear, WHATEVER IS, IS RIGHT. CEP; EnL; EnLi 1-2; FaBoPV; MBW 1-2; NAWM 1-2; NoP; OAEP; OBEC; PoEL 1-5
The rest is all but leather or prunella. BoLiVe; TrGrPo
Rests and expatiates in a life to come. GoTF
See Cromwell damned to everlasting fame! ViBoPo
The soul, uneasy, and confined from home,/Rests and expatiates in a life to come. TreF; ViBoPo
Then drop into thyself, and be a fool! ExPo; FiP
Thus God and Nature link'd the gen'ral frame,/And bade Self-love and Social be the same. CEP
Till tired he sleeps, and life's poor play is o'er. FiP; TrGrPo
'Tis this, Though man's a fool, yet God is wise. GoTL
'Twas all for fear the knaves should call him Fool. ViBoPo
Without this just gradation could they be/Subjected, these to those, or all to thee? HeIP

Essay on Marriage. Anne Finch, Countess of Wilchilsea. We must achieve what we expect. FaBoTw

Essay on Memory. Robert D. Fitzgerald. in older abyss where time slept stirless yet. BoAV

Essay on Psychiatrists. Robert Pinsky.
Blind women, tireless, and the blind little boy. PoA
Son's head impaled on the stiff spear clutched/In her own hand soiled with dirt and blood. HaCAP

Essay on Rime (excerpt). Karl Shapiro.
Its poems appear as nameless synonyms/In the faint collective effort of our art. PP
Unmasks the character and lays bare the face/Which legend, out of goodness, often hides. PP

An Essay on the Fleet Riding in the Downes. Anonymous. That we may finde the same Powers on the Main,/Secure three Kingdoms in the Oak again. CoMu

An Essay on the Genius of Pope (excerpt). Charles Lloyd. Howe'er strong talents exercise their skill. OBRV

An Essay on Translated Verse (excerpt). Wentworth Dillon, Earl of Roscommon. For Truth shines brightest through the plainest dress. FaBoUs

An Essay on Woman. Mary Leapor. Unhappy woman's but a slave at large. NOEC

An Essay upon Satire. John Sheffield. Learn to write well, or not to write at all. APAS

Essence. Samuel Greenberg. Through scepters create emotional resist. MoPo; NePA

Essential oils–are wrung. Emily Dickinson. Makes summer when the lady lies/In ceaseless rosemary. AmPP; CBEP

Essentials. Samuel Greenberg. The bathers fought the ocean's hurl. LiTA

Essex Regiment March. George Edward Woodberry. We march, we sail, whoever fail, the Flower/of Essex goes. PAH

Estat ai en greu cossirier. Beatriz de Dia. if you'd promise me to do/everything I'd want you to. ErPo

The Estate: "Waking by Night'. Charles Brasch. I hear that fathomless ocean breaking about us/In sleep, and all things borne to dissolution. AnNZ

Euclid Avenue. Charles Simic. its screendoor screeching,/endlessly screeching. LCAP

Eudaimon. Kathleen Raine. There one; on earth alone/I lie, you free. PBWP

Eugene Delacroix Says. Edward Dorn. and, I have to add, I hope those satraps/do not wake in time. NoAm

Eugenia: Presage of Storme. George Chapman. But in fresh deluge, Heav'n it selfe came downe. FaBoEn

Eugenio Pacelli. Francis Neilson. His birthright name Pacelli will be sung/In glad Te Deums by celestial choirs. GoYe

The Eugenist. Robert Graves. And Germans with no envy in their souls. FaBoEE

Eulalie. A Song. Edgar Allan Poe. While ever to her young Eulalie upturns her violet eye. EvOK; LaNeLa; Par

Eulogy for a Tough Guy. Daniel L. Klauck. none of us could remember who charlie was. LFAC

Eulogy for Alvin Frost. Audre Lorde. We need you/and there are so few/left. CNA

Eulogy for Hasdai Ibn Shaprut. Anonymous. Once more to trust, once more his/God to love. TrJP

Eulogy for Populations. Ron Welburn. will be buried with secrets/This scares me. PoBA

Eulogy to the Bow and Arrow. Anonymous. And it gained the title of Yellow Bow. WTO

Eumares. Asclepiades. For nothing shalt thou find but bones and dust. AWP

The Eumenides at Home (parody). James Agate. That what was good enough for Aeschylus is by no means/Good enough for me! BXAP

Eunice in the Evening. Gwendolyn Brooks. (And each of us has leave to take/A ginger cookie, too.) TiPo

Euphoria, Euphoria. Mark DeFoe. and me splendid with love for all. AMV-80

Eureka! Alfred Denis Godley. And our efforts success will assuredly bless if we only are/faithful to Soccer! CenHV

Eureka. Ruth O. Maunders. not from her tongue/but from her mind. AMV-80

Euridice Saved. Linda Gregg. Art, I was thinking, is the imitation/of what we called nothing when we lived on the earth. NPGG

Euroclydon. Abbie Huston Evans. And pants against my door./Old tiger, hail! NePoAm

Europa. William Johnson Cory. Your name's the name which half the world divided/Henceforth shall bear. NBM

Europa. William Plomer. Out, far out, by the Thunderer/To sea on a great white bull. MoBS

Europa. Stephen Henry Thayer. That we may see! AA

Europa. Derek Walcott. the hooves and horn-points anagrammed in stars. NoP

Europe. John Ashbery. followed by a long beam of/light skyward, slowly sweeping in a circle/the breath. CoPo

Europe. Louis Dudek.
kings fall with their crowns, poets sink with their laurels. OBCV
...who learn of happiness/from the report of their own actions. OBCV; PeCV

Europe and America. David Ignatow. as guns pounded on the shore. AmFN; NNaP; UnPo

The European Night. Stanislav Vinaver. It would like to light up expanses/And to chase away apparitions. VWA

The European Shoe. Michael Benedikt. Gaily it sets out into the depths of my profoundest/closet, to do battle with the dusts of summer. AmPA; ConAP; TwCP

Eurydice. Francis William Bourdillon. And then I saw no more the sun,/And lost were life and love. HBV 1-2

Eurydice. Hilda ("H. D.") Doolittle. hell must open like a red rose/for the dead to pass. VGW

Eurydice. Linda Gregg. near the opening which is the way in for you/and was the way out for me, my love. NPGG

Eurymachus's Fancy. Robert Greene. And swore no thing so sweet and sour as love. OBSC

Eurynome. Jay Macpherson. Oh who would not sleep with a snake? NMP; OBCV; PV

Eutaw Springs. Philip Freneau. A brighter Phoebus of their own. AA; BeLS; PAH

Euthymiae Raptus. George Chapman. And is the yellow Autumns Nightingall. PoEL 1-5

Eutopia. Francis Turner Palgrave. Or the songs of the butterflies be. OBVV

Eutychides. Lucilius [(or Lucillius)]. Where's a poor tortured soul to dwell? UnS

Ev'ry Time I Feel de Spirit. Anonymous. I feel de spirit, move-in' in my heart,/I will pray Jordan pray. BoAN 1-2

Eva's Lament (excerpt). Anonymous. For I have towchyd his owyn dere tre. AtBAP

Evacuation of New York by the British. Anonymous. Health, peace, and joy to Washington! PAH

Evadne. Hilda ("H. D.") Doolittle. that great arm-full of yellow flowers. BoWoP; MAPA

Evanescence. Frederic William Henry Myers. His swiftest and his sweetest thought/Can never poet say. OBVV

Evanescence. Harriet Prescott Spofford. So are lilies, so are roses! AA

Evangeline. Henry Wadsworth Longfellow.
The deep-voiced neighboring ocean/Speaks, and in accents disconsolate answers the wail of the forest. BeLS
"Father, I thank thee!" AA
Leaped like the roe when he hears in the woodland the voice of the huntsman? WBLP
Leaving behind them the dead on the shore, and the village in ruins. AnNE
Lighted her soul in sleep with the glory of regions ce-/lestial. PoEL 1-5
List to a Tale of Love in Acadie, home of the happy. GoTF; TreF
Numberless noisy weathercocks rattled and/sang of mutation. AA
Sounds of a horn they heard, and the distant/lowing of cattle. AA
Speaks, and in accents disconsolate answers the wail of the forest. AnNE; SpRo
That which the fountain sends forth returns again to the/fountain. PoToHe
While they repeated his prayer, and said, "O Father, forgive/them!" TreF

Evangeline. Norma E. Smith. Tonight you walk these fields again. CaP

The Evangelist. Donald Davie. Each does us credit, and we know it too. NePoEA

The Evangelist. Bennie Lee Sinclair. but always his skill is superior. TAT

Evangelize! Henry Crocker. Evangelize! Evangelize! BLRP

The Evans Country. Kingsley Amis.
A bit on the grand side. What about you? NOBL
He thought, ringing the bell for more of both. NOBL
Style's something else again. NOBL
Tall hotels ablaze with neon/Magnetise the sons of Dai. NOBL
When he touched Dilys up with his gloves on. NOBL
Who's doing better, then? What about you? NOBL
You'll know me easy, because/I'm wearing a black tie, love.' NOBL

Evaporation Poems. Kathleen Norris. The chill settles in around the place where I have moved/with everything. IHMS

Evarra and His Gods. Rudyard Kipling. Maker of Gods in lands beyond the sea. MoBrPo

An Evasion. Douglas Livingstone. He does not choose to cause her life to stop. PeSA

Evasion. Blanaid Salkeld. she might have to acknowledge her latest face. NeIP

Eve. Anonymous. Hell and pain and terror, I. BIrV

Eve. Arthur J. Bull. Innocent as the rose/Then, each rejoicing Spring. UnPo

Eve. Jakov Fichman. ...Eden is enchanted/only till night awakes the shadow in the brush. VWA

Eve. David Gascoyne. In whose black sex/Our ancient culpability like a pearl is set. GTBS-P

Eve. Oliver Herford.
Meseems your "Garden" never could have grown. OBAL
The most Eve did was to display/Contributory negligé. HBMV; YaD

Eve. Ralph Hodgson. "Eva!" again. ALV; AnFE; BoLiVe; BrPo; EvOK; HBV 1-2; LiTB; LiTM; MoAB; MoBrPo; OnMSP; SeCeV; TrCP; TrGrPo; UnPo

Eve. Rainer Maria Rilke. and she had as yet hardly known God. MoRP

Eve. Christina Georgina Rossetti. Grinned an evil grin and thrust/His tongue out with its fork. CH; FM; GTBS-P; NBM; NIP; OxBoCh; PoEL 1-5; SeCeV

The Eve. Howard Schwartz. And all of us will dance in a circle/And sing. VWA

Eve. Robert Leopold Wolf. He ploughed, all glowing, and planted/The apples of her breast. HBMV

Eve Am I, Great Adam's Wife. Anonymous. There'd be no Hell, there'd be no grief,/there'd be no terror, but for me. NOBI

Eve in My Legend. Denis Devlin. Nothing to know that is not she/Nor she know anything but me. IPY

Eve in Old Age. Rob Holland. The dark passed through her into the dark. NIP

Eve in Reflection. Jay Macpherson. And Adam walks in the cold night/Wilderness, waste wood. OBCV

Eve: Night Thoughts. Judson Jerome. By night, as he dreams, I am inventing the lie. SM

The Eve of Bunker Hill. Clinton Scollard. The men whose might made strong the height on the eve of/Bunker Hill! MC; PAH

The Eve of Crecy. William Morris. Ah! qu'elle est belle La Marguerite. OBVV; VLP

Eve of Easter. Bernadette Mayer. I lost the prejudice of paradise/And wound up caring for the babies of these guys. APU

The Eve of Saint John. Sir Walter Scott. That nun was Smaylho'me's Lady gay,/That monk the bold Baron. EnRP; PoEL 1-5

The Eve of St. Agnes. John Keats. The Beadsman, after a thousand aves told,/For aye unsought-for slept among his ashes cold. AtBAP; BeLS; BoLiVe; DiPo; DTo; EnL; ERoP 1-2; ExPo; FiP; GoTL; HAP; HBV 1-2; HoPM; LiTL; MasP; MBW 1-2; MyFE; NIP; NoP; OAEL 1-2; OAEP; OBNC; OBNV; OBRV; PoEL 1-5; PoLf; SeCeV; TEP; TreF; TrGrPo; ViBoPo; WHA

The Eve of St. Mark. John Keats. Then lastly to his holy shrine,/Exalt amind the tapers' shine/At Venice,– EnRP

Eve's Advice to the Children of Israel. Joachim Neugroschel. I often dream of paradise. VWA

Eve's Birth. Kim Chernin. and breath,/ribbed with mortality. VWA

Eve's Daughter. Edward Rowland Sill. She took a good half-hour to loose and lay/Those locks in dazzling disarrangement so! AmePo

Eve's Lament. *Anonymous.* There would be no fear, if it were not for me. OnYI

Eve's Song in the Garden. Lynn Gottlieb. we had not yet eaten/from the tree in the center of the garden/which taught us/how to know death. VWA

Eve's Version. James Harrison. ...God was right/about him–he wasn't ready to be imperfect. AMV-81

Eve-Song. Mary Gilmore. A thread to bind the heart of man! CBAP; PoAu 1-2

Evelyn. Rossiter Johnson. Let me be dumb! AA

Evelyn Hope. Robert Browning. You will wake, and remember, and understand. BoLiVe; HBV 1-2; TrGrPo; VLP

Even as the Others Mock. Dante Alighieri. And hear my senses clamor in their rout. LiTW

Even during War. Muriel Rukeyser. I have seen a ship lying upon the water/Rise like a great bird, like a lifted/promise. TrJP

Even If. Rachel Fishman. Even a rain. VWA

Even in my dreams. Lady Ise. a face I am ashamed to show. BoWoP

Even in the Darkness. Helene Mullins. As though life had never been found/To progress past the sod to the sun. MoRP

Even in the Moment of Our Earliest Kiss. Edna St. Vincent Millay. I tell you this across the blackened vine. ATP

Even So. Dante Gabriel Rossetti. Could we be so now! NOBE; NOBV; OBNC; VLP

An Even-Song. Sydney Thomas Dobell. Meet, meet me, by the thorn upon the hill! OBVV

Even-Song. George Herbert. And in this love, more then in bed, I rest. AnAnS 1

Even Such Is Time. Sir Walter Ralegh. The Lord shall raise me up, I trust. BLPL; EIL; ExPo; FCP; ForPo; GoTF; HAP; LiTB; OBSP; PoRA; SeCeV; SiPS; TreF; WHA

Even the Best. Gary Allan Kizer. My strong son,/My prince,/My star. LFAC

Even There. Lyn Lifshin. the place that was you/changed to air. IHMS

Even Though. John Stone. It is the only science. AMV-81

Even though my hands. *Anonymous.* My master's son will clasp them/with a heavy, broken, sigh. BoWoP

Evening. Richard Aldington. And here am I looking wantonly at her/Over the kitchen sink. MoBrPo; MOON; SeCePo

An Evening. William Allingham. Sweet Love dead. EnLoPo; IrPN; NOBV

Evening. Harry Behn. Into the happy morning/Of someone else's day. TiPo

Evening. John Clare. It hides from the eagle, and joins with the dove:/In beautiful green solitude. NOBV; VLP

Evening. William Cowper. I slight thee not, but make thee welcome still. OBEC

Evening. Hilda ("H. D.") Doolittle. and leaf shadow are lost. CMoP

The Evening. John Gay. And as the passes open, wind along. EnLi 1-2

Evening. John Keble. Till in the ocean of thy love/We lose ourselves in heaven above. TrPWD; VLP

Evening. King D. Kuka. knowing the sand hills were near. VoR

Evening. Itzik Manger. and our house breathes the peace/and piousness/of ryebread and evensong. VWA

Evening. Mary Matheson. If, when night falls, all is so changed, dear heart? CaP

Evening. Hugh McCrae. As one expectant of her Lord's sweet will. PoAu 1-2

An Evening. Robert Mezey. Understood/By those who understand it not. NaP

Evening. Thomas Miller. When we sleep, or sit, or stand,/Is with us, for He loves us all. OxBChV

Evening. Charles Sangster. Nature and Silence passed in solemn guise. ACV; CaP

Evening. Percy Bysshe Shelley. Which the keen evening star is shining through. SyP

Evening. Edward Rowland Sill. Some musing seraph had let fall a flower. AnAmPo

Evening. Charles Simic. ...It repeats the same word/Again and again, but not too loudly... GeTw

Evening. Edith Sitwell. Sir Rotherham Redde gathers bags of gold/Instead of the cherries ruddy and cold. MoBS

Evening. James Stephens. And then the moon's white circle, faint and thin/Looked steady on the earth–there is no sin,. MoBrPo

Evening. Tristan Tzara. then they remember their calves/let's go VWA

Evening. Victor van Vriesland. In solitude to where the dunes abide. TrJP

Evening. James Wright. The wide earth darkened so. NOBA; NYBP; PrIm

Evening: an Elegy (parody). Horace (or Horatio) Smith. I bless'd with learning, takes a pen and writes. BXAP

Evening, and Maidens. William Barnes. ...var to chatty and zee vo'ke goo by. OBEV; OBVV

An Evening and Morning in June. Gavin Douglas. As menstralis playis "The jolly day now dawis'. BSV

An Evening and Morning in Winter. Gavin Douglas. Shupe with hait flambis to stem the freezing fell. BSV

Evening at the Farm. John Townsend Trowbridge. Murmuring, "So, boss! so!" GN

Evening before Rain. Leonard Alfred George Strong. The gray bull will browse, his back to me, when I go by. OxBTC

An Evening Blessing. James Edmeston. May the morn in heaven awake us,/Clad in bright, eternal bloom. BePJ

Evening Bread. Jacob Glatstein. And unspeaking we eat of love and hatred./Evening bread. VWA

Evening by the Sea. Algernon Charles Swinburne. Low places where the rock-fish feed. FaBoPP; SyP

Evening Ceremony: Dream for G.V. Wendy Rose. pull the stars out/with their teeth. TWSS

The Evening Cloud. John Wilson. And tells to man his glorious destinies. HBV 1-2

Evening Contemplation. George Washington Doane. Jesus, look with pitying eye. BLPA; BLPL; FaBoBe

Evening Dance of the Grey Flies. P.K. Page. shone suddenly like the sun/before you died. NOBC

The Evening Darkens Over. Robert Bridges. Thou art alone, fond lover. CMoP; HAP; NBM; NOBV; PoEL 1-5

Evening Ebb. Robinson Jeffers. ...rehearsing behind/The screen of the world for another audience. NoAm

An Evening Falls. James Stephens. And open it,/And see her children there! SUS

Evening Fantasy. Friedrich Hoelderlin. Age then descends on us, calm, contented. LiTW

Evening Harbour. Tom Paulin. An old woman in a sleep of voices. AMV-81

Evening Hymn. William Henry Furness. Fills the universe around. AA; HBV 1-2

An Evening Hymn. Thomas Ken. Sing to my God a grateful Song. OBS; OxBChV

Evening Hymn. Elizabeth Madox Roberts. Quiet and love and peace/Be to this, our rest, our place. TiPo

Evening Hymn (excerpt). George Macdonald. That so to-day what might have been,/To-morrow may appear. TrPWD

Evening Hymn in the Hovels. Francis Lauderdale Adams. O we who hew, build, deck, shall we not also/The happiness that we have given partake?/Hallelujah!' OxBS

Evening in a Lab. Miroslav Holub. search/and find. SUW

Evening in Camp. Patricia Ledward. If you would rise to the sun like a phoenix. WaP

Evening in England. Francis Ledwidge. I and a marsh bird only make a wail. MCCG

Evening in Gloucester Harbor. Epes Sargent. They felt God is, though inconceivable. EtS

Evening in Paradise. John Milton. ...thir songs/Divide the night, and lift our thoughts to Heaven. LoBV

Evening in the Country. John Ashbery. Turmoil that is to be our route. CAPP

Evening in the Sanitarium. Louise Bogan. Miss R. looks at the mantelpiece, which must mean something. FaBoWP; FYAP; IHMS; MP; SBG; TwCP

Evening in the Suburbs. Stella Barnett. And the drinks are Lilliputian. PV

Evening in the Walls. Jean Wahl. And as I think of you I gather strength. VWA

Evening in Tyringham Valley. Richard Watson Gilder. Oh, let they spirit stay with me, sweet/vale! AA

Evening Landscape. Pol de Mont. Red in the light the dying sun is bleeding. LiTW

Evening Meal in the Twentieth Century. John Holmes. And not frighten my young son? MiAP

Evening Melody. Aubrey Thomas De Vere. Yet mine the steps and portal!'
GoBC; HBV 1-2

Evening Music. Kendrick Smithyman. so very sad his eyes from little boys
and girls. AnNZ

Evening Musicale. Phyllis McGinley. And sixty people trying to relax/On
little rented chairs with gilded backs. OBAL

An Evening of Russian Poetry. Vladimir Nabokov. lubov moya,
oststoopnika prostee. NYBP

The Evening of the Feast-Day. Giacomo Leopardi. With a like sadness
would consume my heart. LiTW

Evening of the Rose. Anthony Rudolf. the unbecoming dead/sang him to
his rest. VWA

The Evening of the Visitation. Thomas Merton. O gentle Mary! Our lovely
Mother in heaven! ISi

Evening on Howth Head. Eileen Brennan. into the cyclamen/arms of the
sea. NeIP

Evening on the Broads. Algernon Charles Swinburne. Ghost or God,
evermore moves on the face of the deep. TEP

Evening on the Harbor. Virginia Lyne Tunstall. The day is gone, and all
the restless night/Is bound about with ribbons of pale stars. HBMV

Evening on the Moselle. Decimus Magnus Ausonius. In thy clear crystal.
AnEnPo; LiTW

The Evening Out. Ogden Nash. ...and then go off and spend the evening at
the Club. MoAmPo

Evening: Ponte al Mare, Pisa. Percy Bysshe Shelley. And over it a space of
watery blue/Which the keen evening star is shining through. CBEP

An Evening Prayer. Anonymous.
Because I know Thou lovest me. STF
Blessed be the blossome that sprange, lady, of the! AtBAP
...who with/Thy Tent/Of Peace dost shelter us that pray, and/all/Thy folk
of Israel, and Jerusalem. TrJP

Evening Prayer. Arthur Fitger. Watchmen of Zion, ye will not betray.
AWP

Evening Prayer. Hermann Hagedorn. And in her eyes I saw a ring/Of
heaven's angels, listening. GoBC

An Evening Prayer. Laura E. Kendall. Receive me, Lord. BLRP

Evening Primrose. John Clare. It faints and withers, and is done.
TrGrPo

The Evening Primrose. John Langhorne. Guard thy emblematic flower.
CEP; OBEC

The Evening Primrose. Dorothy Parker. Oh, I am not like that at all!
ALV; InMe

Evening Quatrains. Charles Cotton.
Till Phoebus, dipping in the West,/Shall lead the World the way to Rest.
ExPo; LoBV
Whilst every house does seem a swarm. EG

Evening Red and Morning Gray. Anonymous. Bring the rain upon his
head. FaBoBe; HBV 1-2; OxNR

Evening Refrain. Sherod Santos. The leaves combing slowly the mild sea-
air. MAYP

An Evening Revery. William Cullen Bryant. Shall journey onward in
perpetual peace. AA

Evening Ride. Jill Hoffman. my own music/creaks from the loving saddle/
under me. PH

An Evening's Love. John Dryden.
And passion made us Cowards grow,/Which made us brave before. CavP
He laughed out with A ha ha ha ha. CavP; FF
We shall have the Devil and all/When we come together. CavP

Evening Schoolboys. John Clare. When joys are yours that never cost a
sigh. GLGT

Evening Shade. Anonymous. O may we in Thy bosom rest,/The bosom of
Thy love. AmFP

Evening Song. Cecil Frances Alexander. They have play and pleasure,/But
not love like ours. OHIP

Evening Song. John Vance Cheney. And stir 'twixt silence and a sound.
AA

Evening Song. Kenneth Fearing. Sleep, McKade./Yawn./Go to sleep.
EAS

Evening Song. Sidney Lanier. Never our lips, our hands. AP; GoTF; PG;
TreFT; UnPo; WHA

Evening Song. John Matthias. Into the darkness/of my/childhood.
AMV-81

Evening Song. Jean Toomer. Lips pressed against my heart. BPo; CDC

Evening Song of Senlin. Conrad Aiken. I will forget these things once
more/In the silence of sleep. HBMV

Evening Songs. John Vance Cheney.
And evening come. AA
Leaving behind low, rippling laughter. AA
Makes the golden guesses what they are. AA

Evening Star. George Barker. Is warm under Maisie's bedcover? ELU;
ErPo; PoCh

The Evening Star. Amy Carmichael. And see in clearness the Evening Star.
TRV

The Evening Star. Henry Wadsworth Longfellow. And from thy darkened
window fades the light. AnNE

Evening Star. Edgar Allan Poe. Than that colder, lowly light. AmP; AP

Evening Star. Sappho. (And men to the arms of their brides.) HW

The Evening Sun. Emily Bronte. Where their bright glories shone at first.
CH

An Evening Thought. Jupiter Hammon. Let us with Angels share. Finis.
PoNe

Evening Twilight. Charles Baudelaire. ...which take light/never so well as
under the deep mourning of the night? SyP

Evening Walk. Sonja Akesson. A dazzling city, suburbia or Jerusalem,/a
mirage in the bleak light. WPOW

An Evening Walk. William Stafford. ...Like you, we are alone. NPAW

An Evening Walk (excerpt). William Wordsworth.
Or yell, in the deep woods, of lonely hound. EnRP
The shepherd, all involved in wreaths of fire,/Now shows a shadowy speck,
and now is lost entire. EiCP
Strong flakes of radiance on the tremulous/stream. CoBE

An Evening Walk in Bengal. Reginald Heber. And He, the bounteous Sire,
has given/His peace on earth,–his hope of Heaven! OBTV

The Evening-Watch. Henry Vaughan. ...The last gasp of time/Is thy first
breath, and mans eternall Prime. NCEP

The Evening Wind. William Cullen Bryant.
And softly part his curtains to allow/Thy visit, grateful to his burning brow.
LaNeLa
He hears the rustling leaf and running/stream. AA; AnNE

Evening without Angels. Wallace Stevens. As we stand gazing at the
rounded moon. MoPo; VGW

Eveningsong 1. Ramona Wilson. already showing the last light/in the grass
long and nodding. VoR

Eveningsong 2. Ramona Wilson. twilight comes/we light all the lamps.
VoR

Evensong. Conrad Aiken. The perfect quiet that comes after rain.
HBMV; PG

Evensong. Carleton Drewry. So soon to slacken, too soon disappear/In
sleep I know not why, you know not how. GoYe

Evensong. Peter Kane Dufault. ...for no reason, and for no reason/taken
away. AMV-80

Evensong. Clive Staples Lewis. Raise us in Thy dawn. TrCP

Evensong. Judith Moffett. Life licks and burns at me. LTB

Evensong. Ruth Schaumann. Music, murmur–'tis His will/Life should
listen and be still. CAW

Evensong. Robert Louis Stevenson. ...I will eat and sleep and will not
question more. GoTF

Evensong. George Tankervil. At last it ringeth to evensong. TRV

Evensong. Ridgely Torrence. And that's the end of night. HBV 1-2

An Event. Edward Field. Playing naked and dirty among the chickens.
CoAP

The Event. Thomas Sturge Moore. That floats like a shell to the shore,/
Both given and found. OBMV

Event. Sylvia Plath. The dark is melting. We touch like cripples. NOBA

Eventide. Caroline Atherton Briggs Mason. I hear His voice among the
trees,/And I am not afraid. GoTF; TreFS

Events. George O'Neil. Still as a sea-rock, sat a toad. HBMV

Ever as We Sailed. Percy Bysshe Shelley. The charmed boat approached,
and there its haven found. SeCePo

An Ever-Fixed Mark. Kingsley Amis. Love never lets you go. ErPo;
NoAm; PeHV

The Ever-Living Church. Charles Wesley. And greet the Blood-besprinkled
bands/On the eternal shore. STF

Ever On. Anonymous. All Thine own, my Lord and King. STF

Ever Present. Philip Ayres. And not she me, but I had murdered her.
OBSP

Ever Since. Elizabeth Jane Coatsworth. ...plowing ever since,/for more
than seven score years! SiSoSe

Ever Since. Archibald MacLeish. Whose past is parting: strangers side by
side. NePA

Ever Since Uncle John Henry Been Dead (with music). Anonymous. Dis
yere hammer, nin-pound hammer,/Kill mah partner, kill Joh Henry,/Kill
him dead. AS

The Ever-Touring Englishmen... Anonymous. With their wires they have
bound the whole world together for/themselves. WTO

Ever Watchful. Ta' Abbata Sharra. When to plunge it in the heart-blood of
the many-mustered foemen. AWP

Everest. Horace Shipp. and beyond all guidance the courage of God for
guide. HaMV

Everglade. Anne Cherner. that it was as you had wished. AMV-81

Evergreen. Ewart Milne. The October reality, the image of spring. OxBI

The Everlasting Contenders. Kenneth Patchen. Who praise not grandly/
But wish they could CrMA; NaP

The Everlasting Forests. Dahlia Ravikovich. ...all your/imaginings/won't pull you out again from the waters. BoWoP

The Everlasting Gospel. William Blake.
But thou read'st black where I read white. OBRV
For dust and clay is the Serpent's meat,/Which never was made for Man to eat. OBRV
I am sure this Jesus will not do,/Either for Englishman or Jew. OBRV
You shall lick the dust for meat;...' OxBoCh

The Everlasting Love. Annie Johnson Flint. And loves us to the end. BLRP

The Everlasting Mercy. John Masefield.
The holy bread, the food unpriced,/Thy everlasting mercy, Christ. BoC; GoTF; ILwL; TreFS; TRV; WGRP
I thought all earthly creatures knelt/From rapture of the joy I felt. TRV
Now get to hell; I want to dress. NoAm
Thy hand on mine upon the hale. AtBAP

The Everlasting Mercy (parody). J. C. Squire. And then turned homeward meditating much/About the single transferable vote. BXAP

The Everlasting Voices. William Butler Yeats. O sweet everlasting Voices be still. AWP

The Everlastings. Norman Dubie. It is the thunder at dawn! GeTw

Every Bush New Springing. Anonymous. O she pulled him down. NCEP; PoEL 1-5

Every Christian Born of God. Anonymous. Let us hear no sound of strife/ In our band of brothers. AH

Every Critic in the Town. Robert Fuller Murray. Every critic–don't you know it?/Is himself a minor poet. PoL

Every Day. Ingeborg Bachmann.
and disregard/of all commands. BoWoP
and for the non-observance/of every order. PBWP

Every-Day Characters. Winthrop Mackworth Praed.
And she was not the ball-room's belle,/But only–Mrs. Something Rogers! EnRP
Vir nulla non donandus lauru.' EnRP

Every Day Thanksgiving Day. Harriet Prescott Spofford. But, with remembered blessings then/Made every day Thanksgiving Day. OHIP

Every Earthly Creature. John Malcolm Brinnin. Who die without a candle, or remain/To citizen the natural state of man. LiTA

Every Land Is Exile. Claude Vigee. Every bird, sky's prey and bereft of origins. VWA

Every morning I get up. Huang O. And once again we fall over/ Overwhelmed with passion. BoWoP

Every Night When the Sun Goes In. Anonymous.
He'll face my door and won't come in. TrAS
I'm going away to Marble town. ABF; FSW

Every One to His Own Way. John Vance Cheney. Qietly looking between the green trees. AA

Every Saturday He Stands. Albert Drake. nor see his smile distort/in the hundred hanging moons. AmC

Every Thing. Harold Monro. And your eventual Rubbish Heap, and mine. AnEnPo; MoBrPo

Every Time I Climb a Tree. David McCord. But still it's pretty good for me/Every time I climb a tree NTCP; SoPo; TiPo

Every Time I Feel the Spirit. Anonymous. I asked the Lord could it be mine. FSW

Everybody but Me. Margaret Goss Burroughs. It will mean me. BlSi; FB

Everybody Eats Too Much Anyhow. Ogden Nash. Next time carry your lunch along. AmC

Everybody Loves Saturday Night. Anonymous. Ev'rybody loves Saturday night. FSW

Everybody Ought to Make a Change. Sleepy John Estes. Because it's soon or late/we have to go down in that old lonesome ground. BluL

Everybody's Welcome. Anonymous. Oh Glory! to the dying Lamb. TrAS

Everybody Works but Father. Charles W. McClintock. Everybody works in our house, but my old man. TreFS

"Everybody Works but Father" as W. S. Gilbert Would Have Written It. Arthur G. Burgoyne. Don't blame us if we meditate a mild attempt at parricide. FiBHP

Everyday Dirt. Anonymous. I could tell you more about him, but there ain't no use. FSW

Everyday Will Be Sunday. Anonymous. And on Labor Day nobody works. TreFT

Everymaid. John Oxenham. Thy temple face is chiselled from within. TrCP

Everyman. Anonymous.
Amen, say ye, for saint charity. EnLi 1-2; MeEV; PoEL 1-5
For Thou upon the Cross hast saved our souls! CAW

Everyman. Siegfried Sassoon. Companion in repose with those who once were men. BoLiVe; MoBrPo

Everyman's Library. John Ashbery. ...You knew that. NoP

Everyman: The Desertion of Beauty and Strength. Anonymous. Yet they promised me fair and lovingly. ACP

Everyone in the World. Joel Dailey. falls asleep and, while dreaming of tomorrow,/wakes to that perfect day. APU

Everyone Sang. Siegfried Sassoon. ;and the song was wordless; the singing will never be done. AnFE; BrPo; FaBV; GTBS; GTBS-P; InvP; LOW; MoBrPo; NOBE; OBEV; OBSP; OBWP; OxBTC; PoPl; PoSC; TrJP; WaP

Everything. Philip Levine. and that's everything. AMV-80

Everything. James Paul. We would have to stop everything to turn it off. HoAn

Everything: Eloy, Arizona, 1956. Florence Anthony ("AI"). He can only hurt me a piece at a time. AmPA; FF

Everything Has Its History. Phillis Levin. Between myself and the place I inhabit. AMV-81

Everything in Its Place. Arthur Guiterman. The birds are in its bushes and the wolf is at the door. NLV; OBAL

Everything in the Air Is a Bird. Barbara Guest. the air is a bird. AmPC

Everything is Plundered. Anna Akhmatova. something not known to anyone at all,/but wild in our breast for centuries. WPOW

Everything Is Possible. Robert Pack. Would that then make us free? PPP

Everything Is Round. Gabriela (Lucila Godoy Alcayaga) Mistral. Waves are circlets of little girls/embracing this world...as they play... PBWP

Everything Is Swimming. Stevie Smith. Elle continua de rire comme une hyene. FaBoNo

Everything Passes and Vanishes. William Allingham. And often you see in a footstep/What you could not see in a face. NOBV

Everything That Acts Is Actual. Denise Levertov. ...What holds you/to what you see of me is/that grasp alone. NoAm

Everything We Do. Peter Meinke. with the salesman lying beside her,/will cry out/our unfamiliar name. GOYP

Eves Apologie. Emilia Lanier. This sinne of yours, hath no excuse, nor end. BoWoP

Evesong. Maureen Duffy. cleft and dimpled/the apples she brings to bed. PeHV

Eviction. Elizabeth Brewster. If the sheriff pain/Had not evicted me. CaP

Evidence. Arthur Kober. Sometimes when I'm deep in love/I don't know what I'm thinking of./Oh, don't I, though! InMe

Evidence at the Witch Trials. James Keir Baxter. Between the faggot and the flame/I see his face return. OxBC

Evidence Read at the Trial of the Knave of Hearts. Lewis (Charles Lutwidge Dodgson) Carroll. Between yourself and me. FaBoNo; FaFP; GTBS-P; NBM; OxBoLi

Evidently Chicken Town. John Cooper Clarke. it fucking gets you fucking down/evidently chicken town. FaBoPV

Evil Days. Boris Pasternak. When the man risen from the dead was trying to get to his feet. MoRP

Evil Devil Woman. (Kansas) Joe McCoy. I tried to be/oh tried to be/tried to be/a man to you/a man to you. BluL

The Evil Eye. John Ciardi. Though I had one already and the other came. AtBAP; MoBS; NAs

Evil-Hearted Man. Anonymous. I am so doggone evil, evil as a man can be. FSW

Evil Is Homeless. D. H. Lawrence. grey evil, which has no path, and shows neither light nor dark/and has no home, no home anywhere. MoRP

Evil Is No Black Thing. Sarah Webster Fabio. a criss-crossed pile of/sun-bleached bones. PoBA

An Evil Man. Richard Beer-Hofmann. A Jew, a Jew, a common vulgar Jew! TrJP

Evil Nigger Waits for Lightnin'. LeRoi (Imamu Amiri Baraka) Jones. describing its own voice/its/reason NoAm; NOBA

Evil Prayer. Douglas Hyde. May they lie low in waves of woe,/And tortures slow each day!/Amen! TW

An Evil Spirit, Your Beauty Haunts Me Still. Michael Drayton. By this good wicked spirit, sweet angel devil. GBL

An Evil World. Anonymous. A world withered, graves in number. OnYI

Evoe! Edith Matilda Thomas. And the god, the true Iacchus,/Hears now this song of mine. HBV 1-2

Evolution. John Blight. don sheets, wear stars in your hair, fix tinsel wings? CBAP

Evolution. Rochelle Owens. o junius bird/who excavated. CoPo

Evolution. Landon Smith. Let us drink anew to the time when you/Were a Tadpole and I was a Fish. HBV 1-2

Evolution. May Swenson. a Feast unknown/to stone/or tree or beast. TrGrPo

Evolution. John Banister Tabb. Out of the dead, cold ashes,/Life again. AA; AnAmPo; GoTF; HBV 1-2; PoPl; TreF

Evolution. Israel Zangwill. That love might come to life. TrJP

Evolution from the Fish. Robert Bly. A fire is passing up through the soles of my feet! NoAm; NOBA

Evolutionary Hymn. Clive Staples Lewis. (Far from pleasant, by our present/Standards, though it well may be). NOBL

Ex-Basketball Player. John Updike. Of Necco Wafers, Nibs, and Juju Beads. CTBA; LiSp; NYBP; SM

Ex Libris. Arthur Upson. Lest of his kind intent some human cry/ Interpret not the Messenger aright. HBV 1-2

Ex Maria Virgine. Norbert Engels. I would have borne Him that age-destined day/In Bethlehem. ISi

Ex Nihilo. David Gascoyne. The hardest stone on which to found/Altar and shelter for Eternity. GTBS-P

Ex Ore Infantium. Francis Thompson. And He will smile, that children's tongue/Has not changed since Thou wast young! FaBV; HBV 1-2; OBVV; OxBChV; SUS

The Ex-Poet. Bill Zavatsky. ...the philosophy/of the saw, the theory of the nail/that holds my world in place. APU

The Ex-Queen among the Astronomers. Fleur Adcock. She brings the distant briefly close/above his dreamy abstract stare. FaBoWP

Ex-Voto. Algernon Charles Swinburne. Alive or dead, take me,/Me too, my mother. MOS

The Exact Same Places. Charles Vandersee. those places, almost the exact same places. AmC

Exaggerator. Mark Van Doren. And resting gently where he chose. AnFE

Exaltation. Franz Werfel. In my hair glimmered ever/A nest, a nest of blue light. TrJP

The Examination. W. D. Snodgrass. ..."One of ours; one of ours. Yes. Yes." CAPP; ConAP

Examination at the Womb-Door. Ted Hughes. Pass, Crow. NAs; OxBC

The Examination of His Mistress' Perfections. Francis Beaumont. Let it run on now: I know what it is. GoBC

Examiner. F. R. Scott. The professional mowers drone, clipping the inch-high/green. PPON

The Example. William Henry Davies. To make a stone a flower. AnFE; HBMV; MoBrPo; TrGrPo; WHA

An Example of How a Daily Temporary Madness Can Help a Man... John Stone. ...deep/and comfortable/as a growl. TAT

An Excelente Balade of Charitie. Thomas Chatterton. Or give the mighty will, or give the good man power. CEP; EBEV; EnPE; EnRP; GoTL; LAuP; LiTB; NOEC; OBEC; SeCePo

An Excellent Memory. Allen Curnow. + November 1974, just about/ midnight, give or take a few minutes. OCNZ

An Excellent New Ballad, Called The Brawn Bishop's Complaint. Arthur Mainwaring. The lady in gratitude grants him the favor. APAS

An Excellent New Ballad Called the Prince of Darkness. Anonymous. There was no other way for mending the breed! APAS

An Excellent New Ballad Giving a True Account of the Birth... Charles, Earl of Dorset Sackville. ...you're desired to dispense/With the want of true grammar, good English, or sense. APAS

An Excellent New Song, Being the Intended Speech of a Famous Orator... Jonathan Swift. And be a true Whig, while I'm not in game. APAS

An Excellent New Song Called "Mat's Peace," or The Downfall of Trade. Arthur Mainwaring. If now we must give up Spain. APAS

An Excellent New Song on a Seditious Pamphlet. Jonathan Swift. In Spight of his Deanship and Journeyman Waters. CoMu

An Excellent New Song upon His Grace...Lord Archbishop of Dublin. Jonathan Swift. As did Methusalem of old, and so I end my SONG. CoMu

Excelsior. Ralph Waldo Emerson. That drop from the angels' shoon. PeD

Excelsior. Henry Wadsworth Longfellow. A voice fell, life a falling star,/ Excelsior! AmePo; FaPoR; GoTF; HBV 1-2; HBVY; OBCA; OnMSP; PaPo; PrIm; SpRo; TreF; WBLP

Excelsior (parody). Anonymous. Which only makes him bawl the more–/ "Excelsior!" BXAP

Except I Love. Robert Parry. Yet had I rather thus for to remain/Than laugh, and live, not feeling lover's pain. EiL

Except the Lord, That He for Us Had Been. Henry Ainsworth. That of the heavens and earth is the maker. AH

Exceptional. Thelma Lewis. As if you hoped, of all mankind, you might/ Escape the infallibility of time. AMV-80

Excerpt from a Report to the Galactic Council. Robert Conquest. Accompanying records show... OxBC

Excerpts from the Notebook of the Poet of Santo Tomas. Richard Shelton. I'm in no hurry to pay it. GP

The Excesses of God. Robinson Jeffers. Humanity can understand, and would flow likewise/If power and desire were perch-mates. MoRP

The Exchange. Samuel Taylor Coleridge. We had exchanged our hearts indeed. FiBHP; HBV 1-2; OAEP

Exchange. George Rostrevor Hamilton. Swung in the rope he found. FaBoEE

Exchange. Sister Mary Dorothy Ann. Himself,/The Bread and Wine. GoBC

Exchange. Dabney Stuart. The fear of death, I mean. HoPM

An Exchange of Hats. Stanley Moss. wearing his own last hat, drinking port/and smoking Ideals forever. GP

Exchanges. Ernest Christopher Dowson. All that you had I found. OBMV

The Exchanges II. Robert Kelly. moving to the hidden rhythm of the real CoPo

Exchanging Glances. William Pitt Root. our life as it is now. MAYP

The Exciseman. Robert Burns. He's danc'd awa' wi' the Exciseman. GoTS

The Excrement Poem. Maxine W. Kumin. I honor shit for saying: We go on. FaBoWP

The Excursion. Tu Fu. By the time we reach the shore, it seems as though the/Fifth Month were Autumn. AWP; SD

The Excursion. William Wordsworth.
Among the unthinking masters of the earth/As makes the nations groan. EnRP
And central peace, subsisting at the heart/Of endless agitation. GoTF; WGRP
And, ere the stars were visible, had reached/A village-inn,–our evening resting-place. EnRP
And sometimes, so relenting justice wills,/From palpable oppression of despair. OBRV
And with that pang I prayed to be no more!–' EnRP
By strict necessity, along the path/Of order and of good.' EnRP
His mind was a thanksgiving to the power/That made him; it was blessedness and love. OBRV
an object like a throne/Under a shining canopy of state/Stood fixed.... BoLiVe
Seems but a fleeting sunbeam's gift, whose peace/The sufferance only of a breath of air!' EnRP
Shouteth faint tidings of some gladder place. OBRV
–so shall thy unfailing love/Guide, and support, and cheer me to the end!' EnRP; NoP
That my particular current soon will reach/The unfathomable gulf, where all is still!' OBRV

The Excuse. Sir Walter Ralegh. I loved myself, because myself loved you. AAS; FCP; SiPS

An Excuse of Absence. Thomas Carew. ...nor dares venture/To wander far from you, the centre. CaPo; SeCP

Excuse Us, Animals in the Zoo. Annette Wynne. Excuse us, Animals in the Zoo,/I'm sure we're very rude to you. TiPo

Exeat. Stevie Smith. Then he may commit suicide, then/He may go. NoAm

An Execration against Whores. John Webster. Which, whosoe'er first stamps it, brings in trouble/All that receive it. TW

An Execration upon Vulcan. Ben Jonson. Thy Wives pox on thee, and Bess Braughtons too. AnAnS 2; SeCP

The Execrators. David Galler. Felled, through which low laughters expire. NMP

The Execution. Alden Nowlan. "Don't make it harder for use,' the hangman whispered. PeCV

Execution. James A. Randall, Jr. Better to die, you think./But nothing happens. BPo

Execution of Alice Holt. Anonymous. A-hanging for the mother's sake/On Chester's fatal tree. OxBoLi

The Execution of Cornelius Vane. Sir Herbert Read. And the birds that sing? BrPo; NoAm

Execution of Five Pirates for Murder. Anonymous. Now, alas, their days are ended; they died on Newgate's gallows/high. OBSS

The Execution of King Charles. Andrew Marvell. But bowed his comely head/Down, as upon a bed. AnEnPo; PoRA

The Execution of Luke Hutton. Anonymous. Receive, O sweet Saviour, my spirit unto thee. OBET

The Execution of Madame du Barry. J. J. Bray. ...Medusa sleeps once/ more. NOAV

The Execution of Montrose. William Aytoun. The work of death was done! HBV 1-2; OnMSP

Executive. Sir John Betjeman. The modern style, sir, with respect, has really come to stay. NOBL

The Executive's Death. Robert Bly. Like the sound of horns, the sound of thousands of small/wings. CoAP; NaP

The Exequies. Thomas Stanley. To Love and Fate an equal Sacrifice. AnAnS 2; MeLP

The Exequy. Kildare Dobbs. We'll follow in our own good year. OBCV

An Exequy. Peter Porter. O guide me through the shoals of fear–/ "Furchte dich nicht, ich bin bei dir." OxBC

The Exequy. To His Matchlesse Never to Be Forgotten Freind. Henry, Bishop of Chichester King. Divided, with but half a heart,/Til we shall meet and never part. AtBAP; BoLoP; ForP; GBL; HAP; HBV 1-2; InPS; InvP; JCP; LiTL; LoBV; MeLP; MePo; NOBE; NoP; OBEV; OBS; PoEL 1-5; PPoe; PrIm; QFR; SeCePo; SeCP; TEP; ViBoPo

Exercise. William Stanley Merwin. until everything is continuous again. NOBA

Exercise. Pat Nolan. again forgetting/what I stood for. APU

Exercise for the Left Hand. Constance Urdang. On the other side of the world. AMV-81

Exercise in a Meadow. Jean Elliot. as a cove where no swimmer is swimming. GoYe

The Exercise of Affection. Ayton [(or Aytoun)] Sir Robert. His courage is as little as his wit. BSV

Exeter Book: Maxims. *Anonymous.* And ever for faint-heart scantest of hoards! AnOE

The Exeter Book: The Wanderer. *Anonymous.* And happy the man who seeketh for mercy/From his heavenly Father, our Fortress and Strength. AnOE

An Exeter Riddle. Gavin Ewart. as though he had never been. Vouchsafe me this vision! OxBC

Exeunt. Richard Wilbur. A cricket like a dwindled hearse/Crawls from the dry grass. BoNaP; ELU; HeIP; NCSH; PoLf; Psk

Exeunt Omnes. Thomas Hardy. Soon one more goes thither! QFR

Exhaustive Experimentation. *Anonymous.* Has proved that the arse of the hedgehog/Can hardly be buggered at all. DBV

Exhortation. Louise Bogan. Come to their terms, your plans unmade,–/And be belied, and be betrayed. QFR

Exhortation. Thomas Hastings. In Christ confide. AA

The Exhortation of a Father to His Children. Robert Smith. Desiring him in all your works/For to direct your ways. OxBChV

Exhortation: Summer, 1919. Claude McKay. Wake from sleeping; to the East turn, turn your/eyes! CDC

Exhortation to Learn by Others' Trouble. Henry Howard, Earl of Surrey. But Wyatt said true, the scar doth aye endure. FaBoEE

Exhortation to Prayer. William Cowper. "Hear what the Lord has done for me!" NOCV

Exhortation to Prayer. Margaret Mercer. Prayer-crowned, on blessed bed. AA

Exigencies. Michael William Gilbert. I want to be the kid/who lives next door. AMV-80

Exile. *Anonymous.* And sail on the first favouring wind? KiLC

Exile. Audrey Beecham. The long-extended arms/Of the dead, stretched wide. NeBP

Exile. Chana Bloch. But we have taken out papers and will become citizens. GP

Exile. Ernest Christopher Dowson. While the sad waters of separation/Bear us on to the ultimate night. BoLoP; BrPo

Exile. Donald Hall. ...evade/Whatever hand might reach and touch our hand. NePA

Exile. George Rostrevor Hamilton. And I lie in the sand. FaBoEE

The Exile. Larry Rubin. The white she wore was like a windless cold. GoYe

Exile. Virna Sheard. He sent him home again! PeCV

Exile. Joseph Stroud. Under the sentence and law of that Medieval light. NPGG

Exile. Ellen Bryant Voigt. the little blue flower everywhere. MAYP

Exile. Jennette Yeatman. Old gods sleep far away. GoYe

The Exile at Rest. John Pierpont. The cloud's deep voice, the wind's low/sigh. AA

Exile from God. John Hall Wheelock. ...for God is life, and death perhaps/Exile from God. GoBC; WGRP

Exile in Nigeria. Ezekiel Mphahlele. Meantime,/let them leave my heart alone! PBA

The Exile of Erin. *Anonymous.* For the tie is unbroken on the Plains of Emu. NOAV

Exile of Erin. Thomas Campbell. Erin mavournin, Erin go bragh! HBV 1-2

Exile of the Sons of Uisliu (excerpt). *Anonymous.* She let her head be driven/against the stone, and made a mass of fragments of it, and she was dead. NOBI

Exile's Letter. Li Po. And send it a thousand miles, thinking. CTC; SeCeV

The Exile's Return. Robert Lowell. Voi ch'entrate, and your life is in your hands. AP; MiAP; NePA; OxBA

The Exile's Reveries. James Kennedy. Patriots drag the felon's chain. NOEC

The Exile's Song. Robert Gilfillan. But the weary ne'er return/To their ain countrie! HBV 1-2

Exile Song. Morris Rosenfeld. Even in death we have no luck. LiTW

Exiled. Edna St. Vincent Millay. I have a need of water near. EtS; MOS; PoRA

The Exiled Heart. Maurice Lindsay. ...where each new hero flings/his careful stone that fades in slow, concentric rings. OxBS

The Exiles. W. H. Auden. Accepting dearth,/The shadow of death. OxBTC

Exiles. William Hamilton Hayne. A bleak Siberia of the soul. AA

Exiles. George William Russell. They carry with them diadem and sceptre/And move from throne to throne. BIrV; MoBrPo

Existence. Sheila Moon. existence is/before it gets wiped off. AMV-80

Existential. William Heyen. ...or does know/and doesn't care, or neither. GeTw

Existentialism. Lloyd Frankenberg. But it's thinking that leads to the grave. FiBHP

Exit. Wilson MacDonald. And bitterly do the grasses/In the churchyard grieve. CaP; ViBoPo

Exit. Edwin Arlington Robinson. May we now venture to be kind. MoAmPo; OBSP

Exit God. Gamaliel Bradford. For though some virtues he might lack,/He had his pleasant side. HBMV; InMe

Exit Line. John Ciardi. Love should intend realities: good-bye! WeW

Exit Line. Howard Nemerov. "Good-bye," said the river, "I'm going downstream." WeW

Exit Lines. George Jonas. It makes sense for me to die for Barbara. NeAC

Exit Molloy. Derek Mahon. But still I can hear the birds sing on over my head. PoL

Exit, Pursued by a Bear. Ogden Nash. And awaits the fireball. NYBP

Exits and Entrances. Naomi Long Madgett. but armed with the invincible sword and shield/of our own names and faces. BlSi

Exodus. George Oppen. Miracle/Of their brilliance Miracle/of GP

Exodus. Anita Endrezze Probst. like your dreams,/it never was quite there. CDW

Exodus. Harvey Shapiro. Why then should they carry history/Like an ark, and the remembering/Already begun? VWA

Exodus 1940. Alfred Wolfenstein. Oh how the deluge of these many years/has driven us apart. VWA

Exodus for Oregon. Joaquin Miller. ...But one, with nothing left/beside/His dog to love, crept down among the ferns and/died. BPAW

Exodus from a Renaissance Gallery. Ellen M. V. Acton. And left us, modern, futile, banished? GoYe

The Exodus from Egypt. Ezekielos. Foremost he marched with swift and/haughty step. TrJP

Exodus to Connacht. Fear O Meallain. Now as we journey Westward into Connacht/old friends we'll leave behind us in their grief. FaBoPV

Exorcism. Oliver St.John Gogarty. May be changed to a reed or a laurel. AnIL

The Exorcism. Theodore Roethke. Cold, in my own dead salt. NoAm

An Expanded Want Ad. Brad Leithauser. ...offering you/drenched fields, nearly drowned in dew. MAYP

The Expanding Universe. Norman Nicholson. With white-hot darkness in his eyes. SeCePo

Expanse Cannot Be Lost. Emily Dickinson. The Tent is listening,/But the Troops are gone! MAmP

Expansion to Aveline's. Jim Brodey. evaporation in ascent. ANYP

Expect No Thanks. Caius Valerius Catullus. ...Now he is/The most implacable of my enemies. DBV

Expect Nothing. Alice Walker. But expect nothing. Live frugally/On surprise. AmPA; FF

Expectancies: The Eleventh Hour. Karla M. Hammond. The immediate is past. AMV-80

Expectans Expectavi. Charles Hamilton Sorley. To Thy great service dedicate. FaBoCh; HBMV; LoGBV; WGRP

Expectant Mother. Penelope Shuttle. a whisper between the night and the day. BrRo

The Expectation. Frederick William Faber. It was Heaven, it was Heaven,/Come before its time to thee. ACP

Expectation. Aliza Shenhar. And your hesitant hands/on my expectant eyes/cease to foresee/the future. VWA

Expectation. Thomas Stanley. And know that Time at last/Will crowne thy hope, or fix thy fear. AnAnS 2; OBS

Expecting. Daniel J. Langton. the beating lushness of the freely given. AMV-81

The Expedition to Wessagusset. Henry Wadsworth Longfellow. All who beheld it rejoiced, and praised the/Lord, and took courage. PAH

The Expensive Wife. Judah Ibn Sabbatai. Instead of a crown, thou shalt wear a/wreath of straw. TrJP

Experience. Ralph Waldo Emerson. The founder thou; these are thy race! AnNE; FPL; LiTA; PoEL 1-5; TAP

Experience. Lesbia Harford. And all the storied, splendid sins. CBAP; PoAu 1-2

Experience. Hugo von Hofmannsthal. With strangely fashioned giant yellow sails. AMV-81

Experience. Aline Kilmer. She knows so much that she did not know. BiCB; HBMV

Experience. John Boyle O'Reilly. And loves for his pleasure, and 'tis time he was dead. ACP; OBVV

Experience. Dorothy Parker. And that cleans up the matter. InMe; PoPl

Experience. James Simmons. –the feel of my own body/New to me, as I struck, as he struck. BIrV; CIP

The Experience. Edward Taylor. I praise Thee, Lord, and better praise Thee/would,/If what I had, my heart might ever hold. AmPP

Experience. Edith Wharton. "Not so," Death answered, "they shall/ purchase sleep." AA

Experiential Religion. Travis Du Priest. I never knew that. A Divinity School at Harvard. AMV-80

The Experiment That Failed. John Logan. and Columbus and the two sons died. NU

The Experiment with a Rat. Carl Rakosi. How did he fall/into my power? GP; PoL

Experts at Veneers. Kenward Elmslie. And I was there, and I was there. ANYP

Experts on Woman. Arthur Guiterman. And can/Be quite as unreliable/ As Man. InMe

The Expiration. John Donne. Being double dead, going and bidding go. AtBAP; CBEP; EIL; MeLP; MePo; OBSP; SeCP

Explaining about the Dachshund. John Stone. mixed in with the other smells. NIP

Explanation. William Barber. Wherever we encounter, there are no categories. PeHV

Explanation. Josh Billings. But the wheel that does the squeaking,/Is the one that gets the grease. GoTF; TreFT

Explanation. Geof Hewitt. their real loves waiting,/indifferent, in far off towns. NeAC

An Explanation of the GrassWalking the Fields. Robert Siegel. The Fairies' Kangaroo. GeTw

Explanation, on Coming Home Late. Richard Hughes. It was their shining made us stay. ELU

Explanations. Lucille Clifton. pray/or promise/or prophesy? GeTw

Explanations of Love. Carl Sandburg. There is a place where love begins and a place where/love ends–and love asks nothing. LiTL; MoLP

An Explanaton of the Grasshopper. Vachel Lindsay. He is the Brownies' racehorse,/The Fairies' Kangaroo. SoPo

Exploration. Daniel Gerard Hoffman. strange to these parts, yet whom the anthill/anticipating, sang. CoAP; CoPo

Explorations. Louis MacNeice. Our end is our own to be won by our own endeavor/And held on our own terms. ChMP; CoBMV

Explorations Bronchitis: The Rosario Beach House. Aleida Rodriguez. the house trembled with my coughs/and the breaths of my phantoms of the night. FIA

The Explorer. Rudyard Kipling. Anybody might have found it but–His Whisper came to Me! WHA

Explorers as Seen by the Natives. Doug Fetherling. We who are only too willing to help NOBC

The Explosion. Philip Larkin. One showing the eggs unbroken. EBEV; FaBoMo; HAP; OxBC; SCV

The Explosion of Thimbles. Pier Giorgio Di Cicco. ...this child in you, this half-assed gesture of an/angel leaving the earth. CaPN

An Expostulation. Isaac Bickerstaffe. But–why did you kick me down stairs? FaBoCo; FiBHP; NIP; PV

The Expostulation. Thomas Shadwell. For should the bow unbended be,/ Yet that can never help the cure. OAEP

Expostulation and Reply. William Wordsworth. And dream my time away. BW 1-2; CBEP; EnL; EnLi 1-2; EnRP; ERoP 1-2; HBV 1-2; OAEP; OBRV

Exposure. Seamus Heaney. The comet's pulsing rose. CIP; IPY

Exposure. Wilfred Owen. But nothing happens. FaBoMo; InPS; MMM; MoVE; NoAm; OBWP; PAI; WaP

Expounding the Torah. Louis Zukofsky. –Also. What we say/Here is heard there. VWA

Express. William Allingham. How much by labour can/The feeble race of man! NOBV

Express. W. R. Rodgers. I may have with me my pities and indignations. MoVE

The Express. Stephen Spender. Breaking with honey buds, shall ever equal. BBV; CMoP; EnLi 1-2; ExPo; GoJo; LiTM; MoAB; MoBrPo; MoVE; MP; NAMP; NIP; NoAm; PoPl; RoGo; SeCeV; TwCP

Express Train. Karl Kraus. Gladly would I be free,/this landscape I would be,/that rushes past! TrJP

Expression. Thom Gunn. ...two pairs of matching eyes/void of expression. OxBC

Expression. Isaac Rosenberg. And smouldering wrong. MoBrPo

Exquisite Lady. Mary Elizabeth Osborn. Remember that Aldebaran is blind. NePoAm-2

The Exquisite Sonnet. J. C. Squire. Smites with her stark immortal palimpsest/The green arcades of immemorial years! HBMV

The Extasie. Abraham Cowley. And mount herself, like Him, to' Eternitie in Fire. AnAnS 2; SeCP

Extempore Effusion upon the Death of James Hogg. William Wordsworth. And Ettrick mourns with her their Poet dead. CBEP; EBEV; ERoP 1-2; FaBoRV; FiP; MyFE; NOBE; NoP; OAEL 1-2; OBRV; SCV

Extempore Verses upon a Trial of Skill.... John Byrom. Who scorn'd any Fence but a jolly Abdomen? OBEC

Extensions of Linear Mobility. Jeanine Hathaway. We pull up the blankets/on spent generations. IHMS

Extermination. Richard D'Alton Williams. And the Molock of tyranny reels on his throne. OnYI

The Extermination of the Jews. Marvin Bell. were defeats with which the Gestapo/continues ceasing and ceasing. VWA

The External Element. David McFadden. I hate poetry with a passion/& write poems. NeAC

Extinct Birds. Judith Wright. the poet vanished, in the vanished forest,/ among his brightly tinted extinct birds? PBWP

An Extra Joyful Chorus for Those Who Have Read This Far. Tomas · Transtromer. All the sleepers in the world join hands. EAS

Extract. Paul Frederic Bowles. and the ocean groans darkly grey in the half-light. PoA

Extract from Memoirs. Howard Nemerov. "You fellows go and figure what it's for." OxBC

Extract the Quint-essence. Francis Daniel Pastorius. As this quaint Quint Essence/Of Time and Patience. SCAP

Extracts from Addresses to the Academy of Fine Ideas (excerpt). Wallace Stevens. Black water breaking into reality. LiTM

Extracts: from the Journal of Elisa Lynch. Maura Stanton. "Look at me! Look at your mother!" AmPA

The Extraordinary Dog. Nancy Byrd Turner. A loud "Kerchoo!"–what would he do,/the pompous Pekinese? TiPo

Extraordinary Will. Will Jackett. I confirm, sign, and seal,/This, the true act and deed of/WILL JACKETT. FaBoUs

Extras. Richard Burton. With heaven's own patience are calm and/sweet. AA

The Extravagant Drunkard's Wish. Edward Ward. Exert our malice, gratify our pride,/And settle Satan's kingdom ev'rywhere. NOEC

Extreme Unction. Ernest Christopher Dowson. And each anointed sense will see. ACP; CAW; MoBrPo; OAEL 1-2; OBMV; VLP

Extreme Unction in Pa. David Ray. like that blind Homer kicked upon the shore, seaweed. AMV-81; FAZ

Extremely Naughty Children. Elizabeth Godley. Will go/To tea/With the children/Again? BBGG

Extremes. James Whitcomb Riley. "She's the stilliest child I ever heard!" HBVY

Extremum Tanain. Horace. Beware!...I shall not always wait/Before thy doors! AWP

Exultation is the going. Emily Dickinson. The divine intoxication/Of the first league out from land? NCEP

Eyam (excerpt). Anna Seward. Dim apparition thou!–and bitter is my tear. NOEC

The Eye. Michael Benedikt. The eye of the realist is inflatable. ConAP

Eye. Gray Burr. Then only, thought may grind/A harder sharper lens. WeW

The Eye. Robert Herrick. Ah! what is then this curious sky/But only my Corinna's eye? CaPo

The Eye. Robinson Jeffers. Eye of the earth, and what it watches is not our wars. AmLP; AP; CrMA; LiTA; LiTM; OxBA; WaP

The Eye. Allen Tate. And calls the crows to peck his head. LiTA

The Eye. Richard Wilbur. That this eye not be folly's loophole/But giver of due regard. FiCP

The Eye. Eithne Wilkins. among the rocks, the desert, and the waves. NeBP

Eye and Tooth. Robert Lowell. I am tired. Everyone's tired of my turmoil. CAPP

Eye of God. Jim Tollerud. Long ago the waves/were saltier/and the People strong. VoR

The Eye of Humility. Kay Smith. in the invaded womb of time. OBCV

The Eye of Love. George Moses Horton. But love was in her eye betray'd. BALP

Eye-Witness. Ridgely Torrence. And earth bore East with all toward the new morning. HBMV

Eyeglasses. Tom Clark. Every two hours I wipe off my glasses. ConAP

The Eyeglasses. William Carlos Williams. tranquilly Titicaca– NoAm

Eyeing the Eyes of One's Mistress. Ebenezer Jones. While thine unfeining lids gloriously upward flew. NOBV

Eyes. William Henry Davies. Have I not proved his wisdom is no fable? BrPo; FM

Eyes. Walter De la Mare. But which, bound hand and foot, he, close on night,/Can only see. BrPo

Eyes. Clarisse Nicoidski. the eye walking/around you/me. VWA

Eyes and Tears. Andrew Marvell. These weeping Eyes, those seeing Tears. MePo

The Eyes Have It. William Stephens. in factories, where the eyes see what they know?) NAMP

The Eyes of Cantonese Schoolmasters Remembered in Hong Kong. Willis Barnstone. We have been living for a long time. GLGT

The Eyes of Children at the Brink of the Sea's Grasp. Josephine Jacobsen. Of shaping danger they go–and widen their eyes/Innocent and voluptuous. NePoAm-2

The Eyes of Flesh.   Sandra Hochman.   ...For/a house/is where/deep/ purposes are/broken/off.   NMM

The Eyes of God.   Hermann Hagedorn.   And glow, beyond all telling bright,/Each time a brave soul dares a flight.   HBMV

Eyes of Men Running, Falling, Screaming.   *Anonymous.*   The eyes of the dying and those of the dead.   OBWP

The Eyes of My Regret.   Angelina Weld Grimke.   --The eyes of my Regret.   CDC

Eyes of Night-Time.   Muriel Rukeyser.   giving us gifts at hand, the glitter of all their eyes.   BoWoP; MiAP; NePA

Eyes of Summer.   William Stanley Merwin.   so that they will forget nothing.   CAPP

The Eyes of Texas.   *Anonymous.*   The eyes of Texas are upon you/Till Gabriel blows his horn.   FSW

Eyes So Tristful.   Diego de Saldana.   Say to what ye have betrayed me.   AWP

The Eyes That Drew from Me.   Petrarch (Francesco Petrarca).   And tears are heard within the harp I touch.   NAWM 1-2

Eyes That Last I Saw in Tears.   Thomas Stearns Eliot.   And hold us in derision.   InPo; NOBE; ViBoPo

Eyes That Queenly Sit.   Elizabeth Daryush.   If but the window/Love illuminate.   QFR

The Eyes, the Blood.   David Meltzer.
   into freeways filled with the starlight of cars.   PoM
   A music once was made./I heard it as a child.   VWA

Eyesight II.   Robert Duncan.   How wonderful in the new eye the world will appear!   EAS

Eyewash.   Niall Montgomery.   (these things are all available to salvation they say).   EAS

Eyewinker.   *Anonymous.*   Guzzlewopper.   OxNR

Eyewitness.   Rodney Hall.   But nothing much unusual occurred;/don't get the wrong idea.   PoAu 1-2

Ezek'l Saw de Wheel (excerpt).   *Anonymous.*   'Way up in de middle of de air.   ExPo

Ezekiel.   Laurence Binyon.   None can repeat you, none complete, nor annul you.   ChMP

Ezekiel.   A. N. Stencl.   And in the link-in-link, the iron,/The coming days he sees.   VWA

Ezekiel Saw the Wheel.   *Anonymous.*   A wheel in a wheel, (wheel in a wheel),/Way in the middle of the air.   FSW

Ezekiel, You and Me (with music).   *Anonymous.*   I'm go'n to reap jus' what I sow.   AS

Ezra Pound.   Robert Lowell.   And he, "To begin with a swelled head and end with swelled feet."   NoAm; NOBA

Ezra Shank.   *Anonymous.*   These bubbles mark/o/o/o/Where Ezra sank.   ShM

Ezry.   Archibald MacLeish.   Giddy with grandeur where you stood.   MoVE; NOBA

F

Fa, Mi, Fa, Re, La, Mi.   *Anonymous.*   O sing this once again, lustily.   InPK

Faberge.   James Schuyler.   I have nothing/to cry about now I have you.   ANYP

Fabien Dei Franchi.   Oscar Wilde.   Thou trumpet set for Shakepeare's lips to blow!   BrPo

Fable.   Joan Aiken.   beg him to take off the spell again.   WSC

Fable.   Maurice James Craig.   But let your enemy present his case/In the least favourable time and place.   NeIP

Fable.   James Facos.   But Edison made light of it.   NLV

A Fable.   John Hookham Frere.   The moral of this tale I could not guess/Till Mr Landor sent his works to press.   FaBoCo

Fable.   Norman Harris.   Especially when those con-/cerned/Possess neither (sang the nightin-/gale).   NYBP

Fable.   Mary Mills.   there read the fable, time is always now.   NePoAm

Fable.   D. J. Opperman.   politely each/greets his own face.   PeSA

Fable.   Dorothy Parker.   Oh, they lied in their teeth when they told me of her!   ALV

Fable.   Janos Pilinszky.   and on into the morning when he was beaten to death.   OBVE

A Fable.   Matthew Prior.   He without hair, and thou without a crown.   NoP

Fable.   Frederic Prokosch.   And my love lies cold in the burning wood.   WaP

A Fable for Critics.   James Fenimore Cooper.   ...he/Has made at the most something wooden and empty.   DBV

A Fable for Critics.   James Russell Lowell.

And she could not have hit a more excellent plan/For making him fully and perfectly man.   AmPP; AP; OxBA

And thinks 'em the best he has tasted this season.   NOBA

Any mirror except her own rivers and lakes.   AA

As quiet and chaste as the author's own life.   AnNE; AP; NOBA; OxBA; TAP

At the head of a march to the last new Jerusalem.   AA; AP; NOBA; OxBA; TAP

But of broad, peaceful oak-leaves for citizens saved!   AnNE; NOBA

The calmest degree that you know is superlative?   AmePo

Her fugitive pieces will find themselves safe.   OBSV

Is that you have your slaves, and the Greek had his helot.   AnNE; NOBA; OxBA

Let that mob be the upper ten thousand or lower.   TAP

A name either English or Yankee,--just Irving.   AnNE

That are trodden upon are your own or your foes'.   AnNE; NOBA

That the music had somehow got mixed with the whole.   AnNE; NOBA

While a cloud that floats o'er is reflected within it.   AnNE; OxBA; TAP

Who spoke out for the dumb and the down-trodden then!   AP; OxBA

Why, he'll live till men weary of Collins and Gray.   PP

Fable II: The Vulture, the Sparrow, and Other Birds.   John Gay.   Within my thatched retreat I find/(What these ne'er feel) true peace of mind.   EiCP

Fable IV: The Eagle, and the Assembly of Animals.   John Gay.   Nor imitate the restless mind,/And proud ambition of mankind.   EiCP

The Fable Merchant.   Charles Dobzynski.   For I sell the future in a mere flower!   VWA

The Fable of Acis, Polyphemus, and Galatea.   John Dryden.   But swiftness is the Vice I only fear.   AtBAP

The Fable of Midas.   Jonathan Swift.   And Midas now neglected stands,/With asses' ears, and dirty hands.   APAS

The Fable of the Magnet and the Churn.   Sir William Schwenck Gilbert.   By no endeavor/Can a magnet ever/Attract a Silver Churn!   OnMSP

The Fable of the Piece of Glass and the Piece of Ice.   John Hookham Frere.   All the boys will tease and scorn ye.   OxBChV

Fable of the Speckled Cow.   D. J. Opperman.   Oh where shall I hide/from the stipples that peck?   PeSA

Fable of the Talented Mockingbird.   Scott Bates.   And sang an original love song/That nobody understood.   BoAnP

A Fable of the War.   Howard Nemerov.   That the great work not falter but go on.   NePoEA; OBWP

Fable of the Water Merchants.   Stephen P. Dunn.   and gave the merchants everything they wanted.   LTB

Fable: "The mountain and the squirrel."   Ralph Waldo Emerson.   If I cannot carry forests on my back,/Neither can you crack a nut.   OBCA

Fable VII: The Lion, the Fox, and the Geese.   John Gay.   Will feed on geese both noon and night.   EiCP

Fable X: The Elephant and the Bookseller.   John Gay.   Wits are game-cocks to one another.   EiCP

Fable XIII: Plutus, Cupid, and Time.   John Gay.   That time (when truly understood)/Is the most precious earthly good.   EiCP

Fable XIII: The Tame Stag.   John Gay.   For custom conquers fear and shame.   EiCP

Fable XLV: The Poet and the Rose.   John Gay.   Must we, to flatter her, be made/To wither, envy, pine and fade?   EiCP

Fable XX: The Old Hen and the Cock.   John Gay.   "I ne'er had been in this condition/But for my mother's prohibition."   EiCP

Fable XXIV: The Butterfly and the Snail.   John Gay.   And all thy race (a num'rous seed)/Shall prove of caterpillar breed.   FM

Fables for the Female Sex, V: The Poet and His Patron.   Edward Moore.   Unthinking fools, alone despise/The arts, that taught them first to rise.   CEP

Fables: The Shepherd and the Philosopher.   John Gay.   And those, without our schools, suffice/To make men moral, good and wise.   CEP

Fables: The Sick Man and the Angel.   John Gay.   Then why such haste? so groan'd and dy'd.   CEP

Fabrication of Ancestors.   Alan Dugan.   although I wear a proof/of the war's obscenity.   NoAm

Fabulary Satire, IV.   Daryl Hine.   But who is seldom mentioned in the fable.   NOBC

The Fabulists.   Rudyard Kipling.   We are not, nor we were not, heard at all.   ChMP

The Fabulous Teamsters.   Judith Johnson Sherwin.   if you're not sent up you never get off the ground.   NYP

A Face.   Robert Browning.   All heaven, meanwhile, condensed into one eye/Which fears to lose the wonder, should it wink.   CTC

A Face.   Marianne Moore.   to my mind, to my sight,/must remain a delight.   OBSP; PoCh

Face.   Robert Morgan.   the Tiger clawing through eastern azure.   GeTw

The Face.   Edwin Muir.   The sun- and star-shaped killers gorge and play.   ChMP; GTBS-P

The Face.   Lucien Stryk.   Whoever holds the/string/will not let go.   GP

Face. Jean Toomer. nearly ripe for worms. CDC; NoP

The Face. Thomas Wade. But which sense cannot note by note define. ERoP 1-2

The Face against the Pane. Thomas Bailey Aldrich. Look beyond the stormy skies,/And they see the beacon light. TreFS

Face in a Mirror. Jack Anderson. The problem is,/if you won't be your own friend/you may never find one. LFAC

The Face in the Mirror. Robert Graves. To court the queen in her high silk pavilion. NoP; WeW

The Face of Jesus Christ. Christina Georgina Rossetti. This face, the face of Jesus Christ. BePJ

The Face of Love. Ingrid Jonker. face of my beloved/the face of love. PeSA

Face of Poverty. Lucy Smith. And your children/Will live. NNP; PoNe

The Face of the Waters. Robert D. Fitzgerald. light and the clear day and so simple a goal. BoAV; CBAP; PoAu 1-2

Face on the Daguerreotype. Norman Rosten. With your one-stringed instrument, our desperate glory. HoAn

Face-Paintings of the Caduveo Indians. William Dickey. ...becomes/only a way I remember people looking. FAZ

Face to Face. Frances Cochrane. Until we meet in Heaven, where all tears have passed away. HBV 1-2

Face to Face. Adrienne Rich. ...behind dry lips/a loaded gun. LiTM; NoP

Face to Face with Reality. John Oxenham. And we thank Him for His grace. WBLP

Face to Face with Trouble (excerpt). Margaret E. Sangster. With an honest heart and a childlike trust/That God will do the rest. PoToHe

The Face Upon the Floor. Hugh Antoine D'Arcy. With a fearful shriek, he leaped and fell across the picture–dead. BeLS; BLPA; FaBoBe; FPL; HBV 1-2; PaPo; YaD

Faces. Jack Anderson. Sweet little babies in his damned freezer.... LFAC

Faces. John Ciardi. You know as much about that face as I do. BiP

Faces from a Bestiary. X. J. Kennedy. Do not repent. It is too late. NePoEA-2

Faces in the Street. Henry Lawson. In that pent track of living death–the city's cruel street. CBAP

Faces (parody). D. C. Berry. And if you can't finish this picture in/the final solution, then, presto grace,/yourselves jump. BXAP

Faces Seen Once. James Dickey. Unbearable memoryless face. UnPo

Facing the Chair. Hugh" (Christopher Murray Grieve) MacDiarmid. The unity of life which can only be forged by love. FaBoMo

Facing the New Year. Anonymous. We shall go forward to the work of another year with steadfastness/and confidence. PGD

Facing the New Year. Mark Guy Pearse. Le us pray: Let us praise. BLRP

Facing West from California's Shores. Walt Whitman. (But where is what I started for so long ago?/And why is it yet unfound?) MoAmPo; TAP

Fact. Kenneth Rexroth. The female hyena, it is/Very large. OBAL

Factories. Edward Hirsch. pumping blood through the stillness of my arteries AMV-81

The Factories. Margaret Widdemer. God of Life! Creator! It was I! It was I! HBV 1-2

The Factory. Olga Cabral. there was the yellow chalk sign/the factory's "X." GP

Factory Girl. Anonymous. Pity me, my darling/And carry me away. ABF; FSW; SaC

The Factory Girl. J. A. Phillips. If she sins to escape her bondage/Is there room for wonder then? SaC

The Factory Girl's Come-All-Ye. Anonymous. Sing dum de whickerty, dum de way. AmFP; OBAL

The Factory Hands. Polycarp Chimedza. The grief-wrung minds are shuttled/Between the agony of the factory/And the misery at home. WhB

A Factory Rainbow. Muslih-ud-Din Sa'di. If I can't have the sunshine,/I can have the rainbow. SaC

Factory Windows Are Always Broken. Vachel Lindsay. End of the factory-window song. CrMA; FaFP; LiTA; NAMP; NePA; OBCA; OBSP

Facts. Lewis (Charles Lutwidge Dodgson) Carroll. 'Twould never reach the nearest star,/Because it is so very far. FaBoUs

Facts. William Henry Davies. In faith that Christ is still alive. BrPo

A faded boy in sallow clothes. Emily Dickinson. Remanded to a ballad's barn/Or clover's retrospect. PoEL 1-5

The Faded Face. Thomas Hardy. Faded Face,/Sorrow-wrung! QFR

A Faded Letter. William J. Fischer. You left me at the parting of the way/And sacrificed the world and all its ken. CAW

Faded Pictures. William Vaughn Moody. A picture keeps its eyes, somehow. AP

Fading Beauty. Anonymous. Beauty does fade, at thirty dies. FaBoEE

Fading Beauty. Giambattista Marino. That springs and parches in the self-same hour. AWP

Fading-Leaf and Fallen-Leaf. Richard Garnett. Fade then and fall–thou hast had all/That Life can give: ask somewhat now of Death.' OBVV

The Fading Rose: Epitaph. Philip Freneau. Or ever all who love, shall gain. AA

The Faerie Queene. Robin Blaser. The queen of faerie guarded by blue winged griffins/Untouched by. CoPo

The Faerie Queene. Edmund Spenser.
All ranged in a ring, and dancing in delight. TrGrPo

All which, and thousands mo do make a loathsome life.' NOBE

And all his sences were with deadly fit opprest. PoEL 1-5

And eke this battels end, will need an-/other place. OAEP

And Natur's selfe did vanish, whither no man wist. OAEL 1-2

And now is come to that same place, where first she weft. OBSC

And on his head a garland well beseene. GN

And then returned, having marched thrice,/Into the inner room, from whence they first did rise. OBSC

And to his law compels all creatures to obey. WHA

As plain as at the first, when they were fresh and green. OBSC

But let us hence depart, whilest wether serves and wind. OAEL 1-2; PoEL 1-5

But when she died, the Fairy Queen it brought/To Fairy Land, where yet it may be seen, if sought. OBSC

The carver Holm; the Maple seldom inward sound. OHIP

Compared to the creatures in the seas entrall. AtBAP

Dead sculs and bones of men, whose life had gone astray. PPP

Decked all with flowers, and wings of gold fit to employ. OBSC

Doth seem to be herself, though darkened be her light. OBSC

Drawn of fair peacocks, that excel in pride,/And full of Argus eyes their tayles dispredden wide. WHA

The dreadfull spectacle of that sad house/of Pride. OAEP

Ease after war, death after life does greatly please. MOS; PoPle; SeCePo

The further he doth goe, the further he doth stray. FaBoEn

Gather the Rose of love, whilest yet is time,/Whilest loving thou mayst loved be with equall crime. FaBoEn; NOBE

He set her on her steede, and forward forth/did beare. OAEP

Her filthie parbreake all the place defiled has. EBEV

I from thenceforth have learned to love more dear/This lowly quiet life, which I inherit here.' OBSC

In which a thousand birds had built their bowers. GN

Is woxen so deformed, that he has quight/Forgot he was a man, and Gealosie is hight. NoP

Long way he traveled, before he heard of ought. ExPo

More mild in beastly kind, then that her/beastly foe. OAEP

Ne rested till she came without relent/Unto the land of Amazons, as she was bent. OAEL 1-2

Nor the fine nets, which oft we woven see/Of scorched deaw, do not in th' ayre more lightly flee. WHA

O horrible enchantment, that him so did blend! EBEV; OBSC

O that great Sabbaoth God, graunt me that Sabaoths sight. OAEL 1-2; PoEL 1-5

O, why should Heavenly God to men have such regard! GoBC; NOCV; OBSC

Or Eden selfe, if ought with Eden mote compaire. FiP

Saint George of mery England, the signe of victoree. FaBoPV

So downe he fell, and like an heaped mountaine lay. WHA

So ended he his tale, where I this Canto end. OAEL 1-2

So forth they went, the Dwarfe them guid-/ing euer right. CoBE; OAEP

So huge their numbers, and so numberlesse their nation. MOS

So leave they take of Coelia, and her daugh-/ters three. OAEP

...So passing forth she him/obaid. OAEP

So turne they still about, and change in restlesse wise. PoEL 1-5

So was the high aspyring with huge ruine humbled. NoP

Such grace now to be happy, is before thee laid. FiP

Such one vile Envy was, that fifte in row did sit. TW

That had achiev'd so great a conquest by/his might. EnLi 1-2; OAEP

That she may hark to love, and read this lesson often. OBSC

Therewith she laught, and did her earnest end in jest. MOS

Thether resortes, and laying his sad dartes/Asyde, with faire Adonis playes his wanton partes. PoEL 1-5

Those glaring lamps were set, that made a dreadful shade. SeCePo

Thus did the battle vary to and fro... HoPM

Thy love is there advanced to be another Grace. OBSC

To future age of her this mention may be made. OAEL 1-2

To reap the ripen'd fruits the which the earth had/yold. GN

Vile Poverty, and lastly Death with Infamy. PoEL 1-5

Well may she speede and fairely finish her intent. OAEL 1-2; OAEP

Where let them wend at will, whilest here I doe respire. OAEL 1-2

Where store they found of all, that dainty/was and rare. OAEP

Which by the houres he measured, besought/Them go to rest. So all unto their bowres were brought. NoP

Which, for my Muse her self now tired has/Unto another Canto I will overpass. HW

The which to heare vouchsafe, O dearest/dread, a-while! EnLit; FiP; OAEP

The whiles the maskers marched forth in trim array. FiP

Whose course in often stayd, yet never is astray. MOS

Whose lives although decayed, yet loves decayed never. OBSC

With that misformed spright he backe re-/turned againe. CoBE

Yet all are in one body, and as one appeare. FaBoEn

Yet nathelesse it could not doe him die,/Till he should die his last, that is eternally. OAEP

Yet nothing did he dread, but ever was ydrad. GoBC

The Faerie's Child. Thomas Caulfield Irwin. Where the weary folk are dreaming. OnYI

The Faery Reaper. Robert Williams Buchanan. They blest the wedding/Of a pure colleen! OBVV

Faery Song. John Keats. Adieu, Adieu! CH

A Faery Song. William Butler Yeats. Thousands of years, thousands of years,/If all were told. ViBoPo

Faeryland. Robert Pinsky. ...harbor/Hard in a cold pale storm that falls all over. MAYP

Faesulan Idyl. Walter Savage Landor. Dropt it, as loth to drop it, on the rest. OBRV; SeCePo

Fag-End. Philip O'Connor. ...hide/your blonde strawed skull from the/white/multitude of drips. EAS

Failed Fathers. Lewis Turco. but where, oh where, do the failed fathers go? AMV-81

Failing the Examination. Meng Chiao. My feelings like a knifeblade's wound. GLGT

Failure. Rupert Brooke. An idle wind blew round an empty throne/And stirred the heavy curtains on the walls. ILwL

A Failure. C. Day-Lewis. There's nothing to do but to set the teeth/And plough it in. NOBE

Failure. Richmond Lattimore. Sweet wind, sweet wind, where have you blown our past? PCP

Failure. E. L. Mayo. The bony structure of the universe. FAZ

Failure. Eithne Wilkins. And who, beside the darkened station lamp,/remembering, started back. NeBP

Failures. Arthur Upson. Or else they nodded when their Master-Chance/Wound his one signal, and went on his way. HBV 1-2; WGRP

Fain I Would. Anonymous. Yet thy thoughts doth not half know her.' EIL

Fain Would I Have a Prettie Thing to Give unto My Ladie. Anonymous. But as pretty a thing as may be. CoMu; EIL; EnPo; InvP; OAEP; ViBoPo

Fain Would I Wed a Fair Young Man. Thomas Campion. As I was by one brought forth I would bring/forth another. UnTE

Fain Would My Thoughts. John Austin. All highest praise, all humblest thanks,/Now and for ever be! OxBoCh

Fainne Gael An Lae. Alice Milligan. And bring the hour of thy conquering power/And the dawning of the day! HBV 1-2

Faint Falls the Gentle Voice. Henry Timrod. To make thee hear our cries for peace. AH

Faint Heart. William James Linton. They lose most who are afraid. OBVV

Faint Heart. Rufinus Domesticus. Or else from joy be ever banished. ErPo

Faint Music. Walter De La Mare. All sounds to silence come. FaBoCh; LoGBV

Faint Yet Pursuing. Coventry Patmore. Within this oak-shade one more minute even,/Hearing the winds their Maker magnify. OxBoCh

Faintheart in a Railway Train. Thomas Hardy. That I had alighted there! CTC; EnLoPo

Faintly and from Far away. Vassar Miller. ...Before it swoops me up,/feather/The hawk of the world's forgetting with the down of/Your memory. CoPo

The Fair Agnete. Agnes Miegel. A wave all white–so white–outside was leaping. CAW

Fair and Fair. George Peele. The fairest shepherd on our green,/A love for any lady. EIL; OBEV; ViBoPo

Fair and Free Elections. Anonymous. Let all stand by the ballot box,/For fair and free elections. FSW

Fair, and Soft, and Gay, and Young. Robert Gould. He, too, will find he is undone,/And that she was not made for one. UnTE

Fair and Softly. Philip Ayres. And gladly drudge at the accustom'd plough. FaBoEE

Fair and Unfair. Robert Francis. We'd make a fairer fairer world of it. VGW

Fair Annet's Song. Elinor Wylie. And neither one will stay. AmLP

Fair Annie. Anonymous.
And my mother will make my portion up/When I return again. OxBB; ViBoFo
And one of them will carry me home,/And six I will give to thee. BSV; CH; HBV 1-2; ViBoFo
And two will carry me home,/And we'll have Lord Thomas burned. BaBo
But thanks to a' the powers in heaven/That I gae maiden hame!' AnFE; BaBo; ESPB; FaBoBa; ViBoFo
The leve I'll keep to your sister Jane,/For tocher she gat nane.' ESPB

To come awa a wedded wife,/Gae hame a maid the morn.' ESPB

Fair Annie of Lochryan. Anonymous. And the King of Heaven will father your bairn/Till love Gregor come hame. AS

The Fair at Windgap. Austin Clarke. And so the commotion arose at the fair. OnYI; OxBTC; SeCePo

The Fair Beauty Bride. Anonymous. My true-love is dead and in her grave, and it's there I long to be. AmFP

Fair/Boy Christian Takes a Break. Jim Harrison. ...pray/the removal of what my troubled eyes have seen. NoAm

Fair Cassidy. Anonymous. And may Christ have mercy on Cassidy. BIrV

The Fair Circassian. Richard Garnett. And beware the wily plans/Of the fair Circassians. HBV 1-2; OBVV

The Fair Damsel from London (The Brown Girl–Pretty Sarah). Anonymous. Her red, rosy cheeks is moulderin' away. AmFP

Fair Days; or, Dawns Deceitful. Robert Herrick. What trust to things below, whenas we see,/As men, the heavens have their hypocrisy? CaPo

Fair Ellender. Anonymous. And place fair Ellender in my arms,/And the Brown Girl at my feet. FSW

Fair England. Helen Gray Cone. Twin strengths, with God to friend! AA

A Fair Exchange. Jean de La Fontaine. And with my Petronella spent the night. UnTE

Fair Fannie Moore. Anonymous. And laid by the side of the fair Fannie Moore. BFSS

Fair Florella (B vers.). Anonymous. Don't put your trust in young men/Or you astray they may lead. BaBo

The Fair Flower of Northumberland. Anonymous.
And you're aye welcome back to Northumberland!' BuBa
Scots were neuer true, nor neuer will be,/To Lord, nor Lady, nor faire England. BaBo; ESPB; OxBB

The Fair-Haired Girl. Anonymous. Woe is me, that e'er my sight/Dwelt on charms so deadly bright! OnYI

Fair Hebe. John West. And Reason confirms me a slave to her charms. HBV 1-2

Fair Helen. Anonymous. Since my Love died for me. FaFP; GTBS; GTBS-P; LiTL; ViBoPo

The Fair Hills of Eire, O! James Clarence Mangan. In the sunlight that shone long ago on the shields/Of the Gaels, on the fair hills of Eire, O! IrPN; OBVV

The Fair Hills of Ireland. Sir Samuel Ferguson. On the fair hills of holy Ireland. AnIV; FaBoPP; IrPN; OBEV; OBVV; OnYI

Fair Ines. Thomas Hood. The smile that bless'd one lover's heart/Has broken many more! EnRP; HBV 1-2; OBEV; OBRV; OBVV

Fair Iris and Her Swain. John Dryden. Thus at the height we love and live,/And fear not to be poor. ViBoPo

Fair Is the Rose. Anonymous. Breathing delight to-day, but none to-morrow. EG; EIL

Fair Isabell of Rochroyall. Anonymous. He has given himself a deadly wound/And word spake never mair]. OxBB

Fair Isle at Sea. Robert Louis Stevenson. ...once or twice/I touched at isles of Paradise. NOBV

Fair Janet. Anonymous.
And a' the birds that flew above,/They changed their notes and sang. ESPB
Out of the tane there grew a birk,/And the tither a bonny brier. BaBo; ESPB; OxBB

The Fair Lady of the Plains. Anonymous. The redcaps have murdered my dear loving wife. BFSS

The Fair Lass of Islington. Anonymous. Out-witted by a Country Girl/About his Pipe of Wine. OxBB

The Fair Maid and the Sun. Arthur William Edgar O'Shaughnessy. O sons of men, that toil, and love with tears! BeLS

The Fair Maid by the Shore. Anonymous. I'm again a fair maid on the shore. AmFP; BaBo

The Fair Maid of the West. Anonymous. But since he did it you restore,/See that you play the fool no more. CoMu

Fair Maiden, Who Is This Bairn? Anonymous. That he will grant us of his grace/In heaven high to have a place! ISi

Fair Margaret and Sweet William. Anonymous.
And by misfortune cut them down,/Or they had now been there. ESPB; OxBB
They grew till they joind in a true/lover's knot,/And then they died both together. BaBo; ESPB; OBET; ViBoFo
Three times he kissed her cold corpy lips,/And he fell in her arms asleep. AmFP

Fair Mary of Wallington. Anonymous. Tho the cradle it be full spread up,/the bride-bed is left bare. ESPB

The Fair Morning. Jones Very. Making the woods reecho with his song. NOBA

A Fair Nymph Scorning a Black Boy Courting Her. John Cleveland. Tears can no more affection win,/Than wash thy Aethiopian Skin. AnAnS 2

Fair Phyllis I Saw Sitting All Alone. Anonymous. When he found her, O then they fell a-kissing. GBL

Fair, Rich, and Young. Martial (Marcus Valerius Martialis). As makes her seem, nor fair, nor rich, nor young. NIP

The Fair Singer. Andrew Marvell. And all my forces needs must be undone,/She having gained both the wind and sun. CavP; CBEP; EG; EnLoPo; LiTL; MeLP; MePo; NOBE; NoP; PoEL 1-5; PoPle

Fair Summer Droops. Nashe [(or Nash)] Thomas. The earth is hell when thou leav'st to appear. ElL; LoBV; OBSP

Fair Sylvia. *Anonymous.* May I again turn Wanderer,/And never settle more. OBS

The Fair Thief. Charles Wyndham. And let her prison be my arms! HBV 1-2

Fair Thou Art. Mordecai Ben Isaac. Each man take his share! TrJP

A Fair Warning. E. L. Mayo. And stays long. FAZ

Fair Weather. Dorothy Parker. That casts upon the heart, as it recedes,/Splinters and spars and dripping, salty weeds. SBG

Faire Virtue, the Mistresse of Phil'arete: Shall I, Wasting in Dispair. George Wither. For, if shee be not for me,/What care I, for whome she be. SeCV 1-2

Fairest between Lincoln and Lindsey. *Anonymous.* I wole mone my song/On wham that it is on ilong. MeEL

The Fairest Flower. John Audelay. As fairest of al,/And ever was and ever shal. OxBM

The Fairest He. Horatius Bonar. I glory in that glorious name/Of matchless worth. BePJ

Fairest Lord Jesus. *Anonymous.* Jesus shines brighter, Jesus shines purer,/Then all the angels heaven can boast. TRV; WGRP

Fairest of Freedom's Daughters. Jeremiah Eames Rankin. Flash it across the waters! PAH

The Fairest of Her Days. *Anonymous.* She is the fairest of her days. ElL

Fairground. W. H. Auden. games that call for patience, foresight, maneuver,/like war, like marriage. NYBP

The Fairies. William Allingham. And white owl's feather! AnEnPo; AnIL; CBEP; EvOK; FaBoCh; FaBoPP; FaBV; HBV 1-2; HBVY; IrPN; LoGBV; NOBE; NOBV; OBEV; OBVV; OnMSP; OnYI; OxBChV; OxBI; PoPle; RoGo; SUS; ViBoPo; WSC

Fairies. Hilda Conkling. There you are, Primrose! I see you, Black Wing! TiPo; WSC

Fairies. Rose Fyleman. Well–it's Me! HBMV; HBVY; OxBChV; SoPo

The Fairies. Robert Herrick. Mab will pinch her by the toe. OBS

The Fairies. Patricia Hubbell. Jump into the thistledown/Sleep all night! WSC

Fairies. Thomas Tickell. The whilst poor mortals startle at the sound/Of unseen footsteps on the haunted ground. OBEC

The Fairies Are Dancing All over the World. Michael Rumaker. They are allies courting in the bloodstreams/welcome them and dance with them. PeHV

The Fairies Break Their Dances. Alfred Edward Housman. The young man feels his pockets/And wonders what's to pay. MoVE; NoAm; OBSP

The Fairies' Farewell. Richard Corbet.
For all the Fairies' evidence/Were lost if that were addle. NOBE
Oh, how the Commonwealth doth need/Such justices as you! LiTB; TrGrPo
Or else they take their ease. CBEP
They never danced on any heath/As when the time hath been. FaBoCh; LoGBV; ViBoPo

The Fairies Feast. Charles M. Doughty. In that they shrunk back, and clapped to their/doors.... CH

The Fairies in New Ross. *Anonymous.* Then we sail o'er yellow waves. OnYI

The Fairies of the Caldon Low. Mary Howitt. For I'm as tired as I can be. BeLS; HBV 1-2; HBVY

The Fairies' Shopping. Margaret Deland. The Fairies' sleep is warm and sweet! HBVY

Fairies' Song. [James Henry] Leigh Hunt. Were it not for stealing, stealing. ALV

The Fairy Artist. Nellie M. Garabrant. Jack Frost, the artist's name. PoPl

The Fairy Book. Abbie Farwell Brown. When Mother takes the Fairy Book/And we curl up to hear. HBV 1-2; HBVY

The Fairy Book. Norman Gale. When we cuddle close together with the happy Fairy-book. HBV 1-2; HBVY; OHIP

The Fairy Fiddler. Nora Hopper. But the wild swans they know me,/And the horse that draws the plough. HBMV; ViBoPo

The Fairy Folk. Robert Bird. Perhaps the little fairy folk/Will visit you to-night. HBV 1-2; HBVY

Fairy Godmothers. Eugene Lee-Hamilton. But bitterer is the cup than can be told. OBVV

The Fairy Harpers. James B. Dollard. On Meelin's mournful mountain where the magic harps make moan! CaP

The Fairy Host. *Anonymous.* At chess-craft they excel the Gael. AnIV

The Fairy King. William Allingham. He lived in woods and bowers. IrPN

The Fairy Lough. Moira O'Neill. An' no one there to see! OBVV

The Fairy Lover. Moireen Fox. If I have but the kisses of his proud red mouth. AnIV

The Fairy Maimoune. John Moultrie. ...and sold/(Like our two Kings) their happiness for gold. OBRV

Fairy Music. Francis Ledwidge. The dewy bells of evening ring,/And all is melody. YeAr

The Fairy Nurse. Edward Walsh. Shuheen, sho, lulo lo! OnYI

The Fairy Queen. *Anonymous.* Yet in the morning may be seen/Where we the night before have been. PoPle

Fairy Song. Felicia Dorothea Hemans. By sweet fount or murmuring shore,/Never more! HBVY

A Fairy Song. John Lyly. Kiss Endimion, kiss his eyes,/Then to our midnight heidegyes. OBSC

Fairy Song. Winthrop Mackworth Praed. Softly, slowly: Minstrel, wake! SeCePo

Fairy Song. William Butler Yeats. The lonely of heart is withered away! MoBrPo; OnYI

Fairy Story. Barbara Euphan Todd. That magic was for yesterday,/And not for our enchanting? BoC

Fairy Story. Robert Penn Warren. Even happiness. NYBP

A Fairy Tale. Kenneth Mackenzie. and not scream in the night–/(I trust. I trust.) PoAu 1-2

A Fairy Tale. John Frederick Nims. And both ride off together down his mind. MiAP

A Fairy Tale. Phyllis Thompson. Prince, still humped like a frog in the slime of sex. DFT

A Fairy Tale. Vitomil Zupan. What a nice fairy tale indeed. DFT

Fairy Tales. Jane Flanders. And draw you up like a bucket/Of fresh water. DFT

Fairy Tales. Itzik Manger. how the beggars were rewarded/with crowns of purest gold. VWA

The Fairy Temple; or, Oberon's Chapel.... Robert Herrick. And, by the glow-worm's light well guided,/Goes to the feast that's now provided. CaPo

The Fairy Thorn. Sir Samuel Ferguson. And ne'er was Anna Grace seen again. AnIV; OnMSP; OnYI; VLP

The Fairy Thrall. Mary C. G. Byron. But my heart is cold in the cold night-tide,/Where the elfins ride. HBV 1-2; HBVY

A Fairy Voyage. *Anonymous.* I'd sit astride the stem and guide/It straight to Fairyland and stay. SoPo

A Fairy Went A-Marketing. Rose Fyleman. Thanked it, and let it go. OxBChV; SoPo; SUS

Fairy Wings. Winifred Howard. And hang them to dry,/On a clear frosty night,/From the beams of the moon. SUS

The Fairy Wood. Arthur Symons. And the peace that is not in the world has flown to me. BoC

Fairyland. Rabindranath Tagore. It is at the corner of the terrace where the pot/of the tulsi plant stands. WSC

Faith. *Anonymous.* And say with joyous heart, "They are with Thee." PoToHe

Faith. Robert Browning. You understand me? I have said/enough? TreFT

Faith. Ada Cambridge. Forgive the anguish of the turning wheel! PoAu 1-2

Faith. Preston Clark. And your sorrows are less than your strength/Which he foresaw. HBMV

Faith. Victor J. Daley. The last god dies/With the last believer. PoAu 1-2

Faith. Marjorie Dunkels. Then I felt peculiar/And found that I couldn't! PH

Faith. Frances Anne Kemble. Better be cheated to the last/Than lose the blessed hope of truth. FaBoBe; HBV 1-2; OBVV

Faith. John Richard Moreland. I see the risen Lord again! OHIP

Faith. Ray Palmer A ransomed soul! AA; HBV 1-2

Faith. Alexander Pope. The strength he gains is from the embrace he gives. WGRP

Faith. Margaret E. Sangster. My Father's hand appointing me/My days and ways, so I am free. TRV

Faith. George Santayana. By which alone the mortal heart is led/Unto the thinking of the thought divine. WGRP

Faith. Louise Morgan Sill. His Father, and his God. CAW

Faith. John Banister Tabb. Is Faith–the fervid evidence/Of loveliness unseen. TRV

Faith. Lorenzo Thomas. But you will not ask me to go. APU

Faith. John Greenleaf Whittier. Fall on the seeming void, and find/The rock beneath. TRV

Faith. Ella Wheeler Wilcox. With my last breath. BLRP; PoToHe

Faith and Freedom. William Wordsworth. ...the faith and morals/hold/Which Milton held. GN

Faith and Sight. Anna M. King. I know He will abide with me today. BLRP

Faith and Works. Muriel Spark. As near as two and two make five. OBSP

The Faith Came First. Sydney Carter. no other rock/but this to/build upon. EBCP

Faith for Tomorrow. Thomas Curtis Clark. That what we hope for cometh with the morn! PoToHe

Faith Healer Come to Rabun County. David Bottoms. O sisters come to the altar, lay your hands on the radio. TAT

Faith Healing. Philip Larkin. Saying Dear child, and all time has disproved. NoAm

Faith, Hope and Love. *Anonymous*. Brings Heaven near. BLRP

Faith, I Wish I Were a Leprechaun. Margaret Tod Ritter. I wish I were a leprechaun/Beneath a hawthorn tree! TiPo

Faith–is the Pierless Bridge. Emily Dickinson. To Our far, vascillating Feet/A first Necessity. AmPP

The Faith of Abraham Lincoln. Abraham Lincoln. And that it may be so I give thanks to the Almighty/and seek His aid. TRV

Faith of Our Fathers. Frederick William Faber. We will be true to thee till death. GoTF; TreFS

A Faith on Trial (excerpt). George Meredith. "Him through handmaiden me." WGRP

Faith's Difficulty. Theodore Maynard. For me the birth,/The sorrows of the crucified? TrPWD

Faith's Vista. Henry Abbey. "You could not reach us if you did not/die." AA

Faith Trembling. Mary Ainge De Vere. And not to me? AA

The Faithful. Jane Cooper. Trembling with passionate pity/At my blameless life and shaking its flamelike head? AmPC; NePoEA-2; SM

The Faithful Few. Chester E. Shuler. They must be very precious to/The blessed Prince of Peace. STF

The Faithful Friend. William Cowper. A prison, with a friend, preferr'd/To liberty without. FM

The Faithful Lover. Robert Pack. Although I love you as I do the spring. NePoEA

The Faithful Shepherdess. John Fletcher.
And not a wave shall trouble thee. OBS
I freely offer, and ere long/Will bring you more, more sweet and strong. ViBoPo
If you crave it. EG
Many a note and many a lay. OBS
On the earth, may still befriend/Thee, and this arbour. OBS; ViBoPo
Sweeter than the silver string. TrGrPo
Thus great Pan is ever sung. TrGrPo
Thus I end my evenings knell. OBS
To kiss her sweetest. ViBoPo
To that place day doth unyoke! EG; OBS

Faithful unto Death. Richard Handfield Titherington. "God reigns and the Republic lives!" PAH

The Faithful Wife. Barbara L. Greenberg. ...I would know him with my other/body,/the one that you have never asked to see. SM

Faithfully Tinying at Twilight Voice. Edward Estlin Cummings. the more than thanks of always merest me. NYBP

Faithless. *Anonymous*. Unhappily we burn, Flaccus and I. UnTE

Faithless. Louis Lavater. Praying to God that we may never meet. PoAu 1-2

Faithless Nellie Gray. Thomas Hood. And they buried Ben in four cross-roads,/With a stake in his inside! BXAP; EnRP; FaBoCo; HBV 1-2; InMe; NA; NOBL; ShM; TreF; VLP

Faithless Sally Brown. Thomas Hood. They went and told the sexton, and/The sexton toll'd the bell. HBV 1-2; NOBL; OBNV; TreFS

A Faithless Shepherd. John Clare. Our souls with God, our bodies clay. VLP

The Faithless Wife. Federico Garcia Lorca.
For she was not unwed. LiTW
when I took her to the river. BoLoP; ErPo

The Fakir. Richard Owen Cambridge. All tortured by choice with th' invisible nail. OBTV

The Falcon. *Anonymous*. The falcon hath borne my Mate away. ACP; EG; InPo; LiTB; NU; SeCeV; ViBoPo

The Falcon. Wilfrid Scawen Blunt. A little while/And thou shalt sail back heavenwards. Woe is me! ACP

The Falcon. Richard Lovelace.
And the poetic Swan shall die,/Only to sing thy elegy. CaPo; PBBP
Then stoop so swift unto our Sence,/As thou wert sent Intelligence. PB

The Falcon. Richard Henry Stoddard. With my own white wings for a shroud. AA

The Falcon. Elinor Wylie. And tell her she is beautiful. LOW

The Falcon and the Dove. Sir Herbert Read. And now the falcon is hooded and comforted away. BrPo; FaBoMo

The Falconer of God. William Rose Benet. My soul still flies above me for the quarry it shall find. CAW; HBMV; PG; TreFT; WGRP

Falconry. Anne Wilkinson. Before I dive, God's mercy in my claws. OBCV

The Fall. William Barnes. Feace after feace, an' smile by smile. NBM; PoEL 1-5

The Fall. Russell Edson. But his parents said look it is fall. LCAP

Fall. Aileen Fisher. I wonder if the ladybugs/Have any place to go! YeAr

Fall. Robert Francis. ...Leave the bars lying. VGW

Fall. Robert Hass. ...Rotting caps/gave off a musky smell of loam. AmPA

Fall. Gabriela Melinescu. not from sin, not from sin,/but from weariness. AMV-80

The Fall. Kathleen Raine. the sea will carry us where tides run and currents flow. MoPo

The Fall. John Wilmot, Earl of Rochester. You love me for a frailer Part. EnLoPo; UnTE

Fall 1961. Robert Lowell. my one point of rest/is the orange and black/oriole's swinging nest! OBWP; VGW

Fall Again. H. R. Coursen. south-bound wedge shatters/down the emerald sky. AMV-81

The Fall Again. Howard Nemerov. And whitebeard falling naked to the floor/Ashamed, who was himself both Flood and Ark. ConAP

Fall Colors. Jerome Mazzaro. Next week, the pearl grey mist of early fall/will mute like Abishag the few leaves left. AMV-81

Fall Comes in Back-Country Vermont. Robert Penn Warren. I touch the hand there on the pillow. NYBP; VGW

Fall Days. Marion Conger. This one makes a perfect pipe,/That a perfect cup. SiSoSe

Fall Down. Calvin C. Hernton. ...You were young/Then/You/Died. CNA; PoBA

Fall In. Lincoln Kirstein. We wish to sink. We do not choose to swim. NoAm

Fall in Corrales. Richard Wilbur. Practise the candor of our bones. CoPo

Fall Journey. William Stafford. And then I stopped: my father's eyes were gray. NaP; Str

Fall, Leaves, Fall. Emily Bronte. Ushers in a drearier day. CH; ELP; EnLi 1-2; FaBoCh; FaBoRV; FaBV; LoBV; LoGBV; OBSP; PoEL 1-5; TrGrPo

Fall Letter. Dave Kelly. Then I will be sane again, I will/sit in a room free of flies and write superbly of snow. FAZ

Fall Lightly on Me. Roger Gaess. as if remembering the way to Spring. LTB

The Fall of Hyperion. John Keats.
And clouded all the altar with soft smoke. OBRV
And made their dove-wings tremble. On he flared. ERoP 1-2; OAEL 1-2
Her planetary eyes, and touch her voice/With such a sorrow... MBW 1-2
...the Naiad 'mid her reeds/Prest her cold finger closer to her lips. EnRP
"The one pours out a balm upon the World,/"The other vexes it.' OBRV
–perhaps no further dare. OAEL 1-2

The Fall of J. W. Beane. Oliver Herford. It is not well to mention names. OBAL; StPo

Fall of Leaves. D. S. Savage. falters, unchanneled to determined fingers. PoA

The Fall of Maubila. Thomas Dunn English. And this is why in cloistered cell/I wait my latter day. PAH

The Fall of Niagara. John Gardiner Calkins Brainard. –a light wave,/That breaks, and whispers of its Maker's might. AmePo

The Fall of Princes: Epilogue. John Lydgate. And where I faile, let Lydgate bere the lak. OxBM

The Fall of Richmond. Herman Melville. God's way adore. MC; PAH

The Fall of Rome. W. H. Auden. Silently and very fast. MAT; OAEL 1-2; OxBTC; PAI; UnPo

The Fall of Tecumseh. *Anonymous*. And the bright-bosomed Thames, in his/majesty, sweeps,/By the mound where his followers bore/him. PAH

The Fall of the City: Voice of the Studio Announcer. Archibald MacLeish. Where noon is the first few stars they see or the last one. HoPM

The Fall of the House of Usher. Reed Whittemore. Which was lucky since the house fell in right after,/Like a ton of brick. GP

The Fall of the House of Usher: The Haunted Palace. Edgar Allan Poe. And laugh–but smile no more. TrGrPo

The Fall of the Leaf. Henry David Thoreau. Discumbered of their Persian luxury. AP

The Fall of the Plum Blossoms. Banko. A fall of purest snow. TiPo

Fall of the Year. Henry Ellison. There let Faith beget on Love/The angel thou shalt be Above! OBVV

Fall Practice. Dabney Stuart. Being primed for the big game, hungering for the cup. SM

Fall Song. Daniel David Moses. ...a star comes/loose, slipping down like a sigh. AMV-81

Fall To. Howard Jones. FOR THE RAISING OF THE SEED/TRIES WAITING EXALTATION. NBP

Fall Wind. William Stafford. Once for thin walls, once for the sound of time. PPJ

The Fallen. Duncan Campbell Scott. Master of Life, we thank Thee/That they were what they were. TrPWD

The Fallen Elm. John Clare. Who glue their vile unsatiated maws/& freedoms birthright from the weak devours. FaBoPV

The fallen flowers seemed. Arakida Moritake. But no, ah no, they're only butterflies. LiTW

Fallen Leaves. Anonymous. Set the tune and I will follow you. LiTW

Fallen Leaves. Kathryn Munro Tupper. You stir and listen in your dreamless sleep. CaP

Fallen Majesty. William Butler Yeats. Once walked a thing that seemed, as it were, a burning cloud. PoA

Fallen Rain. Richard Watson Dixon. And I fall and die/Through a wile. NBM

The Fallen Star. George Darley. All join to chant the dirge of him/Who fell just now from Heaven. AnFE; HBV 1-2; OBEV

The Fallen Tower of Siloam. Robert Graves. An old wives' tale, not ours. WaP

The Fallen Tree. Patrick Maybin. ...light-search of leaf/can bring to this dead beauty some fragment of meaning? NeIP

The Fallen Tree. Andrew Young. More dead than upright post or fence or chair. BoNaP

A Fallen Yew. Francis Thompson. Sad tree, whose perishing boughs/So few birds house! BrPo; MoAB; MoBrPo

The Fallen Zulu Commander. C. M. Van Den Heever. Here where you lay the sheep will browse. PeSA

Falling. James Dickey. Not and tries less once tries tries AH, GOD–LCAP; NYBP

Falling. Bob Kaufman. Cutting off the edge of time, falling, endlessly. PoBA

Falling Asleep. Siegfried Sassoon. I've known/ all fading past me into peace. MCCG; MoBrPo; MoVE; OxBTC

Falling Asleep. Ian Serraillier. ...I could weep/For joy. But I fall asleep. DuDa

Falling Asleep in a Garden. David Wagoner. The night-blooming moon opens its pale corolla. AMV-81

Falling Asleep Over the Aeneid. Robert Lowell. It scowls into my glasses at itself. AP; CoBMV; CrMA; MoAmPo; NoAm; OxBA

Falling down to bed. Nila NorthSun. when i see them/i understand. STE

Falling from the ridge. Emperor Yozei. a deep, still pool. LiTW

Falling in Love. Jon Anderson. I think it would like you to awaken. MAYP

Falling in Love. David Perkins. And the heart's awakening. NCSH

Falling Moon. Roberta Hill. You and I must gather under elms. CDW

The Falling of the Leaves. William Butler Yeats. Let us part, ere the season of passion forget us,/With a kiss and a tear on thy drooping brow. VLP

The Falling of the Snow. Raymond Souster. And the cold silent killer's lips of the guns. CaP

Falling Out. Helen Chasin. ...Outside the gemini kingdom/people are catching. IHMS

Falling Snow. Anonymous. What a pretty sight! SoPo

The Falling Star. Sara Teasdale. And then forever to be gone. BrR; MoShBr; OBCA; SoPo; SUS; TiPo

Falling Upwards. David Shapiro. seized by the boy, falling upwards to some height above the earth. AMV-81

The Fallow Deer at the Lonely House. Thomas Hardy. Fourfooted, tiptoe. AWP; BoANP; CH; CMoP; InPo; MoVE; OBSP

The Fallow Field. Julia Caroline Ripley Dorr. When I give my gold to the golden-rod. AA

Fallow Land. Eunice Clark. Low flying crows. NAMP

The Falls. F. D. Reeve. on the soft white breast of the world. NYBP

The Falls of Glomach. Andrew Young. For rain and wind together/Here through the summer make a chill wet weather. OxBS; PoSH

Falltime. Carl Sandburg. Is there something finished? And some new beginning on the/way? PoA

The False Bride. Anonymous. And adieu to my false love for ever. OBET

False Cadence. Bruce Berger. Afraid of the wrong goodbye, I stay too long. AMV-80

False Country of the Zoo. Jean Garrigue. As our love and our pity are, are. LiTM; MP

False Dawn. Walter De la Mare. Sighs; stares at the ocean–and hastens away. FaBoNo

False Enchantment. Jean Starr Untermeyer. The blood with each revolving of the breath/Cries: "Who will come to kiss me from this sleep?" MoAmPo

The False Favorite's Downfall. Anonymous. Then I the mark of ingratitude stand/For betraying the church and enslaving the land. APAS

The False Fox Came into Our Croft. Anonymous. "Take of my feathers but not of my toe." GBP; OxBM; PBBP

False Friends-Like. William Barnes. An' then, vor all I can but way my hat/An' thank en, I do veel a little shy. NOBV

A False Gallop of Analogies. Warham St. Leger. And you, inspiring chavender,/Stuff'd, chavender, or chub. CenHV; FaBoCo; FiBHP

False Gods. Walter De La Mare. Its. "Why, my God, have I forsaken thee?" EaLo

The False Heart. Hilaire Belloc. "Right as a Ribstone Pippin!' But it lied. FaBoCh; FaBoEE; HBMV; LoGBV; OBSP

The False-Hearted Knight. Anonymous. And your cage shall be made of the finest of gold,/And doors of ivory. BaBo

The False Knight and the Wee Boy. Anonymous. "And ye to be drowned,'/Quo' the wee boy, and still he stude. FaBoCh

The False Knight on the Road. Anonymous. Quoth the wee boy, and still he stood. AmFP; AtBAP; CBEP; EnSB; ESPB; GBP

False Linfinn. Anonymous. And the landlord went a-mourning for his fair ladye. BaBo

False Love. Robert Burns. But my fause luver staw my rose,/And left the thorn wi' me. LiTL

False Love. John Lilliat. False hearts can weep, sigh, swear, and yet deceive. OBSC

False Love. Sir Walter Scott. As you with other maidens rove,/I'll smile on other men. ViBoPo

The False Lover. Anonymous.
But nane but thee for me, bonie lovie,/But nane but thee for me. OxBB
Over this vessel you sail on."/Tri-at-ling, tri-la, tri-lay. BFSS

The False Lover Won Back (B version). Anonymous. There's comfort for the comfortless,/There's nane but you for me.' ESPB

False Luve! and Hae Ye Played Me This? Anonymous. As ye look to ither women,/Sall I to ither men. BSV; GBP; PoL

False Nancy. Anonymous. For many a dark and cloudy morning/Turns to a bright and sunshiny day. AmFP

False Poets and True. Thomas Hood. But only lark and nightingale forlorn/Fill up the silences of night and morn. HBV 1-2; PP

False Prophet. Emanuela O'Malley. with long-familiar promises of more/than trumpet vines and humming birds. AMV-81

The False Summer. Marya Zaturenska. The angel music from a demon's throat. CrMA

False Though She Be to Me. William Congreve. I'm grateful for the past. BoLoP; CBEP; HBV 1-2; NOBE; OBEV

False True Love. Anonymous. Nor have courted no other. FSW

False World, Thou Liest. Francis Quarles. Can these bring cordial peace? False world, thou liest. SeCePo

Falsehood. William Cartwright. And as the stream with murmur pass. OBEV

Falstaff's Lament over Prince Hal Become Henry V. Herman Melville. Here's to thee, Hal! ViBoPo

Falstaff's Song. Edmund Clarence Stedman. As the whoreson knave men laid away/A thousand years ago. AA; HBV 1-2

Fame. Anonymous. Some go in by the door called "push,"/And some by the door called "pull." TreFT

Fame. Robert Browning. How the grey lichens, plate o'er plate,/Have softened down the crisp-cut name and date! PP; SoSe

Fame. Eleanor Hollister Cantus. Winds are cold when it is gone. GoYe

Fame. Robert Herrick. The order, but the sum of things. FaBoEE

Fame. Walter Savage Landor. Scribblers and statesmen! are ye not just so? PV

Fame. Charlotte Mew. The moon's dropped child! BrRo; PBWP; SBG

Fame. Sir Thomas More. Of people in perpetual memory. EnRePo

Fame. Vern Rutsala. O never again/will anyone be anonymous and all our graves/will be national shrines! GP

Fame. John Banister Tabb. How star surpasseth star. AA; AmLP

Fame and Fortune. Michael Drayton. Which, as a map, her regency discovers/In camps, in courts, and in the way of lovers. OBSC

Fame and Friendship. Henry Austin Dobson. Who does his better part recall/And of his fault make funeral. OBEV

Fame is a fickle food. Emily Dickinson. Men eat of it and die. TAP

Fame Is a Food That Dead Men Eat. Henry Austin Dobson. Who doth his better part recall/And of his fault make funeral. GTBS; HBV 1-2

Fame Makes Us Forward. Robert Herrick. Is fame (the breath of popular applause). CaPo

The Familiar Colloquies: Sweet Temper and Mutual Affection. Desiderius Erasmus. An uncommon Felicity is due to such uncommon Vir-/tues. HW

A Familiar Epistle to J.B. Esq.. Robert Lloyd. Methinks I hear son Tom reply,/"I'll be a bishop by and by." NOEC; OBSV

Familiar Faces, Long Departed. Robert Hillyer. And Ganymede gives notice in the skies. NYBP

Familiar Friends. James S. Tippett. With five pups to give me/A surprise. SoPo; SUS

A Familiar Letter. Oliver Wendell Holmes. And music must cure you, so pipe it yourself. FaBoUs; InMe

Familiar Lines. Anonymous. To mansions in the skies. FiBHP

Familiar Music. Bill Berkson. A pair of dark blue panties/among hairbrushes. APU

Familiarity Breeds Indifference. Martial (Marcus Valerius Martialis). And then brought her back as his mistress. UnTE

The Familie. George Herbert. But not to make a constant stay. AnAnS 1

Families. Thomas Blackburn. I see no ending to such plight/Except my usual; more insight. OBSP

The Family. *Anonymous.*
And now you know my familee/And all that does belong to me. TiPo
O break it not, lest all the leaves/Shall scatter like the dust. STF

The Family. Donna R. Lydston. That haunts the house with no one waiting there. PoToHe

Family. Norman MacCaig. ...He stared/beyond the serpent in the apple tree/to the round sweet dangerous apple. FF

Family. Josephine Miles. This is what is called the brotherhood of man. FaBoWP; FYAP; GP; GrPl

Family 8. Lyn Lifshin. but he never had a son. NeAC

A Family Album. Alter Brody. Into the little dark face rimmed lovingly between Uncle Isaac's/coarse hands. VWA

Family Album. Lonny Kaneko. Water. Something we choke on. BrSi

The Family Altar. Georgia B. Adams. We hope you have one too! STF

The Family Cat. Roy Fuller. Which none the less cry out in grief/Beneath the mocking, loving tones. OxBC; TEP

Family Chronicle. Anselm Parlatore. grandmothers, & spinster aunts/& all those babies. SUW

Family Court. Ogden Nash. Were more fun to be with. FiBHP

Family Cups. Steve Orlen. The first sorrow comes from the first hope. Str

Family Evening. Daniel Huws. Whereafter none may part but be/The rat leaving a sinking ship. NYBP

The Family Fool. Sir William Schwenck Gilbert. They don't blame you– long as you're funny! ALV; InMe; NLV

Family Fortunes. C. H. Sisson. And I have a brother who, being alive/ Does not need to be put in a poem. OxBC

The Family Goldschmitt. Henri Coulette. The Family Goldschmitt. CoAP; FF

Family/Grove. Albert Goldbarth. And when I do she's there, held/sure, the very light we see by held steady, longer than even a/life. HaCAP

Family History. Wendy Bishop. We continue their life, fearing their style. AMV-81

Family Life. *Anonymous.* Every time he farts, he shits. DBV

Family Life. Allan M. Laing. He hugs the soul he calls his own. FiBHP

A Family Man. Maxine W. Kumin. This is what comes of snapshots. Of talking in bed. IHMS; TAP

Family Matters. Gunter Grass. sit there in plain glass jars/and worry about their parents' future. ELU

The Family Meeting. Charles Sprague. May each repeat, in words of bliss,/ We're all–all here. HBV 1-2

The Family of Eight. Abraham Reisen. The grave's narrow too/But you lie there alone. VWA

The Family of Nations. Willard Wattles. And in the family the Nations plan/Forgets the boy and finds himself a man! PAH

Family Outing–A Celebration. Nicki Jackowska. Leaving mine empty, the clean scythe in my hands. BrRo

Family Photograph. Gerald Vizenor. half white/half immigrant/taking up the city and losing at cards. VoR

A Family Photograph 1939. James Keir Baxter. And build his clay dungeons inside the roller blind. OxBC

Family Plot. Sarah Singer. ...Is it kin or self we serve? AMV-81

Family Poem. John Holloway. But one that takes no food save blood. NMP

Family Portrait. Leonard Feeney. And she hauls me by the hair/Out of Hell! ISi

Family Portrait. Rebecca Hood-Adams. Captives of the camera. AMV-80

Family Portrait 1933. Peter Oresick. quickly; do what you must do. LTB

Family Prime. Mark Van Doren. And yours, will know the taste of in their time. VGW

Family Reunion. Jim Wayne Miller. fresh as the new flowers in the graveyard. Str

Family Reunion. Hollis Summers. Somewhere, surely, a child was born. GoYe

Family Romance. Larry Levis. I thought: why me, why her, & knew it wouldn't last. MAYP

Family Trees. Douglas Malloch. Bethink the lineage of a Pine. OHIP

A Family Turn. William Stafford. Pause–"And it's never been." CAPP

Famine. Georg Heym. It falls and, falling, feels how terror chokes/The gullet, throttling, with two iron fists. LiTW

The Famine Road. Eavan Boland. "Barren, never to know the load/of his child in you, what is your body/now if not a famine road?" FaBoWP

Famine Song. *Anonymous.* But the Lord in whom we trust/Will yet give us crumb for crust/Over here, over here. WTO

The Famine Year. Lady Jane Francesca ("Speranza") Wilde. And arraign ye as our murderers, O spoilers of our land! OnYI

A Famished End to My Tale This Night. Maghnas O Domhnaill. and nothing tempers hard as grief,/worse, I think, than any famine. NOBI

The Famous Ballad of the Jubilee Cup. Sir Arthur Thomas ("Q") Quiller-Couch. When the Jubilee Cup, with John Jones up, was won upon/ Wooden Spoon. InMe; NA

The Famous Fight at Malago. *Anonymous.* Because with five Frigats we did them destroy. CoMu; OBSS

The Famous Flower of Serving-Men. *Anonymous.* The like before was never seen,/A serving-man to be a queen. ESPB; OBET; OxBB

The Famous Light Brigade. *Anonymous.* When he charged through that Rooshian valley with his famous Light Brigade. ShS

The Famous Outlaw Stops in for a Drink. David James. I see/the image of my gun/on every eye. AMV-81

Famous Poet. Ted Hughes. To blink behind bars at the zoo. LiTM

A Famous Sea-Fight. John Looke. As thou didst for Elisabeth/in the yeare 88. CoMu

The Famous Sea Fight between Captain Ward and the Rainbow. *Anonymous.* Who would have gone unto the sea/And brought proud Ward to me.' OBSS

The Fan. John Gay. From noisy anger to the sullen spleen. ViBoPo

Fan. Walter Lew. Searching its fault for your secret. BrSi

The Fan. Edith Sitwell. Feel the Arabian/Winds floating from the fan. HBMV

Fan-Piece, for Her Imperial Lord. Ezra Pound. You also are laid aside. MoAB

A Fancy. *Anonymous.* The Ox fought with the Humble Bee/And claw'd him by the face. FaBoNo

The Fancy. William Rose Benet. Though faded their glory as fadeth the flower of the grass! SD

Fancy. Robert Creeley. ...a/kind of small/nothing. NOBA

Fancy. John Keats. Pleasure never is at home. EnLi 1-2; LoBV; OBEV

A Fancy. Thomas Lodge.
Before my pen by help of fame/Cease to recite thy sacred name. EIL; LoBV; OBSC
Whether you be the rose, or the rose be you. EIL

Fancy. Jonathan Smedley. Narcissus! and a pail of water! OBSP

Fancy Dress. Dorothea Mackellar. Lady, the Holbein type wears well! NOAV; PoAu 1-2

Fancy Dress. Siegfried Sassoon. In heavens where tomahawks are barred. BrPo

Fancy, Farewell. Sir Edward Dyer. And farewell, fancy, that first wrought my woe. EnRePo

The Fancy Frigate. *Anonymous.* Take compassion all on us and never forget/Those poor pipeclay rangers, so called of late. OBSS

A Fancy from Fontenelle. Henry Austin Dobson. For the Rose is Beauty; the Gardener, Time. HBV 1-2; OBVV

Fancy's Home. William Henry Davies. On wild fruits of wonderment/I have nourished ever since. AtBAP

"The fancy, which that I have served long." Henry Howard, Earl of Surrey. Where I am now, as restless to remain,/Against my will, full pleased with my pain. FCP

Fandango. Stanley Vestal. And this here beauty belongs to me! BPAW

Fane Wald I Luve. John Clerk. Treit weill thyself and stand content,/And latt all uthir luvaris be. OxBS

A Fanfare for the Makers. Louis MacNeice. To make is such. Let us make. And set the weather fair. NOBE

Fannie. Thomas Bailey Aldrich. Ah, there are not many/Half so sly, or sad, or mad,/As my true-hearted Fannie. OBAL

Fanny. Anne Reeve Aldrich. No such lovely flowers as grow/In the South! HBV 1-2

Fanny. Fitz-Greene Halleck. Sacred to Scudder's shells and Dr. Griscom. OBAL

Fanny's Removal in 1714. John Winstanley. And so, to clear herself in time, I leave her. NOEC

Fantasia. Gilbert Keith Chesterton. And keep his head and keep his heart,/And only lose his soul. HBMV

Fantasia. Dorothy Livesay. To all save Undine and her comb... OBCV

Fantasia. Leonard Nathan. they yelped in pain. PPJ

Fantasia on a Wittelsbach Atmosphere. Siegfried Sassoon. "Take them for what they were, they weren't so bad!" MoVE

Fantastic World's End. Erin Moure. the fantastic world's end squeezing your bones CaPN

Fantasy. Gwendolyn B. Bennett. And whistled a song to the dark-haired queen... BlSi; CDC

Fantasy. Giosue Carducci. Is it perhaps Alceus, from battle/Returned to the maidens of Lesbos? LiTW

Fantasy. Gerard de Nerval. And whom I now remember with a sigh. LiTW

Fantasy in Purple. Langston Hughes. To go with me/to the darkness/ where I go. BANP; CDC

Farewell, Sweet Dust. Elinor Wylie. But the leaves of the willow are bright as wine. AnAmPo; LiTA

Farewell, Sweet Mary. *Anonymous.* I am ruined forever,/By the loving of you. AmFP

Farewell the reign of cruelty! Sir Thomas Wyatt. Welcome among my pleasant smart. FCP; SiPS

Farewell This World! *Anonymous.*
Grante in Paradise to have a mansion/That shede His blode for my redempcion! EnPo; OxBM
Humiliatus sum vermis. MeEL

A Farewell to a Fondling. Thomas Churchyard. I muse how she had such a grace/To seem a hawk, and be a kite. EiL

A Farewell to a Southern Melody. Huang O. Ten thousand beautiful sensual/Ways we will make love. BoWoP

A Farewell to Agassiz. Oliver Wendell Holmes. Bless them now and evermore! ImOP

A Farewell to America. Richard Henry Wilde. To leave with them and thee behind! AA

Farewell to Anactoria. Sappho. Beloved, in memory. AWP; LiTW

A Farewell to Arms. George Peele. Goddess, allow this aged man his right/To be your beadsman now that was your knight. BoC; HBV 1-2; NIP; NOBE; OBEV; OBWP; PoPle; PoRA

Farewell to Cuba. Maria Gowen Brooks. Than live in pleasure far away. AA

Farewell to Earth. Elizabeth Doten. "Come up higher!" cry the angels: "come up to the/Royal Arch." PeD

Farewell to England. *Anonymous.* And no one think it worth his while/To take up to defend thee. APAS

A Farewell to English (excerpt). Michael Hartnett.
I think the result was a dead heat. CIP
sniff and stand back and proudly offer you/the celebrated Anglo-Irish stew. NOBI

Farewell to Europe. [(or Pillin)] William Pillen. You have no one to bludgeon but each other! VWA

A Farewell to Fal. Gerald Nugent. Plain of the noblest companies! OnYI

A Farewell to False Love. Sir Walter Ralegh. Dead is the root whence all these fancies grew. BoLoP; EiL; FCP

A Farewell to His Mistress. *Anonymous.* I take my leve a-gaynst my wyll. ABF; AtBAP

Farewell to Ireland. Saint Columcille. Thou waterful land. AWP; LiTW

Farewell to Juliet. Wilfrid Scawen Blunt.
And Heaven and Hell may meet,–yet never we. AnEnPo
It was the reddest rose in all the world. BoLoP; EnLoPo
Speedy oblivion, rest for memory. ViBoPo

Farewell to Kurdistan. Rosemary Tonks. I admit it, at the last. OxBTC

Farewell to Lesbia. Caius Valerius Catullus. Clipped it and left it. LiTW

A Farewell to London In the Year 1715. Alexander Pope. And so may starve with me. CEP

Farewell to Love. John Donne. 'Tis but applying worm-seed to the tail. OAEL 1-2

Farewell to Love. Sir John Suckling. And so I love no more. CaPo

Farewell to Malta. George Gordon, Lord Byron. And bless the gods–I've got a fever. OBTV

Farewell to My Mother. Placido (Gabriel de la Conception Valdes). Mother, farewell! The pilgrimage begins. TTY

Farewell to Narcissus. Robert Horan. Nothing now shall leave, now nothing/more shall enter. NYBP

Farewell to New Zealand. Wynford Vaughan-Thomas. It's under-sized; for God's sake throw it back! DBV; NOBL; OBTV

A Farewell to Patrick Sarsfield, Earl of Lucan. *Anonymous.* The beloved of damsels and dames–/Och, ochone! AnIV

Farewell to Poetry. Oliver Goldsmith. While self-dependent power can time defy,/As rocks resist the billows and the sky. OBEC

A Farewell to Sir John Norris and Sir Francis Drake. George Peele. Whose honour and whose glory you defend. OBSC

Farewell to Summer. George Arnold. Fair but faded Summer,/Sweet, farewell! AA

Farewell to the Court. Sir Walter Ralegh.
Of all which past. LO
To haste me hence, to find my fortune's fold. CBEP; EG; EnRePo; FaBoEn; FCP; OBSC; SiPS

Farewell to the Court (excerpt). John Wilmot, Earl of Rochester. And at mankind rail with my parting breath. TrGrPo

Farewell to the Fairies. Richard Corbet. O how the commonwealth doth need/Such justices as you! EvOK; HBV 1-2; MoShBr

Farewell to the Farm. Robert Louis Stevenson. Good-bye, good-bye, to everything! TiPo

Farewell to the Glen. Dante Gabriel Rossetti. And thy trees whispered what he feared to know. MaVP

A Farewell to the Moon. Ed Ochester. that millennia ago/had disappeared. MOON

Farewell to the Muses. John Hamilton Reynolds. ...Sweet Farewell/Be to the Nymphs that on the old Hill dwell. OBRV

Farewell to the Old Year! Eleanor Farjeon. A wee naked babe in the cold. SiSoSe

Farewell to the World of Richard Bishop. *Anonymous.* Doomed at the age of one and twenty,/To die a dreadful death of scorn. CoMu

Farewell to Tobacco. Charles Lamb. And in thy borders take delight,/An unconquered Canaanite. NBM; OBRV; OxBoLi

Farewell to Town. Laurence Housman. Farther and farther from them yet/The road that lies before us. HBMV

Farewell to Van Gogh. Charles Tomlinson. Await us, weighing the unstripped bough. CMoP; GTBS-P; NMP

Farewell to Winnipeg. Roy Daniells. And mimic armies have begun to form. OBCV

Farewell ungrateful traitor. John Dryden. But dying is a pleasure,/When living is a pain. BoLoP; CBEP; ELP; HAP; InPo; LiTB; NOBE; ViBoPo

Farewell, Unkind! Farewell! to Me, No More a Father! *Anonymous.* Then farewell, O farewell! Welcome, my Love, welcome my joy/for ever! EnLoPo

Farewell Voyaging World! Conrad Aiken. we shall never be older or wiser or dead. NYBP

Farewell with a Mischeife. George Gascoigne. In secrete so, my stomacke will I sterve,/Wishing thee better than thou doest deserve. AAS

Farewells from Paradise. Elizabeth Barrett Browning. Farewell! the birds of Eden/Ye shall hear nevermore! OBEV; OBVV

The Farm. Donald Hall. ...Black horned pout/doze on the bottom. LiTM

The Farm. Vassar Miller. ...rest, rest, rest, oh, filling my heart/full of a sweet emptiness! NCSH

Farm Boy after Summer. Robert Francis. For scarcely all its snows can cool that color. NCSH

Farm Cart. Eleanor Farjeon. So sweet a load as you. BrR

Farm Child. R. S. Thomas. Earth breeds and beckons to the stubborn plough. BoNaP; ChMP

Farm Gate. Uys Krige. I lift the catch...and in my heart/open a gate. PeSA

The Farm Hands. Dilys Bennett Laing. ...They could not escape/the crops even in sleep. SaC

Farm Implements and Rutabagas in a Landscape. John Ashbery. ...it sure was pleasant to spend a day in the country. CoAP; GP; SM

The Farm Near Norman's Lane. Mary Finnin. Flood the sea marsh, salt down another spring. PoAu 1-2

The Farm on the Great Plains. William Stafford. pacing toward what I know. HAP; PoCh; VGW

The Farm on the Links. Rosamund Marriott Watson. Only the old home welcomes them again. OBVV

A Farm Picture. Walt Whitman. And haze, and vista, and the far horizon, fading away. InPS; PAI; PPoe

Farm Wife. Matt Field. the days draw in, the winter has begun. AMV-81

Farm Wife. John Hanlon Mitchell. Came love, and parting, birth and death,/And all that women know. CaP

The Farm-Woman's Winter. Thomas Hardy. And what I love he snatches,/And what I love not, brings. VLP

Farmer. Liberty Hyde Bailey. I come and go/In the calm and the storm and the rain. YeAr

Farmer. Padraic Fallon. So softly down you'll think him the month of May. OxBI

The Farmer. Mary Elizabeth ("E") Fullerton. Next day the miller had the grain. CBAP

The Farmer. Sir Alan Patrick Herbert. For either the rain is destroying his grain/Or the drought is destroying his roots. CenHV

The Farmer. Fredegond Shove. ...when peace shall come/With stillness, and long shivers, after death. MMM

The Farmer. Terry Stokes. The wife rubbed herself with bear grease & waited. PoL

Farmer. Lucien Stryk. ...a skin of wood/as much the earth's as his. FAZ

Farmer and Sailor. Plato. Death keeps open house below. LiTW

The Farmer and the Farmer's Wife. P. G. Herbert. He helps himself to applejack,/And she to Paris Green. FiBHP; NLV

The Farmer and the Shanty Boy (Trenton Town). *Anonymous.* For they cut the pine in the wintertime and drive it in the spring. AmFP

The Farmer Comes to Town. *Anonymous.* For the mortgage man's the one who gets it all. TrAS

Farmer Goes Berserk. Anne Elder. Unto Everyman,/according to his worth, acclaim for his labours. CBAP

The Farmer Is the Man. *Anonymous.* He's forgot that he's the man who feeds them all. FSW

Farmer Jones's Wife. *Anonymous.* She can conquer hell and a husband too,/To-i-lu, and a husband too. BFSS

The Farmer of Tilsbury Vale. William Wordsworth. Will hear the wind sigh through the leaves of a tree. EBEV

The Farmer Remembers the Somme. Vance Palmer. And the dark Somme flowing. NOAV; PoAu 1-2

A Farmer's Boy. *Anonymous.* For he was just a farmer's boy/And she a Jersey cow... OBET; PoPle

The Farmer's Boy. Robert Bloomfield.
Nor quit the woods till oaks can yield no more. OBRV
Thus fools and bravoes kindred pranks pursue;/As savage quite, and oft as fatal too. PBBP

The Farmer's Bride. Charlotte Mew. The brown of her–her eyes, her hair, her hair! BoLoP; ErPo; FaBoWP; HBMV; MoAB; MoBrPo; OxBTC; PoRA; SBG; TrGrPo

The Farmer's Clothes Are Soaked Through and Never Dried. Ise Tayu. that fall without cease,/from a sky with never a rift in the clouds. WPOW

The Farmer's Complaint. Anonymous. Ther wakeneth in the world wondred and wee-/As good is swinden anon as so for to swinke! OxBM

The Farmer's Curst Wife. Anonymous. Sing heigh! diddle-eye, diddle-eye, fie!/Diddle-eye, diddle-eye, day! AmFP

The Farmer's Curst Wife (A version). Anonymous. "I have been a tormentor the whole of/my life,/But I neer was tormented so as with/your wife." BaBo; ESPB; ViBoFo

The Farmer's Curst Wife (B vers.). Anonymous. For you've killed all the devils and rent over Hell."/Scrath-a-fillee, fillee, filiddle, filum. BaBo; ESPB

The Farmer's Daughter. Anonymous. In six short months she was laid by the side/Of her love who gave her such a frightful ride. BFSS

The Farmer's Head. Ron Padgett. He was rapidly shouting this as he ran from/the barn. ANYP

The Farmer's Ingle. Robert Fergusson. And a lang lasting train o' peacefu' hours succeed! BSV; CEP

A Farmer's Son So Sweet. Anonymous. In wedlock she was tied/To the farmer's son. OBET

The Farmer's Wife. Anne Sexton. and she wishes him cripple, or poet,/or even lonely, or sometimes,/better, my lover, dead. HoPM; LiTM; NePoEA-2

The Farmer's Wife and the Raven. John Gay. And you, good woman, saved your eggs. PBBP

A Farmer Went Trotting upon His Gray Mare. Mother Goose. Lumpety, lumpety, lump! TiPo

The Farmer (with music). Anonymous. O, the farmer is the man who feeds them all! AS

Farmers. Thomas Lux. I remember how we called it down, how down/we desired it to fall: the rain. LCAP

Farmers. William Alexander Percy. You know they think their work was done/In partnership with Him. WGRP

Farmers. Hortense Roberta Roberts. to change the green/to gold. AMV-81

Farming. Anonymous. From long ago it has been thus. LiTW

The Farmyard. Anonymous. The cat went fiddle-i-fee, fiddle-i-fee. BFSS; OxNR

Farmyard. Ruth Dallas. Has passed from the dream, passed from the trees' long/shadows. AnNZ

A Farmyard Song. Maria Hastings. Dog, goes bow-wow, bow-wow. SoPo

Farolita. Mei-Mei Berssenbrugge. but it is different light. BrSi

Farragut. William Tuckey Meredith. Daring Dave Farragut/Thunderbolt stroke! AA; EtS; FaBoBe; HBV 1-2; HBVY; PAH

Farrell O'Reilly. Oliver St. John Gogarty. Accept this wild leaf from your own twisted tree. OxBTC

Farther. John James Piatt.
his golden prophecy/Lighting the doorway of the pioneer. AmePo
The world may pardon us to hold thee dear. AA

Farther Along. Anonymous. We'll understand it all by and by. FSW

Farther in summer than the birds. Emily Dickinson. Yet a druidic difference/Enhances nature now. PoEL 1-5; QFR

A Farthing. Anonymous. And all for a farthing. OxNR

The Farwell. Henry, Bishop of Chichester King. The hollow Eccho will reply, 'Twas I. CavP

The Fascinating Chill That Music Leaves. Emily Dickinson. To something upper wooing us/But not to our Creator–. AmePo

The Fascination of What's Difficult. William Butler Yeats. I'll find the stable and pull out the bolt. BIrV; BrPo; PoEL 1-5

Fashion. Ada Cambridge. When selfish greed becomes a social sin/The world's regeneration may begin. NOAV

Fashion in the 70's. May Swenson. ...Like, ugly is beautiful. NYP

The Fashionable Heart. Jack Gilbert. writing red in the spaces where it said red,/yellow where it said yellow. NPGG

Fashions in Dogs. E. B. White. Very few have a pug. FiBHP; GDP

Fast. John Tagliabue. and return like/birds to the flight/on the reflection of heaven. SD

Fast Ball. Jonathan Williams. old solitary Whiff-Beard. NeAP

Fast Bundled Is the Firewood. Anonymous. What will that lovely one be like? HW

The Fastidious Serpent. Henry, Lord Johnstone Johnstone. The snake had often to go without/His breakfast, dinner, and tea, oh. HBV 1-2; HBVY

The Fat Boy's Dream. Richard McCann. But no one, no one, can ever bring me down. GrPI

The Fat Budgie. John Lennon. I love him more than daddie/And I'm only thirty two. NLV

Fat Cat. John Ronan. it's the whole show. AMV-81

Fat Is Unfair. Don (Donald Robert Marquis) Marquis. the feet it has/where eer they go/archy. EvOK

The Fat Man. Vern Rutsala. I eat the world. DFF

The Fat Man in the Mirror. Robert Lowell. Only a fat man/Breaks the mirror, O, it is not I! PoA

Fat Tuesday. W. S. Di Piero. ...mix him with my swallowed/pearls and coins and whiskey and days. MAYP

The Fat White Woman Speaks (parody). Gilbert Keith Chesterton. At the end of the field you are rushing on,/Is waiting for his Old Dutch? SpRo

Fata Morgana. Summer Brenner. Now come to your senses./LO AND BEHOLD. APU

The Fatal Dream; or, The Unhappy Favourite. Emanuel Collins. Then, only then, shall my dear Tysey be/Forgotten by his fond Penelope. NOEC

Fatal Interview. Edna St. Vincent Millay.
...and I shall entomb/What's cold by then in an adjoining room. VGW
As I do now, before the advancing day. VGW
Flattened your words against your speaking mouth. VGW
I tell you this across the blackened vine. VGW
It may well be. I do not think I would. AmLP; HAP
"Look what I have!–And these are all for you." VGW
No one but Night, with tears on her dark face,/Watches beside me in this windy place. HAP
She loves you not; she never heard of love. VGW
We rose from rapture but an hour ago. VGW
Will lie between me and my troubled lord. VGW
Yet come no better off, for my quick ear. VGW

Fatal Love. Matthew Prior. Make love at home, and go to bed betimes. FaBoCo; NLV

The Fatal Sisters. Thomas Gray. Hurry, hurry to the field! CEP; CoBE; EiCP; EnPE; LAuP; OAEP

The Fatal Spell. George Gordon, Lord Byron. And worse, the woes we see not–which throb through/The immediate soul, with heart-aches ever new. OBNC

The Fatal Wedding. W. H. Windom. Of bride and groom, of outcast, and the fatal wedding night. GoTF; TreFS

Fatales Poetae. Henry Parrot. In these respects I may myself intrude/Among the poets' thickest multitude. FaBoEE

Fate. Louis James Block. Know faces seen long before. AA

Fate. James Fenimore Cooper, Jr.. The virtues that a whole world sees,/The by-words of the centuries. HBMV

Fate. Ralph Waldo Emerson. Or say, the foresight that awaits/Is the same genius that creates. ForPo

Fate. Susan Marr Spalding. And die unsatisfied–and this is Fate! AA; BBV; HBV 1-2

Fate and the Younger Generation. D. H. Lawrence. –Well, it won't matter so very much, either. OxBoLi

Fate! I Have Asked. Walter Savage Landor. And check the tear (if tear should start)/Too precious for dull clay. ViBoPo

Fate in Incognito. Michael Benedikt. (Listen o how clever it thinks it is outside our windows coming down/the street again... OBAL

The Fate of a Broom–An Anticipation. Thomas Love Peacock. To sweep, beyond the Stygian lake,/The pavement it has helped to make. CBEP

The Fate of Birds. Kenneth Seib. There should be reassuring voices,/Silent, in the flutters of the heart. AMV-80

The Fate of John Burgoyne. Anonymous. And be the fate of all her foes/The same as here recorded. PAH

The Fate of King Dathi. Thomas Osborne Davis. Last of the Pagan race,/Lieth king Dathi. OnYI

The Fate of Narcissus. William Warner. ...though/they/Have long been dead, haunt now the world, is it we mean to/say. OBSC

The Fate of the Cabbage Rose. Wallace Irwin. She's only been gone an hour. FiBHP

The Fate of the Oak. Barry (Bryan Waller Procter) Cornwall. And to mix with the common mould! OHIP

Fate With Devoted... Arthur Davison Ficke. Was in your cellar, rummaging for beer... AnEnPo

Fates of the Apostles. Cynewulf. Unknown are those dwellings, that region and realm. AnOE

Father. Rose Auslander. fell in love with it/and clung there. VWA

Father. Paul Carroll. This underpass is endless. NeAP

Father. Arthur Davison Ficke. The idiot radiance of Thy dawn. TrPWD

The Father. Donald Finkel. will have made off with my blessings and my daughter. CoPo

Father. Frances Frost. A keen-eyed brown earth-lover. SiSoSe; TiPo

Father. Margit Kaffka. And I am so tired–father. PBWP

Father. Ted Kooser. we laughed till we cried. Str

The Father. Richmond Lattimore. the brown feathers of such a bird as fathered this phoenix? EyDe; NePoAm-2

Father. Jean Lipkin. The sky grows big. PeSA

Father. Myra Cohn Livingston. Your hand in mine keeps us straight ahead. NTCP

The Father. Desmond O'Grady. for good and forever–heavy as turf and heartscalded. NoAm

Father. Robert Pack. I dig the worms and find your embryo. CoPo

Father. Lois Reiner. the crew plans its escape. AMV-80

Father. Mildred Weston. So, when he climbs the slope to meet/The rising sun, they kiss his feet. PoSC

Father. John Wheelwright. come home, dead man, who made your mind my home. UnPo

Father Abraham. *Anonymous*. Sittin' down side ob de Holy Lam'. BoAN 1-2

Father and Child. Gwen Harwood.
no words, no tears can mend. CBAP
owl-blind in early sun/for what I had begun. CBAP

The Father and His Children. *Anonymous*. "Then let us all reflect with pleasure,/That labour is the source of treasure." OxBChV

Father and I in the Woods. David McCord. It's sky and brook and bird/ And tree. SO

Father and Mother. X. J. Kennedy. And folks who sleep here overnight/ Wake up a few quarts lighter. GrPl

Father and Son. Frederick Robert Higgins.
Till death drew its grey blind down his face. BoC; OBMV
Yes, one in a graven silence no bird breaks. ACV; BIrV; OxBI

Father and Son. Stanley Jasspon Kunitz. ...he turned to me/The white ignorant hollow of his face. MP; NoAm; TwCP

Father and Son. Delmore Schwartz. Be guilty of yourself in the full looking-glass. LiTA

Father and Son. William Stafford. ...I hold–whatever tugs/the other end–I hold that string. GP

Father and Son. Ronald Wallace. I didn't try to call him back/from that calm, untroubled sleep. AMV-81

Father and Son: 1939. William Plomer. And man, the self-destroyer, was not lucid in his mind:/With a hey nonny nonny/and a hi-de-ho. NoAm; PeSA

Father and Sons. Harvey Shapiro. How solemn their faces grow. FAZ

Father Coyote. George Sterling. Skims your fate o'er the moonlit grass! BPAW

Father Damien. John Banister Tabb. "A leper white as snow!" ACP

Father, Dear Father, Come Home with Me Now. Henry Clay Work. Please, father, dear father, come home! FSW; TreF

Father Death Blues. Allen Ginsberg. My heart is still, as time will tell. SM

A Father Does His Best. E. B. White. Said the infant's mother: "No." ALV

Father Father Son and Son. Jon Swan. I must not falter on my wall. NYBP

Father Fisheye. Peter Balakian. of fishes that wander slowly out to the far waves. MAYP

Father Greybeard. *Anonymous*. I'll give you my thumb. OxNR

Father Grumble. *Anonymous*.
His wife could do more work in a day/Than he could do in seven. AmFP; ViBoFo
Old Mother Grumble clapped her hands/And said that she was very glad. BaBo

Father, Hear the Prayer We Offer. Love Maria Willis. Father, be thou at our side! AH

Father, How Wide Thy Glories Shine. Charles Wesley. As I remain'd thy single care. TrPWD; TRV

Father! I Own Thy Voice. Samuel Wolcott. And greet her glory's dawn. AH

Father in Heaven. Petrarch (Francesco Petrarca). Show them this day you were on Calvary. NAWM 1-2

Father-in-Law. Derek Mahon. When you lost your balance like Li Po/ They found unfinished poems in your sea-chest. FaBoIP

A Father in Tennessee. J. Edgar Simmons. We are well there is no news./ Dad. TAT

Father in the Railway Buffet. U. A. Fanthorpe. You who never even learned to queue? FaBoWP

Father, in Thy Mysterious Presence Kneeling. Samuel Johnson. Of trust and strength and calmness from above. AH

Father, Into Thy Hands. Thomas B. Pollack. Grace to reach the home on high! BePJ

The Father Knows. F. L. H.. God lives and loves and cares for me. BLRP

Father Land and Mother Tongue. Samuel Lover. We call our language Mother Tongue. HBV 1-2

Father Malloy. Edgar Lee Masters. Through Peter the Flame,/Peter the Rock. OxBA

Father Mapple's Hymn. Herman Melville. His all the mercy and the power. EtS

Father Mat. Patrick Kavanagh.
Or at the undying difference in the corner of a field. MoAB; NMP
Or Venus with her ecstasy. AnIL; CMoP

Father Molloy or, the Confession. Samuel Lover. So, now for your blessin', sweet Father Molloy. HBV 1-2

Father O'Flynn. Alfred Perceval Graves. Kindliest creature in ould Donegal. HBV 1-2; OnYI

The Father of My Country. Diane Wakoski. Father,/have you really come home? NoAm; TAP

Father of the Man. Elizabeth Mabel Bryan. Your embryo knight has never questioned how. GoYe

Father of the Victim. Rae Ballard. The cop at the door unwraps a stick of gum. AMV-80

A Father of Women. Alice Meynell. Approve, accept, know them daughters of men,/Now that your sons are dust. BrRo; SBG

Father Poem. Joel Oppenheimer. the fathers of daughters/cannot say this. PoM

Father Riley's Horse. Andrew Barton ("Banjo") Paterson. That the Devil had been ordered to let Andy Regan out/For the steeplechase on Father Riley's horse! NOAV

The Father's Business. Edwin Markham. His name is whispered in the God's abode. TRV

The Father's Gold. *Anonymous*. The Shining Strand who interlaced our/ Grays/To lift, to hold and beautify always. STF

Father's Gone A-Flailing. *Anonymous*. Baby, baby, will go there. OxNR

A Father's Heart Is Touched. Samuel Hoffenstein. I'm almost glad to see you such/An idiot, they won't hurt you much. FiBHP

A Father's Prayer. *Anonymous*. Dear Lord, kind Lord, remember me. STF

Father's Story. Elizabeth Madox Roberts. And I push my fingers into his skin/To make little dents in his big round face. PoSC

A Father's Testament. Judah Ibn Tibbon. Practise these rules, and more to them/I'll add/For thine instruction if my life endure! TrJP

Father's Voice. William Stafford. in the earth, in the air, in the rock. RFM

Father's Whiskers. *Anonymous*. They hide the dirt on father's shirt,/ They're always in the way. FSW

Father Short. *Anonymous*. For a bad master, and a/worse dame. OxNR

Father Son and Holy Ghost. Audre Lorde. I have not ever seen my father's grave. PoBA

Father Takes to the Road and Lets His Hair down. Alan Chong Lau. and sing this song/he once heard in another village BrSi

Father, Teach Me. Walter M. Lee. I would serve like Jesus. STF

Father, the Year Is Fallen. Audre Lorde. When the last warmth is gone/I shall bear in the snow. PoBA

Father Time. Norman Ault. And why only the short ones are glad. HBVY

Father to Son. Elizabeth Jennings. We each put out an empty hand,/ Longing for something to forgive. GOYP

Father to the Man. John Knight. this is the saddest news...and I/am nearer to death... EaLo

Father, Who Mak'st Thy Suff'ring Sons. Arthur Cleveland Coxe. Who in his poor beheld their Lord. AH

Father William. *Anonymous*. But I'll butter my ears on the Fourth of July,/And then I'll be able to skate. NA

Father William. Lewis (Charles Lutwidge Dodgson) Carroll. Be off, or I'll kick you down-stairs! BiCB; BiP; FaBoNo; FiBHP; FPL; GoJo; HBV 1-2; HoPM; InMe; LBN; LiTB; NLV; PoLf; PoRA; TreF; TrGrPo

The Fatherland. James Russell Lowell. His is a world-wide fatherland! GN; HBV 1-2; HBVY; PGD; PoPl

Fatherland Song. Bjornstjerne Bjornson. For her peace no less. AWP

The Fathers. John N. Morris. Looking out of their eyes/With their eyes, looking before us. GP

The Fathers. Edwin Muir. Until they topple and fall,/And fallen let in the day. OxBS

The Fathers. Benjamin Saltman. while my face of yellow horn plunges in the wind. VWA

The Fathers. Siegfried Sassoon. I watched them toddle through the door–/ These impotent old friends of mine. NoAm

Fathers and Sons. *Anonymous*. Nothing of theirs is ours. KiLC

Fathomless Is My Love. Kalola. Fathomless, deep is my love/To thee, my passion, my mate. WTO

Fatigue. Hilaire Belloc. But Money gives me pleasure all the time. FaBoCo; GoTF; MoVE; NLV; NOBL; OxBTC; PV; TreFT

Fatigues. Richard Aldington. again you will dance and whisper in the wind. BrPo

Fatima. Alfred, Lord Tennyson. Die, dying clasp'd in his embrace. GBL; SeCePo; UnPo; UnTE

The Feast of the Snow. Gilbert Keith Chesterton. The gods lie cold where the leaves are gold,/And a Child comes forth alone. HBV 1-2

Feast on Wine or Fast on Water. Gilbert Keith Chesterton. Heaven sent us Soda Water/As a torment for our crimes. ALV

The Feast-Time of the Year. *Anonymous.* ...makes a feast,/And bids the greatest and the least. OHIP

Feasts of Death, Feasts of Love. Stuart Perkoff. coming together NeAP

The Feather. Lilian Bowes Lyon. It was the breath of change/That breathed them apart. ChMP

The Feather. Vernon Watkins. How could a blind rock satisfy/The hungers of the sea? FaBoTw; MoVE

Feather or Fur. John Becker. Do not stir/Do not stir. TiPo

A Feather's Weight. George Parsons Lathrop. A feather often turns the scale. FaBoUs

Feathered Dancers. Kenward Elmslie. Outside the lunchroom, tufts and air-sacs/swell to the size of fruits bursting with seeds. ANYP

Feathered Faith. *Anonymous.* They have no Heavenly Father/To care for them like you and me. STF

Feathered Friends (parody). Robert Peters. And quivering with Cold. BXAP

Feathers and Moss. Jean Ingelow. And home is silent, and love is clay. SpRo

Feathers of Snow. *Anonymous.* And sending their feathers here away there away. GBP

Feathers or Lead? James Richard Broughton. the dungheap cackled/and slithered out under the door. NeAP

Featherstone's Doom. Robert Stephen Hawker. The wind shall be thy changeful loom,/Thy web, the shifting sand! OBNC

February. Bill Berkson. ...the pigeons were picking/up crumbs in the dark February wind. ANYP

February. John Heath-Stubbs. As wicks of thread which now are lighted up/For ceremonials of Candlemas. OBCP

February. William Stanley Merwin. I know nothing/learn of me NNaP

February. Larry Moffi. to live with more than enough/and everything. AMV-80

February. D. S. Savage. The seeds of Spring lie swelling in their soaking house. NeBP

February. James Schuyler. It's a day like any other. ANYP; NeAP

February. Frank Dempster Sherman. "Will you be my Valentine?" YeAr

February. Adeline D. T. Whitney. The weariest month of the year, love,/Is shortest, and nearest the spring! YeAr

February. Barbara Winder. he was the first and strongest in the barn/when he was stabled. PH

February. Francis Brett Young. With all the joy of spring/And morning in her eyes. HBMV; HBVY

February 11, 1977. Frederick Morgan. while you await me, always young. AMV-80

February 12, 1809. Gail Brook Burket. Or did you cradle in your arms a child/Which God and you were certain would be great? PGD

February 14, 22 B. C. Franklin Pierce ("F.P.A.") Adams. You're the one I'd live for, die for–/And I'll be your Valentine. InMe

February Afternoon. Edward ("Edward Eastaway") Thomas. That we have wrought him, stone-deaf and stone-blind. NoAm

February Birthday. Nancy Byrd Turner. What February can do when/She has a mind to! BiCB

February Evening in New York. Denise Levertov. ...A range/of open time at winter's outskirts. NoAm; PAI

February Margins. Brian Henderson. We would read the limits of ourselves/in the extravagant migration of light. CaPN

February Morning. King D. Kuka. I walked on and thought my way to class. VoR

February Park. Gerald Vizenor. hearts beating against my hands/burst inside VoR

February's Forgotten Mitts. Raymond Knister. Spring has flung forward an unringed hand. NOBC

February, Tall and Trim. Anna Neil Gilmore. ...Winter frown/And the storms of sleet come down? YeAr

February Thaw. G. J. F. Dutton. Others, one day nearer spring. PoSH

February: The Boy Breughel. Norman Dubie. A sunrise. The snow. LCAP

February Twilight. Sara Teasdale. As long as it watched me. OBCA; SoPo; YeAr

The Feckenham Men. John Drinkwater. A fiery-hearted thing to do? GTBS

The Feckless Dinner Party. Walter De la Mare. He who misled them all– the butler, Toomes. FaBoTw

Fecundity. Diane Keating. God, how I long for stars/to mark where/I've taken you in. CaPN

Fed Drapes. Clark Coolidge. remnant face/rubber/the pucker. ANYP

The Federal Constitution. William Milns. The Federal Constitution, boys, and Wash-/ington forever. PAH

The Federal Convention. *Anonymous.* On whose decision hangs Columbia's fate. PAH

Federation. W. T. Goodge. This one solid moral teach us–/That a pile of paradoxes are expected to result! NOAV

Feed. Raymond Knister. Then lean again to scoop up the swill. OBCV; PeCV

Feed Still Thyself. Sir Walter Ralegh. And crie, O Love, O death, O vaine desire,/When thou complainst the heate, and feeds the fire. NCEP

The Feeding. Joel Oppenheimer. ...smiling at her,/pleasantly, and, damn it, without/malice, even. NeAP

Feeding Ducks. Norman MacCaig. Till my gestures enlarged, wide over the darkening land. OxBS

Feeding the Fire. Donald Finkel. it has grown, it is/hungrier than ever VWA

Feeding the Lions. Norman Jordan. and get back/before dark. BOLo; CTBA; NBP; PoBA

Feel Like a Bird. May Swenson. to span A Fate? TrGrPo

Feel Me. May Swenson. ...Feel me, to do right. GP

The Feeling. William Bronk. ...When will it end? VGW

Feeling for Fish. Leonard Trawick. You'll wade out deep for the big one. AMV-81

Feeling Fucked/Up. Etheridge Knight. all i want now is my woman back/so my soul can sing. GP; NNaP

Feeling That Way Too. Arthur Vogelsang. My eyes tear and I really do reach for the switch. MAYP

Feeling the Quiet Strike. James Minor. searching for the current/before heading upstream. WOLT

Feelings of a Republican on the Fall of Bonaparte. Percy Bysshe Shelley. And bloody Faith the foulest birth of time. AnEnPo

Feels. J. C. Milne. But the hulls mak feels o's a'! PoSH

Feet. Dorothy Aldis. Oh, there are things/Feet know/That hands NEVER will. SUS

Feet. Mary Carolyn Davies. And told them, "You are seeking God." WGRP

Feet. Harry". But some day I will grow up and see/faces. TiPo

Feet, a Sermon. James Paul. ...here our bodies assume the plane of the earth. HoAn

The Feet of Judas. George Marion McClellan. Christ washed the feet of Judas. BANP; PoNe

Feigned Courage. Charles and Mary Lamb. And the Black Prince goes whimpering to bed. GN; OxBChV

Felicia Ropps. Gelett Burgess. Goops like that annoy me much! BBGG; TiPo

Felicia's Cafe. Mebdh McGuckian. The part of my eye/That is not golden, sees. FaBoIP

Felicity. Isaac Watts. And all the Heav'n I hope above/Is but to see his face. OxBoCh

Feliks Skrzynecki. Peter Skrzynecki. Further and further south of Hadrian's Wall. CBAP

Felise. Algernon Charles Swinburne. Not while I live, not though I die./Good-night, good-bye. BeLS

Felix Randal. Gerard Manley Hopkins. Didst fettle for the great grey drayhorse his bright and battering sandal! BrPo; DiPo; EBEV; EnL; FaBoMo; GTBS-P; HAP; InPo; InPS; LiTB; LiTM; MoAB; MoBrPo; MoPo; NAMP; NoAm; NOBE; NoP; OAEP; OBEV; OBNC; PAI; PoPle; PoRA; PrIm; RoGo; SOTW; VLP

Felixstowe, or The Last of Her Order. Sir John Betjeman. My heart finds rest, my heart finds rest in Thee. OxBTC

The Felled Plane Tree. Anna Hajnal. ...the fallen tree/weeps silently from dead, fringed eyes. BoWoP

A Feller I Know. Mary Austin. Of Pedro-Pablo-Ignacio-Juan-/Francesco Garcia y Gabaldon. AmFN

Fellow-Citizens. Verner von Heidenstam. Which we are and shall be forever. PoPl

Fellowship. *Anonymous.* When a hand is on your shoulder in a friendly sort o' way. BLPA

The Fellowship of Prayer. Nancy Byrd Turner. Thy fellowship shall keep me strong. BePJ

Felo Da Se. Thomas Blackburn. Just what it means I do not understand. OxBTC

Felo de Se. Richard Hughes. –Thou silly worm, gnaw not/Yet thine intricate cocoon. OBMV

The Female Cabin Boy. *Anonymous.* Why then we must ship some sailors like the handsome cabin boy. OBSS

The Female Friend. Cornelius Whur. While lasting joys the man attend/Who has a polish'd female friend! FaBoCo

Female Glory. Richard Lovelace. Mistress o' th' world and me, and Laura is her name. MyFE

The Female God. Isaac Rosenberg. And you, our rose-deaf prison, are very/pleased with the world,/Your world. FaBoTw

The Female Husband, Who Had Been Married to Another Female.... *Anonymous.* To be fruitful, increase, and multiply, sir. CoMu

The Female of the Species. Rudyard Kipling. That the Female of Her Species is more deadly than the Male. BLPA; FPL; HBV 1-2; TreFS

The Female Parricide. *Anonymous.* Thy chariot drive, winged with ambitious fire,/O'er the dead body of thy mangled sire. APAS

The Female Phaeton. Matthew Prior. Obtained the chariot for a day,/And set the world on fire. HBV 1-2

The Female Principle. A. D. Hope. Bed me and beget my son. OxBC

Female Rain. Laura Tohe. luminescence all around. STE

The Female Sailor. *Anonymous.* May she rest at home contented now, the female sailor bold. OBET

The Female Smuggler. *Anonymous.* Like a war-like hero that never was afraid. AmSS

The Female Transport. *Anonymous.* For fear like us you spend your days upon Van Diemen's shore. NOAV

The Female Warrior. *Anonymous.* You must fight, sink, or swim, or die by the sword. ShS

Femina. Daphne Marlatt. The bones of your face are pinned with autographs. NOBC

Femina Contra Mundum. Gilbert Keith Chesterton. "Thou hast begun to love one of my works/Almost enough." MoRP

Feminine. Henry Cuyler Bunner. "Love, we have lost/a year!" AA

Femme et Chatte. Paul Verlaine. Four sparks of phosphor shone like flame. AWP; OBVE

The Fence. Heather McHugh. I ran between them,/drumming the uprights of the fence. GeTw

A Fence. Carl Sandburg. Death and the Rain and Tomorrow. WeW

A Fence or an Ambulance. Joseph Malins. Better put a strong fence round the top of the cliff/Than an ambulance down in the valley. BLPA

Fence Wire. James Dickey. Whether outside, around, or in. NYBP; VGW

Fencing School. John Streeter Manifold. ...I only feel/The sinews of my wrist assert/The tremor of engaging steel. CBAP

The Feral Pioneers. Ishmael Reed.
...I lie down, my hands/supporting my head. UnPo
tears have pressed white hair/to face. PoBA; PoNe

Ferdinando and Elvira. Sir William Schwenck Gilbert.
And ELVIRA to her FERDINAND's irrevocably mated! FaBoCo; FaBoNo; FiBHP; LBN
And I rushed away, exclaiming, "I have found him! I have/found him!" NA

Fergus and the Druid. William Butler Yeats. Ah! Druid, Druid, how great webs of sorrow/Lay hidden in the small slate-coloured thing! CoBE; VLP

Feri's Dream. Frances Cornford. All among its petals, was his hairy face. BoC

Fern. Ted Hughes. ...like the plume/Of a warrior returning, under the low hills,/Into his own kingdom. NYBP

Fern Hill. Dylan Thomas. Though I sang in my chains like the sea. AtBAP; BiP; CMoP; CoBMV; DiPo; EvOK; FaBoPP; FaBV; FPL; GoJo; GTBS-P; HAP; HeIP; InPK; InPS; LiTB; LiTM; LoGBV; MasP; MoAB; MoBrPo; MoPo; MoVE; MP; NIP; NoAm; NOBE; NoP; OAEL 1-2; OAEP; OxBTC; PAI; PoLf; PoPl; PoRA; PPoe; PPP; RoGo; SoSe; TrGrPo; TwCP; ViBoPo; WeW

Fern House at Kew. Paul Dehn. The little star-crossed boy at play/A continent of years away. ChMP

Fernando. Marci Ridlon. My crazy friend Fernando. NTCP

The Ferry. George Henry Boker. I'd double your pleasure, I'd double my/pain,/This moment forever to bury, AA

Ferry-Boats. James S. Tippett. I'm always sorry/When the ride ends. SoPo; SUS; TiPo

Ferry Hinksey. Laurence Binyon. Till he that lingered lost her/Among the leaves of Spring. HBV 1-2

Ferry Me across the Water. Christina Georgina Rossetti. I'll ferry you. BiP; GoJo; OxBChV; SoPo; SUS

The Fertile Muck. Irving Layton. our fingers touching the earth, like two Buddhas. NOBC; OBCV; PeCV

The Fertile Valley of the Nile. Eve Merriam. upon the bony scruff of your departing neck. IHMS

The Festal Board. *Anonymous.* And sadly mixed with blood and tears. BLPA; TreFS

Festal Song. William Pierson Merrill. As brothers of the Son of Man,/Rise up, O men of God! WGRP

The Festival. Frederic Prokosch. The hatreds of a hundred thousand years. LiTA; WaP

Festoons of Fishes. Alfred Kreymborg. Among the coral crypts that hold the sea/Festoons of fishes weave insanity. HBMV

Festubert: The Old German Line. Edmund Charles Blunden. The gray rags fluttered on the dead. MMM

Festum Nativitatis. Aubrey Thomas De Vere. The children sang. Who Mary love/The long year through have Christmas nigh them! IrPN

Festus: Proem to the Third Edition. Philip James Bailey. ...making clear/His might and love in saving sinful man. VLP

Fetching Cows. Norman MacCaig. The black cow is two native carriers/Bringing its belly home, slung from a pole. BoAnP; OxBC

Fetching the Wounded. Laurence Binyon. The first cock crows: the morrow is begun. MMM

A Fete. Larry Eigner. the bombs showered us in the air. NeAP

Feud. Lew Sarett. Laughing—one round for you, and one for me. AnAmPo

Feuerzauber. Louis Untermeyer. And you become/A goddess standing in a world of fire! TrJP

The Fever. Rosemary Dobson. There is no need for you to answer. FaBoWP

A Fever. John Donne.
Are unchangeable firmament. MyFE
For I had rather owner be/Of thee one hour, than all else ever. DiPo; OAEL 1-2

Fever. Thom Gunn. Feverish people require more sleep than most,/And need to learn all they can about repose. PeHV

Fever 103. Sylvia Plath. (My selves dissolving, old whore petticoats)–/To Paradise. CMoP; FaBoWP; NMP; NoAm; NOBA; VGW

The Fever Toy. Charles Wright. Blue idiom, blue embrace. AmPA

Few Days. *Anonymous.* I am going home. ABF

Few Happy Matches. Isaac Watts. And Cupids yoke the doves. NOEC

A Few Lines to Fill up a Vacant Page. John Danforth. I got safe and firm Anch'rage in a trice,/Within the very inmost Bays of blissfull Paradice. SCAP

A Few Muddled Metaphors by a Moore-ose Melodist. Tom (Thomas Hood, Jr.) Hood. It went and cut a pigeon's-wing! FaBoNo

Few Things Can More Inflame. Cecil Day-Lewis. Naked enough to keep its dignity/Though it eye God askance. OBMV

Few Wholly Faithful. *Anonymous.* Saviour, Thou who thus hast loved me,/Give me love like this. BePJ

Fiametta. John Peale Bishop. Until I shall have rightly praised/Her standing thus with slight arms upraised. LiTA; LiTL

Fiammetta. Giovanni Boccaccio. I dwell, who fain would be where she is gone. GoBC

Fiascherino. Charles Tomlinson. The sea unrolls and rolls itself into the low room. NoAm

Fiat Lux. Lloyd Mifflin. Through vasts unwinnowed by the wings of/eld! AA; AnAmPo

Fickle Hope. Harrison Smith Morris. Wilt flee, or wilt thou stay? AA

Fickle in the Arms of Spring. Susie Fry. russet/amber/and gone. AMV-81

The Fickle One. Pablo Neruda. made for my kisses,/made for my soul. FF; OLR

Fiction: A Message. Gavin Ewart. Ponsonby smiled back. He was above her. Of that he was now sure. OxBC

Fiction and the Reading Public. Philip Larkin. You'll be "truly great'. NOBL; OBSV

A Fiction of Edvard Munch. Mary di Michele. I had to scrape my canvas clean/to begin again with a voluptuous death/posing naked on a bed. CaPN

Fiddle-I-Fee. *Anonymous.* And the cat went fiddle-i-fee. AmFP

The Fiddlehead. David McFadden. anchored glumly in the swirling great joy. NeAC

The Fiddler. Martin Buber. ...Before then, Holy Player,/do not break off! VWA

A Fiddler. Walter De La Mare. But a bird sings on in the almond tree. LOW; UnS

The Fiddler. Edna Valentine Trapnell. And he follows its Gleam from the dawn to the gloaming. HBMV

Fiddler Jones. Edgar Lee Masters. And not a single regret. AmP; CMoP; HBV 1-2; LiTA; LoGBV; NoAm; OxBA; TAP; TrGrPo; UnS

The Fiddler of Dooney. William Butler Yeats. And dance like a wave of the sea. DiPo; FaBoCh; LoGBV; NLV; OBVV; PoPle; TiPo; UnS

'Fiddler's Green. *Anonymous.* And I'll play my old squeezebox as we sail along/With the wind in the rigging to sing me this song. OBSS

Fiddler's Green. Theodore Goodridge Roberts. All grief is done; and never more shall we/Make sail at dawning for the luring sea. CaP

Fidelia: Shall I, Wasting in Despair. George Wither. What care I for whom she be? EIL

Fidelis. Adelaide Anne Procter. I shall nurse my love and keep it/Faithfully, for you, till then. BLPA; FaBoBe

Fidelities. Jean Valentine. ...No one/says anything much. No one leaves anyone. NYP

Fidelity. Jerry Kass. and sank helplessly toward the old dream,/in which Felicia died. AMV-80

Fidelity. Trumbull Stickney. Time is dying. AnFE; CoAnAm; LiTA

Fidelity. William Wordsworth. And gave that strength of feeling, great/Above all human estimate! FM

Fidessa, More Chaste Than Kind, XXXVII. Bartholomew Griffin. And where the little God himself is warden. EG; LO

Fidget. *Anonymous.* As little Jenny Wren/Was sitting by the shed. OxNR

Fingernail Sunrise. Vernon Watkins. Mute, remembered alone by him who made it. NYBP

Fingers in the Door. David Holbrook. We are there in our hundred thousand pieces! NePoEA-2

Finigan's Wake. Anonymous. Isn't all the truth I've told ye,/Lots of fun at Finigan's wake? BLPA

Finis. Waring Cuney. You will not again/Love over much. AmNP; BANP

Finis. George Herbert. Good will towards men. JCP

Finis. Sir Henry Newbolt. Nothing more/Need be said. TiPo

Finis. James (1700-48) Thomson. Till, dying, all he can resign is breath. BSV

The Finished Course. Saint Joseph of the Studium. The sorrows of thy former cup/In full fruition swallowed up. WGRP

A Finished Gentleman. Geoffrey Dutton. ...different/From the hands around me, raising schooners at closing time. NOAV

Finistere. Thomas Kinsella. (I went forward, reaching out). IPY

Finisterra. Bayla Winters. ...lick the salty leg of the/sea with my own grateful tongue. AMV-81

Finite. Power (Haold Caleb Dalton) Dalton. Then I found myself a stranger/In my own town. HBMV

Finite Reason. John Dryden. For what could fathom God were more than He. LoBV

Finland. Robert Graves. And stamps to mark the tune. BrPo

Finnair Fragment. Roald Hoffmann. Or have you, polyvowelled friends/conspired in brief white nights/to make a truly light champagne? SUW

Finnegan's Wake. Anonymous.
Oh it's lots of fun at Finnegan's wake. FaBoBa; FSW; TrAS
Thanan o'n dhoul, do ye think I'm dead?' NLV

The Finnesburh Fragment. Anonymous. Or which of the young men.... OBWP

Finnigin to Flannigan. Strickland Gillilan. Gone agin.–Finnigin. FaBoBe; GoTF; HBV 1-2; StPo; TreF; YaD

Fiorentina. Ernest Myers. The very flame that threaten'd Love/Has lent us light to see him by. OBVV

Fir Forest. Ethel Romig Fuller. And all around me everywhere/A gentle sound like murmured prayer. PGD

The Fir-Tree. Edith Matilda Thomas. In my flight I stir. OHIP

The Fire. Charles G. Bell. Saw now and then how a few last sparks would rise/To their brief ecstasy among the stars. MoLP

The Fire. William Burford. And we stand all bloodied in the light. NePA

Fire. William Carpenter. no refuge from the elements, no fixed address. Psk

The Fire. Robert Creeley. makes of her eyes the simple grace. NOBA

The Fire. Robert Duncan. now new old first day jump. VGW

Fire. Joy Harjo. a night wind woman/who burns/with every breath/she takes. TWSS

Fire. Langston Hughes. Fire gonna burn ma soul! NoAm; NOBA

The Fire. Sir Walter Scott. Nor fail'd old Scotland to produce,/At such high tide, her savoury goose. OBCP

Fire. Dorothy Wellesley. Whether we will or no. OBMV

Fire. M.V. Woodgate. I will not forget Thy word. Amen. BoC

Fire. 10/78. Bart Plantenga. ...a swift kick from a gentle/gust & our fears would all be gone. AMV-80

A Fire a Simple Fire. Frederic Will. Forever after the water tastes fiery. FAZ

Fire and Brimstone; or, The Destruction of Sodom (excerpt). George Lestey. ...for all those things that we have done/At your Command? PeHV

Fire and Ice. Robert Frost. And would suffice. AnFE; AnNE; APA; BiP; CABA; CMoP; CoBMV; DiPo; FaBoEE; FaFP; FaPo; FF; FPL; HBMV; HeIP; HoPM; InPK; LiTA; LiTM; MoAB; MoAmPo; MoVE; NePA; NoAm; NOBA; OxBA; PoPl; PrIm; SoSe; TAP; TreFS; TrGrPo; TW; ViBoPo; WHA

Fire and Ice. Michael Pettit. Your time is up. Thou art a little/soul bearing about a corpse. MAYP

The Fire at Alexandria. Theodore Weiss. ...the flashings/of the fathoms of set eyes. CoPo; NoAm; PoA; TAP

Fire at Murdering Hut. Judith Wright. I do not wish to wake/to the cruel day of love. Leave me my rest. ACV

The Fire Breather, Mexico City. Jaime Jacinto. burning from streetlight/to streetlight. BrSi

The Fire-bringer. William Vaughn Moody.
...everything/As on my heavenly hills. WGRP
Laughter and rallying! BBV

Fire Burial. Edgar McInnis. One with the sunlit air and the calling wind/And the sea for ever. CaP

The Fire Burns Low. John Leax. He relives again the day he died... TrCP

Fire Down Below. Anonymous. Fire in the main well,/The captain didn't know. FSW

Fire! Fire! Anonymous. So will I, said Goody Fry. GBP; OxNR

Fire, Hair, Meat and Bone. Fred Johnson. and/fathers/and fathers to me PoBA

The Fire i' the Flint. Lucy Robinson. And lived more base than that young wife/died true. AA

Fire in My Meditation Burned. Henry Ainsworth. Refresh myself; ere that I go,/And I no more shall be. AH

The Fire in the Snow. Vernon Watkins. Seeing in the firelight the brightness of snow. LiTM; MoVE

Fire Island. Rita Mae Brown. Whose capped and sterile teeth/Whisper the great lie, "Love." IHMS

Fire Island. May Swenson. our little Way the dark/glitter in their sight. PoA; TAP

Fire Island Poem. Diane Wakoski. Try,/just try,/to put fire/in your pocket safely,/young man. BiP

The Fire of Drift-Wood. Henry Wadsworth Longfellow. The drift-wood fire without that burned,/The thoughts that burned and glowed within. AP; BLPL; HBV 1-2; MAmP; NOBA; NoP; OxBA; TAP

The Fire of Frendraught. Anonymous. I wan a sair heart when I married him,/And the day it's well return'd again. ESPB; OxBB; ViBoFo

The Fire of Frendraught (C version). Anonymous. But a' is for my own son dear,/The heir o Rothiemay.' ESPB

The Fire of Love. Charles, Earl of Dorset Sackville. And though the flame be not so great,/Yet is the heat as strong. LiTL; UnTE

Fire on the Hills. Robinson Jeffers. The destruction that brings an eagle from heaven is better than mercy. CMoP

The Fire Place. E. W. Mandel. Flaming curtains issue then,/Thus between the witch's thighs. OBCV

Fire-Queen. Ruth Fainlight. Ambitionless as death, perfect, absorbed/Forever by her silent incantation. PoA

The Fire Ship. Anonymous.
Or else you'll get your cobbles sprung and set on fire too. OBSS
She was a nice girl, a decent girl,/But one of the rakish kind. AmSS

The Fire Side. A Pastoral Soliloquy. Isaac Hawkins Browne. Thus the shepherd; then throwing his crook away steals/Direct to St. James's and takes up the Seals. NOEC; OBEC

Fire: The People. Alfred Corn. ...–love that gives them each a name. MAYP

Fire, the Rope... Nikolay Tikhonov. Those were the days when first it was we learned/Words bitter, beautiful and harsh. LiTW

A Fire-Truck. Richard Wilbur. Your phoenix-red simplicity, enshrined/In that not extinguished fire. NCSH

Firebell for Peace. Joyce Lee. "It's only peace'/he prophesies across my years. NOAV

The Firebombing. James Dickey. The thing itself is in that. CAPP; OBWP

Firebowl. Sydney Clouts. we who dance we find/the/fire/of the fire. VWA

Firebrand. Harry Crosby. In Nine Decades/a Mad Queen shall be born. EAS

The Fired Pot. Anna Wickham. He altered the expression of my face/And gave me back my beauty. FaBoTw; FaBoWP; OxBTC

Fireflies. Edgar Fawcett. These hearts of living fire that beat below! AnAmPo; HBV 1-2

Fireflies. Aileen Fisher. ...play/without bumping their heads/or losing their way. SoPo

Fireflies. Carolyn Hall. each leading its oafishonging/To be a shooting star. FaPON; HBVY

Fireflies. William Sharp. And raised them thus to the outer air. FM

The Fireflies (excerpt). Charles Mair. And dreads its captor and his handsel touch. OBCV

Fireflies in the Garden. Robert Frost. Only, of course, they can't sustain the part. OBSP

The Firefly. Ogden Nash. ...with an unidentified glow/on a person's posteerier. FPL

Firefly. Elizabeth Madox Roberts. To have a little bug all lit/And made to go on wings. GoJo; NTCP; SUS; TiPo

Firefly. George Uba. Some speck of fire the night eclipsed. BrSi

The Firefly Lights His Lamp. Anonymous. And slowly lights his lamp. SoPo

Firelight. Edwin Arlington Robinson. Her thoughts a moment since of one who shines/Apart, and would be hers if he had known. NoAm

Fires. William Heyen. with wild and elemental meanings/from our living sun. MAYP

Fires of Driftwood. Isabel Ecclestone MacKay. What is left is nothing–/Ashes blown along the shore! CaP

The Firetail's Nest. John Clare. And pipes her "tweet-tut' fears the whole day/long. EnRP

Fireworks. Babette Deutsch. Night absorbs them/With the sponge of her silence. NYBP; OFD

Fireworks. James Reeve. When magic trees their petals shake/Upon each gazing eye. OnUR; PoSC

First Love. Sharon Olds. ...pain kept coursing through me like/life, like the gift of life. FYAP

The First Love Poem. Myra Glazer Schotz. ...I would be married to you, bring you/ground to stand on, firmly,/and to plant. VWA

The First Meeting. Edward, Lord Herbert of Cherbury. That all it moves, or is inclin'd,/Comes from the motions of your mind. AnAnS 2

First Miracle. Genevieve Taggard. "However you frown, no matter how,/I will sing as I am singing now." HBMV

First Monday Scottsboro Alabama. Tom Weatherly. from north alabama ridges/over bridges sherman didnt burn. PoBA

The First Note, Simple; the Second Note, Distinct. Conrad Aiken. Urge the vast twilight to immortal bloom. LiTA

The First Nowell. *Anonymous.*
  And with His blood mankind hath bought. TreFS
  Born is the King of Israel. LiTB; PCh; ViBoPo

First of All. Kenneth O. Hanson. ...knowing/after all you have been somewhere. GP

The First of All My Dreams. Edward Estlin Cummings. –how you and i are blossoming NYBP; VGW

The First of May. Barbara Guest. who would roast my bird/and eat it. AmPC

The First of My Lovers. Sydney Carter. And the last of my lovers/I'll light a candle still. OBET

First of Summer, Lovely Sight. *Anonymous.* "First of summer, lovely sight!" NOBI

The First of the Emigrants. *Anonymous.*
  And my girl I will find, the one I left behind,/And I'll make her as happy as can be. OBSS
  Sure I'm the man you don't meet ev'ry day! ShS

The First Olympionique to Hiero. Pindar.
  Beheld thy lovely form; and now, he glowed; ATP
  Where peace, where plenty, is for ever found: ATP

The First Olympionique to Hiero of Syracuse. Pindar.
  And swift to victory his master bore, ATP
  Deceive and captivate the mind: ATP
  Deep in his soul, to win the preferred bride. ATP
  From year to year, the promised nuptials wait ATP
  One cheerful moment to regain: ATP
  Proclaimed unrivalled in my song. ATP
  To gorge the gods and a voracious fire: ATP
  To sing more pleasing, in the joyful hour, ATP
  Unclouded days, and taste the sweets of life, ATP
  Unwearied ever, ever fleet: ATP

The First One Drew Me. Rav Abraham I. Kook. None can disclose the tale/Or even explain it in part. VWA

First or Last. Thomas Hardy. Aye, my dear and tender! CMoP

First Party at Ken Keseys with Hell's Angels. Allen Ginsberg. And 4 police cars parked outside the painted/gate, red lights revolving in the leaves. ConAP

First Pathways. Sidney Royse Lysaght. And that we only saw, where ways were rough,/The flowers about our feet. OBVV

First Philosopher's Song. Aldous Huxley. Earth its home and earth its tomb. AWP; HBMV; InPo

First Photos of Flu Virus. Harold Witt. Viruses when the lens is right/change into a bright bouquet. SM

First Practice. Gary Gildner. ...He said, Now. AmPA; InPK; LiSp; Psk; TW

First Praise. William Carlos Williams. They jostle white-armed down the tent-bordered/thoroughfare/Praising my Lady. VGW

First Precinct Fourth Ward. Daniel Mark Epstein. But some people will bet on anything. TAT

First Pregnancy. Alta. hearing you/beating off under covers. NMM

First Prelude. Dream in Ohio: The Father. John Logan. where absolutely anything goes, and there are no shores. LCAP

The First Proclamation of Miles Standish. Margaret Junkin Preston. And order a washing-day! MC; PAH; YaD

The First Psalm. Bertolt Brecht. ...My heart's a little fast. Otherwise everything's fine. NU

First Rain. Zoë Akins. With freshened winds for warning,/Came water–everywhere! HBMV

First Rainfall. Alan P. Lightman. gurgled in the fog/and freely outgassed. SUW

First Reader. Paris Leary. ...This is the last/lesson in the first book. CoPo

The First Reader. Winfield Townley Scott. Never the dream alone. PoA

First Reunion in New Orleans: The Father as King of Revels. John Logan. Leaving us stark naked there as for making love or art. CAPP

The First Robin. Lilian Leveridge. Of the life that blossoms in Spring land,/And never shall fade away. CaP

First Satire of the Second Book of Horace. Alexander Pope. My Lords the Judges laugh, and you're dismissed. OAEL 1-2; PPP; PrIm

The First Satire of the Second Book of Horace Imitated (excerpt). Alexander Pope. You'll gain at least a knighthood, or the bays. OBSV

First Satire: Prologue.. Persius (Aulus Persius Flaccus). You say they squeak, but they will swear they sing. AWP

First Sight. Philip Larkin. What so soon will wake and grow/Utterly unlike the snow. BoNaP; NCSH; NTCP

First Sight of Her and After. Thomas Hardy. I realize that it, for those,/Has been a common day. PoEL 1-5

First Snow. Marie Louise Allen. Look like somewhere else today. SoPo; TiPo

First Snow. Ivy O. Eastwick. This first snow of winter,/This gentle newcomer. TiPo

First Snow. Ted Kooser. sleepily blinking snowflakes from his lashes. GrPl

The First Snow-Fall. James Russell Lowell. Folded close under deepening snow. AA; AnNE; HBV 1-2; MCCG; TreF

First Snow in Alsace. Richard Wilbur. He was the first to see the snow. AP; NoP; OBWP

The First Snow of the Year. Mark Van Doren. The first snow of the year danced on the lawn. NCSH

First Snow on an Airfield. John Ciardi. Tomorrow's manual of guns to learn. PoA

The First Solitude. Luis de Gongora y Argote.
  All memory lost and forfeited all pride. OBVE
  O hermitage well found/Whatever hour it be!' OBVE
  Your epitaph shall travellers undeceive/Who in few letters many years shall see.' OBVE

The First Song. Richard Burton. But held the first his whole life long/Deep hidden in his heart. AA

First Song. Galway Kinnell. His heart to the darkness and into the sadness/of joy. CAPP; LiTM; NCSH; NePoAm; NoP

The First Spousal. Coventry Patmore. The Son of God and Man. OBVV

The First Spring Day. Christina Georgina Rossetti. Till I too blossom and rejoice and sing. WiR

The First Spring Morning. Robert Bridges.
  And summer soon to be. BoNaP
  The gay time is begun. YeAr

First Star. Dave Smith. Is it wind? Is it distance? Is it anger? AMV-81

The First Step. Andrew Bice Saxton. But never can be quite so any more. AA

First Steps up Parnassus. Michael Drayton. And bound upon Parnassus' bi-cleft top. NOBE

First Surf. Emanuel DiPasquale. fearful for my children. Str

The First Swallow. Charlotte Smith. Low twittering underneath the thatch/At the gray dawn of day. HBV 1-2

The First Test. Susan Fromberg Schaeffer. It christens and blinds. IHMS

The First Thanksgiving. Alice Williams Brotherton. And thanks unto the harvest's Lord who sends our/"daily bread." OHIP

The First Thanksgiving. Jack Prelutsky. and as they were thankful,/we're thankful today. NTCP

The First Thanksgiving. Clinton Scollard. That mounted morn and noon and eve on that first Thanks-/giving Day! MC; PAH

The First Thanksgiving. Nancy Byrd Turner. For men and dreams like these, we make/Thanksgiving every year! YeAr

The First Thanksgiving Day. Margaret Junkin Preston. He muttered, "The good Great Spirit loves His white children/best!" MC; PAH

First Thanksgiving of All. Nancy Byrd Turner. The first Thanksgiving of all. PAL; SiSoSe

First Things. Lucienne Desnoues. Hold on hard, hold on, my stevedore heart. WPOW

First Things First. W. H. Auden. Thousands have lived without love, not one without water. NePoAm-2; NYBP

The First Three. Clinton Scollard. Upon their hillside graves our immortelles! MC; PAH

First Three Verses of an Ode to Cary and Morison. Ben Jonson. Whilst that in Heav'n, this light on earth must shine. AnFE

The First Time. John Newlove. And oh I said yes, trying to think/of anything else at all. NeAC

The First Time. Karl Shapiro. And almost gently asks: Are you a Jew? ErPo; SM; VGW

The First Time Ever I Saw Your Face. Ewan MacColl. And last till the end of time. FSW

The First Time I Met You. Little Brother Montgomery. They give me more hard luck and trouble/than I ever had before. BluL

First to Throw a Stone. *Anonymous.* Let the perfect one among you/Be the first to throw a stone. STF

The First Tooth. Charles and Mary Lamb. It's prized more than my best dancing. OxBChV

The First Tooth. William Brighty ("Matthew Browne") Rands. Put your hand in his mouth! Do you feel? He can bite! HBV 1-2; HBVY

First Travels of Max. John Crowe Ransom. Live there, at least, when any are at home. MoAmPo

First Vision. Tadhg Dall O'Huiginn. My spirit sank and I was left to woe. AnIL; BIrV

The First Voyage of John Cabot. *Anonymous.* Fair fall the shadow-seekers!" quoth the king. MC; PAH

The First Wedding in the World. Joel Rosenberg. and stood before the shimmering light/to make their vows. VWA

First Winter. Gail N. Harada. never gave, not even after a light rain. BrSi

First Winter's Day. Dorothy Aldis. Tomorrow we will slide our sleds. SoPo

First Winter Storm. William Everson. The cottonwoods stood somnolent and still/Beneath the sun. NU

First Woman's Lament. Brenda Chamberlain. My man is a bone ringed with weed. NeIP

First World War. Kenneth Slade Alling. ...I was overcome/By the sudden East. NePoAm

The First Year (excerpt). E. J. Scovell. Familiar rise and fall our care for her, our sounds. FaBoWP

The Firstborn. John Arthur Goodchild. Mine by the chain of love with links unbroken,/Dear Saviour, Thine and mine. HBV 1-2

The Firstborn. Gary Soto. A rooster the winter wind sliced/Through a red fence NPGG

Firstborn (excerpt). Charles Wright. Welcome, sweet Luke, to your life. GP

The Firstborn Land. Ingeborg Bachmann. The wick flares up/should a glance light it. BoWoP

Firstfruits in 1812. Wallace Rice. And she's found the things she sought–/found a prize, a bully battle, and a breeze! PAH

The Firstling. Peter Davison. Dry-mouthed and still/Beneath the charmed hill? WeW

Firwood. John Clare. Winter is almost summer where they grow. EG; TrGrPo

Fisbo (excerpt). Robert Nichols. Certain of one thing, now the worst is passed/The last must be the best because the last. OBSV

The Fish. Elizabeth Bishop. And I let the fish go. ExPo; FaBoWP; GoJo; HAP; HeIP; HoPM; InPK; LiTM; MiAP; MoAB; MoAmPo; MOS; NePA; NoAm; NOBA; NoP; NU; PoPl; TrGrPo; ViBoPo; WeW

The Fish. Rupert Brooke.
The hyaline of drifting glooms... BoC
The light, the cries, and the willow dim,/And the dark tide are one with him. FM; MOS

The Fish. Ralph Gustafson. That doing it, the boy should look away. OBCV

Fish. Daniel Halpern. The fish bending to touch her. AmPA

Fish. Michael Hogan. and no room at all for a Cherry Tyme box/with letters from a face he can't remember. GP

Fish. Larry Levis. and the stars begin moving. AmPA

The Fish. Marianne Moore. The sea grows old in it. AnFE; APA; FaBoWP; MoAB; MoAmPo; MOS; MoVE; NoAm; OxBA

Fish. Joe Rosenblatt. I pitched my wishes back into the black water. NOBC

Fish. W. W. Eustace Ross. the fish dripping/sparkling water. PeCV

Fish. Mario Satz. the moonfish, quiet, lighting the darkness of the tea. VWA

Fish. Takahashi Shinkichi. And, stretching marvellously/Become the tracks of the Tokaido Railway Line. NU

Fish. Emily Townsend. I am no flesh? NYBP

Fish. William Carlos Williams. When they see one of them/they know some boat will be lost. NoAm

Fish. Sandra Witt. and the mouth gaping, a soft wound. AMV-80

The Fish Come in Dancing. Kevin Roberts. it gets harder to love/the things/you kill. WOLT

The Fish Counter at Bonneville. William Stafford. So many Chinook souls, so many Silverside. AmFN

Fish Crier. Carl Sandburg. His face is that of a man terribly glad to be selling fish,/terribly glad that God made fish,... AmFN; OxBA

Fish Food. John Wheelwright. I will not ask any more. You saw or heard no evil. AnFE; LiTA; MOS

The Fish-Hawk. John Hall Wheelock. Heaven, crowded with stars, trembled from rim to rim. AnAmPo; EtS; HBMV

Fish in River. *Anonymous.* Should we two be severed, my death is sure. AnOE

The Fish in the Stone. Rita Dove. He knows why the scientist/in secret delight/strokes the fern's/voluptuous braille. HaCAP

Fish Peddler and Cobbler. Kenneth Rexroth. ...while tired/Savage eyed whores paraded the street. NNaP

Fish Riddle: "Although it's cold no clothes I wear." *Anonymous.* I nothing buy or sell or lack. GBP

Fish Riddle: "The robbers came to our house." *Anonymous.* And we were a' ta'en. GBP

Fish Shop Windows. Geoffrey Dutton. Ichthyos, the sign of Jesus. NOAV

The Fish Sonata. Winfield Townley Scott. And, thinking over what he'd said,/Wished his friends were really there. MP

Fish Story. Richard Armour. And fishermen they fled all day from/(As big as this) and got away from. LiSp

A Fish Story. Charles Fishman. ...after they're caught, fish keep/swimming. WOLT

Fish Story. P. L. Jacobs. it's too close to call. LFAC

Fish Story. B. Jo Kinnick. we swim the watery years. AMV-81

A Fish to Feed All Hunger. Sandra Alcosser. And the lure is the same. WOLT

The Fish Upstairs. William Dickey. Now you will go and look at the fish upstairs. Psk

The Fish Will Swim as Before. Michael Spence. As logs jammed between rocks. AMV-81

The Fisher. Roderic Quinn. He stood entranced, enchained by her/Full-breasted loveliness. BoAV; CBAP; PoAu 1-2

The Fisher Cat. Richard Eberhart. The claws of the beast were wide, long his thrashing tail. GrPl

The Fisher Lad of Whitby. *Anonymous.* And I think of my lover away down in the sea,/For he never, never more will come again to me. OBSS

A Fisher's Apology. Arthur Johnstone. ...either region affords him, now his/day is done, the means of sport. GoTS

The Fisher's Boy. Henry David Thoreau. And I converse with many a shipwrecked crew. AA; AnNE; MOS

The Fisher's Life. *Anonymous.* There are no rent days on the sea! EtS; GBP

The Fisher's Widow. Arthur Symons. And the boats go out and the boats come in,/But there's one away. HBV 1-2

Fisherman. Philip Booth. And the dreamer hawk/high over that pool/in the streaming air/cries high and cool. LiSp; WOLT

The Fisherman. Abbie Farwell Brown. But when I tell of city things,/He sniffs and shuts one eye! EtS

The Fisherman. George Bruce. Now the pier is his, now the tide. BSV

The Fisherman. Susan Fawcett. ...the dying dark/lay still, all fish now. WOLT

Fisherman. Robert Francis. Who erstwhile worked his will on worms. PPJ

The Fisherman. Sam G. Harrison. A band of drunken molecules. AMV-80

The Fisherman. of Tarentum Leonidas. This tomb nor wife nor children raised, but we/His fellow-toilers, fishers of the sea. AWP

The Fisherman. Jay Macpherson. Lets down his hook and hoicks him in. NOBC; PeCV

The Fisherman. David McCord. And he has got my wishing/In an awful knot. TiPo

Fisherman. Sacheverell Sitwell. To drown there, stifling in the stiff, cold air. AtBAP

The Fisherman. Douglas Stewart. And the city is lost in a wind of autumn leaves. ACV

The Fisherman. Dabney Stuart. ...I wait/For whatever spawn or breed/Will take my bait. LiSp

The Fisherman. Will Wells. he sometimes dreamed of losing. AMV-80

The Fisherman. William Butler Yeats. And passionate as the dawn. MBW 1-2

The Fisherman Casts His Line into the Sea. Robert Holland. The fish swim in the dark, and cannot see. AMV-80

Fisherman's Blunder off New Bedford, Massachusetts. Annemarie Ewing. Pity that every song he tried to teach her/Made it more diffifcult for her to sing. NePoAm-2

The Fisherman's Hymn. Alexander Wilson. God bless the fish-hawk and the/fisher! AA; EtS

Fisherman's Luck. Wilfred Wilson Gibson. Till I go to seek it/Fifty fathom deep. EtS

The Fisherman's Son. Charles Bruce. Let herring school through heaven's hot July. CaP

Fisherman's Song. *Anonymous.* We'll go to sea no more! PoPle

The Fisherman's Song. Thomas D'Urfey. Then who a jolly fisherman,... ALV

The Fisherman's Wife. Amy Lowell. Upon the wooden sides of a boat. BoWoP

The Fisherman's Wife. Nora Mitchell. The granite blocks/that line the causeway/flash by like fish. AMV-80

The Fisherman Writes a Letter to the Mermaid. Joan Aiken. and do not doubt, your friend/will come to claim it in the end. WSC

Fishermen. Basil Bunting. we have the sea to stare at–/its treason, copiousness, tedium. PoA

Fishermen. James A. Emanuel. Or stand a fisherman. BP

Fishermen. Gabriel Preil. the clouds are torn asunder/one by one. VWA

The Fishermen. John Greenleaf Whittier. The stars of heaven shall guide us,/The breath of heaven shall speed! EtS

Fishermen at Dawn. William Meissner. something silver and ancient and hungry/rising to swallow them from below. WOLT

The Five Voyages of Arnor. George Mackay Brown. ...Drop my harp/ Through a green wave, off Yesnaby,/Next time you row to the lobsters. NePoEA-2

Five Ways to Kill a Man. Edwin Brock. ...see that he is living somewhere in the middle/of the twentieth century, and leave him there. DL

Five Were Foolish. Arthur J. Hodge. The bridegroom went in,/And the door was shut. AH

Five Words for Joe Dunn on His 22nd Birthday. Jack Spicer. That makes poetry/and moves stars. PoM

Five Years Old. Marie Louise Allen. I'll soon be something else again! BiCB

Five Years Old. Lysbeth Boyd Borie. And when is it too old? BiCB; SiSoSe

Fixer of Midnight. Reuel Denney. And he went to fix it right. OBAL

Fixing to Die. Booker White. And don't leave them screaming and crying/ on the graveyard ground BluL

A Fixture. Bill Berkson. In her partition is the stairway of unhunched love,/a muscular mouth. APU

A Fixture. May Swenson. she is the best dressed. NYBP

The Flag. Harry Lyndon Flash. And Freedom smiles, her fate secure,/ Beneath its steadfast stars. MC

The Flag. James Jeffrey Roche. Only—we couldn't read the chart. PAH

Flag. Reg Saner. On his right hand/and behind/the flag of his office hangs,/a wet 4th of July,/refusing to burn. GP

The Flag. Shel Silverstein. But I forget which ones they are. PoSC

The Flag Goes By. Henry Holcomb Bennett. The flag is passing by! AA; BBV; FaBoBe; FaFP; GN; HBV 1-2; HBVY; OHFP; PAL; PGD; SiSoSe; TreF; WBLP; YaD

The Flag of the Constellation. Thomas Buchanan Read. O'er battles that made us a nation. EtS

Flag Song. Lydia Avery Coonley Ward. The flag that is red, white, and blue. YeAr

The Flag Speaks. Emily Greene Balch. Sister of every flag/In the wide world. PGD

The Flag We Fly. Aileen Fisher. That's what it means, the flag we fly. YeAr

The Flagpole Sitter. Donald Finkel. I shall release my hold, and be blown away. CoAP

Flags. Gwendolyn Brooks. Or like the tender struggle of a fan). AmNP

Flail. Power (Haold Caleb Dalton) Dalton. There are words that must be written,/Songs that must be sung. HBMV

Flake Diamond of/the Sea. Larry Eigner. grass by the sea/in quiet smells/ a little way PoM

The Flame. Ezra Pound. Call not that mirror me, for I have slipped/Your grasp, I have eluded. AnFE

Flame-Heart. Claude McKay. Beneath the poinsettia's red in warm December. AmNP; BANP; CDC

Flaming Creatures. Kenward Elmslie. parachutists gliding down to mined branches, all seen in/mirrors. ANYP

The Flaming Heart. Richard Crashaw. Let me so read thy life, that I/ Unto all life of mine may die. AnAnS 1; AtBAP; CAW; CoBE; GoBC; HAP; LiTB; LoBV; NOBE; OBS; OxBoCh; PoEL 1-5; SeCePo; SeCV 1-2; TEP; TrGrPo; WHA

The flaming sighs that boil within my breast. Sir Thomas Wyatt. Let him thank God and let him not provoke/To have the like of this my painful stroke. FCP

The Flaming Terrapin. Roy Campbell. Red thunderbolts to purify the world. MoBrPo

The Flamingo. Lewis Gaylord Clark. A water bird, a gawky bird, a sing'lar bird, by jingo! NA

Flammonde. Edwin Arlington Robinson. In Tilbury Town, we look beyond/Horizons for the man Flammonde. AnAmPo; CMoP; LiTA; LiTM; MAPA; NoAm; SeCeV

Flannan Isle. Wilfred Wilson Gibson. Who thought on three men dead. CH; MoVE; OBVV; PoRA; StPo

Flannery O'Connor. Dorothy Walters. lighting this one, that one/to a flaming illumination. IHMS

Flash. Stephen Todd Booker. There has been enough tears. LFAC

The Flash. James Dickey. Binding, blood-brotherly/Beyond-speech answer. LCAP

The Flash Colonial Barman. William W. Coxon. A fine flash Yankee barman, and once more cut a shine. NOAV

Flash Crimson. Carl Sandburg. I who have seen the flash of this crimson, I ask God for the last and worst. MoAmPo

The Flash Frigate. Anonymous. And send you an invalid to your own native land. AmSS

Flash Jack from Gundagai. Anonymous. But they know me round the backblocks as Flash Jack from Gundagai. PoAu 1-2

"Flash:" The Fireman's Story. Will Carleton. It'll take the strongest angel to hold the old fellow in. BBV

Flashback. Allen Ginsberg. O women shut up, yelling for baby meat more. CAPP

A Flat One. W.D. Snodgrass. We would/Have killed for you today. AmPC; AP; CAPP; LiTM; NePoEA-2; PoCh; SM

Flathead and Nez Perce Sin-ka-ha. William S. Lewis. Nor be weary/Nor be left behind,/In days of war. BPAW

The Flattered Flying Fish. Emile Victor Rieu. The Moon will not shine on your beauty again! ShM; SO

The Flattered Lightning Bug. Don (Donald Robert Marquis) Marquis. the cat ate him. StPo

Flattery. Jonathan Swift. Yet now and then your men of wit/Will condescend to take a bit. GoTF; TreFT

Flavius, If Your Girl Friend. Caius Valerius Catullus. in a blushing blissful song/that echoes against heaven. ErPo

The Flaw in Paganism. Dorothy Parker. (But, alas, we never do.) DBV; NLV

Flawless His Heart. James Russell Lowell. And sudden-passionate in ebbs and flows. MC

Flax. Ivan Bunin. ...that from the shroud/May spring the sky-blue flax. AWP

The Flea. John Donne. Just so much honor, when thou yeeld's to mee,/ Will wast, as this flea's death took life from thee. AnAnS 1; BiP; BLPL; BoLoP; CABA; CBEP; EBEV; FF; FM; ForPo; HoPM; InPS; JCP; LiTB; LiTL; MAT; MePo; NIP; NLV; OAEL 1-2; PoPle; PPoe; SeCP; SeCV 1-2; SoSe; TEP; TrGrPo

The Flea. Roland Young. But she can tell and so can he. PoPl

The Flea Circus at Tivoli. Nancy Willard. and we go out praising. HoAn

Fleadh. Michael Longley. The chanter, the drones. CIP

Fleance. Michael Longley. Hurried back to the digs where Banquo/Sat up late with a hole in his head. FaBoIP

Fleche... Larry Eigner. it's curious when to die VGW

The Fledgling Bard and the Poetry Society. Part I (excerpt). George Reginald Margetson. As gifted, yet as good as God did ever plan. BANP

Fledglings. Thomas Lake Harris. When stars have set. AA

Fledglings. William Meredith. Is there any plummet or flight as sheer as the fledgling's? GLGT

Flee on Your Donkey. Anne Sexton. Those I loved best died of it—/the fool's disease. NYBP

The Fleece. John Dyer.
Prevent the wingy swarm and scorching heat. FaBoUs
Rich queen of mist and vapors! TrGrPo
Thy bosom to a thousand cares divide. PoEL 1-5
To many a kingdom's rent or tyrant's hoard. NOEC

The Fleet at Santiago. Charles E. Russell. How we thrill with the joy of their fame! MC; PAH

Fleet Street. Shane Leslie. With Heaven's tidings shod/About their brave, unwearied feet. OnYI

Fleeting Restlessness. Juana de Ibarbourou. Afterwards I shall be ashes beneath the black earth. LiTW

Fleeting Return. Juan Ramon Jimenez. What you were like, but only that you were. AMV-80

The Fleggit Bride. Hugh" (Christopher Murray Grieve) MacDiarmid. A fleggit bride's the seilfu' sicht. OxBS

A Flemish Madonna. Charles Wharton Stork. What greater power than this has brush or pen:/To bring the thought of God to simple men? HBMV

Flemish Primitive. G. S. Fraser. For ever with the baby at her breast. BSV

Flesh. Mary Elizabeth ("E") Fullerton. 'Tis but the stopt heart/That Time cannot mend. PoAu 1-2

Flesh. Stan Rice. Would you if Death were Flesh? NPGG

The Flesh. Tiroux Yamanaka. From the vein which twines its tiptoe. LiTW

The Flesh and the Spirit. Anne Bradstreet.
For things unknown, only in mind. AnAmPo
If I of Heaven may have my fill,/Take thou the world, and all that will. AP; APA; LiTA; MAmP; NePA; NOBA; OxBA; SCAP; TAP

Flesh Coupon. Jeff Wright. Here. I insist. I want/to pay them all back. APU

The Flesh-Fly and the Bee. Coventry Patmore. Sneer'd, "What a Transcendentalist!" FaBoEE

The Flesh-Scraper. Andrew Young. See, my hand fits it like a glove. ELU

Flesh Will Heal and Pain Will Fade. Claire Richcreek Thomas. The scar—still lingers there. PoToHe

Fleshflower. William Pitt Root. for its last name is called Gates of Paradise. GeTw

Fleur de Lys. Rayner Heppenstall. This lily trampled underfoot/Not for the last time dare not fade. WaP

The Flicker. Lew Blockcolski. on the screen of the Douglas Art Theatre. VoR

The Flies. Merrill Moore. And rest for the night over the mantel-top. AnEnPo

Floris and Blauncheflour: A Lover's Stratagem. *Anonymous.* Wel aughte ich hir yerne to wive/Whenne hie bit so for my live.' OxBM

The Florist Rose. Robert Graves. Bought as a love-gift, droops within the day. AtBAP

Flos Lunae. Ernest Christopher Dowson. I would not alter thy cold eyes. OBMV

Floss won't save you. Emily Dickinson. Prices reasonable. LiTA; NePA

Flotsam and Jetsam. Edward Estlin Cummings. even whose recktie/are covered by lloyd's. NOBA; OBAL

Flow Not So Fast. *Anonymous.* ...your salt tears/Must still fall, dropping from their spheres. ViBoPo

Flow, O My Tears! *Anonymous.* Whose love did ne'er/Forsake thee. EIL

The Flower. Robert Creeley. like this one. CAPP

The Flower. Lee Wilson Dodd. And to some unexpected lass,/Some gangling lad, she flings–the Flower. HBMV

The Flower. George Herbert. Forfeit their Paradise by their pride. AtBAP; AWP; ELP; FaBoRV; InPo; JCP; MePo; NIP; NOBE; NOCV; NoP; OBS; OxBoCh; PoEL 1-5; PPP; SeCP; SeCV 1-2

The Flower. John Holmes. You were running, running, with a flower for me. LiTL

A Flower. Mvula Ya Nangolo. where I rest but not yet dead/just a flower lad. WhB

The Flower. Samuel Speed. But how can I a weed become/If I am shadowed with the Son? OxBoCh

The Flower. Alfred, Lord Tennyson. And now again the people/Call it but a weed. HBV 1-2

The Flower. Robert Penn Warren. It will rustle all night, darling. PoPl

The Flower. Henrik Wergeland. This flower I give you, beloved. LiTW

The Flower and the Leaf. *Anonymous.* So pleasant a ground of no earthly man. PBBP

The Flower-Boat. Robert Frost. To seek for the Happy Isles together. PoA

The Flower-Cart Man. Rachel Field. When it's just past April/and going on May. SiSoSe; SoPo

Flower Ensnarer of Psalms. Rossana Ombres. and only the holiest/hear it moan. BoWoP

The Flower-Fed Buffaloes. Vachel Lindsay. With the Pawnees, lying low,/Lying low. AmFN; ATP; BPAW; CMoP; ExPo; GoJo; LoBV; LoGBV; MoAmPo; NOBA; OBCA; PPON; RFM; VGW

Flower for a Professor's Garden of Verses. Irwin Edman. And keep for you, though far from clever,/Your job–and what a job!–forever! DBV; InMe

A Flower Given to My Daughter. James Joyce. In gentle eyes thou veilest,/My blueveined child. OBMV; PoPl

Flower Herding on Mount Monadnock. Galway Kinnell. It is a flower. On this mountainside it is dying. ConAP; HeIP; LCAP; NaP; NOBA

Flower in the Crannied Wall. Alfred, Lord Tennyson. I should know what God and man is. BBV; BoNaP; DiPo; FaBV; FaFP; GoTF; InPK; LiTB; MaVP; MCCG; NIP; PoPl; TEP; TreFS; TrGrPo; TRV; WGRP

The Flower Market. Po Chu-i. He was thinking, "A cluster of deep-red flowers/Would pay the taxes of ten poor houses." PPON

The Flower Master. Mebdh McGuckian. Our fontanelle, the trout's dimpled feet. FaBoIP

Flower of Exile. Max Dunn. But through the gate sleeps his lost paradise. BoAV

The Flower of Flame (excerpt). Robert Nichols. And dared not ask her why. OBMV

The Flower of Liberty. Oliver Wendell Holmes. The starry Flower of Liberty! HBVY; MC

Flower of Love. Claude McKay. While we lie loving, passionate and mute. BALP

A Flower of Mullein. Lizette Woodworth Reese. For the sweet surety of the common air. MoAmPo

A flower of waves. Lady Ise. as though a breeze had quickened/the sea and set it blooming. BoWoP

Flower Song. Diane Keating. Among the ash/you'll find my heart,/a peach stone. CaPN

The Flower Vendor. Luis Cabalquinto. And the light in us went from stop to go. BrSi

The Flowering Bars. Charles Donnelly. and among strictness sweetness grew,/mystery of flowering bars. CIP

Flowering Currant. Patrick MacDonogh. And what loss is but one/Of his brides to the Lord? ErPo

The Flowering of the Rod. Hilda ("H. D.") Doolittle. it is the greatest among herbs/and becometh a tree. FaBoMo

The Flowering Urn. Laura Riding. It speaks of fruits that could not be. LiTA

Flowering without End. Stefan Zweig. Up, brothers, march onward, march/onward to God. TrJP

Flowers. *Anonymous.* At midnight blooms the flower of sin. WTO

Flowers. Roo Borson. There are holes in his face. CaPN; NOBC

Flowers. Thomas Hood. But I will plight with the dainty rose,/For fairest of all is she. HBV 1-2

The Flowers. Rudyard Kipling. Masters of the Seven Seas, O, love and understand! OBVV

Flowers. Henry Wadsworth Longfellow. Emblems of the bright and better land. HBV 1-2

Flowers. Stephane Mallarme. Great honey'd blossoms, a balsamic tomb/For weary poets blanched with starless life. SyP

The Flowers. William Brighty ("Matthew Browne") Rands. So red, so ripe, the roses burn'd! OBVV

Flowers and Men. D. H. Lawrence. to the honeysuckle at evening now/pouring out its breath. FaBoEE

Flowers By the Sea. William Carlos Williams. peacefully upon its plantlike stem. AmLP; AnEnPo; CMoP; ExPo; GoJo; MoAB; MoAmPo; NoAm; TAP

Flowers for Luis Bunuel. Stuart Z. Perkoff. Bunuel, Bunuel,/is the world? Did you? NeAP

Flowers for the Altar. Digby Mackworth Dolben. Still the poor and weak and weary/Only, worship and believe. GoBC

Flowers for the Brave. Celia Thaxter. What sweetness can match our love? OHIP

Flowers I Would Bring. Aubrey Thomas De Vere. And love to thee is naught; from passionate mood/Secured by joy's complacent plenitude. HBV 1-2; IrPN

Flowers in the Valley. *Anonymous.* Farewell to the flowers in the valley. AtBAP; OLR; OnMSP; OxBoLi

Flowers in the Ward. Shaw Neilson. Whispering they give back/Young feet to the lame. CBAP

The Flowers of Apollo. Hildegarde Flanner. I will not tell how many times I break/The flowers of Apollo for your sake. HBMV

Flowers of Darkness. Frank Marshall Davis. For what flower, plucked,/Lingers long? AmNP; IDB; NoP; PoBA; PoNe

The Flowers of Politics. Michael McClure. ...And make/the giant bright stroke like that madman Van Gogh. NeAP and spread a radiance from ourselves that melts/in light. NeAP

Flowers of the Foothills & Mountain Valleys. Alice Notley. ...courage/is grey-green growing wild. APU

The Flowers of the Forest. Alison Cockburn. For the flowers of the forest are withered away. BSV; OBEC

The Flowers of the Forest. Jane Elliot. "The Flowers of the Forest are a' wede away." BSV; CH; FaBoCh; FaBoRV; GoTS; OBEC; OxBS

The Flowers That Bloom in the Spring. Sir William Schwenck Gilbert. "Oh, bother the flowers of spring!"/Tra la la-la la. BLSo

The Flowing Summer. Charles Bruce.
And rusty iron in a dusty room. CaP
It's almost time to get the cows and milk. CaP
Lee felt the impulse of a sighted end. CaP

The Flown Soul. George Parsons Lathrop. "Come not! Come not again!" AA

Flush or Faunus. Elizabeth Barrett Browning. Who, by low creatures, leads to heights of love. BoC; FM; NBM

Flushing Meadows, 1939. Daniel Gerard Hoffman. With lightning, lightening in a murmur of summer thunder. CoPo

The Flute. Joseph Russell Taylor. They trod the stained flute where it lay. AA

The Flute: A Pastoral. Jose-Maria de Heredia. Rise, wing'd with music, from the o'er-labored heart. AWP

Flute Notes from a Reedy Pond. Sylvia Plath. And how a god flimsy as a baby's finger/Shall unhusk himself and steer into the air. FaBoMo

The Flute of May. Harry Woodbourne. And I began to play/The bird-sweet flute of May. GoYe

The Flute of the Lonely. Vachel Lindsay. All loved the strain, and all/Looked at the moon! CrMA

Flute Player. *Anonymous.* Let them be burnt with fire/Those bamboos that make the flute. WTO

Flute Players. Jean Rabearivelo. Your flute and his/regret their beginnings/in the songs of both your sorrows. PBA

Flute-Priest Song for Rain (excerpt). Amy Lowell. Wee-kee-kee, oriole,/Pattering rain. UnS

Flute Song. Kavangho Masaveimah. Everywhere, far and near,/It will shine–water-shine. WTO

Flux. Richard Eberhart. Enigma rules, and the heart has no certainty. Psk; VGW

The Fly. William Blake. If I live/Or if I die. BoLiVe; CBEP; DiPo; FM; NLV; TrGrPo

The Fly. Walter De la Mare. And specks of salt as bright to see/As lambkins to a shepherd. OnUR; PoPle

The Fly. Barnabe Googe. And thou should'st wail thy case. CH

Fly. William Stanley Merwin. I who have always believed too much in words NNaP

The Fly. Francisco Gomez de Quevedo y Villegas. I'd rather choose to dye in Wine. OBVE

The Fly.　Karl Shapiro.　And dies between three cannibals.　MiAP; MoVE; NIP

A Fly about a Glass of Burnt Claret.　Richard Lovelace.　Thou wouldst be scorched and drowned again!　CaPo

Fly around My Blue-Eyed Gal.　*Anonymous.*　Fly around my blue-eyed gal,/ You almost drove me crazy.　FSW

Fly away, Fly away over the Sea.　Christina Georgina Rossetti.　Bringing the summer and bringing the sun.　SUS

A Fly Caught in a Cobweb.　Richard Lovelace.　Fall yet triumphant in thy woe,/Bound with the entrails of thy foe.　CaPo; SeCP

Fly-Fishing.　John Gay.　And with the fur-wrought fly delude the prey. SD

Fly from the World.　*Anonymous.*　Strike sayle! go soule! rest followes them that dye.　NCEP

Fly in December.　Robert Wallace.　somehow, the three of us.　NYBP

Fly, Ladybug.　Annette Burr Stowman.　Ladybug, ladybug, I'll see you home.　AMV-80

Fly, Love, That Art So Sprightly.　*Anonymous.*　True widow maid, still followeth Diana.　NCEP

A Fly That Flew into My Mistress's Eye.　Thomas Carew.　Thus she received from Celia's eye/Funeral flame, tomb, obsequy.　CaPo

Fly to Jesus.　Charles Wesley.　Blest to all eternity.　BePJ

Flycatchers.　Robert Bridges.　With all manner of rubbish and all manner of lies.　MoVE

Flyer's Fall.　Wallace Stevens.　We believe without belief, beyond belief. MoAB

Flyfisherman in Wartime.　Leonard Bacon.　And the trout that struck in the thunderlight.　FYAP

Flying.　Henry Carlile.　..."The star that moves–that's your father." AMV-80

Flying.　J. M. Westrup.　Sailing away/Like a toy/Balloon.　OnUR

Flying Blossoms.　William Henry Davies.　That they may think they see in me/Another crop of golden corn!　BrPo

The Flying Bum: 1944.　William Plomer.　Planted bang upon the table/A lightly roasted rump of horse.　DTC

The Flying Change.　Henry Taylor.　sustained in time astride the flying change.　MAYP

Flying Changes.　Mary Wood.　Frisbee and I performed the flying change. PH

The Flying Cloud.　*Anonymous.*
　But die a sad and scornful death down in this foreign land.　AmFP
　Come all young men a warning take/Bid a curse to the pirate sea. BaBo; ViBoFo
　When a bombshell set our ship on fire, we were forced to surrender/ then. ABF

The Flying Cloud (I).　*Anonymous.*　So a warning take by my sad state– beware of piracy!　AmSS; OBET; OBSS; ShS

The Flying Cloud (II).　*Anonymous.*　To the burning shores of Africa where the sugarcane does grow.　ShS

Flying Crooked.　Robert Graves.　Even the acrobatic swift/has not his flying-crooked gift.　FaBoMo; LiTM; MP; OBSP; PCP; TwCP

Flying Crow.　Black Ivory King.　Well I hate to hear/that old fireman when he tones his bell/(oh, ring 'em a long time)/Mmmmm.....　BluL

Flying Deeper into the Century.　Pier Giorgio Di Cicco.　...if only I were less than human, not angry/like a beaten thing.　CaPN; NOBC

The Flying Dutchman.　*Anonymous.*　He tries in vain his oath to keep by ent'ring Table Bay!　OBSS; ShS

The Flying Dutchman.　Edwin Arlington Robinson.　One fog-walled island more.　MOS

The Flying Dutchman.　A. M. Sullivan.　But Vanderdecken himself could tell you more!　EtS

The Flying Fish.　Jack Cope.　the flying fish sing to light.　PeSA

Flying Fish.　Mary McNeil Fenollosa.　Or is it the ghosts/In silver hosts/Of birds that were drowned at sea?　AA

The Flying Fish.　John Gray.
　the bird so fair, for its putrid sake,/is flung to the dogs in the junk's white wake.　LoBV; OBNC
　There are seekers of wisdom no less absurd,/son Hang, than thy fish that would be a bird.　NOBV

Flying Fish.　J. Corson Miller.　Your wild heart beats with the rhythm of spray-flung/hours!　EtS

Flying Fish.　Katherine Kelley Taylor.　May He have mercy on a fish's soul. EtS

Flying Fox.　Thomas W. Shapcott.　and tear through its shallow skin, and feast on it.　CBAP

Flying Foxes and Others.　Kay Boyle.　To the rot of fruit, sweet but invisible, spicing the trails of the /air.　AnAmPo

The Flying Lesson.　Petrarch.　But near the Sacred Feet she sits and waits. CAW

Flying Letters.　Zerubavel Gilead.　until I sank/into darkness.　VWA

Flying Noises.　Thomas Lux.　And behind the curtain one marvelous belly/ or else the wind is bringing the usual.　LCAP

The Flying Pig.　*Anonymous.*　Dickery, dickery, dare.　OxNR

The Flying Tailor (parody).　James Hogg.　On tears, and sighs, and groans, and brains, and blood.　BXAP; Par

The Flying Trapeze.　George Lebourne.　And my love he purloin'd away. GoTF; PSoN; TreF

The Flying Wheel.　Katharine Tynan Hinkson.　You will not trouble me again/In the great peace where I attain.　WGRP

The Flyting o' Life and Daith.　Hamish Henderson.　Quo life, the warld is mine.　OxBS

Flyting of Dunbar and Kennedy.　William Dunbar.　Rottin crok, dirtin dok, cry cok, or I sall quell the.　TW

Foal.　Mary Britton Miller.　And you're only a skittish/Child, after all,/ Little foal.　PH

The Foal.　William Renton.　He must stride/Ere he can feed.　NOBV

Foal.　Vernon Watkins.　And eluding the dead hands, begging him to play. OxBTC

Focus.　Kathleen Norris.　It's almost tender,/The way it's done.　GP

Focus.　Adrienne Rich.　Obscurity has another tale to tell.　FaBoWP

Fod.　*Anonymous.*　It was hard to tell which smelt the worst./Tu rolly day. AmFP

The Foe at the Gates.　John Dickson Bruns.　The last grand holocaust of Liberty.　PAH

Foeda Est In Coitu.　Petronius Arbiter (Caius Petronius Arbiter).　This hath pleas'd, doth please, & long will please; never/Can this decay, but is beginning ever.　LiTW

Foetal Song.　Joyce Carol Oates.　I am waiting for my turn.　IHMS; NAs

Foetus.　Phyllis Haring.　And with humility I hope to die.　PeSA

Fog.　Laurence Binyon.　The baffled hive of helpless man laid bare.　SyP

The Fog.　Robert P. Tristram Coffin.　How life was but a name for loneliness.　CrMA

The Fog.　William Henry Davies.　A blind man led me home.　TiPo

Fog.　Kenneth Patchen.　In a heaven where all we of longing lie, clinging together/as it gets dark.　NaP

Fog.　John Reed.　But lonely bells across gray wastes of sea.　AnEnPo

Fog.　Carl Sandburg.　and then moves on.　AP; FaBV; FaFP; FPL; HBMV; HeIP; InPK; LaNeLa; MCCG; MoAB; MoAmPo; OBCA; PoPl; SoPo; SoSe; SUS; TAP; TiPo

Fog 9/76.　Richard Morris Dey.　At last,/into the fog, I/hurled a lamp. AMV-80

The Fog Dream.　Sandra M. Gilbert.　His words hang in the air, unanswered,/then drift away, slow feathers.　PoA

Fog-Horn.　George Herbert Clarke.　And ever the waste, and the dank mist, and night!　CaP

Fog-Horn.　William Stanley Merwin.　As our cries were swallowed up and all hands lost.　NMP

The Foggy Dew.　*Anonymous.*
　But every time she winks or smiles,/She thinks of the foggy dew.　CoMu; ELP; UnTE
　Just to keep her from the foggy, foggy dew. AS; DTC; FSW; GBP; LiTB; OxBoLi; UnTE
　Oh, in my arms, all her charms/were casted in the foggy dew. FSW
　Why we must leave off kissing/and think of the foggy dew.'　OBET

Foggy Mountain Top.　*Anonymous.*　I'd sail all around this whole wide world/To the girl I love the best.　FSW

The Foiled Reaper.　William Kean Seymour.　Lo, there 'tis Death! How piteously he goes,/Wearily swinging.　HBMV

Foiled Sleep.　Madelaine Marie.　And ah! I cannot sleep at night.　PeHV

The Folded Flock.　Wilfrid Meynell.　And fold at need a straggling one. CAW; GoBC; TrPWD

Folded Power.　Gladys Cromwell.　Lifting them gently through strange delight/To a clearer light.　HBMV

A Folded Skyscraper (excerpt).　William Carlos Williams.　there's no place/ anymore for me to grow/except home.　AnAmPo

Folding a Shirt.　Denise Levertov.　the common rituals of life.　NeBP

A Folding and Unfolding.　Welton Smith.　and touch our damp/cheeks with our/crumbling black fingers.　PoNe

Folding the Sheets.　Rosemary Dobson.　And the faint but perceptible scent of sweet clear water.　NOAV

Folds of a White Dress/Shaft of Light.　Deborah Keenan.　or the strong hand reaching towards/you, about to make you famous/and pregnant. PoDr

Foliage.　Felicia Dorothea Hemans.　Dear friend! our fresh delight in simplest nature's hues!　OBRV

Foliage of Vision.　James Merrill.　Time and disaster and the limping blood. MoPo; VGW

Folk Song.　*Anonymous.*
　Oh, the rustling, rustling of that autumn night by the/pools!　LiTW
　Spareribs are too much for me.　ShM

Folk-Song.　Louis Untermeyer.　"Oh mother–oh mother–you never can know–/I loved him so!"　HBV 1-2

Folk Songs, 1.　*Anonymous.*　But a sadder, to come to die/Before having loved at all.　LiTW

Folk Tale. P. Mustapaa. And so wildly in love. HW

Folk Tune. Esther Raab. dispenser of dreams,/collector of pain. VWA

Folk Tune. Richard Wilbur. To beat the leisured snarling drill. AmFN

The Folk Who Live in Backward Town. Mary Ann Hoberman. And take their walks across the ceiling. OBCA

Folk Wisdom. Thomas Kinsella. ...to find a jewel/Made of pain in his hands. TwCP

Folklore. Cyril Dabydeen. as we are grounded. BrSi

Folks and Me. Lucile Crites. That folks you like will sure like you. WBLP

Foller de Drinkin' Gou'd. Anonymous. "Foller de drinkin' gou'd." ABF

The Follies. Daniel Mark Epstein. waking up everybody's children. MAYP

Follow, Follow. Thomas Campion. Beg for mercy. EnLoPo

Follow Jesus. Anonymous. Dwell thou deep within me,/Prompt me everywhere. STF

Follow Me. Henry Wadsworth Longfellow. From the centuries that are gone/To the centuries that shall be. PGD

Follow Me 'Ome. Rudyard Kipling. Follow me–follow me 'ome! OAEP

Follow the Gleam. Alfred, Lord Tennyson. After it, follow it,/Follow the Gleam. BBV; GoTF; TreFT

Follow the Leader. Harry Behn. All over the farm on a summer day! SoPo

Follow Your Saint. Thomas Campion. I shall suffice that they were breathed and died for her delight. AAS; AtBAP; EBEV; EIL; EnLoPo; ExPo; ForPo; HAP; InPo; OAEL 1-2; SeCePo; TrGrPo; ViBoPo

Follower. Michael Arvey. to places I cannot follow. AMV-80

Follower. Seamus Heaney. It is my father who keeps stumbling/Behind me, and will not go away. FaBoIP; IPY

Following the Sun. Jascha Kessler. "But/who are you!" AmPC

Following Van Gogh (Avignon, 1982). Marla Puziss. in your hair, at night/in the hotel of the world. PoDr

Follows How Dumbar Wes Desyrd to Be Ane Freir. William Dunbar. And I awoik as wy that wes in weir. OAEP

The Folly of Being Comforted. William Butler Yeats. O heart! O heart! if she'd but turn her head,/You'd know the folly of being comforted. AnIL; AnIL 019; AnIV; BrPo; GBL; GTBS; HeIP; MBW 1-2; VLP

The Folly of Brown. Sir William Schwenck Gilbert. You cannot fancy what a fool/Poor rich uneducated Brown is. InMe

Fond Affection. Anonymous. Or kiss the lips you once betrayed. AS

A Fond Greeting, Hillock There. Laoiseach Mac An Bhaird. I am in sorrow for its slopes,/the fair hill that held my love. NOBI

Fond Youth. Samuel Rogers. Glad to conceal her tears, her blushes there. OBRV

The Font in the Forest. Léonie Adams. Lichens in frond with their dim arms adore. CrMA

La Fontaine de Vaucluse. Marilyn Hacker. ...crevice where/azure striation swirls beyond the stones. FYAP

Fontenoy. Thomas Osborne Davis. With bloody plumes, the Irish stand–the field is fought and/won! HBV 1-2; OnYI

Fontenoy. 1745. Emily Lawless. Home to Corca Bascinn, in the morning light. AnIV

Food. Marchette Chute. Oh, there are many things to chew/While walking down the avenue. BrR

Food. Victor M. Valle. Drink water/and you drink sky FIA

Food and Drink (excerpt). Louis Untermeyer. There are as many tastes as tongues! MoAmPo

The Food Drops Off a Fork. Michael Silverton. I thought you was alone. PoL

Food for Fire, Food for Thought. Robert Duncan. flickers of unlikely heat/at the edge of our belief bud forth. NeAP

The Food of Love. Mary di Michele. in the fluted singing/of a voice like polished silver/gleaming from a heap of trash. CaPN

Food of the North. D. H. Lawrence. not with the fat of the pig. FaBoEE

Food Strike. Michael Hogan. the water/spitting rust flecks like blood/on the cellblock floor/finally came back on. GP

The Fool. Padraic Pearse. O people that I have loved shall we not answer together? OnYI

The Fool by the Roadside. William Butler Yeats. A faithful love, a faithful love. MoVE

The Fool of Love. Anonymous. ...The sun above/Laughed down on me, the fool of love. UnTE

The Fool on the Hill. The Beatles. and the eyes in his head see the world spinning round. PPoe

Fool's Blues. Funny Paper Smith. People, it don't seem like to me/that God takes care of old folks and fools BluL

The Fool's Prayer. Edward Rowland Sill. "Be merciful to me, a fool!" AA; AnNE; BeLS; FaBoBe; GoTF; HBV 1-2; OHFP; OnMSP; PG; PoLf; TreF; TrPWD; WBLP; WGRP

Fool's Song. Thomas Holcroft. While the sun a good post-horse is found,/So merrily we'll run round. NOEC

Fool Song. Cornel Lengyel. An old man in May, a boy in December. GoYe

Foolish Child. Anonymous. Father begat me,/A simpleton./Whirr, whirr! PBA

The Foolish Miller. Anonymous. And said he was very well served in his kind. UnTE

Foolish Proverb. Anonymous. It's break of day, and here I am once more. UnTE

Fools. Glenn Hardin. They say the largest catfish wait. AMV-81

The Fools' Adventure: The Seeker. Lascelles Abercrombie. ...though stall'd/In Somewhere, yet a piece of the Everywhere. WGRP

The Fools of Forty-Nine. Anonymous. That they never in the world would make a pile. CoSo

Fools, They Are the Only Nation. Ben Jonson. Oh, who would not be/He, he, he? EIL; InvP

Foot Race Song. Anonymous. Who is this man running with me,/The shadow of whose hands I see? NU; OBVE

Foot Soldiers. John Banister Tabb. And on the other side, you know,/Are six, seven, eight, nine, ten. HBV 1-2; HBVY; OBAL

Football. Walt Mason. ...The half-back/raised his fractured head, and cried: "I/call this fun!" SD

Football and Rowing–An Eclogue. Alfred Denis Godley. Rowing and football I'll forswear, and join the Volunteers! CenHV

Football Field: Evening. J. A. R. McKellar. The relics of a mystery men forget. LiSp

A Football-Player. Edward Cracroft Lefroy. Sinew and breath and body; it would live. LiSp

Football Song. Sir Walter Scott. With heart and with hand, like our fathers before. SD

Footnote. Anthony Delius. Sent a White politician/A green sprig of simile. PeSA

A Footnote to a Famous Lyric. Louise Imogen Guiney. Love's self outdo, dear Lovelace! hold/The pinnacles of song. AA

A Footnote to a Gray Bird's Pause. James (Olumo) Cunningham. droppings on the rocks, and rain/glides slowly down. JB

Footnote to Enright's "Apocalypse." Martin Bell. What have we bought?/What have we paid for? FaBoMo

Footnote to Feynman. Jonathon V. Post. The stars are made of the same atoms as/the Earth. SUW

Footnote to History. Elizabeth Jane Coatsworth. With a slow judicious hand! SiSoSe

Footnote to "Howl." Allen Ginsberg. Holy the supernatural extra brilliant intelligent kindness of the soul! AmPP; CAPP

Footnote to John ii.4. R. A. K. Mason. and tell me stories and tuck me up at night. AnNZ

Footnote to Tennyson. Gerald Bullett. 'Tis better to have loved and lost/Than ever to have loved and won. FiBHP

Footnote to the Lord's Prayer (excerpt). Kay Smith. for Thine is the Kingdom and the Power and the Glory. Amen. TrCP

Footnotes to "The Autobiography of Bertrand Russell." Mona Van Duyn. would gaze at each other with a wild surmise. HAP

Footpath. Stella Ngatho. Return my mother to me. WPOW

The Footpath Way. Katharine Tynan Hinkson. Come, take the footpath way with me! HBV 1-2

Footpaths Cross in the Rice Field. Lin Ling. Even though birds/Are creatures with wings. PBWP

Footprints. Hamish Brown. Where we set blue footprints,/tomorrow, is grass. PoSH

Footprints on the Glacier. William Stanley Merwin. I hear names leaving the bark/in growing numbers and flying north NoAm

Foots It (parody). D. C. Berry. Teddy follows his feet/Like a sneaker. BXAP

Footsteps. Hazel Hall. I am the burden of an old despair!/Footfall... HBMV

The Footsteps. Paul Valery. Your footfall was my own heart's beat. LiTW

Footsteps of Spring. Hayim Nahman Bialik. With shining tears expel my black despair./A different wind. VWA

Footwear. May Justus. Which now and then she changes/For moccasins of snow. SoPo; YeAr

For a Birthday. Elaine V. Emans. Give you such birthday presents, if I could. BiCB

For a Blind Beggar's Sign. Clemente Biondi. Who sins, ye rich, if He stands starving here? CAW

For a Child. Denis Glover. At Sumner on a Sunday. AnNZ

For a Child Expected. Anne Ridler. May she grow to her right powers/Unperturbed by passion of ours. LiTM; MoVE; NeBP; SeCePo

For a Child Gone to Live in a Commune. William Stafford. Those empty spaces. It has found them. CAPP

For a Child's Drawing. Anton Vogt. Then closes the eyes that dare no longer see/Save hooded, their erratic destiny. AnNZ

For a Christening. Anne Ridler. In His terrible mercy, world without end. MoPo

For a Christening. Vernon Watkins. Shining, being raised, where holy water shone. MoRP

For a College Yearbook. J. V. Cunningham. Ever distant and dark, ever returning. NoAm

For a Coming Extinction. William Stanley Merwin. Tell him/That it is we who are important HaCAP; NNaP

For a Copy of Theocritus. Henry Austin Dobson. Thine was the happier Age of Gold! HBV 1-2

For a Daughter Gone Away. William Stafford. ...one moving voice touching whatever is present/or might be, even what I cannot see when it comes. NPAW; SV

For a Dead Lady. Edwin Arlington Robinson. Of what inexorable cause/ Makes Time so vicious in his reaping. AnFE; AnNE; APA; CMoP; CoBMV; DL; ForPo; FYAP; GoTF; HeIP; HoPM; InvP; LiTA; MAmP; MAPA; MoAB; MoAmPo; NOBA; OxBA; PoEL 1-5; PoRA; TreFT; ViBoPo; WHA

For a Dewdrop. Eleanor Farjeon. But just a drop of dew instead/Swinging on a spider's thread. HBVY

For a Far-Out Friend. Gary Snyder. You'll ever give/Or get. NeAP; PoM

For a Father. Anthony Cronin. He smiles with his father's hesitant smile/ And speaks with his voice. FaBoTw

For a Fountain. Bryan Waller Procter. And thank the great god Pan for all! OBEV; OBVV

For a Friend. Ted Kooser. all highways make me think of you. GOYP

For a Friend. Lyn Lifshin. your face/so close to mine/it chilled me NeAC

For a Friend. David Steingass. ...I wash my hands, and calcium/Cysts tick through my fingerjoints. TW

For a Girl in Love. Florence Hynes Willette. Break them, wear them,/ With the blossoms on your breast? GoBC

For a Good Dog. Arthur Guiterman. We'll cherish still/Our own beloved bow-wow. GDP

For a Homecoming. Julia Randall. ...and the wings unfold that cannot make/Any but natural journeys while they wake. NMM

For a Lady I Know. Countee Cullen. While poor black cherubs rise at seven/To do celestial chores. CDC; GoSl; HeIP; IDB; InPK; NIP; OBAL; PoNe; ShM; TAP

For a Lamb. Richard Eberhart. Say, there's a lamb in the daisies. CMoP; LiTM; MiAP; OBSP

For a Little Girl Mourning Her Favorite Cat. John Greenleaf Whittier. Or caught a rat/Requiescat! PoL

For a Little Lady. Fred Saidy. He watched the lark's flight–/I, the dollar's. InMe

For a Man Who Learned to Swim When He Was Sixty. Diane Wakoski. our enemies/who make us heroes. FAZ

For a Marriage. Erica Jong. & for the first time/wanting each other/only. CTBA

For a Masseuse and Prostitute. Kenneth Rexroth. Every hour there is less of that touch in the world. NNaP

For a Mocking Voice. Eleanor Farjeon. Ha, ha, ha, ha, ha! CH; TiPo

For a Moment. *Anonymous.* May have been a dream. PBWP

For a Mouthy Woman. Countee Cullen. Satan has enough in hell. OBAL; PoBA; ShM

For a Musician. George Wither. Where Angels musicke make,/I may aspire,/When I this life forsake. OBS

For a Nativity. Lisel Mueller. we lose our crosses in the dancing crowd. NePoAm-2

For a Neighbor Girl. Yu Hsuan-chi. Why bother with the boy next door? BoWoP

For a New Home. Rosa Zagnoni Marinoni. Within its arms of lumber and of stone. PoToHe

For a Parting. Keith Sinclair. Together, with more memories than I remember. AnNZ

For a Pessimist. Countee Cullen. While on his face a death's head sat/And waved a bit of crape. ShM

For a Picture Where a Queen Laments over the Tomb of a Slain Knight. Thomas Carew. I'll die thy valour's sacrifice. CaPo

For a Plaque on the Door of an Isolated House. William Stafford. But there are little rooms in your life like/this pause at the door, Someone Here. FAZ

For a Poet. Countee Cullen. I have wrapped my dreams in a silken cloth,/ And laid them away in a box of gold. GoSl; PoNe; TTY

For a Second Marriage. James Merrill. Concentric rings, those many marriages/That life on each live thing bestows. NePoEA

For a Shetland Pony Brood Mare Who Died in Her Barren Year. Maxine W. Kumin. all silken on one side,/all mud on the other one. PH

For a Son's Marriage. Martial (Marcus Valerius Martialis). And may it never seem to him that she is also old. HW

For a Statue of Chaucer at Woodstock. Mark Akenside. To tame the rudeness of his native land. SeCePo

For a' That and a' That. Robert Burns. That man to man the warld o'er,/ Shall brothers be for a' that. AnFE; CABA; CoMu; EnLit; FaBoBe; FaBoPV; FaFP; FaPoR; HBV 1-2; HBVY; LAuP; LiTB; MCCG; OAEL 1-2; OAEP; OHFP; TEP; UnTE; WBLP

For A' That and A' That (parody). *Anonymous.* Who stands erect in self-respect,/And acts the man for a that. BXAP

For A' That and A' That (parody). Shirley Brooks. The man's an ass for a' that. FaBoCo; NOBL; Par

For a Venetian Pastoral by Giorgione. Dante Gabriel Rossetti. Life touching lips with immortality. ViBoPo; VLP

For a Very Old Man, on the Death of His Wife. Jane Cooper. Those windless flags you see,/Alone in the dying glare. NePoEA-2

For a Voice That Is Singing. Aldo Camerino. ...And bore/where harmony, clear joy,/is enough, and nothing more is asked. VWA

For a War Memorial. Gilbert Keith Chesterton. How many men of England died/To prove they were not dead. MMM

For a Wife in Jizzen. Douglas Young. Dern frae aa men/the ferlies ye ha seen. OxBS

For a Wine Festival. Vernon Watkins. Take from the glass that shone/The vintage that remains. OxBTC

For a Winnebago Brave. Joseph Bruchac. or die of a broken heart. CDW

For a Young South Dakota Man. Freya Manfred. I no longer want to meet/people who have swallowed no living light from black soil. TAT

For Adolf Eichmann. Primo Levi. Saw it grow dark around him, the air fill with death. VWA

For Alan Blanchard. John Oliver Simon. closing the doors of the sun. NeAC

For All Blasphemers. Stephen Vincent Benét. And I shall be in Hell. AtBAP; OxBA

For All in Pain. Amy Carmichael. Come near, that even so/They may have peace. TRV

For All Mary Magdalenes. Desanka Maksimovic. for their loves naked/and damned–/for all Mary Magdalenes. WPOW

For all my Grandmothers. Beth Brant. Strong enough/to encompass our lives. STE

For All Sorts and Conditions. Norman Nicholson. Then call their darkness–Thee. EaLo

For All That Ever Has Been Ours. Ziche Landau. For all that ever has been ours.... LiTW

For All Things Black and Beautiful. Conrad Kent Rivers. Africa is in your grave and may all the elements find peace/with you. CNA

For All We Have and Are. Rudyard Kipling. Who dies if England live? FaPoR

For Allan. Robert Frost. But nobody may give a tree/Excepting Santa Claus. PCh

For Allen Ginsberg, Who Cut Off His Beard. Sanford Pinsker. Anything to get me over the shock/Of finally meeting you face to face. AMV-80

For Alva Benson, and for All Those Who have Learned to Speak. Joy Harjo. And the ground spinning beneath us/goes on talking. TWSS

For Amy Lowell. Countee Cullen. And questions Him–if he is able/to reassure her Why. PoA

For an Age of Plastics. Plymouth. Donald Davie. Something to build with, take a chisel to. NePoEA-2

For An Allegorical Dance of Women by Andrea Mantegna. Dante Gabriel Rossetti. The heart's each pulse shall keep the sense/it had/With all, though the mind's labour run to/nought VLP

For an Amorous Lady. Theodore Roethke. You are, in truth, one in a million,/At once mammalian and reptilian. NLV

For an Autograph (excerpt). James Russell Lowell. Not failure, but low aim, is crime. MCCG

For an Autumn Festival (excerpt). John Greenleaf Whittier. The early and the latter rain! PGD

For an Early Retirement. Donald Hall. This fitted him to teach Creative Writing. TW

For an Egyptian Boy, Died c. 700 B.C. Mary Baron. Sacred despite disgust, protective, real. HoAn

For an Emigrant. Randall Jarrell. And cry–"You stranger, you damned stranger!" OxBA

For an Epitaph at Fiesole. Walter Savage Landor. And he had lived enough when he had dried her tear. FaBoEE; OBNC; OBRV

For an Eskimo. Annie Charlotte Dalton. Death-defying/Eatna! CaP

For an Ex-Far East Prisoner of War. Charles Causley. Beat them, like sword and ploughshare, into one. OxBC

For an Obligate Parasite. Alan Dugan. ...who needs/them? Wills. Lovers. You. TW

For an Officer. *Anonymous.* And I therefore/express regret. OBVE

For an Old Friend. Norbert Krapf. ...The poem/is always too much after the fact. AMV-81

For Andy Goodman–Michael Schwerner–and James Chaney. Margaret Walker. To love and live with them again! BPo

For Angela. Zack Gilbert. Whatever your music, Angela/We embrace. We condone/And we evolve. PoBA

For Angus MacLeod. Iain Crichton Smith. The truest work is learning to be human/definitive texts the poorest can afford. OxBS

For Ann Scott-Moncrieff. Edwin Muir. Last summer in Princes Street. GTBS-P

For Anna. Irving Layton. whether you will warm my aging limbs as a lover NeAC

For Anne. Leonard Cohen. But I do compare/Now that she's gone. ELU; FF; PoCh

For Anne Gregory. William Butler Yeats. Could love you for yourself alone/And not your yellow hair. BiP; CMoP; DiPo; DTC; ExPo; FaFP; ForPo; InPo; LiTL; LiTM; LoBV; SeCeV; SOTW

For Anne, Who Doesn't Know. Gail Fox. there will never be/enough crying between us. IHMS

For Annie. Edgar Allan Poe. With the thought of the light/Of the eyes of my Annie. AmP; AP; APA; BLPL; HBV 1-2; LiTA; NePA; NOBA; OBEV; OBVV; OxBA; TreFS

For Any Beachhead. Michael Kennedy Joseph. He "lost his life"? He found his death. AnNZ

For Any Member of the Security Police. Josephine Jacobsen. Shaped otherwise, and fashioned for you only? NePoAm

For Artaud. Michael McClure. But icy light icy dark and green wet leaves/above. NeAP

For Arthur Gregor. Edward Field. and fell in the grass and lay there overpowered. FAZ

For Arvia. Edwin Arlington Robinson. For you, and for the rest who cannot share/Your gold of unrevealed awakenings. BiCB

For Avi Killed in Lebanon. Mark Osaki. which fills the enormity of the sky. BrSi

For Beauty Being the Best of All We Know. Robert Bridges. If from man's greater need beauty redound,/And claim his tears for homage of his peace. VLP

For Beauty, We Thank Thee. John Oxenham. For that Thou bearest all that Thou hast made;/We thank Thee, Lord! PGD

For Bill. Geof Hewitt. So don't be short, Bill,/just because you haven't got much sleep. NeAC

For Bill Hawkins, a Black Militant. William J. Harris. Night, let me be part of you/but in my own dark way. PoBA

For Black Poets Who Think of Suicide. Etheridge Knight. And be buried in the dust of marching feet. BP; CNA; HeIP; PoBA

For Both of Us at Fisk. Sharon Scott. the spirit moves on/from within. JB

For Brother Malcolm. Edward S. Spriggs. till our hands & eyes/have strength to mould/the concrete beneath our feet CAD

For C. Philip Whalen. At least I broke and stole that branch with love. NeAP; VGW

For C. K. D. L. Kelleher. May the Man above/Give him a crown! NeIP

For Cal. James (Olumo) Cunningham. to die in public/or in the rain. JB

For Carole. Diane Burns. It's been ten years/since I missed/my last/rodeo TWSS

For Charlie's Sake. John Williamson Palmer. And saved us twice, for Charlie's sake. HBV 1-2

For Chicle & Justina. Diane Bickston. And women, must they wear each other's lies/against familiar breasts? LFAC

For Christmas. Dorothy Aldis. And I want an Elephant/Can sit DOWN behind. ChBR

For Christmas. Rachel Field. And not a child but keeps some trace/Of Christmas secrets in his face. ChBR

For Christmas Day. Eleanor Farjeon. And not till after feast. ChBR

For Christmas-Day. Charles Wesley. Formed in each believing heart. CEP

For City Spring. Stephen Vincent Benét. Yet still we praise that crocus head,/April! BXAP; NLV; PoPl

For Colored Girls Who Have Considered Suicide...(excerpt). Ntozake Shange. she placed the rose behind her ear/& cried herself to sleep. BoWoP

For Communion with God (excerpt). Thomas Shepherd. I find no pleasure here below,/When thou dost veil thy Face. TrPWD

For Cora Lightbody, R.N. John Glassco. I sink my shaft in auriferous mud. PoA

For Dan Berrigan. Etheridge Knight. Maybe you see it all, whiteman, or maybe you blind. NeAC

For Daphne at Lone Lake. John Haines. The cry of the heron, suddenly stilled/as it flies from the landing/over this cold lake at evening. NPAW

For David Shapiro. David Lehman. ...collected prayers–what you once believed. PoA

For Decoration Day: 1861-1865. Rupert Hughes. The peaceful barracks where their bodies/sleep. AA

For Decoration Day: 1898-1899. Rupert Hughes. As the Yankee troops–with glory armed/and shod–/In Grand Review swing past the throne of/ God. AA

For Deep Deer-Copse Beneath Mount Han. Anonymous. in his mode is no crookedness. OBVE

For Deeper Life. Katharine Lee Bates. Deepen our spirits for a love like Thine. TrPWD

For deLawd. Lucille Clifton. just pushing CNA; PoBA; TAP; TwCP

For Delphine. James Simmons. A pair of eyes open and stare back. PoL

For Don Allen. Gary Snyder. ..we don't really/know them; Coyote, as mentioned before. PoA

For Doreen. Donald Davie. And the gardens that pock her face. NMP·

For Dr. and Mrs. Dresser. Margaret Avison. can bid us, in turn, o gentle Saviour:/"take, eat–/live'. PeCV

For Drum Hadley. Harold Littlebird. oh thank you Drum/for bringing us home VoR

For E.C.J. Emmett Jarrett. Bob white! Peas ripe! NeAC

For E.J.P. Leonard Cohen. Something forgets us perfectly NoAm; NoP

For E. McC. Ezra Pound. Behold the shield; He shall not take thee all. LiSp; SD

For Each of You. Audre Lorde. and your mother was/a princess/in darkness. CNA

For Eager Lovers. Genevieve Taggard. I do not want to walk that way again. AnAmPo

For Edward Hicks. David Helwig. the peaceable kingdom/made by your hands. NOBC

For Edwin R. Embree. Owen Dodson. Because these men of strength are with us. CNA

For Eleanor and Bill Monahan. William Carlos Williams. O clemens! O pia! O dolcis!/Maria! VGW

For Elizabeth Bishop. Sandra McPherson. I take the globe and roll it away: where/On it now is someone like you? GeTw; MAYP

For Elizabeth Madox Roberts. Janet Lewis. Tears, and my earliest love, Elizabeth, and changeless art. QFR

For Emily (Dickinson). Maureen Owen. I knew you when you/still had hair! APU

For England, in Grateful Appreciation (excerpt). Anton Vogt. But the most remarkable thing about England,/Was that the bread was white. AnNZ

For Eros II. Audrey Wurdemann. When by the eager wick a spark is set. MoLP

For Esther. Stanley Plumly. ...what you meant/to tell me, out of the body, out of the body travel. LCAP

For Euse, Ayi Kwei & Gwen Brooks. Keorapetse Kgositsile. On to the darkness the eye caresses/In us and into us and ours. PoBA

For Ever, Fortune, Wilt Thou Prove. James (1700-48) Thomson. All other blessings I resign/Make but the dear Amanda mine. CBEP; GTBS; GTBS-P

For-Ever Morning. Laura Riding. Oh, just as the chandler sat down to die. LiTA

For Every Day. Frances Ridley Havergal.
      And wing my words that they may reach/The hidden depths of many a heart. BLRP
      I may stretch out a loving hand/To wrestlers with the troubled sea. BLRP
      In kindling thought and glowing word,/Thy love to tell, Thy praise to show. BLRP
      Thy erring children lost and lone. BLRP
      Thy hungering ones with manna sweet. BLRP
      Thy rest, Thy joy, Thy glory share! BLRP
      A word in season, as from Thee,/To weary ones in needful hour. BLRP

For Every Evil under the Sun. Anonymous. If there be none, never mind it. EvOK; HBV 1-2; HBVY; OxNR

For Every Last Batch When the Next One Comes Along. James Dickey. Would you ever believe the size of his you-know-what! GP

For Every Man. Max Isaac Reich. Thine openings and shuttings/Are always right. STF

For Everything Give Thanks. Helen Isabella Tupper. O Lord, our hearts we lift to thee./For everything give thanks! GoTF; TreFT

For Exmoor. Jean Ingelow. –Buy my cherries, whiteheart, blackheart, golden girls, O/buy! OBEV; OBVV

For Fear. Robert Creeley. to drive again/bent nail/into old hurt? NoAm

For February Twelfth. Muriel M. Gessner. The greatness of his life he gave/To all the world. YeAr

For Forgiveness. John Donne. I fear no more. WGRP

For Fran. Philip Levine. Out of whatever we have been/We will make something for the dark. FF; PoCh; SM

For Freckle-Faced Gerald. Etheridge Knight. who now hover above his track/and at night light upon his back. BPo; LFAC; NeAC

For Gabriel. Laya Firestone. To welcome each and every message/With your hand. VWA

For George Santayana. Robert Lowell. refined by bile as yellow as a lump of gold. CMoP; VGW

For God While Sleeping. Anne Sexton. Now you roll/in your sleep, seasick/on your own breathing, poor old convict. CABA; NePoEA-2

For My Daughter. Weldon Kees. I have no daughter. I desire none. CoAP; SM

For My Daughter. Ronald Koertge. I say yes but it will take a long time. GP; Str

For My Daughter. Ed Ochester. I stand with fists clenched, as rain/carries the sounds of your breathing away. Str

For My Father. Rachel Field. He'd find less changed than his own daughter. InMe

For My Father. Paul Potts. Else, how sir, did you come to be American? FaBoTw

For My Father on His Birthday. Greg Kuzma. To be the things we are. Str

For My Father: Two Poems. David Kherdian.
brought on by my English. GP
...in these/cafes were contained the suffering and/shattered hopes of my orphaned people. GP

For My Funeral. Alfred Edward Housman. Thy creature that thou madest/And wilt cast forth no more. CMoP; TrPWD; ViBoPo

For My Grandfather. Richard Robbins. ...where the twin still/turns your colors, year after yellow year. AMV-81

For My Grandfather. Francis Webb. Rather than time upon my wrist I wear/The dial, the four quarters of your death. BoAV

For My Grandmother. Countee Cullen. She held it as her dying creed/That she would grow again. CDC; GoSl; VGW

For My Grandmother, Bridget Halpin. Michael Hartnett. birches falling down the hillside. BIrV; CIP

For My Husband. Ellen Bryant Voigt. whose sad head/looms over any choice you make? NoP

For My Lover, Returning to His Wife. Anne Sexton. As for me, I am a watercolor./I wash off. HaCAP; IHMS; NMM; UnPo

For My Mother. Louise Gluck. gauze flutterings of vegetation. GeTw; UnPo

For My Mother. June Jordan. a highly inflammable/balloon eclipsed by seminal/and nubile/loving. BoWoP; NMM

For My Mother. Iain Crichton Smith. most loved though most bare,/at the end of a rich season. OxBS

For My Mother, Feeling Useless. Paula Rankin. My husband and children saw me leaving. MAYP

For My Mother: Genevieve Jules Creeley. Robert Creeley. I am here,/and will follow. PoM

For My Newborn Son. Sydney Goodsir Smith. Ma sleepan reid Robin. ACV

For My Own Monument. Matthew Prior. He cares not–yet prithee be kind to his fame. CEP; EiCP; HBV 1-2; LoBV; OBEC; OBEV

For My People. Wendy Rose. losing ourselves/finding CDW

For My People. Margaret Walker. Let a race of men now rise and/take control! AmNP; BALP; CNA; IDB; MoRP; PoBA; PoNe

For My Sister's Sake. Hitomaro. With the dew of the lower boughs! AWP

For My Son. John Frederick Nims. (O reborn poplars) than in Michigan earth. MiAP

For My Son, Born during an Ice Storm. David Jauss. That day, even the lilacs/Were borne down/By the diamonds on their backs. Str

For My Son Noah, Ten Years Old. Robert Bly. And slowly the kind man comes closer, loses his rage,/sits down at table. InPS

For My Son on the Highways of His Mind. Maxine W. Kumin. on the highways of your mind. MAT

For My Students, Returning to College. John Williams. Or know what we can never act,/Or what we cannot say. NePoAm-2

For My Torturer, Lieutenant D–. Leila Djabali. Did you run your fingers through your kids' hair? WPOW

For My Twenty-Fifth Birthday in Nineteen Forty-One. John Ciardi. Acrobat, scavenger, mariner–and me. WaP

For My Unborn & Wretched Children. A. B. Spellman. ...if/want decides, let it be me. CNA; PoBA

For My Wife. Steven Lautermilch. how you shine. AMV-80

For My Wife. Julian Symons. That, where so much is doubtful, certainly is good. NeBP; WaP

For Myself. J. A. Hines. Give me the inspiration/of war mongers/and throw their causes/to the orphans. LFAC

For Natalya Correia. Irving Layton. as if to poke chrysolites from their hiding place NeAC

For Nicholas, Born in September. Tod Perry. ...This time I feel/a wind I never knew blow through my bones. NYBP

For Nijinsky's Tomb. Frances Cornford. Their perfect tribute to Perfection paid. UnS

For No Clear Reason. Robert Creeley. grass, trees, and flower-/ing season, for no clear reason. VGW

For No Good Reason. Peter Redgrove. Across the carpets of my home, my own home. NMP

For No One. Paul and John Lennon McCartney. A love that should have lasted years. WTO

For Nothing. Andres Castro Rios. Only remember these words: we/are fucked. InW

For Nothing. Gary Snyder. Snow-trickles, feldspar, dirt. NNaP

For Now. William Stanley Merwin. Between death's republic and his kingdom CoPo; NaP

For Once, Then, Something. Robert Frost. Truth? A pebble of quartz? For once, then, something. AP; ForPo; NoAm; NOBA

For One Lately Bereft. Margaret E. Bruner. And happiness will come to you again. PoToHe

For One Moment. David Ignatow. your hair grey, your legs weakened/from long standing. NNaP

For One Who Died Young. H. R. Hays. We speak to him and he answers. EAS

For One Who Is Serene. Margaret E. Bruner. With peace, which lends me strength and fortitude. PoToHe

For one who says he feels. Petra von Morstein. ...as/I've done,/with a steady sound BoWoP

For One Who Would Not Take His Life in His Hands. Delmore Schwartz. Through hate we come to love,/No other means is known. NAMP

For Our Lady. Sonia Sanchez. ain't no tellen/where the jazz of yo/songs/wud have led us. IHMS

For Our Lady of the Rocks by Leonardo da Vinci. Dante Gabriel Rossetti. Whose peace abides in the dark avenue/Amid the bitterness of things occult. VLP

For Our Sakes. Oscar Wilde. That when we stabbed Thy heart it was our own real hearts we/slew. PGD

For Our Soldiers Who Fell in Russia. Franco Fortini. Blessed are those who did not pray. VWA

For Paddy Mac. Padraic Fallon. It is only the genuflection that survives. CIP

For Patrick, Aetat: LXX. Sir John Betjeman. Pray go on living to a hundred yet! NAs

For Paul Laurence Dunbar. Countee Cullen. In jest, to hide a heart that bled. BALP; CDC; GoSl

For Perfect Peace. Charles Wesley. And all who know that love of Thine,/The joy of angels know. BePJ

For Peter. Lee Gerlach. Love's long sustaining, and wept impatience here. HoAn

For Pity, Pretty Eyes, Surcease. Thomas Lodge. But unto you pertains the loss. EIL

For Poets. Al Young. Dont forget to fly CNA; DFF; PoBA; RFM

For Posterity. Kathleen Raine. Waiting for tea-time, and shadows growing longer. NeBP

For Prodigal Read Generous. Edward Estlin Cummings. (and close your eyes) NoAm

For Randie. Geof Hewitt. The cockeyed gateman wants to let me know/he's been there too. NeAC

For Randolph Bourne. James Oppenheim. Weaving a wreath of triumph/For Randolph Bourne. AnAmPo

For Real. Jayne Cortez. I confess that this beautiful Nigguh is ready. PoBA

For Refugio Talamante. Ed Ochester. This I have learned/from my daughter. LTB

For Rhoda. Delmore Schwartz. Time is the fire in which we burn. MoAB; MoAmPo; OxBA

For Richard Chase. Jim Wayne Miller. He listens to the shell and says:/"The freeway?" GOYP

For Righteousness' Sake. John Greenleaf Whittier. Ye have the future grand and great,/The safe appeal of Truth to Time! AmePo; PoEL 1-5

For Robert Frost. Galway Kinnell. Down hills floating by heart on the bulldozed land. NOBA; PP; VGW

For Rosa Yen, Who Lived Here. Greg Pape. where you lived Rosa. AmPA

For Ruggiero and Angelica by Ingres. Dante Gabriel Rossetti. Again a woman in her nakedness. VLP

For Sale. Anonymous. For it's a darn good layout/For the shape it's in. BPAW

For Sale. Robert Lowell. as if she had stayed on a train/one stop past her destination. ConAP

For Sale. Shel Silverstein. This crying and spying young sister for sale? CTBA

For Sale, a Horse. Charles Edward Taylor. He'll aid your reading of Horatius. AA

For Sale or Rent. Anonymous. They had each other–God was Good! PoToHe

For Sammy Younge. Charlie Cobb. can only find/the/alley PoBA

For Sapphires. Carolyn M. Rodgers. i wonder what lady does daddy know? CNA

For Saundra. Nikki Giovanni. perhaps these are not poetic/times/at all BPo; TTY

For Scholars and Pupils. George Wither. But let my chief endeavours be,/To know my self, thy will, and Thee. OxBChV

For Sergeant Fetta. Ed Sanders. We enter the FLOOD ANYP

For shamefast harm of great and hateful need. Sir Thomas Wyatt. He that had hid the gold and found it not,/Of that he found he shaped his neck a knot. FCP

For Sheridan. Robert Lowell. that what we intended and failed/could never have happened–/and must be done better. HaCAP

For Simone Weil. Sister M. Therese. If you stopped short of thresholds, did it matter,/If Love leaned down and lifted you across? MoRP

For Sleep, or Death. Ruth Pitter. That when I rise again/I may shine bright,/As the sky after rain,/Day after night. TrPWD

For Snow. Eleanor Farjeon. The falling falling Snow? CH

For Soldiers. Humfrey [(or Humphrey)] Gifford. If we live well, in heaven with Christ our souls shall dwell. CH; ElL

For Some Poets. Mae Jackson. with you Marvin X/poet with you please? BOLo; PoBA

For Sore Eyes. *Anonymous.* I shall lese my right arm! OxBM

For Spring. D. G. Jones. evening/cannot conceal the stark/nudity of trees. NOBC

For St. Bartholomew's Eve. Malcolm Cowley. like ashes in the winds of God. NAMP

For Steph. Wendy Rose. blowing kisses from an/increasing distance. CDW

For Stephen. Christopher Brookhouse. When I was seventeen/I didn't look back either. AMV-80

For Stephen Dixon. Zack Gilbert. How lovely the head/Made gourd. PoBA

For Stephen Drawing Birds. Pattiann Rogers. With his stern golden eye over the entire length of your quilt. MAYP

For Steve. Earle Birney. And blood as proud as yours has built a prouder world. WaP

For Strength. Rabindranath Tagore. And give me strength to surrender my strength to thy will with love. MoRP

For Sue. Phil Hey. and took if off at night so you could see the stars. PPJ

For Summer's Here. Ratcliffe Barnett. The saups are on the heather and the white birds on the sea! PoSH

For That He Looked Not Upon Her. George Gascoigne. Because your blazing eyes my bale have bred. ElL; NoP

For the Altarpiece of the Roseau Valley Church, Saint Lucia. Derek Walcott. looking in at the windows/the real faces of angels. NoP

For the Anniversary of My Death. William Stanley Merwin. And bowing not knowing to what CAPP; CoAP; HaCAP; InPK; NaP; NOBA

For the Baptist. William, of Hawthornden Drummond. Only the echoes, which he made relent,/Rung from their marble caves, "Repent, repent!" BSV; GoTS; HBV 1-2; LoBV; OBS; OxBoCh

For the Barbers. Joel Oppenheimer. oh/professionals what we/should fear. CoPo

For the Bicentenary of Isaac Watts. Norman Nicholson. And halt and hobbled dragged the cars. EaLo

For the Book of Love. Jules Laforgue. Men, be correct! And women, purr and smirk! AWP; ErPo; LiTW

For the Briar Rose. William Morris. And smite this sleeping world awake. NOBV

For the Candle Light. Angelina Weld Grimke. A daisy dead and dry. BlSi; CDC; PoNe

For the Children. Thomas Love Peacock. and dream visions of wa-na-bo-zho/thanking the Great One. VoR

For the Children. Gary Snyder. stay together/learn the flowers/go light. NoP

For the Children or the Grown-Ups? *Anonymous.* The children don't know it, and Santa won't tell. OBCP

For the Coming Year. Peter Everwine. They will sing softly to each other/softly OFD

For the Company Underground. Francis MacNamara. Even then, damn me if I'd work a day/For the Company underground./Nor over ground. NOAV

For the Conjunction of Two Planets. Adrienne Rich. We see the things we long to see/In fiery iconography? ImOP

For the Courtesan Ch'ing Lin. Wu Tsao. My dear, let me buy a red painted boat/And carry you away. WPOW

For the Cultural Campaign. Chimedin Jigmed. Lest we should neglect/But one of these fine things. WTO

For the Death of Vince Lombardi. James Dickey. You're going forever, Vince. LiSp

For the Depressed. Julian Symons. The depressed who are also the defeated. WaP

For the Earth God. *Anonymous.* It is the day of trouble. EaLo

For the Eating of Swine. Rodney Jones. ...raising you/on my fork as all the dead shall be risen? MAYP

For the Eightieth Birthday of a Great Singer. Edward Shanks. And now to us for evermore/The essence of your eighty years. UnS

For the El Paso Weather Bureau. Peter Wild. it never touched down. MAT

For the ERA Crusaders. X. J. Kennedy. a raided crapgame scrambling for its cash. SOTS

For the Fallen. Laurence Binyon. To the end, to the end, they remain. AnFE; NOBE; OBEV; OBWP; OxBTC; ViBoPo

For the Family of Cuchonnacht O Dalaigh. Daibhi O Bruadair. and their sons without one syllable of their secret treasure. NOBI

For the Field. Eric Chock. ...For a minute, she shuts her eyes. BrSi

For the Fly-Leaf of a School-Book. Norman Cameron. And split the last atom/And come unto Me. OxBS

For the Fourth Birthday of My Daughter. George Barker. all for Raffaella/Raffaella Flora. NAs

For the Gifts of the Spirit. Edward Rowland Sill. Thy peace, O God, send down! TrPWD

For the Girls 'Cause They Know. Harold Littlebird. good night my children VoR

For the Goddess Too Well Known. Elsa Gidlow. (For what was done there/I ask no man pardon.) PeHV

For the Grave of Daniel Boone. William Stafford. Here on his grave I put it down. NoP; PoPl

For the Hern and Duck. *Anonymous.* Then long too late we falconers cry hey lo! NCEP; PBBP

For the Holy Family by Michelangelo. Dante Gabriel Rossetti. The Seed o' the woman bruise the serpent's head. GoBC

For the Lady Olivia Porter; a Present upon a New-years Day. Sir William Davenant. Thus Poets like to Kings (by trust deceiv'd)/Give oftner what is heard of, than receiv'd. JCP; MeLP; MePo; OBS

For the Last Wolverine. James Dickey. Lord, let me die but not die/Out. LiSp

For the Lord's Day Evening. Isaac Watts. I may lie down, and wake with God. OxBChV

For the Lost Generation. Galway Kinnell. No generation was so gay as the lost. NePoAm; PPON

For the Magdalene. William, of Hawthornden Drummond. His tear-wet feet still drying with her hair. AtBAP; LoBV; PoEL 1-5

For the Man Who Stole a Rose. Harley Elliott. a touch of wonder/rising in your skull. FAZ

For the Market. Jane Mayhall. to sell to exploiters, and the restless rich. TAP

For the Marriage of Faustus and Helen. Hart Crane. Outpacing bargain, vocable and prayer. AP; FaBoMo; LiTM; NePA; NoAm; NOBA; PAI

For the Marsh's Birthday. James Wright. My Irish cockatoo. NYBP

For the Master's Use. *Anonymous.* And some day He may use me/To water His flowers again. BLRP

For the Minority. Robert Peterson. Even so, perhaps we no longer/belong here. NeAC

For the New Railway Station in Rome. Richard Wilbur. What does it say over the door of Heaven/But homo fecit? NePoEA

For the New Union Dead in Alabama. Edward Dorn. cast us back/into isolation PoM

For the New Year. Robert Creeley. Being unsure, there is the fate/of doing nothing right. NaP

For the New Year. Norman Nicholson. Where through my dormer bay/Drizzles the Milky Way. NeBP

For the Night-Mare. *Anonymous.* Theras Saint Jeorge y-named was,/St. Jeorge. St. Jeorge. St. Jeorge. OxBM

For the Nightly Ascent of the Hunter Orion over a Forest Clearing. James Dickey. In his fabulous, rigid, eternal/Unlooked-for role. TwCP

For the Noun C. BL. Parker Tyler. How far can the noun expand, lacking the lust of the verb. PoA

For the One Who Would Take Man's Life in His Hands. Delmore Schwartz. The infinite task of the human heart. LiTA; LiTM; MiAP; MoAB; MoAmPo; MoVE; NePA; NoAm; VGW; WaP

For the Opening of the Hunting Season. Morris Bishop. Blood streaks his shimmering beauty; in his eyes/Lingers incredulous and shocked surprise. BoAnP

For the Peace of Jerusalem. Charles Wesley. Present us sanctified to God,/And perfected in love below. BePJ

For the Poet Who Said Poets Are Struck by Lightning Only... Peter Klappert. ...(Though each upset/makes me considerably more/concrete than I was before.) NLV

For the Princess Hello. David Shapiro. In its turn will be re-painted. ANYP

For the Queen Mother. Sir John Betjeman. And God Bless the Duke of York/Who chose you as his bride. NAs

For the Rain It Raineth Every Day. Robert Graves. How could that comfort you? NYBP

For the Rebuilding of a House. Wendell Berry. I build the place of my leaving/that the dark may come clean. EyDe

For the Record. Jr, Blount Roy. And leaves the blinking world to Sleep. OBAL

For the Running of the New York City Marathon. James Dickey. All winning, one after one. NYP

For the Sake O' Somebody. Robert Burns. For the sake o' Somebody! AtBAP

For the Sexes: The Gates of Paradise. William Blake. The lost traveller's dream under the hill. LiTB; NoP; PoEL 1-5

For the Sin–. *Anonymous.* ...stoning, burning,/beheading, and strangling. TrJP

For the Sisters of the Hotel Dieu. Abraham Moses Klein. be thanked, O plumage of paradise, be praised. SoSe; WHW

For the Sleepwalkers. Edward Hirsch. and wake up to ourselves, nourished and surprised. FYAP; MAYP

For the Stranger. Carolyn Forche. We will give it to each other. MAYP

For the Student Strikers. Richard Wilbur. And the guardsman's son. GLGT; OxBC

For the Sun Declined. Yitzhak Lamdan. Into the web of being, both radiant and/somber. TrJP

For The Time Being. W. H. Auden.

And at your marriage all its occasions shall dance for joy. AnFE; OAEP; SBVL

And the deadly sins/May be bought in tins,/With instructions on the label. TRV

Bringing the child his body and his mind. PCh

God will cheat no one, not even the world of its triumph. MoAB; OAEL 1-2

Great is Caesar: God must be with Him. LiTM; NePA; SeCeV

We who must die demand a miracle. OAEP

For the Truth. Edward S. Spriggs. in the tea rooms of our revolution. BP

For the Union Dead. Robert Lowell. a savage servility/slides by on grease. AmPP; CoAP; FaBoPV; FYAP; HaCAP; HAP; HeIP; InPS; LCAP; LiTM; MP; NaP; NMP; NoAm; NOBA; NoP; OBWP; PAI; PPoe; PPP; SCV; TwCP; UnPo

For the West. Gary Snyder. all those years. NaP

For the Wine of Circe. Dante Gabriel Rossetti. Where the dishevelled seaweed hates the sea. ATP; VLP

For the Word is Flesh. Stanley Jasspon Kunitz. Man enters hell without a golden bough. AnAmPo; VGW

For the Yiddish Singers in the Lakewood Hotels of My Childhood. Harvey Shapiro. These lights flung like farfel./These golden girls. VWA

For the Young Who Want To. Marge Piercy. ...You have to/like it better than being loved. Psk

For Thee, O Dear Dear Country! John Mason Neale. FOR EVER AND FOR EVER/ARE CLAD IN ROBES OF WHITE! VLP

For Them. Michael Brownstein. Primary among which will be the overwhelming need for a nice/hot drink/And a fire, and a friend. APU

For Them. Eleanor Farjeon. Oh please to give a little glee/To them that go without. ChBR

For Them All. John Hall Wheelock. There alone, at last, I rest. HBMV

....For They Shall See God. Luci Shaw. ...Handling/his word we feel his flesh, his bones, and hear/his voice saying our early-morning name TrCP

For This, the Tide. Val Vallis. Enough that the touch of the shell/Be warm to my hand. BoAV

For Thomas Hardy. Jane Cooper. While over the animal sea my first-drawn sob/Straightened to share your dawn. AmPC

For Those Who Always Fear the Worst. *Anonymous.* Suppose your mother/Was a bullfrog's brother. NLV

For Those Who Died. Thomas Curtis Clark. How crowded is the heavenly House of Light/With those who marched–for us into the night.! PGD

For Those Who Fail. Joaquin Miller. Lo, he is a twin brother of mine. PoToHe

For Though the Caves Were Rabbited. Henry David Thoreau. For every man an idiot was,/And every house a folly. OBSP; PoEL 1-5

For Three Swift Days. Gennady Trifonov. And keep the candle burning. PeHV

For Tinkers Who Travel on Foot. Margaret Avison. He consented, himself, to/the finality of/an event. NoAm

For to Admire. Rudyard Kipling. But I can't drop it if I tried! MoBrPo

For to love her for her looks lovely. Sir Thomas Wyatt. And perils appear too abundantly/For to love her. FCP

For Tom Numkena, Hopi/Spokane. Harold Littlebird. with you and your people./Hau! Hau! Hau! VoR

For Tony, Dougal, Mick, Bugs, Nick et al. Dave Bathgate. but there is no sting in death,/no sting for you. PoSH

For Travelers Going Sidereal. Robert Frost. But on Venus it must be venereal. OBAL

For Tu Fu. Feng Chih. Their crowns and purples in this light/Are shoddy when compared with yours. LiTW

For Two Girls Setting out in Life. Peter Viereck. For heaven and hell are childhood playmates still. MiAP

For Under the Volcano. Malcolm Lowry. ″A corpse should be transported by express,' said the Consul/mysteriously, waking up suddenly. NOBC

For Us No Night Can Be Happier. Nicolaus Zinzendorf. That the poor Babe in homely rags and stable/Is the Lord God. AH

For Vicki at Seven. Sydney King Russell. The answers that/I wish I knew! BiCB

For Victor Jara. Miller Williams. Awful and awful. Good friend. You have embarrassed our/hearts. SM

For Walter Lowenfels. Wendy Rose. the lamp post seems tuned to your key. CDW

For Want I Will in Woe I Plain. Sir Thomas Wyatt. Which lacketh will to change his place. SiPS

For Want of a Nail. *Anonymous.* And all for the want/Of a horse shoe nail. FaBoBe; HBV 1-2; OxNR

For We Are All Madwomen. Barbara Sweeney. held together by/something sweet in the dark. AMV-81

For We Are Thy People. *Anonymous.* We are thine acknowledged people,/thou our acknowledged Lord. TrJP

For What As Easy. W. H. Auden. About heart,/By heart, for heart. NoP

For Whitman. Diane Wakoski. Love being/the unnamed/the unnameable. SUW

For Whom, Pyrrha? Horace. My dank and dropping weeds/To the stern God of Sea. LiTW

For Whom the Bell Tolls. John Donne. It tolls for thee. PoLf; TRV

″For Whom the Bell Tolls″. Gavin Ewart. To cram a lifetime into seven days. WaP

For William Carlos Williams. Galway Kinnell. Drained spittle from his pipe, then scrammed. SM

For William Edward Burghardt Du Bois on His Eightieth Birthday. Bette Darcie Latimer. and the dread beauty of living/crushed us into reverence. PoBA; PoNe

For Wilma. Don Johnson. through rafters,/roof, belfry/and beyond. GOYP

For Windows. Robert Grenier. yet fundamentally/diamond-backed. APU

For Witches. Susan Sutheim. tomorrow/perhaps/i will begin/to find/you. NMM

For X. Louis MacNeice. The power of trains advancing/Further, advancing further. BoLoP; EnLoPo

For Years. Ralph J. Mills, Jr. a tree outside heavy with snow. AMV-80

For You. Ted Berrigan. glad to find release in heaven's care. ANYP

For You. Carl Sandburg. Keepers of the lean clean breeds. MoAmPo; MoRP

For You, Falling Asleep after a Quarrel. Diane Middlebrook. Opening it like the sky, our happiness. AMV-81

For You I Have Emptied the Meaning. Louis Zukofsky. Its trunk and silk mesh of kirtle showed evening. NoAm

For You, My Son. Horace Gregory. Farewell, my brother/Comrade, son. MoAmPo

For You, O Democracy. Walt Whitman. For you, for you I am trilling these songs. TrGrPo

For Your Inferiority Complex. David O'Rourke. her tall boyfriend/with the fast car/and paul newman smile/is no competition AMV-81

For Zbigniew Herbert, Summer, 1971, Los Angeles. Larry Levis. And snow collects in the blind eyes of statues. FYAP; LCAP

For Zorro. Diane Bickston. suffering to find a world that matches/the freedom trapped inside our souls. LFAC

The Foray of Con O'Donnell, A.D. 1495. Denis Florence MacCarthy. Take back, MacJohn, thy matchless hound. OnYI

Forbearance. Ralph Waldo Emerson O, be my friend, and teach me to be thine! AA; AnNE; GN; GoTF; HBV 1-2; HBVY; LaNeLa; LiTA; MCCG; TAP; TreFT; TrGrPo; ViBoPo; WGRP

Forbearance. Della Adams Leitner. And in forbearance love will prove/There is no force so strong. STF

The Forbidden. Phyllis Haring. But my head's a cracking seed which will not grow. PeSA

Forbidden Fruit. Emily Dickinson.

The pod that Duty locks! AnNE

There Paradise is found! AnNE

The Forbidden Lure. Fannie Stearns Davis. By bed and board stands Duty/To snatch my dreams from me! HBV 1-2

Force. *Anonymous.* Since then they've called him Sunny Jim. FaBoUs

Force. Nicolai M. Minsky. And play the cosmic game with idle laughter. LiTW

Force. Edward Rowland Sill. There was never winter/But brought the spring. AA

Force. Derek Walcott. what I will not understand/is the beast who writes this/and claims the centre of life. OxBC

The Force of Love. Samuel Jones. Old Night and Death frail men appal,/Without dismaying you at all. NOEC

The Force That through the Green Fuse Drives the Flower. Dylan Thomas. How at my sheet goes the same crooked worm. ATP; BiP; BLPL; CABA; CMoP; CoBMV; DiPo; EBEV; ExPo; FaBoMo; ImOP; InPo; InPS; LiTB;

The Fossils.   Galway Kinnell.   Over the least fossil/day breaks in gold, frankincense, and/myrrh.   NYBP

Fossils.   James Stephens.   And then she laughed.   OnYI

Fossils.   Arthur Stewart.   with a three- or four-chambered heart/that still sighs with your ear held close.   SUW

Foul Water.   Mordecai Temkin.   I cry out to You/that You should bind them for me,/my Lord.   VWA

Found.   Carol Muske.   and stood calling back/across the water   AmPA

Found.   Sarah Taylor Shatford.   But Shakespeare knows it will be met.) W.S. In spirit (Through S.S.).   PeD

Found in a Storm.   William Stafford.   meanings in search of a world. RFM

Foundation of Faith.   John Drinkwater.   And shall by law deliver us. MoRP

Foundations.   Henry Van Dyke.   God is God forevermore.   TRV

Founder's Day.   Robert Bridges.   He biddeth a prayer to bless his youth/ With Truth, and Purity, mother of Truth.   OBVV

The Foundered Tram.   Harold Monro.   Element to element.   BrPo

The Founders of Ohio.   William Henry Venable.   Behold where monumental States/Immortalize their lives sublime!   MC; PAH

The Fountain.   Donald Davie.   Though that was not what Berkeley meant at all.   GTBS-P; OxBTC

Fountain.   Elizabeth Jennings.   But drawing the water down to the deepest wonder.   BoC; PoCh

The Fountain.   Pavlos Liasides.   come for the cool waters and thirsty men. AMV-80

The Fountain.   James Russell Lowell.   Fresh, changeful, constant,/Upward, like thee!   OBCA

The Fountain.   King of Seville, Mu'tamid.   Hath steel somewhat advantage over water.   AWP

The Fountain.   A. J. M. Smith.   The cold, immortal ghost of day.   CaP

The Fountain.   William Wordsworth.   And the bewilder'd chimes.   GTBS; GTBS-P; OBRV; SeCePo

A Fountain, a Bottle, a Donkey's Ears and Some Books.   Robert Frost.   In time she would be rid of all her books.   VGW

The Fountain at the Tomb.   Nicias.   Which Simus here hath set/His buried child to mourn.   AWP

The Fountain in the Park.   Ed Haley.   I never shall forget that lovely afternoon,/When I met her at the fountain in the park.   FSN

The Fountain of Tears.   Arthur William Edgar O'Shaughnessy.   May He find a place for the tears!   OBVV

Fountain of Tears, River of Grief.   Christine de Pisan.   ...I barely can right myself/fountain of tears, river of grief.   WPOW

The Fountain of Youth.   Hezekiah Butterworth.   His soul had gone forth to discover/The beautiful Fountain of Youth.   PAH

The Fountains.   W. R. Rodgers.   ...like one who at a play/Finds himself all alone, and will not stay.   MoVE; PoL

Fountains.   Osbert Sitwell.   ...Close now your golden wings!   MoBrPo

Fountains.   Sacheverell Sitwell.   Because she will not heed him.   MoBrPo

The Founts of Song.   Fiona Macleod.   In these dumb solitudes.   WGRP

Four.   Elise Gibbs.   And I wish I could stop the clock.   BiCB

The Four.   Geoffrey Grigson.   An image of the dead.   WaP

The Four Ages of Man.   William Butler Yeats.   At stoke of midnight God shall win.   MoRP; TrCP

Four Anacreontic Poems, 1.   Edmund Spenser.   But when he saw me stung and cry,/He tooke his wings and away did fly.   AAS

Four Anacreontic Poems, 2.   Edmund Spenser.   With that love wounded my loves hart,/But Diane beasts with Cupids dart.   AAS

Four Anacreontic Poems, 3.   Edmund Spenser.   Then never blush Cupid (quoth I)/For many have err'd in this beauty.   AAS

Four Anacreontic Poems, 4.   Edmund Spenser.   So now I languish, till he please,/My pining anguish to appease.   AAS

Four and Eight.   ffrida Wolfe.   The Foxglove by the garden gate/Looked down and smiled on Four and Eight.   BiCB; SiSoSe

Four Brothers.   W. S. Di Piero.   owing himself only the need to go and go. MAYP

The Four Calls.   Lydia Hadley.   Without a hope, he died.   STF

The Four Cardinal Times of Day.   Rene Daumal.   Closing my ears I hear her footstep as she does not walk away.   AMV-81

Four Children.   Anonymous.   And called their brother/A shocking bad name.   OxNR

Four Choctaw Songs.   Jim Barnes.
as long/as the wind/sleeps.   STE
his skin/will keep/me warm.   STE
to another corner/of the sky.   STE
we knew the wind.   STE

Four Christmas Carols (excerpt).   Anonymous.   If you want the Lord,/he's in Popayan.   PCh

Four Dates.   Anonymous.   London burnt like rotten sticks.   OxNR

The Four Dears.   Ebenezer Elliott.   Let us still pull together, and we/Shall still rob the dear British nation.   SaC

The Four Deer.   Mary Hoxie Jones.   We, who had known their danger, found a swifter/Hunter beside us when the morning was over.   GoYe

Four Ducks on a Pond.   William Allingham.   To remember with tears! IrPN; NOBI; NOBV; OxBI; PoPle

Four Epitaphs.   Sylvia Townsend Warner.   Early to Bed and Early to Rise. MoBrPo

Four Fawns.   Barbara Howes.   Their disclosure, in nature,/Reminds me of you, of blending.   AMV-80

Four Folk-Songs in Hokku Form, 1.   Anonymous.   The flowing of water, the Way of Love.   LiTW

Four Folk-Songs in Hokku Form, 2.   Anonymous.   How knowest whether this night the tempest will not/come?   LiTW

Four Folk-Songs in Hokku Form, 3.   Anonymous.   But love's way never changes of promising never to/change.   LiTW

Four Folk-Songs in Hokku Form, 4.   Anonymous.   Then, perhaps, in the morning my love will remain.   LiTW

Four for Sir John Davies.   Theodore Roethke.
The body and the soul know how to play/In that dark world where gods have lost their way.   NOBA
It was and was not she, a shape alone,/Impaled on light, and whirling slowly down.   NOBA
The word outleaps the world, and light is all.   AP; CoBMV; MoAmPo; NoAm; NOBA
Yes, I was dancing-mad, and how/That came to be the bears and Yeats would know.   NOBA; UnS

The Four Friends.   A.(lan) A.(lexander) Milne.   But James was only a snail. TiPo

Four Friends.   Leo Ward.   And nature one with God, at Nazareth!   GoBC

Four Glimpses of Night.   Frank Marshall Davis.   At the blaring jazz/Of a morning sun.   AmNP; NoP; PoBA; PoNe

Four Glosses.   Anonymous.   -a blackbird, a branch/a mass of yellow. NOBI

Four Haiku.   Richard Wright.   And I have no thoughts.   NoAm

Four Heads & How to Do Them.   John Forbes.
...The artist changes genre.   CBAP
...the genitals mark his centre exactly.   CBAP
Good luck!   CBAP
It's called "Pillow Talk"   CBAP

The Four Horses.   James Reeves.   Stands Brownie the cart-horse,/Whose labor is over.   PH

Four III "here's a little mouse."   Edward Estlin Cummings.   who (look). ,startled.   FaBoMo

Four in the Morning.   Edith Sitwell.   Rhinoceros-black (a flowing sea!). NoAm

Four Japanese Paintings: III The Wave Symphony.   Arthur Davison Ficke. Peace drowning passion, and passion/Leaping from peace.   PoA

Four-Leaf Clover.   Wesley Curtright.   Resigned I'll be...   GoSl

Four-Leaf Clover.   Ella Higginson.   If you work, if you wait, you will find the/place/Where the four-leaf clovers grow.   AA; HBV 1-2

The Four-Leaf Clover.   Monica Shannon.   Because he believed in fairy tales. BrR

The Four-Legg'd Elder.   Sir John Birkenhead.   Th'Assembly having sat Four Years,/Has now brought forth a Whelp.   CoMu

The Four-Legg'd Quaker.   Anonymous.   For if the Quakers be not Gelt/ Your Troopes will have the Staggers.   CoMu

Four Legs, Two Legs, Three Legs.   William Empson.   It is a comfort that the Sphinx took such an answer.   MoPo

Four Little Foxes.   Lew Sarett.   The new little foxes are shivering in the rain-/Step softly.   PoSC; RFM; YeAr

Four Love Poems.   Moses Ibn Ezra.   "Dost thou prefer a widow to a maid?"   TrJP

Four Lovely Sisters.   C. A. Trypanis.   To watch their Highnesses without being tempted.   ELU

The Four Maries.   Anonymous.   And they'll never tell my father or mother/ But that I'm across the sea.   FSW

Four Mountain Wolves.   Leslie Marmon Silko.   her pale lavender outline/ startled into eternity.   VoR

The Four Nights' Drunk.   Anonymous.   And I never seen a cabbage head with a mustache on before.   FSW; OBAL

Four O'Clock Flower Blues.   Anonymous.   Hoo, hoo, Lord, baby June, what a day, what a day!   AmFP

The Four of Them.   Yehuda Karni.   Thus the images/of these four/are engraved/upon me.   VWA

Four-Paws.   Helen Parry Eden.   Then from the swinging lantern's light/ Runs to his Mother in the night.   HBMV

Four Pictures by Juan, Age 5.   David McKain.   the family smiled ear to ear.   PoDr

Four Poems for April.   Louis Adeane.   Frozen for bravery, beautiful. NeBP

Four Poems for Robin.   Gary Snyder.
The first time I have/Ever seen them close.   NOBA; SOTW
I think back when I had you.   NOBA; SOTW

If I am a fool/Or have done what my/karma demands. NOBA; SOTW

Naked under a summer cotton dress. NOBA; SOTW

Four Poems for The St. Louis Sporting News, 4. Jack Spicer. I was not the only one who felt these things. PoM

Four Prayers, I. *Anonymous.* O Spirit Blest, who blesest me,/Rest ye with me. OnYI

Four Prayers, II. *Anonymous.* A hundred praises, Christ, 'tis meet,/For all we drink, for all we eat. OnYI

Four Prayers, III. *Anonymous.* May I not lie with evil,/And may evil not lie with me. OnYI

Four Prayers, IV. *Anonymous.* Three Persons in God; to one God alone we make prayer. OnYI

Four Preludes on Playthings of the Wind. Carl Sandburg.

and even the writing of the rat footprints/tells us nothing, nothing at all MoAB

And the only listeners now are...the rats...and the lizards. AmLP; MoAB; NePA; SeCeV

nothing like us ever was. AmLP; AnAmPo; NePA; SeCeV

What of it? Let the dead be dead. AmLP; AnAmPo; AnFE; AP; BoLiVe; CMoP; MoAB; MoAmPo; NePA; NOBA; SeCeV

Four Quartets. Thomas Stearns Eliot.

And the fire and the rose are one. ExPo; NAWM 1-2

At the still point of the turning world. AtBAP

The life of significant soil. ATP

Of time past and time future. AtBAP

Only through time time is conquered. AtBAP

Point to one end, which is always present. AtBAP

Ridiculous the waste sad time/Stretching before and after. AtBAP

Four Quartz Crystal Clocks. Marianne Moore. ...punctual-/ity is not a crime. AmPP; ImOP; MP; TwCP

Four Questions Addressed to His Excellency, the Prime Minister. James P. Vaughn. the lord chamberlain shivers/a moment sped by AmNP

Four Saints in Three Acts: "Pigeons on the grass alas." Gertrude Stein. ...Let Lucy Lily. CrMA; TAP

Four Seasons. Rowena Bastin Bennett. When stars of frost are glowing. SiSoSe; TiPo

The Four Seasons of the Year. Anne Bradstreet. And all the faults that you shall spy/Shall at your feet for pardon cry. SCAP

Four Seasons of the Year: Spring. Anne Bradstreet. Thy days still lengthen without least decline. AnNE

Four Sheets to the Wind and a One-Way Ticket to France. Conrad Kent Rivers. And I shall die an old Parisian. AmNP; BPo; IDB; NNP; PoBA; PoNe

Four Sides to a House. Amy Lowell. Can you sleep, sleep, Peter? PoRA

Four Sonnets to Helen, 1. Pierre de Ronsard. to see so fair a port, and not to make it! LiTW

Four Sonnets to Helen, 2. Pierre de Ronsard. to die again with no heart left to hurt. LiTW

Four Sonnets to Helen, 3. Pierre de Ronsard. ...where naught else avails, deception's best. LiTW

Four Sonnets to Helen, 4. Pierre de Ronsard. Live, pluck the roses of the world to-day. LiTW

Four Spacious Skies. Susan Astor. And fall into my own backyard,/Clutching Long Island. AMV-80

Four Stories. David Shapiro.

Breathe in–/a large thrush eats the mistletoe. ANYP

The pure-bred animals crossed the/wood in the thundery evening. ANYP

Water collects and then the writer's name appears on the/saucer: a fine gift. ANYP

You are the best. ANYP

The Four Sweet Months. Robert Herrick. ...July comes, and she/More wealth brings in, then all those three. WiR

Four Things. *Anonymous.* And one an altar kept alight. TRV

Four Things. Henry Van Dyke. To trust in God and Heaven securely. AA; BBV; GoTF; HBV 1-2; HBVY; PoLf; PoToHe; TreF; TRV

Four Things Choctaw. Jim Barnes. quick with game, heavy with the wind's wild mint. STE

Four Things Make Us Happy Here. Robert Herrick. Lastly, with friends t' enjoy our days. CaPo

Four Translations from the English of Robert Hershon. Robert Hershon.

and burned a doughnut/on my lawn. NeAC

This permits him time to consider/what he wishes to say to me. NeAC

to be thrown away NeAC

When the sculptors get there/they are surprised. NeAC

Four trees upon a solitary acre. Emily Dickinson. They severally promote or hinder,/Unknown. PoEL 1-5

Four Walls. Blanche Taylor Dickinson. This conscious world with guarded men. CDC

Four Ways of Dying. Steve Chimombo. And thus I die. WhB

The Four Winds. Shane Leslie. A bed of blighted corn. OnYI

The Four Winds. Charles Henry Luders. And stir the petals at her feet, and kiss/The low mound where she lies. AA; HBV 1-2

Four Winds. Hal Porter. how wisely wanton is this epicene! NOAV

Four Winds. Sara Teasdale. When thou art more cruel than he,/Then will Love be kind to thee. HBV 1-2

Four Wise Men on Edward II's Reign. *Anonymous.* For good is dede, the land is sinful. OxBM

Four Women. Nina Simone. What do they call me? My name is "Peaches." MAT

Four Wrens. *Anonymous.* And there are none to show to you. OxNR

Four Years. Dinah Maria Mulock Craik. And I go at Midsummer, when the hay is down. HBV 1-2

Four Years Were Mine at Princeton. John Peale Bishop. But these I wear as a signet set,/As a seal upon my heart. GLGT

The Four Zoas. William Blake.

He knew they were his Children ruind in his ruind world TW

Thus could I sing & thus rejoice: but it is not so/with me.' EnRP; OAEL 1-2; Prf

The winds around on pointed/rocks/Settled like bats innumerable, ready to fly abroad. BoW

Fourpence a Day. *Anonymous.* Then he'll raise us our wages to ninepence a day. OBET

Fourteen Men. Mary Gilmore. The straight up and down/Of each on his tree. CBAP

Fourteenth Birthday. Phyllis McGinley. ...endure/In silence and disdain/ Love's utmost treacheries. NePoAm-2

Fourth Act. Robinson Jeffers. ...but the whole affair is only a hare-/brained episode in the life of the planet. LiTA; WaP

Fourth Dance Poem. Gerald William Barrax. and I was on my way anywhere PoBA

The Fourth Dimension. Leonard Nathan. for a time never to be lived in. AMV-81

Fourth of July. Marchette Chute. But we all like Fourth/Of July a lot. SiSoSe

Fourth of July. Rachel Field. Fourth of July–Hurrah! Hooray! SiSoSe

The Fourth of July. John Pierpont.

Till there's war no more! AnNE; MC; PAH; PAL

When a tyrant's thunder pealed/O'er the trembling seas. YeAr

Fourth of July in Maine. Robert Lowell. ...We turn/our backs and feel the whiskey burn. CAPP

Fourth of July Night. Dorothy Aldis. And I don't ever have to go/To bed, to bed, to bed! SiSoSe; TiPo

Fourth of July Night. Carl Sandburg. The little boat at anchor/in black water sat murmuring/to the tall black sky. OFD

Fourth of July Song. Lois Lenski. For the Fourth so glorious/And our flag so free! SiSoSe

The Fourth Option. Henry Rasof. There is only one way, to be sure/There is a way AMV-80

Fourth Poem. Jorge Carrera Andrade. the mothers of Angola/died together with their sons. WhB

Fourth Sation. Padraic Colum. That grace that brings us revelation! ISi

Fourth Song the Night Nurse Sang. Robert Duncan. from a grave or a bed, from a grave or a bed. VGW

Fourth Station. Paul Claudel. She says no word, but looks on the the crown He has worn... ISi

Fourth Station. William A. Donaghy. He will not heal her withered, widowed heart. ISi

Fourth Station. Ruth Schaumann. I saw your hand ascending/to bid a last adieu. ISi

Fourth Street, San Rafael. Bill Berkson. Stepping up to the adjoining window next in line. APU

Fower-an-Twenty Hielandmen. *Anonymous.* An it's a big lees/Frae the heid tae the tail. FaBoNo

The Fowler. Wilfrid Gibson. I who would house a singing bird/Have caged a broken heart. HBMV

Fowls in the Frith. *Anonymous.* For the best of bone and blood. CBEP; NCEP; OBSP

The Fox. *Anonymous.*

And the little ones chewed on the bones-o. BaBo; StPo

He'd many a mile to go that night,/Before he reached the town-o. FSW

Fox. David Campbell. Where I lie in the bed/Of her still eyes. CBAP

The Fox. John Clare. He lived to chase the hounds another day. BoAnP

The Fox. C. Day-Lewis. But of what, they could hardly say. BoAnP

Fox. Clifford Dyment. From fury into weary/Surrendering of feeling. HaMV; OBSP

The Fox. Phoebe Hesketh. –how the stretch of time/Contracts with the flash of recreation! HaMV

The Fox. Kenneth Patchen. Because there are no proportions in death. AnAmPo

The Fox. Marjorie Somers Scheuer. while warmth of wood/and the sun follow. GoYe

The Fox and the Crow. Jean de La Fontaine. Swore he'd learned his last lesson as somebody's fool. OBVE; PPP

The Fox and the Goose. *Anonymous.* Many bones they must pike/While they lay adowne.' OxBM

The Fox and the Grapes. Marianne Moore. Better, I think, than an embittered whine. FM

The Fox and the Hare. *Anonymous.* She got slowly boiled to death in the copper. OBET

The Fox and the Wolf. *Anonymous.* For he ne fond nones kinnes blisse,/Ne of dintes foryevenesse. OxBM

The Fox at the Point of Death. John Gay. A chicken too might do me good. OBEC

The Fox-Hunters. Ebenezer Elliott. And fain to reap it with a scythe of fire. TW

A Fox Jumped up One Winter's Night. *Anonymous.* And the little ones picked the bones O! BLPA; OxNR; PBBP

The Fox Rhyme. Ian Serraillier. Run, uncle, run/And see what has happened! ELU

The Fox Walked Out, A vers. *Anonymous.* And the youngest says, "Oh, Daddy, go again!/For such good meat from town." BFSS

The Fox Walked Out, B vers. *Anonymous.* Think ye awful lucky in the town-e-o. BFSS

The Fox Who Watched for the Midnight Sun. Norman Dubie. As if the dead hare were soon to awaken! LCAP; MAYP

Foxfire. Nancy Willard. if she could find herself, herself planting/instead of keeping. IHMS

Foxgloves. Ted Hughes. smelling faintly/of Virginia/creepers. LOW

Foxgloves and Snow. Marion Angus. No more I watch the last snows fade/On a dark hill above Glen Doll. PoSH

A Foxhole for the Night. John Robert Quinn. "Gentle Jesus, meek and mild,/Look upon a little child." BoAV

Foxtail Pine. Gary Snyder. and call this other thing, a/foxtail pine. CoPo; NaP; NU

Fr Anselm Williams and Br Leander Neville Hanged by Lutheran... Elizabeth Smither. The tongues would come out later/Into an air gone blue, a world. OCNZ

Fra Bank to Bank. Mark Alexander Boyd. Led by a blind and teachit by a bairn. ExPo; NoP; PPoe; QFR

Fra Lippo Lippi. Robert Browning. Don't fear me! There's the grey beginning. Zooks! BiP; BoLiVe; CABL; CTC; MaVP; MBW 1-2; NoP; OAEL 1-2; OAEP; Prf; TEP; ViBoPo; VLP

Fracture of Light: Song in the Cold Season. Samuel French Morse. the hand gropes on the breast, rewinds the clock. PoA

A Fragment. John Bancks. I burned my hand–to save this bit. NOEC

Fragment. Thomas Lovell Beddoes. That he may hear the devil and his wife/In bed, talking secrets. ELU

The Fragment. Hilaire Belloc. And Juliet answer gently, "I forget." PoL

Fragment. Bruce Berlind. How dare they deserve?/Love, even. FAZ

Fragment. Rupert Brooke. To other ghosts–this one, or that, or I. BrPo

Fragment. George Gordon, Lord Byron. The essence of great bosoms now no more. ERoP 1-2

Fragment. William Cowper. And every muse attend her on her way WGRP

Fragment. Jessie Redmond Fauset. A sharp caught cry. CDC

Fragment. Gerard Manley Hopkins.
Bid joy back, have at the harvest, keep Hope pale. NAMP
The whole landscape flushes on a sudden at a sound. ELU

Fragment. Amy Lowell. Transmuted fall in sheafs of rainbows fraught/With storied meaning for religion's sake. WGRP

Fragment. Hugh McCrae. Stung silent in the martyr's blaze. BoAV

Fragment. Miklos Radnoti. since only he could utter the right curse. VWA

Fragment. Edwin Arlington Robinson. Driving the first of its withered leaves/Over the stones where the fountain broke. MAPA

Fragment. Henry Vaughan. O leave thy cares and follies! go this way,/And thou art sure to prosper all the day. TRV; WGRP

A Fragment. Yvor Winters. They will be done; and let discussion cease. OBSV

Fragment 113. Hilda ("H. D.") Doolittle. of bone and the white shell/and fiery tempered steel. LiTA

Fragment for the Dark. Elizabeth Jennings. May their filaments last till true morning. FaBoWP

Fragment from "Clemo Uti–The Water Lilies." Ring Lardner. When you should of looked after his fold? FiBHP

Fragment from the Elizabethans. W. Bridges-Adams. And cast her reeking fragments on the air. FaBoCo

Fragment: I Saw His Round Mouth's Crimson... Wilfred Owen. The cold stars lighting, very old and bleak,/In different skies. OAEL 1-2

Fragment in Imitation of Wordsworth. Catherine Fanshawe. He'd be four time as tall as me,/And live three times as long. FaBoNo; FaBoPa; HBV 1-2

Fragment: "Mary, I believ'd you quick." Thomas Hood. And I've no plate–but that I'm used to.– NBM

Fragment: "Near where the riotous Atlantic surge." William Allingham. Who tread the mossy track to dip their pails/Into the lonely Spring– IrPN

A Fragment: "Not a drum was heard." *Anonymous.* As his horse on the ramparts we curried... FaBoPa

Fragment of a Character. Thomas Moore. Whatever was the best pye going,/In that Ned–trust him–had his finger. FaBoCo

Fragment of a Greek Tragedy. Alfred Edward Housman. But thine arithmetic is quite correct. CenHV; FaBoNo; NOBL; Par; SpRo

Fragment of a Love Lament. *Anonymous.* In bitter bales she has me brought–/Alas that ever she was unkind!.... OxBM

Fragment of a Pastoral. Barry Schwabsky. to live in this broken world. AMV-80

Fragment of a Song. Lewis (Charles Lutwidge Dodgson) Carroll. I hate such noodles, I do. FaBoNo

Fragment of a Song on the Beautiful Wife of Dr. John Overall... *Anonymous.* As flat as any flounder. BoLoP

Fragment of a Sonnet. Pierre Ronsard. Love poured her beauty into my warm veins. AWP

Fragment of an Agon. Thomas Stearns Eliot. KNOCK/KNOCK/KNOCK LiTB

Fragment of an Anti-Papist Ballad. *Anonymous.* They came to plumo with the Kynges trusty towne. CoMu

Fragment of an Ode to Maia. John Keats. Rich in the simple worship of a day. EnRP; ERoP 1-2; OAEL 1-2; OAEP; OBEV; OBRV; PoEL 1-5

Fragment of Sappho. Ambrose Philips. I fainted, sunk, and dy'd away. OBEC

Fragment: Rain. Percy Bysshe Shelley. The gentleness of rain was in the wind. ChRP

Fragment: "Some pretty face remembered in our youth." John Clare. Seems ever with us whispering love and truth. VLP

A Fragment: "The boy stood on the burning deck. (parody). *Anonymous.* He had no trousers of his own/And so he wore his sister's... FaBoPa

Fragment: The Furl of Fresh-Leaved Dog-Rose Down. Gerard Manley Hopkins. Through the sieve of the straw of his hat. AtBAP

Fragment: "The wing'd seeds with decaying wings." William Allingham. And many seeds like that one seed. IrPN

Fragment Thirty-Six. Hilda ("H. D.") Doolittle. and I lie listening awake? CMoP; OxBA; VGW

A Fragment: To Music. Percy Bysshe Shelley. Where their mother, Care, like a drowsy child,/Is laid asleep in flowers. BoLiVe

Fragment: "–you see." William Allingham. Gables and red tiled roofs and twisted chimneys. IrPN

Fragmenti. Ezra Pound. Marble smooth by flowing waters grown. PoA

Fragments. Corinna.
and the city rejoices mightily/at the keen melody of my voice. PBWP
that she, a woman,/dared take on Pindar. PBWP
You were not like that, Corinna,/in the old days. PBWP

Fragments. John Cotton. We'll play symphonies on the bed springs yet. AMV-80

The Fragments. Peter Dale. The docile bus-queue moons. NOCV

Fragments. Praxilla.
Oh yes, and cucumbers in season,/and apples, and pears. PBWP
there's a scorpion under every stone. PBWP
Your face a virgin's, all beneath a bride. PBWP

Fragments. William Butler Yeats.
God took the spinning-jenny/Out of his side. PrIm
Out of dark night where lay/The crowns of Nineveh. NoAm; PrIm

Fragments of a Lost Gnostic Poem of the Twelfth Century. Herman Melville. The good man pouring from his pitcher clear/But brims the poisoned well. NOBA; NoP; OBSP; PoEL 1-5; ViBoPo

Fragments of Ancient Poetry (excerpt). James Macpherson. ...Let me hear thy voice, as/thou passest, when mid-day is silent around. NOEC

Fragments on the Poet and the Poetic Gift. Ralph Waldo Emerson. And when he goes he carries/No more baggage than a bird. PP

Fragmentum Petronius Arbiter, Translated. Ben Jonson. ...never/Can this decay, but is beginning ever. HeIP

Fragoletta. Algernon Charles Swinburne. And like the panther's feet/The feet of Love. UnTE

A Fragrant Prayer. Biddy Crummy. The Lamb who lay beneath the clay/Was slain for thee. WTO

Fragrant Thy Memories. *Anonymous.* In thee, the toilers cease their weary/quest. TrJP

Fraility. George Herbert. Commodious to conquer heaven and Thee/Planted in me. NOCV; OxBoCh

The Frailty. Abraham Cowley. What wonder is it, if weak I be slain? CavP

The Frailty of Beauty. J. C. And yield more cause of terror than delight. ElL

La Fraisne. Ezra Pound. For we are quite alone,/Here 'mid the ash trees. PG

The Framework-Knitters Lamentation. *Anonymous.* And say my mite I will impart,/To aid the poor distress'd. CoMu

Thc Framework-Knitters Petition. *Anonymous.* And what you give, God will re-pay,/Both here and in the Judgment day. CoMu

France. Oliver Goldsmith. Till, seeming blest, they grow to what they seem. OBEC

France. Langdon Elwyn Mitchell. Felt the first sunshine of the early spring! AA

France: An Ode. Samuel Taylor Coleridge. O Liberty! my spirit felt thee there. ATP; ERoP 1-2; OAEP

France Blues. Sunny Boy. So you can talk with daddy anytime when he's gone BluL

Francis Beaumont's Letter from the Country to Jonson. Ben Jonson. Knowe that it will my greatest comfort bee/T'acknowledge all the rest to Come from thee. SeCP

Francis Jammes: A Prayer to Go to Paradise with the Donkeys. Richard Wilbur. Whose humble and sweet poverty will appear/Clear in the clearness of your eternal love. EaLo

Franciscan Aspiration. Vachel Lindsay. God make us saints, and brave. CAW

A Franciscan Prayer. Enid Dinnis. Then, Sweet Saint Francis, make me mad. CAW

Frangipanni. *Anonymous.* What matters now? I know the poem's done,/ And wonder what the dickens it all means! NA

Frank Albert & Viola Benzena Owens. Ntozake Shange. the carpenter tendin to his own/movin north BlSi

The Frank Courtship. George Crabbe. A few yet lived, to languish and to mourn/For good old manners never to return. OBRV

Frank Drummer. Edgar Lee Masters. Which drove me on trying to memorize/The Encyclopedia Britannica! NoAm

Frank James, the Roving Gambler. *Anonymous.* He's bound for the Frankfort Jail. AmFP

Frank O'Hara. Ted Berrigan. But the people in the sky really love/to have dinner & to take a walk with you. APU

Frank Sinatra. Michael Waters. where Frank Sinatra sang only for them. GeTw

Frankenstein. Edward Field. until trapped at the whirlpool's edge/he plunges to his death. FF

Frankenstein Gets His Man. Frank Carr. "He has his head well screwed on," Flann agreed. AmMo

Frankie and Johnny, I (with music). *Anonymous.* He was her man but he done her wrong, so wrong. ABF; AmFP; AS; ATP; BaBo; BeLS; BiP; BLSo; BluL; FaFP; FF; FSW; LiTL; NIP; NOBA; OxBoLi; TrAS; TreF; TrGrPo; UnPo; ViBoFo; YaD

Frankie's Trade. Rudyard Kipling. Storm along my gallant Captains!/(All round the Horn!) EtS

Frankie Silvers. Frances (Frankie) Silvers. For now I try that awful road. AmFP

Franklin D. Roosevelt's Back Again. *Anonymous.* We've got Franklin D. Roosevelt back again. FSW

Franklin Hyde. Hilaire Belloc. Children in ordinary Dress/May always play with Sand. FaBoUs; NLV

Frascati's. Aldous Huxley. And there we sit in blissful calm,/Quietly sweating palm to palm. InPo; ViBoPo

"Frater Ave Atque Vale". Alfred, Lord Tennyson. Sweet Catullus's all-but-island, olive-silvery Sirmio! ChTr; FaBoPP; GTBS-P; HAP; InPS; MBW 1-2; NoP; OBSP; OBTV; PAI

Fraternitas. *Anonymous.* here the sincerity to rest a man. OBVE

Fraternity. Anne Reeve Aldrich. The solemn "Yea, I understand!" AA

Fraternity. John Banister Tabb. Nor they but vagrant melodies/Till harmonized by me. HBV 1-2

Frau Bauman, Frau Schmidt, and Frau Schwartze. Theodore Roethke. And their snuff-laden breath blowing lightly over me in my/first sleep. CoAP; MoAB; NePoAm; NoAm; NOBA; NYBP; SaC; TAP

Fraudulent Days. Michael Benedikt. In this wholly improvised conviction PoA

Fraulein Reads Instructive Rhymes. Maxine W. Kumin. See how He watches/He snatches the bad ones. NYBP; Psk; SpRo

The Freaks at Spurgin Road Field. Richard Hugo. The dim boy claps because the others clap. LCAP; SM

Freaks of Fashion. Christina Georgina Rossetti. "So we may wear whatever we like,/Anything, everything!" FM

Fred. David McCord. But that's Fred all over. Need I say more? TiPo

Fred Apollus at Fava's. Nicholas Moore. These men/(How vainly!) turn towards me again. ErPo; NeBP

Frederick Douglass. Sam Cornish. the fields and dresses grey with dust PoBA

Frederick Douglass. Paul Laurence Dunbar. And answered thunder with his thunder back. BALP; PoBA

Frederick Douglass. Robert Earl Hayden. fleshing his dream of the beautiful, needful thing. AmNP; BiP; CNA; GP; HaCAP; HoAn; IDB; PoBA; PoNe; TTY

Frederick Douglass: 1817-1895. Langston Hughes. He died in 1895./He is not dead. BPo

Fredericksburg. Thomas Bailey Aldrich. Hark!–the black squadrons wheeling down/to Death! PAH

Free America. Joseph Warren. And fight and shout and shout and fight/ for North Americay! FSW; PAH

Free Enterprise. Charles Stetler. The eternally wilting daisy and sandals are extra. GP

Free Fall. Don Gordon. Meanwhile, I stand with/The free-falling ones/ Who believe the parachutes/Will open some day. AMV-81

Free Fantasia on Japanese Themes. Amy Lowell. And inside, only my books. MoAmPo

Free Grace. Charles Wesley. And claim the crown, through Christ, my own. NOCV

Free Little Bird. *Anonymous.*
   And I ain't going to cry any more. AmFP
   I'll build my nest in the ruffle of her dress/Where the bad boys can never bother me. FSW

Free Martin. Peter Hopegood. and a bonny doe with coat aglow/to rouse me from my sleep. BoAV

A Free Nation. Edwin Markham. Except as he find it/In the security of all. TRV

A Free Parliament Litany. *Anonymous.* From Fools and Knaves, in our Parliament free,/Libera nos, Domine! OxBoLi

Free Silver. *Anonymous.* Regain our precious metal. AmFP

Free Thoughts on Several Eminent Composers. Charles Lamb. Because they're living; so I leave 'em. DBV; FaBoCo; OBRV; OxBoLi

Free Will. Walter Clark. We go these ways. NCSH

The Free Woman. Theodosia Garrison. But I have heard the word she spoke/In her man's arms as the dawn broke. HBMV

A free woman. At last free! *Anonymous.* I am at ease. BoWoP

Freeborn Man. Ewan MacColl. Your travelling days will soon be over. OBET

Freedom. *Anonymous.* Till Thou hast bound me fast, I am not free. PGD

Freedom. Joel Barlow. Kings from the earth and pirates from the waves. AnNE; PAL

Freedom. Ernst. Karl Daniel. Peter Thaelmann Battalion. Ready, forward march. FSW

Freedom. J. Charles Green. used to store muddied pools of rain/to hide the sun from children LFAC

Freedom. Langston Hughes. I want freedom/Just as you. PoBA

Freedom. Abraham Ibn Ezra. He that wealth and power craves,/Shall become a slave of slaves. TrJP

Freedom: A Poem, Written in Time of Recess... Andrew Brice. Clatt'ring within the flabby lean, their pith/Exhaust, and tide of every art'ry frore. NOEC

Freedom and Love. Thomas Campbell. No! nor fetter'd Love from dying/ In the knot there's no untying. BSV; GTBS-P

Freedom For the Mind. William Lloyd Garrison And, in its watches, wearies every star! AA; FaBoBe

Freedom in Mah Soul. David Wadsworth Cannon, Jr.. Freedom in mah soul. PoNe

Freedom Is a Constant Struggle. *Anonymous.* We must be free, we must be free. FSW

Freedom, New Hampshire. Galway Kinnell. And the few who loved him know this until they die. LCAP; NaP

Freedom of Love. Andre Breton. My wife with eyes of water-level of level of air earth and fire. EAS

Freedom of the Hills. Douglas Fraser. "Here is your freedom. Taste–and come again!" PoSH

The Freedom of the Moon. Robert Frost. The color run, all sorts of wonder follow. MOON

A Freedom Song for the Black Woman. Carole C. Gregory. we are the strong women. BlSi

Freely Espousing. James Schuyler. That's their story. ANYP; NeAP; NoP

Freely, from a Song Sung by Jewish Women of Yemen. Stephen Levy. But first/he unbuttoned my gown,/inflamed me. VWA

Freemon Hawthorne. Melvin B. Tolson. In my grandfather's barn/In the Ozarks. FAZ

Freethinkers. Deborah Eibel. They have become a new underworld. VWA

Freeze Tag. Gordon Henry. You wonder/who is/it/now. STE

Freight Boats. James S. Tippett. As they carry anything/From any place you will. BrR

Freight Train. *Anonymous.* And tell them all that I'm gone to sleep. FSW

Freighter. Bruce Ruddick. while boys and tides maraud about her bows. CaP

Freighting from Wilcox to Globe. *Anonymous.* Growing green down on the Gila; there's a home for you and/me. AmFP; CoSo

The French, 1870-1871. *Anonymous.* He crows more loudly in defeat. FaBoEE

French Clock. Hortense Flexner. And hot throats roaring that the King is dead! HBMV

French Cookery. Thomas Moore. Six hundred and eighty-five ways to dress eggs? OBRV

French Desire. Keith Abbott. and it's love me/love me/love me. APU

French Lisette: A Ballad of Maida Vale. William Plomer. 'Tis folly abounding in a strange surrounding/To be divorced from one's pants. ErPo

The French Mood. Abo Stoltzenberg. preserve us also/from the French Mood. VWA

French Peasants. Monk Gibbon. These who go home at dusk,/Along the lane. HaMV; NeIP; OxBI

French Poets. Aram Saroyan. They are gay sons-of-bitches. ANYP

The French Revolution. William Blake. And follow'd the army, and the Senate in peace sat beneath/morning's beam. ChRP

The French Revolution. William Wordsworth. We find our happiness, or not at all! ERoP 1-2; FiP

The Frenchman's Ball. Anonymous. Whacks to the lady to the rum-die-ah. OuSiCo

Frenzy. George Crabbe. Doomed to dismay, disgrace, despair. NOBE

Frere Jacques. Anonymous. ding ding dong, ding ding dong. FSW

Fresco-Sonnets to Christian Sethe. Heinrich Heine. I should dumbfounder every jail-bird there. AWP

Frescoes for Mr. Rockefeller's City. Landscape as a Nude. Archibald MacLeish. There is too much sun on the lids of my eyes to be listening UnPo

Fresh Air. Kenneth Koch. O green, beneath which all of them shall drown! CAPP; NeAP; NNaP; NoAm; PP

The Fresh Air. Harold Monro. But, far and near: "Cuckoo! Cuckoo! Cuckoo!" CH

Fresh Cheese and Cream. Robert Herrick. To your cream here's strawberries. UnTE

Fresh News from the Past. Marvin Bell. ...We loved the word "propellor.." LCAP

Fresh Paint. Boris Pasternak. All will grow white somehow,/Or bandage on a brow. PoPl; TrJP

Fresh Spring. Elizabeth Daryush. Now truly are your haunts their home/Eternal, whom with tears I name. QFR

The Fresh Start. Anna Wickham. I'll write chaste sonnets of imagined Loves. ViBoPo

A Freshet. Antiphilus of Byzantium. I'll see you shrivel yet—the sun can tell/A bastard from a lawful stream full well. LiTW

Freshmen. Barry Spacks. most foul, most foul, the future in your face. NYBP

Freud: Dying in London, He Recalls the Smoke of His Cigar... James Schevill. Love is the fury/To love and find/A single name. TAP

Freya's Spinning Wheel. Adam Oehlenschlager. Spinning thy sparkling wheel on high. LiTW

The Friar. Julian del Casal. The wind that whistles through his empty bag. CAW

The Friar. Thomas Love Peacock. The cry of my dogs was the only choir/In which my spirit did take delight. SD

The Friar and the Fair Maid. Anonymous. For the nimble trick on the friar she played. UnTE

The Friar and the Nun. Anonymous. Each to their cloister did they gone/Sine temptationibus. GBP

A Friar Complains. Anonymous. Men shul finde unnethe a frere/In Englonde within a while. MeEL

The Friar in the Well (A version). Anonymous. Both old and young commended the/maid/That such a witty prank had plaid. ESPB

The Friar in the Well (B version). Anonymous. The friar he walked on the street,/And shaking his lugs like a well-washen/sheep. ESPB

Friar Lubin. Clément Marot. Friar Lubin cannot do it. AWP; DBV

The Friar of Orders Gray. John O'Keeffe. Or knight of the shire/Lives half so well as a holy friar! OnYI; OxBI

The Friar of Orders Gray. Thomas Percy. For since I have found thee, lovely youth,/We never more will part. CEP; HBV 1-2; NOEC; OBEV

The Friar of Orders Grey. Anonymous. And at his heels a stone. ACP; CAW; GoBC

Friars' Enormities. Anonymous. Sle thy fadre and jape thy modre and thay will thee assoile! MeEL

Friday Evening. Julio Marzan. Going nowhere, with nowhere to be from. InW

Friday Night. Kendrick Smithyman. sounds, like shawls falling. OCNZ

Friday Night after Bathing. Stephen Levy. You said, Yes, I do too, we are smooth and smell/so good. VWA

Friday Night's Dream on a Saturday Told. Anonymous. Is sure to come true, be it never so old. HBVY

Friday the Thirteenth. Allen Ginsberg. down thru cloud-floor to Chicago, sunset fire obliterate in black gas. NNaP

Friday. Wet Dusk. Christopher Logue. Outside/they start to shout obscene remarks. OxBTC

Friend. Gwendolyn Brooks. Evening is comforting flame. CNA

A Friend. Santob De Carrion. That friendship surely shun/That feigns to love, and inwardly/Betrays affections won. TrJP

A Friend. Lionel Pigot Johnson. He gave and I, who sing/His praise, bring all I have to bring. HBV 1-2

The Friend. Marge Piercy. Have you cut off your hands yet? NMM

A Friend. Marguerite Power. Your friend!!! FaBoCo; FaFP

A Friend. W. D. Snodgrass. Images fill their vacant eyes. MAT

A Friend. Sir Thomas Noon Talfourd. That a friend is near and feels. PoToHe

A Friend Advises Me to Stop Drinking. Mei Yao Ch'en. I don't know what will happen to me. HoPM

Friend and Lover. Bridges Madeline. But, oh, what anguish to discover/Her lover has become–her friend! AA; HBV 1-2

Friend Cato. Anna Wickham. Cato, in pity, hear our just demur,/Man to be critic, must be connoisseur. MoBrPo

Friend, don't be angry. Mira Bai [(or Mirabai)]. Take her to you. BoWoP

Friend, how can I meet my lord? Mira Bai [(or Mirabai)]. let us never again be torn apart. BoWoP

A Friend in the Garden. Juliana Horatia Ewing. He is a friendly TOAD. OxBChV

Friend Mussunda. Agostinho Neto. O io kalunga ua mu bangele.../We are. WhB

The Friend of Humanity. J. H. Frere and George Canning. Sordid, unfeeling, reprobate, degraded,/Spiritless outcast!' BXAP; CEP; FaBoCo; HBV 1-2; Par

Friend of Souls. Anonymous. An in Thy pardon and Thy care/The heaven of heavens is won. BePJ

A Friend of the Family. Louis Simpson. People live here...you'd be amazed. NNaP

The Friend of the Fourth Decade. James Merrill. –and his lips part/To greet the perfect stranger. NYBP

Friend, on this Scaffold Thomas More Lies Dead. J. V. Cunningham. Who would not cut the Body from the Head. InPK

A Friend or Two. Wilbur D. Nesbit. And heaven will be a better place/For a friend or two. PoLf

A Friend's Greeting. Edgar A. Guest. I'd like to be the sort of friend that you have been to me. BLPA; BLPL

A Friend's Passing. Barclay Sheaks. The memory of your gentleness/remains/with promise. AMV-80

Friend Sparrow. Basho (Matsuo Basho). Among my flowers. AWP

The Friend Who Just Stands By. B. Y. Williams. "God bless the friend who just "stands by"! PoLf; PoToHe

Friend Who Never Came. William Stafford. Sometimes in the sun today I glimpse that world in the blue. FAZ; SM

Friendless Blues. Mercedes Gilbert. I just sit here all a-lone and cry an' moan, cry an' moan. TrAS

A Friendly Address. Thomas Hood. Do what you will, his every want supply,/Keep him–but out of Newgate, Mrs. Fry! PoEL 1-5

The Friendly Beast. Anonymous. I," said the dove from the rafters high. PoSC; SoPo

The Friendly Beasts. Anonymous. The gift he gave Immanuel. BiCB; ChBR; OnMSP; PCh; SiSoSe

The Friendly Blight. Aubrey Thomas De Vere. In God's time cometh the thing God will,/For God is the Lord of all! IrPN

A Friendly Game of Football. Edward Dyson. For the Giant feels he's got a call to plug him if he comes. CBAP

Friends. John Ashbery. The feeling is a jewel like a pearl. LCAP

Friends. Abbie Farwell Brown. A child should never feel a fear,/Wherever he may be. HBV 1-2; HBVY

Friends. Thomas Curtis Clark. The gift of friends, to share the way I go. PoToHe

Friends. Ray Durem. Just the same as if/They was people. PoBA

Friends. Mary Goose. Bomb-pitted with Contentment and the/Pain of Breathing. STE

Friends. Alfred Edward Housman. And I come home to Ludlow/Amidst the moonlight pale. SeCePo

Friends. Lionel Pigot Johnson. I pray you every day. GoBC

Friends. Edward Verrall Lucas. Because he is he and I am I. HBV 1-2

Friends. Richard Moore. ...draws out of the infinite spaces/all things down to its own/niggardly miserable earth. SM

Friends. John Perreault. that is the substance of this shortness. ANYP

Friends. William Stafford. Near things: Friend, here's my hand. PPJ

Friends. William Butler Yeats. So great a sweetness flows/I shake from head to foot. NoAm; WeW

Friends Beyond. Thomas Hardy. And the Squire, and Lady Susan, murmur mildly to me now. CoBMV; FaBoRV; GTBS-P; NOBV; OBEV; OBVV; VLP

Friends Come. Lucille Clifton. they are there. GeTw

Friends in Paradise. Henry Vaughan. And into glory peep. GTBS

From all the jails the boys and girls. Emily Dickinson. Alas! that frowns could lie in wait/For such a foe as this! GLGT

From All These Events. Stephen Spender. In distant worlds, and in years on this world as distant. LiTB; NAMP

From an Asylum: Kathy Chattle to Her Mother, Ruth Arbeiter. Anne Stevenson. Mother, what more? What more? BrRo

From an Elegy upon the Most Incomparable King Charles the First. Henry, Bishop of Chichester King. If Zimri dye in Peace that slew his Lord. OBS

From an Irish-Latin Macaronic. Geoffrey Taylor. And Love, dark head, is all the power/That breaks the green bough into flower. NeIP

From an Old House in America. Adrienne Rich. Any woman's death diminishes me NNaP

From Ancient Fangs. Peter Viereck. "No, not at first." MiAP

From Another Room. Gregory Corso. My feast was in the easy blood that flowed. NeAP

From Battle Clamour. Samuele Romanelli. And home be led in peace. TrJP

From behind the Bars. Fadwa Tuquan. robbing from us the sun, robbing the moon WPOW

From Bethlehem Blown. Mary Sinton Leitch. As sudden on earth's darkness streams a star! PGD

From Bethlehem to Calvary. Meredith Nicholson. Through Calvary's clouds they seek the light that led Him to the/dawn. PGD

From Beyond. Lucia Trent. O God, that men will be so blind! PGD

From Burton the Anatomist. Maurice James Craig. The colours of a million dusks and dawns/Lay low where she was laid. NeIP

From Certain Bokes of Virgiles Aeneais. Henry Howard, Earl of Surrey. Armes unto armes, and offspring of eche race/With mortal warr eche other may fordoe.' EnPo

From Childhood's Hour. Edgar Allan Poe. Of a demon in my view. NePA; PoEL 1-5

From Citron-Bower. Hilda Doolithe. for losing of her maidenhood. AP

From Colony to Nation. Irving Layton. their bones not even picked for souvenirs. NOBC

From Countless Hearts. Gail Brook Burket. We pray for peace to bless the world today. Amen. AH

From Country to Town. Hartley Coleridge. Single am I amid the countless many. CBEP; OBRV

From Creature to Ghost. Pauline Hanson. I die, I live,/in the anguish of both. TAP

From Darkness. Izumi Shikibu. O moon above the mountain crest. PBWP

From Dawn to Noon. Dante Gabriel Rossetti. Those unknown things or these things overknown. MaVP

From Disciple to Master. Monk Gibbon. O wise and travelled souls,/Before I go.' AnIV

From Emily Dickinson in Southern California. X. J. Kennedy. ...Mankind/Seemed elsewhere gone–to Fall– NLV

From Far away. Delmira Agustini. ...like the shadow/Of a flight, pass Storms and Time, Life and Death. PBWP

From Far away. William Morris. To tell of great tidings, strange and true. OHIP

From Far, from Eve and Morning. Alfred Edward Housman. Ere to the wind's twelve quarters/I take my endless way. CMoP; HAP; HeIP; MoBrPo; NBM; NoP; PoEL 1-5; PrIm

From Feathers to Iron. C. Day Lewis. An infant flyaway; but now/We make a man of it. ViBoPo

From: First Aspen. Lynn Strongin. Nervous, earthy woman, you are reaching now/to the marrow of my bone. IHMS

From Four Lakes' Days. Richard Eberhart. Till the twilight folds and all's/As blue as the bluewashed walls. MiAP

From Garden to Garden, Ridge to Ridge. John Muir. Who wouldn't be a mountaineer! RFM

From Garvey's Farm: Seneca, Wisconsin. Ed Hoeppner. young eyes opening to take the cold. AMV-80

From Generation to Generation. William Dean Howells. As your fate is to die, our fate is to be born. AA

From Generation to Generation. Sir Henry Newbolt. Thou too shalt groan at heart that all thy spending/Cannot repay the dead, the hungry dead. FaBoTw

From Ghoulies and Ghosties. *Anonymous.* And all Things that go bump in the Night,/Good Lord deliver us. OFD

From Gloucester Out. Edward Dorn. the whispers of the most flung shores/from Gloucester out CoPo; NoAm; NOBA; PoM

From Government Buildings. Denis Devlin. Fingering the ring with its silver bat, the foreign/And credible Chinese symbol of happiness. IPY

From Greenland's Icy Mountains. Reginald Heber. Redeemer, King, Creator,/In bliss returns to reign. FaPoR; HBV 1-2; TreF; VLP; WGRP

From Greenland to Iceland. *Anonymous.* There are so many people/More clever than I am. FaFP

From Grenoble. James Elroy Flecker. And the rose-garden of my gracious home. OBTV

From Harvest to January. Turner, Charles Tennyson. ...with falling flakes/Shall nurse the soil for next year's scythes and rakes. NOBV

From Heart to Heart. William Channing Gannett. Thou art the ocean, too, and thine,/That ever deepening roll! AH

From Heaven High I Come to You. Martin Luther. A Child so blessed, and full of love,/Sent for your joy from Heaven above. PCh

From Heraclitus. Alan Dugan. ...to give out/all the temporary ornaments I can to peace. PoA

From Here to There. *Anonymous.* When I get there/I'll pull your hair. OxNR

From Here to There. Rachel Korn. without smile,/sadness,/or tears. VWA

From his flock stray'd Coridon. Robert Greene. They woo'd and vow'd, and that they keep,/And go contented to their sheep. EG

From Jerusalem: A First Poem. Gabriel Preil. who dreamed of a village/cool among the stars. VWA

From Le Havre. Charles G. Bell. On the leafwork of a continent axil and veins. NePoAm

From Life. Lazer Eichenrand. Perhaps silence/already climbs up the hour/as the rain climbs upon/the lightning. VWA

From Life. Brian Hooker. As the soft glamor of remembered rain/Hallows the gladness of a sunlit wood. HBV 1-2

From Lois in London. Angela McCabe. regards, Lois. AmPA

From Malay. David Shapiro. If only life and death were an eggshell like Princess Eggshell/Indelible lust (for you). APU

From Mistra: A Prospect. Ted Higgs. for reverie, for freedom, and for love. AMV-80

From Mount Nebo. Karl Wolfskehl. I ask you, mountain, be my final resting place. VWA

From My Arm-Chair. Henry Wadsworth Longfellow. And make these branches, leafless now so long,/Blossom again in song. BLPA

From My Diary, July 1914. Wilfred Owen. Expanding with the starr'd nocturnal flowers. CoBMV; FaBoMo; LiTM; MoAB; MoBrPo

From My High Love. Kenneth Patchen. Let not the bullet go through one before the other. MoAmPo

From My Lai the Thunder Went West. Richard Ryan. from sea to sea drifting,/drops of bright ruby. CIP

From My Mother's Home. Leah Goldberg. The mirror carries on/the family tradition:/that she was beautiful. VWA

From My Rural Pen. T. S. Watt. And if I ever tackle another of these, so am I. FiBHP

From My Thought. Daniel Smythe. The stone and marsh and leaf and spray. GoYe

From My Window. Mary Elizabeth Coleridge. A dreamy watchfulness of tranquil things,/And not unblest. OBNC

From My Window. C. K. Williams. its surface glittering, the dawn, glancing from its glaze, ob-/lique, relentless, unadorned. SV

From Mythology. Zbigniew Herbert. ...They would crush it under their heels and add it/to their dishes. FaBoPV

From Now On. Barefoot Bill. From now on, mama, I said I'm gonna let you go BluL

From Oddity Land. Edward Anthony. He opens it up with a flick of his tail. TiPo

From One of Case's Pill-Boxes. John Case. Enough in any man's own conscience. FaBoUs

From One Who Stays. Amy Lowell. A spectre-horde repeating without change. BoWoP

From Our Album. Lawson Fusao Inada. rats, bedbugs, blacks. AmPA

From Plane to Plane. Robert Frost. Dick said to old Pike, innocent of Shakespeare. MoAmPo

From Potomac to Merrimac. Edward Everett Hale. Whom the land shall bless/In joy and distress/Forever and a day! PAH

From Prologue, Each to the Other. Christopher La Farge. The tune to the reception of your heart. AnAmPo

From Romany to Rome. William Irwin. Upon the road to Romany/The birds are calling still! HBV 1-2

From Rome. For More Public Fountains in New York City. Alan Dugan. and the city's life acknowledge the water of life. NYP; Prf

From Russian Hill. Ina Donna Coolbrith. Below, a sea of stars!/Above, of stars a sea! BPAW

From Sand Creek (excerpt). Simon J. Ortiz. My life. My life. STE

From Scars Where Kestrels Hover. W. H. Auden. And the host after waiting/Must quench the lamps and pass/Alive into the house. FaBoPV

"From sex, this sea...'. D. G. Jones. ...I would find/them also in our mouths NOBC

From Skye, Early Autumn. M. L. Michal. And the sun shining soft/On the loch I have left. PoSH

From Soil Somehow the Poet's Word. Kenneth Leslie. better than day they know the day. OBCV

From Solitude to Solitude towards Life. Paul Eluard. He enjoys and grows by love. LiTW

From Sorrow Sorrow Yet Is Born. Alfred, Lord Tennyson. As when thy moonlights, dim and sweet,/Touch some gray ruin on the hill. OBSP

From St. Luke's Hospital. Madeleine L'Engle. All I can do, and this I do, is love, is pray. CTBA

From Stone to Steel. Edwin John Pratt. The path lies through Gethsemane. NoP; PeCV

From Summer Hours. Albert Samain. In the sick and soundless air? AWP

From Sunset to Star Rise. Christina Georgina Rossetti. My heart goes sighing after swallows flown/On sometime summer's unreturning track. SBG

From That First Night. Izumi Shikibu. Yet I have recklessly/Slept in strange places and strange ways. PBWP

From the Antique. Christina Georgina Rossetti. Shall sleep and sleep for ever. EnLoPo; NOBV

From the Arabic. Percy Bysshe Shelley. Nor claim one smile for all the comfort, love,/It may bring to thee. CBEP; HBV 1-2; OBEV

From the Ballad of Evil. N. P. Van Wyk Louw. Have you looked in the glass/that mirrors you? PeSA

From the Ballad of Two-Gun Freddy. Walter R. Brooks. Sing yip, yip, yippy-doodle-do. SoPo

From the Batter's Box. David K. Harford. A sorrowful strikeout victim/Of daily anticipation. AMV-80

From the Beaumont Series. Dick Gallup. List "a la vie," Tamia. ANYP

From the Brothers Grimm to Sister Sexton to Mother Goose (parody). David Cummings. So much for the Mothers Goose and Earth. BXAP

From the Caledonian Mercury. Gavin Wilson. In Britain none can fit you better/Than can your servant the Bootmaker. FaBoUs

From the Cavities of Bones. Patricia Parker. I, Woman, must be/the child of myself. BlSi

From the Commonwealth. Sandra Maria Esteves. which is the only music I know how to play. LTB

From the Country to the City. Elizabeth Bishop. "Subside,' it begs and begs. CrMA; NYP

From the Crag. Mani Leib. Raised me to praise you from the crag where I cling. VWA

From the Crystal. Sidney Lanier. Jesus, Good Paragon, thou Crystal Christ? BePJ

From the Dark Tower. Countee Cullen. And wait, and tend our agonizing seeds. BALP; BANP; BPo; CDC; IDB; LiTM; PoBA; PoNe

From the Day-Book of a Forgotten Prince. Jean Starr Untermeyer. His gateway is wide and the folk of the moor/Come singing so gaily right up to the door. HBMV

From the Depths. Otakar Fischer. Now from unfathomable distances/God's shadow has fallen on me. VWA

From the Domain of Arnheim. Edwin Morgan. From time the souvenirs are deeds. BSV

From the Dust. Elaine Dallman. I breathe dust spreading down in/a great wing. VWA

From the Embassy. Robert Graves. And shy enquiries for literature/Come in by every post, and the side door. PoA

From the Epigrams of Martial. James Michie.
Booze in the morning–for my sake. FaBoEE
By all means play Lucretia by day. But I need a Lais at night. FaBoEE
Let him believe you're from my farm. FaBoEE
Named me his heir–and promptly rallied. FaBoEE
Remain your only cause for tears. FaBoEE

From the Flats. Sidney Lanier. Bright leaps a living brook! NOBA; OxBA

From the Garden of Heaven. Hafiz. He may find a place in God's Paradise. LiTW

From the German of Uhland. James Weldon Johnson. And will love thee, yes, forever and aye! CDC

From the Grove Press. Anthony Hecht. Based on a volume of/Japanese prints. OBAL

From the Gulf. Will H. Ogilvie. ...by God they'll share! for we've been droving too! PoAu 1-2

From the Harbor Hill. Gustav Kobbe. For I knew o'er the grave o' the Harbor Belle the sea-gulls fly. HBV 1-2

From the Hazel Bough. Earle Birney. or what leans out/from the hazel bough HeIP; NIP

From the Head. Louis Zukofsky. A prayer to the East/Before light–the sun later–/To get over even its chaos early. VWA

From the Highest Camp. Thom Gunn. Born of rejection, of the boundless snow. MP; TwCP

From the House of Yemanja. Audre Lorde. where day and night shall meet/and not be/one. NoP

From the Ice Age. Barbara Bloom. and the woman wrapped in beads/shines in her familiar bones. AMV-81

From the Joke Shop. Roy Fuller. ...Although some boils,/God-given, might more surely make for laughs. OxBC

From the Journals of the Frog Prince. Susan Mitchell. How can I tell her/I am thinking that transformations are not forever? DFT; NIP

From the Narrator's Trance. James (Olumo) Cunningham. oluto/oluto/aaaaaaaaaaah JB

From the Night of Forebeing. Francis Thompson. And in the first does always see the last. OBVV

From the North Saskatchewan. Eli Mandel. what lies north of the river/or past those hills that look like beasts NOBC

From the Notebooks. Theodore Roethke.
Another woman: a change of tears. PoL
Deep in their roots, all flowers keep the light. PoL
Himself the middle of a roaring world. PoL
I'm lost in my name. PoL
I rasp like a sick dog; I can't find my life. PoL
I would be with the wind, in the thump and slam of this/summer joy. PoL

From the Other Shore. William Pitt Root. stones of the river rising up/in the forms of women. MAYP

From the Outside. Mafika Pascal Gwala. dared to stand out/and say/Madaza was a "Wanted." WhB

From the Parthenon I Learn. Willard Wattles. Tells how death can only be/A lovely thing we do not see. HBMV

From the Persian. Kenneth Rexroth. Come to my arms, naked in the dark. FaBoEE

From the Point. Paul Petrie. sidewards–moving–always moving–never resting. AMV-80

From the Prison House. Adrienne Rich. it must forget/nothing NNaP

From the Provinces. Norman Rosten. Expect nothing but advice on metrics. HoAn

From the Rain Down. Rhina P. Espaillat. The starry blossoming of snow. GoYe

From the Rain Forest. Desiree Flynn. coming toward wholeness towards singleness BrRo

From the Righteous Man Even the Wild Beasts Run away. David Bromwich. Over and over they must speak/The water's cadences alone.) PoA

From "The River-Fight." Henry Howard Brownell On fire and sinking! AA

From the Roof. Denise Levertov. ...by design/we are to live now in a new place. NoP

From the Santa-Fe Trail. Vachel Lindsay. And get me a place to sleep in the hay/At the end of a live-and-let-live day. LaNeLa

From the Sea. Sara Teasdale. A heaven of unborn evanescent stars. MoLP

From "The Sinless Child." Elizabeth Oakes Smith Her name of Sinless Child. AA

From the Spanish. Tony Towle. our red mouths visible and the white sky full of clouds. ANYP

From the Sustaining Air. Larry Eigner. I am, finally, an incompetent, after all PoM

From the Triads of Ireland. *Anonymous.* Three services, the worst that a man can serve: serving a bad/woman, a bad lord, and bad land. OnYI

From the Turkish. George Gordon, Lord Byron. False heart, frail chain, and silent lute. HBV 1-2

From the Wash the Laundress Sends. Alfred Edward Housman. And I must get a London one. NoAm

From the Wave. Thom Gunn. Then all swim out to wait until/The right waves gather. NoP

From the Window Down. Louis O. Coxe. The bank undid me to the shore. NYBP

From the Window of the Beverly Wilshire Hotel. Michael McClure. and cases of green eye liner. EAS

From Thee to Thee. Solomon Ibn Gabirol. From Thee I turn to Thee,/And find Love in Thine eyes. EaLo; TrJP

From these high hills... Sir Thomas Wyatt. The first estew is remedy alone. FCP

From Thy Fair Face I Learn. Buonarroti Michelangelo. I rise to God to make death sweet by thee. PeHV

From Tomorrow On. *Anonymous.* Not today. TrJP

From Trollope's Journal. Elizabeth Bishop. ..."Sir, I do declare/everyone's sick! The soldiers poison the air." FaBoPV

From V.C. (a Gentleman of Verona). Gavin Ewart. It's a Public Enemy–to me, you, and Venus a complacent traitor. OxBC

From Venice Was That Afternoon. Jean Garrigue. Sands of our darkening great ills. NOBA

From Vice, 1966. Jim Brodey. directly away from/unsupported world. ANYP

From Whence Doth This Union Arise? Thomas Baldwin. Amen! even so let it be. AH

From Which War. Phillip Yellowhawk Minthorn. from which war I do not know/and I'm terrified. STE

Full Moon at Tierz: Before the Storming of Huesca. John Cornford. For Communism and for liberty. OBWP

Full Moon (fragment). Sappho. Trampling the tender bloom of the soft grass. AWP

Full Moon in Malta. Asphodel. ...Suddenly I saw, looked again and saw/ The merciful corn. BrRo

Full Moon: New Guinea. Karl Shapiro. The bombs are falling darkly for our fate. MiAP

Full Moon, Rising. Jonathan Holden. and feel, for a moment, certain/that as you notice it/you are the only one. GOYP

Full Moon: Santa Barbara. Sara Teasdale. Tracing in crystal the slow way he came. BrR; OBCA

The Full Sea Rolls and Thunders. William Ernest Henley. And in its brotherly unrest/I'll range for evermore. EtS

Full Valleys. F. R. Scott. Long silences/Are of old words and ways/Full valleys. CaP

Full Well I Know. Hartley Coleridge. Revere me for his sake, and love me for my own. NCEP

Full well it may be seen. Sir Thomas Wyatt. Let them enjoy the gain,/ That thinks it worth the pain. FCP; SiPS

Fuller and Warren. Anonymous. As Adam was beguiled by Eve. BeLS

Fuller and Warren. Moses Whitecotton. So those who never marry may well be called wise./So, gentlemen, excuse me; goodbye. AmFP; CoSo; ViBoFo

Fum and Hum, the Two Birds of Royalty. Thomas Moore. Ne'er paused, till he lighted in St. Stephen's lobby.) OBSV

Fun in a Garret. Emma C. Dowd. It's lots of fun–just try it some day/ When it rains too hard to go out to play. SUS; TiPo

The Function Room. Patrice Phillips. so I quit. MAT

The Fundament Is Shifted. Abbie Huston Evans. And not fall. MoRP; NYBP

The Fundamental Project of Technology. Galway Kinnell. ...until the day flashes and no one lives/to look back and say, a flash, a white flash sparkled. SM; SUW; SV

Funebrial Reflections. Ogden Nash. People's friends are people's sarcophagi. ImOP

Funeral. Murray Bennett. There is no pain for me. I am your heart. GoYe

The Funeral. Walter De la Mare. He was so tired, poor thing. CMoP; MoVE

The Funeral. John Donne. That since you would save none of me, I bury some of you. ATP; AWP; BiP; BoLoP; CBEP; CoBE; DiPo; EBEV; EnLoPo; HeIP; InPo; LiTL; MBW 1-2; NAWM 1-2; NoP; OAEL 1-2; OBEV; PoPle; PoRA

The Funeral. Norman Dubie. The cancer ate her like horse piss eats deep snow. MAYP

The Funeral. J. M. And in the cry of the crucified. TrJP

Funeral. Bert Meyer. over the long drawer/they've closed in the earth. PCP

The Funeral. Stephen Spender. Mourned by scholars who dream of the ghosts of Greek boys. CMoP; MoAB; MoBrPo; NAMP; NoAm

Funeral. Joanna Thompson. We crack. We roll away/in waxed limousines, leaving/it all, all, all to the wind. AMV-81

Funeral at Ansley. Don Welch. cottonwoods, and the gray-green/leaves of the buffalo/grass. GP; TAT

Funeral Elegy on the Death of His Very Good Friend Mr. Michael Drayton. Sir Aston Cokayne. But I molest thy quiet; sleep, whilst we/That live, would leave our lives to die like thee. OBS

A Funeral Elogy... John Norton II. Who undertakes this subject to commend/Shall nothing find so hard as how to end. SCAP

The Funeral Home. Robert Mezey. The coffin has sprouted in dark mahogany/Out of them–edged, and shining like a thorn. AmPC; LiTM

Funeral Hymn. Anonymous. As with a robe a mother hides/Her son, so shroud this man, O earth. LiTW

Funeral Hymn. William Walsham Howe. Singing to the Father, Son and Holy Ghost,/Alleluia. Amen. WGRP

Funeral in Hungary. Kay Boyle. Gather my pine-brush and light fires unmolested underneath/my trees. AnEnPo

Funeral Lament from Epiros. Anonymous. Open your eyes! BoWoP

Funeral Notices. Alfonsina Storni. Close to the crosses, my own name dances about. AMV-81

The Funeral of Martin Luther King, Jr. Nikki Giovanni. Where Martin Luther King could have lived and preached/non-violence. BOLo; BPo

Funeral of Napoleon I. Sir John H. Hagarty. For the War-King thunder-stricken from his fiery battle-car! CaP

The Funeral of Philip Sparrow. John Skelton. God send my sparrow's soul good rest. ACP

Funeral of Rufino Contreras. Ruth Wildes Schuler. beneath the shadows/ stetching across/this day of love. SOTS

The Funeral of Time. Henry Beck Hirst Sits, statue-like, alone! AA

The Funeral of Youth: Threnody. Rupert Brooke. All, except only Love, Love had died long ago. SeCeV

A Funeral Oration. David Wright. He hoped to write one good line; died believing in God. MP

Funeral Oration for a Mouse. Alan Dugan. into the common death beyond the mousetrap. AP; HAP; NoAm; PPP

The Funeral Parlor. Henry Johnson. And so it was, all the way back to jail. LFAC

Funeral Poem. LeRoi (Imamu Amiri Baraka) Jones. a bright burst of light and holiness/were/ever CNA

The Funeral Rites of the Rose. Robert Herrick. And closed her up as in a tomb. AnAnS 2; CABA; CaPo; OBEV

Funeral Song. Anonymous. I say to myself he is coming. PeSA

Funeral Song for Mamie Eisenhower. Nellie Wong. my tears brim over the Melmac of decorum. BrSi

Funeral Toast. Stephane Mallarme. The solid sepulchre where lie all things that blight,/Both avaricious silence and the massive night LiTW

A Funerall Song (Lamenting Syr Phillip Sidney). Anonymous. Just grief, heart tears, plaint worthy CH

Fungo. Stanley Plumly. ...I want nothing/empty. AmPA

Funiculi, Funicula. Luigi Denza. Joy is everywhere, funiculi, funicula! TreFT

Funky Football. Fareedah Allah. Hell, no, Baby!/They can't win! BlSi

Funnel. Anne Sexton. to question this diminishing and feed a minimum/of children their careful slice of suburban cake. MoAmPo

The Funnels. Christian Morgenstern. ...making/their woodland way/much brighter,/und so/weit-/er. FaBoNo

Funny Face: The Babbitt and the Bromide. Ira Gershwin. Olive oil! Good-bye! ALV

Funny fantasies are never so real as oldstyle. Lawrence Ferlinghetti. Let's lie down somewheres/baby. ErPo

A Funny Joke. Leon Stokesbury. my father was an employee/of the Atlantic-Richfield Corporation. MAYP

The Funny Old Man and His Wife. Anonymous. And at the end she didn't know a bit/What she'd been laughing at. OnUR; SoPo; SUS

Funny Rigs of Good and Tender-Hearted Masters. Anonymous. It would be such funny rigs/Of good and tender-hearted masters. OBET

Furchte Nichts, Geliebte Seele. Louis Untermeyer. In the absence of a shawl. ALV

"The furious gun in his raging ire." Sir Thomas Wyatt. So now hard force my heart doth all to break. FCP

The Furnace of Colors. Vernon Watkins. Yes, and the field flowers, these deceptive blossoms,/Break from the furnace. NYBP

Furnished Lives. Jon Silkin. I ask you often, but you never say? NePoEA-2; NMP; NoAm

The Furnished Room. James Merrill. What no one else could wreak/On the room's myth. NOBA

Furniture. Chana Bloch. we never heard them go out. GP

Furniture. Phyllis Harris. ...themselves the only/shelter they have found NYBP

The Furniture Man. Dick Gallup. The Canadian border/He holds in his hand ANYP

The Furniture of a Woman's Mind. Jonathan Swift. So, holla boys; God save the King. CEP; PPoe

The Furniture of the Poem. Dennis Saleh. Don't be afraid, Here I am, Here I am! NeAC

Furry Bear. A.(lan) A.(lexander) Milne. I'd sleep all the winter in a big fur bed. SoPo; TiPo

Further Advantages of Learning. Kenneth Rexroth. The opening into that/ Busy place of a better world. TAP

Further in Summer Than the Birds. Emily Dickinson. Yet a Druidic Difference/Enhances Nature now. ForPo; LiTA; MAmP; NOBA; NoP

Further Instructions. Vincent O'Sullivan. Take a look. Let your eye cast its own bronze,/the bronze of pure occasion justify your eye. OCNZ

Further Instructions. Ezra Pound. Or that there is no caste in this family. AnAmPo; MP; TwCP

Further Language from Truthful James. Bret (Francis Bret Harte) Harte. Or is the Caucasian played out? FaBoCo; NOBL

Further Notice. Philip Whalen. Like Yellowstone National Park. PoM; VGW

Fury against the Moslems at Uhud. Hind bint Utba. War will hit you hard/coming at you like lions raging. WPOW

The Fury of Aerial Bombardment. Richard Eberhart. Distinguished the belt feed lever from/the belt holding pawl. AmP; BiP; CMoP; ExPo; FaBoMo; FF; FYAP; HeIP; HoPM; InPK; LiTA; LiTM; MiAP; MP; NIP; NMP; NoAm; NoP; OBWP; PrIm; TAP; TwCP; UnPo; VGW; WaP

The Fury of Cocks. Anne Sexton. blooming, blooming, blooming/into the sweet blood of woman. CAPP

The Fury of Flowers and Worms. Anne Sexton. They slide into the ear of a corpse/and listen to his great sigh. BoWoP

The Fury of Hating Eyes. Anne Sexton. Look! Look! Both those/mice are watching you/from behind the kind bars. TW

Fury's Field. Cecil Bodker. and plough the field of your fury/before they will see your face. PBWP

Fury Said to a Mouse. Lewis (Charles Lutwidge Dodgson) Carroll. I'll try/the whole/cause,/and/condemn/you/to/death. NoP

Fuscara or the Bee Errant. John Cleveland. The Bee committed Paricide. AnAnS 2

De Fust Banjo. Irwin Russell. Fur whar you finds de nigger–dar's de/banjo an' de 'possum! AA; BLPA; HBV 1-2

Futility. Wilfred Owen. –O what made fatuous sunbeams toil/To break earth's sleep at all? AtBAP; CBEP; ChMP; CMoP; CoBMV; FaBoMo; GTBS-P; MMM; MoAB; MoBrPo; NoAm; NoP; OAEP; OBWP; SeCePo; TrGrPo

The Future. Matthew Arnold. Murmurs and scents of the infinite sea. OAEP

The Future. Michael Benedikt. ...we will be/aware as never before of the portability of time. SUW

The Future. George Frederick Cameron. Ye write such words–as these of those who were! OBCV

The Future. James Oppenheim. He did not answer: I started out. TrJP

The Future. Edward Rowland Sill. No curse, no care. AnNE; HBV 1-2

The Future. Vahan Tekeyan. See: with the voice of my past and the face of my soul. AMV-81

The Future and the Ancestor. Andrée Chedid. Let us precede ourselves/across new thresholds. WPOW

Future Blues. Willie Brown. Lord bless that woman/that: put that thing on me BluL

Future generation. Nila NorthSun. he kept thinking of/his own 8 grandchildren. STE

The Future Is for Tomorrow. Anna Greki. The future is for tomorrow. WPOW

The Future Verdict. Ada Cambridge. This wasted chance, and with celestial rage/Cry "O what fools were we!" NOAV

A fuzzy fellow, without feet. Emily Dickinson. To tell the pretty secret/Of the Butterfly! TAP

Fuzzy-Wuzzy. Rudyard Kipling. You big black boundin' beggar–for/you bruk a British square. BrPo; EnLit; HBV 1-2; MCCG; MoBrPo; TrGrPo

Fuzzy Wuzzy, Creepy Crawly. Lillian Schulz Vanada. You were once a caterpillar,/Wriggly, wiggly fellow. SoPo; SUS; TiPo

Fuzzy Wuzzy Was a Bear. Anonymous. Fuzzy Wuzzy wasn't fuzzy,/Was he? NTCP

G

G. Hilaire Belloc. Remember to be thankful for the same. FiBHP

D.G.C. to J.A. Emily Bronte. Me to strike for your life's blood, and you to strike for/mine. BrRo

G. K. Chesterton. Humbert Wolfe. ...when he heard the news/that the place was run by Jews. TrJP

G. K. Chesterton on His Birth. Alfred Edward Housman. Gin on the bun-shops and copy-book stalls. FaBoNo; NLV

G.M.B. Donald Davie. And yet the truth is, fail we must/And be forgiven. OxBC

Gaa-A-Muna, a Mountain Flower. Harold Littlebird. Gaa-a-muna, a mountain flower/With tender blue petals OxBS; VoR

The Gaberlunzie Man. Anonymous. While we shall be merry and sing.' BSV; EnSB; GoTS; OxBB

Gabriel. Adrienne Rich. ...will you stay looking/straight at me/awhile longer VGW

Gabriel. Willard Wattles. That will not fade or vanish/While the arch of Heaven stands. HBMV

Gabriel John. Anonymous. If you please you may, or let it alone,/'Tis all one. CBEP

Gabriel Meets Satan. John Milton. ...fled/Murmuring, and with him fled the shades of night. LoBV

Gabriel's Blues. Calvin Forbes. Dust and dirt blow into my trailing face. PoA

Gadoshkibos. Diane Burns. and he wanders the woods and wonders where the warriors have gone. STE

The Gaelic. Blanche Mary Kelly. Not with my tongue I answer, but my tears. CAW

A Gaelic Christmas. Liam P. Clancy. With a joy untold my kin would rally/To dower with gifts the Lamb of God. ISi

The Gaelic Litany to Our Lady. Anonymous. O Ladder of heaven. CAW; ISi

Gaeltacht. Pearse Hutchinson. because we are strangers. BIrV

Gaffer Gray. Thomas Holcroft. Of his morsel a morsel will give,/Well-a-day. HBV 1-2; NOEC

A Gaggle of Geese, A Pride of Lions. John Moore. and the cubs tangled like liquid buckskin/across the sofa back. DuDa

Gaiety of Descendants. Douglas Newton. To fly me to the Scilly Islands,/Isles of Scilly, Scilly. NeBP

Gaiety: Queer's Song. Richard Howard. Handmaid and Hangman to your need,/Is audience. ErPo

Gaily I Lived. Anonymous. Should think of me, who never thought of him. ELU

Gaily the Troubadour. Thomas Haynes Bayley. Lady love, lady love, welcome me home. BLSo

Gain without Gladness. Liadan. Without his love it cannot last. WPOW

Gal I Left Behind Me. Anonymous. The gal I left behind me. ABF; BPAW; CoSo

Galante Garden. Juan Ramon Jimenez. Spring morning! PoPl

Galatea Again. Genevieve Taggard. And stun you with the quiet gaze of stone. WHA

Gale in April. Robinson Jeffers. From beauty to the other beauty, peace, the night splendor. MoAB; MoAmPo

The Gale of August, '27. Anonymous. O, may we meet together there and dwell in endless peace! ShS

Galete Garden. Juan Ramon Jimenez. And is the illusion no one? WSC

Galileo Galilei. William Jay Smith. At a small secluded doorway/In the ordinary brain. PoCh

Gallant Chateau. Wallace Stevens. The curtains are stiff and prim and still. MoAB; MoAmPo

The Gallant Fifty-One. Henry Lynden Flash. Gallant band of Fifty-one! PAH

The Gallant Fighting "Joe." James Stevenson. We'll follow him with heart and hand,/Wherever he does go. PAH

The Gallant Highwayman. James De Mille. For you can take your lives away/By giving up your purses. WHW

Gallantly within the Ring. John Hamilton Reynolds. Hurl a courageous splendid light/Into the eye,–and then,–the FIGHT! SD

Gallantry. Keith Douglas. (the air commented in a whisper). OBWP

The Gallery. Andrew Marvell. Transplanting Flow'rs from the green Hill,/To crown her Head, and Bosome fill. AnAnS 1; MeLP; NoP; OBS

Gallery of My Heart. King D. Kuka. Walk in, enjoy my treasures. VoR

Gallery Shepherds. Patricia Beer. Kings, entirely urban, whom the artist/Paints as such. OxBC

The Galley. Sir Thomas Wyatt. And I remain despairing of the port. OBSC

The Galley of Count Arnaldos. Henry Wadsworth Longfellow. Only those who brave its dangers/Comprehend its mystery!' OBEV; OBVV

The Galley-Slave. Rudyard Kipling. God be thanked! Whate'er comes after, I have lived and toiled with men! BrPo

The Galley Slave (excerpt). Anonymous. He sigh'd and expired at the oar. PeD

The Galliass. Walter De la Mare. She alone burns none to prove her Sleep.' FaBoTw

Gallop, Gallop to a Rhyme. Monica Shannon. Wind the clock and hear it chime! SiSoSe

A Gallop of Fire. Marie E. J. Pitt. ...Death's own pale horses,/That raced in the tracks behind. PoAu 1-2

Galloping. Cordelia Chitty. And the regular jolt of the horse as he moves. PH

The Galloping Cat. Stevie Smith. To pity a cat like me that/Gallops about doing good. BrRo

Gallow Hill. William J. Tait. In sic a sark o fire, I burn/Trowe Heevin an Aert an Hell! OxBS

The Galloway Shore. Sydney Tremayne. I leaned against a rock, out of the wind. BSV

The Gallows. Edward ("Edward Eastaway") Thomas. On the dead oak tree bough. ChMP; FM; HaMV; InPS; LiTB; MoAB; MoBrPo; NoAm; PAI; UnPo

Gallows and Cross. J. E. H. MacDonald. And heavy was the lowered sky/With sin and pain and loss. CaP

The Gallows Pole. Anonymous. Didn't come to see you hangin'/By the gallows pole. FSW

The Gallows Tree. Frederick Robert Higgins. Creaking, creaking,/High in the hangman's tree. OnYI

Galoshes. Rhoda Warner Bacmeister. All round her galoshes! BrR; NTCP; SoPo; TiPo

Galway. Donagh MacDonagh. A town moored in mud. NeIP

Galway. Louis MacNeice. The war came down on us here. OxBI

Galway. Mary Devenport O'Neill. "Please God, to-morrow!/Then we will work and play." NeIP; OxBI

Galway Races. Anonymous. But failte and hospitality, inducing fresh acquaintance. OxBoLi; SD

The Gambler. Anonymous.
I'm bound to gamble all my life, Du-da, du-da, day. AmFP
I was thinking about that woman that I love,/Run away with another man. FSW
It won't be long till he'll die. ViBoFo

The Gambler's Blues (St. James Infirmary Blues). Anonymous. If anybody happens to ask you,/Then I've got those gambler's blues. TrAS

The Gambler's Repentance. Baron of Offaly, Gerald. In this most vile and sinful cast/Which I will still abhor. AnIV

The Gamblers. Anthony Delius. and pile their silver counters on the beach. PeSA

Gambling. Royall Tyler. Win all your winnings and leave naught,/But sorrow and repentance. TAP

The Gamboling Man (C vers.). *Anonymous.* I'll travel the world over wherever he may roam. AS

The Game. Walker Gibson. On every fall I feel a full year older! NePoAm-2

The Game. Winfield Townley Scott. He goes again–goes his own gait. AnAmPo

Game after Supper. Margaret Atwood. He will be an uncle,/if we are lucky. FaBoWP

A Game at Salzburg. Randall Jarrell. The world whispers: Hier bin i'. MiAP; NoAm

A Game of Chance. Howard Moss. Death is your lover and our body bends/To meet his dark, possessive head. PoA

A Game of Consequences. Paul Dehn. And little Miss Montague screams in her ward. ErPo; FiBHP; NOBL

.The Game of Cricket. Hilaire Belloc. The miserable little Bitch! DBV; FiBHP

A Game of Dice. *Anonymous.* If you could only do as well at night. UnTE

A Game of Glass. Alastair Reid. Which side is the mirror on? NePoEA; PoCh

The Game of Life. John Godfrey Saxe. The victor is he who can go it alone! BLPA; BLPL

Game Out of Hand. Allison Ross. What shall we do to redeem it? GoYe

Game Resumed. Richmond Lattimore. my self. LiSp; NYBP

Gamecock. James Dickey. Battling to the death for what is his. HoPM; UnPo

Games. Sandra McPherson. ...She forgets it easily,/Who never speaks of losing. LCAP

Games, Hard Press and Bruise of the Flesh. R. G. Vliet. not flags of sex even can brag such sport. WeW

Gamesters All. DuBose Heyward. And, down the heat, I heard a woman moaning. HBMV

Gammer Gurton's Needle: Back and Side, Go Bare. William Frederic Stevenson. With jolly good ale and old. EG; EnLi 1-2

Ganga. Thomas Blackburn. For the sake of the bent bow and the silent archer,/Ganga, river of God, come down from the sky.' MoBS

The Ganges. Norman Dubie. Children watering their charges, the black lulled elephants. LCAP

The Gangrel Rymour and the Pairdon of Sanct Anne. Tristan Corbiere. A true sign o the Corse for ye. OBVE

Gangrene. Philip Levine. You are dead. AmPC; VGW

The Gangster's Death. Ishmael Reed. I'm always glad when the chickens come home to roost PoBA

Ganymede. Witter ("Emanuel Morgan") Bynner. Ganymede feels the talons in his spine/Lift him Olympian to lustier wine. AnFE; CoAnAm

Ganymede. William Plomer. BIG BIRD SENSATION, MISSING LOCAL BOY. PeHV

Ganymede and Helen. *Anonymous.* And if ever I should sin so, Lord, have mercy! PeHV

The Gaol Song. *Anonymous.* I'll leave the turnkeys all behind,/The wheel to tread and the corn to grind. GBP

The Gap in the Cedar. Roy Scheele. and then I saw through the swirling. Psk; SM

The Gar. Charles G. Bell. Of the South, you are strong; time is yours; you will/endure. AmFN

Garadh. Padraic Colum. And all the living thoughts I had/Are like far ships at sea! OnYI

A Garage in Co. Cork. Derek Mahon. Not in the hope of a resplendent future/But with a sure sense of its intrinsic nature. FaBoIP

Garage Sale. Karl Shapiro. In this scene nothing serious can go wrong. Psk

Garcia Lorca. Louis Dudek. a child had been taken from bed/and broken in our hands. NOBC

Garcia Lorca Murdered in Granada. John Streeter Manifold. Could not cosset their deformity/Save in a Granada lacking/Federico Garcia Lorca. CBAP

The Garden. Joseph Beaumont. A paradise I planted see/On open Calvary. JCP; OBS; OxBoCh

The Garden. George M. Brady. Or sees the eagles gathering, the farms afire? NeIP

The Garden. Digby Mackworth Dolben. I turned–and so she kissed me. GoBe

The Garden. Hilda ("H. D.") Doolittle. Turning it on either side/Of your path. AnFE; APA; AtBAP; LiTA; MAPA

The Garden. Caroline Giltinan. Love lives in gardens–/God and lovers know! HBMV

The Garden. Louise Gluck. laid like weights on the table. AmPA; FiCP

The Garden. Nicholas Grimald. Seed, leaf, flower, fruit, herb, bee, and tree, and more, then I may sing. OAEL 1-2

A Garden. Andrew Marvell.

And men did rosy garlands wear? HBV 1-2; OBEV; PoPle

How could such sweet and wholesome hours/Be reckoned but with herbs and flowers? AnAnS 1; AnEnPo; AtBAP; AWP; BiP; BLPL; CEP; DiPo; ExPo; ForPo; HAP; HBV 1-2; InPo; InPS; InvP; JCP; LiTB; LoBV; MasP; MeLP; MePo; NIP; NOBE; NoP; OAEL 1-2; OAEP; OBS; PAI; PoEL 1-5; PoLf; PoPle; PoRA; PPoe; PPP; QFR; SeCePo; SeCeV; SeCP; SeCV 1-2; TEP; TrGrPo; ViBoPo; WHA

To live in Paradise alone.... CH

The Garden. Rose Parkwood. Two of Thy children all the days of their life will work in Thy/Garden, Lord! WGRP

The Garden. Ezra Pound. And is almost afraid that I will commit that indiscretion. AWP; CABA 049; HeIP; InPo; LiTA; MoAB; MoAmPo; MP; NIP; NoP; OBSP; PPP; SOTW; TwCP

The Garden. James Shirley. So sad, and true, it may invite/My self to die, and prove mine owne. CavP; OBS

The Garden. Marvin Solomon. With its spears–radios, screen doors, and chromed voices. NePoAm

The Garden. Mark Strand. in the moment before it disappears. GeTw

The Garden. Joshua Sylvester. Rose, lily, violet, marigold, pink, pansies. CBEP

The Garden. Jones Very. No more for sin's dark stain the debt of death to pay. AP; MAmP; OxBA; TAP

Garden at Heidelberg. Walter Savage Landor. From south to north/For this fresh air and fragrant wine. OBTV

The Garden at St. John's. May Swenson. ripping its way through the denim air NePoEA; PoPl

The Garden Boy. Bonisile Joshua Motaung. He never responds,/But says "SHIT!"/Without being heard. WhB

The Garden by Moonlight. Amy Lowell. But who belonging to me will they know/When I am gone. NMM

A Garden by the Sea. William Morris. Once seen, once kissed, once reft from me/Anigh the murmuring of the sea. NOBE; OAEL 1-2; OBNC; PoEL 1-5

Garden Fancies. Robert Browning.

Dry-rot at ease till the Judgment-day! CTC; EnLi 1-2; VLP

Roses, you are not so fair after all! ACV; VLP

The Garden Hose. Beatrice Janosco. I can hear it swallow. NTCP; PoL

The Garden in September. Robert Bridges. Some stormy council hold in the high trees. PoPle

Garden Lore. Juliana Horatia Ewing. 'Twas the bird that sits in the medlar-tree,/Who sang these gardening saws to me. OxBChV

A Garden Lyric. Frederick Locker-Lampson. If you lift a guinea-pig by the tail/His eyes drop out! HBV 1-2; PeD

The Garden of Appleton House, Laid Out by Lord Fairfax... Andrew Marvell. We ordnance plant and powder sow. NOBE

The Garden of Earthly Delights. Charles Simic. I piss in the sink/with a feeling of/eternity. NoP

The Garden of Epicurus. George Meredith. The crucifix that came of Nazareth. ATP

"Garden of Gethsemane." Boris Pasternak. So shall the centuries drift, trailing like a caravan,/Coming for judgment, out of the dark, to me. MoRP

The Garden of God. George William Russell. To sweeten the dead air. WGRP

The Garden of Love. William Blake. And binding with briars my joys and desires. AWP; CABA; DiPo; EnLoPo; EnRP; ExPo; FaBV; GBL; HAP; InPo; LiTB; LiTL; LoBV; MAT; NIP; NoP; SeCeV; SoSe; TEP; ViBoPo

The Garden of Olives. Rainer Maria Rilke. and they are abandoned of their fathers/and shut out of their mothers' hearts. MoRP

The Garden of Proserpine. Algernon Charles Swinburne.

Only the sleep eternal/In an eternal night. AWP; BLPA; BLPL; BoLiVe; DiPo; ExPo; FaBoRV; FaBV; FaPoR; ForPo; HAP; HBV 1-2; InPo; LiTB; MaVP; NOBE; NOBV; NoP; OAEP; OBNC; PoEL 1-5; PoPl; PoPle; PoRA; SCV; SeCePo; SeCeV; TreFT; TrGrPo; VLP; WHA

That even the weariest river/Winds somewhere safe to sea. ViBoPo

The Garden of Shadow. Ernest Christopher Dowson. Nor part in seed-time nor in harvesting. HBV 1-2; OBNC

The Garden of Ships. Douglas Stewart. Now they were strong they could reach it, and they must go. CBAP; PoAu 1-2

A Garden of Situations. Jack Anderson. Bounded on the near side/By uncertain ground/And on the far side by frenzy. PoA

The Garden of the Holy Souls. Harriet Eleanor Hamilton King. To kiss Thy feet. ACP

The Garden Party. Hilaire Belloc. And the flood destroyed them all. DTC; MoVE

The Garden Party. Donald Davie. But theirs is all the youth we might have had. NePoEA

Garden Party. Mary Mills. ...leaving the wet green curly/sod to the six o'clock vultures hovering nearby. NePoAm

Garden Party. Sir Herbert Read. Running over the bright/Green mould of an apple-tree. BrPo

Garden Puzzle. Gray Burr. Wiser than any we know if the solving's a matter/For life, not death. CoPo

The Garden Seat. Thomas Hardy. They are as light as upper air! GoJo; HAP

Garden-Song. James Branch Cabell. Afield is no unpleasant place. HBMV

A Garden Song. Henry Austin Dobson. Find the fair Pierides! BoNaP; HBV 1-2; LoBV; OBEV; OBNC; OBVV

A Garden Song. Thomas Moore. And feel his little silvery feet. BoNaP

A Garden Song. George R. Sims. And watch the product coming up. NOBV

The Garden That I Love. Florence L. Henderson. Sorrow and sighing shall be swept away! HBV 1-2

The Garden Where There is No Winter. Louis James Block. God wills it—for the enchanted Soul's fair/sake. AA

The Garden Year. Sara Coleridge. Chill December brings the sleet,/Blazing fire, and Christmas treat. FaBoBe; GoTF; HBV 1-2; HBVY; TreFT

The Gardener. *Anonymous.*
And aye when you come into my sight/I'll wish you were away. GBP
And your head shall be deckd with the eastern wind,/And the cold rain on your breast. BaBo; CBEP; ESPB

The Gardener. Evelyn Eaton. not yet my Lord's feet. GoYe

Gardener. Ralph Waldo Emerson. See the plum redden, and the beurre stoop. OxBA

The Gardener. Laurence Housman. Uproot and bear me in Thy Breast,/And plant me where it please Thee best! TrPWD

The Gardener. Sidney Keyes. O it is terrible to dream of angels. ChMP; MoAB; MoBrPo

The Gardener. Robert Louis Stevenson. O how much wiser you would be/To play at Indian wars with me! HBV 1-2; HBVY; TreFS

The Gardener. Arthur Symons. And leaves his children to sleep on/In the one quiet bed. BoNaP

The Gardener. John Hall Wheelock. This kiss, father, from him who was your son. NYBP

The Gardener at Thirty. Jascha Kessler. How I died waiting in my dream. AmPC

Gardener Janus Catches a Naiad. Edith Sitwell. Naiad changes–/Quick as these. MoAB; MoBrPo

The Gardener's Cat. Patrick Reginald Chalmers. And if you're humble in estate,/Dream splendidly, at any rate! HBMV; HBVY

The Gardener's Song. Lewis (Charles Lutwidge Dodgson) Carroll. "And all its mystery," he said,/"Is clear as day to me!" HBV 1-2

The Gardener to His God. Mona Van Duyn. ...and it all dies/down, down into the great world's flowering. TrCP; UnPo

Gardeners. David Ignatow. beside her grandfather's elderly puppet walk. PCP

Gardens Are All My Heart. Eve Triem. Saint's grove, my rest at night. GoYe

Gardens No Emblems. Donald Davie. Say, light proceeding edgewise, like a sword. LiTM; NePoEA-2; OAEL 1-2

The Gardens of Alcinous. Alexander Pope. To various use their various streams they bring,/The people one, and one supplies the King. OAEL 1-2

The Gardens of Cymodoce. Algernon Charles Swinburne. Black rocks for thy thorns. FaBoPP

The Gardens of Proserpine. Turner Cassity. She counts the alien seed. PoA

The Gardens of the Sea. George Sterling. When in those gardens of the sea/The lilies of the moon should gleam. EtS; EvOK

Gare du Midi. W. H. Auden. He walks out briskly to infect a city,/Whose terrible future may have just arrived. OBSP

Garfield's Ride at Chickamauga. Hezekiah Butterworth. But floats the flag of forty stars/By Chickamauga River. PAH

Gargoyle. Thomas Rabbit. Their looks are incidental, monumental, sweeping. MAYP

Gargoyle. Carl Sandburg. ...The/fist is pounding and pounding, and the mouth answering. NoAm; NOBA

The Garibaldi Hymn. Luigi Mercantini. The Day is dawning, the Day is dawning, which shall be our own. WBLP

The Garland. Henry Vaughan. A garland, where comes neither rain, nor wind. AnEnPo

The Garland and the Girdle. Buonarroti Michelangelo. What would my arms do in that girdle's place? AWP

Garland for a Propagandist. Ted Pauker. I'll be a Party hack, Sir! NOBL

Garland for a Storyteller. Jessie Farnham. But I would gladly forfeit both/For tales my father told. GoYe

A Garland for Heliodora. Meleager. Queen of them all, the red red rose, the flower which/lovers love. AWP; EnLi 1-2

A Garland of Precepts. Phyllis McGinley. But do not give advice at all. NLV

A Garland of Recital Programs. Franklin Pierce ("F.P.A.") Adams. But he had to git out o' dere. InMe

Garland Sunday. Padraic Colum. Man alive! It comes round again! GoYe

Garlic. Marvin Bell. The herb that beat back fever and sore/went home to its family: the lilies. GP

The Garlic. Bert Meyers. my uncles fill/my mouth with ashes. VWA

Garlic. Justin Richardson. Here today and here tomorrow. PV

Garment. Langston Hughes. For the sky to put on/When the weather's bad. GoSl

The Garment of Good Ladies. Robert Henryson. Her hose of Honesty, I guess,/I should for her provide. ACP

Garnishing the Aviary. Margaret Danner. ...Garnishing/the aviary, burnishing this zoo. BP; BPo

Garnyvillo. Edward Lysaght. Beauty, grave, and virtue wait/On lovely Kate of Garnyvillo! IrPN

The Garret. Ezra Pound. the hour of waking together. PoPl; SOTW

The Garrett. William Makepeace Thackeray. Give me the days when I was twenty-one! HBV 1-2

Garrison. Amos Bronson Alcott. Survived, - its ruin and our peace to see. AA

Garrison Town. Emanuel Litvinoff. ...avarice/Gleams in the commercial eye? WaP

Garryowen. *Anonymous.* Where'er we go they dread the name/Of Garryowen in glory. OnYI

Gary Gotow. George Uba. Nostalgia's throat from ear to ear. BrSi

Gas and Hot Air. Morris Bishop. Outworn, burnt out, exhausted–like the bard. OBAL

Gas from a Burner. James Joyce. And sign crisscross with reverent thumb/Memento homo upon my bum. DBV; TW

Gas Lamp. Willis Barnstone. It's 1893. Sarah dies. My father's born. VWA

Gasbags. *Anonymous.* And light the world with gas. NOBL

Gasco; or, The Toad. Gunter Grass. when he breathes in and out/we can cook ELU

Gascoigne. Thomas, Earl of Dorset Sackville. Then will I laugh and clappe my hands,/As they do now at mee. FaBoEn

Gascoigne's Good Morrow. George Gascoigne. Lord, for thy mercy, lend us might/To see that joyful day! AAS; EnRePo; NOCV

Gascoigne's Lullaby. George Gascoigne. Remember Gascoigne's lullaby. NoP; PoEL 1-5; TrGrPo

Gascoigne's Memories. George Gascoigne.
It is enough and as good as a feast. EnRePo
That haste makes waste, and therefore still I say/No haste but good, where wisdom makes the way. EnRePo
Who spares the first and keeps the last unspent,/Shall find that sparing yields a goodly rent. EnRePo

Gascoigne's Passion. George Gascoigne. Yet grant with me that Gascoignes passions past./Ever or Never. NCEP

Gascoigne's Praise of His Mistress. George Gascoigne. Dame Favor is my mistress' name, Dame Fortune is her/maid. EnRePo

Gascoigne's Woodmanship. George Gascoigne. A tedious tale in rime, but little reason. AAS; EnRePo; QFR

The Gascon Punished. Jean de La Fontaine. And from his presence instantly withdrew. UnTE

Gascoygnes Good Night. George Gascoigne. By whome I hope to ryse againe from death and earthly dust./Haud ictus sapio AAS

The Gash. William Everson. And cup my mouth on the gash of everything I craved,/And am ravaged with joy. GP

Gaspar Becerra. Henry Wadsworth Longfellow. Shape from that thy work of art. AnNE

Gaspara Stampa. William Rose Benet. My words, words you may read when I am dead./But I–would sleep. HBMV

Gastric. C. T. Her bread upon the water. PeD

Gastrology (excerpt). Archestratus. ...Who otherwise shall dine,/Are like a troop marauding for their prey. FaBoUs

The Gate. Yasmeen Jamal. When you forget, you return. LFAC

Gate. David McAleavey. towards a gate past which being/ceases, let us say, to surprise. SUW

The Gate. Edwin Muir. And then behind us the huge gate swung open. CMoP; LiTM

The Gate at the End of Things. *Anonymous.* At the gate at the end of things. BLPA

The Gate of the Year. M. Louise Haskins.
And He led me toward the hills and the breaking of day in the/lone East. TRV
Of things both high and low/God hideth His intention. GoTF; TreFS

The Gate's Open. John Blight. and let us mix a little earth with blood. CBAP

Gateposts. Mebdh McGuckian. And watches for the trout in the holy well. FaBoIP

Gates. Ted Kooser. better to leave it standing wide. GP

Gates. Sister Mary Madeleva. And I have come here, seeking mine,/ Jerusalem, Jerusalem! GoBC

Gates and Doors. Joyce Kilmer. Your breast shall be to-morrow/The cradle of a King. HBV 1-2; HBVY

Gates of Damascus. James Elroy Flecker. Who walks thy garden eve on eve, and bows his head, and calls thee Friend. AnFE; BrPo; HBMV

The Gates of the Year. John Mervin Hull. I find the gates of life. STF

The Gates, VI: The Church of Galilee. Muriel Rukeyser. Let them listen to Galilee. GP

The Gateway. A. D. Hope. The means by which I waken into light. BoLoP; ErPo; UnTE

A Gateway to the Sea–St. Andrews. George Bruce. Before dawn kindles a new day. BSV

Gather Kittens While You May (parody). Oliver Herford. And the Kittens of To-day/Will be Old Cats To-morrow. ElL; SpRo

Gather Ye Rosebuds (parody). Laurence Fowler. I must earnestly warn you that you will eventually lose the habit. BXAP

Gather Ye Roses. Robert Louis Stevenson. Gather ye roses while ye may. GoTF; TreFT

Gathered at the River. Denise Levertov. no memory/of shade,/of leaf,/no pollen. SV

The Gathering. Herbert B. Swett. That freedom's god may lead them on, and/Cuba shall be free. PAH

The Gathering. Dwayne Thorpe. they fused into a single stone that struck/ sparks, the leaping green of cottonwood. AMV-81

Gathering Leaves. Robert Frost. And who's to say where/The harvest shall stop? LOW; VGW

The Gathering on the Plains. William Allen Butler. And forts and frontier settlements will all be scenes of blood. PoOW

Gathering the Bones Together. Gregory Orr. They have become a bridge/ that arches toward the other shore. AmPA; GeTw; Psk

Gathering the Sparks. Howard Schwartz. And the Word/Will be spoken/ Again. VWA

The Gatineaus. James Wreford Watson. ...Swing to its strength,/and let it be the hill in you at length. CaP

Gaudeamus Igitur. Anonymous. Let them ever flourish! GLGT

Gaudeamus Igitur. John Addington Symonds. Die the starch-neck Philistine!/Scoffers and defamers! HBV 1-2

Gauley Bridge. Muriel Rukeyser. These people live here. NNaP

The Gauls Sacrifice. Charles M. Doughty. Their faces dead, turned towards Italia. FaBoTw

Gautama. Thomas S. Jones, Jr. Love's very Heart, wherein all Loves shall live. AnAmPo

Gautama in the Deer Park at Benares. Kenneth Patchen. I think we should all go to sleep now,/And not care anymore. NaP

The Gay. George William Russell. Lest they fly on those wild ways/And life be undone. OBMV

Gay Boys. James Kirkup. They dance together, and are truly gay. PeHV

Gay Epiphany. James Mitchell. Boy, at the lovely tip of your external urethral orifice, all my poetries/terminate PeHV

The Gay Gos-hawk. Anonymous. But I cam' here to bonny Scotland/To the man that I lo'e best! BuBa; GN; HBV 1-2

The Gay Goshawk (A version). Anonymous. An ye may boast in southin lans/Your sister's playd you scorn.' ESPB

The Gay Goshawk (E version). Anonymous. For we left father and mother at ESPB

The Gay Jolly Cowboy Is up with the Sun. Anonymous. A cowboy's life for me. CoSo

The Gay Old Hag. Anonymous. Now you're nearly out of date, says the fine old hag. BIrV; IrPN

Gaze North-East. Anonymous. the tide run to/fulness. BIrV

Gaze Not on Youth. Anonymous. She, onely she, is ever chast,/That is with every looke outfast. NCEP

A Gazelle. Richard Henry Stoddard. Than all the burning words in lovers' songs! AA

The Gazelle Calf. D. H. Lawrence. requiring no shoes, O my children! OxBTC

The Gazelles. Thomas Sturge Moore. ...and has fed/Ineffectual herds of vanished delights. BrPo; OBMV

Gazeteer of Newfoundland. Michael Harrington. Field, Lawn and Cape Onion, Juniper Stump, Turk's Gut, and/Spanish Room. CaP

The Gean Trees. Violet Jacob. And the flame o' the gean tree burnin'/By the Sidlaws' side. PoSH

Gebir. Walter Savage Landor.
And the long moon-beam on the hard wet sand/Lay like a jasper column half uprear'd. EnRP
Ploughs up the silvering surface of her plain. OBRV

Gee, but I Want to Go Home. Anonymous. Gee, but I want to go, Gee, but I want to go home. FSW

Gee Ho, Dobin. Anonymous. Ah poor Roger, flimsy Roger, ah poor Roger, hi ho. CoMu

Gee I Like to Think of Dead. Edward Estlin Cummings. and rosebugs i do HoPM

Gee, Officer Krupke. Steven Sondheim. Gee, Officer Krupke, krup you! OBAL

Gee-Up Dar, Mules. Edwin Ford Piper. Gwan-n, mules! Gee-up dar, mules! YaD

Gee up, Neddy, to the Fair. Anonymous. Gee up, Neddy, to the fair. OxNR

Gee, You're So Beautiful That It's Starting to Rain. Richard Brautigan. Marcia's Long Blonde Beauty/A+! WeW

Geeandess. William Cole. Each thought the other/A bit of a twitch. PV

The Geese. Jorie Graham. this astonishing delay, the everyday, takes place. HaCAP

The Geese. Hyam Plutzik. Value the intermediate splendor of birds. BiP

Gehazi. Rudyard Kipling. Gehazi, Judge in Israel,/A leper white as snow! FaBoPV

Geisha. Gary Gildner. praising all the nipples. GP; PoL

Geist's Grave. Matthew Arnold. The dachs-hound, Geist, their little friend. FM; HBV 1-2; NOBV; TEP

Gellatley's Song to the Deerhounds. Sir Walter Scott. Over bank and over brae,/Hie away, hie away. OBRV

Gellius, What Reason Can You Give. Caius Valerius Catullus. ...Virro's strained thighs/And those white lips of yours have something in common. PeHV

The Gem and the Flower. Alexander Pope. And justly set the Gem above the Flow'r. OBEC

Gemini and Virgo. Charles Stuart Calverley. But make no efforts to propound/Any solution of the question. FiBHP

Gemini Elegy. Margaret Gibson. dark threads, brushed wetly over my hands/like nerves, quickening. MAYP

Gemini Jones. Willard R. Espy. Buzzing about, now to, now from,/All the constellations in God's kingDOM. FaBoUs

The Gemlike Flame. R. P. Lister. And that explains why my old friend Mike/Laid him out with a marlinespike. DBV; FiBHP

Gemwood. Marvin Bell. ...that is nothing/when put next to the last crucial fact/of who is doing the crying. FiCP; LCAP

Genealogical Reflection. Ogden Nash. Was ever lavish. ALV; OBAL

Genealogy. Donald Finkel. and begat/and begat/and begat VWA

Genealogy. Eleni Vakalo. Death has not changed my opinion. PBWP

The General. Siegfried Sassoon. But he did for them both by his plan of attack. BrPo; CMoP; DBV; ELU; FaBV; FiBHP; LiTM; MMM; MoVE; OBSP; OBWP; OxBoLi; OxBTC; TW

The General Armstrong. Anonymous. Then haul'd our wind and stood again for/Freedom's happy shore. PAH

A General Communion. Alice Meynell. For each, the whole of the devoted sun. NOCV

The General Eclipse. John Cleveland. Now e'n John Lilburn take 'em for't. AnAnS 2

The General Elliott. Robert Graves. Whether he died for England's pride/ By battle or by pot. DBV

General Howe's Letter. Anonymous. But, fighting or flying,–I'm your very very/humble. PAH

General John. Sir William Schwenck Gilbert. And Private James, by change of names,/Was Major-General John. NA

General Ludd's Triumph. Anonymous. ...no more/Shall deprive honest workmen of bread. OBET

The General Public. Stephen Vincent Benét. ...He made good sport that night. GLGT

A General Rule for the Epact. Anonymous. Which, rejecting the thirties, gives th' epact you sought. FaBoUs

The General's Death. Joseph O'Connor. His manly face turned to the sky,/ And beaten by the rain. AA

General Store. Rachel Field. "What can I do for you to-day?" SoPo; SUS

A General Summary. Rudyard Kipling. Is to-day official sinning,/And shall be for evermore! HBV 1-2

General Vallancey's Waltz. Paul Durcan. Back to the wall, back to the wall,/To Liberty Hall. FaBoIP

General William Booth Enters into Heaven. Vachel Lindsay. Are you washed in the blood of the Lamb? AmLP; ATP; BoC; CMoP; HBV 1-2; InPo; LiTA; LiTM; MoAB; MoAmPo; MoPo; NoAm; NOBA; OxBA; PoA; SeCeV; TAP; TreFS; TrGrPo; WGRP

General Wonder in Our Land. Anonymous. With general love our voices rise/In one great general peal. NOBI

Generalities. Robert Conquest. With his heart completed/And his words in his arms. OxBC

Generalization. Joseph Capp. I maintain, as a rule,/Man's a fool. TreFT

The Generation Gap. Fareedah Allah. Remember...Tom...and...Aunt Jemima/Bent low to pay your dues. BlSi

Generation Gap. Bronwen Wallace. she reads it/as a metaphor/for her AMV-80

Generations. Joseph Awad. He hangs on tight/As if I might. AMV-81

The Generations.   George M. Brady.   And take from us again our living sons.   OnYI

Generations.   Robert Clark.   ...two children stand/Waiting their turn to work the land.   PoAu 1-2

Generations.   Judy Dothard Simmons.   ...so stay alive/to carry on tradition:/we survive   CNA

Generations.   Moishe Steingart.   I go where the sun with its colors falls down.   VWA

Generosity.   *Anonymous.*   These too would Fionn have given away.   KiLC

A Generous Creed.   Elizabeth Stuart Phelps.   Trust him to God. Dear is the trust.   WGRP

The Generous Years.   Stephen Spender.   Have thoughts yet colder than the thing he is.   PoCh

Genesis.   Brian Higgins.   When, lowering the snake, he sent words to prove the/Fall.   FaBoTw

Genesis.   Geoffrey Hill.   Though Earth has rolled beneath her weight/The bones that cannot bear the light.   ACV; HAP; NePoEA; OAEL 1-2; OxBC

Genesis.   John Hall Ingham.   Might be once more the worm, the rock, the/tree?   AA

Genesis.   Lotte Kramer.   The short word "us" at a table.   VWA

Genesis.   Jules Alan Wein.   And death was but the birthcry of/the morrow.   TrJP

Genesis (excerpt).   *Anonymous.*   Under the black coloured, pitch painted roof/Of the well nailed Ark, when there was no need.   PBBP

The Genesis of Butterflies.   Victor Hugo.   Flutter, and float, and change to butterflies.   AWP

Genesis of Vowels.   James Richard Broughton.   Even crawling inside O/it yowls at U and I.   CrMA

Genesis: The Approach of Pharaoh.   Caedmon.   Howl along the hostile trail–hideous slaughter of the host.   WaaP

Geneva.   Alastair Reid.   time falls, snow falls, words fall.   NYBP

The Genie.   Ann Stanford.   The furious spirit you are letting go.   WSC

Genitori.   David Ray.   While we at home, brother, sister, sucked the bloody air.   TW

Genius.   R. J. P. Hewison.   Will travel much faster than/planes.   FaFP

Genius.   Louis Saunders Perkins.   His body lithe and strong and free as a whip in the wind!   PeHV

Genius.   Edward Lucas White.   Yet, till it is burned out, you must remain.   AA; WGRP

Genius Loci.   Margaret Louisa Woods.   And careless pass him by whose is the gift divine.   HBV 1-2; OBEV; OBVV

Genius Loci of the Morning.   Doug Fetherling.   ...not even the cat, who sleeps/between our sets of feet, will be/disturbed.   NeAC

The Genius of Death.   George Croly.   There fixed till the last thunder's sound/Shall bid thy prisoners be unbound.   HBV 1-2

Genocide.   Nora Dauenhauer.   "Let the Whales Live."   TWSS

Gentian.   Elizabeth Green Crane.   Although sad news to his beloved he bears.   AA

The gentian weaves her fringes.   Emily Dickinson.   And of the breeze–amen!   PoRA

Gentilesse.   Geoffrey Chaucer.   Al were he mytre, croune, or diademe.   AWP; CBEP; OAEL 1-2

Gentle Alice Brown.   Sir William Schwenck Gilbert.   On the promising young robber, the lieutenant of his/band.   FaBoCo; FiBHP; InMe; NA

The Gentle Anarchist.   James Brunton Stephens.   And then it's all up with the fly.   NOAV

The Gentle Check.   Joseph Beaumont.   ...I give/My promise here to strive/Before the lark to be at heav'n tomorrow.   PBBP

A Gentle Echo on Woman.   Jonathan Swift.   What woman is and how to guard her well./Guard her well.   ALV; FaBoCo; FiBHP; LiTL; NLV; NU; OLR; OnYI

A Gentle Heart: Two.   Judith Johnson Sherwin.   white weeds on fire/at the fingertips of each hand shoot/and she's got at least fifty of them   BoWoP

The Gentle Hill.   Salvator Quasimodo.   ...a quivering of human steps/upon the banks among the tender canes.   PoPI

Gentle Jesus.   Charles Wesley.   Make me, Saviour, what Thou art;/Live Thyself within my heart.   OxBChV; OxBoCh; TreFS

Gentle Name.   Selma Robinson.   A friendly, wistful name and airy–/Mary.   BiCB; MoShBr

A Gentle Park.   Moss Herbert.   I walk forever in a gentle park.   GoYe

Gentle River, Gentle River.   *Anonymous.*   And without a groan expired.   AWP; LiTW

The Gentle Snorer.   Mona Van Duyn.   he left us so partisan.   NePA

A Gentle Wind.   Fu Hsuan.   To me they seem no more than weeds or chaff.   AWP

A Gentle Word.   *Anonymous.*   By only a gentle word.   PoToHe

The Gentled Beast.   Dilys Bennett Laing.   a speed beyond my speed.   PH

The Gentleman.   Menahem Lonzano.   Alas! An age that honors clothes/Though worn by horse or ass!   TrJP

A Gentleman of Fifty Soliloquizes.   Don (Donald Robert Marquis) Marquis.   My loves you cannot touch. They're buried deep.   HBMV

A Gentleman of the Old School.   Henry Austin Dobson.   Look down upon your narrow house,/Old friend, and miss you!   EnLit; HBV 1-2

Gentlemen.   Geoffrey Taylor.   Is this not too a temple,/A Holy Place?   FaBoEE

Gentlemen-Rankers.   Rudyard Kipling.   God ha' mercy on such as we,/Baa! Yah! Bah!   NOBV

The Gentlest Lady.   Dorothy Parker.   But oh, her heart was like to break/To count another year.   ISi

Gently He Draweth.   *Anonymous.*   Proving His love again and again!   BePJ

Gently, Johnny My Jingalo.   *Anonymous.*   "Gently, Johnny, my Jingalo."   FSW; OBET

Geo-Politics.   Alvaro Cardona-Hine.   with the accuracy of a Chinese Zen master answering a student/has painted a fly   PoDr

The Geographers.   Karl Shapiro.   Wars cannot change the shapes of continents.   OxBA

Geography.   Michael Dransfield.
in the forest, the uncharted/uplands of the spirit   CBAP
...now rain cleans the air, and falls,/and falls, and will be falling. CBAP

Geography.   Eleanor Farjeon.   The little white-skinned stranger who is in Geography!   BrR

Geography.   Kenneth Koch.   The lake was covered with gloom. Enna plunged into it/screaming.   AmPC; NoAm

Geography: A Song.   Howard Moss.   And silent is/Long Island Sound.   CAD; PV

Geography Lesson.   Carol Rumens.   You're all the hurt geography I own.   FaBoWP

Geological Faults.   Barbara Unger.   The broken wing.   AMV-81

Geometry.   Rita Dove.   They are going to some point true and unproven.   HaCAP

Geometry.   Alfred Kreymborg.   Death being kittens/who once chased their tails.   *AnAmPo

Geordie.   *Anonymous.*   Stole sixteen of the King's royal deer/And he sold them in Gilhooley.   FSW

Geordie (A version).   *Anonymous.*   "The fairest flower o woman-kind/Is my sweet, bonie lady!"   BaBo; ESPB; FaBoBa; OxBB

Geordie (B vers.).   *Anonymous.*   The birds in the air, that fly together pair and pair,/Bear witness, Ann, that I love thee.   BaBo

Geordie (C vers.).   *Anonymous.*   Because he was of that royal blood,/And was loved by a virtuous lady.   BaBo

Geordie (D version).   *Anonymous.*   That I may write into the north/I have wone the life o Geordie'?   ESPB; OBET

Geordie (Georgie).   *Anonymous.*   Saying, "Here lies the body of Georgie.'"   AmFP

George.   Hilaire Belloc.   The moral is that little Boys/Should not be given dangerous Toys.   FiBHP

George.   Dudley Randall.   A long time yet, because you're strong as a mule.   BP; BPo; ConAP; NoAm

George Allen.   *Anonymous.*   The last words that poor Georgie said was, "Nearer, my God, to thee."   AmFP

The George Aloe and the Sweepstake.   *Anonymous.*   This is the last news that I can write to you./To England's coast from Barbary.   BaBo; ESPB; ViBoFo

George Britton.   *Anonymous.*   You're bound to have a hard time wherever you go.   CoSo

George Collins.   *Anonymous.*   He's mourning for his own true love/Just like I mourn for mine.   FSW

George Crabbe.   Edwin Arlington Robinson.
Makes Time so vicious in his reaping.   LiTM
To consecrate the flicker, not the flame. AmePo; AP; BLPL; CMoP; CoBMV; LiTA; MAmP, MoAD, MoAmPo; MoVE; NAMP; NePA; NOBA; NoP; OxBA; PoEL 1-5; PP; TAP

George I,–Star of Brunswick.   William Makepeace Thackeray.   Consistent in his preference for every kind of corruption.   FaBoEE

George II.   William Makepeace Thackeray.   With Pitt on his knees at my dirty feet.   FaBoEE

George III.   Robert Lowell.   morning, noon, and night.   FaBoPV

George III.   William Makepeace Thackeray.   A crazy old blind man in Windsor Tower?   FaBoEE

George IV.   William Makepeace Thackeray.   And the generous aristocracy who admired him.   FaBoEE

George Jones.   *Anonymous.*   They were launched into eternity, and may God grant them rest.   OBSS

George Levison.   William Allingham.   Supernal Wisdom only knows how much.   IrPN

George Ridler's Oven.   *Anonymous.*   Cheek by jowl, my dog and I.   OBET

George Robinson: Blues.   Muriel Rukeyser.   The dust had covered us both, and the dust was white.   NNaP

George Sand.   Dorothy Parker.   (They do those things so well in France).   FiBHP

George the Fourth in Ireland.   George Gordon, Lord Byron.   And Corruption shrunk scorch'd from the glance of his/mind.   OBRV

George the Third.   Edmund Clerihew Bentley.   One can only wonder/At so grotesque a blunder.   DBV; FaBoCo; OxBoLi

George the Third.   George Gordon, Lord Byron.   A lesson which shall be re-taught them, wake/Upon the thrones of earth; but let them quake!'   FiP

George the Third's Soliloquy.   Philip Freneau.   Or share, what still is worse–old Charles's fate.   NOBA

George Towle.   Tony Towle.   which is variable as you drink forever.   ANYP

George Washington.   Anonymous.   This was George Washington.   OHIP

George Washington.   Rosemary and Stephen Vincent Benét.   I'm glad that George was George.   MaC

George Washington.   John Hall Ingham.   The everlasting surges of the tide.   AA; OHIP; PAH; PAL

George Washington.   Shel Silverstein.   And helped us all stay home from school.   PoSC

George Washington.   James S. Tippett.   In all its Valley Forges/As resolute as he.   YeAr

George Washington Goes to a Girlie Movie.   Aram Boyajian.   What are we doing here in the dark?   NeAC

The Georges.   Walter Savage Landor.   (God be praised!) the Georges ended.   ChTr; DBV; FaBoEE; FiBHP; NIP; OBSV

Georges Bank.   Julia Older.   string of pearls with whose final link/their lives, as ours, are irreclaimably fated.   WOLT

Georgia Boy.   Anonymous.   For a lazy man I won't maintain.   OuSiCo

Georgia Dusk.   Jean Toomer.   Bring dreams of Christ to dusky cane-lipped throngs.   AnAmPo; BP; BPo; CDC; NoAm; NoP; PoBA

Georgia Land.   Anonymous.   And I won't be no trouble./Whoa!   OuSiCo

Georgia Towns.   Daniel Whitehead Hicky.   An old man lost in sleep and Time.   AmFN

A Georgia Volunteer.   Mary Ashley Townsend.   Unknown, unnamed, forgotten, lied/A Georgia Volunteer.   AA

The Georgiad.   Roy Campbell.
To dwarf the ox he envies for his size.   MoBrPo
Walk sadly up and down to kill the time.   OxBTC

Georgian Spring.   Roy Campbell.   And all the little sparrows wonder why!   OBSV

The Georgics.   Virgil (Publius Vergilius Maro).
And use thyself betimes to hear and grant our prayers.   AWP
For winter drought rewards the peasant's pain,/And broods indulgent on the buried grain.   EiCP
Heedless of the reins or the charioteer.   LiTW
helpless the charioteer is carried at the will of his horses.   WaaP
So great is their love for praise, their will to win.   SD
That sullen mixture shall at once declare/Winds, rain, and storms, and elemental war.   FaBoUs
There fix their stings, and leave their souls behind.   FaBoUs

Georgie Allen.   Anonymous.   So please, sir, let me be/With the good old engine I loved so well,/One Hundred Forty-three.   BFSS

Georgie Porgie.   Anonymous.   Georgie Porgie ran away.   OxNR

Georgie Porgie (parody).   Franklin Pierce ("F.P.A.") Adams.   Jimmie sees me all the time,–/But Georgie stays away.   HBMV

Georgie Wedlock.   Anonymous.   Now Georgie's a free man in this town,/By the loving of a lady.   AmFP

Georgiques Chretiennes (excerpt).   Francis Jammes.   This turning world, the which like grains we fill.   CAW

Geraldine's Daughter.   Egan O'Rahilly.   That her image must always abide in my heart.   AnIL; OnYI

The Geraldine's Daughter (excerpt).   James Clarence Mangan.   No wonder such heroes and noblemen many/Should cross the blue ocean to kneel at her shrine.   IrPN

Geraldine's Garden.   John Francis O'Donnell.   And a thought I can guess is underneath.   IrPN

The Geraldines.   Thomas Osborne Davis.   Command their son to take the post that fits the/Geraldine.   IrPN

The Geranium.   Theodore Roethke.   But I sacked the presumptuous hag the next week,/I was that lonely.   CoAP; UnPo; WeW

The Geranium.   Richard Brinsley Sheridan.   Oh! who would live if this be death!'   BoLoP; ErPo; UnTE

The Geraniums.   Genevieve Taggard.   They also have good bread.   VGW

The Gerbil Who Got Away.   Judith C. Root.   draughts of vanilla extract.   AMV-81

Gerda, My Husband's Wife.   Eve Triem.   Wailing what you knew–/the love of a stranger/a trapped fox grinning.   GP

The Geriatric Whore.   Pete Winslow.   It's the greatest/Old folks home in the country.   PV

The Germ.   Ogden Nash.   You probably contain a germ.   CenHV; MoShBr

The German Fatherland.   Ernst Moritz Arndt.   All Germany shall be the land!   HBV 1-2

The German Legion.   Sydney Thomas Dobell.   English cot by English water/That shall see the German sea.   PeD

German Shepherd.   Myra Cohn Livingston.   He can never name ocean.   RFM

Germinal.   George William Russell.   He is knit with his doom.   BIrV; MoBrPo; OBEV; OBMV

Germination.   Arlene Stone.   Jehovah the Blind Oculist/saying/You shall be borne.   VWA

Geron and Histor.   Sir Philip Sidney.   To go unto the bride, and use this day/To speak with her while freely speak we may.   SiPS

Geronimo.   Ernest McGaffey.   Mark well his human prototype,/The fierce Apache fettered there.   AA; BPAW; PAH

Geronimo: Old Man Lives On.   Ronald James Dessus.   ...proud–wise and savvy to the white man ways.   LFAC

Gerontion.   Thomas Stearns Eliot.   Thoughts of a dry brain in a dry season.   AP; APA; CMoP; CoBMV; DiPo; EBEV; ExPo; ForPo; GTBS-P; HAP; InPS; LiTA; LiTM; LoBV; MAPA; MoPo; NAMP; NePA; NoAm; NOBA; OAEL 1-2; OAEP; OxBA; PAI; PPP; SBVL; SeCePo; SeCeV; TAP

Gerry's Rocks.   Anonymous.   'Tis the handsome Clara Clark and her true love, brave Monroe.   ABF

Gertrude Stein at Snails Bay.   Peter Porter.   The plane for America is a sort of star   OxBC

Gerusalemme Liberata (excerpt).   Torquato Tasso.   Whilest loving thou mayst loved be with equall crime.   OBVE

A Gest of Robyn Hode.   Anonymous.   For he was a good outlawe,/And dyde pore men moch god.   ESPB; OxBB

Gesture.   Donald Finkel.   softly an inch from your enchanted face.   InPK

Gesture.   Winifred Welles.   They strain out wide and wounded,/Like arms upon a cross.   HBMV

A Gesture by a Lady with an Assumed Name.   James Wright.   To creep outside and see the cops were gone.   ConAP; LiTM

Gestures to the Dead (excerpt).   John Wheelwright.   forever changeless, against a changing sky?   MoVE

Get a Transfer.   Anonymous.   ...the rope,/That lands you at the Station Hope–/Get a transfer.   BLPA; WBLP

Get Into the Boosting Business.   Anonymous.   'Cause he's got the best thing out.   WBLP

Get On Board, Little Children.   Anonymous.   There's room for many a more.   FSW

Get Somebody Else.   Paul Laurence Dunbar.   Nobody else can do the work/That God marked out for you.   BLRP; TRV

Get Stuffed.   Alurista.   long live the revolution   FIA

Get the Gasworks.   David Ignatow.   and papa flings his newspaper outward,/in disgust with discipline.   InPK; PAI

Get Thee Behind Me, Satan.   Millard and Lee Hays Lampell.   I am a Union man,/Gonna leave you behind.   FSW

Get There If You Can and See the Land.   W.H. Auden.   If we don't it doesn't matter, but we'd better start to die.   InPS; NAMP

Get Up.   Philip Levine.   it could be happening to you.   NYP

Get Up!   Joseph Skipsey.   I with a whistle shut the door,/I may not ope again.   NOBV; VLP

Get Up and Bar The Door.   Anonymous.
The barrin' of oor door weel.   BFSS
Get up and bar the door.   ATP; BaBo; BiP; BoLiVe; BSV; EnSB; FaBoBa; GoTS; HeIP; MaC; NoP; OnMSP; OxBS; StPo; TrGrPo; ViBoPo
"John Jones, you have spoken the first word,/Now get up and shut the door."   AmFP

Get Up and Bar the Door (A version).   Anonymous.   "Goodman, you've spoken the foremost/word,/Get up and bar the door."   ESPB

Get Up and Bar the Door (B version).   Anonymous.   "John Blunt, ye hae spoken the fore-/most word,/Ye maun rise up and bar the door."   ESPB

Get Up, Blues.   James A. Emanuel.   Learn what it means/To be up high.   AmNP; BOLo; PoBA

Get Up, Get Up.   Anonymous.   It's nearly time for dinner!   FiBHP; NTCP

Get Up, Jack! John,Sit Down!   Anonymous.   Get up, Jack! John sit down!   ABF

Get You Gone.   Sir Charles Sedley.   For, were I not, you'd leave me too.   ELP

Gethsemane.   Matilda Betham-Edwards.   I weep with thee, and God is here."/Gethsemane!   BePJ

Gethsemane.   Arna Bontemps.   I said your name but silence answered me.   CDC

Gethsemane.   Annette von Droste-Hulshoff.   From out its chaliced pearl the Angel came/To strengthen Him.   CAW

Gethsemane.   Rudyard Kipling.   I drank it when we met the gas/Beyond Gethsemane.   FaBoTw

Gethsemane.   William B. Tappan.   Unheard by mortals are the strains/That sweetly soothe the Saviour's woe.   STF

Gethsemane, Illinois.   Martin Samuel Allwood.   the night of torment cannot grow/into a liberated dawn   LiTW

Gets Hung up on a Dirty, of All Things, Joke (parody).   Henry Taylor.   I shall explain, with love and luck,/Three Chinese sailors and a duck.   BXAP

Gettin' Born.   Anthony Euwer.   He's standin' there out in the air,/A promissory chicken.   PoPl

Getting a Job.   Paul Blackburn.   and the office records it.   NYP

Getting a Poem in the Rain.   Dick Lourie.   and tells me at great length about apples.   NeAC

Getting Across.   Carter Revard.   on the shining girder's side/where he has passed his death.   VoR

Getting at the Root of the Matter (parody).   Henry Taylor.   I found a spring, and cold/clear water tasted good.   BXAP

Getting Back.   Dorothy Brown Thompson.   Getting back together!   SiSoSe

Getting Back to Work.   Leon Baker.   ...and rats running/over my floor (in solitary confinement).   LFAC

Getting by on Honesty.   Stephen E. Smith.   I'd like a rondeau   AMV-80

Getting down to Get over.   June Jordan.   help me/turn the face of history/ to your face.   TAP

Getting Drunk with Daughter.   Robert Huff.   But you and I aren't going to let it rain.   NePoEA-2

Getting Experience.   Miller Williams.   Nobody's going to think you're good and sane and smart.   GP; TAT

Getting inside the Miracle.   Luci Shaw.   Today–another miracle–the feathered/arrows of my faith may link/God's bow and target.   TrCP

Getting Loaded.   Jim Thomas.   and rusty dump rake, the deserted farm house.   AMV-80

Getting Lost in Nazi Germany.   Marvin Bell.   You could swear the voice you hear is kind,/calling you home, little Jewboy in alarm.   VWA

Getting Older Here.   Barbara Hauk.   trying to find/the way back.   AMV-80

Getting On.   Stephen Sandy.   I'll make a smile of teeth. I'll make my mark.   CAD

Getting Out.   J. J. Maloney.   There is openness/wind/trees/children running/To keep appointments I kept long ago.   LFAC

Getting Out.   Cleopatra Mathis.   ...We held on tight, and let go.   MAYP

Getting out of Bed.   Eleanor Farjeon.   Up, sleepy head!   SiSoSe

Getting Serious.   Gary Soto.   Petting one another's love so it won't be sad.   NPGG

Getting Started.   Janet Campbell Hale.   Swept along/and along.   VoR

Getting the Mail.   Galway Kinnell.   ...Kyrie of a chainsaw drifting down off Wheelock Mountain.   UnPo

Getting Through.   Robert P.T. Coffin.   And nothing but opened morning-glories.   AnNE

Getting Through.   Maxine W. Kumin.   they will knock hard to be born.   SUW

Getting Through.   James Merrill.   Cries of snow-crimson children leaving school.   NYBP

Getting to Rome.   Anonymous.   The King you look for here/you won't find unless you bring Him.   NOBI

Getting Under.   Alan P. Lightman.   the bottom.   AMV-81

Getting Up.   Stephen Dobyns.   and the cat takes a half-step, preparing to leap.   MAYP

Getting Up Ahead of Someone (Sun).   Frank O'Hara.   each day's light has more significance these days   ANYP

Getting Up Early.   Robert Bly.   I look up angrily at the light.   NaP

Gettysburg.   James Jeffrey Roche.   The sword of Meade and Lee!   MC; PAH

Gettysburg.   Edmund Clarence Stedman.   "Our grand old Army held the ridge, and/won that glorious day!"   PAH

The Gettysburg Address.   Abraham Lincoln.   shall not perish from the earth.   TRV

Geve Place, Ye Lovers, Here Before.   Henry Howard, Earl of Surrey.   To matche the candle with the sonne.   AAS

Ghaisties.   Robert Garioch.   we'll lauch at daith, an' man, an' the fiend, aw three,/afore we dee.   NeBP

The Ghaists: A Kirk-Yard Eclogue.   Robert Fergusson.   Tell him our ails, that he, wi' wonted skill,/May fleg the schemers o' the mortmain-bill.   OxBS

Ghazal.   Philip Dow.   The dung-beetle is sister to Sisyphus & father/to Ptolemy–in whose mind we lived so long.   NPGG

Ghazal: Japanese Paintbrush.   Randy Mott.   Matisse breathes above his reed brush, while the paint clots and/dries unused.   PoDr

Ghazal of Isa Akhun Zada.   Anonymous.   Beauty with the flame shawl, do not repulse me.   PG

Ghazal XII.   Mirza Ghalib.   no wonder you came/looking for me   LLLT

Ghazals.   Jim Harrison.
...And the inanimate moon/loves him back with silences, and moonbeams made of chalk.   PAI
drags the dead horse away to hollow swelling growls.   NoAm
...Heat comes/out of the center, radiates faintly and no paper will burn.   NoAm
...I'm going to Greenland at dawn.   WeW

A Ghazel of Absence.   Gerrit Lansing.   musicians will play out Gerrit's desire/in the mode of this poem which is like a "gazelle."   CoPo

Gheluvelt.   Robert Bridges.   How we Worcesters lie where we redeem'd the battle.   BrPo

Ghetto Lovesong–Migration.   Carole Gregory Clemmons.   and afterwards,/ sat singing spirituals to sons.   NBP; NMM

Ghetto Summer School.   Douglas Worth.   has anything worth writing down to say.   FF

Ghetto Twilight.   Alter Brody.   Like dry-breasted hags/Welcoming their children to their withered arms.   VWA

Ghost.   Witter ("Emanuel Morgan") Bynner.   Leaving him only motion, only speech.   AnFE

The Ghost.   Charles Churchill.   Features so horrid, were it light,/Would put the Devil himself to flight.   OBSV

Ghost.   Clark Coolidge.   berness/ionalis/deliber.   ANYP

The Ghost.   Hilary Corke.   Whom I have known, but you were not of them.   NYBP

The Ghost.   William Henry Davies.   Confesses to the other's ghost.   BrPo

The Ghost.   Walter De La Mare.
Seem with their quiet to have stilled in/life's dream/All sorrowing now.   OAEP
The sweet cheat gone.   BrPo; CMoP; ELP; EnLoPo; HaMV; HBMV; LiTM; MoAB; MoBrPo; MoVE; NOBE; OAEL 1-2; OxBTC

The Ghost.   Robert Lowell.   Hold: and I grind your manhood bone on bone.   AtBAP; MoVE; PoA

Ghost.   Christian Morgenstern.   A sorrow to the housewife.   WSC

The Ghost.   O'Brien.   Oh! Oh! Oh!   NOEC

Ghost.   John V. A. Weaver.   Oh, God! You think I want to be a ghost?...   HBMV

The Ghost at Anlaby.   Randolph Stow.   I shall go haunting in search of a friend, a friend.   NOAV

Ghost Boy.   Mark Van Doren.   Sometimes a pencil tap.   SO

Ghost-Flowers.   Mary Thacher Higginson.   Forget the vows made in that cloistered/nook.   AA

Ghost House.   Robert Frost.   As sweet companions as might be had.   WSC

The Ghost in the Cellarage.   John Heath-Stubbs.   And the poor ghost under the castle pavement.   NeBP

The Ghost in the Martini.   Anthony Hecht.   Tell her to find her purse.   OxBC

Ghost Night.   Lizette Woodworth Reese.   Although but a ghost/With the ghosts of the year!   HBMV

The Ghost of a Ghost.   Brad Leithauser.   ...a course which homes/outward, and misses nothing at all.   MAYP

The Ghost of an Education.   James Michie.   Scaring strangers, slowing the current, fouling the bed.   NYBP

The Ghost of Lucrece: To Vesta.   Thomas Middleton.   I'll hug thee more than ever I have done.   MOON

The Ghost of the Cargo Boat.   Pablo Neruda.   slow with air and atmosphere and desolate space.   WSC

Ghost Pet.   Horatio Colony.   ...I took it for an omen.   GoYe

Ghost Poem Five.   Mary Norbert Korte.   to make my body full/and moonless light   IHMS

The Ghost's Leavetaking.   Sylvia Plath.   Hail and farewell. Hello, goodbye. O keeper/Of the profane grail, the dreaming skull.   NePoEA-2

The Ghost's Promenade.   Thomas Caulfield Irwin.   Will still remain till I have reached my rest.   IrPN

The Ghost's Song.   Anonymous.   That's to lay me.   FaBoCh; LoGBV

Ghost Story.   Dylan Thomas.   "Let's go in and see if there's any jelly left,'/ Jack said. And we did that.   OBCP

The Ghost That Jim Saw.   Bret (Francis Bret Harte) Harte.   Now I call that meaness!" That's all Jim said.   ShM

The Ghostly Crew.   Anonymous.   I do believe in spirits from that time to this day.   ShS

The Ghostly Father.   Peter Redgrove.   Perhaps one day men would be more spiritual.   MoBS; NePoEA-2

Ghostly Gladness.   Richard Rolle.   But in gladness of God evermore make thou thy glee.   HAP

Ghostly Story.   Milton Acorn.   and a hush as if sparrows were listening.   NeAC

Ghostly Tree.   Léonie Adams.   Or stain a point with blood.   MoAB; MoAmPo

Ghosts.   Elizabeth Jennings.   It is our helplessness they choose/And our refusals that they haunt.   NePoEA-2; PPJ

The Ghosts.   Henry Wadsworth Longfellow.   From the land of the Hereafter.   LoBV

Ghosts.   Ethna MacCarthy.   to lay this cold and lovely dust?   NeIP

Ghosts.   Richard Kendall Munkittrick.   "We are the ghosts of the blossoms/ That died in the early spring."   AA

Ghosts.   Alastair Reid.   Ghost on my desk, speak, speak.   NYBP

The Ghosts of the Buffaloes.   Vachel Lindsay.   Good-night, good-night,...good-night.   MoAmPo; NePA

Ghosts, Places, Stories, Questions.   Vincent Buckley.   ...the few poems/that are the holy spaces of my life.   NOAV

Ghosts' Stories.   Alastair Reid.   The children knew what it was all about.   NePoEA-2

The Ghoul.   Jack Prelutsky.   he hurries to another school/and waits...perhaps for you.   OBCA

Ghoul Care. Ralph Hodgson. You know I'm still your master. AnEnPo; MoBrPo

The Ghyrlond of the Blessed Virgin Marie. Ben Jonson. Of being Daughter, Mother, Spouse of God? ISi

La Gialletta Gallante. Edward, Lord Herbert of Cherbury. And by thy Gold shew like some Copper-mine. AtBAP

Giant Bonaparte. Anonymous. Every morsel snap, snap, snap. OxNR

Giant Decorative Dahlia. Molly Holden. I could not deny it love if I tried. OxBTC

The Giant Puffball. Edmund Charles Blunden. And all my hopes must with my body soon/Be but as crouching dust and wind-blown sand. FaBoTw

Giant's Tomb in Georgian Bay. Katherine"(Amelia Beers Warnock Garvin) "Hale. Out of the naked days. CaP

The Giant Squid of Tsurai. Kirk Robertson. like a revolving door/on a ten-day cycle/and belching. GP

Giant Thunder. James Reeves. Tomorrow you shall have your fill. BoNaP; DuDa

The Giant Tortoise. Edward Lucie-Smith. A ripple in his reverie. BoAnP; PoL

The Giantess. Charles Baudelaire. Like a hushed village underneath a hill. ErPo; OBVE

Giardino Pubblico. Osbert Sitwell. Then in gigantic glory, fade/Sunward through the western glade... ChMP

Gibberish. Mary Elizabeth Coleridge. And when I hear her, I have wings. MoVE

Gibbs (excerpt). Muriel Rukeyser. ...and the refraction carrying fresh clews. ImOP

Gibraltar. Wilfrid Scawen Blunt. To see her red coats marching from the hill. ACP; GTBS; HBV 1-2; OBEV; OBVV

Gibraltar. Richard Chenevix Trench. A glorious picture by the wind unrolled. OBRV; OBTV; OBVV

Gideon at the Well. Geoffrey Hill. ...the armies move,/As out of rock, as floods unfrozen. NePoEA

Gie the Lass Her Fairin'. Robert Burns. An' hey for houghmagandie. CoMu; ErPo

Gife Langour–. Henry Stewart, Lord Darnley. Fairweill. I say no moir. OxBS

Giffen's Debt. Rudyard Kipling. And may in time become a Solar Myth. VLP

The Gift. Anonymous. He moved the gates of heaven apart/And gave to earth–a Mother! PGD

The Gift. Margaret E. Bruner. Here soul meets soul, a precious golden store. PoToHe

The Gift. John Ciardi. That clean white paper waiting under a pen/is the gift beyond history and hurt and heaven. BiP; LiTM; MP; NMP

Gift. Leonard Cohen. and you would hand it back to me. NoAm; SoSe

The Gift. Robert Creeley. ...is/that all, is/that all. NOBA

The Gift. Louise Gluck. At the screen/welcoming each beast/in love's name, Your emissary. FaBoWP; GP

Gift. Judith Hemschemeyer. A poor shawl for your perfect throat. PCP

The Gift. Dick Lourie. there it is: I give you my gift. NeAC

The Gift. Ed Ochester. and the gift of a sweet-faced cat. DFF; GP; Psk

The Gift. George William Russell. And out of hell, beyond its iron bars,/My scorn of all its pains. HBMV

The Gift. Ann Stanford. Fruit, flower, or stone, or given or taken. GP

The Gift. William Carlos Williams. and bowed down/to worship/this perfection. MoRP; NcPoAm-2; PoPl

Gift for the Queen. Anonymous. She gave me a diamond,/As big as my shoe. OxNR

Gift from Kenya. May Miller. That has no end in single flesh/However wound in death. BlSi

Gift Hour. Maria Banus. ...shivering and full like two cups of milk. BoWoP; VWA

Gift of a Mirror to a Lady. David Wagoner. Then shatter the mirror. It was made to shatter. NePoAm-2

The Gift of a Skull. John Skelton. To behold and see/The Trinity. Amen. ACP

A Gift of God. Anonymous. The joy that only Jesus gives/Makes life worth living here below! STF

The Gift of God. Edwin Arlington Robinson. Half clouded with a crimson fall/Of roses thrown on marble stairs. AnAmPo; AP; CoBMV; MAPA; MoAB; MoAmPo; OxBA

The Gift of Gravity. Wendell Berry. This grace is gravity. GeTw

A Gift of Great Value. Robert Creeley. ...and a great/wind we ride. LCAP; NaP

Gift of Sight. Robert Graves. Nor ever before had I been aware of the sky. PCP

The Gift of Song. Anthony Hecht. ...may she by these songs/Know it was love I looked for at her hands. NYBP

The Gift of Song. Horace. By thee I please, by thee I live. LiTW

The Gift of Water. Hamlin Garland. Brothers in bond of the water's ring. AnAmPo; BPAW

The Gift Outright. Robert Frost. Such as she was, such as she would become. AmFN; AP; CMoP; CoBMV; CrMA; InPo; LiTM; LoGBV; MoAB; MoAmPo; NoAm; NOBA; NoP; OxBA; PAL; PPP; WaP

Gift to a Jade. Anna Wickham. At that cold moralist I hotly hurled/His perfect, pure, symmetrical, small world. DBV; ELU; OBSP

The Gift to Be Simple. Howard Moss. And I would remember, now the world is less,/His gentleness. ImOP; MoRP; MP; Psk; TwCP

Gifts. Mary Elizabeth Coleridge. I saw the thing that should have pierced his heart/Turn to a golden staff. PBWP

Gifts. Hazel Harper Harris. Has something special to enjoy. BiCB

The Gifts. John Heath-Stubbs. Making the taste of death/Medicinal, preservative.' OxBC

Gifts. Emma Lazarus. Immortal through the lamp within/his hand. TrJP; WGRP

The Gifts. Charles Levendosky. the shaft of light/thru a chink in roof/falls at your feet. TAT

Gifts. Chauncey R. Piety. And the world is their domain. PGD

Gifts. Karen Snow. We surmount our spoilers, sometimes. FYAP

Gifts. Leon Stokesbury. ...and a little/nearer the vanishing point, thank you. GP

The Gifts of God. George Herbert. If goodness lead him not, yet weariness/May toss him to My breast. GTBS; GTBS-P; TRV

The Gifts of God. Jones Very What none can ever buy for gold. AA

Gifts of Rain. Seamus Heaney. a mating call of sound/rises to pleasure me, Dives,/hoarder of common ground. IPY

The Gifts Return'd. Walter Savage Landor. And all the kisses, to the last. OBVV

Gig at Big Al's. Heather McHugh. my lover comes to watch. GeTw

Gigha. W. S. Graham. The sun with long legs wades into the sea. NeBP

Gil Brenton. Anonymous. "Gil Brenton is my father's name." BaBo; ESPB; OxBB

Gil Morrice. Anonymous. Gin I had kend he'd bin your son,/He'd neir bin slain for mee. OxBB

Gil, the Toreador. Charles Henry ("John Paul") Webb. None know what woman died when fell/Gil, the Toreador. AA

Gila Monster Route. L. F. Post. They were off–down the Gila Monster Route. ABF

Gilbertian Recipe for a Politician. J. A. Lindon. And a party political man is the dregs! DBV

The Gilded Boys. Felice Picano. to dance with every weekend/to prove that they're alive. PeHV

Gilderoy. Anonymous. He was my sovereign, my heart's delight, my charming young/Gilderoy. OBET

Giles Corey. Anonymous. But wickedly he dyed. PAH

Giles Corey of the Salem Farms: Prologue. Henry Wadsworth Longfellow. When in all lands, that lie within the sound/Of Sabbath bells, a Witch was burned or/drowned. PAH

Giles Johnson, Ph.D. Frank Marshall Davis. because he wouldn't teach/ and he couldn't porter. BPo; PoBA

Gilgamesh Laments the Death of Engidu. Anonymous. And haste away over the steppes. LiTW

Gilgamesh: The Seduction of Engadu. William Ellery Leonard. Engadu forgot where he was born. ErPo

Gill Boy. Dennis Schmitz. so cruel no one could love you/& want to survive. NPGG

The Gilliflower of Gold. William Morris. Hah! Hah! la belle jaune giroflee. AnFE; WHA

Gimboling. Isabella Gardner. the floating ashore into sleep and to morning. ErPo; WeW

Gimel. Stuart Z. Perkoff. to be man/within the totality/of his functioning VWA

Gimme de Banjo. Anonymous. Dance, gal, gimme de banjo! ShS

Gimme Yo' Han'. Anonymous. Yes, you mus' be lovin' at God's comman'. BoAN 1-2

Gin I Were a Doo. Anonymous. Wi' ilka neebor doo/On the lums of Balgedie. GBP

Gin the Goodwife Stint. Basil Bunting. Twa pund emigrant/On a C.P.R. packet. CTC; TW

Ginevra. Samuel Rogers. Fasten'd her down for ever! BeLS; PoLf

Ginevra (excerpt). Percy Bysshe Shelley. She shall sleep. ChRP

Ginger Bread Mama. Doughtry Long. trying not to wake up the sun. BPo; PoBA

The Gingerbread House. John Ower. We gobble up our child. AMV-80; DFT

The Gingerbread Man. Anonymous. And sugar horses painted red. OxNR

Gingilee. Moishe-Leib Halpern. He has himself begun to crow,/To himself "Good morning" said. TrJP

Ginkgoes in Fall. Howard Nemerov. Alone and bare, dynastic diagrams/Of their distinguished genealogies. GP; HaCAP

Gioconda. Thomas MacGreevy. Bluish snakes slid/Into the dissolution of a smile. OnYI

Giorno dei Morti. D. H. Lawrence. The candle-flames beside the surplices. BrPo; FaBoRV; NOBE; SeCePo

Giotto's Campanile. Guy Butler. None, none peals now, deep bells of love and pity. PeSA

Giotto's Tower. Henry Wadsworth Longfellow. But wanting still the glory of the spire. EyDe

Giovanni da Fiesole on the Sublime or Fra Angelico's "Last Judgment." Richard Howard. ...The world must be its own/witness, we judge ourselves, raise your hands. Prf

Giovinette, Che Fate All'Amore. Lorenzo Da Ponte. Ah! let us carol and dance and be gay,/la-la-re-la-la. TrJP

Gipsies. John Clare. A quiet, pilfering, unprotected race. CH; NBM; PoEL 1-5

The Gipsies. Richard Scrace. They laugh at wiser men. CaP

The Gipsie Girl. Ralph Hodgson. –But oh, the den of wild things in/The darkness of her eyes! EnLit; MCCG; MoBrPo

The Gipsy Laddie. Anonymous.
But now I've come to an old straw pad/With the gipsies dancing round me. FaBoCh; LoGBV; OxBoLi
A fair young wanton lady. BSV

Gipsy Love Song. Harry Bache Smith. Can you hear the song that tells you/All my heart's true love? FSN

Gipsy Queen. John Alexander Chapman. White in a face of stone. Sister, cold lover, come. OBEV

The Gipsy's Warning. Anonymous. Lies the gipsy's only child. BeLS

Gipsy Song. Ben Jonson. And the luckier lot betide you! FaBoCh; LoGBV

The Gipsy Trail. Rudyard Kipling. And the world is all at our feet! HBV 1-2; PoRA

The Giraffe. Nikolai Gumilev. An exquisite beast, the giraffe. LiTW

Giraffe. Stanley Plumly. Will stand all night/so tall/the sun will rise. AmPA

The Giraffe. Marvin Solomon. Standoffishness will kill the buff giraffe. NePoAm-2

Giraffe and Tree. Walter James Turner. Stood the Giraffe beside a Tree. CH; GrPl

The Giraffes. Roy Fuller. Those creatures walking without pain or love. ChMP; NeBP; NoAm

Girandole. Dorothy Donnelly. ...and the world–what a sight!–/is a girandole, a ring of things–all lights. NYBP

A Girl. Babette Deutsch. Will pillow your bright head/By the incurious dead. HBMV

Girl. Dom Moraes. Wished that I too could turn to stone. NePoEA-2

A Girl. Ezra Pound. And all this is folly to the world. MoAB; MoAmPo

Girl. A. W. Purdy. ...searching/for what's missing/in both of us NoAm

Girl at the Seaside. Richard Murphy. I'll drop through the sea-air/Till everything stops. BIrV; NMP

Girl Athletes. Haniel Long. Rooted in rock beyond the eye,/Their giant forms emerge. HBMV

Girl Betrayed. Hedylos. That she was sleeping and he was merciless. LiTW

A Girl Combs Her Hair. Kimiko Hahn. By her sandals she notices an orchid/in white tissue. She reaches. BrSi

The Girl Describes Her Fawn. Andrew Marvell. Had it lived long, it would have been/Lilies without–roses within. GTBS

Girl Friday. Elaine Equi. soon it will be time for another job. APU

Girl Held without Bail. Margaret Walker. I like it fine in Jail/And I don't want no Bail. BPo; CNA; PoBA

Girl Help. Janet Lewis. The great white lilac bloom/Scented with days to come. HeIP; QFR

The Girl I Call Alma. Linda Gregg. and that it's the others who scar me/not you. AmPA; NPGG

The Girl I Left Behind Me. Anonymous. Don't be lazy, do-si-do, and a little more dough... AmFP

The Girl I Left behind Me. Thomas Osborne Davis. To Ireland bound–nor message need/From the girl I left behind me. FaFP; OnYI; TreF

The Girl I Left behind Me. Samuel Lover. For evermore I'll gladly stay/With the girl I left behind me. FSW

The Girl I Left behind Me (My Parents Raised Me Tenderly). Anonymous. For as sure as you go rambling,/She'll marry another man. AmFP

The Girl I Love. Jeremiah Joseph Callanan. Then my dear may I drink a fond deep health to thee! IrPN; OnYI

The Girl I Took to the Cocktail Party. Trevor Williams. Miss Wagnalls! Look! It's me! FiBHP

Girl in a Black Bikini. Allan Brown. lake sweat, sperm-wet from that first/renewal, thoughtless, paphian. AMV-80

A Girl in a Library. Randall Jarrell. The Corn King beckoning to his Spring Queen. NoAm; NOBA; NoP

Girl in a Nightgown. Wallace Stevens. Either now or tomorrow or the day after that. OxBA

Girl in a White Coat. John Malcolm Brinnin. ...in you I love/All that our faith must find, or wisdom give. SaC

A Girl in a Window. James Wright. She gave, and did not know she gave. ErPo

Girl in Front of the Bank. Robert Wallace. Yet, girl, we hold love's possibility. DFF

The Girl in the Carriage. Anonymous. All that was told of her is true. LiTW

The Girl in the Foreign Movie. Patricia Goedicke. The wonderful tart flavor that was waiting for me/Under the stubby fingers of the leaves. FAZ

The Girl in the Lane. Anonymous. Went hobble, hobble, hobble. OxNR

The Girl in the Willow Tree. Carolyn Maisel. to touch herself. IHMS

Girl in White. Stephen Dobyns. ...she hears/someone crying, then her father's voice raised in anger. MAYP

Girl of Constant Sorrow. Sara Ogan Gunning. And I am sure if there's a heaven/That the miners will be there. FSW

A Girl of Pompeii. Edward Sandford Martin. And, quit of earth's corruptions, shape/Itself, imperishably pure. AA; HBV 1-2

Girl of the Lovely Glance. Praxilla. your face is virgin; lower down you are a married/woman. WPOW

Girl of the Red Mouth. Martin MacDermott. Oh, girl of the low voice, love me! HBV 1-2; OnYI

The Girl on the Greenbriar Shore. Anonymous. Never trust a girl on the greenbriar shore. FSW

Girl Powdering Her Neck. Cathy Song. Two chrysanthemums/touch in the middle of the lake/and drift apart. MAYP

The Girl's Lamentation. William Allingham. For my innocent days will come back no more. SeCePo

A Girl's Mood. Lizette Woodworth Reese. I would give him all these,/Myself, and the sun! HBMV

Girl's Song. Anonymous. Shoots fire into my bones. LLLT

A Girl's Song. Katharine Tynan Hinkson. I heap the stones to make his cairn/Where many sleep as sound as he. OnYI

Girl's Song. Marya Zaturenska. And locked rivers open, run/In the full mid-day sun. OLR

Girl Sitting Alone at Party. Donald Justice. This is that other music, to which/I embrace your shadow. DFF

The Girl Takes Her Place among the Mothers. Marya Zaturenska. "Child, as it was with others, so with you." HBMV

The Girl/The Girlie Magazine. Pat Gray. turning the slick, creased page. AMV-81

Girl to Soldier on Leave. Isaac Rosenberg. I let you–I repine. MMM

Girl to Woman. Nixeon Civille Handy. They crown my daily intent. AMV-80

Girl Walking. Charles G. Bell. Your destiny waddling before you down the road? ErPo; NePoAm-2

The Girl Who Had Borne Too Much. John Woods. and a lean christ lie back at ease/in the fat-rinded murderer. GP

The Girl Who Learned to Sing in Crow. Paul Mariani. ...We know/just as they do it's the song birds make good eating. GeTw

The Girl with 18 Nightgowns. Gregory Orr. that only come out at night. PoL

Girl with Doves. Stephen Gray. ...And the doves will/suddenly fly out of her hands. PeSA

Girl with Long Dark Hair. Stephen Gray. I knew how dark it was. PeSA

Girl with the Green Skirt. Dana Naone. Falling into the deep grass/they want to live with green forever. CDW

The Girl Writing Her English Paper. Robert Wallace. stars would be overhead,/their light come in. Psk

Girls. Pablo Neruda. she who will be fused/with me/in life or death! OLR

Girls. Kenneth Rosen. O oxygen, pinkness, protein, hair, and bone,/a stump in the meadow, river, and stone. AmPA

Girls and Boys, Come out to Play. Mother Goose. And we'll have a pudding in half-an-hour. BrR; TiPo

The Girls around Cape Horn. Anonymous. A health to the dashing Spanish girls I met around Cape Horn. AmFP

Girls from Home. Abraham Reisen. What slaves you have become now! Who/Shall take you to the King again? VWA

Girls Going to the Fair. William Allingham. And Biddy enters Lisnamoy in pride. IrPN

Girls in Their Seasons. Derek Mahon. And keep me warm/Before we go plunging into the dark for ever. BoLoP

Girls' Names. Eleanor Farjeon. And there's Joan, like Joan. BiCB; SUS; TiPo

Girls on Saddleless Horses. R. G. Vliet. what a procession of greenery. PH

Girls' Voices. Brendan Gill. It is to girls' voices he listens and not his own. PoL

Glasgow (excerpt). John Mayne. But peace and plenty gar them sing/Frae year to year! BSV

Glasgow Peggie. *Anonymous.* An I am the earl o the Isle o Sky,/And surely my Peggie will be calle BaBo; ESPB

Glasgow Schoolboys, Running Backwards. Douglas Dunn. Forwards in reverse, always holding their caps. OxBC

Glasgow Street. William Montgomerie. "But why were all the poets dumb?" OxBS

Glasgrion. *Anonymous.* Thorrow that falsenese of that lither ladd/These three liues werne all gone. OxBB

Glass. Robert Francis. And if the glass, only the glass,/Could be removed, the poem would remain. DFF; PP

Glass. Brendan Galvin. and be let in. LTB

Glass. Takako U. Lento. the thin but inevitable glass/between me and your world. BoWoP

Glass. William Stanley Merwin. ...try to call to them/far in the empty face. EAS

The Glass Blower. James Scully. preserving remnants of a model ship. MP; NYBP; TwCP

The Glass Bubbles. Samuel Greenberg. ...each bubble/Contains a complete eye of water. LiTA; NePA

Glass Dialectic. Howard Nemerov. And powerless, you cannot be recalled. WaP

The Glass Door. Robert Watson. Everything we cannot see is here. GP

The Glass Eaters. George Jonas. In the full heat of the sun. NeAC

Glass Houses. Edwin Arlington Robinson. That you may not be here a thousand years. MoRP

A Glass of Beer. James Stephens. The High King of Glory permit her to get the mange. AnFE; CMoP; DBV; DTC; ExPo; FaBoCo; FiBHP; GoTF; InPK; NCSH; NLV; NoAm; OBMV; OBSP; OxBTC; SeCePo; TreFT; TW

The Glass of Pure Water (excerpt). Hugh" (Christopher Murray Grieve) MacDiarmid. To end all movements save movements like these. BSV

The Glass of Water. Wallace Stevens. One would continue to contend with one's ideas. AtBAP; CoBMV; MoAB; MoAmPo; MoPo; OxBA; TAP

The Glass Town. Alastair Reid. and the moment broke with my/breath. NYBP

Glass was the street. Emily Dickinson. It is the past's supreme italic/Makes the present mean. OxBA

Glass World. Dorothy Donnelly. lights up like a chandelier/in a flash of opals and amber. NCSH

Glauce. Aubrey Thomas De Vere. And would that such a life were mine and thine! IrPN

Glaucopis. Richard Hughes. John died, of no complaint,/With owl-eyes too. OBMV

The Glaucous-Gull's Death. D. J. O'Sullivan. Cast them now on the new tidal line,/All that was left of gull and mine. NeIP

The Glazier. Stephane Mallarme. Takes its shirt dazzled/Off the glazier's back. OBVE

Glazunoviana. John Ashbery. Rivers of wings surround us and vast tribulation. LCAP

The Gleaner. Jane Taylor. O no, I would rather work hard all the day,/My little blue apron to fill.' OxBChV

Glee for King Charles. Sir Walter Scott. Here's a health to King Charles! CoBE

A Glee for Winter. Alfred Domett. Make sweet May of Winter weather. HBV 1-2

Glee–The Ghosts. Thomas Love Peacock. ...we'll think it good sport/To be laid in that Red Sea. ViBoPo

Glen-Almain, the Narrow Glen. William Wordsworth. ...Ossian, last of all his race!/Lies buried in this lonely place. GTBS

Glen Lough. Geoffrey Grigson. To see who made those ringing noises in that summer/bay. FaBoPP; OBTV

The Glen of Silence. Hugh" (Christopher Murray Grieve) MacDiarmid. –The tragedy of an unevolved people. CMoP; NeBP

Glen Pean. Denis Rixson. Enclosing us, cutting us from them personally. PoSH

Glen Rosa. William Jeffrey. Mind's aim or what bright beings fill/The corries of the heart and will. PoSH

Glenara. Thomas Campbell. Now joy to the house of fair Ellen of Lorn! HBV 1-2

Glenaradale. Walter Chalmers Smith. We leave thy green valley,/Glenaradale. OBVV

Glenarm. John Lyle Donaghy. With hazel woods in his two eyes. NeIP

Glencoe. Gilbert Keith Chesterton. As if Christ stood on yonder clouded peak/And turned its thousand waters into wine. PoSH

Glencoe. Douglas Stewart. But terrible things were done/Long, long ago. CBAP

Glenfinlas; or, Lord Ronald's Coronach. Sir Walter Scott. We ne'er shall see Lord Ronald more! GoTL

Glengormley. Derek Mahon. ...By/Necessity, if not choice, I live here too. CIP; FaBoIP

Glenkindie. William Scott. We saw them fade within the mist,/And never saw them more. HBV 1-2

Glenlogie. *Anonymous.* "O binna feared, mither, I'll maybe no dee." HBV 1-2

Glenlogie, or, Jean o Bethelnie (A version). *Anonymous.* Bonnie Jean of Bethelny was scarce fif-/teen year auld. ESPB; GN

Glenlogie, or, Jean o Bethelnie (B version). *Anonymous.* Of bonnie Jeanie Melville, who was scarce/sixteen years old. BuBa; ESPB

Glenn Miller's Music Is a Trunk. Carmen Valle. that stores a childhood/crushed to smithereens. InW

Glenpool. Annette Arkeketa West. we are not/alone TWSS

The Glens. John Hewitt. offers in shape and colour all I need/for sight to torch the mind with living light. NeIP

Glimmers. Jack Marshall. This moment/is not enough?–then/eternity won't be either. APU

A Glimpse. Frances Cornford. The same since I was born, the same to be/When all my children's children grow old men. OBMV

Glimpse. Pearl Cleage Lomax. i saw you/on my walk last/night./Running. PoBA

A Glimpse. Walt Whitman. There we two, content, happy in being together, speaking little, perhaps not a word. AmPP; NePA; OxBA; PeHV; PPP

The Glimpse of a Plain Cap. *Anonymous.* Enough! Let us two be one. LiTW

A Glimpse of the Body Shop. Stephen Berg. His helpers wash and bow, laughing. NaP

A Glimpse of Time. Laurence Binyon. Time's stony palace crumbled down/Before that instant kiss. AnFE

Glimpses. Roy Helton. The unimportant beauty of the moon. HBMV

Glimpses # xii (excerpt). Lawrence McGaugh. But that is not today... BOLo

Glints of the Year–from a Window. Thomas Caulfield Irwin. Where the sombrous red moon sets afar/Past the booming line of the surging bar. IrPN

Glitter of Pebbles. Dom Moraes. With all around the ache of space, the glare/Of heat, and at my feet the stone, the stone. ACV

Gloaming. Robert Adger Brown. Silver the hills where the moon climbs over. HBV 1-2

Gloire de Dijon. D. H. Lawrence. Mellow as the glory roses. BrPo; CMoP; ELP; EnLoPo; GBL; NoAm; OAEP

The Gloomy Night Is Gath'ring Fast. Robert Burns. Farewell, my bonie banks of Ayr. MCCG

Gloria in Excelsis. *Anonymous.* Thou only, O Christ, with the Holy Ghost, art most high in/the glory of God the Father. WGRP

The "Gloria Patri." John Heywood. That to hear him speak all degrees do disdain. ACP

Gloriana Dying. Sylvia Townsend Warner. Nor the long, dreaming country lad who lies/Scorching his book before the dying brand. FaBoWP

The Glorious Game. Richard Burton. And kick their heels at heaven a hundred happy ways,/Sky-larking down the days! HBMV

The Glorious Gift of God. Benjamin Beddome. It never should from thence depart. BePJ

The Glorious Name. Amos R. Wells. No other high redeeming name wherein we must be saved. BePJ

Glorious Things of Thee Are Spoken. John Newton. And as priests, His solemn praises/Each for a thank-offering brings. NOCV; WGRP

The Glorious Twelfth. Robert Greacen. After hatred's harvest joy will march, shrouded, to Finaghy. NeIP

The Glorious Victory of Navarino! *Anonymous.* And to the men on board each ship who courage have displayed. CoMu

Glory. D. H. Lawrence. Yet all of these drink blood. OBSP

Glory. Marianne Moore. for rushing to the rescue/as if you'd heard yourself performing. NYBP

Glory. Harvey Shapiro. And heard her say, kiss my ass. PoL

The Glory. Edward ("Edward Eastaway") Thomas. ...I cannot bite the day to the core. OxBTC

Glory. Joseph Wise. Glory sing to the Lord. AH

Glory Be to God for Dappled Things. Diane Keating. I await your dark claw. CaPN

Glory, Glory to the Sun. John Alford. round up their flocks and shout/and scour the land. HBMV

Glory Hallelujah! or John Brown's Body. Charles Sprague Hall. Now for the Union let's give three rousing/cheers,/As we go marching on./Hip, hip, hip, hip, Hurrah PAH

The Glory of God in Creation. Thomas Moore. And all things fair and bright are Thine. OHIP

The Glory of Hanalei Is Heavy Rain. Alfred Alohikea. She and I are two,/Three with the rustle of sea-spray. WTO

The Glory of Lincoln. Thomas Curtis Clark. But who for fellow men endured the shame/Shall have eternal glory for his own. PGD

The Glory of Nature. Frederick Tennyson. Use arms the Soul–anon there moveth by/A more majestic Angel–and we die! OBNC

The Glory of the Day Was in Her Face. James Weldon Johnson. Are one with all the dead, since she is gone. BANP; CDC; IDB; PoBA

The Glory of the Garden. Rudyard Kipling. And the glory of the Garden it shall never pass away! EBCP

The Glory of Toil. Edna Dean Proctor. For both have reared the minster that shrines the sacred fire. PGD

Glory of Women. Siegfried Sassoon. His face is trodden deeper in the mud. MMM; OBWP

De Glory Road. Clement Wood. An' ride ter Hebben up de Glory Road? HBMV; YaD

Glory to the Name of Jesus! A.B. Simpson. Till earth's saved and ransomed millions/Join to praise the Savior's name. BePJ

The Glory Trail. Badger Clark. And if I never lay him low,/I'll never turn him loose! BPAW; PH; StPo

Gloss. Padraic Fiacc. Turn the page. Turn the page. CIP

Gloss. David McCord. My digent self is sertive, choate, loof. OBAL

Gloucester Harbor. Elizabeth Stuart Phelps Ward. There breaks in every Gloucester wave/A widowed woman's heart. AA

Gloucester Moors. William Vaughn Moody. And nothing to say or do? AP; HBV 1-2; NOBA; OxBA; TreFT; WGRP; WHA

Gloucestershire Wassail. Anonymous. For to let these jolly wassailers in. OBET

The Glove. Harold Bond. cowhide, rabbit fur, the five fingers of my hand. NYBP

The Glove. Ben Jonson. That was thy mistress, best of gloves. EiL

The Glove. Richard Lovelace. Are still allowed to fiddle with the case. ALV; EG

The Glove and the Lions. [James Henry] Leigh Hunt. "No love," quoth he, "but vanity, sets love a task like that." BeLS; GN; GoTF; HBV 1-2; HBVY; MaC; TreF; WBLP

Glove Glue. Ken Belford. there was nothing. NeAC

The glow and beauty of the stars. Sappho. when in her roundness she burns silver/about the world. BoWoP

The Glow-Worm. Johnny Mercer. Glow, little glow-worm, glow. OBAL

Glow Worm. Lila Cayley Robinson. Light the path below, above, and lead us on to love! BLSo

The Glow-Worm. Edward Shanks. Round the light of the burning glow-worm, steady and clear. WHA

The Glow-Worm. Charlotte Smith. –So turn the World's bright joys to cold and blank disgust. FM

Glowworm. David McCord. No. Just say/Helloworm! NTCP

Gluggity Glug. George Coleman the Younger. I wish I were over a bottle,/Which goes gluggity, gluggity–glug–glug–glug! HBV 1-2

Gluskap's Hound. Theodore Goodridge Roberts. The black hound running in fierce despair,/With his grief of a thousand year. WHW

A Glut on the Market. Patrick Kavanagh. ...Now I may ride him/Every land my imagination knew. OnYI

The Glutton. Robert Graves. Loathing each other's carrion company. CMoP; TW

The Glutton. John Oakman. And leave to the glutton his pudding and pie. OxBChV

The Glutton. Karl Shapiro. And leave of his volume only the mould of his girth. DFF

Glycerin. Frank Lima. And the circles are hardly warm. ANYP

Glycine's Song. Samuel Taylor Coleridge. To-day! to-day! CH; OBEV; PoPl

Glyph. Anonymous. My sky is full of the dreadful sound/Of the wings of unsuccesses. LiTA

A Gnarled Riverina Gum-Tree. Ernest G. Moll. Stretched up thin to catch the sun. PoAu 1-2

The Gnat. Joseph Beaumont. And out doth keep/All feare. CBEP; FM; LoBV; OBS

Gnat on My Paper. Richard Eberhart. He could not say it. DFF

Gnat-Psalm. Ted Hughes. Your dancing/Rolls my staring skull slowly away into outer space. NoAm

Gnawing the Breast. Sandra McPherson. And the hill might even move a little, feeling the kick/of a child. LCAP

Gnome. Samuel Beckett. Through a world politely turning/From the loutishness of learning. BIrV; OBSP

The Gnome. Harry Behn. Looking things over/On his way home. SoPo; TiPo

The Gnomes. Beth Bentley. ...peering/near-sightedly down its furthest reaches. SaC

Gnomic Lines. Anonymous. Winter shall pass, fair weather return,/The sun-hot summer, the restless sea. LiTW

Gnomic Verses. William Blake. Go, love without the help of anything on earth.' OBRV; TrGrPo

Gnosis. Christopher Pearse Cranch. Melting, flowing into one. AnAmPo; HBV 1-2

Gnostics on Trial. Linda Gregg. ...Try/To keep from happiness. Just try. AMV-80; NPGG

Gnostology. Sam Hamill. I kneel and bow. AMV-81

The Gnu. Hilaire Belloc. Meanwhile the distant Gnu with grateful eyes/Observes his opportunity and flies. BoAnP

The Gnu Wooing. Burges Johnson. Beneath the yew the glad day through/There romps a little gnuey new. HBVY

Go Ahead; Goodbye; Good Luck; and Watch Out. William Bronk. No kind of balm. You look, though. Let me know. GP

Go and Catch a Falling Star. John Donne. Yet she/Will be/False ere I come, to two or three. BiP; FaBV; FF; LiTB; LiTL; NAWM 1-2; PoRA; TEP

Go back to the Country. Jazz Gillum. Plant you forty acres of cotton/and try to do yourself some good BluL

Go Bring Me Back My Blue-Eyed Boy (with music). Anonymous. Around my grave go build a fence,/To show this world I had no sense. AS

"Go Bring Me," Said the Dying Fair. William Hunter. And drop for me the burning tear,"/She said, and sunk away. AH

Go By. Alfred, Lord Tennyson. Pass on, weak heart, and leave me where I lie:/Go by, go by. OBNC

Go-d'ling. Anonymous. I'll lay a man a pint o'rum,/There are no more than thirty-two. BFSS

Go Down Death. James Weldon Johnson. She's resting in the bosom of Jesus. AnAmPo; DL; PoBA; TRV

Go Down, Moses. Anonymous. "Let my people go!" BoAN 1-2; BPo; EaLo; EBCP; FSW; NOBA; TrAS; TreF

Go Down, Ol' Hannah. Anonymous. If you rise in the mornin',/Set the world on fire. OuSiCo; TTY

Go Down, Old Hannah. Anonymous. Nobody feels sorry/For the lifetime man. AmFP

Go Down, You Little Red Rising Sun. Anonymous. And I ain't did no man,/Great Godamighty, no crime. OuSiCo

Go Down You Murderers. Ewan MacColl. Saying, "Go down, you murderer, go down." FSW

Go Far, Come Near. Walter De La Mare. Have mercy on your miseries and your sins. CoBMV

Go Fly a Saucer. David McCord. But Earth has specialized in little men. ImOP

Go, Forget Me. Charles Wolfe. Glory's burning, generous swell,/Fancy, and the poet's shell. HBV 1-2

Go Get the Axe. Anonymous. But a boy's best friend is his mother. AS; TrAS

Go, Grieving Rimes of Mine. Petrarch (Francesco Petrarca). And draw me to her in the blessed place! NAWM 1-2

Go, Happy Rose. Martial (Marcus Valerius Martialis). So, from this hour,/Be love's own flower. PeHV

Go Heart, Hurt with Adversity. Anonymous. "Fare wel my joy and welcom pain/Til I see my lady again!" MeEL; OxBM

Go, Heart, unto the Lamp of Licht. Anonymous. Go, heart, unto thy Saviour. BSV; GoTS

Go Home. Janet Reed McFatter. welcome home; welcome home. GrPl

Go, ill-sped book. John Berryman. and that are fair to see. BoLoP

Go, Little Book. Robert Louis Stevenson. A nightingale in the sycamore. MoBrPo; PoRA

Go Little Ring. Anonymous. "My master would that he were I." CBEP

Go Not, Happy Day. Alfred, Lord Tennyson. Roses are her cheeks,/And a rose her mouth. LiTL

Go not near a house of rose. Emily Dickinson. In insecurity to lie/Is joy's insuring quality. BoLiVe; MoAB; MoAmPo

Go, Ploughman, Plough. Joseph Campbell. The strength you sweat/Shall blossom yet/In golden glory to the sun. HBMV

Go, Rose. John Gay. You die with envy, I with love. CBEP

Go Round. Laura Chester. ...So ashes breathe–Around me now. NPGG

Go, Sad Complaint. Charles, duc d' Orleans. Go! dull complaint, my lady this report. MeEL

Go Sleep, Ma Honey. Edward D. Barker. Go sleep, ma honey, m–m. AA

Go Slow. Langston Hughes. Slow?/????/???/??/? LiTM

Go Take the World. Jay Macpherson. Say: Wisdom is a silver fish/And Love a golden hook. OBCV

Go Tell. Anonymous. Our Jesus Christ is born. EBCP

Go Tell Aunt Rhody. Anonymous. The whole family's weeping/Because the mama's dead. AmFP

Go Tell It on the Mountain. Anonymous. Go tell it on the mountain,/Our Jesus Christ is born. FSW

Go Tell Old Nancy. Anonymous. With a misery in her head. LaNeLa

Go Tell Them That Jesus Is Living. Anonymous. For Christ is risen today! BePJ

Go, Then. Edith Bruck. Think of this and you'll understand,/sweet friend. VWA

Go Then, My Dove, but Now No Longer Mine. Cotton Mather. Rich Words! Heav'n will make amends/For all. SCAP

Go Throw Them Out. Moishe Leib Halpern. and, like children paddling in summer brooks,/dabble their pretty feet in your heart's blood? VWA

Go to Bed First. *Anonymous.* Go to bed third/A golden bird. GBP; OxNR

Go to Bed Late. *Anonymous.* Grow very tall. OxNR

Go to Old Ireland. *Anonymous.* And it's down, down, down derry down. AmFP

Go to Sleepy. *Anonymous.* All de horses in de stable/B'longs ter mammy's little baby. AS; TrAS

Go to the Ant. Stanley J. Sharpless. It's got Solomon beat–and no sweat. NOBL

Go to the Shine That's on a Tree. Richard Eberhart. Be wild aware of light unseen,/And unheard song along the air. UnS

Go Way F'om Mah Window. *Anonymous.* Dan we bofe can haul. ABF; AS

Go where Glory Waits Thee. Thomas Moore. Oh! then remember me. OBNC; TreFS

The Goal and the Way. John Oxenham. Who falters now shames God, and dies. PGD

The Goal of Intellectual Man. Richard Eberhart. The truth of the positive hour/Composing all of human power. MoPo

The Goat. *Anonymous.* Coughed up those shirts and flagged the train. BLPL; OnUR; PoLf

The Goat. Umberto Saba. I heard the lament of all other pain,/all other life. VWA

The Goat. Roland Young. Let's hope she has no sense of smell. BoAnP

Goat Dance. Ron Loewinsohn. The law of the blood,/like you said, "Infinitely personal." GP

The Goat Paths. James Stephens. Something lying on the ground,/In the bottom of my mind. AnIV; AWP; CH; GoJo; LiTB; OxBI; PG; UnPo; WHA

Goat's-Leaf. Marie de France. To you the truth I reported/Of the lay here unfolded. PBWP

Goat-Woman Dares. Judith Mountain Leaf Volborth. waits for crickets/to answer. TWSS

The Goatherd. Grace Hazard Conkling. There were a thousand, more or less! TiPo

Goats. Charles Erskine Scott Wood. They seek the mountain and the tumbling flood. AnEnPo

The Goblin. Rose Fyleman. A goblin lives in our house all the year round. NTCP; TiPo

The Goblin Goose (parody). *Anonymous.* While that Goose says, "Eat no more." FaBoPa

Goblin Market. Christina Georgina Rossetti. To strengthen whilst one stands. AtBAP; BrRo; DTo; EBEV; GoTL; NOBV; OAEP; OBNV; PeHV; SBG; VLP

A Goblinade. Florence Page Jaques. And he dances all day, and/He likes himself. TiPo

God. Gamaliel Bradford. Is a keen, enormous, haunting, never-sated thirst for God. TRV; WGRP

God. Alphonse Marie Louis de Lamartine. The earth sees his works, and heaven knows his/name! ILwL

God. Isaac Rosenberg. Ah! this miasma of a rotting God! MoPo; VWA

God. Boris Slutsky. We were all under God./Ours were the steps he trod. VWA

God. John Banister Tabb. Behold, I breathe and touch Thee too. GoTF; TreFT

God and Man. Samuel Hazo. without a script and fretting for directions. ELU

God and Nature. Musa Moris Farhi. as I kiss her womb/on a beach/by the tideless Aegean VWA

God and the Holy Ghost. D. H. Lawrence. and once done, there is no remedy, no salvation for this,/nonentity is our portion. MoRP

God and the Soldier. *Anonymous.* God is neglected–/The old soldier slighted. GoTF; TreFS

God and the Soul. John Lancaster Spalding.
And man's immortal soul is turned to/clay. AA
No power from you my heart can ever wean. AA
Whence light he draws as from the sun/night's Queen. AA
Where love divine is the infinite prize. AA

God and the Strong Ones. Margaret Widdemer. Reap what ye have sown!" saith God. HBMV

A God and Yet a Man? *Anonymous.* Suffre the paynes that I may; it is my fader wyll. EnPo

God Be in My Head. *Anonymous.*
God be at my end and at my departing. BoC; EaLo; OxBoCh; TRV

God Be With You. *Anonymous.* As your inner, golden ray. PoToHe

God Be with You Till We Meet Again. Jeremiah Eames Rankin. God be with you till we meet again! AH; TreFS

God Bless America. Irving Berlin. God bless America, My home sweet home. BLSo; TreFT

God Bless America. John Fuller. Then, perhaps then, God Bless America. OBSV

God Bless This House from Thatch to Floor. *Anonymous.* All to watch me while I sleep. OxNR

God Bless You. *Anonymous.* Then art thou safe forever. PoToHe

God Bless You, Dear, To-Day! John Bennett. God bless you, dear, to-day! AA

God Cares. Helen Annis Casterline. God cares, He always cares! BLRP

God Cares. Marianne Farningham. O, rest in peace, for the Lord doth care. BLRP

God Does Do Such Wonderful Things! Angela Morgan. God does do such wonderful things! TRV

God Doeth All Things Well. *Anonymous.* Content to know He doeth all things/well. STF

God Don't Like It. *Anonymous.* God don't like it, no, no,/It's a scandalous and a shame. OuSiCo

God Don't Never Change. Blind Willie Johnson. God don't never change/Ohhhh-ahh/Always will be God BluL

God Everywhere. Abraham Ibn Ezra. My every thought, Eternal God of/Heaven,/Ascends to Thee, to whom all praise/be given. TrJP

God (excerpt). Alexander McLachlan. God of the worlds which Death reveals/To all our race.... CaP

God Fashioned the Ship of the World Carefully. Stephen Crane. And there were many in the sky/Who laughed at this thing. MOS

God Forward. A. R. G. And, by God's help, I will. BLRP

God from His Throne with Piercing Eye. Joseph Steward. Nor God the rage or fire control. AH

God Give to Men. Arna Bontemps. God suffer little men/the taste of soul's desire. BANP; BPo; CDC; PoNe

God, Give Us Men! Josiah Gilbert Holland. Wrong rules the land and waiting Justice sleeps. BLPA; GoTF; PAL; TreF; WBLP

God Gives Them Sleep on Ground, on Straw. Roger Williams. O how should that God worship be,/who is but One and True? SCAP

God Has Pity on Kindergarten Children. Yehuda Amichai. so that their happiness may protect us/now and on other days. VWA

God Has Spoken. Paul Verlaine. Of blood dripped, piteous friend, who seekest me in vain? SyP

God Hasn't Made Room. Mririda n'Ait Attik. When I fall asleep on the terrace/On a warm summer night. PBWP

God, How I Hate You. Arthur Graeme West. The bloody fields of Flanders He so loves. MMM

God! How I Long for You... Kenneth Mackenzie. my murdered body and your body's ghost. CBAP

God in the Nation's Life. *Anonymous.* And putting it there in a style to stay. BLRP; WBLP

The God in Whom We Trust. *Anonymous.* Full acceptance in His favor,/And among His sons a place. STF

A God in Wrath. Stephen Crane. "Ah, what a redoubtable god!" OBSP; TAP

God Incarnate. Ruth M. Williams. Some day we'll crown You our Lord and King. BePJ

God Is a Distant–Stately Lover. Emily Dickinson. "Miles", and "John Alden" were Synonyme– AmePo; SoSe

God Is a Masturbator. Gregory Corso. and she and she/for a me and me– GP

God Is at the Anvil. Lew Sarett. He is fashioning a frame/For the shimmering silver beauty of the evening stars. HBMV; TRV; WGRP

God Is Faithful. Frances Ridley Havergal. God is all-sufficient/For the coming year. BLRP

God Is Here Again. Charles Angoff. ..and God is here again, and/all His angels. AMV-80

God Is in Every Tomorrow. Laura A. Barter Snow. Through all eternity–NOW! BLRP; STF

God is indeed a jealous God. Emily Dickinson. That we had rather not with Him/But with each other play. NOBA

God, Is, Like, Scissors. Jose Garcia Villa. He, there, me, here. EaLo

God Is Love. John Bowring. God is wisdom, God is love. FaBoBe

God Is Nigh. *Anonymous.* Safely rest, all is well! God is nigh. TRV

God Is There. Walter E. Isenhour. For the God of earth and heaven/Always meets His children there. STF

God Is with Me. Oswald J. Smith. He will keep me by His pow'r. STF

God Is Working His Purpose Out. A. C. Ainger. When the earth shall be filled with the glory of God as the/waters cover the sea. BLRP; FaPoR

God Keep You. Mary Ainge De Vere. God keep you every time and every-/where. AA

God Know What He's About. *Anonymous.* Only God can understand. STF

God Knoweth Best. *Anonymous.* Satisfied the way He taketh/Must be always best. WBLP

God Knows the Answer. F. B. Whitney. A ministering angel fair,/In answer to my faithful prayer. STF

God Leads the Way. Cleanthes. A recreant, I needs must follow still. EaLo

God Lyaeus. John Fletcher. God of youth, let this day here/Enter neither care nor fear. OBEV; ViBoPo

God Made a Little Gentian. Emily Dickinson. "Creator! shall I bloom?" AA; FaBV

God Made a Trance. *Anonymous.* When you lies upon the bier. OBET

God Made the Bees. Mother Goose. But the miller makes the money. SaC

God Made Trees. *Anonymous.* God made little lads/To kiss pretty wenches. LO

The God-maker, Man. Don (Donald Robert Marquis) Marquis. I will bow down where my brothers bow,/Humble, but open-eyed! HBV 1-2; WGRP

God Makes a Path. Roger Williams. Where God shall sweetening be. PAH; TRV; WGRP

God Moves on the Water. *Anonymous.* God moves on the water,/And the people had to run and pray. OuSiCo

God of Abraham, of Isaac, and of Jacob. *Anonymous.* And what you dole will be my stay/Today and every day. TrJP

The God of Bethel Heard Her Cries. Richard Allen. The God of Bethel heard. AH

The God of Comfort. *Anonymous.* Our God can give songs in the night. STF

The God of Galaxies. Mark Van Doren. And say it without voice. Praise universes/Numberless. Praise all of them. Praise Him. ImOP; MoRP

God of Mercy. (or Molodovski) Kadya, (or Kadia) Molodovsky. Take back the gift of our separateness. WPOW

God of Might, God of Right. *Anonymous.* Earth around will resound/Joyful hymns to heaven. TrJP

God of Our Fathers. Melancthon W. Stryker. Yea, all her peoples shout to thy name. AH

God of Our Fathers, Bless This Our Land. John Henry Hopkins, Jr. Thine be the glory,/Now and forever. AH

God of Our Fathers, Whose Almighty Hand. Daniel C. Roberts. And glory, laud, and praise be ever thine. AH

God of Peace, in Peace Preserve Us. Ernst W. Olson. Peace on earth, good will toward men. AH

God of the Earth, the Sky, the Sea. Samuel Longfellow. Th' in-dwelling God, proclaimed of old. TRV

The God of the Living. John Lodge Ellerton. That body, soul, and spirit be/Forever living unto thee! WGRP

God of the Nations. Walter Russell Bowie. God of thy people, hear us cry to thee. AH; TrPWD

God of the Nations, Near and Far. John Haynes Holmes. And speed, O speed the blessed day/Of justice, love, and peace. AH

God of the Prophets! Bless the Prophets' Sons. Denis Wortman. A weary world awaits thy reign sublime! AH

God of the Strong, God of the Weak. Richard Watson Gilder. And knowing, we may sow the seed/That blossoms through eternity. AH

God of the World. Israel Najara. Angelic hosts and all the sons of man! TrJP

God of the World, Thy Glories Shine. Sewall Sylvester Cutting. The rest of life–the whole of heaven. AH

God of Visions. Emily Bronte. And tell why I have chosen thee! TrGrPo

The God of War. Bertolt Brecht. And every five minutes he assured his public that he would/take up very little of their time. FaBoPV

A God Once Commanded Us. Leah Goldberg. until I meet/that flickering lantern/at the corner of the street. VWA

God Our Help. *Anonymous.* Our crookedness Thou canst make right,/Glory to Thee for aye. Amen. OxBoCh

God Our Refuge. Richard Chenevix Trench. That we could not flee from Thee anywhere,/We fled to Thee. EBCP; GoTF; OxBoCh; TreFT

God Pity Him. *Anonymous.* And Jesus says, "As you've done to them,/You've done it unto me." STF

God Poem. Stanley Moss. ...Who breathes/Comes to nothing: absence, a world. VGW; VWA

God Prays. Angela Morgan. I know at last 'tis God who prays. WGRP

God Provides. St. Matthew Bible, N.T.. Even Solomon in all his glory was not arrayed like one of these. BLRP

God Rest You Merry, Gentlemen. Dinah Maria Mulock Craik. For Jesus Christ, our Saviour,/Was born on Christmas Day. FaFP; FSW; GN; HBV 1-2; HBVY; LiTB; OHIP; TreFS; ViBoPo

God's A-Gwineter Trouble de Water. *Anonymous.* Wade in de water, children,/God's a-gwineter trouble de water. BoAN 1-2

God's Acre. Witter ("Emanuel Morgan") Bynner. And God's name written there–"John Doe." AnEnPo

God's-Acre. Henry Wadsworth Longfellow. This is the place where human harvests grow. HBV 1-2

God's Blessing on Munster. Saint Patrick. On slopes, on plains,/On mountains, or peaks. OnYI

God's Call. *Anonymous.* I have heard Thy voice, I have met Thy/call. STF

God's Controversy with New-England. Michael Wigglesworth. Still in New-England shall be my delight. SCAP

God's Dark. John Martin. All in the Dark, He watches/And guards us while we rest. PoLf

God's Determinations. Edward Taylor.
I do in thee Delight. PoEL 1-5
That now his brightest diamond is grown/Darker by far than any coalpit stone. AmPP; HAP; NOBA
Then halter up this Cur that is so Curst. PoEL 1-5
These therefore and their journey now do come/For to be treated on, and Coacht along. PoEL 1-5

God's Dominion and Decrees. Isaac Watts. Beneath my Lord the Lamb. CEP; OBEC

God's Education. Thomas Hardy. Forsooth, though I men's master be,/Theirs is the teaching mind! MoRP

God's Eye Is on the Sparrow. Bertha Meyer. So I'll trust Him, ever trust Him,/Since I know He cares for me. STF

God's First Creature Was Light. Winifred Welles. Light, the first creature, softly went. ImOP

God's Funeral. Thomas Hardy. Mechanically, I followed with the rest. WGRP

God's Garden. Richard Burton. And make them rose-like in His name. TRV; WGRP

God's Gifts. Jakov De Haan And God alone has saved me from my sins. VWA

God's Goin' to Set This World on Fire (A vers.) (with music). *Anonymous.* All you sinners gonna turn up missing,/One o' these days! AS

God's Goin' to Set This World On Fire (B vers.) (with music). *Anonymous.* Every round goes higher higher,/Some o' these days. AS

God's Goodness. C. D. Martin. God will take care of you. WBLP

God's Grandeur. Gerard Manley Hopkins. World broods with warm breast and with ah! bright wings. AnFE; AWP; BBV; BiP; BLPL; BoC; BrPo; CMoP; DiPo; EBCP; ExPo; FaFP; FF; ForPo; HAP; ILwL; InPK; InPo; InvP; LiTB; LiTM; LoBV; MoAB; MoBrPo; MoPo; MoRP; MoVE; NoAm; NOBE; NOBV; NoP; OAEL 1-2; OBNC; OxBoCh; PPP; PrIm; SeCeV; SoSe; SOTW; TEP; TrCP; TreFT; TrGrPo; UnPo; VLP

God's Harp. Gustav Falke. Hark, what a tone of love passed through the night. AWP

God's Ideal Mother. Cora M. Pinkham. She is her God's ideal. STF

God's Judgment on a Wicked Bishop. Robert Southey. For they were sent to do judgment on him! HBV 1-2; HBVY; OBRV; OnMSP

God's Key. *Anonymous.* That He at last when just He sees 'tis/best/Will give it thee. STF

God's Language. Ruth Fainlight. Until the day that he/Pronounce the name: Messiah. VWA

God's Little Mountain. Geoffrey Hill. And who will prove the surgeon to this stone? NePoEA

God's Love. *Anonymous.* There's more–there's more! BLRP

God's Mother. Laurence Housman. Three bowers of love/Won Christ from Heaven above. ISi

God's Pay. *Anonymous.* Who does God's work will get God's pay. STF

God's Pity. Louise Driscoll. And smile upon us when we meet/And greet so pleasantly. WGRP

God's Plans. *Anonymous.* But thou alone to Him wert dear. BLRP

God's Plans. May Riley Smith. Time will reveal the calyxes of gold. BLRP

God's Presence Makes My Heaven. Oswald J. Smith. His presence makes my heaven/And I am satisfied. STF

God's Promises. *Anonymous.* Upon whose golden rungs we step by step arise. BLRP

God's Residence. Emily Dickinson. His furniture is love. TRV

God's Saints. Henry Vaughan. They are that City's shining spires/We travel to. TRV

God's Sunshine. John Oxenham. For His love is always shining. WBLP

God's Trails Lead Home. John R. Clements. The land of love,/Where all unknown are tears. BLRP

God's Treasure. A.M. N. Read, mark, and learn to obey. STF

God's Trombones: Listen, Lord. James Weldon Johnson. To wait for that great gittin'-up morning–Amen. BANP

God's Unspeakable Gift. Macey P. Sealey. No words can ever express the thought–/It's "God's Unspeakable Gift." BePJ

God's Virtue. Barnabe Barnes. And all in all things with God's virtue filled. NOCV; OBSC

God's Ways Are Strange. Margaret E. Bruner. God's ways are strange. PoToHe

God's Will. Charles E. Guthrie. God's will to love. BLRP

God's Will. Mildred Howells. Deep in the earth's dark breast. HBV 1-2

God's Will. Robert Louis Munger. And lassies laugh and women weep,/And God knows why. AA

God's Will. Edwin H. Nevin. When one with Thee, my life shall be/Attuned to gladsome Melody. BLRP

God's Will for Us. *Anonymous.* This is God's will, for you and me. BLRP; SoSe; WBLP

God's Will is Best. *Anonymous.* Thy Will is best for me. BLRP

God's Will Is Best. Thelma Curtis. Hold Him gently by the hand/And know His will is best. STF

God's Word. John Clifford. But though the noise of falling blows was heard/The anvil is unchanged; the hammers gone. TRV

God's Work. Charlotte Cushman. He peopled it with living beings, that was the/grand, divine, eternal drama. TreFT

God's World. Mildred Keeling. Where the God of Heaven is hovering/About me everywhere. BLRP

God's World. Edna St. Vincent Millay. My soul is all but out of me,–let fall/No burning leaf; prithee, let no bird call. BLPL; CMoP; FaBoBe; FaBV; HBV 1-2; MCCG; MoAmPo; MoRP; PoPl; PoSC; TrCP

God Said, "I Made a Man". Jose Garcia Villa. "Give thy name!'–"Sir! Genius.'" AnFE

God Save Elizabeth! Francis Turner Palgrave. Her's ever and her's still, come life, come death!/God save Elizabeth! HBV 1-2

God Save Great Thomas Paine. Joseph Mather. Paine and his "Rights of Man'/shall be my song. FaBoPV; NOEC

God Save Ireland. Timothy Daniel Sullivan. "O what matter, when for Erin dear we fall!" OnYI

God Save Our President. Francis DeHaes Janvier. God save our president! PAH; PAL

God Save the Flag. Oliver Wendell Holmes. Washed with its stains in the blood of the brave! FaFP; OHFP

God Save the King. Henry Carey. To sing with heart and voice,/God save the King! HBV 1-2; OBEC; PeD; WBLP

God Save the King, That King That Sav'd the Land. Benjamin Harris. And God and Angels, guard his Tent and Throne. SCAP

God Save the Nation. Theodore Tilton. Clothe Thou the fiels, as in the prophet's/vision,/With peace Elysian. AA

God Save the People. Ebenezer Elliott. God save the people! WBLP

God Save the Plough. Lydia Huntley Sigourney. God save the plough! OBAL

God-Seeking. William Watson. And yellowing either bank the king-cups blow. WGRP

God Send Easter. Lucille Clifton. ...as we/glory in our skin CNA

God Send Us Men. F. J. Gillman. These are the bulwarks of the State. TRV

God Set Us Here. Nicasius de Sille. The glory, Lord, we give to thee alone. AH

God Sour the Milk of the Knacking Wench. Alden Nowlan. Let maggots befoul her alive in bed,/and dibble thorns in her tongue. PeCV

God Speed the Plough! *Anonymous.* And long good life to lede/All that for plowmen pray. OxBM

God Supreme! To Thee We Pray. Penina and Edward N. Calishch Moise. Heavenly Father be it so. AH

God That Doest Wondrously. Moses Ibn Ezra. Pardon at Thy people's cry,/As the closing hour draws nigh. TrJP

God the Architect. Harry Kemp. Thou hast put an upward reach/Into the heart of man. HBMV; TRV; WGRP

God, the Artist. Angela Morgan. How did you think of a star? BLPA; PoToHe

God the Omniscient. James Cowden Wallace. That Love is ever nigh. BLRP

God, the Port of Peace. John Walton. Refut overt to wreches in distresse,/And al comfort of mischief and misese. OxBM

God, through All and in You All. Samuel Longfellow. The Indwelling God, proclaimed of old. TrPWD

God to Be First Served. Robert Herrick. Thee to adore thy God, the first of all. OxBChV

God to Man. Talmud. Even as the pool cleanses the defiled! TrJP

God to Thee We Humbly Bow. George Henry Boker. In defeat or victory! AH

God Wants a Man. *Anonymous.* And proves his faith by a consistent walk. BLRP

God, Who Hath Made the Daisies. E. P. Hood. "Suffer the little children,/And let them come to Me." OHIP

God, Whom Shall I Compare to Thee? Judah Halevi. The Lord of Hosts! thrice holy is His/name! TrJP

God, You have Been Too Good to Me. Charles Wharton Stork. There still will be too much for me/To hold in one glad heart. TrPWD; WGRP

Godamighty Drag. *Anonymous.* When the Brazis was risin',/Riley walked the water. OuSiCo

The Goddess. Denise Levertov. lie for lie! AP; LiTM; PoCh

Goddess. Judith Johnson Sherwin. i think of you with bitter longing always BoWoP

Goddess of Wisdom Whose Substance Is Desire. Anne Waldman. not a stag, not a suitor in jealous weeds/but optimistic & boosting speech. APU

Goddwyn: Ode to Liberty. Thomas Chatterton. Ten bloody arrows in his straining fist! TrGrPo

Godfrey Gordon Gustavus Gore. William Brighty ("Matthew Browne") Rands. GodFrey Gordon Gustavus Gore! BBGG; HBVY; TiPo

Godfrey of Bulloigne: Armida...Sets out to undo the Crusaders. Torquato Tasso. Alas what hope is left, to quench his fire/That kindled is, by sight: blowne, by desire. OBVE

Godiva. Alfred, Lord Tennyson. ...she took the tax away/And built herself an everlasting name. BeLS; HBV 1-2

Godiva (parody). D. C. Berry. Herr Love, Herr Lucifer,/Your flash/In the pan. BXAP

Godly Casuistry. Samuel (1612-80) Butler. For truth is precious and Divine,/Too rich a Pearl for Carnal Swine. OBS

Godly Girzie. Robert Burns. Whare'er your sinfu' pintle be. CoMu; ErPo; UnTE

Godmother. Phyllis B. Morden. Was a laughing elf-woman/Nobody could see! BrR; SoPo

Godmother. Dorothy Parker. After what she gave me–/Rest her soul! PoRA

The Gododdin (excerpt). Aneirin [(or Aneurin)]. And I, the meanest of them all,/That live to weep, and sing their fall. OBVE; OBWP

Godolphin Horne. Hilaire Belloc. So now Godolphin is the Boy/Who blacks the Boots at the Savoy. CenHV; DTC; FaBoCo

The Gods. Dennis Lee. though I/do not know you. NOBC

The Gods. William Stanley Merwin. These strewn rocks belong to the wind/If it could use them. NaP

Gods. Anne Sexton. At last,/she cried out,/and locked the door. CAPP

Gods. Walt Whitman. Be ye my Gods. AnAmPo

The Gods Are Mighty. N. P. Van Wyk Louw. but blood is manifest, and words are vain. PeSA SCAP

Gods Determinations. Edward Taylor.
Darker by far than any Coalpit Stone. AP
Sing all ore heaven for aye. And that's but all. AP

Gods in Vietnam. Eugene B. Redmond. Their voices choked/In suspicious silence. NBP; PoBA

The Gods Must Not Know Us. Linda Gregg. the gods must not know us well or they would/not dance so openly, so happily before us. NPGG

The Gods of the Copybook Headings. Rudyard Kipling. The Gods of the Copybook Headings with terror and slaughter return! FaPoR; OBSV; OHFP; OxBTC; TW

The Gods of the Earth Beneath. Edmund Charles Blunden. And then's the end of all her mirth. BrPo

The Gods! The Gods! D. H. Lawrence. and like water-lilies. CMoP

Godspeed. Harriet Prescott Spofford. On her untiring wing my love shall follow! EtS

Goethe and Frederika. Henry Sidgwick. So his pardon is lightly spoken. HBV 1-2

Goethe's Blues. Denise Levertov. ...And I'm/driving away from the gates of/Paradise.' FaBoWP

Goethe's Death Mask. Linda Gregg. ...Something ugly, and eaten into. What a mess his eyes are. MAYP

The Goff. An Heroi-Comical Poem (excerpt). Thomas Mathison. The echoing shore resounds Castalio's name. NOEC

The Gofongo. Spike Milligan. Then he runs away–/And joins the Arab Army! AmMo

Goin' Back T'morrer. Hamlin Garland. O we must start back t'night! OBAL

Goin' 'Cross the Mountain. *Anonymous.* Goin' 'cross the mountain/You can hear my banjo tell. AmFP

Goin' Down to Town (with music). *Anonymous.* I'm a-goin' down to Lynchburg town,/To carry my tobacco down. AS

Goin' Home. *Anonymous.* Looks like rain–my Lawd!/Looks like rain–hanh! ABF

Goin' Up the River *Anonymous.* Goodbye, Cynthie Jane. TrAS

Going. Peter Everwine. the cow is a black globe. NNaP

The Going. Thomas Hardy. Not even I–would undo me so! EBEV; ELP; LiTB; NOBE; UnPo

Going. Robert Kelly. how very far away, easily/that much further away. CoPo

Going. Philip Larkin. What loads my hands down? CMoP

Going. James Schuyler. October would look no different than it looks. ANYP

Going A-Nutting. Edmund Clarence Stedman. In the clear October morning. GN

Going and Staying. Thomas Hardy. Alike dissolving. CMoP; NoAm

Going Away. Howard Nemerov. ...before the screen doors/of their suddenly forbidden houses. DFF

Going Away. Ann Stanford. We will forget how large the world was once. GP; PH

Going Away Blues. Lottie Kimbrough. I ain't got nobody to/Really comfort me BluL

Going Back. Salvatore Quasimodo. the light of a firefly. AMV-81

Going Back. George Rachow. and I give heart to you/your own pulsing ember in fluid. LFAC

Golden Moonrise. William Stanley Braithwaite. Turn to silver calm. PoBA

The Golden Net. William Blake. O when will the morning rise? ERoP 1-2

Golden Oldie. Paul Mariani. ...They can dance/on and on as long as the music lasts. GeTw

Golden Pheasant. William Hart-Smith. When she stops, stops running,/he gives her a kick. NOAV

The Golden-Robin's Nest. John White Chadwick. A thing he wrought of white and golden/hair! AA

The Golden Rule. James Wells. Always do unto another/What you'd have him do to you. STF

The Golden Sea-Otter. Wakarpa. And on my high bed,/The bed made for me/I flung myself down. WTO

The Golden Sequence. Pope Innocent III. Guide the steps that go astray. CAW

The Golden Sestina. Giovanni Pico della Mirandola For heaven's sufficed with a single sun. LiTW

The Golden Shower. Roy Campbell. We think the world a beetle on its stalk. OxBTC

Golden Silences. Christina Georgina Rossetti. But whoso reaps the ripened corn/Shall shout in his delight,/While silences vanish away. NBM

Golden Slumbers. Thomas Dekker. Rock them, rock them, lullaby. CH; ELP; HBV 1-2; ViBoPo

A Golden Sorrow. Martial (Marcus Valerius Martialis). All for love–with a two-million dot! LiTW

The Golden Spurs. Anonymous. ...Now they're hers. UnTE

Golden Spurs. Virginia Scott Miner. Golden spurs/For you to find! SiSoSe

The Golden Stallion. Paul Thompson. As swift as a startled bird. BPAW

Golden Stockings. Oliver St. John Gogarty. And the gold-dust coming up/From the trampled buttercup. OxBI

The Golden Targe. William Dunbar. Weel aucht thou be affeirit of the licht. BSV; OxBS; PP

The Golden Vanity. Anonymous. And have proved unto him far better than their word,/As they sailed... ViBoFo

The Golden Vanity (B vers.). Anonymous. And they sunk him in the Low Lands Low. BaBo; CBEP; ELP; FaBoCh; FSW; OBET; PoPle; WiR

The Golden Voyage. Anonymous. Yet men and boys came all safe home again,/Though they had gone through such dangers. OBSS

The Golden Wedding. David Gray. The water of that earlier board/To-night shall turn to wine. FaBoBe; HBV 1-2

Golden Wedding (excerpt). Alan Mulgan. Holy with self-forgotten charities. ACV

The Golden Whales of California. Vachel Lindsay. Gold, gold, gold. AtBAP

Golden Wings. William Morris. Inside the rotting leaky boat/You see a slain man's stiffen'd feet. OBNC; WHA

Goldenhair. John Waller. Christophr Robin is looking for trade. PeHV

Goldenrod. Elaine Goodale Eastman. Type of all the wealth to be,–/Goldenrod! HBV 1-2

The Goldfinches. Richard Jago. And there in secret sadness inly mourned. PBBP

Goldfinches. John Keats. Fanning away the dandelion's down. GN

The Goldfish. Audrey Alexandra Brown. He sets the wave afire and still is cold. CaP

Goldfish. Harold Monro. Like salmon on a heavenly fishing line. BrPo

Goldfish. Howard Nemerov. They cruise the ocean of an alien dream. BoAnP

Goldfish on the Writing Desk. Max Brod.
  The huge, sorrowful human face. TrJP
  The two dark eyes go to and fro. LiTW

The Goldfish Wife. Sandra Hochman. And teach us how to air/Our lives again. NYBP; UnPo

The Goldsmith's Wife. Anonymous. With a face too white/And a cheek too red. KiLC

The Golem. Shlomo Reich. Drowned in the royal court of my ghetto. VWA

Golf Ball. John Delaney. ...But golfers play it as it lies. AMV-81

The Golf Links. Sarah N. Cleghorn. And see the men at play. FaFP; HBMV; InMe; InPK; PoLf; PoPl; PPON

The Golfer's Rubaiyat (parody). H. W. Boynton. And you in your mild Journey pass the Hole/I made in One–ah, pay my Forfeit then! BXAP

Golfers. Irving Layton. And that no theory of pessimism is complete/which altogether ignores them SD

Golfers. John Updike. mere men, old boys, lost, the last hole a horror. LiSp

Golgotha. X. J. Kennedy. The mad in absolute power. NYBP

Golgotha. John Hall Wheelock. I will pour out Thy love upon them in my agony. MoRP

Golgotha Is a Mountain. Arna Bontemps. I think it will be Golgotha. AmNP; CDC; PoNe

Goliath and David. Louis Untermeyer. Come, old Goliath, come and play! TrJP

Goliath of Gath. Phillis Wheatley. "Knit to my soul for ever thou remain/ "With me, nor quit my regal roof again." BALP

Goll Mac Morna Parts from his Wife. Anonymous. I brought him to grief, woman! NOBI

Golly, How Truth Will Out! Ogden Nash. And that is why I can never amount to anything politically or socially. LiTA; MoAmPo

The Gombeen. Joseph Campbell. As poor as one who never knew/The treasure of the early dew. BIrV

Gondibert. Sir William Davenant.
  And hapless Lovers constancy in Love. OBS
  For he who bus'nesse would from storms procure,/Soon his affairs above his mannage findes. SeCV 1-2
  Whose worth they rev'rendly forbear to rate. CEP

Gone. Mary Elizabeth Coleridge. One door alone is shut, one chamber still. HBV 1-2; OBEV; OBNC; OBVV

Gone. Walter De la Mare. But where's the Queen of Sheba?/Where King Solomon? GoJo

A Gone. Larry Eigner. and the awning was still there NeAP

Gone. Ralph Pomeroy. Stones in the high weeds/mark where there was. DFF

Gone. Carl Sandburg. Nobody knows where she's gone. AmP; APA; NOBA

Gone. Joanna Thompson. and turn his wild brown gaze/to mine. AMV-80

Gone Are the Days. Norman MacCaig. ...let me/buy a love potion, a gin, a double. OxBC

Gone Boy. Langston Hughes. Dog-gone!/He ain't gone. NePoAm-2

The Gone Dead Train. King Solomon Hill. 'Cause I'm a traveling man/ boys, I can't stay here BluL

Gone Fishing. Mark Sanders. they will find the sign/we took care to leave behind. WOLT

Gone! Gone! Forever Gone. Gerald Griffin. A prodigal in promise now;/A miser in fulfilling! OnYI

Gone Is the Sleepgiver. Penelope Shuttle. I was losing strength,/or being turned into a bird). BrRo

Gone on the Wind. James Clarence Mangan. And I Hear voices from Hades like bells on the wind. CBEP

Gone Were but the Winter Cold. Allan Cunningham. At the Spring o' the year. CH

The Gone Years. Alice Fulton. letting the gone/years hug her/with his long wool arms. Str

Gonna Lay My Head down on Some Railroad Line. Anonymous. You ain't no friend to you. AmFP

Goober Peas. Pindar. Goodness how delicious, eating goober peas! FSW; PSoN

Good Advice. Mary Wortley, Lady Montagu. In short, my deary, kiss me, and be quiet. PoL

Good and Bad. Edward Wallis Hoch. That it hardly becomes any of us/To talk about the rest of us. GoTF; TreFS

Good and Bad. James Stephens. How to banish good and ill/With the laughter of the heart. MoBrPo

Good and Bad Children. Robert Louis Stevenson. Hated, as their age increases,/By their nephews and their nieces. BBGG; FaBoCh; FaFP; GoTF; HBV 1-2; HBVY; LoGBV; NBM; NLV; OxBChV; TreF

Good and Clever. Elizabeth Wordsworth. For few can be good, like the clever,/Or clever, so well as the good. OxBTC

Good and Great God! Ben Jonson. For weariness of life, not love of Thee. OxBoCh

Good Appetite. Mark Van Doren. ...may you be fond/Of me and these forever, and wood fire. OBSP

Good & Bad Wives. Anonymous. And may those who are married live happy. CoMu

The Good Beasts. Willis Barnstone. ...Its light/rages, illiterate, until they leave. VWA

Good, Better, Best. Anonymous. And "better' "best'. OxNR

The Good Bishop. Anonymous. Happy was Cologne/To be worthy of such a bishop! CAW; WGRP

Good Bishop Valentine. Eleanor Farjeon. Orange-blossom posies/And gold wedding-rings. PoSC

The Good Boy. Anonymous. Will strive for to spell. OxNR

The Good Boy (with music). Anonymous. I shall be an old bum loved but unrespected. AS

Good-By. Margaret E. Bruner. Like suppliants pleading. PoToHe

A Good-By. Ednah Proctor (Clarke) Hayes. Where red death waits without the gates,/Thy knight, and God's,–I go! AA

Good-By. Grace Denio Litchfield. We cry, as to the wanderer for a night–/"Good-by." PoToHe

Good-by and Keep Cold. Robert Frost. But something has to be left to God. CMoP

Good-By er Howdy-Do. James Whitcomb Riley. Ef He's willin', we'll pull through–/Say good-by er howdy-do! CTC

Good-By Liza Jane (with music). Anonymous. But the bridge it wasn't built yet. Oh! it's good-by Liza Jane. AS

Good-By, Mother. Anonymous. An' de grave is nailed over yo' do'. ABF

Good-By, Old Paint. Anonymous.
And we'll ride the prairie that we love the best. CoSo
Good-by, old Paint, I'm a-leavin' Cheyenne. ABF; FSW

Good-By, Pretty Mama. Anonymous. When I go to town. ABF

Good-bye. Ralph Waldo Emerson. When man in the bush with God may meet? AnNE; FaFP; GoTF; HBV 1-2; LiTA; MAmP; TAP; TreF

Good-Bye, Brother (with music). Anonymous. Now God bless you, now God bless you,/If I don't see you more. AS

Good-Bye, Fare You Well. Anonymous. Hurrah, my boys, we're homeward bound! AmSS

Good-Bye for a Long Time. Roy Fuller. Hurt beyond hurting, never to forget. NeBP

Good Bye, My Lady Love. Joseph E. Howard. But some day you will come back to me,/And love me tenderly,/So good bye, my lady love, good bye. FSN

Good-Bye Old Paint. Anonymous. Good morning, young lady, my hosses won't stand. TrAS

Good-Bye to the Mezzogiorno. W. H. Auden. Remember exactly why one was happy/There is no forgetting that one was. OxBTC

Good-bye to the People of Hang-Chow. Po Chu-i. And help a little in a year when things were bad. LiTW

Good Christians. Robert Herrick. Till they be hid o'er with a wood of darts. LiTB

Good Company. Anonymous. But I feel I am in very good company. OBET

Good Company. Karle Wilson Baker. Lord, who am I that they should stoop–these holy folk of/thine? HBV 1-2; WGRP

Good Company. King of England Henry VIII. Virtue to use,/Vice to refuse,/Thus shall I use me. TrGrPo

Good Company, Fine Houses. John Newlove. ...I have slept/in the turning mountain. PeCV

Good Counsel. James I King of Scotland. And for ilk inch he will thee quit a span. ACP

Good Counsel. James Clarence Mangan. ...when her nest has once been/plundered,/Ne'er can build another more. NOBI

Good Counsel to a Young Maid. Thomas Carew. Than his pale cheek should assign/A perpetual blush to thine. AnAnS 2; CaPo; CavP; CBEP; ErPo; OBS

Good Creatures, Do You Love Your Lives. Alfred Edward Housman. And earth's foundations will depart/And all you folk will die. TW

A Good Creed. Anonymous. Shall reap from our glad sowing. PoToHe

The Good Day. Sir Henry Howarth Bashford. Where the two dear hands I love/Poured the wine, and broke the bread. HBV 1-2

The Good Dream. Denise Levertov. meeting in depths of the sea. NNaP

Good for Nothing Man. Kenneth Pitchford.
and one a' them's got a woman/who oughta be in hell. CoPo
her eyes staring clear, through white flakes of sea-salt. CoPo
just a bad man, a thief. CoPo
peeling peeling the onion skin/down to the nothingness within. CoPo
the petalled flesh/of the human rose. CoPo

Good Fortune. Heinrich Heine. Sits by your bed–and brings her knitting. BLPA

Good Frend. Hilda ("H. D.") Doolittle. ...save/us by the grace He gave/to the herb,/rosemary. NOBA

Good Friday. Anonymous.
Rejoice; for Light was slain to-day, yet did not die. BoC
Three a penny fire shovel,/Hot cross buns. OxNR

Good Friday. Arlene De Bevoise. When all this will be explained. AMV-81

Good Friday. John Frederick Nims. Popped in our pouch of spit, a hot-cross bun. TW

Good Friday. Christina Georgina Rossetti. Greater than Moses, turn and look once more/and smite a rock. OFD; PoEL 1-5; TRV

Good Friday. A. J. M. Smith. That is not all unworthy of/The God I mourn? CaP

Good Friday, 1613. Riding Westward. John Donne. Restore Thine image so much, by Thy grace,/That Thou may'st know me, and I'll turn my face. ATP; DiPo; EnRePo; ExPo; InPS; JCP; MePo; NOCV; NoP; OAEL 1-2; OxBoCh; PPP; SeCP; SeCV 1-2; TEP

Good Friday and the Present Crucifixion. Vincent Buckley. The thong and point of rain. CBAP

Good Friday Evening. Christina Georgina Rossetti. To love Thee much, to love Thee more and still/More and yet more. PGD

Good Friday in My Heart. Mary Elizabeth Coleridge. And night and day, since Thou dost rise, are one. PGD

Good Friday: The Madman's Song. John Masefield. Now darkness is upon the face of the earth. ACV

Good Friday: The Third Nocturn. Peter Abelard. To win the laughter of Thine Easter Day. LiTW

Good Gossips Mine. Anonymous. But wine of the best/Shall have no rest,/Good gossipes mine-a... OxBM

Good Grease. Mary Tallmountain. Good grease. STE; TWSS

The Good Great Man. Samuel Taylor Coleridge. Himself, his Maker, and the Angel Death. HBV 1-2

Good Green Bus. Rachel Field. For audience in the good green Bus! BrR

The Good Hour. Louise Driscoll. He can exult and die in the same breath. HBMV

The Good Humor Man. Phyllis McGinley. Unending sweets, imperishable summer. MoShBr

The Good Inn. Herman Knickerbocker Viele. And here's to the friend/Of the journey's end/At the Inn of the Silver Moon. HBV 1-2

The Good Joan. Lizette Woodworth Reese. For Joan of Arc goes riding by. MoShBr

Good King Arthur. Mother Goose. And what they could not eat that night,/The Queen next morning fried. HBVY

Good King Wenceslas. John Mason Neale. Ye who now will bless the poor,/Shall yourselves find blessing. FSW; HBV 1-2; HBVY; OHIP; OnMSP; TreFS

De Good Lawd Know My Name. Frank Lebby Stanton. An' de good Lawd know my name. WBLP

A Good Life. Robert Watson. I am not ready yet to be the past in the past. AMV-81

The Good Little Girl. A.(lan) A.(lexander) Milne. Have you been a good girl, Jane? BBGG

Good Luck and Bad. John Milton Hay. And sits by your bed, and brings her knitting. FaBoEE

The Good Man. Talmud. Who is honorable?/He who treats all men honorably. TrJP

The Good Man in Hell. Edwin Muir. And love and hate and life and death begin. MoBrPo; MoRP; TW

Good Master and Mistress... Anonymous. Pray think of us poor children/Who are wandering in the mire. EvOK

Good Memory. Sotero Rivera-Aviles. a strange sweat that makes one think of travels. InW

Good Men Afflicted Most. Robert Herrick. He never brings them once to th' push of pikes. LiTB

The Good Moolly Cow. Eliza Lee Follen. "Thank you for your milk,/Mrs. Good Moolly Cow." OBCA

Good Mornin', Blues. Anonymous. When the blues overtaken him, he hollered like a newborn child. InPK

Good Morning. Muriel Sipe. And he said, "Cheep, cheep, cheep." SoPo; SUS; TiPo

Good Morning. Mark Van Doren. Morning to all things that ever/Were and will be, and that are. DuDa

Good Morning America (excerpt). Carl Sandburg. Even though the oldest kings had their singers and/clowns calling, "Oh king, you shall live forever OFD

Good Morning, Father Francis. Anonymous. So kiss, kiss, kiss, and away. OxNR

Good Morning Love! Paul Blackburn. & making a cup/of coffee that's all NMP; NoAm

The Good-Morrow. John Donne. If our two loves be one, or thou and I/Love so alike that none do slacken, none can die. AtBAP; AWP; BiP; BoLiVe; BoLoP; CABA; DiPo; EBEV; EG; ElL; EnL; EnLoPo; ExPo; FaBoBe; FaBV; FF; FPL; HBV 1-2; HoPM; InPo; InPS; InvP; JCP; LiTB; LiTL; LoBV; MBW 1-2; MePo; NAWM 1-2; NIP; NoP; OAEL 1-2; OBS; OLR; PAI; PoEL 1-5; PoPle; PoRA; PPP; SCV; SeCeV; SeCP; SeCV 1-2; SoSe; TEP; TreFT; TrGrPo; UnTE; ViBoPo

The Good-Natur'd Man: Prologue. Samuel Johnson. But confident of praise, if praise be due,/Trusts without fear, to merit, and to you. LoBV

Good News. Anonymous. And I don't want it to leave me behind. FSW

Good News Bad News. Keith Abbott. To live and die/Good news bad news. APU

Good News from New-England. Edward Johnson. Error's brought in to blind men damningly. SCAP

Good-Night. Hester A. Benedict. To hear again her low good-night! good-night! HBV 1-2

Good Night. Joel Dailey. My darling house among houses! APU

Good Night. Thomas Hood. There's a puff–and so good night! SiSoSe; SoPo

Good Night. Victor Hugo. Good night! Good night! SiSoSe; SoPo; SUS; TiPo

Good-Night. Silas Weir Mitchell. One brief "Good-night," for thee and me./Good-night. HBV 1-2

Good Night. John Nichol. Good night, my love! good night! OBVV

Good Night. Dorothy Mason Pierce. He bids His world Good Night. BrR; SiSoSe

A Good Night. Francis Quarles. No sleep so sweet as thine, no rest so sure. OBS; TrGrPo

Good-Night. Percy Bysshe Shelley. The night is good; because, my love,/ They never say good-night. HBV 1-2; LiTL; ViBoPo

Good-Night. Jane Taylor. Little baby dear, good-night. HBV 1-2; HBVY

Good-Night. Edward ("Edward Eastaway") Thomas. But it is All Friends' Night, a traveler's good-night. NoP

Good Night and Good Morning. Richard Monckton, Lord Houghton Milnes. "Good morning! good morning! our work is begun!" OxBChV

Good-Night, Babette. Henry Austin Dobson. "I am so old!"..."Good-night, Babette!" HBV 1-2; OBVV

Good Night, God Bless You. Anonymous. Go to bed and undress you. OxNR

Good Night! Good Night! John Holmes. Let this one have an end! PoToHe

The Good-Night or Blessing. Robert Herrick. Thus a dew of Graces fall/ On ye both; Good-night to all. ALV; CaPo

Good Night, Sweet Repose. Anonymous. Half the bed and all the clothes. OxNR

Good-Night to the Season. Winthrop Mackworth Praed. Good-night to the Season!–Good-night! ALV; NOBE; NOBL; OBNC; OxBoLi; PoEL 1-5

Good Ol' Mountain Dew. Anonymous. Of the good old mountain dew?/ WE DO. ABF

The Good Old Days. Barbara Fried. A careless mumble/Of/one/night/ Stands. NLV

The Good Parson. Geoffrey Chaucer. The lore of Christ and his apostles twelve/He taught, but first he followed it himself. WGRP

Good People. Maura Stanton. ...or part of someone dead/Who thought that life was choice, not accident. SM

A Good Play. Robert Louis Stevenson. So there was no one left but me. MoShBr; TiPo

Good Repute Is Water Carried in a Sieve. Lalleswari. will you maybe succeed in keeping your good name/clear. WPOW

A Good Resolution. Roy Campbell. Clear as a milk-white feather in a crow/Or a black stallion on a field of snow. OBSV

The Good Rich Man. Gilbert Keith Chesterton. But these were luxuries not for him who went for the/Simple Life. DTC

Good Riddance to Bad Rubbish O at Last! Paul Goodman. But my way is to be patient, and I have survived/even to this year not worse than the last. TW

The Good Samaritan. John Henry, Cardinal Newman. When comes a foe, my wounds with oil and wine to tend. OBTV

The Good Shepherd. J. Harold Gwynne. They know for them I lived and died. BePJ

The Good Shepherd. Felix Lope de Vega Carpio. With feet nailed to the cross, Thou'rt waiting still for me! BePJ; CAW

The Good Shepherd. Keidrych Rhys. Teacher said I never polish my shoes. NeBP

The Good Shepherd. Clyde Edwin Tuck. And offers to your wayward soul and mine/The shelter of His fold. BePJ

The Good Ship. Michael Stephens. ...any memory I/have of these New York places evaporates with her sweet tongue. APU

Good Ships. John Crowe Ransom. And unto miserly merchant hulks converted. WeW

Good Sportsmanship. Richard Armour. You have to lose to prove you've got it. LiSp

A Good Start. Larry Moffi. I know to greet the day/by listening carefully first. AMV-81

Good Susan, Be as Secret as You Can. Anonymous. Than wearing horns hath caused an aching head. ErPo

A Good Thanksgiving. Annie Douglas Robinson. If you want a good time, then give something away! PoLf

A Good Thing. Ray Mathew. She left the bowl with me. And that is that. CBAP

Good Thoughts. Katherine Maurine Haaff. From which our lives are made. PoToHe

The Good Time Coming. Charles Mackay. 'Twill be strong enough one day,/wait a little longer. PaPo; VLP

The Good Time Is Now. Laura Chester. ...Stunned, as the yellow of the mustard field,/we galloped beside that evening. APU

Good Times. Lucille Clifton. oh children think about the/good times. AmPA; BPo; CNA; FF; GrPl; InPS; NCSH; PAI; PoBA; TAP; TwCP

Good Times & No Bread. Reginald Lockett. articulate chess playin/trump holdin/cities & states CNA

The Good Town. Edwin Muir. These thoughts we have, walking among our ruins. CMoP

Good Tradition. Anonymous. And all men turn you from the door. AnIL

Good Weather. Giuseppe Gioachino Belli. What a perfect day! What crystal! What paradise! AMV-81

Good Wish. Anonymous. Death on the pillow be thine,/Thy Saviour's presence. FaBoCh; LoGBV

The Good Woman. Crystal MacLean. ...the one who left/and stopped screaming FAZ

Goodbat Nightman. Roger McGough. Batman and Robin/are falling asleep. NoAm

Goodby Betty, Don't Remember Me. Edward Estlin Cummings. proving to Death that Love is so and so. CMoP

Goodby "Hello." Philip Dow. ...Eternity is where we forget we are as we call out: Hello! Hello! NPGG

Goodbye. Bella Akhmadulina. my senses leave me. BoWoP

Goodbye. Chana Bloch. ...If you eat this fruit/you will die,/they didn't mean right away. MAYP

Goodbye. Walter De la Mare. Last of all last words spoken is Goodbye. NoP

Goodbye. Galway Kinnell. That is how we have learned, the embrace is all. Str

Goodbye. Bill Knott. ...I am/under their lids, growing black. EAS

Goodbye. Alun Lewis. ...patches that you sewed/On my old battledress tonight, my sweet. OBWP

Goodbye. Sherod Santos. While the one who is saying goodbye/Lets go the hand of the one left standing. MAYP

The Goodbye. Myra Sklarew. ...Yet/this passing has the shape/of farewell. GOYP

Goodbye David Tamunoemi West. Margaret Danner. ...power that formerly came/from the use of Tamunoemi/your African name. BPo

Goodbye, Little Bonnie, Goodbye. Anonymous. Goodbye, little Bonnie, goodbye. FSW

Goodbye, Little Bonny Blue Eyes. Anonymous. I'm a-going to leave this town. AmFP

Goodbye 'Liza Jane. Anonymous. Oh Liza, poor girl,/She died on the train. FSW

Goodbye, My Lover, Goodbye. Anonymous. Goodbye, my lover, goodbye. FSW

Goodbye Nkrumah. Diane Di Prima. ...it is the calm/of the earth itself. PoM

Goodbye Now, or, Pardon My Gauntlet. Ogden Nash. And a flunky thought she said the earl's room. FiBHP

Goodbye, Sally. James Simmons. ...The singer wants applause/not criticism as he leaves the stage. BIrV

Goodbye to Regal. Daniel Huws. For his ignorance I could strike him dead. NYBP

Goodbye to Serpents. James Dickey. The water in the air without support/ Sustained in the serpent's eye. NYBP

Goodbye to the Poetry of Calcium. James Wright. I do not even have ashes to rub into my eyes. CAPP

A Goodly Child. Anonymous. They say, "Glad may this child's friends be/ To have a child so mannerly as he." OxBChV

Goodman's Sauce. Anonymous. Proud are your Berkshire hearts to bleed/ When drest with Goodman's prime Vale Sauce. FaBoUs

Goodmorning with Light. John Ciardi. Machines and morning fixed upon/ The starting spectrum of the dawn. WaP

Goodnight. John Ciardi. If I am not here for breakfast, geologize at will. OBAL

Goodnight. Stevie Smith. ...It was 2 o'clock and Miriam was quite white/ With sorrow. Very well then, Goodnight. FaBoWP

A Goodnight. William Carlos Williams. And the night passes–and never passes– MoAB; MoAmPo

Goodnight Ladies. Anonymous. We're going to leave you now. FSW

The Goods She Can Carry: Canticle of Her Basket Made of Reeds. Gibbons Ruark. Ending I praise her for putting the basket down. MAYP

Goodwill, Inc. Dennis Schmitz. till I stumble & weave/other richer lives on my own. AmPA

Goody Blake and Harry Gill (excerpt). William Wordsworth. His teeth they chatter, chatter still! Par

Goody-by, Steer. Robert V. Carr. And you're on your way to Packin'town. BPAW

Goose. Richard Emil Braun. ...holding an old red pinwheel,/ran ran ran ran. NoAm

The Goose and the Gander. Anonymous. And she laid a white egg in a willow tree root. GBP

The Goose and the Swans (excerpt). Edward Moore. And striving Nature to conceal,/You only her defects reveal. PBBP

The Goose Fish. Howard Nemerov. Along the still and tilted track/That bears the zodiac. CMoP; LiTM; NePoEA; NIP; NMP; NoAm; NoP; SM

The Goose Girl. Dorothy Roberts. For some day the goose girl will marry a king! CaP

Goose Pond. Stanley Jasspon Kunitz. To find what furies made him man. PoA

Gooseberries. Stephen Berg. Rain beat against the window panes all night. NaP

Gooseberries. Peter Wild. ...and his little wife/who baked for him ran out/ and tore up the gooseberries. DFF; GP

Goosepimples. Coleman Barks. stand up and clap PV

Goosey Gander. *Anonymous.* And threw him down the stairs. OxNR

Goosey Goosey Gander. William Percy French. And giblet pie/Is cheap in Rome to-day. CenHV As they wobble from stair to stair. CenHV Propelled him, all pallid and prayerless,/From attic to hall. CenHV So perhaps I'd better drop it. CenHV

Goosey, Goosey, Gander. Mother Goose. I took him by his left leg/And threw him down the stairs. HBV 1-2; PBBP

Gorbo and Batte. Michael Drayton. That's she alone kind shepherd's boy,/ Let us to Daffadill. LoBV

The Gordian Knot. Thomas Tomkis. Thy little world I'll conquer presently. EiL; UnTE

Gordon Childe. David Martin. Man makes himself. Each crest out-tops the last. PoAu 1-2

Gorg, a Detective Story. John Nichol. ...the man picks up the/corpse & exits. NOBC

Gorgio Lad. Amelia Josephine Burr. There are butterfly wings on a gypsy's loving./Gorgio lad, good-bye. HBMV

The Gorilla. Baxter Hathaway. And buses charge to the zoological gardens. HoAn

The Gorilla at Twenty Nine Years. J. D. Reed. they showed the tartar on their teeth,/scratched and grinned. NeAC

The Goring. Sylvia Plath. Blood faultlessly broached redeemed the sullied air, the earth's/grossness. OBTV

Gormley's Laments (excerpt). Gormley. how much better the poets! PBWP

The Gorse. Wilfred Wilson Gibson. Beneath a blinding sky, one blaze of sun. AtBAP

The Goshawk. John Haines. the Goshawk feeds on your timid heart. GP

The Gospel According to You. *Anonymous.* 'Tis the only gospel that some men will/read,/That gospel according to you. BLRP; STF

The Gospel of Labor. Henry Van Dyke. Heaven is blessed with perfect rest,/but the blessing of earth is toil. TRV; WBLP; WGRP

The Gospel of Mr. Pepys. Christopher Morley. When kisses are a shilling each/We should adventure on a few. InMe; NLV

The Gospel of Peace. James Jeffrey Roche. And craven White, to tell the wrong/A prudent nation bore. PAH

The Gospel Train. *Anonymous.* Get on board, little chillun,/There's room for many a more. BLSo; GoSl; TrAS

The Gosport Tragedy. *Anonymous.* And raving, distracted, he died the next night. AmFP

The Gosport Tragedy (A vers.). *Anonymous.* She stript him and tore him, she tore him in three,/Because he had murdered her baby and she. BaBo

The Gossamer. Charlotte Smith. Leave but the withered heath and barren thorn. ViBoPo

The Gossip. Daniel Halpern. When he reaches for us in our sleep. SO

Gossip Grows Like Weeds. Hitomaro. My girl and I/Sleep arm in arm. OLR

The Gossips. *Anonymous.* While they gossiped around/A tea-caddy. OxNR

Got Dem Blues (with music). *Anonymous.* Sweet Daddy! Uh-huh! Trun me down! Uh-huh! AS

Got the Blues, Can't Be Satisfied. Mississippi John Hurt. You got the blues and still ain't satisfied BluL

Gotham. Charles Churchill. Shall Churchill reign, and shall not Gotham sing? NOEC

Gothic. Jean Starr Untermeyer. To ornament the Gothic of my mind. AnAmPo

The Gothic Dusk. Frederic Prokosch. The streets will flicker, the asylums will be still. PoA

A Gothic Gesture. Steve Levine. Green and lumpy landscaping, brooding/ Piano, parodistic weltschmerz. APU

Gothic Landscape. Irving Layton. It is a Christ drained of all blood. TrJP

Gothic Notebook (excerpts). Mario Luzi. wind in the briar is you, you are here/on the grass in this lucid ferment. LiTW

Gotta' Smoke? William Franklin. I know I look/square, but do/you see a humpbacked/Camel/printed on/me? LFAC

The Goulden Vanitie. *Anonymous.* And sink off the Lowlands low. AtBAP

The Gourd Dancer. N. Scott Momaday. ...as long as there/are those who imagine him in his name. CDW; STE

Gourds. Nicander. And curly cabbages, and add them too. FaBoUs

The Gourmand (parody). Harry Graham. The rich man eats them with a fork,/The poor man with a knife. FaBoPa

The Gourmet's Love-Song. P. G. Wodehouse. Do change your mind, and answer, "Yes,'/And save me from starvation. NOBL

Gout and Wings. Turner, Charles Tennyson. A wing was open'd at me everywhere! NOBV

The Gouty Merchant and the Stranger. Horace (or Horatio) Smith. Leaving the gouty merchant in the dark. BeLS

Government. Tuta Nihoniho. Alas! They cannot be shaken! WTO

Government Injunction. Josephine Miles. The plucking of hope from the hand, honor from the complexion,/Sprite from the spell. PoNe

Government Official. Paul Dehn. Guide where our country's redeemer is laid. WaP

The Gowden Locks of Anna. Robert Burns. Had I on earth but wishes three,/The first should be my Anna. CBEP

The Gowk. William Soutar. And gently spak the howie hill/Cuckoo, cuckoo. BSV; NeBP

The Gown. Mary Carolyn Davies. —But every woman there will look at me. HBMV

Goya. Conrad Aiken. And underscribed it,"Let them slumber,/Who if they woke could only weep'... AmLP

Grab-Bag. Helen Hunt Jackson. Of a sad game of Grab-bag—a sad game to see! OBCA

Grace. *Anonymous.* But we hae meat and we can eat,/For which the Lord be thankit! LoGBV

Grace. Ralph Waldo Emerson. Had not these me against myself defended. AmPP; NoP; TrPWD

Grace. George Herbert. Let suppling grace, to crosse his art,/Drop from above. JCP; SeCV 1-2

Grace. Johnstone G. Patrick. Bless to our use, as we peruse, O Lord! TrPWD

A Grace. Thomas Tiplady. And keep our hearts from growing cold. TrPWD; TRV

Grace. Richard Wilbur. Nevertheless, the praiseful, graceful soldier/ Shouldn't be fired by his gun. LiTA

Grace Abounding. Archie Randolph Ammons. ...find one's/misery made clear, borne, as if also, by a hedge of ice. HaCAP

Grace after Dinner. Robert Burns. And Jock bring in the spirit!/Amen. FaBoEE

Grace after Meals. *Anonymous.* Then let us bless the Lord. TrJP

Grace at Evening. Edgar A. Guest. And when another day shall break/ Unto Thy service may we wake. TrPWD; TRV

Grace at Evening. Edwin McNeill Poteat. Unveil our eyes/To recognize/ Thyself, for Thy dear sake. TrPWD

Grace at Kirkudbright. Robert Burns. Sae let the Lord be thankit. OBSP

Grace at the Atlanta Fox. Turner Cassity. States then "There is no God but God..." NIP

Grace before Meat. Robert D. FitzGerald. So then be their masters your son and mine. NOAV

Grace Before Sleep. Sara Teasdale. Accept, O Lord, our thanks to-night. MoRP; TrPWD

Grace Darling. *Anonymous.* And sing of brave Grace Darling, who nobly saved the crew. OBET; OBSS

Grace for a Child. Robert Herrick. For a benison to fall/On our meat and on us all. Amen. AWP; InPo; InPS; LoBV; MoShBr; OAEP; PAI; PoRA; TrGrPo; ViBoPo

Grace for Children. Robert Herrick. And our peace here, like a spring,/ Make it ever flourishing. EBCP; OxBChV; OxBoCh

Grace for Gardens. Louise Driscoll. Bless the orchards/And the grain! TrPWD

Grace: "God bless our meat." *Anonymous.* Our Gracious Queen Elizabeth. OxNR

The Grace-Note. Denise Levertov. ...so he/ornaments his with/fresh contempt. ConAP

The Grace of Cynthia's Maidenhood. Vinnie-Marie D'Ambrosio. and into her eyes/fall the shining feathers/of shyness and pleasure. IHMS

Grace of the Way (excerpt). Francis Thompson. So ready is Heaven to stoop to him. MoAB; MoBrPo

Grace to Be Said at the Supermarket. Howard Nemerov. That we may look unflinchingly on death/As the greatest good, like philosopher should. SoSe

GraceAnAnne. Lysbeth Boyd Borie. About my yelling–"GraceAnAnne!" BiCB

Graceful Acacia. Walter Savage Landor. And may he lend her shade to me! PoEL 1-5

The Graceful Bastion. William Carlos Williams. the cotton clouds/should merely fall. NYBP

Gracey Nugent. Austin Clarke. Empty the rummer while you are able,/ Two Sundays before Lent. CIP

Gracie. Faye Kicknosway. ...chicken/yard, ma's apron an' my head cool in its bonnet. GeTw; NMM

Gracious Goodness. Marge Piercy. Why is there nothing/I have ever done with anybody/that seems to me so obviously right? BoAnP; HoAn; Psk

Gracious Moonlight. Dante Gabriel Rossetti. And chase night's gloom, as thou the spirit's grief. MaVP

Gracious Saviour, We Adore Thee. Sewall Sylvester Cutting. May we follow/In the same delightful way. AH

Gracius and Gay. *Anonymous.* Kysse me yn my way,/Onys ar y wend. SeCePo

The Grackle. Ogden Nash. I cannot help but deem the grackle/An ornithological debacle. DBV; NLV; PV

Gradatim. Josiah Gilbert Holland. And we mount to its summit/round by round. FaFP; GoTF; HBV 1-2; HBVY; OHFP; TreFS; WGRP

The Graduate. Charles Stetler. Every year we're surprised/how this old chestnut still grabs/a couple squirrels. GP

Graduation Day, 1965. Julio Marzan. Drowned out by the winds and a promise. InW

Graffiti. *Anonymous.* But Sartre is smartre. NLV

Graffiti. Alan Bold.
I'm happy I rejoice in drink. PoL
You'd think that even a deity would wonder why. PoL

Graffiti. Edward Field. That shoot great drops of gism through the sky. CoPo

Graffiti for Lovers. Joan Joffe Hall. It's never enough. AMV-80

Graffiti in a University Restroom... Jim Mitsui. that even the creators of soundtracks/could understand. BrSi

Graffito Inscribed on a Wall of the Taj Mahal. *Anonymous.* The last triumphant wonder of the world! OBTV

A Grafted Tongue. John Montague. speech stumbles over lost/syllables of an old order. BIrV; CIP

Graham Bell and the Photophone. George Edgar Montgomery. or, with selenic stealth, intrude to hymn/subversive music to his sleeping love? SUW

The Grail. Sidney Keyes. She alone/Knew from her birth the mystic Avalon. FaBoTw

Grain Elevator. Abraham Moses Klein. ...Because/always this great box flowers over us/with all the coloured faces of mankind... CaP

A Grain of Moonlight. Asya (Asya Gray). From above and below/As if before/Being. VWA

A Grain of Rice. F. R. Scott. We grow to one world through/Enlargement of wonder. PeCV

A Grain of Salt. William Irwin. For in 'is cabin he can sit/And sail and sail–and let 'er knit. HBV 1-2

Gramercy Park Hotel. Dave Smith. I will not be here long, will be/careful, will have no time for the key. NYP

A Grammar. Andrei Codrescu. i am always behind. EAS

Grammar Commences with a 5-line Curse. Palladas. Sad study, grammar! Its whole content's/one long string of accidents! OBVE

Grammar in a Nutshell. *Anonymous.* The Whole are called Nine Parts of Speech,/Which reading, writing, speaking teach. GoTF; HBV 1-2; HBVY; TreFS

Grammar Lesson. Linda Paston. ...change/to the plural/where you will/never be/lonely again. Psk

The Grammar of Love. Pott and Wright. He brings a change of mood. ALV

A Grammarian's Funeral. Robert Browning. Leave him–still loftier than the world suspects,/Living and dying. BoLiVe; DiPo; HBV 1-2; LoBV; MaVP; NOBV; OAEP; VLP; WGRP

The Gramophone. James Reaney. "I'm all alone/By the telephone!" CaP

Grand Abacus. John Ashbery. ...But it is already too late. The/children have vanished. EAS

The Grand Canyon. James Merrill. They have sat a long time/In one of our highest courts. TAP

Grand Chorus of Birds. Algernon Charles Swinburne. That we ARE to you all as the manifest godhead that/speaks in prophetic Apollo? PoEL 1-5

Grand Conversation on Brave Nelson. *Anonymous.* This grand conversation on brave Nelson arose. OBET

The Grand Duke of New York. Dan Pagis. Wrongs fade beyond the shore and time invites/an easy confabulation. VWA

Grand Finale. Irving Layton. and the moon and all the stars come crashing down. NOBC

The Grand Guignols of Love. Michael Benedikt. That they would look at one another. AmPA

Grand Hotel, Calcutta. Layle Silbert. I was all drunk with India that night. AMV-81

The Grand Inquisitor's Song. Sir William Schwenck Gilbert. All possible doubt whatever. OnMSP

The Grand Match. Moira O'Neill. An' the tongue of the woman that owns him. HBMV

The Grand Old Duke of York. Mother Goose. He was neither up nor down. GBP; SoPo; TiPo

Grand Opening of the People's Theatre. O. J. Goldrick. Where, through God's aid, shall ever wave the flag of Washington! PoOW

Grand Rapids. Julia A. Moore. The largest town in west Michigan/Is the city of Grand Rapids. OBAL

Grand Rapids Cricket Club (excerpt). Julia A. Moore. He got struck severe at the fair ground/For which he took a rest. PeD

Grand Street & the Bowery. David Ghitelman. ...filled/with deaf cries, like an invisible river. FAZ

La Grande Jatte: Sunday Afternoon. Thomas Cole. I note with what calm grace the French relax. NePoAm

Grandeur of Ghosts. Siegfried Sassoon. ...the dead have said/What these can only memorize and mumble. AnFE; HaMV; MoBrPo; OBMV

Grandfather. Willis Barnstone. ...The tailor fades/from all of us, forever, stitching sleeves. VWA

Grandfather. George Bowering. in a Catholic hospital of sheets white as his hair NOBC

Grandfather. Mary Joan Coleman. now I am laying a bridge back to you. AMV-80

Grandfather. Michael S. Harper. ...or the film/played backwards on his grandson's eyes. FiCP; GeTw; LCAP; TAP

Grandfather. Lance Henson. i will follow CDW

Grandfather. Derek Mahon. Nothing escapes him; he escapes us all. FaBoIP; OxBC

Grandfather. Joseph Stroud. Singing of home, death, a blossoming tree. NPGG

Grandfather Frog. Louise Seaman Bechtel. Croak–croak–/SPLASH! TiPo

Grandfather Gabriel. Robert Penn Warren. For that other young guy who died too late. AnAmPo

Grandfather in the Old Men's Home. William Stanley Merwin. Beating their little Bibles till he died. ConAP; LiTM; SM

"Grandfather" in.Winter. Frederick Feirstein. Shema. NYP

A Grandfather Poem. William J. Harris. but words like:/Supreme Court/graceful/wise. CNA; PoBA

Grandfather's Clock. Henry Clay Work. But it stopped short–never to go again–/When the old man died. BLPA; BLSo; FaFP; FSW; PSoN; TreF

Grandfather's Heaven. Naomi Shihab Nye. Keep it simple. Down or up. Str

Grandfather Watts's Private Fourth. Henry Cuyler Bunner. And marched off home, nor'-west by nor'. PoSC; StPo; TiPo

Grandfather Yoneh. Emily Borenstein. ...gazing/straight ahead into the uncertain future. AMV-81

Grandfathers. Michael Castro. with a little help, was able/to make/his father one. VWA

The Grandfathers. Donald Justice. Only these blank, oracular/Headshakes or headnods. NCSH

Grandfathers. Dennis Shady. and chiseled generations/from ancient memories. LFAC

The Grandiloquent Goat. Carolyn Wells. I'd like to have served in the can. MoShBr

Grandma Chooses Her Plot at the County Cemetery. Paul Ruffin. ...I want/the coming up easier than the going down. GOYP

Grandma Fire. Charles G. Ballard. And ever uplifting birds to wing! VoR

Grandma's Advice. *Anonymous.* Why, grandma herself would have died an old maid! OBET

Grandma's Lost Balance. Sydney Dayre. You sit still and I'll go and find it. OBCA

Grandma Shorba and the Pure in Heart. Freya Manfred. you burdened heart/of my heart. FAZ

Grandmamma's Birthday. Hilaire Belloc. Although you bore us all to tears. DBV; ELU; FiBHP; PoPl

Grandmither, Think Not I Forget. Willa Sibert Cather. Ye'll know it's under rue an' rose that I would like to be,/That I would like to be. HBV 1-2

Grandmother. Paula Gunn Allen. After her I sit on my laddered rain-bearing rug/and mend the tear with string. STE; TWSS

The Grandmother. Wendell Berry. ...They had to break her/before she would lie down in her coffin. DFF; GP; SaC

Grandmother. Henry Carlile. Wrong since genesis. DFF; GP

Grandmother. John Paul Minarik. ...weathered but not ready/to join the earth/in a last embrace. LFAC

Grandmother. Ray A. Young Bear. stirring ashes/from a sleeping fire/at night. STE

Grandmother and Child. Ruth Dallas. To challenge the child's strength in the hour of fear. AnNZ

Grandmother and Grandson. William Stanley Merwin. ..."Where, where/Does it remind me of?" Till someone comes. NePoEA-2

The Grandmother Came down to Visit Us. Joseph Bruchac. as we left that house. CDW

Grandmother Grace. Ronald Wallace. Let it be summer. Let it be Williamsburg, Iowa. GOYP; SM

Grandmother Jackson. David Jackson. as we lolloped back along the beach. OBCP

Grandmother Poems. Marilyn Chin. white, the pallor of the dead. BrSi

Grandmother, Rocking. Eve Merriam. So I let him go on his way. GrPl; PCP

Grandmother's Apple Pies. Bruce Weston Munro. When I might have devoured more pie. PeD

Grandmother's Story of Bunker-Hill Battle. Oliver Wendell Holmes. That–in short, that's why I'm grandma,/and you children all are here! PAH

Grandmother Sleeps. Liz Sohappy Bahe. I will wait for her to wake. CDW

Grandmother Watching at Her Window. William Stanley Merwin. But all the time you keep going away, away. PrIm; VGW

Grandmothers. Adrienne Rich. ...Amnesia was the answer. HaCAP

Grandpa Bear. Susan Eisenberg. and all my uncles wept. AMV-81

Grandpa Is Ashamed. Ogden Nash. To learn that "Later, dear" means never. PV

Grandpa's .45. W. M. Ransom. I brush my watery eyes, and breathe. CDW

Grandpa's Picture. Paul Ruffin. nor the unseen certain hand/that kept it in its place. Str

Grandparents. Robert Lowell. I doodle handlebar/mustaches on the last Russian Czar. LiTM

Grandser. Abbie Farwell Brown. If I had a son I know he'd run/Like a brook away to sea! HBMV

The Grandson. James Scully. wait for me, dear old days! I'm coming too. NYBP

A Grandson Is a Hoticeberg. Margaret Danner. "RIGHT ON/ MOTHERS/MOTHER,/DYNAMITE..." BlSi; CNA; FB

Grania. Anonymous. His head upon his lover's breast/Of the terrors of the flight. KiLC

Granite and Cypress. Robinson Jeffers. And people are so shaken.) AmPP; AnAmPo

Granite and Steel. Marianne Moore. composite span–an actuality. NYBP

The Granite Mountain. Lew Sarett. Hunted creatures in their flight/Find a refuge for the night. HBMV

Granma's Words. Ted D. Palmanteer. Be strong/in the heart,/nothing lasts/forever. STE

Granny Crack. James Reaney. I am the darling of your god. NOBC

Grant at Appomattox. Gertrude Claytor. Out of the Wilderness, Lord. GoYe

Grape Daiquiri. Tina Koyama. to soften your fall. BrSi

Grape-Gathering. Abraham Shlonsky. Abraham O Lord! When in Thy winepress I am/cast/Shall I e'er find rebirth? TrJP

The Grape-Vine Swing. William Gilmore Simms. Does the maiden still swing in thy giant clasp? AnAmPo; HBV 1-2

Grapes. Anonymous. Now that the grapes are withering and dry. AWP

Grapes. Sister Maris Stella. Suck the sweet grapes out of their juicy blue/ Pockets and let the sun pour down on you. GoBC

Grapes Making. Léonie Adams. The faint leaf vanishes to light. FYAP; MoVE; NePA; UnPo

The Grapevine. John Ashbery. :Whom must we get to know/To die, so you live and we know? ANYP

The Grapevine. Zoe Kincaid Brockman. Singing, a grapevine climbs the sun! GoYe

Graphemics (excerpt). Jack Spicer. That time leave us/Words, loves. VGW

Grasmere Sonnets. David Wright. Devoured by wind and sea in sight of land. NoAm

Grass. Alfred Corn. As the grass stretches and rises,/That will go, too. MAYP

Grass. John Holmes. That grass in your hands. MiAP

Grass. Carl Sandburg. I am the grass./Let me work. AWP; BBV; BLPL; BoLiVe; FaBV; MCCG; MoAB; MoAmPo; MoVE; NoAm; NOBA; NoP; OBWP; OHFP; OxBA; PoLf; PoPl; TrGrPo; WaaP; WHA

Grass. Mary Morison Webster. Till it have made each green cocoon/ Exactly like its brother. PeSA

The Grass, Alas. Dick Emmons. If it isn't somewhat quieter in the city! QQQ

Grass Fingers. Angelina Weld Grimke. With your tiny, timorous toes. CDC

Grass, Grass. George Bowering. & its colour green. NeAC

The Grass Is a Reasonable Colour. John Newlove. The trees bear fruit. NeAC

The Grass on the Mountain. Mary Austin. And the grass on the mountains. AmFN; AWP

Grass on the Prayer Path. Anonymous. And keep a little path open! PeD

The grass so little has to do. Emily Dickinson. The grass so little has to do/I wish I were the hay! GN; HBVY

Grasse: The Olive Trees. Richard Wilbur. And whose great thirst, exceeding all excess,/Teaches the South it is not paradise. NoAm; NOBA; NYBP

Grasses. Ralph J. Mills, Jr. bent by the wind/their edges shine. FAZ

The Grasses Green of Sweet Content. Arthur Hugh Clough. And grasses green of sweet content. VLP

The Grasshopper. Abraham Cowley. Sated with thy summer feast,/Thou retir'st to endless rest. AWP; EnLi 1-2; FM; HBV 1-2; HBVY; OAEL 1-2; WiR

The Grasshopper. Richard Lovelace.
  And all these merry days mak'st merry men,/Thyself, and melancholy streams. OBEV

...he/That wants himself, is poor indeed. MeLP; SeCePo; SeCV 1-2

The Grasshopper. David McCord. And hopped away proper/As any grasshopper. GrPl

A Grasshopper. Richard Wilbur. Peaceful now that its peace/Lay busily hid. HAP; HoPM

Grasshopper Green. Anonymous. Summer's time for fun. FaPON; HBVY; SoPo

The Grasshopper's Song. Hayim Nahman Bialik. "A plenteous feast in field and fen,/Enough for all.–Amen, amen!" YeAr

Grassroots. Carl Sandburg. Grassroots down under put fingers into dark dirt. RFM

Gratiana Dauncing and Singing. Richard Lovelace. The Graces daunced, and Apollo play'd. AnAnS 2; CaPo; CBEP; JCP; LiTL; LoBV; MeLP; MePo; OAEP; OBEV; OBS; SeCV 1-2

Gratitude. Louise Gluck. ...and the bright sun shining on its tusks. FaBoWP; HeIP

Gratitude. Mikhail Yuryevich Lermontov. But heed Thou that I need not thank Thee long. LiTW

Gratitude. Annette Lynch. Let me out,/Let me out! FF

Gratitude. Clyde McGee. We thank the Keeper of our years. BLRP

Gratitude for Work. John Oxenham. For work to do, and strength to do the work,/We thank Thee, Lord! PGD

A Gratulatory to Mr. Ben. Johnson for His Adopting of Him... Thomas Randolph. But if heaven take thee, envying us thy Lyre,/'Tis to pen Anthems for an Angels quire. AnAnS 2; JCP; OBS

The Grauballe Man. Seamus Heaney. with the actual weight/of each hooded victim,/slashed and dumped. CIP

The Grave. Anonymous. And laid to see upon. ACP

The Grave. Robert Blair.
  Evanishes at crowing of the cock. CoBE; NOEC
  Not to return, how painful the remembrance! EnPE
  Then claps his well fledg'd wings and bears away. EnRP
  When it draws near the witching time of night. ViBoPo

The Grave. John Lyle Donaghy. Even now, from scratching ravens of the mind. NeIP

The Grave. Thomas Gwynn Jones. Unless in that damp cell/The dead may have a dream he cannot tell. LiTW

A Grave. Marianne Moore. in which if they turn and twist, it is neither with volition nor con-/sciousness. AnAmPo; CABA; CMoP; CrMA; ExPo; FaBoWP; ForPo; HAP; HeIP; LiTA; MoPo; MOS; MoVE; NoAm; NOBA; PPoe; SeCeV; TAP; UnPo

A Grave. John Richard Moreland. Who knows how wide its realm may be?/Its depths, how deep? HBMV

The Grave. Saul Tchernichovsky. Nor why he was cut down and thrown here before his time. VWA

The Grave. Yvor Winters. For what one is, one sees not; 'tis the lot/Of him at peace to contemplate it not. MoVE; NoAm

The Grave and the Rose. Victor Hugo. The Grave said to the Rose. AWP

Grave at Cassino. Noah Stern. and in the midst,/the grave of a victim. VWA

Grave Clothes. Karen Swenson. a last dressing. AMV-80

A Grave in Hollywood Cemetery, Richmond. Margaret Junkin Preston. What have we given him? Just a/grave! AA

A Grave in Ukraine. Saul Tchernichovsky. Or why he lived, or timeless bit the/ground. TrJP

The Grave of King ARthur. Thomas Warton, Jr.. The daily dirge, and rites divine. CEP; GoTL

The Grave of Love. Thomas Love Peacock. Immutable as my regret. CH; HBV 1-2

The Grave of Rulry. T. W. Rolleston. Slumbering by the young, eternal/ river-voices of the western vale. AnIL; AnIV; IrPN; OnYI

The Grave of Shelley. Oscar Wilde. Or where the tall ships founder in the gloom/Against the rocks of some wave-shattered steep. OBTV

The Grave's Cherub. Sydney Clouts. Of human and angel face. PeSA

The Grave-Tree. Bliss Carman. Waiting till the Scarlet Hunter/Pass upon the endless trail. CaP

The Grave-Yard. Jones Very. for in the body's health the soul's forgot. NOBA

The Gravedigger. Bliss Carman. Shoulder them in to shore. BoNaP

Gravel. Paul Mariah. He knew the whole prison/Yard/By the feel of his tongue/Against each grey rock. LFAC

The Gravel-Pit Field. David Gascoyne. Round which revolves the Sages' Wheel. NeBP

Gravelly Run. Archie Randolph Ammons. hoist your burdens, get on down the road. CoAP; PoA; Prf

Graven on the Palms of His Hands. Charles Wesley. Jesus, Thou canst not pray in vain. BePJ

Graves. Carl Sandburg. I love you and your great way of forgetting. AnEnPo

Graves Are Made to Waltz On. Peter Viereck. And hands reach out to drag us down below. PoA

Graves at Elkhorn.   Richard Hugo.   ...a casual glance/would tell you there could be no silver here.   UnPo

Graves in Queens.   Richard Hugo.   and you don't mean nothing now you're dead.   NYP

The Graves of a Household.   Felicia Dorothea Hemans.   Alas for love, if thou wert all,/And naught beyond, O Earth!   FaPoR; HBV 1-2; VLP; WBLP

Graves of Infants.   John Clare.   White flowers their mourners are, nature their passing–/bell.   ERoP 1-2; OBVV

Graveside.   Don Domanski.   calling down the many birds/to brutalize the air.   CaPN

Gravestones.   Floyd C. Stuart.   In touch, it is the nearest thing to bone.   AMV-80

Gravestones.   Vernon Watkins.   For the dead live, and I am of their kind.   ChMP; TEP

The Graveyard.   Hayim Nahman Bialik.   The tombstones stood dumb, even they/pitied me.   TrJP

Graveyard.   Robert P. Tristram Coffin.   Small wonder the smallest boy behaves!   AmFN

The Graveyard.   Jane Cooper.   As free as if all guilts were closed and done.   NePoEA-2

Graveyard by the Sea.   Thomas Lux.   ...and then go home, alive,/to sleep the sleep of the awake.   LCAP

A Graveyard in Queens.   John Montague.   the slow pride/of a lament.   IPY

The Graveyard Rabbit.   Frank Lebby Stanton.   (May God defend us!) to shield from/ harm.   AA

The Graveyard Road.   Tom McKeown.   ...the loveliness/of her gold rains down.   HoAn

Gravities.   Seamus Heaney.   ...Colmcille sought ease/By wearing Irish mould next to his feet.   NoAm

Gray Days.   Joanne Lawlor.   Remote serenity of something/gray.   AMV-80

The Gray Folk.   Edith Nesbit.   Because I silenced, long ago,/The only voice that they obey.   NOBV

Gray Glove.   Roo Borson.   the one I'd give up my eyes/in order for you to hear.   NOBC

The Gray Goose.   Anonymous.   And he's goin', "Quank, quink-quank,"/ Lord, Lord, Lord.   FSW

Gray Goose and Gander.   Anonymous.   And carry the good King's daughter/Over the one strand river.   OxBoLi; OxNR

The Gray Hills Taught Me Patience.   Allen Eastman Cross.   I must, and so I dare!   AH

The Gray Mare (Young Johnny the Miller).   Anonymous.   So fare you well, Johnny, go mourn for your Kate.   AmFP

The Gray Oak Twilight.   James C. Kilgore.   with my deep/and Black/abiding/LOVE.   SOTS

The Gray Plume.   Francis Carlin.   O'er Cahir O'Dogherty/Red in his tomb.   HBMV

Gray Shore.   James Rorty.   Hush! said the sea, and hush.   EtS

Gray Silk Twisting.   Patrick Lane.   attached to you by hooks,/tearing me as I come.   NeAC

The Gray Squirrel.   Humbert Wolfe.   the squirrel was not/one of those.   GoJo; MoBrPo

The Gray Swan.   Alice Cary.   My dead, my living child!   BeLS; GN

Gray Thrums.   Clara Doty Bates.   Our puss is gray, so of course/She spins gray thrums.   OBCA

Gray Weather.   Robinson Jeffers.   To the bone, the careless white bone, the excellence.   CMoP; NoAm

Grazing Locomotives.   Archibald MacLeish.   Graze the great machines.   PPJ

Greasy Spoon Blues.   Len Gasparini.   To legalize whoredom and abortion.   NeAC

A Great.   Edward Estlin Cummings.   silence) sky;   NYBP

Great A, Little a.   Anonymous.   The cat's in the cupboard/And can't see me.   OxNR

Great A Was Alarmed at B's Bad Behaviour.   Anonymous.   O, P, Q, R, S, T, U, V, W, X, Y, Z.   FaBoUs; OxNR

The Great Adventure.   Henry David Thoreau.   For I will be her champion new,/Her fame I will repair.   HBV 1-2; OBVV

The Great Adventurer.   Anonymous.   But you'll ne'er stop a lover–/He will find out his way.   FaFP; GTBS; GTBS-P

The Great American Bum.   Anonymous.   And the heck with the man that works.   FSW

Great and Mighty Wonder.   Saint Anatolius.   And Christ shall wield His sceptre,/Our Lord and God for aye.   CAW

The Great Auk's Ghost.   Ralph Hodgson.   And muttered, "I'm extinct."   MoShBr; PoPl; PoPle; PV; ShM

Great-Aunt Rebecca.   Elizabeth Brewster.   Soft as silk and tough as that thin wire/They use for snaring rabbits.   NOBC

The Great Aunts of My Childhood.   Alice Fulton.   to scrub the floors/with harsh yellow soap.   Str

Great Bacchus: from the Greek.   Matthew Prior.   The moral says; mix water with your wine.   FaBoCo

The Great Beam of the Milky Way.   Anonymous.   Let them sort out their bullroarers!   NOAV

The Great Bear.   John Hollander.   All hung with stars!), there still would be no bear.   LiTM; MP; NePoEA-2; NoAm; NYBP; TwCP

The Great Bear Lake Meditations (excerpt).   J. Michael Yates.
...I dream I/only dream I am awake.   NOBC
...I should like to be here when you arrive, but in this weather it is necessary to keep moving.   HoPM

The Great Bell Roland.   Theodore Tilton.   Toll! Roland, toll!   PAH

The Great Blue Heron.   Carolyn Kizer.   A handful of paper ashes,/My mother would drift away.   CoAP; NePoEA-2

The Great Breath.   George William Russell.   Neared to the hour when Beauty breathes her last/And knows herself in death.   MoBrPo; OBEV; OBMV; OxBI; WGRP

The Great Brown Owl.   Jane Euphemia Browne (Aunt Effie).   And the great brown owl flew away in her cowl,/With her large, round, shining eyes.   OxBChV

The Great Canzon.   Kenneth Rexroth.   ...as if/She hid a stone in the grass.   NoAm

Great Central Railway, Sheffield Victoria to Banbury.   Sir John Betjeman.   And we leave the old Great Central/line/For Banbury and buns.   NYBP

Great Churches.   Anonymous.   Who press their fortunes to the hilt,/ Respond to duty's call.   STF

Great Day.   Anonymous.
God's gwineter build up Zion's walls.   BoAN 1-2
We call for valiant-hearted men.   FSW

The Great Day.   William Butler Yeats.   The beggars have changed places, but the lash goes on.   BIrV; CMoP; FF; OBSP

Great Day (Union Version).   Anonymous.   The boss will sing a different tune.   FSW

The Great Depression.   Patricia Goedicke.   Like beggars gathering in the dust.   GP

The Great Despair of the London Whigs.   Anonymous.   But let's, like Origen, since other hopes are past,/Hope the poor devil may be saved at last.   APAS

The Great Discovery.   Eleanor Farjeon.   And while seeking for the Khan/Met his first Red Indian.   PoSC

The Great Divide.   Lew Sarett.   When I drift out on the Silver Sea.   HBMV

The Great Farewells.   Amanda Benjamin Hall.   The woman, tearless, lets him go.   GoYe

Great Farm.   Philip Booth.   and sideways a big man with buckets/sets hugely to milk a big cow.   PoPl

A Great Favorit Beheaded.   Luis de Gongora y Argote.   Much Doctrine lyes under this little Stone.   OBVE

A Great Favourite Song, Entitled The Sailor's Hornpipe.   Anonymous.   With a woman's shift and apron you will have to go to sea.   OBSS

The Great Figure.   William Carlos Williams.   and wheels rumbling/through the dark city.   InPK; NoAm; PAI; QFR

Great Fleas.   Anonymous.   While these again have greater still, and greater still, and so/on.   ALV; BXAP

The Great Fountains.   Anne Hebert.   eternal solitude water solitude.   BoWoP

The Great Freight.   Ingeborg Bachmann.   You will drown with open eyes in light,/if behind you the seagull dives and cries.   PBWP

Great Friend.   Henry David Thoreau.   And see this aged nature,/Go with a bending stature.   MAmP; PoEL 1-5

The Great Frost.   John Gay.   And Heber's banks Eurydice returned.   OBEC; SeCePo

The Great Garret; or, 100 Wheels.   James McMichael.   Sheepwalks. Trails. Uncertain rights of drift.   AmPA

The Great Gatsby: Epitaph.   F. Scott Fitzgerald.   Till she cry "Lover, gold-hatted, high-bouncing lover,/I must have you!"   ELU

Great Gawd, I'm Feelin' Bad (with music).   Anonymous.   I ain't got the man that I thought I had!   AS

Great Getting Up Morning.   Anonymous.   Fare you well, fare you well.   FSW

Great God, How Frail a Thing Is Man.   Mather Byles.   To thee my spirit I resign,/Thou maker of my breath.   AH

Great God Paused among Men.   Daniel Berrigan.   permeable world,–all man would come to.   MAT

Great God, Preserver of All Things.   Francis Daniel Pastorius.   ...till I launch/To thee into eternity/That time which has no end.   AH

Great God, the Followers of Thy Son.   Henry, Jr. Ware.   Children of God and heirs of heaven!   AH

Great God, Thy Works.   Mather Byles.   So the touched needle courts the pole.   AH

Great Godamighty.   Anonymous.   He's a-choppin in de new groun',/Great Godamighty.   ABF

Great-Granddad. *Anonymous.* Twenty-one boys and a great-grandson,/He has a terrible time with that one. CoSo

Great-Grandfather. Freda Downie. And great-grandfather will be one of those. FaBoWP

Great-Grandma. Carol Shields. Respectfully/and/or lovingly,/Catherine. Str

The Great-Grandmother. Robert Graves. The intervening generations (drifting/On tides of fancy still), ignore. DTC

Great-Great Grandma, Don't Sleep in Your Treehouse Tonight. X. J. Kennedy. None so tall/Stands in all/Arkansas! GrPl

Great Grief Came over Me. Aleqaajik. Great grief came over me/While I was picking berries on the fell. WTO

Great-Heart. Rudyard Kipling. Now Great-Heart is gone. HBV 1-2

The Great House. Edwin Muir. ...Praise the few/Who built in chaos our bastion and our home. EyDe

The Great Hunger. Patrick Kavanagh.
And some of the saga defied the draught in the open tomb/And was not blown. BIrV
Be easy, October. No cackle hen, horse neigh, tree sough, duck quack. NoAm; OxBTC
The hungry fiend/Screams the apocalypse of clay/In every corner of this land. CIP; FaBoIP
...Three frozen idols of a speechless muse. IPY; MoAB

The Great Hunt. Carl Sandburg. I shall never find any/greater than you. MoLP

The Great Idealist. Jami. ...but they fail to see/The great Idealist who looms behind. LiTW

Great Is My Envy of You. Petrarch (Francesco Petrarca). Me he disdains, and mocks me from her eyes! NAWM 1-2

The Great Lakes of Canada. Gordon Perry. H-O-M-E-S is the 5-letter key. FaBoUs

The Great Lakes Suite. James Reaney.
"And I don't like the way Windsor/Does,either." WHW
And since we won, we knew we were right. WHW
For when you flow into me/You're not at all through. WHW
In the light of the Sun, my grandmother. WHW
That takes the cake/For a grand gigantic thunderous tragic exit. WHW
This poem, for your ear,/My dear Monseer,/Of their blue continual hell. WHW

Great Lord of All, Whose Work of Love. Jacob Duche. To thy bright throne as incense rise. AH

The Great Lover. Rupert Brooke. Praise you, "All these were lovely"; say, "He loved." BoLiVe; BrPo; FaFP; FPL; HoPM; LiTB; LiTM; MCCG; MoBrPo; NAMP; TreF; TrGrPo; WaP

"The great Macedon, that out of Persia chased." Henry Howard, Earl of Surrey. In princes' hearts God's scourge yprinted deep/Might them awake out of their sunful sleep. AAS; FCP

The Great Magicians. C. Day Lewis. This is the fault they may not/Absolve nor remedy. EaLo

A Great Man. Oliver Goldsmith. He still shall live, shall live as long/–As ever dead man did. NA

Great Man. B. S. Johnson. He seemed bored by our/questions, interested/more in our women. ELU

The Great Man. Eunice Tietjens. The glint of golden sunlight on His wings. WGRP

The Great Merchant, Dives Pragmaticus, Cries His Wares. Thomas Newbery. What do you lack, sir? Come hither to me. OxBChV

The Great Misgiving. William Watson. And there, O death, thy sting. HBV 1-2; OBVV

The Great Moth. Robert Gittings. As if with plumes of grace to hover/A spirit took our part. OxBTC

Great Nature Is an Army Gay. Richard Watson Gilder. The infinite army marches on its remorseless way. HBV 1-2

The Great Nebula in Andromeda. Hugh Seidman. ...the noise/I taste and know nothing of/gripping at my ears AmPA

The Great Offence. Abu Nuwas. Especially as I had tied her girdle/With the wrong bow. LiTW

The Great Panjandrum. Samuel Foote. till the gunpowder ran out at the heels of their boots. FaBoCh; FaBoCo; LoGBV; MoShBr; Par; PoLf

The Great Poet. Linda King. the only ape in town who/uses yards and yards of/pink flowered toilet paper GP

The Great Poet. King of Seville Mu'tamid. Death, the great poet, adds the lacking rhyme. LiTW

Great Powers Conference. Edith Lovejoy Pierce. The Commonwealth of Man without the man. PGD

The Great Pretender. Pat Nolan. I wish they made pantyhose. APU

The Great Redeemer Lives. Anne Steele. For Jesus pleads, and must prevail. BePJ

The Great River. Henry Van Dyke. The world is safe because it floats in Thee. TrPWD

The Great Round-Up. *Anonymous.* In that home of the sweet by-and-by. BPAW; CoSo

The Great Sad One. Uri Z. Greenberg. For him it is impossible, for he is God. VWA

The Great Santa Barbara Oil Disaster OR;. Conyus. or the Great Santa Barbara Oil Disaster/OR: AmPA

The Great Scarf of Birds. John Updike. Melting all thought, the southward cloud withdrew into the air. NYBP

Great Shepherd of the Sheep. Charles Wesley. And reign above the sky. BePJ

The Great Silkie of Sule Skerrie. *Anonymous.* He'll shoot both my young son and me.' BaBo; BuBa; ESPB; FaBoBa; FaBoCh; GBP; MAT; MOS; ViBoFo

The Great Society. Robert Bly. While the mayor sits with his head in his hands. CAD; NoAm; NYP

The Great South Land (excerpt). Rex Ingamells. I am the Hunter of grasses and flowers.' CBAP; NOAV

Great Spaces. Howard Moss. "Nothing is unwilling to be born." TwCP

The Great Speckled Bird. *Anonymous.* I will rise up my savior to greet Him,/On the wings of a great speckled bird. FSW

The Great St. Bernard. Samuel Rogers. That plain, that modest structure, promising/Bread to the hungry, to the weary rest. OBTV

The Great Statue of the General Du Puy. Wallace Stevens. Yet the General was rubbish in the end. LiTA

Great Streets of Silence Led Away. Emily Dickinson. For period exhaled. AtBAP; NOCV

The Great Summons. Chu Yuan. O Soul come back to where men honor still/The name of the Three Kings. AWP; LiTW

The Great Swamp Fight. Caroline Hazard. Please God we use, and not abuse/The land so hardly won! PAH

A Great Tempest on the Plain of Ler. *Anonymous.* save me from the awful blast/and this high tempest out of Hell! NOBI

Great Things. William Blake. This is not done by Jostling in the Street. OBSP; PV

Great Things. Thomas Hardy. Great things to me! GoTF; GTBS; GTBS-P; MoVE; NOBE; TreFT

Great Things Have Happened. Alden Nowlan. ..half-tipsy with the wonder/of being alive, and wholly enveloped in love. GOYP

A Great Time. William Henry Davies. May never come/This side the tomb. AnFE; ExPo; LiTB; MoBrPo; MoVE; WHA

Great Titanic. *Anonymous.* Great Titanic out on the ocean, sinking down. AmFP

Great Tom. Richard Corbet. He may call cousin with the bell of France. OxBoLi

The Great Victory. R.V. Gilbert. Resplendent, on that wondrous shore. BLRP

The Great Voices. Charles Timothy Brooks. Contented and calm as the mountains,/And deep as the woods and the sea. HBV 1-2

The Great Wager. G. Anketall "Woodbine Willie" Studdert-Kennedy. I bet my life on Christ, Christ crucified,/Aye risen, and alive forevermore. TrCP

The Great War. Vernon Scannell. Which ended in a sepia November/Four years before my birth. OBWP

The Great Wave: Hokusai. Donald Finkel. Blindly from wave to wave toward Ararat. PoPl

The Great Wave off Kanagwa. Constance Egemo. ...And the men/in their frail boats/bow their heads and wait. PoDr

The Great Wheel. Hugh" (Christopher Murray Grieve) MacDiarmid. "Auch, to Hell,/I'll tak it to avizandum..." OxBS

The Greater Cats. Victoria Mary (Vita) Sackville-West. Ah, may I stay forever blind/With lions, tigers, leopards, and their kind. OBMV; PoPle

The Greater Country. Grace V. Watkins. ...my God shall lead me by the hand/to heaven's shining hills, my fatherland. AMV-80

The Greater Friendship Baptist Church. Carole C. Gregory. another scoop of ice cream/our smiles receive. BlSi

The Greater Gift. Margaret E. Bruner. Yet of this greater gift no word was spoken. PoToHe

Greater Love. Wilfred Owen. Weep, you may weep, for you may touch them not. AtBAP; BrPo; CMoP; EnLoPo; FaBoMo; FaBoRV; FaFP; GTBS-P; LiTB; LiTM; MasP; MoAB; MoBrPo; NAMP; NoAm; OAEP; SeCeV; ViBoPo; WaaP; WaP

The Greater Music. Theodore Weiss. ..his course/the music they drank as from a golden cup. NePoAm-2

The Greater Trial. Anne Finch, Countess of Winchilsea. Or die by self-denial. TrGrPo

The Greatest Battle That Ever Was Fought. Joaquin Miller. I tell you the kingliest victories fought/Are fought in these silent ways. GoTF; TreF

The greatest bore is boredom. *Anonymous.* While you talk about your own. CenHV

The Greatest Person In the Universe. Daniel L. Marsh. And so I sing of Him and onward plod. BLRP

Greatness. *Anonymous.* Teach the fit wayes their fruitlesse scope t' obtaine. OBS

Grecian Kindness. John Wilmot, Earl of Rochester. Lulled her asleep, and then grew drunk. OBSP

Greece. William Haygarth. Beyond the shadows of Aegina's rocks,/Amidst the dark Aegean's distant surge. OBTV

Greed. *Anonymous.* The wren had ate the porridge down. OxNR

Greed. Douglas Blazek. whose sinew conspired from our sperm LTB

Greed, Part 4. The Turtle. Diane Wakoski. You,/landlord/of my heart. NoAm

The Greed Song. Albert Goldbarth. And I want the ducts. AMV-80

The Greedy Fox and the Elusive Grapes. Aesop. Don't try for things too far beyond your reach! MaC

Greedy Jane. *Anonymous.* "Both!" cried Jane,/Quite bold and plain. HBVY; OxBChV

Greedy Richard. Jane Taylor. But rather save my little store/To give poor folks, who want it more.' OxBChV

Greedy Seasons. Eileen Myles. incumbent steps ahead/to winter. APU

The Greedy the People. Edward Estlin Cummings. and they bow to a must/though the earth in her splendor/says May. SoSe

Greedy Tom. *Anonymous.* He supped it all. OxNR

The Greek Anthology (excerpt). *Anonymous.* Just thought of one–and naturally died. ShM

The Greek Anthology (excerpt). Leonard Alfred George Strong. Single 'e bided, and 'e wished/'Is father done the same. DBV

Greek Archipelagoes. Patrick Leigh-Fermor. The fig leaf lays a shadow on the dust. OBTV

Greek Architecture. Herman Melville. But reverence for the archetype. NoP

The Greek Athlete. Euripides. Such would be the greatest good for every Greek. LiSp

Greek Epigram. Ezra Pound. And as the slave that is given in barter. MoAB; MoAmPo

Greek Excavations. Bernard Spencer. When I broke this crust. ChMP

A Greek Gift. Henry Austin Dobson. How pleased she is looking! CenHV

The Greek Room. James W. Thompson. cold as diamond. BPo

Greek Transfiguration. Kimon Friar. like drifting foam upon the endless sea's/indifferent and listless sursurration. HoAn

The Greeks. Tom Clark. Infinite gifts we are unable to behold PoA

Green. William Barnes. Where moss upon the roofstwones' edge wer/ green. VLP

Green. Walter De la Mare. A sight not infrequently seen. FaBoNo

Green. D. H. Lawrence. For the first time, now for the first time seen. ELU; GBL; MoBrPo; PoA

Green. Paul Verlaine. And soothe my senses with a little rest. LiTW; SyP

The Green Afternoon. Henry Rago. ...like/A luminous choice. VGW

A Green and Pleasant Land. John Peale Bishop. Who moved their muscles to another's mind. PoPl

The Green and the Black. Anthony Bailey. All colors in a fountain changing. NYBP

Green and Yellow. *Anonymous.* ...I want to be sick, and lay me down and/ die.' OBET

Green Apples. Dudley Randall. A young man. FB

Green Apples. Ruth Stone. Saying, this is the moment,/Here, now. InPS

The Green Autumn Stubble. Patrick Browne. But now my wits are crazy and leaden is my tongue. OxBI; WTO

The Green Bed. *Anonymous.* With a bottle of good brandy, and on my knee a girl! AmFP

Green Breeks. Douglas Dunn. Go, talk to him, and tell him who you are,/ Face to face, at last, Scott; and kiss his scar. FaBoPV

The Green Briar Shore. *Anonymous.* And turn my back upon them and alter my mind. AmFP

Green Broom. *Anonymous.* There is none like the Boy that sold Broom, green Broom. ALV; StPo

Green Candles. Humbert Wolfe. "And not," said the room, "go out any more." HBMV; MoBrPo; SO

Green Coconuts: Rio. Lawrence Durrell. Green coconuts, green/Coconuts, patrimony of the ape. OBTV

Green Corn. *Anonymous.* Green corn, don't-cha tell Polly./Green corn. FSW

The Green Corn Dance. Alice Corbin. And the rain comes down. BPAW

The Green Door. Leah Bodine Drake. Where was it? . . . and why do I still/remember? BiCB

Green Enravishment of Human Life. Sister Juana Ines de la Cruz. imprison my two eyes in my two hands/and see no other thing than it I touch. WPOW

The Green Estaminet. Sir Alan Patrick Herbert. So Madeleine serves the soldiers still in the Green Estaminet. HBMV

The Green Eye of the Yellow God. J. Milton Hayes. And the Yellow God forever gazes down. BLPA; PaPo

The Green Family. Colleen Thibaudeau. remembering he looked last into the sun/that was a golden gabriel and sang him home. NOBC

The Green Fiddler. Rachel Field. For I have a hidden fairy tune/In the bottom of my heart. StPo

Green Fields of England. Arthur Hugh Clough. Dear home in England, won at last. OAEP

Green Frog at Roadside, Wisconsin. James Schevill. The sunlit air full of leaping chances. TAP

Green Frogs. David Rigsbee. But the surf drowns out what might have been/their battle song, a song beginning "O love..." AMV-81

The Green Gnome. Robert Williams Buchanan. Chime, sing! rhyme, ring! over fields and fells! StPo

The Green-Gown. *Anonymous.* And at Night went away with a Green-Gown. CoMu

Green Grass. *Anonymous.* And we clap hands together. CH; GBP; OxBoLi; OxNR

Green Grass and Sea. George Woodcock. ...I/drown in that/green sea. AMV-81

Green Grass and White Milk. Winifred Welles. For Teeney and Weeney to have for drinking. TiPo

Green Grass Growing. Patrick Evans. Who shall explain the majesty of women/To us? to us? Exaltation, softness, pleasure. NeBP

The Green Grass Growing All Around. *Anonymous.* And the green grass growing all around! FSW; HBVY; MoShBr

Green, Green is El Aghir. Norman Cameron. Are added unto them that have plenty of water. MoBS; OBWP; OxBTC

Green Grow'th the Holly. *Anonymous.* Hope! Saith the holly. PCh

Green Grow the Lilacs. *Anonymous.*
And change the green lilacs to the red, white and blue. FSW
Saying, "You write to your sweetheart and I'll write to mine." BFSS

Green Grow the Rashes. Robert Burns. An' then she made the lasses, O. ALV; CABA; CEP; CoMu; CTC; EiCP; EnLi 1-2; EnPE; ErPo; FaFP; FSW; HBV 1-2; LAuP; LiTL; LiTL; NoP; OAEL 1-2; OBEC; PPoe; PPP; SeCePo; UnTE; ViBoPo; WHA

Green Grow the Rushes O. *Anonymous.* One is one and all alone/And evermore shall be so. FSW; OxBoLi

Green Groweth the Holly. King of England Henry VIII. Green groweth the holly. EBEV; SBVL; TrGrPo

Green Grows the Rashes. *Anonymous.* Yet a the beds is na sae saft/As the bellies of the lasses O. GBP

Green Haven Halls. Charles Culhane. They scattered our bones/in the heart of the gulag. LFAC

The Green Hills of Africa. Roy Fuller. And the emotion brought from a world already/Dying of what starts to infect the hills. NoP; OBTV

The Green Horse. Bin Ramke. ...I was on/the blue horse, you were on the green." To call out. MAYP

The Green Hunters. Florence M. Wilson. For my heart's in his holdin',/ My mind in his mind. AnIV

Green Ice. Vivienne Finch. where there are Druids/rustling in the leaves. BrRo

The Green Inn. Theodosia Garrison. Who come at last from drought and fast/To sit in God's Green Inn. HBMV

Green Island. William Logan. a mote on the horizon, a silent O. MAYP

The Green Isle of Lovers. Robert Charles Sands. The home undisturbed, the green Isle of/the Lover! AA

Green Jade Plum Trees in Spring. Ou Yang Hsiu. ...Swallows, two/By two, nest under the painted eaves. NaP

The Green Knight's Farewell to Fancy. George Gascoigne. I say, God send me better speed; and, Fancy, now/farewell! EnRePo

The Green Lake. Michael Roberts. Listen. There is another voice that speaks. ChMP

The Green Leaf. Louis Zukofsky. as the light's aire from a vault/which has a knob of sun. CoPo; VGW

The Green Leaves All Turn Yellow. James Kenney. For the green leaves all turn yellow.' IrPN

Green Light. Kenneth Fearing. Broken or sold. Or given away. Or used and forgotten. Or/lost. VGW

The Green Linnet. William Wordsworth. The voiceless Form he chose to feign,/While fluttering in the bushes. AtBAP; CBEP; GTBS; GTBS-P; HBV 1-2; PBBP

Green Lions. Douglas Stewart. And men denied the jungle of young years/ Grow taut, and clench their fists. AnNZ

The Green Little Shamrock of Ireland. Andrew Cherry. The sweet little, green little, shamrock of Ireland! HBV 1-2

Green Martyrs. Richard Murphy. She brings me from Knock shrine/John Kennedy's head on a china dish. NOBI

The Green Mossy Banks of the Lee. *Anonymous.* With the adorable gentle Matilda/On the green mossy banks of the Lee. OBET

Green Moth. Charles Simic. And all so still, so still– GeTw; TiPo

Green Mountain Boy. Florida Watts Smyth. stubborn as stone and set to wear out time. GoYe

The Green Mountain Boys. William Cullen Bryant. For the deeds of tomorrow night. AnNE; MC; PAH; PoPl

Green Pastures. Dick Allen. gratefully through it and it parts a little while. AMV-80

A Green Place. William Jay Smith. And thin-ribbed earth pokes out against the snow? GrPl

Green Plumes of Royal Palms. LeRoy V. Brant. Supreme the triumph on the cross! AH

Green Rain. Dorothy Livesay. I remember the rain as the feathery fringe of her shawl. NIP; NOBC

Green Rain. Mary Webb. Hung poised, forgetting how to fall. BoNaP; CH

Green Red Brown and White. May Swenson. I am not lost I am not lost then/only covered for the night. VGW

A Green Refrain. Avraham Huss. The empty conclusion that is rooted/In the convulsion of our lives. Our lives in captivity. VWA

Green Revolutions. Barbara Guest. Now it's green. Now it isn't. FaBoWP

Green River. William Cullen Bryant. An image of that calm life appears/ That won my heart in my greener years. AP; NOBA; OxBA

The Green River. Lord Alfred Bruce Douglas. Or Love that swoons on sleep, or else delight/That is as wide-eyed as a marigold. HBMV; OBEV; OBVV

The Green Roads. Edward ("Edward Eastaway") Thomas. And hear all day long the thrush repeat his song. FaBoPP; NoAm

The Green Shepherd. Louis Simpson. And on the magic mountain nothing moved. MP; NePoEA; NIP; NoAm; NYBP

The Green-Sickness Beauty. Edward, Lord Herbert of Cherbury. And to be gather'd rather then to fall. AnAnS 2

Green Slates. Thomas Hardy. ..."Our home was where you saw her/ Standing in the quarry!" FaBoPP

Green Sleeves. Anonymous. I shall rouse her in the morn,/My fiddle and I thegither. GBP

Green Song. Philip Booth. my feet take root against tomorrow. BoNaP

A Green Stream. Wang Wei. Oh, to remain on a broad flat rock/And cast my fishing-line forever! SD

Green Sunday. Katue Kitasono. Rise, O Muse! LiTW

Green Symphony. John Gould Fletcher. These are tombs and memorials and temples and altars sun-kindled/for me. AnFE; APA; MAPA; MoAmPo; MoVE

Green Things Growing. Dinah Maria Mulock Craik. Though dust to dust return, I think I'll scarcely mourn,/If I may change into green things growing. FaFP; HBV 1-2; HBVY; OHIP

The Green Train. Emile Victor Rieu. So long as the Green Train thunders on into space? SO

The Green Tree. James Reiss. Under-the-Sod, is playing over there by the green tree. AmPA

Green Valley. Dorothy Vena Johnson. And all I could see/Was the green valley/Surrounding me. PoNe

The Green Valley. Sylvia Townsend Warner. Their children. The horn is blown, but I do not hear it. MoBrPo

The Green Willow. Anonymous. Write this on my tomb, that in love I was true. OBSC

Green Willow, Green Willow. Anonymous. I loved a false young man. AmFP

Green World Two. Miriam Waddington. Far above the snow/fills the falling world/to its topmost branches. PeCV

The Greenback Dollar. Anonymous. Where the heart will know no pain. AmFP

Greener Grass. Frank Steele. once to see the sun come up/across his fields. Psk

Greeness. Angelina Weld Grimke. Hushing the heart that beats and beats and beats? CDC

Greenland Fisheries. Anonymous. And the daylight's seldom seen. FSW

The Greenland Men. Anonymous. But expects to return with gold and silver store. OBSS

The Greenland Voyage. Anonymous. But begin with the sun to have done before noon,/That the carts may come down for the blubber. OBSS

The Greenland Whale. Anonymous. It grieved him a damned sight more./ With a fa la la la la la la... GBP

Greenland Whale Fishery. Anonymous.
And daylight's seldom seen. BaBo; OuSiCo; ViBoFo
And for England bore away. AmFP; OBET

Greens. David Ray. But not to read the law, to reap greens, greens/ Forever in her small, pathetic pail. SM; VGW

Greens (with music). Anonymous. They makes me feel just right. AS

Greensleeves and Pudding Pies. Anonymous. Fiddle and aw' together. LO

Greenwich. Anonymous. And fiery billows roll below. AmFP

Greenwich Avenue. James Schuyler. and the doctor from Philadelphia/ nods and speaks of a further bleeding. NYP

Greenwich Observatory. Sidney Keyes. Enfolds the spheric wonder of the sky. MoAB; MoBrPo

Greenwich Village Saturday Night. Irving Feldman. Hand in hand now you now I going on and off. AmPC

Greer County. Anonymous. And quit corn bread for the rest of my life. ABF; CoSo

A Greeting. William Henry Davies. Good morning, Life–and all/Things glad and beautiful. MoBrPo; MoRP

Greeting. Ella Young. I bid them bring to you/Dreams, and strange imaginings, and sleep. AnIV

Greeting Descendants. A. G. Sobin. ...a white look/in the bottom of a pail. FAZ

Greeting from a Distance. Hans Sahl. For life goes on, I say VWA

Greeting from England. Anonymous. The hour that brings us back to back/But harbingers the larger light. PAH

The Greeting of the Roses. Hamlin Garland. It seemed the sun had made them mad. AA

Gregory Griggs. Laura E. Richards. But he never could tell which he liked the best. OxNR; SoPo

Grenada. Mikhail A. Svetlov. Grenada of mine! WaaP

A Grenadier. Anonymous. Get you gone,/You silly blockhead. OxNR

Grenadier. Alfred Edward Housman. Is neither knowledge nor device/Nor thirteen pence a day. EG; OBMV; OBWP

The Gresford Disaster. Anonymous. They'll be damned like the sinners in hell. GBP; OBET

Gretel in Darkness. Louise Gluck. that black forest and the fire in earnest. AmPA; DFT; GP

The Grey Cock. Anonymous.
And the rocks they melt by the heat of the sun.' ELP; OBET
It's better to live single than bound. FaBoBa

The Grey Cock (A vers.). Anonymous. The worms and creeping things are my waiting maids,/To wait on me whilst I am asleep. BaBo

The Grey Cock (B vers.). Anonymous. The lassie thought it day when she sent her love away,/And it was but a blink of the moon. BaBo; ESPB

A Grey Day. William Vaughn Moody. Or wait until its dreams come true. AnFE; APA

A Grey Eye Weeping. Egan O'Rahilly. A old grey eye, weeping for lost renown,/Have made me a beggar before you, Valentine Brown. FaBoPV; KiLC

The Grey-Eyed King. Anna Akhmatova. "He walks on the earth no longer, your grey-eyed king..." PBWP

The Grey Friar. Thomas Love Peacock. Must be more of a lark than an owl. ALV

A Grey Frock. Zenaida Hippius. The girl in a grey frock.... PBWP

The Grey Funnel Line. Cyril Tawney. And sail the grey Funnel Line no more. OBET

Grey Galloway. Thomas S. Cairncross. Silent as light in old grey Galloway. PoSH

Grey Goose. Anonymous. Lawd, Lawd, Lawd. ABF

The Grey Hair. Judah Halevi. But a score of my friends soon will/make mock of thee. TrJP

Grey Him. Paul Mariah. Thanked me for water thru a straw/During the long hot prison summer. LFAC

The Grey Horse. James Reeves. And it's over the hilltop he'd surely be. PH

The Grey Horse Troop. Robert William Chambers. Drink to the troop that never shall die! HBV 1-2; PAH

The Grey Linnet. James McCarroll. For, behold, there's a little grey nun peeping out/From a bunch of green leaves at his side. CaP

Grey October. "The Critics." ...while we stand by/And shake the killer by the hand. OBET

The Grey Ones. Louis MacNeice. A beggar with a flaming sore. CMoP

The Grey Wolf. Arthur Symons. This time, unless I feed you with my heart? BrPo; FaBoTw

Grey Woman. Gladys Cardiff. Her spirit stands unhoused before my door. CDW; TWSS

Greyport Legend. Bret (Francis Bret Harte) Harte. Drawing the soul to its anchorage. EtS; GN; MOS

Greystone Cottage. Richard Hugo. He sang to himself and I still remember the tune. NPAW

Grid Erectile. Christopher Dewdney. Because it is primitive. CaPN

Grief. Wendell Berry. ...turn back to their day, their grieving and staying. GeTw

Grief. Elizabeth Barrett Browning. If it could weep, it could arise and go. AnFE; FPL; GTBS; HBV 1-2; HeIP; InPK; LoBV; NOBV; OBEV; OBNC; OBVV; PoLf; SBG; TrGrPo; VLP

The Grief. Rainer Maria Rilke. which one like a city of white/stands in the sky at the end of its light... AMV-81

A Grief Ago. Dylan Thomas. And close her fist. AtBAP

Grief and God. Stephen Phillips. Small wonder thou dost shudder at His kiss. WGRP

Grief-In-Idleness. Thomas Lovell Beddoes. To the blushed brim. AtBAP

Grief of a Girl's Heart. Augusta Gregory, Lady Gregory. And my fear is great that you have taken God from me! GBL; OLR; PBWP

The Grief of Cafeterias. John Updike. the servers attend to each other, forever. PPJ

The Grief of Our Genitals. Henry Carlile. At midnight no remedy for this but strong spirits/and in the cure the flaming penance. GP

Grief Plucked Me out of Sleep. Jill King. my night shaped by grief–/for whom? for whom? PeSA

The Griefs of Women (parody). David R. Slavitt. We're really better than they are. BXAP

Griesly Wife. John Streeter Manifold. He'll not be back any more. ATP; MoBrPo; MoBS

A Grievance (parody). James Kenneth Stephen. Nor what I "wished to say" a while ago. BXAP; FaBoPa; HBV 1-2; Par

Grieve Not, Dear Love. John Digby, Earl of Bristol. Doth keep us daily schooled and exercised/Lest that the fright thereof should overbear us. OBSP

Grieve Not for Beauty. Witter ("Emanuel Morgan") Bynner. Mourn not!–yield only happy tears/To deeper beauty than appears! PoA

Grieve Not for Me. Anonymous. For I must go and live with she! ShM

Grieve Not, Ladies. Anna Hempstead Branch. And in your loved one's arms, remember. AnAmPo; FaFP; HBV 1-2

Grieve Not the Holy Spirit. George Herbert. Lord, pardon, for thy sonne makes good/My want of tears with store of bloud. AnAnS 1

Grig's Pig. Anonymous. And all the fun was over. OxNR

The Grimsby Fisherman. Anonymous. Until our rent is all spent and then we look for more. OBSS

The Grimsby Lads. Anonymous. Her sons from the waters return once again. OBSS

The Grinders, or the Saddle on the Right Horse. Anonymous. Who grinds his own bones and his child's for bread?/Tally hi-o, the grinder! GBP

Grinding. Anonymous. Your mill grinds rats and mice. OxNR

Grinding Vibrato. Jayne Cortez. is it too late for the mother tongue in your womanself to insurrect BlSi

The Grip. Brendan Kennelly. But a good grip/Will break the heart/Of the best hound in the land. CIP

Grisaille with a Spot of Red. Samuel Yellen. Flashes an auto, red as blood. NePoAm-2

La Grisette. Oliver Wendell Holmes The wreaths of Pere-la-Chaise! AA; HBV 1-2

Grizzel Grimme. Anonymous. To bed with such a bitch! FaBoEE

Grizzly. Bret (Francis Bret Harte) Harte. Yet remain an outlaw still! AA; AnAmPo; BPAW

Grizzly Bear. Anonymous. Oh, the grizzly, grizzly, grizzly bear. FSW

Grizzly Bear. Mary Austin. You will never meet another grizzly bear. BPAW; GoJo; OnUR; SoPo; TiPo

The Grizzly Bear is huge and wild. Alfred Edward Housman. He has been eaten by the bear. CenHV

The Groaning Board. Pink". Oo! How I love 'em! Oo! Oo! OO! InMe

The Grocer and the Gold-Fish. Wilfrid Thorley. Than a pound of Cheddar? BrR

Grog-an'-Grumble Steeplechase. Henry Lawson. An' The Screamer put his tongue out, and he won/by half-a-tongue. PH

Grongar Hill. John Dyer. Hears the thrush, while all is still,/Within the groves of Grongar Hill. CEP; FaBoPP; GoTL; LAuP; LoBV; NOEC; NoP; OBEC; PoEL 1-5; SeCePo; TrGrPo; ViBoPo

The Groom's Lament. Robert Peterson. I'm getting too old for it. NeAC

Gross, Coarse, Hideous. D. H. Lawrence. the nudity of a Lawrence nude! FaBoEE

Grotesque. Robert Graves.
Hissed like a snake, and swallowed him at one mouthful. DTC
Then put it back again with a slight frown. DTC

Grotesque. Amy Lowell. On your forehead/While you dance? BoWoP

A Grotesque Love-Letter. Anonymous. Youre swete love with blody nailes,/Whiche fedeth mo lice than quailes. MeEL

Grotesques. Robert Graves. Warned by a speaking mare since turned silentiary. CMoP

Grotesques (excerpt). Don (Donald Robert Marquis) Marquis. People think I drink, or something. FiBHP

The Grotto. Ray Fraser. to keep kids from shitting in the chapel/like they used to do NeAC

The Grotto. Francis Scarfe. And never a dawning day will break as pure/As our grave adoration, immature. NeBP; PoA

A Grouchy Good Night to the Academic Year. Ted Pauker. But good night to the Session, good night! NOBL

Groun' Hog. Anonymous. They went a-hog-huntin' hard as they could stave. ABF

Ground for the Floor. Anonymous. And a neat little cottage that's ground for the floor. OBET

Ground Hog. Anonymous. He's eat till his pants won't button at all./Ground hog. TrAS

Ground Hog Day. Marnie Pomeroy. He waddles through the ditch to look for spring. PoSC

Ground Swell. G. Stanley Koehler. as if it would always move, to inner/music, and of its own passion. NePoAm-2

The Ground-Swell. Edwin John Pratt. His harvest-sweepings on a winter sea/To feed the primal hungers of a reef. CaP

Groundhog. Anonymous. Went a-hog hunting as hard as they could stave,/Groundhog. FSW

The Groundhog. Richard Eberhart. Of Saint Theresa in her wild lament. AmLP; CMoP; DTC; ExPo; FaBoMo; FaFP; LiTA; LiTM; MasP; MiAP; MoAB; MoAmPo; MoPo; MoVE; NePA; NoAm; NoP; NU; PPoe; SeCeV; TAP; UnPo; WaP

The Groundhog. Luci Shaw. ...that He who designed/all simple wonderers, may have had me in mind. TrCP

The Groundhog Foreshadowed. Steven Sher. I am no father to this spring. AMV-80

The Grove. Edwin Muir. There was no road except the smothering grove. LiTM; MoPo

Grove and Building. Edgar Bowers. Lose their umbrageous choice within your eyes. NePoEA

Grover Cleveland. Joel Benton. Who went at dawn to that high star/Where Washington and Lincoln are. PAH

The Groves of Blarney. Richard Alfred Millikin. 'Tis in every feature I would make it shine. CBEP; FaBoPP; HBV 1-2; IrPN; OnYI; OxBI; OxBoLi

Growing. Frances Frost. How will my pup, if I'm so tall,/Reach up to kiss me on the nose? BiCB

Growing Gray. Henry Austin Dobson. When neither Time nor Tide can grant/Belief with wishes. HBV 1-2

Growing in Grace. Jack R. Clemo. O Shepherd/Of green pastures! NOCV

Growing in the Vale,. Christina Georgina Rossetti. Sweet Daffadowndilly. BrR; TiPo

Growing Old. Anonymous. My love is still the same. ErPo; KiLC

Growing Old. Matthew Arnold. To hear the world applaud the hollow ghost/Which blamed the living man. EnLi 1-2; FaFP; FiP; HBV 1-2; MaVP; NOBV; OAEL 1-2; PoEL 1-5; VLP

Growing Old. Douglas Fraser. Something that served me well,/And I am quite content. PoSH

Growing Old. Rose Henderson. And down her cheeks are cunning piles/Of little ripples when she smiles. BiCB

Growing Old. Walter Learned. Sweet sixteen is shy and cold,/Calls mesir," and thinks me old. HBV 1-2

Growing Old. Rollin J. Wells. "I live because he has passed my way." BLPA; GoTF; TreFT; WBLP

Growing Old. Ella Wheeler Wilcox. We two pass on–or but one alone. BLPA; FPL

Growing Smiles. Anonymous. Let's smile and smile, and not forget/That smiles go everywhere! PoLf

Growing Together. Joyce Carol Oates. a completion like the exhaling/of a single breath IHMS

Growing Up. Anonymous. And I'm bigger than Bob-tail the puppy,/Who used to be bigger than me. BiCB

Growing Up. Harry Behn. They couldn't hide tigers/Or me any more. BiCB; SiSoSe; SoPo

Growing Up. Linda Gregg. Then turn it off and go on reading. NPGG

Growing Up. Arthur Guiterman. Then I'll be twelve and won't that be fine! BiCB

Growing Up. A.(lan) A.(lexander) Milne. Who's coming out with me? BiCB

Growing Up. Edna Kingsley Wallace. But, oh, I wish my bones would wait/Till I grow up inside me! BiCB

Growing Wild. Jim Wayne Miller. that drag down sheep and cattle between the rivers. GP

Growltiger's Last Stand. Thomas Stearns Eliot. And a day of celebration was commanded in Bangkok. FaBoCh; LoGBV; OBCA; PoPle; RoGo

Grown and Flown. Christina Georgina Rossetti. Sweet sweet love was,/Now bitter bitter grown to me. NOBV

Grownups. William Wise. I'd like to be/A grownup soon. TiPo

The Growth of Love: O Weary Pilgrims. Robert Bridges. And question with the God that I embrace. MoAB; MoBrPo; NoAm

The growth of Sym. C. J. Dennis. "Why, sunlight and worms!' said the little blue wren. ACV

A Grub Street Recessional. Christopher Morley. And land in some Anthology! InMe

Grubber's Day. Jay G. Sigmund. With hill-clay always victor in the game. AnAmPo

Gruesome. Roger McGough. The very next day he.... AmMo

The Grumble Family. Anonymous. We'll never belong to the family of Grumble! WBLP

The Grumbling Hive: or, Knaves turn'd Honest. Bernard Mandeville. Blest with Content and Honesty. CEP

Grunion. Myra Cohn Livingston. catch/catch/catch/(if you can) RFM

Grunion. Wendy Rose. the grunion are building/a star tunnel CDW

Gryll's State. Jr, Blount Roy. Gryll/Will/Be borne out by history yet. OBAL

Guadalajara Hospital.   Ai.   Tear me apart with your holy, invisible hands.   MAYP

Guadalupe, W.I.   Nicolas Guillen.   the Frenchmen strolling and taking it easy/and the sun/burning.   TTY

Guantanamera.   Jose Marti.   Guantanamera guajira Guantanamera.   FSW

Guard.   Michael C. Martin.   Just one of God's creatures, a creature fair.   WaP

The Guard at the Binh Thuy Bridge.   John Balaban.   He aims. At her. Then drops his aim. Idly.   FYAP

A Guard of the Sepulcher.   Edwin Markham.   For we, who all the Wonder might have told,/Kept silence, for our mouths were stopped with gold.   WGRP

Guard Thy Tongue.   Alice M. Barr.   And when you of your neighbor speak/Use words of charity.   STF

The Guarded Wound.   Adelaide Crapsey.   Too heavy!   AnAmPo

The Guardian Angel.   Robert Browning.   This is Ancona, yonder is the sea.   GoBC; HBV 1-2

Guardian Angel.   John Henry, Cardinal Newman.   Thy wings shall waft me home.   GoBC

The Guardians.   Geoffrey Hill.   Gather the dead as the first dead scrape home.   NePoEA-2; NoP

Guardianship.   Georgia Douglas Johnson.   'Tis his to forge the master-key/That wields the locks of destiny!   GoSl

Gubbinal.   Wallace Stevens.   The world is ugly,/And the people are sad.   SOTW

The Gude and Godlie Ballatis: Quhy Sowld Nocht Allane Honorit Be?   Anonymous.   Quhy sowld nocht Allane honorit be?   OxBS

The Gude and Godlie Ballatis: The Reid in the Loch Sayis.   Anonymous.   For tyme sic caussis hes reparit.   OxBS

The Gude and Godlie Ballatis: Till Christ.   Anonymous.   Till Christ, quhome I am haldin for to lufe.   OxBS

Gude Wallace (A version).   Anonymous.   And gainst the morn at twelve o'clock./He dined with his kind Scottish men.   BaBo; ESPB

Gude Wallace (G version).   Anonymous.   The goodwife was a Scots woman,/And she came to his hand.   ESPB

Gudveig.   Francis Berry.   The ghost of a woman, her body overboard/Laid, in the waters around/GREENLAND.   OBTV

The Guerdon of the Sun.   George Sterling.   And after-glows that crown his labor done.   HBMV

Guernica.   James Lewisohn.   and being one of them/leaves his shadow closer to the ground.   LFAC

La Guerre.   Edward Estlin Cummings.   the night utter ripe unspeaking girls.   MoAmPo

The Guerrilla.   Frelimo.   "I bring freedom for all."   WhB

Guerrilla.   Cosmo Pieterse.   to which our suffering needs/even and all our death must lead.   WhB

A Guerrilla Handbook.   LeRoi (Imamu Amiri Baraka) Jones.   We must convince the living/that the dead/cannot sing.   PoBA

Guerrilla Promise.   Mvula Ya Nangolo.   waiting in my sheath/only for your death.   WhB

Guess Who.   Fred Chappell.   ...haven't seen an Elm/in thirteen American Years.   NLV

Guessing.   Anonymous.   It is hard to guess.   PBWP

The Guest.   Anonymous.   And, as at first, still lodge Him in the manger.   BoC; EaLo; EBCP; EvOK; GoBC; OBS; Oxboch; TrCP

The Guest.   Wendell Berry.   ...He's the guest/of my knowing, though not asked.   AP

Guest.   D. J. Enright.   I am the guest, the one to be indulged.   OxBC

The Guest.   Harriet McEwen Kimball.   Lo, my Master/Was the Guest that supped with me!   AA

Guest.   E. A. Lacey.   And I were to spend myself in his torn body/As morning gritted on his eyes.   PeHV

The Guest.   Pentti Saarikoski.   ...whose breasts/are "so moist and tender, you can eat them like candy."   PV

Guest Lecturer.   Darwin T. Turner.   Which has no stage.   BALP

The Guests.   Louis Zukofsky.   two chairs/standing/for the ever-returning/guests.   CoPo

De Guiana, Carmen Epicum.   George Chapman.   The world to her, and both at her blest feet,/In whom the circles of all Empire meet.   OBSC

The Guide.   Arthur Gregor.   To help an ignorant earthling on/to the radiance that he—the bodiless/—is now possessed of!   GP

A Guide to Familiar American Incest: Inventing a Family.   Dennis Saleh.   There's Mother. There's Sister.   NeAC

Guide to Jerusalem.   Dennis Silk.   I enjoy a small enclave of the sun.   VWA

Guide to the Perplexed.   David Malouf.   ...we praise it, wishing at each season,/our friends, in life, in love, the lucky break.   NOAV

Guide to the Ruins.   Howard Nemerov.   ...cloud-reflecting lakes/In the old mountains of time.   EyDe

Guide to the Symphony.   Weldon Kees.   ...The concertmaster rubs a little resin on his bow.   VGW

Guided Missiles Experimental Range.   Robert Conquest.   "O-barren daughters of the fruitful night."   OxBC

Guild's Signal.   Bret (Francis Bret Harte) Harte.   Guild lay under his engine dead.   PaPo

Guilielmus Rex.   Thomas Bailey Aldrich.   'Tis he alone that lives and reigns!   AA; AnNE

Guilt.   Lorenzo Thomas.   But all I want to talk about/Would be unspeakable things.   APU

Guilt and Sorrow.   William Wordsworth.   From lamp of lonely toll-gate streamed athwart the night.   FaBoPP

Guilty.   Marguerite Wilkinson.   O costly valor never won!   TRV

"Guilty or Not Guilty?"   Anonymous.   Himself, the "guilty" child!   BeLS; BLPA

Guinea.   Jacques Roumain.   ...the hard ancestral stone/where your head will rest at last.   TTY

The Guinea Pig.   Anonymous.   And as I'm told by men of sense,/He never has been living since!   NA; OxNR

A Guinea-Pig Song.   Anonymous.   He never has been living since.   OxBChV

Guitar.   Federico Garcia Lorca.   Heart heavily wounded/by five sharp swords.   InPK

Guitar.   David St. John.   I have always loved the word guitar.   MAYP

The Guitarist Tunes Up.   Frances Cornford.   Before they started, he and she, to play.   ELU; SoSe

The Gulf.   Denise Levertov.   no place to go.   NNaP

The Gulf.   Derek Walcott.   age after age, the uninstructing dead.   NoP

The Gulf Stream.   Henry Bellamann.   Sinking and fading as it nears the sun/In this relentless river of desire.   EtS

Gulf Stream.   Susan (Sarah Chauncey Woolsey) Coolidge.   I am most her lover or her foe.   AA; EtS

Gulf-Weed.   Cornelius George Fenner.   Grace informing with silent soul.   EtS

The Gulistan.   Muslih-ud-Din Sa'di.
And clangs the door upon the wolf outside.   AWP
And o'er her tomb wild brambles creep.   AWP
And surely on her threshold dying fall.   AWP; LiTW
A fool among the ruins findeth gold.   AWP; LiTW
He will constrain thee to depart unheard.   AWP; LiTW
Help whom thou may'st—for surely unto thee/Sharp need of help will e'er the end be borne.   AWP
In straits which no escape afford/The hand takes hold of the edge of the sword.   AWP
No voice can answer from the dead again.   AWP; LiTW
Perchance a lurking tiger sleeps therein.   AWP; LiTW
Vile belly! take the crust! 'tis nobler food/Than all the capons plucked in servitude.   AWP
Whilst he who lacks that which the world commends/Must pace a stranger, e'en in his own lands.   AWP
Who did not see in his own house the knave that kissed/his wife?   AWP

The Gull.   Nakasuk.   Your wings/Are red/Up there—in the coolness.   WTO

Gull.   William Jay Smith.   What a wonderful life has he!   TiPo

The Gull Decoy.   Anonymous.   They call me the Gull Decoy.   ShS

A Gull Goes Up.   Léonie Adams.   Desire it is that flies; then wings are freight/That only bear the feathered heart no weight.   WHA

Gull Lake Reunion.   Kelly Ivie.   the land barely speaks.   AMV-81

A Gulling Sonnet.   Sir John Davies.   By their decree he soon transformed was/Into a patient burden-bearing Ass.   EiL

Gulliver.   Sylvia Plath.   The shadow of this lip, an abyss.   NOBA

Gulliver.   Kenneth Slessor.   For God's sake, call the hangman.   ACV

Gulls.   E. A. Muir.   A night, surrounded by such cries.   NCSH

Gulls.   William Carlos Williams.   the gulls moved seaward very quietly.   NoP; OxBA

Gulls and Dreams.   Lionel Stevenson.   Nor mortal minds aspire to know,/The universal loveliness.   CaP

Gulls in an Aery Morrice.   William Ernest Henley.   The way of a man with a maid!   PBBP

The Gully.   Furnley Maurice.
Not knowing it will some day move with wings.   BoAV
Or link by precious link forge chains that hold/The wandering passions of men in one vast fold.   BoAV
Where all things go that die/Like flame and sound, and mist and minstrelsy.   BoAV

Gun Teams.   Gilbert Frankau.   Know the worth of humble servants, foolish-faithful to their gun.   OxBTC

Gunfighter.   Gerald Locklin.   but especially those that can't tell/murder from phenomenology.   AMV-80

Gunga Din.   Rudyard Kipling.   You're a better man than I am, Gunga Din!   BBV; BrPo; FaFP; FPL; GoTF; HBV 1-2; LiTB; MCCG; MoBrPo; OBTV; OnMSP; PoPl; TreF; VLP

Gunnar's Howe above the House at Lithend.   William Morris.   For here day and night toileth the summer/lest deedless his time pass away.   OBTV

H

Had There Been Falsehood in My Breast. Emily Bronte. These tears had never flowed. NOBV

Hadad: The Demon-Lover. James Abraham Hillhouse. Where, where, in what abyss shall I be/groaning. AA

Hadrian's Address to His Soul When Dying. Emperor (Publius Aelius Hadrianus) Hadrian. No more with wonted humour gay,/But pallid, cheerless, and forlorn. OBVE

Haec Olim Meminise Iuvabait. Deems Taylor. And F. P. A. ran a piece of mine in the New York Evening/Mail. InMe

Haemorrhage. Padraic Fiacc. The moon light gets an un-/earthly white Belfast man. CIP

The Hag. Robert Herrick. Called out by the clap of the thunder. CaPo; EnL; FaBoCh; LoGBV; PoSC; WiR; WSC

The Hag and the Slavies. Jean de La Fontaine. To exchange the cock for old Sibylla/Was From Charybdis into Scylla. AWP; OBVE

The Hag of Beare. John Montague. Where once was life's flood/All is ebb. BIrV; CIP; NOBI; OBVE; PBWP

Hag-Ridden. Robert Graves. Did you ride your madman? BIrV

Hagar. Francis Lauderdale Adams. The east sky glints with light,/And it is Christmas Day! OxBS

Hagar. Elisabeth Eybers. been tempered to a man's defiant hate. PeSA

Hagar and Ishmael. Else Lasker-Schüler. And bit their white teeth in the hot sand. BoWoP; VWA

Hagar to Ishmael. Deborah Eibel. You and I must wait for God,/My Ishmael,/Must wait for God. VWA

Hagiograph. Rayner Heppenstall. The saint Pygmalion, saint, beggar and thief. NeBP

Hai. Stuart Z. Perkoff. the waters move & i am alive VWA

Haidee. George Gordon, Lord Byron. ...to spring/On the first foe whom Lambro's call might bring. OBNC; SeCePo

Haifa. Dovid Knut. The penetrating Biblical cold. VWA

Haiku. Gerald Vizenor. once or twice a summer/old school bell VoR

Haiku: "A balmy spring wind..." Richard Wright. I cannot recall. FAZ

Haiku: "A bare pecan tree." Etheridge Knight. a moonlit snow slope. NeAC; SM; TAP

Haiku: "A bitter morning:". J. W. Hackett. without any necks. BoAnP

Haiku: "After a long winter, giving." Chiyo. with blossoms in our hands. BoWoP

Haiku Ambulance. Richard Brautigan. so what? InPK

Haiku: "An empty sickbed..." Richard Wright. In weak winter sun. FAZ

Haiku: "Autumn's bright moon." Kaga no Chiyo. in an unknown sky. PBWP

Haiku: "Being newly-married before all the world." Anonymous. About the quarrels over water. HW

Haiku: "Cherry-blossoms, more." Onitsura. Oh, Horses have four!!! LiTW

Haiku: "Coming from the woods..." Richard Wright. Dangling from a horn. FAZ

Haiku: "Death it can bring." Issa. It's a pretty thing! LiTW

Haiku: "Deep in a windless." Buson (Taniguchi Buso). Something is afraid. WSC

Haiku: "Did I see her." Anonymous. The bride hides herself. HW

Haiku: "Don't dress for it." Chiyo. those darling rags. BoWoP

Haiku: "Eastern guard tower." Etheridge Knight. like lizards on rocks. NeAC; SM; TAP

Haiku: "Even in my village..." Kyorai. like a traveler. FAZ

Haiku: "Fish shop..." Basho (Matsuo Basho). of the salted bream. FAZ

Haiku, for Cinnamon. Lillie D. Chaffin. Across the meadows, we are one/Graceful movement. PH

Haiku: "For some time." Anonymous. The new bride wants/To run into the house. HW

Haiku: "Grasshoppers." Kawai Chigetsu-Ni. Chirping in the sleeves/Of a scarecrow. WPOW

Haiku: "Green weeds of summer." Basho (Matsuo Basho). once used to shimmer. InPK

Haiku: "Hardly Spring, with ice." Chiyo. the kisses are bitter. BoWoP

Haiku: "I called to the wind." Kyorai. still knocks at my gate. WSC

Haiku: "I would like a bell..." Richard Wright. Over willow trees. FAZ

Haiku: "In the August grass." Etheridge Knight. The cracked teacup screams. NeAC; SM; TAP

Haiku: "In the old stone pool." Basho (Matsuo Basho). splishhhhh. InPK

Haiku: "into a forest." Otsuji. was no voice I knew. WSC

Haiku: "Just enough of rain..." Richard Wright. From the umbrellas. FAZ

Haiku: "Making jazz swing in." Etheridge Knight. No square poet's job. NeAC; SM; TAP

Haiku: "Moor:". Basho (Matsuo Basho). where birds sing. FAZ

Haiku: "Morning sun slants cell." Etheridge Knight. On Jailhouse floor. NeAC; SM; TAP

Haiku: "Neither earth nor sky." Hashin. Falling fast oh fast. WeW

Haiku: "No need to cling." Joso. floating frog. FAZ

Haiku: "No one spoke." Ryota. The white chrysanthemums. LiTW

Haiku: "On a withered branch." Basho (Matsuo Basho). Autumn nightfall too. WeW

Haiku: On Her Child's Death. Kaga no Chiyo. My little boy–who ran away. LiTW

Haiku: "On this road." Basho (Matsuo Basho). In the autumn evening. LiTW

Haiku: "Once my parents were older." Chiyo. same cicadas. BoWoP

Haiku: "Once upon a time". Issa. a dry tuft of grass. WSC

Haiku: "Pluck a daisy here–." Robert Phillips. a great star trembles. GrPl

Haiku: "Plum-viewing..." (Taniguchi Buso) Buson. sashes are chosen. FAZ

Haiku: "Sandy shore: and why." Shiki. The midsummer moon? WeW

Haiku: "Seaweed..." Kito. forgotten tides. FAZ

Haiku: "So the spring has come?" Basho (Matsuo Basho). In the morning mist. WeW

Haiku: "Sprayed with strong poison." Paul Goodman. in the crystal vase InPK

Haiku: "Spring rain." Kaga no Chiyo. Everything just grows/More beautiful. PBWP

Haiku: "Spring rain! And as yet." Buson (Taniguchi Buso). Haven't got wet! LiTW

Haiku: "That duck, bobbing up". Joso. has seen something strange... WSC

Haiku: "That early riser." Robert Phillips. ...stands on a footstool/to observe the day. GrPl

Haiku: "That silver balloon." Robert Phillips. ...drifts free of Him/whose breath gave it shape. GrPl

Haiku: "The bride." Anonymous. Of the butterfly wine. HW

Haiku: "The bride puts them away." Anonymous. The lingering scent. HW

Haiku: "The cat spreads herself." Robert Phillips. ...like pea-/nut butter on bread. GrPl

Haiku: "The crow flew so fast..." Richard Wright. Behind in the fields. FAZ

Haiku: "The dew of the rouge-flower." Kaga no Chiyo. When it is spilled/Is simply water. PBWP

Haiku: "The dog's violent sneeze..." Richard Wright. On his mangy back. FAZ

Haiku: "The falling flower." Moritake. Was a butterfly. SoSe

Haiku: "The falling snow flakes." Etheridge Knight. Match the steel stillness. NeAC; SM; TAP

Haiku: "The first night." Anonymous. The elopers/Stay at the beautiful place. HW

Haiku: "The hair ornament of the sun." Mitsuhashi Takajo. into the legendary sea. BoWoP

Haiku: "The halo of the moon." Buson (Taniguchi Buso). Rising up to heaven? MOON

Haiku: "The lightning flashes!" Basho (Matsuo Basho). A night-heron's screech. SoSe

Haiku: "The long, long river." Boncho. On the snowy plain. LiTW

Haiku: "The piano man." Etheridge Knight. his songs drop like plum. NeAC; SM; TAP

Haiku: "The young bride's present." Anonymous. A living Nyorai. HW

Haiku: "The young wife's dreams." Anonymous. Over the corridor. HW

Haiku: "These branches..." Joso. falling blossoms. FAZ

Haiku: "Things long forgotten–". Shiki. this spring day. FAZ

Haiku: To Her Husband, at the Wedding. Kaga no Chiyo. Marriage is even so. HW

Haiku: "To write a blues song." Etheridge Knight. and pluck gems from graves. NeAC; SM; TAP

Haiku: "To write too many." Robert Phillips. ...is to be nibbled/to death by small fish. GrPl

Haiku: "Tow-head dandelions." Robert Phillips. So soon we vanish! GrPl

Haiku: "Under moon shadows." Etheridge Knight. Slices star bright ice. NeAC; SM; TAP

Haiku: "When the daughter." Anonymous. Her mother feels relieved. HW

Haiku: "Whether I sit or lie." Ukihashi. My empty mosquito net/Is too large. WPOW

Haiku: "Why is the hail so wild..." Richard Wright. Only to lie so still. FAZ

Haiku: "winter midnight." Otsuji. Sound like my own. LiTW

Haiku: "Winter rain at night..." Richard Wright. And spicing the soup. FAZ

Hail and Farewell. Anne Higginson Spicer. "God keep you safely, brother,/Who go to die for me." HBMV

Hail! Columbia. Joseph Hopkinson. As a band of brothers joined,/Peace and safety we shall find. AA; BLSo; FaBoBe; FaFP; HBV 1-2; MC; PAH; PAL; TreFS; YaD

Hallowe'en 1971. Michael Dennis Browne. American ghosts running toward them/through the dark, with open hands. AmPA

Hallowe'en Indignation Meeting. Margaret Fishback. I'm scareder of kids than they are of me! PoSC

Hallowed Ground. Thomas Campbell. And your high priesthood shall make earth/All hallowed ground. BLPA; HBV 1-2

Hallowed Places. Alice Freeman Palmer. I read you everywhere. HBV 1-2

Halloween. Robert Burns. They parted aff careerin/Fu' blythe that night. OBEC

Halloween. Marie A. Lawson. Don't you know it's Halloween? SiSoSe; TiPo

Halloween. Myra Cohn Livingston. Hush, child, listen, and believe. OFD

Halloween. Marnie Pomeroy. With the dark so deep I dare not sleep/All night on Halloween. PoSC

Halloween Concert. Aileen Fisher. Halloween, Halloween,/scritch,/scratch,/squeak. SiSoSe

Halloween Witches. Felice Holman. How many brooms will sweep the sky? WSC

Hallucination: I. Arthur Symons. One blood-red petal stained the Baudelaire. SyP

Halo. Ralph Nixon Currey. White as the celluloid about his throat. PeSA

A Halo. Ralph Salisbury. And spreads against the dark. FAZ

The Halt. Josephine Miles. The blind, blundering in his black, black, black need. ELU

Halt and Parley. George Herbert Clarke. Poor clod–while you've parried and parleyed out there. CaP

Haltersick's Song. John Pikeryng. With "Hey, trim' and "Trixy' too/Their banners they display. OBSC

Ham Hound Crave. Rube Lacy. And I rock you easier/than your straight chair ever done BluL

Hamasah: His Children. Hittan of Tayyi. Mine eye says no to slumber all night long. AWP

Hamatreya. Ralph Waldo Emerson. My avarice cooled/Like lust in the chill of the grave. AmPP; AnNE; AP; HeIP; MAmP; MAT; NOBA; NoP; OxBA; PoEL 1-5; PrIm; SeCeV; TAP

The Hambone and the Heart. Edith Sitwell. ...I can but fortell/The worm where once the kiss clung, and that last less chasm-/deep farewell. OBMV

Hambone Blues. Ed Bell. She got the same jelly roll/She had/forty years ago BluL

Hame, Hame, Hame. Allan Cunningham. "I'll shine on ye yet in yere ain countrie." BSV; CH; HBV 1-2; OBEV; OBRV

Hamewith. Sydney Goodsir Smith. Man in dust is lain/And exile wins hame. BSV

Hamilton Greene. Edgar Lee Masters. All honor to them/For what service I was to the people! NoAm; OxBA

Hamlet. Emmett Jarrett. they are all beautiful too. NeAC

Hamlet. William Shakespeare.
And bowl the round nave down the hill of heaven,/As low as to the fiends! Par
And fall a-cursing, like a very drab,/A scullion! TreFT
And flights of angels sing thee to thy rest! DL; FaBoRV; FiP
At his heels a stone. LO
Farewell; my blessing season this in thee! MasP
God ha' mercy on his soul! InPo; TrGrPo; ViBoPo
My thoughts be bloody, or be nothing worth! BiP; HoPM; WaaP
O, that that earth, which kept the world in awe,/Should patch a wall t' expel the winter's flaw! DL
O, there be players that I have seen play, and heard others praise, and that highly, not to speak.. TreFS
the paragon of animals! TreF
So hallow'd and so gracious is the time. FaBoRV; GN; OFD; PCh
So runs the world away. CoBE
Thou canst not then be false to any man. FaFP; GN; GoTF; LiTB; OHFP; PoPl; TreF; TrGrPo; TRV
An thou hadst not come to my bed. UnTE
To give them seals, never, my soul, consent! TreFT
Which bewept to the grave did go/With true-love showers. AnFE; EBEV; EnLoPo; GBL; GoBC; InPo; LiTB; LiTL; OBSC; PoRA; QFR; TrGrPo; ViBoPo
With this regard their currents turn BiP; DiPo; FaFP; HoPM; LiTB; MasP; OHFP; PoPl; TreF; WBLP; WHA

Hamlet in Russia, A Soliloquy. Boris Pasternak. To live a life is not to cross a field.' FaBoPV

The Hamlet of A. MacLeish (excerpt). Archibald MacLeish. As the whole night now/Made visible behind this darkness seems/To beckon to me.... AnAmPo

Hamlet (parody). Stanley J. Sharpless. And he did–nine soliloquies later. BXAP

Hamlet's Soliloquy Imitated (parody). Richard Jago. With this regard from Dodsley turn away,/And lose the name of authors. FaBoPa

The Hammam Name. James Elroy Flecker. The water froze. BrPo; PeHV

The Hammer. Clark Coolidge. gong/steam end/end. ANYP slaps hasps soon. ANYP

Hammer. Erica Funkhouser. every nail slides down/its passageway as if/that destination/had been chosen. AMV-81

Hammer and Anvil. Samuel Valentine Cole. Men's hammers break. God's anvil stands. PoLf

Hammer Man (with music). Anonymous. See the boss man comin' down the line. AS

Hammer, Ring. Anonymous. Won't you ring, old hammer?/Hammer, ring. AmFP

Hammer Song. Anonymous. Hammer ring. ABF

Hammerin' Hank. D. Roger Martin. "Here's a kid who/really has a chance to be/a white Henry Aaron." SOTS

The Hammers. Ralph Hodgson. Silent hammers of decay. GoJo; MoBrPo; NOBE; OxBTC

Hammerstoke. Don Domanski. the fine blue dust that a god leaves/when it is flying toward new worlds/to be born. CaPN

Hampstead: The Horse Chestnut Trees. Thom Gunn. hardening tender green/to insensate lumber. NoP

Hanabi-ko. Wendy Rose. Is this my mother/this rain wind touch of sound? TWSS

The Hand. Brian Fawcett. What should I do/with these hands? NOBC

The Hand. Irving Feldman. I breathed, and this truth burned up my breath. AmPC

The Hand. Ebenezer Jones. For heaven shouldn't purchase/That little sister hand. OBVV

The Hand. Howard Moss. And I must know more than I know. TAP

Hand. Edouard Roditi. ...until they fade into the blue depth of/space. EAS

A Hand. Bernard Spencer. To hunt, to hold its mark/–This loved hand. NeBP

The Hand. R. S. Thomas. Messenger to the mixed things/of your making, tell them I am.' NOCV; OxBC

The Hand and Foot. Jones Very. Bids spheres and atoms in just order move. AP; NePA

The Hand at Callow Hill Farm. Charles Tomlinson. ...whose calm concealed/The tutelary of that upland field. NePoEA-2

Hand by Hand We Shall Us Take. Anonymous. And Goddes son is maked our make. OxBM; SBVL

Hand-Clapping Rhyme. Anonymous. Saw a long-legged sailor/Kiss his long-legged wife! NTCP

Hand-Jive. Sandie Castle. and spend the night mothering them instead. APU

Hand Me Down My Walking Cane. Anonymous. 'Cause all my sins are taken away. FSW

A Hand-Mirror. Walt Whitman. Such a result so soon–and from such a beginning! CBEP; MAmP; OxBA; TW

The Hand of Lincoln. Edmund Clarence Stedman. Since through its living semblance passed/The thought that bade a race be free! AA; OHIP; PGD

A Hand of Snapshots (excerpt). Louis MacNeice. And the ancient cross on the hillside meant myself. FaBoIP

A Hand of Solo. Thomas Kinsella. ...My throat filled/with a rank, Arab bloodstain. NOBI

Hand Saw. Erica Funkhouser. the heat of steel/aging as it passes through/throbbing cells. AMV-81

The Hand That Held It. W. G. Elmslie. The hand that held it scarce was seen. TRV

The Hand That Rocks the Cradle Is the Hand That Rules the World. William Ross Wallace. For the hand that rocks the cradle/Is the hand that rules the world. BLPL; FaFP; PoLf; TreF; WBLP

The Hand That Signed the Paper. Dylan Thomas. Hands have no tears to flow. HaMV; InPo; MoAB; MoBrPo; MoPo; MoRP; NoAm; NOBE; NoP; OBWP; SeCePo; TrGrPo; WaP; WeW

The Handball Players at Brighton Beach. Irving Feldman. festive, clear, crowded with delight. NYP

Handbook of Versification. Gilbert Sorrentino. ...the true/true image of what happened: of the blank world. PoA

The Handcart Song. Anonymous. So merrily on our way we go, until we reach the valley-o. AmFP

Handful of Ashes. Ilya Rubin. Sodom enveloped in human flames,/our unloved, our native home... VWA

A Handful of Dust. James Oppenheim. Who is trying to speak to us? TrJP

A Handful of Small Secret Stones. Chris Bursk. He went to look for bigger rocks. AMV-81

Handfuls. Carl Sandburg. Handfuls again. AP

Handicapped. Daniel Berrigan. in an eye's wink/the kingdom of light FAZ

Handling Synne. Robert De Brunne. Englishmen in ennui. DBV

Handlining Tockers & Gizmos.   Allen Planz.   you'll lose sleep but not food or dreams if kept/tight as shark or ship at either end.   WOLT

The Handloom.   Judith Rodriguez.   the fitter and turner, his wife who sings, and their child.   FaBoWP

The Handmaid of Religion.   Edgell Rickword.   as must, for this wise Prelate's part,/be supreme arbiters of Art.   OBSV

Hands.   Dorothy Aldis.   "Oh, there are things/Hands do/That feet NEVER can."   SUS

Hands.   Frederick Cloud.   That gives to the sightless,/Light.   LaNeLa

Hands.   Donald Finkel.   when the two of you are equally beautiful.   CoAP; InPK; MAT

Hands.   Alex Glasgow.   Just hands, hands, hands, lad,/Hands, hands, hands.   OBET

The Hands.   Tony Harrison.   Heavily weighted, they struggled well,/kicking up the water, then went down.   FaBpTw

The Hands.   Denise Levertov.   ...testing/their diagonals, in common clothes.   NeAP; PoM

The Hands.   William Stanley Merwin.   and I bend to hear who is beating   CAPP

The Hands.   Daniel David Moses.   than you who have eyes.   AMV-80

Hands.   Louis Untermeyer.   Curved in a smile. The mystery remains.   AnAmPo 013; MoLP

The Hands-Across-the-Sea Poem.   J. C. Squire.   Stand by us in the hour of need/And we shall stand by you.   HBMV

Hands Clenched under My Shawl...   Anna Akhmatova.   He said, "Don't stand in the chill."   PBWP

The Hands of God.   D. H. Lawrence.   Let me never know myself apart from the living God!   MoRP

Hands up.   Anthony Rudolf.   ...Oh, say a prayer/for one only kid, son of Our Father/Avraham, who wandered like a gypsy.   VWA

The Handsome Cabin Boy.   Anonymous.   And here's hoping for a jolly lot more/like the handsome cabin boy.   FSW

Handsome Friend, Charming and Kind.   Beatrice de Dia.   but only under the condition/that you swear to do my bidding.   WPOW

Handsome Molly.   Anonymous.   Handsome Molly! Little Molly darling!)   FSW

The Handwriting on the Wall.   Knowles Shaw.   While the Hand is writing on the wall?   AmFP; BLPA

Handy Dandy.   Anonymous.   Which hand will you have,/High or low?   OxNR

Handy Spandy.   Mother Goose.   And out he came, hop, hop, hop.   SoPo

Handyman.   Homer Phillips.   He'll stay right with it/Till it's fixed beyond repair.   QQQ

The Hang-Glider's Daughter.   Marilyn Hacker.   ...We're here, on top of the hill.   MAYP

Hang It on the Wall.   Charlie Patton.   Sweet mama, won't you let it fall   BluL

Hang Me, O Hang Me, and I'll Be Dead and Gone.   Anonymous.   It's layin' in the grave so long.   AmFP

Hang out the Flags.   James S. Tippett.   Let them hang free.   SiSoSe

Hang to Your Grit!   Louis E. Taylor.   To laugh at pain and trouble and keep up his grit.   WBLP

Hang up the Baby's Stocking!   Anonymous.   ...just cram her/stocking with goodies, from the top/clean down to the toe!   OBCP

A Hanging.   Frank Mkalawile Chipasula.   before the sandbags dragged his compressed body/into the dark hole, into total oblivion.   WhB

The Hanging.   J. E. H. MacDonald.   I hang, behead, electrocute.   OBCV

Hanging Fire.   Audre Lorde.   and momma's in the bedroom/with the door closed.   NIP; NoP

Hanging from the branches of a green willow tree.   Lady Ise.   is a/thread of pearls.   BoWoP

Hanging Johnny.   Anonymous.   So hang, boys, hang!   AmSS; FSW; GBP; ShS

The Hanging Man.   Sylvia Plath.   If he were I, he would do what I did.   HaCAP

The Hanging of Sam Archer.   Anonymous.   Upon your knees for mercy cry,/Before, like Archer, bound to die.   AmFP

The Hanging of the Crane.   Henry Wadsworth Longfellow.   And rolled on its harmonious way/Into the boundless realms of space!   GN

Hanging Out the Linen Clothes (with music).   Anonymous.   A-wearing of the linen clothes, a-wearing of the linen clothes.   AS

Hanging Scroll.   Gerald Stern.   like a worried spirit/waiting for love.   PoDr

Hangman.   Florence Anthony ("Ai").   sending tiny slivers of straw into his eyes.   AmPA

The Hangman's Love Song.   Stanley Moss.   and the hangman sings.   VGW

The Hangman's Tree.   Anonymous.   Nor have I come to see you hanging/On the gallows tree.   ExPo

Hangman's Tree.   Lillian Zellhoefer White.   Two phantom bandits swing and sway.   AmFN

Hangman (with music).   Anonymous.   She'll never break this heart of mine.   AS

Hangover Cure.   Alexis.   And there's an end of your headache.   FaBoUs

Hangover Cure.   Amphis.   For that at once all languor will dispel,/As sure as cabbage.   FaBoUs

Hangover Cure.   Nicochares.   Which equally rid you of all your sorrow.   FaBoUs

Hangtown Girls.   Anonymous.   Ha, ha, ha! Hangtown gals.   FSW

Hannah Bantry.   Anonymous.   How she clawed it,/When she found herself alone.   OxNR

Hannah Binding Shoes.   Lucy Larcom.   Hannah's at the window, binding shoes.   GN; HBV 1-2

Hans Beimler.   Ernst Busch.   Nor the enemy forgiven,/Hans Beimler, our Comrade.   FSW

Hans Breitmann's Party.   Charles Godfrey Leland.   All goned afay mit de lager beer-/Afay in de ewigkeit!   CenHV; FaBoCo; HBV 1-2; NOBL; OBAL

Hans Christian Andersen in Central Park.   Hy Sobiloff.   And though you are bronzed with age/They know you are theirs.   PoPl

Hansel and Gretel.   Anne Sexton.   like something religious.   InPS

Hansel and Gretel Return.   David Ray.   You see the jewels you brought gleam/On the dead as they go on talking.   DFT

Hansom Cabbies.   Wilfrid Thorley.   And flunkeys galore/Poll-powdered, receive them at Paradise door.   HBMV

Hanukah.   Jakov De Haan.   "The voice of the poet is the voice of God."   VWA

Hanukkah Hymn.   Anonymous.   That the time is nearing/Which will see/All men free,/Tyrants disappearing.   GoTF; TreFT

Hap.   Thomas Hardy.   These purblind Doomsters had as readily strown/Blisses about my pilgrimage as pain.   AWP; CABA; CMoP; CoBMV; EaLo; InPo; MoBrPo; NIP; NoAm; NoP; OAEL 1-2; OAEP; PPON; PPP; TEP; VLP

The Happening.   Mary Aldis.   But if she gave to his satiety/To no avail, what then? It had to be.   HBMV

Happening.   Edwin Honig.   ...When I turned, the house/Had opened its face, gray as a man's.   NePA

Happening In.   Mark Sanders.   his invitation to stay a while longer/in this place.   WOLT

The Happiest Day, the Happiest Hour.   Edgar Allan Poe.   A soul that knew it well.   AmPP; LITA; NePA; OxBA

The Happiest Heart.   John Vance Cheney.   And left to Heaven the rest.   AA; AnAmPo; APA; GoTF; HBV 1-2; HBVY; TreFS; WGRP

Happiness.   William Dickey.   I won't ever stop until the word gets to you.   Psk

Happiness.   John Dryden.   Tomorrow, do thy worst, for I have liv'd today.   GoTF; TreF

Happiness.   Louise Gluck.   How calm you are. And the burning wheel/passes gently over us.   MAYP

Happiness.   Walter E. Isenhour.   This brings a happiness so sweet,/And springs up from within!   STF

Happiness.   Priscilla Leonard.   No one ever finds them all.   BLPA; PoToHe

Happiness.   A.(lan) A.(lexander) Milne.   And that/(Said John)/Is/That.   BoC; TiPo

Happiness.   Carl Sandburg.   And I saw a crowd of Hungarians under the trees with/their women and children and a keg of beer...   OxBA

Happiness Amidst Troubles.   Immanuel Di Roma.   For me that place hath chiefest charms,/That brings me, dearest, to thine arms.   TrJP

Happiness Dependent on Ourselves.   Oliver Goldsmith.   Leave reason, faith, and conscience, all our own.   OBEC

Happiness Found.   Augustus Montague Toplady.   Real Bliss I then shall prove;/Heav'n below, and Heav'n above.   TrPWD

Happiness in the Trees.   Joseph Ceravolo.   in the velocity of rest.   ANYP

Happiness Makes up in Height for What It Lacks in Length.   Robert Frost.   We went from house to wood/For change of solitude.   MoAB; MoAmPo; MoPo

Happiness of 6 A.M.   Harvey Shapiro.   ..."This is the gift/I was going to give you forever."   NYBP

Happy Are Those Who Have Died.   Charles Peguy.   Happy the ripe stalks and the harvested grain.   WaaP

Happy at 40.   Peter Meinke.   your life depends on it/if you want to be happy/at 40.   GP

The Happy Beggarman.   Anonymous.   And at night in the alehouse I'll stay and pay like a man.   OnYI

The Happy Bird.   John Clare.   ...till gusts arise/More boisterous in their play, then off she flies.   PBBP

Happy Birthday.   Frank Bidart.   they didn't plan it that way.   HaCAP

Happy Britannia.   James (1700-48) Thomson.   The Dread of Tyrants, and the sole Resource/Of those that under grim Oppression groan.   OBEC

The Happy Child.   William Henry Davies.   But not like what the child has seen.   AtBAP

A Happy Christmas.   Frances Ridley Havergal.   His kingdom in thy heart shall never pass away.   BLRP

Happy Christmases (excerpt). John Francis O'Donnell. A faint star cafavan. IrPN

The Happy Countryman. Nicholas Breton. That may breed love's delights?... CH

Happy Day. James (Olumo) Cunningham. right down/right down here JB

Happy Death. John Freeman. Oh, that with them I had fought my fill/ And found like cover! HBMV

Happy Endings. Gail White. it was what she was used to. DFT

The Happy Family. John Ciardi. Sweetly screaming to be fed. DuDa

Happy He. Anonymous. Who, known to all, unknown to himself dies. EiL

The Happy Hen. James Agee. Heads swiftliest for the state of grace. ErPo 064

The Happy Husbandman; or, Country Innocence. Anonymous. Every Night with our Beauties lie. CoMu

Happy Insensibility. John Keats. Was never said in rhyme. GTBS; GTBS-P

Happy Is the Country Life. Anonymous. Age is no pain, and Youth no snare. OBS

The Happy Life. Sir Henry Wotton. Lord of himself, though not of lands,/ And having nothing, yet hath all. MyFE; WGRP

The Happy Life (excerpt). William Thompson. And a chaste, laughter-loving lass. ViBoPo

The Happy Life of a Country Parson (parody). Alexander Pope. And shake his head at Doctor Swift. BXAP

Happy Lifetime to You. Franklin Pierce ("F.P.A.") Adams. And I hope you'll like your baseball suit. InMe

A Happy Man. Carphyllides. Leave me to my quiet rest/In the region of the blest. AWP; LiTW

The Happy Man. Gilbert Keith Chesterton. Three persons and one god. EBCP

The Happy Miner. Anonymous. And I've got plenty! Will you drink lager beer with me? CoSo

Happy Myrtillo. Henry Carey. He had his fill, Oh,/Of what he pleased. SeCePo

Happy New Year, Anyway. Joanna Cole. So Happy New Year, anyway./ You might as well pretend. NTCP

A Happy New Year (excerpt). W. H. Auden. In Russia they've got some ripping new rears.' OBSV

The Happy Night. John, of Buckingham Sheffield. ...does spare/This child of hers, that most deserves her care. UnTE

The Happy Night. J. C. Squire. I am happy to-night: I have laughed to-night at death. HBMV

The Happy Nightingale. Anonymous. And ward off all impending ill/ Which over vice prevails. OxBChV

The Happy Pair (excerpt). Sir Charles Sedley. And gilded pills, though bitter, may delight/The liquorish lust of wav'ring appetite. OBSV

The Happy Poem. Thomas Brush. Coming home to roost. LTB

Happy, Saviour, Would I Be. Edwin H. Nevin. Trust thee all my journey through. AH

The Happy Sheep. Wilfrid Thorley. The carpet underneath their feet. SoPo

The Happy Swain. Ambrose Philips. Since she did herself resign/To my vows, for ever mine. EnLoPo

Happy the Man. John Dryden. But what has been, has been, and I have had my hour. FaPoR

Happy the Moment When We Are Seated in the Palace, Thou and I. Jalal ed-Din or al-Din Rumi. ...for Non-existence/Proclaims in organ tones, "To Him we shall return." ILwL

Happy Thought. Robert Louis Stevenson. I'm sure we should all be as happy as kings. FaBoBe; HBV 1-2; HBVY; OxBChV; TiPo; TreFS

The Happy Tree. Gerald Gould. There on the happy tree they hung/The Savior of mankind. WGRP

A Happy View. C. Day-Lewis. And hardy fingers find an eagle's hold. CMoP

The Happy Wanderer. Percy Addleshaw. Until tired, wise, content, he halts before/The sign o' The Grave, a cool and quiet inn. OBVV

Happy Were He. Robert Devereux, Earl of Essex. Where harmless robin dwells with gentle thrush. EiL; OBSP

Harald, the Agnostic Ale-Loving Old Shepherd... George Mackay Brown. From up to bottom of my glass/Clung a shining fleece. NePoEA-2

Harangue on the Death of Hayyim Nahman Bialik. Cesar Tiempo. In Tel-Aviv there was a poet./And now? TrJP

Harbingers. Basho (Matsuo Basho). plum tree and moon. PoPl

Harbor. Nancy Price. I catch myself. IHMS

The Harbor. Carl Sandburg. Veering and wheeling free in the open. NCSH; PoPl; TAP

The Harbor at Seattle. Robert Hass. ...and that was/how they built the harbor in Seattle. NPGG

The Harbor Dawn. Hart Crane. Turns in the waking west and goes to sleep. AmP; NePA; OxBA

The Harbor of Illusion. Charles Bernstein. ...tour the template, thoroughfare/of noon's atoll. APU

Hard, Ain't It Hard. Anonymous. Hard and it's hard ain't it hard, great God,/to love one that never will be true. FSW

Hard Country. Philip Booth. of shadow and/light. CoAP

Hard Daddy. Langston Hughes. I'd scratch out both his eyes. BANP

A Hard Frost. C. Day Lewis. Grip on the seed and lets our future breathe. HaMV

Hard Frost. Andrew Young. In the long war grown warmer/The sun will strike him dead and strip his armour. BoNaP; MoVE

Hard Heart of Mine. Henry Alline. Their work be my employ. AH

Hard Is the Fortune of All Womankind. Anonymous. And if you won't love him, he'll call you a whore. FSW

Hard Lines. Tom Robinson. No matter how old I get,/She'll always be older. BiCB

The Hard Listener. William Carlos Williams. ...unspoiled/by insects and waiting/only for the cold. OBSP

The Hard Lovers. George Dillon. It is that they together/Share deeply one distress. AnAmPo; PoA

Hard Questions. Margaret Tsuda. a bosom/not his own? RFM

Hard Rock Returns to Prison from the Hospital for the Criminal Insane. Etheridge Knight. The fears of years, like a biting whip,/Had cut grooves too deeply across our backs. BP; ConAP; InPS; LFAC; NIP; NNaP; NoAm; TAP; UnPo

Hard Strain in a Delicate Place. Janet Sylvester. The sky looked faultless, empty. MAYP

The Hard Summer. Mebdh McGuckian. ...folds in your palm/That fall aside like breasts,/Creating the letter M. FaBoIP

Hard Time Killin' Floor Blues. Skip James. Hard times will drive you, from door to door BluL

Hard Times. Anonymous.
   And it's hard, hard times. ABF
   And so it is hard times wherever you go. AmFP

Hard Times, But Carrying On. Dave Smith. ...while all around the bags/ crank up slack as widow's dugs in rain. TAT

Hard Times in the Country. Anonymous. It's a hard times in the country,/ Out on Penney's farm. OuSiCo

Hard To Be A Nigger. Anonymous. For you cain't get yo' money when it's due. ABF

Hard to Bear. Tudor Jenks. I believe that I'm not given to croaking,/But you'll admit that it's provoking! OBCA

Hard Traveling. Woody Guthrie. And I've been doing some hard traveling, Lord. FSW

Hard Trials. Anonymous. Ise bound to leave this world. ABF

Hard Way to Learn. James Hearst. —but no one gave me/a diploma when I was born. AMV-80

The Hard-Working Miner. Anonymous.
   And take him at last/Up to heaven with Thee. AmFP
   His mining's all over, poor miner farewell. ABF; AmFP

Hardcastle Crags. Sylvia Plath. She turned back. GoYe

Harden Now Thy Tired Heart. Thomas Campion. Too oft, I fear thou wilt remember me. AAS; NCEP

The Harder Task. Anonymous. And make me more than conqu'ror in the strife. BLRP

Hardly a Man Is Now Alive. Ring Lardner. A joke on his doctor, who'd thought that he was well. OBAL

Hardly Think I Will. Anonymous. But I hardly think I will. ABF

The Hardness Scale. Joyce Peseroff. Diamonds are forever so I give you softer things. LLLT

Hardon ("get one today"). Ian Wedde. could be happy to just go on missing out/on all the fun/"out there" OCNZ

The Hardship of Accounting. Robert Frost. What he did with every cent. FaBoCh; FaBoCo; FaFP; LoGBV; OBAL

Hardweed Path Going. Archie Randolph Ammons. hardening through the mind and night of the first freeze. HaCAP; UnPo; VGW

Hardy Perennial. Richard Eberhart. Discovering subtleties and profundities in/Any slightest gesture, or delicate glance. GOYP

Hardy's Plymouth. Geoffrey Grigson. As if your town were now re-paved with all/The more aching recollections of your stay. FaBoPP

The Hare. Anonymous. And whelpes play with my skin.' OxBM

Hare. Archestratus. As if they were preparing cat's meat. FaBoUs

The Hare. Walter De la Mare.
   She fled, and left the moonlight there. TiPo
   ...thy foe/Roves Eden, as did Satan, long ago. EBEV

Hare. Molly Holden. make him stand up and fight. TEP

The Hare. Stanley Snaith. And run into our lives and hide. HaMV

The Hare and the Tortoise. Ian Serraillier. I galloped so fast I'm seeing twice double. SO

Hare-Hunting. William Somervile. ...with infant Screams/She yields her Breath, and there reluctant dies. OBEC

Hare in Winter. Marge Piercy. Suddenly my tongue/floats in blood. NeAC

Harvest. Edith Sitwell. ..."Our Christ is arisen, He comes to give a/sign from the Dead." CoBMV; OAEP

Harvest and Consecration. Elizabeth Jennings. The wine and bread protect our ecstasy. NePoEA-2

The Harvest Bow. Seamus Heaney. Yet burnished by its passage, and still warm. FaBoIP

The Harvest Dawn Is Near. George Burgess. But he shall come at twilight's close,/And bring his golden sheaves. AH

The Harvest Elves. Wilfrid Thorley. Just as the harvesters have said. BrR

Harvest Home. Henry Alford. Bid us sing thy Harvest Home! WGRP

Harvest Home. John Dryden. And merrily roar out Harvest Home. PrIm

Harvest Home. Arthur Guiterman. The woods are waving, "Farewell, Summer." YeAr

Harvest Home. Frederick Tennyson. And echoes of the Harvest-home. OBVV

Harvest Hymn. John Greenleaf Whittier. Thanksgivings for the golden hours,/The early and the latter rain! OHIP

The Harvest Moon. Henry Wadsworth Longfellow. And pipings of the quail among the sheaves. AP; GN; MAmP

The Harvest of the Sea. John McCrae. The half-hushed sobbing of the hearts that weep. EtS

Harvest of the Sea. Maire Mhac an tSaoi. And the hare-lip was hidden below the coffin-lid!/And Ochone! PBWP

The Harvest of Time. Harold Trowbridge Pulsifer. Oh, speed the blown chaff down the smoking sky! HBMV

Harvest Poem. David Fisher. the old men gather the vines for burning. NPGG

Harvest Song. Joseph Campbell. And praise Mary's Child/That the harvest is done. OFD

Harvest Song. Richard Dehmel. Grind, O mill, keep grinding! AWP; LiTW

Harvest Song. Ludwig Heinrich Christoph Holty. Home they go, yo ho! AWP

Harvest Song. Jean Toomer. ...It will not bring me knowledge/of my hunger. NoP

Harvest Time. Star Powers. It is the season, it is harvest time! GoYe

Harvest Time. G. A. Watermeyer. and every sickle-arm's left far,/far back to graze the crop. PeSA

A Harvest to Seduce. Melville Cane. What is past is past. NYBP

The Harvest Waits. Lloyd Mifflin. Whirl the spurned chaff adown the void of Time! HBV 1-2

The Harvester. Terry Lawrence. I taste honey and wine. AMV-80

The Harvesters. Mary Gilmore. In separateness they turn, and to the cook-house go. NOAV

Harvesting. Selma Robinson. Cherry and pear, and me, myself,/Pasting a name on each. InMe

The Harvesting of the Roses. Menahem Ben Jacob. Amidst the rage of murderous blows/They were in death to him restored. TrJP

Harvesting Wheat for the Public Share. Li Chu. We will turn it in as the public share. BoWoP; PBWP

Harvey Always Wins. Jack Prelutsky. it isn't that he's better,/it's that Harvey always cheats. NTCP

Harvey Logan. Anonymous. O my babe, my honey babe. OuSiCo

Has Been. Alice F. Worsley. "Your shooting star is dead." AMV-80

Has no one seen my heart of you? Thomas Lovell Beddoes. So Christians fair, farewell. EG

Has Sorrow Thy Young Days Shaded? Thomas Moore. I'll weep with thee, tear for tear. OxBI

Hasbrouck and the Rose. Howard Phelps (Phelps Putnam) Putnam. "O Jesus, Hasbrouck, am I drunk or dead?" CoAnAm; MoVE; OxBA; ViBoPo

The Haschish. John Greenleaf Whittier. The hempen Haschish of the East/Is powerless to our Western Cotton! OBAL

Hasidic Jew from Sadagora. Rose Auslander. So danced the Sadagora Hasid/with the other Hasidim. VWA

Hasidim Dance. Nelly Sachs. On the menorah/the Pleiades pray– VWA

Haskell. Witter ("Emanuel Morgan") Bynner. And then it shadows, and he darts,/With head hung, to the dormitory. GLGT

Hassan's Serenade. James Elroy Flecker. Will come the Gardener in white,/and gather'd flowers are dead, Yasmin! OBEV

Hast Never Come to Thee an Hour. Walt Whitman. To utter nothingness? CBEP

Hast Thou Heard It, O My Brother. Theodore Chickering Williams. Trusting God and in each other,/We are children of the day. AH

Hast Thou Heard the Nightingale? Richard Watson Gilder. Yes, I have heard the nightingale. AA

Hast Thou Not Seen an Aged Rifted Tower. Hartley Coleridge. Yet, to the last, a rugged wrinkled thing/To which young sweetness may delight to cling! EnRP

Hast Thou Seen Reversed the Prophet's Miracle. Frederick Goddard Tuckerman. And in the day's young sunshine, seeking still/For earliest flowers and gathering to the east. NOBA

Haste to the Wedding. Alex Comfort. how finish better than that? ErPo

Hastings Mill. Cecily Fox-Smith. (Shipmate, my shipmate!) and the late dusk falling! HBV 1-2

The Hasty-Pudding. Joel Barlow.
  And the new crop exterminates the old. AP
  To that loved bowl my spoon by instinct floes. AnNE; AP; LoGBV; NOBA; OBAL; OxBA; TAP
  Wakes every child and gladdens every mouse. AmPP
The wide mouth'd bowl will surely catch them all! AmPP; AnNE; AP

Hat Bar. Mildred Weston. With but a single/Thought! FiBHP

The Hatch. Norma Farber. and saw another lining/inside a further sky. SO

Hate! Antokolsy. ...then drops in/dread/And cannot cover his despair. TrJP

Hate. James Stephens. I might have kissed him as I would a maid. MoAB; MoBrPo; OBVV

Hate and Debate Rome through the World Hath Spread. Sir John (1561-1612) Harington. For out of backward love all hate doth grow. TW

The Hate and the Love of the World. Max Ehrmann. And I have cried in my heart, "The world is love!" PoToHe

Hate Mail. Steve Kowit. Dear C, you are a ca-ca pee-pee head. APU

A Hate-Song. Percy Bysshe Shelley. 'Gainst a woman that was a brute. EnLoPo

Hate Whom Ye List. Sir Thomas Wyatt. But love whom ye list; for I care not. EnRePo; FCP; SiPS

Hath Any Loved You Well, Down There. Arthur William Edgar O'Shaughnessy. Your soul through faithless hours. EnLoPo

Hatikvah–A Song of Hope. Naphtali Imber. "Tis then our Hope shall cease to be/With Israel's last son!" TrJP

Hatred. Gwendolyn B. Bennett. And you will understand/My hatred. BANP; BlSi; CDC; PoBA

Hatred of Men with Black Hair. Robert Bly. From the stockade, over the snow, the trail now lost. NaP; TW

Hats. R. H. W. Dillard. How her hands are safe/As the eyelids of birds. GP

Hattage. Sir Alan Patrick Herbert. Meanwhile, I'll buy it back again. Good day. FiBHP

Hatteras Calling. Conrad Aiken. that man in terror may learn once more to be/child of that hour when rock and ocean meet. BoNaP; NoAm; NOBA; TAP

The Hatters. Nan McDonald. From the love of death, dear Lord, deliver me. NOAV; PoAu 1-2

Hauf-Roads Up Schiehallion. Donald Campbell. Here I am–HAUF-ROADS UP PIGGIN SCHIEHALLION/Aa for the guid o my health! PoSH

Haufi. Anonymous. till I see the grass/waving on her tomb. BoWoP

The Haughty Snail-King. Vachel Lindsay. "I wish I had a yellow crown/As glistering...as...the moon." LOW; SO

Haul away, Joe. Anonymous. Away, haul away, Oh, haul away, Joe! AmSS; ShS

Haul away, My Rosy. Anonymous. Haul away, my Johnsy-o. AmFP; FSW; OuSiCo

Haul on the Bowline. Anonymous. Haul on the bowline,/So early in the morning. AmSS; FSW; ShS

The Haunch of Venison, A Poetical Epistle to Lord Clare. Oliver Goldsmith. You may make a Mistake–and think slightly of This. CEP

Haunted. Siegfried Sassoon. And at his heart the strangling clasp of death. CMoP

Haunted Country. Robinson Jeffers. banked back/By the older flood of the ocean, to swallow it. OxBA

The Haunted Garden. Henry Treece. Like a boy searching for his dog? NeBP

The Haunted House. Robert Graves. Do flowers and butterflies belong/To a blind December? OxBI

The Haunted House. Thomas Hood. The place is Haunted! AnEnPo; EBEV; MyFE; NBM; SeCePo; WiR

The Haunted House. George Sylvester Viereck. I hear strange voices calling through the night. AnAmPo

Haunted House. Valerie Worth. Sleeping on the cellar/Shelf like this/Empty/Jelly jar. WSC

Haunted Houses. Henry Wadsworth Longfellow. Wander our thoughts above the dark abyss. AnNE

The Haunted Oak. Paul Laurence Dunbar. On the trunk of a haunted tree. BANP; UnPo

Haunted Odysseus: The Last Testament. Horace Gregory. We shall wait for you behind an open door/And in your shadow as you walk the stairs. MoVE

The Haunted Oven. X. J. Kennedy. Emitting crumby titters. WSC

The Haunter. Thomas Hardy. Still that his path may be worth pursuing,/ And to bring peace thereto. AtBAP; NOBE; PoPle; QFR

The Haunting. Irving Layton. and as if I had lived all my life in arrears NeAC

The Haunts of the Halcyon. Charles Henry Luders. To dream sweet, idle dreams of having/strayed/To Arcady, with all its golden lore. AA

Hava Na Shira. *Anonymous.* Hava na Shira Shire Hallelujah. FSW

Hava Nagila. *Anonymous.* Uru a chim uru a chim b'lev sameach. FSW

Havana Blues. Henry Carlile. A small imperfect replica of you. SM

Havana Dreams. Langston Hughes. (Quien sabe? Who really knows?) GoSl; PoNe

Havdolah. Susan Litwack. We are falling from this life/into the next. VWA

Havdolah Wine. Miriam Ulinover. Only fright can make it bristle. VWA

Have-at a Venture. *Anonymous.* again I'le put it in. CoMu; ErPo

Have Courage, My Boy, to Say No! L. M. Hilton. Have courage, my boy, to say no. WTO

Have Faith. Edward Carpenter. ...as if you were a very Cain flying from/ His face? WGRP

Have Faith in God. Joe Budzynski. Jesus said, "I'll never leave thee,/But will guide while passing through." STF

Have I Done My Best for Jesus? Edwin Young. The world is dying now for the want of/someone/to tell them of the Saviour's matchless/love. STF

Have I Got Dogs! William Cole. I holler "CHOW!" and then I RUN! GDP

Have I, This Moment, Led Thee from the Beach. Walter Savage Landor. I curse it present, I regret it past. GBL

Have Sky. Lewis MacAdams. through the fir trees and pine, through the flush blue sky. ANYP

Have We Not Seen Thy Shining Garment's Hem. Amy Carmichael. O Christ, our King, our Lord whom we adore. TRV

Have You Any Work for a Tinker, Mistris. *Anonymous.* For I am old, and very very cold, and never wear a Jerkin. OBS

Have You Been at Carrick? *Anonymous.* A myriad of welcomes, dear maid of my heart, to thee! AnIV; BIrV

Have You Got a Brook. Emily Dickinson. Beware, lest this little brook of life/Some burning noon go dry! FaBV

Have you heard? The troubles of the road. Sulpicia. It came from nowhere,/luckily for you. BoWoP

Have You Lost Faith? *Anonymous.* When faith in God goes, man, the mortal, loses his only hope. WBLP

Have You Noted the White Areas. Carlyle Reedy. clouds gather behind them. PPJ

Have You Seen the Lady? John Philip Sousa. She's the mint in the julep of joy. OBAL

Have You Thanked a Green Plant Today. Don Anderson. (Now I hereby bequeath to you/A life supply of CO2.) QQQ

Have You Watched the Fairies? Rose Fyleman. I have, I have; I've been there! SoPo; TiPo

Havelok: Havelok at Grimsby and Lincoln. *Anonymous.* Alle him loveden that him sowe,/Bothen heye men and lowe. OxBM

Haven. Donald Jeffrey Hayes. With proud and tilted chin...! AmNP; PoNe

Haverhill, 1640-1890. John Greenleaf Whittier. I pray, God bless the good old town! MAmP

Having a Wonderful Time. Dominic Bevin Wyndham Lewis. The Chim-pan-zee can-not forget. FiBHP

Having Climbed to the Topmost Peak of the Incense-Burner Mountain. Po Chu-i. Then, with lowered head, came back to the Ants' Nest. SD

Having Eaten Breakfast (parody). D. C. Berry. Of the Kyoto days,/ Meditated,/Masa painted BXAP

Having No Ear. Donald Davie. That Edward Taylor's Paradise was seen/ By other light than day? AMV-81

Having Read Books. Heather McHugh. ...I take/the risk of you in the hay's rot. GeTw

Having Replaced Love with Food and Drink. Diane Wakoski. this pasta, green and garlicky/made with my own hands. NAs

Hawaii Dantesca. Charles Wright. When I get there, I hope they forgive me if the knot I tie is/the wrong knot. HaCAP; LCAP

The Hawk. Raymond Knister. Along the soundless horizon. OBCV

The Hawk. William Butler Yeats. A pretence of wit. AtBAP; PoA

Hawk and Snake. Leslie Marmon Silko. I peer out from my rocks/coiled in noontime shade. VoR

The Hawk in the Rain. Ted Hughes. Smashed, mix his heart's blood with the mire of the land. ACV

Hawk Nailed to a Barn Door. Peter Blue Cloud. I look at your beautiful wings/and sense your flight. VoR

Hawk Roosting. Ted Hughes. I am going to keep things like this. CMoP; GTBS-P; HAP; HeIP; LiTM; MP; NePoEA-2; NMP; OxBTC; PB; PPP; TwCP; UnPo

Hawk's Eyes. Yvor Winters. So my course turns/Where I walk each day. PoA

Hawk's Way. Ted Olson. On the empty way the hawk in his beauty went. HoPM

The Hawkbit. Sir Charles G. D. Roberts. Become more fragile and more fine/Breathing the atmosphere divine. HBV 1-2

Hawke. Sir Henry Newbolt. When Hawke came swooping from the West. BBV

Hawking. Michael Drayton. When he his quarry makes upon the grassy plain. SD

Hawking for the Partridge. Thomas Ravenscroft. And sport with them in those delights,/And oft in other things. NCEP; OxBoLi

Hawks. James Stephens. Guard the poor from treachery. HBMV

Hawktree. Dave Smith. in the desert wind, in the wordless/emptied gnarling he had become. HaCAP

Haworth Churchyard (excerpt). Matthew Arnold. Sleep, or only for this/ Break your united repose! FaBoPP

The Hawthorn. *Anonymous.* The fairest of earthkin/My leman she shall be. GBP; OxBM

Hawthorn Dyke. Algernon Charles Swinburne. ...and man and flower/and bird/Here are one at heart with all things seen/and heard. VLP

The Hawthorn Hath a Deathly Smell. Walter De la Mare. Wreathed shall with incense be/Thy sharp-thorned may. AtBAP; BrPo

The Hawthorn Hedge. Judith Wright. The hawthorn hedge took root, grew wild and high/to hide behind. PoAu 1-2

The Hawthorn Tree. Willa Cather. Not what he said to me! HBMV

Hawthorne. Amos Bronson Alcott. Whilst 'neath our pines thou feignest/ deathlike sleep? AA

Hawthorne. Henry Wadsworth Longfellow. The unfinished window in Aladdin's tower/Unfinished must remain! MAmP; NCEP; PoEL 1-5

A Hawthorne Garland. Richard Harter Fogle.
And cured the poor girl of her life. OBAL
For your quite unoriginal sin. OBAL
It was a great treat/To his lofty New-England nose. OBAL
Though some have complained of tenuity. OBAL

A Hawthorne Garland: Scarlet Letter. Richard Harter Fogle. That I've finally managed my A. OBAL

Hay, Ay, Hay, Ay. *Anonymous.* Make we merry as we may. SBVL

Hay for the Horses. Gary Snyder. And dammit, that's just what/I've gone and done.' ConAP; CTBA; GrPl; InPS; NaP; PAI

The Hay Hotel. *Anonymous.* So much depends on bed and board/They give them in the Hay Hotel. BIrV

Hay Is for Horses. *Anonymous.* And wash for old sows. OxNR

Hay's Wharf. Richard Church. Over the Bridge and past Hay's Wharf! HaMV

Hay Scuttle. Robert Morgan. Only way out to the sun is down/through the exquisite filth. MAYP

Hay-Time; or The Constant Lovers. A Pastoral. Josiah Relph. Up, Cursty, up; for God's sake let me gang,/For fear the maister put us in a sang. NOEC

The Hayeswater Boat (excerpt). Matthew Arnold. All else, black water: and afloat,/One rood from shore, that single boat. FaBoPP

Haying. John Frederic Herbin. With hissing stir, among the dusty beams. CaP; PeCV

Hayll, Comly and Clene. *Anonymous.* And go to the tenys. AtBAP; OxBoLi

Haymakers, Rakers. Thomas Dekker. Now the deer falls; hark, how they ring! ELP; ViBoPo

Haymaking. Edward ("Edward Eastaway") Thomas. Immortal in a picture of an old grange. AnFE; BrPo; MoAB; MoBrPo; SeCePo

The Haymow. Luella Markley Mockett. And there they lived–till the rain was over. BrR

The Hayseed. Arthur L. Kellog. The monopolies banded together/To beat a poor hayseed like me. FSW

Hayseed (with music). *Anonymous.* This hayseed was strictly dead in it. AS

The Haystack. Andrew Young. Where cow and horse will eat wall, roof and gable. PoL

The Haystack in the Floods. William Morris. This was the parting that they had/Beside the haystack in the floods. BeLS; CABA; EBEV; ExPo; HAP; LiTL; LoBV; NBM; NoP; OAEL 1-2; OAEP; OBNC; OBNV; PoEL 1-5; PoRA; SeCeV; VLP; WHA

Haywood. Harold LaMont Otey. i know. LFAC

Hazard. Nils Petersen. I only know your head is at my shoulder,/and that we are so small, so insect-small... LiTW

The Hazard of Loving the Creatures. Isaac Watts. For we have all in thee. CEP

Hazardous Occupations. Carl Sandburg. Do the bones repeat: It's a good act–/we got a good hand....? SaC

Haze. Henry David Thoreau. Establish thy serenity o'er the fields. HeIP; InPo; NoP; PoPl

A Hazel Stick for Catherine Ann. Seamus Heaney. a tiny brightening den lit the eye/in the blunt cut end of your stick. FaBoIP

Hazlitt Sups.   Katharine Day Little.   looked prodigiously/like a tree. GoYe

He.   John Ashbery.   He is dangerous even though asleep and unarmed. SOTW

He.   Lawrence Ferlinghetti.   Death   NeAP; PoM

He.   Ronald Koertge.   My mother dials and says,/"Here he is."   Str

He.   Stanley Jasspon Kunitz.   Redemption hangs upon the nails.   CrMA; VGW

He Abjures Love.   Thomas Hardy.   A few sad vacant hours,/And then, the Curtain.   OBNC

He accepts the circle, speech and so.   Anne-Marie Albiach.   formulae/the one for place   BoWoP

He and I.   Dante Gabriel Rossetti.   Even in my place he weeps. Even I, not he.   MaVP; NBM

He and She.   Mrs. Major Arnold.   And know that, though dead, I have never died.   BLPA

He and She.   Eugene Fitch Ware.   I'd ever want another man/Like you? PoLf; YaD

He Approacheth the Hall of Judgment.   Book of the Dead.   Yea. Millions-of-Years, O my Mother, my Heart!   AWP

A He as O.   Edward Estlin Cummings.   ...ca/n/is/ell drunk if i/be pencils InPS; PAI

He Asked about the Quality.   Constantine P. Cavafy.   Quickly, secretly, so the shop owner sitting at the back/wouldn't realize what was going on. PeHV

He Asketh Absolution of God.   Book of the Dead.   That thou and I henceforth may be at peace!   AWP

He ate and drank the precious words.   Emily Dickinson.   What liberty/A loosened spirit brings!   AA

He Bare Him Up, He Bare Him Down.   Anonymous.   By that bed's side there stands a stone,/"Corpus Christi" writ thereon.   MeEV

He Biddeth Osiris to Arise from the Dead.   Book of the Dead.   Come forth, O Quiet Heart,–I have avenged thee.   AWP

He Bringeth Them Unto Their Desired Haven.   Lewis Frank Tooker.   Until for them the very ground/Doth blossom with his fame.   HBV 1-2

He Came to Visit Me.   Martin Seymour-Smith.   The endless drummers of subtracting night.   FaBoTw

He Came Too Late.   Elizabeth Bogart.   She nerved her heart with woman's pride,/And spurned his fickle love.   AA

He Came Unlook'd For.   Sara Coleridge.   Or still in night's dark prison stay.   OBRV

He Cares.   Owen C. Salway.   Wherever you meet Him, He's waiting/there. STF

He Careth.   Marianne Farningham.   Oh, rest in peace, for the Lord will care!   WBLP

He Charges Her to Lay Aside Her Weapons.   Pierce Ferriter.   Oh, lay those arms of yours aside.   AnIL; LiTW; OnYI

He Comes among.   George Barker.   Turning and burning through slow leaves of vague/Urge, shall, until age.   OBMV

He Cometh Forth into the Day.   Book of the Dead.   In the beautiful world by the bright Lake of Horus,/Riseth the Day.   AWP

He Commandeth a Fair Wind.   Book of the Dead.   And I sail in a boat named the Assembler of Souls.   AWP

He Cool, Baby.   Rob Penny.   that's why we/ain't got nuthin   PoBA

He Could Have Found His Way.   Kathleen Dalziel.   ...he felt that spell begin/To work, not needing words.   PoAu 1-2

He'd Nothing But His Violin.   Mary Kyle Dallas.   And I my sweet love-song.   AA; HBV 1-2

He Defendeth His Heart against the Destroyer.   Book of the Dead.   I am the Flower-Bush that blooms for ever.   AWP

He Did Not Know.   Harry Kemp.   And knew that he was dead.   WGRP

"He Didn't Oughter..."   Sir Alan Patrick Herbert.   Why can't he wait till I've gone up to bed?   ALV; FiBHP

He Died for Me.   George Washington Bethune.   For I, thy Saviour, died for thee.   BePJ

He "Digesteth Harde Yron".   Marianne Moore.   This one remaining rebel/is the sparrow-camel.   CMoP; NoAm

He Doeth All Things Well.   Anne Bronte.   O let me serve Thee now! TRV

He Done His Level Best.   Mark (Samuel Langhorne Clemens) Twain.   No matter what his contract was,/HE'D DO HIS LEVEL BEST.   BPAW

He Drunken Rose.   Amarou.   So, busy jargoner, silent for ever more. AWP

He Embarketh in the Boat of Ra.   Book of the Dead.   In thy Boat, O Traveler!   AWP

He Entereth the House of the Goddess Hathor.   Book of the Dead.   For lo, I too would follow/Hathor, who is Love.   AWP

He Establisheth His Triumph.   Book of the Dead.   Open wide the Gate of Death/For me who bear the Rod of Gold/Victorious through the Dark! AWP

He Fell Among Thieves.   Sir Henry Newbolt.   Over the pass the voices one by one/Faded, and the hill slept.   BBV; FaPoR; HBV 1-2; HBVY; OBEV; OBVV; OBWP; OnMSP; OxBTC

He Fishes with His Father's Ghost.   Lewis Nordan.   We sop up with warm white bread.   AMV-81

He Fumbles at Your Soul.   Emily Dickinson.   When Winds take Forests in their Paws–/The Universe–is still–.   AmePo; NOCV

He Gave Himself for Me.   Anonymous.   To sing throughout eternal years,/He gave Himself for me.   STF

He Gives His Beloved Certain Rhymes.   William Butler Yeats.   Live but to light your passing feet.   EG

He Giveth.   Annie Johnson Flint.   He giveth and giveth and giveth again.   BLRP; TRV; WBLP

He Has Fallen from the Height of His Love.   Wilfrid Scawen Blunt.   ...woman half so sweet,/Or death so bitter, or at such dear feet?   ViBoPo

He Has Observ'd the Golden Rule.   William Blake.   Till he's become the Golden Fool.   PV

He Has Served Eighty Masters.   Lesbia Harford.   What sort of thing men who are masters grow.   PoAu 1-2

He Hears the Cry of the Sedge.   William Butler Yeats.   your breast will not lie by the breast/Of your beloved in sleep.   OxBTC

He Hears with Gladdened Heart the Thunder.   Robert Louis Stevenson.   Expectant of the certain end.   GoTF; TreFT

He Held Radical Light.   Archie Randolph Ammons.   ...demanded he/was like any one of us.   NoAm

He Hides Within the Lily.   William Channing Gannett.   Thy purpose crowning all!   AH

He Holdeth Fast to the Memory of His Identity.   Book of the Dead.   Let me remember then the name I bore!   AWP

He Is a Path.   Giles the Younger Fletcher.   A pleasure without loss; a treasure without stealth.   TRV

He Is Coming.   Gladys M. Gearhart.   But to know that He is coming/Fills the soul with pure delight.   STF

He Is Coming, Adzed-Head.   Anonymous.   and his people will answer/ "Amen, amen."   NOBI

He Is Declared True of Word.   Book of the Dead.   And make me thy Beloved.   AWP

He Is Far.   Anonymous.   Now I sike and mourne stille,/For he is far. OAEL 1-2; OxBM

He Is Like the Lotus.   Anonymous.   I blossom in the Field.   EaLo

He Is Like the Lotus.   Book of the Dead.   I blossom in the Field.   AWP

He Is Like the Serpent Saka.   Book of the Dead.   Even as I die and am born.   AWP

He Is More Than a Hero.   Sappho.   ...At such times/death isn't far from me.   PBWP

He Is My Countryman.   Antoni Slonimski.   He is my brother-man. He is humanity.   TrJP

He is not dead that sometime hath a fall.   Sir Thomas Wyatt.   And eke the willow that stoopeth with the wind/Doth rise again, and greater wood doth bind.   AAS; FCP; OBVE

He Is Our Peace.   Molly Anderson Haley.   Owning no rule save his can set men free!   PGD

He is the Lonely Greatness.   Madeleine Caron Rock.   Those darkened eyes. CAW; CH

He Kindleth a Fire.   Book of the Dead.   In peace the Eye of Horus liveth. AWP

He Knoweth Not That the Dead Are Thine.   Mary Elizabeth Coleridge.   They do not know/Life from its ghost.   ELU; OBNC

He Knoweth the Souls of the East.   Book of the Dead.   The Fields of Peace have been given to me as my City.   AWP

He Knows the Way.   Anonymous.   I'll see the face/Of Him who journeyed on before–/Saved by His grace.   STF

He Leadeth Me.   H. H. Barry.   Why in His wisdom He hath led me so. BLRP

He Leadeth Me.   Joseph Henry Gilmore.   Since 'tis my God that leadeth me!   AH; BLRP; WBLP; WGRP

He Leads Us Still.   Arthur Guiterman.   The Nation Lincoln died for cannot fail!   OHIP

He Lifted from the Dust.   Helen Rogers Smith.   Our hope and stay along a war-worn way,/Whose end is–Christ!   BePJ

He Liked the Dead.   Malcolm Lowry.   nor was sun, sun; rose, rose; smoke, smoke; limb, limb.   OxBTC

He Lived a Life.   H. N. Fifer.   I only know he lived a life, a life, in deed! PoToHe

He Lived amidst th' Untrodden Ways.   Hartley Coleridge.   It's still in Longman's shop, and oh!/The difference to him!   FaBoCo; Par

He Lives! He Lives to Bless!   Dorothy Conant Stroud.   Then all of heaven's blessedness/Into your heart He'll bring!   STF

He Lives Long Who Lives Well.   Thomas Randolph.   I say he only WAS– he did not LIVE.   WBLP

He Liveth Long Who Liveth Well.   Horatius Bonar.   And find a harvest-home of light.   HBV 1-2; HBVY

He loved three things in life. Anna Akhmatova. ...And I was his wife. BoWoP

He Loves and He Rides Away. Sydney Thomas Dobell. And come out of my grave and bear the awful eyes. OBNC

He Loves Me. *Anonymous.* But he can't/So he don't. OxNR

He Made the Night. Lloyd Mifflin. He snatched a remnant flying into light/And strewed it with the stars, and called it Night. HBV 1-2

He Made Us Free. Maurice Francis Egan. And rise,–be free! AA

He Maketh Himself One with Osiris. Book of the Dead. Beareth me with him. AWP

He Maketh Himself One with the God Ra. Book of the Dead. The Child of Light who findeth his Father in the/Evening. AWP

He Maketh Himself One with the Only God, Whose Limbs Are the Many God. Book of the Dead. Shall drag me back from my immortal path! AWP

He Maketh No Mistake. A. M. Overton. He made not one mistake. STF

He May Be Envied, Who with Tranquil Breast. Charlotte Smith. Knows, in refined retirement, to possess/By friendship hallow'd–rural happiness! SBG

He Meditates on the Life of a Rich Man. Augusta Gregory, Lady Gregory. What are you better after tonight/Than Ned the beggar or Seaghan the fool? OBMV

He Met Her at the Green Horse... Peter Levi. or like walking/past shut doors/in a never quiet street and talking. NePoEA-2

He Never Did That to Me. Noel Coward. He never did that to me. NLV

He Never Expected Much. Thomas Hardy. And hence could stem such strain and ache/As each year might assign. NAs; NoAm; OxBTC; SCV

He Never Smiled Again. Felicia Dorothea Hemans. He never smiled again! HBV 1-2

He Never Will Forget. M. G. H. And He'll soon come back to take me/Where with Him I'll always be. STF

He Overcometh the Serpent of Evil in the Name of Ra. Book of the Dead. Behold I am Ra of the Eastern and Western Skies! AWP

He Paid Me Seven (parody). *Anonymous.* An' if I hadn't tuck dat, I wouldn' git none. BPo

He Poet in His Poverty. Nizami. For I shall look upon thee, if thou seest not me. LiTW

He Praises Her Hair. *Anonymous.* A breast for men to love. AnIL

He Praises His Wife When She Had Gone from Him. Robin Flower. A lonely shell in place/Of that unrivalled grace. OxBI

He Praises His Wife When She Has Left Him. *Anonymous.* Of that unrivalled grace. AnIL

He Praises the Trees. *Anonymous.* proudly the tangle/of the wind. BIrV

He Prayeth for Ink and Palette That He May Write. Book of the Dead. And thou shalt find that I have written truly. AWP

He preached upon breadth. Emily Dickinson. What confusion would cover the innocent Jesus/To meet so enabled a Man! NAWM 1-2; NOCV

He Puts Me to Rest. David Ignatow. He puts me to rest. VGW

He Raise a Poor Lazarus. *Anonymous.* Git ready and let us go home. AH

He Records a Little Song for a Smoking Girl. James Whitehead. ...Forgive, forgive/My cigarettes, I swallowed smoke alive. GP

He Remembers Forgotten Beauty. William Butler Yeats. Brood her high lonely mysteries. CTC; LLLT

He Renounceth All the Effects of Love. Thomas, Lord Vaux. I make the fire and burn myself with sparks. EnRePo

He Resigns. John Berryman. ...I must start/to sit with a blind brow/above an empty heart. OBSP; SM; WeW

He Resolves to Say No More. Thomas Hardy. And show to no man what I see. TEP

He Roman Road. Thomas Hardy. We walked that ancient thoroughfare,/The Roman Road. InPo

He Runs into an Old Acquaintance. Alden Nowlan. that she would have smiled and said, "Yes,"/if I had asked; and I didn't know. GOYP

He's a Fool. *Anonymous.* He's a fool for not joining the union. FSW

He's Come! The Saviour Has Come! Alice Mortenson. "He 's come! The Saviour has come!" BePJ

He's Coming. Mark Van Doren. Where? O you the south wind,/Keep soft and strong today. FaBV

He's Doing Natural Life. Conyus. dining at the white house PoBA

He's Gone away. *Anonymous.* Look away, look away over Yandro. FSW; TrAS

He's Gone Away (with music). *Anonymous.* But he's comin' back if he goes ten thousand miles. AS

He's Got the Whole World in His Hands. *Anonymous.* He's got the whole world in His hands. BLSo; FSW

He's Jus' de Same Today. *Anonymous.* An' de God dat lived in Daniel's time is jus' de same today. BoAN 1-2

He Said. Jean Valentine. ...and some days all/I can want is sleep. TAP

He Said He Had Been a Soldier. Dorothy Wordsworth. I gave him a piece of cold bacon/And a penny. SaC

He Said: "If in His Image I Was Made." Trumbull Stickney. But God was seen no longer any more. AnFE; APA; LiTA

He Said, Lying There. Alta. "i love you, alta" his voice/in my whole body like a blessing. GP

He Said That He Was Not Our Brother. John Banim. Let him come, the Brigand! let him come! OnYI

He Said the Facts. Merrill Moore. The only things that concern me are the acts.' CrMA

He Satisfies. Frederick William Faber. There's not a wish the heart can have/Which Thou dost not fulfill. BePJ

He Saw Far in the Concave Green of the Sea. John Keats. Where through some sucking pool I will be hurl'd/With rapture to the other side of the world! EtS

He Says He Wrote by Moonlight. Katharyn Machan Aal. I haven't seen the moon in two years. AMV-81

He scanned it, staggered, dropped the loop. Emily Dickinson. Caressed a trigger absently/And wandered out of life. PoEL 1-5

He Sees through Stone. Etheridge Knight. he sees through stone. BALP; ConAP; LFAC; NBP; NNaP

He Shall Speak Peace. Thomas Curtis Clark. For He shall speak peace. WBLP

He Shall Speak Peace Unto the Nations. Lila V. Walters. In His own time "He shall speak peace." BePJ; WBLP

He Shot at Lee Wing. *Anonymous.* A slight but regrettable/Slip of the Tong. ShM

He Singeth a Hymn to Osiris, the Lord of Eternity. Book of the Dead. Where I may sow and reap those sunny fields of wheat/and barley. AWP

He Singeth in the Underworld. Book of the Dead. And goest on thy way. AWP

He Sits down on the Floor of a School for the Retarded. Alden Nowlan. huddled together for a little while by the fire/in the Ice Age, two hundred thousand years ago. GOYP

He Speaks of His Condition through Love. Folcachiero de' Folcachieri. On him who is burned up, yea, visibly. AWP

He Sports by Himself (parody). Susan Miles. And with nine phasms zestless play/That grin and rave. BXAP

He That Fights and Runs Away. *Anonymous.* Will never rise to fight again. TreF

He That Hath No Mistress. *Anonymous.* False Cupid, I will have thee whipped, and have thy mother/carted. GBL; OBSP

He That Is Near Me Is Near the Fire. Origen. He that is far from me is far from the Kingdom. TRV

He That Loves. Sir Philip Sidney. Hath no warrant to aqquire/The dainties of his chaste desire. ErPo

He That Marries a Merry Lass. *Anonymous.* He had better be without her. ALV

He That Ne'er Learns His ABC. *Anonymous.* But he that learns these letters fair/Shall have a coach to take the air. GBP; GLGT

He That Never Read a Line. *Anonymous.* Doth in eternal glory shine. AnIL

He That Would Thrive. *Anonymous.* He that will never thrive/May lie till eleven. HBV 1-2; HBVY; OxNR

He the Beloved (excerpt). Qorratu'l-Ayn. Break it, and hold at last my soul's clear pearl. WPOW

He Thinks of His Past Greatness... William Butler Yeats. Must I endure your amorous cries? DTC; OAEP; PoEL 1-5

He Thinks of Those Who Have Spoken Evil of His Beloved. William Butler Yeats. Their children's children shall say they have lied. CTC; ELU; NOBV

He Told His Life Story to Mrs. Courtly. Stevie Smith. But we can have some conversation before it is too late.' NLV

He Told Me His Name Was Sitting Bull. Joy Harjo. his name will follow me on the interstate/all the way into the center of oklahoma. TAT

He Took Her. Tom (Thomas Lansing Masson) Masson. And finally he took her. OBAL

He Took My Place. Horatius Bonar. I take the gift, Lord, look on me/As one who has Thy gift received. BePJ

He Tries out the Concords Gently. Edward (Edward Dzyubin) Bagritsky. Bursts in unexpected laughs? TrJP

He Understands the Great Cruelty of Death. John Millington Synge. ...and he got up in the way, like an armed robber, with a pike in/his hand. BIrV; OBMV

He Visits a Hospital. Rolfe Humphries. For otherwise, how could I shrink/At entering these walls? AnAmPo

He Waiata mo Te Kare. James Keir Baxter. ...Te Kare,/Is that you are not beside me. OCNZ

He Walketh by Day. Book of the Dead. My spirit is God. AWP

He Walks at Peace. Tao Te Ching. Because he walks at peace with life/And death. TRV

He Was. Richard Wilbur. And the found voice of his buried hands/Rose in the sparrowy air. NCSH; SaC

He Was a Friend of Mine. *Anonymous.* He was a friend of mine. FSW

He Was Formidable. Robert Penn Warren. To that clobber, and slobber, and scream, between the boxcars? LiSp

He Was Not Willing. Lucy R. Meyer. Banish our worldliness, help us to ever/Live with eternity's values in view. STF

He Was Weak. Emily Dickinson. We didn't do it–tho'! PeD

He Who Binds to Himself a Joy. William Blake. But he who kisses the joy as it flies/Lives in eternity's sun rise. EBEV

He Who Has Lost All. David Diop. Tom-toms of my nights, tom-toms of my fathers. TTY

He Who Has Never Known Hunger. Elizabeth Jane Coatsworth. The kindliness of food. TiPo

He Who Hath Loved. Walter Malone. And winged through ever-blooming fields/of heaven. AA

He Who in His Pocket Hath No Money. Anonymous. Should, in his mouth, be never without honey. HBV 1-2

He Who Knows. Anonymous. He who knows, and knows that he knows, is wise, follow him. BLPA

He Who Stole My Virginity. Silabhattarika. Narmada in/the Vindhya mountains. WPOW

He Whom a Dream Hath Possessed. Shaemas O'Sheel. And rides God's battle-field in a flashing and golden car. AnIV; HBV 1-2; HBVY; TRV; WGRP

He Will Give Them Back. George Klingle. That for a little while we were so sad. BLRP

He Wishes for the Cloths of Heaven. William Butler Yeats. Tread softly because you tread on my dreams. CMoP; NOBV; OLR; SOTW

He Wishes He Might Die and Follow Laura. Petrarch (Francesco Petrarca). Oh, what a sweet death I might have died this day three/years to-day! OBMV

He Wore a Crown of Thorns. Alice Mortenson. That when He calls I'll worthy be/To wear a crown of light. BePJ

He Would Have His Lady Sing. Digby Mackworth Dolben. So we the Doom may pass,/And see Him in the Face. CAW; EBEV; GoBC

He Would Not Stay for Me. Alfred Edward Housman. And went with half my life about my ways. PeHV

The Head. Padraic Fallon. What happens and the happening/That will never come to pass. CIP

A Head. James Schuyler. ...So what/if it fades and dies? NoAm; PoM

Head and Bottle. Edward ("Edward Eastaway") Thomas. Quiet in the yard where tree trunks do not lie/More quietly. BrPo

Head Bumper. Anonymous. Gully, gully, gully. OxNR

Head Couples. William H. Matchett. Our lives, in a slow quadrille, have intertwined. NYBP

The Head Is a Paltry Matter. Pier Giorgio Di Cicco. and their lips set to ignite one future after another. NOBC

Head of Medusa. Marya Zaturenska. Emptied of all its sorrow and its dread! MoAmPo

The Head-Stone. William Barnes. When tha be dead that lov'd it. OBVV

The Head That Once Was Crowned with Thorns. Thomas Kelly. Their joy the joy of heaven. TRV

Heading for Eugene. Lorenza Schmidt. Heading for Eugene FIA

Headland. Brewster Ghiselin. The sea-rocks dolphin-dark the green wave frays. PoA

The Headless Gardener. Ian Serraillier. He never sent up his address. BoC

Headline History. William Plomer. "Not End of World,' says Well-Known Red. FaBoCo

Headlined in Heaven. Paul L. Grano. THEY WEPT UPON THE STOCK EXCHANGE. NOAV

Headsong. Joseph Bennett. One side in death; the other burning. NePA

The Healer (excerpt). John Greenleaf Whittier. The Healer by Gennesaret/Shall walk the rounds with thee. PGD

Healing. Charlotte De Clue. it means gathon ihn don....tomorrow. TWSS

Healing. Abraham Reisen. And perhaps I'll be a fool/Again, and young. LiTW; TrJP

The Healing of the Leper. Vernon Watkins. "Be nothing first; and then, be love." FaBoTw

Healing Song. Anonymous. They walk uncertainly,/That is all. OBVE

Healing the Wound. Heinrich Heine. And what long kisses and what delight/In such a night may be! UnTE

Health. Stewart Parker. And the lifting of arms to embrace. CIP

A Health. Edward Coate [(or Coote)] Pinkney. That life might be all poetry,/And weariness a name. AA; AmePo; AnAmPo; GoTF; HBV 1-2; TreFS

Health. Edward ("Edward Eastaway") Thomas. Though scarce this Spring could my body leap four yards. SeCePo

Health and Fitness. J. B. Morton. Now masseur's in the cold, cold ground. FaBoCo

A Health at the Ford. Robert Cameron Rogers. But tell her that I love her, and say I drank/her health/To-day at Deadman's Bar. AA; FaBoBe

Health Counsel. Sir John (1561-1612) Harington. Joy, Temperance and Repose/Slam the door on the doctor's nose. GoTF; TreFT

Health Food. Anonymous. An apple a day/Keeps the doctor away. FaBoUs

A Health Note. Walter Hard. Then I do when I'm well. AnNE

Health of Body Dependent on Soul. Jones Very. And made the body's health depend/Upon the living soul. WGRP

A Health to the Tackers. Anonymous. That who is not still for conformity bill/Will be surely a rogue on occasion. APAS

A Healthy Spot. W. H. Auden. Alone, ironically enough, stands up for. EnLit

The Heap of Rags. William Henry Davies. To many bitter fears/To make a pearl from tears? BrPo

Heap on More Wood. Sir Walter Scott. The boisterous joys of Odin's hall. OBCP; TiPo

Heaps on Heaps. Matthew Concanen. And Heaps on Heaps in wild Disorder fall. SD

Hear, Hear, O Ye Nations. Frederick Lucian Hosmer. And lead the world-triumph of peace and good will. AH

Hear Me Yet. Anonymous. And now leave me to my despair. EIL

Hear, O Israel. Andre Spire. To arms! TrJP; VWA

Hear, Sweet Spirit. Samuel Taylor Coleridge. The boatmen rest their oars and say,/Miserere Domine! ViBoPo

Hear the Bird of Day. David Campbell. What's matter but a hardening of the light? GTBS-P; NOAV

Hear the Voice of the Bard! William Blake. The wat'ry shore,/Is giv'n thee till the break of day. CBEP; ELP; EnPE; NOBE; NU; OBEC; OBEV

Hear Us, in This Thy House. Philip Doddridge. And sleep in death, to rest with God. BePJ

Heard in a Violent Ward. Theodore Roethke. And that sweet man, John Clare. HaCAP; NoAm

Heard in the Cougate. Robert Garioch. "Ah ddae-ken whu' the pplace is comin tae/wi aw thae, hechyuch! fforeign po'entates." OxBTC

Heard on the Mountain. Victor Hugo. The vintage-chant of nature with the dirging cry of/humankind? AWP

Hearing Men Shout at Night on MacDougal Street. Robert Bly. The first New England slave-ship with the/Negroes in the hold. CAD; InPS

Hearing of the End of the War. Richard Tillinghast. flutter/and shatter/against the Great Divide. MAYP

Hearing Russian Spoken. Donald Davie. She trades on broken English with success/And, disenchanted, I'm enamoured yet. GTBS-P; NePoEA-2

Hearing Steps. Charles Simic. Until the last word and the last sound/Of this language I am speaking is forgotten. HaCAP

Hearing That His Friend Was Coming Back from the War. Wang Chien. So that suddenly I might find you standing at my side! LiTW

Hearing the Early Oriole. Po Chu-i. The bird would sing as it sang in the Palace of old. UnS

Hearing the Wind at Night. May Swenson. soothing themselves to sleep. BoNaP

The Hearse Song. Anonymous. And you look like hell when they're through with you. ABF; DTC; FSW; OxBoLi

The Hearse Song (with music). Anonymous. And the worms crawl out and the worms crawl in/And your limbs drop off of you limb by limb. AS

The Heart. Anonymous. "Are you hurt, my lad, are you hurt at all?/O, my own!" MaC

Heart. MacKnight Black. And stirs, remoteas south wind, through your breast. AnAmPo

The Heart. Stephen Crane. And because it is my heart. HoPM; InPK; MoAmPo; TW

The Heart. David Ignatow. that open on the day, fresh and willing/from having studied the heart. VWA

Heart. Joan LaBombard. And it keeps Time for you/with all the impartiality of a judge or a good watch. PPJ

The Heart. Harvey Shapiro. The crazed and hooded creatures of the heart. HoPM

The Heart. Jakov Steinberg. Its youthful dreams, its secret bliss. TrJP

The Heart. Francis Thompson. And all man's Babylons strive but to impart/The grandeurs of his Babylonian heart. BoLiVe; OBMV

Heart and Mind. Edith Sitwell. Will the fire of the heart and the fire of the mind be one AtBAP; ChMP; MoPo; MP; OAEP; OxBTC; SiPS; TwCP

The heart and service to you proffered. Sir Thomas Wyatt. Reward your servant liberally. FCP

The Heart Asks Pleasure First. Emily Dickinson. The liberty to die. AmPP; AnNE; CMoP; InPo; MoAB; MoAmPo; NOBA; NoP; OxBA; PPP; PrIm; SBG; TrGrPo

Heart Burial. Geoffrey Grigson. Earth fell on the box and the biscuit tin. PoL

The Heart Flies Up, Erratic as a Kite. Delmore Schwartz. Light! Light like the deathless past remains. PoA

Heart for All Her Children. Albert J. Hebert, Jr. ...and in all those strange/And varied lands, men were her children, and men had her love. ISi

The Heart Has Its Reasons. Anonymous. Let not its mockery hurt you. Ah, sing low. GoBC

The Heart Has Its Reasons. Felice Picano. For that I could never forgive you. PeHV

Heart-Hurt. *Anonymous.* And all the city heard him moan. TreFT

The Heart Is Deep. Roger Wolcott. ...Tis he alone that can/Find out Cursed Policies of Man. SCAP

A Heart Made Full of Thought. Maghnas O Domhnaill. –such my parting, in troubled tiredness,/from the partner of my heart. NOBI

The Heart Mountain Japanese Relocation Camp: 30 Years Later. Charles Levendosky. their silences burn like pine knots/campfire on a cold night. TAT

The Heart of a Girl is a Wonderful Things. *Anonymous.* For the heart of a girl is a wonderful thing! BLPA

The Heart of a Woman. Georgia Douglas Johnson. While it breaks, breaks, breaks on the sheltering bars. BANP; BlSi; CDC; PoLf; PoNe

The Heart of All the Scene (From "Woodnotes"). Ralph Waldo Emerson The clay of their departed lover. AA

The Heart of God. W. E. Littlewood. Till our souls should rest, in peace, on His breast,/In the heavenly home! BePJ

The Heart of Herakles. Kenneth Rexroth. The tipping earth, the swarming stars/Have an eye that sees itself. NU

Heart of Light. David Campbell. And let such days atone/For those when we are many and alone. BoAV

The Heart of Midlothian. Sir Walter Scott. "Welcome, proud lady".' BSV; EnRP; OAEP

Heart of My Heart. *Anonymous.* That there was not a single hour/We might have kissed, and did not kiss! HBV 1-2

Heart of Oak. David Garrick. We'll fight and we'll conquer again and again. HBV 1-2; NOEC; OBEC; OxBoLi

Heart of Oak. Charles Henry Luders. Ere thy whole soul be slain by cankerous sin. AA

Heart-of-the-Daybreak. Eugene Marais. the small footprints of Nampti/that make my heart sing.' PeSA

The Heart of the Night. Dante Gabriel Rossetti. This soul may see thy face, O Lord of death! MaVP

The Heart of the Tree. Henry Cuyler Bunner. A nations's growth from sea to sea/Stirs in his heart who plants a tree. OHFP; OHIP; PGD

The Heart of the Woman. William Butler Yeats. My breath is mixed into his breath. GTBS

Heart of the Woods. Wesley Curtright. Lost so long ago–/In the Heart of the Woods. GoSl; PoNe

The Heart of the World. Nahman of Bratzlav. And each day comes with its own/songs,/According to the day. TrJP

The Heart of Thomas Hardy. Sir John Betjeman. Died away in the night as frost will blacken a dahlia. TW

Heart Oppress'd with Desperate Thought. Sir Thomas Wyatt. Wherefore all joy I do refuse,/And cruel will thereof accuse. SiPS

The Heart Recalcitrant. Leonora Speyer. A treasure-ship that journeys/Across its own oblivion? PG

The Heart's Abysses. Walter Savage Landor. To see the abysses of the human heart. FaBoEE; OBSV

The Heart's Anchor. William Winter. Is honor rich enough for me. PoToHe

Heart's Compass. Dante Gabriel Rossetti. Stakes with a smile the world against thy heart. MaVP; WHA

Heart's Content. *Anonymous.* And win no more the port of home–/The only Heart's Content! HBV 1-2; PoLf

The Heart's Friend. Mary Austin. She, my heart's friend. BPAW

The Heart's Location. Peter Meinke. and a poem full of ordinary words/about simple things/in the inconsolable rhythms of the heart. GOYP

The Heart's Low Door. Susan Mitchell. And find where Love's red embers glow/A home, who ne'er had home before. HBMV

Heart's Music. *Anonymous.* Love alone to Him is ever pleasing. CAPP; OBEV

Heart's Needle. W. D. Snodgrass.
And you are still my daughter. AmPC; CoPo; SM
because a cricket, who/had minstrelled every night outside/her window, died. NePoEA
Because when they come to full flower/I will be off away. NePoEA
Conceded to the jaw/Of toothed, blue steel. AP
I hold you in my hands. NCSH; NMP; NoPoEA
...Indeed our sweet/foods leave us cavities. NePoEA; NoAm
...We try to choose our life. ConAP; NePoEA

The Heart's Proof. James Buckham. By a thousand, thousand things! BLRP; WBLP

The Heart's Summer. Epes Sargent In our hearts 'tis summer still. AA

The Heart's Wild Geese. Henry Treece. As heart returns to home, year upon year. WaP

Heart Specialist. Elias Lieberman. A wastrel who can spend no more. ImOP

Heart-Summoned. Jesse Stuart. Accompanied, perhaps, by/cloud or star. GoYe

A Heart That's Been Broken. Maureen Owen. swings open & shut/like a gate. LLLT

A Heart That Weeps. Oswald J. Smith. Souls, precious souls, my ceaseless cry. STF

The Heart to Carry On. Bertram Warr. And not lie dead in Germany. PeCV

A Heart to Praise Thee. George Herbert. But such a heart whose Pulse may be/Thy Praise. TRV

Heart, We Will Forget Him. Emily Dickinson.
I may remember him! AA; LiTL; OLR; ViBoPo
I remember him! LLLT

Heart Wounds. Claire Richcreek Thomas. The scar–will long remain. PoToHe

Heartbreak Camp. Roy Campbell. A far hyaena drilling/His company of stars. OxBTC

Heartbreak Road. Helen Gray Cone. I knew I walked that weary way/In a great company. HBMV

Hearth and Home. Stoddard King. Humble, yes, but not unsung,/Strictly modern 5-rm. bung.! OBAL

Hearth Song. Robert Underwood Johnson. Where's an older friend than fire? YeAr

Hearthside Story. X. J. Kennedy. O mistress mine, my kindling wood. CoPo

Hearthstone. Harold Monro. I want nothing now but your fire-side, friend. OBMV

Hearts and Flowers. Mary Dow Brine. Let my heart your garden be/Give the seeds of love to me. FSN

Hearts-Ease. Walter Savage Landor. Bring it; and bring enough for two. EnRP

Hearts, Like Doors, Will Ope with Ease. *Anonymous.* Are "I thank you" and "If you please." HBVY; OxNR

Hearts Were Made to Give Away. Annette Wynne. Hearts were made to give away/On Valentine's dear day. TiPo

Heartsearch. Evelyn K. Gibson. Following in Thy perfect way. STF

Heat. Anacreon. Love's the high fever of the mind. UnTE

Heat. Archibald Lampman. My thoughts grow keen and clear. CaP; NOBC; OBCV; PeCV

Heat. Kenneth Mackenzie. ...his hope/that heat would be arrested on its shore. AP; PoAu 1-2

Heat and Sweat. Mongane Wally Serote. move, child, move/if we don't get there/nobody must... WhB

The Heat in the Room. Weldon Kees. ...flames/Roared like a white-hot furnace, and she screamed. EAS

The Heath. Thomas Boyd. ...sudden clank of his horse's hoof/Frightens the Wanderer aloof. OnYI

The Heathen Chinee. Bret (Francis Bret Harte) Harte. The heathen Chinee is peculiar–/Which the same I am free to maintain. BPAW; CTC; FaBoCo; InMe

A Heathen Hymn (excerpt). Sir Lewis Morris. I know not what to fear or hope,/Nor aught but that Thy will is best. TrPWD

The Heathen Pass-ee. Arthur Clement Hilton. Which the same I am free to maintain. CenHV; FaBoCo; NOBL

The Heather. Steen Steensen Blicher. Larks thrill the waste with a rapture of song. LiTW

The Heather. Neil Munro. And still content, I'd find a bedding cheery/Where'er the heather grew! OBVV

Heather Ale. Robert Louis Stevenson. The secret of Heather Ale. AnEnPo

Heav'n Boun' Soldier. *Anonymous.* Hold out yo' light,/You heav'n boun' soldier,/Let yo' light shine a-roun' de world. BoAN 1-2

Heave Away. *Anonymous.*
And away, my jolly boys, we're all bound to go! ShS
Heave away! yellow gal I want to go. ABF; TrAS

Heave away, My Johnny. *Anonymous.* Where you get soft tack every day and none of your yellow meal. OBSS

Heaven. *Anonymous.*
I'd show you a good way to get in it. UnTE
Of waking up, and finding it Home. PoLf

Heaven. Rupert Brooke. There shall be no more land, say fish. AnFE; BrPo; EBEV; ExPo; HoPM; LiTB; LiTM; MoBrPo; NOBE; PoPle; PoRA; SeCeV; WGRP

Heaven. Martha Gilbert Dickinson. Dead for each other's sake. AA; HBV 1-2

Heaven. Digby Mackworth Dolben. And see him in the Face. BoC

Heaven. George Herbert. Echo. Ever. AnAnS 1; BoLiVe; SeCP; TrCP; TrGrPo

Heaven. Langston Hughes. "Well! And you?" GoSl

Heaven. Philip Levine. and no one to believe/that heaven was really here. LCAP; NaP

Heaven. Gary Soto. But still singing,/"Baby, baby, o baby." NPGG

Heaven and Earth. Frederic Thompson. And in a minute wander centuries away/In the deep sky. CAW

Heaven and earth and all that hear me plain. Sir Thomas Wyatt. Cruel, unkind! I say farewell, farewell! FCP; SiPS

Heaven and Hell. *Anonymous.* and when they snap at it, a puff of dust/ comes out of their dry throats. DL

Heaven and Hell. ·Francis Thompson. But ah, how few the God that loves! OBSP

Heaven-Haven. Gerard Manley Hopkins. And out of the swing of the sea. ACP; BrPo; CAW; CoBE; DiPo; GoBC; HeIP; LoBV; MoAB; MoBrPo; MOS; NoAm; NOBE; NOCV; OAEP; OBEV; OBNC; OBSP; SoSe; SOTW; TrGrPo; ViBoPo; VLP

Heaven in Ordinarie. Daniel Wolff. We live in a time gone black with bravery. SM

Heaven Is Heaven. Christina Georgina Rossetti. I know not if earth is merely earth,/Only that heaven is heaven. YeAr

Heaven Is Here. John G. Adams. This is heaven, its peace, its beauty,/ Radiant with the love of God. AH

Heaven Is Not Far. Christina Georgina Rossetti. O Lord, how long? OxBoCh

Heaven–Is What I Cannot Reach! Emily Dickinson. Enamored–of the Conjuror–/That spurned us–Yesterday! MAmP; NOCV

Heaven, O Lord, I Cannot Lose. Edna Dean Proctor. Thy Heaven, O Lord, I shall not lose! AA

The Heaven of Animals. James Dickey They rise, they walk again. AP; CAPP; CoAP; HeIP; LiTM; NCSH; NoAm; NOBA; TAP

Heaven Overarches Earth and Sea. Christina Georgina Rossetti. What though to-night wrecks you and me,/If so to-morrow saves? HBV 1-2

Heaven's Last Best Work. Alexander Pope. Shakes all together, and produces–You. OBEC

Heaven's Magnificence. William Augustus Muhlenberg. And robe me for that world of light. AA

Heaven Will Protect the Working Girl. Edgar Smith. But Heaven will protect the working girl. FaFP; FiBHP; TreF

The Heavenly Aeroplane. *Anonymous.* We'll blend our voices with the heavenly throng/And praise our Savior as the years roll on. NOCV

The Heavenly Banquet. Saint Brigid. I would like to be watching Heaven's family/drinking it through all eternity. OnYI

The Heavenly City. Stevie Smith. Gold are all heaven's rivers,/And silver her streams. FaBoTw

"Heavenly Father," take to thee. Emily Dickinson. We apologize to Thee/ For Thine own duplicity. AmePo; ILwL; PoEL 1-5

The Heavenly Foreigner. Denis Devlin.
Against the fortress of the Snow Princess. CIP
Nor oblique eyesight deciding other objects were there. CIP

A Heavenly Friend. Paul Tucker. If with our soul 'tis well. BePJ

Heavenly Grass. Tennessee Williams. But they still got an itch for heavenly grass. PoPl

The Heavenly Humor. David Shapiro. And with sparkling desire expected to come crashing through/the floor. ANYP

The Heavenly Jerusalem. Giles the Younger Fletcher. As in his burning throne he sits emparadis'd. OxBoCh

Heavenly Jerusalem, Jerusalem of the Earth. Leah Goldberg. Swallow with no nest./Arrested flight./What now? VWA

The Heavenly Pilot. Cormac Mac Cuilenan. God! wilt Thou grant aid to me/Who came o'er th' upheaving main? CAW; OnYI

The Heavenly Stranger. Ada Blenkhorn. And sing the glad story again and again. BLRP

The Heavenly Tree Grows Downward. Gerrit Lansing. Who bury the dead/to rise again. CoPo

Heavenly Vision. *Anonymous.* And who shall be able to stand? AmFP

The Heavens Are Our Riddle. Herbert Bates. Expectant of the silence of the skies. AA

Heavens Bright Lamp, Shine Forth Some of Thy Light. George Alsop. Heaven I hope will seat him on his Throne. SCAP

The Heavens Declare Thy Glory, Lord! Isaac Watts. But the blest volume thou has writ/Reveals thy justice and thy grace. TreFT

The Heavens Do Declare. *Anonymous.* ...and from the heat/Thereof is hid nothing. AH

Heavenward. Carolina Oliphant, Lady Nairne. Come life and light. HBV 1-2

Heavier the Cross. Benjamin Schmolck. Till for the cross my crown I wear. BePJ

The Heaviest Cross of All. Katherine Eleanor Conway. The crosses we make for ourselves,alas!/are the heaviest ones of all. AA

Heaving the Lead. J. Pearce. We hear the seaman with delight/Proclaim,– "All's well!" EtS

Heaving the Lead Line. *Anonymous.* Throw the lead line over–/No bottom here. AmFP

"The heavy bear who goes with me." Delmore Schwartz. The scrimmage of appetite everywhere. AmLP; LiTM; MiAP; MoPo; MP; NePA; NIP; NoAm; NOBA; TAP; TrJP; TwCP; UnPo

Heavy-Hearted. Judah Al-Harizi. Since from my hair they fled. TrJP

Heavy Heavy Heavy. John Malcolm Brinnin. "What shall ye do to redeem it?" NYBP

Heavy, Heavy–What Hangs Over? Kenneth Burke. A gust in the big tree/ splatters raindrops/on the roof PoL

Heavy-Hipted Woman. *Anonymous.* I won'be back, oh, babe, I won'be back. ABF

Hebe. James Russell Lowell. Follow thy life, and she will sue/To pour for thee the cup of honour! AA; AnFE; AnNE; APA; HBV 1-2

Hebrew Lesson. Max Brod. And our ancient God calling from the mountain. AMV-80

Hebrew Letters in the Trees. J. Rutherford Williams. And the sun was the same as yesterday. VWA

The Hebrew of Your Poets, Zion. Charles Reznikoff. none are like you, Shulamite. VGW

Hebrew Script. Tali Loewenthal. raining arrows of fire/into the great darkness. VWA

The Hebrew Sibyl. Ruth Fainlight. no-one will call me insane–/but God's great sibyl. VWA

Hebrews. James Oppenheim. Is a well in Asia. TrJP

The Hecatomb to His Mistress. John Cleveland. And makes the World but her Periphrasis. AnAnS 2

Hector. Valentin Iremonger. An upturned, dented helmet. CIP; NeIP; OxBI

Hector and Andromache. Alexander Pope. The first in Danger as the first in Fame. OBEC

Hector Protector Was Dressed All in Green. Mother Goose. So Hector Protector was sent back again. HBV 1-2; HBVY; MoShBr; OxNR

Hector the Collector. Shel Silverstein. And all the silly sightless people/ Came and looked...and called it junk. CTBA

Hector the Dog. Kate Barnes. But he'll miss him once the old dog's dead. GDP

A Hedge before Me. Saint Columcille. I write in a shady seat. BIrV

Hedge Life. James Dickey. King-walking hill after hill. LCAP

The Hedge Schoolmasters. Seumas MacManus. Who gathered their ragged classes behind a friendly hedge. CAW

The Hedgehog. John Clare. Though black and bitter and unsavoury meat. SeCeV

Hedgehog. Paul Muldoon. We forget that never again/Will a god trust in the world. BIrV

Hedges Freaked with Snow. Robert Graves. Hedges freaked with snow. OxBTC

Hedro's Lamp. Dante Gabriel Rossetti. O brother, what brought love to them or thee? MaVP

Heedless o' My Love. William Barnes. I can now wipe em away. GBL

Hegel. LeRoi (Imamu Amiri Baraka) Jones. I am wrong, but give me someone/to talk to. CoPo

A Heifer Clambers Up. Gary Snyder. fat/with the baby happy land NoAm; NOBA

Heigh Ho! My Heart Is Low. *Anonymous.* And T for my love Tom. OxNR

Heigh-Ho on a Winter Afternoon. Donald Davie. The bird will call at longer intervals. NePoEA-2; OxBTC

The Height of the Ridiculous. Oliver Wendell Holmes. And since I never dare to write/As funny as I can. AA; AmePo; AnNE; FaFP; FiBHP; FPL; HBV 1-2; MCCG; MoShBr; OBAL; OBCA; PoPl; TreFT; YaD

Heinrich Heine. Ludwig Lewisohn. The child of a diviner will. TrJP

Heir and Serf. Don (Donald Robert Marquis) Marquis. But a knot in the tangled skein of things where chance and/chance combine? HBMV

The Heir of Linne. *Anonymous.*
But lang ere he came down again/Was convoyed by lords fifeteen. BaBo; ESPB
"A curse light on me if ever again,/My lands be in jeopardy!" BuBa; ESPB

Heir to Several Yesterdays. Parham J. Kelley. And mourn my wasted, would-be, bright/Heritage. AMV-80

Heiress and Architect. Thomas Hardy. To hale a coffined corpse adown the stairs:/For you will die. VLP

Heirloom. Leonard Cohen. There is an heirloom somewhere. NOBC

Heirloom. Abraham Moses Klein. A white hair fallen from my father's beard. NIP; NOBC; OBCV; PeCV; TrJP

Helas! Oscar Wilde. And must I lose a soul's inheritance? AnIV; BrPo; GTBS; MoBrPo; TEP; UnTE; VLP

The Helbatrawss. Kingsley Amis. Them uge great vings balls up his plates, yer see. NOBL

Helen. Susan (Sarah Chauncey Woolsey) Coolidge. By wisdom learned since we were dead. AA

Helen. James Harrison. ...even though/it was a woman to blame as usual, died. NLV

Helen. Mary Ann Lamb. Helen, grown old, no longer cold,/Said, "you to all men I prefer." OBRV

Helen. Edward A.U. Valentine. And Helen feeds the flames as long ago! AA

Helen and Corythos. Walter Savage landor. ...and cypresses/From Ida waiting for dissever'd friends. LoBV

Helen Grown Old. Janet Lewis. ...The fading sound/Is blent of falling embers, weeping kings. QFR

Helen Hunt Jackson. Ina Donna Coolbrith. With love, upon her bier. AA

Helen in Egypt. Hilda ("H. D.") Doolittle.
  I only remember the shells,/whiter than bone,/on the ledge of a desolate beach. NOBA
  is it Death to know/this immaculate purity,/security? MOON

Helen Keller. Edmund Clarence Stedman. Not thou, not thou–'tis we/Are deaf, are dumb, are blind! AA

Helen of Kirconnell. Anonymous. And I am weary of the skies,/For her sake that died for me. AnFE; AWP; BSV; CBEP; CH; ELP; GoTS; HBV 1-2; InPo; LiTB; LoBV; OBEV; PoPle; SeCeV; TreFT

Helen–Old. Isabel Ecclestone MacKay. ...But Helen stayed/In Troy...I know...Cease, child–you trouble me! CaP

Helen's Scar. Alden Nowlan. I did it;/and I don't even remember the plum tree. Str

Helen, the Sad Queen. Paul Valery. Stretch toward me their indulgent, graven arms. AWP; CAW

Helen Was Just Slipped into Bed. Matthew Prior. Alas! no eyebrows for tomorrow. EiCP

Helena Embarks for Palestine. Cynewulf. And many a gem in its jeweled setting/Gleamed in that war-host, the gift of a lord. AnOE

Helicon. John Hollander. With night coming on like a death, a ruby of blood is a treasure. NoAm

Heliodore. Andrew Lang. It is not mine. OBVV

Heliodore. J. D. Logan. Dear dreams of our first Love–lost Heliodore! CaP

Heliogabalus. John Hollander. Problems beneath his Im-/Perial drag. NLV; OBAL

Helios. Joel Elias Spingarn. I shall cry out to heaven, "The sun! the/sun!" AA

Heliotrope. Harry Thurston Peck. Of the dead spray of heliotrope/That once she gave the old professor. AA; HBV 1-2

Hell. Anonymous. Ah! my crop had better thriven/Had I sown and ploughed for heaven. WTO

Hell and Heaven. Anonymous.
  I been talked 'bout sure as you're born. ABF
  Me an' my God's gwinter do as we please! OxBoLi

The Hell-Bound Train. Anonymous. For he never rode the hell-bound train. BeLS; BLPA; BPAW; CoSo

Hell Gate. Alfred Edward Housman. But the city, dusk and mute,/Slept, and there was no pursuit. NoAm; UnPo

Hell Hath No Fury... Charles Bukowski. I got into the orange Volks and we/drove off together. GP

Hell in Texas. Anonymous.; "I've a hell on the inside as well as without." ABF; BPAW; CoSo

Hell's Bells. Margaret Fishback. It picks up one person and knocks down a couple. ShM

Hell's Pavement. John Masefield. To sleep on, when his watch was through,–/So he did. BrPo

Hell, Well, Heaven. Mongane Wally Serote. Hell, well, Heavens! WhB

Hellas: Chorus. Percy Bysshe Shelley. Oh, might it die or rest at last! AtBAP; AWP; ChTr; EBEV; EnLit; ERoP 1-2; ExPo; FiP; HAP; HBV 1-2; HeIP; InPo; MyFE; NOBE; NoP; OAEL 1-2; OAEP; OBEV; PoEL 1-5; SeCePo; SeCeV; TrGrPo

The Hellenics. Walter Savage Landor. To find set duly on the hollow stone. EnRP

Hellenics: Blue Sleep. Winifred Bryher. Am I lifted/To the porch of Aphrodite on your wings? PoA

Hellhound on My Trail. Robert Johnson. All I need my little sweet woman/and to keep my company/hmmm hmmm hmmm hmmm/my company BluL

Hello. John Berryman. direction and velocity, to accommodate you, dear. NAs

Hello. Gregory Corso. In the great serenade of things,/am I the most cancelled passage? PoM

Hello! Louise Ayres Garnett. 'phoning the news/through a daffodil. SiSoSe

Hello, Girls (with music). Anonymous. Get up and get my breakfast, you good-for-nothing thing! AS

Hello Goodbye. Sharon Thesen. In the lateness of it all/a numbing silence & the rhythm/of another word written,/and another. CaPN

Hello, Hello. William Matthews. my lungs are thick with the smoke of your absence. PCP

Hello, Ma Baby. Howard. Joseph E. Emerson. Ida. Oh, baby, telephone and tell me I'm your own. BLSo; FSN

Hello, Sister. Mark Saylor. One favor before you go? Smile for me. AMV-80

Hello, Somebody. Anonymous. Hello, Somebody, hello. ShS

Hello There (parody). Brian S. Salome. And sound as this egg on my tray. BXAP

Hello up There. Marge Piercy. but only a huge bobbin of black wire unwinding. NLV

Hellvellyn. Sir Walter Scott. With one faithful friend but to witness thy dying,/In the arms of Hellvellyn and Catchedicam. FM; TEP

The Helmet. Philip Levine. and because they had/to sit up straight/so they could eat. LCAP

Helmet Orchid. Douglas Stewart. Silence like music flowed. BoAV

The Helmets, a Fragment. Thomas Penrose. O shield my suffering country!–shield it!', prayed/The agonising priest. NOEC

The Helmsman. Hilda ("H. D.") Doolittle. we have always known you wanted us. AnAmPo; CMoP; OxBA

The Helmsman: An Ode. J. V. Cunningham. Naked thou liest in an unknown grave! MoVE

Help from History. William Stafford. a past that redeems any future. AMV-81

Help, Good Shepherd. Ruth Pitter. Come then and help us, or we die. OxBoCh

Help Is on the Way. Herbert Scott. ...You may need help. GP

Help, Lord, Because the Godly Man. Francis Rous. That hath been purified. AH

Help Me Today. Elsie Robinson. Help me today. PoToHe

Help Thy Servant. Andrew Broaddus. Lord, we beg, for Jesus' sake/A sweet refreshing shower. AH

Help Us to Live. John Keble. To live more nearly as we pray. TRV

Help Wanted. Franklin Waldheim. Will pay compensation/Of seventeen dollars a week. BLPA

Helpe Me to Seke. Sir Thomas Wyatt. It was myn hert. I pray you hertely/Helpe me to seke. AAS

A Helping Hand. Georgia B. Adams. And if we really care enough/We'll stop to help our brother. STF

Helpmate. Henry Chapin. After, if you must,/you can talk of fate/and all that stuff. FAZ

Hem and Haw. Bliss Carman. And over the quavering voice of Hem/Is the droning voice of Haw. AnAmPo; HBV 1-2

The Hem of His Garment. Anna E. Hamilton. It can endure and suffer much. TrPWD

Hematite Lake. James J. Galvin. Not even nightfall, whose gold we are, can find us. AMV-80

The Hemingway House in Key West. Philip Schultz. All my life I have wondered what he meant to tell me. MAYP

The Hemingway Syndrome. Adrian C. Louis. I touch my groin. STE

Hemlock Mountain. Sarah N. Cleghorn. For all the summer islands where the gulf tides flow. HBV 1-2

The Hemorrhage. Stanley Jasspon Kunitz. We read that day what blotted out the news. NYP; WaP

The Hen. Oliver Herford. No wonder, Child, we prize the Hen,/Whose Egg is Mightier than the Pen. LBN; NA

Hen and Cock. Anonymous. Sell your eggs, and buy shoes. GBP

The Hen and the Carp. Ian Serraillier. What a hullabaloo there'd be. OnUR

The Hen and the Oriole. Don (Donald Robert Marquis) Marquis. the sad advice/of your ugly friend/archy. EvOK; FiBHP

Hen Dying. Alasdair MacLean. For a week or two I'll miss her. BoAnP

The Hen It Is a Noble Beast. William McGonagall. With a leg at every corner. NLV

The Hen Keeper. Anonymous. Go to thy nest and lay. OxNR

Hen's Nest. John Clare. But naught is found and all is given o'er/Till the young brood come chirping to the door. PBBP

Hen Under Bay-Tree. Ruth Pitter. The plant of honour is her house. OxBTC

Hen Woman. Thomas Kinsella. It was a simple world. CIP; IPY

Hence, Away, You Sirens! George Wither. That all your labours will be vain. EIL

Hence These Rimes. Bert Leston Taylor. 'Cause it pleases the eye,/And I like the effect. FiBHP

Henceforth, from the Mind. Louise Bogan. Henceforth, henceforth/Will echo sea and earth. LiTA; MoPo; MoVE; NePA; QFR

Henceforth I Will Not Set My Love. Sir Arthur Gorges. Yet will she wear the sweet woodbine,/The primrose and the violet. GBL

The Henchman. John Greenleaf Whittier. But, at her feet, how blest were I/For any need of hers to die! HBV 1-2; OBEV; OBVV

Hendecasyllabics. Algernon Charles Swinburne. All whose flowers are tears, and round his temples/Iron blossom of frost is bound for ever. FaBoRV; SyP; VLP

Hendecasyllabics. Alfred, Lord Tennyson. Maiden, not to be greeted unbenignly. EBEV; FaBoCo; NOBL; VLP

Hendecasyllables, Help! Caius Valerius Catullus. Say, "Pure, sweet lady, please do give them back." DBV

Hengest Cyning. Jorge Luis Borges. And no one dared ever betray me. NYBP

Henley, July 4: 1914–1964. L. E. Sissman. Blades of a feather. PrIm

Henley on Taieri. Charles Brasch. In the bitter and formless/Light-engulfing/Pit of the desolate sea. AnNZ

A Henpecked Husband. *Anonymous.* I dare not sayn when she saith "Pes!" OxBM

Henry Adams. W. H. Auden. He sat quiet as a mouse. OBAL

Henry and Mary. Robert Graves. Then let us play at queen and king/As down the garden walks we go. BrPo; GoJo; LOW; SO

Henry Before Agincourt. John Lydgate. To give our King the victory.... CH

Henry C. Calhoun. Edgar Lee Masters. And the children of them and their chil-/dren/Wear the envenomed robe. AmP; LiTA; LiTM

Henry Green. *Anonymous.* "In Heaven meet me, Henry!" and she sweetly smiled and died. BaBo

Henry Hudson's Quest. Burton Egbert Stevenson. "God's crypt is sealed! 'Twill stand revealed in His own/good time," quoth he. HBV 1-2; MC; PAH; PAL

Henry James. Clifton Fadiman. Is not always too deuced/Lucid. FiBHP

Henry James. Robert Louis Stevenson. Comes (best of all) himself–our welcome James. OBNC

Henry James at Newport. Weldon Kees. The stone-walled fields are featureless. PoA

Henry K. Sawyer. *Anonymous.* Now think on this widow and on her distress,/And make her a present, and God will you bless. AmFP

Henry King. Hilaire Belloc. With that the Wretched Child expires. BBGG; CenHV; DTC; FaBoUs; HBMV; NLV

Henry Martyn. *Anonymous.*
For all the brave lives of the mariners lost,/That are sunk in the watery main. BaBo
O the tidings be sad that I bring. CBEP

Henry Martyn (A vers.). *Anonymous.* And tell my brothers as they pass by/I've done robbing around the salt sea. ViBoFo

Henry Martyn (E version). *Anonymous.* That he may reign king of the merry/dryland,/But that I will be king of the sea.' ESPB

Henry Miller: A Writer. Carol Lem. is my eye open? AMV-80

Henry My Son. *Anonymous.* And I want to lie down–for ever.' OBET

Henry Purcell. Gerard Manley Hopkins. ...but meaning motion fans fresh our wits with wonder. TEP; UnS; VLP

Henry's Secret. Dorothy Kilner. Since my exercise done, I am ever prepared,/And have leisure remaining for play.' OxBChV

Henry's Understanding. John Berryman. into the terrible water & walk forever/under it out toward the island. CAPP; NoAm; NOBA

Henry the Fifth's Conquest of France. *Anonymous.* To the Rose of England I will give free.' OBET

Henry to Rosamond. Michael Drayton. My Heart remains (deare Paradise) in thee. AnAnS 2

Henry Turnbull. Wilfrid Gibson. With tuppence change till Doomsday on his eyes. ELU; FaBoTw

Henry VIII. *Anonymous.* One died, one survived, two divorced, two beheaded. FaBoUs

Henry VIII. Eleanor and Herbert Farjeon. For this time it was Henry who/Hopped the twig, and a good job too. StPo

Henry Wadsworth Longfellow. Henry Austin Dobson. While song yet speaks an English tongue/By Charles' or Thamis' wave! HBV 1-2

Henry Ward Beecher. Charles Henry Phelps. Wherever men lay bound he clave. AA

Hens. Alden Nowlan. and then the hens–quite calmly–pecked him dead. PoL

The Hens. Elizabeth Madox Roberts. But nothing answered anything. GoJo; HBMV; OBCA; SoPo; SUS; TiPo

The Henyard Round. Donald Hall. deaf, unable to feed herself, demented... Psk

Hep-Cat. John L. Sellers. but spring was gone from his step. LFAC

The Heptalogia. Algernon Charles Swinburne. Till the heart-beats of hell shall be/hushed by a hymn from the hunt that/has harried... OAEP

Heptonstall Old Church. Ted Hughes. The moorland broke lose. InPS

Her, A Statue. Thomas Stoddart. A love-wing'd spirit glide in glory by,/Striking the tent of its mortality! OBNC

Her Absent Lord (excerpt). Ugga Byan. With such fond hopes, for you have not come back. LiTW

Her Answer. John Bennett. And dreams 't is all to-day. AA; BLPA

Her Application to Elysium. Kathleen Norris. And her eyes would not stop shining IHMS

Her Apron through the Trees. Roger Weingarten. ...She died/"of malaria." Elmira would. AmPA

Her Beauty. Max Plowman. And hearing a new music, miss the theme. HBMV

Her Birthday. Harold Witt. and I watch her as the wheels spin her away. AMV-80

Her breast is fit for pearls. Emily Dickinson. Sweet of twigs and twine/My perennial nest. PeHV

Her careful distinct sex whose sharp lips comb. Edward Estlin Cummings. the face in a hoop of grim ecstasy ErPo

Her Courage. William Butler Yeats. Who have lived in joy and laughed into the face of/Death. LiTB

Her Courtesy. William Butler Yeats. Thinking of saints and of Petronius Arbiter. LiTB

Her Dairy. Peter Newell. "Are growing in my garden-plot, and this I call my dairy." NA

Her Dancing Days. Anna Adams. We was both seventeen. BrRo

Her Dead Brother. Robert Lowell. ...Brother, my heart/races for sea-room–we are out of breath. NePoEA

Her Dilemma. Thomas Hardy. Where Nature such dilemmas could devise. BrPo; NOBV

Her Dwarf. George P. Elliott. He brays like a man. MAT

Her Dwelling-Place. Ada Foster Murray. A flame as fragrant as his own. HBV 1-2

Her Epitaph. Thomas William Parsons And Love no longer be a thing to weep. AA; HBV 1-2

Her Eyes. John Crowe Ransom. I apprehend will get some blame/On her good name. LiTM; NePA; OBAL; PoPl

Her Eyes Are Wild. William Wordsworth. And there, my babe, we'll live for aye. NAs

Her Eyes Don't Shine Like Diamonds. David Marion. I love my mother,/And she's my sweetheart. FSN

Her Face Her Tongue Her Wit. Sir Arthur Gorges. to serve to trust to fear. GBL

Her face was in a bed of hair. Emily Dickinson. Who witnesses, believes. NU

Her Fair Inflaming Eyes. Thomas Campion. Till I found 'twas to no end/With a Spirit to contend. LiTL

Her Fairness, Wedded to a Star. Edward J. O'Brien. And innocence doth slumber now/Upon her candid April brow. FaBoBe; HBMV

Her Faith. Hilaire Belloc. Say that's true now, and I'll believe it then. GoBC

Her Favorites. Mattie Lee Hausgen. Ha! I go barefoot all the day! PoPl

Her Garden. Freda Downie. Sour as social justice, on the wash-house wall. FaBoWP

Her Going. Shirley Kaufman. feel the small shape of light/going out of my arms. PCP

Her Hair. *Anonymous.* But rather will in that sweet bondage die/Than break one hair to gain its liberty. LiTL

Her Hair. Charles Baudelaire. Oasis of my dreams, and gourd from whence/Deep draughted wines of memory will flow. NAWM 1-2

Her Hair. Sir Robert Chester. Able to lull asleep a pensive heart/That of the round world's sorrows bears a part. EIL

Her Heart. Bartholomew Griffin. What have I not, if I have but her heart! TrGrPo

Her Horoscope. Mary Ashley Townsend. The rose one leaves in some forgotten book. AA

Her Husband. Ted Hughes. Goes straight up to heaven and nothing more is heard of it. OxBC

Her Kind. Anne Sexton. I have been her kind. CAPP; CoAP; FF; HaCAP; HeIP; LiTM; MP; PPP; TAP; TwCP; WPOW

Her Kisses. Thomas Lovell Beddoes. When heaven is brimful of starry night. AtBAP; LO

Her–"last Poems". Emily Dickinson. What, and if, Ourself a bridegroom–/Put Her down–in Italy? SBG

Her Legs. Robert Herrick. Which is as white and hair-less as an egge. SpRo

Her Letter. Bret (Francis Bret Harte) Harte. And you've struck it,–on Poverty Flat. HBV 1-2; PoLf

Her Lips. *Anonymous.* Whether the roses be your lips or your lips the roses. EG; LiTL

Her Lips Are Copper Wire. Jean Toomer. and press your lips to mine/till they are incandescent NoAm

Her Lips They Are Redder Than Coral. *Anonymous.* My beautiful Georgian rose! FaBoCo

Her Longing. Theodore Roethke. Or beating against the black clouds of the storm,/Protecting the sea-cliffs. NU

Her Love Poem. Lucille Clifton. or hate you but i will have you/have you have you. GP

Her Merriment. William Henry Davies. But laughing gaily, her delighted breasts/Sent ripples down her body to her knees. EnLoPo

Her Mood around Me. Brewster Ghiselin. But up what corridors thrums the flood's growl? LiTL

Her Mother. Alice Cary. She is my mother: you will agree/That all the rest may be thrown away. OHIP

Her Mouth. Richard Aldington. The memory of her kissing mouth/Burns me to gladness. BrPo

Her Music. Martha Gilbert Dickinson. Of violets and love and death. AA

Her Pedigree. Arthur Davison Ficke. Have woven round you, in the burning Now,/A lure unknown to Helen's Phidian brow. HBMV

Her Polka Dots. Peter Newell. And straightway all her polka-dots began a lively dance. NA

Her Praises. Anthony Skoloker. To see, feel, taste, and love earth's rarest jewel. EIL

Her Race. William Butler Yeats. With her dead brother's valour/For an example still? LiTB

Her Rambling. Thomas Lodge. And Neptune, glad and fain,/Yields up to her his reign. LoBV; OBSC

Her Sacred Bower. Thomas Campion. And though not in her bower, yet I/Shall in her temple rest. HBV 1-2

Her Shadow. Elisabeth Cavazza Pullen. I, too, a shade! AA

Her Sister. Moira O'Neill. 'Tis the quare pity o' Brigid MacIlray. OxBTC

Her Skin Is So White as a Lily. Padraic Colum. Do watch her to madness when woonce she do move. LO

Her Story. Naomi Long Madgett. Next time I'll try a gun. IHMS; PoBA

Her Story. Monty Reid. and I also know/they can't help it. CaPN

Her Strong Enchantments Failing. Alfred Edward Housman. But you will die to-day. CBEP; FaBoTw; MAT; NOBE; NOBV; OAEL 1-2

Her Sweet Voice. Thomas Carew. So may you, when the musick's done,/Awake and see the rising sun. LiTL

Her sweet weight on my heart a night. Emily Dickinson. A Fiction superseding Faith–/By so much–as 'twas real– PeHV

Her True Body. Jerred Metz. though touching far from her true body,/make the loveliest of maps. VWA

Her Voice Could Not Be Softer. Austin Clarke. Her voice could not be softer/When she told it in confession. NOBI

Her Way. William Rose Benet. With this you light the dust/That clouds my road. HBMV

Her Whole Life is an Epigram. William Blake. Platted quite neat to catch applause, with a sliding noose at the end. InPK; NIP

Her Window. Robert Leigh. Its fair Course still begun/By Her and by the Sun. CavP

Hera, Hung from the Sky. Carolyn Kizer. I dangle, drowned in fire. NMM

Heracles. Yvor Winters. And Deianira, an imperfect shade,/Retreats in silence as my arc descends. QFR

Heraclitus. William Johnson Cory. For Death, he taketh all away, but them he cannot take. AWP; CBEP; ELU; FaBoEE; FaPoR; GoTF; GTBS; HBV 1-2; NOBE; OBEV; OBNC; OBSP; OBVV; PeHV; PoRA; SeCePo; TreF; ViBoPo; VLP

Heraclitus in the West. Charles G. Bell. Gulls to the landless drop of the wind-gray cloud. NePoAm

The Herald Crane. Hamlin Garland. The voice of hope and dauntless will,/And breaks the spell of dreams. HBV 1-2

Heralds of Christ. Laura S. Copenhaver. ...strife shall cease/Upon the highway of the Prince of Peace. AH

Herb-Leech. Joseph Campbell. For I have the gift/Of the Murrain Stone! AnIL; OnYI

Herbert Street Revisited. John Montague. ...lifting/their hooves through the moonlight. CIP; FaBoIP; IPY

Herbert White. Frank Bidart. –Hell came when I saw/MYSELF.../and couldn't stand/what I see... AmPA

Herbs in the Attic. Marilyn Waniek. Dream music fills the air/like the scent of dried herbs. AMV-81; MAYP

Hercules Furens, IV: Chorus. Seneca (Lucius Annaeus Seneca). Goe see the angry kynges. OBVE

Hercules Oetaetus, II: Chorus. Seneca (Lucius Annaeus Seneca). Straught of her wits, and ful of furius yre. OBVE

The Herd. Frances Cornford. They being, like the stars "preserved from wrong." FM

The Herd Boy. Haniel Long. While mother-naked after/A laurel branch I bore. HBMV

The Herdman. Anonymous. Though poor and plain his diet,/Yet merry it is and quiet. NOBE; OBSC

The Herds. William Stanley Merwin. And the water preparing its descent/To the first dead. NaP; NYBP

Herdsman. Michael Pettit. ...There is no hope unless/I give in and never go back. MAYP

Here. Marvin Bell. when you mistook being here for being there. AmPA

Here. Robert Creeley. Live/on the edge,/looking. NOBA

Here. Philip Larkin. Facing the sun, untalkative, out of reach. CMoP

Here. R. S. Thomas. I must stay here with my hurt. GTBS-P

Here Am I, Little Jumping Joan. Mother Goose. I'm always alone. TiPo

Here and Now. Catherine Cater. No gazer in the crystal ball can see/The future as we see the now and here. AmNP; PoNe

Here and Now. Philip Levine. Nothing needs to be said. PoA; VWA

Here and There. Jon Stallworthy. ...I lie still/In a green sack on a green hill. NoAm

Here and There: Nocturnal Landscape. Malcolm Cowley. Her eyes were fixed and mad, like mine and the panthers.' PoA

Here are fine gifts, children. Sappho. yet I love refinement, and beauty and light/are to me the same as desire for the sun. BoWoP

Here Are the Lady's Knives and Forks. Anonymous. And here is the baby's cradle. OxNR

Here, as in a Painting, Noon Burns Yellow. Natalya Gorbanyevskaya. Am I living or dead, am I leaves or grass? BoWoP; PBWP

Here Awa', There Awa'. Anonymous. Ilka thing pleases while Willie's at hame. OBS

Here Be Dragons. Ginny Friedlander. The spar/is in my hand. AMV-80

Here Begins the Continuation of the Cook's Tale (parody). William Zaranka. May Goddes body fede us everichoon! BXAP

Here Come Three Merchants A-Riding. Anonymous. The fairest one that I can see, sir,/Innamen, senaman, see. TrAS

Here Comes a Wooer. Anonymous. Lily bright and shine-a. OxNR

Here Comes My Lady with Her Little Baby. Anonymous. Here comes old Jack with a broken pack,/A gallop, a gallop, a gallop. OxNR

Here Do I Put My Name for to Betraye. Anonymous. The thief yt steals my book away. FaBoUs

Here Followeth the Songe of the Death of Mr. Thewlis. Anonymous. Lyke co(n)stansie till death/and in heaven be our end! CoMu

Here Have I Been These One and Twenty Years. Arthur Hugh Clough. Heart emptied, and scarce hoping to amend. NAs

Here Have I Dwelt. Anonymous. Now have good day! MeEV

Here Huntington's Ashes Long Have Lain. Ambrose Bierce. Whatever he gained, the loss was ours. DBV

Here I Am. Abraham Sutzkever. A not knowing why. TrJP

Here I Sit Alone. Anonymous. for thu art he that hath all wrought,/and I thi moder alone.' OxBoCh

Here I Sit in My Infested Cubicle. Theresa Greenwood. are but outward symbols of/my inner ghetto. CTBA

Here in Katmandu. Donald Justice. Comes down,/As soon it must, from the mountain. CoAP; ConAP; HeIP; LiSp; NIP; RFM

Here Is a Song. John Peck. Till Christ on high shall rend the sky,/And bid the dead arise. AH

Here Is a Toast That I Want to Drink. Walter Lathrop. Who takes my place when I'm gone. PoLf

Here Is the Abattoir Where. Michael Smith. And, more often, thunderous falls of black stars. CIP

Here Is the Church, and Here Is the Steeple. Anonymous. And here he is a-saying his prayers. OxNR

Here Is the Place Where Loveliness Keeps House. Madison Cawein. Shouting, beneath the leaves' tumultuous green. HBV 1-2

Here Is the Tale. Anthony C. Deane. But, ah, my litle readers, will you mark and understand? InMe; NA

Here Is Your Realism. Maxwell Bodenheim. And for an instant new resentments kill/The swollen wraiths of guiltand perfidy. AnAmPo

Here Lie I, Martin Elginbrodde. George Macdonald. And ye were Martin Elginbrodde. HBV 1-2

Here Lies... Stevie Smith. ...In Death's clime/There's no pen, paper, notion–and no Time. PoA

Here Lies a Lady. John Crowe Ransom. After six little spaces of chill, and six of burning. AnAmPo; AWP; CMoP; CoBMV; EvOK; ForPo; HAP; HBMV; InPo; InvP; LiTM; MoAB; MoAmPo; NAMP; NoAm; PoRA; TAP; VGW

Here Lies a Prisoner. Charlotte Mew. Quieter now than he used to be, but listening still to the magpie chatter/Over his grave. MoBrPo

Here Lies Fierce Strephon. Anthony Hecht. A fate he shared–it bears much thinking on–/With certain persons at the Pentagon. TW

Here Lies My Wife. J. V. Cunningham. ...Eternal peace/Be to us both with her decease. NIP

Here Lies Sir Tact. Timothy Steele. Whose silence was not golden, but just yellow. NLV; TW

Here Lieth Love. Thomas Watson. Whose foolish fault to death himself hath done.' EIL

Here, Lord, Retired, I Bow in Prayer. Matthew Bolles. Then take me to thyself above. AH

Here Pause: The Poet Claims at Least This Praise. William Wordsworth. O wretched man, the throne of tyranny! EnRP

Here's a Health to Them That's Awa'. Robert Burns. May they never eat of her bread! HBV 1-2

Here's a Poor Widow. Anonymous. Come choose the one/You love the best. OxNR

Here's a String o' Wild Geese. Anonymous. They're a' flown frae me! PBBP

Here's the Tender Coming. Anonymous. Here's the tender coming, full of red marines. GBP

Here's to the Ranger! Anonymous. Our safety from the savage,/The guardian of our home. CoSo

Here She Is. Mary Britton Miller. You can see the tiger blaze/In her tiger eyes, her tiger face. TiPo

Here She Stands. Jean Rabearivelo. Like a clump of unwinding seaweed/ And perhaps some grains of salt. PBA

Here Sits the Lord Mayor. Mother Goose. Chin chopper, chin chopper, chin chopper, chin. ExPo; HBV 1-2; HBVY; OxNR

Here the Frailest Leaves of Me. Walt Whitman. And yet they expose me more than all my other poems. AP

Here the Trace. Boris Pasternak. As they drain the vast vault of the night, drop by drop. LiTW

Here/There. Ken Norris. as our lovers walk slowly towards us across a sun-dappled room. CaPN

Here Too the Spirit Shafts. Mechtild of Magdeburg. O finer far, not gems/ But their eternal parts. WPOW

Here We Come A-Piping. Anonymous. And bells beyond the sand. CH; ExPo; PoPle; SiSoSe; TiPo

Here We Come A-Wassailing. Anonymous. And God send you a Happy New Year. PCh

Here We Go Dancing Jingo-Ring. Anonymous. About the merry-ma-tanzie. OxNR

Here We Go Looby Loo. Anonymous. Here we go looby loo,/All on a Saturday night. FSW

Here We Go Round Ring by Ring. Anonymous. And a curtsey to the ground, sir. OxNR

Here We March All Around in a Ring. Anonymous. Kiss her slow and let her know/How you come to love her so. AmFP

Here We Were Born. Marcelin Dos Santos. carry on man's work/the great design of life. WhB

Here Where Coltrane Is. Michael S. Harper. ...the browns/of these men and their music. CNA; PoBA

Here, where the Red Man Swept the Leaves away. Frederick Goddard Tuckerman. As though I walked the wood with sagamore George. NOBA; TAP

Hereafter. Harriet Prescott Spofford. Floating, floating, one forever, in the light of God's great/smile. HBV 1-2

Heredity. Thomas Bailey Aldrich. To one, the cool and reasoning brain;/ To one, the quick, unreasoning heart. AA; AnAmPo

Heredity. Arthur Guiterman. There's nothing at all that will make them respect us. OBAL

Heredity. Thomas Hardy. The eternal thing in man,/That heeds no call to die. CBEP; CTC; EBEV; ImOP

Heredity. Lydia Avery Coonley Ward. No legacy of sin annuls/Heredity from God. HBV 1-2

Heresy for a Class-Room. Rolfe Humphries. O Jean, look out the window at the trees! GLGT

The Heretic. Bliss Carman. By daring love and blameless awe. WGRP

The Heretic's Tragedy. Robert Browning. God help all poor souls lost in the dark! OAEL 1-2

Heretics All. Hilaire Belloc. Because of the love that I bore them, Dona Eis Requiem. ACP

Heriot's Ford. Rudyard Kipling. You've finished with the Flesh, my lord! PoRA

Heritage. Gwendolyn B. Bennett. Hidden by a minstrel-smile. BANP; BlSi

Heritage. Mary Gilmore. Not of ourselves are we strong. CBAP

Heritage. Linda Hogan. From my family I have learned the secrets/of never having a home. TWSS

The Heritage. James Russell Lowell. A heritage, it seems to me,/Well worth a life to hold in fee. HBV 1-2; HBVY

Heritage. Dorothea Mackellar. But the dead women in my soul/Knew all that summer knows. NOAV

The Heritage. Edward Bliss Reed. To hear bleak winds go moaning down the sand,/By the wild sea. EtS

Heritage. Augustus Young. Allow the country die for you. CIP

Heritage: What Is Africa to Me? Countee Cullen. Spicy grove, cinnamon tree/What is Africa to me? FaBV

Herman Altman. Edgar Lee Masters. I would be the untarnished possession forever/Of those for whom I lived. OxBA

Herman Melville. Conrad Aiken. and in the Item loved the Whole. NoAm; NOBA; TAP

Herman Melville. W. H. Auden. And sat down at his desk and wrote a story. LiTA; NePA; OAEP; OxBA

Herman Moon's Hourbook. Christopher Middleton.
Crushed by the silence, bolt it down. NePoEA-2
Draughts of tomorrow/drawn slow/into empty lungs. NePoEA-2
Happy with friends to watch the turning of the stars. NePoEA-2
Harder day comes (Purity. Purity!)/With sweetly reeking coins. NePoEA-2
It is not meant for you. NePoEA-2
One: scattering the blind swarms that drink at the carcass. NePoEA-2

Hermann Ludwig Ferdinand von Helmholtz. Peter Meinke. they glorify the spell of light on/water. SUW

The Hermaphrodite's Song. Lorna Mitchell. And she gently gently gently/ Touched my cheek. BrRo

Hermaphroditus. Algernon Charles Swinburne. But Love being blind, how should he know of this? SyP; TEP; VLP

Hermes came to me in a dream. Sappho. along the banks of Acheron, river of Hell. BoWoP

Hermes of the Ways. Hilda ("H. D.") Doolittle. where sea-grass tangles with/shore-grass. LiTA

Hermetic Bird. Philip Lamantia. forever in the sweat of fire VGW

Hermione. Bryan Waller Procter. This is all we ask, from thee,/Hermione, Hermione! OBVV

Hermit. David Baker. as if they too knew exactly what they sought. AMV-80

Hermit. James Keir Baxter. His spent soul to that river where none grow old. AnNZ

The Hermit. William Henry Davies. Comes like a tiger crunching through the stones. BrPo; MoBrPo

The Hermit. Daniel Halpern. You can't leave a house of air. AMV-80

The Hermit. Hsu Pen. Year follows year,/And life goes on. RFM

The Hermit. Howard Moss. O miseries and appetites of the world. NePoAm

The Hermit. Thomas Parnell. And pass'd a life of piety and peace. GoTL

The Hermit. Sir Walter Ralegh. And at my gate despair shall linger still/ To let in death when love and fortune will. OBSC

The Hermit Cackleberry Brown, on Human Vanity:. Jonathan Williams. ...to hold the world together/like hooved up ground/thats what OBAL; PoM

The Hermit Has a Visitor. Maxine W. Kumin. he will itch. BoWoP

Hermit Hoar... Samuel Johnson. "Come, my lad, and drink some beer." EnLi 1-2; NLV; PV; ViBoPo

The Hermit Marban. Anonymous. all claims to the hour of death,/to be with you, Marban! NOBI

The Hermit Picks Berries. Maxine W. Kumin. and walk to town for some cream. RFM

The Hermit's Song. Anonymous.
And I to be sitting for a while/Praying God in every place. KiLC; OnYI
Swans call, river water falling/Is calling too. KiLC
where a man all day prepared his dying. BIrV

The Hermit Wakes to Bird Sounds. Maxine W. Kumin. one-of-a-kind machines fall silent. GrPl; Psk; WeW

Hermontimus. Ayton [(or Aytoun)] Sir Robert. Tho' but now the spirit of a flower. OBVV

Hernando de Soto. Rosemary and Stephen Vincent Benét. (I hope someone looked after the pigs.) NLV

Herndon. Silas Weir Mitchell. To show that life has naught to match/Such knighthood as the grave can give. PAH

A Hero. Florence Earle Coates. That he sublimed defeat. OHIP

The Hero. Robert Graves. And far worse damage done to bigger boys. PCP

The Hero. Leroy F. Jackson. She's even afraid of the bark of a tree. SiSoSe

The Hero. Robert Nicoll. Then come, and to my hero bend/Upon the grass your knee! HBV 1-2

The Hero. Siegfried Sassoon. Except that lonely woman with white hair. OBWP

Hero and Leander. George Chapman.
All might be seen beneath the waves to swim. EBEV
Fear fills the chamber. Darkness decks the bride. OAEL 1-2
The field his arms. EG
Made them all shrieke, it lookt so ghastly black. AtBAP

Hero and Leander. Thomas Hood.
And Hero's name dies bubbling on her lips. EnRP
O Death, be gracious to my dying suit!' EnRP

Hero and Leander. Christopher Marlowe.
And all that view'd her were enamour'd on her... LoBV
And as he spake, upon the waves he springs. NOBE
And her all naked to his sight display'd. UnTE
And, looking in her face, was strooken blind. HoPM
And with still panting rocked, there took his rest. FaBoEn; WHA
And wound them on his arm, and for her mourned. GBL
Breathed darkness forth (dark night is Cupid's day). SeCePo
Then muse not Cupids sute no better sped,/Seeing in their loves the Fates were iniured. PoEL 1-5
Till she, o'ercome with anguish, shame, and rage,/Danged down to hell her loathsome carriage. AAS; CABA; EBEV; NoP; OBSC; TEP
'Tis wisdom to give much, a gift prevails,/When deep persuading Oratory fails. PeHV
Whence his admiring eyes more pleasure took/Than Dis, on heaps of gold fixing his look. ErPo; OAEL 1-2; TEP
Where kindly Neptune and this traine abode. AtBAP
Who ever loved, that loved not at first sight? AtBAP; BLPL; BoLiVe; FaBoEn; NOBE; TrGrPo; ViBoPo; WHA

Hibernia. Stuart Howard-Jones.
  Preferred to drown than visit it again. DBV; NOBL
Hibiscus and Salvia Flowers. D. H. Lawrence. And still I cannot bear it/
  That they take hibiscus and the salvia flower. FaBoPV
Hibiscus on the Sleeping Shores. Wallace Stevens. And roamed there all
  the stupid afternoon. InPS; PAI
Le Hibou et la Poussiquette. Francis Steegmuller. Dansa au clair de la
  lune. NYBP
Les Hiboux. Charles Baudelaire. That makes the wind change and the
  grasses. AWP
Hic, Hoc, the Carrion Crow. Anonymous. Or else the poor sow's heart will
  down. OxBoLi
Hic Jacet. Louise Chandler Moulton. And yet, had Love been Love, he
  had not/died. AA; AnAmPo; APA
Hic Liber Ad Me Pertinet. Robert Barclay. Non illam preciptorum/Shal
  gar et his ain. FaBoUs
Hic Me, Pater Optime, Fessam Deseris. Lucy Robinson. Should still be
  tossing on the open sea. AA
Hic Vir, Hic Est. Charles Stuart Calverley. Your "poor moralist" betake
  me,/In my "solitary fly." NBM; OxBoLi
The Hicche-Hykeres Tale (parody). W. F. N. Watson. So mote he bere hir
  ful to Marlborrowe. BXAP
Hickenthrift and Hickenloop. X. J. Kennedy. Ate straight through
  Hickenthrift. WSC
Hickety, Pickety, I-Silicity. Anonymous. Every man who has no hair/
  Generally wears a wig. OxNR
Hickory, Dickory, Dock. Mother Goose. Hickory, dickory, dock.
  FaBoBe; FaFP; HBV 1-2; HBVY; OxNR; PoPl; SoPo; TiPo
Hickory Stick Hierarchy. Len G. Selle. To spare the child and spoil the
  rod! AMV-80
Hidden Bow. Mordecai Temkin. oh, fearsome hunter,/Your hidden bow.
  VWA
The Hidden Line. Joseph Addison Alexander. And harden not your heart.
  BLPA
The Hidden Truth. Jami. And from the force that works within the
  stream/The hidden working of the "Truth" may learn. LiTW
Hidden Valley. E. G. Burrows. or sailed off on the broad back of a swan.
  HoAn
The Hidden Weaver. Odell Shepard. Only the fugitive shapes are we,/
  Wrought in the web of eternity. WGRP
Hide and Seek. Robert Graves. Mad monsters of no kind? NTCP
Hide and Seek. Dan Pagis. you can see that I've given up. AMV-81
Hide in the Heart. Lloyd Frankenberg. The infantry of rain and the strong
  wind. AnFE
Hide, O Hide Those Hills of Snow. John Fletcher. But first set my poor
  heart free,/Bound in those icy chains by thee. HBV 1-2; ViBoPo
The Hide of My Mother. Edward Dorn. tail end of a dust storm/somehow
  battered up from Kansas. NeAP
Hide Thou Me. Anonymous. Hide Thou me, Rock of Ages, safe in Thee.
  AmFP
The Hidebehind. Michael Rosen. the Hidebehind's behind you. AmMo
Hidesong. Aig Higo. Alone I tow my death along. TTY
Hiding. Dorothy Aldis. And they were so surprised to find/Out it was me!
  SoPo; SUS; TiPo
Hiding in the Cucumber Garden. Vidya. rattles them to scare off/foxes
  there in the dark. WPOW
Hiding Place. Richard Armour. And if I die,/At least I'll keep. NIP
Hie to the Market, Jenny Come Trot. Anonymous. Jenny came home with
  an empty can. OxNR
Hieland Laddie. Anonymous. Hey ho, away we go,/My Bonnie Hieland
  Laddie. FSW
Hierarchie of the Blessed Angels (excerpt). Thomas Heywood. Grant that
  our willing, though unworthy quest/May, through thy grace, admit
  us 'mongst the blest. WGRP
Hieroglyph. Paul Auster. This knife/I hold against your throat. VWA
Hieroglyphic. Myra Sklarew. unexpected footprints/erased by the sea.
  SUW
Higgledy-Piggledy. E. William Seaman. "Here's my Fifth Symphony:/Duh,
  duh, duh, DUM!" PV
Higgledy, Piggledy, My Black Hen. Mother Goose. Higgledy, piggledy, my
  black hen. FaBoBe; HBV 1-2; PBBP; TiPo
Higgledy, Piggledy! See How They Run! Kate Greenway. Who can say
  what may not happen to-day? TiPo
High. John Perreault. O what endless Hydrox cookies! ANYP
High and Low. James H. Cousins. With joy that one so low should rise so
  high. HBMV; OnYI; OxBI
High and Low. John Banister Tabb. The Slipper went off to the ball.
  BrR
The High Barbaree. Anonymous. Cruising down along the coast of the
  High Barbaree! AmSS; FSW; OuSiCo; ViBoFo
The High Barbaree. Laura E. Richards.
  For you may save the life of/A pretty Muffin Bird! SoPo

"Sailing down along the coast/Of the High Barbaree." BaBo; SUS
The High Bridge above the Tagus River at Toledo. William Carlos Williams.
  ...peacefully continuing in his verse forever. CTC
High Brow. Robert Fitch. And claimed it was mind/Over Matterhorn.
  SD
High-Cool/2. James (Olumo) Cunningham. needs no medicine JB
High Country Weather. James Keir Baxter. Your heart of anger. · AnNZ
High Dive. William Empson. Drink deep the image solid of the bone.
  AtBAP
High Diver. Robert Francis. ...Rippling and responsive lies the water/For
  him to contemplate, then powerfully to enter. LiSp; NePoAm; SD
High Fidelity. Thom Gunn. Surrounded in that played-out pose of age/By
  notes he was, but cannot be again. PoA
High Field–First Day of Winter. Gary Eddy. I feel footsteps moving under
  mine. AMV-80
High Flight. John Gillespie Magee, Jr. Put out my hand, and touched the
  face of God. BBV; FaFP; GoTF; MaC; PGD; TreFS; TRV
High Germany. Anonymous.
  And sent them to the cruel wars in High Germany. CBEP; FSW; WaaP
  I'll think upon my own true love in the Isle of Germany. OBET
High Germany. Edward Shanks. We're going to the merry wars/In Low
  Germany.' OBMV
High Heels. Ron Padgett. You were to put the pink and blue/on the
  beachball on the next page. APU
The High Hills. Ivor Gurney. But the speed, the swiftness, walking into
  clarity,/Like last year's briony, are gone. FaBoPP
High Island. Richard Murphy. Tacking air, quicker and quicker/To rock,
  sea and star. CIP; NOBI
The High Jump. Anonymous. Foeman and friend were flying when he flew.
  LiSp
High-Life Low-Down. Justin Richardson. In front of the sink and said,
  "Kid, this is IT." PV
The High-Loping Cowboy. Curley W. Fletcher. I'm a high-lopin' cowboy,
  an' a wild buckeroo. BPAW
The High Mind. Samuel Daniel. And bears no venture in impiety.
  AnEnPo
High O'er the Hills. William Walker. I'll sing, and be forever blest,/Find
  sweet and everlasting rest. AH
High O'er the Poop the Audacious Seas Aspire. William Falconer. And
  nature, shuddering, feels the horrid roar. EtS
High on the Hog. Julia Fields. And I want/High on the Hog. CNA
High Overhead My Little Daughter. Thomas Edward Brown. That cod!/O
  God!/O God! NOBV
High Pitched Whale. Clark Coolidge. and are if is a the this the the is it.
  ANYP
A High Place. Eithne Wilkins. aloft, the wild hawks clashed. NeBP
High Plains Harvest. Bruce Morton. ...walking the hard straw-strewn
  beach. AMV-81
High Poetry and Low. Wallace Stevens. With the broken statues standing
  on the shore. PoA
High Price Blues. Roosevelt Sykes. It's giving us so much trouble/I
  wonder: what shall we do? BluL
The High Priest. Anonymous. ...and may the affliction of our/souls be our
  atonement. TrJP
High Renaissance. George Starbuck. Sign it "El Greco.' I'll/Slap on a
  frame." NLV; OBAL
High Resolve. Anonymous. Perhaps I'll see the hearts of men. PoToHe
The High Sailboat. Salvatore Quasimodo. I want to go, I want to leave this
  island."/And she: "O my dear, it is late; let us stay." LiTW
The High School Band. Reed Whittemore. And the silences after their
  partings are very deep. GLGT; NCSH
High Sheriff Blues. Charlie Patton. Mr. Purvis on his mansion/He doesn't
  pay no mind BluL
High Summer. Ebenezer Jones. Each muscle sink to itself, and separately
  enjoy. NOBV
High Summer. Jascha Kessler. who can claim the strange harvest of this/
  incessant wintry assault on ourselves? AmPC
High Summer. Guy Rotella. that seems for all the world/as though in
  celebration. AMV-80
High Summer on the Mountains. Idris Davies. And old men in the
  morning/Telling the town their dreams. OxBTC
High-Tide. Jean Starr Untermeyer. She walked the deep fields of the sky.
  MCCG; MoAmPo
The High Tide at Gettysburg. Will Henry Thompson. Lamenting all her
  fallen sons! AA; BeLS; BLPA; FaBoBe; HBV 1-2; MC; PAH; PAL; PaPo;
  TreFS
The High Tide on the Coast of Lincolnshire. Jean Ingelow. Come uppe
  Jetty, follow, follow,/Jetty5 to the milking shed.' BeLS; FaBoPP; GN;
  GTBS; HBV 1-2; NBM; OBVV; OnMSP; PaPo
High to Low. Langston Hughes. we have our problems,/too, with you.
  HaCAP

A High-Toned Old Christian Woman. Wallace Stevens. Wink as they will. Wink most when widows wince. AP; CMoP; CoBMV; MoVE; NoAm; NOBA; TAP

A High-Toned Old Fascist Gentleman (parody). William Zaranka. Incarnadine, the carnage of the swans. BXAP

High Up on Suilven. Norman MacCaig. The old spider outside space/Runs down it–and where's raven? Or where's hill? PoSH

High Water Everywhere. Charlie Patton.
I couldn't see no body home and/Wasn't no one to be found BluL
I'm going back to the hilly country/Won't be worried no more BluL

High Wheat Country. Elijah L. Jacobs. Still, the dust devils swirl, the old wind blows. AmFN

High Wind at the Battery. Ralph Pomeroy. means that we're that much nearer to slow-coming spring. NYBP

High Windows. Philip Larkin. And beyond it, the deep blue air, that shows/Nothing, and is nowhere, and is endless. FaBoMo

High Wonders (parody). Naomi Marks. It's time I got off my arse. BXAP

Higher. Anonymous. And there was no more use for him to be sayin'/ "Higher!" FiBHP

The Higher Calling. W. M. Czamanske. The gift to be a miracle/Shall never pass away. STF

The Higher Catechism. Sam Walter Foss. The greatest joy of joys shall be the joy of going on. WGRP

The Higher Empiricism. Francis C. Golffing. And burnt by adequate objects of desire. PoA

The Higher Good. Theodore Parker And lead still further on such as thy kingdom seek. AA; FaBoBe; HBV 1-2

Higher Love. Jeff Wright. that spits on night's/conditioned surrender. APU

The Higher Pantheism. Alfred, Lord Tennyson.
But if we could see and hear, this Vision–were it/not He? EnLi 1-2; HBV 1-2; MaVP; SpRo; TRV; VLP
For if He thunder by law the thunder is yet His voice. WGRP

The Higher Pantheism in a Nutshell. Algernon Charles Swinburne. Fiddle, we know, is diddle: and diddle, we take it,/is dee. ALV; BXAP; FaBoNo; HBV 1-2; NA; Par; SpRo

Highest Divinity. Anonymous. Worshipped eternally,/Lord of Infinity! TrJP

The Highest Wisdom. Jacopone da Todi. All Bologna's lore were vain,/To increase his mastery. CAW

Highland Cattle. Dinah Maria Mulock. Down the cattle come again! GN

Highland Harry Back Again. Robert Burns. For Highland Harry back again. EBEV

Highland Laddie. Anonymous. Ay, ay, and away she goes,/Bonnie Hieland laddie! ShS

Highland Loves. Rennie McOwan. but is love itself/realised. PoSH

Highland Mary. Robert Burns. But still within my bosom's core/Shall live my Highland Mary. AnFE; AWP; BoLiVe; GoTF; GTBS; GTBS-P; HBV 1-2; InPo; OAEP; OBEC; OBEV; TreFS; TrGrPo; ViBoPo; WBLP

Highland Region. Victor Price. One look into those sad and haughty eyes/ Tells me she never can be truly mine. PoSH

Highland Shooting Lodge. Maurice Lindsay. ...the drifting shroud/of everything men once had thought they owned. PoSH

The Highland Tinker. Anonymous. And half a yard of parkin hanging down below his knee CoMu

The Highlands' Swelling Blue. George Gordon, Lord Byron. The north and nature taught me to adore/Your scenes sublime, from those beloved before. OBRV

Highly Educated Man. Anonymous. Fighting skeeters down in sunny Tennessee. ABF

The Highway. Louise Driscoll. Love laughs glad in the paths aside. HBV 1-2

The Highway. William Channing Gannett. Highway still must lead to thee! WGRP

The Highway. William Stanley Merwin. ...wherever/It heads for it must get there burning. PoA

Highway Blues. Lightning Hopkins. Reason why I was mad/I didn't know what she done it for BluL

Highway Construction. Carol Earle Chapin. Centuries hence, this scavenged place/May spring again in grass! QQQ

Highway: Michigan. Theodore Roethke. One driver, pinned beneath the seat,/Escapes from the machine at last. AmC

Highway Patrol Stops Me, Going Too Slow. Robert Peterson. Give it a free trial in the privacy/of your own home. NeAC

The Highwayman. Alfred Noyes. Plaiting a dark red love-knot into her long black hair. BeLS; FaBV; FaFP; FPL; GoTF; GTBS; HBV 1-2; HBVY; MaC; MCCG; OBNV; OHFP; PoLf; TreFS

The Highwayman's Ghost. Richard Garnett. But, woe is me, I have never a pocket! StPo

The Highwaymen. John Gay. Our fire their fire surpasses,/And turns all our Lead to Gold. WiR

The Hike. Neil Weiss. ...the/mountain shakes us very gently. SD

Hiking. Joseph Bruchac. an old birch tree. CDW

Hiking up Hieizan with Alam Lau/Buddha's Birthday 1974. Garrett Kaoru Hongo. means to praise the earth and those we love? BrSi

Hilaire Belloc. Humbert Wolfe. Now he has his chance to choose/between the devil and the Jews. FaBoEE

The Hill. Rupert Brooke. –And then you suddenly cried, and turned/away. EnLit; GTBS; HBV 1-2; LiTL; MoBrPo; MoLP; OxBTC; ViBoPo

The Hill. Robert Creeley. which is in me/like a hill. ConAP; NoAm

A Hill. Anthony Hecht. I stood before it for hours in wintertime. CoAP; NYBP

The Hill. Horace Holley. And God, the soul's desire. WGRP

The Hill. Edgar Lee Masters. Of what Abe Lincoln said/One time at Springfield. AmLP; AmP; CMoP; ExPo; FYAP; LiTA; LiTM; NePA; NoAm; NOBA; OxBA; SeCeV; TAP; ViBoPo

The Hill Above the Mine. Malcolm Cowley. your white bones drifting like herons across the moon. NAMP; PoPl; SaC

The Hill Burns. Nan Shepherd. Invisible in itself,/Seen only by its movement. PoSH

The Hill Farmer Speaks. H. S. Thomas. Is, Listen, listen, I am a man like you. GTBS-P; HaMV

Hill Hunger. John Foster West. he was seen way over yander/in Oklahomie. TAT

Hill Love. James Macmillan. in the bracken, by starlight,/had found our peace. PoSH

The Hill of Intrusion. W. S. Graham. Crowded in a gesture/Of homesickness. NePoEA

Hill People. Harriet Gray Blackwell. And obdurate as stone. AmFN

The Hill Pines Were Sighing. Robert Bridges. And the shadowy pine-trees sighed. EG; ExPo; OAEP

Hill-Side Tree. Maxwell Bodenheim. With a whisper that holds the smile you cannot/shape. MAPA

The Hill Wife. Robert Frost.
And he learned of finalities/Besides the grave. CMoP; HAP; InPS; LiTM; NePA; NoAm; NoP
They learned to leave the house-door wide/Until they had lit the lamp inside. VGW

Hillcrest. Edwin Arlington Robinson. No louder now than falling leaves. AP; CoBMV; MAmP; MoAB; OxBA; PPoe

The Hillman Looks Back. Rennie McOwan. All these, sear and grasp, and the hillman knows/Their eternal clasp. PoSH

The Hills. Berton Braley. The spell that shall not fail. MCCG

The Hills. Frances Cornford. The enormous power of their peacefulness. MoBrPo

The Hills. Julian Grenfell. All wrath to power, all yearning/To truth, thy dwelling-place. HBV 1-2

Hills. Arthur Guiterman. God, give me hills to climb,/And strength for climbing! HBVY

Hills. Robin Munro. Wherever hills grow hard, put them to the test. PoSH

The Hills and the Sea. Wilfred (William Wilfred Campbell) Campbell. Where the one wise word and the strong word/Is the word that the great hush saith. CaP

Hills Brothers Coffee. Luci Tapahonso. it sure does it for me. STE

Hills o' My Heart. Ethna (Anna Johnston MacManus) Carbery. On every starry moorland loch, and every shadowy glen,/Hills o' my heart! HBV 1-2

The Hills of Cualann. Joseph Campbell. Two moons of ice. AnIV

The Hills of God. A. A. Buist. My gold-bright maid, her dark-browed shepherd,/Enfolded in the hills of God. PoSH

Hills of God, Break Forth in Singing. John Wright Buckham. Joy! for Christ the Lord is come. AH

The Hills of Pomeroy. Ewart Milne. Full of meaning and shining, the kingdom to which I awoke. NeIP

The Hills of Rest. Albert Bigelow Paine. Nor pause, nor heed, till I behold/The happy, happy Hills of Rest. HBV 1-2; WGRP

Hills of Salt. Dahlia Ravikovich. our bodies two salt hills and our feet seaweed. WPOW

The Hills of Sewanee. George Marion McClellan. And makes its burden less to bear. BANP

Hills of the Middle Distance. Archie Mitchell. Hills of the middle distance: storm and calm,/each with its friendliness. PoSH

The Hills of Tsa la gi. Robert J. Conley. in the safety of the hills of Tsa la gi. STE

Hills picking up the moonlight. Nina Cassian. smashes my forehead/the moon BoWoP

Hillside. Alexander Craig. Whose good and evil no man can foresee. PoAu 1-2

A Hillside Farmer. John Farrar. But, oh, how far we see! HBMV

Hillside Pause. Catharine Morris Wright. "A late apple's good," I say,/ laying down the core. GoYe

A Hillside Thaw. Robert Frost. The thought of my attempting such a stay! CMoP; DiPo; ExPo

Hilo, Hanakahi, Rain Rustling Lehua. *Anonymous.* Tell the refrain, rain rustling lehua. WTO `

Him Evermore I Behold. Henry Wadsworth Longfellow. To the centuries that shall be! TRV

Himalayan Balsam. Anne Stevenson. that says "yes" to the coming winter and a summoning odour of/balsam. FaBoWP

Himself. Daniel Gerard Hoffman. Whose gifts are greater than his own. AMV-80

Himself (excerpt). Edwin John Ellis. I pray that e'er this world be done,/ Christ may relieve his piteous pain. OBMV

The Hind. Sir Thomas Wyatt. "Noli me tangere, for Caesar's I am,/And wild for to hold, though I seem tame." EnPo; OBSC; SeCeV; SiPS; TrGrPo

The Hind and the Panther. John Dryden.
And cou'd not bear the Burd'n of a class. OBS
And thy blest Saviour's blood discharge the mighty sum. FiP
For what my senses can themselves perceive/I need no revelation to believe. OBS
The Hind did first her country Cates provide;/Then couch'd her self securely by her side. PoEL 1-5
The lady of the spotted muff began. CEP; CoBE; FiP; PoEL 1-5; SeCV 1-2; TrPWD
The modesty of fame conceals the rest. OBSV
A second century not half-way run/Since the new honours of her blood begun. OBS
The self same doctrin of the Sacred Page/Convey'd to ev'ry clime, in ev'ry age. OBS
To show the change of winds with his prophetic bill. SeCV 1-2

Hind Etin. *Anonymous.* Where the good priest them christened/And gave her good kirking. OxBB

Hind Etin (A version). *Anonymous.* And when her father wad deceasd,/ Heir of the crown was she. BaBo; ESPB

Hind Etin (B version). *Anonymous.* And now I am the wife of Hynde Etin,/Wha neer got christendame.' ESPB

Hind Horn (A vers.). *Anonymous.* But young Hind Horn he took her to bed. ATP; BaBo; ESPB; ViBoFo

Hind Horn (B vers.). *Anonymous.* And the bride frae the bridegroom was stown awa. BaBo; ESPB

Hind Horn (In Scotland Town). *Anonymous.* "I'll follow my true love wherever he may go,/If I have to beg my food from door to door." AmFP

The Hindoo: He Doesn't Hurt a Fly or a Spider Either. A. K. Ramanujan. in murder, make love with hate,/or simply stalk a local fly. OxBC

The Hinds of Kerry. William S. Wabnitz. Working, working near. GoYe

The Hinge. Sheila Cowing. ...To survive the daily/low tide becomes hard work. AMV-81

Hinky Dinky. *Anonymous.* Hinky dinky parlay-voo. ABF; AS; TrAS

A Hint from Herrick. Thomas Bailey Aldrich. Thus by design or chance did he/Drop anchors to posterity. HBV 1-2

Hint from Voiture. William Shenstone. Yet must it still forever pose him/ To match–what Celia never shows him. EnLoPo

A Hint o' Snaw. William Soutar. On the high hills/A hint o' snaw. PoSH

A Hint to the Wise. Pringle Barret. ...A little bird/May cause a lot of trouble by/Repeating what he's heard. HBVY

A Hinted Wish. Martial (Marcus Valerius Martialis). You must be mad beyond redress,/If my next wish you cannot guess! AWP; LiTW

Hints on Pronunciation for Foreigners. *Anonymous.* I'd mastered it when I was five! FaBoUs

Hinx, Minx. *Anonymous.* You or I must be he. OxNR

Hip Shakin' Strut. Hokum Boys: Georgia Tom. (Say, big boy, what did the elephant say to the cat?) BluL

Hippety Hop to the Barber Shop. Mother Goose. And one for Sister Mandy. SoPo; TiPo

Hippies. Barry Dempster. they drew a figure of an angel/braiding daisies in the hair of God. CaPN

Hippity Hop to Bed. Leroy F. Jackson. Go hippity hop to bed. TiPo

The Hippo. Theodore Roethke. Some time I think I'll live that way. VGW

Hippocrene. Amy Lowell. And, with a fine brush,/trace little pictures/To show when you return. MoLP

Hippodromania; or Whiffs from the Pipe (excerpt). Adam Lindsay Gordon. God send me an ending as fair as his/Who died in his stirrups there! CBAP

Hippolytus. Euripides.
And Earth, the ancient life-giver, increaseth/Joy among the meadows, like a tree. AWP
from his own gates? AWP

Hippolytus Temporizes. Hilda ("H. D.") Doolittle. beneath quivering of molten flesh,/of veins, purple as violets?) SBG

Hippopotamothalamion. John Hall Wheelock. Milton, thou should'st be living at this hour. FiBHP; FYAP; NePoAm-2

The Hippopotamus. Hilaire Belloc. his hide is sure to flatten 'em. FiBHP; InPK; PoPl

Hippopotamus. Joanna Cole. "My," fish say, "he eats a lot-of-us!" NTCP

The Hippopotamus. Georgia Roberts Durston. If you touched the Hippo,/ Hippo-pot-a-mus. TiPo

The Hippopotamus. Thomas Stearns Eliot. While the True Church remains below/Wrapt in the old miasmal mist. AnAmPo; AWP; HoPM; LiTB; NAMP; OBMV; PoPl; VGW

The Hippopotamus. Oliver Herford. But why they called that thing a horse,/That's what is Greek to me. NA

The Hippopotamus. Ogden Nash. As you no doubt delight the eye/Of other hippopotami. FaBV; OnUR

Hipporhinostricow. Spike Milligan. The creature is protected you see/From silly people like you and me. AmMo

Hiraeth in N.W.3. Wynford Vaughan-Thomas. All the raptures of love from a Bangor B.A.! NOBL

Hiram Powers' "Greek Slave." Elizabeth Barrett Browning. By thunders of white silence, overthrown. SBG; VLP

The Hired Man on Horseback. Eugene Manlove Rhodes. "To the Master of the Workmen, with the tally of/his work!" BPAW

The Hired Man's Way. John Kendrick Bangs. He's always glad to stop his work/And come and talk to me. OBCA

Hiroshige. Mark M. Perlberg. The fog-blurred grave. NYBP

Hiroshima. Margaret Rockwell. The moment that would force the world to love. PPON

Hiroshima Exit. Joy Kogawa. That outside this store/Is another door BrSi

A Hiroshima Lullaby. Joseph Langland. We fold your paper cranes. PPON

His Adoration. David Morton. Aware of One most pleased at what I do. ISi

His Age. Robert Herrick. The cole once spent, we'l then to bed,/Farre more than night bewearied. CaPo; SeCP

His Answer. Clara Ann Thompson. His heart had learned, through weariness and care,/The patience, that he deemed he'd sought in vain BlSi

His Are the Thousand Sparkling Rills. Frances Alexander. That parched dry Lip, that fading Face,/That Thirst were all for me. OxBI

His Banner over Me. Gerald Massey. But, as I lift mine eyes above,–His banner over me is love. HBV 1-2; WGRP

His Being Was in Her Alone. Sir Philip Sidney. As all the rest, so now the stone/That tombs the two is justly one. ELP

His Best. *Anonymous.* "Well done! you did your best." STF

His Body. Sandra McPherson. Each lonely and earthly, wanting to be celestial. AmPA; GeTw; GP

His Cavalier. Robert Herrick. Ay, and a world of pikes pass through! CaPo; GoJo

His Charge to Julia at His Death. Robert Herrick. As Love shall helpe thee, when thou do'st/go hence/Unto thy everlasting residence. SeCV 1-2

His Content in the Country. Robert Herrick. And like our living, where we're known/To very few, or else to none. CaPo; EnLit; SeCV 1-2

His Creed. Robert Herrick. Lastly, that JESUS is a Deed/Of Gift from God: And here's my Creed. SeCeV

His Delight. Meilir ap Gwalchmai. the nightingale's rapturous song is an ode that/ceases not. LiTW

His Desire. Robert Herrick. Tickling the cittern with his quill. CABA; OAEP; OBSP

His Dream of the Sky-Land: A Farewell Poem (excerpt). Li Po. Gone was the radiant world of gossamer. WSC

His Ejaculation to God. Robert Herrick. Speak but the word, and cure me quite. SeCV 1-2

His Face. Florence Earle Coates. His the divinest face I ever looked into! OHIP

His Fare-well to Sack. Robert Herrick. :what's done by me/Hereafter, shall smell of the Lamp, not thee. AnAnS 2; CaPo; OAEP; SeCP; SeCV 1-2

His Farewell to His Unkind and Unconstant Mistress. Francis Davison. Loving not me alone. ElL; OBSC

His Father's Hands. Thomas Kinsella. countless little nails/squirming and dropping out of it. FaBoIP

His Further Resolution. *Anonymous.* Then if others share with me,/ Farewell her! whate'er she be! HBV 1-2

His Garments. Esther Lloyd Hagg. White garments from Thy stainless life/Oh, give me, Lord, to wear! PGD

His Gift and Mine. Edith B. Gurley. And I am debtor in His sight. BLRP

His Glory Tell. Horatius Bonar. Great Prince of Peace! BePJ

His Grange, or Private Wealth. Robert Herrick. Where care/None is, slight things do lightly please. AnAnS 2; CaPo; FM; GoJo; OAEP; SeCV 1-2

His Hand Shall Cover Us. Isaac Ben Samuel. Lord, now let our crying reach Thee. TrJP

His Hands. John Richard Moreland. Whom these frail, broken/Hands hold fast. TRV

His Heart Was True to Poll. Sir Francis Cowley Burnand. So he back to Bristol bolted,/For his heart was true to Poll. HBV 1-2

His Hope or Sheet-Anchor. Robert Herrick. ...I'm one/Wildered in this vast watery region. CaPo

His Immortality. Thomas Hardy. Dying amid the dark. CMoP; PoPle

His Lachrimae or Mirth, Turn'd to Mourning. Robert Herrick. And turn'd my voice/Into the noise/Of those that sit and weep. SeCV 1-2

His Lady's Cruelty. Sir Philip Sidney. Do they call "virtue" there–ungratefulness? OBEV

His Lady's Death. Pierre Ronsard. And for Death's sake, I am in love with Death. AWP

His Lady's Tomb. Pierre Ronsard. That dead, as living, she may be with roses. AWP

His Last Week. Elinor Lennen. And those who had doubted remembering words/he had spoken. PGD

His Legs Ran About. Ted Hughes. Rushing through the vast astonishment. LLLT

His Life Is Ours. Dorothy Conant Stroud. Sin, shame, and death; His life is ours/Whatever may befall! STF

His Living Monument. Minna Irving. And every black he freed is now/His living monument. PGD

His Lunch Bucket. Doug Cockrell. With all he left her then/to lay open/bitten. Psk

His Majesty. Theron Brown. And nobody ask me why. AA

His Majesty the Letter-Carrier. Emanuel Carnevali. Oh, never mind–tomorrow,tomorrow! AnAmPo

His mansion in the pool. Emily Dickinson. Demosthenes has vanished/In Waters Green– OBAL

His Metrical Prayer: Before Execution. James Graham. And confident thou'lt raise me with the just. OxBS; PrIm

His Metrical Vow. James Graham. I'll tune Thy Elegies to Trumpet-sounds,/And write Thy Epitaph in Blood and Wounds! OxBS; ViBoPo

His Mother in Her Hood of Blue. Lizette Woodworth Reese. But mothers never change at all./Jesus! ISi; OHIP

His Mother-in-Law. Walter Parke. And then, at the risk of breaking his neck,/Turned somersaults home to tea. FiBHP

His Mother's Joy. John White Chadwick. That love had triumphed over death. AA

His Mother's Love. Noah Stern. After to scald him, until he fled despairing to his room–to the fist of/his cruel fate. VWA

His Mother's Service to Our Lady. Francois Villon. And in this faith I choose to live and die. AWP; CAW; CTC; ISi; LiTW

His Muse Speakes to Him. William Habington. Dead in loves firmament, no starre shall shine/So nobly faire, so purely chaste as thine. AnAnS 2

His Name Is at the Top. Anonymous. My Lord must have the most–because/His name is at the top! STF

His Necessary Darkness. Nancy Sullivan. ...let our black ashes/celebrate his necessary darkness. TAP

His Own Epitaph. Thomas (Tom) Brown. The Rose in Wood Street kill'd me. FaBoEE

His Own Epitaph. Robert Herrick. But age hath brought me right to bed. CaPo

His Own Epitaph, When He Was Sick, Being Fellow in New College... John Hoskyns. Part of the dust of so worthy a college. FaBoEE

His Own True Wife. von Eschenbach, Sir Wolfram Love so sweet bestows in all men's sight his own true/wife! AWP

His Parting from Her. John Donne. And, Dearest Friend, since we must part,/drown night/With hope of day; burdens well borne are/light CoBE

His Parting with Mrs. Dorothy Kennedy. Robert Herrick. (And Love will swear't) my dearest did not so. MyFE

His Petition to Queen Anne of Denmark (1618). Sir Walter Ralegh. Who brings us equal, if not greater, bliss. SiPS

His Picture. John Donne. To feed on that which to disused tastes seems tough. CBEP

His Plan. Anonymous. Our purchased souls Him first and last/Love, trust, obey, adore. STF

His Plan for Me. Martha Snell Nicholson. Take me and break me, mould me to/The pattern Thou hast planned. STF

His Plans for Old Age. William Meredith. ...If only his energy lasts. TAP

His Poetry His Pillar. Robert Herrick. Here is my hope,/And my pyramides. AnAnS 2; CaPo; EG; EnL; JCP; LoBV; MyFE; OBS; QFR; SeCP

His Prayer for Absolution. Robert Herrick. That one of all the rest shall be/The glory of my work and me. AnAnS 2; EnL; EnLi 1-2; OxBoCh; SeCV 1-2; TrPWD; TRV

His Prayer to Ben Jonson. Robert Herrick. And thou, Saint Ben, shalt be/Writ in my psalter. AnAnS 2; BoLiVe; CaPo; CavP; JCP; NoP; OAEP; OBS; OBSP; OxBoLi; PP; SeCeV; SeCV 1-2; TrGrPo

His Presence. Dale Schulz. And no good thing withheld from me/As I walked in His own way. STF

His Promises. Martha Snell Nicholson. And He will keep His word! BePJ

His Quest. Lewis Frank Tooker. He searched, but never searched his heart. AA

His Request. Owen Roe O'Sullivan. ...the whole to have/Harmony like a bell. BIrV

His Request to Julia. Robert Herrick. Better 'twere my book were dead/Than to live not perfected. CaPo; OBS

His Return to London. Robert Herrick. Give thou my sacred relics burial. AnAnS 2; CaPo; EnLit; FaBoPP; FF

His Sailing from Julia. Robert Herrick. Work that to life, and let me ever dwell/In thy remembrance (Julia). So farewell. PoEL 1-5

His Saviour's Words, Going to the Cross. Robert Herrick. What bitter cups had been your due,/Had He not drank them up for you. NOCV

His Shield. Marianne Moore. ...Don't be envied or/armed with a measuring-rod. DTC; LiTM; NePA

His Side/Her Side. Jeffrey Skinner. Answer the question, bastard. Don't waste my life. AMV-81

His Sleep. Constance Urdang. And squint wryly into the light/Of our common life. AMV-81

His Son. Callimachus. This grave a father's hopes doth hide. AWP

His Sovereignty. Kalonymos Ben Moses. And He will answer, He will say,/"Forgiven." TrJP

His Statement of the Case. James Herbert Morse. But you shall see gray beards in a long row,/Upon the rustic roads where I now go. AA

His Swans. Geoffrey Grigson. One by one his white birds/Falter, and fall, out of the sky. FaBoRV

His Sweetheart Slain. Anonymous. But Crist ich hire biteche/That was my lemman. OxBM

His Task–and Ours. Dorothy Gould. Undaunted, plan/To make the world/A Home for Man. PGD

His Tears to Thamasis. Robert Herrick. Receive this vow, So fare ye well for ever. FaBoPP; OAEP

His Throne Is with the Outcast. James Russell Lowell. His throne is with the outcast and the weak. TrCP

His Toy, His Dream, His Rest. John Berryman.
And never again can come, like a man slapped,/news like this. FaBoMo; NOBA
and refuses to come home. NOBA
Delmore, Delmore! FaBoMo; NOBA
when he was young & gift-strong. NOBA

His Trees. Mark Van Doren. As ever a second childhood understands. AnFE

His Wife. Rachel Blaustein. but my fetters of iron are stronger–/sevenfold! WPOW

His Wife. Shirley Kaufman. Testing her own lips then,/the coolness, till/she could taste the salt. LCAP

His Will Be Done. Annie Johnson Flint. His tender, loving, joyous will–be done"? BLRP

His Winding-Sheet. Robert Herrick. To be revealed/Next at that great Platonic Year,/And then meet here. AnFE; CaPo; HBV 1-2; OBEV

His Wisdom. Nicholas Breton. And thou wert free and I were still in bond. ALV; OBSC

His Wish to God. Robert Herrick. Reading Thy Bible, and my Book; so end. AnAnS 2; OxBoCh

Hist, oh hist. Thomas Lovell Beddoes. The wildest bee in black and yellow. EG

Hist Whist. Edward Estlin Cummings. devil/devil/wheeEEE OFD; SO

An Historic Moment. William J. Harris. and did a full somersault. BOLo

Historical Incidents. Clarence Day. Muttering and poking spears/At every fish he found. InMe

The Historical Judas. Howard Nemerov. To make our meanness look like justice in/All histories commissioned by the winners. NoP

Historical Museum, Manitoulin Island. Lisel Mueller. warm rooms, soft speech, long years. PoA

An Historical Poem. Anonymous. If a king's brother can such mischief bring,/Then how much greater mischief as a king? APAS

Historical Reflections. John Hollander. Save for this trivial/Idiosyncrasy,/Didn't a much. DBV; NIP; OBAL

The Historie of Squyer William Meldrum: Squire Meldrum at..... Sir David Lindsay. And to the ship he rowit fast. OxBS

Historiography. Lorenzo Thomas. ...in the dull asylum/Of our own enslavements. But Bird was a junkie! APU

History. Robert Fitzgerald. Loving what he beheld and will behold. FYAP; MoVE

History. Robert Francis. and watch the riffraft driftwood floating by? LCAP

History. Jorie Graham. ...The ones where simple/crumbs over the forest/floor endure/to help us home? NPGG

History. Arthur Gregor. ...neither moves toward us/nor falls into watery wastes as we pass? TAP

History. Art Lange. ...It's great,/but not for me. APU

History. D. H. Lawrence. Till at length they mate. BrPo

History. James Liddy. "Let us steal softly out of town,/Oisin, until we reach my place." CIP

History. Robert Lowell. O there's a terrifying innocence in my face/drenched with the silver salvage of the mornfrost. CAPP; HaCAP; TAP

History. Gary Soto. The places/In which we all begin. GP

History. Paul Tanaquil. How once a woman's breast was white. HBMV

History. Robert Penn Warren. Our hearts with fable gray. NoAm

A History. John Williams. And saw at last his God's dark purblind heart/In the lion's eyeball, like a wet coal. NePoAm-2

History and Abstraction. Thomas Lux. in the red vase behind you. AmPA

History Lesson. Mark Van Doren. Then lighted strength; and then the letting go. NYBP

History Lesson for My Son. Ted Kooser. around my feet, my bare feet, where they lay. PoL

History: Madness. Stan Rice. I suffered facts,/And have the bloody photographs to prove it. NPGG

History of a Literary Movement. Howard Nemerov. And Impli, though one of my/Dearest friends, can never,/I have decided, become great. NePoEA; PP

The History of Arizona: How It Was Made and Who Made It. Charles O. Brown. For with his own realm it compares so well/He feels assured it surpasses hell. BPAW

A History of Civilization. Albert Goldbarth. In the fern bar a hand tries a knee, as if unplanned. HaCAP; MAYP

The History of Communications and a Running Account. Pien Chih-lin. I keep for you a running account. LiTW

History of Education. David McCord. And that's what teaching is and was. NIP; OBAL

History of France. Kenward Elmslie. At lunchtime, they take it out,/the tongue-shaped wooden box;/today is beautiful. ANYP

History of Ideas. J. V. Cunningham. Love is God, and sex conversion. NIP

The History of Insipids. John Freke. Mankind, like miserable frogs,/Is wretched, kinged by storks or logs. APAS

A History of Lesbianism. Judy Grahn. ...it's the question/of male domination that makes everybody/angry. PeHV

A History of Love. William Carlos Williams. while a bird jigs and ol' Bunk/Johnson blows his horn. VGW

History of My Heart. Robert Pinsky. The pure source poured altogether out and away. NPGG

A History of Peace. Robert Graves. And of Jane Reece whom Thomas kept in dread/By Pax Romana of his board and bed. HBMV

A History of Photography. Albert Goldbarth. they did it by hand. MAYP

The History of Prince Edward Island. Anonymous. My verse is done, my song is sung, Prince Edward Isle, adieu! ShS

The History of the Flood. John Heath-Stubbs. Merciful and gracious/Bang Bang Bang Bang. MoBS; OxBTC

The History of the Human Body.... Elinor Nauen. I like those goddamn green bananas APU

History of the Modern World. Stanton A. Coblentz. And sees man's slave the master of mankind. PGD

A History of the Pets. David Huddle. ...Goat. Skunk. Some snakes. PPJ

The History of the U.S. Winifred Sackville Stoner. And we are praying that she'll stay forever in our U.S.A. TreF; YaD

The History of the World as Pictures. Nancy Sullivan. How to realize his question/Let alone his answer? CoPo

The History of Truth. W. H. Auden. A nothing no one need believe is there. FaBoMo

History of World Languages. D. J. Enright. And they were down to earth. OxBC

The Hit. John Drinkwater. and it is hot, hotter than ever/and I like it. FaPON

A Hit at the Times. A. O. McGrew. For the subject I've touched, will make us root hog, or die. PoOW

Hit or Miss. Lewis (Charles Lutwidge Dodgson) Carroll. All owls are satisfactory;/Some excuses are unsatisfactory. FaBoNo

Hitch Haiku. Gary Snyder.
breakfast in Elko. LCAP
by moving a single board. LCAP
falling six miles. LCAP
forty miles from farms. LCAP
in the Wobbly hall. LCAP
men all eating lunch. LCAP
mudflats of Willapa Bay. LCAP
the noon whistle. LCAP; SM
out packed in the rain. LCAP

over blackberries. LCAP
Queets Indian Reservation in the rain. LCAP
shattered obsidian. LCAP
Smoke Creek desert. LCAP
soaking in summer rain. LCAP
steep travel a-/head. LCAP
through the dark stony desert. LCAP
too tired to talk. LCAP
the twang of a bowstring. LCAP

Hitchhiker. Jack Marshall. I feel the moon's hub unhinge from center/And roll berserk. NYBP

Hither We Come, Our Dearest Lord. Enoch W. Freeman. What can we do but follow thee. AH

Hitherto and Henceforth. Annie Johnson Flint. And His grace is all sufficient/For the needs of you and me. BLRP

Hitherto Hath the Lord Helped. Anonymous. Ans ia "the same today." BLRP

Hitler, Frothy-Mouth. Anonymous. He's so scared his buttocks quake. WTO

Hits and Runs. Carl Sandburg. ...and the umpire's throat fought in the dust for a/song. SD

The Hittites. Roy Fuller. Whose precise nature never will be known. OBSP

Hmmmm, 8. Leslie Scalapino. the woman's mouth makes a sound like the word Mama. NPGG

Hmmmm, 9. Leslie Scalapino. Seriously, I am fascinated by the way a seal moves. NPGG

Hmmmm, 10. Leslie Scalapino. ...only the muscles/of her haunches appearing to move. NPGG

Hmmmm, 13. Leslie Scalapino. an oyster will cover the irritant in him by coating it over and over. NPGG

Hmmmm, 14. Leslie Scalapino. pebbles and grains will be modifed put in human form. NPGG

Hmmmm, 15. Leslie Scalapino. I took a glance around before I wiped my mouth. Feeling weary. NPGG

Hmmmm, 19. Leslie Scalapino. I wish that I could make you yelp just once. NPGG

Hmmmm, 21. Leslie Scalapino. ...By morning, naturally, I was sated. NPGG

Hmmmm, 22. Leslie Scalapino. as I parted her labia, and finally gently entered her female part. NPGG

Hmmmm, 22. Leslie Scalapino. putting our arms around the necks of the men, began kissing them. NPGG

Ho. Al Young. heaven aint the only H in the dictionary GP; NPGG

Ho, Brother Teig. Anonymous. So I levelled my gun and I shot him dead. GBP

Ho, Everyone That Thirsteth. Alfred Edward Housman. The lad that hopes for heaven/Shall fill his mouth with mould. OAEL 1-2

Ho Ho Ho Caribou. Joseph Ceravolo. ,but/die in you and am/never born again in/the same place; never/stop! ANYP

Ho! Westward Ho!. Ossian E. Dodge. Soon the world shall know/That all is grand in the western land;/Ho! westward Ho! BLSo

Ho! Ye Sun, Moon, Stars. Anonymous. Make its path smooth—then shall it travel/beyond the four hills! PrIm

Hoarded Joy. Dante Gabriel Rossetti. And the woods wail like echoes from the sea. MaVP

Hob Gobbling's Song. James Russell Lowell. And to all such I give fair warning/Of nightmares ere to-morrow morning. OBCA

Hob, Shoe, Hob; Hob, Shoe, Hob. Anonymous. And that's well shod. OxNR

Hob upon a Holiday. Anonymous. For Hob is Cupid in disguise. NOEC

Hobart Town, Van Diemen's Land. Hal Porter. Watchman Death—eternal cown–/Crows the hour through Hobart town. NOAV

Hobbes, 1651. John Hollander. ...nowhere beneath the gray/Sky would be much safer seemed very plain. NoAm

The Hobbit (excerpt). J. R. R. Tolkien. We must away, ere break of day,/To win our harps and gold from him! WSC

Hobie Noble. Anonymous. Before I were ca'd traitor Mains!/That eats and drinks of meal and maut. BaBo; ESPB; OxBB; ViBoFo

Hobo's Lullaby. Anonymous. Well, that's the hobo's lullaby. FSW

Hobson and His Men. Robert Loveman. Hobson and his men. PAH

The Hobthrush. Anonymous. An' I'll be wi' thee–noo. GBP

Hoc Cygno Vinces. Henry Hawkins. O make them white, that they may singing die! ACP

Hoc Est Corpus. Alex Comfort. time like a permanent stone, its cold weight judging. LiTB; LiTM

Hoccleve's Humorous Praise of His Lady. Thomas Hoccleve. And as the jeet hir yen glistren ay. OAEP

The Hock-Cart, or Harvest Home. Robert Herrick. Not sent ye for to drown your pain,/But for to make it spring again. AnAnS 2; CaPo; EBEV; FaBoPV; JCP; OAEP; OBS; SeCP; SeCV 1-2; ViBoPo

Hoddley, Poddley, Puddle and Fogs. Anonymous. What will become of the mice and rats? FaBoNo; OxNR

Hoelderlin's Old Age. Stephen Spender. Burning intensely in the centre of a cold sky. NoAm

Hog at the Manger. Norma Farber. I'll make you a small/silk purse. PCh

Hog Drovers. *Anonymous.* By bringing a prettier one here. AmFP

The Hog-Eye Man (with music). *Anonymous.* Her golden hair hanging down to her knees. AS

Hog-Eye (with music). *Anonymous.* Ro-ly-bo-ly sho-ly hog-eye! AS

Hog Meat. Daniel Webster Davis. Sum souse or pork or chidlins, sum sphar-rib, or de chine. BANP

Hog Rogues on the Harricane. *Anonymous.* Up come Bob and Stokes a-walking on their heels. OuSiCo

Hogamus, Higamus. *Anonymous.* Women monogamous. ELU

Hogarth. Charles Churchill. Which you had never seen, or could not taste. DBV

A Hoggie Dead! *Anonymous.* Come try! come try! come try! PBBP

Hogwash. Robert Francis. Daisies, daisies, in a field of daisies? LCAP

Hogyn. *Anonymous.* Or else your breath is wonder strong,/Hum, ha, trill go bell. GBP

Hogyn cam to bower's dore. *Anonymous.* Or elles your breth ys wonder strong,/Hum, ha, trill go bell.' EnPo

Hohenlinden. Thomas Campbell. And every turf beneath their feet/Shall be a soldier's sepulchre. BeLS; CBEP; FaBoCh; FaBoRV; FaPoR; GN; GTBS; GTBS-P; HBV 1-2; NOBE; OBNC; OBRV; OBWP; OnMSP; RoGo; TreF; WaaP; WBLP; WHA

Hokey, Pokey, Whisky, Thum. *Anonymous.* Says the King of the Cannibal/Islands. OxNR

Hokkaido. Jim Trifilio. sister by sister around the fire/that no one watches go out. FAZ

Hokku: In the Falling Snow. Richard Wright. Until they are white IDB

Hokku Poems. Richard Wright. That he left his lonely caw/Behind in the fields. AmNP; PoBA

Hokusai's Wave. Olga Cabral. there is only one wave/in the universe/and Hokusai is/master of it. PoDr

Hol' de Win' Don't Let It Blow. *Anonymous.* Hol' de win'! Hol' de win' don't let it blow. BoAN 1-2

Hold. Patrick Reginald Chalmers. Sir Guy's tall phantom stoops to pat/His little phantom hound! HBV 1-2

Hold Back Thy Hours. Francis Beaumont and John Fletcher. Stay, and hide all:/But help not, though she call. ViBoPo

Hold Fast Your Dreams. Louise Driscoll.
For little dreams to go. BiCB; SoPo; TiPo
Hold fast–hold fast your dreams! BLPA; FaBoBe; FPL; HBMV

Hold Hard, These Ancient Minutes. Dylan Thomas. Your sport in summer as the spring runs an–/grily. CoBE

Hold, Men, Hold! *Anonymous.* Hold, men, hold! ChBR

Hold My Hand. Edmund Pennant. to gods who don't mind being photographed,/who have the aplomb of models. PoDr

Hold On. *Anonymous.* Keep your hand on that plow, hold on. FSW

Hold on, Abraham. *Anonymous.* Uncle Sam's boys are coming right along, six hundred thousand/ strong. ABF

Hold the Fort. *Anonymous.* Side by side we battle onward,/Victory will come. FSW

Hold the Fort. Philip Bliss. "By Thy Grace, we will." FSW

Hold the Wind. *Anonymous.* Tell um 'bout the world I just come from. GBP

Hold Thou Me Fast. Christina Georgina Rossetti. So earth shall know at last and heaven at last/That I am Thine. BePJ

Hold-Up. Louis MacNeice. ...The conductress/Was dark and lost, refused to change. FaBoIP

Hold up Your Head. *Anonymous.* Mend your clothes. OxNR

Holderlin. Delmore Schwartz. This is eterntiy! Eternity is now! MoRP

Holding Hands. Lenore M. Link. They're holding hands/By holding tails. MoShBr; NTCP; SoPo

Holding On. Richard Jackson. loud kite in a remembered sky. AMV-80

Holding-paddock. William Hart-Smith. and thistles inside. AnNZ

Holding the Mirror up to Nature. Howard Nemerov. the buzzard circles like a clock. PoA

Holding the Sky. William Stafford. Those dark mountains have never wavered. RFM

A Hole in the Floor. Richard Wilbur. Inflaming the damask love-seat/And the whole dangerous room. NoAm; NOBA; SoSe

The Hole in the Sea. Marvin Bell. Courage is in that bottle,/the driest thing there is. NYBP

The Holes. Stephen Berg. Sometimes I want to die because of this. NaP; NYBP

Holes in the Sky (excerpt). Louis MacNeice. Man is a spirit,/Let the bells ring. TRV

The Holiday. Thomas Frank Bignold. And to that end as swiftly as I can/Shall take this copy to the "Englishman'. OBTV

Holiday. John Davidson. Challenge Fate to throw the main. OBVV

Holiday. Horace. Until our weary singing ends/In lullabies to-night. AWP

Holiday. Henry Dawson Lowry. Dance the gay daffodils in smocks of gold. OBVV

A Holiday. Lizette Woodworth Reese. And I its happy guest. AA

Holiday. Adrienne Rich. The long walk back to winter, leagues away. MoLP

Holiday in Reality. Wallace Stevens. And I taste at the root of the tongue the unreal of what is real. NePA; OxBA

Holiday Inn at Bemidji. Gerald Vizenor. molded orchards in the concrete STE

A Holiday Task. Gilbert Abbott A Becket. Change hands ma'am/Celere–run away, just in sham. NA

Holidays. Henry Wadsworth Longfellow. The secret anniversaries of the heart. PoToHe

Holidays. Eva Mylonas. I have no continuity/coherence/conventions. BoWoP

Hollandaise. Sharon Bryan. that assume a willing suspension of despair. MAYP

Hollin, Green Hollin. *Anonymous.* To live at large with liberty,/Birk and green hollin. GBP

The Holloe Menne (parody). Harrison Everard. Noe bangen butte wampere inferled BXAP

The Hollow at Ilbalintja Soak. *Anonymous.* Impenetrable hollow! NOAV

The Hollow Flute. Avner Strauss. Dry bones make good flutes. VWA

The Hollow Land. William Morris. Where the hills are blue. AtBAP; PoEL 1-5

The Hollow Men. Thomas Stearns Eliot. Not with a bang but a whimper. AP; APA; BiP; CoBMV; DiPo; ForPo; InPS; LiTA; LiTM; MAPA; MBW 1-2; MoAB; MoAmPo; NAMP; OAEL 1-2; OBMV; PAI; PoPl

The Hollow Thesaurus. Roger McDonald. This has not happened before. CBAP

A Hollow Tree. Robert Bly. ...In the silence/many feathers. GP; NNaP

The Holly. Walter De la Mare. With berries burning through! CMoP

The Holly. King of England Henry VIII. Who hath my heart truly,/Be sure, and ever shall! CTC; OBSC

The Holly. Edith King. When the ground glitters white with the fresh fallen snow. ChBR

Holly against Ivy. *Anonymous.* So wold I that every man had/That with Ivy will hold! MeEL

Holly and His Merry Men. *Anonymous.* Non but the howlet that cry "How, how!" OxBM

Holly and Ivy. *Anonymous.*
Non but the owlet/That creye, "How! how!" MeEL
Say me no villainy/In lands where we go.' CBEP; OxBM

Holly and Mistletoe. Eleanor Farjeon. That boys shall kiss their share. PCh

The Holly and the Ivy. *Anonymous.*
The holly bears the crown. ELP; GBP
In the holly colour,/The everlasting green. OBET
Sweet singing in the choir. FSW; PCh

Holly Beareth Berries (excerpt). *Anonymous.* She would not for a hundred pounds/Serve Holly so. PBBP

The Holly Bough. Charles Mackay. And join in our embraces/Under the holly bough. OBVV

Holly Fairies. Aileen Fisher. because the fairies/still are there/beneath the red and green. ChBR

The Holly Tree. Robert Southey. That in my age as cheerful I might be/As the green winter of the Holly Tree. EnRP; HBV 1-2

A Hollyhock. Frank Dempster Sherman. And sound of dancing on the floor. AA

The Hollyhocks. Craven Langstroth Betts. And round us is the court of Day! AA

Hollywood. Don Blanding. Perhaps you're a goddess that bears a bright beacon. YaD

Hollywood. Karl Shapiro. This is a soul, a possible proud Florence. LiTM; OxBA

Holocaust 1944. Anne Ranasinghe. Intoning the blessing/Blessed be the Lord... VWA

Holstenwall. Sidney Keyes. Have pity, master. This is a wicked land. FaBoTw

Holy angels, in envy I cast no sigh. Gaspara Stampa. your glory is eternal and fixed in space,/while mine can pass by in a few days. BoWoP

Holy Baptism. George Herbert. Childhood is health. HBV 1-2; PoEL 1-5

Holy Bible, Book Divine. John Burton. Precious treasure, thou art mine. BLRP; WBLP

The Holy City. Frederic Edward Weatherly. Hosanna for evermore! BLRP; WBLP

Holy Cross. *Anonymous.* And sweeter be the burden that hangs upon thee. ACP; CAW

Holy-Cross Day. Robert Browning. A trophy to bear, as we march, thy band,/South, East, and on to the Pleasant Land! VLP

The Holy Earth: In the Immense Cathedral. John Hall Wheelock. Save as it serve the many, mysteriously made One. MoRP

The Holy Eclogue. Sister, Francisca Josefa del Castillo. Let me not stray again, but keep/Me folded fast amid Thy little sheep. CAW

The Holy Eucharist. Pedro Calderon de la Barca. Life and Sacrament to me. CAW

The Holy Fair. Robert Burns. An' monie jobs that day begin,/May end in houghmagandie/Some ither day. CEP; EiCP; EnRP; LAuP; OAEP; OBSV

Holy Family. Muriel Rukeyser. Born, born, we know how it goes. MoAmPo

Holy Father, Great Creator. Alexander V. Griswold. Great Jehovah, great Jehovah,/Form our hearts and make them thine. AH

The Holy Field. Henry Hart Milman. The bones that underneath thee lie/Shall live for Hell or Heaven! OxBoCh

Holy Ghost. *Anonymous.* Roll this golden chariot along,/And I won't stand back behind. OuSiCo

Holy God, We Praise Thy Name. Clarence A. Walworth. Holy, holy, holy Lord. AH; TreFT

The Holy Grail: The Book of Gawain (excerpt). Jack Spicer. I, Gawain, who once was a knight of the Grail in a dark forest. PoM

The Holy Ground. *Anonymous.* And when our money is all spent we'll go to sea once more. OBSS

A Holy Hill. George William Russell. The wrath of stone. AWP

Holy, Holy, Holy. Reginald Heber. God in Three Persons, Blessed Trinity! HBV 1-2; OHIP; TreFT; VLP

The Holy Innocents. Robert Lowell. Lamb of the shepherds, Child, how still you lie. ATP; ConAP; InPo; InvP; MoAB; MoAmPo; NePoEA; OBCP; OxBC; SBVL

The Holy Innocents. Prudentius (Aurelius Clemens Prudentius). And Father and the Paraclete,/The while the endless ages run! CAW

Holy Innocents. Christina Georgina Rossetti. Until thou wake to light/And love and warmth to-morrow. HBV 1-2; HBVY

The Holy Land of Walsingham. Benjamin Francis Musser. The beauty that was Walsingham, that patience/that is Rome. ISi

The Holy Longing. Johann Wolfgang von Goethe. you are only a troubled guest/on the dark earth. NU

The Holy Man. *Anonymous.* Whoso doth the will of the King. OnYI

Holy Matrimony. John Keble. Till to the home of gladness/With Christ's own Bride they rise. AMEN. HBV 1-2; VLP

Holy Night. Nathaniel A. Benson. When man and star stood marvelling at His birth. CaP

Holy Night. Lucille Clifton. joseph, i shine, oh joseph, oh/illuminated night. GeTw

Holy Numbers Litany to the Holy Spirit (excerpt). Robert Herrick. When to Thee I have appealed,/Sweet Spirit comfort me! EnLit

The Holy Nunnery. *Anonymous.* But she softly whispered him,/"I darena this avow." BaBo; ESPB

The Holy of Holies. Gilbert Keith Chesterton. Adonai Elohim! MoRP; TRV; WGRP

The Holy Office. James Joyce. My soul shall spurn them evermore. FaBoTw; NoAm; OxBTC

The Holy Ones, the Young Ones. Chayyim Zeldis. until/their lives burst TrJP

Holy Order. John Basil Boothroyd. That even recording angels find it best/To keep us alphabetical. FiBHP

Holy Poems. George Barker. Cruel to be kind to all his kind is he. MoPo

The Holy Rose. Vyacheslav Ivanov. And seething overflow...Hosanna, Lord! AWP

Holy Satyr. Hilda ("H. D.") Doolittle. answering note for note. MoAmPo

Holy Sonnets, I. John Donne. And thou like Adamant draw mine iron heart. EBEV; EG; MeLP; NOBE; NOCV; NoP; OAEP; OBS; OxBoCh; PoEL 1-5; SeCP

Holy Sonnets, II. John Donne. And Satan hates mee, yet is loth to lose mee. MasP; OBS

Holy Sonnets, III. John Donne. Th'effect and cause, the punishment and sinne. MasP; OBS

Holy Sonnets, IV. John Donne. Or wash thee in Christ's blood, which hath this might/That being red, it dyes red souls to white. EBEV; JCP

Holy Sonnets, V. John Donne. And burn me, O Lord, with a fiery zeal/Of Thee and Thy House, which doth in eating heal. MyFE; TEP

Holy Sonnets, VI. John Donne. For thus I leave the world, the flesh, the devil. EBEV; JCP; LoBV

Holy Sonnets, VII. John Donne. Teach me how to repent; for that's as good/As if thou hadst sealed my pardon, with thy blood. ATP; DiPo; HAP; HeIP; JCP; MBW 1-2; NoP; PPP

Holy Sonnets, VIII. John Donne. ...Then turne/O pensive soule, to God, for he knowes best/Thy true griefe, for he put it in my breast MasP

Holy Sonnets, IX. John Donne. I think it mercy if thou wilt forget. ATP; BiP; EBEV; JCP; NoP; OBS; PPP

Holy Sonnets, X. John Donne. And death shall be no more; death, thou shalt die. AtBAP; BiP; DiPo; EnRePo; ForPo; HAP; HBV 1-2; HeIP; InPS; JCP; LoBV; MBW 1-2; MeLP; NAWM 1-2; NOBE; NoP; OAEP; OBS; PoEL 1-5; PPoe; PPP; SeCP; TrCP; TRV; ViBoPo

Holy Sonnets, XI. John Donne. God cloth'd himselfe in vile mans flesh, that so/Hee might be weake enough to suffer woe. MasP; OBS

Holy Sonnets, XII. John Donne. But their Creator, whom sin nor nature tied,/For us, His creatures, and His foes, hath died. JCP; NOCV; TrCP

Holy Sonnets, XIII. John Donne. This beauteous form assures a piteous mind. EBEV; HeIP; JCP; MBW 1-2; NOCV

Holy Sonnets, XIV. John Donne. Nor ever chaste except you ravish me. BiP; DiPo; EBEV; ForPo; HAP; HeIP; HoPM; InPS; JCP; NoP; PPoe; PPP; TrCP

Holy Sonnets, XVI. John Donne. Thy law's abridgment and Thy last command/Is all but love; oh let that last will stand! JCP

Holy Sonnets, XVII. John Donne. But in thy tender jealosy dost doubt/Least the World, Fleshe, yea Devill putt thee out. MasP; OAEP

Holy Sonnets, XVIII. John Donne. Who is most trew, and pleasing to thee, then/When she'is embrac'd and open to most men. MasP; MeLP; OAEP; OBS

The Holy Spirit. Evelyn Underhill. And bring Thy seed to flower. BoC

Holy Spirit, Faithful Guide. Marcus Morris Wells. Follow me, I'll guide thee home! AH

Holy Spirit, Lead Me. *Anonymous.* That my life may please Him/Everywhere I go. STF

Holy Spirit, Truth Divine. Samuel Longfellow. Be my law, and I shall be/Firmly bound, forever free. AH

Holy Spring. Dylan Thomas. If only for a last time. WaP

The Holy Star. William Cullen Bryant. And send its glorious beams afar/To fill the world with light. BePJ

Holy Thursday. William Blake.
Babe can never hunger there,/Nor poverty the mind appal. CEP; EnLi 1-2; EnPE; FF; InPS; NoP; PAI; TEP
Then cherish pity, lest you drive an angel from your door. BoC; CBEP; DiPo; EnPE; HBV 1-2; InPS; NAWM 1-2; NOBE; NoP; OAEL 1-2; OBEC; OFD; PAI; SCV; TEP; TrCP

Holy Thursday. Charles Wright. What the hymns say, the first page and the last. GeTw

The Holy Tide. Frederick Tennyson. Till the lamp flickers and the memory fails. OBEV; OBVV

The Holy Viaticum Comes to Me. Giovanni Prati. I pardon all and thus Thy pardon prize. CAW

Holy Was Demeter Walking th' Corn Furrow. Edward Sanders. ahh what a thrill/is a god grope PoM

Holy water. Judith Fitzgerald. my love's under-rated CaPN

The Holy Well. *Anonymous.*
"Although you are but a maiden's child,/You are the King of Heaven!" NOCV; OxBoCh
For there are many of those infants' souls/Crying out for the help of Me. BaBo; FaBoCh; GBP; LoGBV
That is passed from sweet Jesus Christ.' OBET

Holy Willie's Prayer. Robert Burns.
And a' the glory shall be thine,/Amen, Amen! BSV; CEP; EBEV; EnL; EnPE; EnRP; GoTS; InPS; LAuP; NOEC; NoP; OAEL 1-2; OBSV; OxBoLi; OxBS; PAI; PoEL 1-5; PPP; TW; ViBoPo
While I can either sing, or whistle,/Your friend and servant. EnRP

Holyhead. Sept. 25, 1727. Jonathan Swift. I'd go in freedom to my grave,/Than rule yon isle and be a slave. BIrV; NOBI

Homage. Helen Hoyt. Even lowlier bowed my head, and bowed my heart. AnAmPo

Homage. Gustave Kahn. of singing thy perfumed grace,/and queenly beauty of thy face. TrJP

Homage. George O'Neil. The creature nodded, and he went away. AnAmPo

Homage. R. J. Schoeck. Homage I pay, my Lord, that now am free. GoYe

Homage and Lament for Ezra Pound in Captivity. Robert Duncan. still, as still as everness returning. NOBA

Homage of War. Bruce Williamson. As if grateful for his stark historic fading. NeIP

Homage to a Government. Philip Larkin. All we can hope to leave them now is money. EBEV; FaBoPV

Homage to Arthur Waley. Weldon Kees. "By misty waters and rainy sands, while the yellow dusk thickens." NaP

Homage to Chagall. Duane Niatum. Our bodies turn into reeds, our eyes into nomads. CDW

Homage to David Smith. John Haines. five fixed and glowing figures/who are not men. LCAP

Homage to Edward Hopper. Emery George. An ancient land lies silent, and is sage. HoAn

Homage to Elvis, Homage to the Fathers. Bruce Weigl. I believe the world will rip apart/From the inside/Of our next moment alive. MAYP

Home Song. Henry Wadsworth Longfellow. To stay at home is best. GN

Home, Sweet Home. *Anonymous.* But I'd give my pony and saddle to be at home, sweet home. CoSo

Home, Sweet Home. Henry Cuyler Bunner.
All you have to pay me is to take in my romanza. CenHV
At home alone. CenHV; InMe
For the soul and the mind that repose not,/O, give us a rest! InMe
Gimme them, and the feelin' of solid domestic comfort. CenHV
The griddle-cake's thar, anyway. InMe
His pristine peace of mind's his final prayer. CenHV; InMe
Or sing at the Cytherean's shrine. CenHV
Yon hearken to the melody of my steam-calliope/Yawp! BXAP; InMe

Home, Sweet Home. John Howard Payne. There's no place like home, oh, there's no place like home! AA; BLPA; BLSo; FaBoBe; FaFP; GoTF; HBV 1-2; PaPo; PSoN; TreF; WBLP

Home Thoughts. Denis Glover. I think of what will yet be seen/In Johnsonville and Geraldine. AnNZ

Home Thoughts. Claude McKay. Oh something's happening there this very minute! GoSl

Home Thoughts. Carl Sandburg. Speak to me... MoLP

Home Thoughts. Odell Shepard. The magic of her cry. HBMV

Home Thoughts From Abroad. Robert Browning. –Far brighter than this gaudy melon-flower! AnEnPo; AWP; BBV; BoLiVe; BoNaP; DiPo; FaBoBe; FaBV; FaFP; FaPoR; FiP; FPL; GoTF; GTBS; HBV 1-2; HBVY; HeIP; InPo; LiTB; MaVP; MBW 1-2; MCCG; NOBE; NOBV; NoP; OAEP; OBEV; OBNC; OBTV; OBVV; PoLf; PoRA; PrIm; SeCeV; TEP; TreF; TrGrPo; WHA

Home-Thoughts from France. Isaac Rosenberg. ..lure and sadden/My heart with futile bounds. MMM

Home-Thoughts, from the Sea. Robert Browning. While Jove's planet rises yonder, silent over Africa. AWP; CBEP; FaBoCh; FaPoR; FiP; GTBS; InPo; MaVP; MBW 1-2; MOS; NOBE; OAEP; OBEV; OBSP; OBVV

Home Thoughts in Laventie. Edward Wyndham Tennant. Home–what a perfect place! HBMV

The Home Winner. Gene Lindberg. She was mother, wife and partner–/ Every inch a pioneer. PoOW

A Home without a Bible (excerpt). Charles D. Meigs. Compass lost and rudder broken,/Drifting, drifting, thoughtlessly. WBLP

Homecoming. *Anonymous.* And the tuft of his nightcap lay red in the west. AnIV

Homecoming. James Keir Baxter. On reef and cave the sea's hexameter beating. AnNZ

Homecoming. Bruce Dawe. –they're bringing them home, now, too late, too early. CBAP

Homecoming. Stefan George. And the first star of sunset greets you/As if you'd only gone a day. AMV-81

Homecoming. Anna Margolin. Oh why do you tremble, child, as I draw near? VWA

Homecoming. Sonia Sanchez. ain't like they say/in the newspapers. PoBA

Homecoming. Karl Shapiro. The imprisoned souls of soldiers and of me. MiAP

Homecoming. Wislawa Szymborska. Looks upon life as upon cast-off trials. AMV-81

Homecoming. John Thompson. And the past is dead and buried and as buried as a root. MAT

Homecoming. Peter Viereck. But, of course, they couldn't hear me. No one could. CoAP

Homecoming Blues. Vassar Miller. I wish I could call my mother/or eat death like candy. GP

Homecoming Celebration. Rosemary Catacalos. when we will have sung ourselves/gently free of our shells. AMV-80

Homecoming in Storm. Bernice Lesbia Kenyon. Moveless with joy, to know you near once more. EtS

Homecoming–Massachusetts. John Ciardi. Nothing in our beginnings knows our ends. NYBP

The Homecoming of Emma Lazarus. Galway Kinnell. It fades, and the wounds of all we had accepted open. NaP

The Homecoming of the Sheep. Francis Ledwidge. And the climbing moon grows small. EnLit; HBMV

The Homecoming Singer. Jay Wright. I close my eyes and listen,/as she goes out to sing this city home. PoBA

The Homeland. Hugh Reginald Haweis. Christ bring us all to the Homeland/Of His eternal love. BLRP

The Homeless. Joan Joffe Hall. which meant suffering for others,/subdued rejoicing. AMV-81

Homeless Blues. Lil' Son Jackson. You know I ain't got no true religion, baby/mmmm well, I don't want to be baptized BluL

Homer. Albert Ehrenstein. For all thoughts and all acts/Trouble the limpid eyes of the world. TrJP

Homer. Dick Gallup. With a gasp we/realize that the temperature stands at 18 degrees. ANYP

The Homer Mitchell Place. John Engels. However brightly leap the brass-hinged bone,/Beam and rafter, joist and cellar-stone? SM

The Homeric Hexameter, Described and Exemplified. Samuel Taylor Coleridge. Nothing before and nothing behind but the sky and the/ocean. FaBoUs

Homeric Hymn to Neptune. George Chapman. Lend All, submitted, to thy drad Command. EtS

Homeric Hymns: Hymn to Aphrodite (abridged). *Anonymous.* Hail to you, goddess, Lady of stately Cypros... LiTW

Homeric Hymns: Hymn to Mercury. *Anonymous.* His sweeter voice a just accordance kept. LiTW

Homeric Unity. Andrew Lang. The crown that burns on thine immortal head/Of indivisible supremacy! HBV 1-2

The Homes. Anne Pitkin. room to start again. AMV-80

The Homes of England. Felicia Dorothea Hemans. Where first the child's glad spirit loves/Its country and its God! FaPoR; PaPo; SBG

Homes of the Cliff Dwellers. Stanley Wood. With the mist, long ages past begotten,/Of the Sun. PoOW

Homesick. Else Lasker-Schüler. Their prayers have gone down in the holy river. PBWP

Homesick Blues. Langston Hughes. I opens ma mouth an' laughs. CDC; MoAmPo; PoPl

Homesick Song. William Haskel Simpson. Ah! then I knew;/Knew why it sang in my heart. BPAW

Homestead-Winter Morning. Mary Ballard Duryee. Trifles deleted and the strength recorded. GoYe

Hometown. Luis Cabalquinto. And a warm dog, snuggled by my feet BrSi

Hometown Piece for Messrs. Alston and Reese. Marianne Moore. watching everything you do. You won last year. Come on. OBAL

The Homeward Bound. Bill Adams. For the packet they watched, "homeward bound"/At the breakin' of day. EtS

Homeward Bound. William Allingham. Round the world and home again,/That's the sailor's way! FaBoBe; HBV 1-2; HBVY

Homeward Bound. Jim Brodey. to blow the dust from my family crest, my cup. ANYP

Homeward Bound. Ezekiel Mphahlele. –you need not look just the way I want. WhB

Homeward Bound. D.H. Rogers. For the girls have got the tow-rope, an' they're hauling in the slack. AnNZ; EtS

Homeward Bound. Robert Southey. And watched, all anxious, every wind that blows. EtS

Homeward Bound. Lewis Frank Tooker. Thine eyes now wait to welcome me/Back where my heart has longed to be. EtS

The Homeward Journey. Leonard Aaronson. ...must wait till/sunlight wakes/Knowledge of what was known, and/then descend.' TrJP

Homework for Annabelle. Phyllis McGinley. But the hearts of the young are brittle as glass. GLGT

Homing. Arna Bontemps. Riding the wind/And screaming bitterly? CDC

Homing. P. C. Bowman. in the place I am meant for/where air collapses. AMV-81

The Homing. John Jerome Rooney. Our men, as of old, are men in/truth! AA

Homing. Reg Saner. ...reading/even humming, the one book. NPAW

The Homing Heart. Daniel Henderson. How swift at dusk my paths run to/The lights of home, the arms of you! HBMV

Homing Pigeons. Ted Walker. they clatter back in the hanging dark. NYBP

Hominization. Miroslav Holub. And maybe they'll find us one day,/when people finally exist. SUW

L'Homme Moyhen Sensuel (excerpt). Ezra Pound. All the same style, same cut, with perfect loathing.' OBSV

Homo Sapiens. John Wilmot, Earl of Rochester. Who was so proud, so witty, and so wise. NOBE

Homosexual Sonnets. Kenneth Pitchford.
for a dozen naked hours of coming and coming. GP
...I can't/think of anything like us before. No wonder it scares me. GP
That's the dream denied us in one-night stands of first/names only. GP
to lay aside their weapons and sleep in each other's arms. GP

Homosexuality. Frank O'Hara. and I want to be wanted more than anything else in the world. NYP; PeHV; PoA; TAP

Homunculus et la Belle Etoile. Wallace Stevens. The torments of confusion. MoAB; MoAmPo

Hon. Mr. Sucklethumbkin's Story. Richard Harris Barham. So–my Lord Tomnoddy went home to bed! OBRV

Honest Abe Lincoln. Max Shulman. Howcome you pulled the trigger on me,/John...Wilkes...Booth? OBAL

Honest Fame. Alexander Pope. Oh grant an honest fame, or grant me none! OBEC

The Honest Whore, I, 1604. Thomas Dekker. It is the honey 'gainst a waspish wife. ViBoPo

Horace, Book V, Ode III. Charles Larcom Graves. And she cows me with the lashing of her tongue. CenHV

"Horace: Book V, Ode III." Ronald Arbuthnott Knox. oculus me tamen ardens et iniquae flagra linguae/agitant exanimatum. CenHV

Horace, Epistle VII, Book I, Imitated. Jonathan Swift. Pray leave me where you found me first. CEP

Horace I. Eugene Field. To-morrow, when the headache comes–well, then I'll/satirize ye! ALV

Horace Kephart. Robert Morgan. ...like a wounded/dove out through scrub and leaves to the creek. MAYP

Horace Paraphrased. Isaac Watts. "Drank up their drink and gone to bed." LoBV

Horace the Wise. Morrie Ryskind. Ain't I been through it? HBMV

Horae Canonicae (excerpt). W. H. Auden. there would be no agents. SaC

Horas Tempestatis Quoque Enumero: The Sundial. John Hollander. Measuring always this moment. NePoEA

Horat. Ode 29. Book 3. Paraphras'd in Pindarique Verse. John Dryden. With friendly Stars my safety seek/Within some little winding Creek;/And see the storm a shore. SeCV 1-2

Horatian Epode to the Duchess of Malfi. Allen Tate. And the katharsis fades in the warm water of a yawn. FaBoMo

Horatian Ode. Joseph Warren Beach. ...subvert/Our state with fears that do not touch the soul? PoA

An Horatian Ode upon Cromwell's Return from Ireland. Andrew Marvell. The same arts that did gain/A power, must it maintain. AnAnS 1; EBEV; FaBoPV; FaBoRV; GTBS; GTBS-P; HAP; HBV 1-2; InPS; JCP; LoBV; MePo; NOBE; NoP; OAEL 1-2; OBEV; OBS; OBWP; PAI; PoEL 1-5; SeCP; SeCV 1-2; ViBoPo

Horatian Variation. Leonard Bacon. Visit my shack! We'll dream we drink/The true Falernian. NYBP

The Horatians. W. H. Auden. but from a sober perspective. NYBP

Horatio Alger Uses Scag. LeRoi (Imamu Amiri Baraka) Jones. in the arab getup, is yo man, rocky, makin/the whole thing/perfect. FaBoCh; GP; LoGBV

Horatius. Thomas Babington, Lord Macaulay. How well Horatius kept the bridge/In the brave days of old. BBV; BeLS; FaFP; FaPoR; HBV 1-2; HBVY; MCCG; OBNV; OBWP; OHFP; PoLf; TreF; VLP

The Horizon Is Definitely Speaking. Diana Chang. and we are on edge BrSi

Horizon Thong. George Abbe. the sun-knot tightens to dark. GoYe

Horizon without Landscape. Tom Lowenstein. The night was with you as you searched,/Without a hat, sawn-off binoculars. VWA

Horizontal World. Thomas Saunders. Somehow, catch all the height and breadth of sky. CaP

The Horn. Léonie Adams.
The heart set beating in the side/Has but the wisdom of a hare? AnAmPo; MoAB; MoAmPo
Since bones have caught their marrow chill. InPo

Horn. Anonymous. ,with sounding voice/Put foemen to flight. Now ask what I'm called. AnOE

Horn. James Hayford. With his own intricate/Simplicities of horn. NePoAm-2

The Horn. James Reaney. To show the sun's fistful of golden darts. OBCV; PeCV

The Horn. James Reeves. For ever be folded, protecting and warm. SO

The Horn Blow. Jeff Tagami. baring their crooked grins. BrSi

Horn, Mouth, Pit, Fire. William Dickey. will be easily as large/and as ambiguous as the rest. AMV-81

Horned Lizard. Charles Molesworth. the sea that fled this hovering vengeance. GrPl

Hornpipe. Edith Sitwell. Are hot as any hottentot and not the goods for me!' FaBoMo; GTBS-P; MoVE; OAEL 1-2; SeCePo

Hornpout. Prescott, Jr Evarts. and I fought to cut it out. WOLT

The Horny-Goloch. Anonymous. It has two horns, an' a hantle o' feet,/An' a forkie Tailie. AmMo; FaBoCh

Horologium: The Mother of God. Anonymous. Him, upon Him, prithee, call,/For to save us one and all. ISi

Horoscope. J. V. Cunningham. ...the storm/That piled them deep will keep them warm. NePoAm

The Horrible Decree (excerpt). Charles Wesley. Lift up the Standard of thy cross,/Draw all men unto Thee. NOCV

Horrible Things. Roy Fuller. "Your face, as you tell/Of all the horriblest things you've seen." OnUR

The Horrid Voice of Science. Vachel Lindsay. And I hope all men/Who think like this/Will soon lie/Underground. PoA

Horror. Peter Baum. Twin carrion birds/Then o'er the churchyard fly. AWP

Horror. Henry Treece. And stops, aghast, to see his own shade propped/Stiff at the board. EAS

Horror Comic. Robert Conquest. Laughter shakes his tonsil/As at a theatre. OxBTC

Horror Movie. Howard Moss. There's a little death in every body. NePoEA-2

A Horror Story Written for the Cover of a Matchbook. Chuck Wachtel. broken light bulb/for her contact lens. APU

Hors d'Oeuvre. Deems Taylor. "But–supper, darling, still is in the pot." UnTE

Horse. Gerard Benson. Less actual, more magical, as shadow horses in some/awed dreaming. PH

Horse. Randy Blasing. weightless, it/could fly. PH

The Horse. Alfred Edgar Coppard. And today or tomorrow it will abandon you. BoAnP

The Horse. Jose Maria Eguren. ...retreats/through ruined squares,/desolate streets. WSC

Horse. Louise Gluck. What is the animal/if not passage out of this life? MAYP

Horse. Jim Harrison. how can I believe/you ran under a low maple limb/to knock me off? BoAnP; PH

The Horse. Faye Kicknosway. as we walked in the slow dark/toward home. GeTw

The Horse. Philip Levine. that the rage had gone out of/their bones in one mad dance. CoAP

The Horse. William Stanley Merwin. beginning to remember/as its leaves fell. GP

The Horse. Francis Ponge. –interrupted during his mass, he turned his byzantine/eyes toward us... NU

Horse. Elizabeth Madox Roberts. He said for me to run along/And not to bother him any more. PH; TiPo

The Horse. Naomi Royde-Smith. And one of them is rather coarse. FaBoCo; FiBHP

The Horse. Shel Silverstein. The horse, of course. PH

A horse and a flea and three blind mice. Anonymous. The flea said, "Whoops, there's/a horse on me." FaFP; NTCP

The Horse and His Rider. Joanna Baillie. It is a British soldier, armed for war! NOEC

The Horse and the Mule. John Huddleston Wynne. That "slow and sure goes far at last'. OxBChV

The Horse and the Whip. Eliezer Steinbarg. You let yourself be harnessed–nag! VWA

Horse Chestnut. Gary Miranda. ...And/no one I've ever loved has died,/exactly. SM

The Horse Chestnut Tree. Richard Eberhart. Which we held in idea, a little handful. AtBAP; CMoP; CrMA; LiTM; MoAB; MoAmPo; NePA; NePoAm; PoPl

Horse-Girl. Henry Petroski. Karen can stand still, Karen can/Pose like a weather vane. PH

Horse Graveyard. Fred Lape. And at the end is a granite boulder with no name,/laid by the man for Dan, best loved of his horses PH

Horse Guards Parade. Thomas (Tom) Brown. Where, free from duns, they may securely dine. FaBoEE

Horse in a Field. Walter De La Mare. Dark head, dark eyes, slim shoulder.../God speed, K. M. HBMV

The Horse in the Drugstore. Tess Gallagher. dimes and to carry the inscrutable bruise like a bride. AmPA

The Horse Named Bill (with music). Anonymous. And your toothbrush–and everything–/That's helpless. AS; FSW

Horse & Rider. Wey Robinson. the horse/Is more so ( ) BXAP; SD

Horse Sense. Anonymous. Just pull an honest load, and then/There'll be no time for kicking. BLPA; GoTF; TreFT; WBLP

The Horse Show. William Carlos Williams. ...I wish you had been/there, I was so interested to hear about it. CMoP; NOBA; TAP; VGW

The Horse Show at Midnight. Henry Taylor. I believe in the singing, and sleep. PH

The Horse Thief. William Rose Benet. String me up, Dave! Go dig my grave! I rode him across/the skies! BBV; BPAW; HBMV; MoAmPo; OnMSP

The Horse Trader's Song. Anonymous. God knows I've been all around this world–/And started around again. AmFP

A Horse Would Tire. Elizabeth Jane Coatsworth. And seek my harbor/Halfway round the world. TiPo

The Horse Wrangler. D. J. O'Malley. Then cut your throat with a barlow knife–/For it's easier done that way. CoSo

The Horseman. Walter De la Mare. And the horse he rode/Was of ivory. GoJo; SoPo; SUS; TiPo

The Horseman on the Skyline. Henry Lawson. The rider on the skyline/Is scouting to the east. CBAP

The Horsemen. Gene Baro. a cry is at the lips, and then is gone. NePoEA-2

Horses. Richard Armour. They're worse to get on. PoPl

Horses. Robert Patrick Dana. And the one horse in the heart/that runs/and runs PH

The Horses. Ted Hughes. Hearing the horizons endure. NoAm; PH

Horses. Rudyard Kipling. And die dumb-mad in the breaking-yard. BoAnP; PoL

The Horses. Maxine W. Kumin. and rub dry their old kisses. DuDa

Horses. Louis MacNeice. Circle around/A spangled lady. PH

The Horses. Edwin Muir.
Our life is changed; their coming our beginning. ACV; CMoP; HaMV; HAP; MoBrPo; NMP; NoAm; NOBE; NoP; OAEL 1-2; OxBTC; PPoe; TEP
Where the blank field and the still-standing tree/Were bright and fearful presences to me. CMoP; FaBoCh; LoGBV; MoVE; OAEL 1-2; PoPle; SeCePo

Horses. Myra von Riedemann. And the closeness of dry earth,/Is horses. OBCV

Horses. Dorothy Wellesley. The welkin flash and thunder to the hoofs/Of Dawn's tremendous team? ChMP; OBMV; OxBTC

Horses Aboard. Thomas Hardy. ...they appear wrenched awry/From the scheme Nature planned for them,–wondering why. BoAnP; FM

Horses and Men in the Rain. Carl Sandburg. ...and all the/olden golden men who rode horses in the rain. PoLf

Horses at Valley Store. Leslie Marmon Silko. So they pause and from their distance/outside of time/They wait. VoR

Horses Chawin' Hay. Hamlin Garland. They ain't no sound that gits me/Like horsus chawin' hay! OBAL

Horses Graze. Gwendolyn Brooks. the Immediate arc, alone, of life, of love. CNA; GP

The Horses of Marini. Tania Van Zyl. when will the unfathomed cave/of a thousand shades stable you? PeSA

The Horses of the Sea. Christina Georgina Rossetti. While the foaming sea-horses/Toss and turn over. GoJo; NTCP; SUS

Horses on the Camargue. Roy Campbell. And loved to course with tempests through the night. AtBAP; GTBS-P; OBTV; PeSA; PoPle; SeCePo

Horsey Gap. Anonymous. Shall feast on the corpses that float by the ferry. FaBoPP; GBP

Hos Ego Versiculos. Francis Quarles. The beauty fades, and man's life ends. OBS

Hosanna. Thomas Traherne. His Laws require His Creatures all to prais/His Name, and when they do 't be most my Joys. PoEL 1-5; SeCV 1-2

Hosanna to Christ. Isaac Watts. Lest rocks and stones should rise and break/Their silence into songs. NOCV

Hose and Iron. Greg Kuzma. I am dying of wisecracks MAT

Hospital. Wilfred J. Funk. A shaft of glory from the throne of God. PoToHe

The Hospital. Patrick Kavanagh. Snatch out of time the passionate transitory. BIrV; CIP; FaBoIP

Hospital. G. C. Millard. The old man had loved more than he could say. PeSA

A Hospital. Alfred Noyes. Looks, through men's eyes, on His own children then. PoPl

Hospital. Karl Shapiro. Are, for the most part, human but unbandaged. VGW

Hospital Barge at Cerisy. Wilfred Owen. Kings passed in the dark barge which Merlin dreamed. CBEP; OBTV

Hospital Evening. Gwen Harwood. who walking makes no footprint and/no shadow on soft-fallen snow. FaBoWP

Hospital for Defectives. Thomas Blackburn. What is it that you say? GTBS-P; OxBTC

Hospital Observation. Julian Symons. ...The wind/blows through/The window beside me, fresh and cool. WaP

Hospital/Poem. Sonia Sanchez. begin the talk/of HYenaaaAAS. BPo; PoBA

Hospital Poems: Transfusion. Merrill Moore. And does the miracles men say it does. PoA

The Hospital–Retrospections. Kenneth Mackenzie. where bodies are made whole/as in the woman bodies are made, whole. CBAP

The Hospital Waiting-Room. William Henry Davies. Until a welcome voice cried–"Next!" BrPo; CBEP

The Hospital Window. James Dickey. I have just come down from my father. BiP; CoPo; HaCAP; HeIP

Hospitality in Ancient Ireland. Anonymous. 'Tis not the guest that will be without it,/But Jesus, Mary's Son. OnYI

Hossolalia. Mildred Luton. He can read my mind/through my knees and heels. PH

The Host of the Air. William Butler Yeats. And never was piping so gay. BrPo; CH; OnYI; SeCeV

The Hostage and His Takers. Sharon Olds. ...stop it so they can/have some peace. SOTS

The Hostess' Daughter. Ludwig Uhland. And I will love thee forever, and aye. AWP

Hostia. Irving Layton. The queer bites on her voluptuous thighs. PV

The Hosting of the Sidhe. William Butler Yeats. And Niamh calling Away, come away. NoAm

The Hosts. George M. Brady. You, the ghost, or I, the living man? NeIP

The Hosts. William Stanley Merwin. this bottle has been in the cave all the time/we have been together. GP

The Hosts of Faery. Anonymous. Masterly at making songs,/Skilled at playing chess. OnYI

Hot Afternoons Have Been in West 15th Street. Paul Blackburn. that all things may be resolved correct and dead . VGW

Hot-Cross Buns. Mother Goose. Give them to your sons. OxNR; SoPo

The Hot Day and Human Nature. Gordon Johnston. And their opposable thumbs. AMV-81

Hot Day at the Races. Tom Raworth. ...the lark's beak neatly pierces his eye. EAS

A Hot Day in Sydney. Anonymous. Convinc'd that, of all the earth's nations,/Not one would be faultless to/Q. NOAV

A Hot Engagement between a French Privateer and an English Fireship. Anonymous. But till then he could never believe it/That Strumbolo lay in the straits. OBSS

Hot Ir'n! Squire Omar Barker. Hey, cowboy! Bring 'em HOT!/HOT IR'N! PoOW

Hot Line. Louella Dunann. "I can't tie mine up, Mom,/I might get a call." QQQ

Hot Night on Water Street. Louis Simpson. And bought the New York Times, and went to bed. MP; TwCP

The Hot Pease Man. Anonymous. Hot are my pease, hot. OxNR

Hot Springs. Earle Birney. they casually shoot every general/and strip the laughing ladies OxBC

Hot Stuff. Edward Botwood. So at you, ye bitches, here's give you Hot/Stuff. PAH

Hot Sunne, Coole Fire, Temperd with Sweet Aire. George Peele. Nor pierce any bright eye,/That wandreth lightly. GBL; NoP; PoEL 1-5; TEP

A Hot Time in the Old Town. Joe Hayden. In the chorus all join in,/there'll be a hot time in the old town tonight. FSN; YaD

Hot Weather in the Plains–India. E. H. Tipple. Oh! it's there my soul shall wander, though it's here my/bones must lie. HBV 1-2

A Hot-Weather Song. Don (Donald Robert Marquis) Marquis. It would break with the weight of a thought! HBMV; YaD

The Hotel. Harriet Monroe. but ever alive, struggling and rising again, seeking/the light, freeing the world. AnAmPo

Hotel. Adam Wazyk. I turn over to my third side. VWA

Hotel Continental. William Jay Smith. P–lease! P–lease! P–lease! WaP

Hotel de l'Univers et Portugal. James Merrill. Sleep, by a strange bed in the dark of dreaming. MoAB; NePoAm; NePoEA-2; PoA

Hotel Fire: New Orleans. Paul Ruffin. the leap the only faith that's left. AMV-81

Hotel in Paris. Dennis Trudell. ...and the terrible strength/of each merciful, tucked wing. PoA

Hotel Paradiso e Commerciale. John Malcolm Brinnin. and pardon this one. HoAn; MP; NoAm; NYBP; PoCh; TwCP

Hotel Sierra. David St. John. Drawn simply by the seasons, by their lives. MAYP

Hotel Transylvanie. Frank O'Hara. to know who I am/why I came there/what and why I am and/made to happen NeAP; PoM

Hotels. David Donnell. and the great bars that go on forever. AMV-81

The Hottentot. Thomas Pringle. His Master cries–"he has no gratitude!" OBRV; OBTV

Hottest Brand Goin'. Smoky Babe. Now you want your car super serviced/Get your super right there/(Talking 'bout the Conoco station) BluL

Houdini. Eli Mandel. like the bound crowds who sigh, who sigh. NIP; NOBC

The Hound. Babette Deutsch. The quarry goes to Autumn, let Spring die. HBMV

The Hound. Robert Francis. Meanwhile I stand/And wait the event. SoSe

The Hound of Heaven. Francis Thompson. Thou dravest love from thee, who dravest Me. ACP; ATP; BLPL; BrPo; CAW; FaBV; FaFP; GoBC; GoTL; GTBS; HBV 1-2; ILwL; LiTB; LiTM; LoBV; MasP; MCCG; MoAB; MoBrPo; OAEP; OBMV; OxBoCh; PoEL 1-5; SeCePo; SeCeV; TreF; TrGrPo; TRV; ViBoPo; VLP; WGRP; WHA

Hound on the Church Porch. Robert P. Tristram Coffin. And every inch of him filled out with pride. GDP

Hound Voice. William Butler Yeats. And chants of victory amid the encircling hounds. SyP

The Hounded Lovers. William Carlos Williams. The movement of benediction/does not turn back/the cold wind. MoLP; NYBP; TrGrPo

The Hounds. Patric Dickinson. Has nobody got a fire to light? ChMP

The Hounds. John Freeman. The unneighboured and uncomforted cold sea. OBMV; OBSP

The Hounds of the Soul. Louis Ginsberg. Where dawnlight flushes the breathless/verge of the loftiest height! TrJP

Hounslow Heath. Anonymous. Now you have seen all that is here/Have patience till another year. APAS

How I'd Have It. John Stone. And then exit all/STAGE RIGHT AMV-81

How I Escaped from the Labyrinth. Philip Dacey. I kept losing my way. PoL; PPJ

How I Got Ovah. Carolyn M. Rodgers. I have shaken rivers/out of my eyes. CNA

How I Was Her Kitchen-Boy. Gunter Grass. ...her grief/left no after-taste. AMV-81

How I wish I had known. *Anonymous.* I would have dyed a robe for you! BoWoP

How Infinite Are Thy Ways. William Force Stead. Lo I, somehow,/Am Thou. OBMV

How It Goes On. Maxine W. Kumin. O lambs! The whole wolf-world sits down to eat/and cleans its muzzle after. FAZ; FiCP

How It Is. Uri Z. Greenberg. How wan they are, and shrunken, when they come back! VWA

How It Strikes a Contemporary. Robert Browning. Let's to the Prado and make the most of time. CABL; CTC; FaBoPV; GTBS-P; MaVP; MBW 1-2; OAEL 1-2; PP; VLP

How Jack Found that Beans May Go Back on a Chap. Guy Wetmore Carryl. She recognized the symptoms as her own. ALV; HoPM

How Lies Grow. Maxine Chernoff. Someday he'll leave me: then what will I do? APU

How Lillies Came White. Robert Herrick. Fell down on you,/And made ye white. AnAnS 2; CaPo

How Long Hast Thou Been a Gravemaker? David Perkins. And picked his own spot, for somebody else to dig. NCSH

How Long, Jehovah? Henry Ainsworth. For bounteously hath he/Rewarded unto me. AH

How Long Shall I Give? *Anonymous.* "Just give till the Master stops giving to you." BLRP

How Long Will It Last? Lady Horikawa. This morning my thoughts are as tangled/as my black hair. WPOW

How Looks the Night? Gerard Manley Hopkins. Where the stint compass of a skylark's wings/Would not put out some tiny golden centre. OBSP

How Low Is the Lowing Herd. Walt Kelly. "Have you heard sheep? is right!" FiBHP

How Many Bards Gild the Lapses of Time! John Keats. Make pleasing music, and not wild uproar. EnRP

How Many Days Has My Baby to Play? Mother Goose. Saturday, Sunday, Monday. OxNR; TiPo

How many evenings in the arbor by the river. Li Ch'ing-chao. startle a shoreful of herons by the lake. BoWoP

How Many Fires. George Reavey. where stay a firebrand heart/in its nomad blaze. EAS

How Many Heavens... Edith Sitwell. He is the core of the heart of love, and He, beyond laboring seas, our/ultimate shore. MoRP; TrCP

How Many Miles to Babylon? Mother Goose. You may get there by candle-light. ExPo; GBP; OBSP; OxNR

How Many Miles to Barley-Bridge? *Anonymous.* But the one that is hindmost/Will meet with a great mistake.' OxBoLi

How Many Moments Must(Amazing Each. Edward Estlin Cummings. ...such mysteries as men/do not conceive—let ocean grow again PoA

How Many New Years Have Grown Old. *Anonymous.* Whether your servant love or no. EiL

How Many Nights. Galway Kinnell. from a branch nothing cried from ever in my life. CAPP; MAT; NaP

How Many Paltry Foolish Painted Things. Michael Drayton. Still to survive in my immortal song. EnLoPo; GBL; NIP; PrIm; TEP

How Many Seconds in a Minute? Christina Georgina Rossetti. No one knows the rhyme. SiSoSe

How many times these low feet staggered. Emily Dickinson. Indolent Housewife—in Daisies—lain! AmPP; HAP; PoEL 1-5

How many wise men and heroes. Ch'iu Chin. And bearing brilliant and noble human beings. BoWoP

How McClellan Took Manassas. *Anonymous.* Tell on shaft and storied brasses/How he took the famed Manassas. PAH

How McDougal Topped the Score. Thomas E. Spencer. For we played Molongo cricket—and McDougal topped the score! PoAu 1-2

How Morning Glories Could Bloom at Dusk. Jorie Graham. But no one said how slow, how willing. NPGG

How Much Longer? Robert Mezey. the rest of her, beached on the mud, was horribly burned. OBWP

How Much Longer Will I Be Able to Inhabit the Divine Sepulcher... John Ashbery. Of the long sepulcher that hid death and hides me? NeAP; NoAm; PoM

How Much Wood Would a Wood-Chuck Chuck. Mother Goose. If a wood-chuck could chuck wood. TiPo

How Music's Made. Dilys Bennett Laing. How music's made is not a thing of luck. ELU

How My Father Died. Nissim Ezekiel. I only felt the breath of his love/but did not hear a word. VWA

How My Songs of Her Began. Philip Bourke Marston. And at His will my lyre grew audible. HBV 1-2

How Night Falls in the Courtyard. Christine Rimmer. ...we bask in the light/and pass the pipe around. AMV-80

How No Age Is Content. Henry Howard, Earl of Surrey. ...their time most happy is,/If, to their time, they reason had, to know the truth of this.' LiTB; LoBV

How Odd. W. N. Ewer. To choose/The Jews. FaBoEE

How of the Virgin Mother Shall I Sing? Saint Ennodius. Mother and Virgin, Jesus born of thee/Is guardian of thine intact purity. ISi

How Oft Has the Banshee Cried. Thomas Moore. So long shall Erin's pride/Tell how they lived and died. AnIV; AWP

How oft have I, my dear and cruel foe. Sir Thomas Wyatt. And yours the loss and mine the deadly pain. AAS; FCP

How Often (parody). Ben King. How often, oh! how oft. HBV 1-2

How Old Are You? H. S. Fritsch. You are not old. PoLf; PoToHe

How Old Brown Took Harper's Ferry. Edmund Clarence Stedman. May trouble you more than ever, when you've nailed his/coffin down! HBV 1-2; MC; OnMSP; PAH; PoNe

How Old's the Moon? *Anonymous.* Dog-skins squashed and beaten flat. MOON

How on Solemn Fields of Space. Elizabeth Daryush. Soul's vague lily scents the void. NOCV

How One-Thumb Willie Got His Name. John L. Sellers. 'cause they never did find willie's thumb. LFAC

How One Winter Came in the Lake Region. Wilfred (William Wilfred Campbell) Campbell. Fast fell the driving snow. CaP; NOBC; OBCV; PeCV

How Our Forefather Got His Wife. Eda Lou Walton. There he changed into a man again/And carried her off like a sack of hay. BPAW

How Paddy Stole the Rope. *Anonymous.* Than when they broke into a church to try and steal a rope. BLPA

How Placidly Shine. Rosalia de Castro. Will there not be a tomb for me?/For me, no. PBWP

How Pleasant Is This Flowery Plain. *Anonymous.* Monarchs, whom Cities and Kingdoms obey,/Are not half so contented, or happy as they. OBS

How Pleasant to Know Mr. Lear. Edward Lear. How pleasant to know Mr. Lear! CBEP; ChTr; EBEV; FaBoCo; FiBHP; HAP; NOBE; NOBL; NOBV; NoP; SpRo; VLP

How Robin Hood Rescued the Widow's Sons. *Anonymous.* They hanged the proud sheriff on that,/And released their own three men. StPo

How Roses Came Red. Robert Herrick. The Roses first came red. CaPo; CavP; EnL; SoSe

How's My Boy? Sydney Thomas Dobell. How's my boy—my boy? CH; EtS; GN; HBV 1-2; OHIP

How Samson Bore Away the Gates of Gaza. Vachel Lindsay. Let Samson/Be coming/Into your mind. MoRP

How Shall a Man Fore-Doomed. Hartley Coleridge. Till at the last he purged away his sin/By loving all the joy he saw within. NCEP

How Shall I Build. Wilfrid Scawen Blunt. Lord, here is darkness. Yet this heart unwise,/Bruised in Thy service, take in sacrifice. CAW

How Shall We Honor Them? Edwin Markham. Flatter their souls with deeds, and all is said? PGD

How Shall We Rise to Greet the Dawn? Osbert Sitwell. We must create and fashion a new God. WGRP

How She Resolved to Act. Merrill Moore. And her tongue raced like a squirrel in the park. MoAmPo

How Should I Rule Me? *Anonymous.* Lest they falle down into thy ey/The spones that above thee be. OxBM

How Singular. Tom (Thomas Hood, Jr.) Hood. And all the rest is only batter. FaBoNo

How Sleep the Brave! William Collins. And Freedom shall awhile repair,/To dwell a weeping hermit there! GN; GoTF; HBV 1-2; HBVY; NOBE; OBEV; TreF

How Small Is Man. John Stuart Blackie. Taught by the vastness of God's pictured plan/In the big world how small a thing is man! PoSH

How Stands the Glass Around? James Wolfe. A bottle and a kind landlady/Cure all again. PAH

How Stars and Hearts Grow in Apples. Virginia Elson. —and spit out stars/by the mouthful, eating the heart out. AMV-81

How Still, How Happy! Emily Bronte. Then let us sit and watch the while/The blue ice curdling on the stream. NOBV; OBNC; VLP

How Still the Hawk. Charles Tomlinson. The shrivelled circle/Of magnetic fear. LiTM

How Strange Love Is, in Every State of Consciousness. Delmore Schwartz. Possessed and blessed by the power which flowers as a fountain/flowers! MoLP

How Strangely This Sun Reminds Me of My Love. Stephen Spender. And the lark ascends, and his voice still rings, still rings. PeHV

How Sweet I Roam'd. William Blake. Then stretches out my golden wing,/And mocks my loss of liberty. CBEP; SeCePo; TreFT

How Sweet Is the Language of Love.　Oliver Holden.　Assured of sweet pardon and peace,/And wholly conformed to thee.　AH

How Sweet Thy Precious Gift of Rest.　Ben Makhir.　Fat capons, quails and fish,/Each upon a lordly dish.　TrJP

How the Bulls Were Begotten: The Two Bulls.　*Anonymous.*　idol of the ox herd/the prime demon Finnbennach.　NOBI

How the Cumberland Went Down.　Silas Weir Mitchell.　And shook their rusty brands,/As the Cumberland went down.　MC; PAH

How the Death of a City Is Never More Than the Sum of the Deaths...　Victor Coleman.　I pictured it with cock/& balls that weighed on me for days.　NOBC

How the Doughty Duke of Albany Like a Coward Knight...(excerpt).　John Skelton.　Of vermin and of lice/And of all manner vice?　OBSV

How the Fire Queen Crossed the Swamp.　Will H. Ogilvie.　..."Twas the Devil that pulled him through!"　PoAu 1-2

How the First Hielandman of God Was Made of Ane Horse Turd...　*Anonymous.*　Sa lang as I may gear get to steill/Will I never work.　FaBoCo; GBP; OBSV

How the Flowers Grow.　(Thomas Nicoll Hepburn) "Setoun. Gabriel"　I have watched them and I know.　SoPo

How the Great Guest Came.　Edwin Markham.　I was the child on the homeless street!　BeLS; BLPA; BLPL

How the Helpmate of Blue-Beard Made Free with a Door.　Guy Wetmore Carryl.　A stern and dreadful lesson learn/When, as you've read, they're cut in turn.　InMe

How the Hen Sold Her Eggs to the Stingy Priest.　Nancy Willard.　beating and beating the gold alive.　LCAP

How the Invalids Make Love.　Susan Feldman.　the shadow of the black bee.　AmPA

How the Joy of It Was Used Up Long Ago.　Linda Gregg.　A filth on the floor of that room.　NPGG

How the Laws of Physics Love Chocolate!　Reg Saner.　a consort of blue trombones.　GP

How the Leaves Came Down.　Susan (Sarah Chauncey Woolsey) Coolidge.　"It is so nice to go to bed!"　HBV 1-2; HBVY

How the Little Kite Learned to Fly.　*Anonymous.*　"And all because I was brave, and tried."　HBV 1-2; HBVY

How the Money Rolls In.　*Anonymous.*　My God, how the money rolls in.　GoTF; TreFT

How the Old Horse Won the Bet.　Oliver Wendell Holmes.　A horse can trot, for all he's old.　AnNE

How the Ploughman Learned His Paternoster.　*Anonymous.*　Unto the which He us bringe/That in heven reigneth eternal Kinge!　OxBM

How the Sky Begins to Fall.　Joan Colby.　...beginning to fall/into my arms like a solar panel/melting with friction.　AMV-81

How the waters closed above him.　Emily Dickinson.　Whose unclaimed Hat and Jacket/Sum the History–　DL; PoEL 1-5

How They Bite.　*Anonymous.*　Wind from the west, bite the best.　SD

How They Brought the Good News by Sea.　Norma Farber.　Hear all about it! News! they cried.　PCh

How They Brought the Good News From Ghent to Aix.　Robert Browning.　Was no more than his due who brought good news from Ghent.　BeLS; BLPL; FaBoBe; FaFP; FaPoR; GN; HBV 1-2; HBVY; HoPM; MCCG; PaPo; RoGo; SpRo; TreF

How They Came from the Blue Snows.　Arnold Kenseth.　We do not understand, we do not follow.　PPON

How They Killed My Grandmother.　Boris Slutsky.　That's how they did it to her.　VWA

How Things Fall.　Donald Finkel.　a feast of heavenly mortar/an orgy of stones.　VWA

How to Amuse a Stone.　Richard Shelton.　amused and free and going home　AMV-80

How To Be Happy.　*Anonymous.*　Do something for somebody, quick!　BLPA

How to Be Old.　May Swenson.　And in time, in time, the doll–/like new, though ancient–will be found.　MAT; UnPo

How to Build a Ha-Ha.　William Mason.　As, round some citadel, the engineer/Directs his sharp stoccade.　FaBoUs

How to Catch a Trout.　Thomas Barker.　But the chief point of all is the cookery.　FaBoUs

How to Catch Unicorns.　William Rose Benet.　The Unicorn is not carnivorous!　HBMV

How to Change the U.S.A.　Harry Edwards.　Just as a gesture/of good faith.　NBP; TW

How to Choose a Horse.　*Anonymous.*　Knock him on the head and feed him to the crows.　FaBoUs

How to Choose a Wife.　*Anonymous.*　Her lips as red as a cherry.　FaBoUs

How to Conceive Boys.　Claude Quillet.　Such Care to propagate the Male obtains,/And through each Species undistinguish'd reigns.　FaBoUs

How to Cure Hops and Prepare Them for Sale.　Christopher Smart.　She cull'd suspicious–lo! she starts, she frowns/With indignation at a negro's nail.　FaBoUs

How to Eat Alone.　Daniel Halpern.　The company is the best you'll ever have.　MAYP

How to Fertilize Soil.　James Grainger.　With weeds, mould, dung, and stale, a compost form,/Of force to fertilize the poorest soil.　FaBoUs

How to Fertilize Soil.　John Scott.　Amends alike the arable and lawn.　FaBoUs

How to Find Your Way Home.　Mario Petaccia.　...Do not look/back. The bridge is a clock.　LFAC

How to Fly by Standing Still (excerpt).　James Keir Baxter.　...When our bones rise again/It will be the everlasting springtime.　OCNZ

How to Forget.　Rebecca Foresman.　Because he's busy being wrong.　PoToHe

How to Get On in Society.　Sir John Betjeman.　Beg pardon, I'm soiling the doileys/With afternoon tea-cakes and scones.　NOBL; OBSV; OxBTC

How to Get There.　Frank O'Hara.　for a couple of hours, but I am not that person.　NoP

How to Get to Canada.　Ted Berrigan.　15 cents is plenty to keep you in the sky.　APU

How to Get to New Mexico.　John Brandi.　I can leave you now.　TAT

How to Give.　*Anonymous.*　Give as you would of your substance/If his hand the offering took.　BLRP

How to Go and Forget.　Edwin Markham.　But I do not know yet/How to go and forget!　HBMV

How to Hide Jesus.　Steve Turner.　Quick, let's hide him.　EBCP

How to Keep Accounts.　*Anonymous.*　By strict observance of this rule, keep good accounts/you may.　FaBoUs

How to Kill.　Keith Douglas.　...A shadow is a man/when the mosquito death approaches.　ChMP; FaBoMo; NOBE

How to Measure a Cat.　Louis Johnson.　their sinuous silhouettes serve/as barometers, define like mirrors.　OCNZ

How to Meditate.　Jack Kerouac.　So I don't have to think/any/more　PoM

How to Murder Your Best Friend.　Diana O Hehir.　And before I can count to ten she raises it high,/Slices it into my chest.　NPGG

How to Own Land.　Susan Farley.　the land will be yours　AMV-80

How to Paint a Perfect Christmas.　Miroslav Holub.　next time/I shall paint/the most perfect Christmas/that ever was.　OBCP

How to Raise a Son.　Martial (Marcus Valerius Martialis).　You'll have to make the boy, I fear,/An architect or auctioneer.　LiTW

How to Reach the Moon.　Marsha Pomerantz.　How do you carry your spores,/the stars, and will you/let them go?　VWA

How to Read Me.　Walter Savage Landor.　Believe that all my griefs were true/And all my joys were dreamt.　NOBV

How to See Deer.　Philip Booth.　...See/what you see.　Psk

How to Start a War.　Phyllis McGinley.　As each drew his sword/On the side of the Lord.　DBV; OBSV

How to Swing Those Obbligatos Around.　Alice Fulton.　I said how many years do you get/if they give you life.　LTB

How to Tell Goblins from Elves.　Monica Shannon.　So you can't mistake a goblin,/When a goblin you have found.　TiPo

How to Tell Juan Don from Another.　Gardner E. Lewis.　...It/Enthralled me, Don Quixote.　FiBHP

How to Tell the Top of a Hill.　John Ciardi.　The next step up is sky.　SoPo

How to Tell the Wild Animals.　Carolyn Wells.　If there is nothing on the tree,/'Tis the Chameleon you see.　FaFP; FiBHP; HBVY; MaC; NLV; TiPo

How to the Singer Comes the Song?　Richard Watson Gilder.　Life of his life, and soul of all his song!　WGRP

How to Treat Elves.　Morris Bishop.　I lifted up my foot, and squashed/The God damn little fool.　DBV; FiBHP; OBAL; OBCA; PoPl

How to Walk in a Crowd.　Robert Hershon.　she'll get/a ticket　FF

How to Write a Letter.　Elizabeth Turner.　Though silent your tongue, you can speak with your pen.　MoShBr; OxBChV

How to Write a Poem about the Sky.　Leslie Marmon Silko.　You see the sky.　NoP

How Totally Unpredictable We Are to One Another.　Robert Sward.　I want to begin immediately.　PoL

How Tuesday Began.　Kathleen Fraser.　and said, "I don't see/so good myself."　CTBA; NYBP

How Violets Came Blue.　Robert Herrick.　Her blows did make ye blue.　CaPo; EnL

How Was Your Trip to L.A.?　Philip Whalen.　Our city tends to disappear in cold weather.　TAT

How We Beat the Favourite.　Adam Lindsay Gordon.　...And that's how the favourite was beat.　CBAP

How We Became a Nation.　Harriet Prescott Spofford.　And that great day the Port Bill passed/Made us a nation hard and fast.　MC; PAH

How We Built a Church at Ashcroft.　Jack Leahy.　Who thought on failure of our church to perpetrate a joke.　PoOW

How We Burned the Philadelphia.　Barrett Eastman.　And troubled his soul no more.　PAH

How We Drove the Trotter. W. T. Goodge. Moses, what a smash! NOAV; PH

How We Heard the Name. Alan Dugan. all of you ba-bas/will hear of as a god. CoAP; NMP; NoAm

How We Learn. Horatius Bonar. And the soul feels it has not wept in vain. HBV 1-2

How We Logged Katahdin Stream. Daniel Gerard Hoffman. And we'll drink to the health of Bold Gattigan, and his gallant/lumbering crew! MaC

How Well for the Birds. Anonymous. Rising and setting he fills all my dreaming. KiLC; WTO

How Will You Call Me, Brother? Mari E. Evans. Have you armed your children? BlSi

How will you cross. Princess Oku. even when we went/together. BoWoP

How Will You Manage. Princess Daihaku. Even when we went the two of us together? AWP

How You Get Born. Erica Jong. She opens her legs to your coming. UnPo

Howard Lamson. Edgar Lee Masters. My dream is what the hillside dreams! NAMP; ViBoPo

Howdy, Honey, Howdy! Paul Laurence Dunbar. Howdy, honey, howdy, won't you step right in? PoLf

Howl, I. Allen Ginsberg. ...butchered out of their/own bodies good to eat a thousand years. NeAP

Howl, II. Allen Ginsberg. ...Down to the/river! into the street! NeAP; PoCh

The Howling of Wolves. Ted Hughes. The night snows stars and the earth creaks. OxBTC

A Hub for the Universe. Walt Whitman. And there is no object so soft but it makes a hub for the wheeled/universe. FaFP

Hubert Horatio Humphrey (1911-1978). Martin Galvin. ...jingling golden/ in otherwise empty pockets. SOTS

Hubert's Museum. Louis Simpson. who "faced a firing squad, received 8 bullets/through the body and head, yet LIVED!" OxBC

Huck Finn at Ninety, Dying in a Chicago Boarding House Room. James Schevill. Through the frontier dream... TAP

Huckleberry Hunting. Anonymous. To me Hilo, me Ranzo boy! ShS

The Huckster's Horse. Julia Hurd Strong. That switched his slim legs like a hula skirt. GoYe

Hudibras. Samuel (1612-80) Butler.
And therefore vulgar authors name/Th'one Good, the other Evil Fame. OBSV

And what men say of her they mean/No more, than that on which they lean. OBSV

For a large conscience is all one,/And signifies the same with none. OBSV
Whil'st still the more he kick'd and/spurr'd,/The less the sullen jade has stirr'd. SeCV 1-2

The Hudson. George Sidney Hellman. And saw his mother waiting at the door. AA

Hudson Ferry. James Schuyler. ...The City Hall all clean/gleams like silver like the magnolias in the moonlight. NYP

Hudson Hornet. William W. Cook. God save the Sundays where he rode. AMV-80

A Hue and Cry after Blood and Murder. Anonymous. And let him take a warning by his friend. APAS

A Hue and Cry after Fair Amoret. William Congreve. And, while she laughs at them, forgets/She is the thing that she despises. CEP; NOEC; OBEC; OBEV

Huesca. John Cornford. Don't forget my love. BoLoP; ChMP

Huey. Etheridge Knight. comes/Revolution. NNaP

Hug o' War. Shel Silverstein. And everyone cuddles,/And everyone wins. NTCP

Hugging the Jukebox. Naomi Shihab Nye. this is not the end of the island, or the tablets this life has been/scribbled on, or the song. MAYP

Hugh Maguire. Eochy O'Hussey. And from his wrists the flame/Thaws manacles of ice. KiLC

Hugh Selwyn Mauberley. Ezra Pound. ...the case presents/No adjunct to the Muses' diadem. NOBA

Hugh Selwyn Mauberley, III. Ezra Pound. What god, man, or hero/Shall I place a tine wreath upon! CoBMV; NOBA

Hugh Selwyn Mauberley, IV. Ezra Pound. laughter out of dead bellies. CoBMV; NOBA; OxBA; VGW

Hugh Selwyn Mauberley, V. Ezra Pound. For a few thousand battered books. CoBMV; NOBA; OxBA

Hugh Selwyn Mauberley, VI: Yeux Glauques. Ezra Pound. At her last maquero's/Adulteries. NOBA

Hugh Selwyn Mauberley, VII: Siena mi fe'; disfecemi maremma. Ezra Pound. Neglected by the young,/Because of these reveries. NOBA

Hugh Selwyn Mauberley, VIII: Brennbaum. Ezra Pound. Level across the face/Of Brennbaum "The Impeccable." NOBA

Hugh Selwyn Mauberley, X. Ezra Pound. The door has a creaking latch. CoBMV; NOBA

Hugh Selwyn Mauberley, XI. Ezra Pound. No instinct has survived in her/ Older than those her grandmother/Told her would fit her station. CoBMV; NOBA

Hugh Selwyn Mauberley, XII. Ezra Pound. The sale of half-hose has/Long since superseded the cultivation/Of Pierian roses. CoBMV; NOBA

Hugh Selwyn Mauberley, XIII: Envoi. Ezra Pound. Till change hath broken down/All things save Beauty alone. LiTA

Hugh Spencer's Feats in France (A version). Anonymous. That there shall neuer be open warres/kept in my land/Whilest peace kept that there may/ bee.' ESPB

Hugh Spencer's Feats in France (B version). Anonymous. Then hold thy hand, Spencer,/I dearly thee pray. ESPB

Hugh Stuart Boyd: His Blindness. Elizabeth Barrett Browning. Scarce plainer than Heaven's angels on the/wing! VLP

Hughie at the Inn. Elinor Wylie. Be provident, and pray for cowardice/ And the loaded pair of dice. NYBP

Hughie Graham. Anonymous. And when they meet the bishop's cloak,/to mak it shorter by the hood.– OxBB

Hughie Grame (A version). Anonymous. And when thou comst to the border-side,/Remember the death of Sir Hugh of/the Grime.' ESPB

Hughie Grame (C version). Anonymous. It was you berievt me o my life,/ An wi the bishop playd the w ESPB

Hughley Steeple. Alfred Edward Housman. And I shall ne'er be lonely/ Asleep with these or those. FaBoPP

A Huguenot. Mary Elizabeth Coleridge. As I sang, "None maketh me afraid!" OBVV

Hull's Surrender. Anonymous. By our fathers we swear it shall dwell here no more. PAH

Hullabaloo Belay. Anonymous. Because me mother come back the very next day. FSW

"Hullo!" Sam Walter Foss. Then the souls you've cheered will/know/Who ye be, an' say "Hullo!" PaPo

Humaine Cares. Nathaniel Wanley. And as if wanting griefe he must/Go take up sorrow upon trust. OBS

The Human Abstract. William Blake. There grows one in the Human brain. BiP; DiPo; EnRP; PPP

The Human Animal. Jane Mayhall. ...And passing still/go on to learn what's gone; and what I will. TAP

The Human Being Is a Lonely Creature. Richard Eberhart. The human being is a lonely creature. NePoAm

The Human Cry. Alfred, Lord Tennyson. Hallowed be Thy name– Halleluiah! ILwL

Human Cylinders. Mina Loy. Destroy the Universe/With a solution. AnAmPo

Human Debasement. A Fragment. Edward Rushton. Ah, all these works are thine! NOEC

Human Dilemma. Jim Rosemergy. Changing until we find that which/ cannot be changed. AMV-80

The Human Fold. Edwin Muir. To lay my head in the light's lap'. LiTM

Human Frailty. William Cowper. The breath of Heaven must swell the sail,/Or all the toil is lost. HBV 1-2

Human Frailty. Philip Freneau. Discharge the debt, and walk away. AnAmPo

Human Geography. Gloria Fuertes. Look at my contained continent. BoWoP

Human Geography. Ruth Whitman. ripening by the black wall. AMV-80

Human Greatness. Edwin Barclay. You are but dust and even Caesar died. PBA

The Human Heart. Frank Carleton Nelson. When He made the heart of man. PoToHe

Human Life. Aubrey Thomas De Vere. Not for their sake, but His who grants them or denies them. HBV 1-2; OnYI

Human Life. Matthew Prior. Wake, eat, and drink, evacuate, and sleep. FaBoEE

Human Life: On the Denial of Immortality. Samuel Taylor Coleridge. Thy being's being is contradiction. ChRP

The Human Mind. Ai Shih-te. but the human mind existed before/there was worship or righteousness. TrJP

Human Needs. E.M. Walker. Some food, some sun, some work, some fun, some-one. PoL

The Human Outlook. John Addington Symonds. Transcending aught we gaze upon. WGRP

The Human Plan. Charles Henry Crandall. But, after all, what may be Heaven indeed? AA

The Human Races. R. P. Lister. Their nature uniformly base is. FiBHP

Human Relations. Emmett Jarrett. while everyone else shouts helpfully to the gears to shift. NeAC

Human Relations. C. H. Sisson. While the other imaginatively rifles your drawers. PoL; TW

The Human Seasons. John Keats. Or else he would forego his mortal nature. CoBE; EnRP; FaFP; GTBS; GTBS-P; HBV 1-2; OBRV; WiR

Human Soul. Rene Maran. Or if all my love's been effaced. TTY

Hush, My Baby, Do Not Cry. *Anonymous.* Hi cockalorum, jig, jig, jig. OxNR

Hush Thee, My Babby. *Anonymous.* So hush-a-bye, babby, lie still. OxNR

Hush Thee, Princeling. Anna Elizabeth Bennett. Hush thee, princeling,/ God's own blessed Son. AH

Hushed by the Hands of Sleep. Angelina Weld Grimke. By the beautiful hands of sleep. CDC

Hushie Ba, Burdie Beeton. *Anonymous.* To wrap your bonnie boukie in. OxNR

Husky Hi. Rose Fyleman. Here comes Keery galloping by! TiPo

Hustle and Grin. *Anonymous.* ...you are out of rhyme/With the busy, hustling throng. WBLP

The Hustler. *Anonymous.* And I would make the Supreme Court eat shit from/a spoon. TW

Hustlers. Dennis Cooper. You know. You're inside us. APU

Hut. G. J. F. Dutton. somebody else's photograph. PoSH

The Hut. Avigdor Hamameiri. Perhaps, perhaps, perhaps, Thou'llt not move me again? LiTW

The Hut. Hilda Van Stockum. We smiled through strands of dripping hair,/Because we felt so dry. BrR

Hut Near Desolated Pines. Alistair Campbell. Sheeting an old man's agony. AnNZ

Hut Window. Paul Celan. Bet–this is/the house where the table stands with/the light and the light. VWA

Huxley Hall. Sir John Betjeman. ...not my lime-juice minus gin,/Quite can drown a faint conviction that we may be born in Sin. OBSV

Hyacinths to Feed Thy Soul. Muslih-ud-Din Sa'di. Buy hyacinths to feed thy soul. BLPA; BLPL; FaBoBe; TRV

The Hyaenas. Rudyard Kipling. Nor do they defile the dead man's name–/That is reserved for his kind. OBSV

Hyd, Absolon, Thy Gilte Tresses Clere. Geoffrey Chaucer. My lady cometh, that all this may disteyne. ExPo; HAP; WeW

Hyder Iddle. *Anonymous.* A tailor's goose will never fly. NA; OxNR

The Hydra of Birds. Nikos Engonopoulos. That it might bind on my face the mask of birds. LiTW

The Hydraulic Ram. Charles Tennyson Turner. As this imprisoned engine, night and day,/Piles its dull pulses in the darkness there? NBM

Hydro Works. J. R. Hervey. The hard core of the purpose and will of man. AnNZ

Hydrographic Report. Frances Frost. Hold on:/off the coast,/glass falling. EtS

Hye Nonny Nonny Noe. *Anonymous.* By being so frank of her/hye nonny nonny noe. FaBoCo; NOBL

Hyena. *Anonymous* Son of the darkness walker. TTY

Hyena. Carol Muske. It is her laughter on the slopes/at night. AmPA

Hygiene Sonnet. Dick Gallup. Than shit as they do, foully, and moistly give vent to their/asses ANYP

Hyla Brook. Robert Frost. We love the things we love for what they are. AnNE; APA; BoNaP; MAPA; SoSe

Hylas. Sextus Propertius. For fortune often mocks the careless lover's eyes. AWP

Hymen: Never More Will the Wind. Hilda ("H. D.") Doolittle. Like a light out of our heart,/You are gone. TrGrPo; ViBoPo

Hymeneal. Caius Valerius Catullus. Sing "Hymen, Hymen', sing/The god of marrying! PeHV

An Hymeneal Song on the Nuptials of the Lady Anne Wentworth and... Thomas Carew. And we from their conjunctions take/Rules to make love an almanac. CaPo

An Hymeneall Dialogue. Thomas Carew. Each by contraction multiply'de. AnAnS 2; SeCP

Hymmnn. Allen Ginsberg. ...Blessed be Death on us All! NOBA

Hymn. Archie Randolph Ammons. and if I find you I must stay here with the separate leaves ConAP

Hymn. Elizabeth Barrett Browning. And when our flesh is only dust,/Abide our souls with Thee. TrPWD

Hymn. Wathen Mark Wilks Call. I praise thee, God. OBVV

Hymn. John Chadwick.
Give or withhold, let pain or pleasure be,/Enough to know that we are serving Thee. TrPWD
We cannot wish for more. TrPWD

Hymn. Stephen Crane. "O God, save us!" MoAmPo

Hymn. Philip Doddridge. And Each the Bliss of all shall view/With infinite Delight. CEP; OBEC

Hymn. Paul Laurence Dunbar.
But in thy presence ever blest,/O God of my salvation. TrPWD; TRV
My greater, guiding star! TrPWD
"O Shepud, I's a-comin' quick"–/O li'l' lamb! AA

Hymn. John Haynes Holmes.
The meek are haloed by thy light. TrPWD
That our quick day, from error free,/May live in Thine eternity. TrPWD

Hymn. Philip Howard With heart and hand, with mind, and all/Which we from Thee possess. ACP; CAW

Hymn. Francis Scott Key. Let my life show forth thy praise. TrPWD

Hymn. Lucy Larcom. Life's murmuring waves a song divine/Shall chant, O God, to Thee! OHIP

A Hymn. Nikolai Nekrasov. Entrust the flag of liberty/At last, to Russian hands. LiTW

Hymn. Louise Townsend Nicholl. Oh, love, take all the faithfulness/Of my unfaithful heart! EaLo

Hymn. Otto Orban. ...as long/as eternal earth rolls, spokes groaning, from cell to cell. VWA

Hymn. Josephine Preston Peabody. And bid them fly unto the day/That Thou hast need of me. TrPWD

Hymn. Edgar Allan Poe. Let my future radiant shine/With sweet hopes of thee and thine. ISi

A Hymn. James Shirley. When all the shadows do increase. GoBC

Hymn. Harriet Beecher Stowe. Disturbs the Sabbath of that deeper sea. PoToHe

Hymn. Synesius. Unknown, unmarked by others/But to my God laid bare! CAW

Hymn. Andrew Young. Lord, give them back when at thy holy altar/We feed on thee, who are the living bread. EaLo

A Hymn: "A hymn of glory let us sing." The Venerable Bede. May all our glory be in Thee! WGRP

A Hymn About a Spoonful of Soup. Jozef Wittlin. Which I want to give you on this day in vain. VWA

Hymn Against Pestilence. Saint Colman. May Jesus with His apostles/Be for our help against danger! OnYI

Hymn before Sunrise, in the Vale of Chamouni. Samuel Taylor Coleridge. Earth, with her thousand voices, praises GOD. EnRP; ERoP 1-2; MCCG; OAEP; OxBoCh; WGRP

Hymn: "Brightest and best of the sons of the morning." Reginald Heber. Dearer to God are the prayers of the poor. NBM

Hymn: Crucifixus Pro Nobis. Patrick Carey. Sigh out a groan, weep down a melting tear. OxBoCh

Hymn: "Eternal Father, strong to save.". William Whiting. And ever let there rise to Thee/Glad hymns of praise from land and sea. NBM

Hymn (excerpt). Richard Watson Gilder. Not ours, O God! the craven part,/To shut one human soul from hope. TrPWD

Hymn for a Household. Daniel Henderson. O Man of Nazareth, be our guest! HBMV

Hymn for Atonement Day. Judah Halevi. Our father, from Thy children's plea/Turn not, we implore Thee! TrJP

A Hymn for Canada. Albert Durrant Watson. Lord of the worlds, make all the lands Thine own! CaP

Hymn for Christmas. Felicia Dorothea Hemans. Oh! clear and shining light! GN

Hymn for Christmas Day. John Byrom. Sav'd by his Love, incessant we shall sing/Of Angels, and of Angel-Men, the King. NOCV; OBEC; PoEL 1-5; SBVL

Hymn for Easter Morn. *Anonymous.* To Thee our praise that we may pay,/To whom our laud is due–for aye. TrCP

Hymn for Lanie Poo. 4. Each Morning. LeRoi (Imamu Amiri Baraka) Jones. This is known/as genealogy. NNP

Hymn for Laudes: Feast of Our Lady, Help of Christians. *Anonymous.* And our lips in echoing song. Amen. ISi

Hymn for Laudes Feast of Our Lady of Good Counsel. *Anonymous.* One God in three Persons. Amen. ISi

Hymn for Nations. *Anonymous.* Work beside me, O my brother,/All for one and one for all! FSW

Hymn for Pentecost. James Clarence Mangan. And thus complete for earth mankind's triumphal arch. CAW

Hymn for Second Vespers;Feast of the Apparition of Our Lady of Lourdes. *Anonymous.* With Their swift Spirit winged with love for Both,/Three-always-One! ISi

Hymn for St. John's Eve. *Anonymous.* Whilst each glad parent told and blessed/The secrets of each other's breast. AWP

Hymn for the Church Militant. Gilbert Keith Chesterton. Sow in our souls like living grass,/The laughter of all lowly things. OxBoCh

Hymn for the Close of the Week. Peter Abelard. Through whom, the Spirit, with these ever one. TrCP

Hymn for the Dedication of a Church. Andrews Norton. And raise to thee still holier prayers! AA

Hymn for the Eve of the New Year. Abraham Gerondi. Begin, New Year–and bring that/joyous day! TrJP

Hymn for the Feast of the Annunciation. Sir Aubrey De Vere. Between those two great beams on plumes outspread/Hovers and gleams the everlasting Dove! ISi

Hymn for the Lighting of the Lamps. Saint Athenogenes. Therefore in all the world, thy glories, Lord, they own. CAW

Hymn for the Slain in Battle. William Stanley Braithwaite. They make the greatest sacrifice. BALP

Hymn: "Framer of the earth and sky." Saint Ambrose of Milan. Faith revives when faith was/failing. TrCP

Hymn from the French of Lamartine (excerpt). John Greenleaf Whittier. ...that I might lose/Myself in finding Thee! TrPWD

Hymn: "Hush! oh ye billows." Joseph Sheridan Lefanu. Angels watch over thee,/Mary, be kind! OnYI

Hymn in Columbus Circle. Stephen Vincent Benét. And every gazer applauds/The tremendous rubber tire. OBAL

Hymn: "My God, I love thee, not because." Robert Francis. Solely because thou art my God,/And my eternal King. WGRP

Hymn: "Now we must praise heaven-kingdom's Guardian." Caedmon. eternal Lord, afterwards made–/for men earth, Master almighty. TrCP

A Hymn–O God of Earth and Altar. Gilbert Keith Chesterton. Lift up a living nation,/A single sword to thee. GoTF; TreFT

Hymn: "O Thou who camest from above." Charles Wesley. And make thy sacrifice complete. SeCePo

The Hymn of Adam. Joost van den Vondel. And language not involved in dark! CAW

Hymn of Apollo. Percy Bysshe Shelley. Victory and praise in its own right belong. EnL; EnLit; ERoP 1-2; HBV 1-2; MBW 1-2; OAEL 1-2; OAEP; OBRV

Hymn of Dedication. Elizabeth E. Scantlebury. May Thy love, O Father, bind this place about. BLRP

The Hymn of Empedocles (excerpt). Matthew Arnold. Because thou must not dream, thou need'st not then despair. OBEV

A Hymn of Form. Gordon Bottomley. As if, after all, God is and is about to speak. BrPo

Hymn of Gratitude. Anonymous. Let all the people worship Thee. BLRP

The Hymn of Hate. Joseph Dana Miller. From blood-drenched shore to shore! PGD

An Hymn of Heavenly Beauty (excerpt). Edmund Spenser. Thy straying thoughts henceforth forever rest. WGRP

Hymn of Joy. Henry Van Dyke. Joyful music lifts us sunward/In the triumph song of life. TRV

Hymn of Man. Algernon Charles Swinburne. Glory to Man in the highest! for Man is the/master of things. VLP; WGRP

A Hymn of Nature. Robert Bridges. And drinks from the rocky rills/The laughter of life. YeAr

Hymn of Pan. Percy Bysshe Shelley. At the sorrow of my sweet pipings. AtBAP; ERoP 1-2; ExPo; FaBoCh; HBV 1-2; LoGBV; MyFE; OAEP; OBEV; OBRV; PoEL 1-5; SeCeV

A Hymn of Praise, on a Recovery from Sickness. Benjamin Colman. Take hence my life an happier State,/More Heav'nly, more Sublime. SCAP

The Hymn of Saint Thomas in Adoration of the Blessed Sacrament. Richard Crashaw. And for thy veil gave me thy FACE. MeLP; OBS

Hymn of Sivaite Puritans. Anonymous. And thus where'er I go/I ever worship God. WGRP

A Hymn of Thanksgiving. Wilbur D. Nesbit. Have them and hold them over-long,/Out of Thy wondrous treasures. OHIP

Hymn of the Alamo. Reuben M. Potter. Like brothers died, and their expiring breath/Was Freedom's breath of life! BPAW

Hymn of the Angels and Sibyls. Gil Vicente. Are there peaks or vales or rills/Beautiful as She? CAW

Hymn of the City. William Cullen Bryant. The vast and helpless city while it sleeps. AmePo

Hymn of the Earth. William Ellery Channing, II. Are mirrored in its round abode. AA; AnNE

A Hymn of the Incarnation. Anonymous. Him bare a maide-moder, Marye. MeEL

Hymn of the Moravian Nuns of Bethlehem. Henry Wadsworth Longfellow. The warrior took that banner proud,/And it was his martial cloak and shroud! PAH

A Hymn of the Sea. William Cullen Bryant. Swept by the murmuring winds of ocean, join/The murmuring shores in a perpetual hymn. MOS

Hymn of the Waldenses. William Cullen Bryant. And thy delivered saints shall dwell in rest. AnNE

Hymn of the West. Edmund Clarence Stedman. Land of the new and lordlier race! HBV 1-2; PAH

The Hymn of the World's Creator (excerpt). Caedmon. He, Lord everlasting, Omnipotent God! CAW

A Hymn of Touch. Gordon Bottomley. Of all senses magnificent. BrPo

Hymn of Trust. Oliver Wendell Holmes. Content to suffer while we know,/Living and dying, Thou art near! AA; TrPWD

A Hymn of Trust. Nettie M. Sargent. In quietness and confidence/Shall be the strength I know. BLRP

Hymn of Unity. Anonymous. But thou wilt abide and see them all/to fade, for thou livest and/endurest to all eternity. TrJP

Hymn of Victory: Thutmose III. Amon-Re. Thutmose, living forever. WaaP

Hymn of Weeping. A. Ben Shefatiah. For unto Thee our eyes turn evermore. TrJP

A Hymn on Froude and Kingsley. William Stubbs. And Kingsley goes to Froude for history. FaBoEE

Hymn on Solitude. James (1700-48) Thomson. Nor by a mortal seen, save he/A Lycidas or Lycon be. NOEC Then shield me in the woods again. CEP; OBEC

Hymn on the Morning of Christ's Nativity. John Milton. Bright-harnest Angels sit in order serviceable. NOBE; OBEV Isis and Orus, and the dog Anubis haste. WHA

An Hymn on the Omnipresence. John Byrom. And the Darkness, to Thee, is as clear as the Light. CEP; TrPWD

A Hymn on the Seasons. James (1700-48) Thomson. Come then, expressive Silence, muse HIS Praise. LAuP; OxBoCh

Hymn: "Sing, my tongue, the Saviour's glory." Saint Thomas Aquinas. Be salvation, homour, blessing,/Might and endless majesty. Amen. WGRP

Hymn Sung at the Completion of the Concord Monument April 19, 1836. Ralph Waldo Emerson. Bid Time and Nature gently spare/The shaft we raise to them and thee. PoPl

Hymn: "The Church's Restoration. (parody). Sir John Betjeman. Look up! and oh how glorious/He has restored the roof! FaBoPa

Hymn: "Thou hidden love of God, whose height." John Wesley. To taste thy love, be all my choice. NOEC

Hymn to Adversity. Thomas Gray. What others are, to feel, and know myself a Man. CEP; GTBS; GTBS-P; OBEC

Hymn to Amen Ra, the Sun God. Anonymous. This is the end,/in peace,/ as it was found. WGRP

Hymn to Artemis, the Destroyer. Marya Zaturenska. Ever for your presence sighs. MOON

Hymn to Athena. Anonymous. Nor thine nor others' praise shall unremembered be. AWP

A Hymn to Bacchus. Robert Herrick. Urge no more, and there shall be/ Daffodils given up to thee. JCP

Hymn to Castor and Pollux. Anonymous. And plow the quiet sea in safe delight. AWP

Hymn to Charity and Humility. Henry More. Lord thrust me deeper into dust/That thou may'st raise me with the just. OxBoCh

A Hymn to Christ at the Author's Last Going into Germany. John Donne. And to 'scape stormy days, I choose/An Everlasting night. AnEnPo; DiPo; EBEV; EnRePo; FaBoRV; JCP; LiTB; OAEP; OBS; OxBoCh; ViBoPo

Hymn to Christ the Saviour. Clement of Alexandria (Titus Flavius Clemens). Praise we our God again,/Lord of our Peace! CAW

Hymn to Colour. George Meredith. ...Death met I too,/And saw the dawn glow through. OBNC

Hymn to Comus. Ben Jonson. Thou break'st all thy girdles, and break'st forth a god. ElL; OAEP

A Hymn to Contentment. Thomas Parnell. And find a life of equal bliss,/ Or own the next begun in this. CEP; NOEC; OBEC

Hymn to Darkness. John Norris. And those that weary are of light, find rest in thee. GTBS 'Tis just we should adore, 'tis just we should thee sing. MePo; OBS; OxBoCh

Hymn to Diana. Caius Valerius Catullus. The lineage of Romulus! AWP

Hymn to Dispel Hatred at Midnight. Yvor Winters. Grief will not turn again. TW

Hymn to Earth. Elinor Wylie. Sleeps as thy lover for a little while. AmLP; LiTM; MoAB; MoAmPo; MoPo; MoVE; NePA

Hymn to Earth the Mother of All. Anonymous. Nor thou nor other songs shall unremembered be. AWP

Hymn to Evil. Louis Ginsberg. Holy is the deed you do! PoA

A Hymn to God in Time of Stress. Max Eastman. God, a motion of thy lip! TrPWD

Hymn to God My God, in My Sickness. John Donne. Therefore that he may raise, the Lord throws down. CABA; DiPo; DTC; EBEV; EnL; GoBC; InPS; LoBV; NIP; NoP; OAEL 1-2; OAEP; OxBoCh; PPP

A Hymn to God the Father. John Donne. And having done that, thou hast done;/I fear no more. AWP; BiP; DiPo; EBCP; EBEV; EnLit; EnRePo; ForPo; GoBC; HAP; HBV 1-2; InPo; JCP; LiTB; LoBV; NoP; OAEL 1-2; OBS; OxBoCh; PoRA; PPoe; SCV; SeCeV; TrCP; TrGrPo; ViBoPo

Hymn to God the Father. Samuel Wesley. Whom none but Thy essential Word/And Spirit comprehend. OxBoCh

Hymn to Her Unknown. Walter James Turner. Printed the foot of Venus/ Where bloomed this asphodel. LiTL; OBMV

Hymn to Horus. Mathilde Blind. And with thy mystic spouses/Rest from the long, long way! OBVV

Hymn to Intellectual Beauty. Percy Bysshe Shelley. To fear himself, and love all human kind. AnEnPo; BiP; BLPL; BoLiVe; EnL; ERoP 1-2; HAP; HeIP; MBW 1-2; NoP; OAEL 1-2; OAEP; OBNC; OBRV

A Hymn to Jesus. Richard of Caistre. And spare that they han done amiss./Amen. MeEL

Hymn to Joy. Julia Cunningham. Announce our love! Amen. PCh

Hymn, to Light. Abraham Cowley. From thence took first their Rise, thither at last must Flow. AtBAP; MeLP; MePo; OBS; SeCV 1-2

That inlet to severe magnificence/Stood full blown, for the God to enter in. OBRV

Which eagles cleave upmounting from their nest. ATP

While his bow'd head seem'd list'ning to the Earth,/His ancient mother, for some comfort yet... ExPo

Hypnopompic Poem. William Cole. That is a convention/I cannot attend. PoL

Hypochondriacus (parody). Charles Lamb. Lucifer teareth me–/Jesu! Maria! liberate nos ab his diris tentationibus/Inimici. BXAP

The Hypocrite. Ben Kalonymos. And he is ever a sad disgrace/To Jewish creed and Jewish race. TrJP

The Hypocrite. John Caryll. Who, though he ulcers have in ev'ry part,/Is nowhere so corrupt as in his heart. APAS

Hypocrite Auteur. Archibald MacLeish. Invent the age! Invent the metaphor! AmPP; MoVE; NePA

Hypocrite Swift. Louise Bogan. Hypocrite Swift sent Stella a green apron/And dead desire. PoA; SBG

Hypocrite Women. Denise Levertov. ...clipped them like ends of/split hair. CAPP; MAT; NMM; PoM

Hypodermic Release. Del Corey. and bones/of those I love. AMV-81

Hyssop." Walter De La Mare. "Why, house-leek," said the Bishop. "That's all." BoC

Hysteria. Chu Shu chen. ...I watch the sun set beyond/The roofs of the women's quarters. NaP

I

I, a Most Wretched Atlas. Heinrich Heine. And lo! now art thou wretched. TrJP

I Accept. Harold Trowbridge Pulsifer. To live as though a pleasant land/Lay just beyond an open door? HBMV

I Am. John Clare. The grass below–above the vaulted sky. CBEP; EBCP; EBEV; ERoP 1-2; GTBS-P; HAP; LiTB; NBM; NOBE; NOBV; NoP; OAEL 1-2; OBNC; PG; PoEL 1-5; PoPl; Prf; PrIm; TrGrPo; VLP; WHA

I Am. Hilda Conkling. I am a very small violet/Thinking of May. TiPo

I Am. Bill Kushner. ...here's a flower not in bloom/here in the glorious East where I rent a small room. APU

I Am 25. Gregory Corso. Then at night in the confidence of their homes/rip out their apology-tongues and steal their poems. CoPo

I Am a Black Woman. Mari E. Evans. Look/on me and be/renewed CNA; NMM

I Am a Book I Neither Wrote Nor Read. Delmore Schwartz. To prove the reality of endless love? TAP

I Am a Brisk and Sprightly Lad. Anonymous. With a yeo, yeo, yeo! AmSS

I Am a Cowboy in the Boat of Ra. Ishmael Reed. party pooper O hater of dance/vampire outlaw of the milky way NBP; NoP; PoBA; PrIm

I Am a Dangerous Woman. Joy Harjo. they can't hear the clicking/of the gun/inside my head TWSS

I Am a Horse. Hans Arp. oh wide wide world FaBoNo

I Am a Hunchback. Robert Louis Stevenson. Good woman, take my arm. OBSP

I Am a Jew. David Martin. Dig deep, dig deep,/You will find my bones. VWA

I Am a King. Rimon. I. Z. and finds its peace/in pain/and in the flow of peace/its dying. VWA

I Am a Leaf. Yehuda Amichai. after they hewed the love from it/as from a quarry/already abandoned. VWA

I Am a Lioness. Aisha bint Ahmad. and O! the lions I've turned away! WPOW

I am a little church (no great cathedral). Edward Estlin Cummings. (welcoming humbly His light and proudly His darkness) MoRP; NePoAm-2

I Am a Negro. Muhammad Al-Fituri. Here is Africa the great/Glittering/In the light of dawn. TTY

I Am a Parcel of Vain Strivings Tied. Henry David Thoreau. While I droop here. AnNE; AP; LiTA; MAmP; NOBA; NoP; PoEL 1-5; TAP

I Am a Peach Tree. Li Po. My thought is like the stream; and flows and follows you/on forever. OLR

I Am a Pilgrim. Anonymous. Well, I believe it would make me whole. FSW

"I Am a Sioux Brave," He Said in Minneapolis. James Wright. Or what kind of words to sing/When he dies. ELU

I Am a Victim of Telephone. Allen Ginsberg. ringing at dawn ringing all afternoon ringing up midnight/ringing now forever. GP; NLV; NYP

I am a widow, robed in black, alone. Christine de Pisan. I am a widow, robed in black, alone. BoWoP

I Am a Wild Young Irish Boy. Anonymous. I've died at my post like an Irish lad, or a wild colonial boy. ShS

I Am a Woman (excerpt). Akhtar Amiri. and this is me. WPOW

I am a young girl, gay. Anonymous. God curse the man who saddled me/as Jesus' wife. BoWoP

I Am Afraid. Anonymous. I am afraid. WSC

I am afraid to own a body. Emily Dickinson. And God for a frontier. LiTA

I Am Aladdin. Robert Carlton Brown. Jinn, take her away. AnAmPo

I am alive–I guess. Emily Dickinson. And try another Key– NOBA

I Am Almost Asleep. Eldon Grier. dripping slantwise into my side. PV

I Am Alone. V. Bhanot. Where Earth unknown bleeds life anew. ACV

I Am an American. Elias Lieberman. I am an American. PAL; PoLf; TreFT

I Am an Ancient Mariner. Anonymous. It's up, by Jove, and away we go: it's all right, Jack. OBSS

I Am as I Am. Sir Thomas Wyatt. That I am as I am and so will I be. CBEP; FCP; SiPS

I Am but a Little Woman. Kivkarjuk. As I pluck the buds of willow,/That are furry like the great wolf's beard. WTO

I Am Called Childhood. Sir Thomas More. Whiche lyfe god sende me to myne endyng day. NCEP

I Am Christmas. Anonymous. Yet for my sake make ye good chere;/Now have good day! OxBM

I Am Dark and Fair to See. Anonymous. For I meddle me to know/Love, and naught can cure it. UnTE

I Am Disquieted When I See Many Hills. Hyam Plutzik. Be still the herdsman's boy among these giants/And the ridges of laurel. VGW

I Am Forsaken. Anonymous. When ich have right good wine/Me liste drinke non ale. OxBM

I Am Fur from My Sweetheart. Anonymous. But there ain't none what can compare with my own sweetheart's/curls. CoSo

I am furious with myself. Elsa Tio. I only see time's scar. BoWoP

I Am Glad Daylong. William Stanley Braithwaite. Where dreams come in from the rush and the din/Like sheep from the rains and thunders. GoSl

I Am Going to Sleep. Alfonsina Storni. tell him not to keep trying, for I have left... BoWoP

I Am Goya. Andrei Voznesensky. and hammered stars into the unforgetting sky–like nails/I am Goya OBWP; WeW

I Am Ham Melanite. William Millett. Christ is everyman's skin/you will be with him tonight... GoYe

I Am He That Aches with Love. Walt Whitman. So the body of me to all I meet or know. LLLT

I Am Here. Robert Mezey. I was here with you and your brother. VWA

I am Hermes. Anyte. ...here a fountain/bubbles forth a cold and stainless water. BoWoP

I Am His Highness' Dog at Kew. Alexander Pope. Pray, sir, tell me,–whose dog are you? HBV 1-2

I Am in Danger–Sir–. Adrienne Rich. chose to have it out at last/on your own premises. HaCAP; NOBA

I Am in Great Misery Tonight. Suibne Geilt. I have lost my unequalled looks./Great misery, Son of God! NOBI

I Am Ireland. Augusta Gregory, Lady Gregory. I am Ireland,/Lonelier than the Hag of Beara. OBMV

I Am Like a Book. David Rokeah. The sea is steadfast in its laws–/time too, as it crumbles. VWA

I Am Like a Rose. D. H. Lawrence. Itself more sheer and naked out of the green/In stark-clear roses, than I to myself am brought. OBSP

I Am Like a Slip of Comet. Gerard Manley Hopkins. To not ungentle death now forth I run. VLP

I Am Lonely. George Eliot. And I am lonely. GN; HBV 1-2

I Am Long Weaned. Brother Antoninus. Unbind those breasts. NMP

I Am New York City. Jayne Cortez. citizens/break wind with me. BoWoP

I Am No Subject unto Fate. Anonymous. Elective Monarchs cannot stand,/Nor Loves, without an equal dart. OBS

I Am Not a Camera. W. H. Auden. The camera may/do justice to laughter, but must/degrade sorrow. EyDe

I Am Not Bound to Win. Abraham Lincoln. And part with him when he goes wrong. TRV

I Am Not the Constant Reader. Michael Brownstein. Concerning life in an attempted passage/From ancient history. ANYP

I Am Not Yours. Sara Teasdale. A taper in a rushing wind. VGW

I Am Now So Weary with Waiting. Gaspara Stampa. and he lives happily up in his hills. WPOW

I Am of Ireland. Anonymous. Come ant daunce wyt me/In Irlaunde. GBP; OnYI

I Am of Ireland. William Butler Yeats. And dance with me in Ireland. LiTB; NAMP; OnYI

I Am of the Earth. Anna Walters. She will embrace me for eternity VoR

I Am Partly Moon... Vincente Huidobro. But disguised thus at the Atlantic balls/It is very difficult to single them out LiTW

I Am Raftery.   Derek Mahon.   my back to the wall, taking my cue from a/ grinning disc-jockey between commercials.   CIP

I Am Raftery.   Anthony Raftery.   A-playing music/Unto empty pockets.   LiTW; OnYI

I Am Rose.   Gertrude Stein.   I am Rose like anything   NePA; OBCA; TrJP

I Am Sitting Here.   Yehuda Amichai.   ...my life/pulses close to a huge heart, always within.   VWA

I Am So Far from Pitying Thee.   *Anonymous.*   Thy servant's happier farre then I!   NCEP

I Am So Glad and Very.   Edward Estlin Cummings.   i am through you so i   CMoP

I am so lost.   Narihira (Ariwara no Narihira).   That I can no longer tell/ Dream from reality.   LiTW

I Am Still Rich.   Thomas Curtis Clark.   A segment of Eternity!   PoToHe

I Am Stone of Many Colors.   Tauhindauli.   Like man/we are/eternal in one sense/vulnerable in the next   STE

I Am Suibne the Wanderer.   Suibne Geilt.   "Horn Head' would be better.   NOBI

I Am Sure of It.   Jimmy Santiago Baca.   close or far away, it doesn't matter, I am sure of it.   LFAC

I Am the Autumn.   Itzik Manger.   The grief of all weary steps/That softly come to me.   TrJP

I Am the Beginning.   Isaiah Shembe.   And the moon had not yet shone/In the space of this earth.   WTO

I Am the Blood.   Isaac Rosenberg.   She is my cenotaph.   MoBrPo

I Am the captain of the Pinafore.   Sir William Schwenck Gilbert.   Then give three cheers, and one cheer more,/For the well-bred Captain of the Pinafore!   TreFT

I Am the Cat.   Leila Usher.   I am THE CAT.   BLPA

I Am the Dean of Christ Church, Sir.   Cecil Arthur Spring-Rice.   We are the University.   NOBL

I Am the Door.   Richard Crashaw.   Hath shut these doores of heaven that/ durst/Thus set them ope.   OAEP

I Am the Duke of Norfolk.   *Anonymous.*   You shall be attended,/Now, now, now.   GBP

I Am the Flag.   Lawrence M. Jones.   I AM THE FLAG.   PAL; PGD

I Am the Gilly of Christ.   Joseph Campbell.   And whoso sings the Gilly's Rann/Will never cry for bread.   AnIL; OnYI

I Am the Great Professor Jowett.   *Anonymous.*   And what I don't know isn't knowledge.   FiBHP; PV

I Am the Little Irish Boy.   Henry David Thoreau.   And I'm four years old.   NAs

I Am the Lord.   Alexander Mack.   Your cause shall be protected.   AH

I Am the Monarch of the Sea.   Sir William Schwenck Gilbert.   Whom he reckons up by dozens, and his aunts.   TreFT

I Am the Mountainy Singer.   Joseph Campbell.   And built the nest in the rock!   AnIL; GoBC; HBMV; MCCG; MoBrPo

I Am the One.   Thomas Hardy.   ...He is the one with us/Beginning and end.'   OxBTC

I Am the Only Being Whose Doom.   Emily Bronte.   But worse to trust to my own mind/And find the same corruption there.   MAT; NCEP; TW; VLP

I Am the People, the Mob.   Carl Sandburg.   The mob—the crowd—the mass— will arrive then.   AmPP; OxBA; TAP

I Am the Poet Davies, William.   William Henry Davies.   For how to manage my damned soul/Will puzzle many a flaming devil.   CBEP; OBSP

"I Am the Resurrection and the Life," Saith the Lord!   Robert Stephen Hawker.   The chanting cuckoo's double note!   GoBC

I Am the Rose of Sharon.   Catherine Winkworth.   In heaven at last we bless Thee.   BePJ

I am the sorrow in the wheat fields.   Ellen Bass.   ...the dampness/of sheets and the panic of self, alone and peculiar, entire and full.   NMM

I Am the Walrus.   The Beatles.   GOOOOOOOOOOOJOOOOOB.   PPoe

I Am the Way.   Alice Meynell.   Access, Approach/Art Thou, Time, Way, and Wayfarer.   ACP; CAW; EBCP; GoBC; NOBV; OBMV; OBSP; TRV

I Am the Wind.   Zoë Akins.   You are the surge of deep music,/I—but a cry!   HBV 1-2

I Am Too Near.   Wislawa Szymborska.   on the tip of each, waiting to be counted,/the fallen angels sit.   BoWoP; PBWP

I Am Waiting.   Lawrence Ferlinghetti.   a renaissance of wonder   CAPP; PoPl

I Am Weary of Straying.   Sarah E. York.   While thy word, and thy love, and thy promise are mine.   AH

I Am Weary of These Times and Their Dull Burden.   Lucius Beebe.   Where is thy glory?   RFM

I Am What You Make Me.   Franklin K. Lane.   because you have made them so out of your hearts.   PGD

I Am With Thee.   Ernest Bourner Allen.   In danger be ever nigh!   BLRP

I Am with Those.   Ingrid Jonker.   about love it has no right   BoWoP

I Am with You Alway.   Edwin H. Nevin.   Lighting up the steps of glory/ With Salvation's radiant beam.   BePJ

I Am Your Loaf, Lord.   David Ross.   Shall you wash your hands of me?   GoYe

I Am Your Mother, Your Mother's Mother.   Jalal ed-Din or al-Din Rumi.   ...Look,/if you dare, on your mind's eternal mate.   OBVE

I Am Your Wife.   *Anonymous.*   And, oh, I thank my God tonight I am your wife.   PoToHe

I am yours.   Frau Ava.   You must stay there/forever.   BoWoP

I Am Yours & You Are Mine So.   Michael Silverton.   we will cover each other with little attentions   PoL

I Ask, Who Will Buy a Poem?   Mathghamhain O Hifearnain.   It is all in vain that I ask.   NOBI

I Asked a Thief to Steal Me a Peach.   William Blake.   And still as a maid/ Enjoy'd the Lady.   CABA; CBEP; ExPo; NoP; OBNC; SeCeV; ViBoPo

I Asked for Peace.   Digby Mackworth Dolben.   And thou didst come/To take me home/Within thy heart to be.   EBCP; OxBoCh

I Asked My Fair, One Happy Day.   Samuel Taylor Coleridge.   Only–only call me thine.   HBV 1-2

I Asked My Mother for Fifteen Cents.   Mother Goose.   And never came back 'till the Fourth of July.   FaFP; MoShBr; TiPo

I asked no other thing.   Emily Dickinson.   "But, madam, is there nothing else/That we can show to-day?"   NOBA; OxBA

I Asked the Little Boy Who Cannot See.   *Anonymous.*   And white is a pleasant stillness when you lie/And dream.   OnUR

I Awoke with the Room Cold.   Marge Piercy.   till all of New York was white with pain like snow.   NeAC

I Been a Bad, Bad Girl.   *Anonymous.*   I want to say to all you bad fellas that you are in the wrong.   OuSiCo

I Been Treated Wrong.   Washboard Sam.   (Play it boy, play it, play it)/ (Yes, yes)   BluL

I before E.   *Anonymous.*   As in "neighbour' or "weigh').   FaBoUs

I, Being Born a Woman and Distressed.   Edna St. Vincent Millay.   I find this frenzy insufficient reason/For conversation when we meet again.   BoLoP; NoP

I Believe.   J. B. Lawrence.   To-morrow's Light/Is always burning 'round the rim of night.   BLRP

I Believe.   Saul Tchernichovsky.   And decked with flowers from my/tomb,/ Shall rise up newly-crowned.   TrJP

I Believe a Leaf of Grass...   Walt Whitman.   And a mouse is miracle enough to stagger sextillions of infidels.   TiPo

I Believe I'll Dust My Broom.   Robert Johnson.   If I can't find her on Philippine's Island/she must be in Ethiopia some where   BluL

I Believe Thy Precious Blood.   John Wesley.   For all a full atonement made.   BePJ

I Bended unto Me.   Thomas Edward Brown.   I turned, and saw them whispering about it.   NOBV; NTCP; PeD; PoSC

I Bet God Understands about Givin up Five.   Yasmeen Jamal.   I bet God can dance too.   LFAC

I Bind My Heart.   Lauchlan MacLean Watt.   God! knit Thou sure the cord/Of my thralldom to my Lord.   TRV

I Bless Thee, Lord, for Sorrows Sent.   Samuel Johnson.   The narrow way to love and power.   AH

I Blow My Pipes.   Hugh McCrae.   I am the lord of everything!   PoAu 1-2

I Bore with Thee, Long, Weary Days.   Christina Georgina Rossetti.   A harvest–come and reap.   BePJ

I Break the Sky.   Owen Dodson.   The whiz, the slime–and the sky is whole.   PoBA

I breathed enough to take the trick.   Emily Dickinson.   How numb, the Bellows feels!   NoAm

I Breathed into the Ash.   Roland Robinson.   the ruin of the world.   BoAV

I Bring to You as Offering Tonight.   Emile Verhaeren.   Air and its light and scents are in my flesh.   AnEnPo

I Bring You News.   *Anonymous.*   An icy season./That's my news.   NOBI

"I Broke the Spell That Held Me Long."   William Cullen Bryant.   Recalled me to the love of song.   AmePo

I Built My Hut.   T'ao Chi'en.   Yet when we would express it, words suddenly fail us.   AWP

I Buried the Year.   W. Luff.   The home in the heavens above.   STF

I Burned My Candle at Both Ends.   Samuel Hoffenstein.   I'm paying now in feeling rotten.   ELU; FiBHP

I Call the Old Time Back.   John Greenleaf Whittier.   And loved with us the beautiful and old.   ViBoPo

I Came A-Riding.   Reinmar von Zweter.   If this is true, an ass can sew a cap.   AWP

I Came from Salem City.   *Anonymous.*   A pocket full of rocks bring home, so, brothers, don't you cry.   AmFP

I Came to Jesus.   George White.   Glad am I that I came to Him./And found His truth and grace.   STF

I Came to the New World Empty-Handed.   Hildegarde Hoyt Swift.   It became mine too.   AmFN

I Came to This Country in 1865.   *Anonymous.*   Oh, you're just as bad as we are, perhaps a damn sight worse.   OuSiCo

I Had a Hippopotamus.　Patrick Barrington.　My sorrow for that might-have-been-a-hippopotamother.　CenHV

I Had a Little Husband.　Mother Goose.　And a little handkerchief,/To wipe his pretty nose.　EvOK; ExPo; FaFP; HBV 1-2; HBVY

I Had a Little Nut Tree.　Mother Goose.　And all for the sake/Of my little nut tree.　CBEP; CH; ExPo; OxBoLi; OxNR

I Had a Little Pony.　Mother Goose.　I would not lend my pony now/For all the lady's hire.　SoPo

I Had a Rooster.　Anonymous.　The little rooster went cock-a-doodle doo,/Dee doodle-dee, doodle-dee, doodle-dee doo.　FSW

I Had a Wife.　Anonymous.　Take her out and chop the head of her,/Early in the morning.　FSW

I Had Been Hungry, All the Years.　Emily Dickinson.　The Entering–takes away–.　AmePo; LiTA; LiTM; MoAmPo; SBG

I Had but Fifty Cents.　Anonymous.　Take my advice, don't try it twice/If you've got but fifty cents!　BeLS; BLPA; NLV; TreF

I Had Gone Broke.　J. V. Cunningham.　By Hatred out of Envy by Despair.　OBSP

I had no time to hate.　Emily Dickinson.　Be large enough for Me–　FPL; PoLf

I Had Not Fastened My Sash over My Gown.　Tzu Yeh.　Blame the Spring wind.　WPOW

I Had Not Minded Walls.　Emily Dickinson.　And dragons in the crease!　AWP; CABA; InPo

I Had to Be Secret.　Mark Van Doren.　As to say any moment/Which was which?　SO

I Had Two Pigeons Bright and Gay.　Anonymous.　I cannot tell for I do not know.　OxNR; PBBP

I Hae a Wife O' My Ain.　Robert Burns.　Naebody cares for me,/I care for naebody.　EiCP; LAuP

I Hardly Ever Ope My Lips.　Richard Garnett.　If you are wise, I think you are a fool.　HBV 1-2

I Hate Men.　Cole Porter.　Oh, I hate men!　DBV

I Hate to See You Clad.　Paul Verlaine.　And prelude to the endless rites of love.　UnTE

I Have a Big Favor to Ask You, Brothers.　Ziche Landau.　That's why he turns to you now for advice,/to your deep wisdom and understanding.　VWA

I Have a Blue Piano.　Else Lasker-Schüler.　Heaven's gate to me while I live–/Forbidden though it is.　TrJP

I Have a Friend.　Anne Spencer.　We are such friends.　CDC

I Have a Gentle Cock.　Anonymous.　And every night he percheth him/In my lady's chamber.　CBEP; EBEV; EnPo; HAP; NCEP; NOBE; NoP; OxBM; PBBP; SeCePo; ViBoPo

I Have a King.　Emily Dickinson.　For my will goes the other way,/And it were perjury!　MAPA

I Have a Place.　Lily A. De Young.　and I sort of like them for that.　AMV-80

I Have a Pretty Little Flow'r.　Francis Daniel Pastorius.　So therefore we say all.　SCAP

I Have a Rendezvous with Death.　Alan Seeger.　I shall not fail that rendezvous.　BBV; BLPA; DL; FaBV; FaFP; GoTF; HBV 1-2; MCCG; OHFP; PoPl; ViBoPo; WaP

I Have a Rendezvous with Life.　Countee Cullen.　Lest Death shall greet and claim me ere/I keep Life's rendezvous.　CDC

I Have a Roof.　Ada Jackson.　Lord, with my reckoning half told/I know that I am rich indeed.　TrPWD

I Have a Room whereinto No One Enters.　Christina Georgina Rossetti.　And think how it will be in Paradise/When we're together.　OBNC

I Have a Terrible Fear of Being an Animal.　Cesar Vallejo.　...or let it go/for life with its three possibilities!　EAS

I Have a Young Sister.　Anonymous.　When the maiden hath that she loveth,/She is without longing.　CH; EBEV; EnPo; ExPo; MeEL; NoP; OAEL 1-2; OxBM; PoEL 1-5; SeCeV

I Have Always Found It So.　Birdie Bell.　I have always found it so.　BLRP

I Have Always Heard of These Old Men.　Anonymous.　A young man he come scampering home/Saying, "Kiss me, my dear wife."　AmFP

I Have Approached.　Alan Paton.　The fortresses and bastions of our fears.　PeSA

I Have Been a Forester.　Anonymous.　I shall build me a bower at the woodes end/There to lead my life.　CBEP; EBEV; FaBoRV; GBP; OBSP

I Have Been My Arm.　Margo Taft.　my hand like an animal/that can not see or feel.　NMM

I Have Been Thinking.　Artie Gold.　Make that what.　CaPN

I Have Been through the Gates.　Charlotte Mew.　...beautiful Jerusalem,/Over which Christ wept.　MoAB; MoBrPo; TrGrPo

I Have Bowed before the Sun.　Anna Walters.　My name is "I am living." I am here.　WPOW

I Have Cared for You, Moon.　Grace Hazard Conkling.　As though Earth were/A wonderful place.　HBMV

I Have Come Far to Have Found Nothing.　Cid Corman.　...lost finally/in that absence whose trace is silence.　VGW

I Have Come to the Conclusion.　Nelle Fertig.　After I had broken a few/very fine mirrors/she said.　FF

I Have Cut an Eagle.　James Koller.　I hide & watch/he will never find my wooden legs　PoM

I Have Exhausted the Delighted Range...　Michael Hartnett.　there is no time now for my dream of hawks.　CIP

I Have Felt It as They've Said.　Larry Eigner.　After trying my animal noise/i break out with a man's cry　PoM

I Have Folded My Sorrows.　Bob Kaufman.　The revisited soul is wrapped in the aura of familiarity.　PoBA

I Have Fought the Good Fight.　Jared B. Waterbury.　"Though I die, I shall live; though I fall, I shall rise."　AH

I Have Found Such Joy.　Grace Noll Crowell.　Yet never, through the ages, commonplace.　PoToHe

I have got her.　Fujiwara no Kamatari.　Yasumiko have I got!　LiTW

I Have Got My Leave.　Rabindranath Tagore.　...A summons has come and I am ready/for my journey.　OBMV

I Have Got to Stop Loving You.　Florence Anthony ("Ai").　But I want to look like me.　GeTw

I Have Had Not One Word from Her.　Sappho.　no woodlot bloomed in spring without song...'　PeHV

I Have Heard.　Anonymous.　To lift me up out of the rough/And permit my spirit to soar.　FiBHP

I Have Heard Ingenuous Indians Say.　Roger Williams.　Who dies in sinnes unpaid, that soule/His light's eternall night.　SCAP

I Have Heard Them Knock.　Michael Hartnett.　but I have never known/the eternal word for "open'.　NOBI

I Have Labored Sore.　Anonymous.　and then shall know both devil and man,/what I was and what I am.　WeW

I Have Lighted the Candles, Mary.　Kenneth Patchen.　For His is a kingdom in the hearts of men.　TrCP

I Have Lived This Way for Years and Do Not Wish to Change.　Michael C. Blumenthal.　Help yourself to the jellyfish, the goose down,/the chocolate-covered cotton balls.　HaCAP

I Have Loved Flowers.　Robert Bridges.　Beauty shall shed a tear.　EG; GoJo; MoAB; MoBrPo

I have neither plums nor cherries.　Nicholas Breton.　To be comforted for ever/Or to look for comfort never....　EG

I have never seen volcanoes.　Emily Dickinson.　Will not cry with joy, "Pompeii!"/To the hills return!　PoEL 1-5

I have no embroidered headband.　Sappho.　when our enemies were in exile.　BoWoP

I Have No Pain.　Anonymous.　Just fetch your Jim another quart/To wet the other eye.　FaBoCo

I Have No Strength for Mine.　Joanne Kyger.　and the moons stacked up like shields　PoM

I Have Not Lingered in European Monasteries.　Leonard Cohen.　and all my work goes well.　NOBC

I Have Not So Much Emulated the Birds that Musically Sing.　Walt Whitman.　I have felt to soar in freedom and in the fullness of/power, joy, volition.　RFM

I Have Seen.　Kathleen McCracken.　light/against my skin.　AMV-80

I Have Seen Black Hands.　Richard Wright.　On some red day in a burst of fists on a new horizon!　NoAm; PoBA

I Have Seen Higher, Holier Things Than These.　Arthur Hugh Clough.　Some day thou shalt it view.　OAEP

I Have Seen the Robins Fall.　Louis Dudek.　And all the poems that sang in my heart/Turned to the same white, bitter salt.　CaP

I Have Set My Heart So High.　Anonymous.　For love me hath in bales brought,/Me think it do me good, y-wis.　OAEL 1-2; OxBM

I Have Some Friends Before Me Gone.　Anonymous.　For I have a home up yonder,/Glory Glory.　AH

I Have Something for You to Laugh at, Cato.　Caius Valerius Catullus.　Transfixed him then and there with my own stiff prick!　PeHV

I Have Sought Long with Steadfastness.　Sir Thomas Wyatt.　None other reason can ye lay/But as who saith: "I reck not how."　EnRePo; FCP; SiPS

I Have Sought Thee Daily.　Solomon Ibn Gabirol.　Nay, surely Thy name I will worship, while breath in/my nostrils be.　LiTW

I Have Three Daughters.　Ruth Stone.　And lordy, give us our share.　InPS; NMM

I Have to Have It.　Dorothy Aldis.　I cannot walk without it.　SoPo

I Have Trod the Upward and the Downward Slope.　Robert Louis Stevenson.　And I have lived and loved, and closed the door.　NOBV

I haven't told my garden yet.　Emily Dickinson.　One will walk today!　AA

I Hear a River.　Trumbull Stickney.　A rainbow stands and summer passes under.　NCEP

I Hear a Voice.　Halper Leivick.　And answered with an echo/Like a resounding choir.　VWA

I Hear America Griping. Morris Bishop. Everything is air-conditioned except the air. AmFN; QQQ

I Hear America Singing. Walt Whitman. Singing with open mouths their strong melodious songs. AmePo; AmFN; AWP; FaBoBe; FaBV; FaFP; FF; FPL; HAP; LiTA; LoGBV; MoAmPo; PAL; PoPl; PoSC; SaC; TreFS; TrGrPo; WeW; YaD

I Hear an Army. James Joyce. My love, my love, my love, why have you left me alone? AnIV; AWP; ExPo; LiTL; LiTM; MoBrPo; NAMP; NoAm; NOBE; OxBI; OxBTC; PoRA; PrIm; SyP; ViBoPo

I Hear and See Not Strips of Cloth Alone. Walt Whitman. Discarding peace over all the sea and land. WaaP

I Hear It Said. Barbara Young. Space for his silences, and space for mine. BLPA

I Hear It Was Charged against Me. Walt Whitman. The institution of the dear love of comrades. LiTA; MCCG; MoAmPo; PPP

I Hear That Andromeda. Sappho. the art of lifting her/skirt over her ankles. PBWP

I Hear That Lycoris Has Buried. Martial (Marcus Valerius Martialis). She is not on good terms with my wife. DBV

I Hear the Wave. Anonymous. I understand the shore when I hear its sound. OnYI

I Hear You've Let Go. Rosario Ferre. now cut the cord/climb the wind/ toughen your heart BoWoP

I Heard a Fly Buzz–When I Died. Emily Dickinson. I could not see to see– AmePo; AmLP; APA; BoWoP; CABA; CMoP; DiPo; DL; ExPo; FF; ForPo; HAP; HoPM; InPK; InPo; LiTA; LiTM; MAmP; MasP; MoAB; MoAmPo; MoVE; NAWM 1-2; NePA; NoAm; NOBA; NoP; OxBA; PoRA; PPP; SCV; SeCeV; SOTW; TAP

I Heard a Linnet Courting. Robert Bridges. But unto love/Resign your simple natures/To tender love. BrPo; LiTB; LiTM; OBMV

I Heard a Soldier. Herbert Trench. That grimy soldier with his rifle/Out in the veldt, alone? AnFE; CH; HBV 1-2

I Heard a Young Man Saying. Julia Fields. Something plans these things... NNP

I Heard an Angel Singing. William Blake. And Misery's increase/Is Mercy, Pity, Peace. CBEP

I Heard Christ Sing. Hugh" (Christopher Murray Grieve) MacDiarmid. But I wot he did God's will wha made/Siccar o' Calvary. ACV; NoAm

I Heard Immanuel Singing. Vachel Lindsay. Alone, set free, rejoicing,/ With a green hill for his throne? HAP

I Heard the Bells on Christmas Day. Henry Wadsworth Longfellow. A voice, a chime, a chant sublime,/Of peace on earth, good-will to men! AH; NTCP; PoSC

I Heard the Old Song. B. W. Vilakazi. You strike fire in me, wake me to madness. PeSA

I Heard the Voice of Jesus Say. Horatius Bonar. And in that light of life I'll walk,/Till traveling days are done. BePJ

I Heard You Solemn-Sweet Pipes of the Organ. Walt Whitman. Heard the pulse of you when all was still ringing little/bells last night under my ear. CBEP; NePA; OxBA

I held a jewel in my fingers. Emily Dickinson. And now an amethyst remembrance/Is all I own. WHA

I Held a Lamb. Kim Worthington. And when I gently put it down/It licked me on the hand. SoPo; TiPo

I Held a Shelley Manuscript. Gregory Corso. pour secrecy upon the dying page. VGW

I, Hermes, Have Been Set Up. Anyte [(or Anytes)]. By my cold, clean, whispering spring. OBVE

I Hid You. Miklos Radnoti. I hold you in those arms. LLLT; VWA

I Hoed and Trenched and Weeded. Alfred Edward Housman. And luckless lads will wear them/When I am dead and gone. LiTM; MoAB; MoBrPo; TrGrPo; VLP; WeW

I Hold Him Happiest. Menander And never, never, any greater thing. TreFT

I Hope I Don't Have You Next Semester, But. Edwin Godsey. and see can you make out/any/noises. HoPM

I, Icarus. Alden Nowlan. But I know I flew when I heard them. NCSH; WHW

I, in My Intricate Image. Dylan Thomas. And my images roared and rose on heaven's hill. EAS; LiTB

I in the Grayness Rose. Stephen Phillips. Then with a shuddering heart no more I/read. EnLit

I in Thee, and Thou in Me. Christopher Pearse Cranch. Thine the invisible future, born of the present, must be. HBV 1-2

I Just Walk around, around, around. Moishe Kulbak. it's void and empty,/ and lonely,/and terribly boring,/brrr!... VWA

I Just Wanna Stay Home. Irwin Silber. 'Cause I just wanna stay home. FSW

I Keep Three Wishes Ready. Annette Wynne. Any day a fairy/Coming down the street. SoPo

I Keep to Myself Such Measures. Robert Creeley. I hold in both hands such weight/it is my only description. NoAm

I Kenning Through Astronomy. Edward Taylor. "Eat, eat me, soul, and thou shalt never die." AmPP

I Kissed Pa Twice after His Death. Mattie J. Peterson. We should try to reach the shining shore. PeD

I Kissed You. Anonymous. I presume there are equal facilities yet. BLPA

I Knew a Boy with Hair Like Gold. Melvin Walker La Follette. And the tears of hell cannot heat my heart/When the white winds blow. NePoEA-2

I Knew a Cappadocian. Alfred Edward Housman. "I have been too prolific." FiBHP

I Knew I'd Sing. Heather McHugh. ...I swore,/nothing, but nothing, would be beneath me. GeTw

I knew quite well that some day. Narihira (Ariwara no Narihira). that some day would be today. LiTW

I Know. Elsa Barker. Love told me all these things. HBMV

I Know. Verda Group. But this I know–He'll be with me/Until those years shall end. STF

I Know a Barber. Edward Anthony. For his favorite hobby is trimming goatees. TiPo

I Know a Flower So Fair and Fine. Nicolai Grundtvig. It buds and blows,/Delightful fragrance breathing. AH

I Know a Lady. Joyce Carol Thomas. A careful queen/She bows to no one CNA

I Know a Lovely Lady Who Is Dead. Struthers Burt. Beauty is hers, and she is beauty instead. HBMV

I Know a Man. Robert Creeley. drive, he sd, for/christ's sake, look/out where yr going. AmC; AmPC; CAPP; ConAP; CoPo; InPS; MAT; NOBA; OBSP; PAI; PoM; PPP

I Know a Man. Peggy Steele. She played Bach so that/it was carved and fragrant. PPJ

I Know a Name! Anonymous. That will set those lands on fire. BLRP

I know a place where summer strives. Emily Dickinson. That stiffens quietly to quartz,/Upon her amber shoe. NePA

I Know de Lord's Laid His Hands on Me. Anonymous. I know de Lord's laid his hands on me. BoAN 1-2

I Know de Moonlight. Anonymous. ...my soul and yo' soul will meet in de day/When I lay dis body down. BPo

I Know He Is Real. Anonymous. O praise Him forever! I know He is real! STF

I Know I'm Not Sufficiently Obscure. Ray Durem. ...an autumn leaf/ hanging from a tree–I see a body! BPo; PoBA

I Know Moonlight (with music). Anonymous. When I lay this body down. AS; UnPo

I Know My Love. Anonymous. And if my Love leaves me, what will I do? AnIV; FSW

I Know My Soul. Claude McKay. ...I'm comforted/By this narcotic thought: I know my soul. BPo

I Know Not How It Falls on Me. Emily Bronte. And who can fight against despair? NOBV

I Know Not How That Bethlehem's Babe. Harry Webb Farrington. I only know a living Christ,/Our immortality. AH

I Know Not Where the Road Will Lead. Evelyn Atwater Cummins. I walk the King's highway. AH

I Know Not Whether I Am Proud. Walter Savage Landor. There is an ear that may incline/Even to words so dull as mine. EnRP

I Know Not Why. Morris Rosenfeld. It lies so deep, I know not why. AA

I Know Not Why, but All This Weary Day. Henry Timrod. Like whispers round the body of the/dead. AmP

I Know on a Night Overcast. Hayim Nahman Bialik. And, roaring, set out with his awesome sword! LiTW

I know some lonely houses off the road. Emily Dickinson. Fancy the sunrise left the door ajar! CBEP; MoAB; MoAmPo; OxBA; PoRA; SO; WSC

I Know Something Good About You. Louis C. Shimon. I know something good about you? BLPA; PoToHe

I Know That All beneath the Moon Decays. William, of Hawthornden Drummond. But that, O me! I both must write and love. BSV

I Know That He Exists. Emily Dickinson. Would not the jest–/Have crawled too far! AmePo; AnFE; APA; MAmP

I Know That I Am a Great Sinner. Purohit Swami. O Lord, Thou art my Master/And I Thy slave. OBMV

I Know That I Must Die Soon. Else Lasker-Schüler. Softly I set my foot/ On the path to my long home. TrJP

I Know That My Redeemer Lives. Charles Wesley. I taste unutterable bliss,/And everlasting rest. TreFS

I Know That My Redeemer Liveth. Virginia Frazer Boyle. For God's own angel of the resurrection/Shall rend the grave, and roll the stone away. BePJ

I Know the Reputation. Lady Kii. I will not go near them,/for I would surely wet my sleeves. WPOW

I Know Where I'm Going. Anonymous.

I Love a Flower. Thomas Philipps. "Than may be proved here, anon,/That we three be agrede in on." MeEL

I Love a Hill. Ralph Hodgson. I always take a road that brings/Me halt upon a hill. BrPo

I Love All Beauteous Things. Robert Bridges. Like the empty words of a dream/Remembered on waking. BrPo; CMoP; EBEV; ExPo; HBMV; HBVY; TrCP

I love and fear him. Lady Kasa. Roars on the coast at Ise BoWoP

I Love but Thee. Heinrich Heine. Then I must weep–and bitterly. AWP

I Love Life. Irwin M. Cassel. I love life, I want to live, I love life. BLSo

I Love Little Pussy. Jane Taylor. But Pussy and I/very gently will play. SoPo; TiPo

I Love Little Willie. Anonymous. For he mightn't like it, Mama, Mama. ABF

I Love, Loved, and So Doth She. Sir Thomas Wyatt. To love so well and live in smart. EnPo; FCP; SiPS

I Love My Jesus Quite Alone. Johannes Kelpius. Thou'rt present with assistance. AH

I Love My Life, but Not Too Well. Harriet Monroe. I love my life, but not too well. HBV 1-2

I Love My Love. Helen Adam. Then the living fleece of her long bright hair, she combed with a/golden comb. NeAP; NMM; WPOW

I Love My Love in the Morning. Gerald Griffin. But best of all when evening's sigh/Was murmuring at its close. ACP; GoBC; IrPN; OnYI

I Love Old Women. William Kloefkorn. always and forever and forever moving,/in the wind. AMV-80

I Love Snow and All the Forms. Percy Bysshe Shelley. I love waves, and winds, and storms... TiPo

I Love Somebody (I Love Little Willie). Anonymous. For I don't care, you know, my Ma. AmFP

I Love the Blue Violet. John Clare. And sweeter than rosebuds than red or white clover/Is bonny young Susan to me. AtBAP

I Love the Lord. Anonymous. Because the Lord to thee, himself/Hath bounteously expressed. AH

I Love the Woods. Leib Neidus. No, not the house–the lovely maid/Who lives there quiet and serene. VWA

I Love Thee, Gracious Lord. C. C. Cox. My love is Thine, and e'er shall be,/Because, my King, Thou reign'st o'er me! BePJ

I Love Thee, Lord. Connie Calenberg. The Lover of my soul for evermore! BePJ

I Love Thy Kingdom, Lord. Timothy Dwight. And brighter bliss of heaven. AH

I Love to Steal Awhile Away. Phoebe Hinsdale Brown. Be calm as this impressive hour,/And lead to endless day. AH

I Love to Tell the Story. Katherine Hankey. To tell the old, old story/Of Jesus and his love. TreFT

I Love What Is Not. Manfred Winkler. And the blood flows from the lands of the forest/with smells of animals and drying leaves. VWA

I Love You. Endre Farkas. and in each/see a naked man playing a violin CaPN

I Love You. Ella Wheeler Wilcox. And we'll live our whole young lives away/In the joys of a living love. BLPA; FaBoBe; FPL

I Love You and the Rosebush. Armando Uribe. And the rosebush gives roses. HoPM

I Love You Truly. Carrie Jacobs Bond. For you love me truly, truly, dear. BLSo; FSN; TreFS

I Loved a Lass. George Wither. For mine, alas! hath left me,/Falero, lero, loo! CH; EnLi 1-2; HBV 1-2; NOBE; OBEV; PG; PoPle; UnTE

I Loved Thee, Atthis, in the Long Ago. Bliss Carman. O Atthis, how I loved thee long ago/In that fair perished summer by the sea! CaP

I Loved Thee Once. Ayton [(or Aytoun)] Sir Robert. To love thee still, but goe no more/A begging at a beggars door. LiTL; OBS; ViBoPo

I loved you; even now I may confess. Alexander Pushkin. I pray God grant another love you so. BoLoP

I Loved You Once (From the Russian of Alexander Pushkin). Dudley Randall. I pray to God another love you so. AmNP

I'm 92, Joe Said. Tom Weber. "Sometimes I talk to a seagull," Joe said. CTBA

I'm a Baby. Cid Corman. ...Or dont you yet/get what I'm saying? GP

I'm a Decent Boy from Ireland. Anonymous. Be kind to your old parents, although they're old and poor. ShS

I'm a Dreamer. Kattie M. Cumbo. One who sleeps/away reality. BlSi

I'm a little Hindoo. Anonymous. I make my little skindoo. FaFP

I'm A-Rollin'. Anonymous. I'm a-rollin', through an unfriendly worl'. BoAN 1-2

I'm a Round-Town Gent. Anonymous. I'm a round-town gent, and I don't choose/To work in the mud and do without shoes. GoSl

I'm a Soldier in the Army of the Lord. Anonymous. Just a soldier,/In the army. AmFP

I'm a Stranger Here. Anonymous. I would go home, but honey/I'm a stranger there. FSW; OuSiCo

I'm Agoing to Lay Down My Sword. Anonymous. Ain't going to study war no more. AH

I'm an Old Cowhand. Johnny Mercer. Yippy-I-O-Ki-Ay, Yippy-I-O-Ki-Ay. OBAL

I'm Ashamed of My Thoughts. Anonymous. Thou not thoughtless nor fickle,/unlike to myself. NOBI

I'm Beginning to Lose Patience. W. H. Auden. And they are not cheap. PV

I'm Black and Blue. Heinrich Heine. Or even hated me. AWP

I'm Called by the Name of a Man. Anonymous. With my red target near the house. PBBP

I'm ceded–I've stopped being theirs. Emily Dickinson. And I choose, just a Crown– SBG; ViBoPo; WPOW

I'm Glad. Anonymous. With such a lot of nice fresh air/All sandwiched in between. HBVY

I'm Glad My Birthday Comes in May! Ivy O. Eastwick. I'm glad my birthday comes in May–/it is my VERY LUCKY DAY! BiCB

I'm Glad the Sky Is Painted Blue. Anonymous. With such a lot of nice fresh air/All sandwiched in between. SoPo

I'm Going Down This Road Feeling Bad. Anonymous. And I ain't gonna be treated this a-way. FSW; TrAS

I'm Going to Break Out. Carmen Valle. that which when said/becomes a little/of what is not said. InW

I'm Going to California. Bina Mossman. A scalloped petticoat,/And a short skirt. WTO

I'm Going to Georgia. Anonymous. Where the wild birds and turtledove can hear my sad cry AmFP

I'm Going to Rocky Island. Anonymous. Ride him to Rocky Island, on a long summer day. AmFP

I'm Gonna Move to the Outskirts of Town. Big Bill Broonzy. I swear I don't want no body ooo, lord, baby always hanging 'round BluL

I'm Gonna Run to the City of Refuge. Blind Willie Johnson. I'm gonna run to the city of refuge/I'm gonna run BluL

I.M.H. Maurice Baring. So bitter is the world I cannot live;–/I dare not die. ACP

I'm Happiest When Most Away. Emily Bronte. But only spirit wandering wide/Through infinite immensity. SeCePo

I'm Here. David Ignatow. Then I'll understand that all is well/again for the human and leave,/content with my condition. GP

I'm Here. Theodore Roethke. I'm here!/Here. CoAP; NYBP

I'm Just a Stranger Here, Heaven Is My Home. Carole Gregory Clemmons. Age and need, those simple weeds,/were gathering around and taking you away. PoBA

I'm Leery of Firms with Easy Terms. C. S. Jennison. She didn't come back at all. QQQ

I'm like a skiff on the Ocean tost. John Gay. Revenge, revenge, revenge,/Shall appease my restless sprite. EnLoPo

I'm Like All Lovers. Lesbia Harford. By my unwomanly love that sets you free/Love all myself, but least the woman in me. NOAV

I'm Lucky. Charlotte Mandel. the bone symmetry/of my lovely skull. AMV-81

I'm nobody! Who are you? Emily Dickinson. To tell your name the livelong day/To an admiring bog! AmePo; AnNE; BoWoP; CBEP; DiPo; GoTF; NCEP; NLV; NOBA; OBCA; OBSP; PoPl; SBG; SO; TAP; TreFS; WHA; YaD

I'm Not a Single Man. Thomas Hood. I'm not a single man. HBV 1-2

I'm not here never was. Constanta Buzea. like a twig stuck into a snowman BoWoP

I'm Not Rich. Joseph Rolnik. With all these stains upon me I'll/Arrive in heaven's promised land. VWA

I'm O'er Young to Marry Yet. Robert Burns. I'm o'er young, 'twad be a sin/To tak me frae my mammy yet. ViBoPo

I'm on an Island. Tom Clark. Anywhere in this world. ANYP

I'm On My Way. Anonymous. I'm on my way, and I won't turn back. FSW

I'm on My Way to Canaan. Anonymous. But Patience clips her wings. AH

I'm Only a Broken-Down Miner. Anonymous. How much, Jesus Christ only knows. AmFP

I'm Ridin' Tonight round the Dam Bed-Ground. Anonymous. While you're ridin' on the old bed-ground. CoSo

I'm Sad. Forugh Farrokzad. The bird is to die BoWoP

I'm Sad and I'm Lonely. Anonymous. Ef trouble don't kill me, I'll live a long time. AS; FSW; TrAS

I'm Seventeen Come Sunday. Anonymous. The drum and fife is her delight,/And a merry man in the morning. UnTE

I'm Soaked through with You. Rachel Korn. with the pain/of loving you, beloved man. VWA

I'm Thankful That My Life Doth Not Deceive. Henry David Thoreau. They'll lay another by tomorrow's sun. PoEL 1-5

I'm the Police Cop Man, I Am. Margaret Morrison. Then many little children's feet/Go hippity across the street. SoPo

I Shall Never Go. A. J. Hovde. And that, despite our dreams, the gods prevail. AMV-80

I Shall Not Be Afraid. Aline Kilmer. But how I wish I were afraid again,/ My dear, my dear! HBMV

I Shall Not Care. Sara Teasdale. And I shall be more silent and cold-hearted/Than you are now. AnEnPo; HBV 1-2; MoAmPo; PoPl; TrGrPo; UnPo

I Shall Not Cry Return. Ellen M. Huntington Gates. And so I do my task and wait/The opening of the outer gate. HBV 1-2

I Shall Not Die. Anonymous. I shall not die because of you. KiLC

I Shall Not Die for Thee. Padraic Colum. I shall not die! CTC

I Shall Not Die for Thee. Douglas Hyde. Little palm, white neck, bright eye,/I shall not die for you. OxBI

I Shall Not Pass This Way Again. Anonymous. I shall not pass this way again. BLPA; BLRP; FPL; GoTF; TreF; TreFS; WBLP

I Shall Not Pass This Way Again. Eva Rose York. "Would she could pass this way/again." FaFP; OHFP; WBLP

I Shall Not Want: In Deserts Wild. Charles F. Deems. So long as earth and heaven endure. AH

I Shall Not Weep. Belle MacDiarmid Ritchey. Nor shall I miss you...over-much. HBMV

I Shall Weep. Peretz Hirshbein. And the fire will be quenched no more. TrJP

I Should Be Ashamed. Uvlunuaq. And I stood on the awl-like pinnacle/ And faltered,/And fell! WTO

I should have been too glad. Emily Dickinson. Faith bleats to understand. NOCV

I Should Not Dare to Be So Sad. Emily Dickinson. Begin to perish now. InPo

I Show the Daffodils to the Retarded Kids. Constance Sharp. then he puts the yellow horn to his ear/and listens. DFF

I Sigh, as Sure to Wear the Fruit. Anonymous. If the pleasure/For the measure/Of my treasure goe. NCEP

I Sigh when I Sing. Anonymous. Her soules into sin/For any worldes win,/ That was ere y-boght! OxBM

I sighed and owned my love. Anonymous. She checks the Flame, but cannot quench the Fire. EG

I Sing a Song Reluctantly. Countess Beatriz de Die. Excess of pride can bring the greatest misery. PBWP

I Sing America Now! Jesse Stuart. For time is brief from cradle to the grave. AmFN

I Sing an Old Song. Oscar Williams. Bundle in the bush of radiance: birth-cry of poem! LiTM; NePA

I Sing No New Songs. Frank Marshall Davis. ...but the dreams of Homer neither/grow nor wilt... PoBA; PoNe

I Sing of a Maiden. Anonymous. Well may such a lady Goddes mother be. AtBAP; CABA; CBEP; EBEV; EG; ELP; ExPo; FaBoCh; FF; HAP; InPo; InPS; ISi; LiTB; LoGBV; MeEL; MeEV; NOBE; NOCV; NoP; OAEL 1-2; OxBM; PAI; PoEL 1-5; SBVL; SCV; SeCeV; TreFS; TrGrPo; ViBoPo; WeW

I Sing of Olaf Glad and Big. Edward Estlin Cummings. more brave than me:more blond than you. AmP; HeIP; LiTA; LiTM; NePA; NoAm; NOBA; NoP; OBSV; OBWP; PPON; VGW; WaP

I Sing the Body Electric. Walt Whitman. O I say now these are the soul! CTC; ErPo; MasP

I Sing the Mighty Power of God. Isaac Watts. And everywhere that man can be,/Thou, God, art present there. TRV

I Sit and Sew. Alice Dunbar Nelson. ...God, must I sit and sew? BlSi; CDC; WPOW

I Sit and Wait for Beauty. Mae V. Cowdery. She will ever hide her face/ And elude my grasping hand! BlSi

I Sit with My Dolls. Anonymous. I do not know where my father is. TrJP

I Sit With My Toes in the Brook. Anonymous. Necessity drives me, say I. FaBoNo

I So Liked Spring. Charlotte Mew. But I'll like Spring because it is simply Spring/As the thrushes do. OxBTC

I Sought All over the World. John Tagliabue. ...The children/laughed in the tree. Psk

I Sought On Earth. George Santayana. Heal me, and keep me in thy dwelling-place. AnEnPo

I Sought the Lord. Anonymous. Always Thou lovedst me. TRV

I Sought with Eager Hand. Allan Dowling. and kissed her from her eyelids to her feet. ErPo

I Speak, I Say, I Talk. Arnold L. Shapiro. But I TALK! GrPl

I Spoke to the Violet. John Shaw Neilson. But I like not the coat that you come in—the colour of death. BoAV

I Spread Out unto Thee My Hand. Henry Ainsworth. to have knowledge of/The way that walk I must. AH

I Stand as on Some Mighty Eagle's Beak. Walt Whitman. Seeking the shores forever. RFM

I Stand Corrected. Margaret Fishback. It often makes the world go flat. PoPl

I started Early—Took my Dog. Emily Dickinson. And bowing—with a Mighty look–/At me–The Sea withdrew– AmPP; DiPo; HAP; InPK; LiTA; LiTM; MOS; NCEP; PoEL 1-5; SBG

I Stepped from Plank to Plank. Emily Dickinson. This gave me that precarious Gait/Some call Experience. AmePo; CMoP; MAmP; NOBA; NOCV; OBSP

I Stood in Jerusalem. Zelda. Am I not your quiet/older brother? VWA

I Stood on a Tower in the Wet. Alfred, Lord Tennyson. And New Year blowing and roaring. OBSP

I stood on the bridge at midnight. Anonymous. Because I couldn't sit down. FaFP

I Stood Tip-Toe. John Keats. My wand'ring spirit must no further soar.– EnRP; PBBP

I Stood Upon a High Place. Stephen Crane. One looked up, grinning,/And said: "Comrade! Brother!" AmePo; AmP; LiTA; NePA

I Stood with the Dead. Siegfried Sassoon. "Fall in!" I shouted; "Fall in for your pay!" ChMP

I Stood Within the Heart of God. William Vaughn Moody. The fruits I look for; everything/As on my heavenly hills. AH

I Stroll. Peter Redgrove. Evening mist-tides hissing past my brogues. NePoEA-2

I Substitute for the Dead Lecturer. LeRoi (Imamu Amiri Baraka) Jones. ...And leave/the bones, my stewed black skull,/an empty cage of failure. NOBA

I Suppose Her Mother Told Her. Francine Corcos. But no man has entered/The conversation. AMV-80

I Syng of a Mayden. Anonymous. Wel may swych a lady/Godes moder be. EnPo; OAEP

I Take 'Em and Like 'Em. Margaret Fishback. Has made me receptive to greens. PoPl

I Take Thee Life. Margot Ruddock. Cries out, cries out/For its true mate. OBMV

I Talk to You. John Newlove. and whether it is fit to whisper or to shout. PeCV

I taste a liquor never brewed. Emily Dickinson. To see the little Tippler/ Leaning against the–Sun– AmePo; CMoP; DiPo; FaBV; FF; GoTF; HeIP; LiTA; LiTM; MAmP; MCCG; MoAmPo; NePA; NOBA; NoP; OxBA; PoEL 1-5; SBG; SeCeV; SoSe; TAP; TreFS

I Taught Myself to Live Simply and Wisely. Anna Akhmatova. If you knock on my door/I may not even hear. PBWP

I Taught the Talented. Sappho. Hero, who was a girl/track star from Gyara GLGT

I Tell of Another Young Death. Cesar Tiempo. And that is all?/–That is all. TrJP

I Thank God I'm Free at Las'. Anonymous. I thank God I'm free at las'. BoAN 1-2; BPo; TAP

I Thank Thee, Lord. Anonymous. 'Twas Thy withholding lightened all my cares/That blessed day. BLRP; WBLP

I Thank You God for Most This Amazing. Edward Estlin Cummings. now the eyes of my eyes are opened) BiP; EaLo; ILwL; MoAB; MoRP; TAP; TrCP

I the People. Alice Notley. ...(and I/the people am still parted in/two & would cry). APU

I Think Continually of Those Who Were Truly Great. Stephen Spender. And left the vivid air signed with their honour. AtBAP; CMoP; DiPo; EaLo; ExPo; GoTF; HAP; LiTB; LiTM; MoAB; MoBrPo; MoRP; NAMP; NOBE; NoP; OAEL 1-2; OAEP; OxBTC; PoPl; PoRA; PP; TreFT; TrGrPo; ViBoPo; WaP

I Think I Know No Finer Things Than Dogs. Hally Carrington Brent. I think I know no finer things than dogs. BBV; BLPA

I Think I See Him There. Waring Cuney. What this man speaks is true. CDC

I think of him. Anonymous. When the east brightens, I then would know... BoWoP

I Think of Him as One Who Fights. Anna Hempstead Branch. Who goes on strange adventurous ways/Through tortured days and dangerous nights. HBMV

I Think of Housman Who Said the Poem Is a Morbid Secretion... Judith Kroll. ...stone of considerable size/growing beneath one's/skin?/I see. UnPo

I Think of Oblivion. Yehuda Amichai. Blessed is the memory of my childhood. His childhood. VWA

I Think of Your Generation. Charles Brasch. Rarer than beauty–like genius a gift and equivocal. AnNZ

I Think Sometimes... Michael Hartnett. to blood beneath, my own blood,/ O my sweet wife! CIP

I Think Table and I Say Chair. Gloria Fuertes. ...What/this means is I love you. AMV-81

I Think That God Is Proud. Grace Noll Crowell. Each finds his hurt heart strangely comforted. PoToHe

I Think the New Teacher's a Queer. Perry Brass. ...and I feared/that they'd beat me up/in the boys' room. PcHV

I Thirst... Katherine Bregy. I am the human heart! CAW

I Thought I Saw Stars. R. P. Lister. There came a day when Adam turned his back upon Eve,/and gardened. PV

I Thought It Was Tangiers I Wanted. Langston Hughes. But I thought it was Tangiers I wanted. PoNe

I Thought Joy Went by Me. Willard Wattles. We are crazy fellows,"..../Laughingly Love said. HBMV

I thought that Love had been a boy. Anonymous. Like tales of fairies often told/By doting age that dies for cold. EnLoPo

I Thought You Loved Me. Anonymous. You deceived me. WTO

I threw a penny in the air. Anonymous. I would have watched where it came down. CenHV

I to My Perils. Alfred Edward Housman. So I was ready/When trouble came. EnLi 1-2; ViBoPo; WeW

I to the Hills Will Lift Mine Eyes. Francis Rous. Henceforth thy going out and in God keep for ever will. AH

I to the Lord from My Distress. Anonymous. For all salvation wholly comes/From the almighty Lord. AH

I Told Jesus. Sterling D. Plumpp. ...fire/his white messengers/& come find out/for himself... PoBA

I, Too. Langston Hughes. I, too, am America. CDC; FF; HaCAP; HeIP

I, Too, Know What I Am Not. Bob Kaufman. No, I am not anything that is anything I am not. NBP

I Took a Bow and Arrow. John Ciardi. Whoever saw a Cinnamon Yak/In the middle of Washington Square. EvOK

I Took a Hansom on To-Day. William Ernest Henley. But a longing dead as its kindred sped/A thousand years ago! HBV 1-2

I Took Leave of My Beloved One Evening. At Taliq. They make me remember the one whom I adore! PeHV

I took my power in my hand. Emily Dickinson. Was it Goliath was too large,/Or only I too small? NePA

I Traveled with Them. King of Seville, Mu'tamid. And the morning received those stars from my hand. AWP

I Turn to Jesus. Oswald J. Smith. I worship and adore Him/And praise Him night and day. STF

I turn you out of doors. Alain Chartier. I turn you out of doors/stubborn desire BoLoP

I Turned On the Hot Water. Janine Canan. she sighed voluptuously, voice trailing into the night. APU

I Used to Love My Garden. C. P. Sawyer. For I found a bachelor's button/In black-eyed Susan's bed. FaBoCo

I used to wrap my white doll up in. Mae Jackson. when i was young/and very colored BOLo; PoBA

"I've been going around everywhere without any skin." Josephine Miles. Not my country or climate, this personal flaying. IHMS

I've Been to a Marvellous Party. Noel Coward. I couldn't have liked it more. NLV

I've Been Workin' on the Railroad. Anonymous. "Dinah, blow your horn." BLSo; FaFP; FSW; SaC; TreF

I've Gone and Stained with the Color of Love. Milton Acorn. But sometimes he just sits and watches me work. NeAC

I've Got a Dog as Thin as a Rail. Anonymous. The fleas on the bottom all hop to the top. GDP

I've Got a Home in That Rock. Raymond Richard Patterson. Enough to make him homesick, what home was really like. FF; PoBA; PoNe

I've Got a New Book from My Grandfather Hyde. Leroy F. Jackson. For the book that I got from my Grandfather Hyde. BrR; SiSoSe

I've Got a Rocket. Anonymous. It's Independence Day. SiSoSe; TiPo

I've Got the Giggles. Sir Alan Patrick Herbert. But I've got the giggles today! FiBHP

I've Got the World on a String. Ted Koehler. What a world, what a life, I'm in love. BLSo

I've Got to Know. Woody Guthrie. I've got to know friend, I've got to know. FSW

I've Had Many an Aching Pain. John Clare. The dearest though I keep myself,/I keep for sake o' somebody. NOBV

I've Known a Heaven Like a Tent. Emily Dickinson. Then swallowed up to view. BoLiVe

I've Labored Long and Hard for Bread. Black Bart. You fine-haired sons of bitches. DBV; PV

I've Learned to Sing. Georgia Douglas Johnson. And happiness is love. GoSl

I've Lost My—. Henry Cholmondeley-Pennell. Lost, alas! I've lost—MY SKYE. CenHV

I've Rambled This Country Both Earlye and Late. Anonymous. Brandy in my bottle and money in my purse. OuSiCo

I've Reached the Land of Corn and Wine. Edgar P. Stites. And view the shining glory shore,/My heaven, my home forevermore. AH

I've seen a dying eye. Emily Dickinson. 'Twere blessed to have seen— AmPP; BoWoP; FPL; InPo; MAPA; NePA; NOBA; PoEL 1-5; PoLf

I've Tasted My Blood. Milton Acorn. I've tasted my blood too much/to abide what I was born to. NOBC

I've Thirty Months. John Millington Synge. But there are millions I'd forget/Will have their laugh at passing me. OBMV

I've Worked for a Silver Shilling. Charles W. Kennedy. These were truth,/And a memorable thing. HBMV

I Wage Not Any Feud with Death. Alfred, Lord Tennyson. We cannot hear each other speak. PPON

I Wait My Lord. Anonymous. I wait my friend. AWP

I Wake and Feel the Fell of Dark. Gerard Manley Hopkins. As I am mine, their sweating selves; but worse. CMoP; CoBE; CoBMV; DiPo; ForPo; GTBS-P; HAP; LiTB; NoAm; NOBE; NOBV; NOCV; NoP; OAEL 1-2; OAEP; PoEL 1-5; PoPle; PPoe; PPP; SCV; SeCeV; TW; VLP

I Wake, My Friend, I. Faye Kicknosway. you wont touch me. but you will, my friend, you/will IHMS

I Wakened to a Calling. Delmore Schwartz. Commanding all consciousness forever to rejoice! PoPl

I walk in loneliness through the greenwood. Anonymous. I walk in loneliness through the greenwood/for I have none to go with me. BoWoP

I Walk in the Old Street. Louis Zukofsky. or look tireless to the stars/and a ripped doorbell. VGW

I Walk on the River at Dawn. Joanne Hart. ...how the cold/burned down the canyon, how I wept,/my face north into the blade of wind. PoDr

I Walked in a Desert. Stephen Crane. A voice said: "It is no desert." AmePo

I Walked Out to the Graveyard to See the Dead. Richard Eberhart. And action must be learned from love of man. MiAP; MoPo

I Walked over the Grave of Henry James. Richard Eberhart. I thought, and took a street-car back to Harvard Square. VGW

I Walked with My Reason. Sorley MacLean. ...I should leap from heaven or hell with a/whole spirit and heart. LiTW

I Walkt the Other Day (To Spend My Hour,). Henry Vaughan. At whose dumbe urn/Thus all the year I mourn. MePo; OBS

I Wandered Angry as a Cloud (parody). Paul Dehn. And now my heart in quiet lives,/Made murmurous with sedatives. SpRo

I Wandered Lonely as a Cloud. William Wordsworth. And then my heart with pleasure fills,/And dances with the daffodils. AtBAP; BoNaP; DiPo; ERoP 1-2; ExPo; FaBoPP; HBV 1-2; HBVY; InPK; InPS; LoBV; MasP; MBW 1-2; NoP; OAEL 1-2; OAEP; OBRV; PoPl; PoRA; RoGo; SpRo; SUS; TEP; UnPo; ViBoPo; WHA

I Want a Girl. Harry and Dillon. Will Von Tilzer. I want a girl, just like the girl that married dear old Dad. TreFS

I Want a Tenant: A Satire. John O'Keefe. Live like wild Arab in a tent,/Before Bob Sowden's house you rent! NOEC

I Want God's Heab'n to Be Mine. Anonymous. Yes, I want God's heab'n to be mine,/Save me, Lord, save me. BoAN 1-2

I Want to Be a Cowboy. Anonymous. I'll rope the slant old heathen and yank them straight/to hell. BPAW

I Want to Be Married and Cannot Tell How. Anonymous. Oh! I wish that young fellow was with me now,/On a May day morning early. OnYI

I Want to Die Easy when I Die. Anonymous. I want to die easy, when I die, when I die. BoAN 1-2

I Want to Die while You Love Me. Georgia Douglas Johnson. The glory of this perfect day/Grow dim or cease to be! AmNP; BANP; BlSi; CDC

I Want to Know. John Drinkwater. So I know really, I suppose,/As much as anybody knows. FaPON

I Want to One Morning. Gordon Turner. if the thesis has managed this climb. AMV-80

I Want to Tell You. Sandra Hochman. Let air fly through the body, let all women dance/Into kingdoms of where loving is not getting even GP

I Want to Write a Jewish Poem. Gary Pacernick. Come and worship with me now. VWA

I Want You. Arthur L. Gillom. I want you, want you, want you–all the while. BLPA; FaBoBe

I Wanted to Die in the Desert. Anonymous. Where the buzzards would peck at my bones. BPAW; CoSo

I wanted to see you. Leila Miccolis. Your drawers match your tie. BoWoP

I Was a Brook. Sara Coleridge. To show their forms and hues in the all revealing sun. OBRV

I Was a Bustle-Maker Once, Girls. Patrick Barrington. Things have decayed in the bustle-building trade,/And that's the truth of it. PoPle

I Was a Wandering Sheep. Horatius Bonar. 'Tis He that still doth keep. BePJ

I Was Always Fascinated. Alma Villanueva. these things were death. WPOW

I Was Born about Ten Thousand Years Ago. Anonymous. Chasing skeeters out of sunny Tennessee. AS; FSW

I was born under a kind star. Katharine Tynan. For I was born under a kind star. EG

I Was Born upon Thy Bank, River. Henry David Thoreau. And thou meanderest forever/At the bottom of my dream. ELU; PoEL 1-5

I Was Fair Beat.   Robert Garioch.   and what a time a reel of tape can play!   OxBTC

I Was Lying Still in a Field One Day.   Zhenya Gay.   And I lay still to watch him play.   TiPo

I Was Made Erect and Lone.   Henry David Thoreau.   Take the sap and leave the heart.   PoEL 1-5

I Was Made of This and This.   Gertrude Robison Ross.   (That I had never been made of this–/The angel's prayer, or the gipsy's kiss!)   HBMV

I Was Playing Golf That Day.   Anonymous.   They almost put me off my game.   FiBHP; PV

I Was Sick and in Prison.   Jones Very.   Till earth restores her sons to heaven again.   NOBA

I Was Sitting in McSorley's.   Edward Estlin Cummings.   outside.(it was New York and beautifully,snowing....   NoAm

I Was the Child.   Valerie S. Warren.   If you must go, go ever so slowly/Into that dark and rippled sunshine lake!   Str

I Was Washing outside in the Darkness.   Osip Mandelstam.   the earth's moving nearer to truth and to dread.   FaBoPV

I Wash My Face in a Golden Vase.   Anonymous.   All on a Christmas day.   ChBR

I Wasn't No Mary Ellen.   Linda King.   I didn't want no litter on my hands   GP

I Watched a Blackbird.   Thomas Hardy.   As if so sure a nest were never shaped on spray.   PB

I watched the moon around the house.   Emily Dickinson.   To follow her superior Road–/Or its advantage–Blue–   MOON

I Wear a Crimson Cloak To-Night.   Lois Seyster Montross.   I wear the crimson cloak to-night!   HBMV

I Weep.   Angelina Weld Grimke.   You would not know/I wept.   CDC

I Went Down into the Desert to Meet Elijah.   Vachel Lindsay.   The carrion-birds a-wheeling round your head.   WGRP

I Went Down to the Depot (with music).   Anonymous.   And laid Jesse James in his grave.   AS

I Went into the Maverick Bar.   Gary Snyder.   I came back to myself,/To the real work, to/"What is to be done."   HaCAP; MAT

I Went My Sunday Mornings Rounds.   John Clare.   I wed the maid in just three weeks/From the first day we parted.   NOBV

I Went Out into the Garden.   Moses Ibn Ezra.   And its thunder surged like the cry of a woman that/gives birth!   LiTW; TrJP

I Went to Death.   Anonymous.   I wende to dede, sooth I you tell.   FaBoRV; OxBM

I Went to Heaven.   Emily Dickinson.   Almost contented/I could be/'Mong such unique/Society.   FaBV; NePA

I Went to Noke.   Anonymous.   But I went to Beckley/And they spoke directly.   GBP; OxNR

I Went to See Irving Babbitt.   Richard Eberhart.   Warbling your native foot-notes mild.   GLGT; OBAL

I Went to the City.   Kenneth Patchen.   Can't hold her pure little han'!   PoPl

I Went to the Sea.   Anonymous.   ...if my wife/Was as white as those.   PBBP

I Went to the Toad That Lies under the Wall.   Anonymous.   I tore the bat's wing: what would you have more?   OxNR

I Went to the Valley.   Lucille Clifton.   my soul got happy/and i stayed all day.   TAT

I Wept as I Lay Dreaming.   Heinrich Heine.   And ever they stream in vain.   AWP

I, who cut off my sorrows?   Akazome Emon.   Why do I still long/for the floating world?   BoWoP; WPOW

I, Who Fade with the Lilacs.   William Griffith.   Hitching, forever hitching/Ships–shallops to a star.   HBMV

I Who Had Been Afraid.   Sister Maris Stella.   Alone with the beloved dead found nothing to fear.   GoBC

I Will Accept.   Christina Georgina Rossetti.   Till I infuse love, hatred, longing, will.–/I do not deprecate.   OxBoCh

I Will Be.   Edward Estlin Cummings.   s(oon & there's/a m oo/)n.   VGW

I Will Be What God Made Me, Nor Protest.   Robert Bridges.   My toil is for man's joy, his joy my own.   VLP

I Will Believe.   William H. Roberts.   I will believe.   BLRP

I Will Bow and Be Simple.   Anonymous.   Yea I'll fall upon the rock.   EaLo

I Will Enjoy Thee Now.   Thomas Carew.   This proud usurper and walk free as they.   LiTL; UnTE

I Will Give My Love an Apple.   Anonymous.   And when they're child-making they're seldom crying.   CBEP

I Will Go Away.   Zvi Shargal.   No one will see,/no one will hear/anything.   VWA

I Will Go into the Ghetto.   Charles Reznikoff.   Breathe deeply:/how good and sweet the air is.   VGW

I Will Go with My Father A-Ploughing.   Joseph Campbell.   That joys for the harvest done.   AnIL; GoBC; OFD; OnYI; SiSoSe; TiPo

I Will Have the Whetstone.   Anonymous.   I will have the whetstone and I may.   FaBoNo; GBP

I Will Make You Brooches.   Robert Louis Stevenson.   Of the death.   BrPo

I Will Not Die for You.   Anonymous.   I will not die for you.   NOBI

I Will Not Let Thee Go.   Robert Bridges.   I have thee by the hands,/And will not let thee go.   AnFE; BeLS; BLPL; CMoP; CoBMV; EnLoPo; FaBoBe; LiTL; OBNC

I Will Praise the Lord at All Times.   William Cowper.   Points to an eternal rest.   EiCP

I Will Write.   Robert Graves.   There are no mails in a city of the dead.   PCP

I Will Write Songs Against You.   Charles Reznikoff.   I will marshall against you/the fireflies of the dusk.   VGW

I Wilp Turn Your Money Green.   Furry Lewis.   Woman quit me, throwed my trunk outdoors   BluL

I Wish.   Nancy Byrd Turner.   Go find the answers, right away, and tell me in September!'   SiSoSe

I Wish I Could Lend a Coat.   Akahito (Yamabe no Akahito).   Of the autumn wind.   AWP

I Wish I Was a Little Bird (with music).   Anonymous.   But I can't stay here by myself.   AS

I Wish I Was a Mole in the Ground.   Anonymous.   And I wish I was a mole in the ground.   ABF; AmFP

I Wish I Was Single Again.   Anonymous.   I wish I was single again.   AmFP; AS; BFSS; FSW

I Wish I Was Where I Would Be.   John Clare.   But as the winds the waters stir/The mirrors change & flye.   NOBV

I Wish I Were.   Anonymous.
I can light cheroots and gaspers with my tail.   FaBoNo; OxBoLi
I can play the fiddle with my left/hind-leg.   FaFP

I Wish I Were by That Dim Lake.   Thomas Moore.   Like freezing founts, where all that's thrown/Within their current turns to stone.   NBM

I Wish, I Wish.   Anonymous.   But she will come like me again.   OBET

I Wish My Tongue Were a Quiver.   L. A. MacKay.   Like a woolly caterpillar pinned on its back–man, that would/be sweet.   TW

I Wish Sometimes, Although a Worthlesse Thing.   Giles the Elder Fletcher.   Kisse me sweete love, this favour doe for me:/Then Crownes and Kingdomes shall I scorne for thee.   AAS

I Wish That My Room Had a Floor.   Gelett Burgess.   Is getting to be quite a bore!   ALV; FiBHP; HBV 1-2; OBCA

I Woke Up Revenge.   A. Poulin, Jr.   a stubborn, undissolving vatican.   TW

I, Woman.   Irma McClaurin.   I swear I hear those sisters still humming.   BlSi

I Won't Be My Father's Jack.   Anonymous.   Prithee, love, play me/T'other little tune.   OxNR; UnS

I Wonder as I Wander.   Anonymous.   I wonder as I wander/Out under the sky.   EaLo; PCh

I Wonder How Many People in This City.   Leonard Cohen.   I wonder how many go back to their desks/and write this down.   CAD; ELU

I Wonder How My Home Is.   Anonymous.   And how I used to walk amid my corn/And through my fields. Alas! What can I do?   WTO

I Wonder What Became of Rand, McNally...   Newman Levy.   "You said it, brother," said Mr. McNally.   InMe

I Wonder What It Feels Like to Be Drowned?   Robert Graves.   I wonder what it feels like to be drowned?   BrPo; MoBrPo

I Wonder Why.   Pluvkaq.   I am not good at hunting.   WeW

I/ wonder why.   Tom Poole.   noontime.   BOLo; NBP

I Work All Day Long for You.   Anonymous.   And when they gits to playing with your heart and they starts/blackin' your heart around.   WTO

I Worship Thee, O Holy Ghost.   William F. Warren.   With thee each day is Pentecost,/Each night Nativity.   AH

I Would Be a Painter Most of All.   Len Chandler.   where you dare not even blink   NBP

I Would I Might Forget That I Am I.   George Santayana.   And doomed to know his aching heart alone.   AWP

I Would I Were a Careless Child.   George Gordon, Lord Byron.   To flee away, and be at rest.   ERoP 1-2

I Would If I Could.   Anonymous.   Could you, without you could,/could ye?   OxNR

I Would in Rich and Golden Coloured Raine.   Thomas Lodge.   That whilest I thus in pleasures lappe did lye,/I might refresh desire, which else would die.   AAS

I Would Like My Love to Die.   Samuel Beckett.   mourning the first and last to love me   BIrV; CIP; NOBI

I would Like to be-A Bee.   Dorothy Walter Baruch.   If I were a Bee.   BiCB

I Would Like You for a Comrade.   Edward Abbott Parry.   If I were not a clumsy calf/And you a little girl   OxBChV

I Would Not Ask.   Grace E. Troy.   Lest seeking selfish ease/Thy best I lose.   STF

I Would Not Live Alway.   William Augustus Muhlenberg.   Alleluia–Amen-evermore with the Lord!   AA; AH; HBV 1-2

I Would Not Paint a Picture.   Emily Dickinson.   Had I the Art to stun myself/With Bolts of Melody!   MAmP; NOBA

Idea of a Swimmer.   Jean-Richard Bloch.   That I may lean my elbow on your knee.   TrJP

The Idea of a University.   David Shapiro.   And the hand opens its ten thousand hold.   ANYP

The Idea of Ancestry.   Etheridge Knight.   ...and I have no sons/to float in the space between.   BALP; BPo; CNA; ConAP; LFAC; NIP; NNaP; PoBA; PPoe; SV

The Idea of Detroit.   Jim Gustafson.   sighing deeply, knowing that nothing/can save it now.   APU

The Idea of Entropy at Maenporth Beach.   Peter Redgrove.   The shrugged-up riches of deep darkness sang.   FaBoMo

The Idea of Order at Key West.   Wallace Stevens.   In ghostlier demarcations, keener sounds.   AP; CMoP; CoBMV; FF; ForPo; HaCAP; HAP; HeIP; MoAB; MoAmPo; MoPo; MOS; NAWM 1-2; NIP; NoAm; NOBA; NoP; OxBA; PP; PPP; PrIm; TAP

The Idea of San Francisco.   Jim Gustafson.   city that constantly squirms/but never screams.   APU

The Idea of Trust.   Thom Gunn.   Wild lilac/chokes the garden.   Psk

Idea's Mirrour.   Michael Drayton.   Which name my Muse to highest heaven shall raise/By chaste desire, true love, and virtue's praise.   OBSC

The Ideal.   Charles Baudelaire.   That night of fever fierce and calamitous!   SyP

Ideal.   Padraic Pearse.   To the death that I shall meet.   AnIV; AWP; LiTW; OnYI

The Ideal.   Francis Saltus Saltus.   And to possess it pay its tribute–Death.   AA

The Ideal Age for a Man.   Monica Shannon.   "The ideal age for a man is two,"/That's what I say, when I look at you.   BiCB

Ideal and Reality.   Joseph Campbell.   The tap-tap of a ringmaker is heard,/Beating his penny in a distant wing.   BIrV

Ideal Beauty.   Fernando de Herrera.   The immortal still I seek and follow on to Heaven!   CAW

The Ideal Husband to His Wife.   Sam Walter Foss.   For I am ready to admit/That you are wrong and I am right.   InMe

Ideal Landscape.   Adrienne Rich.   Those gilded trees, those statues green and white.   NoAm

Ideals.   Robert Greene.   Naught so sweet as is true love.   PoToHe

The Ideals of Satire.   Alexander Pope.   The last and greatest art, the art to blot.   FiP

Identification in Belfast (I.R.A. Bombing).   Robert Lowell.   only joke-matches....Then I knew he was Richard.'   OxBC

Identikit.   Jim Brodey.   revolves a once rectumistic joyous reminder   ANYP

Identities.   Al Young.   or reach for the sky/for the 500th time?   NPGG

Identity.   Thomas Bailey Aldrich.   "I only died last night!"   AA; AnNE

Identity.   Robert Friend.   in the cold syllables/of the tongue I love.   GP; VWA

Identity.   Elizabeth Jennings.   Is all we make each other when we love.   NePoEA

Identity.   Sister Mary Helen.   That we love and need her/World without end.   GoBC

Identity Card.   Susan Tichy.   like a bee in a wet spring bloom.   MAYP

The Ides of March.   Roy Fuller.   ...Yet, plucking nervously/The pregnant twigs, I stay. Good morning, comrades.   PoCh

Idiom of the Hero.   Wallace Stevens.   Out of the clouds, pomp of the air,/By which at least I am befriended.   OxBA

The Idiot.   Adele Naude.   Then will she greet the new world with her cry?   PeSA

The Idiot.   Dudley Randall.   ...the good will/of the good white folks downtown,/who hired him.   BPo

Idiot.   Allen Tate.   Covers his eyes with memory like a sheet.   AnAmPo; FaBoMo; LiTA; NAMP

The Idiot.   Keith Wilson.   who is to tell the stories he saw/flashing in the dust?   Psk

Idiot Boy.   Rowland M. Hill.   "You're looking good for your age today, old man."   AMV-81

The Idiot Boy.   William Wordsworth.   –Thus answered Johnny in his glory,/And that was all his travel's story.   OBNV

Idle Charon.   Eugene Lee-Hamilton.   The widow puts no obol, nor the son,/To pay the ferry in the world beneath.   NOBV; OBVV

Idle Chatter.   Charles Cooper.   i'm gonna be/rich/some/day   BOLo

The Idle Flowers.   Robert Bridges.   The land is laid in snow.   BoNaP

The Idle Life I Lead.   Robert Bridges.   That I have known no day/In all my life like this.   EG; LiTM

Idle Verse.   Henry Vaughan.   Winter is all my year.   AtBAP; OAEP

Idle Words.   Walter Savage Landor.   And that a thousand Angels wait/To write them at thy inner gate.   OBSV

Idleness.   Silas Weir Mitchell.   All magic gifts of joy's simplicity.   AA

The Idler.   Elizabeth Jennings.   Composing stillness round their careless will.   NePoEA

The Idler.   Jones Very.   A laborer but in heart, while bound my hands/Hang idly down still waiting thy commands.   AA; HBV 1-2

An Idler's Calendar: January.   Wilfrid Scawen Blunt.   ...Then home in chastened/pride,/With aching heads, our slaughter satisfied.   VLP

Idleset (2).   Thurso Berwick.   Ill's the airt o the Word the day.   OxBS

Idol.   Louise Driscoll.   "While the woman I am/And the man you are/Are as far apart/As star and star."   HBMV

Idolatry.   Arna Bontemps.   And set an old bell tolling on the air.   AmNP; PoNe

Une Idole du Nord.   Francis Stuart.   ...O God, the only summer/Is on her lips, and even they have lied.   NeIP

Idols.   Richard Burton.   Salute the mystery beyond their ken.   TrPWD

Idyl.   Alfred Mombert.   She smiled, and put a rose into her hair.   AWP

An Idyl in Idleness.   Robert Pack.   And something in our flesh was wrong.   NePoEA

Idyl: Sunrise.   Henrietta Cordelia Ray.   "He cometh, so I wait."   BlSi

Idyl: Sunset.   Henrietta Cordelia Ray.   Does it not seem/That love can all control?   BlSi

Idyll.   Stoddard King.   Of a sylphish shellfish weeping/By a selfish shellfish' cell.   NLV

Idyll.   Hugh Macnaghten.   And I a little child who stands/And gravely kisses both her hands.   HBMV

Idyll.   Francis Webb.   Then like the brown fox of copperplate/Made exit over the lazy dog.   PoAu 1-2

Idyll of the Rose.   Decimus Magnus Ausonius.   Mindful the while that thus time flies for you.   AWP

Idylls.   Moschus.
Be kind to Love, that he be kind to you.   AWP
Piping on reeds I had sat, and had lulled my sorrow to/sleep.   AWP

Idylls.   Theocritus.
And thus reward, and practise my Advice.   PeHV
Be steady, or your pranks will rouse the ram.   AWP
The Bridegroom started from his Trance at last,/And piping homeward jocoundly he past.   OBVE
Ease came with song, he could not buy with gold.   AWP; OBVE
Farewel, and you attending Stars that wheel/Round Nights black Axle-tree, bright Stars, farewel.   OBVE
For see the God takes vengeance on my scorn.   PeHV
I wronged the sire: some Satyr he, or an uncouth-limbed/Pan.   AWP
In cittie nor on hill, but all the night must sleep alone.   OBVE
Not die of famine, amid dreams of gold.   AWP
Poppies and cornsheaves on each laden arm.   AWP
That wait upon the car of noiseless Night.   AWP

Idylls of the King.   Geoffrey Hill.   warheads of mushrooms round the filter-pond.   FaBoPV

Idylls of the King.   Alfred, Lord Tennyson.
"All men, to one so bound by such a vow,/And women were as phantoms...."   OAEL 1-2
And beat the cross to earth, and break the Kind/And all his Table'....   OAEL 1-2
And trust me not at all or all in all.   NOBV; TrGrPo
The darkness of that battle in the West/Where all of high and holy dies away.   VLP
For so the whole round earth is every way/Bound by gold chains about the feet of God.   TreF; WGRP
Nay–God my Christ–I pass but shall not die.   TreFS
Till God's love set thee at his side again!   CABA; VLP
To where beyond these voices there is peace.   EnLit; MaVP
...what I saw was veil'd/And cover'd; and this Quest was not for me.   GoBC

If.   John Kendrick Bangs.   To reach all the sugar and things that I can't/Reach now, when I eat at the table!   OBCA

If.   Mortimer Collins.   If wit were always radiant,/And wine were always iced.   FiBHP

If.   Anselm Hollo.   come see the monster.   APU

If.   William Dean Howells.   That drop untasted might be somehow/spilled.   AA

If.   Rudyard Kipling.   And–which is more–you'll be a Man, my son!   BBV; BLPA; FaBoBe; FaFP; FaPoR; FPL; GoTF; HBV 1-2; HBVY; OHFP; OxBChV; OxBTC; PaPo; TreF; WBLP

If.   Patrick Lane.   I am one of those who laughed/when the burro dropped her on the floor.   NOBC

If.   James Jeffrey Roche.   Thou wilt not break thy heart, dear,/No more, I think, shall I!   HBV 1-2

If a Maid Be Fair.   Laura Goodman Salverson.   Pretty maid, be wise, beware,/O, take care!   CaP

If a Man Die–.   John Richard Moreland.   All sepulchers/Are sealed in vain!   PGD

If All the Seas Were One Sea.   Anonymous.   What a splish-splash that would be!   OnUR; OxNR; SoPo

If All the Skies.   Henry Van Dyke.   And rest from weary laughter/In the quiet arms of grief.   WBLP; WGRP

If All the Thermo-Nuclear Warheads.   Kenneth Burke.   What great PROGRESS that would be!   QQQ

If All the Voices of Men. Horace L. Traubel. you will remember that the/ road runs east as well as west. AA

If all the world were apple-pie. Mother Goose. What should we have to drink? FaFP; HBV 1-2; OxNR; SoPo

If All the World Were Paper. *Anonymous.* If this should be, then how should we/Here make an end of singing? CBEP; FaBoCo; FaBoNo; GBP; LoBV; NTCP; PoPle

If Along the Highroad. *Anonymous.* Friendship takes time to overcome. LiTW

If amour's faith... Sir Thomas Wyatt. Yours is the fault and mine the great annoy. FCP

If Any Be Pleased to Walk into My Poor Garden... Francis Daniel Pastorius. A good man's Word exceeds a bad ones Bond. SCAP

If Bees Stay at Home. *Anonymous.* Fine will be the day. OxNR

If Birds That Neither Sow Nor Reap. Roger Williams. Millions of birds and worlds will God,/Sooner than His forsake. AH

If Blood Is Black Then Spirit Neglects My Unborn Son. Conrad Kent Rivers. Let my women mourn for days/in flight. PoBA

If But One Year. *Anonymous.* But try to live each day He sends/To serve my gracious Master's ends. STF

If Buttercups Buzz'd after the Bee. *Anonymous.* If summer were spring, and the other way round,/Then all the world would be upside down. LoGBV

If by Dull Rhymes Our English Must Be Chained. John Keats. So, if we may not let the Muse be free,/She will be bound with garlands of her own. PP

If Candlemas Day Be Dry and Fair. *Anonymous.* The half o' winter's gone at Yule. PoSC

"If care do cause men cry..." Henry Howard, Earl of Surrey. I do bequeath my wearied ghost to serve her afterward. FCP; SiPS

If Chance Assign'd. Sir Thomas Wyatt. My death, or life with liberty. FCP; SiPS

If Christ Were Here To-Night. Margaret E. Sangster. And heaven will be of thy rich life a part. TRV

If Crossed with All Mishaps. William, of Hawthornden Drummond. The fairest rose in shortest time decays. CBEP

"If Cynthia be a Queen..." Sir Walter Ralegh. Thy mind of neither needs, in both seeing it exceeds. FCP; SiPS

If Easter Be Not True. Henry H. Barstow. Worthwhile the struggle, sure the prize,/Since Easter, aye, is true! BLRP; PGD; TRV

If Easter Eggs Would Hatch. Douglas Malloch. My, wouldn't that be funny! SoPo

If Ever I Marry, I'll Marry a Maid. *Anonymous.* And some bachelors hold they are best as they are. EiL

If ever man might him avant. Sir Thomas Wyatt. I must myself therewith content/And bear it as I can. FCP; SiPS

If Ever You Go to Dublin Town. Patrick Kavanagh. Yet he lived happily/ I tell you. AnIL; CIP; CMoP; InPS; IPY; NMP

If Everything Happens That Can't Be Done. Edward Estlin Cummings. alive we're alive)/we're wonderful one times one SoSe; WeW

If fancy would favor. Sir Thomas Wyatt. To have you day and night,/To love me best of all. AAS; FCP; SiPS

If Fathers Knew But How to Leave. *Anonymous.* Or foot, or face, or foolish hand. EG; EiL

If Frequently to Mass. Christianne Pisan. How foolish he who fool calls me,/If frequently to mass I go. PoPl

If God Exists. Ewa Lipska. God will give me medicine from his stocks/and I'll recover/straight after death. VWA

If Grief for Grief Can Touch Thee. Emily Bronte. O I shall surely win thee,/Beloved, again! EnLoPo; OBNC

If He'd Be a Buckaroo. *Anonymous.* With his ring ting tinny,/And his ring ting ho. OuSiCo

If He from Heaven That Filched the Living Fire. Michael Drayton. Thus poor thieves suffer, when the greater 'scape. TEP

If He Let Us Go Now. Shirley Williams. The only answer I get is his back. BoWoP

"If he that erst the form so lively drew." Henry Howard, Earl of Surrey. Thou canst inflame and quench the kindled fire. FCP; SiPS

If I But Knew. Amy E. Leigh. I'd tell my ardent love to you,/If I but knew—if I but knew. AA

If I Can Stop One Heart from Breaking. Emily Dickinson. I shall not live in vain. AH; FPL; GoTF; OHFP; PoLf; PoToHe; TreF; TRV

If I Consider. Lady Ise. Can I hope, though I am burnt,/That spring will come again? WPOW

If I Could Believe That Death. Gaspara Stampa. Thus to undergo less torment I agree/to go on living in this martyrdom. PBWP

If I Could Go On Kissing Your Honeyed Eyes. Caius Valerius Catullus. No, even if the harvest of our kissing/Were richer than the ripe gold ears of the corn. PeHV

If I Could Grasp a Wave from the Great Sea. John Richard Moreland. The face of Him who walked on Galilee. EtS

If I Could Meet God. Dennis Schmitz. his ears erect with certainty NPGG

If I Could Only Live at the Pitch That Is near Madness. Richard Eberhart. And the truth wailing there like a red babe. FF; LiTM; MAT; MiAP; MoAB; PoPl

If I Could Shut the Gate against My Thoughts. John Daniel. And I remain divided from my sin. EiL; HBV 1-2; LoBV; NOCV; OxBoCh

If I Could Tell How Glad I Was. Emily Dickinson. From mathematics further off/Than from Eternity. MAmP

If I Could Touch. William Stanley Braithwaite. Death would be then between us two/The passing of a summer's night. BALP

If I Could Walk out into the Cold Country. Elizabeth Brewster. Their names erased, in an unfrequented way. NOBC

If I Die a Railroad Man (with music). *Anonymous.* And a nine-pound hammer in my hand. AS

If I Ever Grow Old. Elinor Nauen. del tempo felice nella miseria. APU

If I Felt Less. Morris Wintchevsky. And only wait/Till they bury me. TrJP

If I Forget Thee. Emanuel Litvinoff. I shall crown your innocent heads/ with twelve stars of Israel. TrJP; VWA

If I Go Not, Pray Not, Give Not. *Anonymous.* Mine is the sin, and justice fair demands/That I accept the guilt of bloody hands! STF

If I Got My Ticket, Can I Ride? *Anonymous.* Ride away to the heaven that mornin'. OuSiCo

If I Had a Firecracker. Shel Silverstein. And then I'd do it again. PoSC

If I had as much money as I could/spend. Mother Goose. I never would cry old clothes to sell. FaFP; HBV 1-2

If I Had but Two Little Wings. Samuel Taylor Coleridge. Yet while 'tis dark, one shuts one's lids,/And still dreams on. OHIP

If I Had But Two Little Wings. Thomas Hood. Than when I was a boy. CH

If I Had Known. Mary Carolyn Davies. If I had known. BLPA

If I Had My Way. Blind Willie Johnson. Well if I had, that wicked way/If I had/Eh Lord/I'd tear this building down BluL

If I Had Ridden Horses. Theodore Maynard. A joy as cleansing as the wind that fills/The open spaces on the sunny hills. HBMV

If I Have Lifted up Mine Eyes to Admire. Amos N. Wilder. Forgive the world's fond idolatries. TrPWD

If I Have Made, My Lady, Intricate. Edward Estlin Cummings. into the ragged meadow of my soul. CMoP; FaBV; NAMP; NOBA; PoRA

If I Have Sinn'd in Act. Hartley Coleridge. One sinful wish would make a hell of heaven. NCEP

If I Have Wronged You. Trumbull Stickney. Before we soiled our lips with crime,/That you and I went our two ways. NCEP

If I Leave Here Alive. Solomon Mahaka. I may not be a nice person. WhB

If I Only Was the Fellow. Will S. Adkin. Just try to be the fellow that/ Your mother thinks you are. BLPA

If I Owned All of Alba. Colum Cille. Death will come, if it comes,/ through my love for the men of Ireland. NOBI

If I Ride This Train. Joe Johnson. My address will be unknown except to god and the/Boogaman. PoBA

If I Should Cast Off This Tattered Coat. Stephen Crane. What then? AmePo

If I should die. Emily Dickinson. That gentlemen so sprightly/Conduct the pleasing scene! MoAB

If I Should Die To-Night. Ben King. I might arise the while,/But I'd drop dead again. BLPL; FiBHP; GoTF; HBV 1-2; InMe; PoLf; TreFS; YaD

If I Should Die Tonight. Arabella Eugenia Smith. When dreamless rest is mine I shall not need/The tenderness for which I long tonight. BLPA; HBV 1-2; TreF

If I Should Ever By Chance. Edward ("Edward Eastaway") Thomas. I shall give them all to my elder daughter. FaBoCh; GoJo; GTBS; HBMV; LoGBV; MoAB; MoBrPo; MoShBr; OBMV; OxBChV

If i should sleep with a lady called death. Edward Estlin Cummings. an inch of nothing for your soul. BoLoP; VGW

If I shouldn't be alive. Emily Dickinson. You will know I'm trying/With my Granite lip! FM; MAPA; PG

If I Stand in My Window. Lucille Clifton. praying in tongues BPo

If I Went Away. Desmond O'Grady. there's nothing of value here for a man/but the heavy word from everyone's tongue. CIP

If I were a Cassowary. Samuel Wilberforce. Cassock, bands, and hymn-book too. CenHV

If I Were a Pilgrim Child. Rowena Bastin Bennett. Not one of them will wear/Moccasins upon his feet/Or feathers in his hair! YeAr

If I Were a Queen. Christina Georgina Rossetti. I'd make you Queen,/For I'd marry you. SiSoSe

If I Were a Voice. Charles Mackay. Truths which the ages for aye repeat,/ Unknown to the statesmen at their feet. TreF

If I Were Dead. Coventry Patmore. O God, have Thou no mercy upon me!/Poor Child! ACP; CAW; GoBC; HBV 1-2

If I Were King. Justin Huntly McCarthy.

I could not give you any goodlier thing/If I were king. FaFP; GoTF; PoLf; TreF

If Villon were the King of France! HBV 1-2

If I Were King. A.(lan) A.(lexander) Milne. I'd tell the soldiers, "I'm the King!" OnUR

If I Were Old. Will H. Ogilvie. No dark can ever hide this dear loved land from me. PoSH

If I Were Tickled by the Rub of Love. Dylan Thomas. Man be my metaphor. FF

If Ice. W. W. Eustace Ross. on the brown dry/forest-bed. NOBC; OBCV

If "Ifs" and "Ands." Anonymous. There would be no need for tinkers. FaBoBe; HBV 1-2

If in Beginning Twilight. Edward Estlin Cummings. –"dying" the ghost of you/whispers "is very pleasant" my ghost to NYBP

If in the World There Be More Woe. Sir Thomas Wyatt. And unkindness, alas, hath slain/My poor true heart, all comfortless. EG; EIL; FCP; SiPS

If It All Went up in Smoke. George Oppen. and touch the small/distances the poem/begins VWA

If it be so... Sir Thomas Wyatt. And on my faith, good is the reason,/If it be so. FCP

If It Be True. Esther Johnson. What envious Time takes from my face,/Bestow upon my mind. OBSP

If It Comes. Philip Booth. you will wake,/if it comes,/near morning. NCSH

If It Is Not My Portion. Rabindranath Tagore. ...let me carry the pangs/of this sorrow in my dreams and in my wakeful hours. BoC; OBMV

If it is you, there. Lady Ise. "Do not go, linger a while/among us here in this place." BoWoP

If It Looks Like Jelly, Shakes Like Jelly, It Must Be Gel-a-Tine. Charlie Lincoln (Hicks). If it look like jelly, shake like jelly/it must be gel-a-tine BluL

If It Offend Thee... Horace Gregory. At earth, not fire, and it would say, "This will not do." NMP

If It's Ever Spring Again. Thomas Hardy. Summer-time,/With the hay, and bees achime. OxBTC

If It Were Not for the Voice. Nakatsukasa. Know the spring? AWP

If It Were Real. Ono no Komachi. I shrink into misery. WPOW

If It Were Spring. Leonard Cohen. I will see this mercy done. ACV

If It Would All Please Hurry. James Tate. Hold tight, squeeze. MAYP

If, Jerusalem, I Ever Should Forget Thee. Heinrich Heine. As in art, in life the people/Can but kill, they cannot judge us. TrJP

If Jesus Came to Your House. Anonymous. If Jesus came in person to spend some/time with you. STF

If Justice Moved. Bettie M. Sellers. I'd gnaw on it a thousand years. TW

If Life's a Lousy Picture, Why Not Leave before the End. Roger McGough. & we'll ride off/into/our/happy/ending OxBTC

If Lincoln Should Return. Margaret E. Bruner. Distress would somehow know the thing to do. PoToHe

If Lord Thy Love For Me Is Strong. Saint Theresa of Avila. Love on, and turn to love again? AWP; CAW; LiTW; PBWP

If Love, For Love of Long Time Had. John Heywood. And yours to love as lovely. EIL

If Love's a Yoke. D. C. Berry. Pray lightning's flash/be both hope's reins/and hope's light lash. AMV-81

If Love Were Jester at the Court of Death. Frederic Lawrence Knowles. Better a cross, and nails through either hand,/Than Pilate's palace and a frozen soul! HBV 1-2

If Man Him Bethought. Anonymous. I wene non sinne/Shulde his herte winne. OxBM

If Man, That Angel of Bright Consciousness. Conrad Aiken. but, before tears can fall, they are asleep. NePA

If Mr. H.W. Longfellow Had Written Miss Millay's. Franklin Pierce ("F.P.A.") Adams. For its light is the light eternal/That burns at both its ends. OBAL

If my bark sink. Emily Dickinson. Mortality's ground floor/Is immortality. TRV

If, My Darling. Philip Larkin. Might knock my darling off her unpriceable pivot. EBEV; LiTM

If My Hands Were Mute. Manfred Winkler. With rising reluctance he would begin a motion again. VWA

If My Head Hurt a Hair's Foot. Dylan Thomas. And the endless beginning of prodigies suffers open.' NoAm

If my nipples were to drip milk. Sappho. who wears the scent of violets/on her young breasts. BoWoP

If night takes the form of a whale. Isabel Fraire. that devours everything/endlessly BoWoP

If No One Ever Marries Me. Laurence Alma-Tadema. I shall buy a little orphan-girl/And bring her up as mine. BiCB; OxBChV

If Not (parody). H. A. C. Evans. For, take my tip, you'll miss the bus, old boy. FaBoPa

If, on Account of the Political Situation. W. H. Auden. This is the Abomination. This is the wrath of God. LiTA; WaP

If Once You Have Slept on an Island. Rachel Field. But–once you have slept on an island/You'll never be quite the same! BrR

If Only. Christina Georgina Rossetti. Yea, they shall sing for love when Christ shall come. EBCP; OxBoCh; TrCP

If Only the Dreams Abide. Clinton Scollard. I shall be satisfied/If only the dreams abide. HBV 1-2

If Only We Understood. Anonymous. And we'd love each other better./If we only understood. STF

If Only, When One Heard. Anonymous. And refuse to meet him! AWP

If Pigs Could Fly. James Reeves. If only pigs could fly! OnUR

If Poisonous Minerals. John Donne. That thou remember them, some claim as debt,/I think it mercy, if thou wilt forget. LiTB; UnPo

If Pope Had Written 'Break, Break, Break'. Sir John Collings Squire. With hues more rubicund than Cibber's nose... CenHV; FaBoPa

If recollecting were forgetting. Emily Dickinson. That gathered these today! AA

If She Be Made of White and Red. Herbert P. Horne. Bid Love be still, nor ever speak,/Lest he his own rejection seek. HBV 1-2

If She but Knew? Arthur William Edgar O'Shaughnessy. Would she not come? HBV 1-2

If She Sang. Gerald William Barrax. are dimensions with room/for only two CNA

If So It Hap, This Of-Spring of My Care. Samuel Daniel. That she hath done, the motive of my paine;/Who whilst I love, doth kill me with disdaine. AAS

If So the Man You Are. Percy Wyndham Lewis.
I am the man to shun Hamlet's soliloquy. OBSV
If so a man we throw to the dickey-birds! OBSV
The Ronin, the Wave-Men, camp in the ruined door. OBSV

If Some Grim Tragedy. Ninna May Smith. Save for the little rodent cares that make/Me small as they. HBMV

If Someone Asks You. Mitchell Donian. Mr. Someone/Or yourself/Should take a book down from the shelf. PoSC

If Something Should Happen. Lucille Clifton. where will the captains run and/to what harbor? MAT

If Spirits Walk. Sophie Jewett. Keep the old tryst, sweetheart, and thou/shalt know/If spirits walk. AA; HBV 1-2

If the Birds Knew. John Ashbery. But as though the birds were in on the secret. PoA

If the Black Frog Will Not Ring. Ed Roberson. somewhere makes the black frog sing PoBA

If the Heart Be Homeless. Annemarie Ewing. And wiser than I. NePoAm-2

If the Heart of a Man. John Gay. Dissolve us in pleasure, and soft repose. CBEP; ELP; EnLoPo; HeIP

If the Man Who Turnips Cries. Samuel Johnson. 'Tis a proof that he would rather/Have a turnip than a father. HBV 1-2; LBN

If the Oak Is out before the Ash. Anonymous. Then we'll surely have a soak. OxNR

If the Owl Calls Again. John Haines. the cold world awakens. BoAnP; BoNaP; CoAP; ConAP; HeIP; LCAP; NCSH; NU

If the Robin Sings in the Bush. Anonymous. Then the weather will be warm. PBBP

If the Stars Should Fall. Samuel ("Paul Vesey") Allen. Let them buckle and drop. IDB; NNP; PoBA

If There Are Any Heavens. Edward Estlin Cummings. (suddenly in sunlight/he will bow,/& the whole garden will bow) DFF; MoAB; MoAmPo

If There Be Sorrow. Mari E. Evans. Love withheld.../...restrained NNP; PoNe

If There Is a Perchance. Thomas McAfee. To know by the calloused hands steering. AMV-81

If These Endure. Lilith Lorraine. If these endure we have not fought in vain. PGD

If They Honoured Me, Giving Me Their Gifts. Michael (Katherine Bradley and Edith Cooper) Field. Hail, noble bridegroom, hail! OBMV

If They Spoke. Mark Van Doren. And we might listen; and the world/Be uncreated at one stroke. ImOP

If This Be All. Anne Bronte. Or give me strength enough to bear/My load of misery. TrPWD

If This Be Love. Richard Eberhart. If this be love! O I remember/Tempest, and abysm gone. LiTL

If This Little World Tonight. Oliver Herford. "See the pretty shooting star!" ShM

If Thou Indeed Derive Thy Light from Heaven. William Wordsworth. Shine, Poet! in thy place, and be content. EnRP; OBRV; TrCP; VLP

If Thou Must Love Me. Elizabeth Barrett Browning. But love me for love's sake, that evermore/Thou mayst love on, through love's eternity. FaFP

If Thou Wert by My Side, My Love. Reginald Heber. But ne'er were hearts so light and gay/As then shall meet in thee! HBV 1-2

And snore secure on Decks, till rosy Morn. OBVE

...–and still no pause in the fighting. WaaP

And Streams of Sweat down their sow'r Foreheads flow. OBVE

And the white Ruin rises o'er the Plain. OBVE

And then the Greeks, and Trojans both, gave up their horse/and darts. OBS

And there and then twelve of their noblest died/Among their spears and chariots. OBVE

And with a general Sigh her Grief approv'd. OBVE

before I hear your cries as they come to drag you captive. WaaP

Betwixt Atrides Great, and Thetis God-like Son. OBVE

Bright-arm'd, high-crested, and athirst for war. OBVE

But shew'd mixt tongs from many a land of men cald to their/aid. OBVE

carried with her the shining armour, the gift of Hephaistos. NAWM 1-2

come, let us give some man his glory, or make it our own. WaaP

...could put on lookes, of no more overthrow/Than now fraid life. OBS

Crossing a Ford, the Torrent sweeps away,/An unregarded Carcase to the Sea. OBVE

Dispers'd and broken thro' the ruffled Skies. OBVE

Fixt by their cars, waited the golden dawn. OBVE

He spoke, and shouting held on in the foremost his single-foot/horses. NAWM 1-2

Hector withdrew his spear and said/"Perhaps." OBVE

Hera of the gold throne beside/him. NAWM 1-2

...the horses waited for the dawn to mount to her high/place. NAWM 1-2

Let his renowne be cleare as mine, equall his strength in warre.' OBVE

No Gift shall bribe it, and no Pray'r persuade. OBVE

Of Ilion, Paris, sunlike all in arms/Glittering. OBVE

Or let us Glory gain, or Glory give! OBVE

The Prize contended was great Hector's Life. OBVE

Prone on his face, where gasping he expir'd. OBVE

Resistless when he rag'd, and when he stop'd, unmov'd. OBVE

Rush'd forth with Hector to the Fields of Fight. OBVE

She gently touched him with her hand. PoPl

Shine 'twixt the Hills, or wander o'er the Plain. OBVE

So both sides coverd earth with stones, so both for/life contend/To shew their sharpnesse. OBVE

So firmely stood the Greeks, nor fled for all the Ilians' ayd. OBVE

So flourish these, when those are past away. OBVE

So touchly stood these to their taske and made their worke/as even. OBVE

So wedg'd the helmets and boss'd bucklers stood... OBVE

Such the drear roar of battle when they mixt. OBVE

Such was their burial of Hektor, breaker of horses. NAWM 1-2

Thus she mourned, and the women wailed in answer. OBWP

The Toil of thousands in a Moment falls. OBVE

Troopt to these Princes and the Court along th'unmeasur'd/shore... OBVE

where they went to their beds and took the blessing of slumber. NAWM 1-2

Which Night and Day, I wou'd with Tears repeat. OBVE

Who thus inflames them with heroick Fires. OBVE

Iliad. Humbert Wolfe. but only what's sung,/when love's over, endures. MoBrPo

Ilicet. Theodosia Garrison. "Surely the things he loved the best/Are his to-day." PoLf

Ilicet. Algernon Charles Swinburne. The poppied sleep, the end of all. MaVP; NOBV

Ilion, Ilion. Alfred, Lord Tennyson. When wilt thou be melody born? LoBV

Ill. Bernard Spencer. With their weak charms, moving here and there among the/lamps? NeBP

Ill Luck. Charles Baudelaire. Pours forth its fragrant secret yet/Amidst the solitary shades. PoPl

Ill Met by Zenith. Ogden Nash. None does more than Milton can/To justify the Met to man. NYBP

Ill Omens. Thomas Moore. "That love is scarce worth the repose it will cost!" PoEL 1-5

Ille Terrarum. Robert Louis Stevenson. To hearten up a dowie chield,/Fancy's limmer! OxBS

Illegitimate Things. William Carlos Williams. as poems still conserve/the language/of old ecstasies. MoAB; MoAmPo

Illi Morituri. Mary Morison Webster. ...they go out/on a little breath, they do not care. PeSA

The Illiterate. William Meredith. What would you call his feeling for the words/That keep him rich and orphaned and beloved? NoP

The Illumination. Stanley Jasspon Kunitz. And he held up in his hand/the key,/which blinded me. GP; TAP

Illumination and Ecstasy. Baba Kuhi of Shiraz. And lo, I was the All-living–only God I saw. ILwL

Illumination for Victories in Mexico. Grace Greenwood. Light up, light up your homes! PAH

Illusion. Sir Edmund Gosse. Still sat and preened a common songless fieldfare. SyP

Illusion. Jan Rak. to discover the world/in its dazzling nakedness. LiTW

Illusion. Ella Wheeler Wilcox. There is nothing at all but Me. WGRP

The Illustration–A Footnote. Denise Levertov. under the lake where the Muse moves. PoA

Illustrious Ancestors. Denise Levertov. mysterious as the silence when the tailor/would pause with his needle in the air. NoAm; NOBA; VGW

(Im)c-a-t(mo). Edward Estlin Cummings. not/hing had,ever happ/ene/D HAP; WeW

Im Memory of W. B. Yeats. W. H. Auden. Teach the free man how to praise. PPP

Im Traum Sah Ich Ein Mannchen Klein Und Putzig. Heinrich Heine. And countless fiends laughed loud and cried/"Amen!" AWP

Image. Henry Dumas. I see that their arrows/are really boomerangs. BOLo

The Image. Roy Fuller. A half-loved creature, motionless and bloated. ChMP; GTBS-P; OxBTC

The Image. Richard Hughes. ...Linger/And ponder whither has flitted his sitter impassioned. OBMV

Image. Thomas Ernest Hulme. and workmen whistling. InPK; OxBTC

Image. Anna de Noailles. I have languished for their love/And sought their empty shadows with desire. PBWP

An Image from Beckett. Derek Mahon. I hope they had time, and light/Enough to read it. CIP

Image from d'Orleans. Ezra Pound. In the bright new season. LOW

Image in a Lilac Tree. Terence Tiller. where the five tongues of living drink, and are/poem and image. NeBP

Image in a Mirror. Mae Winkler Goodman. we do not recognize in the brief passing/the dim, distorted image is our own! GoYe

Image in the Mirror. Peggy Susberry Kenner. "i feel good." JB

The Image-Maker. Oliver St. John Gogarty. To clothe in perdurable pride/Beauty his transient eyes descried. OBEV; OBMV; PoRA

Image-Nation 13 (the Telephone). Robin Blaser. of the man with a thousand hearts,/he thought PoM

Image-Nation 3. Robin Blaser. flower and youth with an arrow offshot PoM

Image-Nation (the Poésis). Robin Blaser. who is companion blue-hued well-marked PoM

The Image o' God. Joe Corrie. Me! made after the image o' God–/Jings! but it's laughable, tae. OxBS

Image of City. Lance Henson. the cheap hotels stood in shadows of/each/with/a practiced/solemnity VoR

The Image of Death. Thomas, Lord Vaux. As ye of clay were cast by kind,/So shall ye waste to dust. GoTL; OBSC

The Image of Delight. William Ellery Leonard. I lost not thee, nor any shape of thine. AnFE; APA; HBMV

The Image of God. Francisco de Aldana. And owes its being to the gazer's eye. CAW; WGRP

The Image of Irelande (excerpt). John Derricke. They grow through daily exercise/to all iniquity. OBTV

An Image of Leda. Frank O'Hara. a shadow and caress-/ing a disguise! HaCAP

Imagery. Harindranath Chattopadhyaya. Birdlike from a cage in a freedom of flight. ACV

Images. Richard Aldington. Until you return. MoBrPo; PoA

Images. Alistair Campbell. stepping/on velvet MOON

Images. Kathleen Raine. Whose image the fleet waters break but cannot bear away. NYBP

Images. Richard Schaukal. And onward to the dark horizon flew/On their far-shadowing and soundless wings. AWP

Imaginary Elegies, I-IV. Jack Spicer. The birds are still in flight. Believe the birds. NeAP

The Imaginary Iceberg. Elizabeth Bishop. to see them so; fleshed, fair, erected indivisible. FaBoWP; LiTM; MoAB; MoAmPo; MoVE

Imagination. John Davidson. The mood of men, the world's career. MoBrPo

The Imagination of Necessity. Andrei Codrescu. ...taking what's not yours/but fits you & good luck. EAS

The Imaginative Life. Geoffrey Hill. As though the dead had Finis on their brows. NoAm

Imagine a World of People. Ronald James Dessus. p e o p l e. LFAC

Imagine Grass. Knute Skinner. and somewhere in the measured mass/of everything, imagine grass. GP; SM

De Imagine Mundi. John Ashbery. And they stay on to talk it over. FaBoMo

Imagine the South. George Woodcock. They will people your mind. You will never touch/their hands. NeBP; NOBC

Imagined Happiness. Erik Axe Karlfeldt. For happiness is your dower,/Your morning-gift is rest. LiTW; PoPl

Imagining How It Would Be to Be Dead. Richard Eberhart. And then I pressed on eye and cheek/The sightless hinges of eternity/That make the whole world crea LiTA

The Imbecile. Donald Finkel. ...no ark, though the sea/fall back from Ararat, can land/him. NePoEA-2

Imitated from Rime CCLXIX: "The piller pearisht is whearto I Lent. Petrarch (Francesco Petrarca). Till dreadfull death do ease my dolefull state? OBVE

Imitated from Sonetto in Morte '42. Petrarch (Francesco Petrarca). Eche care decayes, and yet my sorow springes. OBVE

Imitation of Chaucer (parody). Alexander Pope. "Then trust on Mon, whose yerde can talke." FaBoPa; Par

Imitation of Julia A. Moore. Mark (Samuel Langhorne Clemens) Twain. When all your friends as fossils sleep,/Immortalized in lime! OBAL

An Imitation of Martial, Book II Ep. 105. Captain H—. In short, be as lewd as a strumpet. NOEC

Imitation of Spenser. John Keats.
Outvieing all the buds in Flora's diadem. EnRP
Through clouds of fleecy white, laughs the coerulean sky. ATP

Imitations Based on the American (parody). Frank Polite. I have wasted my life. BXAP

The Immaculate Conception. John Banister Tabb. A rainbow beauty passion-free/Wherewith was veiled Divinity. ISi

Immaculate Palm. Joseph Joel Keith. You, who gave your Precious Gift. ISi

Immalee. Christina Georgina Rossetti. And even the watchful hare stands not aloof. BoNaP

Immanence. Richard Hovey. The self-same power in yonder sunset glows/That kindled in the words of Holy Writ. TRV; WGRP

Immanent. Walter De la Mare. The fire-doomed Empire of a myriad Ants. PoA

Immensity. Gerald Stern. ...sneezing madly in the midst of that/life of theirs, weighed down by madness and sorrow. AMV-80

Immigrants. Stanley Nelson. Immigrants! AMV-81

Immigrants. Nancy Byrd Turner. Hundred per cent, red-blood American. AmFN

The Immigration Act of 1924. Laureen Mar. you can't just die and take yourself away. BrSi

Immolated. Herman Melville. Snugged in the arms of comfortable night. ViBoPo

Immolation. Robert Farren. with drowning Peter: "Lord delivere me"/by this White Host. OnYI

Immoral. James Oppenheim. Bu joy drops from me like ripe apples. HBV 1-2

The Immoral Arctic. Morris Bishop. But still, it makes you wonder, sort of. FiBHP

The Immoral Proposition. Robert Creeley. ...The unsure/egoist is not/good for himself. LiTM; NeAP; PoM

An Immorality. Ezra Pound. Than do high deeds in Hungary/To pass all men's believing. CMoP; ForPo; GoJo; GrPl; HBV 1-2; LiTL; LiTM; MoAB; MoAmPo; NePA; NOBA; OBAL; OLR; PoPl

The Immortal. William Blake. Or to fall or to swim or to fly,/With ease searching the dire vacuity. LiTB; LoBV

The Immortal. Marjorie Pickthall. And hear new stars come singing from God's hand. CaP

Immortal. Sara Teasdale. A wave that never finds the shore! WGRP

Immortal. Mark Van Doren. It burrowed back with never a sound,/And awoke the thaw. MoAmPo

Immortal Autumn. Archibald MacLeish. I cry to you beyond upon this bitter air. AP; BiP; BoLiVe; CMoP; CoBMV; LiTA; MoAB; MoAmPo; TrGrPo

Immortal Flowers. Wallace Rice. Even as our common doom/Saddens their bloom. AA

Immortal is an ample word. Emily Dickinson. Except for its marauding hand/It had been Heaven below. NOCV

Immortal Israel. Judah Halevi. Endure till day and night shall cease/to be! TrJP

Immortal Love, Forever Full. John Greenleaf Whittier. We test our lives by thine. AH

The Immortal Mind. George Gordon, Lord Byron. A nameless and eternal thing/Forgetting what it was to die. WGRP

Immortal Nature. Erasmus Darwin. And soars and shines, another and the same. OBEC

The Immortal Part. Alfred Edward Housman. And leave with ancient night alone/The stedfast and enduring bone. MasP; MoBrPo; UnPo; VLP

The Immortal Spirit. Stephen Spender. For that flame-winged Creator who fulfils. MoRP

Immortalis. David Morton. Like tapers burning through the windy night. HBV 1-2

Immortality. Ai. If only this were all it took/to live forever. MAYP

Immortality. Matthew Arnold. His soul well-knit, and all his battles won,/Mounts, and that hardly, to eternal life. FiP

Immortality. Richard Henry Dana. To mingle in this heavenly harmony. AA; WGRP

Immortality. Samuel Greenberg. Are not limits the sooth to formulate/Theories thereof, simply our ruler to feel? LiTA

Immortality. Arthur Sherburne Hardy. And pass the sword from hand to hand! AA

Immortality. Frank Horne Trembling breathlessly at the brink/of realization... BANP

Immortality. Joseph Jefferson. And so this emblem shall forever be/A sign of immortality. BLPA

Immortality. Nicolai M. Minsky. Soon we'll be immortal, too. TrJP

Immortality. Susan L. Mitchell. Watch where within a slow dawn lightens up another sky. OnYI

Immortality. Lizette Woodworth Reese.
Not one drop has been spilled. AA; HBMV; HBVY
Peace and a comforter. AA

Immortality. George William Russell. By unnumbered ways of dream to death. AnIV; AWP; OBMV

Immortality Conferred in Vain. Theognis. But, like a child, with words thou cheatest me. LiTW

The Immortality of the Soul. Sir John Davies. ...I know myself a man,/Which is a proud and yet a wretched thing. ViBoPo

The Immortality of Verse. Horace. They had no poet, and are dead. AWP

The Immortals. Isaac Rosenberg. But now I call him dirty louse. FaBoTw; MMM; TrJP

Immustabilis. Alice Learned Bunner. That which Death takes is ours forever-/more. AA

Imogen. Sir Henry Newbolt. Youth undying for hearts that treasure/Imogen dancing, dancing still. HBMV

Imogen—In Wales. Thomas Caulfield Irwin. And the thistle-down went on the wind. IrPN

The Impartial Inspection. *Anonymous.* And whilst they are each other rending,/A third steps in and leaves them none. APAS

Impasse. Langston Hughes. And you don't/Give a damn. LiTM

The Impatient Poet. D'Arcy Cresswell. What men are kings, what women coil their hair! AnNZ

Impatient with Desire. [or Grenville], George, Baron Lansdowne Granville. By our own folly she's unkind. OBSP

Impenitentia Ultima. Ernest Christopher Dowson. For the last sad sight of her face and the little grace of an hour. BrPo; HBV 1-2

Imperator Victus. Hart Crane. Atahualpa,/Imperator Inca-/Slain. OxBA

The Impercipient. Thomas Hardy. Enough. As yet disquiet clings/About us. Rest shall we. OAEP; PrIm; TrGrPo; ViBoPo; WGRP

The Imperfect Artist. George Rostrevor Hamilton. But even there he failed, they say,/To get a likeness once. DBV

The Imperfect Enjoyment. John Wilmot, Earl of Rochester. To do the wrong'd Corinna right for thee. BoLoP; ErPo; UnTE

The Imperfect Lover. Siegfried Sassoon. Unvanquished in my atmosphere of devils. BrPo

Imperfect Sestina. Phyllis Webb. Eden smells of cedar. Raven holds his wings and sucks his stone. NOBC

Imperial Adam. A. D. Hope. And the first murderer lay upon the earth. CBAP; ErPo; HAP; NoAm; NoP; UnTE

Imperial Thumbprint. Tom Weatherly. walk down fifth avenue,hawkbill/in my hand. PoBA

Imperialist. Archie Randolph Ammons. but they I think/resent being owned or/written into roses. GP

Imperious Ox, Imperial Dish: The Buffalo. Marianne Moore. nor with anyone/of ox ancestry. PoA

Impermanence. Lal Ded. For a moment I saw the aunt of a potter's wife. BoWoP

The Impetuous Lover. A. R. D. Fairburn. SPEAK,OR I FIRE! AnNZ

An Impetuous Resolve. James Whitcomb Riley. A-slingin' pie-crust 'long the road/Ferever an' ferever! BiCB

Impetuous Samuel. Harry Graham. So he sha'n't have jam for tea! NA

Impiety (excerpt). Helene Margaret. I have so little time to live;/Thou hast eternity. TrPWD

The Impious Feast. Robert Eyres Landor.
Absolved from guilt, and far remote from shame. OBRV
Far off, with head as high, old Babylon. OBRV
Strives to surpass herself, and still resumes the song. OBRV
Thrice sounded "Nineveh'. OBRV
Two potent sexes all their realms supply,/Whence nature hath its just fertility. OBRV
What were their threats to her, Bel's daughter and his pride! OBRV

Implicit Faith. Aubrey Thomas De Vere. ...whose knowledge hath a touch/Of God's divine simplicity. GoBC

Implora Pace. Charles Lotin Hildreth. "Peace I implore!" and this alone. AA

The Importance of Mirrors. Helga Sandburg. ...The mirror is her open door. IHMS

The Importance of Poetry; or, the Coming Forth from Eternity into Time. Hyam Plutzik. Not for forever, only a day. PP

Important Matters. Charles Mungoshi. It's been a trying day. WhB

Important Statement. Patrick Kavanagh. I'm as happy as I've ever been. PoCh

An Importer. Robert Frost. Teach your grandmother egg suction. FaBoCo

Impossibilities, to His Friend. Robert Herrick. Then there is hope that you may see/Her love me once, who now hates me. OBSP; OLR

The Impossible Dream. Joe Darion. Still strove with his last ounce of courage,/To reach the unreachable stars. BLSo

Impossibly, motivated by midnight. Edward Estlin Cummings. incredible wampum NAMP

Impotence. Marvin Bell. I'm not letting you go. Just turning you over for a while. AmPA

Impotence. Arthur Winfield Knight. "And that's the way it is." SOTS

An Imprecation Against Foes and Sorcerers. Atharva Veda. As Heaven's lightning strikes a tree. WSC

Impression. Sir Edmund Gosse. Ah! for the age when verse was clad,/Being godlike, to be bad and mad. HBV 1-2

Impression. Arthur Symons. Ah, what is this? what wings unfold/In this miraculous rose of gold? SyP

Impression de Nuit: London. Lord Alfred Bruce Douglas. Men creep like thoughts...The lamps are like pale flowers. OBVV

Impression de Paris. Oscar Wilde. Though it be winter, I would break/Into spring blossoms white and blue. SyP

Impression du Matin. Oscar Wilde. With lips of flame and heart of stone. BrPo; CABA; MoBrPo; SyP; VLP

Impression Japonais. Oscar Wilde. Pulling the leaves of pink and pearl/With pale green nails of polished jade. SyP

Impression of a Fountain. Hakushu Kitahara. A dream drips softly. LiTW

Impressionist. Heather McHugh. ...dust/has almost filled/the eyecup of the dead impressionist. MAYP

Impressions. Oscar Wilde.
     Float on the waves like ravelled lace. SyP
     Like little shreds of crimson silk. SyP
     Wrapped in a veil of yellow gauze. SyP
     The young brown-throated reapers pass,/Like silhouettes against the sky. SyP

Impressions, Number III. Edward Estlin Cummings. Bur s/(t into a stale shriek/like an alarm-clock) UnPo

Impressions of Francois-Marie Arouet (de Voltaire) (excerpt). Ezra Pound. Weeping that we can follow naught else. MoAB

Impressions of My Father/I. Country Ways. Marcia Masters. The silence of books settled over the hills. GoYe

L'Imprevisibilite. Zenaida Hippius. My vessel slices/Through the black shadow of uncertainty. PBWP

The Imprisoned. Robert Fitzgerald. Their speech torn to bits in the torrent. MP; TwCP

Imprisoned. Eunice Tietjens. My heart is clumsy, and my speech,/But, brother, hear my cry! HBMV

Impromptu Lines on Being Asked by Sir Thomas Robinson... Philip Stanhope, Earl of Chesterfield. It shall be witty, and it shan't be long. FaBoEE

Improved 4-Way. Tom Veitch. You will never know when a cold may strike. ANYP

The Improved Binoculars. Irving Layton. All this I saw through my improved binoculars. NOBC

Improved Farm Land. Carl Sandburg. to remember once it had a great singing family of trees. RFM

Improvisation on an Old Theme. Dorothy Livesay. The dazzling violence of atomic death. ACV; CaP

Improvisations: Light and Snow (excerpt). Conrad Aiken. I tell you this, young man, so that your expectations of life/Will not be too great. BoNaP

Improvisations on Aesop. Anthony Hecht. Is not that pastoral instruction sweet/Which says who shall be eaten, who shall eat? OBAL

Improvising. Louise Townsend Nicholl. And what it says she never will remember. NePoAm-2

The Impulse of October. W. R. Moses. The careless hand he sickly stings. NCSH

In a Bar near Shibuya Station, Tokyo. Paul Engle. Outside, Toyko growls like a hunting tiger. AmFN; CAD

In a Bath Teashop. Sir John Betjeman. In the teashop's ingle-nook. BoC; ELU; EnLoPo

In a Bed-Sitter. Hal Porter. the gods defrocked, and Troy a rubbish heap. NOAV

In a Boat. Hilaire Belloc. I will hang in your chapel/A ship of pure gold. ISi

In a Bye-Canal. Herman Melville. Brave, wise, and Venus' son. MAmP

In a Cafe. Richard Brautigan. ...or looking/at the photograph of a dead lover. PCP

In a Cafe. Rosemary Dobson. With waves and angels, balanced on a shell. CBAP

In a Cathedral City. Thomas. Hardy. Here might I rest, till my heart shares/The spot's unconsciousness of you! EnLoPo; FaBoPP

In a Cell I Am Bunked. Martial (Marcus Valerius Martialis). Why, the next time I'll visit your trees. DBV

In a Chain-Store Cafeteria. Paul L. Grano. Yes, this is where the People take tea. NOAV

In a Child's Album. William Wordsworth. The Daisy, by the shadow that it casts,/Protects the lingering dew-drop from the sun. GN

In a China Shop. George Sidney Hellman. A star in the Milky Way. AA

In a Churchyard. Richard Wilbur. These unseen gravestones, and the darker dead. HeIP

In a City Square. Eleanor Glenn Wallis. The restless childish hand/Builds dust or sand. NePoAm-2

In a Closed Universe. James Hayford. Whenever god or nation/Moodily says Tut tut. NePoAm-2

In a Copy of Browning. Bliss Carman. Nine years have made you my master still. HBMV

In a Copy of Omar Khayyam. James Russell Lowell Groping, you may like Omar grasp a pearl. AA

In a Corner of Eden... Peter Levi. and breathed a gentle breath such as yellow/fruit or any sleeping beast may. NePoEA-2

In a Country Cemetery in Iowa. Ted Kooser. Just passing through, you'd say/it looks like foolishness. DFF

In a Country Church. R. S. Thomas. ...and a winter tree/Golden with fruit of a man's body. FaBoMo

In a Country Museum. Patricia Beer. And suitably placed among these bright fields of food. FaBoWP

In a Dark Time. Theodore Roethke. And one is One, free in the tearing wind. CAPP; EaLo; HAP; HeIP; MAT; MoAmPo; NoAm; NOBA; NoP; NYBP; PPP; TAP

In a Desert Town. Lionel Stevenson. We do not lack for grace. AmFN

In a Double Rainbow. Harold Littlebird. to make dry arroyos run/as singing summer floods VoR

In a Dream. David Ignatow.
     and I triumph, whirled in the vacuum bag/with my satellite heart, brain, bones and blood. PoA
     Go to hell,/and I walk off. GP

In a Dream. John Millington Synge. That through my grassy grave/Will rack my haunted brain. SyP

In a Dream Ship's Hold. Suzanne Bernhardt. salt end/of the sea dream's/seder/night. VWA

In a Dream, the Automobile. Adrianne Marcus. and we plunge, prison and passenger,/into the thunder!/America! AmC

In a Field. Robert Pack. Never have I wished more/Not to die. MAT; NePoEA-2

In a Garden. Donald Campbell Babcock. An Eden, with my hoe and rake:/the Serpent only God could make. NePoAm

In a Garden. Elizabeth Jennings. ...Sickness for Eden was so strong. NOCV

In a Garret. Elizabeth Akers Allen. And close again the long unopened door. AA

In a Garret. Herman Melville. One dripping trophy! OBAL

In a Ghetto. Jacob Glatstein. is bitten into your believing bones. VWA

In a Glass-Window for Inconstancy. Edward, Lord Herbert of Cherbury. Clearness for me, frailty for her. AnAnS 2; OBSP; SeCP

In a Gondola. Robert Browning. Over your head to sleep I bow. BoLoP; GBL; GTBS; OBEV; OBVV; UnTE

In a Grave-Yard. William Stanley Braithwaite. Dark of night, and light of sun. PoBA

In a Hard Intellectual Light. Richard Eberhart. And brings the solemn, inward pain/Of truth into the heart again. CMoP; LiTM; MoVE

In a Hotel Writing-Room. John Cowper Powys. And we even came to wonder/Where–in the name of thunder–/We had met before this scene. OxBTC

In a Hundred Years. Elizabeth Doten. For 'tis NOT the same in a hundred years! BLPA

In a London Schoolroom. James Kirkup. these last pretenders of an innocence they know is vain. GLGT

In a London Terminus. John Lehmann. That we may grow as we would be. AtBAP

In a Lovely Garden Walking. Ludwig Uhland. He far in the dungeon-tower! AWP

In a Low Rocking-Chair. Helen Coale Crew. Come back along to me. HBMV

In a Maple Wood. Pat Schneider. in ancient cryptic blessing/on our heads. AMV-81

In a Meadow. John Swinnerton Phillimore. These are her gifts which all mankind may use,/And all refuse. OBEV; OBVV

In a Mirror. Marcia Stubbs. The hill steep and slick, and what/One other reason do I fumble over? MAT

In a Mist. Al Young. ...Life is too long and always too short. AMV-80

In a Moonlit Hermit's Cabin.   Allen, Ginsberg.   Setting up the flag!   MOON

In a Motion.   Laura Chester.   ...That's what it's come back for,/to set you on your way, gladly, with a hum–An approval.   NPGG

In a Mountain Cabin in Norway.   Robert Bly.   No one comes to visit us for a week.   RFM

In a Museum.   Babette Deutsch.   Since death is close, and death is death for us.   HBMV

In a Museum.   Thomas Hardy.   In the full-fugued song of the universe unending.   UnS

In a Museum Cabinet.   May Swenson.   as through gray caves of coral by the sea.   WSC

In a Museum in the Capital.   William Stafford.   while an avalanche whispers our names.   LCAP

In a Night.   Ann Marie Savage.   into a whirlpool of dust, stirred up/one mile deep.   AMV-81

In a Parlor Containing a Table.   Galway Kinnell.   You too. You too. You too.   ELU; NLV; OBSP

In a Poem.   Robert Frost.   As surely as it keeps the stroke and time/In having its undeniable say.   PP

In a Prominent Bar in Secaucus One Day.   X. J. Kennedy.   And she blew us a kiss as they copped her away/From that prominent bar in Secaucus, N.J.   ConAP; FYAP; HoAn; HoPM; NIP; NLV; OBAL; PoCh; PPP; UnTE

In a Province.   Frank Templeton Prince.   And under a clear sky, under a clear green sky.   MoVE

In a Railway Compartment.   John Fuller.   Who roared and reached and caught and held her there.   NePoEA-2

In a Remote Cloister Bordering the Empyrean.   Joel Sloman.   Like Samson, I'm in the dark,/and continue to ride the bus.   VGW

In a Rose Garden.   John Bennett.   We'll build one castle more in Spain,/And dream one more dream there.   BLPA; FaBoBe; HBV 1-2

In a Season of Unemployment.   Margaret Avison.   he is feeling/excellent too, I guess, and/weightless and/"smiling'.   NOBC

In a Shoreham Garden.   Laurence Lerner.   The sunshine of achievement/Ripens nothing there.   NePoEA-2

In a Shuttered Room I Roast.   Dylan Thomas.   And the weather drives me pazzo.   OBTV

In a Spring Grove.   William Allingham.   Each and all these,–and more, and more than these!   IrPN

In a Spring Still Not Written Of.   Robert Wallace.   the beautiful and young/all poems are for.   BoNaP; PP

In a Staffordshire Churchyard.   *Anonymous*.   And I be buried here.   PoPle

In a Station of the Metro.   Ezra Pound.   Petals on a wet, black bough.   AmP; AmPP; CAD; ExPo; ForPo; HAP; HeIP; InPK; MoAB; MoAmPo; NIP; NoAm; NOBA; NoP; OxBA; TAP; UnPo; VGW; WeW

In a Surrealist Year.   Lawrence Ferlinghetti.   And lost teacups/full of our ashes/floated by   PPON

In a Town Garden.   Donald Mattam.   As every urchin by my fence/Notes for future reference.   ELU; FiBHP

In a Train.   Robert Bly.   I have awakened at Missoula, Montana, utterly happy.   CAPP; NaP; PoL

In a tyme of a somer's day.   *Anonymous*.   And than ys best: "Revertere."   EnPo

In a U-Haul North of Damascus.   David Bottoms.   ...Could I be moved/to believe in new beginnings? Could I be moved?   FYAP; MAYP

In a Valley of This Restless Mind.   Ewart Milne.   Lit by a lonely wing, gliding small as snowflake and as silently.   NeIP

In a Warm Bath.   Carl Rakosi.   Bless this water./I must bathe more often.   TAP

In a Wine Cellar.   Victor J. Daley.   Pledge deep our land in/Our land's own wine!   PoAu 1-2

In a Wood.   E. J. Scovell.   But gives me love and weeping.   GBL

In a Wood Clearing.   Wilson MacDonald.   And the wash of her hair that fell about me like rain.   CaP

In a World of Change.   Joseph Awad.   O unchanging Truth.   AMV-80

In A Year.   Robert Browning.   Is it God?   AtBAP

In After Days.   George Frederick Cameron.   Are dead and coffined with her foes.   CaP

In After Days.   Henry Austin Dobson.   Will none?–Then let my memory die/In after days!   EnLit; HBV 1-2; OBEV; OBVV; TreFS

In After Time.   Richard Eberhart.   And man shall know again his richness.   MoRP

In Air.   Peter Clarke.   Five gleaming crows/Float blackly/On wide-stretched air.   PBA

In All the Argosy of Your Bright Hair.   Dunstan Thompson.   ...O my heirs,/You of the equal sadness, give him your prayers.   WaP

In All the Days of My Childhood.   Russell Edson.   ...And so it was in all the days of my childhood.   AmPA

In All the Magic of Christmas Time.   John Jacob Niles.   And gentle Mary, mother mild,/Did comfort Christ, the blessed child.   AH

In All These Acts.   William Everson.   Shaping the weasel's jaw in His leap/And the staggering rush of the bass.   NoP

In Allusion to the French Song, N'entendez Vous Pas ce Language.   Richard Lovelace.   This language wants both tongue and voice.   CaPo

In Ampezzo.   Trumbull Stickney.   Parcel of columbines.   AnFE; APA; CoAnAm; CrMA; NCEP

In an Album.   James Russell Lowell.   In vain, "This Lowell, who was he?"   OBAL

In an Alien Place.   Leib Neidus.   as the beginning longs for the end.   VWA

In an Arab Town.   Susan Tichy.   giggling all the way/about some fat unmarried neighbor/or some poor man's cock.   MAYP

In an Arbour Green.   Robert Weever.   In youth is pleasure, in youth is pleasure.   ELP

In an Artist's Studio.   Christina Georgina Rossetti.   Not as she is, but as she fills his dream.   EnLi 1-2; NoP; OAEP

In an Autumn Wood.   William Alexander Percy.   I love thy loveliness that hears no cry.   HBMV

In an Empty Window.   Ray Fraser.   The giant presence of a terrible God.   NeAC

In an Hour the Sun.   Ray Freed.   I won't fish those waters again.   WOLT

In an Iridescent Time.   Ruth Stone.   Brown gingham, pink, and skirts of Alice blue.   MoAmPo; PoPl

In an Old House.   Spencer Brown.   And had a story left out of their lives.   NYBP

In an Old Library.   Yuan Mei.   Ten thousand yesterdays are gathered here.   LiTW

In an Old Nursery.   Patrick Reginald Chalmers.   Like bees that haunt the lavender/Of some walled garden!   HBMV

In an Old Orchard.   Peter Kane Dufault.   ...still pitifully gathering all/windfalls onto its damp lap of graves.   NYBP

In Ancient December.   Alice Notley.   Singing singing? What am I singing?   APU

In and Out.   L. E. Sissman.   Up the airshaft to where I lie, not quite alone.   NYBP

In and Out: Severance of Connections, 1946.   L. E. Sissman.   Selects his Single, and stands out to sea.   TwCP

In and Out the Bushes, Up the Ivy.   Randall Jarrell.   With its last light: the chipmunk/Dives to his rest.   BoAnP

In Answer of an Elegiacall Letter upon the Death of the King of Sweden.   Thomas Carew.   And dance, and revell then, as we doe now.   AnAnS 2

In Answer to a Question.   Wilfrid Scawen Blunt.   –'Tis conscience makes us sinners, not our sin.   ViBoPo

In Answer to Your Query.   Naomi Lazard.   Yours will be filed accordingly,/answered in its turn.   GP; NLV

In Apia Bay.   Sir Charles G. D. Roberts.   The old fire yet survives,/Here in our modern lives,/Of splendid chivalry and valor high!   PAH

In April.   Ethelwyn Wetherald.   Dissolved in blossom dew, and washed away/In delicate spring rains.   CaP

In Arcadia.   Lawrence Durrell.   Something died out by this river: but it seems/Less than a nightingale ago.   MoBrPo

In Arcady.   Cosmo Monkhouse.   Laugh, laugh your loudest.)   OBVV

In Arden.   Charles Tomlinson.   And time itself must beat to the cadence of this river.   OxBC

In Arizona.   Louis Zukofsky.   Warms what one/can imagine to be its ears.   NoAm

In Assisi.   Michael C. Blumenthal.   and all the white doves kissing in its name.   MAYP

In Autumn.   Jon Anderson.   ...must now love/The passage of time.   AmPA

In Autumn.   Barbara Howes.   A stag dormant, antlered?   LiSp

In Autumn When the Woods Are Red.   Robert Louis Stevenson.   In Autumn when the woods are red/And skies are grey and clear.   NOBV

In Back of the Real.   Allen Ginsberg.   This is the flower of the World.   AmPP; HeIP

In Barracks.   Siegfried Sassoon.   The bugle's dying notes that say,/"Another night; another day."   FaBoTw

In Bed.   Myra Sklarew.   ...the afternoon sun/encircling her.   AMV-81

In Bed with a River.   George Bradley.   A tooth, five-cusped: man.   AMV-80

In Bertram's Garden.   Donald Justice.   Naked to the naked moon.   BoLoP; ErPo; NePoEA; VGW

In Between the Curve.   Barbara Bacon.   to dally by the edge of the stream.   AMV-80

In Black Chasms.   Leslie Norris.   For they are needed against ogres.   WSC

In Blanco County.   Russell T. Fowler.   that life, if nothing else,/is something he knows.   AMV-80

In Bloemfontein.   Alan Ross.   But here, in Bloemfontein,/Keep closed the door.   BoLoP

In Blue (parody).   D. C. Berry.   and I'm ringing the blonde's/door bell my eyes are just right   BXAP

In Bohemia. Arthur Symons. And how the sunlight strikes us dumb! BrPo; SyP

In Bondage. Claude McKay. O black men, simple slaves of ruthless slaves. PoBA

In Brittany. Charles Weekes. And you may pray there, sir, for me. OnYI

In Broken Images. Robert Graves. I in a new understanding of my confusion. PPoe

In Brunton Town. Anonymous. The wind did blow and it ain't no wonder/ And they (?) blew them both into their graves. BaBo

In Cabin'd Ships at Sea. Walt Whitman. This song for mariners and all their ships. MOS

In California. Louis Simpson. ...cloud wagons move/outward still, dreaming of a Pacific. NoAm

In Camus Fields. Leonard Alfred George Strong. Something should break, the tunnel or his heart. DBV

In Canterbury Cathedral. E. W. Oldenburg. ...two words/turned sightseers into pilgrims. EBCP

In Carrowdore Churchyard. Derek Mahon. Rinsing the choked mud, keeping the colours new. CIP; FaBoIP

In Celebration. Ellen Bass. I feasted on your vintage. NMM

In Celebration of My Uterus. Anne Sexton. for the correct/yes. CAPP

In Cemeteries. D. J. Enright. Almost see the made souls, in their/Curious glory. If you are old. OxBC

In Chagall's Village. Rose Auslander. golden wolves are/guarding the lambs. VWA

In Childbed. Thomas Hardy. Such strange things did mother say to me. NAs

In Christ. John Oxenham. His service is the golden cord/Close binding all mankind. STF

In Church. Thomas Hardy. That had moved the congregation so. BrPo; DiPo; DTC; SCV

In Cipres Springes (Wheras Dame Venus Dwelt). Henry Howard, Earl of Surrey. My service thus is growne into disdayne. AAS

In City Streets. Ada Smith. Through the peaty soil and tinkling heather-bells. HBV 1-2

In Clementina's Artless Mien. Walter Savage Landor. Ah yes, Lucilla! and their fall/I still deplore. ViBoPo

In Clonmel Parish Churchyard. Sarah Piatt. In the churchyard of Clonmel? AA

In Cnidus Born, the Consort I Became. Heraclides. To Pluto's realm, till he shall join me there. OBVE

In Cold Hell, In Thicket. Charles Olson. precise as hell is, precise/as any words, or wagon,/can be made PoM

In Cold Storm Light. Leslie Marmon Silko. strands of mist/tangled in rocks/and leaves. NoP; VoR

In Columbus, Ohio. John Matthias. ...I start the car and drive on East/as far as Philadelphia. AMV-80

In Come de Animuls Two by Two. Anonymous. I knows it, dem bones gona rise agin. GBP

In Commendation of George Gascoigne's Steel Glass (1576). Sir Walter Ralegh. As for the verse, who list like trade to try,/I fear me much, shall hardly reach so high. SiPS

In Commendation of Music. William Strode. And change his soul for harmony. ELP; OBEV

In Common. Gene Derwood. Souls immortal we descry. NePA; PoPl

In Computers. Alan P. Lightman. Nothing will be lost. SUW

In Conjunction. Charles Madge. Among alarms, rust and the dead, waiting to be blest. NeBP

In Consort to Wednesday, Jan. 1st. 1701... Richard Henchman. Whose full-Possession (to it's utmost Line)/By an Eternal Gift, is firmly Thine. SCAP

In Cool, Green Haunts. Mahlon Leonard Fisher. "A little brown-eyed fawn was born today!" WeW

In Country Sleep. Dylan Thomas. Your faith as deathless as the outcry of the ruled sun. LiTB

In Coventry. James J. Daly. I wonder what is brewing. CAW

In Crisis. Lawrence Durrell. And O the rose grow in the middle of the great world. LiTM

In Dark Hour. Seumas MacManus. Dear God, be kind with the heart-sick child/Who steps on the Lonely Road. WGRP

In Dat Great Gittin' Up Mornin'. Anonymous. In dat great gittin' up mornin'/Fare you well, Fare you well. AA; BoAN 1-2

In Days of New. Elizabeth Bartlett. His eyes now charged with fire/ready to strangle her. AMV-81

In De Vinter Time (with music). Anonymous. Rid de veloc'pede in de vestibule,/Ah, vimmens! Ah, mens! AS

In Deadly Fear. William Blake. Among the Furnaces of Los in the Valley of the Son of Hinnom. SeCePo

In Dear Detail, by Ideal Light. William Stafford. by ideal light all around us. NaP

In Death. Mary Emily Bradley. O Death, the loveliness that is in thee,/Could the world know, the world would/cease to be. AA

In Death Divided. Thomas Hardy. Stretching across the miles that sever you from me. DTC

In Death's Field. Al-Khansa. and every treaty is erased by time. BoWoP

In December. Andrew Young. With her moist mouth through half the year. SeCePo

In Defense of Black Poets. Conrad Kent Rivers. shall survive the then of then,/the now of now. BOLo; BPo

In Defense of Felons. Robert Mezey. Winter and earth to ashes with its love. NePoEA

In Defense of Metaphysics. Charles Tomlinson. ...Stones are like deaths./ They uncover limits. MoBrPo

In Defense of Satire. Sir Carr Scroope. The world's a wood in which all lose their way,/Though by a diff'rent path each goes astray. APAS

In Defense of Superficiality. Elder Olson. Accept this final bubble,/From one drowned. NYBP

In Defiance to the Dutch. Anonymous. So may his high exploits at last make even/With earth his honor, glory with the Heaven. APAS

In Despair. Constantine P. Cavafy. he longs to feel his kind of love once more. PeHV

In Despair He Orders a New Typewriter. Elder Olson. Unmistakable period. AMV-81

In Dessexshire as It Befel. Anonymous. For breaking of the Lord's birthday. GBP

In Detroit. R. R. Cuscaden. Drifting up and down Woodward Avenue. PoL

In Disguise. Joseph Rolnik. By now more than one king/Has wandered in disguise. VWA

In Dispraise of Poetry. Jack Gilbert. It appears the gift could not be refused. PP

In Dispraise of the Moon. Mary Elizabeth Coleridge. That light, reflected, but makes darkness plain. BoNaP; CH; MOON; NBM

In Distress. David Wagoner. Nothing can be done until daylight. SUW

In Distrust of Merits. Marianne Moore. Beauty is everlasting/and dust is for a time. AP; CoBMV; EaLo; LiTA; LiTM; MoAB; MoAmPo; NePA; OBWP; OxBA; SeCeV; TreFT; TrGrPo; ViBoPo; WaaP; WaP

In Dives' Dive. Robert Frost. Let's have a look at another five. VGW

In Dream. John Millington Synge. Might meet their Christ in sleep. SyP

In Dream: The Privacy of Sequence. Ray A. Young Bear. made the boy dream/that he had rubbed his hands/against the sky. CDW

In Due Season. W. H. Auden. ...bearing a message from/The invisible sole Source of specific things. Prf

In Dulci Jubilo. Anonymous. O that we were there! O that we were there! CAW

In Earliest Spring. William Dean Howells. Leafless there by my door, trembled a sense of the rose. AA; FaBoBe

In Early Spring. Alice Meynell. Sweet Earth, we know thy dimmest mysteries,/But he is lord of his. AnFE; HBV 1-2

In Early Summer Lodging in a Temple to Enjoy the Moonlight. Po Chu-i. Such moods as this, how many men know? LiTW

In Earthen Vessels. John Greenleaf Whittier. The blessed Master none can doubt,/Revealed in holy lives. BLRP; TRV

In Egypt. Paul Celan. Behold, I slept with them! VWA

In England's Green &. Jonathan Williams. crawl, all/exits/from/ hibernaculum! CoPo

In eternum I was once determed. Sir Thomas Wyatt. Now in the place another thought doth rest,/In eternum. AAS; FCP; NOBE; SiPS

In Evening Air. Theodore Roethke. How slowly dark comes down on what we do. CAPP; NYBP; TAP

In Every Thing Give Thanks. Anonymous. "In every thing give thanks." STF

In Evil Long I Took Delight. John Newton. That I should such a life destroy,–/Yet live by Him I kill'd! OxBoCh

In Exile. Blanche Edith Baughan. For parting me and you. ACV; AnNZ

In Exile. Emma Lazarus. And truth's perpetual lamp forbid to wane. SBG

In Explanation. Walter Learned. That–what else could I do? AA; HBV 1-2

In Extremis. Margaret Fishback. And that is nothing short of hell. FiBHP

In Extremis. George Sterling. But near the eternal Peace I lay, nor stirred,/Knowing the happy dead hear not at all. HBV 1-2

In faith I wot not well what to say. Sir Thomas Wyatt. But spite of thy hap, hap hath well happed. FCP; SiPS

In Favor of One's Time. Frank O'Hara. and we live outside his garden in our tempestuous rights NeAP; PoA

In February. Henry Simpson. Go, little verse, and lay in vesture meet/Of poesy, my homage at her feet. HBV 1-2

In February. John Addington Symonds. And the year hath not worn to March. YeAr

In Festubert. Edmund Charles Blunden. And sear no more with second sight. OBMV

In Fields of Summer. Galway Kinnell. A lark bursts up all dew. BoNaP; RFM; VGW

In Fine, Transparent Words. David Vogel. Even a little joy/Is too heavy for us to bear. VWA

In Flanders Fields. John McCrae. We shall not sleep, though poppies grow/In Flanders fields. BBV; BLPA; CaP; FaBV; FaFP; FaPo; FaPoR; FPL; GoTF; GTBS; HBV 1-2; MCCG; NOBC; OBCV; OBWP; OHFP; PAL; PeCV; PGD; PoPl; SiSoSe; TreF; ViBoPo

In flight in escape. Nelly Sachs. I clutch the world's mutations. BoWoP

In Foreign Parts. Laura E. Richards. And no more I'll go a-rovering beyond the harbor bar. HBV 1-2; HBVY

In former days we'd both agree. Bhartrihari. That you are you, and I am me? BoLoP

In France. Frances Cornford. The poplars in the fields of France,/Like glorious ladies come to dance. HBMV

In Francum. Sir John Davies. To make myself his wench but one half hour. FaBoEE

In Freiburg Station. Rupert Brooke. I saw a Bishop with puce gloves go by. OBTV

In Front of a Japanese Photograph. John Peck. And looking, that we stand where he had stood. SM

In Front of the Landscape. Thomas Hardy. Whithersoever his footsteps turn in his farings,/Save a few tombs? OBNC

In Front of the Seine, Recalling the Rio De La Plata. Silvina Ocampo. some just discovered face that once was ours. AMV-80

In Fur. William Stafford. They stand together. The future comes. RFM

In Fuscum. Sir John Davies. But falls into a whore-house by the way. FaBoEE

In Gaetam. Thomas Bastard. He swole to be a Lord: and then he burst. FaBoEE

In Galilee. Mary Frances Butts. And still the lilies bloom in Galilee. AA

In Galilee. Jessie MacKay. To stand before their God in Heaven. AnNZ

In Galleries. Randall Jarrell. A quarter's worth of nickel and aluminum. EyDe

In Glencullen. John Millington Synge. I think I robbed your ancestors/When I was young as you. ELU; FM; OBMV; OxBI

In Go-Cart So Tiny. Kate Greenway. Because our trip's always/Put off till to-morrow. TiPo

In God's Eternal Studios. Paul Shivell. While deep within our souls it glows/From all His starry studios! HBV 1-2

In God's Eternity. Hosea Ballou I. A ceaseless song of praise begin,/And shout redeeming grace. AH

In gold sandals. Sappho. dawn like a thief/fell upon me. BoWoP

In Golden Gate Park That Day. Lawrence Ferlinghetti. except a certain awful look/of terrible depression NoAm

In Good Old Colony Times. Anonymous. With the broadcloth under his arm. BFSS

In Goya's Greatest Scenes. Lawrence Ferlinghetti. and engines/that devour America HeIP; NMP; NoAm; TAP

In Grandfather's Glasses. Patricia Peters. Plane clenched in insubstantial clouds tattering like cobwebs/on wings catching flame. Str

In Grato Jubilo. David McCord. The sound as when a time of singing willed it so! UnS

In Green Old Gardens. Violet Fane. To hold my faith, and to live my life,/Making the most of its shadowy day. HBV 1-2

In-Group. Lionel Kearns. Had theirs/nailed down/too. PeCV

In Guernsey. Algernon Charles Swinburne. But grief shone here, while joy was one with/shame,/Beloved and blest. VLP

In Hades. Anna Callender Brackett. He knew the whole–and could not choose/but turn! AA

In Harbor. Paul Hamilton Hayne. The heavenly harbor at last! AA; HBV 1-2

In Harbor. Lizette Woodworth Reese. Yet, Lord, I wait Thy will. TrPWD

In Harbour. Algernon Charles Swinburne. Is grief still sleeping, is joy not sighing/Outside? VLP

In Hardin County, 1809. Lulu E. Thompson. That nothin' happens down this way. PoSC; StPo

In Hardwood Groves. Robert Frost. I know that this is the way in ours. AmLP; HAP

In Harmony with Nature. Matthew Arnold. Fool, if thou canst not pass her, rest her/slave! OAEP

In health and ease am I. Francis Davison. That, dead unto myself, in you I live. EG

In Heaven, I Suppose, Lie down Together. C. Day-Lewis. Promise of ground below the sprawling flood. MoPo

In Heaven Soaring Up. Edward Taylor. As they to glory ride therein. AH

In Heavenly Realms of Hellas Dwelt. Edward Estlin Cummings. soldier,beware of mrs smith NOBA; OBSV

In Heavy Mind I Strayed the Field. James Agee. And all my will was not enough/to hold the heavens out of me. MoAmPo

In Hellbrunn. Georg Trakl. The golden cloud above the pond. LiTW

In Her Boudoir, the Young Lady,–Unacquainted with Grief. Anonymous. Regrets she made her dear husband go to win a fief. OBVE

In Her Only Way. Robert Graves. She both loved you and hurt you/In her only way. OBSP

In Her Praise. Robert Graves. Woman is mortal woman. She abides. BIrV

In Her Song She Is Alone. Jon Swan. I listened, beyond mourning, for her wings. NYBP

In High Places. Harriet Monroe. The spirit-crowded courts of solitude. PoA

In Him. James Vila Blake. Or in the sea each watery spiritual sphere. WGRP

In Him. Annie Johnson Flint. Eternal in the heav'ns this dwelling stands. BLRP; TRV

In Him We Live. Jones Very. Till in thy perfect love I ever live and/move. AmP; OxBA

In His Mental Illness, William Cowper Finds He Is Not Alone. William Cowper. With few associates, and not wishing more. BoC

In His Service. Clarence E. Clar. Content in His love, you will never grow/old. STF

In His Steps. Katharine Lee Bates. Prints of the gentle feet whose passing healed/All blight from Tabor unto Olivet? PGD

In His Utter Wretchedness. John Audelay. Yif thou be nyd night or day,/Say, "Passio Christi conforta me." MeEL

In Hoc Signo. Godfrey Fox Bradby. Its King a servant, and its sign/A gibbet on a hill. TRV

In Honor of St. Alphonsus Rodriguez. Gerard Manley Hopkins. That in Majorca Alfonso watched the door. EBEV; ForPo

In Honour of Christmas. Anonymous. My semely lorde, for your sake:/Good day! MeEL

In Honour of Taffy Topaz. Christopher Morley. What fun to be a cat! TiPo

In Honour of That High and Mighty Princess Queen Elizabeth... Anne Bradstreet. If many worlds, as that fantastic framed,/In every one be her great glory famed. SBG

In Hospital. James Elroy Flecker. And all that lake a dewdrop on a rose. OxBTC

In Hospital. William Ernest Henley.
But her lip was gray and writhen. VLP
Into the wonderful world. BrPo
Life is (I think) a blunder and a shame. VLP
You carry Caesar and his fortunes–steady! VLP

In Hospital: Poona. Alun Lewis.
But love survives the venom of the snake. DTC; NeBP; SeCePo
The heart's calm voice that stills the baying hounds. DTC

In Hotels Public and Private. Ralph Pomeroy. Groom into singing clans. CoPo

In Humbleness. Daniel Gerard Hoffman. Read this in the histories:/Newsweek, or Thucydides. NePA

In Iceland. Howard McCord. or a bottle of good Polish/vodka gone from your tent. GP

In Imitation of Anacreon. Matthew Prior. And lose the Nymph, to gain the Bays. CEP; FaBoEE

In Immemoriam. Cuthbert (Edward Bradley) Bede. O voices all! like you I die! NA

In Impressions of Hawk Feathers Willow Leaves Shadow. Elizabeth Woody. The cry is my own, the force of breath/the last blossoms to grow. STE

In India. Karl Shapiro. Received his blessing and then shot him dead. NYBP

In Innocence. J. V. Cunningham. As mendicants who see/Mimic the blind. OBSP

In Its Place. Carol Stager. the blue settled, finally,/in the sky. AMV-80

In Jail. Juan Antonio Corretjer. your heart, raised high in your hand,/flowers over the wall.) InW

In January, 1962. Ted Kooser. ...hands which lay curled and still/near the soft gray felt hat on the table. Psk

In Jerusalem Are Women. Arye Sivan. of a man who sits among his dead/like me, here, now. VWA

In Judgment of the Leaf. Kenneth Patchen. In the earth of your eyes, in easy wonder building God. VGW

In June. Nora Perry. The plover's piping note, now here, now there. YeAr

In June and Gentle Oven. Anne Wilkinson. Aloof from seasons, flowing. NOBC; PeCV

In Just-. Edward Estlin Cummings. balloonMan whistles/far/and/wee AmPP; FaBV; HeIP; InPK; NCSH; NoP; PrIm; SoSe

In Kansas. Anonymous. They just tumble into bed, in Kansas. FSW

In Kensington Gardens. Arthur Symons. Hey for the heart's delight! EnLoPo

In Kerry. John Millington Synge. Had built this stack of thigh-bones, jaws and shins. AWP; FaBoPP; GBL; MoBrPo

And at the spiritual prime/Rewaken with the dawning soul. OBNC
Reawaken with the dawning soul. VLP

In Memoriam A.H.H., XLIV. Alfred, Lord Tennyson. My guardian angel will speak out/In that high place, and tell thee all. VLP

In Memoriam A.H.H., XLV. Alfred, Lord Tennyson. Had man to learn himself anew/Beyond the second birth of Death. VLP

In Memoriam A.H.H., XLVI. Alfred, Lord Tennyson. A rosy warmth from marge to marge. VLP

In Memoriam A.H.H., XLVII. Alfred, Lord Tennyson. "Farewell! We lose ourselves in light." VLP

In Memoriam A.H.H., XLVIII. Alfred, Lord Tennyson. ...that dip/Their wings in tears, and skim away. VLP

In Memoriam A.H.H., XLIX. Alfred, Lord Tennyson. Whose muffled motions blindly drown/The bases of my life in tears. VLP

In Memoriam A.H.H., L. Alfred, Lord Tennyson. And on the low dark verge of life/The twilight of eternal day. ELP; NAWM 1-2; PoEL 1-5; SCV

In Memoriam A.H.H., LI. Alfred, Lord Tennyson. To make allowance for us all. VLP

In Memoriam A.H.H., LII. Alfred, Lord Tennyson. When Time hath sunder'd shell from pearl. VLP

In Memoriam A.H.H., LIII. Alfred, Lord Tennyson. Procuress to the Lords of Hell. VLP

In Memoriam A.H.H., LIV. Alfred, Lord Tennyson. And with no language but a cry. BiP; LoBV; NAWM 1-2; OAEL 1-2; OAEP; OBNC; TreFS; TrGrPo; WGRP

In Memoriam A.H.H., LV. Alfred, Lord Tennyson. And faintly trust the larger hope. HBV 1-2; LoBV; NAWM 1-2; OAEL 1-2; OAEP; OBNC

In Memoriam A.H.H., LVI. Alfred, Lord Tennyson. Behind the veil, behind the veil. HBV 1-2; LoBV; NAWM 1-2; OAEL 1-2; OAEP; OBNC

In Memoriam A.H.H., LVII. Alfred, Lord Tennyson. "Adieu, adieu" for evermore. VLP

In Memoriam A.H.H., LVIII. Alfred, Lord Tennyson. And thou shalt take a nobler leave. VLP

In Memoriam, A.H.H., LIX. Alfred, Lord Tennyson. Could barely tell what name were thine. VLP

In Memoriam A.H.H., LX. Alfred, Lord Tennyson. How should he love a thing so low? VLP

In Memoriam A.H.H., LXII. Alfred, Lord Tennyson. Or in the light of deeper eyes/Is matter for a flying smile. VLP

In Memoriam A.H.H., LXIV. Alfred, Lord Tennyson. "Does my old friend remember me?" VLP

In Memoriam A.H.H., LXV. Alfred, Lord Tennyson. A part of mine may live in thee/And move thee on to noble ends. VLP

In Memoriam A.H.H., LXVII. Alfred, Lord Tennyson. Thy tablet glimmers to the dawn. LoBV; OAEL 1-2; OAEP; SeCePo

In Memoriam A.H.H., LXVIII. Alfred, Lord Tennyson. That foolish sleep transfers to thee. VLP

In Memoriam A.H.H., LXIX. Alfred, Lord Tennyson. The words were hard to understand. VLP

In Memoriam A.H.H., LXX. Alfred, Lord Tennyson. And thro' a lattice on the soul/Looks thy fair face and makes it still. NOBV; VLP

In Memoriam A.H.H., LXXI. Alfred, Lord Tennyson. The breaker breaking on the beach. VLP

In Memoriam A.H.H., LXXII. Alfred, Lord Tennyson. And hide thy shame beneath the ground. VLP

In Memoriam A.H.H., LXXIII. Alfred, Lord Tennyson. And self-infolds the large results/Of force that would have forged a name. HBV 1-2

In Memoriam A.H.H., LXXIV. Alfred, Lord Tennyson. Nor speak it, knowing Death has made/His darkness beautiful with thee. LiTB; VLP

In Memoriam A.H.H., LXXV. Alfred, Lord Tennyson. Whate'er thy hands are set to do/Is wrought with tumult of acclaim. VLP

In Memoriam A.H.H.,LXXVI. Alfred, Lord Tennyson. And what are they when these remain/The ruin'd shells of hollow towers? VLP

In Memoriam A.H.H., LXXVII. Alfred, Lord Tennyson. To utter love more sweet than praise. OAEL 1-2; PP

In Memoriam A.H.H., LXXVIII. Alfred, Lord Tennyson. But with long use her tears are dry. NAWM 1-2; OAEL 1-2; OAEP

In Memoriam A.H.H., LXXIX. Alfred, Lord Tennyson. And he supplied my want the more/As his unlikeness fitted mine. OAEL 1-2; OAEP

In Memoriam A.H.H., LXXXI. Alfred, Lord Tennyson. It might have drawn from after-heat. VLP

In Memoriam A.H.H., LXXXII. Alfred, Lord Tennyson. He put our lives so far apart/We cannot hear each other speak. LiTB

In Memoriam A.H.H., LXXXIII. Alfred, Lord Tennyson. That longs to burst a frozen bud/And flood a fresher throat with song. NOBV; VLP

In Memoriam A.H.H., LXXXIV. Alfred, Lord Tennyson. ...and break/The low beginnings of content. VLP

In Memoriam A.H.H., LXXXV. Alfred, Lord Tennyson. The primrose of the later year,/As not unlike to that of Spring. VLP

In Memoriam A.H.H., LXXXVI. Alfred, Lord Tennyson. A hundred spirits whisper "Peace." VLP

In Memoriam A.H.H., LXXXVII. Alfred, Lord Tennyson. And over those ethereal eyes/The bar of Michael Angelo. VLP

In Memoriam A.H.H., LXXXVIII. Alfred, Lord Tennyson. The glory of the sum of things/Will flash along the chords and go. NoP; PBBP; VLP

In Memoriam A.H.H., LXXXIX. Alfred, Lord Tennyson. And buzzings of the honied hours. VLP

In Memoriam A.H.H., XC. Alfred, Lord Tennyson. I find not yet one lonely thought/That cries against my wish for thee. VLP

In Memoriam A.H.H., XCI. Alfred, Lord Tennyson. Come, beauteous in thine after form,/And like a finer light in light. OBNC

In Memoriam A.H.H., XCII. Alfred, Lord Tennyson. And such refraction of events/As often rises ere thy rise. VLP

In Memoriam A.H.H., XCIV. Alfred, Lord Tennyson. They can but listen at the gates,/And hear the household jar within. VLP

In Memoriam A.H.H., XCV. Alfred, Lord Tennyson. To broaden into boundless day. GTBS-P; LoBV; NAWM 1-2; OAEL 1-2; OAEP; PoEL 1-5

In Memoriam A.H.H., XCVI. Alfred, Lord Tennyson. Although the trumpet blew so loud. WGRP

In Memoriam A.H.H., XCVII. Alfred, Lord Tennyson. "I cannot understand: I love." VLP

In Memoriam A.H.H., XCVIII. Alfred, Lord Tennyson. The rocket molten into flakes/Of crimson or in emerald rain. VLP

In Memoriam A.H.H., XCIX. Alfred, Lord Tennyson. They know me not, but mourn with me. VLP

In Memoriam A.H.H., C. Alfred, Lord Tennyson. I think once more he seems to die. VLP

In Memoriam A.H.H., CI. Alfred, Lord Tennyson. And year by year our memory fades/From all the circle of the hills. ELP; FaBoPP; GTBS-P; PoEL 1-5; PoPle; SCV

In Memoriam A.H.H., CII. Alfred, Lord Tennyson. They mix in one another's arms/To one pure image of regret. PoEL 1-5

In Memoriam A.H.H., CIII. Alfred, Lord Tennyson. We steer'd her toward a crimson cloud/That landlike slept along the deep. OAEP; PoEL 1-5

In Memoriam A.H.H., CIV. Alfred, Lord Tennyson. But all is new unhallow'd ground. SBVL; VLP

In Memoriam A.H.H., CV. Alfred, Lord Tennyson. Run out your measured arcs, and lead/The closing cycle rich in good. VLP

In Memoriam A.H.H., CVI. Alfred, Lord Tennyson. Ring in the Christ that is to be. HBV 1-2; NAWM 1-2; OAEL 1-2; OAEP; OFD; TreF; TrGrPo

In Memoriam A.H.H., CVII. Alfred, Lord Tennyson. And sing the songs he loved to hear. SBVL; VLP

In Memoriam A.H.H., CVIII. Alfred, Lord Tennyson. Whatever wisdom sleep with thee. SBVL; VLP

In Memoriam A.H.H., CIX. Alfred, Lord Tennyson. Nor let thy wisdom make me wise. VLP

In Memoriam A.H.H., CX. Alfred, Lord Tennyson. And, born of love, the vague desire/That spurs an imitative will. VLP

In Memoriam A.H.H., CXI. Alfred, Lord Tennyson. Defamed by every charlatan,/And soil'd with all ignoble use. VLP

In Memoriam A.H.H., CXII. Alfred, Lord Tennyson. And world-wide fluctuation sway'd/In vassal tides that follow'd thought. VLP

In Memoriam A.H.H., CXIII. Alfred, Lord Tennyson. And undulations to and fro. VLP

In Memoriam A.H.H., CXIV. Alfred, Lord Tennyson. And knowledge, but by year and hour/In reverence and in charity. VLP

In Memoriam A.H.H., CXV. Alfred, Lord Tennyson. And buds and blossoms like the rest. GTBS-P; HBV 1-2; NOBE; OAEP; OBNC

In Memoriam A.H.H., CXVI. Alfred, Lord Tennyson. Less yearning for the friendship fled,/Than some strong bond which is to be. VLP

In Memoriam A.H.H., CXVII. Alfred, Lord Tennyson. And all the courses of the suns. VLP

In Memoriam A.H.H., CXVIII. Alfred, Lord Tennyson. And let the ape and tiger die. SeCeV; VLP

In Memoriam A.H.H., CXIX. Alfred, Lord Tennyson. And in my thoughts with scarce a sigh/I take the pressure of thine hand. OBNC; PoEL 1-5

In Memoriam A.H.H., CXX. Alfred, Lord Tennyson. But I was born to other things. ImOP; OAEL 1-2; SeCePo

In Memoriam A.H.H, CXXI. Alfred, Lord Tennyson. Thy place is changed; thou art the same. NoP; VLP

In Memoriam A.H.H., CXXII. Alfred, Lord Tennyson. And every thought breaks out a rose. VLP

In Memoriam A.H.H., CXXIII. Alfred, Lord Tennyson. I cannot think the thing farewell. HAP; NOBE; OAEL 1-2; OAEP; SeCePo

In Memoriam A.H.H., CXXIV. Alfred, Lord Tennyson. And out of darkness came the hands/That reach thro' nature, moulding men. VLP

In Memoriam A.H.H., CXXV. Alfred, Lord Tennyson. And whispers to the worlds of space,/In the deep night, that all is well. NOBE; NOCV

In Memoriam A.H.H., CXXVII. Alfred, Lord Tennyson. And smilest, knowing all is well. HBV 1-2; OAEL 1-2; OAEP

In Memoriam A.H.H., CXXVIII. Alfred, Lord Tennyson. ...as in some piece of art,/Is toil cooperant to an end. VLP

In Memoriam A.H.H., CXXIX. Alfred, Lord Tennyson. And mingle all the world with thee. VLP

In Memoriam A.H.H., CXXX. Alfred, Lord Tennyson. I shall not lose thee though I die. HBV 1-2; OAEL 1-2

In Memoriam A.H.H., CXXXI. Alfred, Lord Tennyson. And one far-off divine event,/To which the whole creation moves. OAEP; VLP

In Memoriam (Easter, 1915). Edward ("Edward Eastaway") Thomas. Have gathered them and will do never again. GTBS-P; NOBE; OBWP; OxBTC

In Memoriam F. A. S. Robert Louis Stevenson. And ere the day of sorrow departed as he came. BrPo

In Memoriam Francis Ledwidge. Seamus Heaney. You were not keyed or pitched like these true-blue ones/Though all of you consort now underground. FaBoIP

In Memoriam: Francis Ledwidge. Norreys Jephson O'Conor. The Chiefs of Tyrone and Tyrconnell,/Live on through the years! HBMV

In Memoriam James Joyce (excerpt). Hugh" (Christopher Murray Grieve) MacDiarmid. It cannot be all you assert of it.'/And obviously... FaBoPV

In Memoriam: John Davidson. Ronald Campbell Macfie. The sweet, wild, poignant passion of thy song. GoTS

In Memoriam: Martin Luther King, Jr. June Jordan. deplorable abortion/ more and/more PoBA

In Memoriam Paul Celan. Gad Hollander. ...Eye-deep it led/to the naked and cold. VWA

In Memoriam, Private D. Sutherland. Ewart Alan Mackintosh. For they were only your fathers/But I was your officer. BSV

In Memoriam Rev. J. J. Lyons. Emma Lazarus. And the broad prairie melts in mist of tears. SBG

In Memoriam Roy Campbell. Ralph Nixon Currey. Down the long combers of his pride. ACV; PeSA

In Memoriam S.C.W., V.C. Charles Hamilton Sorley. A sacrificing swift night-shade. MMM

In Memorium. Louisa May Alcott. Out of the finite dark,/Into the Infinite Light. AA

In Memorium. Lewis MacAdams. Killed/Festubert, May 9, 1915–R.I.P. ANYP

In Memorium–Leo: A Yellow Cat. Margaret Sherwood. That life is but one long caress/Of gentle words and gentle hands. BLPA

In Memory. Lionel Pigot Johnson. Those hands to greet,/Us, where love needs no speech. OBNC; PoEL 1-5

In Memory. Katha Pollitt. the calm and serious face. The speaking eyes. MAYP

In Memory, 1978. Judith Kazantzis. she salaams down/on to, dear God, well trodden ground. BrRo

In Memory of a Friend. George Barker. To those that love there are no dead,/Only the long sleepers. OxBTC

In Memory of Anna Hopewell. *Anonymous.* But the skin of the thing that made her go. ShM

In Memory of Arthur Winslow. Robert Lowell. Blood on your finger-tips for Lazarus who was poor. AP; MiAP

In Memory of "Barry Cornwall." Algernon Charles Swinburne. Though the dead to our dead bid welcome, and we farewell. HBV 1-2

In Memory of Basil, Marquess of Dufferin and Ava. Sir John Betjeman. I am deaf to your notes and dead/by a soldier's body in Burma. OBWP

In Memory of Bryan Lathrop. Edgar Lee Masters. The stones shall rise in towers to answer him. PoA

In Memory of Captain Underwood, Who Was Drowned. *Anonymous.* Once Underwood–now under water. FaBoEE

In Memory of Colonel Charles Young. Countee Cullen. A tree with tongues will grow. PoBA

In Memory of David Archer (excerpt). George Barker. ...St. George gives birth to The Dragon. FaBoMo

In Memory of Edward Wilson (parody). James Clerk Maxwell. For me, I ken na ane o' them,/But what the waur am I? BXAP

In Memory of Ernst Toller. W.H. Auden. We know for whom we mourn and who is grieving. AtBAP

In Memory of Eva Gore-Booth and Con Markiewicz. William Butler Yeats. Bed me strike a match and blow. CABA; FaBoPV; MBW 1-2; MoAB; NoAm; OAEL 1-2; OBMV; OxBTC

In Memory of Francois Rabelais. Yunna Moritz. Even our souls may leak away/then, and only return to us/with Hell and horned beasts! VWA

In Memory of G. K. Chesterton. Walter De la Mare. Pity and innocence his heart at rest. GoBC

In Memory of Garcia Lorca. Eldon Grier. Buried,/Is a silver skull. PeCV

In Memory of General Grant. Henry Abbey. In every clime, to every age. AA

In Memory of George Whitby, Architect. Sir John Betjeman. You stand in a long tradition; and we who are left salute you. EyDe

In Memory of James T. Fields. John Greenleaf Whittier. Let thy old smile greet us well. OBVV

In Memory of Jane Fraser. Geoffrey Hill. Dead cones upon the alder shook. NoAm; OxBTC

In Memory of John Lothrop Motley. William Cullen Bryant. Thy memory shall perish only then. AA

In Memory of Kathleen. Kenneth Patchen. Nothing worse that the cold cry of snow. MoAmPo

In Memory of Leopardi. James Wright. When he saw her, naked, carrying away his last sheep/Through the Asian rocks. NaP

In Memory of Major Robert Gregory. William Butler Yeats. ...;but a thought/of that late death took all my heart for speech. AnIL; DiPo; EBEV; OAEL 1-2; OAEP

In Memory of Marie A. Bertolt Brecht. And yet that cloud bloomed only for a minute/And as I looked up vanished in the wind. LiTW

In Memory of My Arab Grandmother. Evelyn Arcad Zerbe. Your heart offered in sacrifice. WPOW

In Memory of My Dear Grandchild Elizabeth Bradstreet. Anne Bradstreet. Is by His hand alone that guides nature and fate. AP; NOCV

In Memory of My Feelings. Frank O'Hara. and save the serpent in their midst. NeAP; PoM

In Memory of My First Chapatis. Diane Di Prima. bursting the air with perennial desperations. PoM

In Memory of My Mother. Patrick Kavanagh.
And you smile up at us–eternally. CIP; FaBoIP; NoAm
Through you I knew Woman and did not fear her spell. BIrV

In Memory of My Uncle Timothy. Alastair Reid. Anyway, now Tim's dead. NePoEA-2

In Memory of Radio. LeRoi (Imamu Amiri Baraka) Jones. An evil word it is,/This love. NeAP; NIP; NoP; PoM

In Memory of Robin Hyde, 1906-39. Charles Brasch. the darkness they command/Is utter, and their kiss a final calm. AnNZ

In Memory of Sigmund Freud. W.H. Auden. Sad is Eros, builder of cities,/And weeping anarchic Aphrodite. AtBAP; CoBMV; HAP; LiTB; OAEL 1-2; OxBA

In Memory of the Circus Ship Euzkera, Wrecked in the Caribbean Sea... Walker Gibson. To see the bunting and the blue balloons. NCSH; NePoAm

In Memory of the Moon. (A Killing.). Charlotte DeClue. the hated dog killed the Moon. STE; TWSS

In Memory of the Utah Stars. William Matthews. how we metabolize loss/ as fast as we have to. GeTw; MAYP; NPAW; Psk

In Memory of the Vertuous and Learned Lady Madre de Teresa. Richard Crashaw. Must learne in life to dye like Thee. AnAnS 1

In Memory of Those Murdered in the Dublin Massacre, May 1974. Paul Durcan. ...and the waitresses too,/flying breasts and limbs,/For a free Ireland. FaBoIP

In Memory of Two Sons. Russell Stellwagon. Though others may perhaps forget,/I give my all to Thee. STF

In Memory of V. R. Lang. Mac Hammond. ...Your beautiful eyes,/Full of the tears of the ages, said everything dies. PoA

In Memory of W. H. Auden. David R. Slavitt. humming in the dark the songs he'd have sung. SM

In Memory of Walter Savage Landor. Algernon Charles Swinburne. Mix with thy name/As morning-star with evening-star/His faultless fame. HBV 1-2; PoEL 1-5

In Memory of Your Body. David Shapiro. And here I beg/permission to close a chapter of still life. ANYP

In Mercy, Lord, Incline Thine Ear. Isaac M. Wise. Devoted, Lord, to thee. AH

In Mexico. Evaleen Stein. In olden ages, long ago,/In Mexico. AA

In Mind. Denise Levertov. but she is not kind. NMM; PAI

In Missing. Ray A. Young Bear. saying she had buried somebody/into the earth with her red/hands. CDW

In Misty Blue. Laurence Binyon. The day my love came home to me. HBMV

In Moncur Street. Dorothy Hewett. she turns upon her other side. NOAV

In Montecito. Randall Jarrell. That surrounds Montecito like the echo of a scream. CoAP; MAT; NoP; NYBP; VGW

In Mortem Venerabilis Andreae Prout Carmen. Francis Sylvester ("Father Prout") Mahony. The bad man's death it well becomes to weep,–/Not so the just. IrPN; NBM

In Mutual Time. Steven Lavoie. rugged canyons smooth into valleys/while shards reform their urn. APU

In My Boat That Goes. Saigyo Hoshi. The cry of the first wild-goose. AWP

In My Craft or Sullen Art. Dylan Thomas. Who pay no praise or wages/ Nor heed my craft or art. BoLoP; ChMP; CMoP; DiPo; GTBS-P; HAP; HeIP; InvP; LiTM; MAT; NeBP; NIP; NoAm; NoP; OAEP; PP; SeCeV; WeW

In My Crib. Joseph Ceravolo. I am sitting/in my house. ANYP

In My Dreams. Stevie Smith. I am glad, I am glad, that my friends don't know what I think. FaBoWP

In My Dreams I Searched for You. *Anonymous.* But I did not find even the echo of your steps. WTO

In My End Is My Beginning. Rosemary Dobson. Saint Christopher, be with me still. BoAV

In My Father's House (with music). *Anonymous.* O there's peace, peace, ev'rywhere! AS

In My First Hard Springtime. James Welch. but choose amazed to ride you down with hunger. AmPA; CDW

In My Heart's Depth. Akazome Emon. like a snipe scratching its feathers. WPOW

In My Lifetime. James Welch. are never wrong and I am rhythm to strong/medicine. CDW; STE

In My Merry Oldsmobile. Vincent Bryan. You can go as far as you like with me,/In my merry Oldsmobile. FSN

In My Mind. Norman MacCaig. on a dead hand/and a book fallen from it. OxBC

In My New Clothing. Basho (Matsuo Basho). I must/Look like someone else SoPo

In My Old Verses. Charles Guerin. Why couldn't I have stayed a poet/ Thus naive! CAW

In My Own Album. Charles Lamb. Go, shut the leaves, and clasp the book. CBEP; OBRV

In My Own Twentieth Century. Natalya Gorbanyevskaya. as, after the screaming of jets,/the trump of Jericho. PBWP

In My Place. Esther Archibald. And I the race might win. STF

In Mysterious Ways. Faye Kicknosway. But no one/believes her; no one. GeTw

In Nakedness. Marnie Pomeroy. You, lion in nakedness,/As citizen must pose. ErPo

In Nature There Is Neither Right nor Left nor Wrong. Randall Jarrell. I've dreamed of my first love, the subtle serpent. OxBC

In Neglect. Robert Frost. And try if we cannot feel forsaken. OBSP; VGW

In New Ross. Valentin Iremonger. ..the oiled machinery of nature shunts/ Day down for repairs. Silently, the night's technicians hunt NeIP

In Nine Sleep Valley (excerpt). James Merrill. Centimeters deep yawns the abyss. HaCAP

In No Way. David Ignatow. ...In no way shall death part us. AMV-81

In North Great George's Street. Seumas (James Starkey) O'Sullivan. ...They lie forever, each in a forgotten grave. BIrV

In November. Anne Reeve Aldrich. My Love and I are living now in May! AA

In November. Archibald Lampman. A pleasure secret and austere. NOBC; OBCV

In Nunhead Cemetery. Charlotte Mew. If he would dig it all up again they would not die. FaBoWP

In Obitum Ben. Jons. Mildmay Fane, Earl of Westmoreland. ...He could no longer tarry,/But was returned again unto the quarry. OBSP

In Obitum M.S., X Maii 1614. William Browne. Mine only died. JCP; NOBE; SeCeV

In Obitum Promi. Henry Parrot. (The Butler gone) the keys are left behind. FaBoCo

In October. Bliss Carman. When all the woods are marching/In triumph of the year? YeAr

In October.... Michael Hamburger. We are only the bed, not the source or the giver.' NePoEA

In Ohio. James Wright. A widow on a front porch puckers her lips/And whispers. NNaP

In Old Tucson. Charles Beghtol. Where purple shadows slanting fall–/In Old Tucson. BPAW

In Old Tucson. Harrison Conrard. The long, lone days, O Time, speed on! BPAW

In Old Tucson. Sharlot M. Hall. The gray street and a crumbling wall. BPAW

In One Battle. LeRoi (Imamu Amiri Baraka) Jones. ...now my fingers eagerly/toward the machine BPo

In One Place. Robert Wallace. ...birds/in it don't remember/it wasn't there. Psk

In Orangeburg My Brothers Did. A. B. Spellman. ...beast's most fatal message/that we die to learn it well. BPo; PoBA

In Orbit (parody). Henry Taylor. I shout three green cheers for myself. BXAP

In Order To. Kenneth Patchen. I didn't want any job that bad. NaP

In Orknay. William Fowler. I change bot seas, bot cannot change my love. GoTS; OxBS

In Our Boat. Dinah Maria Mulock Craik. Speak not, ah, breathe not– there's peace on the deep. HBV 1-2

In Our Lane. *Anonymous.* But they are not like Shu,/So beautiful, so brave. LiTW

In Our Time. Michael Roberts. And folly cannot die, but cannot grow for ever. WaP

In Oxford City *Anonymous.* So let me beware of cruel jealousy. OBET

In Pace In Idipsum Dormiam Et Requiescam. Patrick O'Connor. Of sleep, our peacefullest sea–save blessed death. CAW

In Panelled Rooms. Ruth Herschberger. Frankincense, flowers, upon touching her. LiTA

In Paradise. Arlo Bates. Though thou hast won to Paradise! AA

In Parenthesis. David Jones.
It's cushy enough. FaBoMo
morning sun and smilingly, to wait for the bearers. FaBoMo
Pass it along to Stand-to. NoAm
So double detonations, back and fro like well-played-up-to service/at a net, mark left and right... NoAm
–where it rises to his wire–and Sergeant T. Quilter takes/over. OBWP

In Paris. Thomas Macdonagh. Four hundred and fifty years ago/He wrote that Testament. OnYI

In Passing. Roy Helton. A child's first finger exercise/Before her on the music stand. HBMV

In Passing. Gerald Jonas. What a way to go! GrPl

In Passing. J. Barrie Shepherd. when all our yearly tributes/are delivered and set free. AMV-81

In Perspective. Robert Graves. Even the blind will sense that something's wrong. OBSP

In Peterborough Churchyard. *Anonymous.* And what I was is no affair of yours. NOBL

In Phaeacia. James Elroy Flecker. And in her eyes the forest pool. HBMV

In Philistia. Bliss Carman. They wear the gowns of Gibson. ALV

In Piam Memoriam. Geoffrey Hill. Like a revealed mineral, a new earth. NePoEA-2; OxBC

In Pilgrim Life Our Rest. Edwin Sandys. ...O Thou, our works/To happiest end address. AH

In Place of a Curse. John Ciardi. ...who gambled nothing,/gave nothing, and could never receive enough. HoAn

In Pleasant Lands Have Fallen the Lines. James Flint. While here their name and race shall last. AH

In Populated. Lucille Clifton. their shimmering voices/singing. GeTw

In Portugal, 1912. Alice Meynell. The wine-press holds the unbidden Christ. NOCV; OxBoCh

In Postures That Call. Oscar Williams. But that world can only be better/ That knows they have died in vain. WaP

In Prague. Paul Celan. in which we swam, two dreams now, tolling/ against time, on the squares. VWA

In Praise of a Gentlewoman. George Gascoigne.
Enshrined with snakes within his tomb, did yield her part–/ing breath. EnRePo
She will be stung to death with snakes, as Cleopatra was. EnRePo

In Praise of a Guilty Conscience. Wislawa Szymborska. Nothing is more bestial/than a clear conscience/on the third planet of the Sun. AMV-81

In Praise of Aed. *Anonymous.* Acclaim Aed and his pleasures. AnIL

In Praise of Ale. Thomas Bonham. Oh, give me ale! ALV; FaBoCh; OBS; TrGrPo; ViBoPo

In Praise of Antonioni. Stephen Holden. in the darkness under the searchlights. NYBP

In Praise of Ben Avon. Brenda G. Macrow. ...and their unshifting feet rooted/forever in the mountain's heart. PoSH

In Praise of Beverly. Steve Orlen. I found my own in my good time. GP; MAYP

In Praise of Blur. G. S. Sharat Chandra. You've brought me/the tranquillity of a snail/contemplating its snout... FAZ

In Praise of Clothes. Erica Jong. How it heartens us to strip you off!/& this is no matter of fashion. MAYP

In Praise of Cocoa, Cupid's Nightcap. Stanley J. Sharpless. Cocoa coursing through their veins. ErPo; FiBHP; NLV

In Praise of Commonplace. Sir Owen Seaman. Not half so much for what they said/As for the jolly way they said it. InMe

In Praise of Country Life. Robert Chamberlain. Doth neither wish, nor fear, his dying day. CavP

In Praise of Fidelia. Mildmay Fane, Earl of Westmoreland. In my Fidelia I'll find more. OBSP

In Praise of His Daphnis. Sir John Wotton. Then here conclude/Fair Daphnis' praise. EIL

In Praise of His Lady. Matthew Grove. And till that death our bodies two shall part. EIL

In Praise of His Loving and Best-Beloved Fawnia. Robert Greene. O glorious Sun! imagine me the West,/Shine in my Arms, and set thou in my Breast. PoEL 1-5

In Praise of Ivy. *Anonymous.* For there shall we nothing lack./Veni, coronaberis. MeEL

In Praise of Laudanum. William Harrison. And everything but Mira is forgot. NOEC

In Praise of Limestone. W. H. Auden.
...what I hear is the murmur/Of underground streams, what I see is a limestone landscape. CMoP; CoBMV; FaBoPV; FYAP; HAP; MoAB; MoVE; NePA; NoAm; NoP; OAEL 1-2; PPP
With which we have nothing, we like to hope, in common. CABA

In Praise of Llamas. Arthur Guiterman. In Bolivia, Peru and Ecuador! FiBHP

In Praise of Mary. *Anonymous.*
Levedy, bring us to thine bolde/And shild us from helle wrake./Amen. MeEL
That hath y-dit the foule pit/Inferni. NOBE

In Praise of May. *Anonymous.* Delicate-hued, delightful May. AnIV

In Praise of Music in Time of Pestilence. Daryl Hine. the rebellious angels play with fire. OBCV

In Praise of Neptune. Thomas Campion. The praise of Neptune's empery. BoNaP; CBEP; NOBE; WiR

In Praise of Old Women. Marya Fiamengo. because the highest manifestation of/Hagia Sophia/is old and a woman. WPOW

In Praise of Robert Penn Warren. David Lehman. And beyond the primitive powers of pain and lament. AMV-81

In Praise of Seafaring Men, in Hopes of Good Fortune. Sir Richard Grenville. To purchase fame I will go roam. OBSS; OBTV

In Praise of the Sun. A. W. And yet these Dames, that shine so bright,/Are but the shadow of thy light. CTC; OBSC

In Praise of Three Young Men. Lochlann Og O Dalaigh. Telling of them is dear. NOBI

In Praise of Virginity. Hroswitha von Grandersheim. you, whom he chose in love–/no one will thrust away. PBWP

In Praise of Water-Gruel. Matthew Green. And by swift currents throws off clean/Prolific particles of spleen. FaBoUs

In Praise of Winchester. *Anonymous.* The town is ruled upon skille. OxBM

In Praise of Wisdom. Solomon Ibn Gabirol. I will not rest until I find her source. TrJP

In Praise of Wyatt's Psalms. Henry Howard, Earl of Surrey. Mought them awake out of their sinful sleep. SiPS

In Prison. William Morris. Westward the banner rolls/Over my wrong. AtBAP; NBM

In Procession. Robert Graves. This Town of Hell/Where between sleep and sleep I dwell. MP; TwCP

In Progress. Christina Georgina Rossetti. And her eyes lightnings and her shoulders wing BoWoP

In Provence. Jean Aicard. Come there as to a Paradise. CAW

In Pursuit of Love. Ken Norris. ...& being tired of the mystic rose you wear in your/hair. CaPN

In Quest to Have Not. Edwin Honig. to dive into the eye of the needle. LiTA

In Railway Halls. Stephen Spender. This Tinme forgets and never heals, far less transcends. EnLit; FaBoMo

In Rain. Wendell Berry. for I will rest/in an easy bed tonight. GeTw

In Rainy-Gloomy Weather. Sir John Davies. Now grates upon the gravel of my grave. CBEP

In Rama. George Alfred Townsend. They tell me time is time,/And only heaven mature. AA

In Random Fields of Impulse and Repose. Jeanine Hathaway. shovel across the breast of earth and her/ragged history, home. AMV-81

In Rebellion. John Millington Synge. Toward God high taunts I hurled,/With cursing parched my tongue. SyP

In Reference to Her Children, 23. June, 1656. Anne Bradstreet. I happy am, if well with you. BoWoP; SBG; TAP

In Respect of the Elderly. Thomas Love Peacock. brother owl has told me/respect your elders VoR

In Respectful Memory of Mr. Yarker. John Close. Hark to the tolling bell! FaBoCo

In Response to a Rumor That the Oldest Whorehouse... James Wright. And nobody would commit suicide, only/To find beyond death/Bridgeport, Ohio. CAPP; CoAP; NNaP; TW

In Response to Executive Order 9066: ALL AMERICANS OF JAPANESE... Dwight Okita. when the first tomato ripens/to miss me. BrSi

In Ringlets Curl'd Thy Tresses Flow. Mary Balfour. And warblers chaunt their lov'd notes round. IrPN

In Robin Hood Cove. Marsden Hartley. of nothings in their tuneful/prime. AnFE; CoAnAm

In Roman. Sir John (1561-1612) Harington. For out of backward love, all hate doth grow. PV

In Romney Marsh. John Davidson. The beach, with all its organ stops/Pealing again, prolonged the roar. BSV; FaBoPP; GoTS; OBVV; OxBTC; PoPle; ViBoPo

In Ruin Reconciled. Aubrey Thomas De Vere. One Gael, one Norman; both discrowned. BIrV; IrPN

In Salem. Lucille Clifton. as she beats her ordinary bread. AmPA

In Santa Maria del Popolo. Thom Gunn.

...and was strangled, as things went,/For money, by one such picked off the streets. NMP

Resisting, by embracing, nothingness. CMoP; FaBoMo; GTBS-P; NePoEA-2; OxBC; QFR

In Saram. John Cotton. Go then, Sweet Sara, take thy Sabbath Rest,/With thy Great Lord, and all in Heaven Blest. SCAP

In School-Days. John Greenleaf Whittier Like her - because they love him. AA; AnNE; BLPA; FaBoBe; FPL; GLGT; OBCA; OxBChV; PoPl; TreF

In Scorching Time. Alex Stevens. and that some day, when the sands turn over, will resume sway. AMV-81

In Scotland. *Anonymous.* Ye'll get a whippie/And a supple Tam! OxNR

In Search of a Short Poem for My Grandmother. Louise Hardeman. mouth open to these syllables of praise. AMV-81

In Secreit Place This Hyndir Nycht. William Dunbar. Bot now I luif that graceles gane.' OxBoLi

In Sepia. Jon Anderson. ...He was reading a story so hopeless,/so starless, we all belonged. PoA

In Service. Winifred M. Letts. But her heart is some place far away upon the Wexford/shore. HBMV

In Shadow. Hart Crane. But her own words are night's and mine. NOBA

In Shadow. Caroline Hazard. I was awake/In Gethsemane. GoBC

In Shame and Humiliation. James Wright. The pure, the pure! will never live so long. CAPP

In Sickness. Jonathan Swift. Expir'd To-day, entomb'd To-morrow,/When known, will save a double Sorrow. CEP; NOEC; OBEC

In Sleep. Alice Meynell. And saw Himself, as one looks in a glass,/In those impassioned eyes. BrRo

In Small Townlands. Seamus Heaney. A new world cools out of his head. CIP; NoAm

In Snow. William Allingham. ...this is but an Afghan youth/Shot by the stranger on his native hills. IrPN

In Solitary Confinement, Sea Point Police Cells. C. J. Driver. and leave only the rise and the fall of the seas'/far Atlantic roll. PeSA

In Some Seer's Cloud Car. Christopher Middleton. and ate an egg. TwCP

In Some Way or Other the Lord Will Provide. Mrs. M. A. W. Cook. Yes, we'll trust in the Lord,/And he will provide. AH

In Sorrow. Thomas Hastings. We awake among the blest. AA; HBV 1-2

In Space-Time Aware–. Abbie Huston Evans. Here in the whelming abyss/As it were in the crook of an arm. GP

In Spain. Emily Lawless.
The sun shines last in the West! AnIV
Yet the devil may hold all your blue and your gold/Were I only once back there! AnIV

In Spain. Sir Thomas Wyatt.
If that for weight the body fail, this soul shall/to her flee. FCP
Of mighty love the wings for this me give. OBSC; SeCePo

In Spite of All This Much Needed Thunder. Zack Gilbert. Trembling the night waves, rocking boat and barge. PoNe

In Spite of His Dangling Pronoun. Lyn Lifshin. they were still going to town in/novels she never had time to finish IHMS

In spite of my efforts. Taira no Kanemori. "Is something bothering you?" LiTW

In Spite of Sorrow. Adoniram Judson. We sow on Burmah's barren plain,/We reap on Zion's hill. TRV

In Spring. Li Po. Why part the silk curtains by my bed? LiTW

In Spring in Warm Weather. Dorothy Aldis. There's hardly a baby that hasn't been born. BiCB

In Springtime. Rudyard Kipling. Can you tell me aught of England or of Spring in England now? BrPo

In State (excerpt). Forceythe Willson. And everlasting Canopy and starry Arch/and Shield of All. AA

In Stone Settlements When the Moon Is Stone. Peter Levi. we wither and flourish. EBEV

In Summer. *Anonymous.* "I thynk hit is a fulle fayre tyme/In a mornynge of May." CH

In Summer. Trumbull Stickney. And memory falls from the mast of thought. NCEP

In Summer. Charles Hanson Towne. Bid me farewell when the last stars awake,/Or else my wounded heart will break, will break! HBMV

In Sweet Communion. John Newton. And possess in sweet communion joys which earth cannot afford. TRV

In Sylvia Plath Country. Erica Jong. what could we tell you/after you dove down into yourself/& were swallowed/by your poems? IHMS

In Tall Grass. Carl Sandburg. ...under the hanging/honeycomb the bees come home and the bees sleep. PoA

In Teesdale. Andrew Young. Tonight I fear the fabulous horses/Whose white tails flash down the steep/water-courses. FaBoPP; OBSP

In Temptation. Charles Wesley. Rise to all eternity! NOEC; PoEL 1-5

In Tenebris. Thomas Hardy.

Get him up and be gone as one shaped awry; he disturbs the order here.
BrPo; CMoP; LiTB; LiTM; NoAm; NOBE; NoP; OAEP; PrIm;
SeCePo; TreFS; VLP

One who, past doubtings all,/Waits in unhope. OAEL 1-2

Then might the Voice that is law have said "Cease!' and the ending have
come. OAEL 1-2

In Terror of Hospital Bills. James Wright. For your sake, oh my secret,/
My life. GP

In Tesla's Laboratory. Robert Underwood Johnson. Listen! that murmur is
of angel's wings. AA

In Texas Grass. Quincy Troupe. waiting, waiting for rusted/trains in texas
grass PoBA

In Thankfull Remembrance for My Dear Husband's Safe Arrivall.... Anne
Bradstreet. Impossible for to recount/Or any way expresse. TrPWD

In That Dark Cave. Shel Silverstein. The bone-filled suit of armor/That
lies rusting at his door. ELU

In That Dim Monument Where Tybalt Lies. Arthur Davison Ficke. And
come, with terrible silence in your eyes,/To that dim monument where
Tybalt lies. HBMV

In the Annals of Tacitus. Philip Murray. That history pauses still upon
their noble names. NePoAm

In the Attic. Donald Justice. And the chin settles onto palms above/
Numbed elbows propped on rotting sills. SM

In the Azure Night. Bartolome Galindez. Of the pilgrim of Thebais/Faded
from sight! CAW

In the Backs. Frances Cornford. Why is this air so sacred and so still?
BrRo

In the Backs. James Kenneth Stephen. And certainly she was not beautiful.
NOBV

In the Badlands. David Wagoner. For the sake of the sun. UnPo

In the Baggage Coach Ahead. Gussie L. Davis. But baby's cries can't
waken her,/In the baggage coach ahead. FSN; TreFS

In the Baggage Room at Greyhound. Allen Ginsberg. hurt my knee and
scraped my hand and built my pectoral muscles/big as vagina. NaP; NoP

In the Balance. Anonymous. You're vanquished by the might of Venus.
OLR

In the Bar. Robert Vander Molen. Do you understand? you/Horses ass
TAT

In the Barrio. Alurista. –the one that courses through my veins FIA

In the Basement of the Goodwill Store. Ted Kooser. and the things you
once thought/you were rid of forever/have taken you back in their arms.
GOYP

In the Bayou. Don (Donald Robert Marquis) Marquis. Snakelike over the
secret it hides. AmFN

In the Beach House. Anne Sexton. while summer is hurrying its way in
and out,/over and over,/in their room. PPP

In the Beginning. Rachel Fishman. This is the dawn/The beginning/Again.
VWA

In the Beginning. Daniel Gerard Hoffman. their frenzy's spell unbroken/
defines the topgallant soul. PP

In the Beginning. Harriet Monroe. When first the ocean spoke unto the
sun. AA

In the Beginning. Jenny Lind Porter. And the warmth began, and the chill.
GoYe

In the Beginning. Valerie Sinason. "What will happen?' pleads Eve. BrRo

In the Beginning. Dylan Thomas. Blood shot and scattered to the winds of
light/The ribbed original of love. MoRP

In the Beginning Was a Word. Robert Graves. With saints' and sinners'
lies and laws,/For a new everlasting reign. PoA

In the Beginning Was the. Lee Murchison. and always the beautiful/
trajectories. SD

In the Beginning Was the Bird. Henry Treece. I see it prophesy the path
winds take. LiTB; WaP

In the Bistro. Gwen Harwood. ...One thinks of the small dangling/forelegs
of the flesh-eating dinosaurs. FaBoWP

In the Black Camaro. David Bottoms. a truck backed into a thicket a half-
mile downstream. AmC

In the Bleak Mid-Winter. Christina Georgina Rossetti.
Give my heart. BoC; OxBoCh; TRV
In the bleak mid-winter/Long ago. SUS

In the blue distance. Nelly Sachs. and the stone dancing/changes its dust
to music. BoWoP

In the Breeze. Boris Pasternak. To-day the garden is gazing/With eyes like
anemones. TrJP

In the Cabinet. Shlomo Vinner. The dust of ruins settles in my lungs,/The
key in my hand. VWA

In the Cafe. Roo Borson. If a man could measure up/even to his clothes.
PPJ

In the Cage. Robert Lowell. ...Fear,/The yellow chirper, beaks its cage.
FF; NOBA; SM; SyP

In the Canadian Rockies. Virginia Shearer Hopper. Ball, Columbia,
Eisenhower. AMV-80

In the Carolinas. Wallace Stevens. The white iris beautifies me. VGW

In the Carpenter's Shop. Sara Teasdale. Little faith were the angels
keeping/All the years. HBMV

In the Case of Lobsters. Petra von Morstein. put it in cold/then bring to
the boil BoWoP

In the Catacombs. Harlan Hoge Ballard. United States ahead, by thunder!
YaD

In the Cathedral. Patricia Beer. You take and hold my dead fingers/
Declaring summer. OxBC

In the Cathedral Close. Edward Dowden. And in your wings a light and
wind/Shall move from the Maestro's soul. NBM; OBVV; OxBI

In the Caves of Auvergne. Walter James Turner. O Hunter, your own
shadow stands/Within your forest lair! HBMV

In the Cellars. Jiri Gold. and we choke on the hot/quivering air VWA

In the Cemetery. Thomas Hardy. And as well cry over a new-laid drain/
As anything else, to ease yourpain! BrPo

In the Cemetery of the Sun. Wilfred Watson. Wording me even to the
spring of doom PeCV

In the Cheviots. Maurice Lindsay. Distance re-inflates the hills. PoSH

In the Children's Hospital. Hugh" (Christopher Murray Grieve)
MacDiarmid. But would the sound of your sticks on the floor/Thundered
in her skull for evermore! NoP

In the Children's Hospital. Alfred, Lord Tennyson. The Lord of the
children had heard her, and Emmie had/passed away. HBV 1-2

In the Churchyard. Eleanor Ross Taylor. The nirds eat out one's hands!
UnPo

In the Churchyard at Cambridge. Henry Wadsworth Longfellow. In your
own secret sins and terrors! AP; PoEL 1-5; TAP

In the City. Israel Zangwill. How sweet is human brotherhood,/And all
the common daily life! WGRP

In the City of Bogota. Greg Pape. each one a word resisting/everything
that conspires to silence. MAYP

In the Coach: Conjergal Rights. Thomas Edward Brown. Theer then! theer!
No, I'll have none of your/goodnights.../Congergal rights! conjergal rights!
VLP

In the Cool of the Evening. Alfred Noyes. Softly rustling as He cometh
o'er the far green hill. HBV 1-2

In the Corn Land. Quentin R. Howard. that them two bucks will grow up
wild as/sassafras patches? TAT

In the Courtyard. Miriam Ulinover. Then all the egg yolks will bear/The
dreaded blood spot. VWA

In the Dark. George Arnold. Grant me to see the light! HBV 1-2

In the Dark. Frances Louisa Bushnell. To breathe and blossom in the dark!
AA

In the Dark. Mary Thacher Higginson. Again it will be grasped by thine,
before/My steps can lose the way. AA

In the Dark. Sophie Jewett. Thou wilt avail me in the lonely end.
TrPWD

In the Dark Caverns of the Night. Henry Treece. And heart's
incompetence. NeBP

In the Dark, in the Dew. Mary Newmarch Prescott. Beat for you, and
bleed for you,/In the dark, in the dew! HBV 1-2

In the Dark None Dainty. Robert Herrick. The chosen ruby and the
reprobate. CaPo; CBEP; ELU; PoPle

In the Dawn. Odell Shepard. We may never live to reach it. Ah, but we
have seen the goal! WGRP

In the Days of Old. Thomas Love Peacock. Wiser were the lovers/In the
days of old. HBV 1-2

In the Days of Old Rameses (with music). Anonymous. Are you on, are
you on, are you on? AS

In the Days of Rin-Tin-Tin. Daniel Gerard Hoffman. And overlook the
Little Fellow on his way to school. CoPo; SM

In the Dead of the Night. Norman Dubie. Black, something very bright,
from inside him. AmPA

In the Deep Channel. William Stafford. which tugged at the tree roots
below the river. NaP

In the Deep Museum. Anne Sexton. We have kept the miracle. I will not
be here. MoAmPo; Prf

In the Depths of Night. Manuel Gutierrez Najera. Appease the waves
where there was tumult late! CAW

In the Desert. Stephen Crane. Because it is bitter,/And because it is my
heart. AmePo; LiTM; NOBA; OBSP; TAP

In the Dials. William Ernest Henley. Look on dispassionate–critical–
something 'mused. BrPo

In the Discreet Splendor. Avner Strauss. its light extinguished by a breath
of night,/glows with a radiance that is the moon's. VWA

In the Distance. H. L. Van Brunt. The only beautiful things on earth/turn
into themselves. FAZ

In the Distress upon Me. Henry Ainsworth. Jehovah, my God, makes my
darkness bright. AH

In the Dock. Walter De La Mare. When howls man's soul, it howls
inaudibly. ChMP; LiTM

In the Dome Car of the ″Canadian′. Sid Marty. As he dances in the aisles, for joy NOBC

In the Doorway. Robert Browning. Whom Summer made friends of, let Winter estrange! NCEP

In the Dordogne. John Peale Bishop. delicately bordered by poplars. AnAmPo; OBWP; VGW

In the Dream of the Body. David Keller. beyond the woodpile, the air I could almost hold. AMV-80

In the Dry Riverbed. Zelda. Women faint from sweet scents/and hot fear. VWA

In the Due Honor of the Author Master Robert Norton. John Smith. To th′Honor of our Nation, that thy Paynes/Transcends all former, and their glory staines. SCAP

In the Dumps. Anonymous. And the houses are built without walls. FaBoCo; NA; OxNR

In the Dusk the Path. Izumi Shikibu. That hang across it/Like threads of sorrow. WPOW

In the Dusky Path of a Dream. Rabindranath Tagore. One lamp had flickered in the evening breeze and died. OBMV

In the Dying of Daylight. Walter De La Mare. As if she, too, had heard. ACV

In the Egyptian Museum. Janet Lewis. Pierces me with ″Alas/That the beloved must die!″ NYBP; QFR

In the Elegy Season. Richard Wilbur. And azure water hoisting out of wells. InPK; MoAB; NePoEA; NYBP

In the Emptied Rest Home. Bella Akhmadulina. of the black woods, the vegetable gardens, the sun. BoWoP

In the End. Peter Everwine. —What′s done is done. NNaP

In the Evening. Thomas Hardy. Enough. You have returned. And all is well. ImOP

In the Evening by the Moonlight. James A. Bland. As we sang in de ebening by de moonlight. FSW; PSoN; TreFS

In the Evening from My Window. Anonymous. Plunging into darksome tunnels with a roar. SUS

In the Face of Grief. Sister Juana Ines de la Cruz. My broken heart thy piteous fingers bore. CAW

In the Fall. Hugh″ (Christopher Murray Grieve) MacDiarmid.
Darkens and deepens and takes/Tints of purple-maroon, rose-madder and straw. FaBoMo
In open country again watching an aching spargosis of stars. InPS

In the Fall. Alina Rivero. goes to the window and lets them flow/into the ochres of the afternoon. AMV-81

In the Fall o′ Year. Thomas S. Jones, Jr. Long ago was buried here–/Long ago, with you! HBV 1-2

In the Far Years. Wilson MacDonald. And carry that bread past your door,/Singing a sweet carol. CaP

In the Field. Phyllis Janik. while I′m out hunting tigers–/not for dinner, just for tigers. IHMS

In the Field. Richard Wilbur. And is ourselves, and is the one/Unbounded thing we know. NYBP

In the Field Forever. Robert Wallace. But the stars! all night long the stars are clover,/Over, and over, and over! PPJ

In the Fields. Charlotte Mew. Over the fields. They come in Spring. BoNaP; MoAB; MoBrPo

In the Firelight. Eugene Field. And ″Now I lay me down to sleep!″ AA

In the First Cave. Seymour Mayne. Bow your forehead/like a headstone sinking/towards the sun and rising winds. VWA

In the First House. Joseph Joel Keith. we never did; we had no right to stars. GoYe

In the first place of my life. Ray A. Young Bear. in that it came from the beginnings/unlike ours STE

In the Fishing Village. Sheila Nickerson. And release them from cradles of cold. WOLT

In the Fleeting Hand of Time. Gregory Corso. and leads me into conditional life. NAs

In the Flight of the Blue Heron: To Montezuma. Anita Endrezze Probst. the loom stands like a skeleton/across the Aztec sky. CDW

In the Flowering Season. Michael Roberts. And with no visible horror. FaBoTw

In the Footsteps of the Walking Air. Kenneth Patchen. Unknown roads for sleep to walk upon. EAS

In the Forest. George Bowering. But there are the trees,/darling, over there. NOBC

In the Forest. Russell Edson. ...even as the/evening slowly took the forest LCAP

In the Forest. Sandor Petofi. And I who fondly trusted to their truth/By suffering found that falsehood in them lies. LiTW

In the Forest. Pinhas Sadeh. And then rises. See him: he is a child again. VWA

In the Forest. Oscar Wilde. I track him in vain! SyP

In the Forest of Your Eyes. Arlindo Barbeitos. in your eyes/of the leopard/only the forest is seen. WhB

In the Garden. Ernest Crosby. ″If I smell just as sweet to you/As you smell sweet to me!″ HBV 1-2; HBVY

In the Garden. Richard Eberhart. Stored world of melos appetite. NePoAm-2

In the Garden. C. Austin Miles. Through the voice of woe,/His voice to me is calling. GoTF; TreFT

In the Garden. Tom Schmidt. Emerson′s the last famous poet/I thought I′d ever meet. NeAC

In the Garden at Swainston. Alfred, Lord Tennyson. Three dead men have I loved,/And thou art last of the three. GoBC; OBEV; OBNC; OBVV; VLP

In the Garden of the Lord. Helen Keller. I have strayed into the holy temple of the Lord. TRV; WGRP

In the Garden of the Turkish Consulate. Pinhas Sadeh. So, in silence, slowly, they surrounded me/and tore me to pieces. VWA

In the Garden There Strayed. Anonymous. And was buried before she was born. LO

In the Garden: Villa Cleobolus. Lawrence Durrell. The natural history of the human wish. ChMP

In the gathering dew. Lady Sagami. On the autumn moor/young deer cry. BoWoP

In the Gazebo (parody). Philip Appleman. I lose. Goodbye Broadway,/Hello Rilke. BXAP

In the Ghetto. Hugo Sonnenschein. So as to become a homesickness of the kind/That must bring to the world the Messiah! VWA

In the Gloaming. James C. Bayles. And the pimpernell pellets of Pangipoo. NA

In the Gloaming. Charles Stuart Calverley. As I sit alone at present, dreaming darkly of a Dun. ALV; BXAP; InMe; NOBL

In the Gloaming. Meta Orred. Best for you and best for me. BLSo; FaFP; FSW; TreF

In the Glorious Epiphanie of Our Lord God. Richard Crashaw. Pointing us Home to our own sun/The world′s and his HYPERION. PoEL 1-5

In the Gold Mines. B. W. Vilakazi. Under the green hills of the sky. TTY

In the Gold Room. Oscar Wilde. With the spilt-out blood of the rose-red wine. SyP

In the Good Old Summer Time. Ren Shields. That she′s your tootsey wootsey in The good old summer time. BLSo; FSN; GoTF; TreF

In the Gorge. William Stanley Merwin. Have you left us nothing but your blindness? AmPC

In the Grass. Annette Von Droste-Hulshoff. For every joy the seedling of a dream. PBWP

In the Grass. Hamlin Garland. To bask in the light of your sky! AA

In the Grave No Flower. Edna St. Vincent Millay. There/No flower. CrMA

In the Half Light of Holding and Giving. John Wieners. Past all endurance, existing. CoPo

In the Half-Point Time of Night. Ann Menebroker. and I, bursting with flowers. AMV-80

In the Hamptons. John N. Morris. The snazzy summer theatre takes us in. NYP

In the Heart of Contemplation. C. Day-Lewis. Nothing is innocent now but to act for life′s sake. MoPo; MP

In the Heart of Jesus. Muireadhack Albanach O Dalaigh. So that ere my life be spent/Thou′lt have sent and cleared my way. CAW

In the Heart of the Hills... Anonymous. Passion comes flooding and thrilling again. WTO

In the Heartland. Mark Vinz. as easily as pebbles slipping into still water. GP

In the Heat of the Morning. Anne Szumigalski. ...and left/me alone in this social blaze while you rest in your/cool tombs FaBoWP

In the Hedge-Back. Hugh″ (Christopher Murray Grieve) MacDiarmid.
Kept juist eneuch underneath us to ken/That a warl′ used to be. BSV; NeBP

In the Hellgate Wind. Madeline Defrees. ...routine/as the river I cross over. NYP

In the Henry James Country. William Abrahams. He placed the jewel in the casket and lay down to sleep. WaP

In the Highlands. Robert Louis Stevenson. Only winds and rivers,/Life and death. ACV; BrPo; BSV; FaBoCh; FaBV; GoTS; HBV 1-2; OBEV; OBVV; OxBS; PoSH

In the Hole. John Ciardi. Damn my neighbors. Damn Brewster Diffenbach. HoAn

In the Holy Nativity of Our Lord God. Richard Crashaw. Our selves become our best sacrifice. PoEL 1-5; SBVL; SeCeV; SeCV 1-2

In the Holy Nativity of Our Lord: Shepherds′ Hymn. Richard Crashaw. Made His own bed ere He was born. TrGrPo

In the Home of the Scholar Wu Su-chiang from Hsin-an... Wu Tsao. And the moss on the shore burning red. BoWoP; WPOW

In the Hospital. Arthur Guiterman. ...I know/There is God. WGRP

In the Hospital. Mary Woolsey Howland. These stripes as well as stars/ Lead after Him. HBV 1-2

In the Hospital. Laura Jensen. of the cupboards resting in the snow? AmPA

In the Hospital of the Holy Physician. Nancy Willard. In the pulse of my ruin/I make my cure. IHMS

In the House of Idiedaily. Bliss Carman. O, but life went gaily, gaily,/In the house of Idiedaily! OBVV

In the House of the Dying. Jane Cooper. Upstairs she lies, washed through by the two miracles. NMM

In the House of the Judge. Dave Smith. to hear breathing in the still house of the Judge/where I live. MAYP

In the Huon Valley. James Philip McAuley. The sheds are noisy with packing. CBAP

In the Inner City. Lucille Clifton. like we call it/home CNA; HeIP

In the Interest of Black Salvation. Don L. Lee. Jesus saves–S & H Green Stamps. BP

In the Interstices. Ruth Stone. Who, with their floodgates sundered, drowned when they/were stormed. ErPo

In the Isle of Dogs. John Davidson. A simple tune and great,/The fittest utterance of the voice of earth. OBNC; VLP

In the Jury Room. Hodding Carter. "All right," he said, "he's guilty–let's go home." MAT

In the Ladies' Room at the Bus Terminal (parody). William Zaranka. ...tipping/his hat/in a place like that. BXAP

In the Lake Country. Kay Wissinger. The daffodils beside the lake in spring. AMV-80

In the land of dwarfs. Forugh Farrokhzad. Bloody race of flowers, do you know? BoWoP

In the Land of Magic. Henri Michaux. Strange wounds, suffering on deserted walls, that you/come upon with loathing and nausea... LiTW

In the Land Where We Were Dreaming. Daniel B. Lucas. And left us nothing real but the dead,/In the land where we were dreaming. PAH

In the Lane. Leonard Alfred George Strong. Watching me, and judging me. HaMV

In the Last Few Moments Came the Old German Cleaning Woman. Jane Cooper. When mop in hand the old world through/The door pressed, dutiful, idiot. SM

In the Last Flicker of the Sinking Sun. Peretz Markish. To whom can I belong? VWA

In the Library. Elizabeth Brewster. And think more respectfully of the fox's sincerity. OBCV

In the Library. Michael Patrick Hearn. I'd never get through that at all! NTCP

In the Library. Ed Ochester. conscious of her reed neck/that the smallest stone can break. Psk

In the Lilac-Rain. Edith Matilda Thomas. Mine, a swift pleasure-pain/ None other knows. HBV 1-2

In the Local Museum. Walter De la Mare. Plautus impennis, the extinct Great Auk. HAP

In the Longhouse, Oneida Museum. Roberta Hill Whiteman. without oil, hasp or uranium. STE

In the Madison Zoo. Roberta Hill. bright and fleeting as the path of a snail. CDW

In the Madness of Love. Gary Soto. And the clouds begin to move. NPGG

In the Marble Quarry. James Dickey. But the spirit of this place just the same,/Felt here as joy. AmFN; NoP

In the Matter of Two Men. James David Carrothers. I know! Ah, Friend, I know! BANP

In the Middle of August. Edward Hirsch. Everyone believes in his own luck. MAYP

In the Mines. John Swett. To the loved ones left at home/Throbbing hearts are ever turning. BPAW

In the Mirror. Elizabeth Fleming. What can she be/Looking at? OnUR

In the Monastery. Norreys Jephson O'Conor. Cold is the wind. CAW

In the Month of Green Fire. Sophie Himmell. Dusk-surfeit of linden and yarrow,/Wood sparrow. GoYe

In the Mood of Blake. William Soutar. But when they fear no brother's face/Truth walks about the market-place. HaMV

In the Moonlight. Norreys Jephson O'Conor. Oh, let me fly across the world/To where the Fairies are! HBMV; SoPo; SUS

In the Moonlight. David McKee Wright. O moonlight, bear my message of love to the heart that beats/for me. AnNZ

In the Morgue. Israel Zangwill. "I am more dead than you,/Because, alas, I know it!" TrJP

In the Morning. Jayne Cortez. In the morning in the morning in the morning BlSi

In the Morning. Paul Laurence Dunbar. "Gin us peace an' joy. Amen!" BPo; GoSl

In the Morning All Over. William Stafford. Many ways to go, the best wall is the wind. FAZ

In the Morning I Will Pray. William Henry Furness. Thou wilt peace around diffuse,/Gently as the evening dews. AH

In the Motel. X. J. Kennedy. What a bang-up holiday! Str

In the Mountain Tent. James Dickey. "I shall rise from the dead," I am saying. CAPP

In the Mountains on a Summer Day. Li Po. A wind from the pine-tree trickles on my bare head. AWP; SD

In the Mourning Time. Robert Earl Hayden. but man/permitted to be man. BPo

In the Museum. Isabella Gardner. Then quick I seized my husband's hand while he stared at his/bride. ELU; NYBP

In the Naked Bed, in Plato's Cave. Delmore Schwartz. Again and again,/ while History is unforgiven. ExPo; LiTA; LiTM; MiAP; MoAB; MoAmPo; MoVE; NePA; NoAm; NOBA; PoA; VGW

In the Name of Jesus Christ. Claudia Cranston. To whom the four winds of Heaven/Are but a lullaby for sleeping. HBMV

In the Name of Our Sons. Dorothy Gould. We vow, in tears: It shall not be again! PGD

In the National Gallery. Siegfried Sassoon. The Art Collection of the English Nation. NoAm

In the Neolithic Age. Rudyard Kipling. "And–every–single–one–of–them– is–right!" NOBV

In the New Sun. Philip Levine. ...it was always winter/and a dark snow. NNaP

In the Night. Elizabeth Jennings. I turn and the world turns on the other side. MP; NePoEA; NYBP

In the Night. Elizabeth Madox Roberts. And turned my face against the wall. WSC

In the Night. James Stephens. They terrify my soul! They tear/My heart asunder! OBMV

In the Night Field. William Stanley Merwin. ...A man cannot live by bread/Alone. AP; PoCh

In the Night of the Full Moon. Carl Busse. And I feel in my own breast/ Tears withholden wildly burning. AWP

In the Night Watches. Sir Charles G. D. Roberts. And your pillow wet with tears. PeCV

In the Nuptial Chamber. Thomas Hardy. And it's he I embrace while embracing you! BrPo

In the Old Churchyard at Fredericksburg. Frederick Wadsworth Loring. "Here lies a bearer of the pall/At the funeral of Shakespeare." AA

In the Old City. Yehuda Amichai. two light auras surround their dark bodies. VWA

In the Old City. Jacob Fichman. ...and his cup of/sad enchantments/hold out to me, and it thus far still/sounds and is flowing. TrJP

In the Old Guerilla War. Linda Pastan. I will be a field/where all the flowers/on my housedress/bloom at once. TW

In the Old House. Joan Aiken. that called him so briefly/from his deep/ deep sleep? WSC

In the Old House. Donald Hall. He opened the door and met the young/ woman who waited for him. NePoEA-2

In the Old Jewish Cemetery, Prague, 1970. Edward Lowbury. ...in tune with the sentence that confines/Gentile and Jew to the ghetto of this world. VWA

In the "Old South." John Greenleaf Whittier And plead for the rights of all! AA

In the Old Theatre, Fiesole. Thomas Hardy. The power, the pride, the reach of perished Rome. OBTV

In the Open Fields. Hugo Sonnenschein. But I walked ahead on the open road/into the day that was breaking. VWA

In the Operating Room. Alden Nowlan. I discover/they've strapped/my arms/to the table. NOBC

In the Orchard. Robert Friend. And she laughed back–as if her name were Eve. GP

In the Orchard. Henrik Ibsen. ...what matter/Who may revel with the rest? AWP

In the Orchard. James Stephens. Round by the lilac bushes back to you! LOW; RoGo; SO; WSC

In the Orchard. Muriel Stuart. "Yes. Well, I'll be going. Kiss me..." "Good/night"..."Good night." ErPo; FF; OxBTC

In the Orchard. Algernon Charles Swinburne. Ah God, ah God, that day should be so soon. BoLoP; UnTE

In the Oregon Country. William Stafford. gorged with yew trees that were good for bows. AmFN

In the Orpheum Building. Kit Robinson. Maybe's both ways, be simpler catching a bucket. APU

In the Palms of Ancient Bodhisattvas. John Tagliabue. We progress from one mystery to another like ageless/grasshoppers summoned precisely. AMV-81

In the Pantry. Hugh" (Christopher Murray Grieve) MacDiarmid. For the sicht o'ts eneuch/To turn my soul nesh! NoAm

In the Park. Gwen Harwood. To the wind she says, "They have eaten me alive." CBAP

In the Park. Helen Hoyt.   And yet it was my heart that wanted to stay. HBMV

In the Past. Trumbull Stickney.   That boatman am I.   NOBA; OxBA

In the Pauper's Turnip-Field. Herman Melville.   My heavy hoe/That earthward bows me to foreshow/A mattock heavier than the hoe.   OBSP; PoEL 1-5

In the Person of Woman Kind. Ben Jonson.   And having pleas'd our art wee'll try/To make a new, and hang that by.   NIP; SeCP; SeCV 1-2

In the Pines. *Anonymous.*   And I shivered the whole night through. AmFP; FSW

In the Pink. Siegfried Sassoon.   And still the war goes on; he don't know why.   CMoP

In the Place Where Her Breasts Come Together. Judy Grahn.   "swim' she told me and I/did, I did.   PeHV

In the Planetarium. Siv Cedering Fox.   when I leave one space/for another/space.   LTB

In the Plaza We Walk. Nephtali De Leon.   In the plaza we walk/under tangerine moons.   FIA

In the Pocket. James Dickey.   Now.   LiSp

In the Prison Pen. Herman Melville.   Dead in his meagreness.   PoEL 1-5; TAP

In the Proscenium. Gene Derwood.   Natural as the veronica and the verbena,/In agricultural health.   LiTA

In the Public Garden. Marianne Moore.   ...Art, admired in general,/is always actually personal.   NOBA

In the Public Gardens. Sir John Betjeman.   Ausgang we were out of love/Und eingang we are in.   NYBP

In the Queen's Bedroom. Norman Cameron.   Tell me, Queen, am I irredeemably spoiled?   GTBS-P; OxBTC

In the Ravine. W. W. Eustace Ross.   into the stream/into the stream PeCV

In the Redwood Forest. Ralph Pomeroy.   the brown, clear stream/that cuts its lifetime into/the dimming strata.   CoPo

In the Restaurant. Thomas Hardy.   Let us go, and face it, and bear the shame.   BrPo

In the Ringwood. Thomas Kinsella.   I took my love in my icy arms/In the Spring on Ringwood Hill.   CMoP; FaBoIP; NMP; OxBI

In the Room. James (1834-82) Thomson.   Of births and deaths and bridal nights.   NOBV; OBVV

In the Room of the Bride-Elect. Thomas Hardy.   Good God—I must marry him I suppose! BrPo

In the Root Cellar. Maxine W. Kumin.   Bite me and be born.   FaBoWP

In the Round. Theodore Weiss.   nightlong at its tongs and bones.   NMP

In the Rude Age. Henry Howard, Earl of Surrey.   His livelie face thy brest how did it freate,/Whose cynders yet with envye doo the eate.   AAS; FCP; NCEP

In the Rut. Hamish Brown.   I would have stayed a stag.   PoSH

In the Sea of Tears. Naomi Replansky.   And make no move; but armies come inside.   BrRo; GP

In the Season of Wolves and Names. Marieve Rugo.   for fear the children might hear me.   AMV-80

In the Secret House. Christopher Middleton.   The one note, not lost, for nothing FaBoMo

In the Secret Rose Garden. Sa'd ud-din Mahmud Shabistari.   Yet the Lord of both worlds will enter there.   LiTW

In the Selkirks. Duncan Campbell Scott.   The stream rushes on.   CaP

In the Seraglio. David R. Slavitt.   down on the cushions, a-tremble with dread/while the others hide their eyes.   ErPo; PeHV

In the Servants' Quarters. Thomas Hardy.   And he droops, and turns, and goes.   MoAB; MoBrPo; MoRP

In the Seven Woods. William Butler Yeats.   A cloudy quiver over Pairc-na-lee.   CMoP; LoBV; NoAm

In the Shade of the Old Apple Tree. Harry H. Williams.   I'll be waiting for you,/In the shade of the old apple tree.   FSN; TreFT

In the Shadows. David Gray.   O peevish and uncertain soul! obey/The law of life in patience till the Day.   OxBS

In the Shadowy Whatnot Corner. Robert Silliman Hillyer.   The only world that lasts—of porcelain.   NePoAm

In the Shelter. C. Day Lewis.   Cradling your spark through blizzard, drift and tomb.   BoC

In the Silence. Stephany.   I roamed/a thousand miles/before you came. BPo

In the Silent Midnight Watches. Arthur Cleveland Coxe.   Jesus waited long to know thee,/But he knows thee not.   AH

In the Silent Night. Isaac L. Peretz.   Has my sobbing ever/Waked you from your sleep?   TrJP

In the Silks. Diane Ackerman.   a man's body, or a memory, either one a whip.   MAYP

In the Sitting Room of the Opera. Criss E. Cannady.   the browns built up to show/the monotony of waiting.   PoDr

In the Sky, Clearest Blue. Rosalia de Castro.   While the bitter bile/Overflows in my breast.   PBWP

In the Small Boats of Their Hands. Pamela Kircher.   folds her fingers around it.   AMV-80

In the Smoking Car. Richard Wilbur.   Failure, the longed-for valley, takes him in.   ConAP; LiTM; MoAmPo

In the Snack-Bar. Edwin Morgan.   Dear Christ, to be born for this!   FF

In the Snake Park. William Plomer.   The girl who screamed had fallen in a faint.   NoAm; NYBP; OxBTC

In the Snowfall. Gwerfyl Mechain.   I had no hope of getting home. BoWoP

In the Soul Hour. Robert Mezey.   voices at night/carried across the blowing water.   AmPA; NaP

In the Sprightly Month of May. Sir John Vanbrugh.   They fell together by the ears,/And ne'er were fond again.   UnTE

In the Spring. William Barnes.   An' oh! 'tis the maid I'm a-hopen/to wed in the Spring.   GBL

In the Spring. Meleager.   And sweeter than the violet!   AWP

In the Spring. Alfred, Lord Tennyson.   In the Spring a young man's fancy lightly turns to/thoughts of love.   BoNaP

In the Stable. Elizabeth Goudge.   They knew He was God the Almighty/Come love to seek.   ChBR

In the States. Robert Louis Stevenson.   To-morrow for the States—for me,/England and Yesterday.   BrPo

In the Still, Star-Lit Night. Elizabeth Stoddard   How could the spirit flee? AA

In the Street. Shaw Neilson.   I saw the mark/Of tears upon her, as she stept/Into the dark.   CBAP

In the Streets of Catania. Roger Casement.   Almond and citron bloom quivering at start,/Ends in pure snows.   AnIV

In the Study. Thomas Hardy.   But fresh and honey-like; and Need/No household skeleton at all.   BrPo

In the Suburbs. Louis Simpson.   To the temple, singing.   CAPP; ELU; MAT

In the Subway. Juan Ramon Jimenez.   He goes on talking soundlessly, moving his raised hands furiously, a final spark of blood...   NYP

In the Summer of Sixty. *Anonymous.*   Goin' down the Platte River for death or for life.   CoSo; PoOW

In the Surgery. J. M. Ditta.   ...fall/of seeds and sleet, petal and limb. AMV-80

In the Swamp in Secluded Recesses. Walt Whitman.   Sings by himself a song.   RFM

In the Tail of the Scorpion. Genevieve Taggard.   And whiffs of autumn fleck canary paint.   VGW

In the Tank. Thom Gunn.   And where he must re-enter and re-enter. NoAm

In the Taxidermist's Shop. Siv Cedering Fox.   mortality is there.   AMV-81

In the Third Year of War. Henry Treece.   Only seeking, seeking without finding.   WaP

In the Thirtieth. J. V. Cunningham.   And with my death it dies with me. PoL

In the Time of Revolution. Julius Lester.   nail ourselves to/crosses he must be there,/pinioned,/because/atlanta, georgia/november 20, 1966.   PoBA

In the Time of the Rose. John Savant.   We pause to contemplate/The dancing we have done.   AMV-81

In the Time of Trouble. Leslie Savage Clark.   O Father, gently lead all hearts/That newly come to sorrow!   TrPWD

In the Town. *Anonymous.*   Where I with friends around me/May lay my burden down.   OBCP; PCh

In the Township. Denis Glover.   And his shovel was lashed to his pack. AnNZ

In the Trades. C. Fox Smith.   Down below the keel of her the lost ships lying/In the weed and the coral, far below...   EtS

In the Tree House at Night. James Dickey.   I move at the heart of the world.   NoP

In the Tree-Top. Lucy Larcom.   Rock-a-by, baby! wake by-and-by!/Rock-a-by!   OBCA

In the Trench. Leon Gellert.   I'll lie and feed my sheep/On a green Lawn. BoAV; PoAu 1-2

In the Trenches. Richard Aldington.   And crush the spring leaf with your armies!   MMM

In the Tub We Soak Our Skin. Edward Newman Horn.   The since neglected and unwanted.   ELU

In the Turkish Ward. Peter Balakian.   nothing—plashing water, wind in the moorings.   MAYP

In the Twilight. James Russell Lowell   Long ago!   AA; HBV 1-2

In the Twilight (excerpt). John Francis O'Donnell.   'Tis Earth, though the air and the water be black/with the blackness of Doom!   IrPN

In the Valley of Cauteretz. Alfred, Lord Tennyson.   The voice of the dead was a living voice to me.   BoLoP; NOBE; OBVV; VLP

In the Valley of the Elwy. Gerard Manley Hopkins.   Being mighty a master, being a father and fond.   EG; InPo; NOBV; NOCV; ViBoPo

In the Van Gogh Room. Traise Yamamoto.   The fine bones of my hand/have nothing to say about God.   BrSi

In the Vaulted Way. Thomas Hardy. The thing is dark, Dear. I do not know. BoLoP; OLR

In the Vices. Donald Evans. And soon upon a harlot's house I came–/Within I found him playing at solitaire! HBMV

In the Waiting Room. Elizabeth Bishop. and it was still the fifth/of February, 1918. FaBoWP; HeIP; InPS; LCAP; NOBA; Prf

In the Web. E. L. Mayo. Crows for a dawn he shall not see again/And cannot but desire. MiAP

In the Week When Christmas Comes. Eleanor Farjeon. This is the week when Christmas comes. ChBR; PCh; SiSoSe

In the White Giant's Thigh. Dylan Thomas. And the daughters of darkness flame like Fawkes fires/still. AtBAP; LiTB

In the Wicker Fish-Trap. *Anonymous.* Her escort is like a river. HW

In the Wide Awe and Wisdom of the Night. Sir Charles G. D. Roberts. And knew the Universe of no such span/As the august infinitude of man. CaP

In the Wilderness. Robert Graves. Tears like a lover wept. BoC; EaLo; MoAB; MoBrPo; OxBI; SeCePo

In the Wilderness. Edith Lovejoy Pierce. O Lord, be lost with us,/And then we shall be found. TrPWD

In the Winter of My Thirty-Eighth Year. William Stanley Merwin. While they drift farther away in the invisible morning NOBA

In the Woods. Frederick George Scott. And every cloud a solace and a balm. ACV; CaP

In the Wracks of Walsingham. *Anonymous.* Sathan sittes wher our Lord did swaye/Walsingham oh farewell. NCEP

In the Year of Many Conversions and the Private Soul. John Ciardi. Picking the horn of plenty's garbage can. MiAP

In the Year of Two Thousand. Menke Katz. you are beyond my last night, my first dawn. AMV-81

In the Yellow Light of Brooklyn. Al Lee. I love you. Goodbye. Goodbye. NYP

In the Yucca Land. Madge Morris. The world is so new you could talk with God,/In the Yucca land. BPAW

In the Zoo. Solomon Mahaka. Our minor zoos/Will love to mushroom/In this great zoo. WhB

In These Dissenting Times. Alice Walker.
And how he would like/All eternity to stare/It down. PoBA
And let her pick/Out/A pig. PoBA
And stood around waiting/In their/Brown suits. PoBA
I ponder the exchange/Itself/And salvage mostly/The leaning. PoBA
Knew the arsonist/Of the church? PoBA
Leaving all/The weeds. PoBA
Somctimes/A dime. PoBA
Without knowing a page/Of it/Themselves. PoBA

In These Fair Vales. William Wordsworth. May have a gentle sigh for him,/As one of the departed. CBEP

In Thine Arms. Oliver Wendell Holmes. As Thou didst keep Thy folk of old. TRV

In Thine Own Heart. (Johanne Scheffler) "Angelus Silesius" The cross in thine own heart/Alone can make thee whole. TRV

In This City. Alan Brownjohn. And who has just switched off the light/Forgetting she was there. CAD

In This Dark House. Edward Davison. I shall come back at last/In this dark house to die. OBMV

In This Deep Darkness. Natan Zach. all that is forever homeless/in this deep heavy darkness. VWA

In This Hotel. Emanuel Carnevali. May I ask for a job/As headwaiter/Of this hotel? AnAmPo

In This Hour. Josephine Winslow Johnson. This stone on the mouths of the silent? MoRP

"In This House, There Shall Be No Idols". Carolyn M. Rodgers. when they came./i had spaced. JB

In This Life. Robert Mezey. blossoms of mercy/in the midst of the holocaust. SUW

In This River. Valentin Iremonger. Harvest lost, and all our store-houses empty. NeIP

In This Shanty Shebeen without You. Richard Augustine Chima. But honestly/Don't come/If they have improved you. WhB

In This Strange House. Carleton Drewry. But mind from its fire, a phoenix, fly. MoRP

In This World's Raging Sea. William, of Hawthornden Drummond. And doth again in seas his burden throw. CBEP

In Time. Robert Graves. Befriend us, Time, Love's gaunt executor! FaBoEE

In Time. Kathleen Raine. his face, wounded by us, for us and over us watches. NeBP

In Time Like Air. May Sarton. For us, more human and less holy,/In time like air is essence stated. MoLP; NYBP

In Time Like Glass. Walter James Turner. Fast-fixed as they in Time like glass. MoBrPo; NAMP; OBMV

In Time of Crisis. Raymond Richard Patterson. And build their anger, stone on stone–/Each silently, but not alone. IDB

In Time of Gold. Hilda ("H. D.") Doolittle. ...spoil/what may be vision of a Pharaoh's face. PoA

In Time of Grief. Lizette Woodworth Reese. After a fall of rain. AA; ATP

In Time of Need. Katharine Tynan Hinkson. O Child, come to our hour of dearth/And bid the dead heart live. TrPWD

In Time of Need. William Stafford. holding a calm face against the opening world. UnPo

In Time of Silver Rain. Langston Hughes. When spring/And life are new. GoSl; SoPo; TiPo

In Time of "The Breaking of Nations." Thomas Hardy. War's annals will fade into night/Ere their story die. AnEnPo; BoLoP; CMoP; CoBMV; EBEV; EnLit; ExPo; ForPo; GoTF; GTBS; HAP; LiTB; LiTM; LoBV; MMM; MoAB; MoBrPo; MoRP; NoAm; NOBE; NoP; OAEL 1-2; OAEP; OBEV; OBWP; PoL; PPP; QFR; SeCeV; TreF

In Time of War. W.H. Auden.
Against the poet and the legislator. CMoP
And envied his few friends, and chose his love. CMoP
And hated life with heart and soul. CMoP
And knew himself as one of many men. CMoP
And ravished the daughters, and drove the fathers mad. CMoP
And tyrants held him up as an example. CMoP
But trembled if one passed him with a frown. CMoP
A mountain people dwelling among moun-/tains. EnLit
Mountains and houses, may be also men. CMoP
Nor feel the love that he knew all about. PoPl; SCV

In Town. *Anonymous.* Whee-oop! Whoop-eee! ABF

In Town. David McKee Wright. Old Memory's rich flood-tide. ACV

In Tribute. Vernal House. Come back, old graying guides,/That I, in tribute, may atone. CaP

In Trouble and Shame. D. H. Lawrence. And seeing my cast-off body lying like lumber,/I would laugh with joy. OBMV

In Trust. Mary Mapes Dodge. For God who sendeth/He only lendeth. SiSoSe

In Tyme the Strong and Statlie Turrets Fall. Giles the Elder Fletcher. Thus all (sweet faire) in tyme must have an end:/Except thy beautie, vertues, and thy friend. AAS

In Utrumque Paratus. Matthew Arnold. "I, too, but seem." MaVP; OAEP; OBNC; PoEL 1-5; VLP

In Vain. Rose T. Cooke. I want but one such memory! AA

In Vain Was I Born. Nezahualcoyotl. Let not our hearts be troubled/Close to and beside the giver of life! ILwL

In Vinculis: The Deeds That Might Have Been. Wilfrid Scawen Blunt. The dreamer of brave deeds that might have been,/Shall cureless ache with wounds forever green. TrGrPo

In Vistas of Stone. Abo Stoltzenberg. by all our roots connected/with the deepest wells/of the world. VWA

In War. Mason Jordan Mason. floating with/their broken plums PoNe

In Waste Places. James Stephens. Until I dare my fear and call/The lion out to lick my hand. GTBS; MoAB; MoBrPo; MoVE

In Weather. Robert Hass. curled in the dark of a winged pod/knows flourishing. AmPA; GeTw

In Westminster Abbey. Sir John Betjeman.
And, even more, protect the whites. ExPo
And now, dear Lord, I cannot wait/Because I have a luncheon date. CMoP; DBV; FaBoCo; InPK; NIP; NLV; NOBL; OAEL 1-2; OBSV

In What Manner the Body Is United with the Soule. Jorie Graham. flies off, blue and white and host/to a freedom/it knows nothing of. NPGG

In Which She Satisfies a Fear with the Rhetoric of Tears. Sister Juana Ines de la Cruz. ...for now you see my heart which met/your touch–and so is shattered in your hands. BoWoP

In White Tie. David Huddle. ...I'd/been through enough of a/war to know courage/when I saw it. Str

In Wicklow. Rhoda Coghill. Thoughts that were once her own. NeIP

In Windsor Castle. Henry Howard, Earl of Surrey. To banish the less, I find my chief relief. NOBE; OBSC; SeCePo

In Winter. Paul Blackburn. or else the snow. NYP

In Winter. C. H. Bretherton. Spring with triumph–and our old black hen/(Thank the Lord!) will begin to lay. BiP; InMe; MAPA; SeCeV

In Winter. Michael Ryan. despite mistake after mistake after mistake. MAYP

In Winter. Arthur Symons. As I wait for my love in the fir-tree alley alone with the sun. BrPo

In Winter. Robert Wallace. ...Some/things/are, even if no one comes. BoNaP

In Winter in my Room. Emily Dickinson. This was a dream– AmPP; BiP; ErPo; LiTA; NoAm; NOBA; OxBA

In Winter in the Woods Alone. Robert Frost. Or for myself in my retreat/For yet another blow. HeIP

"In winter's just return..." Henry Howard, Earl of Surrey. But to the heavens, lo, it fled, for to receive his doom. AAS; FCP; SiPS

In Winter, When the Fields Are White. Lewis (Charles Lutwidge Dodgson) Carroll. I tried to turn the handle, but– EBEV; NOBV

In Wonted Walks. Sir Philip Sidney. "Infected minds infect each thing they see." CABA Thought, reason, sense, time, you, and I, maintaine. PoEL 1-5

In Yellow Meadows I Take No Delight. Sir Thomas Browne. Let me have those which are most red and white. FaBoEE

In Your Absence. Elizabeth Baxter. Are many as the things I hear and see. PoToHe

In Your Arms. Miklos Radnoti. In your arms I'll/survive death./It's a dream. VWA

In Your Arrogance. Lynne Lawner. This is not your harvest, these are not your fields! ErPo

In Your Bad Dream. Richard Hugo. Anything. Anything. Ridicule my arm. LCAP

In Youth. Evaleen Stein. O God,–not, not for death! AA

Inadequate Aqua Extremis. Ruth M. Walsh. Or we'll find our country going from/One ex-stream to another! QQQ

Inanna and An. Enheduanna. Who can understand you? BoWoP

Inanna and Ebih. Enheduanna. The dancing city is filled with storm,/ driving young men to you, captive. BoWoP

Inanna and Enlil. Enheduanna. and walk toward you along a path/from the house of enormous sighs. BoWoP

Inanna and Ishkur. Enheduanna. On your harp of sighs/I hear your dirge. BoWoP

Inanna and the Anunna. Enheduanna. Who has ever denied you homage,/ lady, supreme over the land? BoWoP

Inanna and the City of Uruk. Enheduanna. Who dares not worship you? BoWoP

Inanna and the Divine Essences. Enheduanna. You have gathered the holy essences and worn them/tightly on your breasts. BoWoP

Inanna Exalted (excerpt). Enheduanna. My Lady wrapped in beauty Inanna be praised! WPOW

Inanna's Song. *Anonymous.* He is lettuce planted by the water. LLLT

Inapprehensiveness. Robert Browning. I said "Vernon Lee?" NOBV; VLP

Inasmuch! William E. Brooks. Inasmuch as ye did it not to them/Ye did it not to Me. PGD

The Inca Tupac Upanqui. William Hart-Smith. They look like shepherds moving on a plain. NOAV

Incandescence. Lucille Clifton. lucille/we are/the Light GeTw

The Incantation. Amergin. Pleaders, blend pray'r in./So we seek Erinn– OnYI

Incantation for Rain. *Anonymous.* The waters of the dark mists drop, drop. ExPo

Incantation to Get Rid of a Sometime Friend. Emanuel DiPasquale. Dry up/like/unwatered/weed TW

Incantation to Oedipus. John Dryden. Answer me, if this be done?/'Tis done. OFD; WSC

Incanto. Stan Rice. No more death. NPGG

Incarnate Love. Wilbur Fisk Tillett. When God through thee hath spoken,/Love's message is complete. BLRP

Incarnatio Est Maximum Donum Dei. William Alabaster. How might this goodness draw our soules above/Which drew downe God with such attractive Love. MePo

The Incarnation. Charles Wesley. JESUS is our Brother now,/And GOD is All our own! NOCV

The Incarnation and Passion. Henry Vaughan. ...for Love/Is only stronger far than death. TrCP

Incarnation Poem. John Leax. God and flesh were one. TrCP

Incendiary. Vernon Scannell. ...content with one warm kiss/had there been anyone to offer this. OxBC

Incense. Vachel Lindsay. Where all Faiths kneel, as brothers, in one place. MoRP

Incense. Louise Townsend Nicholl. Does the one tempo of the movement flow. NePoAm-2

The Incentive. Sarah N. Cleghorn. –Even as he spoke, the sun's one spark/ Withdrew, and left the dusk more dark.– HBMV

The Incentive. Martial (Marcus Valerius Martialis). Everyone wants to get at her. UnTE

An Inch of Air. Robyn Sarah. ...And moves/an inch over, to put some token air/between her back and his. CaPN

The Inchcape Rock. Robert Southey. And the vessel sinks beneath the tide. PoPle The Devil below was ringing his knell. BeLS; FaBoBe; GN; HBV 1-2; HBVY; OBNV; OBRV; PaPo; TreFS

Incident. Countee Cullen. Of all the things that happened there/That's all that I remember. BiP; BPo; CDC; CTBA; FF; GoSl; IDB; NoAm; NTCP; OBCA; PoBA; PoNe; SoSe; VGW

Incident. LeRoi (Imamu Amiri Baraka) Jones. ...we know nothing. NoAm

Incident. Karl Kopp. how he turned without a word/followed him back to the highway. GOYP

An Incident. Douglas LePan. Again stands superb as a temple. ACV; PeCV

Incident. Norman MacCaig. I give you one/with a hand that trembles/ with a human trembling. FF

Incident. Harvey Shapiro. Slowly I begin to rehearse it. FAZ

An Incident. Frederick Tennyson. ...dying Lord to me has spoken,/At His own Holy Table, face to face! GoBC

Incident at Bruges. William Wordsworth. Fresh from the beauty and the bliss/Of English liberty? OBTV

Incident at Imuris. Alberto Rios. And drinking too much from the town well. APU

Incident at Matauri. Kendrick Smithyman. Rocking and distant the islands slept. AnNZ

Incident at Mossel Bay. Mary Balazs. I let the whole sea/wash in. AMV-81

Incident Characteristic of a Favourite Dog. William Wordsworth. Until her fellow sinks to re-appear no more. FM

An Incident Here and There. Hilda ("H. D.") Doolittle. what saved us? what for? CrMA

Incident in a Rose Garden. Donald Justice. I take it you are he? NCSH

An Incident in the Early Life of Ebenezer Jones, Poet, 1828. Sir John Betjeman. ...to hear a boy's heart break. CMoP; NoAm

Incident of the French Camp. Robert Browning. Smiling, the boy fell dead. BeLS; EnLi 1-2; FaPo; FaPoR; GN; HBV 1-2; HBVY; MaC; MaVP; MBW 1-2; MCCG; OBWP; RoGo; TreF; TrGrPo

An Incident of the Occupation. Ira Gershwin. "Molodyets, ti–moyo mat'!" OxBoLi

Incident on a Front Not Far from Castel di Sangro. Harry Brown. And dust that sifted toward the unseen, unmoved stars. NYBP

Incident on a Journey. Thom Gunn. I would regret nothing. NePoEA

Incidental Pieces to a Walk: for Conrad. James (Olumo) Cunningham. I/ swear/nothing JB

Incidents in Playfair House. Nicholas Moore. Blindingly behind each lover's eye! ErPo; NeBP

Incidents in the Life of My Uncle Arly. Edward Lear. (But his shoes were far too tight). FaBoNo; FPL; MoShBr; NA; NBM; OAEL 1-2; OxBoLi; TrGrPo

Incipience. Adrienne Rich. over the scarred volcanic rock CAPP

Incipit Vita Nova. William Morton Payne. That life renewed whereof the Florentine/Sang ere he wrote the Comedy Divine! AA

Inclusions. Elizabeth Barrett Browning. Nor hands nor cheeks keep separate, when soul is join'd/to soul. HBV 1-2; OBVV; UnTE

Incognita. Henry Austin Dobson. And I sorrow in sackcloth and ashes,/ Longing to see her again. CenHV

Incognita of Raphael. William Allen Butler. The kindred rapture of the heart! AA

The Incomparable Light. Richard Eberhart. Our mystery of time, the only hopeful light. MoRP

Incompatibility. Aubrey Thomas De Vere. O gentle Death, how dear thou makest the dead! IrPN

The Incomprehensible. Isaac Watts. To Thee th' Eternal Fair, the Infinite Unknown. CEP; WGRP

An Inconclusive Evening. Frances Bellerby. I heard that cry as though/It were of a heart-moving voice long dead/The deathless echo. FaBoTw

Inconsistencies. Michelle Roberts. until your face falls against Big Brother's boot. LFAC

Inconsistent. Mark Van Doren. Why do I contradict/Myself? Do not inquire. ELU

Inconstancy's the Greatest of Sins. Edward, Lord Herbert of Cherbury. Like the same body in another place. OBSP

An Inconvenience. John Raven. We gon have/mo room! BPo

An Incorrigible Music. Allen Curnow. A big one! A big one! OCNZ

The Incredible Yachts. Philip Booth. ...none of them/cared to know in truth/what harbor they were in. GP

The Incubation. Al Zolynas. stepping out of the shells/of the only life it's never known. LTB

The Incurables. Arthur Upson. Where young and old and fair and foul are one. AnAmPo

Indecision. Helen Pinkerton. Or we may wait the death none can refuse/ Which will, itself, be in time's disposition. QFR

Indecsion Means Flexibility. Elliot Abhau. "Old Dobbin" will wait/for this headless horseman/to take hold of his fate. PH

Indeed Indeed, I Cannot Tell. Henry David Thoreau. One iota to abate/Of a pure impartial hate. TW

Independence. *Anonymous.* It is God's victory! WTO

Independence. Nancy Cato. ...alone/On the vast plains, with night and rain coming on. PoAu 1-2

Independence. Adebayo Faleti. Let all our people be free. PBA

Independence. Mary Elizabeth ("E") Fullerton. Yet is a secret lute/Awake in my heart. BoAV

Independence. Guy Mason. ` And find a hundred Edens at our feet. CaP

Independence. Roy McFadden. Enraptured child still fond enough to sing. OxBI

Independence. Tobias George Smollett. Immortal Liberty, whose look sublime/Hath bleached the tyrant's cheek in every varying clime. OBEC

Independence. Henry David Thoreau. Wears its emblazonry. AnNE; TreFS

Independence Bell—July 4, 1776. *Anonymous.* Which, please God, shall never die! BLPA; FaBoBe; FPL; MC; PAL

Independence Day. Wendell Berry. ...the bobwhite's/whistle opens in the air, broad and pointed like a leaf. OFD

Independence Day. William Jay Smith. The wind, an Indian paintbrush, sweeps the sky. MP; TwCP

Independence Day. Royall Tyler. Thus we drink and dance away,/This glorious INDEPENDENCE DAY! PAH

The Independent. Phyllis McGinley. Sweeping him bare of all opinion. · FaBoFE

Index. Bernadette Mayer. thigh/Tradition/tuck ANYP

India. Walter James Turner. They hunt, the velvet tigers in the jungle. MoBrPo

The India Guide. Sir George Dallas.
And surely, myself, I'd the voyage have declined/If half what I suffred I e'er had opined! OBTV
Who ploughs foaming billows in search of adventure! NOEC

India the Magic. H. A. Jules-Bois. And he who sees no longer fears to die! CAW

Indian. Jeanne Doriot. as the Indian rocks and stares and waves one hand at me. AMV-81

Indian. Laura Jensen. loose my braid to fly my hair. AmPA

The Indian. Thomas Reed. ...I tell them I will share/my string of beads/if they give me Manhattan. AMV-81

Indian america. Mah-do-ge Tohee. in jicarilla, the apaches run their own bar. STE

An Indian at the Burial-Place of His Fathers. William Cullen Bryant. The realm our tribes are crushed to get/May be a barren desert yet. HeIP

Indian Blood. Mary Tallmountain. with moons of dark/Indian blood. STE; TWSS

The Indian Burying Ground. Philip Freneau. And Reason's self shall bow the knee to shadows and delusions here. AA; AnAmPo; AP; APA; ForPo; HAP; HBV 1-2; HeIP; LiTA; MAmP; NePA; NOBA; NoP; OxBA; PoEL 1-5; PoLf; PoPl; TAP

Indian Camp. Janet Reed McFatter. When these people are gone/they will have taken the land/with them. GrPl

Indian Children. Annette Wynne. What a different place to-day/Where we live and work and play! SoPo; SUS; TiPo

The Indian Convert. Philip Freneau. ...a place/Where there's nothing to eat and but little to steal. TAP

Indian Dance. Frederick Niven. "Just looking at the Indian dance." CaP

Indian Death. Alice Corbin. Not now–but then... BPAW

Indian Death. Eda Lou Walton. Walking I come to you. BPAW

Indian Education. Adrian C. Louis. I love school. STE

The Indian Elephant. C. J. Kaberry. In the Irrawaddy. FiBHP

The Indian Emperor. John Dryden. For all the happiness mankind can gain/Is not in pleasure, but in rest from pain. FiP

The Indian Ghost Dance and War. W. H. Prather. They only ask and pray to God to make John hold his base. PoOW

The Indian Graveyard. Ramona Weeks. never said how. TAT

Indian Guys at the Bar. Simon J. Ortiz. my heart is staggering somewhere in between. STE

The Indian Hunter. Eliza Cook. To find that the white man wrongs the one/Who never did harm to him. BLPA

The Indian Lass. *Anonymous.* Here's a health, a good health, to that Indian lass. OBET

Indian Love Song. Lew Blockcolski. and found his fingers grafted to their backs. VoR

Indian Macho. Louis (LittleCoon) Oliver. She leaned over and whispered: "You go with me." STE

The Indian Maid. Edward Thompson. And when she moves, her mien and grace/Prove her the goddess of the place! NOEC; OBTV

The Indian Mohee. *Anonymous.* I'll turn my course backward across the salt sea,/And there I will dwell with the little Mohee. BFSS

An Indian Mother about to Destroy Her Child. James Montgomery. Her child, her sex, her tyrant, and herself. PaPo

Indian Mounds. Angela Peace. Out our death and yours. AMV-80

Indian Names. Lydia Huntley Sigourney. Your mountains build their monument,/Though ye destroy their dust. AmFN; HBV 1-2; MC; OBCA; PAH; PoLf

Indian Night Tableau. Hyman Edelstein. Panorama of ghostly Indian battles/Re-fought in Canadian skies. CaP

Indian Painting, Probably Paiute, in a Cave near Madras, Oregon. Jarold Ramsey. ...I follow you into stone. TAT

Indian Pipe and Moccasin Flower. Arthur Guiterman. Indian pipe and moccasin flower/Scattered among our hills. BrR; SUS

Indian Pipes. Winifred Welles. Leaf, stem and cup, but could not last the night. AnAmPo

Indian Prayer. Chief Joseph Strongwolf. O Thou Kitchi Manito, hear us! TRV

The Indian Queen: Song of Aerial Spirits. John Dryden. They slide to us and Air. AtBAP

Indian Reservation: Caughnawaga. Abraham Moses Klein. ...About them watch/as through a mist, the pious prosperous ghosts. LiTM; NOBC; NoP; OBCV

Indian Rock, Bainbridge Island, Washington. Duane Niatum. Leaving you alone to bend like the reed. CDW

The Indian's Grave. G. J. Mountain. What will be yours, ye powerful, wealthy, wise,/By whom the heathen unregarded dies? CaP

The Indian's Welcome to the Pilgrim Fathers. Lydia Huntley Sigourney. Say, who shall welcome thee? AA

Indian School. Norman H. Russell. i am not wise enough to know/gods purpose in him. MAT

The Indian Serenade. Percy Bysshe Shelley Oh! press it to thine own again,/Where it will break at last. ATP; AWP; BLPL; BoLiVe; EnLi 1-2; EnLit; EnRP; ExPo; GoTF; GTBS; HoPM; InPo; LiTB; LiTL; LoBV; MCCG; OAEP; OBEV; OBRV; PG; PoPl; TreF; TrGrPo; UnTE; ViBoPo

Indian Sky. Alfred Kreymborg. The same shawl/Wraps them around. BPAW

Indian Song. Willard Johnson. The campfire, flaring to a star,/Fans the wind where hunters are. BPAW

An Indian Song. William Butler Yeats. Dropping at eve in coral bays/A vapoury footfall on the ocean's sleepy/blaze. VLP

Indian Song: Survival. Leslie Marmon Silko. I am the lean gray deer/running on the edge of the rainbow. CDW; VoR

The Indian Student. Philip Freneau. The shepherd of the forest went. OxBA

Indian Summer. Gray Burr. Letting it pass away, becoming myth,/And memory, and finally this sleight. AMV-80

Indian Summer. Wilfred (William Wilfred Campbell) Campbell. Wild birds are flying south. CaP; NOBC; OBCV; PoPl; WHW

Indian Summer. Emily Dickinson. Taste thine immortal wine! AnNE; BoLiVe

Indian Summer. A. S. Draper. ...beneath the blankets/They have spread, until they are fast asleep. YeAr

Indian Summer. Barbara Howes. A golden cataract that comes/Out of the cornucopia of dream. IHMS

Indian Summer. William Ellery Leonard. While still so many yet must come to birth. HBMV; PG

Indian Summer. Susanna Moodie. 'Tis Beauty sleeping on her bier. CaP

Indian Summer. John Banister Tabb. The smoke of many a calument/Ascends to heaven again. AA

Indian Summer, 1927. Anne Hussey. softly tracing the mortar with our fingers. AMV-81

An Indian Summer Day on the Prairie. Vachel Lindsay. He builds him a crimson nest. BPAW; RFM; SoPo

Indian Summer Here, You in Honolulu. Donald Johnson. ...But the wind/In the wake of her skirts is cold. AMV-80

Indian Summer: Montana, 1956. W. M. Ransom. At daybreak I chose a longer, dustier way home. CDW

Indian Summer: Vermont. Anne Stevenson. In the grey desolation/the land was its stones. NCSH

The Indian to His Love. William Butler Yeats. Where eve has hushed the feathered ways,/And drop a vapoury footfall in the water's/drowsy blaze. VLP

The Indian upon God. William Butler Yeats. His languid tail above us, lit with myriad spots of light. MoBrPo; WGRP

Indian Woman's Death-Song. Felicia Dorothea Hemans. One moment, and that realm is ours. On, on, dark rolling stream! SBG

The Indian Women Are Listening: To the Nuke Devils. Wendy Rose. break from electric trees/their tops, fall completely and forever/into star dust. TWSS

Indians. John Fandel. Suns before this morning. AmFN; NYBP

Indians. Charles Sprague. Beyond the mountains of the west,/Their children go to die. GN

Indians at the Guthrie. Gerald Vizenor. new parties in the corporate hills STE; VoR

The Indians Count of Men as Dogs. Roger Williams. To take away Peace from Earthly Men,/They must Each other kill. SCAP

The Indians on Alcatraz. Paul Muldoon. That they would not attack after dark. CIP

The Indians Prize Not English Gold. Roger Williams. The English knowing prize it not,/But fling't like drosse away. SCAP

The Inheritance.   David Ignatow.   I am going to sell your shop,/you to be remembered in my lines.   CAPP

Inheritance.   Frank O'Connor.   Hang them, sweet Christ, all three.   DBV; TW

An Inheritance.   Naomi Replansky.   My father's frown divides my face.   GP

The Inheritors.   Gary Geddes.   We were the inheritors, we/couldn't leave fast enough.   NOBC

The Inheritors.   Dorothy Livesay.   Bound by the heart-beat pulse of a drum!   CaP

Inhuman Henry or Cruelty to Fabulous Animals.   Alfred Edward Housman.   So now be kind to unicorns.   BBGG; FiBHP; NLV

The Inhuman Wolf and the Lamb Sans Gene.   Guy Wetmore Carryl.   The public bar-lamb's worse!   ALV; AmePo

Inis Fal.   Egan O'Rahilly.   ...nothing/Remains to us of all that was our own.   BIrV; OBMV

Inisgallun.   Darrell Figgis.   And the Earth will never find peace again.   OnYI

Inishkeel Parish Church.   Tom Paulin.   There was an enormous sight of the sea,/A silent water beyond society.   FaBoIP

Initial.   Arthur Boyars.   Now like lovers stumbling because of their locked fingers/And their gaze   NePoEA-2

Initial Response.   Katherine Soniat.   lightning striking all the way.   AMV-80

Initials.   Michael S. Glaser.   he's just as good as free.   AMV-81

The Initiate.   William Stanley Merwin.   not even an eye/do we need to take with us/into the light   NNaP

Initiation.   Jayne Cortez.   take us to the place for the new birth blood.   PoBA

Initiation.   Rainer Maria Rilke.   then tenderly your eyes will let it go...   TrJP

Injured Maple.   Ronald G. Everson.   I stand here fearful at dusk under the primitive active tree   NOBC

The Injured Moon.   Charles Baudelaire.   She cunningly powders the breast that nourished you.   MOON

The Injury.   William Carlos Williams.   (if you can find any way) that is/ the only way left now/for you.   AP

Inland City.   John Crowe Ransom.   Moor in my little boats vigilantly!   CMoP

The Inland Lighthouse.   James McMichael.   He is not to leave.   AmPA

Inland Passages, I: The Long Hunter.   Wendell Berry.   he saw a place green as welcome/on whose still water the sky lay white.   GP

The Inn of Care.   Samuel Waddington.   It is the "Inn of Care".   OBVV

The Inn of Earth.   Sara Teasdale.   But the Host went by with averted eye/And barred the outer door.   LiTA

The Inn That Missed Its Chance.   Amos R. Wells.   The birthplace of the Messiah, had I known!   TrCP

Innate Helium.   Robert Frost.   Some gas like helium must be innate.   ImOP

Inner Brother.   Stephen Stepanchev.   To take my troubling, grisly, inner brother!   WaP

Inner-City Lullaby.   Russell Atkins.   ...cat, contrary to being put out,/is brought in/and fed for sleep   CNA

The Inner Light.   Frederic William Henry Myers.   Yes, and in hell would whisper, I have known.   HBV 1-2; WGRP

The Inner Man.   Plato.   Grant me to be beautiful in the inner man.   PoPl

The Inner Part.   Louis Simpson.   As black as death, emitting a strange odor.   PAI

The Inner Significance of the Statues Seated Outside the Boston...   Walter Conrad Arensberg.   Hast thou an easy stool?   AnAmPo

The Inner Silence.   Harriet Monroe.   There where no thought may follow me,/Nor stillest dreams whose pinions plume the way.   HBMV

The Inner Source.   Andrei Codrescu.   Let's hash the hush.   APU

The Inner Vision.   William Wordsworth.   The Mind's internal heaven shall shed her dews/Of inspiration on the humblest lay.   GTBS; GTBS-P; HBV 1-2

Inniskeen Road: July Evening.   Patrick Kavanagh.   ...I am king/Of banks and stones and every blooming thing.   FaBoIP; IPY; NoAm; NoP

Innocence.   George S. Chappell.   I was wrong, I'm glad to say.   YaD

The Innocence.   Robert Creeley.   What I come to do/is partial, partially kept.   NeAP; NoAm

Innocence.   Thom Gunn.   As melting quietly by his boots it fell.   LiTM; NePoEA-2; NoAm

Innocence.   Patrick Kavanagh.   I cannot die/Unless I walk outside these whitethorn hedges.   FaBoIP

Innocence.   Norman MacCaig.   Moused in the dark for what she once had been.   NMP

Innocence.   James Scully.   You could not, could not tell/my heart from my hand.   LTB

Innocence.   Anne Spencer.   'Twas a star-lance in her side!   CDC

Innocence.   Thomas Traherne.   I must becom a Child again.   AnAnS 1

The Innocent.   Gene Derwood.   Life, life, you will not let me die.'   NePA; WaP

The Innocent Breasts.   Joel Oppenheimer.   ...the/breasts hung innocent/in the morning light.   PoM

The Innocent Country-Maid's Delight.   Anonymous.   Through frost and snow, when winds do blow,/To carry the milking-payl.   CoMu

The Innocent Gazer.   John, Lord Cutts.   And I had rather torture mine,/Than rob you of one minute's rest.   CavP

Innocent Landscape.   Elinor Wylie.   Go hence, for it is useless to pretend.   OxBA

Innocent Play.   Isaac Watts.   There's none but a madman will fling about fire,/And tell you, "'Tis all but in sport."   NOEC

Innocent's Song.   Charles Causley.   Herod is his name.   GTBS-P; OBCP

The Innocent Spring.   Edith Sitwell.   But a small wind sighed, colder than the rose/Blooming in desolation, "No one knows."   NOBE

The Innocents.   Jay Macpherson.   Where Herod bleeds his rage away/And wrings his bloodless hands.   OBCV

The Innovator.   Stephen Vincent Benét.   But–Lord, how usual!   EyDe

The Innumerable Christ.   Hugh (Christopher Murray Grieve) MacDiarmid.   On coontless stars the Babe maun cry/An' the Crucified maun bleed.   EaLo; EBEV; NoP; OxBS

Inordinate Love.   Anonymous.   Or withoute quiete to have huge labour.   EBEV; MeEL

The Inquest.   William Henry Davies.   Perhaps my mother murdered me.'   CBEP; DTC; GTBS-P; NOBE; OxBTC

Inquests Extraordinary, III: On the Same.   Anonymous.   Verdict–Ennui, so little work to do.   FaBoEE

Inquietude.   Pauli Murray.   I sink and let the silver tide/Engulf me.   BlSi

Inquisitive Barn.   Frances Frost.   Pokes its red head/Into the sun.   BrR

The Inquisitors.   Robinson Jeffers.   And trampled their watchfire out and went away southward, stepping across the/Ventana mountains.   MoAmPo

The Insatiable Priest.   Matthew Prior.   He can be content with two thousand a year.   OBSP

Insatiableness.   Thomas Traherne.   Sure there's a God (for else there's no delight)/One infinite.   OxBoCh

The Insatiate.   Johannes Secundus.   All attend the steps of age.   UnTE

Inscape.   Susan Litwack.   When a woman opens the heart/she is praying for her soul.   VWA

Inscribed in Melrose Abbey.   Anonymous.   The earth says to the earth, All this is ours.   FaBoEE; FaBoRV

Inscribed upon a Rock.   William Wordsworth.   With shapeless ruin spread around!   SyP

Inscriptio.   Alexander Pope.   Here Dullness reigns, with mighty wings outspread,/And brings the true Saturnian age of lead.   OBSP

An Inscription.   Anonymous.   Winds' stability,/Is mortality.   EIL

The Inscription.   Elsa Barker.   Unto all love-inscriptions that abide,/Power and dominion over life and death.   HBMV

Inscription.   Ebenezer Elliott.   And would not let him have his way.   FaBoEE

Inscription.   Ann Hamilton.   Back to the rose. I cannot see/When sunlight is so close to me.   HBMV

Inscription.   Donald Jeffrey Hayes.   And warms to a spectral fire....   CDC

An Inscription.   Stanislav Vinaver.   And a frightening clarity set in.   VWA

Inscription above the Entrance to the Abbey of Theleme.   Sir Thomas Urquhart.   Gold give us, God forgive us.   FaBoRV

Inscription at Mount Vernon.   Anonymous.
And in the hope of religion, immortality.   MC; OHIP
Who, when he had won all, renounced all, and sought in the/bosom of his family and of nature...   PGD

An Inscription by the Sea.   Edwin Arlington Robinson.   And where it was the ship went down/Is what the sea-birds know.   AWP; ELU; FaBoEE

Inscription for a Fountain on a Heath.   Samuel Taylor Coleridge.   Or passing gale or hum of murmuring bees!   ERoP 1-2; MCCG; OAEP

Inscription for a Grotto.   Mark Akenside.   ...chiefly, if thy name/Wise Pallas and the immortal Muses own.   CEP; NOEC; OBEC; PoEL 1-5

Inscription for a Headstone.   Austin Clarke.   Scrawled in a rage by Dublin's poor.   BIrV; CIP

Inscription for a Mirror in a Deserted Dwelling.   William Rose Benet.   The past unpiteous to your need!   MoAmPo

Inscription for a Statue of Love.   Voltaire (Francois Marie Arouet).   He is, he was, or is to be.   LiTW

Inscription for a Tablet on the Banks of a Stream.   Robert Southey.   Go Stranger, sojourn in the woodland cot/Of INNOCENCE, and thou shalt find her there.   OBEC

Inscription for a Wayside Spring.   Frances Cornford.   I AM THE COLD WATER/THAT RESTORES YOUR SOUL   BrRo

Inscription for an Old Bed.   William Morris.   Right good is rest.   OBEV; OBVV; WiR

Inscription for Arthur Rackham's Rip Van Winkle.   James Elroy Flecker.   Sane men have worshipped stranger Gods than these.   BrPo

Inscription for Marye's Heights, Fredericksburg.   Herman Melville.   Of more than victory the monument.   UnPo

Interview with Doctor Drink. J. V. Cunningham.   ...Who but I/Coil there and squat, and pay your fee? NMP; OBSP; TW; VGW

Intery, Mintery, Cutery Corn.   Mother Goose.   And one flew over the goose's nest. TiPo

Intery, Mintry, Cutery, Corn. *Anonymous.* O-U-T, and in again. OxNR

Inteview. Dorothy Parker.   So far, I have had no complaints. InMe

Intimacy. Al Young. Follow your nose, follow the sun or/follow the dreaming sea, but follow! NPGG

Intimate Associations.   Charles Baudelaire.   that describe the voyages of the body and soul. NU

Intimate Parnassus. Patrick Kavanagh.   Passive, observing with a steady eye. MoBrPo

Intimate Supper. Peter Redgrove.   Walked in his garden in the cool of the evening, waited. FaBoMo; OxBC

Intimates. D. H. Lawrence.   and that held her spellbound for two seconds/ while I fled. BoLoP; NLV; OBSP

Intimations. Alma Johanna Koenig. And this was reward and more for all. VWA

Intimations of Immortality from Recollections of Early Childhood.   William Wordsworth.
And hear the mighty waters rolling evermore. BoC
But trailing clouds of glory do we come. ATP
Though nothing can bring back the hour/Of splendour in the grass, of glory in the flower; ATP
Thoughts that do often lie too deep for tears. ATP; BoLiVe
Where is it now, the glory and the dream? ATP

Intimations of Mortality.   Phyllis McGinley.   Be quiet. You need not tell me. MoAmPo

Into & At. Edmund Pennant.   goats of cast bronze danced into/sunlight on the window sill. SOTS

Into Battle. Julian Grenfell.   And Night shall fold him in soft wings. FaPoR; HBV 1-2; LoBV; MMM; OBEV; OBMV; OBWP; OxBTC; WaaP

Into Blackness Softly. Mari E. Evans.   the/receiving/blackness/sigh PoBA

Into Fish. Sheryl L. Nelms.   he glides/sleek in the spirit/of fish. GOYP

Into Slumbers. John Fletcher.   And kiss him into slumbers like a bride. SeCePo

Into the Book. Martin Grossman.   their machines humming/like locusts in a swarm. VWA

Into the Dark. Paul Monette.   like lovers. Or brothers. Brothers, if you like. AmPA

Into the Future. Harold Witt.   and somewhere Ray Bradbury and Arthur C. Clarke,/under first stars, dream up tomorrow's news. SOTS

Into the Glacier. John Haines.   and we, naked and alone,/awakening forever... CoAP

Into the Noiseless Country. Thomas William Parsons   "Oh, that hushed forest! - soon may I/be there!" AA

Into the Salient. Edmund Charles Blunden.   Into seven days of country where you come out any door. ViBoPo

Into the Twilight. William Butler Yeats.   And hope is less dear than the dew of the morn. HBV 1-2

Into the Wind. Winfield Townley Scott.   Of the cold and mensal, unmentionable moon. NMP

Into the Woods My Master Went. Sidney Lanier.   'Twas on a tree they slew him last,/When out of the woods he came. AH

Into the World and Out. Sarah Piatt.   The children cried so when his eyes were shut. HBV 1-2

Into Their True Gentleness. Pearse Hutchinson.   into their true gentleness,/ even with us. CIP

The Intoxicated Rat. *Anonymous.* Well the cat jumped over and the rat got sober,/Ran back to his hole again. FSW

Intramural Aestivation; or, Summer in Town, by a Teacher of Latin. Oliver Wendell Holmes.   Depart,–be off,–excede,–evade,–crump! FaBoNo

Introducing a Madman. Keith Waldrop.   clever lady (with a/strength which seemed incredible). TW

An Introduction. Kamala Das.   ...no/Aches which are not yours. I too call myself I. WPOW

The Introduction. Louis MacNeice.   They were introduced in a green grave. FaBoIP

Introduction. Clere Parsons.   ...the ballet-dancer/sustains her still mercurial pose in air. FaBoTw

The Introduction. Anne Finch, Countess of Winchilsea.   Be dark enough thy shades, and be thou there content. SBG; WPOW

Introduction of the Shopping Cart. Gerald Costanzo.   The shopping cart. P. T. Barnum./The sky. MAYP

Introduction. Poems, 1831. Edgar Allan Poe.   And even the greybeard will o'erlook/Connivingly my dreaming-book. NOBA

An Introduction to Dogs. Ogden Nash.   But that's probably because they are sensibler. MoShBr

An Introduction to Some Poems. William Stafford.   Good: now it is time. CAPP

Introductory Lines (excerpt). William Butler Yeats.   Poured out wine for the high invisible ones. NU

Introspective Reflection. Ogden Nash.   Were it not for making a living, which is rather a nouciance. NLV

Introversion. Evelyn Underhill.   When first we begin/To speak one with another. WGRP

Intruder. Susan Feldman.   may enjoy our filets of mackerel, our dishes of cream. AmPA

The Intruder. Carolyn Kizer.   She washed and washed the pity from her hands. BoWoP; GP; NePoEA-2

The Intruder. James Reeves.   Not a creature lingers by,/When clumping Two-boots comes to pry. OnUR

The Intruder. Marya Zaturenska.   The flowering love. OLR

Intrusion. Denise Levertov.   something my former eyes had wept for/came asking to be pitied. CAPP

Intuition. Anthony Delius.   The sun goes down, the wind's/Self says No. PeSA

The Inundation. Howard Sergeant.   ...they have taken the cities/who were no enemies. EAS

The Invaders. John Haines.   their cannon and blue flares/pumping fear into the night. TAT

Invalid. Audrey McGaffin.   And healing upon this festering of blame. NePoAm-2

Invasion. Hubert Witheford.   And all the night in natural jubilee/Over a sea of blood rings the heart's revelry. AnNZ

Invasion Exercise on the Poultry Farm. Sir John Betjeman.   I've trussed your missing paratroop. He's waiting for you here.' NOBL

Invasion North. Richard Hugo.   roots and dry meat, enough to last fifty years. GP

Invasion on the Farm. R. S. Thomas.   ...The patched gate/You left open will never be shut again. PoL

Invasion Song. *Anonymous.* And now secure in jail they rest,/The debt of blood, unpaid. PoOW

Invasion Summer. Laurie Lee.   she has no honour and she has no fear. OBSP

Invasion Weather. Douglas Newton.   The ghost of Agamemnon, like a bee,/Hums in the groining of his vaulted tomb. NeBP

Invective against Ibis (excerpt). Ovid (Publius Ovidius Naso).   About thy caryan corps shall have, continuall debate. OBVE

An Invective Against the Wicked of the World. Nicholas Breton.   Yet virtue makes the truest kings and queens. ViBoPo

Invented a Person. Lenore G. Marshall.   And in fear for that one. GoYe

Invention. William Watson.   This, or a kindred rapture, let me own,/I covet ceaselessly! HBV 1-2

The Invention of Astronomy. William Matthews.   The eyelids fall, the star-charts. PoL

The Invention of Comics. LeRoi (Imamu Amiri Baraka) Jones.   my dark and sultry/love. AmNP; CAPP; LiTM; PoBA

The Invention of Fire. Andrew Taylor.   and children clap at the incense of small fires CBAP

The Invention of New Jersey. Jack Anderson.   a faintly bilious look/ perpetually on her face. InPS; PAI; TAT; TW

The Invention of the Telephone. Peter Klappert.   But he wanted you to be/ proud of him, so he invented/the telephone before he called. AmPA; PPJ

The Invention of Zero. Constance Urdang.   I am amazed anew/At the inexhaustible fertility of the natural world. VWA

Inventions. Samuel (1612-80) Butler.   But pass for theirs who had the luck to light/Upon them by mistake or oversight. PV

The Inventor's Wife. Mrs. E. R. Corbett.   Or think it strange I often wish I warn't an inventor's wife? PoLf

The Inventory. Robert Burns.   Then know all ye whom it concerns,/ Subscripsi huic, CABL; FaBoUs

Inventory. Dorothy Parker.   Laughter and hope and a sock in the eye. AnAmPo; NLV

An Inventory of the Furniture of a Collegian's Chamber. John Winstanley.   His INVENTORY thus is ended. OBSV

Inventory–to 100th Street. Frank Lima.   jingling/on the rusty-green/of yesterday's/fire-escapes. ANYP

Inverberg. J. F. Hendry.   Interpreting man's fretted cuneiform. NeBP

Inversnaid. Gerard Manley Hopkins.   Long live the weeds and the wilderness yet. ACP; BLPL; BrPo; CMoP; FaBoMo; FaBoPP; GTBS-P; LiTB; LiTM; LoBV; MoAB; MoBrPo; NoAm; NoP; OAEL 1-2; PoRA; PoSH; UnPo

The Inverted Torch. Edith Matilda Thomas.
Along the old deeps of being, the old/heights? AA
So I awoke, to find me still Time's thrall,/Time's sport,–nor by thy warm, safe/presence stayed. AA
That's heart-break, heart-break! AA
The unreverberant Profound/That hath no name nor mete! AA

Investigation. Julia Vinograd.   What else is war for/but to amuse the dead? IHMS

Investigator. Miriam Waddington. A long lean lap-eared dog sitting on a roof/Blinks wet eyes at me. CaP

Investiture. Brian Henderson. ...I see the/gods themselves rolled crashing down the great steps of the/temple in the darkness. CaPN

The Investiture. Siegfried Sassoon. You roam forlorn along the streets of gold. NoAm

The Investment. Robert Frost. But get some color and music out of life? CMoP; OxBA

Investor's Soliloquy. Kenneth Ward. And lose the name of/Profits. FaFP; FPL

Invictus. William Ernest Henley. I am the captain of my soul. AnEnPo; BLPA; FaBoBe; FaBV; FaFP; FaPo; FaPoR; FPL; GoTF; GTBS; HBV 1-2; HBVY; HoPM; LiTB; MCCG; MoBrPo; NOBE; OBEV; OBMV; OBVV; OHFP; PoPl; TEP; TreF; TrGrPo; ViBoPo; VLP; WGRP; WHA

Inviolable. Daniel Gerard Hoffman. Breaking/Your laws. GrPl

The Invisible. Richard Watson Gilder. One are we with the ever-living One. WGRP

The Invisible Bride. Edwin Markham. Softly she comes to me,/And goes to God again. HBV 1-2

The Invisible Bridge. Gelett Burgess. I fear that I Should Be! NA; TreFT

Invisible, indivisible Spirit. Hilda ("H. D.") Doolittle. it was an ordinary tree/in an old garden-square. BoWoP

The Invisible King. Johann Wolfgang von Goethe. The boy lay dead in the father's arms. NU

Invisible Landscape. Charles Wright. ...the lost/Moment that stopped to grieve and moved on... LCAP

The Invisible Man. T. S. Matthews. These facts I know but find it difficult to understand. PoL

Invisible Trumpets Blowing. Edwin John Pratt. ...hammered/By Roman nails and hung on a Jewish hill. CaP

The Invisible Woman. Robin Morgan. Only the strong can know that. IHMS; NMM

Invitation. Anonymous.
May we not err of layman sort,/When priests and parsons fall? WTO
Or lend my soul seraphic wings,/To get to Thee. OxBoCh

Invitation. Harry Behn. So come have your breakfast, and fly away! SoPo

The Invitation. Tom Buchan. and to be alive/Means having to go away. ACV

Invitation. Victor Contoski. I had holes in my feet/from the nails. PV

The Invitation. Thomas Godfrey. And calm my transports with thy song! AnFE; APA

The Invitation. George Herbert. Where is all, there all should be. AnAnS 1

The Invitation. Robert Herrick. I'le bring a fever; since thou keep'st no fire. CaPo; OAEP

Invitation. Solomon Ibn Gabirol. God's servant, born of Bethlehem! TrJP

The Invitation. Charles Kingsley. Leaving fops and fogies/A thousand feet below. NOBV

The Invitation. Donagh MacDonagh. Leap girl upon his back/And he will race for ever. OnYI

The Invitation. Leonard Welsted. You know your friends; you know your bill of fare. NOEC

The Invitation (abridged). Gronwy Owen. My Christ, who reigns in heaven above,/Receive us to his breast of love! LiTW

The Invitation in It. Kay Boyle. ...their hearts each the flame of a candle/That his breath can extinguish at will. NMM

Invitation of the Mirrors. Tom McKeown. balancing on the horizon. AMV-81

Invitation Standing. Paul Blackburn. take a leaf and/come/just come VGW

Invitation to a Mistress. Anonymous. Come, precious–I'm not good at waiting. UnTE

Invitation to a Sabbath. Harry Mathews. The ash tree stands in the stars. ANYP

Invitation to a Spirit. Anonymous. But descend and enter into your embodiment. WTO

An Invitation to an Invitation. Caius Valerius Catullus. I think of you, and mercy! my/Tunic's got a tent-pole in it. ErPo

Invitation to Dalliance. Anonymous. Come bill, and kiss, and I'll show you. FaBoEE

Invitation to Eternity. John Clare. We are wed to one eternity. NCEP; PoEL 1-5

Invitation to Hsiao Ch'U-Shih. Po Chu-i. And find your way to the parlour of Government House. OBVE

Invitation to Juno. William Empson. Could not Professor Charles Darwin/Graft annual upon perennial trees? AtBAP; CMoP; FaBoMo

An Invitation to Lubberland. Anonymous. Make haste away together. CoBE; FaBoNo; GBP

An Invitation to Madison County. Jay Wright. when people, who have only themselves to give,/offer you their meal. PoBA

Invitation to Miss Marianne Moore. Elizabeth Bishop. from Brooklyn, over the Brooklyn Bridge, on this fine/morning,/please come flying. MoVE

Invitation to the Bee. Charlotte Smith. And that garden shall supply/Thy delicious alchemy. OxBChV

Invitation to the Dance. Anonymous Sport and folly are youth's own,/Tender youth and ruddy. UnTE

Invitation to the Dance. Sidonius Apollinaris. And in garment let each man/Be a Dionysian! AWP

Invitation (To the Night and All Other Things Dark). Ronda Davis. when u save me/from myself? JB

An Invitation to the Zoological Gardens. Anonymous. To witness the bub-bub-beautiful pip-pip-pel-/ican swallow the l-l-ive little fuf-fuf-fish! BoAnP

Invitation to Youth. Anonymous. Old men frighten love away/With cold frost and dry decay. UnTE

Invites His Nymph to His Cottage. Philip Ayres. Thy powers of love, or this my amorous flame. EnLoPo

Inviting a Friend to Supper. Ben Jonson. Shall make us sad next morning, or affright/The liberty that we'll enjoy tonight. AnAnS 2; AWP; BiP; EnRePo; JCP; LiTB; LoBV; NIP; NOBE; NoP; OAEL 1-2; OAEP; OBS; OxBoLi; PoEL 1-5; PPP; SeCP; SeCV 1-2

Invocation. George Gordon, Lord Byron. Its very courage stagnates to a vice. LoBV

An Invocation. William Johnson Cory. Two minds shall flow together, the English and the Greek. HBV 1-2; OBVV

Invocation. Carleton Drewry. The lowliest weed could tell at what terrible cost. MoRP

Invocation. John Drinkwater. Make me immoderately wise. HBMV; PoA

Invocation. Max Eastman. More sacred than the pleasing of a friend. WGRP

Invocation. Horace. All the wars and plagues we're blessed with.) AWP

Invocation. Valentin Iremonger. By these aboding mountains, this lovely glen. BIrV

Invocation. Helene Johnson. Grow high above my head. BANP; PoNe

Invocation. Denise Levertov. that it return to us when we return. PoA

Invocation. of Berditshev, Levi Isaac. "Glorified and sanctified be His great name!" EaLo

Invocation. Arthur J. Little. Haply to mind them that your love endures. ISi

Invocation. Louis MacNeice. Fetch me far and far away. SO

Invocation. Vassar Miller. my foot finds your lintel. NCSH

Invocation. Nakasuk. They pale,/They turn white. WTO

Invocation. Ogden Nash. Smut if smitten/Is front-page stuff. OBAL

An Invocation. Bishop Patrick. be my comrade crowned/with a thousand blessings./Thus the prologue. NOBI

Invocation. Thomas Randolph. To borrow his dog to lead the spheres a-begging. MOON

Invocation. Siegfried Sassoon. And stillness from the pools of Paradise. MoBrPo

Invocation. Edith Sitwell. From the darkened hands of the universal Cain. AtBAP

Invocation. Wendell Phillips Stafford. Be lightning for the land we love! TrPWD

Invocation. Edmund Clarence Stedman. Still be thou kind, for still thou wast most/dear. AA

An Invocation. John Addington Symonds. Or, if I strive, still must I blindly follow. TrPWD; TRV; WGRP

Invocation. Gilbert Thomas. Sir! Quicken us again,/Spirit of Life within! TrPWD

Invocation. Chad Walsh. ...and if all faces are your own/And places, then I worship you alone. TrCP

Invocation and Prelude. Stefan George. To blessed islands and a port of peace. AWP

Invocation before the Rice Harvest. Anonymous. The real brightness is the brightness of my child. WTO

An Invocation (excerpt). Muhammad Iqbal. I will be to him both idol and worshipper. ACV

Invocation (excerpt). Theodore Spencer. Empty me of myself, that when I work,/All that I work for, never concerns me. TrPWD

Invocation for a Storm. Anonymous. Ye rains arise, ye winds arise,/Arise! Arise! WTO

Invocation for the New Year. Margaret D. Armstrong. That never fails, nor stops to count the/cost. STF

Invocation from a Lawn Chair. Mary Jean Irion. trophic ambush of the moon. AMV-80

Invocation of Silence. Richard Flecknoe. Seize our tongues, and strike us dumb! OBSP

Invocation (parody). Samuel Hoffenstein. Delightful Muse, and be my love. BXAP

Invocation to Ireland. Amergin. I invoke the land of Ireland! AnIV; OnYI

Invocation to Rain in Summer. William C. Bennett. O gentle, gentle summer rain! GN

Invocation to Sappho. Elsa Gidlow. do we not touch/across the censorious years? IHMS

An Invocation to the Goddess. David Wright. Plunge and thrash salty hair. NMP; NoAm

Invocation to the Muse. Richard Hughes. You won't be well paid./Aetat. 6 MoBrPo

Invocation to the Social Muse. Archibald MacLeish. Is it just to demand of us also to bear arms? LiTM; NAMP

Invocation to the Wind. Joseph Kalar. or flowers creeping over Mojave! AnEnPo

Invocation to Youth. Laurence Binyon. If Winter come to Winter,/When shall men hope for Spring? OBEV; OBVV

The Invoice. Robert Creeley. And, why don't you get with it. AmPC; VGW

The Inward Light. Henry Septimus Sutton. My life to deepest holiness to lead. WGRP

The Inward Morning. Henry David Thoreau. The harbingers of summer heats/Which from afar he bears. AP; MAmP

Io Victis. William Wetmore Story. Or the Persians and Xerxes? His judges, or Socrates?/Pilate, or Christ? AA; HBV 1-2; WGRP

Iolanthe. Sir William Schwenck Gilbert.
As in King George's glorious days. TrGrPo
ditto, ditto my song–and thank good-/ness they're both of them over! CoBE
Or else a little Conservative!/Fal lal la! EnLi 1-2

Iona. Arthur Cleveland Core Shall brighten evermore. AA

Iona. Frederick Tennyson. In whom all saints are one for evermore! GoBC

Iona: The Graves of the Kings. Robinson Jeffers. What suspicion-agonized eyes, what jellies of arrogance and terror/This earth has absorbed. PrIm

Ione. Aubrey Thomas De Vere. The wild swan's, chanting her death melody. IrPN

The Ionian Islands (excerpt). Richard Monckton, Lord Houghton Milnes. Will bear the fruit of many an after-thought,/Bright in the dubious track of after-years. OBTV

Ioolas' Epitaph. William, of Hawthornden Drummond. A purple Flowre see of this Marble borne. AtBAP; PoEL 1-5

Iowa. Michael Dennis Browne. on their hills are strangely childlike. NYBP

Iowa, June. Michael Dennis Browne. In the house, the tower of the house. AmPA

Iowa Land. Marvin Bell. And he has something to do and what's/to die from–who's close to many, closer. SaC

Ipecacuanha. George Canning. My Damon, I am sick. FaBoNo

Iphigeneia in Aulis: Chorus. Euripides. nor in the poets/nor the songs.' AWP; OBVE

Iphione. Thomas Caulfield Irwin. Remote and lonely, dim, divine. EnLoPo; IrPN

Ipomadon: Ipomadon Plays the Fool at Court. Anonymous. With trenchours and with broken mete/They sayd that noble knight. OxBM

Ipsey Wipsey. Anonymous. Ipsey Wipsey spider/Climbing up again. OxNR

Ipswich Bar. Esther and Brainard Bates. Where cold and still, old Heartbreak Hill/Looks down on Ipswich Bar. HBMV

Irapuato. Earle Birney. do they look like small clotting hearts? NIP; PeCV

Ire. R. S. Thomas. You welcome your man from his long mowing/Of the harsh, unmannerly, mountain hay? OBSP

Ireland. Stephen Lucius Gwynne. Keep me in remembrance, long leagues apart. HBV 1-2

Ireland. John Hewitt. that cries far out and calls us to partake/in his great tidal movements round the earth. CIP; FaBoPP

Ireland. Barten Holyday. Are counted Ireland's earth, mistake, curse, shame. FaBoEE

Ireland. Lionel Pigot Johnson. Sorrows and hates, home to Hell's waste and wild. HBV 1-2

Ireland. John James Piatt. Fields without walls that all the people/own!' AA

Ireland. Richard Ryan. till dawn finds/field is bog, bog lake. CIP

Ireland. Dora Sigerson Shorter. I have left you at last. OBEV; OBVV; OxBI

Ireland. Francis Stuart. Sea-birds' shelter, our shelter and ark. NeIP

Ireland. Jonathan Swift. 'Tis pre-engaged and in his room/Townshend's cast page or Walpole's groom. FaBoPV

Ireland 1972. Paul Durcan. The grave of my firstlove murdered by my brother. FaBoIP

Ireland 1977. Paul Durcan. Do you hear me bawling to you across the hearthrug?' FaBoIP

Ireland, Ireland. Sir Henry Newbolt. Ireland, Ireland, green and sad. FaPoR

Ireland Lake. Robert Hershon. we are making/back from ireland lake NeAC

Ireland Weeping. William Livingston. without breath, and their blood humming on the/ground! GoTS

Ireland with Emily. Sir John Betjeman. Sings its own seablown Te Deum,/In and out the slipping slates. GTBS-P; OxBTC

The Iris. Gasetsu. The colour of the sky. TiPo

Iris. David St. John. In the wake of a woman who's just swept past you on her way/Home/& you remain. LCAP

Iris. William Carlos Williams. startling us from among/those trumpeting/petals. InPS; LCAP; PAI; WeW

Irises. Padraic Colum. Light-plumed Irises, where are they now? BoNaP

Irish. Paul Celan. on the heart slope,/tomorrow. OBVE

Irish. Edward J. O'Brien. For it is Irish, too. SiSoSe

An Irish Airman Foresees His Death. William Butler Yeats. In balance with this life, this death. AnEnPo; CoBMV; EnL; FaBoCh; FaBoMo; GoJo; GTBS-P; HeIP; HoPM; LiTM; LoGBV; MMM; MoAB; MoBrPo; NoAm; NOBE; NoP; OBMV; OBWP; PoPl; PPP; SCV; TrGrPo; WaaP; WaP; WeW

Irish-American Dignitary. Austin Clarke. ...that day in Cork/Had scarcely time for knife and fork. BIrV

Irish Antiquities. Thomas Moore. They put Lord Roden in the van. FaBoEE

Irish Astronomy. Charles Graham Halpine. But, faith, he fears the Irish knack/Of handling the shillaly. HBV 1-2

An Irish Blessing. Joan Murray. may the land rest easy/without your step. LTB

The Irish Cliffs of Moher. Wallace Stevens. A likeness, one of the race of fathers: earth/And sea and air. LCAP; NOBA; VGW

The Irish Council Bill, 1907. Anonymous. Must I go on feeding these?/Says the Shan Van Vocht? OnYI

Irish Dancer. Anonymous. Come and dance with me/In Ireland. AnIL; EnL; FaBoCh; LoGBV; NOBE; OBEV; OxBM; SeCePo

The Irish Franciscan. Rosa Mulholland. Swingeth he as the moon goes down. CAW

The Irish Girl's Lament. Anonymous. He bid her adieu. Then I withdrew from Erin's flowery vale. ShS

Irish Grandmother. Katherine Edelman. When she was a child in Ballybree. AmFN; SiSoSe

The Irish Harper and His Dog. Thomas Campbell. I can never return with my poor dog Tray. CH

Irish History. William Allingham. These can yet sting the patriot thoughts which turn/To Erin's past, and bid them weep and burn. IrPN

Irish Hotel. David Wevill. Our hard bed of dreams, his sea flaw-/less. NYBP

The Irish Hurrah. Thomas Osborne Davis. Of the Saxon reserve at The Irish Hurrah! OnYI

Irish Hymn to Mary. Anonymous. Was the world betrayed and ruined–was by woman's hand/set free. CAW

The Irish Lady. Anonymous. My follies ten thousand times over I see. OuSiCo

An Irish Lake. W. R. Rodgers. Like trout among their grim stony gazes. BIrV

An Irish Lamentation. Johann Wolfgang von Goethe. The Chieftain's pride, his heir, is dead. AWP

The Irish Language. James Clarence Mangan. Shall through Thee call on men to rejoice and/adore! VLP

Irish Lords. Charles H. Souter. When last we camped at Irish Lords, on the road to Ivanhoe. PoAu 1-2

An Irish Love-Song. Robert Underwood Johnson. You gave me my Katherine–leave me my Kate! HBV 1-2

An Irish Lullaby. Alfred Perceval Graves. My precious one, you'll step to shore/On Mother's knee. HBV 1-2

Irish Molly O. Anonymous. ""MacDonald lost his life for love of Irish Molly O!" HBV 1-2

The Irish Mother in the Penal Days. John Banim. Whose mother still must weep o'er him the tears I weep o'er/thee! AnIV

Irish Music. Larry Levis. Up to the empty summit. MAYP

The Irish Peasant Girl. Charles Joseph Kickham. For the lily of the mountain foot/That withered far away. AnIV

The Irish Peasant to His Mistress. Thomas Moore. Where shineth thy spirit, there liberty shineth too! ACP

An Irish Picture. J. Stanyan Bigg. Smoking contented in the falling rain. NOBV

Irish Poetry. Michael Longley. Lost minerals colouring/The initial letter, the stance. CIP

The Irish Rapparees. Charles Gavan Duffy. The men that rode by Sarsfield's side, the roving Rapparees! AnIV

An Irish Satire. Anonymous. This song is y-said of me;/Ever y-blessed mot ye be! OxBM

The Irish Schoolmaster. James A. Sidney. Jist tell them 'twas from Paddy Blake,/Of Bally Blarney College. FiBHP

The Irish Schoolmaster (parody). Thomas Hood. But wears a floury head, and sings in flow'ry speech! BXAP

Irish Song: Rosie O'Grady. Noel Coward. With a Heigho, maybe Begorrah, and certainly Fiddlededee. NLV

The Irish Wife. Thomas D'Arcy McGee. In death I would be near her,/ And rise beside my Irish wife. HBV 1-2

An Irish Wild-Flower. Sarah Piatt. Where you have fallen–is this the/thing that grows? AA

An Irish Wind. Zelma S. Dennis. The Irish wind on old St. Patrick's/Day/ Is magical and surely full of blarney. AMV-80

An Irish Wish. Anonymous. May God bless you always. GoTF; TreFT

The Irish Wolf-Hound. Denis Florence McCarthy. Not Bran, the favorite dog of Fin,/Could rival John MacDonnell's hound. GDP

The Irishman and the Lady. William Maginn. The hearts of the maids, and the gentlemen's heads, were/bothered I'm sure by this Irishman. HBV 1-2

An Irishman in Coventry. John Hewitt. our hearts still listen for the landward bells. BIrV; CIP

An Irishman's Christening. Anonymous. Oh! could that be a wonder, my boy? OnYI

Iron. Walter De La Mare. Stares in upon his ghastly stock/And opens Monday's till? NOBL

Iron-Door-Woman. Judith Mountain Leaf Volborth. Crows await your eyes. TWSS

Iron Eyes. Terence Winch. Okay, you said, c'mon:/dominate the night for me. APU

The Iron Gate (excerpt). Oliver Wendell Holmes The curfew tells me - cover up the fire. AA

Iron Heaven. Betti Alver. it wants to shiver with the passion/of the earth/ and feel its wings of weakness. BoWoP

Iron Landscapes (and the Statue of Liberty). Thom Gunn. Lorn, bold, as if saluting with her fist. FaBoPV; OBTV

The Iron Lung. Stanley Plumly. you could lie down where you were and listen to the dead. AmPA; GeTw; LCAP

The Iron Music. Ford Madox Ford. But I'm with you up at Wyndcroft,/ Over Tintern on the Wye. HBMV

Ironic:LL.D. William Stanley Braithwaite. Whose meaning, charlatan history, tells! BANP

An Ironical Encomium. Anonymous. For he's a raving Nimrod will not start/To bathe his hands in such a royal heart. APAS

Ironwood. Don Domanski. against the never-ending inroad/of North Atlantic weather. CaPN

Irony. Louis Untermeyer. But Man is great and strong and wise–/And so he dies. TrJP

Irony of God. Eva Warner. And had a friend/Named Mary Magdalene. TrCP

Irradiations. John Gould Fletcher.
And a cause worth losing, and a good song to sing! AnAmPo; MoAmPo; NePA
And sit puffing smoke in the air and never say a word. LaNeLa
The fountain tosses pallid spray/Far in the sorrowful, silent sky. AnFE; APA; CoAnAm
I am a drowsy grass-blade/In the greenest shadow. MAPA

Irrational. Philip Lamantia. Jones Very above all. APU

Irreconcilables. Arthur Gregor. nothing in us could explain. NYBP

Irrevocable. Mary Wright Plummer. For what thou hast done thou hast done. WGRP

Irrigation. Susan Tichy. And there are many gods in this green tree. MAYP

Irritable Song. Russell Atkins. Tomorrow, tomorrow/in today? AmNP

Is. Patrick Kavanagh. I'll die in harness with my scheme. FaBoTw

Is 5. Edward Estlin Cummings.
(dreaming,/et/cetera, of/Your smile/eyes knees and of your Etcetera) AnAmPo
punished bottoms interrupt philosophy. AnAmPo
(smoking sawdust/cigarettes in the/middle of the night) AnAmPo

Is It a Month. John Millington Synge. And we took the starry lane/Back to Dublin town again. BIrV

Is It a Sin to Love Thee? Anonymous. In the starlit world above us, call me thine–forever thine! BLPA

Is It Because I Am Black? Joseph Seamon, Jr Cotter. Is it because I am black? BANP

Is It Because of Some Dear Grace... Louis Golding. To bring forth tears again. TrJP

Is It Far to Go. Lewis, Cecil Day. Quick, Rose, and kiss me. AtBAP

Is It No Dream That I Am He. Walter Savage Landor. O tell me, tell me soon. GBL

Is It Not Sure a Deadly Pain. Anonymous. It is a pain that most I rue. CBEP; EnLoPo

Is It Nothing to You? L. James Kindig. You choose by the Master with whom you ally. BePJ

Is It Nothing to You? May Probyn. ...in what measure/Do you more than we? GoBC; OBEV; OBVV

Is It Really Worth the While? Anonymous. Go the route, old scout, and be merry,/For tomorrow you may die. BLPA

Is It the Morning? Is It the Little Morning? Delmore Schwartz. Of the slow light that ascends to the blaze's lightning! ELU

Is It True? Sarah Williams. We should just see God and die? BLPA

Is It True That You Live Where There Is Sorrow. Anonymous. We must go to your house: O my friends, let us re-/joice! ILwL

Is It True, Ye Gods, Who Treat Us. Arthur Hugh Clough. It may be, and yet be not. VLP

Is It Well-Lighted, Papa? James Bertram. Is it well-lighted, Papa? SM

Is John Smith Within? Anonymous. Here a nail and there a nail,/tick, tack, too. OxNR

Is Life Worth Living? Alfred Austin. And men are free to think and act/ Life is worth living still. FaPoR; GoTF; TreFS

Is Love Not Everlasting? Ronald McCuaig. Of moving worlds to this eclipse/Not returning. BoAV

Is Love, Then, So Simple. Irene Rutherford McLeod. Many things, as I sit quite still,/With Eternity in my hand. HBMV; WHA

Is My Lover on the Sea? Barry (Bryan Waller Procter) Cornwall. And there bid him rest! EtS

Is There a Voice (parody). Philip Appleman. The end of the mantic Muskrat and the Seal/Is the end of you, my inarticulate friends. BXAP

Is There Life across the Street? Robert Watson. The street and back to my brick house, my sleeping wife. GP

Is There No Balm in Christian Lands? Anonymous. Open his heart thy love to know,/And bid his brother live. AH

Is This a Holy Thing to See. William Blake. It is a land of poverty! SCV

Is This Africa? Roland Tombekai Dempster. to note the part you play/for your sons and daughters/still washed in tears. PBA

Is This Land Your Land? Anonymous. Then this land will be for you and me. FSW

Is This the Time To Sound Retreat? Charles Sumner Hoyt. Whose love imperial is, whose power sublime. BLRP

Isaac. Stanley Burnshaw. Of the wrong of worshipping the blood's terror of sacrifice. VWA

Isaac. Amir Gilboa. And there was no blood left/in my right hand. VWA

Isaac. Haim Guri. But that hour/he bequeathed to his descendants/still to be born/a knife/in the heart. VWA

Isaac. Barry Holtz. ...And calmed,/He sinks deep into innocent sleep. VWA

Isaac. A. C. Jacobs. And our father, the old God-fearing man, has been dead many years. VWA

Isaac and Archibald. Edwin Arlington Robinson. And I may laugh at them because I knew them. MAmP; OxBA

Isaac and Esau. Rose Drachler. For the customary ram/Familiar to our darkness. VWA

Isaac Leybush Peretz. Moishe Leib Halpern. Like red fire,/Like gold,/Like blood. VWA

Isabel. Anonymous. Never again to the top came he/(By the water's edge, the water's edge) WHW

Isabel. Sydney Thomas Dobell. And dying by its own excess of light,/ Isabel. OBVV

Isabella: or, the Morning (excerpt). Sir Charles Hanbury Williams. Guiltless they'll gaze, and innocent adore. NOEC

Isabella, or The Pot of Basil. John Keats. To steal my Basil-pot away from me!' EnRP; ViBoPo

Isabelle (parody). James Hogg. For they are coming, and they are three! BXAP; Par

Iscah. Howard Schwartz. And all the kinds of wood/Put forth/Fruit. VWA

Ishmael. Gabriel Levin. Bushels they take/And spread over the streets. VWA

Ishmael. Herbert Palmer. And kept his faith with God. And he will reign. OBEV

Isidor. Louis Simpson. "Praise God, may His Name be exalted!" GP; NNaP

Isis Wanderer. Kathleen Raine. That he who lived on the first may rise on the last day. OxBS

The Island. James Dickey. And danced, unimagined and free,/Like the sun taking place on the sea. SM

Island. Langston Hughes. Good morning, daddy!/Ain't you heard? HaCAP

The Island. Sean Jennett. and the singing voice has only songs that wound/with bitterness. The land is dead. NeIP; SeCePo

The Island. Edwin Muir. And with our wild succession braid/The resurrection of the rose. OAEL 1-2

The Island. Robert Southey. They'll stand up for his right,/And their own, to the tight little Island. CoBE

The Island. Giuseppe Ungaretti. The hands of the shepherd were like glass/Polished with glimmering fever. LiTW

An Island. Shawn Wong. into the folds of the sheets. BrSi

The Island. George Woodcock. We left the island to the mice and birds. NeBP

The Island and the Cattle. Nicholas Moore. There was no girl, there were no cattle, and it was day. EAS

It Is Not Beauty I Demand. George Darley. That when my spirit won above/Hers could not stay for sympathy. ERoP 1-2; HBV 1-2; LiTL; OAEL 1-2; OBRV

It is Not Death to Die. George Washington Bethune To reig with thee on high. AA; BePJ

It Is Not Enough. David Henderson. Red China is not allowed in the league/unless she attacks... PPON

It Is Not Likely Now. Frances Bellerby. Before you have finished, again evening will have come. ChMP

It Is Not So with Me. William Blake. ...but it is not so with me. SeCePo

It Is Not Sweet Content, Be Sure. Arthur Hugh Clough. They only study the disease,/Alas, who live not to detect. VLP

It Is Not Too Late. Lucia Trent. For a world without greed, without guns. PGD

It Is Raining. Lucy Sprague Mitchell. that's where I'd like to be. BrR; SoPo; TiPo

It Is So Long Since My Heart Has Been with Yours. Edward Estlin Cummings. filled with skilfully stuffed memories NoAm

It Is That Bane of Self in Love. Richard Eberhart. Curled, rolled, woven, lover. LiTL

It Is the Celestial Ennui of Apartments. Wallace Stevens. As morning throws off stale moonlight and shabby sleep. NePa

It Is the Reed. Sister Maris Stella. It is the reed, it is the reed that sings. GoBC

It Is the Season. Josephine Jacobsen. Say nothing yet./Prepare. TAP

It Is the Sinners' Dust-Tongued Bell Claps Me to Churches. Dylan Thomas. Who have brought forth the urchin grief. OxBTC

It Is the Stars That Govern Us. Michael Magee. now let them gaze at your great constellation. PoA

It Is the Time of Rain and Snow. Izumi Shikibu. And watch the frost/Frail as your love/Gather in the dawn. WPOW

It Is Time. Ted Joans. It's time it is time to straighten up and fly right tonight NNP

It Is Too late! Henry Wadsworth Longfellow. Completed Faust when eighty years were past. BLPL; PoLf

It Is Too late to Call Thee Now. Emily Bronte. For God alone doth know how blest/My early years have been in thee! NOBV

It Is Toward Evening. Anonymous. Make Thou it perfect with Thy perfect life. BePJ

It Is True. Federico Garcia Lorca. Oh, what an effort it is/to love you as I do! OLR

It Is Well for Small Birds That Can Rise up on High. Anonymous. O God in Your Heaven give ease to my pain! NOBI

It Is When the Tribe Is Gone. Duff Bigger. On a night like this one Van Gogh dug in into his bla/and died FAZ

It Is Winter, I Know. Merrill Moore. To rattle the sycamore tree's dry-shriveled seeds. MoAmPo

It Isn't Far to Bethlehem. Arthur R., Jr. Macdougall. In Christ, its comradeship with men. PGD

It Isn't the Church–It's You. Anonymous. It isn't the church–it's you. BLPA; WBLP

It Isn't the Cough. Anonymous. It's the coffin/They carry you off in. FaFP; ShM

It Isn't the Town, It's You. R. W. Glover. It isn't your town–it's you. BLPA

It Makes No Difference Abroad. Emily Dickinson. To him–sums Misery– DiPo

It May Be. Max Jacob. That scorn which is but a dream/Of the shepherd prouder than a king. PoPl

It May Be Good. Sir Thomas Wyatt. For dread to fall I stand not fast. AAS; EnRePo; FaBoPV; FCP; SiPS

It May Be So with Us. John Masefield. Even if we cease life is a miracle. ATP

It May Not Always Be So. Edward Estlin Cummings. Then shall i turn my face, and hear one bird/sing terribly afar in the lost lands. BoLoP; FaBV

It Might Be a Lump of Amber. Walter De la Mare. But what we have to remember, ma'am,/Is to keep our eye on the moral. FaBoNo

It Might Have Been Worse. George William ("A.E.") Russell. Things are far from being as bad/As they easily might have been. PoToHe

It Moves Across. Bernadette Mayer. near a patch of grass. ANYP

It Must Be Summer. Sandor Csoori. With a throaty swan song. AMV-81

"It Out-Herods Herod, Pray You Avoid It." Anthony Hecht. Who could not, at one time,/Have saved them from the gas. CoAP; NCSH; NIP; NoAm; NOBA; OxBC

It Pays to Advertise. Anonymous. Which only goes to show you/That it pays to advertise. GoTF; TreFT

It Pleases. Gary Snyder. The world does what it pleases. TAT

It Rains. Edward ("Edward Eastaway") Thomas. The past hovering as it revisits the light. MoVE; OxBTC

It Really Happened. Elizabeth Henley. And small John's kiss, three times. BiCB

It Rolls On. Morris Bishop. Discovering truths I do not care to know. ImOP

It's A. Kit Robinson. best recollection's/opposite number/on a ordinary day. APU

It's a Different Story When You're Going Into the Wind. David McFadden. ...three pairs of eyes/on him. NeAC

It's a Far, Far, Cry. Patrick Macgill. For my heart is more than often back/By the hills of Donegal. HBMV

It's a Fib. Elspeth. Never to her dying day/Knew one from the other. ALV

It's a Gay Old World. Anonymous. The thing it must be/In its glooom or its glee/Depends on yourself alone. FaFP

It's a Long Way. William Stanley Braithwaite. Thus down the tide of Time shall flow/My dreams forevermore. GoSl

It's a Queer Time. Robert Graves. It's a queer time. MCCG; MoAB; MoBrPo

It's a Terrible Thing! Everett Hoagland. (it's a terrible thing!) BPo

"It's a Whole World, the Body. A Whole World!" David Young. a swami, a world,/seldom whole. FF

It's All the Same. Thadious M. Davis. Tell the Gospel Truth, Rev. BlSi

It's Almost Day. Anonymous. Children are all happy/On Christmas Day. FSW

It's Almost Done. Anonymous. And I ain't gonna see those pretty gals no more. FSW

It's Already Autumn. Elio Pagliarani. overturning the bowl/with his trembling hands. PCP

It's an Owercome Sooth for Age an' Youth. Robert Louis Stevenson. But the nearest friends are the auldest friends/And the grave's the place to seek them. NOBV

It's Cold in China Blues. Isaiah Nettles. If he's so reckless, he's my baby child BluL

It's Comforting. Judy Dothard Simmons. o god/the dreaming CNA

It's Easy to Invent a Life. Emily Dickinson. There–leaving out a Man–. AmePo

It's Fine Today. Douglas Malloch. Ain't it fine today? BLPA

It's Food. Cid Corman. ...Come and/get it. GP

It's Fun to Go out and Buy New Shoes to Wear. Mary Ann Hoberman. It's fun to go shopping for shoes. TiPo

It's G-L-O-R-Y to Know I'm S-A-V-E-D. Anonymous. but it's v-i-c-t-o-r-y to know I've Christ within. FSW

It's Halloween. Jack Prelutsky. For oh tonight/it's Halloween! NTCP

It's Hard on We Po' Farmers. Anonymous. It's hard on we po' farm(ers),/It's hard. OuSiCo

It's Hard to See but Think of a Sea. Louis Zukofsky. I turn to last/Perhaps. VGW

It's Here In The. Russell Atkins. as to harden the unhard and unhard/the hardened. AmNP; PoBA

It's in the Egg. Joe Rosenblatt. ...the toast/dipped in the yolk of the egg, in the yolk that tells all. NOBC

It's in the Name. Kitty Tsui. blood, bone, breath. BrSi

It's in Your Face. Anonymous. You don't have to tell it, it shows in your face. PoLf

It's Just the Same to Me. Hermann Hesse. Feel I but His hand. ILwL

It's Me, O, Lord. Anonymous. It's me, it's me, it's me O, Lord,/An I'm standin' in the need of prayer. BoAN 1-2; FSW

It's Nation Time. LeRoi (Imamu Amiri Baraka) Jones. get up got here bow/It's Nation/Time! NoP

It's nice that though you are casual about me. Sulpicia. I might tumble into bed with a nobody. BoWoP

It's No Good! D. H. Lawrence. but the women are my favorite vessels of wrath. InPS; PAI; PV

It's No Good. Ian Young. (That/was someone else's idea). NeAC

It's No Use Raising a Shout. W. H. Auden. But what does it mean? What are we going to do? OBMV

It's Not Bad Once the Water Goes Down. Thomas Reiter. with its fry still live in its mouth. WOLT

It's Not the Heat So Much as the Humidity. James Tate. A rollerskate collides with a lunchpail. NoAm

It's Once I Courted as Pretty a Lass. Anonymous. And I'll never go there any more. OxNR

It's Over a(See Just. Edward Estlin Cummings. big sound on the ground OxBA; VGW

It's Over Now; I've Known It All. Emily Bronte. With thoughtful heart and tearful eye/I sadly watched that solemn sky. NOBV

It's Raining, It's Pouring. Anonymous. It's raining, it's snowing, the old man is growing. TrAS

It's Raining, It's Raining. Anonymous. And all the little ladies/Are picking up their frocks. OxNR

It's Simply Great. Sidney Warren Mase. To work and win–it's simply great! PoToHe

It's Spring Returning, It's Spring and Love. Anonymous. It's off in the woods for me. HAP

It's Such a Little Thing to Weep. Emily Dickinson. And yet–by Trades–the size of these/We men and women die! AmePo; AmP

It's the Same at Four A.M. Joy Harjo. But he wants the other half TWSS

It's the Syme the Whole World Over. *Anonymous.* Now, a'nt that a blinkin' shyme! AS; BeLS; FSW; GoTF; TrAS; TreFS; UnTE

It's Three No Trumps. Guy Innes. A comrade peered–"Yes, he'd 'a' got 'em!" FiBHP

It's True I'm No Miss America. Stephanie Slowinsky. While blowing kisses through my hoary hair. AMV-80

It's up Glenbarchan's Braes I Gaed. Sir Walter Scott. Right seldom would I fail. PBBP

It's Wonderful. Walter E. Isenhour. That we are soldiers for our Lord/ Beneath His flag unfurled. STF

It's You. L. A. McDonald. It isn't your church, it's you. STF

It Says. Jon Silkin. ...adding/that for the tear she dropped/the man dies. VWA

It Scarcely Seems Worth While. Vladislav Khodasevich. With what a swift astonished tenderness. LiTW

It Seems That God Bestowed Somehow. Amanda Benjamin Hall. I ask you, Sirs, what thought you then/On Christmas long ago? AH

It Should Be Easy. Mark Van Doren. ...waves/Wash once again on straight and silent ground. CrMA

It sifts from leaden sieves. Emily Dickinson. Then stills its artisans like ghosts,/Denying they have been. DiPo; PoPl; SoSe

It sounded as if the streets were running. Emily Dickinson. Nature was in an opal apron,/Mixing fresher air. NePA; OBSP; PBWP

It Started. Jimmy Santiago Baca. I burn these words in praise,/of our meeting, our friendship. LFAC

It struck me every day. Emily Dickinson. But Nature lost the date of this/ And left it in the sky. PPP

It troubled me as once I was. Emily Dickinson. Why heaven did not break away/And tumble blue on me. ImOP

It Was a' for Our Rightfu' King. Robert Burns. The lee-lang night, and weep. EnRP; GoTS; PoEL 1-5

It Was a Funky Deal. Etheridge Knight. It was a funky deal. BOLo; BPo; PoBA

It Was a Goodly Co. Edward Estlin Cummings. to the god of things like they err CrMA; LiTA; LiTM; MoVE; WaP

It was a Special Treat. Luci Tapahonso. we went back to sleep until we reached home. STE

It Was All Very Tidy. Robert Graves. It was all very tidy. OxBTC

It Was an April Morning. William Wordsworth. When they have cause to speak of this wild place,/May call it by the name of EMMA'S DELL. FaBoPP

It Was Far in the Night and the Barnies Grat (parody). Gerry Hamill. The mither beneath the mools knows that. BXAP

It Was for Me. Eva Gray. O glorious day, eternity/With Him, the blessed One in Three. STF

It Was Gentle. Hedva Harkavi. a yellow night/in another kingdom. VWA

It Was in Vegas. J. V. Cunningham. It was enough to stop a man from girling. UnTE

It Was Miss Scarlet with the Candlestick in the Billiard Room. Bernadette Mayer. Plus we see Peggy. APU

It Was My Choice. Sir Thomas Wyatt. There is no way that is so just/As truth to lead, though t'other fail,/And thereto trust. EnRePo; FCP; QFR; SiPS

It Was Not Death, for I Stood Up. Emily Dickinson. Or even a Report of Land–/To justify–Despair. AmePo; AtBAP; BiP; CBEP; MAPA; MasP; MoPo; NePA; NOBA; NoP

It Was Not Fate. William H. A. Moore. And find holiness, love and the peace which passeth under/standing. BANP

It Was Not Strange. Esther Lloyd Hagg. Should find in Bethlehem/The Lamb of God! PGD

It Was Not You. Andre Spire. The days have fled,/My well-beloved. TrJP

It Was the Last of the Parades. Louis Simpson. Another war? No thanks. NYBP

It Was the Lovely Moon. John Freeman. Wonderful in the silvery shine/ Of the round, lovely, thoughtful moon. BoNaP

It Was the Morning. Petrarch (Francesco Petrarca). How craven so to strike me stricken so,/Yet from you fully armed conceal his bow! NAWM 1-2

It Was the Time of Roses. Thomas Hood. We plucked them as we passed."... CH

It Was the Worm. James Richard Broughton. What else gives light to Eternity?/the worm, smiling, said to me. GP

It Was Wrong to Do This, Said the Angel. Stephen Crane. Waging war like the lambkins. AmP; LiTA; NePA

It Was You, Attis. Sappho. But you forget everything. PeHV

It Was Your Song. Steve Kowit. Cavafy, it was your song/from which I borrowed/both the manner & the courage. APU

It Will Not Shine Again. Emily Bronte. I have seen the last ray wane/Of the cold, bright sun. NOBV

It would be wrong for us. Sappho. for mourning to enter a home of poetry. BoWoP

It would have starved a gnat. Emily Dickinson. To gad my little Being out–/And not begin–again– MoVE; NAWM 1-2; SBG

Italia, Io Ti Saluto! Christina Georgina Rossetti. And the sweet name to my mouth. OBTV; OBVV

The Italian Air. Lewis MacAdams. The draught from the leaves sifts down and shakes your hands ANYP

An Italian Chest. Marjorie Allen Seiffert. Now lock the chest, for we/Are dead, and lose the key! HBMV

Italian Extravaganze. Gregory Corso. And ten black cadillacs to haul it in. CoPo

The Italian in England. Robert Browning. So much for idle wishing–how/ It steals the time! To business now. FaBoPV; MaVP; OAEP; OBNV

Italian Music in Dakota. Walt Whitman. Listens well pleas'd. AmePo; AmP

Italian Opera. James Miller. Make Love in Tune, or thro' the Gamut rant. OBEC; UnS

Italian Poppies. Joel Elias Spingarn. And Roman Antony saw you bloom,/ Flaming, on Cleopatra's ships. HBMV

Italian Rhapsody. Robert Underwood Johnson. Oh, let me join the faithful shades that throng that rount/above. HBV 1-2

The Italian Soldier Shook My Hand. George Orwell. No bomb that ever burst/Shatters the crystal spirit. OBWP

Italian Woman. Diane Wakoski. ...centuries of crushed shells,/plus the new. GrPl

Italy. Vincenzo da Filicaja. Victor or vanquished, thou the slave of friend or foe. AWP

Italy and Britain. Joseph Addison. And makes her barren Rocks and her bleak Mountains smile. OBEC

Italy Versus England. George Gordon, Lord Byron. And wish they were not owing to the Tories. NOBE

Ite. Ezra Pound. And take your wounds from it gladly. HAP; MoAB; MoAmPo; PP

ITEM. Edward Estlin Cummings. (exit the hors d'oeuvres) MoAB; MoAmPo

Iter Boreale. Robert Wild. But who shall find a pen fit for thy glory,/Or make posterity believe thy story?/Vive St. George! APAS

Iter Supremum. Arthur Sherburne Hardy. And night at the gates where a soul would/go. AA

Ithaca. Constantine P. Cavafy. that already you will have understood these Ithacas,/and what they mean. LiTW

Ithocles, VI (excerpt). John Addington Symonds. All Crete shall bless the marriage of tonight.' PeHV

Itiskit, Itaskit. *Anonymous.* A little boy came along/Put it in his pocket,/ Pocket, pocket. TrAS

Its a Good Thing to Join a Union. *Anonymous.* It's a fine, fine thing to join a union,/For it will help you. FSW

Its Ain Drap o' Dew. James Ballantine. But ilka blade o' grass/Keps its ain drap o' dew. HBV 1-2

Its Name Is Known. D. L. Kelleher. Some call it love, some grace. NeIP

'Ittle Touzle Head. Ray Garfield Dandridge. Mah 'ittle Touzle Head. BANP

Itylus. Algernon Charles Swinburne. But the world shall end when I forget. GTBS; HBV 1-2; WHA

Iulus. Eleanor Glenn Wallis. And watched as fallen warriors, each in turn,/Became a stillness at the whirlwind's core. NePoAm-2

IV. Joseph Bruchac. in the last days of April CDW

Ivanhoe. Chapt. 39: Rebecca's Hymn. Sir Walter Scott. A contrite heart, a humble thought,/Are mine accepted sacrifice. EnRP

Ives (excerpt). Muriel Rukeyser. naming the instruments we all must hold. UnS

Ivesiana. Bill Berkson. We stopped for a drink/and stayed a year. ANYP

An Ivied Tree-Top. *Anonymous.* It is bright as a garden,/and with no fence around it! NOBI

The Ivory Bed. Winfield Townley Scott. So peace begins the winsome day. ErPo

The Ivory, Coral, Gold. William, of Hawthornden Drummond. That I would wish me thus to dream and die. ELP

The Ivory Dog of My Sister. Mary Tallmountain. Out of dark and different time. TWSS

The Ivory Gate: Stanzas. Thomas Lovell Beddoes. Such antediluvian ocean's stream,/Haunts shadowy my domestic mood. EG; TrGrPo

Ivory Masks in Orbit. Keorapetse Kgositsile. i know how you be tonight! PoBA

Ivory Paper Weight. Adrien Stoutenburg. the papers on my blowing desk,/ and my beast-haunted mind. GP

The Ivory Tower. Robert Hillyer. I note it has outlasted all the bombings. NYBP

Ivry. Thomas Babington, Lord Macaulay. And glory to our Sovereign Lord, King Henry/of Navarre! FaBV; GN; HBV 1-2; HBVY; OBRV

Ivy and Holly. E. H. W. Meyerstein. The village burns us on its tongue,/ And all the tale is true. ELU

Ivy Crest. Anonymous. And everlasting light shines here. AnIL

The Ivy Crown. William Carlos Williams. We will it so/and so it is/past all accident. NoP; PrIm

The Ivy Green. Charles Dickens. A rare old plant is the Ivy green. BoNaP; HBV 1-2; HBVY

The Ivy-Wife. Thomas Hardy. Being bark-bound, flagged, snapped, fell out-/right,/And in his fall felled me! VLP

Izaac Walton, Cotton, and William Oldways. Walter Savage Landor. Just like these idle waves, son Cotton! NBM; PoEL 1-5

J

J. A. G. Julia Ward Howe. The hero's garland his, the martyr's crown. PAH

J'Accuse. Peter Klappert. long forgotten comme tout le monde je les en accuse. AMV-81

J.B. Henry Cuyler Bunner. "A thought of Brougham."–/And that is Fame! AA

J.B. (excerpt). Archibald MacLeish. But we do. That's the wonder. EaLo

J. J. Walter De la Mare. And wonder from which of his old friends in Sinder/Had burst out that muffled, "Old Jones!" FaBoNo

J. Milton Miles. Edgar Lee Masters. Nor even, at last, the voice that I should have known. CrMA

Ja, Ja, Ja! Anonymous. Vell, ve'll git up on der shteeples and ve'll spit down on der peoples,/Mitsch mein ja, ja, ja! ShS

Jabber-Whacky. Isabelle Di Caprio. All Pillsbury were the Taystee loaves,/ And in a Minute Maid. QQQ

Jabberwocky. Lewis (Charles Lutwidge Dodgson) Carroll. And the mome raths outgrabe. ALV; AmMo; BiP; DiPo; EBEV; FaBoBe; FaBoCo; FaBoNo; FaBV; FaFP; FF; FiBHP; FPL; GoJo; GoTF; HBV 1-2; HeIP; HoPM; InPK; InPS; LBN; LiTB; NA; NAMP; NBM; NIP; NLV; NOBE; NOBL; NOBV; NoP; NTCP; OAEL 1-2; OxBChV; PAI; PoPl; PoRA; PPoe; PPP; SeCeV; SpRo; TEP; TiPo; TreF; TrGrPo; VLP

Jabberwocky. Junius Cooper. Till all the woods re-echoed loud, "Callooh! Callay!" InMe

Jacaranda. Roo Borson. on which time/in luminous drops/is raining down. CaPN; NOBC

Jack. Louis Goldberg. This dead moist smell of rain! TrJP

Jack. Charles Henry Ross. We'll find out tomorrow,/And beat him today. OxBChV

Jack, Afterwards. Philip Dacey. Not even my mother knew, when she could see. SM

Jack and Dinah Want Freedom. Anonymous. De nex' day de hide drap off'n yo' back. BPo

Jack and Gye. Anonymous. And we'll bring him up/As other folks do. OxNR

Jack and His Father. John Heywood. Since all these ease not, best ye hang awhile. DiPo

Jack and His Pony, Tom. Hilaire Belloc. Kindness to animals should be/ Attuned to their brutality. BoAnP; PH

Jack and Jill. Anonymous. At see-saw across the gate. OxNR

Jack and Jill. Harriet S. Morgridge. And in this simple story lies concealed/The germ of half that's plucked in fiction's/field. AA

Jack and Jill. Mother Goose.
And Jill came tumbling after. SoPo
And went to bed to mend his head/With vinegar and brown paper. FaFP; HBV 1-2; HBVY; OxBoLi

Jack and Jill (parody). Charles Battell Loomis. Job's patience or Solomon's wisdom, and I love attributes./Whoop!!! BXAP

Jack and Jill (parody). Charles Powell. "There, too, the simple wench will follow after." BXAP

Jack and Joan. Thomas Campion Yet, for all your pomp and train,/ Securer lives the silly swain. EG; EnL; FaBoCh; FaPoR; HBV 1-2; OAEP

Jack and Roger. Benjamin Franklin. And with the self-same weapon, too!' ChTr

Jack Be Nimble. Mother Goose. And Jack jump over/the candlestick. OxNR; SoPo; TiPo

Jack Creamer. James Jeffrey Roche. And the Nation was close to its Maker then. MC; PAH

Jack Donahoe. Anonymous. For we scorn to live in slavery, bound down with iron/chains. CoSo

Jack Frenchman's Defeat. William Congreve. Thou hadst better disband,/ For old Bully, thy doctors are gone. APAS; CoMu

Jack Frost. Helen Bayley Davis. They vanished one by one! SoPo

Jack Frost. (Thomas Nicoll Hepburn) "Setoun, Gabriel" And when you wake you see again/The lovely things you saw in dream. HBV 1-2; HBVY

Jack Frost. Celia Thaxter. Far away out of sight of your mischief! I give you no/welcome, not I! OBCA

Jack Haggerty. Anonymous. Just think of Jack Haggerty and the Flat River girl. AmFP; ShS; ViBoFo

Jack Hall. Anonymous. And the devil of a word said I coming down. OBET

Jack-in-the-Box. Elder Olson. The angel, treed, was trembling, that had promised peace. NePA

Jack in the Pulpit. Anonymous Sold his wife for a minikin pin. OxNR

Jack-in-the-Pulpit. Ivy O. Eastwick. and the gentle tinkle/of falling rain. YeAr

Jack Is Every Inch a Sailor. Anonymous. Then go sailing with his heart still free. FSW

Jack Monroe (Jackie's Gone A-Sailing). Anonymous. This couple they got married, and why not you and me? AmFP

Jack o' Diamonds. Anonymous. Jack o' Diamonds is a hard card to play. OuSiCo

Jack O' Diamonds; or, The Rabble Soldier. Anonymous. Do make me a pallet, I'll lie on the floor. CoSo

Jack O'Lantern. Anna Chandler Ayre. And saucily laughed at him. SoPo

Jack of Diamonds. Anonymous. How bad I do feel! AmFP

Jack Rabbit. Adrien Stoutenburg. My car, a thundering shepherd, coaxed/ him over the hill, and I went on. BoAnP

Jack Robinson. Anonymous. And he was off before you could say Jack Robinson. OBET

Jack Rose. Maxwell Bodenheim. For some time she sat stiffly in the chair,/ Then slowly raised her hand and stroked his hair. HBMV

Jack's Fidelity. Charles Dibdin. And live and die constant to Poll. EtS

Jack Sprat Could Eat No Fat. Mother Goose. They licked the platter clean. FaBoBe; FaFP; HBV 1-2; HBVY

Jack Sprat (parody). Henry Hetherington. They both licked their plates clean. FaBoPa

Jack Sprat's Cat. Anonymous. It went to buy butter/When butter was dear. OxNR

Jack Sprat's Pig. Mother Goose. Says little Jack Sprat. BrR; OxNR

Jack Tar. Anonymous.
And we get nothing for it but toil and vexation.' OBSS
For to wed with a poor country girl/That's no fortune to be had? ShS

Jack the Giant Queller. An Antique History. Henry Brooke. And Truth, from this approving stage,/Shall beam through every act and age. NOEC

Jack the Guinea Pig. Anonymous. Still from care and thinking free,/Is a sailor's life at sea. AmSS

Jack the Jolly Tar. Anonymous.
"I came up and pulled the string, and you came down and let/me in." BaBo
She loved the tarry sailor well,/And told the squire to go to hell. AmFP

Jack Was Every Inch a Sailor. Anonymous.
He caught the whale all by the tail and turned him inside out. WHW
He was born upon the deep blue sea. FSW

Jack Wrack. Anonymous. But get married, my boys, and have all night in, and go to sea no more! ABF

The Jackdaw. William Cowper. For such a pair of wings as thine,/And such a head between 'em. HBV 1-2; HBVY; PB; PBBP

Jackdaw. Tom Earley. Monoglot, that you would speak Welsh. BoAnP

Jacket So Blue. Anonymous. And she'll never put a stain on my jacket so blue. BFSS

The Jackfruit. Ho Xuan Huong. the rich juice will gush and stain your hands. PBWP

Jackie. King D. Kuka. like a beautiful butterfly/leaving a/lonely smile. VoR

Jackie Frazier. Anonymous. In some far-off land,/Oh, in some far-off land. BFSS

Jackie Tar. Anonymous. And the sailor kissed his bride with his trousers on. OBSS

Jacklight. Louise Erdrich. How deep the woods are. TWSS

Jackrabbits. Squire Omar Barker. They say what makes him flee so fast/Is fleas–because he's got 'em! BPAW

Jackson. Anonymous. A bottle of good brandy and on each arm a girl. FSW

Jackson at New Orleans. Wallace Rice. Led by our battle-loving Andrew Jackson,/Blest of Jehovah. PAH

Jackson, Mississippi. Margaret Walker. And the birthing stools of grannies long since fled. FB

Jackson State Prison. Leon Baker. buzzards ride their back. LFAC

Jacksonville Blues. Nellie Florence. But the man I'm loving lives/down in Jacksonville BluL

Jacky, Come Give Me Thy Fiddle. Anonymous. My fiddle and I have had. OxNR; UnS

January. William Carlos Williams. And the wind,/as before, fingers perfectly/its derisive music. MoAB; MoAmPo

January 1. Marnie Pomeroy. Like every January first,/Brand-new in your old name. PoSC

January 15 as a National Holiday. Carter Revard. ...We hit one slot, in Las Vegas, for fifty cents. VoR

January 18, 1979. John Yau. someone half in love with herself/and half in love with the world. APU

January 1939. Dylan Thomas. Over the past table I repeat this present grace. EAS

January 1940. Roy Fuller. But the appearance of choice/In their sad and fatal voice. LiTM; SeCePo; WaP

January 1st. Anne Sexton. I will not speculate today/with poems that think they're money. HaCAP

January 25th. Maxine W. Kumin. barely, barely repeating/themselves enough to hang on. SM

January 3, 1970. Mae Jackson. slavery never did impress me. PoBA

January Brings the Snow. Mother Goose. Blazing fire and Christmas treat. TiPo

January Eclogue. Edmund Spenser. Whose hanging heads did seeme his carefull case to weepe. FiP

January Is Here. Edgar Fawcett. A frost-mailed warrior striding/A shadowy steed of snow. YeAr

January Man. Dave Goulder. ...starting each and every year/Along the way for ever. OBET

A January Morning. Archibald Lampman. With frost-fringed flanks, and nostrils jetting steam. ACV; OBCV

January Morning. William Carlos Williams. Well,/that's the way it is with me somehow. InPS; PAI; SOTW

January Snow. Aileen Fisher. nobody, nobody ever can/count them all...if he counts all day. YeAr

January Wraps up the Wound of His Arm. Charles Henri Ford. like a tear that has changed its mind. EAS

Janus. Madeline Mason. Split as we are in twain,/With cloven core? GoYe

Japan. Anthony Hecht. It shall be buried in excelsior. CrMA; LiTA; LiTM

Japan That Sank under the Sea. Satoru Sato. It is too early to reveal itself. PoPl

The Japanese. Ogden Nash. "So sorry, this my garden now." DBV; InMe

Japanese Beetles. X.J. Kennedy.
 Enough confusion of my own, I've got. HoAn; OBAL
 His own tongue only, and of it not much. HoAn; OBAL
 I could read what page eight had said to try. HoAn; OBAL
 Meek got a word in edgewise after all. HoAn; OBAL
 Or back outside you shall hang by a thread. HoAn; OBAL
 So keep a straight face and sit tight on yours. HoAn; OBAL
 Those bosom chums to whom you're known as "Who?" HoAn; OBAL
 The very mice go down upon their knees. HoAn; OBAL
 When there's some urgent duty I dislike. HoAn; OBAL
 Would starve the horse to death and prize his turds. HoAn; OBAL

A Japanese Birthday Wish. Thomas Burnett Swann. To make of night/A forest flowered with light. GoYe

The Japanese Consulate. Frank Polite. I don't see it that way, O my Kamikaze heart. APU

Japanese Fan. James Kirkup. The paper windows of a soul. GrPl

Japanese Fan. Margaret Veley. I'm translating: this is only/Japanese. NBM

Japanese Girl with Red Table. Stephen Dobyns. ...as he tries/hopelessly to hold his cup steady and make no face. MAYP

Japanese Hokku. Lewis Alexander. O that I were blind! CDC

A Japanese Love-Song. Alfred Noyes. And your face and the flowers/Faint away in the moon. OBVV

The Japanese Lovers. Anonymous. With a paper-muslin ghost. BeLS; BLPA

Japanese Print. Austin Clarke. Sharako, Hokusai! IPY; NOBI

Japanesque. Oliver Herford. And is she not my Japan niece? FiBHP

The Jar. Richard Henry Stoddard. Let the jar be filled with wine! AA

The Jar of Nations. Alfred Edward Housman. And quarrelsome chaps in charnels/Must bear it as best they can. LiTB

Jarama Valley. Anonymous. Let's remember our glorious dead. FSW

Jarcha: "I will make love." Anonymous. touch the jewelry/on my ankles. BoWoP

Jarcha: "If you really care for me." Anonymous. and kiss/my small mouth of cherries. BoWoP

Le Jardin. Oscar Wilde. The roses lie upon the grass/Like little shreds of crimson silk. SeCePo

Jardin de la Chapelle Expiatoire. Robert Finch. And shaded by historic woes/A mother mops her infant's nose. PeCV

Jardin des Fleurs. Charles David Webb. And I will join you there. NePoAm-2

Jardin du Palais Royal. David Gascoyne. Walls of the haunted Memory's arcade. MoPo

Jars. Paul Raboff. Of rocks in the desert/Is mad as a dervish. VWA

Jason. Anthony Hecht. Triumphs in gardens full of marigold. CoPo

Jason and Medea. John Gower. And wax all fresh and green again. ACP

Jason and Medea. Alun Lewis. And in a nest of snakes he courted her. CBEP

Javanese Dancers. Arthur Symons. Like painted idols seen to stir/By the idolators in a magic grove. VLP

Javier. Jose Y., Jr. Teran. who loved to play cars/with empty cartons of milk. LFAC

Jay A-Pass'd. William Barnes. When did my jay all pass me by? NOBV

Jay Gould's Daughter. Anonymous. See the drivers roll. FSW

Jay Gould's Daughter (with music). Anonymous. Le 'em put their trust in the hands of God. AS

Jazz. Frank London Brown. What's going on in there? PoNe

Jazz. Carolyn M. Rodgers. wah wah weeeeeeeeeeeeeeee. JB

Jazz Band in a Parisian Cabaret. Langston Hughes. Can I go home wid yuh, sweetie?"/"Sure." BANP; MoAmPo

Jazz Fantasia. Carl Sandburg. Go/to it, O jazzmen. AnFE; CoAnAm; MoAB; MoAmPo; PoNe

Le Jazz Hot. Anselm Hollo. he had discovered something called "le jazz hot'/& found it of some interest. PoM

The Jazz of This Hotel. Vachel Lindsay. That seems so hot, but is so hard and cold. ATP; PoPl

Jazzonia. Langston Hughes. Six long-headed jazzers play. BANP; NIP

The Je Ne Scay Quoi: A Song. William Whitehead. In short, 'tis that provoking Charm/Of Caelia all together. OBEC; SoSe

Je Ne Veux de Personne aupres de ma Tristesse. Henri de Regnier. Must hear that whisper when his hour has come. AWP

Je Suis une Table. Donald Hall.
 Habit of conversation/(thickly turned thing) may make none. NePoEA
 ...nothing/to relieve on principle/now this intense thickening. EAS

Je T'Adore. Thomas Kinsella. We praise Love the limiter. NoAm

Jealosie. John Donne. As the inhabitants of Thames right side/Do Londons Mayor; or Germans, the Popes pride. AnAnS 1

Jealous Adam. Itzik Manger. he felt like burying his head/and sobbing in the grass. TrJP

The Jealous Brothers. Anonymous. It rained and it hailed and a storm o'ercame them,/Both a watery grave in all the sea. AmFP

The Jealous Enemy. Petrarch (Francesco Petrarca). Nay ev'n the hopes I form'd: and on them fell/E'en in mid way, like some arm'd foe in wait. LiTW

The Jealous Lover. Anonymous. Then she closed her eyes and died. ShS

The Jealous Lover (A vers.). Anonymous. There sleeps that fair Florilla,/So silent in her tomb. BaBo; ViBoFo

The Jealous Lovers. Donald Hall. Her eyes have not shut all night. NYBP

A Jealous Man. Anonymous. Who do you think would want/Such an ugly face? KiLC

A Jealous Man. Robert Graves. His war was not hers. CMoP

The Jealous Wife. Vernon Scannell. At last her fears are justified. ErPo

Jealousie is the Rage of a Man. Anne Finch, Countess of Winchilsea. No wonder, that th' experienc'd Hebrew sage,/Of Man, pronounc'd it the extremest Rage. FM

Jealousy. Anonymous.
 Jealousy when it strikes/Sticks in the marrowbone. KiLC
 Whose ring is that upon your finger? WTO

Jealousy. Mary Elizabeth Coleridge. "Even so!' said the Queen. EnLoPo; NBM; OBNC

Jealousy. Rachel DeVries. ...squinting your eyes/against the sun that glints/too brightly off the hard-packed/snow. AMV-81

Jealousy. Esther Johnson. Or tell me, tyrants, have you both agreed/That where one reigns the other shall succeed? OBSP

Jealousy. Stephen Vincent. There is nothing between us. NeAC

Jeames of Buckley Square. William Makepeace Thackeray. And so, Miss Mary Hann, forget/For hever Jeames of Buckley Square. VLP

Jean. Robert Burns. That nane can be sae dear to me/As my sweet lovely Jean! GTBS; GoTF; GTBS-P; MCCG; OBEV; TreFS; TrGrPo

Jean. Paul Potts. So useless and so void. NeBP

Jean Richepin's Song. Herbert Trench. "Are you hurt my child, are you hurt at all?" OBMV; OxBI

Jeane Dixon's America. Gerald Costanzo. don't look for this to happen any time soon. MAYP

Jeanie Morrison. William Motherwell. Did I but ken your heart still dreamed/O' bygane days and me! HBV 1-2

Jeanie with the Light Brown Hair. Stephen Collins Foster.
 Floating, like a vapor, on the soft summer air. BLSo
 Never more to find her where the bright waters flow. FaFP; FSW; GoTF; TrAS; TreF

Jeanne d'Arc. Louise Gluck. ...and thank/the enemy to whom I owe my life. GeTw

Jeannette. Otto Julius Bierbaum. Jeannette! Jeannette! AWP

Jeannette and Jeannot. Charles Jeffries. Why, let them who make the quarrel be the only men to fight. BLPA

Jeannie Marsh. George Pope Morris. A dimple in the smile of nature. AA

Jeannot's Answer. Charles Jeffries. Were only kings themselves to fight, there'd be an end to war. BLPA

Jeans. J. V. Brummels. They're a one-man dog/And, once broken, will bite another. GP

A Jeat Ring Sent. John Donne. She that, Oh, broke her faith, would soon breake/thee. PoEL 1-5

Jeep. Charles Stetler. ...but your many busts will/always have a place in my Hall of Fame. GP

Jeff Buckner. Frank Beddo. And we were there, but we never said a word. WTO

Jefferson and Liberty. Anonymous. But join with heart and soul and voice/for Jefferson and Liberty. FSW; TrAS

Jefferson D. Henry Sylvester Cornwell. And declare that rebellion no longer shall be!/Jefferson D.! PAH

Jefferson Davis. Walker Meriwether Bell. A relic and a shrine! PAH

Jefferson, Texas. Naomi Shihab. you just cross TAT

Jefferson Valley. John Hollander. ...the lack/Of a singular green is what we mean by black. PPP

Jehovah. Israel Zangwill. Which may not flood the earth but only steal in/Through rifts in your souls. WGRP

Jehovah Buried, Satan Dead. Edward Estlin Cummings. Who dares to call Himself a man. NePA

Jehovah, God, Who Dwelt of Old. Lewis R. Amis. We'll enter, with triumphant song,/The house not made with hands. AH

Jehovah, Lord and Majesty. Conrad Weiser. For thy name's sake, O hear us. AH

Jehovah Our Righteousness. William Cowper. The Lord shall be my righteousness;/The Lord for ever mine. NOCV

Jehovah-Rophi. William Cowper. Oh! send us not despairing home,/Send none unhealed away. EiCP

Jehu. Louis MacNeice. ...unable to imagine/The meaning of the flood tide. LiTM; MoAB; WaP

Jellon Grame (A version). Anonymous. The place my mother lies buried in/Is far too good for thee. BaBo; EBEV; ESPB; OxBB

Jellon Grame (B version). Anonymous. For killing of my mother dear,/And her not hurting thee. ESPB

The Jelly Fish. Robert P. Tristram Coffin. And in this frail transparency/God moves essentially and whole. CAW

Jelly Jake and Butter Bill. Leroy F. Jackson. Poor Jelly Jake and Butter Bill. BBGG

A Jellyfish. Marianne Moore. you abandon your intent. OBSP; PCP

The Jellyfish. William Pitt Root. that slid from the ocean without a sound. BoAnP

Jemmy Dawson. Anonymous. And then he bought a cradle. OxNR

Jennifer Gentle and Rosemary. Anonymous. As the doo flies owre the mulberry tree. OxBoLi

Jenny. Dante Gabriel Rossetti.
Jenny, you know the city now. NBM
Only one kiss. Good-bye, my dear. MaVP; PoEL 1-5

Jenny Kiss'd Me. [James Henry] Leigh Hunt. Jenny kiss'd me. ALV; BiCB; BLPA; EnLi 1-2; FaBoBe; FaFP; FPL; GoTF; HBV 1-2; InMe; LiTL; NLV; NOBE; NTCP; OBEV; OBVV; PoPl; PoRA; SpRo; TreF

Jenny's Ribbons. William Barnes. An' she, a-smilen wi' her bow/O' blue, look'd roun' an' nodded, No. VLP

Jenny wi' the Airn Teeth. Alexander ("Surface man") Anderson. Bigger bogies, bigger Jennies,/Frichten muckle men. HBV 1-2

Jenny Wren. Anonymous. Fie upon you,/Bold-faced jig! EvOK

Jenny Wren. William Henry Davies. Had starlings chattering without stop. MoBrPo

Jeny Kiss'd Me When We Met. Paul Dehn. Say I've had a filthy cold/Since Jenny kiss'd me. FiBHP

Jephthah's Daughter. Charles Heavysege. Nor, walking in the winter, woo the sun. CaP

Jephthah's Daughter. Yehoash. The voice of her they rue! TrJP

The Jerboa. Marianne Moore.
between leaps to its burrow. AtBAP; FaBoWP; FYAP; MoPo
...;but one would not be he/who has nothing but plenty. CMoP

Jeremiad. Oscar Williams. The Red Sea running down the heart of God. LiTA

Jeremiah. Witter ("Emanuel Morgan") Bynner. He pulls mankind in after him, to die. CrMA

Jeremiah, Blow the Fire. Anonymous. Then you blow it rough. OxNR

Jeremy. Jeffrey Miller. & Jeremy, where are you/all these scams seem orphaned. APU

Jeremy's Secrets. Barbara Euphan Todd. No, things don't count till you're really old–/A witch told Jeremy. He's not told! BiCB

Jericho. Willard Wattles. The leveled walls of Jericho,/Jericho, Jericho, Jericho.... HBMV

Jericho's Blind Beggar. Henry Wadsworth Longfellow. He pistis sou sesoke se. WBLP

Jerked Heartstrings in Town. E.B.C. Jones. I turned,–a tawdry simpering little dowd/Passed by, and left me trembling on the curb. HBMV

Jerome. Randall Jarrell. And the lion licks the man's hand with his tongue. PPP

Jeronimo's House. Elizabeth Bishop. I take these things,/not much more, from/my shelter from/the hurricane. MiAP; NoP

Jerry an' Me. Hiram Rich. Who hear the breakin' bar an' think/O' Jerry home an'–me. HBV 1-2

Jerry, Go an' Ile That Car (with music). Anonymous. Oh, Jerry, go and ile that car-r-r! AS

Jerry Hall. Anonymous. A rat could eat him,/Hat and all. OxNR

Jerry Jones. Anonymous. And now he's bones himself. ShM

Jersey Bait Shack. Peter Balakian. how long it waits to soak beneath the bait. MAYP

Jersey Belle Blues. Lonnie Johnson. Boys, it's a very tough titty/but the milk is so doggone good BluL

Jersey Cattle. Ralph Nixon Currey. As they pad through the village street/With a sound like heavy rain. OxBTC

The Jersey Marsh. David Galler. How they no longer have/Much to do with each other. NYBP

Jerusalem. Rose Auslander. Coevals/we have a game/in the air VWA

Jerusalem. William Blake.
And the bitter groan of a Martyr's woe/Is an arrow from the Almighty's bow. OBRV
Both heart in heart and hand in hand. FaBoPV; OBNC; OBRV
Built in Jerusalem's wall. OBRV
A little sound it utters, and its cries are faintly heard. OBRV; ViBoPo
Receive the Lamb of God to dwell/In England's green and pleasant bowers. EaLo; EvOK; FaPoR; NOBE; NOCV; NoP; OBNC; OBRV; PPON; WaaP
Till they have had Punishment enough to make them commit/Crimes. OBNC
Without the Gate of Los, among the dark Satanic wheels. OBRV

Jerusalem. Ruben Kanalenstein. and the beginning of reason,/the inauguration of hope. VWA

Jerusalem. (or Molodovski) Kadya, (or Kadia) Molodovsky. On the verge of the infinite/In Jerusalem. AMV-81

Jerusalem. John Mason Neale. O realm and home of life! HBV 1-2; OBVV

Jerusalem. Jon Silkin. is lift you to where this illumination/overfills with space. VWA

Jerusalem. Antoni Slonimski. As in a Polish countryside, the flies drone in Jerusalem. VWA

Jerusalem. Shlomo Vinner. Jerusalem 1967,/The former address of God. VWA

Jerusalem Delivered (excerpt). Torquato Tasso. And fill these lines with other praise than thine. CAW

Jerusalem in the Snow. Anath Bental. But muddy for hours and days/When it melts. VWA

A Jerusalem Notebook. Harvey Shapiro. crowding east where the sun waits. AMV-81

Jerusalem, Port City. Yehuda Amichai. Jerusalem is the Venice of God. VWA

Jerusalem Sonnets. James Keir Baxter.
His silent laugh still shakes the hills at dawn. NoP; OCNZ
If the fish are to be drawn in at all. OCNZ
Rule over myself He has taken away from me. OCNZ
That His true weight is heavy on your back. OCNZ
Their Master and Maker, drunkards of the sky. OCNZ

Jerusalem the Dismembered. Uri Z. Greenberg. And slay myself and let my blood flow/upon the cliffs! TrJP

Jerusalem, the Golden. Bernard of Cluny. Thou shalt be and thou art. CAW; WGRP

The Jervis Bay. Anonymous. They gave their lives that November day,/Those heroes of the Jervis Bay. OBSS

Jesous Ahatonhia. Jesse Edgar Middleton. Jesus is born;/In Excelsis Gloria! CaP

Jess's Dilemma. Anonymous. Then go up the trail every chance in the spring. CoSo

Jesse James. Anonymous.
And came from a solitary race. BeLS; UnPo
He said there is no man with the law in his hand/Can take Jesse James when alive. AmFP

Jesse James. Rosemary and Stephen Vincent Benét. He earned his outlaw fame. BPAW

Jesse James. William Rose Benet. (Hear that Missouri roll!). BBV; BPAW; FYAP; MoAmPo; NAMP; StPo; TrGrPo

Jesse James (A vers.). *Anonymous.* But that dirty little coward that shot Mr. Howard/And laid poor Jesse in the grave! ABF; AmFN; AS; BaBo; BFSS; CoSo; FaBoBe; FSW; MaC; TrAS; TreFS; ViBoFo; WiR; YaD

Jesse James (B vers.). *Anonymous.* A cowboy drunk his heart did plunk./As you do you'll git according. BaBo; ViBoFo

Jesse James. (Version B). *Anonymous.* While de wind blows down de chimney we will shake with fright. ABF

Jessie. Thomas Edward Brown. A stone remote in some bleak gully of the hills! HBV 1-2

Jessie. Eugene Field. Of all the husbands in the land/There's none so fierce as Jessie's. InMe

Jessie. Bret (Francis Bret Harte) Harte. Jessie is a little child! GN

Jessie Mitchell's Mother. Gwendolyn Brooks. Her exquisite yellow youth... BoWoP; NAs; NMM

Jessie, the Flower o' Dunblane. Robert Tannahill. If wanting sweet Jessie, the Flower o' Dunblane. HBV 1-2

Jessy. Nora Dauenhauer. and my line hooks/on underbrush. TWSS

The Jest. Austin Clarke. Invisible ink. BIrV

Jest 'Fore Christmas. Eugene Field. Jest 'fore Christmas be as good as yer kin be! ChBR; FaBV; FaFP; FPL; HBV 1-2; HBVY; OHFP; PoLf; TreF

The Jester in the Trench. Leon Gellert. They left him–dead. PoAu 1-2

The Jester's Plea. Frederick Locker-Lampson. Forgive the bells their jingle. CenHV

The Jester's Sermon. George Walter Thornbury. And why? Because the motley Fool so wise a sermon made. BeLS; TreFS

Jesu. George Herbert. And to my whole is JESU. EBCP; MeLP

Jesu Christ, My Leman Swete. *Anonymous.* When thou suffredes ded for me. OxBM

Jesu, Come on Board. Johann C. Pyrlaeus. Soldiers on his side. AH

Jesu Dulcis. Saint Bernard of Clairvaux Make of me Thy darling/That I Thee love over all thing. CAW

Jesu, Joy of Man's Desiring. Robert Fitzgerald. The girl, the singing, and the Christmas child. NYBP

Jesu! Send Us Peace. *Anonymous.* Blessed Jesu! MeEL

Jesu, Swete Sone Dere. *Anonymous.* And wite thee from the colde. EnL

Jesu, to Thee My Heart I Bow. Nicolaus Zinzendorf. My only glory be thy cross! AH

Jesukin. Saint Ita. Jesukin is on our breast. CAW; OnYI

Jesus. Francis Lauderdale Adams. They've made God of his carrion/And labelled it "Christ!" OxBS

Jesus. James Philip McAuley. And told them nothing that they wished to know. CBAP

Jesus. Theodore Parker Nor our weak orbs look through immensity. AA

Jesus. Ramon Pimentel Coronel. Yea, Jesus, Son of God, has not a stone/Whereon to lay His head! CAW

Jesus a Child His Course Begun. Margaret Fuller. His yoke to bear, his work to do,/Study his life to learn his will. AH

Jesus and His Mother. Thom Gunn. "I am my own and not my own." EaLo; OxBC

Jesus and I. Dan Crawford. But He never gives in, so we two shall win–/Jesus and I. BLRP; TRV

Jesus Bids Man Remember. *Anonymous.* Thenk well who me rente on the Rode. MeEL

Jesus Borned in Bethlea. *Anonymous.* Jesus borned in Bethlea, and in the manger lay. AmFP

Jesus, Child and Lord. Frederick William Faber. For Thou must one day wake for me/To suffer and to weep! BePJ

Jesus Christ. Woody Guthrie. And a dirty little coward named Judas Iscariot/Has laid Jesus Christ in His grave. WTO

Jesus Comes on Clouds Triumphant. Godfrey Thring. Till the dawn of endless day. BePJ

Jesus Comforts His Mother. *Anonymous.* But singe this song, "By, by, loullay,"/To drive away all heivynis.' MeEL

Jesus Contrasts Man and Himself. *Anonymous.* Hevene blisse I shall yeve thee,/That lasteth ay and oo.' MeEL

Jesus, Deliverer. Saint Anatolius. "Peace! It is I!" BePJ

Jesus Drum. Pearl Cleage Lomax. and Jesus fell like silver/from their mouths. CNA

Jesus, Enthroned and Glorified. Zachary Eddy. Thy living temples let us be,/Thine everlasting rest. AH

Jesus First and Jesus Last. Thomas MacKellar. Let us see Thee, and adore. BePJ

Jesus Himself. Henry K. Burton. And all Thou hast, and all Thou art is mine! BLRP

Jesus, How Much Thy Name Unfolds! Mary Peters. The chiefest of ten thousand, Thou;/The chief of sinners, we. BePJ

Jesus, I Come to Thee. Nathan S. S. Beman. I'll trust alone in thee. AH

Jesus, I Live to Thee. Henry Harbaugh. My life in thee, Thy life in me,/Makes heaven forever mine. AH

Jesus, I Love Thy Charming Name. Philip Doddridge. And, dying, clasp Thee in my arms,/The antidote of death. BePJ

Jesus, in Sickness and in Pain. Thomas H. Gallaudet. In joy or sadness, weal or woe,/Jesus, I'll turn to thee. AH

The Jesus Infection. Maxine W. Kumin. we're leaning on/the everlasting arms. AmC

Jesus Is Coming Soon. Blind Willie Johnson. Said the people in the cities dying/'Counta their wicked ways BluL

Jesus Is Near. Robert Cassie Waterston. Gladly I follow Heaven's command,/With Jesus near! BePJ

Jesus, Keep Me Near the Cross. Fanny J. Crosby. Till my raptured soul shall find/Rest beyond the river. AH

Jesus Lives, and So Shall I. Chr. Furchtegott Gellert. Jesus is the Christian's Trust. BePJ; PGD

Jesus, Lover of My Soul. Charles Wesley. Rise to all eternity. HBV 1-2; WGRP

Jesus Loves Me, This I Know. Anna B. Warner. Yes, Jesus loves me,/The Bible tells me so. AH

Jesus Make Up My Dying Bed. Blind Willie Johnson. Oh well/Done gone over/Make up my BluL

Jesus, Master, O Discover. *Anonymous.* Conscious of our pleasing God. AH

Jesus, Merciful and Mild! Thomas Hastings. Till I reach heaven's blissful shore. AH

Jesus, My God and My All. Frederick William Faber. Time cannot hold Thy wondrous growth,/No, nor eternity. BePJ

Jesus, My Saviour, Look on Me! John MacDuff. Through life, in death, eternally,/Thou art my All. BePJ

Jesus, My Sweet Lover. *Anonymous.* Whon thou soffredest deth for me. MeEL

Jesus Never Fails. Walter E. Isenhour. For He dearly loves His children/And will lead them safely through. STF

Jesus of Nazareth Passeth By. Lydia Sigourney. "Jesus of Nazareth passeth by." BePJ

Jesus Only. Elias Nason. Jesus only, I will, joyous,/Through eternal ages sing. BePJ

Jesus Only. A.B. Simpson. And my hopes are anchored,/Safe within the veil. BePJ

Jesus Reassures His Mother. *Anonymous.* As I lay this Yolisday,/Alone in my longing. MeEL

Jesus Reproaches His People. *Anonymous.* And on an hey hil thu henge me,/All the werld on me to wonder. MeEL

Jesus Return. Henry Van Dyke. Today, to all who need Thee most,/In silent ways, return! TRV

Jesus, Saviour, Pilot Me. Edward Hopper. "Fear not, I will pilot thee." AH; BLRP

Jesus Shall Reign. Isaac Watts. And all the sons of want are blest. BePJ; WGRP

Jesus, Shepherd of Thy Sheep. George Washington Bethune. Take these lambs within thine arms,/Gently to thy bosom pressed. AH

Jesus Spreads His Banner O'er Us. Roswell Park. May we, Lord, remember thee. AH

Jesus Tender Shepherd. Mary L. Duncan. Take me when I die to heaven,/Happy there with Thee to dwell. BLRP

Jesus the Carpenter. Catherine C. Liddell. Unexpected, you know! HBV 1-2

Jesus, the Name Most High. Charles Wesley. Behold, behold the Lamb! BePJ

Jesus, the Soul of Our Joys. Charles Wesley. And sing, with all the heavenly choir,/That endless song above. BePJ

Jesus, These Eyes Have Never Seen. Ray Palmer. The rending veil shall thee reveal,/All-glorious as thou art. AH

Jesus, Thou Art the King. Charles Wesley. Conqu'ring and to conquer go. BePJ

Jesus, Thou Divine Companion. Henry Van Dyke. Lead us to our Sabbath rest. AH

Jesus, Thou Joy of Loving Hearts. Saint Bernard of Clairvaux. Shed o'er the world thy holy light. WGRP

Jesus! Thy crucifix. Emily Dickinson. Mind thee in Paradise/Of our's! MoVE

Jesus to Those Who Pass By. *Anonymous.* To mine herte is made a wounde. MeEL

Jesus Understands. *Anonymous.* Troubled soul–he understands. BLRP

Jesus Was Crucified or: It Must Be Deep. Carolyn M. Rodgers. catch yuh later on Jesus, i mean motha!/it must be/deeeeeep... BlSi; PoBA

Jesus, Won't You Come B'm-By?(with music). *Anonymous.* De Lord knows de world's gwine to end up,/Jesus, won't you come b'm-by? AS

Le Jeune Homme Caressant Sa Chimere. John Addington Symonds. The boy, the myrtle boughs, the triple spell/Of moth and snake and white witch terrible. OBVV

Jew. Pierre Morhange. I embraced in my heart that they hate/The diamond of justice VWA

Jew. James A. Randall, Jr. Felt the bewilderment of one/Who has recalled his murdering. BPo

The Jew. Isaac Rosenberg. Then why do they sneer at me? MoBrPo; VWA

Jew. Karl Shapiro. Where we suffer to die by the hands of ourselves, and to kill. VWA

The Jew at Christmas Eve. Karl Shapiro. Who shakes the fire on the snowy pave. VGW

The Jew of Malta: The Song of Ithamore. Christopher Marlowe. Thou in those groves, by Dis above,/Shalt live with me and be my love. WHA

The Jew to Jesus. Florence Kiper Frank. A thousand times have we been crucified. HBMV; TRV; WGRP

A Jew Walks in Westminster Abbey. Aubrey Hodes. here, in the suburb of the cruel city/and the swift tide out to sea. TrJP

Jewboy. Julian Tuwim. We singing Jews, we Jews possessed... VWA

The Jewel. James Wright. My bones turn to dark emeralds. CAPP; CoAP

The Jewel Stairs' Grievance. Li Po. And watch the moon through the clear autumn. NOBA; OBVE

The Jewels. Charles Baudelaire. It drowned in blood that amber-coloured skin. BoLoP; ErPo

The Jewels. Austin Clarke. God lay upon this tongue. MoAB

Jewish Arabic Liturgies. Anonymous. Return the exiles, the people oppressed/and humble. TrJP

Jewish Ballad. Anonymous. If mine are really worse,/with my hands I'll kill myself. BoWoP

The Jewish Cemetery. Cesar Tiempo. confident that life will not begin tomorrow.... VWA

The Jewish Cemetery at Newport. Henry Wadsworth Longfellow. And the dead nations never rise again. AnNE; AP; ForPo; HAP; HeIP; HoPM; MAmP; NOBA; NoP; OxBA; PPON; TAP

A Jewish Cemetery Near Leningrad. Joseph Brodsky. A couple of miles from the tram terminus. VWA

A Jewish Child Prays to Jesus. I. Blumenthal-Weiss. Has nailed us suffering Jews/Onto the cross once more. VWA

The Jewish Conscript. Florence Kiper Frank. He also died in vain. TrJP

The Jewish Lady. Anonymous. And a bible at my head. BaBo

Jewish Main Street. Irving Layton. Tomorrow some angry potentate/Shall declare null and void. CaP; VWA

The Jewish May. Morris Rosenfeld. Ye shall find the embers burning,/Still, upon the ruined hearth! TrJP

A Jewish Poet Counsels a King. Santob De Carrion. Both fool is called and knave. TrJP

The Jewish Woman. Gertrud Kolmar. The shaking earth will wreck/Its cities: I am greatest. I am all. VWA

The Jews. George Herbert. And by that cry of her dear Lord obtain/That your sweet sap might come again. JCP

The Jews. Mieczyslaw Jastrun. Under it pickets–/To complete the chant for the dead. VWA

The Jews. Henry Vaughan. ...and so heal/The lost Son by the newly found. OBS

Jews at Haifa. Randall Jarrell. Search for one doubt, and whisper: "Truly, we are not dead." MoAmPo

The Jews in Hell. Isaac Goldemberg. Kafka tilts his telescope/and bursts out laughing. VWA

Jezebel. Scudder Middleton. We are, awhile, like happy, armored men/God's searching whip of anger cannot sting! HBMV

Jezebel: Her Progress (excerpt). Gillian E. Hanscombe. She expunges evil/by creating missiles. BrRo

Jezreel. Thomas Hardy. Yea, strange things and spectral may men have beheld in Jezreel! NoP

Jig. C. Day-Lewis. Like fishes for ever, so take it to heart. OxBI

Jig for Sackbuts. Dominic Bevin Wyndham Lewis. Plainly not knowing/Its symbolism. ErPo

Jig Tune: Not for Love. Thomas McGrath. If he were alive we could kill him again. VGW

Jigsaw III. Louis MacNeice. Shuddering through the shuddering main. HaMV

Jigsaw Puzzle. Russell Hoban. He said, "Put it together; the world's like that too." NTCP

Jill. Ronald David Laing. I'll never forgive you for not forgiving me WeW

Jill, Afterwards. Philip Dacey. When they whine, I tell them: climb a hill. SM

Jill Came from the Fair. Eleanor Farjeon. With her toys and her joys/Jill came from the Fair. TiPo

The Jilted Funeral. Gelett Burgess. I wouldn't want to undertake her! ShM

The Jilted Nymph. Thomas Campbell. With proper young men and tall. EnLoPo

Jim. Bret (Francis Bret Harte) Harte. Long-legged Jim. AA

Jim. Barbara Howes. In a folding chair/Waiting for his father? GP

Jim at the Corner. Eleanor Farjeon. And the world nods to him. SoPo; SUS

Jim Bludso of the Prairie Belle. John Milton Hay. And Christ ain't a going to be too hard/On a man that died for men. AA; AnAmPo; BBV; FaBoBe; FaFP; HBV 1-2; MaC; MCCG; PaPo; TreFS; YaD

Jim Crack Corn. Anonymous. Jim crack corn I don't care,/Ole Massa gone away. PSoN

Jim Crow. Anonymous. I do just so. OxNR

Jim Desterland. Hyam Plutzik. The doors, the little doors, swing wide. VGW

Jim Farrow. Anonymous. And this ends my song concerning the Farrows. CoSo

Jim Fisk. Anonymous. But never go back on the poor. AS; ViBoFo

Jim Haggerty's Story. Anonymous. He won't take the advantage no more. ABF

Jim Jay. Walter De la Mare. Poor Jim Jay. BrPo; CenHV; HBMV; SiSoSe; SO

Jim Jones. Anonymous. They'll yet regret they sent Jim Jones in chains to Botany Bay. CBAP; GBP; PoAu 1-2

Jim the Splitter. Henry Clarence Kendall. There's nothing this planet can show him! PoAu 1-2

"Jim, Who Ran Away from His Nurse and Was Eaten by a Lion." Hilaire Belloc. And always keep a-hold of Nurse/For fear of finding something worse. EvOK; OxBChV; ShM

Jimmy Bruder on Quincey Street. Carol Artman Montgomery. your arm in a tee shirt/out the window. AMV-81

Jimmy Jet and His TV Set. Shel Silverstein. And now instead of him watching TV/We all sit around watching him. CTBA; OBCA

Jimmy Judge. Anonymous. I hope his soul's in Heaven for now and eternity. AmFP

Jimmy's Enlisted; or, The Recruited Collier. Anonymous. And I'll lie in the cold, cold grave,/For of single life I'm weary. CoMu; EBEV

Jingle Bells. James S. Pierpont. Oh! what fun it is to ride in a one-horse open sleigh! BLSo; FaFP; FSW; GoTF; OxNR; PSoN; TreF; YaD

Jingle Mammy Song (with music). Anonymous. Nicolay mah lun dee. AS

Jinnie Jinkins. Anonymous. Roll, Jinnie Jinkins, roll! AmFP

Jinny Git Around. Anonymous. Want to git your eye knocked out,/Git on the mountain mill. OuSiCo

Jinny the Just. Matthew Prior. And make thy Concern by reflexion his own. CABL; CEP; NOBE; NOEC; OBEC; OBEV; PoEL 1-5

The Jinx Blues. Son House. Well when I leave this time/I'm gonna hang crepe on/Your door BluL

Jippy and Jimmy. Laura E. Richards. Bow-wow! bow-wow! bow-wow-wow! bow-wow! SoPo; TiPo

Jis' Knowin'. Thomas G. Nickens. draggin' his claws/down a mirror glass. LFAC

Jitterbugging in the Streets. Calvin C. Hernton. Jitterbugging/in the streets. PoBA

Jittery Jim. William Jay Smith. But we'll shut the door on him! BBGG

Jo Jo, My Child. Anonymous. Your mother will dress/Her head with flowers. TrJP

Joan Brown, about Her Painting. Kathleen Fraser. describing the familiar bow-wow/as I make my plans. NPGG

Joan Miro. Ruthven Todd. His people dead, his gay pots broken. EAS

Joan of Arc: Introduction. Hugh McCrae. Wherefore to Chinon? Wherefore I"? PoAu 1-2

Joan of Arc to the Tribunal. Anthony Frisch. Old men, I shall grow older/Than you, when men look back! CaP

Joan's Door. Eleanor Farjeon. You ought to be four. BiCB

Joan to Her Lady. Anonymous. Then what odds 'twixt you and Joan?/Truly in my judgment, none. UnTE

Job. Eli Mandel. Constructing puzzled strictures for his God. PeCV

Job Hunting. Tom Hennen. Across the sky/Rain turning to snow. EaLo; GP; OuSiCo

Job's Ancient Lament. Owen Dodson. God, why have you ruined us? FB

The Job That's Crying to Be Done. Rudyard Kipling. For the glory of the garden glorifieth every one. TRV

Jobson's Amen. Rudyard Kipling. And–the feet of my Beloved hurrying back through Time! AnFE; OBTV

Jock o' the Side. Anonymous. But thou's as weil at thy ain ingle side/Now sitting, I think, 'twixt thee and me! OxBB

Jock o the Side (A version). Anonymous. Thou hast feitched vs home good Iohn/oth Side,/That was now cleane ffrom vs gone. ESPB; ViBoFo

Jock o the Side (B version). Anonymous. And thus the night they a' hae spent,/Just as they had been brither and/brither. ESPB

Jock of Hazeldean. Sir Walter Scott. She's o'er the Border, and awa'/Wi' Jock of Hazeldean! BeLS; BFSS; EnLit; GN; GTBS; GTBS-P; HBV 1-2; MCCG; OAEP; OBRV; OxBS; TEP

Jock the Leg and the Merry Merchant. Anonymous. In brough or land, wherever we meet,/A rank thief I'll call thee.' ESPB

Jockie, Thine Hornpipe's Dull. Anonymous. Us two to all the parish! NCEP

Joculator Domini. Sister Mary John Frederick Teach us who had forgot to pray:/"God give you peace!" GoBC

Jodrell Bank. Patric Dickinson. How lonely all men are. SUW

Joe. David McCord. And waiting there for Joe to go/Is pretty cold work in the snow. TiPo

Joe Bowers. *Anonymous.*
And, more than that, the baby's hair was inclining to be red. ATP
It only said its cussed hair was inclined to be red. ABF; AmFP; BaBo; BFSS; CoSo; FSW; TrAS; TreFS; ViBoFo

Joe Brainard's Painting "Bingo". Ron Padgett. She had misunderstood what I had said. ANYP

Joe Gillon Hypnotizes His Son. Albert Goldbarth. You won't remember any of this. SM

Joe Hill. Alfred Hayes. "I never died," says he. UnPo

Joe Tinker. Amanda Benjamin Hall. Such fools we women are who weep/For men not worth a tear! HBMV

Joe Turner Blues. *Anonymous.* Dey tell me Joe Turner he done come/Come with fohty links of chain. AS; TrAS

Jog on, Jog on, the Footpath Way. *Anonymous.* We'll frolic with sweet Dolly. GBP

A Jog-Trot Pair. Thomas Hardy. Onerous to satiate souls, increased their buoyance. PeD

The Jogger: Denver to Kansas City. David Ray. And he thinks of that secret room, half-way. FAZ

Jogging. Gary Stein. ...Why twhen/you run out of a body for miles/is there any more? AMV-81

Jogging at Dusk. Andrew Grossbardt. and the sad soft light of evening guides me in. AMV-80

Johann Gaertner (1793-1887). Gary Gildner. to make his own hole/and one for his wife as well. FAZ

Johann Joachim Quantz's Five Lessons. W. S. Graham. ...Do not expect applause. FaBoMo

Johannes Agricola in Meditation. Robert Browning. Paying a price, at his right hand? MaVP; OAEL 1-2; OBVV

Johannes Milton, Senex. Robert Bridges. Confiding always on His excellent greatness. CMoP; LiTB; NAMP; PoEL 1-5; PoPl

John Adams. Rosemary and Stephen Vincent Benét. –And this is John Adams who started them all. PAL

John Adkins' Farewell. *Anonymous.* That pardons poor drunkards, and crowns them above. AmFP

John Anderson My Jo. Robert Burns. And sleep thegither at the foot,/John Anderson my jo! AWP; BoLiVe; BoLoP; CABA; CBEP; CEP; CoMu; EiCP; EnLi 1-2; EnPE; ErPo; FaBV; FF; FSW; GTBS; GTBS-P; HBV 1-2; HeIP; InPK; InPo; LAuP; LiTB; LiTL; MCCG; NOBE; NOEC; NoP; OAEP; OBEC; OBEV; OxBS; PG; PrIm; TreFT; TrGrPo; UnTE; ViBoPo; WBLP; WHA

John B. Sails. *Anonymous.* I feel so break-up, I want to go home. AS; FSW

John Barley-Corn, My Foe. Charles Follen Adams. Their greatest curse has been removed,/John Barley-Corn, my foe! OBAL

John Barleycorn. *Anonymous.* Without a little of Barleycorn. OBET

John Barleycorn. Robert Burns. And may his great posterity/Ne'er fail in old Scotland! FaBoCh; HBV 1-2; LoGBV; SeCeV

John Baynham's Epitaph. Thomas Dermody. ..."how dare you write/Such stuff on me, as dead outright;.... OnYI

John Betjeman's Brighton (parody). Gavin Ewart. Still a memory we cherish though the recollection/pales. FaBoPa

John Bright. Francis Barton Gummere. Joining with freedom's deathless song thy/deathless name. AA

John Brown. Harry Lyman Koopman. Our tossing bark of Progress sunward/steers. AA

John Brown. Vachel Lindsay. Old John Brown. AnAmPo; MoAmPo

John Brown. Edna Dean Proctor. John Brown's soul not a higher joy can crave,/Freedom reigns to-day! PAH

John Brown: A Paradox. Louise Imogen Guiney. Christianity's flood-tide and Chivalry's sunset/In the old broken heart of our hanged John/Brown! PAH

John Brown's Body. Stephen Vincent Benét.
And his dad'll bring him a partridge nest,/As soon as his dad comes back. MoAmPo
And how his heart contained its bitterness,/He will not tell us. AmFN
And some with your feet on lions? It is time that you were at rest. MoAmPo
Each dusty road leads to Appomattox now. BeLS
...He hardly knew the man/But it felt funny to leave him just lying there. PoLf
I wondered that I still breathed. AmP
Nor "It is blest," but only "It is here." WHA
Ran into Mississippi and were drowned. AmFN
(The sky is falling, my son.) TreF
Will not forget His foes. AtBAP; PoNe

John Brown's Body. Charles Sprague Hall. As we go marching on! ABF; BLSo; FaFP; FSW; MC; ShS; TrAS

John Bun. *Anonymous.* But Wood would not rhyme with gun, but Bun would. NLV, PoPle; ShM

John Burns of Gettysburg. Bret (Francis Bret Harte) Harte. You'll show a hat that's white, or a feather. HBV 1-2; MC; OHIP; PAL

John Butler Yeats. Jeanne Robert Foster. "Myself seen through a glass darkly." GoYe

John Button Birthday. Frank O'Hara. ...arguing about their/favorite mountain and the million reasons for them both. NAs

John Carey's Second Song. Thomas McGrath. And go in there. And sleep. FAZ

John Chapman. Richard Wilbur. To the rude, forked, and ever savage root. OxBC

John Charles Fremont. Charles F. Lummis. When God sent Opportunity/and Benton found the Man! PAH

John Cherokee. *Anonymous.* With a hauley high, and a hauley low,/Alabama, John Cherokee. GBP

John Clare. Jon Anderson. In it will be a light the color of steel/& landscape, into which the traveler might set out. AmPA

John Clare. Mark Halperin. If we are both John Clare/why does he go away?/and where? and where? SM

John Coil. *Anonymous.* But this here air was too hot for him. ShM

John Coltrane an Impartial Review. A. B. Spellman. you want help. you are sorry you are born with ears. CNA; NNP; PoBA

John Darrow. Donald Davidson. The curse, the hope, the beauty/That never must be told. HBMV

John Donne. James Simmons. You, having once made such a lovely fuss/on Love's behalf, betrayed her, worse than us. CIP

John Donne's Defiance. J. R. Hervey. This death, this fitful dark declaring light. AnNZ

John Donne's Statue. John Peale Bishop. ...the sun/Whose laurel a green summer wears. EyDe

John Dory. *Anonymous.* John Dory at length, for all his strength,/Was clapt fast vnder board-a. BuBa; ESPB; OBSS

John Endicott: Prologue. Henry Wadsworth Longfellow. And persecute the dead for conscience' sake. PAH

John Evereldown. Edwin Arlington Robinson. And that's why I'm going to Tilbury Town.' CMoP; NePA; OxBA

John Filson. William Henry Venable. His name from blank oblivion,/Who never had a grave. PAH

John Fitzgerald Kennedy. John Masefield. The promise of his spirit be/fulfilled. PAL

John Garfield. Nicholas Christopher. And watches rain come down/On a southbound express. MAYP; NYP

John Garner's Trail Herd. *Anonymous.* Just ask him about the time we all went up the trail. CoSo

John Gilbert Was a Bushranger. *Anonymous.* With not the least demurring word/Ought we to interfere? NOAV

John Gorham. Edwin Arlington Robinson. As on two that have no longer much of any-/thing to tell. MAPA; MoAB; MoAmPo; NoAm

John Graydon. Wilson MacDonald. And you can own, as I, these gardens old/John Graydon bought with gold. CaP

John Grumlie. *Anonymous.* But henceforth I maun mind the plow,/And ye maun bide at hame. GBP

John Grumlie. Allan Cunningham. If my wife should na win a penny a day/She's aye her will for me. HBV 1-2; PoLf

John Hardy. *Anonymous.*
John Hardy, that's the last of you. AmFP
You ought to seen John Hardy getting away. FSW

John Hardy (A vers.). *Anonymous.* Than the rocks in the bottom of the sea. BaBo

John Hardy (B vers.). *Anonymous.* Lord, Lord! was "I want to go to heaven when I die." ViBoFo

John Henry (A vers.). *Anonymous.*
Lord, I've hammered my insides in two. BaBo
There's a roarin' in my head, O Lord,/There's a roarin' in my head. ViBoFo

John Henry (B vers.). *Anonymous.* "John Henry I've been true to you." BaBo

John Henry (C vers.). *Anonymous.* Oh, he died with his hammer in his hand. ViBoFo

John Henry (D vers.). *Anonymous.* I cain't stay, no–I cain't stay. ViBoFo

John Henry (E. vers.). *Anonymous.* If he asks you wuz I running/Tell him no, tell him no. ViBoFo

John Henry (F vers.). *Anonymous.* Going, buddy, to my country,/Somebody dying every day. ViBoFo

John Henry in Harlem. M. B. Toleson. Till you conquer de lan' an' conquer de ocean! GoSl

John Henry (variant). *Anonymous.* Yes, old Rattler was a-barkin' at the moon. ABF

John Hielandman. *Anonymous.* What do a care if my belly be fu'? GBP

John Horace Burleson. Edgar Lee Masters. "Roll on, thou deep and dark blue Ocean, roll!" CrMA

John J. Curtis. Joseph Gallager. So be kind-hearted while you can/To the miner from Morea. AmFP

John Jacob Jingleheimer Schmidt. *Anonymous.* "John Jacob Jingleheimer Schmidt!"/Dah, dah, dah, dah, dah, dah. FSW

John Jiggy Jag. *Anonymous.* So, Johnny, how dost thou now? OxNR

John-John. Thomas Macdonagh. God bless and keep you far, John-John!/ And that's my prayer. AnIV; AWP; HBMV; OnYI; OxBI

John Kinsella's Lament for Mrs. Mary Moore. William Butler Yeats. What shall I do for pretty girls/Now my old bawd is dead? AtBAP; CMoP; DTC; LiTM; MoAB; NoP; OAEL 1-2; OAEP

John Knox. Iain Crichton Smith. The shearing naked absolute blade has torn/through false French roses to her foreign cry. OxBS

John L. Sullivan Enters Heaven (parody). Robert Frost. Ring the bells of Heaven! Sound the gladsome chimes! BXAP

John Landless Leads the Caravan. Yvan Goll. Salt from my weak moist hand/The strength of my religion TrJP

John Marr (excerpt). Herman Melville. To hear your chorus once again! ViBoPo

John Maynard. Horatio, Jr Alger. God rest him! Never hero had/A nobler funeral pyre! BeLS; BLPA; FaBoBe

John Mouldy. Walter De la Mare. In the dusk he sat a-smiling,/Smiling there alone. NCSH; OxBChV; PoPle

John Nobody. Dom Moraes. ...a gesture of the hands/Can hardly hold so vast an emptiness. NoAm

John o' Dreams. Theodosia Garrison. ...and yet it seems/Sometimes that you surely found it,/John o' Dreams. HBMV

John O'Dwyer of the Glen. *Anonymous.* Take this parting tear. AnIV

John of Hazelgreen (A version). *Anonymous.* And thou's get all thy father's lands,/And dwell in Hasillgreen.' BaBo; ESPB; ViBoFo

John of Hazelgreen (C vers.). *Anonymous.* And forty times he kissed her ruby lips/And let his lady in. BaBo

John of Hazelgreen (E version). *Anonymous.* And aye she loot the tears down fa/For John o Hazelgreen. BFSS; ESPB

John of Tours. *Anonymous.* For you must shut the baby there. AWP

John Otto. William Stanley Merwin. Your eyes of a promise in the land? AP

John Peel. John Woodcock Graves. Or a fox from his lair in the morning. CH; SD

John Pelham. James Ryder Randall. He, with the martyr's amaranthine wreath,/Twining the victor's crown! AA; PAH

John Plans. Dorothy Mason Pierce. And wait for Father! BiCB

John Quincy Adams 1767-1848. Stephen Vincent Benét. The Adamses have always been/Remarkably like that. NAMP; OBCA

John Riley. *Anonymous.*
And I shall never deceive you any more. FSW
They're living together, doing well. OuSiCo

John Rogers' Exhortation to His Children. *Anonymous.* That I may meet you in the heavens,/where I do hope to rest. OBCA

John's Song. Joan Aiken. and listen for my voice, if for no other/when you're all alone. DuDa

John Saw the Holy Number. *Anonymous.* John saw the holy number sitting on the golden altar. BoAN 1-2

John Skelton. Robert Graves. Old John, you do me good! BrPo

John Smith, Fellow Fine. *Anonymous.* That's to make him pace weel, pace/weel, pace weel. OxNR

John Smith Is My Name. *Anonymous.* When this you see, remember me,/ Though I am long forgotten. FaBoUs

John Smith of His Friend Master John Taylor. John Smith. So rare a Fleet, was never made nor man'd. SCAP

John Smith's Approach to Jamestown. James Barron Hope. And breathed her fragrance on the lofty pines. MC; PAH

John Standish, Artist. Kenneth Fearing. Follow him till he sleeps, and kill him with a stone. AnAmPo

John Sutter. Yvor Winters. What calm catastrophe will yet assuage/This final drouth of penitential tears. MoAmPo; MoVE; NoAm; NOBA; PoPl; QFR

John the Baptist. Louis Simpson. And came to shallow Jordan, where began/The matter of the platter and the sword. NePoEA

John Thomson and the Turk (A version). *Anonymous.* John Thomson's gay lady they took,/And hangd her on yon greenwood/tree. ESPB

John Thomson and the Turk (B version). *Anonymous.* And sae hae they that ill woman,/Upon a scrogg-bush him ESPB

John, Tom, and James. Charles Henry Ross. They've all grown up ugly, and nobody cares. NLV; OxBChV

John Underhill. John Greenleaf Whittier. Frailest and bravest! the Bay State still/Counts with her worthies John Underhill. PAH

John Was A-Writin'. *Anonymous.* Lord told John, "Don't you write no more." OuSiCo

John Wasson. Edgar Lee Masters. If Harry Wilmans who fought the Filipinos/Is to have a flag on his grave/Take it from mine! LaNeLa

John Watts. *Anonymous.* What harm is a little brown mouse? OxNR

John Webster. Algernon Charles Swinburne. Frail, on frail rafts, across wide-wallowing waves,/Shapes here and there of child and mother pass. InvP

John Wesley Gaines. *Anonymous.* Come in, John Wesley/For it rains. ELU; FiBHP

John Wesley's Rule. John Wesley. As long as ever you can. GoTF; HBVY; TreFT

John Winter. Laurence Binyon. John Winter coiled the anchor ropes/ Among his mates once more. MOS

John without Heaven. John Malcolm Brinnin. ...Johnny Damnation, that's me! NoAm

Johnie Armstrong (A vers.). *Anonymous.* Who vowed if ere he lived for to be a man,/O' the treacherous Scots revengd hee'd be. ViBoFo

Johnie Armstrong (B vers.). *Anonymous.* Whyle Johnie livd on the border-syde,/Nane of them durst cum neir his hald. ViBoFo

Johnie Blunt. *Anonymous.* Aha, Johnie Blunt! ye hae spoke the first word,/ Get up and bar the door, O. OxBB

Johnie Cam to Our Toun. *Anonymous.* Then O as he kittled me–/But I forgot to cry. GBP

Johnie Cock (A vers.). *Anonymous.* And many ae was the well-wight man/ At the fetching o Johny away. BaBo; ViBoFo

Johnie Cock (B vers.). *Anonymous.* And his bodie lies dead in Durrisdeer,/ And his hunting it is done. ViBoFo

Johnie Cock (D version). *Anonymous.* Upon thy head be a' this blude,/For mine, I ween, is free.' ESPB

Johnie Cock (K version). *Anonymous.* As dip its wing in the wan water/ An straik it on his ee-bree.' ESPB

Johnie Scot. *Anonymous.* I only seek your daughter fair,/Whose love has cost her dear. BaBo; ESPB

Johnnie Bought a Ham. *Anonymous.* Go see 'em in the room! OuSiCo

Johnnie, Cock up Your Beaver. Robert Burns. Cock up your beaver! AtBAP

Johnnie Cope. Adam Skirving. So I wish you a gude morning.' OxBS

Johnnie Crack and Flossie Sanail. Dylan Thomas. Always used to say that stout and ale/Was good for a baby in a milking pail. GoJo; LOW

Johnnie Norrie. *Anonymous.* And in at a paper doorie. OxNR

Johnny. Emma Rounds. He'd stood up straight–it broke his back! ShM

Johnny and the Highwayman. *Anonymous.* You shall have for your share."/It's down, down, derry derry down. BFSS

Johnny Appleseed. Rosemary Benet. But he has his apple trees still in bloom./Johnny Appleseed! Johnny Appleseed! TrAS

Johnny Appleseed. Arthur Stanley Bourinot. And apple trees/To scent the breeze/In blossom time. CaP

Johnny Appleseed. William Henry Venable. He served his kind by Word and Deed,/In God's grand greenwood chapel. PAH

Johnny Appleseed's Hymn to the Sun. Vachel Lindsay. Our God, the beginning and end! MoRP

Johnny Armstrong. *Anonymous.*
Ring the bell, the calf is dead. OxNR
Then I'll rise and fight again. MaC

Johnny Boker. *Anonymous.* Do, my Johnny Boker, do! AmSS; FSW

Johnny Bull, My Jo, John. *Anonymous.* And haste to thy fast-anchored isle,/O Johnny Bull, my jo. FSW

Johnny Carroll's Camp. *Anonymous.* And before we'll face for home, brave boys, we'll sing the lumbering theme. AmFP

Johnny Come Down to Hilo. *Anonymous.* Poor old man. ABF

Johnny Dyers. *Anonymous.* There's more grief at my heart than my poor tongue can tell. AmFP

Johnny Faa, the Gypsy Laddie. *Anonymous.* With the gypsies dancing round me. AtBAP

Johnny Faa, the Lord of Little Egypt. *Anonymous.* And were all put down for one light wife:/The Earl of Cassilis' honey. EnSB

Johnny Fife and Johnny's Wife. Mildred Plew Merryman. And round and round the world they went/And also stayed at home. SoPo; TiPo

Johnny German. *Anonymous.* You remind me of some flower/Where love and beauty grows. BFSS

Johnny Germany. *Anonymous.* We will live together till death us part. AmFP

Johnny Get Your Gun. F. Belasco. Johnny get your gun, get your gun! PSoN

Johnny, I Hardly Knew Ye. *Anonymous.* Och, Johnny, I hardly knew ye. AnIV; BIrV; ELP; FaBoBa; GBP; OnYI; OxBoLi; WaaP

Johnny, I Hardly Knew Ye: Miltonese (parody). Oliver St. John Gogarty. Met, reaching to great fame by Fortitude. OnYI

Johnny, I Hardly Knew Ye: Swinburnese (parody). Robert Yelverton Tyrrell. For the change of the face of thy colour I know thee not who/thou art. OnYI

Johnny McCardner. *Anonymous.* Get beat like the devil and flogged with the broom–/And it's hard times. OuSiCo

Johnny Morgan. *Anonymous.* Selling of pigs' tails. OxNR

Johnny O Dutchman. *Anonymous.* Sing, "Fol do ra dowdy, oh, fol do ra dowdy O day." BFSS

Johnny Raw and Polly Clark. *Anonymous.* So now once more I'm bang up prime,/Ri tol de lol. CoMu

Johnny Rich. Will Carleton. Yes, I hear it; 'tis somebody that's callin' out for help. PeD

Johnny's Hist'ry Lesson. Nixon Waterman. An' Washington couldn't tell a lie,/In fourteen ninety-two. FPL; PoLf

Johnny Sands. *Anonymous.* For you have tied my hands. AmFP; CoMu; OBET; ViBoFo

Johnny Scot. *Anonymous.* You can make it the heir of all your land/And she your gaily dee. BaBo

Johnny Shall Have a New Bonnet. *Anonymous.* And why may not I love Johnny,/As well as another body? HBV 1-2; HBVY

Johnny Stiles; or, The Wild Mustard River. *Anonymous.* We buried him down by the river/Where the larks and the whippoorwills sang. OuSiCo

Johnny Todd. *Anonymous.* Do not leave your love like Johnny,/Marry her before you go. FSW

Johnny Walk along to Hilo. *Anonymous.* Then Johnny walk along to Hilo,/Oh, poor old man! ShS

Johnny Went to Church One Day. *Anonymous.* And threw them at the people. BBGG

Johnshaven. *Anonymous.* My mou was never even/Since I cam by Johnshaven. GBP

Johnson. *Anonymous.* Who did see this awful murder/and watch poor Johnson die? FSW

The Johnson Boys. *Anonymous.* Shame, shame, the Johnson boys. FSW

Johnson on Pope. David Ferry. ...of folly he made beauty. PP

Johnson's Ale. *Anonymous.* When Johnson's ale was new, my boys,/When Johnson's ale was new. FSW

Johnson's Cabinet Watched by Ants. Robert Bly. ...their five long toes trembling in the soaked earth. NoAm; NOBA

Johnson's Motor Car. *Anonymous.* And we gave three cheers for the I.R.A./and Johnson's Motor Car. FSW

Johnsonian Poem in Progress: "I put my hat upon my head" (parody). F.A.V. Madden He whom you dubbed unclubbable/Don't say the same of you!' BXAP

Johnsonian Poem in Progress: "I put my hat upon my head." (parody). Peter Veale. And even Boswell when we met,/Would not believe a word. BXAP

Johny Faa. *Anonymous.* And we are a' put down for ane,/the earl of Cassilis' lady. OxBB

Joie de Vivre. Joel Dailey. Inhale now. APU

Joined the Blues. John Jerome Rooney. We're never North or South again–he/kissed the Book for both! AA

The Joining. Gerda Norvig. cold, dark and untouchable/in the night/sky. VWA

A Joke Versified. Thomas Moore. "Why so it is, father,–whose wife shall I take?" FaBoCo

The Jokesmith's Vacation. Don (Donald Robert Marquis) Marquis. How I wept and I wept and I wept and I wept! ALV; FiBHP

The Jolly Beggar. *Anonymous.*
And we'll gang nae mair a roving. OxBB
Not a beggar maid but a gay lady,/Your daughter comes back to thee. BFSS

The Jolly Beggar. King of Scotland James I, Let the moon shine ne'er so bright. CoMu

The Jolly Beggars. Robert Burns.
Let them cant about decorum/Who have characters to lose. NLV
One and all cry out Amen! EnRP

The Jolly Cowboy. *Anonymous.* But I'll quit the herd of longhorns for the sake of my little wife. CoSo

The Jolly Driver. *Anonymous.* ...coachman,/That understood driving so fair. UnTE

The Jolly Farmer. *Anonymous.* While my jolly little farmer goes whistling to his plow. BFSS

Jolly Jack. William Makepeace Thackeray. We all were happier, if we all/Would copy Jolly Jack. HBV 1-2

Jolly Jankin. *Anonymous.* Alas! I go with child./Kyrieleison. GBP; NoP; OxBM; OxBoLi

The Jolly Old Pedagogue. George Arnold. This jolly old pedagogue, long ago! HBV 1-2; TreFS

The Jolly Pinder of Wakefield (A version). *Anonymous.* Then would I set as little by him/As my master doth set by me.' BaBo; ESPB

The Jolly Pinder of Wakefield (B version). *Anonymous.* I'le take my benbowe in my hande,/And come into the grenwoode to/thee.' ESPB

The Jolly Plowboy. *Anonymous.* Since she found the bonnie laddie she adores. AmFP

The Jolly Sailor's True Description of a Man-of-War. *Anonymous.* Such rogues there can't be worser. OBSS

The Jolly Shepherd Wat. *Anonymous.* Can I not sing but "hoy"/When the jolly shepherd made so much joy? NOBE; OxBM; SBVL

The Jolly Shilling. *Anonymous.* And nothing at all to carry home to my own dearest wife. OBET

Jolly Soldier. *Anonymous.*

And I'll still be the jolly, jolly soldier. AmFP; OFD
And they'll fight for the pretty girls, for rights and liberty. AmFP

The Jolly Tester. *Anonymous.* I love nothing better than my wife. OxNR

The Jolly Thresherman. *Anonymous.* There are few such noblemen here to be found. AmFP

The Jolly Trades-Men. *Anonymous.* May use my Needle at a pinch,/And do themselves great Pleasure. CoMu

The Jolly Waggoner. *Anonymous.* And many a lad will take his lass/And sit her on his knee. OBET

The Jolly Wagoner. *Anonymous.* Who wouldn't lead the life of a jolly wagoner? TrAS

The Jolly Woodchuck. Dorothy and Marion Edey Grider. He snores in his sleep and rubs his nose. TiPo

The Jolly Young Sailor and the Beautiful Queen. *Anonymous.* And a happier wedding scarce ever was seen,/Than a jolly young sailor to a beautiful queen. ShS

The Jolly Young Waterman. Charles Dibdin. And how should this waterman ever know care,/When he's married and never in want of a fare? NOEC; PoPle

Jonah. *Anonymous.* but God is ever dear. ACP

Jonah. Randall Jarrell. And also much cattle? MoRP

Jonah and the Whale. *Anonymous.* Her jag, her jag, her jagged tail. BLPA

Jonah and the Whale. Viola Meynell. Jonah's thoughts flying through his being. EtS

Jonah Is Cast into the Sea. *Anonymous.* And graunted hym on to be God, and graythly non other. OxBM

Jonah's Gourd Vine: I Vision God. Z. N. Hurston. And the other He clapped across the moon. TTY

Jonathan. Rose Fyleman. And John's old cow/Did nothing but laugh. TiPo

Jonathan. Rachel (Rachel Blumstein). We all must pay with the current coin/of life/For the honey that we taste. TrJP

Jonathan Bing. Beatrice Curtis Brown. For home's the best place for/All people like me! OnMSP; SiSoSe; SoPo; TiPo

Jonathan Gentry, III: Tom's Sleeping Song. Mark Van Doren. And the heart be moulded. LOW

Jonathan Houghton. Edgar Lee Masters. And himself desiring The Hill! OxBA

Jonathan Swift Somers. Edgar Lee Masters. Be thankful if in that hour of supreme vision/Life does not fiddle. OBAL

Jonathan to John. James Russell Lowell. "But nothin' else than wut he sells/Wears long, an' thet J.B./May larn, like you an' me!" PAH

Jone o' Grinfield. *Anonymous.* An' hoo says hoo can tell when hoo's hurt. VLP

Joseph, Jesus and Mary. *Anonymous.* And keep Christ in remembrance/Till seed time comes again. OHIP

Joseph Mary Plunkett. Wilfrid Meynell. "But empty sends the rich away." ISi

Joseph Mica. *Anonymous.* All he want is boiler hot,/Run in there 'bout four o'clock. ViBoFo

Joseph Rodman Drake. Fitz-Greene Halleck. The grief is fixed too deeply/That mourns a man like thee. BLPA

Joseph's Suspicion. Rainer Maria Rilke. he was gone. He pushed his heavy/cap slowly off. Then he sang praise. MoRP; TrCP

Joseph Was an Old Man. *Anonymous.* O the sun and the moon, mother,/shall both rise with me. OBCP

Joses, the Brother of Jesus. Harry Kemp. But never to catch the vision which glorified his clay. HBMV

Joshua Fit de Battle of Jericho. *Anonymous.* And de walls come tumbling down. BPo; MaC; TAP; TrGrPo

Joshua Hight. *Anonymous.* "For I can see it blazing!" ShM

Joshua's Face. Amir Gilboa. high over many lives/may he be raised and glorified. VWA

Josie (with music). *Anonymous.* "He'll be your man, but he'll not come home." AS

Josina, You Are Not Dead. Samora M. Machel. Your life continues in those who continue the Revolution. WhB

Jottings of New York. William McGonagall. ...I sailed from New York/For Bonnie Dundee, my heart it felt as light as a cork. OBTV

Journal. John Ciardi. We fail the sick, but still may raise the dead. PoA

Journal (excerpt). Edna St. Vincent Millay.
All this time–the Bugaboo! ImOP
And from the twentieth story hurls/To the pave the factory girls. SaC

A Journal from France: Seamstress at St. Leon. Gillian Clarke. ...Bats are shuttling/their delicate black silks to mesh/that dark doorway on her absence. OBTV

Journal of a Tour through the Courts of Germany (excerpt). James Boswell. His cringing courtiers played the shameful farce,/But I still seemed to bid him kiss my a—. OBTV

The Journal of Albion Moonlight (excerpt). Kenneth Patchen. The word is the web we take from the womb. NaP

The Journal of Society.   Godfrey Turner.   The man who wears the high-crowned hat and patent-leather boots.   NOBL

Journal of the Storm.   Greg Kuzma.   ...I do not own/these things. I watch them, and forget.   AmPA

Journal, Part IV.   Gayl Jones.   They're all crooked.   BlSi

Journal to Stella.   Morton Dauwen Zabel.   Before man's laughter hunts our fear!   PoA

Journey.   Rodney Hall.   ...Spellbound I relax–/the knife steady, a precious bond.   NOAV

The Journey.   Mary Berri (Chapman) Hansbrough.   I woke–and found the coach had missed/the train!   AA

Journey.   Sam Harrison.   elude me and go drifting out of sight/like the receding fields.   NeIP

The Journey.   David Ignatow.   Going to bed was a journey.   Psk

The Journey.   Henry Johnson.   pretending that he rode/the back of a bronco/as wild as thunder.   LFAC

The Journey.   Scudder Middleton.   Yet never doubt that Sisyphus/Achieved at last the mountain top.   HBMV

Journey.   Raymond Thompson.   I'll learn the art of prayer/And be properly pardoned/ In time/   LFAC

Journey.   Diane Wakoski.   I must have dropped it when transfering.   IHMS

The Journey.   Yvor Winters.   In naked sunlight, on a naked world.   MoVE

The Journey and Observations of a Countryman (excerpt).   John Hawthorn.   I would excuse a man that blood did spill,/Before a wretch that used his parents ill...   NOEC

Journey Back to Christmas.   Gwen Dunn.   "Yes, Tim, you would."   OBCP

Journey from New Zealand.   Robin Hyde.   And the Templar stars in their order said: "Rise and go."   AnNZ

Journey in the Orient.   Maria Luisa Spaziani.   ...and my mother who bakes the bread.   BoWoP

The Journey into France.   Anonymous.   Then was his Father King Henry,/Who (men thought) did the same.   CoMu; FaBoBa; OBTV

Journey: IV.   Erik Lindegren.   (In a shimmer of melting winters/A breast that was never extinguished.)   LiTW

The Journey nears the Road-End.   Rabindranath Tagore.   Your hands are filled with treasure.   DL

Journey of the Magi.   Thomas Stearns Eliot.   I should be glad of another death.   BoC; DiPo; DTC; EaLo; EBCP; FaBoCh; FaBoMo; FaFP; HAP; HeIP; InPK; InPo; LiTA; LiTM; LoGBV; MoAB; MoAmPo; MoRP; MP; NePA; NIP; NOCV; OAEP; OBCP; OBMV; OxBTC; PCh; PPoe; SBVL; SoSe; TAP; TrGrPo; TwCP

The Journey of the Suicides.   Marilyn Bowering.   but these travellers have received a pardon,/and pass freely among the ruins.   CaPN

The Journey Onwards.   Thomas Moore.   We turn to catch one fading ray/Of joy that's left behind us.   GTBS; GTBS-P; HBV 1-2; SeCePo

Journey Round the World.   Ingrid Jonker.   go out/make fruitful the earth   PBWP

Journey's End.   Humbert Wolfe.   You are not called when journey's/done.   TrJP

A Journey through the Moonlight.   Russell Edson.   He floats through high dark branches, a corpse tangled in a tree on a river.   LCAP

Journey through the Night.   John Holloway.   Now, where in the world to go.   NePoEA

Journey to a Parallel.   Bruce McM. Wright.   Now that I can teach Upjohn.   PoNe

The Journey to Golgotha.   K. Raghavendra Rao.   mercy for the body burning in the wind of time!   ACV

A Journey to Hell.   Edward Ward.   Shameful to own and scandalous to hear.   NOEC

Journey to Iceland.   W. H. Auden.   ...again some writer/runs howling to his art.   OBTV; PoA

The Journey to the Insane Asylum.   Alfred Lichtenstein.   Invisible behind enormous trees,/in an incredible calm,/appraches the great horror.   VWA

Journey toward Evening.   Phyllis McGinley.   But not to sleep. He finds it hard to sleep.   GoYe; NYBP

The Journey with Hands and Arms.   Benjamin Saltman.   the arm must be bound/and bound again   VWA

The Journeyman.   Anonymous.   My heart will sink whenever I think/Of the journeywork I'm leaving.   KiLC

The Journeyman.   Ralph Hodgson.   Too late for blaming then.   AtBAP

The Journeyman Tailor.   Anonymous.   Was the journeyman tailor and the beautiful queen.   BFSS

Journeys.   Gary Snyder.   ..."This is the/way to the back country."   NU

Les Jours Gigantesques / The Titanic Days.   Kathleen Fraser.   and becomes the third,/the knowing, between them.   NPGG

Jove for Europaes Love Tooke Shape of Bull.   Barnabe Barnes.   To kisse her lippes, and lye next at her hart,/Runne through her vaynes and passe by pleasures part   AAS

The Jovial Marriner; or, The Sea-Man's Renown.   John Playford.   He scorneth once to shrink or start for any stormy wind.   CoMu

The Jovial Tinker; or, The Willing Couple.   Anonymous.   I hope she will not now complain/to high, to low, to high, to low, to low.   CoMu; UnTE

Jowl, Jowl and Listen.   Anonymous.   Like a mother knaas hor young 'uns.   OBET

Joy.   Gavin Bantock.   and we have no way of following the wind/to the world's end.   OxBTC

Joy.   Clarissa Scott Delany.   Too long stumbled down a maze/Bewildered.   CDC; PoNe

Joy.   Robinson Jeffers.   :yet at length quietness/Will cover those wistful eyes.   CMoP

Joy and Dream.   Johann Wolfgang von Goethe.   And every joy but as one kiss.   LiTW

Joy and Peace in Believing.   William Cowper.   For while in him confiding,/I cannot but rejoice.'   NOCV; TRV

Joy and Pleasure.   William Henry Davies.   But Pleasure then is cold and dumb,/And sings and laughs with strangers near.   OBMV

Joy Enough.   Barrett Eastman.   Above–the firmament?   AA

Joy Is the Blossom.   Walter Savage Landor.   ...and worms are the root.   DBV; HBV 1-2

Joy May Kill.   Buonarroti Michelangelo.   Lest joy so poignant slay a soul so weak.   AWP

Joy-Month.   David Atwood Wasson.   They utter the heart in me.   HBV 1-2

Joy o' Living.   Amanda Benjamin Hall.   To cool in some blue distant place/Till death or dawn should find my face.   HBMV

The Joy of a Singer.   Piuvkaq.   So that we stand/Like a bright flame/Over the plain.   WTO

The Joy of Church Fellowship Rightly Attended.   Edward Taylor.   While in this Coach these sweetly sing,/As they to Glory ride therein.   AmP; CBEP; MAmP; OxBA; SCAP

The Joy of Cooking: Conserves.   David Mus.   There is no ideal time for canning.   PoA

The Joy of Giving.   John Greenleaf Whittier.   The more of your heart's possessing/Returns to make you glad.   ChBR

The Joy of Incompleteness.   Albert Crowell.   Life would be disenchanted.   PoToHe

Joy of Knowledge.   Isidor Schneider.   pull petals from the sun,/and atoms pick apart.   TrJP

Joy of Life.   Moses Ibn Ezra.   And wealth to the poor, and healing/to the sick.   TrJP

The Joy of Love.   Allan Dowling.   and teach new wonders of unselfishness.   BoC; ErPo

Joy of My Life!   Henry Vaughan.   ...This beame/Will guide him In.   OBS; SeCV 1-2

Joy of the Morning.   Edwin Markham.   But had no throat like yours, my bird,/Nor such a listener.   HBV 1-2

Joy's Peak.   Robert Farren.   Or maybe yet–/Olivet?   ISi

Joy's Treachery.   Wilfrid Scawen Blunt.   Dead joys unburied breed us death and pain.   VLP

Joy, Shipmate, Joy!   Walt Whitman.   Joy, shipmate, joy!   AmP; GoTF; HBVY; MCCG; MoAmPo; MOS; OHIP; TAP; TreFT

The Joy So Short Alas, the Pain So Near.   Sir Thomas Wyatt.   Thus brought from wealth, alas, to endless pain,/That undeserved, causeless to remain.   SiPS

Joy Sonnet in a Random Universe.   Helen Chasin.   la la la la la la la la la la. Yeah yeah yeah.   HeIP; NIP

Joy to the World.   Anonymous.   It's now He offers pardon/And gives joy where grief has been.   STF

Joy to the World.   Isaac Watts.   And wonders, wonders, of His love.   FSW

Joyce Kilmer.   Amelia Josephine Burr.   For death to you was one more victory.   HBMV

A Joyful New Ballad.   Anonymous.   On Sion hill may sing the praise of our most mighty Lord.   CoMu; OBSS

A Joyful New Ballad.   Thomas Deloney.   To God, to Her, and to the land/Wherein you nursed were.   ViBoPo

A Joyful Noise.   Donald Finkel.   let each one and his brother turn up his scrubbed, gleaming/face to the sun, and yell.   CoAP

Joyful Prophecy.   Vassar Miller.   who can hold its heartiness/fermented to a man's delight,/if he is held in love.   CoPo

A Joyful Sound It Is.   George Strebeck.   Shall never cease to praise.   AH

The Joyful Wisdom.   Coventry Patmore.   And all grace is the grace of God.   HBV 1-2

Joyfully, Joyfully Onward I Move.   William Hunter.   Joyfully, joyfully, safely at home.   AH

The Joys of Art.   Rachel Annand Taylor.   My soul exults before the Art, the magian Art of old.   OBVV

Joys of Childhood.   John Clare.   And ragwort blooming on when others fade away.   ERoP 1-2

The Joys of Heaven.   Thomas a Kempis.   Always health and joy undying,/To them every good supplying.   CAW

The Joys of Marriage.   Charles Cotton.   Yet, uneasy is his life/Who is married to a wife.   InMe

The Joys of Mary. *Anonymous.* Through Father, Son, and Holy Ghost/ And Christ Eternity.] AmFP

The Joys of Paradise. Saint Augustine. Thou, my everlasting life! CAW

The Joys of the Road. Bliss Carman. These are the joys of the open road–/ For him who travels without a load. HBV 1-2; HBVV; OBVV

Juan Belmonte, Torero. Donald Finkel. In their soft slippers and their bravery. NePoEA

.Juan Murray. *Anonymous.* For if you start to rustling you will surely come to see/The State of Sonora–be an outcast like me CoSo

Juan Quintana. Alice Corbin. And they'll have to get a muchacho/To help with the flock next year. BPAW; HBMV

Juan Rulfo Moved Away. Alberto Rios. Because he was a bad man. APU

Juan's Song. Louise Bogan. Who is it, then, that love deceives? NYBP

Juana. Alfred de Musset. For you that not remember it. AWP

Juanita. Joaquin Miller. Rhymes of battle for the Right! AA

Juanita. Carolina Elizabeth Sarah Norton. Nita! Juanita! Be my own fair bride. FSW

Juanita, Wife of Manuelito. Simon J. Ortiz. That is what I want to teach my son. MAYP

Jubalee; or, What Is de Matter wid de Mourners. *Anonymous.* O, my Lord! Jubalee, Jubalee,/O, Lord! Jubalee. BoAN 1-2

Jubilate. George Arnold. For God is good, and, lo, my ships/Are coming home from sea! EtS

Jubilate Agno. Christopher Smart.
For he can creep. CTC
For I bless God for every feather from the wren in the sedge to the/ CHERUBS and their MATES. AtBAP
For I paid for my seat in St. Paul's, when I was six years old, and took possession against the evil AtBAP
For secondly he kicks up behind to clear away there. NCEP
For the Fatherless Children and widows are never deserted of the Lord. NCEP
For the Poorman's nosegay is an introduction to a Prince... AtBAP
Let Buz bless with the Jackall–but the Lord is the Lion's provider. NCEP

Jubilate Canis. Erica Jong. & may I praise God always/as a dog. MAYP

Jubilate Herbis. Norma Farber. ...The/hang of its waxen cloud exalts this house. PCh

Jubilation T. Cornpone. Johnny Mercer. The pants blown off his seat. OBAL

Jubilee. *Anonymous.* Live and learn, Jubilee. FSW

Jubilee before Revolution (parody). Andrew Lang. And I trow that another were fitter to sing you a song for a Queen. BXAP

Jubilo. Allen Tate. Beyond the Day of Jubilo. WaP

Judaeus Errans. Louis Golding. For he is sadder than God knows. TrJP

Judah in Exile Wanders. George Sandys. ...all her sweets convert to gall. AH

Judaism. John Henry, Cardinal Newman. No hopeful answer came–a Price more rare/Already shed in vain. ACP

Judas. *Anonymous.* Thou wolt fursake me thrien ar the coc him crowe. ViBoFo

Judas. Vassar Miller. ...never see me where/I hang, huge teardrop on the cheek of night. MoAmPo

The Judas Goat. Susan Musgrave. I prayed I had not become human. NOBC

Judas Iscariot. Robert Williams Buchanan. Iscariot washes the Bridegroom's feet,/And dries them with his hair. OBVV; OxBoCh

Judas Iscariot. Countee Cullen. And all the love he had. PoLf

Judas Iscariot. Margaret Nickerson Martin. What was left in the world for me/After the Light was out? PGD

Judas Iscariot. R. A. K. Mason. and would sing like the thrush/ that sings in the thicket. AnNZ

Judas Iscariot. Stephen Spender. ...We stare/Across two thousand years, and heaven and hell,/Into each other's gaze. MoAB; NIP

Judas, Joyous Little Son. Norma Farber. Who's to say/what follows after? AMV-80

Judas, Peter. Luci Shaw. do you love me AMV-80

Judean Summer. Fay Lipshitz. Here and there, defiant,/A shout of gold. VWA

Judeebug's Country. Joe Johnson. 3/4 man and the Parthenon is crumblin' PoBA

A Judezmo Writer in Turkey Angry. Stephen Levy. stop I'll get/all of it published yet/I'll get them all VWA

The Judge. Karl Kopp. It's damned good land Judge you/got a bargain. TAT

The Judge. Kenneth A. McClane. which need not break. AMV-81

Judge Harsh Blues. Furry Lewis. Lots of people had justice, they'd be in the penitentiary too BluL

The Judge is Fury: Epigraph. J. V. Cunningham. Experience is defendant, and the jury/Peers of tradition, and the judge is fury. QFR

Judge Kroll. Barbara L. Greenberg. and hears the knuckle-cracking in his brain/turning his hairs white. AMV-81

Judge Me, O God. Joel Barlow. And my triumphant songs shall praise/ The God that rules the skies. AH

Judge Not According to the Appearance. Christina Georgina Rossetti. And hear it, "Fear not: it is I." TrPWD

Judge Somers. Edgar Lee Masters. Wherein Nature, in a mood ironical,/ Has sown a flowering weed? FaBoEE; OBSV

The Judge with the Sore Rump. St. George Tucker. And let me get out of the bar. OBAL

Judged by the Company One Keeps. *Anonymous.* And the pig got up and slowly walked away. BLPA; FPL; NLV; YaD

The Judgement. Dora Read Goodale. Till that judge forgive thee. AA; AnAmPo

Judgement. George Herbert. There thou shalt finde my faults are thine. AnAnS 1; SeCP

Judgement Day. *Anonymous.* Don't you hear them sinners cryin'? WTO

The Judgement of Desire. Edward, Earl of Oxford De Vere. Then to injoye what others misse,/Laridon, tan, tan, Tedriton teight.' EnPo

The Judgement of God. William Morris. For even if I beat, their hate/Will grow to more than this mere grin. OBVV

The Judgement of Tiresias. Hildebrand Jacob. That sex does Venus most befriend,/That party best obtains its end.' NOEC

Judges, Judges. Gene Baro. Let flesh swing open! Let the ghost abide! NePoEA-2

Judgment. *Anonymous.* "Thou didst thy best–that is success!" AnAmPo; GoTF; TreFT

Judgment. William Rose Benet. Like to a man who stands with smoking knife/Above his dead, and sees the rising moon. AnAmPo

Judgment. Grace Ellery Channing-Stetson. As he gazed:–"Be praised, great God,"/he said,/"For a glorious victory!" AA

The Judgment. Kathleen Spivack. clear, trembling, tart as fresh pineapple. BoWoP

Judgment Day. Giuseppe Belli. they will blaw out the caunnles, and guid-nicht. OBVE

Judgment Day. William Dean Howells. He lifted up the pity of His face. AA

Judgment Day. John Oxenham. Doth but borrow/Sorrow. TRV

A Judgment in Heaven. Francis Thompson.
Lo! They were standing by His side! MoAB; MoBrPo
The Poet drew, in the thunderous blue in-/volved dread of those mounted pinions. CoBE

The Judgment of Paris. William Stanley Merwin. whose roots are said to dispel pain NNaP

The Judgment of the May. Richard Watson Dixon. But now thou seemest far away. OBNC

A Judicious Observation of That Dreadful Comet. Ichabod Wiswall. My Heart is cold, my Quill grows dry,/And must a while in silence lie. SCAP

Judith. William Young. And those that follow will ride as free/As ever of old rode Marion's men. AA

Judith of Bethulia. John Crowe Ransom. Yes, and chilled with fear and despair. CrMA; DTC; FaBoMo; FYAP; LiTA; LiTM; MoPo; NePA; NoAm; NOBA

Judith of Minnewaulken: Judith Remembers. Maxwell Anderson. Only dark answering day? WHA

Judith Recalls Holofernes. Maura Stanton. something that sounds like a thousand/transparent wings rising behind my eyes. AmPA

Judy-One. Don L. Lee. always going somewhere/strongly. TAP

Jug Brook. Ellen Bryant Voigt. it is you I look for/in the slate face of the water. MAYP

The Jug of Punch. *Anonymous.* A kerry pipin and the crack and crunch,/ And on the table a jug of punch. FSW

A Juggle of Myrtle Twigs. Edward Codish. While he had strength, and you/Know that all that love can do. VWA

Juggler. Richard Wilbur. Who has won for once over the world's/weight. AmP; CMoP; LiTM; MoAB; NCSH; NePA; NePoEA; NYBP; TAP

Juggling Jerry. George Meredith. Drop me a kiss–I'm the bird dead-struck! BeLS; HBV 1-2; OAEP; SeCePo; VLP

Juggy's Christening. *Anonymous.* Once more to my Juggy's labour.' NOEC

The Jugs. Paul Celan. and do not flow over like you or like me. OBVE

Jugurtha. Henry Wadsworth Longfellow How cold are thy baths, Apollo! AA; AP

JuJu. Askia Muhammad Toure. A LOVE SUPREME.... PoBA

A Juju of My Own. Lebert Behune. Me no care fe fum-fum/come Juju come... PAI; PoBA; PoNe

Juke Box Love Song. Langston Hughes. Dance with you, my sweet brown Harlem girl. GrPl; IDB; OLR; PoBA

Julia. Wendy Rose. lioness/with cub. STE; TWSS

Julia Miller. Edgar Lee Masters. Be with me in paradise. MoVE

Julia's Petticoat. Robert Herrick. But ah! I co'd not: sho'd it move/To Life Eternal, I co'd love. AnAnS 2; CaPo

Julian and Maddalo (excerpt). Percy Bysshe Shelley. The following morning, urged by my affairs,/I left bright Venice.... OAEL 1-2; OBTV

Julian Barely Misses Zimmer's Brains.   Paul Zimmer.   Spring/Has come and I am alive/With the sense that I am still alive.   GOYP

Julian Grenfell.   Maurice Baring.   And you will speed us onward with a cheer,/And wave beyond the stars that all is well.   HBMV

Julian M. and A.G. Rochelle.   Emily Bronte.   The soul to feel the flesh and the flesh to feel the chain!'   BrRo

Juliana.   Cynewulf.   Grant us, Great God,/Thou Joy of men, that we find Thy face/Mild with mercy on that Great Day! Amen   AnOE

Julie Ann Johnson.   *Anonymous.*   Gwineter hug my Julie,/Oho!   ABF

Julie-Jane.   Thomas Hardy.   She chose her bearers before she died/From her fancy-men.   MoVE

Juliet.   Hilaire Belloc.   Juliet was next me and I do not know.   BoLoP; ELU; EnLoPo

Julio.   Kell Robertson.   "Here lay Julio/He were crazy for Truck."   TAT

Julius Caesar.   *Anonymous*   Squashed his wife with a lemon-squeezer.   InPK

Julius Caesar.   William Shakespeare.
   ...and put a tongue/In every wound of Caesar that should move/The stones of Rome to rise and mutiny   LiTB
   And say to all the world "This/was a man!"   FaFP; TrGrPo
   And we must take the current when it serves,/Or lose our ventures. PoPl; TRV
   He thinks too much: such men are dangerous. TreFS
   Here is himself, marred, as you see, with traitors. FaPoR
   ...Mischief, thou art afoot./Take thou what course thou wilt! GoTF; TreF
   Seeing that death, a necessary end,/Will come when it will come. FF
   That this foul deed shall smell above the earth/With carrion men, groaning for burial. TreFS
   Upon what meat doth this our Caesar feed,/That he is grown so great? GoTF; TreFS

Julius Caesar and the Honey-Bee.   Charles Tennyson Turner.   I might have set the honey-maker free.   FM; NBM

July.   W. Ralph Johnson.   Whatever good I have is what you gave.   AMV-81

July.   Susan Hartley Swett.   It is July.   GN

July.   John Greenleaf Whittier.   And sunset splendour of July.   YeAr

July 1914.   Anna Akhmatova.   the Mother-of-God will spread/a white shroud over these great sorrows.   WPOW

July 1st, French Creek.   Kevin Roberts.   Hell we may as well/be doing this/as anything else/as silly.   WOLT

July 31.   Norman Jordan.   and all old men/are hip to it.   PoBA

July 4th.   May Swenson.   ...And we want more: red giant,/white dwarf, black hole dense, invisible, all in one.   PoA

July 4th.   Anne Waldman.   a child can wave as the boats go by.   APU

July Dawn.   Louise Bogan.   When curved toward the full it sharpens.   NePoAm-2

A July Dawn (excerpt).   John Francis O'Donnell.   The sun was up, the country woke!   IrPN

July in Indiana.   Robert Fitzgerald.   A warm full moon will rise/out of the mothering dust, out of the dry corn land.   NYBP

July in the Jardin des Plantes.   Claire McAllister.   But the summerdusk darkens; leaves turn red overnight.   NePA

July in Washington.   Robert Lowell.   that only the slightest repugnanace of our bodies/we no longer control could drag us back.   LCAP; NaP; Prf

July Meadow.   Louise Driscoll.   When little white-tailed rabbits/Make their swift way through.   YeAr

A July Storm: Johnson, Nemaha Country, Nebraska.   Steve Hahn.   the damp terror of space.   AMV-81

July the First.   Robert Currie.   ...the stars/a bright one in the west/pulsing like a heart.   Psk

July Wakes.   *Anonymous.*   Weavin' fifty-one weeks of bread/An' one of life.   OBET

Jumbled in the Common Box.   W. H. Auden.   Rude and ragged rascals run.   PoRA

The Jumblies.   Edward Lear.   And they went to sea in a sieve.   BLPL; EBEV; EnLi 1-2; EvOK; FaBoBe; FaBoNo; FaFP; GoJo; HBV 1-2; HBVY; LBN; LiTB; MOS; NA; OnMSP; OxBChV; OxBoLi; PoRA; SeCeV; SoPo; TEP; TiPo; WiR

Jumbo Jee.   Laura E. Richards.   And flung their crowns at the rising moon.   SUS

Jump Cabling.   Linda Pastan.   I thought why not ride the rest of the way together?   AmC

Jump Jim Crow.   Thomas D. Rice.   Ebry time I wheel about,/I jump Jim Crow.   BLSo

Jump–Jump–Jump.   Kate Greenaway.   And all come home/Some other day.   TiPo

Jump or Jiggle.   Evelyn Beyer.   Lions stalk–/But–I walk!   SoPo; TiPo

Jump-Rope Rhyme.   *Anonymous.*   "Kachoo, kachoo, kachoo, sir."   NTCP

The Jump Shooter.   Dennis Trudell.   breathe deeply and begin/to whistle/as I walked back home.   LiSp

Jump-to-Glory Jane.   George Meredith.   It is a lily-light she bears/For England up the ladder-stairs.   VLP

Jumpin' Judy.   *Anonymous.*   All over dis worl',hanh, all over dis worl',hanh!   ABF

Jumping Joan.   *Anonymous.*   When nobody's with me/I'm all alone.   OxNR

Junction.   John Pass.   lightning in one hand,/the unthinkable/stone in the other.   WOLT

Juncture.   Rea Lubar Duncan.   ...seep/slow pain on our joy and stain our sleep.   PoNe

June.   William Cullen Bryant.   To hear again his living voice.   AA; HBV 1-2

June.   Mary Carolyn Davies.   And we fly through the air on the merry-go-round!   SiSoSe; TiPo

June.   Elaine Feinstein.   how each Summer day is won/from soil, the old clay soil/and that long, cold kingdom.   BrRo

June.   Nora Hopper.   That's the way of June.   YeAr

June.   Francis Ledwidge.   Even the roses spilt on youth's red mouth/Will soon blow down the road all roses go.   BBV; BIrV; HBMV; HBV 1-2; NOBI

June.   Wilson MacDonald.   or make me unremember choirs/that sang for me in June.   CaP

June.   Douglas Malloch.   The fairy month, the merry month, the laughter/of the year!   YeAr

June.   Mebdh McGuckian.   ...we are Kay/And Gerda, under a white tent.   FaBoIP

June.   Harrison Smith Morris.   All the new is over-old./Heigh ho!   HBV 1-2

June.   Theodore Harding Rand.   Life and sweet earth are young, God grows not old!   CaP

June.   James Reaney.   The garter snake leaves behind/One of his silver glittering crystal annual sleeves.   WHW

June 10.   Marcos Rodriguez Frese.   Fierce party in the streets. The evening falls.   WPOW

June Bracken and Heather.   Alfred, Lord Tennyson.   As the green of the bracken amid the gloom of the heather.   EnLoPo; PPoe

A June Day.   Sara Teasdale.   Then blue night, and the day was ended/That never will come again.   YeAr

June Fugue.   Thomas W. Shapcott.   you will get the dark all over you.   NOAV

June in Wiltshire.   Geoffrey Grigson.   In the bland hedge thick as a mound.   WaP

June Is Bustin' Out All Over.   Oscar, II Hammerstein.   Jest because it's June! June! June!   BLSo

June Morning.   Hugh McCrae.   ;travel the wholesome road/And give my body to the sun.   BoAV; PoAu 1-2

June Night.   Hazel Hall.   She went as though with a quick fear/Of the eternal winter here.   HBMV

June Rapture.   Angela Morgan.   That I might know the passion of this day!   HBMV

June Song.   Abby Rosenthal.   I doubt I could do it again.   AMV-81

June Song of a Man Who Looks Two Ways.   Leslie Daiken.   June, fuchsia and ear-lobe,/Snapdragon and bee.   NeIP

June Thunder.   Louis MacNeice.   Now if now only.   CMoP; MoPo

June Twenty-First.   Bruce Guernsey.   The sun refuses to set,/bright as a penny in a loafer.   PPJ

June Twilight.   John Masefield.   Love, can this beauty in our hearts/End?   GoYe

The Jungle.   Diane Di Prima.   that the block of ice which binds us/binds us both.   PoM

The Jungle.   Louis Dudek.   to be drowned in space where all that was/is sound in a deaf ear, fear in a forgotten dream.   PeCV

Jungle.   Phyllis Haring.   Yammering fearfully at the sound of drums.   PeSA

The Jungle.   Alun Lewis.   ...struggle end/With the last kindness of a foe or friend?   MoPo

Jungle.   Mary Carter Smith.   No one sheds a tear.   PoNe

The Jungle.   William Carlos Williams.   a girl waiting/shy, brown, soft-eyed–/to guide you/Upstairs, sir.   CABA

The Jungle (excerpt).   Archibald Fleming.   Thick with power oozed over branches.   NAMP

The Jungle Husband.   Stevie Smith.   ...So no more now, from your loving husband, Wilfred.   FaBoWP; NLV

Jungle Taste.   Edward S. Silvera.   Dark hidden beauty/In the faces of black women,/Which only black men/See.   CDC

Junglegrave.   S. E. Anderson.   Send me no flowers, man, send me no flowers   PoBA

Junior Addict.   Langston Hughes.   Sunrise, please come!/Come! Come!   BPo; CNA

Juniper.   Eileen Duggan.
   In the shelter sweet of the juniper tree!   ChBR; PCh
   You will answer for your fool.   CAW

Juniper.   Robert Francis.   I speak for it, its silence speaks for me.   VGW

Juniper.   Laurie Lee.   between our banks of steep embraces.   NeBP

The Juniper Tree. Wilfred Watson. O never you will, said she WHW

Junk. Richard Wilbur. And Wayland's work/is worn away. HAP; NoP; SaC; SM; WeW

Junk. William Zaranka. He smiles at the prize: it sparkles: junk. AMV-80

The Junk Shop. Henri Coulette. These bronze, unbarbered heads are not our kings/But subjects of our thought. NYBP

Junker Schmidt. Kozma Prutkov. Summer will return. ELU

A Junkie with a Flute in the Rain. David Fisher. a junkie with a flute in the rain NPGG

Junkyards. Julian Lee Rayford. all the parts of motors/rusting FAZ; PPJ

Juno, That on Her Head. Fulke, Lord Brooke Greville. Repentance still becomes desires mother. NCEP

Jupiter and Ganimede. Thomas Heywood. Let him be brought to wait on us at table. PeHV

Jupiter and Ten. James Thomas Fields. We perused the printed label,/ And 't was Jupiter and Io! OBAL

Jurgis Petraskas, the Workers' Angel, Organizes... Anthony Petrosky. ...troopers kneel hunched over/their black Fords, tipped off, waiting. FYAP

Just. Judith Johnson Sherwin. ...what is it/makes you take love so hard? TAP

Just a Closer Walk with Thee. Anonymous. To Thy shore, dear Lord, to Thy shore. FSW

Just a Few Scenes from an Autobiography. John Tagliabue. and my wife and I travel in love FAZ

Just a Smack at Auden. William Empson. Waiting for the end, boys, waiting for the end. FaBoCo; LiTM; MoBrPo; UnPo

Just a Wearyin' for You. Frank Lebby Stanton. Just a wearyin' for you. GoTF; TreF

Just a While. Frantisek Gottlieb. window lit into darkness–/under the light of the family circle. VWA

Just About Asleep Together. Molly Peacock. ...And blankly/shifting and waking without waking/is that much touch that is our sleep making. SM

Just after Noon with Fierce Shears. Tram Combs. once in a life/such wonder. MP; TwCP

Just an Old Man. Mary Goose. From both I learn. STE

Just an Old Sweet Song. Donagh MacDonagh. ...the waters/Advance on the earth as the war tides recede. CIP

Just As I Am. Charlotte Elliott. O Lamb of God, I come! HBV 1-2; VLP

Just as the Small Waves Came Where No Waves Were. Pamela Millward. rolled effortless and mammoth through the night. NU

Just as the Tide Was A-Flowing. Anonymous. Success to the girl that will do so/Just as the tide was a-flowing. OBET

Just As Thou Art. Russell Sturgis Cook. O needy sinner, come, O come. AH

Just Be Glad. James Whitcomb Riley. And through all the coming years, just be glad! WBLP

Just Because. Moishe Leib Halpern. Why?/Just because. VWA

Just before Dawn. Roo Borson. full of letters lying in the dark,/from the world to the world. CaPN

Just before the Battle, Mother. George Frederick Root. But, oh, you'll not forget me, mother,/If I'm numbered with the slain. FSW; PSoN; TreFS

Just Beguiler. Thomas Campion. Yet not still secure. AtBAP

Just behind the Battle, Mother. Anonymous. But never, never with the slain. FiBHP

Just California. John S. McGroarty. Just California stretching down/The middle of the world. BPAW

Just Dropped In. William Cole. Which he certainly knew you knew, U Nu. FiBHP; GoJo; PoL; PoPl

Just Folks. Edgar A. Guest. Because from friends we're never/parted. FaFP; TreFS

Just for the Ride. Anonymous. "I don't know–I just came for/the ride." FaFP

Just for To-day. Sybil F. Partridge. But keep me, guide me, love me, Lord,/Just for to-day. HBV 1-2; TreF; TRV

Just Forget. Myrtle May Dryden. Forget when traveling or at home. WBLP

Just Friends. Robert Creeley. Everything is water/if you look long enough. NeAP

Just from Dawson. Anonymous. And sent the miner home that night to Deadwood on the hills. ABF

Just Keep On. Clifton Abbott. An' a place where things come right. STF; WBLP

Just Like Me. P.W. Sinks. And the gain to our church–what would it be. BLRP

Just Lost, When I Was Saved! Emily Dickinson. Slow tramp the Centuries,/And the Cycles wheel! AA; AmePo; AnFE; APA; MoAmPo; NOBA; NOCV; Prf

Just Making It. Richard Thomas. Enough to hush the screams within PoNe

Just One Book. Anonymous. There's just one Book. BLRP

Just One Signal. Anonymous. For the way to fight is to fight. PAH

Just Taking Note–. Sharon Scott. only seems like now, they ain't so/ revolutionary anymore. JB

Just Tell Them That You Saw Me. Paul Dresser. Just whisper if you get a chance to mother dear, and say,/I love her as I did long, long ago. FSN; GoTF; TreFS

Just the Same Today. Anonymous. And the God that lived at Pentecost,/Is just the same to-day. BLRP; WBLP

Just Then the Door. Merrill Moore. Just about the time the morning broke. AnEnPo

Just Think. Paul Celan. name-alert, hand-alert/forever,/from the unburiable. VWA

Just This. Istvan Vas. nothing but this, and only this. VWA

Just to Be Glad. Merlin G. Miller. Asking for lives filled with sweetness,/ Gratitude, gladness and praise. STF

Just To Be Needed. Mary Eversley. "Than any freedom in this world could be." PoToHe

Just Try This. Anonymous. An' keep on keepin' on. WBLP

The Just Vengeance (excerpt). Dorothy L. Sayers. Give me the confused self that you can do nothing with;/I can do something. BoC

Justice. Langston Hughes. Her bandage hides two festering sores/That once perhaps were eyes. BPo

Justice. Petra von Morstein. even/if I only/pass them BoWoP

Justice Denied in Massachusetts. Edna St. Vincent Millay. And a blighted earth to till/With a broken hoe. MoAmPo; SBG

Justice Is Reason Enough. Diane Wakoski. ...Justice is/reason enough for anything ugly. It balances the beauty in the /world. AmPA; CoPo

The Justice of the Peace. Hilaire Belloc. Moreover, I have got the upper hand,/And mean to keep it. Do you understand? NOBV; OBSV

Justice to Scotland. Anonymous. An' cleek my duds for auld lang syne. InMe; NLV

The Justified Mother of Men. Walt Whitman. The justified mother of men. OHIP

Justine, You Love Me Not! John Godfrey Saxe. Justine, you love me not! HBV 1-2

Jutacula Rock. Robert Morgan. in text and context, history, word? SUW

The Jute Mill Song. Anonymous. There's no' much pleasure livin' aff'n ten and nine. OBET

Juvenal's Sixth Satire. John Dryden.
And much good love, without a feather-bed. OBSV
Goes flaunting out, and, in her trim of pride,/Think all she says or does, is justified. OBSV

Juvenal's Tenth Satire Translated (excerpt). Henry Vaughan. And in a tide of tears grow old and die. OBSV

Juvenile Court. Sara Henderson Hay. Released them to their parents, on probation. DFT

Juventius, Could You Not Find in This Great Crowd of Men. Caius Valerius Catullus. And whom you prefer to me, though you don't know how much it/hurts? PeHV

Juventius, My Honey. Caius Valerius Catullus. I shan't steal kisses from you any more. PeHV

Juxta. Grover Jacoby. A spring gale/Eddying amidst the scrap iron. GoYe

K

The K.K.K. Disco... Noah Mitchell. We are perceiving an end/to Me, You, Us, and Them. LFAC

Ka 'Ba. LeRoi (Imamu Amiri Baraka) Jones. ...What will be/the sacred words? BPo; CAPP; CNA; TAP

The Kabbalist. Deborah Eibel. He mastered men and trees and birds and winds. VWA

Kaddish. Allen Ginsberg.
...–Death, stay thy phantoms! NeAP; NOBA; PoM; VWA
Lord Lord Lord caw caw caw Lord Lord Lord caw caw caw Lord NeAP
Love,/your mother'/which is Naomi– AmPC; HaCAP
size of the tick of the hospital's clock on the archway over the/white door– NeAP
with your Death full of Flowers NeAP

Kaddish. David Ignatow. and I am safe and always have been. NU; VWA

Kaddish. Levi Yitzhok. Magnified and sanctified be His great/Name! TrJP

Kadia the Young Mother Speaks. Jessie Sampter. Baby! TrJP

Kafka's Other Metamorphosis. Len Gasparini. And had a chancre the size/Of a chrysalis on her crotch. NeAC

Kafoozalum. Anonymous.

Keep It Clean. Charlie Jordan. takes soap and water/for to keep it clean. BluL

Keep It Dark. *Anonymous.* It's all out and about!/Keep it dark! PBA

Keep Love in Your Life. Thomas Curtis Clark. Keep love in your life alway. WBLP

Keep Me As Your Servant, O Girdhar. Mira Bai [(or Mirabai)]. At midnight on the banks of Jumna/give me your vision. PBWP

Keep Me f'om Sinkin' Down. *Anonymous.* Keep me f'om sinkin' down f'om sinkin' down. BoAN 1-2

Keep Me, Jesus, Keep Me. Waverly Turner Carmichael. Keep me, Jesus, keep me. BANP

Keep Me Still, for I Do Not Want to Dream. Larry Eigner. the flowers are hidden lately NeAP

Keep My Skillet Good and Greasy. *Anonymous.* Good and drunk and goozy all the time. FSW

Keep on Praying. Roger H. Lyon. His heart divine/Will enter thine, and lead the way/To blissful day. BLRP

Keep on Pushing. David Henderson. I know we can make it/With just a little bit of soul. PoBA

Keep Smiling. *Anonymous.* "Here is that very selfsame smile/Come back with us to bed." WBLP

Keep Sweet. *Anonymous.* Jesus, keep me sweet. STF

Keep the Glad Flag Flying. *Anonymous.* Help him play a manly part. FaFP

Keep the Sea. *Anonymous.* Which peace men shuld enserch with bisinesse/And knit it sadly, holding in holynesse. OxBM

Keep Thou My Way, O Lord. Fanny J. Crosby. O bear me safe o'er death's cold wave/To heaven, my blissful home. TrPWD

Keep Ye Holy Sabbath Rest. *Anonymous.* Day of rest, God hath blest Israel's/Sabbath day. TrJP

Keep Your Eyes on the Prize. *Anonymous.* Keep your eyes on the prize,/Hold on. FSW

Keep your eyes open when you kiss. John Berryman. You do, you do, and I look into them. BoLoP

Keep Your Kiss to Yourself. *Anonymous.* I'll love no woman young or old/because her kiss is–what it is! NOBI

Keep Your Lamp Trimmed and Burning. *Anonymous.* Keep your lamp trimmed and burning,/For this old world it is almost gone. FSW

The Keeper. *Anonymous.* Hey down (Ho down)! Derry, derry down./Among the leaves so green, O. FSW

The Keeper. William Carpenter. It would be I who kept on living here/and kept forgetting. Psk

The Keeper of the Midnight Gate. George Mackay Brown. You'd be better in the silver cage of a merchant. OxBC

Keeping Christmas. Eleanor Farjeon. Do not keep but give away. OBCP

Keeping Hair. Ramona Wilson. washed my hair in willows/may also keep my heart. VoR

Keeping Their World Large. Marianne Moore. ...Shine, O shine/unfalsifying sun, on this sick scene. WaP

Keeping Things Whole. Mark Strand. I move/to keep things whole. CoAP; HaCAP; HeIP; LCAP; NoAm; PPP; TAP

Keeping Victory. Walter E. Isenhour. Knowing that His hand will lead you/Up the way that saints have trod. STF

Keeping You Alive. Tess Gallagher. :..who sings/and sings in the deepending well/of your sleep. GP

The Keepsake Corporation. David Fisher. It's getting so you can't even take a military jet/home to hunt ducks. NPGG

Keepsake from Quinault. Dorothy Alyea. The ripest fruit you must eat from the spray. GoYe

Keine Lazarovitch. Irving Layton. While all the rivers of her red veins move into the sea. ACV

Keith of Ravelston. Sydney Thomas Dobell. The sorrows of thy line! CH

Kelly. Robert Hershon. and we played all night. NeAC

Kellyburnbraes. *Anonymous.* An' the thyme it is wither'd and rue is in prime. OxBB

Kelp. Nora Dauenhauer. unrolled by the hands/of the waves. TWSS

Kelpius's Hymn. Arthur Peterson. As downward to this world of night/The New Jerusalem they bring! AA

Kemp Owyne (A version). *Anonymous.* And smilingly she came about,/As fair a woman as fair could be. BaBo; BoLiVe; BuBa; EnSB; ESPB; SeCeV; ViBoFo

Kemp Owyne (B version). *Anonymous.* An relieved sall she never be,/Till St. Mungo come oer the sea.' ESPB

Kennedy. Michael Heffernan. light of day held darkness back like the whole Atlantic. AMV-80

Kennedy Airport. Aaron Kramer. her five American children and their mates/never did grow quite prosperous enough to send). AMV-80

Keno. Dara Wier. Every night it's not like life. MAYP

The Kent State Massacre. Barbara and Jack Warshaw Dane. Till we sink this murdering system/In the darkest pits of hell! FSW

Kent State, May 4, 1970. Paul Goodman. ...Call the soldiers back. MAT

Kentucky Babe. Richard Henry Buck. Close yo' eyes in sleep. AA; FSN; HBV 1-2

Kentucky Belle. Constance Fenimore Woolson. Ah! we've had many horses, but never a horse like her! BeLS; BLPA; FaBoBe; MaC; PAH; PH; StPo

Kentucky Birthday. Frances Frost. Abraham Lincoln, seven. SiSoSe; YeAr

Kentucky Blues. Little Hat Jones. 'Cause I don't play the dozen, I declare, man, and neither the ten BluL

Kentucky Bootlegger. *Anonymous.* They'll be selling each other I do declare. FSW

Kentucky Moonshiner. *Anonymous.* Their breath smells as sweet as the good old moonshine. AS; OBAL; TrAS

Kentucky Mountain Farm. Robert Penn Warren.
The apple falls, falling in the quiet night. MoVE
In a whispering tree, like cedar, evergreen. MoVE

Kentucky Philosophy. Harrison Robertson. Ef you don't want a lickin' all over, be sho dat dey allers/go "punk!" HBV 1-2

The Kentucky Thoroughbred. James Whitcomb Riley. And next my wife, and then I fall/Down on my knees and love the hoss. ELU

Kept for Jesus. Edith E. Cherry. I would be "nothing, nothing,"/Thou shalt be "all in all." BePJ

Keramos. Henry Wadsworth Longfellow. And all are ground to dust at last,/And trodden into clay! MAmP; PoEL 1-5

Keraunograph. Hayden Carruth. The rites uninterrupted by our arrival/Or departure. NMP

Kerchoo! Margaret Fishback. And Dature starts her Highlad Flig. PoSC

Kerr's Ass. Patrick Kavanagh. And the God of imagination waking/In a Mucker fog. FaBoIP; NOBI

The Kerry Dance. James Lyman Molloy. ...gone, alas! like our youth too soon. OnYI

The Kerry Lads. Theodosia Garrison. And what's a careless kiss or so/To one remembered song? HBMV

The Kerry Recruit. *Anonymous.* And contented with shellocks I live on half pay./With me kerry-ay-ay, fa la de ral lay. FSW

Kevin Barry. Terence Ward. For the evil crew who murdered Kevin Barry/That day in November? OnYI

Kevin Barry: Died for Ireland,/1st November, 1920. *Anonymous.* Lads like Barry will free Ireland,/For her sake they'll live and die. AS; FaBoBa; FSW

The Key. John Oxenham. Of Life reborn of Death. BePJ

The Key-Board. William Watson. Touched to immortality/By her finger-tips. HBV 1-2

The Key to Everything. May Swenson. of course I'd/be gone by then I'd/be far away IHMS; NePoEA

Key West. Hart Crane. Where gold has not been sold and conscience tinned. CMoP

The Keyhole in the Door. *Anonymous.* I took up my position by the keyhole in the door. CoMu

Keys. Glen Rockwell. it would be impossible/to lose a key here. AMV-81

The Keys of Canterbury. *Anonymous.* If you will be my joy, my sweet and only dear,/And walk along with you anywhere. AmFP

The Keys of Morning. Walter De la Mare. And that, when beckoning, he should wag/The littlest in the air. AtBAP; MoVE; NoP

The Keys of the Jail. *Anonymous.* ...I mean, with/those four red wheels. OuSiCo

Khamsin. Clinton Scollard. The scourge from the desert, blew in! AA

Khristna and His Flute. Laurence Hope. To save thee from the magic/Of Khristna and his flute. HBV 1-2

Kibbutz Sabbath. Levi ben Amittai. I thank thee for the slice of bread and the prayerful mood. EaLo

Kick a Little Stone. Dorothy Aldis. Along the sidewalk over the cracks/The shadow bounces too. SoPo

Kicking from Centre Field. David McFadden. & a clarity/that pierced through to the other world. NeAC

The Kicking Mule. *Anonymous.* I ain't got time to kiss you now,/I'm busy with this mule. AmFP

Kicking the Leaves. Donald Hall. ...taking/the step they will follow, Octobers and years from now. GLGT

Kid. Robert Earl Hayden. taunts them and scampers off,/laughing as he goes. CAD; NCSH

The Kid Has Gone to the Colors. W. M. Herschell. Was changed by the Flag to a man! PoLf

The Kid's Last Fight. *Anonymous.* I looked again–the Kid was dead! GoTF; TreF

Kid Stuff. Frank Horne. Kid Stuff/born two thousand years ago. AmNP; PCh; PoBA; PoNe

The Kid: The Awakening (excerpt). Conrad Aiken. and I open my eyes: and the world looks in! MoVE

Kidnap Poem. Nikki Giovanni. yeah if i were/a poet i'd kid/nap you BPo; GOYP; NoAm; TAP

Kidnaper.　Tess Gallagher.　"You must have given me up."　AmPA

The Kidnapping of Sims.　John Pierpont.　At us let angels hiss/From heaven that fell!　PAH

Kilaben Bay Song.　*Anonymous.*　People all eating/Camp quiet again. NOAV

Kilcash.　*Anonymous.*　And from that to the deluge of waters/In bounty and peace remain.　BIrV; KiLC; OBMV; OxBI

The Kilfenora Teaboy.　Paul Durcan.　But Oh it's the small bit of furze between two towns/Is what makes the Kilfenora teaboy really run. FaBoIP

Kilimandjaro.　Bayard Taylor.　Father of Nile and Creator of Egypt.　AmP

The Kilkenny Boy.　Eileen Shanahan.　Of the days when she/Was too young for a name.　NeIP

The Kilkenny Cats.　*Anonymous.*　Instead of two cats, there warnt/any. FaFP; GoTF; ShM; TreF

Kill a Robin or a Wren.　*Anonymous.*　Never prosper, boy or man.　PBBP

Killarney.　Edward Falconer.　Beauty's home, Killarney, ever fair Killarney. TreFS

Killarney.　William Larminie.　Still, though many an age be gone,/Round Killarney lingers.　AnIV

Killed at the Ford.　Henry Wadsworth Longfellow.　And the neighbors wondered that she should die.　AP; OHIP

Killed in Action.　Terence Tiller.　they know the lion's power.　NeBP

Killer.　*Anonymous.*　With my bronco called Apache and Adolphus-that's my gun.　ABF; CoSo

Killer Diller.　Memphis Minnie.　I'm a killer diller from the South　BluL

The Killer Too.　Walker Gibson.　His own bombs burst on his own tomb. FF

Killers.　Carl Sandburg.　I am the killer who kills today for five million killers who wish/a killing.　MoVE

"The killers that run...'.　Leonard Cohen.　which goes on gaily/quite unchecked/until everyone is dead　NOBC

Killing.　Samuel Greenberg.　While David held the head/For those who stood by.　LiTA

The Killing.　George MacBeth.　...nor pity the/Man imprisoned for stealing/Fire from heaven. He, too, is guilty.　FaBoMo

The Killing.　Edwin Muir.　By chance, he on his road and I on mine? ACV; ChMP; MoRP; PoPl

Killing a Whale.　David Gill.　Dead whales are rendered down,/Give oil. BoAnP

Killing No Murder.　Sylvia Townsend Warner.　Save doing nothing, to undo a heart.　MoBrPo

The Killing of the Birds.　Shirley Williams.　...At the window Daddy was screamin/bout some man and Mamma was cryin.　BoWoP

Killing Rabbits.　Ed Ochester.　your capped teeth flash and tear flesh. LTB

Killing the Rooster.　Sheryl L. Nelms.　out among the rows of green onions Str

Killyburn Brae.　*Anonymous.*　When they go down to hell they are thrown out again.　OnYI

Kilmallock.　Sir Aubrey De Vere.　The charnel of yon desecrated fane! IrPN

Kilmeny.　James Hogg.　She left this world of sorrow and pain,/And return'd to the land of thought again.　CABL; HBV 1-2; OBEV; OBRV

Kilmeny.　Alfred Noyes.　And nobody knew where Kilmeny had been. EnLit

Kilroy.　Eugene McCarthy.　absent without leave/from Vietnam.　NIP

Kilroy.　Peter Viereck.
And in the suburbs Can't sat down and cried.　MoAmPo; NIP; PoRA
He was there, he was there, he was there!　FF

The Kilruddery Hunt.　Thomas Mozeen.　Thus ended at length a most delicate chase,/That held us five hours and ten minutes' space.　BIrV

Kiltartan Legend.　Padraic Fallon.　And humbly, or most royally, adds her own.　NOBI

Kimono.　Jorie Graham.　loosens her stays/pretending she's alone.　MAYP

Kin.　Michael S. Harper.　and the worn body you will carry/as your own birthmark of his scream.　LCAP

Kinaxixi.　Agostinho Neto.　too simple/for he who is tired and has to walk on.　WhB

Kinchinjunga.　Cale Young Rice.　And till no sacrificial suffering,/On any shrine is left to tell life's sting.　AnAmPo; HBV 1-2

Kincora.　James Clarence Mangan.　Dead, oh, Kincora!　AnIV; OnYI; OxBI

Kind.　Archie Randolph Ammons.　as finished as you/and with a flower. NoP; PrIm

Kind Are Her Answers.　Thomas Campion.　Never were days yet called two,/But one night went betwixt.　AnFE; BoLoP; EG; ELP; FaBoEn; HBV 1-2; LiTL; SeCeV; TrGrPo

Kind Hearts.　*Anonymous.*　For only in darkness/Grow hatred and strife. HBV 1-2

A Kind Inn.　George Dillon.　Trust me: I know these waterways.　GoYe

Kind Lovers, Love On.　John Crowne.　There soon would be nothing but trees.　InvP

Kind Miss (with music).　*Anonymous.*　What do I care for your world of pleasure,/When all I want is a handsome man.　AS

The Kind of Act of.　Robert Creeley.　...There is no more giving in/when there is no more sin.　NeAP

Kind of an Ode to Duty.　Ogden Nash.　...Thou must,/this erstwhile youth replies, I just can't.　TrGrPo

The Kind of Poetry I Want (excerpt).　Hugh" (Christopher Murray Grieve) MacDiarmid.　May be conditioned by traces/Of a derivative of phenanthrene!　PAI

The Kind of Waters, the Sea Shouldering Whale.　William Wood.　These waterie villagers with thousands more,/Do passe and repasse neare the verdant shore.　SCAP

Kind Robin Lo'es Me.　*Anonymous.*　Kind Robin lo'es me.　BSV

Kind Sir: These Woods.　Anne Sexton.　Still, I search in these woods and find nothing worse/than myself,...　GoYe

Kind Words Can Never Die.　Abby Hutchinson.　Kind words can never die, no, never die.　AH

Kindergarten.　Dennis Schmitz.　a child's unfinished body,/waxy & insistent. NPGG

Kindertotenlieder.　Michael Longley.　Everywhere, teethmarks on this and that.　CIP

Kindle the Taper.　Emma Lazarus.　Where are the lion warriors of the Lord?　AH

The Kindly Neighbor.　Edgar A. Guest.　When man has made the man next door his friend.　PoToHe

Kindly Unhitch That Star, Buddy.　Ogden Nash.　That's the way they are. LiTA; PoPl

Kindly Vision.　Otto Julius Bierbaum.　Full of beauty waiting till we enter. AWP

Kindness.　*Anonymous.*
And pussy will love me/Because I am good.　OxNR
The best little donkey that ever was born.　OxNR
Lest soon, they whom thou holdest/dearest/Be past thy need.　STF

Kindness.　Catherine Davis.　To be again of a like mind.　NYBP

Kindness.　Thomas Sturge Moore.　Which sails for the islands of balm/Luxuriant and warm.　OBMV

Kindness.　Sylvia Plath.　You hand me two children, two roses.　BoC; FaBoWP

Kindness during Life.　*Anonymous.*　I'd rather have one blossom now/Than a truck load when I'm dead.　STF

Kindness to Animals.　*Anonymous.*　Nor do these gentle creatures wrong. FaBoUs; HBV 1-2; HBVY; SoPo

Kindness to Animals.　Joseph Ashby-Sterry.　Be always kind to animals wherever you may be.　InMe; NA

Kindness to Animals.　Laura E. Richards.　And I rinse him all off in the sinkie.　NTCP; SoPo; TiPo

Kinds of Shel-Fish.　William Wood.　To dive for Cocles, and to digge for Clamms,/Whereby her lazie husbands guts shee cramms.　SCAP

The Kine of My Father.　Dora Sigerson Shorter.　Bitter is your trouble–and I am far from you.　OnYI; OxBI

Kineo Mountain.　Celeste Turner Wright.　And other cliffs impossible to climb.　Psk

Kinfauns Castle (excerpt).　William Montgomerie.　...because a sage/Here dwelling taught the wisdom of the coming age.　OxBS

The King.　Mary Elizabeth Coleridge.　But the man went out to die. OBVV

The King.　Rudyard Kipling.　"Our King was with us–yesterday!"　CABA; VLP

The King.　Douglas Livingstone.　to smile full-faced and yellowly/at a thousand box cameras.　BoAnP

King Alfred Answers the Danes.　Gilbert Keith Chesterton.　Yet by God's death the stars shall stand/And the small apples grow.'　OxBoCh

The King and the Clown.　*Anonymous.*　I choose (and I thank you) to die of old age.　MaC

King Arthur.　*Anonymous.*　The Queen next morning fried.　NA; OxNR

King Arthur.　John Dryden.　And as these Excel in Beauty,/Those shall be Renown'd for Love.　CEP

King Arthur and His Round Table: Bees and Monks.　John Hookham Frere. The Belfry swarm'd with Monks; it seem'd alive.　OBRV

King Arthur and King Cornwall.　*Anonymous.*　He put the head upon a swords point,...　ESPB

King Arthur's Death.　*Anonymous.*　The rites of the Church bestow on me. ACP

King Arthur's Dream.　*Anonymous.*　The Lion and the Sovereign Leech also.　ACP

King Arthur's Waes-Hael.　Robert Stephen Hawker.　And learn the lip of Bethlehem's child.　ISi; OBEV; OBVV; OxBoCh

King Berdok.　*Anonymous.*　Thocht lufe be sweit, oft syis it is full sour. OxBS

King Billy. Edwin Morgan. Deplore what is to be deplored,/and then find out the rest. BSV

King Borborigmi. Conrad Aiken. But has bad dreams; I fear he has bad dreams. MAPA

King Cahal Mor of the Wine-Red Hand. James Clarence Mangan. Of the time and reign/Of Cahal Mor of the Wine-red Hand. AnIV; GoBC

King Christian. Johannes Evald. And war and victory, be thine arms/My grave! AWP

King Cophetua and the Beggar Maid. Don (Donald Robert Marquis) Marquis. Oh, Virtue always wins, I sing,/If Wisdom's mingled in it! HBMV; InMe

King David. Stephen Vincent Benét. (And the Lord is King above all gods!) HBMV

King David and King Solomon. James Ball Naylor. And King David wrote the Psalms. CenHV

King David Dances. John Berryman. all the black same I dance my blue head off! OBSP; OxBC

King Duffus. Sylvia Townsend Warner. Could I not stay at least until dewfall? FaBoWP

King Edward the Fourth and a Tanner. Anonymous. If ever thou comest to merry Tamworth,/thou shalt have clouting-leather for thy shone. BaBo; ESPB

The King Enjoys His Own Again. Martin Parker. Else never rejoice, till I hear the voice,/That the King enjoys his own again. OBS

King Estmere. Anonymous. And brought her home to merry England,/With her to lead his life. BuBa; ESPB; OBNV; OxBB

The King-Fisher Song. Lewis (Charles Lutwidge Dodgson) Carroll. So get you gone—'tis too absurd/To come a-courting me!' FaBoNo

King George V. Charles W. Hayward. And in his leisure moments potted pheasants/And perseveringly collected stamps. NOAV

King Harald's Trance. George Meredith. Strained he, staggered, broke/Doubled at their feet. VLP

King Hart: Hart's Castle. Gavin Douglas. That for thair reird they micht nocht heir the sound. AtBAP

King Henry. Anonymous. But never before wi a courteous knight/That ga me a' my will. BaBo; ESPB; OxBB

King Henry Fifth's Conquest of France (A vers.). Anonymous. And the finest flower that is in all France/To the Rose of England I will give free. BaBo

King Henry Fifth's Conquest of France (B vers.). Anonymous. And the finest flower in all French land,/Five tons of gold now is his fee. BaBo

King Henry IV. William Shakespeare.
...an accusation/betwixt my love and your high majesty. WaaP
I think there's no man speaks better Welch. NAs
Uneasy lies the head that wears a crown. FiP; MOS

King Henry to Rosamond. Michael Drayton. For though in France awhile my body be,/My heart remains (dear Paradise) in thee. OBSC

King Henry V. William Shakespeare.
And hold their manhoods cheap, whiles any speaks/That fought with us upon Saint Crispin's day. FaPoR
The bidding of a monarch, and his countenance/Enforces homage. PH
Cry "God for Harry, England, and Saint George!" TreF; WaaP
Delivering o'er to executors pale/The lazy, yawning drone. GN
Gently to hear, kindly to judge, our play. SCV
Holding due course to Harfleur. MOS
A little touch of Harry in the night. FaBoRV
Minding true things, by what their mockeries be. WaaP
Which oft our stage hath shown; and for their sake/In you fair minds let this acceptance take. CTC

King Henry VI. William Shakespeare.
His body couched in a curious bed,/When care, mistrust, and treason waits on him. TreFS
So is the equal poise of this fell war. MOS

King Henry VIII. William Shakespeare.
And when he falls, he falls like Lucifer,/Never to hope again. GoTF
...He would not in mine age/Have left me naked to mine enemies. TrGrPo
Killing care and grief of heart/Fall asleep or hearing, die. GN; OAEP; OBS
Shall see this, and bless Heaven. WGRP
This little one shall make it Holy-day. NAs

King I Sit. Anonymous. "Ich shal be king, that men shulle see,/When thou, wreche, ded shalt be." OxBM

The King in His Beauty. James G. Deck. Till I, in robes of white arrayed,/Thy face in glory see. BePJ

The King in May. Michael Dennis Browne. I am becoming a vegetable/of stiff gold. NYBP

King James and Brown. Anonymous. I might be likened to a bird,'/Quoth he, "that did defile it nest." ESPB

King James II. John Dryden. He looked into himself, and was deceived. ACP

King John. William Shakespeare.
...Misery's love,/O, come to me! TreFT

To seek the beauteous eye of heaven to garnish,/Is wasteful and ridiculous excess. TreFT

King John and the Abbot of Canterbury. Anonymous. Thou hast brought him a pardon from good King/John. GN; HBV 1-2

King John and the Bishop. Anonymous. I neuer knew shepeard that goot such a liuinge/But David, the shepeard, that was a king. BaBo

King John's Castle. Thomas Kinsella. The cold, the crowded, the crying, this is not their fortress. OxBI

King Lear. William Shakespeare.
And show the heavens more just. TrGrPo
Crack nature's molds, all germins spill at once/That make ingrateful man! TW
...he hates him/That would upon the rack of this tough world/Stretch him out longer. FiP
How sharper than a serpent's tooth it is/To have a thankless child! Away, Away! TreFT
Lest my brain turn, and the deficient sight/Topple down headlong. FaBoPP
No cause, no cause. Prf
Or ere I'll weep, O fool, I shall go mad! TreFT
That thou mayst shake the superflux to them,/And show the heavens more just. PPON

King Lives. Jill Witherspoon Boyer. crowd murmuring popeyes/for the last look CNA

King Lot's Envoys. Drummond Allison. Waited with ale and girls for what came next! OBSP

King Midas. Howard Moss. Dear Dionysus, give me back again/Ten fingertips that leave the world alone. CoAP; TAP

King Midas Has Asses' Ears. Donald Finkel. ...they know/Us better than we know ourselves, and rightly so. NePoEA-2

The King o' Spain's Daughter. Jeanne Robert Foster. And never again in a pool of black water/Have I seen the blue eyes of the King o' Spain's daughter. HBMV

King Oedipus. Sophocles. Why should we honor the gods, or join the sacred dance? LiTW

The King of Ai. Hyam Plutzik. And the vultures circle the sky at eventide. LiTM; VWA

The King of Brentford. William Makepeace Thackeray. And envy times departed,—that knew a reign like his. HBV 1-2; OBNV

The King of Canoodle-Dum. Sir William Schwenck Gilbert. But none of them wept for their FREDDY, except/HUM PICKITY WIMPLE TIP. CenHV

The King of Cats Sends a Postcard to His Wife. Nancy Willard. catnip from the other side. OBCA

The King of China's Daughter. Edith Sitwell. When I hung my cap and bells upon/Her nutmeg tree. FaBoMo; MoBrPo

The King of Connacht. Anonymous. "All that we saw/Was his shadow under his shield." KiLC

The King of Denmark's Ride. Carolina Elizabeth Sarah Norton. Dear steed! our ride hath been in vain/To the halls where my love lay dying. GN; HBV 1-2

The King of Dreams. Clinton Scollard. Every man is a King of Dreams! HBV 1-2

The King of France. Anonymous. they all came down again. OxNR

The King of Harlem. Federico Garcia Lorca. past your noble and desperate king/whose beard-lengths go down to the sea. NYP

King of Ireland's Son. Nora Hopper. He follows after shadows-the King of Ireland's Son. AnIL

The King of Kings. Lon Woodrum. He sits upon the throne of hearts! BePJ

The King of Love. Sir Henry William Baker. Good Shepherd, may I sing Thy praise/Within Thy house forever. BePJ

The King of Sunshine. Michael Silverton. he seems odd in the forest. PV

King of the Belgians. Marion Couthouy Smith. Silence that shines, and speech that is proud/and tender! PAH

King of the Castle. Anonymous. Get down you dirty rascal. OxNR

The King of the Cradle. Joseph Ashby-Sterry. Leave tears, sweet, for to-morrow! HBV 1-2

The King of the Hobbledygoblins. Laura E. Richards. And we never shall see you again, dears! OBCA

The King of Thule. Johann Wolfgang von Goethe. Nor drop did he ever drink more. AWP

The King of Ulster. Anonymous. In Autumn God/Heeds how He drops/The golden fruit. KiLC

The King of Yellow Butterflies. Vachel Lindsay. And hide them in the hay. OBCA

The King of Yvetot. Pierre Jean de Beranger. This jolly little king! AWP

The King on the Tower. William Makepeace Thackeray. And list to their loudest song? OBVV

King Orfeo. Anonymous. He's taen his lady, and he's gaen hame,/An noo he's king ower a' his ain. BuBa; ESPB; OxBB; OxBoLi

King Philip's Last Stand. Clinton Scollard. And yet what one of us would not/Do battle for his own! PAH

King Pippin. *Anonymous.* You ne'er saw the like. OxNR

King Richard II. William Shakespeare. ...and with a little pin/Bores through his castle-wall, and–farewell king! HoPM

King Rufus. Y. Y. Segal. What a fiery/Potentate! WHW

The King's Answer. John Wilmot, Earl of Rochester. Thanks you as much as if he did. FaBoCo

The King's Ballad. Joyce Kilmer. (Hark to the thrush's trilling). HBV 1-2

The King's Breakfast. A.(lan) A.(lexander) Milne. I do like a little bit of butter to my bread!' CenHV; OxBChV

King's College Chapel. Charles Causley. They sit in their white lawn sleeves, as cool as history. BoC

The King's Disguise (excerpt). John Cleveland. The princely eagle shrunk into a bat. JCP

The King's Dochter Lady Jean. Anonymous. He sank into his sister's arms,/And they died as white as snaw. ESPB

The King's Highway. John S. McGroarty. With the breath of God about us on the King's Highway. BLRP; BPAW; HBV 1-2; TRV

The King's Men. William Heyen. ...They will keep on, lowering/their barred visors against the setting sun. PoA

The King's Missive. John Greenleaf Whittier. And the freedom of soul he prophesied/Is gospel and law where the martyrs died. PAH

The King's Own Regulars. Anonymous. For if they beat us in the fight, we beat them/in the race. PAH

The King's Ring. Theodore Tilton. "Even this shall pass away.'" GoTF; TreFS

The King's Son. Thomas Boyd. He gallops; and the dark wind brings;/His lonely human cry. AnIV; OBMV; OxBI

King Saul. Allan Kolski Horvitz. Characteristically,/Saul only admires/their thick souls. VWA

A King Shall Reign in Righteousness. Sebastian Streeter. The words of life from Christ the Lamb. AH

King Triumphant. Isaac Watts. And infant voices shall proclaim/Their early blessings on his name. BLRP

King William and King James. Anonymous. As they left the cold Bine Waters. BFSS

King William's Dispatch to Queen Augusta... Coventry Patmore. Thank God from whom all blessings flow! FaBoEE

King William the Third to Himself. Anonymous. The self-same thing will be. FaBoEE

King William Was King George's Son. Anonymous.
And follow on to the fife and drum. AmFP
Hug her neat and kiss her sweet,/Then you may rise upon your feet. OuSiCo

King Wind. Mark Van Doren. Forever. Motion is all. NCSH

Kingcups. Sacheverell Sitwell. Make summer with their wide-eyed gold. MoBrPo

The Kingdom. Louis MacNeice.
Belongs, though he never knew it, to the Kingdom. LiTM
...;such a church/Bears in its lines the trademark of the Kingdom. ChMP

The Kingdom. Jon Swan. He is not at home. NYBP

Kingdom Coming. Henry Clay Work. It mus' be now de kingdom comin',/an' de year of Jubilo! BLSo; PSoN

The Kingdom of God. Rab. in that day/shall the Lord be One,/and His name one. TrJP

The Kingdom of God. Francis Thompson. And lo, Christ walking on the water/Not of Gennesareth, but Thames! AtBAP; BrPo; EaLo; FaPoR; GoBC; GTBS-P; ILwL; NOCV; OxBoCh; PoPle; SeCeV; TRV

The Kingdom of God. Richard Chenevis Trench. That this is blessing, this is life. WBLP

Kingdom of Heaven. Léonie Adams. I am Gabriel. MoAB; MoAmPo

The Kingdom of Poetry: Swift. Delmore Schwartz. I am a Fool. PoA

The Kingfisher. Amy Clampitt.
but, down on down, the uninhabitable sorrow. HaCAP

The Kingfisher. William Henry Davies. A lonely pool, and let a tree/Sigh with her bosom over me. MoVE; NOBE; OBEV

The Kingfisher. Blanche Mary Kelly. Bear them along the way of God's behest,/Breast on His breast. GoBC

The Kingfisher. Andrew Marvell. Charm'd with the Saphir-winged Mist. AtBAP; PB

Kingfisher Flat. William Empson. Each holds that bruise to her heart like a stone/And aches for rain. PoM

The Kingfishers. Charles Olson. I hunt among stones CMoP; InPS; NeAP; NOBA; PoM

The Kingis Quhair: The Coming of Love. King of Scotland James I, My hert, my will, my nature, and my mynd/Was changit clene rycht in ane other kind. GoTS

The Kingly Lyon, and the Strong Arm'd Beare. William Wood. The Civet sented Musquash smelling ever. SCAP

The Kings. Louise Imogen Guiney. Die, driven against the wall.' GoBC; HBV 1-2

Kings and Queens: "First William the Norman." Anonymous. Now God's sent Elizabeth:/All of us love her. OxNR

The Kings and Queens of England. Anonymous.
Leaving George and Liz the Second. FaBoUs
Prince of Orange Will., Mary, Anne, G.G., G. Billy/Victor. FaBoUs

Kings and Stars. John Erskine. Stars beget journeys. TrCP

Kings Came Riding. Charles Williams. They shone like the gleaming/Stars in the sky. OBCP

The Kings From the East. Alexander Gray. The kings begoud their singin'. ACV; GoTS

The Kings of Europe A Jest. Robert Dodsley. Supply the honest jester's place. CEP

Kings of France. Mary W. Lincoln. The throne is now vacant, and no one can tell/The name of the next, so I'll bid you farewell. BLPA

The Kings of the East. Katharine Lee Bates. There beams above a manger/The child-face of a star. WGRP

The Kings of the World... Rainer Maria Rilke. which will close again behind it. NU

Kings River Canyon. Kenneth Rexroth. Over the cobbles, in a lost Spring. NaP

The Kingship of the Hills. Will H. Ogilvie. And only a step from their cottage doors/The rough hill-shepherds are emperors. PoSH

The Kinkaiders. Anonymous. She is the queen of all the rest. CoSo

The Kinkaiders (with music). Anonymous. And for the homestead law he made,/This noble Moses P. Kinkaid. AS

Kinloch Ainort. Sorley MacLean. flat-rock snoring of high mountains. PoSH

Kinmont Willie. Anonymous. I wad na have ridden that wan water/For a' the gowd in Christentie. BaBo; BSV; ESPB; OxBB

Kinnaird Head. George Bruce. You yield to history nothing. BSV; NeBP

Kinneret. Judith Herzberg. for each light there is another light/wanting to stifle it. VWA

Kinnereth. Rachel Bluwstein. Were you, indeed? Or did I dream a dream? LiTW; TrJP

Kinship. Seamus Heaney. how the goddess swallows/our love and terror. IPY

Kinship. Sir Charles G. D. Roberts. To the wisdom and the stillness/Where thy consummations are. CaP

Kiph. Walter De la Mare. ...Oh, if/I could but find again/That stone called Kiph! TiPo

Kirk Lonegren's Home Movie Taking Place Just North of Prince George... Sharon Thesen. ...That was the end, and/what a crazy image of love. NOBC

The Kirk of the Birds, Beasts and Fishes. Anonymous. The howlet read the order,/They held a bonnie work. GBP

The Kirk's Alarm. Robert Burns. Your muse is a gipsy, e'en tho' she were tipsy/She cou'd ca' us nae waur than we are. OxBoLi

The Kirkyaird by the Sea (excerpt). Paul Valery. aa gangs to grund and comes again in play. OBVE

A Kiss. Anonymous.
I send this/Kiss for him. KiLC
Till she do kiss me as she kissed me then. OnYI; OxBI

A Kiss. Henry Austin Dobson. Will she kiss me to-morrow? ALV; CenHV; HBV 1-2

A Kiss. William, of Hawthornden Drummond. Hark, happy lovers, hark! EiL

The Kiss. Ben Jonson. That I might die kissing! HBV 1-2; UnTE

The Kiss. Walter Savage Landor. Give her as sweet and pure a kiss. OBVV

The Kiss. Thomas Moore. You know 'twas in the dark you taught me! EnLoPo

The Kiss. Ned O'Gorman. ...It rimes with tiger/and the gallow tree. FYAP

The Kiss. Robert Pack. sweeter than any apple I have known. AMV-81

The Kiss. Coventry Patmore. He thought I thought he thought I slept.' ALV; BoLoP; EnLoPo; FiBHP; LiTL; NOBV; OBVV; PoPle

The Kiss. Siegfried Sassoon. Quail from your downward darting kiss. MMM

The Kiss. Anne Sexton. Pure genius at work. Darling, the composer has stepped/into fire. NIP

The Kiss. Claude Clayton Smith. black & white/over & over/again. PoDr

The Kiss. Sara Teasdale. Think you that I could let a beggar enter/Where a king stood before? HBV 1-2

The Kiss. John Yau. ...until they began turning themselves, faster/and faster, as if a destination would arrive. APU

Kiss. Al Young. who touch my body with a silence/more beautiful than poetry PoBA

The Kiss and the Cup. Anonymous. And drink me at one draught! UnTE

Kiss'd Yestreen. Anonymous. Sic kindly kisses as he gae me. ErPo; GBP; PoL

The Kiss-Fest. Irwin Edman. What do we care for their sneers and their hisses so/Long as we run up a goodly amount? InMe

A Kiss in the Morning Early. *Anonymous.* That you met in the morning early.' GBP

A Kiss in the Rain. Samuel Minturn Peck. She says I am her rain beau since/I kissed her in the rain. OBAL

Kiss in the Ring. *Anonymous.* Kiss your bride and come out of the ring. OxBoLi

Kiss Me Again. Henry Blossom. Kiss me again! GoTF; TreFT

Kiss Me, Dear. John Dryden. Kiss'd him up and eas'd his pain. UnTE

Kiss Me Quick and Go. Silas S. Steele. To cheat surprise and prying eyes,/ Why, kiss me quick, and go! BLSo

The Kiss of God. G. Anketall "Woodbine Willie" Studdert-Kennedy. And then the waking to an everlasting Love. BLRP

The Kisse: A Dialogue. Robert Herrick. Love, honie yeelds; but never stings. CavP

Kisses. *Anonymous.* Another give me for that bite. WTO

Kisses. Thomas Campion. Kisses make men loth to go. ElL; OBSC

Kisses Desired. William, of Hawthornden Drummond. After one kiss, but still one kiss, my dear. EnLoPo

Kisses in the Train. D. H. Lawrence. Like a magnet's keeper/Closing the round. MoAB; MoBrPo

Kisses Loathesome. Robert Herrick. What should poking-sticks make there,/When the ruff is set elsewhere? CaPo; LiTL; OBSP; UnTE

Kissie Lee. Margaret Walker. On Talladega Mountain in the likker raids. BlSi; NMM

Kissin'. *Anonymous.* Puir folk couldna' hae it. FiBHP; GoTF; LiTL; TreF

Kissing. Fred Emerson Brooks. But makes a curtsey to the heart. PeD

Kissing. Edward, Lord Herbert of Cherbury The Kiss alone./So 'tis enough. EnLoPo; LiTL; ViBoPo

Kissing and Bussing. Robert Herrick. We busse our wantons, but our wives we/kiss. OAEP

Kissing Game. Bob Rosenthal. and you forever will be/the words and kisses/spinning the bottle. APU

Kissing Helen. Plato. Oh, cruel I, to intercept it! OBVE

Kissing Natalia. Eldon Grier. I remember now, and your mouth left the slightest aftertaste of/earth. NOBC

Kissing's No Sin. *Anonymous.* If it wasna plenty,/Puir folk wadna get it. HBV 1-2; UnTE

Kissing the Dancer. Robert Sward. words sweet words,/learn wings instead. CoPo

Kissing the Toad. Galway Kinnell. to love on, oh yes, to love on. DFT

Kit Carson's Last Smoke. Stanley Vestal. God send the West a many such/To make our country thrive! PoOW

Kit Carson's Ride. Joaquin Miller. Poor, burnt, blinded Pache. I love him.../That's why. BPAW; TreFS

Kit Hath Lost Her Key. *Anonymous.* So either go or stay. UnTE

Kit Logan and Lady Helen. Robert Graves. Weeping, they kiss; to the Squire's lasting shame,/Who broke the heart in both. HBMV

The Kitchen Chimney. Robert Frost. ...remind me/Of castles I used to build in air. EyDe

Kitchen Door Blues. Tennessee Williams. so for God's sake lock/that kitchen door! GrPl; OBAL

A Kitchen Memory. Roy Scheele. The only sound is the fan stirring the heat. Str

Kitchen Poem. Francis Scarfe. I give you my kitchen poem,/Immortal TRISTAN. EAS

A Kitchen Prayer. M. Petersen. May they find naught but joy and peace/ And happiness therein. STF

Kitchen Song. Jeannine Dobbs. Here's a slice/of sun and a song. Str

Kitchen Tables. David Huddle. mother and father sit at a small, round table. Str

Kitchen Window. Ruth N. Ebbers. And I shall conquer any dread of night. AMV-80

Kitchen Window. J. E. H. MacDonald. Or if for me they rise and pass. CaP

Kitchenette Building. Gwendolyn Brooks We think of lukewarm water, hope to get in it. BALP; BPo; FaBoWP; FF; NoP; PoNe

The Kitchie-Boy. *Anonymous.* Bat lettel did the old man keen/It was his ain kittchen-boy. BaBo; ESPB

A Kite. *Anonymous.* Whichever way I chanced to blow. SoPo; TiPo

The Kite. Harry Behn. When it flaps on a string/In the top of a tree. TiPo

Kite. Laura Jensen. ...a celebrity who tells/what it is like in the altitude. LCAP

The Kite. Adelaide O'Keeffe. And, like a flock of wild geese, sweeps its flowing tail. OxBChV

The Kite. Mark Strand. Slowly beginning to wake. NYBP

Kite Days. Mark Sawyer. O boy, O boy! I call that Spring! BrR; SiSoSe; TiPo

A Kite Is a Victim. Leonard Cohen. to make you worthy and lyric and pure. NOBC; SD

Kite Poem. James Merrill. And kissed and kissed, as though to escape on a kite. MP; TwCP

Kites. Michael Brownstein. She returns to Andre with the sails. ANYP

Kithairon sang of cunning Kronos. Korinna. Insanely he shouted and lobbed the rock/down on thousands of mortals below! BoWoP

A Kitten. Eleanor Farjeon. and he drops off to sleep/With one paw on his nose. TiPo

The Kitten. Ogden Nash. Eventually it becomes a/CAT. DFF; MoShBr

The Kitten and the Falling Leaves. William Wordsworth. Over wealthy in the treasure/Of her own exceeding pleasure! HBVY; PBBP; PCat

Kitty. Elizabeth Payson Prentiss. But she got away from kitty,/Long time ago. MoShBr

Kitty Bhan. Edward Walsh. And, pulse of my heart! what gloom is thine? ACP

The Kitty-Cat Bird. Theodore Roethke. –Or you'll end like the Kitty-Cat Bird. OBAL

Kitty, Kitty Casket. *Anonymous.* S'all full o' mud, I tossed it away. OuSiCo

Kitty Kline. *Anonymous.* Oh how I love that girl. AmFP

Kitty Morey. *Anonymous.* I titty-atty-ing 1-o. AmFP

Kitty Neil. John Francis Waller. "Dance light, for my heart it lies under your feet, love!" HBV 1-2

Kitty of Coleraine. Charles Dawson Shanly. The devil a pitcher was whole in Coleraine. HBV 1-2; MCCG; OnYI; StPo

Kivers. Ann Cobb. "The kiver's favoring your face to-day!" AmFN

The Kiwi Bird in the Kiwi Tree. Charles Bernstein. ...The first fact is the social body,/one from another, nor needs no other. APU

Klabauterwife's Letter. Christian Morgenstern. Your dutiful Klabauterfrau. WSC

Klaxon. James Reaney. Everyone wished to walk. AmC

Kleomedes. David Wright. "The last of the heroes was Kleomedes." NoAm

Kleptomaniac. Leonora Speyer. She did not want it, but she stole. AnAmPo; HBMV

The Klondike. Edwin Arlington Robinson. Looking each his own way to find the golden/river. PAH

Knapweed. Arthur Christopher Benson. Thou hast brave health and fortitude/To live and die alone! HBV 1-2

Kneading. Barbara Crooker. Think of wheatfields/rippling like oceans/and spreading/in the flat Kansas sun. SOTS

Knee Deep. Ted Joans. and I drown/in my own/juices/of/joy. GP

Knee-Deep in June. James Whitcomb Riley. I'll git down and waller there, And obleeged to you at that! AmePo; OHFP

Knee Lunes. Robert Kelly. after silence your legs/break open/the final measure CoPo

The Knee on Its Own. Christian Morgenstern. It's not a tent, it's not a tree,/A knee and nothing more. FaBoNo

The Kneeling Camel. Anna Temple Whitney. Assured that He no load too great/Will make thee bear. BLPA

Kneeling Here, I Feel Good. Marge Piercy. sweet black mother of our food/you will have the rest. NeAC

The Knell. Muhammad Al-Fituri. closed down the hatch of his vault/and slept. TTY

The Knife. Juan Gelman. with a kind of light like the knife that you used/ while it was in your hand. VWA

The Knife. Milton Kaplan. (Have mercy on us) we must use the/knife. TrJP

The Knife. Richard Tillinghast. ...old like rain/older than anything that dies can be. MAYP

The Knife. Jean Valentine. ...And someone will be at the door. LCAP

Knife and Sap. Kenneth Leslie. with warm tears for healing. PoL

The Knight. Rainer Maria Rilke. And play/And sing. AMV-81

The Knight and Shepherd's Daughter (A version). *Anonymous.* He had both purse and person too,/And all at his command. ESPB

The Knight and Shepherd's Daughter (B vers.). *Anonymous.* She proved to be the King's daughter,/And he but a blacksmith's son. BaBo; ESPB

The Knight and the Shepherd's Daughter. *Anonymous.* And he but a blacksmith's son./Ri fol diddle O day. AmFP; BaBo; ViBoFo

The Knight, Death, and the Devil. Randall Jarrell. And the body underneath it says: I am. CrMA; WeW

The Knight Fallen on Evil Days. Elinor Wylie. With whom the Angels deigned to measure swords! MoAmPo

The Knight in Disguise. Vachel Lindsay. Yea, ere we knew, Sir Philip's sword was drawn/With valiant cut and thrust, and he was gone. HBV 1-2

The Knight in the Wood. John Byrne Leicester Warren, Lord De Tabley. Feared to advance, feared to return–That's all. NCEP; NOBV; VLP

The Knight of Curtesy: The Eaten Heart. *Anonymous.* With woe and pain my life is spent. TrGrPo

A Knight of Ghosts and Shadows. Dunstan Thompson. And I imagine roses for a moment on the winter hills. NePA

The Knight of Liddesdale. *Anonymous.* "It is for the Lord of Liddesdale/ That I let all these teares downe fall." ESPB

The Knight of the Burning Pestle. Francis Beaumont and John Fletcher. And thither will we go now! OBS
But I would eat and drink of the best, and no work would I do. OBS
For him that was of men most true. AtBAP
The more he laughs, the more he may! TrGrPo

Knight Olaf. Heinrich Heine. I also bless the eldertree/Where you surrendered, dear, to me. HW

The Knight's Ghost. *Anonymous.* The ane a duke, the second a knight,/ And third a laird o lands sae free.' ESPB

The Knight's Leap. Charles Kingsley. For such a bold rider's soul. StPo

The Knight's Tomb. Samuel Taylor Coleridge. His soul is with the saints, I trust. CBEP; ERoP 1-2; FaBoCh; GN; LoGBV

Knight, with Umbrella. Elder Olson. Even for a cab. FiBHP

The Knight Without a Name. *Anonymous.* To seek a name in the seas. WiR

The Knightly Code. Eustache Deschamps. Thus, a knight like Alexander/ May you hope in time to be. CAW

Knights Errant. Sister Mary Madeleva. Love, thou wilt break my heart! CAW

The Knights to Chrysola. Rachel Annand Taylor. O Dream undying,/ Chrysola! OBVV

Knightsbridge of Libya. Sorley MacLean. ...but that/my darling should be crooked and a liar. NeBP

The Knitters. Padraic Colum. These knitters at their doors. SaC

Knock at the Doorie. *Anonymous.* Clean yir feeties,/An' walk in. OxNR

Knock on Wood. Henry Dumas. me and willie play togetherin/and we don't miss CNA; PoBA

Knocking at the Door. John Freeman. And she and I each listen in vain! HBMV

Knockmany. Richard Ryan. forward, clutching the twitching/shape, humming...humming... CIP

Knole. C. H. Sisson. Those others will die at this or the next year's turn/ And find the resurrection encased in sleep.' NOCV

The Knot. Tom Clark. who/has had a hand in it. HoAn

The Knot. Stanley Jasspon Kunitz. I shake my wings/and fly into its boughs. HAP

The Knot. Adrienne Rich. Little wonder the eye, healing, sees/for a long time through a mist of blood. CAPP

The Knot. Henry Vaughan. Which us in Him, and Him in us,/United keeps for ever. ISi

The knot which first my heart did strain. Sir Thomas Wyatt. Since well ye know this painful fit/Hath last too long. FCP; SiPS

The Know. Kathleen Fraser. this message is a conviction/from someone sprung into the joy of not knowing NPGG

Know It Is Christmas. Lois Snelling. Christmas...Christmas!/Timeless hour! BiCB

Know Thyself. Kenneth Burke. I'm flunking my Required Course/In Advanced Burkology. OBAL

Know Ye Not That Lovely River. Gerald Griffin. Know ye not that lovely river? OnYI

Know Ye the Land? George Gordon, Lord Byron. Are the hearts which they bear and the tales which they tell. MCCG

Knowest Thou Isaac Jogues? Francis W. Grey. As one who shunneth honor–"I am he." CAW

Knowing. Mary Coghill. without you all the grains will fall through. BrRo

Knowing I Live in a Dark Age. Milton Acorn. as a poem erases and rewrites its poet. NOBC

Knowledge. *Anonymous.* Is in the Book our mothers read. PoToHe

Knowledge. Louise Bogan. Trees make a long shadow/And a light sound. HBMV

Knowledge. Nina Cassian. No one fears me/except Error,/who is everywhere. BoWoP

Knowledge. Harold M. Grutzmacher. As I rested and gathered and waited/For another time, another chance. AMV-81

Knowledge, Acquaintance. John Skelton. For I have gravyd her wythin the secret wall/Of my trew hart, to love her best of all! NCEP

Knowledge after Death. Henry Charles Beeching. And we, being they, are still ourselves made whole. OBVV

Knowledge and Reason. Sir John Davies. But read not those which in our hearts are writ. OBSC

Knowledge of Age. Margaret Avison. Anatomist, make distinct this bone from the/Bone of the uncorrupted dead. PeCV

The Knowledge of Light. Henry Rago. Answering a child's candor/Beyond the child's PoCh; VGW

The Knowledge That Comes Through Experience. Jane Cooper. It seems to me I may be capable/Once I'm a skeleton, of love and wars. NMM

The Knowledgeable Child. Leonard Alfred George Strong. And, where they've children, nobody/Will let me next or nigh them/For fear I'll say good-bye to the OBMV

Knowlt Hoheimer. Edgar Lee Masters. Bearing words, "Pro Patria.'/What do they mean, anyway? OxBA

Known. Joel Dailey. When that butt/goes out/the World ends, O.K.? APU

The Known Soldier. Kenneth Patchen. That men might not live? WaaP

The Known World. Brewster Ghiselin. There is no jungle, sighed the striped mind. MoVE

Knoxville Girl. *Anonymous.* Because I murdered that Knoxville girl,/The girl I loved so well. FSW

Knoxville, Tennessee. Nikki Giovanni. not only when you go to bed/and sleep BlSi; BPo; CNA; PAI; PoBA; SO

Koala. Alan Ross. Sun-doped and happy, a gnawed twig in your paw like/ a pen. BoAnP; OBTV

Kob Antelope. *Anonymous.* Your neck seems long, long/To the covetous eyes of the hunter. WTO

Kochia. Thomas Hornsby Ferril. They are not wonder. NePoAm-2

A Kodak; Tregantle. Horatio Brown. And I thanked the God that made him and the land and sea and me. PeHV

Koheleth. Louis Untermeyer. While any dog living/Outroars a dead lion. TrJP

Kohoutek. Richard Ryan. A faint odour of bone/Withers quickly, my brain is stone. CIP

Koina ta ton Philon. John Addington Symonds. Like dews that drop on hills unknown,/To feed a lordly river. OBVV

Kojiki: Metal Hoe Hill. *Anonymous.* How I would dig it up! HW

Koko. Ann Downer. not knowing a word for zebra. SUW

Kol Nidra. Joseph Leiser. Breathing but the breath of ages. AA; TrJP

The Kola Run. *Anonymous.* Up our duff, Jack, for spewing up our duff, Jack. OBSS

Kolendy for Christmas. *Anonymous.* And thou, His Mother, His weeping calm. CAW

The Kona Sea. *Anonymous.* Your tabu is gone! your holy of holies invaded!/Broke down by a stranger! WTO

The Koocoo. *Anonymous.* At last, kooke, kooke, kooke; six kookes to one koo. GBP

Kookaburra. *Anonymous.* Stop! Kookaburra, stop! Kookaburra,/Leave some there for me. FSW

Kopis'taya. Paula Gunn Allen. ...Let's dance/the dance of feathers, the dance of birds. STE; TWSS

Kora for March 5th. Lewis MacAdams. Dana/and me/in wet fear/walking to the parking lot/gray lines of/soaked cars. ANYP

Kore. Robert Creeley. "O love,/where are you/leading/me now?" ConAP; CoPo; InPS; NMP; PAI

Kore. Ezra Pound. And wept, and weep until she come again. HBV 1-2; LoBV

Korea. Vincent Buckley. And Eve with cities tumbling from her flesh? BoAV

Korea Bound, 1952. William Childress. the pale, amorphous masks of prisoners,/whose lack of freedom guar- antees their lives. AmFN

A Korean Woman Seated by a Wall. William Meredith. Shiver the porcelain fable to green shards. NePoEA

Korf's Clock. Christian Morgenstern. time (as Korf intended)/neutralizes time. FaBoNo

Korf's Enchantment. Christian Morgenstern. Kidnapped from Odeliseluse/ To a New World in air.... WSC

Korf's Joke. Christian Morgenstern. smiling sweetly like a well-fed baby. ELU

Koskiusko. Samuel Taylor Coleridge. In the mere wilfulness, and sick despair of soul! EnRP

KRAA. William Pitt Root. Above curve the dark glittering twin suns. SM

The Kraken. Alfred, Lord Tennyson. In roaring he shall rise and on the surface die. AmMo; CABA; NoP; OAEL 1-2; OBNC; OBRV; PoEL 1-5; SyP; VLP; WiR; WSC

Kral Majales. Allen Ginsberg. Thus I have written this poem on a jet seat in mid Heaven. GP; PoM

The Krankenhaus of Leutkirch. Richmond Lattimore. sit on the mushroom circles of the forest floor. NYBP

Kree. Armistead Churchill Gordon. Dat side de river, again I'll be/Wid my boy Kree. AA

Kreutzer Sonata. Ted Hughes. To need to corner all the meat in the world,/Even from your own hunger. FaBoMo

Kris Kringle. Clinton Scollard. We're glad to have Kris Kringle come. ChBR

Krishnakali. Rabindranath Tagore. her black gazelle eyes I have seen. ACV

Kriss Kringle. Thomas Bailey Aldrich. Dropped a handful of flakes in the oriole's empty nest. HBVY

The Kropotkin Poems (excerpt). Phyllis Webb. in Adam's garden/he plants all his blood. NOBC

Ku Kluck Klan. Lawrence Gellert. Ku Kluck Klan, Ku Kluck Klan,/ Lowest down creeper in de lan'. TrAS

Ku Klux. Madison Cawein. And for a word too much men oft have/died. AA; PAH

Ku Klux. Langston Hughes. And tell me you believe in/The great white race. BPo

Ku Li. Robin Hyde. And burnt in the immortal tiles forever. AnNZ

Kubla Khan. Samuel Taylor Coleridge. For he on honey-dew hath fed,/And drunk the milk of Paradise. AtBAP; AWP; BiP; BoLiVe; CH; DiPo; ELP; ERoP 1-2; ExPo; EyDe; FaBoBe; FaBoCh; FaBV; FaFP; FF; FiP; ForPo; FPL; GN; GoJo; GoTF; GTBS; HAP; HBV 1-2; HeIP; HoPM; InPK; InPo; InPS; InvP; LiTB; LoBV; LoGBV; MaC; MasP; MAT; MBW 1-2; MCCG; MyFE; NAWM 1-2; NIP; NOBE; NoP; OAEL 1-2; OAEP; OBEV; OBNC; OBRV; PAI; PoEL 1-5; PoPl; PoRA; PP; PPoe; PrIm; RoGo; SCV; SeCeV; SoSe; SyP; TEP; TreFS; TrGrPo; UnPo; ViBoPo; WeW; WHA; WSC

Kula...A Homecoming. Diane Mei Lin Mark. "United in strength." BrSi

Kum Ba Yah (Come By Here). Anonymous. O Lord, Kum ba yah. FSW

The Kumulipo: Birth of Sea and Land Life. Anonymous. The Time passes, this night of Kumulipo/Still it is night WTO

The Kumulipo: The Dawn of Day. Anonymous. Man spread abroad, man was here now/It was Day WTO

Kunai-Mai-Pa Mo. Ethel Anderson. And much afraid, much afraid,/Followed Mo through the shade. PoAu 1-2

Kyoto: March. Gary Snyder. And wake and feed the children/and grandchildren that they love. PPP

Kyran's Christening. Alden Nowlan. ...When the salt is put in her mouth she doesn't cry. NeAC

"Kyrie, so Kyrie.'. Anonymous. Deo gracias therto–alas, I go with chylde!/"Kyrieleyson." EnPo

Kyrielle. John Payne. All things must end that have begun. HBV 1-2

Kyrielle: Party Politics. Frederick T. Macartney. Society has to organize. NOAV

Kythans. Stewart McGavin. roun the pinnacles/mak kythans. PoSH

L

A la Bourbon. Richard Lovelace. Or like th' offended sky/Frown death immediately. CaPo

A la Claire Fontaine. Anonymous. And we would walk together/Lovers the same old way. FSW

La, La, La! Thomas M. Disch. Lie down, lie down, lie down NLV

A La Promenade. Paul Verlaine. With a shy pity pouting in the mouth. AWP; OBVE

Labor. Anonymous. Good God, we ha' bought it fair. PGD

Labor. Lucille Day. Outside the sky will clear./By noon/someone will be born. VWA

Labor and Capital: Impression. William Dean Howells. But they seemed to have frozen there ere they ran,/The Company's man. AmePo

Labor and Love. Sir Edmund Gosse. Labor and love! then fade without a sigh,/Submerged beneath the inexorable wave. AMV-81; HBV 1-2

Labor Day. Gary Pacernick. And Tom, the neighborhood maniac, hops the bus to/the Ohio State Fair. TAT

Labor Day. Marnie Pomeroy. To see such silver and gold on things/Makes us all richer than queens and kings. PoSC

Labor Not in Vain. Anonymous. In twenty years, the whole wide world/May look and see and know. STF

Labor of Fields. Elizabeth Jane Coatsworth. Once more, once more men gather in the hay. TiPo

The Laboratory. Robert Browning. But brush this dust off me, lest horror it brings/Ere I know it–next moment I dance at the King's! ATP; BoLiVe; OBEV; OBVV

The Laboratory Midnight. Reuel Denney. All the loam loaned to spine and ligament. ImOP; NePA

Laboratory Poem. James Merrill. Easy in the presence of her lover. InPK; MAT; MP; NePoEA-2; TwCP

The Laborer. Samuel Chimsoro. But the sweet taste of wine/Aging in the landlady's glass. WhB

The Laborer. Richard Dehmel. To be bold as the birds through the air that drive:/Only time! AWP

The Laborer. Jose-Maria de Heredia. In sunless fields of Erebus forlorn. AWP

Laborers of Christ! Arise. Lydia Sigourney. And the blessed gospel's saving health/Repay your arduous toil. AH

Laborers Together with God. Lucy Alice Perkins. Since I may work with thee! BLRP

Laboring and Heavy Laden. Jeremiah Eames Rankin. Here I fix my habitation,/In thy sheltering love at home. AH

The Labors of Hercules. Marianne Moore. that the German is not a Hun. AnAmPo; OxBA

The Labors of Thor. David Wagoner. And match her knee for knee, grunting like thunder. GP

Labour. M. Saint-Marthe. The sooner he'll behold the Promis'd Day. FaBoUs

Labour of the Brain, Ballad of the Body. Nicole Forman. God might suffocate/between these fingers. NMM

The Labourer in the Vineyard. Stephen Spender. Flesh filled with statue, as the grape with wine. NeBP

The Labouring Man. Anonymous. They can't do without the labouring man. OBET

The Labyrinth. W. H. Auden. Looked up and wished he were the bird/To whom such doubts must seem absurd. LiTA; NePA

The Labyrinth. Edwin Muir. ...I did not know the place. MoBrPo

Lac Courte Orielles: 1936. Phyllis Wolf. laying on his hairless chest/inches of it. STE

The Lace Curtains. Lewis MacAdams. I can still see her, patially./through the lace curtains streaming through the window. ANYP

Lace Tell. Anonymous. We'll have a pudding in half an hour. OBET

The Lacemaker (Vermeer). Anne Marx. Das Ding an sich is all of life,/a task to be dispatched. GoYe

Lachesis. Victor J. Daley. Me, and my dreams, and my life,/All into a worsted stocking. CBAP

Lachesis. Kathleen Raine. Who must about our necks the millstone bear. NYBP

Lachin Y Gair. George Gordon, Lord Byron. The steep frowning glories of dark Loch no Garr. OxBS

Lachlan Gorach's Rhyme. Anonymous. Follow through/The country dance. PoPle

Lachrimae. Anonymous. Feel not the world's despite. AtBAP

Lachrimae Amantis. Geoffrey Hill. "tomorrow I shall wake to welcome him." NOCV; NoP

Lachrymae. David Gascoyne. They are Thy tears which fall. AtBAP; BoW

Lack Wit. Anonymous. For the longer I live/The more fool am I. OxNR

Lackey Bill. Anonymous. For the dearest girl in all the world has gone square back on me. CoSo

The Lacking Sense. Thomas Hardy. For thou art of her clay. CMoP; PoEL 1-5

The Lacquer Liquor Locker. David McCord. In that lacquer liquor locker which a liquor lackey locked. FiBHP; InMe

Lacrimae Musarum. William Watson. Master who crown'st our immelodious days/With flower of perfect speech. HBV 1-2

Lacrimas; or, There Is a Need to Scream. K. Curtis Lyle. by a soundless crystal/of cocaine PoBA

Lad of Athens, faithful be. Emily Dickinson. All the rest is Perjury. FaBoEE

Lad of the Curly Locks. Anonymous. As I mind my father's house/At morning and at evening. KiLC

Lad's Love. Esther Lilian Duff. I picked them in a posy/And I offered it to you. HBMV

The Ladder. Gene Baro. rises a silken ladder/into the depthless air. NePoEA-2

The Ladder. Leonora Speyer. I kissed the foot that bruised me as it passed. HBMV; PG

The Ladder Has No Steps. Jorge Plescoff. the sun repeating/its tender warmth VWA

The Ladder of St. Augustine: The Heights. Henry Wadsworth Longfellow. But they, while their companions slept/Were toiling upward in the night. GoTF; TreF

The Ladies. Rudyard Kipling. For the Colonel's Lady an' Judy O'Grady/Are sisters under their skins! ALV; EnLit; GoTF; MoBrPo; TreFT

The Ladies' Aid. Anonymous. That men will get the toil and sweat, and the Ladies' Aid the Rest. PoLf

Ladies and Gentlemen This Little Girl. Edward Estlin Cummings. like Coney island in winter CMoP

Ladies' Eyes Serve Cupid Both for Darts and Fire. A. W. What better place can Love require,/Than that where grow both shafts and fire? OBSC

Ladies in the Dinin' Room. Anonymous. Kiss your darlin' honey. OuSiCo

The Ladies of St. James's. Henry Austin Dobson. ...Phyllida/Is all the world to me! HBV 1-2; PoRA

A Ladies Prayer to Cupid. Giovanni Battista Guarini. Well practis'd in love's schoole, let him within/Weare all his beard, and none uppon his chinn. OBVE

Ladies That Have Intelligence in Love. Dante Alighieri. Commend thou me to each, as doth behove. LiTW

Ladies' Voices. Gertrude Stein. Yes masked balls./Poor Augustine. SOTW

The Lads in Their Hundreds. Alfred Edward Housman. The lads that will die in their glory and never be old. ATP; CoBMV; MasP; MoBrPo; OxBTC; VLP

The Lads of the Village. Stevie Smith. Or upon any field of experience where pain makes patterns/the poet slanders. OBSP

The Lads of Wamphray. Anonymous. "For of a' the lads that I do ken,/ The lads o Wamphr BaBo; ESPB

Lady... Anonymous. Queen. OxNR

Lady. Ted Berrigan. Everything you are gone slightly mad./America. APU

The Lady. Elizabeth Jane Coatsworth. And take off your hats,/you filthy things! MaC

A Lady. Amy Lowell. Gather it up from the dust,/That its sparkle may amuse you. MAPA; MoAmPo

A Lady. W. D. Snodgrass. ...I know she wipes her hands. TW

The Lady A. L., My Asylum in a Great Extremity. Richard Lovelace. And hast but showed me how I may resign/Possession of those things are none of mine. CaPo

The Lady Again Complains. Henry Howard, Earl of Surrey. Do your good will to cure a wight that liveth in distress. SiPS

Lady Alice (A version). Anonymous. Sure never were seen such true lovers/before,/Nor eer will there be again. ESPB

Lady Alice (B version). Anonymous. Which never there was seen before,/ And it never will again. ESPB

Lady Alice (C version). Anonymous. And twisted and twined in a true-lover's/knot, which made all the parish admire. ESPB

Lady Alice (George Collins), I. Anonymous. And may you be as true to your love/As I have been to mine. AmFP

Lady Alice (George Collins), IV. Anonymous. So why not me, why not me for mine? AmFP

Lady and Crocodile. Charles Burgess. (Though only if you feel you must)/ begin your walk again.... NePoAm-2

The Lady and the Bear. Theodore Roethke. As he went on fishing his way. GoJo; NLV; SO

The Lady and the Dwarf-King. Anonymous. The seventh was her comfort, for he in time/Will surely avenge his father's crime. BaBo

Lady Anne Bathing. Anthony Delius. The tree, the peak and all beyond it shiver. PeSA

Lady April. Richard Le Gallienne. I love best thee–/Thou pretty pretty lady! YeAr

Lady Bates. Randall Jarrell. You're fast asleep, you're fast asleep. MiAP

Lady Byron's Reply to Lord Byron's Fare Thee Well. Anonymous. If thou canst–be happy still. BLPA

Lady Clara Vere De Vere. Alfred, Lord Tennyson. Pray Heaven for a human heart,/And let the foolish yeoman go. HBV 1-2

A Lady Comes to an Inn. Elizabeth Jane Coatsworth. Has forgotten those men and that beautiful bride. MoAmPo; SO; StPo

Lady Day. Padraic Fallon. No planet in your sunken house. NeIP

Lady Day in Harvest. Sheila Kaye-Smith. And light the way to our native town. ISi

Lady Diamond. Anonymous. For there never was man of woman born/Sae fair as him that is slain. BaBo; ESPB

A Lady Dying in Childbed. Robert Herrick. But so as still the mother's power/Lives in the pretty lady-flower. EG

Lady Elspat. Anonymous. Ye's get as mieckle o my free lan/As he'll ride about in a summer's/day.' BuBa; ESPB

Lady Feeding the Cats (excerpt). Douglas Stewart. And so she is, she is trembling with love and/power. BoAnP

Lady Flower. Anonymous. And never slight a soldier because he's so poor. BFSS

The Lady Fortune. Anonymous. Ne truste no man to this wele, the wheel it turneth so. HeIP; NIP

Lady Franklin's Lament (I). Anonymous. He's left his home to return no more. OBSS; ShS

Lady Franklin's Lament (II). Anonymous. Oh, Arctic seas, what you have sealed/At the judgment-day will be revealed! ShS

Lady Geraldine's Courtship. Elizabeth Barrett Browning. And I shall not blush in knowing that men call him lowly born. DTo

Lady Godiva. Edward Shanks. Then smiled as she thought that there had been one/And that Peeping Tom was better than none. HBMV

Lady, I Thank Thee. Anonymous. Reste and blisse gif thou me,/My levedy, then ich deye. OxBM

Lady in a Distant Face. James Welch. past for ladies up like smoke in narrow wind. AmPA

The Lady in Kicking Horse Reservoir. Richard Hugo. and their tongues are teasing oil from whales. CoAP; LCAP; NoP

The Lady in Love. Anonymous. Hoogh, quoth he. OxNR

The Lady in the Barbershop. Raphael Rudnik. She sweeps herself up into the line/Of darkness that is her discipline. NYBP

The Lady in the Pink Mustang. Louise Erdrich. I don't sell for nothing less. TWSS

The Lady in the Wood. Anonymous. Ich am a maide–that me ofthunche!/ Leef me were gome boute gile.' OxBM

The Lady Is a Tramp. Lorenz Hart. That's why the lady is a tramp! OBAL

Lady Isabel. Anonymous. But a' was for that ill woman,/In the fields mad she gaed. BaBo; ESPB

Lady Isabel and the Elf-Knight. Anonymous.
Lye ye here, a husband to them a'.' FaBoBa; OAEP
Your cage will be made of the glittering gold,/And hung on yon willow tree. FSW

Lady Isabel and the Elf-Knight (A vers.). Anonymous. "If seven king's-daughters here ye hae slain,/Lye ye here, a husband to them a'." BaBo; ESPB; ViBoFo

Lady Isabel and the Elf-Knight (B vers.). Anonymous.
And there they have buried false Sir John,/For fear he should be seen. BaBo
I called upon your pretty Caroline/For to drive the old cat ViBoFo

Lady Isabel and the Elf Knight (B version). Anonymous. She thanked God most cheerfully/The dangers she oercame. ESPB

Lady Isabel and the Elf Knight (H version). Anonymous. And where I gave a pickle befor/It's now I'll give you three.' ESPB

Lady Isabel and the Elf Knight (Pretty Polly). Anonymous. "And your nest shall be made of leaves of gold,/Instead of the green willow tree." AmFP

The Lady Isabella's Tragedy. Anonymous. And made the simple scullion boy/the heir to all his land. GBP

Lady Jane. Sir Arthur Thomas ("Q") Quiller-Couch. Difficult though its meter was to tackle,/I'm glad i wrote it. FiBHP; InMe

The Lady Jane: A Humorous Novel in Rhyme (excerpt). Nathaniel Parker Willis. 'Tis woman's love. This I believe. Amen. OBAL

Lady, Lady. Anne Spencer. Where the good God sits to spangle through. BlSi; PoBA

Lady Lazarus. Sylvia Plath. And I eat men like air. CAPP; ConAP; FaBoWP; HaCAP; MAT; NaP; NIP; NoAm; NOBA; NoP; PPoe; PrIm; TAP; VGW

Lady Lost. John Crowe Ransom. And her right home and her right passion. AnFE; MoAB; MoAmPo; TrGrPo; UnPo

Lady Love. Paul Eluard. Speak when I have nothing to say OBVE

Lady Luck. Ann Gottlieb. ...and we walk off arm in arm,/each other's windfalls, dodging the pigeons. NMM

Lady M. M—'s Farewell to Bath. Mary Wortley, Lady Montagu. John, bid the Coachman drive. CEP

Lady Maisry. Anonymous.
And the lord he died on Sunday next/Before the prayer begun. OBET
For my young lord is coming,/I hear his bugle blow. BaBo

Lady Maisry (A version). Anonymous. An the last bonfire that I come to,/ Mysel I will cast in.' BaBo; ESPB; OxBB; ViBoFo

Lady Maisry (B version). Anonymous. And mony wife be made a widow,/ And mony ane want their son.' ESPB

Lady Margaret. Anonymous. No, Little Margaret's in her cold black coffin/ With her pale face to the wall. FSW

Lady Maria, in You Merit and Distinction. Bieiris de Romans. for in you are gaiety and happiness,/and all good things one could ask of a woman. PeHV

Lady Moon. Richard Monckton, Lord Houghton Milnes. Lady Moon, Lady Moon, whom are you loving?/"All that love me." MoShBr; OxBChV

Lady Moon. Christina Georgina Rossetti. Wane, be at rest. OxBChV

Lady My Treasure. Sir Philip Sidney. O the fair nymph born to do women honour,/Lady my Treasure. GBL

Lady, of Anonymous Flesh and Face. J. V. Cunningham. I sit with beer and bourbon at this bar. HoPM

The Lady of Arngosk. Anonymous. "I winna gang wi you,' she said,/"Nor ony Highland loon.' ESPB

Lady of Carlisle. Anonymous. Saying, "Here is the prize that you have won." AmFP; FSW; OuSiCo

Lady of Castlenoire. Thomas Bailey Aldrich. Would seem cast in gentler mould, would seem full of love and spring. BeLS

Lady of Heaven. Guittone d'Arezzo. As nail from out a plank is struck by nail. CAW

A Lady of High Degree. Anonymous. My lady and love to be. AWP

Lady of Letters. Raymond F. Roseliep. and incarnate raptly, once again,/ the Word. ISi

Lady of Lidice. Fray Angelico Chavez. forever the lover/of every small town. ISi

The Lady of Life. Thomas Michael Kettle. I heard new feet sound in the statued porch/And salutations I had heard before. ACP

Lady of Miracles. Nina Cassian. No, there's just your cruelty circling/my head like a bright stinking halo. WPOW

Lady of O. James J. Galvin. O ineffable Lady of O. ISi

Lady of Peace: Cathedral: Honolulu.. Fray Angelico Chavez. And lay your leis where I lie,/and peace. ISi

The Lady of Shalott. Alfred, Lord Tennyson. God in his mercy lend her/grace,/The Lady of Shalott. ATP; BeLS; BLPL; DiPo; EnLit; FaFP; FiP; GN; GTBS; HBV 1-2; InPS; MaC; MaVP; MBW 1-2; MCCG; NOBE; OAEL 1-2; OAEP; OBEV; OBNV; OBRV; OBVV; SeCeV; TEP; TreF; VLP; WHA; WiR

Lady of Shrouding Hair. *Anonymous.* your throat so ringed about/it is in chains for certain... NOBI

The Lady of the Castle. John Hollander. ...hers is the/Linear kingdom. GP

Lady of the Ferry Inn. Gwerfyl Mechain. sing intimate songs/and pour the mead. BoWoP

The Lady of the Lake. *Anonymous.* No more we'll have to sigh and sob beneath the willow tree. ShS

The Lady of the Lake. Sir Walter Scott.

And for a father hear a child!/'Ave Maria!' EnRP; ISi

And morning dawn'd on Benvenue. EnRP

And now 'tis silent all–Enchantress, fare thee well! OAEP; ViBoPo

Ben-an heaved high his forehead bare. PoEL 1-5

But breathless all, Fitz-James arose. OxBS

But merrier were they in Dunfermline gray,/When all the bells were ringing. HBVY

Emblem of hope and love through future years. ViBoPo

Enchantress, wake again! ViBoPo

For at dawning to assail ye/Here no bugles sound reveille. OBRV; TrGrPo

Here's no war-steed's neigh and champing,/Shouting clans, or squadrons stamping. GN

Hunters watch so narrowly.' EnRP

Like the bubble on the fountain,/Thou art gone, and for ever! BSV; OBRV; TreFS; TrGrPo; WHA

Nor rush nor bush of broom was near,/To hide a bonnet or a spear. OBRV

"Roderigh Vich Alpine dhu, ho! ieroe!" EnRP; PoEL 1-5; ViBoPo; WHA

Sweet Marjorie's the word, and a fig for the vicar! NBM; ViBoPo

Time rolls his ceaseless/course. ViBoPo

The Lady of the Lambs. Alice Meynell. A shepherdess of sheep. GTBS; OBEV

The Lady of the Manor. George Crabbe. Tears, true as those, which, ere she found her grave,/The noble Lady to our sorrows gave.' NOBE; OBNC

The Lady of the Pearls (excerpt). Alexandre Dumas. It is what I shall be when you are there no more. TTY

The Lady Pitcher. Cynthia Macdonald. To make sure/She couldn't/Hold anything for long. Psk

The Lady Poverty. Alice Meynell. And slender landscape and austere. GTBS; NOBV; OBMV

The Lady Prayeth the Return of Her Lover Abiding on the Seas. *Anonymous.* That rather had to die in troth than live forsaken so. ElL; GBL

Lady Ralegh's Lament. Robert Lowell. Down and down; the compass needle dead on terror. OBSP

A lady red upon the hill. Emily Dickinson. As if the resurrection/Were nothing very odd! AA; BoNaP; HBV 1-2; OHIP

Lady "Rogue" Singleton. Stevie Smith. What I feel for the elephants and the miasmas/And the general view. FaBoWP; OBSP

The Lady's Complaint. John Heath-Stubbs. For after death there's a judgement due.' MP; TwCP

The Lady's Diary. Charles Dibdin. And Monday morn stepped in a chaise/and ran away with Captain Clackit. NOEC

The Lady's Dressing Room. Jonathan Swift. Such gaudy Tulips rais'd from Dung. ErPo; NCEP; NoP; TEP

The Lady's-Maid's Song. John Hollander. For though we throw the dog his bone/He wants it back with interest. LiTM; MP; NePoEA; TW; TwCP

A Lady's Prayer to Cupid. Thomas Carew. ...let him within/Wear all his beard, and none upon his chin. CaPo; OBSP

The Lady's Receipt for a Beau's Dress. *Anonymous.* He's not one jot better than monsieur Pantin. CoMu

The Lady's Resolve. Mary Wortley, Lady Montagu. He comes too near that comes to be denied. BoWoP; OBSP

The Lady's Song. John Dryden. When Pan, and his Son, and fair Syrinx, return. LoBV; SeCeV

The Lady's Song in Leap Year. *Anonymous.* While you and I, diddle diddle, keep the bed warm. GBP

The Lady's Third Song. William Butler Yeats. All the labouring heavens sigh. FaBoTw

The Lady's Yes. Elizabeth Barrett Browning. And her yes, once said to you,/SHALL be yes for evermore. HBV 1-2; LiTL

Lady Sara Bunbury Sacrificing to the Graces, by Reynolds. Daryl Hine. Remark in dance on the shaven lawn/Rustics, Death and Sin. EyDe

A Lady Stood. Sir Dietmar von Aist. I grudge them not the men their arms caress. AWP; LiTW

Lady Tactics. Anne Waldman. not to be confused with sentimental/or sly PoM

Lady That Hast My Heart. Hafiz. So echoes of desire his bosom fill. LiTW

Lady, the Silly Flea. *Anonymous.* Were I a flea in bed I would not bite you,/But search some other way for to delight you. NCEP

A Lady Thinks She Is Thirty. Ogden Nash. How old is Spring, Miranda? PoPl

A Lady to a Lover. Roden and Wriothesley Berkeley Noel. And I in arms of thine, my friend,/In dying arms of thine! OBVV

The Lady Venetia Digby. Ben Jonson. The vision of Our Saviour, face to face... GoBC

Lady, Weeping at the Crossroads. W. H. Auden. Find the penknife there and plunge it/Into your false heart. MoVE

The Lady Who Loved a Swine. *Anonymous.* "Humph!" said he. OuSiCo

The Lady Who Offers Her Looking Glass. Matthew Prior. Venus, let me never see. CBEP; FaBoEE; NOEC; OBEV; OBSP; ViBoPo

A Lady with a Falcon on Her Fist. Richard Lovelace. And in that just dominion bred/In which the nobler is the she. CaPo

The Lady with Technique. Hughes Mearns. I love 'em when they get that way! FiBHP

The Lady with the Unicorn. Vernon Watkins. He looks, and she looks forth: there are no other eyes. LiTB; MP; TwCP

The Ladybird. *Anonymous.* And bring down eleven. GBP

Ladybird. Clive Sansom. No tenderer creature/Beneath the sky. GrPl

Ladybird! Ladybird! Emily Bronte. Ladybird! Ladybird! haste! fly away! OnUR

Ladybird, Ladybird. Mother Goose. And she crept under a pudding-pan. CBEP; SoPo

The Ladybirds. Edward Lucie-Smith. They are ungrateful. What a relief/Never to find expected grief! BoAnP

Ladybug. Robert Sund. "That don't give 'em/much of a chance, does it!" BoAnP

Ladybug's Christmas. Norma Farber. a ruby sequin/over his heart. PCh

Lafayette to Washington. Maxwell Anderson. ...Even so the kingdoms falter/and go down of themselves! PAL

The Lagoon. Ashton Greene. Learn, for who of us can ever make a sterile land a/lagoon? NePoAm

Lagoons, Hanlan's Point. Raymond Souster. moving with wonder/through the antechamber/of a waking world. NOBC

Laguna Blues. Charles Wright. Whatever it is, it bothers me all the time. GeTw

Laguna Perdida. Maynard Dixon. And the skull that lies by its salt-dry verge/Gleams pale to the death-pale moon. BPAW

Laid in My Quiet Bed. Henry Howard, Earl of Surrey. If, to their time, they reason had to know the truth of this. EnRePo; FCP; InvP

Laid Off. Francis Webb. Castles crane forward, puff themselves up, and watch/For the foolhardy twinkle of my match. BoAV

Laid on Thine Altar. *Anonymous.* But, gaining back my will, may find it thine. TrPWD

Laieikawai's Lament after Her Husband's Death. *Anonymous.* My heart is darkened/With love./Alas, my husband! WTO

Laila Boasting. Laila Akhyaliyya. when we wail with the first knives/of dawn. BoWoP

The Laily Worm and the Machrel of the Sea. *Anonymous.* An he has tane that gay lady,/An ther he did her burne. ESPB; InvP; LoBV; OxBB; PoEL 1-5

A Laird, a Lord. *Anonymous.* A stealer of beef. OxNR; SaC

The Laird O' Cockpen. Carolina Oliphant, Lady Nairne. But as yet there's nae chickens appear'd at Cockpen. BeLS; BSV; HBV 1-2; OBRV

The Laird o Drum. *Anonymous.* Then I'll tak back my word again,/And the Coutts will come and see me.' ESPB

The Laird o' Logie. *Anonymous.* The wanton laird of young Logie. CBEP; CH

The Laird o Logie (B version). *Anonymous.* And now the lady has gotten hir luve,/The winsom laird of Ochiltrie. ESPB

The Laird o' Ochiltree Wa's. *Anonymous.* And I hae tane awa' the bonniest lass/That is in a' the north countrie. OxBB

The Laird of Logie. *Anonymous.* And she's gotten a father to her bairn,/The wanton laird of Young Logie. BaBo; ESPB

The Laird of Wariston (A vers.). *Anonymous.* And sae brak out the feud/That gard my dearie die. BaBo; ESPB

The Laird of Wariston (B vers.). *Anonymous.*

And tie a handkerchief round my face,/That the people may not see.' ESPB

He had the wyte o his ain death,/And bonny lady"s overthrow." BaBo

The Lairdless Place. Kate Rennie Archer. Black Angus, wagging his tail by the white laburnums,/Greet their Laird's shade! GoYe

The Lairig. J. C. Milne. Dyod, fa kens fut wis in His croon! PoSH

Lais. Hilda ("H. D.") Doolittle. wishing to see that face and finding this. MoAmPo

Lais. Elaine Feinstein. a holy trimmer in this Protestant city:/you cannot hide the evidence of grace. FaBoWP

Lais to Aphrodite. Edwin Arlington Robinson. And what I am I will not see. FaBoEE

Lak of Stedfastnesse. Geoffrey Chaucer. And wed thy folk agein to stedfastnesse. AWP

The Lake. Matthew Arnold. And let the peaceful be! CBEP

A Lake. Thomas Lovell Beddoes. A lake/Is a river curled and asleep like a snake. NOBV

The Lake. Louis O. Coxe. ...one dark more to coil/Around them, perfect still until the last. MoVE; NYBP

The Lake. Ted Hughes. Battering it to death with sticks and stones. FaBoTw; NYBP

The Lake. Edgar Allan Poe. An Eden of that dim lake. OBRV

Lake. R. A. Simpson. ...and soon his line/Is holding the lake exactly. CBAP

The Lake. James Stephens. And a mad moon glared at Him. AnEnPo; MoBrPo

The Lake. John Banister Tabb. To clasp in love's captivity,/And keep them one–is mine. AmP

The Lake above Santos. Keith Wilson. Over buried, drowned Santos, Hill/Town, a moon rises. GP

Lake Chelan. William Stafford. where what comes finds a brim gravity exactly requires. BiP; NaP

Lake Chemo. James Wilton Rowe. Outshining in brilliance the rays of the sun. AmFP

The Lake: Coda. Tom Clark. And lights rising throne on throne HoAn

Lake Harriet: Wind. Laurie Taylor. cares nothing/for the flicker of my warmth. AMV-81

Lake Harvest. Raymond Knister. And diamonds and pieces of a hundred rainbows are strown/around. PeCV

The Lake in the Sky. John Haines. ...the light/from the ring on your finger darkens... LCAP

The Lake Isle. Ezra Pound. ...profession of writing,/where one needs one's brains all the time. CABA; CrMA; FaBoCo; HBV 1-2; OBSP; PoA

The Lake Isle of Innisfree. William Butler Yeats. I hear it in the deep heart's core. BoC; BrPo; CMoP; CoBMV; DiPo; FaBoPa; FaBoPP; FaBV; FaFP; FaPoR; FPL; GoTF; GTBS; InPK; InPS; LiTM; MBW 1-2; MCCG; MoAB; MoBrPo; NoAm; NOBE; NoP; OAEP; OBEV; OBVV; OnYI; OxBTC; PAI; PoPl; PoRA; PrIm; RoGo; TEP; TreF; TrGrPo; VLP; WeW; WHA

Lake Leman. George Gordon, Lord Byron. –'twould disarm/The spectre Death, had he substantial power to harm. OBNC

Lake Michigan Blues. Yank (James) Rachel. Says I hope some day my/baby want to cross Lake Michigan too BluL

Lake, Mountain, Tree. Denis Glover. –Lake, mountain, tree,/sings Harry. AnNZ

The Lake of Gaube. Algernon Charles Swinburne. If the soul that we live by never, For aught that a lie saith, fear. OAEL 1-2; VLP

The Lake of the Caogama. Anonymous. But the darndest lake among them is the lake of the Caogama. WTO

The Lake of the Dismal Swamp. Thomas Moore. And paddle their white canoe! BLPA

Lake-Song. Jean Starr Untermeyer. The fertile tears of women/That water the dreams of men. AnAmPo; HBMV; TrJP

Lake Success. Robert Conquest. Fall in Long Island. OxBC

Lake Superior. Samuel Griswold Goodrich. Deems as a bubble all your waves! AA

Lake Superior. Lorine Niedecker. We watched a gopher there. FaBoWP

Lake Walk at New Year's. Leigh Perez-Diotima. Hand in hand we begin the walk across Wonder Lake/walking on water. AMV-81

The Lakers: Prologue (excerpt). James Plumptre. The natives by the name of Lakers call. NOEC

Lakes. W. H. Auden. Just reeling off the names is ever so comfy. NePA; NePoAm

Lakeshore. F. R. Scott. Watching the whole creation drown/I muse, alone, on Ararat. NOBC; OBCV

Lakeside Incident. Robin Skelton. Only a tattered rag/of blue hangs on a thorn. NOBC

Lakshmi. Padraic Fallon. On her right hand it rides, and earth/Turns quietly on the spindle. NOBI

Lalai (Dreamtime). Sam Woolagoodjah. Her name is Dragon Fly. NOAV

Laleham: Matthew Arnold's Grave. Lionel Pigot Johnson. But he, who loved them, is at rest. FaBoPP

Lalela Zulu. Anonymous. Ha! they finished them off! PeSA

Lalique. Hal Porter. iris, jonquil, fragile, spare,/pricked on silk and champagne air. PoAu 1-2

Lalla Rookh. Thomas Moore.
The antelope, whose feet shall bless/With their light sound thy loneliness. BIrV
Of lovers' hearts, when newly blest,/Too newly to be quite at rest! OBNC
Oh misery! must I lose that too?... SpRo
Sublime, from that valley of bliss to the world! TEP
They'll weep for the Maiden who sleeps in this wave. OBNC
Think, think what a heaven she must make of Cashmere! EnRP

Laly, Laly. Mark Van Doren. Laly, Laly,/So young were we. SO

The Lama. Ogden Nash. There isn't any/Three-l lllama. FaBoCh; FiBHP; PV

Lamarck Elaborated. Richard Wilbur. The voice of Sirens gave us vertigo. AP; NePoEA

The Lamb. William Blake. Little Lamb, God bless thee! BLPL; BoLiVe; CAW; DiPo; EaLo; EBCP; EnPE; ExPo; FaBoBe; FaBoCh; GoJo; GoTF; HBV 1-2; HeIP; InPS; LiTB; LoBV; LoGBV; NAWM 1-2; NIP; NoP; OAEL 1-2; OBEC; OxBChV; OxBoCh; PAI; PoPl; SBVL; SeCeV; SoSe; SUS; TEP; TrCP; TreF; TrGrPo; TRV; UnPo; WGRP; WHA

Lamb. Michael Dennis Browne. Saw a lamb being born! NU

The Lamb. Keith Wilson. I walked, my face roughening in the cold. Psk

The Lamb-Child. John Banister Tabb. For love of her, each mother-sheep/And baby-lamb He blessed. ChBR

The Lamb Was Bleating Softly. Juan Ramon Jimenez. I opened the barn door to see if/He was there./He was! NU; PCh

Lambeth Lyric. Lionel Pigot Johnson. "Have at the Faith!" each cries: "good bye till our/Next merry meeting!" NOBV

Lambkin. Anonymous. And the false nurse will be burned, such a villain is she.' OBET

Lambs Frolicking Home. Fred Lape. like pollen from the stamens of a flower. BoAnP

The Lambs of Grasmere, 1860. Christina Georgina Rossetti. Yet not forget this flooded spring/And scarce-saved lambs of Westmoreland. FM

The Lambs on the Green Hills Stood Gazing on Me. Anonymous. For that's the best way to forget her. AnIV

Lame Angel. Donald Finkel. a worm rehearsing perpetually the life of a butterfly/but a worm to the end VWA

A Lame Beggar. John Donne. "To stand or move!" If he say true, he lies. FF

The Lame One. Sherwood Anderson. My city is a murmur of voices coming out of a pit. AnAmPo

The Lame Soldier. Anonymous. Go sail with your soldier, he'll find you a home. OuSiCo

The Lamed-Vow. Rose Auslander. We do not know them/we never recognize the/36 just men VWA

Lament. Yehuda Amichai. makes the circle endless/and godless. VWA

A Lament. Margaret Avison. The viscera still shine/with sun, by weed and silver riverflow. HAP

Lament. Laurence Binyon. Frail violets, freshly born. MoVE

Lament. Gelett Burgess. Get off the stage ere we begin our booing! InMe

Lament. Brenda Chamberlain. My man is a bone ringed with weed. NeBP; WPOW

A Lament. William, of Hawthornden Drummond. Moeliades sweet courtly nymphs deplore/From Thule to Hydaspes' pearly shore. LoBV

A Lament. Wilfred Wilson Gibson. Nor feel the heart-break in the heart of things? MMM; OxBTC

Lament. Gudmundur Gudmundsson. But in by the dark hearth-fire/My hopes lay ashen and dead. LiTW

Lament. Matangi Hauroa. Your name will live/In this place/And perhaps in this poor house of proverbs here. WTO

Lament. Dorothy Livesay. So your hand; your dead hand, my dear. CaP

Lament. Denis Florence Maccarthy. And sorrow whistles/O'er desert plains. OBVV

Lament. Edna St. Vincent Millay. Life must go on;/I forget just why. DL; PoPl

Lament. Yonathan Ratosh. at the crossroads paved/with bones. VWA

Lament. Rainer Maria Rilke. in the sky at the end of the beam of light... PoPl; TrJP

Lament. George Roberts. ...and my heart is the reverse of yours/sister it is growing smaller GOYP

Lament. Anne Sexton. ...the sun/unaccustomed to anything else/goes all the way down. ConAP

A Lament. Percy Bysshe Shelley. No more–O never more! AtBAP; ChRP; EG; EnLi 1-2; GTBS-P; LoBV; NOBE; OAEP; OBRV; PoRA; TEP; TreFT; TrGrPo; WHA

Lament. Joseph Stroud. No need to weep NPGG

Lament. Dylan Thomas. And all the deadly virtues plague my death! ErPo; MasP; PPP

Lament. Edward Walsh. And O, my wreck'd hope,/That the cold earth's your dwelling! OBVV

Lament. William Carlos Williams. with long nose and clear blue eyes,/secure... VGW

A Lament: 1547. Alexander Scott. I say no moir. CH

Lament after Her Husband Bishr's Murder. Al-Khirniq. How could they recover from the sword? BoWoP

Lament City. Thomas Lux. we love it so much! AmPA

Lament for a Cricket Eleven. Kenneth Allott. When shall I burn this negative/And hang the receiver up on grief?' OxBTC

Lament for a Dead Lover. Siraad Haad. The dates on their way from Basra cut off by the seas. WTO

Lament for a Husband. Anonymous. You will sing out for yams,/the food of the living. BoWoP

Lament for a Poor Poet. Myles Connolly. For they, at least, remembered Him/While other songs forgot. CAW

Lament for a Sailor. Paul Dehn. But you are the quietest fish in the sea. WaP

Lament for a Warrior. *Anonymous.* Will the earth's womb not be filled,/ will the grave have never done! PeSA

Lament for Adonis. Bion. "Woe for Cytherea, for Adonis' beauty dead!" LiTW

Lament for Adonis. Elizabeth Barrett Browning. And weep new when a new year refits thee for weeping. ATP

Lament for Apirana Ngata. Arnold Reedy. But you have gone, old one, into the night–alas. WTO

The Lament for Art O Laoghaire (excerpt). Eibhlin Dubh O'Connell. –ere he enter that school/not for study or for music/but to bear clay and stones. NOBI

The Lament for Art O'Leary. *Anonymous.* But to prop the earth and the stone. AnIL; KiLC

Lament for Azazel. Francis Landy. They cast lots between blood and blood./Both are for Azazel. VWA

Lament for Banba. Egan O'Rahilly. For the still proud people of Banba! AnIV; AWP

Lament for Barney Flanagan. James Keir Baxter. And let light perpetual shine upon him. NoP

Lament for Better or Worse. Gene Baro. The bats have fled the tower. Now hoots the sleepless/hour. NePoEA-2

A Lament for Bion. Moschus. Ah, and had my song power, I too to Pluto had sung. AWP; EnLi 1-2

Lament for Captain Paton. John Gibson Lockhart. For it ne'er shall see the like of Captain Paton no mo! OBRV

Lament for Chaucer. Thomas Hoccleve. O maister, maister, God thy soule reste! OBEV

Lament for Chaucer and Gower. Thomas Hoccleve. To thee, in faith I can no nerther seye:/His creatures mosten thee obeye. OxBM

Lament for Corc and Niall of the Nine Hostages. Torna. Mourns Lea Mogha, ruined too! OnYI

Lament for Culloden. Robert Burns. That ne'er did wrang to thine or thee.' CBEP; GTBS; GTBS-P; HBV 1-2; OBEV

Lament for Daphnaida. Edmund Spenser. Weep Shepheard weep, to make mine undersong. FiP

Lament for Fearghal Ruadh. Tadhg O'g O Huiginn. –the wall of learning is broken. NOBI

Lament for Glasgerion. Elinor Wylie. To watch me wither and grow old. AmLP; PoA

Lament for Ignacio Sanchez Mejias. Federico Garcia Lorca. and I remember a sad breeze through the olive trees. LiTW It was five in the shadow of the afternoon! OBVE

Lament for Lost Lodgings. Phyllis McGinley. I'll motor no more, Miranda. NYBP; SpRo

Lament for Mafukuzela. *Anonymous.* Mofukuzela, son of Dube, hero of heroes! WTO

The Lament for O'Sullivan Beare. *Anonymous.* With the red wounds of fear/Of Muirtach Og/Our O'Sullivan Beare! AnIV

Lament for Pasiphae. Robert Graves. Dying sun, shine warm a little longer! FaBoTw

Lament for Richard Rolston. Osbert Sitwell. On the grass, thinking of the sea always, of the ship plunging. ChMP

Lament for Sean. D. J. O'Sullivan. Strong, strong, strong! NeIP

Lament for Sean MacDermott. Seumas (James Starkey) O'Sullivan. And your hand even now grips mine as though there never/were a grave. AnIV

Lament for Taramoana. Makere. Then shall Venuku eat men/Till none remain. WTO

Lament for the Alamo. Arthur Guiterman. Pay your debt of blood and tear/For those who died in the Alamo! AmFN

Lament for the Cuckoo. Alcuin. Sometimes remember us. Love, fare you well. PeHV

Lament for the Death of Eoghan Ruadh O'Neill. Thomas Osborne Davis. But we're slaves, and we're orphans, Eoghan!–why did you/die? AnIv; IrPN; NOBI; OnYI; OxBI

Lament for the Death of Thomas Davis. Sir Samuel Ferguson. And if God grant this, then, under God, to Thomas Davis/Let the greater praise belong! AnIV; BIrV; IrPN; NBM; NOBI; OnYI; OxBI

Lament for the Dorsets. Al Purdy. After 600 years/the ivory thought/is still warm. NoP

Lament for the European Exile. Avner Strauss. Atonement for your blood/ At the hands of the world/That shed it. VWA

Lament for the Great Music (excerpt). Hugh" (Christopher Murray Grieve) MacDiarmid. Or a piper coming from far away? OxBTC

Lament for the Great Yachts. Patric Dickinson. Shamrock, Westward, Lulworth, Britannia. HaMV

Lament for the Makaris. William Dunbar. Timor mortis conturbat me. ACP; AtBAP; BSV; CBEP; EBEV; GoTS; NoP; OAEL 1-2; OAEP; OBEV; OxBS; PoEL 1-5; PP; ViBoPo

Lament for the Non-Swimmer. David Wagoner. They splash ashore, pretending to feel buoyant. DFF

Lament for the O'Neills. John Montague. The Flight of the Earls. CIP

Lament for the Poets: 1916. Francis Ledwidge. In Derry of the little hills. AnIV; AWP; OnYI; OxBI

A Lament for the Princes of Tyrone and Tyrconnel. *Anonymous.* And render light the chain that binds/Our fallen land! AnIV

Lament for the Woodlands. *Anonymous.* Shaun O'Dwyer of the Valley/ Your pleasure is no more. KiLC

Lament for Thomas MacDonagh. Francis Ledwidge. Lifting her horn in pleasant meads. AnIV; BIrV

Lament for Turlough O'Carolan. David Hopes. ...the wind's not come quiet/though the harper's gone who lied through it. SM

The Lament for Urien. Ernest Rhys. Thy brothr shall rise from his sleep in might. OBMV

The Lament for Yellow-Haired Donough. *Anonymous.* Not grudging any his share of it. KiLC

Lament in Autumn. Harold Stewart. But still we cling, and still regret, regret.... PoAu 1-2

Lament my loss... Sir Thomas Wyatt. And keep them free from all such pain and care. AAS; FCP

Lament of a Last Letter. Janet E. Harrison. tail, eyes...wings and from these letters flew. AMV-80

Lament of a Man for His Son. Mary Austin. What is my life to me, now you are departed! AWP; BPAW

Lament of a Mocking-Bird. Frances Anne Kemble Through the grim northern winter drear/and dark. AA; HBV 1-2

Lament of an Idle Demon. R. P. Lister. That men make hotter hells than ever he did. DBV; FiBHP; NOBL

Lament of Anastasius. William Bourne Oliver Peabody. Since thou art where the ills o live can/never reach thee more. AA

The Lament of Edward Blastock. Edith Sitwell. Could I but know she was not this,–not this! OBMV

Lament of Granite. David Ross. Than granite remembered of man. PG

Lament of Hsi-Chun. Hsi-chun. Would I were a yellow stork/And could fly to my old home! BoWoP

The Lament of Maev Leith-Dherg. *Anonymous.* On the Hill of Cucorb's Fate/High his Cromlech raise. OBWP; OnYI

The Lament of Saint Ann. *Anonymous.* For even this earth bears its fruits in due season and blesses/Thee,/O Lord! CAW

The Lament of the Border Widow. *Anonymous.* Wi' ae lock o' his yellow hair/I'll chain my heart for evermair. CH; GBP; HBV 1-2; OxBB

The Lament of the Damned in Hell. Edward Hilton Young. When I have rav'd ten thousand years in fire,/Ten thousand thousand, let me then expire.' OxBoCh

The Lament of the Flowers. Jones Very. To glad the heart and save from harm. MAmP; NOBA; OxBA

Lament of the Flutes. Christopher Okigbo. Sing a new note. PBA

Lament of the Frontier Guard. Li Po. And we guardsmen fed to the tigers. AP; CoBMV; OBVE; OBWP; VGW; WaaP

Lament of the Irish Emigrant. Helen Selina Sheridan. And the springin' corn, and the bright May morn,/When first you were my bride. HBV 1-2; OBVV

Lament of the Jewish Women for Tammuz. Charles Reznikoff. Now they are scattered over the pavements–/the delicate skeletons of the leaves. VWA

Lament of the Mangaire Sugach. Andrew Magrath. Receive him, like Peter, to dwell in THY HOUSE at last! OnYI

Lament of the Master of Erskine. Alexander Scott. Fare weel and have gude nicht:/I say no more. BSV; GBL

Lament of the Virtues and Verses on Account of the Death of Don Guido. Antonio Machado. and the Andalusian gentleman/on his best behaviour. OBVE

The Lament of the Voiceless. Laura Bell Everett. They mourn for you, your sons who never were. PGD

Lament over the Ruins of the Abbey of Teach Molaga. James Clarence Mangan. Resounded in mine ears like to a dirge/The roaring of the wave. NOBI

A Lament to My Mother. Guy C. Z. Mhone. Black mother, I still am/One of the soil. WhB

Lament to Nana of Erech. *Anonymous.* Oh queen, as in thy chamber thou didst perish, so do/thou thyself make them ashamed. LiTW

Lament while Descending a Shaft. *Anonymous.* I envy the man with the hoe. AmFP

Lament, with Flesh and Blood. Sandra McPherson. Still you brood in the lake like wild rice. SM

Lament: "Within my bosom stirs once more tonight." Princess Zeb-un-Nissa. And, wing-clipt and imprisoned, my heart's bird/Flutters against his barriers, wild for flight. LiTW

The Lamentable Ballad of the Bloody Brook. Edward Everett Hale. And never shall the Bridegroom return to his Bride,/From that dark and cruel Day,–cruel Day! HBV 1-2; PAH

A Lamentable Case. Charles Hanbury-Williams. Or Chloe in the morning. ErPo; UnTE

A Lamentation.   Thomas Campion.   Since more him none shall see.   CH; OHIP

Lamentation.   Nissim Ezekiel.   And let my leaf be green with love/And let me live.   VWA

A Lamentation.   James Clarence Mangan.   Or was't but the night-wind sweeping/Down the hollow glen?   IrPN

Lamentation.   Harold LaMont Otey.   knowing when to respect the anguish of timeless/time.   LFAC

A Lamentation.   Carl Rakosi.   you, wretched man,/are already on your way into the earth.   VWA

The Lamentation for Celin.   Anonymous.   "Let me kiss my Celin, ere I die!– Alas! alas for/Celin!"   AWP

The Lamentation of Chloris.   Anonymous.   For you cannot deny but my shepherd's to blame.   CoMu

Lamentation of Nippur.   Anonymous.   When the word of Enlil rushes forth, eye cannot be-/hold it.   LiTW

The Lamentation of the Old Pensioner.   William Butler Yeats.   I spit into the face of Time/That has transfigured me.   HAP; InPK; NoAm; PPON; TW; VLP; WeW

A Lamentation on My Dear Son Simon Who Dyed of the Small Pox...   John Saffin.   But that which Crowneth all the Rest/In his own language better is Exprest.   SCAP

Lamentation on the Death of the Duke of Wellington.   Anonymous.   To see him laid down in his tomb will be a solemn sight.   OBET

Lamentations.   Alter Brody.   The bits of a photograph lie on the/dresser...   TrJP; VWA

Lamentations.   Louise Gluck.
   Above the churned reeds, the leaves let go/a slow moan of silver.   MAYP
   the earth, that first time/seen from the air. BoWoP; HaCAP; MAYP
   Far away, in the void that he had shaped,/he turned to his angels. MAYP
   there was no authority above them. MAYP

Lamentations.   Siegfried Sassoon.   Such men have lost all patriotic feeling.   OBSV

Lamentations of an Au Pair Girl.   Susan Feldman.   in short: the poet.   AmPA

The Lamenting Maid.   Anonymous.   And I'll wear it for my dear Johnson's sake.   OBET

Lamenting Tauaba.   Laila Akhyaliyya.   while one dove on a branch mourns/or birds fly.   BoWoP

Lamia.   John Keats.
   And, in its marriage robe, the heavy body wound.   CABL; ERoP 1-2; OAEP
   Might fancy-fit his brows, silk-pillowed at his ease. SeCePo
   Shut from the busy world of more incredulous. CABL

Lamkin (A version).   Anonymous.   But sairer grat the nourice,/when she was tied to the stake.   BaBo; CBEP; ESPB; FaBoBa; OxBB; ViBoFo

Lamkin (B vers.).   Anonymous.   For Falseness and Lamkin/Deserved well to die.   BaBo

Lamkin (C vers.).   Anonymous.   And the false nurse was burnt/To a stake standing by.   AmFP; BaBo; ESPB

Lamkin (K version).   Anonymous.   And see your mother's heart's blood,/so freely running.   ESPB

Lamorna Cove.   William Henry Davies.   Each furious thought that's driving through my brain/Screams in its fresh young wonder and delight.   BrPo

The Lamp.   Sarah Pratt McLean Greene.   When thou shalt hand, so tremblingly,/Thy empty lamp to Him.   AA

The Lamp.   Sara Teasdale.   Knowing how well on earth your love sufficed me,/A lamp in darkness.   MoLP

The Lamp.   Charles Whitehead.   Alas! to know that the consuming mind/Shall leave its lamp cold, ere the sun appear.   OBEV; OBVV

The lamp burns sure, within.   Emily Dickinson.   Unconscious that the oil is out/As that the slave is gone!   LiTA

The Lamp in the West.   Ella Higginson.   Dear God, wilt thou not set a lamp/Low in the West for me?   AA; HBV 1-2

The Lamp Now Flickers.   Alfred Grunewald.   See how you wrote it once in sand/And soon no trace of it remains.   VWA

The Lamp of Poor Souls.   Marjorie Pickthall.   Cling to His arms and sleep, and sleeping, dream,/And dreaming, look for me.   HBV 1-2

The Lamp's Shrine.   Dante Gabriel Rossetti.   My heart takes pride to show how poor it is.   MaVP

The Lamplighter.   Seumas (James Starkey) O'Sullivan.   Before the chilly dawn can blight/The delicate frail buds of light.   BIrV; OxBI

The Lamplighter.   Robert Louis Stevenson.   O Leerie, see a little child and nod to him to-night!   FaFP; OxBChV; SaC; TreF

The Lamps Are Burning.   Charles Reznikoff.   in the morning, afternoon, and/evening–/be at ease in Zion.   TrJP

Lan Nguyen: The Uniform of Death 1971.   David Mura.   Who wears the uniform of death?   BrSi

Lancashire Born.   Anonymous.   Where they sup sour milk in a ram's horn.   GBP

Lancashire Lads.   Anonymous.   But we'll ne'ver forget sweet Manchester and the girls we leave/behind.   CoMu

The Lancashire Puritane.   Anonymous.   Hee is a bisconted Hypocrite.   CoMu

Lancashire Winter.   Tony Connor.   who, against pikes and burning brands,/built the future with bare hands.   OxBTC

Lancaster County Tragedy.   W. Lowrie Kay.   But he went the house cat in.   ShM

Lancelot.   Arna Bontemps.   Least of all in the day of falling fruit.   CDC

Lancelot and Guinevere.   Gerald Gould.   Where with him, with him, all the way,/Went the sad eyes of Guinevere.   HBV 1-2

Lancer.   Alfred Edward Housman.   Oh who would not sleep with the brave?   EnLit; InPS; MoBrPo; OBWP

The Lancet.   Denis Devlin.   Bear fruit of me.   NOBI

Land.   Carroll Arnett.   Without this/what is/worth doing.   VoR

The Land.   Struthers Burt.   But now, even more widely scattered lie our dead.   HBMV

The Land.   Rudyard Kipling.   For whoever pays the taxes, old Mus' Hobden owns the land.   MoBrPo; OnMSP

The Land.   Victoria Mary (Vita) Sackville-West.
   And the lapwings crying free above the plough.   PeHV
   Till each was both or either, and the soul/Was not afraid.   AtBAP

The Land behind the Wind.   David Wagoner.   There lay the wind at their feet like a pathway.   NPAW

The Land Called Scotia.   Donatus.   a people renowned in war and peace and faith.   NOBI

Land-Fall.   George M. Brady.   ...the tears of those/Who live between the breaking and the broken leaf.   NeIP

The Land-Mine.   George MacBeth.   If it shall come, will find me on my knees.   OBWP

A Land Not Mine.   Anna Akhmatova.   the secret of secrets is inside me again.   NU

The Land o' the Leal.   Carolina Oliphant, Lady Nairne.   In the land o' the leal.   GTBS; GTBS-P; HBV 1-2; MCCG; WBLP

The Land of Beginning Again.   Louisa Fletcher.   And never be put on again.   BLPA

The Land of Cockayne.   Anonymous.
   Thus he may to that land win.   MeEV
   Y-dight in stew ful swithe wel,/Powdred with gilofre and canel. OxBM

The Land of Cokaigne.   Anonymous.   Rich meat to princes and kings.   CAW

The Land of Cokaygne.   Anonymous.   Let's pray God that so it be/Amen, for holy Charity.   BIrV; NOBI; OAEL 1-2; OnYI

The Land of Counterpane.   Robert Louis Stevenson.   The pleasant land of counterpane.   BrPo; EBEV; FaBoBe; FaFP; GoTF; HBV 1-2; HBVY; NLV; NTCP; OxBChV; PoPl; SoPo; TreF

The Land of Dreams.   William Blake.   Above the light of the morning star.   BeLS; CH; OBRV

The Land of Dreams.   Henry Martyn Hoyt.   On wind-swept uplands, yearning toward the dawn.   HBMV

The Land of Heart's Desire.   Emily Huntington Miller.   "But I have entered in."   HBV 1-2

Land of Hope and Glory.   Arthur Christopher Benson.   God, who made thee mighty, make thee mightier yet.   FaPoR

The Land of Indolence.   James (1700-48) Thomson.   But whate'er smack'd of Noyance, or Unrest,/Was far far off expell'd from this delicous Nest.   OBEC

Land of Little Sticks, 1945.   James Tate.   ...forehead/against his forearm, leaning up against the barn.   MAYP

Land of My Heart.   William Dudley Foulke.   That thou shalt be a fitting messenger/To carry hope to all the sons of men.   PAL

Land of Nations (excerpt).   Gertrude Stein.   Climate and the affections. Jews quote that.   AtBAP

The Land of Story-Books.   Robert Louis Stevenson.   And go to bed with backward looks/At my dear Land of Story-books.   FaBoBe; HBV 1-2; HBVY; TiPo; TreFS

The Land of the Evening Mirage.   Anonymous.   In the land of the evening mirage.   WGRP

Land of the Free.   Sister Mary Honora.   ...guarding a costly orchid tuft,/plebeian in our land.   NePoAm-2

Land of the Free.   Arthur Nicholas Hosking.   Our lives we consecrate to thee, our guide the Might of Right.   BLPA; PAL

Land of the Free.   Archibald MacLeish.   We don't know/We're asking   AmFN; MoAB

Land of the Wilful Gospel.   Sidney Lanier.   And Fashion, in freedom, will die of the lie/in her face.   PAH

Land's End.   Stanton A. Coblentz.   Gods speak from the torn waves' droning eloquence.   BPAW; EtS

The Land That Is Not.   Edith Sodergran.   And there comes an answer: I am the one you love/and always shall love.   HW

The Land War.   Seumas (James Starkey) O'Sullivan.   And the sons have remembered their deeds/As the fields have remembered the corn.   OxBI

The Land Where Hate Should Die.   Denis A. McCarthy.   Of this great Land in which we live!   PGD

Land Where the Columbines Grow. Arthur J. Fynn. Softly sings where the columbines grow. PoOW

Landcrab. Margaret Atwood. face in the mirror,/my tiny nightmare. SoSe

Landed: A Valentine. Richard Howard. ...take/Soon the mouth out of my very words. PoA

Landeys. Anonymous. A trimmed tree/is no place for song birds. PBWP

Landfall. Anonymous. O spirit of the earth! The stranger humbly offers his/ heart as food for thee. WTO

The Landfall. James Dickey. That child, never touched by the rays of the sun,/Might rise, because of love. PoA

Landfall in Unknown Seas. Allen Curnow. The stain of blood that writes an island story. AnNZ

Landfill. Michael S. Harper. and will be taken to the landfill, and filled, and filled. LCAP

The Landing. Daniel Halpern. and yet take them in. AmPA

The Landing of the British Settlers of 1820 (excerpt). Alex Wilmot. The Kafir"s Fiery Cross illumes the midnight skies. ACV

The Landing of the Pilgrim Fathers. Felicia Dorothea Hemans. Freedom to worship God. BeLS; BLPA; FaBoBe; FaBV; FaFP; FaPo; GN; GoTF; HBV 1-2; HBVY; MC; OHIP; PAH; PAL; PaPo; PGD; SBG; TreF; WBLP

Landing on the Moon. May Swenson. ...Dare we land upon a dream? MOON; TAP

Landlady. P. K. Page. and palm the dreadful riddle of their skulls–/hoping the worst. CaP; SoSe

Landlord Fill the Flowing Bowl. Anonymous. Does a very foolish thing, and seldom gets another. FSW

The Landlord's Wife. Marilyn Chin. The man from above, from Yenan. BrSi

The Landlubber's Chantey. James Stuart Montgomery. Heave, ye rollers, heave! HBMV

The Landmark. Dante Gabriel Rossetti. As here I turn, I'll thank God, hastening,/That the same goal is still on the same track. MaVP; NBM

Landor. John Albee. Or chant some line of cadenced, classic/hymn. AA

The Landrail. John Clare. And hid, and all my dinner eat,/Till four o'clock was gone. PBBP

The Landrail. Sir Aubrey De Vere. And visions of pure love in amaranthine bowers! IrPN

A Landscape. John Cunningham. Closing in an azure sky. CEP

Landscape. David Gascoyne. Only a dusty statue lifts and drops its hand. FaBoMo

Landscape. William Mason. Wash, with the crystal coolness of its rills,/ Some mouldring abbey's ivy-vested wall. OBEC

Landscape. Octavio Paz. The crags weigh/No more than our shadows. OBVE

Landscape. Alfred W. Purdy. Snow and the threat of snow.... CaP

Landscape. Abraham Sutzkever. Birds fly by like falling stars. VWA

Landscape and Figure. Thomas Kinsella. ...The protecting flesh/When it falls will melt away in a kind of mud. IPY

Landscape as a Nude. Archibald MacLeish. She has brown breasts and the mouth of no other country. CMoP

Landscape as Metal and Flowers. Winfield Townley Scott. The whistle fades,dragging freight cars,day coaches and/the caboose. AmFN; GoJo; MiAP

Landscape, Deer Season. Barbara Howes. While the blood-red target-sun, over our hill,/Topples to death. GoJo; LiSp; PoL

Landscape I. Charles Madge. ...the ruling laws of the globe in reference to its veins of water. EAS

The Landscape Lies Within My Head. Gervase Stewart. I paint the slums, the countryside. WaaP

Landscape near a Steel Mill. Herschel Horn. crying: Fools! Where is our bread? PPON

The Landscape Near an Aerodrome. Stephen Spender. Religion stands, the church blocking the sun. AnEnPo; CoBMV; LiTM; MoAB; MoBrPo; MoVE; NoAm; OAEP; OxBTC

Landscape, New Mexico. Kell Robertson. celebrate the end of anything. TAT

The Landscape of Love. Thomas Cole. ...she/Is all of darkness in the dark. NePoAm

Landscape of Screams. Nelly Sachs. hung up to be dried by God/in the cosmos– NYBP

The Landscape of the Heart. Geoffrey Grigson. And the whole heart of man. LiTB; WaP

Landscape of the Vomiting Multitudes. Federico Garcia Lorca. did the city swarm out to the rails of the jetty, as one. NYP

Landscape of Violence. Ralph Nixon Currey. And every rider caught outside/Must pray between his horse's knees. PeSA

Landscape with Figures. Keith Douglas. I am the figure writhing on the backcloth. NePoEA

Landscape with Figures. Theodore Enslin. I see/no more. CoPo

Landscape with Figures. A. R. D. Fairburn. and plays at Walton Heath, and drives a sports. AnNZ

Landscape with Leaves and Figure. Olga Broumas. you said I know that/day BoWoP

Landscape with Little Figures. Donald Justice. And the pieces of sky that will go on falling for days. LCAP

Landscape with Minute Wildflowers. Hugh Maxton. I return lowly, blind, at work too. CIP

Landscape with Next of Kin. Olga Broumas. ...is/there anything you won't forgive/her/him. BoWoP

Landscape with the Fall of Icarus. William Carlos Williams. this was/ Icarus drowning. NIP

Landscape with the Giant Orion: Orion Seeks the Goddess Diana (excerpt. Sacheverell Sitwell. And look upon these blossoms of so long ago. MoVE

Landscape with Tractor. Henry Taylor. and to know she will stay in that field till you die? MAYP

Landscape Workers. Harley Elliott. like myths/awaiting an occasion. LTB

Landscapeople. John Ashbery. Until it ceases to be a problem. HaCAP

Landscapes. Thomas Stearns Eliot.
The hermit's chapel, the pilgrim's prayer. BiP; LoGBV
No concurrence of bone. BiP; LoGBV
The palaver is finished. BiP; LoGBV
Red river, river, river. LoGBV
Swing up into the apple-tree. BiP; GTBS-P
Where the roads dip and where the roads rise BiP

Landscapes. Richard Hugo. ...and the man inside who sold it/long ago, forgot he made the deal and will not move. GP

Landscapes. Louis Untermeyer. Good God, and what is all this beauty for? HBV 1-2

The Lane. Andrew Young. That knit hills closer than loose stones. HaMV

Lang Johnny More. Anonymous. The English lady, and little wee boy,/ Went a' to Benachie. ESPB

Langaig. Richard Hugo. we recover, and hum when alone, and hum wrong. WOLT

Langley Lane. Robert Williams Buchanan. For the sake of the pleasure one cannot hear,/And the pleasure that only one can see? HBV 1-2

Langston. Mari E. Evans. ...he/told it like it/was... BOLo; CNA

Langston Blues. Dudley Randall. long gone song/for Langston Hughes CNA; FB

Langston Hughes. Lew Blockcolski. I taped the book back together/for my sleeping children. VoR

Langsyne, When Life Was Bonnie. Alexander ("Surface man") Anderson. For noo, alas, 'tis winter/That gangs a twalmonth roun'. HBV 1-2

The Language. Robert Creeley. ...Speech/is a mouth. CAPP; CoPo; TAP

The Language. Anselm Hollo. that moves, is born,/& leads a life,/& gives it on. APU

Language Has Not the Power to Speak What Love Indites. John Clare. The Soul lies buried in the ink that writes. ELU; OBNC

Language Lesson, 1976. Heather McHugh. and let me be/the one you never hold. MAYP

Language of Ancients. Hayim Lenski. Like the names of the ancients, like Hayman, Halevi. VWA

The Languages We Are. F. J. Bryant. We cling to our frosty vapors and/ Melt it with hate-heat eyes for warmth. NBP

Lanigan's Ball. Anonymous. And that put an end to Lanigan's ball. OxBoLi

Lantern. Frank Polite. a horse, plunging into darkness,/kicks a stone out of its path. GP

Lantern. Gary Soto. And suddenly saw them for the first time/By the same light that gave you away. Str

The Lantern out of Doors. Gerard Manley Hopkins. Their ransom, their rescue, and first, fast, last friend. CMoP; LiTB; OxBoCh; TrCP; VLP

Lao-Tse. Thomas S. Jones, Jr. Silent with peace he had not understood. AnAmPo

Lao-Tzu. Po Chu-i. How comes it that he wrote a book/Of five thousand words? LiTW

Laocoon. Don Gordon. To light in the mind the violent statue, to unwind the Laocoon. WaaP

Laocoon. Donald Hall. And smothered truth to win a war for Greece. NePoAm-2

Laodamia. William Wordsworth. A constant interchange of growth and blight! EnRP; ERoP 1-2; OAEP

The Lapful of Nuts. Sir Samuel Ferguson. That sat with thy white lap full of nuts/Beneath the hazel tree. IrPN; VLP

Lapidary. Bonnie L. Alexander. When you breathe again/your breath will blow the stone in two. AMV-80

Lapis. Shawn Wong. a liquid hand. BrSi

Lapis Lazuli. William Butler Yeats. Their ancient, glittering eyes, are gay. CMoP; CoBMV; DTC; FaBoMo; FaBoTw; FF; ForPo; InPK; InPS; LiTB; LiTM; MAT; MoPo; MoVE; NAWM 1-2; NoAm; NOBE; NoP; OAEL 1-2; OAEP; PAI; PP; PPoe; TEP

Lapsus Linguae. Richard Howard. ...Slips of our mother tongue. NoAm

Last Night in Calcutta. Allen Ginsberg. sticking morphine in the arm and eating meat. NoAm

Last Night in Sisseton, S. D. Mary Goose. sounds of tents flapping/in the background. STE

Last Night My Soul Departed. Muireadhach Albanach O Dalaigh. –my pain it is not beneath my head! NOBI

The Last Night That She Lived. Emily Dickinson. And then an awful leisure was,/Our faith to regulate. AmP; AmePo; AnFE; APA; BoWoP; CMoP; CoAnAm; DiPo; ExPo; ForPo; LiTA; MAmP; NePA; OxBA; PoEL 1-5; QFR; SOTW

Last Night There Was a Cricket in Our Closet. Leroy V. Quintana. trying to find you/that cricket in the other's closet. GP

Last Night They Heard the Woman Upstairs. Leslie Ullman. She must make love slowly, the way/she climbs the stairs. AMV-80

Last night thin rain, gusty wind. Li Ch'ing-chao. By now/they're/fat/ green/and skimpy/red. BoWoP

Last Night We Had a Thunderstorm in Style. Robert Louis Stevenson. The strenuous faithful buckled to their prayers. NOBV

The Last o' the Tinkler. Violet Jacob. But the trayv'lin's near its endin',/ An' the end's aye the best. OxBS

The Last of His Tribe. Henry Clarence Kendall. Like a marvellous dream in his face? CBAP; PoAu 1-2

The Last of the Fire Kings. Derek Mahon. Not to release them/From the ancient curse/But to die their creature and be thankful. FaBoIP; FaBoPV

The Last of the Grand Old Masters. Tom Patey. For the toothless old tykes of tomorrow/Were the Tigers of Yesterday. PoSH

Last of the Poet's Car. Tony Connor. ...I bought the car/with dollars I earned from the sale of love poems. OxBTC

The Last of the Princes. A. K. Ramanujan. has telegraphed thrice already for money. OxBC

The Last One. William Stanley Merwin. The lucky ones with their shadows. LCAP; NoAm; VGW

The last one. Nelly Sachs. will speed its freight/dismal time/to its sodden grave. BoWoP

The Last Ones. Dan Pagis. Am I it? I am./There is no time to explain. VWA

The Last Picnic. Stanley Jasspon Kunitz. Yesterday we had a world to lose. NoAm

Last Plea. Jean Starr Untermeyer. Ballast by Your bright strength my failing might. TrPWD

Last Poem. Ted Berrigan. Let none regret my end who called me friend. APU

Last Poem. Charles Donnelly. ...you give/Like Raleigh, Lawrence, Childers, your services but not yourself. BIrV

Last Poems. Alfred Edward Housman.
The heart of man has long been sore/And long 'tis like to be. OAEP
Keep we must, if keep we can,/These foreign laws of God and man. OAEP
Shoulder the sky, my lad, and drink/your ale. OAEP
The Spartans on the sea-wet rock sat/down and combed their hair. OAEP
To air the ditty,/And to earth I. OAEP
Walk the resounding way/To the still dwelling. OAEP

The Last Post. Robert Graves. ...the red sunset flare/Was blood about his head as he stood there. MMM

A Last Prayer. Helen Hunt Jackson. Let me repentant work for thee! AA; TrPWD; TRV

Last Quarter. John Hollander. a part of life/begins MOON

The Last Quarter Moon of the Dying Year. Jonathan Henderson Brooks. Would God that I shall seem/So beautiful in death. CDC

The Last Quatrain of the Ballad of Emmet Till. Gwendolyn Brooks. Chaos in windy grays/through a red prairie. CNA; PoBA

The Last Redoubt. Alfred Austin. And none, till the judgment trump and shout,/Shall drive her out of the last redoubt. HBV 1-2

Last Refuge. Buonarroti Michelangelo. Wells in the heart when all thy truth appears,/Lest death should vanquish love. LiTW

The Last Refuge. Augustus Young. slippers and hatchet before the television. BIrV

The Last Republicans. Austin Clarke. The Special Branch castled their plans,/Quicklimed the last Republicans. CIP

The Last Reservation. Walter Learned. Moved on–and, thank God, forever at/rest/In the last reservation. AA; PAH

The Last Resort. Robert Willson. No one felt a tug. FAZ

The Last Ride Together. Robert Browning. Ride, ride together, for ever ride? BoLiVe; BoLoP; CenHV; FiP; GTBS; HBV 1-2; LiTB; LoBV; MaVP; OAEP; OBEV; OBVV; PoEL 1-5; UnPo; VLP; WHA

The Last Ride Together (From Her Point of View) (parody). James Kenneth Stephen. It's the very devil that you and he/Ride, ride together, forever ride. BXAP; FaBoCo; Par; UnPo

The Last Rite. Richard Frost. "For our sake, brother, eat it all." AMV-80

Last Rite. John V. Hicks. soft as a sigh, the sift of the first snow. AMV-81

Last Rites. David Citino. let the darkness race across your body. AMV-80

Last Rites. Christina Georgina Rossetti. Raise him a tombstone of snow. OxBChV

The Last Romantic. Alexander Laing. Deepen to purple, and are one with night. AnAmPo

The Last Round. Anna Wickham. And crown the fight. MoBrPo

Last Sheet. Roy Fuller. Played gently while the beauteous statue reconciled/The jarred generations, and Sicily and Bohemia. TEP

Last Snow. Andrew Young. Stabbing a dead leaf from below/Kills winter at a blow. OxBTC

The Last Song. Eileen Duggan. I shall not sing again. CAW

Last Song. James Guthrie. A fond goodnight/Wherever you are. TiPo

The Last Song. Joy Harjo. oklahoma will be the last song/i'll ever sing. TAT; TWSS

Last Songs. Galway Kinnell. reinvent it on earth/as song. CAPP

Last Speech to the Court. Bartolomeo Vanzetti. that agony is our triumph. NAMP

Last Statement. Vladimir Mayakovsky. I could tell it to the world right now. FaBoPV

The Last Summer. Vivian Smith. while like a knife a scarlet bird/sings deserts in the lemon-trees. PoAu 1-2

The Last Supper. Stan Rice. Get a sponge. Get a shovel. Call God. Soup's on. NPGG

The Last Supper. Rainer Maria Rilke. and try to find a way out. But he/is everywhere like a twilight-hour. MoRP; OFD

The Last Supper. Oscar Williams. The day lay in the glass and the blood was gone. FaFP; LiTA; LiTM; MoRP; NePA

Last Things. Bill Manhire. ...The stone like stone/hit bottom and was obsolete. OCNZ

Last Things. William Meredith. Event he foresees for each of us–a reckoning, our own. NoAm

Last Things. Kathleen Raine. We what we are. NYBP

Last Things, Black Pines at 4 a.m. Robert Lowell. ...Valery/and Trollope the huntsman are happy to drop out. NOBA

The Last Time. Tom Veitch. After it was over everybody puked/And left. ANYP

The Last Time I the Well Woke. Anonymous. with-outen he fynde hit mylke and pap/a long while-ey./Byuan hys my name iet. NCEP

The Last Tournament. Alfred, Lord Tennyson.
Ay, ay, O ay–the winds that move the mere. FaBoRV
Far over sands marbled with moon and cloud,/From less and less to nothing. FaBoPP

The Last Tourney. Frederic F. Van de Water. And as I fall hear through the evening air/The distant horn of Roland, faintly blown. HBMV

The Last Trail. Stanton A. Coblentz. He slipped away like one who went/ To a lovers' rendezvous. BPAW

The Last Trial. Anonymous. Set me to these, or any other trial,/Except my Mistress' anger and denial. OBSC

The Last Turn. William Carlos Williams. the pigment the genius of a world/artless but supreme... NYP

The Last Utterance of the Delphic Oracle. Anonymous. ...The garrulous/ Water has dried up at last. OBVE

Last Verses. Thomas Chatterton. And this last act of wretchedness forgive. TrGrPo

Last Verses. William Motherwell. It were in vain,–for Time hath long been knelling,–/"Sad one, depart!" HBV 1-2

The Last Violet. Oliver Herford. And happy dreams, we'll meet again next year! OHIP

Last Visit. Robert Finch. And nothing has changed except what brought us here. NOBC

The Last Voyage. Katharine Tynan Hinkson. And find my ship with sails all set/By the dim quayside, and embark. HBMV

The Last Voyage of the Fairies. William Henry Davenport Adams. And lost to mortals evermore! HBVY

The Last War. Kingsley Amis. And soon they'll all smell alike, he thought, and felt sick,/And went to bed at noon. OBSV; OxBC; SoSe

The Last Warmth of Arnold. Gregory Corso. And it was about airplane glue he was thinking/when he fell and died beneath the Brooklyn Bridge. CoPo; NoAm

Last Week I Took a Wife. M. Kelly. To lose my wife? A trifle! BLSo

The Last Whiskey Cup. Paul Engle. Across the grassy ranges of the world. ATP; YaD

A Last Will and Testament. Anonymous. Unto Heven on high my soule I bequeth. MeEL

A Last Will and Testament. John Winstanley. My life is done,/And so I think to leave it. OBSV

The Last Will and Testament of Anthony, King of Poland. Anonymous. Since you into a hole did tumble. APAS

Last Will of the Drunk. Myra von Riedemann. Give me a drink. OBCV

The Last Wish. Edward Robert Bulwer, Earl of Lytton. The all-endured this nothing-done costs me. OBSP; OBVV

The Last Wolf.   Mary Tallmountain.   I know what they have done.   TWSS

The Last Word.   Matthew Arnold.   .When the forts of folly fall,/Find thy body by the wall.   BoLiVe; CABA; EnLi 1-2; FiP; HBV 1-2; NOBE; OAEL 1-2; OBNC; OBVV; PG; PoEL 1-5; TreFT; VLP; WHA

The Last Word.   Peter Davison.   Nick through your flesh and creak into the block.   InPK

A Last Word.   Ernest Christopher Dowson.   ...O pray the earth enfold/Our life-sick hearts and turn them into dust.   MoBrPo; SyP; VLP

The Last Word.   Frederic Lawrence Knowles.   Even an endless sleep would be/Stirred by the dreams of you!   HBV 1-2

A Last Word.   May Sarton.   To open up a simple world of praise!   GLGT

The Last Word of a Bluebird.   Robert Frost.   And perhaps in the spring/He would come back and sing.   GoJo; GrPl; SO; TiPo

Last Words.   Annette von Droste-Hulshoff.   For then I greet you from the stars.   CAW

Last Words.   John Hollander.   Verses a–CRASH! BANG! BLURP!/GLUB"...(end of quote).   OBAL; PV

The Last Words.   Maurice Maeterlinck.   Do not let him weep.   AWP; PoPl

Last Words.   James Merrill.   Part looks into your light/And lives to tell you so.   TAP

Last Words.   Sylvia Plath.   And the shine of these small things sweeter than the face/of Ishtar.   FYAP

Last Words, 1968.   Lance Henson.   I am ready to begin again   CDW

Last Words before Winter.   Louis. Untermeyer.   For I spy the woolly, woolly wolf.   MoAmPo

The Last Words of Don Henriquez.   Zalman Schneour.   The Lord our God is One God!'   TrJP

The Last Words of My English Grandmother.   William Carlos Williams.   Trees! Well, I'm tired/of them and rolled her head away.   SOTW

Last Words on Greece.   George Gordon, Lord Byron.   So strong thy magic or so weak am I.   ERoP 1-2

Last Words to a Dumb Friend.   Thomas Hardy.   Showing in the autumn shade/That you moulder where you played.   FM; OAEP; PCat

Last Words to Miriam.   D. H. Lawrence.   I should have been cruel enough to bring/You through the flame.   CoBMV

A Last World.   John Ashbery.
And the truth is cold, as a giant's knee/Will seem cold.   ANYP
As we gallop into the flame.   PoM

Last Year's Discussion: The Nobel Russian.   Phyllis McGinley.   In Bronxville, Chicago, Butte, Fond du Lac?   FaBoEE

The Last Years.   William Henry Davies.   And Death takes all of us as one.   FM

Lat Noman Booste of Konnyng Nor Vertu.   John Lydgate.   Al stant on chaung like a mydsomyr rose.   AtBAP

Late.   Louise Bogan.   You look upon the air.   PBWP; VGW

Late.   Daniel Halpern.   I sit with you here, waiting for you to turn/ again from that window and talk to me.   AMV-81

Late.   Helen Salz.   Oh embassy of doves/you are late/flying!   GoYe

Late Abed.   Archibald MacLeish.   You lie there/thinking of nothing/ watching the sky...   NCSH

Late Afternoon.   Elizabeth Sullam.   Before light withdraws we would like to say/unforgettable words.   AmC

Late Afternoon on a Good Lake.   Dara Wier.   ...luck is/shaking a cup of ice, I want/to drink that water.   MAYP

Late Again.   Gabriel Zaid.   But we/ruminate with our heads.   AMV-81

Late Air.   Elizabeth Bishop.   ...Phoenixes/burning quietly, where the dew cannot climb.   PoPl

Late at Night.   William Stafford.   We live in a terrible season.   NNaP; PoL; RFM

Late at Night during a Visit of Friends.   Robert Bly.   The human face shines like a dark sky/As it speaks of those things that oppress the living.   InPS

A Late Aubade.   Richard Wilbur.   And some blue cheese, and crackers, and some fine/Ruddy-skinned pears.   SM; SoSe

Late Autumn.   William Allingham.   ...but no vain terror thrills/His perfect harvesting; he sleeps at ease.   IrPN

Late Autumn.   A. M. Sullivan.   For Nature has a bitter season/When she informs upon her own.   GoBC

Late Autumn.   Andrew Young.   Till I saw that slant-legged robin/With autumn on his chest.   HaMV; MoVE

Late Autumn Walk.   J. D. McClatchy.   As nutskin, tobacco, cider, plum.   AMV-80

Late Comer.   Fanny de Groot Hastings.   And being neither part nor parcel of/Its tranquil beauty know herself in love.   GoYe

Late Corner.   Langston Hughes.   Oh, lonely Cross!   NePoAm-2

Late Dandelions.   Ben Belitt.   and a scarab aloft on the stem revelation had hollowed!   NYBP

Late-Flowering Lust.   Sir John Betjeman.   At all the thoughts that in us spring/From this late-flowering lust.   CMoP; ErPo; NMP; TW

Late Game.   B. H. Fairchild.   and one pale cry leaps/toward the stars.   AMV-81

Late Gothic.   Phyllis Gotlieb.   reaching blackened arms of the chimneys on the other.   NOBC

The Late Hour.   Mark Strand.   And, finally, without warning or desire,/the lonely and the feckless end.   HaCAP

Late in Fall.   Ramona Wilson.   singing on fine and shivering limbs/of spread and open trees.   VoR

Late Last Night.   Arthur Gregor.   the singleness in every name.   VGW

Late Last Night.   Langston Hughes.   So I was cryin'/On account of/You!   NoAm

The Late, Last Rook.   Ralph Hodgson.   Or ghostly scarecrows walk his dream.   MoBrPo

Late Late.   George Starbuck.   the box is a box is a box.   PPON

Late Leaves.   Walter Savage Landor.   And spring and summer both are past/And all things sweet.   HBV 1-2

Late Light.   Edmund Charles Blunden.   Penitential low recall.   EnLoPo

Late Light.   Barbara Bellow Watson.   all dice were cast.   NYBP

Late Lights in Minnesota.   Ted Kooser.   pulling an old woman downstairs to the toilet/among the red eyes of her cats.   TAT

Late Lunch, San Antonio.   Vincent O'Sullivan.   In the glare of such election, slap backs, call each other/Moses.   OCNZ

A Late Manuscript at the Schocken Institute.   Gabriel Preil.   their frozen stream flowing/from Mantua to Amsterdam.   VWA

Late Moon.   Philip Levine.   and in darkness/nothing falls/staining her lap.   LCAP

The Late Mother.   Cynthia Macdonald.   Becoming her mother and my own.   Psk

Late November in a Field.   James Wright.   I wish they were/Grass.   CAPP; NNaP

Late October.   Sara King Carleton.   And the dancing light of the/lantern, homeward bound.   GoYe

Late October.   Sara Teasdale.   The others thought of tomorrow, but they/Only remembered yesterday.   PoSC; YeAr

The Late Passenger.   Clive Staples Lewis.   Because of you the Ark must sail without the Unicorn.'   EBCP; TrCP

Late, Passing Prairie Farm.   William Stafford.   ...When you pass here, traveler,/you too can't keep from making sounds,/like theirs, that will last   GOYP

Late Reflections.   Babette Deutsch.   After a death in the house, mirrors be covered.   NYBP

Late Rising.   Jacques Prevert.   in the memory/of a man who is hungry.   CAD

The Late Show.   William Heyen.   ...The old flicks/are followed by the news.   GLGT

The Late Show.   Janet Sylvester.   I want her to find the place under my eye/where someone once connected.   MAYP

The Late Snow and Lumber Strike of the Summer of Fifty-Four.   Gary Snyder.   And stand in lines in Seattle./Looking for work.   NaP; NMP

Late Sonnet.   Hayden Carruth.   Nor is it essential to be young.   SM

Late Spring.   John Gill.   ...rooted by his lightning/sheathed and unsheathed.   NeAC

Late Spring.   Robert Hass.   ...the/rhythm will keep me awake, changing.   GeTw; MAYP

A Late Spring.   James Scully.   The roots shaken with water and dirt/Torn from a long sleep.   NYBP

A Late Spring Day in My Life.   Robert Bly.   A horse gazes steadily at me.   NCSH

A Late Spring: Eastport.   Philip Booth.   the whole/room will/bloom.   Psk

Late Starting Dawn.   Richard Brautigan.   ...a deer/standing alone in a meadow.   PCP

Late Tutorial.   Vincent Buckley.   ...You and I/Follow but feebly where our words aspire.   PoAu 1-2

Late Winter.   Hazel Hall.   April, when you dance down these ways/Hush your awakening feet.   HBMV

Late Winter.   James Philip McAuley(What joy I found/Mounting that tiny/Stair of sound.   PoAu 1-2

Late Wisdom.   George Crabbe.   When all these tyrants rest, and thou/Art warring with the mighty dead?   HBV 1-2; OBEV; TrGrPo

Lately, Alas, I Knew a Gentle Boy.   Henry David Thoreau.   Nor mortals know a sympathy more rare.   AP; MAmP; PeHV

Lately I've felt a grave concern.   Countess Beatriz de Die.   you must obey my every need.   BoWoP

Later Life, VII.   Christina Georgina Rossetti.   And death and torment, rightly understood.   LO

A Later Note on Letter #15.   Charles Olson.   The poetics of such a situation/are yet to be found out   CAPP

The Lateshow Diorama.   Christopher Dewdney.   As if you had left a trace, a phantom in time at which the/olfactory dog continued to bark.   CaPN

The Latest Decalogue.   Arthur Hugh Clough.
At any rate shall never labour/More than thyself to love thy neighbour.   BiP; DBV; GTBS-P; HAP; NOBE; OAEL 1-2; OAEP; OBNC; OBSV; TRV; ViBoPo; VLP

Thou shalt not covet, but tradition/Approves all forms of competition. CABA; EBEV; ExPo; FaBoCo; FF; GoTF; HoPM; InMe; LoBV; NBM; NIP; OBVV; PPP; TreFT; WGRP

Latet Anguis. *Anonymous.* You and I, my lyf, and Amyas OBEV

Latimer's Light. *Anonymous.* Latimer's Light is here to stay/Till the trump of a coming judgment day. TRV

Latin. *Anonymous.* Now it's killing me. ChTr; PoPle

Latin Hymn. Winthrop Mackworth Praed. Ave Mary! take my child! CoBE

Latin Lullaby. *Anonymous.* "Gentle dreams, steal over Thee." CAW

The Latin Tongue. James J. Daly. In sacred Embassies from pole to pole. CAW; GoBC

Latter Day Psalms. Cliff Ashby. My mind is melancholic,/I cannot praise my maker. NOCV

The Latter Part of the Third Book of Lucretius... John Dryden. Who dyes to-day, and will as long be so,/As he who dy'd a thousand years ago. FaBoRV

A Latter Purification. Haim Guri. You are a line and yet another line. VWA

The Latter Rain. Jones Very. And all that once received the early rain/Declare to man it was not sent in vain. AmP; GN; OxBA

The Lattice at Sunrise. Charles Tennyson Turner. And, at prime hour, behold!-He follows me/With golden shadows to my secret rooms! OBVV

The Laud of Saint Catherine. Algernon Charles Swinburne. A God beheld in dreams that were/Beheld of her! CAW

Lauda. Girolamo Beneveni. Pierced on the cruel cross,/At peace shall never be. CAW

Laudanum. *Anonymous.* Command your sleepy poet to descend. NOEC

Laudate for Christmas. Prudentius (Aurelius Clemens Prudentius). Unto God the One and Three/Through the ages evermore! CAW

Lauds. W. H. Auden. Among the leaves the small birds sing:/In solitude, for company. TrCP

Lauds. John Berryman. permissive, smiling on our silliness You forged. HAP

Laugh and Be Merry. John Masefield. Laugh till the game is played; and be you merry, my friends. EnLit; FaFP; MoBrPo; PoPl; TreFT

Laugh It Off. Henry Rutherford Elliot. There's no recipe like laughter-/Laugh it off. WBLP

Laughing Backwards. Jim Hall. ...slinging cherry bombs/at all those tragic fools picking their way forward. GOYP

The Laughing Faces of Pigs. Fred Lape. Maybe the earth herself had a good belly laugh/the era that she first gave birth to pigs. BoAnP

The Laughing Hyena, by Hokusai. D. J. Enright. ...It, at least,/Knows exactly why it laughs. MP; TwCP

Laughing Song. William Blake. To sing the sweet chorus of "Ha, Ha, He!" BrR; CBEP; DiPo; EnLi 1-2; GoJo; NLV; OxBChV; PoSC; SoPo; SUS; TiPo

Laughing Time. William Jay Smith. Hee! Hee! Hee! Hee! Ha! Ha! Ha! Ha! Ha! SoPo

The Laughing Willow. Oliver Herford. Would make a weeping willow laugh. HBV 1-2

Laughter. Isabella Valancy Crawford. Nor will under stormy sky/Laughter's airy music ring. CaP

Laughter. Miriam Waddington. and we laugh/laugh laugh. WHW

The Laundress. Thomas Kinsella. She searched in her basket/And fixed her ruffled sheet. IPY

Laundromat. David McCord. I'm glad the spinning earth can't throw us out into the/night! QQQ

Laundry & School Epigrams. Bernadette Mayer. They'll get a chance to meet/The female police/& eat Chicken McNuggets. APU

Laura. Robert Tofte. Which you in breast, hair, heart, and face, may see. EIL

Laura Cashdollars. Bernadette Mayer. to mix the fourth with. ANYP

Laura's Song. Oliver Madox Brown. Cling closer, love, and close thine eyes. OBVV

Laura Sleeping. Charles Cotton. And all Mankind her Creatures are. CavP; ELP; LoBV; OBS; ViBoPo

Laura Sleeping. Louise Chandler Moulton. Thus, from the Night, Dawn's sunlit beauty/breaks. AA

Laura Waits for Him in Heaven. Petrarch (Francesco Petrarca). that I should be making haste for ever. OBMV

Laurana's Song. Richard Hovey. Till he grow weary with the over-sweet,/And die, or kill. AA

The Laureate. Robert Graves. That glitter a cold span above the sea. BIrV; FaBoTw; OBSV

The Laureate (parody). William Aytoun. And nothing to do but to pocket my gold! BXAP; Par

The Laurel Tree. Louis Simpson. It is so that spiritual messengers/Deliver their meaning. NNaP

Laurels and Immortelles. *Anonymous.* And crowned him with death's immortelles. BLPA

Laurence Bloomfield in Ireland. William Allingham.

And firesides buried under fallen thatch. BIrV

And Paudeen Dhu, with meekly dismal face,/Receives the full possession of the place... NOBI

Here, every thought and mood and fancy rise/From common earth, and soar to mystic skies. IrPN

Laurentian Shield. F. R. Scott. From millions whose hands can turn this rock into children. NOBC; OBCV

Lauriger Horatius. John Addington Symonds. If we may not kiss the girls,/Drink while time's a-flying? HBV 1-2

Laus Deo. Robert Bridges. For God requires no more than thou hast done,/And takes thy work to bless it for his own. VLP

Laus Deo. John Greenleaf Whittier. Tell the nations that He reigns,/Who alone is Lord and God! AmP; AnNE; AP; MC; PAH

Laus Infantium. William Canton. And left, O little child, its reflex there. HBV 1-2

Laus Mortis. Frederic Lawrence Knowles. In His unwithering sheaves, O bind my heart! HBV 1-2

Laus Veneris. Louise Chandler Moulton. There she sits in the picture,/Daughter of foam and fire. AA; HBV 1-2

Laus Veneris. Algernon Charles Swinburne. Until God loosen over sea and land/The thunder of the trumpets of the night. MaVP; VLP

Laus Virginitatis. Arthur Symons. And thou dost give, with thy own loveliness,/My beauty back to me. EnLoPo

Lausanne. Thomas Hardy. "Truth like a bastard comes into the world/Never without ill-fame to him who gives her birth'?" FaBoRV; FaBoTw; OBTV

Lavender Blue. *Anonymous.* You must love me, dilly dilly,/'Cause I love you. CH; FSW; LiTL

The Lavender Cowboy. Harold Hersey. But only two hairs on his chest. BPAW; CoSo; FSW

Lavender's for Ladies. Patrick Reginald Chalmers. For when she calls lavender summer must die! HBMV

Lavinia. James (1700-48) Thomson. Thoughtless of Beauty, she was Beauty's Self,/Recluse amid the close-embowering Woods. OBEC

Lavish Kindness. Elinor Wylie. And none has fathomed their intent. AtBAP; CrMA

The Law. Samuel (1612-80) Butler. While it condemns a less delinquent for 't. NLV

The Law. Albert Haynes. While the rest of us are beaten/into pebbles, plowshares, and fossils. NBP

The Law. Abraham Ibn Ezra. With joy and awe Thy name to bless. TrJP

The Law. Grace Schulman. "Fathers, forgive me. I cannot follow." GP

Law in the Country of the Cats. Ted Hughes. And one man bursting into the police station/Crying: "Let Justice be done. I did it, I." TW

Law Like Love. W. H. Auden. Like love we seldom keep. CMoP; CoBMV; FaBoMo; NoP

The Law of Averages. Troubadour". Not always nothing to a pair;/But pretty nearly. FiBHP; InMe

The Law of the Jungle. Rudyard Kipling. But the head and the hoof of the Law and the haunch/and the hump is-Obey! LiTB; PoEL 1-5

The Law of the Yukon. Robert W. Service. This is the Will of the Yukon-Lo! how she makes it plain! CaP; HBV 1-2; TreFS

The Law West of the Pecos. Squire Omar Barker. West of the Pecos law was law! BPAW

Lawd, Dese Colored Chillum. Fareedah Allah. Lawd, dese Chillum won't let you be/White for nothing. BlSi

Lawn-Mower. Dorothy Walter Baruch. Across the grass./Zwuzz, wisssh. SoPo; SUS

Lawn Order. William Franklin. 'Cause it's snitch on your neighbor time. LFAC

The Lawn Roller. Robert Layzer. Cold as the face of Helen in her distress,/Was looking through the branches, hard and alone. NePoEA

A Lawn-Tennisonian Idyll (parody). *Anonymous.* She laughed, he frowned;/I turned and went my way. FaBoPa

Lawrence: The Last Crusade (excerpt). Selden Rodman. This strip of sand, with hedge on every side... NAMP

Lawyer Clark Blues. Sleepy John Estes. He say if I just stay out of the grave/Old John I see you won't go to the pen BluL

The Lawyer's Invocation to Spring. Henry Howard Brownell. Hail, as aforesaid, coming Spring! PoLf

The Lawyers Know Too Much. Carl Sandburg. The lawyers-tell me why a hearse horse snickers hauling a lawyer's bones. BiP; CMoP; DBV; HBMV; YaD

Lay Dis Body Down. *Anonymous.* Lay dis body down. ABF

Lay of Ancient Rome. Thomas Russell Ybarra. Of far away B. C./From us of Anno Domini. HBV 1-2; InMe

The Lay of Prince Marvan. *Anonymous.* With Colman's glorious heritage I'd part/To bear thee company! AnIV

The Lay of St. Cuthbert (excerpt). Richard Harris Barham. And Cecily Roumeli came to this nation/With William the Norman, and laid its foundation. NBM

A Lay of St. Gengulphus (excerpt). Richard Harris Barham. But remember Gengulphus's wife!–and reflect/On the moral enforced by her terrible tale! VLP

The Lay of the Battle of Tombland. Dunstan Thompson. "rest," they ordered, "the rest is ours." LiTA; NePA

The Lay of the Captive Count. Johann Wolfgang von Goethe. And I inherit Strength and Spirit. AWP

The Lay of the Cid: Pawning the Coffers of Sand. *Anonymous.* He is gone out from Burgos... LiTW

Lay of the Deserted Influenzaed. Henry Cholmondeley-Pennell Ad I shall dever see her bore,/By beautiful! by owd!! InMe

Lay of the Ettercap (parody). John Leyden. And bake him in a pye. BXAP

A Lay of the Famine. *Anonymous.* And the pale corpse of a maiden young stretched on a new-made grave. OnYI

Lay of the Forlorn. George Darley. Farewell to Ierne! Ierne, farewell. OnYI

The Lay of the Labourer. Thomas Hood. The Spital, or the Gaol! SaC

Lay of the Last Frontier. Harold Hersey. And all thuh host who rode thuh range/Now ride thuh Last Frontier. PoOW

The Lay of the Last Minstrel. Sir Walter Scott.

And, home returning, soothly swear,/Was never scene so sad and fair! FaBoPP; OBRV

And strives to trim the short-liv'd blaze. OBRV

And thus I love them better still,/Even in extremity of ill. BSV

The Bard may draw his parting groan. FaBoPP; OBRV

Be THOU the trembling sinner's stay,/Though heaven and earth shall pass away! OBRV

The dirge of lovely Rosabelle. BSV

Enough, he died with conquering Graeme. OBRV

For love is heaven, and heaven is love. BSV; ViBoPo

For Love shall still be lord of all! ATP; OBRV

From Warkworth, or Naworth, or merry Carlisle. OBRV

Gentle lords and ladies gay. TrGrPo

Their name unknown, their praise unsung. OBRV

Though there, forgotten and alone,/The Bard may draw his parting groan. EnRP; FaBoPP; OBRV

Unwept, unhonored, and unsung. BLPA; FPL; GN; OAEP; OHFP; OxBS; TreF; TrGrPo

Which heart to heart, and mind to mind,/In body and in soul can bind. OBRV

The Lay of the Levite. William Aytoun. And listen to the distant cry/Of "Clo!–old Clo!" HBV 1-2

The Lay of the Lovelorn. Sir Theodore and Aytoun, William E. Martin. Rest thee with thy yellow nabob, spider-hearted Cousin/Amy! FaBoCo; VLP

The Lay of the Trilobite. May Kendall. To be a simple Trilobite/In the Silurian seas.' CenHV

The Lay of the Vigilantes. *Anonymous.* But we left him alone with the Devil. PoOW

The Lay of Thrym. *Anonymous.* And for many rings the might of the hammer. LiTW

The Lay Preacher Ponders. Idris Davies. And all my spare time to God.' ACV; OxBTC

Lay Your Arms Aside. Pierce Ferriter. Gentlest of women, lay your arms aside. BIrV

Lay Your Head on My Shoulder. Yehuda Amichai. Rest, rest your head, therefore. VWA

Lay Your Sleeping Head, My Love. W. H. Auden. Watched by every human love. BoLiVe; BoLoP; ChMP; CoBMV; LiTB; MoAB; MoBrPo; MoPo; MoVE; SeCePo; TEP

Lay Your Weapons Down, Young Lady. Piaras Feiritear. But add an "a' or an "e'/and it gives your Christian name away... NOBI

The Layers. Stanley Jasspon Kunitz. I am not done with my changes. AMV-80

Laying By. Randall Williams. You are sure of that. AMV-80

Laziness and Silence. Robert Bly. After sleeping all night by the lake. PPP

Lazy Lou. Mary Mapes Dodge. I'd change my ways. That's what I'd do. BBGG

Lazy Man's Song. Po Chu-i. So even he was not so lazy as I. OBVE

Lazy Mary. *Anonymous.* Yes, mother, I will get up,/I will get up today. AmFP

The Lazy People. Shel Silverstein. I'm much too tired today. NTCP

The Lazy Pussy. Palmer Cox. Yet she's a good-for-nothing cat,/As all the world may see. OBCA

The Lazy Roof. Gelett Burgess. They do Not Have Much Fun! NA

The Lazy Writer. Bert Leston Taylor. We've really had no fall at all. ALV

The Lea Rig. Robert Burns. To meet thee on the lea-rig,/My ain kind dearie, O! BSV

Leac A'Chlarsair. Lucy Taylor. And living presence of sweet music stirs/By Leac a' Chlarsair. PoSH

Lead. Jayne Cortez. to hear Lead Belly/spit the Blues out PoBA

Lead, Kindly Light. John Henry, Cardinal Newman. Which I have loved long since, and lost/awhile. BLPL; FaBoBe; FaPoR; GoTF; MyFE; TreF

Lead On, O King Eternal. Ernest W. Shurtleff. The crown awaits the conquest; Lead on, O God of might. AH

Lead Us, O Father, in the Paths of Peace. William Henry Burleigh. Until our lives are perfected in thee. AH

Leadbelly Gives an Autograph. LeRoi (Imamu Amiri Baraka) Jones. ...An/old deaf lady/burned to death/in South Carolina.) CNA

The Leaden Echo and the Golden Echo. Gerard Manley Hopkins. Yonder. BrPo; CMoP; CoBMV; DTC; EnLi 1-2; FaFP; GTBS-P; LiTB; LiTM; LoBV; MasP; MoAB; MoBrPo; MoVE; NOBV; OAEP; OBMV; OBNC; SOTW

The Leaden-Eyed. Vachel Lindsay. Not that they die, but that they die like sheep. ATP; BoLiVe; CMoP; ELU; FaBoEE; LiTA; MoRP; NAMP; NePA; OBSP; PPON

A Leaden Treasury of English Verse. Paul Dehn.
And the other ranks might have got worried. DBV
A fission! A fission!/We all fall down. QQQ
(A Mr. Hutton had pressed the wrong button/On the coast of Maine.) DBV; QQQ
What mortal hand could put its thumb/So neatly on uranium? QQQ
Which, because of radiation/Will be cared for by the nation.) DBV

The Leader. Hilaire Belloc. We lost her in the dawn. ACP

The Leader. Dorothy Livesay. till flowers are black mouths/and the stones bleed my song. PeCV

A Leader. George William Russell. Sorrow we could understand/And the mystery told in tears. HBMV

Leaders. *Anonymous.* We need your help in every place–/Before, behind, beside. WBLP

The Leaders of the Crowd. William Butler Yeats. And heartier loves; that lamp is from the tomb. EBEV; EnLit; MoAB; MoBrPo

The Leadsman's Song. Charles Dibdin. We hear the seaman with delight/Proclaim–"All's well." HBV 1-2

Leady-Day, an' Ridden House. William Barnes. Zoo ridden house is such a caddle,/That I would rather keep my staddle. VLP

The Leaf. William Carson Fagg. I watch it through wire mesh/and move my animal instincts/safely to a snot-covered corner. LFAC

Leaf. John Hewitt. Let me narrow in on my night/with that effortless certainty. NeIP

A Leaf. Ludwig Uhland. So much that was most dear to me. AWP

The Leaf. John Williams. That none or all/Might disappear. NePoAm-2

Leaf After Leaf..... Walter Savage Landor. Should we, her wiser sons, be less content/To sink into her lap when life is spent? TRV; ViBoPo

Leaf-Eater. Thomas Kinsella. ...then gropes/Back on itself and begins/To eat its own leaf. FaBoIP

The Leaf-Makers. Harold Stewart. Seldom would trees have anything to wear! PoAu 1-2

The Leaf-Picking. Frederic Mistral. The two are now together. AWP

A Leaf-Treader. Robert Frost. Now up, my knee, to keep on top of another year of snow. MoAmPo

Leafless Trees, Chickahominy Swamp. Dave Smith. in the dead miles nothing explains or changes or relieves? MAYP

Leaflets. Adrienne Rich. ...I am thinking how we can use what we have/to invent what we need. NoAm

Leaflight. Dorothy Donnelly. dropping gold foil/on field and wall. NCSH

The League of Nations. Mary Siegrist. A Cain without a country, a Judas at the board! MC; PAH

The League of Selves. Alvin Toffler. trigger pulled,/now dies. AMV-80

Leah. Shirley Kaufman. and I swim raging/against the stream. VWA

The Leak in the Dike. Phoebe Cary. So long as the dikes of Holland/Divide the land from the sea! FaFP; PaPo; TreF

A Lean Day in a Convict's Suit. Jean Wahl. And too, some images of hair and lips. VWA

Lean Gaius, Who Was Thinner Than a Straw. Lucilius [(or Lucillius)]. THE DEATH OF NOTHING, FUNERAL OF GAIUS! OBVE

Lean Street. G. S. Fraser. The fat sky gurgles like a swollen bladder/With the foul rain that rains on poverty. NeBP; OxBS

Leander Stormbound. Sydney Goodsir Smith. Or maybe hear the thunderan sea/...Wantan me. OxBS

Leaning on a Limerick. Eve Merriam. But it's got to come out liverwurst. TDH

The Leap. James Dickey. While I examine my hands. NIP

Leap-Centuries. Paul Celan. cold start/with haemoglobin. OBVE

A Leap for Life. Walter Colton. And folded to his heart his boy–/Then fainted on the deck. PaPo

Leap in the Dark. Roberta Hill. it sings of its needles of ice, sings because of the scars. WPOW

Leap in the Smoke. John Buchan. Dear city of my pilgrimage. PoSH

The Lesson. Edward Lucie-Smith. Pride, like a goldfish, flashed a sudden fin. NCSH; OxBTC; TwCP

The Lesson. Paul Mariani. ...the eyes turning as the/fingers tighten on the scrawny neck. MAYP

The Lesson. Elizabeth Peterson. "Never anything happens you can't wear jeans." AMV-80

The Lesson. Larry Rubin. The formic wine within the purple grail. GoYe

The Lesson. Charles Simic. I burst out laughing. HaCAP

Lesson for a Boy. Samuel Taylor Coleridge. See a man who so loves you as your fond S. T. COLERIDGE FaBoUs

Lesson for Dreamers. Paul B. Janeczko. and finally my face. PCP

A Lesson for Mamma. Sydney Dayre. Now, mamma, couldn't you? OBCA; OxBChV

The Lesson for Today. Robert Frost. I had a lover's quarrel with the world. LiTA; LiTM; NePA; WaP

A Lesson from Van Gogh. Howard Moss. Van Gogh was saying, "I am not a tree,/A fish, a serpent, lion, pig, or jay." MoAB

A Lesson in Detachment. Vassar Miller. She'll cup no joy now in her palm,/But perch it on her knuckle.. NePoEA-2

A Lesson in Hammocks. James Schevill. His cigar on fire for the sensual life. FAZ

A Lesson in Handwriting. Alastair Reid. Tomorrow, words begin. NYBP

A Lesson in Love. Philip Hobsbaum. Truth lies between your legs, and so do I. OxBTC

A Lesson in Oblivion. Dabney Stuart. ...Except I'd have your tongue cut out. GP

A Lesson in Translation. Gabriel Preil. Did I learn a lesson in translation? VWA

The Lesson of the Water-Mill. Sarah Doudney. "The mill cannot grind/With the water that is past." HBV 1-2; PoToHe; TreFS

Lessons. Louis Untermeyer.
And if you do it, do it today. TiPo
Keep count of only shining hours. TiPo
To give–and forgive–/Is a good way to live. TiPo
Too little wrought. TiPo

Lessons. Helen Weber. Hunger for bread and peace. PGD

Lessons from the Gorse. Elizabeth Barrett Browning. Drops be on our cheeks–O world, they are not tears but dew. HBV 1-2

Lessons in History. Robert Penn Warren. And who know, or guess, what, long ago, happened there? AMV-80

Lessons of the War. Henry Reed.
At seven o'clock from the houses, is roughly a distance/Of about one year and a half. GTBS-P; NIP
That battle-fit we lived, and though defeated,/Not without glory fought. OBWP

Lessons of the Year. Anonymous. And out of our loss is gain. BLRP

Lest any doubt that we are glad that they were born Today. Emily Dickinson. Without the date, like Consciousness or Immortality– NAs

Lest Thou Forget. William L. Stidger. Hearing the Infinite whisper there. PoToHe

Lester Leaps In. Al Young. in order to blow what it's like being born. NPGG; SM

Lester Tells of Wanda and the Big Snow. Paul Zimmer. It don't snow like that no more. Too bad. FAZ

Lester Young. Ted Joans. Angels of Jazz–they don't die–they live/they live–in hipsters like you and I AmNP

Let All Created Things. Artis Seagrave. And to restore/All things, he rose/To die no more. AH

Let America Be America Again. Langston Hughes. All, all the stretch of these great green states–/And make America again! PoNe

Let Be. Anonymous. What's the good of irritatin'?/Let 'im be. WBLP

Let Christian Hearts Rejoice Today. Jean de Brebeuf. Jesus Christ of Bethlehem. AH

Let Dreamers Wake. Lilith Lorraine. Chart the tides of millennium! PGD

Let Erin Remember the Days of Old. Thomas Moore. Thus, sighing, look through the waves of time/For the long-faded glories they cover. EnRP

Let Go: Once. Gerald Fleming. ...Past that/is relaxation, like a swimmer/climbing onto shore. AMV-81

Let Go the Reef Tackle. Anonymous. Let go the reef a-tayckle,/My sheets, they are jammed! ShS

Let Her Give Her Hand. Anonymous. For be the old love ne'er so true,/She is ever for the new. ELP

Let Heroes Account to Love. Alan Dugan. Vomit your essence, Hercules. Be me: NoAm

Let Him Return. Leona Ames Hill. Poised on a curve of gusty autumn sky. PoToHe

Let Him with Kisses of His Mouth. Anonymous. The virgins love thee well. AH

Let It Go. William Empson. You don't want madhouse and the whole thing there. FaBoMo; OBSP; OxBTC

Let Me Be a Giver. Mary Carolyn Davies. Some lonely soul to bless. PoToHe

Let Me Be Held When the Longing Comes. Stephany. a warmth and a blossom/of a feeling, sweetly,/gladly, home. BPo

Let Me Be to Thee as the Circling Bird. Gerard Manley Hopkins. Love, O my God, to call Thee Love and Love. VLP

Let Me Enjoy. Thomas Hardy.
I'll pour out raptures that belong/To others, as they were my own. FaBV
I will lift glad, afar-off eyes,/Though it contain no place for me. AnFE; AWP; HBV 1-2; InPo; MoRP; NoAm; ViBoPo

Let Me Flower as I Will. Lew Sarett. God, let me flower as I will! TrPWD

Let Me Fly. Anonymous. Now let me fly unto Mount Zion, Lord, Lord. FSW

Let Me Go. Anonymous. "Let me go, mother, let me go/To my wife's country." WTO

Let Me Go Back. Mary E. Albright. He is "with me always" there! BLRP

Let Me Go down to Dust. Lew Sarett. Gives its worn body back to earth again. TrPWD

Let Me Go Warm. Luis de Gongora y Argote. And let the world laugh, an' it will. AWP

Let Me Go Where Saints Are Going. Lewis Hartsough. Bear me over angel pinions,/Longs my soul to be away. AH

Let Me Grow Lovely. Karle Wilson Baker. Why may not I, as well as these,/Grow lovely, growing old? BLPA; FaBoBe; HBMV; TrPWD

Let Me Lift Jesus, Lord. Jo Gardner. That I am yielded fully to Thy power/Dynamic and serene. BePJ

Let Me Live but from Year to Year. Henry Van Dyke. My heart will keep the courage of the quest,/And hope the road's last turn will be the best. GoTF; TreFT

Let Me Live Out My Years. John G. Neihardt. Let me be as a tune-swept fiddle-string/That feels the Master Melody–and snaps! GoTF; HBMV; TreFS; YaD

Let Me Look At Me. Bessie June Martin. I'll turn my eyes away from him,/And look instead at me. STF

Let Me Love Bright Things. A. Newberry Choyce. And one with white hands/To comb her gleaming hair! HBMV

Let Me Not Die. Edith Lovejoy Pierce. Sweeps down and down and down into the pit. TrPWD

Let Me Put It This Way. George Jonas. Suits me just fine. NeAC

Let me see you. Mira Bai [(or Mirabai)]. She spends her days looking for crows. BoWoP

Let Me Speak of Pure Things. Ho Chih-Fang. Under the blue sky–this serenity! LiTW

Let Mine Eyes See Thee. Saint Theresa of Avila. Let mine eyes see Thee and then see death. AWP; CAW

Let Minions Marshal Every Hair. Anonymous. But they want nothing that are drunk. ALV

Let No Charitable Hope. Elinor Wylie. And none has quite escaped my smile. AnAmPo; HBMV; LiTA; LiTM; MoAB; MoAmPo; NePA; OBSP; OxBA; PBWP; SBG; TrGrPo; VGW

Let Not One Sparke of Filthy Lustfull Fyre. Edmund Spenser. Only behold her rare perfection,/And blesse your fortune's fayre election. TEP

Let Not the Sluggish Sleep. Anonymous. More vent'rous is than he that sleeps/With twenty mortal foes! OBSP; OxBoCh

Let Not Thy Beauty. Aurelian Townsend. And every tongue that wags will grace/Thy vertue with a story. AnAnS 2; JCP

Let Not Your Heart Be Troubled. Alice Mortenson. For as He ascended to heaven/So will your King reappear! BePJ

Let Other People Come as Streams. Charles Reznikoff. trodden under foot today/and here tomorrow morning. VGW

Let Others Sing of Knights and Palladines. Samuel Daniel. Though th' error of my youth in them appeare,/Suffice, they shew I lov'd and lov'd thee deere. AAS

Let's Do It. Cole Porter. Let's do it, let's fall in love. OBAL

Let's Forget. Charles L. H. Wagner. And in meeting it be great. PoToHe

Let's Get Going. Leyla Hanim. Enjoy yourself in this world,/Never mind what they say. PBWP

Let's Go to the Wood, Says This Pig. Anonymous. Kiss her to death, says this pig. OxNR

Let's Talk, Mother. Edith Bruck. doesn't take flight anymore/on wings of innocence. VWA

Let Some Great Joys Pretend to Find. Thomas Shadwell. No empty space in life be found,/But one continued joy go round. OAEP

Let the Dead Depart in Peace. Anonymous. Leave your arrows in the quiver,/And let the dead depart in peace. WTO

Let the Deep Organ Swell. Charles Constantine Pise. And hearken to their humble prayer. AH

Let the Florid Music Praise. W. H. Auden. And my vows break/Before his look. MoPo

Let the Light Enter. Frances E. W. Harper. Then be blessed with light, more light. PoNe

Let the Rest of the World Go By. J. Keirn Brennan. And let the rest of the world go by. UnPo

Let the Wind Blow High or Low. *Anonymous.* I'll roll my lass all in the grass,/Let the wind blow high or low. OBET

Let Them Alone. Robinson Jeffers. Hemingway play the fool and Faulkner forget his art. AP

Let There Be Law. Mark Van Doren. Let law be father of our peace. MoRP

Let There Be Light. William M. Vories. God, give thy wayward children peace! AH

Let There Be New Flowering. Lucille Clifton. let love be/at the end. GP; PPJ

Let This Be My Parting Word. Rabindranath Tagore. ...and if the end comes here, let it come–let this be/my parting word. MoRP

Let Thy Kingdom. *Anonymous.* The good shepherd feeds his sheep. AH

Let Tyrants Shake Their Iron Rod. William Billings. Loud hallelujahs let us sing,/And praise his name on every chord. AH

Let Us All Be Unhappy on Sunday. Lord Charles Neaves. But of course they can sit still at home,/And get dismally drunk upon whisky. FaBoCo

Let Us Break Bread Together. *Anonymous.* Oh, Lord, have mercy if you please. AH; FSW

Let Us Declare! (excerpt). Angela Morgan. The coming of that age/When man shall find his wings! PGD

Let Us Drink. Alcaeus. In sportive chase the last pursue. AWP

Let Us Forget. Agnes Mary Frances (Mme Emile Duclaux) Robinson. Without to-morrow, without yesterday. WHA

Let Us Gather at the River. Marge Piercy. ...songs/in praise of the green brown river/flowing clean through the blue green world. GeTw

Let Us God, Then, Exploring. Virginia Woolf. Life, Life, Life! cries the bird/As if he had heard.... BoNaP

Let Us Have Faith That Right Makes Might. Abraham Lincoln. let us to the end dare to do our duty/as we understand it. TRV

Let Us Have Peace. Nancy Byrd Turner. Let us have peace! PoToHe

Let Us Keep Christmas. Grace Noll Crowell. Let us get back our childlike faith again. TRV

Let Us Laugh. Zvi Shargel. Until the grief is gone/and you, its messenger,/and I. VWA

Let Us Learn. Melech, Ravitch. and nothing comes between the sons of Adam and God. VWA

Let us not Pretend. Ray Mathew. To the crow's eyes. BoAV

Let Us Now Praise Famous Men. C. Day-Lewis. ...and stand a moment in silence/For the passing of an era, at their own funeral. BiP; CMoP

Let Us Rise Up and Live. Francis Sherman. ...Let us rise up and live! CaP

Let Us Sing Unto the Lord a New Song. Denise Levertov. the singing begins. CAPP

Let Us Smile. Wilbur D. Nesbit. It's worth a million dollars, and it doesn't cost a cent. WBLP

"Let us suppose the mind." Barbara Moraff. when, extending its antennae it discovers/not god/but its own miracle. IHMS

Let Us with a Gladsome Mind. John Milton. For his mercies aye endure,/Ever faithful, ever sure. TRV; WGRP

Let War's Tempests Cease. Henry Wadsworth Longfellow. Till Thou shalt reign alone,/Great King of Kings. OHIP

Let Your Pastor Know. *Anonymous.* But the pastor–for not knowing,/Simply "gets it in the neck." STF

Let Zeus Record. Hilda ("H. D.") Doolittle. to freighted ships baffled in wind and blast. MoAmPo

Let Zulu Be Heard. Isaiah Shembe. You young men of Shaka/Before the uMsindisi. WTO

The Lethal Thought. Mary Boyd Wagner. And writhed to see its lethal sting/Destroying you. GoYe

Lethe. Hilda ("H. D.") Doolittle. without question,/without kiss. AmLP; CMoP; FaBoWP; LiTM; MoAmPo; PG; PoRA; TrGrPo; VGW; ViBoPo; WHA

Lethe. Georgia Douglas Johnson. To sink in quiet seas. CDC

Lethe. Edna St. Vincent Millay. Dip the song in the stream. PG

The Letter. *Anonymous.* So precious to me are the fourscore words,/That each letter changes into a bar of gold. LoBV

The Letter. W. H. Auden. Always afraid to say more than it meant. FaBoTw; NoAm

The Letter. Patricia Beer. But drops caught up in the bough/Fall murderously on me now. OxBC

Letter. Alexander Bergman. that must be said to them, to me/or anyone alive? What?/Love,/Abraham. TrJP

The Letter. Paul Blackburn. By this hand, the third day of August .'55/from the ARSIA/in a timeless sea . CoPo

The Letter. John Blight. I have it pressed to me, this hour, with love. CBAP

Letter. Philip Dow. Last time together we bathed each other, chaste. I remember as I masturbate. NPGG

A Letter. Ralph Waldo Emerson. And aim a telescope at the inviolate sun. OxBA

Letter. William Empson.
And hide a tumult never to be told. ChMP; LiTB
Or call the tune to make the dancing throng/Free only as they aloof compose it and are strong. LiTB

A Letter. Anthony Hecht. The endless repetitions of his own murmurous blood. NYBP; OxBC

The Letter. John Holmes. But one is currency. One is mine. One. NePoAm

A Letter. Rachel Korn. Because the envelope–is empty. VWA

Letter. William Stanley Merwin. I tell you HAP

The Letter. Beatrice M. Murphy. You see, it is my heart. PoNe

A Letter. King of Seville Mu'tamid. Make bold to write upon my telltale cheek/In a clear hand the things I dare not speak. LiTW

A Letter. Sir Arthur Thomas ("Q") Quiller-Couch. And come–you will come? to Commem. CenHV

The Letter. Charles Reznikoff. smelling a pungent weed, noting a bird's/two notes. VWA

The Letter. Elizabeth Riddell. Always with love, with love. NOAV

A Letter. Anne Ridler. And since you, loiterer, did compose this wonder,/be with me still, and may God hold his thunder. LiTL

Letter. Mark Strand. It is all I have. I give it all to you. Yours, NoAm

The Letter. John Tatham. Goe and prosper for a space,/Till I rob thee of thy place. CavP

The Letter. John Hall Wheelock. The words: "My darling, my beloved one." AnEnPo; LiTL

Letter 27. Charles Olson. backwards I compell Gloucester/to yield to Maximus, to/change/Polis/is this. CoPo

Letter #8. Dennis Brutus. And it is the brusque inquiry/and threat/that I remember of that night/rather than the stars. WhB

Letter Across Doubt and Distance. M. Carl Holman. Calmed, as that gray church tower/Checks the wild pigeons taking them to breast. AmNP; PoNe

A Letter Catches Up with Me. Eric Chaet. As for love: it overwhelms my fear. VWA

Letter Containing a Panegyric on Bath. Christopher Anstey. Who says, There is neither Transgression nor Sin;/A Doctrine that brings many Customers in. OBEC

The Letter Edged in Black. *Anonymous.* When he handed me that letter edged in black. FSW

A Letter for Allhallows. Peter Kane Dufault. who, one way or another, were made ghosts/in all their country's wars. NYBP

Letter for Duncan. Larry Eigner. you'll always go to sleep/more times than you'll wake PoM

A Letter for Marian. Thomas McGrath. But not so easy. VGW

Letter for Melville 1951. Charles Olson. He'll not say a word because he need not, he said so many. CoPo

Letter from a Black Soldier. Bill Anderson. ...falling/petal by petal on the muzzles of the transfigured/horses. VGW

Letter from a Contract Worker. Antonio Jacinto. and I–oh, the hopelessness–I can't write. WhB

Letter from a Coward to a Hero. Robert Penn Warren. Honor, for death shy valentine. MoAmPo

Letter from a Death Bed. John Ciardi. to praise you as you are from all I leave. NCSH

A Letter from a Friend. Carolyn Maisel. At night the birds and insects will hide/in you. IHMS

A Letter from a Friend. John N. Morris. The dead and the serious old/Do not expect the main thing from us. CABA

A Letter from a Girl to Her Own Old Age. Alice Meynell. With morning tears thy mournful twilight blesses. FaBoRV; GoTL; LiTB; MoBrPo; SBG; ViBoPo

Letter from a State Hospital. Frank Mundorf. and I marvel at men never gentle until they are old. GoYe

Letter from a Wife. S. Carolyn Reese. Apart-from-you takes half my strength/The rest I need for waiting. PoNe

Letter from a Working Girl. Herbert Scott. I will finish this letter later. GP

Letter from an Institution, III. Michael Ryan. You start to want to crazy. AmPA

Letter from an Island. John Malcolm Brinnin. I've never been more serious./Love, J. TAP

A Letter from Aragon. John Cornford. It will be as a heap of ruins with us workers beneath it.' OBWP

A Letter from Artemisa... John Wilmot, Earl of Rochester. But you are tir'd, and so am I./Farewel. SeCV 1-2

A Letter from Berlin. Jon Stallworthy. ...a trench, filled/not with snow only, east of Buchenwald. NoAm; OBWP; OxBC

Letter to My Sister. Anne Spencer. The gods their god-like fun. AmNP; BlSi; PoBA; PoNe

Letter to My Wife. Roy Fuller. Always and have no consolation from the ghosts? NeBP

Letter to My Wife. Miklos Radnoti. the light of 2 x 2 is raining down on me. VWA

Letter to My Wife. Keidrych Rhys. When bombs come shrieking down, pray men's minds might be/unfurled. WaP

Letter to Myself (parody). Christopher Reid. I could run on till Doomsday in this shrill,/Pindaric fashion, and, dear Clive, no doubt I will. FaBoPa

Letter to N. Y. Elizabeth Bishop. nevertheless I'd like to know/what you are doing and where you are going. LiTL; MP; NoP; NYP; TwCP

Letter to P. Robert Friend. I do not utter now/the word "love." NYBP

Letter to Pasternak. Ralph Pomeroy. internally, secretly, as unrestricted as a stallion's shadow. CoPo

A Letter to Paul Celan in Memory. Jerome Rothenberg. "drunk/"blest/ "gebentsht VWA

Letter to Pearse Hutchinson. Eilean Ni Chuilleanain. Do not expect to feel so free on land. FaBoWP

A Letter to Peter. Fay Chiang. see you soon. love, fay 1/17/78. BrSi

Letter to R. Willard Maas. ...the need/Which grows from the arms' want through desolation. WaP

Letter to Reed from Lolo. Richard Hugo. ...I will write some more forever though only poetry and therefore always/failure. Dick. NNaP

Letter to Robert. Mary Fabilli. ₆(This is what I think of the international situation–very/lucid, is it not). IHMS

Letter to Robert Fergusson. Alexander Scott. And here's my ain–Yours, Alexander Scott. OxBS

A Letter to Robert Frost. Robert Hillyer. Since I write oftener than you, I vow/Another letter twenty years from now. MoAmPo

A Letter to Ron Silliman on the Back of a Map of the Solar System. Dennis Schmitz. to eat or forget our real origins. LCAP

Letter to Scanlon from Whitehall. Richard Hugo. Say yes. Be nice. Love. Dick. NNaP

Letter to Seamus Heaney. Michael Longley. And prolong this sad recital/ By leaving careful footprints round/A wind-encircled burial mound. FaBoIP

Letter to Sir H. Wotton at His Going Ambassador to Venice. John Donne. And to send you what I shall begge, his staires/In length and ease are alike every where. OBS

A Letter to Sir Robert Walpole. Henry Fielding. To take your humble servant lower. CEP

Letter to Statues. John Malcolm Brinnin. My next companion shall be flesh and bone. EyDe

Letter to the City Clerk. Frederick A. Wright. That nothing there is ever killed or sold. FaFP

A Letter to the Countess of Denbigh. Richard Crashaw. He is repuls'd indeed, but You're undone. MePo; SeCP

Letter to the Front. Muriel Rukeyser. As I now send you, for a beginning, praise. WaP

Letter to the Governors, June 8, 1783. George Washington. we can never hope to be a happy nation. TRV

Letter to the Night. Lloyd Frankenberg. For all our songs are to the night. AnAmPo

Letter to the Revolution. Susan Griffin. I find your presence/everywhere, but nowhere/do I find your heart. NPGG

A Letter to Three Irish Poets. Michael Longley. Claim this my country, though today/Timor mortis conturbat me. BIrV

Letter to Tina Koyama from Elliot Bay Park. Jim Mitsui. asking why we should expect to translate/the hunger of poetry. BrSi

Letter to Viscount Cobham. William Congreve. And all the Golden Age, is but a Dream. LoBV

Letter to Wagoner from Port Townsend. Richard Hugo. We are called human. C'iao. Dick. NNaP

Letter to Welch from Browning. Richard Hugo. ...Take care, Chief Boiling/Whiskey. Dick. NNaP

A Letter to Wilbur Frohock. Daniel Gerard Hoffman. my accent's improving. CoPo

A Letter to William Carlos Williams. Kenneth Rexroth. ...one who creates/Sacramental relationships/That last always."/With love and admiration... NNaP; PP

Letter V. W. S. Graham. Reply. Present your world./Gannet of God, strike. OxBTC

Letter VI. W. S. Graham. What shall I answer for? ChMP; FaBoMo

Letter VIII. Randall Swingler. That death himself brings nothing to an end. WaP

Letter with a Black Border. Sandra McPherson. But you do not know/A single one of the mourners. GeTw

Letter Written on a Ferry Crossing Long Island Sound. Anne Sexton. good news, good news. CoAP; MP; NYBP; TwCP

Letters. Charles Bukowski. ah, she has such a beautiful soul! GP

Letters. Ralph Waldo Emerson. That the word the vessel brings/Is the word they wish to hear. OBSP

Letters. Bernard Spencer. utter the clothed or the naked man? NeBP; WaP

The Letters. Alfred, Lord Tennyson. There comes a sound of marriage bells. HBV 1-2

The Letters at School. Mary Mapes Dodge. And kissed the Vowels, for, you see,/They couldn't do without them. OBCA

Letters for the New England Dead. Mary Baron. The winged skulls shriek: None shall escape the wrath/Of the King of Terrors. HoAn

Letters Found near a Suicide. Frank Horne.
...and thought only of her? BPo
and want me back... BPo; PoNe
hurtling/through the tape/to victory... BPo; PoNe
Is that thin sound I hear/Your applause?... CDC
over the line/to victory... BPo; PoNe

Letters from a Father. Mona Van Duyn. So the world woos its children back for an evening kiss. FYAP

Letters from an Irishman to a Rat. Christopher Logue. whereas in my house there are only five. BoAnP

Letters from Birmingham. Harold Bond. hearing church organs grind out canticles/for all souls dynamited into heaven. TAT

Letters from Kazuko (Kyoto, Japan–Summer 1980). Alan Chong Lau. shaking the air around me BrSi

Letters from the Astronomers, I: Nicholas Copernicus (1473-1543). Siv Cedering Fox. An armillary sphere? An astrolabe? SUW

Letters from the Astronomers, II: Johannes Kepler (1571-1630). Siv Cedering Fox. Geometry indeed is God. SUW

Letters from Vicksburg, XII. Gary Gildner. we leave our arms and some come cleare acrost. SM

The Letters of a Name. Colette Inez. Tomorrow I will let you take my name away. AMV-81

The Letters of Summer. Christopher Buckley. the lines will be fulfilled–this is all they're saying. AMV-80

The Letters of the Book. Rose Drachler. The sharp-toothed father/Of our fathers/Who was wont to gore in the past VWA

Letters & Other Worlds. Michael Ondaatje. the blood searching in his head without metaphor NOBC; NoP

Letters to a Stranger. Thomas James. But the snow keeps whispering of you over and over. AmPA

Letters to Live Poets. Bruce Beaver.
and the empty, ocean-hymning shells. CBAP
not all writers, yet all conscious/of the gift of the living word. CBAP
room by room like a shabby genteel boarding house, age. CBAP
...taking stock of/Monkey, Piggsy, Sandy's belt of skulls. CBAP
that some men, early or late, may listen? CBAP
...Tomorrow we'll talk of life and sundry other things. CBAP; NOAV
...Why don't I/reflect some therapeutically?/You tell me. CBAP

Letters to My Daughters. Judith Minty. two fingers to hold a fork, a pen, nothing more. AMV-81

Letters to Walt Whitman. Ronald Johnson.
Arus-eyed & insistent. VGW
bound up in the unquenchable flames of double suns. VGW
I, too, have plucked a stalk of grass/from your ample prairie, Walt. VGW
that surrounds us,/singing. VGW

Lettice. Dinah Maria Mulock Craik. Life bears Love's cross, death brings Love's crown. HBV 1-2

Letting Go. Richard Shelton. it will last long enough AMV-81

Letting My Feelings Out. Yu Hsuan-chi. Half-drunk, I get up and comb my hair. BoWoP

Letty's Globe. Charles Tennyson Turner. Bright over Europe fell her golden hair. CBEP; HBV 1-2; NOBV; OBEV; OBVV; OnUR

Leukothea. Keith Douglas. only the little bones and the great ones, disarranged. NeBP

Levant. Lawrence Durrell. Something money or promises can buy. OBTV

A Levantine. William Plomer. He has no principles at all. OBMV

Levavi Oculos. Marion Campbell. "I, too, joyfully trod my hills and came away,/"And bore a Burden up a stony road.' PoSH

Levee Camp Blues. Anonymous. I'm 'fraid he might kick me an' I might die. OuSiCo

Levee Camp "Holler." Anonymous. Um–m, cain' see nothin' but de stars an' moon. ABF

Levee Camp Moan. Texas Alexander. Lord if she don't come on the big boat/I mean she better not land BluL

Levee Moan (with music). Anonymous. O honey, your hair grows too long, O honey, your hair grows too long. AS

The Level and the Square. Robert Morris. "We meet upon the Level and we part upon the Square." BLPA

The Levelled Churchyard. Thomas Hardy. From zealous Churchmen's pick and plane/Deliver us O Lord! Amen!' NOBL

Leves Amores. Arthur Symons. ...and you are mine; my sweet! AnEnPo; UnTE

Leviathan. *Anonymous.* Thus, thus the Calf's-Head-Club shall sing,/ Leviathan, our god and king. APAS

Leviathan. William Stanley Merwin. ...And he waits for the world to begin. ConAP; NePoEA; NoAm; NOBA

Leviathan. Kenneth Pitchford. home to the coral fathoms of my day. CoPo

Leviathan. Peter Quennell. Such pitiless disharmony of shapes. MoBrPo

Levitation. Alvin Aubert. ...my heart/soars with that intrepid flyer. GP

Lewd Love is Loss. Robert Southwell. In which to live is death, to die is Hell. ACP

Lewesdon Hill. William Crowe. To climb, as now, to Lewesdon's airy top. NOEC

Lewis and Clark. Rosemary and Stephen Vincent Benét. And it spread out an Empire before us. BPAW

Lewis Carroll. Eleanor Farjeon. Allow me to tell you a couple!' OxBChV

Lewti. Samuel Taylor Coleridge. To-morrow Lewti may be kind. EnRP

Lexington. Oliver Wendell Holmes. Wide as o'er land and sea/Floats the 'fair emblem her heroes have won! MC; PAH

Lexington. Sidney Lanier. As Harrington came, ye likewise came/And died at the door of our House of Fame. PAH; PAL

Lexington. John Greenleaf Whittier. The lion of our Motherland! MC; PAH

The Lexington Miller. *Anonymous.* I warn all men and maidens, to all their vows prove true. BaBo

The Lexington Murder. *Anonymous.* Don't ever let the devil get/The upper hand on you. BaBo; OuSiCo

LI. Ted Berrigan. Gus Cannon gulping, "I called myself Banjo Joe!" ANYP

Li'l' Gal. Paul Laurence Dunbar. Dat's de reason I's a-sighin' an' a-singin' now fu' you,/Li'l' gal. GoSl

Li'l Liza Jane. *Anonymous.* Oh! Eliza, Li'l Liza Jane. BLSo

Li Po. Ruth Gilbert. A young moon on his breast. AnNZ

Liadan Laments Cuirithir. Liadan. I will not live without him. BIrV; NOBI; OnYI; PBWP

Liady-Day an' Ridden House. William Barnes. That I wou'd rather kip my staddle. OBRV

The Liar. *Anonymous.* Were the lies killed overnight/Rising from the dead with dawn. KiLC

The Liar. Robert Earl Hayden. When they say, "It is Roi/who is dead?" I wonder/who will they mean? AmPP; NOBA

Liard Hot Springs. Gordon Massman. We were like two fish/darting/in and out of the water/before dawn. CTBA

Libation. Denise Levertov. After these months of pain we begin/to admit our new lives have begun. GP

A Libel on D. Jonathan Swift. And, Statesmen by ten thousand odds/Are ANGELS, just as--are GODS. NCEP

Liberace. Jonathan Holden. Thank you very much. MAYP

Liberal or Innocent by Definition. James Philip McAuley. That's not my point, and where are we at.' NOAV

Liberation. Diane Mei Lin Mark. the retreat of tide from shore BrSi

Liberation. Ruth Stone. The spider with her web across our lips. BoWoP

The Liberator. Emily Holmes Coleman. all of us/shall/dance/within. EAS

The Liberator. Lucien Stryk. Work done, betrayals yet to come. GP

The Libertine. Louis MacNeice. O leave me easy, leave me alone. DTC; NoAm

Liberty. John Milton Hay. And though thou slay us, we will trust in/thee! AA

Liberty. Edward ("Edward Eastaway") Thomas. And this moon that leaves me dark within the door. MoAB; OAEL 1-2

Liberty. Sir Thomas Wyatt. For I am now at liberty. OBSC

Liberty and Independence. *Anonymous.* Rang out loudly "INDEPENDENCE,"/Which, please God, shall never die. TreFS

Liberty and Peace. Phillis Wheatley. And heavenly freedom spread her golden ray. BlSi; SBG

Liberty Enlightening the World. Edmund Clarence Stedman. Till the last sun grow pale/Let there be Light! PAH

Liberty (excerpt). William Wordsworth. The bed we give him, though of softest down. FaBoCo; FiBHP; Par

Liberty for All. William Lloyd Garrison. And, by a mighty hand, th' oppressed HE yet shall save! AA; AmePo

The Liberty Pole. *Anonymous.* And, huzzah for King George and our coun-/try forever!/Derry down, down, hey derry down. PAH

The Liberty Song. John Dickinson. Not as Slaves, but as Free men our money we'll give. BLSo; TrAS

Liberty Tree. Thomas Paine. Let the far and the near, all unite with a cheer,/In defence of our Liberty Tree. MC; PAH

The Librarian. Charles Olson. ...Who is/Frank Moore? CAPP; CoPo

Library. Louis Jenkins. ...and crews with/chain saws and representatives of the paper company. NU

The Library. John Logan. ...made of the bent bodies/of fabulous, elongate beasts AMV-80

The Library. Mary Mills. where the lions of Judah lie in their fusty lair. NePoAm

The Library. Frank Dempster Sherman. Hic habitat Felicitas! AA

The Lice-Finders. Arthur Rimbaud. Ceaselessly heave and swoon a wish to cry. SOTW; SyP

Lichen. Mary Elizabeth ("E") Fullerton. Delicate beauty/Trembles and goes. PoAu 1-2

The Licht Nichts. Violet Jacob. I' the licht nichts o' the year. ACV

Lichtenberg. Rudyard Kipling. The smell of the wattle by Lichtenberg,/ Riding in, in the rain! EnLit

Licia (excerpt). Giles the Elder Fletcher. Except thy beauty, virtues, and thy friend. EBEV

The Licorice Fields at Pontefract. Sir John Betjeman. And wound with flaming ropes of hair. CMoP; NMP

Liddell and Scott. Thomas Hardy. I feel as hollow as a fiddle,/Working so many hours,' said Liddell. OxBoLi

The Lido. Edmund Wilson. Exhaled from open flanks, the sea. ErPo

The Lie. Rudyard Kipling. And ring-fence-deer-park Lie. NOBL

The Lie. Al Lee. Everyday now are as unreliable/As their eyes. AmPA

The Lie. Howard Moss. Lie to me. And lie to me. AtBAP; LiTM; MoAB; NePoAm

The Lie. Sir Walter Ralegh. No stab the soul can kill. AAS; AtBAP; CBEP; CTC; EBEV; ExPo; FaBoPV; FCP; ForPo; HAP; HBV 1-2; InvP; LiTB; MasP; NOBE; NoP; OAEP; OBSC; PoEL 1-5; PPoe; PPON; QFR; SCV; SeCeV; SiPS; TEP; TreFT; TrGrPo; ViBoPo

Lie Closed, My Lately Loved. John Woods. ...Around/His yellow mouth hang crumbs of flowers. ConAP

Lie on the Sand. Alistair Campbell. Where perfect thoughts like bees in amber lie. AnNZ

Lied in Crete. Alvaro Mutis. In that certitude I rest./In happiness. AMV-80

Lies and Gossip. Raymond Ringo Fernandez. and it's his turn/to tell a lie.... LFAC

Life. Franklin Pierce ("F.P.A.") Adams. Entered I into the subway station/Known as Cathedral Parkway. InMe

Life. *Anonymous.* To accept justly what is right. PoToHe

A Life. Chana Bloch. ...foxheads,/sharp-nosed,/amber-eyed,/dreaming her dreams. MAYP

Life. Alice Brown. My champion, Death! AA

Life. Samuel Taylor Coleridge. And thought suspended lie in Rapture's blissful/trance. EnRP

Life. George Crabbe. But what still deepening clouds of Care survive! OBEC

Life. Margaret Deland. Men's hungry souls have called that great Heart, GOD! WGRP

The Life. Philip Dow. paying back the sea. AmPA

Life. Paul Laurence Dunbar. And that is life! AmNP; CDC

Life. Artie Gold. You have dropped your handkerchief. NOBC

Life. Amory Hare. For one the mire, the hurry and the throng. HBMV

Life. George Herbert. Since if my scent be good, I care not, if/It be as short as yours. AnAnS 1; CBEP; EG; FaBoRV; HBV 1-2; JCP; LiTB; MeLP; MePo; NoP; OBS; PoPle; SeCeV; SeCP; SeCV 1-2

Life. Alfred Kreymborg. I agree with you cheerfully, ladies. ELU

A Life. Sylvia Plath. And a drowned man, complaining of the great cold,/ Crawls up out of the sea. NOBA

Life. Nan Terrell Reed. Where is that gown I could fashion–alone? BLPA

Life. Edward Rowland Sill.
And Time is conquered, and thy crown is won. TRV
So live each day that God shall say,/"Well done!" at last. BLRP

Life. Grace Treasone. and laughs, not tears, will start. PeD

Life. Jones Very. Who will not hear and make his word their friend. AP

Life. Ella Wheeler Wilcox. Down to the grave–ARE ITS HOPES IN VAIN? PoToHe

A Life. George Edward Woodberry. My bare poles dip, through sun and spray,/The dim marge of God's outer sea. EtS

The Life. James Wright. And it is/The last time. LCAP; NaP

Life, A Question. Corinne Roosevelt Robinson. Life is the test of us! HBV 1-2

The Life above, the Life on High. Saint Theresa of Avila. I'm dying of desire to die. WGRP

Life After Death. Pindar. Burned for the glory of Heaven continually. EaLo

Life after Death. Richard W. Thomas. And that is the way it suppose to/ be in this house of sweat and horizons. PoBA

The Life and Character of Dean Swift (excerpt). Jonathan Swift. He grew, or else his comrades lied,/Confounded dull before he died. NOBI; NOBL

Life and Death. William Ernest Henley.
Coming up from Richmond,/On the way to Kew. OBNC
I am the womb and the grave,/The Now and the Ever. OBNC

O, let me be at peace with it. BoAV; PoAu 1-2

On the vast wave of life go by/That, reared, shall never reach the shore. BoAV

That act of mine the ultimate stars/Shall look on sprang in primal ooze. BoAV; PoAu 1-2

There Time shall be/Marshal to Eternity. PoAu 1-2

Through battle climbed to battle, free/To grapple God up there. PoAu 1-2

Life's Work. Maxine W. Kumin. lovesong is the dry aftersound/of your long nails clicking. GP

Life Sculpture. George Washington Doane. Our lives, that angel-vision. BLPA; OHFP; WBLP

Life Story. J. Kates. on any object for the chance/to breed. AMV-81

Life Story. Tomioka Taeko. I've turned into a boy for my lover/and won't let him talk back to me WPOW

Life Story. Tennessee Williams. and that's how people burn to death in hotel rooms. PeHV

Life Studies. Peter Schjeldahl. How do you explain this? ANYP

Life Study. Steve Orlen. Not mine, not hers, belonging to nothing and no one. MAYP

The Life That Counts. A.W. S. That is the life that counts. FaFP; WBLP

Life the Beloved. Dante Gabriel Rossetti. And the red wings of frost-fire rent the sky. MaVP

Life the Very Gods in My Sight Is He Who. Sappho. I can feel that I have been changed, I feel that/death has come near to me. WPOW

The Lifeboat. George R. Sims. He's allus the first aboard her when the lifeboat wants a crew. PaPo

The Lifeguard. James Dickey. And hold in my arms a child/Of water, water, water. CoPo; LiSp; NoP; NYBP

Lifelines. Gavin Ewart. In a field of alien corn a girl was reaped. EAS

Lifelines. T. R. Hummer. Down through the streams of my palms,/The deep lifelines. AMV-80

Lifelong. Rachel Boimwall. My wholeness is being destroyed/through the swift passage/of time. VWA

Lifesaving. Sandra McPherson. And you said, "So that's what love is." MAYP

A Lifetime Devoted to Literature. Judith Rodriguez. ...a sitter on Boards/ preparing to live for ever. NOAV

The Lift. Raymond Souster. the French probably have/an expression for it. PoL

Lift Every Voice and Sing. James Weldon Johnson. True to our native land. FaBV; FSW; GoSl; PoNe

Lift Up Your Heads, Rejoice. Thomas Toke Lynch. Redemption draweth nigh. TrCP; VLP; WGRP

Lift Your Glad Voices in Triumph on High. Henry, Jr. Ware. For Jesus hath risen, and man shall not die. AH

Lifting and Leaning. Ella Wheeler Wilcox. Or are you a leaner who lets others bear/Your portion of worry and labor and care? BLPA; WBLP

Lifting Illegal Nets by Flashlight. James Wright. ...something/Is gone lonely/Into the headwaters of the Minnesota. NNaP

The Liftman. H. A. C. Evans. Just up and down and up and down. PoL

Light. Carol Coates. against the pattern of the pillow,/sleeping. CaP

Light. Hermann Hagedorn. But to the wide, clear-windowed room/It is rebirth. MoRP

The Light. John Holloway. Barriers that divide/And therefore also join,/ Crazy things and holy. NePoEA

Light. John Milton. ...that I may see and tell/Of things invisible to mortal sight. OBEV

Light. Jon Silkin. And what single light is not drowned/In the glut of the sea's dark sound? NoAm

Light, 2. Richard Eberhart. such peace/has no need/to figure/out who pulled/the trigger. NoAm

Light, 4. Louis Zukofsky P.S. I want to resign. NoAm

Light a Candle. Zelda. and in her hand/the sinking sun... VWA

Light and Dark. Barbara Howes. The spell of the world is loosed, it is time to go. MoVE

The Light and Glory of the World. William Cowper. It gives, but borrows none. TRV

Light and Love, Hope and Faith. Eva Gray. Charts the course of every Christian,/Leads us on to paradise. STF

Light and Rejoicing to Israel. Anonymous. Merciful One and All-holy,/ Praised for ever and ever. TrJP

Light Another Candle. Miriam Chaikin. sing yet another song, hoi!/chirry, birry, bin. NTCP

Light at Equinox. Léonie Adams. And netherwards for partner draws her shade. CrMA

Light Baggage. Alice Walker. a slouched back against the shoulders/of the world. LTB

Light Breaks Where No Sun Shines. Dylan Thomas. Above the waste allotments the dawn halts. CMoP; EnL; FaBoMo; LiTB; LiTL; MoAB; MoBrPo; OAEP; OxBTC; SeCePo; ViBoPo

A Light Breather. Theodore Roethke. A small thing,/Singing. NoP

Light Casualties. Robert Francis. Did a few tears fall? PPJ

A light exists in spring. Emily Dickinson. As Trade had suddenly encroached/Upon a Sacrament. BoWoP; ExPo; LiTA; NOBA; OxBA

The Light from Within. Jones Very. And lit, as by a lamp from heaven,/ The world's track of sin. WGRP

The Light-Hearted Fairy. Anonymous. With a hey and a heigh and a ho! SUS

Light in the Darkness. Aileen Fisher. The light of the Captain's faith! YeAr

Light in the Open Air. Annie Dillard. This causes a very peculiar sensation,/difficult to describe. SUW

The Light in the Temple. William Rose Benet. Good tidings of great joy. MoRP

A Light Left On. May Sarton. And by that light found out. MoLP

Light, Light of My Eyes. Sextus Propertius. Since that day I have had no pleasant nights. LiTW

Light Listened. Theodore Roethke. Light listened when she sang. BiP; MoAmPo; UnTE

Light Lover. Aline Kilmer. Oh, I think you had better go back to sea! HBMV

Light mist, then dense fog. Li Ch'ing-chao. I am more frail than the orchid petals. BoWoP

Light Morning Snow, We Wait for a Warmer Season. John Garmon. falling, delicate, merging. AMV-80

The Light Now Shineth. Anonymous Souls in conflict, burdened, sighing,/ Jesus came to save. STF

The Light of Asia. Sir Edwin Arnold.
...the boy attained thereat/Dhyana, first step of "the path." VLP
The heart of it is Love, the end of it/Is Peace and Consummation sweet. Obey! VLP

The Light of Asia (excerpt). Mrs. Major Arnold. And gateways, to the river and the bridge/Under the city walls. OBTV

The Light of Bethlehem. John Banister Tabb. The lordliest, earthward bending, hail/The Light of Bethlehem! CAW

The Light of Faith. Edgar Dupree. Revealing with it God's great providence. BLRP

Light of Judea. Claude Vigee. Jerusalem of the future/Which the glare/Of the summer snow unveils. VWA

The Light of Life. Hugh" (Christopher Murray Grieve) MacDiarmid. –Then be life's locht, my wife!... CMoP

The Light of Stars. William Henry Furness. Let them shine serene and still,/And with light my being fill. TrPWD

Light of the Soul. Edward Caswall. All glory with the Father be,/And Holy Ghost, eternally! BePJ

The Light of the World. B. (Eliezer Blum) Alquit. The hand of creation/ weeps. VWA

Light of the World. Slyvester Judd. Hope spreads on heavenward wing. BePJ

Light of the World. John S. B. Monsell. Rise in the new creation/Which springs from love and Thee. TrPWD

The Light on Cape May. Anonymous. On our passage home from Liverpool to Philadelfiee. ShS

The Light'ood Fire. John Henry Boner. And a red, rousing light'ood fire. AA

Light or Sheade. William Barnes. Words alwone vrom her a-vallen,/Would be jay vor all the night. NOBV

The Light Passages. Debora Greger. goes to the piano/and begins to play. MAYP

Light Rain. Christopher Buckley. and I am thinking–it is a light rain, just after... AMV-81

Light's Glittering Morn. John Mason Neale. An Angel robed in light hath said,/"The Lord is risen from the dead." EBCP; OxBoCh

Light Shining Out of Darkness. Jane Borthwick. Thou wilt perform unto the end the work thou hast begun. BLRP

Light Shining Out of Darkness. William Cowper. And he will make it plain. AtBAP; EaLo; SeCePo

Light Showers of Light. Kathryn Lindskoog. It is the only art. AMV-80

The Light That Came. Lucille Clifton. "you might as well answer the door, my child,/the truth is furiously knocking." GeTw

Light the Lamps Up, Lamplighter. Eleanor Farjeon. Because the night is here. CH; SiSoSe; TiPo

Light under the Door. Marilyn Waniek. I remember Mama's voice humming mezzo/as I walked out into the light. MAYP

Light-Winged Smoke, Icarian Bird. Henry David Thoreau. And ask the gods to pardon this clear flame. AP; MAmP; NOBA; OBSP; TAP; ViBoPo

A Light Woman. Robert Browning. Here's a subject made to your hand! HBV 1-2; VLP

The Light Woman's Song. Judith Johnson Sherwin. what shall I hunger for/and not let go TAP

The Light Year. John Ridland. and still so far/from any neighboring star/ in the spacious/dark OFD

The Light Yoke and Easy Burden. Charles Wesley. And fill me with Thy perfect peace. BcPJ

Lighten Our Darkness. Lord Alfred Bruce Douglas. And knew them all for liars, rogues and knaves. HBMV

Lighthearted William. William Carlos Williams. twirling his green moustaches. LOW; SO

The Lighthouse. John Seller Anson. and drowned it with my call. AMV-80

A Lighthouse in Maine. Derek Mahon. Out you get and/Walk the rest of the way. FaBoIP; OBTV

Lighthouse in the Night. Alfonsina Storni. A crow digs endlessly/but no longer bleeds. BoWoP

The Lighthouse Invites the Storm. Malcolm Lowry. What good spirit undulates you still like kites that/Children are guardians of in cold blue?... NOBC

The Lighthouse Keeper's Offspring. James Richard Broughton. and all of earth's dry murder thrown/overboard with ease. CrMA

Lighting the Night Sky. Kenneth O. Hanson. "and shaped like the top of a table." FYAP

Lightly Like Music Running. Jean Garrigue. ...in the green fables/Of the dogdays, in early youth. MoVE

Lightly stepped a yellow star. Emily Dickinson. "Father," I observed to Heaven,/"You are punctual!" MoAmPo; MoShBr; OxBA

Lightness Remembered. Nancy Willard. there's no saving you. LCAP

Lightning. Witter ("Emanuel Morgan") Bynner. Followed by the sight of you when you are gone. MoLP

Lightning. D. H. Lawrence. Home, away home, ere the lightning floated forth again. CMoP; LiTL; MoAB; MoBrPo; UnTE

Lightning Bug. Robert Morgan. the edge of the orchard country. GeTw

The Lightning Flash. Anonymous. We join our hands in wedlock bands, but her face I ne'er can see! AmFP

The lightning is a yellow fork. Emily Dickinson. The Apparatus of the Dark/To ignorance revealed. InPK

Lightning of the Abyss. Jules Laforgue. Ah, to become nothing again, irrevocably spent! SyP

Lightning Rides. P. Wolny. a single geranium. PPJ

Lights among Redwood. Thom Gunn. ...we stand/and stare–mindless, diminished–/at their rosy immanence. OBTV

The Lights Go On. Mark McCloskey. I follow her outside like a white flag. AMV-80

The Lights in the Hallway. James Wright. ...longing/For the red spider who is God. CAPP

Lights in the Quarters Burnin' Mighty Dim. Anonymous. Captain, can't you see this four o'clock trouble 'bout to kill poor me? OuSiCo

Lights Out. Edward ("Edward Eastaway") Thomas. Its silence I hear and obey/That I may lose my way/And myself. BrPo; MMM; NOBE

LII. Ted Berrigan. you have kept up with the times and I am glad! ANYP

LIII. Ted Berrigan. Fucking is so very lovely/Who can say no to it later? ANYP

Like a Beach. Harvey Shapiro. Whose happiness/Even here/Is being sacrificed? VWA

Like a Field Waiting. Raquel Chalfi. and there are so many things/a field can wait for when/predators wait at her edge. VWA

Like a Great Rock, Far out at Sea. Lady Sanuki. Is never for a moment dried. AWP

Like a Laverock in the Lift. Jean Ingelow. Sitting by the golden sheaves on our wedding-day. HBV 1-2

Like a Midsummer Rose. John Lydgate. Of whos five woundes print in your hert a rose. OxBM

Like a mountain whirlwind. Sappho. love shattered my heart. BoWoP

Like a Mourningless Child. Kenneth Patchen. I am so close to good. I have no need to see God. MoAmPo

Like a Pearl. Hayim Naggid. And fade/Like the luster of a pearl. VWA

Like a Pearl Dropped. Trumbull Stickney. Your face possesses my despair. NCEP

Like a ravaged sea. Lady Ise. the sleeve I pressed to it/would float back moist with foam. BoWoP

Like a Silkworm Weaving. Mahadevi (Mahadeviyakka). O lord white as jasmine. PBWP

Like a sweet apple reddening on the high. Sappho. ...lying trampled on the earth/yet blooming purple. BoWoP

Like a wave crest. Emperor Uda. One white egret/Guards the harbor mouth. LiTW

Like a Whisper. Ethan Ayer. Must make an end of something–even change. GoYe

Like a Woman. Uri Z. Greenberg. Tortured with longing/As though he had sent me a love letter. VWA

Like a Young Levite. Osip Mandelstam. Lit up the night of Jerusalem and the smoke of nonexistence. VWA

Like an Adventurous Sea-Farer Am I. Michael Drayton. Thus in my Love Time calls me to relate/My tedious Travells and oft-varying Fate. EtS; MOS

Like an April Day. Johan Sebastian C. Welhaven. The flower will then reveal its blossom-heart. LiTW

Like an Elephant. Mahadevi (Mahadeviyakka). Call me: Child, come here,/come this way. PBWP

Like an Ideal Tenant. Ruth Daigon. it wraps itself in silence/closing in on death AMV-81

Like an Old Proud King in a Parable. A. J. M. Smith. Like an old proud king in a parable. OBCV

Like Any Other Man. Gregory Orr. So many years/before the soft key of your tongue/unlocked my body. FF

Like as a Huntsman. Edmund Spenser. So goodly wonne with her own will beguiled. BoLiVe; GBL; SeCePo

Like as the bird in the cage enclosed. Sir Thomas Wyatt. By loss of life liberty, or life by prison? FCP; SiPS

Like as the Damask Rose. Francis Quarles. So Man that dies, shall live again. CBEP; LoBV

Like as the Dove. Sir Philip Sidney. More happy I, might I in bondage bide! SiPS

"Like as the Lark." Thomas William Parsons And whom Heaven crowns with greater/length of days. AA

Like as the swan towards her death. Sir Thomas Wyatt. I do bequeath my very breath/To cry: "I died and you regard it not." FCP; SiPS

Like Barley Bending. Sara Teasdale. Change my sorrow/Into song. HBMV

Like Birds of a Feather. Ralph Schomberg. Sister, brother,/We bespatter one another. TrJP

Like Children of the Summertime Playing at Cards. Julie Herrick White. to wait for the next big draw. AMV-80

Like David. Gabriel Preil. and even the sun, small as David the shepherd boy,/withholds its light from me. VWA

Like Dolmens Round My Childhood, the Old People. John Montague. I felt their shadows pass/Into that dark permanence of ancient forms. EBEV; FaBoIP; IPY

Like Flowers We Spring. Anonymous. Unto our silent graves mournfully wending. CBEP; EIL

Like Ghosts of Eagles. Robert Francis. those mighty whisperers/Missouri Mississippi. LCAP

Like Groping Fingers. Abraham Sutzkever. And they grasped the sense of words/molten in lead. TrJP

Like Gulliver. Nina Cassian. I laugh at you through strings and snakes/of blood, my furious lovers with your tiny bows. BoWoP; VWA

Like Loving Chekhov. Denise Levertov. ...a pain and fear/familiar in the love of the unreachable dead. InPS

Like Musical Instruments. Tom Clark. And then you do PPoe

Like Noah's Weary Dove. William Augustus Muhlenberg. The ark shall ride the sea of fire,/Then rest on Sion's hill. AH

Like Odysseus under the Ram. Archilochus. Dark of heart, dark of mind. OBVE

Like Ripples on the Water. Anonymous. He is like a rippling wave/That passes by. WTO

Like Rousseau. LeRoi (Imamu Amiri Baraka) Jones. They wait and touch and watch their dreams/eat the morning. PoA

Like Smoke. Mririda n'Ait Attik. Their promises are like smoke,/like smoke, like smoke. PBWP

Like Snow. Robert Graves. Holding the histories of the night/In yet unmelted tracks. AtBAP

Like the Eyes of Wolves. Nachum Yud. Comes a flash from my world,/A cutting cold light. TrJP

Like the Honeycomb Dropping Honey. Hildegard von Bingen. In a flock of virgins/She spread about her. WPOW

Like the Idalian Queen. William, of Hawthornden Drummond. A hyacinth I wish'd me in her hand. BSV; GoTS; SeCePo

Like the Prime Mover. Mehdi Ali Seljouk. My tribute from the lustrous barons of the sky. ACV

Like the Touch of Rain. Edward ("Edward Eastaway") Thomas. And will not open again. BoLoP; EnLoPo; GBL

Like They Say. Robert Creeley. ...And/why not, I thought to/myself, why/not. ELU

Like This Together. Adrienne Rich. grip earth and let burn. CoPo; VGW

Like Those Boats Which Are Returning. Saigyo Hoshi. Scatheless through the storms of life. AWP

Like Those Sick Folks. Sir Philip Sidney. Bitter grief tastes me best, pain is my ease,/Sick to the death, still loving my disease. OBSP

Like to a Coin. Arlo Bates. Its tracings firm as when they first were set. AA

Like to the Grass That's Green Today. Peter, the Younger Bulkeley. But it may clip thee in thy prime. AH

Like to the seely fly. Francis Davison. But I my burning and my death foresee. EG

Like to the Thundering Tone. Richard Corbet. E'en such is he who died and yet did laugh/To see these lines writ for his epitaph. NA

Like to These Unmeasurable Mountains. Sir Thomas Wyatt. And I always plaints that pass thorough my throat. AAS; CABA; FCP

Like trains of cars on tracks of plush. Emily Dickinson. Oh, for a bee's experience/Of clovers and of noon! MoAB; MoAmPo

Like Treasure Hidden in the Ground. Mahadevi (Mahadeviyakka). the ways of our lord/white as jasmine. WPOW

Like Water Down a Slope. Zalman Schneour. Would that I were as clear and/transparent as the water streaming/down a mountain-slope... TrJP

Like Weary Trees. Jacob Glatstein. Like weary trees,/interlaced,/shadowy we fell asleep. VWA

Like Wings. Philip Schultz. ...my mouth frozen/round the sound of your name. MAYP

A Likeness. Robert Browning. A thing of no value! Take it, I supplicate!' CTC; PAI; VLP

A Likeness. Willa Cather. Not even,–luckier than this other–/His sorrow in a marble face. HBMV

The Likeness. Arthur Gregor. I shape with bare/and desperate hands/its likeness in myself. VGW

The Likeness. Martial (Marcus Valerius Martialis). For then, I swear, the world today/No rarer picture could display. PeHV

The Likeness. Leonard Nathan. And that's all you can say. GP

Lilac. Frank Stewart Flint. And the butterfly does not fear you. HBMV

The Lilac. Humbert Wolfe. and each dew-note had a/lilac in it. HBVY

Lilac Time. Piet Hein. what's easier done than said. PV

Lilacs. Amy Lowell. Since certainly it is mine. AtBAP; BLPL; LaNeLa; MoAmPo; MoVE; OxBA

The Lilacs and the Roses. Louis Aragon. Like far-off conflagrations: roses of Anjou. OBWP

Lilian. Alfred, Lord Tennyson. Like a rose-leaf I will crush thee,/Fairy Lilian. HBV 1-2; PeD

Lilian's Song. George Darley. From the sun-cloud trills the lark. OBNC

The Lilies. Wendell Berry. ...they breathe their light/into the mind, year after year. GeTw

Lilies. Padraic Colum. That turns the natural/Into supernal. NePoAm

Lilies. John Francis O'Donnell. Be patient, spring is coming quick, and ye/Shall rise again. IrPN

Lilies. Shiko. White lilies in a row! SUS; TiPo

Lilies Are White. Anonymous. If you will have me,/I will have you. PoPle

Lilies for Neal. James Minor. from the emptying/bottle of bourbon. WOLT

The Lilies of the Field. Compton Mackenzie. The certain faith of a March daffodil. OBVV

Lilies of the Valley. Jo Gardner. His presence brings forth fragrance without fail. BePJ

Lilies of the Valley. Jon Silkin. Memorable as the skin/Of a fierce animal. NoAm

Lilith. Ruth Fainlight. Good wives make amulets/Against her, to protect themselves./Lilith is jealous. VWA

Lilith. Ruth Feldman. my frail progeny will fade and die/as her brood grows rosier. VWA

Lilith. Donald Finkel. twenty years/of sweat and bread/and everything to lose VWA

Lilith. Yvan Goll. Closing the compass of its legs/In a prayer to the Absolute VWA

Lilith. Linda Gregg. First for food and then also for flowers. WPOW

Lilith. Allen Grossman. I spread my hair over them. VWA

Lilith. X. J. Kennedy. Second came she whom he begot us by. UnTE

Lilith. Primo Levi. The rest is will o' the wisp and pale light. VWA

Lilith: Adam to Lilith. Christopher John Brennan. ...just the great wings spreading wide. PoAu 1-2

Lilith on the Fate of Man. Christopher John Brennan. and I shall muse above the little dust/that was the flesh that held my world in trust. PoAu 1-2

Lilith's Child. Edward Francisco. The cry of Lilith's child. DL

Lilith: The Anguish'd Doubt Broods over Eden. Christopher John Brennan. to take unto itself some olden word: PoAu 1-2

Lilium Regis. Francis Thompson. What I sang when Night was on the waters! HBMV

Lilli Burlero. Anonymous. Lilli burlero, bullen a la. FSW; NOBI

Lillian's Chair. Olga Cabral. Left us this empty chair. GP

Lilliburlero. Anonymous. For Talbot's de dog, and James is de ass. ViBoFo

Lilliburlero (A New Song). Thomas, Marquess of Wharton. By Chreist and St. Patrick, the nation's our own! APAS

Lilliput Levee. William Brighty ("Matthew Browne") Rands. Such was the custom in Lilliput-land. CenHV

A Lilliputian Ode on Their Majesties' Accession. Henry Carey. God send/No end/To line/Divine/Of George and Caroline! NOEC

Lilliputian's Beer Song. Septimus Winner. Let me wind up with my rhyme/And I'll sing some other time. OBAL

Lilly Dale. H. S. Thompson. Now the wild rose blossoms o'er her little green grave,/'Neath the trees in the flow'ry vale. BLSo

The Lilly in a Christal. Robert Herrick. Then will your hidden Pride/Raise greater fires in men. AnAnS 2; AtBAP; NoP; PoEL 1-5; SeCePo; SeCP

Lilly's Song. Evan Zimroth. My lover, childbride. AMV-81

Lilt Your Johnnie (parody). Anonymous. Amang the thummart dawlit wa'/To lilt your Johnnie. BXAP

Lily. Rosanna Warren. summer uncoiling in which we are/farther and farther apart. MAYP

Lily Adair. Thomas Holley Chivers. For my beautiful, dutiful Lily Adair. OBAL

The Lily Bed. Isabella Valancy Crawford. With cedar paddle, scented, red,/He pushed out from the lily bed. PeCV

Lily Flower. Michael Brownstein. You have your own telephone ANYP

Lily, Germander, and Sops-in-Wine. Anonymous. With sweet-briar/And bon-fire/And strawberry wire/And columbine. AnFE

Lily, Lois & Flaubert: The Site of Loss. Kathleen Fraser. remembered barks form a discourse that still perforates the common silence. NPGG

Lily Munro. Anonymous. Oh, lay the lily ho! OuSiCo

The Lily of the Valley. Thomas Lovell Beddoes. Sign the warrant for its death. EG

The Lily of the West. Anonymous. I never can forgive her, the Lily of the West. AmFP; BFSS; FSW

The Lily of Torrow. Henry Van Dyke. He has discovered it first, and perhaps I/shall find it to-morrow. AA

The Lily-White Rose. Anonymous.
And ever she sang: MeEL
And I must home gone. EG

Limb and Mind. John Waller. And the mind drives/To the lovers' schism. NeBP

The limb of forests rises up. Yvonne Caroutch. Nothing can ever cloud/its incorruptible retina BoWoP

Limbo. Anonymous. And I paid them for laying me in Limbo. OBET

Limbo. Samuel Taylor Coleridge. A fear–a future state;–'tis positive Negation! ERoP 1-2; OAEL 1-2

Limbo. Seamus Heaney. Even Christ's palms, unhealed,/Smart and cannot fish there. CIP; OxBC

Limbo. Marieve Rugo. ...our coins/for the guardian of that last river which was the first. AMV-81

The Lime Avenue. Sacheverell Sitwell. And so the long morning/Wept itself away. LOW

The Limejuice Tub. Anonymous. Drive me back to the lime-juice tub. NOAV

Limeraiku: "There's a vile old man." Ted Pauker. "Where's your bloody fan?" NOBL

Limerick: "A beautiful lady named Psyche." Anonymous. Is his beard, which is dreadfully spyche. LiBL; TDH

Limerick: "A big bull-dyke, surly and sallow." Anonymous. (That's something I find hard to swallow.) PeHV

Limerick: "A bigamist born in Zambezi." David McCord. I choose to be twozi not threezi. InMe

Limerick: "A boot and a shoe and a slipper." John Banister Tabb. The slipper went off to the ball. TDH

Limerick: "A Boston boy went out to Yuma." D. D.. And a puma in very good huma. ShM

Limerick: "A bright little maid in St. Thomas." Ferdinand G. Christgau. But I'm sure that these garments St. Mhomas. HBV 1-2; TDH

Limerick: "A Briton who shot at his king." David Ross. I'm getting the hang of the thing! ShM

Limerick: "A bugler named Douglas MacDougal." Ogden Nash. Thus saving the price of a bugle. NePA

Limerick: "A bull-voiced young fellow of Pauling." Morris Bishop. But the hogs find it simply appalling. TDH

Limerick: "A camel, with practical views." Oliver Herford. Little dreaming their souls they would lose. TDH

Limerick: "A canary, its woe to assuage." Oliver Herford. "But it's far in advance of the age." TDH

Limerick: "A canner, exceedingly canny." Carolyn Wells. But a canner can't can a can, can he? HBV 1-2; HBVY; LiBL; YaD

Limerick: "A cannibal bold of Penzance." Anonymous. And now he can't button his pants. LiBL

Limerick: "A canny old codger at Yalta." Anonymous. He's just like rock of Gibraltar. LiBL

Limerick: "A careless young driver, McKissen." Lee Blair. Now lissen! McKissen is missen. TDH

Limerick: "A careless young lad down in Natchez." Anonymous. On the seat of his pants he wears patchez. TDH

Limerick: "A careless zookeeper named Blake." *Anonymous.* "Very nice, but I still prefer steak." TDH

Limerick: "A certain old party of Moultrie." Jr, Blount Roy. And half of the biddies in Moultrie. TDH

Limerick: "A certain young fellow, named Bobbie." *Anonymous.* He replied: "But, you see, it's my hobby." LiBL

Limerick: "A certain young gourmet of Crediton." Charles Cuthbert Inge. His tomb bears the date that he said it on. CenHV; LiBL; TDH

Limerick: "A certain young man of great gumption." *Anonymous.* They say 'twas a case of consumption. ShM

Limerick: "A chap has a shark up in Sparkill." Morris Bishop. He'd make every beast in the Ark ill! TDH

Limerick: "A charming young woman named Pat." *Anonymous.* So imagine her meaning of that. NIP

Limerick: "A Clergyman out in Dumont." Morris Bishop. It seems to be just what they want. LiBL

Limerick: "A clergyman told from his text." *Anonymous.* Got rattled, and shouted, "Who's next?" TDH

Limerick: "A clumsy young laddie was Mulligan." J. B. Lee. And landed ker-plunk on his skulligan. TDH

Limerick: "A cold had a corpulent pig." Marnie and Harnie Wood. Ad wodt let be taste, shell or sig! TDH

Limerick: "A coloratura named Luna." J. F. Wilson. And now she can't carry the tuna. TDH

Limerick: "A Conservative, out on his motor." A. W. Webster. So I don't blame myself one iota. TDH

Limerick: "A decrepit old gas man named Peter." *Anonymous.* And, as anyone can see by reading this, he/also destroyed the meter. LiBL; SoSe

Limerick: "A distinguished old one-legged colonel." *Anonymous.* And cried, "The expense is infolonel!" TDH

Limerick: "A dragon, who was a great wag." Carolyn Wells. A dragon a-draggin' a drag? TDH

Limerick: "A farmer once called his cow 'Zephyr'." *Anonymous.* Which made him considerably dephyr. TDH

Limerick: "A farmer's boy, starting to plough." D. S. Martin. To prove what I meant it to shough. TDH

Limerick: "A father once said to his son." *Anonymous.* And I shall begin when you've done. TDH

Limerick: "A Fire Island pixie called 'Mary.'". *Anonymous.* So I want to warn you to be wary.' PeHV

Limerick: "A flea and a fly in a flue." *Anonymous.* So they flew through a flaw in the flue. LiBL

Limerick: "A ghoulish old fellow in Kent." Morris Bishop. "I was careful, my dear,/To follow your natural bent." ShM

Limerick: "A greedy small lassie once said." *Anonymous.* At which point everyone fled. TDH

Limerick: "A guy asked two jays at St. Louis." Ferdinand G. Christgau. Said the guy, "If you fellows St. Whouis?" TDH

Limerick: "A half-baked potato, named Sue." George Libaire. "I'm damned if I don't–or I do." LiBL

Limerick: "A handsome young gent down in Fla." *Anonymous.* And shot him. Now what could be ha.? TDH

Limerick: "A handy old guide from the Bosphorous." *Anonymous.* And lighted the way clear across for us. TDH

Limerick: "A hearty old cook of Lithonia." Jr, Blount Roy. "I bet I can eat a lot monia." TDH

Limerick: "A heathen named Min, passing by." Oliver Herford. The mince pie that Min spied was Min's pie. TDH

Limerick: "A hermaphrodite fairy of Kew." *Anonymous.* Of a bisexual built for two. PeHV

Limerick: "A hippo decided one day." *Anonymous.* And fell back with a splash in the bay. TDH

Limerick: "A housewife called out with a frown." *Anonymous.* But she slipped on the stairs and came down. TDH

Limerick: "A is the autograph bore." Oliver Herford. They'd deplore even more than before. TDH

Limerick: "A jolly young artist called Bruno." *Anonymous.* Quickly tucked him away in his–"you know!" TDH

Limerick: "A jug and a book and a dame." Edwin Meade Robinson. What you say, it's a great little game! HBMV

Limerick: "A king, on assuming his reign." *Anonymous.* That I haven't been born with a breign. TDH

Limerick: "A lady there was of Antigua." Cosmo Monkhouse. Or do you refer to my figure? HBV 1-2

Limerick: "A lady track star from Toccoa." Jr, Blount Roy. She survived–sadder, wiser and sloa. TDH

Limerick: "A lady who lived at Bordeaux." *Anonymous.* For the corn is gone (so is her teaux). TDH

Limerick: "A lady who lived in Uganda." William Jay Smith. On an air-conditioned veranda. TDH

Limerick: "A lady who signs herself 'Vexed.'". Edward Gorey. But I feel I am coming unsexed. OBAL

Limerick: "A lady whose name was Miss Hartley." William Jay Smith. So they had to give up with Miss Hartley. TDH

Limerick: "A large, colored dyke from Atlanta." *Anonymous.* It's a project that's sponsored by ANTA.' PeHV

Limerick: "A leopard when told that benzine." Oliver Herford. Of a spot (or a leopard) was seen. TDH

Limerick: "A Lesbian born under Pisces." *Anonymous.* And gives all her girlfriends surprises. PeHV

Limerick: "A lesbian girl of Khartoum." *Anonymous.* Who does what, and with which, and to whom?' NOBL

Limerick: "A lieutenant who went out to shoot." Morgan Taylor. For that was the Riff in the Lieut. LiBL

Limerick: "A limerick packs laughs anatomical." *Anonymous.* And the clean ones so seldom are comical. LiBL

Limerick: "A maiden caught stealing a dahlia." *Anonymous.* They'll send you to jail, you bad gahlia. TDH

Limerick: "A major, with wonderful force." *Anonymous.* So just rhododendron, of course. TDH

Limerick: "A man hired by John Smith and Co." Mark (Samuel Langhorne Clemens) Twain. The drivers, therefore, didn't do. FaBoNo; TDH

Limerick: "A man to whom illness was chronic." *Anonymous.* "No, no," said the Doc, "that's Teutonic." LiBL

Limerick: "A Martian named Harrison Harris." Al Graham. And that's why he's now on Polaris. QQQ

Limerick: "A mathematician named Bath." J. F. Wilson. And choked. What a sad afterMATH. TDH

Limerick: "A matron well known in Montclair." William Jay Smith. And ran a bell cord through her hair. TDH

Limerick: "A merchant addressing a debtor." R. C. And the sooner he pays it the bebtor. TDH

Limerick: "A mother in old Alabama." William Jay Smith. With big brother's chisel and hammer! TDH

Limerick: "A new servant maid named Maria." *Anonymous.* Her position by now is much higher! TDH

Limerick: "A nice old lady named Tweedle." *Anonymous.* And was deftly pulled out by the beadle. LiBL

Limerick: "A patriot, living at Ewell." Langford Reed. A measure effective though cruel. TDH

Limerick: "A Phoenician called Phlebas forgot." Wendy Cope. And been left in the ocean to rot. FaBoWP

Limerick: "A pointless old miser named Quince." John Ciardi. And dropped dead, which he's been ever since. TDH

Limerick: "A Potsdam, les totaux absteneurs." George Du Maurier. Grand manchons, et terribles duffeurs. CenHV; LiBL

Limerick: "A precocious, impulsive young Mr." *Anonymous.* I'm to you nothing more than a sr. TDH

Limerick: "A pretty young actress, a stammerer." Eille Norwood. The rest of the story's "in camera." CenHV

Limerick: "A pretty young school mistress named Beauchamp." *Anonymous.* And with tears in my eyes I beseauchamp. TDH

Limerick: "A prominent lady in Brooking." *Anonymous.* And tell which was which without looking. TDH

Limerick: "A railway official at Crewe." *Anonymous.* It cut him–it cut him in two! TDH

Limerick: "A rheumatic old man in White Plains." *Anonymous.* And that's all he gets for his pains. LiBL

Limerick: "A salmon remarked to his mate." Norman R. Jaffray. But they're claiming, right now, you were eight. TDH

Limerick: "A schoolma'am of much reputation." Minnie Leona Upton. She said, "Yes, but not during vacation!" TDH

Limerick: "A senator, Rex Asinorum." *Anonymous.* then laconically scribbled, "I'm forum." TDH

Limerick: "A skeleton once in Khartoum." *Anonymous.* As to which should be frightened of whom. ShM

Limerick: "A smooth-bottomed fellow named Fritz." *Anonymous.* He can't find a penis that fits. PeHV

Limerick: "A staid schizophrenic named Struther." *Anonymous.* But then, I still have each other. NIP

Limerick: "A strong-minded lady of Arden." Morris Bishop. And never begs anyone's pardon. TDH

Limerick: "A surgeon once owned a big ape." *Anonymous.* But the surgeon cut off his escape. TDH

Limerick: "A swimmer whose clothing was strewed." *Anonymous.* You expected this line to be lewd. NIP

Limerick: "A taxi-cab whore out at Iver." Victor Gray. And a ten-shilling tip to the driver. NOBL

Limerick: "A thrifty soprano of Hingham." Ogden Nash. So that when they wore out she could singham. TDH

Limerick: "A thrifty young fellow of Shoreham." *Anonymous.* to pick up a pin, then he toreham. TDH

Limerick: "A trendy young girl from St. Paul." *Anonymous.* Front page, sporting section, and all. NIP

Limerick: "In the wax works of Nature they strike." Anthony Euwer. There are no two exactly alike. HBMV

Limerick: "In this book every line has been clean." *Anonymous.* Or snafu– if you know what we mean. LiBL

Limerick: "It etait un Hebreu de Hambourg." George Du Maurier. Un Dimanche, au milieu d'Edimbourg. CenHV

Limerick: "It's time to make love: douse the glim." Conrad Aiken. and the loin lies down with the limb. FaBoNo; NLV

Limerick: "It was a refractory gnu." *Anonymous.* But we must give our gnu to some zu. TDH

Limerick: "Jerome was a dizzy giraffe." *Anonymous.* Did it cover Jerome? Only half! TDH

Limerick: "Lucasta," said Terence O'Connor." Edwin Meade Robinson. Bu gosh! how I'm stuck on my honor! HBMV

Limerick: "Miss Minnie McFinney of Butte." Carolyn Wells. I'm a peach, and that's all there is tutte. LiBL; TDH

Limerick: "Mussolini's pet Marshal, Graziani." Thomas Russell Ybarra. And twenty-five times in the fanny. LiBL

Limerick: "My name's Mister Benjamin Bunny." Frederic Edward Weatherly. It's convenient, but certainly funny! CenHV

Limerick: "N is for naughty young Nat." Isabel Frances Bellows. He said he supposed 'twas the cat. TDH

Limerick: "No matter how grouchy you're feeling." Anthony Euwer. Thus preserving the face from congealing. HBMV; LiBL

Limerick: "No water. dry rocks and dry throats." Wendy Cope. I hope you'll make sense of the notes. FaBoWP

Limerick: "Now the ears, so I always had thunk." Anthony Euwer. As racks for the Jooler-man's junk. HBMV

Limerick: "Now the sneeze is a joy-vent, I s'pose." Anthony Euwer. But you want to watch out where it goes. HBMV

Limerick: "O God, inasmuch as without Thee." *Anonymous.* May know nothing whatever about Thee. LiBL

Limerick: "O limerick, Learest of lyrics." David McCord. Whose apteryx rhymed with apteryx! InMe

Limerick: "O's Operatic Olivia." Isabel Frances Bellows. They don't care for that in Bolivia. TDH

Limerick: "O was an ossified oyster." Carolyn Wells. For his home in the sea, which was moister. TDH

Limerick: "Of inviting to dine, in Epirus." Carroll Watson Rankin. To feed such a freak you can't hire us. TDH

Limerick: "Oh, King of the fiddle, Wilhelmj." Robert Jones Burdette. Wilhelmj, I think it would killmj. TDH

Limerick: "Oh, there once was a merry crocodile." Gerturde E. Heath. Oh, this tearful, snaky, smiling crocodile! TDH

Limerick: "On pianos and organs she lbs." *Anonymous.* As he goes on his lone nightly rds. TDH

Limerick: "On the deck of a ship called the Masm." Conrad Aiken. And the old salt replied to her, Yas'm. FaBoNo

Limerick: "Once a Frenchman who'd promptly said "oui'." *Anonymous.* Was a tipple no stronger than toui. TDH

Limerick: "Once a grasshoper (food being scant)." Oliver Herford. "It's an uncle you need, not an ant." TDH

Limerick: "Once a pound-keeper chanced to impound." Oliver Herford. Since he'd only one ounce in his pound. TDH

Limerick: "One evening a goose, for a treat." Oliver Herford. And for hissing was thrown in the street. TDH

Limerick: "One morning old Wilfrid Scawen Blunt." Victor Gray. –Your wage is a social affront!' NOBL

Limerick: "Our ambassador to Venus, Mz Abner." *Anonymous.* While the masculine weenies were grabbin' er! PeHV

Limerick: "Our Vicar is good Mr. Inge." *Anonymous.* And pulled at each end of the string. TDH

Limerick: "Q is a quoter who'll cite." Oliver Herford. But a second-hand-dealer in light. TDH

Limerick: "Quoth a cat to me once: Pray relieve." Oliver Herford. I replied, "Quite a few, I believe." TDH

Limerick: "Quoth the bookworm, "I don't care one bit." Oliver Herford. As completely as I can bore it. TDH

Limerick: "Said a cat, as he playfully threw." *Anonymous.* I only was artesian you. TDH

Limerick: "Said a fellow from North Philadelphia." Berton Braley. Till the church bells are ringing a knellphia. TDH

Limerick: "Said a gabby old queer in Saint-Lo." *Anonymous.* I'm a bit of a bisexual, you know.' PeHV

Limerick: "Said a girl from beyond Pompton Lakes." Morris Bishop. When I mixed up the gas and the brakes. LiBL

Limerick: "Said a lachrymose Labrador seal." Oliver Herford. To magnificent pearls they congeal. TDH

Limerick: "Said a lady who wore a swell cape." Oliver Herford. But copy the things that I wear! TDH

Limerick: "Said a maid, "I will marry for lucre." *Anonymous.* I notice she did not rebuchre. TDH

Limerick: "Said a saucy young skunk to a gnu." Gerard Neyroud. I'd hate to be me, were I you. TDH

Limerick: "Said a sporty young person named Groat." *Anonymous.* But my horse always takes table d'oat. TDH

Limerick: "Said an asp to an adder named Rhea." Joseph S. Newman. Oh, venom I next gonna see you? TDH

Limerick: "Said Nero to one of his train." *Anonymous.* From burning my city again. LiBL

Limerick: "Said old Peeping Tom of Fort Lee." Morris Bishop. And I find 'em all peeping at me. LiBL

Limerick: "Said the crab: "'Tis not beauty or birth.'" Oliver Herford. Then go sidewise for all you are worth. TDH

Limerick: "Said the elephant to the giraffe." Charlotte Osgood Carter. At others you'd better not laugh. TDH

Limerick: "Said the mole: "You would never suppose." Oliver Herford. On William the Conqueror's nose. TDH

Limerick: "Said the mouse with scholastical hat." A. B. P. Much quicker than you could say "Scat!" TDH

Limerick: "Said the Reverend Jabez McCotton." James Montgomery Flagg. To the pure almost everything's rotten. LiBL

Limerick: "Said the spider, in tones of distress." Oliver Herford. I never can have a new dress. TDH

Limerick: "See that senor so amorous and menacing." Ogden Nash. The duenna won't let him duennacing! TDH

Limerick: "She sat in a mighty fine chair." Wendy Cope. Bad as Albert and Lil–what a pair! FaBoWP

Limerick: "Should a plan we suggest, just that minute." *Anonymous.* And he's got the game fixed so he'll win it. LiBL

Limerick: "Sir Bedivere Bors was a chivalrous knight." Frederick B. Opper. He really presented a comical sight. TDH

Limerick: "So tall was a cowboy called Slouch." *Anonymous.* Slouch three days later said, "Ouch!" TDH

Limerick: "Some Harvard men, stalwart and hairy." Edward Gorey. "Come on out, we are burning a fairy!" OBAL

Limerick: "T was a tidy young tapir." Carolyn Wells. For he wiped his feet clean on the scraper. TDH

Limerick: "Teacher Bruin said, "Cub, bear in mind." Mark Fenderson. "Not," said the cub, "when I'm ink-lined." TDH

Limerick: "That famous old pederast, Wilde." *Anonymous.* Whenever you sucked off the child. PeHV

Limerick: "That the Traylee's the best cigarette." R. Rhodes. Two good "lines'–one you give, one you get. FaBoUs

Limerick: "The ankle's chief end is exposiery." Anthony Euwer. The part called the calf with the toesiery. HBMV

Limerick: "The babe, with a cry brief and dismal." Edward Gorey. For the depth of the font was abysmal. OBAL

Limerick: "The bachelor growls when his peace is." J. Adair Strawson. Although they're preserving the creases. TDH

Limerick: "The breasts of a barmaid of Crale." *Anonymous.* Was the same information in Braille. NOBL

Limerick: "The British in branding their betters." David McCord. But after their names, not on sweaters. InMe

Limerick:: "The cautious collapsible cow." *Anonymous.* And sinks fore and aft with a bow. LiBL

Limerick: "The daughter of debate." Queen of England Elizabeth I. Hath taught still peace to grow. LiBL

Limerick: "The fabulous wizard of Oz." Anonymous. He wasn't the wiz that he woz. QQQ; TDH

Limerick: "The girl with the theater hat." Carolyn Wells. But she didn't care much about that. TDH

Limerick: "The hands they were made to assist." Anthony Euwer. And are hitched to the end of the wrist. HBMV

Limerick: "The heavyweight champ of Seattle." *Anonymous.* And deflowered a whole herd of cattle. OBAL

Limerick: "The ladies inhabiting Venus." Al Graham. And nothing but space is between us! QQQ

Limerick: "The life boat that's kept at Torquay." *Anonymous.* And as smart and as brave as can buay. LiBL

Limerick: "The poor benighted Hindoo." Cosmo Monkhouse. For pants he makes his skindoo. HBV 1-2

Limerick: "The Reverend Henry War Beecher." Oliver Wendell Holmes. And thus did the hen reward Beecher. CenHV; FaBoNo; HBVY

Limerick: "The S & M bar, oh my dears." *Anonymous.* The thrill of your gayest young years! PeHV

Limerick: "The styles that at present are regnant." *Anonymous.* But I think they are simply repugnant. LiBL

Limerick: "The sultan got sore on his harem." *Anonymous.* (The confusion is called harem scarem.) GoTF; TDH; TreFT

Limerick: "The Thames runs, bones rattle, rats creep." Wendy Cope. Wei la la. After this it gets deep. FaBoWP

Limerick: "The treatment by old Mr. Mears." *Anonymous.* Can it be he is one of those queers? PeHV

Limerick: "The young things who frequent picture-palaces." *Anonymous.* They cling to their long-standing fallacies. NOBL

Limerick: "Then the pair, followed Pa to Manhasset." *Anonymous.* And as for the bucket Manhasset. GoTF; LiBL

Limerick: "There is a creator named God." James Whistler. That he does no great credit to God. LiBL

Limerick: "There is a young artist named Whistler." Dante Gabriel Rossetti. Come equally handy to Whistler. LiBL

Limerick: "There is an old he-wolf named Gambart." Dante Gabriel Rossetti. Will be ground by the grinders of Gambart. CenHV

Limerick: "There is little in afternoon tea." Gelett Burgess. A cow might enjoy in a tree. FaBoNo

Limerick: "There lived an old woman at Lynn." *Anonymous.* This charming old woman of Lynn. OxBChV

Limerick: "There once was a bonnie Scotch laddie." *Anonymous.* What had 'e had? Had 'e had haddie? LiBL

Limerick: "There once was a girl of New York." Cosmo Monkhouse. Before she went out for a walk. LiBL; NA

Limerick: "There once was a girl of Pitlochry." *Anonymous.* Of the ten times more usual crochry. CenHV

Limerick: "There once was a guy named Othello." Edwin Meade Robinson. That bird wasn't black, he was yellow! HBMV

Limerick: "There once was a happy hyena." Carolyn Wells. He carelessly stuck a verbena. TDH

Limerick: "There once was a kind armadillo." Oliver Herford. Pray rest on my shell as a pillow. TDH

Limerick: "There once was a man, named Power." John White. Now you see him every hour on the hour. ShM

Limerick: "There once was a man of Bengal." *Anonymous.* But a dog ate him up in the hall. CenHV; OnUR; OxBoLi

Limerick: "There once was a man of Calcutta." *Anonymous.* And b-b-b-b-b-b-butta. LiBL

Limerick: "There once was a man who said: "Damn!" Maurice Evan Hare. I'm not even a bus, I'm a tram.' CenHV; NOBL; OxBoLi

Limerick: "There once was a man who said, 'God.'. Ronald Arbuthnott Knox. When there's no one about in the Quad.' FaBoCo; NLV; NOBL; OxBoLi; PoPle

Limerick: "There once was a man who said, "How." *Anonymous.* 'Twould make such a terrible row. LiBL; NA

Limerick: "There once was a man who said, 'Oh.'. Carolyn Wells. And calmly responded, "Why, No!" TDH

Limerick: "There once was a Master of Arts." Cosmo Monkhouse. But he still was a Master of Arts. TDH

Limerick: "There once was a peach on a tree." Abbie Farwell Brown. And turned to a squash! O dear me! TDH

Limerick: "There once was a person of Benin." Cosmo Monkhouse. A word of inscrutable meanin'. LiBL; NA

Limerick: "There once was a pious young priest." *Anonymous.* And I want to get started, at least. NIP; TDH

Limerick: "There once was a popular crooner." M. B. Thornton. And I wish he had landed there sooner. LiBL

Limerick: "There once was a Renaissance man." *Anonymous.* And "I will if I must' on his can. PeHV

Limerick: "There once was a sculptor called Phidias." Oliver Herford. Which shocked all the pure and fastidious. LiBL

Limerick: "There once was a sensitive cat." Alice Brown. But don't be so rude as all that! TDH

Limerick: "There once was a spinster of Ealing." *Anonymous.* So she kept her eyes trained on the ceiling. NIP

Limerick: "There once was a warden of Wadham." *Anonymous.* But be a fine fellow at bottom. PeHV

Limerick: "There once was a wonderful wizard." Conrad Aiken. and farted a forty-day blizzard. FaBoNo

Limerick: "There once was a young man named Hall." *Anonymous.* But he didn't–he died in the fall. ShM

Limerick: "There once was an old man of Lyme." Cosmo Monkhouse. And bigamy, sir, is a crime. LiBL; NA

Limerick: "There once were some learned MD's." Oliver Herford. Allowed one to catch it with ease. LiBL

Limerick: "There once were two cats of Kilkenny." *Anonymous.* Till instead of two cats there weren't any. CenHV

Limerick: "There's a combative Artist named Whistler." Dante Gabriel Rossetti. Offer varied attractions to Whistler. CenHV

Limerick: "There's a lady in Washington Heights." Morris Bishop. Of showers of meteorites. QQQ

Limerick: "There's a Portuguese person named Howell." Dante Gabriel Rossetti. For living is lying with Howell. CenHV; DBV

Limerick: "There's a sensitive man in Toms River." Morris Bishop. And also is fine for the liver. TDH

Limerick: "There's a vaporish maiden in Harrison." Morris Bishop. Who suffers, I fear, by comparison. LiBL; TDH

Limerick: "There's a wonderful family called Stein." *Anonymous.* And no one can understand Ein. DBV

Limerick: "There was a brave girl of Connecticut." Ogden Nash. But deplorable absence of ecticut. NePA

Limerick: "There was a brave knight of Lorraine." Mary Mapes Dodge. This noble young knight of Lorraine. TDH

Limerick: "There was a bright fellow named Peter." Marie Bruckman MacDonald. For the 'skeeter was fleeter than Peter. TDH

Limerick: "There was a composer named Bong." *Anonymous.* With occasional thumps on the gong. TDH

Limerick: "There was a dear lady of Eden." *Anonymous.* And then both skedaddled from Eden. LiBL; NA

Limerick: "There was a fair maid from Decatur." *Anonymous.* Where a dozen fat savages ate her. LiBL

Limerick: "There was a faith-healer of Deal." *Anonymous.* I dislike what I fancy I feel.' CenHV; FaBoCo; LiBL

Limerick: "There was a frank lady of Dedham." X. Y. Z. And the sound of her accents just sped 'em. TDH

Limerick: "There was a gay damsel of Lynn." *Anonymous.* To fit this slim person of Lynn. LiBL; NA

Limerick: "There was a good Canon of Durham." William Ralph Inge. But I fear we may have to inter'm.' CenHV

Limerick: "There was a painter named Scott." Dante Gabriel Rossetti. On the part of the painter named Scott. CenHV

Limerick: "There was a princess of Bengal." Walter Parke. To do without eating at all! NA

Limerick: "There was a professor called Chesterton." Sir William Schwenck Gilbert. As it ruined for life his digesterton. TDH

Limerick: "There was a professor of Beaulieu." C.E.M. Joad. Distressed the New Forest unduly. FaBoCo

Limerick: "There was a queer fellow named Woodin." Cuthbert (Edward Bradley) "Bede. That imprudent old fellow named Woodin. CenHV; TDH

Limerick: "There was a sick man of Tobago." *Anonymous.* "To a roast leg of mutton you may go'. OxBChV

Limerick: "There was a sightseer named Sue." *Anonymous.* "It's not an old beast, but a gnu." TDH

Limerick: "There was a trim maiden named Wood." William A. Lockwood. 'Tis time I did things which I could. LiBL

Limerick: "There was a young bard of Japan." *Anonymous.* But I make a rule of always trying to get just/as many words into the last line as I/possibly can. CenHV

Limerick: "There was a young belle of old Natchez." Ogden Nash. She drawled, When Ah itchez, Ah scratchez! LiBL; NLV; NoP

Limerick: "There was a young boy of Quebec." Rudyard Kipling. But we don't call this cold in Quebec.' FaBoNo

Limerick: "There was a young critic of Kings." Arthur Clement Hilton. And exclaim: "It is biggish for King's!" CenHV

Limerick: "There was a young curate of Hants." Edward Valpy Knox. Of this regular army of ants!' CenHV

Limerick: "There was a young curate of Kidderminster." *Anonymous.* When he quite inadvertently slid ag'inst her. TDH

Limerick: "There was a young curate of Salisbury." George Libaire. Till the vicar compelled him to Walmisbury. FaBoCo; LiBL

Limerick: "There was a young fellow called Crouch." Victor Gray. Christ's sake shut your trap while I–ouch! NOBL

Limerick: "There was a young fellow from Boise." John Straley. To what people in Brooklyn called Joise. TDH

Limerick: "There was a young fellow from Fife." Thomas Russell Ybarra. One ear, seven teeth–and his life. LiBL

Limerick: "There was a young fellow named Dice." *Anonymous.* For the plural of spouse, it is spice. LiBL

Limerick: "There was a young fellow named Hall." J. F. Wilson. How I fell in the spring in the fall. TDH

Limerick: "There was a young fellow named Hatch." *Anonymous.* Sit down, and I'll play you a snatch. LiBL

Limerick: "There was a young fellow named Nutz. *Anonymous.* Than ever got in through your guts.' PeHV

Limerick: "There was a young fellow named Shear." John Ciardi. But the rest of the way through is clear. TDH

Limerick: "There was a young fellow named Sydney." Don (Donald Robert Marquis) Marquis. But he'd a good time doin' it, did'ney? LiBL

Limerick: "There was a young fellow named Tait." Carolyn Wells. And his tete-a-tete ate at 8.08. HBV 1-2; HBVY

Limerick: "There was a young fellow named West." *Anonymous.* Had fallen asleep on his chest. TDH

Limerick: "There was a young Fellow of Caius." *Anonymous.* And pay less attention to these.' NOBL

Limerick: "There was a young fellow of Ceuta." *Anonymous.* I ought to have sounded my hooter.' CenHV

Limerick: "There was a young Fellow of King's." *Anonymous.* With a bum like a jelly on springs. NOBL

Limerick: "There was an auld birkie ca'ed Milton." Andrew Lang. Sae slicht was the Gaelic he built on. CenHV

Limerick: "There was an exclusive old oyster." Laura A. Steel. That very retiring old oyster. TDH

Limerick: "There was an old cat named Macduff." J. G. Francis. That their cheeks got a permanent puff. TDH

Limerick: "There was an old fellow of Lynn." Anonymous. Said, "It's never too late to begin." LiBL

Limerick: "There was an old Fellow of Trinity." Arthur Clement Hilton. And so had to leave the vicinity. CenHV; LiBL

Limerick: "There was an Old Lady named Crockett." William Jay Smith. And came roaring back down like a rocket! ShM

Limerick: "There was an old lady of Chertsey." Edward Lear. Which distressed all the people of Chertsey. OxBChV

Limerick: "There was an old lady of Dover." Carolyn Wells. The overturn of her turnover. TDH

Limerick: "There was an old lady of Harrow." Anonymous. "They build these 'ere churches too narrow." TDH

Limerick: "There was an old looney of Rhyme." Anonymous. For I'm never "all there' at a time!" TDH

Limerick: "There was an old man by Salt Lake." William Jay Smith. And they said, "Aw, go jump in the lake!" TDH

Limerick: "There was an old man from Darjeeling." Anonymous. So he stood up and spat on the ceiling. NTCP

Limerick: "There was an old man in a Barge." Edward Lear. Which helped that Old Man in a Barge. EBEV

Limerick: "There was an old man in a boat." Edward Lear. That unhappy Old Man in a boat. EBEV; FaBoNo; HBV 1-2; WiR

Limerick: "There was an Old Man in a pew." Edward Lear. That cheerful Old Man in a pew. MoShBr

Limerick: "There was an Old Man in a tree." Edward Lear. It's a regular brute of a bee! FaBoNo; HBV 1-2; InvP; LBN; LiBL; NoP; OxBChV; TEP

Limerick: "There was an old man in a trunk." Ogden Nash. And he answered: "It's just as I thunk." CenHV; FaBoCo

Limerick: "There was an old man of Bengal." Thomas Anstey Guthrie. For he never played cricket at all. CenHV

Limerick: "There was an old man of Blackheath." Anonymous. I have bitten myself underneath!' CenHV

Limerick: "There was an old man of Boulogne." Anonymous. But the horrible double entendre. CenHV; FaBoCo; OxBoLi

Limerick: "There was an old man of Calcutta." Ogden Nash. To a soft, oleaginous mutta. NoP

Limerick: "There was an old man of Cape Horn." Edward Lear. That dolorous Man of Cape Horn. EBEV

Limerick: "There was an old man of Cape Race." Anonymous. And imagined that Wells was a place. FaBoCo

Limerick: "There was an Old Man of Dumbree." Edward Lear. That amiable Man of Dumbree. NBM; OxBChV

Limerick: "There was an old man of Dunblane." Edward Lear. To request you won't stay in Dunblane?' EBEV

Limerick: "There was an Old Man of Dundee." Edward Lear. And exclaimed, "I'll return to Dundee." FaBoNo

Limerick: "There was an old man of El Hums." Edward Lear. In the roads and the lanes of El Hums. FaBoNo

Limerick: "There was an old man of Girgenti." Edward Lear. That susceptible man of Girgenti. FaBoNo

Limerick: "There was an old man of Hawaii." Anonymous. Without even saying, "Good-baii!" TDH

Limerick: "There was an Old Man of Hong Kong." Edward Lear. That innocuous Old Man of Hong Kong. FaBoCo; NBM

Limerick: "There was an old man of Ibreem." Edward Lear. You disgusting Old Man of Ibreem!' EBEV

Limerick: "There was an Old Man of Kamschatka." Edward Lear. To all the fat dogs in Kamschatka. NA; NOBL

Limerick: "There was an old man of Khartoum." William Ralph Inge. But I never can recollect whom.' LiBL; NOBL; OxBoLi

Limerick: "There was an Old Man of Leghorn." Edward Lear. Who devoured that Old Man of Leghorn. NA

Limerick: "There was an Old Man of Madras." Edward Lear. That it killed that Old Man of Madras. FaBoNo

Limerick: "There was an Old Man of Melrose." Edward Lear. You stupid Old Man of Melrose. LBN

Limerick: "There was an old man of Nantucket." Dayton Voorhees. And as for the bucket, Nantucket. HBV 1-2; LiBL

Limerick: "There was an old man of Peru." Edward Lear. That intrinsic Old Man of Peru. EBEV; TDH

Limerick: "There was an old man of Spithead." Edward Lear. That doubtful old man of Spithead. FaBoNo

Limerick: "There was an old man of Tarentum." Cosmo Monkhouse. Said, "I really can't tell, for I rent 'em!" HBV 1-2; InvP; LBN; LiBL

Limerick: "There was an old man of the Cape." Anonymous. But they keep such a beautiful shape. LiBL

Limerick: "There was an Old Man of the Coast." Edward Lear. And called for some hot buttered toast. CenHV; LiBL; MoShBr

Limerick: "There was an Old Man of the Dee." Edward Lear. Which grieved that Old Man of the Dee. FaBoNo

Limerick: "There was an Old Man of the East." Edward Lear. That it killed that Old Man of the East. EBEV

Limerick: "There was an Old Man of The Hague." Edward Lear. That deluded Old Man of The Hague. EvOK; TDH

Limerick: "There was an old man of the Nile." Edward Lear. Of sharpening one's nails with a file! TDH; VLP

Limerick: "There was an old man of the West." Edward Lear. That uneasy Old Man of the West. EBEV

Limerick: "There was an Old Man of Thermopylae." Edward Lear. You shall never remain in Thermopylae.' CenHV; EBEV; EvOK; FaBoNo; LBN; LiBL; NA; NBM; NOBL

Limerick: "There was an old man of Three Bridges." Edward Lear. Which relieved that old man of Three Bridges. FaBoNo

Limerick: "There was an old man of Toulon. William Jay Smith. So they chased that man out of Toulon. TDH

Limerick: "There was an Old Man of Vesuvius." Edward Lear. That morbid Old Man of Vesuvius. FaBoNo; GLGT; LiBL

Limerick: "There was an old man of West Dumpet." Edward Lear. And was heard through the whole of West Dumpet. EBEV

Limerick: "There was an Old Man of Whitehaven." Edward Lear. So they smashed that Old Man of Whitehaven. EBEV; NBM; VLP

Limerick: "There was an Old Man on some rocks." Edward Lear. You will pass all your life in that box.' NOBV

Limerick: "There was an Old Man on the Border." Edward Lear. Which vexed all the folks on the Border. CenHV; EBEV

Limerick: "There was an old man said, "I fear.'". Walter De la Mare. And chopped off his head with a shubble. TDH

Limerick: "There was an old man who said, "Do." Anonymous. But I fear that is almost too few. LiBL; NA

Limerick: "There was an Old Man who said: "How." Edward Lear. Which may soften the heart of that cow.' EvOK; OxBChV

Limerick: "There was an Old Man who said, "Hush!" Edward Lear. It is four times as big as the bush! FaBoCo; GoJo; HBV 1-2; NA; NBM; NOBL; OxBChV; OxBoLi; TEP

Limerick: "There was an Old Man who screamed out." Edward Lear. And continued to knock him about. EBEV; NOBV

Limerick: "There was an Old Man who supposed." Edward Lear. While that futile Old Gentleman dozed. LBN; LiBL; NA; NOBV; NoP

Limerick: "There was an old man whose despair." Edward Lear. Which partly assuaged his despair. FaBoNo; VLP

Limerick: "There was an old man with a beard." Edward Lear. Have all built their nests in my beard!' FaBoCo; FaBoNo; HBV 1-2; LiBL; NOBL; NoP; NTCP; OnUR; OxBChV; TEP; TiPo

Limerick: "There was an old man with a gong." Edward Lear. So they smashed that Old Man with a gong. GoJo; TDH

Limerick: "There was an Old Man with a poker." Edward Lear. But knocked them all down with his poker. HBV 1-2

Limerick: "There was an old man with a ribbon." Edward Lear. This is quite the best use for my ribbon.' FaBoNo

Limerick: "There was an old miser at Reading." Anonymous. The poor creature could scarce get her head in. OxBChV

Limerick: "There was an old monk of Siberia." Anonymous. And eloped with the Mother Superior. LiBL

Limerick: "There was an Old Person of Anerley." Edward Lear. But returned in the evening to Anerley. FaBoCo; LiBL

Limerick: "There was an old person of Bar." Edward Lear. That placid old person of Bar. FaBoNo

Limerick: "There was an old person of Basing." Edward Lear. And escaped from the people of Basing. EBEV

Limerick: "There was an old person of Blythe." Edward Lear. That lively Old Person of Blythe. EBEV

Limerick: "There was an old person of Bow." Edward Lear. You will go back directly to Bow!' EBEV; VLP

Limerick: "There was an old person of Bradley." Edward Lear. That melodious old person of Bradley! UnS

Limerick: "There was an Old Person of Bromley." Edward Lear. That unpleasing Old Person of Bromley. NBM

Limerick: "There was an old person of Brussels." Edward Lear. Which distressed all the people of Brussels. FaBoNo

Limerick: "There was an old person of Burton." Edward Lear. That distressing Old Person of Burton. EBEV

Limerick: "There was an old person of Cassel." Edward Lear. Which perplexed that Old Person of Cassel. EBEV

Limerick: "There was an old person of Cromer." Edward Lear. Which concluded that person of Cromer. TDH

Lincoln. James Russell Lowell. New birth of our new soil, the first American. AnNE; HBVY; MC

Lincoln. Silas Weir Mitchell. Who always on earth's little ones hath/ smiled. PAH

Lincoln. James Whitcomb Riley. And will us, through the sacrifice/Of self, his peaceful life. OHIP

Lincoln. Corinne Roosevelt Robinson. A Nation's Cross to a new Calvary! OHIP

Lincoln. John Townsend Trowbridge. Has reared his monument and crowned him saint. PGD

Lincoln. Nancy Byrd Turner. "There's light upon it still." TiPo

Lincoln and Liberty. F. A. Simpson. The pride of the Suckers so lucky,/ For Lincoln and Liberty, too. AS; FSW; TrAS

Lincoln at Gettysburg. Bayard Taylor. "We consecrate ourselves to them, the Con-/secrated!" PAH

The Lincoln-Child. James Oppenheim. Work wrought through Love! HBMV

Lincoln, Come Back. Thomas Curtis Clark. Lincoln, come back, rebuild our broken world. PGD

Lincoln Leads. Minna Irving. For Lincoln leads them all. OHIP

Lincoln Monument: Washington. Langston Hughes. Timeless walls/Of time–/Old Abe OFD

Lincoln's Birthday. John Kendrick Bangs. A loved immortal rose/All glorified! PGD

The Lincoln Statue. W. F. Collins. As one who trusted, one who knew/ The common heart. OHIP; PGD

Lincoln, the Man of the People. Edwin Markham. And leaves a lonesome place against the sky. HBV 1-2; MC; MCCG; MoAmPo; OFD; OHFP; OHIP; PAH; PAL; PGD; TreFS; TrGrPo

The Lincolnshire Poacher. Anonymous. Oh, 'tis my delight on a shining night/In the season of the year! CH; FSW; GBP; OnMSP; OxBoLi; SD

Lincolnshire Remembered. Frances Cornford. Nor, if they have finished work,/ are they afraid. HaMV

A Lincolnshire Shepherd. Anonymous. So we can count our lambing times as I am counting sheep. OBET

Lindbergh. Anonymous. And his name will go down through the ages, as the bravest hero of them all. AmFP

Lindedi Singing. Innocent Banda. In the wind/I hear her cry still. WhB

Lindeman. Mary Jane White. I thought probably I would hate you, but I have not. AMV-81

The Linden Tree. Aist, Dietmar von. My griefs been all too long. PoPl

The Line-Gang. Robert Frost. They bring the telephone and telegraph. OBSP

Line Like. Nelly Sachs. But such is love–– BoWoP

The Line of an American Poet. Reed Whittemore. Poems uniform, safe and pure. MoVE; PPON

The Line of Beauty. Arthur William Edgar O'Shaughnessy. God become human and man grown divine. OnYI

The Line to Heaven by Christ Was Made. Anonymous. The Train will stop and take you in. BXAP; PeD

The Line-Up. Joan Swift. having to accuse/and accuse. FiCP; SM

Line-Up for Yesterday. Ogden Nash. These men are the game. SD

Lineage. Robert Farren. And cringe in the town. CoBE

Lineage. Reba Terry. I shall give birth to my daughter here,/holding up the sky. AMV-81

Lineage. Margaret Walker. My grandmothers were strong./Why am I not as they? BlSi; BOLo; CNA; NMM; PBWP; PoBA

The Linebacker at Forty. Jon Wallace. rising within a circle of light/like a star. AMV-81

Linen Bands. Vance Thompson. God hath the soul. AA

Linen Town. Seamus Heaney. Take a last turn/In the tang of possibility. CIP

The Linen Weaver. Anonymous. ...I'll go serve,/With willing mind, his majesty King George.' NOEC

The Linen Workers. Michael Longley. And into his dead mouth slip the set of teeth. FaBoIP

The Liner She's a Lady. Rudyard Kipling. 'Ome an' friends so dear, Jenny, waitin' in the cold! FaBV

Lines. Ada Sister Mary. Which e'en the Angels, high in Heaven,/Might lean to earth to hear. BlSi

Lines. Stopford Augustus Brooke. We shall not know that all is lost,/So great shall be our bliss. IrPN

Lines. Hartley Coleridge. You'd give your love to me, poor elf,/Your praise to my great father. NBM; PoEL 1-5

Lines. Aubrey Thomas De Vere. You can forget: ah then, forgive! IrPN

Lines. Michael Drayton. That it receiv'd too large a share/From Nature's rich perfumes... LoBV

Lines. Gavin Ewart. The seven dwarfs were singing these mystical motifs. EAS

Lines. Paul Goodman. for I have learned by the unlikely way/of deficiency and excess temperance. PeHV

The Lines. Randall Jarrell. The longest of their lives, the men are free. CrMA

Lines. Herbert Martin. The heart must beat as the times require. PoBA

Lines. Mary Ada, Sister. ...that this/Accused thing, this Achan in our camp,/May be removed. BlSi

Lines. Heather McHugh. ...man with a hearing-aid walks/without aim, happy just to be alive. MAYP

Lines. George Meredith. As a sea-shell of the sea/Ever shall I sing of thee. HBV 1-2

Lines. Brian Swann. They fit & fit & fit... AMV-81

Lines Addressed to a Seagull. Gerald Griffin. She smiles like a victor, serene on the world! OnYI

Lines by a Fond Lover. Anonymous. Now forever fare thee well! NA

Lines by a Medium. Anonymous. If I may, can, shall–still/I might, could, would, or should! NA

Lines by a Person of Quality. Alexander Pope. Melody resigns to fate. InMe; NA

Lines Composed a Few Miles above Tintern Abbey. William Wordsworth. And rolls through all things. NU
And this green pastoral landscape, were to me/More dear, both for themselves and for thy sake! BiP; DiPo; ERoP 1-2; ExPo; FaBoPP; FF; FiP; ForPo; GoTF; GoTL; HBV 1-2; HeIP; InPS; LoBV; MasP; MBW; MCCG; 1-2; NAWM 1-2; NIP; NoP; OAEL 1-2; OAEP; OBNC; OBRV; PAI; PoEL 1-5; PPP; PrIm; SeCePo; SeCeV; TEP; TreFS; TrGrPo; WHA
The guide, the guardian of my heart, and soul/Of all my moral being. WGRP
That on the banks of this delightful stream/We stood together. Prf

Lines Concerning the Unknown Soldier: "Arteries juicy with blood." Osip Mandelstam. The centuries surround me with fire. NAs

Lines Declining a Transatlantic Dinner Invitation. Marilyn Hacker. pour one more brandy, as it were, on me. MAYP

Lines Descriptive of Thomson's Island. Benjamin Lynde. For here with joy and dutiful regard/In all my rural comforts he had shared. SCAP

Lines for a Christmas Card. Hilaire Belloc. Noel, Noel, Noel, Noel. TW

Lines for a Dead Poet. David Ferry. We were his citizens, and stayed/In a country that his poems made. PP

Lines for a Drawing of Our Lady of the Night. Francis Thompson. Then rest a little; and in sleep/Forget to weep, forget to weep! ISi

Lines for a Feast of Our Lady. Sister Maris Stella. the litany that climbs and grows/upon the lattice of the Rose. ISi

Lines for a Friend Who Left. John Logan. Write/or come back, before I forget/what we both look like. DFF

Lines for a Hard Time. Gena Ford. ₆...And send our sons/to walk out in open day. IHMS

Lines for a Sundial. Thomas Herbert Warren. OF ETERNALLE. OBVV

Lines for a Wedding Gift. Wesley Trimpi. That is, that each shall understand. NePoEA

Lines for a Worthy Person Who Has Drifted by Accident... Sir Alan Patrick Herbert. And what my father used to say,/Is good enough for me. NOBL

Lines for a Young Wanderer in Mexico. John Logan. Falls back on this rain wet, brick real street. PoA

Lines for an Eminent Poet and Critic. Patric Dickinson. For fear he is the flea. PV

Lines for an Interment. Archibald MacLeish. Now you are dead... CMoP; NOBA

Lines for an Old Man. Thomas Stearns Eliot. Tell me if I am not glad! FaBoTw; TW

Lines for Cuscuscaraway and Mirza Murad Ali Beg. Thomas Stearns Eliot. How unpleasant to meet Mr. Eliot!/(Whether his mouth be open or shut). FiBHP; NLV; OBAL; PoPl; SpRo

Lines for Marking Time. Roberta Hill. Indians know how to wait. BoWoP; CDW; TWSS

Lines for Michael in the Picture. John Logan. what was locked is yours, Michael, as much as mine. CAPP

Lines for My Father. Patrick Worth Gray. Their crests tousled by the fight,/Like your unruly hair. AMV-81

Lines for the Ancient Scribes. Harvey Shapiro. Though ash lay on the altar stone. VWA

Lines for the Hour. Hamilton Fish Armstrong. Knowing the slow mutations of the soul. HBMV; MC

Lines for the Margin of an Old Gospel. Sheila Wingfield. And night is freezing. ChMP

Lines for the Planned Parenthood Clinic. Linda Westfall Spurrier. ...some/ wait alone/for conspicuous men/to come. SOTS

Lines for Those to Whom Tragedy Is Denied. Joyce Carol Oates. As certain birds bred for color and song and beyond/Their youth's charm. IHMS

Lines from a Misplaced Person. Jeanne Hill. and the Black Rock Canal bleeds in my skin FAZ

Lines from an Elegy on the Death of His Wife. Hitomaro. And sorrow darkens all the day. LiTW

Lines Written at Cambridge, to W. R., Esquire. Phineas Fletcher. Thou Chame, and Chamish nymphs, bear witness of my vow! EiL

Lines Written at the Grave of Alexander Dumas. Gwendolyn B. Bennett. And silence never moves,/Nor speaks nor sings. CDC; PoNe

Lines Written at the Temple of the Holy Sepulchre. George Sandys. I may be known and entertained for Thine. BePJ

Lines Written beneath a Picture. George Gordon, Lord Byron. For by the death-blow of my Hope/My Memory immortal grew. OBSP

Lines Written by a Bear of Very Little Brain. A.(lan) A.(lexander) Milne. That these are whose–but whose are these?/On Friday– FaBoNo

Lines Written during a Period of Insanity. William Cowper. I, fed with judgment, in a fleshly tomb, am/Buried above ground. EBEV; FiP; HAP; InPo; NoP; OAEL 1-2; PPP; Prf; TW

Lines Written Immediately after Parting from a Lady. Sir Samuel Egerton Brydges. On delusion my raptures arose! NOEC

Lines Written in a Country Parson's Orchard. Leslie Daiken. How little reaped where they had sown–/The generous Ascendancy. OnYI

Lines Written in a Mausoleum. Lillian Grant. Nor symmetric/stillness prove/the finality/of love. GoYe

Lines Written in Dejection. William Butler Yeats. I must endure the timid sun. MBW 1-2; NAs

Lines Written in Early Spring. William Wordsworth. Have I not reason to lament/What man has made of man? ACV; CBEP; EnLi 1-2; ERoP 1-2; FPL; HBV 1-2; MBW 1-2; MCCG; OAEL 1-2; OAEP; OBRV; PG; PoLf

Lines Written in Kensington Gardens. Matthew Arnold. Calm, calm me more! nor let me die/Before I have begun to live. EnLi 1-2; FaBoPP; NIP; TrPWD

Lines Written in Oregon. Vladimir Nabokov. Esmeralda, immer, immer. NYBP

Lines Written in the Album at Elbingerode, in the Hartz Forest. Samuel Taylor Coleridge. Himself our Father, and the World our Home. OBTV

Lines Written in the Bay of Lerici. Percy Bysshe Shelley. Destroying life alone, not peace! ERoP 1-2; OAEL 1-2

Lines Written in the Dog-Days. William Woty. How charming now, and cool it is! NOEC

Lines Written in the Front of a Well-Read Copy of Burns's Songs. Anonymous. Nor creesh, nor blot, not rend, nor spoil it. FaBoUs

Lines Written near Linton, on Exmoor (parody). Daniel Gerard Hoffman. Dissolves my dream, his task, and the name/Of the wretched place from whence he came... BXAP

Lines Written near Richmond, upon the Thames, at Evening. William Wordsworth. –The evening darkness gathers round/By virtue's holiest powers attended. OBEC

Lines Written on a Seat on the Grand Canal, Dublin. Patrick Kavanagh. O commemorate me with no hero-courageous/Tomb–just a canal-bank seat for the passer-by. BIrV; CIP; CMoP; InPS; IPY; NOBI

Lines Written on a Very Boisterous Day in May, 1944. John Clare. To rest my weary limbs amid the storms of May. OBSP

Lines Written on a Window at the Leasowes at a Time of Very Deep Snow. William Shenstone. My few sincerer friends detain,/And keep false friends away. OBSP

Lines Written on a Window-Shutter at Weston. William Cowper. Whose friend was God, but God swore not to aid me! EiCP; LAuP

Lines Written on Hearing the News of the Death of Napoleon. Percy Bysshe Shelley. And weave into his shame, which like the dead/Shrouds me, the hopes that from his glory fled.' ChRP; ERoP 1-2

Lines Written on November 15, 1933 by a Man Born November 14, 1881... Clayton Hamilton. But–what of me?/And–what of you? InMe

Lines Written on the Antiquity of Microbes. Strickland Gillilan. Adam/Had 'em. AtBAP; GoTF; PoEL 1-5; TreFT

The Lingam and the Yoni. A. D. Hope. While, in its secret valley,/Withers the herb of joy. MAT; NoAm; WeW

Lining Track. Anonymous. Hey boys, can't you line, ho boys, just a hair. AmFP

Link O' Day. Anonymous. Run yeh! Run yeh! 'Fo' do link o' day. TrAS

Links. Turner Cassity. And might bring off the tricks he used to do. SM

Links. Barry Dempster. ...horse hooves mixed/with the howling of a piano. CaPN

Links. Ricardo Pau-Llosa. sprouting through scales in the new coolness of the weather. AMV-81

The Linnet. Robert Bridges. Resign your simple natures,/To tender love. LiTL; OBEV

The Linnet. Walter De La Mare. And, at a flutter of wing,/Might vanish in song. HBMV; LiTB; LoBV

The Linnet in the Rocky Dells. Emily Bronte. There is no need of other sound/To soothe my Lady's dreams. BrRo; VLP

Linnets. Larry Levis. and the father of that silence. LCAP

Linota Rufescens. John Lyle Donaghy. ...I found you, sepulchred/in silver, in the fork of the birch– OnYI

Linstead Market. Anonymous. Oh what a Saturday night. FSW

Lintie in a Cage. Alice V. Stuart. Will ring even-on i' my ear/Till the close o my mortal times. OxBS

The Lion. Hilaire Belloc. And a good little child will not play with him. NLV

Lion. Mary Elizabeth ("E") Fullerton. Leaves flung from his flanks/In terrible unknowing! PoAu 1-2

The Lion. Vachel Lindsay. And all is family peace again. HBMV; ShM

The Lion. Ogden Nash. Up and swallowed Bryan's Bryaness. CenHV; ShM

Lion. May Swenson. is sweet as yearling's blood/in the corners of your lips LiTM; SoSe

The Lion. Walter James Turner. Into some midnight lair/Leapt from the printed page. MoBrPo

The Lion and Albert. Marriott Edgar. "What, waste all our lives raising children/To feed ruddy Lions? Not me!" OBNV

The Lion and O'Reilly. Richard Weber. Splitting the board with a final hit. PPON

Lion and Rabbit. Eliezer Greenberg. Pity rather the rabbit who even when free/Keeps trembling in his skin. BoAnP

The Lion and the Cub. John Gay. But know, what stupid asses prize,/Lions and noble beasts despise. GN; HBV 1-2

The Lion and the Mouse. Jeffreys Taylor. Nor shall we ever, if we're wise,/The meanest, or the least despise. HBV 1-2; HBVY; OnMSP

The Lion and the Unicorn. Mother Goose. Some gave them plum cake,/And sent them out of town. EvOK; HBV 1-2; OxBoLi

The Lion and the Wave. William Allingham. ...At last into his cave/This Lion cowering crept, lay down, and died. FM

The Lion at Noon. Victor Hugo. If he should move his massive paw,/Lo, what a cloud of flies! LiTW

The Lion for Real. Allen Ginsberg. Your starved and ancient Presence O Lord I wait in my room at/your Mercy. HaCAP

Lion Gate. Vera Rich. And strong eyes questing distances where crowd/Mist-shapes like unknown beasts half-hid in cloud. PoSH

Lion & Honeycomb. Howard Nemerov. Perfected and casual as to a child's eye/Soap bubbles are, and skipping stones. PP

The Lion-House. John Hall Wheelock. Paces your burning thought,/For the delight of Whom? HBMV

The Lion-Hunt. Thomas Pringle. And talk of our deeds o'er a flask of old wine. OBTV

Lion Hunts. Patricia Beer. It must always be the animal who dies. OxBTC

The lion is a beast to fight. Sir Arthur Thomas ("Q") Quiller-Couch. He runs with all his mane. CenHV

Lion, Leopard, Lady. Douglas Le Pan. Again in fleecy skies the lilies wave. OBCV

A Lion Named Passion. John Hollander. ...Jackels attend/The offal. And new cities raven and distend. NePoEA-2

The Lion over the Tomb of Leonidas. Anonymous. Whose bones I guard, bestriding this his grave. AWP

The Lion Roars at the Enraging Desert. Wallace Stevens. Caparison elephants, teach bears to juggle. NePA

The Lion's Bride. Gwen Harwood. Come soon, my love, my bride, and share this meal. BoWoP

The Lion's Cub. Maurice Thompson. She bore one cub, one only, but it wears/the lion's mane! AA

The Lion's Nature. Anonymous. If we harken to His word, that we go nowhere astray. MeEV

The Lion's Skeleton. Charles Tennyson Turner. The claws remain, but worms, wind, rain, and heat/Have sifted out the substance of thy feet. FM; NBM; NOBV; VLP

Lions and Gruel and Uncles. Lewis (Charles Lutwidge Dodgson) Carroll. "Well, then your uncles are–" FaBoNo

Lions in Sweden. Wallace Stevens. The vegetation still abounds with forms. BiP

The Lions of Fire Shall Have Their Hunting. Kenneth Patchen. And their terrible eyes are watching you. VGW

The Lip and the Heart. John Quincy Adams. The silence of the heart. AA; AmLP

Lips and Eyes. Giambattista Marino. Weeping or smiling pearles to Celia's face. OBVE

The lips of the one I love are my perpetual pleasure. Hafiz. His evening lectionary, and reciting the Book at dawn. BoLoP

Lips That Touch Liquor. George W. Young. And the lips that touch liquor must never touch mine. NLV; PaPo; TreFT

Lips Tongueless. Robert Herrick. This the lips we will permit/For to tell, not publish it. CaPo

Liquor and Longevity. Anonymous. And some of them, a very few,/Stay pickled till they're ninety-two. FPL

Lis'en to de Lam's. Anonymous. Lord, I wan'ta go to heaben when I die. BoAN 1-2

Lisa. Constance Carrier. yet interpose no barrier between them,/that she may move in both. SoSe

Lisbon. Anonymous. May great success attend them/Till they return again. AmFP

The Lisbon Packet. George Gordon, Lord Byron. Even on board the Lisbon Packet? NLV

Lise. Rose T. Cooke. May move thee to sigh once more. AA

Lisnagade. Anonymous. But my lady Mary fell asleep and the cowards ran away. WTO

Lispy Bails Out. David Barker. one hand clutching your little nursebag/ and the other the ripcord. GP

The List. Michael McClure. Glittering/gold/trembling/on darkness. NU

List of Prepositions. Benjamin Hall Kennedy. When 'state', not 'motion', 'tis they mean. FaBoUs

Listen. Edward Estlin Cummings. they don't want/to/no WaaP

Listen. Jessica Hagedorn. and listen/always listen/to the silent air. WPOW

Listen! Lilian Moore. Whatever in the world/is she having for lunch? NTCP

Listen. Charles Patterson. Then open time's doors and let loose/Your misery and awaken deaf mute men NBP

Listen Children. Lucille Clifton. we have always loved each other/children all ways/pass it on CNA; PoBA

Listen. Put on Morning. W. S. Graham. Waken into falling light. FaBoTw; LiTM; MP; NMP

Listen to the Bird. Laya Firestone. The shape of the land/Takes form. VWA

Listen to the Mocking Bird. Alice Hawthorne. Listen to the mocking bird,/Still singing where the weeping willows wave. BLSo; FSW; PSoN; TrAS; TreFT

Listen to the People: Independence Day, 1941 (excerpt). Stephen Vincent Benét. That's our Fourth of July. PoSC

Listenen to Big Black at S.F. State. Sonia Sanchez. loud with blk/nation/ hood/builden. BPo

A Listener's Guide to the Birds. E. B. White. And dozens of other inspired phrases. NYBP

The Listeners. Walter De la Mare. When the plunging hoofs were gone. AWP; BBV; BLPL; BrPo; CMoP; CoBMV; FaFP; GoTF; GTBS; HAP; HBV 1-2; HBVY; HeIP; HoPM; InvP; LiTB; LiTM; MaC; MoAB; MoBrPo; MoPo; MoVE; NAMP; NCSH; NoAm; NOBE; NoP; OAEP; OBEV; OBMV; OBVV; OnMSP; PoPl; PoPle; PoRA; SeCeV; SoSe; TreF; TrGrPo; ViBoPo; WeW; WHA; WSC

Listening. Alice Corbin. Who come out of the silence? BPAW

Listening. Aileen Fisher. he seldom hears/my voice at all. NTCP

Listening. Hanny Michaelis. for the no man's land/of my existence/breaks out anew. VWA

Listening. Nancy Passy. I listen/for my name. AMV-81

Listening. William Stafford. ...something in the night/will touch us too from that other place. RFM

Listening-Post. Martin C. Rosner. I have/No dominion. AMV-80

Listening to a Broadcast. John Streeter Manifold. There is no siding for the brain. WaP

Listening to a Confucious. Henryk Grynberg. because you will not gain will not buy a thing/beyond what she herself can offer you VWA

Listening to Beethoven on the Oregon Coast. Henry Carlile. the night cries of birds drown in the surf's roar. Psk

Listening to Foxhounds. James Dickey. Making no outcry, no matter/Who may be straining to hear. LiSp; PAI

Listening to Grownups Quarreling. Ruth Whitman. and I was shaken, shaken/like a mouse/between their jaws. NTCP

Listening to Her. Natan Zach. ...keeps/sleep from the eyes, to listen to her/otherwise unheard, at least now. VWA

Listening to the Music of Arsenio Rodriguez Is Moving Closer... Victor Hernandez Cruz. Are the windows opened?/Has it rained? APU

Listens, Too (parody). D. C. Berry. I leave on the canvas such weight/it is only my knuckles popping. BXAP

Liszt. Edmund Clerihew Bentley. That was the way/He used to play. UnS

Lit'le David Play on Yo' Harp. Anonymous. Lit'le David play on yo' harp, halleluja. BoAN 1-2

The Litanie. John Donne. As sinne is nothing, let it no where be. AtBAP; PoEL 1-5

The Litanies of Julia Pastrana. Thomas W. Shapcott. Give thanks never to have/seen them/real and alive/among/us. CBAP; NOAV

Litany. Charles Angoff. O Lord, remember us. TrPWD

The Litany. Charles Cotton. From His Highness, and the Devil,/Libera nos, etc. OBSV

A Litany. Sir Philip Sidney. Who Love can temper thus,/Good Lord, deliver us! OBSC; UnPo

Litany For Dictatorships. Stephen Vincent Benét. Our children know and suffer the armed men. AnEnPo; NAMP; OxBA

Litany for Halloween. Anonymous. And THINGS/That go BUMP in the night,/Good Lord, deliver us! SiSoSe; SoPo

A Litany for Latter-Day Mystics. Cale Young Rice. And that, thro' the wide universe,/Well-being's breath distills. WGRP

A Litany for Old Age. Una W. Harsen. Then from the craven fear of death/Good Lord, deliver me. TrPWD

Litany for Peace. Leslie Savage Clark. Be with us, Lord! PGD

A Litany in Time of Plague. Nashe [(or Nash)] Thomas. Brightness falls from the air. CABA
I am sick, I must die./Lord, have mercy on us. CABA; DL; EnLi 1-2; ForPo; NIP; NoP; OAEL 1-2; PoRA; PPP; PrIm

Litany of Sleep. Tristan Corbiere. SLEEP, ON WAKING, SAYS TO ME: YOU HAS SAWN ME APART. OBVE

The Litany of the Dark People. Countee Cullen. When Bethlehem and Calvary/Are merged in Paradise. EaLo; MoRP; TrPWD

Litany of the Heroes. Vachel Lindsay. God help us to be brave. MoRP

Litany of the Lost. Siegfried Sassoon. Deliver us from ourselves. MoRP

Litany of the Rooms of the Dead. Franz Werfel. O pity the dead! We shall soon be/among them. TrJP

Litany to Our Lady. Caryll Houselander. Lady, giver of Bread,/Christ-bestowing. ISi

Litany to Satan. Charles Baudelaire. My soul may sit, that cries upon thee now. AWP; SyP

Litany to the Holy Spirit (excerpt). Robert Herrick. Sweet Spirit comfort me! CoBE; OBEV; PoPle

Literary Criticism. Myles Na Gopaleen. My reference is to Ezra . DBV

Literary Dinner. Vladimir Nabokov. and I stowed all the studs on the edge of my plate. FiBHP; OBAL

Literary Gruk. Piet Hein. Like a man in a book on a book on a book. LiTW

Literary Importation. Philip Freneau. And say what they think in a handsomer stile. TAP

Literary Landscape with Dove and Poet. Phyllis McGinley. ..."Coo, Coo" is Metahysics. NePoAm-2

Literary Life in the Golden West. Philip Whalen. Drinking muscatel and swapping stories/Until the buttons drive us home. NAs

Literary Love. Harry Kemp. I thought, "What lovely poems this will make!" HBMV

A Literary Squabble. James Robinson Planché. By giving three cheers for "Lord §Hough-Howé ton!" CenHV

Literary Zodiac. R. A. Piddington. While the tax gatherer spiders for his prey. PV

Little. Dorothy Aldis. But every morning he still is/Too little to look. NTCP; SUS; TiPo

Little Ah Sid (with music). Anonymous. Sang little Ah Sid, this Chinese kid,/As he played the long summer day. AS

Little Air. Stephane Mallarme. In the billow become you/Your nude jubilation PoPl; SyP

Little and Great. Charles Mackay. Ye were but little at the first,/But mighty at the last. HBV 1-2; HBVY; PoLf

The Little Angels. Jacopone da Todi. The sweetness of His face. CAW

Little Annie Rooney. Michael Nolan. Little Annie Rooney is my sweetheart! FSN; GoTF; TreF

Little Ball of Yarn. Anonymous. It was then I spun her little ball of yarn. FSW

The Little Beach-Bird. Richard Henry Dana. Where birds for gladness sing! AA; AnAmPo; AnNE; APA; EtS; HBV 1-2

Little Bell. Thomas Westwood. ...Love, deep and kind,/Shall watch around, and leave good gifts behind,/Little Bell, for thee. GN; HBV 1-2

Little Bessie. Anonymous. I was going when you called me,/When you came and kissed my hand. AmFP

Little Big Horn. Ernest McGaffey. The shades of the dead through the ages lie/dreaming. PAH

Little Billee. William Makepeace Thackeray. But as for little Bill he made him/The Captain of a Seventy-three. CenHV; EtS; FaBoCh; FaBoCo; HBV 1-2; HBVY; LBN; LoGBV; MOS; NA; NOBL; PoPle; ShM; TreFS

Little Billy. Anonymous. For telling such lies o' the kirk. GBP

Little Birches. Mary Effie Lee Newsome. Their violet velvet shadow robes/ Beside them on the grasses. PoNe

The Little Bird. Anonymous.
And this is what happened. PBA
But he shook his little tail/And away he flew. OxNR

The Little Bird. Walter De La Mare. In from the dark ivy hopped a/Wee small bird.And that was Me. BiCB; BrR; NAs

A Little Bird. Aileen Fisher. and orange juice--for him! SoPo

Little Bird, Go through My Window. Anonymous. Go through my window, my little bird,/And buy molasses candy. OuSiCo

A Little Bird I Am. Jeanne Marie Guyon. And in thy mighty will to find/ The joy, the freedom of the mind. WGRP

Little Birdie. Anonymous. I've a short while to be here,/And a long time to be gone. FSW

The Little Birds. Anonymous. All mouth that once had been all egg. NTCP

Little Birds. Lewis (Charles Lutwidge Dodgson) Carroll. When the bells have tinkled,/And the Tale is told. FaBoNo; OxBoLi

Little Birds. Jacob Sternberg. And of a strange bird that chirps/With a foreign sound. TrJP

The Little Black Boy. William Blake. And be like him, and he will then love me. AtBAP; AWP; BiP; CABA; DiPo; EnPE; HBV 1-2; HeIP; InPo; LoGBV; MyFE; NAWM 1-2; NoP; OAEL 1-2; OBEC; OBEV; OxBChV; OxBoCh; PoNe; SeCeV; TreFS; TrGrPo

Little Black Bug. Margaret Wise Brown. Said little old mouse./Squeak-eak-eak-eak-eak. NTCP

The Little Black Dog. Elizabeth Gardner Reynolds. And followed Him quite to the cross. PoLf

The Little Black Dog Ran Round the House. Anonymous. Who cracked his throat with crowing. OxNR

Little Black Man with a Rose in His Hat. Audrey Wurdemann. Goes back like a lord, alone. YaD

Little Black Rose. Anonymous. every mountain valley and bog in Ireland will shake/one day, before she shall perish, my Roisin Dub NOBI

The Little Black Sheep. Paul Laurence Dunbar. An'–dat lil' brack sheep–wuz–me! WBLP

The Little Black Train. Anonymous. There's a little black train a-comin',/An' it may be here tonight. AmFP; OuSiCo

Little Blue Ben. Anonymous. Where shall I find the little Blue/Ben? OxNR

Little Blue Betty. Anonymous. And she tumbled down and broke her head. OxNR

Little Blue Ribbons. Henry Austin Dobson. When "Little Blue Ribbons" prefers it so. BiCB

Little Blue Shoes. Kate Greenaway. Blue Shoes may go quite alone. TiPo

Little Bo-Peep. Anonymous. To tack again each to its lambkin. OxNR; SpRo

Little Bo-Peep. Mother Goose.
And bring their tails behind them. SoPo
That each tail should be properly placed. HBV 1-2; HBVY

The Little Boats of Britain. Sara E. Carsley. And the little boats of Britain shall go sailing by their side! CaP

Little Boxes. Malvina Reynolds. And they all look just the same. FSW

Little Boy Blue. Guy Wetmore Carryl. The farmer take offense. ALV

Little Boy Blue. Eugene Field. Since he kissed them and put them/there. AA; BeLS; FPL; GoTF; OBCA; PoLf

Little Boy Blue. Robert Lockwood. My baby, she gone and left me/She left me all a lone BluL

Little Boy Blue. Mother Goose. For if I do, he'll be sure to cry. FaFP

Little Boy Blue. John Crowe Ransom. He rubbed his eyes again and went to sleep. LiTM

The Little Boy Found. William Blake. Her little boy weeping sought. CBEP; NoP

A Little Boy in the Morning. Francis Ledwidge. Barefooted in the shining grass? MCCG; OnYI

Little Boy Lost. William Blake.
And away the vapour flew. CBEP; NoP
Are such things done on Albion's shore? CEP; ViBoPo

A Little Boy Lost. Jerome Rothenberg. ...,and I/have no way of turning now, no door. CoPo

The Little Boy Lost. Stevie Smith. But darker days and hungrier I must spend/Till hunger and darkness make an end. FaBoTw

A Little Boy's Vain Regret. Edith Matilda Thomas. I think I should be a better boy. AA

The Little Boy to the Locomotive. Benjamin R. C. Low. I hardly dare come close to you. HBMV

Little Boys of Texas. Robert P. Tristram Coffin. Sadder, wiser, and plumb dead! ShM

Little Brass Wagon. Anonymous. Fare you well, my darling. FSW

Little Breeches. John Milton Hay. Is a derned sight better business/Than loafin' around The Throne. AA; FaBoBe; HBV 1-2; PaPo; TreFS

Little Britain. Anonymous. Where birds escape the fatal gun,/And men alone are shot at. NOEC

Little Brother. Aileen Fisher. "EVERYthing's robins/when you're still just three." BiCB; DTC

The Little Brother. James Reeves. Hear the lost sisters innocently tease. OxBTC

A Little Brother of the Rich. Edward Sandford Martin. The trials of abounding wealth. AA; HBV 1-2

The Little Brother Poem. Naomi Shihab Nye. when you need it, and you don't have so much time. Str

Little Brother's Secret. Katherine Mansfield. O the darling! NAs; TiPo

Little Brown Baby. Paul Laurence Dunbar. Little brown baby wif spa'klin'eyes! BANP; NoP; PoNe

The Little Brown Bulls. Anonymous. We will drink to the health of the little brown bulls. AmFP; BaBo; OuSiCo

Little Brown Church in the Vale. William S. Pitts. No spot is so dear to my childhood/As the little brown church in the vale. TreFT

Little Brown Dog. Anonymous. And him that tells a bigger tale/Would have to tell a lie./Sing taddle-o-day. FSW

Little Brown Jug. Joseph E. Winner. Ha! ha! ha! you and me, little brown jug don't I love thee! ABF; BLSo; FaFP; FSW; OBAL; PSoN; TrAS; TreF

Little Buttercup. Sir William Schwenck Gilbert. Come, of your Buttercup buy! GoTF; TreFS

A Little Cabin. Charles Bertram Johnson. Dat's de deed to it. BANP

Little Candle. Carl Sandburg. So does nay little candle/speaking for itself in its personal corner. GoYe

The Little Car. Guillaume Apollinaire. And although we were both grown men/We had just been born SOTW

A Little Carol of the Virgin. Felix Lope de Vega Carpio. let my child sleep,/hold back the branches. PCh

The Little Cart. Arthur Waley. They stand hesitating in the lonely road and their tears fall like/rain. AtBAP; LoBV

The Little Carved Bowl. Margaret Widdemer. But today someone gave me/A little carved bowl. BrR

The Little Cat Angel. Leontine Stanfield. For the name of the kitten was Love. BLPA

Little Catkins. Alexander Blok. Rise to greet you, Willow Sunday,/Holy day. EaLo; OFD

The Little Chap Who Follows Me. Anonymous. A little fellow follows me. PoToHe

Little Charlie Chipmunk. Helen Cowles LeCron. Oh, little Charlie Chipmunk was a very tiresome child! SoPo; TiPo

A Little Cheat! Anonymous. No true Malayan maid is she,/But just an arrant little cheat. WTO

The Little Child. Albert Bigelow Paine. For the thorns that it must wear. AA

A Little Child, a Limber Elf. Samuel Taylor Coleridge. So talks as it's most used to do. LoBV

The Little Child's Faith. Louis Edwin Thayer. Believing his daddy's all right. PoToHe

The Little Chisel. N. P. Van Wyk Louw. with a crack that from my chisel blow/runs to the furthest star. PeSA

Little City. Robert Horan. By night we cannot see the flies' faces/and the spider, rocking. CrMA; NePA

The Little Clan. Frederick Robert Higgins. Then mourn no less/The living glory of/Each Gaelic word! OBMV

Little Clown Puppet. Carolyn Haywood. But the little clown puppet, he parachuted! BrR

Little Cock Robin. Anonymous. He'll hide his head under his wing. PBBP

A Little Cock Sparrow Sat on a Green Tree. Anonymous. So he clapped his wings and away he flew. OxNR

The Little Commodore (parody). J. C. Squire. When the Pegasus came sailing from the West. HBMV

Little Cosmic Dust Poem. John Haines. my voice, your face, this love. SUW

The Little Cradle Rocks Tonight in Glory. Anonymous. Don't you hear His foot on the treetop,/Soft like the south wind blow? AmFP

The Little Creature. Walter De La Mare. My great grandam–She was a Witch. EvOK

The Little Dancers. Laurence Binyon. Their eyes shining, grave with a perfect pleasure. CH; MoBrPo; MoVE; OBVV; OxBTC

Little Dandelion. Helen Barron Bostwick. Little winged Dandelion/Soareth away. HBV 1-2; HBVY

The Little Dandelion. Lula Lowe Weeden. And leave it with a bald head. CDC

The Little Dark Rose. Owen Roe MacWard. Some day ere shall perish my Little Dark/Rose! OnYI

Little David. Anonymous. Little David, play on yo' harp, Hallelu! FSW; GoSl; TrAS

Little Dirge. Jean Starr Untermeyer. My youth is slipping out the door. HBMV

A Little Dog-Angel. Norah M. Holland. The little dog-angel's eager bark/Will comfort his soul in the shivering dark. PoLf

The Little Dog under the Wagon. Anonymous. He follows on his horny toes,/The little dog under the wagon. PoLf

The Little Doll. Charles Kingsley. Yet for old sakes' sake she is still, dears,/The prettiest doll in the world. OxBChV

The Little Donkey. Francis Jammes. and peasant women such as she/who sells pine logs for firewood. PCh

The Little Dove. Anonymous. There I'll meet Mary and my Jane. AmFP

The Little Drummer. Anonymous. Five thousand a year as long as they lived,/And it's oh, my good fortune. AmFP

The Little Drummer. Richard Henry Stoddard. Sat the little drummer, fast asleep,/With his rat-tat-too. PAH

The Little Duck. Joso. --that is the look/on the little duck's face. SoPo

Little Dunkeld. Anonymous. Dung doun the steeple, and brucken the bell. GBP

A Little Dutch Garden. Hattie Whitney. And Gretchen is holding it fast. AA

Little Eclogue. Elinor Wylie. Let men inquire, and gods obscurely know. NMM

Little Elegy. Denis Devlin. For no reason that I can tell. NOBI

Little Elegy. X. J. Kennedy. And for her sake trip up Death. CoAP; ConAP; ELU; GoJo; HoPM; NCSH

Little Elegy. Elinor Wylie. And you nowhere. LOW

The Little Elf. John Kendrick Bangs. "I'm quite as big for me," said he,/"As you are big for you." AA; BiCB; FaBoBe; HBV 1-2; HBVY; NTCP; OBCA

Little Epithalamium. Chester Kallman. I say them in ceremony again:/Oak, fern, ivy and pine. CrMA

Little Exercise. Elizabeth Bishop. think of him as uninjured, barely disturbed. CoAP; CrMA; MoAB; MoAmPo; NCSH; NYBP; UnPo

The Little Factory Girl to a More Fortunate Playmate. Anonymous. And at my work I'll think of them and holidays to come! SaC

The Little Family. Anonymous. He'll bid us live forever where pleasure never dies. BaBo; BFSS

Little Fan. James Reeves. Watch now, or she'll be gone for ever/To the rocks by the brown sandy shore. SO

The Little Farm; or, The Weary Ploughman. Anonymous. Although I'm young and in my prime my courage is pull'd down. CoMu

Little Father Poem. Marvin Bell. the sand smooth because soft. LCAP

Little Feet. Elizabeth Akers. And pray that He who feeds the crying ravens/Will guide the baby's feet. HBV 1-2

Little Fish. D. H. Lawrence. their little lives are fun to them/in the sea. OxBTC; SOTW

The Little Fish That Would Not Do as It Was Bid. Jane and Ann Taylor. "Dear mother, had I minded you,/I need not now have died." OHIP

Little Fishes in a Brook. Anonymous. Johnnie eats them like a man. OxNR

The Little Fox. Dorothy and Marion Edey Grider. I like to be only/Squat and bunchy—/Do You-oo-oo-oo, too? TiPo

Little Fred. Anonymous. And always said his prayers. HBV 1-2; HBVY

Little Friend. Anonymous. To find the apple, quince, and pear. OxNR

Little Gal at Our House. Anonymous. Fat as she can waller. ABF

The Little General. Edwin Muir. Fast in the little General's fragile hand. BSV

Little General Monk. Anonymous. Now little General Monk is dead. OxNR

The Little Gentleman. Anonymous. Seek in all things that you can/To be a little gentleman. HBV 1-2; HBVY

The Little Ghost. Katharine Tynan Hinkson. For she has seen the mothers' children/And knows that it is well. HBV 1-2

The Little Ghosts. Thomas S. Jones, Jr. Do they come back to you? HBV 1-2

Little Giffen. Francis Orrery [(or Orray(] Ticknor. The whitest soul of my chivalry,/For Little Giffen of Tennessee. AA; HBV 1-2; MaC; MC; PAH; TreFS

A Little Girl. Charles Angoff. She is/The constellation/Of all creation. GoYe

A Little Girl. Anonymous.
And we made merry work. OxNR
Thank you, Grandam. OxNR

The Little Girl. Nicholas Moore. And the big, grown-up, cold-looking feet. ErPo; NeBP

Little Girl, Be Careful What You Say. Carl Sandburg. be what you wish to be. GoYe

The Little Girl Found. William Blake. Nor the lions' growl. CBEP; DiPo

The Little Girl Lost. William Blake. And naked they convey'd/To caves the sleeping maid. DiPo

Little Girl, My Stringbean, My Lovely Woman. Anne Sexton. you will strike fire,/that new thing! NYBP

A Little Girl on Her Way to School. James Wright. Following the white swan through the hedge. GLGT

A Little Girl's Dream World. Della Burt. Could it be that/it never/was? BlSi

The Little Girl with Bands on Her Teeth. Genevieve Taggard. I travel the risk of the end. O perilous love. VGW

The Little Golden Ring. Anonymous. To think of me while gazing on that little golden ring. ShS

Little Gray Songs from St. Joseph's, XLVII. Grace Fallow Norton. Yet here it weeps–long blind, long blind–/And cannot understand. HBV 1-2

Little Gray Songs from St. Joseph's, XXX. Grace Fallow Norton. I see mine own face over me,/With tears upon its cheek. HBV 1-2

The Little Green Blackbird. Kenneth Patchen. And our only crime, that we are here to serve it. PoCh

The Little Green Orchard. Walter De La Mare. Someone is waiting and watching there,/In the little green orchard. EvOK

Little Gregory. Theodore Botrel. "Jesu Domine!" CAW

Little Guinever. Annie Fields. For Guinever is but a child. AA

Little Gustava. Celia Thaxter. And oh, her breakfast is sweet indeed/To happy little Gustava! HBV 1-2; HBVY

Little Hands. Laurence Binyon. More, more than wisdom understands/And love, love only knows. HBV 1-2

The Little House in Lithuania. Samuel Marshak. A woman said: "Farewell, my son!" VWA

The Little Hunchback. James Whitcomb Riley. They's nary angel 'bout the place with "curv'ture of/the spine." PeD

Little Hundred. Anonymous. Five's a little hundred. OxNR

Little Hunger. Richard Murphy. and pick a hearthstone from a rubble fragment/to make it integral. BIrV

Little Husband. Anonymous. And a little silk handkerchief/to wipe his pretty nose. OxNR

Little Ivory Figures Pulled with String. Amy Lowell. The murmur of it is loud–loud. AnFE; APA; MAPA; NAMP; ViBoPo

Little Jack Dandy-Prat. Anonymous. A little pig on a string/Cost him five shilling. OxNR

Little Jack Frost. Anonymous. That Little Jack Frost was glad to go. SoPo

Little Jack Horner. Mother Goose. And said, "What a good boy/am I!" FaBoBe; FaFP; HBV 1-2; HBVY; SoPo; SoSe

Little Jim. Edward Farmer. In heaven, once more to meet again,/Their own poor Little Jim. PaPo

Little Joe Gould Has Lost His Teeth and Doesn't Know Where. Edward Estlin Cummings. but it's more fun to be more to be fun to be little joe gould) NoAm

Little Joe the Wrangler. N. Howard Thorp. For our little lost horse herder, wrangler Joe. BPAW; CoSo; FSW

Little John a Begging (A version). Anonymous. I shold haue purcchased three of the/best churches/That stands by any highway.' ESPB

Little John a Begging (B version). Anonymous. 'Tis of Robin Hood, that archer good,/And how Little John went a begging. BaBo; ESPB

Little John Nobody. Anonymous. But little John Nobody, that dare not once speak. OxBoLi

The Little Johnny Mine. Daisy L. Detrick. That a certain FIRE made him a danged millionaire! PoOW

Little Johnny's Confession. Brian Patten. they have my lollypops. CAD

Little Katy. Anonymous. Little Katy bit his head off. ShM

A Little Kingdom I Possess. Louisa May Alcott. And dare to take command. AH

The Little Knight in Green. Katharine Lee Bates. I kiss her feet and deem it sweet/To perish for my queen. AA

Little Lad. Anonymous. Is the bonny bowl/They breakfast in. BiCB; OxNR

The Little Lady. Russell Edson. Now, and forever, my love, she says with the puppet master/making her voice with his falsetto... GP

The Little Lady Lairdie. Anonymous. If it wasn't for your cold nose/I would kiss thee now-o. OxNR

Little Lady Wren. Tom Robinson. And will not bob it when I say,/"Bob it now!"? TiPo

The Little Land. Robert Louis Stevenson. And just come back, a sleepy head,/Late at night to go to bed. SoPo

Little-League Baseball Fan. W. R. Moses. ...And my God, who could connect/With those impossible curves? LiSp; NCSH

Little Libbie. Julia A. Moore. To welcome home friends once more. ATP; OBAL; PeD

Little Light. Jim Brodey. to dry my glazed flesh with/some of your happy brilliance. APU

A Little Litany to St. Francis. Philip Murray. ...larks at/Portiuncula singing when you died,/Pray for us,/AMEN NePoAm

The Little Lost Child. Edward B. Marks. Left me at home deserted, alone, and took,/And took you, my child, away. TreFS

Little Lost Pup. Arthur Guiterman. Oh, the blithest of sights in the world so fair/Is a gay little pup with his tail in the air! BBV; GoTF; TreFS

The Little Lough. John Hewitt. but sheltered only from the ruffling wind. NeIP

The Little Love-God. Meleager. fear not, with my Zenophile/remain thou here to dwell. AWP

Little Lover. Leonora Speyer. Left you to grieve to heights again. HBMV

Little Lullaby. Irving Feldman. Bodies approach; they wish to fulfill you. NYBP

Little Lute. Richard Corbet. That in her heart would be content/To be at his commandement. FaBoEE

Little Lyric (of Great Importance). Langston Hughes. Was heaven sent. NLV; OBAL

A little madness in the spring. Emily Dickinson. This whole Experiment of Green–/As if it were his own! MAmP; TAP

Little Maggie. Anonymous. And a banjo on her knee. FSW

A Little Maid. Anonymous. And fastened the door with a skewer. OxNR

The Little Maid. Anna Maria Wells. I only wipe one teacup,/And set it on the shelf. OBCA

Little Maid, Pretty Maid. Anonymous. When I send for thee/Then come thou. OxNR

The Little Man and the Little Maid. *Anonymous.* And could have of a cat but her skin, skin, skin. OxNR

The Little Man Who Wasn't There. Hughes Mearns. I wish, I wish, he'd go away. FaFP; SoPo

Little Marble Boy. James Wright. in an everlasting gesture/to catch a white fish. EyDe

Little Mary Cassidy. Francis A. Fahy. I never would feel lonesome with the two of us alone. HBV 1-2

Little Mathiue Grove. *Anonymous.* And to-morrow I will have to die. BaBo

The Little Milliner. Robert Williams Buchanan. To ashes, like the chestnuts, close together! BeLS

Little Miss and Her Parrot. John Marchant. Is it not absurd,/That a senseless bird,/Which knows not a word,/My mind should rule? OxBChV

Little Miss Muffet. Mother Goose. And frightened Miss Muffet away. FaBoBe; FaFP; HBV 1-2; HBVY; SoPo; TiPo

Little Miss Muffet (parody). *Anonymous.* She–shrieking–turned and fled. BXAP; FaBoPa

Little Miss Pitt. William Wise. When it's time he was upstairs in bed? TiPo

Little Mohee. *Anonymous.* I'll go spend my days with/My little Mohee. ABF; AmFP; AmSS; BaBo; FSW

Little Moppet. *Anonymous.* And stole my little moppet/away. OxNR

A Little More About the Brothers and Sisters. Sharon Scott. only about what the people are doing. JB

A Little Morning Music. Delmore Schwartz. Gazing and blazing, blessing and possessing all vividness/and all darkness. BoNaP; NYBP

Little Moses. *Anonymous.* And rested in Heaven above. FSW

Little Mousgrove and the Lady Barnet. *Anonymous.* Then let us call for grace/That we may shun this wicked vice/And mend our lives apace. OxBB

Little Musgrave and Lady Barnard. *Anonymous.* But lay my lady on the upper hand,/For she came of the better kin. BaBo; CABL; ESPB; FaBoBa; InvP; OBET

Little Musgrave and Lady Barnard (B version). *Anonymous.* For which Ile repent all the dayes of/my life,/And god be with them all three!' ESPB

Little Musgrave and Lady Barnard (Little Matthy Groves). *Anonymous.* Today I've killed two true lovers,/And tomorrow I must die! AmFP

Little Nag. *Anonymous.* And trotted out of town. OxNR

The Little Nipper an' 'Is Ma. George Fauvel Gouraud. An' yer should o' 'eard 'im larf. AA

Little Ode. Paul Goodman. we deviate straight forward to immortal death. PoA

Little Ode for X. Maura Stanton. ...an equation for X,/as it, too, now grows by substitution. MAYP

The Little Old Lady in Lavender Silk. Dorothy Parker. There was nothing more fun than a man! InMe; NLV; YaD

The Little Old Sod Shanty. *Anonymous.* And we'd see the old sod shanty on our claim. AmFP; AS; BFSS; BPAW; CoSo; FSW

The Little Ones' A.B.C. Noel Coward. And Mother'd like to slit your throats! NLV

Little Orphant Annie. James Whitcomb Riley. Er the Gobble-uns'll git you/Ef you don't watch out! AA; BBGG; FaFP; HBV 1-2; HBVY; MoShBr; NLV; OBAL; OBCA; OxBChV; PaPo; TiPo; TreF

Little Pagan Rain Song. Frances Shaw. Song of my soul that will not forget/The sleeping body of me. HBMV

A Little Page's Song. William Alexander Percy. He'd love me sure–/And maybe praise! HBV 1-2

Little Papoose. Arthur Chapman. Little papoose, we die! BPAW

A Little Parable. Anne Reeve Aldrich. I should have made a lighter cross/To bear up Calvary! AA; HBV 1-2

The Little Peach. *Anonymous.* Attendez a mon narration triste! NA

The Little Peach. Eugene Field. Ah, well, its mission on earth is through./Adieu! LBN; OBAL; ShM

Little People. Isaac L. Peretz. And Time, untiring, never late,/Sweeps by on great steel wings,/entirely out of rhyme. TrJP

A Little Person. Brian Hooker. God one morning, glad of heaven,/Laughed–and that was you! HBMV

Little Phillis. Kate Greenaway. I think it only came. BiCB

Little Phoebe. *Anonymous.* And give him a dip upon the lip,/and the blood run to his toes. FSW

Little Pig. *Anonymous.* Great big Thumbo,/father of them all. OxNR

The Little Pig. Ziche Landau. And it's as tender and as innocent/as your lines, divine Verlaine! VWA

A Little Pig Asleep. Leroy F. Jackson. He had shellac on all his feet/And rubber in his nose. BrR

Little Piggy. Thomas Hood. Well, I never before saw a pig dance a jig! SoPo

The Little Poem of Life. John Oxenham. Till younger lives come all their love to prove. TRV

Little Political Poem. Edward Hirsch. through so many different countries... AMV-81

Little Polly Flinders. Mother Goose. For spoiling her nice new clothes. HBV 1-2; HBVY

Little Ponds. Arthur Guiterman. Oh, happy little ponds to be/So well deceived! HBMV

A Little Pretty Bonny Lass. *Anonymous.* I swore I would, yet still she said I should not/Do what I would, and yet for all I could not. EIL; NCEP

Little Pretty Nancy Girl. *Anonymous.* She was not very lusty. OxNR

Little Pudding (parody). Mary M. Roberts. ...when the idea of eating/and the idea of pudding/are one. BXAP

Little Puppy. Hilda Faunce Wetherill. And the square cornbread is in the ashes,/Waiting our return. TiPo

Little Rain. Elizabeth Madox Roberts. And I got some rain in my hair. SoPo; SUS

Little Raindrops. Jane Euphemia Browne (Aunt Effie). Why can't you play on that?' HBV 1-2; HBVY; OxBChV

The Little Red Lark. Alfred Perceval Graves. And dew-drops glisten,/Laughing on every spray. HBV 1-2

The Little Red Ribbon. James Whitcomb Riley. The little red ribbon, the ring and the rose! HBV 1-2

Little Red Riding Hood. Olga Broumas. peopled with wolves and our lost,/flower-gathering/sisters they feed on. DFT

Little Red Riding Hood. Guy Wetmore Carryl. If a swallow cannot make a summer,/It can bring on a summary fall! FiBHP

Little red riding hood. Nila NorthSun. babe was the only one/who came to visit gramma. GP

Little Red Riding Hood. Anne Sexton. from their going down/and their lifting up. DFT

Little Red Riding Hood and the Wolf. Roald Dahl. She said, "Hello, and do please note/My lovely furry wolfskin coat." DFT

The Little Red Sled. Jocelyn Bush. We'll go like a fairy,/So light and so airy! SoPo; TiPo

A Little Rhyme and a Little Reason. Henry Anstadt. Surely God should have our service now and evermore./Amen. BLRP

Little Roach Poem. C. W. Truesdale. into a blaze of sunlight/over a blue sea. PoDr

The Little Road. Nancy Byrd Turner. "That's why I brought you home." TiPo

Little Roads to Happiness. Wilhelmina Stitch. There's always the self same mind to lead us home at/night. PoToHe

Little Robin Redbreast. *Anonymous.* And poop went his hole. PBBP

The Little Rose Is Dust, My Dear. Grace Hazard Conkling. The rose, the little wind and you/Have gone so far away. HBV 1-2

The Little Rose Tree. Rachel Field. I wonder if the gardener knows,/Or if he calls each just a rose? SUS; TiPo

Little Rosewood Casket. *Anonymous.* Oh, dear sister, do not weep. FSW

Little Saling. Olaf Baker. Though the sun at Little Saling/Lies warm upon the leads. HBMV

Little Sally Racket. *Anonymous.* With a haul-ey hi-ho/Haul 'em away. FSW

Little Sally Sand. *Anonymous.* Turn to the east and turn to the west,/And turn to the one that you love best. TrAS

Little Sally Waters. Mother Goose. Fly to the one that you love best. AmFP; FSW; TiPo

Little Satellite. Jane W. Krows. I would only soar from sight/If I could return each night. SoPo

Little Scotch-ee (with music). *Anonymous.* For I'm afraid you will sarve me like you sarved/Your little Scotch-ee,/Your little Scotch-ee. AS

A Little Scraping. Robinson Jeffers. And gathers multitudes like game to be hunted when the season comes. NoAm

The Little Searcher. Donna Bowen. And in the twilight let me in the smallest gate. AMV-80

A Little Sequence (excerpt). Francis Burdett Money-Coutts. For God has something still to teach/In that diviner vale. OBVV

The Little Shepherd's Song. William Alexander Percy. For I think there must be/Inside of me/A bird! YeAr

The Little Shoes That Died. Mary Gilmore. Then from the shoes they slipped her feet,/And the little shoes died. NOAV

The Little Shroud. Letitia Elizabeth Landon. And only asked of heaven its aid/Her heavy lot to bear. PaPo

Little Sir Hugh. *Anonymous.* Besides, a penknife sticks in my heart,/So out I cannot creep.' OBET

Little Sis. David Kherdian. brush against our one innocent/life. AMV-80

The Little Sister of the Prophet. Marjorie Pickthall. Will he touch my cheek as he used to, and laugh and be/kind? HBV 1-2

Little Sleep's-Head Sprouting Hair in the Moonlight. Galway Kinnell. ...the wages of dying is love. LCAP

Little Snail. Hilda Conkling. I saw that it was his umbrella! TiPo

A Little Something for William Whipple. Dave Oliphant. worth finishing with a stigma C. FAZ

Little Son. Georgia Douglas Johnson. The very world epitomized/In turmoil and delight. CDC

A Little Song. Robert Grosseteste. Forgive, and make me whole. ISi

A Little Song. Charles O. Hartman. ...You'll hear in high limbs/voices of dry leaves. SM

A Little Song of Life. Lizette Woodworth Reese. Is to see that we grow Nearer the sky. BrR; GoTF; HBMV; OBCA; TiPo; TreFT

A Little Song of Spring. Mary Austin. Woolly clouds come creeping. YeAr

Little Song of the Maimed. Benjamin Peret. and a wooden leg OBWP

A Little Song of Work. Sarah Elizabeth Sprouse. The gift of work; its fellowship/And rugged fruitfulness. BLRP

Little Songs. Marjorie Pickthall. ...men will go singing still/Of little dawns of springtime above an English hill. CaP

Little Sparrow (Come All You Young and Handsome Ladies). Anonymous. So I'll sit down all broken-hearted/And try to pass my troubles by. AmFP

The Little Star. Anonymous. He could not determine his journey's direction/But for your bright scintillating protection. InMe; SpRo

Little Steamboat. Oscar Williams. And beats the thin, tin sides of time/With hot and foggy hands. PoPl

Little Sticks. Eric Rolls. Then may it leap and catch a heart/And set it burning bright. PoAu 1-2

A Little Talk wid Jesus Makes It Right. Anonymous. Thank God, I'll always find,/Dat a little talk wid Jesus, makes it right. BoAN 1-2

A Little Te Deum of the Commonplace (excerpt). John Oxenham. For all that childhood teaches us of Thee:/We thank Thee, Lord! TRV

Little Tee-Wee. Anonymous. My story's ended. OxNR

Little Theocritus. Caroline Wilder (Fellowes) Paradise. To listen to your singing through its/tears. AA

Little Things. Anonymous.
But little things are seen by God/From His watchtower in heaven. STF
That make life worth the fight. PoToHe
"Ye have done it unto Me." STF

Little Things. Julia A. Fletcher Carney.
Help to make the earth happy/Like the heaven above. HBV 1-2; HBVY
Make the mighty ages/Of eternity. FaFP

The Little Things. Elizabeth Isler. That burn unnoticed, quietly. PoToHe

Little Things. Orrick Johns. Than a tall stone temple that may stand too long. AnAmPo; PG

Little Things. James Stephens. Little creatures, everywhere! AnEnPo; MoBrPo; SiSoSe

Little Things. Marion Strobel. Love that's fragile,/Love that's old. HBMV

Little Thomas. F. Gwynne Evans. Who, alas! departed from us/In that noisy way. BBGG

The little tigers are at rest. Tom (Thomas Hood, Jr.) Hood. The all-embracing bounteous bear/Dreams sweetly in his lowly lair. CenHV

Little Tiny Puppy Dog. Spike Milligan. Or else he'll start to sleep much thinner. GDP

The Little Toil of Love. Emily Dickinson. The little toil of love, I thought,/Was large enough for me. LiTL

Little Tommy Tucker. Mother Goose. How shall I marry/Without any wife? HBVY

Little Tommy Yesterday. Alex Glasgow. Little Tommy Nowadays, canny little man,/Buys some plastic roses as a present for his mam. OBET

Little tree. Edward Estlin Cummings. we'll dance and sing/"Noel Noel" LOW; NTCP; OBCP; PCh; RoGo

Little Trotty Wagtail. John Clare. So, little Master Wagtail, I'll bid you a good-bye. CBEP; OnUR; PB; UnPo

A Little Tumescence. Jonathan Williams. limp,/simply ErPo; NeAP; PoM

The Little Turtle. Vachel Lindsay. But he didn't catch me. GoJo; NTCP; OBAL; OBCA; SoPo; SUS; TiPo

The Little Vagabond. William Blake. But kiss him, & give him both drink and apparel. CBEP; CEP; NLV; OBSV; SeCeV

Little Viennese Waltz. Federico Garcia Lorca. violin and sepulcher, the ribbon of the waltz. SOTW

The Little Waves of Breffny. Eva Gore-Booth. And the Little Waves of Breffny go stumbling through my/soul. AnIV; HBV 1-2; HBVY; OnYI

A Little Way. Frank Lebby Stanton. They would be kissed by thine! AA

The Little Wee Man. Anonymous. I turned about, and gave a look,/Just at the foot of Benachie. BuBa

A Little While. Don (Donald Robert Marquis) Marquis. the shadows gather...what comes after/No man knows! HBV 1-2

A Little While. Dante Gabriel Rossetti. I'll tell thee, when the end is come,/How we may best forget. ViBoPo; VLP

A Little While, a Little While. Emily Bronte.
And given me back to weary care. OBNC; OxBI; ViBoPo
My hour of rest had fleeted by,/And back came labour, bondage, care. OAEP

A Little While I Fain Would Linger Yet. Paul Hamilton Hayne. A little while I still would linger here. AA; HBV 1-2

A Little While to Love and Rave. Samuel Hoffenstein. Accept my praise now–I'd rather/Never meet the gifted Author! ALV

The Little Whistler. Frances Frost. And I can whistle now! SoPo; TiPo

The Little White Cat. Anonymous. The little white cat, snowy white/That was drowned in a trench. OnYI

Little White Fox. David Rowbotham. I am grateful to him. BoAV

Little White Lily. George Macdonald. Little White Lily is happy again. HBV 1-2; HBVY

Little White Schoolhouse Blues. Florence Becker Lennon. Roll, Missouri, roll. PoNe

Little Wild Baby. Margaret Thomson Janvier. Little wild baby, lie still! Lie still and sleep.) AA; HBV 1-2

Little Willie. Anonymous.
Ain't he cute? He's only six! GoTF; NA; TreFS
"He's really nicer than he seems." ShM
"It's so hard to raise a daughter." ShM
"'Twas a chilly day for Willie/When the mercury went down." MoShBr; PoPle; ShM

Little Willie. Gerald Massey. Little matters though the door/Be a workhouse grave. PaPo

Little Willie's My Darlin'. Anonymous. If you think I don't love her,/Got a foolish idea. OuSiCo

Little Wind. Kate Greenaway. Little wind, blow off the rain. GoJo; SUS

The Little Woman and the Pedlar. Anonymous. This is none of I! OxNR

A Little Word. Anonymous. And bear sweet sunshine in the face. STF

Little Words. Benjamin Keech. Two fond hearts were mended. PoToHe

Little Yellow Leaf. James Tate. ...failure/the first day of the rest of our lives. NoAm

Littoral. Hjalmar Flax. One by one/I fill my heart with them. InW

The Litttle Black-Eyed Rebel. Will Carleton. Thought the little black-eyed rebel, with a/twinkle in her eye. PAH

Liu Ch'e. Emperor Wu-Ti. A wet leaf that clings to the threshold. OBVE

Live Acts. Charles Bernstein. ...binding up in an unlimited way what/otherwise goes unexpressed. APU

Live Blindly. Trumbull Stickney. And all his island shivered into flowers. AmLP; APA; LiTA; NePA; TrGrPo

Live Christ. John Oxenham. That fruit through all eternity. BLRP

Live Not, Poor Bloom, but Perish. Anonymous. Lingering death with teares invoked. NCEP

Live while You Live. Philip Doddridge. I live in pleasure, when I live to Thee. OxBoCh

The lively sparks that issue from those eyes. Sir Thomas Wyatt. For after the blaze, as is no wonder,/Of deadly "nay" hear I the fearful thunder. FCP

Liverpool. Anonymous. Your joys on earth will soon be/gone,/Your flesh in dust be laid. AmFP

Liverpool Girls. Anonymous. And pay no attention to runner or whore/When yer hat's on yer head and yer feet's on the shore. OBSS

Liverpool John. Anonymous. Longed to see the sun again, so he sailed from Birkenhead. OBSS

Lives. Cyril Dabydeen. I am topsy-turvy once more. BrSi

Lives. Gerald Dawe. for others to live in/before moving somewhere else. AMV-81

Lives. Derek Mahon. Let him revise/His insolent ontology/Or teach himself to pray. FaBoIP

Lives. Henry Reed. To cross it you have to bridge it, and it will not flow uphill. BoNaP; LiTB

The Lives of Famous Men. Jack Gilbert. and go on pulling at the long rope. NPGG

Lives of Great Men. Anonymous. That we're apt to leave behind us/Letters that we ought to burn. FaFP; GoTF; TreFT

The Lives of Gulls and Children. Howard Nemerov. And paced by the sweet shrieking of the quick. NePoEA

Lives of the Poet. Ron Miles. More meek, more natural than a third-hand version. AMV-81

Lives of the Saints. Jon Anderson. Give me a little time,/Eternity,/& I will mend. FiCP

The Livid Lightnings Flashed in the Clouds. Stephen Crane. And all the being is still to hear. AmePo

Living. Anonymous. To thrill with all the sweets of life–is living. BLPA; FaBoBe; GoTF; TreFS

A Living. W. S. Di Piero. There I stand. There I be. AMV-80

Living. William Dean Howells. To hurl myself into the changeless grave! AmePo

A Living. D. H. Lawrence. –And we, we get it all from them for nothing. RFM

Living. Denise Levertov. Each minute the last minute. VGW

Living. Harold Monro. Back to your rampart, Death. LiTB; SeCePo

Living. D. S. Savage. Another year burns down to stub and ash,/And I am older. NeBP

Living among the Dead. William Matthews. I almost never dream of anyone,/except my sons,/who is still alive. GeTw

The Living Book. Charlotte Fiske Bates. But, like the eyes that mark great Guido's/fame,/It follows every one, as if by name. AA

Living Bread. Eva Weaver Sefton. Herein the gospel mystery lies,/Through Christ revealed by sacrifice. BePJ

Living by the Red River. James Wright. Walls that still hold the whole prints/Of ancient ferns. NNaP

The Living Chalice. Susan Mitchell. Master of Life take me, Thy Cup am I. HBMV

The Living Dog and the Dead Lion. Thomas Moore. Who'll feed on them living, and foul them when dead. OBRV

The Living God. Daniel Ben Judah. And let His praise resound for/evermore. TrJP

The Living God. Charlotte Perkins Stetson Gilman. And I do not stand alone! WGRP

The Living God. Abraham Ibn Ezra. O Thou, who openest graciously/Thy hand to all that live. TrJP

Living in Sin. Austin Clarke. For every infant severed from the breast. ELU

Living in Sin. Adrienne Rich. she woke sometimes to feel the daylight coming/like a relentless milkman up the stairs. FF; IHMS; NePoEA; NoP; NYBP; SoSe; TAP; UnPo

Living in the Boneyard. John Oliver Simon. middle of the first/line maybe no one/will notice NeAC

Living in the Moment. Marilyn Hacker. wrap up in flannel for the night that started/thousands of miles before, hundreds of times away. NYP

Living in the Present. Clarinda Harriss Lott. you dream you dream/that you are sleeping AMV-81

Living in the World. Alan Chong Lau. the only light on the block BrSi

Living Marble. Arthur William Edgar O'Shaughnessy. That sleep indeed were endless, even as death. VLP

A Living Memory. William Augustus Croffut. So softly out of mine! AA

Living? Our Supervisors Will Do That for Us! David Holbrook. And probably rather hard up out of the bargain. NePoEA-2

A Living Pearl. Kenneth Rexroth. ...Next week/She will be one year old. LiTM

Living Poetry. Hugo Margenat. as out of its own mouth the river's body flows. InW

The Living Room. Gjertrud Schnackenberg. And Paradise a figuring of air. FYAP

The Living Statue. Anonymous. And all the waves toss wildly at the sight. UnTE

The Living Temple. Oliver Wendell Holmes And mould it into heavenly forms! AA; AmePo; AP; WGRP

Living Tenderly. May Swenson. My flesh lives tenderly/inside its bone. BoAnP; OBCA

Living Together. Tomioka Taeko. Your freedom too/Was no better than a fool's story WPOW

The Living Truth. Sterling D. Plumpp. dubois returning condemned lives/to pure glories... PoBA

Living Water. Ruth M. Williams. Their thurst unto him bring. BePJ

Living Waters. Caroline Spencer. Even the great and loving heart of God,/Whereby all love doth live. HBV 1-2

Living with Children. Jim Wayne Miller. "Don't touch this or you'll die!"/It's too late. GOYP

Living with Chris. Ted Berrigan. For god's sake, is there anyone out there listening?/If so, Peace. NoAm

Living with Others. Al Zolynas. I live for such moments. LTB

Living with You. Angela Langfield. Yet every time I am caught,/every time waved down,/and taken for questioning. FF

Le Livre Est sur la Table. John Ashbery.
In the waves' minutes, or did the land advance? ANYP; EAS
the woman gone/Into the house, from which the wailing starts? ANYP

A Liz-Town Humorist. James Whitcomb Riley. And you'd orto' heerd 'em yell! AmePo

Liza Jane. Anonymous. She died on the train. ABF; AS

Lizard. D. H. Lawrence. If men were as much men as lizards are lizards/they'd be worth looking at. BoAnP

The Lizard. Ruth Lechlitner. "So now we know." AMV-81

The Lizard. Edwin Markham. The circle of eternal youth. BPAW

Lizard. Alan McLean. ...and I'd just as soon/You hadn't to do that. BoAnP

The Lizard. Rona Murray. he is not dead. NOBC

The Lizard. Theodore Roethke. Don't Poke more than Twice/At an Intimate Place like his Gizzard. GrPl

Lizards and Snakes. Anthony Hecht. And swinges the scaly horror of his folded tail. CoPo; FaBoMo; NCSH; TwCP

The Lizards of La Brea. Marc De Baca. brittle as jelly jars. AMV-80

Lizie Lindsay (A version). Anonymous. "The ladys of Edinburgh city,/They neither milch goats nor kie." ESPB

Lizie Lindsay (B version). Anonymous. For ye're great Macdonald's braw lady,/And will be to the day that ye dee.' ESPB

Lizie Wan. Anonymous.
"The sun and the moon shall dance on/the green/That night when I come hame." BaBo; ESPB; ViBoFo

"When the sun and the moon set on yonders green hill,/And I'm sure that never can be." AmFP; BaBo

Lizzie Borden. Anonymous. She gave her father forty-one. DBV; GoTF; ShM; TreFS

The Llama. Hilaire Belloc. The Mongol of the Monastery of Shan. EvOK; FaBoCh; FiBHP; LoGBV

Llanberis Summer. Marianne Loyd. A rockslide of agate. AMV-81

Llangollen Vale (excerpt). Anna Seward. While all who honour Virtue, gently mourn/LLANGOLLEN's vanish'd Pair, and wreath their sacred urn. PeHV

LLewellyn and the Tree. Edwin Arlington Robinson. May be as far off as a moral. BeLS; HBMV

La Llorona. Greg Pape. saying "Oh my son my son" AmPA

LMFBR. Gary Snyder. robes and garbs/of the Kali-yuga/end of days. PoM

Lo! As the Potter Mouldeth. Anonymous. Thy bond regard, let sin be veil'd from/Thee. TrJP

Lo, for I to Myself Am Unknown. Jalal ed-Din or al-Din Rumi. I was born not in China afar, not in Saqsin and not/in Bulghar. ILwL

Lo! how I seek and sue to have. Sir Thomas Wyatt. In joy or pain for to endure. FCP; SiPS

Lo, I Am Stricken Dumb. Anonymous. In the havoc of their transgression/a whirlwind swallows me up. TrJP

Lo! Leman Sweet. Anonymous. And I aske the noght elles. CoBE

Lo Que Digo (with music). Anonymous. You will know I love you,/And fear I do not know. AS

Lo, What Enraptured Songs of Praise. Sebastian Streeter. In swelling notes of ceaseless praise. AH

Lo, what it is to love! Sir Thomas Wyatt. Lo, what it is to love! FCP

Lo, Who Could Stand. Anonymous. O Lord, the shield and buckler/of my need. TrJP

Lo-Yang. Emperor Ch'ien Wen-ti. And the girls with their high baskets full of fruit. AWP

Load. John Hewitt. on wither'd goldenrod and snapdragon/and tarnisht marigold. OnYI

The Loadstone of His Love. Charles Wesley. O may we all the loving mind/That was in Thee receive. BePJ

Loam Norton. Gwendolyn Brooks. I am not remote,/not unconcerned.... BP

The Loan of a Stall. James L. Duff. And she took the loan of a stall. ISi

Lob. Edward ("Edward Eastaway") Thomas. Young Jack perhaps, and now a Wiltshireman/As he has oft been since his days began. MoVE

Lobo. Charles Lillard. You're not the survivor. NOBC

Lobotomy. Kenneth Pitchford. the waking truth in dying eyes, like frost. PoA

Lobster Cove Shindig. Lillian Morrison. What a brawl until the sun appears/Majestic, like the law. BoNaP

The Lobster Pot. John Arden. There was not. ELU

The Lobster Quadrille. Lewis (Charles Lutwidge Dodgson) Carroll. Will you, won't you, will you, won't you, won't you join the/dance? MoShBr; OxBChV; Par; PoPle

Lobsters in the Window. W. D. Snodgrass.
Hear what the newsboys shout,/Or see the raincoats pass. BiP; BoAnP; NCSH; NYBP; TAP
Starting to swell and ache/With that thick peg in the wrist. HeIP

Local Habitation: On Inhabiting an Orange. Josephine Miles. Making down the roads of earth/Endless detour. PoA

A Local Man Remembers Betty Fuller. James Whitehead. ...I'm satisfied she can't. GP

Local Note. Arthur Guiterman. Whose name supplies the long-sought rhyme/for "orange'. NLV

Local Places. Howard Moss. What songs they sing they always sing again. NePoEA-2

Local Politics. Robert Pinsky. The wild bird with its hardware in its claws. MAYP

A Local Storm. Donald Justice. Still, how nice for our egos. NCSH

A Local Train of Thought. Siegfried Sassoon. "That train's quite like an old familiar friend," one feels. AtBAP

Locale. Penelope Shuttle. Only bitter and wise blood,/the shorn fleece of the womb. BrRo

Localities. Carl Sandburg. I know how the fingers of late October/Loosen the hazel nuts". AmFN

Location. Knute Skinner. these near, immediate thickets where we hide? MAT

The Location of Things. Barbara Guest. who do not fear the melancholy of the stair. NYP

Locations. Kathleen Fraser. These acts of attention to fill in/all the gaps/where his body keeps going away NPGG

Locations. Jim Harrison. beyond, a green continent. AmPA

Loch Coruisk (Skye). William Sharp. Scarce living sound is heard, save high/The eagle's scream or wild swan's cry. SyP

Loch Leven. Sydney Goodsir Smith. And kent the glorie and the gleen/ Was but the waukenin o' her een? BSV

Loch Lomond. Lady John Scott.
And the world does not know how we are greeting. TreFS
On the bonnie, bonnie banks of Loch Lomond. FSW; GoTF

Loch Luichart. Andrew Young. With the slow motion of my prow/And dripping oar. PoSH

Loch Ossian. Syd Scroggie. That Summer seemed in love with idle days. PoSH

Lochaber No More. Allan Ramsay. An' then I'll leave thee an' Lochaber no more. HBV 1-2

Lochan. Roger Smith. Encapsulated everything we sought to find/And never felt to end. PoSH

Lochiel's Warning. Thomas Campbell. Look proudly to Heaven from the deathbed of/fame. EnRP

The Lochmaben Harper. Anonymous.
For thou shall get a better mare,/And weel paid shall thy cowte foal be. ESPB; OxBB
Then back to Henry, the English king,/Restored the stately Wanton Brown. BaBo

The Lochmabyn Harper. Anonymous. He was paid for the foal he had never lost,/And three times o'er for the good grey mare. BuBa

Lock the Dairy Door. Anonymous. I haven't got a key! OxNR; PBBP

Lock the Door, Lariston. James Hogg. "Elliot of Lariston, Elliot for aye!" BSV; GoTS; OxBS

Lock the Place in Your Heart. Zindzi Mandela. breathe into it and let my secrets go LLLT

The Lockless Door. Robert Frost. And alter with age. NOBA; WSC

Locks. Kenneth Koch. And, when I am not, the lock on my sleep, that keeps me/from waking and finding you are not there. CoAP

Locks and Bolts. Anonymous.
And all young men who get such wives/Should fight till you overcome them. TrAS
Fight on and take another. FSW; OBET

Locksley Hall. Alfred, Lord Tennyson.
And the kindly earth shall slumber, lapt in universal law. GoTF; WBLP
For the mighty wind arises, roaring seaward,/and I go. BLPL; CABA; DiPo; EBEV; FaBoBe; FaFP; HBV 1-2; MaVP; MBW 1-2; OAEL 1-2; OAEP; VLP; WHA
In the Parliament of man, the Federation of the world. PoLf

Locksley Hall Sixty Years After. Alfred, Lord Tennyson. Then I leave thee lord and master, latest lord of/Locksley Hall. EnLi 1-2

The Locomotive to the Little Boy. Benjamin R. C. Low. God and His heaven are globed in you. HBMV

The Locus. Cid Corman. an ideal the wisest man/has not yet formulated/into truth,/as the earth has. VGW

Locus. Robert Earl Hayden. ...Old Testament battleground/of warring shades whose weapons kill. FYAP

The Locust Hunt. Philip Murray. But none of us desired to have them again. NePoAm-2

The Locust Tree in Flower. William Carlos Williams. white/sweet/May/ again SOTW

Locusts of Silence. Seymour Mayne. buzz with prayer/in the forsaken silences VWA

The Lodge Room over Simpkins' Store. Lawrence N. Greenleaf. In plainest Lodge room in the land–up over Simpkins' store. PoOW

The Lodger. Michael Longley. Careful not to curtail our lives/Or change the names he has given us. FaBoIP

Lodgers. Julian Tuwim. Terrible burghers in terrible lodgings. VWA

The Lodging. George Mackay Brown. If the queer pair below/Will pay their lodging. BSV

A Lodging for the Night. Elinor Wylie. And ravished the poor soul you never wanted. ErPo

The Lodging-House Fuchsias. Thomas Hardy. They cut back all the flowery mass/In the morning. OBSP

Lodging with the Old Man of the Stream. Po Chu-i. "Privy Councillors do not sleep in barns." AWP

Loft. Michael Dransfield. the first morning of winter CBAP

Lofty Lane. Edwin Gerard. Before you halt at the lines again! PoAu 1-2

Logan at Peach Tree Creek. Hamlin Garland. As on the day McPherson died. MC; PAH

Logan Braes. John Mayne. Revered by friends, and far frae faes,/We'd live in bliss on Logan Braes. OxBS

Logging (excerpt). Gary Snyder.
Hovering over ten thousand acres/Of young fir. NOBA
Taurus by nightfall. NMP

Logic. Anonymous. Ergo, Good wine carrieth a man to heaven. FaBoUs

Logic. Calvin Murry. laid low by a trumpet, or a dream. LFAC

A Logical Song. Anonymous. 'Tis better repenting a sin/Than regretting the loss of a pleasure. ErPo

The Logical Vegetarian. Gilbert Keith Chesterton. So very, very, very Vegetarian. CenHV

The Logs. Sir Charles G. D. Roberts. The huge tide hurries them away. ACV

Lohengrin. William Morton Payne. To dim the memory of that love outpoured/Upon thee by thy stainless knight and/lord. AA

Lois in Concert. Charles Moorman. "Doesn't it seem to you she's fumbling/About up there?" AMV-81

Loitering with a Vacant Eye. Alfred Edward Housman. And I stept out in flesh and bone/Manful like the man of stone. WeW

Lollay, Lollay, Little Child! Anonymous. When he of the appel ete and Eve it him betaughte. OxBM

Lollingdon Downs. John Masefield.
And the night is full of the past. GoYe
Is one, always the same, one life, one fire? LiTB
To nothing, not even Death, not even tears. ChMP

Lollocks. Robert Graves. And to pay every debt/As it falls due. DTC; EvOK

Lolly-Too-Dum. Anonymous. Ha ha ha, you pretty young girls,/that feeling's off of me. FSW

Lolly Trudom. Anonymous. Lolly trudom, trudom, trudom, a lolly day. BFSS

The Lollypops. Cordia Thomas. for who would want a lollypop/To chase one, don't you know? SoPo

Lolo Died Yesterday. Cyn Zarco. died dancing/on treasure island BrSi

London. William Blake. And blights with plagues the Marriage hearse. AtBAP; AWP; CABA; CBEP; DiPo; EnPE; ExPo; FaBoPP; FaBoPV; FF; HAP; HeIP; InPK; InPo; InPS; LiTB; MAT; NAWM 1-2; NIP; NOBE; NoP; OBNC; PAI; PPoe; PPON; PrIm; SCV; SeCePo; SeCeV; TEP; UnPo; ViBoPo

London. John Davidson. The heart of London beating warm. NOBE; OBNC

London. Manmohan Ghose. This is London. I lie, and twine in the roots of things. ACV

London. J. R. Rowland. Poisonously green and bursting with the wet. CBAP

London. T. P. Cameron Wilson. Oh! keep it unharmed, dear London town! HBMV

London: A Poem in Imitation of the Third Satire of Juvenal (excerpt). Samuel Johnson. The groom retails the favours of his lord. OBSV

London Adulterations. Anonymous. Here's wishing all rogues their deserts they must have. OBET

London after the Great Fire, 1666. John Dryden. Charmed with the splendour of this northern star,/Shall here unlade him and depart no more. NOBE

London and Bristol Delineated. Richard Savage. As full of turbulence as void of sense. FaBoPP

London Bells. Anonymous. And here comes a chopper to chop off your head. LiTB; OxBoLi

London Bridge. Anonymous. Huzza! 'twill last for ages long,/With a gay lady. CH; EyDe; GBP; OxBoLi; OxNR

London City (B vers. with music). Anonymous. Upon my breast place a turtle dove,/To show the world I died for love. AS

London Despair. Frances Cornford. Why cannot all of us together–why?–/ Achieve the one simplicity: to die? OBMV

A London Fete. Coventry Patmore. Went forth to fight, with murderous faces. HAP; NBM

London, Hast Thou Accused Me. Henry Howard, Earl of Surrey. That so hath judged Babylon,/Immortal praise with one accord. AAS; FCP; OAEP

London Interior. Harold Monro. The sunlight lays a streak upon the floor. BrPo

London Is a Fine Town. Anonymous. They can't resist the charm. CoMu

London Lickpenny. John Lydgate. For whoso wants Money with them shall not speed. GoTL; MeEV; OxBM

London Night. Kathleen Raine. Elsewhere and far He died, but here, oh at heart, He rises! NeBP

London Nightfall. John Gould Fletcher. To pour the thick night out upon the earth. MoAmPo

London Pavement Artist. James Schevill. Art is the pavement that eats you... TAP

A London Plane-Tree. Amy Levy. But she has listen'd to the voice/On city breezes borne. OBVV

London Poets. Amy Levy. No more he comes, who this way came and went. OBVV

The London Prentice. Anonymous. And what this Couple did, Sir,/Alas I dare not Name. CoMu; UnTE

London Rain. Louis MacNeice. Falling asleep I listen/To the falling London rain. HeIP; NoP

London's Bridge Is A-Burning Down. Anonymous. Hug her nice and kiss her twice/For the prettiest girl I know. AmFP

London Sad London. Anonymous. But if he comes not what becomes of London?/Undone. OBS

London Snow. Robert Bridges.` At the sight of the beauty that greets them, for the charm they have broken. AnFE; BoNaP; BrPo; CMoP; CoBMV; EBEV; FaBoPP; GTBS-P; LiTB; LiTM; LoBV; MoAB; MoBrPo; NBM; NoAm; NOBE; NOBV; OAEL 1-2; OBNC; OxBTC; PoEL 1-5; SeCePo; SeCeV; TrGrPo; VLP; WiR

A London Sparrow's If. J. A. Lindon. An' when they 'atch, your be cock-sparrers, sce? BoAnP

London Spring. Antoni Slonimski. Know that I watch, and that I wake. TrJP

London Tom-Cat. Michael Hamburger. He conjures tangled forests in a furnished flat. BoAnP

London Town. Lionel Pigot Johnson. And we shall know. FaBoPP

London Voluntaries. William Ernest Henley.
And memories of gold and golden dreams. BrPo
Thus vicious and thus patient, sits him down/To the black job of burking London Town? BrPo; VLP

The Londoner in the Country. Richard Church. To feel that great heart beat,/And recognise my own. HaMV

The Lone Biker. R. Wayne Hardy. and becomes another star/in the distant night. LFAC

Lone Dog. Irene Rutherford McLeod. Wide wind, and wild stars, and hunger of the/quest! CoSo; GDP; MCCG; TiPo

Lone Founts. Herman Melville. Wise once, and wise thence evermore. AnFE; LiTA; ViBoPo

Lone Gentleman. Pablo Neruda. black roots shaped like fingernails and shoes. ErPo

Lone Huntsman. Christie Jeffries. When the chase ends. GoYe

The Lone Prairie. Anonymous. No sunbeams rest on a prairie grave. ViBoFo

The Lone Star Trail. Anonymous.
I woke up broken-hearted with a yearling by the tail. CoSo
To drive away the thoughts of the darling girl that was so dear to me. BFSS

The Lone Star Trail (with music). Anonymous. I'll quit punching cows in the sweet by and by. AS

A Lone Striker. Robert Frost. Come get him–they knew where to search. SaC

The Lone Wild Fowl. H. R. MacFayden. Great Spirit, come and rest in me. AH

Loneliness. Edwin Essex. The stricken silences,/When Thou art dumb! TrPWD

Loneliness. Brooks Jenkins. I understand these people better, now I know. CTBA

Loneliness. Sandra McPherson. Maybe just listen to my voice. AMV-80

Loneliness. Franz Werfel. To search in darkness out of limits/The gleam of truth within myself. TrJP

Loneliness. Al Young. the gunshot he fires/up into the silent air/is to awaken PoBA

Loneliness: An Outburst of Hexasyllables. Hayden Carruth. What good is it to know? SM

Loneliness and July Ninth. Claribel Alegria. where old people stand around/with bluish hands. BoWoP

The Loneliness of the Long Distance Runner. Alden Nowlan. I silently curse her. InPK; PV; TW

Lonely. Bloke Modisane. inbred deformiteis of loneliness? PBA

The Lonely. George William Russell. A child lay weeping. AWP; OnYI

Lonely. Andre Spire. And the proud sweat glued to my skin. AWP; TrJP

Lonely Are the Fields of Sleep. Mary Newton Baldwin. To wander unremembered ways/With consciousness undone. GoYe

Lonely Beauty. Samuel Daniel. How most it hurts that most delights the sense. CTC; OBSC

The Lonely-Bird. Harrison Smith Morris. And I, in thee, have uttered what I am! AA

The Lonely Bugle Grieves. Grenville Mellen. And high above the fight the lonely bugle grieves! AA

The Lonely Death. Adelaide Crapsey. And draw the sheet under my chin. AnFE; APA

The Lonely Dog. Margaret E. Bruner. He only craved an understanding friend. PoToHe

Lonely House. Emily Dickinson. Think that the sunrise left the door ajar! AnEnPo

The Lonely Isle. Claudian (Claudius Claudianus). Where those curved arms shut in a tranquil sea. AWP

The Lonely Land. A.J.M. Smith. broken by strength/and still strong. CaP; NOBC

Lonely Love. Edmund Charles Blunden. But shared with me the strangest happiness. OxBTC

Lonely Lover. Robert P. Tristram Coffin. And plays the lonely lover under his mows. MoLP

The Lonely Man. Randall Jarrell. Opening in a good firm for a former cat. OxBC

The Lonely Month. Ruthven Todd. This long and lonely month. NeBP

The Lonely Mother. Fenton Johnson. Swaying for her son who walks in sorrow. GoSl; PoNe

Lonely Night. Sappho. Time passes–yet I lie alone. LiTW

A Lonely Pond in Age-Old Stillness Sleeps. Basho (Matsuo Basho). Suddenly into it a lithe frog leaps. AWP

Lonely Road. Peter Abrahams. Bitter sadness,/That's the road I go. PBA

The Lonely Road. Kenneth Rand. Yet I await what hope the turning yields/And beg with empty hand. HBV 1-2

The Lonely Scarecrow. James Kirkup. Why do you always fly away? GrPI

The Lonely Shell. Martha Eugenie Perry. Fashioned of pearl and rose/This lonely shell. CaP

The Lonely Street. William Carlos Williams. they mount the lonely street. MP; PoA; TwCP

The Lonely Traveller. Kwesi Brew. Meandering his weary way/On the green and golden hills of Africa. PBA; TTY

Lonesome Dove. Anonymous.
Lie mouldering away in the cold ground. AmFP
We'll press for Canaan's shore. AmFP

The Lonesome Dream. Lisel Mueller. still innocent of us. CoAP

The Lonesome Grove. Anonymous. I once like you did have a mate,/But like you now I'm desolate. TrAS

Lonesome in the Country. Al Young. all that hilly sweetness wasting MAT; NPGG

Lonesome Road (with music). Anonymous. Before I seen your smilin' face/An' heard your lyin' tongue. AS

Lonesome Valley. Anonymous. He's got to go there by himself. FSW

Lonesome Water. Roy Helton. I'm bound to the hills. AmFN; MoAmPo

Long Ago. Syd Scroggie. Of aromatic larch below/The breast of Broad Cairn, long ago. PoSH

Long and Lazy. Robert Herrick. Lazy to others, but be long to me. FaBoEE

The Long and Lonely Winter. Dave Goulder. The long and lonely winter will be here. OBET

Long Are the Hours the Sun Is Above. Robert Bridges. That I sit so much by myself alone. EG

Long as the Darkening Cloud Abode. George Richards. Is vast creation's deathless theme. AH

Long Barren. Christina Georgina Rossetti. Feed Thou my feeble shoots. PBWP; TrCP; VLP

Long Betwixt Love and Fear. John Dryden. Let me die ere I see/That I'm forsaken. LiTL; ViBoPo

Long-Billed Gannets. Frances D. Emery. And the flutter of wings in our minds. GoYe

Long-Distance. Carol Burnes. the long, deep shiver. AMV-81

Long Distance. Dana Naone. All the cobras came to the phone/flaring and hissing. CDW

Long Distance. William Stafford. You think they are. ELU; SO; WSC

Long Distance Moan. Blind Lemon Jefferson. This long distance moan/about to worry me to death this time BluL

Long Division: A Tribal History. Wendy Rose. I suckle coyotes/and grieve. TWSS

Long Feud. Louis Untermeyer. And then the small grass covers him. AnAmPo; APA; MoAmPo

The Long Garden. Patrick Kavanagh. Where the sun was always setting on the play. FaBoIP; IPY

Long Gone. Anonymous. He's gone John,/He's long gone. ABF

Long Gone. Sterling A. Brown. To be Long Gone... BALP; BANP; BPo

Long Hair. Gary Snyder. And deer bound through my hair. NOBA

A Long & Happy Life. Simon Schuchat. And I will never read what's written/In another's solid hands. APU

The Long Harbour. Mary Ursula Bethell. still undiscovered shore. ACV; AnNZ

The Long Hill. Sara Teasdale. The rest of the way will be only going down. HBMV; LiTA; MoAmPo; PoPl

Long History of the Short Poem. Paul Hoover. It was then, of course, they knew she was pregnant. APU

Long I Thought That Knowledge Alone Would Suffice. Walt Whitman. It is to be enough for us that we are together–We never separate/again. NOBA

Long Island Springs. Howard Moss. The stone, the stone parentheses of years. GP; HoAn; UnPo

Long John. Anonymous. He's long gone, He's long gone John. FSW

Long John. Padraic Fallon. As well as mother's lullabies.' NeIP

The Long Joke. R. T. Smith. following the bird with no name. STE

Long-Legged Fly. William Butler Yeats. Like a long-legged fly upon the stream/His mind moves upon silence. CMoP; FaBoMo; FaBoTw; ForPo; InPS; LiTM; NoAm; NOBE; NoP; PAI; PPoe; TEP

Long-Line Skinner. Anonymous. Lookin' for the woman/Lord, that'll love me the best. FSW

Long Lines. Paul Goodman.

...the dreary snowflakes do not cease/drifting past my window in the demi-dark. NMP; VGW

...It's I who say/the words like "I love you' or "thank you.' PeHV

Long Live Our Dear and Noble Queen. Edward Edwin Foot. ...With fortitude/The ceremony she withstood. FaBoCo

Long Live the Weeds. Theodore Roethke. These shape the creature that is I. NoAm; NOBA; PoA

Long Lonely Lover of the Highway. Frederic Will. until the first rays of morning. AMV-81

Long Lonesome Road. *Anonymous.* Hang down your head and cry. OuSiCo

Long, Long Ago. Thomas Haynes Bayly. Blest as I was when I sat by your side,/Long, long ago, long ago. BLSo; BrR; ChBR; FSW; OHIP; PCh; PoSC; PSoN; TreF

A long, long sleep. Emily Dickinson. To bask the centuries away/Nor once look up for noon? NCEP

Long May. Rosalia de Castro. My happiness came with you,/It fled again with you. PBWP

Long Neglect Has Worn away. Emily Bronte. Swiftly flew the fingers fine/When the pen that motto drew. NOBV; NoP

The Long Night. Harry Bache Smith. Then fade as doth a silenced song. AA

The Long Night Home. Charles F. Gordon. grows stoutly toward our future... NBP

The Long Night Moon: December. Frances Frost. ...children wait with dreaming faces/the Eve when The Child is born. YeAr

A Long Overdue Thankyou Note to the Girl Who Taught Me Loving. Tom Schmidt. If she has to ask she'll never/know. NeAC

The Long Parenthesis. Roberta Hill Whiteman. one after the other shimmer boldly in the wind. TWSS

Long Person. Gladys Cardiff. May your channels never break. CDW; STE; TWSS

The Long Picnic. Russell Edson. What is written on it is that the summer is over.... LCAP

Long Plighted. Thomas Hardy. Till the last crash of all things low and high/Shall end the spheres? NOBV

A Long Prologue to a Short Play... Sir Henry Sheers. You'll keep a wind, as long as he did fight. APAS

Long Pursuit. *Anonymous.* Worn out with coaxing, sleep. UnTE

The Long Race. Edwin Arlington Robinson. It seemed as if the little horse had won. CrMA

The Long River. Donald Hall. ...Now/the wood is dark/with old pleasures. ConAP; LCAP; NePoEA-2; SM

The Long Road West. Henry Herbert Knibbs. Running on forever, down the long road west. BPAW

Long Roads. Mikhail Matusovsky. And only alien cities lie ahead. LiTW

The Long Season. James Haug. Let us talk, lean on each other's voices/in this long season of killing. AMV-81

Long Since Last. Ruth Miller. O lost to the bliss of any more remembering. PeSA

The Long Small Room. Edward ("Edward Eastaway") Thomas. The hundred last leaves stream upon the willow. BrPo

Long Song. Yityangu ("New") Ejong. right in the water CBAP

Long Summer. Laurie Lee. The gold earth turned to good–forever. BoNaP

Long Summer Day. *Anonymous.* Long summer day. OuSiCo

Long Summer (excerpt). Robert Lowell. ...love-longing/mists the windshield, soothes the eye with milk. CAPP

Long Tail Blue. *Anonymous.* I'll sing a song not very long,/About my long tail blue. BLSo

Long Term Suffering. Richard Eberhart. And note how strangely you had to act. GLGT; GP

Long Time a Child. Hartley Coleridge. Time is my debtor for my years untold. CBEP; HBV 1-2; NBM; NCEP; PoEL 1-5

A Long Time Ago. *Anonymous.* Long time ago. ABF; AmSS; ShS

A Long Time Ago. T'ao Ch'ien. So I went home/And lived in idleness. LoGBV

Long Tom. Wilfrid Gibson. And why they'd love him all his brief life through. OxBTC

Long, Too Long America. Walt Whitman. (For who except myself has yet conceiv'd what your children en-masse/really are?) NoAm

Long Trip. Langston Hughes. A wilderness of water. MOS

The Long Voyaage. Malcolm Cowley. foam brightens like the dogwood now/at home, in my own country. AnFE; NePA

A Long Walk before the Snows Began. Robert Bly. open places like the plains of North China,/where the mice have been, just a half hour ago. LCAP

Long Walks in the Afternoon. Margaret Gibson. still find my way back. AMV-81; MAYP

The Long War. Li Po. They have accomplished nothing! WaaP

The Long Waters. Theodore Roethke. I embrace the world. NaP; NYBP

A Long Way Outside Yellowstone. Thomas McGrath. Wondering if hers is among them. Or perhaps not. VGW

The Long White Seam. Jean Ingelow. Her wedding gown it was she wrought,/Sewing the long white seam. GN; HBV 1-2; NOBV

The Long Word. Deirdre Ballantyne. and be able to finish/your poem. AMV-80

Longer to muse. Sir Thomas Wyatt. And perdy to forget. FCP; SiPS

Longface Mahoney Discusses Heaven. Horace Gregory. not even a girl there. ExPo; VGW

Longfellow's Visit to Venice. Sir John Betjeman. Are melodiously mingled in my warm New England breast. NOBL

A Longford Legend. *Anonymous.* Learn to ease her, and stop her, and back her astern. OnYI; StPo

Longing. *Anonymous.* How is it you cannot hear/Your loved yoke-fellow? WTO

Longing. Matthew Arnold. For then the night will more than pay/The hopeless longing of the day. CBEP; FPL; HBV 1-2; LO; OAEP; PoLf

The Longing. William Goodreau. Reaching that seasoned door I can clasp and open. AMV-80

Longing. Judah Halevi. Mine eyes would never yearn to look/beyond. TrJP

Longing. George Herbert.
And heal my troubled breast which cryes,/Which dyes. AnAnS 1
Thy pile of dust, wherein each crumme/Sayes, Come? SeCV 1-2

Longing. Rachel Korn. that now, at any moment,/you may come, come, come. VWA

The Longing. Theodore Roethke. I'll be an Indian./Ogalala?/Iroquois. NaP

Longing for Jerusalem. Judah Halevi. Moisten thy holy dust with wet cheeks/streaming free. TrJP

Longing for the Emperor. Empress Iwa no Hime. Can my love fade too? BoWoP

Longing for the Persimmon Tree. Millen Brand. You get old/and friends die. TAT

Longjaunes His Periplus (excerpt). Howard McCord. Everywhere the solemn/malignancy of life/is the burden/to be carried into the mountains. GP

Longshore Intellectual. Sean Lucy. And their girl-friends lonely–we have our consolations. CIP

Lonnie Kramer. Geary Hobson. full of Indians street-people/and other workers of the world. STE

Loo-Wit. Wendy Rose. Loo-wit sings and sings and sings. STE

Looby Loo. *Anonymous.* Shake yourself a little, and turn yourself about. SoPo

The Look. Elizabeth Barrett Browning. And filled the silence, weeping bitterly. TrCP; TRV

The Look. Elizabeth Daryush. Where's no tale, no track,/But a flash, a sigh. PoA

Look. William Stafford. This bubble here is always ready, for you. FAZ

The Look. Sara Teasdale. Haunts me night and day. ALV; HBV 1-2; LiTL

Look-a How Dey Done My Lord. *Anonymous.* He bow'd his head an' died, head an' died, head an' died, head an' died, head an' died. BoAN 1-2

Look at All Those Monkeys. Spike Milligan. While an elephant raised his hat. OnUR

Look at My Face. Carolyn M. Rodgers. bits of me splintered in to a mirror/falling falling rolling,/in... JB

Look at That Gal. Julian Bond. We cannot all be/Martin Luther King. PoNe; TTY

Look away/Look away. Stephen Todd Booker. Bang! dixieland. LFAC

Look Back. Carroll Arnett. something bad/is going to keep on/happening. STE

Look Closely. Morton Marcus. If you look closely/you can see it. FF

Look down Fair Moon. Walt Whitman. Pour down your unstinted nimbus sacred moon. MOON

Look down That Lonesome Road. *Anonymous.*
Darlin', what have,/Have I done? OuSiCo
You caused me to walk and talk with you,/Like I ne'er done before. BLSo

Look, Edwin! Edna St. Vincent Millay. Well, he was born in Paris, France. GoJo

Look for Me on England. H. B. Mallalieu. As if in braille, your face. WaP

Look Home. Robert Southwell. He should, he could, he would, he did the best. NOCV

Look, How Beautiful. Robinson Jeffers. Look how beautiful are all the things that He does. His signature/Is the beauty of things. MoRP

Look, I Have Thrown All Right. L. A. MacKay. Lifting a mute and horrible face still towards you. PeCV

Look, in the Labyrinth of Memory. Delmore Schwartz. Look, reader, how we stare at an abyss! TrJP

A Look into the Gulf. Edwin Markham. Her weary lips beat on without a sound. AA

Look Not in My Eyes, for Fear. Alfred Edward Housman. A jonquil, not a Grecian lad. PeHV; PoEL 1-5

Look Not to Me for Wisdom. Charles Divine. For oh, she talks of wisdom/With challenge in her eyes. HBMV

Look on Him Whom They Pierced, and Mourn. Isaac Watts. And deep repentance drown mine eyes/In undissembled woe. NOCV

Look on Me with Thy Sweet Eyes. *Anonymous.* Rest and bliss give thou me,/When I die, Lady meet. MeEV

Look or You Leap. Jasper Heywood. See all! say nought! hold thee content! EIL

Look Out Below! Charles R. Thatcher. And the cry "Look out below." PoAu 1-2

Look Out There. *Anonymous.* it is swollen/to full flood! NOBI

Look over Yonder. Lawrence Gellert. Just like I do,/Oh my Lord, just like I do. TrAS

Look, Stranger. W. H. Auden. And all the summer through the water saunter. CoBMV; InvP; MoAB; MoBrPo; OAEP; TrGrPo

Look to the Back of the Hand. Judith Minty. "Hair on the back of the hand/denotes extreme cruelty in a woman." PoA

Look to the Leaf. *Anonymous.* When the leaf decides to fly/Kiss your love goodbye. UnTE

Look Up! Edward Everett Hale. And lend a hand. FaBoBe; FaFP

Look Up. Martha Snell Nicholson. With ear of faith, His footfall drawing near! BePJ

Look up to Pentland's Tow'ring Tap. Allan Ramsay. To plague us wi' your whining cant. BSV

Look, You Have Cast Out Love! Rudyard Kipling. It may be they shall give me greater ease/Than your cold Christ and tangled Trinities. OBSP

Look You, My Simple Friend. Arthur Hugh Clough. Where He again is visible, tho' in anger. VLP

The Lookers-On. Jasper Heywood. See all, say nought, hold thee content. ACP

Lookin' for the Bully of the Town. *Anonymous.* An' it was the last of that bully of this town. BaBo

Looking at a Dead Wren in My Hand. Robert Bly. ...The black spot on your head is your own mourn-/ing cap. GP; NNaP

Looking at a Dry Canadian Thistle Brought in from the Snow. Robert Bly. ...it is my/mother. NNaP

Looking at a Picture on an Anniversary. Thomas Hardy. ...little I care/To live myself, my dear,/Lone-labouring here! EyDe

Looking at Each Other. Muriel Rukeyser. Yes, we were looking at each other NNaP

Looking at Henry Moore's Elephant Skull Etchings in Jerusalem... Shirley Kaufman. our skulls/much smaller than theirs/begin to shine. BoWoP; LCAP

Looking at New-Fallen Snow from a Train. Robert Bly. The sword by his side breaks into flame. NaP

Looking at Pictures to Be Put away. Gary Snyder. Bodies thick with food and lovers/After twenty years. FF; InPS; NNaP; PAI

Looking at Power. Warren Woessner. we close wire gates when we leave. AMV-80

Looking at Quilts. Marge Piercy. she seized her time and made new. SaC

Looking at Some Flowers. Robert Bly. Only free of the sea for five or six thousand years. NaP; NOBA

Looking at the Empire State Building. Ralph Pomeroy. or spot lovely Melisande leaning out from an upper floor/to let down her long golden hair. GP

Looking at Wealth in Newport. James Schevill. As Jame's home flickers transformed into a Funeral Parlor. TAT

Looking at Your Face. Galway Kinnell. ...trying to read/the white chiselings of the poem/in the white stone. PPJ

Looking Back (excerpt). Henry Vaughan. Chasing that shade/Which my sins made,/While I so spring, as if I could not fade! FaBoPP

Looking Both Ways. Jane O. Wayne. Somewhere a door must be fanning the air,/someone practicing an exit,/a girl looking both ways. GOYP

Looking Both Ways before Crossing. John Woods. and in a still place in the wind,/be what I have become. ConAP

Looking down a Hill. A. R. Thompson. we make our mountains as we climb. PoSH

Looking Down on Mesopotamia. Mary Ursula Bethell. Night has fallen. Earth sleeps wrapped round/with the sure purpose of eternity. AnNZ

Looking Down on West Virginia. John Dickson. of new steel and sulphur and coal/and grey trains/and home. AMV-81

Looking for a Country under Its Original Name. Colleen J. McElroy. their mysteries so perfect even their undoings/seem as planned as way signs on a map BlSi

Looking for a Home. Bert Stern. To watch the October leaves/In the dark FAZ

Looking for a Rest Area. Stephen P. Dunn. I keep asking. AmPA

Looking for a Ship. *Anonymous.* I had a look for a wes'ly ship,/I had a look. OBSS

Looking for Buddha. Jaime Jacinto. spun from our impermanence/our celebration. BrSi

Looking for Maimonides: Tiberias. Shirley Kaufman. Some sticky coins/compose their prayers./He is not there. VWA

Looking for Mountain Beavers. David Wagoner. ...swinging our flashlights/Up and around our heads like holes in the night. VGW

Looking for Mushrooms at Sunrise. William Stanley Merwin. Where else am I walking even now/Looking for me. NaP; NOBA

Looking for My Old Indian Grandmother in the Summer Heat of 1980. Diane Glancy. I want to know what rock it is/she left upturned. STE

Looking for the Buckhead Boys. James Dickey. "Fill 'er up. Fill 'er up, Charlie." LiSp

Looking for the Melungeon. Dave Smith. ...pines sieving/air, the cleat ringing like small jewelry. HaCAP

Looking for Work. Raymond Carver. My new shoes wait by the door./They are gleaming. GeTw

Looking Forward. Robert Louis Stevenson. And tell the other girls and boys/Not to meddle with my toys. BrPo; NLV; OxBChV

A Looking-Glass. Thomas Carew. One beam of love will soon destroy/And melt that ice to floods of joy. CaPo

The Looking-Glass. Rudyard Kipling. More hard than any ghost there is or any man there was! EvOK; FaBoTw; GTBS; OBMV

The Looking Glass. James Shirley. And make them fair in soul as well as face. LiTL

A Looking-Glass for Smokers (excerpt). Lawrence Spooner. Or go about my business well abroad,/And naught to hinder... NOEC

Looking into a Face. Robert Bly. Through which the body moves like a sliding moon. NOBA

Looking into a Tide Pool. Robert Bly. ...as the/healer sings wildly, shouting to Jesus and his dead mother. CAPP; MAT

Looking into History. Richard Wilbur. That draws all waters toward/Its live formality. VGW

Looking On. Anthony Thwaite. In whose arms she will flourish/Or else will die. NePoEA-2

Looking Out. Helen Chasin. they are my battle. NMM

Looking Up at Down. Big Bill Broonzy. Yeah, poor me's down so low, baby/ooo lord gal, Big Bill is looking up to down BluL

Looking Up at Leaves. Barbara Howes. Balanced between reflection and reflection. BoNaP

Looking West. William Stafford. and glowed a long time before it went out. NYBP

The Lookout. William Collins. 'Twas but the hand of God upon the deep. EtS

The Looks of a Lover Enamoured. George Gascoigne. To look again, and link with me in heart. EIL; SeCePo

The Loom of Dreams. Arthur Symons. And who knows but that God, beyond our/guess,/Sits weaving worlds out of loneliness? VLP

The Loom of Time. *Anonymous.* For the pattern which He planned. BLPA

The Loon. Theodore Harding Rand. The echo of thy flout of Noah's ark! CaP

The Loon. Lew Sarett. A hermit-soul gone raving mad,/And beating at his bars. HBMV

The Loon. Alfred Billings Street. Till in chains no more to him the lake/yields watery boon. AA

A Loon Call. Richard Eberhart. Praise to the cry that I cannot understand. AMV-80

A Loon I Thought It Was. *Anonymous.* But it was my love's splashing oar. OBVE

Loony, 29: The Good Folks at the Camp Meeting. William Kloefkorn. all slightly disconnected in the head/and needing mercy. GP

Loony, 51: During the War. William Kloefkorn. like Axis Sally herself,/on out of town tires. GP

A Loose Saraband. Richard Lovelace. Leave me but love and sherry. CaPo; CavP; PoEL 1-5

Loose Woman. X. J. Kennedy. Was one thing more we never did find out. WeW

Loose Woman Poem. Sharon Thesen. something that her moons/can waylay waylay waylay/in the dark. CaPN; NOBC

Loot. Thom Gunn. with the blood toward my hands, through/me to retain possession. ErPo; NePoEA-2

Looting. Jascha Kessler. Condemned to live, I speak now HoAn

The Lord. Jose Maria Gabriel y Galan. There with His arms stretched wide– CAW

Lord Abbott. Hilaire Belloc. There is a picture of the incident. FaBoNo

Lord Alcohol. Thomas Lovell Beddoes. Lord Alcohol, the drunken fay,/Lord Alcohol alway! WiR

Lord Arnaldos. James Elroy Flecker. "I only tell my song to those/Who sail away with me." StPo

Lord, At This Closing Hour. Eleazar Thompson Fitch. Let glory from the Church arise/Through Jesus Christ our Lord. AH

Lord Banner. *Anonymous.* And place my fair lady by my side and Young Lagrue at my/feet. BaBo

Lord Barrenstock. Stevie Smith.
Be good, my Lord, since you cannot be pretty. OBSV
That is the root of my profound aversion. FaBoNo; NLV

Lord Bateman. *Anonymous.* And I'll go marry the Turkish lady/That crossed the roaring sea for me. AmFP; FSW; OBET

Lord Beichan and Susie Pye. *Anonymous.* "Oh, I'll range no more in foreign lands,/Since Susie Pye has cross'd the sea." GN

The Lord Chancellours Villainies Discovered. *Anonymous.* With pox o' Chancellour, villanous Chancellour,/Damnable Chancellour, oh. CoMu

Lord Coningsby's Epitaph. Alexander Pope. The rest God knows–so does the Devil. FaBoEE

Lord Cozens Hardy. Sir John Betjeman. That first Lord Cozens Hardy,/The Master of the Rolls. OxBTC

Lord, Dear God! To Thy Attending. Heinrich Otto. Bless the labor of my hand. AH

Lord Delamere. *Anonymous.* But I wish that every honest man might/enjoy his own.' ESPB

Lord, Deliver, Thou Canst Save. Eliza Lee Follen. Burst the bonds that we abhor. AH

Lord Derwentwater (A version). *Anonymous.* There's other fifty pounds in my left/pocket,/Divide it from door to door.' BaBo; ESPB

Lord Derwentwater (D version). *Anonymous.* And a' ye lords o merry Scotland/Be kind to my ladie!' ESPB

Lord Derwentwater (The King's Love-Letter). *Anonymous.* For all my steeds and the rest of my property/We'll retain to her lady's side. AmFP

The Lord Descended from Above. Thomas Sternhold. And have not wavered wickedly/Against my Lord and God. AH

Lord Epsom. Hilaire Belloc. He had the Hunter led away. PH

Lord Finchley. Hilaire Belloc. It is the business of the wealthy man/To give employment to the artisan. DTC; ELU; FaBoCo; FaBoEE; FiBHP; NLV; NOBL; OxBoLi

Lord Fluting Dreams of America on the Eve of His Departure... Paul Zimmer. And gold is strained like sunshine/Through the heath. VGW

Lord Galloway. Robert Burns. So ended in a mire! DBV

Lord God of Hosts. Shepherd Knapp. Until in all the earth thy kingdom come. AH

The Lord God Planted a Garden. Dorothy Frances Gurney. One is nearer God's heart in a garden/Than anywhere else on earth. BLPA; FaBoBe; FPL; HBMV; WGRP

Lord Gorbals. Harry Graham. I've a mind to raise your rent! FaBoCo

Lord, Grant Us Calm. Christina Georgina Rossetti. Still let the earth abide to set Thee forth,/Or vanish like a smoke to set forth Thee. OxBoCh

The Lord Has a Child. Langston Hughes. Every place, everywhere, every day. AH

Lord, Hear My Prayer. John Clare. But still regard the destitute. NOCV; NoP; TrCP

Lord Heygate. Hilaire Belloc. I do not think you want to hear/About this unimportant Peer. OxBoLi

Lord High-Bo. Hilaire Belloc. Disturb the privacy of those/About to wash or change their clothes. FiBHP

Lord, How Shall I Me Complain. *Anonymous.* By this example you may see/That when I sleep I may not wake. CBEP

Lord, I Am Thine. Samuel Davies. And on that grace I dare depend. AH

Lord, I Know Thy Grace Is Nigh Me. Hervey Doddridge Ganse. I will teach the blind to find Him/Who can turn their night to day. AH

Lord, I Want to Be a Christian. *Anonymous.* Lord, I want to be a Christian,/In-a my heart. AH; BoAN 1-2

Lord, If Thou Art Not Present. John Gray. Loving Thee, find Thee; love Thee, finding Thee. CAW; TrPWD

The Lord in the Wind. James Picot. My prayer, keep dew and anthem in my heart! PoAu 1-2

Lord, In thy Presence Here. Jesse L. Holman. The Lord indeed is here. AH

Lord Ingram and Chiel Wyet. *Anonymous.* All for the good and honorable marriage/At Mary Kirk he gave me. BaBo; ESPB

Lord Ingram and Chiel Wyet (B version). *Anonymous.* But a' was for the bonnie babe/That lay blabbering in her bleed. ESPB

Lord Ingram and Chiel Wyet (C version). *Anonymous.* To father my bairn on Auld Ingram,/An Lord Wayets beside!' ESPB

The Lord into His Garden Comes. *Anonymous.* Where we shall part no more. AH

The Lord Is King. *Anonymous.* Forever shall the Lord be King! TrJP

The Lord Is My Shepherd. John Knox. His rod and His staff will uphold me. BePJ

Lord, It Belongs Not to My Care. Richard Baxter. But 'tis enough that Christ knows all,/And I shall be with him. EBCP; OxBoCh

Lord! It Is Not Life to Live. Augustus Montague Toplady. Peace and happiness are Thine,–/Mine they are, if Thou art mine. OxBoCh

Lord, It's All, Almost Done. *Anonymous.* Nothin' but to bring them yallow womens over here. huh! OuSiCo

Lord Jesus Christ, We Humbly Pray. Henry Eyster Jacobs. When thou shalt spread thy heavenly feast. AH

Lord! Lead the Way the Saviour Went. William Croswell. If given for the Saviour's sake,/They lose not their reward. AH

Lord, Listen. E. Lasker-Schuler. And everywhere, in every core, there's bitterness. VWA

Lord Livingston. *Anonymous.* And wi' a crack her heart did brake;/And sae this ends my sang. ESPB; OxBB

Lord Lovel. *Anonymous.*
For all lover true to admire. BLPA
Which true lovers always admire. AmFP; FSW

Lord Lovel (A vers.). *Anonymous.*
So there entwined in a true lovier's knot,/For all true lovier's to admire, ire, ire... ViBoFo
To cut off a branch of that true-lover's knot,/And buried them both in one grave. BaBo

Lord Lovel (B version). *Anonymous.* That ilka ane might plainly see/They war twa lovers sweet. ESPB

Lord Lovel (D version). *Anonymous.* Lady Nancie died for pure, pure love,/Lord Lovel for deep sorraye. ESPB

Lord Lovel (parody). *Anonymous.* He threw the baboon heels over head,/And there he stuck tight in the mire, -ire, -ire... ViBoFo

Lord Lucky. Hilaire Belloc. He only once indulged the whim/Of asking Meyer to lunch with him. NLV

Lord Lundy. Hilaire Belloc. And gracious! how Lord Lundy cried! FaBoCo; OBSV; OxBoLi

Lord, Make a Regular Man Out of Me. Edgar A. Guest. Lord, make a regular man out of me. BLPA; BLPL

Lord, Many Times. Richard Chenevix Trench. Lord, Holy One! if thou who knowest worse/Should loathe us too! BePJ; OBRV

Lord, Many Times Thou Pleased Art. George Wither. And they and we, who now are here./Together still remain. AH

Lord Maxwell's Last Goodnight. *Anonymous.* Lord Maxwell has te'n his last good-night. BaBo; OxBB

Lord, My Weak Thought in Vain Would Climb. Ray Palmer. Thy sovereign wisdom I adore,/And calmly, sweetly, trust thee still. AH

Lord North's Recantation. *Anonymous.* Our glory at most/Is only that–tyrants recant. PAH

The Lord of All. Edwin Markham. They saw Apollo come again, and heard/His name cried in the porches of the sun! CAW

Lord of All I Survey. Keith Sinclair. Mother I am monarch of all I survey. AnNZ

Lord of All Pots and Pans and Things. Cecily Hallack. Accept this service that I do, I do it unto Thee. TRV

Lord of Each Soul. Paul Engle. Lord of our hand and lord of head. Amen. AH

Lord of Eden. Marie de L. Welch. Lion! Eagle! Serpent!...Eve! AnAmPo

The Lord of Heaven to Earth Came Down. Kathryn Blackburn Peck. He rules today with great renown/The Kingdom of the Spirit! BePJ

Lord of Life, All Praise Excelling. Clement Clarke Moore. To the poor belongs the treasure/Of the scattered ears behind. AH

The Lord of Lorn and the Fals Steward. *Anonymous.* For God may suffer for a time/But will disclose it in the end. OxBB

The Lord of Lorn and the False Steward. *Anonymous.* To see these two children sett vpp/In their seats of gold full royallye. ESPB

Lord of My Heart's Elation. Bliss Carman. Lord of the world's elation,/Thou breath of things unseen. AH; HBV 1-2; NOBC; OBCV; TrPWD

Lord of the Dance. Sydney Carter. I am the Lord/Of the Dance, said he. OBET

The Lord of the East. Chu Yuan. Hidden in darkness, I make my way to the east. LiTW

Lord of the Far Horizons. Bliss Carman. To walk with the Sons of Morning/Through the glory of Earth the fair. TrPWD

The Lord of the Isle. Stefan George. Departed with a muffled cry of pain. AWP

The Lord of the Isles (excerpt). Sir Walter Scott. To that dark inn, the Grave! BSV

Lord of the Winds. Mary Elizabeth Coleridge. Tossed by the waters, at Thy feet I fall. OxBoCh; TrPWD

Lord of the World. *Anonymous.* The Lord with me,–no fears my soul/can shake. TrJP

The Lord of the World. G. Anketall "Woodbine Willie" Studdert-Kennedy. 'Tis the Lord of the World you see. PGD

Lord of the Worlds Below! James Freeman. To thee, dread King,/We homage bring,/And own thy power. AH

The Lord Our God Alone Is Strong. Caleb T. Winchester. To seek the God that faith hath found. AH

Lord Randal. *Anonymous.*
For I'm sick at the heart, and I fain wald lie down. AtBAP; ATP; AWP; BaBo; BSV; DiPo; EBEV; ESPB; FaBoBa; FF; ForPo; FPL; HAP; HBV

1-2; HeIP; HoPM; InPo; LiTB; LiTL; LoBV; MaC; NIP; NoP; OAEL
1-2; OxBB; OxBS; SeCeV; TreF; TrGrPo; ViBoFo; WeW
For she was the cause of my lying down. AmFP

Lord Randal (B vers.). *Anonymous.* And lat her hang there for the poysoning o me. BaBo; ESPB

Lord Randal (C vers.). *Anonymous.* Oh mak my bed, mammy, now, now, oh mak my bed, mammy,/now! BaBo; ESPB; ViBoFo

Lord Randall. *Anonymous.* Oh, what will you leave your sweetheart, my son?/A rope that will hang her. FSW

Lord Rendal. *Anonymous.* For I'm wearied with hunting and fain would lie down.' EnSB

The Lord's Chameleons. Peter Klappert. and they were left to hug what was, and ate the air. AmPA

The Lord's My Shepherd, I'll Not Want. Francis Rous. And in God's house forevermore/My dwelling-place shall be. AH

The Lord's Prayer in Verse. Aaron Hill. Nor, when we meet with evil, let us fall. FaBoUs

Lord Saltoun and Auchanachie. *Anonymous.* And he died in the chamber that Jeanie died in. BaBo; ESPB

Lord, Save Us, We Perish. Christina Georgina Rossetti. Be Thy Love before, behind us,/Round us, everywhere. TrPWD

Lord Shaftesbury. John Dryden. And once in twenty years, their scribes record,/By natural instinct they change their lord. LoBV

The Lord Sits with Me Out in Front. Jack Gilbert. ...The tape finishes again/and we sit on. Unable to find things to say. NPGG

Lord Tennyson and Lord Melchett. D. H. Lawrence. I lick the cream off property! that's what it seems to say! FaBoEE

Lord–Thine the Day. Dag Hammarskjöld. And I the day's. EaLo

Lord Thomas and Fair Annet. *Anonymous.* And by this ye may ken right weil,/They ware twa luvers deare. EnLit; ESPB; FaBoBa; OxBB; ViBoFo

Lord Thomas and Fair Annet (B vers.). *Anonymous.* There was never three lovers that ever met/More sooner they did depart. BaBo; ESPB

Lord Thomas and Fair Annet (I version). *Anonymous.* For or the morn at ten o clock/Ye's deal'd as fast at mine.' ESPB

Lord Thomas and Fair Annet (The Brown Girl). *Anonymous.* And the brown girl at my feet. AmFP

Lord Thomas and Fair Ellender. *Anonymous.* I want fair Ellender in my arms,/The brown girl at my feet. AmFP

Lord Thomas and Fair Ellinor. *Anonymous.* For all true loves to admire. OBET

Lord Thomas and Lady Margaret. *Anonymous.* And when that my good lord comes home/I will say thou's my sister's son. BaBo; ESPB

Lord Thomas Stuart. *Anonymous.* "I'm feared it's mony unco lords/Havin my love to the clay. BaBo; ESPB

Lord, Thou Clepedest Me. *Anonymous.* And "those a little' a long way is. OBSP

Lord, Thou Hast Promised. Samuel K. Cox. And still thy richer gifts repeat/Till grace in glory is complete. AH

Lord, Thou Hast Suffered. Amy Carmichael. Eternal Comforter. TRV

Lord Ullin's Daughter. Thomas Campbell. And he was left lamenting. BeLS; FaPoR; GN; GTBS; GTBS-P; HBVY; OBRV; RoGo; TreF; WBLP

Lord Vyet. Arthur Christopher Benson. And yet the furthest star/Is not so far as I.' OBVV

Lord Walter's Wife. Elizabeth Barrett Browning. Come, Dora, my darling, my angel, and help me to ask him to dine. BeLS; HAP

Lord Waterford. *Anonymous.* With a nice resarved sate, says the Shan Van Vocht. ChTr; GBP

Lord, When the Wise Men Came from Far. Sidney Godolphin. Then, though we do not know, we love. HAP; MeLP; NOCV; OBS

Lord, Where Shall I Find Thee? Judah Halevi. And Thou upholdest them all! TrJP

Lord, while for All Mankind. John R. Wreford. Be Thou her refuge and her trust,/Her everlasting Friend. TrPWD

Lord! Who Art Merciful as Well as Just. Robert Southey. My nothingness, my wants,/My sins, and my contrition. TrPWD

Lord, Who's the Happy Man. Nicholas and Nahum Tate Brady. When earth's foundation shakes, shall stand,/By providence secured. AH

Lord William, or, Lord Lundy. *Anonymous.* Commend me all to my good-mother,/At night when ye gang home.' ESPB

Lordings, Listen to Our Lay. *Anonymous.* May joy come from God above,/To all those who Christmas love. OHIP

The Lordly and Isolate Satyrs. Charles Olson. They go. And the day CABL; CoAP; NeAP; PoM

The Lordly Hudson. Paul Goodman.
Be patient. Paul! home! home! NYP
Be quiet, heart! home! home! CoAP; NMP; VGW

The Lords of Creation. *Anonymous.* Shall the very last woman obey. PoLf

The Lords of the Main. Joseph Stansbury. The first-born of Neptune are Lords of the/Main! PAH

Lords of the Wilderness. John Leyden. They scorn to yield their ancient sway to man. OBRV

Lore. R. S. Thomas. Live large, man, and dream small. OxBC

Lorena. *Anonymous.* 'Tis dust to dust beneath the sod,/But ther, up ther, 'tis heart to heart. BFSS

Lorena. H. D. L. Webster. But there, up there, 'tis heart to heart. BLPA; FSW; PSoN

Lorraine Loree. Charles Kingsley. And no one but the baby cried for poor Lorraine, Loree. BBV

Los Angeles. Eloise Klein Healy. and loved you all night,/completely out of proportion. GP

Los Cuatro Generales. *Anonymous.* They did not disgrace you... FSW

Los Mineros. Edward Dorn. every window has been abused with the rocks of departing children. PoM

Los Pastores. Edith Agnew. And they all went kneeling, kneeling/At the manger in Belen. ChBR; PCh

Losers. Jonathan Holden. ...relieved/of their secrets, are as honestly/miserable as they look. MAYP

Losers. Carl Sandburg. "Come on, you...Do you want to live forever?" CMoP; HBMV; MoAB; MoAmPo; MoVE; NoAm; TrGrPo

Losing a Slave Girl. Po Chu-i. Nor any knows, save the bright watching moon. AWP

Losing the Straight Way. Ian Wedde. their blood ran on in silence. OCNZ

Losing Track. Denise Levertov. a light growth of green dreams drying. HeIP; NaP; NoAm; NOBA; PoM

Losing Track. Cathy Song. dotting the points to a constellation/you had yet to name. BrSi

Loss. Richard Aldington. The white slim body my senses fed upon/And all the secret shadows shot with fire? BrPo

Loss. Archie Randolph Ammons. to float/off their stems/and go ConAP

Loss. Julia Johnson Davis. But in her room...an empty room.../She had no pride. HBMV

Loss. Alex Kuo. there in the beginning. BrSi

Loss. Charles Madge. For yesterday is always sad, its nature/Darker than love would wish in every feature. FaBoMo

Loss in Delay. Robert Southwell. Happy man, that soon doth knock/Babble babes against the rock! OBSC

Loss! Loss! Rhoda McMahon. Ice tolled fey moon-scenes! WeW

Loss of an Oil Tanker. Charles Causley. A drowned fish and a sea-bird's feather. OxBC

The Loss of Strength. Austin Clarke. ...slime steps on stone,/I count them–not my own. IPY

Loss of the Amphitrite. *Anonymous.* Lamenting sore for those no more on board the Amphitrite. OBSS

The Loss of the Birkenhead. Sir Francis Hastings Doyle. Joint-heirs with Christ, because they bled to save/His weak ones, not in vain. HBV 1-2

The Loss of the Cedar Grove. *Anonymous.* Our brave and honored captain who died all in command. ShS

The Loss of the Druid. *Anonymous.* For Jackson swears he'll never send/The Druid to sea again! ShS

The Loss of the Due Dispatch. *Anonymous.* To God alone our praise we give/Who safely brought us there. AmFP

The Loss of the Evelyn Marie. *Anonymous.* Pray for the six skippers who are lost out at sea/In this ill-fated trawler, the Evelyn Marie. OBSS

The Loss of the New Columbia. *Anonymous.* And send his blessing on these poor people who have lost their sons in such/distress. AmFP

Losses. Randall Jarrell. We are satisfied if you are; but why did/I die? AmP; CoBMV; HaCAP; LCAP; LiTM; MoVE; OxBA; PoA; TAP; UnPo; WaP

Lost. Alfred Alvarez. Hers. Not yours, my love. Hers. NMP

The Lost. *Anonymous.* Like pigeon in quest of a mate that is lost. WTO

Lost. W. H. Auden. Who ferries no one to a happy shore. FaBoEE

Lost. Millen Brand. No, they might not be there at all/But that one sees the flames go out. NYBP

Lost. Chu Shu-chen. And I wipe away my tears with my sleeve. BoWoP

Lost. David Fisher. o little lost poet with/many fine doctors and one celestial pillow. NPGG

Lost. Charles, duc d' Orleans. The man forlost, that wot not where he goth.' OxBM

Lost. Carl Sandburg. And the harbor's eyes. AmPP; BrR; CMoP; PoPl; WHA

The Lost. Jones Very. That now to them dost all thy substance give. MAmP; NOBA

Lost. David Wagoner. ...The forest knows/Where you are. You must let it find you. GP; PoA

Lost Acres. Robert Graves. To walk there would be loss of sense. NoAm

Lost after All. Charlie D. Tillman. Bitter the wail of a spirit;/Lost after all. PeD

Lost Anchors. Edwin Arlington Robinson. Telling of much that once had come to pass/With him, whose mother should have had no sons. CMoP; MAmP

Lost and Found. George Macdonald. A light I knew not till my soul was dark. TRV; WGRP

Lost and Given Over. Edwin James Brady. Ho! Bullee in the Al-lee. PoAu 1-2

The Lost Angel. Philip Levine. and gives me back my life. NOBA

The Lost Baby. *Anonymous.* Poor little lost baby, baby, poor little lost babe! AmFP

The Lost Baby Poem. Lucille Clifton. always for your never named sake BlSi

The Lost Ball. Lucy Sprague Mitchell. Come here, my peek-a-boo ball! TiPo

Lost Beliefs. William Dean Howells. The desolate nest is broken/And torn with storms and rain! AmePo

Lost But Found. Horatius Bonar. I love, I love his home. HBV 1-2

Lost, But Won. Henry J. Von Schlichten. God the Son/Brought my release. BePJ

The Lost Carnival. Fred Chappell. ...tigers/pad soft and restless through the falling flakes. GOYP

The Lost Child. James Reaney. And lo! Cities and gardens, shepherds and smiths. NOBC

The Lost Children. Richard Eberhart. ...Let us go,/And hold close our loves. NePoAm-2

The Lost Children. Randall Jarrell. But the child keeps on playing, so I play. CoAP; PrIm; TAP

The Lost Children. Gregory Orr. eidolons, adrift on the night air. GeTw

A Lost Chord. Adelaide Anne Procter. It may be that only in Heaven/I shall hear that grand Amen. CAW; FaFP; GoTF; HBV 1-2; PaPo; TreF; VLP; WBLP; WGRP

Lost Cinderella. Edith Weaver. sobbing over the fallen sparrow/in your belled hand's cradle? DFT

Lost City. Ingrid Jonker. orange poppy of the sky PeSA

The Lost Colors. Elizabeth Stuart Phelps Ward. For your sake storm we any height. AA; HBV 1-2; HBVY

Lost Companions. Helen Bryant. I cannot believe them old. AMV-80

Lost Contact. William Cole. the contact lens/you are looking for! PoL

Lost Contact. Sylvia Wheeler. Odds are on rape. FAZ

The Lost Continent. Jenny Joseph. The curled-up figure of the woman lies/And lost within that passive sea my words. BrRo

The Lost Dancer. Jean Toomer. The diamond body of his being. BALP; PoBA

The Lost, Dancing. Edward Field. and turn and wave goodbye/to the Alexandria you are losing. GP

Lost Desire. Meleager. Cease thy vain dreams of beauty's warmth–forget/The face thou longest for! AWP

Lost Dog. Frances Rodman. And rushes at a call to meet the one/Who of his tiny universe is sun. GDP

The Lost Doll. Charles Kingsley. The prettiest doll in the world. MoShBr; SoPo

Lost Explorer. Edmund Pennant. No talisman, tongue-sinew, signet-ring? Nothing? GoYe

Lost For a Rose's Sake. *Anonymous.* That my love Marie/Might love me yet. AWP

Lost Garden. Katherine"(Amelia Beers Warnock Garvin) "Hale. Only these lines remain! CaP

The Lost Genius. John James Piatt. I saw the Ghost of Youth! AA

A Lost God (excerpt). Francis William Bourdillon. Yet real somewhere. WGRP

The Lost Heifer. Austin Clarke. And her voice coming softly over the meadow/Was the mist becoming rain. BIrV; OxBI

The Lost History Plays: King Canute (parody). Stanley J. Sharpless. Thou rul'st the waves; my task's to waive the rules. BXAP

The Lost History Plays: King Ethelred the Unready (parody). Bill Greenwell. And fall upon mine sword, when I'm/not ready? BXAP

The Lost History Plays: Savanarola (parody). Max Beerbohm. Then shall you see a cinder, not a man,/Beneath the lightnings of the Vatican. BXAP

A Lost Illusion. George Du Maurier. Near the nice little man in blue goggles. That's me. CenHV

Lost Illusions. Georgia Douglas Johnson. Veils that hung low o'er the blaze of the truth! BANP

Lost in a Blizzard. Arthur W. Monroe. No, it's Bill, my friend. PoOW

Lost in a Corridor of Power. Michael Brownstein. Back into the seat and push off. ANYP

Lost in a Norther. Hamlin Garland. And cloudless, soft, serene as May,/Opened the jocund day. BPAW

Lost in Heaven. Robert Frost. Let's let my heavenly lostness overwhelm me. MoAmPo

Lost in Translation. James Merrill. ...turns the waste/To shade and fiber, milk and memory. FYAP; HaCAP

Lost in Yucatan. Tom McKeown. And an altar of sacrifice, between the ocean/And the hidden quarry of the gods. HoAn

The Lost Ingredient. Anne Sexton. ...,as if salt or money or even lust/would keep us calm and prove us whole at last. CoPo

A Lost Jewel. Robert Graves. "Turn to me, sweetheart! Why do you not turn?" EnLoPo; NYBP

Lost Jimmie Whalen. *Anonymous.* And wide is the gulf, love, between you and I... ABF I will sigh till I die by the side of your grave! AmFP; BaBo

Lost Johnny. *Anonymous.* To the road where my Johnny is. AmFP

The Lost Lagoon. [(Emily(] Pauline Johnson. I hear the call of the singing firs/In the hush of the golden moon. BPAW

The Lost Language. Irving Feldman. Where are you, o liebe breyt? AmPC

The Lost Leader. Robert Browning. Pardoned in heaven, the first by the throne! EnL; FaBoPV; GoTF; GTBS; HBV 1-2; MBW 1-2; MCCG; TreFS; TrGrPo; ViBoPo; VLP

The Lost Leader. Douglas Fraser. Leave him spreadeagled on Rubicon Wall! PoSH

Lost Letter to James Wright, with Thanks for a Map of Fano. Gibbons Ruark. Toward the river ferry taking sounding after sounding. MAYP

Lost Light. Elizabeth Akers. The window is dark and the night is cold,/And the story forever told. HBV 1-2

Lost Lines from Chaucer's Prologue to The Canterbury Tales. *Anonymous.* He had a eunuch cat hight Ganymed. PeHV

The Lost Little Sister. William Barnes. Vrom stwone to stwone the water's bed. PoEL 1-5

Lost Love. *Anonymous.* For yellow, fresh and full-blown once it bloomed. WTO

Lost Love. Robert Graves. Without relief seeking lost love. AWP; CH; FaBoCh; LoGBV; MoAB; MoBrPo; NoP

Lost Love. Andrew Lang. In dreams doth he behold her/Still fair and kind and young. BSV; HBV 1-2

A Lost Love. Henry Francis Lyte. Till we shall meet again. GTBS

Lost Lover Blues. Blind Boy Fuller. And I ain't got no loving baby now. BluL

The Lost Man: A Crocodile. Thomas Lovell Beddoes. Tearing the hairy leeches from his throat. AnFE

The Lost Mistress. Robert Browning. I will hold your hand but as long as all may,/Or so very little longer! BoLoP; CBEP; FiP; HBV 1-2; NOBE; OBEV; OBNC; OBVV; PoPle

A Lost Mohican Visits Hell's Kitchen. A. K. Redwing. "You can't get something for nothing" daydreams. VoR

Lost Moment. Hoyt W. Fuller. to walk the empty plains of hell/forever and ever/more. PoBA

Lost Moments. Glover Davis. glistens on the crushed cups/and papers floating by. SM

Lost Month. William Stanley Merwin. We keep discovering parts of ourselves which came/to exist under this influential sign. AmPC

The Lost Mr. Blake. Sir William Schwenck Gilbert. And I should like to know where in the world/(or rather, out of it) they expect to go. EnLi 1-2; InMe

Lost Objects. Diana O Hehir. My father's eyesight, my oldest child's talent, the key to/my house, the short way home. AMV-80

The Lost Occasion. John Greenleaf Whittier. ...as if to manifest/Thy nobler self, thy life at best! BLPL; NOBA

Lost on September Trail, 1967. Alberto Rios. ...her knees/which looked up at opposite ends/of the sky. FYAP

The Lost Orchard. Edgar Lee Masters.
And I have seen them merge in their leafy sky/Till they became the light of the full moon. LaNeLa; MoPo
Over the tree tops to predestined mates. CMoP

The Lost Parasol (excerpt). Sandor Weores. the sleek silk vanishes into foaming shade. OBVE

Lost Parents. Lawrence Ferlinghetti. in a Jungian search/for lost parents/their own age AmC; GP; PoM

Lost Picture. Ray Fraser. to the farm down the long dirt road/by the river. NeAC

The Lost Pictures. Hollis Summers. "Here we are," you can say,/Knowing you aren't. HoPM

The Lost Pilot. James Tate. ...or that misfortune/placed these worlds in us. CoAP; NoP; OBWP; TwCP; UnPo

The Lost Playmate. Abbie Farwell Brown. But oh! I miss the little moon/Who played there in the afternoon. HBVY

The Lost Pleiad. William Gilmore Simms From the lone sphere they blest! AA

The Lost Range. Henry Herbert Knibbs. Wishing him luck on The Lost Range down yonder against/the sky. BPAW

The Lost Shipmate. Theodore Goodridge Roberts. Shall I find you south of the Gulf?–or are you dead in my heart? CaP

Lost Ships. Thomas Hornsby Ferril. I fled under a hill that hid the sky. EtS

The Lost Shoe. Walter De la Mare. For her lost shoe. BrR

Lost Silvertip. J. D. Reed. the honey crystallized,/and the honey-lover smoke. NYBP

The Lost Son. Theodore Roethke. Be still./Wait. AP; CAPP; CoBMV; HaCAP; HAP; LiTM; MiAP; MoPo; NePA; VGW

Love. Jones Very. The prints where first she trod, a child of mortal birth. AP

Love. William Watson. But hush! Remind not Eros of his wings. TrGrPo

Love, 20c the First Quarter Mile. Kenneth Fearing. ...and a few reporters, if anything should break. HAP; WeW

A Love Affair. Arnold Bennett. Lo! In due time she returned to the clod./ She was missed. OxBTC

Love among the Manichees. William Dickey. Smiling, "Now you have come." PoCh

Love Among the Ruins. Robert Browning. Love is best. BoLiVe; EnLit; FaBV; HAP; HBV 1-2; MBW 1-2; MCCG; NOBE; OAEL 1-2; OAEP; OBEV; OBVV; PoEL 1-5; PrIm; VLP

Love and a Question. Robert Frost. The bridegroom wished he knew. MoBS

Love and Age. Walter Savage Landor. Quite beyond recall, but not forgotten quite. GBL

Love and Age. Thomas Love Peacock. When our young days of gathering flowers/Will be a hundred years ago. HBV 1-2; NOBV; OBEV; OBNC; PoPle; ViBoPo

Love and Death. Caius Valerius Catullus. Thy love is sweet and sweeteneth/The very bitterness of death. AWP

Love and Death. Margaret Deland. Nor know great Death is kind! AA; HBV 1-2

Love and Death. Rosa Mulholland. Now the summer air is sweet with the rose's fragrant breath/That conquered Death. HBV 1-2

Love and Death. John Frederick Nims. Without the assuring skull beneath the lip. HoPM; SM

Love and Death. George Gordon, Lord Byron. To strongly, wrongly, vainly love thee still. EBEV; NOBE

Love and Debt Alike Troublesom. Sir John Suckling. As good stuff under Flanel lies, as under Silken clothes. AnAnS 2; CavP

Love and Discipline. Henry Vaughan. And all the year have some green ears. TrPWD

Love and Folly. Jean de La Fontaine. Let Folly be the guide of Love,/ Where'er the boy may choose to go. AWP

Love and Fortune. Fulke, Lord Brooke Greville. Fortune, adieu! OBSC

Love and fortune and my mind... Sir Thomas Wyatt. And all my thoughts are dashed into dust. FCP

Love and Friendship. Emily Bronte. He still may leave thy garland green. VLP

Love and Hate. Frank O'Connor. This is all my song,/I will love only hate. KiLC; TW

Love and Honour. Fulke, Lord Brooke Greville. "How fatal are blind Cupid's ways." OBSC

Love and Hope. Dante Gabriel Rossetti. Scorn-fired at length the illusive eyes of Hope. MaVP

Love and Jealousy. Robert Greene. Swearing, no greater mischief could be wrought/Than love united to a jealous thought. EIL

Love and Jealousy. William Walsh. The blaze grows greater, but 'tis sooner out. BoLoP

Love and Language. Louisa S. Bevington. When I offered you my soul/ Heard you what I said? NOBV

Love and Liberation. John Hall Wheelock. Ride over them with love! MoAmPo

Love and Liberty. A Cantata. Robert Burns. Churches built to please the priest. NOEC

Love and Life. Julie Mathilde Lippmann. Said Life:–"Here's grief." AA; HBV 1-2

Love and Life. John Wilmot, Earl of Rochester. This live-long minute true BoLoP; CavP; CEP; ELP; EnLoPo; GBL; HAP; HBV 1-2; LiTL; LoBV; MePo; NIP; NOBE; OBEV; OBS; PoEL 1-5; SeCV 1-2; TrGrPo; ViBoPo

Love and Lust. Isaac Rosenberg. Finding love was lust. ChMP; TrJP

Love and Marriage. Ray Mathew. But she it is who names the wedding-day. PoAu 1-2

Love and Music. Anonymous. Come, let us go and listen to his flute. WTO

Love and Poetry. Louis Simpson. And everything else is prose. PPoe

Love and Poverty. Elisabeth Cavazza Pullen. "It was Poverty who went!" AA

Love and Reason. Matthew Prior. And blind Himself, conducts the dazl'd Guide? OBEC

Love and Respect. Pathericke Jenkyn. I will render thee the guerdon/Of a never-dying love. CavP

Love and Sacrifice. Bernard O'Dowd. And, till its burden goes,/Our work is–where it bleeds. BoAV

Love and Sleep. Algernon Charles Swinburne. And glittering eyelids of my soul's desire. BoLoP; UnTE; VLP

Love and Time. Beatrix Demarest Lloyd. Across the gardens of Life they go. AA

Love and Wine. Thomas Shadwell. Nor would kings rule the world but for love and good drinking. UnTE

Love, as a Warrior Lord. Ovid (Publius Ovidius Naso). The vassal world is then thy own. LiTW

Love at Large. Coventry Patmore. Out of the North, where life did freeze,/Into the haven where they would be. NOBV

Love at Roblin Lake. Al Purdy. and forgotten everything after/on our journey into the dark. NoP

Love at Sea. Theophile Gautier. Lies where no man will steer,/No maiden land. AWP; HBV 1-2

Love at the Door. Meleager. Safe harbor from the whistling gale! AWP

Love Beleaguered. Katherine Garrison Chapin. To share this last joy, sweet and desperate. MoLP

Love between Brothers and Sisters. Isaac Watts. May grow to clubs and naked swords,/To murder and to death. FaBoUs

The Love Bit. Joel Oppenheimer. ...i,e. we make it crazy or/no, and sometimes in the afternoon. CoPo; PoM

Love–bittersweet, irrepressible–. Sappho. To chase Andromeda, you leave me. BoWoP

Love Breathing Thanks and Praise (excerpt). Richard Baxter. And as a dying man to dying men. TRV

Love by the Water-Reeds. Anonymous. Lo, prince and princess stir in their sleep! WTO

Love Calls Us to the Things of This World. Richard Wilbur. And the heaviest nuns walk in a pure floating/Of dark habits,/keeping their difficult balance. AmPP; CAPP; CMoP; HAP; HeIP; InPS; MoAmPo; NePA; NePoEA; NIP; NoAm; NIP; PoRA; PPP; PAI; TrGrPo; UnPo; VGW

Love Came Back at Fall o' Dew. Lizette Woodworth Reese. This the word that brake his heart–/Yet it brake mine, too! HBV 1-2

Love can do all but raise the dead. Emily Dickinson. And so abets the shining fleet/Till it is out of gaze. LiTA; NePA

Love Cannot Live. Anonymous. Hope cannot give/That hap denies. EIL

Love Charm. Anonymous. By virtue of the invocation "There is no God but/Allah and Muhammad is His Prophet." WTO

Love-Charms. Thomas Campion. In vain are all the charms I can devise;/ She hath an art to break them with her eyes. NOBE

Love Child–a Black Aesthetic. Everett Hoagland. ...godly milky/nascency succulent miracle BPo

Love Comes Quietly. Robert Creeley. able to go/alone all the way. LLLT

Love Constraining to Obedience. William Cowper. Changes a slave into a child,/And duty into choice. NOCV

Love Continual. John Heywood. As ye perceive by me doth fall,/And yours to love as lovingly. CBEP

Love Dialogue. Anonymous. "Yea, in good fayth. Then am I yours/alsoo." CoBE

Love Dirge. Anonymous. ...I, like a/Fish out of water, am dangling in the sun. WTO

A Love Dirge to the Whitehouse (or It Soots You Right). Bob Fletcher. and soon we come/to bury the hatchet NBP

Love Dislikes Nothing. Robert Herrick. I'm a man for ev'ry Sceane. AnAnS 2; CBEP

Love Divine, All Loves Excelling. Charles Wesley. Lost in wonder, love, and praise! NOCV

Love doth again. Sir Thomas Wyatt. She shall my heart obtain. FCP; SiPS

Love Enthroned. Richard Lovelace. Her crowned self submits to her own laws. CaPo

Love Equals Swift and Slow. Henry David Thoreau. The hunter and his game. NoP

Love (excerpt). Alice Walker. He has no teeth/But is kind. NMM

Love-Faith. Harry Kemp. Dear, I still believe in love,/But no more–in you! HBMV

Love Fallen to Earth. Paul Verlaine. Brightening the littered leaves upon the ground? SyP

The Love Feast. W. H. Auden. Make me chaste, Lord, but not yet. ErPo

Love Flows from God. Mechtild of Magdeburg. And all the strings must sound/Which are strung in love. WPOW

Love for a Beautiful Lady. Anonymous. For hire love mourning I make,/ More ins mon. MeEL

Love for a Hare. Melvin Walker La Follette. ...I heard him squeal/Before he died beneath my wheel. NePoEA-2

Love for Instance. Dan Gerber. and tell me/what's the difference FAZ

A Love for Patsy. John Thompson, Jr. In all the world no two things match/But the green eyes of Patsy. LiTA; LiTL; NePA; WaP

Love (fragment). Sappho. Falling upon me, shakes me leaf and bough. AWP

Love from My Father. Carole Gregory Clemmons. but my father brings fresh glazed donuts in a white bag. CNA; PoBA

Love Guards the Roses of Thy Lips. Thomas Lodge. But if thou do not, Love, I'll truly serve her/In spite of thee, and by firm faith deserve her. EIL

Love Has Eyes. William Forster. ...and my delighted eyes/Throb as with beams intense, and splendour of the skies. CBAP

Love Longs to Touch. Carol Lee Sanchez. we hated more fiercely. TWSS

Love! Love! Rhoda McMahon. How her heart hums! WeW

Love, Love! What Nonsense It Is. Natalya Gorbanyevskaya. How low are the ceilings. WPOW

Love Made in the First Age. Richard Lovelace. Enjoying of myself I lie. AnAnS 2; CaPo; JCP; OAEL 1-2; SeCP

Love Made Me Such That I Live in Fire. Gaspara Stampa. I'll not repent of burning as I love. PBWP

Love Making. James Tate. ...you/who are now my enemy, leave me. EAS

The Love-Making: His and Hers. Eve Merriam. My Venus My Venice I cannot forget/my lake of desire I dip my oar UnTE

Love Me! Stevie Smith. That the rocks will harp on for ever, and my Love me never be/heard. OBSP

Love Me. Maria Wine. always let some of my blond hair/be free PBWP

Love Me Again. Anonymous. And sure, methinks, I have great wrong/If that I be not loved again. EIL

Love Me and Never Leave Me. Ronald McCuaig. They were buried side by side. BoAV; PoL

Love Me, and the World Is Mine. David Reed, Jr. Love me, and the world is mine. TreFT

Love Me at Last. Alice Corbin. Love me at last–I am but sliding water/Over a stone. HBMV

Love Me Little, Love Me Long. Anonymous.
Love me little, love me long,/Is the burden of my song. BLPA; EIL; FaBoBe; FaFP; LiTL; TreF
So to thee farewell. CBEP; NoP

Love Me Little, Love Me Long. Robert Herrick. ...desire/Grown violent does either die or tire. CaPo

Love Me, Love My Dog. Isabella Valancy Crawford. "Ho!" thought the page, "she loves his hound,/So this is Lady Clare!" WHW

Love Me or Not. Thomas Campion. So would I love that neither should repent. EIL; HBV 1-2; ViBoPo

Love Medicine. Eda Lou Walton. And laugh when I see her hiding/From my mocking eyes all day. BPAW

Love Medley: Patrice Cuchulain. Michael S. Harper. ...blood, veins,/machinery and love: our names. GeTw

Love, Meet Me in the Green Glen. John Clare. Meet me in the green glen. ELP

The Love-Moon. Dante Gabriel Rossetti. The love-moon that must light my soul to Love? MaVP

Love much. Earth has enough of bitter in it. Ella Wheeler Wilcox. There is no thing which love may not achieve. PoToHe

Love, My Machine. Louis Simpson. I am going into the night to find a world of my own. CAPP

Love Necessitates. Eugene B. Redmond. Precise preparation (mercy!)/For the Academy of Hard Knocks. CNA

Love Not. Carolina Elizabeth Sarah Norton. Faultless, immortal, till he change or die./Love not! HBV 1-2; IrPN; OBVV

Love Not Me for Comely Grace. John Wilbye. To doat upon me ever! ALV

Love of Fame, The Universal Passion. Edward Hilton Young.
Sales, races, rabbits, and (still stranger!) pews. OBSV
They'll find that their religion has been one. OBSV

The Love of God. John Audelay. I love His love for evermore. OxBM

The Love of God. Bernard Rascas. Except the love of God, which shall live and last for aye! CAW; WGRP

The Love of Hell. Abraham Burstein. Thine is the joy and the charm and/the glory! TrJP

Love of Nature. James (1700-48) Thomson. When Angels dwelt, and GOD himself, with Man! OBEC

The Love of Older Men. James Kirkup. but there are no young angels/like the one I was in my golden days. PeHV

The Love of the Father. Anonymous. The love of the Father eternal/Is over us all the way. BLRP

Love on the Farm. D. H. Lawrence. Against him, die, and find death good. CMoP; ErPo; FaBV; FF; MoAB; MoBrPo; TrGrPo

Love on the Mountain. Thomas Boyd. To the East or the West I will follow/Till the dusk of my day. AnIV; HBV 1-2; OxBI

Love Once Was Like an April Dawn. Robert Underwood Johnson. Yet with what words I'd welcome thee–/Couldst thou return, dear mystery! HBV 1-2

Love Perfumes All Parts. Robert Herrick. Nor can Juno sweeter be,/When she lies with Jove, than she. UnTE

Love Pictures You as Black and Long-Faced. Lance Jeffers. in your wheat-strewn bed's the planetary gust/of your people's victory! FB

Love Play. William Cavendish, Duke of Newcastle. Yet both of us will find it... ErPo

A Love Poem. John Ashbery. Our notes to each other, always repeated, always the same. HaCAP

Love Poem. Rosemary Aubert. and I want to be/your final adventure. AMV-80

Love Poem. Robert Bly. And the small mainstreets abandoned all night. BiP; PAI; PCP

Love Poem. Alex Comfort. And I will ride her thighs' white horses. ErPo

Love Poem. Maurice James Craig. Where the sweet water meets the salt. NeIP

Love Poem. Judson Crews. And all/that there is/Is/Between them. UnTE

Love Poem. Lauris Edmond. something very light and fragile to carry. OCNZ

Love Poem. Yuri Kageyama. nothing's changed BrSi

Love Poem. Janet Lewis. The vintner, and his heavy head/In vineyards overgrown. QFR

Love Poem. John Logan. I died mimicking the dead. CAPP

Love Poem. Gary Miranda. made me think just now of you untangling/blueberries, carefully, from their dense branches. SM

Love Poem. John Frederick Nims. All the toys of the world would break. FF; HoPM; MiAP; SoSe

Love Poem. Gregory Orr. a telephone number: yours. GeTw

Love Poem. Ron Padgett. ...blazing/with kisses that smoulder toward heaven. APU

Love Poem. Kathleen Raine. Lost, in the heart's worship, and the body's sleep. LiTB; MoAB; MoBrPo; MoPo; NeBP

Love Poem. Susan Irene Rea. ...The sun paints/our bodies simple and shining. AMV-80

Love Poem. Leslie Marmon Silko. when the rain smell comes with the wind. UnPo; VoR

Love Poem. Linda Wagner. as this your silvered body/brings/&/shares FAZ

Love Poem. Chris Wallace-Crabbe. And love breaks on my cold hills like the sun. PoAu 1-2

Love Poem. Miller Williams. Sands run through the children in their sleep. MAT

Love Poem. Jiri Wolker. And to the ground be hurled/Before my eyes? LiTW

Love Poem–1940. Miriam Hershenson. These soothing hands of light will never/Massage oblivion into your bones. GoYe

Love Poem for Lin Fan. Marilyn Bowering. My mind goes no further. CaPN

A Love Poem for My Country. Frank Mkalawile Chipasula. And I will emerge from the night breaking into song/Like the sun, blowing out these evil stars. WhB

Love Poem Investigation for A.T. Frank Frate. Smouldering in a self-made cave, like a sold son. AMV-80

Love Poem: "Less the dog begged to die in the sky." George Barker. To mitigate my sorrows. NeBP

Love Poem on Theme by Whitman. Allen Ginsberg. nude ghosts seeking each other out in the silence. CAPP; NaP

Love Poem: The Dispossessed. T. R. Hummer. God knows why/Anyone would bother/To forward such a thing. MAYP

Love Pursued. Anonymous. Carry my holla, holla, ce,la,ho,ho,hu. GBL

Love Redeemed. William Baylebridge.
More sure in this, my full devotion's done–With spirit and sense, by love annealed, at one. BoAV
So has our love. BoAV; PoAu 1-2
So senses you, none breathes who's less alone! CBAP
With flesh the imminent two converts one. PoAu 1-2
Yea, flesh itself is bursting into song! PoAu 1-2

Love Rejected. Lucille Clifton. their country don't love them. BPo

Love Restored (excerpt). Ben Jonson. Would die a destin'd sacrifice/Than live at home and free. UnS

Love's Alchemy. John Donne. Hope not for mind in women; at their best/Sweetness and wit, they are but mummy, possessed. CABA; LiTL; NoP; OAEL 1-2; OAEP; SUW; ViBoPo

Love's Apparition and Evanishment. Samuel Taylor Coleridge. In the chill'd heart by gradual self-decay. EnRP

Love's Arithmetic. Sir Edward Sherburne. Thousand torments, thousand kisses.' CavP

Love's Assize. Guido Cavalcanti. As no god, saving only Death, can save. LiTW

Love's Baubles. Dante Gabriel Rossetti. Follies of love are love's true ministers. MaVP

Love's Calendar. William Bell Scott. For Love hath made but one of twain. HBV 1-2

Love's Caution. William Henry Davies. But do not breathe at home one word of this! ChMP

Love's Change. Anne Reeve Aldrich. With that awful change in his face? AA

Love's Clock. Sir John Suckling. Strange blisses,/And what you best like. CaPo

Love's Coming. Shaw Neilson. Love came so lightly/I knew not that he came. PoAu 1-2

Love's Consolation. Richard Watson Dixon. ...wherefore thus I cross/All lovers pale and starving with their loss. OBNC

Love's Cosmopolitan. Annie Matheson. Ambassador of God, great-hearted Jew! OBVV

Love's Courtship. Thomas Carew. Maids often lose their maidenhead/Ere they set foot in nuptial bed. UnTE

Love's Deity. John Donne. If she whom I love, should love me. ATP; AWP; DiPo; EIL; EnLit; EnRePo; GBL; InPo; LiTB; LiTL; OAEP; SeCePo; WHA

Love's Despair. Richard Lynch. And yet nor die, nor draw a life-like breath. EIL

Love's Despair. Diarmad O'Curnain. For aye, thy leal and silent lover. OnYI; OxBI

Love's Emblem. John Clare. Her beauty conquers all. NIP

Love's Emblems. John Fletcher. "Ladies, if not plucked, we die." BoLoP; EG; EIL; HBV 1-2; NIP; NOBE; OBEV; UnTE

Love's Ending. Anonymous. Death was the end of every such desire. OBSC

Love's Entreaty. Buonarroti Michelangelo. And he who fain would find it, first must die. AWP

Love's Epitaph. William Cavendish, Duke of Newcastle. Next lover may he be love-curst,/As I the first. CBEP; OBSP

Love's Exchange. John Donne. Racked carcasses make ill anatomies. LiTL

Love's Fancy. John Dryden. Ah, what a joy to hear, "Shall we again?" ErPo

Love's Fatality. Dante Gabriel Rossetti. Life's iron heart, even Love's Fatality. MaVP

Love's Flight. Else Lasker-Schüler. Only my soul was tired and tame. TrJP

Love's Fool. John Rosenthal. I was a perfect fool a long time ago and sang/Wise songs to girls under the ridiculous moon. AMV-81

Love's Force. Thomas Carew. ...then the noblest breast first felt/Itself for its own proper object melt. CaPo

Love's Franciscan. Henry Constable. Thy arrows quiver, and thy relics shine. ACP; GoBC

Love's Glory. Fulke, Lord Brooke Greville. Love being placed above these middle regions/Where every passion wars itself with legions. OBSC

Love's Grave. Thomas Watson. "Here lieth Love, of Mars the bastard son,/Whose foolish fault to death himself hath done." OBSC

Love's Growth. John Donne. No winter shall abate the spring's increase. JCP; MBW 1-2; NoP

Love's Guerdons. Edith Nesbit. Do not call her–let the strangers pass! NOBV

Love's Horoscope. Richard Crashaw. Love shall live, although he die! HBV 1-2

Love's Immaturity. E. J. Scovell. ...Oh, life should give/Light till we understand they live, they live. GBL; LiTB

Love's Immortality. Elsa Barker. Enough that we have justified our birth,/Ere entering the inscrutable abode. HBMV

Love's Infiniteness. John Donne. ...so we shall/Be one, and one another's all. LiTL

Love's Insight. Anonymous. No looks proceed/From those fair eyes but to me wonder breed. GTBS

Love's Justification. Buonarroti Michelangelo. That breathes on earth the air of paradise. AWP

Love's Kiss. Helen Hay. And in the grave one may forget–forget. AA

Love's Labour Lost. Robert Tofte. Like hardened rock that force nor power can move. EIL

Love's Labour's Lost. William Shakespeare.
Else none at all in aught proves excellent. PP
For still her cheeks possess the same/Which native she doth owe. CTC
No thought can think, nor tongue of mortal tell. EIL; InvP
That show, contain, and nourish all the world. GBL
Turning mortal for thy love. GTBS; HBV 1-2; ViBoPo
Unpleasing to a married ear. BiP; DiPo; EG; EIL; ExPo; FF; FiP; HAP; HBV; 1-2; HeIP; InPK; InPo; LoBV; NIP; NLV; NOBE; NoP; OAEL 1-2; OBEV; OBSC; PBBP; PoEL 1-5; PoPle; PoRA; PrIm; SeCePo; SeCeV; SoSe; TEP; TreFT; TrGrPo; UnPo; ViBoPo
...what fool is not so wise/To lose an oath to win a paradise? ViBoPo
While greasy Joan doth keel the pot. AWP; BiP; BoNaP; DiPo; EIL; ExPo; FaBoCh; FaBoEn; FF; FiP; GN; GoJo; GTBS; GTBS-P; HAP; HBV 1-2; HeIP; InPK; InPo; LiTB; LoGBV; MCCG; NIP; NOBE; NoP; OAEL 1-2; OBEV; OBSC; PAI; PBBP; PoEL 1-5; PoSC; PrIm; RoGo; SeCePo; SeCeV; SoSe; TEP; TreFS; TrGrPo; UnPo; ViBoPo; WeW; WHA; WiR

Love's Land. Isabella Valancy Crawford. Love's solid land is everywhere! CaP

Love's Language. Donagh MacDonagh. Veil from our eyes that/Time is in flight. NeIP

Love's Last Suit. Thomas Davidson. Proudly give the churl his own,/And forget me when I'm gone! BSV

Love's Likeness. George Darley. And yet will have him woo! OBVV

Love's Limit. Anonymous. Tell her, Good faith, good faith, good faith–not I! EG; TrGrPo

Love's Longing. Anonymous. Lost in day-dreams and vain desires of bliss. UnTE

Love's Lord. Edward Dowden. My spirit must lose itself in Thee,/Crying a name–Life, Light, or Love. HBV 1-2

Love's Lovers. Dante Gabriel Rossetti. Seals with thy mouth his immortality. MaVP

Love's Martyrs. John Ford. Love's Martyrs must be ever, ever dying. NOBE

Love's Matrimony. William Cavendish, Duke of Newcastle. Only they not embrace,/We face to face. SeCePo

Love's Memories Haunt My Footsteps Still. John Clare. Sad disappointment waits for ever NOBV

Love's Mortality. Richard Middleton. And we but fretful shades that dreamed before/That love, and are no more. WHA

Love's night & a lamp. Meleager. witness her lying/–in other arms. BoLoP

Love's Nightingale. Richard Crashaw. There all the year/Love's nightingales shall sit and sing. LoBV

Love's Nobility. Ralph Waldo Emerson. He serves all who dares be true. GoTF; TreF

Love's Offence. Sir John Suckling. And others doth offend when 'tis let loose. CaPo

Love's Old Sweet Song. G. Clifton Bingham. Still to us at twilight comes love's old song,/Comes love's old sweet song. BLSo; FaBoBe; FSN; GoTF; TreF

Love's Own Form Is Sufficient Unto. R. G. Vliet. love made these poems. I don't know why. PoL

Love's Pains. John Clare. I tried to throw away the bud,/But the blossom would remain. NOBV

Love's Philosophy. Percy Bysshe Shelley. What are all these kissings worth,/If thou kiss not me? AtBAP; BLPA; BLPL; BoLoP; EnLi 1-2; FaBoBe; FaBV; GoTF; GTBS; GTBS-P; HBV 1-2; HoPM; LiTL; OAEP; OBRV; OLR; PG; TreFT; TrGrPo; UnTE; ViBoPo

Love's Prayer. James Whitcomb Riley. This vast treasure of content/That is mine to-day! AA

Love's Prerogative. John Oxenham. For this is Love's prerogative–/To give–and give–and give. BLRP

Love's Prisoner. Mariana Griswold Van Rensselaer. Sweet Love has freed my eyes, but they are wet. HBV 1-2

Love's Progress. John Donne. He that doth not, his error is as great/As who by clyster gave the stomach eat. LiTB; ViBoPo

Love's Protestation. Thomas Lodge. Cease to recite thy sacred name. ACP

Love's Pursuit. Robert Browning. While the one eludes, must the other pursue. TreFT

Love's Rebel. Henry Howard, Earl of Surrey. Strive not with Love; for if ye do, it will ye thus befall. OBSC

Love's Remorse. Edwin Muir. "Eternity alone our wrong can right,/That makes all young again in Time's despite." LiTL; OxBTC

Love's Resume. Heinrich Heine. For she herself, my Queen of Love,/Is Rose, and Lily, and Sun, and Dove! TrJP

Love's Resurrection Day. Louisa May Alcott. By a way Love knows. AA; HBV 1-2

Love's Rosary. Alfred Noyes. And–a dream may bring him back to me/About the break of day. HBV 1-2

Love's Rosary. George Edward Woodberry. "Bid me not live," I sigh, "till all be gone." AA

Love's Secret. William Blake. O, was no deny. EnLoPo

Love's Servile Lot. Robert Southwell. For Love is full of showers. ACP

Love's Slavery. John, of Buckingham Sheffield. While I endure her Chains. CEP

Love's Snare. Sir Thomas Wyatt. But ha! ha! ha! full well is me,/For I am now at liberty. LiTL

Love's Spite. Aubrey Thomas De Vere. Men loved: but hope they deemed to be/A sweet Impossibility! HBV 1-2

Love's Stratagems. Donald Justice. Arms cut off at the elbow. NYBP

Love's Stricken "Why." Emily Dickinson. The hugest hearts that break. BoLiVe

Love's Testament. Dante Gabriel Rossetti. Draw up my prisoned spirit to thy soul! MaVP

Love's Torment. Anonymous.
Almost as great as indigestion. UnTE
Shall I be refused your bed? UnTE

Love's Tribute. Lorena W. Sturgeon. A living tribute to that love–/A faithful memory. PGD

Love's Trinity. Alfred Austin. Wide as the realms of air or planet's curving sweep. OBVV

Love's Triumph. Ben Jonson. Who had the power and virtue to remove/Such monsters from the labyrinth of love. EnRePo

Love's Victories. James Shirley. And, when he please, cold rocks inflame. GoBC

Love's Vision. Edward Carpenter. He the Eternal appeared. WGRP

Love's Votary. George Augustus Simcox. Love give me all for all. NOBV

Love's Will. Lewis Warsh. I crave the moments that pass me by. APU

Love's Wisdom. Margaret Deland. And, by my silence, I do prove/ Wisdom and Love! AA

Love's Witchery. Thomas Lodge. Each hour,/That hath bewitched me. ElL

Love's without Reason. Alexander Brome. Something there is moves me to love, and I/Do know I love, but know not how, nor why. OBS

Love's Witness. Aphra Behn. And last, when Words are into Clouds devolv'd. BoWoP

Love's Young Dream. Thomas Moore. Oh! 'twas light that ne'er can shine again/On life's dull stream. HBV 1-2; WBLP

The Love Secret. Anonymous. Deeds shall be done for her none ever did. AWP

Love Serviceable. Coventry Patmore. He does not rightly love himself/Who does not love another more. EnLoPo

Love Should Grow Up Like a Wild Iris in the Fields. Susan Griffin. tender, blinks, and opens/face up to the skies. NPGG

The Love-Sick Frog. Anonymous. Heigh ho! says Anthony Rowley. OxNR

The Love-Sick Lass. Hugh (Christopher Murray Grieve) MacDiarmid. Lies sabbin' noo! BSV

Love Sleeping. Plato. ...bees with their noise invade/His rest, and on his lips their honey made. AWP; FaBoEE

Love Somebody, Yes I Do. Anonymous. Love somebody, but I won't tell who. FSW

Love Somebody, Yes I Do (with music). Anonymous. Love somebody, yes I do,/'Tween sixteen and twenty-two. AS

Love Song. Judah Al-Harizi. Softly will I drop beside thee like/the dew upon Hermon. LiTW; TrJP

Love Song. Samuel ("Paul Vesey") Allen. Still hell is an entrancing place/ Because you're going there. NNP

Love-Song. Anonymous.
   And his sorrow and sighing have pass'd away. AWP
   And I am the wild bird/Tempted by the toothsome trap. TTY
   The dying quarry/Looked at me with my love's eyes. AWP; LiTA
   If I might find again/My hand upon her breast. LiTW
   A kiss for him! AnIL
   Oh my slender boy! BoWoP
   One regardeth her going forth abroad/Even as hers yonder, the Only One. LiTW
   We shall be safe, diddle, diddle,/Out of harm's way. OxNR

Love Song. Hayim Be'er. Rabbi Nachman blesses her with the gift/of good life/until it becomes day. VWA

Love Song. Kosrof Chantikian. to be touched/by you AMV-81

Love Song. Gavin Ewart. in your army of lovers/I am a private soldier. OxBTC

The Love Song. Ivor Gurney. Man may conquer, a girl surrender her sweet EnLoPo

Love Song. Judah Halevi.
   Laying his caressing hand/Underneath my burning head. TrJP
   Marvellous is Thy love! TrJP

A Love Song. W. F. Hawley. Will give old Time his silken wings. OBCV

A Love Song. Else Lasker-Schüler.
   In the high reeds behind this world. BoWoP
   Only our shoulders still like butterflies/are playing. TrJP

Love Song. Luis Ponce de Leon. O lady, slumbering be thine/alone where the cold couch is dressed? TrJP

Love Song. Joseph Gordon ("Adam Drinan") MacLeod. The false sea likes to be visited. NeBP

Love Song. Dorothy Parker. And I wish somebody'd shoot him. InMe

A Love Song. Raymond Richard Patterson. Do I love you? BOLo

Love Song. Flavien Ranaivo. For dreams are your life/In the night/And my hope in the day. PBA

Love Song. Margot Ruddock. I will give/It back to Thee. OBMV

Love Song. Anne Sexton. that field of ponies. NCSH

A Love-Song. Hales Thomas of. There where he sits in Heaven's high/ sphere. MeEV

A Love-Song. Walter James Turner. I do but pass that Image on/For new eyes to discover. OBMV

A Love Song. Royall Tyler. ...love is like a dizziness,/Wont let a poor man go about his business. TAP

Love Song. Reed Whittemore. You still-or so thou tellest me?-mean? AmFN

Love Song. William Carlos Williams. a burst of fragrance/from black branches. MoAB; MoAmPo

Love Song. Elinor Wylie. And I shall love you, keeping/His word, and no more weeping. BLPL

Love Song. Bob Zmuda. one must die for love. AMV-81

A Love-Song by a Lunatic. Anonymous. As flies run up the window-pane,/ So fly my thoughts, dear love, to thee! NA

Love Song for a Tyrant. Marion Brimm Rewey. with songs that must shatter/on stone. AMV-81

Love Song for the Future. Vassar Miller. Wolf and lamb lie down together. NCSH

Love Song from New England. Winifred Welles. My heart is breaking in the snow? HBMV

Love Song: I and Thou. Alan Dugan. a help, a love, a you, a wife. AP; CAPP; FF; HoPM; InPK; NoAm; SoSe

Love Song: "I passed by the house of the young man who loves me." Anonymous. In order to catch another glimpse of my lover... TTY

Love Song: "My boat sails downstream." Anonymous. Placed before the god with the handsome countenance. TTY

Love Song: "My loved one is unique, without a peer." Anonymous. She is such an unrivalled goddess in appearance. TTY

The Love Song of J. Alfred Prufrock. Thomas Stearns Eliot. Till human voices wake us, and we drown. AP; APA; ATP; AWP; BiP; CMoP; CoBMV; DiPo; EBEV; ExPo; FF; ForPo; HAP; HBMV; HeIP; HoPM; InPK; InPo; InPS; LiTB; LiTM; MAPA; MBW 1-2; MoAB; MoAmPo; MoVE; MP; NAWM 1-2; NePA; NIP; NoAm; NOBA; NOBE; NoP; OAEL 1-2; OAEP; OxBTC; PAI; PoA; PoRA; PPP; PrIm; SeCeV; SoSe; SOTW; TAP; TreFT; TrGrPo; TwCP; ViBoPo

The Love Song of J. Alfred Prufrock (parody). J. Walker. Soft fruit also filled him with dread. BXAP

Love-Song of the Water Carriers. Anonymous. For the hearts of these others are double. PeSA

Love Song out of Nothing. Vassar Miller. Who, minus you, am nothing but a nought. NePoEA

Love Song: "The little sycamore." Anonymous. Love, it is love that gives me strength,/Averting the perils of the river. TTY

Love Song to Eohippus. Peter Viereck. Dance on in this museum case. MoAmPo

Love Song to King Shu-Suen. Kubatum. youth, I am in love with you! WPOW

Love Song to Lucy. Helen Ehrlich. A parent-link to all that lies before. SUW

Love Songs. Anonymous.
   and those who see us/will think we are lovers. BoWoP
   I remember/your black mustache. BoWoP
   Let our enemies go blind. BoWoP
   like the helpless nightingale/you locked in a cage. BoWoP
   My husband says not a word and my mind is withering. WTO
   With a handsome lover/you can stand pain. BoWoP

Love-Songs. Moses Ibn Ezra. Like nursing mothers, to their babes/that croon. TrJP

Love Songs. Mina Loy.
   Printed in blood on its wings. AnAmPo
   Prolonging flight into the night/Never reaching. VGW

Love Songs, At Once Tender and Informative. Samuel Hoffenstein.
   And let the deeps behind them be/For sturdier fish the fatal sea? OBAL
   And when your mouth is mine, I miss/The wistfulness of wanting you. OBAL
   Anger will make easy yet/The bitter footfalls of regret. OBAL
   Beneath the moon I know her equals. OBAL
   From which but fools like me would roam! OBAL
   Have fallen on another's sight/And been broken! OBAL
   I should like to know with whom. OBAL
   Introduce me to your friend. OBAL
   My all-if you were ever home! OBAL
   None but a better man shall part/What God has joined together. OBAL
   Oh, the blunder of it! OBAL
   Say she doesn't think at all. OBAL
   That poor Cupid have his vision/Back again? OBAL
   We'll both be friendly and untrue. OBAL
   We may then conclude our love/With a profitable deal. OBAL
   Were I not born to be in Dutch. OBAL
   When we were sure no sword could sever/Two people born to love forever. OBAL
   Who says two sexes aren't enough? OBAL
   The years their disappointments waste/On a memory so chaste. OBAL
   You always see me not at all. OBAL
   You stood with women in a row. OBAL
   Your little mind! NLV; OBAL

Love Songs in Age. Philip Larkin. It had not done so then, and could not now. PPP

A Love Sonnet. George Wither. Since she, alas! hath left me,/Falero, lero, loo! ElL; FaBoPP; GBL; LiTL; OBS; ViBoPo

Love Sonnets. Zora Cross.
   And lack myself, that which yourself supplies. CBAP
   And soul from soul the secret seems to keep. CBAP

Love Sonnets, VIII. Charles Harpur. Chime up like silver-winged dreams in flight. PoAu 1-2

Love Speaks at Last. Edward, Lord Herbert of Cherbury. 'Tis not enough that trees do stand,/If their fruit fall and perish too. AnAnS 2

A Love Story. Robert Graves. Paid homage to them of unevent. AtBAP; CMoP; FaBoTw; LiTB; MoVE

The Love Suicides at Sonezaki (excerpt). Chikamatsu Monzaemon. They thus become a model of true love. DL

Love, Sweet Love. Felix McGlennon. That is love, that is love! PaPo

A Love Symphony. Arthur William Edgar O'Shaughnessy. Longer I could not stay, and so/I fled back to your feet. HBV 1-2

The Love-Talker. Ethna (Anna Johnston MacManus) Carbery. Pray for the soul of Maire Og at dawning of the day! AnIV; OnYI; OxBI

Love, that dwarfs our life. Akahito (Yamabe no Akahito). even though you cover it/with careful wrappings. LiTW

Love That Is First and Last. Algernon Charles Swinburne. Gleams like a glorious emerald Guenevere's. LiTL

Love That's Pure, Itself Disdaining. Johann A. Gruber. And your heart and house would be/From within swept clean and free. AH

Love the Beautiful. Moses Mendelssohn. Wish for the good,/And the best do. GoTF; TreFT

Love, the Delight of All Well-Thinking Minds. Fulke, Lord Brooke Greville. To set all women light, but only she. GBL

Love, the Light-Giver. Buonarroti Michelangelo. Alone; for lo! our eyes see nought in heaven/Save what the living sun illumineth. AWP; LiTW

Love the Ruins. Malka Tussman. Then gather up the splinters,/and love the ruins,/my God. VWA

Love the Wild Swan. Robinson Jeffers. Hear the music, the thunder of the wings. Love the wild swan. AnFE; HeIP; MoAB; MoAmPo; PAI; TW

LOVE TIGHT. Ted Joans. LIONS IN LOVE/FOREVER CNA

Love, Time and Death. Frederick Locker-Lampson. Ah me, for Love—will Death my Love restore? HBV 1-2

Love to Faults Is Always Blind. William Blake. And forges fetters for the mind. ViBoPo

Love to My Lord. Louisa Van Plettenhaus. Long, louder, sweeter, fuller still–/Love to my Lord! BePJ

The Love Token. Anonymous. Saying, "If I had staid there seven years longer,/No girl but you could have married me." BaBo

Love Triumphant. Frederic Lawrence Knowles. Dear, how long ago we knew! GoTF; HBV 1-2; TreFT

Love U.S.A. Kathleen Spivack. like in the/poems/let's/pretend. BoWoP

Love Unchangeable. Rufus Dawes. Nor ask for more above. AA

Love Undeclared. Anonymous. Then shall I chaunge for no newe. OxBM

The Love Unfeigned. Geoffrey Chaucer. And sin he best to love is, and most meke,/What nedeth feyned loves for to seke? NOBE; OBEV

Love Unknown. Samuel Crossman. I all my days/Could gladly spend. BoC

Love Unknown. George Herbert. Who fain would have to be new, tender, quick. JCP; Prf

Love Unlike Love. Anonymous. And love in love shall make it fine. MeEL

Love Unsought. Emma Catharine Embury Thy pathway like a distant star. AA

Love Vagabonding. William, of Hawthornden Drummond. Tell her he nightly lodgeth in my heart. EG

Love Was Once Light as Air. Cecil Day Lewis. Shadows my noontime still/And haunts my night. OAEP

Love Wears Roses' Elegance. Sister Bertken. What mind can follow, proving? LLLT

Love What It Is. Robert Herrick. In the same sweet eternity of love. AnAnS 2; FaBoEE; GBL

Love Which Frees. Gloria Fuertes. now I'm the sweet child/and no longer the bitter woman. WPOW

Love Which Is Here a Care. William, of Hawthornden Drummond. Eternal joy which nothing can molest. OxBoCh

Love Who Will, for I'll Love None. William Browne. In love with all, yet lov'd of none. CavP; HBV 1-2

Love, Whose Month Was Ever May. Ulrich von Liechtenstein [(or Lichten Stein)]. Love inconstant I forbear. AWP

Love Will Find Out the Way. Anonymous. Love will find out the way. CBEP; FaBoCh; GBL; GN; HBV 1-2; LiTL; LoGBV; OBEV; TreFS; WiR

Love without Hope. Robert Graves. Singing about her head, as she rode by. BoLoP; ELU; FaBoEE; GBL; GTBS-P; OAEL 1-2; OxBI

Love without Longing. Anonymous. Quan the mayden hayt that sche lovit,/sche is without longyng. OxBoLi

Love without Love. Luis Llorens Torres. the dog of my heart will not bark. InW

Love You Alone Have Been with Us. Jalal ed-Din or al-Din Rumi. you give light to those on earth/beauty and splendor of the age LLLT

Love, You've Been a Villain. James Robinson Planché. Cenotaph'd, and paragraph'd,/And reckon'd quite a bore. NOBL

Love Your Enemy. Yusef Iman. But when will we love ourselves? BPo; TTY

Lovebirds. William Jay Smith. And the pure sunlight is all from heaven. ErPo

Loved of My Soul. Israel Najara. And have compassion as in days/gone by. TrJP

The Loved One. Joseph Hansen. Soap-scented hands, another birthday card. NYBP

Loveliest of Counties, Shropshire Now (parody). Ian Sainsbury. Shropshire may soon be known as the Deserted County. BXAP

Loveliest of Trees. Alfred Edward Housman. To see the cherry hung with snow. AWP; BiP; BLPL; BoLiVe; BoNaP; CMoP; CoBMV; DiPo; ELP; FaBoBe; FaBV; FaFP; FF; GoTF; GTBS; HAP; HeIP; InPK; InPo; InPS; LiTB; LiTM; MasP; MoAB; MoBrPo; NAs; NoAm; NoP; OAEL 1-2; OHIP; OxBTC; PoLf; PrIm; SoSe; TEP; TreFT; TrGrPo; ViBoPo; VLP

Loveliest of What I Leave behind Is the Sunlight. Praxilla. but also cucumbers that are ripe, and pears, and apples. WPOW

Lovelight. Georgia Douglas Johnson. And love the light between. AmNP

Loveliness. Hilda Conkling. Comes alive when I remember. TiPo

The Loveliness of Love. George Darley. Hers could not stay, for sympathy. EG; GTBS-P

Lovelocks. Walter De la Mare. Yet still she twisted, sleeked and tossed/Her beauteous hair about. MoVE

The Lovely Delightful Song of Thy Sister. Anonymous. I have found that Amon is given to me thereby/For ever and ever. LiTW

The Lovely Etan. Anonymous. But I know the lovely Etan/will not be sleeping alone. NOBI

Lovely Girls with Flounder on a Starry Night. Anselm Parlatore. like those girls. SUW

The Lovely Lass o' Inverness. Robert Burns. For mony a heart thou has made sair,/That ne'er did wrang to thine or thee! GoTS

A Lovely Lass to a Friar Came. John Wilmot, Earl of Rochester. I must own, Sir, but I blush indeed with Shame,/Your Pennance is prevailing. CoMu

A Lovely Love. Gwendolyn Brooks. Definitionless in this strict atmosphere. BPo

Lovely Mary Donnelly. William Allingham. But blessings be about you, dear, wherever you may go. AnIV; HBV 1-2; IrPN

The Lovely Rivers and Lakes of Maine. George B. Wallis. The Cosbosecontic and Millenkikuk! BLPA

A Lovely Rose Is Sprung. Anonymous. A little child she bore us/E'en in the deepest night. AWP

The Lovely Shall Be Choosers. Robert Frost. "Trust us," the Voices said. AmP; CoBMV; MoAB; MoAmPo; NOBA; OxBA

Lovely Tear of Lovely Eye. Anonymous. The devel is shent,/Crist, through the might of thee. OxBM

The Lovely Village Fair; or, I Dont Mean to Tell You Her Age. Anonymous. And that day I will tell you her name. CoMu

A Lovely Young Moor. Anonymous. and went toward the door,/which I opened all the way. BoWoP

The Lovely Youth. Aneirin. Sooner to be food for ravens than to the funeral rites. LiTW

Lovelye William. Anonymous. And the grave is the first place I expect to find rest. AmFP

The Lovemaker. Robert Mezey. As left you in that place,/Restless, unsatisfied. CABA; NePoEA-2

Lovemusic. Carolyn Kizer. Remembered cinnamon and lime/Will fructify a bleaker time. ErPo

The Lover. Robert Duncan. ...Now I am mistaken, often,/seeing his wraith in faces passing. PeHV

The Lover. Richard Henry Stoddard. Becomes the night of snow! AA

The Lover: A Ballad. Mary Wortley, Lady Montagu. We harden like trees, and like rivers grow cold. CEP; NoP; OBEC

The Lover Abused Renounceth Love. George Turberville. Such as do make a man but smart/For bearing them a faithful heart. EIL

The Lover Accusing Hys Love for Her Unfaithfulnesse... Anonymous. Therwith to trayn the Grekish host/From Troyes return where they wer lost. EnPo

The Lover and Birds. William Allingham. Most comforting and gentle thoughts I had. OBVV

Lover and Echo. Carroll O'Daly. Farewell and adieu./Echo: Adieu! OnYI

The Lover and the Beloved. Ramon Lull. "To my Beloved." CAW

The Lover and the Nightingale. Anonymous. A new, new love it is wherewith I die! UnTE

The Lover and the Syringa Bush. Herman Melville. While here by Eden's gate I linger/Love's tryst to keep, with truant Eve. OBAL

The Lover Beseecheth His Mistress Not to Forget... Sir Thomas Wyatt. Whose steadfast faith yet never mov'd:/Forget not this! ViBoPo

The Lover Compareth Himself to the Painful Falconer. Anonymous. "Wo ho ho!' I crie; "I come," then saie,/Make me as glad as hee! EnPo; PBBP

The Lover Compareth His State to a Ship in Perilous Storm...   Petrarch (Francesco Petrarca).   And I remain despairing of the port.   EIL; EnPo; GBL; HeIP; PoEL 1-5

The Lover Complaineth the Unkindness of His Love.   Sir Thomas Wyatt.   My lute, be still, for I have done.   AtBAP; EIL; EnPo; FaBoEn; GBL; OAEP; PoEL 1-5; TrGrPo; ViBoPo

The Lover Consults with Reason.   Thomas Carew.   The wheel of Fortune, not the sphere of Love.   TrGrPo

The Lover Disceived by His Love Repenteth Him of the True Love ...   Anonymous.   And not to flete from feare to feare,/Such anker hold I have.   EnPo

The Lover Exhorteth His Lady to Be Constant.   Anonymous.   So shall you not be shent/But worthily praised,/As you have deserved.   OBSC

The Lover Exhorteth His Lady to Take Time, While Time Is.   George Turberville.   Which if you pluck not from the stalk, will fall within/this hour.   EnRePo

The Lover Freed from the Gallows.   Anonymous.   And now to show that I am true to my lover,/I'll wed my darling at the blooming spring.   BFSS

The Lover, Having Dreamed of Enjoying His Love....   Sir Thomas Wyatt.   Such mocks of dreams do turn to deadly pain.   AAS; CoBE; WHA

The Lover in Liberty Smileth at Them in Thraldom.   Anonymous.   Lo, such is hap! Mark well my song!   EIL

The Lover is Near.   Johann Wolfgang von Goethe.   The sun is set, I wait the rise of starlight,/Starlight and–you!   LiTW

A Lover Left Alone.   Anonymous.   It were in vain/To say again/Fortune's will.   MeEL

The Lover Mourns for the Loss of Love.   William Butler Yeats.   She has gone weeping away.   WeW

A Lover of Peace.....   Samuel Gorton.   Youle find that all compulsion, is nought but that Nim-rod.   SCAP

Lover of the Lord.   Anonymous.   Or you can't go to heaven when you die.   AmFP

The Lover Proved False.   Anonymous.   Excepting he was up on yonder gallows tree/And my faith could bring him down.   AmFP

The Lover Rejoiceth the Enjoying of His Love.   Sir Thomas Wyatt.   Of my soveraigne I have redresse,/And I content me with my hire.   FaBoEn

The Lover Remembereth Such as He Sometimes Enjoyed...   Leon Stokesbury.   Luck is something I do not understand.   SM

A Lover's Anger.   Matthew Prior.   And forgot every word I designed to have said.   ErPo; UnTE

The Lover's Appeal.   Sir Thomas Wyatt.   Say nay! say nay!   GTBS; GTBS-P

The Lover's Arithmetic.   Anonymous.   Heigho, dot and go one,/Fal lal de ral de ra, &c.   OxBoLi

The Lover's Choice.   Thomas Bedingfield.   She shines intrinsically fair.   HBV 1-2

A Lover's Complaint.   William Shakespeare.   And new pervert a reconciled Maide.   NCEP

A Lover's Confession.   Charles, duc d' Orleans.   I stale a coss of gret sweetnesse.   NOBE; OxBM

A Lover's Curse.   Meleager.   Let him fall asleep,/Locked in her arms, a second Endymion!   LiTW

A Lover's Envy.   Henry Van Dyke.   I only ask to give to her/All that her heart desires.   HBV 1-2

The Lover's Farewell.   James Clarence Mangan.   Warden, wilt thou softly close the gate/When thou knowest I leave my heart behind?   IrPN

The Lover's Gifts.   Anonymous.   When the wool is on the sheep's back, there is no thread.   OxNR

The Lover's Invitation.   John Clare.   And I'll ever after love thee.   VLP

A Lover's Lament.   Anonymous.
My true love's in her grave and I wish I was there.   AmFP
Oh, my little breath, now I go there alone in sorrow.   AWP

The Lover's Lament (A vers. with music).   Anonymous.   And so must you and I.   AS

The Lover's Lament for Her Sailor.   Anonymous.   For the blue waves to roll over her pretty blue eyes.   AmFP

Lover's Lane.   Paul Laurence Dunbar.   'Dout a lovah's lane.   BANP

The Lover's Leap. A Tale.   Andrew Macdonald.   Miss Lucy to Ringwood, the very next day,/Was given in a matrimonial way.   NOEC

A Lover's Lullaby.   George Gascoigne.   And when you rise with waking eye,/Remember then this lullaby.   HBV 1-2; OBEV

Lover's Meeting.   Ray Mathew.   because there is nothing to be said.   CBAP

A Lover's New Year's Gift.   John Lydgate.   And conferme fully up my choise ay from yere to/yere.   PoEL 1-5

A Lover's Plea.   Thomas Campion.   Do not mock me in thy bed,/While these cold nights freeze me dead.   NOBE

The Lover's Posy.   Rufinus Domesticus.   So must you too, haughty maid.   AWP

The Lover's Prayer.   Anonymous.   Do not let me wait in vain.   WTO

Lover's Reply to Good Advice.   Richard Hughes.   It bears all away.   MoBrPo

The Lover's Resolution.   George Wither.   For if she be not for me,/What care I for whom she be?   AWP; BoLoP; GoTF; HBV 1-2; InMe; LiTL; NOBE; OBEV; PG; TreFS

The Lover's Song.   Alfred Austin.   Who calls his love his own?   OBVV

The Lover's Song.   Edward Rowland Sill.   If there is hope for me at all,/She must be blind like thee.   AA; HBV 1-2

The Lover's Tasks.   Anonymous.   And you shall be a true lover of mine.   OxNR

A Lover's Words.   Vernon Watkins.   Twined, hidden from sight/With blind-moles under the hill.   DTC

The Lover Sendeth Sighs to Move His Suit.   Sir Thomas Wyatt.   With pitiful complaint and scalding fire,/That from my breast deceivably doth start.   LiTL

The Lover Sheweth How He Is Forsaken of Such as He Sometime Enjoyed.   Sir Thomas Wyatt.   How like you this, what hath she now deserved?   AAS; AtBAP; EIL; ELP; EnPo; FaBoEn; GBL; HoPM; InPS; OAEP; PAI; PoEL 1-5; PoRA; TrGrPo; ViBoPo

The Lover Tells of the Rose in His Heart.   William Butler Yeats.   For my dreams of your image that blossoms a rose in the deeps of my/heart.   CMoP; ViBoPo

Lover That I Hope You Are.   Milton Acorn.   and lost, lives for the next total throw.   NeAC

The Lover Thinks of His Lady in the North.   Shaemas O'Sheel.   Ah, so my love and longing must be known, Dear Heart, to/you!   HBV 1-2

The Lover to Himself.   David Phillips.   on your shadow, the one/that kisses back   NeAC

The Lover to His Lady.   George Turberville.   Would I were heaven! I would behold/Thee then with all mine eyes.   CTC; FaBoEE; FF; OBSC

Lover to Lover.   David Morton.   I shall have need of them, when you are gone.   HBMV

The Lover to the Thames of London.   George Turberville.   Have power for aye in wonted gult to glide.   EIL; NoP; OBSC

A Lover, upon an Accident Necessitating His Departure....   Thomas Carew.   For my just hand may sometime move/The wheel of Fortune, not the sphere of Love.   CaPo

The Lovers.   Conrad Aiken.   punctually, at a certain hour, on a certain date.   AP; NYBP

The Lovers.   George Gordon, Lord Byron.   Their hearts the flowers from whence the honey sprung.   LiTL

The Lovers.   Phoebe Cary.   And she answered, "I promised to cleave, and I've cleft."   HBV 1-2

The Lovers.   Alex Comfort.   like water falling under the night's drum.   NeBP; PoA

Lovers.   Mary Elizabeth ("E") Fullerton.   The one integrity/Of soul is to be lone,/Inviolate, and free.   BoAV; PoAu 1-2

The Lovers.   Joan Murray.   For them/there is no/embarrassment.   LTB

The Lovers.   W. R. Rodgers.   Poured up one outward and widening wave/Of eager and extravagant anger.   BIrV; OBSP

The Lovers.   William Jay Smith.   They stare, a sheet loose-folded round their knees,/Off into space, as from Etruscan tombs.   MoAmPo

The Lovers.   Marya Zaturenska.   What the eye loses, let the heart recover.   MoAmPo

Lovers, and a Reflection.   Charles Stuart Calverley.   How much fewer volumes of verse there'd be!   FaBoCo; FaBoPa; NA; SpRo; VLP

Lovers Conceits Are Like a Flattring Glasse.   Anonymous.   But now I finde the glasse abused me.   OBS

The Lovers' Death.   Charles Baudelaire.   ...re-light/the tarnished mirrors and the flames blown to the night.   SyP

Lovers' Debouchment (parody).   William Zaranka.   Drowns us in drouth, nor no man ever loved.   BXAP

The Lovers Go Fly a Kite.   W. D. Snodgrass.   On an invisible staff/To run up an allegiance!   NYBP

Lovers How They Come and Part.   Robert Herrick.   Where e're they met, or parting place has been.   AtBAP; GBL; OBSP; OxBoLi; PoEL 1-5

Lovers in Winter.   Robert Graves.   And still with branches green/Ride our ill weather out.   FaBoEE; NYBP

The Lovers Melancholy.   John Ford.
So to conclude calamity in rest.   PoEL 1-5
...there's no mirth/Which is not truly season'd with some madness. PoEL 1-5

The Lovers of Marchaid.   Marjorie Pickthall.   All above the wind-washed graves where dead seamen lie.   HBV 1-2

The Lovers of the Poor.   Gwendolyn Brooks.   Try to avoid inhaling the laden air.   BiP; CAPP; NoAm; NOBA

Lovers Relentlessly.   Stanley Jasspon Kunitz.   The secret lords, whom only death can change.   UnTE

Loves End.   Edward, Lord Herbert of Cherbury.   It be a Temple, but without a Saint.   AnAnS 2; SeCP

Loves Heretick.   Thomas Stanley.   Every beauty takes my minde,/Tied to all, to none confin'd.   CavP

The Loves of the Birds.   Anonymous.   'Tis clear the peacock is a fool.   WTO

The Loves of the Plants. Erasmus Darwin. And drink the floods of odour and of song. PeD

Loves of the Puppets. Richard Wilbur. And made the birds explode for miles around. CoPo; OxBC

The Loves of the Triangles (excerpt). John Hookham Frere. And wanton OPTICS roll the melting eye! FaBoNo

Loves She Like Me? Samuel Woodworth. Loves she like me? AA

The Loves Who Many Years Held All My Mind. Walter Savage Landor. Not one, the latest of the flight, is seen. GBL

Loves World. Sir John Suckling. It may fall out some honest Lover/The rest hereafter will discover. SeCV 1-2

Lovesick. Anonymous. And lie beside you all the night. UnTE

The Lovesick Cowboy. Anonymous. I ask God to help you and bid you farewell. CoSo

The Lovesleep. Gavin Ewart. no one can sleep in the arms of an enemy, however charming. OxBC

Lovesong. Rainer Maria Rilke. O sweet song. OLR

Lovest Thou Me? William Cowper. Oh for grace to love thee more! HBV 1-2; OBEC; TrPWD

Lovewell's Fight. Anonymous.
They safe arriv'd at Dunstable, thirteenth/day of May. BaBo; HBV 1-2; PAH
When Lovewell brave 'gainst Paugus went,/With fifty men from Dunstable. PAH

Loving. Shirley Kaufman. when I wake before dawn/the room is already light VWA

Loving. Jane Stembridge. I wish we could do it all again,/with clown hats on. NMM

Loving and Beloved. Sir John Suckling. Love's triumph must be Honour's funeral. CaPo; OBS

Loving and Liking. Dorothy Wordsworth. But like it, enjoy it, and thankfully eat. OxBChV

The Loving Ballad of Lord Bateman. Charles Dickens. Now that Sophia has crossed the sea. BeLS; BLPA; CoBE

Loving Henry. Anonymous. So I'll fly to the tops of some tall tree/And there I'll sit and sing. BaBo

Loving She Stood Apart. Patrick Lane. and I was blind to/her but O the night NeAC

Loving the Rituals That Keep Men Close. Palladas. signs for the distant and disconsolate heart. OBVE

Low-Anchored Cloud. Henry David Thoreau. Bear only perfumes and the scent/Of healing herbs to just men's fields! ImOP; NoP; ViBoPo

The Low-Backed Car. Samuel Lover. Though it beat in a low-backed car! HBV 1-2

Low Barometer. Robert Bridges. ...and thrust/The baleful phantoms underground. CMoP; CoBMV; ForPo; LiTB; NoAm; NOCV; QFR

Low Church. Stanley J. Sharpless. But the choir-boy is happy and gay. NLV

Low Doun in the Broom. Anonymous. For he's low doun, he's in the broom,/That's waitin' on me. BSV; GoTS

Low down Chariot. Anonymous. Oh, low down the chariot, let-n me ride. OuSiCo

The Low-Down, Lonesome Low. Anonymous. And he drowned in the low-down, lonesome low. OuSiCo

Low Fields and Light. William Stanley Merwin. Neither what is nor what was, but the flat light rising. ConAP; LCAP

A Low Prayer, a High Prayer. Anonymous. Arrange them Thyself, O Thou King of Grace. WTO

The Low Road. Marge Piercy. and know who you mean, and each/day you mean one more. LTB

Low Tide. Lynette Roberts. Each beating hour/Rings false. NeBP

Low Tide. Warren Woessner. Lakes faintly shine through/like white stones/or fish. WOLT

Low Tide on Grand-Pre. Bliss Carman. In grief the flood is bursting home! CaP; NOBC; OBCV; PeCV

A Low Trick. Gelett Burgess. It was a horrid thing to do! OBCA

Lowdown Dirty Blues. Anonymous. I been doin' all I can, honey,/Just tryin' to get along with you. AmFP

Lowdown Rounder's Blues. Peg Leg Howell. I feel so disgusted/I've got them lowdown rounder blues BluL

Lower Court. Carolyn Baxter. recite her life back, (in the) same order. LFAC

The Lower Criticism. John Hollander. Nothing much happens and/Nobody screws. DBV; PV

Lower Forms of Life. Mary Winter. Who wear our bones inside. GoYe

Lower the Standard: That's My Motto. Karl Shapiro. ...As the lad said: We must/love one another or die. NoAm

Lowery Cot. Leonard Alfred George Strong. Be overstrong for mortal clay. MoBrPo

The Lowest Place. Christina Georgina Rossetti. Where I may sit and see/My God and love Thee so. EnLi 1-2; NOBV; TrPWD

The Lowest Trees Have Tops. Sir Edward Dyer. They hear and see, and sigh; and then they break. AtBAP; CBEP; EG; EiL; FaBoEn; HAP; InPo; OBSP; PoEL 1-5; PoRA; WeW

Lowlands. Anonymous.
Lowlands, lowlands, away, my John. TrAS
My Lowlands a-ray. AmSS; FSW; GBP; OxBoLi

The Lowlands o' Holland. Anonymous. And he's drowned in the sea. AmSS; CH

The Lowlands of Holland. Anonymous. Since cruel seas and angry winds parted my love and me. AmFP

Lowly Bethlehem. Nicolaus Zinzendorf. Thence came Jesus to release us,/Favored Bethlehem. TrAS

The Lowly Peasant. Anonymous. You will see your woman with another, and your children at/my table! PBWP

Lowriders #2. Reyes Cardenas. everything/makes/its music FIA

Lowshot Light. William Barnes. An' plough, in my sweet fancy, now do sheen. VLP

The Lowveld. Charles Eglington. And understand the cruel and lucid tongue/Directing the migration of the herds. PeSA

Loyal. William Matthews. ...fiction/that there is work to be done,/and almost inconsolably. MAYP

Loyal Effusion. Horatio and James Smith. And, oh! in Downing Street should revel Old Nick revel,/England's prime minister, then bless the devil! OBRV

The Loyal General: Prologue. John Dryden. And Act your selves the Farce of your own Age. SeCV 1-2

The Loyal Scot (excerpt). Andrew Marvell. ...in a Baron Bishop you have both/Leviathan served up and Behemoth. ViBoPo

Loyal Sins. Jacob Glatstein. You're my fate./My blessing. VWA

Loyalty. Berton Braley. Because—well, because he's my friend. BLPA

Loyalty. Allan Cunningham. Hame, hame, hame, to my ain countrie! GN

Loyalty. William Henry Davies. Can sing without his robe or glass. BrPo

Loyalty Confin'd. Sir Roger L'Estrange. My King can only captivate my mind. OBS

Luath. Robert Burns. Hung owre his hurdies wi' a swirl. GDP

Lubber Breeze. Thomas Sturge Moore. Laughs in his sleeve. CH

Lubly Fan. Cool White. Den lubly Fan will you cum out tonight,/An' dance by de lite ob de moon. TrAS

Lucasia, Rosania and Orinda Parting at a Fountain, July 1663. Katherine ("Orinda") Philips. So let our hopes to meet allay,/The fears and Sorrows of this day. PeHV

Lucasta Laughing. Richard Lovelace. For the unjustest act/Is still the pleasant'st jest. PoEL 1-5

Lucasta's Fan, with a Looking-Glass in It. Richard Lovelace. ...vows herself accursed/If hence she dress herself but in his eyes. CaPo

Lucasta's World. Richard Lovelace. Thus Earth from flames and Ice repreev'd,/E're since hath in her Sun-shine liv'd. CaPo; SeCP

Luchow's and After. L. E. Sissman. ...the lethal weapon of/The gift of things and not the gift of love. NYP

The Luciad. Luís de Camoens. So toyl the Nymphs, to snatch and to defend/The men of Lusus from a dismal end. OBVE

Lucifer. Maxwell Anderson. And my son Prometheus shall rise against me/Armored, bearing my name. MoRP

The Lucifer. Guy Glover. He had many true-loves–but never one. CaP

Lucifer. D. H. Lawrence. coming like the ruby in the invisible dark,/glowing with his own annunciation, towards us. OAEP

Lucifer in Starlight. George Meredith. The army of unalterable law. AnEnPo; AWP; BoLiVe; CBEP; ExPo; FF; ForPo; GoTF; HAP; HBV 1-2; InPo; LiTB; LoBV; NOBE; NOBV; NoP; OAEL 1-2; OAEP; OBEV; OBNC; OBVV; PoEL 1-5; PPoe; SeCeV; TreFT; TrGrPo; UnPo; ViBoPo; VLP; WeW

Lucifer in the Train. Adrienne Rich. After our weary transit, find us rest. EaLu; NePoEA-2

Lucina Schynning in Silence of the Night... Eilean Ni Chuilleanain. Again the chirp of the stream running. CIP

Lucinda Matlock. Edgar Lee Masters. It takes life to love Life. CMoP; FaBV; FF; HAP; LaNeLa; LiTA; LiTL; LiTM; MCCG; MoAmPo; MoVE; NoAm; NOBA; OxBA

Luck. Elaine Epstein. it is what we mistake for love. AMV-81

Luck. Wilfred Wilson Gibson. Well, still I've got my old jack-knife. EtS; MoShBr; OBMV

Luck. Langston Hughes. To others/Only heaven. MoLP

Luck. Evan V. Shute. Each in an empty frame! CaP

The Luck of Edenhall. Henry Wadsworth Longfellow. One day like the Luck of Edenhall! AWP; StPo

Luckes, my fair falcon, and your fellows all. Sir Thomas Wyatt. Ye be my friends, and so be but few else. AAS; FCP

"Luckies". Reginald Gibbons. The years are smoke. MAYP

Lucky. Cathy Song. it was his first alphabet. BrSi

The Lucky Chance: Song. Aphra Behn. Cheerer of age, youth's kind unrest,/And half the heaven of the blest. WPOW

The Lucky Coin. Austin Clarke. How shall we praise the men that freed us/From everything but thought. NeIP

Lucky Lion! *Anonymous.* How blessed it is,/Lion. WTO

The Lucky Marriage. Thomas Blackburn. Who have no wedding ring or mutual bed? GTBS-P

The Lucky Sailor. *Anonymous.* Let's not forget now we're come home/Each bold sailor's pretty lass. OBSS

Lucretius. Alfred, Lord Tennyson. Thy duty? What is duty? Fare thee well!' OAEL 1-2; VLP

Lucretius Versus the Lake Poets. Robert Frost. God bless the Dean and make his deanship plenary. GLGT

Lucy. Walter De la Mare. I would that all remembrances/As gently pierced my breast! CMoP; EnRP; NOBE; OBEV; TrGrPo

Lucy. William Wordsworth.
But she is in her grave, and O,/The difference to me! BLPA; FaBV; FPL; GoTF; LoBV; MaC; OBEV; TreF; TrGrPo
...the last green field/That Lucy's eyes surveyed. OBEV; TrGrPo
The memory of what has been,/And never more will be. GN; OBEV; TrGrPo
Roll'd round in earth's diurnal course,/With rocks, and stones, and trees. AnFE; HBV 1-2; LiTL; OBEV; TrGrPo

Lucy and Kitty. *Anonymous.* Only ribbon round it. OxNR; TiPo

Lucy Answers. Helen Ehrlich. So tides will turn and sweep him, too, away. SUW

Lucy Gray. William Wordsworth. And sings a solitary song/That whistles in the wind. BeLS; EnRP; ERoP 1-2; FiP; GTBS; HBV 1-2; MBW 1-2; OAEL 1-2; OAEP; OBRV; OxBChV; SeCeV; TEP; TreFS

Lucy Lake. Ogden Nash. And let's lynch Lucy! ShM

Lucy Lake (parody). Newton Mackintosh. Few people knew she died, but oh,/The difference to her! BXAP; HBV 1-2; SpRo

Lucy Lavender. Ivy O. Eastwick. For–"I can't stay quiet,"/Little Lucy said. BiCB; SiSoSe

Lucy Locket and Kitty Fisher. *Anonymous.* But the devil a penny was there in it/Except the binding round it. OxBoLi

Lucy McLockett. Phyllis McGinley. And the lady/Who taught kindergarten. BiCB

Lucy Taking Birth. Diana Scott. Lucy has survived this night/And has one created days hard grace BrRo

The Ludlow Massacre. Woody Guthrie. And then I hung my head and cried. FSW

Ludwig's Death Mask. Ted Hughes. In union with the communion of angels. NoAm

The Lugubrious Whing-Whang. James Whitcomb Riley. Tickle me, love, in these lonesome ribs. NA; YaD

Luis de Camoes. Roy Campbell. And taught his gorgon destinies to sing. FaBoTw; PeSA

Luke 11: "Blessed be the paps which Thou hast sucked'. Richard Crashaw. The mother then must suck the Son. JCP

Luke Havergal. Edwin Arlington Robinson. There is the westrn gate, Luke Havergal–/Luke Havergal. MAmP

Lula Vires. *Anonymous.* And he never returned to stand trial/For the awful deed that he had done. AmFP

The Lull. Molly Peacock. ...Life's cache/is flesh, flesh, and flesh. MAYP

Lulla La, Lulla Lulla Lullaby. William Byrd. O joy, and joyful happy day, when wretches want their will. SBVL

Lullaby. Léonie Adams. Here is the pillow./Rest. AmLP; MoAB; MoAmPo

Lullaby. *Anonymous.*
And the dark blue waves rolling over me. AmFP
If thou'lt sleep as I bid thee, my own/little boy. TrJP
So on mine, my baby, thou./Puva...puva...puva. SUS

Lullaby. William Barnes. Lullaby, Lilibrow. Lie asleep;/Blest be thy rest. VLP

Lullaby. Elinor Chipp. Rest, little baby, rest! HBMV

Lullaby. Elizabeth Jane Coatsworth. Sleep, mouseling, sleep. SiSoSe

Lullaby. Paul Laurence Dunbar. Po' little lamb. GoSl

Lullaby. Frederick Eckman. ...Would you go to sleep, go to sleep? FAZ

Lullaby. Kenneth Fearing. the bars of the Tombs. CMoP

Lullaby. Max Harris. The thorn and the storm your eyes have shed/and they are in me and you are dead. BoAV

Lullaby. Robert Hillyer. No one, not even you. DuDa; LOW

Lullaby. Samuel Hoffenstein. So, be wise, my lamb, and sleep. TrJP

Lullaby. Josiah Gilbert Holland. Into the lily world gone. AA; HBV 1-2

A Lullaby. Randall Jarrell. And his dull torment mottles like a fly's/The lying amber of the histories. HaCAP; OxBC

A Lullaby. Janet Lewis. She could not love Him more,/But loved Him just the same./Lullee, lullee, lullay. NOCV

The Lullaby. Félix Lope de Vega Carpio. Bend down the branches yonder/To shield my Darling's rest. CAW

Lullaby. Seumas MacManus. Leanbhain O, Leanbhain O! AnIV

Lullaby. Dom Moraes. You will not hear it. Sleep, my darling. NePoEA-2

Lullaby. Carolina Oliphant, Lady Nairne. And O may its wakening be blither than mine! HBV 1-2

Lullaby. Nohomaiterangi. Take them, lest they disappear. WTO

Lullaby. Seumas (James Starkey) O'Sullivan. In the heart of a country of gold. OnYI

Lullaby. Sue Owen. And a few of the nails. AMV-80

Lullaby. John Phillip. Thy nurse will tend thee, as duly as may be. EIL

Lullaby. Quandra Prettyman. sleep, love, sleep. BOLo

Lullaby. Christina Georgina Rossetti. Sing it high, sing it low,/Love me–I love you. PoPle

Lullaby. Anne Sexton. while the goat calls hush-/a-bye. NoAm

Lullaby. Edith Sitwell. And with the Ape thou art alone–/Do,/Do. AtBAP; ChMP; CMoP; LiTM; SBVL; WaP

Lullaby. Gilles Vigneault. And the snow is deep/sleep... WHW

Lullaby. Shlomo Vinner. The pining body;/Just sleep. VWA

Lullaby. Miriam Waddington. far from snows of winnipeg/and seven sister lakes. CaP

Lullaby. William Butler Yeats. From the limbs of Leda sank/But not from her protecting care. BoLoP; FaBoTw; OBMV

Lullaby: "Come sleep, and with the sweet deceiving." Francis Beaumont and John Fletcher. O let my joyes, have some abiding. FaBoEn

Lullaby: "Dormi, Jesu, mater ridet." *Anonymous.* "Sandman steal Thee, little One!" ISi

Lullaby for an Emigrant. Benjamin Fondane. Next year in...where?/Fie, fie! VWA

Lullaby for Ann-Lucian. Calvin Forbes. They recognize his color and his greed. PoBA

Lullaby for Miriam. Richard Beer-Hofmann. Life of me, Miriam, my child–sleep on! VWA

Lullaby for My Dead Child. Denise Jallais. To console you for being little/And dead. BoWoP

Lullaby in Auschwitz. Pierre Morhange. They never told me I might turn back VWA

Lullaby in Bethlehem. Sir Henry Howarth Bashford. Thou art mine–and fast I hold Thee,/Baby dear. HBV 1-2; HBVY

Lullaby, O Lullaby. William C. Bennett. Sleep, then kiss those blue eyes dry./Lullaby! O lullaby! HBV 1-2

Lullaby of an Infant Chief. Sir Walter Scott. For strife comes with manhood, and waking with day. HBV 1-2; OxBChV

Lullaby of the Iroquois. [(Emily)] Pauline Johnson. Little brown baby of mine, go to sleep. ACV

A Lullaby of the Nativity. *Anonymous.* Graunt hem his blissing,/That now maken chere. MeEL

Lullaby of the Woman of the Mountain. Padraic Pearse. Stir not to-night till the sun whitens over you. OnYI

Lullaby Town. John Irving Diller. But to frolic and sing and then go off to sleep! BLPA

Lullabye. Kathryn Stripling. and I had wished the sky to fall. AMV-80

Lullay, lullay. *Anonymous.* That peine vs helpe ay to fle,/The wikkede fendes lore. Amen. OxBoCh

Lullay, Lullay. John Skelton. Ywis, poule-hachet, she blerid thine i. EnPo; PoEL 1-5

Lullay, My Child. *Anonymous.* Fader of Grace,/Whether thou has/Forgeten thy litel sone?'... OxBM

Lullay My Liking. *Anonymous.* God grant them all his blessing/That now maken cheer. EG; ELP

Lully, Lulley. *Anonymous.* The faucon hath borne my make away. AtBAP; DiPo

Lulu. *Anonymous.* The other one got away. ABF; CoSo

The Lumber Camp Song ("The Shanty Boy's Song"). *Anonymous.* Hundreds of able-bodied men are wanted on the drive. ShS

Lumber of Spring. Anne Ridler. And severed from that element for ever. NYBP

The Lumberman's Alphabet. *Anonymous.*
At the woodsman's shanty there's nothing goes wrong. AmFP
Zed for Zero, in the cold winter time,/And now I have brought all these letters in rhyme. ShS

The Lumberyard. Ruth Herschberger. Silent as we, but crazed, crazed as the flame. LiTA; LiTL

Lumen de Lumine. Percy Bysshe Shelley. ...like a star,/Beacons from the abode where the Eternal are. GoBC

Lumiere. H. L. Van Brunt. bearing up the light. AMV-81; LTB

The Luminous. Barbara Guest. blazes from the paper without lifting your hands. PoM

Luminous Night. Louis Simpson. This world so many have left. CAPP

Lump. Robert Phillips. Learn to take one's lumps. AMV-80

Lumumba's Grave. Langston Hughes. Space is his grave. CNA

Lunar Baedeker. Mina Loy. the fossil virgin of the skies/waxes and wanes. VGW

Lunar Eclipse. Diane Glancy. It remains to orbit the earth/only occasionally reminded it is outranked. STE

The Mad-Merry Pranks of Robin Good-Fellow. *Anonymous.* And beldams old my feats have told,/So vale, vale; ho, ho ho! CBEP

A Mad Negro Soldier Confined at Munich. Robert Lowell. ...Each subnormal boot-/black heart is pulsing to its ant-egg dole. FaBoMo; NMP; OxBC

The Mad Rapist of Calaveras County. Pete Winslow. "Let me go you fool!" and "Hot dog!" PV

The Mad Scene. James Merrill. As the lean tree burst into grief. CoAP; NoAm; NOBA; PoA; TAP

Mad Song. William Blake. For light doth seize my brain/With frantic pain. CEP; ERoP 1-2; NOEC; OAEL 1-2; PoEL 1-5; PoRA; PrIm; TEP; TrGrPo

Mad Song. Denise Levertov. How am I to be cured against my will? TAP

Mad Song. Hester Sigerson. I hear what she is saying! AnIV

Mad Sonnet 1. Michael McClure. ...And the walking Virtue/that you are! PoM

Mad Sweeny. John Montague. The whole world/turning in wet/and silence, a/damp mill wheel. FaBoIP

The Mad Woman of Punnet's Town. Leonard Alfred George Strong. The singing children of her brain. MoBrPo

The Mad Yak. Gregory Corso. How many shoelaces will they make of that! CoPo; NoAm

Madaket Beach. Isabel Harriss Barr. The spindly sandpiper stopped short and leapt/To air, while time rose, circled and was gone. GoYe

Madam and Her Madam. Langston Hughes. If I love you! BALP

Madam and the Minister. Langston Hughes. So I ain't in no mood/For sin today. NOBA

Madam Eglantine. Geoffrey Chaucer. And after Amor vincit omnia. NOBE

Madam Gabrina, or the Ill-Favour'd Choice. Henry, Bishop of Chichester King. ...No cunning curse/Can mend that Night-peece: That is, Make her worse. CavP

Madam Hickory. Wilbur Larremore. For Mistress Andrew Jackson. AA

Madam Life. William Ernest Henley. And your little job is done. CABA; InPK; MoBrPo; NBM; TrGrPo

Madam Mouse Trots. Edith Sitwell. All's well with the world! SyP

Madam's Past History. Langston Hughes. Madam to you. NoAm

Madam, withouten many words. Sir Thomas Wyatt. Ye shall another man obtain,/And I mine own and yours no more. CBEP; FCP; NoP; OBSP

Madame D'Albert's Laugh. Clément Marot. But only that sweet laugh wherewith she slays me. ALV; AWP

Madame Dill. *Anonymous.* And waddles through the Louvre. FiBHP

Madame, I Have Come A-Courting. *Anonymous.* She's a greenhorn, you're another."/Fal tum a link tum, a tu rye day. AmFP

A Madame, Madame B. Beaute Sexagenaire. Charles, Earl of Dorset Sackville. You'll find her somewhere in the litany/With pride, vainglory, and hypocrisy. APAS

Madboy's Song. Muriel Rukeyser. Fly down, Death. MoAmPo; TrJP

Madchen Mit Dem Rothen Mundchen. Heinrich Heine. And my tears for very rapture./On that wee white hand should fa'. AWP

Made in Heaven. Peter Porter. The apotheosis of the young wife and mediocre dancer. PPON

The Made Lake. Louise Townsend Nicholl. On whose new margins children greet the swans. NePoAm-2

Made Shine. Josephine Miles. Leaped and made shine the dark face in its sleep. NoAm

Made to See. John Nist. And it's for this/our eyes were made to see. AMV-80

Madeleine in Church (excerpt). Charlotte Mew. Again, again it would speak as it has spoken to me of things/That I shall not see! MoAB; MoBrPo; SBG

Mademoiselle from Armentieres. *Anonymous.* For we'll be back in a few short years./Hinky, dinky, parley voo. BLSo; FSW; OBAL

Mademoiselle Richarde. Edith Sitwell. And she has her own resting-place at last. MoVE

Madge Wildfire's Death Song. Sir Walter Scott. The owl from the steeple sing/Welcome, proud lady! HAP; NOBE; OBNC

Madhouse. Calvin C. Hernton. To drive us mad. IDB; NNP; PoNe

Madison Square. Glanz-Leyeles. A. Whose passion in one stormy moment spent/Bore giant sons of iron and cement. VWA

Madly Singing in the Mountains. Po Chu-i. I choose a place that is unfrequented by men. CBEP

The Madman. S. J. Pretorius. ...Insane/is he,/the other, Me. PeSA

The Madman. Constance Urdang. Ran screaming from the mirror, and was mad. PoPl

The Madman's Song. John Webster. And die in love and rest. EiL

Madman's Song. Elinor Wylie. After the milk-white hounds of the moon. LOW; MoAB; MoAmPo; MOON; PoRA

The Madman's Wife. Steve Orlen. ...Oh, poor us, I begin. MAYP

Madness. James Dickey. Help help madness help. NYBP

Madness. Sachiko Yoshihara. O everything each and everyone so pitiful. BoWoP

Madness One Monday Evening. Julia Fields. And made mermaids come from the sea. NIP; NNP

Madonna: 1936. John Louis Bonn. And metal snake doth magnify my name. ISi

La Madonna dell' Acqua. John Ruskin. And of God's voice, when man's is comfortless. NOBV

Madonna di Campagna. Alfred Kreymborg. Except to raise some earth to shelter those/Whom the Madonna gathers for respose? HBMV

La Madonna di Lorenzetti. John Williams Andrews. And neighbors toiling up the terraced land. HBMV

Madonna Mia. Algernon Charles Swinburne. She is more strong than death,/Being strong as love. HBV 1-2

Madonna Natura. Fiona Macleod. ...take me by the hand/And guide me onward to thy Promised Land! WGRP

Madonna of the Dons. Arthur MacGillvray. Cover the words we form with flesh. ISi

Madonna of the Empty Arms. Maurice Francis Egan. "I clasp you all; my own Child waits,' she said. ISi

Madonna of the Evening Flowers. Amy Lowell. While all about us peal the loud, sweet, Te Deums of the/Canterbury bells. AmLP; PeHV; TreFT

Madonna of the Exiles. James Edward Tobin. He rose. There are things men can never slay. ISi

Madonna of the Hills. Paula Gunn Allen. and her son who walked around dead. TWSS

The Madonna's Lamp. Prince of Sweden, Wilhelm. Still, still the mild Madonna face will glow,/Although the lamp has darkened long ago. CAW

Madonna's Lullaby. Saint Alphonsus Liguori. Your gaze enkindles me somehow. ISi

Madrid. Pai Wei. Your labour which has exceeded that of St Mary. PBWP

Madrid, Iowa. Ron Ikan. a disposition lower than Australia. PPJ

Madrigal. John Frederick Nims. Virus of love, whose counter-dose alone/Is faucet of cut vein or ripsaw bone. MiAP

Madrigal: "A sparrow hawk proud did hold in wicked jail." *Anonymous.* To let a thousand such enjoy their quiet. PBBP

Madrigal: "Ay me, alas, heigh ho, heigh ho!" Thomas Weelkes. She will sit and cry,/Fie fie fie fie fie! OxBoLi

Madrigal: "Come, doleful owl, the messenger of woe." *Anonymous.* Which having heard, I'll do the like for thee. PBBP

Madrigal: "Come, sable night." John Ward. Whilst all his hopes do faint, and life is failing. EnRePo

Madrigal: "Come, woeful Orpheus." William Byrd. And I'll thereto compassionate my voice. EnRePo

Madrigal: "Crabbed age and youth." William Shakespeare. O sweet shepheard, hie thee,/For methinks thou stay'st too long. GTBS; GTBS-P

Madrigal: "Dainty sweet bird." Thomas Vautor. Thou livest singing, but I singing die. EnRePo

Madrigal de Verano. Federico Garcia Lorca. I will eat the apple./Let me! ErPo

Madrigal: "Dear, if you change." John Dowland. Ere I prove false to faith, or strange to you. EnRePo

Madrigal: "Dear, when I did from you remove." Edward, Lord Herbert of Cherbury. Heaven's lights and you to me will shine. EiL

Madrigal: "Eyes that are clear, serene." Gutierre de Cetina. Look angrily then if you must–but look at me! LiTW

Madrigal: "Flow forth, abundant tears." John Attey. ...this for thy sake/Shall honor all my life. EnRePo

Madrigal: "Flow not so fast." John Dowland. Gentle springs, freshly your salt tears/Must still fall dropping from their spheres. EnRePo

Madrigal: "Go, nightly Cares." John Dowland. And thus and thus, vain world, again adieu. EnRePo

Madrigal: "Ha ha! ha ha! This world doth pass." Thomas Weelkes. Fara diddle dyno,/This is idle fyno. OxBoLi

Madrigal: "Have I found her." Francis Pilkington. Chain me to thee with that hair. EnRePo

Madrigal: "How should I love my best?" Edward, Lord Herbert of Cherbury. In love you some other wise,/Believe't, I will. PoEL 1-5; SeCP; ViBoPo

Madrigal: "I always loved to call my lady Rose." *Anonymous.* My rose was gone, and nought but prickles left me. EiL

Madrigal: "In nets of golden wire." Thomas Morley. Ere long, alive, alas, thou shalt not see me. EnRePo

Madrigal: "Is Love a boy?" William Byrd. Power of my life, let here thy grace be shown. EnRePo

Madrigal: "Ladies, you see time flieth." Thomas Morley. Nor be so dainty/Of that which you have plenty. EnRePo

Madrigal: "Lady, the birds right fairly." *Anonymous.* To love your sleep it may not be. PBBP

Madrigal: "Lais now old." Orlando Gibbons. Nor dare she look upon her winter face. EnRePo

Madrigal Macabre. Samuel Hoffenstein. But I, who have but thinly thrived,/Should much prefer to be revived. ShM

The Maiden and the Lily.   John Fraser.   O doctor, where's my lily?   HBV 1-2

The Maiden City.   Charlotte Elizabeth Tonna.   Yet the Maiden on her throne, boys, shall be a maiden still.   HBV 1-2

Maiden Eyes.   Gerald Griffin.   But that which looks from maiden eyes/ Should last of all be broken.   HBV 1-2

The Maiden Hind.   *Anonymous.*   Lucky the lad who from trouble can fly! LiTW

Maiden in the Mor.   *Anonymous.*   The rede rose an te lilye flowr.   AtBAP; BuBa; LoBV; MeEL; NCEP; PoEL 1-5

Maiden Lane.   Al Lee.   The wheels squealing like the hull/Of a submarine about to burst.   NYP

A Maiden Lies in Her Chamber.   Heinrich Heine.   Its skull keeps nodding and nodding/Crazily under the moon.   AWP

Maiden Name.   Philip Larkin.   With your depreciating luggage laden. GTBS-P

The Maiden of the Smile.   Alfred Austin.   But the sweetest smile she ever wore/Was the smile she wore in death.   TEP

The Maiden's Best Adorning.   *Anonymous.*   Thy soul shall fly to paradise above.   OxBChV

The Maiden's Choice.   *Anonymous.*   If she's a knave, the fool.   ALV

The Maiden's Complaint.   *Anonymous.*   I daily weep/And keep my sheep/ That feed upon the down.   OLR

A Maiden's Denial.   *Anonymous.*   And then at cards we better shall agree. ErPo

A Maiden's Ideal of a Husband.   Henry Carey.   Never tyrannical,/But ever true.   HBV 1-2

A Maiden There Lived.   *Anonymous.*   With his pick-axe, sexton, coffin, funeral, skeleton,/and bone-house.   NOBL

Maidenhood.   Henry Wadsworth Longfellow.   For a smile of God thou art. HBV 1-2

The Maidens Came.   *Anonymous.*
After ther liff grant them/A place eternally to sing. Amen.   PoEL 1-5
The lily, the rose, the rose I lay.   AtBAP; CBEP; EG; GBL; ViBoPo

The Maids Conjuring Book.   *Anonymous.*   Then send for me with speed. CoMu

The Maids of Elfin-Mere.   William Allingham.   And the tall reeds sigh as the wind doth blow.   IrPN; OnYI

The Maids of Honour.   *Anonymous.*   But shee'le gett one to starch her Ruffe/That never troubles mee Boy.   CoMu

The Maids of Simcoe.   *Anonymous.*   And when our money it is all spent, we'll hunt the woods for more.   ShS

Maids When You're Young, Never Wed an Old Man.   *Anonymous.*   So, maids when you're young, never wed an old man.   FSW

The Mail Boat, Leinster.   *Anonymous.*   In the cold and changeless waters of the Irish sea so deep.   OBSS

Mail Call.   John Bensko.   the instinct of their hands to block out pain. MAYP

Mailed to G. B.   Gene Derwood.   You light my page, but no light leaps its rim.   NePA

Mailligh Mo Stor.   George Ogle.   "Si Mailligh mo stor.   IrPN

The Mailman.   Victor Contoski.   trying to make me believe/my friends have forgotten me.   GP

The Maimed Debauchee.   Alexander Pope.   Thus far was right, the rest belongs to Heaven.   CABA

The Main-Deep.   James Stephens.   Hush–hushing...   MoBrPo; MOS; OBMV; UnPo

Main Man Blues.   Eugene B. Redmond.   Slap-a-hand, lend-a-hand, main man?   GP

The Main-Sheet Song.   Thomas Fleming Day.   Yo ha! Yo ho! Come down with a will/And bring the main-sheet aft.   EtS

The Main-Truck; or, A Leap for Life.   George Pope Morris.   Then folded to his heart his boy,/And fainted on the deck.   BLPL; PoLf

Maine.   Philip Booth.   ..Maine trades/in staying power, not shiftless drives. AmFN

Maine.   Elinor Nauen.   like songs/my mother/sang–happy/& betrayed. APU

Maine Sea Gulls.   Russell Hoban.   "Ayeh," they both agree, and flap away. BoAnP

The Maine Trail.   Gertrude Huntington McGiffert.   Come haste! the hour sets its face/Unto great Happenings.   HBV 1-2

Mainline.   John Ditsky.   ...Not/far, the pusher lurks.   AMV-80

Mainsail Haul.   *Anonymous.*   Oh, it's about ship, stations, boys, be 'andy./ All raise tacks, sheets, and mainsl' 'aul!   ShS

The Mainspring.   Martha Eugenie Perry.   This is the ultimate steel!   CaP

Maintenance.   Robyn Sarah.   I mean the thread that breaks./The dust between/typewriter keys.   CaPN

Maire My Girl.   John Keegan Casey.   Dwells she in beauty there,/Maire my girl.   AnIV; IrPN; OnYI

Maisrie.   Jessie MacKay.   For the fisher-wife an' the weary lady,/Maisrie, Maisrie!"   AnNZ

Majestic Sweetness.   Stennett Samuel.   Had I a thousand hearts to give,/ Lord! they should all be Thine.   BePJ

The Majesty and Mercy of God.   Sir Robert Grant.   With true adoration shall lisp to Thy praise.   OHIP; WGRP

The Majesty of God.   Thomas Sternhold.   And he, as sovereign Lord and King/Forevermore shall reign.   WGRP

Major Andre.   *Anonymous.*   Success to the brave Americans, the sons of liberty.   BFSS

Major Andre (Arnold's Treason).   *Anonymous.*   Every man wished Andre clear, and Arnold in his stead.   AmFP

Major Macroo.   Stevie Smith.   To cherish them and be neglected and not think it inhuman.   NLV; SBG

Majuba Hill.   Roy MacNab.   Saw how remote were the dead asleep.   PeSA

The Makar.   William Soutar.   though aa his feres were fremmit men/wha cry: Owre late, owre late.   OxBS

Make Believe.   Alice Cary.   You are jesting with my pain.   HBV 1-2

Make Friends.   Ali Ben Abu Taleb.   And he who has one enemy shall meet him everywhere.   TRV

Make Love Not War.   Howard Nemerov.   (Or, roughly, the peace that passeth understanding.)   NAs; NoAm

Make Me a Garment.   *Anonymous.*   My true love died the other day/I believe I'll die tomorrow.   OuSiCo

Make Me a Pallet on Your Floor.   Ma (and Jimmy) Yancey.   That you made me that pallet/Down upon your floor   BluL

Make Me Hear You.   Reginald Gibbons.   ...Oh, love, I would/never have seen that without you.   MAYP

Make Music with Your Life.   Bob O'Meally.   howlin/Like a guitar player CNA

Make Way!   Florence Crocker Comfort.   The flame that lights the candles in men's eyes.   PGD

Make Way.   Steven Lavoie.   neither aging nor desire/makes enough time. APU

Make Way!   Ada Negri.   of a flying strophe, a splendid sheath/of thunderbolts and flowers!   PBWP

Make Way for Liberty.   James Montgomery.   Thus Death made way for Liberty!   TreFS

Make Ye a Joyful Sounding Noise.   *Anonymous.*   And unto generations all/ Continue doth his verity.   AH

The Maker.   R. S. Thomas.   And dry hearts smoked in its wake.   ELU

Maker of Songs.   Hazel Hall.   Weave through the pattern every fragment/Of glittered breath that you have known.   HBMV

The Makers.   David Galler.   ...He made that craft this art.   NYBP

The Makers.   Richard Kell.   The poem is plain, final, able to please,/Clear of the hungers that made it what it is.   CIP

The Makers.   Nan McDonald.   No more the singer, but the song.   ACV

The Makers.   Howard Nemerov.   And stops of breath we build our Babels of.   FYAP

Makhno's Philosophers.   John Streeter Manifold.   His soul is back again among the sabres/Yelling, "The Deed!ç The Deed!"   CBAP; NOAV

Making.   Phyllis Webb.   And for our dubious value it will do./It always does.   PoCh

Making a Door.   Dennis Schmitz.   I hand her the saw.   LCAP

Making a Fist.   Naomi Shihab Nye.   clenching and opening one small hand. MAYP

Making a Man.   Nixon Waterman.   Until he wins–nervous prostration and death.   BLPA

Making an Impression.   William Jackson.   and no need of teeth.   AMV-80

Making Chicago.   Dennis Schmitz.   the sun leaves a virgin spot/of joy. LCAP; NPGG

Making Contact.   John Streeter Manifold.   That at any moment I could put my head in her lap and weep.   CBAP

Making Feet and Hands.   Benjamin Peret.   ...they chase dragonflies/without caring what people will say.   EAS

Making It Simple December 8, 1969.   David McElroy.   the seventeen days till Christmas.   AmPA

Making Land.   Thomas Fleming Day.   "All right! Lay down on deck!" EtS

Making Love, Killing Time.   Anne Ridler.   And with no wish to escape it, then and there/Loved what we were.   NMP

Making Love outside Aras an Uachtarain.   Paul Durcan.   And, levelling an ancient rifle, he says "Stop/Making love outside Aras an Uachtarain." FaBoIP

Making Miso.   Lawson Fusao Inada.   All you have to do/is do it,/with your full being,/and know how to love, and eat, and laugh.   GP

Making Music.   Judith Minty.   and the static rock beat out of the radio. GeTw

The Making of Birds.   Katharine Tynan.   Bade them soar and sing for His joy.   HBMV; OxBI

The Making of Color.   Hugh Seidman.   Conflagrant world against world AmPA

The Making of Man.   John White Chadwick.   Shock and strain and ruin are/Friendlier than the smiling days.   AA

The Making of the Cross. William Everson. ...the rattler/Filmed his glinty eye, and found his hole. VGW

Making Port. James T. McKay. And more I'd give to hold her hand,/And look into her eyes! -EtS

Making up for a Soul. David Wagoner. To stop the gaps in ourselves, like better halves. VGW

Malachi. Earl Bowman Marlatt. "Must worship Him in spirit/"And in truth." MoRP

Malacoda. Samuel Beckett. all aboard all souls/half-mast aye aye/nay CIP

The Maladjusted: A Tragedy (excerpt). Morris Bishop. The Body Shop would not receive his body. NLV

The Malady of Love Is Nerves. Arbiter (Caius Petronius Arbiter) Petronius. I follow after Love, lord of my will. AWP

Malaga. Pearse Hutchinson. lies lost in a strength of jasmine down a summer beach. BIrV

Malawi. Innocent Banda. Malawi, your name means tomorrow! WhB

Malcolm. Lucille Clifton. and from their holes black eagles flew/screaming through the streets CNA

Malcolm. Kattie M. Cumbo. you who made me see have gone from sight. BOLo

Malcolm. Sonia Sanchez. floods the womb until I drown. BP

Malcolm. Welton Smith. in my heart there are many/unmarked graves. BPo

Malcolm, a Thousandth Poem. Conrad Kent Rivers. Your articulation is a silent, Amen. CNA

Malcolm's Katie. Isabella Valancy Crawford.
All else is mortal but immortal–Love!' OBCV
And beat within his knotted, naked breast... OBCV

Malcolm X. Gwendolyn Brooks. who was a man. BALP; BP; CNA; OFD; PoBA; TTY

Malcolm X–An Autobiography. Larry Neal. and I bear witness–all praise is due Allah! BPo

Malcom, Iowa. Charles Itzin. the relics of generals and kings/still abdicate FAZ

The Malcontent. John Marston.
And all is raked in ashy heaps of beastliness. TW
Whilst others beds are downe, his pillowes stone. PoEL 1-5

The Maldive Shark. Herman Melville. Pale ravener of horrible meat. AP; LoGBV; MAmP; MOS; NePA; NOBA; NoP; OxBA; PoEL 1-5; TAP; TW

Male and Female Created He Them. Aldous Huxley. Say, is it possible...to love too much? ALV

Male Rage Poem. Pier Giorgio Di Cicco. Take it like a man. NOBC

Male Rain. Laura Tohe. then rides away leaving/his enemy behind STE

La Male Regle de T. Hoccleve. Thomas Hoccleve. Wherfore I was the welcomere algate,/And for a verray gentil man y-holde. EnPo

Male Torso. Christopher Middleton. And the small horned worms walk high with hope. NePoEA-2

Malediction. Phyllis McGinley. Perhaps that will instruct them to/Ravage a poet's favorite view. DBV

Malediction. Barry Spacks. A discard, your dense self your last/Enormity. TW

Malediction upon Myself. Elinor Wylie. Descends in silver to his proper bride. AnAmPo

The Malefic Return. Ramon Lopez Velarde. ...and a profound reactionary sorrow. OBVE

The Malefic Surgeon. Gerrit Lansing. Drifting in his watery nursery/of brazen pomps, old nightmares stink romantic. CoPo

A Malemute Dog. Pat O'Cotter. If I lose out that pal-loving feeling/Of a malemute's nose on my hand. BLPA

Malest Cornifici Tuo Catullo. Allen Ginsberg. & when they have eyes for me it's Heaven. NeAP

The Malfeasance. Alan Bold. And the people found each other/And thereby hangs a tail. AmMo

Malice Domestic. Ogden Nash. "She should have thought of the chance she took,/Making a pass at a poet's cook." DBV

The Malice of Innocence. Denise Levertov. ...writing/details of agony carefully into the Night Report. NNaP

Malison of the Stone-chat. Anonymous. Wha my eggs wad tak, tak! GBP

Malisons, Malisons, More Than Ten. Anonymous. That harry the Lady of Heaven's hen. PBBP

Mallee in October. Flexmore Hudson. ...nest of twigs so few/that both the sky and the eggs show through. PoAu 1-2

The Maltworm's Madrigal. Henry Austin Dobson. For when my tongue is loosed most, then most I lose my/speech. HBV 1-2

Malum Opus. James Appleton Morgan. Mehercle! You're gratus to that! FaBoCo; NA

Malvern Hill. Herman Melville. Leaves must be green in Spring. AP; FPL; MAmP; MC; PAH; TAP

Malvern Hills. Joseph Cottle. On that vast ocean death conducts us to. NOEC

Malvern Waters. Anonymous. Is famed for containing just nothing at all. FaBoEE

Malvolio (parody). Walter Savage Landor. And furthermore I do hereby pronounce/Divorce between the nightingale and thee. Par

Mama and Daughter. Langston Hughes. Turn around!/So I can brush your back, I say! UnPo

Mama Don't 'Low. Anonymous. Mama don't 'low no singin' round here. FSW

Mama Have You Heard the News?(B vers. with music). Anonymous. "We'll all draw a pension from Casey's death." AS

Mama Knows. Sharon Scott. that's why all our/lies and/covering over/are all so/very very/good. JB

Mama's Advice. Kurt M. Stein. A gute Noodlesupp' tut Wunders workeh. InMe

Mama's God. Carolyn M. Rodgers. didn't and ain't got/no color. GP

Mamana Saquina. Jose Craveirinha. and achieved the miracle of one hundred and fifty-/five bales of cotton. WhB

Mamano. Jose Craveirinha. in that fatal night that deported/fifty-three women/to the plantations of Sao Tome? WhB

Mamba the Bright-Eyed (excerpt). George Gordon McRae. Attracted every wondering glance. PoAu 1-2

Mamma! Frank Horne. I scampered/and fell.../–Mamma!...Mamma!... BPo

Mamma, Mamma. Anonymous. Mamma, but it's so many bullies don't go at all. OuSiCo

Mamma's Gone to the Mail Boat. Anonymous. Mamma's gone to the mail boat,/Bye. OuSiCo

Mamma Sings. Samuel Hoffenstein. For if you bawl, you bawl alone. DBV

A Mammon-Marriage. George Macdonald. Motionless sit the bridegroom and bride/On the Dead-Sea-shore. BoLoP; CBEP; NBM; OBVV

Mammy Hums. Carl Sandburg. Then the face of sleep must be the one face you were looking/for. PoNe

Mamparra M'gaiza. Jose Craveirinha. Stupid cattle/mine cattle/cattle of Africa, marked and sold. WhB

The Man. Michael Dennis Browne. He tears the stocking from his head/& is the girl of your dreams. GP

The Man. Robert Creeley. no see before/come down on him. OBAL

Man. Sir John Davies. Which is proud, and yet a wretched thing. EIL; OBEV

Man. Samuel Greenberg. Time loses thine eye! CrMA

Man. George Herbert.
And both thy servants be. AnAnS 1; InPo; MePo; NoP; OAEP; PoEL 1-5; SeCP; TrGrPo; TrPWD
...Man is one world, and hath/another to attend him. SeCV 1-2

A Man! Clinton Scollard. The flower imperishable of this valiant age,–/A true American! OHIP

Man. Henry Vaughan. God order'd motion, but ordain'd no rest. AnEnPo; CBEP; ForPo; HBV 1-2; MeLP; MePo; NOBE; NOCV; OBEV; OBS; PoEL 1-5; SeCV 1-2

Man. Humbert Wolfe. and space is but the span/of the long love of man. MoBrPo

A Man about the Kitchen. Rodney Hobson. We still seem to spend an/Eternity in it! QQQ

A Man Adrift on a Slim Spar. Stephen Crane. God is cold. MOS

The Man Against the Sky. Edwin Arlington Robinson. Where all who know may drown. AP; APA; CMoP; CoBMV; LiTA; MAPA; MoVE; NAMP; OxBA

A Man All Grown Up Is Supposed To. Terry Stokes. no one ever there when you need them. AmPA

Man Alone. Louise Bogan. Strangers lie in your arms,/As I lie now. NYBP

Man Alone. Denise Levertov. So it is with the gods,/and with the halfgods,/and with the heroes. CAPP

Man and Bat. D. H. Lawrence. But I am greater than he.../I escaped him. BoAnP

Man and Beast. Clifford Dyment. You the hunter, or I the prey? BoAnP

Man and Cows. Andrew Young. ...we both were held divine/In Egypt these, man once in Palestine. EBEV

Man and Dog. Edward ("Edward Eastaway") Thomas. Together in the twilight of the wood. FM

The Man and His Image. Jean de La Fontaine. Needless to say, I mean your Maxim Book. OBVE

Man and Machine. Robert Morgan. And by morning the fields were new. Str

Man and Nature. Robert Kelley Weeks. That your lives are not thus/Prevented, but made strong! AA

Man and the Ascidian. Andrew Lang. Blind, deaf, and indolent, does Man/Revert to the Ascidian. HBV 1-2

The Man and the Weasel. Phaedrus. Would boast the merit of a friend. AWP

Man May Work from Sun to Sun. ·Anonymous. But woman's work is never done. SaC

Man Meeting Himself. Howard Sergeant. I do not know their language! EAS

The Man-Moth. Elizabeth Bishop. cool as from underground springs and pure enough to/drink. LiTA; LiTM; MAT; MiAP; MoAB; MoAmPo; NoAm; NOBA; NYP; PoCh; PPP

A Man Named Hods. Anonymous. And now they say he's senator, but of that I shore don't know. CoSo

Man, Not His Arms. Selden Rodman. Remember only, for your own salvation,/Your brotherhood, and give it to the world. WaP

Man O'War Bird. Derek Walcott. ...somewhere is an Eye/That weighs the world exactly as it pleases. TTY

A Man of Action. Charles Stetler. It was the only thing he ever shoved down my throat. GOYP

The Man of Calvary. Anonymous. I will fly to the arms of Jesus and be at rest. OuSiCo

The Man of Calvary (Easter Day Service). Anonymous. How can I die while Jesus lives? AmFP

Man of Constant Sorrow. Anonymous. I'll meet you on God's golden shore. FSW

Man of Crete. J. R. Hervey. I came not for this. AnNZ

A Man of Culture. Arthur Seymour John Tessimond. Echo of echoes, shadower of shades! HaMV

Man of Derby. Anonymous. And that is how he served me. OxNR

A Man of Experience. Laoiseach Mac an Bhaird. Lord, look at the state you're in! KiLC

Man of Galilee. Mary Louise Deissler. Come walk with me! Come walk with me! BePJ

The Man of Kerioth (excerpt). Robert Norwood. ...A spirit must be free/To tread the upper air of day with him. CaP

Man of Letters. Warren Knox. Resolved the problem PDQ,/Then told me where to go. QQQ

The Man of Life Upright. Thomas Campion. The earth his sober inn/And quiet pilgrimage. AAS; EIL; OAEP; PoRA; ViBoPo

A Man of Men. Leonard Charles Van Noppen. Rugged and resolute, a man of men! PGD

Man of My Time. Salvatore Quasimodo. black birds, the wind, cover their heart. PoPl

The Man of O. Marina Rivera. "No, next!" FIA

The Man of Peace. Bliss Carman. To be made sweet and strong of heart/In Lincoln's brotherhood. OHIP

The Man of Prayer. Christopher Smart. Where knock is open wide. BBV; LiTB

A Man of Rain. Arlindo Barbeitos. a man of rain/lies dead on the ground of decayed leaves. WhB

A Man of Sense. Richard Eberhart. He made it in his senses by imagination free. MiAP

The Man of Sorrows. Anonymous. In every man that suffers, he, the Man of Sorrows, stands! PGD

The Man of Taste. James Bramston. This is true taste, and whoso likes it not,/Is blockhead, coxcomb, poppy, fool, and sot. FaBoCo

The Man of the House. Katharine Tynan Hinkson. Guard me mine and my own rooftree./"Man of the House!" CAW

The Man of the North Countrie. Thomas D'Arcy McGee. Between the South and the North Countrie. OnYI

The Man of the Open West. Arthur W. Monroe. Spirit of the rugged ranges,/Soul of the open West. PoOW

Man of the World. Michael Hamburger. And wake to serve his master loyally. NePoEA-2

A Man of Thessaly. Anonymous. He jumped into another bush/And scratched them in again. CBEP; FaBoCo; OxNR

The Man of Valour to His Fair Lady. William Dunbar. Best now I luif that graceles gane.' MeEL

The Man-of-War's Garland. Anonymous. And each brave jolly tar/That boldly faced their enemies/In the time of the war. OBSS

A Man of Words. Anonymous. You're dead, and dead, and dead indeed. CBEP; FaBoBe; FaBoCh; FaFP; FF; GoTF; HBV 1-2; LoGBV; OxBoLi; TreFS

A Man of Words. John Ashbery. And the past slips through your fingers, wishing you were/there. PoA

Man on Move Despite Failures. Jeffery Alan Triggs. because I'm breathing an absurd music/that will not stop. AMV-80

The Man on the Bed. Debora Greger. beating and beating its wings/against the glass. MAYP

The Man on the Dump. Wallace Stevens. Where was it one first heard of the truth? The the. HAP; NAWM 1-2

The Man on the Flying Trapeze. George Leybourne. His movements are graceful, all girls he does please, and my move he has stolen away. BLSo; FaBoBe

Man on Wheels. Karl Shapiro. You get yourself a shell or else. PCP

A Man's a Man for A' That. Robert Burns. Shall brithers be for a' that. BoLiVe; CoBE; EnLi 1-2; EnPE; FSW; InPo; LoBV; MasP; OxBS; TrGrPo; ViBoPo

Man's Amazement. Anonymous. Yea from his own mouth he will freely unfold,/The sum and the substance of what I have told. CoMu

Man's Anxious, but Ineffectual Guard Against Death. Thomas Lovell Beddoes. And every breath of her's as full of ghosts/As a sunbeam with motes. ChRP

A Man's Bread. Josephine Preston Peabody. Yea, and in quiet sleep/When all is done. YeAr

Man's Days. Eden Phillpotts. A li'l lew corner o' airth to lie in. HBV 1-2; OBEV; OBVV; OxBTC

Man's Dying-Place Uncertain. Robert Herrick. ...but he/Never can tell where shall his landing be. CaPo

Man's Going Hence. Samuel Rogers. Like setting suns or music at the close! OBNC

Man's Inhumanity to Man. Robert Burns. Man's inhumanity to man,/Makes countless thousands mourn. BLPA; FaFP

Man's Littleness in Presence of the Stars. Henry Kirke White. What art thou in the scale of universe?/Less, less than nothing! WBLP

A Man's Love. Tove Ditlevsen. Now the dark does his longing enfold. LiTW

Man's Medley. George Herbert. Hath found the art/To turn his double pains to double praise. ViBoPo

Man's Mortality. Simon Wastell.
The snow dissolves–and so must all! HBV 1-2
The swan's near death; man's life is done! WBLP

A Man's Need. Anonymous. So a man cannot fall asleep without a girl. WTO

Man's Pillow. Irving Browne. Such his last pillow. AA

The Man's Prayer. Thomas Augustin Daly. For time and strength, O Lord! on Thee,/My spirit calls. TrPWD

A Man's Sliding Mood. Mary Elizabeth ("E") Fullerton. Some stilly shaping thing that bides and broods? CBAP

Man's Way. Leonard Alfred George Strong. Forgive it, Kitty,/'Tis man's way. HBMV

A Man's Woman. Mary Carolyn Davies. And neither earth nor sea nor sky shall rob me then of him. PoLf

Man's World Dissolving. Derek Butler. and on the other terror has rained/reigned/long enough. LFAC

A Man Said. Stephen Crane. "The fact has not created in me/A sense of obligation." FF; GoTF; ImOP; LiTM; NCEP; OBAL; OBSP; OBSV; PrIm; TAP; TreFT; WeW; YaD

Man Sails the Deep a While. Robert Louis Stevenson. And fifty fathom deep/Your colours still shall fly. MOS

A Man Saw a Ball of Gold. Ron Padgett. Ay, by the heavens, it was a ball of gold. ANYP; EvOK; LiTA; NePA; PoPl

The Man Sentenced to Death. Jean Genet. My God, I'm going to croak without once being able/To hold you close to my cock and my heart! PeHV

The Man She Called Honey, and Married. Alberto Rios. to put his pictures on her/with his hands. MAYP

The Man That Hails You Tom or Jack. William Cowper. To pardon or to bear it. PoL

The Man That Lives. Anonymous. Our lives shall not endure. OBET

The Man That Waters the Workers' Beer. Anonymous. And I waters the workers' beer. FSW

Man the Enemy of Man. Sir Walter Scott. At first the bloody game begun. WBLP

Man Thinking about Woman. Don L. Lee. ...a blackbird resting/on a telephone wire that moves/quietly with the wind./a southwind. CNA; NoAm

Man to Man. John McClure. Of love and lovers' ecstasy/At dawn or evening. HBMV

The Man to the Angel. George William Russell. Rest the lips of the Unknown/Tenderest upon my brow. OBVV

The Man under the Bed. Erica Jong. I breathe into his mouth/& make him real AmPA

Man Unto His Fellow Man. Norman Corwin. Music: Man unto his fellow man,/a friend forever. TrJP

The Man Upright. Thomas Macdonagh. But like a man with nothing to do/Except walk straight upright like me and you. BIrV

A Man Walking and Singing. Wendell Berry. at his momentary song. AP

A Man Walks in the Wind. Maurice Lesemann. And always the room will throb quietly and slow. AnAmPo; LiTL

A Man Was Drawing Near to Me. Thomas Hardy. The man revealed himself to me. InPo

Man was Made to Mourn, A Dirge. Robert Burns. That weary-laden mourn! CEP

The Man Watching. Rainer Maria Rilke. This is how he grows: by being defeated, decisively,/by constantly greater beings. NU

Man White, Brown Girl and All That Jazz. Gloria C. Oden. We have had the best of it. PoBA

The Man Who Broke the Bank at Monte Carlo. Fred Gilbert. At the man who broke the bank at Monte Carlo. FSN; FSW; TreF

The Man Who Buys Hides. Dennis Schmitz. ...only the head/drags & the eyes roll/over, counter to the earth. LCAP

The Man Who Dreamed of Faeryland. William Butler Yeats. The man has found no comfort in the grave. CMoP; NoAm; NoP; OAEP; PoPle

The Man Who Dreamt He Was Turquoise. Wendy Rose. holding the planet/in place. TWSS

The Man Who Finds That His Son Has Become a Thief. Raymond Souster. It could hardly be otherwise. NOBC; OBCV

The Man Who Frets at Worldly Strife. Joseph R., and Halleck, Fitz-Greene Drake. "Good Lord! what fools ye be." AA

A Man Who Had Fallen Among Thieves. Edward Estlin Cummings. a million billion trillion stars. AP; CoBMV; HAP; LiTM; MoVE; NoAm; NOBA; OxBA; TAP

The Man Who Hid His Own Front Door. Elizabeth MacKinstry. There stood that little Elvish man/And smiled to see her, too! TiPo

The Man Who Invented Las Vegas. Gerald Costanzo. was a thing some of the people/who live on earth for a while/could believe in. TAT

The Man Who Jumped. Anonymous. He fell down and broke his bones. OxNR

The Man Who Knew Too Much. David Wojahn. ...weary/of the dialogue, tired enough for home. MAYP

The Man Who Married Magdalene... Anthony Hecht. She hath her reward. CoPo

The Man Who Married Magdalene. Louis Simpson. The loose behavior of the bone/And the immodest thigh. NePoEA; NoAm; SM; TAP

The Man Who Named Children. Alberto Rios. each in his turn. LTB

The Man Who Owned Cars. Elliot Fried. Nights in his corrugated harem he had so many lovers/it was nearly impossible to choose. GOYP

The Man Who Rode to Conemaugh. John Eliot Brown. "Run for your lives to the mountain side!" PAH

The Man Who Sang the Sillies. John Ciardi. And The Sillies are the sweetest that I know. OBCA

The Man Who Thought He Was a Horse. Thomas Hornsby Ferril. And a patch of oats grew up out of his blood. NePoAm-2

The Man Who Wanted to be a Seagull. J. R. Hervey. He smiled, expecting wings of liberty. AnNZ

A Man Whom Men Deplore. Alfred Kreymborg. Call him high Shelley now and praise his wake. HBMV

The Man Whom the Sea Kept Awake. Robert Bly. The nine steps to the bottom of the sea. NePoEA

The Man with Nought. Anonymous. And never looked behind him. OxNR

Man with One Small Hand. P. K. Page. ...See how it will fit/so sweetly, sweetly in the infant's glove. OBCV

The Man with the Blue Guitar. Wallace Stevens.
   A composing of senses of the guitar. CMoP
   The imagined pine, the imagined jay. LiTA
   It cannot be nothing else. CMoP
   Of a man that plays a blue guitar. CMoP; UnS
   Of things exactly as they are. CMoP; NoAm

The Man with the Hoe. Edwin Markham. After the silence of centuries? AA; AmLP; AnAmPo; AnFE; APA; BLPA; BLPL; EaLo; FaFP; GoTF; HBV 1-2; LiTA; MCCG; MoAmPo; OHFP; PPON; PrIm; SaC; TreF; TrGrPo; TRV; WBLP; WGRP

The Man with the Hoe: A Reply. John Vance Cheney. But follow sorry phantoms to and fro,/And let a kingdom go. HBV 1-2

The Man with the Hollow Breast. Tania Van Zyl. the richest one that ever such a load/could find but that was not to be. PeSA

The Man with Three Friends. Dora Greenwell. And if it be death, I will die with thee,/Or for thee, as it may befall.' OBVV

The Man Within. Annemarie Ewing. Your other half, mesdames, the man within. NePoAm-2

The Man without a Road: X. Erik Lindegren. as if the world had disappeared traceless like a dream/and rests within us finally secure LiTW

The Man Without Faith. Richard Church. He has forestalled death. MoRP

Man without Sense of Direction. John Crowe Ransom. ...as men are served by women/Who comfort them in darkenss and in sun. LiTM; OxBA

A Man Young and Old: The Friends of his Youth. William Butler Yeats. And he that shrieks from pride. AtBAP

Mana Aboda. Thomas Ernest Hulme. Josephs all, not tall enough to try' FaBoMo

The Managers. W. H. Auden. Look, nor would they thank you if you said/you were. EnLit

Mananitas (with music). Anonymous. With the one I'd say, "How are you?"/With the other, "Good bye to you." AS

Manassas. Catherine Ann Warfield. And shrunk from battle's wild affray/At Manassas. MC; PAH

The Manatee. Carey Blyton. It suffers from brainstorms/And hangs upside down in a tree. AmMo

Manchan's Prayer. Anonymous. and I seated somewhere/praying to God a while. NOBI

Mancheser by Night. Mathilde Blind. As life exchanges semblances with death. SBG

The Manchester Ship Canal. Anonymous. And sure we've had enough of that,/At least within this town, sir. OBET

Manchouli. William Empson. So too to extract false comfort from that word. CoBMV

Mandala. Patrick Boland. A part of love, the heart of love, and center.' LiTA

Mandalay. Rudyard Kipling. An' the dawn comes up like thunder outer China 'crost the Bay! ATP; BrPo; EnLit; FaBV; FPL; GoTF; HBV 1-2; LiTB; MoBrPo; NOBE; OBTV; TreF; TrGrPo

Mandelstam. Richard Burns. Fly to the city and stand there and wait/For the beggar at the gate VWA

Mandelstam. David Young. it's a stiff, black world/you left behind. AmPA

Mandoline. Paul Verlaine. Into the rose and gray/Ecstasy of the moon. AWP; OBMV

The Mandrake Hert. Sydney Goodsir Smith. And the bluid rins aye frae the torn ruit. AtBAP; OxBS

Mandrake's Song. Thomas Lovell Beddoes. But the owl's brown eye's the sky's new blue./Heigho! Foolscap! NBM

Mandrakes for Supper. James Keir Baxter. ...travelling light by mountain roads/To Elsewhere; drank at desert wells; gained strength. OxBC

Manerathiak's Song. Anonymous. Swept away by winds. Eya-ya-ya... WHW

Manere of the Crying of Ane Playe. William Dunbar. Slynk first to me the can. AtBAP

Manet: The Execution of Emperor Maximilian. W.D. Snodgrass. Whoever he was, is now all finished being. AmPC

Manfred: An Incantation. George Gordon, Lord Byron. And the day shall have a sun,/Which shall make thee wish it done. DBV; EnRP; OAEL 1-2; OBRV

Mangers. William Henry Davies. is known as Christ to every man,/And Jesus to a little child. MoRP

The Mango Tree. Eric Chock. ...And he's making sure no more extra branches getting in/the way. BrSi

Mangrove. John Blight. troops of the mangroves, uniform, everywhere. NOAV

Mangrove in Crome. Clark Coolidge. shoot shot shout/ scup. ANYP

Manhattan. Morris Abel Beer. Behold the city street! AmFN

Manhattan. Lorenz Hart. We'll turn Manhattan/Into an isle of joy. OBAL

Manhattan. H. R. Hays. My body is full of windows. EAS

Manhattan Lullaby. Rachel Field. And boys like you are born. AmFN

Manhattan Menagerie. Joseph Cherwinski. And stalk these trees of glass, these caves of stars. GoYe

Manhole Covers. Karl Shapiro. Strong with its cryptic American,/Its dated beauty. AmFN; GoJo; GP; NCSH

Manhood. Oliver Wendell Holmes. And wallowing hateful in the eye of day! AP

Manhood. Sir Thomas More. But what no force, his reason is no better. EnRePo

Manhood End. Anthony Thwaite. My head full of the smell my nostrils smelt. NMP

The Maniac. Thomas Russell. Thou'rt gone for evermore! OBEC

The Manichaeans. Gary Snyder. And keep back the cold. VGW

Manichean Geography I. Tom Paulin. And the chosen people will serve/Themselves with orange jube-jubes/In a brand-new discount warehouse FaBoIP

Manifest Destiny. Anselm Hollo. wipe out poverty everywhere in the world/in its most obvious form, the poor. APU

Manifest Destiny. Anita Endrezze Probst. and he has yet to live. CDW

Manifesto. Paris Leary. and turns to the cool hills singing in procession. CoPo

A Manifesto for the Faint-Hearted. Carole Oles. Store advice/in a cool, dry place. SM

Manifesto of the Soldier Who Went Back to War. Angel M. Queremel. A secret!/Know this. WaaP

Manikin and Minikin. Alfred Kreymborg. I can't say it!/Manikin! MAPA

Manila. Eugene Fitch Ware. And do we feel discouraged? We do not think we do! FiBHP; InMe; PV; YaD

Manila Bay. Arthur Hale. But don't forget our chaplain/With his head out of the port. PAH

Manitou. Ron Ikan. but still, like the heat lightning you've/only skirted, within striking distance. PPJ

Mankind. Anonymous. So men; some stiff, some loose, some firm: All earth! FaBoEE

The Manless Society. Pierre Unik. ...immense pinned butterfly/at the entrance of a motionless station. EAS

The Manlet (parody). Lewis (Charles Lutwidge Dodgson) Carroll. He hies him once more to the runlet,/To fetch her the Drake! BXAP; Par

Manly Diversion. Karl Kopp. my son puzzled by the grown-up fun/ beyond the ken of Mrs. Roybal GP

Manly Ferry. John Philip. support the green entablature of boys and dogs and grass. NOAV

The Manly Man. Anonymous. When the manly man goes forth to hold his own on land or sea! BLPA; WBLP

Mannahatta. Walt Whitman City nested in bays! My city! AA; EyDe; HBV 1-2; MoAmPo; NYP

Mannequins. Daniel Mark Epstein. kiss me, you desecration of a man. MAYP

The Manner of a Poet's Germination. Jose Garcia Villa. he lived outside of books. PP

Mannerly Margery Milk and Ale. John Skelton. With Mannerly Margery Milk and Ale. FaBoNo; NoP

Manners. Elizabeth Bishop. so we all got down and walked,/as our good manners required. CTBA; GOYP; NCSH; OxBC

Manners. Howard Nemerov. And that is all it's ever going to be. NLV

Manners. Mariana Griswold Van Rensselaer. He says, How do you do? HBMV; HBVY

Manners at Table When away from Home. Anonymous. Then men will say thereafter/That "A gentleman was here." OxBChV

Manners in the Dining-Room. Anonymous. You shan't have none at all. OxNR

The Manoeuvre. William Carlos Williams. that's what got me–to/face into the wind's teeth. LOW; PCP

Manomin. Phyllis Wolf. manomin on blackened tongue. STE

Manong Benny. Virginia Cerenio. in our every breathing BrSi

Manong Federico Delos Reyes and His Golden Banjo. Al Robles. oh god, how i love my music! BrSi

Manong Jacinto Santo Tomas. Al Robles. the rice and fish taste better dat way. BrSi

The Manor Farm. Edward ("Edward Eastaway") Thomas. This England, Old already, was called Merry. ExPo; HaMV; SeCeV

The Manor Garden. Sylvia Plath. The small birds converge, converge/With their gifts to a difficult borning. FaBoWP; LCAP

Manor Water. Anonymous. They wad get grist eneugh. GBP

Manos Karastefanis. James Merrill. I've brought you a white cheese/From my island, and the sea's/Voice in a shell. TAP

Mans Restlesse Soule Hath Restlesse Eyes and Ears. Roger Williams. Make glad the English, and the Indian. SCAP

A Mantelpiece of Shells. Ruthven Todd. Into the vast spiral that will throw up others. NYBP

Mantis. David McCord. Leads with its left and not the chin. OBAL

Mantis. Louis Zukofsky. And build the new world in your eyes, Save it! PoA

The Mantis Friend. Vincent McHugh. I suppose where all the rest of us must go. NePoAm-2

Mantle. William Heyen. now a fastball, now a slow/curve hanging/like a model's smile. MAYP

The Mantle of Mary. Patrick O'Connor. Little blood-brother of the Crucified. ISi

The Mantle So Green (Lovely Nancy). Anonymous. You're welcome, lovelye Nancy, to my arms once more. AmFP

Mantova. James Wright. The best days are the first/To flee. LCAP; NNaP

The Manual. Larry Rubin. And quietly closed the drawer, and lied. GP

Manuelzinho. Elizabeth Bishop. Again I promise to try. FaBoWP; NYBP

Manufactured Gods. Carl Sandburg. The same as a big wooden god or a brass/Or dough-face god with golden ear-rings. WGRP

The Manuscripts of God. Henry Wadsworth Longfellow. And read what is still unread/In the manuscripts of God. TRV

Many a Mickle. Walter De La Mare. Mother, the fading wall, the dream,/ The drowsy bed. FaBV

Many a Phrase Has the English Language–. Emily Dickinson. Hush–Only to me! DiPo

Many Are Called. Edwin Arlington Robinson. To cling where mostly its infrequent rays/Fall golden on the patience of the dead. MAmP; MoVE; OxBA

Many Birds. Anne Welsh. And the fleeting is gathered into the glory. PeSA

Many Die Here. Gayl Jones. You, who have let my people die without a name. BlSi

Many Happy Returns. W. H. Auden. Follow your own nose. NAs

Many Indeed Must Perish in the Keel. Hugo von Hofmannsthal. And my own portion of this common life/Is more than taper flame or slender lyre. AWP; TrJP

Many Red Devils. Stephen Crane. To write in this red muck/Of things from my heart. TAP

Many Things. Oliver Wendell Holmes. Is half so sweet as love. PoToHe

Many Things Thou Hast Given Me, Dear Heart. Alice Wellington Rollins. But simply as the natural and sweet/Continuance of days spent here with thee. AA

Many Thousand Gone. Anonymous. Many thousand gone. ABF; FSW

Many Wagons Ago. John Ashbery. ...But we stay behind, among them,/ The injured, the adored. HaCAP

Many Wings. Isabel Fiske Conant. Be kind to many wings,/Air, water, fire. HBMV

Many without Elegy. W. S. Graham. Nor fret for few who die before I do. OxBS

Many Workmen. Stephen Crane. But some had opportunity to squeal. LiTA; NePA; TAP

Many Years Ago. Arlindo Barbeitos. with such a drought/that the land ate the lakes/and the men ate the land. WhB

Manyoshu: Spring Is Passing. Empress Jito. apparel spread for drying–/ heavenly Kaguyama. PBWP

Manyoshu: To Love Someone. Lady Kasa. Back behind a starving god/ Within a Buddhist temple. PBWP

Manyoshu: Waiting for the Emperor Tenji. Nukada. Princess. the autumn wind is blowing. PBWP

Manyoshu: When, Loosened from the Winter's Bonds. Nukada. Princess For me, the autumn hills! PBWP

The Manzanita. Yvor Winters. This is the shadow of the vast madrone. VGW

Manzini: Escape Artist. Gwendolyn MacEwen. but listen, it was thursday, there was this boy,/Manzini– NOBC

A Maori Girl's Song. Alfred Domett. And quite forget this feeling–O, this sad, sweet pain! OBVV

The Map. Elizabeth Bishop. More delicate than the historians' are the map-makers' colors. LoGBV; NOBA

The Map. Gloria C. Oden. Will you, because you might not/particularly care to see it so? AmNP; NNP; PoNe

The Map. Gary Soto. And Molina calls it his place of birth. MAYP

The Map. Mark Strand. Perfect distance from what is. NYBP

The Map of Mock-Begger Hall. Anonymous. For mock begger hall stands empty. CoMu

A Map of Montana in Italy. Richard Hugo. ...But last night the Italians/ cheered the violence in one of our westerns. LCAP

Map of My Country. John Holmes. Famous for nothing, except that I have been happy in/them. AmFN; MiAP

The Map of Places. Laura Riding. Holes in maps look through to nowhere. LiTA; NoAm

A Map of the Western Part of the County of Essex in England. Denise Levertov. ...and remembers/the walls of the garden, the first light. CoAP; ConAP

A Map of Verona. Henry Reed. And what good Arms shall take them away again? ChMP

Map Reading. David Citino. I'm about to show you a mighty river. AMV-81

Map Reference T994724. John Pudney. ...the sun's bright finger/On a dead face. WaP

Maple and Sumach. C. Day-Lewis. Speak in me now for all who are to die! CoBMV; FaBoMo

Maple Feast. Frances Frost. From maple sweetness, maple wonder! SiSoSe

The Maple Hangs Its Green Bee Flowers. John Clare. And be my own dear maid! AtBAP

Maple Leaf Rag. Sydney Brown. For there's not a stunt that's in it with the Maple Leaf Rag. BLSo

Maple Leaves. Thomas Bailey Aldrich. Like coins between a dying miser's fingers. AnNE; GN

Maple Leaves. Shiko. red leaves that fall. SoPo

Maples (parody). Philip Appleman. If you have to ask,/You can't afford it. BXAP

The Mapmaker on His Art. Howard Nemerov. Where, till the day I die, I will not go. NYBP

Mapooram. Anonymous. Why, that's two tree boughs rubbing in the wind. NOAV

Mappemounde. Earle Birney. Adrcam in that mere we drift toward map's end. OBCV; PeCV

Maps. Robert Hass. The long ripple in the swamp grass/is a skunk/he shuns the day NPGG

Maps. Dorothy Brown Thompson. For home-staying/Vagabonds! BrR

Maps for a Son Are Drawn as You Go. Samuel Hazo. And so do I. AMV-81

Maps to Nowhere. David Rosenberg. and beyond the little picture show/of stars and galaxies/cheapened by superstition. VWA

Maquillage. Arthur Symons. Fade in a fragrant mist of tears away/When weeping noon leads on the altered day. OBSP; VLP

Marginalia (excerpt). W. H. Auden. for lone survivors like him/who remember its virtues. FaBoEE; OAEL 1-2

Mari Magno. Arthur Hugh Clough. And with one clear departure hence/ The quietude is more intense. OBTV

Maria. George Alexander Stevens. Unless here tomorrow you'll give me relief. UnTE

Maria Bright. Walther von der Vogelweide. Didst bear a happy burden, oh maiden undefiled! ISi

Maria Jane. Alfred Scott-Gatty. What will you eat at twenty? BBGG

Maria Wentworth, Thomae Comitis Cleveland... Thomas Carew. ...where vertue must/Fraile as our flesh, crumble to dust. AnAnS 2; ATP; CaPo; JCP; MeLP; MePo; SeCV 1-2

Mariale (excerpt). Bernard of Cluny. Mary leads him home at last. CAW

Marian. George Meredith. She can wage a gallant war,/And give the peace of Eden. HBV 1-2

Marian at the Pentecostal Meeting. Alden Nowlan. Christ pity her and let her ride/God's carousel forever. ELU

Marian Drury. Bliss Carman. And never the burning heart within you/ Stirs in your sleep by the roving tide. HBV 1-2

Mariana. Alfred, Lord Tennyson. O God, that I were dead! AWP; BiP; CABA; CBEP; CH; ChRP; GTBS; HBV 1-2; InPo; InPS; LiTL; MaVP; MBW 1-2; MyFE; NOBE; NoP; OAEL 1-2; OAEP; OBEV; OBNC; OBRV; OBVV; PAI; PoEL 1-5; PoPle; TEP; TrGrPo; UnPo; ViBoPo; VLP; WiR

Mariana in the South. Alfred, Lord Tennyson. To live forgotten, and love forlorn.' MaVP; VLP

Marianne Moore (1887-1972). Raymond F. Roseliep. honor and point of dust. SOTS

Marie Curie Contemplating the Role of Women Scientists... Robert Frazier. Across the night-black templates/Of an open prairie. SUW

Marie Magdalen's Complaint at Christ's Death. Robert Southwell. Though my life thou drav'st away,/Maugre thee my love shall stay. AnAnS 1; MePo

Marie Magdalene. George Herbert. And yet in washing one, she washed both. AnAnS 1

The Marigold. Thomas Ford. That is our Queen, the Marigold. ACP; CAW

Marigold. Richard Garnett. And all the Toms, though never so bold,/ Quailed at the martial Marigold. PCat

Marigold. John Haines. and the dusty bees are dozing/like pardoned sinners. PoL; PPJ

The Marigold. George Wither. I never follow an inferior way. CBEP; OBS

The Marigold So Likes the Lovely Sun. Thomas Watson. When my She-sun doth either laugh or lour... AtBAP; LO

Marigolds. Robert Graves. Love must ever yet return. BrPo

Marin. Philip Booth. and is more Maine/than Maine. NYBP

Marin-An. Gary Snyder. ...thousands/and thousands of cars/driving men to work. TAT; WeW

Marina. Thomas Stearns Eliot. And woodthrush calling through the fog/ My daughter. AmP; CMoP; FaBoMo; GTBS-P; HeIP; InPo; LiTA; MBW 1-2; MOS; NOBE; NOCV

The Mariner. Allan Cunningham. Then leave nae mair my heart to break/ 'Mang Scotland's hills behind. EtS

The Mariner's Bride. James Clarence Mangan. I'll go where the mariner's going;/And be the mariner's bride. IrPN

The Mariner's Dream. William Dimond. O sailor boy! sailor boy! peace to thy soul! BeLS; HBV 1-2

The Mariner's Song. Sir John Davies. There is no fishing to the sea, nor service to the king. OBSC

The Mariner's Wife. William Julius Mickle. There's nae luck about the house,/When our gudeman's awa. ViBoPo

Mariners. David Morton. And a lone ship that rides there with the moon. EtS

The Mariners. Margaret Louisa Woods. The mariners sleep by the sea. OBVV

Mariners' Carol. William Stanley Merwin. O star, shine before us! EaLo

The Marines' Hymn. Anonymous. They will find the streets are guarded/By United States Marines. BLSo; GoTF; PAL; TreF; YaD

The Marionettes. Walter De La Mare. And affrights even fear. AtBAP; MMM

The Mariposa Lily. Ina Donna Coolbrith. Thou winged bloom! thou blossom—butterfly! AA; BPAW

Maritae Suae. William Philpot. With that old silver heart I gave,/My first gift—and my last. OBVV

Maritimes. Penelope Shuttle. fed on the salt and blood of me. BrRo

Marius Victor. Sir Walter Raleigh. In vice we dwell, in sin that hath no end. FCP

Mariushka's Wedding Song. Anonymous. I have caught the shining falcon. HW

The Mark. Louise Bogan. And all at length are gathered in. MoPo; MoVE

Mark. Ernest McGaffey. The whippoorwills complain beside/The lonely Kankakee. AA

Mark Anderson. Wilfred Wilson Gibson. But only gaze upon the glass/Of water that he could not drink. MMM

Mark Anthony. John Cleveland. Never Mark Anthony/Dallied more wantonly/With the fair Egyptian Queen. ALV; EG; InvP; OAEL 1-2; SeCP; ViBoPo

Mark Van Doren. James Worley. we were but windfall parties to those falls. AMV-81

Mark You How the Peacock's Eye. Gerard Manley Hopkins. The pupil, plays its liquid jet/To win a look of violet. FM

The Market. Gary Snyder.
how can I tell   NaP
I came to buy/a few bananas by the ganges/while waiting for my wife. CoPo

Market Day. Abigail Cresson. Not every time, but now and then? HBMV

Market Day. Mary Webb. Would make an end of poverty. CH

The Market Economy. Marge Piercy. Don't read the fine/print, there isn't any. GeTw

Market Square. A.(lan) A.(lexander) Milne. 'Cos they haven't got a rabbit, not anywhere there! TiPo

The Market-Square's Admiring Throngs. Johann Wolfgang von Goethe. Sing to others if you'll tarry/Silent with your serving boy. PeHV

The Market Town. Francis Carlin. A ploughing match with a guinea's prize/For the skill of your hands and eyes. HBMV

Market Women's Cries. Jonathan Swift.
And I must maintain them. AnIV
But think it as sweet as her own. AnIV
Or, like my own herrings, I soon shall be dead. AnIV

The Marketwoman. Agostinho Neto. –Buy oranges! WhB

Marking Time. Peter Steele. that someone is condoning lust,/drugs, and a merry life. NOAV

Markings. Frank Steele. I find I have one leaf/to throw away/and one to keep. Psk

Marks. Linda Pastan. ...Wait 'til they learn/I'm dropping out. NIP

Marlborough (excerpt). Charles Hamilton Sorley. The thing that all can feel, but none can tell. WGRP

Marlburyes Fate. Benjamin Tompson. New England will be prosperous once at length. SCAP

Marlow and Nancy. Sandra McPherson. Pushing me away but blue, so blue. AmPA

Marlowe. Arthur Bayldon. A scullion fleeing with a bloody knife. PoAu 1-2

Marm Grayson's Guests. Mary E. Wilkins Freeman. "My sons, I've told you many times that signs are naught," said she. OBCA

Marmion. Sir Walter Scott.
And ne'er held marble in its trust/Of two such wondrous men the dust. BSV; FaBoPP; OBRV
And shout of loud defiance pours,/And shook his gauntlet at the towers. OHFP
And still the scatter'd Southron fled before. OBRV
The bars descending razed his plume. WHA
The busy day and social night. OBRV
Flow on, flow unconfin'd, my Tale! OBRV
Gladly I turn me from the sight,/Unto my tale again. BSV
A ministering angel thou! TreFS
Never, O never! OBRV; ViBoPo
That to the cottage, as the crown/Brought tidings of salvation down. GN
We'll keep our Christmas merry still... PCh
Where shiver'd was fair Scotland's spear,/And broken was her shield! ELP; EnRP; PoEL 1-5
Whose islands on its bosom float,/Like emeralds chas'd in gold. FaBoPP

Marquette on the Shores of the Mississippi. John Jerome Rooney. Seeking the long-lost children of his God. CAW

The Marquis of Carabas. Robert Barnabas Brough. Chapeau bas!/Gloire au Marquis de Carabas! FiBHP; HBV 1-2

Marrakech. Ralph Nixon Currey. Backwards and forwards to the Muslim hour. PeSA

Marrakech. Richard Eberhart. And all is made whole in the heart and time. LiTM

Marrakesh Women. Lyn Lifshin. dark blood strands of wool   LTB

Marriage. Anonymous.
And be a good and faithful wife. AmFP
And draw an adder or an eel. GBP

A Marriage. Anthony Barnett. For/know/he lived   VWA

Marriage. Raymond Carver. ...ponds of silver water/that shiver and can't understand their being here. GeTw

Marriage. Austin Clarke. With guilty hope at every change of moon! BIrV; GTBS-P

Marriage. Mary Elizabeth Coleridge. All for her sake must the maiden die! PeHV

Martial in London. Mortimer Collins. And I'll envy no Rothschild his million. ALV; InMe

Martial's Quiet Life. Henry Howard, Earl of Surrey. Neither wish death, nor fear his might. OBSC

"Martial, the things for to attain." Henry Howard, Earl of Surrey. Contented with thine own estate,/Neither wish death nor fear his might. FCP

A Martian Sends a Postcard Home. Craig Raine. and read about themselves–/in color, with their eyelids shut. NoP

Martin Buber in the Pub. Max Harris. Exchanging shells, which placed against the ear,/Occasionally echo the throbbing of a heart. BoAV; NOAV; PoAu 1-2

The Martin Cat Long Shaged of Courage Good. John Clare. Left free from boys and dogs and noise and men FM

Martin Luther at Potsdam. Barry Pain. And yet, like my title, have nothing to do! ALV; NA

Martin Luther King Jr. Gwendolyn Brooks. So it shall be spoken./So it shall be done. BOLo; CNA; PoBA

Martin's Blues. Michael S. Harper. Yes we did!/Yes we did! CNA; HaCAP; PoBA

Martin Said to His Man. Anonymous. Who's the fool now? FaBoNo; NA

The Martyr. Natalie Flohr. Another cross loomed dark against the sky. PGD

Martyr. Mary Elizabeth ("E") Fullerton. Though waves climbed upward o'er her shining face. CBAP

The Martyr. Herman Melville. When they bare the iron hand. AmePo; PoEL 1-5; TAP; TrGrPo

The Martyr and the Army. Jock Henderson. With the rigor mortis of military design. AMV-81

The martyr poets–did not tell–. Emily Dickinson. Some seek in art–the Art of peace– EyDe

A Martyr's Death. Menahem Ben Jacob. And died for them a martyr's death. TrJP

A Martyr's Mass. Alfred Joseph Barrett. ...how his sealed lips sang/The Ite, Missa Est! GoBC

Martyr's Memorial. Louise Imogen Guiney. Of all his dear domain to live forgot. AA

Martyrdom. Rufus Learsi. The Peak still glimmers: thrill, my/spirit, thrill! TrJP

Martyrdom. Richard W. Thomas. Blamed your death on (IT! PoBA

The Martyrdom of Becket. Anonymous. Contra regis consilia. EnPo

Martyrdom of Father Campion. Henry Walpole. Hath reaped a joy, which never shall have end. GoBC

The Martyrdom of Mary, Queen of Scots. Robert Southwell. His axe cut off my cares from cumberd breast. ACP

The Martyrdom of St. Teresa. A. D. Hope. Pours down on every true believer/The mystic blood of martyrdom. CBAP

Martyrdom of Two Pagans. Philip Whalen. For we took our shoes off/As we fell. NeAP

The Martyred Democrat. C. J. Dennis. In Lady Lusher's drawing-room, one summer afternoon. CBAP

The Martyred Earth. Ewart Milne. Nothing buried remains. The dust is moving fast. BIrV

The Martyrs of the Maine. Rupert Hughes. No! Bring them home! PAH

A Marvel. Carolyn Wells. Old Ptolemy Copernicus/Flammarion McGower. OBCA

Marvel No More Although. Sir Thomas Wyatt. For such a pleasant chance,/To sing some pleasant song. AAS; SiPS

Marvel of Marvels. Christina Georgina Rossetti. Cold it is, O my King, how cold alone on the wold. NOBE; OBVV; OxBoCh; WGRP

Marvell's Garden. Phyllis Webb. where they have wept without/and I within. OBCV

Marvell's Ghost. John Ayloffe. Or such as did in fury turn/Th' Assyrian's palace to his urn. APAS

Marvellous Martin. Charles Harpur. Their slimy embryos came in youthful Lottery's brain. CBAP

Marvelous. Allan Kaplan. And Tania's over forty! PoL

Marvels. Anonymous. Save us and send us some drink or we dey! OxBM

Marx, the Sign Painter. Edgar Lee Masters. I'd like to see the signs. NoAm; TAP

Mary. Fray Angelico Chavez. Pendant for my lips, Maria! ISi

Mary. Robert Farren. God's Heaven,/for Heaven's where's God. ISi

Mary Ackerman, 1938, Eugene Buechel Photograph Museum of Modern Art... Diane Glancy. photographs still reflect a young girl/before an awkward car. STE

Mary Ames. Anonymous. I never saw Mary more provoked. NA

Mary an' Martha Jes' Gone 'Long. Anonymous. Free grace an' dyin' love,/To ring dem charmin' bells. BoAN 1-2

Mary and Gabriel. Rupert Brooke. The air was colder, and grey. She stood alone. ISi

Mary and Her Son Alone. James Ryman. I will arise by my grete might/And confort thee alone.' OxBM

Mary and Martha. Annie Johnson Flint. These are the things we can keep. STF

Mary and the Baby, Sweet Lamb. Anonymous. Oh, Mary and the Baby, sweet Lamb. AmFP

Mary and the Bramble. Lascelles Abercrombie. ...I bid thee know/That answering God's own love thy womb shall throe.' OBMV

Mary and the Lamb. Frank Dempster Sherman. He makes a nice dish in this region/To eat in the spring! InMe

Mary Ann. Anonymous. Did you ever feel the pain, my dear, Mary Ann. FSW

Mary Ann. Joseph Tabrar. He's going to marry Mary Ann! PV

Mary Arnold the Female Monster. Anonymous. Binding black beetles round its eyes/Placed in walnut shells. GBP; OBET

Mary at the Cross. Clyde McGee. And grant their dead shall not have died in vain. PGD

Mary Beaton's Song. Algernon Charles Swinburne. The next, that saw not love, saw me/Between the sea-banks and the sea. HBV 1-2

Mary Booth. Thomas William Parsons Now cover it in earth, - her earth no more. AA

Mary Complains to Other Mothers. Anonymous. Wounded and dedd my dere sone, dere. MeEL

Mary Desti's Ass. Frank O'Hara. that was love but I kept on traveling ANYP

The "Mary Gloster." Rudyard Kipling. Never seen death, yet, Dickie? ...Well, how is your time to learn! BeLS

Mary Gulliver to Captain Lemuel Gulliver. Jonathan Swift. So might I find my loving spouse of course/Endued with all the virtues of a horse. OAEL 1-2

Mary Had a Baby. Anonymous. The people keep a-coming and the train done gone. BoAN 1-2; FSW

Mary Had a William Goat (with music). Anonymous. Shirts can do no harm inside, but the oyster can. AS

Mary Hamilton. Anonymous. What lands I was to tread in/Or what death I should dee.' NOBE; OxBB

Mary Hamilton (A version). Anonymous. There was Marie Seton, and Marie/Beton,/And Marie Carmichael, and me.' AmFP; BaBo; ESPB; FaBoBa; NoP; OAEP; ViBoFo

Mary Hamilton (B version). Anonymous. An ye had a mind to save my life,/Ye should na shamed me here.' CBEP; ESPB

Mary, Helper of Heartbreak. Margaret Widdemer. (Mary, helper of heartbreak, send him to me to-night!) HBMV

Mary Hynes. Padraic Fallon. That he was bred a poet whose selfish trade it is/To keep no beauty to himself. AnIV; OxBI

Mary Hynes. Anthony Raftery. And King of Glory, dry up the roadway/Till I find my posy at Ballylee! KiLC

Mary Immaculate. Eleanor C. Donnelly. The peerless splendors of thy soul by far/Outshine the glow of heaven's serenest star. CAW

Mary in the Silvery Tide. Anonymous. His last words were for Mary in the rolling silvery tide. OBET; ShS

Mary Is with Child. Anonymous. The King of Heven's Sonne.' MeEL

Mary Jane. Anonymous. Oh, poor Mary! oh, poor Jane! NA

Mary Jane, the Milkmaid. Anonymous. "Oh, the farther the better, kind sir," she said. BFSS

Mary Le More. George Nugent Reynolds. And sigh'd for the wrongs of poor Mary le More. OnYI

Mary Lifted from the Dead. William Alfred. Lifted our perished hearts toward you. AH

Mary Magdalene. Kassia. Do not overlook me, your slave,/in your measureless mercy. BoWoP

Mary Magdalene. Dante Gabriel Rossetti. He needs me, calls me, loves me: let me go!' GoBC; MaVP

Mary Magdalene. Leonora Speyer. I know the woman well. HBMV

Mary, Mary (parody). Anthony C. Deane. And lo! the Garden is a Paradise! FaBoPa

Mary, Mary, Quite Contrary. Mother Goose. And pretty maids all of a row. TiPo

Mary Middling. Rose Fyleman. Now what would you give for a pig like that? SUS

Mary Mild, Good Maiden. Colum Cille. So I'll pray while I live. NOBI

Mary Modyr, Cum and See. Anonymous. And bring us to blys that is abone./Amen, amen, amen, for charite. OxBoCh

Mary Morison. Robert Burns. The thought o' Mary AnFE; BoLiVe; CEP; EG; GTBS; GTBS-P; HBV 1-2; InPo; MCCG; OAEP; OBEC; OBEV; OxBS; TreFT; TrGrPo; WHA

Mary, Mother of Christ. Countee Cullen. That night she kissed his coral lips/How could she know the rest? PCh

Mary of Bethlehem. Mary King. Because she had been one of them/And greatly loved in Bethlehem. ISi

Mary of the Wild Moor. Anonymous. Saying, "There Mary died, once the gay village bride,/From the winds that blew across the wild moor." BaBo; BFSS

Mary on Her Way to the Temple. Ruth Schaumann. To wait till time shall reach its fruitfulness. ISi

Mary Passed This Morning. Owen Dodson. Goodnight, goodnight./signed Joseph. PoBA

Mary Passes. *Anonymous.* Upon the thorn-boughs roses stood. ISi

Mary, Queen of Heaven. *Anonymous.* There to love our God most glorious.'/Ecce virgo, radix Jesse. MeEL

Mary, Queen of Scots. Henry Glassford Bell. Then weigh against a grain of sand the glories of a throne. BeLS; BLPA; FaBoBe

Mary Queen of Scots. Charles Tennyson Turner. To clear her fame, yea, very babes have yearned/Over this saddest story of the isles. HBV 1-2

Mary's a Grand Old Name. George M. Cohan.
And there is something there that sounds so fair, it's a grand old name! BLSo; FSN; GoTF
Don't ever fear sweet Mary, beware of sweet Marie! TreFT

Mary's Assumption. Alfred Joseph Barrett. There was silence in heaven; as if for half an hour/No angel breathed. ISi

Mary's Baby. Shaemas O'Sheel. Suddenly on Calvary all the olives wept. CAW; HBV 1-2; HBVY

Mary's Ghost. Thomas Hood. They haven't left an atom there/Of my anatomie. FiBHP

Mary's Girlhood. Dante Gabriel Rossetti. Because the fullness of the time was come. CAW; GoBC; ISi; MaVP; WGRP

Mary's Lamb. Sarah Josepha Hale.
And make it follow at your call,/If you are always kind. FaBoBe; FaFP; HBV 1-2; HBVY; OBCA; OxBChV
"Oh, Mary loves the lamb, you know,"/The teacher did reply. OxNR; SoPo; TiPo

Mary's Lullaby. Ivy O. Eastwick. Little Treasure,/Little Boy. ChBR

Mary's Son. Lucia Trent. Let us remember You as one who died/For love of every comrade at his side. PGD

Mary's Song. Marion Angus. Tho' he be nae mine, as I am his. BSV

Mary's Song. Charles Causley. That all the world/May enter in. OBCP

Mary's Song. Sylvia Plath. O golden child the world will kill and eat. CAPP; FaBoMo; FaBoWP

Mary's Vision. *Anonymous.* "True is that vision, Mother." ISi

Mary Shepherdess. Marjorie Pickthall. All to Mary Shepherdess they'd fold their hands and pray. ISi

Mary Speaks to Jesus. Barry Dempster. ...I couldn't help wishing/you'd rolled it down into the city,/sun setting, caving in the crowds. CaPN

Mary Suffers with Her Son. *Anonymous.* So lat us deiyen bothen isame. MeEL

Mary the Cook-Maid's Letter to Dr. Sheridan. Jonathan Swift. And so I remain in a civil way, your Servant to command/Mary. LoBV; OnYI; OxBoLi

Mary Tired. Marjorie Pickthall. Near the Ransom of the World. ACV; PeCV

Mary Was a Red Bird. *Anonymous.* Mary was a red bird/All day long! OuSiCo

Mary Was Watching. *Anonymous.* Bees bring you honey from their hoard,/When you awake. ISi

Mary Weeps for Her Child. *Anonymous.* Ther shall I be,/Man to restore,/Naylit full sore/Upon a tre.' OxBoLi

Mary Winslow. Robert Lowell. "Come, Mary Winslow, come;I bell thee home." AnNE; MiAP; MoVE; PPP

Mary Wore Three Links of Chain (with music). *Anonymous.* All my sins been taken away, taken away. AS

Mary Wyatt and Henry Green. *Anonymous.* He, too, must close his youthful life, and slumber with the dead."] AmFP

The Maryland Battalion. John Williamson Palmer. And fair Freedom is singing Sweet Home in the West. AA; HBV 1-2; MC; PAH

Maryland, My Maryland. James Ryder Randall. She breathes! She burns! She'll come! She'll come!/Maryland, my Maryland! FaPo

Maryland Resolves. *Anonymous.* From real griefs, from factious elves,/Will speedily relieve ye. PAH

The Maryland Yellow-Throat. Henry Van Dyke. Sing, merry bird, the charm's complete,/"Witchery-witchery-witchery!" HBV 1-2

Masada. Isaac Eichanan Mozeson. Bt those who chose/To survive survival. AMV-81

Masar. Walter Savage Landor. Yet was not courage wanting in the child...' LoBV

Mashkin Hill. Louis Simpson. And there is no God for Levin/but the quietness of his house. SaC

The Mask. Elizabeth Barrett Browning. Whom sadder can I say? she said. CBEP; OBNC; OBVV

Mask. Elizabeth Cox. The call boy rudely raps. GoYe

The Mask. Clarissa Scott Delany. I turned aside until the mask/Was slipped once more in place. CDC; PoNe

The Mask. Patty L. Harjo. And I cried VoR

The Mask. Irma McClaurin. carving out my heart with yesterday's pain. BlSi

Mask. Stephen Spender. As man behind his mask still wears a child. MoAB; MoBrPo

The Mask and the Poem. Alejandra Pizarnik. she will be taken to a temple in ruins/she will be left/alone. VWA

Mask-Maker. Michael Jackson. and to us all the curse of secrecy. OCNZ

The Mask of Anarchy. Percy Bysshe Shelley. Ye are many—they are few.' CABL; LoBV; OBSV; SCV

Mask of Love. Thomas Kinsella. Reddening, and disappears. CMoP; NMP

Mask of Stone. Henry Johnson. pretending the wind's/blown something/into my eyes. LFAC

The Mask the Wearer of the Mask Wears. William Bronk. look lovingly, look long, on what there is. GP

A Maske for Lydia. Thomas Randolph. Still such an Ethiope be. AnAnS 2

The Masked Shrew. Isabella Gardner. The helpless, hungry, nervous shrew/lives for a year of hurly-burly/and dies intolerably early. ImOP

Masked Woman's Song. Louise Bogan. And not in those roped arms. NMM

Masks. Thomas Bailey Aldrich. How wan her cheeks are, and what heavy/tears! AA

Masks. Elizabeth Fenton. My nakedness the mask itself. NMM

Masks. Brian Swann. ...Into a night/that is not dark/but masked. AMV-81

The Masochist. Maxine W. Kumin. as if they never called you mine,/mine, mine. IHMS; PoA

Masochistic Tendencies. Carolyn Baxter. jingling,/like the smallest,/cowbell/on the junkman's wagon,/in the distance. LFAC

The Mason. Robert Farren. Leave me not a stone in thine enemies' hand! OnYI; OxBI

Mason Jar. David Steinberg. the maple tree wept down. AMV-81

The Masque of Balliol (excerpt). Henry Charles Beeching. My gown, the wonder of beholders,/Hangs like a footnote from my shoulders. GLGT

The Masque of Christmas. Ben Jonson. O but Log was too heavy to dance it. OxBoLi

Masque of Cupid: Up, Youths and Virgins, Up, and Praise. Ben Jonson. Shine, Hesperus, shine forth, thou wished star! HW

Masque of Hymen: Glad Time Is at His Point Arrived. Ben Jonson. And though full years be told,/Their forms grow slowly old. HW

A Masque of Life and Death. Witter ("Emanuel Morgan") Bynner. And kissed me with her lips. AnAmPo

The Masque of Queen Bersabe (excerpt). Algernon Charles Swinburne. And light, and thunder of the tides. AtBAP

The Masque of Queenes. Ben Jonson. Fire above, and fire below,/With a whip i' your hand, to make him goe. FM; OFD; WSC

A Masque of Reason: God's Thanks to Job. Robert Frost. And as such I promote you to a saint. MoRP

The Masque of the Inner-Temple and Gray's Inne. Francis Beaumont.
And keep him ever by 'em. OBS; TrGrPo
Each Song a Sacrifice. OBS
That we his Priests should all absolve. OBS

Masque of the Virtues against Love. From Guarini. Mary Monck. Yours be the advantage all; for we/Claim naught but th' honour of the victory. NOEC

A Masque Presented at Ludlow Castle (Comus). John Milton.
And give resounding grace to all Heaven's harmonies! BoLiVe; ExPo; NOBE; OBEV; SeCeV; TrGrPo; ViBoPo
Come, knit hands, and beat the ground/In a light fantastic round. BoLiVe; NOBE; OBEV; PPoe; SeCeV; TrGrPo
Gentle swain at thy request/I am here. EBEV; EG; GN; NOBE; OBEV; OBS; SeCeV
Listen and save. ViBoPo
Think what, and be adviz'd, you are but young yet. AtBAP; PoEL 1-5
To gaze upon the sun with shameless brows. ViBoPo
To touch the prosperous growth of this tall Wood. AtBAP
To wait in Amphitrite's bower. AtBAP
What hath night to do with sleep? EG; WHA

Masquerade. Carolyn M. Rodgers. ultimately realize the specific beautiful or ugly/innards of/our/selves. BlSi

The Masquerader. Aline Kilmer. Can you forgive our foolish condescension,/Now you are gone? HBMV

Masques. Ben Jonson. Your sheepe, and you they will deceave. AnAnS 2

Mass at Dawn. Roy Campbell. Never was wine so red or bread so white. PeSA

Mass of Love. *Anonymous.* Instead of Amen, Amen,/They sang Amor, Amor. LiTW; PoPl

Massa's in de Cold, Cold Ground. Stephen Collins Foster. Pickin' on de old banjo. TreF

Massachusetts Song of Liberty. Mrs. Mercy Warren. But swear to defend her,/And scorn to survive, if unable to save. PAH

Massachusetts to Virginia. John Greenleaf Whittier. No fetters in the Bay State—no slave upon our land! AnNE

The Massacre of the Innocents. William Jay Smith. How beautiful it might have been to live. EaLo

The Massacre of the Innocents: The Devil's Doubts. Giambattista Marino. These are the knotty Riddles, whose darke doubt/Intangles his lost Thoughts, past getting out. OBVE

The Massacre of the Macpherson. Ayton [(or Aytoun)] Sir Robert. Here's your fery good healths,/And tamn ta whusky duty! BXAP; CenHV; FaBoCo

Massada. Yitzhak Lamdan. Behind the future's screen a great dawn watches,/Keeping guard on Massada. VWA

The Massasauga. Hamlin Garland. Death waits and watches where he lies AA; BPAW

Massenet/Never wrote a Mass in A. Antony Butts. It'd have been just too bad,/If he had. FiBHP

The Master. C. G. L.. "What would I give to hear Wood Jones on this!" ImOP

The Master. William Stanley Merwin. Our reality and its insupportable innocence. NePoEA

The Master. S. D. Robbins. And when Thy kingdom unto us shall come,/Our servant be! BePJ

The Master. Edwin Arlington Robinson. And have one Titan at a time. AmP; HBV 1-2; LiTA; MoAB; MoAmPo; OHIP

Master and Man. Anonymous. Draggle tail, dreary dun. NA; OxNR

Master and Man. Sir Henry Newbolt. 'Twull be best, sir, for you to be fushin'/And me wi' the gaff. OxBTC

Master Canterel at Locus Solus. David Shapiro. Nights the mirror shines west/And directly receives the sun ANYP

Master Charge Blues. Nikki Giovanni. gonna take my master charge/and get everything in town OBAL

The Master City. Rose J. Orente. I start again, to build, to stay. GoYe

Master Hugues of Saxe-Gotha. Robert Browning. Do I carry the moon in my pocket? OAEL 1-2

Master I Have, and I Am His Man. Mother Goose. Higgledy, piggledy, niggledy, niggledy,/Gallop a dreary dun. TiPo

The Master Mariner. George Sterling. Then gaze again to sea–and sigh. HBV 1-2

Master McGrath. Anonymous. "Long live the Republic,' said Master McGrath. OBET

Master, No Offering. Edwin Pond Parker. Dear Lord, to thee. AH

The Master of Laborers. George Edward Day. Thou Son of God! Thou Son of Man! PGD

The Master of the Golden Glow. James Schuyler. More litter, less clutter. ANYP

The Master of Time. Jan van Nijlen. He made my home till Death should call me thence. LiTW

The Master-Player. Paul Laurence Dunbar. And brought forth music sweet and strong. TRV

The Master's Call. Oswald J. Smith. Answer quickly, "Lord, send me!/To the lands beyond the sea"? STF

Master's in the Garden Again. John Crowe Ransom.
Now he will defer to the house and to her. NoAm
Play sweeter than pray, that the darkened be gay. AP

The Master's Invitation. Anson Davies Fitz Randolph. If thou but follow me! AA

The Master's Touch. Horatius Bonar. Complete Thy purpose, that we may become/Thy perfect image, O our God and Lord! BePJ; HBV 1-2; TrPWD

The Master Singers. Rhys Carpenter. God in his heaven bidding light arise. WGRP

Master Skylark. John Bennett.
Hio, hark away! AA
When spring-time cometh with/the summer at her heels. AA

The Master Spirit. George Chapman. He goes before them and commands them all,/That to himself is a law rational. EtS

The Master Weaver. Anonymous. But trust the Master Weaver/And His steady, guiding Hand. STF

The Masterful Man. Henry Tyrrell. The red blood of the people, warm, sincere,/Blending of Puritan and Cavalier. PGD

The Masterpiece. Walter Conrad Arensberg. The supreme poet who imagined God. AnAmPo

The Masterpiece. Walter Malone. A masterpiece of God. PGD

Masters. Kingsley Amis. And we are taken if we wish to give,/Are needed if we need. NePoEA; PoPl

The Masters. Laurence Hope. My hope is but in song to show/How honored and how dear you are. HBV 1-2

The Masters. Margaret Widdemer. How to bear the blackened night/And the dreadful dawn. HBMV

Masters in This Hall. William Morris. For today are poor fold raised up/and cast a-down the proud. FSW

Mastery. Sara Teasdale. Of my own spirit let me be/In sole though feeble mastery. HBV 1-2; WGRP

Mastrim: A Meditation (excerpt). Hugh Maxton. and neutral voices, seen and never heard. CIP

The Matadors. Josephine Jacobsen. Toro, toro! Venga! TAP

The Match. Andrew Marvell. And have within our Selves possest/All Love's and Nature's store. EBEV

A Match. Algernon Charles Swinburne. And I were king of pain. ALV; ELP; EnLi 1-2; GTBS; HBV 1-2; LiTL; NOBV; OBVV

A Match with the Moon. Dante Gabriel Rossetti. She kissed me for good-night. So you'll not tell. NCEP; NOBV; VLP

Mater Amabilis. Sir Aubrey De Vere. Her anthem, "Salve, Redemptoris Mater." ISi

Mater Amabilis. Emma Lazarus. Whom she crooned to sleep and rocked upon/her knees. OHIP

Mater Dei. Padraic Fallon. How huge a body she was, how she corrected/The very tilt of the earth on its new course? NOCV

Mater Dei. Katharine Tynan Hinkson. Since God Himself played by her gown. ISi

Mater Desiderata. Winthrop Mackworth Praed. With all the quiet of a thought/And all the passion of a dream/Link'd in a golden spell together. OBVV

Mater Dolorosa. William Barnes. Mother, never mourn. CH; HBV 1-2; OBEV

Mater Dolorosa. John Banister Tabb. Who died upon a Tree. AnAmPo

Mater Incognita. Sister Mary Benvenuta. In reparation for the days/Of empty grief–before I knew. ISi

Materia Nupcial. Pablo Neruda. blind fish or balls of dense water. ErPo

Materialized into an owl. Louis (LittleCoon) Oliver. Old man Choska had died. STE

Maternal Despotism; or, The Rights of Infants. Richard Graves. And boys and kings thenceforth you'll see/Enjoy complete Equality. NOEC

Maternal Lady with the Virgin Grace. Mary Ann Lamb. ...they wish to be/A Catholic, Madonna fair, to worship thee. ISi

Maternity Gown. David Holbrook. As you saw the love in mine–as you do now, say you do! OxBTC

A Mathematical Problem. Samuel Taylor Coleridge. 'Tis rais'd upon A.B. the straight, the given line. FaBoUs

Mathematics. Joel Oppenheimer. there are no horses we will use/the dogs. they will do. CoPo

Mathematics of Encounter. Isabella Gardner. and the equation solved. ErPo

Mathematics of Love. Michael Hamburger. The links are chance, the chain is fate. NePoEA-2

Mathematics or the Gift of Tongues. Anna Hempstead Branch. The Lord of Love is whole again. ImOP

The Mathmid. Chaim Nachman Bialik. And earth and all her fullness are forgotten... AWP

Matilda. Hilaire Belloc. And therefore when her Aunt returned,/Matilda, and the House, were Burned. CenHV; FaBoCh; LoGBV

Matilda. F. Gwynne Evans. Nothing but naughty temper killed her. BBGG

The Matin Pandemoniums. Richard Eberhart. Where is there deeper secret revelation than among/The early morning pandemoniums of the birds? NYBP

Matin Song. Nathaniel Field. For the gray morn breaks from thine eyes. HBV 1-2

Matinal. Cilla McQueen. repairing her small wounds. OCNZ

Matinees. James Merrill. Ever gratefully, Your little friend... HaCAP; NOBA; Prf

Mating Answer. Ronald Bottrall. Down to soft welcoming feathers, warm eggs. PoA

Mating the Goats. Aliki Barnstone. or be a goat. AMV-81; BoWoP

Matins. Denise Levertov. Thrust close your smile/that we know you, terrible joy. AmPP; CoPo; FaBoWP; IHMS; NoAm; NOBA

Matins–Friday. John Henry, Cardinal Newman. To whom all worship shall be done/In every time and place. VLP

Matins, or Morning Prayer. Robert Herrick. Thy golden censers filled with odours sweet/Shall make thy actions with their ends to meet. CaPo

Matisse. Edward Hirsch. All my life I dream of dancers whirling/Through the trees like colorful wild beasts. PoDr

Matisse Tits. David Barker. sophisticated as hell. GP

Matlock Bath. Sir John Betjeman. A sense of doom, a dread to see/The Rock of Ages cleft for me. NYBP

Matmiya. Mary Tallmountain. I see you sitting. TWSS

Matrimony. John Williams. Where the ploughshares are hot, and your faith is not real. NOEC

Matrix (excerpt). Dorothy Wellesley. And cast out the soul. OBMV

Matrix III. Ed Lipman. will boost my grip in holding onto dreams/I must remember. LFAC

The Matron of Jedborough and Her Husband (excerpt). William Wordsworth. Beneath worse ailments of the mind. PeD

Matronita. Dennis Silk. She alone unfolds the town-plan,/sculling away on water. VWA

May-June, 1940. Robinson Jeffers. It will not be in our time. LiTA; MoAB; MoAmPo; NePA; WaP

The May Magnificat. Gerard Manley Hopkins. In God who was her salvation. AtBAP; ISi; VLP

May Margaret. Theophile Marzials. The dearer for the tears. HBV 1-2

May Morn. Michael McClure. there are doors of tissue gold... EAS

May Morning. Celia Thaxter. That I may be a child again this blissful/ morn of May. AA

May Mornings. Ivy O. Eastwick. Go dancing to school. BrR; SiSoSe

May-Music. Rachel Annand Taylor. Lo, I follow thee. HBV 1-2

May My Heart Always. Edward Estlin Cummings. pulling all the sky over him with one smile. MoRP; OBSP

May No Man Sleep in Your Hall. Anonymous. To drive away the flies, madam. GBP; NCEP

May Poems. Anonymous.
And ar in mirth ay mair and mair/Thruch glaidnes of this lusty May. OxBS
The planeitis for to agif us licht. OxBS
This foirsaid flour that wes so fair. OxBS

May Song. Anonymous. And if we live to tarry the town,/We'll call another year. OBET

May Song. Wendell Berry. ...-a beauty/we have less than not/deserved. AP

A May Song. Violet Fane. My love (who loves me not) and I. OBVV

The May Sun Sheds an Amber Light. William Cullen Bryant. Low in her grave. AA

A May Sunday. Thomas Caulfield Irwin. The wind begins to sound along the bar. IrPN

May the Ambitious Ever Find. Charles, Earl of Dorset Sackville. Her eyes shall give me brighter days,/Her arms much softer nights. UnTE

May the man who gained my trust yet did not come. Ryojin Hisho. Then he would sway and shiver as he walked. BoWoP

May the Men Who Are Born. Hitomaro. Such as mine has been! AWP

May Thirtieth. Anonymous. You must keep their memory green. PoSC

May Time. Sir Thomas Wyatt. Rejoice! let me dream of your felicity. OBSC

The May Tree. William Barnes. His limbs wer a-fringed wi' the vrost or the snow. LiTB; LoBV

May Trees in a Storm. Geoffrey Grigson. HALT glitters, but I choose/ Your way. GBL

May with Its Light Behaving. W. H. Auden. How insufficient is/The endearment and the look. EBEV

May You Always Be the Darling of Fortune. Jane Miller. wholly evident: the rain in the white basin, and I/vigilant. AMV-80

Maybe Alone on My Bike. William Stafford. and I hear in the chain a chuckle I like to hear. NYBP

Maybe Love. Allen Ginsberg. Love's death, & body's end. PeHV

Maybe You Cannot Comprehend. Salvador Villanueva. and our house, like the century,/is falling to pieces... InW

Mayday. Ed Roberson. kindling floor of your dreaming PoBA

The Mayers' Song. Anonymous. And send you a joyful May. GBP

Mayflower. Conrad Aiken. this holy land, our faith itself, to share again/ with our godfathers, Will and Ben. MP

The Mayflower. Erastus Wolcott Ellsworth. Over the bay, and over the ship Mayflower. AA; FaBoBe; HBV 1-2; MC; PAH

Mayflower. John Boyle O'Reilly. Mayflower! Foremost and best of our/ ships! AA; PAH

A-Maying, A-Paying. Nashe [(or Nash(] Thomas. So merrily trip and go! EiL

Maymie's Story of Red Riding-Hood. James Whitcomb Riley. An' story's honest truth-an' all so, too! DFT

Mayor of Lagos. Anonymous. So may you handle Lagos with care. WTO

The Mayor of Scuttleton. Mary Mapes Dodge. But the worst of it all was, nobody knew/What the Mayor of Scuttleton next would do. NA

The Mayors. William Blake. Good English hospitality, O then it did not fail! CH

A Maypole. Jonathan Swift. I mean the church, the king, and me. CBEP; NCEP

Maystress Jane Scroupe. John Skelton. She flourisheth fresh and new/In beauty and virtu. EG

Maytime. Anonymous. Nor make the watch-dog bark/Under my lattice dark. AWP

Maze. Richard Eberhart. And the lake of my eyes is a cheat. AnAmPo

Mazeppa. George Gordon, Lord Byron. The king had been an hour asleep. EnRP; OBRV

Mazeppa. Roy Campbell. With truth a silver trumpet at his lips. AnFE

McAfee's Confession. Anonymous. But on heaven's bright and flowery plain/I hope to meet you all again. AmFP

McAndrew's Hymn. Rudyard Kipling. What your good leddy costs in coal?...I'll burn 'em down to port. CABL; OxBTC

McCaffery. Anonymous. For bloody lies and tyranny/Have made a murderer of McCaffery. OBET

McDonogh Day in New Orleans. Marcus B. Christian. How dear comes beauty when a skin is black. AmNP; PoNe

McIlrath of Malate. John Jerome Rooney. And valor claimed her own! PAH

McKinley. Anonymous. And with new yearnings in her eyes/Climbs to her watch-tower–reassured. MC; PAH

McKinley Brook. Anonymous. And Satan's kingdom soon shall fall! ShS

McLean's Welcome. James Hogg. Strong arms and broad claymores, three hundred and ten! OxBS

MCMXIV. Philip Larkin. Never such innocence again. EBEV; OBWP

McNaughtan (Johnny Scot). Anonymous. The vict'ry's into Scotland gane,/ Tho' sair against their will. OxBB

Me. Walter De la Mare.
Always just me. FaPON
And the spirit within it/Is gone. BiCB; TiPo

Me. Hughes Mearns. My truest friends, a loyal set,/Are all the folks I've never met. InMe

Me Alone. Lula Lowe Weeden. I felt myself so much riding in a King's coach,/Me alone. CDC

Me and My Chauffeur Blues. Memphis Minnie. Then he can be my little boy/Yes I'll treat him good BluL

Me and My Dog. Anonymous. Me and my dog/don't care whether/we get any work/or not. PoAu 1-2

Me and Prunes. Rupe Sherwood. We'd prospect there for sulphurets–and find 'em, too. Hey,/Prunes? PoOW

Me and Samantha. Pyke Johnson, Jr. But I know I would like you much better,/If you'd be a good girl, and shut up. GDP

Me and the Devil Blues. Robert Johnson. So my old evil spirit/can get a Greyhound bus and ride BluL

Me and the Mule. Langston Hughes. You got to take me/Like I am. IDB

Me, Colored. Peter Abrahams. You talk too much. Go'n wash up. PBA

Me from myself–to banish. Emily Dickinson. How this be/Except by Abdication–/Me–of Me? NoAm; SBG

Me Happy, Night, Night Full of Brightness. Ezra Pound. If she give me many,/God am I for the time. InvP

Me Imperturbe. Walt Whitman. To confront night, storms, hunger, ridicule, accidents, rebuffs, as the/trees and animals do. NOBA

Me, in Kulu Se & Karma. Carolyn M. Rodgers. ...its me being music/in kulu se & karma land PoBA

Me Johnny Mitchell Man. Anonymous. I'm say "No, sir, Joe come out on shtrike,/Me Johnny Mitchell man!" TrAS

Me List No More to Sing. Sir Thomas Wyatt. For I reck not a bean:/I wot what I do mean. AAS; FCP; SiPS

Me to You. Alastair Reid. Write, and I'll come. NYBP

Me Up at Does. Edward Estlin Cummings. You wouldn't have NYBP; OBSP; WeW

Mea Culpa. Ethna (Anna Johnston MacManus) Carbery. I lay a lonely heart/Before Thy feet. CAW; TrPWD

The Meadow. John Wieners. Words from our poems/Menace the night. CoPo

Meadow Grass. Michael Mott. under a shifting, mostly indifferent sky AMV-80

The Meadow Lark. Hamlin Garland. And work for the time is a pleasant thing. AA

The Meadow Mouse. Theodore Roethke. All things innocent, hapless, forsaken. HeIP; NaP; PPoe

Meadowland. Anonymous. We, the peoples of the land of Soviets. FSW

Meadowsweet. William Allingham. Our Streamlet curved, as now, through grass and wheat. OBNC

Mean Drunk Poem. Sharon Thesen. The Gap is real & there is no such thing as/female intelligence. We're dumber than hell. CaPN; NOBC

Mean Mistreater Mama. Leroy Carr. When the one that you love,/Baby, is loving someone else? BluL

Mean Old Twister. Kokomo Arnold. Says I got everybody happy/'round here in my neighborhood BluL

Meandering Wye. Robert Bloomfield. And shout, "Delicious WYE, farewell!" OBNC

The Meaning. Ralph Gustafson. Where the oak is, the woodbird heedless/ Hammers at my final house. OBCV

The Meaning of a Letter. Anonymous. Promoter of Mutual Acquaintance/ Of Peace and Good Will. PoToHe

The Meaning of Africa. Abioseh Nicol. And a small bird singing on a mango tree. PBA

The Meaning of Love. Anonymous. That's the meaning of love in the soul. WTO

The Meaning of the Look. Elizabeth Barrett Browning. "Because I KNOW this man, let him be clear.'" TrCP; TRV

The Meaning of Violence. John Williams. Beyond self's vanquishment/We feed upon our kill. NePoAm-2

The Meanings in the Pattern. Judy Grahn. It takes three days and nights to tell it. APU

Meditation on a Bone. A. D. Hope. What bone shall speak for me? TW

Meditation on a Memoir. J. V. Cunningham. Who knows what themes,/What lunar senses,/Compel his dreams? QFR

Meditation on Communion with God. Judah Halevi. "Blest be Thy glorious Name, O Lord!" TrJP

A Meditation on John Constable. Charles Tomlinson. ...The artist lies/For the improvement of truth. Believe him. NePoEA-2

A Meditation on Rhode Island Coal. William Cullen Bryant. And melt the icicles from off his chin. TAP

Meditation on Statistical Method. J. V. Cunningham. Will average out. CoAP; ForPo; QFR; VGW

Meditation on the BMT. Paul Blackburn. if they relieve their bladders against some/crappy wall or other. CoPo

Meditation on the Nativity. Elizabeth Jennings. A maid, a child, God young. NAs

Meditation under Stars. George Meredith. Half strange seems Earth, and sweeter than/her flowers. OAEP

A Meditation upon the Toothache. Laurence Lerner. The imagination hurts, like fear: or toothache. NePoEA-2

A Meditation: What is a Stocking in Eternity? Lewis MacAdams. The/day most clearly begins. ANYP

Meditations. Solomon Ibn Gabirol. And guide thee at last to the heavenly/garden. TrJP

Meditations. Edward Taylor.
Eate, Eate me, Soul, and thou shalt never dy. AmP; AP; LiTA; NoP; TAP
The Guests that Come hereto shall swim in bliss. TAP
I'll wagon-loads of love and glory bring. AnNE; AP
Let me thy Angell bee, bee thou my Lord. AP; LiTA; TAP
Lord, blow the coal, Thy love enflame in me. AnNE
My bells shall then thy praises bravely chime. NoP
Shall be the psalms sung forth in gracious lays. AnNE
Thy bottle make my soul, Lord, it to hold. LiTA
Thy Glory then I'le make my fruits and Crop. AP
Thy wrath, slay sin, and in they Love mee bench. AP
Which can thy glorious praises sing out best. AP
With my strong Wings whose Feathers are thine own. AP

Meditations for a Savage Child. Adrienne Rich. why should the wild child/weep for the scientists/why. LCAP

Meditations for August 1, 1666. Philip Pain. No More! O solemn sound: This night I may/Be struck by Death, and never see the day. SCAP

Meditations for July 19, 1666. Philip Pain. This day is past; but tell me, who can say/That I shall surely live another day. SCAP

Meditations for July 25, 1666. Philip Pain. Lord, as thou givest me more hours to live,/So with it, Oh do thou thy grace me give. SCAP

Meditations for July 26, 1666. Philip Pain. Lord, let thy Terrours every day cause me/To prepare for my end, and ready be. SCAP

Meditations in an Emergency. Frank O'Hara. Turning, I spit in the lock and the knob turns. CAPP; TAP

Meditations in Time of Civil War. William Butler Yeats.
Befitting emblems of adversity. CABL
But take our greatness with our bitterness? CABL; MoVE
Come build in the empty house of the stare. CABL
In the cold snows of a dream. BIrV; CABL; NOBE
Juno's peacock screamed. CABL
Suffice the ageing man as once the growing boy. CABL
These stones remain their monument and mine. CABL

Meditations of a Hindu Prince. Sir Alfred Comyn Lyall. With the dirge, and the sound of lamenting and voices of/women who weep? WGRP

Meditations of a Tortoise Dozing under a Rosetree... Emile Victor Rieu. There is no one like me. FiBHP

Meditations of an Old Woman. Theodore Roethke.
Even the stones speak. NaP
I am still happy. AP; LCAP; NaP; NOBA
If the wind means me,/I'm here!/Here. NaP
A light wind rises: I become the wind. NaP
Unprayed-for,/And final. NaP

Meditations on the Sepulchre in the Garden. Philip Doddridge. Though mine own sepulchre can see/A paradise reserved for me. NOCV; NOEC

Mediterranean. Israel Pincas. It's like a thousand years ago,/Now, this evening. VWA

The Mediterranean. Allen Tate. Rot on the vine: in that land were we born. AP; ExPo; FaBoMo; HAP; InPo; LiTA; LiTM; MoAB; MoAmPo; MOS; MoVE; NePA; OxBS; PoCh; SeCePo; SeCeV; VGW; WeW

Mediterranean. Ruth Whitman. A rosy air washes his absence. VWA

The Medium. Elaine Feinstein. ...Perhaps you should talk to them? BrRo

The Medium IV Sights. Carl Rakosi. beholds the hairy/pappus of a dandelion. PAI

Medium Poem. Eileen Myles. ...And I am never/sure. And I am always here. APU

Medlars and Sorb-Apples. D. H. Lawrence. Intoxication of final loneliness. OAEL 1-2

Medley. *Anonymous.* And struck up a bit of a jig. OxNR

Medoro's Inscription for a Cave. John Stewart of Baldynnis And unmolestit be your silver spring. BSV

Medusa. Louise Bogan. And does not drift away. AWP; BoWoP; HoPM; InPo; MoAB; MoAmPo; MoVE; NMM; NoP

The Medusa. Guy Davenport. a ferociousness of light/in the cold dark of the seas. GP

Medusa. Sylvia Plath. There is nothing between us. CAPP

Medusa. Robert Kelley Weeks. O love that turns to stone! AA

Medusa's Hair Was Snakes. Was Thought, Split Inward. Kathleen Fraser. ...a regularity from which the clouds drift/into their wet embankments. NPGG

The Meek and the Proud. Abraham Ibn Chasdai. But 'neath its wrath the proudest/cedars fall. TrJP

Meet Me in St. Louis. Andrew B. Sterling. Meet me at the fair. FSN; FSW; GoTF; OBAL; TreFT

Meet Me in the Primrose Lane. John Clare. And silence sleeps about the glen. AtBAP

Meet Mr. Universe. Edward Estlin Cummings. who made the world's best one hand snatch OBAL

Meet the Supremes. David Trinidad. ...Then, at least for Flo,/begins the long and painful process of letting go. APU

Meet We No Angels, Pansie? Thomas Ashe. But–meet no we angels, Pansie? HBV 1-2; OBVV

The Meeting. Louise Bogan. ...Like a faithless brother/You take and drop my hand. NePoAm-2; NYBP

The Meeting. Gerald Constanzo. the ashes you leave behind are/your name. MAYP

Meeting. George Crabbe. And now let naught in memory live/But that we meet, and that we love. HBV 1-2; OBEV

A Meeting. C. Day Lewis. ...Nature, it seems, can afford/Such wastefulness–not we. NYBP

The Meeting. Tess Gallagher. ...Early/and late, this hour has closed/around us. GeTw

Meeting. Sam Harrison. knowing that this/was holy ground, that no pursuing ghost/could claim us now. NeIP

A Meeting. Daniel Gerard Hoffman. Or wings singed in the sun. CoPo

The Meeting. Jocelyn Hollis. then you came forth, and all the earth was light! AMV-80

The Meeting. Nicki Jackowska. ...The life not yet/invented. BrRo

The Meeting. Pierre Louys. and we will give them roses for each night's/reward.' PeHV

The Meeting. Howard Moss. It was there, I think, we finally met. GOYP; HoAn; NYBP

Meeting. Christina Georgina Rossetti.
...and I felt my hair/Put on a glory, and my soul expand. HBV 1-2
Never to part more. GBL

The Meeting. Muriel Rukeyser. And all the birds fly out of my scene. MoAmPo; TrJP

Meeting. William Saphier. at a solemn farewell meeting. AnAmPo

The Meeting. Kathleen Spivack. and kicked/their mothers with joy and/evangelical fervor. NMM

The Meeting. Ramona Wilson. shards of reasonable nights. VoR

Meeting a Bear. David Wagoner. Meanwhile, move off, yielding the forest floor/As carefully as your honor. HAP

Meeting After Long Absence. Lilla Cabot Perry.
Heart has found rest on heart. AA
You come–a stranger from your eyes/Looks out–and, meeting, first we part. AA

Meeting after Separation. Marula. And in an instant the doe-eyed girl/Was completely merged in my heart. BoWoP

Meeting Anais Nin's Elena. Gene Frumkin. ...fled from me/to tear at love, devour its cold meat. AMV-81

Meeting and Passing. Robert Frost. Afterward I went past what you had passed/Before we met and you what I had passed. OxBA

Meeting at Night. Robert Browning. Than the two hearts beating each to each! AWP; BoLiVe; BoLoP; CBEP; DiPo; ELP; FaBV; FF; FiP; GBL; GTBS; HBV 1-2; HeIP; InPo; InPS; InvP; LiTL; MaVP; MBW 1-2; MCCG; MOS; NOBE; NOBV; OAEP; OBEV; OBNC; OBSP; OLR; PAI; PoPl; PoRA; SCV; SeCePo; SoSe; TreFT; TrGrPo; UnPo; ViBoPo; VLP; WeW

Meeting at the Building. *Anonymous.* All over this world. FSW

A Meeting at the Crossroads. Joseph Bruchac. ...As I go past them I can see/the tail light of the Chevy blinking on and off/in ecstacy. AmC

Meeting at the Local. Tom Parson. I am one on earth talking with you. SOTS

Meeting by the Gjulika Meadow. Geoffrey Grigson. The lemon sun again, and the scent/And magenta of cyclamens. WaP

Meeting Halfway. R. Wayne Hardy. won't you move over.../just a little closer? LFAC

Meeting-House Hill. Amy Lowell. With dull, sea-spent eyes. LoGBV; MoAmPo; OxBA; SBG

Memoria Technica for the Plays of Shakespeare. *Anonymous.* Romeo, Macbeth, Cleopatra, Caesar, Coriolanus. FaBoUs

Memorial. Mae Winkler Goodman. The grave marked only by the green/ Memorial of grass! PGD

Memorial. Robert Pinsky. No hospital beds, but a lifting of metal wings. HaCAP; SM

Memorial Sonia Sanchez. i'll send my ass C.O.D./to any Revolutionary,/u dig? BlSi

Memorial Couplets for the Dying Ego. George Barker. I burn like St Catherine's wheel/Spun on fires I cannot feel. EBEV

Memorial Day. William E. Brooks. ...Will we grant them/sleep? PAL; PGD

Memorial Day. Laureen Ching. Just platoons of Scouts/planting flags. AMV-80

Memorial Day. Theodosia Garrison. The spirit of America today is marching by! OHIP; PoSC

Memorial Day. Richard Watson Gilder. His grave was deckt with flowers by strangers' hands/to-day. OHIP

Memorial Day. Emma A. Lent. Let music sound, and flowers be laid/ Upon each resting-bed. WBLP

Memorial Day. Josephine Miles. All these camellias overgrown and wasting? NoP

Memorial Day. Annette Wynne. And be ourselves, in turn, the brave! OHIP

Memorial Day: A Collaboration. Ted and Anne Waldman Berrigan. & the hole is closed & the boat has left & the day is closed. EAS

Memorial Lines on the Gender of Latin Substantives. Benjamin Hall Kennedy. Est summum nefas fallere:/Deceit is gross impiety. FaBoUs

The Memorial Pillar. Felicia Dorothea Hemans. Mother and child!–your tears are past–/Surely your hearts have met at last. SBG

Memorial Poem. Roy Fuller. The strange emaciated brown-faced fiend lay dead. OBSP

Memorial Poem. Jacob Glatstein. an eternal deathday light/forever flickering? VWA

Memorial Rain. Archibald MacLeish.
Aud suddenly, and all at once, the rain! OBWP
He rests, he is quiet, he sleeps in a strange land. BoLiVe; CMoP; LiTA; MoAB; MoAmPo; NoAm

Memorial Service. Ursula Vaughan Williams. and greets her friends as deaths' new wife. PoL

Memorial Service for the Invasion Beach Where the Vacation.... Alan Dugan. and barely can not hear them calling, "Here's one." MP; NMP; TwCP

Memorial Sonnet. Marjorie Meeker. By any pledge of any God or man. AnAmPo

Memorial Thresholds. Dante Gabriel Rossetti. Or mocking winds whirl round a chaff-strown floor/Thee and thy years and these my words and me. MaVP

Memorial to D.C. Edna St. Vincent Millay. Once the ivory box is broken,/ Beats the golden bird no more. OxBA

Memorial to the Great Big Beautiful Self-Sacrificing Advertisers. Frederick Ebright. There is a dignity in silence. WaP

Memorial Verse.. Matthew Arnold. ...for few or none/Hears thy voice right, now he is gone. CABA; FiP; HBV 1-2; OAEL 1-2; OAEP; PP; VLP

Memorial Verses for Travellers. Sir Anthony Fitzherbert. Make merry, sing an thou canst, take heed to thy geer, that/thou lose none. FaBoUs

Memorial Wreath. Dudley Randall. Our hearts beat prouder for the blood we inherit. CNA; IDB; NNP; PoBA; PoNe

Memorials: On the Slain at Chickamauga. Herman Melville Make this memorial due. AA

Memories. Thomas Bailey Aldrich. The thrill that shook you at your child's/first cry. AA

Memories. George Denison Prentice. Like other dreams must fade! AA

Memories. Arthur Stringer. This many a year–this many a year! HBV 1-2

Memories. Walt Whitman. ...their loves, joys, persons, voyages. PCP

Memories of a Lost War. Louis Simpson. They will be proud a while of something death/Still seems to need. NePoAm; OBWP; VGW

Memories of Aunt Maria-Martha (parody). William Zaranka. To drink the brack that Ahab spit at heaven. BXAP

Memories of Verdun. Alan Dugan. I was afraid of a nothing, a death;/they were afraid of less, its lieutenant. OBSP

Memories of West Street and Lepke. Robert Lowell. hanging like an oasis in his air/of lost connections. AmPP; CAPP; CMoP; ConAP; InPS; NaP; NOBA; PAI

A Memory. Marvin Bell. You were put in the hole for good reason. GP

A Memory. Rupert Brooke. Takes all too long to lay asleep again. BrPo

Memory. William Browne. Then be an age! that we may never try/More grief in parting, but grow old and die. HBV 1-2

The Memory. Robert Creeley. Did wonder pour down/on the whole goddamn town. CAPP; VGW

Memory. Babette Deutsch. Yet there delight blooms in remorseless cold. PoA

The Memory. Edward John, Lord Dunsany. But an emperor of Tartary has died for love of me. OxBI

Memory. Michael Hamburger. It was the herbs and the hazc. OxBTC

Memory. Helen Hoyt. I cannot remember our love. PoLf

A Memory. Frederic Lawrence Knowles. Till a hundred nests gave music,/ And the East was gray. HBV 1-2

Memory. Walter Savage Landor. It hurries down to wither on the strand. EBEV; NOBV; OAEL 1-2

Memory. Abraham Lincoln. I'm living in the tombs. BLPA; FaBoBe; FPL; WBLP

Memory. Arthur Rimbaud. My fixed canoe, its chain eternally drawn down/deep in this edgeless eye of water–to what slime? LiTW

Memory. Christina Georgina Rossetti. My heart dies inch by inch; the time grows old,/Grows old in which I grieve. OBNC

Memory. Dante Gabriel Rossetti. Or the one flower of ease in bitterest hell? CBEP; OBSP

Memory. Erik Johann Stagnelius. Till I, a shade in heaven, clasp her, a shade. AWP

A Memory. Leonard Alfred George Strong. Yet life is often queer like that. FaBoCo; NOBL; PoPl

Memory. Joseph Stroud. Home, a sound of bells,/In the huge, quiet night. NPGG

A Memory. Katharine Tynan. God send fine weather to carry home the sheaves!' OxBI

Memory. William Butler Yeats. Where the mountain hare has lain. BIrV

Memory, a Small Brown Bird. Rich Ives. There is no one to keep her from leaving. AMV-81

Memory Air. Charles Dobzynski. You breathe me I inscribe you/circular memory VWA

Memory as Memorial in the Last. Edward Marshall. but in memory and oblivion only at the/last in the nothingness that is everything. CoPo

Memory Gardens. Allen Ginsberg. Everything else, drunken/dumbshow. NNaP

Memory Movie. Diane Webster. And today takes charge. AMV-81

Memory of a Porch. Donald Justice. The sighing of ferns/Half-asleep in their boxes. NCSH

Memory of a Scholar. Richmond Lattimore. Never forget. For there was none like you. GLGT

Memory of Another Climate. Gabriel Preil. and the landscape remained lucid in the eye/even in the rain. VWA

The Memory of Boxer Benny (Kid) Paret. Frank Lima. Benny's an/empty bag. PoNe

Memory of Brother Michael. Patrick Kavanagh. Shall we be thus for ever? FaBoIP; MoAB; OnYI; OxBI

A Memory of Earth. George William Russell. Death made wide a million gates/So to close her tragic story. OBVV

The Memory of Elena. Carolyn Forche. ...bells/waiting with their tongues cut out/for this particular silence. MAYP

Memory of Hills (excerpt). Rex Ingamells. wrinkled acknowledgement of the moon's clarity. CBAP

The Memory of Kent. Edmund Charles Blunden. One primrose from my Kentish home/Is worth all these to me. HBMV

Memory of My Father. Patrick Kavanagh. "I was once your father." FaBoIP; InPS

The Memory of the Dead. John Kells Ingram. And true men be you, men,/Like those of Ninety-Eight! AnIV; HBV 1-2; OnYI; OxBI

A Memory of the Players in a Mirror at Midnight. James Joyce. Pluck forth your heart, saltblood, a fruit of tears./Pluck and devour! InvP; NoAm; ViBoPo

Memory of the Present. David Shapiro. You hate the flow, and yet it flows. APU

A Memory-Picture. Matthew Arnold. Quick, thy tablets, Memory! VLP

Memphis Blues. Sterling A. Brown. De win' sing sperrichals/Through deir dus'. BANP

Memphis Minnie-Jitis Blues. Memphis Minnie. I heard my companion say/ I won't see your smiling face again BluL

Men. Archibald MacLeish. We have lived a long time in this land and with honor. AmFN; MoAB; YaD

Men. Dorothy Parker. They make me sick, they make me tired. DBV

Men against the Sky. John Haines. and one old windmill,/its broken arms/ clattering in the darkness. LCAP

Men Are Children of This World. Moses Ibn Ezra. But their thirst would remain/unquenched forever. TrJP

The Men Are Coming Back! Barry Cole. Dye across their untouched lips. OxBTC

Men Are the Devil. Mary Carolyn Davies. But what are you going to do in spring? HBMV; YaD

Men at Forty. Donald Justice. Behind their mortgaged houses. GP; LCAP; PPP; Prf

The Men behind the Guns. John Jerome Rooney. Shall the voice of peace bring sweet release to the men be-/hind the guns! AA; BLPA; EtS; FaBoBe; HBV 1-2; MC; PAH; YaD

Men Fade Like Rocks. Walter James Turner. Smoother than river-rain/Falls chime on chime. OBMV

Men Fishing in the Arno. Elizabeth Jennings. Yet not surprised should the river suddenly/Yield a hundredfold, every hunger appeased. OBTV

Men Improve with the Years. William Butler Yeats. A weather-worn, marble triton/Among the streams. MBW 1-2

Men in Green. David Campbell. With fifteen spitting tommy-guns/To keep a jungle back. BoAV; PoAu 1-2

Men in the City. Alfonsina Storni. crossing back and forth/the men... PBWV

Men Loved Wholly Beyond Wisdom. Louise Bogan. Music in the granite hill. AnAmPo; HBMV; InPo; LiTA; LiTL; LiTM; NePA; PBWV; VGW

Men Made out of Words. Wallace Stevens. The whole race is a poet that writes down/The eccentric propositions of its fate. MoAB; NOBA; OBSP; TAP; VGW

Men Marry What They Need. I Marry You. John Ciardi. Men marry what they need. I marry you. MoLP

Men May Talk of Country-Christmasses. Philip Massinger. ...I dare swear the cook that dressed it/Was the devil, disguised like a Dutchman. OBCP

The Men of Old. Richard Monckton, Lord Houghton Milnes. Remembering distance leaves a haze/On all that lies below. GTBS
They went about their gravest deeds/As noble boys at play. OBEV; OBVV

The Men of the Alamo. James Jeffrey Roche. "Thermoplylae left one alive–the Alamo/left none." BPAW; PAH

Men of the High North. Robert W. Service. Let's have a rouse that will ring round the earth. ACV

The Men of the Maine. Clinton Scollard. The whole land bound in closer amity! MC; PAH

The Men of the Merrimac. Clinton Scollard. Shame upon us, shame upon us, should the/nation e'er forget! PAH

Men of the North. John Neal. Upon our haughty foe! AA

Men of the North and West. Richard Henry Stoddard. Strike! Men of the North and West. PAH

Men of the Rocks. Adam Drinan. taste of resignation, sweet! OxBS

Men of the Rocks. Joseph Gordon ("Adam Drinan") MacLeod.
The false sea likes to be visited. OxBS
Happy our hill then/feed her children. OxBS

The men of valor. Akahito (Yamabe no Akahito). Over the clean sea-beach. AWP; LiTW

Men Only Pretend. Anonymous. Begeled, parde,/Withouten grace. MeEL

Men's Impotence. Anonymous. Curling downwards at the corners,/Like a bent twig/For a kayak rib. WTO

Men's Loving Is a False Affection. Anonymous. God help who follow in my footsteps. NOBI

The Men's Room in the College Chapel. W. D. Snodgrass. returning, masterless and twisted. GP; MoAmPo; PPP; TW

Men's Voices. Inger Christensen. why have they wakened me? BoWoP

Men Say They Know Many Things. Henry David Thoreau. Is all that any body knows. AnNE; ImOP; PoPl

Men tell and talk. Nia Francisco. and the woman's pregnancy STE

The Men That Don't Fit In. Robert W. Service. He's a man who won't fit in. BLPA; BLPL

Men Told Me, Lord! David Starr Jordan. I could no more through all eternity! WGRP

Men Walked To and Fro. Blanaid Salkeld. catholic/pleasure/treasure. NeIP

The Men Who Come Behind. Henry Lawson. But we'll leave it to be hackneyed by the fellows in the rear. NOAV

Men Who March away. Thomas Hardy. Men who march away. MMM; OBWP

Men Working. Edna St. Vincent Millay. They were putting in the poles: bringing the electric light. SaC

The Menagerie. William Vaughn Moody. There may be hidden meaning in his grin. AP; YaD

Menaphon. Robert Greene.
As behoves/Shepheards loves. AtBAP
Labour for me; love rest in prince's bower. LoBV; OBSC
When thou are olde, ther's grief inough for thee! AtBAP
Wherefore no time my banning prayers shall pause,/till proud she repent. OBSC
Yeeld to Samela. AtBAP

Mendacity. Alfred Edgar Coppard. Little love, my love, come to me. LiTL; OBMV

Mendax. Gotthold Lessing. Why, don't you see, my friend, the fellow's talking. PV

Mendel's Law. Peter Meinke. completely new, yet linked to paradise. SUW

The Mendicants. Bliss Carman. Then supperless he laid him down/That night, and slept beneath the stars. HBV 1-2

Mending Crab Pots. Dave Smith. "Them poets, goddam 'em, always/in school with their white hands." GeTw

Mending Sump. Kenneth Koch. "We'd better leave him in the sump," he said. BXAP; HeIP; InPK; NeAP; NoAm; PV

Mending the Adobe. Hayden Carruth. I remember my mother. EyDe; Psk

Mending the Bridge. Douglas Stewart. Monstrous against the marshes of the night. AnNZ

Mending Wall. Robert Frost. He says again, "Good fences make good neighbors." AmFN; AnNE; AP; CMoP; CoBMV; DiPo; ExPo; FaBoPV; FaBV; FaFP; FPL; HAP; HBV 1-2; HeIP; HoPM; InPK; InPo; InPS; LaNeLa; LiTA; LiTM; MCCG; MoAB; MoAmPo; MoVE; NePA; NoAm; NOBA; NoP; OHFP; OxBA; PAI; PrIm; SCV; SeCeV; SoSe; TAP; VGW; ViBoPo; WHA

Mendings. Muriel Rukeyser. "The war will be over before your work is ready." SaC

Mene, Mene, Tekel, Upharsin. Madison Cawein. Thou art weighed in the scales and found/wanting, the balance of God, O Spain! PAH

Menelaus and Helen. Rupert Brooke. And Paris slept on by Scamander side. SeCePo

Menodotis. Leonidas of Alexandria. How very like to all the world, except/Menodotis. AWP; LiTW

Menses. Edna St. Vincent Millay. ...and damn/To tedious Hell this body with its muddy feet in my mind! NMM

Mental Cases. Wilfred Owen. Pawing us who dealt them war and madness. BiP; BrPo; CMoP; FaBoMo; MMM; NoAm; WaP

Mental Health. Elliot Fried. Be screwed up or warped or sick/but don't explain yourself away. GP

The Mental Hospital Garden. William Carlos Williams. ...her mind/drinks up/the full meaning/of it/all! FYAP

The Mental Traveler. William Blake. And all is done as I have told DiPo; EnRP; ERoP 1-2; LAuP; MasP; OAEL 1-2; PoEL 1-5

Mentis Trist. Robert Hillyer. Daily cup, the Holy Grail. HBMV

Mentreche il Vento, Come Fa, Si Tace. Delmore Schwartz. –Consent, consent, consent to be/My many-branched, small and dearest tree. AnFE; CoAnAm

The Menu. Thomas Bailey Aldrich. With "Not at Home" to anyone/Excepting Alfred Tennyson. HBV 1-2

The Mer-Man and Marstig's Daughter. Anonymous. They dance wi' nae sic unco man. AWP

Mercado. Greg Pape. one bright horn/that lifts the sky. AmPA

Merce Cunningham and the Birds. Lisel Mueller. ...and then disappear into nowhere. GrPl

Merce of Egypt. Charles Olson. when the spring comes, and flood, the tassels/rise, as my head. NoP

Merced. Adrienne Rich. ...that is unable/to hate, therefore to love. NOBA

Mercedes. Elizabeth Stoddard Now she knows her lover's fate! AA

Mercedes, Her Aloneness. Colette Inez. in the singular print of her palm,/anointing aloneness. IHMS

Merchandise. Sean Jennett. ...but those dark men/looked at his load and laughed, and turned away. NeIP

Merchandise. Amy Lowell. All made out of nothing,/And so beautiful! LaNeLa; MAPA

The Merchant and the Fidler's Wife. Anonymous. That Gamesters Drink, and Fidlers Wives,/They are ever Free and Common. CoMu; OxBB

Merchant Marine. Josephine Miles. A rendable tissue of sea lanes, there is the heart. TAP; VGW

The Merchant of Venice. William Shakespeare.
Ding, dong, bell. BoLiVe; CTC; DiPo; EG; ElL; ELP; EnLi 1-2; EnRePo; GoTF; GTBS; GTBS-P; InPo; LiTB; OAEL 1-2; OAEP; OBEV; OBSC; PoEL 1-5; SeCeV; TreFS; TrGrPo; ViBoPo; WHA
Fare you well; your suit is cold.' CTC
No better a musician than the wren. PB
So be gone; you are sped.' CTC
Still quiring to the young-ey'd cherubims. BoC; FaBoRV; FiP; GBL; GN; GoBC; GoTF; OHFP; PoPle; TreFS; TrGrPo; WHA
When mercy seasons justice. BBVV; FaFP; GoTF; LiTB; OHFP; TreF; TrGrPo; TRV; WBLP
Which, hearing them, would call their brothers fools. TrGrPo

The Merchant Shipping Act. Anonymous. Because they know by doing so they'd be breaking of the ac'. OBSS

The Merchantman. John Davidson. And death draws nigh. OBVV

Merchants from Cathay. William Rose Benet. Lest once more those mad Merchants come/chanting from Cathay! HBMV; MoAmPo

The Merchants of London. Anonymous. So merrily march the merchantmen. GBP

Mercian Hymns (excerpt). Geoffrey Hill.
...he entered into the last dream/of Offa the King. FaBoMo; HAP
he left behind coins, for his lodging, and traces of/red mud. NoP

Mercies and Blessings. Anonymous. He is my Shepherd indeed! STF

The Mercies of the Year, Commemorated.   John Danforth.   And see, your Future Lives, Jehovah Praise.   SCAP

Merciless Beauty.   Geoffrey Chaucer.
Since I am free, I count him not a bean.   CBEP
So woundeth it throughout my hearte keen.   ACP

Mercury Bay Eclogue.   Michael Kennedy Joseph.   Where Kupe and where Cook have trod.   AnNZ

Mercury. On Losing my Pocket Milton...   Robert Andrews.   Phoebus ordained: presenting, see,/The laurel never sere.'   NOEC

Mercury's Song to Phaedra.   John Dryden.   The Legend of Love no couple can find/So easie to part, or so equally join'd.   OBSP; SeCV 1-2

Mercury Shew'd Apollo, Bartas Book.   Nathaniel Ward.   Let Men look to't, least Women wear the Spurrs.   SCAP

Mercy.   Anonymous.   Mercy asketh but Godes wille.   OxBM

Mercy and Love.   Robert Herrick.   And with the last he still directs the Just.   SeCV 1-2

A! Mercy, Fortune.   Anonymous.   And sende me joy where I am nowe in pain.   MeEL

Mercy Is Most in My Mind.   Anonymous.   Sa that I may thi mercy syng/in thi blys with-owten ende.   CoBE

Mercy to Animals.   Martin Farquhar Tupper.   And man at least, if not his beast,/Shall bless me for my verses.   PeD

The 'Mergency Man.   John Millington Synge.   And the 'mergency man in two days and a bit/Was found in the ebb tide stuck in a net.   PoPle

Meridian.   Brewster Ghiselin.   And what does not die.   AMV-80

Merie Sungen the Muneches.   Anonymous.   And here we thes muneches sang.   AtBAP

Merits of Laughter and Lust.   Eli Mandel.   Jove built Arcady again, and so today I love/the white round shoulder of the distant sky.   PeCV

Merlin.   Ralph Waldo Emerson.
As the two twilights of the day/Fold us music-drunken in.   AnNE; AP; CTC; EBEV; EnLi 1-2; EnLoPo; HAP; MAmp; NOBA; NoP; OxBM; PoEL 1-5
Nor sword of angels could reveal/What they conceal.   AA; AnNE; AtBAP; BoLoP; NOBA; OxBA

Merlin.   Geoffrey Hill.   And over their city stands the pinnacled corn.   InPK; PoL

Merlin.   Edwin Muir.   And Time locked in his tower?   CBEP; FaBoTw; OxBS

Merlin and the Gleam.   Alfred, Lord Tennyson.   Follow The Gleam.   MaVP; OAEL 1-2; OAEP; VLP

Merlin and the Snake's Egg.   Leslie Norris.   He has found the snake's egg.   WSC

Merlin Enthralled.   Richard Wilbur.   The sky became a still and woven blue.   CMoP; NePoEA; NYBP

Merlin in the Cave: He Speculates without a Book.   Thom Gunn.   This is an end, and yet another start.   NePoEA

Merlin's Apple-Trees.   Thomas Love Peacock.   On my new-born apple-trees.   OBRV

Merlin, They Say.   Fulke, Lord Brooke Greville.   "Yet you would laugh as heartily, as I."   NCEP

The Mermaid.   Anonymous.
Ere lang the waves war foamin'.   ·CH
They may look, they may wait till the cold water rise,/They may look to the bottom of the sea.   AmFP
This night we all must start/To heaven or else to hell.   OuSiCo

The Mermaid.   Ben King.   Oh, no. By Jove! There comes the white hippocampus.   OBAL

The Mermaid.   Alfred, Lord Tennyson.   All looking down for the love of me.   GN; WSC

The Mermaid (B version).   Anonymous.   For the want of a life-boat they all went/down,/And she sank to the bottom of the sea.   AmFP; BaBo; ESPB; FSW; TreF; ViBoFo

A Mermaiden.   Thomas Hennell.   Later near by they hung a passing bell/Hard by a charted rock: which tolls the rising swell.   FaBoTw

The Mermaidens.   Laura E. Richards.   And never feel tired a bit.   BrR; OBCA

The Mermaids.   Walter De la Mare.   From the darkling caves.   BrPo

The Merman.   Alfred, Lord Tennyson.   We would live merrily, merrily.   GN; WSC

Merops.   Ralph Waldo Emerson.   One word, no more, to say.   AmePo; AnFE; APA; OxBA

Merrily Danced the Quaker's Wife.   Anonymous.   Merrily danced the Quaker.   OxNR

Merritt Parkway.   Denise Levertov.   gliding/north & south, speeding with/a slurred sound–   AmC; AmPP; NeAP; PoM

Merry Are the Bells.   Anonymous.   With a merry ding-dong, happy let us be!   HBV 1-2; HBVY; MoShBr; TiPo

The Merry Bagpipes.   Anonymous.   and thou shalt Pipe, and I'll Dance to thee,/To thee, to thee, derry, derry, to thee &c   CoMu

A Merry Ballad of Vintners.   John Payne.   The vintners that put water in our wine.   ALV

A Merry Bee.   Joseph Skipsey.   Pluck'd and placed in Annie's bosom,/Hums the bee!   OBVV

Merry Christmas!   Elder Olson.   Better be blind than see what we must see.   FAZ

The Merry Cuckold.   Anonymous.   And he thats no Cuckold, in ·Countrey or City,/However lucke hold, will buy this our Ditty.   CoMu

Merry-Go-Round.   Dorothy Walter Baruch.   Around/And round/And/Round.   BrR; SoPo; SUS; TiPo

Merry-Go-Round.   Langston Hughes.   Where's the horse/For a kid that's black?   CTBA; PoNe

Merry-Go-Round.   Oliver Jenkins.   Carrying us giddily away and over/The bright, green terraces of summer.   GoYe

Merry-Go-Round.   James Philip McAuley.   New-comers clamber on as these are going/Reluctantly to join the crowd outside.   CBAP

The Merry-Go-Round.   Rainer Maria Rilke.   And oftentimes a blissful dazzling smile/vanishes in this blind and breathless game.   CAD; WeW

Merry-Go-Round.   Mark Van Doren.   Oh, music, oh, mine.   SO

The Merry Hay-Makers.   Anonymous.   And when they are Crack'd, away they are pack'd,/for Virgins, away to the City.   CoMu; ErPo

The Merry Hoastess.   Anonymous.   My Ale was tunn'd when I was young,/and a little above my knee.   CoMu

Merry It Is.   Anonymous   Sorrow and mourn and fast.   HAP

The Merry Jovial Beggar.   Peter Casey.   But the soul that courts it, it must die, a low unlovely thing.   WTO

The Merry Little Maid and Wicked Little Monk.   Anonymous.   And– goodness gracious!   ErPo

·The Merry-ma-Tanzie.   Anonymous.   We pray this couple may kiss together,/About the merry-ma-tanzie.   GBP

The Merry Man of Paris.   Stella Mead.   Oh! what a merry little fat grey man!   SUS

Merry May the Keel Row.   Anonymous.   Merry may the keel row,/The ship that my love's in.   GBP

The Merry Minuet.   Sheldon Harnick.   What nature doesn't do to us, will be done by our fellow/man.   DBV; TW

The Merry Month.   Anonymous.   But it's just a headache to any teacher.   InMe

Merry Old Souls (excerpt).   Morris Bishop.   And then they heated Florence with old Savonarola.   DBV

The Merry Window.   Francis Scarfe.   since even her own self has forgotten her.   EAS

The Merry Wives of Windsor.   William Shakespeare.   Till candles and starlight and moonshine be out.   ViBoPo

Merthymawr.   George Woodcock.   Wind dries the blood on the moving sand.   NeBP

Meru.   William Butler Yeats.   His glory and his monuments are gone.   NoAm; OAEL 1-2; PAI; PoA

A Mery Gest How a Sergeaunt Wolde Lerne to Be a Frere.   Sir Thomas More.   Now make good chere,/And welcome everychone.   AAS

Meson Brujo.   E. A. Lacey.   ...build the log pyramid/in my cold chambers at the Meson Brujo.   PeHV

Mesopotamia.   Rudyard Kipling.   Shall we leave it unabated in its place?   MMM

Mess Deck Casualty.   Alan Ross.   ...cursing, stumble out like ghosts into the frozen dark.   WaP

The Mess of Love.   D. H. Lawrence.   And we've made a great mess of love, mind-perverted, ego-/perverted love.   OAEL 1-2

The Message.   John Donne.
Or prove as false as thou art now.   EiL; EnLit; MBW 1-2; MeLP; OBS; ViBoPo; WHA .

Message.   Allen Ginsberg.   I will be home in two months and look you in the eyes   ConAP; NeAP; VGW

The Message.   Heinrich Heine.   But never speak a word.   AWP

The Message.   Thomas Heywood.   And when you hear her kind reply,/Return with pleasant warblings.   HBV 1-2

A Message.   George Ives.   And bend and kiss you, bid you follow me.   PeHV

The Message.   Meleager.   And I'm going to get there ahead of you!   LiTW

Message.   Renata Pallottini.   What in you were words/in them shall be roots.   WPOW

A Message.   Elizabeth Stuart Phelps.   Dying, kiss your pictured faces,/Wishing they'd been better men?   PAH

The Message.   Jacques Prevert.   The hospital where someone's dead.   WeW

Message.   Gyorgy Raba.   here's where I live/number 1 number 1   VWA

Message.   Dorothy M. Richardson.   How each hour moves toward their awakening?   PoA

Message at Sunset for Bishop Berkeley.   Heather McHugh.   ...the sky/is really something.   GeTw

Message Clear.   Edwin Morgan.   i am the resurrection and the life.   NIP

Message from a Cross.   Max Harris.   ...and showed/its claws streaking the gentle groins/and panting and panting.   NOAV

Message from Home.   Kathleen Raine.   The birds that call to you, and all the shoals/That swim in the natal waters of her ocean.   ImOP

It is his singing/Outshines the noise/Of leaves clashing in the wind. MoAmPo

Outshines the noise/Of leaves clashing in the wind. MoAB; OxBChV

Metrical Feet. Samuel Taylor Coleridge.
Strikes his thundering hoofs like a proud highbred racer. HBV 1-2; OxBChV

With a leap and a bound the swift Anapests throng. SoSe

...you would not from its whole ridge/See a man who so loves you as your fond S. T. COLERIDGE. NIP

A Metrical Index to the Bible. Josiah Chorley. And then his letter seals. FaBoUs

A Metrical Version of the Bible....(excerpt). *Anonymous.* David alone, with sling and stone, ten thousand kill'd or/more. FaBoUs

Metroliner. Jack Du Vall. the arbitrary skylines of the cities/they join. AMV-80

Metropolitan Night. Jorge Guillen. Upon the living stars! NYP

Metropolitan Nightmare. Stephen Vincent Benét. He pried from the insect jaws the bright crumb of steel. ImOP; NYBP

The Metropolitan Railway. Baker Street Station Buffet. Sir John Betjeman. Thou art the worn memorial, Baker Street. EBEV; OxBTC

Metrum Parhemiacum Tragicum. Pope Eugenius III. To dwell a ghost amid the ghosts. WaaP

The Mewlips. J. R. R. Tolkien. You go to find the Mewlips–and the Mewlips feed. AmMo; SO; WSC

Mews Flat Mona. William Plomer. Oh, Mona! that accounts for you now! FaBoTw

Mexican Market Woman. Langston Hughes. And the sun has made/Her skin so brown. SaC

Mexican Quarter. John Gould Fletcher. Babylon and Samarkand/Are mud walls in a waste of sand. BPAW

A Mexican Scrapbook. Dave Oliphant. unmarked on any map or guide. FAZ

Mexican Serenade. Arthur Guiterman. So I guess that you had better/Go to sleep. FiBHP

Mexico. Robert Lowell.
feeding our minds...the mind which is also flesh. BiP

What is history? What you cannot touch. HaCAP

Mexico City: 150 Pesos to the Dollar. Jim Mitsui. A shadow empties the bottom of the moon. BrSi

Mexico City Blues. Jack Kerouac.
Accept as thus–the Truth. NeAP

and safe in heaven dead NeAP

But Deadbelly get Ahead/Ha ha ha NeAP

Center of lake of light NeAP

Down to Kill Roy NeAP

dreadful murderer/B U D D H A NeAP

...harder yet/are the chances, for a man/to be reborn a man/in this Karma earth PoM

I've lost my way. NeAP

Like kissing my kitten in the belly/The softness of our reward NeAP

meaning–you just/numbly dont get there NeAP

No no? No such thing as no. NeAP

one dinner NeAP

Praised be my fellow man/For dwelling in milk NeAP

Mexico City Hand Game. Rayna Green. these Indians tilt the odds/in a lottery/you can't buy tickets for TWSS

De Mexico Ha Venido. *Anonymous.* "Before I'd marry that kind, I'd rather die!" TrAS

Mexico Is a Foreign Country, IV: The Mango on the Mango Tree. Robert Penn Warren. Blest in that blasphemy of love we cannot now repeat. NoAm

The Mexico Trail. *Anonymous.* Where the girls are few and always true,/And my falsehearted love I'll forget I knew. BFSS

Mezzo Cammin. Henry Wadsworth Longfellow. The cataract of Death far thundering from the heights. AmePo; CBEP; FPL; NoP; TAP

Mezzo Cammin. Judith Moffett. The grass is green here too; I call/My draw a fair one. SM

Mi Abuelo. Alberto Rios. ...see a/ripple-topped stream in its best suit, in the ground. MAYP

Mi Caballo Blanco. *Anonymous.* My horse, my horse is galloping,/My horse, my horse goes on and on. FSW

Mi Corazon. Gordon W. Norris. "Mi amor, mi corazon!" BPAW

Mi Y'Malel. *Anonymous.* Redeem itself through deed and sacrifice. FSW

Mia Carlotta. Thomas Augustin Daly. Carlotta./I gotta! GoTF; InMe; NLV; TreFS

Miami. Daniel Mark Epstein. ...the garden/where jets flash like swords above your head? MAYP

Mice. Rose Fyleman. But I think mice/Are nice. EvOK; NTCP; SoPo; SUS; TiPo

The Mice at the Door. Vincent McHugh. "This man/"is immortal' NePoAm-2

Mice in the Hay. Leslie Norris. whispering worshipping OBCP; PCh

Michael. Sandra McPherson. And now again–though celestiality maroons you–as/a heron opens rising from a snag. LCAP

Michael. William Wordsworth. Beside the boisterous brook of Green-head Ghyll. DiPo; EnL; ERoP 1-2; GoTL; OAEL 1-2; OAEP; WHA

Michael Angelo: A Fragment (excerpt). Henry Wadsworth Longfellow. Quickened are they that touch the Prophet's bones. MAmP

Michael Finnigan. *Anonymous.* Poor old Michael, please don't begin ag'in. FSW

Michael Robartes and the Dancer. William Butler Yeats. They say such different things at school. OAEL 1-2

Michael Robartes Bids His Beloved Be at Peace. William Butler Yeats. And hiding their tossing manes and their tumultuous feet. BrPo; NoAm

Michael, Row the Boat Ashore. *Anonymous.* Michael, row the boat ashore, Alleluya. BLSo; FSW

Michael's Room. Reginald Gibbons. and you stare at his hand holding yours. AMV-81

Michael Walked in the Wood. Robert Greacen. And they walked as they talked/Among ferns and bracken and clover. NeIP

Michaelmas. Norman Nicholson. St. Michael's victory in the purged and praising rain. MoBrPo

Micheal Mac Liammoir. Paul Durcan. ...A green carnation/For you all, dear boy; If you must weep, ba(w)ll;/Slan agus Beannacht: Micheal FaBoIP

Michelangelo's Kiss. Dante Gabriel Rossetti. What holds for her Death's garner? And for thee? MaVP

Michelangelo: "The Creation of Adam." Gregory Djanikian. would he begin to doubt his purpose here/before that light touch binds him to those eyes? AMV-81

Michie Preval. *Anonymous.* Danse calinda, bou-doum, bou-doum,/Danse calinda, bou-doum,bou-doum. ABF

Michigan I-O. *Anonymous.* To that God-forsaken country-o called Michigan I-O. AmFP

Mick. James Reeves. And right through the flower-beds see him go! GDP

Mickleham Way. Ivy O. Eastwick. With blackberries large/And ripe and sweet. BrR

The Microbe's Serenade. George Ade. We'll sit beneath some fungus growth/Till dissolution claims us both. OBAL

Microcosm. Bertram Dobell. Nature's most noble offspring–yet her worst! OBVV

Microcosmos. Nigel Heseltine. ...and in the black space/of the sky down twinkled the stars like a gentle loving face. NeBP

Microcosmos. "Susan Miles." Beautiful and appalling. OxBTC

Microcosmus. Nashe [(or Nash(] Thomas. More light, ye spheres/in concord sound/And with your music fill this round! UnS

Micromutations. James Wright. Till we struck stone at last, to lie/Here on the frozen floor of hell. NYBP

The Microscope. Maxine W. Kumin. That's how we got the microscope. QQQ

Mid-August. Louise Driscoll. Of bins for the fruit/And death for the flower. YeAr

Mid-August at Sourdough Mountain Lookout. Gary Snyder. Through high still air. HAP; MAT; NaP; NCSH; NoP; TAP

Mid-Century. Mary Elizabeth Osborn. Behind drawn curtains; play a harpsichord/And circumvent the storm. NePoAm

Mid-Country Blow. Theodore Roethke. But my ear still kept the sound of the sea like a shell. BoNaP

Mid-Ocean in War-Time. Joyce Kilmer. On waves that shroud a thousand newly dead! MOS

Mid-Plains Tornado. Linda Bierds. drawn back again. AMV-80

Mid-Term Break. Seamus Heaney. A four foot box, a foot for every year. NCSH; NoP

Mid-Winter Walking. Robert Graves. But found no winter anywhere to see. MoAB

Midcentury Love Letter. Phyllis McGinley. In no such winter can survive alone. MoLP; ViBoPo

Middle Age. Patricia Beer. The one who is not lying there/Could have been. FaBoWP

Middle-Age. E. B. C. Jones. And sometime water gushes from/Fountains that have long been dry. HBMV

Middle Age. Rudolph Chambers Lehmann. And still the distant peaks have/The glow of twenty-two. HBV 1-2

Middle Age. Paula Rankin. What a mess they leave. MAYP

The Middle-Aged. Adrienne Rich. Upon what terms, with how much left unsaid. HaCAP; NePoEA-2

Middle-Aged Child. Inez Hogan. But I do/The best I can/For a middle-aged child. BiCB

Middle-Aged Conversation. Arthur Seymour John Tessimond. Better than the summit raptures/And the deep-sea sorrows? No. PoL

The Middle Ages. John Haines. the reins still taut in that armored fist. LCAP

Middle Ages. Siegfried Sassoon. And the moon sank red. SO

Miners. Wilfred Owen. But they will not dream of us poor lads/Lost in the ground. BrPo; MoAB; MoBrPo; NOBE

Miners. James Wright. I can hear cars, moving on steel rails, colliding/ Underground. ConAP; CTBA

Miners' Wives. Joe Corrie. What more do they want? what more can they take?/Unless our eyes, and leaves us blind. OxBS

Ming the Merciless. Jessica Hagedorn. there's always hot water/in this house BrSi

Mingled Yarns. X. J. Kennedy. Young Al the old lamp-rubber. OBCA

Mingling My Prayer. Saigyo Hoshi. Lo, ten times I have recited the/ Honorable Name. AWP

Mingus. Bob Kaufman. To the light/Of imaginary night. PoBA

Miniature. Eden Phillpotts. Holds up his little crumb of crust/And cries, "Behold the loaf!" OBSP

Miniatures IV. Mute the Hand Moves from the Heart. Lynn Strongin. giving psalm/and ease. IHMS

The Minimal. Theodore Roethke. Cleaning and caressing,/Creeping and healing. BiP; HaCAP; NoAm; NOBA

Minimum Security. James Lewisohn. At last I have the night flowers/to tend and the morning hills/to haul into sleep. LFAC

A Minion Wife. Nicholas Udall. Else is he a man unkind. EiL

The Minister. Fenton Johnson. Such is religion. AnAmPo

Miniver Cheevy. Edwin Arlington Robinson. Miniver coughed, and called it fate,/And kept on drinking. AnNE; AWP; CMoP; CoBMV; FaBoCh; FaBV; FaFP; FaPo; FF; ForPo; FPL; GoTF; HBV 1-2; HeIP; InMe; InPo; LiTA; LoGBV; MaC; MCCG; MoAB; MoAmPo; NAMP; NePA; NIP; NLV; NoAm; NOBA; NoP; OBSV; OxBA; PoEL 1-5; PoLf; PoPl; PoRA; SCV; SeCeV; SpRo; TAP; TreF; TrGrPo; WHA; YaD

Miniver Cheevy, Jr. (parody). David Fisher Parry. Miniver sighed, and read some more/F. Scott Fitzgerald. BXAP; SpRo

Minna. Maxwell Bodenheim. Blending the arrested figures upon the arched/sarcophagus of pain. MAPA

The Minneapolis Poem. James Wright. ...mysterious lives/Of the unnamed poor. FYAP; NoAm; UnPo

Minnesota Camp Grounds. Gerald Vizenor. back from the dead lake water/one at a time STE

Minnie. Thomas Caulfield Irwin. O Lady Moon. IrPN

Minnie and Her Dove. Charles Tennyson Turner. Until the full-grown wings of human grief/Eclipse thy memory of the kite and dove. FM

Minnie and Mattie. Christina Georgina Rossetti. Half of primroses. GoJo; InvP; SUS; TiPo

Minnie and Mrs. Hoyne. Kenneth Fearing. Alone in the broom closet on the forty-third floor. AnEnPo; PoRA

Minnie and Winnie. Alfred, Lord Tennyson. Wake, little ladies! The sun is aloft. HBV 1-2; HBVY; NA; OxBChV

Minnie Morse. Kaye Starbird. Unless you live on oats and hay–/And whinny. PH

Minnows. John Keats. The while they cool themselves, they freshness/ give,/And moisture, that the bowery green may live. GN

A Minor Bird. Robert Frost. In wanting to silence any song. CMoP; LOW; PB

Minor Elegy. Henriqueta Lisboa. Then the dubious smell/of flowers placed under circling flies. BoWoP

Minor Key. Teller. J. L. When your stones hit my window/I won't care. VWA

A Minor Victorian Painter. John Hewitt. making ready the subjects/for the long afternoon. CIP

Minot's Ledge. Fitz-James O'Brien. Within, there is the peace of God. OnYI

Minotaur. Robert Fisher. I am...waiting AmMo

The Minotaur. Robert Gibb. ...her hair/Reverberates with light. FAZ

Minotaur Poems. E. W. Mandel.
And who wiped god from off his eyes and face? OBCV
I came upon a man with the face of a bull. OBCV
Last Saturday we saw him at the horizon/screaming like a hawk as he fell into the sun. OBCV

The Minstrel. James Beattie.
And shrill lark carols clear from her aerial tower. ViBoPo
Whom Nature's charms inspire, and love of humankind. CEP; EnPE; NOEC

The Minstrel. Johann Wolfgang von Goethe. And thank your GOD as I thank ye/For this delicious wine-cup! AWP

The Minstrel-Boy. Thomas Moore. They shall never sound in slavery. ACP; AnIL; CoBE; FaBoBe; FaFP; FSW; GN; GoBC; GoTF; HBV 1-2; OAEP; OnYI; PrIm; RoGo; TreF

The Minstrel Responds to Flattery. Sir Walter Scott. All mourn the minstrel's harp unstrung,/Their name unknown, their praise unsung. OBNC

The Minstrel's Last Lay. John Barth. I hump the jug and fill her up with fiction. OBAL

The Minstrel's Song. Thomas Chatterton. Thus the damsel spake and died. LoBV

Minstrel's Song. Ted Hughes. The star is standing over the animal shed. OBCP

The Mint Julep. Charles Fenno Hoffman When Jove himself added a handful of hail. AA; AmePo

The Minuet. Mary Mapes Dodge. Just to feel like those who met/In the graceful minuet–long ago. OHFP

Minuet in a Minor Key. Phyllis Janowitz. taking no notice of posted limits or/signs of treacherous soft shoulders,/frost heaves ahead. AmC

A Minuet on Reaching the Age of Fifty. George Santayana. And close our eyes, still smiling, on the/dance. BLPL; FaFP; HBMV

Minus One. John Ciardi. ...and whose/hawk is this now? unchosen? come to choose? HoAn

The Minute. Karl Shapiro. Rise and sweep past me, spinning threads of fear. ATP; LiTA; MiAP; MoVE

The Minute before Meeting. Thomas Hardy. Thereby denying to this hour of grace/A full-up measure of felicity. VLP

The Minute-Men of North-Boro'. Wallace Rice. And take the plough again in peace, their/warrior's duty done. PAH

Minutes. Denis Johnson. make it enough/make it enough/or eat/suffering without end MAYP

Minutes of Gold. *Anonymous*. Hopelessness somewhere, and bring me a friend. PoToHe

The Minyan. Jack Myers. sleeping on half a bed, hoping the other half/ isn't earth. VWA

Mips and Ma the Mooly Moo. Theodore Roethke. What footie will do will be final. NLV

Mir Traumte Von Einem Konigskind. Heinrich Heine. I burst for thee, and thy dear love. AWP

Mir Traumte Wieder Der Alte Traum. Heinrich Heine. Superfluous was the bite. AWP

Mira is dancing with bells tied. Mira Bai [(or Mirabai)]. Only he/is her ultimate protector. BoWoP

Mira's Will. Mary Leapor. In body healthy, and composed in mind. NOEC

The Mirabeau Bridge. Guillaume Apollinaire.
The days go I remain OBVE
Within your shadow I am bound. BoLoP

Mirabell, Book 9 (excerpt). James Merrill. ...till the given/Moment comes to render what we owe. HaCAP

The Miracle. Liberty Hyde Bailey. I wonder what will next be there! OHIP; YeAr

The Miracle. Walter De La Mare. As if, like Chaucer's child, he thought/ All but "O Alma!" nought. CoBE; LiTB; UnPo

The Miracle. Allan Dowling. first in my heart of all her sweet warm body/ are those two human breasts. ErPo

The Miracle. Ralph Waldo Emerson. Nay, God is witness, gave the names. FM

The Miracle. Elsie Melchert Fowler. MY BIRTHDAY CAKE! BiCB

The Miracle. Chaim Grade. Thus I live like a war invalid/with sensations of shot-off fingers. VWA

The Miracle. Caelius Sedulius. It poureth out as purest wine. CAW

The Miracle. Sir John Suckling. Making ice another burn,/Whilst itself doth harder turn! CaPo

A Miracle for Breakfast. Elizabeth Bishop. as if the miracle were working, on the wrong balcony. AmP; LiTA; MiAP

A Miracle Indeed. Purohit Swami. I asked a little power,/Thou gavest me a begging-bowl. OBMV

The Miracle of Dawn. Madison Cawein. That line of rose no more be drawn/Above the ocean's spray! HBV 1-2

Miracle Play. *Anonymous*. A King of Bliss that hight Jesus. ACP

Miracle Play: Satan and Pilate's Wife. *Anonymous*. Your striff and your strength shall be stroyed. ACP

Miracle Play: The Lament of Eve. *Anonymous*. Ye must delve and I shall spin/In care to ledyn our life. ACP

Miracles. Conrad Aiken.
And slowly descend the hill, through dew-wet grass. HBMV
Clear things may not be seen. MoAmPo

Miracles. Arna Bontemps. Walking on the sea. GoSl; PoNe

Miracles. Walt Whitman. What stranger miracles are there? BBV; HBVY; LaNeLa; MoRP

Miracles at the Birth of Christ. Isaac Watts. Our souls adore the eternal God/Who condescended to be born. NOCV

Mirage. Christina Georgina Rossetti. ...mine own self, are changed/For a dream's sake. BoLoP; EnLi 1-2; LLLT; PoRA

A Mirage. Ruth Setterberg. Dew falls from frosty reed, and flowers bend in the wind. AMV-80

The Mirage. Oscar Williams. And I awoke on the starved pavements of no love. CrMA; LiTL; LiTM; NePA

Miramar Beach. J. V. Cunningham. In the warm wonder of winter sun. PoA

The Miramichi Fire. *Anonymous*. Such another horrid fire,/See again I do not wish. AmFP

Miramichi Lightning. Alfred Goldsworthy Bailey. as the rancour of a cloud broke off and fell/into the back of town and foundered there. OBCV

Miriam: Chorus. Lady Elizabeth Carew. For in a wife it is no worse to find/A common body, than a common mind. LiTL

Miriam Tazewell. John Crowe Ransom. For weeks she went untidy, she went sullen. TW

The Mirror. Edgar Bowers. He stands, who was my future, claiming me. QFR

Mirror. Tada Chimako. with only wind blowing in the mirror. BoWoP

Mirror. Peter De Vries. And when I turn they see death in my face. PoA

The Mirror. Louise Gluck. as a man bleeding, not/the reflection I desire. FaPON; GP; MAYP

The Mirror. Blanche Mary Kelly. Nor note the glass/That shows Thy Face. GoBC; TrPWD

Mirror. James Merrill. Echo of mine, I am amenable. CoAP; NePoEA-2; SM

The Mirror. John N. Morris. Perhaps is the child, perhaps the summer and sea. PoA

Mirror. Sylvia Plath. ...and in me an old woman/Rises toward her day after day, like a terrible fish. FaBoWP; HAP; NYBP; SoSe

The Mirror. Dante Gabriel Rossetti. And must seek elsewhere for his own. SyP

A Mirror for Poets. Thom Gunn. You cannot smile at me and make an end.' LiTM; NePoEA

Mirror for the Barnyard. Jack Myers. or conquer others was the only difference between us. AmPA

Mirror Images. Laurel Speer. And just the beginning of liver spots./Oh God. AMV-80

Mirror in February. Thomas Kinsella. Not young, and not renewable, but man. CIP; FaBoIP; GTBS-P; NoAm

The Mirror in the Front Hall. Constantine P. Cavafy. proud to have embraced/total beauty for a few moments. PeHV

The Mirror in Which Two Are Seen as One. Adrienne Rich. your nerves the nerves of a midwife/learning her trade NNaP

Mirror, Mirror. Robert Graves. Or shall I marry old knives-and-scissors/Shouting through the town? HBMV

The Mirror Perilous. Alan Dugan. possessed of an echo but not a fate. LiTM; MP; TwCP

Mirrorment. Archie Randolph Ammons. and flowers perched birds. PCP

The Mirrors. Sophia de Mello Breyner Andresen. Light torn from/Within a cold glassy fire. PBWP

Mirrors. Elizabeth Jennings. ...But love/Perceives without a mirror in the hands. NePoEA

The Mirrors of Jerusalem. Barbara F. Lefcowitz. that everywhere poke from the roadside. AMV-80; VWA

Mirth. Robert Herrick. The sweetest solace is to act no sin. LiTB

Mirthful Lunacy. Thomas Stoddart. One as a lonely shadow, one star! OBNC

Mis' Smith. Albert Bigelow Paine. "I'm ready as I'll ever be,/I reckon." PoLf

Misadventures at Margate. Richard Harris Barham. Give my respects to Mrs. Jones, and say I'm pretty well! HBV 1-2

Misanthropos (excerpt). Thom Gunn. ...But/at times I am ravenous. OxBC

Misapprehension. Paul Laurence Dunbar. "Ay, brother,–'tis well writ,/But where's the joke?" BPo

Miscarriage. Michael Longley. My son or my daughter. PoL

The Miscegenous Zebra. Roland Young. He's more contented in the zoo. BoAnP

The Mischievous Raven. Anonymous. Lumpety, lumpety, lump! OxNR

A Misconception. James Russell Lowell. Does himself all the good he can by stealing. OBAL

Misconceptions. Robert Browning. Love to be saved for it, proffer'd to, spent on! AtBAP; OBEV; OBVV

Misdemeanor. Eve Triem. the lipstick stain/I could not wipe away/tells me and tells/joy of the marble/is in the waiting. GP

Mise en Scene. Robert Fitzgerald. By what grand eye were these images summoned there? NYBP; VGW

Miser. Gordon LeClaire. To stalk their prey from room to haunted room. CaP

Miser. Harold Vinal. I am a miser/Counting my gold. MCCG

La Misere (parody). Philip Appleman. it is a very/Zen/experience / this death BXAP

Miserere. David Gascoyne. And all they see their vision sanctifies. NeBP

Miserere. Gaspar Nunez de Arce. As through the scattering mists of day/Came a far locomotive's shout. CAW

Miserere mei, Domine. Sir Thomas Wyatt. And thus beginneth his song therewithal. FCP

Miserere, My Maker. Anonymous. Miserere, miserere, I am dying. NOCV

Misericordia! James Lipton. Can't we just quietly/Swallow The Pill?' NLV

Misericordia. Margaret Mead. Of chiselled boughs against the winter night! PoA

Miserie. George Herbert. My God, I mean my self. PoEL 1-5

Miserly Paron. Anonymous. A cow! AnIL

Misery. John Holmes. Cherish the cure, as if it were good to keep. NYBP

The Misery of Mechanics. Philip Booth. But nothing that he can fix. MAT

The Misfit-1939-1945. C. Day Lewis. For the first step along the Calvary road? BoC

Misfortunes Never Come Singly. Harry Graham. All the toast was burnt with/nurse. FaFP; NA; TreFT

The Misfortunes of Elphin: The War-Song of Dinas Vawr. Thomas Love Peacock. And his overthrow, our chorus. AWP; MyFE; WaaP

Misgivings. Herman Melville. The hemlock shakes in the rafter, the oak in the driving keel. AP; MAmP; NePA; NOBA; OxBA

Mishka. John Gray.
And his body is bathed in grass and sun. VLP
Her touch is a perfume, a melody. NOBV; SyP

Mismatch. Carl Lindner. ...hanging on until the end. AMV-80

Misogynist. Richard Conniff. A woman fit to be reproduced. DBV

The Misogynist. Jean Morgan. A hand in winter, resisting the glove. FF

Misplaced Sympathy. Charles Follen Adams. "Little lion in the corner,/Mama, isn't gettin' any!" OBAL

Miss Ada. Christophr Fahy. Last night we had our first snow of the season. TAT

Miss Alderman. Robert Winner. and buttoned her dress/afterwards. GP

Miss Betty's Singing-Bird. John Winstanley. All these and more will surely bring/To girls, if good, this coming spring. NOEC

Miss Biddy Fudge to Miss Dorothy (excerpt). Thomas Moore. And romance, and high bonnets, and Madame Le ROI! NBM

Miss Bitter. N. M. Bodecker. "Want some tea?" NTCP

Miss Buss and Miss Beale. Anonymous. Miss Beale and Miss Buss. CenHV; PoPle

Miss Cho Composes in the Cafeteria. James Tate. ...You jot/it down, jump up, look/at me and giggle. SM; WeW

Miss Creighton. Henry Taylor. ...the horses/slowly turned and moved toward the barn. GrPl

Miss Crustacean. Robert Phillips. my entire shell will crack and bust. GeTw

Miss Ellen Gee of Kew. Anonymous. I'll change your singing Q.' FaBoNo

Miss Euphemia. John Crowe Ransom. And she sits with us only/Till next Pentecost. CMoP

Miss Fogerty's Cake. Anonymous. While every man swore he was poisoned/By eating Miss Fogerty's cake. BLPA; NLV

Miss Gee. W. H. Auden. And a couple of Oxford Groupers/Carefully dissected her knee. OxBTC

Miss Grant. Freda Downie. In Gaelic, as big as a tombstone/And appropriately black. FaBoWP

Miss James. A.(lan) A.(lexander) Milne. They called her Diana Fitzpatrick Mauleverer James. MoShBr

Miss Jennian Jones. Anonymous. I dreamt I saw a ghost last night/Under the apple tree! AmFP

Miss Kilmansegg and Her Precious Leg. Thomas Hood.
And that was the end of the Christening. NOBV
And the Quaker was hoarse with cheering! VLP
"Because her own Leg had killed her!" NOBV
She stood on a Member that cost as much/As a Member for all the County! NOBV
With virus ta'en from the best-bred cow/Of Lord Althorpe's–now Earl Spencer. NAs

Miss Kilmansegg's Birth. Thomas Hood. It's ten to one she had had to make shift/With rickets instead of rockets! OxBoLi

Miss Kilmansegg's Honeymoon. Thomas Hood. For she dreamt she had married the Devil! NBM

Miss Lavender. Jon Stallworthy. ...Those/died after for no reason, or/for want of a Spanish imperative. OxBC

Miss Loo. Walter De la Mare. Asked nothing else, if she had you. CMoP; HBV 1-2; OxBTC

Miss Marnell. Austin Clarke. All signed–"Yours Gratefully, In Jesus Christ." IPY

Miss Melerlee. John Wesley Holloway. Farewell, Miss Melerlee! BANP; PoNe

Miss Millay Says Something Too. Samuel Hoffenstein. I want to live like the sober herring,/And die as pickled when die I must. NLV

Miss Nancy's Gown. Zitella Cocke. Are blooming bright as the night/She danced the minuet! AA

Miss Packard and Miss Giles. Owen Dodson. And all the Aprils we assemble here. GLGT

Miss Pheasant. Walter De la Mare. As espying a lady named Pheasant. FaBoNo

Miss Rosie. Lucille Clifton. I stand up. AmPA; BlSi; CNA; NMM; PoBA; TwCP

Miss Snooks, Poetess. Stevie Smith. But went on being awfully nice/And took a lot of prizes. PV

Miss T. Walter De La Mare. Whatever Miss T. eats/Turns into Miss T. CenHV; FaBoBe; GoJo; GrPl; MoShBr; NTCP; OnUR; SoPo; SUS; TiPo

Miss Twye. Gavin Ewart. A wicked man in the bathroom cupboard. ErPo; FiBHP; NeBP; NOBL; PV

Miss You. Anonymous. The world is full of folks, it's true,/But there was only one of you. PoToHe

Miss You. David Cory. Only that 'twas heaven/Just to be with You. BLPA; FaBoBe; GoTF; TreFS

Missa Papae Marcelli. James Philip McAuley. Magog, looming at the gate,/When music sounds, forgets his hate. BoAV

The Missal. Rosemary Dobson. Before the Voice of Man was heard;/In the beginning was the Word.' BoAV

The Missal. Ruth Pitter. Man may not see that innocence again. CAW

The Missel-Thrush's Nest. John Clare. She lays six eggs in colours dull,/Blotched thick with spots of burning red. VLP

The Misses Poar Drive to Church. Josephine Pinckney. Better to pray for the Restoration/Than the overseer of a patch-work nation. AnAmPo

Missing. Anonymous. "None shall pluck them from My Hands." WGRP

Missing. W. H. Auden. Must quench the lamps and pass/Alive into the house. OxBTC

Missing. A.(lan) A.(lexander) Milne. Hasn't anybody seen my mouse? MoShBr

Missing. John Pudney. The ocean lifted, stirred,/Leaving no word. HaMV; OxBTC

Missing. John Banister Tabb. Fold close my little one! TrPWD

Missing Beat. Carolyn M. Rodgers. i can only bougaloo & bop JB

Missing Dates. William Empson. The waste remains, the waste remains and kills. CMoP; CoBMV; ForPo; HAP; LiTB; LiTM; MoAB; MoBrPo; MoPo; NoAm; NOBE; NoP; OAEL 1-2; UnPo; ViBoPo

The Missing Link. Oliver Herford. And that's the way it comes to-day/The MISSING LINK is missing. CenHV

Missing My Daughter. Stephen Spender. The roses raced around her name. AtBAP; GTBS-P; Str

The Missing Person. Donald Justice. This last disguise, himself. NYBP

Missing the Children. Paul Zimmer. But I am far away, searching the rooms/Of my house, looking for my children. Str

Mission. Anonymous. But never knew substantial joys,/Until I heard my Savior's voice. AmFP

Mission Bay. John Koethe. With no more distance than the earth can bear. PoA

The Mission Bells of Monterey. Bret (Francis Bret Harte) Harte. O Mission bells of Monterey! PeD

Mission Tire Factory, 1969. Gary Soto. "Buy some sandwiches. You guys saved my life." NPAW; NPGG

Missionaries in the Jungle. Linda Piper. Administering to garrulous black ghetto residents. BlSi

The Missionary Visits Our Church in Scranton. Jay Parini. They were said to be wishing us well in Scranton. MAYP

Missions. Anonymous. Both at home and o'er the sea. STF

Mississippi Blues. Anonymous. See you in nineteen and forty-fo'. AmFP

Mississippi Born. Pearl Cleage Lomax. sister sister./another child has come. CNA

Mississippi Mornings. Tom Dent. soon everything moving & the/hustle is on/toward busy new/early early. APU

Mississippi Sawyer. Anonymous. Honor partners, balance all. AmFP

Mississippi Sounding Calls, I. Anonymous. Quarter twain. AmFP

The Missive. Sir Edmund Gosse. And your life is but a roses's. HBV 1-2

A Missouri Maiden's Farewell to Alabama. Mark (Samuel Langhorne Clemens) Twain. Ere, dear Alabama! They turn cold on thee! InMe

Missouri Sequence: Nightfall. Brian Coffey. when the priest elevates/the Saviour of the world. CIP

Missouri Town. John Palen. a dry old clerk in sleeves gathers it all. AMV-80

A Missouri Traveller Writes Home: 1830. Robert Bly. And start to westward through the heavy grass. NePoEA

A Misspelled Tail. Elizabeth T. Corbett. Back two his home at last. OBCA

Missy Sick. Anonymous. You shall give it me every night Sir CoMu

Mist. Gill Man. The valley floor appears. PoSH

Mist. Henry David Thoreau. Of healing herbs to just men's fields. AA; AmePo; AmLP; AWP; InPo; OxBA

Mist. Andrew Young. And leave me here alone/To tread this mist where earth and sky are one. PoSH

The Mist and All. Dixie Willson. I like the fall–/The mist and all.– BrR; SoPo; YeAr

Mist Forms. Carl Sandburg. A riddle is here no man tells, no woman. CMoP; HBMV

The Mist over Pukehina. Anonymous. This is my farewell of love to thee. WTO

The Mist Rauk Is Hanging. John Clare. And in drab frock on monday/Goes milking the cows. NOBV

Mistakable Identity. Elaine V. Emans. No–seven young icicles taking leave/on their eave. AMV-80

The Mistake. Anonymous. None needs our pity half so much/As idlers,–always pity such. PaPo

The Mistaken Resolve. Martial (Marcus Valerius Martialis). ...send/Me such a cook or coachman, but no friend. PV

Mistakes. George W. Swarberg. The mark we leave, by word or deed,/Cuts deep in someone's heart. STF

Mistakes. Ella Wheeler Wilcox. The sorrow of our sad mistakes. PoToHe

Mister Charlie. Lightning Hopkins. I got a home for you long/as the day BluL

Mister Frog Went A-Courting (with music). Anonymous. There's bread and cheese upon the shelf,and if you want any just help yourself. AS

Mister Johnson. Ben Harney. Oh! Mister Johnson made him good. OBAL

Mister Tambourine Man. Bob Dylan. In the jingle, jangle morning I'll come followin' you. NIP

Mistletoe. Walter De la Mare. Lips unseen–and kissed me there. SO

The Mistletoe Bough. Thomas Haynes Bayly. The bride lay clasped in her living tomb! BLPA; GoTF; HBV 1-2; PaPo; TreFS; VLP

Mistletoe Sprites. Solveig Paulson Russell. Good luck comes with mistletoe! ChBR

Mistral. Barbara Howes. Bent low, deafened, I plunge/On, blind in the face of the storm. NYBP

The Mistress. Joan Barton. "Dear wife'..."devoted mother'.../"Beloved child'... OxBTC

The Mistress. Sir William D'Avenant. And, nature failing, want no arts.' JCP

The Mistress: A Song. John Wilmot, Earl of Rochester. And make us blest at last. CavP; EBEV; MePo; NOBE; OBS

The Mistress Addresses the Wife. Naomi Replansky. Let your eyes just once/Fasten upon mine. GP

The Mistress (excerpt). John Wilmot, Earl of Rochester.
And haunts my breast by absence made/The living tomb of love. ViBoPo
You had gone mad like me. AtBAP

Mistress Hale of Beverly. Lucy Larcom. Whose unobtrusive excellence awed back/delusion's tide! PAH

Mistress of the Matchless Mine. Clyde Robertson. To the Mistress of the Matchless Mine. PoOW

The Mistress of Vision. Francis Thompson.
Music in the holy poets to my wistful want, I doubt me! BrPo; OBVV
Thrice-threefold walled with emerald from our mortal morn-/ings grey... CH

Mistress, Since You So Much Desire. Thomas Campion. I climb to crown my chaste desire. OAEL 1-2

A Mistress without Compare. Charles, duc d' Orleans. The which hath whool my service and mine hert. MeEL

Mistresses. Anonymous. But nonetheless important. KiLC

Mistrustful Minds Be Moved. Sir Thomas Wyatt. Thereof God send them part. FCP; SiPS

Mists and Rain. Charles Baudelaire. For two to sleep with sorrow on a hazardous Bed. SyP

The Mists Are Rising Now. Hasye Cooperman. The evening mists are rising now. GoYe

The mists rise over. Akahito (Yamabe no Akahito). Pass away so easily. HoPM

The Misty Island. Anonymous. And we in dreams behold the Hebrides. PoSH

Misunderstanding. Irving Layton. I could see/her devotion/to literature/was not/perfect. PV

The Mither's Lament. Sydney Goodsir Smith. And wersh the wine o' victorie! ACV; OxBS

The Mitherless Bairn. William Thom. That God deals the blow, for the mitherless bairn! HBV 1-2

Mithridates. Ralph Waldo Emerson. Vein and artery, though ye kill me! AP; NOBA

The Mitten Song. Marie Louise Allen. Fingers all together! BrR; NTCP; SoPo; SUS; TiPo

Mix a Pancake. Christina Georgina Rossetti. Catch it if you can. NTCP; SoPo; SUS

Mixed Feelings. John Ashbery. As we babble about the sky and the weather and the/forests of change. GP; HAP

Mixed Media. James Schevill. To find the right mixture that cures my specialized life. AMV-81

Mixed Sketches. Don L. Lee. wondering, how did we survive? BPo

The Mixer. Louis MacNeice. And often spoken but no longer heard. FaBoTw

Miyoko San. Mary McNeil Fenollosa. And I have painted Miyoko San. AA

Mizpah. Julia Aldrich Baker. He blesseth thee, He blesseth me,/And we are near. BLPA; FaBoBe

The MJQ. Joyce Carol Thomas. Then Delicate pasticios/Say Travel a little higher CNA

MMDCCXIII 1/2. Lorenzo Thomas. The cruelties of ages past affect us now. APU

Mnemosyne. Trumbull Stickney. It rains across the country I remember. AmePo; AnFE; CoAnAm; CrMA; LiTA; NCEP; NOBA; OxBA; ViBoPo

Mnemosyne Lay in Dust. Austin Clarke. The house in which his mother was born. CIP; CMoP; IPY

Moan, Moan, Ye Dying Gales. Henry Neele. O, let us think of those/Whose lives are lost in woes,/Whose cup of grief runs o'er. HBV 1-2

Moanish Lady! (with music). Anonymous. When the good Lord shall call you home. AS

Moby Dick: The Whale. Herman Melville. I give the glory to my God,/His all the mercy and the power. TrGrPo

A Mock Charon. Richard Lovelace. And softly, softly breathe, lest you infect us, too. CaPo

A Mock Invocation to Genius (excerpt). William Woty. And on thine anvil shall I hammer out/The thought chaotic to prefulgid form. NOEC

Mock On, Mock On, Voltaire, Rousseau. William Blake. Where Israel's tents do shine so bright. AtBAP; BiP; HAP; LAuP; NAWM 1-2; NoP; OAEL 1-2; OAEP; OBNC; OBRV; OBSP; OxBoCh; PoEL 1-5; PPoe; PPP; PrIm

Mock Orange. Louise Gluck. How can I be content/when there is still/that odor in the world? MAYP

A Mock Song. Richard Lovelace. For our Dragon hath vanquished the St. George. CaPo

Mockery. William Blake. But still in Israel's path they shine. TrGrPo

Mockery. Katherine Dixon Riggs. And poking through the window was her bold gold head! BrR

The Mockery of Life. Wilfrid Scawen Blunt. We conquer fate and half forget our tears VLP

The Mocking Bird. Anonymous. You'll still be the sweetest little/Baby in town. AmFP

The Mocking-Bird. Ednah Proctor (Clarke) Hayes. Pours the whole forest from one tiny/throat! AA

The Mocking Bird. Sidney Lanier. How may the death of that dull insect be/The life of yon trim Shakespeare on the/tree? AA

The Mocking-bird. Frank Lebby Stanton. Fer there warn't no use in stayin'/When one bird could sing fer all! AA

The Mocking-bird. Henry Jerome Stockard. The birds, but notes of thine imperial own! AA

The Mocking Fairy. Walter De la Mare. The Fairy mimbling mambling in the garden. MoBrPo; MoShBr

Mocking Song against Qaqortingneq. Piuvkaq. Words melt away/Like hills in fog. WTO

The Mockingbird. Randall Jarrell. Which one's the mockingbird? which one's the world? DuDa; NYBP; RFM

Mockingbird, Copy This. Jack Myers. Then sing. AMV-81

Mockingbird in Winter. Ernest Kroll. Because the time was wrong. AMV-80

Model. Archie Randolph Ammons. ...what/can't be reconciled is/home and steady at work. FAZ

A Model for the Laureate. William Butler Yeats. Keep his lover waiting. CMoP

A Model Sermon. Anonymous. Thou art the man, and thou alone will make/A Felix tremble, and a David quake! FaBoUs

Model T. Adrien Stoutenburg. grapple with pride/the thin and perilous wheel. CTBA

Moderation. Robert Herrick. Kings ought to shear, not skin their sheep. FaBoEE

Moderation: Odes. Horace. Nor plagues that haunt the rich man's door/Embittering all his state. PoToHe

Modern American Nursing. Lucy Hricz. savior, who indeed would never think of saving herself. AMV-80

Modern Architecture. Norman Nathan. freezing wet or hot humid black/in a dragon's belly. AMV-81

The Modern Baby. William Croswell Doane. The Websters and the Lincolns and the Roosevelts, you know. BLPA; YaD

A Modern Ballad. Caroline D. Emerson. Fly through the air, perhaps it is–that elevator car! BrR

Modern Beauty. Arthur Symons. ...Still am I/The torch, but where's the moth that still dares die? EnLit; HBV 1-2

The Modern Chinese History Professor Plays Pool Every Tuesday... James Baker Hall. the Professor, or his wife, or the young lady. TAT

Modern Critics. Samuel Taylor Coleridge. Cool, sober murderers of their neighbours' fame. FaBoEE

Modern Declaration. Edna St. Vincent Millay. Shall love you always. MoLP

A Modern Dragon. Rowena Bastin Bennett. And all the earth trembles when he rushes by. SoPo; TiPo

The Modern Fine Gentleman (excerpt). Soame Jenyns. Fierce without strength; o'erflowing, though not full. OBSV

The Modern Fine Lady. Soame Jenyns. And with true scorpion rage she stings herself to death. NOEC; OBSV

Modern Grimm. Dorothy Lee Richardson. Only the wind. DFT

The Modern Hiawatha (parody). George A. Strong. Why he turned them inside outside. BBV; FaBoCo; FaBoPa; FaFP; FiBHP; GoTF; HBV 1-2; InMe; MoShBr; NA; Par; SpRo; TreFS; YaD

The Modern Jonas. Anonymous. Returned back,/From not one third their number. PAH

Modern Kabbalist. Marcia Falk. What shall I do/with these/small/inviolate/knives/that scar the mind. VWA

Modern Love. J. V. Cunningham. Without a simultaneous plop. PoL

Modern Love. John Keats. That ye may love in spite of beaver hats. CBEP; OBNC

Modern Love. Gerald Stern. in the stunted remains of last summer's silk forest. AMV-80

Modern Love, I. George Meredith. Each wishing for the sword that severs all. EnLoPo; HBV 1-2; HeIP; NBM; NOBV; NoP; OAEL 1-2; OAEP; PoEL 1-5; VLP

Modern Love, II. George Meredith. And smote himself, a shuddering heap of pain. EnLi 1-2; HBV 1-2; OAEP; VLP

Modern Love, III. George Meredith. The hour has struck, though I heard not the bell! HBV 1-2; VLP

Modern Love, IV. George Meredith. Little avails that coinage to the old! OAEP; VLP

Modern Love, V. George Meredith. A wave of the great waves of Destiny/Convulsed at a checked impulse of the heart. NOBV; VLP

Modern Love, VI. George Meredith. They sat, she laughing at a quiet joke. NOBV; ViBoPo; VLP

Modern Love, VII. George Meredith. The former, it were not so great a curse/To read on the steel-mirror of her smile. NOBV; VLP

Modern Love, VIII. George Meredith. Speak, and a taste of that old time restore! OAEP; VLP

Modern Love, IX. George Meredith. I might, and yet thou goest safe, supreme. NOBV; VLP

Modern Love, X. George Meredith. Her much-adored delightful Fairy Prince! NBM; PoEL 1-5; VLP

Modern Love, XI. George Meredith. Within it, featured even in death divine,/Is lying a dead infant, slain by thee. VLP

Modern Love, XII. George Meredith. So shorten I the stature of my soul. TEP; ViBoPo; VLP

Modern Love, XIII. George Meredith. When the renewed for ever of a kiss/Whirls life within the shower of loosened hair! OBNC; VLP

Modern Love, XIV. George Meredith. The game you play at is not to my mind. HBV 1-2; VLP

Modern Love, XV. George Meredith. The words are very like: the name is new. VLP

Modern Love, XVI. George Meredith. Now am I haunted by that taste! that sound. EnLi 1-2; HBV 1-2; NOBV; VLP

Modern Love, XVII. George Meredith. Dear guests, you now have seen Love's corpse-light shine. BoLoP; HeIP; NOBV; NoP; OAEP; VLP

Modern Love, XVIII. George Meredith. 'Tis true that when we trace its source, 'tis beer. NBM; PoEL 1-5; VLP

Modern Love, XIX. George Meredith. Still rubs his hands before him, like a fly,/In a queer sort of meditative mirth. VLP

Modern Love, XX. George Meredith. Have I not any charity to give? VLP

Modern Love, XXI. George Meredith. Her lost moist hand clings mortally to mine. NOBV; VLP

Modern Love, XXII. George Meredith. Yours is a lower, and a happier star! VLP

Modern Love, XXIII. George Meredith. My feet were nourished on her breasts all night. NOBV; VLP

Modern Love, XXIV. George Meredith. Never! though I die thirsting. Go thy ways! VLP

Modern Love, XXV. George Meredith. And life, some think, is worthy of the Muse. NOBV; VLP

Modern Love, XXVI. George Meredith. You must bear all the venom of his tooth! HBV 1-2; VLP

Modern Love, XXVII. George Meredith. ...Shouldst thou wake/The passion of a demon, be not afraid. VLP

Modern Love, XXVIII. George Meredith. I feel the promptings of Satanic power,/While you do homage unto me alone. VLP

Modern Love, XXIX. George Meredith. And eat our pot of honey on the grave. OAEP; VLP

Modern Love, XXX. George Meredith. Lady, this is my sonnet to your eyes. HAP; NBM; NoP; OAEP; PoEL 1-5; ViBoPo; VLP

Modern Love, XXXI. George Meredith. And yet I do prefer it. What's my drift? NOBV; VLP

Modern Love, XXXII. George Meredith. Shrieking Bacchantes with their souls of wine! VLP

Modern Love, XXXIII.   George Meredith.   My wife, read this! Strange love-talk, is it not?   VLP

Modern Love, XXXIV.   George Meredith.   Niagara or Vesuvius is deferred.   NOBV; VLP

Modern Love, XXXV.   George Meredith.   Save her? What for? To act this wedded lie!   VLP

Modern Love, XXXVI.   George Meredith.   ...At the two I stand amazed.   NOBV; VLP

Modern Love, XXXVII.   George Meredith.   Our tragedy, is it alive or dead?   NOBV; VLP

Modern Love, XXXVIII.   George Meredith.   Oh, when you counsel me, think what you/mean!   VLP

Modern Love, XXXIX.   George Meredith.   God, what a dancing spectre seems the moon!   VLP

Modern Love, XL.   George Meredith.   The dread that my old love may be alive/Has seized my nursling new love by the throat.   VLP

Modern Love, XLI.   George Meredith.   ...O, look we like a pair/Who for fresh nuptials joyfully yield all else?   HBV 1-2; VLP

Modern Love, XLII.   George Meredith.   "You love...?love...?love...?' all on an indrawn breath.   NOBV; ViBoPo; VLP

Modern Love, XLIII.   George Meredith.   We are betrayed by what is false within.   AnFE; EnLoPo; HBV 1-2; InPo; NBM; NOBE; OAEP; OBNC; PoEL 1-5; SeCeV; TEP; VLP

Modern Love, XLIV.   George Meredith.   Never, she cries, shall Pity soothe Love's thirst,/Or foul hypocrisy for truth atone!   VLP

Modern Love, XLV.   George Meredith.   These are the summer days, and these our walks.   NBM; PoEL 1-5; VLP

Modern Love, XLVI.   George Meredith.   While with a widening soul on me she/stared.   OAEP; VLP

Modern Love, XLVII.   George Meredith.   The swan sail with her young beneath her wings.   AnFE; EnLoPo; GTBS; GTBS-P; NOBE; NOBV; OAEL 1-2; OBNC; SeCeV; ViBoPo; VLP

Modern Love, XLVIII.   George Meredith.   I feel the truth; so let the world surmise.   EnLi 1-2; NoP; OAEL 1-2; OAEP; VLP

Modern Love, XLIX.   George Meredith.   Lethe had passed those lips, and he knew all.   EnLi 1-2; HBV 1-2; NoP; OAEL 1-2; OAEP; VLP

Modern Love, L.   George Meredith.   To throw that faint thin line upon the shore!   AnFE; EBEV; EnLi 1-2; EnLoPo; GoTF; GTBS; GTBS-P; HAP; HBV; InPo 1-2; NBM; NOBE; NOBV; NoP; OAEL 1-2; OAEP; OBNC; PoEL 1-5; SeCeV; TreFT; TrGrPo; ViBoPo; VLP; WHA

Modern Love Poems.   Anonymous.   O God, forgive me my shortcomings.   WTO

Modern Love Songs.   Faarah Nuur.   Give me treatment, but don't put me in hospital!   TTY

Modern Midnight Conversation: Between a Contractor and His Wife.   Anonymous.   I'll think of what must soon approach,/And fit myself to fit a coach.   NOEC

Modern Midnight Conversation: Between an Unemployed Artist...   Anonymous.   Thither we all, alas! must go,/Where death will quickly end my woe.   NOEC

Modern Ode to the Modern School.   John Erskine.   So Jim never said anything.   YaD

Modern Poetry.   Anita Skeen.   the challenge of the line, not even the title/of a single poem.   IHMS

A Modern Romance.   Paul Engle.   It was an All-American day.   PoPl

Modern Romance.   William J. Harris.   fell to her death/from a great height/in Arizona.   GP

The Modern Romans.   Charles Frederick Johnson.   Turning the Fenian down once more to be/"bossed by a Dago'"   AA

The Modern Woman to Her Lover.   Margaret Widdemer.   I shall not lie to you ever again–/Will you love me still?   HBMV

The Modern World.   Colin Ellis.   Too poor to tax, too numerous to feed.   FaBoEE

The Modernists.   Tom MacInnes.   Maybe earlier in Ur!   CaP

Modes of Pleasure.   Thom Gunn.   The will awaits its gradual end.   PeHV; PPP

The Modes of the Court.   John Gay.   But shift you, for money, from friend to friend.   HeIP

The Modes of Vallejo Street San Diego, Los Angeles (excerpt).   Hugh Seidman.   had tried deeply but could not/so that that was why   UnPo

A Modest Wit.   Seelleck Osborn.   "Pray, why did not your father make/A gentleman of you?"   BLPA; HBV 1-2

Modesty.   Aaron Hill.   And she who means no mischief does it all.   OBSP

Modo and Alciphron.   Sylvia Townsend Warner.   Dead is the holy Alciphron!   MoBrPo

Modyr Whyt as Lyly Flowr (excerpt).   Anonymous.   Thy lullyng lessyth my langowr.   AtBAP

Moenkopi.   Arthur Sze.   out of sand, barren sand.   BrSi

Mog the Brunette.   Anonymous.   To his sorrow he finds with his match he has met,/And wishes the devil had Mog the Brunette.   CoMu

Moggy and Me.   James Hogg.   You'll learn it by lookin' at Moggy an' me.   HBV 1-2

Moggy's Wedding.   Charles R. Thatcher.   And stretch'd blind drunk beneath the table/Was how she spent her widding night.   NOAV

Moguls and Monks.   Lewis MacAdams.   Fates, be kind.   APU

Mohammed and Seid.   Harrison Smith Morris.   Thus said, and made the slain a martial/grave.   AA

Mohammed Ibrahim Speaks.   Martha Beidler.   And her eyes were like black pearls/Within their shells.   FF

Mohini Chatterjee.   William Butler Yeats.   Men dance on deathless feet.'   MoRP; NoAm

Moire.   Michael McClure.   82. MY WHISKERS–THE WOLF'S BEARD.   EAS

Moist Moon People.   Carl Sandburg.   They were all there; the clock ticks spoke with castanet clicks.   MoAmPo

Mojo Hiding Woman.   Blind Boy Fuller.   I done sting my baby/and she won't stay away from me.   BluL

Molasses River.   Richard Kendall Munkittrick.   That's corked with an old corn-cob.   OBCA

The Mole.   John Clare.   Where taste admires and thy still labour thrives.   SeCeV

The Mole.   John Haines.   as the rising sun slowly dries/his strange, unruly wings.   NCSH

The Mole.   Dennis Schmitz.   I will die just once gnawing/the sober radish of the heart.   AmPA

The Mole and the Eagle.   Sarah Josepha Hale.   And God formed each, and formed their sphere,/And thus his goodness doth appear.   OBCA

Mole Catcher.   Edmund Charles Blunden.   There's not a peal in England sounds so well.   OBMV

Mole in the Ground.   Anonymous.   If I was a mole in the ground.   FSW

Mole Talk.   Leo Kennedy.   To lift a stiffened limb, or pluck/The seaming of a shroud.   PeCV

Molecatcher.   Albert D. Mackie.   Binnae the mowdie-man's.   GoTS

Moles.   William Stafford.   and I rumple on through sorrows.   NYBP; RFM

Moll-in-the-Wad and I Fell Out.   Anonymous.   It's an old soldier's button, says/Moll-in-the-Wad.   OxNR

Mollesse.   Josephine Jacobsen.   Of course you can keep spring, says the invisible bush.   NePoAm-2

Molly Asthore.   Sir Samuel Ferguson.   But one kiss from her honey mouth/Would make me whole again!   IrPN

Molly Bawn.   Anonymous.
And through his misfortune it was poor Molly Bawn.   ViBoFo
He shot and killed me and now I am gone.   BaBo

Molly Bawn and Brian Oge.   Anonymous.   We'll get wed–behave you villain–Brian Oge.   OnYI

Molly Bond.   Anonymous.   Molly's ghost will stand before you like a mountain of snow.   BFSS

Molly Brannigan.   Anonymous.   When I hear ye cryin' o'er me, "Arrah! why did ye die?"   FSW

Molly Malone.   Anonymous.   Cryin', "Cockles and mussels, alive, alive, oh!"   FSW; MaC

Molly Means.   Margaret Walker.   Lean is the ghost of Molly Means.   AmNP; BlSi; NMM; PoNe; StPo

Molly Mog: or, The Fair Maid of the Inn.   John Gay.   And so I shall lose Molly Mog.   CEP; CoMu

Molly Moor.   George Farewell.   And sit on Proserpina's throne,/When she is up to Ceres gone.   NOEC

Molly of the North Country.   Anonymous.   And a pretty maid's beauty it will soon fade away.   OBET

Molly Pitcher.   Laura E. Richards.   To hold the name of Molly Pitcher.   PAH; YaD

Molly Pitcher.   Kate Brownlee Sherwood.   And the army was wild with cheers.   MC; PAH; PAL

Moly.   Thom Gunn.   Dreaming the flower I have never seen.   HAP; NoAm; PrIm

Moly.   Edith Matilda Thomas.   Hermes' moly, growing solely/To undo enchanter's wile!   HBV 1-2

Mom I'm All Screwed Up.   Frank Lima.   isn't mamacita's heart going to/kiss mom/good night/no/no/no.   ANYP

Mom's Homecooked Trees.   Michael Stephens.   ...and she knows they/will answer: Hoy, hoy, hoy!   APU

A Moment.   Stopford Augustus Brooke.   Do I not know her lips are cold.   IrPN

Moment.   Robert Creeley.   except the body is moved,/still, to some other use.   CAPP

The Moment.   Theodore Roethke.   We end in joy.   NYBP

The Moment.   David Rowbotham.   When the world is known not to be green forever.   BoAV

The Moment.   Kendrick Smithyman.   None is revealed.   AnNZ

The Moment.   William Stafford.   they don't have it.   NNaP

The Moment before Conception.   Eve Merriam.   touch me constantly!   UnTE

Moment by Moment.   Daniel W. Whittle.   Jesus, my Saviour, abides with me still.   BLRP

Since woman is the helpmeet made for man? VLP

Though there be nothing new beneath the sun. VLP

Monna Lisa. James Russell Lowell. Makes it seem sweeter to be hers! AmLP

Monoagram 23. Martina Werner. in vain in vain the/moment/gone BoWoP

The Monochord. Dante Gabriel Rossetti. And in regenerate rapture turns my face/Upon the devious coverts of dismay? MaVP

Monochrome. Louise Imogen Guiney. And Self begin to be. AnAmPo

Le Monocle de Mon Oncle. Wallace Stevens. That fluttering things have so distinct a shade. AP; APA; CoBMV; LiTM; MAPA; MoAB; NoAm

Monody. Herman Melville. Glazed now with ice the cloistral vine/That hid the shyest grape. AP; LiTA; MAmP; NCEP; OBSP; PoEL 1-5

Monody on a Century. Earle Birney. And men with boots will put an end/To making similes. CaP

Monody to the Sound of Zithers. Kay Boyle. Friended thus, I have let nothing pass. PoA

Monogamania. Eve Merriam. I hoe in one furrow/And heap all my fill. UnTE

Monogamy (excerpt). Gerald Gould. And read a book on sexual morality. OxBTC

Monogram 4. Martina Werner. blue forget-me-nots/glaze cracked BoWoP

Monogram 29. Martina Werner. the trees/reproduce/more humanely. BoWoP

Monologue of a Deaf Man. David Wright. Involved like them in the not unhearing air. MP; NoAm

Monologue of the Rating Morgan in Rutherford County. C. F. MacIntyre. Lord, is there nothing left for a horse/but a daily quota of intercourse? PH

Monologue of Two Moons, Nudes with Crests. 1938. Norman Dubie. Twigs, leaves and an infinite black string. FiCP

Monologue through Bars. Nelson Hubbell. she fed me cartridges, she clicked my safety off. AMV-81

Monseigneur Plays. Theodosia Garrison. Monseigneur plays his new gavotte. HBMV

Monserrat. William Edwin Collin. God is–and in the morning fire. CaP

Monsieur McGinte. Anonymous. Habille dans sa meilleure costume. NA

Monsieur Pussy-Cat, Blackmailer. Stevie Smith. Take care you don't pousser trop/The one who gives you such jolis plats. PCat

Monsieur Qui Passe. Charlotte Mew. God! but the night is cold! SBG

Monsoon. Kenneth Slade Alling. And the gharri so slow in getting you there. NePoAm

Monsoon. David Wevill. Where the scorpion hungers, carrying his bruise down. NYBP

The Monster. Greg Kuzma. To hear them howling/In the hills. AmPA

The Monster. Edward Lowbury. If he weren't, we'd be in a mess. AmMo

The Monster. Henry Rago. "Monster!" I cried. And "Monster!" cried the mouse PoA

Monster Alphabet. Robert Fisher. Zobo bird–so/who are you? AmMo

The Monstrous Marriage. William Carlos Williams. ...a leather belt made/upon which he perched to enjoy her. MoPo

Mont Blanc. Percy Bysshe Shelley. If to the human mind's imaginings/Silence and solitude were vacancy? EnRP; ERoP 1-2; InPS; NIP; NoP; OAEL 1-2; OBTV; PP; TEP

Montalbert (excerpt). Charlotte Smith. Nor is the deepest shade, the keenest air,/Black as my fate, or cold as my despair. BoWoP

Montana Eclogue. William Stafford. one flake at a time teaches/grace, even to stone. NYBP

Montana Fifty Years Ago. J. V. Cunningham. This was Montana fifty years ago. Prf

Montana Pastoral. J. V. Cunningham. But fear, thirst, hunger, and this huddled chill. MAT; MoAmPo; PrIm; VGW

Montana Remembered from Albuquerque; 1982. Ron Rogers. Greater/than a moth's wing, or a human heart. STE

Montana Wives. Gwendolen Haste. I couldn't help it! I just laughed and laughed. AmFN

Montcalm and Wolfe. Anonymous. Then says this brave youth, "I quit this earth with pleasure." AmFP

Monte Alban. Joseph Stroud. Ghosts of black hands through the ruins NPGG

Montefiore. Ambrose Bierce. And in a moment was a lonely man! AA; AnAmPo

Monterey. Charles Fenno Hoffman. Than not have been at Monterey? AA; FaBoBe; HBV 1-2; MC; PAH

Montgomery. Anonymous. And they must drink or die. AmFP

Montgomery. Sam Cornish. my feet two hundred years old CNA; PoBA; Psk

Montgomery. H.A.C. Evans. They are all on secret missions for Montgomery the/Tops. GDP

Montgomery. J. C. Hall. Hither and thither crying. ChMP

Montgomery at Quebec. Clinton Scollard. Honor, then, for all time be/To the brave Montgomery! PAH

The Month of Falling Stars. Ella Higginson. These things are. August's own. YeAr

Month of January. Frankie Armstrong. And the beauty of a fine young man will all soon fade away. BrRo

The Month of the Thunder Moon. Marion Doyle. One may find on every side/Signs of Nature's wonder. YeAr

The Months. Anonymous. December: And a Cristesmasse I drinke red wine. OxBM

The Months of the Year. Richard Grafton. And all the rest have thirty-one. FaBoU

Montreal. Abraham Moses Klein. Here in these beating valves, you will/For all my mortal time reside! CaP; OBCV

Montrose to His Mistress. James Graham. That puts it not unto the Touch,/To win or lose it all. OxBS

Monument. Milton Acorn. the ghosts stood gossiping. NeAC

The Monument. Elizabeth Bishop. ...Watch it closely. HaCAP; LiTA; MoPo; NoAm; NOBA; PP; PPoe

A Monument. Charles Madge. Of evils on the watching shore. FaBoMo

Monument. A. M. Sullivan. Pounds the tombs of the world into dust and loosens the dust/of Jan who sleeps... GoYe

The Monument. Samuel Wesley. Pity a wretch like him should ever live! OBSP

The Monument and the Shrine. John Logan. His wheels click in the single road. LCAP

Monument Mountain. William Cullen Bryant. Is called the Mountain of the Monument. BeLS

Monument to a Boxer. Lucilius [(or Lucillius)]. For making their work one hell of a lot lighter. LiSp

Monument to Pushkin. Joseph Brodsky. is more comfortable/than standing/on pedestals. VWA

A Monumental Memorial of Marine Mercy &c. Richard Steere. O who can tast thy Good, and not Thanksgiving Raise. SCAP

The Monuments of Hiroshima. D. J. Enright. –who might have wished for something lasting,/Like a wooden box. OBSP

Monumentum Aere, Etc. Ezra Pound. To keep grass/Over your grave. NOBA

Moo! Robert Hillyer. Summer is over, summer is over. OBAL

The Moo-Cow-Moo. Edmund Vance Cooke. But our hired man he sets close by/An' squirts an'squirts an' squirts. FaFP; MoShBr

Moochie. Eloise Greenfield. And every time she gets the hiccups/I laugh NTCP

A Mood. Winifred Howells. My spirit it was that fell. AA

The Mood. Quandra Prettyman. I could not/be saved. PoBA

A Mood. Amelie Troubetzkoy. Fetterless, lawless, a maiden free! AA

A Mood Apart. Robert Frost. For any eye is an evil eye/That looks in on to a mood apart. OBSP

The Moods. Fannie Stearns Davis. The Moods have drawn swift fingers through my heart. HBV 1-2

Moods. Leib Kwitko. And I join the procession,/And my child follows behind. TrJP

The Moods. William Butler Yeats. What one in the rout/Of the fire-born moods/Has fallen away? CTC; VLP

Moods of Rain. Vernon Scannell. Sighing you into sleep/Where peace prevails and only soft rains fall. BoNaP

The Moon. Charles Best. So as you come, and as you do depart,/Joys ebb and flow within my tender heart. OBSC

The Moon. Bhasa. The moon in truth, proud of its brilliance, doth lead/astray all this world. LiTW

The Moon. Robert Creeley. and felt as if someone/were there, waiting, alone. VGW

The Moon. William Henry Davies. Who worships thee till music fails/Is greater than thy nightingales. BrPo; MoBrPo; MoVE

The Moon. Eliza Lee Follen. That small twinkling star/Is your little baby. HBV 1-2; HBVY

The Moon. Louise Ayres Garnett. Trailing a Hundred Stars/Over the Night. SiSoSe

The Moon. Donald Hall. in the void branches/of a tree, beside/a cold kettle. NCSH

Moon. Frances Horovitz. no more than a thumbprint/on the edge of the sky BrRo

Moon. Henry Rowe. While o'er thy myrtled lawns I stray/Beneath, O maiden Moon! thy ray. OBEV

The Moon. Ryuho. Spilled it on the grass SoPo

The Moon. Percy Bysshe Shelley.

And ever changing, like a joyless eye/That finds no object with its constancy? FaBoCh; LoGBV; OBEV

The moon arose up in the murky East,/A white and shapeless mass–. BoLiVe

That gazes on thee till in thee it pities... ChRP

Moonlight in Autumn. James (1700-48) Thomson. And hung on every Spray, on every Blade/of Grass, the myriad Dew-Drops twinkle round. OBEC

Moonlight in Italy. Elizabeth Clementine Kinney The sense of worship into uttered praise. AA

Moonlight Night: Carmel. Langston Hughes. And beating the land's/Edge into a swoon. MOS

Moonlight Night on the Port. Sidney Keyes. For some are lucky, leaving their curved faces/Propped in the moonlight while their bodies drown. DTC

Moonlight on Lake Sydenham. Wilson MacDonald. To light the first thin taper of the dawn. CaP

Moonlight...Scattered Clouds. Robert Bloomfield. Scatter'd immensely wide from east to west,/The beauteous' semblance of a Flock at rest. OBNC

Moonlight Song of the Mocking-bird. William Hamilton Hayne As if the vanished soul of Keats/Had found its new birth in a bird. AA

Moonlight (with music). Anonymous. I would fly to the arms of my darling/And there I would stay till I die. AS

Moonlit Apples. John Drinkwater. On moon-washed apples of wonder. BoNaP; OBMV; OxBTC; PoRA

Moonlit Night in Kansas. Victor Contoski. An old Indian recites/meaningless words:/Topeka, Manhattan, Wichita. TAT

Moonrise. Hilda ("H. D.") Doolittle. She is great,/we measure her by the pine-trees. PoA

Moonrise. Gerard Manley Hopkins. Parted me leaf and leaf, divided me, eyelid and eyelid of/slumber. FaBoPP; MoAB; MoBrPo; MOON; NOBV; SeCePo

Moonrise. D. H. Lawrence. In this odd life will tarnish or pass away. LiTM; MOON; PoA

Moonrise. Frank Dempster Sherman. That hangs between the darkness and the/light. AA

Moonrise in the Rockies. Ella Higginson. And a million firs stand tipped with/lucent fire. AA

Moonset, Gloucester, December 1, 1957, 1:58 AM. Charles Olson. I can die now I just begun to live CAPP

The Moonsheep. Christian Morgenstern. His body's white, the sun is red./The Moonsheep. FaBoNo; MOON

Moonshine. Sonny Boy Williamson. Now that is the reason why/I believe I'll make a change BluL

Moonshiner. Anonymous. And if moonshine don't kill me, I'll live till I die. FSW

Moonshot. Robert Kelly. shaping the matter of all energies/to our one energy MOON

Moonshot Sonnet. Mary Ellen Solt. [concrete poem] BoWoP

The Moonstar. Dante Gabriel Rossetti. Lady, not thou but she was glorified. MaVP

Moontan. Mark Strand. invisible/as anyone. NYBP

Moonwalk. John Engels. and the manshaped night remaining total MAT

The Moor. Ralph Hodgson. Unbody me–I'm tired–and get me home. MoBrPo

Moorburn in Spring. Anonymous. Or wander mid the deepenings of the glens. PoSH

The Moorhen Pond. Tom Earley. Welsh fish are not fussy. BoAnP

Moorings. Norman MacCaig. Longing to clear the hurdles/That ring the Point of Stoer. OxBTC

Moorland Night. Charlotte Mew. Oh! then, to me. ChMP; ViBoPo

Moorlands of the Not. Anonymous. And pause betimes in gnostic rimes/To woo the Over Soul. NA

Moors, Angels, Civil Wars. Keith Sinclair. Doctors' medicines; sweet swallow down. AnNZ

The Moose. Elizabeth Bishop. then there's a dim/smell of moose, an acrid/smell of gasoline. FaBoWP

Moose. Robert Wiljer. straight man in a masterly gag. AMV-81

Moose Lake State Hospital. Dennis Shady. And we will talk of old days again. LFAC

Moosehead Lake. Anonymous. Lovely fa-de-little-aro, sing tooral all day. OuSiCo

Mopoke. Louis Lavater. Blots for a moment/My sleepy star. PoAu 1-2

The Moral. Bernard Mandeville. A Golden Age, must be as free,/For Acorns, as for Honesty. CEP

The Moral. Theodore Weiss. ...the passionate failures,/the perfect despairs, these never fail us. Prf

A Moral Alphabet (excerpt). Hilaire Belloc. Remain there; do not fool around. NOBL

The Moral Bully. Oliver Wendell Holmes. And bait his homilies with his brother worms? AnNE

Moral Essays. Alexander Pope.
Alive ridiculous, and dead forgot. ExPo
And fame, this lord of useless thousands ends. ExPo; FiP
Just is the twig is bent, the tree's inclined. GoTF
"Oh, save my Country, Heav'n!" shall be your last. CEP
Prov'd, by ends of being, to have been. CoBE

These are Imperial Works, and worthy Kings. CABL; PoEL 1-5
You hold him no Philosopher at all. LiTB

A Moral in Sevres. Mildred Howells. She glances back with bashful eyes. AA; HBV 1-2

Moral Ode. D. Rosenmann-Taub. how you puncture bloods/and fingernails. VWA

A Moral Poem. J. V. Cunningham. Nor live curiously,/Cheating providence. VGW

A Moral Poem Freely Accepted from Sappho. James Wright. And in virtue. CAPP

Moral Story II. David Wright. And lineaments of desire lit the old hag. ChMP; PeSA

The Moral Taxi Ride. Erich Kastner. And kick a hole in his hat. ErPo

The Moral Warfare. John Greenleaf Whittier. The Light, and Truth, and Love of Heaven! AnNE; PAL; TreFT

Morality. Matthew Arnold. 'Twas when the heavenly house I trod,/And lay upon the breast of God. GTBS; HBV 1-2

Morality. Jean Garrigue. Smile as you say this who will be/Dust when these stones still mark the Sacred Way. ELU

The Morality of Poetry. James Wright. A blue sea-poem, joy, moon-ripple on wave. PP

Morals. James Thurber. Never serve a rabbit stew before you catch the rabbit. FaBV

Mordent for a Melody. Margaret Avison. Pas de million until our singeing-day. ACV

A More Ancient Mariner. Bliss Carman. Then loafs all winter upon his hoard,/With the mercury at zero. OBAL

More Clues. Muriel Rukeyser. ...somewhere in me, clues IHMS

More Distant Than the Dead Sea. Nadia Tueni. There was/a woman like a departure in a fragment of/landscape. PBWP

More Foreign Cities. Charles Tomlinson. It commands vacancy. NePoEA-2

More Good Whiskey Blues. Peetie Wheatstraw. Well, since you has come back to me/ooo well well, I hope you have come to stay BluL

The More It Snows. A.(lan) A.(lexander) Milne. How cold my/TOES-tiddely-pom/Are/Growing. NTCP

More Letters Found Near a Suicide. Frank Horne. Through the tape/To victory... BANP

"More Light! More Light!" Anthony Hecht. And settled upon his eyes in a black soot. CoAP; ConAP; HAP; NePoEA-2; NoAm; NOBA; NoP; OBWP; SM; SoSe; TwCP; UnPo; VGW; VWA

More Love. Anonymous. How can ye love God,/Whom ye have not seen? AH

More Love to Thee, O Christ. Elizabeth Payson Prentiss. More love, O Christ, to thee,/More love to thee. AH

More Lovely Grows the Earth. Helena Coleman. More conscious of the Love that glorifies/The common ways and makes them holy ground? CaP

The More Loving One. W. H. Auden. Though this might take me a little time. HoPM

More Nudes for Florence. Harold Witt. we ring, like bells of Florence, renaissance. ErPo

More of a Corpse Than a Woman. Muriel Rukeyser. we've a new race to start. NMM

More of Thee. Horatius Bonar. More of Thy love and truth, Incarnate Word. BLRP

More (parody). Philip Appleman. We bomb ourselves back/To the stone age. BXAP

More Power. Egan O'Rahilly. A year from today; together/With all whom we like. BIrV; OnYI

More Prayer. Anonymous. "The deepest need of men–/"More prayer!" STF

More Reformation. Daniel Defoe. For it will all the power of art outdo/To join the new reformer and the beau. OBSV

More Scraps of Lear: "Hassall irritates me." Edward Lear. ...and 2 Thermometers stewed in treacle/for supper. FaBoNo

More Sonnets at Christmas. Allen Tate.
The Huns gelded and feeding in a ring. LiTA; NePA
...these are the better notions. LiTA; SBVL
This crucial day, whose decapitate joke/Languidly winds into the inner ear. LiTA; NePA
While the sun squats upon the waveless seas. LiTA; LiTM; NePA; WaP

More Strong Than Time. Victor Hugo. My soul more love than you can make my soul forget. AWP

More Than. Susan Fitzpatrick. The world broken open, spilling life. AMV-80

More Than Fifty. Jack Gilbert. So what, I think happily. So what! NPGG

More Than Flowers We Have Brought. Nancy Byrd Turner. And our promise, too, we leave/With the flowers. SiSoSe

More Than Most Fair. Fulke, Lord Brooke Greville. Honour the shrine where you alone are placed. EiL

A Morning Kiss. Andrew McCord Jones. and the pain speaks clearly. LFAC

A Morning Letter. Robert Duncan. This is early morning in a world of kings. PoA

Morning Light. Louis Dudek. inside my room. AMV-80

Morning Light. Mary Effie Lee Newsome. And making a morning path to the light/For the tropic traveler! PoNe

The Morning Light. Louis Simpson. And my life, pitilessly demar.ding,/Rises forever in the morning light. NNaP; NoAm

The Morning Light Is Breaking. Samuel Francis Smith. Stay not till all the holy/Proclaim, "The Lord is come!" AH; WGRP

Morning Light Song. Philip Lamantia. From flying straight to Your Heart Whose Rays conduct me to/the SONG! NeAP

Morning Light the Dew-Drier. Mary Effie Lee Newsome. After the dews of blood? AmNP; CDC; PoBA

'Morning, Morning. Ray Mathew. ...I don't hear the calling/And dancing of cockatoo-crested morning. PoAu 1-2

Morning, Noon, and... Hawley Truax. before it turns up-/side down with the lark. NYBP

The Morning of the Red-Tailed Hawk. Bettie M. Sellers. between my trembling hands. AMV-80

Morning on the Lievre. Archibald Lampman. Till we only hear their whir/In behind a rocky spur,/Just ahead. SD

Morning on the Shore. Wilfred (William Wilfred Campbell) Campbell. A dead, drowned face stares up immutably. NOBC

Morning on the St. John's. Jane Cooper. And shakes a man as dawn shakes birds and flowers. NYBP

Morning Once More. Joy Harjo. and my whole life/a rider. TWSS

A Morning-Piece; or, An Hymn for the Hay-Makers. Christopher Smart. and we'll dance to the tune of the stream. NOEC

Morning Poem. Jennivien-Diana Beenen. and little russian dolls/conversing in wooden cabinets. AMV-81

The Morning Porches. Donald Hall. Two billion particles make up a bird. NePoAm-2

Morning Prayer. Anonymous. If these, my loved ones, were not here with me. PoToHe

Morning Prayer. Aua. Towards the whitening dawn. WTO

Morning Prayer. Nissim Ezekiel. To make it human good. ACV

Morning Prayer. Ogden Nash. Today, O Lord, for your dear sake,/I'll try to keep them when awake. GrPl; OxBChV

A Morning Prayer. Betty Perpetuo. I pray that Thou wilt find me, Lord,/Waiting patiently. STF

A Morning Prayer. Ella Wheeler Wilcox. "The world is better that I lived today." PoToHe

The Morning Prayers of the Hasid, Rabbi Levi Yitzhok. Phyllis Gotlieb. Miriam the Prophetess will dance before us/at that Festival VWA

The Morning Purples All the Sky. Roman Breviary. On Earth, in heaven, to God most high,/For Christ's great victory! BePJ

Morning Rush. Constance Clark. and never going fast enough. AmC

Morning Serenade. Madison Cawein. Arise! come down! loved that thou art! HBV 1-2

Morning Song. Karle Wilson Baker. Never so glad as we're going to be! HBMV

Morning Song. Henry Blakely. twice the numbered sands of deserts/and lengths of beaches. CNA

Morning Song. Charlotte DeClue. Tomorrow,/she will die. STE; TWSS

Morning Song. Alan Dugan. I shall walk out bravely into the daily accident. CAD; ELU

Morning Song. Afanasy Afanasyevich Foeth. But a song is lifting its wings. AWP

Morning Song. Solomon Ibn Gabirol. So will I thank Thee, praising, while/there dwelleth/Yet the breath of God in me. TrJP

Morning Song. Gregory Orr. the way swordblades/pierce a magician's box. MAYP

Morning Song. Sylvia Plath. the clear vowels rise like balloons. BoWoP; HaCAP; HeIP; IHMS; InPK; InPS; LCAP; NAs; NOBA; PAI; PrIm; SBG

Morning Song. Kurt M. Stein. Eh's melten tut, arise! FiBHP

Morning Song. Leon Stokebury. The beads of dew on these most secret places. AMV-80

Morning Song. Sara Teasdale. Only the lonely are free. MOON

A Morning Song for Imogen. William Shakespeare. Arise, arise. AnEnPo

Morning Star. Thomas Hornsby Ferril. Once I loved until I could not breathe. VGW

Morning Star. James J. Galvin. I'll snuff the stars about Her head/And wither Paradise. ISi

The Morning Star. Primus St. John. I vote for Mr. Anderson. PoBA

Morning Star Man. George Keithley. ...Look up-It is I! It is I! NPGG

Morning Star, O Cheering Sight! Anonymous. Fill my heart with light divine. AH

Morning Sun. Louis MacNeice. That forming on a cigarette covers the red. MoAB; MoBrPo; MP

Morning Swim. Maxine W. Kumin. ...I was the well/That fed the lake that met my sea/In which I sang Abide With Me. LiSp; SM

The Morning They Shot Tony Lopez, Barber and Pusher Who Went Too Far. Gary Soto. ...slide/In the same blood you closed your eyes to. MAYP

A Morning to Remember; or, E. Pluribus Unum. Edward Dorn. ...No son, Big Novelist said/it's lonely up here NoAm

The Morning Track. Edward Parone. Just this side of stillness and of death. NYBP

Morning Vigil. Phil George. We endure./We sing. VoR

The Morning Watch. Henry Vaughan. My lamp, and life, both shall in thee abide. BoC; LiTB; LoBV; MePo; OBS; OxBoCh; SeCePo; ViBoPo

Morning Work. D. H. Lawrence. And laughing with work, living their work like a game. MoAB; MoBrPo

Morning Workout. Babette Deutsch. Odor of earth/Enriches azuring air. LiSp; NePoAm-2; SD

Morning Worship. Mark Van Doren. Leave them all there/Old lover. Live on. NePoAm-2

The morns are meeker than they were. Emily Dickinson. I'll put a trinket on. BoNaP; HBV 1-2; OBCA; PoPl; TiPo; TreFT; YeAr

The Moron. Anonymous. My God! perhaps I am! CenHV; GoTF; TreFT; YaD

Morrissey and the Russian Sailor (with music). Anonymous. To brave Jack Morrissey and Paddies evermore. AS

The Morrow's Message. Dante Gabriel Rossetti. And thrice,–whereby the shadow of death is dead. MaVP

Mors et Vita. Richard Henry Stoddard. Certain is nothing but Death! AA

Mors et Vita. Samuel Waddington. ...but will death let/Our eyes the longed-for vision see?/We know not yet. HBV 1-2

Mors Iabrochii. Anonymous. Et profugi gemitus exgrabuere rathae. NA

Mors, Morituri Te Salutamus. Francis Burdett Money-Coutts. Hoves thy black flag!...Therefore I hate thee, Death! OBVV

Mort aux Chats. Peter Porter. Death to all cats! The Rule/of Dogs shall last a thousand years! OxBC

La Mort d'Arthur (parody). William Aytoun. Whereon no canker lighted, for they bore/The magic stamp of MECHI'S SILVER STEEL. FaBoPa

Mortal Combat. Mary Elizabeth Coleridge. And be a man like other men. OBVV

Mortal Combat. Alice Fay Di Castagnola. And no one can foretell which side will win. GoYe

Mortal Love. Basil Dowling. Nor they with their batteries,/Nor death, can move it. AnNZ

Mortal, Sneer Not at the Devil. Heinrich Heine. And to-morrow thou must borrow,/As thou borrow'st yesterday. TrJP

Mortality. Anonymous. Wind's stability,/Is mortality. CBEP

Mortality. James Devaney. Life is no more. BoAV; PoAu 1-2

Mortality. Naomi Long Madgett. When hope starts staggering. NNP; PoBA

Mortally. James Kirkup. creep into the season's river/and the ruin. NeBP

De Morte. Anonymous. ...i' the fifth diseases clog/And trouble him; then death's his epilogue. OBSP

De Morte. Sir Henry Wotton. ...then Death's his Epilogue. OBS

Morte Arthur (excerpt). Anonymous. The vesere, the aventaile, his vesturis riche,/With the valiant blode was verrede all over. PoEL 1-5

Morte D'Arthur. Alfred, Lord Tennyson.
And on the mere the wailing died away. AnEnPo; DL; DTo; FaBoBe; FiP; HBV 1-2; NIP; NOBV; OAEL 1-2; OBNV; PoEL 1-5; SeCeV; WHA
Bound by gold chains about the feet of God.... GoBC
The clear church-bells ring in the Christmas-/morn. OAEP; TRV; VLP
Where I will heal me of my grievous wound. RBV

Mortem, Quae Violat Suavia, Pellit Amor. William Johnson Cory. And fear of death, like childish dream,/Will pass and flee, when thou art here. NBM

Mortification. George Herbert. That all these dyings may be life in death. AnAnS 1; MePo; OAEP; SeCP; ViBoPo

The Mortified Genius. James Graeme. Spurning true genius prostrate at his feet. NOEC

A Mortifying Mistake. Anna Maria Pratt. For I thought of my doll and–sakes/alive!–I answered, "Mary Ann!" AA; HBV 1-2; HBVY

Mortmain. Robert Penn Warren. Naked in that black blast of his love. NOBA; PoCh; Prf

Les Morts Vont Vite. Henry Cuyler Bunner. Clasps thee with arms that cling like/Death's embrace:/Les morts vont vite! AA

De Mortuis Nil Nisi Bonum. Richard Realf. Plant daisies at his head and feet. HBV 1-2

Morvin. John Fuller. The poking finger to a nervous age. NePoEA-2

Morwennae Statio. Robert Stephen Hawker. The changeless God's eternal fane. GoBC

Mos' Done Toilin' Here. Anonymous. Hm Lord, I'm mos' done toilin' here. BoAN 1-2

The Mosaic Worker.   Arthur Wallace Peach.   Under the Craftsman's sure and knowing hand/Become a life made beautiful!   BLRP

Mosby at Hamilton.   Madison Cawein.   We felt the South still had some sons/She would not scorn to bury.   PAH

Moschatel.   D. J. O'Sullivan.   I dream that I'm a tree!   NeIP

Moschus Moschiferus.   A. D. Hope.   Accept this song I too have made for you.   CBAP; GrPl

Moscow Nights.   *Anonymous.*   This most beautiful Moscow night.   FSW

Moses.   Amir Gilboa.   I am still a child.   VWA

Moses.   Sydney Tremayne.   For the chosen have no choice.   OxBS

Moses' Account.   Milan Fuest.   And I shall never see your Promised Land.   VWA

Moses and Jesus.   Israel Zangwill.   In one strange, silent, piteous gaze,/and dim/With bitter tears of agonized despair.   TrJP

Moses and Joshua.   Else Lasker-Schüler.   When his soul, a weary lion, cried to God.   VWA

Moses on Mount Nebo.   Abraham Regelson.   And my soul trembles with the stillness.   VWA

Moses Supposes His Toeses Are Roses.   *Anonymous.*   As Moses supposes his toeses to be.   OxNR

The Mosquito.   Rodney Jones.   How she thrills to my life, how she sings for the harvest.   MAYP

The Mosquito.   D. H. Lawrence.   Queer, what a dim dark smudge you have disappeared/into!   BoAnP; PoPle

Mosquito.   John Updike.   The small welt of remorse subsides as side/By side we, murderer and murdered, sleep.   BoAnP

Moss.   Nancy Willard.   ...laid low/and still blossoming/under the snow.   HoAn

Moss-Gathering.   Theodore Roethke.   As if I had committed, against the whole scheme of life, a desecration.   CoBMV; RFM; VGW

The Moss of His Skin.   Anne Sexton.   how I hold my daddy/like an old stone tree.   CoAP; IHMS; SM

The Moss-Rose.   Sir Henry Newbolt.   And the morning shadows of youth, and the night that fell/thereafter.   HBV 1-2

The Moss Supplicateth for the Poet.   Richard Henry Dana.   To die when he awakes in God!   AA

Mossbawn: Two Poems in Dedication.   Seamus Heaney.
   sunk past its gleam/in the meal bin.   CIP
   With all of us there, our anonymities.   CIP; FaBoIP

The Most Acceptable Gift.   Matthis ("Asmus") Claudius.   Our humble, thankful hearts.   BLRP

The Most Alluring Clouds That Mount the Sky.   William Wordsworth.   The house that cannot pass away be ours.   NOBV

The Most Beautiful Girl in the World.   Lorenz Hart.   Which side?/This side.   OBAL

The Most Beautiful Woman at My Highschool Reunion.   Ellen Marie Bissert.   like the woman waiting for me tonight/does to mine.   PeHV

Most beutiful of things I leave is sunlight.   Praxilla.   then ripe cucumbers and apples and pears.   BoWoP

The Most Expensive Picture in the World.   Howard Nemerov.   "It is the most expensive picture, yes,/But only in the world."   EyDe

Most Like an Arch This Marriage.   John Ciardi.   in faultless failing, raised by our own weight.   MoLP; PoPl; WeW

Most Lovely Shade.   Edith Sitwell.   Shall pour such splendour as your heart to me.   AtBAP; FaBoTw; GTBS-P

The Most of It.   Robert Frost.   And forced the underbrush—and that was all.   BiP; CABA; CrMA; HAP; MoPo; NePA; NoP; NU; PPoe

Most Quietly at Times.   Casar Flaischlen.   It pales and passes, fading when it came.   AWP

The Most-Sacred Mountain.   Eunice Tietjens.   For once I stood/In the white windy presence of eternity.   HBMV; MoRP

Most Souls, 'Tis True, but Peep Out Once an Age.   Alexander Pope.   And, close confin'd to their own palace, sleep.   ELU

Most Sovereign Lady.   *Anonymous.*   Tresore full dere, gronded with grace.   MeEL

The Most Vital Thing in Life.   Grenville Kleiser.   The most vital thing in life.   PoToHe; SoSe

Most Weeds, Whilst Young.   Francis Daniel Pastorius.   'Tis hard to Root it out.   SCAP

Mot Eran Dous Miei Cossir.   Arnaut Daniel.   To enhance thy dignities.   AWP

Motels, Hotels, Other People's Houses.   H. L. Van Brunt.   where little was said/and less was known   FAZ

A Motet.   John Amner.   And teach me how I may Thy dwelling find.   OBSP

Motets, II.   *Anonymous.*   God's curse on him who made me a nun.   PBWP

Motets: "My love, how could your heart consider."   *Anonymous.*   for my heart heeds nothing, only loving you.   PBWP

A Moth.   Henry Bellyse Baildon.   And mass her conquering glooms, then rise and flit/A shadow through the shades!'   NOBV

The Moth.   Walter De la Mare.   In ecstasy swirls and sways/To her stange tryst.   BrPo; MoVE

Moth.   Lance Henson.   hanging from the/old/sky   VoR

The Moth.   Vernon Scannell.   An appetite that must/Make do with such rough food as she, too, must.   OxBC

The Moth and the Flame.   George Taggart.   That's the tale of the Moth and the Flame!   FSN; TreF

Moth-Song.   Ellen Mackay Hutchinson Cortissoz.   –Dim as a ghost he flies/Through the night mysteries.   AA

Moth-Terror.   Benjamin De Casseres.   Night-Moth, Change-Moth, Time-/Moth, eaters of dreams and of me!   TrJP

The Mother.   *Anonymous.*
   The fair report of seven good children's deeds.   OHIP
   For she, who made of home a Heaven,/Wakes–to find Heaven her home!   PGD
   Your love still close and watching through the years.   PoToHe

The Mother.   Gwendolyn Brooks.   I loved you all.   BlSi; BPo; FaBoWP; GP; NMM

Mother.   Aldo Camerino.   maternal love, filial love/in the old place, desecrated by barbarians.   VWA

Mother.   Thomas Curtis Clark.   Queen of my heart,/My Mother.   PGD

The Mother.   Sara Coleridge.   No murmuring streams her grief assuage.   OBVV

Mother.   Barry Dempster.   babes dropping quietly to the ground.   AMV-80

Mother.   Philip Dow.   oh, so that's who you are, my Mother: Mother:/Father's-old-widow.   NPGG

Mother.   Max Ehrmann.   Let me sleep on, dear God, if I but dream.   PoToHe

Mother.   Rose Fyleman.   It's like a lovely fairy/Dropped in to say good-night.   SiSoSe

The Mother.   S. S. Gardons.   Where she moves by habit, hungering and blind.   NePoEA-2

Mother.   Seamus Heaney.   Stuffs air down my throat.   NAs

Mother.   Theresa Helburn.   ...men do not celebrate in rhyme/Their daily bread.   OHIP

Mother.   D. L. Kelleher.   The skilled musicians there,/Around him in the nimble air.   NeIP

Mother.   Sharon Mayer Libera.   You read and doze, too real for me, too deep.   IHMS

The Mother.   Catulle Mendes.   Should say: "Sleep in my bosom, O my/child!"   TrJP

Mother.   Jose Montoya.   That woman–she only complains/in her sleep.   FIA

Mother.   Nagase Kiyoko.   If I move she quickly breaks,/and the splinters stab me.   BoWoP

The Mother.   Nettie Palmer.   Into realms of pain I bring/You for joy's own offering.   PoAu 1-2

The Mother.   Padraic Pearse.   My sons were faithful, and they fought.   OnYI

The Mother.   Kathryn White Ryan.   To him life I gave, on him life I thrust–/Was it–death–too?   CAW

Mother.   Anwar Shaul.   Oh, Mother, is there anyone to plead on our behalf?   VWA

Mother.   Keith Sinclair.   A moon to her sun and his star   AnNZ

Mother.   Emily Taylor.   He is heard to speak through a mother's love.   PGD

Mother.   Julian Tuwim.   But the corpse of my name/Lies there till this very day.   VWA

Mother.   Stephen Vincent.   ...I float/like a swan/over 30/white lakes.   NeAC

Mother–a Portrait.   Ethel Romig Fuller.   Of women, best/And loveliest.   PGD

Mother, among the Dustbins.   Stevie Smith.   Can you question the folly of man in the creation of God?/Who are you?   PBWP

Mother and Child.   Ivy O. Eastwick.   O happy Mother, to possess/So loving-kind a boy!   SiSoSe

The Mother and Child.   Vernon Watkins.   Springs like a star to her milk, is not for the grave.   NeBP

The Mother and Her Son on the Cross.   *Anonymous.*   Thou bring us into Hevene light./Amen.   MeEL

Mother and Poet.   Elizabeth Barrett Browning.   Let none look at me!   HBV 1-2; SBG

Mother and Sister of the Artist.   Olga Cabral.   I have set you in the exact corner/of cruel time/From which there is no escape.   PoDr

Mother and Son.   William Heyen.   ...Tell her, if you can,/that I have seen her there, and know.   GeTw

Mother and Son.   Allen Tate.   The bright wallpaper, imperishably old,/Uncurls and flutters; it will never fall.   LiTA; MoAB; MoAmPo; MoVE

A Mother before a Soldier's Monument.   Winnie Lynch Rockett.   ...the costly price/I paid for laurel wreath and marble shaft!   PGD

Mother Bombie: Fools in Love's College.   John Lyly.   Nay, 'tis confessed/That fools please women best.   TrGrPo

Mother Carey's Chicken.   Theodore Watts-Dunton.   Prophetic Nature bares the secret of the story/That holds the spheres in song!   OBVV

Mother Cat. John Montague. already fierce/at the trough. NOBI

The Mother Country. Benjamin Franklin. Which nobody can deny, deny,/ Which nobody can deny. PAH

Mother Country. Christina Georgina Rossetti. Vanity of vanities,/As the Preacher saith. OxBoCh

The Mother Crab and Her Family. L. T. Manyase. So manners win our admiration/And the best manners are imitation. PeSA

Mother Dark. Francesca Yetunde Pereira. For her children now/Oppress her children. PBA

Mother darling, I cannot work the loom. Sappho. broken me with love for a slender boy. BoWoP

Mother Dear, O! Pray for Me. Anonymous. That paints with gold the flowery mead,/Which blossoms in our way. AH

Mother/Deer/Lady. Harold Littlebird. I love you forever, always and in all ways VoR

Mother Doesn't Want a Dog. Judith Viorst. She will not want this snake. NLV

Mother Doorstep. Victor J. Daley. Old Mother Doorstep had nursed him well. NOAV

Mother Earth. Anna Margolin. And half awake, half dreaming I/Aspire through you to heaven high. VWA

Mother Earth: Her Whales. Gary Snyder. In the sparkling whorls/Of living light. LCAP

Mother England. Edith Matilda Thomas. At cry of thine, how proudly would they dare!' AA; HBV 1-2

Mother Goose. Anonymous. On a very fine gander. SoPo

Mother Goose (circa 2054). Irene Sekula. All the Super's polariscopes/ Couldn't revitalize his isotopes. QQQ; ShM

Mother Goose Rhyme. Kenneth Rexroth. Said, "Ladies, don't you know we are all in Hell?" ErPo

Mother Goose's Garland. Archibald MacLeish. We die of vertigo. OBAL

Mother Goose Up-to-Date. Louis Untermeyer.
   And the echoes edged back still further/As the silence gathered them in. MoAmPo
   And Tom went roaring down the street. MoAmPo
   Grinly I tell you this. And this is all. MoAmPo
   in that country... MoAmPo
   That ninety million think the same–including Eddie Guest. MoAmPo

Mother, Home, Heaven. William Goldsmith Brown. There we shall meet, when life is o'er,/In that blest Home, to part no more. FaBoBe; HBV 1-2

Mother, I Am. Lucille Clifton. someone of it is answering to/your name. GeTw

A Mother in Egypt. Marjorie Pickthall. ...lest the wrath of that Other/ Should reach to him there! CaP; HBV 1-2

Mother, in the 45 cent Bottle. Paul Blackburn. stiffening of old men NYP

The Mother in the House. Hermann Hagedorn. You are lovelier than ever, I do believe. HBMV; OHIP

The Mother in the Snow-Storm. Seba ("Major Jack Downing") Smith. The babe looked up and sweetly smiled! PaPo

A Mother Is a Sun. Peggy Bennett. (Haunted by that gentle fire). PoSC

Mother Love. Janie Alford. And lo, it was there I could best compare/My mother's love for me! PGD

Mother Marie Therese. Robert Lowell. My mother's hollow sockets fill with tears. CoPo

Mother Most Powerful. Giovanni Dominici. Shows thou wert mortal,– Mother,–yea, and more! CAW

Mother, Mother, Are You All There? Felicia Lamport. The pattern of Oedipus wrecks. NLV

Mother, Mother, Make My Bed. Anonymous. And the rose it clung round the sweet briar. ELP

Mother Niddity Nod. Anonymous. Before she got half-way there. OxNR

Mother o' Mine. Rudyard Kipling. Mother o' mine, O mother o' mine! FaFP; TRV; WBLP

Mother of Fishermen. H. Roland-Holst. ...as if that habit of expecting nothing/will die with me, and that hopeless peace. PBWP

The Mother of God. William Butler Yeats. And bids my hair stand up? SBVL

Mother of Man. Vesna Parun. It's bitter to be a man, while the knife is the brother of man. PBWP

Mother of Men. Brian Hooker. Praise we today in sturdy chorus,/Mother of Men–Old Yale! HBMV

Mother of Men. Stephen Southwold. I lay until I slept; and when the day/ Found us, my soul knelt at our feet to pray. HBMV

Mother of Ten. Leonard Alfred George Strong. And, obedient, learned to dread/Grave no more than marriage bed. DBV

Mother of the Groom. Seamus Heaney. The wedding ring/That's bedded forever now/In her clapping hand. OBSP

The Mother of Us All. "We cannot retrace our steps." Gertrude Stein. My long life, my long life. CrMA

Mother Poem. Joel Oppenheimer. ...refusing the/only thing that will/ comfort him at all. PoM

Mother-Prayer. Margaret Widdemer. Leaving to God/His own task for them. HBMV

Mother's Advice. Anonymous. That you learn from your mother at home. AmFP

A Mother's Birthday. Henry Van Dyke. Bless her in earth and heaven. OHIP

Mother's Day. Sandie Castle. Motion denied mother-fucker! APU

Mother's Day. Jerome Sala. and ALL the mothers in the world today/ hiding tactical weapons/in their babushkas! APU

Mother's Habits. Nikki Giovanni. and like my mother i shall fade/into my dreams/no longer caring/either BlSi

Mother's Hands. W. Dayton Wedgefarth. No touch that brings such perfect peace as Mother's hands. PoToHe

The Mother's Hymn. William Cullen Bryant. In ways of Love and Truth and Right. OHIP

Mother's Inheritance. Abu Khalid. Fawziyya. But they failed to reach/the glistening silk that nestles/the twin doves/in my breast. WPOW

A Mother's Lament for the Death of Her Son. Robert Burns. O, do thou kindly lay me low/With him I love at rest. HoPM

Mother's Love. Ross B. Clapp. That one is your dear mother. WBLP

Mother's Love. F. Montgomery. The warmest love that can grow old–/ This is mother's love. PGD

The Mother's Lullaby. John Clare. But God has heard, and the storm is gone, so hush and/lullaby! NAs

The Mother's Malison, or, Clyde's Water. Anonymous.
   he plunged in,/But never raise again. ESPB
   Ther mideers went up and doun the water,/Saying, Clayd's water din us wrong! ESPB

A Mother's Name. Anonymous. Has ever reached half high enough/To write a mother's name. PGD

Mother's Nerves. X. J. Kennedy. I gave it a bang and in she dove. GrPl

Mother's Party. Aileen Fisher. "What's your age?"/and/"What's your name?" BiCB

A Mother's Picture. Edmund Clarence Stedman. The fair, young Angel of my infancy. OHIP

A Mother's Prayer. Jeanette Saxton Coon. I need Thee greatly–now. STF

A Mother's Prayer. Margaret E. Sangster. But never let me lose my song/ Before the hardest day is through. TrPWD

The Mother's Prayer. Dora Sigerson Shorter. Oh, 'tis lonely, lonely, by the little grave! HBV 1-2

The Mother's Sacrifice. Lydia Sigourney. Like Abraham's faith, was counted righteousness. PaPo

Mother's Song. Anonymous.
   And it's O! sweet, sweet! and a lullaby. GN; HBV 1-2
   I ask you, cranes,/to warm my child in your wings. BoWoP
   Is it strange if I start to cry with joy? OBCP; WTO

The Mother's Song. Virginia Woodward Cloud. When the grinding shall cease! AA

A Mother's Song. Francis Ledwidge. Go headlong down among the deep/ Whales. EtS

The Mother's Tale. Eleanor Farjeon. "Once in a stall/In Bethlehem..." BiCB

Mother Sarah's Lullaby. Itzik Manger. and took away in his little pipe/ Mother Sarah's song. TrJP

Mother Shake the Cherry-Tree. Christina Georgina Rossetti. Six for father, hot and tired,/Knocking at the door. TiPo

Mother Shipton's Prophecies. Charles Hindley. The world then to an end shall come/In Eighteen Hundred and Eighty-one. BLPA

Mother Shuttle. Anonymous. And who was the gainer by that? OxNR

A Mother Speaks: The Algiers Motel Incident, Detroit. Michael S. Harper. "Oh I'm so sorry,/officer, I broke your gun." AmPA; BPo

Mother Superior. George MacBeth. ...Your duty is not to the/Sick but to the unborn. Perform it. NMP

Mother Tabbyskins. Elizabeth Anna Hart. For all doctors are not mice,/ Some are dogs, you see! CenHV; OxBChV

Mother the Wardrobe Is Full of Infantrymen. Roger McGough. mother don't lie there say something please MAT

A Mother to Her Waking Infant. Joanna Baillie. Go to thy little senseless play–/Thou dost not heed my lay. NOEC

Mother to Son. Langston Hughes. And life for me ain't been no crystal stair. AmNP; CDC; CTBA; GoSl; NTCP; OBCA; PoNe; SO; TTY

Mother Wept. Joseph Skipsey. Father hid his face and sigh'd,/Mother turn'd and wept. HBV 1-2; OBVV; VLP

Motherhood. Josephine Dodge Daskam Bacon. He only knows his mother– give him back. HBV 1-2

Motherhood. Charles Stuart Calverley. "My hen has laid an egg, I know;/ And only hear the noise she's making!" FM

Motherhood. Karl M. Chworowsky. While Love still spends itself in Motherhood. PGD

Motherhood. Agnes Lee. "I am the mother of Iscariot." BLPA; HBMV

Motherhood. Susan Ludvigson. what grace warms the air like steam. AMV-81

Mountain Song. Harriet Monroe. Over the Great Divide I go. HBV 1-2

Mountain Study. Peter Van Toorn. or those fish spread flat on newspaper,/ something for the eye. NOBC

Mountain Talk. Archie Randolph Ammons. so I went on/counting my numberless fingers. HaCAP

The Mountain That Got Little. William Stafford. no matter how little it is. FAZ

The Mountain to the Pine. Clarence Hawkes. And the infinite stars in heaven are old to/me. AA

A Mountain-Toilet Thief. Al Robles. Wiped Buddha clean with toilet paper/and threw it to the wind. BrSi

Mountain Top. *Anonymous.* If a tree don't fall on me/I'll live until I die. AS

Mountain Town–Mexico. Eldon Grier. an orange cat comes snaking through the door in search of food. NOBC

The Mountain Tree. Hugh Connell. Under this rock they met together. NeIP

Mountain Vigil. Douglas Fraser. The full measure/Of cool pleasure,/The secret shared. PoSH

The Mountain Whippoorwill. Stephen Vincent Benét. An' then the noise of the crowd began. StPo; TrGrPo; YaD

A Mountain Wind. George William Russell. Leave me, O sky-born powers,/Brother to grass and stones. AWP

The Mountain Woman. DuBose Heyward. Then, like a creature with a mortal hurt,/She fell, and wept away the afternoon. AnAmPo

The Mountaineer. Robert Nathan. He found one shelter–in a caravan/ Bound for the hills. TrJP

Mountaineering Bus. Rennie McOwan. The climbers will change, the hills remain. PoSH

The Mountaineers. Dannie Abse. The more we climb the further we have to go. PP

Mountains. W. H. Auden. Five minutes on even the nicest mountain/Are awfully long. FaBoPV

The Mountains. Walter De la Mare. An still my ghost sits at my eyes/And thirsts for their untroubled snows. BrPo

The Mountains. Louis Dudek. ...while we gaze and gaze/at the low valleys, and the meandering rivers. CaP

The Mountains. Walker Gibson. Oh how he wishes he were there again! SD

Mountains and Other Outdoor Things. Ruth Good. live on elevations/ gravity can't reach. PoDr

The Mountains Are a Lonely Folk. Hamlin Garland. They fold their forests round their feet/And bolster up the sky. GoTF; TreFT

Mountains Are Steadfast but the Mountain Streams. Hwang Chin-i. And the great heroes, famous for a day,/they die, they die. PBWP

The mountains grow unnoticed. Emily Dickinson. For fellowship at night. MoAB; MoAmPo; TrGrPo

The Mountains in the Desert. Robert Creeley. and all the habits of it. CoPo

The Mountainy Childer. Elizabeth Shane. While the crack o' a laugh came back to me. HBMV

The Mountebanks. Charles Henry Luders. Moved from us like a moving crowd. AA

Mourn for Yourself. Geoffrey Keating. Yet you would mourn for evermore. BIrV

Mourn Not the Dead. Ralph Chaplin. Who see the world's great anguish and its wrong/And dare not speak! HBMV; ViBoPo

The Mourners. Bevil Higgons. Though now you mourn, 't had lessened much your woe/Had Sorrel stumbled thirteen years ago. APAS

The Mourners Came at Break of Day. Sarah Flower Adams. An angel sits beside the tomb. HBV 1-2

The Mournful Dove (The False True-Lover). *Anonymous.* There's a curley headed girl just a-roaming in the world,/I'll always call her mine. AmFP

Mourning. Andrew Marvell. But sure as oft as Women weep,/It is to be suppos'd they grieve. CABA; SeCP

Mourning. Josephine Van Fossan. And reshaped it, as though it were soft/ supple clay,/Into peace from His merciful throne. STF

Mourning and Melancholia. Alfred Alvarez. ...Now I'm cold like him/Cold and untameable. Will have to be put down. VWA

The Mourning Bride. William Congreve. Married in haste, we may repent at leisure. GoTF; TreF; ViBoPo

The Mourning Conquest. *Anonymous.* And leave his foe to sigh and cry/ Alas poor thing CoMu

A Mourning Letter from Paris. Conrad Kent Rivers. or one forgets the joy to which we were born. BPo

Mourning Letter, March 29 1963. Edward Dorn. associate me with no other honor. ConAP

Mourning Pablo Neruda. Robert Bly. No one lays flowers/on the grave/of water,/for it is not/here,/it is/gone. LCAP

Mourning Picture. Adrienne Rich. and leave this out? I am Effie, you were my dream. CoAP

Mourning Poem for the Queen of Sunday. Robert Earl Hayden. who would have thought she'd end that way? HaCAP; HoAn; NoP; PoBA

A Mourning-Song for Rangiaho. Te Heuheu Herea. Like the splume of a wave/Into the eye of the void. WTO

Mourning Women. Mathilde Blind. But souls ye have none fit for Paradise. SBG

Mourningsong for Anne. David Posner. I suppose, by one of those tall, dark, handsome/Gentlemen the Victorians were so crazy about. FAZ

The Mouse. Elizabeth Jane Coatsworth. But no little feast/Is spread any more. MoShBr; OBCA; SoPo; SUS; TiPo

Mouse. Hilda Conkling. And who dresses you in gray velvet? SoPo; TiPo

The Mouse. Jean Garrigue. Praise him who sweetens/On a small hate. MP; TwCP

The Mouse. Hugh McCrae. I thought of you, dear Dorothy! PoAu 1-2

The Mouse. Laura E. Richards. Oh, I'll NEVER come back any more. ma'am! OBCA

Mouse and Mouser. *Anonymous.* And I'll eat you too, good body. OxNR

The Mouse and the Cake. Eliza Cook. Or the best of our pleasures may turn into pain. OxBChV

The Mouse Dinners. Russell Edson. ...and sees this only now that/he has himself become a mouse... SoSe

Mouse Night: One of Our Games. William Stafford. Duck and cover! It takes a man/to be a mouse this night," he said. NCSH

The Mouse's Lullaby. Palmer Cox. And bring to my baby a fresh penny roll. OBCA

Mouse's Nest. John Clare. And broad old cesspools glittered in the sun. ExPo; InPK; LiTB; LoBV; SeCeV; VLP

The Mouse's Petition. Anna Laetitia Barbauld.
Casts round the world an equal eye,/And feels for all that lives. OxBChV
May some kind angel clear thy path,/And break the hidden snare. FM

The Mouse That Gnawed the Oak-Tree Down. Vachel Lindsay. And started on another tree. LOW

The Mouse Whose Name Is Time. Robert Francis. Nobody living knows. LOW

Mousemeal. Howard Nemerov. and that his crudest and most terrifying dreams/will not return with such wide publicity. MP; NCSH; TwCP

Mouth. Clarisse Nicoidski. nothing more than writing/which is silent VWA

The Mouth and the Ears. Shem-Tob Palquera. A single mouth, friend, but a pair of/ears. TrJP

Mouth of the Amazon. R. P. Gira. in your laughing eyes. AMV-80

The Mouth of the Hudson. Robert Lowell. in the sulphur-yellow sun/of the unforgivable landscape. AmFN; CAD; CoPo; NaP; NYP

Mouth to mouth recitation. Judith Fitzgerald. not to interpret roses/but to accelerate/breathless art CaPN

Mouths. Louis Dudek. in that greater mouth/nothing can still or fill. PeCV

The Move Continuing. Al Young. as tho tonight were only the beginning/ of all those/yester-/days PoBA

Move On, Yiddish Poet. Jacob Glatstein. Veiled in her royal darkness,/ your crown city of Safed/is waiting for you. VWA

Moved by Her Music. Richard Gillman. Intently, silently involved in being all/Of her earth-altering ambition. NePoAm-2

Moved Towards a Future. Laura Chester. ...And over the left/shoulder is our distance. NPGG

Movement. Denise Levertov. ...the outflying spirit's/vertical trampoline. LLLT

The Movement of Fish. James Dickey. And, of its one movement, the depth. NYBP; VGW

Movement Song. Audre Lorde. saying we cannot waste time/only ourselves. CNA

Movements. Norman MacCaig. ...the cursive adder writes/Quick V's and Q's in the dust and rubs them out. OxBC

Movie Actors Scribbling Letters Very Fast in Crucial Scenes. Jean Garrigue. Pours from the blood into ink. TAP

Movie-Going. John Hollander. These fade. All fade. Let us honor them with our own fading/sight. CoAP; NYP; PPP

Movie Queen. James P. Vaughn. stuck/at the foot of her head. NNP

Movies. Clark Coolidge. a looseness. ANYP

The Movies. Jack Gilbert. so long now these people were the only family he had. NPGG

Movies for the Home. Howard Moss. Only as they were, if that is where you are. NePoEA-2; NYBP

Movies, Left to Right. Robert Sward. I look back. Nowhere. Meanwhile, one or more wives/Go on stilts for the mail. NYBP

Moving. Barbara Crooker. shake violently in the wind. AMV-80

Moving. Darrell Gray. Goodbye, goodbye. It/seemed so real. APU

Moving. Randall Jarrell. She holds the cat so close to her he pants. DFF

Moving. William Matthews. We twist away like a released balloon. PoL

Moving. Janet Reed McFatter. Already the spiders are hunched/and spinning new webs. GrPl

Mr. Roosevelt Regrets. Pauli Murray. "Mr. Roosevelt regrets......" PoBA

Mr. Secretary. Karl Patten. ...or death's/Handshake, in gray gloves, hidden. SOTS

Mr. Slimmer's Funèral Verses for the Morning Argus. Charles Heber Clark. Drop him in the sepulchre/With his Uncle Jerry. OBAL

Mr. Smith. William Jay Smith. How rewarding to know Mr. Smith! FiBHP; SpRo

Mr. Strugnell (parody). Wendy Cope. Enjoying perfect boredom up in Hull. FaBoPa

Mr. Symons at Richmond, Mr. Pope at Twickenham. Julian Symons. Thinking deceit and friendship and malice/By the river at Richmond. WaP

Mr. T. S. Eliot Cooking Pasta. Jozsef Tornai. in that, somehow,/one recognizes oneself. GrPl

Mr. Thomas Shepheard...Hee a Man of a Thousand. Edward Johnson. Oh Christ, why dost thou Shepheard take away,/In erring times when sheepe most apt to stray. SCAP

Mr. Tom Narrow. James Reeves. Till he sold his barrow/For half a crown. SO

Mr U Will Not Be Missed. Edward Estlin Cummings. not excluding mr u. VGW

Mr. Vachel Lindsay Discovers Radio (parody). Samuel Hoffenstein. Who would have thought that a guy like that/Had the radio under his hat? BXAP

Mr. Walter de la Mare Makes the Little Ones Dizzy (parody). Samuel Hoffenstein. The rabbits, the oak and the walnut trees. Par; SpRo

Mr. Ward of Anagrams Thus. Nathaniel Ward. Can let out an Anagram/even as he list. SCAP

Mr. Wells. Elizabeth Madox Roberts. I do not have to look to know/That Mr. Wells is coming in. HBMV; HBVY

Mr. Whittier. Winfield Townley Scott. –No more begrudge their freedom than his tears. CrMA; VGW

Mr. Z. M. Carl Holman. "One of the most distinguished members of his race." SoSe

Mririda. Mririda n'Ait Attik. Nothing like it ever heard in this valley. WPOW

Mrs. Albion You've Got a Lovely Daughter. Adrian Henri. Mrs Albion you've got a lovely daughter. OxBTC

Mrs. Alfred Uruguay. Wallace Stevens. The ultimate elegance: the imagined land. AP; MoPo; MP; NePA; PAI; TwCP

Mrs. Applebaum's Sunday Dance Class. Philip Schultz. the room everywhere filled with light! AMV-81; MAYP

Mrs. Asquith Tries to Save the Jacarandas. Harold Witt. Some spirit dies with the murdering of trees. AMV-81

Mrs. Barks. Rose Fyleman. And says, "Good-morning, love," to me. BrR

Mrs. Brown. Rose Fyleman. I sometimes wonder if I know/When I have gone to sleep. OxBChV; TiPo

Mrs. Brown and the Famous Author. Stoddard King. The hostess reads, with gentle zest,/The poetry of Edg-r Gu-st. ATP

Mrs. Busk. Osbert Sitwell. Fresh Codfish, Fine Codfish!' OxBTC

Mrs. Crudeman. Osbert Sitwell. But a second look at Felicity,/Who resembled her mother,/Was less reassuring. HaMV

Mrs. Frances Harris's Petition. Jonathan Swift. Or the Chaplain (for 'tis his trade,) as in duty bound,/shall ever pray. CBEP; CEP; OxBI

Mrs. Golightly. Gertrude Hall. The time has come to speak. AA

Mrs. Green. David Huddle. ..to walk/softly into/that lady's/kitchen. PPJ

Mrs. Hamer. Jane Stembridge. all of us/is tired. NMM

Mrs. Hen. Anonymous. The nicest in the town. OxNR

Mrs. Jaypher. Edward Lear. "From the Jaypher Wisdom-Boat."' FaBoNo

Mrs. Jaypher on Lemons. Edward Lear. And then to go at once to bed. FaBoNo

Mrs. Johnson Objects. Clara Ann Thompson. An' jest let me ketch you chasin'/Aft' them white trash any mo'. BlSi

Mrs. Judge Jenkins. Bret (Francis Bret Harte) Harte. "It is, but hadn't ought to be." BXAP; CABA; FiBHP; HBV 1-2

Mrs. Kriss Kringle. Edith Matilda Thomas. None to talk with–always single! OBCA

Mrs. Loewinsohn &c. Ron Loewinsohn. to take your oviform invention from you, for the world. NeAP

Mrs. Macintosh. Rodney Hall. All day her hymns escape the house. CBAP

Mrs. Malone. Eleanor Farjeon. There's room for another/One, Mrs. Malone.' OxBChV

Mrs. Mason's Basin. Anonymous. Threw the basin on the bricks. OxNR

Mrs. McGrath. Anonymous.
Lav beg, the Cracker, O. OnYI
Wid yer too-ri-aa, fol-the-did-dle-aa./Too-ri-oo-ri-oo-ri-aa. FaBoBa; FSW

Mrs. Peck-Pigeon. Eleanor Farjeon. Mrs. Peck-Pigeon/Goes picking for bread. NTCP; OnUR; SoPo; SUS; TiPo

Mrs. Sadie Grindstaff, Weaver and Factotum, Explains... Jonathan Williams. could do a little/of/mebby OBAL

Mrs. Santa Claus' Christmas Present. Alice S. Morris. The reindeer lift their heads to hear/The happiest laugh of all the year. PoSC

Mrs. Saunder's Experience. Anonymous. And trust in God whose grace alone/Can set a captive free. AmFP

Mrs. Severin. Winfield Townley Scott. ...on a diningroom-table,/naked confronted her unanswering Lord. NePoAm

Mrs. Seymour Fentolin. Oliver Herford. Is Seymour really her first name,/And has the printer spelt it right? HBMV

Mrs. Smith. Frederick Locker-Lampson. I know that when they walk in grass/She wears balmorals. HBV 1-2

Mrs. Snipkin and Mrs. Wobblechin. Laura E. Richards. And out of the window a-tumble she did go. OxBChV; SoPo; TiPo

Mrs. Southern's Enemy. Osbert Sitwell. For Dust is insatiate and invincible. AtBAP; ViBoPo

Mrs. Trollope in America. Helen Bevington. And spit whenever we wanted to. NLV; OBAL

Mrs. Vickers' Daughter. Anonymous. Johnny's got the sweetest girl,/Mrs. Vickers' daughter. AmFP

Mrs. Walpurga. Muriel Rukeyser. and Mrs. Walpurga and we may wake. NMM

Mrs. Williams. Edgar Lee Masters. Do you think that Spoon River/Had been any the worse? NAMP

Mswaki. Jim Brodey. yupi tas yi chauntra/sticks/oa ANYP

The Mu'Allaqa of Antar. Antar [(or Antana)]. ...father/carrion for the wild beasts and all the great vultures. TTY

The Mu'allaqat: Ode. Imr el Kais. While the wild beast corpses, grouped like great bulbs/up-torn, cumbered the hollow places,... AWP

The Mu'allaqat: Pour Us Wine. Ibn Kolthum. Without her I am sad as an old mother/Hearing of the death of her many sons. AWP

Much Ado about Nothing. William Shakespeare.
Converting all your sounds of woe/Into Hey nonny, nonny, ALV; AWP; BoLiVe; CTC; DiPo; ELP; ExPo; FF; FiP; GoTF; HBV 1-2; InMe; InPo; LiTB; LiTL; MCCG; OAEP; OBSC; PoEL 1-5; SeCeV; TreFS; TrGrPo; ViBoPo
Hang thou there upon the tomb,/Praising her when I am dumb. CTC; OBSC; ViBoPo
This is an accident of hourly proof,/Which I mistrusted not. TrGrPo

Much Ado about Nothing in the City (parody). Anonymous. Converting all your notes of woe/Into hey money, money. FaBoPa

Much Distressed. Anonymous. The Queen is much distressed. CBAP

Much Has Been Said... Anonymous. And ask the fair creature herself if it's true,/Which I'm certain shee won't deny. CoMu

Much madness is divinest sense. Emily Dickinson. Demur–you're straightway dangerous–/And handled with a Chain– AmPP; BoWoP; CBEP; CMoP; DiPo; ELU; HeIP; LiTA; LiTM; MAT; NAWM 1-2; NoAm; NOBA; NoP; OxBA

Much of Me. Chuck Eggerth. And home is something/I carry within me. AMV-80

Muckers. Carl Sandburg. Ten others, "Jesus, I wish I had a job." CTBA; SaC

Muckish Mountain (The Pig's Back). Shane Leslie. And the Heavens for a sty! AnIV

Muckle-Mou'd Meg. James Ballantine. Elibank hunt again, Wat's snug at hame. HBV 1-2

Muckle-Mouth Meg. Robert Browning. To Muckle-mouth Meg in good earnest! HBV 1-2

Mud. Polly Chase Boyden.
How nice mud feels/Between the toes. NTCP; SoPo; TiPo
I'd rather wade in wiggly mud/Than smell a yellow rose. FaBV

The Mud Turtle. Howard Nemerov. ...He takes/A secret wound out of the world. NYBP

The Muddy Rat. Horiguchi Daigaku. Sleeps with his mate in his arms. LiTW

The Mudtower. Anne Stevenson. flicker as snow flickers, blown from those inland hills. HoAn

The Mufadaliyat: Gone Is Youth. Son of Jandal, Salamah. So stand we, great in men's eyes: our ladies ne'er turn/aside whenso they travel from Khatt... AWP

The Mufaddaliyat: His Camel. Alqamah. I bring her to drink the dregs of cisterns all mire and/if she mislikes it... AWP

Mugford's Victory. John White Chadwick. And who brought him, though dead, to his own! PAH

The Mugger. Robert Pack. My plans are coming true. Nothing can stop me now. GP

Mugging (excerpt). Allen Ginsberg. ...my shoulder bag with 10,000 dollars/full of poetry left on the broken floor– HaCAP

Muhammedan Call to Prayer. Bilal. Arise to prayer. Arise to divine service. TTY

Muirland Meg. Robert Burns. That is the measure of Muirland Meg. ErPo

Le Musee Imaginaire.   Charles Tomlinson.   it forbids us to approach it.
   NePoEA-2.

The Muses.   *Anonymous*.   Musa, Musa,/Made by Cupid's mamma.
   FaBoNo

The Muses.   Edith Matilda Thomas.   "They lightly serve who serve us best,/
   Nor know they how the task was done!"   HBV 1-2

The Muses Elizium.   Michael Drayton.
   For our Tita is this day/Married to a noble fay.   HW
   So my gallant Youths farewell. AnAnS 2
   That many a glorious age their captives were. AnAnS 2; OAEL 1-2
   There to live an Anchorite. AnAnS 2

The Museum.   William Abrahams.   Whispering, consoling, promising: I am
   Love.   WaP

Museum.   Robert Hass.   ...the green has begun to emerge from the rind of/
   the cantaloupe, and everything seems possible.   NPGG

Museum of Cruel Days.   Richard Hugo.   ...Buy whatever hunger/looks good
   on the stand.   NPAW

Museum of Man.   Earle Birney.   & try on everything for size.   OxBC

The Museum of the Second Creation.   Sandra McPherson.   Their sparkle's
   on his broomstraws.   LCAP

Museum-Piece.   Audrey Alexandra Brown.   And all humanity a jest.   CaP

Museum Piece.   Lawrence P. Spingarn.   Piling the golden fleeces at her feet.
   GoYe

Museum Piece.   Richard Wilbur.   To hang his pants on while he slept.
   CMoP; ConAP; FaBoMo; MiAP; NePA; NIP; PoPl; PPoe; TAP

Museum Piece No. 16228.   Elaine Watson.   "Remember me?"   AMV-81

Museum with Chinese Landscapes.   Walter Cybulski.   Who will remember
   this music/if the reeds forget when the wind stops?   AMV-81

Museums.   Louis MacNeice.   Any number of consumptive Keatses and
   dying Gauls.   MoBrPo; NAMP

Musgrove.   *Anonymous*.   I soon the day shall shortly see,/That will land my
   soul in eternity.   AmFP

The Mushroom Gatherers.   Donald Davie.   Surely these acres are Elysian
   Fields.   NePoEA-2

Mushroom Hunting in Late August, Peterborough, N.H.   Michael C.
   Blumenthal.   And I eat.   MAYP

The Mushroom Is the Elf of Plants–.   Emily Dickinson.   That Mushroom–it
   is Him!   DiPo; NePA

Mushrooms.   Sylvia Plath.   Our foot's in the door.   BoNaP; FaBoWP;
   NePoEA-2; WeW; WPOW

Music.   *Anonymous*.
   The flying bird turned back to hear.   WTO
   So is a strain of music with pleasant/wine. TrJP

The Music.   Charles Baudelaire.   Lull and annul me–and become
   monstrously the mirrors/Of my insensate errors!   SyP

A Music.   Wendell Berry.   but is a singing in a dark place.   VGW

Music.   Alice Dunbar-Nelson.   Music! With you, soul on your parted lips!/
   Music–is you!   BlSi

Music.   Ralph Waldo Emerson.   There alway, alway something sings.
   AnNE; FaBV; WGRP

Music.   Eleanor Farjeon.   To dance and sing,/To sing and dance.   TiPo

Music.   John Fletcher.   Fall asleep, or, hearing, die.   FaBoCh; LoGBV

Music.   Robert Herrick.   Thy circumfused rapture much more then/Must
   move to love us softer-moulded men.   CaPo

The Music.   Everett Hoagland.   playing your blue steel/guitar book-long
   song/crazy!   CNA

Music.   Amy Lowell.   And I go to sleep, dreaming.   AnAmPo; YaD

Music.   Naomi Shihab Nye.   The second lesson was long.   Str

Music.   Frank O'Hara.   and the stores stay open terribly late.   NoP; NYP

Music.   Charles Phillips.   The beauties of my Father's house, which shall/
   No more be shut from me!   CAW

Music.   Anne Ryan.   Be still the speech that silence narrows/Into fresh
   song!   CAW

Music.   William Bell Scott.   Dear old Ions was asleep.   NOBV

Music.   Percy Bysshe Shelley.   ...Care, like a drowsy child,/Is laid asleep in
   flowers.   TrGrPo

Music.   Edith Matilda Thomas.   The God of Music dwelleth out of doors.
   HBV 1-2

Music.   Tony Towle.   As his music is a preservative, for him not you.
   ANYP

Music (after Sully Prudhomme).   George Du Maurier.   Drift on through
   slumber to a dream, and through a/dream to death.   CBEP

Music Alone Shall Live.   *Anonymous*.   Music alone shall live, never to die.
   FSW

Music and Drum.   Archibald MacLeish.   Music's begun.   MoRP

Music and Memory.   John Albee.   Still bringing all the pain they cost.   AA

Music and Words.   Elizabeth Jennings.   We think we can forget/If we sing
   loud enough.   UnS

Music at Twilight.   George Sterling.   Or Silence lay her kiss on Music's
   mouth!   HBV 1-2

Music by the Waters.   John Hay.   I pick them and they sing.   AMV-81

The Music Crept by Us.   Leonard Cohen.   I will place my/paper hat on
   my/concussion and dance   FF

Music God.   Mark Van Doren.   Or so we say of three clear tones/That in
   eternal quiet lie.   UnS

Music in an Empty House.   Hugh Sykes Davies.   The tattered/tapestry/
   hold/many/moths.   EAS

Music in Camp.   John Reuben Thompson.   Who still, 'mid War's embattled
   lines,/Gave this one touch of Nature.   AA; BLPA; HBV 1-2

Music in the Air.   George Johnston.   Quack! in the dark, says he.   PeCV

Music in the Air.   Ronald McCuaig.   When Jack had his girl/On Friday
   night.   ErPo

Music in the Night.   Harriet Prescott Spofford.   And vanishes among the
   stars.   AA

Music in the Rec Hut.   Hubert Creekmore.   And the sting of night and
   starlight in every heart.   WaP

Music in Venice.   Louis Simpson.   Even to Envy, sharpening a knife,/His
   interest.   NYBP

The Music of a Tree.   Walter James Turner.   With throbbing heart, tip-toe I
   stole away.   MoBrPo

Music of Colours: the Blossom Scattered.   Vernon Watkins.   And the two
   feasts, where light and darkness meet.   ACV; LiTB

Music of Colours–White Blossom.   Vernon Watkins.   Utterly secret. I know
   you, black swan.   LiTM; WaP

The Music of His Steps.   Samuel Wakefield.   And loved and blessed them all
   in death.   AH

Music of Hungary.   Anne Reeve Aldrich.   God made my soul for Hungary!
   AA

Music of the Dawn.   Virginia Bioren Harrison.   Seems the music made when
   God's own hands His mighty/harpstrings sweep.   HBV 1-2

The Music of the Future.   Oliver Herford.   But to fugues and sonatas that
   possibly hide/Uncomposed in her–well–in her tuneful inside.'   CenHV

Music of the Night.   John Neal.   And rival minstrels meet.   AA

The Music of the Spheres.   Marvin Bell.   They gave us guilt and the past,/
   and we sing what we know best.   PoA

Music's Duel.   Richard Crashaw.   (That liv'd so sweetly) dead, so sweet a/
   grave!   CoBE; GoTL; OBS; PBBP; SeCP; SeCV 1-2

Music Stirs Me.   Ricarda Huch.   Beauty is everywhere kin.   PBWP

Musica No.   Richard Duerden.   in the sacred bulb/the sea cave.   NeAP

A Musical Critic Anticipates Eternity.   Siegfried Sassoon.   "The music was
   devoid of all divinity!"   UnS

A Musical Instrument.   Elizabeth Barrett Browning.   As a reed with the
   reeds in the river.   EnLi 1-2; FaBoBe; GTBS; HBV 1-2; HBVY; MCCG;
   NoP; OAEL 1-2; OAEP; OBEV; OBVV; OnMSP

The Musical Lion.   Oliver Herford.   And flee at the very first note!   OBCA

The Musical Orchard.   Douglas Dunn.   The music inside fruit!   FaBoMo

Musical Shuttle.   Harvey Shapiro.   Love in his season/Had moved me with
   that song.   VWA

Musician.   Louise Bogan.   And, under the palm, the string/Sings as it
   wished to sing.   GoJo; NYBP; UnS

The Musician.   R. P. Lister.   And in deep memory his bent fingers play/
   Long after the sunset of his piping day.   UnS

The Musician at His Work.   Robert Currie.   felt the pain/greater than pain/
   knew exactly/what it meant   Str

A Musician Returning from a Cafe Audition.   Michael D. Minard.   A blight
   on cafe owners, the entire crop.   AMV-80

Musicians wrestle everywhere.   Emily Dickinson.   Some think it service in
   the place/Where we, with late, celestial face,/Please God, shall ascertain
   UnS

Musings.   William Barnes.   The summer when our life was fair.   HAP;
   NOBE; OBNC

Musk Oxen.   Igjugarjuk.   Far from our dwellings/In the regions of happy
   summer hunting.   WTO

Musketaquid.   Ralph Waldo Emerson.   Yet envies none, none are
   unenviable.   AP

Muskrat.   *Anonymous*.   It's a wonder I don't die.   FSW

The Musmee.   Mrs. Major Arnold.   Heaven have her in its tender care!/O
   medeto gozarimas!   OBTV

Musophilus.   Samuel Daniel.   To do worthy the writing, and to write/
   Worthy the reading, and the world's delight?   FaBoRV

Muss I Denn.   *Anonymous*.   I'll return, my love, to you.   FSW

Mussel Hunter at Rock Harbor.   Sylvia Plath.   –this relic saved/face, to face
   the bald-faced sun.   NYBP

Musselburgh Field.   *Anonymous*.   Wee chased them to D   ESPB

Mussels.   Mary Oliver.   ...as they lean/into the rocks, away/from my
   grasping fingers.   NU

Must.   Alun Lewis.   Go to making/Dust?   ELU

Must Be the Season of the Witch.   Alurista.   her children suffer: without her
   FIA

Must I Go Bound?   *Anonymous*.   And I love the lad would break my heart.
   WTO

A Mustacheless Bard.   J. Gordon Coogler.   Unless they believe that kisses
   are sweeter/From lips that bear a mustache.   OBAL

My brother has on a thin robe. Lady Otomo of Sakanoe . O Sao wind, don't blow hard/till he is home. BoWoP

My Brother Was Silent. Amir Gilboa. And his blood cried out of the ground. VWA

My Brothers... Anna Walters. I am ashamed/for soon I will be as you.... VoR

My Burial Place. Robinson Jeffers. I should be pleased to lie in one grave with'em. AP

My Buried Friends. *Anonymous.* With songs I sent her in love's day and live with my loved friends forever. AmFP

My Butterfly. Robert Lee Frost. I found it with the withered leaves/Under the eaves. AmePo

My Cabinets Are Oyster-Shells. Margaret Cavendish, Dutchess of Newcastre. And thus with waters am I crowned. ELP

My Camping Ground. Morris Rosenfeld. Oh, make my sad heart sing anew;/make warm, make sweet, my camping/ground! TrJP

My Candidate. Norman H. Crowell. But take it from me...he gets my vote! YaD

My Captain. Dorothea Day. Christ is the Captain of my soul. BePJ; BLPA

My cat and I. Roger McGough. Then my cat and i go back inside/And talk about the past. OxBTC; PoL

My Catbird. William Henry Venable. He snarls, and mews, and flies. AA; HBV 1-2

My Cats. Stevie Smith. That sit on tombstone for your mats. FaBoNo

My Cheap Lifestyle. Eileen Myles. I expect the stars will be bright/The woods full of bears. APU

My Child. Susan Griffin. these things we never show/and children suffer. NPGG

My Child. John Pierpont. 'Twill be our heaven to find that–he is there! AA; HBV 1-2

My Child Came Home. Stefan George. My own and yet, how very far from me! LiTW

My Childhood's Bedroom. Charles P.R. Tisdale. Let me tumble at your feet. AMV-80

My Children's Book. John N. Morris. ...This/Is the exciting part, do not interrupt me. AMV-80

My Choice. Grace B. Renfrow. I'd rather have Jesus, there's nothing beside. BePJ

My Christmas: Mum's Christmas. Sarah Forsyth. snow to play in getting soaked and frozen whenever outside. OBCP

My Church. E., O. G. For fear, I would seem to limit/The love of the illimitable God. BLPA; SoSe

My City. James Weldon Johnson. To be dead, and never again behold my city! BANP; CDC; PoNe

My Claw Is Tired of Scribing! Colum Cille. Hence my claw is tired of scribing. NOBI

My Cobra Girl. *Anonymous.* You are coming very slowly, why do you delay/O my black cobra? WTO

My Companion. Joyce Ramage. This Saviour who still lives today,/The Christ of Calvary. BePJ

My Companion. Charles Wesley. And search the oracles divine,/Till every heartfelt word is mine. STF

My Company. Sir Herbert Read. And share their doom. BrPo; MMM

My Comrade. Edwin Markham. For she can take away the dread of things. AA

My Comrade. James Jeffrey Roche. The steel, if cold, is one, and strong and/pure. AA

My Correspondent's Last Ride. George Alfred Townsend. He fell the day that Richmond fell,/And took the first despatch. AA

My Country. Mikhail Yuryevich Lermontov. The tramp and whistle of the dance, and hear/The drunken babble round. LiTW

My Country. Dorothea Mackellar. I know to what brown country/My homing thoughts will fly. PoAu 1-2

My Country (excerpt). George Edward Woodberry. These thy foundations are, O firm-set State! AA

My Country Is the World. Robert Whitaker. When man with man shall mate/O'er all the world. PGD

My country need not change her gown. Emily Dickinson. There's something in their attitude/That taunts her bayonet. AmFN

My Country, Right! Thomas Curtis Clark. Thus may our meekness make her great,/Worthy in Freedom's eyes. PGD

My Country 'Tis of Thee. Ambrose Bierce. Whips to the Quaker's hide/And made him spring! YaD

My Country, to Thy Shore. Theodore Chickering Williams. Until, in God's own day,/Mankind be one. AH

My Cousin Agueda. Ramon Lopez Velarde. in the ebony of an ancient cupboard. OBVE

My Cousin German Came From France. *Anonymous.* That's the way the Polka goes. FaBoCh; LoGBV

My Cow. Howard McCord. smiling like an old man. GP

My Creed. Alice Cary. I know the blood about his heart/Is dry as dust. WGRP

My Creed. Jeanette Gilder. 'Tis what we do, not what we say, that makes us worthy of His/grace. WGRP

My Creed. S. E. Kiser. Could learn to shape my action to it. PoToHe

My Creed. Howard Arnold Walter. I would look up–and laugh–and love–and lift. FaFP; PoLf; WBLP

My Crime. Barefoot Bill. It ain't no fine for you/Get ready for the electric chair BluL

My Cross. Zitella Cocke. Had He not met me on the road/And helped me on the way! HBV 1-2

My Dad and Mam They Did Agree. *Anonymous.* When one was in a passion/The other could forbear. PoL

My Dad's Dinner Pail. Edward Harrigan. The drink would taste sweeter from dad's dinner pail. BLPA

My Daily Creed. *Anonymous.* Let me think more of my neighbor/And a little less of me. TRV

My Daily Prayer. Eva Gray. For 'tis in Jesus' name I pray. Amen. STF

My Daily Prayer. Grenville Kleiser. Lord, show me how. BLRP

My Dame Hath a Lame Tame Crane. *Anonymous.* Feed and come home again. OxNR

My Dancing Day. *Anonymous.*
May come unto the general dance. OxBoLi
This have I done for my true love. CBEP

My Dark Fathers. Brendan Kennelly. ...in a place/Of unapplauding hands and broken song. BIrV; CIP

My Darling Dear, My Daisy Flower. John Skelton.
Thou sleepest too long, thou art beguiled. HAP
Ywis, pole hatchet, she bleared thine eye. NoP

My Daughter Considers Her Body. Floyd Skloot. ...Learning to touch her wounds comes first. SM

My Daughter Louise. Homer Greene. But she rests, at the end of the path, in the city/Whose "builder and maker is God." HBV 1-2

My Days among the Dead Are Past. Robert Southey. Yet leaving here a name, I trust,/That will not perish in the dust. EnRP; HBV 1-2; OBRV; TEP

My Days Are Gliding Swiftly By. David Nelson. And just before the shining shore,/We may almost discover. AH

"My days' delight, my springtime joys fordone." Sir Walter Ralegh. Who have brought glory and posterity/Unto this widow land and people hopeless? FCP

My Days Have Been So Wondrous Free. *Anonymous.* I lent a sigh to them. TrAS

My Days of Love Are Over. George Gordon, Lord Byron. To have, when the original is dust,/A name, a wretched picture, and worse bust. OBNC

My Dead. Frederick Lucian Hosmer. For God hath given to Love to keep/Its own eternally. WGRP

My Dead. Rachel (Rachel Blumstein). What I have lost: what I possess forever. VWA

My Dear and Only Love. James Graham. And love thee more and more. BSV; CavP; JCP; OBS

My Dear, Do You Know. *Anonymous.* And don't you remember/The babes in the wood? PBBP

My Dear Lady. *Anonymous.* My dear lady. EIL

My Dearest Rival. Sir John Suckling. For no one stock can ever serve/To love so much as shee'l deserve. MeLP

My Dearling. Elizabeth Akers Allen. But it shall never bring to you/The hapless fate of Anne Boleyn! AA

My Death. A. J. M. Smith. Is what I've been always wanting. OBCV

My Death. Carl Zuckmayer. Within my father's house. Within my/mother's arms./High in years–! TrJP

My Definition of Poetry. Douglas Blazek. always I would acquire/its perfectly realized/experience. LTB

My Delight. Gamaliel Bradford. Climbing up to heaven above/Night and wind and storm. HBMV

My Delight and Thy Delight. Robert Bridges. Heart to heart as we lay/In the dawning of the day. AnFE; CMoP; GTBS; HBV 1-2; LiTL; NBM; NOBE; OAEP; OBEV; PoEL 1-5

My Diet. Abraham Cowley. And all beyond is vast eternity. LiTL

My Dim-Wit Cousin. Theodore Roethke. I heard your laughter rumble from my belly. DFF

My Dog. John Kendrick Bangs. The other open, ready for/His master coming through the door. BLPA; BLPL; FaBoBe

My Dog. Marchette Chute. Oh, puppy, I love you so. SoPo; TiPo

My Dog. Tom Robinson. He cuddles up and laps my hand/And tells me he can understand. SoPo

My Dog Dash. John Ruskin. I'll praise him to the very last. FM

My Dog Jock. Hayden Carruth. like the Indians now, and God,/and everyone. FAZ

My Dog Ponto. Edgar Lee Masters. And keep as all my own this higher music. FM

My Dog Tray.   John Byrom.   ...Tray/Be as dull as his Master, when Phebe's away?   SeCePo

My Donkey.   Rose Fyleman.   And little shoes of lavender,/To keep him from the cold.   TiPo

My Doves.   Elizabeth Barrett Browning.   My spirit and my God shall be/My seaward hill, my boundless sea.   VLP

My Dream.   *Anonymous.*   I asked him to lend me eighteenpence,/But he borrowed a shilling of me.   NA

My Dream.   Lew Blockcolski.   I woke up.   VoR

My Dream.   Christina Georgina Rossetti.   And tell it as I saw it on the spot.   BrRo; VLP

My Dream by Henry James.   Michael Ryan.   and everything I felt in the world was love for her.   SV

My Dreams, My Works, Must Wait Till after Hell.   Gwendolyn Brooks.   My taste will not have turned insensitive/To honey and bread old purity could love.   NoP

My Drinking Song.   Richard Dehmel.   Above this life to which our lives are clinging!/Hail!   AWP

My Early Home.   John Clare.   My early home was this.   HBV 1-2; PoLf

My Elbow Ancestry.   Larry Mollin.   still trying/to steer things/his own way   NeAC

My Enemy.   Alice Williams Brotherton.   Adieu, dear Death—one kiss! We/part.   AA

My Epitaph.   H. J. Daniel.   And died regardless of his fate or fame.   FaBoEE

My Epitaph.   David Gray.   In Eden every flower is blown: Amen.   OBVV

My Erotic Double.   John Ashbery.   Thank you. You are too.   LCAP

My Estate.   John Drinkwater.   Tom Squire, my gray dog Timothy,/My wife and Master Candleshine.   HBMV

My Evening Prayer.   Charles H. Gabriel.   Help me to live.   BLPA; FaBoBe

My eyes are thirsty.   Mira Bai [(or Mirabai)].   She is his slave for many lives.   BoWoP

My Face.   Anthony Euwer.   It's the people in front get the jar!   FaFP; PoLf

My Face Is My Own, I Thought.   Tom Raworth.   taking the scissors/began to trim off the baby's fingers.   EAS

My Fair Lady.   *Anonymous.*   Under the leaves so green.   UnTE

My Fairy.   Lewis (Charles Lutwidge Dodgson) Carroll.   Moral: "You mustn't."   FaBoNo

My Faith.   Ananda Acharya.   ...to the/All-soul's temple of rest.   WGRP

My Faith Looks Up to Thee.   Ray Palmer.   O, bear me safe above,/A ransomed soul.   AH; BLSo; WGRP

My Familiar.   John Godfrey Saxe.   Who never, never goes!   AnNE; GoTF

My Family's under Contract to Cancer.   Greg Simison.   another reunion table/minus one more chair.   AMV-80

My Father.   Abraham Chalfi.   The one who is missing/was myself.   VWA

My Father.   Rae Dalven.   we wouldn't give in.   GoYe

My Father after Work.   Gary Gildner.   fallen out of it/and vanished.   AMV-80; Psk

My Father Died.   *Anonymous.*   And half a ha'penny candle.   PoPle

My Father Died This Spring.   Joanne Kyger.   but strange how blood brings curiosity.   PoM

My Father Dragged by Horses.   T. Alan Broughton.   to flailing hooves and a hundred sharp suns.   AMV-80

My Father Dreams of Baseball.   Laurence Lieberman.   The features are fixed with the dull metallic glow/of an ancient face, cast in bronze or brass.   LiSp

My Father Gave Me a Lump of Gold.   *Anonymous.*   For I have jined this low-down gang,/And no one cares for me.   OuSiCo

My Father in the Night Commanding No.   Louis Simpson.   "Listen!" the wind/Said to the children, and they fell asleep.   CoAP; ConAP; HeIP; LCAP; MP; NePoEA-2; NoAm; NOBA; NYBP; SM; TAP; TwCP; VGW

My Father Is the Nightingale.   *Anonymous.*   She who sings her melodies/In the deep sea...   LO

My Father Kept a Horse.   *Anonymous.*   Had a nip from the flea, had a bite from the louse.   GBP

My Father Kept His Cats Well Fed.   Kenneth Sherman.   before the startling ring/and the long unwinding of curses/and cloth.   HeIP

My Father Knows.   Wilbur Fisk Tillett.   With love for all his heart o'erflows!   BLRP

My Father Moved through Dooms of Love.   Edward Estlin Cummings.   love is the whole and more than all   AmP; AtBAP; CMoP; CoBMV; CrMA; FYAP; HAP; LiTA; MoAB; MoPo; MoVE; NoAm; NOBA; NoP; OxBA; PoCh; TAP; UnPo

My Father, My Son.   John Malcolm Brinnin.   They were so bad I cried.   NYBP

My Father: October 1942.   William Stafford.   ...He just wins or loses.   CAPP; NaP

My father owns the butcher shop.   *Anonymous.*   And I'm the little hot dog/That runs around the street.   FaFP

My Father Paints the Summer.   Richard Wilbur.   Riding the palest days/Its perfect blaze.   NCSH; NOBA

My Father's at the Helm.   *Anonymous.*   To that blest port of endless rest,/Where storms shall never come.   BePJ

My Father's Child.   Gertrude Bloede.   The soul, through gates rolled open wide,/Passed into Paradise.   AA

My Father's Close.   *Anonymous.*   He hath it still complete.   AWP

My Father's Cot (parody) (excerpt).   J. C. Squire.   A craven spirit and a heart/That never will be whole.   BXAP

My Father's Country.   Joyce Lee.   Safe from death, I keep them in endless summer.   NOAV

My Father's Eye.   Eleni Vakalo.   I became suspicious even of those who had real eyes.   BoWoP

My Father's Ghost.   David Wagoner.   I hold/My father's ghost in my arms in his dark doorway.   Str

My Father's Heart.   Stuart Friebert.   ...fancied/this little father of mine an object/of universal desire.   Str

My Father's Leaving.   Ira Sadoff.   no words from a woman/I loved were strong enough to make me stop.   AmPA

My Father's Martial Art.   Stephen Shu Ning Liu.   this oncoming traffic with your hah, hah, hah.   BrSi

My Father's Song.   Simon J. Ortiz.   and my father saying things.   MAYP; STE

My Father's Voice in Prayer.   Mary Hastings Nottage.   My father's voice in prayer.   BLRP

My Father's Watch.   John Ciardi.   I saw my Father's face frown through the glass.   ImOP

My Father's Wedding 1924.   Robert Bly.   His two-story house he turned/into a forest,/where both he and I are the hunters.   InPS

My Father & the Figtree.   Naomi Shihab.   emblems, assurance/of a world that was always his own.   GP

My Father Was a Frenchman.   *Anonymous.*   He cut it through the middle.   OxNR

My Father, Who's Still Alive.   Jose Kozer.   ...my father/who was a tailor and a communist.   VWA

My Fatherland.   William Cranston Lawton.   To tell us we have found our father-/land?   AA

My Fathers Came from Kentucky.   Vachel Lindsay.   Under the redbird's wings/Was peace and honeycomb.   AmFN; HBMV

My Fault's Small, About the Size of a Pin Prick.   Jeffrey Miller.   and in awe by the colossal beauty/of an empty room.   APU

My Feet.   Gelett Burgess.   They Ride me Everywheres.   NA

My Feet.   Louis Jenkins.   ...wondering which steps/to take across the snows/of this first long winter/in the new world.   GP

My Feet They Haul Me 'Round the House.   Gelett Burgess.   I only have to steer them and/They ride me everywhere.   HBV 1-2

My, Fellowship, With, God.   Jose Garcia Villa.   Unalphabeted.   EaLo

My Fiddle.   Leib Kwitko.   May it be his for many a long year!   VWA

My First Love.   Harry Graham.   I always eat bananas now!   FiBHP

My Fixed Abode Is Glen Bolcain.   Suibne Geilt.   good its yews among all yew-trees,/and its sweet birches better!   NOBI

My Flying Machine.   Louis Daniel Brodsky.   Each song I write leaves in its wake.   AMV-80

My Folk, What Have I Done Thee?   William Herebert.   Gin nouthe and answere thou me.   OxBM

My Former Hopes Are Fled.   William Cowper.   I'll gaze upon it while I run/And watch the rising day.   OxBoCh

My Friend.   Samuel ("Paul Vesey") Allen.   Instead of him.../My friend.   FB

My Friend.   Marjorie Lorene Buster.   He's been there many times before.   STF

My friend must be a Bird.   Emily Dickinson.   Ah, curious friend!/Thou puzzlest me!   TAP

My Friend (parody).   Philip Appleman.   Velvet-green—this landscape perfectly/Moss?   BXAP

My Friend the Wind.   King D. Kuka.   and we will fly to a very happy land.   VoR

My Friends Are Little Lamps to Me.   Elizabeth Whittemore.   For every time I lose a friend/A little lamp goes out.   PoToHe

My Friends, This Storm.   Kizito Z. Muchemwa.   ...dies/unspoken and unspeaking/lily-white.   WhB

My Gal Sal.   Paul Dresser.   But dead on the level was my gal Sal.   BLSo; FSN; TreFT

My Galley.   Sir Thomas Wyatt.   And I remain despairing of the port.   AAS; BiP; CABA; CBEP; DiPo; FCP; HAP; InPS; LiTB; MOS; NoP; OAEL 1-2; PPP; TEP; WeW

My Gang.   Jack Kerouac.   ...I'll/be cruel, I'll be cruel   PoM

My Garden.   Thomas Edward Brown.   'Tis very sure God walks in mine.   BLPL; EBCP; EnLit; FaBV; GTBS; HBV 1-2; HBVY; InPK; OBEV; OBVV; PeD; PoLf; TreF; TRV; WBLP; WGRP

My Garden.   William Henry Davies.   He swallows his own face in half a second!   BoNaP

My Garden. J. A. Lindon. 'Tis very sure my garden's full of snails! DBV; InPK; PoL

My Garden. Janice Appleby Succorsa. Finding our way to Beauty–and to God! HoPM

My Garden Is a Pleasant Place. Louise Driscoll. And grant me grace, and make you hear! BLPA; FaBoBe

My Garden, My Daylight. Jorie Graham. ...For free he says/so that I can't refuse. HaCAP; MAYP

My Ghostly Father. *Anonymous*. My ghostly father, I me confess/First to God and then to you. BoLoP; CBEP; EnLoPo; GBL

My Gift. Christina Georgina Rossetti. I will give Him my heart. BrR; ChBR; SiSoSe

My Glass Is Half Unspent. Francis Quarles. O spare till then; and then I die contented. OxBoCh

My God. Solomon Ibn Gabirol. For past is now thy wrath, and thou/dost comfort me. TrJP

My God, How Wonderful Thou Art. Frederick William Faber. The love of my poor heart. GoBC

My God, I Thank Thee. Andrews Norton. Let kneeling faith adore thy will. AH

My God, My God, Look upon Me. Chad Walsh. "Into thy hands," and he was dead. TrCP

My God, You Have Wounded Me with Love. Paul Verlaine. But what I have, my God, I give to you. ILwL

My Good Old Man. *Anonymous*. The best old man a-living in the land,/ The best old man for life. BFSS

My Grace Is Sufficient for Thee. *Anonymous*. "His grace was sufficient for me." BLRP
When the evening shadows lengthen,/Thou shalt lay thy burden down. BePJ

My Grandaddy Mostly with His Knife. David Huddle. There'll be A Hot Time/In The Old Town/Tonight. GrPl

My Grandfather Always Promised Us. Liam Rector. while the fields of his century move far,/& then farther away. AMV-80

My Grandfather Burning Cornfields. Roger Sauls. the wind finally bearing away/the darkness that is/a flock of small birds. Str

My Grandfather Dying. Ted Kooser. ...His breath/was as sour as an orchard/after the first frost. Str

My Grandfather in Search of Moonshine. George Ella Lyon. turning like a twig on a spider strand/hung plumb-bob for the web. GOYP

My Grandfather's Church Goes Up. Fred Chappell. when the Willer so willeth works his wild wonders. SM

My Grandfather's Days. *Anonymous*. Where children you may get by steam, such pretty little things. OBET

My Grandfather's Funeral. James Applewhite. Toiling in the sacrament of seasons. TAT

My Grandfather Was a Quantum Physicist. Duane Big Eagle. My grandfather knew this. STE

My Grandmother. Perseus Adams. ...the huge mountain/Of rectifying darkness, now all but level with her sight. PeSA

My Grandmother. Karl Shapiro. ...confusing/The tongues and tasks of her children's children. VGW

My Grandmother and the Voice of Tolstoy. Steve Orlen. ...tugging/The eye of the world open and it saw me. AMV-81

My Grandmother Green. *Anonymous*. Then she, too, would have been an old maid! AmFP

My Grandmother Had Bones. Judith Hemschemeyer. Did her raw wristbone scrape against my hair? DFF

My Grandmother's Funeral. Jascha Kessler. And I say, "Taking Humanities?" AmPC

My Grandmother's Love Letters. Hart Crane. With such a sound of gently pitying laughter. BLPL; CMoP; FaBoBe; MoAB; NoAm; NOBA; NoP

My Grandmother Sent Me a New-Fashioned Three-Cornered Cambric... *Anonymous*. But a new-fashioned three-cornered cambric country-cut handkerchief. OxNR

My Grandpa Died Today. Joan Fassler. And we went on with the game. DL

My Grave. Thomas Osborne Davis. If one were sure to be buried so. ACV; OnYI

My Great-Grandfather's Slaves. Wendell Berry. We cannot be free of each other. GeTw

My Great Great etc. Uncle Patrick Henry. James Tate. Well then think of your great great etc. Uncle/Patrick Henry. GP; OBAL

My Grief on Fal's Proud Plain. Geoffrey Keating. And sent safe into exile over the waves of/Cliodhna! OnYI

My Grief on the Sea. *Anonymous*. His breast to my bosom./His mouth to my mouth. AnIL; LiTW; NOBI; OnYI; WTO

My Grief on the Sea. Douglas Hyde. His mouth to my mouth. OBEV; OBVV; OxBI

My Guardian Angel Stein. Philip Schultz. like love & family romance, has neither beginning, middle nor end. MAYP

My Hairt Is Heich Aboif. *Anonymous*. And thay will on you rew, as mine hes done one me. OxBS

My Hand Has a Pain. Saint Columcille. That is why my hand has pain! BIrV

My Hands Are Withered. *Anonymous*. –there's a bit on stone, a bit on bone/and a bit on this withered hand.' NOBI

My Handsome Gilderoy. *Anonymous*. My winsome Gilderoy. AtBAP; CH

My Happiness. Greg Pape. and she was saying oh honey. MAYP

My Happy Life. Mildmay Fane, Earl of Westmoreland. More than a thousand others blest. CavP

My Hat. Stevie Smith. Go home, you see, well I wouldn't run a risk like that. BrRo

My hated birthday is here, and I must go. Sulpicia. and, being forced, I cannot be myself. BoWoP

My Head on My Shoulders. Jeremy Ingalls. Though boots, though knife shall fail us, fear no death. GoYe

My Heart and I. Elizabeth Barrett Browning. I think, we've fared, my heart and I. HBV 1-2

My Heart Belongs to Daddy. Cole Porter. So Da-da-da-daddy might spank. OBAL

My Heart Burns for Him. *Anonymous*. Where in the forest will I find my madman? WTO

My Heart, How Very Hard It's Grown! Cotton Mather. My heart, once by thy plowshare broke,/Will entertain thy word. AH

My heart I gave thee... Sir Thomas Wyatt. For he that believeth bearing in hand,/Ploweth in water and soweth in the sand. FCP

My Heart Is a Lute. Lady Anne Barnard. Lest the strings should break, and the music be done. HBV 1-2

My Heart Is Heich Above. *Anonymous*. And they will on you rue,/As mine has done on me. AtBAP; BSV; ErPo; GoTS; OBEV

My Heart Is in the East. Judah Halevi. As a treasure of beauty I prize. TrJP

My Heart Is Woe. *Anonymous*. Then came Longeus with a spere and cleft His hart in sonder.' OxBM

My Heart Leaps Up. William Wordsworth. And I could wish my days to be/Bound each to each by natural piety. AtBAP; BiP; BoLiVe; DiPo; ERoP 1-2; ExPo; FaBV; FaFP; GoTF; GTBS; GTBS-P; InPK; InPo; InPS; LoBV; MBW 1-2; MCCG; NOBE; NoP; OAEL 1-2; OAEP; OBNC; OBRV; OBSP; PoPl; SoPo; TEP; TiPo; TreF; TrGrPo; TRV; ViBoPo

My Heart Moves as Heavy as the Horse That Climbs the Hill. *Anonymous*. And many, many troubled thoughts are quite breaking my/heart. ELU

My Heart, My Heart Is Mournful. Heinrich Heine. I would he shot me dead! PoPl

My Heart's Desire. *Anonymous*. Wilt Thou receive them, Lord of grace,/ And give to me a crown? STF

My Heart's in the Highlands. Robert Burns. My heart's in the Highlands, wherever I go. AnEnPo; AWP; CoBE; FaBoBe; FaBoPP; FaFP; GN; HBV 1-2; InPo; LiTL; PoPl; PoPle; SD; TreFT

My Heart Shall Be Thy Garden. Alice Meynell. Flit to the silent world and other summers,/With wings that dip beyond the silver seas. HBV 1-2

My Heart Stood Still. Lorenz Hart. I never lived at all until the thrill of that moment when my heart stood still. BLSo

My Heart, Thinking. Lady Otomo of Sakanoe. Will still break through. AWP; LiTW

My Heart Was Wandering. Christopher John Brennan. my heart still walks a thing apart,/my heart is restless as of old. BoAV; PoAu 1-2

My Hereafter. Juanita De Long. I shall become a part of them. WGRP

My Hero. Benjamin Brawley. And Galahad to me. BANP; PoNe

A! My Herte, A! What Aileth The. Sir Thomas Wyatt. A! my herte,a! what aileth thee? AtBAP

My Hiding Place. Kathryn T. Bowsher. I have found Thee–/My Hiding Place! STF

My Hobby Horse. *Anonymous*. And dance to the bag-pipes and beating of the drum. OxNR

My Home. *Anonymous*. I shoot wild ducks down deep snake-holes,/And drink gin-sling from two-quart bowls. NA

My Home's across the Smokey Mountains. *Anonymous*. I'll never get to see you any more. AmFP; FSW

My Honey, My Love. Joel Chandler Harris. My honey my love, my heart's delight–/My honey, my love! FaBoBe

My Honeyed Languor. Edward (Edward Dzyubin) Bagritsky. In heavy drops perpetually flow, flow,/flow. TrJP

My hope, alas, hath me abused. Sir Thomas Wyatt. And I remain all comfortless. FCP; SiPS

My Hope, My Love. *Anonymous*. And death shall never approach us/In the bosom of the fragrant wood! BIrV

My Hopes Retire; My Wishes as Before. Walter Savage Landor. The shore repels it; it returns again. GBL; OBNC

My Horses. Jean Jaszi. North and South and every way/Every day. SoPo

My Horses Ain't Hungry. *Anonymous*. But a false hearted lover will lead you to the grave. FSW

My House. Robert Adamson. I must get those jeans taken up CBAP

My House. George Bruce. Unworried and/Warm–secure. OxBS

My House. Jane W. Krows. And I'll get/I bet–a pet. SoPo

My House. Claude McKay. But things for him will not be what they seem/To average men since he has dreamt his dream! CDC

My House, I Say. But Hark to the Sunny Doves. Robert Louis Stevenson. Who now, deposed, surveys my plain abode/And his late kingdom, only from the road. FM; NOBV

My Husband. *Anonymous.* At night he comes home and f–ks me. CoMu

My husband is the same man. Sila. in endless evenings of making love. BoWoP

My Indian Girl. Ali Sedat Hilmi Torel. O lei, O lei, O lei.... PeD

My Influence. *Anonymous.* Lord, may my life help others lives,/It touches by the way. STF

My Infundibuliform Hat. Charles Follen Adams. And she smashed my infundibuliform hat. OBAL

My Inmost Hope. Sarah Copia Sullam. And show the spiteful sland'rer by this/sign/That you will shield me with your/endless might. TrJP

My Invention. Shel Silverstein. But the cord isn't long enough. PV; QQQ

My Jack. John Francis O'Donnell. Low laughters and the lamp-lit room. IrPN

My Jacket Old. Herman Melville. Ere Work, alack, came in with Wail. SaC

My Jesus, As Thou Wilt. Benjamin Schmolck. "My Lord, Thy will be done." BePJ

My Johnny. *Anonymous.* So blow gently the winds on the ocean/And send back my Johnny to me. OBET

My Joy, My Jockey, My Gabriel. George Barker. But always and for ever he/At night will sleep and keep by me. MoAB; MoBrPo

My Kate. Elizabeth Barrett Browning. She has made the grass grener even here with her grave–/My Kate. OBVV; OHFP; WBLP

My Kin Talk. Anna Margolin. my voice is not my own–/my kin talk. VWA

My Laddie. Amelie Rives. An' close, an' close into your ear/I'll tell ye how I lo'e ye, dear. HBV 1-2

My Laddie's Hounds. Marguerite Elizabeth Easter. Wha is it hunts my laddie's hounds/Till fa' o" day? AA

My Ladies Haire Is Threeds of Beaten Gold. Bartholomew Griffin. But ah the worst and last is yet behind,/For of a Gryphon she doth beare the mind. AAS

My Lady. Philip James Bailey. And I, like Earth all budding out with love. OBVV

My Lady Carenza of the lovely body. *Anonymous.* ...Please ask the king of glory, when/you enter heaven, to join us once again. BoWoP

My Lady Has the Grace of Death. Joseph Mary Plunkett. She took my sword from her side all bloody/And died for love. OxBI

My Lady Nature and Her Daughters. John Henry, Cardinal Newman. Ladies rule where hearts obey. GoBC

My Lady's Tears. *Anonymous.* O! strive not to be excellent in woe,/Which only breeds your beauty's overthrow. NOBE; OBEV

My Lady Takes the Sunlight for Her Gown. Thomas Cole. She sings and threads her antique tapestry. NePoAm

My Lady Wind. *Anonymous.* Remember what old nurse has sung/Of busy Lady Wind. HBV 1-2; HBVY

My Land. Thomas Osborne Davis. Yes, she'a a rare and fair land–/This native land of mine. HBV 1-2; PAL

My Land Is Fair for Any Eyes to See. Jesse Stuart. The snow flakes drifting through green tops of pine. TiPo

My Language. Heinz Politzer. I go with you through dusk and tide. LiTW

My Last Afternoon with Uncle Devereux Winslow. Robert Lowell. Uncle Devereux would blend to the one color. ForPo; NoP; VGW

My Last Duchess. Robert Browning. Which Claus of Innsbruck cast in bronze for me! AWP; BeLS; BiP; DiPo; ExPo; FaBoPV; FaFP; FF; FiP; ForPo; FPL; GoTF; GTBS-P; HAP; HBV 1-2; HeIP; HoPM; InPK; InPo; InPS; LiTB; MasP; MAT; MaVP; MBW 1-2; MCCG; NIP; NOBE; NOBV; NoP; OAEL 1-2; OAEP; OBNC; PAI; PoEL 1-5; PoLf; PoPle; PPP; PrImr; SCV; SeCeV; SoSe; TEP; TreFS; TrGrPo; VLP; WeW; WHA

My Last Illusion. John Kaye Kendall. I wonder what became of Molly! FiBHP

My Last Terrier. John (G. Forrester Scott) Halsham. And through the dim Elysian bounds/Leads all his cry of little hounds. HBV 1-2

My Latest Sun Is Sinking Fast. Jefferson Haskell. O, bear me away on your snowy wings/To my immortal home. AH

My Legacy. Helen Hunt Jackson. ..."Join heir/With Christ make hast to ask him for thy share." HBV 1-2

My Legs Are So Weary. Gelett Burgess. It Sticks to my Head! LBN

My Letter. Grace Denio Litchfield. Straight, swift, and sure, it brought me/word! AA

My Li'l John Henry. *Anonymous.* Oh, my li'l John Henry,/Godamighty know. ABF

My Life by Somebody Else. Mark Strand. Somebody else has arrived. Somebody else is writing. GP

My life closed twice before its close. Emily Dickinson. Parting is all we know of heaven,/And all we need of hell. AA; APA; AtBAP; BoLoP; BoWoP; DiPo; GBL; GoTF; HeIP; LiTA; LiTM; MAPA; MoAB; MoAmPo; MoVE; NePA; NIP; NoAm; NOBA; OBSP; OLR; OxBA; PoPl; PPP; SBG; SCV; SoSe; TreFT; TrGrPo; ViBoPo; WHA

My Life had stood–a Loaded Gun. Emily Dickinson. For I have but the power to kill,/Without–the power to die– AmPP; HAP; NAWM 1-2; NoP; SBG; WeW; WPOW

"My Life Has Been the Poem..." Henry David Thoreau. But I could not both live and utter it. AmePo

My Life Is a Bowl. May Riley Smith. Home, dear heart,/To you. BLPA

My Life Is Like the Summer Rose. Richard Henry Wilde. But none, alas! shall mourn for me! HBV 1-2; TreFT

My Life Like Any Other. Philip Levine. ...nothing, except the life I'd entered. AMV-81

My Life's Delight. Thomas Campion. Come, then, and make thy flight/As swift to me, as heavenly light. TrGrPo

My Life, the Quality of Which. Etheridge Knight. But you have to feel for it NNaP

My Limbs I Will Fling. William Strode. Is much better far/Than a careful chair/And a wreath of thorns without. CBEP

My Little Buckaroo. *Anonymous.* So go to sleep,/My little buckaroo. BPAW

My Little Cow. *Anonymous.* and there's my song all. OxNR

My Little Dreams. Georgia Douglas Johnson. Tonight, within my heart! BANP; BlSi; CDC; GoSl; PoNe

My Little Girl. Samuel Minturn Peck. Who has my love and prayers! AA

My Little Lodge. *Anonymous.* And no forbidding fence in sight! OnYI

My Little Love. Charles B. Hawley. "Good night! Sweet dreams! God keep you everywhere!" HBV 1-2

My Little Love Lies on the Ground. Larin Paraske. Crawl through muddy marshes/Wallow in foul waters. PBWP

My Little Maid. *Anonymous.* And some she gave to the truckler's/dog. OxNR

My Little Neighbor. Mary Augusta Mason. And chatters wondrous things to me. AA

My Little Old Man and I Fell Out. *Anonymous.* And get you gone, you little old/man! OxNR

My Little Pretty Mopsy. *Anonymous.* And ever your own ye shall me find,/At all times redy to kiss you.' OxBM

My Little Soul, My Vagrant Charmer. Emperor (Publius Aelius Hadrianus) Hadrian. And not so witty as you were? OBVE

My Little Wife. *Anonymous.* She sat by the fire/And told many a fine tale. OxNR

My Lodge at Wang-Ch'uan after a Long Rain. Wang Wei. Why should I frighten sea-gulls, even with a thought? LiTW

My Lodging It Is on the Cold Ground. Sir William D'Avenant. For thou art the man that alone art/The cause of my misery. JCP

My Lord. Martha Snell Nicholson. How they might come to Thee,/My Lord, my Lord. BePJ

My Lord's A-Writin' All de Time. *Anonymous.* My Lord's a-writin' all de time yes, all de time. BoAN 1-2

My Lord Says He's Gwineter Rain Down Fire. *Anonymous.* Take yo' net an' foller me. BoAN 1-2

My Lord Tomnoddy. Robert Barnabas Brough. He's the Earl of Fitzdotterel's eldest son. FiBHP; VLP

My Lord, What a Mornin'. *Anonymous.* When de stars begin to fall,/When de stars begin to fall. BoAN 1-2

My Lord, What a Morning. Waring Cuney. Keep him, Lord/As you made him,/Big, and strong, and black. TTY

My Lost Youth. Henry Wadsworth Longfellow And the thoughts of youth are long, long/thoughts. AA; AmPP; AnFE; AnNE; AP; APA; AWP; EtS; ExPo; FaBoBe; FaBV; FaFP; FaPoR; FPL; GoJo; HBV 1-2; LaNeLa; LiTA; MAmP; MCCG; NePA; NOBA; OBEV; OxBA; PoEL 1-5; PoLf; PoRA; RoGo; SeCeV; TAP; TreF; ViBoPo

My Love. Edward Estlin Cummings. thy eyes are the betrayal/of bells comprehended through incense ErPo; LiTL; LiTM; VGW

My Love. James Russell Lowell. Sweet homes wherein to live and die. BLPL; FaBoBe; HBV 1-2

My Love. Ono-no-Yoshiki. There is none that knows. AWP; LiTW

My Love. Richard Shelton. I touch you/as a blind man touches the dice/ and finds he has won. GOYP

My Love and I for Kisses Play'd. William Strode. Take your own kisses, give me mine again. FaBoEE

My Love behind Walls. Heather Spears. Suffer me thus secure, to his return. OBCV

My Love for All Things Warm and Breathing. William Kloefkorn. ...into the/boundless lust of all things bound but gathering. AMV-81

My Love for Thee. Richard Watson Gilder. While comrade flags flame forth on wall and towers! HBV 1-2

My Love I Gave for Hate. *Anonymous.* my love I gave for hate. BIrV

My Love in Her Attire. *Anonymous.* But Beauty's self she is,/When all her robes are gone. BLPL; EG; FF; GTBS; HeIP; LiTB; NIP; OBSP; ViBoPo

My Love Is a Tower. Lewis, Cecil Day. And pull the earth apart. AtBAP

My Love Is Dead. Thomas Chatterton. Gone to his death-bed/All under the willow tree. WiR

My love is in my house. Mira Bai [(or Mirabai)]. She takes him inside. BoWoP

My Love Is Like the Sun. *Anonymous.* And a woe that no mortal can cure. AnIV

My love is like unto th' eternal fire. Sir Thomas Wyatt. By whom hell may be felt or death assail! FCP

My Love Is Past. Thomas Watson. I know by proof that love is long annoy. PBBP

My Love Is Playing... *Anonymous.* O broken and blind may be the eyes/Of any girl that looks at him. WTO

My Love Is Sleeping. Kenneth Leslie. where her hand yearns, but not to touch my hand. OBCV

My Love Is Young. Earle Birney. that i'm to die/or she's to leave me NOBC

My Love, Oh, She Is My Love. *Anonymous.* But if she soften not her eye/I know that life and I must part. AnIV

My Love's Guardian Angel. William Barnes. When you, wi' me, mid speak to her ear/–in the night. AtBAP; GBL; NBM; PoEL 1-5

My Love, She Passed Me By. *Anonymous.* There's not a boy in a thousand/That a young girl can trust. AmFP

My Love, She's but a Lassie Yet. Robert Burns. He could na preach for thinkin o't. ViBoPo

My Love She's But a Lassie Yet. James Hogg. For all I see/Are naught to me,/Save her that's but a lassie yet. HBV 1-2

My Love-Song. Else Lasker-Schüler. Like a hidden spring/Murmurs my blood. TrJP

My Love Sways, Dancing. Moses Ibn Ezra. A zephyr light its secret would disclose. LiTW

My Love Wants to Park. Eloise Klein Healy. Try to stay away from the back seat. GP

My Love Was Light. Thomas Lanier Williams. Light was my love and better dead! PoA

My Love When This Is Past. Stephany. I will be more/and not alone. BPo

My Lover Capable of Terrible Lies. Kaccipettu Nannakaiyar. like a water lily/gnawed by a beetle. WPOW

My Loves. John Stuart Blackie. Pallas? Juno? Venus?–he/Should have chosen all the three! OBVV

My Lulu (with music). *Anonymous.* Says, "Good -by, honey," that's all. AS

My Lute and I. Sir Thomas Wyatt. Shall us apply/to sigh and mone. MeEL

My Luve's in Germany. *Anonymous.* Willie's slain! CH

My Luve's Like a Red, Red Rose. Robert Burns. Though it were ten thousand mile. BoLiVe; FaBoBe; FPL; GTBS-P; HoPM; PoSC; TrGrPo

My Madonna. Robert W. Service. And she hangs in the church of Saint Hilaire,/Where you and all may see. BLPA

My Maid Mary. *Anonymous.* Whilst I am singing and mowing/my corn. OxNR

My Makeup. Rochelle Kraut. for lipstick/I wear my lips. APU

My Mama Moved among the Days. Lucille Clifton. right back on in BlSi; PoBA

My Mammy's Maid. *Anonymous.* She stole oranges,/I do believe. OxNR

My Mammy Was a Wall-Eyed Goat. *Anonymous.* Ma-ha-mee! FaBoNo

My Man John. *Anonymous.* And I will go a-walking with you anywhere.' OBET

My Many-Coated Man. Laurie Lee. and, hooded by a smile, commits/his private murder to the mind. NYBP

My Marriage with Mrs. Johnson. Jack Gilbert. ...everyone gaping/and elaborate Louis Quatorze wondering at his envy. NPGG

My Maryland. James Ryder Randall. Maryland, My Maryland! AA; AnAmPo; FaBoBe; FaFP; HBV 1-2; MC; PAH; TreF

My Master and I. *Anonymous.* I can promise you we shall not get first in a rage. CoMu; OBET

My Master Hath a Garden. *Anonymous.* And the gentle sounding flute. AtBAP

My Master Was So Very Poor. Harry Lee. He gave His all and knew no loss. TRV

My Mate Bill. George Herbert Gibson ("Ironbark"). As'll make them toney seraphs sit back on their thrones an' stare! PoAu 1-2

My Midnight Meditation. Henry, Bishop of Chichester King. And all those weeping dewes which nightly fall,/Are but the tears shed for thy funerall. MePo; OBS

My Mind Keeps out the Host of Sin. Edmund Elys. Refine my Heart; and that it be/Kept Pure, O Lord, I give it Thee. NCEP

My Mind to Me a Kingdom Is. Sir Edward Dyer. Would all did so as well as I! BLPL; CoBE; EIL; EnLi 1-2; FaBoBe; GoTF; HBV 1-2; LiTB; MCCG; NIP; NOBE; PG; TreFS; TrGrPo; ViBoPo; WGRP

My Mirror. Aline Kilmer. My dead child's face look out at me. AnAmPo

My Mistress. William Warner. So smooth, so soft, as this. EIL

My Mistress Makes Music. *Anonymous.* And I will play as much as she'll desire. UnTE

My Mistress's Boots. Frederick Locker-Lampson. Set your dainty hand awhile/On my shoulder, Dear, and I'll/Put them on. HBV 1-2

My Money! O, My Money! Mavimbela. Let us go then to Durban/Where we shall get a better woman. WTO

My Morning Song. George Macdonald. Therefore I stir my inmost heart to worship fervently. TRV

My Most. My Most. O My Lost. Jose Garcia Villa. The beautiful, the terrible Accost. BoW

My Mother. *Anonymous.* But no one else's mother/Is quite so dear as mine. STF

My Mother. Amelia Josephine Burr. How shall I dare to dream that I enclose/Her Maker in the mind she overflows? HBMV

My Mother. Josephine Rice Creelman. My precious mother is with me. OHIP

My Mother. Francis Ledwidge. ...God who such a mother gave/This poor bird-hearted singer of a day. HBMV; OHIP

My Mother. Claude McKay. Beneath its breast my mother lies asleep. AnEnPo

My Mother. Robert Mezey. that's what I say,/love,/Mother NaP; SM

My Mother. Hayim Naggid. In my sleep flags of blackness/Are folded and put away. VWA

My Mother. Bertha Nolan. "God bless and keep you," mother dear, today. PGD

My Mother. Ann Taylor. If ever I could dare despise/My Mother? OHIP; OxBChV; PaPo

My Mother. Jane Taylor. And tears of sweet affection shed,–/My Mother. BLPA; BLPL; TreF

My mother always said. Sappho. but a garland of fresh flowers. BoWoP

My Mother and My Sisters. Simon J. Ortiz. She can always tell. GP

My Mother Bids Me Bind My Hair. Anne Hunter. Now Lubin is away. CBEP; HBV 1-2; OBEC

My Mother on an Evening in Late Summer. Mark Strand. It is much too late. FYAP; GeTw

My Mother Once Told Me. Yehuda Amichai. But my hands, clinging,/Remain/Clinging. NYBP

My Mother Pieced Quilts. Teresa Acosta. knotted with love/the quilts sing on. FIA; WPOW

My Mother's Bible. George Pope Morris. In teaching me the way to live,/It taught me how to die. BLRP; PaPo; WBLP

My Mother's Birthday: "I used to watch you sleeping." Kathleen Raine. For that unwanted babe, for comfort too long ago, too/far away. NAs

My Mother's Childhood. Barry Spacks. she waited,/and was good. GP

My Mother's Death. Judith Hemschemeyer. But who will help me. Str

My Mother's Feet. Stanley Plumly. every step of the way shining out of them. GeTw

My Mother's Garden. Alice E. Allen. Sweet as the breath of roses blown,/The fragrance of her life. BLPA; BLPL; FaBoBe

My Mother's House. Eunice Tietjens. It still exists in some dim way/While I remember it," she said. HBMV

My Mother's House (excerpt). Leah Goldberg. And the mirror maintains/The family tradition:/That she was very beautiful. PBWP

My Mother's Life. William Meredith. I think she gives the right answer, before/the light dims, bluing, then purpling the retina. AMV-81

My Mother's Love. *Anonymous.* And through the changing scenes of life/I find a haven there. STF

My Mother's Prayer. T. C. O'Kane. Daily calling me to heaven,/Even from my trundle bed. BLPA; FaBoBe

My Mother's Shoes. Rayzel Zychlinska. At night I come back/in my mother's shoes/bedecked with the patient dust of years. VWA

My Mother's Sister. C. Day-Lewis. How can this be justified, how can it/Be justified? OxBTC

My Mother's Table. Hy Sobiloff. Where I climbed a ladder of birthdays,/Reading my father's face. NePA

My Mother Said. *Anonymous.* I shall never come back. LoGBV; OBSP; OxNR; PoPle

My Mother Shoots the Breeze (excerpt). Fred Chappell. He still called me Annie Mexico. NLV

My Mother Takes a Bath. Yuri Kageyama. With the water singing koto strings in her ears. BrSi

My Mother Was a Lady. Edward B. Marks. And you wouldn't dare insult me, Sir, if Jack were only here. TreF; YaD

My Mother, Who Came from China, Where She Never Saw Snow. Laureen Mar. Dull thunder passes through their fingers. WPOW

My Mother Would Be a Falconress. Robert Duncan. talking to myself and would draw blood. PoM

My Mothers Maydes when They Did Sowe and Spynne. Sir Thomas Wyatt. Graunt theim, goode lorde, as thou maist of thy myght,/To frete inward for losing suche a losse. AAS

My Mouth Is Often Joined against His Mouth. Arthur Rimbaud. 'Tis the tube where descends the celestial breath/Feminine Canaan in the protruding halves. PeHV

My Mouth Is Very Quiet. Jose Garcia Villa. But he holds to his North or South/Blows–and again is quiet. AnFE; CoAnAm

My Muse and I, Ere Youth and Spirits Fled. George the Younger Colman. Simply because my fire is going out. ELU

My Muse, What Ails This Ardour? Sappho. To think a soare so deadly/I should so rashly ripp up. OBVE

My Naked Aunt. Archibald MacLeish. Till love's put off and pain/and wish and death. NePA

My Name and I. Robert Graves. Than ever I for him. NoAm; NYBP

My Name Is Afrika. Keorapetse Kgositsile. To every birth its pain/All else is death or life PoBA

My Name Is George Nathaniel Curzon. Anonymous. I dine at Blenheim once a week. NOBL

My Name Was Legion. Hildegarde Hoyt Swift. To build a world for the free. AmFN

My Nannie's Awa'. Robert Burns. The dark, dreary winter, an' wild-driving snaw,/Alane can delight me–now Nannie's awa'. GN; HBV 1-2

My Need. Anonymous. But all is found in Christ my Lord. STF

My Neighbor's Reply. Anonymous. Spreads joy abroad and doubles all his own. PoToHe

My Neighbor's Roses. A. L. Gruber. Is grown for you upon your neighbor's vine? BLPA; PoToHe

My New Garden Field. Anonymous. And to all other young men I now bid adieu. AmFP

My New World. Irving Browne. Thou let me live a day/In my new world. AA

My New Year Prayer. Anonymous. And make me, Lord, the instrument/To lead their hearts to thee. STF

My Nightingale. Rose Auslander. in the garden of my sleepless dream. VWA

My November Guest. Robert Frost. And they are better for her praise. AnFE; APA; BLPL; BoLiVe; HBMV; MoVE; OxBA; PoLf; ViBoPo

My Object All Sublime. Sir William Schwenck Gilbert. With a twisted cue,/And elliptical billiard balls! TreFT

My Old Beaver Cap. Anonymous. La tul da rol de day. BFSS

My Old Bible. Anonymous. Though surrounded by care,/While possessing this blessing Divine. BLRP; STF

My Old Black Billy. Edward Harrington. Indispensable,/Old black billy. PoAu 1-2

My Old Cat. Hal Summers. Well died, my old cat. OxBTC; PCat

My Old Counselor. Gertrude Hall. Lift up thy heart! Exult that it is so! AA

My Old Dutch: A Cockney Song. Albert Chevalier. There ain't a body livin' in the land/As I "swop" for my dear old Dutch! VLP

My Old Hammah (with music). Anonymous. Yes, be so col'! AS

My Old Kentucky Home. Stephen Collins Foster. For the old Kentucky home, far/away. AA; AnAmPo; APA; BLSo; FaBoBe; FaBV; FaFP; GoTF; PoLf; PSoN; TreF; TrGrPo

My Old Straw Hat. Eliza Cook. Farewell, till spring days come again–/My Old Straw Hat! BrRo

My Old True Love. Anonymous. My rosy red lips will never be kissed till you return again. OuSiCo

My Old Wife's a Good Old Cratur. Anonymous. But none of them have got such spouses,/No such baccy, no such beer. OBET

My Olson Elegy. Irving Feldman. Now you are heavier than earth, everything/has become lighter than the air. Prf

My Only Star. Francis Davison. Which in your bosom seeks his only shrouding? ElL

My Orcha'd in Linden Lea. William Barnes. To where, vor me, the apple tree/Do lean down low in Linden Lea. NOBV

My Other Chinee Cook. Brunton Stephens. For I'm sure they know the story of the so-called "rabbit pie". PoAu 1-2

My Other Me. Grace Denio Litchfield. Send back my other Me! AA; HBV 1-2

My Owen. Ellen Mary Patrick Downing. More than the wisest know your heart shall preach to me. HBV 1-2

My Own Brand. Art Cuelho. a chance to put on my own brand. TAT

My Own Cailin Donn. George Sigerson. Is the joy around your footsteps, my own Cailin Donn! FaBoBe; HBV 1-2

My Own Dark Head (My Own, My Own). Anonymous. he would have no heart who denied you love. NOBI

My Own Epitaph. John Gay. I thought so once; but now I know it. FaBoEE; FF; GoTF; NIP; NOEC; SeCePo; SeCeV; TreFT

My Own Hallelujahs. Zack Gilbert. Shouting my own/Hallelujahs. PoBA

My Own Heart Let Me More Have Pity On. Gerard Manley Hopkins. Bctweenpie mountains–lights a lovely mile. CoBMV; FaBoMo; InPS; LiTM; NOBV; NoP; PAI; VLP

My Own Hereafter. Eugene Lee-Hamilton. That is the only after-life I need. WGRP

My Own House. David Ignatow. ...completing this/poem, would be like entering my own house. AMV-80

My Ox Duke. John Dyer. The honest ox, rejoiced, into the shade. NOEC

My Papa's Waltz. Theodore Roethke. Then waltzed me off to bed/Still clinging to your shirt. AmP; CAPP; CMoP; CrMA; CTBA; FF; HaCAP; HAP; HeIP; HoPM; InPK; InPS; LCAP; LiTM; MiAP; MoAB; NCSH; NIP; NLV; NoAm; NOBA; NoP; PAI; PPoe; PPP; PrIm; SM; TAP; VGW; WeW

My Parents Kept Me from Children Who Were Rough. Stephen Spender. I longed to forgive them, but they never/smiled. OAEP

My Past. Dennis Cooper. ...Who knows where that/man and that feeling are now. APU

My Past Has Gone to Bed. Siegfried Sassoon. Simplicities unlearned long since and left behind. AtBAP

My "Patch of Blue." Mary Newland Carson. We'll find our "Patch of Blue." BLPA

My Peace I Give unto You. G. A. Studdert Kennedy. And find the path that, piercing it,/Leads through to Peace again. EBCP

My Penis. Ed Ochester. even on lonely winter evenings refusing/not to point to the stars. GP

My People. Margery Himel. What unites us is not our past/but our future. IHMS

My People. Else Lasker-Schüler. The brittle rock of bone,/My people,/Cries out to God. WPOW

My Period Had Come for Prayer. Emily Dickinson. I worshipped–did not "pray"– EaLo

My Physics Teacher. David Wagoner. One foot forever into the wastebasket. SUW

My Picture. Adelaide Anne Procter. It shall stay and cheer the end! PeD

My Picture Left in Scotland. Ben Jonson. And all these through her eyes have stopped her ears. AnAnS 2; EnRePo; ForPo; LiTL; MePo; PoEL 1-5; QFR; SeCP; SeCV 1-2

My Place. David Ignatow. having located himself/through my place. CAPP

My Plan. Marchette Chute. And all the Hudson River/In which to wash my dishes. BiCB; BrR

My Playmate. John Greenleaf Whittier. The moaning of the sea of change/Between myself and thee! AP; APA; HBV 1-2; NOBA; OBVV

My Poem. Nikki Giovanni.
if i never do/anything/it will go on BOLo; PoBA
the revolution it will go on BPo

My Poker Girl. Tom (Thomas Lansing Masson) Masson. Forever, on a OBAL

My Policeman. Rose Fyleman. But I like mine best of course. SoPo; TiPo

My Polish Grandma. Edward Field. speaking a different language and forgetting/why it was so important/to go to a new country. Prf

My Political Faith. George Frederick Cameron. And give each tyrant to his grave/And freedom to each lovely land. PeCV

My portion is defeat–today. Emily Dickinson. Who to have had it, would have been/Contenteder–to die– OBWP

My Portrait. Moishe-Leib Halpern. If life is battle and love/Then my blood is boiling hot. TrJP

My Prayer. Anonymous.
And break thy schemes of earthly joy,/That thou may'st seek thine all in Me. STF
Let my life help the other lives it touches by the way! BLRP
More dear, more intimtely nigh/Than e'en the sweetest earthly tie. BePJ; BLRP

My Prayer. Horatius Bonar. Be still alone with Thee. BLRP

My Prayer. Henry David Thoreau. That I thy purpose did not know,/Or overrated thy designs. HBV 1-2; HBVY; PoPl

My Pretty Little Miss. Anonymous. "Down to the river to water my geese,/And over the river to Charlie." BFSS

My Pretty Little Pink (with music). Anonymous. Where the girls are sweet as sweet can be/And the boys like sugar candy. AS

My Pretty Pink. Anonymous. And the girls as sweet as candy. AmFP

My Pretty Rose Tree. William Blake. And her thorns were my only delight. BoLoP

My Puppy. Aileen Fisher. It's funny/my puppy/knows such a great deal. OnUR

My Purse. Anonymous. As I played me with a bow/I said: "God, what is al this?" OxBM

My Queen. Anonymous. Ere I cease to love her, my queen, my queen! HBV 1-2

My Queen. William Winter. And I a monarch–at thy feet! AA

My Ramblin' Boy. Tom Paxton. May all your ramblin' bring you joy. FSW

My Recollectest Thoughts. Charles Edward Carryl. That I'm the sole survivor of/The famous Forty Thieves! HBV 1-2; HBVY; NA

My Regrets. Michael André. fragrant as the rose at dawn in spring etc. APU

My Relatives for the Most. Frederick B. Hudson. stop the white man's mule stop/in his traces. AMV-80

My Return to Czechoslovakia. Murray Edmond. –right through into Czechoslovakia. OCNZ

My Rival. Rudyard Kipling. Just think, that She'll be eighty-one/When I am forty-nine! OxBTC

My Road. Oliver Opdyke. 'Tis the road to you and the road for me. HBV 1-2

My Rose. Hildegarde Hawthorne. Begging one rosebud–but my rose was/dead. AA

My Sabine Farm. Eugene Field. And what's, oh, what's a Sabine farm to me without Maecenas! InMe

My Sad Captains. Thom Gunn. and turn with disinterested/hard energy, like the stars. CMoP; FaBoMo; LiTM; NePoEA-2; PAI; PoCh

My Sad Self. Allen Ginsberg. where all Manhattan that I've seen must disappear. NoAm; UnPo

My Sadness Sits Around Me. June Jordan. My sadness sits around me BPo

My Sailor of Seven. Gerald Brenan. Your voyage be happy, my sailor of seven! BiCB

My Samsons. Haim Guri. Behold, my Samsons are returning in the thick of the night/Lit up by the flaming foxes. VWA

My Sense of Sight. Oliver Herford. But could not hear its peak. HBMV; HBVY

My Shadow. Robert Louis Stevenson. Had stayed at home behind me and was fast asleep in bed. FaBoBe; FaBV; GoTF; HBV 1-2; HBVY; OnUR; OxBChV; SoPo; TEP; TiPo; TreF

My Share of the World. Alice Furlong. I would give up all but God/For my share of the world! HBV 1-2; OBVV

My Shepherd Is the Living Lord. Thomas Sternhold. That in thy house for evermore/My dwelling place shall be. AH

My Ship and I. Robert Louis Stevenson. And to fire the penny cannon in the bow. SUS

My Ship Is on de Ocean. Anonymous. My ship is on de ocean,/Po' sinner, fare-you-well. BoAN 1-2

My Ships. Ella Wheeler Wilcox. But bring my love-ship home to me. PoLf

My Shoes. Charles Simic. With your mute patience, forming/The only true likeness of myself. CoAP; HaCAP

My Silks and Fine Array. William Blake. True love doth pass away! BoLiVe; CBEP; ELP; GBL; TEP; UnPo

My Singing Aunt. James Reeves. But poor old uncle's groaning. ShM

My Sins in Their Completeness. Mael Isu O Brolchain. I would not take a day of drink/for these tears upon my cheek. NOBI

My Sister. Alfonsina Storni. ...I know everything, but she's/like heaven and knows nothing. Which is her fate. BoWoP

My Sister Jane. Ted Hughes. My sister's nothing but a great big crow. OnUR; SO

My Sister Laura. Spike Milligan. She must have something heavy inside. NTCP

My Sister, My Self. Raymond Filip. A doll found in the river. CaPN

My Sister's Sleep. Dante Gabriel Rossetti. "Christ's blessing on the newly born!" EnL; ExPo; LoBV; MaVP; MyFE; OAEP; SeCeV; VLP

My Sisters. Bill Kushner. Around & around some imaginary dancefloor & I'd/Look up into their eyes, their eyes so far away. APU

My Six Toothbrushes. Phyllis McGinley. Against the cool, reflective tiles. GoYe

My Son. James D. Hughes. And cheer for him whose work is done. BLPA

My Son and I. Philip Levine. and sway toward the bed/in a last chant before dawn. FAZ; GP; NYP

My Son and I. Rosemary Norman. But my will runs to waste/In incontinent tears. BrRo

My Son Doesn't See a Thing. Tomas Rivera. Let's go home,/you can't see a thing. FIA

My Son, Forsake Your Art. Mahon O'Heffernan. The making of a poem shall profit not. BIrV

My Son, My Executioner. Donald Hall. And name with my imperfect breath/The mortal paradox. NePoEA Observe enduring life in you/And start to die together. InPK; SM

My Son, My Son... Seymour Cain. Breathe./Make./Be. AMV-81

My Song. Hayim Nahman Bialik. I swallowed sighs that seeped into my bones. VWA

My Song. Hazel Hall. It would not let the darkness heal/About my heart. HBMV

My Song. King D. Kuka. He has sung. VoR

My Song. Rabindranath Tagore. ...my song will speak in your living heart. OHIP

My Song Is Love Unknown. Samuel Crossman. In whose sweet praise/I all my days/Could gladly spend. OxBChV

My Song of Today. Saint, of Lisieux Therese. There shall I sing in bliss amid angelic lyres,/The eternal, glad today! CAW

My Song to the Jewish People. Leib Olitski. Before our eyes there stand/somewhere, in freer lands, the/children Jacob's goodly tents!... TrJP

My Songs Are Poisoned. Heinrich Heine. And, love, among them–thee! AWP

My Sons. Ron Loewinsohn. ...to fill our days with beauty/from whatever faucet's available. DFF; NeAP

My Sore Thumb. Burges Johnson. An' that'll keep up int'rest some/In my poor thumb! HBVY

My Sorrow. Seumas (James Starkey) O'Sullivan. 'Tis there I would nestle at rest till the quivering moon/Uprose in the golden quiet over the hill. HBV 1-2

My Sorrow, Donncha. Padraig O Heigeartaigh. –but the One who framed us of clay on earth/not so has ordered. NOBI

My Sort o' Man. Paul Laurence Dunbar. That's one of earth's most blessed things/They can't monopolize. AmNP

My Soul Before Thee Prostrate Lies. C. F. Richter. And quicken this dead heart of mine. AH

My Soul Doth Pant towards Thee. Jeremy Taylor. That in thy arms, for ever, I/May lie. TrPWD

My Soul Hovers Over Me. Joshua Tan Pai. drop by drop/without restraint/forever– VWA

My Soul in the Bundle of Life. Anonymous. In the assemblies, I will bless thy/Name! TrJP

My Soul Is Robbed. Isaac Rosenberg. And takes unto itself the strangest of strange lands. MoPo

My Soul's Been Anchored in de Lord. Anonymous. God knows my soul's been anchored in de Lord. BoAN 1-2

My Soul Shall Cling to Thee. Charlotte Elliot. While, as my strength, my rock, my all,/Saviour! I cling to Thee? BePJ

My Soul Thirsts for God. William Cowper. None proves less grateful to His care/Or yields him meaner fruit than I. TrCP

My Soul, Weigh Not Thy Life. Leonard Swain. And on thy head shall quickly shine/The diadem of God. AH

My Soul Would Fain Indulge a Hope. Joseph Steward. Shine through a dark, benighted soul,/And bid a sinner live. AH

My South. Don West. Cumberlands/Smokies/Unakas– PoNe

My Specialty Is Living Said. Edward Estlin Cummings. one pair of trousers (which had died) MoVE; NOBA

My Spectre around Me Night & Day. William Blake. This the Wine & this the Bread CBEP; NCEP; OAEL 1-2; OxBoCh

My Spirit. Thomas Traherne. Exalted there they ought to Shine. SeCV 1-2

My Spirit Will Not Haunt the Mound. Thomas Hardy. If otherwise, then I shall not,/For you, be there. MoBrPo; OBNC; QFR

My spouse, Chunaychunay. Anonymous. For today my heart was brought to tears. BoWoP

My Spring Thing. Everett Hoagland. grass in the splendor/of thighs/without wings–/worth BPo

My Springs. Sidney Lanier. For when He frowns, 'tis then ye shine! UnPo

My Star. Robert Browning. Mine has opened its soul to me; therefore I love it. BoLiVe; EvOK; HBV 1-2; MBW 1-2; OAEP; SoSe; TrGrPo

My Star. Plato. Heaven, with a host of eyes to gaze on thee. EnLi 1-2

My Stars. Abraham Ibn Ezra. If I suddenly decided to sell shrouds,/People would suddenly stop dying. OFD

My Stearine Candles. James Henry. Gives me just what I want, and asks back nothing. NOBV

My Strawlike Hair. Asya (Asya Gray). And suddenly recognize/Who I am. VWA

My Street Baby's Lament. William Franklin. It's the cocaine talkin', and street-baby dreams. LFAC

My Style. Charles Bukowski. some would claim that I have succeeded/in this. AMV-81

My Subtle and Proclamant Song. Sean Jennett. my subtle and proclamant song. NeIP

My Sun-Killed Tree. Marguerite Harris. how nearer by a universe/to their divinity. GoYe

My Sweet Gazelle! Immanuel Di Roma. Beside those eyes all other beauty's/vain. TrJP

My sweet old etcetera. Edward Estlin Cummings. Your smile/eyes knees and of your Etcetera) AmPP; CMoP; FF; HeIP; InPS; NAMP; NePA; OBAL; OBWP; OxBA; PAI; PPP; SOTW; WaaP; WaP

My Sweet Sweeting. Anonymous. For none I find CH

My Sweetest Lesbia. Thomas Campion. And crown with love my ever-during night. AAS; AtBAP; AWP; BiP; ElL; FF; GBL; HAP; HeIP; InPS; LoBV; NIP; NoP; OAEL 1-2; PoRA; PrIm; TEP; TrGrPo; UnTE

My Sweetheart in the Rippling Hills of Sand. Princess Likelike. We delighted in the forest. WTO

My Sweetheart's the Mule in the Mines. *Anonymous.* On the bumper I sit, and I chew and I spit./All over my sweetheart's behind. AmFP; BPAW; FSW

My Teeth. Ed Ochester. to taste its own power/at last. DFF; GP

My Thing Is My Own. *Anonymous.* My thing is my own, and I'll keep it so still,/Until I be Marryed, say Men what they will. CoMu

My Thirty Years. Juan F. Manzano. For her–oh, God!–who brought this torment to me. TTY

My Thought Was on a Maid So Bright. *Anonymous.* With that maid that is so bright,/Redemptoris Mater. ISi

My Thoughts Are Winged with Hopes. George, Earl of Cumberland Clifford. Till Cynthia shine as she hath done before. EiL

My Thoughts Are Winged with Hopes, My Hopes with Love. Sir Walter Ralegh. Till Cynthia shine as she hath done before. GBL

My Thread. David Hofstein. My thread for the new wick/Of freedom's torch,/Oh world! TrJP

My Three Wives. *Anonymous.* The third for a warming-pan,/Doctress, and nurse. FaBoEE

My Thrush. Mortimer Collins. Sing on, dear Thrush, amid the limes! HBV 1-2

My Triumph. John Greenleaf Whittier. My freehold of thanksgiving. AnNE; NOBA

My triumph lasted till the drums. Emily Dickinson. A Bayonet's contrition/Is nothing to the Dead. OBWP; WaaP

My True Love. Ivy O. Eastwick. So you I'll never wed! SiSoSe

My True Love Hath My Heart and I Have His. Mary Elizabeth Coleridge. I love no love but thee. BoLiVe; BoLoP; CH; DiPo; FaBoBe; GBL; HBV 1-2; LiTL; OAEP; PoEL 1-5; PoPle; SeCeV; TrGrPo; ViBoPo; WHA

My True Love Makes Me Happy. Beatrice de Dia. No matter what pain that brings you. WPOW

My True Memory. Asya (Asya Gray). Arching her back,/She hissed/And slipped out of the house. VWA

My True Sailor Boy. *Anonymous.* And it was, as you may understand,/Written in blood by the lady's hand. BFSS

My Trundle Bed. J. G. Baker. "Father, do Thou bless my child." BLPA; FaBoBe

My Trust. John Greenleaf Whittier. My mother's chastening love I own. OHIP; PGD

My Twelve Oxen. *Anonymous.* I have twelve oxen, and they be fair and rede,/And they go a-grasing down by the mede. OxBM

My Uncle Jehoshaphat. Laura E. Richards. And they both rode to town on the brindled calf,/To carry it home to its mother. OxBChV

My Uncle Joe. Robert B. Smith. Finally, he became a perfect gentleman/just in time for rigor mortis. LFAC

My Uncle Paul of Pimlico. Mervyn Peake. They smile (while purring the refrains),/At little thoughts that cross their brains. OnUR

My Uninvited Guest. May Riley Smith. To every door, O Pain, thou hast a key! AA; WGRP

My Valentine. Kitty Parsons. "To you, with Love from Me." SoPo

My Valentine. Robert Louis Stevenson. I will make a palace fit for you and me/Of green days in forests and blue days at sea. GrPl; OFD; SiSoSe

My Voice. Oscar Wilde. ...music of the sea/That sleeps, a mimic echo, in the shell. BrPo

My Wage. Jessie B. Rittenhouse. Life would have paid. BLPA; PoToHe

My Way Is in the Sand Flowing. Samuel Beckett. and live the space of a door/that opens and shuts NOBI

My Way Is Not Thy Way. D. H. Lawrence. For all we are worth. CMoP

My Way's Cloudy. *Anonymous.* Go sen'-a dem angels down, O, bretheren. BoAN 1-2

My White Book of Poems. Rachel (Rachel Blumstein). and the grief of a heart/going under/everyone now/can calmly finger. VWA

My Wicked Uncle. Derek Mahon. More wicked already than ever my uncle was. FaBoIP; OxBC

My Wife. Robert Louis Stevenson. The august Father/Gave to me. DL

My Wife Is My Shirt. Stephen Tropp. & finally button her blood around my hands InPK; PeD

My Wife's a Wanton Wee Thing. *Anonymous.* I took a rung and I claw'd her,/An' a braw guid bairn was she. CoMu

My Wife's a Winsome Wee Thing. Robert Burns. She is a lo'esome wee thing,/This sweet wee wife o' mine. HBV 1-2; LiTL

My Wild Irish Rose. Chauncey Olcott. She may let me take/The bloom from my wild Irish rose. BLSo; FSN; FSW; GoTF; TreFT

My Wind Is Turned to Bitter North. Arthur Hugh Clough. Returns no more, no more. OAEP; VLP

My Winsome Dear. Robert Fergusson. That fill Edina's street/Sae thrang this day. SeCePo

My Winter Past. Eldon Grier. in the licorice veins of my sensuality. NOBC

My Wish for My Land. Randolph Stow. under the far far harking of the crows. NOAV

My Wish for You. Rabi'a of Balkh. think of me, and know the worth you've lost. WPOW

My Wishes. Patrick Healy. No–I warrant she'll like me the better. OnYI

My Woman. Caius Valerius Catullus. write on the wind, write on the rushing waves. PoPl

My Woman. A. D. Winans. my woman needs no introduction. AMV-80

My Woodcock. Patrick Reginald Chalmers. I shall hear the click-click of the gun I'd/Omitted to load! CenHV

My Yellow Gal. *Anonymous.* My yellow, yellow, yellow, yellow gal. ABF

My Young Mother. Jane Cooper. calling me from sleep after decades. FaBoWP

My Zipper Suit. Marie Louise Allen. Zip it up, and zip it down,/And hurry out to play. BrR; SUS; TiPo

The Myall in Prison. Mary Gilmore. And the black feet of its night/Go walking through my room. BoAV; CBAP; PoAu 1-2

Mycenae. David Fisher. my small black dog lies there... NPGG

Mycerinus. Matthew Arnold. Mix'd with the murmur of the moving Nile. MaVP

Mye Love Toke Skorne My Servise to Retaine. Sir Thomas Wyatt. For as there is a certeyne tyme to rage,/So ys there tyme suche madnes to asswage. AAS

Myfanwy. Sir John Betjeman. Ringleader, tom-boy, and chum to the weak. BoLoP

Mynstrelles Songe. Thomas Chatterton. Thos the damselle spake, and dyed. AnFE; EnLoPo; OBEC

Myrtle. Ted Kooser. a yellow candle flame/no wind or weather dare extinguish. GOYP

Myrtle for Two. George F. Whicher. Myrtle suits me, rather. NLV

Myself. Edgar A. Guest. Whatever happens, I want to be/Self-respecting and conscience free. BLPA; BLPL

Myself When I Am Real. Al Young. I long to fade back/into this door of sun forever CNA; PoBA

Myself when Young (parody). Tom Donnelly. Well, there are other Mermaids on the Beach. BXAP

The Mysteries. Leonard Alfred George Strong. And reckon bravely in a row/The things I am afraid to know. HaMV

Mysteries. Terence Winch. ...collaborate/on a series of detective stories in which/the murderer is always an orangutan. APU

The Mysteries Remain. Hilda ("H. D.") Doolittle. I am the vine,/the branches, you/and you. NOBA; TAP; VGW; WPOW

Mysterious Biography. Carl Sandburg. honorable distinguished Christofo Colombo. OFD; SiSoSe

Mysterious Britain. Amy Clampitt. There are some things, it seems,/you just can't get close to. AMV-81

The Mysterious Cat. Vachel Lindsay. Oh, what a proud mysterious cat./Mew...Mew...Mew. GoJo; OBCA; SoPo; TiPo

Mysterious East. William Cole. Then an old friend kindly/Chopped off his head. OBAL

Mysterious Landscape. Hans Carossa. Bearing back the perished form. LiTW

The Mysterious Music of Ocean. *Anonymous.* That thus the watery realm cannot contain/The joy they breathe? EtS

Mysterious Presence! Source of All. Seth Curtis Beach. Let living psalms of praise be heard. AH

Mystery. Elizabeth Barrett Browning. And widen, so, the broad life-wound/Which soon is large enough for death. OBVV

The Mystery. Ralph Hodgson. And His own face to see. HBV 1-2; MoAB; MoBrPo

The Mystery. Douglas Hyde. Who teaches the place where couches the sun?/(If not I) OnYI; OxBI

The Mystery. Sara Teasdale. Can I ever know you/Or you know me? HBMV

The Mystery. Lilian Whiting. Am I bringing you lilies to-day. AA

Mystery. Yehoash. Long, long I heard both voices/blending,/Uncomprehending. TrJP

"Mystery Boy" Looks for Kin in Nashville. Robert Earl Hayden. We'll go and find them, we'll go/and ask them for your name again. LCAP; NoAm

The Mystery of Cro-A-Tan. Margaret Junkin Preston. Sphinx-like untold, the ages hold/The tale of CRO-A-TAN! PAH

The Mystery of Emily Dickinson. Marvin Bell. I won't say anything would have happened/unless there was time, and eternity's plenty. LCAP

The Mystery of Life. John Gambold. Where in their bright result shall rise/Thoughts, virtues, friendships, griefs and joys. NOEC

The Mystery of the Caves. Michael Waters. wanting so much to come home. GeTw; MAYP

The Mystery of the Innocent Saints (excerpt). Charles Peguy. And I his adversary desire that he shall gain. CAW

Mystery Story. Howard Nemerov. I can't remember what he done. NLV

The Mystic. Witter ("Emanuel Morgan") Bynner. But I inclined to every kind,/All seven on one hill. HBV 1-2

Mystic. D. H. Lawrence. Hogging it down like a pig I call the feeding of corpses. WeW

Mystic. Sylvia Plath. The heart has not stopped. NYBP `

The Mystic. Cale Young Rice. Only to stand at last on the strand/Where just beyond lies God. WGRP

The Mystic. Alfred, Lord Tennyson. Investeth and ingirds all other lives. OAEP; VLP

Mystic and Cavalier. Lionel Pigot Johnson. To make with you my home. MoBrPo; SeCePo; VLP

A Mystic as Soldier. Siegfried Sassoon. O music through my clay,/When will you sound again? WGRP

The Mystic Borderland. Helen Field Fischer. Across the distance, in the same old way. WBLP

The Mystic Drum. Gabriel Okara. and turned away; never to beat so loud any more. TTY

The Mystic Magi. Robert Stephen Hawker. And now–once more to die.' OBCP

Mystic River. John Ciardi. That breaks,but calls a million birds to/flight. AmP; NYBP

The Mystic's Prayer. William Sharp. That, when I wake, clear eyed may be/My soul's desire. HBV 1-2; TrPWD; WGRP

Mystical Poets. Amado Nervo. Hath loved your tangled locks enwound. CAW

Mysticism Has Not the Patience to Wait for God's Revelation. Richard Eberhart. The tug of laughter and of irony. MoPo; NoAm

A Myth. Charles Kingsley. The wind will blow, the dawn will glow,/Ere thou hast sailed them through. GN

The Myth. Edwin Muir. Guarding the invisible sheaves/The risen watchers stand. CMoP

Myth. Muriel Rukeyser. ...She said, "That's what/you think." FaBoWP; IHMS; NNaP

The Myth of Arthur. Gilbert Keith Chesterton. You shall not be a myth, I promise you. HBMV

Myth on Mediterranean Beach: Aphrodite as Logos. Robert Penn Warren. And leaves them naked to the day. HAP

The Mythical Journey. Edwin Muir. He builds in faith and doubt his shaking house. NoAm; OxBS

Mythics. Helen Chasin.
–alien, determined/to make it out of this dreary household. DFT
drop into living with my blind, punished hero. DFT
her scaly heart flaking until dawn. DFT
I kept my king, gold, child, and secret. DFT
Now, rewarded, I submit to his transfiguration. DFT
this perpetual ecstasy denies. DFT

Mythmaking. Kathleen Spivack. and all the world fall shadow/to the crumpling of that sheet. NMM

Mythological Sonnet XVI. Roy Fuller. In time fused with divine breasts, buttocks, arms. ErPo

Mythological Sonnets, VIII: "Suns in a skein." Roy Fuller. What fearful monsters slouched about the sky? GTBS-P

Mythology. Lawrence Durrell. O men of the Marmion class, sons of the free. DTC; OxBTC

Mythology. Earle Thompson. I understand my childhood. STE

Mythology. Michael Waters. I already knew the answer. MAYP

The Mythos of Samuel Huntsman. Hyam Plutzik. Who will deal alone with God? LiTM

Myths. Guy Butler. Both eternally lost to news or rumours of spring. PeSA

Myths. Daniel L. Klauck. the most corruptible metaphor/of a faltered humanity LTB

Myths and Texts. Gary Snyder.
All but/Coyote. CAPP; NaP
It was so quiet we could hear the birds. CAPP; NaP
The sun is but a morning star NaP; NeAP; NoP; PoM
Until the deer come down to die/in pity for my pain. CAPP

Myxomatosis. Philip Larkin. If you could only keep quite still and wait. CMoP; ELU; NMP; NoAm; NoP

N

N. Hugh Seidman. Such is the illusion of the stones that challenge air PoA

N. B., Symmetrians. Gene Derwood. The temperate zones are yet more fully manned. LiTA; NePA

N.Y. Ezra Pound. And thou shalt live for ever. NYP

The Nabara. C. Day Lewis. Long after Nabara's passion was quenched in the sea's/heart. HaMV; OBNV

Naboth's Vineyard. John Caryll. And so he left them thunderstruck and dumb,/Stung with their present guilt, and fate to come. APAS

Nache-born Easman. Anonymous. Nachel-born easman ev'ywhere I go. ABF

De Naevo in Facie Faustinae. Thomas Bastard. I know not, but it is a spotless spot. FaBoEE

Nahant. Ralph Waldo Emerson. The sea-beat scorns the minster clock/And breaks the glass of Time. AmPP

Nails. Gary Gildner. Like building dream houses–/no one knows what you mean. TAP

The Naked and the Nude. Robert Graves. How naked go the sometime nude! NYBP; SoSe

Naked I Came. Palladas. Why toil I, then, in vain distress,/Seeing the end is nakedness? NIP

Naked in Borneo. May Swenson. new spirit sneaked in. NYBP

The Naked Land. Kenneth Patchen. ...O gently silent forms/Of the last spaces. EAS

Naked Poetry. Peter Cooley. Screw poetry. Screw flicks. I want you. Write,/XXX Henry SM

The Naked Seed. Clive Staples Lewis. –Because the heaven, moved moth-like by thy beauty, goes/Still turning round the earth. TrCP

Naked War (parody). Michael Heffernan. Walruses idled in the estuaries. BXAP

The Naked World. Rene Sully-Prudhomme. Outward forms, too beautiful, beget only sorrows. ImOP

Nam. Mike Lowery. arms and legs can't be/spliced from old MGM movies Psk; SOTS

Nam Semen Est Verbum Dei. Louise Imogen Guiney. Vows that pure Seed some harvest, ere the snow. CAW

Namaqualand After Rain. William Plomer. The pretty loxia weaves. ACV

Namby-Pamby. Henry Carey. Let the poets, one and all,/To his genius victims fall. FaBoNo; FaBoPa; NOEC; OBSV; Par

The Name. Anonymous. No one knows our name until our last breath goes out. NU

A Name. Maxine Chernoff. ...It was his parents' fault. They/called him Dirk. APU

The Name. Robert Creeley. ...I cannot/be more than the man/who watches. CoPo

The Name. Eileen Duggan. You soon will touch the skies. ISi

The Name. Sara Henderson Hay. What daily chaff and straw they've spun to gold. DFT

The Name. Don (Donald Robert Marquis) Marquis. "All names mean God, perchance!" HBV 1-2

A Name for All. Hart Crane. Struck free and holy in one Name always. PP; VGW

Name Giveaway. Phil George. TWO SWANS ASCENDING FROM STILL WATERS/must be a name too hard to remember. VoR

A Name in the Sand. Hannah Flagg Gould. For glory or for shame. AA

The name–of it–is "Autumn." Emily Dickinson. Then–eddies like a Rose–away–/Upon Vermilion Wheels– InPS; PAI

The Name of Jesus. Annie Johnson Flint. For every danger, every fear,/Our shield and our defender. BePJ

The Name of Jesus. John Newton.
And may the music of thy name/Refresh my soul in death. NOEC; OBEC; TrPWD
'Tis manna to the hungry soul,/And to the weary rest. STF

The Name of Mother. George Griffith Fetter. The blessed name of Mother. PGD

The Name of Our Country. Dennis Schmitz. ...the senses crawl slowly/over the surface not heavy/enough to sink. AmPA

The Name of Washington. Arthur Gordon Field. And bless the name of Washington. PAL; PGD

The Nameless Doon. William Larminie. No faintest sigh of story lisps the wave. AnIL; BIrV; IrPN; NBM; OxBI

A Nameless Epitaph. Matthew Arnold.
Are God's worst portion to mankind. FaBoEE
Remember each unto the end. VLP

Nameless Journey (excerpt). Leah Goldberg. Sometimes I think without a name/of him whose name I don't know. BoWoP

The Nameless Maiden. Anonymous. "Oh there! just there! Oh there! just there!" ErPo

A Nameless One. Margaret Avison. over rips and tears and/thin places. HeIP; NOBC

The Nameless One. James Clarence Mangan. He too had tears for all souls in trouble/Here and in Hell. ACP; BIrV; EnRP; GoBC; HBV 1-2; IrPN; NBM; NOBI; OBEV; OBVV; OnYI; OxBI

The Nameless Ones. Conrad Aiken. and, on a park bench, come to a last decision. NePA; OxBA

A Nameless Recognition. Arthur Gregor. have reached had our shyness and/each other's namelessness been breached. GP

The Nameless Saints. Edward Everett Hale. Count me among all Faithful Souls. WGRP

Names. Dorothy Aldis. Softly,/On a summer's day. SUS

The Names. Lauris Edmond. ...They will sound/in the dreams of your children's children. OCNZ

Names. D. J. Enright. Whose names are on monthly cheques, who have/ succeeded. FaBoCo

Names. Jorge Guillen. But the names still remain. LiTW

Names From the War. Bruce Catton. America's most profound and touching mystery. AmFN

Names in Monterchi: To Rachel. James Wright. ...the rest of/Piero's name is a secret. NNaP

The Names of Georgian Women. Bella Akhmadulina. Natella! a voice answered. BoWoP

Names of Horses. Donald Hall. O Roger, Mackerel, Riley, Ned, Nellie, Chester, Lady Ghost. HAP; LCAP; LLLT; PH

The Names of the Humble. Les A. Murray. I want to speak the names of all the humble. CBAP

The Naming. Terry Hummer. They gave the calf my name. AMV-81

Naming. Joseph Stroud. Catch of night, as slowly he began to name/The far off, alien stars. NPGG

The Naming of Cats. Thomas Stearns Eliot. Deep and inscrutable singular Name. NLV

Naming of Parts. Henry Reed. For to-day we have naming of parts. DTC; FF; GoJo; HeIP; HoPM; InPK; InPS; LiTB; LiTM; MP; NOBE; NoP; PAI; PrIm; SeCePo; SoSe; UnPo; WaP

Naming of Private Parts (parody). John Lloyd Williams. That little room I showed you is not made of perspex. BXAP; FaBoPa

The Naming of the Beasts. Francis Sparshott. the inarticulate brute/finds names for them all. NOBC

Naming Power. Wendy Rose. ...a thirty year old woman/is waiting for her name. TWSS

Naming the Baby. May Richstone. And now we call him by such names/ As "Cookie," "Sugarplum," and Snooks!" BiCB

Naming the Rain. Annette Arkeketa West. I can only roll you under/the carpet now TWSS

Namkwin Pul. Bernard Gutteridge. ...white bottoms–a hundred of them–/ Shock the Burmese lasses. WaP

Nana Kru. *Anonymous.* Nana, I paid/My dowry for you,/Nana, Nana Kru. PBA

Nanak and the Sikhs (excerpt). *Anonymous.* ..how many/shall be emancipated in company with them! WGRP

Nancy Cock. *Anonymous.* Before her old grandmother/Grows a young man. OxNR

Nancy Dawson. Herbert P. Horne. You are Nancy, that old Nancy;/ Nancy Dawson. HBV 1-2

Nancy Hanks. Rosemary and Stephen Vincent Benét. Did he get on? FaBV; LaNeLa; NTCP; PoPl; SiSoSe; TiPo

Nancy Hanks. Harriet Monroe. A battle-flag/And the victor's bays! OHIP

Nancy Hanks, Mother of Abraham Lincoln. Vachel Lindsay. Nancy Hanks had the loveliest face! CMoP

Nancy Lee. *Anonymous.* The sailor's wife his star shall be! AmSS

Nancy, You Dance. Michael L. Johnson. once we have done our dance. AMV-81

Nani. Alberto Rios. Even before I speak, she serves. GP; SM

Nanny. Francis Davis. Queen of the pure hearts, do I love thee! HBV 1-2

Nanny's Sailor Lad. William Allingham. The wave may flow, the breeze may blow,/They'll carry me no more! IrPN

Nano's Song. Ben Jonson. O, who would not be/He, he, he? BoLiVe; LoBV

Nansen. Gary Snyder. And your three-year life has been full/Of mild, steady pain. InPS; PAI

Nantucket. William Carlos Williams. –And the/immaculate white bed. HAP; OxBA; SOTW; TAP; WeW

Nantucket / Mussels / October. Stephen Lewandowski. they steam in wine & anise,/are eaten with butter. WOLT

Nantucket's Widows. Richard Foerster. and race with dolphins at the prow. AMV-81

Nantucket Whalers. Daniel Henderson. Such fortitude and grace/As grudging ocean yields a conquering race. EtS

Nanye'hi (Nancy Ward), the Last Beloved Woman of the Cherokees... Rayna Green. Their silence all these years/doesn't fool anyone TWSS

Naomi Wise. *Anonymous.*
  Don't listen to the story some villain's tongue will tell/Or you are sure to meet Naomi's fate. AmFP
  He owned he was the man that killed poor Oma Wise. BaBo
  The jury correctly the murder did tell. ViBoFo
  No doubt but the jury their minds they could tell. BaBo

Napa, California. Ana Castillo. and the land/that in turn waits/for us... WPOW

Naphtha. Frank O'Hara. but I have to smile ANYP

Napkin and Stone. Vernon Watkins. Here it is found. NYBP

Naples. Samuel Rogers. Still wandering in a City of the Dead! OBTV

Naples Again. Arthur Freeman. may set its simpler meaning over mine. NYBP

Napoleon. Walter De La Mare. Soldiers, this solitude/Through which we go/Is I.' FaBoCh; FaBoTw; LoGBV; MoVE; NOBE

Napoleon and the British Sailor. Thomas Campbell. But never changed the coin and gift/Of Bonaparte. BeLS

Napoleon Hoped That All the World Would Fall beneath His Sway. *Anonymous.* Have thought the thing Napoleon thought was to their/ interest. FaBoCo

Napoli Again. Richard Hugo. Take the extra coin. I only came/to see you living and the fountains run. LCAP

Nappy Edges (A Cross Country Sojourn). Ntozake Shange. this is my space/i am not movin BlSi

Nappy Head Blues. Bobby Grant. And you must want me to lay/down and die for you BluL

Narcissa. Gwendolyn Brooks. While sitting still, as still, as still/As anyone ever sat! GrPl; NTCP

Narcissus. Alistair Campbell. O Echo, Echo. AnNZ

Narcissus. Charles Gullans. What life could not provide/Nor love endure. NePoEA

Narcissus. Donald Petersen. By day the world pursued him and he fled/To its dark night where the clear waters start. NePoEA-2

Narcissus. John Press. My own reflection in wide-opened eyes. UnTE

Narcissus. Paul Valery. As you within the waters, my illimitable soul! AWP

Narcissus and Some Tadpoles. Victor J. Daley. And, like a kite without a tail,/He flops into the hollow vale. PoAu 1-2

Narcissus, Come Kiss Us! *Anonymous.* "Narcissus, shan't miss us, and be by our side!" ErPo

Narcissus in a Cocktail Glass. Frances Minturn Howard. Sleep came instead, in a three-cornered skull/Shaped much like death's, and oddly beautiful. GoYe

Narcissus in Camden (parody). Helen Gray Cone. Paumonikides/So long! BXAP

Narcissus: To Himself. David Galler. That sometimes show what's left of me! PoA

Narrative. Russell Atkins. "if's, in, ss'd/shsh" erced/"ft/"isk PoBA

Narrative. Louis Dudek. That here we cannot live or love the same again. CaP

Narrative. Elisabeth Eybers. ...this tranquil strength/is better than the thing she's waiting for. PeSA

The Narrative Hooper and L.D.O. Sestina with a Long Last Line. James Whitehead. "Peace, Sheriff," said the hairy man, "I'm no hooper–I'm/from Dumas, Arkansas." HoPM; TAT

The Narrow Door. Charlotte Mew. And one pays down with pebbles from the shore. SBG

The Narrow Doors. Fannie Stearns Gifford. The Doors that let the dark leap in/Across my sunny life! HBMV

A narrow Fellow in the Grass. Emily Dickinson. And Zero at the Bone– AmPP; AtBAP; BoWoP; CMoP; DiPo; ExPo; FaFP; FM; FPL; GoJo; HAP; HoPM; LiTA; LiTM; MAmP; MAPA; MoAB; NIP; NOBA; NoP; OBCA; OxBA; PoEL 1-5; PoLf; PPoe; PPP; SeCeV; SoSe; TAP; WeW

The Narrow Sea. Robert Graves. Death's narrow but oppressive sea/Looks not unnavigable to me. FaBoEE; FaBoMo; MOS

The Narrows. Joseph Bruchac. twin magnets/drawing each other towards sunset. FAZ

The Narrows of Birth. William Everson. Warring in the narrows of this birth. PoM

Naseby: Late Autumn. Basil Dowling. Musing on man and mineral, and take/This gleam of greed home in an envelope. AnNZ

Nashville Stonewall Blues. Robert Wilkins. I get out I'm going to that woman, I'll/be right back again BluL

Naso, You're All Men's Man. Caius Valerius Catullus. Although you try your best to please/Any man–on your hands and knees. DBV

Nat Turner. Samuel ("Paul Vesey") Allen. let him come. CNA; FB

Natalya Nikolayevna Goncharov. Don Coles. Bless it. Soon. Can she talk? NOBC

Nathan Hale. *Anonymous.* No fears for the brave; no fears for the/brave. PAH

Nathan Hale. Francis Miles Finch. The name of HALE shall burn! MC; PAH; PAL

Nathan Hale. William Ordway Partridge. But one poor life, that my own land may live! PAL

Nathaniel Lee to Sir Roger L'Estrange, Who Visited Him in His Madhouse. Nathaniel Lee. I am strange Lee altered; you are still L'e-Strange. FaBoEE

Nation. Charlie Cobb. Nation/Strength/People/(now) PoBA

Nation. Mendel Naigreshel. He is the primal rock. VWA

A Nation Once Again. Thomas Davis. When my dear country shall be made/A Nation once again. NOBI

A Nation's Strength (excerpt). Ralph Waldo Emerson. And lift them to the sky. AmFN; PAL; PGD; TRV

A Nation's Wealth. John Dyer. ...and the wide main/Wooes us in ev'ry port? OBEC

A Nation Wrapped in Stone. Roberta Hill. and time to watch rain soak the trees. BoWoP; CDW

National Cold Storage Company. Harvey Shapiro. ...all the years of our lives. MAT; NYP; VGW

The National Gallery. Louis MacNeice. ...rekindle a/pentecost in Trafalgar Square. EyDe

A National Hymn. John William DeForest. God stand its sentinel/For evermore. PAL

The National Miner. Anonymous. There the miners are a-digging, digging in the cold, damp ground. AmFP

The National Ode. Bayard Taylor. And the greater task, for thee to live! PAH

National Presage. John Kells Ingram. They know not what—but surely something great. OnYI

National Song. William Henry Venable. Imperial to save! MC; PAH

National Winter Garden. Hart Crane. Lug us back lifeward—bone by infant bone. AmP; ErPo; LiTM; OxBA

Nationalism. Harry Roskolenko. And we'll dance internationally. Dance! Dance! Dance! AMV-80

Nationality. Mary Gilmore. This loaf is my son's bread. BoAV; CBAP; PoAu 1-2

Nations. Michael Brownstein. Little tables around the world. ANYP

Nations That Long in Darkness Walked. John Barnard. His reign forever shall endure. AH

The Native. William Stanley Merwin. Like air rising through thin ice, feed themselves forth/To inherit the earth. NePoEA-2

Native African Revolutionaries. Paul Jones. At dawn there are no ripe mangoes/for miles. AMV-80

Native-Born. Eve Langley. And native with night, that land from whence they came. BoAV; PoAu 1-2

The Native Irishman. Anonymous. They rule themselves they'll be as good,/Almost, as Englishmen! OnYI

Native Moments. Walt Whitman. I will be more to you than to any of the rest. NePA; OxBA

Native Origin. Beth Brant. They tend the fire, and wait. STE

Native Working on the Aerodrome. Roy Fuller. For bombers; and bears the earth upon his head. NeBP

The Natives. David Mura. the hair on our shoulders dangles and shines. BrSi

The Natives of America. Ann Plato. Remember this, though I tell no more. BlSi

Nativitie. John Donne. With his kinde mother, who partakes thy woe. AnAnS 1; OBS

The Nativity. Anonymous. He us all to Heven bring,/Qui mortem Cruce voluit. MeEL

Nativity. Gladys May Casely Hayford. And kissed their motherhood into his mother's eyes. CDC

Nativity. Linda Hogan. The smell/comes from stone. TWSS

A Nativity. Rudyard Kipling. It is well—it is well with the child! NAs

The Nativity. Clive Staples Lewis. Oh that my baa-ing nature would win thence/Some woolly innocence! EBCP; TrCP

Nativity. James Montgomery. Worship Christ the new-born King. NOCV; OBRV

Nativity. W. R. Rodgers. And in its head set the heart's singing birds. NeBP

Nativity. May Sarton. Here is love, naked, lying in great state/On the bare ground, as in all human faces. NePoAm-2

The Nativity. Henry Vaughan. And say once more, Let there be light. SBVL

The Nativity. Charles Wesley. Peace on earth, and mercy mild;/God and sinners reconciled. BLRP

The Nativity Chant. Sir Walter Scott. Keep the house frae reif and wear. FaBoCh; LoGBV; NAs

Nativity Ode. Saint Cosmas. "God of our Fathers! Thou art blessed!" CAW

The Nativity of Christ. Luis de Gongora y Argote. That flower had fallen,—that crimson blossom. CAW

The Nativity of Christ. Robert Southwell. O happy field wherein this fodder grew,/Whose taste doth us from beasts to men renew. EBCP

Nativity Song. Jacopone da Todi. O King, in my hour of danger,/Wilt thou be strong for me? OHIP

Natura Naturans. Arthur Hugh Clough. Or ever yet to young desire/Was told the mystic name of Love. HAP; NOBV; VLP

Natura Naturans. Kathleen Raine. Empty chrysalids of that bright ephemerid the soul. NYBP

Natural Architecture. John Hay. Or else, how should we bless what we receive? NePoAm

Natural Causes. Winfield Townley Scott. Of the girl running toward me forever through the/cloversunned field. LiTL

Natural History. Anonymous. That's what young women are made of. OxNR

Natural History. Laura Fargas. ...bigger than/this poem, smaller than the whole world. SUW

Natural History. Richard Howard. The heart of our green season. TAP

Natural History. Robert Penn Warren. They must learn to stay in their graves. That is what graves are for. FF

Natural History (excerpt). Harold Monro. The vixen woman/Who came my way. OBMV

A Natural History of Dragons and Unicorns My Daughter and I Have Known. William Pitt Root. held in that eye of his, which is every bit as real/as he is invisible. AMV-81; SM

The Natural History of Pliny. Vincent McHugh. Why do I watch your face? NePoAm-2

A Natural History of Southwestern Ontario, III. Christopher Dewdney. Who would have abandoned so young a child this deeply in the/woods? CaPN

Natural Law. Babette Deutsch. Sir Isaac said nothing of. MoLP

Natural Magic. Robert Browning. A fairy-tale! Only—I feel it! VLP

The Natural Order of Things. Harley Elliott. beginning a new row. NeAC

Natural Selection. Summer Brenner. In Oaxaca I was loudly scolded for feeling pineapples too long. APU

The Naturalist's Summer-Evening Walk. Gilbert White. Leander hastened to his Hero's bed. NOEC; PBBP

Naturally. Audre Lorde. Proud beautiful black women/Could better make and use/Black bread. BlSi; CNA

Naturally the Foundation Will Bear Your Expenses. Philip Larkin. (He once met Morgan Forster)/My contact and my pal. FaBoPV

Nature. John Clare. But there are souls that in this lovely hour/Know all I mean, and feel whate'er I feel. CBEP

Nature. George Herbert. And a much fitter stone/To hide my dust then thee to hold. OAEP

Nature. Henry Wadsworth Longfellow. How far the unknown transcends the what/we know. AA; AmePo; AmLP; AnNE; AP; AWP; FaBoBe; FPL; GoTF; InPo; PoLf; TAP; TrGrPo; TRV; WHA

Nature. Walter Stone. But found themselves beguiled, beguiled/By her indifferent breast. NYBP

Nature. Henry David Thoreau. To have one moment of thy dawn,/Than share the city's year forlorn. BLPL; FaBoBe; HBV 1-2

Nature. Jones Very. Hear from his Father's lips that all is good. AP; HBV 1-2

Nature. Alfred de Vigny. And by my breast and brows the airs be riven. AWP

Nature and the Poets. James Beattie. Teach beauty, virtue, truth, and love, and melody. OBEC; SeCePo

Nature at Three. Bettye Breeser. The brand new world of Nature holds/So much for him to see! BiCB

Nature Be Damned. Anne Wilkinson. Then roused from this reality I saw/Nothing, anywhere, but snow. NOBC; OBCV; PeCV

Nature Green Shit. Gary Snyder. hey that's my cat!/Coming home. LCAP

Nature in Couplets. Charlton Ogburn. Before I die, a book-eared dog. GrPl

Nature in Her Working. Richard Stanyhurst. Her vertu meriteth more prayse, than parlye can utter. NCEP

Nature in War-Time. Herbert Palmer. But little recks the world in its distress/The sorrow that is silent on the hill. HaMV

"Nature" Is What We See. Emily Dickinson. So impotent Our Wisdom is/To her Simplicity. MAmP

Nature Morte. Louis MacNeice. Exudes from the dried fish and the brown jug and the bowl. NoAm

Nature Note. Arthur Guiterman. They hop because they do not choose/To run. SUS

Nature Notes (excerpt). Louis MacNeice. We have to surrender, finding/Through that surrender life. FaBoIP

The Nature of an Action. Thom Gunn. Only my being there is different. ACV; NePoEA

The Nature of Jungles. W. R. Moses. Every day, walking the city jungles. NCSH

The Nature of Love. James Kirkup. Can split the infinite of light/That shutters nothing out. EaLo

The Nature of Man. C. H. Sisson. If we have reasons, they lie deep. FaBoTw

The Nature of the Eagle. Anonymous. And he can take the food for his soul,/Through the grace of our dear Lord. PBBP

The Nature of the Turtle Dove. Anonymous. His hated foes to hell shall fare,/His lovers to his realm. PBBP

Nature's Charms. James Beattie. Flocks, herds, and waterfalls, along the hoar profound! OBEC

Nature's Cook. Margaret Cavendish, Duchess of Newcastle. When with salt rheum and phlegm they powdered are. PBWP

Nature's Creed. *Anonymous*. For in all of these appeareth clear/The handiwork of God. OHIP

Nature's Easter Music. Lucy Larcom. And double its gladness so. OHIP

Nature's Hymn to the Deity. John Clare. The first link in the mighty plan/Is still–and all upbraideth man. EBCP; VLP

Nature's Influence on Man. Mark Akenside. And form to his the relish of their souls. CEP; OBEC

Nature's Key-Notes. Thomas Caulfield Irwin. The Cricket cheers the dusk with mirth. IrPN

Nature's Lineaments. Robert Graves. Whose fish, fish. FaBoTw

Nature's Questioning. Thomas Hardy. And Earth's old glooms and pains/Are still the same, and Life and Death are neighbors nigh CoBMV; InPo; MoPo; TEP; VLP

Nature's Travail. *Anonymous*. ...then ceased from bearing evermore. AWP

Nature Study, after Dufy. Helen Bevington. The look of April, after this,/When it, too, is hypothesis. NYBP

Nature, that gave the bee so feat a grace. Sir Thomas Wyatt. In change whereof I leave my heart behind. FCP

Nature, That Washed Her Hands in Milk. Sir Walter Ralegh. Shuts up the story of our days. CABA; FCP; NoP

Nature: The Artist. Frederic Lawrence Knowles. The careless carpentry of snow! AA

The Naughty Blackbird. Kate Greenaway. And what shall we do to the Blackbird/Who listens unawares? HBVY

Naughty Boy. Robert Creeley. ...Uncle Jim's deep-fired, all-fat, real gone/whale steaks. NoAm

The Naughty Lord & the Gay Young Lady. *Anonymous*. And beat old Mr December,/Who seduced young Lady May. CoMu

The Naughty Preposition. Morris Bishop. And yet I wondered: "What should he come/Up from out of in under for?" FiBHP; NLV; NYBP; PV

Nausea. Catherine Davis. And feeds itself alone. NePoEA

Nausea. E. L. Mayo. ..."Get about your business, Paraclete!" MiAP

Nausicaa. Irving Layton. but on her or my raincoat go roughly to it. ErPo

Nausicaa with Some Attendants. Tom Lowenstein. these were whispered/to have dull authority. VWA

A Nautical Extravaganza. Wallace Irwin. But I ain't worth a darn, at spinnin' a yarn/What wanders away from the truth. StPo

Nauty Pauty Jack-a-Dandy. *Anonymous*. And away did hoppy-hop. OxNR

Nauvoo. Bayard Taylor. So that thy brethren may see it and say, "Go thou and do likewise!" OBAL

The Navajo. Elizabeth Jane Coatsworth. You may pass close by their encampments and never/know. AmFN

Navajo. William Haskel Simpson. What it has found out, running,/Is not told to me,/Though I ask. BPAW

Navajo Song. Maynard Dixon. Go, stepping soft in your star-buttoned moccasins, A-zlay. BPAW

Naval Engagement. Tom Veitch. Tee hee. ANYP

The Navigators. Walter James Turner. Slow winding silver tracks of slime/Showed bright where came back none. OBMV

Nay, Ivy, Nay. *Anonymous*. Let Holly have the mastery as the manner is. CBEP; CH

Ndaaya's Kasala (excerpt). Citeku Ndaaya. Mbombo/silence PBWP

Ne Plus Ultra. Samuel Taylor Coleridge. Save to the Lampads Seven,/That watch the throne of Heaven! ERoP 1-2; OAEL 1-2

Neaera's Kisses. Johannes Secundus. Yes, my Neaera! yes, 'tis thee! UnTE

Neaera When I'm There Is Adamant. George Buchanan. But that my pain is unenjoyed. OBVE

Neanderthal. Michael Jackson. are buried here. OCNZ

Near. Abba Kovner. where are you/and me. VWA

Near. William Stafford. but nothing will happen until we pause/to flame what we know, before any signal's given. ConAP

Near a Waterfall at Ryumon. Lady Ise. displaying to us her white robes? BoWoP

Near an Old Prison. Frances Cornford. Or through thick time must we reach back in vain/To inaccessible pain? OBMV

Near Avalon. William Morris. In all their heaumes some yellow hair. CBEP; OAEL 1-2

Near Barbizon. Galway Kinnell. ...this intellectual, this rich American, this/fascist boss! NePoAm-2

Near Dover, September, 1802. William Wordsworth. Only, the nations shall be great and free. EnLi 1-2; EnRP; MBW 1-2

Near Drowning. Ralph Pomeroy. holding,/holding/to keep. DFF

Near Helikon. Trumbull Stickney. And the girl closed her window not to hear. AnFE; LiTA; NCEP

Near Lanivet, 1872. Thomas Hardy. Some day.–Alas, alas! AWP; CMoP; LoBV; NoAm

Near Neighbors. Martial (Marcus Valerius Martialis). Must be his neighbor or his lodger. AWP

Near Perigord. Ezra Pound. A broken bundle of mirrors....! CABL; FaBoMo; LiTA; LiTM

Near the Base Line. Samuel L. Albert. Death will be lurking near the base lines. NePoAm-2

Near the Border of Insanities. Dannie Abse. where the sad journey home is no journey,/but a reawakening still yet in dream. PoA

Near the Death of Ovid. Robert Conquest. Was their passion for sex or reason a sharper/Edge to the great gift?–Yes. NoAm

Near the Lake. George Pope Morris. It taught me how to die. AA

Near the Ocean. Robert Lowell. till time, that buries us, lay bare. NOBA

Near the School for Handicapped Children. Thomas W. Shapcott. leaving us all behind like a skimming tambourine/brittle with music. CBAP

Nearer. Judith Herzberg. ...as stake/for a new start only the fact/that scorched earth can still be used. BoWoP; VWA

Nearer Home. Phoebé Cary. On the rock of a living faith! AA; AnAmPo; BLRP; FaFP; HBV 1-2; TreF; WBLP; WGRP

Nearer, My God, to Thee. Sarah Flower Adams. Nearer, my God, to thee,/Nearer to thee. FaBoBe; FaFP; FSW; GoTF; HBV 1-2; PoLf; TreF; VLP; WBLP; WGRP

The Nearest Friend. Frederic W. Faber. But when I sleep, Thou sleepest not,/But watchest patiently. TreFS

Nearing Again the Legendary Isle. C. Day-Lewis. From purple rhetoric of evening skies. CoBMV; FaBoTw; LiTB; MoAB; MoBrPo

Nearing La Guaira. Derek Walcott. Nothing is bitter and is very deep. TTY

Nearing Winter. Ernest Sandeen. to forgive an earth that shakes so/with savage important noise? NYBP

Nearly Everybody Loves Harvey Martin. William D. Barney. How are the mighty fallen/and the weapons of war, are they perished! LiSp

Nebraska. Jon Swan. This was the bed of forgotten seas; this wheat is/blossoming. RFM

Nebuchadnezzar. Irwin Russell. By now I 'spect he's grazin'/On de odder side de creek. HBV 1-2

Nebuchadnezzar. Elinor Wylie. But the clover is honey and sun and the smell of sleep. MoAmPo; SBG

Nebuchadnezzar's Kingdom-Come. David Rowbotham. ...beasts set free/On captured innocence in the den,/Confounding deities, not men. NOAV

A Necessary Miracle. Eda Lou Walton. This shall be called the laying on of hands/and a farewell. NYBP

A Necessitarian's Epitaph. Thomas Hardy. Till they sink down and feel no more. FaBoEE

Necessities of Life. Adrienne Rich. like old women knitting, breathless/to tell their tales. HaCAP; NIP; NoAm; NOBA

Necessity. Harry Graham. But I had to stop her snoring! FaBoCo

Necessity. Langston Hughes. Which is why I reckon I does/have to work after all. NOBA

The Necessity of Rejection. James Schevill. My body shakes with the will to endure. FAZ

Nechama. Shirley Kaufman. like a hole in the ice/where a child fell in. LCAP

Neckwear. Michael Silverton. a view to being recalled as one/of Fashion's tragic figures. PV

The Necromancers. John Frederick Nims. The princess flings our halo, knife by knife. PoCh

Necropolis. Karl Shapiro. But only multiply in the green grass. MoAB; PoA

Ned Braddock. John Williamson Palmer. Steeple and State!" said the Axe to the Sword. MC; PAH

Ned Bratts. Robert Browning. Where Bunyan's Statue stands facing where stood his Jail. CABL; VLP

Ned Christie. Robert J. Conley. he was a blacksmith/and was/a brave/man. STE

Ned's Delicate Way. Henry Lawson. "Try a smoke, and let's know what you think of it." CBAP

Ned Vaughan. Walter De la Mare. And folded both sheepdog/And Shepherd in Sleep. FaBoEE

Neddy Nibble'm and Biddy Finn. *Anonymous*. And I'm dashed if ever I do, sirs,/O! no I won't. GBP

Need. Babette Deutsch. Who with each heartbeat fight the fear of change. MoLP; PCP

The Need. Siegfried Sassoon. O move in mercy among us. Grant accepted grace. TrPWD

Need Is Our Name. Luci Shaw. Triumph/Is Yours. TrCP

Need of an Angel. Raymond Souster. Who lead through forests of darkness to the dawn? CaP

The Need of Being Versed in Country Things. Robert Frost. One had to be versed in country things/Not to believe the phoebes wept. NoAm; NOBA; OxBA; UnPo

Need of Loving. Strickland Gillilan. Folks need a lot of loving all the while. BLPA; PoToHe; WBLP

The Need of the Hour. Edwin Markham. The power to be alone and vote with God. PAL

The Need to Love. Shlomo Vinner. The ability to love is the ability to leave/And move on. VWA

The Needle. Grace Cornell Tall. In triumph through the needle's/ Microscopic arch. GoYe

The Needle. Samuel Woodworth. The needle directed by beauty and art. GN; HBV 1-2

Needle and Thread. Pan Chao. They may carve monuments yet lack all understanding. WPOW

The Needle's Eye. Anonymous. You, oh you, because I wanted you. AmFP

Needle Travel. Margaret French Patton. But the trip around the garment's hem/Is not the path I tread. HBMV

Needles and Pins. Mark Van Doren. And off went Rumpelstiltskin, mumbling. SO

The Needles' Lighthouse from Keyhaven, Hampshire. Charles Tennyson Turner. ...Those who dwell/Near these great beacons are instructed well. FaBoPP

The Needless Alarm. John Ruskin. of of FM

Needless Worry. Ralph Waldo Emerson. But what torments of grief you endured/From evils which never arrived! GoTF; TreFT

Needs. Archie Randolph Ammons. I want to mow while riding. NIP; OBAL

Needs. Elizabeth Rendall. Cotton threads and clear clean water and jesting and a/friend. HBMV

Needs Must I Leave, and Yet Needs Must I Love. Henry Constable. For as my heart is love, love not in me,/So beauty thou, beauty is not in thee. InvP

Negative Passage. Michael Newman. The creatured Image became the Likeness. PoA

The Negatives. Philip Levine.
...caught in a strange country/for which no man would die. NePoEA-2
...knowing our pain/is not theirs or caused by them. NePoEA-2
listen that old command/dreaming of authority. NePoEA-2
...The one word/my mouth must open to is why. NePoEA-2

Negatives. Charles Wright. The blackout like scarves in our new hair. PoA

Neglectful Edward. Robert Graves. "Have you nothing better for Nancy?" BrPo; MoBrPo

Negritude. James A. Emanuel. Black the way a hero dies. BPo; CNA

The Negro. James A. Emanuel. A-ness never/Had a chance. BPo; HoPM

A Negro Cemetery Next to a White One. Howard Nemerov. Separate but equal where it counts. OBSP

Negro Dreams. Doughtry Long. to shack with history/for the night. PoBA

Negro Hero. Gwendolyn Brooks. To the continuation of their creed/And their lives. CAPP

A Negro Judge. Frederick Seidel. Brownish white, whitish brown—and sings. CoPo

A Negro Love Song. Paul Laurence Dunbar. Jump back, honey, jump back. BANP; PoNe

A Negro Peddler's Song. Fenton Johnson. And also sweet potat-y. AmNP

Negro Poets. Charles Bertram Johnson. And point our souls the way? BANP

Negro Reel (with music). Anonymous. Kiss him twice and hug him, too. AS

The Negro's Tragedy. Claude McKay. This Negro laughs and prays to God for Light! BPo

Negro Serenade. James Edwin Campbell. An' stops dis ha't f'um sighin'! BANP

Negro Servant. Langston Hughes. O, sweet relief from faces that are white! VGW

The Negro Singer. James David Corrothers. Nor my dark face dishonor any song. BANP

A Negro Soldier's Viet Nam Diary. Herbert Martin. Have you prayed, lately, for that? PoBA

The Negro Soldiers. Roscoe Conkling Jamison. That those who mock might find a better way! BANP

The Negro Speaks of Rivers. Langston Hughes. My soul has grown deep like the rivers. AmFN; AmNP; BANP; BPo; CDC; GoSl; HaCAP; HAP; HeIP; IDB; NIP; NoAm; NOBA; NoP; OBCA; PoBA; PoNe; TAP; TTY

Negro Spiritual. Perient Trott. Oh, sable is my throat! PoNe

Negro Spirituals. Rosemary and Stephen Vincent Benét. But David's harp was gold. AmFN

Negro Woman. Lewis Alexander. Like the quiver of a Negro woman's eyelids cupping/tears. CDC; PoBA

Negroes. Maxwell Bodenheim. Like a quavering, feverish laugh/Softened in a long-forgotten cradle. PoNe

Nehi Blues. Blind Willie (Joe) Reynolds. They work hard all the time trying to stay in these young men's ways/Mmmmmmmmmmmmmmmnmmmmm BluL

Neighbor. Charles Waterman. little long necks stretching to the sun. GP

The Neighbor. Miller Williams. he's set about building something in his barn/and it's big. GP

Neighborly. Violet Alleyn Storey. 'Cause that way we get two desserts/ Instead of only one! TiPo

Neighbors. David Allan Evans. Now they are waving/to each other/with rags,/not smiling. Psk

Neighbors. Marilyn Francis. The chimney smoke we saw was bramble fire. GoYe

The Neighbors. Theodosia Garrison. I watched them through the swinging gate—the dawn/Stayed till the last had gone. HBMV

Neighbors. Lennox.
Furthermore, he stutters. DBV
Think that I am not so torrid. InMe

Neighbors. Charles Malam. Characteristic of his neighbors. AMV-80

Neighbors. Anne Spencer. You must have a soul to clutch. CDC

The Neighbors Help Him Build His House. Anonymous. And here be the house of the Lord! LiTW

The Neighbors of Bethlehem. Anonymous. A palace fair for greatest king! OHIP

Neighbour. J. R. Hervey. The news is spoken. AnNZ

The Neighing North. Annie Charlotte Dalton. "Thule? Thule? There's no Ultima Thule for man!" CaP

Neila. Yvan Goll. God's ancient cry VWA

Neither Blemish This Book, Nor the Leaves Double Down. Anonymous. And each book in my study your pleasure attends. FaBoUs

Neither Here Nor There. W. R. Rodgers. Though at night there is the smell of morning. LiTB; LiTM; MoAB; MoBrPo; NeBP; ViBoPo

Neither Hook nor Line. John Bunyan. Or they will not be catch'd, whate'er you do. LiSp; SD

Neither Out Far Nor In Deep. Robert Frost. But when was that ever a bar/To any watch they keep? AmP; AP; CoBMV; CrMA; DiPo; HAP; LiTA; MoAB; MOS; NoAm; NOBA; NoP; TAP; WeW

Neither Shadow of Turning. Jack R. Clemo. HIS gifts never mystified. NOCV

Neither Spirit Nor Bird. Anonymous. That was my heart you heard/ Leaping under the willows. AWP; BPAW; PG

Neither This Nor That. Luis Palés Matos. one half Spanish,/the other African. InW

Nekros. John Banister Tabb. Arise! thou has inherited the sky. AmP

Nell Flaherty's Drake. Anonymous.
And so ends the song of my beautiful drake. AnIV
On the monster that murdered Nell Flaherty's drake. OnYI
There ends the whole tale of Nell Flaherty's drake. TW

Nell Gwynne's Looking-Glass. Laman Blanchard. Was that face by beauty's spell/To the honest soul of Nell. HBV 1-2

Nelly Bly. Stephen Collins Foster. I'll sing for you and play for you/A dulcet melody. FSW

Nelly Trim. Sylvia Townsend Warner. And afraid of the dark,/As his fathers were. ErPo; MoAB; MoBrPo

Nelson's Death. Anonymous. All the world with Lord Nelson they would not compare. OBET

Nelson's Death and Victory. Anonymous. May this turn the heart of our enemy./Huzza, my brave boys. OBSS

Nelson Street. Seumas (James Starkey) O'Sullivan. "There's a Land that is Fairer than This." OxBI

Nemea. Lawrence Durrell. Quiet, Quiet, Quiet. ChMP; FaBoTw; GTBS-P

Nemea 11 (excerpt). Pindar. and be a theme of elaboration in the deep, sweet singing. SD

Nemean Ode: VI. Pindar. a man to guide the strength in a boy's hands. LiTW

Nemesis. Ralph Waldo Emerson. Tighter wind the giant coils. AtBAP; NOBA

Neni, Coronaberis. Anonymous. Thus endeth the song of great sweettness,/ Veni, coronaberis. BoW

Neo-Classical Poem. William Jay Smith. He is. As you imagined Him. WaP

Neo-Thomist Poem. Ernest Hemingway. ...I shall not/want him for long. OBAL

Neoplatonic Soliloquy. Donald Campbell Babcock. O Soul, within thine house make room. NePoAm

Nepenthe. George Darley.
Ceaseless her joyful deathwail she/Sang to departing Araby! OBNC; OBRV
Far athwart his lair I run. NBM; OBNC; OBRV; PoEL 1-5
Hoopoe, if of that tribe which sing/Articulate in the desert ring! OBNC; OBRV; PBBP
Make rich the winds with minstrelsy. OBNC

New Jersey Turnpike. Richard Cumbie. I paid graciously to be allowed Delaware. NLV

New Jersey White-Tailed Deer. Joyce Carol Oates. It will not melt but must be chewed.) GeTw

The New Jerusalem. *Anonymous.* Would God my woes were at an end,/ Thy joys that I might see. HBV 1-2; OBEV; OxBoCh; ViBoPo

The New Jewish Hospital at Hamburg. Heinrich Heine. With which he often wept the vast/and hopeless/Incurable affliction of his brothers. TrJP

New King Arrives in His Capital by Air... Sir John Betjeman. Where a young man lands hatless from the air. OxBoLi

A New Leaf. Kathleen Wheeler. "Do better, now, my child." PGD; WBLP

New Leaves. Juan Ramon Jimenez. Look how the golden children/Are climbing the silver poplars to the sky! PoPl

New Life. Amelia Josephine Burr. Raise a slender stalk of words/From a root unseen. HBV 1-2

New Life. Joseph E. Kariuki. And life is born anew. TTY

New Lines for Cuscuscaraway and Mirza Murad Ali Beg. Louis Simpson. I will sing unto the Lord/In a voice that is cheerfully dry. OBAL

The New Litany. Rita Mae Brown. As Venus in her ascendency/Draws triangulations on reality. PeHV

A New Litany in the Year 1684. *Anonymous.* And from the Star Chamber in Westminster Hall,/Libera nos Domine. APAS

The New London. John Dryden. And gently lay us on the Spicy shore. FaBoCh

New Love. Martial (Marcus Valerius Martialis). When in his arms young Ganymede/Snuggles and lifts warm lips to kiss. PeHV

New Love, New Life. Amy Levy. But this time is the last. OBVV

The New Man. Jones Very. And bid them seek with morn the hills and fields once more. AP; NOBA

The New Manong. Luis Syquia. burning the/bleeding/sun BrSi

The New Married Couple. *Anonymous.* If I can, my Wife will hold almost a year,/this Riddle me Riddle nine months will clear. CoMu

The New Mars. Florence Earle Coates. For peace on earth–a lasting peace, and just! PGD

New Maths. Tom Lehrer. It's so simple, so very simple/That only a child can do it! FaBoUs

New Mexican Desert. Witter ("Emanuel Morgan") Bynner. Out of the desert, out of sight,/Into the solid sky. BPAW

New Mexican Mountain. Robinson Jeffers. ...remember that/civilization is a transient sickness. InPS; NoAm; PAI

New Mexico. Polly Chase Boyden. Then outdoors is Out West,/But indoors is Home. TiPo

New Mexico and Arizona. George Canterbury. I'll take, to prove myself sincere,/My "davy'–on a Mormon Bible. PoOW

New Minglewood Blues. Noah, Jug Band Lewis's. They got womens in the camp don't/mean no man no good BluL

The New Mistress. Alfred Edward Housman. And the enemies of England, they shall see me and be sick. MoBrPo

The New Moon. Edmund Charles Blunden. Fearing the firmament to be the Khan/Of grotesque Caliph or blotched Caliban. BrPo

The New Moon. Kobayashi Issa. How keen the cold! MOON

New Moon. D.H. Lawrence. brings a fresh fragrance of heaven to our senses. BoNaP

The New Moon. Sara Teasdale. When a maiden moon wakes up in the sky? MOON

New Moses. Michael Kennedy Joseph. The cherub with the fiery sword/ Was waiting there as well. AnNZ

The New Mothers. Carol Shields. the fathers/are coming Str

New Music. Gwen Harwood. pierced by a brilliant nerve of sound. CBAP

New National Anthem. *Anonymous.* But hell, we'll take the pike/If this don't stop. CoSo

New National Hymn. Francis Marion Crawford. Take Thou, at last, our souls to Thine eter-/nal peace. PAH

The New Navigation. *Anonymous.* For the cut of all cuts is a Birmingham cut. OBET

The New Negro. James Edward McCall. Holding his destiny within his hands. CDC

The New Neighbor. Rose Fyleman. Do you think your mother/Will ask me in to tea? SoPo; TiPo

New Night Thoughts on Death. A Parody. William Whitehead. Fools banter heav'n itself, O Young!–and thee! NOEC

The New Notebook. Maria Banus. only of waves/which come and go. PBWP

New Numbers: Foreword. Christopher Logue. but most of all I want my poems sung/unthinkingly between your lips like air. OxBTC

The New Nutcracker Suite (excerpt). Ogden Nash. And the toys came dancing from the Christmas tree/To celebrate the famous victory. PCh

The New Order. Phyllis McGinley. And the Kennedys talk on TV. AmFN

A New Order of Chivalry. Thomas Love Peacock. May have more of King Richard than Moses and Co. CenHV

New Orleans. Hayden Carruth. O King of the Zulus, consecrate me! AmFN

New Orleans. Joy Harjo. dancing with a woman as gold/as the river bottom. STE; TWSS

A New Orleans Balcony–1880. Dorothy Haight. Framing her like the borders of a valentine! CAW

A New Patriotism. Chauncey R. Piety. And as deep as the Kingdom of God. PGD

The New Physician. Stephen Chalmers. Such things made even half-real, 'twere not vain/To be a poet ministering to pain! HBMV

The New Pieta: For the Mothers and Children of Detroit. June Jordan. he moves no more PoBA

The New Platform Dances. Jack A. Mapanje. ...Haven't I/Danced the bigger dance?/Haven't I? WhB

The New Poem. Charles Wright. It will not be able to help us. GeTw; HaCAP

A New Poem (for Jack Spicer). Robert Duncan. a bird I cannot name crows. NNaP; PoM

A New Poet. William Canton. We two have made the angels smile! HBV 1-2

A New Poet Arrives. Gavin Ewart. Change, in the Arts, is nearly always good. OxBTC

New Potatoes. Ken Belford. Left from even/The most casual touch? NeAC

New Prince, New Pomp. Robert Southwell. And highly praise his humble pomp,/Which he from heaven doth bring. AnAnS 1; EG; ELP; GN; NOBE; NOCV; OBSC; OHIP; SBVL; TrCP

New Proverb. Shirley Brooks. Is the way to feel stupid and have red eyes. FaBoNo

The New Ring. Karl Shapiro. ...and the body hangs from/the nail, and the nail holds. MoLP

The New River Head, a Fragment. E. Dower. I leaned upon my staff and fell asleep.' NOEC

New River Train. *Anonymous.* It's soon gonna carry me away. FSW

New Romance. Nellie Wong. study, cook oxtail stew, and walk on picket lines. BrSi

The New Roof. Francis Hopkinson. Our government firm, and our citizens free. PAH

The New Saddhus. Robert Pinsky. Pack straps and belts, fading from their embarrassed bodies! MAYP

New Sea Song. *Anonymous.* But we will spend them on shore with our sweethearts and wives. OBSS

New Season. Philip Levine. ...all/the small secret mouths are feeding/on the green heart of the plum. NNaP

A New Shirt! Why? Paul L. Grano. and forget the shirt. PoAu 1-2

New Shoes. Marjorie Seymour Watts. I listen to its happy squeak. SoPo

New Shoes. Alice Wilkins. Whenever I wear my new shoes/I always have to sing! SUS; TiPo

A New Siege: An Historical Meditation (excerpt). John Montague. (a flock of swans)/drives forward CIP

A New Simile in the Manner of Swift. Oliver Goldsmith. Our modern bards! why what a pox/Are they but senseless stones and blocks? LAuP

New Skills. Naomi Shihab Nye. And I am not yet ready to go home. PH

The New-Slain Knight. *Anonymous.* And if I live and brook my life/Ye'se never hae cause to rue.' ESPB

New Snow. Catharine Bryant Rowles. The wonder of winter/And new white snow! YeAr

The New Song. Arthur Gordon Field. Till all the world is fired/With love that shall not fail. PGD

A New Song. Seamus Heaney. A vocable, as rath and bullaun. FaBoTw

A New Song: "As near beauteous Boston lying." *Anonymous.* Tell your masters they were dreamers,/When they thought to cheat the brave. PAH

A New Song, Call'd The Red Wig. *Anonymous.* And wish little Charley and his colleagues safe in hell. CoMu

A New Song Called The Curling of the Hair. *Anonymous.* But never a lad that ever I found,/Was able to Curl my Hair'o./Finis CoMu

A New Song, Called the Frolicsome Sea Captain, or Tit for Tat. *Anonymous.* So we are the cuckolds, boys, all in a row. OBSS

A New Song Called the Gaspee. *Anonymous.* Though he should offer fifty fold. PAH

A New Song Composed on the Death of Lord Nelson. *Anonymous.* Mourn, England, mourn, mourn and complain,/For the loss of Lord Nelson who died on the main. CoMu

A New Song Entitled the Warming Pan. *Anonymous.* Drive Pretender to the D–l, keep K. George in his place,/Derry Down. CoMu

A New Song: "Has the Marquis La Fayette." Joseph Stansbury. Witness Burgoyne, and two famous Bro-/thers! PAH

A New Song of an Orange. *Anonymous.* And many besides may at last loose their own/for an Orange. CoMu

A New Song of Mary. *Anonymous.* And wept water full bitterly,/And teres of blod ever among. MeEL

A New Song of New Similes. John Gay. When I am rotten as a pear,/And mute as any fish. FaBoCo; NOBL

A New Song of Wood's Halfpence. Jonathan Swift. Or, egad, if you don't, there's an end of your credit:/Which nobody can deny. OxBoLi

A New Song on the Birth of the Prince of Wales. *Anonymous.* The bedsteads and the tables, kitchen pokers, and the floors. CoMu; FaBoBa; NOBV; VLP

A New Song on the Blandford Privateer. *Anonymous.* To Bristol Town then haste ye down,/Your sweethearts to revive all. OBSS

A New Song on the Taxes. *Anonymous.* There never was such taxes in Ireland before. WTO

A New Song on the Total Defeat of the French Fleet. *Anonymous.* And let them know we always will be masters of the main. OBSS

A New Song to an Old Tune. *Anonymous.* Shots in my locker yet remain,/John Bull, Esquire, my jo! PAH

A New Song to Sing about Jonathan Bing. Beatrice Curtis Brown. "I wrap it up neatly and send it by post/To my friends and relations who need it the most." SoPo

New Spring. Juan Ramon Jimenez. Pain whistled in my blood. OLR

A New Spring. Albert D. Mackie. Aathing comes back–my heart is howe!–/Aathing but you, my dear. OxBS

New Storefront. Russell Atkins. he dared their margins with silver FB

A New Story. Simon J. Ortiz. "No," I said. No. STE

New Strain. George Starbuck. as if the air/might hold some further thing/for the listening. MP; TwCP

New Students. Marvin Bell. That is why this circumstance of energy/is recorded as glory and passes into study. GLGT

The New Style. David O'Bruadair. But their tongue gets caught in his "Hms' and "Haws'. BIrV

The New Sun. John Wain. Let our firm hearts pray to be orphaned! NePoEA-2

The New Tenants. Edwin Arlington Robinson. What ultimate insolence would soon be theirs. NoAm

New Territory. Eavan Boland. By peering down the unlit centuries/He glimpsed the holy boy. CIP

The New Testament. *Anonymous.* Hebrews, James, Peter, and John,/Jude and Revelation. FaBoUs

The New Testament. Thomas Russell. When Christ, and Christ alone, shall be/The trembling sinner's stay. TreFS

New Testament: Revised Edition. Sister Mary Catherine. And let a Child turn homeless from our door. ISi

New Things and Old. Sister Mary Madeleva. And a woman who ponders/On all these things. GoBC

New Time. *Anonymous.* And he will ensure thee/A Happy New Year. BLRP

The New Trinity. Edwin Markham. Bread, Beauty and Brotherhood. PGD

The New Vestments. Edward Lear. "Any more, any more, any more, never more!" NOBV

The New Vicar of Bray. Colin Ellis. I'm for the people that pay, sir! NOBL

The New Victory. Margaret Widdemer. The stable world itself is her great monument. WGRP

The New View. John Holmes. For sorrow, and a new view past where the tree fell. MiAP

The New Vintage. Douglas Le Pan. And shimmered with unheard-of consummations sterile. OBCV

A New War Song by Sir Peter Parker. *Anonymous.* The continent, whole,/We will take, by my soul,/If the cowardly Yankees will let us. PAH

The New Warden. Jimmy Santiago Baca. One old convict ended up marrying the governor's mother. LFAC

The New Wife. *Anonymous.* How I long to take you/All to myself/As a mother takes her child. WTO

A New Wind A-Blowin'. Langston Hughes. And we'll show 'em what free men can really do! TrAS

New Wine, Old Bottles. Colin Newbury. No answer; this, at least, was as before. AnNZ

New Words for an Old Song. Babette Deutsch. Joy comes late. NePoAm

New Words to the Tune of "O'Donnel Abu." Jim Connell. Till Labour has triumphed and Ireland is Free! OnYI

The New World. Paul Engle. Out of the ripping pain of war/A new world nation... AmFN

New World. Brewster Ghiselin. Then day surrounds us like an empty room. MoVE

The New World. LeRoi (Imamu Amiri Baraka) Jones. ...a strong strong man/older, but no wiser than the defect of love. NoAm; NoP

The New World. Jones Very. Their strong foundations laid and held by God's right hand. AA; AnNE; AP

New World. Derek Walcott. So both made the New World. And it looked good. OxBC

The New World (excerpt). Edgar Lee Masters. But this New World is forever new to hands that keep it/new. AmFN

New World of Will. David Shapiro. on this same spot again I hinder you. ANYP

A New World Symphony. Kit Wright. as, happily, we/freely may. NLV

The New World: The New God. Witter ("Emanuel Morgan") Bynner. Can God be God till we ourselves are whole! WGRP

New Year. *Anonymous.* Let the Old Year out and the New/Year in. OxNR

The New Year. Charles Cotton. We better shall by far hold out,/Till the next Year she face about. GoTL

The New Year. Dinah M. Mulock Craik. He is the wonderful glad New Year. BrR; YeAr

A New Year. Mary Carolyn Davies. It's not a year only,/But a world/For You! YeAr

New Year. Gail N. Harada. The new year arrives,/deaf, smelling of gunpowder. BrSi

The New Year. Homera Homer-Dixon. We shall not fear! BLRP

The New Year. Horatio Nelson Powers. Beyond tomorrow's mystic gates. PoToHe

A New Year. Dora Sigerson Shorter. My little lambs shall play/Beneath the sun. YeAr

New Year. Stephen Spender. Effect their beauty without robbery. AWP

The New Year. J. D. Templeton. All that I ask–you keep the faith unbroken! PGD

A New Year Carol. *Anonymous.* And the bugles they do shine. AtBAP; CH; OxBoLi; PoSC

The New Year for Trees. Howard Schwartz. That all fruit that follows/Belongs to the new year/To come. VWA

A New Year Idyl (excerpt). Eugene Field. Thou shouldst not, gentle roachling, be/Forlorn and gaunt and weak and sad. PoSC

New Year Letter. W. H. Auden. O da quod jubes, Domine. FaBoRV; NoAm

New Year on Dartmoor. Sylvia Plath. ...You are too new/To want the world in a glass hat. FaBoWP

New Year's. Charles Reznikoff. our God Who imprisons in coffin and grave/and unbinds the bound. OFD You have inherited. VGW

New Year's 1978. Howard Nemerov. Why our eyes come shaped like footballs from God's passing/hand. SOTS

A New Year's Burden. Gerard Manley Hopkins. The love once ours, but ours long hours ago. AtBAP

New Year's Carol. *Anonymous.* Come all you heavy laden/I'll ease you of your pain.' OBET

New Year's Day. Richard Crashaw. His Persian lovers all shall leave him/And swear faith to Thy sweeter powers. JCP

New Year's Day. Rachel Field. A new one's come to stay. SoPo; TiPo

New Year's Day. Robert Lowell. The Child is born in blood, O child of blood. AmPP; ConAP; LiTM; NePoEA; PPoe

New Year's Eve. John Berryman. We clasp upon the stroke, kissing with happy cries. LiTM; NMP

New Year's Eve. Thomas Hardy. And went on working evermore/In his unweeting way. MoBrPo; NoAm

New Year's Eve. Alfred Edward Housman. And I left them there at their altars/Ringing their own dead knells. VLP

New Year's Eve. D. H. Lawrence. As the firelight falls and leaps/From your feet to your lips! BoLoP; ErPo

New Year's Eve. H. B. Mallalieu. My glass lies shattered at your feet. Resolve. WaP

New Year's Eve, 1938. John Frederick Nims. the waif appeal from lackland hearts/to Sallys name or perhaps anothers MiAP

New Year's Eve in Solitude. Robert Mezey. Give me my robes of earth/and my black milk. NaP; VWA

New Year's Eve in Troy. Adrienne Rich. This year draws up whose belly sings/with some three hundred ruinous days. NePoEA-2

A New-Year's Gift Sent to Sir Simeon Steward. Robert Herrick. And thus, throughout, with Christmas plays/Frolic the full twelve holy-days. CaPo

The New Year's Gift to Phyllis. Matthew Prior. And in return of it will take/Some levity from you. CBEP

New Year's Poem. Margaret Avison. Which mirrors quietly the light/Of the snow, and the new year. LiTM; NOBC; OBCV

A New-Year's Promise. *Anonymous.* And I will give thee rest. BLRP

A New-Year's Sacrifice. Thomas Carew. Behold the blaze of thy immortal name. CaPo

New Year's Song. Ted Hughes. Though the worst cold's to come. OBCP; OFD

New Year's Water. *Anonymous.* Open you the east door, and let the New Year in. GBP; OFD; PoL

A New Year's Wish. S., J. H.. Shall dawn the glory of eternal light. BLRP

New Year's Wishes. Frances Ridley Havergal. This will ensure thee/A Happy New Year. BLRP; STF

Newsboy. Irving Layton. Finally enfold the season's cloves,/Cover a somnolent face on Sundays. CaP

Newsletter from My Mother. Michael S. Harper. The Panthers are surrendering/1 at a time. PoBA

The Newspaper. George Crabbe. So wise their counsel, their reports so just!– PPON

Newspaper. Aileen Fisher and never once thinks of being Daddy to me. SoPo

Newspaper Hats. Jim Howard. ...hoping to see/how we wear the things that happen in the world. AMV-81; FAZ

Newsreel. C. Day-Lewis. You'll know you slept too long. MoAB; MoBrPo

Newstead Abbey. George Gordon, Lord Byron. But the wreck of the line that have held it in sway. ChRP

The Newt. David McCord. He's never spry–/Don't ask me why. TiPo

Newton's Third. Jake T. W. Hubbard. And five cards up. AMV-80

Newton to Einstein. Jeannette Chappell. Let's talk of Relativity. GoYe

Next. Tina Koyama. swallowing old questions with a numbing tongue. BrSi

Next Day. Randall Jarrell. Confused with my life, that is commonplace and solitary. HAP; NoAm; NoP; NYBP

Next Door to Monica's Dance Studio. Barbara Smith. This pen into magic, this paper to dance. AMV-81

The Next Market Day. Anonymous. "Till he larns me that tune called the next market day." FSW

Next of Kin. H. B. Mallalieu. To you each one commits his debt today. WaP

Next of Kin. Christina Georgina Rossetti. Yea, we twain shall sleep together in an equal bed. HBV 1-2

Next, Please. Philip Larkin. ...In her wake/No waters breed or break. EiCP; HeIP; MoBrPo; NePoEA

The Next Table. Constantine P. Cavafy. Naked I can see again the limbs I loved. PeHV

Next Time. Laura Simmons. They cannot make us ope His wounds again–/"Next time"! PGD

The Next Time You Were There. Samuel Hazo. That man is you. FAZ

Next to of Course God America I. Edward Estlin Cummings. He spoke. And drank rapidly a glass of water. AmFN; AmP; AnNE; BiP; ExPo; FaBoPV; InPo; LiTM; NCSH; NePA; NLV; NoP; OBWP; OFD; OxBA; TAP; VGW; WaaP; YaD

Next unto Him Was Neptune Pictured. Edmund Spenser. ...;but the white fomy creame/Did shine with silver, and shoot forth his beame. EtS

The Next War. Robert Graves. Playing at Royal Welch Fusiliers. BrPo

The Next War. Wilfred Owen. He wars on Death–for Life; not men–for flags. AnEnPo; WaP

The Next War. Osbert Sitwell. And the children/Went.... MMM

Next Year. Nora Perry. TODAY, TODAY! PoToHe

Next Year, in Jerusalem. Shirley Kaufman. I hear myself hearing/my breathing. Loud. VWA

Ngoni Burial Song. Anonymous. we all shall enter the earth. PeSA

NHR. Jack Hirschman. lighting up from within/with the real thin/bones of the rainbow/body. VWA

Niagara. Richard Emil Braun. lower, to swim secretly. NoAm

Niagara. Lydia Huntley Sigourney. As if to answer to its God through thee. AmLP

Niagara Falls. Alan Dugan. The falls, of course, continued with great dignity. PoA

Niagara Falls. Philip Parisi. How the rooms are full of those waiting to be laughed at. FAZ

Niagara Falls Nocturne. Len Gasparini. our honeymoon was nothing more/than breakfast in bed. NeAC

A Nice Correspondent. Frederick Locker-Lampson. Love, some day they'll print it, because it/Was written to You. HBV 1-2

Nice Day for a Lynching. Kenneth Patchen. I shall be forever killing; and be killed. PoNe

A Nice Part of Town. Alfred Hayes. Full of real death and enormous explosions that actually go bang. NYBP

The Nicest Phantasies Are Shared. Brian Coffey. in every difference/love decrees CIP

Nicholas Ned. Anonymous. So he thought it was night, and he went to bed. NTCP

Nicholas Nye. Walter De La Mare. Would brood like a ghost, and as still as a post,/Old Nicholas Nye. HBMV; HBVY

Nichols Fountain. Virginia Scott Miner. Stay away from this fountain/if you must have something pretty. FAZ

The Nicht Is Neir Gane. Alexander Montgomerie. The nicht is neir gane. AtBAP; BSV

Nick and the Candlestick. Sylvia Plath. You are the baby in the barn. CAPP; CoAP; LCAP; PBWP

A Nickle Bet. Etheridge Knight. But for a day the nickle bet/Made your hopes ten feet tall. CAD

Nicolas Gatineau. Arthur Stanley Bourinot. More profit than he ever hoped to gain–/The increment of immortality. CaP

Niddle Noddle. Anonymous. Wiggle waggle went his tail. OxNR

Nievie Nievie Nick Nack. Anonymous. I'll beguile ye if I can. OxNR

Nigerian Unity/or little niggers killing little niggers. Don L. Lee. suppose those/who made/wars/had to fight you. NeAC

The Nigga Section. Welton Smith. i hope you are smothered/in the fall of a huge yellow moon. BPo

Nigger. Frank Horne. Nigger...nigger...nigger... BANP; CDC

Nigger. Sonia Sanchez. my man/you way behind the set BPo

Nigger. Karl Shapiro. And is Jesus riding to raise your wage and to cut that cord? OxBA

Nigger's Leap, New England. Judith Wright. Night floods us suddenly as history/that has sunk many islands in its good time. NOAV

Nigger Song: An Odyssey. Rita Dove. We croon, "yeah." AmPA

The Night. Al-Khansa. The night was pain. BoWoP

The Night. Hilaire Belloc. And cheat me with thy false delight,/Most Holy Night. HBV 1-2; OBEV; OBVV

Night. William Rose Benet. Kneel to your overlord,/Children of night! MoAmPo

Night. Chaim Nachman Bialik. There let men hear thee, O my song, until/Thy tears are ended and my pain is stilled. AWP; LiTW

Night. Hayim Nahman Bialik. Thy tears are ended and my pain is stilled. AWP; LiTW

Night. William Blake. "As I guard o'er the fold." AtBAP; BLPL; BoNaP; CBEP; EnRP; FaBoBe; HBV 1-2; HBVY; MyFE; OBEC; OBEV; OxBChV; OxBoCh; PoLf; TreFT; WiR

Night. Robert Bly. ...and soon to be swallowed/Suddenly from beneath. NaP

Night. Louise Bogan. That more things move/Than blood in the heart. UnPo

Night. John Brown. ...and imag'd the still voice/Of quiet whispering in the ear of Night. OBEC

Night. Aldo Camerino. night fluid like a smooth sea. VWA

Night. Hartley Coleridge. Oh! that I were the happy dream that creeps/To her soft heart, to find my image there. NCEP

Night. Victor J. Daley. The marching melody of stars and suns. PoAu 1-2

Night. Peter Everwine. and we eat. NNaP

Night. Donald Jeffrey Hayes. It will drift into this room/In an hour..... CDC

Night. Charles Heavysege. I took thee for an angel, but have wooed/A cacodaemon in mine ignorant mood. OBCV

Night. Hermann Hesse. Speaks at this hour my name within her heart. AWP

Night. Solomon Ibn Gabirol. My heart, a hero, chafes and breaks/its bonds. TrJP

Night. Jami. Roll up your mattresses, ye nightly-dead, and neglect/not prayer! LiTW

Night. Robinson Jeffers. And death is no evil. AP; AWP; CoBMV; InPo; LiTA; MoAmPo; MoPo; NOBA; OxBA; WHA

Night. Glyn Jones. Back on the Pasc of this raw dawn./Llanon. NeBP

Night. Richard Lovelace. Whilst the scorched shiv'ring world new-born/Now feels it all the day one rising morn. CaPo

Night. Lois Weakley McKay. Whose touch is soft as fur. SiSoSe

Night. Gabriela (Lucila Godoy Alcayaga) Mistral. The earth too, as my cradle swung,/Drifted into slumber deep. LiTW

Night. James Montgomery. Think of heaven's bliss, and give the sign/To parting friends;–such death be mine! HBV 1-2

Night. Joyce Carol Oates. You've always had a queer imagination, she is told. GeTw

Night. Henri de Regnier. Yea, and with more abiding memories fraught. AWP

Night. Thomas William Rolleston. For me, the death of all desires/In deep, eternal calm. HBV 1-2

Night. Sir Philip Sidney. My soul is blest, sense joy'd, and fortune raised. SiPS

Night. Robert Southey. How beautiful is night! GN

Night. Sam Duby R. Sutu. That I too may let my light shine through the dark. PeSA; TTY

Night. John Addington Symonds. Lift thou the soul to spheres that gave her birth! HBV 1-2

Night. Sara Teasdale. It never will be far. BrR; SoPo; SUS; TiPo

Night. Edward Hilton Young. And can Eternity belong to me,/Poor Pensioner on the bounties of an Hour? OBEC; SeCePo

The Night a Sailor Came to Me in a Dream. Diane Wakoski. Perhaps you told me/you were not/dead. TAP; VGW

Night after Night. Gertrude Bloede. And with glad voices cry, "Awake! awake!" AA

Night Airs. Walter Savage Landor. Washed white in the cold moonshine on gray cliffs. BoNaP

Night Mail. W. H. Auden. For who can bear to feel himself forgotten? OxBTC The typed and the printed and the spelt all wrong. GrPl

The Night-March. Herman Melville And back through all that shining host/His mandate sends. AnFE; CoAnAm; LiTA

Night Mare. Anita Endrezze-Danielson. It's alright. You're almost there. STE

The Night Mirror. John Hollander. ...huge/, on the pillow's dark side. NYBP; Prf

Night Mists. William Hamilton Hayne. For they are Nature's dreams. AA

The Night Moths. Edwin Markham. Do they go lost and aimless to the deep? HBMV

Night Music. Chester Kallman. Will know, will know, will know. PoPl

Night-Music. Philip Larkin "Blow bright, blow bright/The coal of this unquickened world." InPS; PAI

Night-Music: Time Exposures. Muriel Rukeyser. while strength and hours run/checkless downhill. PoA

Night Musick for Therese. Dachine Rainer. On the black horse of midnight I ride. NePoAm-2

The Night Nurse Goes Her Round. John Gray. and dreams are what a dream should be, or true. LoBV; OBNC

Night of Battle. Yvor Winters. The dark blood of the folk. PoA

Night of Frost in May. George Mcredith. ...the sparkle-crest/Seen spinning on the bracken-crook. VLP

The Night of Marvels. Sister Violante Do Ceo. A mortal man becomes a God! CAW

Night of Rain. Bernice Lesbia Kenyon. Rain in my heart, and at my window rain. HBMV

Night of Sine. L. Sedar-Senghor. To live before I sink, deeper than the diver, into the lofty/depth of sleep. PBA

Night of Spring. Thomas Westwood. We would learn and know! CBEP; OBVV

The Night of the Dance. Thomas Hardy. That she will return in Love's low tongue/My vows as we wheel around. BrPo

Night of the Immaculate Conception. Juan Maragall. O night so clear, so fair to see!– CAW

Night of Wind. Frances Frost. Bodies of little foxes may hide and sleep. TiPo

Night on Clinton. Robert Mezey. and was not speaking to me. AmPA; NaP

Night on the Prairie. Rufus B. Sage. Thus chamber'd here, may not kings envy me? PoOW

Night on the Prairies. Walt Whitman. I see that I am to wait for what will be exhibited by death. MoRP; RFM

Night on the Shore. Heinrich Heine. And we easily catch a divine catarrh,/And an immortal cough. LiTW

Night opens like an almond. Yvonne Caroutch. In our cold beds we pursue/the endless fall of silences. BoWoP

Night Out. R. A. Simpson. All roads and found them safe as far as they could see. PoAu 1-2

Night Out, Tom Cat. Charles deGravelles. the flesh of dark. AMV-81

Night-Piece. Léonie Adams. Which star he sees since Hesper set. MoAB; MoAmPo

Night Piece. James Joyce. Voidward from the adoring/Waste of souls. NoAm; PoA; SyP

Night Piece. John Streeter Manifold. As the three came past with the step of kings. LiTM; MoBrPo; WaP

Night-Piece. Raymond Richard Patterson. Lonely, sleepless and dumb. CAD; PoBA; WSC

A Night Piece. Edward Shanks. Silence. We do not know. HBMV

Night Piece. Mark Strand. ...as if/the city, finally, were singing itself to sleep. NYP

A Night-Piece. William Wordsworth. Is left to muse upon the solemn scene. EnRP; MOON

A Night-Piece on Death. Thomas Parnell. And mingle with the Blaze of Day. CEP; NOEC; OBEC; OnYI; SeCePo

A Night-Piece; or, Modern Philosophy. Christopher Smart. And next morn pored in Plato for more. NOEC

The Night-Piece, to Julia. Robert Herrick. My soul I'll pour into thee. AnFE; AtBAP; ATP; CaPo; ELP; HBV 1-2; InvP; JCP; LiTB; LiTL; LoBV; NoP; OAEL 1-2; OAEP; OBEV; OBS; PoEL 1-5; PoPle; PoRA; SeCeV; SeCP; SeCV 1-2; TreFT; WHA

Night Plane. Frances Frost. ..."Put out your lights,/children of earth. Sleep warm." TiPo

Night Poem. Wayne Dodd. Let it go on forever. AMV-80

Night Poem in an Abandoned Music Room. [(or Pillin)] William Pillen. I lay silently, waiting, waiting... VWA

Night Quarters. Henry Howard Brownell. And the great maze of lifts and shrouds! GN

Night's Ancient Cloud. Thomas Keohler. Revels in night's ancient cloud. AnIV

Night's Fall. W. S. Graham. The friendly thief sea wealthy with the drowned. NeBP

Night's Mardi Gras. Edward J. Wheeler. Each one, in form grotesque, playing its part/In the fantastic Mardi Gras of Night. HBV 1-2

Night Scenes. Robert Duncan. we return to her parvis. VGW

The Night Serene. Luis Ponce de Leon. Re-echoing vales where every balm distils! CAW; TrJP

Night Shift. Naomi Shihab. I will do it over & over/as long as it needs to be done. GP

Night Shore. Barry O. Higgs. and shlopped my head into the billow. PeSA

Night Singers. Sappho. adorned with violets. HW

The Night Sits in This Chair. Alice Notley. ...When my face/comes back I sip more of the wine. APU

Night Slivers. Darwin T. Turner. and red-necked laughs still promise patient dawn. NBP

Night Song. Frances Cornford. And other distant dogs respond/Beyond the fields, beyond, beyond. FM; GDP

Night Song. A. R. D. Fairburn. and dress your hair for Judgment morn. AnNZ

Night Song. Louise Gluck. You'll get what you want. You'll get your oblivion. MAYP; SV

Night Song. Wallace Gould. ah, sing to him, nigger. AnAmPo

Night Song. Lisel Mueller. the one that sings was mine. AMV-80

Night Song at Amalfi. Sara Teasdale. But how can I give silence/My whole life long? MoAmPo

Night Song for a Child! Charles Williams. Princes, round his final bed/Be your great protection shed. OBEV

Night Song for a Woman. Al Purdy. –if anyone were to listen/they'd know/about humans NOBC

Night Song for an Old Lover. Susan Glickman. ...for whoever joins me/in the ceremony of dreams. AMV-81

Night Song for Two Mystics. Paul Blackburn. tho Llull remain a lover. NeAP

Night Song from Backbone Mountain. Daniel Mark Epstein. I have been happy, so long. TAT

Night Songs. Thomas Kinsella. A woman lay with golden skin. ACV

Night Sowing. David Campbell. I meet you as a lover. BoAV; CBAP; PoAu 1-2

Night, Stars, Glow-Worms. Halper Leivick. (Poor,/poor wolf.) LiTW

Night Storm. William Gilmore Simms. And see, the boy still sleeping at your side! EtS; MOS

Night Sweat. Robert Lowell. ...as you bear/this world's dead weight and cycle on your back. TAP; VGW

Night Teeth. Peter Brett. arm in arm under a sliver of blazing/moon– forever night blooms. AMV-80

Night the Ninth Being the Last Judgment. William Blake. The dark Religions are departed & sweet Science reigns/END OF THE DREAM OAEL 1-2

The Night There Was Dancing in the Streets. Elder Olson. The fruits of Necessity ripen in all weathers. NePA

Night Thought. Gerald Jonas. and trying to yield/is like trying to fall/asleep, or trying not to. NYBP

Night Thought of a Tortoise Suffering from Insomnia... Emile Victor Rieu. There is no doubt of that. FiBHP

Night Thoughts. Henri Coulette. What are we if not wholly catholic? FYAP

Night-Thoughts. Solomon Ibn Gabirol. Still am I lord, and will in freedom/strive. TrJP

Night Thoughts: Baby & Demon. Gwen Harwood. Be sure I'll have your heart, my love,/when all your loving's done. CBAP

Night Thoughts in Age. John Hall Wheelock. All night, in a half dream, I have lain here listening. MoVE; NYBP

Night Thoughts over a Sick Child. Philip Levine. ...unseen in the frozen snow. NePoEA-2; SM

Night Thoughts While Travelling. Tu Fu. ...I am like a gull/Lost between heaven and earth. BrPo

Night Train. Mary C. Fineran. and you listen to the sounds of this journey/to nowhere you know. AMV-81

Night Train. Robert Francis. I must be sometime taking. DuDa; LOW

Night Trip across the Chesapeake and After. Sydney Lea. A cold breath swept the bay. MAYP

Night up There. G.D. Valentine. The noise of the mad torrent in the vale/Is faint indeed–and how the dawn delays! PoSH

A Night Vigil in the Left Court of the Palace. Tu Fu. All night I ask what time it is. LiTW

Night Visitors. Molodovsky (or Molodovski) Kadya (or Kadia). and outside the door I heard him crying. VWA

The Night-Walker. Horace Gregory. ...has deceived/The unwary into an immoderate love of death. MOON

Night Walkers. Kendrick Smithyman. warning no calm is without pain and death upon the flood? AnNZ

The Night Was Clear and the Moon Was Yellow. Jeffrey Miller. ...and you gave me a hand job as I/tooled on happily. APU

The Night Was Growing Old. *Anonymous.* And her shoes were full of feet. FaBoNo; NLV

The Night Was Smooth. James Bertolino. But the baby wasn't right. PoL

A Night Watch. *Anonymous.* Short, night, to-night, and length thyself to-morrow. OBSC

Night Watch. Margo Magid. that lap like tidepools/the walls of its cave NMM

The Night Watch. William Winter. When will the morning break? AA

Night Watchmen. Wymond Garthwaite. But nobody dares/Because of the bears! BrR

The Night Will Never Stay. Eleanor Farjeon. Like sorrow or a tune. CH; HBMV; NTCP; OxBChV; SiSoSe; SoPo

The Night Wind. Emily Bronte.
And thou for being alone.' ChRP; NCEP; RoGo; TEP; VLP
Who once lives, never dies!' OAEP

Night-Wind. Beatrix Demarest Lloyd. And to the earth are wafted down his sighs. AA

Night Wind. Fyodor Tyutchev. For Chaos stirs when you have sounded. LiTW

Night Wind in Fall. W. R. Moses. Every lake in Canada under the stars. NCSH

Night Winds. Adelaide Crapsey. They tell the clattered trees that I/Should weep? QFR

A Night with a Holy-Water Clerk. *Anonymous.* Thought I on no gile. MeEL

Nightbreak. Adrienne Rich. Time for the pieces/to move/dumbly back/toward each other. IHMS

Nightdream. Charles Wright. ...each/In a soft hat, fill/With dust-dolls their long boxes). LCAP

Nightfall. Kalidasa. As he sets kisses on her face. LiTW

Nightfall. Elder Olson. I move in darkness till he finds his light. DFF

Nightfall. Antonio de Trueba. Oh, what despairing morrows,/If nought to us replies!– CAW

Nightfall. Fyodor Tyutchev. as though the waters of a spring/had come to touch her burning feet. LiTW

Nightfall in Dordrecht. Eugene Field. "Sleep, little tulip, sleep!" AA

Nightfall in Inishtrahull. D. J. O'Sullivan. Venus shines bright, night falls at Inishtrahull! NeIP

Nightfall in Soweto. Mbuyiseni Oswald Mtshali. "Open up!" he barks like a rabid dog/thirsty for my blood. WhB

Nightfall on Sedgemoor. Andrew Young. But long June evenings when I came this way. FaBoPP

The Nightfishing (excerpt). W. S. Graham. ...And we went keeled over/The streaming sea. BSV

Nightflight and Sunrise. Geoffrey Dutton. From light, so with their substance he awaits the night. BoAV

Nightgown, Wife's Gown. Robert Sward. Arms around her, I caress her wings. ELU

The Nightingale. Mark Akenside. And pity nature's common cares,/Till I forget my own. HBV 1-2; OBEV

The Nightingale. *Anonymous.*
To become the prey of a shark or whale,/With my drownded shipmates of the Nightingale. ShS
To rock your young baby, hear the nightingales sing! AmFP; BaBo; UnTE

The Nightingale. Richard Barnfield. Even so, poor bird, like thee/None alive will pity me. AWP; EG; GTBS-P

The Nightingale. Richard Brathwaite. I am not as I wish. ElL

The Nightingale. Samuel Taylor Coleridge. Sweet Nightingale! once more, my friends! fare well. EnRP; ERoP 1-2; FM; OBRV; PBBP

The Nightingale. Marie de France. Breton poets rhymed the tale,/Calling it The Nightingale. BoWoP

The Nightingale. Edward Moxon. Prophetic to have mourned of man the fall. OBRV

The Nightingale. Petrarch (Francesco Petrarca). How few its joys, how little they endure! LiTW; PoPl

The Nightingale. Famianus Strada. So far even little soules are driven on,/Struck with a vertuous emulation. OBVE

The Nightingale and Glow-Worm. William Cowper. Peace both the duty and the prize/Of him that creeps and him that flies. HBV 1-2; OnMSP; PBBP

The Nightingale near the House. Harold Monro. Now is a raging fire, then is like ice,/Then breaks, and it is dawn. HBMV; MoBrPo

The Nightingale's Song. King of Scotland James I And thankit Lufe that had thair makis wunne. OxBM

Nightingale Weather. Andrew Lang. In the dawn, 'twixt him and me. ACV

Nightingales. Robert Bridges. Dream, while the innumerable choir of day/Welcome the dawn. AtBAP; BrPo; CMoP; CoBMV; ExPo; ForPo; HBMV; LiTB; LiTM; MoAB; MoBrPo; MoPo; NOBE; OAEL 1-2; OBEV; OBMV; OBNC; OBVV; PBBP; PoPl; SeCeV; TrGrPo; UnPo; VLP

Nightingales. Grace Hazard Conkling. Or some shy angel calling me/To follow far away? HBMV

Nightingales Are Not Singing. Moshe Dor. mitigates the battles of salt and/gold. VWA

The Nightingales of Spring. *Anonymous.* Of the nightingales of spring–welcome, my dear! AmFP

Nightletter. Charles Wright. ...The thing that is not left out always/is what is missing. Everything's certain. PoA

A Nightly Deed. Charles Madge. And fetch him winter fuel. NeBP

Nightmare. James A. Emanuel. He just laughed/At my tears. BPo

Nightmare. Edward Field. I was firmly convinced that if I ran away/nobody anywhere wanted me. Str

Nightmare. Isabella Gardner. The red-haired dreamer wakens. CoAP

A Nightmare. Sir William Schwenck Gilbert. ...–and thank goodness they're/both of them over! NOBL; OxBoLi

The Nightmare. Jascha Kessler. O you! Hybrid! Roar, bitch! Blast! Make me–pure! AmPC

The Nightmare. Sorley MacLean. Too late, you fool. NeBP

Nightmare Abbey: Three Men of Gotham. Thomas Love Peacock. And our ballast is old wine. MyFE

Nightmare at Noon. Stephen Vincent Benét. I shall not sleep tonight when I hear the plane. OxBA

Nightmare Begins Responsibility. Michael S. Harper. nightmare begins responsibility. GeTw; HaCAP; LCAP; TAP

Nightmare Inspection Tour for American Generals. Gibbons Ruark. The dead pride of our own/Mother country, weeping/To be let down. TW

Nightmare Number Three. Stephen Vincent Benét. But, if it's got so they like the flavor...well... MaC; MoAmPo; SaC

Nightmare of a Cook. Chester Kallman. Nothing of me, when you are done, my friends. CrMA

Nightmare of Mouse. Robert Penn Warren. And I wasn't, so didn't–till teeth crunched on my skull. SO

Nightmare on Rhum. James Macmillan. Or have the mountains eaten me? PoSH

Nightmare, with Angels. Stephen Vincent Benét. Where he sowed them, the green vine withered, and the smoke/and the armies sprang up. MAT

Nightmares. Siv Cedering Fox. the calmer sea, that bring/all other dreams to me. WSC

Nightmares: Part Three. Lynn Moskowitz. sweats in frightened endurance of her own sudden emotions. AMV-81

Nightpiece. Lewis Turco. ...Chimes reach,/like lianas, from life to death, room to room. SOTS

Nights. Cyn Zarco. or an open book/lying next to me. APU

Nights in Hackett's Cove. Mark Strand. this turning away, this longing to be there. GeTw

Nights in the Gardens of Port of Spain. Derek Walcott. As daylight breaks the Indian turns his tumbril/of hacked, beheaded coconuts towards home. OxBC

Nights on the Indian Ocean. Cale Young Rice. When under the shadow of death's shore/We drop its ended dream. EtS

Nights Passed on Ward's Island, Toronto Harbour. Doug Fetherling. saved from extinction by a puff at the last possible/moment. NeAC

Nights Primarily III. Ed Lipman. they got this poet/only by flashlight/they got this poet. LFAC

The Nights Remembered. Harold Vinal. Perchance, beloved, when the years have lengthened–/They will remember us. HBMV

Nightsong. Philip Booth. there is no dark, nor death. MoLP

Nightsong. Louis O. Coxe. and our hands deadly/and the dead, friends. FYAP

Nightswim. William Pitt Root. ...glancing at the dark, waiting/for another scrap of it/to seek him out. MAYP

Nightwalker. Thomas Kinsella. I think this is the Sea of Disappointment. BIrV; IPY

Nightwood. William Jay Smith. While clothed in soft, white light, the dark wolf digs. PoA

Nihil Humani Alienum. Titus Munson Coan. From nothing human let us hold apart! AA

Nihon Shoki: Dawn Song. *Anonymous.* The day has dawned, my beloved. HW

Nijinsky. Doris Ferne. Paying you tribute with our wild applause! CaP

Nijinsky. Parker Tyler. Dream: and the great anthropomorphic rose. PoA

Nike. Adam Wazyk. over your folded wings, which will soar tomorrow. VWA

The Nike of Samothrace. Hilda Morley. knows of/no water unstirring FAZ

Nikki-Rosa. Nikki Giovanni. all the while I was quite happy BlSi; BP; CAD; HeIP; IHMS; NBP; NoAm; NYP; PoBA; TAP

Nikolina. Celia Thaxter. But the child that stands amid the blossoms gay/Is sweeter, quainter, brighter e'en than they. GN; HBV 1-2

Nikos Painting. Kenneth O. Hanson. Nikos loves you. FAZ

No Holes Marred.   Suzanne Douglass.   And a stamped, return envelope–/ Too small to hold it.   QQQ

No, I Am Not as Others Are.   Francois Villon.   Yes, or else go alive to 'heaven.   AWP

No Idle Boast.   Edward C. Lynskey.   On my third cast I hooked/the largemouth bass.   WOLT

No Images.   Waring Cuney.   And dish water gives back no images. AmNP; BANP; CDC; GoSl; MAT; TTY

No! Indeed.   Sir Thomas Wyatt.   Be in my minde withoute recure?/What no, perdy!   MeEL

No Irish Need Apply.   *Anonymous.*
But to me it is an honour/To be born an Irishman.   WTO
Saying, "When next you want a beating,/Write "No Irish need apply.'" FSW

No Job Blues.   Ramblin' (Willard) Thomas.   I got to get me another meal-ticket woman/so I won't have to work no more   BluL

No-Kings and the Calling of Spirits.   Nancy Willard.   our holding on/and our letting go/and our letting go.   LCAP

No Labor-Saving Machine.   Walt Whitman.   For comrades and lovers. PCP

No Laws.   Brian Allwood.   Not always: there may not be room.   WaP

No Less Than Prisoners.   Frederick T. Macartney.   Though we take separate pathways evermore.   CBAP

No Loathsomeness in Love.   Robert Herrick.   She's to me a paragon. AnAnS 2; GBL

No Lock Against Lechery.   Robert Herrick.   The whore to come out, or the lecher come in.   CaPo

No Longer Mourn for Me.   William Shakespeare.   And mock you with me after I am gone.   BoLiVe

No Love, to Love of Man and Wife.   Richard Eedes.   No thine, no mine, may other call,/Now all is one, and one is all.   InvP

No Madam Butterfly.   Louise Hajek.   I know a thousand others just like you.   AMV-80

No Man, If Men Are Gods.   Edward Estlin Cummings.   To hold a mountain's heartbeat in his hand   InvP; MoPo; NePA; VGW

No Man Knows War.   Edwin Rolfe.   ...dead beside you,/his shared cigarette still alive in your lips.   TrJP; WaP

No Man's Land.   Eric Bogle.   For, William McBride, it all happened again/ And again and again and again and again.   OBET

No-Man's Land.   J. H. Knight-Adkin.   For the lone patrol, with his life in his hand,/Is hunting for blood in No-Man's Land.   MCCG

No Marvel Is It.   Bernard de Ventadour   Of my pure faith, I'd give the whole.   AWP; LiTW

No Matter.   Paulus Silentiarius.   Thou knowst its use. It hides–no matter whom.   AWP; EnLi 1-2

No Mean City.   Patrick MacDonogh.   We cut, to make wit's reputation,/ Our total of two friends by half.   BIrV; OBSP

No Miracle.   Daniel Corkery.   And his heart blazed while his hand smote. AnIV

No Mixed Green Salad for Me, Thanks.   Georgie Starbuck Galbraith.   Food rife with chlorophyl/Is orophyl!   QQQ

No Money in Art.   Jim Gustafson.   No Money in Art!   APU

No Moon, No Chance to Meet.   Ono no Komachi.   A running fire in my breast/That turns my heart to ashes.   WPOW

No Moon, No Star.   Babette Deutsch.   And vanish.   NYBP

No More.   Carl Clark.   I damn your gods,/And thank you too.   JB

No More Auction Block.   *Anonymous.*   No more driver's lash for me,/Many thousand gone.   BPo

No More Beneath the Oppressive Hand.   *Anonymous.*   Behold the smiling happy land,/That freedom calls her own.   AH

No More Booze.   *Anonymous.*
Got to get your can filled Monday.   OBAL
O fireman! save my child!   TrAS; TreF

No More Destructive Flame.   Francis X. Connolly.   No more destructive flame but light.   ISi

No More Good Water.   Jaybird Coleman.   Hey pretty mama/Tell me what have you done   BluL

No More Love Poems #1.   Ntozake Shange.   i cdnt stand bein sorry & colored at the same time/it's so redundant in the modern world   BlSi

No More, O Maidens.   Alcman.   sacred, his plumage as purple as waves, and his heart/never burdened.   LiTW

No More Soft Talk.   Diane Wakoski.   I will not make it easy for you/ anymore.   FF; IHMS

No More Than Five.   Fred Levinson.   good friends/who console her/by growing old/simultaneously   AmPA

No More the Slow Stream.   Floris Clark McLaren.   Spun in the current, swept toward no visible ocean.   OBCV

No More the Thunder of Cannon.   Julia Caroline Ripley Dorr.   Will wear in your hearts forever/The glory of long ago!   OHIP

No More Will I Endure Love's Pleasing Pain.   *Anonymous.*   Nor round my heart's leg tie his galling chain.   FaBoCo

No More Women Blues.   Texas Alexander.   Lord, I walked all last night/ and all last night before.   BluL

No More Words.   Franklin Lushington.   Now play out the game!   PAH

No More Words! To the Field, to Arms!   Veronica Franco.   we'd die together shot down by one shot.   PBWP

No Names.   *Anonymous.*   But the force of her farts/Is like stones from a sling.   KiLC

No, Never Think.   Alexander Pushkin.   To share, unwilling, yet to share at last my passion!   ErPo

No New Music.   Stanley Crouch.   the beasts blow through/their corncob pipes.../No new music   PoBA

No New Thing.   Vincent Buckley.   The building of the honeycomb.   CBAP

The No-Night.   Irving Feldman.   You gone too, nothing yourself.   NoAm

No No Blues.   Willie Baker.   I long to hear some good gal call my good gal call my name   BluL

No, No, Poor Suffering Heart.   John Dryden.   Love has found out a way to live by dying.   LiTB; LiTL; LoBV; QFR; ViBoPo

No Occupation.   George Rostrevor Hamilton.   So be it, without end! FaBoEE

No Offence.   D. J. Enright.   And fed into the mouth of a large cylinder/ Labelled "Lufthansa."   OxBTC

No One Cares Less Than I.   Edward ("Edward Eastaway") Thomas.   The call that I heard and made words to/early this morning.   MoVE

No One Ever Walking This Our Only Earth.   Muriel Rukeyser.   As air is given to the mouth of all?   NNaP

No One in Particular.   John Perreault.   If so,/at least no one can be hurt/by such slight deceptions.   ANYP

No One Is Asleep.   Michelle Roberts.   when no one is asleep/even while dreaming.   LFAC

No One Remembers Abandoning the Village of White Fir.   Duane Niatum. "Niatum! Niatum!"   CDW

No One So Much As You.   Edward ("Edward Eastaway") Thomas.   A pine in solitude/Cradling a dove.   ChMP; GBL

No One Talks about This.   Carl Rakosi.   If I forget you, may my eyes/lose their Jerusalem.   GP

No Other Choice.   *Anonymous.*   I serve thee with my heart,/And fall before thee.   NOBE; TrGrPo

No Pains Comparable to His Attempt.   *Anonymous.*   Examples be of mine estate, though there appear no wound.   PBBP

No passenger was known to flee.   Emily Dickinson.   Contrives that none go out again–   MoVE

No Place So Grand.   *Anonymous.*   Fightin' like divils for concilialtion,/And hatin' each other, for the love of God.   WTO

No Platonique Love.   William Cartwright.   They only find a Med'cine for the Itch.   CABA; GBL; InvP; JCP; LiTB; OAEL 1-2; PoEL 1-5

No Pleasure Without Some Pain.   Thomas, Lord Vaux.   ...Nay, death you may call/That feels each pain and knows no joy at all.   ElL; EnRePo

No Possum, No Sop, No Taters.   Wallace Stevens.   But at a distance, in another tree.   AmP; HaCAP; MoVE; OxBA; TAP; VGW

"No Quarrel."   Sir Alan Patrick Herbert.   But it would seem some major operation/(On head and heart) may be the only way.   DBV

No Question.   George Dillon.   Why birds must fly, seeing the flight of birds. AmLP

No Rack Can Torture Me.   Emily Dickinson.   Captivity is Consciousness–/ So's Liberty.   MAmP; MoAB; MoPo

No Regret.   Rochelle Kraut.   and know the names/of many of these/wild flowers.   APU

No Remedy.   Drummond Allison.   No remedy for our split mind.   OxBTC

No Return.   Vassar Miller.   Our apples rotted, only His crosstree/Bears crimson fruit. But no hand plucks it down.   CoPo

No Road.   Philip Larkin.   Willing it, my ailment.   EBEV; MoBrPo

No Room.   Dorothy Conant Stroud.   Then oh, the glory we shall know/ Which cannot wane or dim!   STF

No Room at the Inn.   *Anonymous.*   Come welcome, sweet Jesus, and lodge in our hearts.   FSW

No Season for Our Season.   Willard Maas.   Against the enemy before the gate.   AnAmPo

No Second Troy.   William Butler Yeats.   Was there another Troy for her to burn?   BrPo; CMoP; EnLoPo; GTBS-P; MBW 1-2; NoAm; NOBE; OAEL 1-2; OxBTC; PoEL 1-5; PPP; SeCePo; WeW

No Sect in Heaven.   Elizabeth H. Jocelyn Cleaveland.   For all had put on Christ's righteousness.   BLPA; TreFS

No Sense Grieving.   Ilya Rubin.   I am nothing but a weight on His scales. VWA

No Shop Does the Bird Use.   Elizabeth Jane Coatsworth.   and a star is his candle/to light him to bed.   OBCA

No Sickness Worse Than Secret Love.   *Anonymous.*   there lives not, never did, nor will,/one who more gravely stole my love.   NOBI

No Signal for a Crossing.   Rhoda Donovan.   that point on the far/horizon, the last stop.   AMV-80

No Single Hour Can Stand for Naught.   John Clare.   And there my love will live.   OBNC

No Single Thing Abides. Lucretius (Titus Lucretitus Carus). How beautiful thy feet are on the hills! AWP; ImOP; PG

No, Sir, No. *Anonymous.* And she answered, "No, sir, no." AmFP

No Sky At All. Hashin. the snowflakes fall... SoPo

No Snake in Springtime. Elizabeth Jane Coatsworth. The supple definitions of his strength. AnAmPo

No Speech from the Scaffold. Thom Gunn. As he rests there, while/he is still a human. OxBTC

No Such Thing. Marcia Southwick. You proceed with caution, as though you were an endless night/scarcely touching the earth. AMV-81

No Sufferer for Her Love. *Anonymous.* I'm no sufferer for her love. AnIL

No Swan So Fine. Marianne Moore. The king is dead. AmLP; AP; CoBMV; EyDe; NoP; OxBA; PoA; PrIm; UnPo

No Sweeter Thing. Adelaide Love. The story of a Babe whose humble birth/Became the loveliest of truths we know. PGD

No teacher I of boys or smaller fry. Allen Beville Ramsey. To teach men how to teach men how to teach. CenHV; PV

No, Thank You, John. Christina Georgina Rossetti. Here's friendship for you if you like; but love–/No, thank you, John. TEP

No Thanks. Edward Estlin Cummings. you're divine!said he/(you are Mine said she) UnTE

No Theory. David Ignatow. no theory that does not grow sick/at the odor escaping. NNaP

No, Thou Hast Never Griev'd but I Griev'd Too. Walter Savage Landor. ...The sun himself can give/But little colour to the desert sands. GBL

No Time. Terence Tiller. You will not see the sorrow of no time. NeBP

No Time Ago. Edward Estlin Cummings. made of nothing/except loneliness. OBSP

No Time For God. Norman L. Trott. Will He–Should He,/Have time for you? BLRP

No Time for Poetry. Julia Fields. Midnight is not time for Poetry AmNP

No Truer Word. Walter Savage Landor. Than that the largest heart is soonest broken. GoTF; TreF

No Trust in Time. William, of Hawthornden Drummond. And twice it is not given thee to be born. LoBV

No Uneasy Refuge. Blanaid Salkeld. who has done with all his enemies before he entered. AnIV

No Use. W. D. Snodgrass. No use...No use... BoLoP

No Voice of Man. Raymond Falconer. o emigrant ships stoked/wi misery. PoSH

No White Bird Sings. John Ciardi. which are never entirely accidents. Not when one sings. AMV-80

No Woman Born. Robert Farren. There is, to be named one with her, no woman born. OxBI

No Woman No Nickel. Bumble Bee Slim. Lord you know I want a friend/like the one what Adam had BluL

Noah. Chana Bloch. The last/waters go on rocking/in the conch of the ear. VWA

Noah. Roy Daniells. Leaned from the admiral's walk and watched them drown. PeCV; WHW

Noah. Hermann Hagedorn. Build you an ark! I tell you, it's going to rain. MoRP

Noah an' Jonah an' Cap'n John Smith. Don (Donald Robert Marquis) Marquis. Swappin' yarns an' fishin' in a little River! LoGBV; PoLf

Noah and the Waters: Chorus. Cecil Day Lewis. And believe that beyond this flood a/kinder country lies. OAEP

Noah in New England. Tom Lowenstein. Caulk the draughty shingles/With threads of rock. VWA

Noah's Ark. Marguerite Young. And dust implicit with lilies of His skull. MoPo

Noah's Carpenters. *Anonymous.* And only those will be secure./Who shelter 'neath Christ's blood. STF

Noah's Flood. Michael Drayton. That living idly without taking paine/(Like to the first) made every man a Caine. PBBP; PoEL 1-5

Noah's Prayer. Carmen B. Gastold. Lead me until I reach the shore of Your covenant./Amen TrCP

Noah's Raven. William Stanley Merwin. Hoarse with fulfilment, I never made promises. AmPC; HaCAP

Noah's Song. Evan Jones. Tomorrow I'll send out the dove and raven. PoAu 1-2

Nobility. Alice Cary. For he who is honest is noble,/Whatever his fortunes or birth. OHFP; WBLP

The Noble Balm. Ben Jonson. For men to use their fortune reverently,/Even in youth. OBEV

The Noble Duke of York. *Anonymous.* But when you're only halfway up,/You're neither up nor down. FSW

The Noble Fisherman, or Robin Hood's Preferment. *Anonymous.* An habitation I will build,/Where they shall live in peace and/rest.' ESPB

Noble Love. Richard Flecknoe. Until it all like incense burns/And unto melting sweetness turns. ACP

The Noble Nature. Ben Jonson. And in short measures life may perfect be. GN; GoBC; GTBS; GTBS-P; HBV 1-2; HBVY; MCCG; PG; TreFT

Noble Sisters. Christina Georgina Rossetti. If thus you shame our father's name/My curse go forth with you. CoBE

The Noble Tuck-Man. Jean Ingelow. Wildly then shake hands all four/(Hum and Ho, the end is Hi). NA

The Nobleman and Thresherman. *Anonymous.* To maintain thy wife and thy loving family.' OBET

A Nobleman's House (excerpt). May Sarton. ...the garden/A little overgrown now/Despite the freshly raked sand. EyDe

The Nobleman's Wedding. William Allingham. For she was a young and a sweet noble lady,/The fairest young bride that I ever have seen. IrPN

The Nobleman's Wedding. *Anonymous.* Thinking she might come to life again. AnIV

Noblesse Oblige. Jessie Redmond Fauset. Pride is with me yet! CDC

Noblesse Oblige. Celeste Turner Wright. Sometimes a frog becomes a prince.../But often he does not. Psk

Nobody. Robert Burns. If nobody care for me,/I'll care for nobody. LiTL

Nobody Comes. Thomas Hardy. And nobody pulls up there. BiP; MoVE

Nobody Knows But Mother. Mary Morrison. Nobody knows but Mother. BLPA

Nobody Knows de Trouble I See. *Anonymous.* Nobody knows de trouble I see, Glory, hallelujah! AH; BLSo; BoAN 1-2; FSW

Nobody Lives on Arthur Godfrey Boulevard. Gerald Costanzo. ...mouthing our own sad psalms. MAYP

Nobody Loses All the Time. Edward Estlin Cummings. (and down went/my Uncle/Sol/and started a worm farm) AnNE; CMoP; DL; FaBoCo; FF; LiTM; MP; NLV; NOBA; TwCP

Nobody Riding the Roads Today. June Jordan. But I hear the living rush/far away from my heart BPo

Nobody's Child. Phila H. Case. I am sure I shall then be somebody's child. TreF

Nobody will open the door for you. Blanca Varela. You, small worm, worm-mouth, worm-hate, master/of death and/life. You can't go in. They say. BoWoP

Nocht o' Mortal Sicht. Bessie J. B. Macarthur. It is a ghaist that walks the hoose/And casts its shadow on the wa'. OxBS

Nocturn at the Institute. David McElroy. It is nothing, nothing at all,/for the cabbage down the hall. Psk

Nocturn Cabbage. Carl Sandburg. series of little silver waterfalls in the moon. DuDa

Nocturnal. Os Marron. So must her dreams be... NeBP

Nocturnal Heart. Anne-Marie Kegels. We float, forgotten by day. BoWoP

A Nocturnal Reverie. Anne Finch, Countess of Wilchilsea. Or pleasures, seldom reach'd, again pursu'd. CEP; EBEV; FaBoEn; GoTL; LoBV; NOEC; NoP; OBEC; PBWP; PoEL 1-5; SBG; SeCePo

A Nocturnal Sketch. Thomas Hood. That upward goes, shows Rose knows those bows' woes! FaBoCo; FiBHP; NBM

Nocturnal Sounds. Kattie M. Cumbo. Sleep comes to close the ears of/the mind to night sounds of this world. BlSi

Nocturnal Thoughts. Avraham Huss. And we have fosaken the day,/And we have forgotten. VWA

A Nocturnal upon St Lucy's Day, Being the Shortest Day. John Donne. Both the year's, and the day's deep midnight is. AnAnS 1; AtBAP; BoW; CBEP; EBEV; EnRePo; GBL; JCP; LiTB; MeLP; MePo; NOBE; NoP; OAEL 1-2; OBS; PoEL 1-5; PoPle; PPP; SeCP; SeCV 1-2; TEP

Nocturnal Visitor. Carolyn Miller. Asleep, this stupid boy is beautiful. AMV-80

Nocturne. Thomas Bailey Aldrich. Ah, me! it was he that won her/Because he dared to climb! HBV 1-2

Nocturne. Gwendolyn B. Bennett. Chilled to crystal tears. BANP

A Nocturne. Wilfrid Scawen Blunt. When the long night is done/Then shall ye sleep. OBMV

Nocturne. Amelia Josephine Burr. Silence of a world asleep–/And...your breast. HBV 1-2

Nocturne. Roussan Camille. and with all these worlds prostrated before the night's black prairies. TTY

Nocturne. Richard Church. ...It is through you/That beauty lives, you make the midnight sing! ChMP

Nocturne. Edward Davison. For ever be my ghost. CH

Nocturne. Frances Frost. while the sun-warmed beaches and the sea/thunder their slow, eternal wars. BoNaP

Nocturne. Richard Garnett. And stillness falls on all the night. OBVV

Nocturne. Crosbie Garstin. In the star-chamber of the Wild. CH

Nocturne. Donald Jeffrey Hayes. Lullaby..... CDC

Nocturne. Robert Hillyer. That I may meet you there. FYAP

Nocturne. Victor Hugo. "It is the Lord! It is the Lord Most High!" CAW

Nocturne. Pinkie Gordon Lane. and the color of blue/everywhere BlSi

Nocturne. Naomi Long Madgett. You lie! BALP

Nocturne.　Richard Murphy.　It's all over over over　IPY

Nocturne.　Kathleen Raine.　somewhere the islands of the blest.　ChMP

Nocturne.　John V. A. Weaver.　Nothin' to you, and everythin' to me?　AnAmPo; HBMV

Nocturne at Bethesda.　Arna Bontemps.　You are sad. It is the same with me.　BALP; BANP; CDC; PoNe

Nocturne, Central Park South.　L. E. Sissman.　...Doubt/Is the house dick and time whistles taxis.　NYP

A Nocturne for October 31st.　Yvor Winters.　You made your calm patrol.　PoA

Nocturne for the U.S. Congress.　Victor Contoski.　And darkness descends on the Department of Justice.　GP

Nocturne: Georgia Coast.　Daniel Whitehead Hicky.　I cannot say if their catch is shrimp,/Or fireflies buring clear.　AmFN

Nocturne: Homage to Whistler.　Ruth Feldman.　who flung a pot of paint in the public's eyes/and opened mine.　AMV-81

Nocturne II.　Ruben Dario.　Which penetrates and stirs my own heart.　AMV-81

Nocturne–III.　Jose Asuncion Silva.　Oh, the shadows which seek each other in nights of sad-/ness and tears!　LiTW

Nocturne in a Deserted Brickyard.　Carl Sandburg.　Make a wide dreaming pansy of an old pond in the night.　MoAmPo

Nocturne in G Minor.　Karl Gustave Vollmoeller.　The nightwind storms and shivers through the reeds.　AWP; LiTW

Nocturne in the Women's Prison.　Maria Beneyto.　still loving, and ageing by centuries...　WPOW

Nocturne: Lake Huron.　Conor Kelly.　as we move slowly round to greet the dawn.　AMV-80

Nocturne of Birth and Water.　Don Domanski.　making the sound of heavy keys/along a thin brass ring.　CaPN

Nocturne of Remembered Spring.　Conrad Aiken.　And then we laugh, with shadows in our eyes.　HBMV

Nocturne of the Self-Evident Presence.　Thomas MacGreevy.　I see alps, ice, stars and white starlight/In a dry, high silence.　BIrV; CIP

Nocturne of the Wharves.　Arna Bontemps.　And I have broken down before the wind.　BANP; BPo; PoNe

Nocturne Varial.　Lewis Alexander.　I came as a shadow,/to dazzle your night!　PoBA; PoNe

Nod.　Will Bennett.　I wave my arm like someone drowning;/achieve motion as a statue might,/by innuendo.　APU

Nod.　Walter De La Mare.　"Rest, rest, and rest again."　AtBAP; HBMV; MoAB; MoBrPo; OxBTC

Nodes.　Alice Corbin Henderson.　Beside God's ancient everlasting rune.　WGRP

Noel.　Hilaire Belloc.　And the small child Jesus smile on you.　HBMV

Noel.　Gail Brook Burket.　And blessed are all hearts today/Which turn toward Bethlehem.　PGD

Noel.　Richard Watson Gilder.　And Christ, the flower of all.　AA

Noel: Christmas Eve, 1913.　Robert Bridges.　Heark'ning in the aspect/of th'eternal silence.　CAW; LiTB; MoVE; NOCV; OBCP; OxBoCh; PoEL 1-5

Noel! Noel!　Laura Simmons.　How close the Christ Child comes! how near the Star!　PGD

Noel Tragique.　Ramon Guthrie.　The tragickest durn thing I ever heard!　ErPo

Noh Play.　Jim Brodey.　No rhythm. No melody./No words.　APU

Noise Grimaced.　Larry Eigner.　gripping the shoulders/before or after our deaths　NeAP

The Noise of the Village.　Anonymous.　The noise/Of the village.　OBVE

The Noise That Time Makes.　Merrill Moore.　Over the earth brushing the eternal grass.　MoAmPo; TrGrPo; YaD

Noises.　Fred Johnson.　connecting youtometoyoutometo/you to me/to you.　CNA

Nomad Exquisite.　Wallace Stevens.　Forms, flames, and the flakes of flames.　AtBAP

Nomen.　Naomi Long Madgett.　and having no need to let myself be robbed/a second time.　BlSi

Non Amo Te.　Thomas (Tom) Brown.　I do not love thee, Dr. Fell.　AWP; ImOP

Non Dolet.　Oliver St. John Gogarty.　Nor, after Caesar, skulk in Rome.　OBMV; OnYI; OxBI

Non-Euclidean Elegy.　John Frederick Nims.　Tea rooms teeter like kites.　MoVE

Non Nobis.　Henry Cust.　Let Hell afford/The pavement of her Heaven!　OBEV; OBVV

Non Nobis Domine.　Rudyard Kipling.　Not unto us the Praise!　EBCP

Non Piangere, Liu.　Peter Porter.　The fire will come out of the sun/and I shall look in the heart of it.　OxBC

Non Que Je Veuille Oter La Liberte.　Pernette de Guillet.　But I would wish, to both our hearts' delight,/For his will to be joined with my desire.　WPOW

A Non Sequitor.　Elizabeth T. Corbett.　To see the rainbow's wheel ganne, made of flax.　FaBoNo

Non Sum Qualis Eram Bonae Sub Regno Cynarae.　Ernest Christopher Dowson.　I have been faithful to thee, Cynara! in my fashion.　AWP; BLPA; BoLoP; BrPo; EnLoPo; FaBoBe; FaFP; FPL; GBL; GoTF; GTBS-P; HAP; HBV 1-2; HeIP; InPo; LiTL; MoBrPo; NOBE; NoP; OAEL 1-2; OBEV; OBMV; OBNC; OBVV; PG; PoPl; PrIm; TEP; TreF; TrGrPo; ViBoPo; VLP

Non Sum Qualis Eram in Bona Urbe Nordica Illa.　John Hollander.　Lord, may we live to spend next year/In Copenhagen!　ErPo

Non Ti Fidar.　Louis Zukofsky.　A song that lovers' heads/Ear to, and on ear foretell.　VGW

None.　Josephine Miles.　Toppled in that void tossed there, and woke.　VGW

None Can Experience Stint.　Emily Dickinson.　The Poverty that was not Wealth–/Cannot be Indigence.　MAmP

None Is Happy.　Hartmann von Aue.　Such as that which I confess/Is my furnace of distress.　AWP

None of Self and All of Thee.　Theodore Monod.　Grant me now my soul's desire,/"None of self and all of Thee."　BLRP

None Other Fame Mine Unambitious Muse.　Samuel Daniel.　Avon shall be my Thames, and she my Song,/No other prouder Brookes shall heare my wrong.　AAS

None Other Lamb, None Other Name.　Christina Georgina Rossetti.　Nor heaven have I, nor place to lay my head,/Nor home, but Thee.　OxBoCh; TrPWD; TRV

Nones.　W. H. Auden.　Or the deer who shyly from afar/Peer through chinks in the forest.　CoBMV

Nongtongpaw.　Charles Dibdin.　Good night t' ye, Mounseer Nongtongpaw!　HBV 1-2

Noni Daylight Remembers the Future.　Joy Harjo.　to know/that we're alive/we are alive.　TWSS

The Nonny.　James Reeves.　And if she goes too far, explodes.　AmMo

Nonpareil.　Matthew Prior.　Grows a fair plant, bears flowers and fruit.　EnLoPo

The Nonpareil's Grave.　M. J. McMahon.　And in the fields of Oregon,/Unmarked, leave Dempsey's grave.　SD

Nonsense.　Anonymous.
　The milner said: "Shew, henne, shew!/I may not shake my bagge for you."　OxBM
　Shall be made friends in a left handed trance. FaBoNo; NA
　So they that suffered wrong and were upbraded/Shall be made friends in a left-handed trance. FaBoNo; NA

Nonsense.　Elizabeth T. Corbett.　Even such is man, who died and then did laugh/To see such strange lines writ on's epitaph.　FaBoNo

Nonsense.　Thomas Moore.　God bless me, what a deal you've seen!　FaBoEE; InMe; NA

Nonsense.　Robert Haven Schauffler.　See the stubble turn gold and the wormwood bear roses/of song?　HBMV

A Nonsense Alphabet.　Edward Lear.　Tinkly, minkly,/Piece of zinc!　SoPo; SUS

A Nonsense Carol.　Anonymous.　The cow brake loose, the rope ran home,/Sir, God give you good-morrow!　OxBoLi

A Nonsense Song.　Stephen Vincent Benét.　–Rosemary, Rosemary, let down your bright hair!　OBAL

Nonsense Verses.　Charles Lamb.　Remember the loss is her own if she lose it.　NA

The Noodle-Vendor's Flute.　D. J. Enright.　In real cities, real houses, real time.　NoP

Nooksack Valley.　Gary Snyder.　...The dog/Turns and turns about, stops and sleeps.　NaP

Noon.　John Clare.　Caring not to stir at all,/'Till the dew begins to fall.　OBRV; SeCePo

Noon.　Michael (Katherine Bradley and Edith Cooper) Field.　...Sharply on my mind/Presses the sorrow: fern and flower are blind.　NOBV

Noon.　Robinson Jeffers.　Full of the God, having drunk fire.　MoAmPo

Noon Glare.　Matthew Brennan.　Sunshine, blinding as daybreak in Sahara glares.　AMV-80

Noon of the Sunbather.　Marge Piercy.　But the ashes dance. Each ashfleck leaps at the sun.　NMM

Noon Quatrains.　Charles Cotton.　In a more mild and temp'rate ray/We may again enjoy the day.　LoBV

Noon's Dream-Song.　Eugene Lee-Hamilton.　While fades the song of what but seems.　NOBV

The Noonday April Sun.　George Love.　and then run down in rivers to the sea of dreams　IDB; NNP

Noonday Sun.　Kathryn and Byron Jackson.　And she'll never more come to my call.　TiPo

Noone and a Star Stand, Am to Am.　Edward Estlin Cummings.　both and)Self adventures deathlessness　NePoAm-2

"Noone" Autumnal This Great Lady's Gaze.　Edward Estlin Cummings.　...so unimaginably young a star　CrMA

The Noosing of the Sun-God. Jessie MacKay. Evermore was the flight/Of the fire-bird of Rangi. ACV

Nor'Easter. Bianca Bradbury. Roaring pirate tunes/On down the dunes. EtS

Nor House Nor Heart. Elinor Lennen. Nor house nor heart shall know the Christmastide! PGD

Nor Mars His Sword. Dunstan Thompson. I believe, even our deaths are forgiven. NePA

Nor Will These Tears Be the Last. Johann Wolfgang von Goethe. Ah, how the long, deep agony/Lasts here, under the sun. LiTW

Nora. Dora Sigerson Shorter. I, hungry, kissed the brogue upon her mouth. HBMV

Norah. Zoë Akins. But where in the world is the path for me/Except the river that runs to the sea! HBV 1-2

Norembega. John Greenleaf Whittier. He needs the earthly city not/Who hath the heavenly found. PAH

Norfolk. Sir John Betjeman. Of unkept promises and broken hearts. ChMP

The Norfolk Girls. Anonymous. Here's a health to all the Norfolk girls,/ And Portsmouth maidens, too. AmSS

The Norfolk Rebellion: The Rebels' Rhyme. Anonymous. And you must thank us for that. GBP

The Norfolk Rebellion: The Slaughter of the Rebels. Anonymous. Shall fill the vale of Dussindale/With slaughtered bodies soon. GBP

Normal as Two Ships in the Night. Walta Borawski. ...violent passions/ composed for solo insruments. AMV-81

The Norman Baron (excerpt). Henry Wadsworth Longfellow. Knocking at the castle-gates. PeD

Norman Morrison. Adrian Mitchell. put on a new skin of flame/and became/Vietnamese. FF

Norris Dam. Selden Rodman. ...and the power/Stokes the atomic ovens at Oak Ridge. PoNe

Norse Lullaby. Eugene Field. Sleep, little one, sleep. SUS

Norse Sailor's Joy. Wilfrid Thorley. And in their eyes the promise of delight/Round the warm ingle at the fall of night. EtS

The Norsemen. John Greenleaf Whittier. Through the mind's waste of woe sin,/Of an immortal origin! PAH

North. Philip Booth. love is twice warm in a cold place. NePoEA; PoPl

North. Lance Henson. flower into a cold wind that smells/of the moon STE

The North. Barry McKinnon. a kind of ownership/not to care NOBC

North American Sequence: Journey to the Interior. Theodore Roethke. And the dead begin from their dark to sing in my sleep. LCAP

North and South. Claude McKay. O sweet for quiet dreams are tropic lands! AmPP; GoSl

The North and the South. Elizabeth Barrett Browning. –"Alas, but must you take him again?'/Said the South to the North. OBVV

North Atlantic. Carl Sandburg. I am a son of the sea/and the sea's wife, the wind. MOS

North Clark Street. Raymond Thompson. and never got out alive. LFAC

The North Country. D. H. Lawrence. With violent achings heaving to burst the/sleep that is now not long. OAEP

North Country. Kenneth Slessor. Dripping red with blood. CBAP

The North Country Collier. Anonymous. And I am but a sheep-girl and who can me blame? OBSS

The North Country Maid. Anonymous. Are all growing green in my north country. OBET

North Express. Joyce Mansour. Cobra WPOW

North Haven. Elizabeth Bishop. ...Sad friend, you cannot change. HaCAP

North Infinity Street. Conrad Aiken. You hear that contrapuntal pawnshop beat. AP

North Labrador. Hart Crane. No birth, no death, no time nor sun/In answer. CMoP; FaBoMo; PoL

North of Berwick. Sydney Tremayne. Through all our absences the long tide surges. BSV

North of Santa Monica. Carter Revard. and the lines of white surf come in. VoR

The North of Wales. Herbert Morris. among the weathers of their loveliness. NePoAm-2

North Philadelphia, Trenton, and New York. Richmond Lattimore. and the bright winter sky as from a tube of indigo is squeezed away. NYBP

A North Pole Story. Menella Bute Smedley. But looked, and changed their mind! OxBChV

The North Sea (excerpt). Heinrich Heine. Where the voice of her lover sounds even sweeter/Than fiddles and flutes. AWP

North Sea Off Carnoustie. Anne Stevenson. candles in the windows of a safe earth. HoAn

The North Sea Undertaker's Complaint. Robert Lowell. Melted the hammer of his heart to fire. NePoEA

North Shore. Peter Davison. Death, do you hear me singing in your key? CoPo

North to Milwaukee. Gerald Vizenor. the phlegm of last rites/stains the sleeves of the survivors VoR

The North Wind Came Up Yesternight. Robert Bridges. The dawning's crimson flush. SeCeV

The North Wind Doth Blow. Mother Goose. Will hide his head under his wing,/Poor thing! HBV 1-2

North Wind in October. Robert Bridges. He passeth, and all again for awhile is bright. VLP

Northboun'. Lucy Ariel Williams Holloway. An' Hebben is up,/I'm upward boun'. BANP; BlSi; CDC; GoSl; PoNe

Northern Boulevard. Edwin Denby. Anyone's life is greater than his care. CrMA

The Northern Cobbler. Alfred, Lord Tennyson. Fur I weänt shed a drop on 'is blood, noa, not fur Sally's oan kin. EBEV

Northern Farmer, New Style. Alfred, Lord Tennyson. Proputty, proputty, proputty–canter an' canter/awaay. BiP; BoLiVe; MBW 1-2; NOBV; OAEP; VLP

A Northern Hoard. Seamus Heaney.
And stop my ears against the scream. CIP
infected sutures/and ill-knit bone? CIP

Northern Ireland: Two Comments. Seamus Deane. There is the gaunt power/That sucks men for their marrow. CIP

A Northern Legion. Sir Herbert Read. The legion now is lost. None will follow. SeCePo

Northern Pike. James Wright. I am so happy. CAPP

The Northern Seas. William Howitt. Where the pelican of the silent North/Sits there all silently. GN

A Northern Spring. Gene Baro. though my mother will stand in her doorway/and pass half an hour away. NePoEA-2

The Northern Star. Anonymous. And the waves have spread/The sandy bed/That holds my Love from me. HBV 1-2

A Northern Suburb. John Davidson. Whose prize for unremitting care/Is only not to be disgraced. NBM; NOBV; OBNC

A Northern Vigil. Bliss Carman. Where the caldron mantles and spills/ Another dawn on the world! OBEV; OBVV; PeCV

Northern Water Thrush. D. G. Jones. and the flawed human world/return with his delicate bone. PeCV

Northfield. Anonymous. And bring the promised day. AmFP

Northhanger Ridge. Charles Wright. It sleeps as it's always slept, without/ Shadow, waiting for nothing. HaCAP

Northumberland Betrayd by Dowglas. Anonymous. They landed low by Barwicke side;/ ere Douglas] landed Lord Percye. ESPB; OxBB

Northward. Dominick J. Lepore. When time was always within/The purview of my telescopic eye. AMV-80

Northwest Airlines. Fred Chappell. And I thought, O God, please. Please! HoPM

Northwind. Gene Baro. and the year's cruel turning on the merciless. NePoEA-2

Norway. Norman Dubie. In the early spring rain that has turned to hail. GeTw

Nosce Teipsum: An Acclamation. Sir John Davies. And are astonisht when they view the same. SiPS

Nose, Nose, Jolly Red Nose. Mother Goose. And they gave me this jolly red nose. BrR; FaBoCh

Nosegay. Elizabeth Jane Coatsworth. your grandchildren's children/will hold to their noses. OBCA

A Nosegay. John Reynolds. (Ah, Gillyflower, ah Daisy!) with a grace/Like stars divine! OBEV

A Nosegay Always Sweet, for Lovers to Send for Tokens of Love... William Hunnis. On ground he takes his rest. EIL

Nostalgia. Walter De La Mare. Where Dark doth dwell. CoBMV; LiTM

Nostalgia. D. H. Lawrence. I wish with my breast I could crush it, perish it all. PoA

Nostalgia. Louis MacNeice. But earth and will are stronger/And nearer– and we stay. OnYI

Nostalgia. Gertrude Millard. the woman's laughter holds the lilt/Of the wench she used to be.) BPAW

Nostalgia. Karl Shapiro. Let the wind blow, for many a man shall die. AP; CMoP; CoAP; CoBMV; MP; NePA; TrJP; TwCP; WaaP

Nostalgia for 70. Jim Wayne Miller. ocean will lie on the horizon, a destination. AmC; AMV-81

Nostalgias. Derek Mahon. A lost tribe is singing "Abide With Me'. FaBoIP

Nostalgie d'Automne. Leslie Daiken. Here on a barrow/In Theobald's Road. NeIP

Not a Sou Had He Got (parody). Richard Harris Barham. And we left him alone in his glory. HBV 1-2

Not All Sweet Nightingales. Luis de Gongora y Argote. Making music for her I love. CAW

Not All There. Robert Frost. God found I wasn't there–/At least not over half. FaBoCo

Not Alone for Mighty Empire.   William Pierson Merrill.   Till it find its full fruition/In the brotherhood of man!   AH; TrPWD

Not Any More to Be Lacked.   Emily Dickinson.   Plated the residue of Adz/ With Monotony.   MAmP

Not Any Sunny Tone.   Emily Dickinson.   How dead we are.   AnFE; APA; MAPA

Not as Wont.   Joseph Skipsey.   We'd met, but not as wont we'd met. NOBV

Not because of you, not because of me.   Natalya Gorbanyevskaya.   and since then, like a naked torch,/I have been steeped in pitch.   BoWoP

Not Being Oedipus.   John Heath-Stubbs.   It vanished from history, as from legend.   OxBC; TEP

Not Being Wise.   Virginia Elson.   Not hunger, not heart–just a matter/of my not being wise in the ways of water.   AMV-80

Not Blindly in the Dark.   Robert M. Stanley.   For a dimness worse than under floors.   AMV-81

Not by Bread Alone.   James Terry White.   Only the heart, with love afire,/ Can satisfy the soul's desire.   GoTF; PoLf; TreFT

Not Changed, But Glorified.   Anonymous.   Since thou hast left us–all alone with/sorrow/And blind with tears?   STF

Not Dead.   Robert Graves.   Over the whole wood in a little while/Breaks his slow smile.   HBMV

Not Drunk Is He.   Thomas Love Peacock.   ...who prostrate lies,/Without the power to drink or rise.   ViBoPo

Not Even in Dreams.   Lady Ise.   I turn away in shame.   WPOW

Not Every Day Fit for Verse.   Robert Herrick.   So the fancy cools, till when/That brave spirit comes again.   PoRA

Not for Its Own Sake...   Hazel Littlefield.   Of finite space and mortal discipline.   GoYe

Not for That City.   Charlotte Mew.   Too sound for waking and for dreams too deep.   MoBrPo

Not from This Anger.   Dylan Thomas.   Shall her smile breed that mouth, behind the mirror,/That burns along my eyes.   LiTB; PoA

Not Going with It.   Zali Gurevitch.   ...only tomorrow I could/write this. VWA

Not Gone Yet.   John Swanick [(or Swanwick)] Drennan.   And silently the ship is put about.   IrPN

Not Heat Flames Up and Consumes.   Walt Whitman.   Wafted in all directions O love, for friendship, for you.   NePA

Not Heaving from My Ribb'd Breast Only.   Walt Whitman.   Need I that you exist and show yourself any more than in these songs.   NePA

Not Her, She Aint No Gypsy.   Al Young.   She aint sold out yet & her tongue's still flapping   GP

Not Here.   Edmund Wilson.   Not here, old shadows–I know you, all too well!   PoA

Not Honey.   Hilda ("H. D.") Doolittle.   And fiery tempered steel.   AnFE; APA; CoAnAm; MAPA; MoPo

Not I.   Anonymous.   Not I, but Christ/In every thought and word.   BLRP

Not I.   Robert Louis Stevenson.   Some like chaff;/Not I.   NA; NOBL

Not I, But God.   Annie Johnson Flint.   I know not, but He knows.   STF

Not Ideas about the Thing but the Thing Itself.   Wallace Stevens.   ...It was like/A new knowledge of reality.   HaCAP; HAP; LCAP; TAP; ViBoPo

Not in Dumb Resignation.   John Milton Hay.   Thy righteous will be done. WGRP

Not in India.   Jalal ed-Din or al-Din Rumi.   Soul and body transcending I live in the soul of my/Loved One anew!   ILwL

Not in Narrow Seas.   Allen Curnow.
   But age-soured infancy, a darkened dawn.   AnNZ
   Cold hands carve and sprinkle/To blue-lipped silt below. AnNZ

Not in the Guide-Books.   Elizabeth Jennings.   A simple life or death. LiTM; MP; NePoEA

Not in the Poet.   George Barker.   ...foreseeing/its purpose is to haunt the shell like singing.   OBSP

Not in Vain.   Anonymous.   "Christ has risen from the dead!"   BLRP

Not Iris in Her Pride.   George Peele.   Ye may not see, for peeping flowers, the grass.   ViBoPo

Not Just Yet.   Carter Revard.   and Billy Don was dancing/half buried in the sagging blonde/when the state patrolman went in.   VoR

Not Knowing.   Mary Gardiner Brainard.   So I sent the coming tears back with the/whispered word, "He knows."   AA; TRV

Not-Knowing.   Dawn Hinshaw.   It means everything.   AMV-81

Not Late Enough.   Hazel Townson.   Gabbling wild lies of ruffians, skids or snow.   PV

Not Like a Cypress.   Yehuda Amichai.   dust rises in many myriads of grains.   VWA

Not Lost, But Gone Before.   Carolina Elizabeth Sarah Norton.   Not lost, but gone before.   BLRP; PaPo; WBLP

Not Lost in the Stars.   Bruce Bliven.   And saddening those waiting to be born.   QQQ

Not Lotte.   Katherine Hoskins.   I fear Iambus would have grabbed his clothes/And written the ode at Weimar.   ErPo

Not Marble.   William Shakespeare.   You live in this, and dwell in lovers' eyes.   AnEnPo

"Not Marble Nor the Gilded Monuments".   Archibald MacLeish.   Look! It is there!   AP; BoLoP; CMoP; CoBMV; HoPM; LiTL; MoAB; MP; NIP; PoRA; TwCP; ViBoPo

Not Marching away to Be Killed.   Jean Overton Fuller.   Peace is the man I love not/Marching away to be killed.   FF

Not My Best Side.   U. A. Fanthorpe.   What, in any case, does it matter what/You want? You're in my way.   FaBoWP

Not of All My Eyes See.   Gerard Manley Hopkins.   ...it is old earth's groping towards the steep/Heaven whom she childs us by.   OBSP

Not of Itself but Thee.   Anonymous.   By it perfumed, but it perfumed by thee.   AWP

Not of School Age.   Robert Frost.   He bet it was out today,/And would I see if he was right?   GLGT

Not Often.   Ray Fraser.   it hasn't happened often.   NeAC

Not on Sunday Night.   Anonymous.   But not on Sunday night.   STF

Not One Is Turned away from God.   Dorothy Conant Stroud.   And we, with them one day shall stand/Before Him, face to face!   STF

Not Only in the Christmas-Tide.   Mary Mapes Dodge.   For Christ, who lived for all the world,/Was part of all the year.   ChBR

Not Only Where God's Free Winds Blow.   Shepherd Knapp.   There, most of all, thou art.   AH

Not Ours the Vows.   Bernard Barton.   Made by adversity sublime,/By faith and hope immortal.   HBV 1-2

Not Palaces.   Stephen Spender.   Death to the killers, bringing light to life. CMoP; FaBoMo; LiTB; LiTM; MoAB; MoBrPo; NoAm; NoP; WaP

Not Quite Fair.   Henry Sambrooke Leigh.   "Why am I so intensely plain?" InMe

Not Quite Spring.   Lyn Lifshin.   then hugs her huge body to sleep.   NeAC

Not Ragged-and-Tough.   Anonymous.   First cousin to Ragged-and-Tough. FaBoNo

Not Saying Much.   Linda Gregg.   ...The men/did not talk to them much, and neither time/nor that fine place gave them a sweetness.   NPGG

Not Seeing Is Believing.   Paul Petrie.   who is walking a small, white dog/ through the plum-brown, silvery trees.   TAP

The Not-So-Good Earth.   Bruce Dawe.   wiping out in a blue flash and curlicue of smoke/600 million Chinese without a trace...   CBAP

Not Such Your Burden.   Agathias.   And there our thoughts are dull enough, God knows!   AWP

Not That Far.   May Miller.   Is this home/There's fog over the harbor/And I can't see   BlSi

Not That, If You Had Known.   Trumbull Stickney.   Loving what was not, might not be, nor is.   NCEP

Not the Arms Race.   Sam Abrams.   finally/a clear sign.   APU

Not There.   Anonymous.   And no risen Redeemer/Had waited for her. STF

Not Thinking of America.   Judith Kroll.   set in a ring of mountains, a hard cold ring.   AmPA

Not This Leaf Haunts Me.   Tony Cosier.   And this our stay on earth essential as our going.   AMV-81

Not Thou But I.   Philip Bourke Marston.   Thou hadst the peace and I the undying pain.   BLPA; BLPL

Not Three–But One.   Esther Lilian Duff.   But you shall not tell the gray from the gold/Or the stone from the shining hair.   HBMV

Not to Be Ministered To.   Maltbie Davenport Babcock.   Not to be loved, but to love.   TrPWD

Not to Forget Miss Dickinson.   Marshall Schacht.   ...beleaguered/Up to its sills by the gnawing fact.   LiTM

Not to Keep.   Robert Frost.   They had given him back to her, but not to keep.   AnAmPo; CMoP; OxBA

Not to Love.   Robert Herrick.   Little thou'lt love, or not at all.   CaPo; OAEP

Not to March.   Kris Hackleman.   Lion,/Lamb–/hang on to my soul. AMV-80

Not to sigh and to be tender.   Aphra Behn.   Thou'dst better part with Flesh and Blood,/Than be, where Life's not understood.   BoWoP

Not to Us, Not unto Us, Lord.   Anonymous.   ...bless the Lord both now/ And ever henceforth. Praise the Lord!   AH

Not Tonight, Josephine.   Colin Curzon.   ...Not tonight, Josephine.   ErPo

Not Understood.   Thomas Bracken.   And understood.   BLPA

Not unto the Forest.   Margaret Widdemer.   There is a memory in the forest. HBMV

Not Wanting Myself.   Linda Gregg.   The only lover my mind has left/ separates my mind, like milk.   NPGG

Not Waving but Drowning.   Stevie Smith.   I was much too far out all my life/And not waving but drowning.   FaBoWP; FF; GTBS-P; HAP; HeIP; NoAm; NOBE; NoP; OAEL 1-2; OxBTC; PoL; PPP; PrIm; SBG; TEP

Not Wholly Lost.   Raymond Souster.   And nothing can take them from us or change them/Unless it is death.   OBCV

Not with a club.   Emily Dickinson.   To sing unto the stone/Of which it died.   LiTA; WHA

Not without Beauty. John A. B. McLeish. And the street slumbers on. CaP

Not Yet. Joanne Kyger. center upon center unfold, lotus petals,/the boundless wave of bliss. APU

Not Yet Dead, Not Yet Alone. Osip Mandelstam. And poor indeed he who, half-alive,/Begs favour of a shadow. OBVE

Notation in Haste. Elias Lieberman. I am the Whom It May Concern. GoYe

Note. Frank Lima. And I am an ape in half the world. ANYP

The Note-Book of a European Tramp (excerpt). Michael Hamburger. When all the nightmares he most feared/Prosper in daylight and endure. NePoEA

Note Delivered by Female Impersonator. Heather McHugh. You interest me. AmPA

Note from an Exhibition. Albert Goldbarth. ...small ocean, small mercator. AMV-81

Note from an Intimate Diary. Emanuel Litvinoff. it will be the day when we remember. NeBP

A Note from the Pipes. Leonora Speyer. Your wood, your nymph, your kiss, your rhyme,/And all your godlike summer-time! HBMV

Note in a Sanitorium. Ray Amorosi. Blue halo. Me. No hand, no wife, no song. FAZ

Note in Lieu of a Suicide. Donald Finkel. I have in Kerioth a wife and two kids/who but for me would be living on the state. CoPo

A Note Left in Jimmy Leonard's Shack. James Wright. The poor old man. HaCAP; NoP

A Note of Humility. Arna Bontemps. We may come back to triumph mournfully/An hour or two, but it will not be soon. PoNe

Note on Feeding. *Anonymous.* Breast/Is best. FaBoUs

Note on Intelligence. W. H. Auden. A man who's untrue to his wife. FiBHP; PoPl

A Note on Lizards' Feet. James Van Rensselaer. And it wouldn't of hurt God/To give 'em all wings! BPAW

Note on Local Flora. William Empson. As this in Kew thirst for the Red Dawn. AtBAP; EBEV; FaBoMo; MoVE

A Note on Master Crow. Jean Garrigue. As of broad-backed bishop/Or of crook. BoAnP

Note on Modern Journalism during the Last Campaign. E. L. Mayo. And we publish whatever/You want us to utter. FAZ

Note on Propertius 1.5. Fleur Adcock. And she compliant to his every wish. BoLoP

A Note on The Hunted City, 1939-1967. Kenneth Patchen. They were writers, and they wrote. NaP

A Note on Wyatt. Kingsley Amis. God bless you, dear, and all who sail in you. WeW

Note to Gongyla. Sappho. Back to me once more-of all girls the one I/Yearn most to look on. LiTW

Note to the Previous Tenants. John Updike. and dried in the air like the floor. GOYP

Note to Wang Wei. John Berryman. Be dust myself pretty soon; not now. NYBP

Notes after Blacking Out. Gregory Corso. Nothing sits on nothing in a nothing of many nothings/a nothing king. NeAP

Notes for a History of Poetry. David Daiches. And memory's fabled daughter/Is Silence in the end. PoA

Notes for a Lecture. David Ignatow. ...You have a costume,/you have meaning. NNaP

Notes for a Movie Script. M. Carl Holman. Cut-with no music-on her smile. AmNP; PoBA; PoNe; WeW

Notes for a Revised Sonnet (parody). Edward Pygge. ...while the liquor flows like lava/In the parlour of the Marchioness of Dufferin and Ava. BXAP

Notes for a Sonnet (parody). Edward Pygge. ...But there will be/Fifty-six new sonnets by tomorrow night. BXAP

Notes for a Southern Road Map. Phyllis McGinley. Look away, Dixieland, from the smokehouse door. NLV

Notes for a Speech. LeRoi (Imamu Amiri Baraka) Jones. as any other sad man here/american. CoPo

Notes for Albuquerque. Roberta Hill Whiteman. Only owls have homes. STE

Notes for Echo Lake 11. Michael Palmer. ...Poems will sometimes overcome them, or else stones. APU

Notes for Echo Lake 5. Michael Palmer. ...An outstretched arm offers me its hand. NPGG

Notes for My Son. Alex Comfort. you will gather the spit of your chest/and plant it in their faces. LiTM; MoBrPo; NeBP; SeCePo

Notes for the Chart in 306. Ogden Nash. He enters without knocking. NYBP

Notes from a Journey. Sam Hunt. It was a steep, slow climb. OCNZ

Notes from a Slave Ship. Edward Field. The shore a fading memory and the direction lost. PP

Notes from an Analyst's Couch. Anita Endrezze Probst. Tie your notes into one smooth ribbon/and let me hang. CDW

Notes: II. Jane Heap. Where go the birds? PoA

Notes Made in the Piazza San Marco. May Swenson. ...they/are touching hips and shifting on the single-footing waves. CoAP

Notes of an Interview. William Johnson Cory. To the splendour breaking from you, though you veil it. NBM

Notes on a Certain Terribly Critical Piece. Reed Whittemore. I am busy writing a critical piece. PP

Notes on a Child's Coloring Book. Robert Patrick Dana. And line with line, color with color strives. PoPl

Notes on a Girl. Peter Kane Dufault. and will not let us see His face. ErPo

Notes on a Life to Be Lived. Robert Penn Warren.
But you believe nothing, with the evidence lost. NoAm
...The child's cry comes from the house. NoAm
The light above the mountain is/Now beyond sight. NYBP
Teach me, my son, the ways of day. NoAm

Notes on a Long Evening. David Phillips. expect/nothing NeAC

Notes on a Track Meet. David McCord. And times his quarters on the dial/That measures two feet to the mile. SD

Notes on My Father. Katrina Anghelaki-Rooke. from under begins/the ascent of fate. PBWP

Notes on the Post-Industrial Revolution. Edward Morin. Even a good wind blows some ill. FAZ

Notes to the Reader. Robert Bringhurst. It is possible to use, to this/purpose, only certain postures. NOBC

Notes Toward a Supreme Fiction: The President Ordains the Bee to Be. Wallace Stevens. Booming and booming of the new-come bee. AtBAP; LiTA; LiTM; MoPo; NOBA

Notes towards a Poem That Can Never Be Written. Margaret Atwood. Elsewhere you must write this poem/because there is nothing more to do. NOBC

Nothing. Julia de Burgos. let's drink to the splendor of not being our bodies. BoWoP

Nothing. Walter De la Mare. Scampered a shape that never was seen. WSC

Nothing. Barrie Reid. it is the lightening, fading star of morning. BoAV

Nothing. Charles Simic. ...hovering/So still, in the windless sky. NNaP

Nothing. Burns Singer. And you are me, and we are two/Demonstrations that nothing is true. OxBS

Nothing-At-All. *Anonymous.* And down at one gulp house and old/woman went. OxNR

Nothing Better. *Anonymous.* to know some word of mine had won/And saved a soul from death? STF

Nothing Between. C.A. Tindley. Keep the way clear! Let nothing between! BePJ

Nothing but a man. Nadia Tueni. It was simple in the deep earth/and brief. BoWoP

Nothing but Death. Pablo Neruda. where death is waiting, dressed like an admiral. EAS

Nothing but Image. Jody Swilky. like men lost in the heart/of New York, in an almost memorable past. AMV-81

Nothing but No and I, and I and No. Michael Drayton. Then answer no and I, and I and no. GBL

Nothing Fair on Earth I See. Angelus Selesius (Johannes Scheffler). See Thee truly as Thou art! BePJ

Nothing Gold Can Stay. Norma Farber. ...Let me gather gold. AMV-81

Nothing Gold Can Stay. Robert Frost. Nothing gold can stay. BoLiVe; GrPl; MoAB; MoAmPo; NCSH; NOBΛ; SoSe; TAP; VGW; WHA

Nothing in Heaven Functions As It Ought. X. J. Kennedy. You'll hear an instant click, a tear will start/Imprinted with an abstract of his case. SM

Nothing in Rambling. Memphis Minnie. Well I believe I'll marry/Oooooo oooo, lord, and settle down BluL

Nothing Inside and Nothing Out. Ray Amorosi. ...anxious/for another night, singing. FiCP

Nothing Is. Sun-Ra. And the fire are really the same-/Upon different degrees. PoBA

Nothing Is Enough. Laurence Binyon. Nothing is enough! MoBrPo

Nothing More Will Happen. Marge Piercy. The heavy iron gates/are closing in my breasts. NeAC

Nothing Move Thee. Saint Theresa of Avila. God alone suffices. PBWP

Nothing New. Robert Herrick. There's no vice now but has his president. CaPo

Nothing Sacred. Roger Woddis. Soon they'll play it in the nude! NOBL

Nothing Strange. Tom Kryss. watching the grass that/has grown. NeAC

Nothing To Be Said. Philip Larkin. And saying so to some/Means nothing; others it leaves/Nothing to be said. OxBTC

Nothing to Do? Shel Silverstein. Now go upstairs and take a nap. BBGG

Nothing to Fear. Kingsley Amis. As cold as ice, but just as set on me. DBV; ErPo; OxBC

Nothing to Save. D. H. Lawrence. like the eye of a violet. SOTW

Nothing to Say, You Say? Conrad Aiken. And what we thought, and silenced, none shall know. LiTA

Nothing to Wear. William Allen Butler. If he married a woman with nothing to wear? HBV 1-2; OBAL; PoLf

Nothing to Wish or to Fear. John Newton. And prisons would palaces prove/If Jesus would dwell with me there. BePJ

Nothingness. Aharon Amir. and I no longer knew who or what I was/and I was no more VWA

Notice. David McCord. I've got a frog/Inside my hat. SoPo

Notice the Convulsed Orange Inch of Moon. Edward Estlin Cummings. Then you will slowly kiss me. VGW

Notice What This Poem Is Not Doing. William Stafford. Notice what this poem has not done. LCAP

The Notorious Glutton. Ann Taylor. To learn the disgrace in which gluttony ends. OxBChV

Notre Dame. Osip Mandelstam. The more I thought: I too one day will create/Beauty from cruel weight. OBVE

Notre Dame des Petits. Louis Mercier. When her Jesus, too, was small. ISi

Notre Dame Perfected by Reflection. Harold Witt. a wavering vision entranced to glass and stone. HoAn

Notre Dames des Champs. John Millington Synge. Sisters of Mercy, to love is delight! SyP

Nottamun Town. *Anonymous.* Ten thousand got drowned that never were born. FaBoNo; NCEP; OxBoLi

Nottingham Fair. *Anonymous.* With my hat in my hand to keep my head warm. AmFP

The Nottinghamshire Poacher. *Anonymous.* And all into pieces she ought to be torn. OBET

Nova. Robinson Jeffers. ...and die without grief or/fear knowing it survives us. HAP

Nova. Charles Levendosky. stain/red novae/from/my thighs. SOTS

The Novel. Denise Levertov. back into life, back to the gods. AP; NoAm

Novelettes III: The Gardener. Louis MacNeice. To find the Walls of Derry/Or the land of the Ever Young. FaBoIP

Novella. Adrienne Rich. Outside, separate as minds,/the stars too come alight. PPP

The Novelty Shop. Duane Niatum. ...Eagle Runner/Abandons the city of red rain, and dives/Into the sea at the end of the pier. CDW

Novembeer Fugitive. Henry Morton Robinson. And loneliness more fleet. GoYe

November. Margaret Atwood. it is always heavier than you thought. NOBC

November. Laurence Binyon. Houses and sky, a dream, a dream! SyP

November. Robert Bridges. Shall dream a dream crept from the sunless pole/Of how her end shall be. NBM; OBNC; PBBP; PoEL 1-5

November. Alice Cary. Think how the roots of the roses/Are kept alive in the snow. OBCA

November. C. L. Cleaveland. We still will find a cheerful mind/Around the fire at home! HBV 1-2

November. Elizabeth Jane Coatsworth. And earth sinks to rest/Until next spring. YeAr

November. Hartley Coleridge. Wrap their old limbs with sombre ivy twine. LoBV; OBRV

November. Elizabeth Daryush. the roving spirit/stay her and return. QFR

November. Aileen Fisher. ...Winter/with a cold red nose! SiSoSe; TiPo

November. Mahlon Leonard Fisher. It is such sound as death; and, after all,/'Tis but the forest letting dead leaves fall. HBV 1-2

November. Frederick William Harvey. How thin he dangles/In these gray rains! OxBTC

November. Ted Hughes. Patient to outwait these worst days that beat/Their crowns bare and dripped from their feet. CMoP; GTBS-P; NePoEA-2; NMP; NoP

November. John Keble. As his when Eden held his virgin heart. OBEV; OBVV

November. William Morris. These outstretched feverish hands, this restless heart? GTBS

November. Christina Georgina Rossetti. Trackless and noiseless through the/keen night air. YeAr

November. Elizabeth Stoddard The loss of beauty if not always loss! AA

November. Frederick Goddard Tuckerman. Till all the world is harsh and cold and gray. NOBA

November. Samuel S. Turner. these dark days toward spring. AMV-80

November, 1806. William Wordsworth. And honour which they do not understand. OBRV; OBWP

November, 1941. Roy Fuller. Whose fathers made both myth and progeny. MoPo

November 1967. Paul Durcan. "He was pure straight; God rest him; not like us." FaBoIP

November 1968. Adrienne Rich. starting to give yourself away/to the wind CAPP; NMM

November 2 A.M. Conspiracy. Sara Bard Field. Lest I, discovered, perish as a spy. AnEnPo

November Afternoons. Sister Mary Madeleva. At peace with beauty and needing no song at all. GoBC

November Blue. Alice Meynell. The throng go crowned with blue. MoBrPo

November Cotton Flower. Jean Toomer. Beauty so sudden for that time of year. CDC; NoAm; UnPo

November Day at McClure's. Robert Bly. we are sailing on skeletal eerie craft over the buoyant ocean. NU

November: Epping Forest. John Davidson. ...and all the forest rocked and sang. GTBS

November Eves. James Elroy Flecker. Is it the mist or the dead leaves,/Or the dead men–November eves? MoVE; SyP

November Garden. Louise Driscoll. Swinging there alone/As if to challenge you! YeAr

November Morning. Evaleen Stein. Oh! can it be that darkness/Is ever anywhere? YeAr

November Night. Adelaide Crapsey. The leaves, frost-crisp'd, break from the trees/And fall. AnAmPo

November Night, Edinburgh. Norman MacCaig. The fog unfolds its bitter scent. BSV; NMP

November Poppies. Hilary Corke. And they flower like clockwork in her bitterest hour. NYBP

November Rain. Maud E. Uschold. A tree could never/Hold them all. YeAr

November Snow. E. J. Carson. not before/or after AMV-81

November Song. Mark Vinz. the wind is an old beggar/rattling our bones in his cup. Psk

November Sun. Elizabeth Daryush. Back to the alien dungeon, where all night/Unseen he burns. PBWP

November Sunday Morning. Alvin Feinman. I sit/And smoke, and linger out desire. CoAP

November Surf. Robinson Jeffers. the dignity of room, the value of rareness. CrMA; MoPo; OxBA

November the Fifth. Leonard Clark. Must wait a year now to remember/Another fifth of November. OnUR

November through a Giant Copper Beech. Edwin Honig. ...braces for throat-/cutting ice, bandaging snow. NoAm; NYBP

November Twenty-Sixth Nineteen Hundred and Sixty-Three. Wendell Berry. no longer the keeper/of what he was. LiTM

November Walk. Susanne Doyle. or seeing, saw as deadly company AMV-81

November Wears a Paisley Shawl. Hilda Morris. She rustles, rustles through the town. YeAr

Novembers or Straight Life. Maureen Owen. "Yes," said Uncle Alfred, "This is Raven Brook,/and here is Jake waiting for us." APU

The Novice. Edward Davison. All round the valley?–Lost, O, lost! ErPo

The Novices. Denise Levertov. ...listening/to the hum of the world's wood. NaP

Now. Robert Browning. While cheeks burn, arms open, eyes shut and lips meet! CBEP; VLP

Now. Mary Barker Dodge. That only Death can earn! AA

Now. Christopher Gilbert. so I hand him half. MAYP

Now. Thomas Ken. A thousand thanks to GOD I paid,/That my sad Never was delay'd. OxBoCh

Now. Harriet Monroe. It is creation's morning–/Now is the world begun. HBV 1-2

Now. William Stafford. They ask how we are. It is this year. NNaP

Now Ain't That Love? Carolyn M. Rodgers. and think it's my heart that i/hear/in my ears. uh. now ain't that love? BPo

Now all of change. Sir Thomas Wyatt. To quit the craft that me beguiled. FCP; SiPS

Now all that sound of laughter, sound of singing. Rosalia de Castro. This solitude's my home. BoWoP

Now and Afterwards. Dinah Maria Mulock Craik. Pardon those erring prayers! Father, hear these! HBV 1-2; PoLf; WGRP

Now and Again. Roo Borson. ...let somebody else/run their little way into the future. AMV-81

Now and Then. Ian Hamilton. ...young men who have come to nothing. NoAm

Now and Then. Margaret E. Sangster. And the Lord can make them anywhere,/His "desert place apart." TRV

Now as Then. Anne Ridler. "Lord turn us again, confer on us victory." WaP

Now Be the Gospel Banner. Thomas Hastings. The song responsive raise. AH

Now, before Shaving. Aaron Kramer. A drowned face waits at the mirror. AMV-81

Now Behold the Saviour Pleading. John Leland. Now he calls thee to his arms. AH

Now Blue October. Robert Nathan. Will make its summer in the heart again. FYAP

Now Christmas Is Come. *Anonymous*. Let us make them such cheer,/As will keep out the wind and the weather. PCh

Now Close the Windows. Robert Frost. But see all wind-stirred. LOW

Now come, my boon companions. Thomas Randolph. And then prepare to kiss. EG

Now Comes the Blast of Winter. *Anonymous* Soregh and murne and fast. SeCePo

Now Does Our World Descend. Edward Estlin Cummings. –arise, my soul; and sing. AP; NYBP

Now Dreary Dawns the Eastern Light. William Butler Yeats. Has had no luck at all. CMoP

Now Evening Puts Amen to Day. Paul Horgan. All things whisper in the blood,/Wondrous is God's sovereign will. AH

Now Every Child. Eleanor Farjeon. Little Christ Jesus/Our Brother is born. BiCB; SUS

Now from Labor and from Care. Thomas Hastings. O accept the song of praise. AH

Now from the East. Masahongva. Dwell the shower maidens,/Cold, cold!/Cold, cold! WTO

Now Goeth Sun under Wood. *Anonymous*. me reweth, marie, thi sone and the. CBEP; NCEP

Now He Is Dead. Alistair Campbell. And into a white cauldron dives. AnNZ

Now Help Us, Lord. *Anonymous*. With one united voice! AH

Now I Am a Man. Russell Marano. but with no one to blame. AMV-80

Now I Have Come to Reason. C. Day-Lewis This architecture will stand. CMoP

Now I Have Forgotten All. David Vogel. Goes running on,/From nowhere to nowhere,/Without me. VWA

Now I Have Found a Friend. Henry Hope. Thou mad'st my soul embrace/Jesus as mine. BePJ

Now I Have Nothing. Stella Benson. I am glad–I am glad–the stone is of your choosing... OxBTC

Now I knew I lost her. Emily Dickinson. But the Restitution/Of Idolatry. PeHV

Now I Lay Me. *Anonymous*. And wake me with the morning light./Amen. SoPo

Now I Lay Me Down to Sleep. *Anonymous*. If I should die before I wake/I pray The Lord my soul to take. FaFP; GBP; GoTF; OxNR; TreF

Now I'm Easy. Eric Bogle. But it's nearly over now, and now I'm easy. OBET

Now I Set Me. Reinhold W. Herman. I have mate, but need copilot. QQQ

Now, If You Will Look in My Brain. Jose Garcia Villa. Carve, inflict upon this brow/The majesty of its doomed Now. AnFE; CoAnAm

Now in my heart. Sappho. etched/by love. BoWoP

Now in the Bloom. Florence Kiper Frank. But hears the proud dead/Whimpering. GoYe

Now in the Palace Gardens. Trumbull Stickney. Would I were with the leaves that thread by thread/Soften to soil, I would that I were one. AnFE; CoAnAm; LiTA; NCEP

Now in the Time of This Mortal Life. Norman Nicholson. And feel the Flesh becoming Word. NeBP

Now in This Long-Deferred Spring. Sylvia Townsend Warner. Farewell, and overlook/these white ashes among the black. FaBoWP

Now Is Farewell. Blanaid Salkeld. You lift those eyes that praise the sea,/Freezing my corpse. NeIP

Now Is the Accepted Time. Charles Wesley. Melt down my spirit, Lord, and mould/Into Thy perfect love. BePJ

Now Is the Cherry in Blossom. Mary Eleanor Wilkins. And you and I in the world togethr. AA

Now Is the High-Tide of the Year. James Russell Lowell. Lie deep 'neath a silence pure and smooth,/Like burnt-out craters healed with snow. TreFS

Now Is the Month of Maying. *Anonymous*. Shall we play barley-break./Fa la la! EBEV

Now Is the Time of Christmas. *Anonymous*. For now is the time of Christmas. MeEL; OxBM

Now Is Yule Come. *Anonymous*. This ends my carol with care away. OxBM

Now Israel May Say, and That Truly. William Whittingham. His name hath saved us from these wicked men. AH

Now It Can Be Told. Philip Levine. though dull and ancient, I still gleam,/like worn cloth, not like a woman's eyes. VWA

Now It Is Broccoli. Jeff Tagami. behind the box of frozen peas/and ice cubes. BrSi

Now Jentil Belly Down. *Anonymous*. Down, down,/Now jentil belly down. GBP

Now Kindness. Peter Viereck. Killed and redeeming, shines from all pale girls. LiTA

Now Let Our Hearts Their Glory Wake. Elizabeth Scott. And here, O great Jehovah, fix/Thy pleasant, lasting rest. AH

Now Lift Me Close. Walt Whitman. So long!–And I hope we shall meet again. DFF

Now Look What Happened. Molly Peacock. as you may be sorry about a chance you lost/or a way or a coin or a limb you lost. MAYP

Now Must I Learn to Live at Rest. Sir Thomas Wyatt. But once to have the liberty/That I have lack'd so long. AAS; FCP; SiPS

Now, My Usefulness Over. Edwin Honig. ...this cruel and absolute/jewel of your life. NoAm

Now or Never. Astra. and i deserved something/better/for myself/now/or never BrRo

Now or Never. Judith Moffett. ...now you conclude or never. SM

Now Our Meeting's Over. *Anonymous*. Then we'll land on the shore and we'll shout forever more! ABF

Now Philippa Is Gone. Anne Ridler. And take our tea and melons in the shade. FaBoTw

Now Poem. For Us. Sonia Sanchez. ...tell us of their juju years/so ours will be that much stronger. CNA; PoBA

Now She Is Like the White Tree-Rose. C. Day-Lewis. She has at heart a certain dawn. CMoP; FaBoTw; MoBrPo

Now Sleep My Little Child So Dear. Casper Kriebel. Before in infancy/The world you first did see. AH

Now Sleeps the Crimson Petal. Alfred, Lord Tennyson. Into my bosom and be lost in me. BoLiVe; ELP; ExPo; GBL

Now Sleeps the Gorge. Alistair Campbell. Walks or flies but in its living grace. AnNZ

Now Springs the Spray. *Anonymous*. All for love I am so sick/That sleep I never may. MeEV; OAEL 1-2; OxBM

Now Sprinkes the Spray. *Anonymous*. Yif I may, it shal him rewe,By this day. ABF; AtBAP; PoEL 1-5

Now Strike Your Sailes Ye Jolly Mariners! Edmund Spenser. Better safe port, then be in seas distrest. EtS

Now Thank We All Our God. Martin Rinkart. And free us from all ills/In this world and the next. GoTF; TreFS

Now That Can Never Be Done. Sister Maris Stella. ...one by one/I should write them down. Now that can never be done. GoBC

Now That I Am Forever with Child. Audre Lorde. You...flowing through selves/toward you. PoBA

Now That My Father Lies down Beside Me. Stanley Plumly. who lies deeper in the drifting dark than life. GeTw

Now That the Flowers. Cullen Jones. It is only the wind that you hear sighing. GoYe

Now That the Truth Is Tried. Thomas Whythorne. If not performed at last. EIL

Now That the Winter's Gone. Thomas Carew. Now do a choir of chirping minstrels bring/In triumph to the world the youthful Spring. PoSC

Now That Your Shoulders Reach My Shoulders. Robert Francis. Where is a weight to lift as welcome? Str

Now the Day Is over. Sabine Baring-Gould. And to thee, blest Spirit,/Whilst all ages run. OxBChV

Now the Earth, the Skies, the Air. *Anonymous*. No birds sings/But notes of misery. EIL

Now the Holy Lamp of Love. Patrick MacDonogh. God's own fox will have his way/This night or some other night. BIrV

Now the Laborer's Task Is O'er. John Lodge Ellerton. Father, in Thy gracious keeping/Leave we now Thy servant sleeping. BLPA; GoTF; HBV 1-2; TreFS; WGRP

Now the Leaves Are Falling Fast. W. H. Auden.
None may drink except in dreams. CMoP
Whose white waterfall could bless/Travellers in their last distress. CoBMV

Now the lotuses in the imperial lake. Wang Ch'ing-hui. And ask her to permit me/To follow her to safety. BoWoP

Now the Most High Is Born. James Ryman. (Scripture seith thus)/Nunc natus est Altissimus. MeEL

Now the Noisy Winds Are Still. Mary Mapes Dodge. April's coming up the hill! YeAr

Now the People Have the Light. Charles G. Ballard. For now the people have the light VoR

Now There Is Nothing Left. L. A. MacKay. And learn, like many more, that life's a cable/Twisted of tedious, small, unfinishing dyings. CaP; PeCV

Now Thrice Welcome Christmas. *Anonymous*. And everyone now/Is a king in conceit. OHIP

Now through Night's Caressing Grip. W. H. Auden. Let them lie, then gently wake. PoRA

Now We've Met. *Anonymous*. With a headstone for his bride. OBET

Now When So Much Has Passed. George Seferis. Shall we be able to die according to the rules? LiTW

Now while the night her sable veil hath spread. William, of Hawthornden Drummond. I wake, muse, weep, and who my heart hath slain/See still before me to augment my pain. AAS; AtBAP; EBEV; EG; EIL; ELP; HeIP; LoBV; NoP; PoRA; QFR; SeCePo; TEP; ViBoPo

Nutting Time. Emilie Poulsson. Strong old North Wind from the branches/Shakes the nuts; 'tis nutting time! BrR

NW5 & N6. Sir John Betjeman. I caught her terror then. I have it still. SCV

Nydia's Song. Edward Robert Bulwer, Earl of Lytton. Its proof is–to die! OBVV

A Nymph and a Swain. William Congreve. And the nymph may be chaste that has never been tried.' ALV; UnTE

The Nymph Complaining for the Death of Her Faun. Andrew Marvell. For I would have thine Image be/White as I can, though not as Thee. AnAnS 1; AtBAP; CBEP; CH; FM; GoTL; HBV 1-2; HeIP; LoBV; MePo; OAEL 1-2; OBS; PoEL 1-5; SeCP; SeCV 1-2

Nymph of the Garden where All Beauties Be. Sir Philip Sidney. And I do swear, even by the same delight,/I will but kiss, I never more will bite. InvP

A Nymph's Disdain of Love. Anonymous. And so think I, with a down, down, derry! EIL

A Nymph's Passion. Ben Jonson. If love or fear would let me tell his name. EnLit; OBEV

Nymphidia. Michael Drayton. Which thing was done with good intent,/And thus I left them feasting. OAEP

Nymphing through Car Windows. Greg Keeler. ...It's almost night. WOLT

A Nympholept. Algernon Charles Swinburne. And nought is all, as am I, but a dream of/thee. VLP

Nymphs and Satyrs. Gavin Ewart. The inside of the nymph is as wet and pink/As the lustful lips of the satyr. PV

The Nymphs (excerpt). [James Henry] Leigh Hunt. While her tired husband and her children sleep. OBRV

Nystagmus. Joseph Matuzak. ...could not/bear my eyes to break you apart. SUW

The Nyum-Nyum. Anonymous. And with this verdict I conclude/One portion of my song. NA

O

O. Rita Dove. ...and nothing's/like it used to be, not even the future. HaCAP; MAYP

O. Salvador Villanueva. the life of a man is a single and continuous journey of blood. InW

O. Richard Wilbur. No hawk or hickory to true my run. LiTA; MoPo

O Aa the Manly Sports. J. K. Annand. For wale o aa the manly sports/Climbin bears the gree. PoSH

O All Down within the Pretty Meadow. Kenneth Patchen. To just such golden ones as these HAP

O All You Little Blackey-Tops. Anonymous. Then you must fly and I must run,/Shu-a-O! Shu-a-O! PBBP

O Amber Day, Amid the Autumn Gloom. William Talbot Allison. And falling leaves saw old unhappy loves. CaP

O! Are Ye Sleepin, Maggie? Robert Tannahill. What care I for howlet's cry,/For boor-tree bank, or warlock craigie?' OBRV; OxBS

O Artemis and your virgin girls. Telesilla. Run swiftly to escape/the rape of the hunter Alpheus. BoWoP

O Atthis. Ezra Pound. I long for thy narrow breasts,/Thou restless, ungathered. PoA

O-Bar Cowboy. Anonymous. I will drag up the yearlings in the O-Bar pen. CoSo

O, Be Not Too Hasty, My Dearest. Robert Henry Newell. And, after we've taken our doses,/Suppose we swear off, for a year. OBAL

O Beautiful Calm. Tu-kehu and Wetea. From the kelp and its hold-fast/On rocks firmly anchored. WTO

O Beautiful My Country. Frederick Lucian Hosmer. And on thy shining forehead/Be peace the crowning gem! AH; MC; PGD

O, Beautiful They Move. [(or Pillin)] William Pillen. I clack, clack/into the veins of all Creation. VWA

O Billows Bounding Far. Alfred Edward Housman. Farewell, thou humid main. BoNaP

O Bird, So Lovely. Louis Golding. Like a flock of snowflakes drifting/towards a down bank of snows. TrJP

O Black and Unknown Bards. James Weldon Johnson. You sang a race from wood and stone to Christ. BANP; BPo; HeIP; PoBA; PoNe; TTY; UnPo; UnS

O Blessed House, That Cheerfully Receiveth. Karl J. P. Spitta. Rejoice in Thee, O blessed Lord, in Thee. TrPWD

O Blest Estate, Blest from Above. George Sandys. ...and joy which shall forever, ever last. AH

O Blest Unfabled Incense Tree. George Darley. Mourned by the desert where she dies! AtBAP; FaBoCh; FaBoRV; LoGBV

O Blisful Light: Troilus and Criseide. Geoffrey Chaucer. To which gladnesse, who nede hath, God him bringe! AtBAP

O Boy Cutting Grass. Hitomaro. Of my Lord who is going to deign to come. AWP

O Boys! O Boys! Oliver St. John Gogarty. But Boys! O Boys! O Boys! OBMV

O Brazil, the Isle of the Blest. Gerald Griffin. And he died on the waters, away, far away! ACP

O briar-scents, on yon wet wing. George Meredith. My thirst to bite where she had bit. EG

O Brother Man. John Greenleaf Whittier. And in its ashes plant the tree of peace. TRV

O Brother Tree. Max Michelson. Reveal to me thy serene knowledge. TrJP

O Brothers, Why Do You Talk. Mahadevi (Mahadeviyakka). she has lain down/with the lord, white as jasmine,/and has lost caste. WPOW

O Bruadair. James Stephens. So I'll sing no more songs for the men that care nothing/for me. BIrV; OxBI

O Bury Me Beneath the Willow (with music). Anonymous. And perhaps he'll think of me. AS

O By the By. Edward Estlin Cummings. and will somebody tell/me why people let go OxBA

O California. Alejandro Murguia. Let's go to California FIA

O Canada! Adolphe Routhier. As waiting for the better day/We ever stand on guard. FSW

O Carib Isle! Hart Crane. Sere of the sun exploded in the sea. AP; MoPo; NePA; NoAm; PoA; VGW

O Catch Miss Daisy Pinks. Alistair Campbell. Crackles like paper money. AnNZ

O Child of Beauty Rare. Johann Wolfgang von Goethe. He looked upon the twain, like Joseph standing by. ISi

O Child of Lowly Manger Birth. Ferdinand Q. Blanchard. Teach us to share thy ageless power. AH

O Children, Would You Cherish? Christopher Dock. And every lamb of Jesus/Shall then receive his crown. AH

O Christ of Bethlehem. H. Glenn Lanier. The blessing of thy holy Name/Grace every village home. AH

O Christ of Calvary, This Lent. Alice Mortenson. Thy resurrection day will dawn/With deeper meaning now. BePJ

O Christ, Thou Art within Me Like a Sea. Edith Lovejoy Pierce. Thou art within me like a sea at dawn. TrPWD

O Christ, Who Died. John Calvin Slemp. And let you die with bleeding heart. TrPWD

O Christmas Night. Henricus Selyns. For they, the after-life, shall live/With him, in New Jerusalem. AH

O City, Cities! (excerpt),. R. Ellsworth Larsson. as winds unravel vagrant bells. AnAmPo

O Come Out of the Lily. Ruth Pitter. As once in the garden, walk again,/Centre and spirit of human kind. AnFE

O! Come to the Greenwood Shade. Alexander McLachlan. If freedom be but there. PeCV

O Come with Me, Thus Ran the Song. Emily Bronte. And thou hast toiled and laboured long/With aching head and weary eye. NOBV

O'Connor the Bad Traveler. Peter Klappert. That's my song: a couple of mouthfuls of air,/a serenade, by bulblight. FiCP

O Could I Find from Day to Day. Benjamin Cleavland. And when my flesh dissolves in death/My soul shall love thee more. AH

O Country People. John Hewitt. or when the last lint's carted round the bend. ACV

O Crimson Blood. Hildegard von Bingen. The winter-storm the serpent breathes/Has never withered. WPOW

O Cuckoo. Anonymous. In the midst of my love! AWP

O.D. Zack Gilbert. Turn from this/Death/sleep. CNA

O Daedalus, Fly Away Home. Robert Earl Hayden. O fly away home fly away BiP; HAP; IDB; NCSH; PoBA; PoNe; WeW

O Day of God, Draw Nigh. Robert B. Y. Scott. Let there be light again, and set/Thy judgments in the earth. AH

O Day of Light and Gladness. Frederick Lucian Hosmer. Who fillest from thy fullness/Time and eternity. AH

O Day of Rest and Gladness. Christopher Wordsworth. We reach the rest remaining/To spirits of the blest. WGRP

O Dear Life, When Shall It Be? Sir Philip Sidney. At her lips, my nectar drinking. EnRePo

O Dear O. Anonymous. My husband got no courage in him/O dear O! ErPo

O Death. Anonymous. Can't you spare me over for another year? TrAS

O Death, Rock Me Asleep. Anne Boleyn. Death doth draw nigh;/There is no remedy. EIL; FF

O Death, Rock Me Asleep. George Boleyn. For now I dye,/I die, I die. EnPo; FaBoRV

O Desolate Eves. Christopher John Brennan. ...,yet I draw courage to front the/way. CoBE; PoAu 1-2

O Deus, Ego Amo Te. Gerard Manley Hopkins. What must I love thee, Lord, for then?/For being my king and God. Amen. TrPWD

O Dirty Bird Yr Gizzard's Too Big & Full of Sand. James Koller. this the fellow/made the world/what it is PoM

O Divine Star of Heaven. John Fletcher. Make me by thy answer blessed. GBL

O do not grieve, Dear Heart, nor shed a tear. Margaret Canvendish, Duchess of Newcastle. When in your hate a devil's shape I take. EnLoPo

O Do Not Prize Thy Beauty. *Anonymous* Some even to themselves seem strange/Thorough their own delay. LiTL

O Doctor Dear My Love. Anne Halley. O dear my doctor, love, be still/ Hush, surgeon, little friend, come fast. NMM

O'Donnell Aboo. Michael Joseph McCann. Strike for your country, "O'Donnell Aboo!" FSW; OnYI

O dream from the blackness. Sappho. Now may I have/all these things. BoWoP

O Dream, Where Art Thou Now? Emily Bronte. Thou canst not shine again. NOBV

O Dreams, O Destinations. C. Day-Lewis We settle, but like feathers on time's flow. MoPo

O'Duffy's Ironsides. *Anonymous.* The Fascists sing the ancient hymn,/"The Peeler and the Goat." OnYI

O Earnest Be. *Anonymous.* O never be faint hearted. AH

O Earth! Art Thou Not Weary? Julia Caroline Ripley Dorr. O Earth! art thou not weary of thy dead? AA

O Earth, Sufficing All Our Needs. Sir Charles G. D. Roberts. But here I find Him, in your quickening dust. CaP

O Earth, Turn! George Johnston. My why and how are me. WHW

O Ease My Spirit. Hugh" (Christopher Murray Grieve) MacDiarmid. As on my sweetheart's head, and draw it to me. BSV

O'er Continent and Ocean. John Haynes Holmes. O'er sea and shore and continent,/To all the sons of men. AH

O'er the Water to Charlie. Robert Burns. And live and die wi' Charlie. FaBoCh

O'er Waiting Harp-Strings of the Mind. Mary Baker Eddy. An offering pure of love, where to/God leadeth me. AH

O Fairest of the Rural Maids. William Cullen Bryant. Of those calm solitudes, is there. AA; AmLP; AnAmPo; LaNeLa

O Faithless Thorn. *Anonymous.* O faithless thorn. WTO

O Fearfull, Frowning Nemesis. Samuel Daniel. As we, so they that treate us thus,/Must one day perish like to us. PoEL 1-5

"O Felix Culpa!" *Anonymous.* Therefore we must singen/Deo Gratias. ACP; CAW

O Flame of Living Love. Saint John of Damascus. How delicately thou teachest love to me! AWP; CAW

O Fly My Soul. James Shirley. Poor Pilgrims needs must lose their way,/ When all the shadowes do encrease. AtBAP; OBS; OxBoCh

O Fond, but Fickle and Untrue. Walter Savage Landor. And Love goes too...but goes the last. GBL

O For a Booke." *Anonymous.* For a jollie goode Booke whereon to looke,/is better to me than Golde. CH; PoSC; SiSoSe

O, for Ane-and-Twenty. Robert Burns. I'm thine at ane-and-twenty, Tam. BSV

O For Doors to Be Open. W.H. Auden. The six beggared cripples. AtBAP; CoBMV; OAEP; ViBoPo

O for the Happy Hour. George Washington Bethune. Then shall our people all be thine,/Our church, like that above. AH

O Friends! Who Have Accompanied Thus Far. Walter Savage Landor. Of youth; without it life and death are one. GBL

O Friendship! Friendship! the Shell of Aphrodite. Walter Savage Landor. Lies always at the bottom of thy warm and limpid waters. GBL

O, Gambler, Git Up Off o' Yo' Knees. *Anonymous.* End o' dat mornin' when de Lord said to hurry. BoAN 1-2

O Gather Me the Rose. William Ernest Henley. The memories that follow! MoBrPo

O Gentle Love. George Peele. I take the wound, and die at Venus' foot. EIL

O Gentle Ships. Meleager. While Zeus breathes friendly on your sails. AWP

O Girl, You Torment Me... *Anonymous.* So will I snare you, for I have caught a thousand so. WTO

O Glorious Childbearer. Joseph Campbell. Immaculate of man's infirmities. OnYI

O Glorious Christ of God; I Live. Cotton Mather. Oh, for an Healed Soul! SCAP

O Glory of Virgins. Saint Venantius Fortunatus. Glory to You forever and ever. Amen. ISi

O God, Above the Drifting Years. John Wright Buckham. To build a kingdom yet to be. AH

O God, Accept the Sacred Hour. Samuel Gilman. And humbly learn, like him, to give/Our powers, our wills, to thee. AH

O God, Great Father, Lord, and King. E. Embree Hoss. And bring them all to heaven at last. AH

O God! Have Mercy in This Dreadful Hour. Robert Southey. O God! have mercy on the mariner! MOS; TrPWD

O God, How Many Years Ago. Frederic William Henry Myers. Wherever there is misery,/Wherever there are men. HBMV

O God, I Cried, No Dark Disguise. Edna St. Vincent Millay. And let the face of God shine through. AH

O God, in Restless Living. Harry Emerson Fosdick. Enrich our souls in secret/With abundant life. AH

O God, in Whom the Flow of Days. Donald Campbell Babcock. Forbid that we should vainly rove/Beyond the freedom of thy love. AH

O God, in Whose Great Purpose. James G. Gilkey. O God of strength, be thou to us/Our fathers' God again! AH

O God! O Montreal! Samuel (1835-1902) Butler. O God! O Montreal! FaBoCo; NBM

O God of Bethel. Doddridge. Philip Logan. John And at our Father's loved abode/Our souls arrive in peace. WTO

O God of My Salvation, Hear. Joel Barlow. Recall my wandering thoughts to mourn. AH

O God of Stars and Distant Space. John Franzen. And when the evening shadows fall/Bestow thy blessing on us all. AH

O God of Youth. Bates G. Burt. When all its kingdoms shall his kingdom be. AH

O God Our Help in Ages Past. Isaac Watts. And our eternal home! BLRP; EaLo; FaPoR; HBV 1-2; OxBoCh; WGRP

O God, Send Men. Elizabeth Burrowes. Each making answer, Here am I, send me. AH

O God, the Rock of Ages. Edward Henry, Bishop of Exeter Bickersteth. And let Thy Spirit brighten/The hearts Thyself hast blessed! BLPA; FPL

O God, Though Countless Worlds of Light. James D. Knowles. In many a heart now dead in sin,/A living temple rear. AH

O God Whose Presence Glows in All. Nathaniel Langdon Frothingham. And we can need no other rest. AH

O Golden Fleece. George Barker. Adorning the head that destiny never worried. MoAB; MoBrPo

O Gongyla, my darling rose. Sappho. ...you whom of all women/I most desire. BoWoP

O goodly hand. Sir Thomas Wyatt. And rid it out of pain. FCP; InvP; SiPS

O Gracious Father of Mankind. Henry Hallam Tweedy. Content to pray in life and love/And toil, till all are thine. AH

O Gracious Jesus, Blessed Lord! Andrew Fowler. We may awake to see thy face. AH

O Gracious Shepherd. Henry Constable. Then know Thy sheep, which knows his Shepherd's voice. OxBoCh

O'Grady's Goat. Will S. Hays. Was Mag McGinty's bushtlefast,/That inded Grady's goat. PoLf

O Grief! *Anonymous.* My cries and weeping. EIL

O Hark to the Herald. Eleazar Ben Kalir. The leaves of the Arabah are struck/thrice. TrJP

O Have You Caught the Tiger. Alfred Edward Housman. And that is why the noble beast/Has bitten off your head. BXAP; FaBoNo; SpRo

O Hear My Prayer, Lord. John Craig. Let thy good sprite conduct/Me to the land of right. AH

O Heart, Small Urn. Hilda. Doolithe. or dried up in the bleak drought/of bitter thought. AtBAP

O Heaven Indulge. Stephen Tilden. O might we live to him alone,/And nevermore transgress. AH

O Heavy Step of Slow Monotony. Ernst Toller. Nowhere blossoms Miracle. TrJP

O Holy City Seen of John. Walter Russell Bowie. And where the sun that shineth is/God's grace for human good. AH

O Holy, Holy, Holy Lord. James Wallis Eastburn. ...thy praises flow/From saint and seraph's burning tongue. AH

O Holy Water. Margot Ruddock. I weep and bleed/To follow thee. OBMV

O How I Love Thy Law. Isaac Watts. And there I write Thy praise. STF

O How Sweet Are Thy Words! Anne Steele. Teach me to love Thy Sacred Word/And view my Savior here. BLRP

O'Hussey's Ode to the Maguire. James Clarence Mangan. But the memory of the lime-white mansions his right hand/has laid/In ashes warms the hero's heart! AnIV; IrPN; NOBI; SeCePo; TW

O Hymen! O Hymenee! Walt Whitman. you would soon certainly kill me? ErPo

O I Won't Lead a Homely Life. Thomas Hardy. And sunk and sad was she! UnS

O It's Best Be a Total Boor. Daibhi O Bruadair. since the prime of life– that I might have spent as a boor. NOBI

O Jesu Parvule. *Anonymous.* My bairn sleep softly now. ISi

O Nightingale! Thou Surely Art.   William Wordsworth.   That was the Song—the Song for me!   AtBAP; HBV 1-2; PBBP

O No, John!   *Anonymous.*   O no, John! No, John! No, John! No!   ErPo; UnTE

O Now the Drenched Land Wakes.   Kenneth Patchen.   From this white grove/Where all nouns grieve.   PoA

O, Open the Door to Me, O!   Robert Burns.   My true love! she cried, and sank down by his side/Never to rise again, O!   FaBoCh; LoGBV

O Paradise! O Paradise!   Frederick William Faber.   In God's most holy sight.   WGRP

O people who live in the world.   Andal.   give away our possessions and live for him.   BoWoP

O Pine-Tree Standing.   Hakutsu.   The men of old time.   AWP

O Pioneers!   John Peale Bishop.   ...A continent they had/To ravage, and raving romped from sea to sea.   VGW

O Pity Our Small Size.   Benjamin Rosenbaum.   We are so weak. O pity our small size.   TrJP

O Powers Celestial, with What Sophistry.   Barnabe Barnes.   The land unknown, to rest and comfort me.   EnLoPo

O Realm Bejewelled.   Forugh Farrokhzad.   propagandizing our projects for stability,/and silence   WPOW

O'Reilly's Reply.   Richard Weber.   Perhaps it's unlikely, but I'd like to stay.   NMP

O Ride On, Jesus.   *Anonymous.*   Want t' go t'hebb'n in de mo'nin'.   AH

O Risen Lord upon the Throne.   Louis F. Benson.   Refresh us from thy wells of peace.   AH

O, Rocks Don't Fall on Me.   *Anonymous.*   O, rocks, don't fall on me,/Rocks an' mountains don't fall on me.   BoAN 1-2

O Rose, O Rainbow.   Nicholas Moore.   Mr. Orlimpit imagines his daybreak, its limpid, purely/Crystalline virtue.   NeBP

O Sailor, Come Ashore.   Christina Georgina Rossetti.   Feeble insects made it/In the stormy sea.   BrR; FM

O Saviour of a World Undone.   Leonard Withington.   My tears shall mingle with his blood.   AH

O, Saw Ye the Lass.   Richard Ryan.   To my dear one, the lass wi' the bonny blue een.   FaBoBe; HBV 1-2

O say, dear life, when shall these twinborn berries.   *Anonymous.*   Then be thou kind-bestow them free on me.   EG

O Say, My Brown Drimin.   *Anonymous.*   When the flint-hearted Saxons they've chased far away.   OnYI

O Sheriffs.   Drummond Allison.   Them string up undecayed and stellify.   OBSP

O Ship of State.   Henry Wadsworth Longfellow.   Our faith triumphant o'er our fears,/Are all with thee,—are all with thee!   FaFP

O Simplicitas.   Madeleine L'Engle.   Wiser than all men's knowing.   EBCP; OBCP; PCh

O Sing to Me of Heaven.   Mary Stanley Bunce Dana.   In heaven above, where all is love,/There'll be no sorrow there.   AH

O Sing unto my Roundelay.   Thomas Chatterton.   All under the willow-tree....   CH; LiTB

O Sion, Haste, Thy Mission High Fulfilling.   Mary A. Thomson.   Tidings of peace;/Tidings of Jesus,/Redemption and release.   AH

O Sleep.   Grace Fallow Norton.   Bear me now in thy deep/Bosom, Sleep,/O Sleep.   HBV 1-2

O Sleep, My Babe, Hear Not the Rippling Wave.   Sara Coleridge.   As when it deeply sighs/O'er autumn's latest bloom.   OBNC; OBRV

O Softly Singing Lute.   Francis Pilkington.   Yea, love through heart it dies—it dies.   OAEP

O Solitary of the Austere Sky.   Sir Charles G. D. Roberts.   Then shall this atom of the Eternal Soul/Encompass thee in its benign control!   CaP

O Son of God, Afflicted.   *Anonymous.*   Lord, may a love replying,/Within my soul awake.   STF

O Son of God, It Would Be Sweet.   Colum Cille.   To stay with Comgall, to visit Caindech,/it would be sweet.   NOBI

O Son of Man, Thou Madest Known.   Milton S. Littlefield.   Thy purpose for thy world we share.   AH; TrPWD

O Sons of Earth.   Alexander Pope.   Reason's whole pleasure, all the joys of sense,/Lie in three words–Health, Peace, and Competence.   TreFT

O Soul, With Storms Beset.   Solomon Ibn Gabirol.   Then will His angels come and lead/thee in/To Paradise.   TrJP

O Sower of Sorrow.   Joseph Mary Plunkett.   Withered leaves you shall find/And shall lose after finding.   CAW

O Spacred Head! Now Wounded.   Paul Gerhardt.   For he who dies believing/Dies safely in Thy love!   BePJ

O Spirit of Venus Whom I Adore.   *Anonymous.*   A striken deer, I seek the forest zones.   PeHV

O Spring, Come Prettily In.   Adolf Strodtmann.   Come in, O Spring, come prettily in/All human hearts, I pray!   CAW

O Star of Galilee.   Girolamo Savonarola.   And the kingdom come of peace.   ISi

O! Start a Revolution.   D. H. Lawrence.   but to abolish the working classes for ever/and have a world of men.   FaBoEE

O Stay, Sweet Love.   *Anonymous.*   I never meant to live and die a maid.   EG; TrGrPo

O Strassburg.   *Anonymous.*   "Farewell, farewell, my darling,/I'll never see thee more!"   WaaP

O Strong to Bless.   Elizabeth Daryush.   ...now we,/Mother, yet once more/come home to thee.   QFR

O! Susanna.   *Anonymous.*   I've come from Alabama/Wid my banjo on my knee.   GoTF

O Sweet Anne Page.   William Shenstone.   O sweet! O sweet Anne Page!   SeCePo

O Sweet Delight.   Thomas Campion.   Which till their eyes ache, let iron men envy!   EG

O sweet is love, and sweet is lack!   Francis Thompson.   Call the tired Love back!   EG

O Sweet Spontaneous.   Edward Estlin Cummings.   thou answerest/them only with/spring).   AnNE; NoAm; NoP; OxBA; PrIm; TrGrPo

O Sweetheart, Hear You.   James Joyce.   So he who has sorrow/Shall have rest.   FaBoRV; GBL; HBMV; MoBrPo

O. T.'s Blues.   Waring Cuney.   Well his wife and his mother naturally cried.   MAT

O Tan-Faced Prairie-Boy.   Walt Whitman.   When lo! more than all the gifts of the world you gave me.   OxBA; PeHV

O Taste and See.   Denise Levertov.   hungry, and plucking/the fruit.   NoP; PBWP; PPP; TAP

O Tell Me How to Woo Thee.   Robert Graham.   For thy dear sake, nae care I'll take,/Tho' ne'er another trow me.   OBEC

O Tender under Her Right Breast.   George Barker.   As now, the day is over.   MoAB; MoBrPo

O Terrible Is the Highest Thing.   Kenneth Patchen.   So be the angels blinded in her new holiness.   VGW

O Terry.   Ruth Herschberger.   Instead of angry animals.   PoL

O, That I Had Some Secret Place.   *Anonymous.*   I hope I shall with Jesus reign,/And therefore I will serve him.   AmFP

O That I Had Wings Like a Dove.   *Anonymous.*   Stretch forth Thy arm from out the ark,/And take me to Thy rest.   OxBoCh

O That My Love Were in My Arms.   *Anonymous.*   Where would your lover go to sleep?/Upon your bosom 'tween your breats.   WTO

O the Chimneys.   Nelly Sachs.   And Israel's body in the smoke through the air!   VWA

O the Little Rusty Dusty Miller.   *Anonymous.*   I would give it all/To my dusty miller.   OxNR

O, the Marriage!   Thomas Osborne Davis.   The ladies that ride in their carriage/Might envy my marriage to me.   OBVV

O Thirsty Wind.   *Anonymous.*   There stands bird-haunted Lehua.   WTO

O, Thou Eternal One!   Derzhavin.   The soul shall speak in tears of gratitude!   WGRP

O Thou Eternal Source of Life.   Rolland W. Schloerb.   But feels the death that all must die/As fuller life is won.   TrPWD

O Thou Eternal Victim Slain.   Charles Wesley.   My God, who dies for me, for me.   NOCV

O Thou Immortal Deity.   Percy Bysshe Shelley.   By all that he has been and yet must be.   TrPWD

O Thou Most High Who Rulest All.   Anne Bradstreet.   Let not thine own inheritance/Be sold away for nought.   AH

O Thou That Sleep'st.   Sir William Davenant.   Good nut-brown ale and toast.   CBEP; InvP

O Thou to Whom the Musical White Spring.   Edward Estlin Cummings.   i. spill my bright incalculable soul.   InPo

O Thou Who Art Our Author and Our End.   Sir John Beaumont.   For lower I can find no place to stand.   GoTF; TreFT

O Thou, Who Didst Ordain the Word.   Edwin Hubbell Chapin.   Give him the victor's glistening robe,/The palm-wreath and the crown.   AH

O Thou Whose Feet Have Climbed Life's Hill.   Louis F. Benson.   Thy name, proclaimed by every lip,/The Master of our schools.   AH

O Thou Whose Gracious Presence Blest.   Louis F. Benson.   This home we consecrate to-day/Will be a Holy Place.   TrPWD

O Thou Whose Gracious Presence Shone.   Marion Franklin Ham.   That lifts the world to realms divine.   AH

O Thou Whose Image.   Arthur Hugh Clough.   I will not ask to feel thou art.   TrPWD

O Thou Whose Pow'r.   Boethius.   From thee, great God, we spring, to thee we tend,/Path, motive, guide, original, and end.   TrPWD

O Thou! Whose Presence Went Before.   John Greenleaf Whittier.   And to his fettered soul be given/The glorious freedom of the just.   AH

O Thought!   Von Trimberg Susskind.   o bear me to the spirit's haunts!   TrJP

O to Be a Dragon.   Marianne Moore.   Felicitous phenomenon!   CTC; GoYe; NMM; PoPl

O to Be Up and Doing.   Robert Louis Stevenson.   Ye call me by the ear and eye!   GoTF; TreFT; TRV

O'Tuomy's Drinking Song.   John O'Tuomy.   This, this is my grand recreation!   OnYI

O Turn Onee More. Duncan Campbell Scott. O turn once more. CoBE
O Turn Ye, O Turn Ye. Josiah Hopkins. And prove that his mercy is boundless and free. AH
O-U-G-H. Charles Battell Loomis. He taught no more, I held him fast,/And killed him wiz a rough. NLV
O Virgin. Anonymous. And when I die may I say the pater,/Virgin Mary. WTO
O Virtuous Light. Elinor Wylie. ...radiance/Which is engendered of its own! AnAmPo; MoAB; MoAmPo; MoPo; NePA
O Waly, Waly Up the Bank. Anonymous. For a maid again I'll never be. EnLoPo; FaBoBa; GBP; OBS
O, Wasn't Dat a Wide River! Anonymous. Dere's one mo' river to cross. BoAN 1-2
O Wearisome Condition. Fulke Greville, Lord Brooke. To hate those errors which herself doth give. CBEP
O Were My Love Yon Lilac Fair. Robert Burns. Till fley'd awa by Phoebus' light! BSV; GBL; HBV 1-2; OBEV
O Wert Thou in the Cauld Blast. Robert Burns. The brightest jewel in my Crown/Wad be my Queen, wad be my Queen. BoLiVe; EBEV; EnL; EnPE; HeIP; NOBE; NoP; OAEP; OBEC; OxBS; TrGrPo; WHA
O Western Wind. Anonymous. Christ, that my love were in my arms,/And I in my bed again. HoPM; LiTB; PoPle; TrGrPo; UnTE
O Wha's the Bride? Hugh" (Christopher Murray Grieve) MacDiarmid. My virgin womb ha'e met.... AtBAP; BoLoP; BSV; CMoP; ErPo; FaBoTw; GTBS-P; LiTM; NeBP; NoAm; OBMV; OxBS
O What if the Fowler. Charles Dalmon. I'll weep all the day by my red fuchsia tree! CH
O What Pleasure 'Tis to Find. Aphra Behn. Her pride in her denial lies/And mine is in my victories. UnTE
O What's the Rhyme to Porringer. Anonymous. A psalm-book, and a Presbyter. GBP
O What Transparent Waves, What a Tranquil Sea. Vittoria da Colonna. the soul still catches sight of its faithful star. PBWP
O Where Are You Going? W. H. Auden. As he left them there, as he left them there. CMoP; LiTB; MoVE; NOBE; SoSe
O, Where Were We before Time Was. Max Dunn. and that whoever seeks to know/all of the loved will see love die? NOAV
O White Mistress. Don Johnson. O indoctrinated cattle of an illusion. NNP
O Whither Shall I Fly? Francis Quarles. ...my wings shall be/Stretch'd out no further than from thee to thee. OxBoCh
O Whose Are These Children. Richard Snyder. And the Lord of the Flies must leer/At such outpouring. SOTS
O Why Should the Spirit of Mortal Be Proud? William Knox. Oh, why should the spirit of mortal be proud? WGRP
O Why Was I Born with a Different Face? William Blake. When Elate I am Envy'd, When Meek I'm despis'd. PoL
O Wind, Why Do You Never Rest. Christina Georgina Rossetti. From the dim north bringing snow? TiPo
O, Woman! Sir Walter Scott. When pain and anguish wring the brow,/A ministering angel thou! GoTF
O Woman Full of Wile. Geoffrey Keating. O woman full of wile! OnYI
O Word of God Incarnate. William Walsham How. Till, clouds and darkness ended,/They see Thee face to face. TRV
O World. George Santayana. Unto the thinking of the thought divine. FPL; GoTF; HBV 1-2; PoLf; TreFS; TrGrPo; TRV
O World, Be Nobler. Laurence Binyon. O World, be nobler, for her sake! GTBS; HBV 1-2; MoBrPo; OBEV
O World, Be Not So Fair. Grace Fallow Norton. O world, be not so fair. HBV 1-2
O Wretch, Beware. William Dunbar. Vanitas Vanitatum, et omnia Vanitas. BSV
O Ye Sweet Heavens! Thomas William Parsons As I, O Pleiades! your beauty scan? AA
O Years Unborn. John Richard Moreland. The star that led to Bethlehem! PGD
O You among Women. Frederick Robert Higgins. As a coy star is there in the quiet/Of the wood's blue eye. BIrV
O You Chorus of Indolent Reviewers. Alfred, Lord Tennyson. So fantastical is the dainty metre. PV
O Young and Fearless Prophet. Samuel Ralph Harlow. Triumphantly to lead us/Along God's holy way. AH; TrPWD; TRV
O Youth with Blossoms Laden. Arthur Wallace Peach. Have pity–and remember/How soon thy roses die! HBMV
Oak. Philip Child. Returns the whispered message of the leaves. CaP
The Oak. John Dryden. Supreme in state, and in three more decays. OHIP
The Oak. Alfred, Lord Tennyson. Trunk and bough,/Naked strength. PoPl
Oak and Olive. James Elroy Flecker. Was I not bred in Gloucestershire,/One of the Englishmen! HBMV

The Oak and the Ash. Anonymous. Oh the oak and the ash and the bonnie ivy tree,/They flourish at home in my own country. FaBoCh; FSW; LoGBV
The Oak and the Brere. Edmund Spenser. Such was th' end of this ambitious Brere,/For scorning eld. OBSC
The Oak and the Olive. George Barker. ...Why, then, should I find/a child's face bright with tears haunting my mind? FaBoMo; OBTV
The Oak-Tree. William Barnes. Var I da love noo tree so well/'S the girt woak tree that's in the dell. OBVV
The Oakey Street Evictions. Anonymous. Alang wi' the twenty candymen an' Johnny that carries the bell. OBET
Oasis. Edward Dowden. Long since,–I know not when. OxBI
The Oasis of Sidi Khaled. Wilfrid Scawen Blunt. Oh this is rest. Oh this is paradise. OBTV
The Oath. Allen Tate. Then Lytle turned with an oath–By God it's true! FaBoMo; LiTM; NoAm; OxBA; VGW
Oatmeal Deluxe. Stephen Dobyns. what trouble would I make for you, a woman? AMV-81
Obatala, the Creator. Anonymous. You have twenty or thirty children waiting for me./Whom I shall bear! WTO
Obedience. George Herbert. They were by winged souls/Entred for both, farre above their desert! AnAnS 1
Obedience. George Macdonald. And I walk in a light divine/The path I had feared to see. BePJ; BLRP; TreFT; TRV; WGRP
The Obelisk Inscriptions (excerpt). Hatshepsut. On the Horus throne of all the living, eternally like Re. WPOW
Oberammergau. Leonora Speyer. Lord, help Thou mine unbelief! AnAmPo; HBMV
Obermann Once More. Matthew Arnold. High in the Valais-depth profound,/I saw the morning break. PoEL 1-5
Oberon's Feast. Robert Herrick.
   ...The feast is ended. BoLiVe; CaPo; OAEP; SeCV 1-2; TrGrPo
   ...some store/Of emmit's eggs; what would he more? ViBoPo
Oberon's Palace. Robert Herrick. ...This flax is spun. CaPo
Oberon, the Fairy Prince: A Catch. Ben Jonson. Else it was he. EIL; FM
Obit. Robert Lowell. After loving you so much, can I forget/you for eternity, and have no other choice? HaCAP
Obit on Parnassus. F. Scott Fitzgerald. To linger till ninety, like Landor. InMe; NLV; NYBP; PrIm
Obituary. Max (Charles Heber Clark) Adeler. Drop him in the sepulchre/With his Uncle Jerry. DTC
Obituary. Anthony Brode. It's sad kind words are seldom said/Until a rake is safely dead. FiBHP
Obituary. Kenneth Fearing. You were his true-blue pal. VGW
Obituary. Weldon Kees. And a black wreath decorates the door. BoAnP
Obituary. Thomas William Parsons But - kiss me, darling! dear old Smiler's dead. AA; HBV 1-2; HBVY
Obituary in Bitcherel. Conrad Aiken. And this be it known is all that we know. OBAL
The Objection to Being Stepped On. Robert Frost. The first tool I step on/Turned into a weapon. NLV
Objects. W. H. Auden. Extols the silence of how soon a loss. NePoAm-2
Objects. Richard Wilbur. The Cheshire smile–which sets me fearfully free. FF; NoP
The Objects of the Summer Scene. Thomas Caulfield Irwin. The tinkle of the dead leaf by the lone/Sea road, the sad look of the setting star. IrPN; NBM
Objets d'Art. Cynthia MacDonald. You'll know it by the three gold ones over the door. NMM
Oblation. A. Newberry Choyce. And little golden heads for when your head is gray. HBMV
The Oblation. Algernon Charles Swinburne. Mine is the heart at your feet/Here, that must love you to live. EnLit; GTBS; HBV 1-2; VLP
Obligations. Jane Cooper. And death and all we came here to evade. AmPC; NePoEA-2
Obligatory Love Poem. P. L. Jacobs. how do angels learn to sing? LFAC
Oblique. Archibald Rutledge. We only know they shall arrive. TRV
Oblique Birth Poem. Ann Darr. he sings in his cracked voice and we/are all laughter. GP
Oblivion. Jessie Redmond Fauset. Oblivion–the shroud and envelope of happiness. BANP; PoNe
Oblivion. Ellis Ayitey Komey. Before they die and turn to mud/And I have gone. PBA
Oblivion! Nelly Sachs. The dead dance/flower stalks of the wind– PBWP
Oboe. Laurence McKinney. "It's an ill wood wind no one blows good." NLV
Obon by the Hudson. Richard Oyama. stepping in the twin moons of the dance BrSi
The Obscene Caller. Philip Dacey. It will be he/who hangs up first. AmPA
The Obscene Caller. Cheri Fein. He preses down on my face/Ringing again and again. TW

Obscene Phone Call #2. Joy Harjo. None of your voices is enough/to fill this woman up. TWSS

The Obscure Night of the Soul. Saint John of Damascus. Among the lilies, and forgetting them. AWP; CAW; OBMV

The Obscure Pleasure of the Indistinct. Bin Ramke. ...Sounds/from the kitchen again are muffled, vague. MAYP

The Obscured Prince; or, the Black Box Boxed. *Anonymous.* And after Charles, who wrongs you of your crown,/Shall cut a million of true English down. APAS

Obsequies of Stuart. John Randolph Thompson. Shall lead his horsemen headlong on the foe,/In victory careering! PAH

The Obsequies of the Lord Harrington. John Donne. Doth practice dying by a little sleep. MyFE

Obsequies to the Lady Anne Hay. Thomas Carew. Thus even by Rivals to be Deifide. AnAnS 2

Observation. Robert Herrick. His Bed, Male children shall beget. FaBoUs

Observation. Dorothy Parker. Because I do not give a damn. FiBHP; InMe

Observation. Richard Weber. Women together/Little Better. PoL

Observation. Derk Wynard. How water must do just that for stone. AMV-80

Observation at Dawn. Abba Kovner. Then my finger taps on your throat/groping like a blind man's cane. VWA

Observation Car. A. D. Hope. But something went wrong with the plan: I am still on the train. NoAm

Observation Car and Cigar. William Stafford. ...our loves are brought/before us and followed securely into a new evening. LCAP

Observation of a Bee. Leah Goldberg. Fear kills./Watch out. WPOW

Observation of Facts. Charles Tomlinson. Those facets of copiousness which I proposed/Exist, do so when we have silenced ourselves. NePoEA-2

Observations in a Cornish Teashop. Kenneth Rexroth. Would be nicer to be/Fed intravenously? OBAL

The Observatory Ode. John Frederick Nims. No heat like science and poetry when they kiss. SUW

Observe the Whole of It. Thomas Wolfe. It's your oyster–yours to open if you will. TreFT

The Observer. David C. Yates. ...He is/the observer. He watches, He does not interfere. AMV-81

Observing a Vulgar Name on the Plinth of an Ancient Statue. Walter Savage Landor. Let Britons paint their bodies blue/As formerly, but touch not you. EyDe

The Obsession. Rosy Liggett. Together when he walked to the end of our hall. AMV-80

Obsessions. Denise Levertov. where the city's ashes that we brought with us/flew into the intense sky still burning. LiTM; NePoEA-2; SM

Obsessive. Marvin Bell. the father of a friend just sickened and sickened. LCAP

Occam's Razor Starts in Massachusetts (parody). Edward Pygge. And sees Narcissus making up his face. BXAP

The Occasional Yarrow. Stevie Smith. Bless thy sweet name and all who praise/The Occasional Yarrow. FaBoNo

Occasioned by General Washington's Arrival in Philadelphia... Philip Freneau. And all the pageant scene expires. PAH

Occasioned by Seeing a Walk of Bay Trees. Mildmay Fane, Earl of Westmoreland. His year's all spring, and hath no fall. OBSP

Occupation: Housewife. Phyllis McGinley. ...And with Contract she delays/The encroaching desolation of her days. DBV

Occupational Hazards. David Young. the fallen trees/keep ringing. FiCP

Ocean. Robinson Jeffers. Greatness is but less little; and death's changed life. AP; CoBMV

The Ocean. Moschus. ...where the brook's murmuring/Moves the calm spirit, but disturbs it not. AWP

Ocean. Robert Pollok. Thy great obeisance. EtS

The Ocean. George Denison Prentice. I go–I go–dear Ocean, fare thee well! EtS

The Ocean. Laura St. Martin. and the moon casts a furious gleam on the many-knuckled sea FF

The Ocean. John Augustus Shea. Be more mighty, more lasting,/More chainless than thou! EtS

The Ocean Burial. *Anonymous.* They buried him there in the deep, deep sea. PSoN; ShS; ViBoFo

The Ocean-Fight. *Anonymous.* Full many a bard shall chant his lays,/Their requiem. PAH

The Ocean Is Like a Wreath. Kuapakaa. As you paddle to destruction at the point of Lehua,/Ualapue, Kaluaaha, Molokai. WTO

An Ocean Lullaby. Charles Augustus Keeler. The ship is your cradle, the sea is your home. EtS

The Ocean Said to Me Once. Stephen Crane. "Until he stands like a child/"With surplus of toys." MOS

The Ocean Spills. Samuel Hoffenstein. The sands are dry, the ocean filled. ALV

The Ocean Wanderer. *Anonymous.* Death like pomatum, tea, and crabs must fall. NA

The Ocean Wood. John Byrne Leicester Warren, Lord De Tabley. Will bring no comfort home to me. CBEP

Oceana and Britannia. John Ayloffe. And by her oracles the world shall sway. APAS

Oceans. Juan Ramon Jimenez. and are we standing now, quietly, in the new life? NU

The Ochil Hills. *Anonymous.* Nane, nane on earth that wander. PoSH

The Ocotillo in Bloom. Marilla Merrimar Guild. They flutter there/And poise in air. BPAW

October. John Bayliss. Have we not learnt our histories? NeBP

October. Bill Berkson. ...and the stone/of your words as they pass, as I do not hear them. ANYP

October. Robert Frost. For the grapes' sake along the wall. GoJo; MAmP

October. Rose Fyleman. But isn't it lovely/Kicking up leaves! SiSoSe; TiPo

October. Judith Goren. to romp in the falling leaves. AMV-81

October. Steve Hahn. the hats of small barbarians/who lie drunken in the leaves. PPJ

October. Patrick Kavanagh. And my nineteen years weigh heavily on my feet. CIP; GTBS-P

October. Fredric Koeppel. darkened to slate by melting frost. AMV-80

October. Greg Pape. Night after night/the drunks and the dancers/hold still/in the ruined walls. AmPA

October. Barry Spacks. My wife sits reading in a garden chair. PoA; SM

October. Dylan Thomas. ...sun of October/Summery/On the hill's shoulder. YeAr

October. Edward ("Edward Eastaway") Thomas. And this mood by the name of melancholy/Shall no more blackened and obscured be. ChMP; MoVE; NoAm

October. Jones Very. To bid me heed before the approach of winter's sterner day. AnNE

October. Thomas Wolfe. ..and they will think of things they have no words to utter. AnEnPo

October 1. Karl Shapiro. What shall uproot a house and bring this care into his eye? MoAB; MoAmPo; PoA

October 14. 1644. Edward, Lord Herbert of Cherbury. And bring my Soul to its desired place. AnAnS 2

October 16: The Raid. Langston Hughes. Perhaps/You will recall/John Brown. BOLo; PoBA

October 1803. William Wordsworth. I tremble at the sorrow of the time. EnRP

October 1942. Roy Fuller. ...a streaming wound which heals in evil. WaP

October and November. Robert Lowell. artist and office-holder to a claque of less/than fifty souls...to each his venomous in-group. MAT

October Dusk. C. Stephen Finley. And into the ground. AMV-80

October Elegy. Margaret Gibson. ...fire cracks/from common stone, a sunrise in evening. FYAP

October Flies. Jascha Kessler. –to give/thanks, I say, that, distracted, He clap not His/Hands! AmPC

October, Hanson's Field. Roo Borson. Past sunset they send up their shadows/to lean against the trees,/like holograms. CaPN

October Hill. R. Wayne Hardy. and defecated by the raw land/and its wild secret. LFAC

October in Tennessee. Walter Malone. October, like a King resigned to fate,/Dies in his forests with their sunset fire. AA

October Journey. Margaret Walker. stagnant, and green, and full of slimy things. AmNP; IDB; PoBA; PoNe

October Maples, Portland. Richard Wilbur. They could not choose but to return in blue. CoPo

October Morning. John James Piatt. Good, our first fire is lighted! YeAr

October Night. Agnes Louise Dean. The cold stars are bright. YeAr

October Poems: The Garden. Robert Penn Warren. All things that fed luxurious sense/From appetite to innocence. PoA

The October Redbreast. Alice Meynell. This singing-bird's a lad, a lad. MoBrP

October's Bright Blue Weather. Helen Hunt Jackson. Love loveth best of all the year/October's bright blue weather. AmePo; BLPA; BLPL; FaBoBe; GN; GoTF; HBVY; PoSC; TreFT

October's Party. George Cooper. And then the party ended/In jolly "hands around." BrR; HBV 1-2; HBVY; PoLf; SiSoSe

October's Song. Eleanor Farjeon. The greenleaf is flowing/In flame out of sight! PoSC

October Winds. Virginia D. Randall. Then gently shoo the flocks away,/Before the winter comes to stay. YeAr

October XXIX, 1795. William Stanley Braithwaite. Because he played with Beauty for a toy!' CDC

Ode on Melancholy. John Keats. And be among her cloudy trophies hung. AtBAP; BoLiVe; DiPo; ERoP 1-2; ExPo; FiP; ForPo; HAP; LiTB; MAT; MBW 1-2; NAWM 1-2; NIP; NOBE; NoP; OAEL 1-2; OAEP; OBEV; OBNC; PAI; PoEL 1-5; PoPle; PoRA; PPP; PrIm; SeCeV; TEP; TreFS; TrGrPo

An Ode on Miss Harriet Hanbury. Sir Charles Hanbury Williams. A beauty, that can charm like you. OBEC

Ode on Science. Jezaniah Sumner. All haughty tyrants we disdain,/And shout "Long live America!" TrAS

Ode on Solitude. Alexander Pope. Steal from the world, and not a stone/ Tell where I lie. ATP; AWP; DiPo; ExPo; FiP; GoBC; GoTF; HBV 1-2; HBVY; HeIP; InPo; NIP; OAEP; OBEC; PoPl; PoPle; PoRA; PPoe; Prf; SeCeV; TEP; TreFS; ViBoPo

Ode on St. Cecilia's Day. John Dryden.
And seems to shake the spheres. GN
Charge, charge! 'tis too late to retreat. GN

An Ode on the Birth of Our Saviour. Robert Herrick. And plaster'd round with amber. GN; SBVL

Ode on the Death of a Favorite Cat, Drowned in a Tub of Gold Fishes. Thomas Gray. Nor all that glisters, gold. CEP; EBEV; EiCP; FaBoBe; FaBoCo; FM; GTBS; HoPM; InPS; LAuP; NLV; NOBE; NOBL; NOEC; NoP; OAEP; OBEC; PCat; PoEL 1-5; PPP; TEP

An Ode on the Death of Mr. Henry Purcell (excerpt). John Dryden. And list'ning and silent, and silent and list'ning,/and list'ning and silent obey. PBBP

Ode on the Death of the Duke of Wellington. Alfred, Lord Tennyson. God accept him, Christ receive him. ACV; OBVV; VLP

Ode: On the Death of William Butler Yeats. A. J. M. Smith. To the tumultuous throng/Of the sky his cold and passionate song. OBCV; PeCV

Ode on the Departing Year. Samuel Taylor Coleridge. Glitter green with sunny showers. FaBoPP

An Ode on the Despoilers of Learning in an American University (1947). Yvor Winters. Of Learning is its own/Inscrutable old Bar. ExPo

Ode on the Pleasure Arising from Vicissitude. Thomas Gray. And tastes it as it goes. CEP; EiCP; GTBS; GTBS-P; LAuP; NOEC; OBEC

Ode on the Poetical Character. William Collins. Or curtain'd close such Scene from ev'ry future View. CEP; EiCP; EnPE; EnRP; ERoP 1-2; LAuP; NOEC; NoP; OAEL 1-2; OAEP; PoEL 1-5; TEP

An Ode on the Popular Superstitions of the Highlands of Scotland... William Collins. And, touch'd with love like mine, preserve my absent friend. CEP; EiCP; EnPE; LAuP; NOEC; OAEL 1-2; OAEP; OBEC

Ode on the Spring. Thomas Gray. We frolic, while 'tis May. CEP; EiCP; GTBS; GTBS-P; HBV 1-2; LAuP; NOEC

Ode on Theoxenos. Pindar. Grace and Persuasion dwell in young Theoxenos. PeHV

Ode on Zero. Phoebe Pettingell. Must both, in total, be THE GREAT ZERO. PoA

Ode: "Once more the country calls." Allen Tate. Go kill the dying swan! WaP

Ode: "Peer of gods he seemeth to me." Sappho. Caught by pains of menacing death, I falter,/Lost in the love-trance. LiTW

Ode: "Poor bird, I do no envy thee." George Daniel. ...Pretty redbreast, sing/What I would speak. PBBP

Ode Recited at the Harvard Commemoration. James Russell Lowell. But ask whatever else, and we will dare! AA; AP; HBV 1-2; MAmP; NOBA; OBWP; OHIP; PAH

Ode: Salute to the French Negro Poets. Frank O'Hara. and dying in black and white we fight for what we love, not are NeAP; NNaP; PoM; PoNe

An Ode: Secundum Artem. William Cowper. To bind the poet's brow, or please the critic's nose. PP

Ode: "Sire of the rising day." John Byrne Leicester Warren, Lord De Tabley. Abash'd before the perfect crowning sleep. OBVV

Ode: "Sleep sweetly in your humble graves." Henry Timrod. By mourning beauty crowned! MAmP; NOBA; OxBA; TAP

Ode: Solitude, at an Inn. Thomas Warton, Jr.. Thy presence is, sweet Solitude. CEP

Ode Sung at the Opening of the International Exhibition. Alfred, Lord Tennyson. And gathering all the fruits of earth and/crown'd with all her flowers. VLP

Ode Sung in the Town Hall. Ralph Waldo Emerson. Ere freedom out of man. AnNE

Ode: "Tell me, thou soul of her I love." James (1700-48) Thomson. Oh visit thou my soothing dream! OBEC

Ode: "That I have often been in love, deep love." John Wolcot. Go, Wedlock, to the men of leaden brains,/Who hate variety, and sigh for chains. NOEC

An Ode: "The merchant, to secure his treasure." Matthew Prior. And Venus to the Loves around/Remarked how ill we all dissembled. InPo; NOEC; NoP; PoRA; ViBoPo

Ode: The Spirit Wooed. Richard Watson Dixon. When the voice has ceased to cry? OBNC

Ode: "They journeyed." Ibn al-Arabi. Is it not enough? AWP; LiTW

An Ode: "Thou Dome, where Edward first enroll'd." Thomas Tickell. To Him, through every rescu'd land,/Ten thousand Living trophies stand. OBEC

Ode to a Beautiful Woman. Carl Clark. Come close, warm me, even/If I die in the flame. JB

Ode to a Butterfly. Thomas Wentworth Higginson. Symbol of life, me with such faith endow! AA; FaBoBe; HBV 1-2

Ode to a Country Hoyden. John Wolcot. Clip thy wild tongue, and tie thee to the table. NOEC

Ode to a Dead Dodge. David McElroy. ...Very good, I've heard, for tea. AmC; AmPA; DFF

Ode to a Dental Hygienist. Earnest Albert Hooton. She sees how much of me is rotten. FiBHP

Ode to a Ditch. Anonymous. And offal and filth of all manner in heaps. PeD

Ode to a Dressmaker's Dummy. Donald Justice. Prim ghost the evening light shone through. DFF

Ode to a Fat Cat. Annabel Farjeon. And so I sing/To matchless Maud/ Squatting in a drawer in Spring. PCat

Ode to a Friend. William Mason. Will heave one tuneful sigh, and sooth my hov'ring Shade. OBEC

Ode to a Homemade Coffee Cup. Marine Robert Warden. so that you may share with me/a moment of morning silence. AMV-81

Ode to a Lady Whose Lover Was Killed by a Ball... George Gordon, Lord Byron. Thou too hast kept thy plight full well,/As many a baffled Heart can tell. ERoP 1-2

Ode to a Lebanese Crock of Olives. Diane Wakoski. Thank you, Aunt Libby,/from a failed beach girl,/out of the West. GP

Ode to a Lost Cargo in a Ship Called Save. Jose Craveirinha. And the cargo of young people, uninsured but liberated/From the hellish hold of the burned boat. WhB

Ode to a Model. Vladimir Nabokov. by removing you bodily/from back numbers of Sham? OBAL; PoPl

Ode to a Nightingale (parody). Roy Kelly. Immortal, they may rest sublime,/though beauty burns and love goes wrong. BXAP

Ode to a Nightingale: The Nightingale. John Keats. Charmed magic casements, opening on the foam/Of perilous seas, in faery lands forlorn. FaBV

Ode to a Pig While His Nose Was Being Bored. Robert Southey. To think that for your master's good you die? NOBL

Ode to a Skylark. Percy Bysshe Shelley. The world would listen then–as I am listening/now. BoLiVe; MBW 1-2; NOBE

Ode to a Vanished Operator in an Automatized Elevator. Loyd Rosenfield. Both Up and Down wish you were here. QQQ

Ode to a Young Lady, Somewhat Too Sollicitous about Her Manner... William Shenstone. So Laura's words be not unkind. CEP

Ode to Anactoria. Sappho. Till, as one about to die, I linger/Paler than grass is... AWP

Ode to Aphrodite. Sappho. ...O Aphrodite,/Fight by my shoulder! AWP; EnLi 1-2

Ode to Apollo. John Keats. From thee, great God of Bards, receive their heavenly/birth. ERoP 1-2

Ode to Arnold Schoenberg. Charles Tomlinson. ...cradling space/and then/ filling it with verdure? NePoEA-2

Ode to Beauty. Ralph Waldo Emerson. Unmake me quite, or give thyself to me! AP; ForPo; PoEL 1-5

Ode to Bohemians. Ron Padgett. ...Thank you, anyway,/colorful individuals. APU

Ode to Chloris. Charles Cotton. Love or Death should set me free. CavP

Ode to Cupid. Charles Cotton. Two Loves would make all women mad. CavP

Ode to Duty. William Wordsworth. And in the light of truth thy Bondman let me live! AWP; BiP; EnLit; ERoP 1-2; FPL; GoTF; GTBS; GTBS-P; HBV 1-2; HBVY; InPo; NoP; OAEL 1-2; OBEV; OBRV; TreFS; TRV; WGRP

Ode to England. William Wilberforce Lord
Doth yield to Immortality. AA
Through its deep night, that kindled as he/fell. AA

Ode to Ethiopia. Paul Laurence Dunbar. And proudly tune their lyres to sing/Of Ethiopia's glory. BALP

Ode to Eve. Edwin Meade Robinson. Of gains unsought your apple brought, to stagger a re-/vivalist!) InMe

Ode to Evening. William Collins. And hymn thy fav'rite name! AnEnPo; AnFE; ATP; AWP; EBEV; EG; EiCP; EnPE; EnRP; ExPo; FaBoBe; GTBS; HAP; HBV 1-2; InPo; LAuP; LoBV; MasP; NOBE; NOEC; NoP; OAEL 1-2; OAEP; OBEV; PoEL 1-5; PPP; SeCePo; SeCeV; TreFT; TrGrPo; ViBoPo; WHA

Ode to Evening. Joseph Warton. That fills with farewell notes the dark'ning plain. ATP

Ode to Fanny. John Keats. Love! on their lost repose. ChRP

Ode to Fear. William Collins. And I, O Fear, will dwell with Thee! CEP; EiCP; EnPE; LAuP; NOEC; OAEP; TrGrPo

Ode to Fidel Castro. Edward Field. The way you meant to be. CoPo

Ode to Food. Darrell Gray. Come into me, and I will make you full. APU

Ode to Fortune. Joseph R. and Halleck, Fitz-Greene Drake. 'T were cruelty to tumble down. AA

Ode to Freedom. Aaron Zeitlin. Like a bad dream on memory's ebbtide drifting. VWA

Ode to Jamestown. James Kirke Paulding. He is a bastard if he dare to mock/Old Jamestown's shrine or Plymouth's/famous rock. PAH

Ode to Joy. Daniel Gerard Hoffman. Nothing else there was that we need know. AMV-81

Ode to Joy. Michael McClure. What joy to be in flight. GP

Ode to Joy. Frank O'Hara. No more dying NeAP; PPP

Ode to Joy. Friedrich von Schiller. See, above the starry clime/God a great reward preparing. LiTW

Ode to Leven Water. Tobias Smollett. The blessings they enjoy to guard. BSV; CEP; OBEC

Ode to Liberty. Percy Bysshe Shelley. As waves which lately paved his watery way/Hiss round a drowner's head in their tempestu-/ous play. MBW 1-2

An Ode to Master Endymion Porter, upon His Brother's Death. Robert Herrick. Thanks to the generous vine/Invites fresh grapes to fill his press with wine. CaPo

Ode to Me. Kingsley Amis. But not all that many. Cheers! NAs

Ode to Memory. Alfred, Lord Tennyson. I faint in this obscurity,/Thou dewy dawn of memory. VLP

Ode to Mercy. William Collins. Thou, thou shalt rule our queen, and share our monarch's throne! EiCP; LAuP

Ode to Michael Goldberg's Birth and Other Births: "I don't remember." Frank O'Hara. "no excuses, now" NAs; NeAP

Ode to Miss Hoyland (parody). Thomas Chatterton. And make thy Baker blest? BXAP

Ode to Moderation (excerpt). Annabella Plumptre. Then if thy victims pause, prepare th' eternal chain. NOEC

An Ode to Mr. Anthony Stafford to Hasten Him into the Country. Thomas Randolph. And Doric music make/To civilize with graver notes our wits again. AnAnS 2; OBS; ViBoPo

Ode: To My Lovers. Paul Verlaine. And make a feast of shit and cum, of ass and thighs! PeHV

Ode: To My Pupils. W. H. Auden. We shall lie out there. MoBrPo

An Ode to Myself. Thomas Dermody. Never shall lingering honour quit/Thy heart sincere. OnYI

Ode to Naples (excerpt). Percy Bysshe Shelley. ...even as the Power divine/Which then lulled all things, brooded upon mine. FaBoPP

Ode to Nea. Thomas Moore.
Along that wild and lonely shore,/Such walks will be our ruin! OBNC
I'll praise, admire, and worship thee,/But must not, dare not, love again. OBNC

Ode to New York. Reed Whittemore. Would you buy these woids? NYP

Ode: "To orisons, the midnight bell." William Beckford. He turned, and vanished in the bright'ning dell. OBTV

Ode to Peace. Anonymous. Which erring made mankind arise,/To deeds of sin, to blood and wars. PAH

Ode to Pity. William Collins. Till, virgin, thou again delight/To hear a British shell! CEP; EiCP; EnPE; LAuP

Ode to Popularity. Winthrop Mackworth Praed. And hang, to dry upon the shore,/My trowsers and my jacket. VLP

Ode to Pornography. Jack Anderson. our species can be best and/blessed when we are most at play. PoA

Ode to Psyche. John Keats. A bright torch, and a casement ope at night,/To let the warm Love in! CABA; CBEP; DiPo; ERoP 1-2; HBV 1-2; InPS; LiTB; LoBV; MBW 1-2; NOBE; NoP; OAEL 1-2; OAEP; OBEV; OBNC; OBRV; PAI; PoEL 1-5; PP; PPP; WHA

Ode to Quinbus Flestrin. Alexander Pope. Lofty poet! touch the sky! OAEP

Ode to Salt. Pablo Neruda. but the inward flavor of the infinite. NU

Ode to Simplicity. William Collins. And all thy Sons, O Nature, learn my Tale. CEP; EiCP; EnLi 1-2; GTBS; LAuP; NOBE; OBEC; OBEV; TEP

Ode: To Sir William Sydney, on His Birth-Day. Ben Jonson. The Birth-day shines, when logs not burne, but/men. NAs

Ode to Solitude (excerpt). James Grainger. Bend, great God, before thy shrine,/The bournless macrocosm's thine. ViBoPo

An Ode to Spring in the Metropolis. Sir Owen Seaman. I ought to know! FiBHP

Ode to Terminus. W. H. Auden. self-proclaimed poets who, to wow an/audience, utter some resonant lie. HAP

Ode to the Alien. Diane Ackerman. I am life, and life loves life. SUW

Ode to the Cameleopard. Thomas Hood. And staring round him with a brace of beads! FaBoNo

Ode to the Chinese Paper Snake. Richard Eberhardt. And you increase his inviolability. CrMA

Ode to the Confederate Dead. Allen Tate. Sentinel of the grave who counts us all! AP; FaBoMo; HeIP; InPo; LiTA; LiTM; MoAB; MoAmPo; MoPo; MoVE; NoAm; NOBA; NoP; OBWP; OxBA; PrIm; SeCeV; TAP; UnPo; ViBoPo

Ode to the Confederate Dead in Magnolia Cemetery. Henry Timrod. There is no holier spot of ground/Than where defeated valor lies,/By mourning beauty crowned! PAL; TreFT

Ode: To the Cuckoo. Michael Bruce. Companions of the spring. NOEC; OBEC; PBBP

Ode to the Day. Ken Norris. as the world turns once and we manage it,/only rarely getting dizzy. CaPN

Ode to the End of Summer. Phyllis McGinley. Summer, farewell, farewell. NLV

Ode to the Evening Star. Mark Akenside. Till I forget my own. CEP; OBEC

Ode to the Finnish Dead. Chad Walsh. Bloom in th beauty of your giving, each/By each, in mankind's heart, brave Finnish dead. HoAn

Ode to the Fourth of July. Daniel George. Shout! Shout! Columbia's name, Columbia's name. TrAS

An Ode to the Framers of the Frame Bill. George Gordon, Lord Byron. Who, when asked for a remedy, sent down a rope. CoMu; SaC

Ode to the German Drama. Anonymous. To low-born arrogance to bend,/Established order spurn, and call each outcast friend. NOEC

Ode to the Hayden Planetarium. Arthur Guiterman. The drama of the world's annihilation! ImOP

Ode to the Human Heart. Laman Blanchard. And die ere man can say "Long live the Queen!" InMe; NA; NOBL

Ode to the Inhabitants of Pennsylvania. Anonymous. Our inexperienced troops inspire,/And conquest's laurels gain! PAH

Ode to the Lake of Geneva. William Parsons. More rapturous far were their delight/Could all partake the common right! OBTV

Ode to the Last Pot of Marmalade. "John." But leave me one spoonful of Bonnie Dundee. OBTV

Ode to the Medieval Poets. W. H. Auden. ...the knowledge/that you would have wrought them so much better. PoA

Ode to the Moon. Thomas Hood. And close his eyelids with thy silver wand! OBVV

Ode to the Muse on Behalf of a Young Poet. David Wagoner. The forgeries of death. AMV-80

Ode: To the Nightingale. Joseph Warton. No more to visit vale or shade,/Some barbarous virgin's captive made. PBBP

Ode to the North-East Wind. Charles Kingsley. Blow, thou wind of God! FaPoR; GN

Ode to the Norther. William Lawrence Chittenden. Here's to the strong, gray weather/That makes the heart of oak! BPAW

Ode to the Protestant Poets. Paul Hoover. stiff as nurses and slow as metaphysicians. APU

Ode to the Sea. Howard Baker. Burdened, yet to the nascent future bound! OxBA

Ode to the Setting Sun: The Sun. Francis Thompson. Before thy ark Earth keeps her sacred dance. GoBC; InMe; MoAB; MoBrPo; OBNC; WHA

Ode to the Spirit of Earth in Autumn. George Meredith. The spirit of the red man/Is welcomed by his fathers up on high. TEP; VLP

Ode to the Virgin. Petrarch. Receiving my last breath in peace. ISi

Ode to the Watermelon. Pablo Neruda. turned itself into a single/drop of water. EAS; NU

Ode to the West Wind. Percy Bysshe Shelley. If Winter comes, can Spring be far behind? AnEnPo; AWP; BiP; BoNaP; DiPo; EBEV; EnL; ERoP 1-2; ExPo; FaBoBe; FaBV; FaFP; FiP; ForPo; FPL; GTBS; GTBS-P; HAP; HBV 1-2; HeIP; InPo; InPS; LiTB; LoBV; MBW 1-2; MCCG; MOS; NAWM 1-2; NIP; NOBE; NoP; OAEL 1-2; OAEP; OBEV; OBNC; OBRV; OHFP; PAI; PoEL 1-5; PoLf; PoRA; PPoe; PPP; PrIm; SeCeV; TEP; TreFS; TrGrPo; ViBoPo; WHA

Ode to Tobacco. Charles Stuart Calverley. Here's to thee, Bacon! ALV; FaBoCo; FiBHP; HBV 1-2; InMe

Ode to Venice. George Gordon, Lord Byron. One freeman more, America, to thee! CABL

Ode to Walt Whitman. Federico Garcia Lorca. that a negro boy would tell the golden Whites/of the coming of the reign of the ears of corn. PeHV

Ode to Winter. Thomas Campbell. No bounds to human woe. GTBS; GTBS-P

Ode to Wisdom. Elizabeth Carter. That all but VIRTUE's solid joys,/Are vanity and woe. OBEC

Ode to Work in Springtime. Thomas Russell Ybarra. (To end this otherwise would be/Immoral!) HBMV

Ode to Zion. Judah Halevi. Rejoicing find amid the joy of thee/returned unto thine olden youthful/time. TrJP

An Ode upon a Question Moved, Whether Love Should Continue For Ever? Edward, Lord Herbert of Cherbury. One would have thought some influence/Their ravish'd spirits did possess. AnAnS 2; JCP; MeLP; MePo; OBS; SeCP; ViBoPo

Oedipus. Edwin Muir. Our natural steps and the earth and skies from harm. CMoP

Oedipus at Colonus. Sophocles.
...following/The hundred-footed sea-wind and the gull. LiTW
Of horses and horses of the sea, white horses. OBVE

Oedipus at Colonus. William Butler Yeats. The second best's a gay goodnight and quickly turn away. OBMV

Oedipus at San Francisco. Donald Finkel. and there's no getting around it, I am a bastard. CoPo

Oedipus Rex: Chorus. Sophocles. And faith is sapped, and Heaven defied. WGRP

Oedipus to the Oracle. Wesley Trimpi. ...I am free to go/From darkness into darkness to my peace. NePoEA

Oenone. Alfred, Lord Tennyson. All earth and air seem only burning fire. EnLi 1-2; MaVP; MBW 1-2; OAEP; OBRV; ViBoPo; VLP

Oenone's Complaint. George Peele. That all the world may see how false of love/False Paris hath to his Oenone been. EIL; OBSC

Of a Certain Green-Eyed Monster. Esther Lilian Duff. But he did give Elizabeth a Dodo/And he never even offered one to me. HBMV

Of a Contented Mind. Thomas, Lord Vaux. The sweetest time in all my life/To deem in thinking spent. CoBE; EIL; EnRePo; GoBC

Of a Daw. John Heywood. A daw is a daw, and a daw shall be ever.' PBBP

Of a Fair Lady Playing with a Snake. Edmund Waller. A marble one so warm'd would speak. PoEL 1-5

Of a Fair Shrew. Sir John (1561-1612) Harington. As makes her seem, nor fair, nor rich, nor young. FaBoEE

Of a Lady That Refused to Dance with Him. Henry Howard, Earl of Surrey. It boots me not that for my wrath I should disturb the same.' SiPS

Of a Little Take a Little. Anonymous. 'Tis manners so to do. OxNR

Of a Mistress. Sir Aston Cokayne. The world shall never say I love in vain. CavP

Of a Mouse and Men. A. J. Hovde. To find our suicidal surrogate no longer there. AMV-81

Of a Poet Patriot. Thomas Macdonagh. And his deed the echoes fill/When the dawn is come. CAW; HBMV; OnYI; OxBI

Of a Rich Miser. George Turberville. Which makes thee wealthy to thine heir,/a beggar to thy self. EnRePo

Of a Rose, a Lovely Rose. Anonymous. And schild us fro the fendes hand. AtBAP; OBEV; OxBM; OxBoCh

Of a Spider. Wilfrid Thorley. While fairies ride the silver ferry/Between the rose-bud and the cherry. BrR

Of A' the Airts the Wind Can Blaw. Robert Burns. There's not a bonie bird that sings,/But minds me o' my Jean. AWP; EiCP; EnLi 1-2; GoTS; InPo; LoBV; NoP; OAEP; OBEC; OxBS; ViBoPo

Of a Woman, Dead Young. Dorothy Parker. Where is Their pride, and Their vengeance? SBG

Of a Zealous Lady. Sir John (1561-1612) Harington. Did take a priest at last for pure devotion. FaBoEE

Of All Our Bath-House Thieves the Cleverest One. Caius Valerius Catullus. That hairy rump won't make you any money. DBV; PeHV

Of All Plants, the Tree. Mary Jane White. Into which the leaves push out/And fall away. AMV-80

Of All the Birds That I Do Know. Anonymous. Philip will crie still: yet, yet, yet. CH; NCEP

Of All the Gay Birds That E'er I Did See. Anonymous. And when the night comes away flies she. PBBP

Of All the Men. Thomas Moore. I've seen him but three times today! FiBHP

Of All the Sayings in This World. Anonymous. Till trouble troubles you. OxNR

Of All the Seas That's Coming. Anonymous. I would to God that he were hang'd/That does not love a coney. EBEV

Of All the Souls That Stand Create. Emily Dickinson. To all the lists of clay! AA; AmePo; AnNE; APA; DiPo; MAmP; NePA; TrGrPo

Of All the Sounds Despatched Abroad. Emily Dickinson. Then knit, and passed/In seamless company. AnFE; APA; MAPA

Of All Things for You to Go Away Mad. Joanne Kyger. ...You read/a lot of books. PoM

Of an Ancient Spaniel in Her Fifteenth Year. Christopher Morley. But I was always ready to bark–/And so was she. GDP

Of an Heroical Answer of a Great Roman Lady to Her Husband. Sir John (1561-1612) Harington. The bottom with your ballast full was laded.' BoLoP; ErPo

Of an Old Con. George, Jr Mosby. other than all the love he can muster/and all the man he can be. LFAC

Of an Old Song. William Edward Hartpole Lecky. Some sudden thought, some careless rhyme/Still floats above the wrecks of Time. WGRP

Of an Orchard. Katharine Tynan Hinkson. And in his orchard talk with God. GoBC; HBV 1-2; OBVV; WGRP

Of Angels. E. L. Mayo. One will be leaving any minute now. FAZ

Of Astraea. John Davies. And be refined with burning. TrGrPo

Of Autumn. Veronica Porumbacu. King Herod of the Autumn massacred hundreds/of leaves with his words. BoWoP; VWA

Of Baiting the Lion. Sir Owen Seaman. You met a Lion unaware,/And felled him flying through the air. NA

Of Ballad-Singers. John Gay. And Greece and Troy retreat on either side. EnLi 1-2

Of Beauty. Sir Richard Fanshawe. Love may return but never lover. BoLoP; InMe

Of Birds and Birders. John Heywood. Better for birders, but for birds not so good. PBBP

Of Books. John Florio. Show how they lived; the other where they lie! EIL

Of Boston in New England. William Bradford. Doe throw you downe from your high estate,/And make you low and desolate. SCAP

Of bronze and blaze. Emily Dickinson. An island in dishonored grass,/Whom none but daisies know. MAmP; MAPA; MoPo

Of Caution. Francesco da Barberino. Be free of fruit to all. AWP

Of Certain Irish Fairies. Arthur Guiterman. So I will catch the Cluricawne and you shall have them all. PoLf

Of Change of Opinions. Victor Plarr. For old gray death upon his crutch/To rake into his Bag of Nought. NOBV

Of Clementina. Walter Savage Landor. And Modesty who, when she goes,/Is gone for ever. HBV 1-2; OBEV

Of Commerce and Society. Geoffrey Hill.
At times it seems not common to explain. PPoe
...The bull and the great mute swan/Strain into life with their notorious cries. PPoe
By all means let us appease the terse gods. PPoe
Resonant with tributes and with commerce. NePoEA-2; PPoe
The sea creaked with worked vessels. PPoe
The sea decent again behind walls. PPoe

Of Common Devotion. Francis Quarles. Our God's forgotten, and our soldiers slighted. FaBoEE; OBSP

Of Corinna's Singing. Thomas Campion. E'en from my heart the strings do break. EnLit; HBV 1-2

Of Course I Know. Ziche Landau. I/am/lost forever. VWA

Of course–I prayed. Emily Dickinson. Merry, and Nought, and gay, and numb–/Than this smart Misery. BoWoP; MoAmPo

Of Crossing the Street. John Gay. Amazed, on Scylla's craggy dangers run. EnLi 1-2

Of Cynthia. Anonymous. But their hearts, they do not so/In their love and duty. OBSC

Of Dancing. Alan Brownjohn. ...Those who can move need not/dance. FaBoMo

Of Dandelions & Tourists. Joe Rosenblatt. to the earth alive with blissful fur. NOBC

Of De Witt Williams on His Way to Lincoln Cemetery. Gwendolyn Brooks. Nothing but a plain black boy. NoAm; NOBA

Of Death. Samuel Harding. Who shall his corpse in the best dish present. CBEP

Of Death. Mary Herbert, Countess of Pembroke. That not one grief remaineth. EIL

Of Difference Does It Make. Tom Paulin. like a mild and patient prisoner/pecking through granite with a teaspoon. FaBoIP

Of Disdainful Daphne. M. H. Nowell. Woe worth such choosing! EIL

Of Drunkenness. George Turberville. Then hatred is in head. NLV; NoP

Of Dying Beauty. Louis Zukofsky. A sun-god in a temple of decay. PoA

Of Edmund Spenser's Fairy Queen... Sir Walter Ralegh. Where Homer's sprite did tremble all for grief,/And cursed th' access of that celestial thief. FCP

Of England, and of Its Marvels. Petrarch. Which might be fair to tell but which I hide. AWP

Of English Verse. Edmund Waller. But as long-lived as present love. AnAnS 2; CavP; OAEL 1-2; OBS; PP; SeCP

Of Few Words, Sir, You Seem to Be. Anonymous. Content you with Nay, for you get no more. SiPS

Of Flowers. Alan Loney. remind ya of women,don't they' OCNZ

Of Fortune. Thomas Kyd. He only that no death doth dread/Doth live at rest. EIL

Of Fortune. Sir Thomas More. And take no thing at all, or be content/With such reward as Fortune hath you sent. CoBE

Of God We Ask One Favor. Emily Dickinson. We reprimand the Happiness/That too competes with Heaven. EaLo

Of Gods Omnipotencie. Alexander Hume. Ye love that God which bought you deare. NOCV

Of Her Breath. Robert Herrick. That all the spices of the East/Are circumfused there. EG

Of Himself. Meleager. Salute my garrulous old age, and be/Thine own what now thou honorest in me. AWP

Of His Cynthia. Fulke, Lord Brooke Greville. Yet without love nought worth to me. EIL; ELP; NoP

Of His Death. Meleager. Even this, oh Love, for thee to Death! AWP

Of the Incomparable Treasure of the Scriptures. *Anonymous.* Read not, but first desire God's grace/To understand thereby. TRV

Of the Last Verses in the Book. Edmund Waller. Leaving the old, both Worlds at once they view,/That stand upon the threshold of the New. AnAnS 2; EBEV; FaBoRV; HAP; HBV 1-2; MePo; NoP; OAEP; OBS; SeCP; SeCV 1-2; ViBoPo

Of the Loss of Time. John Hoskyns. Not here he lives: but here he dies. FaBoEE

Of the Lost Ship. Eugene Richard White. "Fell through a crack in the Floor of the/Sea"? AA

Of the Mathematician. Alice Clear Matthews. The world is capable of, the infinite/Pattern of truth the poet rearranges. GoYe

Of the Nativity of the Lady Rich's Daughter. Henry Constable. So many hearts already she hath slain,/As few behind to conquer shall remain. OBSC

Of the New Prosody. Brewster Ghiselin. The power and the heartbeat and male music of our being. MoVE

Of the Night, Let the Bridegroom Sing. Statius Publius Papinius. Of the night, let the bridegroom sing. HW

Of the Principal and Vice-Principal of the Ladies' College, Cheltenham. *Anonymous.* How different from us,/Miss Beale and Miss Buss. FaBoEE

Of the Pythagorean Philosophy. John Dryden. So Coral soft, and white in Oceans Bed,/Comes harden'd up in Air, and glows with Red. FM

Of the Scythians. Katha Pollitt. or seen in the wind their glittering wild hair flow? SM

Of the Surface of Things. Wallace Stevens. The moon is in the folds of the cloak. ELU

Of the Terrible Doubt of Appearances. Walt Whitman. He ahold of my hand has completely satisfied me. NePA

Of the Theme of Love. Margaret Cavendish, Duchess of Newcastle. But now thy tree is left so bare and poor/That they can hardly gather one plum more. OBSP

Of This World's Theater in Which We Stay. Edmund Spenser. She is no woman, but a senseless stone. NIP

Of Thomas Traherne and the Pebble outside. Sydney Clouts. This heathen bit of the world lies warm in my palm. VWA

Of Those Who Walk Alone. Richard Burton. Earth's wrongs are ended. HBV 1-2

Of Three Damsels in a Meadow. John Payne. ..."Who would fly/From such a fortune sure were scant of wit." OBVV

Of Three or Four in a Room. Yehuda Amichai. and remain sealed, like letters which have no/address and no one to receive them. VWA

Of Time and the Line. Charles Bernstein. ...it takes two lines to make/an angle but only one lime to make/a Margarita. APU

Of Treason. Sir John (1561-1612) Harington. Why, when it prospers, none dare call it treason. ALV; ExPo; FaBoEE; FF; InPK; NLV; OxBoLi

Of True Liberty. Sir John Beaumont. Thus still the poore man hath the better part. OBS

Of Tyndarus. Richard Stanihurst. Hardlye ye may kisse mee, where no such gnomon apeereth. BIrV

Of Use. John Heywood. At last, cuck, cuck, cuck–six cucks to one coo. FaBoEE; PBBP

Of Watchmen. John Gay. This work shall shine, and walkers bless my name. EnLi 1-2

Of Women. *Anonymous.* With you at night, about you at sunrise. ErPo; PV

Of Women. Richard Edwards. Ha, ha! methinks I make a lie. EIL

Of Women No More Evil. *Anonymous.* Love them or hate, 'twere little matter then. AnIL

Of Wonder. Mary Gilmore. So to my heart brought full beatitude. BoAV

Of Wounds. Sister Mary Madeleva. I know now that they are beautiful as God. ISi

Of Wounds and Sore Defeats. William Moody. Down the gray disastrous morn,/Laughter and rallying! HBV 1-2

Of You, If Anyone, It Can Be Said. Caius Valerius Catullus. Open your mouth; you'll do it with one breath. DBV

Of Your Father's Indiscretions and the Train to California. Lynn Emanuel. ...you were the girl in the dress/Red as a house burning down. MAYP

Ofay-Watcher Looks Back. Mongane Wally Serote. I want to look at what happened. WhB

Off a Puritane. *Anonymous.* then downe shee Layd, & since tis sayd,/shee quencht his spirits motion. CoMu

Off Banks Peninsula. Denis Glover. Wind whispers in: and the yacht again/Asserts direction on the trackless tide. AnNZ

Off Brighton Pier. Alan Ross. They'll pension me off to go fishing.' OBWP

Off from Boston. *Anonymous.* Never stain its bosom more. MC; PAH

Off from Swing Shift. Garrett Kaoru Hongo. No one speaks a word. MAYP

Off Manilly. Edmund Vance Cooke. For us fellers, what was dyin'/And a-soakin' in the water of Manilly. PAH

Off Molokai. Norman Hindley. They're pulled from the green ground of the sea,/Big as a six pound rose. WOLT

Off Riviere Du Loup. Duncan Campbell Scott. Soft blowing from the pleasant plain. EtS; IIBV 1-2; MCCG; OBCV

Off Saguenay. Alfred Goldsworthy Bailey. become the night's blown wave. ACV

Off the Back of a Lorry. Tom Paulin. I must return to/like my own boke. FaBoIP

Off the Ground. Walter De la Mare. You danced us square. Turvey;/Off the ground! StPo

Off to Patagonia. Theodore Weiss. ...doing your best/to remember that, so far, you have returned. TAP

Off to Sea Once More. *Anonymous.*
No more, no more, don't go to sea no more. OBSS
"There goes Jack Rack, poor sailor lad, he must go to sea once more!" ShS

Off to the Fishing Ground. L. M. Montgomery. And we envy no landsman his dream and sleep/When we're off to the fishing ground! CaP

Off Viareggio. Kenneth Pitchford. bear still the weight of a real sun on their shoulders,/and endure. CoPo

Off Womanheid Ane Flour Delice. *Anonymous.* She is my soverene and serene,/Off womanheid the flour delice. OxBS

The Offended. Anne Hebert. that the cry FIRE burst from its heart/as its speech. BoWoP

The Offender. Denise Levertov. ...The eye/luminous, price of solitude. NePoEA-2

The Offensive. Keith Douglas. the quiet like a curtain/when the piece is complete. NeBP

An Offer. Arthur Guiterman. I may give, O Lord, for Thee,/One-sixteenth in Charity. DBV; TrJP

Offering. *Anonymous.* I have made my prayer sticks into something alive. NU

Offering. Thomas Macdonagh. To her who gave me all I give these songs. ACV

The Offering of the Heart. Rolfe Humphries. Innocence; mystery: an Age of Science/Would hardly understand. FYAP

The Office of Poetry. Nathaniel Whiting. Ere Hopkins and Sternhold knew how to scan. OBS

Office Party. Phyllis McGinley. And the plump blonde from Personnel/Is sick behind the water cooler. OBSV

Officer Brady. Robert William Chambers. An' tether 'im out on the Bloomin'dale route/Like a loonytick goat! Whurroo!' InMe

Officers. Josephine Miles. Since then, I have not met an officer/That I can call by name. FaBoWP

Officers' Mess. Gavin Ewart. Yes, I think you can count on that, old boy–tonight'll be a thick/night. OxBTC

Officers' Mess. Harold Monro. Among men waiting to be dead. BrPo

An Officers' Prison Camp Seen from a Troop-Train. Randall Jarrell. ...guns learn everything/From your thin body pinned against the light. WaP

Offshore. Philip Booth. ...we crewed with Arc-/turus, Vega, Polaris,/ tacking into the dark. SD

Offshore Breeze. Milton Acorn. that red jag of a headland, to harbor. NeAC

Offspring. Naomi Long Madgett. Her very individual,/Unpliable/Own. FB

Oft have I sigh'd for him that heares me not. Thomas Campion. For him that can breake vowes but not returne. FaBoEn

Oft in My Thoughts. Charles, duc d' Orleans. God have her soul, I can no better say. NoP

Oft in the Silent Night. Otto Julius Bierbaum. Oft in the silent night. AWP

Oft, in the Stilly Night. Thomas Moore. Sad Memory brings the light/Of other days around me. AnFE; BLPL; CBEP; FaBoBe; GoBC; LiTB; LoBV; MCCG; OAEP; OBNC; OBRV; OxBI; PoEL 1-5; Prf; WHA

The Oft-Repeated Dream. Robert Frost. Was afraid in the oft-repeated dream/Of what the tree might do. PG

Often I Am Permitted to Return to a Meadow. Robert Duncan. everlasting omen of what is. CAPP; CMoP; HeIP; NOBA; NU

Often I Compare My Lord to Heaven. Gaspara Stampa. a horrid winter overtakes my soul. PBWP

Often Rebuked, Yet Always Back Returning. Emily Bronte. Can center both the worlds of Heaven and/Hell. EnLit

Often when alone I liken my lord. Gaspara Stampa. leaving me despoiled of my glorious hours. BoWoP

The Oftener Seen, the More I Lust. Barnabe Googe. Such pleasures rife shall I obtain/When distance doth depart us twain. InvP

Ogier the Dane: Song. William Morris. Kiss me, love! for who knoweth/ What thing cometh after death? OAEP; ViBoPo

Ogres and Pygmies. Robert Graves. Reading between such covers he will likely/Prove his own disproportion and not laugh. CABA; CMoP; FaBoMo; LiTB; LiTM; NoAm; SeCePo; SeCeV

Oh, Absalom, My Son. *Anonymous.* Oh, Absalom, my son, my son. FSW

Oh Ambulance Man. Memphis Jug Band. I mean my weary/sooooooul. BluL

Oh, Babe, It Ain't No Lie. Elizabeth Cotton. This life I'm livin' is very hard. FSW

Oh, Baby, Baby, Baby Dear. Edith Nesbit. Only content and we are here,/My baby dear. NOBV

Oh Beach Love Blossom. Judson Crews. and I kiss but a mouthful of sand UnTE

Oh! Blame Not the Bard, If He Fly to the Bowers. Thomas Moore. Shall pause at the song of their captive and weep! NOBI; OnYI

Oh, Breathe Not His Name. Thomas Moore. Shall long keep his memory green in our souls. AnIL; CoBE; HBV 1-2; TreFS

Oh Bright Oh Black Singbeast Lovebeast Catkin Sleek. Michael McClure. The only vision sight-sense. CoPo

Oh, Bury Me Not on The Lone Prairie (with music). Anonymous. His bones now rot on the lone prairie. AS

Oh But It Was Good... Harold Littlebird. and we tracked wearily down that two-lane highway/back to Santa Fe VoR

Oh Captain! My Captain! Walt Whitman. Fallen cold and dead. LoGBV

Oh Come, Little Children. Phyllis McGinley. At six o'clock some Christmas morning. FaBV

Oh, Come to Me when Daylight Sets. Thomas Moore. When smoothly go our gondolets/O'er the moonlight sea. EnRP

Oh Cruel Was the Press-Gang. Anonymous. Now he is forced to fiddle-scrape,/And I am forced to beg. GBP

Oh, Day of Days. Leroy V. Brant. See! Shining still the sweet star's holy fires. AH

Oh, Dear! What Can the Matter Be? Anonymous. Johnny's so long at the fair. CH; FaBoNo; FSW; LiTL; PoPle

Oh, Dem Golden Slippers. James A. Bland. Golden slippers I,m gwinter wear,/To walk de golden streets. GoSl; PSoN

Oh Did You Hear? Shel Silverstein. April Fool! PoSC

Oh, Earlier Shall the Rosebuds Blow. William Johnson Cory. The dead must rest, the dead shall rest. HBV 1-2

Oh Ease Oh Body-Strain Oh Love Oh Ease Me Not! Wound-Bore. Michael McClure. LET PURE BLACK WORDS MOVE FROM THOUGHT/BEHIND. CoPo

Oh, England. Sick in Head and Sick in Heart. Anonymous. And yet sicker thou art still/For thinking, that thou art not ill. FaBoEE

Oh Fair Enough Are Sky and Plain. Alfred Edward Housman. A silly lad that longs and looks/And wishes he were I. MCCG

Oh, Fair to See. Christina Georgina Rossetti. Oh, fair to see! OHIP; TiPo

Oh Father. Wendy Rose. oh father, who am I? CDW

Oh, for a Pentecost! Anonymous. Oh, for a Pentecost! BLRP

Oh! for a Steed. Thomas Osborne Davis. For freedom's right;/In flushing fight/To conquer if then to fall. IrPN

Oh, for the Time When I Shall Sleep. Emily Bronte. And never suffer more! ATP

Oh Freedom. Anonymous. And go home to my Lord/And be free. FSW

Oh, Give Me the Hills. Anonymous. Oh, there let me live till I die. AmFP

Oh, Give Us Back the Days of Old. John Mason Neale. By all Thy woes, by all Thy joys, Lord Jesus grant them peace. NOCV

Oh, Hear Me Prayin'(Lord, Feed My Lam's). Anonymous. Oh, hear me prayin',/I want to be more holy ev'ry day. BoAN 1-2

Oh, Hollow! Hollow! Hollow! Sir William Schwenck Gilbert. Even in colocynth and calomel?/I cannot tell. FaBoNo

Oh, How My Love with a Whirling Power. Tu-kehu and Wetea. I mourn for house, and tribe, and home. WTO

Oh, I Wish I Were Single Again. Anonymous. Oh, I wish I were a single girl again. AmFP

Oh, I Would Be a Cowboy and with the Cowboys Stand. Anonymous. And spur him in the shoulder, with my silver spurs, of course. CoSo

Oh, If They Only Knew! Edith L. Mapes. The mantle of self-righteousness? BLRP; WBLP

Oh! Isn't It a Pity. Harriet H. Robinson. For I'm so fond of liberty/That I cannot be a slave. SaC

Oh, It's Nine Years Ago I Was Digging in the Land. Anonymous. A right tur-a-naddy, mish-n-darn tur-nan. AmFP

Oh King of Saints, How Great's Thy Work, Say We. Edward Johnson. Abide, and crowne thy Head with lasting glee. SCAP

Oh, Lawd, How Long? Anonymous. An' soon she'll sing dat heavenly song-oh, Lord, how long? ABF

Oh, Let Thy Teachings. Immanuel Di Roma. Ever to make all men in soul and body/free. TrJP

Oh, Let Us Howl Some Heavy Note. John Webster. We'll sing like swans to welcome death/And die in love and rest. InvP

Oh Light Was My Head. Cecil Day Lewis. Old follies returning grow wise at last. OAEP

Oh, Little Town of Bethlehem. Lewis H. and Philip Brooks Redner. Oh come to us, abide with us,/Our Lord Immanuel! FSW

Oh, Lovely Appearance of Death. Anonymous. It never shall flutter again. OuSiCo

Oh Lovely Fishermaiden. Heinrich Heine. And many a pearly treasure/Burns in the depths below. AWP

Oh, Lovely Rock. Robinson Jeffers. Felt its intense reality with love and wonder, this lonely rock. NoAm; NU

Oh Lucky Jim. Anonymous. Oh lucky Jim, how I envy him! GBP

Oh, Mary Don't You Weep. Anonymous. Oh, Mary don't you weep. FSW

Oh moon, oh moon! Anonymous. She gave me these two secrets–/but don't ask why. BoWoP

Oh Mother of a Mighty Race. William Cullen Bryant. And, as they fleet,/Drop strength and riches at thy feet. AP; FaBoBe; HBV 1-2; HBVY; PAH; PAL

Oh, My Darling Clementine. Percy Montross. Dreadful sorry Clementine. FaBoBe

Oh, My Geraldine. Sir Francis Cowley Burnand. Oh! rum! tum!! tum!!! my Geraldine. NA

Oh, My Good Lord, Show Me de Way. Anonymous. Oh, my good Lord, show me de way,/Enter de chariot, travel along. BoAN 1-2

Oh, My Liver and My Lungs. Anonymous. There is naught but anguish ev'rywhere/As on through life we go. OuSiCo

Oh My People I Remember. Wendy Rose. I have not forgotten. CDW

Oh No. Robert Creeley. and they will likewise all have places. AmPC; HeIP; InPK; NaP; SM

Oh, No! Mary Mapes Dodge. And greased it nice/With camphor-ice. BBGG

Oh, No Cross That I May Carry! Alice Mortenson. Just because He loved me so. BePJ

Oh No John. Anonymous. Oh no John, no John, no John, no. OBET

Oh, No! We Never Mention Her. Thomas Haynes Bayly. But if she loves as I have loved, she never can forget. PaPo

Oh, Noa, Noa! William Cole. Alas! I'm told in no vicinity/Is such a thing as blessed twinnity! NLV

Oh Oh Blues. Bert Mays. I went out to the stable, I found a mule dying/he must have had 'em too BluL

Oh, oh, you will be sorry for that word! Edna St. Vincent Millay. I shall be gone, and you may whistle for me. BoWoP

Oh, Please Don't Get Up! Ogden Nash. Why woman is a wow, or should I say a wowess. NePA

Oh Promise Me. Clement Scott. Oh promise me! Oh promise me! BLSo; FaFP; FSN; GoTF; TreF

Oh, Roll on, Babe. Anonymous. When the sun goes down, you'll roll no more. OuSiCo

Oh, See How Thick the Goldcup Flowers. Alfred Edward Housman. "Good-by, young man, good-by." EnLi 1-2; FaBV; MoBrPo

Oh send to me an apple that hasn't any kernel. Anonymous. And when we were in love there was grace and good temper. FaBoCh; LoGBV

Oh, Sing to God. Jacob Steendam. Who through the billows/Did make a road and to dry land did lead you. AH

Oh, Sleep, Fond Fancy. Anonymous. Thy master's head hath need of sleep and resting. ElL

Oh, Sleep Forever in the Latmian Cave. Edna St. Vincent Millay. Whereof she wanders mad, being all unfit/For mortal love, that might not die of it. ExPo; LiTM; MoAmPo; MoVE; NoAm; NoP; SeCeV; ViBoPo

Oh, Slow Up, Dogies, Quit Your Roving Round. Anonymous. Lay still, little dogies, lay still. OuSiCo

Oh, Stop Being Thankful All Over the Place. Ogden Nash. There but for the grace of God speak I. NePA

Oh, Susan Blue. Kate Greenaway. Down in the meadow where th cowslips grow! TiPo

Oh, Susanna. Anonymous. I come from Alabama with a banjo on my knee. FSW

Oh! Susanna. Stephen Collins Foster. And when I'm dead and buried,/Susanna, don't you cry. OBAL

Oh, Sweet Content. William Henry Davies. Twitch with the stars that shine in thousands there. CH

Oh Tannenbaum. Anonymous. Your leaves will teach me, also. FSW

Oh That I Were. Anonymous. And where I would be/I can not. OxNR

Oh, the Funniest Thing... Anonymous. And it took seven stitches in the tomcat's toe. EvOK

Oh the Inconstant. N. P. Van Wyk Louw. between her bestowal and her desire. PeSA

Oh! the time that is past. Anonymous. Thou hast slighted the critical minute of love. BoLoP

Oh, The Wild Joy of Living. Robert Browning. All the heart and the soul and the senses forever in joy! GoTF; TreFT

Oh There Is Blessing in This Gentle Breeze. William Wordsworth. ...or shall some floating thing/Upon the river point me out my course? TreFT

Oh, Think Not I Am Faithful to a Vow! Edna St. Vincent Millay. I am most faithless when I am most true. FaBV

Oh, Thou! Who Dry'st the Mourner's Tear.   Thomas Moore.   As darkness shows us worlds of light/We never saw by day!   TrPWD

Oh! To Have A Birthday.   Lois Lenski.   Happy heart so light!   BiCB

Oh! Weary Mother.   Barry Pain.   (Oh! weary mother, drive the cows to roost.)   NA

Oh! Weep for Those.   George Gordon, Lord Byron.   Mankind their country–Israel but the grave!   AnEnPo

Oh, What a Plague Is Love!   Anonymous.   Phyllida flouts me.   InvP

Oh, when I was in love with you.   Alfred Edward Housman.   And miles around they'll say that I/Am quite myself again.   BoLiVe; BoLoP; FaBV; LiTB; LiTL; MoBrPo; NBM

Oh, When Shall I See Jesus?   Anonymous.   When I hear the trumpet sound in that morning.   AH

Oh! Where Do Fairies Hide Their Heads?   Thomas Haynes Bayly.   No keyhole will be fairy-proof,/When green leaves come again.   HBV 1-2; HBVY

Oh! Where's the Slave So Lowly.   Thomas Moore.   Farewell, Erin! farewell all,/Who live to weep our fall!   NOBI

Oh Who Is That Young Sinner with the Handcuffs on His Wrists?   Alfred Edward Housman.   He can curse the God that made him for the colour of his hair.   AtBAP; FaBoTw; NOBV; PeHV; SoSe

Oh, Who Regards.   Anonymous.   No sad relation/Can melt our frozen hearts into compassion,/Into compassion.   EIL

Oh, Would That I Knew.   Al-Samua'al Ibn Adiya.   Yet needed no reminder to give theirs/to others.   TrJP

Oh, Ye Censurers.   Al-Samua'al Ibn Adiya.   I ne'er feared to give defiance to my/oppressor.   TrJP

Oh––-Yeah!   Sharon Scott.   about what they/believe/is/themselves.   JB

Oh Yes.   William Matthews.   Don't cry. Your wounds are/beautiful if you'll love mine.   AmPA

Oh, Yes! Oh, Yes! Wait 'Til I Git on My Robe.   Anonymous.   Wait 'til I git on my robe,/Oh, yes.   BoAN 1-2

Oh Yield, Fair Lids.   Richard Brinsley Sheridan.   Till her eyes shine, 'tis night within my heart.   OnYI

Oh, You Wholly Rectangular.   E. R. Cole.   unravelling deserts behind.   GoYe

Oh young men oh young comrades.   Stephen Spender.   no ghost ever had, immured in his hall.   NAMP

Ohio.   John Updike.   ...the empty road/soared east and west. No static. Air.   AMV-80

Ohio Valley Swains.   James Wright.   I'll kill you.   NNaP

Ohioan Pastoral.   James Wright.   And now it hisses among the green rings/On fingers in coffins.   LCAP

Ohms.   Irving Layton.   ...even he/is gibberish to their ears   NeAC

Oil.   Linda Hogan.   getting fat on the outside/while inside we grow thin.   TWSS

Oil.   Gary Snyder.   steel plates and/long injections of pure oil.   LCAP

Oil and Blood.   Gary Allan Kizer.   This joker god with a spastic/Twitch said away with the bitch/And gave his snake a break.   LFAC

Oil Painting of the Artist As the Artist.   Archibald MacLeish.   Than under the whole damn range (he finds) of the/Big Horns   NAMP

L'Oiseau Bleu.   Gordon Bottomley.   The bird drops home.   BrPo

L'Oiseau Bleu.   Mary Elizabeth Coleridge.   It caught his image as he flew.   CH

Oiseaurie (parody).   Margaret Widdemer.   I scrabble my toes.../Glunk!   BXAP

Oisin.   Anonymous.   Once they were quick to follow/The shadow of golden Fionn.   KiLC

Oisin in the Land of Youth.   Michael Comyn.   And return from aye from the Land of Youth!   AnIL

Ojibwa War Songs.   Anonymous.   I strike for life.   AWP

Ojisan after the Stroke: Three Notes to Himself.   Tina Koyama.   and into the rest of darkness.   BrSi

Ojistoh.   [(Emily)] Pauline Johnson.   "My Mohawk's pure white star, Ojistoh, still am I."   NOBC

Okay–.   Sharon Scott.   over the absence of/revival meetings/and/home.   JB

Okay "Negroes."   June Jordan.   Come a little closer./Where you from?   BPo

Okeechobee.   John Allison.   but lost somewhere in space the whooping crane's/final cry is speeding toward a star.   GrPl

Okefenokee Swamp.   Daniel Whitehead Hicky.   Trembles red-eyed before the claws of death.   AmFN

Okinawa Kanashii Monogatari.   Geraldine Kudaka.   bird wings clipped, birds feet chained   BrSi

De Ol' Ark's A-Movering' an' I'm Goin' Home.   Anonymous.   De ol' ark's a-moverin',/An' I'm goin' home.   BoAN 1-2

Ol' Bunk's Band.   William Carlos Williams.   ...These are men!/Men!   NOBA

Ol' Clothes.   Anonymous.   Ol' woes!   PoToHe

Ol' Doc' Hyar.   James Edwin Campbell.   Een de mighty fine house on de mighty high hill!   BANP

Ol' Dynamite.   Phil Le Noir.   Then turning slides his saddle off,/An' quickly disappears.   BPAW

Ol' Hag, You See Mammy?   Anonymous.   Row boat for catfish, row boat.   OuSiCo

Ol' Hannah.   Doc Reese.   I say it don't make no difference/'cause they both life time   BluL

The Ol' Jinny Mine.   Daisy L. Detrick.   They dug out a lot from that Ol' Jinny mine.   PoOW

Ol' John Brown.   Anonymous.   But he must shovel coal to make the engine smoke.   ABF

Ol' Man River.   Oscar, II Hammerstein.   But ol' man river, he jus' keeps rollin' along.   BLSo

Ol' Mother Hare.   Anonymous.   Settin' in corner,/Smokin' my seegar.   ABF

Ol' Rattler.   Anonymous.   Heah, Rattler, heah.   ABF

De Ol' Sheep Done Know De Road.   Anonymous.   De ol' sheep done know de road,/De young lam's mus' fin' de way.   BoAN 1-2

Old.   Ralph Hoyt   By the wayside, on a mossy stone.   AA

The Old.   George, Jr Mosby.   releases smoke like grey stone/and old hair.   LFAC

The Old.   Roden and Wriothesley Berkeley Noel.   After noise, tranquillity.   OBVV

Old Abe Lincoln Came out of the Wilderness.   Anonymous.   Old Abe Lincoln came out of the wilderness,/Many long years ago.   AS; FSW; TrAS

The Old Adam.   William Rose Benet.   His heart held breathless with beatitude.   YaD

The Old Adam.   Denise Levertov.   What have I done with my life?   NaP; UnPo

Old Adam (with music).   Anonymous.   If he'd only had a mammy/For to hold him on her knee.   AS

Old Age.   Son of Ya'fur Al-Aswad.   Low speech they murmur, in tones that bear no secrets/abroad: they gain their ends without toil...   AWP

Old Age.   Anonymous.
And still their leaves are full of life/But there is none in my old body.   WTO
No lover peaceful while the rival weeps. WTO

Old Age.   E. Keary.   Out of this outside me, shall wing/Itself fair and free.'   NOBV

Old Age.   Sophocles.   Blown from night and the North.   LiTW

Old Age.   Frederick Tennyson.   Laughter is dead. There is no mirth in boys.   NOBV

Old Age Compensation.   James Wright.   They don't need my candle/But I do.   NNaP

The Old Age Home.   Theodore Holmes.   It is the water that bubbles up in the fountains in our studies.   CoPo

Old Age in His Ailing.   Herman Melville.   As, reduced to skimmed milk, to slander the cream.   TAP

The Old Age of Michelangelo.   Frank Templeton Prince.   Do not forget the poor old man.   PeSA

Old Age Pensioner.   Joseph Campbell.   A Lear at last come to his own.   AnIL

Old Age Sticks.   Edward Estlin Cummings.   &)youth goes/right on/gr/owing old   InPS; PAI

An Old Air.   Frederick Robert Higgins.   And she took herself to the woods of Gort!   AnIL

Old Amusement Park.   Marianne Moore.   when the triumph is reflective/and confusion, retroactive.   NYBP

Old and New.   Anonymous.
I see that the new will not compare with the old.   AWP; LiTW
Rules he who notes the sparrow's fall. BLRP

Old and New Art.   Dante Gabriel Rossetti.   The hand which after the appointed days/And hours shall give a Future to their Past?   MaVP

The Old and the New.   Queenie B. Mills.   in the starlit night.   SoPo

The Old and the New Courtier.   Anonymous.   By the poor Courtier of the King's, and the King's poor Courtier.   CoMu

The Old and Young Courtier.   Anonymous.   Or the King's young courtiers.   ViBoPo

The Old Angler.   Walter De La Mare.   He muttering squats, aloof, forlorn,/Dangling a baitless hook.   OAEP

The Old Anguish.   Chu Shu-chen.   ...I sit with my/Old anguish as the evening fades.   BoWoP

Old Apple Trees.   W. D. Snodgrass.   It seemed better that we kept alive.   CAPP; FYAP; SV

Old Argonaut.   Sara Saper Gauldin.   Now make your unwavering last stand.   AMV-81

The Old Ark's A-Moverin'.   Anonymous.   The old ark's a-movin and I thank God.   FSW

Old Arm-Chair.   Eliza Cook.   My soul from a mother's old arm-chair.   ATP; BrRo; InPK; PaPo; WBLP

The Old Astronomer to His Pupil.   Sarah Williams.   I have loved the stars too fondly to be fearful of the night.   BLPA; TRV

An Old Atheist Pauses by the Sea.   Thomas Kinsella.   And then the will, and then the consciousness.   ELU

The Old Athens of the West Is Now a Blue Grass Tour.   James Baker Hall.   we saved a shitload of that old elegance—   TAT

Old Australian Ways.   Andrew Barton ("Banjo") Paterson.   You then might see what Clancy saw/And know what Clancy knew.   NOAV

Old Bachelor.   Anonymous.   From matrimony free.   ABF

Old Balaam.   Anonymous.   At thoughts of what e'en mules may dare/In this great country of light air!   PoOW

Old Bandy Legs.   Anonymous.   I tripped up his heels and he fell on/his nose.   OxNR

Old Bangham.   Anonymous.   Derrum, kimmy quo qua.   FSW; OuSiCo

Old Bangum.   Anonymous.   They raced the wild boar to his den,/And found the bones of a thousand men.   BaBo

The Old Bark Hut.   Anonymous.   Remember Bob the Swagman, and the old bark hut.   PoAu 1-2

The Old Battalion.   Anonymous.   I've seen them,/Hanging on the old barbed wire.   OBET

Old Beard A-Shakin'.   Anonymous.   I pushed him in the well, and he wished me in hell,/With his old gray beard a-shakin'.   BFSS

The Old Beauty.   Phyllis McGinley.   And keeps her stubborn suitor, Death,/Moping upon the stair.   FaBoEE

Old Ben Golliday.   Mark Van Doren.   Who will sew your buttons on?/My, my, my!   SO

Old Bibles.   Marilyn Waniek.   little ash ascensions/of the Word.   MAYP

Old Bill.   Anonymous.   Dis mornin', dis evenin', so soon.   ABF

Old Bill's Memory Book.   William Rose Benet.   And Laura had measles/And wanted to die!   InMe

The Old Biograph Girl.   Margaret Benbow.   my face once glowed in the dark.   AMV-81

Old Black Joe.   Stephen Collins Foster.   I hear their gentle voices calling "Old Black Joe."   FaFP; GoTF; PSoN; TreFS

Old Black Men.   Georgia Douglas Johnson.   And they have learned to live it down/As though they did not care.   CDC; PoBA; PoNe

Old Black Men Say.   James A. Emanuel.   whatever they raised—/them old Black men.   PoBA

Old Blue.   Anonymous.
    Saying, "Come on, Blue, finally got here too."   GDP; OuSiCo; SD
    Singin' ya old Blue, you good dog you.   FSW

Old Boards.   Robert Bly.   As the rooster walks away springily over the dampened hay.   NaP

The Old Boast.   William Stanley Merwin.   from the harpist's fingers/rain   NOBA

The Old Boat.   Lenore Pratt.   The wing feather of a sea-bird fiercely wild.   CaP

Old Boniface.   Anonymous.   He slept without a shirt on.   OxNR

The Old Books.   Vernon Scannell.   You'll never know. My God, they were beautiful, the old books.   OxBC

Old Books Are Best.   Beverly Chew.   Old Books are best.   HBV 1-2

Old Botany Bay.   Mary Gilmore.   The knotted hands/That set us high!   PoAu 1-2

Old Brass Wagon (with music).   Anonymous.   Promenade around the Old Brass Wagon,/You're the one, my darling.   AS

The Old Bridge at Florence.   Henry Wadsworth Longfellow.   And when I think that Michael Angelo/Hath leaned on me, I glory in myself.   EyDe

Old Brown's Daughter.   Anonymous.   But, by jingo, next election/I shall put up as MP.   OBET

The Old Brown Schoolhouse.   Anonymous.   Old schoolhouse! a blessing on thee!   TreF

Old Buck's Ghost.   Frank Benton.   And that's the cause, says Packsaddle, that I have told this tale.   PoOW

An Old Buffer.   Frederick Locker-Lampson.   And I'll find her a wholesome corrective in Birch.'   CenHV

The Old Bullock Dray.   Anonymous.   So come and take possession/Of my old bullock dray.   PoAu 1-2

The Old Burying-Ground.   John Greenleaf Whittier.   And over both is Heaven.   AP

The Old Cabin.   Paul Laurence Dunbar.   Roun' dat po' ol' cabin do'.   PoLf

The Old Casa.   Torrey Connor.   And I am here to see the last rose fall!   BPAW

Old Cat Care.   Richard Hughes.   But I never heard/He caught the Blue Bird.   OBMV

An Old Cat's Confession.   Christopher Pearse Cranch.   But I own that I love a good fire,/And occasional herring and mouse.   OBCA

An Old Cat's Dying Soliloquy.   Anna Seward.   Since thou, her more loved master, art not there.'   NOEC

An Old Charcoal Seller.   Po Chu-i.   Half a length of red lace, a slip of damask/Dropped on the ox—is payment in full!   SaC

The Old Chartist.   George Meredith.   I'll preach you to the British nation.   NBM

The Old Chisholm Trail.   Anonymous.   Com-a-ti-yi yippi, yippi yea.   AmFP; BeLS; BFSS; BPAW; CoSo; FaBoBe; FSW; TreFT

Old Christmas.   Anonymous.   One pye-meat spiced brave I see,/One which, I must not leave alone.   OHIP

Old Christmas.   Mary Howitt.   For he doth more good unto the poor/Than many a crowned king!   GN

An Old Christmas Greeting.   Anonymous.   And so let's all be jolly.   TiPo

Old Christmas Morning.   Roy Helton.   I'm laying there dead at his side.   MoAmPo

Old Christmas Returned.   Anonymous.   Plum-pudding, goose, capon, minced pies, and/roast beef.   GN; OHIP

The Old Churchyard of Bonchurch.   Philip Bourke Marston.   They shall lie there, together.   HBV 1-2; NBM; OBNC; OBVV

The Old City.   Ruth Manning-Sanders.   Fly, fly, from the old city/Into the field!   CH

The Old Cloak.   Anonymous.   And I'll take my old cloak about me.   BuBa; OBEV; OBSC; TrGrPo

The Old Clock on the Stairs.   Henry Wadsworth Longfellow.   "Forever—never!/Never—forever!"   HBV 1-2; WBLP

Old Clothes.   Phil Hey.   to forgive you once more/your merely human shape?   GOYP

Old Colony Times.   Anonymous.   Three roguish chaps fell into mishaps,/Because they could not sing.   BLSo

The Old Conservative.   Lewis Frank Tooker.   And make the "vasty deep' a boulevard/For motors and joy-riders! All it's worth."   EtS

The Old Cottagers.   John Clare.   And filled the neighbouring village with their praise.   OBRV

Old Counsel of the Young Master of a Wrecked California Clipper.   Herman Melville.   All hands save ship! has startled dreamers.   FaBoRV

Old Country Talk.   Endre Farkas.   The one here/is accented by fur & fire   CaPN

Old Countryside.   Louise Bogan.   The thin hound's body arched against the snow.   AmLP; HAP; LiTA; NePA

The Old Couple.   F. Pratt Green.   The way, on windy nights, linoleum lifts.   OxBTC

Old Couple.   Charles Simic.   I know that his hand has reached hers/Just as she was about to turn on the lights.   HaCAP

The Old Couple, III, i: Love's Prime.   Thomas May.   Then lose no time, for Love hath wings,/And flies away from aged things.   EG

The Old Cove.   Henry Howard Brownell.   "All that I axed vos, let me alone."   PAH

The Old Cow Died.   Anonymous.   The old cow died, sail a-round.   FSW

The Old Cowboy.   Anonymous.   But the old cowboy will soon be gone,/Just like the buffalo.   CoSo

The Old Cowboy's Lament.   Robert V. Carr.   And I've got to be a-movin'—movin' on.   BPAW; PoOW

Old Crabbed Men.   James Reeves.
    Reducing the stubbornest beauty to nakedness.   ErPo
    Something pleasing perhaps to former minds or eyes.   ChMP

An Old Cracked Tune.   Stanley Jasspon Kunitz.   I dance, for the joy of surviving,/on the edge of the road.   GP; SM

Old Creation Chant.   Anonymous.   Moving is the great earth of Kane...   WTO

Old Crumbly Crust.   Anonymous.   She kicked old Crumbly on the chin,/And blood ran to his toes.   BFSS

The Old Cumberland Beggar.   William Wordsworth.   So in the eye of Nature let him die!   CABL; ERoP 1-2; LaA; MBW 1-2

Old Damon's Pastoral.   Thomas Lodge.   Who dare trust upon to-morrow,/When nor time nor life sojourns not?   OBSC

Old Dan'l.   Leonard Alfred George Strong.   Old Dan'l's out again.   ELU; MoBrPo; PoSC

Old Dan Tucker.   Daniel Decatur Emmit.   Old Dan Tucker your to late to come to supper.   ABF; BLSo; FSW; PSoN; TrAS

Old Dan Tucker (Down Rent Verses).   Anonymous.   Get out the way, Big Bill Snyder,/We'll tar your coat and feather your hide, sir.   TrAS

Old Devil.   Bo Carter.   you don't need no man, baby/don't know you in the dark when he feel   BluL

Old Doc.   Mark Vinz.   nor was there when his stroke came around.   Psk

Old Dog.   Raymond Souster.   defying him/through this poem of pain.   GDP

Old Dog.   William Stafford.   I gave her something the vet had given,/and patted her still, a good last friend.   BoAnP; GDP

Old Dog Blue.   Jim Jackson.   Blue treed a possum in Noah's ark   BluL

The Old Dog in the Ruins of the Graves at Arles.   James Wright.   ...Nobody can tell me/The old dogs don't know.   NNaP

Old Dog, New Dog.   Sydney Lea.   pursue downhill, half blind with my own laughter.   MAYP

Old Dog Tray.   Stephen Collins Foster.   I'll never never find/A better friend than old dog Tray.   FSW; GDP

Old Dominion.   Robert Hass.   ...people in tennis/whites who look so graceful from this distance.   MAYP

Old Dubuque.   Dave Etter.   like my dead grandmother/loved her steins of Star beer.   AmFN

Old Ego Song.. ᴊ John Minczeski.   I suppose we should leave him there,/ alone, nodding off to sleep, dreaming.   AMV-80

Old Ellen Sullivan.   Winifred Welles.   The clothes like blossoms, all sweet and fresh and fluffy.   TiPo

Old Emily.   Hyacinthe Hill.   it rained and I cried and daddy bought me a gun.   GoYe

Old England.   Nahum Tate.   Then Asaph's song shall be like Doeg's rhyme. APAS

Old England Forever and Do It No More.   *Anonymous.*   The Queen and Prince Albert, and do it no more.   GBP

Old English Charm Song.   *Anonymous.*   In the name of sweete Jesus/I take thee from the ground.   CAW

Old English Prayer.   *Anonymous.*   It is the music of the soul.   GoTF; TreFT

Old Essex Door.   Agnes MacCarthy Hickey.   ...What narrow things/Doors are, that a Soul's wings/Must fold to stoop beneath!   GoYe

The Old Familiar Faces.   Charles Lamb.   All, all are gone, the old familiar faces.   AWP; BLPA; FaBoBe; FaBoRV; FaFP; FaPoR; FPL; GTBS; GTBS-P; HBV 1-2; NBM; NOBE; OBEV; OBRV; PG; PoPl; TreF; ViBoPo

Old Farmer Alone.   Robert P. Tristram Coffin.   A warm place there for him and love and sleeping.   MoLP

The Old Farmer and His Young Wife.   *Anonymous.*   If ever I go out from home a cuckold I come in.   GBP

Old Farmer Giles.   *Anonymous.*   Took a run, and jumped clean over. OxNR

Old Fashioned Fun.   William Makepeace Thackeray.   And this would cause a roar,/When your old joke was new.   InMe

The Old-Fashioned Garden.   John Russell Hayes.   And naught is heard except the frogs'/small choir in distant meads.   AA

Old-Fashioned Love.   *Anonymous.*   Say, wilt thou, my dear?" And she wilted.   MaC

The Old-Fashioned Pitcher.   George E. Phair.   The stout-hearted pitcher/ Who finished the game.   SoSe

An Old-Fashioned Poet.   Ada Foster Murray.   O muse immortal, singer true,/What harmonies unite the two!   HBV 1-2

Old Father Annum.   Leroy F. Jackson.   ...I hope to be proud/Of the little rascal when I come back.   SiSoSe

Old Fellow.   Ernest Walsh.   I should be more than a page of print she knows by heart.   ErPo

Old Fence Post.   Leigh Hanes.   And an old fence post, and a little brown wren/That may any moment fly out again!   GoYe

An Old Field Mowed.   William Meredith.   Second growth and second growth.   NYBP

The Old Figurehead Carver.   H. A. Cody.   And the Marco Polo leading/ With my carving in her teeth.   EtS

The Old Filthy Beer Pail.   Katie V. Hall.   And then a glad victory song may be sung.   PeD

Old Fisherman with Guitar.   George Mackay Brown.   ...and gathered the mouth of Thora/to his mouth.   BSV

The Old Flag.   Henry Cuyler Bunner.   Teach him to hold it holy and high/ For the sake of its sacred dead.   PAL; PGD

The Old Flagman.   Carl Sandburg.   Ruddy as a hard nut, hair in his ears, clear sea lights in his eyes.   YaD

The Old Flame.   Robert Lowell.   as it tossed off the snow/to the side of the road.   BoLoP; NoAm; NOBA

Old Flemish Lace.   Amelia Walstein Carpenter.   To Olde Sainte Marke's i' the Bowerie,/Dear Hal,–with thee!   AA

Old Florist.   Theodore Roethke.   Or stand all night watering roses, his feet blue/in rubber boots.   CTBA; NCSH; OBSP; PCP; SaC

The Old Folk.   Tove Ditlevsen.   With no one can they talk about/this great/at-birth-ordained/event.   PBWP

Old Folks at Home.   Stephen Collins Foster.   Far from de old folks at home.   AA; BLSo; FaBoBe; FaFP; FSW; GoTF; HBV 1-2; PSoN; TreF; WBLP

An Old Folks Home.   Paul Lake.   The green fruit ripen, or the rotten drop? AMV-81

Old Fort Meigs.   *Anonymous.*   When we fought here with Harrison,/A long time ago.   MC; PAH

Old Fortunatus.   Thomas Dekker.   And some with adoration crown her fame.   ViBoPo

Old Forty-Five Per Cent.   *Anonymous.*   Great God! can such a soul be saved?   FaBoEE

Old Furniture.   Thomas Hardy.   He should not continue in this stay,/But sink away.   MoVE; OxBTC

The Old Garden.   Baron Joseph von Eichendorff.   And, through the garden, through the glen/A wondrous music rings.   LiTW

Old Gardens.   Arthur Upson.   I pluck a rose–to let it fall/And perish in the gloom.   HBV 1-2

The Old General.   Sir Charles Hanbury Williams.   He strains his crippled knees, and struts along.   OBEC

The Old Ghost.   Thomas Lovell Beddoes.   At his yearning desire and agony. WiR

The Old Girl.   Gary Lenhart.   She stood on her head while Aunt Lily/Hung buckets full of water from her feet,/to no avail.   APU

The Old Gods.   Edwin Muir.   And vast compassion curving like the skies. BSV; EaLo

The Old Gospel Ship.   *Anonymous.*   I'm gonna shout and sing, until the bells do ring,/When I'm sailing through the sky.   FSW

Old Gramophone Records.   James Kirkup.   And the turntable turns on a ghost of the ghosts of the past.   NYBP

Old Grandpaw Yet.   *Anonymous.*   There's plenty all around the chair. AmFP

Old.Gray Beard A-Shaking.   *Anonymous.*   I bid him farewell and I wished him in hell/With his old gray beard a-shaking.   AmFP

Old Gray Goose.   *Anonymous.*
Because their mother's dead.   ABF
She's left five little goslings/to scratch for their own bread.   GBP

The Old Gray Mare.   *Anonymous.*   The old gray mare, she ain't what she used to be,/Many long years ago.   AS; FSW; GBP

Old Grey.   Fred Lape.   ...and so foiled to the end/his ancient enemy. BoAnP

The Old Grey Wall.   Bliss Carman.   Who rests on this old grey wall/Lays a hand on the shoulder of God!   CaP

Old Grimes.   Albert Gorton Greene.
And everybody said he was/A fine old gentleman.   AnAmPo; GoTF; HBV 1-2; HBVY; InMe; TreFS
Than loafin' around The Throne.   BeLS

An Old Habitant.   Frank Oliver Call.   And in the orchard fruit begins to fall.   CaP

Old Hannah.   *Anonymous.*   Well, it seems like everything/That I do is wrong.   FSW

The Old Hokum Buncombe.   Robert E. Sherwood.   The moss-covered buncombe we all love so well.   InMe; NLV

The Old Home.   Madison Cawein.   In boyhood I knew them, and still they call to me.   HBV 1-2

Old Homes.   Edmund Charles Blunden.   And in your pastoral still my life has rest.   MoVE

The Old House.   William Barnes.   Zoo, iff 'twer mine, I'd let aluone/The girt wold house o' mossy stuone.   OBVV

The Old House.   George Edward Woodberry.   Now falls the evening light. God give thee peace!   HBMV

Old House Place.   Velma Sanders.   Remembering that once it sheltered love. AMV-80

Old Houses.   Homer D'Lettuso.   An old house knew my mother's lovely face.   PoToHe

Old Houses.   Jennie Romano.   Knowing so many things they never have told.   PoToHe

The Old Houses of Flanders.   Ford Madox Ford.   They are no more, the old houses of Flanders.   CTC

Old Humpy.   *Anonymous.*   The old woman went off ti-hippity-hop, ti-hippity-hop,/Hey, hey, ti-hippity-hop, ti-hippity-hop.   AmFP

Old Hundred.   Mark Van Doren.   As they sailed on, as they sailed on,/Over his unmoving mound.   UnS

The Old Hundredth.   William Kethe.
From men and from the angel-host/Be praise and glory evermore.   FaPoR
Praise Father, Son and Holy Ghost.   BLSo

The Old Hymns.   Frank Lebby Stanton.   To "Canaan's fair and happy land, where my possessions/lie."   BLRP

Old I Am.   Herman Charles Bosman.   On a lost field and slept among/His neighbour men.   PeSA

Old I Am.   Thomas Stanley.   Old I am, and therefore may,/Like Silenus, drink and play.   AWP

Old Indian Trick.   Rayna Green.   visions of light and spirit/to wipe terror away   TWSS

An Old Inmate.   Kenneth Mackenzie.   and the futile difficult sounds of his old girl's crying.   PoAu 1-2

Old Inn on the Eastern Shore.   William H. Matchett.   And, knowing yourself no sinner,/Will go in to bathe before dinner.   NePoEA

The Old Inn-Sign.   Wilfrid Thorley.   Before the old Inn-sign.   BrR

An Old Irish Blessing.   *Anonymous.*   And up and off and on its way to God. TRV

Old Iron.   Douglas Stewart.   Like seeing in the rain at night a woman's face. BoAV

Old Ironsides.   Oliver Wendell Holmes.   And give her to the god of storms/ The lightning and the gale!   AA; AmePo; AmLP; AnNE; AP; BLPA; EtS; FaBoBe; FaFP; FaPo; FPL; GN; GoTF; HBV 1-2; HBVY; MaC; MC; MCCG; MOS; PAH; PAL; PoPl; TAP; TreF; YaD

Old January.   Edmund Spenser.   And blow his nails to warm them if he may.   YeAr

Old Jewish Cemetery in Worms.   Alfred Kittner.   and no new graves will be dug here.   VWA

The Old Jockey.   Frederick Robert Higgins.   Light leaps on his face. AnIV; OBMV; OxBI; OxBTC

The Old Man Who Lived in a Wood. *Anonymous.* She should ne'er be ruled by he. MoShBr

The Old Man Who Lived in the Woods. *Anonymous.* He swore she could do more work in a day/Than he could do in seven. OnUR

Old Man with a Mowing Machine. May Carleton Lord. he merely mows and leaves no unsightly scars. GoYe

Old Mansion. John Crowe Ransom. To dip, alas, into some unseemlier world. HeIP; NOBA

Old Maps. Eunice Tietjens. I find my pleasure as a rule/Is quite diminished. BrR

Old Maps and New. Norman MacCaig. Here live monsters. OxBC

The Old Mare. Elizabeth Jane Coatsworth. Finding any motherhood/Most sweet. MoAmPo

The Old Marlborough Road. Henry David Thoreau. You may go round the world/By the Old Marlborough Road. PoEL 1-5

The Old Marquis and His Blooming Wife. *Anonymous.* And with the Yorkshire blade/She danced a jig at night. CoMu

The Old-Marrieds. Gwendolyn Brooks. But in the crowded darkness not a word did they say. AmNP; PoBA

Old Marse John. *Anonymous.* Yes, mourner, you shall be free,/When the good Lord sets you free. TTY

The Old Masters. Emile Verhaeren. Between two drinking-bouts a masterpiece. AnEnPo

Old May Song. *Anonymous.* To draw you these cold winters away. AtBAP

The Old Men. Cid Corman. black buckles dangling/from dusty black vests PCP

The Old Men. Walter De la Mare. Yet reluctant we go. MoAB; MoBrPo

The Old Men. Irving Feldman. Down down into the earth! MP

The Old Men. Alexander Javitz. Why do your eyes pity me? TrJP

Old Men. Nancy Keesing. Waits the last wisdom, the merging of the past with whole. BoAV

The Old Men. Rudyard Kipling. That he who hath not endured to the death, from his birth he hath never/endured! OBSV

Old Men. Ogden Nash. But the old men know when an old man dies. DFF; EvOK; InPS

Old Men. Alicia Ostriker. It seems the way to talk about old men. AMV-81

The Old Men. Charles Reznikoff. and the watermelon too many seeds. DFF

The Old Men Admiring Themselves in the Water. William Butler Yeats. "All that's beautiful drifts away/Like the waters." FaBoCh; GoJo; LoGBV; PCP

Old Men and Old Women Going Home on the Street Car. Merrill Moore. Saying, "This tastes so good!" or, "This smells so sweet!" MoAmPo

Old Men on the Blue. Thomas Hornsby Ferril. At night the old men sleep in houses that/Will always have geraniums in the windows. PoOW

Old Men Pitching Horseshoes. X. J. Kennedy. ...kick dust with all the force/Of shoes still hammered to a living horse. AMV-81

Old Men's Ward. Elma Dean. Spare him the pity–he departed whole,/ spitting the dear brown weed, owning his soul. GoYe

Old Men, White-Haired, beside the Ancestral Graves. Basho (Matsuo Basho). Stand lonesome, leaning on their staves. AWP

Old Men Working Concrete. Phil Hey. They talk. They dip snuff./They are happy. FiCP

Old Michael. George M. Brady. His clay to nourish yet the longing root/Of the wild daffodil, the ivy leaf. NeIP

The Old Mill. Thomas Dunn English And the wheel moves slowly round. AA

The Old Miner. *Anonymous.* Now who'll replace this old coal miner/When I've paid God my fare? OBET

The Old Miner's Refrain. *Anonymous.* And we'll row you to the bright celestial shore. AmFP

Old Miniatures. Leo Vroman. and a trail of gold weaves/away under weeds and thorns. VWA

Old Moll. James Reeves. Most ree-markable old party. WSC

Old Montague. Michael Kennedy Joseph. Game of chess, which he will always win. AnNZ

Old Moon My Eyes Are New Moon. Allen Ginsberg. to turn back to sleep in my dark bed on earth. VGW

Old Mortality. Sir Walter Scott. Was never wight so starkly made,/But time and years would overthrow. EnRP

The Old Mother. *Anonymous.* For her children are grown and her work is done. PoToHe

Old Mother Goose. *Anonymous.* Would ride through the air/On a very find gander. PBBP

Old Mother Goose and the Golden Egg. *Anonymous.* And mounting its back,/Flew up to the moon. OxNR

Old Mother Hubbard. *Anonymous.* And built him a monument/When he was dead. HBV 1-2; HBVY; OnMSP; OxNR

Old Mother Hubbard. Mother Goose. And so the poor dog had none. FaBoBe; SoPo; TiPo

Old Mothers. Charles Sarsfield Ross. Old garden walks, old roses, and old loves. PoToHe

Old Mountain Road. Charles Simic. Knowing myself a born doubter. FYAP

The Old Mountaineer. W. K. Holmes. Oh may my spirit still by memory share/The high serenity that blessed me there! PoSH

Old Movies. John Cotton. I feel nostalgic. FF

The Old Munro Bagger. *Anonymous.* It is not the ones left that are keeping me going/But the new ones they are making me do.' PoSH

Old Nick in Sorel. Standish O'Grady. And now 'tis resolved that this frightful new-comer/Will winter in hell and be here in the summer. OBCV

The Old Nudists. Joan Colby. ...They know/what's going on/inside us. AMV-80

The Old O. O. Blues. Al Young. We out to smash your bourgeois ass/and by we I mean The Community! NPGG

The Old Oak Tree. *Anonymous.* Nor none was found to bless the ground/ Beneath the old oak tree. ShS

The Old Oaken Bucket. Samuel Woodworth. The moss-covered bucket which hangs in the well. BLPA; BLSo; FaBoBe; FaFP; FPL; FSW; PaPo; PSoN; TreF; WBLP

Old October. Thomas Constable. Thank goodness, old October's here! HBV 1-2

The Old One and the Wind. Clarice Short. Is rife with excitements of the world's beginning/And its end. IHMS

The Old Orange Flute. *Anonymous.* Toora lu, toora lay, oh, it's six miles/from Bangor to Donnahadee. FSW 'Twas the old flute still whistling "The Protestant Boys'. FaBoBa; GBP

The Old Ox. George Rostrevor Hamilton. Deep-lowing for his deep content. FaBoEE

The Old Pack. *Anonymous.* For they have the dogs, and are riding tantivy. APAS

Old Paintings on Italian Walls. Kathleen Raine. Have faded from our ken, we from their knowledge fallen. NYBP

The Old Parish Church, Whitby. Hardwick Drummond Rawnsley. A ship that meets all storms, rides out all gales. OBVV

The Old Pastor. John Banister Tabb. Have entered, and I am/Alone, and it is late. AmP

The Old Peasant in the Billiard Saloon. Huw Menai. Having found none worthier of his confidence! ACV

The Old Peasant Woman at the Monastery of Zagorsk. James Schevill. Her silent fury of bones hammering the boards. NMP

The Old Pensioner. William Butler Yeats. The well-known faces are all gone,/and the fret is on me. InPK

Old People. Myra Cohn Livingston. Talking and talking and talking and talking and talking. CTBA

The Old People Speak of Death. Quincy Troupe. ...spirit/now less than bone CNA

Old People Working (Garden, Car). Gwendolyn Brooks. A way of greeting or sally to the world. SaC

Old Photo, 1942. George Uba. appears the exact color of earth. BrSi

Old Photographs. David Harsent. their blurred smiles meant for no one. PoL

An Old Picture. Howard Nemerov. The bridal bed already made,/The crypt also richly arrayed. OBSP

Old Pictures in Florence. Robert Browning. At least to foresee that glory of Giotto/And Florence together, the first am I! VLP

The Old Pilot. Donald Hall. there are the wings of a thousand biplanes. LCAP

The Old Pines. Cid Corman. meaningless–/buried mouths. GP

The Old Place. Blanche Edith Baughan. The place that's broken my heart– the place where I've lived/my life. AnNZ

An Old Polish Lesson. Deanna Louise Pickard. and the willow limbs will dance the mazurka with the wind. AMV-81

The Old Pond. Basho (Matsuo Basho). The sound of water. SoPo

The Old Pope is Comforted by the Thought of the Young Pompilia. Robert Browning. Presently when I follow if I may! BoC

Old Poulter's Mare. *Anonymous.* She was in wretched case. PeD

The Old Prison. Judith Wright. cried as the wind now cries/through this flute of stone. PoAu 1-2

The Old Pro's Lament. Paul Petrie. no net, no ball, no game–/and still playing/to win. LiSp; TAP

Old Pudding-Pie Woman. *Anonymous.* You may follow her by the smell. OxNR

The Old Quartermaster. Gordon Grant. Except by ancient crabs like me, who served/their time in sail. EtS

Old Quin Queeribus. Nancy Byrd Turner. He only let them grow! EvOK; SoPo; TiPo

Old Rattler. *Anonymous.* Here, Rattler, here. FSW

Old Red Hoss Mountain. Cy Warman. Down in the ragged canyon where "Martha's younket" sleeps. PoOW

The Old Repair Man. Fenton Johnson. It is good we have the Old Repair Man. AmNP

Old River Road. Blanche Whiting Keysner. The new highway's for going. GoYe

The Old Road. Jones Very But he shall walk with Me, his God. AA

Old Road Song Poem. Artie Gold. though no more than a hair/discovered in a gravy. CaPN

The Old Road to Paradise. Margaret Widdemer. For the old road to Paradise,/That's a crowded way! HBMV

Old Roads. Eilean Ni Chuilleanain. Slowly the old roads lose their grip. CIP

Old Roadside Resorts. Molly Peacock. ...the vacant stateliness of claw-footed chairs. MAYP

Old Robin of Portingale. Anonymous. And he went him into the holy land,/Wheras Christ was quicke and dead. ESPB

Old Roger. Anonymous. Which made the old woman go Hipertihop,/He Hi, Hipertihop. OxBoLi

The Old Room. William Stanley Merwin. if I called It is not me would it reach/through the bells NYBP

Old Rosin the Beau. Anonymous.
And do not forget to scratch on them/The name of old Rosin, the Beau. BLSo; CoSo; FSW
Nor even old Rosin the beau. PSoN

Old Rowley the King. Anonymous. And when I've done,/My brother and son/May end their tricks in a string. APAS

The Old Rugged Cross. George Bennard. I will cling to the old rugged cross,/And exhange it some day for a crown. AH

The Old Sailor. Glenn Ward Dresbach. He blusters still and walks with seaman's legs. EtS

The Old Sailor. A.(lan) A.(lexander) Milne. He did nothing but basking until he was saved! CenHV

The Old Saint. Muriel Stuart. You have lost Egypt though you saved your ships. HBMV

Old Sam's Wife. Anonymous. And the devil sent him Anna. ChTr

The Old Santa Fe Trail. Richard Burton. Lo! brightsome fruits to feed a mighty folk. BPAW; PAH

Old Santa Is An Active Man. Lois Lenski. And then goes climbing back! ChBR

Old Scent of the Plum Tree. Fujiwara Ietaka. Alas...the cold moon of spring... AWP

The Old School List. James Kenneth Stephen. But we're all in the old school List. CenHV

The Old Scottish Cavalier. Ayton [(or Aytoun)] Sir Robert. Of the last old Scottish cavalier/All of the olden time! GN; HBV 1-2

The Old Scout's Lament. Anonymous. And now, our West, good-by. CoSo

An Old Seaport. Anonymous. In one wide zone of rest, glooms the gray evenfall. EtS

Old Seawoman. Gordon LeClaire. The ships forever gone. CaP

The Old Section Boss. Anonymous. You see; dat's de way de Hoosiers feeds way out in Arkansaw. BPo

The Old Sergeant. Forceythe Willson. "Bless you!" gasped the old, gray Sergeant, and he lay and said no more! AA; BeLS

The Old Settler's Song. Francis Henry. As I think of my pleasant condition,/Surrounded by acres of clams. BPAW

The Old Sexton. Park Benjamin. Gather–gather–gather them in. AA; HBV 1-2

De Old Sheep Dey Know de Road. Anonymous. Young lambs must find de way. BPo

Old Shellover. Walter De La Mare. "Ay!" said Creep. AtBAP; OxBChV; PoPle

Old Shepherd's Prayer. Charlotte Mew. I wud sooner sleep. EaLo; MoAB; MoBrPo; OxBTC

Old Ship Riggers. H. A. Cody. Maybe there'll be work for riggers,/In the Port, beyond the blue. EtS

The Old Ships. James Elroy Flecker. And the whole deck put on its leaves again. AnFE; BrPo; EtS; EvOK; FaBoRV; GTBS; MoBrPo; MOS; MoVE; OBMV; PoPle; PoRA; RoGo; WHA

Old Ships. Louis Ginsberg. They fall to dreaming of the days long past. HBMV

Old Ships. David Morton. Blowing in mists, their spectral sails like light. BBV; EtS

Old Shoes and Leggin's. Anonymous. With his old shoes on and his leggin's. OuSiCo

Old Skinflint. Wilfrid Gibson. Old daddy Skinflint, the father of me. OBMV

Old Smoky. Anonymous.
Last night I were with her, but to-night she is gone. BaBo
She's as true as your mountains/And as pure as the dove. AmFP

Old Soldier. Padraic Colum. So it is to be an Old Soldier. OBMV

Old Soldiers Home at Marshalltown, Iowa. Jim Barnes. But somewhere in your head the old soldiers/are dying, dying into the fullness of spring. AMV-80; FAZ

Old Soldiers Never Die. Anonymous. Old soldiers never die,/They just fade away. FSW

An Old Song. Solomon Blumgarten (Yehoash) And one who sings her child to sleep. LiTW

The Old Song. Gilbert Keith Chesterton. Had shown under the shattered sky a people that were/free. FaBoTw

Old Song. Louis Dudek. nor waste your lips to count them. ACV

Old Song. Edward Fitzgerald. And away to the meadows,/The meadows again! GN; OBEV; OBVV

The Old Song. Charles Kingsley. God grant you find one face there/You loved when all was young! CBEP; OBVV; PG

Old Song. F. R. Scott. only a moving/with no note/granite lips/a stone throat PeCV

An Old Song. Yehoash. A running lake, a flock of sheep,/And one who sings her child to sleep. AWP; LiTW

An Old Song Ended. Dante Gabriel Rossetti. Say I'm looking in his eyes/Though my eyes are dim.' BoLoP

An Old Song Re-sung. John Masefield. The broken glass was chinking as she sank among the wrecks. EvOK; ExPo; LiTB

An Old Song Resung. Charles Larcom Graves. I hope to win her in the end–/My daughter. CenHV

An Old Song Reversed. Richard Henry Stoddard. There's a loss for every gain! AA

Old Song Written during Washington's Life. Anonymous. Long live great Washington!/Huzza! Huzza! OHIP

The Old Songs. Sir Owen Seaman. Who never made, or saw, a joke. InMe

An Old Souldier of the Queens. Anonymous. And the Queen's old Souldier. OBS

The Old Squire. Wilfrid Scawen Blunt. I like to be as my fathers were,/In the days e'er I was born. FaPoR; HBV 1-2; OBEV; OBVV; SD

The Old Stoic. Emily Bronte. Through life and death, a chainless soul,/With courage to endure! EnLi 1-2; EnLit; FaPoR; FPL; GoTF; NOBE; OAEP; OBEV; OBNC; OBVV; OxBI; PoLf; PoPl; TreFT; TrGrPo; ViBoPo

The Old Stories. Gene Frumkin. ...there is/no other way, academically, to settle their likenesses/but by brutal dislocation. AMV-80

Old Storm. David Phillips. in the hunger/of his blizzard NeAC

The Old Story. Marcus Argentarius. Must you find only at the end/That who has nothing has no friend? AWP; LiTW

Old Story. Lance Henson. cloud your eyes/with/pain VoR

An Old Story. Rena Lee. Adam was/busy busy busy/dressing and keeping the garden/for God. VWA

The Old Story. Louis MacNeice. Massing for action on the cold horizon. GBL

An Old Story. Edwin Arlington Robinson. I never knew the worth of him/Until he died. AnNE; GoTF; HBMV; MoAmPo; OBSP; TreFS

The Old Story over Again. James Kenney. They will tell us the old story over again. OnYI

An Old Street. Virginia Woodward Cloud. "It is too late for laughter,–or for love." AA

Old Stuff. Bert Leston Taylor. Jill must have her pair of Jacks. HBMV

The Old Summerhouse. Walter De la Mare. That music, remote, forlorn. CMoP; FaBoPP; FaBoRV; GTBS-P; MoPo

Old Susan. Walter De la Mare. And rooted in Romance remain. CMoP; GoTF; MoBrPo; TreFS

The Old Sussex Road. Ian Serraillier. Help pull out my horse. He's down below. NTCP

An Old Sweetheart of Mine. James Whitcomb Riley. To greet the living presence of that old sweetheart of mine. BeLS; BLPA; FPL; TreFS

The Old Swimmer. Christopher Morley. And though I kiss the salt no more/Other swimmers will. LiSp; SD

The Old Swimmin'-Hole. James Whitcomb Riley. And dive off in my grave like the old swimmin'-hole. BeLS; FaFP; HBV 1-2

Old Tennis Player. Gwendolyn Brooks. He leans to life, conspires to give and get/Other serving yet. LiSp; SD

The Old Testament. Thomas Russell. And Malachi with garments rent,/Concludes the ancient Testament. TreFS

Old Testament Contents. Anonymous. And all the books are twenty-seven. BLPA

The Old Testament (excerpt). Anonymous. To the land of milk and honey. FaBoUs

Old-Testament Gospel. William Cowper. Oh grant that I may faithful be/To clearer light vouchsafed to me! TrCP

Old Thad Stevens. Kenneth Porter. Some day when men have half their evens/we'll dare talk proudly of Old Thad Stevens. NePoAm-2

An Old Thought. Charles Henry Luders. The other marks them crumble, silently. AA

Old Timbrook Blues. John Byrd. Old Missus went to the race track/and lost all-a her mon' BluL

The Old-Time Cowboy. Anonymous. When the wicked rise from heaven and the weary are at rest. CoSo

Old-Time Service. Thomas Churchyard. The greatest lady in a shire/She might have served seven year. OBSC

Old Timers. Carl Sandburg. I am an ancient reluctant conscript. AnAmPo; NoAm; YaD

The Old Times Were the Best. James Whitcomb Riley. Yet a feeling's ever present/That the Old Times were the best. FaFP

Old Tippecanoe. *Anonymous.* And "go it for" Tyler and "Tippecanoe." PAH

Old Tityrus to Eugenia. Charles Cotton. T' oblige the world, bright nymph, thou sure wast born. ViBoPo

Old Trail Town, Cody, Wyoming. John Garmon. the sign says/donations/ will be appreciated TAT

The Old Tree. Andrew Young. A pillar of damp fire. GoJo

Old Triton Time. Vernon Watkins. He suddenly seems young, the water old. OBSP

The Old Trouper. Don (Donald Robert Marquis) Marquis. both our professions/are being ruined/by amateurs. FaBoCo

An Old Tune. Andrew Lang. In some forgotten life, long time gone by. AWP; HBV 1-2

The Old Vicarage, Grantchester. Rupert Brooke. And is there honey still for tea? BrPo; DBV; FaBoPP; FaBV; MoBrPo; MoVE; OBTV; OxBTC; PoRA

The Old Violin. Maurice Francis Egan. A master-touch!–its sweet soul wakes/and sings. AA

Old Virginny. James A. Bland. There's where we'll meet and we'll never part no more. FaBV

Old Voyager. Walter Blackstock. The port was known–the reckoning was true. GoYe

The Old Walking Song. J. R. R. Tolkien. And whither then? I cannot say. RFM

Old Walt. Langston Hughes. Old Walt went seeking/And finding. HeIP

Old War-Dreams. Walt Whitman. I dream, I dream, I dream. OBSP

An Old Waterford Woman. Mary Devenport O'Neill. "And what,' she said,/"Are the dead/But earth?' NeIP

The Old Wharves. Rachel Field. How can they stand so patiently! SoPo

The Old Whim Horse. Edward Dyson. Nigh a shattered drum and a king-post rotting/Are the bleaching bones of the old grey horse. CBAP

The Old Whore Speaks to a Young Poet. Dave Smith. But fight back, gambol/while you can, then go with grace in your prime. SM

Old Wichet. *Anonymous.* Old Wichet went a noodle out, a wise man he came home. StPo

The Old Wife. Rolly Kent. and find just the sun on a dry, old head. FF

The Old Wife and the Ghost. James Reeves. And a tidy big cat she fetches back/To keep the mice from her kitchen. ShM

Old Wife in High Spirits. Hugh" (Christopher Murray Grieve) MacDiarmid. As kythed in that wild auld carline that day! CMoP; NMP; OxBTC

The Old Wife's Tale. George Peele.
And every sheave a golden tree. OBSC
And never be we mute. OBSC
She could not live a maid. ALV; AtBAP; OBSC

Old Winter. Thomas Noel.
But we care not a whit, as we jovial sit/Before our blazing fire. PoSC
From our snug fire-side this Christmas-tide/We'll keep old Winter out. GN; HBV 1-2

Old Witherington. Dudley Randall. As if the world compressed to one old man/Who was the sun, and he sole faithful planet. ConAP; NoAm; TW

The Old Wives Prayer. Robert Herrick. Drive all hurtfull Feinds us fro,/ By the Time the Cocks first crow. SeCV 1-2

An Old Woman. *Anonymous.*
And yet this old woman/Could never keep quiet. OxNR
He never took toll/Of a mouse in his life. OxNR
Laws a mercy on my soul, I think at last I hear you. AmFP
May I go with you? Aye, by-and-bye. OxNR

The Old Woman. John Bunker. Twilight and silence and a heart at peace. CAW

The Old Woman. Joseph Campbell. And her thoughts as still/As the waters/Under a ruined mill. ACV; AWP; GoBC; HBMV; MCCG; MoBrPo; OnYI; OxBI; OxBTC; TreFT; ViBoPo

Old Woman. Linda Pastan. When my griefs sing to me/from the bright throats of thrushes/I sing back. FiCP

The Old Woman. Beatrix Potter. That little old woman was/Surely a mouse! GoJo; NTCP

An Old Woman. Charles Henry Ross. You could not have kept her a week on a penny. OxBChV

The Old Woman. Marjorie Allen Seiffert. I've somebody sleeping/In every bed! AnAmPo

An Old Woman. Edith Sitwell. Forgive and bless all men like the holy light. CoBMV; MoPo

Old Woman. Iain Crichton Smith. too many waves to mark two more or three. BSV; FaBoTw; OxBTC

Old Woman All Skin and Bone. *Anonymous.* "Yes, my darling, by and by." BOO! TrAS

Old Woman Awaiting the Greyhound Bus. Duane Niatum. And chews time like a white rabbit. CDW

The Old Woman in a Shoe. *Anonymous.* She whipped them all soundly and put them/to bed. OxNR

An Old Woman Laments in Spring-Time. Edith Sitwell. ...Death seemed but the shade/That those heavenly branches made. ViBoPo

Old Woman of Beare. *Anonymous.* Changes with the ebbing tide. AnIL; KiLC; OnYI

The Old Woman of Beare Regrets Lost Youth. Frank O'Connor. What was water far and wide/Changes with the ebbing tide./Ebbtide. OBMV

The Old Woman of Berkeley. Robert Southey. And children at rest at their mothers' breast/Started, and scream'd with fear. OBRV

An Old Woman of the Roads. Padraic Colum. Out of the wind's and the rain's way. BoC; CAW; FaBoBe; FYAP; GoBC; GoTF; GTBS; HBMV; MoBrPo; NOBI; OBEV; PG; PoRA; TreFS; WHA

Old Woman, Old Woman. *Anonymous.* Now I hear you clearly. OxNR

An Old Woman, outside the Abbey Theater. Leonard Alfred George Strong. They'd run like hell from in the slums. DBV; FiBHP; MoBrPo

An Old Woman Remembers. Sterling A. Brown. "And then/There wasn't any riot any more." CNA; PoBA

The Old Woman Remembers. Lady Gregory, Augusta Gregory. So may God give to them and all/The blessing of His lasting peace! OnYI

An Old Woman's Answer to a Letter from Her Girlhood. Susan L. Emory. And see God's face, Ancient of Days, Eternal! CAW

An Old Woman's Song. Akjartoq. while the sun rides up the sky/in the cool morning./in the cool morning! WPOW

Old Woman's Song. Thomas Cole. Who grows the roses/Of Paradise. NePoAm-2

The Old Woman's Three Cows. *Anonymous.* Rosy and Colin and Dun. OxNR

The Old Woman Sits. Leasa Davis. She knits the only warmth/she will receive all winter. CTBA

An Old Woman Speaks of the Moon. Ruth Pitter. And I took it as good, and a happy omen to me. BoC

The Old Woman Who Bought a Pig. *Anonymous.*
Now there lays the lonely three,/Old man, old woman, and little piggy, uh-uh-huh! BFSS
So it's all over, and the old woman's home again now. OxNR

The Old Woman Who Lived in a Shoe. *Anonymous.* And when she came back she found 'em all a-loffing. OxBoLi

The Old Woman Who Went to Market. *Anonymous.* "Oh, Lord have mercy on me! Can this be I?"/Fol-lol, diddle, diddle, diddle, dol. BFSS

The Old Women. George Mackay Brown. An undersong of terrible holy joy. NePoEA-2; OxBS

Old Women. Babette Deutsch. Old women, pitying all that age can kill,/ Lie quiet, wondering that they are old. HBMV

Old Women beside a Church. Keith Wilson. the wind brushes adobe walls away/grain by grain. Psk

Old Women of Toronto. Miriam Waddington. and partial view, at least, of the bright lake. NOBC

The Old Women Still Sing. Charles H. Rowell. Singing their lives, yours and mine. CNA

Old World, New World. Harry Roskolenko. With curators on every corner and a red light. AMV-81

An Old-World Thicket. Christina Georgina Rossetti. Still journeying toward the sunset and their rest. SBG

The Old Year. John Clare. The eve of New Year's Day/Left the Old Year lost to all. NOBV; OBCP; PG

The Old Year. Clarence Urmy. Close it and lay it in God's hand. PGD; PoToHe

The Old Year and the New. Annie Johnson Flint. Faith, Hope, and Love–abide. BLRP

The Old Year's Prayer. Minna Irving. Bring faith in God, a beacon in the night/To guide mankind aright. PGD

Old Zip Coon (Turkey in the Straw). Bob Farrell. And de bery nex President, will be Zip Coon. TrAS

The Olden Days. Joseph Hall. Then farewell, fairest age, the world's best days,/Thriving in ill, as it in age decays. OBSC

Olden Love-Making. Nicholas Breton. Or leave the lover's state. DiPo; OBSC

Older Grown. Kate Greenaway. Shake hands, good-bye, and have no fear/ To welcome well another year. BiCB

Older Now. Dave Gingell. amongst the solitude of hills/that kept their faith with me. PoSH

The Oldest Soldier. Robert Graves. The oldest soldier of the row. DTC

Ole Moke... Harold Littlebird. accept this universal prayer VoR

Oleanna. *Anonymous.* Ole, Ole, Ole, Ole, Ole, Ole anna. FSW

The Oleaster. Robert Graves. Though in rock rooted like an oleaster. OBTV

Olga Poems. Denise Levertov. ...in back of their hard, or veiled, or shining/unknowable gaze... LCAP; NNaP

Oliphaunt. J. R. R. Tolkien. And I never lie. AmMo

On a Window at the Four Crosses. Jonathan Swift. Put up your wife, she's crosser than all four. FaBoEE

On a World War Battlefield. Thomas Curtis Clark. The pure white flag of love and brotherhood. PGD

On a Young Lady's Going into a Shower Bath. Francis Scott Key. ...a refuge find/From the rude napkin's irreligious touch. UnTE; YaD

On a Young Man and an Old Man. Edward May. They both grew friends, and drank their liquor off. OBSP

On Addy Road. May Swenson. ...and saw/in the dew of the sandy road/faint print of a fox's paw. GOYP

On Aesthetics, More or Less. Peter Kane Dufault. They do say only the lun-/atic stares at the bare moon. NYBP

On Alexander and Aristotle, on a Black-on-Red Greek Plate. Alan Dugan. to Porus and the elephants/and drunkenness in Babylon. PPP

On Alexis. Plato. Who snatcheth it–lost we not Phaedrus so? AWP

On Amaryllis A Tortoyse. Marjorie Pickthall. Take Heart of me, who by His Grace,/Slough'd off my Pris'n and won my Race. PeCV

On an Aberdeen Favourite. Anonymous. An extraordinary thing for Aberdeen. FaBoEE; FaBoPP

On an Air of Rameau. Arthur Symons. It is the melancholy of ancient death/The harpsichord dreams of, sighing in the room. OBNC

On an American Soldier of Fortune Slain in France. Clinton Scollard. Though your pulseless clay may moulder/In the Forest of Argonne! MC

On an Anniversary after Reading the Dates in a Book of Lyrics. John Millington Synge. ...What year will they write/For my poor passage to the stall of Night? FaBoEE; NOBI; OBMV; PoL

On an East Wind from the Wars. Alan Dugan. ...as it cuts/your children's new names in the tombstone of thin air. AP

On an Engraved Gem of Leander. John Keats. He's gone: up bubbles all his amorous breath! CBEP

On an Engraving by Casserius. A. D. Hope. ...till the deep/Dawns with that unimaginable day.' CBAP

On an Houre-Glasse. John Hall. How art thou Nothing when th' art most of all! MeLP; MePo

On an Ill-Managed House. Jonathan Swift. Sloth, Dirt, and Theft, around her wait. AnIV

On an Indian Tomineois, the Least of Birds. Thomas Heyrick. But in Return did make the work more Rare. FM

On an Infant Dying as Soon as Born. Charles Lamb. A more harmless vanity? GTBS; GTBS-P; OBEV; OBRV

On an Insignificant Fellow. George Nathanial, Marquis Curzon. Colley was living, Colley's dead. PV

On an Intaglio Head of Minerva. Thomas Bailey Aldrich. To have his carven agate-stone/On such a bosom rise and fall so! HBV 1-2; InMe

On an Invitation to the United States. Thomas Hardy. And their experience count as mine. AWP; InPo

On an Island. John Millington Synge. And Jude, now you're married, will stretch on the floor. BIrV; MoBrPo; OBSP; OBVV

On an Italian Hillside. Richard Weber. On the secret, slate-dark, flowering, flooded sea. NMP

On an Old Horn. Wallace Stevens. Pipperoo, pippera, pipperum...The rest is rot. LiTA

On an Old Muff. Frederick Locker-Lampson. Still I must go and weed/Hard in my garden. CenHV

On an Old Sun Dial. Anonymous. Love is forever over all. GoTF; TreFT

On an Old Toper Buried in Durham Churchyard, England. Anonymous. And then his bier took him. ShM

On an Old Woman. Lucilius [(or Lucillius)]. She buys them black, they therefore need/No subsequent immersion. AWP; LiTW

On an Upright Judge. Jonathan Swift. To cut his throat before he married. ALV; DBV

On Andrew Turner. Robert Burns. And ca'd it Andrew Turner. DBV; PV

On Another. Hilaire Belloc. Cannot express my thoughts on birds. FaBoEE

On Another's Sorrow. William Blake. He doth sit by us and moan. AWP; CBEP; CEP; EBCP; EnRP; FaBV; ViBoPo

On Apis the Prizefighter. Lucilius [(or Lucillius)]. who never by any chance hurt one of them. WeW

On Apples. David Ross. But you must smell them. NYBP

On Approaching My Birthday. Vassar Miller. when I grew up to wither into truth. IHMS; NMM

On Archaeanassa. Plato. What flames felt you who saw her noon of light? AWP

On Arrival. Richard Howard. and it will never have been written. TAP

On Arthur Hugh Clough. Algernon Charles Swinburne. As belongs to believers in Clough. FaBoEE

On Ascending a Hill Leading to a Convent. Francisco Manuel de Mello. Hope is reality and time is life. CAW

On Australian Hills. Ada Cambridge. But trust the guidance of the One Who Knows. PoAu 1-2

On Authors and Booksellers. Alexander Pope. So pimps grow rich, while gallants are undone. FaBoEE

On Autumn Lake. John Ashbery. In each the potential is realized, the two wires/Are crossing. LCAP

On Barclay's Apology for the Quakers. Matthew Green. The crows, that brought him bread and meat.' NOEC

On Bassa. Martial (Marcus Valerius Martialis). With males renounced, adultery can flourish. PeHV

On Beauty. A Riddle. Matthew Prior. Of Idle Tales, and foolish Riddles. CEP

On Becoming Man. R. P. Lister. I sometimes longed to be a fish again. PV

On Behalf of Some Irishmen Not Followers of Tradition. George William Russell. The golden heresy of truth. AnIL; PoLf

On Being a Woman. Dorothy Parker. Yet do you up and leave me–then/I scream to have you back again? FPL; PoLf

On Being Asked for a Peace Poem. Howard Nemerov. With the fierce gaze and implacable small smile. OxBC

On Being Asked for a War Poem. William Butler Yeats. Or an old man upon a winter's night. MoVE; NIP; OBWP; PP

On Being Brought from Africa to America. Phillis Wheatley. Remember, Christians, Negroes, black as Cain,/May be refin'd, and join th' angelic train. RALP; FF; HeIP; NOBA; NOEC; SBG; TAP; TTY

On Being Head of the English Department. Pinkie Gordon Lane. I am selfish. I am cruel./I am love. BlSi

On Being Invited to a Testmonial Dinner. William Stafford. my head may twitch for itself, and those kings die. NePoAm-2

On Being Much Better Than Most and Yet Not Quite Good Enough. John Ciardi. Who swam ten miles out–and nine back. GOYP

On Being Photographed. William H. Gass. ...As a harmless cloud. AMV-81

On Being Sixty. Po Chu-i. Not to complain of three-score, "the time of obedient/ears." AWP

On Being Told That One's Ideas Are Victorian. Sara Henderson Hay. If the lady's not willing/She's just old fashioned! InMe

On Bell-Ringers. Voltaire (Francois Marie Arouet). That ye wore round your necks what you hold in your/hand! ShM

On Ben Dorain. Duncan Ban MacIntyre. Scenes of my spring-time and its joys–for ever fare/you well. PoSH

On Ben Jonson. Sidney Godolphin. Here lies Ben Jonson, every age will look/With sorrow here, with wonder on his book. CBEP

On Ben Jonson, in Westminster Abbey. Sir John Young. O rare Ben Jonson! FaBoEE

On Bertrand Russell's "Portraits from Memory'. Donald Davie. Her sheaves too heavy for the talkers there. FaBoTw

On Blenheim House. Abel Evans. That 'tis a house, but not a dwelling. CBEP; OBEC

On Board the '76. James Russell Lowell. Himself our bravest crown. MOS

On Board the Cumberland. George Henry Boker. A monument, that needs no scroll,/For those beneath the wave! PAH

On Board the Leicester Castle. Anonymous. And when the singing and dancing it was all over/We raised our ports and sang out with good cheer. OBSS

On Botching. John Heywood. God wrought as like a botcher, as God might do. FaBoCo

On Burning a Dull Poem. Jonathan Swift. Though born in snow, it died in flame. TW

On Burroughs' Work. Allen Ginsberg. Don't hide the madness. NoAm; NOBA

On Button the Grave-Maker. Anonymous. Are graves become but Button-holes? FaBoEE

On Buying a Dog. Edgar Klauber. If he could talk, I'll guarantee/He'd never speak to you or me. GDP; NTCP

On Buying a Horse. Anonymous. Take off his hide and feed him to the crows. NLV; PH

On Calamy's Imprisonment and Wild's Poetry. Hudibras" The squire of Newgate rock them on a sledge. APAS

On Calvary's Lonely Hill. Herbert Clark Johnson. On some high lonely hill/Before the cleansing's done. PoNe

On Catching a Dog-Daisy in the Mower. Peter Redgrove. "I'd better pick the white bits up,/And put them on the heap, for tidiness." NePoEA-2

On Catullus. Walter Savage Landor. Sprinkles another's laughing face/With nectar, and runs on. OBEV; ViBoPo

On Censure. Jonathan Swift. The most effectual way to balk/Their malice, is–to let them talk. CBEP

On Certain Days of the Year. Nancy Simpson. ...believing I could give him/the sun and the moon. AMV-81

On Certain Ladies. Alexander Pope. And haunt the places where their honour died. FaBoCo

On Certain Mornings Everything Is Sensual. David Jauss. Even the alarm clock/Had its hands all over me. GOYP

On Certain Wits. Howard Nemerov. ...the prophets of Baal/Were aesthetically significant, while Elijah's were very plain. HaCAP; OxBC

On Change of Weathers. Francis Quarles. We know not what to have, nor how to ask. OBSP

On Christmas Day. *Anonymous.* For ploughing on Our Lord's birthday. OBET

On Christmas Day. Clement Paman. On such a ground, music 'twill be to die. OxBoCh

On Christmas-Day. Thomas Traherne. The Minster rings. OBS; OxBoCh; PoEL 1-5

On Christmas Eve. W. S. Di Piero. and we all emerge entirely where we are. AMV-81

On Christmas Eve. Edith Lovejoy Pierce. They troubled not the little Jesus' sleep... MoRP

On Christopher Wordsworth, Master of Trinity. Benjamin Hall Kennedy. I wrote Who wrote Icon Basilike? FaBoCo

On City Streets. Margaret E. Bruner. We fear to change the old, established way. PoToHe

On Clarastella Singing. Robert Heath. To glorifie her after death, She'll ne'er/Need Change; She's Angel now, and Heav'n is here. OBS

On Clarastella Walking in Her Garden. Robert Heath. To tell us She their sweets did give. CavP; OBS

On Clark Street in Chicago. George Keithley. no more no more no more. NPGG

On Clergymen Preaching Politics. John Byrom. If these good folks would keep within their tether! SeCePo

On Clinton Edward Dawkins, Commoner of Balliol. J. W. Mackail. Spell Him with a capital. FaBoEE

On Colley Cibber's Declaration That He Will Have the Last Word... Alexander Pope. For know, the last word is the word that lasts longest. FaBoEE

On Communists. Ebenezer Elliott. ...he is willing/To fork out his penny and pocket your shilling. NLV; NOBL

On Corwen Road. Jay Ames. though 50 years and more/have passed/dry-sapping this older tree. AMV-80

On Court-Worme. Ben Jonson. Which was a cater-piller. So t'will dye. SeCP

On Death. John Keats. ...nor dare he view alone/His future doom which is but to awake. SyP

On Death. Anne Killigrew. When Canaan did with Milk and Honey flow. BoWoP

On Death. Walter Savage Landor. ...all I know/Is, there is not a word of fear. BoLiVe; TrGrPo

On Death and Love. Janet Campbell Hale. And listen/To his heart/beat. VoR

On Death (excerpt). Anghelos Sikelianos. Listen to the roar of your liberation... LiTW

On Delia. Sir Hildebrand Jacob. A pious, sordid, drunken scold. FaBoEE

On Dennis. Alexander Pope. Secure in dullness, madness, want, and age. FaBoEE

On Descending the River Po. William Parsons. Felt my own littleness, and want of strength,/And thought no more to aim at works of length. OBTV

On Devenish Island. Frank Ormsby. I keep what you gave. CIP

On Digital Extremities. Gelett Burgess. I'll be Awfully Sad, when it Goes! HBVY

On Disbanding the Army. David Humphreys. Thither by death-tides borne, as ye full soon/have been. PAH

On Discovering a Butterfly. Vladimir Nabokov. red label on a little butterfly. NYBP

On Diverse Deviations. Maya Angelou. Where love is the scream of anguish/And no curtain drapes the door. BlSi

On Dives. Richard Crashaw. Spare this one Jewel; I'll be Dives still! ACP

On Doctor Fuller. *Anonymous.* Here lies Fuller's/Earth. FaBoEE

On Don Juan del Norte, Not Don Juan Tenorio del Sur. Alan Dugan. or verbalize his failure by the traveller's success. ErPo

On Don Surly. Ben Jonson. Surly, use other arts, these only can/Style thee a great fool, but no great man. FaBoEE

On Donne's Poem "To a Flea." Samuel Taylor Coleridge. In purgatory fire on Bardolph's nose. FM

On Donne's Poetry. Samuel Taylor Coleridge. Wit's forge and fire-blast, meaning's press and screw. CBEP; ERoP 1-2; InvP; NoP; OAEL 1-2; OAEP; PP

On Dr. Chard. *Anonymous.* Who fill'd half of this churchyard. FaBoEE

On Dr. Evans Cutting down a Row of Trees at St. John's College... *Anonymous.* And bears the like antipathy to trees. FaBoEE

On Dr. Keene, Bishop of Chester. Thomas Gray. If you scratch him will fester. FaBoEE

On Dr. Lettsom. *Anonymous.* Why, what care I, I lets 'em. FaBoEE

On Dr. Samuel Ogden. R. P. Arden. So wrapt his thoughts in Arabic/And bid 'em all defiance. FaBoCo

On Dreams. Jonathan Swift. Flirts from his Cart the Mud in Walpole's Face. BIrV

On Dreams and Mexican Songs. Tom Dent. Shed no tears, that's the way it is. APU

On Dressing to Go Hunting. *Anonymous.* But I'll keep up the struggle for as long I dare. PH

On Drinking & a New Moon through the Window. Keith Wilson. Instead I have this bent body/haunted by a thousand lives. GP

On Dulcina. Sir Walter Ralegh. Foregoe me now, come to me soon. CoMu

On Dwelling. Robert Graves. Like trees they murmur or like blackbirds sing/Courtesies of good-morning and good-evening. CBEP; CMoP; FaBoMo; MoVE; OBSP

On Earth. Forugh Farrokhzad. What good is a star? BoWoP

On Earth There Is a Lamb So Small. Nicolaus Zinzendorf. It may behold thy holy face/And all its radiance truly. AH

On Easter Day. Celia Thaxter. Christ is risen for all time! YeAr

On Easter Morning. Eben E. Rexford. And lo! the Christ they sing of is here in our midst to-day. BLRP

On Eastnor Knoll. John Masefield. A land of shadows. CH; MCCG

On Editing Scott Fitzgerald's Papers. Edmund Wilson. But only spell and point and punctuate. CrMA; NYBP

On Edmund Burke. Oliver Goldsmith. To eat mutton cold and cut blocks with a razor. FaBoEE

On Edward Seymour, Duke of Somerset. *Anonymous.* Eschew the golden hall, thy thatched house is best. OBSC

On Eleanor Freeman. *Anonymous.* She'll rise a star that fell a flower. OBEV

On Elizabeth Ireland. *Anonymous.* Here lie I as warm as they. FaBoEE

On Ellson Fell. William Landles. Still in the quiet o the hills. PoSH

On English Monsieur. Ben Jonson. Daily to turn in Paul's, and help the trade. NLV; NoP

On Entering a Forest. Elinor Lennen. Irrevocable judgments/Of the parliament of trees. PGD

On Even Keel. Matthew Green. Life's voyage to the world unknown. OBEC

On Evolution. John Ciardi. could he see us, would reject us. OBAL

On Exodus, III, 14, I Am That I Am. Matthew Prior. And his enlarg'd Ideas found the Road,/Which Faith had dictated, and Angels trod. CEP

On Falling. Andrew Greig. Their eyes are calm/surviving smoothly/in a monstrous environment.... PoSH

On Falling Asleep by Firelight. William Meredith. ...dust/Isaiah said would be the serpent's meat. NoAm; NYBP

On Falling Asleep to Birdsong. William Meredith. Yet all of a piece and clever/And at some level, true. PoCh

On Fame. John Keats.
Make your best bow to her and bid adieu,/Then, if she likes it, she will follow you. CBEP; EnLit; NCEP
Why then should man, teazing the world for grace,/Spoil his salvation for a fierce miscreed? CABA; EnLit; NCEP

On Fanny Godwin. Percy Bysshe Shelley. This world is all too wide for thee. ChRP; OBNC

On Fell. Gotthold Lessing. And got well, while the scorpion died of the bite. ShM

On File. John Kendrick Bangs. Then go out and burn the file. PoToHe; WBLP

On Finding a Small Fly Crushed in a Book. Charles Tennyson Turner. Yet leave no lustre on our page of death. FM

On Finding the Truth. Jones Very. And Man and Nature lived again for aye. TrCP

On First Entering Westminster Abbey. Louise Imogen Guiney. Above the oval sea of ended kings. AA

On First Hearing Beethoven. George Barker. Deaf dumb and blind can only stare at the sky. UnS

On First Looking in on Blodgett's Keats's "Chapman's Homer." George Starbuck. that great whales' blanket party hump and hump. NIP; OBAL; PP

On First Looking into Chapman's Homer. John Keats. Silent, upon a peak in Darien. BiP; BLPA; BoLiVe; DiPo; ERoP 1-2; ExPo; FaBoBe; FaBoCh; FaBV; FaFP; FaPo; FF; FiP; ForPo; FPL; GN; GoTF; GTBS; GTBS-P; HAP; HBV 1-2; HBVY; HeIP; HoPM; InPK; InPo; LiTB; LoBV; LoGBV; MBW 1-2; MCCG; NAWM 1-2; NIP; NOAV; NOBE; NoP; OAEL 1-2; OAEP; OBEV; OBNC; OBRV; PoEL 1-5; PPoe; PrIm; RoGo; SeCeV; SoSe; TEP; TreF; TrGrPo; ViBoPo; WHA

On First Looking into Chapman's Homer I (parody). T. Griffiths. 'Cos Pope does a lot but Chapman more/(If you can't read Homer in Greek). BXAP

On First Looking into Chapman's Homer II (parody). Peter Peterson. the only/one his returning master/actually to recognize. BXAP

On First Looking into Chapman's Homer (parody). W. S. Brownlie. Looking at the sea and wondering what its name is. BXAP

On First Looking into Loeb's Horace. Lawrence Durrell. Indifference and success had crowned them all. FaBoMo; LiTM

On First Looking into Michael Grant's Cities of Vesuvius. Gavin Ewart. but with the blue sea and sky there was always benevolent sun. OBTV

On First Looking into the Dark Future. Roger Lancelyn Green. Silent upon a spike in Magpie Lane. CenHV

On Fleas. Augustus De Morgan. While those again have greater still, and greater still, and so on. TreFS

On Fleas. Jonathan Swift. And so proceed ad infinitum. GoTF; TreFS

On Flower Wreath Hill (excerpt). Kenneth Rexroth. Playing soundlessly in the/Circle of dancing gopis. GP

On Foinaven. Donald G. Saunders. ...I'm/prey too, picked-/out on stone, from time. PoSH

On Forelands High in Heaven. Alfred Edward Housman. And blots the foolish faces/Of my poor friends and me. PAI

On Fort Sumter. *Anonymous*. Who says, with "SOUTHERN DARING,"/ "I'LL FIND A WAY, OR MAKE IT!" MC; PAH

On Fortune. Queen of England, Elizabeth I. Where virtue's force can cause her to obey. PBWP

On Friendship. William Cowper. Be very much his friend indeed/To pardon or to bear it. GoTF; TreFT

On Friendship. William Whitehead. The pang which parts us from our weeping friends. OBEC

On Frosty Days. David Campbell. And here's my horse, my dog and I. CBAP

On Frozen Fields. Galway Kinnell. O only universe we know, forgive us. CAPP

On Fruition. Sir Charles Sedley. All in the ecstasy of doing. ErPo

On Galveston Beach. Barbara Howes. Before striking out in their sea. MoAmPo

On Gaulstown House. Jonathan Swift. I wish then, dear George, it were better or worse. CBEP

On Gay Wallpaper. William Carlos Williams. the sound of rain. MoAB; MoAmPo; TAP

On Getting a Natural. Dudley Randall. I know/I'm black/AND/beautiful. FB; PoBA

On Giles and Joan. Ben Jonson. I know no couple better can agree! NOBL

On Glaister's Hill: Carlyle on Burns. William Jeffrey. Alack, there's naething but the waukrife cheep/O' Smith, Ricardo, Bentham and their peers. OxBS

On Going Home. Marjorie L. Agnew. The person I have become now/Can be found. GoYe

On Going to the Wars. Earle Birney. And win the wide sundrenched Pacific. WaP

On Growing Old. John Masefield. Even the night will blossom as the rose. CMoP; CoBE; FaFP; FPL; GoTF; HBMV; LiTB; LiTM; MoAB; MoBrPo; MoRP; PG; PoLf; PoRA; TreFS; ViBoPo; WHA

On Growing Old. Srinivas Rayaprol. Like women. ACV

On Growing Old in San Francisco. Jack Gilbert. two girls barefoot never coming back NPGG

On Gustavus Adolphus, King of Sweden. Sir Thomas Roe. While Victory lay weeping by his side. FaBoEE

On Gut. Ben Jonson. Lust it comes out, that gluttony went in. AnAnS 2; JCP; NoP

On Halloween. Shel Silverstein. And wear a wig of sauerkraut. PoSC

On Hampstead Heath. Wilfred Wilson Gibson. Sits, tight-lipped, quaking, eager-eyed and pale,/Beneath her purple feather. HBV 1-2

On Hardscrabble Mountain. Galway Kinnell. To a dormouse with a paunch and large ears like/leaves or wings. RFM

On Harting Down. Thomas Sturge Moore. Parked therein, numerous, timid, dumb/Musings retired or neared. OxBTC

On Having Grown Old. Ernest G. Moll. Then, on my slab, while stars put on their white/Uniforms, yield myself to absolute night. BoAV

On Having Piles. Sir Walter Scott. Slice bullock's rumps–but spare the rump of man. FaBoEE

On Hearing a Beautiful Young Woman Describe Her Class... A. J. Hovde. She sighs, then tags a femur, pondering the remains. AMV-81

On Hearing a Broadcast of Ceremonies in Connection with.... Denis Wrafter. Than that of growing grass/Or lambs or infant joys! NeIP

On Hearing a Flute at Night from the Wall of Shou-Hsiang. Li Yi. And someone somewhere, playing a flute,/Has made the soldiers homesick all night long. UnS

On Hearing a Lady Praise a Certain Reverend Doctor's Eyes. George Outram. And when he preaches he shuts mine. DBV; GoTF; TreFT

On Hearing a Symphony of Beethoven. Edna St. Vincent Millay. Music my rampart, and my only one. LiTA; LiTM; MasP; MoAB; MoAmPo; NePA; TrGrPo; UnS

On Hearing It Has Been Ordered in the Chapterhouses of Ireland... Padraigin Haicead. merely condemn the herd of narrow censors/and the hate they bear my people, O my God. NOBI

On Hearing Mrs. Woodhouse Play the Harpsichord. William Henry Davies. Has made this poet my dumb slave. BrPo

On Hearing Prokofieff's Grotesque for Two Bassoons...(parody). Louis Untermeyer. Abandon the jig. BXAP

On Hearing That the Students of Our New University Have Joined... William Butler Yeats. Restraining reckless middle-age? NoAm

On Hearing the Airlines Will Use a Psychological Profile... Stephen P. Dunn. knowing, in a sense, there is no such thing/as the wrong man. AmPA

On Hearing the First Cuckoo. Richard Church. Not the flesh, but the mind, Menelaus, is frail. OBMV

On Hearing the Marsh Bird's Water Cry. Duane Niatum. Listen to the shamans roam through stars. CDW

On Heaven. Ford Madox Ford. In the cool of the even/In front of a cafe in Heaven. CTC; ViBoPo

On Hedylus. Martial (Marcus Valerius Martialis). ...yet I'd swear/That his cloak's much less worn than the hole in his rump. PeHV

On Her Coming to London. Edmund Waller. Nor envy's blast, nor fortune's rage/Shall ever work you ill. HBV 1-2

On Her Dancing. James Shirley. So nimbly with a marble heart. PoPle

On Her Loving Two Equally. Aphra Behn. If Damons, all my Hopes are crost;/Or that of my Alexis, I am lost. SBG

On Himself. *Anonymous*. Who was not even an Academician. FaBoEE

On Himself. Charles Churchill. Taste with contempt beholds, nor deigns to place/Amongst the lowest of her favour'd race. OBEC

On Himself. Walter Savage Landor. Or they will take thee for an owl. FaBoEE

On Himself. William Oldys. And one friend Old is worth a hundred new. FaBoEE

On Himself. Matthew Prior. Can Stuart, or Nassau go higher. FaBoEE

On Himself. Dante Gabriel Rossetti. And that saved the rear of Rossetti. FaBoEE

On Himself. Jonathan Swift.
AETATIS ANNO LXXVIII FaBoEE
I pay my club, and so good-bye. AnIV

On Himselfe. Robert Herrick.
But Ile spend my comming houres,/Drinking wine, and crown'd with flowres. FaBoEE; SeCV 1-2
The Muses will weare blackes, when I am dead. CaPo; SeCP

On His 86th Birthday. Thomas Hardy. As each year might assign. ACV 010

On His Books. Hilaire Belloc. "His sins were scarlet, but his books were read." ACP; FaBoCo; FaBoEE; GoTF; NLV; OxBoLi; PoPl; TreFT; WeW

On His Dog. John Gay. Who fawn'd like man, but ne'er like man betray'd. ALV

On His Exile to Iona. Saint Columcille. I should die of the love that I bear the Gael! CAW; LiTW

On His Friend, Joseph Rodman Drake. Fitz-Greene Halleck. None named thee but to praise. OBVV

On His Garden Book. Francis Daniel Pastorius. Perhaps we shall be One at once. SCAP

On His Lady's Waking. Pierre Ronsard. With breast as marble cold, as marble pure. AWP

On His Late Espoused Saint. Sir Kenelm Digby. All the light and beauty that she had is gone. ACP

On His Love. Daqiqi. O God! I would there were no life for me. LiTW

On His Mistress. John Donne. Think it enough for me to have had thy love. AnAnS 1; BoLoP; LiTB; PoEL 1-5; SeCeV; ViBoPo

On His Mistress Drown'd. Thomas Spratt. These Tears, these Tears shall mend thy Way. ATP; EnLoPo

On His Mistress Going from Home. *Anonymous*. So does the short enjoyment of such bliss,/And till restored, continual torment is. OBS

On His Mistress Looking in a Glass. Thomas Carew. ...and your face/Shall shine with an immortal grace. CaPo

On His Mistress, the Queen of Bohemia. Sir Henry Wotton. Oh tell if she were not designed/The eclipse and glory of her kind? AnAnS 2; EG; EiL; EnLoPo; GBL; HAP; JCP; LoBV; MeLP; MePo; MyFE; NoP; OBS; SeCP; TrGrPo; ViBoPo

On His Mistresse Going to Sea. Thomas Cary. Whilst both contribute to your own undoing. OBS

On His Mistris that Lov'd Hunting. *Anonymous*. Thou needst not fear no other ill/Than Turtles suffer when they Bill. OBS

On His Own Agamemnon and Iphigeneia. Walter Savage Landor. I am tragedian in this scene alone. OBRV

On His Own Deafness. Jonathan Swift. I hardly hear a Woman's Clack. BIrV; FaBoEE

On His Portrait. William Cowper. And hardly know, at the first view,/If I were here, or there. EyDe

On His Publisher. Alfred, Lord Tennyson. Ancient Pistol, sealskin Payne. FaBoEE

On His Queerness. Christopher Isherwood. And am not even sorry that I know nothing–/About fish. OxBTC; PeHV

On His Royal Blindness Paramount Chief Kwangala. Jack A. Mapanje.
...We should not wait for the children to/Tell us about our toothless gums
or our showing flies. WhB

On His Seventy-Fifth Birthday. Walter Savage Landor. It sinks, and I am
ready to depart. AnEnPo; AWP; BLPL; BoLiVe; EBEV; GoTF; InPo;
LiTB; OAEL 1-2; OAEP; SeCeV; TreF; TrGrPo; WHA

On His Writing Verses. John Hawthorn. And so NOEC

On History. Paul Hoover. sometimes later, they zig-zag crazily back/in no
decided direction. APU

On Honour. Bernard Mandeville. Because none e'er lay in her bed,/Unless
they first were knocked o' th' head. NOEC

On Hope. Richard Crashaw. True Hope's a glorious huntress, and her
chase/The God of Nature in the field of Grace. MePo; NOBE

On Hot Days. James Reiss. ...just as the El burst overhead/like a
thunderclap. AmPA

On How the Cobler. *Anonymous.* Though big with art, they Cannot
Overtopp/the spirits teaching in a Coblers Shopp. SCAP

On Hurricane Jackson. Alan Dugan. to the statistical Sparta of the
champs. CoAP; LiSp; NCSH; PoL; SD

On Hygiene. Hilaire Belloc. ...for now we know/Both how to make men
sick and keep them so. DBV

On Imagination. Phillis Wheatley. Cease then, my song, cease the unequal
lay. BlSi; PoNe

On Imitation. Samuel Taylor Coleridge. Yet all like Fox can game–like Pitt
can drink. OBSP

On Independence. Jonathan Mitchell Sewall. Keep us from invaders by
land and by sea,/And from all who'd deprive us of our liberty. PAH

On Installing an American Kitchen in Lower Austria. W. H. Auden. To
hold her Thermopylae. NYBP

On J. W. Ward. Samuel Rogers. He has a heart, and gets his speeches by
it. ALV; DBV

On Jacob Tonson, His Publisher. John Dryden. With frowzy pores, that
taint the ambient air. FaBoEE; OBSV

On Jam. Hilaire Belloc. And that is all I know of Jam. NLV

On James Grieve, Laird of Boghead, Tarbolton. Robert Burns. Then
welcome, hail! damnation. DBV

On Jocky Bell. *Anonymous.* Take this stane aff my wame, and lay it on o'
thine. FaBoEE

On John Adams, of Southwell. George Gordon, Lord Byron. He could not
carry off, so now he's carri-on. PV

On John Donne's Book of Poems. John Marriot. You have him living to
Eternity. CH

On John So. *Anonymous.* And so let him lie. FaBoEE

On John William Mackail, Fellow of Balliol. *Anonymous.* I'm Mackail–and
who are you? FaBoEE

On Jordan's Bank. George Gordon, Lord Byron. How long thy temples
worshipless, Oh God? ChRP

On Judas Iscariot. Francis Quarles. God knows, some curse themselves, in
cursing him. FaBoEE

On Keats Who Desired That On His Tomb Should Be Inscribed–. Percy
Bysshe Shelley. A scroll of crystal, blazoning the name/Of Adonais!
FaBoEE

On King Richard the Third, Who Lies Buried under Leicester Bridge. Sir
John Suckling. Judgement must come, and water then will be/A heaven to
thee in hellish misery. CaPo

On Kingston Bridge. Ellen Mackay Hutchinson Cortissoz. The quick and
dead together talked,/On Kingston Bridge. AA

On Knighthood. Folgore da San Geminiano. And all who in that following
went with her. AWP

On Knowing Nothing. A.J.M. Smith. As deep, as nothing, as the grave.
PeCV

On Ladies' Accomplishments. *Anonymous.* Sweet lady, tell me–can you
make a pudding? FaBoUs

On Lady Anne Hamilton. Richard Brinsley Sheridan. With a muff and a
cloak and a tippet–poor Anne. FaBoEE

On Lady Gregory's Search for Talent. James Joyce. When thousands of
students/Cried "All we are in that category!" FaBoEE

On Lady Poltagrue, a Public Peril. Hilaire Belloc. To his extreme
annoyance, tempted him. ALV; FaBoCo; GoTF; PoL; PV; TreFT

On Lake Pend Oreille. Richard Shelton. At her pathetic signnal/the
aristocracy of leaves/will begin to let go. NYBP

On Lavater's Song of a Christian to Christ. Johann Wolfgang von Goethe.
He would not be so violent in his repetition/if it were not a questionable
proposition. ELU

On Laying the Corner-Stone of the Bunker Hill Monument. John Pierpont.
And thy right hand shall guard their fame. AnNE; PAH

On Laying up Treasure. Lois Smith Hiers. In a season of snow, they shall
batter my door to/borrow/A sip of my wild sweet grape. GoYe

On Leander's Swimming over the Hellespont to Hero. Thomas Warton, Jr..
Drown me on my return–but spare me as I go. FaBoEE

On Leaping over the Moon. Thomas Traherne. As o'er our heads, a place
of bliss. AtBAP; LiTB; LoBV; MOON; SeCV 1-2

On Learning That Certain Peat Bogs Contain Perfectly Preserved Bodies.
Susan Ludvigson. or the features of the man/who should be bones.
MAYP

On Learning to Adjust to Things. John Ciardi. "The climate's very healthy
once you're used to being dead." OBCA

On Learning to Play the Guitar. Ray Fraser. you left behind immortal
lines/for other happy singers. NeAC

On Leaving Baltimore. Duane Niatum. Bursting from the rip in the sun.
CDW

On Leaving Bruges. Dante Gabriel Rossetti. And have its will upon the
extreme seas. CBEP

On Leaving Cuba, Her Native Land. Gomez de Avellaneda Gertrudis.
...and trembling, the ship/cuts through the waves and flies in silence!
WPOW

On Leaving Holland (excerpt). Mark Akenside. He reigns not but by her
preserving voice. OBTV

On Leaving Mrs. Brown's Lodgings. Sir Walter Scott. But all's one for
that, since I must and will away. NBM

On Leaving Prison. Luis Ponce de Leon. Spends his life in solitude,/
Neither envied nor envious. ILwL

On Leaving Ullswater. Kathleen Raine. Only myself how strange/to the
strange present come! NeBP

On Lebanon. David Gray. O Maiden of the Maronites! AA

On Lending a Punch-Bowl. Oliver Wendell Holmes –My dear, where have
you been? AA

On Liberty and Slavery. George Moses Horton. And in thy shades the
storm shall calm,/With songs of Liberty! PoNe

On Lieutenant Shift. Ben Jonson. Lent him a pocky whore. She hath paid
him. OBSV

On Linden Street. Shelley Ehrlich. I find on my street the new/breath, the
silenced hammer. AMV-80

On Lisa's Golden Hair. Roy Campbell. Or Tantalus, with streams that
shone as golden. AtBAP

On Listening to the Spirituals. Lance Jeffers. ...a passionate heaven rose
no/God in heaven could create! PoBA

On Living with Children for a Prolonged Time. Mark Lowey. as I dipped
my hands/in the bullrush slaughter. AMV-81

On Looking at a Copy of Alice Meynell's Poems. Amy Lowell. The living
have so much to do. SBG

On Looking at an Old Climbing Photograph. Douglas Fraser. What need–
so long as they can climb again? PoSH

On Looking at Stubbs's Anatomy of the Horse. Edward Lucie-Smith. I
gape for anecdote, absurd detail,/Like any yokel with his pint of ale.
NePoEA-2

On Looking into E. V. Rieu's Homer. Patrick Kavanagh. Joking on the
fabulous mountain-side. NOBI

On Looking into Henry Moore. Dorothy Livesay. Woman in man, and
man in womb. OBCV

On Looking up by Chance at the Constellations. Robert Frost. That calm
seems certainly safe to last tonight. CMoP; NePA

On Lord Galloway. Robert Burns. Not one of them a knave. FaBoEE

On Lord Holland's Seat near Margate, Kent. Thomas Gray. And foxes
stunk and littered in St. Paul's.' CABA; LAuP; NOEC; OAEL 1-2;
SeCeV; TW

On Love. Kyogoku Tamekane. till my thoughts are worn out/and I no
longer hate you LLLT

On Lucy Countesse of Bedford. Ben Jonson. My Muse bad, Bedford write,
and that was shee. AnAnS 2; EnRePo; OAEP; OBS; SeCP; SeCV 1-2

On Lydia Distracted. Philip Ayres. And with each motion she ensnar'd a
heart. EnLoPo

On Maids and Cats. Henricus Selyns. How e'er it hits, there is no dough.
SCAP

On Man. Walter Savage Landor. The present hour was ever markt with
shade! NBM; OBNC; OBRV

On Marcus the Physician. Nicarchos [(or Nicarchus)]. We're burying the
statue today. LiTW

On Margaret Ratcliffe. Ben Jonson. Earth, thou hast not such another.
SeCP

On Marriage. Richard Crashaw. I would be married to a single life.
FaBoEE; HW

On Marriage. Thomas Flatman. Good faith, Mr. Parson, excuse me from
that! ELU; FaBoUs; FiBHP; NOBL

On Mary Magdalen. William, of Hawthornden Drummond. –Thus sighed
to Jesus the Bethanian fair,/His tear-wet feet still drying with her hair.
OAEL 1-2

On Maurus the Rhetor. Palladas. I was impressed. LiTW

On May-Day, When the Lark Began to Ryse. *Anonymous.* And let my
mouth thy preising now bewrye. LO

On Measure. Keith Waldrop. praying, "Lord, grant her/wings." InPK

On Meesh-e-gan. *Anonymous.* You sure get bit on Meesh-e-gan. ABF;
TrAS

On Startling Some Pigeons.　Charles Tennyson Turner.　An eagle, weary of his mighty wings,/With anxious inquest fills his mortal span?　PB

On Stella's Birthday.　Jonathan Swift.　To split my worship too in twain.　InPK; NIP; NOBI; OAEL 1-2

On Stripping Bark from Myself.　Alice Walker.　as I see I must.　LTB

On Sturminster Foot-Bridge.　Thomas Hardy.　As a lattice-gleam when midnight/moans.　FaBoPP; OAEP; OBSP

On Such a Day.　Mary Elizabeth Coleridge.　Rejoice a moment–then/ Remember.　MoVE

On Such a Windy Afternoon.　Theodore Enslin.　Such wind.　AMV-80

On Sunday in the Sunlight.　William Rose Benet.　And teach me the true language/Of silentness!　HBMV

On Supporters of the Baconian Theory.　Alfred, Lord Tennyson.　But make him kick the dead.　FaBoEE

On Sweet Killen Hill.　Tom MacIntyre.　That love lacks surveillance/On sweet Killen Hill.　CIP; NCSH

On Sympathisers with the American Revolution.　Charles Wesley.　O let them all thy love receive,/And saved, with us, for ever live!　NOCV

On Taine.　Alfred Ainger.　When–Enter Taine!–and all is entertaining.　ALV

On Teaching David to Shoot.　Walter McDonald.　And he takes aim. And fires.　AMV-80

On Teaching the Young.　Yvor Winters.　Laurel, archaic, rude.　NoAm; NOBA

On the 25th Anniversary of the Liberation of Auschwitz...　Eli Mandel.　a body melting　NOBC

On the American Rivers.　James Smith.　And Mrs. Sippy rolls her tides/ Responsive to Miss Souri.　FaBoUs

On the Annunciation of Fra Angelico.　Manuel Machado.　Like vivid sunburst on some crystal sphere.　CAW

On the Apparition of Oneself.　William Burford.　Our brother, friend, or a creature even of this flesh.　PoA

On the Appeal From the Race of Sheba: II.　Leopold Sedar Senghor. ...came the classical murmurous movement of a hundred herds.　TTY

On the Army of Spartans Who Died at Thermopylai.　Anonymous.　We kept the Spartan code, and here we lie.　FaBoEE

On the Astrologer and Almanac Maker, John Partridge.　Jonathan Swift. As he himself could, when above.　FaBoEE

On the Asylum Road.　Charlotte Mew.　To them, yes, every pane! MoBrPo

On the Athenian Dead at Ecbatana.　Plato.　and so we seize the moment/to tell the sea Goodbye.　PoPl

On the Author of the Treatise of Human Nature.　J. H. Beattie.　And yet the huge bulk of a sinner/Said there was neither spirit or matter.　FaBoCo

On the Balcony.　D. H. Lawrence.　The boat has gone.　BrPo; GBL

On the Banks of Salee.　Anonymous.　But we'll not sport together on the banks of Salee.　AmFP

On the Banks of the Little Eau Pleine.　Anonymous.　But I'll never forget Johnny Murphy, on the banks of the Little Eau Pleine.　AmFP

On the Banks of the Wabash, Far Away.　Paul Dresser.　On the banks of the Wabash, far away.　BLSo; FSN; FSW; GoTF; TreFT

On the Baptized Aethiopian.　Richard Crashaw.　And now, I doubt not, the Eternal Dove/A black-fac'd house will have.　FaBoEE; NoP; SeCV 1-2

On the Beach.　Charles Stuart Calverley.　Fate should snatch from me the jewel/Which I bought for one and sixpence on the beach.　ALV; FiBHP

On the Beach.　Frances Cornford.　Supremely calm, though just a little late. BoAnP

On the Beach.　Pati Hill.　freshly escaped from the drygoods factory/across the bay　FAZ

On the Beach at Fontana.　James Joyce.　Ache of love!　AnEnPo; MoBrPo; OBMV; PoA; SoSe

On the Beach at Night Alone.　Walt Whitman.　And shall forever span them and compactly hold and enclose them.　NePA; TAP

On the Benefactions in the Late Frost, 1740.　Alexander Pope.　To take the only way to be forgiven.　NOEC; OBSP

On the Big Horn.　John Greenleaf Whittier.　O wild, waste lands that await/The harvest exceeding great,/Break forth into praise of God!　PAH

On the Birth of a Posthumous Child, Born in Peculiar Circumstances... Robert Burns.　And from thee many a parent stem/Arise to deck our land. NAs

On the Birth of Dan Goldman.　Daniel Berrigan.　...solve/resolve the mystical dance.　NAs

On the Birth of His Son.　Su Tung-p'o.　Then he will crown a tranquil life/ By becoming a Cabinet Minister.　AWP; LiTW; OBVE; OFD; TRV

On the Birth of My Son, Malcolm Coltrane.　Julius Lester.　for the/life that we,/in our killing,/failed/to give them.　PoBA

On the Bleeding Wounds of Our Crucified Lord.　Richard Crashaw.　Nere was't thou in a sence so sadly true,/The well of living Waters, Lord, till now.　SeCV 1-2

On the Blessed Virgin's Bashfulness.　Richard Crashaw.　'Twas once look up, 'tis now look down to/heaven.　EnLi 1-2; HAP; ISi; OAEP; OBSP

On the Breaking-Up of a School.　Tadhg O'g O'Huiginn.　The wall of learning has broken.　AnIL

On the Bridge of Athlone: A Prophecy.　Donagh MacDonagh.　Lot's daughters with no Lot and no wine-cup/To get them a son.　OxBI

On the Bright Side.　Carter Revard.　as the sun got out of our eyes/and into our hungry bellies.　VoR

On the Brink of Death.　Buonarroti Michelangelo.　Whose arms to clasp us on the cross were spread.　AWP

On the British Invasion.　Philip Freneau.　Will bring them to an early grave/On the shores of Pensacola.　PAH

On the British King's Speech.　Philip Freneau.　And Whitehead, thou to write his epitaph.　PAH

On the Building of Springfield.　Vachel Lindsay.　While countless generations pass away.　MoRP; NAMP; OHFP; WHA

On the Burial of His Brother.　Catullus.　And, brother, for all time, hail and farewell.　AWP; EnLi 1-2

On the Bust of Helen by Canova.　George Gordon, Lord Byron.　Behold the Helen of the heart!　EyDe

On the Campagna.　Elizabeth Stoddard　Deep in the shadow of Rome!　AA

On the Candidates for the Laurel.　Alexander Pope.　Oh! save the salary, and drink the sack!　FaBoEE

On the Capture and Imprisonment of Crazy Snake, January, 1900.　Alexander L. Posey.　I bow to him, exalt his name!　BPAW

On the Capture of the Guerriere.　Philip Freneau.　Long, too long our seamen's jailors,/Dacre and the Guerriere!　PAH

On the Cards and Dice.　Sir Walter Ralegh.　An herald strange, the like was never born,/Whose very beard is flesh, and mouth is horn.　EnRePo; FCP

On the Charlie So Long.　Anonymous.　'Case he been on the Charlie so long. AS

On the Circuit.　W. H. Auden.　God bless the U.S.A., so large,/So friendly, and so rich.　NOBL; OxBTC

On the Circumsision: New Years Day.　Luke Wadding.　No other new years gift/Doth he require from us.　NOBI

On the Clerk of a Country Parish.　William Shenstone.　No music like a bell.　FaBoEE

On the Cliff.　Hal Summers.　And let the judging mind be still.　ChMP

On the Cliffs.　Algernon Charles Swinburne.　And in thine heart, where love and song make/strife,/Fire everlasting of eternal life.　VLP

On the Closing of Millom Ironworks.　Norman Nicholson.　When whichever way it blows it's a cold wind now.　FaBoTw

On the Coast near Sausalito.　Robert Hass.　Creature and creature,/we stared down centuries.　WOLT

On the Coast of Coromandel.　Osbert Sitwell.　Any music save by Handel/ On the coast of Coromandel!　MoBrPo; SeCePo

On the Collar of Mrs. Dingley's Lap-Dog.　Jonathan Swift.　Whose heart in this four-footed thing lies.　FaBoEE; FM

On the College Archery Range.　Robert Wallace.　The beauty is, how wholly/they attend their huntings here.　LiSp

On the Completion of the Pacific Telegraph.　Jones Very.　The dawn on earth of Freedom's perfect day.　AP; TAP

On the Couch.　Oscar Williams.　Crashing, as I lie here, stretched out, running running.　WaP

On the Countess Dowager of Pembroke.　William Browne.　Both her mourner and her tomb.　AWP; CABA; EnLi 1-2; GoTF; HAP; InvP; JCP; NoP; OBEV; PoEL 1-5; SeCeV; TreFS; ViBoPo; WeW

On the Countess of Dorchester.　Charles, Earl of Dorset Sackville.　At once both stink and shine.　APAS; CavP

On the Crocodile.　Thomas Heyrick.　They are conjoyn'd in Man, as well as Me!　FM

On the Croun o Bidean.　J. K. Annand.　Sin the blude of my Norse forebears/Melled the mountain dew and the brine.　PoSH

On the Crucifix.　Buonarroti Michelangelo.　The soul now turning to the Love Divine,/That oped, to embrace us, on the Cross its arms.　CAW

On the Crucifixion.　Giles the Younger Fletcher.　Why stay'st thou then my soul; o fly, fly, thither haste thee.　EBCP; OxBoCh

On the Cuckoo.　Francis Quarles.　Ere we have left to feed it, feeds on us. PBBP

On the Curve-Edge.　Abbie Huston Evans.　Relishing life, sucking the honeycomb.　NYBP

On the Danger of War.　George Meredith.　In peril of his blood his ears incline/To drums whose loudness is their emptiness.　CoBE; PPON

On the Dangers Attending Altruism on the High Seas.　Gilbert Keith Chesterton.　but–if you find a fish on land,/oh throw it in the sea. FaBoNo

On the Danube.　Robert Conquest.　Looking through a spring rain and imagining love.　NMP

On the Dark, Still, Dry, Warm Weather ...　Gilbert White.　...down rush the showers,/And float the deluged paths and miry fields.　NOEC

On the Dates of Poets.　Michael L. Johnson.　the consummate symmetry of the dead.　AMV-80

On the Day of Atonement.　Yehuda Amichai.　He too lowered the shutter and locked the door,/and with all those who prayed, I went home.　VWA

On the Dead. Walter Savage Landor. Death follows with uplifted dart. NBM

On the Death-Bed. Thomas Hardy. Though it be burning for evermore. BrPo

On the Death of a Cat. Christina Georgina Rossetti. Softly, softly let him tread,/Nor disturb her narrow bed. PCat

On the Death of a Child. Edward S. Silvera. So you stole away in the dark. PoNe

On the Death of a Favourite Old Spaniel. Robert Southey. Of their own charity, may envy thee. FM

On the Death of a Journalist. Roy Campbell. Than could a saint with fifty lives. CoBE

On the Death of a Lady's Dog. Wentworth Dillon, Earl of Roscommon. What we then envy'd, now we mourn! CavP

On the Death of a Lady's Owl. Moses Mendes. She wept upon thy tomb. TrJP

On the Death of a Metaphysician. George Santayana. Bubble from depths of the Icarian sea. AA; AmLP; APA; ViBoPo

On the Death of a Monkey. Thomas Heyrick. H'had Shows of Reason, and few Men have more. FM; MePo

On the Death of a New Born Child. Mei Yao Ch'en. Her breasts are still filling with milk. NaP

On the Death of a Nightingale. Thomas Randolph. Shall flock about thee, and keepe time with kisses. AnAnS 2; PBBP

On the Death of a Pious Lady. Olof Wexionius. The saint heaven hath, the mother once they had. AWP

On the Death of a Prince: A Meditation. Thomas Philipott. It shall be freed from foreign injury. JCP

On the Death of a Recluse. George Darley. And she is all thine own. CBEP; OBVV; OxBI

On the Death of a Young and Favorite Slave. Martial (Marcus Valerius Martialis). Mine be as lowly and as green a tomb! AWP; LiTW

On the Death of an Emperor Penguin in Regent's Park, London. David Wright. A smashed world whirl away in stinging snow. NYBP

On the Death of an Epicure. Richard Graves. 'Tis time to part, but oh! what is to pay? CBEP

On the Death of Anne Bronte. Charlotte Bronte. Must bear alone the weary strife. ViBoPo

On the Death of Benjamin Franklin. Philip Freneau. And turned the lightning's darts aside! PAH

On the Death of Captain Nicholas Biddle. Philip Freneau. The bursting Randolph ruin spread,/And lost what honor won. PAH

On the Death of Catarina de Attayda. Luîs de Camoens. Sighed o'er the ruin, and returned to heaven! AWP

On the Death of Commodore Oliver H. Perry. John Gardiner Calkins Brainard. Yet there are spirits here that to the strain/Would send a still small voice responsive back/again. PAH

On the Death of Dermody, the Poet. Henry Kirke White. Yet may the lily and the rose/Bloom on my grassy bed. PeD

On the Death of Doctor Swift. Jonathan Swift.
Forgetting his own flesh and blood! ViBoPo
"It is not yet so bad with us!" ViBoPo
That kingdom he had left his debtor,/I wish it soon may have a better. EiCP; OnYI; ViBoPo
We hope he's in a better place. ViBoPo
Which Pope must bear as well as I. ViBoPo

On the Death of Donne. Thomas Carew. Adored again with new apostasy. NOBE

On the Death of Dr. Robert Levet. Samuel Johnson. And free'd his soul the nearest way. CEP; EBEV; EiCP; HBV 1-2; HeIP; InPS; LAuP; NOBE; NOEC; NoP; OAEL 1-2; OBEC; OBEV; PAI; PoEL 1-5; PPP; SCV; TEP; ViBoPo

On the Death of Echo. Hartley Coleridge. And to no call can Echo more reply– BoAnP; GDP

On the Death of Edward III. Anonymous. And now her los biginneth to swage,/That selde y-seye is soone foryete. OxBM

On the Death of Elizabeth, Queen of Henry VII... Anonymous. God grant her now hevyn to encrese/and owr kyng Harry long lyff and pease FaBoRV

On the Death of Emperor Tenji. Anonymous. I saw my Lord,/The one I love,/Last night..in sleep. BoWoP

On the Death of Francis Thompson. Alfred Noyes. How grandly glow the bays! OBVV

On the Death of Friends in Childhood. Donald Justice. Come, memory, let us seek them there in the shadows. ConAP; LCAP; NCSH

On the Death of Her Mother. Muriel Rukeyser. ...and you/are/Dead, and here is your gift: my life which is my home. SM

On the Death of His Child. Faydi. ...O thou whose cheeks and body were as/jasmine, how art thou? LiTW

On the Death of His Son. Lewis Glyn Cothi. Farewell, whilst I live below,/my merry darling, my Sion. PoPl

On the Death of His Son. Charles Wesley. And see him with our Angel stand,/To waft, and welcome us to land. NOCV

On the Death of His Son Vincent. [James Henry] Leigh Hunt. And blest, as saviours from the one dire pang/That mocked the will to move it. NOBV

On the Death of His Wife. Frank O'Connor. That woman's hand–can it be true?–/No more beneath my head will lie. BIrV; CIP

On the Death of His Wife. Muireadhach Albanach O Dalaigh. No more beneath my head will lie. BIrV; CIP

On the Death of Ho Chi Minh. Eli Mandel. you cannot touch his body now/or burn his poems. NIP

On the Death of Jackson. Anonymous. "Jackson and victory!" PAH

On the Death of Joseph Rodman Drake. Fitz-Greene Halleck. That mourns a man like thee. AA; AmLP; GoTF; HBV 1-2; PAH; PoEL 1-5; TreFS

On the Death of Karl Barth. Jack R. Clemo. In deeps or shallows, all projections of the divine. NOCV

On the Death of Keats. John Logan. Oh Keats, the violet. The violet. The violet/was your favorite flower. Prf

On the Death of Lisa Lyman. Della Burt. Talk is too unreal. BlSi

On the Death of Little Mahala Ashcraft. James Whitcomb Riley. And the katydids and crickets hollers/"Haly!" all the night. AA

On the Death of M. D'Ossoli and His Wife, Margaret Fuller. Walter Savage Landor. Take we our seats and let the dirge begin. PAH

On the Death of Mary. Rainer Maria Rilke. Man, kneel down, look after me and sing. ISi

On the Death of Mistress Mary Prideaux. William Strode. They well are fitted: both are but a span. JCP

On the Death of Mr. Crashaw. Abraham Cowley. 'Twill learn of things Divine, and first of Thee to sing. AnAnS 2; GoBC; MeLP; MePo; OBS; SeCP; SeCV 1-2; ViBoPo

On the Death of Mr. Pope. Anonymous. His works are the apocalypse of verse. NOEC

On the Death of Mr. Purcell. John Dryden. The Gods are pleas'd alone with Purcells' Layes,/Nor know to mend their Choice. NOBE; UnS

On the Death of Mr. William Hervey. Abraham Cowley. Where Grief and Mis'ery can be join'd with Verse. AnAnS 2; CBEP; EBEV; FaBoRV; GTBS; NOBE; OBEV; OBS; SeCP; SeCV 1-2; ViBoPo

On the Death of Mrs. Bowes. Mary Wortley, Lady Montagu. With fellow-angels you enjoy it now. BoWoP

On the Death of Mrs. Felicia Hemans (excerpt). Lydia Huntley Sigourney. As for a florist fallen. PeD

On the Death of Mrs. Throckmorton's Bullfinch. William Cowper. His head alone remained to tell/The cruel death he died. HBV 1-2; NOEC; PBBP; PPP

On the Death of My Son Charles. Daniel Webster. My son! my father! guide me there. AA

On the Death of Neruda. Olga Cabral. Never again to leave Chile/never in exile again. SOTS

On the Death of Neruda. H. L. Van Brunt. but out of fear/of the unknown. LTB

On the Death of Old Bennet the News-Crier. Anonymous. Homer was blind, and Bennet could not read.' NOEC

On the Death of Parents. Alfred Barson. They shall rise up from this knowledge. AMV-80

On the Death of Phillips. Anonymous. The lowering lute lamenteth now therefore/Phillips her friend that can her touch no more. OBSC

On the Death of President Garfield. Oliver Wendell Holmes. And autumn's golden sun beholds/A nation bowed, a world in tears. PAH

On the Death of Pym. William, of Hawthornden Drummond. To whom a devil–"This is the Lower House. ALV

On the Death of Robert Browning. Algernon Charles Swinburne. And life and death but shadows of the soul. EnLit

On the Death of Robert Lowell. Eileen Myles. The old white haired coot./Fucking dead. APU

On the Death of Sir Philip Sidney. Henry Constable. And now begin to weep, when they have done. GoBC; OBEV

On the Death of Southey. Walter Savage Landor. ...who ran/The race we run, when Heaven recalls him hence. OBVV

On the Death of Squire Christopher, a Remarkably Fat Sportsman. John Wigson. Life breeds a throng; and Death must come/To thrust some out, to make more room. OBSP

On the Death of Sylvia Plath. Judith Herzberg. It must find refuge with the wolves/if such motherly wolves/still exist. VWA; WPOW

On the Death of the Evansville University Basketball Team... Robert W. Hamblin. to question the betraying earth? AMV-80

On the Death of the Giraffe. Thomas Hood. But then in spots she was so rich,–/I wonder which? FaBoEE

On the Death of the Great Chef Alexis Soyer. Anonymous. Indeed, indeed, great Pan is dead. FaBoEE

On the Death of the Lord Treasurer. Anonymous. He would have spared thee, and tak'n a bribe. FaBoEE

On the Death of William Edward Burghardt Du Bois... Conrad Kent Rivers.
which now and forever hold communion over/you. NBP; PoBA

On the Deaths of Thomas Carlyle and George Eliot. Algernon Charles
Swinburne. The light of little children, and their love. HBV 1-2

On the Debt My Mother Owed to Sears Roebuck. Edward Dorn. and she
was part of that stay at home army to keep/things going, owing that debt.
ConAP

On the Decease of the Religious and Honourable Jno Haynes Esqr.... John
James. Let me my wishes on them Spend/That they poor Souls may live
and mend. SCAP

On the Defeat at Ticonderoga or Carilong. *Anonymous* Soon shall proud
Carilong be humbled low/Nor Montcalm's self, prevent th' avenging/blow.
PAH

On the Defeat of Henry Clay. William Wilberforce Lord. His god-like
image, till it sinks where blends/Time's dim horizon with Eternity. PAH

On the Defeat of Ragnall by Murrough King of Leinster A.D. 994.
Anonymous. As they flee across Aughty in the late evening. OnYI

On the Democracy of Yale. Frederick Scheetz Jones. That He uses with
Hadley and Dwight! HBV 1-2; YaD

On the Departure of Sir Walter Scott from Abbotsford, for Naples. William
Wordsworth. Wafting your Charge to soft Parthenope! EBEV; EnRP

On the Departure of the British from Charleston. Philip Freneau. "These
for their country fought and bled." PAH

On the Departure Platform. Thomas Hardy. –O friend, nought happens
twice thus; why,/I cannot tell! NOBE; OBNC; OxBTC

On the Deputy of Ireland's Child. Sir John Davies. Nature, my nurse, had
me to bed betimes. FaBoEE

On the Desert. Stephen Crane. Is in the dance of the whispering snakes.
LiTM

On the Detraction which Followed upon My Writing Certain Treatises. John
Milton. But from that mark how far they rove we see/for all this waste of
wealth, and loss of blood. ATP; ExPo; FaBoPV; SeCeV

On the Disadvantages of Central Heating. Amy Clampitt. by mere affect,
the perishing residue/of pure sensation AMV-80

On the Discoveries of Captain Lewis. Joel Barlow. Let our occident stream
bear the young hero's/name,/Who taught him his path to the sea. AmPP;
MC; PAH

On the Doorstep. Thomas Hardy. And forth I stride. MoVE

On the Duke of Buckingham. James Shirley. The great man's volume, all
time's story. FaBoEE

On the Duke of Buckingham, Slain by Felton... Owen Felltham. They oft
decline into the worst of ill/That act the people's wish without law's will.
JCP

On the Earl of Leicester. *Anonymous.* Here lieth the Earl of Leicester,/
Whom all the world did hate. FaBoEE

On the Eclipse of the Moon of October 1865. Charles Tennyson Turner. So
perfect was the silence Nature kept. OBNC

On the Edge. Frank Dwyer. ...like taking/candy from a baby. AMV-81

On the Edge. Philip Levine. Whose page is blanker than the raining skies.
CoAP; TAP

On the Edge at Santorini. Michael C. Blumenthal. fall like rain to the
hungry sea. AMV-80

On the Edge of a Safe Sleep. Teresa D. Cader. always like this, on the
edge/of a safe sleep, lost in flight. AMV-81

On the Edge of the Copper Pit. Pauline Henson. And I'm but a breath on
the steps of Heaven–/If I'm at all! GoYe

On the Edge of the Pacific. Theodore Maynard. Eager to reach the land of
Prester John. CAW

On the Edition of Mr. Pope's Works with a Commentary and Notes.
Thomas Edwards. Dragged to oblivion by the foundering weight. TW

On the Emigration to America. Philip Freneau. And happier systems bring
to view,/Than all the eastern sages knew. PAH; TAP

On the Erection of Shakespeare's Statue in Westminster Abbey. Alexander
Pope. Enter Shakespear, with a loud clap. FaBoEE

On the Esplanade des Invalides. David Fisher. I will come like the stars/in
the similitude of white fowl. NPGG

On the Eve of a Birthday. Geoffrey Grigson. So was I. NAs

On the Eve of Our Anniversary. Gary Margolis. this spring these plants
our rings Str

On the Eve of the Feast of the Immaculate Conception: 1942. Robert Lowell.
Man eats the Dead/From pole to pole. WaaP

On the Eve of the Plebiscite. Kenneth Rexroth. By whose indifferent
consent they rule. NNaP

On the Eve of War. Danske Dandridge. Be with us still,–be with us still!
PAH

On the Extinction of the Venetian Republic. William Wordsworth. Men
are we, and must grieve when even the/shade/Of that which once was great
is passed away. BoLiVe; EnL; FaBoRV; FaPo; GTBS; GTBS-P; HBV 1-2;
LoBV; MBW 1-2; MCCG; NOBE; NoP; OAEP; OBEV; OBNC; OBRV;
TrGrPo; ViBoPo

On the Farm. R. S. Thomas. The shrill sentence: God is love. OxBTC

On the Farm. Barbara Winder. in an instant all the junk/will burst into a
flame. PH

On the Fifth Anniversary of Bluma Sach's Death. Vinnie-Marie D'Ambrosio.
how the bright rooms laughed with music/while we wept! IHMS

On the Fine Arts Garden, Cleveland. Russell Atkins. and then the golden
lamps/the while/slowly filtering– PoBA

On the First of March. *Anonymous.* With October's wind and rain.
OxNR

On the Flightiness of Thought. *Anonymous.* They are neither fickle nor
inconstant–not as I am. OnYI

On the Fly-Leaf of a Book of Old Plays. Walter Learned. I'm back in
those forgotten days,/And watch her at her binding. HBV 1-2

On the Fly-Leaf of Manon Lescaut. Walter Learned. They hold the mirror
up to you. AA

On the Fly-Leaf of Pound's Cantos. Basil Bunting. ...There are the Alps,/
fools! Sit down and wait for them to crumble! FaBoTw; NoAm; OxBTC

On the Following Work and Its Author. Jonathan Mitchell. Reader, think
oft, and help thy thoughts thereby. SCAP

On the Founding of Liberia. Melvin Tolson. A moment of the conscience
of mankind! UnPo

On the Frequent Review of the Troops. M". Let casuists tell us, if they
can,/Is England's welfare furthered? NOEC

On the Friendship betwixt Two Ladies. Edmund Waller. Are so choicely
matched a pair,/Or with more consent do move. PeHV

On the Frozen Lake. William Wordsworth. Till all was tranquil as a
dreamless sleep. FaBoCh; LoGBV

On the Gift of a Knife. Muireadhach Albanach O Dalaigh. works hard,
my knife, till all are served. NOBI

On the Glorious Assumption of Our Blessed Lady. Richard Crashaw.
Sweet Angels come, and sing the rest. ISi; OBS

On the Grand Canal. David Gascoyne. As the boat's motion swept her
from my sight. SeCePo

On the Grasshopper and the Cricket. John Keats. The grasshopper's
among some grassy hills. BiP; BoC; BoLiVe; DiPo; ERoP 1-2; ExPo;
FaBoBe; GN; HBV 1-2; InPo; LiTB; MBW 1-2; NIP; OAEL 1-2; SeCeV;
TrGrPo

On the Grave of a Young Cavalry Officer Killed in the Valley... Herman
Melville. His happier fortune in this mound you see. AP

On the Great Fog in London, December 1762. James Eyre Weeks. Or
corks afloat upon the sullen flood. NOEC

On the Great Plateau. Edith Wyatt. Down the Santa Clara Valley through
the world from far/away–/Far and far away–far away. HBMV

On the Hall at Stowey. Charles Tomlinson. Facing the empty house and its
laden barns. CMoP; NoAm

On the Happy Corydon and Phyllis. Sir Charles Sedley. And something
else, but what I dare not name. BoLoP

On the Hazards of Smoking. Leah Goldberg. Isn't it an oppressive spring!
I told you: Don't smoke. AMV-81

On the Heart's Beginning to Cloud the Mind. Robert Frost. Far into the
lives of other folk. CMoP

On the Height. Eunice Tietjens. A bird dipped wing, and, swift and white,/
Peace brooded there. HBMV

On the Heights. Lucius Harwood Foote. Sees far below the steadfast lands.
AA

On the Heights. W. K. Holmes. And, past philosophy's surmisings, know!
PoSH

On the Heights. Walter Savage Landor. The heavy-hooft below. FaBoEE

On the High Cost of Dairy Products. James McIntyre. How dear it is, they
mutter. FiBHP

On the Hill. William Soutar. The banners o' Scotland flaunter by/And the
buskit buglers blaw. PoSH

On the Hill below the Lighthouse. James Dickey. Coming back, coming
back, going over. NePoEA-2; SM

On the Historians Freeman and Stubbs. J. E. Thorold Rogers. Stubbs
butters Freeman, Freeman butters Stubbs. FaBoEE

On the holy day of your going out to war. Mahodahi. and the sun on its
longer voyage/is melancholy. BoWoP

On the House of a Friend. John Logan. with the smile of your own face.
DFF

On the Hurry of This Time. Henry Austin Dobson. We may not work–ah!
would we might!–/With slower pen. HBV 1-2

On the Ice Islands Seen Floating in the German Ocean. William Cowper.
In no congenial gulf for ever lost! OAEL 1-2; PrIm

On the Imprint of the First English Edition of.... Max Beerbohm. This
plain announcement, nicely read,/Iambically runs. InPK; PV

On the Inconstancy of Women: From the Latin of Catullus. George Lamb.
Should be inscribed upon the air,/Or in the running stream. PV

On the Ineffable Inspiration of the Holy Spirit. C Greiffenberg. The moon;
then turns about, and earthward, too, is clear. PBWP

On the Infancy of Our Saviour. Francis Quarles. The Weed not being, I
may adore the Wearer. OBS; OxBoCh; SeCePo

On the Instability of Youth. Thomas, Lord Vaux. And able age, to do Thy holy will. EnRePo

On the Irish Club. Jonathan Swift. To rail at men by nature fools:/But * * * * * * * * * * * * OBSV

On the Island. Dennis Brutus. and we knew another week would have to pass. WhB

On the Island. L. E. Sissman. As I can profit by a visit to/The fish-shaped island, population two. NYBP

On the Jewish Day of Judgment in the Year 1942. Jozef Wittlin. Exiles, sons of Eve, the accursed seed of Cain. VWA

On the Jubilee of Queen Victoria (excerpt). Alfred, Lord Tennyson. Dawns into the Jubilee of the Ages. UnPo

On the Lacedaemonian Dead at Plàtaea. Simonides (of Ceos). By the celebrant above, they are raised, Valor's breath. WaaP

On the Lake. Victoria Mary (Vita) Sackville-West. The small, immediate candle in the prow/Burns brighter in the water than any star. ChMP; MoVE; OBMV; SBG

On the Lake Poets. Charles Townsend. For poems diluted with plenty of water. FaBoEE

On the Lakes of Ponchartrain. Anonymous. I'll drink to the health of the Creole girl on the lakes of Ponchartrain. AmFP

On the Land. Ray Lindquist. John Deere, Farm-All, Oliver, Massey-Ferguson. TAT

On the Last Page of the Last Yellow Pad in Rome before Taking Off... Miller Williams. I know. I know. AMV-80

On the Late Engagement in Charles Town River. Anonymous. Who now is venturing their lives in North America. OBSS

On the Late Massacre in Piedmont. John Milton. Early may fly the Babylonian woe. ATP; AWP; BiP; DiPo; EnL; EnLit; ExPo; FaPo; GTBS; GTBS-P; HAP; HBV 1-2; HeIP; InPo; JCP; LiTB; LoBV; MBW 1-2; NIP; NOBE; NOCV; NoP; OAEP; OBWP; PoEL 1-5; PPoe; PPP; SeCeV; UnPo; ViBoPo; WaaP; WeW

On the Late Metamorphosis of an Old Picture.... Anonymous. The devil mob had here no more to say,/But charmed at William's name marched all away. APAS

On the Late S. T. Coleridge. Washington Allston. Of all he loved: thy living Truths are/left. AA

On the Late Successful Expedition against Louisbourg. Francis Hopkinson. He guides the conq'ring sword, he governs in/the fight. PAH

On the Latest Crisis of Confidence. Haywood Jackson. Me: I won't even let them/take my blood/pressure/now. SOTS

On the Latin Gerunds. Richard Porson. She mourn'd in silence, and was Di-do-dum. FaBoUs

On the Lawn at Ira's. Gregory Orr. it suddenly flies, unwavering, away. GeTw

On the Lawn at the Villa. Louis Simpson. So we sat there all afternoon. CoAP; LCAP; OBAL; OxBC; PPP

On the Life-Mask of Abraham Lincoln. Richard Watson Gilder. A power was his beyond the touch of art/Or armed strength–his pure and mighty/heart. AA; HBV 1-2

On the Lord Gen. Fairfax at the Siege of Colchester. John Milton. ...In vain doth Valour bleed/While Avarice, and Rapine share the land. OBS

On the Lord Mayor and Court of Aldermen... Andrew Marvell. I see who e'ers freed, you for Slaves are decreed/Until you burn again, burn again. CoMu; FaBoBa

On the Loss of the "Royal George." William Cowper. And he and his eight hundred/Must plough the wave no more. AnFE; EBEV; EtS; FiP; GN; HBV 1-2; InPo; MyFE; NOBE; OAEP; OBEC; RoGo; TrGrPo

On the Loss of U.S. Submarine S4 (excerpt). Harry Clifford Canfield. More for the Pleasure than the Vice. FaBoCo

On the March. Richard Aldington. Party–HALT! BrPo

On the Margin: "An anniversary approaches of the birth of God." David Wright. And very much like what we have to put up with daily. NAs

On the Marginal Way. Richard Wilbur. May that vast motive wash and wash our own. CAPP; CoAP; NOBA

On the Margins of a Poem. Jiri M. Langer. Indeed/they are pure,/but they are also/broken. VWA

On the Marriage. Francis Beaumont. ...the amorous vine/Did with the fair and straight-limbed elm entwine. LiTL; ViBoPo

On the Marriage of a Virgin. Dylan Thomas. The other sun, the jealous coursing of the unrivalled blood. EnLoPo; HW

On the Marriage of T. K. and C. C. the Morning Stormy. Thomas Carew. Which shall confound with its loud whistling noise/Her pleasing shrieks, and fan thy panting joys. BoLoP

On the Masquerades. Christopher Pitt. But the chaste Muse, with blushes covered o'er,/Retires confused, and will reveal no more. NOEC

On the Meadow. Katri Vala. this is the road of life! PBWP

On the Meanness of Lord Eldon. Anonymous. Verdict–Confined a week in Eldon's larder. FaBoEE

On the Meatwheel. Dick Gallup. You're a pip/They say/If you can breathe. APU

On the Meetings of the Scotch Covenanters. Anonymous. Lest, if thou slip, thou fall to hell. FaBoEE

On the Memory of Mr. Edward King Drown'd in the Irish Seas. John Cleveland. We floating Islands, living Hebrides. AnAnS 2; OAEL 1-2; OBS; SeCP

On the Miracle of Loaves. Richard Crashaw. Thou to their teeth hast proved Thy Deity. ACP; OBSP

On the Moor. Cale Young Rice. There was no heart to break if death/For me had made demanding. HBV 1-2

On the Moor of Kasuga. Hitomaro. and must be boiling them. AWP

On the Morning of the Third Night above Nisqually. W. M. Ransom. Tonight she comes for me. CDW; NU

On the Motor Bus. Alfred Denis Godley. Domine, defende nos/Contra hos Motores Bos! NLV

On the Mountain. Michael Kennedy Joseph. Before the children's bones, on the holy mountain. AnNZ

On the Mountain. Reuental. Sir, Neidhart von All the young ones into the bushes. AWP; LiTW

On the Mountain. Ruth Stone. For the flare, polestar, pulley toward the edge. BoWoP

On the Mountains. Alcman. And milked a lioness with your hands, to make/A round of silver-bright cheese-cake. LiTW

On the Move. Thom Gunn. One is always nearer by not keeping still. CMoP; ForPo; HAP; LiTM; MP; NePoEA-2; NIP; NMP; NoP; OAEL 1-2; OxBTC; PPP; TwCP

On the Murder of Sir Edmund Berry Godfrey. Anonymous. The devil's an ass, for Jesuits on this spot/Broke both the neck of Godfrey and their Plot. APAS

On the Name of Jesus. Richard Crashaw. And breake before thee. AnAnS 1

On the Naming Day. Johari M. Kunjufu. as the guinea corn is finely ground/in the way of a thousand stones/we take our own CNA

On the Nativity of Christ. William Dunbar. He that is crownit abone the sky/Pro nobis Puer natus est! OBEV; OxBoCh

On the Nativity of Christ Our Lord. Joseph Bennett. The congressed candles fuming in the nave. NePA

On the Nativity of Our Saviour. Thomas Philipott. For here the sun was followed by a star. JCP

On the Nature of Love. Wilfrid Scawen Blunt. –Nay, give me any love, so it be love of thee. ViBoPo

On the Needle of a Sun-Dial. Francis Quarles. It finds no rest on earth, makes no abode,/In any Object, but his heav'n, his God. OBS; TrGrPo

On the New Forcers of Conscience Under the Long Parliament. John Milton. New presbyter is but old priest writ large. CABA; FaBoPV

On the New Laureate. Anonymous. That Cibber may serve both for fool and for poet. FaBoCo

On the New Road. Lyn Lifshin. I button and unbutton/what I feel NeAC

On the Night. Ivor Gurney. Or a frightened rook-wheeling plain once bed of the sea? OBSP

On the Night Express to Madrid. Lora Dunetz. I stare into the dark of night and see/Myself reflected, staring back at me. AMV-81

On the Night in Question. Patricia Goedicke. To the dim brackets of a house,/The dark period of a door. TAP

On the Night Train from Oxford. E. L. Mayo. ...even/to one on this night train. FAZ

On the Ocean Floor. Hugh" (Christopher Murray Grieve) MacDiarmid. On the ocean floor as the foraminifera die. FaBoMo; HAP

On the Origin of Evil. John Byrom. And when the life of Christ in men/Revives its faded image, then/Will all be Paradise again. NOEC

On the Oxford Book of Victorian Verse. Hugh" (Christopher Murray Grieve) MacDiarmid. Smiffkins, Pimple, and Jingle. Oh Lord! how long? MoBrPo

On the Oxford Carrier. John Milton. Only remains the superscription. NA

On the Painter Val Prinsep. Dante Gabriel Rossetti. Reflects little credit on God. FaBoEE

On the Park Bench. Kenneth Slade Alling. He'll only be deported. NePoAm

On the Passion. Anonymous. If ich of love can. OxBM

On the Path. Avner Strauss. God, who bade me walk,/sets in my path an angel for my devil. VWA

On the Pavement. David A. Sam. and protest only to the jackhammer. AMV-80

On the Photograph of a Man I Never Saw. Hyam Plutzik. Is the glance softened?/Bowed the face? VWA

On the Phrase, "To Kill Time." Voltaire (Francois Marie Arouet). I think I can be even with mankind. ALV; PV

On the Physician to Chelsea Hospital by Himself. Messenger Mounsey. To let the old carcase of Mounsey be quiet. FaBoEE

On the Picture of a "Child Tired of Play." Nathaniel Parker Willis. Thou wilt sink to sleep on thy mother's breast. HBV 1-2

On the Picture of the Three Fates in the Palazzo Pitti, at Florence. Arthur Henry Hallam. More this grand sadness tells, than forms of fairest life. OBRV

On the Pilgrim's Way in Kent, as It Leads to the Coldrum Stones. Asphodel. And if I die tomorrow, will I be gone? BrRo

On the Pilots Who Destroyed Germany in the Spring of 1945. Stephen Spender. Assumes their guilt, honours, repents, prays for them. NeBP

On the Plains. Francis Brooks. Only the hawk moves, fain to kill,/Circling on high. AA

On the Planet of Flies. Christian Morgenstern. we're not mistakenly swallowed/or cooked in their pies. FaBoNo

On the Plough-Man. Francis Quarles. T'one's at God's finding; t'other at his owne. OBS

On the Poet O'Shaughnessy. Dante Gabriel Rossetti. To the fancy of Arthur O'Shaughnessy. ChTr

On the Poet's Leer. David Ray. wondering/how far the fat-cheeked/boy's hands/have plowed/by now. NePoEA-2

On the Pole. Uri Z. Greenberg. It is good to descend, to rake in the remnants of honey/and the white milk–in the final place. VWA

On the Porch at the Frost Place, Franconia, NH. William Matthews. and since nothing stopped/my sight, I let it go. MAYP

On the Porch of the Antique Dealer. Paul Ramsey. Shine/In the sun. FAZ

On the Portrait of a Woman About to be Hanged. Thomas Hardy. And a thing of symmetry, seemly to view,/Brought to derision! CMoP

On the Power of Sound. William Wordsworth. And vanish, though the heavens dissolve, her/stay/Is in the WORD, that shall not pass away. VLP

On the Princess Mary. John Heywood. Her honest fame shall ever live/Within the mouth of man. OBSC

On the Projected Kendal and Windermere Railway. William Wordsworth. Speak, passing winds; ye torrents, with your/strong/And constant voice, protest against the wrong. VLP

On the Proposal to Erect a Monument in England to Lord Byron. Emma Lazarus. Hers is the shame if such forgotten be! AA

On the Prorogation. Anonymous. We tyrants love, if we can tyrants be;/If not, next wish is we may all be free. APAS

On the Publication of Diaries and Memoirs. Thomas Hood. Turn'd into cash, they are laid out again! FaBoEE

On the Quay. John Jay Bell. "Always somebody goin' away,/Somebody gettin' home." HBV 1-2

On the Queen's Visit to London. William Cowper. Where George, recover'd, made a scene/Sweet always, doubly sweet. PeD

On the Queens Return from the Low Countries. William Cartwright. ...But being all/Are gone, the Many-headed Beast must fall. MePo

On the Range. Raymond Souster. drifting the summer/labyrinths of love. NOBC

On the Receipt of My Mother's Picture Out of Norfolk. William Cowper. Thyself removed, thy power to soothe me left. CEP; EnPE; EnRP; FiP; HBV 1-2; NOEC; OAEP; OBEC; WHA

On the Reed of Our Lord's Passion. William Alabaster. That all that see this wonder maye expresse/Upon this grounde how well growes barrennes. PoEL 1-5

On the Relative Merit of Friend and Foe, Being Dead. Donald Thompson. One theirs, one ours. But as to which you wore,/No indication. WaP

On the Religion of Nature. Philip Freneau. And man's religion be complete. AmePo; AmPP; MAmP

On the Relinquishment of a Title. Geoffrey Grigson. Discarded ermine to reveal a pig. FaBoEE

On the Resurrection of Christ. William Dunbar. Dispulit of the tresur that he yemit:/Surrexit Dominus de sepulchro. NOCV; OxBS; PoEL 1-5

On the Reverend Jonathan Doe. Anonymous. I can't congratulate the Devil. ChTr; FaBoEE

On the Ridgeway. Andrew Young. The oldest in the world?' "Yes, love.' I said. FaBoPP

On the Rising Generation. Howard Dietz. I'm cold already and I'm fainting. ALV

On the Road. Paul Laurence Dunbar. Dough lone de way, my dearie. AA

On the Road. Tudor Jenks. Said Wisdom to Folly,/"I thought to ask you." NA

On the Road at Night There Stands the Man. Dahlia Ravikovich. And even though I was his eldest daughter/He cannot tell me one word of love. WPOW

On the Road Home. Wallace Stevens. The fragrance of the autumn warmest,/Closest and strongest. NU

On the Road There Stands a Tree. Itzik Manger. Her love prevented my one dream,/To soar across the skies. VWA

On the Road through Chang-Te. Sun Yun-feng. I order the carriage to stop for a while. BoWoP; WPOW

On the Road to Anster Fair. William Tennant. Her clowns, with cobbled shoon stuck full of iron tackets. OBRV

On the Road to California. Anonymous. Far across the Rocky Mountai::s,/Crystal streams and flowing fountains. AmFP

On the Road to Chorrera. Arlo Bates. For the sake of the rider who would /not heed! AA

On the Road to Gundagai. Anonymous. And we tramped from Lazy Harry's, not five miles from Gundagai. PoAu 1-2

On the Road to Paradise. Garrett Kaoru Hongo. Why do I always wish I was Tu Fu? HoAn

On the Road to the Sea. Charlotte Mew. I have made you smile. BrRo; FaBoWP; PeHV

On the Road to Vicenza. Ralph Gustafson. As who should swat a fly/On Titian's Virgin's nose CaP

On the Ruins of a Country Inn. Philip Freneau. Again collect our jovial crew. AA

On the Safe Side. Edward John, Lord Dunsany. Although at Oxford long ago/We held that he was only clay.' OxBI

On the Sale By Auction of Keats' Love Letters. Oscar Wilde. Not knowing the God's wonder, or His woe? AnEnPo

On the Same. Hilaire Belloc. I cost my foolish mistress fifty pound. PoL

On the Same. Roy Campbell. And writing novels with her broom. OxBTC

On the Same. John Milton. For all this waste of wealth and loss of blood. SeCeV

On the Same. Dante Gabriel Rossetti. Were nature's endowments to Val. FaBoEE

On the Sea Wall. C. Day-Lewis. Barbed relics of love's old war. SeCePo

On the Sentence Passed by the House of Lords on Dr. Sacheverell. Anonymous. And pisses on the wretch he scorns to tear. APAS

On the Setting Up of Mr. Butler's Monument in Westminster Abbey. Samuel Wesley. He asked for bread, and he received a stone. PPON

On the Seventh Anniversary of the Death of My Father. Robert Pack. The two of us, at last, together laid. NePoEA

On the Shore of Nawa. Hioki no Ko-okima. Trails over the mountain. AWP

On the Sicilian Strand a Hare Well Wrought. Decimus Magnus Ausonius. Perhaps of Heav'n, if there a Dog-star be. OBVE

On the "Sievering" Tram. Bernard Spencer. ...with the traffic/-gongs ringing like glory. NAs

On the Site of a Mulberry-Tree. Dante Gabriel Rossetti. Whose soul is carrion now,–too mean to yield/Some Starveling's ninth allotment of a ghost. CBEP; NCEP; TW

On the Skeleton of a Hound. James Wright. Knocked down a fence, tore up a field of clover. LiTM; NePoEA

On the Slain Collegians. Herman Melville. Which storms lay low in kindly doom,/And kill them in their flush of bloom. MAmP

On the Slope of the Desolate River. Rabindranath Tagore. ...I stood and watched her little lamp uselessly lost/among lights. OBMV

On the Smooth Brow and Clustering Hair. Walter Savage Landor. Its constancy, its peace, be mine. GBL

On the Snake. Anonymous. For the Head of the Serpent we know should/be bruis'd. PAH

On the Snuff of a Candle. Sir Walter Ralegh. Rather than live in snuff, will be put out. FaBoEE; FCP; SiPS

On the Sonnet. John Keats. She will be bound with garlands of her own. CABA; ERoP 1-2; NIP; NoP; OAEL 1-2

On the South Coast of Cornwall. John Gray. ...no thought but of the strong/Sea, whence their food, their crisp hair, and their song. NOBV

On the South Downs. Sara Teasdale. It was myself that sang in me. MoAmPo

On the Spartan Dead at Thermopylae. Simonides (of Ceos). That here obedient to her laws we lie. WeW

On the Staircase. Eleanor Farjeon. It's horrid on the staircase/Going up to bed. SiSoSe

On the Street. Constantine P. Cavafy. by the so deviate sensual delight he has enjoyed. BoLoP

On the Struma Massacre. Ralph Gustafson. Statistics are become Thine agony,/The ocean designate, Gabbatha, Lord. OBCV

On the Subject of Poetry. William Stanley Merwin. Father, that I do not understand. PP

On the Subject of Waves... Eldon Grier. Is this what you meant by "waves', Li Po? PeCV

On the Suicide of a Friend. Reed Whittemore. Either way, now he is dead and done with that lot. ConAP; NMP

On the Sultan Mahmud. Firdausi. Life, when thou putt'st the helmet on. LiTW

On the Sun Coming out in the Afternoon. Henry David Thoreau. But in the shade I will believe what in the sun I loved. OBSP; PoEL 1-5

On the Supposed Author of a Late Poem "In Defense of Satire." John Wilmot, Earl of Rochester. Made up of all these halves, thou canst not pass/For anything entirely but an ass! APAS

On the Swag. R. A. K. Mason. for this is Christ.' AnNZ

On the Symbolic Consideration of Hands and the Significance of Death. Miller Williams.   old nuns in France who carve beads out of knuckle bones. InPK

On the Telescopic Moon.   John Swanick [(or Swanwick)] Drennan.   And lighting furtive kisses to their mark.   BIrV; IrPN

On the Tercentenary of Milton's Death.   Gavin Ewart.   ...As well as arrogance, beauty.   OxBC

On the Third Day.   Stephen Spender.   And a whole sky floods the pool of one mind.   NeBP

On the Thirteenth Day of Christmas.   Charles Causley.   His eye is dry as the splitting sky/And his face is yellow.   OBCP

On the Threshold.   *Anonymous.*   I'll let you know which shortly–farewell, a long farewell.   BLPA

On the Threshold.   Karl Kraus.   that through the darkness quivered/with those perceiving eyes.   TrJP

On the Threshold.   Amy Levy.   Nor torn from out my heart the old, cold sense/Of your misprision and my impotence.   NOBV

On the Times.   *Anonymous.*   But wel I wot they lake none othes.   OxBM

On the Tombs in Westminster Abbey.   Francis Beaumont.
Buried in dust, once dead by fate.   ACP; CH; GTBS; GTBS-P; HBV 1-2; OBEV; PoPle; TrGrPo; ViBoPo
Yet to this shape all must be brought. LoBV; NOBE

On the Tower.   Annette von Droste-Hulshoff.   Dreams shake my loosened hair–the wind/Lone listener to my spirit wild.   PBWP; WPOW

On the Trail to Idaho.   *Anonymous.*   Go 'long, Blue Dog.   CoSo

On the Train.   Rachel McAlpine.   people are good to her   OCNZ

On the Translation of Anacreon.   Horace Walpole.   And drunkenness grows sober as she reads.   FaBoEE

On the Triumph of Rationalism.   Alfred Ainger.   And Paul's will peter out. FaBoCo

On the Twenty-Fifth of July.   David Cornel DeJong.   a message I sent to/ the beetles of Japan.   NYBP

On the Twenty-Third Psalm.   *Anonymous.*   And in the blest hereafter I shall know,/Why, in His wisdom, He hath led me so.   TRV

On the Uncleanly Habits of Sir Charles Wetherell.   *Anonymous.*   Verdict– Had tried to wash a shirt marked Wetherell.   FaBoEE

On the Uniformity and Perfection of Nature.   Philip Freneau.   Is order all, and all is right.   AmePo; AmPP

On the Universality and Other Attributes of the God of Nature.   Philip Freneau.   For them in life, or death provides.   AP; ForPo

On the University Carrier Who Sickn'd in the Time of His Vacancy...   John Milton.   Hobson has supt, and's newly gone to bed.   MePo

On the University of Cambridge's Burning the Duke of Monmouth's... George Stepney.   Melt down their Sejanus to pots and brass kettles. APAS

On the Unusual Cold and Rainie Weather in the Summer, 1648.   Robert Heath.   Nothing but lightning and Heav'ns fire/Can purge our pestilential aire.   OBS

On the Upside.   G. E. Murray.   ...old lovers/Tossing again in a warehouse loft, straining free.   MAYP

On the Use of Jayshus.   Oliver St. John Gogarty.   It is not always from devotion.   FaBoEE

On the Vanity of Earthly Greatness.   Arthur Guiterman.   And I don't feel so well myself.   BXAP; HeIP; HoPM; InPK; NAMP; NIP; NLV; OBCA; PoPl; PV; TrJP

On the Vanity of Man's Life.   *Anonymous.*   Did dreadful death forbear his fume/For beauty, pride, or lust?   OBSC

On the Verge.   William Winter.   The shattered ship that sails tonight!   AA

On the Victory of Poland and Her Allies over the Sultan Osman, 1621. Casimir Sarbiewski.   His pillow haunted–.   CAW

On the "Vita Nuova" of Dante.   Dante Gabriel Rossetti.   Christ, charging well his chosen ones, forbade/Offence: "for lo! of such my kingdom is." MaVP; VLP

On the Wall.   Immanuel Di Roma.   Wake, if thou'rt sleeping still!   TrJP

On the Wall.   Louise Johnson.   Well I'm gon' leave here   BluL

On the Wallowy.   Laura Chester.   Nothing trembles/but the memory of us. NPGG

On the Way.   Mordechai Husid.   ...who is it/on his way now moves/and plays havoc with my footsteps?   VWA

On the Way.   Georg Trakl.   Let go, when drunk with wine your head into the gutter/sinks.   LiTW

On the Way to Language.   Michael Palmer.   crossed by the bridge/of frequent sighs   NPGG

On the Way to the Island.   David Ferry.   My lady, I love you because of the dark/Over which your glass slippers so ignorantly danced!   NePoAm-2

On the Way to the Mission.   Duncan Campbell Scott.   The moon went on to her setting/And covered them with shade.   CaP; NOBC

On the Welsh Marches.   Walter Stone.   And in his depths the first Iberian stirs.   NYBP

On the Wide Heath.   Edna St. Vincent Millay.   Too lonely, to be free. CMoP

On the Wide Stairs.   Yehuda Amichai.   ..."My soul is rent and torn,/like yours, but it is also beautiful,/like lace."   VWA

On the Wing.   Christina Georgina Rossetti.   Bent in a wind which bore to me a sound/Of far-off piteous bleat of lambs and sheep.   SBG

On the Wings of a Dove.   Jim Wayne Miller.   and flew out over the river toward the island.   AMV-80

On the World.   Francis Quarles.   Where, having stayed a while, I pay/Her lavish bills, and go my way.   HAP

On the World.   Jonathan Swift.   I damn such fools!–Go, go, you're bit. AnIV

On the Young Statesmen.   Charles, Earl of Dorset Sackville.   Shifting about, grow less and less,/With here and there a pawn.   APAS

On This Day.   M. B. Goffstein.   how amazed the children/there/will be. NTCP

On This Day I Complete My Fortieth Year.   Peter Porter.   the ghosts of mid-channel, the banging doors/of the state sirocco.   NAs

On This Day I Complete My Thirty-sixth Year.   George Gordon,Lord Byron. Then look around, and choose thy ground,/And take thy rest.   AnFE; CABA; CoBE; ERoP 1-2; FiP; HBV 1-2; MBW 1-2; MCCG; NAs; NoP; OAEL 1-2; OAEP; OBWP; TreFT; TRV; ViBoPo

On This Island.   W. H. Auden.   "What can I do? It's my bread and butter." TRV

On This My Sick-Bed Beats the World.   Jiri Wolker.   Why must I die when I had hoped to fall?   WaaP

On This Sea-Floor.   Ralph Gustafson.   Old Proteus naps.   PeCV

On this wondrous sea.   Emily Dickinson.   Land, ho! Eternity!/Ashore at last!   AA

On Thomas Carew.   *Anonymous.*   As roots on earth embrace to rise/Most lovely flowers in Paradise.   CBEP

On Thomas Hood.   Walter Savage Landor.   Before me on each path there stood/The witty and the tender Hood.   PV

On Thomas Moore's Poems.   *Anonymous.*   So the most recent/Is the least decent.   FiBHP

On Thomas, Second Earl of Onslow.   *Anonymous.*   Yes; drive a phaeton and four.   FaBoCo

On Those That Deserve It.   Francis Quarles.   Durst ye not stoop to play the fooles for him?   MePo; NOCV; OBS

On Those That Hated "The Playboy of the Western World", 1907.   William Butler Yeats.   Even like these to rail and sweat/Staring upon his sinewy thigh.   NOBI

On Time.   Richard Hughes.   Flitted and sipped, and sipped again! MoBrPo

On Time.   John Milton.   Triumphing over Death, and Chance, and/thee O Time.   BLPL; BoC; CABA; DiPo; LiTB; LoBV; MePo; OBEV; OBS; OxBoCh; SeCeV; TRV

On Time with God.   C. D. Nutter.   I'll follow Him at home, abroad/'Til time becomes eternity.   STF

On to Richmond.   John Reuben Thompson.   And a terrible business, McDowell, to you,/Was that pleasant excursion to Richmond.   PAH

On to the Morgue (with music).   *Anonymous.*   That's where we'll all be/One hundred years from now.   AS

On Tobacco.   Charles Cotton.   This satire, perhaps, else had looked like sense.   OBSV

On Tobacco.   Thomas Pestel.   How it befell, when we our foes did choke/ Like bees, and put them pell-mell to the Smoke.   EIL

On Tom Holland and Nell Cotton.   *Anonymous.*   A yard of Holland for an ell of Cotton.   FaBoEE

On Tom Moore's Translation of Anacreon.   Thomas Erskine, Lord Erskine. For we have one Anacreon Moore.   FaBoEE

On Tom-O-Combe.   *Anonymous.*   The devil and he had both one nurse. FaBoEE

On Tom Onslow, Earl of Onslow.   *Anonymous.*   Why, drive a phaeton and four.   FaBoEE

On Tomato Ketchup.   *Anonymous.*   None'll come, and then a lot'll. FaBoUs; NLV

On Top of Old Smoky.   *Anonymous.*
I lost my true lover/For courtin' too slow.   BLSo; FSW
Where the wild birds in heaven can hear my sad cry. FaFP; TreFT

On Top of Troubled Waters.   Dorothy J. Langford.   And know that neither storm nor death/Christ from His people parts.   BePJ

On Trinity Sunday.   John Byrom.   Living relations, evidently Trine.   PeD

On True Worth.   Muslih-ud-Din Sa'di.   Still base as when from earth it came.   LiTW

On Trust in the Heart.   Seng-Ts'an.   ...for what can words tell/Of things that have no yesterday, tomorrow or to-/day?   ILwL

On Two Brothers.   Simonides (of Ceos).   For ever, though they lived so short a time.   AWP

On Two Ministers of State.   Hilaire Belloc.   And Caliban, and Lump and I are all agreed.   PV

On Vacation.   Robert Creeley.   ...until I am/driven by that density home. CAPP

One Morning We Brought Them Order. Al Lee. ...she then/exploded, killing ten. FF

One Morning When the Rain-Birds Call. Lloyd Roberts. And the vanguard of the summer host will camp with us again. CaP

One Need Not Be a Chamber–To Be Haunted. Emily Dickinson. O'erlooking a superior spectre–/Or more–. AmePo; SyP

One Night. Marchette Chute. She must have known before she came/That it was Christmas Eve. ChBR

One Night away from Day. John Digby. While the crowd cowered/In sheer terror beneath them. EAS

One-Night Expensive Hotel. Ronald G. Everson. ...Soon I shall risk the bed,/wriggling down among mute faces of bone. NOBC

One-Night Fair. Nancy Price. ...There's no right name/for how it was. The farm's never looked the same. GOYP

One Night Stand. LeRoi (Imamu Amiri Baraka) Jones. We have come a long way, & are uncertain which of the masks/is cool. NeAP

The One-Night Stand: An Approach to the Bridge. Paul Blackburn. all the picture window/mirrors and maintains ErPo

One No. 7. John Frederick Frank. At TV in Apt. 15b, East 187. GoYe

One of Many. Stevie Smith. Weeping bitterly the little child cries: I die one of many. OxBC

One of the Boys. Philip Dacey. including the amazing/dissolution of walls between rooms. Str

One of the Jews. Constantine P. Cavafy. the hedonism and the arts of/Alexandria/kept him a devoted disciple. TrJP

One of the Many Days. Norman MacCaig. the huge concept of Ben Dorain. PoSH

One of the Principal Causes of War. Hugh" (Christopher Murray Grieve) MacDiarmid. That she wished me a wound far worse to staunch–/And not in the hand! OBSP

One of the Regiment. Douglas Le Pan. No greater excellence the sun encloses. CaP

One of the Seven Has Somewhat to Say. Sara Henderson Hay. And things can gradually slip back to normal. DFT

One of Us Two. Ella Wheeler Wilcox. Oh, God! Oh, God! have pity on that one. PoToHe

One of Wally's Yarns. John Masefield. When the watch went below. BrPo

One Old Ox. Anonymous. Twelve typographical topographers typically translating types. FaBoNo

One Perfect Rose. Dorothy Parker. Ah no, it's always just my luck to get/One perfect rose. ALV; FiBHP; NIP; NLV; NoP; OBAL; OLR

One Poet Visits Another. William Henry Davies. On my own little horse of wind and fire. DTC; TW

One Presenting a Rare Book to Madame Hull Senr: His Vallintine. John Saffin. Leave Her Devoted at Minerva's Shrine SCAP

One Race, One Flag. A. R. D. Fairburn. the bond of kinship, the heritage of Empire. AnNZ

One Rose of Stone. Keith Wilson. then place this stone rose here/on this grave, just to mark a loss? GOYP

One's-Self I Sing. Walt Whitman. The Modern Man I sing. AnAmPo; DiPo; FaBoPV; NOBA; OxBA

One Saturday. Annie Douglas Robinson. And fancied we were queens. AA

One Sea-Side Grave. Christina Georgina Rossetti. But one remembers yet. NOBV

One Sided Shoot-Out. Don L. Lee. only blackpeople play it fair. BPo; PoBA

One Snowy Night in December. John N. Morris. The municipal lions listen/to the snow, that white answer. NYP

The One Song. C. G. Hanzlicek. What else is there to sing about? AMV-80

One Star Fell and Another. Conrad Aiken. All lost for nothing, and ourselves a ghost. MoAmPo

One Step at a Time. Anonymous. "One thing at a time, and that done well,"/Is wisdom's proven rule. WBLP

One Step from an Old Dance. David Helwig. In the calm and peaceable kingdom. WHW

One Step Twix't Me and Death. Roger Williams. How should (when Christ hath both refresh't,)/Thy Love and zeale be more? SCAP

One Sweetly Solemn Thought. Phoebe Cary. Nearer my home today, today,/Than I have been before. AH

One, the Other, And. Wendy Wieber. the greenest/singing leaves/grew/tendresses/of trust NMM

One Thing. Owen Meredith. A harvest of barren regrets. WBLP

One Thing at a Time. Anonymous. As many can tell. OxNR

One Thing at a Time. M. A. Stodart. So work while you work,/And play while you play. PoToHe

One Thing I of the Lord Desire. Anonymous. No matter how, if only sin/Die out in me. STF

The One Thing Needful. Vassar Miller. God knows, no rime nor reason except his. PoCh

The One Thing Needful. Max Isaac Reich. I'm still a pauper here below. BLRP

The One Thing That Can Save America. John Ashbery. Our country, in fenced areas, in cool shady streets. NOBA

One Thing to Take, Another to Keep. Crescenzo Del Monte. ...An art, I tell you,/by no means given to just anyone. VWA

One Thought for My Lady. Bloke Modisane. Always without words. PBA

One Thousand Fearful Words for Fidel Castro. Lawrence Ferlinghetti. I give you my sprig of laurel. CoPo; VGW

One Thousand Feet of Shadow. David Craig. And my friend's face transfixed/In the tearing gasp of his last breath. PoSH

The One Thousandth Psalm. Edward Everett Hale. And to use all things for the good of Thy children. TRV

One Time. Douglas Livingstone. –some time after/and in shallower water. PeSA

One Time Henry Dreamed the Number. Doughtry Long. we laughed/then went to bed/and kept each other warm. BP; BPo; CNA; PoBA

One Times One. Edward Estlin Cummings. the old sixth/avenue/el;in the top of his head:to tell/him CTC

One to Destroy, Is Murder by the Law. Edward Hilton Young. How was I shock'd to think the hero's trade/Of such materials, fame and triumph made! FF

The One to Grieve. Rudy Thomas. anyone could hunt the old dog/if they could find him after that. GOYP

One to Make Ready. Anonymous. And away goes the mare. OxNR

One to Nothing. Carolyn Kizer. Shucks a'mighty. If you're an eagle, you just go. OBAL

One Token. William Henry Davies. To prove death but a veil to hide/Another life on the other side. BrPo

One, Two, Buckle My Shoe. Anonymous. Nineteen, twenty,/My stomach's empty. HBV 1-2; HBVY

One, Two, Buckle My Shoe. Mother Goose. Nine, ten,/A good fat hen. SoPo; TiPo

One, Two, Buckle My Shoe. Ogden Nash. And Happy Birthday, with twice my heart. BiCB

One, Two, Three. Samuel L. Albert. And hurtled him into space forever. NePoAm-2

One, Two, Three! Henry Cuyler Bunner. This dear, dear, dear old lady,/And the boy who was half-past three. HBV 1-2; PoLf

One-Two-Three. Hannah Senesh. The dice were cast. I lost. WPOW

One, Two, Three, Four. Anonymous. Eating cherries off a plate. OxNR

One, Two, Three, Four, Five. Anonymous. The little finger on the right. OxNR

One, Two, Three–Gough! Eve Merriam. But you can often call their blough. NTCP

One, Two, Whatever You Do. Anonymous. Things will come right,/you know, by and by. OxNR

One-Upmanship. Miriam Chaikin. "You win," she called,/but Lou didn't hear. NTCP

One Way Down. David Craig. The pools lie flat and shallow and black/As death, the ultimate absence of qualities. PoSH

One Way Gal. William Moore. She takes the blues away and satisfies my mind BluL

One Way of Looking at It. Arthur Joseph Munby. And wish yourself as free as I am. NOBV

One Way of Love. Robert Browning. Those who win heaven, blest are they! HBV 1-2

One Way of Trusting. Hannah Parker Kimball. They trust it, dear, because they must. AA

One-Way Song. Percy Wyndham Lewis.
I cannot help this. It is noblesse oblige. PP
You will soon discover what we One-ways lack! CTC

One We Knew. Thomas Hardy. Past things retold were to her as things existent,/Things present but as a tale. VLP

One Week. Carolyn Wells. The Coroner upon them/SAT. LBN

One Wept Whose Only Child Was Dead. Alice Meynell. A mother, a mother was born. AnFE; GoTF; TreFT

One West Coast. Al Young. You take trips to contain the mystery. NPGG

The One White Hair. Walter Savage Landor. Fair as she was, she never was so fair! HBV 1-2

The One Who Grew to Be a Wolf. Patricia Monaghan. stabbed with the shadow light of wolves. PoDr

The One Who Is Within. Nia Francisco. the smell of cedar wood and hickory on your clothes STE

The One Who Runs Away. Callimachus. I prefer the nether-treasure of the one who runs away. LiSp

The One Who Struggles. Ernst Toller. I was myself Mother to myself. TrJP

One Who Watches. Siegfried Sassoon. Hoarded like happy summers in my/heart. TrJP

The One Whose Reproach I Cannot Evade. George Hitchcock. ...my thighs/half-eaten by the raging twilight. EAS

One Wife for One Man. Frank Aig-Imoukhuede. Just one wife for one man! PBA

One Winter Afternoon. Edward Estlin Cummings. –i thank heaven somebody's crazy/enough to give me a daisy NCSH

One Winter Night in August. X. J. Kennedy. Our ancient boy (age seven)/ Woke up and went to sleep. OBCA

One Word Is Too Often Profaned. Percy Bysshe Shelley. The devotion to something afar/From the sphere of our sorrow? BLPL; CBEP; GoTF; GTBS-P; LiTB; LiTL; MCCG; OBRV; TreFT; WHA

One Word More. Robert Browning.
  Drew one angel–borne, see, on my bosom! FiP; HBV 1-2; PoEL 1-5; ViBoPo; VLP
  Taught babes in grace their grammar,/And struck the simple, solemn. OAEP

One Writing against His Prick. Anonymous. Or I'll ne'er draw thee, but against a post. TW

One X. Edward Estlin Cummings. hate laugh shimmy. FaBoMo

One Year After. Gary Allan Kizer. Of every sailor who threw his/Bag down on deck, sucked in/Salt and signed himself whole. LFAC

One Year Ago. Walter Savage Landor. Love! broken should have been thy bow/One year ago. EnLi 1-2

One Year Later. Eric Torgerson. Something of you in the mirror changes my face. PoL

One Year to Life on the Grand Central Shuttle. Audre Lorde. it will matter less/what token we pay/for change CNA

One Year to Live. Mary Davis Reed. To serve my gracious Master's ends. PoToHe

Onely the Reverend Grave and Godly Mr. Buckly Remaines. Edward Johnson. It's Buklies joy that Christ his sons new making,/Hath placest in's churches for to shine as Stars. SCAP

The Oneness of the Philosopher with Nature. Gilbert Keith Chesterton. oh photograph me thus! FaBoNo

The Ongoing Story. John Ashbery. The people who own them seem rock-true and marvelously/self-sufficient. HaCAP

The Onion. John Thompson. defeats me, calling me through strange earths/to this place suddenly yours. NOBC

Onion Bucket. Lorenzo Thomas. The vegetables are walking. PoBA

The Onion, Memory. Craig Raine. headless torsos, faceless lovers, friends of mine. NoP

Onion Skin in Barn. Kenneth Slade Alling. It has its palace as it had before. NePoAm

Onions. Philemon. ...for by itself onion/Is bitter and unpleasant to the taste. FaBoUs

Only. Harriet Prescott Spofford. But heaven stooped under the roof on the morn/That it brought them only a baby. HBV 1-2

Only a Baby Small. Matthias Barr. Small, but how dear to us,/God knoweth best. HBV 1-2; HBVY; PaPo

Only a Cowboy. Anonymous. But now he is sleeping on the old staked plains. CoSo

Only a Little Litter. Myra Cohn Livingston. thanks a heap for the rocks. QQQ

Only a Little Thing. M. P. Handy. We may wish it undone someday. PoToHe

Only a Miner. Anonymous. Our Joe, aged just 20, was killed in the mines. AmFP

Only a Smile. Anonymous. I also might take my share. STF

The Only Bar in Dixon. James Welch. and all the saints come back for laughs. AmPA; FF

The Only Daughter. Anonymous. For I am the only daughter. OBET

Only for Me. Mark Van Doren. Only for me, for me she cried. NCSH

The only ghost I ever saw. Emily Dickinson. And God forbid I look behind/Since that appalling day! NePA; WSC

Only in This Way. Margaret Goss Burroughs. For the future...for your century. BlSi

The Only Jealousy of Emer. Anonymous. until all knowledge be known. BIrV

The Only Jealousy of Emer (excerpt). William Butler Yeats. What wounds, what bloody press/Dragged into being/This loveliness? MoAB

Only Jesus Will I Know. Charles Wesley. Only Jesus will I know,/And Jesus crucified. BePJ

Only Joy! Now Here You Are. Sir Philip Sidney. No, no, no, no, my Dear, let be. ElL; EnRePo; GBL; HAP; InvP; UnTE

Only My Opinion. Monica Shannon. That he giggles, as he wiggles/Across a hairy leaf. SoPo; TiPo

The Only Name Given Under Heaven. Steele. The regions of unclouded light–Where joy forever reigns. BePJ

The Only News I Know. Emily Dickinson. If other news there be,/Or admirable show–/I'll tell it you. BoLiVe; NOCV

Only of Thee and Me. Louis Untermeyer. For we are Love, and God Himself is made/Only of thee and me. HBV 1-2

Only One. Ralph Burns. "No," said the little girl, "no, no, no, no, no." PoDr

The Only One. Jo Gardner. And there was His blessing given. BePJ

Only One King. John Richard Moreland. And he wrote only on the sand! PGD

Only One Life. Gladys M. Bowman. To behold the face of Jesus, in/The meeting in the air! STF

Only One Mother. George Cooper. But only one mother the wide world over. SiSoSe

Only Seven (parody). Henry Sambrooke Leigh. And so I'd better call my song/"Lines after Ache-inside." BXAP; HBV 1-2; SpRo

Only Silence. Arthur Stanley Bourinot. And the rafters/Lost all laughter/ Long, long ago. CaP

The Only Son. Sir Henry Newbolt. "Within her heart she rocks a dead child, crying/"My son, my little son.'" HBV 1-2

Only the Beards Are Different. Bruce Dawe. Somewhere the country's saviour cries in his sleep.. PoAu 1-2

Only the Dead. Reed Whittemore. Wiser than the living, they have shown/ How true Nobility is bred in The Bone. NYBP

Only the Heart. Marjorie Freeman Campbell. Only the heart knows its own despair! CaP

Only the Polished Skeleton. Countee Cullen. The worth of all it so despised. PrIm; VGW

Only the Wholesomest Foods You Eat. Samuel Hoffenstein. Renal calculus and gastritis. TrJP

Only Thy Dust... Don (Donald Robert Marquis) Marquis. I will lie down beside thee, love,/And mingle with thy roses. PoLf

The Only Tourist in Havana Turns His Thoughts Homeward. Leonard Cohen. let us maintain a stony silence/on the St. Lawrence Seaway. NoAm

Only Waiting. Frances Laughton Mace. By whose light my soul will gladly/Wing her passage to the skies. BLPA

The Only Way to Have a Friend. Anonymous. And prove that fact be true. PoToHe

The Only Way to Win. Anonymous. Be a man and face the battle–/That's the only way to win. WBLP

Only Years. Kenneth Rexroth. Long rollers wrinkling the dark bay. TAP

The Onondaga Madonna. Duncan Campbell Scott. He draws his heavy brows and will not rest. PeCV

Ons as Me Thought Fortune Me Kyst. Sir Thomas Wyatt. Of my sufferaunce I have redres,/And I content me with my hiere. AAS

The Onset. Robert Frost. And there a clump of houses with a/church. AmP; AnNE; CMoP; CoBMV; MoAB; MoAmPo; OxBA; PPP

Ontogeny. Jarold Ramsey. I leap, for love's ultimate ploy,/crying, "Darling, take me, I'm a changed boy!" NIP

Onward, Christian Soldiers. Sabine Baring-Gould. With the Cross of Jesus/ Going on before. FaBoBe; FaFP; FaPoR; FSW; GoTF; HBV 1-2; TreF; VLP; WGRP

Onward Christian Soldiers! Frank Marshall Davis. 'Tis holier to die/By a Christian gun... FB

Onward, Onward, Men of Heaven. Lydia Huntley Sigourney. And your death is victory. AH

Onwardness. Doris Hedges. And that this strangest spending/Buy survival at the end of time. CaP

The Oocuck. Justin Richardson. Spare me the ingalenight! BoAnP; FiBHP

Open. Joseph Bruchac. feathers of seed/have touched the Earth. FAZ

Open. Larry Eigner. the flowers seem to nod NeAP

An Open Air Performance of "As You Like It." E. J. Scovell. And art delivered up/To nature and the wild again. ChMP

Open and Closed Space. Tomas Transtromer. No, they are moving. EAS

Open Casket. Sandra McPherson. ...It is summer and/vacation there. GeTw

Open Country. Richard Hugo. no captain, and the charts dead wrong. LCAP; NPAW

The Open Door. Anonymous. But I close my door on none/Lest Christ close his door on me. KiLC

The Open Door. Elizabeth Jane Coatsworth. the track of small feet/like dark fern seed. DuDa

The Open Door. Grace Coolidge. Nor fail to show the way/Which leads us home. TRV

Open Dream Sequence. Carol Lee Sanchez. i did not make-up/this time. TWSS

Open Earth. Clarisse Nicoidski. each stone on your roads speaks to us of the beating of/your heart VWA

Open Heart. Michael Salcman. Sending our hearts racing to shore. AMV-80

Open House. Theodore Roethke. Rage warps my clearest cry/To witless agony. AP; CoBMV; NoAm; NOBA; NoP

Open Letter. Owen Dodson. Bury that agony, bury this hate, take our black hands in yours. BALP

Open Letter from a Constant Reader. Mona Van Duyn. ...I bless/all knowledge of love, all ways of publishing it. GP; PoA

An Open-Letter-Poem-Note to Vincent Van G. Bernadine. ...it was bought by the/highest bidder for 5.2 million dollars. LTB

Open My Eyes. Betty Scott Stam. Use me, O Lord, use even me. STF

Open Poetry Reading. Jesus Papoleto Melendez. We would not dress a flower/Before their naked eyes. AMV-81

An Open Question. Thomas Hood. But what is your opinion, Mrs. Grundy? NBM

Open Range. Kathryn and Byron Jackson. And here, by the campfire,/Am I. TiPo

Open Range. Thomas Mitchell. and the walk home always seems longer. AMV-81

Open Roads. David Donnell. ...the truck/was what I missed most when I came to the city of light. Str

The Open Sea. William Meredith. And give thanks it was not I, nor yet one close to me. CoAP; GrPl; MOS; NePoEA; TAP; UnPo

An Open Secret. Caroline Atherton Briggs Mason. Would read the secret in your simple ways. AA

Open the Door. Anonymous. So ope me the door when I tap by and by. WTO

Open the Door. Dorothy and Marion Edey Grider. So early Saturday morning. SiSoSe; TiPo

Open the Door to Me, O. Robert Burns. Never to rise again, O! AtBAP; PoEL 1-5

Open the Door, Who's There Within? Anonymous. You shall not kiss me. EG; EiL; GBL

Open the Gates. Anonymous. Swift to Thy sons who in God rest/secure. TrJP

Open to Visitors. E. V. Milner. No one, no one at all, reveals. ELU

Open Your Eyes. Emma Boge Whisenand. And make you glad and kind and wise. PoToHe

Open Your Hand. Dorothy R. Fulton. our beginning, our conveyance, and our journey's end. AMV-81

Opening of Eyes. Laura Riding. Mutely astonished to rehearse/The unutterable simple verse. NoAm

Opening the Season. Stephen Lewandowski. the prosperous gleaming smelt. WOLT

The Opening Year. Anonymous. That we may praise thee, year by year,/With angel-hosts above. BLRP

Operatic Note. Melville Cane. Were never cursed with feeble lungs. UnS

Operation. Alfred Alvarez. Hold us and pick us to pieces. NMP

The Operation. Robert Creeley. Cruel, cruel to describe/what there is no reason to describe. NaP

The Operation. W. D. Snodgrass. ...the crystal world/Is inverted, slow and gay. InPK; TAP

Operation–Souls. Anonymous. This call to you goes forth today/To rally to the man. STF

Operative No. 174 Resigns. Kenneth Fearing. Herewith, therefore, to take effect at once, I resign. NYBP

Ophelia. Vernon Watkins. Child too soon buried. MoVE

Ophelia's Song. Marya Zaturenska. I shall not come to harm. OLR

Ophra. Judah Halevi. And no other sunshine than her beauty. LiTW; TrJP

Opifex. Thomas Edward Brown. I bid thee carve them, knowing what I know.' OBVV

Opinions of the New Student. Regino Pedroso. Until yesterday I was polite and peaceful... TTY

Opium Clippers. Daniel Henderson. "Where flies the spindrift? Where went the wind?" EtS

The Opium Den. Anonymous. And pipes are the flutes that they play on. WTO

An Opium Fantasy. Maria White Lowell. His silver balls, that, softly dropt,/Ring into golden bowls. AnFE; APA

Opossum. William Jay Smith. The Possum that really was just playing possum/Gets up in a flash and scurries away. TiPo

Oppian's Halieuticks (parody). William Diaper. What great Effects from slender Causes flow! BXAP; FM; NOEC; PeD

The Opponent Charm Sustained. Samuel Greenberg. Thy Nature has cuddled me/That pricks,–to renew its psalm. MoPo

The Opportune Overthrow of Humpty Dumpty. Guy Wetmore Carryl. Gets warmed when coal is fired. BBGG

Opportunity. Berton Braley. The best work hasn't been done. WBLP

Opportunity. Madison Cawein. To know, too late, the Fairy in disguise. AA

Opportunity. Harry Graham. He's publishing a book next May/On "How to Make Bee-keeping Pay'. DTC; FaBoCo

Opportunity. John James Ingalls. I answer not, and I return no more!' AA; FaFP; GoTF; HBV 1-2; HBVY; OHFP; PoLf; TreF; WBLP; YaD

Opportunity. Niccolo Machiavelli. How lightly I have fled beneath thy hand. AWP

Opportunity. Walter Malone. Each night a star to guide thy feet to Heaven. BLPA; BLPL; FaBoBe; WBLP; YaD

Opportunity. William Malone. No shame-faced outcast ever sank so deep/But yet might rise and be again a man! HBV 1-2

Opportunity. Edward Rowland Sill. And saved a great cause that heroic day. AnNE; BLPA; GN; GoTF; IIBV 1-2; HBVY; MCCG; OHFP; TreFS; WGRP; YaD

The Opposite House. Robert Lowell. Viva la muerte! CMoP; NYP

Opposition. Sidney Lanier. To uses, arts, and charities. AnFE; APA; LiTA

Oppression. Langston Hughes. And the song/Break/Its jail. CNA

Ops in a Wimpey. Anonymous. "Who'll come on ops in a Wimpey with me?" CoMu

Optimism. Blanaid Salkeld. My luck will turn when I'm a ghost. NeIP

Optimism. Ella Wheeler Wilcox. And God shall hear your words and make them true. BLPA; BLPL; FaBoBe

The Optimist. Anonymous.
  "All right so far." BLPA; GoTF; TreFT; YaD
  You silly, bloody fool! PV

Optimist and Pessimist. McLandburgh Wilson. The pessimist sees the hole. GoTF; TreFT

Options. O. (William Sidney Porter) Henry. I guess it's cause/Pa never does. FiBHP

Or Ever God Created Adam. Anonymous. We were plighted, I and you! WTO

Or Wren or Linnet. Samuel Taylor Coleridge. No tree, but in it/A cooing cushat. PBBP

The Oracle. Arthur Davison Ficke. "How strange to read it in a book!/I could have told you all of these!" HBV 1-2

Oracle. E. L. Mayo. ...Who hears your voices in their mountains/Shall be ripped like mandrakes shrieking out. MiAP

Oracle at Delphi. Robert Bagg. Sleekly, so blood ran like hot gold in his mouth. NePoAm-2

Oracle: Iwori Wotura. Anonymous. "Beauty and all sorts of good fortunes arrive." WTO

The Oracular Portcullis. James Reaney. Then quite quickly her portcullis closed. ErPo; PeCV

Oraga Haru. Issa.
  Buddha accepts/The money/And the flowers. OFD
  He bows his head/To the sacred offerings/Of the New Year. OFD
  Must be a holiday/Even/For the long rain. OFD

The Orange Bears. Kenneth Patchen. A hell of a fat chance my orange bears had! NaP

The Orange Bough. Felicia Dorothea Hemans. And bind it, mother! on my breast/When I am laid in VLP

Orange Chiffon. Jayne Cortez. and my shadow half the size of two dates/broke BlSi

Orange County Plague: Scenes. Laurence Lieberman. ...I pray for the fantastic/Messages one can learn to receive when the heartbeat skips. CoPo

Orange Jews. Ron Padgett. In Wee-John-Boo, in "Boo-Boo" by John Greenleaf Whittier. EAS

Orange Juice Song. David Phillips. bourbon and orange juice is a rotten way to get drunk. NeAC

The Orange Lily. Anonymous.
  And a sweet orange lily for me. NOBI
  Who bravely wore on Boyne's red shore/The royal loyal Lily O. FaBoPV

The Orange Lily O. Anonymous. There's not a flower in Erin's bower/Can match the Orange Lily O. GBP; IrPN

Orange March. Richard Murphy. Bygone canon, bygone spleen. NOBI

The Orange Tree. John Shaw Neilson. Plague me no longer now, for I/Am listening like the Orange Tree. BoAV; CBAP; PoAu 1-2

The Orange Tree. Ellen Pearce. I don't always understand his business. IHMS

The Oranges. Abu Dharr. The watchers smiled in glad surprise. TTY

Oranges. Jonathan Swift. They'll make a sweet Bishop when Gentlefolks sup. NCEP

Oranges and Lemons. Anonymous. Here comes a chopper to chop off your head. OxNR

Orara. Henry Clarence Kendall. Which keeps the river of the song/A beauty out of sight. CBAP; PoAu 1-2

An Oration, Entitled "Old, Old, Old, Old Andrew Jackson." Vachel Lindsay. Booted and spurred/To ride! YaD

Oration on the Toes. Edward Brynes. to lunge up and make monkeys of us all. AMV-81

Orator. Ralph Waldo Emerson. Because they are not strong. AnNE; OxBA

The Orator. Roy McFadden. We'll need a Sheehy Skeffington. OnYI

Orator Prigg. William Blake. And puffing his cheeks he replied "A great wig." OBSV

The Orator's Epitaph. Lord Brougham. The hole in which my body lies/Would not contain one-half my speeches. NLV

The Orb Weaver.   Robert Weaver.   To thrive in nature and in man's nature.   PPON

Orbiter 5 Shows How Earth Looks from the Moon.   May Swenson.   A man in the moon.   SUW

Orchard.   Hilda ("H. D.") Doolittle.   I bring you as offering.   APA; AtBAP; CMoP; ExPo; LiTA; LiTM; MoAmPo; OxBA

The Orchard.   Gretel Ehrlich.   Tonight so many of them fall.   MAYP

The Orchard.   Michael Spence.   White as bones, white as petals in the grass.   AMV-80

Orchard.   Ruth Stone.   And shook the hills with trumpeting.   PH

The Orchard and the Heath.   George Meredith.   And seemed the desert of the night/Far down with mellow orchards to endow.   OBNC

An Orchard at Avignon.   Agnes Mary Frances (Mme Emile Duclaux) Robinson.   One moment fills the amazed heart,/And never comes again.   HBV 1-2; NOBV; OBTV

The Orchard by the Shore: a Pastoral.   Elinor Sweetman.   In the orchard by the shore!   OBVV

The Orchard-Pit.   Dante Gabriel Rossetti.   And that the same last eddy swallows up.   EnLoPo; NBM; NCEP; OAEL 1-2; PoEL 1-5; SCV; SyP; VLP

Orchard Snow.   J. B. Goodenough.   Pips holding Eve's promise here,/And Adam's grief.   AMV-81

Orchard Song.   Sappho.   ...while from quivering leaves/Streams down deep slumber.   LiTW

Orchestra.   Sir John Davies.
And still the murmur with the daunce doth meete.   FaBoEn
For dancing is love's proper exercise.' UnS
I do aspire the shadow to relate. OBSC
Since when, his brain that had before been dry,/Became the well-spring of all Poetry. EG

Orchestra.   Reg Saner.   if only we had remembered.   AMV-80

The Orchestra.   William Carlos Williams.   It is a design.   HAP

Orchids.   Judith Minty.   she was already floating in air.   GeTw

Orchids.   Theodore Roethke.   Loose ghostly mouths/Breathing.   CMoP; NMP; PPoe

Orchids.   Theodore Wratislaw.   A temple of coloured sorrows and perfumed/sins!   VLP

Ordeal.   Nina Cassian.   and your memories will seem to begin/with the creation of the world.   PBWP

The Ordeal by Fire (excerpt).   Edmund Clarence Stedman.   Before the memories we bear,/The flames leap backward everywhere.   WGRP

An Order for a Picture.   Alice Cary.   If you paint me the picture, and leave that out.   BLPA

Orders.   Abraham Moses Klein.   Let me wonder.   WHW

Ordinance on Winning.   Naomi Lazard.   We advise you to wait patiently/for your prize/which will either come or not.   GP

An Ordinary Day beyond Kaitaia.   Kendrick Smithyman.   You must change your words.   OCNZ

The Ordinary Dog.   Nancy Byrd Turner.   I wish the pompous Pekinese/Could know the Jolly Pup!   TiPo

An Ordinary Evening in Cleveland.   Lewis Turco.   like a blind man eating fish in an empty room.   NYBP

Ordinary People on Sunday.   Tom Veitch.   Yes, ten years of smouldering in jail,/about to erupt in death...   ANYP

The ordinary valour only works.   Christopher Anstey.   Which nothing can intimidate but danger.   CenHV

Ordinary Women.   Marilyn Hacker.
not looking at the sidewalk or the sky.   LTB
up from our terror, with women: me, you. LTB

The Ordinary Women.   Wallace Stevens.   They flitted/Through the palace walls.   OxBA

Ordination.   Sister Mary Immaculate.   And for my hunger, you will give me Bread.   GoBC

Oread.   Hilda ("H. D.") Doolittle.   Cover us with your pools of fir.   AP; AWP; CMoP; ExPo; GoJo; InPS; MoAmPo; MoVE; NoAm; NOBA; OxBA; SBG; TAP; WeW

Oreads.   Kathleen Raine.   Protect us from invading night/And the unbroken silence of the dead.   PoSH

An Oregon Message.   William Stafford.   Burn this.   CoAP; MOON

The Oregon Trail.   Anonymous.   He carried kids until his back was broke on the/Oregon Trail.   BPAW

The Oregon Trail.   Arthur Guiterman.   Two hundred wagons, following a Star!   BPAW

Oregon Trail: 1851.   James Marshall.   Roaring to the sunset on the Oregon Trail!   BPAW

Oregon Winter.   Jeanne McGahey   The farmers clean their boots, and whittle, and drowse.   AmFN

Orestes Pursued.   Charles David Webb.   ...Not sings, mourns.   NePoAm-2

The Organ Cactus.   Dorothy Scarborough.   This organ vast shall play his symphony!   BPAW

The Organ-Grinder.   Jimmy Garthwaite.   He asked me once–and squeaked at me/Because I hadn't any!   BrR

The Organ Grinders' Garden.   Mildred Plew Merryman.   Are pleased to wait serenely/for the coming of the spring.   SoPo

Organ Solo.   Knute Skinner.   hoping that she would understand/and take me quickly into hand.   GP

Organ Transplant.   J. D. Reed.   My blood has adopted a child/who shuffles through my chest/carrying a doll.   PoL

The Organist.   George W. Stevens.   He is the most exciting thing/In town on Sabbath day.   BLPA

The Organist in Heaven.   Thomas Edward Brown.   And moved the balanced stars.   LoBV; OBVV

Orgy.   Gina Labriola.   I am waiting for someone to swallow me up,/but with all my thorns.   WPOW

Orgy.   Norman MacCaig.   ...–having discovered/that the innkeeper was the inn.   OxBC

The Orient Express.   Randall Jarrell.   Behind everything there is always/The unknown unwanted life.   AmP; AP; CMoP; CoAP; CoBMV; NOBA

Orient Ode.   Francis Thompson.   When all thy crying clear/Is but: Lo here! lo there!–ah, me, lo every–/where!   CoBE

Orient Wheat.   Adrienne Rich.   In the green fields they'll be saying/Can never grow again.   NePoEA

An Oriental Apologue.   James Russell Lowell.   Forever for the people's good should spin.   PoEL 1-5

Orientale.   William Ernest Henley.   A touch Sidonian–modern–taking–strange!   PeD

Oriflamme.   Jessie Redmond Fauset.   Still visioning the stars!   BANP; BlSi; PoBA

The Origin of Baseball.   Kenneth Patchen.   So he wanted to throw something/And he picked up a baseball.   LiSp

The Origin of Centaurs.   Anthony Hecht.   Those powerful, clear hoofprints on the path.   NePoEA

The Origin of Cities.   Robert Hass.   ...accounts/are kept carefully, what goes out, what returns.   NPGG

The Origin of Didactic Poetry.   James Russell Lowell.   Put all your beauty in your rhymes,/Your morals in your living.   PoEL 1-5

Origin of Dreams.   Marvin Bell.   ...Then we go looking.   LCAP

The Origin of Species.   Myra Sklarew.   ...not too much/competition, no chance of a favorable/variation.   SUW

The Origin of the Praise of God.   Robert Bly.   ..."Now do you still say you cannot choose/the road?"   NU

Original Child Bomb (excerpt).   Thomas Merton.   ...men seemed to be fatigued by the/whole question.   NAs

An Original Cuss.   Keith Preston.   For cutting loose from habit.   ALV

Original Epitaph on a Drunkard.   Royall Tyler.   He's quaffing in a world of spirits.   OBAL

The Original Lamb.   Anonymous.   "Thanks, teacher dear," the scholars cried, and awe crept/darkly o'er 'em.   InMe

Original Sin.   Robinson Jeffers.   And not fear death; it is the only way to be cleansed.   MoAB; MoAmPo; MoVE

Original Sin.   Alexander Laing.   And a small blue bubble of lead under the skin.   NYBP

Original Sin: A Short Story.   Robert Penn Warren.   Or it goes to the backyard and stands like/an old horse cold in the pasture.   AmP; CrMA; HoPM; LiTA; LiTM; MoVE; NOCV; PPP; SM; TAP

Original Strawberry.   Nancy Willard.   From which constellation shall you sail/to the mandala/that only a knife can find?   LCAP

Originality.   Thomas Bailey Aldrich.   No rose has been original.   AnNE

Origins.   Joy Harjo.   But not very far at all.   TWSS

Origins.   Keorapetse Kgositsile.   what is this thing called/love   PoBA

Origins and History of Consciousness.   Adrienne Rich.   ...and sleeps/like a dumb beast, head on her paws, in the corner.   NIP

The Origins of Escape.   Charles P. R. Tisdale.   ...Under a leaf sit six daddy longlegs,/Sheltered from the rain.   AMV-81

The Origins of Life.   Titus Lucretius Carus.   They give the drafts to others.   LiTW

Oriki Erinle.   Anonymous.   He is the one who looks after my child.   PBA; TTY

Orinda to Lucasia.   Katherine ("Orinda") Philips.   Ev'n thou may'st come too late,/And not restore my life, but close my eyes.   PeHV

Orinda to Lucasia Parting, October, 1661, at London.   Katherine ("Orinda") Philips.   And have more cause than e'er I had before,/To fear that I shall never see thee more.   OBS

Orion.   Paul Engle.   And dip your club three times in fiery answer.   AnAmPo

Orion.   Richard Henry Horne.
And all his laurels deepening but the shade.   VLP
Like glistering stones in the congealing air. VLP

Orion.   Adrienne Rich.   you with your back to the wall.   NIP; NoAm; NoP

Orisha.   Jayne Cortez.   Orisha Orisha Satchmo Orisha   BlSi

Orishas.   Larry Neal.   whose blood is that efficient lackey-tom motherfuckers?   NBP

Orkney Interior. Ian Hamilton Finlay. In a little rock pool that reflects the moon. NMP

The Orlando Commercial. George Macbeth. ...exclusive ORLANDO/the new seamless nylon. NOBL

Orlando Furioso. Lodovico Ariosto.
As doth a glasse the lillies faire and roses. OBVE
Let Hellicon, Pindus, Parnassus hill/Sound Isabella, Isabella still. OBVE
Scriv'ners and clarks, and lawyers and atturneys. OBVE
Till all be spent, and he his number mist. LiTW

Orlo's Valediction. Jon Manchip White. The slavery and precipitancy of his days. NePoEA

Ornamental Water. Louise Townsend Nicholl. The ornamental water of the mind. NePoAm

Ornaments. Frank Ormsby. And today the delft hens have laid delft eggs. CIP

Ornithology in Florida. Arthur Guiterman. And that's what I know about birds. BoAnP; InMe

The Oro Stage. Henry Herbert Knibbs. And the pinto wheeler draggin' in the chains. BPAW

The Orotava Road. Basil Bunting. ...sharing our/desires and lack of faith in desire. NoAm

The Orphan. Anonymous.
And if your mother slight me, her blood on the hearth-/stone! KiLC
Living with my brother and my sister-in-law. PoA

Orphan Born. Robert Jones Burdette. For I will just be gathered to/My incubator. OBAL

The Orphan Boy. Anonymous. And whilst I live shelter I'll give/To a poor little soldier's boy.' OBET

Orphan Boy, Fishing. Albert Goldbarth. Let him come as her answer. WOLT

The Orphan Boy's Tale. Amelia Opie. Your happy, happy, orphan boy! PaPo

The Orphan Girl. Anonymous. And her soul had fled to that home above/Where there's bread and room for the poor. AmFP; AS

The Orphan's Song. Sydney Thomas Dobell. And ho but I love thee dearly! CH; ELP; OBNC

Orphans. David Ray. ...or lay your/life frail as a rose petal against my face. FiCP

Orpheus. Donald Davie. Is that how it was? One hopes so. TEP

Orpheus. J. F. Hendry. And landward through the rains, the sea/unrolls a proud vast tragedy. NeBP

Orpheus. Robert Herrick. And, looking back, that look did sever/Him and Eurydice for ever. CaPo

Orpheus. Elizabeth Madox Roberts. And tap them down with humming words. MoAmPo

Orpheus. W. D. Snodgrass. So night by night, my life has gone. CABA

Orpheus. Yvor Winters. Sang unmeaning down the stream. MoVE; NOBA; VGW

Orpheus and Eurydice. Robert Browning. –no past is mine, no future: look at me! CTC

Orpheus and Eurydice. Geoffrey Hill. His countenance, his hands' motion,/Serene even to a fault. NePoEA-2

Orpheus and Eurydice. Jean Valentine. ...the river/tossing a shoe up, a handful of hair. FaBoWP; LCAP

Orpheus I Am, Come from the Deeps Below. John Fletcher. Till women waft them over in their tears. GBL

Orpheus in Greenwich Village. Jack Gilbert. should notice, suddenly,/they had no ears? NPGG; PoL; PP

Orpheus in the Underworld. David Gascoyne. Cold curtains of rock concealing the bottomless sky. FaBoTw

Orpheus to Beasts. Richard Lovelace. Seeing more harmony/In her bright eye,/Than now you hear. CaPo

Orpheus to Eurydice. Frederick Morgan. and you, already, have been lost again. AMV-80

Orpheus to Woods. Richard Lovelace. Nor carve any from your wombs/Aught but coffins, and their tombs. CaPo

Orphic Interior. Leonardo Sinisgalli. While there wept underground the eyes/Of stone. LiTW

Orsames' Song. Sir John Suckling. The devil take her! AnEnPo

Ortho's Epitaph. Charles Stuart Calverley. Yet the turf that I'm clad with is strange to me quite. FaBoEE

Ortiz. Hezekiah Butterworth. Away with the warrior's plume! PAH

Ortus. Ezra Pound. No portion, but a being. LiTA; NePA

Oscar. Bill Berkson. the whole of the whole the/whole other whole ANYP

Osculation. Henry Sydnor Harrison. While poor Leigh's one vaunted stunt/Was with Jenny. InMe

Oshun, the River Goddess. Anonymous. O, how sweet/Is the touch of a child's hand! WTO

Osip Mandelshtam. Irving Layton. flashing the Jew's will, his mocking contempt for slaves NeAC

Osip Mandelstam. Seamus Deane. ...and wait/For the Gossamer of Paradise/To spider in our dirt-filled eyes. FaBoPV

Osmund Toulmin. Osbert Sitwell. Watching the flushed schoolgirls playing hockey. AtBAP

The Osprey Suicides. Laurence Lieberman. as if deaf to their rising chorus of squawks. HoAn

Ossawatomie. Carl Sandburg. Asking again: Where did that blood come from? OxBA

Ossian (excerpt). John Francis O'Donnell. Say to Patrick, I wait. IrPN

Ossian's Serenade. Calder Campbell. I'll give thee for a playmate sweet. BLPA

The Ossianic Cycle: The Song of Finn. Anonymous. The sea is lulled to rest, flowers cover the earth. OnYI

Ostia Antica. Anthony Hecht. And symbols of endurance, whispers,/"This is love." NePA

'Ostler Joe. George R. Sims. In the arid desert of Phryne's life, where all was parched and hot. BeLS; BLPA; HBV 1-2; TreF

Ostrava. Petr Bezruc. And we take the judgment seat. LiTW

The Ostrich Is a Silly Bird. Mary E. Wilkins Freeman. Without a blessed thing to do/Until he comes in sight. LBN; OBCA; SoPo; TiPo

Ostriches & Grandmothers! LeRoi (Imamu Amiri Baraka) Jones. wondering/at the bar's/delay NeAP

Oterborne (excerpt). Anonymous. And syne my logeyng I haue take/Wyth my brande dubbyd many a knyght.' OxBS

Othello. William Shakespeare.
Farewell! Othello's occupation's gone! TreFT; TrGrPo
Here comes the lady; let her witness it. BoC; EBEV; SCV; TreF
I know not where is that Promethean heat/That can thy light relume. FiP
I took by the throat the circumcised dog/And smote him, thus. FiP; GoTF; TreFS
If I court moe women, you'll couch with moe men. LoBV
It strikes where it doth love. She wakes. BiP
No,–heaven forfend!–I would not kill thy soul. EBEV
O Desdemona, Desdemona! dead!/O! O! O! BiP
Pride, pomp, and circumstance of glorious war! WHA
Robs me of that which not enriches him/And makes me poor indeed. FaFP; GoTF; TreFS
...when they are full,/They belch us. DBV
Yield up, O love, thy crown and hearted throne/To tyrannous hate! TW

Othello Jones Dresses for Dinner. Ed Roberson. my tie becomes crooked but do not/be alarmed i am well mannered. PoBA; PoNe

An Other. Thomas Carew.
The flames, the arrowes, all lye here. AnAnS 2; SeCP; SeCV 1-2
So the faire Modell broke, for want/Of roome to lodge th'Inhabitant. AnAnS 2; SeCV 1-2

The Other. Peter Cooley. You will never have known me. AMV-80; MAYP

The Other. Ruth Fainlight. ...Loving her I shall learn/My own secret at last from the words of her song. BrRo

Other. Lance Henson. thirsty without me VoR

Other Fabrics, Other Mores! Anna Maria Lenngren. Make-up, muslins, brazen talk/Go hand-in-hand with modern days.' PBWP

The Other Fellow's Job. Strickland Gillilan. Keep too busy at your own to want "the other fellow's job." WBLP

The Other Journey. Katherine Garrison Chapin. ...the delicate cross-bow mark/Of bird, left in the ebbing sand. MoVE

Other Lives. Patricia Hooper. ...You enter someone's life/some nights as though his heart beats in your heart. AMV-81; HoAn

Other men are thorn. Mahadevi (Mahadeviyakka). I cannot take/any man in my arms but my lord/white as jasmine. BoWoP

The Other One. Harry Thurston Peck. But oh the ache of the heart that longs/Night and day for the other one! AA

The Other One Comes to Her. Mary Aldis. But when the hour came–to his surprise/She sent him from her with remorseful eyes. HBMV

The Other Person's Place. Donald H. Hover. What kindness, sympathy and grace/Lie in the other person's place! STF

Other Sheep I Have, Which Are Not of This Fold. William Cullen Bryant. And lift to heaven the voice of praise. TrPWD

Other Shore. Anonymous. On the other shore. ABF

The Other Side. Roy Fuller. Of memory of things before, confirm/After-life's ludicrous reality. OxBC

The Other Side. Seamus Heaney. and talk about the weather/or the price of grass-seed? FaBoIP

The Other Side. Thomas Reiter. though he told me he never saw/the same one twice. AMV-80

The Other Side of a Mirror. Mary Elizabeth Coleridge. That heard me whisper, "I am she!" BoWoP; CBEP

The Other Side of Jordan. Anonymous. Oh, Jordan is a hard road to travel, I believe. FSW

The Other Side of This World. Calvin Forbes. Is everything in its place except me? MAYP

Our Lady in the Middle Ages. Frederick William Faber. Then were the natural charites exhaled/Afresh, from out the blessed love of Mary. ACP; CAW; ISi

Our Lady of France. Lionel Pigot Johnson. Nay! here my children/fold/ Their exiled hands in prison, and long for me. ISi

Our Lady of Good Voyage. Lucy A. K. Adee. On boats with sail/And mast. ISi

Our Lady of Mercy. Sister Mary Bertrand. "Most gracious advocate, turn thine eyes this way." ISi

Our Lady of the Libraries. Sister Mary Ignatius. From manuscripts like winding-sheets/Her risen praises steal! ISi

Our Lady of the May. Lionel Pigot Johnson. O Flower of flowers, our Lady of the May! ISi

Our Lady of the Passion. John Mauropus. The whole world's Consolation is my woe! ISi

Our Lady of the Refugees. Sister Maura. guide them in faith beneath familiar stars–/Our Lady of the Refugees. ISi

Our Lady of the Skies. James M. Hayes. Above the world, protecting it,/ Our Lady of the Skies. ISi

Our Lady of the Snows. Rudyard Kipling. Said our Lady of the Snows. ACV

Our Lady of the Waves. George Mackay Brown. Star of the Sea, shine for us. NePoEA-2

Our Lady on Calvary. Sister Michael Marie. Ever Queen and Mother of God. ISi

Our Lady Peace. Mark Van Doren. Our lady lived, fierce in each other's frown. WaP

Our Lady's Labor. John Duffy. She wove for him in darkness, day by day,/Out of the labor of a lovely loom. ISi

Our Lady's Lullaby. Richard Verstegan. Sing lullaby, my life's Joy. ACP; CAW; GoBC; ISi

Our Lady's Salutation. Robert Southwell. God yielding to descend cut off our thrall. ISi

Our Lady's Song. Anonymous. Bote ley thou thi fet to my pappe,/And wite the from the colde. OBEV

Our Lady with Two Angels. Wilfred Rowland Childe. Prepared by the Spouse-Emperor for His Bride. ISi

Our Left. Francis Orrery Tichnor. Honor the brave/Who died to save/ Your all upon "Our Left." MC; PAH

Our Life Is Hid with Christ in God. George Herbert. To gain at harvest an eternal Treasure. OAEL 1-2

Our Light Afflictions. Anonymous. When, folded in His loving arms,/The weary are at rest. BLRP

Our Lips and Ears. Anonymous. Myself and I, and mine and my,/And how I do and did. BLPA; GoTF; TreF; WBLP

Our Little Calf. Dorothy Aldis. You'll be our cow! TiPo

Our Little Ghost. Louisa May Alcott. "God bless our little ghost!" OBCA

Our little kinsmen. Emily Dickinson. And left the little angleworm/With modesties enlarged. ImOP

Our Lives. Sharon Scott. things are/spots/and spaces/people/can't name, Brothers. JB

Our lives are Swiss. Emily Dickinson. Forever intervene! NOBA; PoL; TAP

Our Lord and Our Lady. Hilaire Belloc. But Our Lady stands above the world/With the white Moon at Her feet. GoBC; HBMV; ISi

Our Love Shall Be the Brightness. James Wreford Watson. The brightness from on high/will cover the earth with beauty, and/inhabit the human sky. CaP

Our Love Was a Grim Citadel. R. A. K. Mason. and Chaos bids ten thousand spears/run to erase our straw-built folly. AnNZ

Our Lucy. Paul Goodman. how suddenly! there she was/and now is not in our empty house. GDP

Our Madonna at Home. Rafael Pombo. Nor either mother could my soul resign. CAW

Our March. Vladimir Mayakovsky. Our breasts are as crashing brass. AWP

Our Modest Doughboys. Charlton Andrews. "And am I glad I'm home? Ah, oui!"/Said Private Mike McCann. PAH

Our Mother's Body Is the Earth. Mary McAnally. to hiss and spume her orgasm. AMV-80

Our Mother Tongue; or, An Envoy to an American Lady. Richard Monckton, Lord Houghton Milnes. Forget not it is yours and ours. GN

Our Movement. Paul Eluard. We are born of everywhere are limitless. LiTW

Our Mr. Toad. David McCord. When the dusk draws/nigh/no/near. TiPo

Our Nation Forever. Wallace Bruce. One God and one faith all victorious! OHIP

Our National Banner. Dexter Smith. Wave it, save it, evermore. PAH

Our Orders. Julia Ward Lowe. And God, and Truth, and Freedom die! AA

Our Own. Margaret E. Sangster. To undo the work of the morn. BLPA; PoToHe

Our Parodies Are Ended. Horace Twist. Leave not a groat behind! Par

Our People. Teresa Anderson. and the dust of the dead/sings under the blade of the plow. LTB

Our People. Diane Burns.
and I tighten the black leather brace/that keeps my knife hand steady. TWSS
And rub/the wounds/together. STE

Our Photographs. Frederick Locker-Lampson. To leave my Boots. ALV; DBV

Our Poets' Breed. Luis, Montoto y Rautenstrauch. Refuse us not an alms, for love of God! CAW

Our Polite Parents. Carolyn Wells.
But "Children will be children," Mamma said. BBGG
Grandpapa was quite annoyed. BBGG
Hasn't found the baby yet. BBGG
"I wouldn't do that dear," Mamma said. BBGG
Mamma felt quite irritated. BBGG
Mamma raised her eyebrows slightly. BBGG
Mamma said, "Why, Moses, dear!" BBGG

Our Prayer of Thanks (excerpt). Carl Sandburg. Our prayer of thanks. TRV

Our Presidents. Anonymous. A nation's problems has to face. BLPA

Our Rock. Francis Scott Key. 'Tis gain to die with Jesus nigh–/The Rock of thy salvation. BePJ; STF

Our Saviour's Golden Rule. Isaac Watts. And neither do nor say to men/ Whate'er you would not take again. OxBChV

Our Saviour's Love. Anonymous. Which made hell shake and devils tremble. OBET

Our School Now Closes Out. Edmund Dumas. The house above, when all is love/There'll be no parting there. AH

Our share of night to bear. Emily Dickinson. Afterward–day! AA

Our Ship She Lies in Harbour. Anonymous. I'm married to the lad I love/ And I'm happy in my mind.' OBET

Our Silly Little Sister. Dorothy Aldis. We couldn't think what to say back. EvOK

Our Singing Strength. Robert Frost. And sing the wildflowers up from root and seed. AtBAP

Our Sister. Horatio Nelson Powers. She knew what they alone can know/ Who live above but dwell below. HBV 1-2

Our Smoke Has Gone Four Ways. Lance Henson. keep us strong/to meet the/coming days. CDW

Our States, O Lord. John Mycall. Whilst we glad songs of praise prepare/ For thine almighty name. AH

Our Strange and Lovable Weather. William Matthews. ...we can't/say surely what we've undergone,/and need to know, and need to know. NPAW

Our Sunday morning when dawn-priests were applying. John Berryman. About our pines our sister, wind, is moving. BoLoP

Our Tense and Wintry Minds. Hayden Carruth. Tonight the peace of Christ is born/And joy inviolate. AH

Our Times Are in His Hands. Mary D. Freeze. He'll give His Spirit's grace and power/To fill, to comfort, and direct. STF

Our Traveller. Henry Cholmondeley-Pennell Then, why the dickens don't you go and do it? InMe

Our True Beginnings. Wrey Gardiner. We find the crabbed certainty of our true beginnings. NeBP

Our Two Opinions. Eugene Field. 'Nd I havin' my opinyin uv him. AA

Our Two Worthies. John Crowe Ransom. And Paul, out of Tarsus?/He is our Exegete. OBAL

Our Vegetable Love Shall Grow. Elaine Feinstein. the beauty of its present flesh. PoL

Our Village. Thomas Hood. But I haven't come to that–and I hope I never shall–/and that's the Village Poor House! CBEP; InMe; OBSV; PoEL 1-5; PoPle

Our Visit to the Zoo. Jessie Pope. And we all went home/In a taxi-cab. PoPle

Our Wee White Rose. Gerald Massey. But never, never match our wee/ White Rose of all the world. HBV 1-2

Our Youth. John Ashbery. ...We escape/Down the cloud ladder, but the problem has not been solved. CAPP; ConAP; SOTW; VGW

Ourobouros. Jorge Plescoff. Only then will the return/begin. VWA

Ourselves we do inter with sweet derision. Emily Dickinson. That doubts as fervently as it believes. FaBoEE

Ourselves were wed one summer–dear. Emily Dickinson. But You–were crowned in June– PeHV

Out. Nathaniel Burt. become so shining that we cease to be. MoLP

Out and Fight. Charles Godfrey Leland. And the braggart and the Gascon/Be extinguished from the land. PAH

Out-Dated Poem. Dick Gallup. ...,or cared much like I/Do today whether it rained or not. ANYP

Out Fishin'.   Edgar A. Guest.   A feller's always mostly man,/Out fishin'. BLPL; PoLf

Out Fishing.   Barbara Howes.   ...I do not know him: he does not know me. LiSp

Out from Gloucester.   Harlan Trott.   Boats bound south for Georges/Sway in a slow farewell.   EtS

Out from Lobster Cove.   J. D. Reed.   One thing is done, and it bells/up in the throat.   NeAC

Out Goes She.   *Anonymous*.   Threepence on the railway–out goes she. PoPle

Out in the Cold.   George Starbuck.   those dear, well-meant, unsatisfactory/ approximations of the eventual me?   NYBP

Out in the Country, Back Home.   Jeff Daniel Marion.   nose uplifted to signal/your passing.   PPJ

Out in the Dark.   Edward ("Edward Eastaway") Thomas.   If you love it not, of night.   BrPo; CH; GTBS-P; LiTM; MoAB; MoBrPo; MoVE; NOBE; PoPle

Out in the Fields.   *Anonymous*.   Out in the fields of God.   GoTF; HBV 1-2; HBVY; TreFS; TRV

Out in the Fields with God.   Elizabeth Barrett Browning.   Out in the fields with God!   BLRP; WBLP; WGRP

Out of a War of Wits.   Dylan Thomas.   And be struck dumb, if only for a time.   PoA

Out of Body.   Janice Townley Moore.   My fears walled in his body/must come to a certain stop.   AMV-81

Out of Bounds.   John Banister Tabb.   O comrades, let us one and all/Join in to get Him back His ball!   TRV

Out of Catullus.   Richard Crashaw.   While our joyes so multiply,/As shall mocke the envious eye.   CavP

Out of Chaos Out of Order Out.   Michele Roberts.   who stirs the clutter in her little room   BrRo

Out of Doors.   Walter Conrad Arensberg.   It has itself the old disease of thought.   AnAmPo

Out-of-Doors.   Robert Whitaker.   And challenge all the spaces of the sun. TrPWD

Out of French.   Sir Charles Sedley.   By heaven, I would not live an hour. FaBoEE

Out of Hearing.   Jane Barlow.   She will not wake, mavrone, she will not wake.   HBV 1-2

Out of Luck.   Abraham Ibn Ezra.   Were selling shrouds my business,/No man would ever die!   TrJP

Out of Mourning.   Anthony S. Abbott.   I would feel that touch before another night.   AMV-81

Out of My Soul's Depth.   Thomas Campion.   Their sin-sick souls by him shall be recured.   OxBoCh

Out of My Study Window.   Reed Whittemore.   ...an icicle/Is something about which to be illogical.   PoPl

Out of Our Shame.   Norman Rosten.   it is your own son about to be born. TrJP

Out of Question & Mind...   Noah Mitchell.   that the rush hour/of their birth/is over,/over,/over!/?   LFAC

Out of Sight, Out of Mind.   Barnabe Googe.   When distance doth depart us twain.   EiL; EnRePo; InPS; PAI

Out of Sleep.   Allen Curnow.   You will not grasp the meaning, you will be in it.   AnNZ

Out of Sorts.   Sir William Schwenck Gilbert.   For you're not at all well! ALV

Out of Soundings.   Padraic Fallon.   Good-morning, goodmorning, goodmorning–sir.   NeIP

Out of Superstition.   Boris Pasternak.   And blew the dust away.   LiTW

Out of That Sea.   David Ferry.   We saw how our hands came wrinkled out of that sea.   NePoAm-2

Out-of-the-Body Travel.   Stanley Plumly.   like his hand, in fever, on my forehead.   AmPA; GeTw; LCAP

Out of the corpse-warm vestibule of heaven steps the sun.   Ingeborg Bachmann.   History, has ordained us a grave/from which there is no resurrection.   BoWoP

Out of the Cradle Endlessly Rocking.   Walt Whitman.   The sea whisper'd me.   AA; AP; APA; AWP; DiPo; ExPo; ForPo; GoTF; HAP; HeIP; InPo; MAmP; MoAmPo; NAWM 1-2; NePA; NOBA; NoP; OxBA; PB; PoEL 1-5; PPoe; PrIm; SeCeV; TAP; TreFS; ViBoPo; WeW; WHA

Out of the Dark Wood.   Peter".   ...He has been hiding here for/Many generations.   AmMo

Out of the Darkness.   Frankie Armstrong.   The end won't come in darkness but a/blinding flash of light.   BrRo

Out of the Darkness.   Gertrud Kolmar.   And sleep, my brow inclined to the East,/Until sunrise.   WPOW

Out of the Deepness.   William Jackson.   ...I turn,/and touch my glass to his. AMV-81

Out of the Depths.   Frederic Lawrence Knowles.   Even on Calvary's slope,/ I sing!   TrPWD

Out of the Earth.   Mary Carolyn Davies.   For only men who are brave and good/Can come out changeless from a wood.   HBMV

Out of the Frying Pan into the Fire.   James Henry.   Without being prosecuted as a felon,/Spy, or disturber of the public peace.   NOBV

Out of the Hitherwhere.   James Whitcomb Riley.   Out of the hitherwhere into the yon.   BLPA; FPL

Out of the Hurly-Burly.   Max (Charles Heber Clark) Adeler.   With Jane, Maria, and portions of Hannah.   CenHV

Out of the Italian.   Richard Crashaw.   And to many Deaths renew mee. SeCV 1-2

Out of the Old House, Nancy.   Will Carleton.   Until we commence a-keepin' house in the/house not made with hands.   AA

Out of the Past.   Robert Wallace.   you–someone?–waded, holding up a skirt. PoL

Out of the Rolling Ocean the Crowd.   Walt Whitman.   Every day at sundown for your dear sake my love.   ViBoPo

Out of the Sea.   Witter ("Emanuel Morgan") Bynner.   So silent you vanished, so sweet you endure,/And never a word.   MoLP

Out of the Sea, Early.   May Swenson.   it exposes each silk thread and rumple in the carpet.   RFM

Out of the Strong, Sweetness.   Charles Reznikoff.   a people of love, a compassionate people.   VWA

Out of the Vast.   Augustus Wright Bamberger.   For the God whose love we sing/Lends a little of his heaven/To every living thing.   TRV

Out of the Wilderness.   Ulrich Troubetzkoy.   Kentucky-born, into the wilderness.   GoYe

Out of This Life.   *Anonymous*.   Or shall at last, it be mine to find/That all I'd worked for is left behind?   STF

Out of Time (excerpt).   Kenneth Slessor.   And Time flows past them like a hundred yachts.   CBAP

Out of Tune.   William Ernest Henley.   It were better to die,/And soon! MoBrPo

Out of Whack.   Russell Edson.   Of course, screamed the king and queen, are you blind, can't you see that/our mouths...   LCAP

Out of You.   Rodney Phillips.   slowly slipping away   PoL

Out of Your Hands.   Theodore Weiss.   wise and thoughtless joy.   CoPo

Out of Your Sleep Arise and Wake.   *Anonymous*.   And in thy court to have a place,/That we may there sing noel./Noel!   NoP

Out on Santa-Fe-Blues.   Arthur Petties.   It won't be long till/back up this road I'm gone   BluL

"Out, Out–".   Robert Frost.   And they, since they/Were not the one dead, turned to their affairs.   CABA; DL; FF; HAP; HeIP; OxBA; SoSe; VGW

Out There.   Bill Berkson.   Going on inside.   ANYP

Out There Somewhere.   Henry Herbert Knibbs.   With buds of roses in her hair and kisses on her mouth.   BLPA

Out to Old Aunt Mary's.   James Whitcomb Riley.   Out to Old Aunt Mary's.   FaFP; OHFP

Out West.   Gary Snyder.   wearing those tight blue jeans.   BLPA; BPAW; FaBoBe; FaFP; GoTF; HBV 1-2; NNaP; PoOW; TreF

Outbreak.   Bill Anderson.   Lord, what must she be/to other men?   VGW

Outburst from a Little Face.   John Woods.   I'm tired of sitting on my lap/to reach the cereal.   GP

Outcast.   Claude McKay.   Under the white man's menace, out of time. BALP; BP; PoBA

The Outcast.   George William Russell.   On the outcast majesty/They lean as a friend.   OBSP; OxBI

The Outcast.   Frank Elwood Sanford.   Poor dilapidated, broken,–/Old umbrella.   PeD

The Outcast.   James Stephens.   Is Joy, and gives Joy back to me.   MoBrPo

An Outcry upon Opportunity.   William Shakespeare.   Thy heinous hours wait on them as their pages.   NOBE

The Outdoor Christmas Tree.   Aileen Fisher.   Little hoppy cottontails,/come and see tonight.   SiSoSe

An Outdoor Litany.   Louise Imogen Guiney.   Help me endure the Pit, until/Thou wilt not have forgotten me.   TrPWD

The Outer from the Inner.   Emily Dickinson.   The Star's shole Secret–in the Lake–/Eyes were not meant to know.   MAmP

Outer Space, Inner Space.   Gladys Cardiff.   They stretched until they seemed/to converge where we began.   TWSS

Outgrown.   Julia Caroline Ripley Dorr.   As plainly, perhaps, and as bluntly as I might in our earlier/youth.   HBV 1-2

The Outlanders.   Andrew Glaze.   In all the level stare that met our stare. NYBP

Outlanders, Whence Come Ye Last?   William Morris.   Minstrels and maids, stand forth on the floor.   OxBoCh

The Outlandish Knight.   *Anonymous*.
And the doors of the best ivory.'   OBET
She rode till she came to her father's hall,/Three hours before it was day. ShM

Outlaw.   John Giorno.   was killed/last night/by the police.   ANYP

The Outlaw.   Seamus Heaney.   Who, in his own time, resumed the dark, the straw.   NoAm; OxBC

The Outlaw Murray. *Anonymous.* Sic favour get before a king/As did the Outlaw Murray of the for-/est frie? ESPB; OxBB

The Outlaw of Loch Lene. Jeremiah Joseph Callanan. The birds go to sleep by the sweet wild twist of her song. AnIV; BIrV; CH; GBL; IrPN; OBEV; OBRV; OnYI; OxBI

The Outlaw's Song. Joanna Baillie. And use it as ye may. OBEV

Outlook Uncertain. Alastair Reid. lugubrious ending,/new lives pending? NePoEA-2

Outside. Phyllis Beauvais. there isn't any/where to go. IHMS

Outside. Audre Lorde. who are come to make our shattered faces/whole. NIP

Outside. William Stafford. Coyotes are circling around our truth. NePoAm-2

Outside Baby Moon's. Paul Violi. Faithless Reader, you'll still feel like a leaf/lost in a pile of gloves. APU

Outside Dunsandle. Sacheverell Sitwell. Waiting for lost travellers to come by. ChMP

Outside Every Window Is a Flowering Thing. Anita Skeen. ...let us say/how our lives have changed. AMV-81

Outside Fargo, North Dakota. James Wright. I nod as I write good evening, lonely/And sick for home. LCAP; NNaP

Outside the Chancel Door. *Anonymous.* But here I lie as warm as they. ShM

Outside the Door. Annette Wynne. Until a puffing wind comes by. SoPo; SUS

Outside the Holy City. James G. Gilkey. O God, give us the strength to build/With Christ that city here! AH

Outside the Supermarket. Roy Fuller. He weeps for a single neck. OxBC

Outside the Window. Thomas Hardy. And he steals off, leaving his stick unclaimed. BrPo

Outside White Earth. Gordon Henry. on the paint/of a peeling wall. STE

Outward. John G. Neihardt. I am Wind and Sky and Sea! HBV 1-2

Outward. Louis Simpson. Sinuously it swims through the stars. NYBP

Outward Bound. Thomas Bailey Aldrich. Ionian isles are thine, and all the fairy/shores! AA; EtS

Outward Bound. Edward Sydney Tylee. Only our love and prayers. PAH

The Outward Man Accused. Edward Taylor. If no, thy tongue belies itself, for lo/Thou saidst thy heart was dressed from sin also. LiTA

The Outwit Song. Daniel Gerard Hoffman. But I can outwit him. SaC

Outwitted. Edwin Markham. We drew a circle that took him in! AnAmPo; BLPA; ELU; FPL; GoTF; MCCG; MoAmPo; TreFT; TRV

Ovedue Balance Sheet. Therese Plantier. and all at once caught sight of night. BoWoP

The Oven Bird. Robert Frost. Is what to make of a diminished thing. AP; AWP; CoBMV; CrMA; ForPo; HeIP; InPo; MAPA; NoAm; NOBA; NoP; OxBA; PPP; TAP; UnS

Over. R. S. Thomas. Consider it, then,/A finished performance. FF

Over 2000 Illustrations and a Complete Concordance. Elizabeth Bishop. –and looked and looked our infant sight away. HaCAP; LCAP; NoAm

Over All the Face of Earth Main Ocean Flowed. John Milton. The dry land Earth, and the great receptacle/Of congregated waters He call'd Seas. EtS

Over and Over Stitch. Jorie Graham. ...the dry stalks of daylilies/marking a stillness we can't keep. HaCAP

Over and Under. William Jay Smith. Hear the crack of thunder! TiPo

Over Bright Summer Seas. Robert Hillyer. He slips the mooring of his consciousness. NYBP

Over Case's Door. John Case. Within this place/Lives Doctor Case. FaBoUs

The Over-Heart. John Greenleaf Whittier. And trust the unknown for the known. NOCV; TRV; WGRP

Over in the Meadow. *Anonymous.* So they beaved all day in a cozy wee den. SoPo

Over in the Meadow. Oliver A. Wadsworth. So they toiled and were wise,/Where the men dig and delve. MoShBr

Over Jordan. *Anonymous.* I'm just a-going over home. OuSiCo

Over Saleve. George Herbert Clarke. The little lark knows all her loveliness. CaP

Over Sir John's Hill. Dylan Thomas. Stone for the sake of the souls of the slain birds sailing. CABL; DiPo; LiTB; MoAB

Over the Bridge. Li Kwang-T'ien. No answer, hand in hand, we cross the bridge. LiTW

Over the Coffin. Thomas Hardy. Had lived like the wives in the patriarchs' days. BrPo

Over the Dark World Flies the Wind. Alfred, Lord Tennyson. And still divide the rapid mind/This way and that in search of ease. FaBoRV

Over the fence. Emily Dickinson. Oh, dear,–I guess if He were a Boy–/He'd–climb–if He could! SBG

Over the Great City. Edward Carpenter. And other love is pain, but this is joy eternal. WGRP

Over the Heather the Wet Wind Blows. W. H. Auden. I shall do nothing but look at the sky. EnLi 1-2; PoRA

Over the Hill to the Poor-House. Will Carleton. That you shall never suffer the half I do today. BeLS; BLPA; FaFP; PaPo; TreF

Over the Hills and Far Away. William Ernest Henley. Over the hills and far away. HBVY; TreF

Over the Phone. Mekeel McBride. shaped like a Tiffany lamp and shining. MAYP

Over the River. Nancy Woodbury Priest. The angel of death shall carry me. HBV 1-2

Over the Sea to Skye. Robert Louis Stevenson. All that was me is gone. EtS; MOS

Over! The Sweet Summer Closes. Alfred, Lord Tennyson. And winter again and the snows. GBL

Over the Wall: Berlin, May 1975. C. H. Sisson. Yet the afternoon sun falls upon faces/Less tame than tigers. OBTV; OxBC

Over the Water to Charlie. *Anonymous.* To make a white cake for my Charlie. OxNR

Over the Wintry Threshold. Bliss Carman. Whose hearts have lain a moment/On that eternal breast. HBV 1-2

Over Their Graves. Henry Jerome Stockard. "Come let us clasp your hands, we're/brothers all,/Over their graves!" AA; OHIP

Over Three Nipple-Stones. Paul Celan. you hold it to/a clock-shadow's ear/at dusk. VWA

Over to God. Stephen Harrigan. that is so deadly/but so cruel to withhold. FAZ

Overcoats. Larry Kramer. By then, everyone would be looking. AMV-80

Overflow. John Banister Tabb. O'er grief and wrong. CAW; HBV 1-2

The Overgrown Back Yard. John Holmes. Begins to take shape. CrMA; NePoAm

Overheard. Denise Levertov. ...a great/bough or beam/unaware it had/spoken. PoM

Overheard in a Barbershop. Irving Layton. Death's/little victory flags. NMP

Overheard in an Orchard. Elizabeth Cheney. That they have no heavenly Father/Such as cares for you and me. BLRP; TRV

Overheard in the Louvre. X. J. Kennedy. What winning's worth this loss of face? ELU

Overheard on a Saltmarsh. Harold Monro. Give them me. Give them./No. CH; GoJo; MoShBr; SO; TiPo; WSC

Overheard over S.E. Asia. Denise Levertov. I decorate it in black, and seek/the bone.' BoWoP

Overland to the Islands. Denise Levertov. –"every step an arrival." ConAP; UnPo

The Overlander. *Anonymous.*
For tonight we'll drink the health/Of every overlander. PoAu 1-2
I can find a job with a crawling mob/On the banks of the Maranoa. NOAV

Overlooking the River Stout. Thomas Hardy. O never I turned, but let, alack,/These less things hold my gaze! FaBoPP

Overlord. Bliss Carman. Earth to my mother earth,/Spirit to thee. CaP

Overnight, a Rose. Caroline Giltinan. May, some day, bear a rose for Him/It took my life to grow. HBMV

Overnight Guest. Ramona Wilson. imagining that curve/to this night. VoR

Overripe Fruit. Kasmuneh. A nameless "him' my eyes in vain salute. TrJP

Overseer of the Poor. James Hayford. God of the rich there never was. NePoAm-2

The Overtakelessness of Those. Emily Dickinson. Beyond the hope of touch. MoRP

The Overthrow of Lucifer. Phineas Fletcher. His net is broke, the fowl go free, the fowler ta'en. OBS

Overtones. William Alexander Percy. Yet this was but a simple bird,/Alone, among dead trees. HBMV; HBVY

An Overture. Michael Knoll. but wishing us well,/wishing us a life/in another story. LFAC

Overture to Strangers. Phyllis Haring. Or a calabash of teeth and dry wind and whispers. PeSA

Overtures to Death. C. Day Lewis. Mister, you can rely on us/To execute your will. CMoP

The Overturned Lake. Charles Henri Ford. as the mind is overturned by memory, the heart by dread. EAS

An Overworked Elocutionist. Carolyn Wells. So long as I declaim with oratorical display. BLPA; BLPL

The Ovibos. Robert Beverly Hale. He's fair to look on as the rose/And gentle as a kitzen. FiBHP

Ovid. Richard Pevear. "Forgive me, Caesar, I want to come home." AMV-81

Ovid in the Third Reich. Geoffrey Hill. ...I, in mine, celebrate the love-choir. FaBoMo; NoAm; PoL

Ovid, Meet a Metamorphodite. Jonathan Williams. the cream of/genes! PoM

Ozymandias Revisited. Morris Bishop. Mr. and Mrs. Dukes, and Oscar Baer/Of 17 West 4th St., Oyster Bay. NLV

P

P.C. Plod Versus the Dale St. Dog Strangler. Roger McGough. ...he might/well be a cocker spaniel. NoAm

The P'eng That Was a K'un. Lao Tse [or Lao Tzu]. Though, indeed, neither started as a fish. AmMo

P Is for Paleontology. Milton Bracker. Without ever knowing the head or the tail of it. FiBHP; InMe

P.S. Jascha Kessler. –but /perhaps (though how was one to believe it?)/ only because it was one's own? AmPC

P.S. James Russell Lowell An' leaves me frontin' South by North. AA

P's the Proud Policeman. Phyllis McGinley. And he points the way politely/To the playground or the park. SoPo; TiPo

Pa. Leo Dangel. ...Anyway, you should have been home/half an hour ago. AMV-81; Str

Pa, Pa, Build Me a Boat. Anonymous. Pa, Pa, build me a boat/To sail across the ocean. AmFP

Pacchiarotto and Other Poems: Epilogue. Robert Browning. I'll posset and cosset them, nothing loth,/Henceforward with nettle-broth! VLP

Pacelli and the Ethiop. Turner Cassity. The pontiff washes in the silver bowl that saves. GP

Pachuco Remembered. Tino Villanueva. in your wicked/stride... FIA

Pachuta, Mississippi / A Memoir. Al Young. Cool as sundown/I lived there too. TAT

Pacific Door. Earle Birney. lie the bleak and forever capacious tombs of the sea PeCV

Pacific Epitaphs. Dudley Randall.
And another with a submachine gun. NoAm
And severed my medical career. NoAm
But struck one target. NoAm
Kilroy/Is/Here. NoAm
Now I lie silent here. NoAm
Than the girl I raped. NoAm

The Pacific Highway. C. R. Ballard. And Nations shall learn war no more. PAH

Pacific Sonnets. George Barker.
And so we are perfect sacrifice to nothing. LiTM
The perfect and nonexistent obsequies. LiTM; MOS
...the stance of vague/Horror; paralysed with mere pity's peace? LiTM
To the mouth of the death for which no one is ready. LiTM

Pacified. Thomas G. Nickens. (stopping of course for ice cream popcorn 'n coke)/to watch the late movie. LFAC

The Pacifist. Hilaire Belloc. But Roaring Bill (who killed him) thought it right. MoVE

Pacifists. George Woodcock. As the weak sun breaks on the land without a hill. NOBC

Pack, Clouds, away, and Welcome, Day! Thomas Heywood. Sing, birds in every furrow. EG; EIL; GBL; GTBS-P; SoSe; ViBoPo

The Pack Rat. Robert Pack. Forebear, survivor, have I lost my way? PPP; WeW

The Package. Aileen Fisher. oh, what CAN the package be? SoPo

Packard. David Barker. Together we shall travel very far indeed. AmC; DFF; GP

Packet of Letters. Louise Bogan. There, still in murderer's guise, two stand embraced, embalmed. GrPl; LiTL; PCP

Packin' Trunk Blues. Leadbelly. Get you half a gallon of whiskey and get on you a big drunk BluL

Packing a Photograph from Firenze. William H. Matchett. In the fall of this house all houses stand condemned. NePoEA

Packing in with a Man. Judith McCombs. Less shelter, more fear LTB

Pact. Kenneth Fearing. And on that day, and in that place, we will try again, and this time we/shall win. CMoP

A Pact. Ezra Pound. Let there be commerce between us. AmPP; ELU; LiTA; NePA; NoAm; NOBA; OxBA; PoPl; TAP

The Pact. Larry Rubin. Once again, I trace my signature in red. AMV-81

Pad, Pad. Stevie Smith. The years have taken from me. Softly I go now, pad pad. ELU

The Padda Song. Anonymous. Doun i' the meadow, where we twa met. GBP

Paddle Your Own Canoe. Sarah Knowles Bolton. But, if you succeed, you must/Paddle your own canoe. FaFP

Paddling Song. Anonymous. They are all crying. PBA

Paddy Biran's Song. Paddy Biran. dynamite which exploded CBAP

Paddy Doyle. Anonymous.
And pay Paddy Doyle for his boots. AmSS

We'll bowse her up and be done! ShS

Paddy, Get Back. Anonymous.
Oh, wasn't that a bunch of hoodlums/For to take a ship around Cape Horn! AmFP; AmSS
Rise tacks 'n' sheets, 'n' main s'l haul! ShS

Paddy Murphy. Anonymous. They drank his health in ice-cold beer that/ night! PV

Paddy O'Rafther. Samuel Lover. In feeding the hungry and cheering the sad,/Paddy O'Rafther! HBV 1-2; StPo

Paddy's Metamorphosis. Thomas Moore. "Good Lord! only think,–black and curly already!" OnYI

Paddy West. Anonymous.
And we'll think of the cold nor'westers/That we had in Paddy West's! ShS
If he'll ask you: "Were you ever at sea?' tell him: "Three times/around Cape Horn.' OBSS

Paddy Works on the Railway. Anonymous. Oh, poor Paddy works on the railway. AmSS

Padraic O'Conaire–Gaelic Storyteller. Frederick Robert Higgins. And only the young winds cry. OBMV; OnYI; OxBI

The Padstow Night Song. Anonymous. On the merry morning of May. GBP

Paean. Jonathan Henderson Brooks. Oh, heaven is where she stands! CDC

Paean to Eve's Apple. James Liddy. And rechart the stars and the sins. CIP

Pagan Epitaph. Richard Middleton. Dreaming, dreaming pleasantly. OBVV

The Pagan Isms. Claude McKay. ...He will lead me and no man/Can violate or circumvent His plan. BPo

Pagan Prayer. Alice Brown. March with us, heroes! WGRP

A Pagan Reinvokes the Twenty-Third Psalm. Robert Leopold Wolf. The cup that runneth over still remains. HBMV; TrPWD

The Pagans Wild Confesse the Bonds. Roger Williams. Of divine Nature of his God,/And blest eternall Maker. SCAP

Page. Sandra McPherson. ...lest he believe you say more than an ingenuous alpha-/bet, a cruel child of a language. PoA

Page from a Diary. Desmond O'Grady. And shut the lot out in firm precaution. NoAm

The Page of Illustrations. Peter Schjeldahl. You know it–you are welcome to it. I close, and go in peace. ANYP

A Page's Road Song. William Alexander Percy. A singing page I'll be/ Here, in Thy springtime,/Jesu. TrPWD; YeAr

The Pageant. John Greenleaf Whittier. The living jewels of the spring! AmLP

The Pageant of Seaman. Mary C. G. Byron. To the sun unsetting their flag is streaming, answering/flame with flame. HBV 1-2

Pageant Verses. Sir Thomas More. Qui dabit eternam nobis pro munere vitam/In permansuro ponite vota deo. AAS

Pagett, M. P. Rudyard Kipling. And I prayed to the Lord to deliver another one into my hand. BrPo

Pain. Thomas Edward Brown. ...giving us the poles/That are His own, not merely balanced strife. PeD

Pain. James Henry. Only take thy fingers off me.' NOBV

Pain. St. John Lucas. Grant me, O Gods, to prize aright/Sorrow, since sorrow gives me sight. HBV 1-2

Pain. Elsie Robinson. Opportunity, a privilege, a challenge–to the God that/gropes within me. PoToHe

Pain. George William Russell. Yet his soul within is sweet. MoBrPo

Pain. Edith Sodergran. love, solitude, and the face of death. PBWP; WPOW

Pain. Leonora Speyer. Blinded, I grope along–/To song! HBMV

Pain. Alfonsina Storni. to feel the perennial forgetfulness of the sea. WPOW

Pain. Robert Wrigley. and another creature's belly forever. AMV-81

Pain for a Daughter. Anne Sexton. and I saw her, at that moment,/in her own island, and I knew that she/knew. SoSe

Pain Has an Element of Blank. Emily Dickinson. New periods of pain. CBEP; DiPo; LiTM; MoAB; MoAmPo

Pain in All Love. Coventry Patmore. To the thorn'd brow that makes the heavens pale. FaBoEE

Pain Paint. Peter Minck. All as to the benefit/Derived by the use of PAIN PAINT. FaBoUs

A Painful Love Song. Yehuda Amichai. stuck deeply into the world's flesh,/each one at his place. LLLT

The Painful Plough. Anonymous. Not a man that you can mention/Can live without the plough. OBET

Painkillers. Thom Gunn. –of feeling no pain? AMV-81

Painlessly out of Ourselves. William Page. Like two black birds in flight. AMV-81

Pains and Gains. Edward, Earl of Oxford De Vere. But who sits still and holdeth fast the nets. ElL

The Pains of Sleep. Samuel Taylor Coleridge. And whom I love, I love indeed. CBEP; ERoP 1-2; NCEP; OAEP; OBNC; OBRV; SeCePo; SyP; TEP

The Paint Box. Emile Victor Rieu. Watching a unicorn drinking the dew. SO

The Painted Ceiling. Amy Lowell. It is only because you are short. OBAL

A Painted Fan. Louise Chandler Moulton. The soft, south wind of memory blows. AA

Painted Head. John Crowe Ransom. The olive garden for the nightingales. AP; CoBMV; CrMA; LiTA; LiTM; MoAB; MoAmPo; MoPo; MoVE; NoAm; NOBA; NoP; OxBA

The Painted Hills of Arizona. Edwin Curran. Like some great colored wall of sudden lightning! BPAW; HBMV

The Painted Lady. Margaret Danner. ...my huge/peach paper rose, or lavender sea-laced fan? BPo

Painted Passages. Gail N. Harada. to another side/of home. BrSi

A Painted Whore, the Mask of Deadly Sin. William Lithgow. Sweet fair without, and stinking foul within. OBTV

The Painter. John Ashbery. As though his subject had decided to remain a prayer. HaCAP; NOBA; NoP; SOTW

The Painter. Robert Fitzgerald. And art unfleshed desire. MoVE

The Painter Dreaming in the Scholar's House. Howard Nemerov. The same dream that then flared before intelligence/When light went forth looking for the eye. PoDr

A Painter in New England. Charles Wharton Stork. But the landscape of New England holds a rapture hard/to win. HBMV

The Painter in the Lion Cage. Betti Alver. yet never will be saved from the majestic brute/I drew myself. BoWoP

The Painter's Mistress. James Elroy Flecker. And in dark hollow tresses, gold. BrPo

The Painter Who Pleased Nobody and Everybody. John Gay. Each found the likeness in his thought. BeLS

The Painters. Judith Hemschemeyer. ...sealed thick and tight and safe/with paint and piss and lemonade. Psk

Painters. Muriel Rukeyser. a woman among them, painting. EyDe

Painting. A. C. Jacobs. What he utters/Will touch/The depths of survival. VWA

Painting by Chimes. Bernadette Mayer. a line without position/has brushed a stroke with its return. ANYP

Painting of a Lobster by Picasso. Hy Sobiloff. On a checkered table cloth, blue and white. NePA

Painting of a White Gate and Sky. Louise Erdrich. You sister/You heart of grey snow. TWSS

Painting of my Father. Padraic Fallon. ...taking over/The whole south of England at a blow. NOBI

Painture. Richard Lovelace. But perish they and their effigies. CaPo

A Pair. Karl Gjellerup. Lo! the world is born again. PoPl

A Pair. May Swenson. as when light-/browed, swimming,/he leads. RFM

A Pair of Fireflies. Stephen Shu Ning Liu. her eyes blink, tirelessly winking. BrSi

A Pair of Lovers. Jeanne Robert Foster. The resurrection will be/Finding myself yours again. HBMV

A Pair of Wings. Stephen Hawes. Crye (thee/Hy MeEL

Paired Lives. W. R. Rodgers. ...and in/Its own reticence rests. CIP

The Paisley Ceiling. Lila Arnold. a coral paisley cobra. IHMS

The Paisley Officer. *Anonymous.*
And as their life's blood ebbed away it mingled in one stream. ShS
So they closed their eyes to the earth and skies on India's burning shore. ShS

Paistin Fionn. Sir Samuel Ferguson. If you would come with me, brown girl, sweet. OxBI

Paiute Ponies. Jim Barnes. then drop once more into centuries or dreams. CDW

Palabras Carinosas. Thomas Bailey Aldrich. I'll have to say Good-night again! AA; HBV 1-2

Palabras Grandiosas. Bayard Taylor. Yet I am yourn, and you are mine! OBAL

Palace. Dorothy Vena Johnson. And spooky shadows creep. GoSl

Palace Dancer, Dancing at Last. Rayna Green. ...stories/that made us dream over her/shattered breath TWSS

The Palace for Teeth. Abigail Luttinger. think of your roots. AMV-80

The Palace of Art. Alfred, Lord Tennyson.
A haunt of ancient Peace. UnPo
Perchance I may return with others there/When I have purged my guilt. EnLi 1-2; MaVP; OAEP; VLP
Their moon-led waters white. FaBoPP

The Palace of Honor. Gavin Douglas. Thus I bewaill my faitis repugnant,/Inconstant warld and qwheill contrarious. PoEL 1-5

The Palace of Humbug. Lewis (Charles Lutwidge Dodgson) Carroll. That horrid dream of marble halls! FaBoNo

The Palace of Truth. William Langland. And may lead in whom she loveth as her love liketh. ACP

A Palace Poem. Hsueh Feng. Eunuchs in court-dress preparing a bed. LiTW

Palaces of Gold. Leon Rosselson. Invisible fingers will mould/Palaces of gold. OBET

Palais des Arts. Louise Gluck. ...begin/as male and female, thrust and ache. MAYP

Palamon and Arcite, III: "Parts of the whole are we; but God the whole. John Dryden. To make a vertue of Necessity. NAs

The Palatine. Willa Cather. Back to your play, little brother. HBMV

The Palatine. John Greenleaf Whittier. Of the blazing wreck of the Palatine! EtS; MOS

The Pale Blue Casket. Oliver Pitcher. Rock, rock, rock the casket here in the moonlight. NNP; PoBA; TTY

Pale Is Death. Joachim Du Bellay. Like death, but seeing it, affects a soul/Of gentleness, if sweet death seek that goal. LiTW

Palermo, Mother's Day, 1943. William Belvin. ...the vibrations/Of distant propellers meaning no malice but death. PoPl

Palestine. John Greenleaf Whittier. On the heart's secret altar is burning the same! WBLP

Palimpsest. Hyman Edelstein. ...Is it Codes Ur? Or Codex Babylon? CaP

Palindrome. Lisel Mueller. with both of us looking the other way. IHMS

A Palinode. Edmund Bolton. O! what is praise, pomp, glory, joy, but so/As shine by fountains, bubbles, flowers, or snow? ElL; InvP; OBSC; PoEL 1-5; PrIm

Palinode. Oliver St. John Gogarty. "A gentle man on Earth/And gentle 'mid the Shades. OBMV

A Palinode. Robert Greene. My time is loosely spent, and I undone. OBSC

Palinode. James Russell Lowell Floats down, - "Auf Wiedersehen!" AA

Palinode. Maura Stanton. my mother, combing her long hair, looking/curiously at the white, shrouded branches. MAYP

Palladium. Matthew Arnold. And while it lasts, we cannot wholly end. GTBS-P; MaVP; OAEL 1-2; OAEP; OBNC; PPP; VLP

Pallid Cuckoo. David Campbell. And fill and overflow the heart. CBAP; PoAu 1-2

The Pallid Thunderstricken Sigh for Gain. Alfred, Lord Tennyson. And skins the colour from her trembling lips. TW

Pallor. Agnes Mary Frances (Mme Emile Duclaux) Robinson. Nor shall the lutes of Eden avail/To let them dream they are not dead. NOBV

The Palm. Roy Campbell. To sing with the silver hosannahs of rain. MoBrPo

Palm House, Botanic Gardens. George Hetherington. This tomb, this dungeon: O castrated trees! NeIP

Palm Leaves of Childhood. G. Adali-Mortti. those whispering leaves behind the slit/on the cabin wall of childhood's/dreaming and becoming. PBA

The palm of my hand. Fumi Saito. it becomes cold and hardened/and only slightly shrunken. BoWoP

Palm of the Hand. Rainer Maria Rilke. fills them with having arrived. NU

Palm Sunday. Francis Jammes. And where I heard the good priest say the Passion. CAW

Palm-Sunday. Henry Vaughan. But one green Branch and a white robe. AtBAP

A Palm-Sunday Hymn. William Herebert. Queme thee thenne, milsful King, oure offringe of this song. MeEL

Palm Sunday: Naples. Arthur Symons. Carry a palm for me. BrPo

The Palm Tree. Abd-ar-Rahman I. May the beneficent rains besought by the poor/Never forsake you. AWP

The Palm-Tree and the Pine. Richard Monckton, Lord Houghton Milnes. As these young lovers face to face/Renew their early vows! HBV 1-2

Palm Trees. Rex Warner. across the tremendous oceans of the Milky Way. OBTV

The Palm Willow. Robert Bridges. There the Spring-goddess cowers in faint attire/Of frightened fire. VLP

The Palmer. William Langland. And walked full wide in wet and in dry. ACP

The Palmer's Ode. Robert Greene. The way to good is never late.' CTC; EnRePo; OBSC

Palms and Myrtles. Eleazar Ben Kalir. "Blessed art Thou for evermore." TrJP

Palo Alto: The Marshes. Robert Hass. ...Citizens are rising/to murder in their moral dreams. NPGG

The Palomino Stallion. Alden Nowlan. fighting and pleading/to be let out. BoAnP; PH; PoL

The Paltry Nude Starts on a Spring Voyage. Wallace Stevens. Across the spick torrent, ceaselessly,/Upon her irretrievable way. HaCAP

Pamela in Town. Ellen Mackay Hutchinson Cortissoz. And won her faith, her love, her beauty. AA; HBV 1-2

Pan and Luna. Robert Browning. ...what the after age/Knows and names a pine, a nation's heritage. VLP

Pan and Syrinx. W. R. Rodgers. Her only answer from the reed he blew. NMP

Pan and the Cherries. Paul Fort. Let us adore Pan, god of the world! AWP

Pan-Asian Holiday Tour. Luis Syquia. of human joy &/sorrow... BrSi

Pan Cogito's Thoughts on Hell. Zbigniew Herbert. ...His artists are guaranteed peace,/good food and total isolation from infernal life. FaBoPV

Pan in Wall Street. Edmund Clarence Stedman. The quarter sounded from the steeple. AA; AnAmPo; HBV 1-2

Pan Loved His Neighbour Echo–but That Child. Moschus. That when ye love, the like return ye prove not. OBVE

Pan-Pipes. Patrick Reginald Chalmers. Piping a magic of March,/Just as he did long ago! HBMV

Pan Piping. Thomas Stanley. In a well order'd measure beat the ground. FaBoEE

Pan's Song. John Lyly. That still my Syrinx' lips I kiss. ELP; OBSC; ViBoPo

Pan with Us. Robert Frost. Play? Play?–What should he play? OxBA

Panama. Amanda T. Jones. Let all men pass who come in love. PAH

Panama. James Jeffrey Roche. But–the hand that ope'd the gate/Shall forever hold the key! MC; PAH

The Panama Limited. Booker White. The train/I'm riding, it don't burn no coal/Mmmmmmmmmmmmmmmmmmmm. BluL

The Pancake Collector. Jack Prelutsky. It is time that I pour out the batter/and bake up a few hundred more. OBCA

The Panchatantra: Fool and False. Anonymous. Shun him from the start. AWP

The Panchatantra: Kings. Anonymous. And rivers, and women, and kings. AWP

The Panchatantra: Poverty. Anonymous. 'Twas better to be dead than poor. AWP

The Panchatantra: The Penalty of Virtue. Anonymous. The world takes rare and little note/Of any plucky deed. AWP

The Panchatantra: True Friendship. Anonymous. 'Tis death, death only, sets a measure. AWP; LiTW

Pancho Villa. Lou Lipsitz. So, old truculence–our thundercloud, our rainbow. NCSH

Pandora and the Moon. Merrill Moore. And if she succeeds in that then she succeeds. MoAmPo

Pandora's Song. William Vaughn Moody. As on my heavenly hills. AnFE; APA

Pandosto: In Praise of his Loving and Best-Beloved Fawnia. Robert Greene. Shine in my Arms, and set thou in my Breast. AtBAP

A Panegyric. John Grubham, and Henry Hall. Howe. Must serve their masters, though they damn their souls. APAS

Panegyric. Harris Lenowitz. Feet for glue or cloven feet or hooves/that split the world from knowing too much VWA

A Panegyric on Geese. Francis Sylvester ("Father Prout") Mahony. Encourage peace, and take to heart/A goose. OnYI

A Panegyric on Nelly (excerpt). John Wilmot, Earl of Rochester. She who no equal has, must be alone. UnTE

A Panegyric on the Author of "Absalom and Achitophel." Anonymous. And reign the Prince o'th' Air in which it flies. APAS

A Panegyric to Sir Lewis Pemberton. Robert Herrick. And when wise poets shall search out to see/Good men, they find them all in thee. CaPo

A Panegyric upon Oates. Richard Duke. Oates being to this happy nation/The mystic emblem of salvation. APAS

A Panegyrick to My Lord Protector. Edmund Waller. While all your Neighbor Princes unto you/Like Joseph's Sheaves pay reverence and bow. OBS

Panegyrick upon O. Cromwell. Edmund Waller. With bending Sails each vessel of our Fleet: SeCV 1-2

Pangloss's Song. Richard Wilbur. And gained in service of our fair/And universal Queen. AP; NePoAm-2; NLV; NoAm; OxBC

The Pangolin. Marianne Moore. that comes into and steadies my soul. AP; CoBMV; CrMA; FaBoWP; HAP; NoAm; NOBA; PBWP

Pangur Ban. Anonymous. I get wisdom day and night/Turning darkness into light. AnIL; FaBoCh; LoGBV; NOBI; OnYI; OxBI

Panhandle Cob. Anonymous. How Cob gave his life for the kiddy an' went straight up to glory. CoSo

Panic. Lloyd Davis. If this is where I die/I want someone to know. WOLT

Panic. Archibald MacLeish.
Man's fate is a drum! MoAmPo
What shadow hidden or/Unseen hand in our midst/Ceaselessly touches our faces? MoAmPo

Pannyra of the Golden Heel. Albert Samain. Pannyra naked in a flash divine! AWP

Panope. Edith Sitwell. And the first music heard among the trees. MoAB; MoBrPo

Pans Anniversarie. Ben Jonson. This is the Shepherds Holy-day. OBS

The Pansy. Samuel Hoffenstein. And that you got it from your mother. DBV

Pansy. Mary Effie Lee Newsome. Of the softest flower that grows! CDC

The Pansy and the Prayer-Book. Mathilda Betham Edwards. Come like this flower between thy God and thee.' OBVV

The Panther. Anonymous. And when the poor elephant suffers from bile,/Then tenderly lace up his stays! NA

Panther. Sam Cornish. his life runs through/them PoBA

The Panther. Ogden Nash. Don't anther. MoShBr; OBAL; OBCA; SoPo; TiPo

The Panther. Rainer Maria Rilke. And ceases, in the heart, to be. LiTW; NU; PoPl

Panther and Peacock. Gwen Harwood. ...feathers, glistening warm/with his own heartstain, fell through infinite space. CBAP; PoAu 1-2

Panther Man. James A. Emanuel. if THAT'S the way he is/even yr GHOST/can take m. BPo

Pantisocracy. Samuel Taylor Coleridge. And see the rising Sun, and feel it dart/New rays of pleasance trembling to the heart. EnRP

Pantomime. Paul Verlaine. And in her heart a voice that sighs. AWP; SyP

Pantomime Diseases. Dannie Abse. and not hooked by Captain Hook but by/that ponce, Peter Pan! All the rest is fiction. DFT

Pantoum. John Ashbery. For they must have motion/Through the vague snow of many clay pipes. SM

Papa above. Emily Dickinson. While unsuspecting Cycles/Wheel solemnly away! AmPP; FM

Papa John. Jorge De Lima. It looks like the witchcraft of Papa John. TTY

Papa Love Baby. Stevie Smith. But I think I was somewhat to blame. DBV; SBG

Papa's Letter. Anonymous. "Papa's letter" was with God. WeW

Paper Anarchist Addresses the Shade of Nancy Ling Perry. George Woodcock. Terrible children, comrades, enemies. NOBC

The Paper Cutter. David Ignatow. "I will buy a house/and then I will lie down in it/and not get up all day," he laughs. CTBA

The Paper Kite (excerpt). Samuel Bowden. With her alike concludes th' advent'rous flight. NOEC

The Paper Lantern. Tennessee Williams. My sister was quicker at everything but I. CTBA

Paper Matches. Paulette Jiles. We come bearing supper,/our heads on fire. NOBC

Paper Men to Air Hopes and Fears. Robert Francis. A smooth folder in a steel file. LCAP

Paper Mill. Joseph Kalar. "Who could believe it? Who could believe it?" AnAmPo

The Paper Nautilus. Marianne Moore. ...as if they knew love/is the only fortress/strong enough to trust to. FaBoWP; VGW

Paper of Pins. Anonymous. And I'll not marry you. ABF; AmFP; BFSS; BLSo; FSW

Paper Words. William Franklin. I still take tigers/safely home. LFAC

Papermill Graveyard. Ben Belitt. ...and delivers/our unhaunted world to the Prince of Darkness! NYBP

The Paperweight. Gjertrud Schnackenberg. Still, I must try to think a little of it,/With so much winter in my head and hand. SM

Paperweight Escape. Stephen Todd Booker. thank you, my friend./thank you. LFAC

Paphnutius (excerpt). Hroswitha von Grandersheim. till she sheds her rough goatskin/and puts on the soft fleece of a lamb WPOW

Paphos. Lawrence Durrell. May taste in its reproachful roar/The ancient relish of her sun. NYBP

Papio. Eric Chock. and she wants you still. BrSi

The Paps of Dana. James Stephens. I think the mountains ought to be/Taught a little modesty. NoAm

The Paps of Jura. Andrew Young. Who climb, a desperate lover,/With hand and knee. PoSH

Parable. W. H. Auden. If it were not reminded/By days when I forget to wind it. FaBoCo

Parable. Peggy Bennett. Their fathers' mothers, daughters, and wives. ELU

A Parable. George L. Kress. And I blow horns–and I can't hear. STF

A Parable. James Russell Lowell. "The images ye have made of me!" PGD

Parable. Robert Pack. And the animals came forth and licked my hands. NePoEA-2

Parable. William Soutar. They curse; they strike; they break the wall/Which buries them beneath its fall. HaMV

Parable. Richard Wilbur. ...his horses's shoes/Were heavy, and he headed for the barn. OBSP

Parable: November. Stephen Tapscott. sack beside the fragrant apple/bushel under my back stoop! FAZ

The Parable of the Old Man and the Young.   Wilfred Owen.   But the old man would not so, but slew his son,/And half the seed of Europe, one by one.   FaBoRV

Parabola.   A. D. Hope.   I have this thing, and only this, to do.   NOAV; PoA

Paracelsus.   Robert Browning.
As when a queen, long dead, was young.   AnFE; GTBS; MyFE; OBEV; OBRV; WHA
Our work is done; we have no heart/to mar our work, we cried.   OBRV
Who should be saved by them and joined with them.   WGRP
Whom the shy fox from the hill/Arouses...   OBRV

Parachute.   Dwight Okita.   A nightlight turns its seashell back to the room.   BrSi

Parachute.   Stanley Snaith.   Down to firm, century-anchored earth, to pace/In safety amid the treacheries of space.   HaMV

Parachute Descent.   David Bourne.   ...So you can stay/In the sky, boy, and have no fear.   WaP

Parachutes, My Love, Could Carry Us Higher.   Barbara Guest.   ...I am closer to you/Than land and I am in a stranger ocean/Than I wished.   NeAP

Parachuting Thoor Ballylee (parody).   William Zaranka.   Heart, star, rood, rose, swan, gyre, and Ballylee.   BXAP

The Parachutist.   Jon Anderson.
...as those/who imagine the silence of a guest/to be mysterious, or wrong.   NYBP
who imagine the silence of a guest/to be mysterious, or wrong.   AmPA; LiSp

The Parade.   Ashton Greene.   World of make-believe, live as children–the/Parade.   NePoAm

A Parade.   Mary Catherine Rose.   A-rum-a-tee-tum-a-tee-tum-/a-tee-tum.   SoPo

Parade's End.   Barbara Guest.   if I can squeeze out of my eyes/enough water. Water.   PoM

Paradigm.   Babette Deutsch.   Tree, tree in the darkness/Of air, of water. Still. And alone.   TrJP

The Paradigm.   Allen Tate.   Hate is its ignorant paradigm.   NOBA

Paradigms of Fire.   Brian Swann.   of skin the broken interdiction/of touch   AmPA

Paradise.   Willis Barnstone.   He saw Flame/he saw flame.   VWA

Paradise.   Chana Bloch.   We keep our heads down like burrowing animals/that can't see in the daylight.   VWA

Paradise.   Immanuel Di Roma.   Homely old hags always snoring?   TrJP

Paradise.   Frederick William Faber.   All rapture through and through,/In God's most holy sight.   HBV 1-2

Paradise.   George Herbert.   And such beginnings touch their END.   BoLiVe; OAEL 1-2; SeCP; TrGrPo

Paradise.   Christina Georgina Rossetti.   To have my part with all the saints,/And with my God.   HBV 1-2; OxBoCh; WGRP

Paradise.   E. N. Sargent.   Put your arms around me. Our winter is real.   NYBP

Paradise: A Hindoo Legend.   George Birdseye.   "Begone! we'll have no fools in paradise!"   HBV 1-2

Paradise Lost.   John Milton.
Abject and lost, lay these, covering the flood,/Under amazement of their hideous change.   LiTB
Abominable, inutterable, and worse/Than fables yet have feign'd, or fear conceiv'd.   MyFE
Accursed, and in a cursed hour he hies. ATP; EBEV; EnLi 1-2; OAEP; WHA
Adorns him, colour'd with the Florid hue/Of Rainbows and Starrie Eyes.   PB
...Advise if this be worth/Attempting, or to sit in darkness here/Hatching vain empires.   FaBoPV
...After short silence then/and summons read, the great consult began.   OAEL 1-2
Amongst innumerable stars.   WHA
...and in the ascending scale/Of heaven the stars that usher evening rose.   NIP
And justify the ways of God to men. FaBoRV; FiP; NAWM 1-2; PoEL 1-5
...and never shall my harp thy praise/Forget, nor from thy Father's praise disjoin.   ILwL
And o'er the dark her Silver Mantle threw.   FaBoRV; MOON
And of their vain contest appeared no end.   EmL; MBW 1-2; NoP; OAEL 1-2; TrCP
And summons read, the great consult began.   ATP; MBW 1-2; OAEP
And sweet, reluctant, amorous delay.   ErPo
And waking cri'd, This is the Gate of Heav'n.   EBEV
And what is else not to be overcome?   WHA
As Man ere long, and this new World shall know.   BiP; LiTB
At thy right hand voluptuous, as beseems/Thy daughter and thy darling, without end.'   OAEL 1-2
Blest pair; and O yet happiest if ye seek/No happier state, and know to know no more.   BiP; HW; MBW 1-2; POEL 1-5

Both her first born and all her bleating Gods. EBEV
...but fled/Murmuring, and with him fled the shades of night. OAEL 1-2; WHA
But Mercy first and last shall brightest shine. ExPo
By conquering this new world, compels me now/To do what else though damned I should abhor. TW
By their rebellion, from the Books of Life. FiP
...by what means he shall achieve/Mankind's deliverance. FaBoPV
Cast forth redounding smoke and ruddy/flame.... EnL
Draws in, and at his Trunk spouts out a Sea. MOS
Ev'ning and morn solemnized the fifth day. PBBP
Fawning, and licked the ground whereon she trod. FM
For thou art heavenly, she an empty dream. ChTr; EBEV; FaBoPV; FiP; MBW 1-2; OAEL 1-2
...for whom/This glorious sight, when sleep hath shut all eyes? TrGrPo
Founded in righteousness and peace and love/to bring forth fruits joy and eternal bliss. FaBoPV
Frighted the reign of Chaos and old Night. TrGrPo
From what high state of bliss, into what woe!' NOCV
Gorgons and Hydra's, and Chimera's dire. AtBAP; OBS
...happiest if ye seek/No happier state, and know to know no more. EBEV
The haunt of seals and orcs, and sea-mews' clang. FaBoPV
...heard this heavy curse,/Servant of servants, on his vicious race. FaBoPV
His wrath which one day will destroy ye both. EBEV
Hurling defiance toward the vault of Heav'n. PoEL 1-5
Hymns of high praise, and I among them chief. ILwL
I may assert Eternal Providence,/And justify the ways of God to men. NoP; SCV
If not, what resolution from despair. MyFE
In Vallombrosa, where th'Etrurian shades/High overarch't imbowr. FaBoPP
The latter quick up flew, and kickt the beam. SCV
Led on th' eternal Spring. PPP
The middle Tree and highest there that grew,/Sat like a Cormorant... ExPo
Of sorrow unfeigned, and humiliation meek. OAEL 1-2
Of things invisible to mortal sight. AtBAP; ExPo; MBW 1-2; OAEL 1-2; OAEP; SCV; WHA
Regain'd in heav'n, or what more lost in hell? MyFE
Reserved from night, and kept for thee in store.' OAEL 1-2
Save he who reigns above, none can resist. DL
Sense of new joy ineffable diffused... ATP
...sent forth from hearts contrite, in sign/Of sorrow unfeigned, and humiliation meek. NAWM 1-2
The starry flock, allured them, and with lies/Drew after him the third part of Heaven's host. MBW 1-2
That day and night of his destruction/wait!... CoBE
Their number last he sums. MyFE
There wanted yet the master work... FM
They hand in hand with wandering steps and/slow,/Through Eden took their solitary way. EnL; FaBoRV; FiP; HeIP; MyFE; NAWM 1-2; NOCV; OAEL 1-2; PoEL 1-5; SCV
They taste and die: what likelier can ensue? ATP
Uncertain which, in ocean or in air. NIP
Unweaned, unobnoxious to be pain'd/By wound, though from their place by violence mov'd. ExPo
We now debate; who can advise, may speak. NIP
...what may be yet/Regain in Heav'n, or what more lost in Hell? EBEV
When Charlemagne with all his peerage fell/By Fontarabbia. WHA
When Satan still in gaze, as first he stood,/Scarce thus at length failed speech recovered sad. FaBoPV
Who durst defy th' Omnipotent to arms. NIP
Who now triumphs, and in th'excess of joy/Sole reigning holdst the Tyranny of Heav'n. SCV

Paradise Lost: V.   Anthony Hecht.   Given to lewdness and/Rodomontade.   NLV

Paradise Regained.   John Milton.
Affirming it thy star, new-graven in heaven,/By which they knew thee King of Israel born.   PCh
And now wild Beasts came forth the woods to roam.   CABL
Both Paynim, and the Peers of Charlemane.   OBS
For what concerns my knowledge God reveals.   OBS
Home to his Mothers house privat returnd.   CABL
I seek not mine but his/Who sent me, and thereby witness what I am.   LiTB; OBS
...a king complete/Within thyself, much more with empire joined.   ViBoPo
Man fall'n shall be restor'd, I never more.   OBS
Meekly composed awaited the fulfilling.   ISi
On David's Throne, be propheci'd what will.   OBS
So fares it when with truth falsehood contends.   CABL
These only with our Law best form a king.'   OAEL 1-2; OBS
These rules will render thee a king complete/Within thy self, much more with empire joined.   OBTV

This wounds me most (what can it less) that Man,/Man fallen shall be restored, I never more. LiTB

To gain a Scepter, oftest better misst. CABL

Paradise Saved. A. D. Hope. Sterile and impotent and justified. OxBC

Paradisi Gloria. Thomas William Parsons Through the bright, busy, and eternal day. AA

The Paradox. *Anonymous.*
Props of the church, and pillars of the throne? APAS
You may find this advertisement: "Wanted–A girl to/cook." ShM

Paradox. Benjamin K. Bennett. that what counts in a poem is brevity. PoL

The Paradox. John Donne. Here dead men speake their last, and so/do I;/Love-slaine, loe, here I lye. OAEP

The Paradox. Paul Laurence Dunbar. Down where the Dream Woman dwells. PoBA

Paradox. Angelina Weld Grimke. As kisses are to love. CDC

Paradox. Vassar Miller. So will Your gifts of sight and hearing plunder/My eyes with lightning and my ears with thunder. NePoEA

A Paradox. William Herbert, Earl of Pembroke. Ethiopes' lips are soft as thine. EIL

The Paradox. Francesca Yetunde Pereira. ...And gods/are silent. PBA

A Paradox. Aurelian Townsend. 'Tis much to dye; 'tis more to fynde/Two of my minde. AnAnS 2; SeCP

The Paradox of Time. Pierre Ronsard. Alas, Time stays,–we go. AWP

Paradox: That Fruition Destroys Love (excerpt). Henry, Bishop of Chichester King. As warm our hands by putting out the fire. ErPo

Paradox: The Birds. Karl Shapiro. To love you for your turn and wheel and glide and song. CrMA

Paradoxes and Oxymorons. John Ashbery. ...The poem is you. NoP

A Paragraph. Hayden Carruth. ...we are your brothers and sisters/only a minute away, a second, a song... FAZ

A Paragraph Made Up of Seven Sentences Which Have Entered My Memory... Chuck Wachtel. ...Atomic Energy, The Circus, Abominable Snowman, Napo/leon and More... APU

Parallax. Maxwell Anderson. Than light that left Andromeda/Nine hundred thousand years ago. NYBP

Parallel Texts. Robert Kelly. yielding to dark:/the carolla. CoPo

Paralytic. Sylvia Plath. Drunk on its own scents,/Asks nothing of life. FaBoWP

Paranoia. Michael Dennis Browne. you know you have died. AmPA

Paranoia in Crete. Gregory Corso. I forfeit the Echinadian Isles– NeAP

Paraphrase. Hart Crane. Among bruised roses on the papered wall. MoVE

A Paraphrase from the French. Matthew Prior. Whilst you, great sir, at Notre Dame,/Te Deum sing in quiet!' OxBoLi

Paraphrase of Luther's Hymn. Frederic Henry Hedge His Kingdom is forever. AA

A Paraphrase on Thomas a Kempis. Alexander Pope. Speak, gracious Lord, oh speak; Thy servant hears. GoBC; OBEC; TrPWD

Parasitosis. Ronda Davis. been operating on nubs since it first called us niggahs. JB

Paratrooper. John Giorno. the point/to pull/the ripcord. ANYP

The Parcae, or Three Dainty Destinies: The Armillet. Robert Herrick. "I care not now how soon 'tis done/Or cut, if cut by you." CaPo

Parchman Farm Blues. Booker White. But I hope some day/I will/overcome BluL

Parcy Reed. *Anonymous.* Whae ever rides i' the Border side/Will mind the laird o' the Troughend. OxBB

Pardon. Julia Ward Howe. Turns the reft bosom of Nature, his mother,/low sighing,/Greatest, forgive! PAH

The Pardon. Richard Wilbur. I beg death's pardon now. And mourn the dead. NePoEA; NIP; NoAm; NOBA; NoP

Pardon, Old Fathers. William Butler Yeats. Nothing but that to prove your blood and/mine. OAEP

The Pardoner's Sermon. Sir David Lyndsay. I trow ye be nocht wyse. BSV

Parentage. Alice Meynell. And she who slays is she who bears, who bears. SBG

Parentage. William Stafford. I'd just as soon be pushed by events to where I belong. BiP

The Parental Critic. Keith Preston. We lay it gently on our lap/And dust its little jacket. NLV

A Parental Ode to My Son. Thomas Hood. I cannot write unless he's sent above. FiBHP; HBV 1-2; PoLf

Parenthood. John Farrar. We, too, will have children who do not behave! OHIP

Parents. Vincent Buckley. ...barely/Visible in the window's copper sheen. CBAP

Parents. William Meredith. to our uncomprehending children and grandchildren. FYAP

The Parents of Psychotic Children. Marvin Bell. are just practical and do not sing,/like the crazy birds, to their offspring. SUW

The Parents-Without-Partners Picnic. Ted Schaefer. our cigarettes so crazy in the dark. FAZ

Parfum Exotique. Charles Baudelaire. Mixed in my soul with the song the mariner sings. AWP

The Pariah's Prayer. Johann Wolfgang von Goethe. We others too, to sing your praises/Need to hear just such a wonder. ILwL

Paring the Apple. Charles Tomlinson. Compelling a recognition. CMoP; NePoEA-2; NMP; OxBTC

Paris. Gregory Corso. Dollhouse of Mama War. VGW

Paris. Jane Garnett. and holds his hand out for a franc. AMV-80

Paris. Gertrud Kolmar. Like the head of an adder,/Black with veins, a fist... PBWP

Paris. Arthur Symons. Offers herself, a rose, and craves of us/A rose's place among our memories. NOBV; SyP

Paris at Night. Tristan Corbiere. On a bed of the Morgue...With his eyes wide open! SyP

Paris by Night. Joseph Milbauer. The river and all that it contains,/Including my own reflection. VWA

Paris in the Snow. L. Sedar-Senghor. Also because of the hands of dew that lie on my burning cheeks/at night. PBA

A Paris Nocturne. William Sharp. And the sands of the dunes are scattered/In the scud of the spray. SyP

Paris: The Seine at Night. Charles Divine. Soul of you that comes by night, never goes away. HBMV

Paris: This April Sunset Completely Utters. Edward Estlin Cummings. Night, argues/with certain houses NAMP; SOTW

Parish. Norman Dubie. Or passing through it, all signs/Of them vanishing into the hills. MAYP

The Parish Church. Julio Herrera Reissig. While through the vestry doorway come the cries/From out the barnyard and the gallant crowing. CAW

The Parish Register. George Crabbe.
And consolation for their sorrow found. EnPE; OAEL 1-2; OBRV
Half his delighted offspring mount his knees. OBRV
I preach for ever; but I preach in vain! OBRV

Parisian Dream. Charles Baudelaire. And a grey sky was drizzling down/Upon this sad, lethargic world. NAWM 1-2

A Parisian Idyl (excerpt). George Moore. ...and we will pass a pleasant week/Together, watching the falling of the leaves. SyP

Parisian Nectar. Gelett Burgess. I prefer another diet. FaBoNo

Parity. Kenneth Rexroth. And pause or stagger slightly/And go about his business. GP

The Park. Robin Blaser. Jessie Whitehead told me they sometimes choose a tree/and kill it, they so mire the branches. CoPo

Park. David Ignatow. ...feel the quiet/and stability they make,/and lasting custom. Psk

The Park. James S. Tippett. As dandelions/On a hill. BrR; SUS; TiPo

The Park at Evening. Leslie Norris. As the park turns gently into evening. DuDa

Park Avenue. Robert Fitzgerald. Sheathing speed in sleep. NYP

The Park in Milan. William Jay Smith. Music fades; the streets are black with flies. CAD; CoAP

Park Pigeons. Melville Cane. Rooks circle in the sun. CAD

Park Poem. Paul Blackburn. to prepare/love later. CoPo

The Parklands. Stevie Smith. High the sun stood in the heavens,/But no shadow followed him. MoBS

Parks and Ponds. Ralph Waldo Emerson. Nor my unseasoned step disturbs/The sleeps of trees or dreams of herbs. PoEL 1-5

Parlement of Foules. Geoffrey Chaucer. And driven awey the longe nightes blake! ATP; CTC; SeCePo

Parley of Beasts. Hugh" (Christopher Murray Grieve) MacDiarmid. At hame it's hard to feel. BoAnP; MoBrPo; NoAm; NoP; OBMV

A Parley with His Empty Purse. Thomas Randolph. Gape on, as they do to be paid, gape on! JCP; OBS

Parleyings with Certain People of Importance in Their Day. Robert Browning. "Omnia non omnibus"–no harm is meant! VLP

The Parliament Dissolved at Oxford. John Ayloffe. Making the people happy, monarch great. APAS

Parliament Hill. Sir Henry Howarth Bashford. Bending like a finger-tip, and beckoning to you. BrR

Parliament Hill Fields. Sir John Betjeman. Sheaves of drooping dandelions to the courts of/Kentish Town. FaBoTw; HaMV; NOBE

Parliament Hill Fields. Sylvia Plath. I enter the lit house. HaCAP

The Parliament of Bees. John Day.
All this I'll do that men with praise may crown/My fame for turning the world upside-down. ViBoPo
As thou in service true shalt be/Unto our crown and royalty. ViBoPo
The blacker are their crimes, he louder sings. ViBoPo

Parliament of Cats. D. J. Enright. Who was a Saint of course! (Genuflecton.) NMP

The Parliament of the Three Ages (excerpt). *Anonymous.* Bedraggled from their dunking when the ducks took to the water. PBBP

The Parliament Soldiers. *Anonymous.*
   The Parliament soldiers are all to be hang'd. GBP
   To see the parliament soldiers go by. OxNR
Parnell. Thomas Michael Kettle. Limned in his blood across your clearing skies/Look up and read: Parnell! AnIV
Parnell. William Butler Yeats. "Ireland shall get her freedom and you still break stone." CMoP
Parochial Theme. Wallace Stevens. Piece the world together, boys, but not with your hands. LiTA
A Parodie. George Herbert. Thou com'st and dost relieve. AnAnS 1; OBS
Parodies of Cole Porter's "Night and Day". Ring Lardner. There's a voice telling me I'm he, the good little egg you meant. OBAL
Parody. Martha Paley Francescato. The eye in the leaf/Wombs BoWoP
A Parody on A Psalm of Life. Oliver Wendell Holmes. Some forlorn and henpecked brother,/When he sees, shall crow again. BLPA
Parody on Thomas Hood's "The Bridge of Sighs." *Anonymous.* Get his half-dollah back,/zzZ. FiBHP
Parole Board. Derek Butler. And they sit there and tell me/I haven't been here long enough. LFAC
Parole Denial. J. Charles Green. i have lost my/stomach/among dead fish LFAC
Paros. Robin Macgowan. ...head, dis-/Membered, floats out over the singing stones. EAS
Parrhasius. Nathaniel Parker Willis May spend itself - what thrice-mocked/fools are we! AA
Parricide. Julia Ward Howe. And the captive's friend/From his ashes makes us freemen still. PAH
The Parrot. Thomas Campbell. Flapped round his cage with joyous screech,/Dropt down, and died. FM; PB
The Parrot. James Elroy Flecker. But that was long ago! FaBoTw
The Parrot. Wilfrid Gibson. Before his soul was stolen by the sea. OBMV
The Parrot. Edward Lucie-Smith. And all the neighbors/Know you swear. BoAnP; SO
The Parrot. John Skelton. Pomp, pride, honor, riches and worldly lust,/Parrot saith plainly shall turn all to dust. ACP
Parrot and Dove. Walter Savage Landor. And every Muse in every tongue/Has heard and prais'd her nightly song. PB
The Parrot and the Carrot We May Easily Confound. Robert Williams Wood. For carrots are unable to engage in conversation. PV
The Parrot Cry. Hugh" (Christopher Murray Grieve) MacDiarmid. For fegs, it's aye high time/The claith was owre the parrot! OxBS
The Parrot Fish. James Merrill. And throwing back its head the sea began to sing. NOBA
Parrot, Fish, Tiger and Mule. Eliezer Greenberg. The mule is a hard worker–and an imbecile. BoAnP
The Parrots. Wilfred Wilson Gibson. And jangling like a bell. CH; RoGo
Parsifal. Paul Verlaine. And oh! the chime of children's voices in the dome. SyP
Parsley. Rita Dove. ...He will/order many, this time, to be killed/for a single, beautiful word. HaCAP
The Parsnip. Ogden Nash. Myself, I find this claim incredible. NePA
Parson Allen's Ride. Wallace Bruce. The parson who came in his one-horse chaise. MC; PAH
Parson Gray. Oliver Goldsmith. But ah! poor parson! when he died,/His breath he could not draw! NA
The Parson Grocer. *Anonymous.* Must be a wretch–a villain,/For any mischief rife. CoMu
Parson's Pleasure. Barry O. Higgs. To allow the spider/To seek its pleasure. PeSA
The Parsons. Thomas Edward Brown. The same's the drones is livin' on the beeses honey. DBV
Part for the Whole. Robert Francis. Part may be more than whole, least may be best. PoA
Part of a Letter. Richard Wilbur. Ca, c'est l'acacia. CMoP
Part of a Novel, Part of a Poem, Part of a Play: The Hero. Marianne Moore. ...This then you may know/as the hero. PoA
A Part of an Ode. Ben Jonson. Who, ere the first down bloomed on the chin,/Had sow'd these fruits, and got the harvest in. OBEV
The Part of Fortune. Ann Sanfedele. I would not have it so/But for the stars. AMV-81
Part of Mandevil's Travels. William Empson. Adam come here for; and recités my motto.). AtBAP
Part of Plenty. Bernard Spencer. No, but lovely in that way. ErPo; GBL; LiTB; LiTL; LiTM; MoLP
Part of the 9th Ode of the 4th Book of Horace... Horace. That Man is ready to defend/With Life his Country, or his Friend. OBVE
Part of the Darkness. Isabella Gardner. Bereaved, we started home, leaving that animal there. BoAnP
Part of the Vigil. James Merrill. Nothing else mattered. NoAm

A Part-Sequence for Change. Robert Duncan. and the ascendancy of the shadow/in the blossoming mass. VGW
Part Winter. Marilyn Bowering. We meet at the white where hill and sky meet,/and black birds gather in and storm. CaPN
Parta Quies. Alfred Edward Housman. Sleep on, sleep sound. NOBE; TEP
Parted Love. Dante Gabriel Rossetti. And thy heart rends thee, and thy body endures. MaVP
Parted Lovers. Judah Halevi. Of thy desire, and to the land of thy true belonging. LiTW
Parted Souls. Edward, Lord Herbert of Cherbury. Death unto us must be freedom and rest. AnAnS 2; SeCP
The Parterre. E. H. Palmer. With Madame who is too more sweet/Than every roses buttoning there. FaBoCo; NA; NOBL
The Parthenon. John Heath-Stubbs. Owl-clawed, hooks to the heart. OBTV
Parthenope. Barnabe Barnes. England, in one small subject, such contains. CBEP
Partial Comfort. Dorothy Parker. May view John Knox in paradise. FaBoCo; OBAL
Partial Draft. Robert B. Shaw. before pursuing its scratchy path again. AMV-81
Partial Eclipse. W. D. Snodgrass. Next morning you had gone. MOON
The Partial Explanation. Charles Simic. To eavesdrop/On the conversation/Of cooks. FiCP; NoP
Partial Resemblance. Denise Levertov. shone in the opening and shutting of your/ingenious blindness. CoAP; NaP
Parting. *Anonymous.* Ah! years may pass, and moons may fleet how many,/Ere we fond lovers meet again. WTO
Parting. Alice Corbin. We shall both lie down/At the foot of the hill, and sleep. BPAW
Parting. Judah Halevi. Of thy departure, when thou wentest forth, it went out/after thee. AWP
Parting. Michael Hogan. If you ever get there, think of me. GP
The Parting. Elizabeth Jennings. The strangeness our last meeting had/And try to force it back. NePoEA-2
Parting. Gerald Massey. One little corner of thy light. HBV 1-2
Parting. Coventry Patmore. Night and day, regret should walk. PoToHe
Parting. Gabriel Preil. she cannot reach me. VWA
Parting. Kathleen Raine. I offer what I can, my living moment,/My human span. LiTL
Parting. William Caldwell Roscoe. I too lie safe beneath his wing. OBVV
The Parting. Sappho. by the brook where we two were not side by side... LiTW
Parting. Shlomo Vinner. Visions of an autumn evening. VWA
A Parting. Wang Wei. But O my prince of Friends, do you? LiTW
Parting. William Butler Yeats. I offer to love's play/My dark declivities. FaBoTw
Parting: 1940. John Frederick Nims. The blood flows one imposed way, and no other. PoA
Parting: A Game. Lynn Sukenick. Double/the empty spaces. NMM
Parting after a Quarrel. Eunice Tietjens. And in my heart I heard the little click/Of a door that closes–quietly, forever. HBMV
Parting as Descent. John Berryman. And shriek with joy in that place beyond prayer. LiTA; MoAmPo
Parting at Dawn. *Anonymous.* 'Tis day and we must part. WTO
Parting at Dawn. John Crowe Ransom. Philosophy was wrong, and you may meet. AnAmPo
Parting at Morning. Robert Browning. And the need of a world of men for me. AWP; CBEP; DiPo; FaBV; FF; FiP; GTBS; HBV 1-2; HeIP; MaVP; MBW 1-2; MCCG; MOS; NOBE; OAEP; OBEV; OBNC; OBSP; OBVV; SoSe; TreFT; UnPo; VLP; WiR
Parting at Morning. Sir Dietmar von Aist. Alas, thou takest all my joy with thee! AWP
Parting Friends. *Anonymous.* I hope we'll meet on Canaan's shore. ABF
Parting from My Son. Evangeline Paterson. your dreams are not enough/to keep me warm. AMV-80
Parting Gift. Elinor Wylie. Put it into your left-hand pocket/And never look inside. LOW; OxBA
The Parting Glass. Philip Freneau. May heaven forbid the Parting Glass! AA; AmP
A Parting Guest. James Whitcomb Riley. "Thanks.–So fine a time! Good night." HBV 1-2; TreFT
The Parting Hour. Olive Custance. Ah! bitter word "Farewell." HBV 1-2
A Parting Hymn. Charlotte Forten. And may we meet again where all/Are blest and freed from every thrall. BlSi
A Parting Hymn We Sing. Aaron R. Wolfe. Until we join the church above,/And know as we are known. AH
Parting in Wartime. Frances Cornford. And now we three in Euston waiting-room. FaBoWP; NIP
The Parting Injunctions. Clarence Day. Are one of those functions/That poison their lives. DBV

Parting is Hard. *Anonymous.* In a murky dream, I see your face again. BoWoP

The Parting of the Ways. Joseph B. Gilder. Be godlike in the will to serve! AA; HBV 1-2; PAH

The Parting Verse, the Feast There Ended. Robert Herrick. Herrick shall make the meddow-verse for/you. SeCV 1-2

Parting with Lucasia: A Song. Katherine ("Orinda") Philips. Since we our Passion have subdu'd,/Which is the strongest thing I know. PeHV

Parting, without a Sequel. John Crowe Ransom. And cold as any icicle. DTC; LiTL; MoAB; MoAmPo; MoVE; OxBA; SoSe

Partings. Charles Guerin. ...bids/Silence, and drinks our soul through closed eye-lids. AWP

Partings. Maria Jane Jewsbury. A heart-sick yearning for the time/When it should never more be spoken. OxBChV

Partly to My Cat. Ellen Bass. I will run,/like you cat,/making deep snow prints,/hearing the crunch. NMM

Partridges. John Masefield. The twilight hears and darkness hears them call. LiSp; OxBTC

Parts. Ziche Landau. they remind me of good friends, old letters,/and of her who gave me my life. VWA

Parts Man. Michael West. hear all the wheels/hiss in the street, turning/anxiously into themselves. AmC

The Parts of a Poet. Wendy Rose. ...parts of me/are a woman who judges. TWSS

The Party. Margaret Avison. No alien unthought breath corrupts/This decorously airless air. PoA

Party. Constance Carrier. What is the archaic now, in a world all future and space? NePoAm-2

The Party. Paul Laurence Dunbar. An' dey ain't no use in talkin', we jes' had one scrumptious/time! AmNP

Party. Donald Justice. Leer and Pinch Me and their kind/Are taking possession of/Our crowded rooms, our empty persons. GP

A Party. Laura E. Richards. While they were quarreling, ate it all. BiCB; SiSoSe; SoPo

The Party. W. R. Rodgers. ...And far doors bang in mind, idly. BIrV

The Party. Jerome Sala. Certain they are blue, without ever looking up at the sky. APU

The Party. Reed Whittemore. "That did be fun!" the youngest shouted, and/ate pies/With wild surmise. CAD; CoAP; ConAP; NCSH

Party at Bannon Brook. Alden Nowlan. ...the icicles/stroked by an amorous sun. NeAC

Party at Hydra. Irving Layton. When she vanishes your hand is a river you swim in forever. HeIP

The Party at the Contessa's House. Brian Robertson. city lights mark the horizon. AMV-80

Party Going. Bill Manhire. going outside with all the others. OCNZ

Party in Winter. Karl Shapiro. Into the castle of the birthday party. PCP

Party Knee. John Updike. A buffered aspirin for a splitting leg. FiBHP

Party Piece. Brian Patten. And all there was between them then/was rain. BoLoP

Parvuli Ejus. Aubrey Thomas De Vere. "God reigns: at His feet earth's Destiny sleeps like a/child." IrPN

Pas de Deux for Lovers. Michael Dransfield. ...Day/is so deep already with involvement. CBAP

Pasa Thalassa Thalassa. Edwin Arlington Robinson. Down where he lies to-night, silent, and under the storms. EtS; LaNeLa; MOS

Paschal Lamb. Robert Hass. ...take them down to the department secretary and have her put/them in the mail. NPGG

Pasquin to the Queen's Statue at St. Paul's, during the Procession... William Shippen. And Mahomet and Mustapha prepare/To stem by force his madness and despair. APAS

The Pass. John Logan. to walk back/alone toward the rock. LCAP

Pass around Your Bottle. *Anonymous.* I spent it for drink, but I never did think/That my fun would ever end. OuSiCo

Pass forth, my wonted cries. Sir Thomas Wyatt. And render love for love,/Which is a just reward. FCP; SiPS

Pass It On! *Anonymous.* How sweet to know the Saviour was/pleased–to see you pass it on! STF

Pass It On. Henry K. Burton. Live for Him, with Him you reign–/Pass it on. BLRP

Pass it on grandson. Ted D. Palmanteer. something/like a hint,/from an/Old Warrior. STE

The Pass of Kirkstone. William Wordsworth. Thy lot, O Man, is good, thy portion, fair! HBV 1-2

Pass to thy Rendezvous of Light. Emily Dickinson. Who slowly ford the Mystery/Which thou hast leaped across! NAWM 1-2

Passage. Hart Crane. Memory, committed to the page, had broke. CMoP; ExPo; MoVE; NoAm; NOBA

Passage. Richard Eberhart. We can't see it, but we feel it all the time. FAZ

Passage. John M. Roderick. "Not yet," he said/And squeezed a thumb into its throat until/I could not breathe. GOYP

Passage of an August. Eithne Wilkins. she was no stranger, love. And none/can drive her out. NeBP

Passage Over Water. Robert Duncan. and within the indestructible night I am alone. NoAm; NOBA

Passage Steamer. Louis MacNeice. And the world and the day are grey and that is all. MOS

Passage to India. Walt Whitman.
O farther, farther, farther sail! AmePo; DiPo; MoRP; PoEL 1-5; TrPWD; TRV; WGRP
The Younger melts in fondness in his arms. ILwL

Passages. Larry Eigner. the grounding of arms/toys, and the blinding gulls NeAP

Passages. David Walker. ...A taking/pains: as though seeing the light. AMV-80

Passenger Pigeons. Robert Morgan. To echo the birdstorms of those early/sunsets, what high river of electron, cell and star? GeTw; MAYP

Passenger Train. Edith Newlin Chase. With its wheels still singing the clickety-clack/Of a hurrying passenger train. SoPo

The Passengers. David Antin. a window an orange a shadow of an/odor. NYBP

Passengers. Denis Johnson. to open its grace and incredible harm/over my life, and I will never die. MAYP; SM

The Passenjare. Isaac H. Bromley. Punch, boys, punch, punch with care,/All in the presence of the passenjare. FiBHP

The Passer. George Abbe. as true as metal, as deftly as surgeon's wrist. LiSp; SD

A Passer By. Robert Bridges.
In the offing scatterest foam, thy white sails crowding. BoC; CMoP; CoBMV; EtS; ForPo; GTBS; HBV 1-2; LiTB; LiTM; MoAB; MoBrPo; MOS; NBM; OAEL 1-2; OAEP; OBEV; OBNC; OBVV; OxBTC; PoPle; SeCeV; WiR
Or lest the burly oarsman turn his prow/Within your guardian isle. BrPo

Passer Mortuus Est. Edna St. Vincent Millay. Just because it perished? CMoP; FaBoWP; MoAmPo; OxBA

Passin Ben Dorain. Alastair Mackie. Aa I can dae/is to pint in homage to the poem/as we drave by its theme and variations. PoSH

Passing and Glassing. Christina Georgina Rossetti. Our doings have been done,/And that which shall be was. OBNC

Passing Away. Christina Georgina Rossetti. Then I answer'd: Yea. GoBC; NoP; OAEL 1-2; OBVV

The Passing Bell. Thomas Heywood. For hark! still, still the bell doth toll/For some but now departed soul. FaBoRV

The Passing Bell. James Shirley. Sad Bell-wether to the rest. ACP

The Passing Bell at Stratford. William Winter. The path whereon his footsteps go. AA

The Passing Flower. Harry Kemp. And still a kiss is sweet! HBMV

Passing into Storm. Patrick Lane. coming like madness in the snow. NOBC

Passing It On. Reg Saner. ...the way/his eyes beat and grow secret/under this strange love/shaken into me. GP

Passing Love. Langston Hughes. You will not stay when summer goes. BiP

The Passing of a Dream. John Clare. When shall my mind awake/In its own loved scenes again. NOBV

The Passing of Arthur. Alfred, Lord Tennyson. And the new sun rose bringing the new year. EBEV; FaBoRV; GTBS; OBNC

The Passing of Arthur (parody). J. C. Squire. That in his final act our old friend Malory/Was obviously playing to the gallery. BXAP

The Passing of Lydia. Horace. And who would hold so cold and old a thing? UnTE

The Passing of March. Robert Burns Wilson. She cast her violets underneath his feet. HBV 1-2

The Passing of the Buffalo. Hamlin Garland. Now, they are gone! BPAW

The Passing of the Forest. William Pember Reeves. For Man's dominion–beauty swept away! AnNZ

The Passing of the Poets. Fear Flatha O Gnimh. Today as in the past/our hopes are with the blood of Rogh. NOBI

The Passing of the Shee after Looking at One of A.E.'s Pictures. John Millington Synge. The weazel, lark and crow. BIrV; FaBoEE; OnYI

The Passing of the Unknown Soldier. Vilda Sauvage Owens. Offer a prayer–a tear. MC

Passing Out. Philip Levine. "Oh, my dark one,/tell of the coming of cold/and of Kings, ancient and ruined." AmPC

Passing Remark. William Stafford. there are so many things admirable people/do not understand. GP

Passing Strange. Alan Bernheimer. Material needs a life of fact/to make a spectacle of/one of these days. APU

The Passing Strange. John Masefield. Our joy, a rampart to the mind. BoLiVe; LiTB; MoAB; MoBrPo; MoPo; OBEV

Passing the Graveyard. Andrew Young. You undressed first and went to bed. DTC

Passing the Masonic Home for the Aged. Herbert Scott. ...Inside, the faces/of ten thousand winters press the panes. PPJ

Passing Through. Annie Johnson Flint. For he saith, "Tjou passest through." BLRP

Passing Visit to Helen. D. H. Lawrence. Break in by making any reply! CMoP

Passion. Galway Kinnell. My new eyes searched the passion of the stars. NePoAm

The Passion. Ralph Knevet. As blood and water issued from thy wound,/ So with thy blood, do Thou my tears compound. JCP

The Passion and Exaltation of Christ. Isaac Watts. And Angels sound with endless Joy/The Saviour and the King. NOCV

Passion and Worship. Dante Gabriel Rossetti. This harp still makes my name its voluntary. MaVP

The Passion Drinker. Anita Endrezze-Probst. But the dead say only the earth endures. VoR

The Passion-Flower. Margaret Fuller. My love gave me a passion-flower. HBV 1-2

The Passion of Christ. Denis Devlin. Oh, come, Unworldly, from the World within! IPY

The Passion of Jesus. *Anonymous.* My saule with sanctes, Salviour resaif,/ Sen that thy Passioun purged my trespas. MeEL

The Passion of Our Lady. Charles Peguy. He had saved the world. ISi

The Passionate Encyclopedia Britannica Reader to His Love. Maggie". That is, I hope, how I'm to you. InMe

The Passionate Pilgrim. William Shakespeare.
Bad is the best, though excellent in neither. EIL
For methinks thou stay'st too long. EIL; FaBoEn; GBL; LiTB; TreFS; UnTE
For now my song is ended. EIL
Thy discontent thou didst bequeath to me. EIL

The Passionate Professor. Bert Leston Taylor. But after dark all cats are gray./Love, it is night! NLV

The Passionate Reader to His Poet. Richard Le Gallienne. And I will give my days i' the sun/For that great song of thine. HBV 1-2

The Passionate Shepherd. Nicholas Breton. Are not these with thousands moe/Than the court of kings do know? ViBoPo

The Passionate Shepherd to His Love. Christopher Marlowe. Then live with me and be my Love. AAS; AnEnPo; AWP; BiP; BoLoP; CTC; DiPo; EIL; ELP; EnL; ExPo; FaBoBe; FaFP; FCP; FF; FPL; GoTF; GTBS; GTBS-P; HAP; HBMV; HBV 1-2; HeIP; HoPM; InPK; InPo; InPS; LiTB; LiTL; LoBV; NIP; NLV; NOBE; NoP; OAEL 1-2; OAEP; OBEV; OBSC; OLR; PAI; PG; PoLf; PoRA; PPoe; PPP; SCV; SeCePo; SeCeV; TreF; TrGrPo; UnTE; ViBoPo; WHA

The Passionate Shepherd to His Love. Delmore Schwartz. And be my night, my warmth, my wife. NIP

The Passionate Sword. Jean Starr Untermeyer. Swing it straighter and higher! HBMV; TrJP; TrPWD

The Passions. William Collins. Confirm the tales her sons relate! EiCP; GoTL; GTBS; GTBS-P; HBV 1-2

The Passions That We Fought With. Trumbull Stickney. That power was once our torture and our lord. NCEP

Passiontide Communion. Katharine Tynan Hinkson. Thou art content and sleepest well. TrPWD

Passive Resistance. Joseph Bruchac. the last coil of wire/was gone, flushed down/a thousand prison toilets. SOTS

Passivity. Mary Elizabeth ("E") Fullerton. Angels nor devils are of these–/ The castaways on velvet ease. BoAV

Passover. Rose Auslander. Plagues and miracles/sand snakes/The lamb the lamb VWA

Passover Dachau. B. Z. Niditch. round an Egyptian wound. AMV-81

Passover Eve. Fania Kruger. And winds are whispering in every shutter. GoYe

The Passover in the Holy Family. Dante Gabriel Rossetti. And Mary culls the bitter herbs ordained. GoBC; MaVP

The Past. William Cullen Bryant. Fills the next grave - the beautiful and young. AA

The Past. Ralph Waldo Emerson. Alter or mend eternal Fact. AmePo; FaBoCh; FPL; LiTA; LoGBV; PoEL 1-5; TAP

Past. John Galsworthy. The stars have twinkled, and gone out. HBV 1-2

The Past. Ralph Hodgson. The Past comes back in the mouth with blood. PoL

Past. Winifred Howells. And to be idle once was no distress. AA

The Past. William Oandasan. and tears stream down laughing Yuki faces/ tens of thousands of years old STE

Past and Present. R. E. Egerton Warburton. Shot like a pellet from his own pop-gun. NOBV

The Past Is Dark with Sin and Shame. Thomas Wentworth Higginson. And man's true aim shall yet be won! AH

The Past Is the Present. Marianne Moore. the occasion and expediency determines the form. PP

Past Love. Anne Keiter. and I catch your eye/in the silver reflection/of my wine goblet. GOYP

Past Time. Harvey Shapiro. Out of ignorance not love. PoL

Pastel. Francis Saltus Saltus. Time having blurred it like that pale/pastel! AA

A Pastel. Paul Verlaine. Tall, slim, amid the statues and the trees. SyP

Pastel: Masks and Faces. Arthur Symons. ...a flush/Ruddy and vague, the grace/(A rose!) of her lyric face. NOBV; SyP

Pastime. King of England Henry VIII. Thus shall I use me. CTC; EBEV; OBSC

The Pastime of Pleasure. Stephen Hawes.
And that I may myselfe well apply,/Thy sone and thee to laude and magnify. PoEL 1-5
At last the belles ringeth to evensong. MyFE
The outwarde countenance I made gladde and light. PoEL 1-5
That after your life, fraile and transitory,/You may than live in joye perdurably. PoEL 1-5

The Pastor. William C. Summers. They rejoiced on their way. STF

The Pastor's Friend. *Anonymous.* And to him–there wasn't a single thing/ wrong! STF

The Pastor Speaks Out. David Fisher. The collection plate hangs/at the end of the verger's arm like a leech. NPGG

A Pastoral. *Anonymous.* "Come, play with me, my treasure!" AWP; UnTE

A Pastoral. Nicholas Breton.
That may breed true love's delights? ELP
Thou shalt hear so sweet a sung/Never shepherd sung the like. E1L
Was made the lady of the May. TrGrPo

A Pastoral. John Byrom. Take Heed, all ye Swains, how you love one so fair. OBEC

Pastoral. Alan Creighton. They munch along their quiet search. CaP

Pastoral. Norman Dubie. The vigil of astonishment. AmPA

Pastoral. Clifford Dyment. Hands plucking and twisting the stems,/Came the sauntering sorrowful stranger. MoVE

Pastoral. Gavin Ewart. he rode contented through a summer idyll. OxBC

A Pastoral. Norman Gale. Love played at Find-me-for-you-May/In Mary's breast. HBV 1-2

A Pastoral. Geoffrey Hill. Evidently-veiled griefs; impervious tombs. NePoEA-2

Pastoral. Robert Hillyer.
And the watchdog with a nervous bark/Halts an imaginary thief. LOW
How spring, inviting bloom and rhyme,/Defeats the orchard men of time. BoNaP
Lovers under the hemlock lie. MoAmPo

Pastoral. Ron Loewinsohn. which from a distance looked like/a field of wild buttercups. NeAP

Pastoral. Robin Magowan. among almonds/a ploughman whistles. PoDr

A Pastoral. Theophile Marzials. Methinks the birds will scarce be home/ To wake our wedding-day! HBV 1-2

Pastoral. Kenneth Patchen. Flashing like silver teeth in the sun. AtBAP; NaP

Pastoral. Lawrence Raab. or a different season, or another life. AmPA

Pastoral. Charles Simic. And light her way NNaP

A Pastoral. George Alexander Stevens. Fatigu'd with dirt, drink, and embrace. CoMu; ErPo

Pastoral. Marion Strobel. ...and the sun/Falls in little sprays, to be picked by anyone! PoA

Pastoral. Allen Tate. Lay at her wandering side. AP

Pastoral. Ellen Bryant Voigt. weighing a handful of berries,/a handful of stones. MAYP

Pastoral. William Carlos Williams.
No one/will believe this/of vast import to the nation. AmPP; OxBA
These things/astonish me beyond words. MP; TwCP

Pastoral. David Wright. And the round earth turn a shoulder/Into mustering gloom. NYBP

Pastoral Ballad: Absence. William Shenstone. Soft hope is the relique I bear,/And my solace wherever I go. OBEC

A Pastoral Ballad. By John Bull. Thomas Moore. That you'd all of you know, as you sped,/Where a bullet of sense ought to hit. BIrV; OBSV

A Pastoral Ballad in Four Parts. William Shenstone.
And my solace wherever I go. CEP
But their love is not equal to mine. CEP; OBEC
Or sure I must envy the song. CEP
Was faithless, and I am undone. CEP

A Pastoral Courtship. John Wilmot, Earl of Rochester. So kisses to a lover's guest/Are invitations, not the feast. UnTE

A Pastoral Courtship (excerpt). Thomas Randolph. In one good manners grant me all. ViBoPo

Pastoral Dialogue Castara and Parthenia. Thomas Flatman. If our Lamps be extinguisht at midnight or noon. CEP

A Pastoral Elegy. Albius Tibullus. Wealth I despise in easy competence. AWP

Pastoral Hymn. Joseph Addison. And Streams shall murmur all around. OBEC

Pastoral Hymn. John Hall. Yet in them all thy name dost write. OxBoCh; TrPWD

A Pastoral. In the Modern Style. Worcester". Adieu, my goats; for ne'er shall rural muse/Your philosophic beards to stroke refuse. NOEC

Pastoral Landscape. Ambrose Philips. And, see, the Boys their Flocks to Shelter drive. OBEC

A Pastoral of Tasso. Samuel Daniel. But when as our short light/Comes once to set, it makes eternal night. OBSC

The Pastoral on the King's Death. Written in 1648. Alexander Brome. Down scrip and sheep-hook goes,/When foxes Shepherds be. OBS

Pastoral Poesy. John Clare. Of humble quietness. ACV; ERoP 1-2; OAEL 1-2

Pastoral Song for the Nuptials of Charles, Duke of Lorraine... Pierre de Ronsard. Now return, my children, to your pastures green/And your fellow shepherds. May your life be serene. HW

Pastoral: The Tenth Eclogue. Michael Drayton. The faithful swain here lastly made an end,/Whom all good shepherds ever shall defend. JCP

Pastorale. Robert A. Davis. Like a hooded nun telling her beads/In the twilight of a vast cathedral. GoSl

A Pastorall Dialogue. Thomas Carew.
Griefe, interrupted speach with teares supplyes. AnAnS 2; SeCP
The Nymph fled fast away. AnAnS 2

Pastorals: Summer. Alexander Pope. On me love's fiercer flames for ever prey,/By night he scorches, as he burns by day. CEP

Pastourelle. Anonymous.
"I pray you, sir, let me go milk my cow." OBSC
I wis my mother then shall us see. LO

Pastourelle. Donald Jeffrey Hayes. To the fullness of the heart...! AmNP

The Pasture. Robert Frost. You come too. AnNe; BiP; BLPL; BoC; CMoP; DiPo; GoJo; LaNeLa; MoAB; MoAmPo; MoShBr; NOBA; OxBA; PoPl; SoPo; SoSe; SUS; TiPo; ViBoPo

A Pasture. Frederic Lawrence Knowles. Well, maybe–I'm not city-bred. AA

Pastures of Plenty. Woody Guthrie. I come with the dust and I'm gone with the wind. WTO

Pat-a-Cake, Pat-a-Cake, Baker's Man. Anonymous. Put it in the oven for Tommy and me. OxNR

Pat Cloherty's Version of the Maisie. Richard Murphy. Kerrigan's wife was brought from Cross/home to Inishbofin/and she's buried there. IPY

Pat Works on the Railway. Anonymous. To work upon the railway. FSW; TrAS

Pat Young. Kenneth Mackenzie. which all her composition proves/–Glory be! PoAu 1-2

Patapan. Bernard De La Monnoye. Dance, and make the village hum! ChBR; PCh

A Patch of Old Snow. Robert Frost. The news of a day I've forgotten–/If I ever read it. CMoP; OBSP

Patch-Shaneen. John Millington Synge. You'll hear Patch-Shaneen cry. LoBV

Patches of Sky. Debora Greger. asking who she belonged to,/the other answering, "Whom?" MAYP

A Patching Together: The Cell Lay inside Her Body. Murray Edmond. I give him my hand. He bites it. NAs

The Patchwork Quilt. Dora Sigerson Shorter. So I have a coverlet for my narrow bed. HBMV

Pater Filio. Robert Bridges. I forgave, but tell the measure/Of her crime in thee, my treasure. CMoP; OBEV; OBVV; ViBoPo

The "Pater Noster". Anonymous. Let never the fiend with false fending/Cumber us in no shame. ACP; CAW

Pater's Bathe. Edward Abbott Parry. Is to take a dip from the side of a ship, in the trough of the rolling/sea. OxBChV

Pater Vester Pascit Illa. Robert Stephen Hawker. Thou didst provide, e'en for this nameless bird,/Home, and a natural love, amid the surging seas. CAW; CoBE

Paternal. Ernest J. Wilson, Jr. Ah'm gonna send you off to school. PoNe

Paterson. William Carlos Williams.
–and still the roar in his mind is/unabated. AtBAP
black plush, a dark flame. CMoP
blest, as am I, and humbled/by such ecstasy. MoLP
But/only one man–like a city. TAP
Earth, the chatterer, father of all/speech . . . . . NoAm
I thought I should never/see you again. MoLP
or Mezz Mezzrow... CMoP
shells and animalcules/generally and so to man,/to Paterson. CMoP; NoAm; NOBA
to the attentive/and obedient mind. OxBA
...when the word, a supple word,/lived in it, crumbled now to chalk. PP

The Path. William Cullen Bryant. The tangled swamp, through which a pathway strays/Becomes a garden with strange flowers and sprays. MAmP

The Path. Edward ("Edward Eastaway") Thomas. And stay; till, sudden, it ends where the wood ends. BrPo; MoVE; NoAm

Path Flower. Olive Dargan. And humble as a wondering child/I watched her vanishing. HBMV

The Path of the Padres. Edith D. Osborne. The little path, forgotten,/Winds on in beauty still. AmFN

The Path of the Stars. Thomas S. Jones, Jr. And were forever in a wakened world. MoRP; WGRP

The Path of Wisdom. Anonymous. For the things that are pleasing to/God are made known unto us. TrJP

The Path That Leads Nowhere. Corinne Roosevelt Robinson. On the path that leads to Nowhere/I have sometimes found my soul! BLPA; HBMV

Pathedy of Manners. Ellen de Young Kay. Her meanings lost in manners, she will walk/Alone in brilliant circles to the end. SoSe

The Paths of Prayer. Edouard Roditi. And, added to a myriad others,/Bring promised peace to all who live. VWA

Paths They Kept Barren. John Garmon. ...then we have nightmares/even the huge storms of the prairies cannot overcome. AMV-81

Paths to God. Musa Moris Farhi. mine is through/the flesh VWA

Patience. Bartola Cattafi. the patience that wears out the flesh/in order for the bone to shine. AMV-81

Patience. Elaine Feinstein. to make peace with her own monstrous nature. BrRo; FaBoWP

Patience. Harry Graham. And I may have to wait for years/Till either of them reappears. FiBHP; MoShBr

Patience. Frank Horne. and shake the very pillars/of the everlasting heavens... BPo

Patience. G. Anketall "Woodbine Willie" Studdert-Kennedy. Until we stand upon the height,/And see the perfect day. TrPWD

Patience: Bunthorne's Recitative and Song. Sir William Schwenck Gilbert. Why, what a most particularly pure man/this pure young man must be! CoBE

Patience, for I have wrong. Sir Thomas Wyatt. Hereafter comes not yet. FCP; SiPS

Patience for My Device. Sir Thomas Wyatt. Patience, with a good will,/Is easy to fulfil. FCP; SiPS

Patience, Hard Virtue. Daniel Berrigan. The children live, the children/rise from My Lai ditch. LFAC

Patience Is a Virtue. Anonymous. Make a very pretty face. OxNR

Patience of a People. F. J. Bryant, Jr. ...a/Fall bonfire in summer that only/Lets one eye sleep CNA

Patience of all my smart. Sir Thomas Wyatt. But note I will this text,/To draw better the next. FCP; SiPS

Patience on a Monument. Mary di Michele. your basic igneous boulder with a hole for music/drilled into her heart. CaPN

Patience Taught by Nature. Elizabeth Barrett Browning. But so much patience as a blade of grass/Grows by, contented through the heat and cold. EBCP; OxBoCh

Patience Though I Have Not. Sir Thomas Wyatt. Patience without offence/Is a painful patience. FCP; NoP; OBSC; SiPS; TrGrPo

Patience With the Living. Margaret E. Sangster. Be patient with the living. PoToHe

The Patient. Nicholas Moore. I can't remember, he said, but I'm all right. EAS

The Patient Church. John Henry, Cardinal Newman. True Seed! thou shalt prevail! GoBC

Patient Griselda. Geoffrey Chaucer. And let him mope, and wring his hands, and wail. PoRA

The Patient Is Rallying. Weldon Kees. Like spines of air, frozen in an ice cube. NaP

The Patient: Rockland County Sanitarium. Calvin C. Hernton. Immobile, terrified eyes. PoBA

Patmos. Friedrich Hölderlin. With the All-Highest's Son, inseparable from Him... OBVE

Patmos. Edith Matilda Thomas. Who would hold perpetual lease/Of an isle in seas of peace. HBV 1-2

The Patriarch. Robert Burns. The patriarch he coost the sark/And up and till't like fire!!! CoMu

The Patricians. Douglas Dunn. Their middle-aged children from the new estates. OxBC

Patrick Ewing Takes a Foul Shot. Diane Ackerman. and pupils jump/because he jumps MAYP

Patrick Sarsfield, Lord Lucan. Anonymous. And Patrick Sarsfield, Ireland's darling. KiLC

Patrico's Song. Ben Jonson. To the jealous his own false terrors. LoBV

The Patriot. Robert Browning. 'Tis God shall repay: I am safer so. PoRA; TrGrPo

The Patriot. J. C. Milne. For Lochnagar? Wi' clook and claw! PoSH

The Patriot Game. Anonymous. I'm sorry my rifle has not done the same,/For the quisling who sold out the patriot game. FSW

Patriotic Ode on the...Persecution of Charlie Chaplin. Bob Kaufman. Come on, Chaplin, we mean business. PoBA

The Peddler and His Wife. *Anonymous.* here thieves disturb them now no more,/For all is peace and love. AmFP

The Pedestrian's Plaint. Edward Verrall Lucas. When the Armstrongs cease from siddling/And the Royces roll no more. CenHV

The Pedigree. Thomas Hardy. And the stained moon and drift retook their places there. CoBMV

Pedigree. Mary Mills. Wisdom has a hard mouth. NePoAm

The Pedigree of Honey. Emily Dickinson.
A clover, any time, to him,/Is aristocracy. FaBV; NoAm; YaD
The right of way to Tripoli/A more essential thing. BLPL; NOBA

Pediment: Ballet. Louise Townsend Nicholl. And only music stays. UnS

Pedlar. *Anonymous.*
all that you ever said/and for the worse,/an end. OBVE
Of me a grain! OBEV; PoPle; WiR

The Pedlar. Charlotte Mew. Take it. No, give it back! HBMV

Pedlar. Sharon Nelson. pedlar arise a new day a new day/to be/hocked/in the streets VWA

A Pedlar of Small-Wares. Sir John Suckling. And wish, against himself, that they may have the knack. CaPo

The Pedlar's Caravan. William Brighty ("Matthew Browne") Rands. Just like the Travels of Captain Cook. OxBChV

The Pedlar's Song. William Shakespeare. Buy Lads, or else your Lasses cry: Come buy. CH

Pedra. John William Burgon. A rose-red city half as old as Time. BLPA

Pedro. Phoebe W. Hoffman. Each week he lives one brief and glorious day. GoYe

Pedro. Luis Omar Salinas. silence within silence FF

Peek-A-Boo. Robert Lowenstein. He would surely ordain a Fourth Amendment for the sky. AMV-81

Peekaboo, I Almost See You. Ogden Nash. ...and pass my declining years/saluting strange women and grandfather clocks. PoLf

Peeler and the Goat. *Anonymous.* Oh! it's then I'd be the dandy O. AnIL

The Peeler's Lament. *Anonymous.* For the devil, after prospectin' round, called it a damn poor place for/hell. CoSo; WTO

Peeling Onions. Adrienne Rich. These old tears in the chopping-bowl. BoWoP; CAPP; HaCAP; TAP

The Peeper. Peter Davison. I love at eyes' length! ErPo

The Peepers in Our Meadow. Archibald MacLeish. Or are they silenced by that silence out beyond?/Struck dumb? NCSH

Peeping Tom. Francis Hope. Her beauty, not his sin, had struck him blind. ErPo

Peer Gynt. Charles Hamilton Sorley. And he whom we had hated, waxen weak,/First in his weakness learns a little love. HBMV

Peer of the Gods Is That Man. Sappho. ...I grow paler/than dry grass and lack little/of dying. OBVE

Peewits on the Hills. Alice V. Stuart. Crying, world without end? ACV

Peg. *Anonymous.* Her leg was drowned first, and/her head followed after. OxNR

Peg-Leg's Fiddle. Bill Adams. When the bell strikes the dog-watch, and the moon is on the/sea. BBV; EtS

Peg Leg Snelson. Melvin B. Tolson. To his ability to make a deacon's wife the first night. FAZ

Peg of Limavaddy. William Makepeace Thackeray. And till I expire,/Or till I grow mad, I/Will sing unto my lyre/Peg of Limavaddy! OBTV

Pegasus. Lewis, Cecil Day. Of both, can ride me. Bellerophon, I am yours. AtBAP; PoPle

Pegasus. Patrick Kavanagh. Every land my imagination knew. FaBoIP; MoAB; OxBI

Pegasus Lost. Elinor Wylie. Between sun-wilted hedgerows into town. MoAmPo

Peggu's Wedding. Thomas Edward Brown. And, Misthriss! no more weddin's, aw good/sakes! no, no more weddin's for me! EnLit

Peggy. Allan Ramsay. With innocence, the wale of sense,/At wauking of the fauld. OBEV; ViBoPo

Peggy. Blanaid Salkeld. And a girl of twenty/Who has loved no man, loves me. OnYI

Peggy Browne. Turlough O'Carolan. I wake alone, sighing for Peggy Browne. BIrV

Peggy-o. *Anonymous.* And he's buried in the Louisiana Country-o. FSW

Peggy Said Good Morning. John Clare. But she's been gone some ten years since, and I know not what to do. ELP

Peking Man, Raining. Katharine Auchincloss Lorr. or branches of a tall tree deep in the middle/of a forest. SUW

The Pelican. *Anonymous.* I'm darned if I know how the helican. GoTF; TreFS

The Pelican. Greg Kuzma. glad to be flying. AmPA

The Pelican Chorus. Edward Lear. We think so then, and we thought so still! FaBoNo; PB

Pelicanaries. J. Patrick Lewis. they sleep on two too little feet. PPJ

Pelicans. Robinson Jeffers. He is weary of nothing; he watches air-planes; he watches/pelicans. FM; MoAmPo

The Pelicans My Father Sees. Sister Maris Stella. After the long dark winter. After the night. GoBC

The Pell Mell Celebrated. John Gay. And o'er thy head destructive tiles impend. EnLi 1-2

Pelleas and Ettarre (excerpt). Alfred, Lord Tennyson. He dies who loves it,-if the worm be there. PoEL 1-5

Pelters of Pyramids. Richard Henry Horne. Upon the glistening silence of the sands/Whereon no trace of mortal dust was seen. OBTV

Pelvic Meditation. Bruce Smith. the woman as witness, the clamor of crickets. AMV-80

The Pen-Guin. The Sword-Fish. Robert Williams Wood. The Sword-fish mightier than the Penguin. NLV

Pen Hy Cane. Mason Jordan Mason. and never remember/to fill his pen/again PoNe

Penal Law. Austin Clarke. When hands are joined and head bows in the dark. BoLoP; ELU; GTBS-P; IPY; NoAm; NOBI

Penal Rock: Altamuskin. John Montague. ...so I melt a ball of snow/From the hedge into their rusty tin before I go. FaBoIP

Penal Servitude for Mrs. Maybrick. *Anonymous.* So stick close to your husband and keep clear of Berry's/drop. OxBoLi

The Penalties of Baldness. Sir Owen Seaman. Sent forth an angel flying through it. FiBHP

The Penalty for Bigamy Is Two Wives. William Matthews. ...the silence for which/the mouth slowly opens. AmPA

The Penance. Nahum Tate. That failing would incense her more/Than all his trespasses before. CavP

Pendant Watch. Madeline Defrees. And the captain knows. And I know. We have it timed to the second. NMM

Pendulum Rhyme. Selma Robinson. I'll wait until eleven strikes-/Perhaps a little after. InMe

Penelope. Monique Laederach. "This place isn't for you," he says, "I am/their host.") BoWoP

Penelope, for Her Ulysses' Sake. Edmund Spenser. Whose fruitless work is broken with least wind. NIP

Penetration and Trust. George Meredith. And never a corner for serpent sin. VLP

A Penguin. Oliver Herford. Un-til they are so weak, they float/With-out re-sis-tance down his throat. FiBHP; PV

Penguin on the Beach. Ruth Miller. ...He eats/Fish from his Saviour's hands, and it tastes black. PeSA

Penguins in the Home. Helen Bevington. I like to sit around with mammals. OBAL

Penicillin. Frank Lima. Because I have copied everything I have seen. ANYP

The Peninsula. Seamus Heaney. Water and ground in their extremity. FaBoIP

The Penitent. Edna St. Vincent Millay. "But if I can't be sorry, why,/I might as well be glad!" ALV; YaD

The Penitent. Jeremy Taylor. And then one Drop of Balsam will suffice. OBS; OxBoCh

A Penitent Considers Another Coming of Mary. Gwendolyn Brooks. Mary would not punish men-/If Mary came again. NoAm; PCh

The Penitent Hopes in Mary. *Anonymous.* Jesu have mercy of me,/That all this world honoures/Amen. MeEL

The Penitent Nun. John Lockman. "But first let's do as Jane has done." UnTE

The Penitent Palmer's Ode. Robert Greene. Man is sin, and flesh is grass. LoBV; OBSC

Penitential Psalm. *Anonymous.* Tears doth he weep, laments doth he pour forth. WGRP

Penitential Psalm to the Goddess Anunit, IV. *Anonymous.* As a mother who hath borne children, as a father who hath/begotten (them), may it be glad! WGRP

Penitential Psalms: Introduction. Sir Thomas Wyatt. With tender heart, lo, thus to God he sings: FCP

Penmanship. Tom Clark. And you go on choosing me/Over and over again/Irrespective of merit ANYP

The Penn Central Station at Beacon, N.Y. Ed Ochester. Manhattan Manhattan Manhattan Manhattan TAT

Pennies. Joyce Kilmer. What is the key to Everlasting Life?/A blood-stained Cross. CAW

Pennines in April. Ted Hughes. Carrying the larks upward. PPP

Pennsylvania Academy of Fine Arts. Ernest Kroll. Filled in the fine detail complete/To the least flower, to the last leaf. AMV-80

Pennsylvania Deutsch. Christopher Morley. Grandma is a widow. NLV

Pennsylvania Places. Thomas Augustin Daly. No? I could if I had time. OBAL

Pennsylvania Song. *Anonymous.* Nor slaves nor cowards we will prove,/Great Britain soon shall see. PAH

Pennsylvania Station. Langston Hughes. To glorify the earth-and you-and me. AmNP

Pennsylvania Winter Indian 1974.　Harold Littlebird.　...rambling and singing in her hills and/open valleys, bathing in all her beauty　VoR

Penny and Penny.　*Anonymous.*　Who will not save a penny/Shall never have many.　OxNR

Penny Is a Hardy Knight.　*Anonymous.*　"He was a man, let him go'.　OxBM

Penny Trumpet.　Raphael Rudnik.　Lips, breasts–led me to rooms/Where trumpets play all night.　MAT; NYBP

The Penny Whistle.　Edward ("Edward Eastaway") Thomas.　Says far more than I am saying.　MoAB; MoBrPo

Penny Whistle Blues.　E. H. L. Island.　I'm feeling very blue,/And unhappy.　InMe

The Pennycandystore beyond the El.　Lawrence Ferlinghetti.　Too soon! too soon!　BiP; CAD; CAPP; CTBA; HeIP; TAP

Penological Study: Southern Exposure, 3. Wet Hair...　Robert Penn Warren.　Again he had come late to supper,/Then lied, to boot.　NoAm

Pensees de Noel.　Alfred Denis Godley.　Christmas comes but once a year.　DBV; InMe

Pensionnaires.　Paul Verlaine.　And, blushing, smiled innocently.　PeHV

Pent-Up Aching Rivers (excerpt).　Walt Whitman.　...you children prepared for,/And you stalwart loins.　ViBoPo

Pentachromatic.　Julia de Burgos.　then take Julia de Burgos by force.　InW

Pentagonia (parody).　G. E. Bates.　Who work in the Pentagon Building　NYBP; SpRo

Pentecost.　Florence Anthony ("Ai").　If you suffer in the grave,/you can kill from it.　LTB

Pentecost.　John Bennett.　it brings the Glory that all men may share.　EBCP

Pentecost.　Adelbert Sumpter Coats.　Make every day a Pentecost.　TrPWD

The Pentecost Castle (excerpt).　Geoffrey Hill.　my desire dying/as I desire　HAP

Pentimento.　Lori Fisher.　marble hides nothing.　PoDr

The Pentland Hills.　*Anonymous.*　Pastured with sheep, forever green.　GBP

Pentucket.　John Greenleaf Whittier.　Whose grass-grown surface overlies/The victims of that sacrifice.　MC; PAH

Penumbra.　Pierre Louys.　but men shall know nothing thereof.　PeHV

Penumbra.　Dante Gabriel Rossetti.　Bewail one hour the more, when sea/And wind are one with memory.　VLP

The Penurious Quaker; or, The High Priz'd Harlot.　*Anonymous.*　Farewel you Puritannick Prig,/I scorn to take your Shilling.　CoMu

A Peony for Apollo.　Charles Edward Eaton.　Give us the courage of our leisure/To make the unimagined world more real.　GoYe

The People.　Tomasso Campanella.　To tell this truth, it kills him unforgiven.　AWP; DBV

The People.　Robert Creeley.　some god looks/truly down/upon them.　VGW

People.　Orhan and Halman Veli Kanik.　The way I watched people/When I was small.　LLLT

People.　D. H. Lawrence.　They ever should be.　BrPo

People.　Lois Lenski.　These make a town.　SoPo

The People.　Elizabeth Madox Roberts.　And in between are the people.　GoJo; SoPo; TiPo

The People.　William Butler Yeats.　After nine years, I sink my head abashed.　CMoP

People.　Yevgeny Yevtushenko.　I make my lament against destruction.　DL

The People at the Party.　Lisel Mueller.　...toward the unsatable/Inexorable wilderness of feeling.　NePoAm-2

People Buy a Lot of Things.　Annette Wynne.　And then I'd open wide the cage, and set the singer free.　SoPo

People Do Gossip.　Sappho.　hidden under/wild hyacinths　PBWP

The People (excerpt).　Robin Hyde.　Honour meant most. She listened by the door/For who'd betray it; but too spent to care　AnNZ

The People Has No Obituary.　Eunice Clark.　When death dries out the special planted man.　NAMP

People Hide Their Love.　Emperor Wu-Ti.　Like a flower that seems too precious to be picked?　LiTW; OLR

The People in the Park.　Léonie Adams.　Where it is nothing, one with its assent.　MoVE

People, male and female.　Mahadevi (Mahadeviyakka).　...what can you/cover and conceal?　BoWoP

The People of Blakeney.　*Anonymous.*　And crack hazel-nuts/With a five-farthing beetle.　GBP

People of the Future.　Ted Berrigan.　you didn't write them,/I did.　APU

People of the South Wind.　William Stafford.　"No One, No One, No One."　NNaP

People on Sunday.　Edwin Denby.　And turned its head away without the least surprise.　ANYP

The People's Choice: The Dream Poems II.　LeRoi (Imamu Amiri Baraka) Jones.　...I feel no single/treachery but what you are having been these few seconds/something like my self　BiP

The People's King.　Lyman Whitney Allen.　And virtue the cornerstone.　PGD

The People's Petition.　Wathen Mark Wilks Call.　Give us our daily bread!　OBVV

The People, the People.　George Oppen.　...Will she not rot/Without us and die/In childbed leaving/Monstrous issue–　GP

People Trying to Love.　Stephen Berg.　they touch you.　NaP

The People vs. the People.　Kenneth Fearing.　"An Omnibus Guide to Chance and Superstition," by One Who Knows.　MoAmPo

The People Went to War.　Antonio Jacinto.　I do know: the people will come back.　WhB

People Who Died.　Ted Berrigan.　My friends whose deaths have slowed my heart stay with me/now.　APU

People Who Went by in Winter.　William Stafford.　"In every storm I hear them pass."　GP

People Will Talk.　*Anonymous.*　Oh, yes, they must talk, you know.　GoTF; TreFS

People Will Talk.　Samuel Dodge.　But don't think to stop it, it is of no use,/For people will talk.　WBLP

The People, Yes.　Carl Sandburg.
...and every one missed him.　LiTA; MoAmPo
The hallelujah chorus forever shifting its star soloists.　BBV; NAMP
held up by slow friendly winds.　CMoP
"I want to know!"　AmFN
The people move/in a fine thin smoke,/the people, yes.　FYAP
"Small men never feel small."　OBAL
"Where to? what next?"　BoLiVe; MoAB; MoAmPo; NoAm; NOBA; TrGrPo
"Which way to the post office, boy?"/"I don't know." "You don't know/much, do you?"...　OBAL
"Why did the children/pour molasses on the cat/when the one thing we told the children/they must...　OBAL

Pep.　Grace G. Bostwick.　You'll get the best of the whole show–/That's pep!　WBLP

Peppergrass.　Stanley Plumly.　blowing the lights out, one by one.　LCAP

Pepsi Generation.　Walasse Ting.　Day and night/Eat fish　MAT

Pepys Bar, West Forty-Eight Street, 8 a.m.　L. E. Sissman.　An iron spider waits for his successes.　NYP

Per Amica Silentia Lunae.　Ronald de Carvalho.　like a dead fruit, a useless fruit/that rots,/and falls....　LiTW

Per Ardua ad Astra.　John Oxenham.　I somewhat grace Thy fosterings/And climb Thy loftier Way.　TrPWD

Per Aspera.　Florence Earle Coates.　Arcturus and the Pleiads beckon him.　HBMV

Per Diem et per Noctem.　Mary Stanley　I wish all his tomorrows fair.　AnNZ

Per Iter Tenebricosum.　Oliver St.John Gogarty　And Lesbia's sparrow-all alone?　AnIL; OBMV; OxBI

Per Pacem ad Lucem.　Adelaide Anne Procter.　Lead me, Oh Lord–till perfect Day shall shine,/Through Peace to Light.　TrPWD

Perambulator Poem.　David McCord.　I let them know/that I was christened.　OFD

Perception of an Object Costs.　Emily Dickinson.　And then upbraids a Perfectness/That situates so far–　MAmP; NOBA

Percolating Highway.　Michael Castro.　I'm running from myself & I feel like dying.　VWA

Percussions.　Ron Welburn.　and horns beat on/brightly you know for song.　CNA

Percy/68.　Glenn Myles.　"Just like Daniel Boone, coming back to/Work these bears."　NBP

Percy Shelley.　John Peale Bishop.　Did Percy Bysshe have any balls?　ErPo

Perdido, Duke?　Robert McGovern.　You're encased in vinyl.　SOTS

Perdita.　Florence Earle Coates.　And as the wild rose, fair.　AA

Perdita.　John Swanick [(or Swanwick)] Drennan.　Shook down the shining shadow of her hair,/And nothing said.　IrPN

Perdita.　Louis MacNeice.　Among the clank of cans and the roistering files/Of steam the caterpillars wait for wings.　PoA

Perdy, I said it not.　Sir Thomas Wyatt.　And her I have reserved/Within my heart forever.　FCP; PoEL 1-5

Pere Lalement.　Marjorie Pickthall.　Thy rod my guide and comfort, underneath/Thy everlasting arms.　CaP; NOBC; OBCV; PeCV

Le Pere Severe.　*Anonymous.*　"'Tis better far the cold to dree/Than give my true love up for thee."　AWP

Peregrine.　Elinor Wylie.　I'm a good hater,/But a bad lover.　BLPL; HBMV

Peregrine Prykke's Pilgrimage (parody).　Clive James.　I'll have to learn to leave myself alone.　FaBoPa

Peter Rabbit. Sandra McPherson. They will make us wash the green/From our hands and our knees. LCAP

Peter Rabbit Sex Poem. Marilyn Bowering. and to feel it beginning/to burn its way through from the core. CaPN

Peter's Tears. Thomas Hood. He's laying her dust, for fear of it rising. GoTF; TreFT

Peter Stuyvesant's New Year's Call. Edmund Clarence Stedman. And on he pushed, a two-miles' tread,/To breakfast at his Bouwery. PAH

Peter White. *Anonymous.* And that stands all awry. OxBoLi; OxNR

Peterhead in May. Burns Singer. Unused but significant/Of something to come. OxBS

Peterhof. Edmund Wilson. Said the Great Dane to Peter the Great. GoJo

Petit, the Poet. Edgar Lee Masters. Tick, tick, tick, what little iambics,/While Homer and Whitman roared in the pines? AnFE; APA; CMoP; CoAnAm; InPo; LaNeLa; LoGBV; MoAmPo; MoVE; NoAm; NOBA; OxBA; PPON; TAP

A Petite Histoire of Red Fascism. Andrei Codrescu. will henceforth be em-/ployed to make statues/of the brass. APU

A Petition. Thomas Bailey Aldrich. I beg you very gently break the news. AA

Petition. W. H. Auden. New styles of architecture, a change of heart. CMoP; CoBMV; LiTB; MoPo; OAEP

Petition. John Drinkwater. He had a heart to praise, an eye to see,/And beauty was his king. TrPWD

Petition. Harold McCurdy. Love on the Cross and in our star-crossed faces. AMV-81

Petition. Eleanor Slater. Always in/Superlative. TrPWD

Petition. R. S. Thomas. ...that truth should defer/To beauty. It was not granted. FaBoMo

Petition for a Miracle. David Morton. Shining through/The thing I wrought.) ISi

The Petition for an Absolute Retreat. Anne Finch, Countess of Winchilsea. When all Heaven shall be survey'd/From those Windings and that Shade. OBEC; PoEL 1-5; SBG; TrGrPo

A Petition from the Chain Gang at Newcastle to Captain Furlong... Francis MacNamara. And as in duty bound we all/Will ever pray. NOAV

The Petition of the Gray Horse, Auld Dunbar. William Dunbar. For with my hand I have indost/To pay quhatevir his trappouris cost. OxBS

The Petition of the Orangemen of Ireland. Thomas Moore. For which your petitioners ever will pray,/&c. &c. &c. &c. &c. NOBI

The Petition of Tom Dermondy to the Three Fates in Council Sitting. Thomas Dermody. Magnific Fame! And let fat Plenty/Marry one Poet out of Twenty! AnIV

Petition of Youth before Battle. John Bunker. Give me a faint glimpse of Heaven. CAW

Petition to the Queen. Sir Walter Ralegh. Of her we had, but praise our living Queen,/Who brings us equal, if not greater, bliss. FCP

Petrarch. Giosue Carducci. Breaks from her tuneful lips, "Rome! Italy!" AWP

The Petrified Fern. Mary Bolles Branch. Sweetly to surprise us the last day. AA

The Petrified Leaf. Mary Bolles Branch. So, I think, God hides some souls away,/Sweetly to surprise us, the last day. HBV 1-2

The Pets. Robert Farren. Then the fly. CoBE; OxBI

The Pettichap's Nest. John Clare. A spot like this would be her chosen home. PBBP

A Petticoat. Gertrude Stein. A light white, a disgrace, an ink spot, a rosy charm. NMM

The Pettitoes Are Little Feet. *Anonymous.* And the pettitoes to the little pig. OxNR

The Petty Officers' Mess. Roy Fuller. Like ours at what their strange captivities/Invisibly engender. ChMP

The Pewee. John Townsend Trowbridge. Is solace to the pensive ear:/"Pewee! pewee! peer!" HBV 1-2

Pewter. Jack Gilbert. to praise her, to tell of me, yes, and of you, my King. NPGG

Peyote Poem. Michael McClure.
becoming an osprey frozen skyhigh/to challenge me. NeAP; PoM
...I visit/among the peoples of myself and know all/I need to know. PoM

Peyote Vision. Lew Blockcolski. to watch his head become an explosion/of dream daisies. VoR

Phaedra. Hilda ("H. D.") Doolittle. fades and shrinks, a red leaf/drenched and torn in the cold rain. SBG

Phaedra. Osip Mandelstam. And cool the black sun/Of a savage, insomniac, passion. OBVE

Phaedra: The Conquest of Love. Jean Baptiste Racine. ...Diddain not my ill-uttered plea,/Which would not have been made, except to thee. LiTW

Phaeton. Eli Mandel. And take me with him by the ten taut reins/Of my skinned and burning hands. PeCV

Phallic Root. Shiraishi Kazuko. then I would vastly hold/and embrace you. WPOW

The Phallic Symbol. Nicholas Moore. And then I knew I had no hope at all. NeBP

Phallus. Shiraishi Kazuko. I would wish to catch in my arms,/Endlessly,/One such as you. BoWoP

Phantasia for Elvira Shatayev. Adrienne Rich. We have dreamed of this/all of our lives LiSp

Phantasus. Arno Holz.
Burst your bowels! LiTW
A dreamer and a prodigal. AWP
my clever little eyes/raisins! LiTW; PCh

Phantasy. *Anonymous.* But that we done for God's love have we no mair. ACP

A Phantasy of Heaven. Harry Kemp. ...and He/Will only laugh, remembering, once/He was a boy in Galilee! HBMV

Phantom. Samuel Taylor Coleridge. She, she herself, and only she,/Shone through her body visibly. ERoP 1-2; OAEL 1-2; OBSP; PoEL 1-5

The Phantom Bark. Hart Crane. Imprisoned never, no not soot or rain. CMoP

The Phantom Horsewoman. Thomas Hardy. Draws rein and sings to the swing of the tide. CMoP; FaBoPP; NOBE; PoEL 1-5; WSC

The Phantom Light of the Baie des Chaleurs. Arthur Wentworth Hamilton Eaton. Cold as the winter moon that lies/On the Baie des Chaleurs. CaP

Phantom or Fact. Samuel Taylor Coleridge. And 'tis a record from the dream of life. EnRP; ERoP 1-2

The Phantom Ship. J. W. De Forest. To fell and fiery disaster/Right off the Block Island shore. EtS

The Phantom Ship. Henry Wadsworth Longfellow. He had sent this Ship of Air. EtS

The Phantom-Wooer. Thomas Lovell Beddoes. Ever singing "die, oh! die." EnRP; ERoP 1-2; OBRV; TrGrPo; ViBoPo; WiR

Phantoms. Harry McGuire. God, forgive! CAW

Phantoms All. Harriet Prescott Spofford. The Navy of Old Spain! AA

Phantoms of the Steppe. Alexander Pushkin. Chill my heart with fear to-night! WSC

Phar Lap in the Melbourne Museum. Peter Porter. ...be proud/Of a thoroughbred bay gelding who ran fast. PoAu 1-2

Pharao's Daughter. Michael Moran. "Tare-an-ages, girls, which o'yees own the child?" BIrV

Pharaoh and Joseph. Else Lasker-Schüler. Thus my lips indite/Great sweetnesses/In the wheat of our morning. VWA

Pharaoh's Army Got Drownded (with music). *Anonymous.* O Mary, don' you weep, don' you mo'n. AS

Pharsalia: The Rivalry between Caesar and Pompey. Lucan (Marcus Annaeus Lucanus). And saw the ruin with rejoicing eyes. OBVE

The Phases of Darkness. Paul Petrie. and those black spaces in between that peer/so strangely at me through half-opened doors. TAP

Phases of the Moon. Robert Browning. Goes dispiritedly, glad to finish. MOON

The Pheasant. Robert P. Tristram Coffin. He lay in jewelled feathers, dead. TiPo

Pheasant. Zulfikar Ghose. Before he died. ACV

Pheasant. Sidney Keyes. Exotic bird, haunter of autumn hedgerows. HaMV

The Pheasant Hunter and the Arrowhead. Julian Gitzen. with the dust of thousands of game-bird bones. AMV-80

Phenomena. Robinson Jeffers. It slides into a cloud over Point Lobos. NoAm; NOBA; OxBA

Phenomenal Survivals of Death in Nantucket. Louise Gluck. My second in the sea. AmPA; SM

The Phenomenon. Karl Shapiro. Her faulty snowfall brilliantly denied. CMoP; NMP; NYBP

The Phi Beta Kappa Poem. Richmond Lattimore. and the way up to the light still there for you to find. GLGT

Phil. Ted Kooser. the black bird of your death flaps,/calling our names. AMV-81

Philadelphia. *Anonymous.* And the pretty girls are plenty. AmFP

Philadelphia. Rudyard Kipling. They are all in Pennsylvania this morning! OBTV

Philander. Donald Hall. He went to bed with what he thought the girls were symbols of. ELU; ErPo

The Philanderer. Moses Mendes. With you I'll toy, and kiss and play,/But hang me if I marry! TrJP

Philarete Praises Poetry. George Wither. Let my life no longer be/Than I am in love with thee. OBS

Philarete to His Mistress (excerpt). George Wither. Win and wear thee he that may. PeD

Philatelic Lessons: The German Collection. Lawrence P. Spingarn. The Prussian boundaries were drawn by Polish chaps. NYBP

Philatelist Royal. Robert Graves. To say what he honestly/Thought of Philately. FaBoCo

Philemon and Baucis. Arthur Golding. ...and honour/due/Be given to such as honour him with fear and reverence true.' OBSC

Philip, My King. Dinah Maria Mulock Craik. As thou sittest at the feet of God victorious,/"Philip, the king!" HBV 1-2

Philippine Madonna. Louise Crenshaw Ray. We saw Our Lady in the candle-light/Her raiment dry, no water on the floor! ISi

Phillada Flouts Me. *Anonymous.* And all for that my dear/Phillada flouts me. HBV 1-2; OBEV; TrGrPo; ViBoPo

Phillis. *Anonymous.* You'd cry aloud, "The next is me!" UnTE

Phillis and Corydon. Arthur Colton. Corydon made his choice and took– Well, which do you/suppose? HBV 1-2

Phillis's Resolution. William Walsh. That he who once has been my slave/ Should ever be my king. OBSP

Philocles. of Tarentum Leonidas. An offering from Philocles. AWP

Philoctetes. John Byrne Leicester Warren, Lord De Tabley. The Gods are just, and compensation comes. NOBV

Philoctetes. Thomas Russell. That parts fam'd Trachis from th'Euboic shore. LoBV

Philological. John Updike. As every school child ought to know. ELU

Philomel. Richard Barnfield.
All thy fellow birds do sing/Careless of thy sorrowing.... NOBE
None alive will pity me. CH; GTBS; HBV 1-2; OBEV

Philomel to Corydon. William Young. That woman likes a slave–but loves a/master. AA

Philomela. Matthew Arnold. Eternal pain! AtBAP; BoLiVe; EnLi 1-2; GTBS; HBV 1-2; MaVP; MCCG; OAEL 1-2; OAEP; OBEV; PBBP; PPP; SeCeV; UnPo; VLP; WHA

Philomela. John Crowe Ransom. Unto more beautiful, persistently more/ young,/Thy fabulous provinces belong. AmP; CMoP; FaBoPP; MoVE; NoAm; NOBA; OBAL; OBSV; OxBA

Philomela. Sir Philip Sidney. Thy thorn without, my thorn my heart invadeth. HBV 1-2; NOBE; OBEV

Philomela's Ode in Her Arbour. Robert Greene. Though love be sweet, learn this of me/No love sweet but honesty. OBSC

Philomela's Second Ode. Robert Greene. Here he paused and did stay,/ Sighed, and rose, and went away. OBSC

Philomela, the Nightingale (excerpt). Patrick Hannay. And thus her passion paints. PBBP

Philomena Andronico. William Carlos Williams. Fall/loosely/(waiting)/at her sides. FaBoMo

Philon the Shepherd–His Song. *Anonymous.* Your mind is light, soon lost for new love. ALV; NOBE; OBSC

Philonous' Paradox. Christopher Gilbert. "he who doubts all things" FAZ

A Philosopher. John Kendrick Bangs. Somewheres about if I took care/To strike a match and find out where. HBV 1-2

A Philosopher. Sam Walter Foss. An' fold his arms an' shet his eyes,/An' set, an' set, an' flosserfize. OBAL

The Philosopher. Edna St. Vincent Millay. So wisely and so well? CMoP

The Philosopher. Sara Teasdale. Till he was ninety-two. PoToHe

The Philosopher and Her Father. Shirley Brooks. "You bad old man to sit and tell/Such gibberybosh about a Bell!" CenHV

The Philosopher and the Birds. Richard Murphy. ...But at Rossroe hordes/ Of village cats have massacred his birds. CIP

The Philosopher and the Lover to a Mistress Dying. Sir William Davenant. Since Knowledge is but Sorrow's spy,/It is not safe to know. MePo; NOBE; Prf

The Philosopher's Scales. Jane Taylor. While the scale with the soul in't so mightily fell/That it jerked the philosopher out of his cell. HBV 1-2

The Philosopher to His Mistress. Robert Bridges. To happy worlds, where I/Still in thy love belong. LiTM; OAEP; PoEL 1-5

Philosopher, Whom Dost Thou Most Affect." Richard Garnett. With those to study, and with these to dine. HBV 1-2

Philosophers Have Measured Mountains. George Herbert. Yet few there are that found them; Sin and Love. TRV

The Philosophic Apology. Samuel Greenberg. That judgement soothes, thy dusty heart-speck's tear. MoPo; NePA

The Philosophic Flight. Giordano Bruno. If death so glorious be our doom at all! AWP

The Philosophic Pill. Sir William Schwenck Gilbert. Should always gild the philosophic pill! GLGT

Philosophy. John Kendrick Bangs. Where I may sleep and dream there's Light again. PoToHe

Philosophy. Paul Laurence Dunbar. But hit's mighty ha'd to giggle w'en dey's nuffin in de/pot. BPo

Philosophy. Dorothy Parker. And what if I don't, and what if I do? InMe

Philosophy Is Born. Christian Morgenstern. I might in fact be seeing my first sheep. FaBoNo

Philotas: Chorus. Samuel Daniel. It is that height of fortune doth undo/ Both her own quietness and others' too. OBSC

Phineas Pratt. Gloria MacArthur. Nor worth the forty years I died. GoYe

Phineas within and without. Paul Zimmer. He died amidst their whole. VGW

Phoebe Dawson. George Crabbe. Nor let me preach for ever and in vain! EBEV; GoTL

Phoebe in a Rosebush. Clyde Watson. But you're the one for me NTCP

Phoebe on Latmus. Michael Drayton. Under a poplar, shadowed from the sun,/Where merrily to court him she begun. OBSC

Phoebe's Sonnet. Thomas Lodge. And so sing I, with a down a down. ViBoPo

Phoebus, Arise. William, of Hawthornden Drummond. And ev'ry thing, save her, who all should grace. BSV; ElL; GoTS

Phoebus with Admetus. George Meredith. The day is never darken'd/That had thee here obscure. EnLi 1-2; NOBE; OBEV; OBVV

The Phoenix. *Anonymous.* ,and attain thereafter/Bliss on high in the heavenly home. AnOE

Phoenix. Rose Auslander. Beyond the wall of tears/the phoenix period/in flames VWA

The Phoenix. Arthur Christopher Benson. And are with gazing most content. OBEV; OBVV

The Phoenix. J. V. Cunningham. Your mute voice on the crystal embers flinging. NoAm; QFR

The Phoenix. George Darley.
As to sip fast that nectarous shower/A thirstier minstrel drew in me! CBEP; OAEL 1-2; OBEV; OBVV
Mourn'd by the desert when she dies. EG; LoBV; WiR

The Phoenix. Robert Fisher. look in the fire-light/and a phoenix may come to rest. AmMo

The Phoenix. Matti Megged. And return/With wings scorched. VWA

The Phoenix. Ogden Nash. Out pops itselve. CenHV; NePA

The Phoenix. Howard Nemerov. Himself his father, son and bride/And his own Word LiTM; NePA

Phoenix. W. H. Oliver. And angered, soul's harsh prize. AnNZ

Phoenix. Carolyn M. Rodgers. and i shall/travel with the wind/no more. JB

The Phoenix. Theodore Spencer. Flared better than it knew. CrMA

The Phoenix and the Turtle. William Shakespeare. For these dead birds sigh a prayer. CABA; CBEP; FaBoEn; LiTB; LiTL; LoBV; MasP; MePo; MyFE; NOBE; NoP; OAEL 1-2; OBEV; OBSC; PoEL 1-5; SeCePo; SeCeV; TEP

The Phoenix Answered. Anne Ridler. All that I praise and bless. ChMP

A Phoenix at Fifty. Lawrence Ferlinghetti. Yet will arise NAs

The Phoenix (excerpt). *Anonymous.*
Eternal is the Prince who grants such bliss. PBBP
His body renewed by the birth of fire,/Taint of evil all taken away. LiTW
Singing and caroling to meet the sun.... OAEL 1-2

The Phoenix of Mozart. Claude Vigee. when the rings of the wind on our upturned wrists/revolve their strange fires. VWA

Phone Call. Tom Crawford. I love you AMV-81

Phone Call to Rutherford. Paul Blackburn. ...You have...made/a record in my heart./Goodbye. CTBA; PoM

Phone Number. Jack Collom. I used to get there on my bike. APU

A Photo of Miners. Brendan Galvin. who thinks he will croon his way/out of this? LTB

Photogenes and Apelles. Matthew Prior. And in their working, took great care/That all was full, and round, and fair. GoTL

Photograph. Quandra Prettyman. We see a hand and we call it love. PoBA

Photograph at the Cloisters: April 1972. Helen Chasin. like stars for words for doing something terrible. NMM

Photograph in a Stockholm Newspaper for March 13, 1910. Don Coles. ...They persuade me/all will be well. NOBC

Photograph of Haymaker, 1890. Molly Holden. ... uncovered them, succulent and straight,/immediate with moon-daisies. OxBTC

Photograph of My Father in His Twenty-Second Year. Raymond Carver. And do not even know the places to fish? WOLT

The Photograph of Myself. Jon Anderson. to whom I speak and listen. AmPA

The Photograph the Cat Licks. Beatrice Walter. ...Only the cat,/who misses her,/licks it now and then. NMM

Photographer. Philip Booth. I keep for life/how light/shapes how/lives deepen. EyDe

The Photographer. Roger Pfingston. light that draws from him/like a poultice/some essence of himself. PoDr

The Photographer's Wife. Janet Beeler. But a chance lens flare/surrounds her face/with a rim of fire. AMV-81

The Photographer Whose Shutter Died. William Meissner. ...he cannot stop from staring/all the way to the back of his brain. PoDr

Photographic Plate, Partly Spidered, Hampton Roads, Virginia... Dave Smith. ...one face/that is mine, that is going to wheel at me the secrets of many. MAYP

Photographing the Facade–San Miguel de Allende. Betsy Colquitt. we searcha by camera eye for Gothic things. AMV-80

Photographs. William Peskett. the love conceals/the care. AMV-81

Photographs. Charles Wright. And we hold such poses forever. HoPM

Photographs: A Vision of Massacre. Michael S. Harper. now slightly pink,/and never to be used. PoBA

The Photos. Diane Wakoski. How I hate my destiny. NIP

The Photos from Summer Camp. Izora Corpman. I said, "SO"/when I was 8. FAZ

Photos of a Salt Mine. P.K. Page. the filter here, not innocence but guilt. NOBC

Phraseology. Jayne Cortez. the impulsive foam/of a spastic BlSi

Phryne. John Donne. Only in this, that you both painted be. FaBoEE

Phyllida and Corydon. Nicholas Breton. And Phillida with garlands gay/ Was made the Lady of the May. EG; EIL; FaBoEn; OAEP; SeCePo; TrGrPo

Phyllida's Love-Call to Her Corydon, and His Replying. Anonymous. Heaven keep our loves away. AnFE; EIL; OBEV; OBSC

Phyllidula. Ezra Pound. If she does not count this blessed/Let her change her religion. FaBoTw

Phyllis. Anonymous. I am young and young are you:/'Tis the time for playing. UnTE

Phyllis. Nicholas Breton. For as on you our Muse begun, in you all music endeth!' OBSC; TrGrPo

Phyllis. Thomas Lodge.
  In spite of thee, and by firm faith deserve her. EG
  Nor grace to those that crave it. ACP
  Pray her, before I die she will come see me. EIL

Phyllis. Thomas Randolph. Unless you meet again tomorrow. BoLoP

Phyllis. Sydney King Russell. Lay and stared and could not weep. ErPo

Phyllis Corydon clutched to him. Caius Valerius Catullus. Could Venus yield more love-delight/than here she grants in Love's requite? BoLoP

Phyllis Knotting. Sir Charles Sedley. Phyllis, without frown or smile,/Sat and knotted all the while. NOBE

Phyllis; or, The Progress of Love. Jonathan Swift. Are cat and dog, and rogue and whore. OAEL 1-2; OBSV

Phyllis's Age. Matthew Prior. And Phyllis is some Forty-three. CEP; FaBoEE

Phyllyp Sparrowe (excerpt). John Skelton. That he coulde there espye/ With his wanton eye. PB

Physical for My Son. Barbara Smith. And I wanted somewhere to save your blood. AMV-80

Physical Geography. Louise Townsend Nicholl. This room would not confine us as before/Since cyclones and tornadoes had begun. ImOP

Physical Universe. Louis Simpson. and she continued to breathe evenly/ from the depths of sleep. InPS

A Physics. Heather McHugh. above ourselves because we meant,/in time, to measure up. MAYP

The Physics of Ochun. Victor Hernandez Cruz. and rushed home sparkling in/her yellow dress. APU

The Piano. Frank Davey. & hide my fists/in my hands. NOBC; WHW

Piano. D. H. Lawrence. Down in the flood of remembrance, I weep/like a child for the past. BLPL; CBEP; CMoP; GrPl; GTBS-P; HAP; HeIP; InPK; InvP; LiTB; MoAB; MoBrPo; NIP; NoAm; NOBE; NoP; OAEL 1-2; OAEP; OBSP; PoPle; UnPo; WeW

Piano. Lisa Russ. Light strikes the face of the sleeper. PPJ

The Piano. Paul Verlaine. And on the way towards the window dies,/Half-open on the little garden-close? LiTW

Piano after War. Gwendolyn Brooks. And stone will shove the softness from my face. AmNP

Piano and Drums. Gabriel Okara. wandering in the mystic rhythm/of jungle drums and the concerto. NIP; PBA; TTY

Piano at Evening. Palea. Again I chant my refrain/Of long ago and a piano singing/Far into the night. WTO

Piano Lessons. Baron Wormser. ...the piano stood/For all that we wanted to do yet never would. MAYP

Piano Pieces (excerpt). Thomas W. Shapcott. breaking a flower/from its green stem. CBAP

Piano Practice. Howard Moss. ...Now your hands/Are on the mysteries of the commonplace. NYBP

Piano Practice. Ian Serraillier. "Aha-there isn't any water!" BBGG

Piano Practice. Derek Walcott. with stones like white sheep in its pastures/ by a silver-circletted sea. NYP

Piano Recital. Babette Deutsch. She stoops–to drink the meaning/At the still brink of song. NePoAm

The Piano Tuner. W. Atmar Smith, II. "thank you." AMV-80

Piano Tuner, Untune Me That Tune. Ogden Nash. Well, I wish him a thousand harems of a thousand wives apiece,/and a thousand little ones by each.. UnS

Piazza Di Spagna. Willard M. Grimes. Keats wrote in water that engulfed the world. GoYe

Piazza di Spagna, Early Morning. Richard Wilbur. Perfectly beautiful, perfectly ignorant of it. GrPl; InPS; OBSP; PAI; SM; VGW

Piazza Piece. John Crowe Ransom. I am a lady young in beauty waiting. AP; BoLoP; CoBMV; GoTF; HeIP; InPo; MoAB; MoAmPo; MoVE; NoAm; NOBA; NoP; OxBA; SoSe; TAP; TreFT; TrGrPo

A Piazza Tragedy. Eugene Field. To die!/O my! FiBHP; NLV

Piazzas. Barbara Guest. and no one walks the piazza. NeAP

Pibroch. Ted Hughes. This is where all the stars bow down. FaBoMo; NePoEA-2; OAEL 1-2; PoCh

Pibroch of Donald Dhu. Sir Walter Scott. Pibroch of Donuil Dhu,/Kneel for the onset! EnLi 1-2; FaBoCh; FaPoR; HBV 1-2; InPo; NBM; OxBS; PoEL 1-5

The Picador Bit. Bink Noll. thrills every male groin while he swings there/ and, helpless, spills the fire of his urine. LiSp

Picasso and Matisse. Robert Francis. Peacefully pursue their war. NePoAm

Picasso's Women. Olga Cabral. under the grave eyes of women forbidden to age. PoDr

Piccadilly. Thomas Burke. And why we love you last and best/Whose hearts were broken on your breast! HBMV

Piccante. Mary Di Michele. ...wrestling/with strangers on the couch. AMV-81

"Picciola". Robert Henry Newell. But 'tis the tenderest reed of all/That trembles first when Earth is shaken. AA

Piccola Commedia. Richard Wilbur. But the heat! I can feel it yet,/And that conniving cold. GP

Pick-A-Back. Anonymous. And I'll get over the misty moor. OxNR

Pick a Bale of Cotton. Anonymous. Oh, Lordy, pick a bale a day. ABF; FSW

Pick a Fern, Pick a Fern, Ferns Are High. Anonymous. (no one feels half of what we know). OBVE

Pick a Quarrel, Go to War. W. H. Auden. No one guesses you are weak. PV

The Pick-Up. J. V. Cunningham. Hysteric in the elemental act. UnTE

Pick-up at Chef Rizal Restaurant. Virginia Cerenio. by rizal weeping verses BrSi

Pick upon Pick... Alex Comfort. to hear the prisoners singing in the sea. NeBP

Pickers. Peter Brett. ...full of/the night in their faces. AMV-81

The Picket Fence. Christian Morgenstern. The architect, however, flew/to Afri-or Americoo. GrPl

The Picket-Guard. Ethel Lynn Beers. The picket's off duty forever. HBV 1-2; MC; PAH

The Picket Line Song. Anonymous. Come and picket on the picket line. FSW

Picketing Supermarkets. Tom Wayman. All this food is grown in the store. NIP

The Pickety Fence. David McCord. Pickety/Pickety/Pick. NTCP; TiPo

Pickin Em Up and Layin Em Down. Maya Angelou. gettin to the next town/Baby. NLV

Picking Apples. Maurice Lindsay. and shrill among the leaves, children impatiently calling. BSV

Picking Grapes in an Abandoned Vineyard. Larry Levis. Carry the grapes up into the solemn house,/Where I was born. MAYP

Picking Lilies. Anonymous. And I'll think on her when she's dead and gone. OBET

A Picnic. Aileen Fisher. NOW all we want/is another one! SoPo

Picnic. Hugh Lofting. Fancy, Nancy/What a spree! GoJo; SUS

The Picnic. John Logan. To play the school games with the others. ConAP; CTBA; NCSH; NePoEA-2

Picnic. Ray Mathew. For I will never come again/With you, with love, to such a time. BoAV

Picnic Day. Rachel Field. And cherries overhead! SiSoSe; SoPo; TiPo

Picnic: The Liberated. M. Carl Holman. Privileged prisoners in a haunted land. PoBA; PoNe

Pico della Mirandola. Mason Jordan Mason. Man or not PoNe

Pictor Ignotus. Robert Browning. Tastes sweet the water with such specks of earth? CTC; TEP; VLP

The Picture. Anacreon. All of her, but voice, is here. UnTE

A Picture. D. C. Cuthbertson. An aspen, quivering there beside the burn,/ And perfect peace. PoSH

The Picture. Robert Lowell. still over us, still in parenthesis. NoAm

A Picture. Howard Nemerov. Seriously running. OxBC

Picture Collection. Marjorie Welish. carrying crossbows, seeing it lead/and finesse the climactic horse. APU

Picture Framing. Bert Meyers. I drive home/the proud cattle of my hands. ELU

A Picture from Life's Other Side. Anonymous. It's a picture from life's other side. FSW

Picture of a Castle. William Meredith. Where a sweet particular girl will say the truth/Over and over until I take it in. NePoEA

Picture of a Nativity. Geoffrey Hill. Freeze into an attitude/Recalling the dead. NoAm; OxBC

The Picture of Her Mind. Ben Jonson. But such a mind, mak'st God thy guest. GoBC

The Picture of J. T. in a Prospect of Stone. Charles Tomlinson. her doom (unknown),/her unmown green. PoCh; PPP

The Picture of Little J.A. in a Prospect of Flowers. John Ashbery. And only in the light of lost words/Can we imagine our rewards. ConAP; PPP

Picture of Little Letters. John Koethe. A peculiar name flickers in the mirror, and then disappears. AMV-81

The Picture of Little T. C. in a Prospect of Flowers. Andrew Marvell. Nip in the blossom all our hopes and thee. AnAnS-1; CBEP; ExPo; GTBS; HBV 1-2; JCP; LiTB; MeLP; MePo; NOBE; NoP; OAEL 1-2; OBEV; OBS; PPP; PrIm; SeCeV; SeCP; SeCV 1-2

Picture of Loot. Alan Sillitoe. The sack of rich great London. OxBTC

A Picture of Okinawa. Dennis Schmitz. only thirty years to come down human. LCAP; NPGG

Picture of Seneca Dying in a Bath. Matthew Prior. And lives and speaks, restor'd and whole. CEP

Picture People. Rowena Bastin Bennett. If I should play a minuet/Upon an old-time spinet. YeAr

Picture Postcards. Miklos Radnoti. Blood mixed with mud was drying on my ear. VWA

Picture-Show. Siegfried Sassoon. And life is just the picture dancing on a screen. CMoP

The Picture That Is Turned toward the Wall. Charles Graham. And a picture that is turned to the wall. GoTF; TreF

Pictures. C. Fox Smith. You paint me a ship as is like a ship...an' that'll do/for me!' EtS

Pictures at an Exhibition. Nathan Rosenbaum. Here is the alchemy of art that brings to this room/The face and the spirit of Israel. GoYe

Pictures from Brueghel. William Carlos Williams.
center of/their workaday world PPP
no time for any-/thing but his painting. LCAP
a splash quite unnoticed/this was/Icarus drowning. LCAP; PPP
a winter-struck bush for his/foreground to/complete the picture... LCAP

Pictures in the Smoke. Dorothy Parker. And after that, I always get them all mixed up. NLV

Pictures of a Gone World. Lawrence Ferlinghetti.
And night's trees stood up PoM
and sung/a sweet high hungry/single syllable HoPM

Pictures of the Rhine. George Meredith. And bridal vines drink in his juices on each side. OBTV

Pictures on the Wall. Zvi Shargel. show me the other side of passing,/the other side of death. VWA

Picturesque; a Fragment. John Aiken. ...these the mental eye/Suffice to charm, and all it sees is good. NOEC

Pie in the Sky. Anonymous. And you'll eat in the sweet bye and bye. GBP

A Pie Sat on a Pear Tree. Anonymous. Thrice so merrily hopped she,/Heigh O, heigh O, heigh O! PBBP

A Piece of Black Bread. Edward (Edward Dzyubin) Bagritsky. And the trumpet's song, till in woods/they are drowned. TrJP

A Piece of Shrapnel. David Ray. begging not to be stolen still again from/this grave, which is in a field of clover. NIP

Pied Beauty. Gerard Manley Hopkins. He fathers-forth whose beauty is past change:/Praise Him. AnEnPo; ATP; AWP; BiP; BoLiVe; BrPo; CMoP; CoBMV; DiPo; EaLo; EBCP; FaBoMo; FaFP; GoJo; GTBS-P; HAP; HeIP; HoPM; InPK; InPo; InPS; InvP; LiTB; LiTM; MoAB; MoBrPo; MoRP; MoVE; NAMP; NIP; NoAm; NOBE; NOBV; NoP; OAEL 1-2; OAEP; OBEV; OBMV; OBNC; OBSP; PAI; PoPl; PoRA; PPP; PrIm; SCV; SoSe; SOTW; TEP; TreFS; TrGrPo; TRV; ViBoPo; VLP; WeW

The Pied Piper of Hamelin. Robert Browning. If we've promised them aught, let us keep our promise. BBV; BeLS; BiP; BLPL; FaBoBe; FaBoCh; FaFP; FaPo; GN; HBV 1-2; HBVVY; LoGBV; OBNV; OxBChV

Pier delle Vigne. Dante Alighieri. one who lies prostrate from the blows of Envy. HoPM

The Pier-Glass. Robert Graves. True life, natural breath; not this phantasma. CMoP; CoBMV; MoAB; NoAm

The Piercing Chill I Feel. Buson (Taniguchi Buso). under my heel... InPK

Piere Vidal Old. Ezra Pound. Ha! this scent is hot! MoAB

Pierrette in Memory. William Griffith. But going, took the stars and moon/And sun away with her. HBV 1-2

Piers Gaveston. Michael Drayton. Or doe you sporte at my calamitie? PeHV

Piers Plowman (excerpt). Anonymous. And wept and wrung her hands when she was/taken. EnLit

Piers the Ploughman. William Langland.
For in his Logic, he used even the least of birds. PBBP
Where neither man nor beast could get near their birds. PBBP

Piers the Plowman's Creed. Anonymous. Each word by itself, and all if it need be. MeEV

Pieta. James Philip McAuley. Clean wounds, but terrible,/Are those made with the Cross. CBAP; PoAu 1-2

Pieta. Rainer Maria Rilke. now I can no longer/give you birth. OFD

The Pieta, Rhenish, 14th C., the Cloisters. Mona Van Duyn. But unmanned spirit or unfleshed man/I cannot cradle. Child, no one can. Prf

Pig. Anthony Hecht. O Swine that takest away our sins/That takest away OxBC

The Pig. Ogden Nash. I call it stupid-of the pig. DBV; FPL

Pig Poem. Cary Waterman. They have never been christianized. GP

Pig Song. Margaret Atwood. This is a hymn. NoP

A Pig-Tale. Lewis (Charles Lutwidge Dodgson) Carroll. And still he sits, in miserie,/Upon that ruined Pump! WiR

A Pig Tale. James Reeves. And that's the end of my little pig tale. SoPo

Pigeon. Roy Fuller. All who will closely look at once espy/A geometrical and insane eye. PB

Pigeon. Elouise Loftin. But dont run/I wont just think pigeon CNA

The Pigeon-Feeders in Battery Park. Julia Cooley Altrocchi. It is the old who must give what they have,-to a dove. GoYe

Pigeons. Richard Kell. one quick gust/They fountain into air. BoAnP

Pigeons. Bert Meyers. they moan and I'm there/and it's still like that. EAS

Pigeons. Marianne Moore. ...this is a dainty breed. PoA

Pigeons. Alastair Reid. as though forever, his appointed pigeon. MP; NePoEA; NYBP; NYP; TwCP

Pigeons. Robert F. Whisler. Yet I cannot help but wonder why/a pigeon struts when he can fly. AMV-80

Pigeons in Prison. Derek Butler. Returning wings promise/one more day/one more day. LFAC

Pigmeat. Leadbelly. Take that bowl to chiny/stand a test just any where BluL

Pigmies and Cranes. Walter Savage Landor. But show me the more tricky if you can. NOBV

Pigs. John Cotton. A roof with a pig under it/Means home. BoAnP

The Pigs. Geoffrey Lehmann. Watching the men who calmly watched my death. CBAP

The Pigs. Jane Taylor. And then he may laugh at the pigs. FM

The Pigs for Circe in May. Joanne Kyger. and the Great Pigs waddle off in the sky– PoM

Pigs o' Pelton. Anonymous. There's five black swine and never an odd one. GBP

Pigwiggin Arms Himself. Michael Drayton. He scarce could stand on any ground,/He was so full of mettle. MoShBr

The Pike. Edmund Charles Blunden. And the miller that opens the hatch stands amazed at the whirl in the water. AnFE; LiTM; MoVE

The Pike. John Bruce. How pure brave my wet thrasher, my enemy. LiSp

Pike. Ted Hughes. That rose slowly towards me, watching. CMoP; FaBoMo; HAP; HeIP; InPS; LiTM; MAT; NCSH; NePoEA-2; NMP; OxBTC; SoSe

Pike's Peak. Anonymous. But you'd be a bigger tract of land/If you were thin out-spread. BPAW

The Pike's Peakers. Lawrence N Greenleaf. And gave him just ten minutes to skedaddle. PoOW

The Pilgrim. Emma Catharine Embury. Through Christ, the Way–the Truth–the Life. OBCA

The Pilgrim. Sarah Hammond Palfrey. Forever of my company! AA

The Pilgrim. Richard Wightman. The pines, the patient stars,/And the new day. WGRP

The Pilgrim and the Herdboy. Robert Williams Buchanan. But no City, great or small,/Have I ever seen at all! OBVV

Pilgrim at Rome. Anonymous. Unless thou bring Him with thee, thou wilt not find. AnIL

The Pilgrim Fathers. Leonard Bacon. And spring adorns the earth no more. WGRP

The Pilgrim Fathers. John Pierpont. Shall foam and freeze no more. AA; HBV 1-2; MC; PAH

The Pilgrim Fathers. William Wordsworth. Concord and Charity in circles move. PAH

The Pilgrim from the East. Gustave Kahn. beside the sweet and delicate face/that by thy hearth-stone smiles. TrJP

The Pilgrim of a Day. Thomas Campbell. To night and silence sink for evermore! OBRV

Pilgrim's Problem. Clive Staples Lewis. ...But the experienced walker knows/That the other explanation is more often true. TrCP

The Pilgrim's Progress. John Bunyan.
He'll labour night and day/To be a Pilgrim. EBCP; EBEV; WiR
Here little, and hereafter Bliss,/Is best from age to age. EBEV; HBVY
Some, though they shun the Frying-pan,/Do leap into the Fire. EBEV

Pilgrim's Song. Bernard S. Ingemann. And the end of toil and gloom. WGRP

Pilgrim Song. Florence Earle Coates. Strong with love's humility. OHIP

The Piper on the Hill. Dora Sigerson Shorter. The wind, the wind, the wind, the wind,/May blow her home again. HBV 1-2; HBVY; OnYI

The Piper's Progress. Francis Sylvester ("Fathus Prout") Mahony. Can't I soften the heart of a/stone! FiBHP

The Pipes. Lou Lipsitz. They say only those pipes are real. LTB

The Pipes at Lucknow. John Greenleaf Whittier. But the"sweetest of all music/The pipes at Lucknow played! GN; HBVY

The Pipes o' Gordon's Men. J. Scott Glasgow. Dinna ye hear th' bagpipes play? HBV 1-2

Piping Down the Valleys Wild. William Blake. And I wrote my happy songs/Every child may joy to hear. EnPE; FaBoCh; FaBV; GoTF; InvP; LoGBV; NOBE; OBEC; OnUR; PoPle; TreFS; UnS

Piping Peace. James Shirley. Who is the Master of our spring/And all the bloom we owe. ACP; LoBV; NOBE; OBEV

Pipings. J. Paget-Fredericks. As blossoms blow on window panes. BrR

Pippa Passes. Robert Browning. All's right with the world! ATP; BLPL; BrR; EBCP; FaFP; GoJo; GoTF; GTBS; LiTB; MCCG; NTCP; OBEV; OBVV; OHIP; PoPl; PoToHe; TEP; TrCP; TreF; TRV; UnPo; WGRP

Pippa Passes, but I Can't Get around This Truck. Margaret Blaker. But I'm still in Fairport. NLV

The Pirate Don Durk of Dowdee. Mildred Plew Merryman. The Pirate Don Durk of Dowdee. OnUR; SoPo; TiPo

The Pirate (excerpt). Sir Walter Scott. Eagle of the north-west, thou hast heard/the voice of the Reim-kennar. OΛEP

The Pirate of High Barbary. Anonymous. Sailing down the coast of High Barbary. EtS

Pirate Story. Robert Louis Stevenson. The wicket is the harbour and the garden is the shore. BeLS; TiPo

Pirate Treasure. Abbie Farwell Brown. "Hey! Jolly Roger, O." EtS

Pirate Wind. Mary Jane Carr. And laugh to see you run! BrR; SiSoSe

Pirates. Elizabeth Jane Coatsworth. Died upon those wind-blown gallows/At twenty-one or so! EtS

Pirates. Alfred Noyes. Come, old friend, come thro' the darkness and let us be/playmates again. MCCG

The Pirates of Penzance. Sir William Schwenck Gilbert.
...As I was merciful to/you just now, be merciful to me! NAs
I am the vey model of a modern Major-/General. CoBE
A policeman's lot is not a happy one. TrGrPo

Pirouette. Audre Lorde. I cannot return. NNP

The Pisan Cantos (excerpt). Ezra Pound.
But oblivion, not thy forgiveness, FRANCE. FaBoTw
Here error is all in the not done,/all in the diffidence that faltered. FaBoTw; NOBE

Pisanello's Studies of Men Hanging on Gallows. John Wheatcroft. across from the muddy town square in Milano. FAZ

Piscatorie Eclogues. Phineas Fletcher. Well may I pitie; she must cure thy pain. SeCV 1-2

Pisces. R. S. Thomas. In the delicate flesh/And the tooth that bruises. OxBC

Pisces Child. Sandra McPherson. You will never run dry. NMM

Pisgah. Willard Wattles. Knowing each painful step I trod/Hath brought me daily home to God. WGRP

Pistol Slapper Blues. Blind Boy Fuller. that's a lying woman/and a monkey man./Mmmmmmmmmmmmmmmmmm..... BluL

The Pit of Bliss. James Stephens. And, in cloud, and clod, to Sing/Of Everything, and Anything. AnFE

Pit, Pat. Anonymous. Gone into the cherry tree. OxNR

Pit Viper. N. Scott Momaday. Mere hunger cannot urge him from this drowse. CDW

Pit Viper. George Starbuck. they aren't small-/time haters/that joined up. NYBP; SUW

The Pitch Piles Up in Part. Desmond O'Grady. for whatever new comes from it/something old died. CIP

Pitch Seven. Hamish Brown. Take in the tangled slack! PoSH

Pitcher. Robert Francis. Making the batter understand too late. LiSp; NePoAm; OBSP; PP; SD; SoSe

The Pitcher. Yuan Chen. Streamed from my eyes and fell on the collar of my dress. AWP

A Pitcher of Mignonette. Henry Cuyler Bunner. In the tenement's highest casement. AA; HBV 1-2

The Pitt-Rivers Museum, Oxford. James Fenton. For his father had protected his good estate. FaBoMo

Pittsburgh. Witter ("Emanuel Morgan") Bynner. Mornings naked on a rock. AmFN

Pittsburgh. Hy Sobiloff. And raked the quarry to stoke his volcanic heart. NePA

Pity. Babette Deutsch. But the young must eat pomegranate seeds in the darkness under the/earth. WHA

Pity and Love. Anonymous. I love with pity, pity me with love. ALV

Pity Ascending with the Fog. James Tate. ...weather/is far too clear for me to think of/anything but august comedy. NoAm

Pity Me Not. Edna St. Vincent Millay. ...heart is slow to learn/What the swift mind beholds at every turn. AnNE; CMoP; MoAB; MoAmPo; NePA; OxBA; TrGrPo

Pity Not. William Haskel Simpson. If they rise again,/Love folds them then. HBMV

The Pity of It. Thomas Hardy. And their brood perish everlastingly. CMoP; LiTM; WaP

The Pity of Love. William Butler Yeats. All threaten the head that I love. AnIV; CMoP; NOBV; VLP

The Pity of the Leaves. Edwin Arlington Robinson. They fluttered off like withered souls of/men. AA; MoAmPo

Pity Poor Labourers. Anonymous. When we'll have the farmers all under our thumbs. OBET

Pity the Down-Trodden Landlord. Arnold Clayton. And don't be behind with the rent. FSW

Pity this busy monster, manunkind. Edward Estlin Cummings. —listen:there's a hell/of a good universe next door;let's go. AmP; AmPP; AP; CoBMV; CrMA; LiTA; LiTM; MoVE; NePA; NOBA; OxBA; PPP; TAP

A Pity. We Were Such a Good Invention. Yehuda Amichai. We even flew a little. BoLoP

Piute Creek. Gary Snyder. Watch me rise and go. CAPP; CoAP; ConAP; NaP; NOBA

Piyyut for Rosh Hashana. Haim Guri. The curtains billow and the doors move on their hinges. OFD

Pizen Pete's Mistake. Merrill Honey. And then his voice came drifting back: "My name is Billy the Kid." BPAW

A Pizza Joint in Cranston (parody). Craig Weeden. ...leaving you/with stomach cramps on the black streets of Cranston? BXAP

A Place (Any Place) to Transcend All Places. William Carlos Williams. very, very specially, heaped/about the roots for nourishment. NYP

The Place at Alert Bay. Muriel Rukeyser. Form that is energy from these seas risen,/Identified. Resumed in God. PoA

A Place by the River. William Keens. baptism by immersion and the glorious hysteria. TAT

A Place in Thy Memory. Gerald Griffin. A smile and kind word when we meet,/And a place in thy memory. HBV 1-2

Place Me in the Breach. Yehuda Karni. and from their strength my bones will/sing, that pine/to greet the Messiah. TrJP

Place Me under Your Wing. Hayim N. Bialik. And allow your breast to shelter my head,/The nest of my deepest prayers. VWA

Place-Names of China. Alan Bennett. Cold the seat and loud the cistern/As I read the Harpic tin. FaBoPa; NOBL

The Place of Backs. William Stanley Merwin. as we grow smaller because of the melting of our bones. HoPM

A Place of Burial in the South of Scotland. William Wordsworth. ...and neighbouring thickets/ring/With jubilate from the choirs of spring! VLP

Place-of-Many-Swans. Charlotte DeClue. Who weeps over fallen trees? STE; TWSS

The Place of O. Ray A. Young Bear. a woman's dream for her/daughter is much stronger/than your death. VoR

The Place of Pain in the Universe. Anthony Hecht. The pain is life-like in that waxwork tear. CrMA; LiTA

The Place of Peace. Edwin Markham. I have a place where my spirit sings,/In the hollow of God's Palm. GoTF; TreFT; TRV

The Place of Rest. George William Russell. The Mother takes her child again. WGRP

The Place of the Damned. Jonathan Swift. How happy for us, that it is not at home! FaBoEE; OBSV

The Place of the Fian Is Bare Tonight. Anonymous. And Cailte wept bitterly. NOBI

The Place of the Solitaires. Wallace Stevens. Which is to be a place of perpetual undulation. SyP

The Place of V. Ray A. Young Bear. is walking away in his/father's hands in the form/of four sticks. VoR

Place Pigalle. Richard Wilbur. ...now shall I gently seize in my/Desperate soldier's hands which kill all things. HeIP

A Place to Live. Martin Grossman. And not turn away. AMV-80

Places and Ways to Live. Richard Hugo. a world the color of salt with no young music in it. GP

Places I Have Been. Joyce M. Volk. These places I have known. AMV-80

Places, Loved Ones. Philip Larkin. Your person, your place. CMoP; NePoEA

Places of Nestling Green. [James Henry] Leigh Hunt. The slender trunks, to inward peeping sight/Thronged in dark pillars up the gold green light. OBRV

A Placid Man's Epitaph. Thomas Hardy. Who might have meetly used it. MoBrPo

Placing a $2 Bet for a Man Who Will Never Go to the Horse Races ... Diane Wakoski. A certain spirit/I hope/you've passed on to me. UnPo

Plague of Dead Sharks.   Alan Dugan.   what the sun burns up of it, the moon puts back.   AP; LiTM; NoAm

A Plague of Starlings.   Robert Earl Hayden.   chitter and quarrel/in the piercing dark/above the killed.   HoAn

The Plaidie.   Charles Sibley.   Wha kens but it may rain?   HBV 1-2

Plain.   Miller Williams.   I am not alone.   TAT

Plain-Chant for America.   Katherine Garrison Chapin.   Died for and sung for and fought for,/And worked for,/Is living yet.   PAL

Plain Dealing.   Alexander Brome.   I'll love my Country, Prince, and Laws; and those, that love/the King.   OBS

Plain Dealing's Downfall.   *Anonymous.*   While Knavery, laughing, rung her passing bell.   OBSV

Plain Fare.   Daryl Hine.   The way that I could not afford to go.   CoAP

The Plain Golden Band.   *Anonymous.*   The pride of the valley, the girl I adore.   ShS

Plain, Humble Letters.   David Vogel.   My sister, hidden/In Bessarabian evenings.   VWA

Plain Language from Truthful James.   Bret (Francis Bret Harte) Harte.   Which the same I am free to maintain.   BeLS; BLPA; BPAW; CTC; FaBoBe; FaBoCo; HBV 1-2; InMe; NOBL; OBAL; TreF; YaD

A Plain Man's Dream.   Frederick Keppel.   Love they would learn full soon without/my teaching!   AA

The Plain of Adoration.   *Anonymous.*   worshipped such stones until/the coming of good Patrick to Armagh.   BIrV

The Plain Sense of Things.   Wallace Stevens.   Required, as a necessity requires.   HaCAP; PAI

Plain Song.   Jean Cocteau.   I am your divine name.   PoPl

Plain Song.   Benjamin Fondane.   and I can no longer hide from death.   VWA

Plain Song Talk.   Richard Eberhart.   And of death the less said the better.   PoA

Plain Talk.   William Jay Smith.   That's how he felt–that's how I feel.   DBV; FiBHP; MoAmPo

Plainness.   Jorge Luis Borges.   like stones of the road, like trees.   NYBP

Plains.   W. H. Auden.   ...nothing is lovely,/Not even in poetry, which is not the case.   NePA

The Plains.   Maynard Dixon.   Trail of my own lost footprints–I go to the plains!   BPAW

The Plains.   Roy Fuller.   and at the end of every day is night.   MoPo

The Plains of Mexico; or, Santa Anna.   *Anonymous.*   Along the plains of Mexico!   AmSS

The Plains of Waterloo.   *Anonymous.*   ..."You're welcome, lovely William, from the plains of/Waterloo."   OBET

Plaint.   *Anonymous.*   And I pretty wench can get none.   OxNR

Plaint.   Ebenezer Elliot.   That God is All, His shadow shows.   OBEV; OBVV

Plaint.   Charles Henri Ford.   Do angels pick the cherry-blood of folk like me, Lord?   AtBAP; EAS; MoVE; PPON

The Plaint of the Camel.   Charles Edward Carryl.   Any shape does for me!   AnAmPo; EvOK; HBV 1-2; HBVY; SoPo

The Plaint of the Wife.   W. R. S. Ralston.   Driven out, thrown away, married too soon!   AWP

Plainview: 3.   N. Scott Momaday.   a prairie fire.   CDW

The Plan of Salvation.   John Milton.   Adore the Son, and honour him as me.   WGRP

A Plan to Live My Life Again.   Diana O Hehir.   Particles scraping against an interior lining.   NPGG

Les Planches-en-Montagnes.   Michael Roberts.   Here untended roar machines/In mastery of black ravines.   OBMV

The Plane: Earth.   Sun-Ra.   T, then, is a symbol for the plane earth.   PoBA

Plane Geometer.   David McCord.   To box the crazy compass of bad dreams.   NYBP

Plane Geometry.   Emma Rounds.   And the ang-gulls convex'd.   ImOP; QQQ; SpRo

Plane Wreck at Los Gatos.   Woody Guthrie.   And all they will call you will be deportee.   InPK; PrIm; WTO

The Planet.   Josephine Jacobsen.   and water, water: the innocent planet,/shining and shining.   GP

A Planet of Descendance.   William Frederick Stevenson.   And invalid's puissancy.   NOBV

The Planet on the Table.   Wallace Stevens.   Of the planet of which they were part.   HaCAP; HAP

Planetarium.   Adrienne Rich.   ...for the relief of the body/and the reconstruction of the mind.   CAPP; FaBoWP; HaCAP; NIP; NoAm; NOBA

The Planetary Arc-Light.   August Derleth.   "I see they've put a new streetlight out there."   GoYe

Planetary Exchange.   LeRoi (Imamu Amiri Baraka) Jones.   ...Through the dazzling/lives of the planets and stars. I am. sings.   CAPP

The Planets Line Up for a Demonstration.   Josie Kearns.   lifting us higher than fear.   SUW

Planh for the Young English King.   Bertrand.   There where there is no grief, nor shall be sadness.   LiTW

Plankton.   Ruth Miller.   Apart, we left the strange sea/Within each other.   PeSA

Planning the Perfect Evening.   Rita Dove.   ...And how hulking/you are, my dear, my sweet black bear!   MAYP

Plans.   Helen Morgan Brooks.   may pause and look back/to toss their bouquet.   NNP; PoNe

Plans.   Dorothy Brown Thompson.   Won't it be nice?   BiCB

Plans for Altering the River.   Richard Hugo.   Just when the water was settled and at home.   FYAP

The Planster's Vision.   Sir John Betjeman.   "No Right! No Wrong! All's perfect, evermore."   PoPl

Plant a Tree.   Lucy Larcom.   And his work its own reward shall be.   HBVY; OHFP; PGD; WBLP

The Plantation.   Seamus Heaney.   To be pilot and stray–witch,/Hansel and Gretel in one.   FaBoIP

Plantation Bitters.   *Anonymous.*   Nine pounds avoirdupois is added to my weight.   FaBoUs

A Plantation Ditty.   Frank Lebby Stanton.   Oh, wait, good Lawd, 'twell ter-morrer!   AA; HBV 1-2

Plantation Play-Song.   Joel Chandler Harris.   Hop light, ladies,/Oh, Miss Loo!   MCCG

The Planter's Daughter.   Austin Clarke.   And O she was the Sunday/In every week.   CIP; OxBI; OxBTC

The Planticru.   Robert Rendall.   Nor kens hoo firm she heads b' siklike toil/Man's aald inheritance o' sea and soil.   OxBS

The Planting.   Harley Elliott.   ...searching a place/in my arm.   NeAC

Planting a Magnolia.   W. D. Snodgrass.   And will survive us./Before it dies.   NoAm

Planting a Tree.   Nancy Byrd Turner.   Grow well, good tree!   YeAr

Planting Flowers on the Eastern Embankment.   Po Chu-i.   Sits till evening and will not move from the place!   BoNaP

The Planting of the Apple-Tree.   William Cullen Bryant.   On planting the apple-tree.   AA; AnNE; GN; HBV 1-2; HBVY; LaNeLa; OHIP; PoSC

Planting Trees.   Violet Helen Friedlaender.   Some thanks for every lovely tree/That dead men grew for me.   BoNaP

Planting Trout in the Chicago River.   Dennis Schmitz.   ...the gills/have an almost human grin.   NPGG

The Plants.   Michael Dennis Browne.   whose pages turn without me.   GP

Plants Don't Talk, People Say.   Rosalia de Castro.   without it/how shall I live?   WPOW

Plaque.   Bruce Ruddick.   The passing freight flutters the laundry hung out like cliches.   CaP

...Plashes the Fountain.   Paul Celan.   the pair of eyes that lay ready there as/tear-upon-/tear.   OBVE

Plastic Jesus.   *Anonymous.*   Plastic Jesus is a holy bar.   FSW

Platform Goodbye.   H. B. Mallalieu.   My love is in all you do,/Yours with me wherever I go.   WaP

Plato, a Musician.   Leontius.   For in his heart and in his hand there lingered/Some remnant of the ancient melodies.   UnS

Plato in London.   Lionel Pigot Johnson.   In as august a sphere:/Perchance, far higher.   VLP

Plato Instructs a Midwest Farmer.   David Palmer.   "I don't think it's gonna make it."   SUW

Plato To Theon.   Philip Freneau.   To Jove, dear Theon, be resigned.   AA

Plato Told.   Edward Estlin Cummings.   avenue/el;in the top of his head:to tell/him   AmFN; AmPP; CrMA; MoVE; NoAm; NOBA; NYP; OxBA; WaP

The Platonic Lady.   John Wilmot, Earl of Rochester.   These are the only sweets of love.   UnTE

Platonic Love.   Abraham Cowley.   My mistress and at th' instant he/Should steal her quite from me.   NoP; SeCV 1-2

Platonick Love.   Edward, Lord Herbert of Cherbury.   My chief contentment I will entertain.   AnAnS 2; OBS

The Platypus.   *Anonymous.*   ...They showed me/the way Djanbun went across the mountain range.   NOAV

The Platypus.   Oliver Herford.   Or-in-tho-rhyn-chus Par-a-dox-us.   FiBHP; NA

The Plaudite, or End of Life.   Robert Herrick.   It is the last commends the play.   CaPo

Play.   Archie Randolph Ammons.   is allowed, considering   PoA

Play.   Frank Asch.   I'll hold the string said I.   NTCP

The Play.   C. J. Dennis.   "Peanuts or lollies!" sez a boy upstairs.   PoAu 1-2

The Play.   Charles Otis Judkins.   The full moon sank beneath the sea.   PeD

The Play.   James Benjamin Kenyon.   Nor know they play Life's Comedy of Tears.   HBV 1-2

Play about, Do.   Basho (Matsuo Basho).   Jewels of dew!   SoPo

Play-Acting.   Frances Barber.   And scandal left her presence/For person more endowed!   GoYe

Play Ball! Robert Francis. Star in his casket. AMV-80

The Play-House. Joseph Addison. And in his own vile tatters stinks again. APAS

A Play of Opposites. Gray Burr. There is no luck out there beyond earshot. CoPo

The Play of the Four P.P.: The Palmer. John Heywood. And at Our Lady that standeth in the Oak. ACP; CAW

The Play of the Weather: The English Schoolboy. John Heywood. And to hear the birds how they flicker their wings/In the pitfall! I say it passeth all things. ACP

Play-Song. Anonymous. –He drove a white horse and went splash in the sea. LiTW

Play Song. Peter Clarke. Or up to the hill where the daisies grow,/There's where we will go. PBA

Playboy. Richard Wilbur. Consents to his inexorable will. FF; NoAm; NOBA; NoP; WeW

The Playboy of the Demi-World: 1938. William Plomer. He'd shrivel up at once or turn to stone. OxBTC; PeHV; TW

Player. Stephen Dunning. helping us keep time FAZ

Player Piano. John Updike. Misstrums me, or tries a new tune. WeW

The Players Ask for a Blessing on the Psalteries and Themselves. William Butler Yeats. But bless our hands that ebb away. UnS; VLP

Playgrounds. Laurence Alma-Tadema. I wish that I were very tall,/High up above the trees. HBV 1-2; HBVY

Playing Catch. Keith Moul. we have broken into dreams. AMV-80

Playing House. Jack Gilbert. Not needing to touch the other's arm first? NPGG

Playing Pocahontas. Lew Blockcolski. and no one noticed. VoR

Playing the Bones. Elizabeth Brewster. tapped out long ago/for a child. AMV-81

Playmates. Lillian Everts. the evidence inviting me to trace/it where it was before it left its place. GoYe

Plays. Walter Savage Landor. How many prompters! what a chorus! HBV 1-2; NLV; OBSP; OxBoLi; PV

Playthings. William Cowper. Because men suffer it, their toy the world. WaaP

Playwright. John Woods. Then, safe until the matinee. CoPo

Plaza Real with Palmtrees. Paul Blackburn. All of it gentle NoAm

Plea. John Ciardi. –or starve yourself, and starve me, and be right.' OBSP

The Plea. John Drinkwater. On these, and make those gardens mine. MoRP

Plea for a Captive. William Stanley Merwin. Kill it at once or let it go. NePoEA-2; NoAm; NYBP

A Plea for a Plural. Rudolph Chambers Lehmann. How oft your pellets pass them/Is singular–like grouse. CenHV

A Plea for Flood Ireson. Charles Timothy Brooks. Shall cleanse the stain and expiate all. PAH

A Plea for Haste. Petronius Arbiter (Caius Petronius Arbiter). So come to bed; there's time for dawdling after. UnTE

Plea for Hope. Francis Carlin. He lost that hope which, having gained,/We too would lose in Thee attained. TrPWD

A Plea for Mercy. Kwesi Brew. But we have come in tattered penury/Begging at the door of a Master. PBA

A Plea for Postponement. Petronius Arbiter (Caius Petronius Arbiter). Our deepest need until...until...until... UnTE

A Plea for Promiscuity. Edmund Waller. Take advice of present love. UnTE

Plea For Tolerance. Margaret E. Bruner. And lifted upward to a saner view. PoToHe

A Plea for Trigamy. Sir Owen Seaman. I will marry no wife, since I can't do with one less/Than three. NOBL

The Plea of the Midsummer Fairies. Thomas Hood.
And Time is reckon'd a discarded thing.' OBNC
And we will muffle up the sheepfold bell/Whene'er thou listenest to Philomel.' OBRV
And with a ragged edge cut heart from heart. OBRV
And youth's warm gracious heart is harden'd quite. OBNC
O then I clap aloft my brave broad wings,/And make the wide air tremble while it rings!' OBNC
Till shrill larks warn them to their flowery cells.' OBNC; OBRV

A Plea to Boys and Girls. Robert Graves. And call the man a liar who says I wrote/All that I wrote in love, for love of art. GTBS-P

Plea to Eros. Anonymous. On my body there's no part/But bears a scar for every dart. UnTE

A Plea to My Sister Carolyn Cunningham: the Artist. James (Olumo) Cunningham. paint me JB

Plea to Those Who Matter. James Welch. happy for the snow clean hands of you, my friends. AmPA

Plead for Me. Emily Bronte. Speak, God of Visions, plead for me/And tell why I have chosen thee! EnLi 1-2; PoEL 1-5

The Pleaders. Peter Davison. We are among you; we are going to stay. NYBP

Pleading Voices. Shalom Katav. let all people live/In peace.../Peace. VWA

Pleasant and Delightful. Anonymous. And if ever I return again I will make you my bride.' OBET; OBSS

Pleasant Changes. Jane Euphemia Browne (Aunt Effie). Are we knowing/Where we're going,/What we're doing here? OxBChV

The Pleasant Comedie of Old Fortunatus. Thomas Dekker.
Let us sing merrily, merrily, merrily. AtBAP
Vertues braunches wither, Vertue pines. AtBAP

Pleasant Comedie of Patient Grissill. Thomas Dekker. Then hey noney, noney: hey noney, noney. AtBAP

The Pleasant Life in Newfoundland. Robert Hayman. (I doe beleeve) they'd live no other where. NOBC

Pleasant Memories: The Meadow-Field. Charles Sangster. Mary, do yo remember? OBCV

A Pleasant New Ballad of Two Lovers. Anonymous. "Complaine, my lute, complaine with me,/Untill that he doth come againe." CoMu

A Pleasant New Court Song. Anonymous. Rewards me with a kisse,/and thanks me for my paine. CoMu

Pleasant Sounds. John Clare. the dew flashes from its brown feathers! CBEP

Pleasant the House. Anonymous. twenty, her noble doorway. BIrV

Please. Ronald Koertge. ...Come back, bitch. Eat me alive. GP

Please Excuse Typing. John Basil Boothroyd. Splendid. FiBHP

Please Forward. James Welch. ...Grave mama, I caught/the silliest and it was me. CDW

Please keep an eye on my house for a few moments. Vidya. with their sharp and broken stalks,/which may scratch my breasts. BoWoP

Please Master. Allen Ginsberg. over & over, bamming it in while I cry out your name I do love you. PeHV

Please Say Something. Tomioka Taeko. and give it good thought/OK? WPOW

Please Tell Me Just the Fabuli. Shel Silverstein. And kindly, kindly spare me/All this insignifigancia. ELU

Please to Ring the Belle. Thomas Hood. "The next time you come, love, pray come with a ring." HBV 1-2

Pleasent Delusion of a Sumpteous Citty. Sarah Kemble Knight. They'r very fine! sais my deluded eye. SCAP

The Pleasing Constraint. Richard Brinsley Sheridan. You may think what you please–but they both were content. ALV

Pleasure. Anonymous. If a man were married to/Anyone but his wife. UnTE

Pleasure It Is. William Cornish. And thank Him than. CBEP; CH; MeEL

The Pleasure of Ruins. J. D. McClatchy. aligned like pillars to shade what gods may yet arrive. PoA

The Pleasure of Walking through an Alley. John Gay. Here roams uncombed the lavish rake, to shun/His Fleet Street draper's everlasting dun. EnLi 1-2

Pleasure Reconciled to Virtue: A Masque. Ben Jonson. Tis only she can make you great,/Though place here make you knowne. AnAnS 2

Pleasures. Albert Goldbarth. rub his face in, real, and warm, and nubbled lovely. GeTw

Pleasures. Denise Levertov. opens blue and cool on a hot morning. CAPP; NeAP; NoAm; NOBA

Pleasures, Beauty. John Ford. In the game are felt no pains,/For in all the loser gains. LiTL; ViBoPo

The Pleasures of Hope. Thomas Campbell. Her name, her nature, wither'd from the world! EnRP

The Pleasures of Imagination. Mark Akenside.
And tune to Attic themes the British lyre. OBTV
To guard the sacred volume of the laws. EnPE; EnRP

The Pleasures of Love. Wilfrid Scawen Blunt. Dear endless argument! yet sometimes we/Even as we argue kiss. There! Let it be. HBV 1-2

The Pleasures of Melancholy. Thomas Warton, Jr.. Of wood-hung Meinai, stream of Druids old. CEP; EnRP; LAuP; NOEC

The Pleasures of Merely Circulating. Wallace Stevens. Yet that things go round and again go round/Has rather a classical sound. LiTA; LOW; MAT; OBAL

Pledge. Avraham Shlonsky. Lest now I learn nothing, again. VWA

The Pledge at Spunky Point. John Milton Hay. But ez fur myself, I thank ye,/I'll not take any in mine. OBAL

Pledge of Allegiance. Anonymous. with liberty and justice for all. TRV

The Pleiades. Mary Barnard. What girl or star sings now/like a swan on the Yellow River? NYBP

The Pleiades. Elizabeth Jane Coatsworth. Only to name the little stars, the pretty Pleiades. ImOP

Plenary. Anonymous. Ye living men, come, view the ground/Where you must shortly lie. AmFP

Plenty. LeRoi (Imamu Amiri Baraka) Jones. ...The/real breadth of where we move toward, the perfection/of space. CAPP

Plexus and Nexus. Judson Jerome. Experience runs through me like a tape. AMV-81

The Plight. James W. Thompson. And gods are supposed/but flowers be BPo

Plighted. Dinah Maria Mulock Craik. but each unto each, as in Thy sight, one. HBV 1-2

Pliny Jane. Mildred Luton. picking her way through a field/of imaginary violets. PH

The Plodder Seam. *Anonymous.* Oh, I'd rather sweep the streets than have/To burrow like a mole. ELP

The Plot against Proteus. A. J. M. Smith. Cast off, and nab him; when you have him, call. OBCV; PeCV

The Plot against the Giant. Wallace Stevens. It will undo him. CMoP; FF; OxBA

Plot Improbable, Character Unsympathetic. Elder Olson. Took aim and shot him dead. NePA

The Plot to Assassinate the Chase Manhattan Bank. Carl Larsen. and sea-foam, and the earth. FF; PPON

The Plough-Hands' Song. Joel Chandler Harris. My honey, my love! AA

The Plough-Horse. Rhoda Coghill. As a sleepwalking monk would carry his girdle and habit. OnYI

The Ploughboy. John Clare. Then off behind the plough afield/He goes, the whalebone whip to yield. PoEL 1-5

The Ploughboy in Luck. *Anonymous.* Blossy boys, bubble oh!/Over the brow. OxNR

The Plougher. Padraic Colum. And the thrones of the gods and their halls, their chariots, purples and splendors. AnFE; GoBC; GTBS; HBMV; MoBrPo; OnYI

Ploughing on Sunday. Wallace Stevens. The wind pours down. AmLP; GoJo; NCSH; PoPl; SOTW

The Ploughman. *Anonymous.* I will wash the ploughman's clothes,/And dry them on the dyke, O. GBP O' a' the trades that I do ken,/Commend me to the ploughman. CoMu

The Ploughman. Karle Wilson Baker. He will not let my field lie fallow. WGRP

The Ploughman. Gilbert Thomas. Unseen, undreamt, there still may toil/The patient plough of Hope. HBMV

Ploughman at the Plough. Louis Golding. The Earth poised on his broad hands. HBMV; OHIP

The Ploughman, in Imitation of Milton. Samuel Jones. Lies sheltered only in her shift below him. NOEC

Plow. *Anonymous.* If he handles me right who is my ruler. AnOE

The Plow. Richard Henry Horne. Plow deep and straight with all your powers. HBV 1-2

Plowing at Full Moon. Leo Dangel. Drinking the moon. AMV-80

The Plowman. *Anonymous.* There'll be two losses for one winter. APAS

The Plowman. Robert Burns. He sheds the roughness, lays it by,/And boldly plows his day there. UnTE

The Plowman. Max Harris. and your coarse hands helpless, singing at a plow. BoAV

Plowman. Sidney Keyes. ...Now I keep company/Only with seasons and the cold crazy moon. MoAB; PoRA

The Plowman. Raymond Knister. But I shall not, doing it, look backward. OBCV; PeCV

Plowman's Song. Raymond Knister. Turn under, plow,/Turn under. CaP

Plowmen. Robert Frost. Unless in bitterness to mock/At having cultivated rock. SaC

Pluck the Fruit and Taste the Pleasure. Thomas Lodge. Joy and pleasure is there none. ElL

Plucking out a Rhythm. Lawson Fusao Inada. and the figure is completely/out of sight. AmPA

Plucking the Rushes. *Anonymous.* You and I plucking rushes/Had not plucked a handful when night came! BoLoP; OBVE; OLR

A Plum. Leib. ...Until there remained in his hands/the skin, the pit, and clinging foam. VWA

The Plum-Blossom. Akahito (Yamabe no Akahito). It was only that snow had fallen! AWP

Plum Blossoms. *Anonymous.* Could paint the scent as well. SoPo

Plum Blossoms. Basho (Matsuo Basho). A delicate pink veil. SUS

Plum Blossoms. Chu Shu-chen. Still drowsy with wine. PBWP

The Plum-Cake. Ann Taylor. "Do not be such a glutton again." HBVY

The Plum Gatherer. Edna St. Vincent Millay. But they do not sing. NoAm

The Plum Tree. James Reaney. Only he hears, and farther away,/Some happy animal's slow, listless moo. CaP

The Plum Tree by the House. Oliver St. John Gogarty. And I am turned to sleep. OBEV; PoRA

The Plumber Arrives at Three Mile Island. Robert Stewart. ...it used to be/a plumber always had a place to wash/when he was through to tally up the costs. AMV-81; FAZ

The Plumpuppets. Christopher Morley. The little Plumpuppets plump-up it! TiPo

Plunder. Archie Randolph Ammons. ...my mind's indicted by all I've taken. NoAm

Plunger. Carl Sandburg. Take a long breath and let yourself go. BoLiVe

The Pluralist and Old Soldier. John Collier. And when I die, may I still numbered be/With the rough soldier, to eternity. NOEC

Plus Ca Change... Philip Whalen. Certainly not. Just what shall we tell the children? WeW

Plus Ultra. Algernon Charles Swinburne. Fade at forethought's touch of life's unknown/surprises/Far beyond. VLP

Plutarch. Agathias. Their lives have parallels, but thine has none. AWP

Pluto's Council. Edward Fairfax. Between the solid earth and welkin flit. OBSC

Pluviose. Julian Bell. The stream that to the water meadows/Runs, and floods blue. ChMP

Plymouth Harbor. Mrs. Ernest Radford. Oh, what know they of harbors/Who toss not on the sea! HBV 1-2

Pneumonia Blues. Blind Lemon Jefferson. Tell my good gal I'm going but I'm/still a-standing pat BluL

Po" Boy. *Anonymous.*
It's hard times, po' boy. ABF
Nobody knows my name. TrAS

Po' Boy Blues. Langston Hughes. I wish I'd never been born. BANP

Po' Boy (with music). *Anonymous.* Hung down my head and cried, po' boy! AS

Po' Farmer. *Anonymous.* Dey git all de farmer make. OuSiCo

Po' Laz'us. *Anonymous.* Wo–Lawdy, well, next pay day. OuSiCo

Po' Laz'us (Poor Lazarus). *Anonymous.* "Dat's my only son, Lawd, Lawd, dat's my only son." ABF

Po' Mourner's Got a Home at Las'. *Anonymous.* Po' mourner's got a home at las'. BoAN 1-2

The Poacher. *Anonymous.* And I hallede to the hokes and the hert smote. OxBM

Poaching in Excelsis. G. K. Menzies. Tae win awa' tae Africa an' poach a rhinocerious. FaBoCo

The Pobble Who Has No Toes. Edward Lear. That Pobbles are happier without their toes. AmMo; FaBoCh; FaBoCo; FaBoNo; HBV 1-2; HBVY; LBN; LoGBV; MaC; MoShBr; NA; OxBChV

Pocahontas. George Pope Morris. An angel kneels, in woman's form,/And breathes a prayer for him. MC; PAH

Pocahontas. William Makepeace Thackeray. How a daughter of their sires/Saved a captive Englishman. AmFN; GN; MC; OnMSP; PAH; PAL

Pocahontas to her English husband, John Rolfe. Paula Gunn Allen. ...taking/certain life from the wasting of my bones. STE

Pocket Guide for Servicemen. Hubert Creekmore. ...too much to build/Respect where none has been, or been owed. WaP

Pocket Poem. Ted Kooser. ...I want to be so close/that when you find it, it is warm from me. PPJ

Pockets. Howard Nemerov. What is a pocket but a hole? NIP

Pockets. Susan Adger Williams. And one for hoptoads! BrR

Pocomania. Derek Walcott. High overhead the crow of night/Patrols eternity. NoAm

Pod of the Milkweed. Robert Frost. ...reason why so much/Should come to nothing must be fairly faced. LiTM

Poe at Tea. Barry Pain. But he always came home to tea, tea, tea, tea,/Tea to the n-th. HBV 1-2

A Poe-'em of Passion. Charles F. Lummis. In her solemn sepulcher, Me. BXAP; ShM

Poe's Cottage at Fordham. John Henry Boner. Have cenotaphed his fame. AA

Poem. Robin Blaser.
Listen./The words/sure as a scream. NeAP
when young will end as such. NeAP

Poem. Jim Brodey. the price of my poems is one hamburger! ANYP

The Poem. Babette Deutsch. The logic of the poem is not ours. PoA

Poem. Blanche Taylor Dickinson. Into the brush of another day. CDC

Poem. Langston Hughes. Beautiful, also, are the souls of my people. CDC

The Poem. Galway Kinnell. driven crazy on a locust/post. NaP

Poem. Frank Lima. Light/twelve/Candles/In/My/Head. ANYP

Poem. Pearl Cleage Lomax. the poem sits/smiling/just/behind my lips. CNA

Poem. R. A. K. Mason. but handy for the crucified. ACV

Poem. Bernadette Mayer. To get out of this seaport/You must be a cutter of networks. ANYP

A Poem. Richard Meltzer. faster than a novel PoL

The Poem. William Stanley Merwin. And the lark take the keys/And hang them in heaven. PP

A Poem. Ezekiel Mphahlele. sing the blues/so pain will bleed and let the islands in. WhB

The Poem. David Schloss. I have come to rest beneath its sheer net. PoA

Poem. James Schuyler.   You lack charm.   ANYP

Poem. Charles Simic.   I will look into the earth.   NNaP

Poem. Keith Sinclair.   For when flesh fell/In my arms, soul did as well.   ACV

Poem. Josephine Strongin.   and you seem One?   AnAmPo

Poem. Charles Tomlinson.   To your own meaning, yourself alone.   CMoP

Poem. Tony Towle.
The air comes with us,/a warm halo of fog and icy water with no sense of motion.   ANYP
The remaining years are disappointing.   ANYP

Poem #18.   *Anonymous.*   Once our love is cemented/Let no parting break!   HW

Poem, 1972.   Syd Scroggie.   Obedient to the living God,/His judgment and his laws.   PoSH

Poem: "A clitoris is a kind of brain."   Alice Notley.   ...are there/misprints in the Manhattan Telephone Directory?   APU

Poem: "A frail sound of a tunic trailing."   Antonio Machado.   and the bells dream.   AWP

Poem about a Seashell.   Ranice Henderson Crosby.   it is rough/like my edges   NMM

A Poem about Beauty, Blackness, Poetry.   Linda Brown Bragg.   ...bones of Black strength/have always been/poems for our people.   CNA

A Poem about Breasts.   James Wright.   And round again, and, again, round.   TAP

A Poem about Love.   G. S. Fraser.   And made me cry aloud?   NeBP

Poem about Morning.   William Meredith.   But there is a great deal about it you don't understand.   NYBP

Poem about People.   Robert Pinsky.   All dream it, the dark wind crossing/The wide spaces between us.   NPGG

A Poem about Poems about Vietnam.   Jon Stallworthy.   the mikes that hung upon your lips/when you were at the Albert Hall.   NoAm

Poem: "About the size of an old-style dollar bill."   Elizabeth Bishop.   the yet-to-be-dismantled elms, the geese.   FYAP; HaCAP

Poem About Waking.   David Ferry.   And thus in rage/I loved, alas!   NePoAm-2

Poem About Your Face.   Nathan Alterman.   you were lit to terror by God's image/reflected in his worlds of pallid stone.   VWA

Poem after a Speech by Chief Seattle, 1855.   Charles Brashers.   It is the beginning of survival.   AMV-81

Poem after Apollinaire.   Ira Sadoff.   I just need a few moments to recover   AmPA

Poem: "After your death."   Bill Knott.   a round animal, nameless.   EAS

Poem against Catholics.   James and Fenton Fuller.   John   God–they ate Catholics and their Catholic God!   OBSV

A Poem against Rats.   Fred Levinson.   he never would have waxed in my care   AmPA

Poem against the British.   Robert Bly.   It is also good to be poor, and listen to the wind.   ConAP; PAI

Poem against the Rich.   Robert Bly.   The stones bow as the saddened armies pass.   NMP; NoAm; NOBA

Poem and Message.   Dannie Abse.   And I call your name as loud I can/and give you all the light I am.   TEP

Poem: "As rock to sun or storm."   Niall Sheridan.   The dire and sweet alarm/Of beauty that outruns the eager eye.   OnYI

The Poem as Striptease.   Philip Dacey.   as to just how far/she went.   PPJ

Poem: "As the cat."   William Carlos Williams.   into the pit of/the empty/flowerpot   InPK; InPS; LOW; PAI

Poem at Equinox.   Hilary Corke.   green bubbles bursting in the powdery air/for love!   NYBP

Poem: "At night Chinamen jump."   Frank O'Hara.   we couple in the grace/of that mysterious race.   NoAm; NOBA; SM

Poem at Thirty.   Sonia Sanchez.   i am not afraid/of the night.   BlSi; BPo; CNA; NMM; PoBA

Poem at Thirty.   John Woods.   Send us one such morning to grow on.   CoPo

Poem: "At your light side trees shy."   Bill Knott.   A kneeling enters them.   EAS

The Poem Becomes Canadian.   Pier Giorgio Di Cicco.   ...At this moment/the poem will be happy forever.   CaPN

Poem Beginning "The."   Louis Zukofsky.   Myriad upon myriad shall be.   CoPo

Poem Beginning with a Line by Cavafy.   Derek Mahon.   Cartridges on a deserted rifle range.   FaBoIP

A Poem beginning with a Line by Pindar.   Robert Duncan.   clockwise and counter-clockwise turning.   ConAP; NeAP; NMP; NNaP; PoM

Poem by a Perfectly Furious Academician.   Shirley Brooks.   Then nobody will buy.   FiBHP; NOBV

Poem by the Bridge at Ten-Shin.   Li Po.   With her hair unbound, and he his own skiffsman!   OBVE

Poem by the Charles River.   Robin Blaser.   No agony/as if/my mind had eaten death   NeAP

Poem by the Clock Tower, Summer.   James Keir Baxter.   Again the dark Dove nestles in my breast.   ACV

Poem Called Poem.   James Whitehead.   ...This poem is an ancient form.   GrPl

(Poem) (Chicago) (The Were-Age).   Bill Knott.   To tame these dead bodies and wet ashes.   EAS

The Poem Circling Hamtramck, Michigan All Night in Search of You.   Philip Levine.   ...A strange star is born/one more time.   NNaP

Poem: "Come, brother, and tell me your life."   Jorge Rebelo.   In our land/Bullets are beginning to flower.   WhB

Poem Composed in Rogue River Park...   Tom Wayman.   Let me stay in Grants Pass, Oregon, forever.   PoL

A Poem Containing Some Remarks on the Present War.   *Anonymous.*   Their raptur'd tongues do tell/Their joys great.   PAH

Poem: "Disturbing to have a person."   Barbara Guest.   Ain't nothin' like river trout.   FaBoWP

Poem/Ditty-Bop.   Carolyn M. Rodgers.   Let's grow in love.   JB

Poem Ending with an Old Cliche.   Paul Zimmer.   Life is precious.   AMV-81

Poem: "Entombed in my heart."   Margery Dodson.   ...walk hand in hand/each long and lovely day, the rutted rue.   AMV-80

A Poem Entreating of Sorrow.   Sir Walter Ralegh.   Cleaves to mischance and unrepaired loss./For tender stalks–   SiPS

A Poem (excerpt).   Oliver Wendell Holmes.   We own the love that calls us back to Thee!   TrPWD

Poem Following Discussion of Brain.   Stan Rice.   and I wake from and into/dream.   NPGG

Poem for a Christmas Broadcast.   Anne Ridler.   Then even sin contrives your greater glory.   NeBP

Poem for a "Divorced" Daughter.   Horace Coleman.   cause I do/where I am   LTB

Poem for a Neighbor.   Pat Therese Francis.   the mosaic of a common light.   AMV-81

A Poem for a Poet.   Don L. Lee.   the way of the Sun/as to make them/blacker.   PoBA

A Poem for a Poet.   Audre Lorde.   And what piece of me is it then/Buried down in North Carolina.   NMM

Poem for a Singer.   Milton Acorn.   we ought to die/is the only way we might live.   NeAC

Poem for a Song.   Heather Cadsby.   what have I made.   AMV-80

Poem for a Suicide.   George Economou.   wrapped up in blankets.   DFF

A Poem for Anton Schmidt.   [(or Pillin)] William Pillen.   among clockwork robots/and malevolent puppets.   VWA

Poem for Aretha.   Nikki Giovanni.   think about it   BPo; PoBA

Poem for Ben Barney.   Leslie Marmon Silko.   sunshine not yet through.   CDW; VoR

Poem for Black Boys.   Nikki Giovanni.   You just invent your own games and teach us old ones/how to play   BPo

A Poem for Black Hearts.   LeRoi (Imamu Amiri Baraka) Jones.   ...and white men call us faggots till the end of/the earth.   BP; CAPP; IDB; PoBA; PoM; SOTW

Poem for Carroll Descendant of Chiefs.   Lance Henson.   while the bone moon/watches from a windless sky   VoR

A Poem for Christmas.   C. A. Snodgrass.   Most any soul with God's Good Will.   PoToHe

Poem for David Janssen.   R. T. Smith.   you have found the one-armed man/and found him certain kin.   AMV-81

A Poem for Diane Wakoski.   Ray A. Young Bear.   they merge from your ears and infect love.   CDW

Poem for Dorothy Holt.   Susan Irene Rea.   the grasses vanish.   AMV-81

Poem for Easter.   Robert Kelly.   to find that he is not alone.   VGW

Poem for Easter.   Laurie Lee.   waiting the dawn to fly its bird of god.   BoC

A Poem for Ed "Whitey" Ford.   Jonathan Holden.   Our beauty pure expertise.   MAYP

Poem for Edie Sedgwick.   Stewart Brisby.   & after fifty requests/you got your wish.   LFAC

Poem for Epiphany.   Norman Nicholson.   Only my two eyes and the wild skies to see.   PoPl

Poem for Etheridge.   Sonia Sanchez.   blue / indigo /bodies............   BPo

Poem for Flora.   Nikki Giovanni.   i want to be/like that   PoBA

Poem for Friends.   Quincy Troupe.   too save our children/too save yourself   PoBA

Poem for Garcia Lorca.   George Woodcock.   Remember Lorca, who died only for being Lorca.   NOBC

Poem for Good Friday.   D. G. Jones.   In the wind a part of April, now.   PeCV

Poem for Half-White College Students.   LeRoi (Imamu Amiri Baraka) Jones.   you might be surprised right out the window, whistling dixie on the/way   BPo; CAPP; TAP; UnPo

Poem for Hemingway & W. C. Williams.   Raymond Carver.   they disappear again/into the fading trees/& fields & light/upstream.   WOLT

A Poem for Heroes. Julia Fields. Blood will not serve. CNA

A Poem for Integration. Alvin Saxon. beyond the flicker of/a puffed-out candle PoBA

Poem for J. Wendell Berry. She has taken back into her flesh,/and made light, the dark seed of her pain. GeTw

Poem for Jacqueline Hill. *Anonymous.* for me, the death in darkness; to you, now, a hard dawn. BrRo

Poem for Jan. Joseph Bruchac. forever looking back/over his stooped shoulder CDW

Poem for John My Brother. William Aberg. We both know all we can ask/Is to pass God's steady test of endurance. LFAC

Poem for L. C. Peter Klappert. ...My figure has led you to briars. AmPA

Poem for Lorry. Gerald Hausman. ...She was on the bed/crying. CTBA

Poem for Marc Chagall. Leonard Cohen. And fill their mouths with good bread,/And his happy song. OBCV

A Poem for Max Nordau. Edwin Arlington Robinson. Dun shades quiver down the lone long fallow. AmePo

Poem for Mother's Day. Margaret Fishback. Otherwise I think I could/Dress in ermine, mink or sable. InMe

A Poem for Museum Goers. John Wieners. and streaming in/flames. NeAP

Poem for My Dead Husband. Sheila Roberts. and hobbled off/on mean and crooked feet. AMV-80

Poem for My Family: Hazel Griffin and Victor Hernandez Cruz. June Jordan. I see my self/Alive/A life BPo

A Poem for My Father. Sonia Sanchez. ...i cros myself/with her confessionals. BPo; IHMS

Poem for My Father. Annette Arkeketa West. and the proud hunger/of eyes/I will never know TWSS

Poem for My Father's Ghost. Mary Oliver. A brother who has walked his thousand miles. InPS; Str

Poem for My Grandfather. A. C. Jacobs. For me you are a light on the mantelpiece,/A half shadow on the wall. VWA

Poem for My Mother. Siv Cedering Fox. and stand behind your chair,/brushing the stars out of your hair. Str

Poem for My Mother. Lowell Jaeger. that's the price you pay raising the kind of bird/that flies. AMV-80

Poem for My Thirty-Second Birthday. John Ciardi. Your unknown twin in the debris of time. MiAP

Poem for My Twentieth Birthday. Kenneth Koch. the man standing upright in the dream. PoA

Poem for Myself and Mei: Abortion. Leslie Marmon Silko. and the iridescent wings/flutter and cling/all the way home. VoR

Poem for Nana. June Jordan. God knows I hope he's right. BlSi

Poem for Otis Redding. Joyce Carol Thomas. doing the Hucklebuck CNA

A Poem for Painters. John Wieners. blood already running there. NeAP; PoM

Poem for Pat. Paula Gunn Allen. ...what magic materialized out of that wind,/and if it rained. TWSS

Poem for People Who Are Understandably Too Busy to Read Poetry. Stephen P. Dunn. There's an awful shrug and, suddenly,/you're beautiful for as long as you live. GOYP

A Poem for Players. Al Young. They'll let you play anybody but you,/that's pretty much what they will do. GP

A Poem for Positive Thinkers. Barbara Mahone. which means I can just be me. PoBA

Poem for Roslyn. James Lewisohn. it is the last day and the first. LFAC

Poem for Some Black Women. Carolyn M. Rodgers. a little less a little more/add here detract there/.lonely. BlSi

A Poem for Speculative Hipsters. LeRoi (Imamu Amiri Baraka) Jones. Like,/he was really/nowhere. NoAm; NOBA

Poem for the Atomic Age. Emanuel Litvinoff. but worst was the silence whose words/stung like whips and remained unspoken. NeBP

Poem for the Conguero in D-yard. Raymond Ringo Fernandez. you bring me closer/to home.... LFAC

Poem for the Creative Writing Class, Spring 1982. Merle Woo. Who can keep us caged? BrSi

A Poem for the Insane. John Wieners. We ride them/and Tingel-Tangel/in the afternoon. NeAP; PoM

A Poem for the Meeting of the American Medical Association. Oliver Wendell Holmes. Where'er the eagle spreads his wings,/From northern pines to southern roses! PoEL 1-5

A Poem for the Old Man. John Wieners. home in the hands/of strangers NeAP

Poem for the Year Twenty Twenty. Al Lee. I rejoice that my soul and I/Are mortal and will not last. AmPA

Poem for the Young White Man Who Asked Me How I, an Intelligent... Lorna Dee Cervantes. but in this country/there is war. WPOW

Poem for Thel–the Very Tops of Trees. John Major. a wreath of/green-green melodies. NBP

A Poem for Trapped Things. John Wieners. I watch you/all morning/long./with my hand over my mouth. NeAP; PoM

Poem for Unwed Mothers. Nikki Giovanni. it was good for the virgin mary/its good enough for me OBAL

Poem for viet nam. Ray A. Young Bear. ...the children/growing up drunk. STE

Poem for Vladimir. G. Ripley. When time said you were dead. AMV-81

Poem for You. Robert Pack. And nothing really matters, except to you. NePoEA

Poem: "Form is the woods." Jim Harrison. the spoor of feathers/and slight, pink bones. VGW

Poem from Deal. David Shapiro. WALK ON THE MATTRESSES;DON'T WAKE THE BABIES. ANYP

Poem from Llanybri. Lynette Roberts. ...send an ode or elegy/In the old way and raise our heritage. NeBP

Poem from London, 1941. George Woodcock. Moulding from the burning voice a phoenix day. NeBP

Poem from the Empire State. June Jordan. No rhyme can be said./where reason has fled. BPo

Poem from "The Revolution." Ilya Rubin. My tragedy a speck/in your radiant hand! VWA

Poem: "Geranium, houseleek, laid in oblong beds." John Gray. ...And I/Yield to the strait allure of simple things. SyP

Poem: "Get your tongue." Ted Kooser. I'm kissing you/goodbye. PoL

A Poem–Good or Bad–A Thing–With One Attribute–Flat. Melech Ravitch. ...And what can be flatter than a flat poem? VWA

Poem H. Vicente Rodriguez Nietzche. we give to the world every second/as a gift... InW

Poem: "Hasten on your childhood to the hour." Pablo Picasso. sand earth song sand of the earth afternoon sand earth. EAS

Poem: "Hate is only one of many responses." Frank O'Hara. if felt by me, will be smilingly deflected/by your mysterious concern NeAP; SOTW

Poem: "He lying spilt like water from a bowl." Alison Boodson. and peace is in his kiss. NeBP

Poem: "He watched with all his organs of concern." W. H. Auden. ...distorted features/That wept, and grew enormous, and cried Woe. PoA

Poem: "High on a ridge of tiles." Maurice James Craig. His face is deadly pale. BoAnP; NeIP

The Poem I Am Writing. Artie Gold. for it seems to me and him/that America/happened most there. CaPN

Poem: "I believe the yellow flowers think with me." Alice Notley. To say the closure will be a little, just a little, like this. APU

Poem: "I burn for England with a living flame." Gervase Stewart. In a war for freedom, who were never free. WaP

Poem: "I cannot tell, not I, why she." Walter Savage Landor. Dark look, and overhanging thorn. OAEL 1-2

Poem: "I do not want only." Colleen Thibaudeau. I want it to be like a lacy Breughel. NOBC

Poem: "I do not want to be your weeping woman." Alison Boodson. pinning you to me on a sword of tears. NeBP

Poem: "I heard of a man." Leonard Cohen. it is because I hear a man climb stairs/and clear his throat outside our door. ELU

Poem: "I keep feeling all space as my image." Sanders Russell. three elements of recognition become new numbers. EAS

Poem: "I knew a woman, lovely in her bones." Theodore Roethke. (I measure time by how a body sways.) TrGrPo

Poem: "I know not if from uncreated spheres." Niccolo Machiavelli. Can this be, Master, what thine eyes have done? AWP

Poem (I Lived in the First Century). Muriel Rukeyser. I lived in the first century of these wars. UnPo

Poem: "I loved my friend." Langston Hughes. I loved my friend. DFF; NTCP

Poem: "I met Mother on the street." Lennart Bruce. I'm so proud of you my son! PoL

The Poem: "I sing th' adventures of mine worthy wights." Thomas Morton. There Caron Cerberous and the rout of/feinds,/Had lap enough and so their pastims ends. SCAP

Poem: "I take four devils with me when I ride." Gervase Stewart. Takes off the prize, who is no more than ghost. WaP

Poem: "I walk at dawn across the hollow hills." Ruthven Todd. I walk at midnight on the trampled ferns. EAS

Poem: "I watched an armory combing its bronze bricks." Frank O'Hara. which willfully parades in/its room, refusing to move. NoP

Poem: "I Will Always Love You." Frank O'Hara. I will always love you LLLT

A Poem in Black and White. Mongane Wally Serote. yet, alexandra's night shadow is soaked and drips with my tears. WhB

A Poem, in Defence of the Decent Ornaments of Christ-Church..(excerpt). *Anonymous.* Know this was meant a Poem not a Tract. OBS

Poem in June. Milton Acorn. my trees lean into summer. WHW

Poem in Karori. Louis Johnson. another, another, will follow his fright up the street. AnNZ

Poem in May. John Hewitt. a pebble wakens in a sleepy pond. NeIP

Poem in Nueva York. Cyn Zarco. en mi poema/sorpresa. APU

Poem in October. Dylan Thomas. On this high hill in a year's turning. BiP; BoC; CoBMV; DiPo; LiTB; MoVE; NAs; NeBP; OAEP; PoA; PoPl; PoRA; PrIm; SeCePo; SoSe

A Poem in Praise of Colum Cille. Dallan Forgaill. No slight news out of Niall's people. NOBI

Poem in Prose. Archibald MacLeish. If giver could. LiTL; MoLP; PoPl

Poem: "In secret." Pablo Picasso. in a cafe last summer/in Barcelona. EAS

Poem: "In the corner a violet jug." Pablo Picasso. very white sun the intensely white sun. EAS

Poem: "In the early evening, as now, a man is bending." Louise Gluck. it is spring, the pear tree/filming with weak, white blossoms. HaCAP

Poem: "In the earnest path of duty." Charlotte Forten. We would win a wreath immortal/Whose bright flowers ne'er fade and die. BlSi

Poem in the Matukituki Valley. James Keir Baxter. Of what's eternal shake his grave of time. AnNZ

The Poem in the Park. Peter Davison. ...I'd left the poem/seated motionless upon a wooden bench/with tears in its eyes. GOYP

Poem: "In the stump of the old tree." Hugh Sykes Davies. ...but you'll never want/to eat with it again. EAS

Poem in Three Parts. Robert Bly. And live forever, like the dust. CAPP; ConBMV; NaP; NOBA

Poem in Time of War. William Abrahams. Under the helmet is friend or fatal face. WaP

Poem in Time of Winter. Ray Mathew. But I don't give a damn,/I don't give a river,/I don't give a duck. NOAV

Poem in Which My Legs Are Accepted. Kathleen Fraser. in the first floating and rising of/water. AmPA; LLLT; NMM

A Poem in Yellow after Tristan Tzara. Jerome Rothenberg. my yellow dingdong PoM

A Poem Intended to Incite the Utmost Depression. Samuel Hoffenstein. What the deuce do you expect? FaBoCo

Poem: "Is to love, this–to nurse a name." Rhoda Coghill. Accept the implication of a curve, subdued to the wave's beauty. NeIP

Poem: "It doesn't look like a finger..." Hugh Sykes Davies. AND ANYTHING YOU SEE WILL BE USED/AGAINST YOU. EAS

Poem: "It's a dull poem." Steve Jonas. centrally lo-/cated under 21/white males/& i'll be yr slave. PeHV

Poem: "Khrushchev is coming on the right day!" Frank O'Hara. I am foolish enough always to find it in wind NeAP; PoM

Poem: "Lana Turner has collapsed!" Frank O'Hara. oh Lana Turner we love you get up CAPP; VGW

Poem: "Like a deaf man meshed in his endless silence." John Wain. Everything is known to a god. The gods are desperate. PoCh

A Poem Like a Grenade. John Haines. one hard piece of metal flying off/ might even topple a government. EAS

Poem: "Little brown boy." Helene Johnson. ...You're/All right with me,/ You are. PoBA

Poem: "Look at Me 8th Grade." Sonia Sanchez. while america wanders/ dumb with her wet bowels. PoBA

A Poem Looking for a Reader. Don L. Lee. i/don't love. BP

Poem: "Love being what it is, full of betrayals." Ruth Herschberger. Their hopes are retinal. HoAn

Poem near midway truck stop. Lance Henson. and look west toward home STE

Poem near the Sea. Frelimo. Near the sea,/a new poem/for new men. WhB

Poem, Neither Hillaryous Norgay. Gardner E. Lewis. You'll nEverest if you're Tensing."; FiBHP

Poem No. 21. Doughtry Long. and still as someone/first touching their blackness. CNA

Poem (No Name No. 2). Nikki Giovanni. Get Black Bitterness/NOW BOLo

Poem: "O gentle queen of the afternoon." W. S. Graham. On so sweet an archipelago/As love on love. NeBP

Poem: "O men, walk on the hills." Maxwell Bodenheim. Life escapes defiantly/From the old, sleek tyrannies of earth. TrJP

Poem: "O who can ever praise enough." W. H. Auden. And in the pit of terror thrown/Shall bear the wrath alone. PoA

A Poem of a Maid Forsaken. Anonymous. Till that she was close closed under ground. PBBP

Poem of Angela Yvonne Davis. Nikki Giovanni. to myself just make it easy/on yourself PoBA

A Poem of Broken Pieces. Andrew McCord Jones. for we are the poets/ writing poems by/paying the rent/with our lives. LFAC

Poem of Circumstance. Jean Cocteau. For you can watch it grow. CAW

Poem of Distant Childhood. Noemia da Sousa. And it will be like a new childhood shining for everyone... PBWP

Poem of Explanations. Dahlia Ravikovich. I'm not an apple that never ripens. BoWoP

Poem of Holy Madness, IV. Ray Bremser. to gestures,/and love! NeAP

The Poem of Joao. Noemia De Sousa. who can take the multitude and lock it in a cage? WhB

Poem of Pathos. Tadeusz Rozewicz. it is monstrous/and does not die. FaBoPV

A Poem of Privacy. John Addington Symonds. Of lips, arms, and hidden charms. ALV

A Poem of Sir Walter Rawleighs. Sir Walter Ralegh. When we have wandred all our wayes/Shutts up the story of our dayes. AAS

Poem of the Conscripted Warrior. Rui Nogar. With yellow beaks/And red tails... TTY

The Poem of the End (excerpt). Marina Tsvetayeva. This is delirium,/ please say this bridge cannot/end/as it ends. BrRo; OBVE; PBWP

A Poem of the Forty-Eight States. Kenneth Koch. You and I will go there when Kenneth is dead. NNaP; OBAL

Poem of the Future Citizen. Jose Craveirinha. I!/A man among many/ citizens of a Nation which has yet to exist. TTY

Poem of the Intimate Agony. Julia de Burgos. This my heart so flowing and so lasting! InW

Poem of the Mother. Myra Sklarew. so when his time comes/he can leave me. AMV-80; Str

Poem of the Son. Gabriela (Lucila Godoy Alcayaga) Mistral. Should I die tonight, let me be Thine. PoPl

A Poem of Towers. James Wright. ...over the East River/That loves them and drowns them. CAPP

Poem: "Old man in the crystal morning after snow." Delmore Schwartz. I near you, you near him, all of us must die. PoA

Poem on Azure. Anna de Noailles. Like a white cemetery exposed by the Bosphorus... WPOW

Poem on Canada: Cold Colloquy. Patrick Anderson. to flash at last, sparking the mountain falls/of Restigouche–spawning a silver million. CaP; NOBC; PeCV

A Poem on Elijahs Translation.... Benjamin Colman. And Faith their Consolation did afford,/Elijahs more Illustrious Second Coming with/his Lord. SCAP

A Poem on England's Happiness. Anonymous. So shall the land be truly blessed: he reign/For our protection; we his rights maintain. APAS

Poem: "on getting a card." William Carlos Williams. his style/has other outstanding/virtues/which delight me. VGW

Poem on Hampstead Heath. Louis Adeane. The loss of what is born, the lapse of what is old. NeBP

Poem on His Birthday. Dylan Thomas. As I sail out to die. DiPo; NAs

A Poem on Inter-Uterine Device. A. Rasheed Ghazi. Just who cares to come with me. PeD

The Poem on Our Mother, Our Mother Rachel. Avot Yeshurun. ...As meadows/so we wore this Land. VWA

Poem on the End of Sensation. Ken Stange. abrupt conclusions. AMV-80

The Poem on the Guilt. Avot Yeshurun. and lay on the floor and lay on the child and died of longing. VWA

The Poem on the Jews. Avot Yeshurun. ...and look/upon me as someone they didn't see awhile. VWA

Poem on the Suicide of My Teacher. Joseph Stroud. To open a vault in you, as the one in me. NPGG

Poem; or, Beauty Hurts Mr. Vinal. Edward Estlin Cummings. ono./comes out like a ribbon lies flat on the brush AmP; InPS; MoAB; MoAmPo; MoVE; NIP; OBAL; OxBA; PAI; PPoe

Poem out of Childhood. Muriel Rukeyser. the childhood, the gestures, the rigid travellers. NMM

Poem: "Pity, repulsion, love and anger." Roy Fuller. Or made it an image of their heart. NeBP

Poem Proud Papa. Endre Farkas. Suddenly/bloody & beautiful/she is here CaPN

A Poem Put into My Lady Laiton's Pocket. Sir Walter Ralegh. But yet amongst those cares which cross my rest,/This comfort grows, I think I love thee best. FCP; SiPS

Poem Read at Joan Mitchell's. Frank O'Hara. happiness/the least and best of human attainments ANYP

The Poem: "Rise Oedipeus, and if thou canst unfould." Thomas Morton. With proclamation that the first of May,/At Ma-re Mount shall be kept hollyday. SCAP

The Poem Rising by Its Own Weight. Denise Levertov. holds you,/holds you/close and tenderly before he vanishes. GP

Poem Rocket. Allen Ginsberg. back to sleep in my dark bed on earth. CoPo

A Poem Sacred to the Memory of Sir Isaac Newton. James (1700-48) Thomson. Sleeps with her kings, and dignifies the scene. CEP

Poem: "So many pigeons at Columbus Circle." Arthur Gregor. the madonnas at noon.... VGW

Poem: "So they begin." Boris Pasternak. So verses start them on their way. TrJP

Poem: "Some are too much at home in the role of wanderer." Denise Levertov. Can now take root in life, inherit love? NeBP

Poems. Gary Gildner. ...but it makes you/feel so good in your bones and it's all free! Psk

Poems. Antonio Machado.
The afternoon has gone to sleep/and the bells dream. LiTW
feels the dampness of the garden like a caress. AWP; LiTW
their shadows grow monstrous. LiTW
What do you seek,/poet, in the sunset? LiTW

Poems, I. Philip O'Connor. ...and crowded with gesticulating poetesses. EAS

Poems, II. Philip O'Connor. sufficient to take Britain which they did. EAS

Poems, III. Philip O'Connor. ...the cold pigeons/rested upon his shoulder. EAS

Poems, IV. Philip O'Connor. unborn children in Midnight Market. EAS

Poems, V. Philip O'Connor. thinking hard. EAS

Poems, VI. Philip O'Connor. ...knitted a pair of thoughtful brows. EAS

Poems, VII. Philip O'Connor. ...He then flew into his friend's apartment/through the willingly open window. EAS

Poems, VIII. Philip O'Connor. ...God had/thrown a lamp-post at the Captain, temporarily disabling/him. EAS

Poems, IX. Philip O'Connor. for indeed and forever would he be/to them/just dad. EAS

Poems, X. Philip O'Connor. the even tenour of her ways. EAS

Poems, XI. Philip O'Connor. and could not should as he had broken the even tenour of her/ways. EAS

Poems, LVIII. "Twenty years hence my eyes may grow." Walter Savage Landor. And I shall catch, ere you can pass,/That winged word. PG

Poems, XCIII: "Mother, I cannot mind my wheel." Walter Savage Landor. He always said my eyes were blue,/And often swore my lips were sweet. PG

Poems, XCVIII: "In spring and summer winds may blow." Walter Savage Landor. (When it was full and at the lip) struck down. PG

Poems, CXL: "The burden of an ancient rhyme." Walter Savage Landor. Seizing my forelock...it was gone. PG

Poems about Playmates. Ronda Davis.
carrying groceries/on Saturday mornings. JB
i can still smell him/in my dreams. JB

Poems: Birmingham 1962-1964. Julia Fields.
In their efferevescent youth/And for indifferent seasons. PoBA
Nor dreamed to know, nor wished to learn thereof. PoBA

Poems Chiefly of Early and Late Years: Prelude. William Wordsworth. For benefits that still survive, by faith/In progress, under laws divine, maintained. VLP

The Poems Come Easier. Ray Mathew. bring yellow-sun pollen/with song to the comb. BoAV

Poems for My Brother Kenneth. Owen Dodson. Unconcerned with the morning star. IDB; PoBA; PoNe

Poems for My Daughter. Horace Gregory. He is my flesh and I/am what he was. MoAmPo

Poems for the New. Kathleen Fraser. In snow, in light,/we are about to become! IHMS; NMM

Poems from a First Year in Boston. George Starbuck. hold in the faces of inheritors/a tight precarious old man's embrace. NePoEA-2

Poems from a Greek Anthology (excerpt). Decimus Magnus Ausonius. ...It's what I wanted,/If not what I want. NNaP

Poems from a Greek Anthology (excerpt). Martial (Marcus Valerius Martialis).
...I can't/Understand, Vacerra, why,/You don't have more money. NNaP
...only this stone,/Out in the fields, ever bring forth a tear. NNaP

Poems from a Greek Anthology (excerpt). Palladas. The old sickness overcomes me. NNaP

Poems from Prison. J. J. Maloney. In the Drill cage at the zoo. FAZ

Poems from the Coalfields, 1: Air Shaft. Ian Healy. ...for the lungs/Are dusted with the particles of death. PoAu 1-2

Poems from the Coalfields, 2: Advice from a Nightwatchman. Ian Healy. ...go/Find a park. PoAu 1-2

Poems from the Greek Anthology. of Tarentum Leonidas. Here Klito spent eighty years. NNaP

Poems from the Greek Anthology (excerpt). Asclepiades. Now she hangs her weapon in/The midst of your golden gate. NNaP

Poems from the Greek Anthology (excerpt). Johannes Secundus. Lais can no longer see/Lais in Lais herself. NNaP

Poems in Praise of Practically Nothing. Samuel Hoffenstein.
And what thanks do you get? The gate–I know it! InMe
And what thanks do you get? You're just as dirty! InMe
A complex, or assistant foreman! InMe
What thanks do you get for it? Me don't ask it! InMe
What thanks do you get? She beats you to it! InMe
What thanks do you get? The pants get shiny. InMe
When night comes around you've got to undress yet. EvOK; FiBHP; InMe

Poems of My Lambretta. Paul Goodman. and you have gone to Bloomington. NMP

Poems of Night. Galway Kinnell. The river leaning like a wave towards the emptiness. NaP

The Poems of Our Climate. Wallace Stevens. Lies in flawed words and stubborn sounds. AmP; MoPo; MP; NoP; OxBA; PP; TrGrPo; TwCP

Poems of Passion, Carefully Restrained So as to Offend Nobody. Samuel Hoffenstein. And love you, whom I ought to swat. InMe

Poems of the Arabic (excerpt). *Anonymous.* "Suit thy gree the stroke!" and I–"Suit thy gree!" ErPo

Poems to a Brown Cricket. James Wright. In a book that is shining. NaP; NYBP

The Poet. Joel Benton. He sleeps like fair Endymion. WGRP

The Poet. Elizabeth Barrett Browning. And praise his world for ever, as thou bidst. VLP; WGRP

The Poet. William Cullen Bryant. That sway from mood to mood the willing/mind. AA; AP; MAmP

The Poet. Witter ("Emanuel Morgan") Bynner. What would they do to you and me/If we should say we knew him? WGRP

The Poet. Lucille Clifton. tap dancing for my life DFF; GP

The Poet. William Henry Davies. All crazy for my burning crown. DTC

The Poet. C. Day-Lewis. Short, short is the time. OxBI

The Poet. Paul Laurence Dunbar. A jingle in a broken tongue. BPo

The Poet. Ralph Waldo Emerson.
Through worlds and races and terms and times/Saw musical order and pairing rhymes. PP
To mask a king in weeds. AnNE; OxBA; PCP

The Poet. Padraic Fiacc. Christ on a tree for you and me/And none of the worlds between! CIP; NeIP

The Poet. Anita Grannis. While I, at whom their grim lips curled, live on/And will be young when their last dust is gone! HBMV

A Poet. Thomas Hardy. It will be word enough of praise. NoAm

Poet. Donald Jeffrey Hayes. He knew me intimately too...! AmNP

The Poet. John Keats.
Comes articulate and presseth/On his ear like mother-tongue. PP
Till such unearthly intercourses shed/A visible halo round his mortal head. ERoP 1-2

The Poet. James Kirkup. His singular way, a gentle lunatic at large/In the societies of cross and reasonable men. PP

The Poet. Mary Sinton Leitch. A song of faith and youth and love/He sings at the gates of death. HBMV

The Poet. Haniel Long. I know a thing too strange for knowing,/I, the clay. HBMV

The Poet. Amy Lowell. Life's loneliness of dreaming ecstasy. WGRP

The Poet. Edwin Markham. O men of earth, that wandering voice/Still goes the upward way: rejoice! WGRP

The Poet. Cornelius Mathews. Closing their lids, bestow a dirge-like death! AA

The Poet. Angela Morgan.
Drowning thy music with their cry for gold! WGRP
List'ning with eager ears that understand. TrPWD

The Poet. Yone Noguchi. And move upward to the woodland. WGRP

Poet. Linda Pastan. all the letters of the alphabet/to choose from. DFF

The Poet. Thomas Randolph. A witty man, or one that's out of's wits. PoL

Poet. Karl Shapiro. And none shall speak his name. AnFE; CMoP; LiTM; MoAB; MoAmPo; NoAm

The Poet. Alfred, Lord Tennyson. She shook the world. EnL; OAEP; PP

Poet. Peter Viereck. And all things are because he willed them so. HoPM; MiAP; MoAmPo

The Poet. William Watson. Towers to a lily, reddens to a rose. TrGrPo

The Poet. Walt Whitman. This is what I have learnt from America–it is the amount, and it I teach again. MoAmPo

The Poet: A Rhapsody. Mark Akenside. To warn thee from the service of the ingrate. PP

Poet and Critic. Samuel Daniel. Whereby we come to bury our deserts/In th' obscure grave of singularity. OBSC

Poet and Goldsmith. Vernon Watkins. Night speaks, the artificer, beating out gold.' PoCh

The Poet and His Book. Edna St. Vincent Millay. Yellow clay on dust! AmLP; MoAmPo; NePA

Poet and Lark. Mary Ainge De Vere. Content to dream, and sing no more. AA; HBV 1-2

Poet and Peasant. R. H. Long. More peasant in the soul of one,/More poet in the other. PoAu 1-2

The Poet and the Child. Winifred Howells. The poet and the child walked hand in hand. AA

The Poet and the Dun. William Shenstone. Fate, Fate has ordained us to plague one another. PP

The Poet and the Wood-Louse. Helen Parry Eden. Reflecting where our scaly heart is/Some skyey grace. HBV 1-2

The Poet and the World. George Gordon, Lord Byron. That goodness is no name, and happiness no dream. SeCePo

The Poet at Fifty. Laurence Lerner. Of chatter from the reasonable young/ Who love each other so. PeSA

The Poet at Night-Fall. Glenway Wescott. Like a wind-bell/On a porch where no wind ever blows? PoA

The Poet at Seven. Arthur Rimbaud. and he lay alone on pieces of unbleached canvas,/violently breaking into sail. NaP

A Poet at Twenty. Donald Hall. ...And when I look in his eye, it/is not his eye that I see. EAS

The Poet Confides. Herbert T. J. Coleman. For I am the soul of man. CaP

The Poet Describes His Love. Robert Nathan. All joy, all grief, all beauty to her lover. HBMV

The Poet Haunted. Wendy Rose. Ghost of my self TWSS

A Poet!–He Hath Put His Heart to School. William Wordsworth. But from its own divine vitality. EnRP; VLP

Poet-Hearts. Baron Joseph von Eichendorff. Wonderfully God endows/ Poet-hearts that give Him pleasure. CAW

The Poet Imagines His Grandfather's Thoughts on the Day He Died. Wing Tek Lum. Dear ancestors, all this is still one in my mind. BrSi

The Poet in Old Age Fishing at Evening. Desmond O'Grady. He merges awhile into the lie/Of his own silhouette. CIP

Poet in Residence at a Country School. Don Welch. And in all that silence, neither of us/can imagine where he'd rather be. GOYP

Poet in Winter. Edward Lucie-Smith. As a false snowstorm falls upon a stage. TwCP

The Poet Is Dead. William Everson. Shearwaters, insatiable,/Stun themselves in the sea. NoP

The Poet Laments the Coming of Old Age. Edith Sitwell. And the great heart that the first Morning made/Should wear all Time's destruction for a dress. NoAm

The Poet Lives. Jacob Glatstein. The coffin-birds will peck at you/but they'll never, God forbid, wish you a living year. VWA

The Poet Loosed a Winged Song. Joseph Campbell. If needs be, Christ, to set us free!/To set us free! OnYI

The Poet Loves a Mistress, But Not to Marry. Robert Herrick. Who having two or three,/Will be content with one? ALV; CaPo; ErPo

The Poet Loves from Afar. Desmond O'Grady. ...a night's wild loving/ With that young one I saw at the crossroads dance. NoAm

The Poet of Bray. John Heath-Stubbs. That howsoever taste may veer/I'll be in the swim, sir. NOBL

Poet of Earth. Stephen Henry Thayer. To voice the deeper tones, and lead the way/To immortality, through life and death! AA

The Poet of Gardens. Daniel Henderson. Poet, see your sylvan view/Fresh with an eternal dew! HBMV

A Poet of One Mood. Alice Meynell. And in mine arms, clasped, like a child in tears. HBMV; SBG

The Poet on the Island. Richard Murphy. Doctors were called, and he agreed to sail. CIP; NMP

The Poet Prays. Grace Noll Crowell. Gather the fragrant petals of my life/ And crush them, Lord, then help me sing the song. TrPWD

The Poet Questions Peace. George Chapman. Till all be ordered with confusion. JCP

A Poet Recognizing the Echo of the Voice. Diane Wakoski. you have used our skulls/for ashtrays. NIP

Poet's Bread. Sister Mary Philip. Make hunger-bread of/Beauty and tears. GoBC

The Poet's Call. Thomas Curtis Clarke. "God sends a Voice, a Voice!" WGRP

The Poet's Day. Richard Weber. When his language dies and our atom of Earth is finally/split. CIP

A Poet's Epitaph. Kingsley Amis. You should have stuck to spewing beer, not ink. DBV

A Poet's Epitaph. William Wordsworth. Or build thy house upon this grave. EnRP; OBRV

The Poet's Farewell to His Teeth. James Dickey. toast me just once in the local anaesthetic. DFF; GP; PoA

The Poet's Fate. Thomas Hood. Gives it a wipe–and all is gone. ELU; FiBHP; PV

The Poet's Final Instructions. John Berryman. near Cedar on Lake Street, where the used cars live. SM; VGW

A Poet's Grace. Robert Burns. The friend we trust, the fair we love,/And we desire no more. TrPWD

The Poet's Harvesting. Charles J. O'Malley. Restlessly throb in my soul, and shape themselves into/measure. CAW

A Poet's Hope. William Ellery Channing. If my bark sinks, 'tis to another sea. AA; AnAmPo

A Poet's Household. Carolyn Kizer. On the porch, the fierce poet/Is chanting words to himself. PoL

The Poet's Journal (excerpt). Bayard Taylor. Thou dost punish us with blessing! TrPWD

Poet's Lament on the Death of His Wife. Raage Ugaas. Have I broken my shin, a bone which cannot be mended? WTO

The Poet's Lot. Oliver Wendell Holmes. O rather sleep in churchyard clay,/With urn and cherub o'er thee! PoEL 1-5

The Poet's Prayer. *Anonymous*. And let me be rather but honest with no wit,/Than a noisy nonsensical half-witted poet. OBSV

Poet's Prayer. Adelaide Love. To sing my faith! To sing my faith/Unto the hearts of men! TrPWD

The Poet's Prayer. Stephen Philipps. And men not measure from what height I fell. WGRP

Poet's Prayer. M. L. Sussman. With music chanting like a whippoorwill. AMV-80

A Poet's Progress. Michael Hamburger. ...hospitable to all/who can endure the cold intensity of art. NePoEA; PP

Poet's Protest. Doris Hedges. Words were meant/To catch meanings in. CaP

The Poet's Prothalamion (Excerpt). J. W. Scholl. ...My lips touched/Its faultless agent. PeD

A Poet's Proverbs. Arthur Guiterman.
Before the Second Word. TiPo
Forget Yourself and think of Those Around. TiPo
...what you Give/Is that which proves your Right to Live. TiPo

The Poet's Request. *Anonymous*. I demand a high chair/cushioned with down. BIrV

The Poet's Secret. Elizabeth Stoddard The secret each alone must learn. AA

The Poet's Shield. Archilochus. A new one's just as good. LiTW

The Poet's Simple Faith. Victor Hugo. My future is not one of my concerns. TRV; WGRP

The Poet's Song. Alfred, Lord Tennyson. For he sings of what the world will be/When the years have died away.' ELP; FiP; VLP

The Poet's Song to His Wife. Bryan Waller Procter. They tell how much I owe/To thee and Time! HBV 1-2

The Poet's Use. Alexander Pope. And Heav'n is won by violence of Song. OBEC

The Poet's Voice. William Blake. Is giv'n thee till the break of day.' ChTr

The Poet's Welcome to His Illegitimate Child. Robert Burns. 'Twill please me mair to hear and see't/Than stockit mailins. BoC

A Poet's Welcome to His Love-Begotten Daughter. Robert Burns. But be a loving father to thee,/And brag the name o't. LiTB; NAs; NOEC; OxBoLi; PoEL 1-5; ViBoPo

Poet's Wish. Valery Larbaud. On All Saint's Day with a simple ornament, a little moss. GrPl

A Poet's Wish: An Ode. Allan Ramsay.
And always hope the best. CEP
I'll fairly and squairly/Quite a' and seek nae mair. OBEC

Poet Songs. Karle Wilson Baker. Men heed them not–they only make/My soul turns herself more fair. HBMV

The Poet Speaks. Georgia Douglas Johnson. And loving only giving. AmNP

A Poet Speaks from the Visitors' Gallery. Archibald MacLeish. Whose songs are marble/and whose marble sings. NYBP

A Poet Thinks. Lui Chi. Stay with me tonight,/Old songs. AWP; LiTW; PG

Poet to Dancer. Bernice Kavinoky. o, could the word/so speak,/reply,/be heard! UnS

A Poet to His Beloved. William Butler Yeats. I bring you my passionate rhyme. BrPo

Poet to His Love. Maxwell Bodenheim. And then it has no need for ringing,/For your voice takes its place. PoPl

The Poet to the Birds. Alice Meynell. ...for me/There is no peace but one. FM

The Poet to the Sleeping Saki. Johann Wolfgang von Goethe. Still quaffing, to my lip I place a finger,/Lest waking he should freshen my delight. PeHV

Poet-Tree. Earle Birney. they just need me & maybe you OxBC

The Poet Tries to Turn in His Jock. David Hilton. The shot goes in. LiSp

Poet, Whoe'er Thou Art. John Wilmot, Earl of Rochester. Go hang thyself, and burn thy Mariamne. DBV

Poet Woman's Mitosis: Dividing All the Cells Apart. Wendy Rose. like sores that grow and burst/no matter what. TWSS

Poet Wondering What He Is Up To. D. J. Enright. The eccentric circle of your years. OxBC

Poeta Fit, non Nascitur. Lewis (Charles Lutwidge Dodgson) Carroll. But, when he thought of publishing,/His face grew stern and sad. FaBoNo; NBM; OBSV

Poeta Loquitur. Algernon Charles Swinburne. When their Muse, as such trollops will truly,/Sails too near the wind.] OAEL 1-2

The Poetaster. Ben Jonson.
Nor her peevishness annoy me. EG
...Others fight below/With gnats, and shaddowes, others nothing know. PoEL 1-5

The Poetess Ko Ogimi. Helen Chasin. ...Unless/this here is a hereafter/ death will get her to. NMM

The Poetess's Bouts-Rimes. *Anonymous.* I'll tell the rhymes and drop the rest: NOEC

Poeti-c Art. Arudra. there is/no cart/moving PCP

The Poetic Land. William Caldwell Roscoe. And in my heart a sound, a voice, a name/Hangs, as above the lamp hangs the expiring flame. OBVV

Poetic Tale. Grace Maddock Miller. Tails set atilt for/Wagging! GDP

Poetic Thought. *Anonymous.* If ever I'll gaze on thy glorious behind. FiBHP

Poetical Economy. Harry Graham. And share with me the grave respons./ Of writing this amazing nons.! CenHV; FaBoCo; TreFS

Poetical Numbers. Alexander Pope. And what Timotheus was, is Dryden now. OBEC; SeCePo

Poetics. Archie Randolph Ammons. from the self not mine but ours. NoP

Poetics. Andre Spire. And your lips, by themselves, will then/Begin to sing young songs. VWA

Poetics against the Angel of Death. Phyllis Webb. long lines, clean and syllabic as knotted bamboo. Yes! NOBC

Poetry. Lucius Harwood Foote. If the heart of the minstrel is mute. AA

Poetry. Mary Elizabeth ("E") Fullerton. And in God's house are many scansions. NOAV

Poetry. Nikki Giovanni. which is all we poets/wrapped in our loneliness/ are trying to say. NIP

Poetry. Ella Heath. I am God's soul, fused in the soul of man. HBV 1-2; WGRP

Poetry. Greg Kuzma. ...listening hard for voices/to come out of them. And they do. PoA

Poetry. Edwin Markham. From worlds before and after. AA

Poetry. Marianne Moore.
discovers in/it, after all, a place for the genuine. OBSP
...genuine, you are interested in poetry. BiP; CMoP
...then you are interested/in poetry. AmP; AP; APA; ATP; BiP; BLPL; BoWoP; CoAnAm; CoBMV; ExPo; FaBoWP; FF; HAP; HeIP; InPo; LiTA; LiTM; MoAB; MoAMPo; NAMP; NePA; NIP; NoAm; NOBA; NoP; OxBA; PP; TAP; TreFT; UnPo; ViBoPo

Poetry. Frank O'Hara. ...as if/you would never leave me/and were the inexorable/product of my own time. HaCAP

Poetry. Carl Rakosi. unchanged under the ash of Herculaneum. GP

Poetry. William Soutar. ...the gift which gives/A vision of the beautiful. HaMV

Poetry. Abraham Sutzkever. ...Touch it without/letting it show the print of your fingers. VWA

Poetry. Claude Vigee. throughout the night/in summer. VWA

Poetry, a Natural Thing. Robert Duncan. his only beauty to be/all moose. CAPP; NoAm; NOBA

Poetry and Philosophy. Thomas Randolph. What foot through heaven hath worn the milky way! OBS

Poetry and Science. Walter James Turner. They fill me with new joy–this is my dream. SeCePo

Poetry and the Poet. Henry Cuyler Bunner. Out on important business– back at 6. OBAL

Poetry and Thoughts on Same. Franklin Pierce ("F.P.A.") Adams. In the editorial room/Of the New York Tribune. HBMV

Poetry Concert. Michael S. Harper. and on the assembly line/of Cadillac I heard you sigh. TAP

Poetry Defined. John Holmes. And what worked with these/Can with any words, I say. GrPl; PP

Poetry for Supper. R. S. Thomas. ...while the talk ran/Noisily by them, glib with prose. OxBC

Poetry Is... Bruce Bennett. Silent the sea/the wind and the well. AMV-81

Poetry Is a Destructive Force. Wallace Stevens. It can kill a man. OxBA

Poetry is Death Cast Out. Sydney Clouts. A little further than I had thought/To go, a stream with a singing sound. PeSA

Poetry Is Happiness. Wrey Gardiner. Poetry is life and life lies lazy in the sun. NeBP

Poetry Is in the Darkness. Aram Boyajian. –and a last glance back at the sea/full NeAC

The Poetry of a Root Crop. Charles Kingsley. Who mute upon her tomb doth pray,/Till the resurrection day. LoBV

Poetry of Departures. Philip Larkin. Books; china; a life/Reprehensibly perfect. CMoP; FF; HeIP; MP; NMP; OxBC; PrIm; TwCP

Poetry Paper. Andrei Codrescu. the silence of my surroundings and go to sleep forever. EAS

Poetry Perpetuates the Poet. Robert Herrick. When all now dead shall re- appear. FaBoEE

The Poetry Reading. Bill Manhire. In which they have chosen to make their homes. OCNZ

Poetry Reading. Eileen Myles. ...I was/pretty happy to be with my/friends. APU

Poetry Reading. Vernon Scannell. There are more women here than men. NOBL

Poetry's a Gift Wherein but Few Excell. Nathaniel Ward. And he doth best, that passeth all the rest. SCAP

Poetry Today. John Heath-Stubbs. But I never heard/That the frogs stopped croaking. PoL

Poetry Workshop in a Reform School. Betty Adcock. And I have come away peeled to the bone,/having given away all my weapons. AMV-80

Poets. Mark Akenside. ...and changeful Time/Sees him at will keep measure with his flight,/At will outstrip it. OBEC

Poets. Hortense Flexner. The last to come will make his little tune,/And think it new–about the weary moon! HBMV

Poets. Joyce Kilmer. They only sing who are struck dumb by God. AnAmPo; WGRP

The Poets. Scudder Middleton. Give us again the solace of belief. HBMV

The Poets. David Wevill. And build our crude villages under the frown/Of friendlier hills, where the vultures eat vegetables PP

The Poets Agree to Be Quiet by the Swamp. David Wagoner. Stoop, and begin the ancient croaking. CoAP; VGW

Poets and Linnets (parody). Thomas Hood. Well, there's my musing ended. CenHV; HBV 1-2

Poets and Their Bibliographies. Alfred, Lord Tennyson. Had swamped the sacred poets with themselves. PP

The Poets at Tea. Barry Pain.
Allons, from all bat-eyed formula. HBV 1-2; Par
And do not make it strong. Par
For ever let Britannia wield/The tea-pot of her sires! Par
Mix a' thegither. Par
Oh, hear us, our handmaid unheeding,/And take it away! Par
Tea to the n–th. Par
"You bade me speak the truth." Par

Poets' Corner. Robert Graves. Long, Long before his Debts are Pay'd. FaBoEE

Poets Hitchhiking on the Highway. Gregory Corso. We ended by melting away,/hating the air! AmC; NeAP; NoAm; PoM

Poets in Africa. Roy Campbell. Who in more fiendish war-paint shine? ACV

Poets in Time of War. Bertram Warr. Serenely, our visionary heritage has flowered. CaP

The Poets Light but Lamps. Emily Dickinson. Disseminating their/ Circumference. AmePo; HeIP; PP

Poets Lose Half the Praise. Edmund Waller. Could it be known what they discreetly blot. PP

Poets Love Nature. John Clare. For where they bloom God is, and I am free. CBEP; ERoP 1-2; OAEL 1-2

Poets Observed. Francis Coleman Rosenberger. A few survive in deeps, very/Wily, large, and solitary. AMV-80

The Poets of Hell. Karl Shapiro. And spits into the constellated skies. NYBP

The Poets of the Nineties. Derek Mahon. And rest assured, the day/Will be all sunlight, and the night/A dutiful spectrum of stars. FaBoIP

The Poets' Paradise. Michael Drayton. Where he provides with pastoral strains,/In Lyrics to delight you. WiR

Poets Seven Years Old. Arthur Rimbaud. Below, alone, lying on pieces of unbleached/Canvas, with a violent premonition of sails!... SOTW

Poets to Come. Walt Whitman. Expecting the main things from you. AnAmPo; FF; LiTA; TrGrPo; YaD

Poggio. Lawrence Durrell. Married unwisely, yes, but died quite well. OxBTC

Pogroms. Andre Spire. Protect us more than your sword! VWA

Poietes Apoietes. Hartley Coleridge. Or sour the sweetness that in thee I tasted. OBNC

The Point. Evan Jones. without it no people, no life, no art. NOAV

The Point. John Montague. Alone, but equal to the morning. IPY

The Point. Gary Soto. And Molina's eyes are lost/Between the blue of two stars. MAYP

Point Grey. Daryl Hine. A beauty of sorts is nearly always within reach. NOBC

Point of No Return. Mari E. Evans. ....too late/....alas NNP

Point of No Return. Robert Graves. Till he has won a second soul for glory,/At the point no return. BIrV

Point Shirley. Sylvia Plath. Against both bar and tower the black sea runs. NIP; NoP

The Point, the Line, the Surface and Sphere. Claude Bragdon. In seed, stem, leaf, and fruit appear. ImOP

The Pointed People. Rachel Field. And shaking with silent laughter. WSC

The Pointless Pride of Man. *Anonymous.* Wald slepe thee with/A night under shete. MeEL

Points of View. Amy Lowell. Age lights the candle and hobbles to/bed. LOW

Poison Ivy! Katharine Gallagher. For she grows Poison Ivy! SiSoSe

The Pontoon Bridge Miracle.   Vachel Lindsay.   Come let us be bold with our songs.   LoBV; NePA

Pontoosuce.   Herman Melville.   She vanished, leaving fragrant breath/And warmth and chill of wedded life and death.   MAmP; NOBA

The Pony Blues.   Son House.   You know/the way he can travel/is a low down/old dirty shame   BluL

The Pony Express.   Dorothy Brown Thompson.   When swift-thudding hoofs won the long race with fear.   AmFN

Pony Girl.   Jane P. Moreland.   Pick your speed, pick your steed.   PH

Pooh!   Walter De La Mare.   And these pronounced "Pooh!"   FiBHP; HAP

The Pool.   Robert Creeley.   for which he cannot find/a means or time.   CoAP

The Pool.   Hilda ("H. D.") Doolittle.   What are you–banded one?   CMoP; ExPo

The Pool.   E. L. Mayo.   All are compact of pity and of fear/As we are, only real.   MiAP

Pool.   Carl Sandburg.   Writhed into a stiff pool.   AP

A Pool.   Thomas Whitbread.   I am midway somewhere.   Where, I do not know.   NYBP

The Poolhall.   Don Burt.   the parable that time told in that room.   AMV-80

Poop.   Gerald Locklin.   already it is true.   Str

The Poor.   Speer Strahan.   Beggar am I that wait and pray/To feast my soul on His beauteous Face.   CAW

The Poor.   Emile Verhaeren.   On earth's far plains of sun and wind.   AWP

The Poor.   William Carlos Williams.   turning his corner has/overwhelmed the entire city   MoAB; MoAmPo; NoP; PPP

Poor Angels.   Edward Hirsch.   Let what rises live with what descends.   MAYP

Poor Boy.   Anonymous.   Bow down your head and cry.   FSW

Poor Boy Blues.   Ramblin' (Willard) Thomas.   Poor boy. Poor boy. Poor boy long way from home.   BluL

Poor Brother.   Anonymous.   Should have his head upon one end,/His feet upon the other.   NA

Poor but Honest.   Anonymous.   Isn't it a blooming shame?'   NLV; OxBoLi

The Poor Can Feed the Birds.   Shaw Neilson.   The poor can feed the birds.   PoAu 1-2

The Poor Children.   Victor Hugo.   And finds them ragged babes that weep!   AWP

A Poor Christian Looks at the Ghetto.   Czeslaw Milosz.   And he will count me among the helpers of death:/The uncircumcised.   NIP

Poor Crow!   Mary Mapes Dodge.   I'm honest, and really/I've come a long way.   OBCA

Poor Dear Grandpapa.   D'Arcy Wentworth Thompson.   He's broken his leg in trying to spell/Tommy without a T.   NA

Poor Devil That I Am, Being So Attacked.   Palladas.   1. The Iliad and 2. the wife!   OBVE

Poor Ellen Smith.   Peter Degraph.   Oh, I do appeal to the Justice of Time!   AmFP

Poor Fool.   Evan V. Shute.   Stranger to drop it–as each mortal must!   CaP

Poor for Our Sakes.   Mary Brainerd Smith.   Are rich beyond all counting and all dreams.   BLRP

The Poor Ghost.   Christina Georgina Rossetti.   Let me sleep now till the Judgment Day.'   GBL

The Poor Girl's Meditation.   Padraic Colum.   This I can say, O lad,/I am fitted to lie my lone.   BIrV; OBMV; OLR

Poor Grandpa.   R. C. O'Brien.   'Cause it was the last vacation/Grandpa ever had.   ShM

Poor Henry.   Walter De La Mare.   Sleek with the bloom/Of health next week!   HBMV

Poor Howard.   Anonymous.   Left me here to sing this song.   FSW

The Poor in Church.   Arthur Rimbaud.   Their long yellow fingers kissing the holy waters.   LiTW

Poor Is the Life That Misses.   Anonymous.   Shall I a virgin die?   Fie no!   EIL; UnTE

Poor Jack.   Charles Dibdin.   For the same little cherub that sits up aloft/Will look out a good berth for poor Jack!   BeLS; HBV 1-2

Poor Kid.   William Cole.   Can't make a buck!   OBAL; PV

Poor Kings.   William Henry Davies.   God's pity then, say I,/On some poor king.   HBV 1-2

Poor Kitty Popcorn (with music).   Anonymous.   And she fell into the column with a low, glad cry,/"Me-o-o-w!"   AS

Poor Lil' Brack Sheep.   Ethel M. C. Brazelton.   An' de lil' brack sheep–is me!   BLPA

Poor Little Jesus.   Anonymous.   Wasn't that a pity and a shame?   FSW

Poor Little Johnny.   Anonymous.   He won't get his hundred here today.   AmFP

Poor Lonesome Cowboy.   Anonymous.   And a long ways from home.   ABF; CoSo; TiPo

Poor Lonesome Cowboy (with music).   Anonymous.   I ain't got no sweetheart,/To sit and talk with me.   AS

Poor Man Blues.   Anonymous.   No, this song ain't nothin'/But a poor man singin' the blues.   FSW

Poor Man Blues.   Henry Townsend.   I done give you my money/I done give you most anything   BluL

The Poor Man Pays for All.   Anonymous.   For still 'tis found too true a case,/That poor men pay for all.   OBET

The Poor Man's Pig.   Edmund Charles Blunden.   And sulky as a child when her play's done.   MoBrPo

The Poor Man's Province.   John Wright.   And if the Lord be pleased to make me one/Of his poor flock, I shall not be undone.   NOEC

A Poor Man's Work Is Never Done.   Anonymous.   Well now, away with my wife and welcome,/Then my troubles will have an end.   OBET

Poor Matthias.   Matthew Arnold.   What are left, will hardly be/Better than we spent with thee.   FM; PoEL 1-5

Poor Me.   Anonymous.   Poor me, I brood.   ErPo

Poor Movies.   Will Bennett.   ...unemployed/with no prospects for work.   APU

The Poor of London.   William Forster.   And brandish vested rights to pillage and devour.   CBAP

Poor Old Horse.   Anonymous.   Poor old horse, let him die.   CH; OBET

Poor Old Horse.   David Holbrook.   With a soft-footed child skipping jump on the quay at the/Mill.   NePoEA-2

Poor Old Lady.   Anonymous.   She died, of course.   OBCA; SoPo

Poor Old Man.   Anonymous.   If you growl too loud your head they'll bust./Oh, poor old man!   ShS

The Poor Old Man (parody).   J. C. Squire.   Thank God I'm not/That poor old man.   HBMV

The Poor Old Prurient Interest Blues.   John Hartford.   Have mercy on my poor old prurient interest.   MAT

Poor Omie.   Anonymous.   I murdered my own true lover; I'll never reach the sky.   PrIm

Poor Poll.   Robert Bridges.   just as that monkey would, poor Polly, have done for you.   EBEV; MoPo; OxBoLi; OxBTC

A Poor Relation.   Audrey McGaffin.   Perhaps Aunt Ellie smiles to see/What she had never, when alive.   NePoAm-2

The Poor Relation.   Edwin Arlington Robinson.   From which there will be no more flying.   AnAmPo; MAPA

The Poor Scholar.   Abraham Ibn Chasdai.   And stores of gold lie buried in the/ground.   TrJP

A Poor Scholar of the 'Forties.   Padraic Colum   As in wild earth a Grecian vase!   AnIL; GLGT; NOBI; OxBI

The Poor Shammes of Berditchev.   Rochelle Ratner.   thus dividing the part which loved/from the mind not worthy.   VWA

Poor South! Her Books Get Fewer and Fewer.   J. Gordon Coogler.   She was never much given to literature.   FaBoCo; FiBHP

Poor Vaunting Earth, Gloss'd with Uncertain Pride.   George Alsop.   Tophet was made for such Supremacy.   SCAP

The Poor Voter on Election Day.   John Greenleaf Whittier.   A man's a man today!   PAL

Poor Wat.   William Shakespeare.   For misery is trodden on by many,/And being low never relieved by any.   OBSC

A Poor Wayfaring Stranger.   Anonymous.   I'm only going over home.   AmFP; BFSS; BLSo; TrAS

Poor Wolf Speaks.   Poor Wolf.   ...For doing so Crow Breast, the/Gros Ventre chief, called me a fool.   NU

The Poor Working Girl (with music).   Anonymous.   My God! do you wonder at crime!   AS

Pop.   David McFadden.   that characteristic POP of a burst balloon/followed by no crying.   NeAC

Pop! Goes the Weasel.   Anonymous.   Pop! goes the weasel.   BLSo; FaBoNo; FSW; OxNR; PoPle; PSoN; SoPo; TreFT

The Popcorn-Popper.   Dorothy Walter Baruch.   Soft white/Popcorn.   BrR

The Pope from Penance Purgatorial.   George Buchanan.   Freed some, but Martin Luther freed them all.   OBVE

The Pope He Leads a Happy Life.   Charles James Lever.   And when my cheery glass I tope,/I'll fancy then I am the Pope.   HBV 1-2

The Popish Plot.   John Dryden.   Believing nothing or believing all.   ACP

The Poplar.   Richard Aldington.   Will you always stand there shivering?   HBMV

Poplar.   Gottfried Benn.   dead space opposing,/to and fro.   PoPl

The Poplar Field.   William Cowper.
    Have a being less durable even than he.   CH; ELP; FaBoPP; FaBoRV; FiP; ForPo; HAP; HBV 1-2; InPo; LAuP; NOBE; NOEC; OBEC; PoEL 1-5; RoGo; SeCeV; TrGrPo; WiR
    Have a still shorter date, and die sooner than we.   GTBS; GTBS-P

The Poplar's Shadow.   May Swenson.   The poplar plume belongs/to what enormous wing?   NYBP

Poplar Tree.   Padraic Colum.   With furrowed bole and black the Poplar stands.   NePoAm

The Poplars.   Theodosia Garrison.   Look down with gracious mien.   HBMV; OHIP

Posthumous. Henry Augustin Beers. The breath that gave it life was thine. AA

Posthumous Coquetry. Theophile Gautier. His mouth upon my mouth has said/Pater and Ave for my peace. AWP

Posthumous Keats. Stanley Plumly. to what is already overwhelming. GeTw; SV

Posthumous Rehabilitation. Tadeusz Rozewicz. the dead will not rehabilitate us. FaBoPV

The Postilion Has Been Struck by Lightning. Patricia Beer. Having seen every sight/But never anyone struck by lightning. OxBC

Postlude. William Carlos Williams. Blue at the prow of my desire. AnAmPo

Postlude: for Goya. Ramon Guthrie. We have won if we can believe/that this is not an end. NMP

The Postman. Laura E. Richards. I wish you'd go away. SoPo; TiPo

Postman Cheval. Andre Breton. ...as woman delights to see man/After having made love. EAS

The Postman's Bell Is Answered Everywhere. Horace Gregory. ...these are the last/words I shall write. MoAmPo; MoVE; NYBP

Postscript. Sandra Hochman. ...my life/Is just about over. NMM

Postscript. Mary Mills. ...the very sea/moves over mountains man has never known. NePoAm

Postscript. R. S. Thomas. Sound was the lament of/The poets for deciduous language. FaBoMo; OxBC

Postscript: For Gweno. Alun Lewis. Among the glittering stars your voices named. BoLoP; GTBS-P

Postscript, on a Name. Stephen Ratcliffe. Concentrates what Time forgave! AMV-80

Postscript to a Pettiness. Arthur Seymour John Tessimond. Promise to keep no diary of/Days when I fail, dear love, to love! OBSP

Postscript to Die Schone Mullerin. R. P. Llster. They take to filtering the water. PoL

A Postscript to Verses on the History of France. Anonymous. And without God's help/the divill will have all. NOBI

The Postures of Love. Alex Comfort. ...and no tree stands/ever, forever–moving, lifeless, alone. NeBP

The Posy of Thyme. Anonymous. And are forced to sing lullaby/And like me wear the posy of thyme. OBET

The Posy Ring. Clément Marot. And stayed, whose names hereon I've writ. AWP

Pot and Kettle. Robert Graves. And my fond heart beats time with yours and cries,/"Cuckoo! Cuckoo!" HBMV

The Pot-Bellied Anachronism. Ann Darr. ...That I can be any/shape I want, even pudding-shaped and/nobody can stop me. GP

The Pot of Flowers. William Carlos Williams. and there, wholly dark, the pot/gay with rough moss. QFR

Pot of Tea. Susan Griffin. A wet heat rises up in the/air and touches us. NPGG

Pot Shot. Padraic Fallon. ...I tame/The world around me till it names my name. CIP

Potato. Richard Wilbur.
Awkward and milky and beautiful only to hunger. CAPP; CrMA; LiTA; MoAB
Vestigial virtues, are eaten; we shall survive. TrGrPo

The Potato Eaters. Frank Graziano. Good-bye, with a handshake,/Vincent. PoDr

The Potato Harvest. Sir Charles G. D. Roberts. ...Down the dusk hillside/Lumbers the wain; and day fades out like smoke. CaP; NOBC

Potatoes. David Donnell. the potatoes sit quietly on top of each other growing eyes. NOBC

The Potatoes' Dance. Vachel Lindsay. The beauteous Irish lady,/Who/Gives/Potatoes/Eyes. SUS

The Potomac. Karl Shapiro. And embassies dissolve to molecules. AP; CoBMV

Potomac Town in February. Carl Sandburg. I know why; I'll see you tomorrow; I'll tell/you everything tomorrow. EvOK

Potpourri from a Surrey Garden. Sir John Betjeman. Pam and I, as the organ/Thunders over you all. CenHV; FiBHP

The Potter. Anonymous. I stumbled like a drunkard. TTY

The Poultries. Ogden Nash. What a conundrum! CenHV

Poultry. Diana Der Hovanessian. What is this peck,/peck, peck? GrPl

Pound at Spoleto. Lawrence Ferlinghetti. His voice/went on/and on/through the leaves.... CAPP; PoM

Pounds and Ounces. Michael Brownstein. Baby Egypt damp with glee ANYP

Pour Down. John Holmes. The wells of his offering,/Pour down. NePoAm

Pourquoi. Anonymous. I'm glad you greased/My little dog's nose with tar. GDP

Poussin. Louis MacNeice. And thus we dally and dip our spoon. EyDe

Poverty. Charles Simic. It is a gift/Which I am no longer afraid/to open. MAT

Poverty. Theognis. Death is the lighter evil of the two. AWP

Poverty. Thomas Traherne. But now I have a deity. OxBoCh; Prf; TEP; TrCP

Poverty, in Imitation of Milton. Samuel Jones. Most venerable Poverty! to thee all hail! NOEC

Poverty Knock. Anonymous. When ah hear me shuttle/Go poverty, poverty knock! OBET; VLP

Povre Ame Amoureuse. Louise Labe. Grant to my poor soul amorous the dark gift of this/illusion. AWP

Power. Thomas Stephen Collier. That move unceasing toward the gate of/Death. AA

Power. Matthew Prior. Frail as the Cord, and brittle as the Urn. LoBV

Power. Adrienne Rich. her wounds came from the same source as her power TAP

Power and Peace. Robert Herrick. Power and Peace to keep one throne. CaPo

The Power and the Glory. Siegfried Sassoon. To fill my dark with fire, my heart with faith? OBMV

Power-Cut. Mebdh McGuckian. The door-butler lets the strangers in. FaBoIP

Power Failure. Michael Dennis Browne. We must be brave in our dark. AmPA

Power Failure. Josephine Jacobsen. ...And recognize its strong/shape under the gathered stars. FAZ

The Power in the People. Robert Herrick. The saucy subjects will bear the sway. CaPo

The Power of Fancy. Philip Freneau. You and I will walk alone. AP

The Power of Innocence. C. G. H. Ye that have passions for a tear,/Give nature vent, and drop it here! NOEC

The Power of Interval. John Byrne Leicester Warren, Lord De Tabley. Her burning eyes on her forgetful hands. NOBV; OBSP; VLP

The Power of Littles. Anonymous. Eternity in heaven. TreFT

The Power of Love. John Fletcher. Ilion, in a short hour, higher/He can build, and once more fire. HBV 1-2; UnTE

The Power of Love He Wants Shih (Everything). Rochelle Owens. What is that?/the pigeons? NMM

The Power of Malt. Alfred Edward Housman. Look into the pewter pot/To see the world as the world's not. HBV 1-2

The Power of Maples. Gerald Stern. you have to plant your table under its leaves and begin eating. NU

The Power of Music. Thomas Lisle. Such power hath music in hell! NOBL

The Power of Music (excerpt). Pindar. Drooping his swift wings on either side. UnS

The Power of Prayer. Sidney and Clifford Lanier. Yea, Dinah, whar 'ould you be now, exceptin' fur dat pra'r? HBV 1-2

The Power of Silence. William Henry Davies. No more of bangle, scarf or feather. BrPo

The Power of the Dog. Rudyard Kipling. Should we give our hearts to a dog to tear? BLPA; BoAnP; GDP

The Power of Thought. Von Trimberg Susskind. A thought can glide through stone,/and steel, and iron chain. TrJP

The Power of Time. Jonathan Swift. When my old cassock (said a Welsh divine)/Is out at elbows, why should I repine? CBEP; FaBoEE; PV

The Power Station. James Merrill. The blind delirium that still utters it. ConAP

Power Station. T. W. Ramsey. To the cross that crowns the spire. HaMV

The Power to Change Geography. Diana O Hehir. Promising/To take a shape. NPGG

Power to the People. Howard Nemerov. That we may lick their hinder parts and/thump their heads. PoL

The Powerful Eyes O' Jeremy Tait. Wallace Irwin. But rarest of all is the pearls that fall/From a truthful mariner's lips. FiBHP; StPo

The Powerline Incarnation. Les A. Murray. It who feels nothing It who answers prayers. CBAP

Powers and Times Are Not Gods. W. H. Auden. Let us pray. MoRP

The Powers of Love. George Moses Horton. O what is there like love. BALP

The Powers of the Pawn. David Solway. and ponder how he died. AMV-81

The Powte's Complaint. Anonymous. And send thy sands to make dry lands,/when they shall want fresh water. GBP

Powwow. W. D. Snodgrass. Of grasshoppers and dragonflies/That go with us, that do not live again. GrPl; NYBP

Powwow 79, Durango. Paula Gunn Allen. exploding color in the light. STE

Powwow Remnants. Lew Blockcolski. Small sparrows have left droppings to be remembered by. VoR

Practical Concerns. William J. Harris. Very little about technique. PoBA

Practical People. Robinson Jeffers. Make it a difficult world...for practical people. NAMP

A Practical Program for Monks. Thomas Merton. Thank you. Even though the nights are never danger-/ous, I have one of everything. CoPo

A Practical Woman. Thomas Hardy. And used him till he'd done his job,"/Was all thereon she said. NAs

The Practice of Absence. Robert Friend. of woman or pebble/the body of the dark. VWA

The Practice of Magical Evocation. Diane Di Prima. what rhythm add to stillness/what applause? PoM

Practicing. Sonia Gernes. And then you will go. AMV-80

A Praefatory Poem to the Little Book, Entituled, Christianus per Ignem. Nicholas Noyes. Mean while what warms me I have blest. SCAP

Praetorium Scene: Good Friday. Elinor Lennen. The scarlet robe the military wore/Put on the Prince of Peace, for mockery! PGD

Prague Spring. Tony Harrison. The last snow of this year's late slow thaw/dribbles as spring saliva down his jaw. OBTV

Prairie. Herbert Bates. Back to the old eternity/Of placid, all-consoling sea. AA

Prairie. K. N. Llewellyn. Anguish, tough wood, and earth, remain. YeAr

Prairie. Carl Sandburg. I am the dust of men. LaNeLa

The Prairie Dog. Arthur Guiterman. It needs just a little hypocrisy/To make the world safe for democracy. BPAW

Prairie-Dog Town. Mary Austin. That are under the mound/In Prairie-Dog Town. BPAW; TiPo

Prairie Fires. Hamlin Garland. A fiery furnace where the cattle trod. OBCA

Prairie Graveyard. Anne Marriott. in the centre of the huge lone land and sky. CaP; NOBC; OBCV

Prairie Lullaby. Anonymous. Tumble in bed, my baby,/My little sleepy head,/To a prairie lullabye. BPAW

A Prairie Ride. William Vaughn Moody. Neigh to the pastured mothers of the race. AnEnPo

The Prairie Schooner. Edward Everett Dale. It will be a prairie schooner/ With the tongue a-pointing west. BPAW

Prairie Spring. Edwina Fallis. Only a prairie child/Knows such sweet hours. SUS

A Prairie Water Colour. Duncan Campbell Scott. Of shadow in the slew. OBCV

Prairie Wind. Duncan Campbell Scott. To the dead pale prairie grasses? ACV

Prairie Wolves. Robert V. Carr. They wail a curse against their fate. BPAW; PoOW

The Prairies. William Cullen Bryant. And I am in the wilderness alone. AP; MAmP; NOBA; OxBA; PoEL 1-5; TAP

Praise. Anonymous. The martins and the swallows/Are God Almighty's bows and/arrows. OxNR

Praise. Jane Cooper. who could have foretold/I would live to write at fifty? TAP

Praise. Edith Daley. And crushed within a broken heart/That God bends low to hear. TRV

Praise. R. H. Grenville. Than streams of water in a desert place! PoToHe

Praise. George Herbert. Ev'n eternitie is too short/To extoll thee. AnAnS 1

Praise. William Matthews. ...Say it again and again, the names are/lying down to sleep together. AmPA

Praise. Seumas (James Starkey) O'Sullivan. Sweet, you are praised in a silence,/Sung in a sigh. HBV 1-2

Praise. Rainer Maria Rilke. Becasue I praise. ChTr

Praise. Christopher Smart. The little labourer at his task/Is worthy of his hire. OxBChV

Praise and Love. William Brighty ("Matthew Browne") Rands. And the world with music rang. OBVV

Praise and Prayer. Sir William Davenant. And are, without a beggar's blush, forgiven. GoBC; OBEV

Praise Doubt. Mark Van Doren. Praise him. He dances upon the whitecaps. EaLo; MoRP

Praise for an Urn. Hart Crane. They are no trophies of the sun. AP; ATP; AWP; CMoP; CoBMV; HAP; InPo; LiTM; MoAB; MoAmPo; MoVE; NoAm; NOBA; OxBA; PPP

Praise for Mercies Spiritual and Temporal. Isaac Watts. Then let me love thee more than they,/And try to serve thee best. NOEC

Praise for Sick Women. Gary Snyder. Blood dripping through crusted thighs. NeAP

Praise-God Barebones. Ellen Mackay Hutchinson Cortissoz. "Feel'st not, Sir Dick," say saucy Moll,/"A Pious Melancholy?" AA

Praise Him Who Makes Us Happy. Mark Van Doren. Praise Him, the only good. AH

Praise in Summer. Richard Wilbur. And sparrows sweep the ceiling of our day? CAPP; NoP; PP

Praise Now Your God. H. P. Brucker. Alleluia, Great is God!/Alleluia, Alleluia! AH

Praise of a Child. Anonymous. We need a child to inherit our belongings. WTO

Praise of a Train. Anonymous. Bring them back to their homes. WTO

The Praise of Age. Robert Henryson. The more of age the nearer heavenis bliss.' BSV

The Praise of Ben Dorain. Duncan Ban MacIntyre. In a delirium with the strange prolixity/Of the talking called for, I fear. GoTS

Praise of Ceres. Thomas Heywood. Ceres, Queen of Plenty, hallows/ Growing fields as well as fallows. ElL

The Praise of Derry. Saint Columcille. It is sweeter and dearer to me. CAW

The Praise of Dust. Gilbert Keith Chesterton. To make a fairer face than heaven,/Of dust and nothing more. MoBrPo

Praise of Earth. Elizabeth Barrett Browning. And hail upon the vine! OBVV

The Praise of Fionn. Anonymous. For wisdom, courage and strength/A man the like of Fionn? KiLC

Praise of God. Anonymous. The birds, they never cease/and their souls are only air. NOBI

Praise of Homer. George Chapman. And foolish Fame, deriv'd from thence, despises. OBS

Praise of Ibikunle. Anonymous. Rogi-rogbe!/Terror in battlement. WTO

The Praise of Industry. James (1700-48) Thomson. Has light as Air each Limb, each Thought as clear as Day. OBEC

Praise of Little Women. Juan, Archpriest of Hita, Ruiz. By consequence, of woman-kind be sure to choose the/least. AWP

Praise of Mary. Anonymous. When so great prize is had/For the mere asking. ISi

The Praise of Meaner Wits This Work Like Profit Brings. Sir Walter Ralegh. Of all which speak our English tongue, but those of thy device. SiPS

Praise of My Lady. William Morris. My lady moving graciously./Beata mea Domina! HBV 1-2

Praise of New England. Thomas Caldecot Chubb. Oh, my New England where true worth is valued yet! GoYe

The Praise of New Netherland. Jacob Steendam. And furnish, what the heart with transport fills,/The finest fishing. PAH

The Praise of Philip Sparrow. George Gascoigne. Sweet Philip shall be my bird still. ViBoPo

The Praise of Pindar in Imitation of Horace His Second Ode, Book 4. Abraham Cowley. And there with humble sweets contents her industry. OAEL 1-2

The Praise of Sailors. Anonymous. And as my song beginning had/So must it have an end. OBSS

The Praise of Waterford (excerpt). Anonymous. Then Waterford true shall never decrease–/Quam diu vere intacta manes. NOBI

Praise of Women. Robert Mannyng [(or Manning)]. Ne derer is none in Goddys hurde/Than a chaste womman with lovely worde. OBEV

Praise of Women. Palladas. (2) in the grave. LiTW

Praise of Zeus. Aratus of Soli. So far as it is lawful for you to answer my prayers,/give guidance throughout all my song. ILwL

Praise Song for King Kalakaua. Anonymous. Ka-la-kaua, the illustrious! WTO

Praise the Lord. John Milton. Ever faithful, ever sure. FaBoCh; LoGBV

Praise the Lord and Pass the Ammunition! Frank Loesser. Praise the Lord, and pass the ammunition/And we'll all stay free! YaD

Praise to Jesus! William Ball. And we praise, for grace so free,/Thee, Jehovah-Jesus, Thee! BePJ

Praise to Light. Thomas Cole. ...Greet with an eye to love/The hard or simple chore. NePoAm-2

Praise to the End! Theodore Roethke. The light becomes me. InPS

Praise Ye the Lord, O Celebrate His Fame. Peleg Folger. ...may my soul her nimble journey take/Into the regions of eternity. AH

The Praises. Charles Olson. Every natural action obeys by/the straightest possible process. VGW

The Praises of a Countrie Life. (Horace, Epode 2). Ben Jonson. ...his moneys he gets in with paine,/At th'Calends, puts all out againe. SeCP

Praises of God. Anonymous. And it without a soul but wind. AnIL

Praises of Henry Francis Fynn. Anonymous. Wild animal of the blue ocean. WTO

Praises of King George VI. A. Z. Ngani. share your wisdom with us, your learning, art! PeSA

Praises of the King Dingana (Vesi). Anonymous. they joined in stabbing frogs in the river. PeSA

Praises of the King of Oyo. Anonymous. King of all kings. WTO

Praises of the King Tshaka. Anonymous. he who was like the maned lion. PeSA

Praises of the Train. Demetrius Segooa. What can the road owners do to me, the black centipede,/rushing on, fixed to time? PeSA

Praising the Poets of That Country. Howard Nemerov. While elsewhere the profane crowds would walk/Unthinking their free and many ways to death. PP

The Praties. Anonymous. Will give us crumb for crust,/Over here, over here. FSW

Prattle. John Ciardi. When I'm as big as twenty-five, about? BiCB

Praxis. Sharon Thesen. fragments of bliss & roses/decorating your fists. CaPN

Praxiteles and Phryne. James Russell Lowell The Phryne whom he loved! AA; BeLS

Pray! Irene Arnold. Others will be attracted/From darkness into light. BLRP; STF

Pray! Amos R. Wells. Pray! for Jesus joins your prayer. STF

Pray, Christian, Pray! *Anonymous.* Then pray, Christian, pray! STF

Pray for the Dead. Arthur Wentworth Hamilton Eaton. That they shall be in touch with thee. AA

Pray-Give-Go. Annie Johnson Flint. And pray–that other hearts may Pray! BLRP; STF

Pray On! *Anonymous.* We then shall see Him face to face–/Oh, glorious day of days! STF

Pray Remember the Poor. Christopher Smart. And tell my sire his sons shall be/As charitably great as he. NOEC

Pray to What Earth Does This Sweet Cold Belong. Henry David Thoreau. ...and winter slow/Increase his rule by gentlest summer means. UnPo

Pray Without Ceasing. Ophelia Guyon Browning. And cries, "It shall be done sometime, somewhere." BLPA; BLPL

Prayer. *Anonymous.*
    And age on ages sing Amen. CAW
    Assured that He will grant my quest/Or send some answer far more blessed. STF
    For nothing can untwine/Thy life from mine. STF
    Fulness of joy, and faith, and love/To every waiting heart. STF
    Oh, meet me at the river, I ask in Thy name./Amen. OuSiCo
    One to watch, one to pray,/And two to bear my soul away. OxBoLi
    Still be my vision, O Ruler of all. OnYI
    To grow more loving every day. SoPo

A Prayer. Margaret Bailey. And–please–a twinkle in my eye. Amen. TRV

Prayer. Willem Bilderdijk. Pray Thou Thyself in me and cleanse my prayer. LiTW

A Prayer. Berton Braley. And drop a Regular tear! BLPA

Prayer. Margueritte Harmon Bro. And in the silence here at last I feel/Thy hand upon me, as I kneel. TrPWD

A Prayer. Anne Bronte. Do Thou my Strength, my Saviour be,/And make me to Thy glory live! TrPWD

Prayer. Isabella Maria Brown. It sure is raining hard today. NNP; PoNe

A Prayer. Samuel Butler the Second. I would not be–not quite–so pure as you. FaBoEE

Prayer. Witter ("Emanuel Morgan") Bynner. All ways to enter/And no way to go. EaLo

A Prayer. William Ellery Channing. Passion–that breath of Instinct, and the key/Of Thy dominions, untold Majesty! TrPWD

A Prayer. George F. Chawner. Lead at last to heaven above! BLRP

Prayer. Gilbert Keith Chesterton. A single sword to thee! WGRP

Prayer. Gabrielle Coignard. Ah, do not let me fall in the abyss! WPOW

Prayer. Hartley Coleridge. Then pray to God to cast that wish away. GoTF; TreFT

A Prayer. Joseph Seamon, Jr Cotter. O God, give me words to make my dream-children live. BANP

A Prayer. Digby Mackworth Dolben. Sweet Jesu, deliver/Thy servants ever. GoBC

A Prayer. Lord Alfred Bruce Douglas. And I saw not. Oh! open Thou mine eyes. CAW; TrPWD

A Prayer. John Drinkwater. Give us to build above the deep intent/The deed, the deed. HBV 1-2; OBVV; TrPWD; WGRP

A Prayer. Paul Laurence Dunbar. Thy gracious balm I need. TrPWD

A Prayer. Max Ehrmann. And may the evening's twilight find me gentle still. BLPA; BLPL; FaBoBe; PoToHe

Prayer. Thomas Ellwood. For that is more than I can do. WGRP

Prayer. Gavin Ewart. O Lord in your odd way please do not desert me OxBC

Prayer. James Elroy Flecker. How faint, how loud the bravest hearts have cried. TrPWD

Prayer. Frank Stewart Flint. Give me the vision,/And they may live. TrPWD

Prayer. Hazel J. Fowler. The hollow, famished cup of Love, replete! TrPWD

A Prayer. Norman Gale. And go in hope from this to Thee,/The pupil of Thy country air. TrPWD

A Prayer. Theodosia Garrison. Let me work and be glad. TrPWD

A Prayer. Humfrey [(or Humphrey)] Gifford. As long as thou art on my side,/What need I care for more? OxBoCh

Prayer. Claire Goll. To create you anew out of my love. TrJP

Prayer. Arthur Guiterman. Grant me the grace, I beg upon my knees,/Not to forget that I was one of these. TrPWD

Prayer. Haim Guri. Bless them–for time has come./Thy blessing on the boys. TrJP

A Prayer. Marion Franklin Ham. And give me, in adversity,/The heart that still can trust and sing. TrPWD

A Prayer. Sir William Rowan Hamilton. Yet with an equal joy let me behold/Thy chariot o'er that way by others rolled.' IrPN

Prayer. Doris Hedges. And sing my song of joy in perfect purity. GoYe

A Prayer. Felicia Dorothea Hemans. Be as the meek wild-flower's–if transient, yet not vain. TrPWD

Prayer. Eliza M. Hickok. Or send some answer far more blest. BLRP

A Prayer. Katharine Tynan Hinkson. Thine only till I die. OBVV

Prayer. Langston Hughes. I do not know. CDC; EaLo

A Prayer. Harry Kemp. And thank the kind, benignant God/For what I have not been. HBV 1-2; WGRP

A Prayer. William Laird. Shake hands with elder brother, Doom,/Nor bawl, nor scurry from the room. HBMV

A Prayer. Archibald Lampman. Grant us, O mother, therefore, us who pray,/Some little of thy light and majesty. TrPWD

A Prayer. Richard Le Gallienne. I fain would bring my soul back safe to thee. TrPWD

Prayer. Clive Staples Lewis. My dead lips breathe and into utterance wake/The thoughts I never knew. TrCP

Prayer. May Carleton Lord. But grant my brother's need shall find/I thought of him instead. PGD

A Prayer. George Macdonald. A fool I bring thee to be made a child. TrPWD

Prayer. Lev Mak. Up from the depths of separation,/Float the splinters of my poems. VWA

A Prayer. Edwin Markham. Place where passing souls can rest/On the way and be their best. HBMV; HBVY; PGD; TrPWD; TRV; WGRP

Prayer. Barbara Marr. I'll not need eyes to make me whole. TrPWD

A Prayer. Irene Rutherford McLeod. All sick and sorrowing hearts to fold/In thy enfolding rest. TrPWD

Prayer. Eduard Moricke. Employ me discreetly,/That peace may possess me. TrPWD

Prayer. Stanley Moss. to see the green, that old anarchy. GP; PoL

Prayer. James P. Mousley. the starred night is above/the moving grass beneath me GoYe

A Prayer. Frederic William Henry Myers. Be thou beside us, very near, O God! TrPWD

Prayer. Mike Newell. in midwinter, my love for you always./February 14/Mike AMV-80

A Prayer. Alfred Noyes. Let my love be heard/Whispering in your wings. PoPl

A Prayer. John Oxenham. By grace I may at last/Be with Thee, Lord! BLRP; TRV

Prayer. Edith Lovejoy Pierce. I, the swinging needle in the compass of the world;/Thou, the perpetual North. TrPWD

Prayer. Edward Bliss Reed. When my child's call I hear, I catch her to my heart. HBMV

Prayer. Charles Francis Richardson. The blessing shall not fail. AA

Prayer. Theodore Roethke. Let Light attend me to the grave! MP; TwCP

A Prayer. Christina Georgina Rossetti. Let that cord be love; and some day make my narrow/Hallow'd bed according to Thy Word. Amen. OBVV

Prayer. Avraham Schlonsky. Teach me a roaring like you to your creatures. VWA

A Prayer. Clinton Scollard. That I may be forgiven/For following loveliness! TrPWD

A Prayer. Frank Dempster Sherman. God make me worthy of my friends. GoTF; TreFS

A Prayer. Edward Rowland Sill. Thy garment's hem, which Truth and Good/we name. AA

Prayer. Robert Louis Stevenson. Show me Thyself in all I see,/Thou Lord of all. TrPWD

A Prayer. Sara Teasdale. Oh, let me love with all my strength/Careless if I am loved again. HBMV; TrPWD

A Prayer. Mary Dixon Thayer. To weep for words I never said? HBMV; TrPWD

Prayer. Henry David Thoreau. Or overrated thy designs. AmePo; AnNE

Prayer. Richard Chenevix Trench. And joy and strength and courage are with Thee? BLRP; TRV; WBLP; WGRP

A Prayer. Julian Tuwim. I pray Thee O Lord from the depths of/my heart. TrJP

Prayer. Louis Untermeyer. God, keep me still unsatisfied. MoAmPo; TrJP; WGRP

The Prayer. Jones Very. My spirit loves with thine in peace to dwell. EBCP; OxBA; TrCP; TrPWD

Prayer. George Villiers. O Lord my God, my Lover, and my Friend. TrPWD

Prayer. Thomas Washbourne. Who gave that strength to Samson, can not/Break the cords of Man. WGRP

A Prayer. Vernon Watkins. Like Samson, Tranquil-souled,/Who remained strong, though blind. MoRP; PoPl

Prayer. John Hall Wheelock. Pity Inexorable, Remorseless Love. EaLo; NePoAm

Prayer. Amos N. Wilder. Made of the world a hushed transfigured place. TrPWD

A Prayer. Yehoash. And let Thy step resound upon/Our night-palled earth. TrJP

A Prayer after Illness. Violet Alleyn Storey. Lovely as pansies or a bluebird's wings! TrPWD

Prayer after World War. Carl Sandburg. Out of the storm let us have one star. VGW

Prayer Against Indifference. Joy Davidman. Break roof and let my death come in. AnEnPo; TrPWD

Prayer against Love. Caius Valerius Catullus. O give me health, expel this foul disease,/because my heart sincerely honors you. LiTW

Prayer–Answer. Ednah D. Cheney. God only waited for me till/I prayed the larger prayer. STF

Prayer Answered. *Anonymous.* My prayer was answered. STF

Prayer at Dawn. Diarmuid O'Shea. And even the birds are singing the Lord God's praise! KiLC

Prayer at Dawn. Edwin McNeill Poteat. Now we begin another day together. TrPWD

Prayer before Birth. Louis MacNeice. Otherwise kill me. FaBoIP; GTBS-P; LiTB; MP; NAs; OAEP; TwCP

Prayer before Execution. Queen of Scots Mary. O Jesu, my Savior, I languish for thee! CAW; TRV; WGRP

Prayer before Meat. Una W. Harsen. Linked here by bonds of love, now let us feed/Upon Thy grace and find it meat indeed. TrPWD

Prayer before Sleep. Alice Lucas. And in Thy gracious love hast given/Light upon earth and light in heaven. TrJP

Prayer before Study. Theodore Roethke. Deliver me, O Lord, from all/Activity centripetal. TrPWD

Prayer before Work. May Sarton. Give it strict form. SaC

Prayer: "Bless Thou this year, O Lord!" Andrew S. C. Clarke. Bless Thou this year, O Lord! PGD

A Prayer Brings Rain. Edward Fairfax. And conquer fortune, fate and destiny strange. OBSC

Prayer by Moonlight. Roberta Teale Swartz. No wine but the rich garnet pour of time/Tasting of pain and danger as you will. TrPWD

Prayer during Battle. Hermann Hagedorn. Keep open, oh, keep open/My mind, my heart! TrPWD

Prayer for a Day's Walk. Grace Noll Crowell. In silent sympathy. PoToHe

A Prayer for a Little Home. Florence Bone. God bless thee, when winds blow,/Our home, and all we know. BLPA; FaBoBe; FaFP; GoTF; TreFT

A Prayer for a Marriage. Mary Carolyn Davies. May storm-clouds change the gold of too much sun. TrPWD

Prayer for a New House. Louis Untermeyer. May they be strong to keep hate out/And hold love in. BLPL; PoLf; PoToHe; TrPWD

Prayer for a Pilot. Cecil Roberts. Who ride Thy realms on Birds of Steel. BBV

Prayer for a Play House. Elinor Lennen. Nature, take care! TrPWD

A Prayer for a Preacher. Edward Shillito. Ply them in prison souls to break the bars/And by me, Lord, pass in. TrPWD

Prayer for a Second Flood. Hugh" (Christopher Murray Grieve) MacDiarmid. ...replenish the salt o' the earth/In the place o' their birth. EBEV

A Prayer for a Sleeping Child. Mary Carolyn Davies. Safe from hurt and free from harm. OHIP

A Prayer for a Very New Angel. Violet Alleyn Storey. When she wakes up, do things for her my way! BLPA; GoTF; TreFS

Prayer for All Poets at This Time. Irwin Edman. Angel of poets,/Tell us how/To move men nobly,/To move them now. TrPWD

Prayer for Boom. Robert Grenier. ...thus subject/to death unknown by heart attack in time. APU

A Prayer for Broken Little Families. Violet Alleyn Storey. Growing, day by day, more closely into oneness with each/other. PoToHe

A Prayer for Charity. Edwin O. Kennedy. That does not need a spear-torn side/Or sight of body crucified/To teach me not to be unkind. TrPWD

Prayer for Contentment. Edwin McNeill Poteat. Make me content, O Lord, with daily bread. TrPWD

Prayer for Dew. Eleazar Ben Kalir. And looks to Thee to give the earth her/greeness/With dew. TrJP

Prayer for Dreadful Morning. E. Merrill Root. Than that the world should stay a stuffy room! TrPWD

Prayer for Every Day. *Anonymous.* Blessings be unto Thee! PBA

A Prayer for Every Day. Mary Carolyn Davies. Let me be joy, be hope! Let my life sing! BLPA; FaBoBe; PoToHe

A Prayer for Faith. Buonarroti Michelangelo. Withholding Faith that opes the doors of/heaven. ILwL

A Prayer for Faith. Alfred Norris. The rest–'tis Thine to give or take. BLRP

A Prayer for Faith. Margaret E. Sangster. For if the prayer dies from my heart I will be quite alone. PoToHe

Prayer for Fine Weather. Shane Leslie. Have pity at least on the spuds. PoL

Prayer for Fish. Ronald Wallace. keeping their proper seasons. AMV-80

Prayer for Forbearance. *Anonymous.* But "yiet' and "yiet' was endless,/and "thole a little' a long way is. LoBV

Prayer for Good Dreams. *Anonymous.* Blessid be the blossom that sprang, Lady, of thee!/In nomine Patris et Filii et Spiritus Sancti/Amen OxBM

A Prayer for Indifference. Fanny Macartney Greville. Contented, half to please. LoBV; NOEC; OBEC; OBEV

Prayer for Kafka and Ourselves. Anthony Rudolf. ...The stone/the builders had doubts about/has become the corner-stone VWA

Prayer for Light. Stanton A. Coblentz. O grant him light to see himself as foe! TrPWD

Prayer for Living and Dying. Christopher La Farge. Carve love deep on my death. TrPWD

Prayer for Messiah. Leonard Cohen. after the raven has died for the dove. OBCV

A Prayer for My Daughter. William Butler Yeats. And custom for the spreading laurel tree. BLPL; CABA; CMoP; CoBMV; HAP; LiTB; LiTM; LoBV; MasP; MoAB; MoRP; NAs; NoAm; NoP; OxBTC; PoA; PoLf; PrIm; TEP; TW; ViBoPo

A Prayer for My Son. Yvor Winters. Pity this small and new/Bright soul on hands and knees. CrMA; TrPWD

A Prayer for My Son. William Butler Yeats. Protecting, till the danger past,/With human love. EBEV; NAs

Prayer for Neighborhood Evangelism. Annetta Jansen. That these be brought into the fold/In Jesus' Name we pray. STF

Prayer for Pain. John G. Neihardt. O let me feel the biting strokes/That I may fight again! HBV 1-2; TrPWD; WGRP

Prayer for Peace. Johnstone G. Patrick. Circle my stubborn soul,/Lap it in peace. TrPWD

A Prayer for Peace. Edward Rowland Sill. Through all the darkness, unto the dawning,/To his beloved he giveth sleep. TrPWD

Prayer for Peace: II. Leopold Sedar Senghor. And lo, the serpent of hatred raises its head in my heart, that serpent that I believed was dead. TTY

A Prayer for Pentecost. Catherine Bernard Brown. To labor for eternity,/Our wills all Thine. BLRP

A Prayer for Purification. Buonarroti Michelangelo. So near to death, so far from God, forlorn. AWP

Prayer for Rain. Aqib Abdullahi Jama. It is to you that I have turned for help! WTO

Prayer for Rain. Kalevala. Though the toil of Vainamoinen. WGRP

Prayer for Rain. Herbert Palmer. Send the rain! HaMV

A Prayer for Recollection. *Anonymous.* Nor feeble-willed like me. KiLC

Prayer for Redemption. *Anonymous.* And may the branch (of Jesse)/spring up in Jerusalem! TrJP

Prayer for Rich and Poor. William Langland. Comfort Thy care-stricken, Christ in Thy Kingdom. BoC

A Prayer for Rivers. Keith Wilson. this time, you completely beside me,/riverfrost on your hair, and on mine. GOYP

Prayer for Serenity. Reinhold Niebuhr. And the wisdom to know the one from the other. GoTF

Prayer for Shut-Ins. Ruth Winant Wheeler. Please give fresh courage, ease their load. PoToHe

Prayer for Song. Fay Lewis Noble. Shepherd of things gone wrong,/Mend my broken mood. TrPWD

A Prayer for St. Innocent's Day. Helen Parry Eden. Nazarius, Celsus, Victor, Innocent! CAW

Prayer for Strength. Margaret E. Bruner. And from my heart, Lord, I would rout/All bitterness. This is my prayer. PoToHe

A Prayer for Thanksgiving. Joseph Auslander. We thank Thee for a final golden chance/To rise again and build a nobler world. TrPWD

Prayer for the Age. Myron H. Broomell. Forgive him for his Neolithic sins. TrPWD

Prayer for the Great Family. Gary Snyder. The Mind is his Wife./so be it. HAP; OFD

Prayer for the Home (excerpt). Edgar A. Guest. Let Thy love and Thy grace/Shine upon our dwelling place. TRV

A Prayer for the Household. Robert Louis Stevenson. we beseech of Thee this help and mercy for Christ's sake. TRV

Prayer for the Journey. *Anonymous.* In the name of the Father and the Son/And the Holy Gost, Amen. OxBM

Prayer for the Little Daughter between Death and Burial. Diana Scott. Lady of the shortest day/watch over our daughter/whom we commit to the grass BrRo

A Prayer for the New Year. *Anonymous.* Serve Thee through all this coming year. BLRP

A Prayer for the New Year. Violet Alleyn Storey. In earthly bulbs, spring flowers; in man, the Christ;/In years, eternity. TrPWD

A Prayer for the Old Courage. Charles Hanson Towne. But keep ye white forever–keep ye whole/The battlements of dream within the soul! TrPWD

Prayer for the Royal Marriage. John Masefield. With wind-delighting clamour of glad voice. HW

A Prayer for the Self. John Berryman. ...Lift up/sober toward truth a scared self-estimate. PPP

Prayer for the Speedy End of Three Great Misfortunes. Frank O'Connor. Hang them, oh Christ, all three! DTC; OBMV

Prayer for the Useless Days. Edith Lovejoy Pierce. Do not leave me, God. TrPWD

Prayer for This Day. Hildegarde Flanner. But the patience and poise of flowers from the earth. TrPWD

A Prayer from 1936. Siegfried Sassoon. O heaven of music, absolve us from this hell/Unto unmechanized mastery over life. TrPWD

A Prayer: "Give me work to do." Anonymous. And a friend with whom/I can be silent. PGD

Prayer in a Country Church. Ruth B. Van Dusen. We pray for "peace on earth, good will to men." TrPWD

Prayer in Affliction. Violet Alleyn Storey. For suffering humankind, a wiser pity/For those who lift a heavier cross with Thee! TrPWD

Prayer in April. Sara Henderson Hay. Can I disrust Eternity? TrPWD

A Prayer in Darkness. Gilbert Keith Chesterton. Heard all the crickets singing, and was glad. BoC; FPL; MoBrPo; PoLf; TrGrPo

A Prayer in Late Autumn. Violet Alleyn Storey. My awful dearth just as one pumpkin mocks,/In clownish glee, this frosted field! TrPWD

Prayer in Mid-Passage. Louis MacNeice. Thou my meaning, Thou my death. EaLo

A Prayer in Spring. Robert Frost. But which it only needs that we fulfil. MoRP; TrCP; TrPWD; YeAr

A Prayer in the Prospect of Death. Robert Burns. But, Thou art good; and Goodness still/Delighteth to forgive. HBV 1-2; TrPWD; WGRP

A Prayer in Time of Blindness. Clement Wood. Trudging the hard gay road/Of the clean-souled sons of men. TrPWD

Prayer in Time of War. Henry Treece. Man rock the mountain with his two bare hands! WaP

Prayer Moves the Hand That Moves the World. John A. Wallace. And moves the hand which moves the/world,/To bring salvation down. STF

Prayer of a Beginning Teacher. Ouida Smith Dunnam. Lord, help me to be true;/For I am just beginning, too. TrPWD

Prayer of a Modern Thomas. Edward Shillito. Show me Thy pierced side. PGD

Prayer of a Patriot. Henry J. Von Schlichten. Our humble prayer–/Forever free! BePJ

Prayer of a Soldier in France. Joyce Kilmer. So, let me render back again/This millionth of Thy gift. Amen. CAW; GoBC

Prayer of a Teacher. Dorothy Littlewort. Firm hand and high heart for the further task. TrPWD

Prayer of an Unbeliever. Lizette Woodworth Reese. To stumble to that lodging which is You. TrPWD

Prayer of an Unemployed Man. W. C. Ackerly. Abide with me and be my friend. PoToHe

Prayer of an Unknown Confederate Soldier. Anonymous. I am among all men, most richly blessed. GoTF; TreFT

Prayer of Any Husband. Mazie V. Caruthers. May not the two of us be parted long! PoToHe

The Prayer of Beaten Men. Margaret Louisa Woods. Give us our swords again, and hold thy hand. HBV 1-2

Prayer of Columbus. Walt Whitman. And anthems in new tongues I hear saluting me. ATP; PGD; TrPWD; TRV; WGRP

Prayer of Little Hope. Jean Wahl. And you were never more deaf and more dumb. VWA

Prayer of St. Francis of Assisi for Peace. Pat Therese Francis. And it is in dying that we are born to eternal life. FPL

Prayer of St. Francis Xavier. Alexander Pope. My God, my Father, Maker, and my King! TrPWD

Prayer of Thanksgiving. Theodore Baker. Thy name be ever praised! O Lord, make us free! BLSo

The Prayer of the Donkey. Carmen De Gasztold. And, Lord, one day, let me find again/my little brother of the Christmas crib. PCh

Prayer of the Fishing Net. Anonymous. Free through whom?/Free through Kane. WTO

Prayer of the Five Wounds (excerpt). Anonymous. Whan thow suffredis ded for me. AtBAP

Prayer of the Maidens to Mary. Rainer Maria Rilke. By the same wonder wounded be. AWP

A Prayer of the Night Chant. Anonymous. In beauty it is finished. ExPo

A Prayer of the Peoples. Percy MacKaye. We, who pray, ourselves are fate. TrPWD; WGRP

Prayer of the Young Stoic. Stephen P. Dunn. With thee I cannot live,/And turn from thee–in vain. TrPWD

Prayer on Fourth of July. Nancy Byrd Turner. For peace and blessing may she stand,/America our land! YeAr

Prayer on Making a Canoe. Anonymous. When the storm tosses on all sides. WTO

Prayer on the Night Before Easter. John Holmes. And keep for us, those of us who need it, sleep, and sleep. MoRP

Prayer: "Prayer, the Church's banquet." George Herbert. The land of spices; something understood. NOBE

The Prayer Rug. Sara Beaumont Kennedy. I hold in fief/Four square feet of the orient. HBMV

Prayer That an Infant May Not Die. Francis Jammes. You live forever at Your mother's side! CAW

A Prayer to Be Said When Thou Goest to Bed. Francis Seager. Saying, "To the Lord be all honour and praise/For his defence both now and always!" OxBChV

A Prayer to Escape from the Market Place. James Wright. Only to see him vanishing at the damp edge/Of the road. NaP

Prayer to Go to Paradise with the Asses. Francis Jammes. To mirror their sweet, humble poverty/In the clear waters of eternal love. AWP

Prayer to God. Placido (Gabriel de la Conception Valdes). Lord of my life, work Thou Thy perfect will. CAW; TTY

Prayer to Hermes. Robert Creeley. and will tell of itself/all, all the world. PoM

Prayer to Isis. Christina Walsh. O Isis, mother of God, hear my prayer. BrRo

Prayer to Santa Maria Del Vade. Juan, Archpriest of Hita, Ruiz. From out my weary prison, my life of woes so mean! CAW

Prayer to St. Helena. Anonymous. Now and in the houre of my dede,/And bring my soule to requied. OxBM

Prayer to St. Patrick. Ninine. God be with us, together with the prayer of Patrick, chief/apostle. OnYI

Prayer to the Blessed Virgin. Rodriquez de Padron. That he may harvest for the better time. CAW

Prayer to the Crucifix. Mossen Juan Tallante. Salvation in his grief's confession:/Memento mei. CAW

Prayer to the Father in Heaven. John Skelton. And, after this life, to see thy glorious Face. HoPM; TrPWD

Prayer to the God Thot. Anonymous. when the noisy man comes you remain hidden. TTY

Prayer to the Hunting Star, Canopus. Anonymous. that makes me miss my mark. PeSA

A Prayer to the Lord Ramakrishna. James Wright. Sleep on. NNaP

Prayer to the Mountain Spirit. Anonymous Spirit of the Mountain! BPAW; WGRP

Prayer to the Pacific. Leslie Marmon Silko. swallowing raindrops/clear from China. CDW; NoP; VoR

A Prayer to the Sacrament of the Altar. Anonymous. And blisse with thee that leste shall ay. MeEL

Prayer to the Snowy Owl. John Haines. preserver of whiteness. BoAnP

A Prayer to the Trinity. Anonymous. And on alle that mercy nede for charite./Amen, par amore, Amen. MeEL

Prayer to the Trinity. James Edmeston. Nothing can our peace destroy. HBV 1-2

A Prayer to the Trinity. Richard Stanyhurst. Thee, sacred Spirit, labourers refreshing,/Still be renowned. CoBE; ElL

Prayer to the Virgin. Anonymous.
  That havet hidut the foule put/Inferni. EnLit
  That we may meet with dear Jesus–that is our prayer–hail! OnYI

Prayer to the Virgin of Chartres. Henry Adams.
  The futile folly of the Infinite. CAW; GoBC; ISi
  Listen, dear lady! You shall hear the last/Of the strange prayers Humanity has wailed. AmePo

A Prayer to the Wind. Thomas Carew. Or else quite extinguish mine. AnAnS 2

Prayer to the Young Moon. Anonymous. hai hai!/Young moon PeSA

Prayer to Venus. Geoffrey Chaucer. So that I have my lady in my arms. LiTL

Prayer to Venus. Edmund Spenser. Oh, grant that of my love at last I may not miss! ElL

Prayer under the Pressure of Violent Anguish. Robert Burns. Then man my soul with firm resolves/To bear and not repine. TrPWD

A Prayer unto Christ the Judge of the World. Michael Wigglesworth. And teach the Sons of men thy wayes. SCAP

Prayers. Henry Charles Beeching. Take my spirit to Thee. OBEV; OBVV

The Prayers. Howard Schwartz. With a blessing/From the dark sun/Of their source. VWA

Prayers Must Have Poise. Robert Herrick. ...words ought to have their weight. LiTB

Prayers of a Christian Bridegroom. Pierre Poupo. But he who is well married is near to Paradise. HW

Prayers of Steel. Carl Sandburg. Let me be the great nail holding a skyscraper through blue/nights into white stars. AnAmPo; AP; CMoP; MoAmPo; TrCP; TrPWD; YaD

Prayers to Liberty. Anwar Shaul. They are not to be found/Neither in East nor in West. VWA

Prayerwheel/2. David Meltzer. ...We continue/talking, growing nervous, drinking/too much coffee. NeAP

Praying. P. J. Kavanagh. As horses in fields suddenly stop/Their gallop at a horizon and crop. OBSP

The Praying Mantis. Ogden Nash. And faintly whisper, Lord deliver us. PV

The Praying Mantis Visits a Penthouse. Oscar Williams. I search my mind for possible wounds and feel/The victim's body heavy on the victor's heart. FaFP; LiTM; NePA

Pre Domina. Jean Lipkin. Slept mortal all morning. PeSA

Pre-Existence. Paul Hamilton Hayne. Unknown, scarce seen, whose flickering grace/Faints on the outmost rings of space! HBV 1-2

Pre-History Repeats. Robert J., Jr. McKent. Will rise from their ashes in ten million years? QQQ

Pre-positions. Jose Isaacson. because one March afternoon/you gave me/a between/a beat. VWA

The Preacher. Al-Mahdi. Continuing yet/Not to cut with your own? TTY

The Preacher and the Slave (with music). Anonymous. Chop some wood, 'twill do you good, And you'll eat in the sweet bye and bye. AS; FSW; TrAS

The Preacher's Mistake. William Croswell Doane. "Down here among my people." BLPA; PoToHe

A Preacher's Prayer. Anonymous. I only ask, when I voice the message/My Saviour's heart. STF

The Preacher's Prayer. George Macdonald. And men will hear, or when I sing or preach. TRV

The Preacher's Vacation. Anonymous. "Jesus absent on vacation, heaven closed till his return.'" BLPA; BLPL

The Preacher's Wife. Anonymous. But really, it takes a lot of grace/To be a preacher's wife. STF

The Preacher Sought to Find Out Acceptable Words. Richard Eberhart. Diverted from swimming a moment when he dropped. WaP

The Preachers. Norman Nicholson. As He heard the birds/Preach to St. Francis. NeBP

Preachin' the Blues. Son House. When the spirit comes, sisters,/I want you to jump straight up and down. BluL

Preaching Blues. Robert Johnson. Stay/out/there/all/day BluL

Preachment for Preachers. Alexander Barclay. He betides himself to wake his own body/Before he crow to cause others wake or rise. CAW

Precarious Ground. Leah Bodine Drake. Only upon the slope/Of old catastrophe. GoYe

Precaution. Heinrich Heine. One can catch a cold so quickly/In the absence of a shawl. UnTE

Precedent. Paul Laurence Dunbar. "I will send my dogs to lick your sores!" AmePo

The Precept of Silence. Lionel Pigot Johnson. I have not spoken of these things, Save to one man, and unto God. CAW; HBV 1-2; MoBrPo; ViBoPo; VLP

Precepts He Gave His Folk. Elijah Hazaken. Israel glowed that day, God's Ten/Commandments receiving. TrJP

La Preciosa. Thomas Walsh. But in stone the Virgin listened,–never smiled nor spoke again. ISi

The Precious Blood. Anonymous. All sufficient is the glory/of the Lord's atoning Blood. STF

Precious Child, So Sweetly Sleeping. Anna Hoppe. Endless hymns of praise I sing. AH

Precious in the Sight of the Lord... Anonymous. 'Tis the tenderest token of His love so deep. BLRP

Precious Mettle. Lewis Warsh. I bought a pack of smokes for the journey. APU

Precious Moments. Carl Sandburg. Dying he lives and speaks! MoAmPo

A Precious–Mouldering Pleasure–'tis–. Emily Dickinson. Old volumes shake their Vellum Heads/And tantalize–just so– DiPo

The Precious Name. John Newton. So shall the music of Thy name/Refresh my soul in death. BePJ

The Precious Pearl. Pat Wilson. A perfect grievance–rolled from off the tongue. AnNZ

Precious Stones. Charles Stuart Calverley. I think there possibly might be/E'en greater geese than thou. InMe

Precious Things. Anonymous. But pray don't touch my sweet little lips. GoSl; TTY

Precious to me–she still shall be. Emily Dickinson. When Summer's Everlasting Dower–/Confronts the dazzled Bee. PeHV

Precious Words. Emily Dickinson. A loosened spirit brings! BBV

The Precipice. John Banister Tabb. And who among us knows/How near the brink he goes? AmP

The Precision. Yvor Winters. Suspended on cold iron, branded on air. EAS

Precursors. Louis MacNeice. And–during thunder-storms–the light comes shining/through. OBSP

Predestination. Rudyard Kipling. Even now–even now–even now! LoBV

The Predicter of Famine. William Carlos Williams. ...his eye/alert to the providing water. VGW

The Prediction. Mark Strand. and taking the moon and leaving the paper dark. EAS; LCAP

Preexistence. Frances Cornford. And in my fingers long and brown/The little pebbles lay. HBMV

Preface. W. H. Auden. And the ripeness all. LiTA

La Preface. Charles Olson. The babe/the Howling Babe PoM

Preface. Carol Shauger. into a strange/incomprehensible man. AMV-80

Preface. Theodore Weiss. Darnel, Ragweed, Wortle NMP; VGW

Preface ShrinkLit: Elements of Style William Strunk, Jr. & E. B. White. Maurice Sagoff. "Er–I mean 'Quite!'/Or, simply, 'Right!'" NLV

Preface to a Twenty Volume Suicide Note. LeRoi (Imamu Amiri Baraka) Jones. On she on her knees, peeking into/Her own clasped hands. AmNP; CAPP; InPS; NNP; PAI; PoBA; PoM; PoNe; PPP; TTY

A Preface to the Memoirs. James Merrill. From the eruptions of a court whose pageants/These deep-pitted features chronicle. NOBA

Prefatory Sonnet. Henry Clarence Kendall. And these, at least, though far between and few,/May catch the sense like subtle forest spells. BoAV

Preference. Langston Hughes. When she conversations you/it ain't forever, Gimme! HaCAP; NOBA

Preference. Daniel Sargent. I should rather have one place where I can stand/And gaze at her, than roam all roads in the land. ISi

The Preference Declared. Eugene Field. For me, supine beneath this vine,/Doing my best to get a jag on! NLV

Pregnancy. Sandra McPherson. ...and three/Beings' lives gel in my womb. BoWoP; NMM

Pregnant Image of "Exaggerating the Village." Nora Dauenhauer. lying on/her exaggerated belly/lies/"Lying There." TWSS

Pregnant Teenager on the Beach. Mary Balazs. drops her among stones/and cracked shells. AMV-80

Pregnant Woman. Ingrid Jonker. with my bloodchild under your water...? PeSA

Prehistoric Burials. Siegfried Sassoon. Earth's ignorant nullity made strange with flowers. MoBrPo

A Prehistoric Camp. Andrew Young. Its race of men long flown. CBEP

The Preiching of the Swallow. Robert Henryson. And thus endis the preiching of the Swallow. OxBS

Prejudice. Georgia Douglas Johnson. The fire of whose furnaces may/sleep, but never dies! AmNP; PoBA

The Prejudice against the Past. Wallace Stevens. The Swedish cart to be part of the heart. LiTM

Preliminary Poem. John Heath-Stubbs. Pursue the wild game through thickets of irony. OxBC

Preliminary to Classroom Lecture. Josephine Miles. Querying too, querying, my quiet kin? NoAm

Prelude. Christine Ama Ata Aidoo. You stranger do not know. PBWP

Prelude. Richard Aldington. Yet no god loved as loves this poor frail dust. BrPo

Prelude. Arthur Christopher Benson. I feed the porch with fragrant smoke,/Strew roses on the stair. OBVV

Prelude. Clemens Brentano. "O star and blossom, spirit, robe,/Love, heartbreak, time, eternity." LiTW

Prelude. Stefan George. ...we/are ready to follow him to night or death. WaaP

Prelude. W. W. Gibson. Surge with the life-song of humanity. MoBrPo

Prelude. Patrick Kavanagh. Lovers alone lovers protect. FaBoIP; IPY; NoAm

Prelude. R. A. K. Mason. but it can stab. AnNZ

Prelude. Josephine Preston Peabody. Singing and singing and singing! AA

Prelude. Conrad Kent Rivers. a land apart, to dust, to clay. PoBA

(...Prelude). Rokwaho. naked...the morningstar is born(e)... STE

Prelude. D. Rosenmann-Taub. and a lone body lying in gentleness/silent as light. Afterwards the wind. VWA

Prelude. John Millington Synge. In converse with the mountains, moors, and fens. AWP; BoNaP; FaBoPP; HBMV; MoBrPo; OBMV

A Prelude. Maurice Thompson. Whence perfect wild-flowers leap and shine! AmePo; HBV 1-2

Prelude. John Greenleaf Whittier. The sole necessity of Earth and Heaven! AP

Prelude. Traise Yamamoto. ...None of this prepares you for what you will choose to tell: tell,/and retell. BrSi

Prelude to Akwasidae. Anonymous. Early Early Early/Huuuuuuuuuuuuuuuuuu–beeeeeeeeeeeeeeee TTY

Prelude to an Evening. John Crowe Ransom. Smoothing the heads of the hungry children. AP; CoBMV; EAS; MoAB; MoAmPo; MoPo; MoVE; NePA; OxBA; PoCh

A Pretty Girl. J. Gordon Coogler. And there are no pimples encircling her dimples/As ever, as yet, I have seen. OBAL

The Pretty Girl of Loch Dan. Sir Samuel Ferguson. I'd take the mountainside e'en now,/And walk to Luggelaw again! HBV 1-2

The Pretty Maid. Frederick York Powell. And they are off a-field to work: as they do every day. OBMV

Pretty Maids Beware!!! Anonymous. The traitor lurks, the undermining foe. CoMu

Pretty Mary. Anonymous. He closed his eyes, no more to rise on the sweet Dundee. BFSS

Pretty Molly. Anonymous.
He threw some dirt o'er her and turned to go home,/The birds to weep, nobody to mourn. BFSS
"Jim Lukus has drowned her and then run away." BFSS

The Pretty Ploughboy. Anonymous. And at night she'll return/To her nest back again. GBP

Pretty Polly. Anonymous.
For killin' pretty Polly will send my soul to Hell. AmFP
For killing pretty Polly and running away. FSW; OuSiCo
Left nothing behind but the birds to mourn. AmFP
...she came to her father's house/One hour before it was day. UnTE
So now that she's married, she lives at her ease;/She goes at her will and returns as she pleases. BFSS

Pretty Polly of Topsham. Anonymous. And I never will go near my false Polly any more. AmFP

Pretty Polly (with music). Anonymous. Thy cage shall be made of handbeaten gold,/Thy door of the finest ivory. AS

Pretty Saro. Anonymous. And I'll dream of pretty Saro wherever I go. AmFP; FSW

Pretty Sport. William Habington. Bedlam! this is pretty sport. NOBE

Pretty Twinkling Starry Eyes. Nicholas Breton. Show the praise of your perfections. EiL

Pretty Vomit. Bob Rosenthal. a bucket of steaming water/slop slop. APU

Pretty Wantons. Anonymous. Oh, pretty warbling from a sweet sweet throat! EiL

A Pretty Woman. Simon J. Ortiz. and the land was a pretty woman/smiling at us/looking at her. CDW

Pretty Words. Elinor Wylie. Gilded and sticky, with a little sting. HBMV; YaD

The Pretzel Man. Rachel Field. And this is not the case with kings! SoPo

Prevalent Poetry. Charles Follen Adams. With orthography not so injiouxrious. CenHV

Prevarication. Anonymous. That's what gave me/This jolly red nose. OxNR

Prevision. Ada Foster Murray. We shall not miss the Summer's full-blown grace,/Nor hunger for the swift, exquisite Spring. HBV 1-2

Prewar Late October Sea Breeze. Robert Grenier. ...sallow virginal pools in/windy amber watercolor. APU

Prey to Prey. David Rowbotham. Sea-dead, having died so without even hate. CBAP

Priam and Achilles. Alexander Pope. These Words soft Pity in the Chief inspire,/Touch'd with the dear Remembrance of his Sire. OBEC

Priapus and the Pool. Conrad Aiken.
And leave not in a single crevice/A single leaf. AmLP
"I never loved you so." AmLP; NoAm
Or, if the heart provide, a snake. AnAmPo
This is what you are to me. CMoP; NOBA; TrGrPo

The Price He Paid. Ella Wheeler Wilcox. By the sins of their fathers scarred. WBLP

Price of a Drink. Josephine Pollard. "Five cents a glass!" Does anyone think/That is really the price of a drink. PaPo

The Price of Begging. Emmanuel Frances. Who begs, a thousand times he dies. TrJP

The Price of Paper. Lawrence Russ. or big waves, about to break over him. AMV-81

Prices. Louis Ginsberg. The one that wanted nothing/Took the most of me. TrJP

Pride. Barten Holyday. The peacock's tail is furthest from his sight! FaBoEE

Pride. Violet Jacob. For the warst sin, neebours, is pride, ay, pride! OxBS

The Pride. John Newlove. and in this land we/are their people, come/back to life again. NOBC

Pride and Hesitation. Cerise Farallon. ... my heart would bedded clover become/to blossom beneath your form UnTE

Pride Is Out. Anonymous. That he forgive thee thy pride/And they sins that thou hast do. CBEP

The Pride of a Jew. Judah Halevi. And sing Thy praises, O my song,/alway! TrJP

Pride of Ancestry. Robert Frost. That their descent from such a calorie/Accounts for their genius and love of drink. OBAL

The Pride of Kildare. Anonymous. But my blessings on Susan, the Pride of Kildare. OBET

A Pride of Ladies. Anne Halley. Mariner, Swineherd, King,/and set one free. NMM

La Priere de Nostre Dame. Geoffrey Chaucer. Bring us to that palace that is built/For penitents that be to mercy able./Amen. ISi

Priest and Pagan. Albert Durrant Watson. And poured His blessing on us both. CaP

The Priest and the Mulberry Tree. Thomas Love Peacock. Much that well may be thought cannot wisely be/said. GN; OnMSP; StPo

Priest Lake. William Stafford. ...but I come/back, far down these evenings, faithful, to glean. PoA

The Priest of Christ. Thomas Ken. And wisely fair restoratives supply. TRV

The Priest of Coloony. William Butler Yeats. This way were all reproved/Who dig old customs up. OnYI

The Priest of Felton. Anonymous. And nobody there to help him. OxNR

Priest Or Poet. Shane Leslie. Enhungered, thirsting as they daily sink/Beneath the trampling multitude. CAW; WGRP

The Priest Rediscovers His Psalm-Book. Anonymous. And light my pathway with His face/When the dead flesh is left behind. KiLC

The Priest's Lament. Robert Hugh Benson. Whose shoulder bears the heavier load,–/Is it not Mine? ACP

A Priest's Prayer. Martha Gilbert Dickinson. Kiss me, Jessica! Once for all. AA

The Priesthood. George Herbert. the poor do by submission/What pride by opposition. AnAnS 1

Primary. Abbie Huston Evans. But these tunneled through pit blackness:/Scarlet; yellow; blue. GP

Primary Education. Phyllis McGinley. Or so believes the Board of Ed. GLGT

A Primary Ground. Adrienne Rich. understanding her case, trying to make her understand. NNaP

Primary Lesson: The Second Class Citizens. Sun-Ra. The Advance Prophet transcends the/Law concerning "A prophet." PoBA

Primary Numbers. Edvard Kochek. and yet linked to/pure primary numbers. AMV-81

Primavera. Frank Lima. Hi Monkey/I'm home ANYP

Prime. W. H. Auden. Which the coming day will ask. CMoP

Prime. Langston Hughes. In the section of the niggers/Where a nickel costs a dime. PoBA

The Prime of Life. Walter Learned. Rose came by with a smile for me,/Just as I thought I was getting old. HBV 1-2

A Primer for Schoolchildren. Richard Weber. Who still must ask why it all began. CIP

Primer Lesson. Carl Sandburg. Look out how you use proud words. MoAMPo; MoShBr; PoPl

Primer Lesson. Mark Vinz. into the long Dakota night. TAT

Primer of Consequences. Virginia Brasier. He just goes "fffff-ut!" ShM

Primer of Plato. Jean Garrigue. To be the image each first was. MoVE; NOBA

A Primer of the Daily Round. Howard Nemerov. Peeling an apple somewhere far away. NYBP; SM; WeW

The Primitive. Don L. Lee. they brought us here–/to drive us mad./(like them) BPo

A Primitive Like an Orb. Wallace Stevens. And the giant ever changing, living in change. NOBA

Primitives. Dudley Randall. gas, powder and a/little rubble. BALP; BPo

Primo Vere. Giosue Carducci. Has spring, too, felt the doom of years? AWP

The Primrose. Thomas Carew. I must tell you, these discover/What doubts and fears are in a lover. FaBoUS

The Primrose. Robert Herrick. –These discover/What fainting hopes are in a lover. HBV 1-2; OBEV; ViBoPo

The Primrose Bed. Robert Graves. The other could not mate. TEP

The Primrose, Being at Montgomery Castle, upon the Hill... John Donne. First into this five, women may take us all. FaBoPP; GBL

A Primrose Dame. Gleason White. I almost wish I were a Tory. HBV 1-2

Primroses. Alfred Austin. Go as gently as you came. OBVV

The Prince. Edgar Bowers. Where is the guile enough to comfort me? ConAP

Prince Alfrid's Itinerary (excerpt). Anonymous. Long-living worthies, commerce, wealth. BIrV

Prince Charming. John N. Miller. ...let no slack lips dispel my charm. DFT

Prince Heathen (A version). Anonymous. For hearts will break, and bands will/bow;/So dear will I love my lady now!' ESPB

Prince Heathen (B version). Anonymous. When hearts are broken, bands will bow;/Sae well's he loved his lady now! ESPB

Prince Henry the Navigator. Sydney Clouts. I cross the deliberate gulf of man. PeSA

Private Devotion. Phoebe Hinsdale Brown. And lead to endless day. AA

The Private Dining Room. Ogden Nash. I haven't thought for thirty years/Of Lalage and Barbara. ExPo; NYBP; PoCh

A Private Letter to Brazil. Gloria C. Oden. is not that slight tossing dead Leander? AmNP; NNP; PoNe

Private Means is Dead. Stevie Smith. Who are too old in any case to go to the War. OxBC

The Private Meeting Place. James Wright. ...But now the winter's come. NYBP

The Private of the Buffs. Sir Francis Hastings Doyle. Who died, as firm as Sparta's king,/Because his soul was great. HBV 1-2; OBEV; OBTV; OBVV; PaPo; VLP

Private Pain in Time of Trouble. Kathleen Spivack. It is a false spring this year. AmPA

Private Pantomime. Ruth Stone. And I thrust both my hands into a pair of gloves, tight. PoA

Private Rooms. Diana O Hehir. Down and down her slanting country, her hair straight out behind her/Like a sail. NPGG

Private Transport. Adrian Mitchell. A sneer on four square wheels FaBoEE

Private Worship. Mark Van Doren. Oh, he could see what tears had done to stone. LiTL; MoVE

Privation. Hayden Carruth. weeping in the/spring, summer, fall,/and winter of/humiliation. FAZ

Privilege. Alejandra Pizarnik. you a shadow until the day of days. VWA

Privy-Love for my Landlady. George Farewell. Dear, doting Dick, for O! she saved my life. NOEC

The Prize Cat. Edwin John Pratt. I thought an Abyssinian child/Had cried out in the whitethroat's scream. NoAm; PeCV

Prize for Good Conduct. Kenneth Allott. As they sit in the sunshine, crying no rest for the wicked. OBWP

Prize-Giving. Gwen Harwood. ...a sage fool trapped/by music in a copper net of hair. CBAP

The Prize of the Margaretta. Will Carleton. And the truth was shown, for the world to/read,/That men may follow and boys may lead. PAH

A "Prize' Poem. Shirley Brooks. And now thou seest my soul's angelic hue. FaBoCo; FaBoNo

The Pro. Karen Swenson. She is our first attempt at victory, our final/painted desert of defeat. AMV-81

Pro Femina. Carolyn Kizer.
And the luck of our husbands and lovers, who keep free women. MAT; NMM
Flux, efflorescence–whatever you care to call it! NMM
Springing, full-grown, from your own head, Athena? NMM

Pro Libra Mea. Joseph Ignatius Constantin Clarke. And lift my heart or bear my cross. TrPWD

Pro Patria. Constance Carrier. and the doves come down for bread on the/sun-warmed stone. NePoAm; NYBP

Pro Patria Mori. Thomas Moore. Is the pride of thus dying for thee. GTBS; GTBS-P

Pro Sua Vita. Robert Penn Warren. "So the rigid hills had been forgot/In darkness, if God had wasted not." MoAmPo

Probability and Birds. Russell Atkins. dogs are random CNA; FB

The Probatioun Officeres Tale. Gerard Benson. So be she got hir Pusheres into court. BXAP; NLV

Proberbially Useful Dates for Weathermen. Anonymous. Then hope for a prosperous autumn that year. FaBoUs

Probity. David Swanger. Already they have plans to grow/umbrellas under the side porch. FAZ

The Problem. Paul Blackburn. and know a god/to dedicate it to. NeAP

The Problem. Ralph Waldo Emerson I would not the good bishop be. AA; AnNE; AP; AWP; HBV 1-2; LiTA; MAmP; NePA; NOBA; NoP; OxBA; TAP; WGRP

A Problem in Morals. Howard Moss. With women and men,/A middle ground. ErPo

Problem in Social Geometry–The Inverted Square! Ray Durem. When you tire of pot/Try thought. NBP; PoBA

The Problem of Wild Horses. Barbara Winder. ...sucking the good water/between my teeth. PH

Problems. Alexander Scott. We hae a problem here. FF

Problems of a Journalist. Weldon Kees. The evening paper, in an Irving Place cafe. NaP; NYP

The Problems of a Writing Teacher. David Ray. Screaming across the page, Ahhhhhhhh. NePoEA-2

Proceedings of the Wars. Erin Moure. they labour to find an entrance without stairs CaPN

The Process. Robert Kelly. I am with/the old men/watching one/spring go out. CoPo

Process. Charles L. O'Donnell. After the searching share of pain/Has cut a furrow through my heart. TrPWD

A Process in the Weather of the Heart. Dylan Thomas. And the heart gives up its dead. MoAB; NeBP

The Process of Conception. Claude Quillet. A useful Lesson to the forward Wife. FaBoUs

Process of time worketh such wonder. Sir Thomas Wyatt. Naught helpeth time, humbleness, nor place. FCP; SiPS

The Procession. Margaret Widdemer. Till the snow comes back, and stays/Here for all our winter plays! YeAr

The Procession: A New Protestant Ballad. Anonymous. The Protestant cause let's serve,/And give to the devil the pope. APAS

A Procession at Candlemas. Amy Clampitt. ...and the sorrow/of things moving back to where they came from. FaBoWP; HaCAP

Processional. William Jay Smith. By more than the idiot wind that rakes the pits of Hell. NePoAm

Proclaim the Lofty Praise. Sarah Judson. With all our powers to praise and love/Our Saviour, God, and King. AH

A Proclamation. Anonymous. Fear Bute, fear Mansfield, North and me,/And be as blest as slaves can be. PAH

The Proclamation. Henry Wadsworth Longfellow. O Magistrates, take heed, lest ye be found/As fighters against God! PAH

The Proclamation. John Greenleaf Whittier. And heal with freedom what your slavery/cursed. PAH

Proclamation/From Sleep, Arise. Carolyn M. Rodgers. THE SLAVE PERIOD IS OVER JB

Procne. Peter Quennell. As the branch swung beneath her dancing feet. ChMP; LiTB; LiTM; MoBrPo

Procrastination. Doctor Edward Young. O'er those we love, we drop it in their grave. AnEnPo

Procrastination. Edward Hilton Young. In all the magnanimity of Thought/Resolves; and re-resolves: then dies the same. OBEC

The Prodigal. Elizabeth Bishop. ...But it took him a long time/finally to make his mind up to go home. CoAP; InvP; LCAP; LiTM; MoAB; MP; NYBP; PPP; TwCP

Prodigal. Ellen Gilbert. O hold me to Thy Heart once more,/And hide me from the past. GoBC

Prodigal's Return. Ralph D. Eberly. "My sons! My sons! My sons!" AMV-80

The Prodigal Son. Edwin Arlington Robinson. And I, the ghost of one you could not save,/May find you planting lentils on my grave. MoAmPo

The Prodigal Son. Arthur Symons. Weary and famished, fallen and desolate? BrPo

Prodigals. Charles L. O'Donnell. To His Father's house and festival/And the right-hand seat. HBMV

The Prodigy. Sir Alan Patrick Herbert. And I kissed her at the Zoo. EvOK

Prodigy. Charles Simic. the great ones on several boards/at the same time. GeTw

De Produndis. Dorothy Parker. The tales of girls he used to have? ErPo

De Produndis (excerpt). Elizabeth Barrett Browning. I thank Thee while my days go on. TrPWD

Proem. Madison Cawein. And the world would be richer one poet/the more. AA; BoNaP

Proem. Wilfrid Gibson. The man who hews the coal to feed my fire. HBMV

Proem. Heinrich Heine. Complain, and are not fain/To say what they saw in her heart. AWP

A Proem. Samuel Ward Nor ivory nor gold the Crucifix. AA; AmLP

Proem. John Greenleaf Whittier. As theirs, I lay like them, my best gifts on thy shrine! AA; AnNE; AP; HBV 1-2; NePA; NoP; OxBA; TAP

Proem to Hellenics. Walter Savage Landor. Temper a graver with a lighter song. ViBoPo

Proem to "The Kid." Conrad Aiken. and the locked heart of man his only doubt. MoAB

Proem to the Parlement of Foules. Geoffrey Chaucer. Cometh al this newe science that men lere. FiP

The Profane. Horace. Much will be missing still, and much will be amiss. AWP

The Professional. David Ignatow. ...but of a spirit that demands/to be compensated for its skill. NNaP

Professional Amnesia. Erin Moure. the women are running out of it, into a summer lake of air CaPN

Professional Prisoner. Jessica Scarbrough. will I recognize the woman who stands/at the grave? LFAC

The Professionals. Geoffrey Grigson. ...the children swing in blue/And green, and the wet clouds extend. PoA

Professor Drinking Wine. Alasdair Clayre. thought Clitheroe, with precision, as he poured. PV

Professor Gratt. Donald Hall. Face stuffed and sneering, "Gratt has what it takes." OBAL

Professor Kelleher and the Charles River. Desmond O'Grady. All shadows procession in an acropolis of lights. CIP; NoAm

Professor Noctutus. George Macdonald. I will bury you nicely with my spade and shovel. NOBV

A Professor's Song. John Berryman.　Convulsed, foaming immortal blood: farewell.　HeIP; NoAm; NOBA; OxBC

The Professor Waking.　James Tate.　...If they ask me to run/for President, I might give in!　FF

Professors.　Harold A. Larrabee.　Or just about/Like other folks.　InMe

Proffered Love Rejected.　Sir John Suckling.　When I at first the forty crowns/For one night's lodging bid.　CavP; NCEP

The Proffered Rose.　King of Bohemia Wenceslas.　I might have plucked the rose, and I did not.　LiTW

Profile.　Bronwen Wallace.　when the shutter/reopen　AMV-81

The Profile on the Pillow.　Dudley Randall.　but I keep, against the ice and the fire,/the memory of your profile on the pillow.　BP; BPo; PoBA; TAP

Profiles of My Father.　Rhyll McMaster.　and the Coach's light blue, shot-silk togs.　CBAP

Profit and Loss: An Elegy upon the Decease of Mrs. Mary Gerrish...　John Danforth.　You want her Much: seek her in Christ/And you will find her there.　SCAP

De Profundis.　Hugh" (Christopher Murray Grieve) MacDiarmid.　To the soul the Abyss.　SeCePo

De Profundis.　Christina Georgina Rossetti.　I strain my heart, I stretch my hands,/And catch at hope.　CoBE

De Profundis.　Amos N. Wilder.　Deliver us, O Lord,/With bread of health from life's abundant board.　TrPWD

De Profundis.　Sir Thomas Wyatt.　Then will I crave with sured confidence./And thus begins the suit of his pretense.　FCP

De Profundis Clamavi.　Charles Baudelaire.　...What hides itself/When the skein of Time slowly divides itself?　SyP

Prognosis.　Louis MacNeice.　And his message easy?　CMoP; OxBI

Prognostic.　Samuel Yellen.　Then wastes and crumples it to dry brown sorrow.　NePoAm

A Prognostication on Will Laud, Late Archbishop of Canterbury. Anonymous.　For Church's good; she rises high,/When such as you fall down.　OxBoLi

Program Note on Sibelius.　Donald Campbell Babcock.　Still glides the swan across the mere of magic,/Dark under cypress.　UnS

Progress.　Edith Agnew.　An automobile, I would not trade it/For any burro!　AmFN

Progress.　Anonymous.　We would not long for heaven/If earth held only joy.　STF

Progress?　W. H. Auden.　Man can picture the Absent/and Non-Existent. SUW

Progress.　Sally Belfrage.　Chaps in whose light we are/Now being Conned. PV

Progress.　Suzanne Douglass.　The faster we go, the louder we get.　QQQ

Progress.　Felicia Lamport.　When we're thrown into the hunting of the quark.　QQQ

Progress.　Connie Martin.　the heartwood thrown open against the blade. PPJ

Progress.　David McCord.　Suggest that where he was is where we are. ImOP

Progress.　Peter Meinke.　Libido/ergo sum.　PoL

Progress.　Ella Wheeler Wilcox.　...Be not afraid/To thrust aside half-truths and grasp the whole.　BLPA; FPL

The Progress of a Divine (excerpt).　Richard Savage.　These kill her embryo, and preserve her honour.　OBSV

The Progress of Beauty.　Jonathan Swift.　Send us new nymphs with each new moon.　CABA; ForPo; NCEP

The Progress of Dulness.　John Trumbull.　And wonder what the times will come to!　AnNE

The Progress of Error.　William Cowper.　How much a dunce that has been sent to roam/Excels a dunce that has been kept at home.　OBTV

Progress of Evening.　Walter Savage Landor.　In slow and silent, dim and deepening waves.　OBNC

The Progress of Faust.　Karl Shapiro.　Where, at his back, a dome of atoms rose.　DiPo; MoAB; MP; NYBP

The Progress of Learning: Preface.　Sir John Denham.　To Heaven her branches and to Hell her roots.　OBSP

The Progress of Man.　George Canning.　Starts from his rank, and mars creation's plan.　FaBoNo

The Progress of Marriage.　Jonathan Swift.　But, for a parting present, leave her/A rooted pox to last for ever!　EiCP

The Progress of Photography.　Byron Vazakas.　an illusion the will cannot destroy.　MoPo

The Progress of Poesy.　Matthew Arnold.　And down he lays his weary bones.　EnL; NOBV; PP; VLP

The Progress of Poesy.　Thomas Gray.
　Beneath the good how far–but rise far above the great.　ATP; AWP; CEP; EiCP; EnPE; GTBS; GTBS-P; HBV 1-2; LAuP; NOEC; OAEP; OBEC; OBEV; PP; ViBoPo
　The bloom of young desire, and purple light of love. ATP
　Hyperion's march they spy and glittering shafts of war. ATP
　Or ope the sacred source of sympathetic tears. ATP

The rocks and nodding groves rebellow to the roar. ATP
The terror of his beak, and lightnings of his eye. ATP
They sought, O Albion! next thy sea-encircled coast. ATP
The unconquerable mind, and Freedom's holy flame. ATP
With necks in thunder clothed, and long-resounding pace. ATP

The Progress of Poetry.　Christopher (Christopher St. John Sprigg) Caudwell.　But look at the footprint. There's hair between the toes!'　OxBTC

The Progress of Poetry.　Jonathan Swift.　While from below all Grub Street rings.　CABA; CBEP; EiCP; InvP; NOBI; OnYI

The Progress of Sir Jack Brag.　Anonymous.　But we never will be beat by any mortal foe,/boys!/Tullalo, tullalo, tullalo-o-o-o, boys!　PAH

Progress of Unbelief.　John Henry, Cardinal Newman.　Waits but to burn the stem before her idol's throne.　GoBC

Progress Report.　Charles Simic.　Neither does he, the spellbound one. GeTw

Progression.　Francis Scarfe.　Where love will be almost as simple as it looks.　NeBP

Progression of the Species.　Brian W. Aldiss.　We can manage it for ourselves, thanks/From now on.　FF

The Prohibition.　John Donne.　To let me live, O love and hate me too. EG; EiL; MBW 1-2; MeLP; OBS

Prohibition.　Don (Donald Robert Marquis) Marquis.　denies you the beer/ to cry into.　PoPl

The Project.　Gregory Orr.　But when the flesh was gone,/the light was gone too.　GeTw

A Projection.　Reed Whittemore.　I wish they would make provisions for this,/Those rocket gentlemen.　NePoEA

Proletarian Portrait.　William Carlos Williams.　That has been hurting her OBAL; TAP

Prologue.　W. H. Auden.　The giantess shuffles nearer, cries 'Deceiver'. NoAm

The Prologue.　Anne Bradstreet.　Will make your glistering gold but more to shine.　AP; BoWoP; NOBA; OxBA; SBG; SCAP; TAP

Prologue.　Lazer Eichenrand.　the sorrow of the moments/of His creation. VWA

Prologue.　Archibald MacLeish.　They say there is no end to it.　MoAmPo

Prologue.　Carol Lee Sanchez.　...you come to/Paguate sometimes and visit us...　TWSS

Prologue.　Arthur Symons.　My life is like a music-hall.　BrPo

Prologue.　Edward Taylor　Or as in Jewellary Shops, do jems.　AP

Prologue for a Bestiary.　Ronald Perry.　And the emerald crumbles into dust.　NePoEA-2

Prologue: Moments in a Glade.　Alan Stephens.　...and I have known/That what I will have surely spoken/Abides thus–may be yet thus broken.　QFR

Prologue, Spoken by Mr. Garrick...　Samuel Johnson.　And Truth diffuse her radiance from the stage.　CEP; EBEV; LAuP; NOEC; NoP; OBEC; SeCeV

Prologue to a Saga.　Dorothy Parker.　Gangway, girls: I'll show you trouble. InMe

Prologue to a Translation.　John Trevisa.　And this game rule and leede/ And bring it to a good ende.　OxBM

Prologue to Antonio's Revenge.　John Marston.　Your favour will give crutches to our faults.　LoBV

Prologue to Aureng-Zebe.　John Dryden.　And see us play the Tragedy of Wit.　ATP; CBEP; OBS; OxBoLi; PP; SeCeV

Prologue to General Hamley.　Alfred, Lord Tennyson.　With one gray glimpse of sea.　FaBoPP

Prologue to Hugh Kelly's "A Word to the Wise'.　Samuel Johnson.　And mirth was bounty with a humbler name.　EBEV

Prologue to Love Triumphant.　John Dryden.　An old man may at least good wishes give you.　OxBoLi

Prologue to Mr. Addison's Tragedy of Cato.　Alexander Pope.　As Cato's self had not disdain'd to hear.　CEP

Prologue to the Avowis of Alexander.　John Barbour.　It garris him oft-tymes leif foly,/And all murning of musardy.　OxBS

Prologue to The Tempest.　John Dryden.　Or, if your fancy will be farther led/To find her woman, it must be abed.　EnL

Prologue to the University of Oxford, 1673...　John Dryden.　But 'tis your Suffrage makes Authentique Wit.　OBS; PP

Prologues to What Is Possible.　Wallace Stevens.　The way a look or a touch reveals its unexpected magnitudes.　LCAP; NePoAm

Prolonged Sonnet: When the Troops Were Returning from Milan.　degli Albizzi, Niccolo.　And each as silent as a man being shaved.　AWP; OBVE

Proloug of the Twelfth Buik of the Aenead.　Gavin Douglas.　Forgane thir stannyris schane the beryall strandis.　AtBAP

Promenade.　David Ignatow.　while overhead, ignored in the walk,/are the leaves touching each other and/the sun.　TrJP

Promenades and Interiors.　Francois Coppee.　Mother, blessed among all women may you be!　CAW

La Promessa Sposa.　Walter Savage Landor.　And envy more than they condemn/The rival who avenges them.　NOBV

Prometheus. George Gordon, Lord Byron. And making Death a Victory EnRP; ERoP 1-2; InPS; NOBE; NoP; OAEL 1-2; PAI

Prometheus. Johann Wolfgang von Goethe. All careless of thee too,/As I! AWP

Prometheus. Jenny Mastoraki. you, having discovered fire,/hastily trade your liver. BoWoP

Prometheus. Jonathan Swift. For want of vultures, we have crows. FaBoPV

Prometheus Bound. Aeschylus.
No, not one shift–to rid me of this shame. LiTW
What bitter wrongs I bear! LiTW

Prometheus Unbound. A. D. Hope. Judging that theft of fire from which they died."" OxBC

Prometheus Unbound. Percy Bysshe Shelley.
And I sped to succour thee. ChRP; FiP; LoBV
Ay, many more which we may well divine. WSC
Dizzy, lost, yet unbewailing! FiP; PoEL 1-5
It is the unpastured sea hungering for calm. ChRP
The loftiest star of unascended heaven,/Pinnacled dim in the intense inane. ChRP; FiP
Nurslings of immortality! ViBoPo
So sweet, that joy is almost pain. PBBP; ViBoPo
This is alone Life, Joy, Empire, and Victory. FaBoRV; OAEL 1-2; OAEP; OBRV; SeCeV
...which sinks at length/Prone, and the aerial ice clings over it. PBBP
Which walk upon the sea, and chant melodiously! NOBE; PBBP; ViBoPo

Prometheus, with Wings:. Michael Ondaatje. wooed a host of mermaids after dusk. PeCV

The Promise. Mary B. Fowler. "I'll make you what you want to be." STF

Promise! Mafika Pascal Gwala. OR–who hasn't kept the promise? WhB

The Promise. Johari M. Kunjufu. they will only know me BlSi

Promise. George William ("A.E.") Russell. Thy travel done. BoC

A Promise. Sir Thomas Wyatt. And I content me with my hire. OBSC

The Promise in Disturbance. George Meredith. The rebel discords up the sacred mount. VLP

A Promise Made. Anonymous. Is a debt unpaid. FaFP

The Promise of a Constant Lover. Anonymous. Your faithful friend, and will be to my last. EIL

Promise of Peace. Robinson Jeffers. How shall the dead taste the deep treasure they have? AP; CoBMV; LiTA; LiTM; MoAB; MoAmPo; NePA

Promise Your Hand. Henry Rago. Marvelously catching my flight; containing me. NMP

The Promised Land. Anonymous. I am bound for the promised land. AmFP; TrAS

Promised Land. Mary Engel. How old is the ghetto? Ask the question, nobody knows. AMV-80

The Promised Land. Jessie E. Sampter. But we must hear God's trumpet clear/Sound peace upon His Hill. TrJP

Promises. Ruth Forbes Sherry. Time is mountain's promise and sea's contract. GoYe

Promises Like Pie-Crust. Christina Georgina Rossetti. Many thrive on frugal fare/Who would perish of excess. NOBV

Promises of Freedom. Anonymous. May de Devil preach 'is funer'l song. BPo

Promises, VIII. Founding Fathers.... Robert Penn Warren. For we are their children in the light of humanness, and under the/shadow of God's closing hand. NoAm

The Promissory Note (parody). Bayard Taylor. Where the tempest whispers, "Pay him!" and I answer,/"Nevermore!" BXAP; HBV 1-2; Par; SpRo

The Promontory Moment. May Swenson. ...and the sea robin's arc/now stilled on the rock. NYBP

Promontory Moon. Galway Kinnell. Dissolves at her touch and is weaved anew. MOON

Pronouns. Karle Wilson Baker. Like a shamed schoolboy then I mumbled low,/"We,/Lord." TreFT

The Pronunciation of Erse. A. D. Hope. No fuchulain! PV

The Proof. W. H. Auden. Out into sunlight. OAEL 1-2

Proof. Bessie Calhoun Bird. The intransmutable verity. BlSi

Proof. Ethel Romig Fuller. Why should mortals wonder if God hears prayer? TRV

Proof. Brendan Kennelly. Proof is what I do not need. CIP

Proof. Leslie Ullman. I will eat oranges until my skin is flawless. FAZ

The Proof. Richard Wilbur. Crossed out delete and wrote his patient stet. EaLo; OBSP

Proof Positive. Deems Taylor. And you will learn, my skeptic friend,/The truthfulness of what I've said. UnTE

Proofs of Buddha's Existence. Anonymous. "Here surely lived a Buddha, Lord of Righteousness!" WGRP

Proper Clay. Mark Van Doren. And whence the music no one made? PoRA; TrGrPo

Proper Pride. D. H. Lawrence. they are humble, with a creeping humility, being parasites/or carrion creatures. FaBoEE

A Proper Sonnet, How Time Consumeth All Earthly Things. Thomas Proctor. For all is thine, be it good or bad that grows. FaBoRV; OBSC

Propertian. L. A. MacKay. Nor Elbruz cool his veins with all its snow. PeCV

The Properties of the Shires of England. Anonymous. That Lord that for us all did die/Save all these shires. Amen say I. FaBoPP; GBP

Properzia Rossi. Felicia Dorothea Hemans. Say proudly yet–"'Twas hers who loved me well!" SBG

A Prophecy. Allen Ginsberg. where rockets rise/to take me home TAP

A Prophecy. Arthur Lee. If but the rights of subjects they receive,/'Tis all they ask–or all a crown can give. PAH

A Prophecy. Christopher Levenson. To enter the ruined monastery of sleep. ErPo

Prophecy. Luigi Pulci. But see, the sun speeds on his western path/To glad the nations with expected light. PAH

Prophecy. Jules Supervielle. And say, "Why, it's a goldfinch." AMV-81

A Prophecy. Maurice Thompson. Rally and cheer in freedom's holy name! AA

Prophecy. Gulian Verplanck. And what thou art, America shall be. MC; PAH

Prophecy. Elinor Wylie. To set his mouth against a crack/And blow the candle out. AnAmPo; BLPL; BoWoP; FaBoWP; PrIm; VGW

Prophecy in Flame. Frances Minturn Howard. At that same small, fierce-flickering fire. AmFN

The Prophecy of Dante. George Gordon, Lord Byron. So be it: we can bear. ERoP 1-2

The Prophecy of Famine. Charles Churchill.
Sickly crept on, and, with complainings rude,/On nature seemed to call, and bleat for food. OBSV
They've sense to get, what we want sense to keep. OBSV
Which bends to fashion, and obeys the rules,/Imposed at first, and since observed by fools. NOEC

The Prophecy of Samuel Sewall. John Greenleaf Whittier. And the Lord of the Harvest deign to own/The precious seed by the fathers sown! MAmP

Prophecy on Lethe. Stanley Jasspon Kunitz. Your jelly-mouth and, crushed, your polyp eyes. PoA

The Prophecy Sublime. Frederick Lucian Hosmer. The commonwealth of man,/The City of our God! TrPWD

The Prophet. Abraham Cowley. Hereafter fame, here martyrdom. JCP; TrGrPo

The Prophet. Kahlil Gibran.
And if you sing though as angels, and love not the singing,/you muffle man's ears to the voices... PoToHe
And verily he will find the roots of the good and the/bad, the fruitful and the fruitless,... PoToHe
And when the earth shall claim your limbs, then shall you truly dance. DL
For life goes not backward nor tarries with yesterday... PoPl; PoToHe
...a prayer for the beloved/in your heart and a song of praise upon your lips. PoLf
Therefore give now, that the season of giving may be yours and not/your inheritors'. PoPl

The Prophet. Alexander Pushkin. And burn men's hearts with this, my Word. AWP; EaLo; LiTW; WGRP

The Prophet. Yehoash. "Beware, you are dead sheaves,/I am a flaming fire." TrJP

Prophet and Fool. Louis Golding. And there I hear the flutes of peace,/Being a prophet and a fool. HBMV

The Prophet Jeremiah and the Personification of Israel. Eleazar Ben Kalir. And pity Zion; for the time is/come. TrJP

The Prophet Lost in the Hills at Evening. Hilaire Belloc. ...Stand about my wraith,/And harbour me–almighty God. OxBoCh

The Prophet's Warning; or, Shoot to Kill. Ebon. bringing bullet holes/and death/and apple pie! PoBA

The Prophets. Richard Shelton. letting them go NYBP

Prophets for a New Day. Margaret Walker. And he drives us out of the city/To be stabbed on a lonely hill. BPo

Prophets Who Cannot Sing. Coventry Patmore. Far better be dumb dogs. CoBE

The Prophylactic. Russell Edson. ...and I curse my ancestors for being chickens/rather than horses. GP

Propinquity Needed. Charles Battell Loomis. For love to get well started, really needs propinquity/(Hence my title). InMe

Propitious Days for Weddings. Anonymous. Saturday no luck at all. FaBoUs

Proportion. Amy Lowell. Fluttering about a white azalea bush. BoWoP

Proportions. Joseph Stroud. ...and walk on through a world/Renewed and fresh as far as the mind/Can create. NPGG

Proposal. Anonymous. "Go ask Papa." GoTF; TreFS

Proposal. Robert Sward. ...My consent/Is immediate. Ladies and gentlemen, my wife. ELU

Psalm of Those Who Go Forth before Daylight.   Carl Sandburg.   ...they are brothers of cinders.   AnAmPo; MoShBr; OxBA

Psalm–People Power at the Die-In.   Denise Levertov.   great energy flowed from solitude,/and great power from communion.   FAZ

A Psalm Praising the Hair of Man's Body.   Denise Levertov.   ...as river-/grass on the woven current/indicates ripple./praise.   CAPP

Psalm to My Beloved.   Eunice Tietjens.   And like a tide you have flowed into me.   ErPo

Psalm to the Holy Spirit.   A. M. Sullivan.   "What shall a creature pay Thee in love for the moment of under-/standing?"   TrPWD

A Psalm to the Son.   Marguerite Wilkinson.   Oh, wash my eyes with tears that they may know the light of Thy/love!   TrPWD

Psalme CXXXVII.   George Sandys.   And without pity heare their dying grones.   OBS

Psalmodist.   Leib.   ...to knit/The heart to God, to unbind the sorrow on silent lips.   VWA

Psalms, CXLVII.   Christopher Smart.   Till Jesus make them comprehend/His ways, his truth and light.   NOCV

Psalms of Love.   Peter Baum.   Be thou mine!   AWP

The Psalter of Avram Haktani.   Abraham Moses Klein.
      And the good Lord said nothing, but with a nod/Summoned the angels of Sodom down to earth.   PeCV
      ...yet I/Still cannot fathom how they danced,/Or why.   PeCV

Psalter of the Blessed Virgin Mary.   Saint Bonaventure.   and he will never thirst.   ISi

Pshytik.   Nahum Bomze.   Beyond blue walls/black death is waiting.   VWA

PSI.   Melvin B. Tolson.   ...disappeared in the abyss/(Vanitas vanitatum!)/of white Charybdis.   PoBA

Psittachus Eois Imitatrix Ales Ab Indis.   Sacheverell Sitwell.   Through crystal prisms in a falling rain.   AtBAP; MoBrPo

Pslam XXIV.   Sir Philip Sidney.   Who is this glorious King? The Lord of armies guiding,/Even He the King of glory hight.   FCP

Psyche.   Samuel Taylor Coleridge.   And to deform and kill the things whereon we feed.   ERoP 1-2

Psyche.   Jones Very.   It soared on golden pinions free!   AP

Psyche to Cupid: Her Ditty.   James Richard Broughton.   sing loud the disgraces of exuberant love.   ErPo

Psyche with the Candle.   Archibald MacLeish.   There is no answer other to this mystery.   MoLP; PCP

Psychedelic Firemen.   David Henderson.   of cities insane/   NBP

Psychoanalysis.   Gavin Ewart.   the biggest fish are still outside the nets.   NYBP

Psychological Prediction.   Virginia Brasier.   Puts on rubber gloves when stealing a cookie.   BBGG

Psychology Today.   Judson Jerome.   ...who would expect such/throbbing/from one gland left on earth—my leaden heart?   AMV-81

Psycholophon.   Gelett Burgess.   Sounds make the song, not sense,/Thus I inhibit!   CenHV; NA

Psychometrist.   James Stephens.   Stones shall sing in ecstasy!   NoAm

The Psychonaut Sonnets: Jones.   Albert Goldbarth.   ...Each rung/on the drainrack trumpets swansong, swansong.   SM

Pub.   Julian Symons.   The days are beginning to fall.   LiTB; WaP

Puberty.   Jon Wallace.   water and seed.   AMV-80

Puberty Rite Dance Song.   *Anonymous.*   Through her holy truth/she goes about.   BoWoP

Public Aid for Niagara Falls.   Morris Bishop.   And I watched the tourist stand/Spitting in Niagara Falls.   InMe; NLV

Public Beach (Long Island Sound).   Christopher Morley.   Lo, a new people rises from the sea.   NLV

The Public Garden.   Robert Lowell.   ...Nothing catches fire.   AP; NoP

Public Holiday: Paris.   Joyce Horner.   Before the man with the blown balloons goes home.   GoYe

Public Journal.   Phyllis McGinley.   And the American royalties, and an inherited income,/To keep the wolf at bay.   NLV

Public Library.   Dannie Abse.   Read by whose hostile eyes, in what bed-sitting rooms,/in which rainy, dejected railway stations?   OxBC

Public Library.   Candace Thurber Stevenson.   Eyes advance, waver as they feed/upon the rich succulence/of words.   GoYe

A Public Nuisance.   Reginald Arkell.   But still he stands/Addressing his ball.   LiSp; SD

Public School 168.   Stewart Brisby.   before we met the man who ate glass/& asked about our dreams.   LFAC

Publication Is the Auction.   Emily Dickinson.   But reduce no Human Spirit/To Disgrace of Price–.   AmePo; NoP

Published Correspondence: Epistle to the Rapalloan.   Archibald MacLeish.   There's a word for my praise–if there's a rhyme for/cantos!   PoA

Publisher's Party.   Phyllis McGinley.   Away in haste I slither,/Feeling I need a breather.   OBAL

Publishing 2001.   Bob Rosenthal.   the single chord the wild bar.   APU

Puck Goes to Court.   Fenton Johnson.   (Alas! Where is there sport?)   CDC; GoSl

Puck's Song.   Rudyard Kipling.   But Merlin's Isle of Gramarye/Where you and I will fare!   FaBoCh; FaBV; LoGBV; OxBChV; PoPle

The Puddle.   Eden Phillpotts.   And mark and mirror and contain/The gold and purple, rose and red.   HBMV

The Puddy and the Mouse.   *Anonymous*   Squeak! quo she, I'm weel awa.   GBP

Pudgy.   Frank Lima.   my feet gag my heart/they're cold.   ANYP

The Pueblo Women I Watched Get down in Brooklyn.   Wendy Rose.   they will be cut/or silenced or raped.   TWSS

Puella Parvula.   Wallace Stevens.   ...Hear what he says,/The dauntless master, as he starts the human tale.   HaCAP; LCAP

Puer Aeternus.   Kathleen Raine.   Where all return/spent torch and pilgrim shroud.   NYBP

Puer Ex Jersey.   *Anonymous.*   Est bene for him/Relinqui id alone.   NA

De Puero Balbutiente.   Thomas Bastard.   And when it slideth forth, it goes as nice/As when a man doth walk upon the ice.   OBSP

Puerperium.   Edmund Waller.   Our present joy and our hopes increase.   JCP

Puerto Ricans in New York.   Charles Reznikoff.
      "Ah, tragic, tragic, tragic!"   CTBA
      and he a larger package:/a brand-new windowshade.   CTBA

Puerto Rico Song.   William Carlos Williams.   the evening–/zippe, zappe!–/it goes.   NYBP

Puk-Wudjies.   Patrick Reginald Chalmers.   You'll know the Puk-Wudjies are somewhere around!   HBVY

The Pulkovo Meridian: Leningrad: 1943.   Vera Inber.   It's not the first one in the family.   WaaP

Pull My Daisy.   Jack Kerouac.   let my gap be shut   PoM

The Pulley.   George Herbert.   If goodness lead him not, yet weariness/May toss him to My breast.   AtBAP; ATP; AWP; DiPo; EaLo; EBCP; ExPo; HAP; HBV 1-2; HeIP; InPK; InPo; InPS; LiTB; MePo; NOBE; NOCV; NoP; OAEL 1-2; OAEP; OBEV; OBS; OxBoCh; PAI; PPP; PrIm; SeCeV; SeCP; SeCV 1-2; TEP; TreFT; TrGrPo; ViBoPo; WHA

Pulling Out.   Lyn Lifshin.   nobody can touch them   NeAC

Pulling Weeds.   Eric Chock.   like the white man you hate/in your dreams.   BrSi

A Pulpit to Be Let.   *Anonymous.*   ...for in vain she cares/For wand'ring planets that has fixed stars./Praelucendo pereo.   APAS

The Pulse.   Mark Van Doren.   And neither is young/And neither is old.   MoAmPo; PoPl

The Pulverized Screen.   Edmond Jabes.   a pulverized screen/of patience   VWA

Pumas.   George Sterling.   Man, who is made more terrible far than they,/Dreams he is otherwise!   BPAW

The Pumpkin.   Robert Graves.   Why, there was that pumpkin entire on his stalk!   WSC

Pumpkin.   Robert Morgan.   like planets submerged and rising.   GeTw

The Pumpkin.   John Greenleaf Whittier.
      Golden-tinted and fair, as thy own Pumpkin pie!   OHIP
      In a pumpkin-shell coach, with two rats for her team!   PoSC

Pumpkins.   John Cotton.   Half expecting/To find the garden/Cratered like a moon.   BoNaP

Puna's Fragrant Glades.   Queen Lydia Lili, u-o-ka-lani.   I come quietly to find/A flower to place upon my heart.   WTO

Punch and Judy.   *Anonymous.*   Says Judy to Punch,/My eye is too sore.   OxNR

Punch, Brothers, Punch!   *Anonymous.*   All in the presence of the passinjare.   CBEP

Punchinello.   Hugh de Burgh.   Except that I am a fool.   CAW

The Punching Clock.   Milos Macourek.   to have one's whole life punched by seconds/up to the very end...   LiTW

Punctilio.   Mary Elizabeth Coleridge.   So dull habit shall not be/Wrongly call'd Fidelity.   OBEV; OBVV

Punishment.   Seamus Heaney.   yet understand the exact/and tribal, intimate revenge.   FaBoPV; NoP

Punishment for a Wayward Train.   Antonio Jacinto.   te-quem-tem te-quem-tem te-quem-tem.   WhB

Punk Pantoum.   Pamela Stewart.   Tonight, dragging the white-hot razor across our throats,/and back...   SM

Punk Party. ey Told Me It Was Literary...]   Wendy Rose.   Like any party/they photograph each other but forget/to develop the film.   TWSS

Punkin Pie.   Harry Edward Mills.   Must be a bird at bakin' when it comes to punkin pie.   PeD

Punkydoodle and Jollapin.   Laura E. Richards.   He takes it with brandy, and thinks it no sin./Oh, Punkydoodle and Jollapin!   OBCA

Punto Final.   Shirley Hill Witt.   But I can't: she is me.   TWSS

The Puppet Play.   Padraic Colum.   And he beams on them all, the Old Showman.   RoGo

The Puppet Player.   Angelina Weld Grimke.   Twitching the strings with slow sardonic grin.   CDC

Puppy.   Aileen Fisher.   an ice-cream cone.   SoPo

Puppy. Fred Lape. His heaven would be a place where all day long/he'd lay his head upon somebody's knees. BoAnP; GDP

Puppy and I. A.(lan) A.(lexander) Milne. "I'll come with you, Puppy," said I. OnUR; SoPo; TiPo

Purchase of a Blue, Green, or Orange Ode. Josephine Miles. Sugared, colored, out of a jar, an ode. NoP

Pure Death. Robert Graves. As greeted our love's first accomplishment. AWP; CoBMV; GTBS-P; InPo; MoAB; MoPo

Pure is the Dewy Gem. Jeremiah Joseph Callanan. But O!–what ray ere shone from Heaven/Like God's first smile on a soul forgiven. IrPN

Pure Nails Brightly Flashing. Stephane Mallarme. The frame defines oblivion: against night/a septet of reflections holds the scene. LiTW

Pure Notations. Steve Levine. Something like life's pure notations, being taken. APU

Pure Platonicke. George Daniel. This is pure Platonicke Love. CavP

Pure Products. Denise Levertov. but to live a little, invoking/the old powers. NMP

Pure Simple Love. Aurelian Townsend. Intreat her to excuse mee toe. AnAnS 2; SeCP

Purer in Heart. Anonymous. Purer in heart, help me to be. STF

Purer Than Purest Pure. Edward Estlin Cummings. and every world before silence begins a star. Amen. AH

Purgatorio. Hart Crane. As one whose altitude at one time, was not so. NAMP

Purgatory. William Butler Yeats. Appease/The misery of the living and the remorse of the dead. CMoP

The Purification. Saint Cosmas. "This Bairn is Lord of life and death." ISi

Purification of the Blessed Virgin. Joseph Beaumont. By His own death can make His Mother live. ISi

The Purist. Ogden Nash. "You mean," he said, "a crocodile." DBV; FiBHP; GoJo; InPS; MoAmPo; MoShBr; NLV; OBCA; PV; ShM; TreFT

The Puritan. Karl Shapiro. Fixed like a gargoyle on a cathedral wall. MoAmPo

The Puritan Hacking away at Oak. Todd Gitlin. God hangs tapestries in a worked-out mine, way back in the woods. AMV-80

A Puritan Lady. Lizette Woodworth Reese. Or sleet sharp at a pane? AnAnS; MoAmPo

The Puritan on His Honeymoon. Robert Bly. The monkeys gibbering by our bridal bed. FF; NePoEA

The Puritan's Ballad. Elinor Wylie. Treading as soft as a tiger cat,/To tell me terrible lies? HBMV; LiTL; NMM; PoRA

Purity. Hayim Lenski. Bless us, O burning bush,/With your light, your truth, your peace. VWA

Purity of Heart. John Keble. And for His service and his throne/Selects the pure in heart. BLRP

The Purple Blemish. Par Lagerkvist. the purple plumage of your respendence. AMV-81

The Purple Cow. Gelett Burgess. I'd rather SEE than BE one! AmePo; FaBoCo; FaBoNo; FaFP; FiBHP; FPL; GoTF; GrPl; HBV 1-2; HBVY; LBN; NA; NePA; NLV; NTCP; OBAL; OBCA; PoLf; PoPl; SoPo; TiPo; TreFS; YaD

Purple Dry Buds. Michelle Roberts. the dry/wet buds/and the cut. LFAC

The Purple Island. Phineas Fletcher.
A shepherd's bliss nor stands nor falls to ev'ry tongue. ViBoPo
This tower then only falls when treason undermines. JCP

The Purple, White and Green. L. E. Morgan-Browne. March and fight for our one common right,/CITIZENS TO BE! BrRo

Purpose. John James Piatt. His prow is always there! AA

The Purpose of Altar Boys. Alberto Rios. I would look/with authority down/the tops of white dresses. MAYP

The Purpose of Fable-Writing. Phaedrus. 'Tis but a play to form the youth/By fiction, in the cause of truth. AWP

The Purpose of the Chesapeake & Ohio Canal. Dave Smith. air thickening in still streets and between brown walls. GeTw

The Purse–Seine. Paul Blackburn. I love you and you love me... CoPo

The Purse-Seine. Robinson Jeffers. ...:surely one always knew that cultures/decay, and life's end is death. CMoP; HAP; NoAm; NOBA; NoP; OxBA; PrIm; WeW

Pursuit. Vern Rutsala. He catches them/And makes them pay FAZ

Pursuit. Julian Tuwim. Yea, Mother of Living,/Thou dost not permit!... TrJP

Pursuit. Robert Penn Warren. And rattles her crutch, which may put forth a small bloom, perhaps/white. CrMA; HAP; LiTA; MoPo; MP; NePA; PPP; TwCP

Pursuit from Under. James Dickey. Pitch a tent in the pasture, and starve. HAP; PPP

Pursuit of an Ideal. Patrick Kavanagh. ...Now I woo/The footprints that you make across November. FaBoIP

The Pursuite. Henry Vaughan. Ah! Lord! and what a Purchase will that be/To take us sick, that sound would not take thee? SeCP

Pushcart Row. Rachel Feild. On the cobblestones of Pushcart Row. BrR; SoPo

Pushed to the Scroll. Winifred Hamrick Farrar. pushed to the ultimate end/to leave the naked soul. AMV-80

The Puss and the Boots (parody) (excerpt). Henry Duff Traill. A stout heart, feline cunning, and–who knows? BXAP; Par

Puss in the Pantry. Anonymous. See how she tosses/the mutton, mutton bone. OxNR

Puss up the Plum Tree. Anonymous. Diddlety, diddlety, dumpty. OxNR

Pussy. Anonymous. For pussy don't like to be worried and teased. OxBChV

Pussy Cat. Anonymous. Why did you eat the dumplings? OxNR

Pussy Cat Mole. Anonymous. Until her best petticoat's mended/with silk. OxNR

Pussy-Cat, Pussy-Cat, Where Have You Been? Mother Goose. I frightened a little mouse under the chair. FaBoBe; FaFP; HBV 1-2; HBVY; SoPo; TiPo

Pussy Has a Whiskered Face. Christina Georgina Rossetti. Doggie scampers when I call,/And has a heart to love us all. TiPo

Pussycat Sits on a Chair. Edward Newman Horn. And test their bruised omnipotence/Against the cat's austere defense. ELU

Put Down. Leon Damas. ...a butcher with hands frightfully red/with the blood of their civilization. TTY

The Put-Down Come On. Archie Randolph Ammons. ...but turning the permanent also/into the transient takes up all the time that's left. NoP

Put Forth, O God, Thy Spirit's Might. Howard Chandler Robbins. To serve thee is to reign. AH; TrPWD

Put Forth Thy Leaf, Thou Lofty Plane. Arthur Hugh Clough. Be still, refrain thyself, and wait. EBEV

Put It Through. Edward Everett Hale. Put it through! MC; PAH

Put My Name Down. Irwin Silber. So I'm gonna put my name down. FSW

Put Off Thy Bark from Shore, Though Near the Night. Frederick Goddard Tuckerman. Between the sailing cloud and the seasick sea. MOS

Put Your Finger in Foxy's Hole. Anonymous. Foxy's at the back door,/Picking a marrow bone. OxNR

Put Your Word to My Lips. Rachel Korn. to the border outlined by tears,/frontier at the country of night. VWA

Putney Hymn. Anonymous. Tossed to and fro his passions fly/From vanity to vanity. TrAS

Putting in the Seed. Robert Frost. Shouldering its way and shedding the earth crumbs. ErPo; NoAm; OxBA

Putting on My Shoes I Hear the Floor Cry out beneath Me (parody). Michael Heffernan. Slowly they settled/To the ocean floor/To be found in stone years after. BXAP

Putting on Nightgown. Anonymous. Up he comes, up he comes,/Out at the top. OxNR

Putting on the Style. Anonymous. And as I look around me, I'm very apt to smile,/Because so many people putting on the style. FSW

Putting to Sea. Louise Bogan. And learn with joy, the gulf, the vast, the deep. LiTM; PoA

Puzzled. Langston Hughes. What we're gonna do/In the face of/What we remember. UnPo

Puzzled. Carolyn Wells. And now he's sorely puzzled that no child has ever read it. OBCA

The Puzzled Census Taker. John Godfrey Saxe. "Ich kann nicht Englisch!" civilly said/The lady from over the Rhine. HBV 1-2

The Puzzled Game Birds. Thomas Hardy. They are not those who used to feed us/When we were young–they cannot be! PBBP

A Puzzling Example. Virginia Sarah Benjamin. Till she's as old as brother Jack,/Who now is twice as old as she. BiCB

Pygmalion. Hans Brockerhoff. ...The gods can blow/Life into marble, but not into wood. AMV-80

Pygmalion. Hilda ("H. D.") Doolittle. And my work is for naught? WGRP

Pygmalion. Albert G. Miller. In the parlor after midnight making sheep's-eyes at a/statue. InMe

Pygmalion to Galatea. Robert Graves. Give me an equal kiss, as I kiss you. PG

The Pylons. Stephen Spender. Where often clouds shall lean their swan-white neck. AWP; EnLi 1-2; NoAm

Pyms Anarchy. Thomas Jordan. All things were thus when Pym was King. OBS

Pyramis or The House of Ascent. A. D. Hope. The builders of the pyramid everywhere! PoAu 1-2

Pyramus and Thisbe. Laurence Dakin. The hand that marks the face of time is still,/And all the ages sleep. CaP

Pyramus and Thisbe. Ovid (Publius Ovidius Naso). ...and that which after fire/Remained, rested in one tomb as Thisbe did desire.' LiTW

Pyramus and Thisbe. John Godfrey Saxe. ...accidents often befall/From kissing young fellows through holes in the wall. HBV 1-2; OnMSP

Q

Quebec Liquor Commission Store. Abraham Moses Klein. even for kings, the rag-poor past, the purple that may set.' ACV; OBCV

Queen. Dom Moraes. The fallen rain glitters like stars/In the dark river of her hair. NePoEA-2

The Queen. Pablo Neruda. Only you and I,/only you and I, my love,/ listen to it. OLR

The Queen. Kenneth Pitchford. I on my last descent into the dark. NYBP; NYP

Queen and Slave. Mortimer Collins. And live the life whose love is free/ And never swerve! OBVV

Queen-Ann's-Lace. William Carlos Williams. a pious wish to whiteness gone over/or nothing. AmPP; AP; BLPL; MoAB; MoAmPo; NoAm; NOBA; NoP; PrIm; TAP

Queen Anne. Anonymous.
As fair as a lily, as brown as a bun. ChTr
While we young maidens walk out and in. OxNR

Queen Anne's Lace. June Jordan. Repeatedly/you do revive/arouse alive/a suffering. TAP

Queen Anne's Lace. Mary Leslie Newton. But left her lace to whiten on/ Each weed-entangled way! BrR; MoShBr

Queen Anne's Musicians. Thomas Hennell. Fate's left instead of luck: what's candle lit in sun for? FaBoTw

Queen Cleopatra. Conrad Aiken. Of this and that, and Antony,/And the laugh that will not die. HBMV

Queen Eleanor's Confession (A version). Anonymous. And said, Earl Martial, but for my/oath,/Then hanged shouldst thou be. BaBo; ESPB; OBET; PrIm

Queen Eleanor's Confession (B version). Anonymous. Gin I had na sworn by the croun an the/septer roun,/Eearl Marchell sud ben gared dee.' ESPB

Queen Elizabeth. Anonymous. A face more like/A soup-tureen. DBV

Queen Guennivar's Round. Robert Stephen Hawker. But old Cornwall's bounding daughters/For gray Dundagel's tide. CoBE

Queen Jane. Anonymous. His mother's poor body lay mouldering away. FSW

Queen Mab. Thomas Hood. But good ones love the dark, and find/The night as pleasant as the day. HBV 1-2; HBVY

Queen Mab. Ben Jonson. Some of husbands, some of lovers,/Which an empty dream discovers. HBV 1-2

Queen Mab. Percy Bysshe Shelley.
Some shone like stars, and, as the chariot passed,/Bedimmed all other light. GN
...where/Honour sits smiling at the sale of truth. FF; PPON

Queen Mother to New Queen. Robert Graves. "His Majesty's turned parsimonious/And keeps no whore now but his Consort." OBSV

Queen of Cheese. James McIntyre. About to fall and crush them soon. FiBHP; PeD

The Queen of Courtesy. Anonymous.
For she is Queen of Courtesy. ISi
So fare we all with love and list/To King and Queen by Courtesy. ACP

The Queen of Crete. John Grimes. And the sea forgets and goes to sleep. HBMV

The Queen of Elfan's Nourice. Anonymous. Yon's the road the wicked gae,/An that's the road to hell.' ESPB

The Queen of Elfland's Nourrice. Anonymous. Or his mither take him frae cauld!' FaBoCh

The Queen of Fairies. Anonymous. The glow-worm lights us home to bed. ViBoPo

The Queen of Hearts. Anonymous. I'll forsake them all and follow thee. FSW; OBET

The Queen of Hearts. Mother Goose. And vowed he'd steal no more! FaBoBe; HBVY

Queen of Heaven. Anonymous. Help me to my lives ende,/And make me with thyn Sone y-saught... OxBM

Queen of Heaven Mausoleum. Dennis Schmitz. ...will I cry/to be buried or gratefully begin/to nurse at the world I thirsted for? LCAP

Queen of Horizons. Joseph Dever. And waft me Mary-high again. ISi

The Queen of Lydia. C. H. Sisson. So you see how barbarians are. OxBC

The Queen of Paphos, Erycine. Anonymous. Before my life, my love shall end. ElL; GBL

The Queen of Scotland. Anonymous. She was it pleasd, when she'd a son,/ To hae a pap again. ESPB

The Queen of Seasons. John Henry, Cardinal Newman. But because it comes first,/and is pledge of the rest. GoBC

The Queen of the Angels. Giovanni Boccaccio. Thy Son prepares His flock in recompense. CAW

The Queen of the Nile. William Jay Smith. To the Queen of the Nile/By the green palm tree. GrPl

Queen of the World. Anonymous. Then crown her Queen of the World! PGD

The Queen's Afterdinner Speech (excerpt). Percy French. "In the Irish Times,' sez she.... OxBI

The Queen's Last Ride. Ella Wheeler Wilcox. The Queen in silence is driving by. BLPA

The Queen's Marie. Anonymous. The lands I was to travel in/Or the death I was to die! OBEV; PoPle

The Queen's Men. Rudyard Kipling. Even Belphoebe's, whom they gave their lives for! AtBAP

The Queen's Song. James Elroy Flecker. Content should Time confess/ How sweet you were. BrPo; HBV 1-2

The Queen's Speech. Arthur Mainwaring. So may God direct you in your wise consultations,/To ruin these happy and flourishing nations. APAS

Queen Sabbath. Hayim Nahman Bialik. Depart you in peace, you angels of/peace! TrJP

Queen Victoria. Anonymous. Ladies, help me for to sing,/Victoria, Queen of England. CoMu

Queen Victoria and Me. Leonard Cohen. confusing the star-dazed tourists/ with our incomparable sense of loss NoAm

A Queen Wasp. Walter De La Mare. Back to my self am gone. AtBAP

The Queens. Robert Fitzgerald. Each one has ermine or satin robes, and bears above/A wand and crown. NYBP

Queens. John Millington Synge. ...so you're the Queen/Of all are living, or have been. GBL; MoBrPo; OBMV; OnYI

The Queer. Henry Vaughan. Which makes the high transcendent bliss/Of knowing thee, so rarely known. PoEL 1-5

A Queer Thing. Nancy Keesing. "But I am here.' "You are not,' your mother said. NOAV

Queer Things. Emanuel Carnevali. begging all the world/to enter in it. EAS

Queer Things. James Reeves. Why should he do me any harm?" WSC

Quen Alysandyr Our King Was Dede. Anonymous. That stad is in perplexite. AtBAP

Query. Ebon. moved to the tune/of a different/even Blacker band... PoBA

Query. Mildred Weston. The Blush/Of shame? PoL

The Quest. Ellen Mackay Hutchinson Cortissoz. I look for you with smiles, with tears,/But look for you in vain! HBV 1-2

The Quest. Gladys Cromwell. How I look for your melodies! HBMV

Quest. Naomi Long Madgett. And the golden April rains/Are my tears. BPo

The Quest. Clinton Scollard. Such a golden store of honey! BrR

The Quest. Eliza Scudder. And I must rest at last, in Thee, my home. TrPWD

The Quest. Harold Vinal. Not knowing what we seek--if it be earth/Or love or death or, beyond chaos, heaven. GoYe

The Quest. James Wright. Though bare as rifted paradise. NYBP

The Quest Eternal (excerpt). Brajendranath Seal. The Kingdom come, the Sovereign State of Man! ACV

The Quest of Silence: Fire in the Heavens, and Fire Along the Hills. Christopher John Brennan. in the cicada's torture-point of song. CBAP; PoAu 1-2

The Quest of the Orchis. Robert Lee Frost. Said that the fall might come and whirl of leaves,/For summer was done. AmePo

The Quest of the Sangraal: The Coming of the Sangraal. Robert Stephen Hawker. And, like a drunken giant, sobb'd in sleep! VLP

Questing. Anne Spencer. Leaf from her brow, light from her torched hand. CDC

A Question. Anonymous.
If I really, really love Him,/Can I be afraid? BLRP
Tell me, if it followed you,/Would the world be better? WBLP
Unknown to me; sure Nature's deck/Was ravished from her snowy neck. CBEP

The Question. W. H. Auden. from where did Christ get/that extra chromosome? SUW

The Question. James Beattie. But say, is yours without compare? FaBoCo

A Question. William Cole. The seals/Have the best deals? BoAnP

Question. Norma Craig. On the bottom shelf/In the shoe shop? PoL

The Question. Robert Duncan. to show wherein the spirit had food? NeAP

The Question. Norman Gale. How will you lift that bankrupt head/When all the butterfly beauty's dead? ELU; FiBHP

The Question. Wilfred Wilson Gibson. ...I'll never know/Till Doomsday if the old cow died or not. MMM

The Question. Karla Kuskin. Or maybe I will stay a child. NTCP

A Question. Edna Livingston. And turn to him and be of womankind? GoYe

The Question. Frank Templeton Prince. The thing we know of but we do not know. BoLoP; ChMP; GTBS-P; PeSA

The Question. Muriel Rukeyser. I come with my word alive. IHMS; WPOW

The Question. Percy Bysshe Shelley. That I might there present it:--O, to whom? CH; EnRP; FiP; HBV 1-2; MyFE; OBEV; OBRV; PoPle

Question. May Swenson. With cloud for shift/how will I hide? HeIP; LiTM; NePoEA; PrIm; SM; VGW

A Question. John Millington Synge. That board–you'd rave and rend them with your teeth. MoBrPo; NOBI; OBVV

The Question. Rachel Annand Taylor. Lo! Every soul is Calvary,/And every sin a Rood. HBV 1-2

The Question. Frederick Goddard Tuckerman. With a clover in her hand. AP

Question and Answer. Samuel Hoffenstein. Decent behavior/From a popular savior. DBV; FiBHP; PV

Question and Answer. Langston Hughes. Why take it?/To remake it. BPo

Question and Answer. Kathleen Raine. And with the sun rises perpetual day. MoBrPo

The Question Answer'd. William Blake. The lineaments of Gratified Desire. ELU; ErPo; FaBoEE; GBL; NoP; OBSP; ViBoPo

Question in a Field. Louise Bogan. Or the horrible beautiful kind? NYBP; SBG

The Question, Is It? Alfred Goldsworthy Bailey. to admire the skill of the trailing arbutus/in decanting its fragrance. AMV-81

The Question Is Proof. Elizabeth Bartlett. You have the reply NePoAm-2

Question Not. Adam Lindsay Gordon. Courage in our own. PoToHe

A Question of Form and Content. Jon Stallworthy. They shall be guests at the secret/wedding of form and content. OxBC

Question Time. Jack Lindsay. "Who started the Great War?'/I did, I did, I did. NOAV

Question to Life. Patrick Kavanagh. So be reposed and praise, praise praise/The way it happened and the way it is. MoBrPo

The Question to Lisetta. Matthew Prior. Simplest of swains! the world may see/Whom Chloe loves, and who loves me. OBEV

The Question Whither. George Meredith. And Whither vainer sounds than Whence,/For word with such wayfarers. HBV 1-2; WGRP

Questioning Faces. Robert Frost. to glassed-in children at the window sill. ELU; GrPl; NCSH

The Questionings. Frederic Henry Hedge. Losing still, that I may find/This bounded self in boundless Mind. HBV 1-2

Questions ⅛. Donald Hall.
...Her/changeableness. My unchangingness. FF
Why is she angry? FF

Questions. Dagmar Hilarova. Nothing of this world belongs to me/any more VWA

The Questions. Robert Pinsky. In the office is Mrs. Apostolacos; the bus driver is Ray. NPGG

Questions and Answers. Doris Muhringer. That's the world. AMV-80

Questions and Answers. Diana O Hehir. ...the lover/With a valley full of wheat. NPGG

Questions for the Candidate. John Holmes. ...Would he/Die if it were forbidden him to write? PP

Questions My Son Asked Me, Answers I Never Gave Him. Nancy Willard. At rest on its threads I am learning to fly. LCAP

Questions of Travel. Elizabeth Bishop. ...Should we have stayed at home,/wherever that may be? NOBA

Quha Is Perfyte. Alexander Scott. And evirilk greif is gane/For evir mair. OxBS

Qui Laborat, Orat. Arthur Hugh Clough. So, with Thy blessing blest, that humbler prayer/Approach Thee morn and night. EnLi 1-2; TrPWD; VLP

Qui Perdiderit Animam Suam. Richard Crashaw. By three days' loss eternally to save. ACP

Quia Amore Langueo. Anonymous. In blisse; Quia amore langueo. ACP; AtBAP; CBEP; CoBE; EnLit; ISi; LiTL; MeEL; NOBE; NOCV; OBEV; OxBM; OxBoCh; PoEL 1-5

The Quick. Sean Jennett. shall grow to manhood in a world at war. NeBP

Quick and Bitter. Yehuda Amichai. Had we remained together/We could have become a silence. BoLoP

The Quick and the Dead. Ilarie Voronca. Among whom I go like a secret word threading through my poem? VWA

Quick-Falling Dew. Basho (Matsuo Basho). This wretched life. AWP

Quick, Henry, the Flit! James Schuyler. Slap. Drat the mosquitoes. NoAm

Quick Now, Here, Now, Always–. William J. Rewak. but I am ready against the dark/to listen for more than love. AMV-81

Quick-Step. Robert Creeley. ...in/simple time to/all their graces. VGW

Quickening. Christopher Morley. The stirring of a sonnet still unborn. HBMV

The Quickening. Stella Weston Tuttle. remembering/as something stirred. GoYe

Quickness. Henry Vaughan. A quickness which my God hath kissed. BoC; ELP; LoBV; MeLP; MePo; NOBE; NOCV; OBS; OxBoCh; SeCePo; SeCP; SeCV 1-2

Quicksands (parody). William Zaranka. To sink into the smell of their own farts. BXAP

Quid Non Speremus, Amantes? Ernest Christopher Dowson. Thee may I serve and follow all my days,/Whose thorns are sweet as never roses are! HBV 1-2

Quid Petis, O Fily? Anonymous. Thus saying to our Savior; this saw I in my syght. SeCeV

Quid Sit Futurum Cras Fuge Quaerere. Matthew Prior. Love and life are for to-day. FaBoEE

The Quidditie. George Herbert. I am with thee, and most take all. PoEL 1-5

Quien Sabe? Madge Morris. When the earth was void and the deep was/dumb?"/"Quien sabe?" BPAW

Quiescent, a Person Sits Heart and Soul. Ring Lardner. Neither of them had ever met. OBAL

Quiet. Marjorie Pickthall. Time, like one wrong/Note in a song,/With their bloom, passes. NOBC; OBCV

Quiet. Ernest Radford. The quiet that my dream fulfils/Of Quiet, aching tho' it be. OBVV

Quiet. Brian Swann. That's also why I'm quiet/as an old shoe/happily wrinkled AmPA

Quiet. Giuseppe Ungaretti. With the swallows flees/The final harrowing. PoPl

Quiet By Hillsides in the Afternoon. Martha Lifson. finding shadows to lie down in/and the quiet that finally touches my palms AMV-80

Quiet Days. Mildred T. Mey. Though one lies still, the heart and mind can grow. PoToHe

Quiet Desperation. Louis Simpson. the trees and houses vanishing/in quiet every day. SV

The Quiet Enemy. Walter De la Mare. Hold ajar the wicket gate. BrPo

The Quiet-Eyed Cattle. Leslie Norris. The Child in their stable/Whose name lives forever. PCh

The Quiet Flower. Josephine Winslow Johnson. Which, alone and immaculate and white,/Blossoms beyond the temporal hour. MoRP

The Quiet Fog. Marge Piercy. ...a mirror/tall as childhood/reflecting/nothing. UnPo

Quiet from Fear of Evil. M'K." S.C. Jesus our glorious King. BLRP

Quiet Fun. Harry Graham. He does enjoy his little bit of fun. DBV; ShM

The Quiet Glades of Eden. Robert Graves. In the quiet glades of Eden. BoLoP; ErPo

The Quiet Glen. Douglas Fraser. Life has no need of reasons. PoSH

The Quiet Hour. Louise Hollingsworth Bowman. That speaks the words of life so pure and fair! BLRP

The Quiet House. Charlotte Mew. I do not care; some day I shall not think; I shall not be! BrRo; EBEV; SBG

The Quiet Kingdom. Carl Busse. It will be found, I say to thee/By one who yearneth deep as we. AWP

The Quiet Life. William Byrd. Yet merry it is, and quiet. EiL; GoBC; HBV 1-2

The Quiet Life. Alexander Pope. Tell where I lie. ALV; GTBS-P

The Quiet Life. Seneca (Lucius Annaeus Seneca). Death to him's a strange surprise. LiTW

A Quiet Life and a Good Name. Jonathan Swift. Slaves to their quiet and good name,/Are used like Dick, and bear the blame. CBEP

The Quiet Light of Flies. Natan Zach. and still there's time to rest,/the night drifts. VWA

The Quiet Mind. Anonymous. No wealth is like the quiet mind. OBSC

The Quiet Night. Heinrich Heine. So many a night in the olden years? LiTW

The Quiet Nights. Katharine Tynan Hinkson. The sands upon the shore, I keep/And name my lovely nights of sleep. HBV 1-2

A Quiet Normal Life. Wallace Stevens. But his actual candle blazed with artifice. LCAP

The Quiet of the Dead. Mary Morison Webster. Such quiet as is lent/To stones in winter fields. PeSA

The Quiet Pilgrim. Edith Matilda Thomas. Lord, I go softly all my years! AA

A Quiet Soul. John Oldham. It hardly now enjoys a greater rest. OBEV

Quiet Things. Grace Noll Crowell. The sheltered ways, the quiet ways of peace. PoLf

The Quiet Tide near Ardrossan. Charles Tennyson Turner. But yet more stately were the power and ease/That with a whisper deepen'd all the seas. FaBoPP

Quiet Town. William Stafford. and are dangerous, are bombs exploding/a long time, carrying bombs elsewhere to explode. MAT

Quiet Waters. Blanche Shoemaker Wagstaff. E'er once again we shall drift/On the turbulent, open sea. BLPA

The Quiet Woman. Genevieve Taggard. To kiss my body, quivering and cold. AnEnPo

Quiet Work. Matthew Arnold. Laborers that shall not fail, when man is/gone. EnL; FaBoBe; HBV 1-2; MaVP; MCCG; OAEP

Quietly. Kenneth Rexroth. In their interlocked rhythms, the pulse/In your thigh caressing my cheek. Quiet. ErPo

A Quilled Quilt, a Needle Bed. Brad Leithauser. Yet-perfect intricacies/Of lichens, seeds and crystals. MAYP; SM

Quills. Charlotte Gafford. ...slow, cumbersome,/elegant, coiffed with a headful of poison. AMV-81

The Quilt. Larry Levis. ...even I/will be a believer. MAYP

The Quilt. Mary Effie Lee Newsome. To cover up the tired day/In such a cozy sort of way. CDC

Quilt Song. Mark Vinz. Warmed again, you wait/while snowflakes swirl in golden double loops. GOYP

Quintana Lay in the Shallow Grave of Coral. Karl Shapiro. ...That's why/they're all crusades. VGW

A Quintina of Crosses. Chad Walsh. The life of God must blood this cross for love. TrCP

The Quip. George Herbert. And then they have their answer home. AnFE; JCP; LiTB; OAEP; OBS; OxBoCh; SeCP; SeCV 1-2

Quite Apart from the Holy Ghost. Adrian Mitchell. ...That happens when/A poet engenders generations of advertising men. OBSV

Quite Forsaken. D. H. Lawrence. For which I wanted the night to retreat! BrPo

Quite Shy Actually but Obsessed. Jeffrey Miller. I see hell as a collection of warm fires. APU

Quite the Cheese (parody). H. C. Waring. Oh, he fancies it QUITE THE CHEESE! BXAP

Quits. Thomas Bailey Aldrich. There's many another Inn in town.   AA

The Quitter. Anonymous. You've got to quit your quittin'. BLPA; WBLP

Quivira. Arthur Guiterman. The City of Quivira whose streets are paved/with gold. BPAW; PAH

Quo' the Tweed. Anonymous. For ilka ane that ye droon,/I droon twa. CH

Quo Vadis? Myles Connolly. And even as he goes his Friend/Is knocking at his heart. TRV

Quod Dunbar to Kennedy. William Dunbar. Clym ledder, fyle tedder, foule edder, I defy the. OxBoLi

Quod Tegit Omnia. Yvor Winters. embedded in this crystalline/precipitate of time. MoVE; QFR

Quodlibets. Robert Hayman. Not thick, unwholesome, shuffling, as 'tis here. OBTV

A Quoi Bon Dire. Charlotte Mew. You will have smiled, I shall have tossed your hair. HBMV; OxBTC

Quoits. Mary Effie Lee Newsome. He beats them easily. CDC; GoSl

Quondam Was I in My Lady's Grace. Sir Thomas Wyatt. ...But what altho she had sworn,/Sure quondam was I. EnPo; GBL

Quoniam Ego in Flagella Paratus Sum. William Habington. Once dead, his sin/Men cannot expiate with tears. ACP

A Quotation from Shakespeare with Slight Improvements. Lewis (Charles Lutwidge Dodgson) Carroll. ...this from thee/Will I to mine leave as 'tis left to me.' FaBoNo

Quotations. George Oppen. "Cop's bitch." NNaP

R

R-and-R Centre: An Incident from the Vietnam War. D. J. Enright. We weren't surprised when the Americans didn't win. OxBC

R. B. Samuel Gorton. Know then your selves, that Christ you so will use. SCAP

R-E-M-O-R-S-E. George Ade. The cold, gray dawn of the morning after. ALV; FiBHP; NLV; OBAL; TreFT

R. I. P. Jan Struther. She fell between two stools, and broke her neck. InMe

R is for the Restaurant. Phyllis McGinley. To read ice-cream/Upon the bill-of-fare. TiPo

R.M.S. Titanic. Anthony Cronin. The west is not awake to where Titanic/Smokes in the morning, huge against the stars. BIrV

R-P-O-P-H-E-S-S-A-G-R. Edward Estlin Cummings. rea(be)rran(com)gi(e)ngly/,grasshopper; AmPP; InPK; NoP; PPP

A. R. U. (with music). Anonymous. Ridin' the brake beams close to the wheels. AS

R. W. Artie Gold. even becoming precious, concentrates to burn us where we've/chosen to make our stands. CaPN

Rabbi Ben Ezra. Robert Browning.
   Let age approve of youth, and death complete the same! BBV; BLPL; FaFP; FiP; GTBS; HBV 1-2; MasP; MaVP; MBW 1-2; OAEP; OBNC; OBVV; TEP; WGRP
   Youth shows but half; trust God, see all nor be afraid. BiCB; PoPl; PoToHe; TRV

Rabbi, Where Dwellest Thou? Come and See. Anonymous. Bursts upon the enfranchised Bride/The triumphant "Come and see." BePJ

Rabbi Yom-Tob of Mayence Petitions His God. Abraham Moses Klein. And benedictions on this hallowed/knife/Which pries the door to the eternal life. TrJP

Rabbi Yussel Luksh of Chelm. Jacob Glatstein. There is no black. Is no white./No guilt./All/Are right. TrJP

The Rabbit. Anonymous. When such depravity is found/It only can live underground. DBV; FaBoCo; FiBHP

The Rabbit. William Henry Davies. Until his smiling murderer comes,/To kill him in the morning light. BoAnP

The Rabbit. Georgia Roberts Durston. Twisting in and out and round about,/As safe as it can be. SoPo

The Rabbit. Edith King. As down his hidy-hole he dashes/And disappears from sight. HBMV; SoPo

The Rabbit. Elizabeth Madox Roberts. And I looked back very hard at him. OBCA; SoPo; TiPo

A Rabbit as King of the Ghosts. Wallace Stevens. And the little green cat is a bug in the grass. SOTW

The Rabbit Catcher. Sylvia Plath. The constriction killing me also. SBG

Rabbit Cry. Edward Lucie-Smith. Ajar to the still sky stripped bare of birds. NePoEA-2

Rabbit Foot Blues. Blind Lemon Jefferson. Reason I'm going home with you, sugar, I ain't much hard to be fooled BluL

Rabbit Hash. Anonymous. Oh, rabbit a-hash. ABF

The Rabbit-Hunter. Robert Frost. And deal a death/That he nor it/(Nor I) have wit/To comprehend. GDP; LiSp

The Rabbit Man. Anonymous. The finest Hampshire rabbits/That e'er crept from a hole. OxNR

Rabbits. Dorothy Walter Baruch. And they/Made faces/With their noses/Up and down. SoPo; SUS; TiPo

Rabbits. Dennis Schmitz. ...now your voice/weighs nothing though/you sing. FiCP

The Rabbits' Song outside the Tavern. Elizabeth Jane Coatsworth. We who dance hungry and wild/Under a winter's moon. SUS; TiPo

Rabia. James Freeman Clarke. Will not, in his prayer, recall/That he is chastised at all. HBV 1-2

A Raccoon. Siv Cedering Fox. I stay on my side of the broken line/that divides the going from the coming. AmC

Raccoon on the Road. Joseph Payne Brennan. ...I turned the fragrant earth/And laid him in. GoYe

Raccoon Poem. Miriam Palmer. it is time now to splash through/the thawed ice NMM

Raccoon's Got a Bushy Tail. Anonymous. Before I sing 'em all again/I'd see you all in hell. FSW

The Race of the Oregon. John James Meehan. And the breathless million that looked/upon/The matchless race of the Oregon. PAH

Race Prejudice. Alfred Kreymborg. I won't love you if you are. ELU

The Race Question. Naomi Long Madgett. Nor crown your nakedness/With jewels of my elegant pain. BPo

Race Riot, Tulsa, 1921. Sharon Olds. ...to/darken it more and more toward the color of the human. MAYP

The Racer's Widow. Louise Gluck. How even he did not get to keep that lovely body. AmPA; GeTw; LiSp; NYBP; SM

Rachel. Ruth Gilbert. But you were blind, and slept, and did not know. AnNZ

Rachel. Rachel (Rachel Blumstein). for memories are preserved in my feet/ever since, ever since. VWA

Rachel Goes to the Well for Water. Itzik Manger. If only there were two,/she'd like to have them both. VWA

Rachel's Lament. Linda Zisquit. my name my naked virtue/for your tribes. VWA

A Racing Eight. James L. Cuthbertson. The crew to row, the boat to go,/The eight to win the race. PoAu 1-2

The Racing-Man. Sir Alan Patrick Herbert. I cannot think that they have done/A great amount of riding. BoAnP; FiBHP; PH

Racing, Reckoning Fingers Flick. Palladas. like a soul passing over, to the debit side. OBVE

The Rackets around the Blue Mountain Lake. Anonymous. For you know when I have money the devil's in me./Derry, down, down, down derry down. FSW

Radar. Alan Ross. We cannot see what we do. DFF; FF

Radcliff, Kentucky. Thomas G. Nickens. And the slaughterhouse/is as close/as I/ever/want to be/to the smell of war again LFAC

The Radiance. Kabir. and that's why everything you do has some weird failure in it. LLLT

The Radiance of Extinct Stars. Allan Kolski Horvitz. yours has been the startling flash. VWA

Radiant Is the World Soul. Rav Abraham I. Kook. And find delight in what is truly precious. VWA

Radiant Ranks of Seraphim. Valery Bryusov. And our fiery breasts they cover/As with hidden holy rain. AWP

Radiation Leak. Jody Aliesan. I hold my head in my hands/and bring away hair. LTB

Radiation Victim.   Colin Thiele.   And make mankind its hideous secret torch.   NOAV

Radiator Lions.   Dorothy Aldis.   He hasn't dogs or polliwogs/Like any other child.   SoPo

The Radical.   Waring Cuney.   And they never thank me.   CDC

Radical Coherency.   David Antin.   she might have survived and he would have gotten out/of her bed.   APU

The Radical in the Alligator Shirt.   Lou Lipsitz.   but now I know why: they knew better.   AMV-80

A Radical Song of 1786.   St. John Honeywood.   Stop the courts in each county, and bully the/laws.   PAH

A Radical War Song.   Thomas Babington, Lord Macaulay.   In drinking unexcised gin,/And wooing fair poissardes, sir.   OBSV

Radio.   Frank O'Hara.   ...I think it has an orange/bed in it, more than the ear can hold.   PoA

Radio.   Arthur Seymour John Tessimond.   Sound like a sea to conceal the bone, the broken shell,/the broken ship.   HaMV

The Radio under the Bed.   Reed Whittemore.   Tum-te-tum, tum-te-tum, tum-te-tum, into my grave.   NYBP

Raftery's Dialogue with the Whiskey.   Padraic Fallon.   Listen! I'll drink to that.   DTC

The Raftsmen.   Anonymous.   Bing on the ring! Bing, bang! (Hey)   FSW

Rag Doll and Summer Birds.   Owen Dodson.   The dark stiff little compact spots you see on these white fields/are not shadows.   PoNe

Rag Time Cowboy Joe.   Lewis F. and Grant Clarke Muir.   He's a high-faluting, scooting,/shooting son-of-a-gun from Arizona,/Ragtime Cowboy Joe.   FSW

Ragged and Dirty.   Anonymous.   Mmm, mistreat me, baby,/And I swear I don't mind dying.   AmFP

Ragged Island.   Edna St. Vincent Millay.   Over a sea with death acquainted, yet forever chaste.   NoP

The Ragged Robin Opens.   Miklos Radnoti.   we see yellow autumn, a visitor.   AMV-80

The Ragged Wood.   William Butler Yeats.   No one has ever loved but you and I.   BoC; GBL

Raggedy.   Anonymous.   So union members are we.   FSW

The Raggedy Man.   James Whitcomb Riley.   Raggedy! Raggedy! Raggedy Man!   HBV 1-2; HBVY; OBCA; OxBChV; TiPo; TreFS

The Raggle Taggle Gypsies.   Anonymous.   Along with the raggle-taggle gypsies, O!'   CBEP

Raging Can-all.   Anonymous.   And you'll get an extra dose of the raging can-all.   ABF

Raging Canawl.   Anonymous.   Just call the driver aboard and hitch a lantern on his back.   AS

The Raging Generation.   Mbuyiseni Oswald Mtshali.   Power! Power! Power! To the people!   WhB

Ragout fin de siecle.   Erich Kastner.   So much for that.   ErPo; PeHV

Ragout (parody).   William Zaranka.   And it tastes like nobody but you.   BXAP

Rags.   Edmund Vance Cook.   I'll take my chance in hell.   BLPA

Ragupati Ragava Rajah Ram.   Anonymous.   Puhtita bhavana si ta ram.   FSW

The Rahat.   John Jerome Rooney.   And Earthward he was gone!   AA

The Raid.   William Everson.   And the short quick quench of the sea.   PrIm

Raid on the Market.   Polycarp Chimedza.   As silver bracelets are liberally handed out.   WhB

The Raider.   W.R. Rodgers.   Halt, hang hump-backed, and look into his crater.   AnIL; MoBrPo

The Railroad.   Henry David Thoreau.   And the blackberries a-growing.   FaBV

Railroad Bill.   Anonymous.
I'm gonna ride old Railroad Bill.   FSW
An' that wuz the last of po' Railroad Bill.   ABF

Railroad Bill (with music).   Anonymous.   Well, it's ride, ride, ride.   AS

The Railroad Blues.   Anonymous.   But when a man's in trouble, it's a long freight-train and ride.   AmFP

The Railroad Cars Are Coming (with music).   Anonymous.   The railway cars are coming, humming/Through New Mexico.   AmFN; AS; BPAW; BrR

The Railroad Corral.   Anonymous.
For there's a town that's a trunk by the railroad corral.   CoSo
For we're well on the road to the railroad corral.   FSW
Let them loaf if they will, for the railroad's in sight.   TrAS

Railroad Song.   Thomas Holley Chivers.   Is for Riding on a Rail.   PeD

Railroad to Hell.   Anonymous.   With bonnets and hats, old dresses and brats,/Made up into bundles as you have seen Pat's.   VLP

A Railroader for Me.   Anonymous.   If ever I marry in this wide world,/A railroader's bride I'll be.   AmFP

The Railway Junction.   Walter de la Mare.   And one toward distant seas?   CBEP; OxBTC

Railway Station.   John Hay.   as tracks lead inward to the waiting trains.   WaP

The Railway Stationery.   Kenneth Koch.   Now it screams closer, and he flags it down.   ANYP; NoP

Rain.   Kenneth Slade Alling.   O God, I kneel before the art,/Of this great lyrist, earth.   HBMV

The Rain.   Anonymous.
And rain on the house-top,/But not upon me!   TiPo
A raging dog, gnawing its way to pass out.   WTO
The unjust hath the just's umbrella.   FaBoCo; FaFP

Rain.   Einar Benediktsson.   Each raindrop shares the ocean's fate.   LiTW

The Rain.   Robert Creeley.   Be wet/with a decent happiness.   CAPP; CoAP; ConAP; VGW

The Rain.   William Henry Davies.   'Twill be a lovely sight.   EnLit; OxBTC; TiPo

Rain.   Frank Marshall Davis.   before the boss comes 'round.   GoSl

Rain.   Emanuel DiPasquale.   the rain hushes the surface of tin porches.   InPK; PoL

Rain.   Christopher Fry.   The snail drags his caution into the sun.   BoC

Rain.   Haim Guri.   And a little, falling on the leaves, becomes pearls waiting for the sun.   VWA

Rain.   John Haines.   and our house is a raft of shingles/sunk under leaves and vines.   NPAW

Rain.   Sam Harrison.   clutching a beggar's penny in my hand.   NeIP

Rain.   William Ernest Henley.   In her wet prints a pretty housemaid passes.   SyP

Rain.   Lance Henson.   on a damp/stone/melt   VoR

The Rain.   George Herbert.   And at your lodging with their thanks appear.   BoC

Rain.   Anselm Hollo.   ..."it is for ever/washing the substance of the land into the sea."   PoM

Rain.   Patrick F. Kirby.   We, too, shall be in the rain/A long, long while.   GoBC

Rain.   Vachel Lindsay.   Alone with lost years.   CMoP

Rain.   Sister Mary Lucina.   and rain passing/through uneven light.   AMV-80

Rain.   Howard Moss.   And only the dead are wrong.   ErPo

Rain.   Paul Murray.   among the trees, rain whispers endlessly?   BIrV

Rain.   Vladimir Nabokov.   because the sun is there.   GrPl

Rain.   Seumas (James Starkey) O'Sullivan.   Round the black headlands/ Streaming with rain.   OnYI

Rain.   James Whitcomb Riley.   Why, rain's my choice.   BoNaP

Rain.   Peter Sears.   how far how deep I don't know.   AMV-80

Rain.   Frances Shaw.   O Rain, my mother Rain!   HBMV

Rain.   Robert Louis Stevenson.   And on the ships at sea.   GoJo; NTCP; SoPo; SUS; TiPo

Rain.   Edward ("Edward Eastaway") Thomas.   Cannot, the tempest tells me, disappoint.   OBWP; OxBTC

Rain.   William Carlos Williams.   following/and falling endlessly/from/her thoughts.   AP; CoBMV

Rain.   James Wright.   The sad bones of my hands descend into a valley/Of strange rocks.   NaP

Rain after a Vaudeville Show.   Stephen Vincent Benét.   I stamped the ground in the strong joy of life!   MoAmPo

The Rain and the Rainbow.   Leo Fredericks.   Smell of wet heleniums. The rainbow of roses.   ACV

Rain at Wildwood.   May Swenson.   on the wood's floor released/tangy dews and ozones.   NYBP

Rain before Seven.   Anonymous.   Fair by eleven.   FaBoBe; OxNR

Rain Chant.   Louis Mertins.   Come the little clouds out of the Ice-Caves,/ To bring us rain for our harvests!   BPAW

Rain Clouds.   Elizabeth-Ellen Long.   In green grass silk/With wild-flower frills.   BrR

The Rain Comes Sobbing to the Door.   Henry Clarence Kendall.   The rain comes sobbing to the door.   ACV

The Rain-Crow.   Madison Cawein.   Like some drenched truant, cower.   AA

Rain Down.   Mary Ellen Solt.   [concrete poem]   BoWoP

Rain Falls. It Dries...   Miklos Radnoti.   Listen on to the world's tiny flutters and yelps.   AMV-81

Rain for Ka-waik.   Paula Gunn Allen.   a token for our hearts to drink,/a wakening.   TWSS

Rain Forest.   Eric Rolls.   One might well open a vein/And decorate a bower for dying/With red rosettes.   NOAV

Rain Forest.   Dave Smith.   ...that clapping of hands/before which we may not speak or sing or ever stop.   HaCAP

Rain Has Fallen on the History Books.   David Rosenberg.   spoken words/a wind has blown away.   VWA

Rain in Summer.   Henry Wadsworth Longfellow.   More than man's spoken word.   GN

Rain in the Desert.   John Gould Fletcher.   Whirling, extinguishing the last red wisp of light.   BPAW; NCSH

The Rambling Cowboy. *Anonymous.* For if you ever cross those plains,/ She'll marry another man. BFSS; CoSo

Rambling Gambler. *Anonymous.* If I'm on your book, love, please blot out my name. CoSo

Rambling, Gambling Man. *Anonymous.* I'm a rambler I'm a gambler/And I gamble when I can. FSW

The Rambling Sailor. *Anonymous.* I court them all and marry none,/And still be a rambling sailor. OBSS

The Rambling Sailor. Charlotte Mew. Wi' your head lyin' soft in the sand. HBMV; PoRA

The Rambling Soldier. *Anonymous.* And if you want to know my name/ 'Tis Bill the rambling soldier. OBET

Rambunctious Brook. Frances Frost. all night long! BrR

Rambuncto (parody). Margaret Widdemer. Under the circumstances....What's life for? BXAP

Ramon. Bret (Francis Bret Harte) Harte. Dead as stone! BeLS

Ramon. E. A. Lacey. Seven years ago that sailor set forth for Antarctica. PeHV

The Rampage. C. K. Williams. I'm hungry now I want just to sleep/and they let him GeTw

Rana, I know you gave me poison. Mira Bai [(or Mirabai)]. Mira's lord knows she is his servant. BoWoP

Rana, why do you treat me. Mira Bai [(or Mirabai)]. Mira has her lord Girdhar,/who turns poison into nectar. BoWoP

Ranch at Twilight. *Anonymous.* Rest for the hard-riding waddies, peace and contentment for all! BPAW

The Rancher. Keith Wilson. over the saddlehorn, he led/fall's last drive/ across the hazy range. GP

Ranchers. Maurice Lesemann. They worked a homely hem. BPAW

Random Generation of English Sentences; or, The Revenge of the Poets. William Jay Smith. Where all your hot-rugged brothers and sisters are headed./Madam, good-bye! OBAL

Random Reflections on a Cloudless Sunday. John Hall Wheelock. In Bronx Park when he's feeling so pleased with himself. NePoAm

Random Reflections on a Summer Evening. John Hall Wheelock. The tender cluck of the hen pheasant urging them on. NYBP

Random Wheels,. Terry Borst. nothing/could be easier. AmC

Range-Finding. Robert Frost. But finding nothing, sullenly withdrew. AmLP; CABA; NIP; NoAm; NoP; OBWP

The Range in the Desert. Randall Jarrell. The lizard's tongue licks angrily/ The shattered membranes of the fly. NOBA

The Range Rider's Soliloquy. Earl Alonzo Brininstool. I seem to look through on the glories that lie in that great Home/Corral. PoOW

The Range Riders. *Anonymous.* Just turn your back on her with scorn and disdain. CoSo

Rank. Lincoln Kirstein. Jack and I got see-double drunk. OBWP

The Rann of the Three. *Anonymous.* Three Persons in God, yet only one God is there. CAW

Rannoch Moor. Malcolm MacGregor. As the sun, its globe compressed in/ The mist-sprayed air, sinks lidless down. PoSH

Ranolf and Amohia. Alfred Domett. The genuine passions of the nether pit! ACV; AnNZ; OBTV

Ransi-Tansi-Tay. *Anonymous.* You're all too black and dirty/with a Ransi-tansi-tay! PoPle

The Ransomed Spirit to Her Home. William B. Tappan. And cheer our hearts, Celestial Love! AH

Rant Block. Michael McClure. If there are bastions, let my love be walls! EAS

The Rantin Dog the Daddie O't. Robert Burns. The rantin dog the Daddie o't. OxBoLi; PPP

The Rantin Laddie. *Anonymous.* Ye'll happy be and ye'll happy be,/For they are frank and free. AmFP

The Rantin Laddie (A vers.). *Anonymous.* With a gude claymor in every hand,/And O but they shin'd bonie. BaBo

The Rantin Laddie (B vers.). *Anonymous.* An' hush-a-by, wee babbie O. BaBo

Rantin, Rovin Robin. Robert Burns. Robin was a rovin boy,/Rantin rovin Robin! OxBS

The Ranting Wanton's Resolution; 1672. *Anonymous.* Then there lies a Lady of pleasure. CoMu

Rap Sheet. Paul D. Shiplett. 1982 Employed as a salesman. LFAC

Rape. Tom Pickard. its me next. FaBoTw

Rape. Thomas Rabbit. The men turn away and the boy's death grows. MAYP

Rape. Adrienne Rich. will you swallow, will you deny them, will you lie your way/home? GP

The Rape of Europa. Richard P. Blackmur. —else what is born lies nameless in her lap. CrMA

The Rape of Lucrece. William Shakespeare.
And ever let his unrecalling crime/Have time to wail the abusing of his time. OAEL 1-2
Since men prove beasts, let beasts bear gentle minds.' PBBP

To cheer the plowman with increaseful crops,/And waste huge stones with little water drops. LiTB; PoEL 1-5

To Tarquin's everlasting banishment. BeLS

The Rape of the Lock. Alexander Pope.
And beauty draws us with a single hair. ACP; ViBoPo
And Betty's prais'd for Labours not her own. AtBAP; CABA; CEP; CoBE; DiPo; NOBE
And 'midst the Stars inscribe Belinda's Name. AtBAP; ATP; DiPo
And the long labours of the toilet cease. FaBoPP; OBSV
And tremble at the sea that froths below! ViBoPo
Anxious, and trembling for the Birth of Fate. AtBAP; BiP; CEP; DiPo; EBEV; FiP; ForPo; HAP; MasP; MBW 1-2; MOON; NAWM 1-2; NOEC; NoP; OAEL 1-2; OAEP; OBNV; OxBoLi; PoEL 1-5; SeCeV; TEP; TrGrPo; WHA
Belinda smiled, and all the world was gay... ExPo
Colours that change whene'er they wave their wings. NOBE
The conqu'ring Force of unresisted Steel? AtBAP; CABL; CEP; CoBE; DiPo; EnL
Hairs less in sight, or any Hairs but these! AtBAP; CABL; CEP; CoBE; DiPo
In glitt'ring dust and painted fragments lie! ViBoPo

Rape Poem. Marge Piercy. ...murder those who dare/live in the leafy flesh open to love. Psk

The Raper from Passenack. William Carlos Williams. ...And hatred, hatred of all men/—and disgust. TW

Raphael's San Sisto Madonna. George Henry Miles. ...they are face to face/With the Eternal Father! CAW

The Rapid. Charles Sangster. Mingling their lives with its treacherous spray! CaP; WHW

Rapid Transit. James Agee. That now is tamed, and once was wild. AnAmPo; MoAmPo; NAMP

Rapids at Night. Duncan Campbell Scott. Wild with rushing dreams and deep with the sadness,/That dwells at the core of all things. CaP

A Rapier of Treason. *Anonymous.* Being intelligent, I measure him/by his mere look. BoWoP

The Rapist. Stephen P. Dunn. like this poem/that is already inside you. PoL

Rapist. Jose Y., Jr. Teran. she spills/her last proposition/an abstraction lost in her moan. LFAC

The Rapist's Villanelle. Thomas M. Disch. I couldn't help myself. I had to smile. SM

Rapping along with Ronda Davis. James (Olumo) Cunningham. stranded/ among your hair. JB

The Rapture. Sir Henry William Baker. Thus blest, I scarce one thought should cast away/On heav'n's eternal happiness, or you! NOEC

A Rapture. Thomas Carew. Should make men Atheists, and not women Whores. AnAnS 2; CaPo; CavP; JCP; OAEL 1-2; SeCP

Rapture. Randolph Carlson. For the just shall rise to meet their Lord/In the flicker of an eye. AMV-80

Rapture. Stefan George. And of the eternal voice I am the thunder! AWP

The Rapture. Thomas Traherne. Who rais'd? Who mine/Did make the same? What hand divine? OBS

Rapture: An Ode. Richard Watson Dixon. The new-born soul that height/ By ecstasy hath trod. OxBoCh

Rapunzel. Olga Broumas. upon rows of kisses from all lips. DFT

Rapunzel. Sara Henderson Hay. I might have known I would not be the last. DFT

Rapunzel. Faye Kicknosway. Let 'm pocket-pool. APU

Rapunzel. Eli Mandel. climb toward the turnip-colour sun. DFT

Rapunzel. Anne Sexton. did moonlight sift into her mouth. DFT

Rapunzel. Louis Untermeyer. Let down your hair! DFT

Rapunzel Song. Gerard Previn Meyer. and mounted swiftly into time. DFT

The Raquette River, Potsdam, New York.... Anthony Piccone. We laugh/ at my lack/of fish. WOLT

Rare Moments. Charles Henry Phelps. Rank and tangled vine and jungle block our/pathway to the peak. AA

Rare News. Nicholas Breton. Which, when they fall, then look for a confusion. NIP

Rare Willie Drowned in Yarrow, or, The Water o Gamrie (A version). *Anonymous.* Sine, in the clifting of a craig,/She found him drownd in Yarrow. BaBo; BSV; ESPB; GBP; GoTS

Rare Willie Drowned in Yarrow, or, The Water o Gamrie (B version). *Anonymous.* And she's tied it about sweet Willie's/waist,/An drawn him out o Yarrow. ESPB

Rare Willie Drowned in Yarrow, or, The Water o Gamrie (D version). *Anonymous.* "Baith our miders sall be alike sory,/For we's baith slep soun in Gamry." ESPB

Rare Willy. *Anonymous.* She found him drown'd in Yarrow. OxBB

A Raree Show. Stephen College. And successor has the clap,/With a hey, trany nony nony no. APAS

Raspberries. Laurence Lerner. As I go on eating, waiting for the news. EBEV

The Raspberry in the Pudding. Philip O'Connor. ...He is a sensation,/for newspapers and headaches. He is exploded! EAS

The Rasslers. William D. Barney. Let someone get hurt good. Maybe get killed. LiSp

A Rat. *Anonymous.* Went down a rope to say/his prayers. OxNR

The Rat. William Henry Davies. They'll soon see who was left at home.' OxBTC

The Rat. Arthur Symons. He stirs the dust where the feet of my dreams had passed. SyP

The Rat and the Elephant. Jean de La Fontaine. That a rat is not an elephant. OBVE

The Rat Is the Conciest Tenant. Emily Dickinson. Lawful as Equilibrium. MAmP

Rat Riddles. Carl Sandburg. And the tail of a green-eyed rat/Whipped and was gone at a gray rathole. SO

The Ratcatcher's Daughter. *Anonymous.* So there was an end of Lily white Sand,/His ass, and the Ratcatcher's daughter! GBP; OxBoLi

Ratcliffe Highway. *Anonymous.* We soon bid adieu to fair London/And all the flash girls in the town. OBSS

The Rath in Front of the Oak Wood. *Anonymous.* The rath survives; the kings/are covered in clay. NOBI

Rather Too Good, Little Peggy! Adelaide O'Keeffe. When indiscreet–we're call'd TOO GOOD./Never do so again.' FaBoUs

The Ration Card. Liz Sohappy Bahe. in dance, in song, in that little taste. CDW

Ration Party. John Streeter Manifold. Every imaginable pattern of constraint. WaP

Rats. Walter De La Mare. One, with its forepaws,/Wash its whiskered face. BoAnP

The Rats. Georg Trakl. The icy wind through the darkness whines. LiTW

Rats Away! *Anonymous.* Bothe by dayes and by nightes! et in nomine Patris et/Filii, etc. OxBM

Rattan bed, paper netting. Li Ch'ing-chao. there's/no one/person/to send/ it to. BoWoP

The Rattle Bag. Dafydd Ap Gwillym. Amen, who scared off my girl. NLV; TW

Rattler, Alert. Brewster Ghiselin. My foamless heart, the bloodleap at my wrist. HAP; WeW

The Rattlesnake. *Anonymous.* To my rattle, to my roo-rah-ree! BFSS; CoSo

The Rattlesnake. Robert V. Carr. A challenge full of deathless hate. PoOW

The Rattlesnake. Alfred W. Purdy. Ubiquitous, marvellous grass privateer. WHW

The Rattlesnake. Robert Wrigley. ...his dry music/still singing in our ears. AMV-80

The Rattlesnake Band. Robert J. Conley. the hat with the rattlesnake band/is gathering dust. STE

Rauf Coilyear (excerpt). *Anonymous.* And said: "Ye ar welcum heir,/Be him that me bocht." OxBS

The Ravaged Villa. Herman Melville. Makes lime for Mammon's tower. AP; CTC; MAmP; NOBA; PoEL 1-5

The Raven. Samuel Taylor Coleridge. They had taken his all, and REVENGE it was sweet! WiR

Raven. Duane Niatum. the way the fire cooled to coal. STE

The Raven. Nicarchos [(or Nicarchus)]. The raven dies. AWP; LiTW; UnS

The Raven. Edgar Allan Poe Shall be lifted - nevermore! AA; AnFE; AP; APA; BeLS; BLPA; FaBoBe; FaBoCh; FaBV; FaFP; FPL; GN; GoJo; GoTF; HBV 1-2; LiTA; LoGBV; MCCG; NePA; NOBA; OBCA; OBNV; OHFP; OxBA; PaPo; PoRA; RoGo; TAP; TreF; ViBoPo; WBLP; WHA

The Raven. Adrienne Rich. even as you prime your feathers and set sail. NePoEA-2

Raven at Lemon Creek Jail. Thomas Waltner. each step tuned to the flap of your wings. LFAC

The Raven Days. Sidney Lanier. Begin to gleam across the mournful plain? AmePo; CBEP; NePA; OxBA

Raven/Moon. Anita Endrezze-Probst. Raven listens, whistling in stunted trees. VoR

The Raven Visits Rawhide. *Anonymous.* Slammed the door and was off in flight,/Ridin' the parson's horse. BPAW

Ravenglass Railway Station, Cumberland. Norman Nicholson. Long years after the once tall trunk is down. NYBP

Ravenna. Louis MacNeice. A bad smell mixed with glory, and the cold/ Eyes that belie the tessellated gold. OBTV

Ravens. Ted Hughes. Sitting soft. InPS; NAs

Ravin's of Piute Poet Poe (parody). C. L. Edson. Matting on my chamber floor. BXAP

The Ravine. James Applewhite. Air tasted good when I breathed the cold sun. AMV-80

Raving Warre, Begot. Thomas Campion. Thus still needy dyes/Th' unknowne multitude. AAS

Ravings (parody). Tom (Thomas Hood, Jr.) Hood. Yes:–his pointless perpetual ditty/Perplexes pyramidal piles! BXAP; Par

Ravished by all that to the eyes is fair. Buonarroti Michelangelo. But beauty and the starlight of her eyes. AWP

Ravngard and Memering. *Anonymous.* And clothe thee too in scarlet red,"/Said Dame Gunild. BaBo

Raw Honey. Lewis MacAdams. aching softly asks would I like a piece of fresh-baked bread and/butter?/With a little honey? APU

Ray. Otto Orban. Statues in a museum where no one comes to visit. VWA

Ray Charles. Sam Cornish. & he rolls/up his/sleeves CNA

Raya Brenner. Pinhas Sadeh. I, in a dimness, still, silent,/in the twilight before morning,/expired. VWA

Raziel. Yvan Goll. From earth arose the flaming Name/From floral whorls from spectral horns/On the high hour of death VWA

Razon de Amor (excerpt). Pedro Salinas. As certain of not dying/as is/the immense love of the dead. LLLT

Razor. Robert B. Smith. ...pulling free/to the yearning pulse, the blood/ and the final cleaving. LFAC

The Razor-Seller. John Wolcot. "Made," quoth the fellow, with a smile,– "to sell." HBV 1-2; InMe

Re-Act for Action. Don L. Lee. your/children's graves. BPo; NBP

Re-Birth. *Anonymous.* you told us too that when we died/we should return again. PeSA

The Re-Birth of Venus. Geoffrey Hill. ...approaches all/Stayers, and searchers of the fanged pool. NePoEA

Re-Forming the Crystal. Adrienne Rich. But the energy it draws on/might lead to racing a cold engine, cracking the frozen spiderweb... CAPP; TAP

Re-Statement of Romance. Wallace Stevens. In the pale light that each upon the other throws. MoLP

The Reach of Silence. Charles Black. But winter lasts forever. AMV-81

Reaching. William Carson Fagg. The guard turns, grinning,/and shoots the bird. LFAC

Reaching the Horizon. Robert Mezey. ...and/can think of nothing to say. NaP

The Reactionary Poet. Ishmael Reed. Make it by steamboat/I likes to take it real slow CNA

Read Me, Please! Robert Graves. And the name which you stumble on/Is, alas, your own. NYBP

Read, Sweet, How Others Strove. Emily Dickinson. Passed out of record into renown. AH; NOCV

Read the Bible Through. Amos R. Wells. You will kneel in very rapture,/ When you read the Bible through! STF

Readen Ov a Head-Stwone. William Barnes. When they be dead that loved it. CH; HBV 1-2

The Reader Writes. Carl Crane. To seem more deep than Robert Frost. PoPl

Reading a Medal. Terence Tiller. -my helpless paradox–because FaBoTw; GTBS-P

Reading and Talking. Louis Zukofsky. if tears/show him/to the/letter. VGW

Reading Faust. Judah Goldin. I recall these Mephistopheles lines. AMV-81

Reading in Fall Rain. Robert Bly. the rooster lifting his legs/high in the wet grass. GP; GrPl

Reading in the Night. Roy Fuller. For it to be beyond our human powers/ Even to orchestrate another's fugue. OxBC

Reading in War Time. Edwin Muir. And gather an image whole. WaP

Reading Indian Poetry. Ramona Wilson. Fat, cold-eyed crows lighten our day. VoR

The Reading Lesson. Richard Murphy. If they were pheasants, they'd be in his pot/For breakfast, or if wrens he'd make them king. IPY

The Reading Mother. Strickland Gillilan. I had a Mother who read to me. BLPA

Reading Myself. Robert Lowell. this open book...my open coffin. HaCAP; TAP

Reading Plato. Jorie Graham. trying to slip in/and pass/for the natural world. MAYP

Reading Room, the New York Public Library. Richard Eberhart. In silence and sweet temper, loving the world. GOYP; GP; NYP

Reading Sign. Jack Anderson. The honeysuckle scent,/raspberries–black & red,/greenleaf, rose, & thorn. LFAC

Reading the Books Our Children Have Written. Dave Smith. Under this the other one has answered. See tomorrow. HaCAP

Reading the Brothers Grimm to Jenny. Lisel Mueller. the world as it might be? DFT; NYBP

Reading Time: 1 Minute 26 Seconds. Muriel Rukeyser. aftermath proof, extended radiance. MoPo; NePA; PBWP

Reading Today's Newspaper. Steve Abbott. until we hear in ourselves again/the forgotten song of love. AMV-80

Reading Walt Whitman. Calvin Forbes. Good Langston sat too long to lift me. PoBA

Readings, Forecasts, Personal Guidance. Kenneth Fearing. ...She will communicate with a number of friends/and relatives long deceased. MoAmPo

Readings of History. Adrienne Rich. I take your life into my living head. ConAP

Ready. Phoebe Cary. But there wasn't a man of them that day/Who was fitter to die than he! PAH

Ready, Ay, Ready. Herman Charles Merivale. Be thy first word thy last,– Ready, ay, ready! HBV 1-2

Readymade. John Perreault. They beautify any room in your house. ANYP; EAS

The Reagan (parody). Richard Quick. Quoth the Reagan, "Nevermore!" FaBoPa

Real Deal Revelation. Raymond Ringo Fernandez. can't get loose/can't/be yourself/can't.... LFAC

Real Happiness. Oliver Goldsmith. To different nations makes their blessings even. OBEC

Real Life. Ted Berrigan. As my strength and I walk out and look for you. NoAm

The Real Muse. Fred Muratori. Speeding through white water like a log. AMV-81

The Real Muse. Tom Scott. Frae earth mak you immortal images. PoA

Real Old Mountain Dew. Anonymous. Take off your coat and free your throat/With the real old Mountain Dew. FSW

The Real People Loves One Another. Rob Penny. backwards under the sun. CNA; PoBA

Real Presence. Ivan Adair. My God...my Brother-Man. WGRP

Real Property. Harold Monro. Sometimes when I have found a friend/I give a blade of corn away. BoNaP

A Real Question Calling for Solution. Robert Penn Warren. And the thought that, on your awaking, identity may be destroyed. PPP

A Real Santa Claus. Frank Dempster Sherman. I'll be Santa Claus to him! ChBR

A Real Story. Linda Pastan. tell us a real story. Str

The Real Thing. Ronald Wallace. our tongues blunt as husks in our cheeks? AMV-81

A Real Woman. John Keats. From Pyrrha's pebbles or old Adam's seed. LiTL

Realism. Thomas Bailey Aldrich. The Muse in alien ways remote/Goes wandering. AnNE

Les Realites. Barbara Guest. as this pharmacy/turns our desire into medicines and revokes the rain. AmPC

Reality. Sir Aubrey De Vere. Mortal! Love that Holy One!/Or dwell for aye alone. WGRP

Reality. Martha Gilbert Dickinson. A chord, a dream, a longing, love of Thee! AA

Reality. Frances Ridley Havergal. In the long noon of Eternity/Unveiled, Thy "bright reality"? BePJ; WGRP

Reality. Angela Morgan. In large fulfillment of our biggest hope! WGRP

Reality. Raymond Souster. Holding a box of shoe-laces in unendingly shaking hands. CaP

Reality Is an Activity of the Most August Imagination. Wallace Stevens. Night's moonlight lake was neither water nor air. AmC

Realization. Ananda Acharya. To realize the purpose which Truth proclaims to be the all-/supreme. WGRP

Realization. Mahlon Leonard Fisher. The Fact could not be sadder than the Thought! AnAmPo

The Reaper. Leslie Holdsworth Allen. Yet she has steeds of fire/And men of gold! PoAu 1-2

The Reaper. Robert Duncan. The source of the song will die away. CrMA

The Reaper. John Banister Tabb. To heap with many a harvest-dream/The granary of Sleep. ACP

The Reaper. William Wordsworth. The music in my heart I bore,/Long after it was heard no more. GTBS; GTBS-P

The Reaper and the Flowers. Henry Wadsworth Longfellow. And took the flowers away. AnNE; HBV 1-2

Reapers. Mathilde Blind. But these human creatures cease not from their reaping/While the corn stands high, waiting to be cut SBG

Reapers. Jean Toomer. ...the blade,/Blood-stained, continue cutting weeds and shade. BPo; CDC; HAP; InPK; NoAm; PoBA; PPP

The Reapers. Lauchlan Maclean Watt. We who have looked on the Reapers/Go quietly, all our days. PGD

Reaping. Amy Lowell. Oh, my God! It ain't decent any more either way! SBG

The Reapings. Theodore Weiss. the gifts, the firstlings, weathered/on that forging stone. NMP

The Rear Guard. Irene Fowler Brown. That we were born of those, unflinching,/loyal,/Who wore the gray. PAH

The Rear-guard. Siegfried Sassoon. Unloading hell behind him step by step. ACV; MCCG; MoBrPo; NoAm; OBWP; WaP

Rear Porches of an Apartment Building. Maxwell Bodenheim. The death of the afternoon to them/Is but the lengthening of blue-black shadows on brick walls. AnAmPo

Rear Vision. William Jay Smith. Unwinding still the darkening thread? NYBP

Rearmament. Robinson Jeffers. ...the dance of the/Dream-led masses down the dark mountain. OxBA

Rearrange a Wife's Affection? Emily Dickinson. Leads is through the grave to thee. AnNE; PoEL 1-5

The Reason. Leonard Bacon. We think so much about so little/And think so little of so much. YaD

A Reason. Robert Creeley. Your face is hurt/all the same. NaP

Reason. Josephine Miles. Reason, Reason is my middle name. AmC; InPK; NCSH; NoAm; NoP; PoCh; TAP

The Reason. James Oppenheim. This perfect night could never be/Were we not mated each to each. HBV 1-2

Reason. John Tatham. Reason and Madmen never could agree. CavP

A Reason Fair to Fill My Glass. Charles Morris. And that I think's a reason fair/To fill my glass again. HBV 1-2

Reason for Not Writing Orthodox Nature Poetry. John Wain. And where you love you cannot break away. HaMV; MP; PP

The Reason for Poetry. Nancy Morejo. Please hear me I am alone. WPOW

The Reason for Skylarks. Kenneth Patchen. Out of his pocket he played tune/After until they came up to him. NaP

The Reason for the Pelican. John Ciardi. It's really quite a splendid beak/ In quite a splendid size. PoPI; SoPo

Reason Has Moons. Ralph Hodgson.
But, O! delighting me. FaBoCh; LoGBV; OBSP
God loves an idle rainbow,/No less than labouring seas. MoVE

Reason I Stay on Job So Long. Anonymous. Like she rolls her dough. ABF; GBP

Reason. The Use of It in Divine Matters. Abraham Cowley. And from afar 'tis all Descry'd. AnAnS 2

The Reason Why. Thomas Lovell Beddoes. I know my love can never die. OBRV

A Reasonable Affliction. Matthew Prior. His wife, that he may live. ALV; GoTF; HBV 1-2; NOEC; NoP; ShM; TreFT; TrGrPo

Reasons. Thomas James. ...other strangers/Will put their mouths together. PoA

Reasons For and Against Marrying Widows. Henricus Selyns. But be this so or not, who can take water down him/Another had to drown in? SCAP

Reasons for Attendance. Philip Larkin. If no one has misjudged himself. Or lied. BiP

Reasons for Music. Archibald MacLeish. Meaning/the movement of the sea. NePA

Reasons to Go Home. Greg Forker. you'll have to ride alone tonight. LFAC

Reb Hanina. Paul Raboff. As after fire/Smoking char. VWA

Rebeca in a Mirror. Judith Rodriguez. the unasked bodily friendship/of her first home. CBAP

Rebecca. Joseph Eliyia. But sweeter yet, the sun-beauteous wife of Isaac. VWA

Rebecca's After-Thought. Elizabeth Turner. Loved her better, and forgave her. HBV 1-2; HBVY

Rebecca, Who Slammed Doors for Fun and Perished Miserably. Hilaire Belloc. They never more would slam the Door,/–As often they had done before. NOBL; SO

The Rebel. Hilaire Belloc. But fear perhaps my little son/Should break his hands, as I have done. CoBE

The Rebel. Mari E. Evans. trying to make/Trouble... AmNP; IDB; IHMS; PoBA

A Rebel. John Gould Fletcher. We would have no power left to look on that dead face. MoAmPo

Rebel. Irene Rutherford McLeod. I shall have sung! I shall have sung! HBMV

The Rebel. Padraic Pearse. Ye that have bullied and bribed, tyrants, hypocrites, liars! OnYI

The Rebel. Innes Randolph. I won't be reconstructed and I don't give a damn. NLV; OBAL; OxBoLi

The Rebel General. Chris Wallace-Crabbe. Who bicker till his gavel calls a halt. CBAP

The Rebel Girl. Joe Hill. For it's great to fight for Freedom/With a Rebel Girl. FSW

The Rebel Scot. John Cleveland. ...A poet should be feared/When angry, like a comet's flaming beard. PeD; TW

The Rebel Soldier. Anonymous. I am a rebel soldier and far from my home. LoGBV; OxBoLi

The Rebellious Vine. Harold Monro. And all the time God knew. BrPo

Rebels. Ernest Crosby.
 The lie upon his lips!... MC
 Why, then be rebels for the right/By Aguinaldo's side! PAH

Rebels from Fairy Tales. Hyacinthe Hill. We may begin from the same tadpoles, but/we've thought a bit, and will not turn to men. DFT; SO

Rebirth. Margaret E. Bruner. Who suffer here on earth. PoToHe

Rebirth. Rudyard Kipling. In our own likeness, on the edge of it. GTBS; LoBV; OBNC

Rebirth. Antonio Machado. or the sound of the water when it is flowing. NU

Rebirth. Catriona Stamp. balls of thread growing/from the creative void–/ woven for eternity. BrRo

Rebolushinary x-mas/eastuh julie 4/ etc. etc. etc. etc. Carolyn M. Rodgers. we don't celebrate farts no mo. JB

Reborn. Kingsley Amis. While I every moment am reborn.' OxBC

Rebuff. Samuel L. Albert. Alone and pitched the desert path and gone. NePoAm-2

Rec Room in Paradise. Tom Clark. ...and they/laugh, until they are rolling on the floor/of the heavenly TV lounge. APU

The Recall. James Russell Lowell. To birds and me the need to sing! AP

Recall. Reed Whittemore. "Hip, hip. Eyes front. Chin up," to the tick/Of the marvellous stomach clock. NYBP

Recalling War. Robert Graves. To yet more boastful visions of despair. CMoP; CoBMV; ForPo; LiTM; MMM; NoAm; OAEL 1-2; OBWP; WaP

The Recantation. Albius Tibullus. Fond dream! which now the east and south winds bear/Away to far Armenia's spicy lands. LiTW

The Recapitulation. Richard Eberhart. Accord what is spiritual. MoRP

Recapitulations. Karl Shapiro. Even the women could detect/Their awful fall from intellect. PoNe

A Receipt for Stewing Veal. John Gay. O, then! with what rapture/Will it fill dean and chapter! FaBoUs

Receipt for the Vapours. Mary Wortley, Lady Montagu. I believe the dose will do. PBWP

A Receipt to Cure a Love Fit. Anonymous. And leave all the rest of the work to the string. NOEC

Receiving Communion. Vassar Miller. here on my turbulent dust/ preventing so all fantasy of flesh. NePoEA-2

A Recent Dialogue. Thomas Moore. Snored out (as if some Clerk had given/His nose the cue) "Amen." NBM

The Reception. June Jordan. a true gut-funky blues to make her really dance. FaBoWP; NMM

Recessional. Georgia Douglas Johnson. Within, without, the vassal heart– its reasoning who/knows? CDC; PoNe

Recessional. Rudyard Kipling. Thy Mercy on Thy People, Lord! AWP; BBV; BLPA; BLPL; BLRP; BoLiVe; BrPo; CABA; EnLi 1-2; EnLit; FaBoPV; FaBV; FaFP; FaPo; FaPoR; GN; GTBS; HBV 1-2; HBVY; InPo; LiTB; MCCG; MoBrPo; NOBE; NOBV; NoP; OAEP; OBEV; OBNC; OBVV; OHFP; TreF; TrGrPo; TRV; UnPo; ViBoPo; VLP; WBLP; WGRP; WHA

Recessional. Thomas MacGreevy. The long, silvery roar/Of Mal Bay. CIP

The Recessional. Sir Charles G. D. Roberts. Till remembrance has no longer/Care to laugh or weep. HBV 1-2

Recessional for the Class of 1959... Joseph R. Cowen. They will be a libation/To our cupidity/In our pursuit of happiness. PoNe

Rechargeable Dry Cell Poem. Jim Wayne Miller. Explains why I'm Eveready, why/you're a strange new story every time. GOYP

Recipe. Anonymous. Both are enjoyable only when hot. UnTE

Recipe. Albert Goldbarth. ...a/clear broth–just water/that tastes of these roots. VWA

Recipe for a Pleasant Dinner-Party. Anonymous. Warm plates and hot potaters. FaBoUs

Recipe for an Ocean in the Absence of the Sea. Richard Howard. Serve at once. It does not keep. TAP

Recipe for Living. Alfred Grant Walton. A faith in man, a trust in God. PoToHe

Recipe for Salad. Sydney Goodsir Smith. Fate cannot harm me, I have dined today. FaBoUs

Recipe: To Mak a Ballant. Alexander Scott. Syne rin like hell afore the result explodes! BSV

Reciprocity. John Drinkwater. As little daunted as a star or tree. PoA

Reciprocity. Vassar Miller. When your one need is me to need you still? IHMS; NePoEA

Recital. John Updike. Dy who oompahs on the tubo,/solo, quite like Roger Bubo! OBAL

Recital (excerpt). Louise Townsend Nicholl. And gives back an image, the image of music? UnS

Recitative. Hart Crane. And let us walk through time with equal pride. FaBoMo

Recitative. Ronald McCuaig.

And onward plough and ploughmen go/Into the field where farmers grow. NOAV

Your kiss incurious as the windless air. PoAu 1-2

Recklessly I Cast Myself away. Izumi Shikibu. A heart in love/Becomes a deep ravine? PBWP

The Reckoning. Alice R. Friman. And we, promised by blossoms,/run gathering/bushels of cinders, black and still as nuns. AMV-81

The Reckoning. Theodore Roethke. The penny that usurps the poor. PoA

Reckoning. Fay Zwicky. and in My pain's darkness/trample her glass. NOAV

Reckoning A. M. Thursday after an Encounter.... Doris Turner. I'll pin a lotus in your (hair... JB

Reclaimed Area. Jon Silkin. ...formic acid to bite with as its unregarded jaws grow. NoAm

Reclining Figure. Donald Hall. I anchored,/in the darkness of harbors/ laid-by. ConAP; LCAP

Recluse. Aldo Camerino. I'm not beginning my life over,/but waving to it from a distance. VWA

The Recluse. William Wordsworth. Guide, and support, and cheer me to the end! OBRV

The Recluses. Stuart Z. Perkoff. They are always/inside NeAP

Recognition. John White Chadwick. Some secret sense shall cry, 'Tis you and/–you! AA

The Recognition. Denise Levertov. not bones but the shape of bones. VGW

Recognition. Georgette Perry. a tiny trembling. Day tatters in the wind. AMV-80

The Recognition (parody). Frederick William Sawyer. She knew him–by his appetite! HBV 1-2

Recollection. Anne Reeve Aldrich. For Memory locks her chaff in bins/ And throws away the grain. AA

Recollection. Duane Big Eagle. Arrows to the heart. STE

Recollection. Amelia Walstein Carpenter. Shall whisper, "Hark! who sang that love-/song? Hark!" AA

A Recollection. Frances Cornford. "I know a person who has died." ELU; FaBoWP

Recollection. Dorothy Donnelly. Heel cannot bruise, nor weight break/The shadow shape of gold. NCSH

Recollection. Donald D. Govan. Wolf said we are human. NBP

Recollection. Marilyn R. Mumford. This time we'll see her tip her head and sing. AMV-80

The Recollection. Percy Bysshe Shelley. The lifeless atmosphere.... CH

Recollection Long Ago: Sad Music. Robert Penn Warren. Even now. SV

Recollections of a Day's Journey in Spain. Robert Southey. ...Earth itself/ Appeared the place of pilgrimage it is. OBTV

Recollections of Burgos. Richard Chenevix Trench. Wind far away that poplar-skirted stream. OBRV

Recollections of "Lalla Rookh." John Townsend Trowbridge. Some flowers of rhyme untouched by Time,/And songs that sing forever. OBAL

Recollections of Love. Samuel Taylor Coleridge. Dear under-song in Clamor's hour. ChRP

Recollections of the Arabian Nights. Alfred, Lord Tennyson. I saw him–in his golden prime,/THE GOOD HAROUN ALRASCHID. VLP

Recompense. Nixon Waterman. Because, for just a little while,/The way seemed dark and dreary. HBV 1-2

Reconciled Differences. Roger Sauls. you closing around me/like a cat. AMV-81

The Reconcilement. John, Duke of Buckingham Sheffield. O to be happy– to be kind–/Sure never is too late! CEP; LiTL; OBEV

Reconciliation. Anonymous. so you should give to me your love in the like/ measure. AnIL

Reconciliation. C. Day-Lewis. Appear the argent, swan-assemblied reaches. MP; NoAm; TwCP

Reconciliation. Elizabeth Doten. While men and angels, stars and suns,/ Unite to praise Thee evermore! TrPWD

Reconciliation. Else Lasker-Schüler. A great star has fallen into my lap. PBWP

The Reconciliation. Archibald MacLeish. We touch and by that touching farness are alone. MoAmPo

Reconciliation. Caroline Atherton Briggs Mason. Let there be peace between us ere we/die! AA

Reconciliation. J. U. Nicolson. There shall be peace between us two. HBMV

Reconciliation. D. Rosenmann-Taub. in the infinite/mirror of the breast? VWA

Reconciliation. George William Russell. On the laugh of a child I am borne to the joy of the King. MoRP; OBMV; OxBI; TrCP

The Reconciliation. Alfred, Lord Tennyson. We kissed again with tears. HBV 1-2

Reconciliation. John Hall Wheelock. Emblems of the inexplicable will. CrMA

Reconciliation. Walt Whitman. Bend down and touch lightly with my lips the white face in the coffin. AnEnPo; HAP; MoAmPo; NoP; OBSP; OBWP; OxBA; TrGrPo; WaaP

The Reconciliation: A Modern Version Odes of Horace III, 9. Franklin Pierce ("F.P.A.") Adams. So I will be your Mrs. Q./Horatius. NLV

Reconnaissance. Arna Bontemps. In latitudes where storms are born. AmNP; BPo

Reconsecration. Dorothy Gould. May we greet with joy another year. PGD

Record Perpetual Loss. Mary Stanley. the cold unanswerable logic of a death. AnNZ

A Record Stride. Robert Frost. As if I had measured the country/And got the United States stated. NePA

Recorders Ages Hence. Walt Whitman. while the arm of his friend rested upon him also. MoAmPo; NePA

Recorders in Italy. Adrienne Rich. There were four recorders sweet upon the wind. UnS

The Recovery. Edmund Charles Blunden. But the mouse stays his nibbling, to explore/My eye with his bright eye. CBEP; MoBrPo

Recovery. Patricia Y. Ikeda. I don't know. I don't know. BrSi

Recovery. F. R. Scott. And truth stands naked under the flashing charge. CaP

The Recovery Room: Lying-in. Helen Chasin. this ordeal has almost nothing to do with love. IHMS

Recreation. Audre Lorde. I made you/and take you made/into me. NIP; NoP

Recreation. Jane Taylor. We muffled up in cloak and plaid,/And trotted home behind the lad. NBM; OBRV; OxBoLi

Recrimination. Ella Wheeler Wilcox. Rushed to my arms and spat upon your/face! AA

The Recruit. Robert William Chambers. The Rigiment's flatthered to own ye, me/spark! AA; HBV 1-2

The Recruit. Alfred Edward Housman. Oh, town and field will mind you/Till Ludlow tower is down. FaPoR

Recruiting Drive. Charles Causley. The butcher-bird sings, sings, sings. NePoEA; OxBTC; PPON; PrIm

The Recruiting Sergeant. Anonymous. The sword of war may mow me down. OBET

The Recruiting Serjeant (excerpt). Isaac Bickerstaffe. What a charming thing's a battle! NOEC

The Recruits. Ian Hamilton. ...till/It's perfect night in you. And then you scream. NoAm

Recuerdo. Paula Gunn Allen. pocket bright bits of obsidian and fragments/old potters left behind. STE

Recuerdo. Edna St. Vincent Millay. And we gave her all our money but our subway fares. AmFN; CTBA; EvOK; FaFP; FPL; LiTA; LiTL; LiTM; NoAm; OxBA; PoA; TAP

The Recurrence. Edwin Muir. And counterfeit mortality. MoPo

Red. Countee Cullen. And walked out proud as any queen. GoSl

Red, and White Roses. Thomas Carew. And then they both shall grow together. AnAnS 2

Red Anger. R. T. Smith. the trail of tears never ends. STE

Red Ants. Anonymous. But like flask of rose-water in fashion/Is the cure my dear flame can bestow. WTO

Red Apple Juice. Anonymous. Send you back to your mama some old day. FSW

Red Beauty. Anonymous. As soon as I saw you/My life ached for you, my enemy. WTO

Red Bird. Anonymous. Red bird, red bird soon in the morning. FSW

The Red-Breast of Aquitania. Francis Sylvester ("Father Prout") Mahony. O DELUSIVE DREAM! OnYI

Red Clay. Linda Hogan. We are here, the red earth/passes like light into us/and stays. TWSS

Red Cloud. John G. Neihardt. ...a toothless, ancient squaw/Lifted a feeble fist at him and screamed. BPAW

The Red Cockatoo. Po Chu-i. They took a cage with stout bars/And shut it up inside. LiTW

The Red Cow Is Dead. E. B. White. Toll the bell, young fellow! NLV; NYBP

Red Cross Nurses. Gervase Stewart. Seeing, feeling and hearing the things which are hidden. WaP

The Red Dog. Laura Jensen. to be their hard sounds/as their bodies leave the water. LCAP

Red Dust. Philip Levine. ...having eaten it/all these years. NNaP

The Red Flag. James Connell. We'll keep the red flag flying here. FSW; VLP

The Red Flag. Michael Jackson. covers your father's tracks. OCNZ

Red Geranium and Godly Mignonette. D. H. Lawrence. that blossomed at last, red geranium, and mignonette. GTBS-P

Red Geraniums. Martha Haskell Clark. And red geraniums aflame upon my window sill. BLPA

The Red Ghosts Chant. Lilian White Spencer. Utes are eagles flying high and far...../Hi-yu! Hi-yu! Hi-ya!!! PoOW

A Red Glow in the Sky. Alexander Blok. and the rhythm of life returning. OBVE

The Red-Gold Rain. Sacheverell Sitwell.
Or wind blowing over those hot rocks that hold the water? AtBAP
Will fall one day to flood this tower. AtBAP; MoBrPo

The Red-Haired Man's Wife. James Stephens. Still are secret, unreach'd and untouch'd and not subject/to you. HBMV; MoBrPo; OBVV

Red Hanrahan's Song about Ireland. William Butler Yeats. But purer than a tall candle before the Holy Rood/Is Cathleen, the daughter of Houlihan. ACV; CMoP; FaBoCh; LoGBV; NOBI; OnYI; OxBI

The Red Heart. James Reaney. Beneath the dancing feet of crowds/Of other still-living suns and stars. CaP

The Red Herring. Anonymous. Don't you think I did well with my red herring? FaBoNo

Red-Herring. D. H. Lawrence. we should start an' kick their –ses for 'em/ an' tell 'em to–. NoAm

The Red Herring. George MacBeth. ...And perhaps also/to amuse children. Small children. SO

Red Hugh. Thomas MacGreevy. And out to Simancas all knew/Where they buried Red Hugh. OnYI

Red Indian Corpse. Peter Redgrove. Typed on a tag-label tied to his left big toe. OxBC

Red Iron Ore. Anonymous. Derry down, down, down, derry down. ABF; AS; FSW

Red Jack. Mary Durack. Red Jack and Mephistopheles/Went all their ways alone. PoAu 1-2

Red Jacket. Fitz-Greene Halleck. Thy name, thy fame, thy passions, and/ thy throne! AA

Red Light. LeRoi (Imamu Amiri Baraka) Jones. ...now you think/your way out of this SOTW

The Red Light Saloon. Anonymous. Your muscle is hard from your head to your toe! ShS

Red Lilies. Barbara Guest. The paper folded like a napkin/other wings flew into the stone. PoM

Red lotus incense fades on the jewelled curtain. Li Ch'ing-chao. The next, it weighs on my heart. BoWoP

The Red Man's Wife. Douglas Hyde. For the wife of the Red-haired man. OnYI; OxBI; SeCePo

Red May. Agnes Mary Frances (Mme Emile Duclaux) Robinson. Out of the window the trees in the Square/Are covered with crimson may. HBMV

The Red Men. Charles Sangster. We scan the trail of Thought, but all is overcast. CaP

Red o'er the Forest. John Keble. The laggard body soon will waft to Heaven. OxBoCh

A Red Red Rose. Robert Burns. And I will come again, my Luve,/Tho' it were ten thousand mile! AtBAP; AWP; BiP; BoLoP; BSV; CABA; CBEP; CEP; DiPo; EiCP; EnL; EnLi 1-2; FaBV; FaFP; FF; ForPo; GBL; HAP; HBV 1-2; HeIP; InPo; InvP; LAuP; MCCG; NIP; NOBE; NOEC; NoP; OAEL 1-2; OBEC; OBEV; OLR; OxBS; PG; PoEL 1-5; PoLf; PrIm; SeCeV; SoSe; TEP; ViBoPo

Red Riding Hood at the Acropolis. Myra Sklarew. still wearing her ancient/polka dot dress. DFT

Red Right Returning. Louis O. Coxe. ...find/Known channels with a red nun on my right. MoVE;.; WaP

Red River Shore. Anonymous.
And stay with their husbands the rest of their lives. CoSo
She's the one I will marry on Red River shore. ABF

Red River Valley. Anonymous.
And the pain you are causing to me. FaFP
But remember the Red River Valley,/And the girl that has loved you so true. AS; FaBoBe; TrAS
For they say you are taking the sunshine,/Which has brightened our pathway a while. BLSo
Just remember the Red River Valley/And the cowboy who loves you so true. BPAW; CoSo; FSW; TreFS

The red road. Nila NorthSun. make them aware/it can be done. STE

Red Rock Ceremonies. Anita Endrezze-Probst. I am making the words/ speak in circles. CDW; VoR

The Red Room. Judith Berke. Like that part of the fire that remains longest. PoDr

The Red Sea Place in Your Life. Annie Johnson Flint. A place that His hand has made. BLRP

Red Sky at Morning. Gilbert Thomas. Its naked arms were black as night,/And grim with prophecy. TreFS

Red Sky at Night. Anonymous. Shepherd's warning. OxNR

Red Stockings, Blue Stockings. Anonymous. Till our skirts shall touch the ground. OxNR

The Red Thread of Honor. Sir Francis Hastings Doyle. That crimson thread was twined. BBV

The Red Wheelbarrow. William Carlos Williams. beside the white/ chickens. AmLP; BLPL; CMoP; ForPo; GrPl; HeIP; HoPM; InPS; LiTA; LiTM; MoAB; MoAmPo; NIP; NoAm; NOBA; NoP; PrIm; SoSe; SOTW; TAP; UnPo

Red Whiskey. *Anonymous.* Pretty girls when I'm lonesome and heaven when I die. AmFP

The Red, White and Blue. David T. Shaw. Three cheers for the red, white and blue. WBLP

The Red, White and Red. *Anonymous.* We'll all die defending the Red, White and Red! AmFP

Red White & Another Ism. Harold LaMont Otey. wonderin' whose dream/it'll be to commence/the next pogrom so as/to preserve their/ independence day LFAC

Red Wine. Justin Richardson. The nearer the sweet, the meeter the Beaune. PV

The Red-Wing Blackbird. William Carlos Williams. ...and the o-/dors of the swamp vodka/to his nostrils. DFF

Red Wing Hawk. James Applewhite. As if yellow eyes in sunlight were answering prayer. AMV-81

Redbreast, Early in the Morning. Emily Bronte. But like the shriek of misery/That wild, wild music wailed to me. NCEP

The Redbreast (excerpt). William Wordsworth. Betray the elf that loves to dwell/In Robin's bosom, as a chosen cell. PBBP

Rededication. Emanuel Litvinoff. That understanding will flash through the arrested mind. WaP

The Redeemer. Fiona Macleod. Shout "Thy Redeemer liveth, and calleth for thee!" WGRP

The Redeemer. Kizito Z. Muchemwa. but do not leave your questioning mind, brother,/to be nibbled in this dance of mice. WhB

The Redeemer. Siegfried Sassoon. Mumbling: "O Christ Almighty, now I'm stuck!" MMM; WGRP

Redemption. Stanley Cooperman. be silent. AMV-80

Redemption. George Herbert. Who straight, "Your suit is granted," said, and died. AnAnS 1; CABA; EaLo; EBCP; ExPo; FF; HAP; InPK; InPS; JCP; LiTB; MeLP; MePo; NOBE; NOCV; NoP; OBS; PAI; SCV; SeCeV; SeCP; SeCV 1-2; SoSe; TEP; TrCP

Redeployment. Howard Nemerov. I heard the dust falling between the walls. LiTM; NePA; OBWP; TrJP

Redesdale and Wise William. *Anonymous.* "If there is a gude woman in the world,/Your one sister is she." ESPB

The Redingote and the Vamoose. Richard Kendall Munkittrick. And how long they will run over hill and dell/Is really more than I can tell. OBCA

Rediscovery. Kofi (George Williams) Awoonor. and the halleluyahs of our second selves. TTY

Redo, 1-5. Lyn Hejinian. In a time of brain and desire/patience is the mental equivalent of running. APU

Redondillas. Sister Juana Ines de la Cruz. In her you started first to burn! CAW

The Redshanks. Julian Bell. And knowledge seems no less absurd/If of a mistress, or a bird. OBMV

The Redwing. Patric Dickinson. And I know how I know. BoAnP; HaMV

Redwings. James Wright. And fell asleep by a fire. NNaP

The Redwoods. Louis Simpson. considering whom to please. AmFN; CoAP; PP

The Reed. Henry Bernard Carpenter. Thou shalt bruise them with rod of iron,/and break them like vessels of clay. AA

The Reed. Caryll Houselander. the cradle of God. ISi

The Reed. Mikhail Yuryevich Lermontov. Or have you never suffered/And tasted misery? AWP

A Reed. Osip Mandelstam. Secretly I am envious of everyone,/And with everyone secretly in love. VWA

The Reed-Player. Archibald MacLeish. ...as one who longs/to turn to dreams, and smiled, and played again,/The Song of Songs. HBMV

The Reeds in the Loch Sayis. *Anonymous.* For time sic causis has repairit. BSV; GoTS

Reefing Topsails. Walter Mitchell. Haul taut your bowlines—well all—belay! EtS

The Reek and the Rambling Blade. *Anonymous.* Away goes a reek and the rambling boy. OuSiCo

Reference to a Passage in Plutarch's Life of Sulla. Robinson Jeffers. When life grows hateful, there's power... CrMA

The Refiner's Fire. *Anonymous.* And His gold did not suffer a bit more heat/Than was needed to make it pure. BLRP

Reflecting on the Aging-Process (parody). Robert Peters. ...am no longer/ twenty-five am fat and/turning to stone. BXAP

Reflection. *Anonymous.* With a heart He may always see. STF

A Reflection. Thomas Hood. Than Adam was not adamant! FaBoEE; NBM; PV

Reflection. Kurt M. Stein. And always there is some dam fool who writes them. InMe

The Reflection. Edward Taylor. Enthrone thy Rosy-self within mine Eyes. AmPP; AtBAP; NePA; OxBA

Reflection. Walter James Turner. Leaving their brightness on dead moons/ As suns less heavenly do. OBMV

Reflection: After Visiting Old Friends. John Allison. Inside we breathe though our skins. GrPl

Reflection and Advice. Ezra Pound. You will not lack your reward. OBSV

Reflection by a Mailbox. Stanley Jasspon Kunitz. "Sequence, consequence, and again/consequence." TrJP; WaP

Reflection from Rochester. William Empson. "For hunger or for love they bite and tear." PoA

Reflection from Sea and Sky. Walter Savage Landor. Deep beneath and bright above. FaBoEE

Reflection in a Green Arena. Gregory Corso. The leaves are leaves again no tree forgot. VGW

A Reflection of Night. T. Walking Eagle Marietta. like an owl staring into the eyes/of a hawk. LFAC

Reflection on Babies. Ogden Nash. Is always walcum. FaBoUs; NLV

A Reflection on the Foregoing Ode. William Cowper. And, trusting in his God, surmounts them all. OBVE

Reflections. Anita Barrows. I drained the madness/from your womb. NMM

Reflections. Edna Becker. I must be still. TRV

Reflections. Samuel Taylor Coleridge. Speed it, O Father! Let thy Kingdom come! EnRP; OBEC

Reflections. A. Deshoulicres. Coward! regard it with unhurried breath,/ And know this outrage for the last. PBWP

Reflections. Carl Gardner. I have ordered too many executions. NNP; PoBA

Reflections. Louis MacNeice. At which I cannot write since I am not lefthanded. FaBoIP

Reflections. Merle Molofsky. by that which is and never could be me. AMV-81

Reflections. David R. Pichaske. It is cold, and there is no mail service. AMV-80

Reflections. Vivian Smith. along the failing tightrope of the will. CBAP

Reflections at Dawn. Phyllis McGinley. I wish I didn't talk so much,/ When I am at a party. FiBHP; NLV; NOBL

Reflections (excerpt). Philip Freneau. Speak–for you must–you have no hour to lose. PPON

Reflections in a Hospital. Emanuel Eisenberg. This is what a guy must come to/Ere you yield! ALV

Reflections in a Little Park. Babette Deutsch. Yet cannot blink and cannot bless/God's manifest ungraciousness. ELU; NePoAm

Reflections in a Slum. Hugh" (Christopher Murray Grieve) MacDiarmid. And I am concerned with the blossom. FaBoTw; NMP

Reflections in an Iron Works. Hugh" (Christopher Murray Grieve) MacDiarmid. You fools who equip your otherwise helpless foes! NAMP

Reflections in Bed. Julian Symons. Unripe for revolution or for death. WaP

Reflections of a Trout Fisherman. Andrew Demon. never giving up on living/without a brilliant battle. AMV-80

Reflections on a Womb Which Is Called "Vacant." Jeanine Hathaway. ...This house I live in/has pockets of magic. IHMS

Reflections on Ice-Breaking. Ogden Nash. But liquor/Is quicker. BLPL; FaBoCo; FaFP; LiTM; NePA; NLV; NoP; OBAL

Reflections on the Death of a Parrot. Jaime Jacinto. reflection losing itself in the dark globes of/his eyes. BrSi

Reflections on the River. Andrew Young. As though the heavens were seized with an earthquake. ACV

Reflections on Water. Kenneth Pitchford. The angel that we wrestle is ourselves. CoPo

Reflections outside of a Gymnasium. Phyllis McGinley. How pleasant life was in the eighties! SD

Reflections upon a Recurrent Suggestion by Civil Defense. Reed Whittemore. From the grown-up's house to the child's house, I'll keep. PoCh

Reflections, Written on Visiting the Grave of a Venerated Friend. Ann Plato. We turn to dust, to sleep, repose. BlSi

Reflective. Archie Randolph Ammons. me that/had a/weed in it. HaCAP

Reflexes. Marvin Bell. No one can picture the worst. Str

Reflexions on the Seizure of the Suez.... Howard Nemerov. –Next Time, Go by Pyramid. NLV

Reformation of Manners. Daniel Defoe.
And fain would sin, but nature won't assist. OBSV
And in one act two vices gratified. OBSV
Thus thousands to religion are brought o'er,/And made worse devils than they were before. NOEC

Reformed Drunkard. Vernon Scannell. But that is not/For him to think about, far less to say. AMV-80

The Relic. John Donne. Should I tell what a miracle she was. CABA; EIL; GBL; HAP; LiTB; LoBV; MyFE; NOBE; NoP; OAEL 1-2; PPP; SeCeV; WHA

The Relic. Robert Hillyer. And hide the thrush's skull away. GoYe; UnS

Relics. George Frederick Cameron. ...and this joyless gem/That glittered on her taper finger fair. PeCV

Relics. Suzanne Gegna. the cut of your pattern/like the design in a bolt of memory AMV-81

The Relics. Harry Mathews. Until I know less. ANYP

Relics. David Wagoner. Your heads heavy with promises for another season. FAZ

The Relief of Lucknow. Robert Lowell. As the pipes played Auld Lang Syne. HBV 1-2; StPo

The Relief on Easter Eve. Thomas Pestel. Nightly this repast go take,/Get to relief from thy brake. CBEP; OxBoCh

Relieving Guard. Bret (Francis Bret Harte) Harte. Somehow it seemed to me that God/Somewhere had just relieved a picket. RoGo

Religio Laici. John Dryden.
And all his Righteousness devolv'd on thee. NOCV; OBS
And Epicurus guessed as well as he. ViBoPo
So dies, and so dissolves in supernatural light. FiP
Sufficient, clear, and for that use ordained. OBS; WGRP
Tom Sternhold's or Tom Shadwell's Rhimes will serve. AnAnS 2; CEP; OAEL 1-2; OBS; SeCV 1-2
What farther means can reason now direct,/Or what relief from human wit expect? OxBoCh
Which, from the Universal Church receiv'd,/Is try'd, and after for its self believed. OBS

Religio Novissima. Aubrey Thomas De Vere. And undispensed sustain its discipline! IrPN; IrPN; NBM sustain its discipline!; NBM

Religion. Samuel (1602-80) Butler. The maggots of corrupted texts... DBV

Religion. Heinrich Heine. Your eyes I do believe in–/And in your wicked heart. LiTW

Religion. Henry Vaughan. And turn once more our water into wine! NOCV; OAEL 1-2; OBS; OxBoCh

Religion. Jean Vauquelin de la Fres Why dost thou tread down Death? It is that I/Am Death's own slayer, who can never die. CAW

Religion and Doctrine. John Milton Hay. And what the Christ had done to him,/He knew, and not the Sanhedrim. WGRP

Religion Back Home. William Stafford. And he said, "I always did get/them two guys mixed up." OBAL

Religion Is a Fortune I Really Do Believe. Anonymous. Bow low down in de valley for to pray,/An' I ain't done prayin' yet. BoAN 1-2

The Religion of Hudibras. Samuel (1602-80) Butler. And blaspheme custard through the nose. DBV; InMe

Religious Musings. Samuel Taylor Coleridge.
Flows to the ray and warbles as it flows. EnRP
'Tis the Messiah's destined victory. WGRP

A Religious Use of Taking Tobacco. Robert Wisdome. Thus think, then drink Tobacco. EIL; HBV 1-2; OBS

Reliques. Edmund Charles Blunden. Will square the circle one bright day. ImOP

The Relish of the Muse. Sir John Beaumont. As closing sounds of some delightful bell. PoL

Relocation. David Mura. Bansai tree,/like me you are useless/and a little sad. BrSi

Reluctance. Robert Frost. Of a love or a season? CMoP; ExPo; MoAB; MoAmPo; NOBA; OxBA

Remain, Ah Not in Youth Alone. Walter Savage Landor. Nor go when dust is gone to dust. HAP; OAEP; OBNC

Remainder. Frederika Blankner. And what I saw, I keep/Forever. GoYe

The Remains. Mark Strand. I empty myself of my life and my life remains. NYBP; PPP

Remains of an Indian Village. Al Purdy. I hear their broken consonants... NOBC

Remarkable Art. Gelett Burgess. But imagine the/Ride, when you start. FaBoNo

Remarks from the Pup. Burges Johnson. Mine is the saner attitude. GDP

Remarks of Soul to Body. Robert Penn Warren. In a blinding blaze, from the filth of the world's floor. NAs

Rembrandt's Late Self-Portraits. Elizabeth Jennings. ...You chose/What each must reckon with. EyDe

Remedies. Gary Soto. And Grandma hums prays hums Str

The Remedy Worse Than the Disease. Matthew Prior. I died last night of my physician. ALV; FaBoEE; HBV 1-2; TrGrPo

Remember. William Johnson Cory. And, if you see a beauteous thing, just say, he is not here. OBVV

Remember. Joy Harjo.
Remember the dance that language is, that life is./Remember. STE
Remember/to remember. TWSS

Remember. Georgia Douglas Johnson. Remember through the night. PoNe

Remember. Christina Georgina Rossetti. Better by far you should forget and smile/Than that you should remember and be sad. AnEnPo; AWP; BoLiVe, BoLoP; EnLoPo; FaBV; FPL; GoTF; GTBS; HBV 1-2; MCCG; NOBE; NOBV; NoP; OAEL 1-2; OAEP; OBEV; OBNC; OBVV; PoLf; PoPle; PoRA; SBG; TreFS; TrGrPo; ViBoPo; WHA

Remember Dear Mary. John Clare. And the more I behold–only loves thee the more. WeW

Remember Me. Keith Douglas. and simplify me when I'm dead. NeBP; NePoEA; OxBTC

Remember Me! Thomas Haweis. "Saviour!" with my last parting breath,/I'll cry, "Remember me!" BePJ

Remember Not. Helene Johnson. Let Love's beginning expiate Love's end. BANP; PoNe

Remember or Forget. Hamilton Aïdé. For calmness to remember,/Or courage to forget. HBV 1-2

Remember (parody). Anonymous. I'd rather you'd remember and be sad. ALV; BXAP

Remember Sabbath Days. Larry Eigner. and prepare darkness/among the stars VWA

Remember September. May Justus. And showed a mouse a little house/To keep him through the cold. SiSoSe; YeAr

Remember, Sinful Youth. Anonymous. Your final destiny, 'scape for life! AH

Remember Suez? Adrian Mitchell. And England's trousers falling down. OxBTC

Remember That Country. Jean Garrigue. An unsullied country, almost beyond the stars. VGW

Remember That Night. Anonymous. my fortune in hand/and ready to go. NOBI

Remember the Day of Judgment. Anonymous. Think the blod fro Jesu ran,/Whan he deyed, withouten nay. MeEL

Remember the Ladies. Lyn Lifshin. whether you will/offend a mother or father/who has lost a child LTB

Remember the Last Things. Anonymous. And shild thee fra the Fendis plicht–/Memor esto novissima. MeEL

Remember the Promise, Dakotah. Robert V. Carr. Dance the ghost-dance, O Dakotah!/For to-morrow thy people come home. PoOW

Remember the Source. Richard Eberhart. Every work of noble mind/is a noble work of God. MoRP

Remember thee! remember thee! George Gordon, Lord Byron. Thou false to him, thou fiend to me! BoLoP; MBW 1-2; OBSP; ViBoPo

Remember Thou Me. Anonymous. E'en on death's journey remember thou me. WTO

Remember, Though the Telescope Extend. George Dillon. Remember this and let the world be lost. ImOP

Remember Thy Covenant. Edith Lovejoy Pierce. O God, set thy kiss on the cloud! MoRP

Remember Thy Creator Now. Peter Long. Youth is the day, the precious day,/When mercy may be found. AH

Remember Times for Sandy. Carolyn M. Rodgers. And I would always remember/Times. JB

Remember Way Back. L. C. Green. Well now I love my little woman/I want the whole world to know BluL

Remember Your Lovers. Sidney Keyes. Remember your lovers who gave you more than love. WaP

Remembered Grace. Coventry Patmore. Gaps in the low-hung gloom, and, bright in air,/Orion or the Bear. OxBoCh

Remembering. Akjartoq. While the sun slowly went his way/Across the sky. WTO

Remembering. Maya Angelou. I lie in stolid hopelessness/and they lay my soul in strips. PPJ

Remembering. Clarisse Nicoidski. the road of life/around/my memories VWA

Remembering. Judit Toth. It's to one system the onion/and time curving in the onion's peel belong. VWA

Remembering Althea. William Stafford. you knew, delicately, through amber, that August day. NYBP

Remembering Apple Times. John T. Hitchner. I drift across and dream the time/when ever-after time was mine. AMV-80

Remembering Day. Mary Wight Saunders. For this is our Remembering Day. YeAr

Remembering Fannie Lou Hamer. Thadious M. Davis. But for strong new growth/Under midnight moons BlSi

Remembering Fire. Rodney Jones. ...impalpable country/Of sleep, holding all of this back, drifting toward the unborn. MAYP

Remembering Golden Bells. Po Chu-i. Because, in the road, I met her foster-nurse. AtBAP; AWP

Remembering Him. Joe Reccardi. I loved him so AMV-80

Remembering Home. Susan Petrykewycz. So close in heart and soul. AMV-80

Remembering Lincoln. Frank Mundorf. and tears creep inward, drying on the heart. GoYe

Remembering Lunch. Douglas Dunn. Each squelch of leather on mud complaining, "But where are you going?" OxBC

Remembering Lutsky. Rayzel Zychlinska. I still go there, looking for him/ among the empty tables. VWA

Remembering My Father. Jonathan Holden. I know exactly what I look like. Str

Remembering Mykenai. Alfred Corn. Echo through ruins like yours, Mykenai. SM

Remembering Nat Turner. Sterling A. Brown. The marker split for kindling a kitchen fire. PoBA; PoNe

Remembering Snow. Ralph Nixon Currey. Remembering snow as I remember sun. PeSA

Remembering That Island. Thomas McGrath. ...the lying famous corrupt/ Senators mine our lives for another war. NePoEA; PPON

Remembering the Automobile. Deirdra Baldwin. That re-enters as the children spill from the open car doors. AmC

Remembering the Thirties. Donald Davie. Whose green adventure is to run to seed. FaBoPV; NePoEA; OxBTC; PP

Remembering the Winter. Rowena Bastin Bennett. Oh, wise are the wild things, preparing for the winter! SiSoSe

Remembrance. John Henry Boner. Remember only when her babe first smiled. AA

Remembrance. Emily Bronte. How could I seek the empty world again? BLPL; BoLoP; BoWoP; CH; EBEV; EnLoPo; FaFP; ForPo; GTBS; HAP; HBV 1-2; LiTB; LiTL; MasP; NOBE; NoP; OAEP; OBNC; OxBI; PoEL 1-5; TEP; TreFT; TrGrPo; VLP

Remembrance. Margaret E. Bruner. She waits, from earthly cares forever free. PoToHe

A Remembrance. Willis Gaylord Clarke Throned in my heart I see thee still. AA

Remembrance. Ibnu'l-Farid. And is Shi'b 'Amir prospering since we departed, and/will it one day bring the lovers together? LiTW

Remembrance. Aline Kilmer. For I had always loved it so! CAW

Remembrance. George Parsons Lathrop. You are in heaven now. AA

Remembrance. Antoni Slonimski. Strength ever lessening, hope grown/ever less. TrJP

A Remembrance of a Color inside a Forest. Ray A. Young Bear. "i hope you/don't mind." CDW

A Remembrance of My Friend Mr. Thomas Morley. John Davies. That Nature wrought must unto dust be brought. OBSP

Remembrance of Things Past. Horace Coleman. still trying to get their crisp/black fingers on our white throats FAZ

Remembrances. John Clare.
And winter fought her battle strife and won. SaC
It runs a naked stream, cold and chill. NBM
So it went the common road to decay. CBEP; NCEP

The Reminder. Léonie Adams. A lone, a steadfast eye/Silently looks in. MoVE

Reminder. *Anonymous.* My voice in praise had lifted. STF

The Reminder. Thomas Hardy. Do you make me notice you! CMoP; OBCP

Reminiscence. Thomas Bailey Aldrich. And, with the urn, she bore my heart away! AA; AnAmPo

Reminiscence. Wallace Irwin. It seems I had the best o' him/And him the best o' me. FiBHP; NOBL

A Reminiscence of 1820. H. H. Dugmore. And gird us for our duties. ACV

Reminiscences of a Dancing Man. Thomas Hardy. To a thunderous Jullien air? MoVE

Reminiscences of a Day: Wicklow. John Francis O'Donnell. Vague intimations that made time/A very time of Gold. IrPN

Reminiscent Reflection. Ogden Nash. I hardly ever repent. FaBoCo

Remnant Ghosts at Dawn. Oliver La Grone. Frozen for new eyes/At break of another dawn... FB

Remon. *Anonymous.*
O belle femme qui ca voule mo fai. ABF
O dame Romulus, oh!/How could you be cruel to me? TrAS

A Remonstrance. John Gerrard. Plain virtue, which shall one day vice outshine,/And truth in rags a diamond from the mine. NOEC

Remonstrance. Sidney Lanier. Opinion, damned Intriguer, gray with guile,/ Let me alone. AmePo

Remonstrance. Philodemos of Gadara. Are you a Lover or a Senator? LiTW; OLR

A Remonstrance. James Kenneth Stephen. Why should you not marry me for a change? NOBV

Remonstrance to the King. William Dunbar. Gif that the tryackill cum nocht tyt/To swage the swalme of my dispyt! OxBS

Remorse. Sir John Betjeman. I would listen even again to that labouring breath. MoBrPo; OBSP

Remorse. Richmond Lattimore. to prove that heart, at least, was true. PoA

The Remorse for Time. Howard Nemerov. Which even then washed him away past pardon. NCSH

Remorse–is memory–awake. Emily Dickinson. The Adequate of Hell– NOBA; NOCV; NoP

A Removal from Terry Street. Douglas Dunn. That man, I wish him well. I wish him grass. FaBoMo; OxBC; PoL

Removal: Last Part. Carroll Arnett. it goes on ending/toward another/new ending. VoR

Remove the Predicate. Clark Coolidge. the known is old and we are new. APU

Renaissance. Robert Avrett. And Art knew Titian and the tapestries. GoYe

Renaissance/A Triptych. John Minczeski. now what about this pain/what about this ecstasy. PoDr

The Renaming. Valerie Sinason. she began again/and named the sky/plate. BrRo

Renaming the Evening. Eric Pankey. revealing something hidden. AMV-81

Renascence. Muredach J. Dooher. I wandered soft away. OnYI

Renascence. Edna St. Vincent Millay. And he whose soul is flat–the sky/ Will cave in on him by and by. FaFP; HBV 1-2; MAPA; MoAB; MoAmPo; NePA; OHFP

Rencontre. Jessie Redmond Fauset. My heart that slept so still, so spent,/ Awoke last night,–to break anew! CDC

Render unto Caesar. Rolfe Humphries. Greater than any it ever had before. CrMA

Rendez-vous Manque dans la Rue Racine. John Millington Synge. Lord God, I am slow to learn! BIrV

Rendezvous. Mary Scott Fitzgerald. Hand-in-hand with beauty. PoToHe

Rendezvous. Robert Hillyer. In what age and what country you will come,/That I may meet you there. MoLP

Rendezvous. Edna St. Vincent Millay. And I wish I did not/feel like your mother. NMM

The Rendezvous. Bernard Spencer. city of our rendezvous. GTBS-P

The Renegade Wants Words. James Welch. noon and the eagles–not one good word. CDW

The Renegado (Act V, Scene I). Philip Massinger. ,nor must I think it now,/In you, a work less pious. ACP

Renewal. Gladys Cromwell. Above this hour of bitterness I'll lift/My spirit up and taste my grief again! AnAmPo

Renewal. Michael (Katherine Bradley and Edith Cooper) Field. And I trust myself, as from the grave I may,/To the enchanting miracles of change. OBVV

Renewal. Steve Kowit. I will have no recourse/but to find the little/bitch & scratch her eyes out. APU

A Renewal. James Merrill. Love buries itself in me, up to the hilt. OBSP; PoPl; SM

The Renewal. Theodore Roethke. I find that love, and I am everywhere. VGW

Renewal by Her Element. Denis Devlin. My landscape is grey rain/Aslant on bent seas. CIP

Reno, 2 a.m. Sam Hamill. ...They dream of California/as tho from here/ there is no where else to go. TAT

Renoir's Confidences. J. Michael Pilz. Will they shatter the moment's quiet perfection? AMV-81

Renouncement. Alice Meynell. I run, I run, I am gathered to thy heart. AnFE; BoLoP; CAW; GoTF; GTBS; HBV 1-2; LiTL; MoBrPo; NOBE; OBEV; OBMV; OBNC; OBVV; TreFT; ViBoPo

A Renouncing of Love. Sir Thomas Wyatt. Me list no longer rotten boughs to climb. EnLi 1-2; Enlit; EnPo; FaBoEn; GBL; LiTL; OAEP; SiPS

The Renowned Generations. William Butler Yeats. Drown all the dogs,' said the fierce young woman. OxBoLi

Rent. Jane Cooper. Not a roof but a field of stars. FYAP; TAP

Renunciants. Edward Dowden. –Comrade, it serves to feel/The sackcloth next the skin. OBVV

Renunciation. Wathen Mark Wilks Call. A child of human hopes and human fears. OBVV; WGRP

A Renunciation. Henry, Bishop of Chichester King. Now turn from each: so fare our sever'd hearts/As the divorced soul from her body parts. OBEV

Renunciation. P. H. Pearse. To the deed that I see/And the death I shall die. NOBI

Reparation. Helen Hoyt. All of the earth of love/And love's high heaven! HBMV

Reparation or War. *Anonymous.* Then none but slaves shall bend to tyranny. PAH

Repartee. Charles Follen Adams. "You know I'm D E F!" OBAL

Repartee. *Anonymous.* "Yes, love," said he, "by marriage." GoTF; TreFT

Repast. Gertrude Tiemer-Wille. From can–to can–to can. GoYe

The Repeated Journey. Thomas McGrath. ...years whose casual ignorant lovers/We were for a season. NePoEA

Repeated Pilgrimage. John Gilland Brunini. Would rise to parch my throat–and I would flee. GoBC

Repentance. George Chapman. My soul's dark offspring, willing it should die/To loves, to passions, and society. OBSC

Repentance. George Herbert. Fractures well cur'd make us more/strong. OAEP

Repentance. George Alexander Stevens. Be henceforth Repentance a stranger to Love. NOEC

Repentance. Louis Untermeyer. But first let's learn to do what Jane has done. NLV

Repetition. Wyatt Prunty. Where memory folds like calloused hands. AMV-81

Repetition of Words and Weather. Ruth Stone. It won't be changed with words. BoWoP

Repetitions. Carl Sandburg. Cheap as sunlight,/And morning air. HBMV

Repetitions of a Young Captain. Wallace Stevens. In a beau language without a drop of blood. WaP

The Repetitive Heart. Delmore Schwartz.
And the past is immortal, the future is inexhaustible! ViBoPo
The scrimmage of appetite everywhere. MoVE

Reply. Hartley Coleridge. Tho' love was kind, why should we fear,/But holy death is kinder? OBRV

Reply. Sidney Godolphin. but he by this Diviner Art/makes conquest of the Heavenly part. OBS

The Reply. Philip Levine. Which bears eternity/To the last command. PoA

Reply. Victoria McCabe. ...I'm scratching/for the whole paragraph. PoL

Reply. Sir Walter Ralegh. To live with thee and be thy love. ViBoPo

The Reply. Theodore Roethke. A man, a man alive. NoP; NYBP

A Reply from the Akond of Swat. Ethel Talbot Scheffauer. You know why, and for whom, and for what. FiBHP

The Reply of Socrates. Edith Matilda Thomas. Behold! He, too, hears but the voice of the Laws, the flutes of/the God! WGRP

Reply to a Creditor. George Harding. Dear Messrs. T., I'm yours without a farthing./For executors and self, GEORGE HARDING FaBoUs

Reply to a Marriage Proposal. Irihapeti Rangi te Apakura. The lips are made to taste with/but the body is firmly held. PBWP

A Reply to an Imitation of the Second Ode....of Horace. Richard Bentley. Yet left Content, a Genuine Stoick He,/Great without Patron, rich without South-Sea! OBEC

Reply to Dipsychus. Arthur Hugh Clough. Whom God deludes is well deluded. FaBoCo

Reply to In Flanders Fields. John Mitchell. To you who sleep where poppies grow/In Flanders Fields. BLPA; PAL

A Reply to Lines by Thomas Moore. Walter Savage Landor. It would give me a cough, and a rheumatise too... ChTr

Reply to Mr. Wordsworth (excerpt). Archibald MacLeish. How break and enter what will only bend? ImOP

A Reply to Nancy Hanks. Julius Silberger. He lives in the heart/Of everyone. TiPo

Reply to the Committed Intellectual. Francis Sparshott. of a white face framed in our avid gunsight. NOBC

Reply to the Provinces. Galway Kinnell. Pointing out for each other the brown faces in the leaves. NYBP

Reply to the Question: "How Can You Become a Poet?" Eve Merriam. where there is no leaf left/invent one. DFF

A Reply to Zaidun's Complaint... Wallada. From every cloud, in mighty streams, to refresh it! PBWP

The Report. Jon Swan. And, after the subway, walk up to the night. NYBP

Report from a Far Place. William Stafford. ...they/burn, or don't burn, in their own/strange way, when you say them. CAPP

Report from a Planet. Richmond Lattimore. ...a handful of men./No two from one country. FYAP

Report from California. Lois Moyles. for truly they are soothed with drifting. NYBP

Report from the Carolinas. Helen Bevington. Pines and magnolias. Also, we have lately,/Certain uncertainties–. AmFN

Report from the Correspondent They Fired. David McElroy. ...we could be hams/curing in the shade, good to eat. AmPA

Report on Experience. Edmund Charles Blunden. Over there are faith, life, virtue in the sun. CBEP; FaBoTw; GTBS-P; NOBE; OBMV; OBWP

A Report Song in a Dream, between a Shepherd and His Nymph. Nicholas Breton. But I waked, and all was done. GBL; OBSC; SeCePo

The Reporters. Newman Levy. The bold, reprehensible, brave, indispensable/Sensible lads of the press. InMe

Reportless subjects, to the quick. Emily Dickinson. But like an Oriental Tale/To others, fabulous– NOBA

The Reports Come In. J. D. Reed. and scratching in its underwear,/fumbles for a heritage. NYBP

Reports of Midsummer Girls. Richmond Lattimore. ...to share the light/of lost long days before midsummer ends. PCP

Le Repos en Egypte. Agnes Repplier. Lay stretched o'er-wearied. On my breast of stone/Rested the Crucified. CAW; ISi

Repose. Alfred Lichtenstein. Three children stand around in silence. VWA

Repose of Rivers. Hart Crane. And willows could not hold more steady sound. AP; AWP; CMoP; CoBMV; ExPo; ForPo; InPo; LiTM; MoAB; MoAmPo; NoAm; NOBA; OxBA; SeCeV

Repression. Timothy Corsellis. Here there is a real despair. WaP

Repression of War Experience. Siegfried Sassoon. I'm going stark, staring mad because of the guns. BrPo; CMoP; MMM; NoAm

Reprieve. Barbara Villy Cormack. Thank God,–thank God for rain! CaP

The Reprisall. George Herbert. The man, who once against thee fought. AnAnS 1

Reprisals. William Butler Yeats. Then close your ears with dust and lie/Among the other cheated dead. OBWP

Reproach. Firdausi. Were thy beauty mine own, or thy lips, or thine eyes. LiTW

Reproach to Julia. Robert Graves. Yourself to love, still haggling at the price. ELU; FaBoEE

A Reproach to Morvyth. Dafydd ap Gwilym. ...nay, depart not against my will:/never shouldst thou depart with it! LiTW

La Reproduction Interdite / Not to Be Reproduced. Kathleen Fraser. ...each a potential source of precision/and invention, given a hand to hold it. NPGG

Reproduction of Life. Erasmus Darwin. And breaks in hemispheres the obdurate shell. PBBP

Reproof. Anonymous. "My child," He said, "what could I do?/You never did let go!" STF

The Republic 1939. James Liddy. But dried among the bric-a-brac/On mantlepieces of Peru and Mexico. CIP

Republic to Republic. Witter ("Emanuel Morgan") Bynner. And the name you called me then/I call you now–/O Liberty, my Love! PAH

The Repulse. Thomas Stanley. That I was never blest. AnAnS 2; MeLP; MePo; OBS

The Request. Abraham Cowley. My Verses shall not onely wound, but murther Thee. AnAnS 2

Request for a Song. Julian Tuwim. the bullets of my quick sixshooter glittering song. LiTW

Request for Meat and Drink. Sedulius Scottus. So off to the Bishop, my Muse, and make my request. NOBI

Request for Requiems. Langston Hughes. Cause there ain't a good man/Like me left around. ShM

Request Numbers. G. N. Sprod. And pea-green zombie with X-ray eyes. FiBHP

Request of a Dying Child. Lydia Huntley Sigourney. And from the everlasting hills,/A song of rapture pour'd. OBCA

Request to a Year. Judith Wright. reach back and bring me the firmness of her hand. CBAP; FaBoWP

Requests. Digby Mackworth Dolben. To take me home/Within Thy Heart to be. TrPWD

Requiem. F. Norreys Connell. But I thank Thee, God, for my life! HBV 1-2

Requiem. Kenneth Fearing. And everywhere, on all of it, the brightness of the sun. CMoP

Requiem. Ivor Gurney. My dead friend's face as well. FaBoEE; FaBoTw

Requiem. Joseph Lee. Soldier, sleep sound! OHIP

Requiem. George Lunt His life he gave! AA

Requiem. John Frederick Matheus. But not, my beloved, will fading wither you. CDC

Requiem. Theodore Maynard. Then turn aside and leave my dust in earth. GoBC

Requiem. Martin T. O'Connor. And kind hearts tire/Too soon, too soon. AMV-80

Requiem. Kathleen Raine. Your death my passion. NeBP

Requiem. William Stafford. beyond our hearing is the hearing of the community. NaP

Requiem. Robert Louis Stevenson. And the hunter home from the hill. AnFE; BBV; BrPo; BSV; DL; FaBV; FaPoR; FPL; GoTF; GoTS; GTBS; HBV 1-2; HBVY; MCCG; MoBrPo; NLV; NOBE; NOBV; OBEV; OBNC; OBVV; OHFP; PoLf; PoPl; PoRA; TreF; TrGrPo; ViBoPo; WGRP; WHA

A Requiem. James (1834-82) Thomson. Couched triumphant, calm and brave,/In the ever-holy grave. EnLit; HBV 1-2

Requiem. Stephen Vincent. her four sons, my father/and me NeAC

Requiem. Hamilton Warren. And lies dreaming/Of sunlight on viable water. GoYe

Requiem 1935-1940. Anna Akhmatova. let the prison dove call in the distance/and the boats go quietly on the Neva. BoWoP

Requiem after Seventeen Years. Dahlia Ravikovich. it is the sea/that gives life to the rivers. VWA

Requiem for a River.   Kim Williams.   "We concreted the dam," Bert said./ Thanks.   RFM

Requiem for a Young Soldier.   Florence Earle Coates.   Who, content, to-night are sleeping–/Painless, dreamless, there!   OHIP

Requiem for and Abstract Artist.   Jascha Kessler.   with no address/but this home in time, this I?   AmPC

Requiem for "Bird" Parker.   Gregory Corso.   first and second and third voice/yeah, yeah.   PoNe

Requiem for My Mother.   Keorapetse Kgositsile.   Before they disappear beyond/These white-hooded mountains and appetites.   WhB

A Requiem for Soldiers Lost in Ocean Transport.   Herman Melville.   Nor heed they now the lone bird's flight/Round the lone spar where mid-sea surges pour.   PoEL 1-5

Requiem for Sonora.   Richard Shelton.   yours is the only death I cannot bear.   Psk

Requiem for the Croppies.   Seamus Heaney.   And in August the barley grew up out of the grave.   BIrV; CIP; FaBoIP; FaBoMo; OBWP

Requiem for the Plantagenet Kings.   Geoffrey Hill.   ...the sea/Across daubed rock evacuates its dead.   NoAm

Requiescant.   Frederick George Scott.   O house them in the home of God!   OHIP

Requiescat.   Matthew Arnold.   To-night it doth inherit/The vasty hall of death.   AWP; BoLiVe; ELP; EnLi 1-2; EnLit; FiP; GoTF; GTBS; HBV 1-2; HeIP; InPo; InvP; LiTB; LiTL; MaVP; NOBE; OAEP; OBEV; OBVV; PG; PoRA; TreFS; ViBoPo; WHA

Requiescat.   Katherine Anne Porter.   She has well chosen silence/With her hands crossed.   HBMV

Requiescat.   Rosamund Marriott Watson.   Lest my poor dust should dream of you.   HBV 1-2

Requiescat.   Oscar Wilde.   Heap earth upon it.   BrPo; EnLit; GoTF; GTBS; HBV 1-2; InvP; MoBrPo; OBNC; OBVV; OnYI; OxBI; TreF; TrGrPo; WHA

Required Course.   Frances Stoakley Lankford.   Whose language he would live, upon the way.   GoYe

Required of You This Night.   Peter Redgrove.   Not for you anyway, Peter.   NMP

Requirements.   Rufinus Domesticus.   She consenting, I withstood.   ErPo

De Rerum Natura.   Andrei Codrescu.   ...With this secret method of defying birth controls I popu-/late the world with poets.   APU

De Rerum Natura.   Lucretius (Titus Lucretitus Carus).
And kindle with thy own productive fire.   OBVE
It rises from, and makes up things again.   OBVE
Thou wander'st in the Labyrinth of Life.   OBVE
Walking around in a world which produces plenty.   NAs
What gain to us would all this bustle bring?   CTC
Who dies today, and will as long be so,/As he who died a thousand years ago.   OAEL 1-2

The Rescue.   Robert Creeley.   They are running to arrive.   CAPP

Rescue.   Olive Tilford Dargan.   And a heart that begged to die/is keen again to face/A beckoning life.   GoYe

The Rescue.   John Logan.   it was my self you hauled/back from my despair.   CoAP; NYBP

Rescue.   Dabney Stuart.   Is the only depth I'll sound/That may save me from myself.   NYBP

Rescue.   Ellen Bryant Voigt.   as I wait on the dock,/braiding the long line that knots and tangles.   NoP

Rescue the Dead.   David Ignatow.   You who are free,/rescue the dead.   CAPP; ConAP; PrIm; VGW

The Rescued Year.   William Stafford.   and the sound that followed the couplings back/will ripple forward and hold the train.   LCAP

Resemblance.   *Anonymous.*   In the middle watch of the night.   WTO

Resentments Composed Because of the Clamor of Town Topers...   Sarah Kemble Knight.   O still their Tongues till morning comes!   SCAP

Reservation Special.   Lew Blockcolski.   Then he stuffs his black bag/with our lives and is gone/in his alphabet auto.   VoR

Reserve.   Richard Aldington.   I think of how the dead, my dead, once lay.   BrPo

Reserve.   Lizette Woodworth Reese.   Lacking that word, you shall be poor in-/deed.   AA

Reserve.   Mary Ashley Townsend.   Is greater still in that which he withholds.   AA

Reserved.   Walter De La Mare.   Preparing for the Night.   GTBS-P

The Reservoir.   Edward Field.   will it still be possible to reopen it, and explore?   GP

Residence in France: The Prelude.   William Wordsworth.   His days he wasted, an imbecile mind.   ChRP

The Resident Worm.   James Hayford.   Inhuman are the ways of God.   NePoAm-2

Residential Rhymes (excerpt).   Osman Edwards.   Brother-gods, they wait for me!   OBTV

Residue of Song.   Marvin Bell.   as if for the last time, believing that you will leave me.   AmPA

Resignation.   *Anonymous.*   To have my stars afford the world their shining.   OBSC

Resignation.   Matthew Arnold.
Fate gave, what chance shall not control,/His sad lucidity of soul.   FaBoRV
The something that infects the world.   MaVP; OAEP; VLP

Resignation.   Thomas Chatterton.   Which God, my east, my sun, reveals.   TrCP

Resignation.   Santob De Carrion.   Joy sure shall come behind.   TrJP

Resignation.   Walter Savage Landor.   In this, or in some other spot,/I know they'll shine again.   HBV 1-2; TreFT

Resignation.   Henry Wadsworth Longfellow.
And Christ Himself doth rule.   TRV
The grief that must have way.   HBV 1-2

Resignation.   Sir Thomas Wyatt.   Since women use so much to feign.   OBSC

Resignation: an Ode to the Journeymen Shoemakers (excerpt).   John Wolcot.   A truth that Grandeur wishes not to know.   NOEC

Resignation–To Faustus.   Arthur Hugh Clough.   So leave but perfect to my eye/Thy columns set against thy sky!   VLP

Resigning from a Job in a Defense Industry.   Sandra McPherson.   ...the mania/of waters above torpedoes.   LCAP

The Resolute Courtier.   Thomas Shipman.   When his thin wheyish blood/Is far less comfortable than his tears?   ErPo; GBL

Resolution.   Ted Berrigan.   & Don't You Tread On Me.   ANYP; OFD

Resolution.   William Stanley Merwin.   The clock dropping its shoes and/No floor   NYBP

The Resolution.   Vassar Miller.   The candle in its sconce.   CoPo

Resolution.   Henry More.   Mistrust of GOD's good providence/Doth daily vex their wearied sense.   OxBoCh

Resolution.   Charles L. O'Donnell.   For fear You may not strike again/I will not draw the steel.   GoBC; TrPWD

Resolution.   Wiolar".   Pierrot whistled down the wind–/And of course I went!   InMe

Resolution and Independence.   William Wordsworth.   I'll think of the leech-gatherer on the lonely moor!   BoNaP; CABA; CBEP; DiPo; EBEV; ERoP 1-2; FaBoRV; HAP; InPS; LiTB; MasP; MAT; MBW 1-2; NOBE; NOCV; NoP; OAEL 1-2; OAEP; OBNC; OBRV; PAI; Par; PoEL 1-5; PPP; SpRo; TEP

Resolution in Four Sonnets.   Charles Cotton.
And (which is worse) too modest to consent.   PoEL 1-5
Sh'as no more wit to ask than to deny.   PoEL 1-5; Prf
Though ask'd, I know not how she would resist.   PoEL 1-5
Unless he offer more than she demands.   PoEL 1-5

Resolution of Dependence.   George Barker.   The equation is the interdependence of parts.'   FaBoTw; LiTB; LiTM

Resolutions?–New and Old.   Harvey E. Rolfe.   If only to Jesus you'll yield your all,/He'll give His best unto you.   STF

The Resolve.   Alexander Brome.   Else I'm a servant to the glass/That's with Canary lined.   CavP; EG; LiTL; OBEV

The Resolve.   Mary Lee, Lady Chudleigh.   A Mind, that triumphs over Vice and Fate,/Esteems it mean to court the World for Praise.   OBEC

Resolve.   Charlotte Perkins Stetson Gilman.   Back to the way!   PoToHe; WGRP

The Resolve.   Denise Levertov.   The sound now/is a direct, intense/sound of/direction.   RFM

Resolved.   Ottis Shirk.   Be able every day to live/And be a better man.   STF

Resolving Doubts.   William Dickey.   And should that happen, I will think him you.   ErPo

Resort.   Kendrick Smithyman.   ...What will/the dinghies do then?   OCNZ

Resound My Voyse, Ye Wodes That Here Me Plain.   Sir Thomas Wyatt.   No grace to me from the there may procede,/But as rewarded deth for to be my mede.   AAS; FCP; SiPS

Resounding.   Katherine Soniat.   as a scattering of wild flowers.   AMV-81

Respect for the Dead.   Laura Riding.   Respect for your hate.   LiTA

Respectabilities.   Jon Silkin.   ...a fair if privileged/Mind veined with gold.   NePoEA-2; NoAm

Respectability.   Robert Browning.   Put forward your best foot!   EnLoPo; MBW 1-2; ViBoPo

The Respectable Burgher.   Thomas Hardy.   And read that moderate man Voltaire.   CMoP; NoAm; VLP

Respectable People.   Austin Clarke.   Memory finds beyond that last/ Improvidence, their mad remains.   CMoP; NMP

Respice Finem.   Thomas Proctor.   Your ancient years are but a withered grass.   OBSC

The Respite.   Ingeborg Bachmann.   A harder time is coming.   WPOW

Resplendent Studs of Heaven's Frame.   *Anonymous.*   Fine Lapis tandem coelo descendis ab alto/et fundum rursus, cum gravitate petid.   SCAP

Respondez!   Walt Whitman.   (What/do you suppose death will do, then?)   AmePo; NoAm; PoEL 1-5

Response. Mary Ursula Bethell. And "Everything is for a very short time." FaBoWP

Response. Bob Kaufman. As stars appear/In the dark/Skies. BOLo

Response to Rimbaud's Latter Manner. Thomas Sturge Moore. Which is the sun bound/In the arms of the sea. OBMV; SyP

Responses. Robert Hershon. yes he says/what is it? PoL

Responsibilities. J. C. Hall. I rejoice in their family fealty now. HaMV

Responsibilities: Prologue. William Butler Yeats. I have no child, I have nothing but a book,/Nothing but that to prove your blood and mine. PoEL 1-5

Responsibility. Anonymous. 'Tis a bloody big load to carry. FaBoUs; PV

A Responsory, 1948. Thomas Merton. Spring wine from their ivory/Or roses from their eyes? VGW

Ressaif My Saul. R. Crombie Saunders. Ressaif my saul, and lat it be/At ane with thy felicitie. OxBS

Rest. Anonymous. In this quiet corner, to fold your hands and sit. PoToHe

Rest. Mathilde Blind. But kneel to him she hates to crave/The absolution of the grave. SBG

Rest. John Henry, Cardinal Newman. The verses of that hymn which Seraphs chant above. OBRV; OBVV

The Rest. Ezra Pound. I have beaten out my exile. AmP; MoAB; MoAmPo; NoAm; NOBA; OxBA; PP

Rest. Christina Georgina Rossetti. And when she wakes she will not think it long. EnLi 1-2; HBV 1-2; NOBE; OAEL 1-2; OBEV; OBNC; OBVV; TrGrPo

Rest. Jacob Isaac Segal. on a silvery afternoon/talk is filled with light. VWA

Rest and Silence. Georg Trakl. The Sister appears in autumn and black decay. LiTW

Rest from Loving and Be Living. C. Day-Lewis. Sink lower, fade, as dark womb/Recedes creation will step clear. CoBMV; MoBrPo; OBMV

Rest Hour. George Johnston. Tell the hour of Andrew's resting. WHW

Rest in Peace. Wilfred J. Funk. Shield him with Thy smile. PoLf

Rest Is Not Here. Carolina Oliphant, Lady Nairne. All things around me tell/Rest is found there. HBV 1-2

Rest O Sun I Cannot. Joseph Tusiani. I cannot, till I reconcile my time/With your eternal charity of light. GoYe

Rest of the Weary. Anonymous. Thine to be ever, Savior and Friend. BePJ

Rest Only in the Grave. James Clarence Mangan. That House is narrow, and dark, and small–/But the only Peaceful House of all. BIrV

The restful place, reviver of my smart. Sir Thomas Wyatt. Wherefore with tears, my bed, I thee forsake. FCP; SiPS

Resting Place. Jon Silkin. ...Angel of death/made of desire and mercy raise your wings. VWA

Restless as a Wolf. Moishe-Leib Halpern. The rustle of a tree, a bell's peal,/smoke.... TrJP

The Restless Heart. Anonymous. Have mercy, Tuka says. WGRP

The Restless Heart. Henry Howard, Earl of Surrey. Against my will, full pleased with my pain. SiPS

The Restless State of a Lover. Henry Howard, Earl of Surrey. Rue on my life; or else your cruel wrong/Shall well appear, and by my death be seen. GoTL

Restoration. Woodridge Spears. It was a thrust of light restored him here. GoYe

The Restoration of Enheduanna to Her Former Station. Enheduanna. From the doorsill of heaven came the word:/"Welcome!" BoWoP

Restricted. Eve Merriam. Not/That I'd want my daughters ever to/But still,/Some of my–. TrJP

Restricted. Miriam Waddington. Though we are broken, they are whole. CaP

Results of a Scientific Survey. Bruce Cutler. fleet images frozen forever. AMV-80; FAZ

The Results of Stealing a Pin. Anonymous. So let us avoid all little sinnings,/Since such is the end of petty beginnings. FaBoUs

Resume. Dorothy Parker. You might as well live. ALV; DBV; DL; HeIP; InMe; InPK; NLV; NoP; OBAL; PoPl; ShM; TrJP

Resurgam. Anonymous. The shadow of the great White Throne/Falls broader, deeper, year by year. WGRP

Resurgam. W. Nelson Bitton. Blessed be God, who bides in grace and turns not from our/prayer. BLRP

Resurgam. Struthers Burt. I cannot grasp the rapture now of you,/Who were so close to dawn, and trees, and dew. HBMV

Resurgam. Marjorie Pickthall. Love is the end.' OBCV; TrCP

Resurge San Francisco. Joaquin Miller. Farewell, forever and a day! PAH

Resurgence. Laura Bell Everett. Bring near the Brotherhood of Man. PGD

Resurgence. Jalal ed-Din or al-Din Rumi. Let me be Naught! The harp-strings tell me plain/That "unto Him do we return again!" LiTW

Resurrection. Richard P. Blackmur. Instead there are a thousand in her shrouds/swarming to set the sails that are not there. PoA

The Resurrection. Jonathan Henderson Brooks. That breathed the living breath of spring. AmNP; CDC; PoNe

Resurrection. George Crabbe. And Nature has her types to show/Throughout the varying year. OxBoCh

Resurrection. John Donne. Salute the last, and everlasting day. AnAnS 1; OBS

Resurrection. Kenneth Fearing. As you work, and sleep, and talk, and laugh, and die. CMoP

Resurrection. Frank Horne. and the laws of the prophets. OFD; PoBA

Resurrection. Saint John of Damascus. Our Christ hath brought us over/With hymns of victory. PGD

Resurrection. Marie L. Kaschnitz. Admitted early into a house of light. WPOW

Resurrection. Harry Kemp. And make God's perfect meadows doubly sweet/With rosy vagrancy of little feet. HBV 1-2

Resurrection. Sidney Lanier. Fain, fain am I, O CHRIST, to pass the grave! PoEL 1-5

Resurrection. Robert Pack. The sea sparkles with the sperm/Of his rejected light. NePoEA-2

Resurrection. Lady Margaret Sackville. Lived for a hour–then for all time were dead. HBMV

The Resurrection. William Edward Taylor. And died. AMV-80

The Resurrection. Nathaniel Wanley. Then will I rise and dress me lord for thee/Who did'st by death undress thee lord for me. LoBV

Resurrection–An Easter Sequence (excerpt). W. R. Rodgers. Yes, it was a hard death. ACV

Resurrection: Fragments. Felix Mnthali. and trying to come to terms/with bits of selves/shelved on the day of arrest. WhB

Resurrection Hymn. Michael Weiss. That we all may sing for aye,/Hallelujah! BePJ

Resurrection of Arp. A.J.M. Smith. and death, after all, was only "another room'. NOBC

Resurrection of the Dead. Aliza Shenhar. After all/nothing causes death/and nothing/brings to life. VWA

Resurrection of the Right Side. Muriel Rukeyser. all the blue flowers open LCAP

Resurrection Song. Thomas Lovell Beddoes. And pull up the nostrils! his nose was snub. ELU; ERoP 1-2; FaBoEE; NBM

Resurrexit. Henry Longan Stuart. For Love, that conquers Death and Fear,/Is risen–That was dead. CAW

Resuscitation Team. U. A. Fanthorpe. ...her face/Still in the rictus of victory? FaBoWP

Retaliation. Oliver Goldsmith.
He shifted his trumpet, and only took snuff. CEP; DBV; FaBoPV; LaA; NOBI; NOEC; OxBoLi
"Thou best humour'd man with the worst/humour'd muse." OAEP

The Retarded Children Find a World Built Just for Them. Diana O Hehir. They sing and sing like all the birds of the desert. NPGG

The Retarded Class at F.A.O. Schwarz's Celebrates Christmas. David Fisher. I am not sure I have earned a blue one. NPGG

Retinue. Paul Verlaine. of the insolent approving stare/of her familiar animals. ErPo

The Retired Boxer. Lucilius [(or Lucillius)]. because she never lets up,/even in bed–and she beats him there, too. LiSp

The Retired Cat. William Cowper. Will learn, in school of tribulation,/The folly of his expectation. FM; PCat

The Retired Colonel. Ted Hughes. And the last sturgeon of Thames. NePoEA-2

Retired Farmer. David Allan Evans. he figured he was in motion. Psk

Retired This Hour from Wondering Crowds. Walter Savage Landor. Absorbed, and almost doubting it. GBL

Retirement. Anonymous.
Ah, God, ah God! 'tis food today/That feeds me and not kisses. ErPo; KiLC
Tasting the Glories that shall crown/An endless Life when this is done. OBEC

Retirement. William Cowper.
And what could a remoter scene show more? FaBoPP
Whom I may whisper, Solitude is sweet. BLPA

The Retirement. John Norris. 'Twill not be short, because 'tis all my own. CavP; OBS

Retirement. Richard Chenevix Trench. Keep thou thine heart close fasten'd, unreveal'd,/A fenced garden and a fountain seal'd. OBVV

Retirement, an Ode (excerpt). Thomas Warton, Sr.. Meet to adore some Calf of Gold. ViBoPo

The Retirement of the Elephant. Russell Edson. Goddamn everything! AmPA

Retort. Paul Laurence Dunbar. "Thou art worse than a fool, O head!" AA

Return to Ararat. Martyn Halsall. And his tears were thicker than forty days of rain. TrCP

Return to Astolat. Gail White. for days when it rains too hard/to be trowelling in the garden. AMV-81

Return to Dachau. B. Z. Niditch. and I begin to be afraid. AMV-81

Return to Hinton. Charles Tomlinson. a mill-race for an unglimpsed fish? CMo?

Return to Lake Emily Chequamegon National Forest. Richard Behm. ...dance with them/this silent, simple dance. WOLT

Return to Lane's Island. William H. Matchett. Where I could not escape the rote of the rolling waves. PoPl

Return to Life. Abbie Huston Evans. I make free with myself at last; I see that we are friends. NePoAm

Return to Prinsengracht. Janice Blue-Swartz. and we are seized by the cold terror/and sudden realization of discovery. AMV-81

Return to Ritual. Mark Van Doren. Listen! The dust is humming a song to the men. MoVE

Return to Sirmio. Caius Valerius Catullus. till the Lydian lakes re-echo all the laughter in my home. LiTW

Return to Spring. Florence Ripley Mastin. You who perceive this thing, you shall return to spring. GoYe

A Return to the Tree of Time. Vesna Parun. but let me sing and return/to the root of my song, the deepest to me. WPOW

Return to the Valley. Elfreida Read. And marvel at the simple amnesty of soil. AMV-80

The Return to Work. William Carlos Williams. slapping her thighs. CTBA; NYBP

Returned to Frisco. W.D. Snodgrass. Stood like the closed gate of your own backyard. AP

Returned to Say. William Stafford. Our moccasins do not mark the ground. ConAP; NaP

Returning. Ruth Guthrie Harding. Let me lie till Thine Own Springtime with the pines be-/side my bed! HBV 1-2

Returning at Night. Jim Harrison. in the third phase/of the moon. VGW

Returning from Harvest. Vernon Watkins. Full harvest tilted high/In the ruts of tomorrow's ice. NYBP

Returning Home. Joachim Du Bellay. Sooner my Lyre, than all Mount Palatine,/Mild Anjou's air, than all the salt sea spate. LiTW

Returning Spring. Baron Joseph von Eichendorff. Oh, not for me/Comes spring a-winging. CAW

Returning to Roots of First Feeling. Robert Duncan. and restore lasting melodies of his desire. PoA

Returning to Store Bay. Barbara Howes. Alive in the muscular sea. Psk

Returning to the Fields. T'ao Ch'ien. Now I have turned again to Nature and Freedom. LiTW

Returning to the Town Where We Used to Live. Susan Musgrave. I wanted to be held/and to hold you like this. NOBC

Returning to the World. Laura Chester. ...streaming over the/roof of this room, and I am deep in my comforter. NPGG

Returning, We Hear the Larks. Isaac Rosenberg. Or her kisses where a serpent hides. BrPo; FaBoMo; MMM; OAEL 1-2; OBWP; VWA; WaaP

Reuben and Rachel. Harry Birch. Better or worse, we're in for life. PSoN

Reuben Bright. Edwin Arlington Robinson. ...and put some chopped-up cedar boughs/In with them, and tore down the slaughter-house. AmP; AnNE; MoAB; MoAmPo; NePA; NOBA; NoP; TAP; TrGrPo

Reuben James. James Jeffrey Roche. For God never ranks His sailors by the Regis-/ter of earth! PAH

Reuben Pantier. Edgar Lee Masters. Dear Emily Sparks! GLGT

Reuben Ranzo. Anonymous.
Ranzo, boys, Ranzo! AmFP; AmSS; ShS
Though Ranzo was no sailor,/He's first mate of that whaler. FSW

Reuben, Reuben. Anonymous. And I'll split with you my money/Every pay-day of my life. FSW

Reuben, Reuben. Michael S. Harper. we've lost a son,/the music, jazz, comes in. GeTw

Reuben's Cabin. Robert Morgan. ...What/are you thinking now in the/ silence circling up near Buzzard Rock? TAT

Reunion. Heather Cadsby. It's time to leave. AMV-81

Reunion. Paul Dehn. You are much uglier...and so am I. PV

Reunion. Carolyn Forche. ...voice/of a woman singing of a man/who could make her do anything. MAYP

Reunion. Judith Herzberg. but I did not know how/with difficult eyes. BoWoP

Reunion. William Stanley Merwin. Would you have known delight/If it had knocked you down? AmPC

Reunion. Edwin Arlington Robinson. But not so friendly and not quite so near. NoAm; NOBA

A Reunion. James Schuyler. You may get to like them. ANYP

Reunion. Cyril Tawney. You'll need to wait a long, long while. OBET

Reunited. Sir Gilbert Parker. My love to yours shall reach, then one deep moan/Of joy, and then our infinite Alone. OBEV; OBVV

Rev. Homer Wilbur's "Festina Lente." James Russell Lowell. And embryo Good, to reach full stature,/Absorbs the Evil in its nature. OBAL

The Rev. Nicholas Noyes to the Rev. Cotton Mather... Nicholas Noyes. New-Englands Thaumatorgos you shall be,/And have the thanks, both of the bond and Free. SCAP

Rev Owl. Abraham Moses Klein. To find them kosher/For an owl. TrJP

Le Reve. Edgar Bowers. Lay him who dreamed me still and, maybe, you. ConAP

Revealed. Harry Lyman Koopman. For they see, hear, smell, feel not/what Heaven reveals all about. AA

Reveille. Audrey Alexandra Brown. We will pass with the sword in the hand and the hand lifted. CaP

Reveille. John Godfrey. ...and I want you never to die. APU

The Reveille. Bret (Francis Bret Harte) Harte. For the great heart of the nation, throbbing, answered,/"Lord, we come!" GN; HBV 1-2; MC; OHIP; PAH; PAL

Reveille. Ted Hughes. Over the ashes of the future. PPP

Reveille. Michael O'Connor. Fall in! Fall in! AA; HBV 1-2

Reveille. Lola Ridge. Till the birds shall fly to the mountains/For one safe bough. AnAmPo; HBMV

Reveille. Louis Untermeyer. We rise, half-shaken, to the challenging hour,/And answer it–and go.... HBV 1-2

The Revel. Bartholomew Dowling. Hurrah for the next that dies! BLPA; HBV 1-2; OnYI

A Revel. Donagh MacDonagh. And I, like them, would be lost in time. NeIP

Revelation. Verne Bright. All things burn with God's white fire. BLRP; WBLP

Revelation. Jerald Bullis. –these, our streets of gold. AMV-81

Revelation. Warren F. Cook. That all is love which brings my Lord to me. BLRP

Revelation. Blanche Taylor Dickinson. But Lucifer saw himself, too, fair. CDC

Revelation. Robert Frost. So all who hide too well away/Must speak and tell us where they are. InPo

Revelation. Sir Edmund Gosse. And dares not clutch what Love was half revealing. OBEV; OBVV

Revelation. Carole C. Gregory. and when am I coming back to stay. BlSi

Revelation. Nancy Keesing. Rests in the earth, absolute and complete. PoAu 1-2

Revelation. Edwin Markham. Saw his bright hand send signals from the suns. WGRP

Revelation. David Meltzer. After dinner &/a Havatampa cigar. NeAP

Revelation. William Soutar. The mourners in the alien street/At their own doorways mourn. HaMV

Revelation. Robert Penn Warren. Something important above love, and about love's grace. AnFE; LiTA; MoPo; NePA; NoAM

The Revelation. William Carlos Williams. To search her eyes/For that quiet look– MoLP

The Revenant. Walter De la Mare. Now wrapt in the gross clay, bereft of life's breath. GBL

The Revenant. Robert Siegel. someday it will return to trouble you. GeTw

Revenge! Horace. A charred and blackened bough. AWP

Revenge. Robert Nugent, Earl Nugent. To speak the very truth of thee. PV

The Revenge. Pierre Ronsard. And I shall laugh my turn. AWP

The "Revenge." Alfred, Lord Tennyson. And the little Revenge herself went down by the island crags/To be lost evermore in the main. BeLS; DTo; FaBoCh; FaPo; HBV 1-2; MaC; MCCG; OAEP; OBWP; OnMSP; PoRA

Revenge Fable. Ted Hughes. His head fell off like a leaf. TW

The Revenge of America. Joseph Warton. The rage that sweeps my sons away,/My baneful gold shall well repay.' OBTV

The Revenge of Hamish. Sidney Lanier. And the wind drove a cloud to seaward, and the sun/ began to shine. AP; PoEL 1-5

The Revenge of Rain-In-The-Face. Henry Wadsworth Longfellow. In the Year of a Hundred Years. BBV; BPAW; PAH

Revenge of the Hunted. R. A. D. Ford. and here the judgment of the wood. LiSp

Revenge to Come. Sextus Propertius. Your beauty waits this ending. Woman, believe–and/fear! AWP; LiTW

The Revenger's Tragedy (excerpt). Cyril Tourneur. You deceive men, but cannot deceive worms. ViBoPo

Revenue Man Blues. Charlie Patton. I have been a good provider, but I/B'lieve I been misled BluL

Reverdure. Wendell Berry. ...Good work done/comes back into the mind,/a free breath drawn. SaC

The Reverend Mr. Higginson... Edward Johnson. Him here retain, blest he whom Christ hath call'd. SCAP

Reverie. Don (Donald Robert Marquis) Marquis. O little sad sardine, I fear/Our world is full of woe! FPL; PoLf

Reverie at Dawn. Egan O'Rahilly. One morning before Titan thought of stirring his feet. AnIL; FaBoPV; KiLC

Reverie of a Mum. Nancy Keesing. And that was my castle in Spain. CBAP; NOAV

The Reverie of Poor Susan. William Wordsworth. And the colors have all passed away from her eyes! CH; ERoP 1-2; GTBS; GTBS-P; HBV 1-2; MBW 1-2; MCCG; OxBoLi; WiR

The Reversible Metaphor. Troubadour". Can make me see each time anew/The beauty of the rose? InMe

Reversion. Barry O. Higgs. Of her wonderful wonderful snout. PeSA

Reversionary. Stevie Smith. The world inherits wormliness. FaBoEE

Revertere. Anonymous. And then is best, Revertere. PBBP

Review from Staten Island. Gloria C. Oden. the unlearned depths of me. NNP; PoBA; PPP

Revised Notes for a Sonnet (parody). Edward Pygge. Then shave myself with Uncle's full-dress sabre. BXAP

Revisiting the Field. Walter Pavlich. Didn't we all block big as trees. AMV-81

The Revival. Henry Vaughan. The lilies of his love appear! BoLiVe; NOCV; OBS; OxBoCh; PoEL 1-5; PoPle; TrGrPo

Revival Hymn. Joel Chandler Harris. Ax de Lord fer ter fetch you up higher! HBV 1-2; MCCG

A Revivalist in Boston. Adrienne Rich. He made us hear the ranks of shining feet/Treading to glory's throne up Tremont Street. EaLo

Revive Us Again. John J. and William Porter Mackay Husband. Hallelujah! Thine the glory,/Revive us again! FSW

Revolt. Rachel (Rachel Blumstein). Lie down in your corner of darkness till I return,/till I return from him. VWA

The Revolt of Islam. Percy Bysshe Shelley.
　And did with soft attraction ever draw/Their spirits to the love of freedom's equal law. ChRP
　Heavily borne away on the exhausted blast. ChRP
　Swayed in the air:– ChRP
　This playmate sweet,/This child of twelve years old. GN
　...Thus the vast array/Of those fraternal bands were reconciled that day. OBWP

The Revolution. Jack Gilbert. Amid the primary colors of the island, he will/become a fine thing, perhaps, but a different one. NPGG

Revolution. Lesbia Harford. Than home or palace gardens/If she is there. PoAu 1-2

Revolution. Alfred Edward Housman. 'Tis silent, and the subterranean dark/ Has crossed the nadir, and begins to climb. BrPo; ImOP; NoP; OBSP

Revolution. Musaemura Bonus Zimunya. I warn you not to be deceived by the top:/vast tumular hordes abound beneath the surface. WhB

The Revolutionaries. R. P. Lister. While we erect in your old places/Something considerably worse. NOBL

Revolutionary. James P. Friel. too young/to ever have given AMV-81

Revolutionary Dreams. Nikki Giovanni. i would have a revolution CNA; GP

Revolutionary Letter #19. Diane Di Prima. you can have what you ask for, ask for/everything IHMS

Revolutionary Letters. Diane Di Prima.
　good morning brother, let me/fight by your side GP
　...heavy deeds/make heavy hearts and to them/life is suffering. stand clear. GP
　our babes toddle barefoot thru the cities of the universe. GP
　the word has power, the chant is going up. GP

Revolutionary Petunias. Alice Walker. "Don't yall forgit to water/my purple petunias." BlSi

The Revolutionary Screw. Don L. Lee. now/that was/revolutionary. GP

The Revolving Door. Newman Levy. While friends, heartbroken, search for Paul/MacGregor James D. Cuthbert Hall. ShM

Revving Up La Reve. Joel Dailey. I dream of/The New Now,/nebulous, nomadic. APU

The Reward of Innocent Love. William Habington. And add a perfume to our dust. ACP

Reward of Service. Elizabeth Barrett Browning. Thou shalt be served thyself by every sense/Of service which thou renderest. BLPA; FaBoBe

Reward of Virtue. Arthur Guiterman. I picked his pocket of his little book. InMe

The Rewards of Farming. Anonymous. Long Life and Success to the Farmer! PoPle

Rex Mundi. David Gascoyne. If you hear it in the distance, do not scorn the herald's note. ChMP

Reynard the Fox. Anonymous. Tally-ho hark-away, Tally-ho hark-away, Tally-ho hark-/away/My boys, away, hark-away! OnYI

Reynard the Fox (excerpt). John Masefield.
　And rest in peace till another day. NAMP; ViBoPo
　He breathed deep pleasure and trotted on. OBNV
　This life was not a dream that passes/To Ock, but like the summer flower. CMoP

Rhapsodies. Cyril Dabydeen. I bang on the empty drums/alone BrSi

Rhapsody. William Stanley Braithwaite. Like sheep from the rains and thunders. BALP; BANP

Rhapsody. Frank O'Hara. ...as I historically/belong to the enormous bliss of American death. NoAm; NYP

A Rhapsody (excerpt). Henry Vaughan. Hunts for a mate, and the tired footman reels/'Twixt chairmen, torches, and the hackney wheels. FaBoPP

A Rhapsody of Old Men, VII. Dimitris Tsaloumas. and the stigma of my shame. CBAP

Rhapsody of the Deaf Man. Tristan Corbiere. Silence is golden–St. John Chrysostom. LiTW

Rhapsody on a Windy Night. Thomas Stearns Eliot. The last twist of the knife. ACV; CMoP; ExPo; HeIP; InPo; InPS

A Rhapsody, Written at the Lakes in Westmorland. John Brown. All things at rest, and imaged the still voice/Of Quiet whispering to the ear of Night. NOEC

A Rhemish Carol. Robert Finch. While you, you have champagne. NAs

The Rhetoric of Langston Hughes. Margaret Danner. and dedicated ourselves/to be unraveling. BlSi; FB

Rhinoceros. William Hart-Smith. Have another cheese straw! BoAnP

The Rhinoceros. Ogden Nash. I'll stare at something less prepoceros. CenHV; FiBHP; MoAmPo; OBAL; OnUR

Rhinoceros. Adrien Stoutenburg. or merely the pause/between monster and monster. BoAnP

Rhoda Pitkin. Edgar Lee Masters. Out of the books which Ezra Fink/ Gave and controlled for Spoon River? NoAm

Rhodanthe. Agathias. And bring us to that haven of her breast. AWP

Rhode Island. William Meredith. ...He just lays there. NoP

Rhododaphne. Thomas Love Peacock.
　But the god the pilot pitied,/Saved, and made him rich and great. OBRV
　Which never more, oh youth! believe,/Shall either earth or heaven unweave. OBRV

The Rhododendron Plant. Allen Katzman. only the beauty is/real. WeW

The Rhodora. Ralph Waldo Emerson The self-same Power that brought me/there brought you. AA; AnNE; AP; APA; AWP; BoNaP; FaBV; FaFP; GN; HBV 1-2; HBVY; HeIP; InPo; LiTA; MAmP; MCCG; NOBA; NoP; OHFP; OxBA; SeCeV; TAP; TreFS; TrGrPo; TRV; WHA

Rhoecus. James Russell Lowell. But from that eve he was alone on earth. AA; MCCG

Rhotus on Arcadia. John Chalkhill. Shrinking beneath the burden of the Flesh. OBS

The Rhyme. Robert Creeley. and behind her there were/flowers, and behind them/nothing. AmPC

A Rhyme-beginning Fragment. Anonymous. Ere I be brought to ground. AnIL

Rhyme for a Chemical Baby. Joseph Cook. Men began to reign. QQQ; SpRo

Rhyme for a Child Viewing a Naked Venus in a Painting... Robert Browning. Amazed, amazed, amazed, amazed. NOBV

Rhyme for a Geological Baby. Joseph Cook. Lias and Trias and that is enough. QQQ; SpRo

Rhyme for Astronomical Baby. Joseph Cook. Mother takes by calculation/ The angle of its inclination. QQQ; SpRo

Rhyme for Botanical Baby. Joseph Cook. She'll make up her mind not to mind them. QQQ; SpRo

Rhyme for Night. Joan Aiken. Without dark, how could we sleep? DuDa

Rhyme for Remembering How Many Nights There Are in the Month. Justin Richardson. And twenty-eight each un-leap year. FaBoUs

Rhyme for Remembering the Date of Easter. Justin Richardson. That Easter on the first Sunday after the full moon/following the vernal equinox doth fall. FaBoUs

Rhyme for Remembrance of May. Richard Burton. May means remembering you! HBMV

Rhyme for the Child as a Wet Dog. Judith Johnson Sherwin. The rabbits' ears, the birds' beaks/on call. TAP

Rhyme from Grandma Goose. Annemarie Ewing. What kind of talent have you got? NePoAm

The Rhyme of Joyous Garde (excerpt). Adam Lindsay Gordon. But to perish as these things perish'd. PoAu 1-2

A Rhyme of Life. Charles Warren Stoddard. Till I have found the gates of pearl,/And anchored there. HBV 1-2

A Rhyme of One. Frederick Locker-Lampson. I'm glad, though I am old, you see,–/While you are One. HBV 1-2

Rhyme of Rain. John Holmes. "What a time to think of that,"/Said the first, and missed the hat. GrPl

The Rhyme of the Chivalrous Shark. Wallace Irwin. Though his record be dark, is the man-eating shark/Who will eat neither woman nor child. ShM

A Rhyme of the Dream-Maker Man. William Allen White. He'd given our dream to you. PoLf

Rhyme of the Fishermen's Children. Anonymous. An' blaw my father heame to my moother. GBP

The Rhyme of the Kipperling. Sir Owen Seaman. And the Fuzzy-wuz took the bag. CenHV

Rhyme of the Rails. John Godfrey Saxe. Bless me! this is pleasant,/Riding on the Rail! InMe; MoShBr; PoLf

The Rhyme of the Rain Machine. F.W. Clarke. And stopped the storm with a single word,/By just predicting–Rain! BoNaP

A Rhyme of the Sun-Dial. William Bell Scott. Hark, the bell tolls! up, sexton and delve! NOBV

The Rhyme of the Three Captains. Rudyard Kipling. "Shall dip their flag to a slaver's rag–to show that his trade is fair!" BeLS

Rhymed Dance Calls. Anonymous. Now the dude of the ballroom./Promenade to seats. CoSo

Rhymed Mnemonic of the Forty Counties of England. Donald Monat. Cornwall, Monmouth–that's enough. FaBoUs

Rhymes (?). Henry Sambrooke Leigh. Melpomene! assist me, please,/To somewhat higher heights to climb. NOBL

Rhymes. Y. Y. Segal. the rhymes were befriended/and my poem is ended. WHW

Rhymes. Frank Steele. "You can cut yourself on a sheet of paper/and your skin's about as thin." PPJ

Rhymes and Rhythms: Prologue. William Ernest Henley. Dear Heart, no more–no more. VLP

Rhymes for a Modern Nursery. Paul Dehn.
And died the following June. FiBHP
Dreadful sorry, Clementine. FiBHP; ShM
And killed my youngest daughter. FiBHP
Which frightened Miss Muffet to bits. FiBHP; ShM
Did you ever see such a neat little growth/On two blind mice? FiBHP

Rhymes of a Rolling Stone. Robert W. Service. Behold it, our Land of Beyond! TRV

Rhymes on the Road (excerpt). Thomas Moore. Some Mrs. Hopkins, taking tea/And toast upon the Wall of China! OBSV; OBTV

Rhymes to Be Traded for Bread: Prologue. Vachel Lindsay. Therefore, to-day the singer/Turns beggar once again. LaNeLa

A Rhymester. Samuel Taylor Coleridge. And only not so fast as we forget 'em. PV

Rhyming a Friend's Poem. Yu Hsuan-chi. And when I'm sad, I take it out again. BoWoP

Rhyming Prophecy for a New Year. Leonard Cooper. Same old names and same old faces; M.P.'s strike for/higher pay. FaBoCo

Rhyming with a Friend. Yu Hsuan-chi. Thready moss grows on the high hill between us. BoWoP

The Rhythm. Robert Creeley. light at the opening,/dark at the closing. CoPo; LiTM

Rhythm. Jean Percival Waddell. Cut the currents of strife. CaP

Rib Sandwich. William J. Harris. and didn't even/need a passport CNA

Ribald Romeos Less and Less Berattle. John Frederick Nims. And such old winter-bitten sticks and stems they/figure the hell with. MAT

The Ribbon-Fish. Robert Adamson. We have crossed the ocean and our paths are wakes of blood. CBAP

A Ribbon Two Yards Wide. Alfred Kreymborg. The king rides like a ghost on exhibition/To feed the faithful eye with superstition. HBMV

Ribh Considers Christian Love Insufficient. William Butler Yeats. How can she live till in her blood He live! TW

Rice. Carol Muske. Day without rice. AmPA

Rice and Rose Bowl Blues. Diane Mei Lin Mark. he'd heard/such a thing BrSi

Rice Pudding. A.(lan) A.(lexander) Milne. What is the matter with Mary Jane? BBGG

Rich and Poor; or, Saint and Sinner. Thomas Love Peacock. And a stench in the nose of piety. FaBoCo

Rich Days. William Henry Davies. And woodnuts rich, to make us go/Into the loneliest lanes we know. BoNaP

The Rich Interior Life. Richard Eberhart. The true heart plays at ease there,/In the music of those mornings. MoRP

A Rich Irish Lady. Anonymous. My follies ten thousand times over I see. FSW

A Rich Irish Lady (Sally). Anonymous. Ten thousand times over your Sally you'll see. AmFP

The Rich Lady from Dublin. Anonymous. Before you'll be through dancing o'er Sally our Queen. BFSS

The Rich Man. Franklin Pierce ("F.P.A.") Adams. You bet I would! FiBHP; InMe; NLV; OBAL

Rich Man. Anonymous. Doctor/Lawyer/Indian Chief. SaC

The Rich Man and the Poor Man. Anonymous. Glory Hallelujah, Hi ro jerum. FSW

Rich Mine of Knowledge. George Chapman. My love to you in my desire to learn. SeCePo

The Rich Old Lady. Anonymous. I love my darlin'-o. OuSiCo

A Rich Old Miser. Anonymous. Leddy and the day, day good day. AmFP

A Rich Tuft of Ivy. Suibne Geilt. I'm a sheep without a fold. NOBI

The Rich Widow. Anonymous. So as you go round, kiss her one, two, three. AmFP

Richard Cory. Edwin Arlington Robinson. And Richard Cory, one calm summer/night,/Went home and put a bullet through his/head. AmP; AnNE; CMoP; DiPo; DL; DTC; ExPo; FaFP; FF; ForPo; FPL; GoTF; HAP; InPK; LiTA; LiTM; LoGBV; MasP; MoAB; MoAmPo; MoVE; NePA; NIP; NOBA; NoP; OxBA; PoLf; PoRA; PrIm; SoSe; StPo; TAP; TreF; TrGrPo

Richard Cory (parody). Paul Simon. Oh I wish that I could be/Richard Cory. InPK

Richard Dick upon a Stick. Anonymous. To buy a horse to plough. OxNR

Richard Hunt's Arachne. Robert Earl Hayden. in the moment's centrifuge of dying/becoming FB

Richard II. William Shakespeare.
Bores through his castle wall, and farewell king! DiPo; DL
Dear for her reputation through the world... FaBV; FaPoR
Spurred, galled, and tired by jaucing Bolingbroke. PoPle
This nurse, this teeming womb of royal kings. FaBoPP

Richard III. William Shakespeare. Which almost burst to belch it in the sea. MOS

Richard Pigott, the Forger (excerpt). William McGonagall. And Parnell's life has been saved, which I consider/no sin. PeD

Richard, Richard: American Fuel. Melvin Dixon. the weighty echoes of Bessie's moan. LTB

Richard Roe and John Doe. Robert Graves. That most of all he wished himself John Doe. CMoP

Richard Somers. Barrett Eastman. His soul will leap to Ocean's arms! AA

Richard Tolman's Universe. Leonard Bacon. Except that I'm stuck for better or worse/In Tolman's elastic universe. ImOP

Richer. Aileen Fisher. but I have a birthday, so.../I feel finer. BiCB

Riches. Anonymous. And nought when old enjoy'd, denied the power. AWP

Riches. William Blake. Nor the secret hoard up in his treasury. BoLiVe; TrGrPo

Richie Story (A version). Anonymous. "For I've gotten my lot and my heart's/desire,/And what Providence has ordered for/me." BaBo; ESPB

Richie Story (B version). Anonymous. Monny an halled that gay lady,/But fue halled Richerd Storry. ESPB

The Rick of Green Wood. Edward Dorn. ...talking/pleasantly, of the green wood and the dry. NeAP; PoM

The Riddle. Anonymous. Be you my Sun, I'll be your Marigold. UnTE

The Riddle. W. H. Auden. Every living creature is/Woman, Man, and Child. EnLi 1-2

The Riddle. Alexander Brome. And let our pains be less, or power more. OBS

A Riddle. William Cowper. And yielded with pleasure when taken by force. HBV 1-2

Riddle. William Heyen. But who killed the Jews? GP; SM

The Riddle. Ralph Hodgson. Guess who knew he'd got them wrong. PoPl

The Riddle. Georgia Douglas Johnson. White men's children in black men's skin. PoBA

A Riddle. Martial (Marcus Valerius Martialis). How can you be a man this morning? PeHV

A Riddle. Cynthia Ozick. Know how I comment,/solve my name in a moment. VWA

A Riddle. William Soutar. Will rive his linty locks awa/And lave him bell and bare. (a dandelion.) OxBS

A Riddle. Charlotte Zolotow. "But I'm not scared now/because of you." NTCP

Riddle #14: A Horn. Anonymous. Off into darkness. Ask my name. DiPo

Riddle 24 (Jay: Higora). Anonymous. ...Now I am named,/As these six letters clearly say. PBBP

Riddle #29: The Moon and the Sun. Anonymous. ...And no one/Knew where the soft-footed thief had vanished. GoJo

Riddle 7 (Mute Swan). Anonymous. I pass like a soul over land and sea. PBBP

Riddle 9 (Cuckoo). Anonymous. She had fewer in spite of all she had done. PBBP

Riddle: "A hill full, a hole full." Mother Goose. Yet you cannot catch a bowl full. SoPo; TiPo

Riddle: "A house full, a hole full." Anonymous. And you cannot gather a bowl full. OxNR

Riddle: "A long white barn." Anonymous. And no door at all, at all. GBP

Riddle: "A riddle, a riddle, as I suppose." Mother Goose. A hundred eyes and never a nose! OxNR; TiPo

Riddle: "A shoemaker makes shoes without leather." Anonymous. And every customer takes two pair. OxNR; SoPo

Riddle: "A white bird featherless floats down through the air." *Anonymous.* And never a tree but he lights there. GBP

Riddle: "A wide mouth, no ears nor eyes." *Anonymous.* Full forty at a meal. CoBE

Riddle: "Around the rick, around the rick." *Anonymous.* And left his body lying. OxNR

Riddle: "Arthur O'Bower had broken his bands." *Anonymous.* Canna turn Arthur O'Bower. GBP; OxNR

Riddle: "As black as ink and isn't ink." *Anonymous.* And hops about like a filly-foal. OxNR

Riddle: "As I was a-walking on Westminster Bridge." *Anonymous.* Now what was the name of this scholar? OxNR

Riddle: "As I was going o'er London Bridge." *Anonymous.* Not a man in all England/Can mend that. OxNR

Riddle; "As I was going o'er Tipple Tine." *Anonymous.* That ever went over Tipple Tine. OxNR

Riddle: "As I was walking in a field of wheat." *Anonymous.* I kept it till it ran alone. OxNR

Riddle: "As I went through a garden gap." *Anonymous.* If you'll tell me this riddle, I'll give you a groat. HBV 1-2; HBVY

Riddle: "As round as an apple, as deep as a cup." *Mother Goose.* And all the king's horses can't fill it up. OxNR; TiPo

Riddle: "As soft as silk, as white as milk." *Anonymous.* And a green coat over me all. GBP; HBV 1-2; HBVY; OxNR; PoPle

Riddle: "Banks fou, braes fou." *Anonymous.* Ye'll no gather your nieves fou. GBP

Riddle. Bible: "A stern destroyer struck out my life." *Anonymous.* I am helpful to men, and am holy myself. EnLi 1-2

Riddle: "Black I am and much admired." *Anonymous.* And take me from my resting bed. OxNR

Riddle: "Black within and red without." *Anonymous.* Four corners round about. GBP; OxNR

Riddle. Bookworm: "A moth ate a word." *Anonymous.* A whit the wiser when the word had been swallowed. EnLi 1-2

Riddle: "Close in a cage a bird I'll keep." *Anonymous.* It's notes yield sweet delight. CoBE

Riddle: "Clothed in yellow, red, and green." *Anonymous.* By lords and knights I am caressed. OxNR

Riddle: "Down by the waterside stand a house and a plat." *Anonymous.* Every one with a bell and a blue hat,/And what is that? GBP

Riddle: "Elizabeth, Lizzy, Betsy and Bess." *Anonymous.* They each took one and left four in it. HBV 1-2; HBVY; OxNR

Riddle: "Every lady in the land." *Anonymous.* All this is true without deceit. OxNR; PoPle

Riddle: "Fatherless an' motherless." *Anonymous.* An' niver spok' sin. GBP

Riddle: "First I am frosted." *Mary Austin.* Fourth, I am eaten. TiPo

Riddle: "First it was a pretty flower." *Christina Georgina Rossetti.* It will make a splendid pie for your/Thanksgiving Spread. SoPo

Riddle: "Flour of England, fruit of Spain." *Anonymous.* I'll give you a ring. HBV 1-2; HBVY; OxNR

Riddle; "Formed long ago, yet made today." *Anonymous.* Nor any wish to keep. HBV 1-2; HBVY; OxNR

Riddle: "Four and twenty white bulls." *Anonymous.* Forth came the red bull/And licked them all. GBP

Riddle: "Four stiff-standers." *Anonymous.* Two crookers,/And a wig-wag. GBP; OxNR

Riddle: "Goes through the mud." *Anonymous.* And only leaves one track. OxNR

Riddle: "He went to the wood and caught it." *Anonymous.* Home with him he brought it. GBP; OxNR

Riddle: "Hick-a-more, Hack-a-more." *Anonymous.* Hung on the kitchen door. OxNR

Riddle: "Higgledy-piggledy here we lie." *Anonymous.* Picked and plucked and put in a pie. OxNR

Riddle: "Higher than a house." *Mother Goose.* Oh! whatever can that be? OxNR; SoPo; TiPo

Riddle: "Hitty Pitty within the wall." *Anonymous.* Hitty Pitty will bite you. OxNR

Riddle: "Hoddy doddy." *Anonymous.* Pray tell me, what is that? OxNR

Riddle: "House full, yard full." *Anonymous.* You can't catch a spoonful. NTCP

Riddle: "Humpty Dumpty sat on a wall." *Anonymous.* Cannot put Humpty Dumpty together again. HBV 1-2; HBVY

Riddle: "I am within as white as snow." *Anonymous.* And yet am lesser than a mouse. GBP

Riddle: "I come more softly than a bird." *Mary Austin.* And children play with me. SoPo; TiPo

Riddle: "I have a little sister they call her Peep-peep." *Mother Goose.* The poor little thing hasn't got but one eye. OxNR; TiPo

Riddle: "I have no wings, but yet I fly." *Mary Austin.* Who lets me quickly go will surest gain. SoPo; TiPo

Riddle: "I'm a strange creature, for I satisfy women." *Anonymous.* Remembers our meeting. Her eyes moisten. PV

Riddle: "I'm called by the name of a man." *Anonymous.* With my red target near the house. OxNR

Riddle: "I never speak a word." *Mary Austin.* And yet great rocks I break. TiPo

Riddle: "I sat wi' my love, and I drank wi' my love." *Anonymous.* I'll give any man a pint o' wine/That'll read my riddle right. GBP

Riddle: "I saw five birds all in a cage." *Anonymous.* Their tails were thirty feet in length. CoBE; GBP

Riddle: "I washed my face in water." *Anonymous.* ...a towel/That was neither wove nor spun. GBP

Riddle: "In marble halls as white as milk." *Anonymous.* Yet thieves break in and steal the gold. GBP; HBV 1-2; HBVY; OxNR; PoPle

Riddle: "In Mornigan's park there is a deer." *Anonymous.* In Mornigan's park she walks alone. GBP; MOON

Riddle: "In Spring I look gay." *Anonymous.* And in Winter quite naked appear. OxNR

Riddle: "It has a head like a cat, feet like a cat." *Anonymous.* A tail like a cat, but it isn't a cat. NTCP

Riddle: "Itum Paradisum all clothed in green." *Anonymous.* Who said it had horns, but was not a beast. GBP

Riddle: "King Charles the First walked and talked." *Anonymous.* Half an hour after his head was cut off. OxNR

Riddle: "Little Billy Breek." *Anonymous.* He has more horns/Than all the king's sheep. OxNR

Riddle: "Little bird of paradise." *Anonymous.* She does the work that no man can. OxNR

Riddle: "Little Nancy Etticoat." *Mother Goose.* The shorter she grows. HBV 1-2; HBVY; NTCP; OxNR; SoPo; TiPo

Riddle: "Lives in winter." *Mother Goose.* And grows with its roots upward! SoPo; TiPo

Riddle: "Long legs, crooked thighs." *Anonymous.* Little head and no eyes. GBP; HBV 1-2; HBVY; OxNR

Riddle: "Make three-fourths of a cross." *Anonymous.* And a circle complete. HBV 1-2; HBVY; OxNR

Riddle of Night. *Jiri M. Langer.* Should I think/of beauty/until it passes/away? VWA

Riddle of Snow and Sun. *Anonymous.* And rode away horseless to the King's white hall. CBEP; NCEP

The Riddle of the World. *John Greenleaf Whittier.* With a child's trust leans on a Father's breast. TRV

Riddle: "Old Mother Twitchet had but one eye." *Mother Goose.* She left a bit of her tail in a trap. HBV1-2; HBVY; NTCP; OxNR; SoPo

Riddle: "On yonder hill there is a red deer." *Anonymous.* You cannot drive that deer away. GBP

Riddle: "Once hairy scenter did transgress." *Anonymous.* Upon a Sabbath day. CoBE

Riddle: "Promotion lately was bestow'd." *Anonymous.* To help him with their kind good will. CoBE

Riddle: "Purple, yellow, red, and green." *Anonymous.* Tell me this riddle while I count eight. OxNR

Riddle: "Red and blue and delicate green." *Anonymous.* Answer this riddle by to-morrow at noon. GBP

Riddle: "Riddle me, riddle me ree." *Anonymous.* I'll give you a groat. OxNR

Riddle: "Runs all day and never walks." *Mother Goose.* It has a mouth, but never eats. TiPo

Riddle: "See, see, what shall I see?" *Anonymous.* A horse's head where his tail should be. OxNR

The Riddle Song. *Anonymous.* A baby when it's sleepin', there's no cryin'. BLSo; FSW

Riddle: "Stiff standing on the bed." *Anonymous.* That would not take it in her hand. GBP; PoL

Riddle. Storm: "At times I am fast confined by my Master." *Anonymous.* Or who stays my course when stillness comes/to me? EnLi 1-2

Riddle: "Take of letters the first." *Anonymous.* But the dunce would produce if he could. CoBE

Riddle: "The beginning of eternity." *Anonymous.* The beginning of every end, and the end of every place. GoTF; TreFT

Riddle: The Book-Worm: "A moth ate a word." *Anonymous.* ...Yet the thief/Was no wiser for the words he gorged. CoBE

Riddle: "The fiddler and his wife." *Anonymous.* And three-quarters of another. OxNR

Riddle: "The land was white." *Anonymous.* It will take a good scholar/To riddle me that. OxNR

A Riddle: The Letter H. *Catherine Fanshawe.* Ah! breathe on it softly, it dies in an hour. GN

Riddle: The Swan: "Silent my robe, when I rest on earth." *Anonymous.* Singing with glorious song as I speed/O'er field and flood, a ghostly wanderer. CoBE

Riddle: "The vase which holds all fat'ning liquor." *Anonymous.* United all denote the name/Of a large town of Christian fame. CoBE

A Riddle: The Vowels. Jonathan Swift. It can never fly from you. GN

Riddle: "Their tongues are knives, their forks are hands and feet." Adrian Mitchell. Two curried lovers on a rice-white sheet. FaBoEE; GBL

Riddle: "There is one that has a head without an eye." Christina Georgina Rossetti. Half the answer hangs upon a thread. OxBChV

Riddle: "There was a girl in our town." *Anonymous.* Guess her name, three times I've telled it. HBV 1-2; HBVY; OxNR

Riddle: "There was a king met a king." *Anonymous.* I've told you already/ And won't tell you again. OxNR

Riddle: "There was a man made a thing." *Anonymous.* But he 'twas made for did not know/Whether 'twas a thing or no. GBP

Riddle: "There was a man rode through our town." *Anonymous.* Three times I've named his name. OxNR

Riddle: "There was a man who had no eyes." *Anonymous.* He took no apples off, yet left no apples on it. OxNR

Riddle: "There was a thing a full month old." *Anonymous.* Adam was years four score. OxNR

Riddle: "There were three sisters in a hall." *Anonymous.* I would say good morrow,/Then, aunts, all three. OxNR

Riddle: "Thirty white horses." Mother Goose. Now they stand still. SoPo; TiPo

Riddle: "Thomas a Tattamus took two T's." *Anonymous.* Tell me how many T's there are in all THAT! HBV 1-2; HBVY

Riddle: "Trip trap in a gap." *Anonymous.* As many feet as a hundred sheep. GBP

Riddle: "Twelve pears hanging high." *Anonymous.* And yet left eleven there. OxNR

Riddle: "Two bodies have I." *Anonymous.* The faster I run. OxNR

Riddle: "Two brothers we are." *Anonymous.* And empty when we go to rest. OxNR

Riddle: "Two legs sat upon three legs." *Anonymous.* And makes him bring back one leg. HBV 1-2; HBVY; NTCP; OxNR

Riddle: What Am I? Dorothy Aldis. But when they lit the candle, then I/ smiled! SoPo

Riddle: "What God never sees." *Anonymous.* Read my riddle, I pray. OxNR

Riddle: "White as snow and snow it isn't." *Anonymous.* Black as tar and tar it isn't. GBP

The Riddles. *Anonymous.* Was no whit the wiser when he swallowed the/ words. EnLit

Riddles. Patrick F. Kirby. Not now would we let down the mind's gates. GoBC

Riddles and Lies. Christine Zawadiwsky. As long as I continue/to kiss you good-bye. AMV-80

The Riddles of Change. Felix Mnthali. and settle like dew/over the crannies/and crevices of all our lives! WhB

Riddles Wisely Expounded. *Anonymous.*
But always, when a lover speaks,/Look kindly and reply. BaBo; ViBoFo
He flew awa in a blazing flame. ESPB; FaBoBa; GBP; HBV 1-2; ViBoFo
I wish that you may constant prove/unto the man that you do love. BaBo; ESPB
Nelle ich speke no more with the! BaBo; ESPB

The Riddling Knight. *Anonymous.*
"And now, fair maid, I will marry with thee." PoEL 1-5
As the dow flies over the mulberry-tree. AtBAP; FaBoCh; LoGBV

Ride. Josephine Miles. But now it's down the road, and we're in it. FaBoWP

Ride a Cock-Horse. *Anonymous.* And a two-penny apple pie. OxBoLi; OxNR

Ride a Cock Horse (parody). Barry Pain. Where she did ride, and he for two-and-six mote go. BXAP

Ride a Cockhorse. Mother Goose. She shall have music wherever she goes. ExPo; FaBoBe; FaFP; HBV 1-2; HBVY; SoPo; TiPo

Ride away, Ride away. Mother Goose. And Johnny shall ride/To see his grandmother. OxNR; TiPo

The Ride-by-Nights. Walter De la Mare. Under the silver, and home again. DuDa; SiSoSe; TiPo; WSC

Ride 'Im Cowboy. A. L. Freebairn. Oh hell—he's throwed you a mile. PH

The Ride of Collins Graves. John Boyle O'Reilly. For he offered his life for the people's/sake! PAH

The Ride of Tench Tilghman. Clinton Scollard. The World Turned Upside Down! MC

Ride On, Moses. *Anonymous.* Ride on, King Emanual,/I want to go home in de mawnin'. BoAN 1-2

The Ride Round the Parapet. Friedrich Rueckert. Wooden Lady Eleanora von Alleyne! AWP

Ride the Turtle's Back. Beth Brant. We listen. STE

The Ride to Cherokee. Amelia Walstein Carpenter. God rest him! I'm the victor, to-day in/Cherokee! AA

The Ride to the Lady. Helen Gray Cone. Now God's great grace assoil the soul/That went out in the wood! AA

The Rider. Leah Bodine Drake. And so we stoned him till he died. NePoAm-2

The Rider at the Gate. John Masefield. The beaten men come into their own. BrPo

The Rider Victory. Edwin Muir. Rider and horse with stony eyes/Uprear their motionless statuary. CMoP; LiTM; WaP

The Riders. Robert Friend. I cannot halt that mindless stream,/whose will is my necessity,/overthrow or victory. GP

Riders. Linda Peavy. Across the phantom acres of the B-Bar-B. PH

The Riders Held Back. Louis Simpson. ...there were many slain/In the dark fields. ConAP

Riders of the Stars. Henry Herbert Knibbs. And a viewless rider swept the sky on the trail of a/shooting star? BPAW

Rides. Gene Derwood. In the cars, to the stars, waves, wars, riding/And questing. LiTM; NePA

The Ridiculous Optimist. *Anonymous.* Because that he could hew/And hammer, he was glad. STF

Ridin'. Charles Badger Clark, Jr. That have wandered out of hell,/And a-ridin'. BPAW

Riding. William Allingham. Creels and all, creels and all. OxBChV

Riding. Harry Amoss. With wind-blown blushes that never bring tears. CaP

Riding. Florence Grossman. It was not my hands on the reins/the horse had obeyed/but his voice. PH

Riding a One-Eyed Horse. Henry Taylor. and see you safely through diminished fields. HeIP; InPK; PH

Riding across John Lee's Finger. Stanley Crouch. A timeless state of mind. PoBA

Riding Adown the Country Lanes. Robert Bridges. O heart! for all thy griefs and pains/Thou shalt be loth to die. VLP

Riding Double. Peter Wild. an iron ship glides into the deserted horizon. AmPA

Riding Down. Nora Perry. The little lass who blushed to see! HBV 1-2

Riding down from Bangor. Louis Shreve Osborne. A tiny little earring in that horrid student's beard. BLPA

Riding in the Rain. Maxine W. Kumin. like lazy mastodons/going from here to there. RFM

Riding Lesson. Henry Taylor. ...When you see/they're gonna throw you, get off. NLV; PH

The Riding of the Kings. Eleanor Farjeon. But rode to find a Child. ChBR; YeAr

Riding Song. Isidor Schneider. ...and death?/will be but a change of the weather. PG

The Riding Stable in Winter. John Tagliabue. But in the winter the children like the calm and the/radiant made me remember these words. PH

Riding the "A." May Swenson. The station/is reached/too soon. CAD

Riding the Blue Sapphire Mountains. Mahadevi (Mahadeviyakka). stripped of body's shame/and heart's modesty? BoWoP; PBWP

Riding the Elevator into the Sky. Anne Sexton. some useful door—/somewhere—/up there. NYP

Riding Together. William Morris. The sweet Saints grant I live not long. NOBE; OAEL 1-2

Riding Westward. Harvey Shapiro. Here in the car and in Queens and in Brooklyn. GP; NYP; VWA

Riding with Kilpatrick. Clinton Scollard. Those who rode with Kilpatrick can never/forget! PAH

Riding with the Fireworks. Ann Darr. the C# moon strikes/a chord across/the sunset clef, and all/is music, music. AmC

Rienzi to the Romans. Mary Russell Mitford. The eternal city shall be free! her sons shall walk with princes. GoTF; TreFS

The Rifleman's Song at Bennington. *Anonymous.* By the rifle, the good rifle!/In our hands it is no trifle! PAH

The Riflemen at Bennington. *Anonymous.* In our hands/Will prove no trifle. FSW

The Rifles. *Anonymous.* To welcome my true love with ten thousand bright joys. OBET

Rift Tide. Ruth M. Walsh. I think we're drifting apart. QQQ

Rigadoon, Rigadoon, Now Let Him Fly. *Anonymous.* Sit him on father's foot, jump him up high. OxNR

Right Apprehension. Thomas Traherne. Those Infant-Days, when I did see/Wisdom and Wealth couch'd in Simplicity. PoEL 1-5

The Right Heart in the Wrong Place. James Joyce. If a Joyce is found cleaning/The boots of a Rumbold. FaBoPV

Right Is Right. F. W. Faber. To falter would be sin. TRV; WBLP

The Right Kind of People. Edwin Markham. "You'll find the people here the same,"/The wise man said. BLPA; FPL; PoToHe

Right Now. William Stafford. my glimpse, this town, our time. NaP

The Right of Way. William Carlos Williams. I saw a girl with one leg/ over the rail of a balcony MoVE

Ripe, Being Plunged into Fire... Friedrich Holderlin. Try to look, but let ourselves be rocked as/In swaying bark on the sea. OBVE

The Ripe Fruit. *Anonymous.* And what man cares for withered fruit? UnTE

Ripe Grain. Dora Reed Goodale. In Heaven stands the ripened grain. HBV 1-2

Ripening. Noelle Caskey. that blood-red wakening. DFT

Ripper Collins' Legacy. Don Johnson. best suited for the match/upcoming with the Masked Executioner. LiSp

Ripperty! Kye! Ahoo! Henry Lawson. And–that's how a good many married folk dwell./Ripperty! Kye! A-hoo! CBAP

A Ripping Trip. *Anonymous.* Finally gets into a fight–rip, goes the engine. CoSo

Riprap. Gary Snyder. all change, in thoughts/As well as things. HaCAP; NeAP; NOBA; PoM

A Rise. Ernest McGaffey. The black bass rises to the fly. AA

The Rise and Fall of Creede. Cy Warman. And men moved on and gave no heed/To life or death–and this is Creede. BPAW; PoOW

Rise and Fall of Valentines. Fairfax Downey. We never sign the valentines we send in February. InMe

Rise and Shine. *Anonymous.* Children of the Lord. FSW

Rise and Shine. Richmond Lattimore. to scarf our loves in paradisial air. NYBP

Rise, Crowned with Light. Alexander Pope. Thy realm shall last, thy own Messiah reigns. GoBC

Rise, Glorious Conqueror! Rise. Matthew Bridges. Brought safely home. BePJ

Rise, Happy Morn. Alfred, Lord Tennyson. O Father! touch the east, and light/The light that shone when hope was born. BePJ

Rise, Lady Mistress, Rise! Nathaniel Field. For grey morn breaks from thine eyes. EiL

Rise Me up from down below. *Anonymous.* Rise me up from down below. ShS

Rise, Mourner, Rise. *Anonymous.* Oh, can't you rise an' tell what de Lord has done for you. BoAN 1-2

Rise, O My Soul! *Anonymous.* To Thee I die; to Thee I only live! OxBoCh

The Rise of Man. John White Chadwick. While the long way behind is prophecy/Of those perfections which are yet to be. AA

The Rise of Shivaji. Zulfikar Ghose. ...They rose then to join/in praise of Shivaji's shrewd sense of politics. MoBS

Rise Oot Your Bed. John Barr. Our Johnnie's no that weel.' AnNZ

Rise Up, O Men of God. William Pierson Merrill. Rise up, O men of God! AH

Rise Up, Shepherd, and Follow. *Anonymous.* Rise up shepherd and follow. BoAN 1-2; FSW

Rise with the Lamb of Innocence. *Anonymous.* To ris with him fra ded to life. MeEL

Rise, Ye Children. Justus Falckner. Victory! our song shall be,/Like the thunder of the sea! AH

Rise You Up, My True Love. *Anonymous.* We'll hug and kiss each other and a-married we will be. AmFP

Risen Matters. Clark Coolidge. And and is the rod without/Which no field. APU

Risen with Healing in His Wings. Saint John of Damascus. And the Pascha of salvation/Hail, with His triumphant band. BePJ

The Rising. Thomas Buchanan Read. A hundred voices answer'd, "I!" PAH; TreFS

Rising High Water Blues. Blind Lemon Jefferson. I leave with a prayer in my heart:/black water won't rise no more BluL

Rising in the Morning. Hugh Rhodes. All the day after, assure thyself,/The better shalt thou speed. OxBChV

The Rising in the North. *Anonymous.*
Men will be men when mony is gone. BaBo; ESPB
The Nortons' ancyent had the cross,/And the five wounds our Lord did bear. ACP

The Rising of the Moon. *Anonymous.* For the pikes must be together/By the rising of the moon. FSW

The Rising of the Moon A.D. 1798. John Keegan Casey. Who would follow in their footsteps/At the risin' of the moon! IrPN; OnYI

The Rising of the Session. Robert Fergusson. We'll gladly prie/Fresh noggans o' your reaming graith/Wi' blythsome glee. OxBS

The Rising Sun Blues. *Anonymous.* Going back to spend the rest of my life beneath that Rising Sun. OuSiCo

The Rising Village. Oliver Goldsmith.
And torn from those who had no power to save. OBCV
Beyond his hopes, with joy and plenty crowned. OBCV
Death bears the blame, 'tis his envenom'd dart/That strikes the suff'ring mortal to the heart. PeCV
He looks to Heaven, and lulls his cares to rest. NOBC
Heightening the horror of its gloomy shades. OBCV
They think their knowledge far exceeds their own. CaP

The Risk. Anne Sexton. and eats up her heart like two eggs. BoWoP

Rispetti: On the Death of a Child. Paul Heyse. I said aloud: "Look out that you don't fall!" PoPl

Rispetto. Agnes Mary Frances (Mme Emile Duclaux) Robinson. While I shall sleep, while I–while I–forget! HBMV

Risposta. John Wilbye. Seldom it comes, to few from heaven sent,/That much in little, all in naught–Content. HBV 1-2

Risselty-Rosselty. *Anonymous.* If you want any more, you can sing it yourself, Willaby-wallaby now, now, now! DiPo; FSW

Rissem. Sandra M. Gilbert. there are no words for "love" or "death." AMV-81

The Rite. Peter Dale. your time about my wrist. NAs

The Rite. Dudley Randall. and drank his blood and ate his heart. HoPM

Rite of Passage. Sharon Olds. ...get down to/playing war, celebrating my son's life. MAYP

Rite of Spring. Seamus Heaney. Her entrance was wet, and she came. OxBC

Rite of Spring. Leo Kennedy. Set them into the earth to sprout and blossom. CaP

Rites for a Demagogue. Anthony Thwaite. The stock-response still raging in the shroud? NePoEA-2

The Rites for Cousin Vit. Gwendolyn Brooks. ...comes haply on the verge/Of happiness, haply hysterics. Is. BPo; HAP; SM

Rites of Passage. Audre Lorde. Quick/children kiss us/we are growing through dream. CNA; PoBA

Rites of the Eastern Star. Janine Pommy-Vega. You could hear the cracking of bones/from the seventh row. APU

Ritratto. Ezra Pound. I never saw her again. PP

The Ritual. Paul David Ashley. And they return. LFAC

The Ritual. Joy Gwillim. the dark bloom of the world. AMV-80

The Ritual. Edwin John Pratt. And with the grind of timbers on the sides/Of cliffs resounding with the march of tides. NoAm

Ritual Not Religion. Telugu E. Indian. ...He's like the stupid swain/Who seeks the lamb his bosom hides. WGRP

Ritual of Departure. Thomas Kinsella. Sourness in the clay. The roots tear softly. CIP; CMoP

The Ritual of Memories. Tess Gallagher. One life I have lived for you. This one/is mine. GeTw

Ritual Three. David Ignatow. for to live is to act in terms of death. ConAP

A Ritual to Read to Each Other. William Stafford. ...the darkness around us is deep. NePA

The Ritualists. William Carlos Williams. rhythms of casting–that slow dance. NYBP

The Rival. Sylvia Townsend Warner. Fond and severe, as looks the groom on bride. MoAB; MoBrPo

The Rival Curates. Sir William Schwenck Gilbert. They think him, all around,/The mildest curate going. CenHV; VLP

The Rival Friends: Have Pity, Grief. Peter Hausted. To take both life and love away. EG

The Rival Sisters, III: Song. Robert Gould. And that she was not made for One. CEP

Rivalry. Alden Nowlan. her own smile becoming tighter and tighter. PoL

The Rivals. James Stephens. So I didn't listen to him/As he sang upon a tree. InvP; MoVE; NoAm; OBEV; OBMV; PoPl

Rivals. William Walsh. I can endure my own despair,/But not another's hope. HBV 1-2; OBEV

Riven Doggeries. James Tate. The ideal pet, however,/is unrecognizable when it arrives/in the river awash in the land afar. MAYP

The Riven Quarry. Gloria C. Oden. wolves sharp-eyed at the/heels of spirit. PoBA

The River. Matthew Arnold. And dead to hopes of future joy. CBEP

The River. Sam Cornish. grandmother/used to chain herself/to the postoffice/for woman rights PoBA

The River. Hart Crane. Meeting the Gulf, hosannas silently below. AP; OxBA; PrIm

The River. Ralph Waldo Emerson. And soon may give my dust their funeral shade. MAmP

The River. D.G. Jones. catches the light/and sends it back. NOBC

The River. Mary Sinton Leitch. The river bears me through the fragrant darkness,/And so I cannot sleep. HBMV

River. Lawrence Locke. The river is always going home. GrPl

The River. Pare Lorentz. before it has picked up the heart of/a continent and shoved it into the Gulf of Mexico. AmFN; NAMP

The River. Patrick MacDonogh. This calm-flowing river. NeIP

The River. Roy MacNab. ...we heard the river roar/To its death trampled in the bloody miles of sea. PeSA

The River. Dabney Stuart. I drink that water, and find it cool and clear. NYBP

The River. Leo Vroman. and it shall never, never end/till I am dead. VWA

The River. Don Welch. There is a single hole/in the clouds through which/time is escaping. Str

River Afram. Andrew Amankwa Opoku. River, I am passing. PBA

The River Again and Again. Linda Gregg. And we would know each other sometimes/with a love that touches indifference. NPGG

The River Boats. Daniel Whitehead Hicky. And all their pilots fast asleep. AmFN

The River Dart. *Anonymous.* Now let me over/To go where I will. GBP

The River Don. *Anonymous.* Each year a daughter or a son. GBP

The River Fight. Henry Howard Brownell.
And the traitor flags come down. PAH
There were thirteen traitor hulls/On fire and sinking! AA; EtS

The River Glideth in a Secret Tongue. Anthony Ostroff. And doth flow deep the summer long. NePoAm-2

The River God. Sacheverell Sitwell. Which, while they also fall, tell time like clocks. MoBrPo

The River God. Stevie Smith. If she wishes to go I will not forgive her. BrRo; FaBoNo; FaBoTw; FaBoWP; PBWP

River God's Song. Anne Ridler. I move and remain. NYBP

A River in Asia. Andrew Grossbardt. gathering at the river's edge FAZ

The River in March. Ted Hughes. A salmon, a sow of solid silver,/Bulges to glimpse it. OxBC

River in Spate. Louis MacNeice. And then the minute after and the minute after the minute/after. FaBoIP

The River in the Meadows. Léonie Adams. Or the bosom it dwelt in, stone. AnAmPo; MoAB; MoAmPo

The River Is a Piece of Sky. John Ciardi. The river has splashes,/The sky hasn't any. PoPl; SoPo

The River Map and We're Done. Charles Olson. old hulk Rocky Marsh. CoPo

River-Mates. Padraic Colum. ...the deep, dark, full and flowing River! AnIV; AWP

The River Merchant's Wife. Li Po. And I will come out to meet you/As far as Cho-fu-Sa. AWP; BoLoP; FYAP; HAP; HeIP; InPK; InPS; LiPo; LiTA; LiTW; MoAmPo; MoPo; MP; NIP; NoAm; NOBA; NOBE; NoP; OBMV; OBVE; PAI; PG; PPoe; PrIm; SOTW; TAP; TwCP; UnPo

The River of Bees. William Stanley Merwin. But we were not born to survive/Only to live HeIP; LCAP

The River of Heaven. *Anonymous.* a cloud is even now passing across the clear face of the/moon. AWP; LiTW

The River of Life. Thomas Campbell. And those of youth, a seeming/length,/Proportion'd to their sweetness. BSV; FaFP; GTBS; GTBS-P; HBV 1-2; LiTB

The River of Rivers in Connecticut. Wallace Stevens. The river that flows nowhere, like a sea. HaCAP; HAP; NOBA; VGW

The River of Stars. Alfred Noyes. Teach me of death, and for ever, and set my feet on the way! OnMSP

River Rhyme. William Carlos Williams. ...a bulk/that writhes and fat-/tens as it speeds. PoA

River Road. Stanley Jasspon Kunitz. through the deep litter of the years. NoAm

River Road Studio. Barbara Guest. careful to replace them/until they are truly quartets. PoM

River Roads. Carl Sandburg. And the mist along the river fix its purple in lines of a/woman's shawl on lazy shoulders. VGW

River Roses. D. H. Lawrence. Here in this simmering marsh. BrPo; CMoP; GBL; OAEL 1-2; ViBoPo

River Skater. Winifred Welles. You see his figure, slanted like a pen,/Writing his own and winter's signature. SD

River Song. Elizabeth Brewster. Oh glory gone. CaP

River Song. Weldon Kees. And I wanted to die, but they left me there. NoAm; PPP

River Sound Remembered. William Stanley Merwin. It will be the seethe and drag of the river/That I will hear longer than any mortal song. SM

The River Swelleth More and More. Henry David Thoreau. Her young disciples leaves behind. NOBA

The River That Is East. Galway Kinnell. The immaculate stream, heavy, and swinging home again. NYP

The River Walk. Padraic Fallon. ...if the girl insist/On love—must be a very pantheist. OxBI

Riverdale Lion. John Robert Colombo. that you are as much a Canadian as they are. PeCV

Riverfront, St. Louis. John Knoepfle. I discover a Roosevelt dime/blackened by many waters. TAT

The Riverman. Elizabeth Bishop. Luandinha seconded it. NYBP

Rivers. Thomas Storer. Take Loire and Po, yet all may not compare/With English Thamesis for buildings rare. EIL

Rivers and Mountains. John Ashbery. Slowly out into the sun-blackened landscape. ANYP; CoAP; NoAm; NOBA

Rivers Arise. John Milton. Or Medway smooth, or royal towred Thame. FaBoPP

Rivers of the West. Sunset Joe". No vale kissed by laughing waters,/Can be lovely as Ouray. PoOW

The Rivers Remember. Nancy Byrd Turner. They bear the glory of Washington! AmFN

Rivers Unknown to Song. Alice Meynell. Ignorant, innocent, instantaneous, free,/Unwelcomed, unrenowned. HBMV

Riverside Drive, November Fifth. Katha Pollitt. —as if he could outpace/darkness drifting home like a flock of crows. AMV-81

Riverton. Edmund Wilson. That holds the splendor though the days depart. AnFE

Rivets. N. S. Olds. But all I'll own of the old man's pride/Are rows of rivets along her side. EtS

Rivulose. Archie Randolph Ammons. what is your time where so much time is saved? SUW

Rizpah. Alfred, Lord Tennyson. I am going. He calls. CABL; PoEL 1-5; VLP

The Roach. John Raven. I know it would've/come right up/and gave me/ five! BPo; HoPM

Roaches. Edward Field. greeting you joyfully. NYP

The Road. Conrad Aiken. I knew my face would not be young again. AP; MoAmPo

The Road. Patrick Reginald Chalmers. Still 'twas me that went wid her right on to the end! HBV 1-2

The Road. John Gould Fletcher. There was my road, and nothing more to say. HBMV

The Road. Helene Johnson. Rise to one brimming golden, spilling cry! BANP; BlSi; CDC; GoSl; PoNe

Road. William Stanley Merwin. I pass thousands of miles of fences PPJ

The Road. Herbert Morris. but for the way the waif befits my life. NePoAm-2

The Road. Edwin Muir. And a blind seed all. BSV; CMoP; FaFP; LiTB; LiTM; ViBoPo

The Road. Nikolay Platonovich Ogarev. The land of my heart. AWP

The Road. Christine Orr. But the Road that runs by Atholl will be doing yet for me. PoSH

The Road. Siegfried Sassoon. The Road would serve you well enough for bed. MCCG

The Road. Zalman Schneour. For them prepare/The road! TrJP

The Road. James Stephens. And learn that we are better than our clay,/And equal to the peaks of our desire. HBMV

The Road along the Thumb and Forefinger. Mark Hickey. If only the eye could hold it. AMV-81

The Road at My Door. William Butler Yeats. And turn towards my chamber, caught/In the cold snows of a dream. LiTB

The Road Back. Anne Sexton. like a persistent rumor/that will get us yet. NYBP

The Road Back and Forth to Ryley." Monty Reid. ...In the morning, driving,/it disappears. CaPN

Road Fellows. Barbara Young. I think they're strolling still. BrR

The Road from Election to Christmas. Oscar Williams. The road to Christmas is clear. NAMP

Road Hazard. Rayna Green. it's not the booze or pick-ups/that will kill me/on this road TWSS

A Road in Kentucky. Robert Earl Hayden. so dark and so dark in the briary light. LCAP; NCSH

A Road in the Weald. Richard Church. Directing another vein the world's heart—Rome! HaMV

The Road Is Wider Than Long (excerpt). Roland Penrose. while Maritza/tunes the two chords of her guitar. EAS

The Road Moves On. Dorothy Nash. We have reached a liberation. PoSH

The Road Not Taken. Robert Frost. And that has made all the difference. AnFE; AnNE; APA; CMoP; CoBMV; DiPo; EvOK; FaBoCh; FaFP; FPL; GoTF; HAP; HeIP; LiTA; LiTM; LoGBV; MAPA; MoAB; MoAmPo; MP; NePA; NoAm; NoP; OxBA; PG; PoLf; PoPl; RFM; SeCeV; SoSe; TAP; TreFT; TwCP

The Road of Birds. Harry Humes. And nothing ever really at dead rest. AMV-80

A Road of Ireland. Charles L. O'Donnell. My father met my mother on the road, in Donegal. HBMV

The Road of Life. William Morris. Till, ere we know it, our weak shrinking feet/Have brought us to the end and all is done. OBNC

The Road of Remembrance. Lizette Woodworth Reese. The old wind blowing up the land,/The old thoughts at our heart. HBV 1-2

Road Runner. Sharlot M. Hall. Then—off like a shot he'll go. BPAW

The Road's End. Theodosia Garrison. "Seeing that true love walked beside her/All of the way, all of the way. HBMV

Road's End. Rolf Jacobsen. —what the hell is this? NU

The Road's End. John Montague. ...and someone/Has propped a yellow cartwheel/Against the door. FaBoIP

Road-Song of the Bandar-Log. Rudyard Kipling. Be sure—be sure, we're going to do/some splendid things! OAEP

The Road the Crows Own. Susan Astor. He waves th frayed emblems of his wings/And warns us off. AMV-81

The Road to Anywhere. Bert Leston Taylor. And blest is he who follows free/The Road to Anywhere. HBMV

The Road to Babylon. Margaret Adelaide Wilson. —Young feet that fretted so to roam/Have missed the road returning home. HBMV

The Road to Bologna. Roy MacNab. Have I anything to declare/to the marshalled dead? PeSA

The Road to Castaly: Revelation. Alice Brown. Child of a starveling sod. WGRP

The Road to Cook's Peak. Anonymous. Those two little mules on the road to Cook's Peak. CoSo

The Road to Dieppe. John Finley. Forget long hates in one consummate faith. MCCG

The Road to France. Daniel Henderson. See, with what proud hearts we advance/To France! HBV 1-2; MC; PAH

The Road to Hate. Patrick Kavanagh. And God visited him every day out of pity/Till in the end he became a most noble saint. TW

The Road to Hogan's Gap. Andrew Barton ("Banjo") Paterson. Along with Hogan's brindled bull/And Hogan's old grey mare! CBAP

The Road to Nijmegen. Earle Birney. in the griefs of the old and the graves of the young. OBCV

The Road to Pengya. Tu Fu. How I'd like to have wings/and fly back to him. Prf

The Road to School. Joy M. Lane. Dew has turned to rime. AMV-81

The Road to Texas. Berta Hart Nance. Before you gave to Texas/The rugged strength of oak. BPAW

The Road to the Bow. James David Corrothers. I hold my head as proudly high/As any man. BANP

The Road to the Pool. Grace Hazard Conkling. Contented like the road that dozes/In panniered gown of briar roses. HBMV

The Road to Vagabondia. Dana Burnet. On the road to Vagabondia that lies across the earth! PoLf

The Road to Zoagli. Max Beerbohm. For dead he lay. FaBoNo

The Roadmenders' Song. Anonymous. Hungry and thirsty we break these stones in the cold of winter. WTO

Roads. George Mackay Brown. Tinkers and shepherds/Have the whole round hill for a road. PoSH

Roads. Ruth Dallas. And tree and singing bird in this still room. AnNZ

Roads. Rachel Field. Lead you back home again! BrR; SoPo; TiPo

The Roads Also. Wilfred Owen. And in passion past the reach of the stairs/To the world's towers or stars. EBEV

Roads Go Ever Ever On. J. R. R. Tolkien. Over grass and over stone,/And under mountains in the moon. TiPo

Roadside Flowers. Bliss Carman. We blossom and ask no reason,/The Lord of the Garden knows. HBMV

Roadside near Moscow. R.A.D. Ford. Nothing but the rain, turning/To snow,–all that I wish to see. PeCV

Roadways. John Masefield. In quest of that one beauty/God put me here to find. GTBS; MCCG

Roan Stallion. Robinson Jeffers. ...The night-wind veering, the smell/of the spilt wine drifted down hill from the house. BeLS; NAMP

Roarers in a Ring. Ted Hughes. ...in the bottomless black/Silence through which it fell. NePoEA-2

The Roaring Days. Henry Lawson. The mighty Bush with iron rails/Is tethered to the world. BoAV

The Roaring Lad and the Ranting Lass. Anonymous. Come Boys a good health to our selves. CoMu

The Roast Beef of Old England. Henry Fielding. And Old England's Roast Beef! CEP; OBEC

Roast Swan Song. Anonymous. Lights flash, teeth clash–I fear the latter./Ouch!...Ouch!... LiTW

Roasted Sucking Pig (parody). Anonymous. And if he a guest should wish,/LET HIM SEND FOR ME! BXAP

Rob Roy. Anonymous. Think nae mair of gauin back,/But tak it for your hame, lady.' ESPB
We will get the bagpipes,/And we'll hae a dance, ladie.' BaBo; ESPB

Rob Roy. Sir Walter Scott And the lake her lone bosom expands to the sky. NBM

Robben Island. Robert Dederick. ...little else to do/But gaze and gaze on a splendid view. PeSA

The Robber. Anonymous. And I've a bonnie laddie noo/And breists for him to sook. OBVE

The Robber. Ivy O. Eastwick. he stole my locket,/my heart as well! SiSoSe

The Robber. Walter James Turner. Behind a cloud, the Robber laughed/In a mad white carouse. MoBrPo

Robbing and Stealing Blues. Gene Campbell. Your women don't know how to rob;/they're too doggone scared to steal BluL

Robene and Makyne. Robert Henryson. Keepand his herd under a heuch,/Amangis the holtis hair. BoLoP; BSV; GoTS

Robens' Promised Land. George Purdom. 'Cotia was a colliery./Her men were true and bold. WTO

Robert Barnes, Fellow Fine. Anonymous. And now, good sir, your horse is/shod. OxNR

Robert Burns. William Alexander. Of that poetic and triumphant peasant/Driving his laureled plow! HBV 1-2

Robert E. Lee. Julia Ward Howe. We honor thee, Virginia's son. MC; PAH

Robert Frost. Robert Lowell. how little good my health did anyone near me. NoAm

Robert Frost's Left-Leaning TRESPASSERS WILL BE SHOT Sign (parody). William Zaranka. But not to make it right, or take it down. BXAP

Robert Fulton. Ann Stanford. ...Robert Fulton/praised it as an instrument/for true liberty and peace. GP

Robert G. Shaw. Henrietta Cordelia Ray. In rev'rent love we guard thy memory. BlSi

Robert Louis Stevenson. Lizette Woodworth Reese. Where do you sing again! HBV 1-2

Robert Lowell. Richard O'Connell. —our anti-Horace/Of the nuclear American Imperium. AMV-81

Robert Lowell Is Dead. Patrick Worth Gray. And I am scared for all of us. SOTS

Robert of Lincoln. William Cullen Bryant. Chee, chee, chee. AnNE; FaBoBe; HBV 1-2; HBVY; OBCA; WBLP

Robert Rowley Rolled a Round Roll Round. Anonymous. Robert Rowley rolled round? OxNR

Robert's Farm. Anonymous. It's hard times in the country, out on Roberts' farm. FSW

Robert's Rules of Order. Robert Peterson. then hot-foot some of them Spanish magistrates FAZ

Robert the Bruce. Edwin Muir. Having outfaced three English kings/And kept a people's faith. OxBS

Robert Whitmore. Frank Marshall Davis. mistook him/for a former Macon waiter. BPo; NoP; PoBA; PoNe

Roberta. Leadbelly.
'Cross the country/with my long clothes on BluL
This man ain't got nobody to/take his troubles to BluL

Robertin Tush. Anonymous. And she galloped after it on a white horse. GBP

De Roberval. John Hunter-Duvar. As 'twas the first, shall be the last to press/This wild and noble shore. A fond farewell! CaP

Robespierre and Mozart as Stage. Robert Lowell. Mozart's barber Figaro could never/cut the gold thread of the suffocating curtain. FaBoMo

Robin. Paula Gunn Allen. Somewhere a hot roof waits/spine thrust into the sky/for your sound. TWSS

The Robin. George Daniel. ...Prettie Redbreast, Sing,/What I would speake. FaBoRV; FM; OBS

A Robin. Walter De la Mare. Calling on all. CMoP; FaBoRV; PB

The Robin. William Bell Scott. He knows as well, it seems, as we/The time is come to fly away. FM

The Robin. Jones Very. Had learned that Heaven is pleased thy simple joys to share. AnNE

Robin-a-Bobbin. Anonymous. Did Robin-a-bobbin/Who bent his bow. OxNR

Robin. A Pastoral Elegy. John Dobson. If yours be wand'ring, quickly call it home.' NOEC

Robin Adair. Caroline Keppel. And will wed none but you,/Robin Adair! FaBoBe; HBV 1-2

A Robin and a Robin's Son. Anonymous. And so they went back home again. OxNR

Robin and Gandelein. Anonymous. That thu hast slawe good Robin/And Gandelin his knave.' OxBM

Robin and Gandelyn. Anonymous. Robin lyeth in greenwood bounden. BaBo; EnSB; ESPB; OxBB

Robin and Richard. Anonymous. And I will come after, on little Jack Nag.' OxBoLi; OxNR

The Robin and the Redbreast. Anonymous. If ye touch one o' their eggs,/Bad luck will sure to follow. PBBP

The Robin and the Wren. Anonymous. Are God's cock and hen. PBBP

Robin at My Window. James Melville. I gave him leif, and furth guid robein furd. BSV

Robin Good-Fellow. Anonymous. So vale, vale; ho, ho, ho! FaBoCh; ViBoPo

Robin Good-Fellow's Song. Anonymous. Tom shall play, I will sing, for all your pleasures. EIL

Robin Hood. Anonymous. He'll come back again/If we are good. OxNR

Robin Hood. Gray Burr. A song more true/Than art or craft/Or history knew. NCSH

Robin Hood. John Keats. Let us two a burden try. AWP; EnLi 1-2; EnLit; InPo

Robin Hood and Allen A Dale. *Anonymous.* And so they returned to the merry green wood,/Amongst the leaves so green. BaBo; ESPB; FaBoBe; GBP; HBV 1-2; MCCG; MoShBr

Robin Hood and Guy of Gisborne. *Anonymous.* But Litle Iohn, with an arrow broade/Did cleaue his heart in twinn. BaBo; BuBa; CoBE; ESPB; OAEP

Robin Hood and Little John. *Anonymous.*
And there in the woods these bold fellows stood,/While this little babe was baptized. AmFP; BaBo; ViBoFo
Yet nevertheless, the truth to express,/Still Little John they did him call. BaBo

Robin Hood and Maid Marian. *Anonymous.* For the people that dwell in the North can tell/Of Marian and bold Robin Hood. BaBo

Robin Hood and Queen Katherine. *Anonymous.* And when Queene Katherine puts up her/finger]/Att her Graces commandement I'le bee.' ESPB

Robin Hood and Queen Katherine (B version). *Anonymous.* We must give gifts to the kings officers;/That gold will serve thee and mee.' BaBo; ESPB

Robin Hood and the Beggar. *Anonymous.*
And Robin took these brethren good/To be of his yeomandrie. BaBo; ESPB
He smil'd to see his merry young men/Had gotten a taste of the tree. BaBo; ESPB

Robin Hood and the Bishop. *Anonymous.* And bade him for Robin Hood to pray. BaBo; ESPB

Robin Hood and the Bishop of Hereford. *Anonymous.* And he made the Bishop to dance in his boots,/And glad he could get so away. BaBo; BuBa; ESPB

Robin Hood and the Butcher. *Anonymous.*
But if Robin walke easte, or he walke/west,/He shall neuer be sought for me.' ESPB
"O have me commended to your wife/at home;'/So Robin went laughing away. BuBa; ESPB

Robin Hood and the Curtal Friar. *Anonymous.*
"Haue done and tell it me;'/"If that thou will goe to merry green-/wood,... ESPB
There was neither knight, lord, nor earl/Could make him yield before. BaBo; ESPB

Robin Hood and the Golden Arrow. *Anonymous.* Now, my friends, attend, and hear the/end/Of honest Robin Hood. ESPB

Robin Hood and the Monk. *Anonymous.* God, that is euer a crowned kyng,/Bryng us all to his blisse! BaBo; ESPB; FaBoBa; MeEV; OBNV; ViBoFo; ViBoPo

Robin Hood and the Pedlars. *Anonymous.* Looke well aboute they are not to stoute,/Or you may have worst of the blowes. ESPB

Robin Hood and the Potter. *Anonymous.* God haffe mersey on Roben Hodys solle,/And saffe all god yemanrey! BaBo; ESPB

Robin Hood and the Prince of Aragon. *Anonymous.* They are gone to the wedding, and so/to bedding,/And so I bid you good night. ESPB

Robin Hood and the Ranger. *Anonymous.* They all did declare, and solemnly swear,/They'd conquer, or die by his side. ESPB

Robin Hood and the Scotchman. *Anonymous.*
Thus ended the fight, and with mickle/delight/To Sherwood they hasted away. ESPB
To give us true peace, that mischief may/cease,/And war may give place unto love. ESPB

Robin Hood and the Shepherd. *Anonymous.* How a shepherd-swain did conquer them;/The like did never none. ESPB

Robin Hood and the Tanner. *Anonymous.* The wood shall ring, and the old wife sing,/Of Robin Hood, Arthur, and John. BaBo; ESPB; MaC

Robin Hood and the Three Squires. *Anonymous.* And they freed their own bold men. EnSB

Robin Hood and the Tinker. *Anonymous.* And with them a part to take,/And so I end my song. BaBo; ESPB

Robin Hood and the Two Priests. *Anonymous.* And he returned to the merry green-wood,/With great joy, mirth and pride. BuBa

Robin Hood and the Valiant Knight. *Anonymous.* Such outlaws as he and his men/May England never know again! ESPB

Robin Hood and the Widow's Three Sons. *Anonymous.* They hang'd the proud Sheriff on that,/And releas'd their own three men. BuBa; EnLi 1-2; ESPB; OnMSP; ViBoFo

Robin Hood Newly Revived. *Anonymous.* If you will have any more of bold Robin Hood,/In his second part it will be. BaBo; ESPB

Robin Hood Rescuing Will Stutly. *Anonymous.* Where we will make our bow-strings twang,/Musick for us most sweet. BaBo; ESPB

Robin Hood, Robin Hood. *Anonymous.* Robin Hood, Robin Hood,/He will fret full sore. OxNR

Robin Hood's Birth, Breeding, Valor, and Marriage. *Anonymous.* And then I'll make ballads in Robin/Hood's bower,/And sing em in merry Sherwood. ESPB

Robin Hood's Chase. *Anonymous.* To pardon his life, and seek no more strife."/And so endeth Robin Hood's chase. BaBo; ESPB

Robin Hood's Death. *Anonymous.*
And lay my vew-bow by my side,/My met-yard wi.... BaBo; ESPB
And there they buried bold Robin Hood,/Within the fair Kirkleys. ESPB; OBET; TrGrPo
That they may say, when I am dead/Here lies bold Robin Hood.' FaBoBa; ViBoFo

Robin Hood's Delight. *Anonymous.* For three dayes space they wine did/chase,/And drank themselves good friends. ESPB

Robin Hood's Funeral. Anthony Munday. And on to Wakefield take your way. WiR

Robin Hood's Golden Prize. *Anonymous.* And hee returnd to the merry green-wood,/With great joy, mirth and pride. BaBo; ESPB

Robin Hood's Progress to Nottingham. *Anonymous.* And they buried them all in a row. BaBo; ESPB; OBET

The Robin in Winter. William Cowper. That tinkle in the wither'd leaves below... BoAnP

The Robin Is the One. Emily Dickinson. Submits that home and certainty/And sanctity are best. FaBV; HBVY

Robin Red Breast. Lula Lowe Weeden. Into my little mouth. CDC

Robin Redbreast. William Allingham. And a crumb of bread for Robin,/His little heart to cheer! FaBoBe; HBV 1-2; HBVY; MoShBr; OxBChV; PBBP

Robin Redbreast. *Anonymous.* Pussy-cat said naught but "Mew," and Robin flew away. HBV 1-2

Robin Redbreast. William Henry Davies. Pretty Robin Redbreast, Come. PB

Robin Redbreast. George Washington Doane. In gentleness and constancy. AA; HBV 1-2; HBVY

Robin Redbreast. Stanley Jasspon Kunitz. I caught the cold flash of the blue/unappeasable sky. Prf

Robin Redbreast's Testament. *Anonymous.* And by came a greedy gled,/And snapt him a' away. GBP

Robin's Come! William Warner Caldwell. Calling from the open door,/With her soft voice, o'er and o'er,/Robin's come! HBVY

Robin's Cross. George Darley. Here lies the little Friend of Man! OnYI

The Robin's Egg. Annie Charlotte Dalton. Why, for an amulet, I fain would beg/The turquoise of some robin's egg. CaP

Robin's Secret. Katharine Lee Bates. And I never, never, never, never, never/meant to tell. AA

The Robin's Song. C. Lovat Fraser. God bless you, and God bless me! MoShBr

Robin's Song. E.L.M. King. Snowdrops a-shivering,/Winter dead. TiPo

Robin the Bobbin. *Anonymous.* And yet he complained/that his stomach wasn't full. OxNR

Robin, Wren, Martin, Swallow. *Anonymous.* Are God Almighty's bow and arrow. GBP

Robins. George Bruce. Present to us their note for maintenance. BSV

Robinson. Weldon Kees. Where trees are actual and take no holiday. NaP; NoAm; NYBP

Robinson at Home. Weldon Kees. And the long curtains blow into the room. CoAP; NYBP

Robinson Crusoe. *Anonymous.* Poor old Robinson Crusoe! OxNR

Robinson Crusoe. Charles Edward Carryl. And particular in turning out their toes. AA; BaBo; BeLS; ESPB; FiBHP; HBV 1-2; HBVY; InMe; MCCG; OxBB; TreFT

Robinson Crusoe Daniel Defoe. Maurice Sagoff. Eventually,/Friday comes. NLV; PoRA

A Robyn Joly Robyn. Sir Thomas Wyatt. At othre fieres thy self to warme/And set theim warme with the. AAS

The Roc. Richard Eberhart. And flew, instinctively, toward the dawn. CMoP

The Roc. Edward Lowbury. Won't even notice when we choose to go. AmMo

The Rock. *Anonymous.* And a sprig of the rosemary. GBL

The Rock. Thomas Stearns Eliot.
The cycles of Heaven in twenty centuries/Bring us farther from God and nearer to the Dust. OBMV; TRV
Familiar with the roads and settled nowhere. TiPo
In an age which advances progressively backwards? TRV
Let the fire not be quenched in the forge. EBCP
O Light Invisible, we give Thee thanks for Thy great/glory! ILwL; OxBoCh
Only for important weddings. NAMP
The perpetual struggle of Good and Evil. TiPo
Their only monument the asphalt road/And a thousand lost golf balls. TRV
...they are not in the City. TiPo
To be filled with a litter of Sunday newspapers? TRV

The Rock. Mary Fabilli. One can't achieve/infrangible solutions/outside the rock. AMV-81

The Rock. William Stanley Merwin. hearing under the breath the stone/that is ours alone. NYP

The Rock. Wallace Stevens. Night's hymn of the rock, as in a vivid sleep. AP

The Rock-A-By Lady. Eugene Field. Comes stealing; comes creeping. HBVY; TiPo

Rock-a-Bye Baby. Effie I. Canning. So rock-a-bye, baby, mother is here. FSN

Rock-a-Bye Baby. Mother Goose. And down will come baby, cradle and all. FaFP; TiPo

Rock-a My Soul. Anonymous. Oh, rock-a my soul. FSW

Rock about My Saro Jane. Anonymous. And rock about, my Saro Jane. FSW

Rock and Hawk. Robinson Jeffers. Which failure cannot cast down/Nor success make proud. MoVE; NoAm; NOBA; OxBA

Rock and Roll. Sibyl James. his old Ford door WIDE OPEN on that/ Promised Land. AmC

Rock away, passenger. Anonymous. Crushed will be the carriages, engine and all. CenHV

Rock, Ball, Fiddle. Anonymous. He that lies in the middle/Shall have a gold fiddle. CBEP; OxBoLi

Rock, Be My Dream. MacKnight Black. Rock, be my dream, a burning fulfilled. PoSH

Rock Carving. Douglas Stewart. And moves like the shadow of a bird across the stone. SeCePo

Rock Climbing. Jane Cooper. And looking back to hillsides build/ Imaginary houses. NMM

The Rock Crumbles. Else Lasker-Schüler. My people,/Cry out to God. TrJP

Rock'd in the Cradle of the Deep. Emma Hart Willard. Rock'd in the cradle of the deep. PSoN

Rock (excerpt). Kathleen Raine. And weather them down to sand on the sea-floor. ImOP

The Rock Island Line. Anonymous. Buy your ticket at the station on the Rock Island Line. AmFP; FSW

Rock Leader. Dave Bathgate. Old climbers never die, they just run out of rope. PoSH

Rock-Lily. Roland Robinson. ...Alone/this spray breaks from the stone. BoAV; PoAu 1-2

Rock Me to Sleep. Elizabeth Akers Allen. Rock me to sleep, mother,–rock me to/sleep! AA; BLPA; BLPL; FaBoBe; FaFP; HBV 1-2; OBCA; PaPo; TreF; WBLP

Rock 'n' Row Me over. Anonymous. Oh, rock 'n' row me over,/One more day! FSW

Rock of Ages. Augustus Montague Toplady. Let me hide myself in Thee. BLRP; BLSo; FaFP; FaPoR; FSW; GoTF; HBV 1-2; NOCV; OxBoCh; TreF; WGRP

The Rock of Cashel. Sir Aubrey De Vere. Or Thebes half buried in the desert sand. IrPN; NBM

Rock of My Salvation. Mordecai Ben Isaac. Thy shepherds seven/Haste to my salvation! TrJP

Rock Painting. Carroll Arnett. From his/hands, it/is in/the stone. VoR

Rock Painting. Jack Cope. do they know he will die? PeSA

Rock Pilgrim. Herbert Palmer. I will plod up the ridge to the right, past the crimson-green holly. OxBTC

Rock, Rock, Sleep, My Baby. Clyde Watson. When your Daddy comes back home/He'll sing a song for you. NTCP

Rock Tumbler. Monty Reid. A woman/fishes in the water/for a stone. CaPN

Rock Water Blues. Bessie Smith. They ain't no place for a poor old girl to go BluL

Rocket Show. James Keir Baxter. Mad as the polar moon, decipherable by none. AnNZ

Rockferns. Norman Nicholson. My soul shall detonate on high/And plant itself in cracks of sky. MoBrPo

Rocking. Archie Randolph Ammons. that earnest little/rooster off again. GP

The Rocking Chair. Abraham Moses Klein. its music moves, as if always back to a first love. CaP; HeIP; NoP; PeCV

Rockingchair. Robert Morgan. ...Quiet/after the stroke, he rocked himself/ through childhood and a second infancy. PPJ

Rocks. Florence Parry Heide. I really hold a million million rocks here in my hand. NTCP

Rocks and Deals. Geoffrey Young. But if the dead could write, would we bother to? APU

Rocks and Gravel. Anonymous. When you lays all night and your Daddy's on benzedrine. FSW

Rocky Acres. Robert Graves. Terror for fat burghers in far plains below. LiTB; NoAm; UnPo

The Rocky Island. Anonymous. To let the wide world know I died for love. AmFP

The Rocky Mountains. Anonymous. Where the wild beasts howls and roars. AmFP

The Rocky Road to Dublin. Anonymous. Down the rocky road and all the way to Dublin./Whack-fol-lol-de-ra. FaBoBa

Rococo. John Payne. In Love's lips my roses lie. OBVV

Rococo. Algernon Charles Swinburne. For one that you remember/And ten that you forget. HBV 1-2; ViBoPo

The Rod. Robert Herrick. The rod doth sleep, while vigilant are men. LiTB

Roddy M'Corley. Anonymous. And young Roddy M'Corley goes to die/On the Bridge of Toome today. FSW

Rodeo Days. Squire Omar Barker. Hi-yip! We've still got the ol' rodeo! PoOW

Rodin to Rilke. Emily Grosholz. you see how it stiffens, fires to a beautiful red. AMV-80

Rodney's Glory. Owen Roe O'Sullivan. And vindicate bold England's right/And die for Erin's glory. OnYI

Rodney's Ride. Anonymous. And the sons of the free may recall with pride/The day of Delegate Rodney's ride. MC; PAH

A Rodomontade on His Cruel Mistress. John Wilmot, Earl of Rochester. But she is worse: in time she will forestall/The Devil, and be the damning of us all. OBSP

Roethke Plain. John Malcolm Brinnin. they look like bunny shoes./Love,/ T. NoAm; TAP

Rogation Days. Kenneth Rexroth. ...or if I just wanted/to go nowhere at all. NaP

Roger and Dolly. Anonymous. ...as you came you may go,/Stumpaty, stumpaty, stump. OxNR

Roger and Dolly. Henry Carey. While Dolly's afraid she shall die an old maid,/Mumpaty, mumpaty, mump. CoMu; NOEC

Roger and Me. Anne Le Dressay. waiting for the chance to run/home free. AMV-81

Roger Francis. Wilfrid Thorley. With a rod, a net,/And a pickle-jar. BrR

Roger Williams. Hezekiah Butterworth. And so the pine boughs cover me. PAH

Rogue Pearunners. Ronald G. Everson. lest the mind open/with intuitions and imaginings. PeCV

Le Roi Est Mort. Agnes Mary Frances (Mme Emile Duclaux) Robinson. Nor is of any creed, and dead/Can never rise again. OBVV

Roisin Dubh. Aubrey Thomas De Vere. But on poisons thrive, and in death survive/Through ghostly night. AnIV

Roisin Dubh. Owen Roe MacWard. Before the day she sinks in death, my Ros geal dubh! OnYI

The Rokeby Venus. Robert Conquest. ...the inhabitants/Of our imaginations and our beds. NoAm

Roll a Rock Down. Richard Burton. And say that I went like a ranger should go. AnAmPo

Roll, Alabama, Roll. Anonymous. The Kearsage won. Alabama so brave/ Sank to the bottom to a watery grave. OBSS

Roll-Call. Nathaniel Graham Shepherd. Numbered but twenty that answered/"Here!". AA; HBV 1-2; OHIP

Roll Call: A Land of Old Folk and Children. Isaac J. Black. my camera cannot shoot. CNA

Roll de Ol' Chariot Along. Anonymous. Roll de ol' chariot along,/Ef you' don't hang on behin'. BoAN 1-2

Roll in My Sweet Baby's Arms. Anonymous. Wouldn't even go my bail. FSW

Roll, Johnny Booger. Anonymous. The boys can't beat our time. BFSS

Roll, Jordan, Roll. Anonymous. I want to go to Heaven when I die/To hear Jordan roll. AA; AH; BoAN 1-2; FSW

Roll, Julia, Roll. Anonymous. Julia, roll! Roll! Julia, roll!/The Liverpool girls they've got us in tow! ShS

Roll On, Sad World! Frederick Goddard Tuckerman. Look, where the gray is white! AnNE; TreFS

Roll on the Ground. Anonymous. Eat soda crackers,/Roll on the ground. AmFP; FSW

Roll Out, O Song. Frank Sewall. Come, let us in Him rest. Amen. AA

Roll Over. Anonymous. And the little one said,/"Good night." FSW

Roll the Chariot (with music). Anonymous. And we won't drag on behind. AS

Roll the Cotton down. Anonymous. Oh, roll the cotton down. AmFP; ShS

Roll the Union On. Lee and Claude Williams. Hays. We're gonna roll the union on. FSW

Rolled over on Europe. Stephen Spender. and these few lines/Written from home, are real. CMoP

Rollicking Bill the Sailor. Anonymous. But we have only one bed!/Cried the fair young maiden. AmSS

The Rollicking Mastodon. Arthur Macy. For Little Peetookle is spared the strain/Of the Rollicking Mastodon over in Spain. NA

The Rolling English Road. Gilbert Keith Chesterton. Before we go to Paradise by way of Kensal Green. EvOK; FaBoCh; HBMV; LoGBV; NOBE; NOBL; OBEV; OBMV; OxBTC; SeCeV

Rolling Home. Anonymous.
Ancient ocean wave to waft us to that well-remembered shore. OBSS
Rolling home to dear New England,/rolling home, dear land, to thee. AmSS; ShS

Rolling 'ome to Merry England,/Where kind friends do await for me. ShS

Rolling Home.　Charles Mackay.　Rolling home, dear land, to thee!　FSW

Rolling John (excerpt).　A. J. Wood.　Rolling John attend my prayer:/Hi ho my bonny boy!　PoAu 1-2

Rolling Log Blues.　Lottie Kimbrough.　Gonna fix it/so I won't have to drift no more/Mmmmmmmm.　BluL

The Rolling Sailor.　Anonymous.　I do love a jolly sailor,/Blithe and merry might he be.　OBSS

Rolling the Lawn.　William Empson.　As martyrs gridirons, when God calls the roll.　MoBrPo

Rolling Thunder.　Phyllis Wolf.　...See the clouds/become deeper as they pass the rise.　STE

Rollo's Miracle.　Paul Zimmer.　But that sun shines on and on–/Bright as a fresh dropped egg.　GOYP

Rolly Trudum.　Anonymous.　Rolly-trudum, trudum, trudum-rolly-day.　AmFP

Roma.　Rutilius.　Joy out of strife by sparing/O'ercamest the sources of terror/In love with all that remains.　CTC

Roma Aeterna.　Adelaide Crapsey.　Thine olden Palatine the birds/Still sing.　QFR

The Roman Calendar.　Benjamin Hall Kennedy.　Make Nones the 7th, Ides the 15th day.　FaBoUs

The Roman Earl.　Anonymous.　Let her hear not sigh nor groan.'　OBVE

Roman Fountain.　Louise Bogan.　After the air of summer.　NoP; SBG; WPOW

Roman History in Rhyme (excerpt).　Edward B. Goodwin.　And Ancus made the Ostian port,/Sublician bridge, and many a fort.　FaBoUs

A Roman Mirror.　Sir James Rennell Rodd.　And sets the dead-land-lilies in her breast.　OBVV

Roman Numerals.　Anonymous.　And L for Fifty, I'll tell you.　FaBoUs

A Roman Officer Writes.　Charles M. Doughty.　Strengthen thee, in this sorrow, I pray the gods!　FaBoTw

Roman Presents.　Martial (Marcus Valerius Martialis).　...it's an act/Of generosity–in point of tact.　OBCP

The Roman Road.　Thomas Hardy.　The Roman Road.　AWP; BrPo; FaBoPP; GoJo; MoBrPo; NOBE

A Roman Roman.　Crescenzo Del Monte.　many houses crumbling, step by step,/while I, thank God, am still on my feet.　VWA

The Roman Stage.　Lionel Pigot Johnson.　The next imperial actor now/Bids the satyric piece begin.　BrPo; NOBV

A Roman Thank-You Letter.　Martial (Marcus Valerius Martialis).　I miss the old four pounds. Let's start again!　OBCP

Roman Wall Blues.　W. H. Auden.　When I'm a veteran with only one eye/I shall do nothing but look at the sky.　DTC

Roman Women.　Thomas Edward Brown.　O Pincian woman, do not come to Rome!　NOBV; OBNC

Romance.　William Ernest Henley.　And they meant it too, by thunder!　EnLit; MC; PAH

Romance.　Mildred Howells.　They see a little dark-eyed girl at play.　AA

A Romance.　Chester Kallman.　He loved, he died. No one knows which came first.　PoA

Romance.　Andrew Lang.　My heart is colder than the clay!　HBV 1-2

Romance.　Edgar Allan Poe.　Unless it trembled with the strings.　AP; APA; AtBAP; BoLiVe; NePA; OxBA

Romance.　Robert Louis Stevenson.　Of the broad road that stretches and the/roadside fire.　BLPL; BSV; GoTS; GTBS; HBV 1-2; LiTL; MoBrPo; OBEV; OBVV; PoRA; PoSC; TrGrPo

Romance.　Walter James Turner.　Chimborazo, Cotopaxi,/They had stolen my soul away!　BiCB; CH; GoJo; HBMV; HBVY; MoBrPo; NOAV; NOBE; OBMV; PoRA; TrGrPo; WHA

The Romance of Citrus.　Christy Sheffield Sanford.　..."would you mind if I changed my name to/Tangerine?"　APU

The Romance of Imprinting.　Christy Sheffield Sanford.　...Pa-/rishioners in Wells, England (1595), marked/with crosses. Numberous scattered...　APU

Romance of the Cigarette.　Mary di Michele.　the heart's a chess game where the queen's lost/or the closest thing to death in life.　CaPN

Romance of the Range.　Robert V. Carr.　An' now we've went an' fixed it so she'll never go away.　PoOW

The Romance of the Rose.　Guillaume de Lorris　So truly set all forth as now/'Tis writ within this book I trow.　EG; EnLi 1-2; OAEL 1-2; PoEL 1-5

The Romance of the Rose: Love vs. Marriage.　Jean de Meung.　Not all the gold of Araby/Or Frisia would pay that fee.　EnLi 1-2

Romance of the Swan's Nest.　Elizabeth Barrett Browning.　She could never show him–never,/That swan's nest among the reeds!　GN

Romance VIII.　Saint John of Damascus.　Wherefore He is called together/Son of God and Son of Man.　ISi

Romans Angry about the Inner World.　Robert Bly.　It is like a jagged stone/Flying toward them out of the darkness.　NoAm; NOBA; PPoe

The Romantic.　Colin Ellis.　To learn the rapture of defeat.　PoL

Romantic.　George Garrett.　Who will be wounded most?　HoPM

Romany Gold.　Amelia Josephine Burr.　And we're taking the road together.　HBMV

The Romaunt of the Rose.　Anonymous.　Men clepen them sirens in France.　PBBP

Rome.　Joachim Du Bellay.
　And that which fleeteth doth outrun swift time.　AWP
　That which is firme doth flit and fall away,/And that is flitting, doth abide and stay.　LiTW

Rome.　Thomas Hardy.
　It is an ample fame.　EnLi 1-2; MoAB
　Through each rent wall their feeble works in-/vade/Once shamed all such in power of pier and/groin.　VLP

Rome.　Marcelino Menendez y Pelayo.　'Twas human glory, or God's majesty?　CAW

Rome.　Panormitanus.　And the ever-moving will remain forever.　OBVE

Rome, Conqueror, Conquered.　Joshua Sylvester.　Sith Time hath conquer'd the world's conqueror?　FaBoEE

Rome Once Alone.　Clark Coolidge.　and the last thing I rob will be a gong.　APU

Rome Remember.　Sidney Keyes.　How alien the lovers of your ghost.　MoAB

Romeo and Juliet.　Howard Phelps (Phelps Putnam) Putnam.　For love of you, old slit, for love of you.　ErPo

Romeo and Juliet.　Fred Newton Scott.　Don't stab ourselves in the left pulmonary,/I'm Romeo, Juliet!　InMe

Romeo and Juliet.　William Shakespeare.
　More light and light: more dark and dark our woes!　GBL; TreFT
　O! That I were a glove upon that hand,/That I might touch that cheek.　BoC; LiTB; LiTL; MaC; MasP; MOON; TreF; TrGrPo; WHA
　...she gallops night by night/Through lovers' brains, and then they dream of love; BoW; FiP; LiTB; MaC; TreF; TrGrPo; WSC
　Then move not while my prayer's effect I take. BiP; SoSe
　This is thy sheath; there rust, and let me die. DL
　Thy drugs are quick. Thus with a kiss I die. FaFP; FiP; GoTF; LiTL; TreFS; TrGrPo; WHA
　To an impatient child that hath new robes/And may not wear them. GoTF; HW; LiTL; TreFS
　Upon the sweetest flower of all the field. FaBoRV; GN
　...you shall not stay alone/Till holy church incorporate two in one. GoBC

The Romish Lady.　Anonymous.　God pardon priest and people and so I bid farewell.　BFSS; OuSiCo

The Romney.　Harriet Monroe.　"Who was this Romney?"　HBMV

Romp.　Dave Etter.　I/am/glad/she/chose/to/run　WeW

Romping.　John Ciardi.　All right. Once more, then. But just once. You hear?　CTBA; NCSH

Ron Mason.　Hone Tuwhare.　...There's/work yet, for the living.　OCNZ

Ronald Wyn.　Robert Bagg.　I grave these rocks with love, in which you are versed.'　MP

The Ronan Robe Series.　Jaune Quick-To-See-Smith.　Stripes going round.　TWSS

Ronas Hill.　Hamish Brown.　marking our beginning/marking our end?　PoSH

The Rondeau.　Henry Austin Dobson.　Behold!–the Rondeau, tasteful, light,/You bid me try!　HBV 1-2

Rondeau.　Charles, Duc d' Orleans.　The year his winter cloak lets fall.　LiTW

Rondeau.　William Jay Smith.　Lord, I'm done!　FiBHP

Rondeau after a Transatlantic Telephone Call.　Marilyn Hacker.　..."Goodnight,/love. It was good."　SM

Rondeau: "By two black eyes my heart was won."　Anonymous.　Thought proper to reward my flame/With two black eyes!　FaBoCo

Rondeau for You.　Mario De Andrade.　The thought, the soul, the grief of you.　TTY

Rondeau: "Homage to change that scatters the poppy seed."　Ronald Bottrall.　It is when hiving brain-cells in us breed/Homage to change.　MoVE

Rondeau in Wartime.　James Bertram.　No nearer home.　AnNZ

Rondeau: "Of Eden lost."　George Ellis.　Finds this fair fruit too well suffice/To pay the peace, and honest praise,/Of EDEN lost.　OBEC

A Rondeau of Remorse.　Burges Johnson.　Oh, miserie! All flesh is grass!/Unhappy I!　HBMV

Rondeau Redouble.　John Payne.　And holdeth in the hollow of his hand/My day and night.　HBV 1-2

Rondel.　Philip Dacey.　As they watch fall the uninvited/And beautiful snow onto their bed.　SM

Rondel.　X. J. Kennedy.　The world is taking off her clothes.　SM

Rondel.　Muriel Rukeyser.　Come and celebrate with me.　FF

Rondel: Autumn.　Matt Field.　and sink at last to the lasting dark.　AMV-80

Rondel: Beside the Idle Summer Sea.　William Ernest Henley.　Beside the idle summer sea.　OBNC

Rondel for Middle Age.　Louise Townsend Nicholl.　We play now very lightly, on the strings.　NePoAm

Rondel for September. Karle Wilson Baker. You thought it was a falling
leaf we heard. HBMV

Rondel: "Good-by, the tears are in my eyes." Francois Villon. Good-by,
the last of my good-bys. AWP

Rondel: "Kissing her hair I sat against her feet." Algernon Charles
Swinburne. Unless, perhaps, white death had kissed me there,/Kissing her
hair? BLPL; FaBoBe; HBV 1-2; ViBoPo

Rondel: "Love, love, what wilt thou with this heart of mine?" Jean Froissart.
Naught see I permanent or sure in thee! AWP

A Rondel of Love. Alexander Scott. Flee always from the snare. BoLoP;
BSV; OBEV; OxBS

A Rondel of Merciless Beauty. Geoffrey Chaucer. Straight through my
heart the wound is quick and keen. TrGrPo

Rondel (parody). Anonymous. Behold the works of William Morris!
BXAP; Par

Rondel: "Strengthen, my Love, this castle of my heart." Charles d'Orleans.
Strengthen, my Love, this castle of my heart. AWP

Rondelay. John Dryden. Kised him up, and eased his pain. ALV; CavP;
DiPo; ViBoPo

Rondo. George Moore. And if love such a thing not be,/I loved not thee.
UnTE

Ronsard. Miriam Allen DeFord. Over whose waves the insect pipes and
drummers/Die in an afternoon. HBMV

Ronsard to His Mistress. William Makepeace Thackeray. And gather in
their blushing prime/The roses of your youth! HBV 1-2

Rontgen Photograph. Elisabeth Eybers. All grief and ecstasy and pain/
were they a phantom of the brain? PeSA

Roof Garden. Raymond Filip. I sweep away blossoms and dust,/Small
claims to my care,/Which lend the sunset its colors. CaPN

The Roof Garden. Howard Moss. And water mains, writhing underfoot.
MAT; NYP

Roof Garden. James Schuyler. a long, long time ago/petunias/adorable,
sticky flower. ANYP

The Roof of the World. Michael Dennis Browne. waiting around minutely,
in baskets,/to be born again. AmPA

Roofs. Joyce Kilmer. But it leads at last to a golden Town where/golden
Houses are. BLPL; PoLf

Rooftop. Willis Barnstone. and forgot to sail back up/in the high open
sunny air. FAZ

The Rooftop. Thom Gunn. Huddled in dark, and hold,/Waiting for when
they fill. NoP

Rooftop Winter. Dwayne Thorpe. ...I hold/whatever offers refuge. Cold is
cold. AMV-80

The Rooftree. Allen Tate.
...a house of strife/Built far back in the fundaments of life. PoA
More spectral than November eve could mix/With sunset, to blaze on her
pale crucifix. PoA
Nor poured out quite when the life-blood has run. PoA
Until he freed his negroes, lest he be/Too strict with nature and then they
less free. PoA
Which brother, you or I, shall swiftly go. PoA

The Roofwalker. Adrienne Rich. fleeing across the roofs. CAPP; CoAP;
PPP

Rookery. Nora Dauenhauer. the beach twitches with life. TWSS

The Rookery at Sunrise. William Sharp. ...they sway/In one black phalanx
towards the day. FM

Rookhope Ryde. Anonymous. To pray for e] singer of this song,/For he
sings to make blithe your/cheer. ESPB

Rookie's Lament. Anonymous. Had to go out and dig another "rear."
ABF

The Rooks. Anonymous. Wi October's wind and rain. GBP; HBMV;
MoBrPo

The Rooks. Jane Euphemia Browne (Aunt Effie). But rooks all talk
together. OxBChV

Rooks. Charles Hamilton Sorley. From day to night, from night to day.
MoBrPo

The Room. Conrad Aiken. I will praise darkness now, but then the leaf.
AP; LiTM; MAPA; MoAmPo; NePA; NOBA

The Room. C. Day-Lewis. ...under the royal action and abstraction/He
lived in, he was real. PoCh

The Room. De Leon Harrison. Nor realizing that without life/there is no
rhythm PoBA

The Room. Elizabeth Jennings. Tomorrow's debris settles here/To make
my art, to alter me. NePoEA-2

Room. Shirley Kaufman. ...He has/gone out of you. NMM

The Room. William Stanley Merwin. You would say it was dying it is
immortal. NaP; NOBA

The Room. Vladimir Nabokov. unknown, unloved–but not alone. NYBP

The Room. Gregory Orr. the white room swallowing what was passed.
GeTw

The Room. William Soutar. Even as the day into this room. EBEV

Room. Ruth Stone. With my ear against the plaster. BoWoP

Room 000. William Stafford. "Why is a hall? is a hall? is a hall?" GLGT

The Room Above the Square. Stephen Spender. Where among stones and
roots, the other/Unshattered lovers are. ChMP; NOBE

The Room above the White Rose. Joseph Stroud. With the faint,
otherworld song of monks/Chanting in the Dragon Temple at dawn.
NPGG

The Room and the Windows. Feng Chih. Which rise from the forgotten
past and the fading future. LiTW

Room for a Jovial Tinker: Old Brass to Mend. Anonymous. And then no
doubt your Mistresses will pay you for it soundly./With hey ho, hey, derry
derry down;. CoMu; OxBB

Room for Jesus. Barbara H. Staples. And He'll conquer every foe! STF

A Room I Once Knew. Henry Birnbaum. Close the front door. This is/
The front porch. Goodnight, house. GoYe

A Room in the Past. Ted Kooser. and wiped out the sink, turning her
back/on the rest of us, forever. Str

A Room in the Villa. William Jay Smith. While, patient in the eaves, the
shadows wait. NYBP

The Room of My Life. Anne Sexton. and the sea that bangs in my throat.
CAPP

Room of Return. Galway Kinnell. Pricking the sky, shelled by the dirty
sea. NYP

A Room on a Garden. Wallace Stevens. He well might find it in this fret/
Of lilies rusted, rotting, wet/With rain. NoP

Room Poems. Eli Bachar. they cover the stains of my presence with clear
dust VWA

The Room's Width. Elizabeth Stuart Phelps Ward. O Lord of life! am I
forbid/To cross the room? AA

Room Service. John W. Moser. ..."If I've got a telephone, a television,/my
Bible, and room service, what more do I need." FAZ

Rooming House. Ted Kooser. under the blind man's door, and all is right.
PoL

Rooming-House Melancholy. Erich Kastner. (But marriage is a yet more
awful doom.) LiTW

Rooms. Charlotte Mew. Out there in the sun–in the rain. PBWP

Roosevelt Considers Catfish Stew. R. T. Smith. Roosevelt, Roosevelt,
where them catfish be? WOLT

Roosters. Elizabeth Bishop. faithful as enemy, or friend. AmLP; CrMA;
LiTM; NePA

Roosters. Elizabeth Jane Coatsworth. "You're right!"/says Rooster Two.
SO

The Roosters Will Crow. Cecilia Meireles. In that soft contour/Of a shell
in the water. PBWP

Root. Miklos Radnoti. A saw wails over my head. VWA

The Root Canal. Marge Piercy. ...a grandiose/talking headstone for my
tooth. DFF; HoAn

Root Cellar. Theodore Roethke. Even the dirt kept breathing a small
breath. AmPP; BoNaP; HeIP; InPK; NoP; PPP

Root Hog or Die. Anonymous. And you land in the calaboose to–Root hog
or die. AmFP; FSW

Root Hog or Die. Floyd B. Small. They were very thick in places
where 'twas root hog or die. PoOW

Roots. Louis Ginsberg. And so I learned how my little tree/Was rooted
deep in Eternity! TrJP

Roots. Seymour Mayne. ...And already begun to grow pale/green roots.
NOBC

Roots and Branches. Robert Duncan. awakening transports of an inner
view of things. VGW

Roots and Leaves Themselves Alone. Walt Whitman. If you become the
aliment and the wet they will become flowers, fruits, tall branches and trees.
NePA

Roots Go Down. Lloyd Frankenberg. the distant dripping of water wasting
through clay. AnEnPo

The Roots of Revolution in the Vegetable Kingdom. Constance Urdang. let
there be only the earth and the seeds/and the harvests thereof. GP

The Rope. Tania Van Zyl. So little/then it matters/what is treasured.
PeSA

Rope and Drum. Robert Currie. the rope burns still/hot on his neck Str

A Rope for Harry Fat. James Keir Baxter. "We will not change our
policy,"/Says Harry Fat the Proud. MoBS

Rope's End. Peter F. Neumeyer. and hauls me gasping sandwards through
his sonnet. WOLT

The Ropewalk. Henry Wadsworth Longfellow. And the spinners backward
go. AP; MAmP

Rorate Coeli Desuper. William Dunbar. Pro nobis Puer natus est. BSV;
SBVL

Rorschach. Laura Fargas. Seeds are falling everywhere. SUW

Rory O'More; or, Good Omens. Samuel Lover. For there's luck in odd
numbers," says Rory O'More. HBV 1-2

Rory of the Hill. Charles Joseph Kickham. The rough and ready roving
boys, like Rory of the Hill. OnYI

Rosa. Anonymous. Rosa, let us get married, O Rosa sweet! TrAS

Rosa Mystica. *Anonymous.* Transeamus! CAW; EG; GoBC; ISi

Rosa Mystica. Gerard Manley Hopkins. Draw me by charity, mother of mine. ACP; GoBC

Rosa Nascosa. Maurice Hewlett. ...there are mines/Far down, whose sacred fee/And golden hold no trammelling can bind. OBVV

Rosa Rosarum. Agnes Mary Frances (Mme Emile Duclaux) Robinson. And o'er that chill and secret wave it throws/A sudden dawn of red. HBMV

Rosabelle. Sir Walter Scott. But the sea-caves rung, and the wild winds sung,/The dirge of lovely Rosabelle. BeLS; EnLi 1-2; GTBS; GTBS-P; HBV 1-2

Rosader's Sonnet. Thomas Lodge. But in thy love I live and die. OBSC

Rosalie. Washington Allston. In music to her soul. AA

Rosalie, the Prairie Flower. George Frederick Root. Sweet Rosalie, "The Prairie Flow'r". BLSo

Rosalind's Scroll. Elizabeth Barrett Browning. And pale among the saints I stand,/A saint companionless. HBV 1-2

Rosalynde. Thomas Lodge.
Heigh ho, my heart! would God that she were mine! EiL; GoBC; GTBS; GTBS-P; LiTB; OBEV; OBSC; TrGrPo; UnTE
Shall true hearts be fancies fuell? AtBAP; EG; PoEL 1-5; TrGrPo
Spare not, but play thee! ALV; EiL; EnLit; GoBC; GTBS; HBV 1-2; InvP; LoBV; NOBE; NoP; OBEV; OBSC; SeCePo; UnTE; ViBoPo

Rosamond's Appeal. Samuel Daniel. Because her griefs were worthy to be known,/And telling hers, might hap forget mine own. OBSC

The Rosarie. Robert Herrick. But forthwith bade my Julia shew/A bud in either cheek. InMe

The Rosary. Sister Maura. Of mystic beauty, day by day, to be/Diadem for the Queen of the Rosary. ISi

The Rosary. Robert Cameron Rogers. I kiss each bead, and strive at last to learn/To kiss the Cross. AA; BLSo; FaBoBe; FSN; HBV 1-2; TreF; WBLP

The Rosary of My Tears. Abram Joseph Ryan. He reaches the haven through tears. HBV 1-2

The Rosciad. Charles Churchill. Live without sex, and die without a name. NOEC

The Rose. Angelus Selesius (Johannes Scheffler). Nor seeks the idle eye to tell its power. CAW

A Rose. Arlo Bates. "Yet at least with the rose/Went a kiss that I'm wearing." HBV 1-2

The Rose. William Browne. God shield the stock! If heaven send no supplies,/The fairest blossom of the garden dies. HBV 1-2; OBEV

The Rose. Robert Creeley. to come home to. AP

A Rose. Sir Richard Fanshawe. Nay, force thy bud to blow; their tyrant breath/Anticipating life, to hasten Death. CavP; HBV 1-2; OBEV; OBS; PoEL 1-5; SeCePo

The Rose. Johann Wolfgang von Goethe. Rose once redly glowing. AWP

The Rose. George Herbert. For my answer is a rose. AtBAP; LiTB; PoEL 1-5

The Rose. Thomas Howell. Of all the pleasant flowers in June/The red rose hath no peer. EiL; OBSC

The Rose. G. A. Studdert Kennedy. I an my rose/Are one. EBCP

The Rose. Thomas Lodge. I think with doubtful view/Whether you be the rose, or the rose is you. OBSC

The Rose. Richard Lovelace. Her bed a rosy nest/By a bed of roses prest. EG

The Rose. Theodore Roethke. Gathering to itself sound and silence–/Mine and the sea-wind's. BiP; CH; HBV 1-2; NaP; NOBA; NYBP; PAI; PPoe

The Rose. Pierre Ronsard. Like roses that were loveliest. AWP

Rose. Lewis Thompson. Such massive sweetness fills no smaller air. AtBAP

The Rose. William Carlos Williams. stillness was an eternity/long since begun NOBA

The Rose and God. Charles Wharton Stork. Whence love to every crimson petal flows. HBMV

Rose and Root. John James Piatt. I know a Rose in overhead. AA

The Rose and the Gauntlet. John Wilson. On the withered leaves and the maiden dead. BeLS

The Rose and the Thorn. Paul Hamilton Hayne. The thorn has pierced her heart. AA; FaBoBe; HBV 1-2

The Rose and the Wind. Philip Bourke Marston. Roses must live and love, and winds must blow. OBVV

Rose Aylmer. Walter Savage Landor. A night of memories and sighs/I consecrate to thee. AWP; BoLiVe; BoLoP; CABA; CH; ELP; EnLoPo; ExPo; FaFP; GoTF; GTBS; HAP; HBV 1-2; HeIP; HoPM; InPo; LiTB; LiTL; LoBV; NOBE; NoP; OAEL 1-2; OAEP; OBEV; OBNC; OBRV; OBVV; PoEL 1-5; RoGo; SeCeV; TEP; TreFS; TrGrPo; WHA

Rose Bay Willow Herb. Judy Ray. rose bay willow herb. AMV-81; FAZ

The Rose-Bud To a Young Lady. William Broome. Queen of Fragrance, lovely Rose. CEP; LoBV; OBEC

Rose-Cheeked Laura. Thomas Campion. Ever perfect, ever in them-/Selves eternal. AAS; AtBAP; EnL; EnLoPo; ExPo; InPK; InPo; InPS; InvP; LoBV; NoP; OAEL 1-2; OAEP; PAI; PoEL 1-5; SeCeV; TrGrPo; ViBoPo

Rose Connoley. *Anonymous.* And gaze upon his own dear son, swinging on the gallows high. AmFP

La Rose des Vents. Richard Wilbur. And tend the true,/The mortal flower. MiAP

The Rose Family. Robert Frost. You, of course, are a rose–/But were always a rose. NIP; OBAL; OBCA; SoSe

A Rose in October. James Whitcomb Riley. For my Rose of October there promised/She'd bloom for me aye, as–my wife. OBAL

Rose in the Afternoon. Jenny Joseph. And only your image waking in the dark. BrRo

Rose in the Garden. *Anonymous.* To court all night and sleep all day. AmFP

The Rose Is a Royal Lady. Charles G. Blanden. I'll find my cap a feather,/And kiss a Highland bride! HBMV

The Rose Is Red, the Grass Is Green. *Anonymous.* And see the cat play with the dog. OxNR

The Rose Is Red, the Rose Is White. *Anonymous.* I would not part with my sweetheart/For tuppence ha'penny farden. OxNR

The Rose Is Red, the Violet's Blue. *Anonymous.* And fortune said it should be you. OxNR

Rose-Marie of the Angels. Adelaide Crapsey. How God will be glad of thee,/Little Sister Rose-Marie! HBV 1-2

The Rose of Eden. Susan K. Phillips. But the hour that brought the scent of rose, she lived it in Paradise. BeLS

The Rose of England. *Anonymous.* Confound his ffoes, Lord, wee beseeche,/And loue His Grace both night and/day! ESPB

The Rose of Life. Luis de Gongora y Argote. ...their tyrant breath,/Anticipating life, to hasten death. AWP

The Rose of May. Mary Howitt. Left, like a noble deed, to grace/The memory of an ancient race. HBV 1-2

The Rose of Peace. William Butler Yeats. A peace of Heaven with Hell. OBVV

The Rose of the World. John Masefield. "O Rose of all the World, O lovely thing." PoRA

The Rose of the World. William Butler Yeats. He made the world to be a grassy road/Before her wandering feet. BoLiVe; BrPo; CMoP; HBV 1-2; MoAB; MoBrPo; OBVV

The Rose of Tralee. C. Mordaunt Spencer. Oh, no! 'Twas the truth in her eye ever dawning,/That made me love Mary, The Rose of Tralee. FSW; OnYI; TreFT

Rose Pogonias. Robert Frost. That none should mow the grass there/While so confused with flowers. MAmP

Rose Red to Snow White. Joan Colby. or sleep grunting all winter. DFT

The Rose's Cup. Frank Dempster Sherman. For that may be the reason/Her lips with dew are wet. AA

The Rose Still Grows beyond the Wall. A. L. Frink. Just as it will for evermore. BLPA

The Rose That Bore Jesu. *Anonymous.* And folwe we this joyful birth:/Transeamus. OxBM

Rose the Red and White Lilly. *Anonymous.* I wonder what would our step-dame say/Gin she this sight did see! ESPB; OxBB

A Rose to the Living. Nixon Waterman. Sumptuous wreaths to the dead. HBV 1-2; PoToHe

The Rose Tree. William Butler Yeats. There's nothing but our own red blood/Can make a right Rose Tree. CMoP; DiPo; ELP; FaBoPV; OBMV

A Rose Will Fade. Dora Sigerson Shorter. A rose will fade in a day! HBV 1-2

Rosebud. Jon Anderson. ...it seems important not to hurt the land. MAYP

The Rosebush and the Trinity. Alfred Joseph Barrett. More about the rose. GoBC

Rosemary Lane. *Anonymous.* So me and my baby/To the workhouse must go. OBET

The Rosemary Spray. Luis de Gongora y Argote. The blue-eyed flower, that blooms to-day,/To honey turns to-morrow. AWP; LiTW

Roses. *Anonymous.* Then may be proved here anon/That we three be agreed in on.' OxBM

Roses. Thomas Campion. And as a rose in Venus' bosom worn,/So doth a bridegroom his bride's bed adorn. OBSC

Roses. J. Corson Miller. You'll hear the roses speak to the moon. CAW

Roses. Pierre Ronsard. Be therefore kind, my love, whilst thou art fair. AWP

Roses. Pierre de Ronsard. That in death as in life thy body may be roses. LiTW

Roses. Thomas Stanley. And a youthful measure tread. AWP

Roses and Revolutions. Dudley Randall. the blood-red flower of revolution. BPo; CNA; ConAP; NIP; NoAm; PoBA; TAP

Roses are Beauty, but I Never See. John Masefield. Pasture to living beauty, life that was. EnLi 1-2

Roses Gone Wild. John Taylor. Wind cries in roses gone wild. AMV-80; FAZ

Roses in December. G. Anketall "Woodbine Willie" Studdert-Kennedy. Forgive, when I remember. BLPA

Roses of Memory. Armistead Churchill Gordon. In the red front of War. AA

The Roses of Queens. Claire Nicholas White. Their hopes have come to rest/in the radiant roses of Queens. NYP

The Roses of Sa'adi. Marceline Desbordes-Valmore. You may take from it now their fragrant souvenir. BoWoP; LiTW; WPOW

The Roses of Thy Cheeks. Rafi of Merv. Thy mart is thronged today, but few will come to-/morrow. LiTW

Roses on the Breakfast Table. D. H. Lawrence. How lovely is the self this day discloses. BrPo

The Roses on the Terrace. Alfred, Lord Tennyson. As this red rose, which on our terrace here/Glows in the blue of fifty miles away. VLP

Roses Only. Marianne Moore. you thorns are the best part of you. AnFE; CoAnAm; LiTM

Roses Red. Arno Holz. Flies the Phoenix bird,/Singing. AWP

Roses, Revisited, in a Paradoxical Autumn. J. W. Cullum. leaving us with old sonnets and our own uncertain wrists. AMV-81

Rosewood Casket. Anonymous. But the golden ring he gave me/From my finger never part. FSW

Rosewood Vision. Jim Brodey. I'm called "The Collision" ANYP

Rosh Pina. Dovid Knut. It's not slaves who die, but people. VWA

Rosie. Anonymous. O Rosie, oh, Lawd, gal. ABF

Rosie Nell (with music). Anonymous. I'd rather be with Rosie Nell, a-swinging in the lane. AS

Rosies. Agnes I. Hanrahan. Since we kep' rakin' in the hay/Thon day–thon day! HBV 1-2

Roslin and Hawthornden. Henry Van Dyke. And rolled the psalm, and poured the/prayer,/From Nature's solemn altar-stair. AA

Ross's Poems. Geoffrey Lehmann.
And the sky is lit by static lightning,/violet flashes. Jack. CBAP
"Someone has to plant them,' she said. CBAP
something we have lost. CBAP
That's our style of funeral. CBAP
Travelling between them/I stay sane. CBAP
You tell me. CBAP

Rossetti at Tea. Barry Pain. (O weary mother, drive the cows to roost). HBV 1-2

Rostov. G. S. Fraser. And says, "Why do you strike me brother? I am Man." WaP

Rosy Apple, Lemon, or Pear. Anonymous. Mother's runaway daughter. CH; PoL

The Rosy Bosom'd Hours. Coventry Patmore. A drizzling rain set in. EnLoPo; NOBV

The Rosy Days Are Numbered. Moses Ibn Ezra. Tell thou their number, then, in cups/of wine! TrJP

Rotation. Julian Bond. in an 8-ball universe built for ivory. FF; NIP; NNP

Rothesay, O. Anonymous. The day we went to Rothesay, O. FSW

Rothiemurchus. Colin Lamont. There's werm air tae lave you and bield fae the storm/Wi its cheated scream. PoSH

Rothko. James Moore. the shape he had made himself of himself. AMV-81

Rotten Lake Elegy. Muriel Rukeyser. beating, up from dead lakes, ascents of fire. MoPo; NePA

Rotten Row. Frederick Locker-Lampson. That I'm not quite so handsome now. ALV

Rouen. May Wedderburn Cannan. And the trains that go from Rouen at the ending of the day. OBWP; OxBTC

Rouge Bouquet. Joyce Kilmer. Shield us here./Farewell! HBV 1-2; MC; PAH; PoPl; TreFS

Rough Winds Do Shake. Louis Simpson. Then she'll lie still, asleep, who now lies ill, awake. ErPo

Roughchin, the Pirate. Arthur Boswell. And says our breakfast will be cold/If we play pirate any more. EtS

Round. Rachel Boimwall. A round tear/drops from your eye. VWA

The Round. Philip Booth. bittersweet, sumac,/snow, and frozen seed. BoNaP; GrPl; NCSH

A Round. William Browne. And plump as the lusty grape. ViBoPo

Round. Weldon Kees. "Wondrous life!" cried Marvell at Appleton House. CoAP; NaP; NoAm

Round about Me (fragment). Sappho. Spreads as a river. AWP

Round about, Round about. Anonymous. Up a bit, up a bit,/In a wee house. OxNR

Round About, Round About, Here Sits the Hare. Anonymous. And this little dog said, Give me a/little bit please. OxNR

Round about the Rosebush. Anonymous. Are sitting/On the doorsteps. OxNR

Round About There Sat a Little Hare. Anonymous. The bow-wows came and chased/him/right up there! OxNR

Round and Round. Dorothy Brown Thompson. Jesus' birthday/Comes again! BiCB; ChBR

Round and Round Hitler's Grave. Anonymous. Gonna lay that poor boy down,/He won't get up no more. FSW

Round and Round the Garden. Anonymous. Tickle you under there! OxNR

Round and Round the Rugged Rock. Anonymous. Now tell me if you can. OxNR

The Round Barrow. Andrew Young. Through the wan mist I journey on,/A clanking skeleton. SeCePo

Round Cape Horn. Anonymous. "Round Cape Horn." EtS

Round Dance, & Canticle. Robert Kelly. walking down to the sea &/back again. CoPo

Round Her Neck She Wore a Yellow Ribbon. Anonymous. She'd saved them for her lover who is far, far away. FSW

A Round Number. Keith Douglas. and Time has reached a round number. NeBP

Round Our Restlessness. Elizabeth Barrett Browning. Round our restlessness, his rest. TRV

Round Robin. Bhartrihari. O fie on her and him and Love and HER and me! LiTW

A Round Song. Rhyll McMaster. World you are good for me. CBAP

The Round Table. Peggy Susberry Kenner. And no one/leaves the round table. JB

The Round Table. [(or Manning)] Robert Mannyng. Evenly all of an assize. ACP

Round the Bay of Mexico. Anonymous.
I'm bound away for the fishing ground. FSW
Oh, Mexico's the place I belong in,/Round the Bay of Mexico. OuSiCo

Round Trip. Stan Rice. Can you stand on your hind legs like an angel and sing/the perfectly circular song? NPGG

The Round-Up. Sarah Elizabeth Howard. The round-up waits another call. PoOW

Round Valley Reflections. William Oandasan. not be the ash of memory in print/but cold mountain water STE

A Roundabout Turn. Robert E. Charles. And give me the Heath; it's flat! MoShBr

Rounded up in Glory. Anonymous. When He rounds you up within the Master's fold. CoSo

Roundel in the Rain. Anonymous. Still we shout with voice emphatic,/Hi! FiBHP

Roundel: "My ghostly fadir, Y me confesse." Charles, duc d' Orleans. First to God and then to you. EnPo

Roundel of Passion-Tide. Anonymous. But, friend of Mine, who wounded, knowest thou,/My hands? CAW

A Roundel of Rest. Arthur Symons. They know who work, not they who play,/If rest is sweet. HBV 1-2

A Roundelay. Michael Drayton. Thy Sylvia is as chaste as fair. EIL

A Roundelay. Edmund Spenser. Now endeth our reoundelay. EIL

The Roundhouse Voices. Dave Smith. ...and I stand down/on my knees to cry Who the hell are you, kid? AMV-80; GeTw; LiSp; MAYP

Rounding the Cape. Roy Campbell. And Night, the Negro, murmurs in his sleep. PeSA

Rounding the Horn. Anonymous. "God bless those pretty Spanish girls we left around Cape Horn." OBSS

The Roundup Cook. Robert V. Carr. We brag upon his chuck and act/Like perfect gentlemen. BPAW; PoOW

A Rouse for Stevens. Theodore Roethke. Brother, he's our father! OBAL

Rousecastle. David Wright. And unfamiliar angles of the under sea. MoBS

The Rousing Canoe Song. Hermia Fraser. Only hide thee, Lost Enchantress! CaP; WHW

Roustabout Holler. Anonymous. Take her down the river further, 'cause they ain't no mo'. OuSiCo

Rout. Philip Booth. flat out, straight/into the continent. FAZ

The Rout of San Romano. Jon Manchip White. Brothers in blood, a beastly, bitter brood. NePoEA

Route. Joseph Ceravolo. Waitress lips are kissing/our cheeks Hurrah! ANYP

Route 29. Catharine Savage Brosman. never the connection, the return. AMV-81

Route 95 North: New Jersey. P. C. Bowman. To flounder where the mountain and the whirlpool meet. AMV-80

A route of evanescence. Emily Dickinson. An easy morning's ride. AmePo; AmLP; ForPo; NoP; PoEL 1-5; SoSe

Route Six. Stanley Jasspon Kunitz. Twenty summers roll by. AMV-80

Routes. Peter Everwine. I race the shadows of the trees. FiCP; NNaP

The Routine. Paul Blackburn. I have watched him grow ELU

The Rover's Apology. Sir William Schwenck Gilbert. And I'll marry that lady to-morrow! ALV

The Rovers: Rogero's Song.   George Canning.   ...never shall I see the U–/–niversity of Gottingen/–niversity of Gottingen.–   CEP; NOEC

A-Roving.   *Anonymous.*   I'll go no more a-roving/With you fair maid.   FSW; ShS; UnTE

The Roving Gambler.   *Anonymous.*   If you ever see me coming back again I'll be with the gambling man.   ABF; AS; TrAS

Roving Gambler Blues.   *Anonymous.*   I am a roving gambler; rambling, gambling man.   FSW

The Roving Shanty Boy.   *Anonymous.*   Take a drink most any time–whiskey clear with me.   AmFP

The Roving Worker.   *Anonymous.*   'Tis the sole hope of the Rover!   OnYI

The Row between the Cages.   Thomas Armstrong.   Wor aud cage sent his notice in,/Just to vex the maisters.   VLP

Row Gently Here.   Thomas Moore.   What angels we should be!   HBV 1-2

Row of Houses.   John Robert Quinn.   To this dismal row/Of houses where only starved/Antennas grow?   AMV-80

A Row of Stalls.   Raymond Knister.   But the colt was too heavy.   OBCV

A Row of Thick Pillars.   Stephen Crane.   That crawls to the cool shadows of the pillars/To die.   AmePo

Row, Row, Row Your Boat.   *Anonymous.*   Life is but a dream.   FSW

The Rowan.   Violet Jacob.   But the rowan's deid.   PoSH

The Rowan County Crew (Tolliver-Martin Feud Song).   *Anonymous.*   It burns the breasts of those who drink it and sends their souls to hell.   AmFP; OuSiCo

The Rowan Tree.   Carolina Oliphant, Lady Nairne.   But hallowed thoughts around thee twine o' hame and in–/fancy,/O rowan tree!   HBV 1-2

The Rowers.   Laura Benet.   What manner of burden was it they proudly bore?   GoYe

Rowing.   Ed Ochester.   the stiff locks squeaking/"I love I love."   Str

Rowing.   Anne Sexton.   This story ends with me still rowing.   BoWoP; CAPP

Rowing Early.   John Peck.   And they part to receive it, unawares.   SM

Rowland's Rhyme.   Michael Drayton.   So that alone her happy sight/Contains perfection and delight.   OBSC

The Rows of Cold Trees.   Yvor Winters.   among the blessed who have Latin names.   NoAm; NOBA

A Roxbury Garden.   Amy Lowell.   And after dinner there are lessons.   LaNeLa

Roy Bean.   *Anonymous.*
   And just now I ain't gonna tell you any more.   ABF; CoSo
   Which concludes this very interesting song.   BeLS; BPAW; OBAL

The Royal Adventurer.   Philip Freneau.   I curse–and quit the land.   PAH

The Royal Angler.   *Anonymous.*   Bait it with whore, and it will hold a King.   OBSV

The Royal Crown.   Solomon ibn Gabirol.   "And unto Thee shall be its desire."   AWP

Royal Education.   Winthrop Mackworth Praed.   Which a well-taught Prince should earn,/With six thousand pounds a year.   OBSV

The Royal Light Dragoon.   *Anonymous.*   They do like to spend a time in a soldier's company.   OBET

The Royal Line.   [James Henry] Leigh Hunt.   And fourth, whom Canning and Sir Will/preserve.   FaBoUs

The Royal Love Scene.   Ernest Christopher Dowson.   And pleasure heightens beauty in our eyes.   UnTE

The Royal Mummy to Bohemia.   Charles Warren Stoddard.   Must gird his marble loins and follow me.   AA

The Royal Palace of the Highest Heaven.   Alexander Montgomerie.   Whose crafty course no cunning can find out.   GoTS

Royal Palm.   Hart Crane.   As though it soared suchwise through heaven too.   AP; CMoP; MoAB; MoAmPo; NoAm; NoP; TrGrPo

A Royal Pickle.   Carlton Talbot.   Goes the great fathingale.   ALV

Royal Presents.   Nathaniel Wanley.   ...and say those Eastern kings/Did not present thee with more precious things.   OxBoCh; TrPWD

A Royal Princess.   Christina Georgina Rossetti.   I, if I perish, perish; in the name of God I go.   BrRo

The Royal Stag.   Hugh" (Christopher Murray Grieve) MacDiarmid.   Like the sight of a Royal with its Rights and Crockets,/Its Pearls, and Beam, and Span.   FaBoMo

The Royal Tour.   Peter Pindar.   Well, make haste home–I've got, I've got no brass.'   NOEC; OxBoLi

The Royal Way of the Holy Cross.   Thomas à Kempis.   ;for the sufferings of this life,...are not worthy to be compared with the glory which shall   BoC

The Royalist.   Alexander Brome.   Let's tipple round; and so 'tis here.   CavP

Royalties.   D. J. Enright.   It was always a buyer's market, always.   NOBL

Royalty.   Arthur Rimbaud.   ...during which they/moved forward toward the gardens of palm trees.   SOTW

Rozhinkes Mit Mandlen.   *Anonymous.*   Shlof-zhe, Yidele, shlot.   FSW

Ruaumoko–The Earthquake God.   Mohi Turei.   Even though I am quiescent as in death/I soar amongst the stars.   WTO

A Rub.   John Banister Tabb.   That they settled it by blows.   OBAL

Rub-a-Dub-Dub.   *Anonymous.*   'Twas enough to make a man stare.   NOBL; OxNR

Rub-a-Dub-Dub.   Mother Goose.   Turn 'em out, knaves all three!   HBV 1-2; HBVY

The Rubaiyat: A book of verses underneath the bough.   Omar Khayyam.   And Bahram, that great Hunter–the Wild Ass/Stamps o'er his Head, but cannot break his Sleep.   EG

Rubaiyat for Sue Ella Tucker.   Miller Williams.   ...She left out/A large part of the story but told it well.   SM

The Rubaiyat of Omar Khayyam.   Edward Fitzgerald.   "I came like Water, and like wind I go."   EBEV; TRV

Rubaiyat of Omar Khayyam.   Omar Khayyam.
   And in the joyous errand reach the spot/Where I made One–turn down an empty Glass!   AnFE; AtBAP; AWP; EBEV; EnL; FaBoBe; FaFP; FaPoR; GoTF; GTBS; GTBS-P; HAP; HBV 1-2; HeIP; LiTB; MasP; NOBV; NoP; OBEV; OBVE; OBVV; PoEL 1-5; PrIm; SeCeV; TreF; TrGrPo; ViBoPo; VLP; WeW; WHA
   And one by one back in the Closet lays.   EaLo; TRV
   The Bird of Time has but a little way/To fluter–and the Bird is on the Wing.   SeCeV
   Drink! for you know not why you go, nor where.   FaBoRV
   For all the Sin wherewith the Face of Man/Is blacken'd, Man's Forgiveness give–and take!   EaLo; LoBV
   The Leaves of Life keep falling one by one.   FF
   ...Man's forgiveness give–and take!   ILwL; SeCeV
   Nor all your Tears wash out a Word of it.   PoPl
   O, Wilderness were Paradise enow!   LiTL; TEP
   Re-mold it nearer to the Heart's Desire!   BiP; EG; FaBV; LiTW; PoPl
   Sans Wine, sans Song, sans Singer, and–sans End!   NOBE; OBNC; OxBI; SeCeV; WGRP
   So late emerged from, shall so soon expire.   WGRP
   That every Hyacinth the Garden wears/Dropt in her lap from some once lovely Head.   SeCePo
   There was–and then no more of Thee and Me.   HoPM

The Rubicon.   William Winter.   Nor sin nor Sorrow, Love nor Hate/Can touch me there.   HBV 1-2

Rubies and Pearls.   Robert Herrick.   To part her lips, and showed them there/The quarrelets of pearl.   HBV 1-2

Rubin.   Charles Cooper.   thanks/rubin/for givin' us/fun   PoBA

The Rubinstein Staccato Etude.   R. Nathaniel Dett.   Ah! Rubinstein only could make such an end!   BANP

Rubric.   Josephine Preston Peabody.   But I shall find the farthest dream/That kisses me, asleep.   AA

Rude Awakenings.   Bob Rosenthal.   To be remembered in love, a clear molting sensation.   APU

Rude Boreas.   *Anonymous.*   Where the tempest now, who feels it? None! the danger's drowned/in wine!   OBET

Rudel to the Lady of Tripoli.   Robert Browning.   But to the East–the East! Go, say this, Pilgrim dear!   LoBV

Rudolph Is Tired of the City.   Gwendolyn Brooks.   Then, all the hours left I'd go/A-SPREADING out-of-doors.   TiPo

Rue.   *Anonymous.*   He'll take what he can find.   FSW

La Rue de la Montagne Sainte-Geneviève.   Dorothy Dudley.   A carven face forever weeping.   HBMV

A Rueful Lamentation on the Death of Queen Elizabeth.   Sir Thomas More.   My palace builded is, and lo now here I lie.   AAS; FaBoRV; LiTB; OBSC

Rufus Mitchell's Confession.   *Anonymous.*   I bowed before the altar,/I laid my banjo by.   AmFP

Rufus Prays.   Leonard Alfred George Strong.   'N a cup for Thee.   MoBrPo

Rufus's Mare.   *Anonymous.*   Of going to Heaven I've heard him boast,/But down in Hell he'll surely roast!   ShS

Rugby Chapel–November, 1857.   Matthew Arnold.   On, to the City of God.   CBEP; MaVP; OAEP; OxBoCh; PoEL 1-5; VLP; WGRP

The Ruin.   *Anonymous.*
   The spot where the hot baths burst into air.   AnOE; PrIm
   ....This was a kingly thing!   EnLit
   Where the baths were... It is an admirable thing!   EBEV

The Ruin.   Richard Hughes.   Cools its small grey feet in the grasses.   OBMV

The Ruin.   Charles Tomlinson.   The effect is nature's/Who ignores it, and in whose impoverishment we domi-/cile.   NePoEA-2

The Ruin of Bobtail Bend.   James Barton Adams.   An' till Gabriel's horn I will sit an' mourn the ruin of Bobtail Bend.   PoOW

The Ruined Cabin.   Alfred Castner King.   For the occupant and house alike grow old.   PoOW

The Ruined Chapel.   William Allingham.   And stars move calmly overhead.   IrPN

A Ruined House.   Richard Aldington.   And a broken toy left by their child...   BrPo

The Ruined Maid.   Thomas Hardy.   ...You ain't ruined,' said she.   BoLoP; BrPo; CABA; CMoP; FiBHP; HeIP; LiTB; NIP; NLV; NOBL; NoP; OxBTC; PPoe; SCV; SeCeV; TEP; WeW

The Ruined Motel.   Reginald Gibbons.   ...hope/was the hollowness in their cold clean skulls.   MAYP

Ruines of Rome.   Joachim Du Bellay.
Again on foot to rear her poulder'd corse.   FaBoPP
And that is flitting, doth abide and stay.   FaBoPP

Ruins at Sunset.   William Allingham.   Slender and tall a Round Tower's pointed crest/Rose dimly black against the gorgeous west.   IrPN

Ruins of a Great House.   Derek Walcott.   "as well as if a manor of thy friend's..."   TwCP

The Ruins of Rome.   John Dyer.   How sweet thy Diapason, melancholy!   OBEC

Ruins of the City of Hay.   Randolph Stow.   And their dogs rejoice in the bones of all my brethren.   CBAP; PoAu 1-2

Ruins under the Stars.   Galway Kinnell.
And up there the old stars rustling and whispering.   LCAP; NaP
Of breaking to a sacred, bloodier speech.   RFM

Rule Britannia.   James (1700-48) Thomson.   "Britons never will be slaves."   CEP; EiCP; EnLi 1-2; FaPoR; GTBS; GTBS-P; HBV 1-2; NOEC; OAEP; OBEC; OBWP; TreF; WBLP

A Rule for Birds' Nesters.   Anonymous.   Bad luck will surely follow!   HBV 1-2; HBVY

A Rule for Shooting.   Anonymous.   All the pheasants ever bred/Won't make up for one man dead.   FaBoUs

The Rule of the Road.   Anonymous.   If you go to the right, you are wrong.   FaBoUs

Rulers: Philadelphia.   Fenton Johnson.   God's blessing on the monarch who rules on Lombard/Street in Philadelphia.   AmFN; GoSl; PoNe

Rules and Lessons.   Henry Vaughan.   Above are restless motions, running lights,/Vast circling azure, giddy clouds, days, nights.   TRV

Rules and Regulations.   Lewis (Charles Lutwidge Dodgson) Carroll.   MORAL: "Behave."   FaBoUs; NOBV

Rules for Daily Life.   Anonymous.   He will thee guard and keep.   STF

Rules for the Road.   Edwin Markham.   The earth is friendly as a mother's breast.   GoTF; TreFT

A Rum Cove, a Stout Cove.   Tom Paulin.   a flightless timorous landrail/whose cry is rusted, hard, like chains.   FaBoIP

The Rum Tum Tugger.   Thomas Stearns Eliot.   And there's no doing anything about it.   EvOK; FaBoNo; FaBV

Rumba.   Jose Z. Tallet.   And pa-ca, pa-ca, pa-ca, pa-ca!/Pam! pam! Pam! TTY

Rumba of the Three Lost Souls.   Charles Madge.   Not all Scotland can recall/What the eagles eat.   NeBP

Rumination.   Richard Eberhart.   To fire my clay, when I am still.   LiTA; LiTM

Rumor Laetalis.   Peter Abelard.   I have only the swindling/Memory of poisoned honey.   LiTW

Rumoresque Senum Severiorum.   Marcus Argentarius.   "Remember, daughter," she bleats, "you and I go halves!"   ErPo; LiTW

Rumors.   Reginald Arkell.   Who knew when the war was going to end.   GoTF; TreFT

Rumors of War in Wyoming.   Tom Rea.   I think of her, each night/dreaming intruders, their bloody forearms raised.   SOTS

Rumpelstiltskin.   Anne Sexton.   one part papa,/one part Doppelganger.   DFT

Rumplestiltskin Poems.   William Hathaway.
brilliant as day and rocks are so ready/for the stamping of little feet.   DFT
Days and nights whirl by to that first kiss/so full of promise and surprise.   DFT
My awful stamp will bury all names still unsung.   DFT
"My name, ho-ho. You'll never know my name!"   DFT
so in seconds is his final, secret name.   DFT

Rumpty-Iddity, Row, Row, Row.   Anonymous.   I could eat it now.   OxNR

Run along, You Little Dogies.   Anonymous.   It's our misfortune we ever did roam.   OuSiCo

Run Come See.   Anonymous.   Run come see Jerusalem.   FSW

The Run from Manassas Junction.   Anonymous.   Moreover, when you've turned your tail,/Won't hesitate to follow.   PAH

Run, Kitty, Run!   Jimmy Garthwaite.   I think I'll go and try it out on mine!   BBGG

Run Little Dogies.   Anonymous.   And tending a baby that's none of your own.   BPAW

Run, Mary, Run (I Know de Udder Worl' Is Not Like Dis).   Anonymous.   I know de udder worl' is not like dis,/Oh, not like dis.   BoAN 1-2

Run, Nigger, Run!   Anonymous.
Dat Nigger tore up de whole co'n field.   BPo
Run, nigger, run, it's almos' day.   ABF

Runagate Runagate.   Robert Earl Hayden.   Mean mean mean to be free.   BALP; BP; BPo; CNA; IDB; InPS; LCAP; PoBA; PoNe

Runaway.   Rhoda Coghill.   I have no wish to hold them.   NeIP; OxBI

The Runaway.   Robert Frost.   Ought to be told to come and take him in.   AnNE; AWP; FaBoCh; GoJo; HaMV; InPo; LoGBV; MCCG; MoAB; MoAmPo; MP; PH; TiPo; TwCP; VGW

The Runaway.   Daniel Whitehead Hicky.   Oh, do not weep for any lad/Lost among the flowers!   BrR

Runaway.   Kim Kurt.   To hold this rampant earth, and fly/My love on the strength of its out-bound stride.   NePoAm-2

The Runaway Slave at Pilgrim's Point.   Elizabeth Barrett Browning.   White men, I leave you all curse-free/In my broken heart's disdain!   BrRo; PoNe; SBG

The Runaways.   Mark Van Doren.   And had again their own high wall and hard.   PoRA

Rune.   Philip Brasfield.   and time is better used/for other rituals–/long nights ahead.   LFAC

Rune.   Muriel Rukeyser.   The word in the word wakes me.   SM

A Rune for C.   Barbara Howes.   Square and oil-shambled, blue between elms, the caboose!   NYBP; SM

The Rune of Hospitality.   Anonymous.   Often, often, often/Goes the Christ in the stranger's guise.   CAW

Rune of Riches.   Florence Converse.   Let's lock our wealth out-doors!   SUS

Runes.   Howard Nemerov.   But being the secret hidden from yourself.   PoCh

Runes for an Old Believer.   Rolfe Humphries.   The wolves of evening will be much abroad.   NYBP

The Runes on Weland's Sword.   Rudyard Kipling.   But for The Thing.   AtBAP; PoEL 1-5

A Runic Ode.   Thomas Warton, Sr..   I smile in the Embrace of Death!   CEP

A Runnable Stag.   John Davidson.   The stag, the runnable stag.   AnFE; BrPo; BSV; EvOK; FaPoR; FM; GoTS; GTBS; HAP; HBV 1-2; OBEV; OBVV; OxBTC; PrIm; SD; WiR

Runner.   W. H. Auden.   Where fate is freedom,/Grace and surprise.   SD

The Runner.   Jerah Chadwick.   the spaces/between them, a distance/we must try to cover.   AMV-81

The Runner.   Gary Gildner.   show the lake all frozen over,/show the mound of snow   TAP

The Runner.   Alexandra Grilikhes.   but his heart runs.   SD

The Runner.   Walt Whitman.   With lightly closed fists, and arms partially rais'd.   InPK; InPS; LiSp; PAI; SD

The Runner in the Skies.   James. James Oppenheim   She hurries through the night to a far lover.   AnEnPo; TrJP

The Runner with the Lots.   Léonie Adams.   And the blind hands bearing the luck of the year.   MoPo; NePA

Running.   Richard Wilbur.
Flying full tilt already.   CoAP
Thinking of happiness, I think of that.   NCSH

Running Back.   Dave Smith.   I don't have to look for what will be/there, dark, pure, calling incomprehensibly.   LiSp

Running Blind.   Nancy Jones.   Unstop her ears, unstitch her eyes/And leave me/To run my life/Alone.   LiSp

Running It Backward.   John N. Morris.   Into the dark and shining/Whirring tiny mouth of the machine.   GP

Running the Batteries.   Herman Melville.   So Porter proves himself a brave man's son.   PAH

Running the Blockade.   Nora Perry.   This "damned Yankee jade"/Who had run the blockade!   PAH

Running the River Lines.   David Baker.   its cry still strung between us like a fine line.   MAYP

Running the Trotline.   Jim Elledge.   and the roots he left behind/tugging, tugging back.   WOLT

Running through Sleep.   Kathleen Norris.   Stuffing its heart with rags   IHMS

Running to Paradise.   William Butler Yeats.   And there the king is but as the beggar.   BoLiVe; LOW; OxBoLi

Running under Street Lights.   Christy White.   To be let go.   AMV-80

Running Vines in a Field.   Robert Carlton Brown.   They forget me for a little pride of old time.   AnAmPo

Runoff.   Archie Randolph Ammons.   the soggy small marsh, nutgrass and swordweed!   PPP

Rupert Brooke.   Wilfrid Gibson.   Tarry by that old garden of your delight.   HBMV

Rural Bliss.   Anthony C. Deane.   As long as Maud is there, you see–what matters all the/rest?   InMe

The Rural Carrier Stops to Kill a Nine-Foot Cottonmouth.   T. R. Hummer.   ...But I felt my spine/Squirm suddenly. I admit it. It was mine.   SM

The Rural Dance about the Maypole.   Anonymous.
And bound themselves by kisses twelve, to meet next/holiday.   OxBoLi
And each a 2 pence, 2 pence, 2 pence gave him and went/away.   GBP

Rural Dumpheap.   Melville Cane.   And, gladly, spring begins.   AmFN

The Rural Lass.   Catherine Jemmat.   This world it should end as begun.   NOEC

Rural Legend.   Mary Elizabeth Osborn.   That the bird has roused the god-with-pointed-/ears?   NePoAm

Rural Life.   George Crabbe.   Exposing most, when most it gilds distress.   NOBE

Rural Lines after Breughel.   Norbert Krapf.
...He dreams/of hunting with hounds in the snow.   PoDr
...Soon they/will be in the field again. PoDr
...That is enough. PoDr
Rural Route.   R. T. Smith.   to a reservoir of heart safe from harm.
AMV-81
Rural Simplicity.   H. J. Byron.   Rather than passing my time/Searching for
"Simple Rurality."   NOBL
Rural Sports.   John Gay.
Upon the burthen'd stream he floating lies,/Stretches his quivering fins, and
gasping dies.   FM
The wood resounds: he wheels, he drops, he dies. PBBP
Rus in Urbe.   Clement Scott.   And build my nest on the nearest tree!
HBV 1-2
The Rush of the Oregon.   Arthur Guiterman.   Of a rush of fourteen
thousand miles/for the chance of a bitter fight!   PAH
Rushing.   Ray A. Young Bear.   the rushing sounds of a river/under our
house.   CDW
Rushmore.   Harold Witt.   temples, obelisks, the statued ages/were equaled
in that democratic rock.   TAT
Rusia en 1931.   Robert Hass.   ...Think of the forty million/families of the
hungry....   MAYP
Russia.   Alexander Blok.   Dearer to me than every other/Are you, my
Russia, even so.   AWP
Russia.   William Carlos Williams.   ...I am the background/upon which you
will build your empire.   VGW
Russia 1812.   Victor Hugo.   ...as he stood/before his butchered legions in
the snow.   OBWP
Russian and Turk.   *Anonymous.*   Kalatalustchuk/Mischtaribusiclup-/Bulgari-
/Dulbary /Sagharimsing. e e n / n   NA
Russian Asylum.   Marilyn Bowering.   writing out love like this.   CaPN;
NOBC
A Russian Cradle Song.   David Nomberg.   In the future must thou battle/
Till the strife is won!   TrJP
A Russian Fantasy.   Nathan Haskell Dole.   Dushka, little soul, when dids't
thou/die?   AA
Russian New Year.   Bill Berkson.   Still we are the same,/Sideways   ANYP
The Russian Soul II.   John Hollander.   Threw in the sponge and was/
Scraped off the tracks.   NLV
A Russian Spring Song with Minaiev.   Thomas Walsh.   For him, sweet
blossomings and death.   GoBC
Russians.   Keith Douglas.   ...Well,/at least forget what happens when it
thaws.   OxBTC
Russians Breathing.   Philip Hammial.   The mouth takes food.   NOAV
Rust.   Mary Carolyn Davies.   I had a heartbreak long ago.   HBMV
Rust.   Michael Hogan.   where there could be a mushroom, pale and
mysterious,/growing out of the concrete floor.   LFAC
The Rusted Chain.   Yosef D. Ben Yeshaq.   Wake up rusting chain, Speak
people of yonderland!   VWA
The Rustic at the Play.   George Santayana.   That prompts the passions of
this strutting world.   HBV 1-2; OBVV
Rustic Childhood.   William Barnes.   O shining grass, and shady bough.
OBNC
A Rustic Song.   Anthony C. Deane.   But I does ma wark, if ma
consonants/Be properly mixed with ma vowels!   FiBHP; InMe
The Rustler.   *Anonymous.*   And I hope to see the hoodoos dead and damn
them all in hell.   CoSo
Ruston, Louisiana: 1952.   Cleopatra Mathis.   or the trees on a familiar
street, repeating/and repeating.   AMV-80
Ruth.   Thomas Hood.   Share my harvest and my home.   BoLoP; EnLoPo;
EnRP; GN; GoTF; HBV 1-2; LiTL; LoBV; NOBE; OBEV; OBNC; OBRV;
OBVV; TreFS
Ruth.   Colleen J. McElroy.   read this/and count them   BlSi
Ruth.   Pauli Murray.   Surrender to none the fire of your soul.   NMM
Ruth and Johnnie.   *Anonymous.*   And John kept going/Ruthlessly.   ShM
Ruth; or, the Influences of Nature.   William Wordsworth.   And all the
congregation sing/A Christian psalm for thee.   ChRP; ERoP 1-2; GTBS;
GTBS-P; PoEL 1-5
Rutherford McDowell.   Edgar Lee Masters.   Which labors and loves and
suffers and sings/Under the sun!   EyDe; LiTA; OxBA
The Rwose in the Dark.   William Barnes.   Ov her bright feace, by mornen
light.   AtBAP; NOBV
Rydal.   Hartley Coleridge.   The Beautiful is good, the good is true.   VLP
Ryder.   John Haines.   and the moon itself,/a pale horse of torment flying...
LCAP
Rye Bread.   William Stanley Braithwaite.   But Dionysus led them home/In
a chariot of pain.   CDC
Rye Whiskey.   *Anonymous.*   You've robbed my poor pockets of silver and
gold.   FSW
Rye Whiskey (Clinch Mountain).   *Anonymous.*   You killed my poor pappy,/
Now, dang you, try me.   TrAS
Rye Whisky.   *Anonymous.*

I surely will die.   ABF; CoSo
'Twill all be forgotten/A hundred years hence. OxBoLi
Ryokan.   William Heyen.   amid peach blossoms by the river.   AMV-81

S

S F.   Ernest Leverett.   And return to Mars/As a Martian/Raccoon.   QQQ
S. P. C. A. Sermon.   Stuart Hemsley.   (And on behalf)/Of the fatted calf.
FiBHP
S. S. City of Benares.   G. S. Fraser.   The small ghosts flicker, whisper,
unconsoled.   NeBP
S. S. "Lusitania."   Matthew Arnold.   "Reached Cape Verde Islands,
"Lusitania."'   CBEP
S.S.R., Lost at Sea–The Times.   Ralph Gustafson.   O let the heart's tough
riggings salvage him,/Only whose lengths can grapple with these dead.
OBCV
S. T. Colerige Dismisses a Caller from Porlock.   Gerard Previn Meyer.
There's only room in poetry/for one of us!   GoYe
Sa-ca-ga-we-a.   Edna Dean Proctor.   "Sho-sho-ne Sa-ca-ga-we-a, who led the
way/to the West!"   PAH
Saadabad.   James Elroy Flecker.   Or remember how his poet took a girl to
Saadabad?   SeCePo
Saadi.   Ralph Waldo Emerson.   That blessed gods in servile masks/Plied for
thee thy household tasks.   AmP; OxBA
Saagin.   Sydney Goodsir Smith.   Nou in saagin my weird rocks.   AtBAP
Sabbath.   Jean Burden.   I will live six days in one,/naming the holy names.
AMV-81
Sabbath.   Jakov De Haan.   Not one of the many, but you, Sabbath, alone.
VWA
Sabbath.   Rivka Fried.   And walked through the gates hearing/the flapping
of many wings/rising upwards.   VWA
Sabbath.   D. Rosenmann-Taub.   ...the face of dusk/wanders between the
never and the never.   VWA
The Sabbath Day Was By.   Howard Chandler Robbins.   And blessed we,
who have not seen,/But love him and adore.   AH
Sabbath, My Love.   Judah Halevi.   Chant: "Come in peace, O blissful/
Seventh Day!"   TrJP
A Sabbath of Rest.   Isaac Luria.   This day is for Israel light and/rejoicing,/
A Sabbath of rest.   TrJP
Sabbath Reflection.   Denis Wrafter.   'Twas so I felt the harlot say/As she
knelt proudly down to pray.   NeIP
Sabbatical.   Linda Zisquit.   to remove the blood/that covers me everywhere.
VWA
The Sabine Farmer's Serenade.   Francis Sylvester ("Father Prout") Mahony.
Don't say nay,/Charming Judy Callaghan.   HBV 1-2
Sacco-Vanzetti.   Moishe Leib Halpern.   With wings outspread forever
greets/Death in fire.   VWA
Sacco Writes to His Son.   Alun Lewis.   And my hand trembles...I am Oh,
so weak....   DTC
The Sack of Baltimore.   Thomas Osborne Davis.   Some cursed him with
Iscariot, that day in Baltimore.   IrPN
The Sack of Deerfield.   Thomas Dunn English.   And, ere dawning of the
morning, I was/twenty miles away.   PAH
The Sacrament.   John Donne.   I do believe and take it.   TRV
The Sacrament of Sleep.   John Oxenham.   To feel the comfort of His soft
embrace.   PoLf
The Sacrament of the Altar.   *Anonymous.*   It is God body and no mo.
MeEL
Sacramento.   *Anonymous.*   Ah, there is lots of gold, oh, so I've been told,/
Upon the banks of the Saccarimento!   FSW; ShS; TrAS
The Sacraments of Nature.   Aubrey Thomas De Vere.   Those abject, who
together have partaken/These Sacraments of Nature–and in vain.   ACP;
CAW
Sacramentum Supremum.   Sir Henry Newbolt.   To the long parting, and the
age to come.   GTBS
Le Sacre-Coeur.   Charlotte Mew.   And this One–He has been dead so long!'
OBTV
Sacred and Profane Love, or, There's Nothing New under the Moon Either.
Peter De Vries.   "For God's sake be careful or someone will hear you!"
NLV
The Sacred Children.   H. R. Hays.   And know that death flies into rooms/
On a bird's wings.   EAS
Sacred Elegy V.   George Barker.   ...Beast, brute, bastard. O dog my God!
MoPo
Sacred Emily.   Gertrude Stein.   A blow is delighted.   OBAL
Sacred Family (excerpt).   Gertrude Stein.   Do I make faces like that at
you./Pinkie.   AtBAP
Sacred Formula to Attract Affection.   *Anonymous.*   I, Gatigwanasti, I take
your soul. Sge!   LiTA

Sacred Formula to Destroy Life. *Anonymous.* And dwindle away,/Never to reappear. Listen! LiTA

A Sacred Grove. Fran Winant. that swayed and sang/when the wind passed through. BrRo

The Sacred Hearth. David Gascoyne. The faithful fire of vision still awaiting our return. FaBoTw

Sacred Objects. Louis Simpson. I sit in a window, combing my hair/day in day out. CAPP

The Sacred Order. May Sarton. Read faith as on a lover's in their faces. ImOP

Sacred Poetry. John Wilson. ...darkness broods/O'er ghastly shapes, and sounds not to be borne. WBLP

The Sacrifice. Chana Bloch. He will remember the blade's/white silence,/ the waiting/under his father's eyes. VWA

Sacrifice. Ralph Waldo Emerson. "'Tis man's perdition to be safe,/When for the truth he ought to die." HBV 1-2; HBVY; TRV

The Sacrifice. George Herbert. Never was grief like mine. AtBAP; PoEL 1-5

Sacrifice. Nana Issaia. as my daily life/took over the room. BoWoP

Sacrifice. Thomas Kinsella. My heart is in your hands: mind it well. IPY

The Sacrifice. Moshe Yungman. There is no escape–/no escape. VWA

Sacrifice of a Red Squirrel. Joseph Langland. The fixed ideas are coming to hunt you down. NYBP

Sacrifice of a Virgin in the Mayan Ball Court. Norman Dubie. ...Returning, and/To kill. Again! GeTw

The Sacrifice to Apollo. Michael Drayton. ...then let the Lyre/Sound, whilst his Altars endlesse flames expire. OBS

The Sacrilege. Thomas Hardy. ...and he will hear that scream/Until his judgment-time. DTo

The Sad Child's Song. Mark Van Doren. Heavy, oh Heavy, is mine to keep. SO

The Sad Day. Thomas Flatman. Persuade the world to trouble me no more! OBEV

Sad Day in Berlin. Sarah Kirsch. ...there must be/other tigers about PBWP

Sad-Eyed Lady of the Lowlands. Bob Dylan. Or, sad-eyed lady, should I wait? BiP

Sad Green. Sylvia Townsend Warner. And the daisies kept under. MoBrPo

Sad Is the Seagull. Larin Paraske. colder am I and wretched/colder still than that. PBWP

Sad Love and Sad Song. Homei Iwano. And I pour it on my own tears. LiTW

The Sad Lover. George Crabbe. Then met his Fanny with a borrow'd smile. OBNC

Sad Memories. Charles Stuart Calverley. In dreams I see that rampant He, and tremble at that Miaow. FM

The Sad Shepherd. Ben Jonson.
Down to the drowned lands of Lincolnshire;/To make ewes cast their lambs. FaBoPP
To fright the frost out of the grave. AtBAP; GoBC

The Sad Shepherd. William Butler Yeats. Among her wildering whirls, forgetting him. MOS; PP

Sad Steps. Philip Larkin. But is for others undiminished somewhere. NoP

Sad Story. Clarence Day. The art of his competitors the day he got the job. InMe

The Sad Story of a Little Boy That Cried. *Anonymous.* It was only a mouth with a border of Jack. BBGG

Sad Strains of a Gay Waltz. Wallace Stevens. ...the music/Will be motion and full of shadows. OxBA

The Sad Tale of Mr. Mears. *Anonymous.* And a madder man than Matthew Mears/You would not wish to see. GoTF; HBV 1-2; StPo; TreFS; YaD

The Sad Years. Eva Gore-Booth. Perhaps...in the coming years... HBMV

The Saddest Words (Addendum). *Anonymous.* It might have been/A great deal worse. PoToHe

Saddle. William Haskel Simpson. With shooting stars, slip loose, let go! BPAW

Saddle and Cell. The Three (Maria Isabel Barreno and Maria Teresa Horta and Maria Velho da Costa) Marias. is to keep that beloved's other face/ clasped in your hands. BoWoP

The Saddled Ass. Deems Taylor. "And on the proof, and whosoever saddled you!" NLV

De Sade. John Fuller. But he's known all the same/As the dark ne plus ultra of Reason. NLV

Sadie and Maud. Gwendolyn Brooks. She is living all alone/In this old house. NoAm; NOBA; TAP

Sadie's Playhouse. Margaret Danner. ...waving cool, green, shady,/over the (dancing now) African ladies. PoBA

Sadie (with music). *Anonymous.* He was Sadie's man, that had done her wrong, he wouldn't come home. AS

Sadness. Barbara Guest. Yet do you know I shall carry always/that blemish on my breast? AmPC

Sadness. Alfred, Lord Tennyson. And I say it, and repeat it,/Immeasurable sadness! FaBoEE

Sadness and Still Life. Bin Ramke. Saturday's light, delicate/membrane still intact. MAYP

Sadness, Glass, Theory. Roy Fuller. Only one other in our life would know us. WaP

The Sadness of the Moon. Charles Baudelaire. And hides it from the Sun, deep in his heart. MOON

The Sadness of Things for Sappho's Sickness. Robert Herrick. But bid good-night, and close their lids for ever. PoPle

Safari West. John A. Williams. in which Dachau is maintained in something of/greater degree. NBP; PAI

Safe. James Walker. Safe in firelight sit. OBCP

Safe for Democracy. Leonard Alfred George Strong. Let but another world-war kill/The rest, it will be safer still. HBMV

Safe in His Keeping. Edgar Cooper Mason. For in His keeping I shall still abide. BLRP

Safe in their Alabaster Chambers. Emily Dickinson.
Ah, what sagacity perished here! AmPP; CBEP; MasP; NAWM 1-2; NIP; NoP
Soundless as dots on a disk of snow. AnFE; APA; MAmP; MAPA; MoPo; NIP; NOBA; NoP; OxBA

Safe Places. Constance Urdang. Or lay behind them, maybe, in the ruined cities. GP

Safed. Dovid Knut. I can hear God, leaning over Safed. VWA

Safed and I. Molly Myerowitz Levine. I'll learn from you,/old witch,/who bewitches men/and women, too. VWA

Safely Home. *Anonymous.* Oh, the joy to see you come! STF

Safety. Rupert Brooke. And if these poor limbs die, safest of all. BrPo; EnLoPo

Safety at Forty; or, An Abecedarian Takes a Walk. L. E. Sissman. Must I confess my weariness/At facing stringent mistresses/And head for haven? Here I come. Prf

Safety or Something. P. L. Jacobs. i am/simply myself/it will find a level. LFAC

Saffold's Cures. Thomas Saffold. Try before you judge and speak as you find. FaBoUs

Sag', Wo Ist Dein Schones Liebchen. Heinrich Heine. And this book is but the urn/Of the ashes of love dead. AWP

The Saga of Gisli (excerpt). *Anonymous.* And my self you solely/Sovereign shall govern.' OBVE

Saga of Leif the Lucky (excerpt). Hervey Allen. He and his golden bearded curls.... EtS

Sagacity. William Rose Benet. And now there is merely silence, silence, silence saying/All we did not know. MoAmPo

Sagamore. Corinne Roosevelt Robinson. For one is gone–who shall not go–/From Sagamore! HBMV

Sage Counsel. Sir Arthur Thomas ("Q") Quiller-Couch. Stay home and learn your catechissum. HBV 1-2; HBVY; LBN; NA; NLV

The Sage in Unison. Harold Stewart. And twenty jangling wires are set at war. NOAV

Sagebrush. Charles Erskine Scott Wood. Christ! for a horse between my legs/And the sagebrush once again. BPAW

The Sages. Adam Mickiewicz. He lives, and peace is in His heavenly realm! CAW

Sagesse. Hilda ("H. D.") Doolittle. and this one's bigger than–than a hundred others,/sparrows, I think it was. NOCV

Sagesse. Paul Verlaine. Where hast thou laid, who comest here,/Thy youth away? EnLi 1-2; SyP

The Sagging Bough (parody). Louis Untermeyer. Or, being near the grave itself, it bent/Because of nothing more than gravity. BXAP

Sagimusume: The White Heron Maiden. Jonny Kyoko Sullivan. and send these skirts/unravelling at my feet. WPOW

The Saginaw Song. Theodore Roethke. All women, O, are beautiful/When they are half-undressed. NLV

Said Agatha Christie. George Starbuck. Rabble?" she groused. OBAL; PV

Said Aristotle Unto Plato. Owen Wister. "Thank you, I prefer the bottle." PoPl

Said death to passion. Emily Dickinson. And the Debate was done. MoVE

Said Hanrahan. Patrick Joseph Hartigan. We'll all be rooned," said Hanrahan,/"Before the year is out." PoAu 1-2

Said J. Alfred Prufrock. George Starbuck. "Pity. Design." PV

Said the Canoe. Isabella Valancy Crawford. Pressed shapes, thin, woven and uncertain/As white locks of tall waterfalls. NOBC

Said the Innkeeper. Myles Connolly. A man must make his living while he may. TRV

Said the monkey to the donkey. *Anonymous.* "I'd like a swig of ink." FaFP

Said the Rose. George Henry Miles. and bid her wear it/For my sake. BLPA

Said the Whisky Flask. *Anonymous.* Shun them as you would shun the devil. STF

A Sail. Mikhail Yuryevich Lermontov. As though in storm were peace. AWP; LiTW; PoPl

Sail and Oar. Robert Graves. Lest man sail, or woman row. MOS

Sail at the Mast Head. *Anonymous.* The sail on the mast flaps, dancing, and "talks' in the wind... WTO

Sail away. Robert Adamson. The black bird sang as if it had a song. CBAP

Sail away Ladies. *Anonymous.* Don't you rock 'im die-dy-o. FSW

Sail Peacefully Home. Simeon S. Frug. And let it at last/Sail peacefully home. TrJP

Sailboat, Your Secret. Robert Francis. Your losses to profit, your wayward onwardness. SD

Sailing after Lunch. Wallace Stevens. And then rush brightly through the summer air. MoPo

Sailing at Dawn. Sir Henry Newbolt. Souls of all the sea-dogs, lead the line today! EtS

Sailing from the United States. Stanley Moss. ...to work myself/As a mine, subject to explosions and cave-in. VGW

Sailing Home from Rapallo. Robert Lowell. The corpse/was wrapped like panetone in Italian tinfoil. HaCAP; NoAm; TAP

Sailing Homeward. Chan Fang-sheng. And moved his brush to write a new song. AWP; FaBoCh; LoGBV

Sailing in Crosslight. Anita Skeen. with your presence, drifting/toward her like smoke IHMS

The Sailing of the Fleet. *Anonymous.* For Sons of Drake are lords of Colon's/world. PAH

The Sailing of the Sword. William Morris. When the Sword came back from sea! CoBE; OAEP; OBVV; TreFS

Sailing, Sailing. Gray Burr. While Captain Slocum's riding lights/Danced a jig between the poles. CoPo; NYBP

Sailing Sailing. Godfrey Marks. For many a stormy wind shall blow/ere Jack comes home again. FSW

Sailing to an Island. Richard Murphy. ...Here is a bed. IPY; NMP

Sailing to Byzantium. William Butler Yeats. Of what is past, or passing, or to come. AnIL; AtBAP; BiP; CMoP; CoBMV; DiPo; ExPo; FaFP; FF; ForPo; FPL; GoTF; GTBS-P; HAP; HeIP; HoPM; InPK; InPo; InPS; InvP; LiTB; LiTM; MasP; MBW 1-2; MoAB; MoBrPo; MoPo; MoRP; MoVE; NAMP; NAWM 1-2; NIP; NoAm; NOBE; NoP; OAEL 1-2; OAEP; OBMV; OxBI; OxBTC; PAI; PP; PPoe; PPP; PrIm; SeCePo; SeCeV; SoSe; TEP; TreFT; UnPo; ViBoPo

Sailing upon the River. George Crabbe. Fluttering they move their weedy Beds among,/Or instant diving, hide their plumeless Young. OBNC

The Sailor. William Allingham. I never more may steer! HBV 1-2

Sailor. Eleanor Farjeon. To marry a Sailor/Who sails on the sea! BrR

Sailor. Langston Hughes. A blue bird in a nest. GoSl; PoA

The Sailor. Goodridge MacDonald. Unpainted, luscious, half-divine/To men who sail in ships. CaP

Sailor. P. K. Page. wilted like foam or daisies from their thirst. ACV

The Sailor. Sylvia Townsend Warner. Lest she should lie awake and tremble/When the great storm-winds blow. OBMV

The Sailor and His Bride. *Anonymous.* "With my soul in heaven and my body in the sea,/And the proud waves rolling over me." AmFP

Sailor and Inland Flower. Hamish Maclaren. And I might be in Atlantis, or any haunted place/Out of time and space. EtS

The Sailor and the Shark. Frederick York Powell. You'd better ship along with him before his love grows cold. OBMV

A Sailor at Midnight. E. N. Sargent. "No, I'm a poet," I said. "Fuck me again." NMM

The Sailor Boy. *Anonymous.* And that's the way a sailor's life/to his sweetheart often goes. ShS

The Sailor Boy. Alfred, Lord Tennyson. Far worse than any death to me.' MOS

The Sailor Cut down in His Prime. *Anonymous.* For these girls of the city were the ruin of me. OBET

Sailor Man. H. Sewall Bailey. The other side of Nowhere/Led somewhere in the end. EtS

Sailor on the Deep Blue Sea. *Anonymous.* For I'm going to end my troubles/By drowning in the deep blue sea. FSW

The Sailor's Alphabet. *Anonymous.* X,Y,Z is the name on our stern. AmFP; OBSS

A Sailor's Apology for Bow-Legs. Thomas Hood. And that's the way, you see, my legs got bowed! EtS; MOS

Sailor's Carol. Charles Causley. In the sea's blue snow. AtBAP; OBCP

The Sailor's Christmas Day. *Anonymous.* Christmastide cheers the heart of a brave British tar. OBSS

The Sailor's Complaint. *Anonymous.* Shall take a full glass, shall take a full glass/To his passage o'er the ferry. OBSS

The Sailor's Consolation. Charles Dibdin. That you and I are sailors. BeLS; FaBoCo; HBV 1-2; TreFS

Sailor's Consolation. William Pitt. Then, Bill, let us thank Providence/That you and I are sailors! EtS; LBN

The Sailor's Consolation (excerpt). *Anonymous.* So, Billy, let's thank Providence/That you and I are sailors.' PoPle

The Sailor's Grace. *Anonymous.* Look in the harness cask and you'll find a horse and shoe! ShS

The Sailor's Grave. *Anonymous.* And many a wild prayer followed the wave/As he sunk into a sailor's grave. ShS

The Sailor's Grave. Eliza Cook. But many a rude player hallowed the wave/That closed above the sailor's grave. BLPA

The Sailor's Lamentation. *Anonymous.* Though he know 'twas our due, 'twould help to increase his store. OBSS

A Sailor's Life. *Anonymous.* "How can I live now my William is gone?" OBSS

The Sailor's Mother (excerpt). William Wordsworth. What clothes he might have left, or other property. Par

A Sailor's Prayer. George Hornell Morris. We give our thanks/That Thou hast made–/The turmoil of the sea! TrPWD

The Sailor's Return. *Anonymous.* Like a Nightingale in spring, Welcome home, my dearest. OxBoLi

A Sailor's Song. Hazel Harper Harri. As I sail home to Galveston/In oleander time! EtS

The Sailor's Sweetheart. Duncan Campbell Scott. And there's no one left to kiss me now/Over my heavy heart. PeCV

The Sailor's Way. *Anonymous.* For around Cape Horn and home again, oh, that is the sailor's way! ShS

A Sailor's Wife. Clara Bernhardt. While I...I suffer wordlessly,/Because he left the sea for me. CaP

The Sailor's Wife. William Julius Mickle. There's little pleasure in the house/When our gudeman's awa'. BeLS; BSV; GN; GTBS; GTBS-P; HBV 1-2

Sailor's Woman. Annette Patton Cornell. I wait again..as I waited then.../as sailors' women wait for their men. GoYe

A Sailor's Yarn. James Jeffrey Roche. For he ain't like some of the swabs I've seen,/As would go and lie to a poor marine. MOS; NA

The Sailor to His Parrot. William Henry Davies. And you tell me to go to hell! BoAnP; EtS; ViBoPo

Sailor, What of the Isles? Edith Sitwell. No more than the father knows of the child, or the sailor of/chartless isles. ChMP

Sailors. Louis Simpson. Threshing the salt green sea. NYBP

Sailors for My Money. *Anonymous.* To sea, to sea, how e'er the wind doth blow. OBSS

Sailors' Harbour. Henry Reed. (For we have to look trim in the port) and in/The high-piled ambiguous cargo. MOS

Sailors on Leave. Owen Dodson. To battle for, to die. AmNP

The Sailors' Wives. *Anonymous.* And in the other corner were battalions forming fours. OBSS

Sails. George Sterling. Under the night's first star I watch you sink,/In the world's twilight fading, fading West. EtS

Sainclaire's Defeat. *Anonymous.* He fell that day amongst the slain, a valiant/man was he. PAH

Saint. Robert Graves. And crept into his grave when he was dead. CMoP

Saint. Stephane Mallarme. Musician of silence. SyP

Saint. Kersti Merilaas. Round about your path the ranks encroach,/Bannered with the grace of angel splendor. LiTW

The Saint. Humbert Wolfe. fire, spoke to fire, and mixed in heaven, Maid. CAW

Saint Apollinare in Classe. R. N. D. Wilson. the gold that clustered then/about the Host? CAW

Saint Brendan's Prophecy. *Anonymous.* And religion's pristine form/Shall give peace and calm the storm. OnYI

Saint Cloud. Sir Walter Scott. And rank among the foremost class/Our evenings at Saint Cloud. OBTV

Saint Coyote. Linda Hogan. always lying/about who created death and light. STE

Saint Erkenwald. *Anonymous.* And all the bells in the city boomed out at once. MeEV

Saint Francis. John Peale Bishop. Saint Francis preaching to the birds. EaLo

Saint Francis and Saint Benedight. *Anonymous.* From curfew time to the next prime. EaLo

Saint Francis and the Birds. Roy McFadden. ...Identity/Lost, he stood in swollen ecstasy. OxBI

Saint Francis and the Sow. Galway Kinnell. the long, perfect loveliness of sow. FYAP

Saint Francis Borgia or a Refutation for Heredity. Phyllis McGinley. But Francis, kneeling/Prays for their souls. NePoAm-2

Saint George of England. Cecily Fox-Smith. He'll come home to rest in England where the golden willows/blow! BBV

Saint Germain-en-Laye. Ernest Christopher Dowson. To death the host of all our golden dreams. SyP ·

Saint Harmony My Patroness. Paul Goodman. ...there is a tear/in my blue eyes for her sake. VGW

A Saint...He Ain't. E. Y. Harburg. And Peale is most appalling. DBV

Saint-Henri Spring. Milton Acorn. stuck to by drab threads of January. NeAC

Saint Ita's Fosterling. Saint Ita. On my breast babe Jesu slumbers,/Yet in heaven his soft feet go. OnYI

The Saint John. George Frederick Clarke. Content, with De Monts and Champlain,/With this, for Cathay. CaP

Saint John. Elizabeth Jane Coatsworth. Till that head from desert sands,/A princess, hot with dancing, carried between her hands. GTBS; MoRP

Saint John the Baptist. William, of Hawthornden Drummond. Rung from their marble caves "Repent! Repent!" CBEP; EaLo; GTBS; GTBS-P; NOBE; OBEV; TrCP

Saint Judas. James Wright. I held the man for nothing in my arms. ConAP; LCAP; NMP; NOBA; SM

Saint-Just 1767-93. Robert Lowell. He did, the scaffold, "Je sais ou je vais." FaBoMo

Saint Leger. Clinton Scollard. And, alas, for the boasting, the vaunting, the/vain/Saint Leger! PAH

Saint-Lo. Samuel Beckett. and the old mind ghost-forsaken/sink into its havoc NOBI

Saint Luke the Painter. Dante Gabriel Rossetti. Ere the night cometh and she may not work. GoBC

Saint Malcolm. Johari (Jewel C. Latimore) Amini. But his word cauterizes our infection/unifying blackness BPo

Saint Mary Magdalene. Richard Crashaw. ...We goe to meet/A worthy object, our Lord's FEET. AtBAP; FaBoCo; MeLP; Par; SeCV 1-2

Saint Nicholas. Marianne Moore. would it not be the most/prized gift that ever was! NYBP

Saint Patrick's Day, 1973. Wendy Rose. the daily flight/at my senses of these couplets. CDW

Saint Paul. Frederic William Henry Myers. Christ the beginning, for the end is Christ. PGD; TRV

Saint Peray. Thomas William Parsons. Send round your bottles, Hal–and set your night. HBV 1-2

Saint Pumpkin. Nancy Willard. because I gave you a false face/and a light of my own making. LCAP

Saint R. L. S. Sarah N. Cleghorn. –The Sister, when she turned his pillow over,/Kissed "Treasure Island" on its well-worn cover. HBMV

The Saint's Delight. Anonymous. I feel like I'm on my journey home. TrAS

Saint's Parade. Robert Layzer. On the gasping red piazza/Where the young men play darts. NePoEA

Saint Stephen and King Herod. Anonymous. And therefore is his even/On Christe's own day. BoLiVe; OxBM; OxBoCh; OxBoLi; TrGrPo

Saint Stephen in San Francisco. Melvin Walker La Follette. I am elemental fire. I burn. CoPo

Saint Thomas Aquinas. Thomas S. Jones. Unveil the hidden beauty of His Face. CAW

Saint Valentine's Day. Coventry Patmore. Or e'er the Snowdrop die! GoBC; OBNC

Sainte Anne de Beaupre. Richard Eberhart. And Bonne Sainte Anne not hunted down/by time. NePoAm

The Saints. Robert Creeley. and laughed back/until my mind cracked. NMP

Saints. George Garrett. ...They love the songs/of joyous saints whose tongues are holy dust. EaLo

Saints, and Their Care. Alberto Rios. To make one look only into the centers of their eyes. APU

Saints in Glory, We Together. Nehemiah Adams. Yesterday, today, forever,/Jesus Christ, the same. AH

Saints Lose Back. Nancy Willard. consider how the other half lives. HoAn

Sair Fyel'd, Hinny. Anonymous. Sair fyel'd, hinny,/Sin' aw ken'd thou. GBP

Sakhara. R.A.D. Ford. The half-starved children/In the desert slums. NOBC

The Sakiyeh. Mathilde Blind. Bound blindfold to the groaning wheel of Time. SBG

Sal Got a Meatskin. Anonymous. Old Liza told me so. FSW

Salaam Alaikum. Anonymous. May the peace of Allah abide with you. PoLf

Salad. Mortimer Collins.
After which I fancy we/Shall want a few bottles of Heidsieck or Roederer. Par
And eggs–boil 'em hard. ALV; Par
Ox-fed orating ominous octastichs. CenHV

Salad La Raza. Janet Campbell Hale. I tried not to think/Of Caesar Chavez. VoR

The Salamanca Doctor's Farewell. Anonymous. To think how they'll truss up the savior o'th'nation. APAS

Salami. Philip Levine. the true and earthy prayer/of salami. NNaP; NOBA; TAP

Salamis. Aeschylus. Perished so vast a multitude of men. WaaP

Salamis. Lawrence Durrell. To remain and realize were the harder task. NYBP

Salangadou. Anonymous.
"Oh, where is my darling gone?"/Salangadou, Salangadou. FSW; TrAS
Salangadou? ABF

Les Salaziennes (excerpt). Auguste Lacaussade. They riveted my youth to an insulting repose. TTY

Sale. Josephine Miles. Implacably shod into the perfect street. PoL

Sale. Miller Williams. and when it's gone it's gone/so hurry/hurry WeW

A Sale of Smoke. Roberta Spear. Her fire has already started. AmPA

The Sale of the Pet Lamb. Mary Howitt. It maketh even the little child with heavy sighs complain. CH

Salem. Robert Lowell. And fought the British Lion to his knees? AnNE; NePoEA

Salem. Edmund Clarence Stedman. The stones of Gallowes Hill shall tread. AA; PAH

Salem, Massachusetts. Edwin Muir. And in the evenings businessmen from Boston/Sit in the beautiful houses, mobbed by cars. OBTV

Sales Talk for Annie. Morris Bishop. All right, go ahead and cry, damn it! NLV

The Salesman. Robert Mezey. I hear the faery spirits shriek in hell. NePoEA

Salesman. Ruth Roston. O Lamb, I praise/the perfect whiteness of your shirt. AMV-80

A Salesman Is an It That Stinks Excuse. Edward Estlin Cummings. or Think We've Met subhuman rights Before AmP; DBV; NIP; NoAm; OxBA; TW

Sally. Paul Durcan. Sally, I was happy with you. FaBoIP

Sally Ann. Anonymous. I'm gonna marry you, Sally Ann. FSW

Sally Brown. Anonymous Spent my money on Sally Brown. AmFP; AmSS; FSW; ShS

Sally Free and Easy. Cyril Tawney. Hope she dies of shame. OBET

The Sally from Coventry. William Thornbury. I've left it rent-paid to the villainous Scot! HBV 1-2

Sally Go Round the Sun. Anonymous. Sally go round the chimney-pots/On a Saturday afternoon. OxNR

Sally Go Round the Sunshine. Anonymous. Every afternoon,/Boom! Boom! OuSiCo

Sally Goodin. Anonymous.
And-a home you go, the old last time,/And you know where. AmFP
Raise corn on the hillside an' the devil in the valley. FSW

Sally in Our Alley. Henry Carey. But not in our alley! AWP; BLPL; BLSo; BoLoP; CBEP; CoMu; FaBoBe; FaFP; FSW; GTBS; GTBS-P; HBV 1-2; InMe; LiTL; NOBE; OBEV; PG; PoPle; PoSC; TreF; ViBoPo

Sally Monroe. Anonymous. And all my life I'll mourn for young Sally Monroe! OBSS; ShS

Sally My Dear. Anonymous. And if I were a wave I'd raise a commotion. FSW

Sally's Garden. Anonymous. Come drink, my boys, you're welcome, for I am young and the world is/wide. AmFP

Sally Simpkin's Lament. Thomas Hood. And would say more, but I am doomed/To break off in the middle.' EnRP; MOS; ShM

Sally Sweetbread. Henry Carey. Can deary be cheated/When nothing is miss'd. CoMu

Sally Waters. Anonymous. And kiss her over/and over again. OxNR

Salmon. Jorie Graham. smiling, faces pressed against the stone. MAYP

The Salmon. Christian Morgenstern. In silence, back to Amst-/-Erdam. FaBoNo

Salmon Cycle. Avner Treinin. a circle more encompassing, enclosing all my life,/from which I shall burst forth no more. VWA

Salmon Draught at Inveraray. R. W. Nunley. The look that seemed reproach was only death. WOLT

Salmon Drowns Eagle. Malcolm Lowry. Any moral to this dins in drowned ears. OBCV

Salmon Eggs. Ted Hughes. And mind condenses on old haws. NAs

Salmon-Fishing. Robinson Jeffers. Race up into fresh water. AnEnPo; SD

Salmon Fly Hatch on Yankee Jim Canyon of the Yellowstone. Greg Keeler. and each will be home. WOLT

Salome. Anonymous. Salome said, Baloney!/And kicked the chandelier. WTO

Salomon. Pierre Morhange. Very far from us/And with no knowledge of how to live VWA

Salt. Lucille Clifton. but what he will/strain the ocean for and/what he needs. GP

Salt. Monk Gibbon. Or perches in the branch her soul has chosen. OxBI

Salt. Ruth Stone. And we all die/On the down side. NMM

The Salt Flats. Sir Charles G. D. Roberts. These marshes pale and meadows by the sea. CaP

The Salt Garden. Howard Nemerov. Where his salt dream lies. NePoEA

Salt Lake City. Hayden Carruth. Ribs, the salt desert, and crazy religion. AmFN

Salt Man. Annette Arkeketa West. we speak/the color/of the/heart TWSS

Salt of the Earth. D. H. Lawrence. Slowly the salt of the earth becomes salt of the sea. NoAm

The Salt Pork. Robert Clayton Casto. we are holy, holy, holy. HeIP

Salt Water Story. Richard Hugo. he is the one who waves. NoP

Salty Dog Blues. *Anonymous.* Honey, let me be your salty dog. CoSo; FSW

Salut Au Monde! Walt Whitman. And distant lands, as real and near to the inhabitants of them/as my land is to me. AtBAP; SUS

Salutamus. Sterling A. Brown. We must plunge onward; onward, gentlemen.... CDC

Salutation. Thomas Stearns Eliot. We have our inheritance. AnAmPo

Salutation. Ezra Pound. And the fish swim in the lake/and do not even own clothing. HeIP; LoGBV; MoAB; MoAmPo; NOBA; OxBA; TAP; VGW

Salutation. George William Russell. One river born of many streams/Roll in one blaze of blinding light! OnYI

The Salutation. Thomas Traherne. That Strangest is of all, yet brought to pass. AtBAP; InvP; NOCV; NoP; OBS; OxBoCh; SeCP; SeCV 1-2

Salutation. Emperor of Abyssinia Zerea Jacob. Give/life to me as thou didst to my fathers and pardon the sins of/all my people! ISi

The Salutation of the Blessed Virgin. John Byrom. The birth of JESUS in the human soul. ISi

Salutation of the Dawn. Kalidasa. Such is the Salutation of the Dawn! GoTF

Salutation the Second. Ezra Pound. Say that you do no work/and that you will live forever. NOBA; OxBA

Salutation to Jesus Christ. John Calvin. Grant us thy Spirit's help, thy will/In every deed to do. WGRP

Salutations to Mary, Virgin. *Anonymous* Speed thanks to Him who swept death's yoke from every town. ISi

Salute. Oliver Pitcher. You could go on...But won't. PoBA

Salute. James Schuyler. ...I salue/that various field. ANYP; FYAP; NeAP

Salute to Life. Dmitri Shostakovitch. And radiant as the morning is our fair land. FSW

Salute to the Elephant. Odeniyi Apolebieji. Primeval leper, animal treading ponderously. WTO

Salute Your Partner. *Anonymous.* Hitch up and promenade to your seats. AmFP

Salvador Dali. David Gascoyne. And lovers float down from the cliffs like rain. EAS; OxBTC

The Salvation of Texas Peters. James W. Foley. For, though killin' 's repperhensible, it's/somethin' ye can stan'. ShM

Salvation Prospect. LeRoy Smith, Jr. Where the red leaves bleed for ever/And never pale. NePoAm

Salve! Thomas Edward Brown. They have a cheerful warmth–those ashes on the stone. HBV 1-2; OBEV; OBVV

Salve Regina. *Anonymous.* O gentle, O tender, O gracious Virgin Mary. ISi

Salvos for Randolph Bourne. Horace Gregory. possibly this is best to be/or not to be. NAMP

Sam. Walter De La Mare. Morning would find me gone. FaBV; MoAB; MoBrPo; OnMSP; TiPo

Sam Bass. *Anonymous.*

But if I'm right in my surmise he's gone the other way. AS; BeLS; BeLS 004; CoSo; FSW

Oh, what a scorching Jim will get when Gabriel blows his horn! AmFP

There'll be a lively mix-up down there among the coals. ViBoFo

Sam Hall. *Anonymous.*

All the whores are down in hell, God damn their eyes. ABF; AmFP; CoSo; FSW; TW; UnPo

And I left him layin' dead, blast his eyes! ViBoFo

Sam's World. Sam Cornish. she wears it proudly/a black and grey/round head of hair CNA

Sam, Sam the butcher man. *Anonymous.* And died with a toothache in his heel. FaFP

Sam, the Sportsman. *Anonymous.* And he'd go and fetch her the drake, drake, drake. OxNR

Samadhi. Conrad Aiken. Stoop, but upon your back be ever conscious/Of sunlight, and a shadow that may grow. MAPA

Samarian Nights. Yaakov Fichman. Mysterious as a primeval night. LiTW

Sambo's Right to be Kilt. Charles Graham Halpine. And give him the largest half! AA

The Same Continued. Wilfrid Scawen Blunt. What else remains of their dark horoscope/But a tall tree and courage and a rope? VLP

The Same Dream. Shlomit Cohen. my image was not on the cloud nor anywhere else. VWA

The Same Forever. Horatius Bonar. Who drinketh shall not drink in vain./I drink and love! BePJ

The Same Gesture. John Montague. the same gesture as/eased your snowbound/heart and flesh. BIrV

The Same Old Jazz. Philip Whalen. "What's wrong with two?" NeAP

The Same Old Story. James J. Montague. The price of meat has made men rage/And always with abundant reason. HBMV

Same Old Trick. William W. Pratt. It was done long ago by a common old cow. QQQ

The Same Side of the Canoe. Alda Espirito Santo. and we sit side by side/together in the canoe of our beaches. PBWP

Same Tits. James Tate. hot as hell outside. FAZ

Same Train. *Anonymous.* Same train be back tomorrer,/Same train, same train. BoAN 1-2

Samela. Robert Greene. For beauty, wit, and matchless dignity,/Yield to Samela. EIL; GBL; HBV 1-2; NOBE; OBEV; OBSC; ViBoPo

Samis Idyll. Dachine Rainer. Here we can love until we have to die. NePoAm

Samos. James Merrill. We shall be dust of quite another land/Before the seeds here planted come to light. HaCAP

The Sampler. Rachel Field. When sampler threads should turn to gray. BiCB

The Sampler. Nancy Byrd Turner. My, little girls were surely clever/When great-grandmother was ten years old! BiCB

Samson. *Anonymous.* He says, "An' now I got-n my way,/I'll tear the buildin' down." OuSiCo

Samson. Amir Gilboa. And the gates of his Gaza are still asleep in the ore./And Delilah VWA

Samson Agonistes. John Milton.

...advise/Forthwith how thou oughtst to receive him. OBS

And calm of mind, all passion spent. BoC; EBEV; ExPo; FaBoRV; FiP; MBW 1-2; MyFE; NOBE; OAEL 1-2; OBEV; OBS; PoEL 1-5; SeCeV

And I shall shortly be with them that rest. EBEV

And now at nearer view, no other certain/Than Dalila thy wife. OBS

Endure it, doubtful whether God be Lord,/Or Dagon. TRV

His message will be short and voluble. OBS

I leave him to his lot, and like my own. EBEV

Into a Dungeon thrust, to work with Slaves? EBEV

Life in captivity/Among inhuman foes. FaBoPV; ViBoPo; WHA

Lose thir defence distracted and amaz'd. OBEV

...not sway'd/By female usurpation, nor dismay'd. OBS

...turn/His labours, for thou canst, to peaceful end. SeCeV

Universally crown'd with highest praises. AtBAP; OBS

Whom patience finally must crown. NOBE; NOCV; SeCeV

Without all hope of day! AnFE

Samson Rends His Clothes. Anadad Eldan. Fragments of suns and chains sank/in the Gaza sea. VWA

Samson to His Delilah. Richard Crashaw. When first I looked on thee I lost mine eyes. TrGrPo

Samuel Allen. *Anonymous.* And there abide the Lord beside, the Father of us all. AmFP

Samuel Brown. Phoebe Cary. To our house in the street down town. OBAL

Samuel Hall. *Anonymous.*

And I feel so God damned proud/That I want to shout out loud, "Fuck 'em all." DBV

Damn your hides! ChTr

Samuel Hearne in Wintertime. John Newlove. and she twisted about them like/an eel, dying, never to know. NOBC

Samuel Hoar. Franklin Benjamin Sanborn. The simple grandeur of thy life and death. AA

Samuel Sewall. Anthony Hecht. Madam, your humble servant, Samuel Sewall. ConAP; LiTM; MP; NePoEA; NLV; PoPl; TwCP

Samurai and Hustlers. Joe Johnson. we are samurai and hustlers/in the rain CNA

A San Diego Poem: January–February 1973. Simon J. Ortiz. ...There are no echoes. CDW

San Francisco. Mary Austin. With a slow sound the ferries pace/A milky way of light. BPAW

San Francisco. John Vance Cheney. Mother, what hast thou done, what hast thou/done! PAH

San Francisco. Joaquin Miller. One solid San Francisco, one,/The fairest sight beneath the sun. PAH

San Francisco. Walter Adolphe Roberts. I think, if I went back, that she/Would take me to her breast. PoNe

San Francisco Arising. Edwin Markham. Build strongly, for her name must be/With Carthage of the sail-white sea. BPAW

San Francisco Bay. Joaquin Miller. Warm as a kiss when love is kind. BPAW

The San Francisco Company. Isaac W. Baker. And then return to where you wish and never want for more. AmFP

San Francisco County Jail Cell B-6. Conyus. who thinks he's a poet PoBA

San Francisco Falling. Edwin Markham. A thousand dreams of joy, or power,/Gone in the splendor of an hour. BPAW

San Francisco from the Sea. Bret (Francis Bret Harte) Harte. But, yielding to the common lot,/Lie unrecorded and forgot. BPAW

San Francisco Poem. John Logan. Two people surface and begin to swim. NNaP

San Juan Capistrano. Alice Cecilia Cooper. Awake in us dear memories of God's peace. GoBC

San Lorenzo Giustiniani's Mother. Alice Meynell. But never the Son who cannot change. HBV 1-2

San Marco Museum, Florence. Sister Maris Stella. ...no tapers here/Were lit but for the spirit's eye and ear. GoBC

San Miguel De La Tumba. Gonzalo de Berceo. Than the bishop, hight Don Tello, has been hurt by hand of/mine. CAW

San Pedro Road. Robert Hass. done with casting, reeling in slowly, casting... GeTw; WOLT

San Sabas. Luis Palés Matos. San Sabas, ample as a tree,/Giving his paternal shade. CAW

San Sepolcro. Jorie Graham. ...something terribly/nimble-fingered/finding all of the stops HaCAP

(San Ysidro, Cabezon). Paula Gunn Allen. and swift winds on the peaks/where the light is clear. TWSS

Sanary. Katherine Mansfield. A scent of dying mimosa flower/Lay on the air, but sweet–too sweet. AnNZ

Sancho. William Edwin Collin. Bemoaning distresses of maidens/In the clump of eucalyptus trees. CaP

Sanct Christopher II. Giuseppe Belli. whit's this I hae upon my back; the Warld?' OBVE

Sancta Silvarum. Lionel Pigot Johnson. Then cast once more your heightening spell. BrPo; VLP

Sancte Confessor. Rhabanus Maurus. With the Blest Spirit, He who filleth all things,/Unity Trinal! CAW

The Sanctimonious Poets. Friedrich Holderlin. energy is needed, people remember yours. NU

Sanctimony. *Anonymous.* But his poor forgetful body swallows spirits by mistake. WTO

Sanctity. Patrick Kavanagh. The agonising pincer-jaws of Heaven. BIrV; ELU; NOBI

Sanctuary. John Basil Boothroyd. What we can't seem to manage for man? FiBHP

Sanctuary. Bruce Boyd. to watch the tall water close over their heads. NeAP

Sanctuary. Louise Imogen Guiney. Float less than April fog below our hermit-/age. AA

Sanctuary. Dorothy Hewett. waiting for a fourth cremation. CBAP

The Sanctuary. Ford Madox Hueffer. Your kind, dear eyes shine in your dear, dear face. PoA

The Sanctuary. Howard Nemerov. ...out of sight/Though not, in time's ruining stream, out of mind. NePoEA

Sanctuary. Dorothy Parker. And sweet's the air with curly smoke/From all my burning bridges. NLV

Sanctuary. Elinor Wylie. How can I breathe? You can't, you fool! BoWoP; MoAB; MoAmPo

The Sanctum. Thomas Augustin Daly. Cry "non sum dignus" o'er and o'er/For her dear sake. TrPWD

Sand-Between-the-Toes. A.(lan) A.(lexander) Milne. Christopher is found with/Sand-between-the-toes. TiPo

Sand Creek. Charles G. Ballard. White Antelope is my name UnPo; VoR

Sand Dunes. Robert Frost. For the one more cast-off shell. MoAB; MoAmPo; RFM

Sand Dunes and Sea. John Richard Moreland. And in my heart the bitter wind of memory blowing. HBMV

The Sand Martin. John Clare. That lone heath and its melancholy pond. PBBP; TEP

The Sand Painters. Ben Belitt. And empties a season of rain. EyDe

Sand Paintings. Alice Corbin. The female moon/Beckons to darkness/And disappears. AnAmPo; BPAW

The Sandgate Girl's Lamentation. *Anonymous.* And I have married a keelman,/And my good days are done. CoMu; ELP; TW

The Sandhill Crane. Mary Austin. When the sandhill crane goes walking. BPAW; TiPo

Sandhill People. Carl Sandburg. , yet a face the beach wears between sunset and/dusk. CMoP

The Sandman. Margaret Thomson Janvier. As shuts the rose, they softly close, when he goes through/the town. HBV 1-2; HBVY

Sandpaper, Sandpiper, Sandpit. Warren Slesinger. if a loved one is lost. See true grief. AMV-80

Sandpiper. Elizabeth Bishop. and mixed with quartz grains, rose and amethyst. HeIP; NYBP

The Sandpiper. Witter ("Emanuel Morgan") Bynner. Vigilant among the grasses,/Where a fledgling bobs and passes. HBMV

The Sandpiper. Celia Thaxter. For are we not God's children both,/Thou, little sandpiper, and I? AA; FaBoBe; GN; HBV 1-2; HBVY; OBCA; OxBChV

Sandpipers. Helen Merrill Egerton. Darkness in the purple rushes–/Weet, a-weet, a-weet, weet weet! CaP

The Sands of Dee. Charles Kingsley. Across the sands of Dee. BeLS; FaBoPP; FaPoR; GN; GTBS; HBV 1-2; MCCG; PoPle; TreF; VLP; WBLP

Sandstone. Anne Marriott. Stands steady the supple new growth/Beyond the strained stretch of the clutching tide. CaP

Sandwich Man. Louis Johnson. and share the crusts of love in fairer weather. AnNZ

The Sandwich Man. Ron Padgett. And the horrible license plate on it ANYP; ConAP

Sandy. *Anonymous.* And the mill belonged to Sandy. OxNR

Sandy Kildandy. *Anonymous.* He gaed tae the byre/And swallowed the coo. OxNR

Sandy Lan'. *Anonymous.* Sandy bottom, sandy lan'. ABF

Sandy Star. William Stanley Braithwaite. With the secret on his brow. BANP; HBMV

Sang: Recoll O Skaith. Sidney Goodsir Smith. I maun loo i the pit o hell. NeBP

Sang: "There's a reid lowe in yer cheek." Robert MacLellan. And the sang ye sing as ye hap me ower/Is meant for him. OxBS

Sans Souci. Lisel Mueller. Negation is equal to love. NePoAm-2

Sant'Angelo D'Ischia. Edwin Denby. On a beach, four males in brilliant weather ANYP

Santa Anna or The Plains of Mexico. *Anonymous.* And Santa Anna ran away,/Along the plains of Mexico! AmSS

Santa Barbara. Francis Fisher Browne. And summer rules the radiant year. AA

Santa Barbara Beach. Ridgely Torrence. "Who dreams my fountain's laughter/Shall feed my wells with tears." HBMV

The Santa Barbara Earthquake. *Anonymous.* But we should all be ready/Before our time has come. AmFP

Santa Caterina. Myra Glazer Schotz. till dreams of power/entered me again/like magma– VWA

Santa Claus. *Anonymous.* Don't you think that Christmas/Is pleasantest of all? SoPo

Santa Claus. Walter De la Mare. There dwells thy loved Santa Claus. PCh

Santa Claus. Dom Moraes. ...invited visitor/Lifted his claws above them, holes for eyes. NoAm

Santa Claus. Howard Nemerov. Just one of the crowd lunching on Calvary. HAP

Santa Claus and the Mouse. Emilie Poulsson. The very stocking with the hole/The little mouse gnawed through. ChBR

Santa Claus in a Department Store. Christopher Hassall. ...No, there's no risk/Of damage. They pack the cuckoo separately. OxBTC

The Santa Fe Trail. *Anonymous.* Just a-janglin' for old Santa Fe. CoSo

The Santa Fe Trail. Arthur Chapman. And one sees o'er the long dead trail/A ghostly caravan. BPAW

Santa Fe Trail. Barbara Guest. O mother of lakes and glaciers save us gamblers/whose wagon is perilously rapt. NeAP; PoM

Santa Lucia. *Anonymous.* Home of fair poesy, realm of pure harmony,/Santa Lucia, Santa Lucia! FSW

Santa Maria del Fiore. George Herbert Clarke. Arno and April and the Apennines! CaP

Santiago. Thomas A. Janvier. So the fight was won that our Sampson planned! MC; PAH

Santo Domingo Corn Dance. R. P. Dickey. there it comes, then it comes, and it comes. TAT

Santorin. James Elroy Flecker. She sank into the moonlight/And the sea was only sea. FaBoTw; GoJo; OBMV

Santos: New Mexico. May Sarton. And pierced with anguish, at last act for love. EaLo

Santy Anno. *Anonymous.* Heave her up and away we'll go,/All on the plains of Mexico. FSW; OuSiCo; ShS

Saon of Acanthus. Callimachus. Asleep, not dead; a good man never dies. AWP; TRV

Sapho's Song. John Lyly. In thee poor Sapho lives, for thee she dies. OBSC

Sapientia Lunae. Ernest Christopher Dowson. And I went reading in that rune of roses/Which to her votaries the moon discloses. EnLi 1-2; HBV 1-2

The Sappa Creek. Gary Snyder. Tending sick and nervous old & cranky ship. NCSH

A Sapphic Dream.   George Moore.   Of sexless love, and strange unreached kisses.   SyP

Sapphic Stanzas.   Alexander Radishchev.   Happy mayst thou be if thou canst be only/Happy without love.   LiTW

Sapphics.   Dominic Bevin Wyndham Lewis.   Casting his bowler glumly on the sideboard:/"Gimme my dinner."   NOBL

Sapphics.   Thomas Morris.   O think on Morris, in a lonely chamber,/Dabbling in Sapphic.   NOEC

Sapphics.   Algernon Charles Swinburne.   Hearing, to hear them.   AnEnPo; PoEL 1-5

Sapphics Against Anger.   Timothy Steele.   If not the holiest of powers, sustaining/Only if mastered.   SM

The Sapphire.   William Stanley Merwin.   As the world's love before the world was.   PoA

Sappho.   Bliss Carman.   Trample and break and charge along the sand!   PeCV

Sappho.   Caius Valerius Catullus.   And rang my ears, and eyes became/Veiled, as in night.   AWP

Sappho.   Jack Cope.   her mouth blooms with a beloved name, her own.   PeSA

Sappho, Be Comforted.   William Carlos Williams.   for all (a second choice) you/present for my passionate caresses.   NePoAm-2

Sappho, if you do not come out.   Sappho.   ...Dearest Atthis,/can you now forget all those days?   BoWoP

Sappho Rehung.   LeRoy Smith, Jr.   Sappho was singing.   NePoAm

Sappho's Death: Three Pictures by Gustave Moreau (excerpt).   Thomas Sturge Moore.   Suspends her yet in immortality.   SyP

Sappho's Reply.   Rita Mae Brown.   An army of lovers shall not fail.   PeHV

Sappho's Tomb.   Arthur Stringer.   In the low-roofed room/That drips with tears!   CaP

Sara in Her Father's Arms.   George Oppen.   Do you suppose, Max, of which she is made.   GP; NNaP

Saragossa.   Henry Sambrooke Leigh.   Vainly–(that sneeze again? Loved one, I'm Off!)   FaBoCo

Sarah.   Edna Aphek.   call her the/laughing one.   VWA

Sarah.   Robin Hyde.   Let some wild/Eclipse of reason build in me/The overthrow of Hagar's child.   AnNZ

Sarah.   Delmore Schwartz.   Love is unjust: justice is loveless.   VWA

Sarah Byng.   Hilaire Belloc.   Confirmed in her instinctive guess/That letters always bring distress.   CenHV; GoJo

Sarah: Cherokee Doctor.   Wendy Rose.   and keep the amulets/intact.   STE

Sarah Cynthia Sylvia Stout Would Not Take the Garbage Out.   Shel Silverstein.   But children, remember Sarah Stout/And always take the garbage out!   BBGG; OBCA

Sarah Hazard's Love Letter.   John Ellis.   For oft beneath fair friendship's specious show/Lurks the false, trait'rous, undermining foe.   NOEC

Sarah Lorton.   Mary Finnin.   They pluck blanched flowers in the valley of the moon,/Sarah Lorton and her death together.   BoAV

Sarah Threeneedles.   Katharine Lee Bates.   Her food was more divine.   HBMV

Sarai.   Joseph Sherman.   and I was beautiful   VWA

Sarajevo.   Lawrence Durrell.   Composed around the echo of a pistol-shot.   GTBS-P; OBTV

Sarasvati.   James Stephens.   This is, naught else is, certainty.   NoAm

Saratoga Ending.   Weldon Kees.   ...on rows of yellow jars/In which the lemon trees were ripening.   NaP

Saratoga Song.   Anonymous.   And vain is their endeavor/Who strive to do us harm.   PAH

Sardanapalus.   Henry Howard, Earl of Surrey.   Murder'd himself, to show some manful deed.   SiPS

Sardis.   Anonymous.   When with Immanuel we reign,/Forever blest.   AmFP

Sarentino–South Tyrol.   Philip Brantingham.   ...I expect at any time/to see a man-bat flap/away from a stony turret.   AMV-80

Sargent's Portrait of Edwin Booth at "The Players".   Thomas Bailey Aldrich.   May know what sweet majestic face/The gentle Prince of Players wore!   AA

Sartorial Solecism.   R. E. C. Stringer.   Besides, it's grand for bailing.   FiBHP

Sasha and the Poet.   Jean Valentine.   "By Shakespeare.' And walked away.   VGW

Saskatchewan Dusk.   C. M. Buckaway.   ...nor the true form/of the prairie gathering in the dusk.   AMV-80

Sassafras.   Samuel Minturn Peck.   Catch the distant klingle-klang/Of the cow-bells tinkling home!   AA

Sassafras Tea.   Mary Effie Lee Newsome.   And that's one thing I really like/That they say's good for me.   CDC; GoSl

Satan.   Michael Madhusudan Dutt.   A phantom of departed splendour lone.   ACV

Satan Is Following Me.   Anonymous.   Here he is near!   WTO

Satan Is on Your Tongue.   George Barker.   Tomorrow they'll find the mess of blood and the feather.   MoAB; MoBrPo

Satan, No Woman.   Fulke, Lord Brooke Greville.   Feare Women that Sweare, Nay; and know they lye.   NCEP

Satan's a Liah (with music).   Anonymous.   Ain' gonna worry my Lawd no mo'.   AS

Satchmo.   Melvin B. Tolson.   "I'd be the greatest trumpeter in the Universe,/if old Satchmo had never been born!"   BPo

Satellites.   Gary Lenhart.   A Sugar Crisp box dropped past their heads/From a few stories up, riling them.   APU

Sather Gate Illumination.   Allen Ginsberg.   who loves himself loves me who love myself.   NeAP

Satie, at the End of Term.   Simon Curtis.   Mercy of irreverence.   NOBL

Satin-Clad.   Stevie Smith.   And she counts them as they fall.   OxBC

The Satin Shoes.   Thomas Hardy.   And her sweet syllables seemed to play/Like flute-notes softly blown.   CoBMV

Satire.   John Donne.
   And constantly a while must keepe his/bed.   OAEP
   And div'st, near drowning, for what's vanished.   OBSV
   And to every suitor lie in every thing,/Like a king's favourite, yea like a king.   OBSV
   ...but my words none draws/Within the vast reach of the huge statute laws.   ViBoPo
   Of my work lessen, yet some wise man shall,/I hope, esteem my writs canonical.   OBSV
   So perish souls, which more choose men's unjust/Power from God claimed, than God himself to trust.   CABA; EBEV; JCP; MeLP; MePo; NoP; OAEL 1-2; OBS; OBSV; PoEL 1-5; SeCP; SeCV 1-2

Satire.   Alexander Geddes.   Dread poetry, and damn the poet.   ACP

Satire.   John Marston.   ...a god that can do villainy/With a good grace and glib facility.   ViBoPo

A Satire.   John Oldham.   Be all but poet, and there's way to live.   ViBoPo

Satire.   Alexander Pope.   All, all but Truth, drops dead-born from the Press,/Like the last Gazette, or the last Address.   OBEC

Satire.   Edward Hilton Young.   What most we wish, with Ease we fancy near.   LAuP

A Satire Addressed to a Friend (excerpt).   John Oldham.   My thoughts and actions are, and shall be free.   AnAnS 1; NoP; OBS; OBSV

A Satire against Reason and Mankind.   John Wilmot, Earl of Rochester.   Huddled in Dirt this reasoning Engine lies/Who was so Proud, so Witty, and so Wise.   SCV

A Satire against Wit.   Sir Richard Blackmore.   Let 'em pound drugs, they have no brains to beat.   APAS

A Satire on Charles II.   John Wilmot, Earl of Rochester.   A merry monarch, scandalous and poor.   OBSV

A Satire on London.   Henry Howard, Earl of Surrey.   Immortal praise with one accord.   SiPS

Satire on Old Rowley.   Anonymous.   Brother to brother should be kind,/Yet bear the Littletons in mind.   APAS

A Satire on Samuel Butler (excerpt).   John Oldham.   And well might bless the fever that was sent,/To rid him hence, and his worse fate prevent.   OBSV

A Satire on the O'Haras.   Tadhg Dall O Huiginn.   O spare this crew of six!   NOBI

A Satire on the People of Kildare.   Anonymous.   This song is isaid of me,/Ever iblessed mote ye be.   OnYI

Satire Septimus Contra Sollistam.   William Rankins.   open that secret coffer we may see,/(if not possesse) that heavenly treasury.   NCEP

A Satire upon the French King.   Thomas (Tom) Brown.   And may all Christian people say amen to 't.   APAS

Satire upon the Heads; or, Never a Barrel the Better Herring.   Thomas Gray.   P.S.–As to Trinity Hall/We say nothing at all.   FaBoCo

Satire upon the Licentious Age of Charles II.   Samuel (1602-80) Butler.   Would drink her down, and turn her into a sow.   NOBL

Satires.   Alamanni.   Rhou shalt be judge how I do spend my tyme.   OBVE

Satires.   Nicholas Boileau-Despréaux.   The Skies, and Stars, his Properties must seem,/And turn-spit Angels, tread the Spheres for him.   OBVE

Satires.   Horace.   With Peace, let Tares and Acorns be my food.   OBVE

Satires.   Juvenal (Decimas Junius Juvenalis).   Go, go from the martial plain which you have forgotten!   PeHV

Satires.   Sir Thomas Wyatt.
   Grant them, good Lord, as thou mayst of thy might,/To fret inward for losing such a loss.   FCP; SiPS
   In this world now, litle prosperity,/And coin to keep as water in a sieve.   EnRePo; FCP; SiPS
   Thou shalt be judge how I do spend my time.   FCP; PoEL 1-5; SiPS

Satires of Circumstance.   Thomas Hardy.   Whom during her life I thought nothing of.   BrPo

A Satirical Elegy on the Death of a Late Famous General.   Jonathan Swift.   From all his ill-got honors flung,/Turned to that dirt from whence he sprung.   CABA; ExPo; FF; HoPM; NIP; NLV; NoP; OBSV; PoEL 1-5; SeCeV

A Satirical Poem about Drink.　Chimedin Jigmed.　Keep yourselves well in hand/And work hard for the State.　WTO

The Satirist.　Harry Lyman Koȯpman.　Then suddenly he reels.　AA

Satisfaction.　Archie Randolph Ammons.　descent's a nasty dinner.　GP

Satisfaction–Is the agent.　Emily Dickinson.　Immortality contented/Were Anomaly.　NOBA

Satisfied.　Samuel Valentine Cole.　In whose dear look thou shalt be satisfied.　BLRP

Satisfied.　Edgar Cooper Mason.　Through life, through death, beyond the sun,/On heaven's eternal shore.　BLRP

The Satisfying Portion.　Anonymous.　Then my joys shall never end.　BLRP

Satori.　Gayl Jones.　and i spring from the/Buddha's forehead/black as jesus.　BlSi

Saturday Afternoon at the Movies.　John Logan.　he should just face the facts/and get his ass home.　NNaP

Saturday Afternoon, when Chores Are Done.　Harryette Mullen.　to keep what we do/from coming apart at the ends.　AMV-81

Saturday Blues.　Ishman Bracey.　Takes all them dogs to/run my women down　BluL

Saturday in the County Seat.　Elijah L. Jacobs.　Down here it is raucous and gritty and crude. I love it.　AmFN

Saturday Market.　Charlotte Mew.　Never again remember the deep green hollow/Or the top of the kind old tree!　HBMV

Saturday Morning.　Richard Howard.　On a wound. You must have/come.　ErPo

Saturday Morning at the Laundry.　Christopher Gilbert.　despite the washers arguing. Imagine that.　MAYP

Saturday Night.　Sir Alan Patrick Herbert.　Nothing-much-matter-day-night!　NLV

Saturday Night.　Langston Hughes.　Till de red dawn come.　MoAmPo

Saturday Night.　Antigone Kefala.　movements following the eternal blueprint.　CBAP

Saturday Night.　James Oppenheim.　And clerk and foreman, peddler and grocer, are in our/Family of God!　HBV 1-2

Saturday Night in the Parthenon.　Kenneth Patchen.　...appears/For a moment on the balconies of my chosen sleep.　EAS

Saturday Night in the Village.　Giacomo Leopardi.　Let it not grieve you,/if the following day is slow to arrive.　OBVE

Saturday's Child.　Countee Cullen.　The only kind of middle wife/My folks could beg or borrow.　LiTM; NAs; OFD; PoBA; SaC

Saturday Shopping.　Katherine Edelman.　Our cupboard is bare!　SoPo

Saturday Sundae.　F. R. Scott.　And cellophane shall wrap the heretic.　CaP

The Saturday Tub.　Mary Gilmore.　The world fell into a blood-bath tub!　NOAV

Saturn Fallen.　John Keats.　"Saturn, sleep on! while at thy feet I weep."　AnEnPo; LoBV

Saturninus.　Katherine Eleanor Conway.　Only the mother, like God, forgives, and/comforts her heart with the past.　AA

Satyr.　Charles Gullans.　...You need/Their answers in the fundamental act.　PoA

The Satyr.　James Stephens.　And disappeared among the greenery.　OnYI

The Satyr in the Periwig.　Edith Sitwell.　Tear off a satyr's periwig!　AnEnPo

A Satyre Entituled the Witch.　Anonymous.　And the whole yeare bee as Halcyons day:/Oh were Canidia gone.　CoMu

A Satyretericall Charracter of a Proud Upstart.　John Saffin.　Then Let my Muse for Thee this Trophy raise.　SCAP

The Satyrs and the Moon.　Herbert Sherman Gorman.　Except their shaggy little child,/Who cried and cried.　HBV 1-2

Satyrs upon the Jesuits: Prologue.　John Oldham.　More dreaded than the Bor, and frighten worse/Than damning Pope's Anathema's, and curse.　CEP; SeCV 1-2

Satyrus Peregrinana.　William Rankins.　Then thought I, Oh there is a Judge above/Will all this wrong with one true sentence move.　OBSV

The Sauchs in the Reuch Heuch Hauch.　Hugh" (Christopher Murray Grieve) MacDiarmid.　Nor frae their ancient amplefeyst/Sall God's ain sel' them wile.　NoAm

The Saucy Sailor.　Anonymous.　...I don't care a single straw, my love,/What the world says of me.'　OBET

Saul.　Nathan Alterman.　So it was. And David heard.　TrJP

Saul.　Robert Browning.
As this moment, had love but the warrant, love's heart to/dispense!　BBV
Brought to blaze on the head of one creature–King Saul!　BoLiVe; FiP
–'E'en so, it is so!'　OAEP; VLP
Shall throw open the gates of new life to thee! See/the Christ stand!'　ILwL; TRV
Till the rapture was shut in itself, and the earth sank to rest.　WGRP

Saul.　Amir Gilboa.　In Beit-She'an the people of Israel wait.　VWA

Saul.　Charles Heavysege.
Now let me die, for I indeed was slain/With my three sons.　PeCV
O leave me, Creator, Tormentor, alone!　OBCV

...when the soul/Hangs poised, with folded wings, 'tween day and night. CaP

Saul.　Else Lasker-Schüler.　And with five hundred thousand men he swings the clubs.　VWA

Saul.　Isaac Rosenberg.　For my soul yearns and fears.　VWA

Saul.　George Sterling.　Whose sword is laid and his armor hung in the House of/Ashtoreth.　HBMV

Saul, afterward, Riding East.　John Malcolm Brinnin.　Damascus! Damascus! HoAn; Prf

Saul's Song of Love.　Saul Tchernichovsky.　Shall then the virgins rejoice? VWA

Sausage.　Axionicus.　...Then do I add a slice/Of tender tripe; and a snout soak'd in vinegar.　FaBoUs

Sausage.　Edgar A. Guest.　For a plate of steaming sausage like the kind my mother fried.　OBAL

A Savage.　John Boyle O'Reilly.　–the woman/reels/And drops without a moan: Dixon is/dead.　AA

The Savage Beast.　William Carlos Williams.　...How many, like/this dog, could I not wish/had been here in my/place, only a little closer!　TW

Savage Portraits.　Don (Donald Robert Marquis) Marquis.
A fellow-angel to that godly bone!　HBMV
...for every pest you slay/Ten more rank flies pollute the breath of day. HBMV
I think they'd both be happier, for the nonce.　HBMV
Kiss her, you crook; it is your life-work: Sweat!　HBMV
She writes, has bunions, and–Good God! her Nose!　HBMV

The Savages.　Josephine Miles.　We cannibals must help these Christians. LiTM

Savannah.　Alethea S. Burroughs.　Oh! come unto thy battle bed,/Savannah! O Savannah!　PAH

Savannah Mama.　Blind Willie McTell.　Well I'd like to love you, baby/but your good man got me barred　BluL

Saved.　Anonymous.　Were "John S. Clark as Acres at the Charing Cross tonight."　FaBoUs

Saved.　Maria Teresa Horta.　now that I am yours/yours and saved PBWP

Saved, but–.　Anonymous.　If Thou callest can I answer,/"Here am I, send me, send me"?　STF

Saving the Fish.　R. T. Smith.　Hope's the strangest game we play.　WOLT

Saving the Harvest.　Geoffrey Lehmann.　And oil burners roaring in the night.　CBAP

Savior! I've No One Else to Tell.　Emily Dickinson.　Is it too large for Thee?　AmePo; TrCP; TrPWD

The Saviour.　Samuel Wesley.　O Lamb of God! was ever pain–Was ever love like Thine?　BePJ

The Saviour Can Solve Every Problem.　Oswald J. Smith.　There is nothing that He cannot do.　BePJ

Saviour, Sprinkle Many Nations.　Arthur Cleveland Coxe.　Till on earth by every creature/Glory to the Lamb be sung.　AH

Saviour, Thy Dying Love.　Sylvanus D. Phelps.　My ransomed soul shall be,/Through all eternity,/Something for thee.　AH

Saviour, Who Died for Me.　Mary J. Mason.　If I may call Thee mine/ Eternally.　BePJ

Saviour, Who Thy Flock Art Feeding.　William Augustus Muhlenberg. Drink the rivers of thy grace.　AH

Saviour, Whose Love Is Like the Sun.　Howard Chandler Robbins.　And opened heaven for our delight.　TrPWD

Savonarola.　Edmund Clerihew Bentley.　To talk of serving God and Mammon.　OxBoLi

Saw God Dead but Laughing.　Jose Garcia Villa.　That could laugh only– after His murder.　AnFE

Saw You My Father.　Anonymous.　So she went her love away,/And it proved but the blink of the moon.　OBET

Saw You My True Love John?　Anonymous.　The lassie thought it day, when she sent her lover away,/And it was but a blink of the moon.　BFSS

Sawney Was Tall.　Thomas D'Urfey.　For now he ne're will be my love agen.　OAEP

The Saws Were Shrieking.　W. W. Eustace Ross.　the sweet spruce,/and the sweet hemlock.　CaP; PeCV

Saxon Grit.　Robert Collyer.　Let us thank God for the Saxon grit.　HBV 1-2

Saxophonetyx.　Cyn Zarco.　and there was nothing left in the room/but mercy.　APU; BrSi

Say "Au Revoir," but Not "Good-Bye."　Harry Kennedy.　I loved you then, I love you yet.　FSN

Say Goodbye to Big Daddy.　Randall Jarrell.　Or else it will be.　LiSp; PoNe

Say Hello to John.　Sherley Anne Williams.　His bright black face above me/saying, Say hello to John.　BlSi

Say, Lad, Have You Things to Do?　Alfred Edward Housman.　"No, my lad, I cannot come."　VLP

Say, Lovely Dream.　Edmund Waller.　Sleep does disproportion hide,/And, death resembling, equals all.　OAEP

Scholars. Walter De la Mare. And wakes to dream all night. NoAm

The Scholars. William Butler Yeats. Did their Catullus walk that way? CMoP; NoP; OAEL 1-2; PoA

A Scholder Indian Poem. Joy Harjo. sips it patiently/between his silver-mirrored teeth. TWSS

Scholfield Huxley. Edgar Lee Masters. And the next day have the worms/ Slipping in and out between your fingers? LiTA; MoPo; TrPWD

School after Christmas. Wymond Garthwaite. I wish–I wish/It came again in June. ChBR

School and Schoolfellows. Winthrop Mackworth Praed. That I could be a boy again,–/A happy boy,–at Drury's. OBRV

School Begins. Nell Goodale Price. "Hi ya, gang!" BrR

School-Bell. Eleanor Farjeon. Nine-o'clock/Bell! BrR; SiSoSe

The School Bus. Larry Eigner. being useful, small FAZ

School Cadets. Anne Elder. Earnestly they are inflated, diminished...and away... CBAP

The School Children. Louise Gluck. bearing so little ammunition. AmPA; HaCAP

School Days. Will Cobb. And you wrote on my slate "I love you, Joe,"/ When we were a couple of kids. FSW

School Days. Will D. Cobb. They've cut them up since those days. GoTF; TreFT

School Days. William Stafford. and fly all alone through the night/toward being the person I am. LCAP

School Days/Rule Days. Derek Butler. Children be children. LFAC

School Dinners. Anonymous. If that don't get you/Then the afters will. WTO

The School for Objects. Paul Hoover. ...They're shifting/monuments, take no risks, are true. APU

School for Scandal. Richard Brinsley Sheridan. I'll warrant she'll prove an excuse for the glass. NOEC; TreF

The School Girl. William Henry Venable. God's wrath must on the miscreant lie/Who dares offend her! AA

The School Globe. James Reaney. But with blood, pus, horror, death, stepmothers, and lies. NOBC

The School Hockey Team in Amsterdam. Frank Ormsby. ...Brothels and Sex Shops everywhere./Wish you were here. OBTV

School Is Out. Frances Frost. ...marked/with well-earned, golden stars! SiSoSe

School Is over. Kate Greenaway. Who'll laugh loudest?/Let us try. TiPo

The School-Master and the Truants. John Brownjohn. And gave him such a lesson as might well suffice for ten. OBCA

The School-Mistress. In Imitation of Spenser. William Shenstone. 'Till reason's morn arise, and light them on their way. CEP; LaA; LAuP

The School of Night. A. D. Hope. And dead sea scrolls that were my heart attest/How once I visited your holy land. PoA

The School of Sorrow. Harold Hamilton. And the cross is exchanged for the crown. BLRP

School's Out. William Henry Davies. Merry mites,/Welcome. BoC; OBMV

The Schoolboy. William Blake. When the blasts of winter appear? BoNaP; CH; FaBoCh; GLGT

The Schoolboy Reads His Iliad. David Morton. He dreams of marbles and of tops, and nods. MCCG

A Schoolboy's Lot. Anonymous. Al day yven agagement/To yiven us strokes grete. OxBM

Schoolboys in Winter. John Clare. In the pale splendour of the winter sun. CBEP; InvP; NBM; PoEL 1-5; VLP

Schoolfellows. Winthrop Mackworth Praed. Where bearded men appear to-day/Just Eton boys grown heavy. NBM

Schoolgirl on Speech-Day in the Open Air. Iain Crichton Smith. The schoolgirl rises–and must do the same. NePoEA-2

Schoolgirls Hastening. John Shaw Neilson. Morning is with me, and the breath/Of schoolgirls hastening down the way. BoAV; NOAV

The Schoolmaster. Anonymous. To skelp the bairns on Monday. GBP; GLGT

Schoolmaster. George Rostrevor Hamilton. For God, the great Headmaster. FaBoEE

The Schoolmaster Abroad. Sir Owen Seaman. With instantaneous Kodak-shots/Secured by ushers on the spots! OBTV

The Schoolmaster Abroad with His Son. Charles Stuart Calverley. On their charms to a dull little varmint/Of seven or eight. NOBL

A Schoolmaster's Admonition. Anonymous. But such as will loiter, and lazy will be,/Shall for their labour be brought on their knee. OxBChV

A Schoolmaster's Precepts. John Penkethman. "Those that want learning, he that seeks to teach,/Himself (though most unlearned) may all outreach OxBChV

Schoolroom: 158–. James E. Warren, Jr. He has a prince's eyes. GoYe

Schoolroom on a Wet Afternoon. Vernon Scannell. Vicious rope, glaring blade, the gun cocked to kill. HaMV

Schoolyard in April. Kenneth Koch. The teachers themselves/stare out of windows,/remembering April. PoA

The Schooner Blizzard. Anonymous. So now you'll please excuse me, for I'm nearly out of breath. ShS

The Schooner Fred Dunbar. Amos Hanson. And when our money is all gone, we'll plough the bay some more. AmFP

The Schooner Kandahar. Anonymous. We were a jolly crew. ShS

The Schreckhorn. Thomas Hardy. When dawn that calls the climber dyes them rose? OAEL 1-2

Schubertiana. Tomas Transtromer. The stubborn humming sound that this instant is with us/upward into/The depths. NU

A Schule Laddie's Lament on the Lateness o' the Season. James Logie Robertson. It pits hiz laddies sair aboot. NOBV

Schwiegermutterlieder. Tony Harrison. Else Crossfield, Dietzsch,/nee Schubert–British bitch! PAI

Science. Robinson Jeffers. ...who would have dreamed this/infinitely little too much? NU; OxBA

Science as Art. Hugh Seidman. like gravity, like weight AmPA

Science Fiction. Kingsley Amis. Worse than their sires, of wider range,/ And much more durable. NePoEA-2

Science Fiction. Reed Whittemore. And return to Mars as himself, a Martian/Raccoon. GP

Science for the Young. Wallace Irwin. Heat creates both light and motion. ShM Yet it proves by demonstration/Newton's law of gravitation. BBGG; DBV; QQQ

Science in God. Robert Herrick. A Substance, not a Qualitie. ImOP

The Science of the Night. Stanley Jasspon Kunitz. And all my hearts in unison strike twelve. MoAmPo; MP; TwCP; UnTE

A science–so the savans say. Emily Dickinson. And countless butterfly! ImOP

Scientia Vincit Omnia? Merrill Moore. Love in a test-tube he knew was a dangerous thing. AnAmPo

A Scientific Expedition in Siberia, 1913. Kelly Cherry. ...and I have/Come with blood in my mouth, my hands sopped/With red snow, to speak and save. SM

Scientific Proof. James W. Foley. It also gives its length and breadth/And what's the price of coal. QQQ

The Scientist. Janet Burroway. By the mystery and the function of his denying. SoSe

Scintilla. William Stanley Braithwaite. At a dead man's door. BANP; CDC

Scissor-Man. George MacBeth. ...I sleep like a weapon/with a yen for a pierced ear. FaBoMo

The Scissor-Man. Madeline Nightingale. Sing to make the work go well,/ Like the Scissor-man. TiPo

Scissors and String, Scissors and String. Anonymous. When a man marries his trouble/begins. OxNR

The Scissors-Grinder. Vachel Lindsay. And there beside the railroad bridge/I saw the Wandering Jew. MAPA

The Scolding Wives Vindication. Anonymous. He shall dig Gravel next Horn-Fair/and that he is like to do. CoMu

Scorned. Alexander Smith. And I am very weary; so, good-night! OBVV

The Scorner. Tchicaya U. Tam'si. I will waltz to the tune of your slow sadness. TTY

The Scorpion. Hilaire Belloc. He is a most unpleasant brute/To find in bed, at night. BoAnP

The Scorpion. William Plomer. A scorpion on a stone. AtBAP; NoAm; OBMV

Scorpion. Stevie Smith. Scorpion so wishes to be gone. EBEV; FaBoWP

A Scot, a Welsh and an Irish Man. Anonymous. But he pulled it out by the tail. GBP

Scotch Rhapsody. Edith Sitwell. That is the place–that is the place–that is the place for me! MP; TwCP

Scotch Song. Thomas D"Urfey. And Pipe a Tune to please me. CEP

Scotch Te Deum. William Kethe. His truth at all times firmly stood/And shall from age to age endure. WGRP

Scotland. Sir Alexander Gray. Kissed by the wind/And caressed by the rain. BSV; GoTS; OxBS

Scotland. William Soutar. Whan ye come hameless here/And ken ye are at hame. OxBS

Scotland, 1941. Edwin Muir. And melt to pity the annalist's iron tongue. BSV; OxBS

Scotland's Burning. Anonymous. Pour on water, pour on water. FSW

Scotland's Winter. Edwin Muir. And are content/With their poor frozen life and shallow banishment. OxBS; OxBTC

Scotland Small? Hugh" (Christopher Murray Grieve) MacDiarmid. Nothing but heather!'–How marvellously descriptive! And/incomplete! PoSH

Scotland Yet. Henry Scott Riddell. We'll drink a cup to Scotland yet,/Wi' a' the honors three. HBV 1-2

The Scots in Berwick. Anonymous. And when he has it,/Gas, dikes him! OxBM

Scots Wha Hae. Robert Burns. Let us do or die! ATP; CEP; CoBE; EnPE; FaPoR; FSW; OAEL 1-2; OAEP; OBEC; OxBS; SeCeV; TEP; WHA

Scottish Castle. Anonymous. Will no' drive Willie Wastle doon. OxNR

A Scottish Cat. Anonymous. I put it in my meal-poke,/to eat it to my bread. OxNR

The Scottish Merchant's Daughter. Anonymous. Will you then my heart decline?"/"No, Sir! no, Sir! no, oh, no, no!" BFSS

The Scottish Mountaineering Club Song. John G. Stott. Memories raise of joyous days/Upon the mountain side. PoSH

A Scottish Proverb. Anonymous.
For when the corn's to shear the bairn's to bear. FaBoUs
One's enough, and twa's too mony. FaBoUs

A Scottish Shoe. Anonymous. The bell rope broke,/And down she fell. OxNR

Scottsboro. Anonymous. Like cat down cellar wit' nohole mouse. InPK

Scottsboro, Too, Is Worth Its Song. Countee Cullen. But they have raised no cry./I wonder why. PoBA

The Scourge. Stanley Jasspon Kunitz. While all my children leaped/Out of the glowing wood. CrMA

The Scow on Cowden Shore. Anonymous. And the title that I give it is "The Scow on Cowden Shore." ShS

The Scow on Cowden Shore (III). Anonymous. And they were hard men to conquer on the scow on Cowen Shore. ShS

Scrap Iron. Raymond Durgnat. This cold steel slowly burns to be a gun. PCP

Scrapbooks. Nikki Giovanni. that perhaps one day i can unfold/for my grandchildren CNA

Scraps. Susannah Fried. like an old leaf/on a path, in winter. VWA

Scraps. Rodger Kamenetz. more Jews are killed/to restore the general complacency. APU

The Scratch. James Dickey. I shall dream of a crown til I do. AP

Scrawled in Pencil in a Sealed Railway Car. Dan Pagis. cain son of man/ tell him that i VWA

A Screamer Discusses Methods of Screaming. James Schevill. The inside scream has no echo. TAP

Screaming Tarn. Robert Bridges. So from his lips the crime returned/To haunt the spot where it was done. ExPo

Screw-Guns. Rudyard Kipling. ...but you can't get away from the guns! ViBoPo

Screw Spring. William M. Hoffman. These walls, this bed/do/not/grow. FF

The Scribblers. Walter Savage Landor. The taller mastiff deems it aptest/ To lift a leg and play the baptist. OBSV

The Scribe. Anonymous. I write well under the greenwood. AnIL; OnYI

Scribe. Paul Auster. a hundred white stones/turn to raging phlox. VWA

The Scribe. Walter De La Mare. All words forgotten–/Thou, Lord, and I. AnFE; AtBAP; CMoP; FaBoCh; LoGBV; MoRP; OBMV; TrCP; TrPWD

The Scribe. Endre Farkas. ends the epic/makes the night lyric CaPN

The Scribe's Prayer. Arthur Guiterman. Guide Thou the pen within my wavering hand! TrPWD

The Scribe's Prayer. Robert W. Service. Yet do I know Thy Love: have mercy, Lord... TrPWD

Scrievin. Alexander Scott. Scrievit by hands sae unlike mine. BSV

Scrimshaw. Michael Hogan. ...I buy a small necklace for/my wife. Promise to write him a poem. LFAC

Scroll. Stanley Moss. So if you must,/Pray standing. VWA

Scroll-Section. Robert Finch. the seal of your mind borrowed and not returned. PeCV

Scroppo's Dog. May Swenson. ...Scroppo's dog forlornly/yodels in time to the village siren sounding noon. GDP

The Scrutiny. Richard Lovelace. I laden will return to thee,/Ev'n sated with variety. AnAnS 2; BoLoP; CaPo; CavP; EnLit; EnLoPo; GBL; MeLP; MePo; NoP; OBS; SeCP; TrGrPo

The Sculptor. Anonymous. And I could change it, nevermore. PoToHe

The Sculptors. Alfred W. Purdy. and I'd like to buy every damn case PeCV

Sculpture. Anonymous. And I could fashion it no more! BLPL; PoLf

Scum o' the Earth. Robert Haven Schauffler. In the wealth of the richest bloods of earth. HBV 1-2

Scunner. Hugh" (Christopher Murray Grieve) MacDiarmid. –And I lo'e Love/Wi' a scunner in't. BSV; FaBoTw

The Scurrilous Scribe. Philip Freneau. The sons of smut and scandal hurt me not. AA

Scylla and Charybdis. Thomas Kinsella. Making a third, to round the simple moral. OxBTC

Scyros. Karl Shapiro. And war began next Monday on the Danes. HoPM; LiTA; LiTM; MoVE; NePA; SeCeV; WaP

The Scythe. Henry Kanabus. It is waving its arms/in a thousand different parodies. APU

Scythe Song. Andrew Lang. Hush, ah hush! and the Scythes are swinging/ Over the clover, over the grass! GN; HBV 1-2

The Scythians. Alexander Blok. Once only the barbarian lyre calls. AWP; WaaP

De Se. John Weever. I'll give the devil two for pay,/If he will fetch the third away. FaBoEE

A Se Stesso. Giacomo Leopardi. And of all things the infinite vanity! AWP

The Sea. Anonymous.
And clumsy sailors tumble in. NA
The sea's in flood! KiLC

The Sea. Barry (Bryan Waller Procter) Cornwall. And Death, whenever he comes to me,/Shall come on the wild, unbounded sea! GN; GoTF; HBV 1-2; HBVY; TreFS

The Sea. Hart Crane. The bottom of the sea is cruel. CrMA

The Sea. William Henry Davies. With savage joy, and efforts wild,/To smash his rocks with a dead child. FaBoTw

The Sea. Lloyd Frankenberg. ,...how perfectly/mirrors God's face, the workings of his mind. AnFE; CoAnAm; MOS

Sea. Don Gordon. And the world of man are the last voids...pendulous,/ unborn. EtS

The Sea. Herman Gorter. Each dune looked up from dreamy memories. LiTW

The Sea. D.H. Lawrence. Sea, you shadow of all things, now mock us to death with/your shadowing. BoNaP; MOS; NAMP

Sea. Bernadette Mayer. Laughed at, one/may be redder; further is a warehouse where... ANYP

The Sea. Ken Noyle. The sea you saw/Is not the same sea/You see. MOS

The Sea. Richard Henry Stoddard. Through the night. AA; HBV 1-2

The Sea. Francis Webb. ...And we/Turn again to our mother, our revels. The sea, the sea! CBAP; PoAu 1-2

Sea and Land Victories. Anonymous. Who witnessed Havre's smoking plains,/And Hampton's female cries. PAH

The Sea and Ourselves at Cape Ann. Lawrence Ferlinghetti. Odyssey turned to Iliad/in parked cars PoM

Sea and Shore. Harry Lyman Koopman. We wait, thy will to do. AA

The Sea and the Eagle. Sydney Clouts. Terribly like a swoop of water. PeSA

The Sea and the Hills. Rudyard Kipling. So and no otherwise–so and no otherwise–hillmen desire their/Hills. FaBV; MOS

The Sea and the Mirror. W. H. Auden.
And the silence ripeness,/And the ripeness all. SeCeV
Roll them overboard and sleep. FaBoTw

The Sea and the Skylark. Gerard Manley Hopkins. To man's last dust, drain fast towards man's first slime. FM; LiTB; OBMV

The Sea and the Tiger. Laurence Collinson. ...and with/their honest mouths eat out my eyes. PoAu 1-2

Sea Bells. Richard Eberhart. Hearing them, year to year, I talk to myself alone. AMV-80

The Sea Bird. Keith Douglas. crept into the dead bird, ceased to exist. ChMP

The Sea Bird to the Wave. Padraic Colum. Art thou gone? EtS; SUS

Sea-Birds. Elizabeth Akers. Where is thy mate, and where thy nest? AA; FaBoBe; HBV 1-2

The Sea Birds. Van K. Brock. And no one shall put salt on their bright tails. NYBP; SM

Sea-Birds. Fray Angelico Chavez. And you upon the quarterdeck/To feed them, Mother Carey. ISi

Sea-Birds. James (1700-48) Thomson. Infinite wings! till all the plume-dark air/And rude resounding shore are one wild cry. EtS

Sea Born. Harold Vinal. I wear the sea as others wear a crown! HBMV

A Sea Boy on the Giddy Mast. John Clare. In every hope appears a grave/ And leaves no hope for me. PPP

Sea Burial. Robina Monkman. Leave him at last to sea-dark sleep, with one clear Har-/bour light/Bright as the pole star over him EtS

Sea Burial from the Cruiser "Reve." Richard Eberhart. She is now water and air,/Who was earth and fire. NYBP

Sea Calm. Langston Hughes. It is not good/For water/To be so still that way. LOW

Sea Canes. Derek Walcott. brings those we love before us, as they were,/ with faults and all, not nobler, just there. HeIP

The Sea Captain. Anonymous.
To roam all alone on the shore? ViBoFo
With ale and beer and brandy I'll drink about galore. BaBo

The Sea-Captain. Gerald Gould. Having her arms about me. And I shall trust her then. EtS

The Sea Cathedral. Edwin John Pratt. Without one chastening fire made to start/From altars built around its polar heart. CaP

Sea-Change. John Masefield. And coming the proud over all o' the birds o' the sea. AtBAP; FaBoTw; MOS; OBMV

Sea-Change. Genevieve Taggard. You are most loved, most lost, most beautiful. EtS

Sea Sonnet. Norma Lay. Tell me I say, who contemplate, aghast,/sky bells now silent, and the channel lost. GoYe

Sea-Sonnet. Victoria Mary (Vita) Sackville-West. And that same moon shall heap the desolate tide/Beneath the night's unchanging architrave. SBG

A Sea-Spell. Dante Gabriel Rossetti. And up her rock, bare-breasted, comes to die? SyP; VLP; WSC

Sea Surface Full of Clouds. Wallace Stevens. Came fresh transfigurings of freshest blue. AP; CMoP; CoBMV; MoAB; MoAmPo; MOS; VGW

Sea Things. Gwendolyn MacEwen. ...and complex hungers/crashing on the high white beaches of the world. FaBoWP

Sea Town. Frances Frost. and windows have seaward eyes. EtS

Sea Turtle. Liston Pope. The blood wrung from the cursing sailors' shirts. AMV-80

The Sea-Turtle and the Shark. Melvin B. Tolson. beyond the stomach walls/of the shark. BP; PoBA

Sea Violet. Hilda ("H. D.") Doolittle. frost, a star edges with its fire. NoP

Sea Voyage. William Empson. We sum in port her banquet of degrees. CMoP; MOS

Sea-Voyage. John Hall Wheelock. A chamber for His splendor, without bound. EtS

A Sea-Voyage from Tenby to Bristol, Begun Sept. 5, 1652... Katherine ("Orinda") Philips. In short, the Heav'ns must needs propitious be,/Because Lucasia was concerned in me. SBG

Sea-Ward, White Gleaming through the Busy Scud. Samuel Taylor Coleridge. Now floats upon the air, and sends from far/A wildly-wailing note. BiP; PBBP

Sea-Wash. Carl Sandburg. The sea-wash repeats, repeats. BrR; OBCA

The Sea-Watcher. Aubrey Thomas De Vere. Free hearth for thee, and honest fame.' IrPN

Sea-Way. Ellen Mackay Hutchinson Cortissoz. Thou shalt lie still and ebb no more. AA

Sea-Weed. D.H. Lawrence. it slips over it as shadows do, without hurting itself. BoNaP; MOS

The Sea-Weed. Elisabeth Cavazza Pullen. "Land ho!" Columbus cried. AA

Sea-Wind. Stephane Mallarme. But, O my heart, hear thou, hear thou, the sailors' song! AWP; SyP

The Sea Wind. Harry Martinson. It's nearly evening now or morning. NU

Sea Words. Mary Sinton Leitch. ...The wash of a liquid moon/against lean bows/Is in them, and sea stillness and sea wonder. EtS

Sea Wrack. Moira O'Neill. The wrack may drift ashore. OnYI

Seabirds. Robert B. Smith. What curse, what blessing have you/laid on me/with white bellies which promise/your secret oceans? LFAC

Seaconk or Rehoboths Fate. Benjamin Tompson. All crueltyes which paper stain'd before/Are acted to the life here ore and ore. SCAP

Seaconk Plain Engagement. Benjamin Tompson. Quickly we pray oh Lord! say thou Amen. SCAP

The Seafarer. *Anonymous.*
cannot allay the anger of God/towards a soul sin-freighted. OBVE
for all time, the Lord eternal./Amen. EBEV
It cries in my ears and it urges my heart/To the path of the whale and the plunging sea. AnOE; EtS; MOS
Over the waves of the sea.... EnLi 1-2
Whets for the whale-path the heart irresist-/ibly,/O'er tracks of ocean... EnL

Seafarer. Archibald MacLeish. And learn to sleep against this ground. NoAm; NoP

The Seafarer. Ezra Pound. His born brothers, their buried bodies/Be an unlikely treasure hoard. AmP; AnAmPo; AP; CTC; ExPo; FaBoTw; HeIP; InPK; LiTA; LiTW; NoP; OxBA

The Seafarer (excerpt). *Anonymous.* No one to comfort my desolate heart. PBBP

The Seagull. Mary Howitt. For the sea is his truest home! OxBChV

Seagulls. Robert Francis. Freedom that flows in form and still is free. RFM

Seagulls. John Updike. beautiful gods stroll unconcerned/among our mortal apprehensions. Psk

Seagulls on the Serpentine. Alfred Noyes. We have all of us lost the sea, and we all remember./But you–have wings. EtS

Seal. William Jay Smith. He plops at your side/With a mouthful of fish! GrPl; RFM

Seal at Stinson Beach. Roberta Hill. In the drawing back, the breathing in, I find my bones. VoR

Seal Lullaby. Rudyard Kipling. Asleep in the arms of the slow-swinging seas. SoSe; TiPo

Seal of Fire. Mordecai Temkin. Why do you conceal Your face,/my Lord? VWA

Seal Pups. Nora Dauenhauer. rolling with the breakers. TWSS

Seal Rock. Sue Baugh. What can be said between one wave and the next? AMV-81

Seal Rock. Katha Pollitt. Whatever their language, they are not speaking to us. MAYP

Seal Rocks: San Francisco. Robert Conquest. We can enjoy the merely/Actual: a good thing for verse. PP

Sealed Bags of Ducats. Martial (Marcus Valerius Martialis). Calenus, you'll die of starvation. LiTW

Sealed Orders. Richard Burton. ...and see the longed-for land/Lie, known and very near. HBV 1-2

Seals at High Island. Richard Murphy. ...till the bitter ocean's tongue/Swells in their cove, and smothers their sweet song. CIP; IPY

The Seals in Penobscot Bay. Daniel Gerard Hoffman. when the boom, when the boom, when the boom/of guns punched dark holes in the sky. MP; TwCP

Seals, Terns, Time. Richard Eberhart. Enticed to the release of the sky. LiTM; MoAB; MoAmPo

Seaman, 1941. Molly Holden. ...as if he'd stayed/a fisherman for life and never gone to war/was not to be expected. FaBoWP

The Seaman's Compass. *Anonymous.* 'Tis pity that they should ever speak word again.' OBSS

A Seaman's Confession of Faith. Harry Kemp. The prayer and faith of seamen will not fail/O God, my God, as long as ships do sail. TrPWD

A Seamark. Bliss Carman. The emerald dragon breaks his teeth. PeCV

Seamas, Light-Hearted and Loving Friend of My Breast (excerpt). Eoghan Rua O Suilleabhain. and I'll save not a halfpenny pay till the day I die! NOBI

The Seamen and Soldiers' Last Farewell to Their Dearest Jewels. *Anonymous.* Farewell, my dearest dear, till our next meeting. OBSS

The Seamen's Distress. *Anonymous.* And we poor seamen do lie on the top,/Whilst the landmen lies below. OBSS

The Seamen's Wives' Vindication. *Anonymous.* May be ashamed of your actions, and thus I bid you adieu. OBSS

Seamen Three. Thomas Love Peacock. And your ballast is old wine. OBRV; WiR

The Seamy Side of Motley. Sir Owen Seaman. With the strain of trying to be/Funny every week. InMe

Seance. William Abrahams. As though I were not beside you, "Yes! Oh, yes!" NYBP

Seance. Francis King. And mine the stiff and automatic hand. PoA

Seance. Edouard Roditi. ...Where the stranger stood the two/men find a railway ticket to an unknown destination. EAS

Search. Claribel Alegria. Each morning I will know it. BoWoP

The Search. Kwesi Brew. Revealed the truth/That they had been/The slaves of fools. PBA

The Search. Thomas Curtis Clarke. The Lord of Love was standing there! WGRP

The Search. Ernest Crosby. I sought my Brother out, and found all/three. AA

The Search. Michael Hamburger. Why, Mors, need we tell you, m o r s, MORS. VWA

The Search. George Herbert. So doth thy nearenesse bear the bell,/Making two one. AnAnS 1

The Search. John of the Cross. Look then on me, thus shrouded, as I cry. BoC

Search. Anne Marriott. I sought–and found Him there. TRV

The Search. Charles Shaw. I'd love to meet that bloke who rode/The big white bull through Wagga. NOAV

Search. Raymond Souster. ...so filled/with such strength, such tenderness of love. ELU; OBCV

The Search. Henry Vaughan. Travels in clouds, seeks manna, where none is. SBVL; SeCP

Search. Margaret Widdemer. And ye shall be with Me. TrPWD

Search for Love. Henry Johnson. To lived unloved, makes us cold; cruel; remote. LFAC

The Search Party. William Matthews. The child was still/alive. Admit you're glad. GeTw

The Searching. Alice S. Cobb. Where she dare preen and reaffirm/Her womanness. BlSi

Searching for Lambs. *Anonymous.* We'll join our hands in a wedded band/And a-married we will be.' OBET

Searching the Desert for the Blues. Blind Willie McTell. tell that same line to somebody else./Lord lord/lord lord lord. BluL

Seascape. Elizabeth Bishop. and when it gets dark he will remember something/strongly worded to say on the subject. FaBoWP; MoAB; MOS; OxBC; PPP

Seascape. Langston Hughes. We saw an Indian merchantman/Coming home. BrR

Seascape. Stephen Spender. While, above them, that harp assumes their sighs. AtBAP; CoBMV; MOS; NoP

Seascape. Francis Brett Young. Until, with day, another blue be born. OxBTC

Seascape with Bookends. Charles Edward Eaton. Here in the book it cannot stay forever and there on the/sea the text is lost. AMV-80

Seashore. Ralph Waldo Emerson. I make some coast alluring, some lone isle,/To distant men, who must go there, or die. OxBA

The Seaside and the Fireside: Dedication. Henry Wadsworth Longfellow. Nor stand as one unsought and uninvited! MAmP

Seaside Golf. Sir John Betjeman. And splendour, splendour everywhere. LiSp; PoPl; SD

Season of Blood. Arnaldo Santos. to tear out my bowels/and hurl them in the face of this season. WhB

The Season of Phantasmal Peace. Derek Walcott. but, for such as our earth is now, it lasted long. NoP

Season's Greetings. Hilaire Belloc. Noel, noel, noel, noel! DBV

The Season's Lovers. Miriam Waddington. Unless you read love's double mind/Or invent its polar map. OBCV; PeCV

Season Ticket. Gloria Frym. Anna Pavlova rises like a phoenix/instead of a swan especially in your honor/tonight. APU

The Season 'Tis, My Lovely Lambs. Edward Estlin Cummings. pulled six months for selling snow. NIP; UnPo

Seasong. Stefan George. What profit has my whole day won/If now the fair child does not come? LiTW

Seasons. Barry Dempster. ...the pattern of your/heart falling into my/soft and empty arms. CaPN

The Seasons. Thomas Holcroft. Then will we, when labour's o'er,/At harvest-home our catches roar. NOEC

The Seasons. Rolfe Humphries. Across the snow—in at the fox's death. NYBP

The Seasons. Kalidasa.
The absent grieving and the pain/Of separated love. AWP
And stirs with lover's fancies fond/The young man's eager heart. AWP
Forget sad thoughts forlorn. AWP
Shower blessings on my wife. AWP
Sweet friends at evening, and a spot/Cool after burning days. AWP
With dreams of loving bliss. AWP

Seasons. Christina Georgina Rossetti. And starved the snow he shines upon. YeAr

The Seasons. James (1700-48) Thomson.
All-beauteous Nature fears to be out-/done. OAEP
And all the fell Society of Night. AtBAP
And ask the helping hospitable hand. FM
And every Man within the Reach of Right. EnRP
And let me never never stray from THEE! CEP
And numberless such offices of love,/Daily and nightly, zealous to perform. EBEV; OAEL 1-2
And once rejoicing never know them more. PoEL 1-5
And pour their Souls in Transport, which the SIRE/Of Love approving hears, and calls it good. EnRP
And property assures it to the swain,/Pleased and unwearied, in his guarded toil. FaBoPP
...and wanton rolls/The glancing eye, and turns the changeful neck. PBBP
Dig for the withered herb through heaps of snow. FM
Mixed in mad tumult and discordant joy. FM
Of those that under grim oppression groan. SeCePo
...or drives them wide-dispersed,/Wounded and wheeling various down the wind. PBBP
Refining still, the social passions work. NoP; SeCePo
The Storms of WINTRY TIME will quickly pass,/And one unbounded SPRING encircle All. CEP; OAEP
Stretch'd out, and bleaching in the northern blast. BSV; EBEV
...such is the force/With which his frantic heart and sinews swell. FM
Then straight air, sea, and earth are hushed at once. OAEL 1-2
Till, more familiar grown, the table crumbs/Attract his slender feet... PBBP

Seasons and Times. William Barnes. When footsteps are few on the ground? NOBV

The Seasons in North Cornwall. Charles Causley. In the sea-roads of the moor. ACV

Seasons of the Soul. Allen Tate.
Him in the empty hall. MoVE; NePA; OxBA
The living wound of love. NePA; OxBA
Put back upon his jaws. NePA; OxBA
Whether your kindness,/mother,/Is mother of silences. AP; CrMA; MoPo; NePA; OxBA

A Seat for Three: Written on a Settle. Walter Crane. Free, equal, and fraternally,/A seat for three. OBVV

Seated on her bed legs spread open. Joyce Mansour. Eaten by a woman/Who saw nothing BoWoP

Seaward. Celia Thaxter. No sadder sound salutes you than the clear,/Wild laughter of the loon. AA

Seaward Bound. Alice Brown. Spread silence round Thee, and dwell there apart,/Awful, alone. TrPWD

Seaway. Grace Wilson. Haul the wind! Put out again to sea! AMV-81

Seaweed. Henry Wadsworth Longfellow. Household words, no more depart. AP; HBV 1-2; MOS; OxBA; TAP

Seaweed, Seaweed. Hannah Tatana. But the spirit curls and sleeps/Huddled up/Within me. WTO

Seaweeds. Sandra McPherson. And I take in their iodine. AmPA; PoA

Seboyeta Chapel. Shirley Hill Witt. And think of gold/At Seboyeta. TWSS

The Second Advice to a Painter. Andrew Marvell. Kings are in war but cards: they're gods in peace. APAS

The Second Angel. Philip Levine. My brother, the angel, has fallen. NaP

The Second Anniversarie. John Donne. Thou art the Proclamation; and I am/The Trumpet, at whose voyce the people came. AnAnS 1; FaBoEn; OAEL 1-2; OxBoCh

The Second Asgard. Matthew Arnold. Death, and the gloom which round me even now/Thickens, and to its inner gulph recalls. FiP

Second Avenue Winter. Charles Simic. Its ritual and secret life/Where I wish to be anointed. NYP

Second Best. Rupert Brooke. O heart, in the great dawn! MoBrPo; OBVV

A Second Birthday. Albert Kayper-Mensah And as he walked past me, I saw my face. ACV

The Second Brother. Thomas Lovell Beddoes. Was but a drop in the world-melting flood. AtBAP

Second Carolina Said-Song. Archie Randolph Ammons. and I/threwed the limb over my shoulder and/carried'em home. OBAL

The Second Coming. Dannie Abse. and one red poppy in the corn. NMP; NoAm

The Second Coming. John William Carrington. and wondered/what would come next HoPM

The Second Coming. Carl Clark. On the third day./Man died. JB

The Second Coming. Norman Gale. So much for Calvary!" He said. HBV 1-2

The Second Coming. William Butler Yeats. And what rough beast, its hour come round at last,/Slouches towards Bethlehem to be born? AtBAP; BIrV; BLPL; CMoP; CoBMV; DiPo; EaLo; EnL; ExPo; FaBoMo; FaBoPV; FF; ForPo; GTBS-P; HAP; HeIP; HoPM; InPK; InPo; InPS; LiTB; LiTM; LoBV; MasP; MAT; MBW 1-2; MoAB; MoBrPo; MoRP; MoVE; NAWM 1-2; NIP; NoAm; NOBE; NoP; OAEL 1-2; OAEP; OxBI; OxBTC; PAI; PPoe; PPP; PrIm; SBVL; SCV; SeCePo; SeCeV; SoSe; TEP; UnPo; WaP; WeW

The Second Crucifixion. Richard Le Gallienne. Yet Christ is with me all the day. HBV 1-2; OBVV; WGRP

The Second Dream. Jean Valentine. Liquid as butterflies, with nothing to do. LCAP

Second Epistle to Robert Graham. Robert Burns. Those cut-throat bandits in the paths of fame. DBV

A Second Epitaph. Anonymous. For my soule to say a Pater Noster and an Ave. MeEL

The Second-Fated. Robert Graves. A moon-warmed world of discontinuance. NoAm

Second Fig. Edna St-Vincent Millay. Come and see my shining palace built/upon the sand! AmP; FaBV; NoP

The Second Generation. Menachem Z. Rosensaft. as we add defiant sparks/to an eternal fire AMV-81

Second Glance at a Jaguar. Ted Hughes. Hurrying through the underworld, soundless. NoAm; NYBP; PrIm

Second Half. David McCord. Nature, it seems, the greatest Healer,/Is even greater as Congealer. SD

Second Honeymoon. Anonymous. The milk-white tooth of passion/is between us. BIrV

Second Horn. W. S. Di Piero. and lets the sparks, all secular and good,/formlessly rain down. MAYP

Second Hymn to Lenin. Hugh" (Christopher Murray Grieve) MacDiarmid. Ah, Lenin, politics is bairns' play/To what this maun be! OAEL 1-2

The Second Hymn to the Night. Novalis (George Friedrich Philipp von Hardenerg). ...you are the messenger who opens/mysteries that unfold forever, but avoids words. NU

The Second Iron Age (1939-1945). Michael Harrington. Man will arise and spit his brackish soul/Out of himself and be a god again. CaP

The Second Life. Edwin Morgan. Slip out of darkness, it is time. OxBS

The Second Life of Lazarus. Gwen Harwood. Reborn in flames, pain cried its price. CBAP

The Second Man. Julian Symons. ...not to see/The private virtue and the public good/As incompatible. WaP

The Second Mate. Fitz-James O'Brien. "Master, I was the second mate!" AA

A Second Molting. Ralph Salisbury. ...the worst/stories we/war-bonneted braves ever had/heard. STE

Second Nature. Diana Chang. Strange to say. BrSi

The Second Night. M. L. Hester, Jr. Halfway up, already full dark. AMV-80

Second Night, or What You Will. Rolfe Humphries. Time will not shift in favor,/Nor circumstance be kind. MoLP

The Second Nimphall. Michael Drayton. So thou'lt leave him and goe with me. AtBAP

Second of August. *Anonymous.* Send peace and contentment to all British tars. OBSS

The Second Part of Absalom and Achitophel. John Dryden. And for my foes may this their blessing be,/To talk like Doeg, and to write like thee. OBSV

The Second Pastoral, or, Alexis: The Argument. Virgil (Publius Vergilius Maro). And find an easier Love, tho' not so fair. PeHV

Second Poem. Peter Orlovsky. ...on a hill a butterfly/makes a cup that I drink from, walking over a bridge of/flowers. NeAP

The Second Poem the Night-Walker Wrote. Johann Wolfgang von Goethe. You too will be silent. NU

The Second Rapture. Thomas Carew. This is true bliss, and I confess/There is no other happiness. CaPo; UnTE

Second Reading. Richard Beyer. and finally go/out of print. AMV-81

A Second Review of the Grand Army. Bret (Francis Bret Harte) Harte. ...and I spake–and lo! that sign/Awakened me from my slumber. HBV 1-2; MC; PAH

The Second Satire of the First Book of Horace (excerpt). Alexander Pope. Better than lust for boys, with Pope and Turk,/Or others' spouses, like my Lord of York.' OBSV

Second Seeing. Louis Golding. For He is God and Ghost and Everyman. WGRP

The Second Sermon on the Warpland. Gwendolyn Brooks. Conduct your blooming in the noise and whip of the/whirlwind. BPo; NOBA; PoBA

Second Shadow. Theodore Roethke. And shake the shade that hugs him close. PoA

The Second Shepherd's Play: Haylle, Comely and Clene. *Anonymous.* Have and play the with-alle/And go to the tenys. BoW; NAs; OBEV

The Second Shepherds' Play. *Anonymous.* To sing ar we bun,/Let take on loft. PoEL 1-5

Second Sight. Michael Longley. "You have crossed the water to visit me." FaBoIP

Second Skins–A Peyote Song. Joseph Bruchac. you are turning in the wind CDW

Second Song–To the Same. Alfred, Lord Tennyson. With a lengthened loud halloo,/Tu whoo, tu whit, tu whit, tu whoo-o-o. PBBP

A Second Stanza for Dr. Johnson. Donald Hall. His head was in his hat. FiBHP; ShM

The Second Thanksgiving, or The Reprisal. George Herbert. Against thee, in thee I will overcome/The man who once against thee fought. OAEP

The Second Violinist's Son. Debora Greger. ...What I heard now/was a kind of completion he found/only outside himself. AMV-80

Second Vision. Tadhg Dall O'Huiginn. And still I wait, for she is wondrous fair. AnIL

The Second Volume. Robert Mowry Bell. Soul, soul, there is a sequel to thy tale! AA

Second Wisdom. Henry Morton Robinson And be as wise as lilies of the field. GoYe

Second Woman's Lament. Brenda Chamberlain. And throw his challenge out in lanes of light. NeIP

Secrecy. Samuel Daniel. And wrong yourselves to do her right. OBSC; OLR

Secrecy Protested. Thomas Carew. The world will see thy picture there. AnAnS 2; CaPo; OAEP; SeCP

A Secret. *Anonymous.*
Shall no man know her name for me. OBSC
Then the whole secret will be out. SoPo; TiPo

Secret. Gwendolyn B. Bennett. I shelter a song for you/Secretly.... BlSi; CDC

The Secret. Jose Joaquin Casas. The saving Wisdom that mankind adores!– CAW

The Secret. John Clare. Are but the recollected choice/Of what I felt for thee. GBL

The Secret. Ralph Spaulding Cushman. You must seek Him in the morning/If you want Him through the day. STF; TRV

Secret. Esther Hull Doolittle. Because the sun has whispered/That Summer's on the way. YeAr

Secret. Catherine Haydon Jacobs. We two have won. GoYe

The Secret. Lonny Kaneko. Good bye. Good bye. BrSi

The Secret. Denise Levertov. for that/most of all. NaP

The Secret. Arthur Wallace Peach. I only know I sing/The song within my heart! HBMV

The Secret. George William Russell. And trails the stars along with them. MoBrPo

The Secret. James Stephens. I had buried it so low/In my mind! WSC

The Secret. Mary Morison Webster. None shall now tell it. PeSA

The Secret Garden. Thomas Kinsella. My hand strays out and picks off one sick leaf. IPY; TwCP

The Secret Garden. Robert Nichols. A snail or a stone under the lowliest leaf. WGRP

The Secret Heart. Robert P. Tristram Coffin. But it shone long enough for one/To know that hands held up the sun. PoSC

Secret Idiom: Sanctuary. Clifford Dyment. ...omnibus/Bullies a passage through congested ways. PoA

The Secret in the Cat. May Swenson. I stroke him/but cannot find the dial. DFF; GP

The Secret Irish. Allen Hoey. ...that you claim/stains my Celtic soul. AMV-81

The Secret Land. Robert Graves. And sometimes we may meet. BoC

Secret Laughter. Christopher Morley. By God, I have a son. FaBV; TreFS

Secret Love. John Clare. The riddle nature could not prove/Was nothing else but secret love. CBEP; ERoP 1-2; FaBV; LiTL; LO; NBM; OAEL 1-2; OBNC; PoEL 1-5; TrGrPo; VLP

Secret-Love. John Dryden.
If Soldier-like, he may have termes to come/With flying colours, and with beat of drum. SeCV 1-2
Those who write not, and yet all Writers nick,/Are Bankrupt Gamesters, for they damn on Tick. SeCV 1-2

The Secret Love. George William Russell. And the throb wherein those old lips met/Is a living music in us yet. HBV 1-2

A Secret Love or Two I Must Confess. Thomas Campion. Judge then what debtor can keep touch truly. AAS; ErPo

The Secret Muse. Roy Campbell. Whose footfall is my beating heart. BoC; PeSA

The Secret of Poetry. Jon Anderson. The secret of poetry is cruelty. MAYP

Secret of Song. Christine White. Christ found my heart full of sorrow,/Cleansed it and filled it with love. STF

The Secret of the Cross. M. J. Clarkson. Till others learn to love thee too/And thus return to God. BePJ

The Secret of the Deeps. Sidney Royse Lysaght. Under the silent roof-tree, over the windy floor. EtS

The Secret of the Sea. Henry Wadsworth Longfellow. Sends a thrilling pulse through me. AnNE; EtS

Secret Parting. Dante Gabriel Rossetti. Nor spire may rise nor bell be heard therefrom. MaVP

The Secret People. Gilbert Keith Chesterton. Smile at us, pay us, pass us. But do not quite forget. FaPoR; OxBTC

The Secret Place. A. A. Pollard. O soul, it is the secret place of prayer! STF

The Secret Place of Prayer. Georgia B. Adams. That's why I love the secret place,/The secret place of prayer! STF

Secret Pleasures. Robert Morgan. ...I offer/the land my leisure. MAYP

Secret Prayer. John Cross Belle. May reach His throne of glory,/Who is mercy, truth and love. STF

The Secret Sits. Robert Frost. But the secret sits in the middle and knows. InPK; LOW; SoPo

The Secret Song. Margaret Wise Brown. I, said the gray fox,/All alone. OBCA

The Secret Town (excerpt). Abraham Sutzkever. beneath my home town that was/slaughtered, was slain. TrJP

Secret Weapon. Ammonides. And the Parthian cavalry/Will stampede at once beyond the last horizon. LiTW

Secretary. Ted Hughes. Hiding her lovely eyes until day break. ErPo

The Secretary. Peter Redgrove. Best lover, secretary, and perfect staff. OxBTC

The Secretary Written at the Hague, in the Year 1696. Matthew Prior. So bless'd as the Englishen Heer SECRETARIS. CEP

Secrets. E. Kathryn Fowler. 'Cause a secret is inside. BiCB; ChBR

Secrets. Linda Pastan. never tell/never tell/never tell. AMV-80

The Secrets of Angling. John Dennys. His mind is rapt above the starry sky. MyFE

The Secrets of the Earth. William Blake. Why a little curtain of flesh on the bed of our desire?' NOBE

Sects. Jack Gilbert. making a sound like some other planet's machinery. NPGG

The Secular. Chris Wallace-Crabbe. And hear the sap leap in trees/Already marked out for death. NOAV

Secular Games. Richard Howard. But unlike God in heaven, come and go. PoA

Secular Litany. Michael Kennedy Joseph. And Saint Billy Bungstarter/Have mercy on him. AnNZ

The Secular Masque. John Dryden.
But neither side a winner,/For things are as they were. OBSP
'Tis well an old age is out,/And time to begin a new. DiPo; ExPo; FaBoRV; HAP; NOBE; OBSP; PoEL 1-5; PrIm; SeCeV; SeCV 1-2; ViBoPo

Security. Denis Glover. Exhorts for God, for freedom, and the ballot box AnNZ

Security. Michael Hamburger. For still my children play,/And shall tomorrow, if the weather holds. NMP; PoCh

Security. Charles L. O'Donnell. But send some kind centurion,/An expert with the lance. TrPWD

Security. Lina Sandell. We may trust His purpose wholly–/'Tis His children's welfare solely. STF

Security. Margaret E. Sangster. And, in his arms, we waken! BLRP

Security. Robert Tucker. Oh, at the gates, they move,/But–fear no evil. PPON

Seder, 1944. Friedrich Torberg. "Why is this night so different from..." VWA

Seder-Night. Israel Zangwill. Its God shall be the God of all the/earth. TrJP

The Sedge-Warbler. Ralph Hodgson. And thousand worlds my silent world would light/Till broke the babel of the summer day. PB

Sedge-Warblers. Edward ("Edward Eastaway") Thomas. What no man learnt yet, in or out of school. PoPle

The Sedges. Seumas (James Starkey) O'Sullivan. Like the little wind that laughing/Across the water blows. AnIV

Sediment. David Ignatow. and I tasting of sediment. NYBP

Seduced Girl. Hedylos. And he was strong–and I was half asleep. BoLoP; ErPo

Seduction. Nikki Giovanni. "Nikki,/isn't this counterrevolutionary...?" NMM

Seduction. Jo Ann Hall-Evans. AW.../SH...IT/SE...DUC...ED!! BlSi

The Seduction. Suzanne Berger Rioff. Make me an animal/who loves its own tongue. NMM

See a Pin and Pick It Up. *Anonymous.*
  All the day you'll have good luck. FaBoBe
  Bad luck you will have all day. HBV 1-2; HBVY

See! Here, My Heart. *Anonymous.* Lo! here my hert. MeEL

See How the Rising Sun. Elizabeth Scott. And in thy presence I would spend/A long eternity. AH

See in the Midst of Fair Leaves. Marianne Moore. an arrow turned inward has/no chance of peace. MoAB

See-Saw, Down in My Lap. *Anonymous.* Blown away in the street. OxNR

See-Saw, Margery Daw. *Anonymous.* And this is it, this is it, this is it. OxNR

See-Saw, Sacradown. *Anonymous.* That is the way to London town. OxNR

See That One? Robert Bagg. Or, curled up in a car, her purr? ErPo

See the Chariot at Hand Here of Love. Ben Jonson. Oh so white, oh so soft, oh so sweet is she! InvP

See the Crocus' Golden Cup. Joseph Mary Plunkett. Earth and heaven's latest born. OnYI

See Where My Love A-Maying Goes. *Anonymous.* And kiss amongst the willows. EIL

Seed. Herman Charles Bosman. The earth renders the farmer in due season/Corn. PeSA

The Seed. Aileen Fisher. where do you suppose/it stores up all/of the things it knows? OnUR

The Seed-Eaters. Robert Francis. Cracked corn, cracked wheat, peanuts and split peas, hail! NePoAm-2

The Seed Growing Secretly. Henry Vaughan. Keep clean, bear fruit, earn life and watch/Till the white winged reapers come! OxBoCh; SeCV 1-2

Seed Journey. Gregory Corso. For some seeds/meal is the end of the journey. VGW

Seed Leaves. Richard Wilbur. Takes aim at all the sky/And starts to ramify. BoNaP; NCSH

The Seed of Nimrod. De Leon Harrison. its movement/& the void PoBA

The Seed of Reality. Max Von Hartmann. For the song/of the meadowlark/is always/new. AMV-80

The Seed-Picture. Medbh McGuckian. Till it catches light, makes women/Feel their age, and sigh for liberation. FaBoIP

The Seed Shop. Muriel Stuart. And in my hand a forest lies asleep. BoNaP; GoTS

Seeds. Walter De la Mare. To bask in sun,/And see the day. TiPo

Seeds. John Oxenham. We know not what we shall be–only this–/That we shall be made like Him–as He is. WGRP

Seeds. Thurmond Snyder. Tiny buds had sprung up among the weeds. NNP

Seeds. Augusta Webster. Half is the hearing. OBVV

Seeds of Lead. Amir Gilboa. After many years this became clear to me/in the gardens of big cities/and in museums. VWA

The Seeds of Love. *Anonymous.*
  Give it time, it will rise up again. FaBoCh; LoGBV; OBET; WiR
  Is all overrun with rue? GBP; OxBoLi
  That first had this heart of mine. CBEP

Seein' Things. Eugene Field. Than I should keep a-livin' on an' seein' things at night! HBV 1-2; HBVY; TreF

Seeing. John Lyle Donaghy. and am at the end of soul's endless journey. NeIP

Seeing and Doing. John Dean. ...Benjamin: six months old. AMV-81

Seeing Auden off. Philip Booth. ...I wave him off, toward Iowa,/tonight. PoA

Seeing Her Dancing. Robert Heath. So undiscern'd she mov'd, that we/Perceiv'd she stirr'd, but did not see. OBS; OBSP

Seeing in the Dark. Matthew Brennan. undeveloped, waiting for/immersion. AMV-81

Seeing Oloalok. Marilyn Bowering. Her eyes kept watch on her people. NOBC

Seeing St. James's. Ray Mathew. ...those whom you saw were those whom you saw and/So understood, not trying to understand. NOAV

Seeing the Plum Blossoms by the River. Lady Ise. I will only wet my sleeve/in impervious waters. BoWoP

Seeing the Returning Geese. Lady Ise. Have they learned to live/in a flowerless country? BoWoP

Seek Flowers of Heaven. Robert Southwell. That worldly weeds needs must be loath/that can these flowers find. TrCP

Seek the Lord. Thomas Campion. Whose fruit so sov'reign is/That all who taste it are from death restored. OxBoCh; TrCP

A Seeker in the Night. Florence Earle Coates. Then draw me close, and hold me fast! TrPWD

The Seekers. John Masefield. But the hope of the City of God at the other end of the road. HBV 1-2; WGRP

The Seekers. Charles Hamilton Sorley. –Yet still they march rejoicing on. WGRP

The Seekers. Victor Starbuck. But did not understand. WGRP

Seeking a Mooring. Wang Wei. Only still bands of desolate mist/And a single fishing boat. BoWoP; WPOW

Seeking God. Edward Dowden. And it sufficed that I was found of Thee. WGRP

Seele Im Raum. Randall Jarrell. "To own an eland! That's what I call life!" CoBMV; LCAP

Seems Like We Must Be Somewhere Else. Denise Levertov. ...Lonesome man, wanted the trains/to speak for him. NePoEA-2

Seen from the Train. C. Day Lewis. And turned my eyes away. BoC

Seen in a Glass. Kathleen Raine. Assume in nature's glass, in nature's eyes. ChMP

Seesaw. Gerardo Diego. Sing yes Sing no LiTW

The Seesaw. Oscar Williams. O pivot's pressure at the heart, through you I hear/The universe hallooing for an end. LiTA

Seferis. Lawrence Durrell. That even to die is somehow to invent. EBEV

Segovia and Madrid. Rose T. Cooke. –Would my soul forget Madrid? AA

Seguidilla. Jose de Valdivielso. Trust not, Mother dear,/Hearts ungrateful here! CAW

Sehnsucht. Anna Wickham. God save us all from death when we are fed. MoBrPo

Sehnsucht, or, What You Will. "Corinna". The answer's yes/To that deep query. FiBHP

Seicheprey. *Anonymous.* And left to shattered Seicheprey/Unending, sweet repose. PAH

Seismograph. Ephraim Auerbach. as I advance,/and I with it,/sullen and sad. VWA

Seizure. Sappho. I must suffer everything, being poor. LLLT

Seizure. James E. Warren, Jr. the bright, clean, strong words still remain. AMV-81

Selah. R. S. Thomas. ...the self/sought for the purpose that had brought it there. FaBoMo

Seldom "Can't." *Anonymous.* Never "sha'n't,"/Never "won't." HBVY

Selective Service. Carolyn Forche. We lie down in the fields and leave behind/the corpses of angels. MAYP

Self. Norman Henry Pritchard II. with fear/of being/uneaten PoBA

A Self Accuser. John Donne. 'Tis strange that she should thus confess it, though't be true. FaBoEE

Self-Acquaintance. William Cowper. And make me Thy belov'd abode,/And let me roam no more. NOCV

Self-Analysis. Anna Wickham. Give me the straight and ordered flame! MoBrPo

The Self and the Weather. Reed Whittemore. Be wet leaves, wet grass, wet laundry, and so on. NMP

Self-Congratulatory Ode on Mr Auden's Election (parody). Ronald Mason. ...and now will be/taught in her/Turn to suck eggs. FaBoPa

Self-Consciousness Makes All Changes Happy. Jonathan Richardson. When conflagration ruins worlds, their God/Regards the heart sincere, sits smiling there. NOEC

Self-Criticism in February. Robinson Jeffers. Justice will soon prevail. I can tell lies in prose. AmPP

The Self-Deceaver. Juan de Montalvan. All thy attempts how can I blame/To work my Death? I seek the same. OBVE

Self-Deception. Matthew Arnold. Some end is there, we indeed may gain? MaVP

Self-Defense. Santob De Carrion. And ask within my whitened head/For wit that is not there. TrJP

Self-Dependence. Matthew Arnold.
...nor pine with noting/All the fever of some differing soul. GoTF
Who finds himself, loses his misery! BBV; HBV 1-2; MaVP; MCCG; OAEP; TreFS; VLP; WGRP

Self Dirge. Wendy Rose. and why pain? CDW

Self-Discipline. George William Russell. And our lofty doom fulfil. MoBrPo

Self-Employed. David Ignatow. for who else could I get in my place/to do the job in dark, airless conditions? NNaP

Self-Examination. *Anonymous.* And make me meet for heaven above,/To join Thy saints in praise and love. FaBoUs

The Self-Hatred of Don L. Lee. Don L. Lee. hatred of/my light/brown/ outer. BPo; TW

Self in 1958. Anne Sexton. if I could remember how/and if I had the tears. HaCAP

Self-Knowledge. Samuel Taylor Coleridge. Ignore thyself, and strive to know thy God! ERoP 1-2; SeCePo

Self-Pity. D. H. Lawrence. without ever having felt sorry for itself. BoAnP; OxBTC

Self-Pity Is a Kind of Lying, Too. James Schuylr. ...one day we'll/just have snow/to wear too. PoM

Self-Portrait. Cecil Bodker. –or perhaps/like gunpowder. BoWoP

Self-Portrait. Nina Cassian. ...then I'm allowed/to be accepted as human– and even beautiful. VWA

Self-Portrait. Edgar Jackson. as we pass in silence towards freedom–/the freedom of choice. LFAC

Self-Portrait. Moses Mendelssohn. Hump and heavy-tongue combined. TrJP

Self-Portrait. Robert Pack. ...Are there eyes beneath the table? Laughter? A nest of birds? CoPo

Self-Portrait. R. S. Thomas. ...The hurrying eyes/pause, waiting for an outdistanced/gladness to overtake them. NAs

Self-Portrait. Judith Mountain Leaf Volborth. sings to the lines/in her face. TWSS

Self-Portrait, 1969. Frank Bidart. ...What reaches him except disaster? HaCAP

Self Portrait 4. Tove Ditlevsen. I loathe her. WPOW

Self-Portrait, as a Bear. Donald Hall. ...and the sun/lifts through a haze every morning/of the summer in the stomach. SO

Self-Portrait in 2035. Charles Wright. Spider recite his one sin. LCAP

Self-Portrait in a Convex Mirror. John Ashbery. Here and there, in cold pockets/Of remembrance, whispers out of time. HaCAP

Self-Portrait with Hand Microscope. Lucille Day. live things. SUW

Self-Projection. Archie Randolph Ammons. ...what more than the self/ sometimes needs the self. FAZ

Self-Protection. D. H. Lawrence. A drab and dingy bird. NoP

Self's the Man. Philip Larkin. Or I suppose I can. NOBL

The Self-Slaved. Patrick Kavanagh. We'll both go off together/In this delightful weather. MoBrPo

The Self Unsatisfied Runs Everywhere. Delmore Schwartz. –But who, being human, wishes to be a gull,/Knows nothing much, though birds are beautiful. PoA

The Self-Unseeing. Thomas Hardy. Yet we were looking away! EBEV; HAP; MoBrPo; NOBE; NOBV; OBNC; PrIm; VLP

The Selfe-Banished. Edmund Waller. For if I breake, you may mistrust/ The vow I made to love you too. MePo; OBS

Selfishness. Margaret E. Bruner. The dead know nought of sorrow. PoToHe

The Selfsame Song. Thomas Hardy. As also are those who heard/That song with me. CMoP; PBBP

Selichos. Francis Landy. Fallow fallow/chance it VWA

Selling Ruined Peonies. Yu Hsuan-chi. Princes would covet what they could not buy. BoWoP

La Selva. Cid Corman. where the trees march firmly/out of rank into the woods. VGW

Semantic. Robert Conquest. And reads dawn lifting from the shadowy hills. TEP

The Semblables. William Carlos Williams. within where the wrapt machines/are praying... AP; FaBoMo; NOBA

Semele Recycled. Carolyn Kizer. its birth and rebirth and decay. InPS

Semen. Coleman Barks. suddenly come alive/and jabber like/foreigners PV

Semen. Martha Paley Francescato. mirrored/calcined/futile/tough BoWoP

Semi-Private Room. Alden Nowlan. "Mr. Nowlan, are you asleep?" NeAC

A Semi-Revolution. Robert Frost. But they're one thing that should be done by halves. LiTM

Seminary. Constance Carrier. almost unconsciously they come/to change One should be to I am. NePoAm

Semmes in the Garden. George Marion O'Donnell. And poised with muscles taut, intent/Upon the passionless descent. NYBP

Sence You Went Away. James Weldon Johnson. Sence you went away. BALP; BANP

Send for Lord Timothy. John Heath-Stubbs. Honey for tea, and nothing/ Will ever really happen again. OxBC

Send Forth, O God, Thy Light and Truth. John Quincy Adams. To him shall thanks and praise ascend,/My Saviour and my God. AH

Send Forth the High Falcon. Léonie Adams. Shall lull both terror and innocence to rest. InPo

Send Me. Christina Georgina Rossetti. Be it a wide or narrow place, 'tis well/So that the work it holds be only done. TRV

Send No Money. Philip Larkin. Tracing the trite untransferable/Truss- advertisement, truth. TW

The Send-Off. Wilfred Owen. Up half-known roads. BrPo; LiTB; MoAB; MoBrPo; MoVE; OBWP; OxBTC; PAI

Seneca. Thomas Merton. For the Night Bird's/Inscrutable cry. CoPo

Seneca Lake. James Gates Percival. And evening tells us toil is o'er. AnNE

De Senectute. Franklin Pierce ("F.P.A.") Adams. Some can be poets, and some can't. HBMV

Senex. Sir John Betjeman. Teach sulky lips to say, my Lord,/That flaxen hair is dust. DTC

Senex to Matt. Prior. James Kenneth Stephen. I knew that once: but now– I think it. CenHV; FiBHP

Senile. Pat Folk. he must have raised/rare orchids/years ago. PCP

Senior Members. Sean Lucy. I am the inheritor. Kneel at my feet. CIP

Senlin. Conrad Aiken.
And daisies burn like stars on the darkened hill. LOW
Repeating three clear tones. LiTM; MoAmPo; NoAm; TrGrPo

Senryu. Pat Nolan. The bed creaks/as I make it. APU

Sensation. Arthur Rimbaud.
And I'll go far, very far, like a gypsy,/Into Nature–happy, as if with a woman. SOTW; SyP
Happy as one walks by a woman's side. AWP

Sensational Relatives. Alexis Krasilovsky. Catfish didn't register/to swim this brook. AMV-80

Sensationalism. Larry Levis. ...it mattered once,/If only to him. And before he turned into paper. MAYP

Sense and Spirit. George Meredith. To read her own and trust her down to death. WGRP

A Sense of Coolness. Quincy Troupe. have pulled down with fangs of poison PoBA

The Sense of Death. Helen Hoyt. O death, that gave my life to me! HBMV

A Sense of Humour. Vachel Lindsay. And fays, or suchlike friendly things,/Throw kisses through the glass. MAPA

The Sense of Responsibility. Harry Mathews. I trace the dancing of their secular swarm. ANYP

The Sense of Smell. Louis MacNeice. How many adieus? NYBP

The Sense of the Sleight-of-Hand Man. Wallace Stevens. ,the life/That is fluent in even the wintriest bronze AP; CABA; CoBMV; HAP; LiTM; MoAB; MoAmPo; MoPo; MP; NOBA; PoA; TwCP

Sensibility. Louis Simpson. this tender girl and I/were married in rain- water. GP

A Sensible Girl's Reply to Moore's. Walter Savage Landor. It would give me rheumatics, and so it would you. FaBoEE

The Sensitive Plant. Percy Bysshe Shelley. No light, being themselves obscure. EnRP; ERoP 1-2; GoTL; OAEL 1-2

Sensitive Sydney. Wallace Irwin. So I knowed I'd brung the joke too far/ And we wasn't friends no more. FiBHP

Sensitiveness. John Henry, Cardinal Newman. I love His precept more. TrCP

The Sensualists. Theodore Roethke. Then each fell back, limp as a sack,/ Into the world of men. ErPo; NePoAm-2; UnTE

Sensuality. Coventry Patmore. But all delights rejoice his days/Who takes with thanks and never seeks. OBVV

Sent Ahead. John Hay. ...I praise the star that slings my body free. NePoAm

Sent from Egypt with a Fair Robe of Tissue to a Sicilian Vinedresser. Thomas Sturge Moore. Like a stripp'd child fain in the sea to dip. OBEV; OBVV

Sent from the Capital to Her Elder Daughter. Lady Otomo of Sakanone [(or Sakanoe)]. Not missing a day,/Not even an hour. BoWoP; WPOW

Sent to a Lady, with a Seal. Robert Lloyd. 'Tis seal'd for ever on my heart. FaBoUs

Sent to a Patient, with the Present of a Couple of Ducks. Edward Jenner. And therefore I've sent her a couple of Quacks. FaBoUs

Sent to Him, as He Whisper'd. Sir Hildebrand Jacob. Who can make soft, simple speeches/Pleases Myra full as well. FaBoEE

Sent to Miss Bell H—, with a Pair of Buckles. John Cunningham. Useless, you'll be thrown aside. FaBoUs

Sent to Wen T'ing-Yun on a Winter Night. Yu Hsuan-chi. Wheeling, evening sparrows wail and sob. BoWoP

Sent with a Rose to a Young Lady. Margaret Deland. Should he send half the whole! AA

Sentence. Witter ("Emanuel Morgan") Bynner. You, my comrade, had to go,/I to stay. HBV 1-2

Sentences (excerpt). Tony Harrison. edible necklaces/and caged red birds. OBTV

Sentience. Sandra McPherson. nor gives me anything I want but myself. PoA

Sentiment. Thomas Chatterton. All to one common dissolution tends. NOEC

Sentimental Conversation. Paul Verlaine. And the night only heard the words they said. SyP; WSC

Sentimental Lines to a Young Man Who Favors Pink Wallpaper... Margaret Fishback. Now do you prefer the blue? FiBHP

The Sentimentalist. Edward Field. crushed the longings of my sentimental heart. PPJ

The Sentiments. *Anonymous.* Though justly we will serve our king,/We'll try a tug with Rome. APAS

The Sentinel. Annie Johnson Flint. For only peace and pardon pass/The watchful guard of prayer. BLRP

A Sentinel's Song. Rarawa Kerehoma. Let them come. The blue heron/Is awake and on guard. WTO

Sentinel Songs. Abram Joseph Ryan. Brave Songs, with sleepless eyes. HBV 1-2

The Sentry. Alun Lewis. In the flower of fury, the folded poppy,/Night. DTC

The Sentry. Wilfred Owen. "I see your lights!" But ours had long died out. AnEnPo; MMM

Senzangakhona. *Anonymous.* Red-spotted black beast of Nobamba/That goes about causing trouble. WTO

Separate Parties. Dabney Stuart. Child, though magician, elf, you're not/My imagination but my daughter. NYBP

Separate Peace. Harrison Smith Morris. The glow of what has gone. MC

Separation. Matthew Arnold. Who, let me say, is this stranger regards me,/With the gray eyes, and the lovely brown hair? HBV 1-2

Separation. Alice Learned Bunner. And I could only look at her–through/tears. AA

A Separation. William Johnson Cory. ...and I,/Content with one such flower, will die. OBNC

Separation. Martha Gilbert Dickinson. So far each heart hath from the other grown,/Alone were less alone. AA

Separation. William Stanley Merwin. Everything I do is stitched with its color. AmPC; HAP; NoP; PCP

Separation. D. S. Savage. Consciousness aches in the void for the physical thud of your/heart. NeBP

A Separation. Stephen Spender. Unchanging love swears all's unchanged, and knows/That what it has not, still stays all it has. MoLP

Separation. P. Wolny. a rose unopened,/blackened by the cold. DFF

A Separation Deed. Sir Lewis Morris. And this Indenture also witnesseth. OBVV

Separation on the River Kiang. Li Po. The long Kiang, reaching heaven. SOTW

Sephestia's Song to Her Child. Robert Greene. When thou art old there's grief enough for thee. ELP; EnLi 1-2; GTBS; HBV 1-2; LoBV; NOBE; OBEV; OBSC; PoEL 1-5; TrGrPo

Sepia Fashion Show. Maya Angelou. I'd remind them please, look at those knees/you got a Miss Ann's scrubbing. BlSi

Sept. 1957. Edward Marshall. like the rest but still for thee. CoPo

September. George Arnold. A future summer gleams,/Passing the fairest glories of the present! HBV 1-2

September. Edwina H. Fallis. Today it is summer,/Tomorrow is fall. SUS; TiPo; YeAr

September. Marilyn Hacker. Two laminated toucans pepper meat/as sunlight sheaths behind the sumac trees. NYP

September. Ted Hughes. And quietly the trees casting their crowns/Into the pools. BoLoP; OLR

September. Aldous Huxley. A chance light shines and suddenly it is spring. EBEV

September. Helen Hunt Jackson. One day of one September/I never can forget. FPL; PoLf

September. Joanne Kyger. and whose skin is made dusky by stars. APU

September. Archibald Lampman. And through the wind-touched reddening woods shall rise/October with the rain of ruined leaves. PeCV

September. Linda Pastan. in the morning the fields were wet/and it was autumn. Psk

September. Boris Pasternak. ...the country house/stares forward, hallucinated, at the road to the metropolis. NaP

September 1, 1939. W. H. Auden. Show an affirming flame. CMoP; CoBMV; ExPo; ForPo; InPo; LiTA; MasP; MoAB; MoBrPo; MoVE; OAEP; OxBA; PrIm; SeCeV; WaP

September 1, 1965. Paris Leary. We need a new chauvinism about existence. CoPo

September, 1913. William Butler Yeats. They're with O'Leary in the grave. BrPo; CMoP; CoBMV; FaBoPV; GTBS-P; HAP; NoAm; PoRA; PPoe

September 2. Wendell Berry. I would sleep, my leaves all dissolved in flight. PoA

September 30. Dick Lourie. with my wife my new wife what skin what hair/what eyes NeAC

September 7. Ellen Bass. held the pebbles in our hands/and ate the freckled pears. NMM

September Afternoon. Margaret Haley Carpenter. More beautiful than summer once had been. GoYe

September Butterfly. Mollie Boring. yawning like a cobweb/stretched across/the bay. AMV-80

September Days Are Here. Helen Hunt Jackson. With summer's best of weather,/And autumn's best of cheer. GoJo; OBCA; TiPo; YeAr

September Evening, 1938. William Plomer. Then arm in arm along the path/Silent they saunter away. SeCePo

The September Gale (excerpt). Oliver Wendell Holmes. My loved! My long-lost breeches! FiBHP

September in Australia. Henry Clarence Kendall. With thy voices for ever! OBVV; PoAu 1-2

September Is Here. Edward Bliss Reed. Fruit will be falling,/September is here. YeAr

September: Last Day at the Beach. Richard Tillinghast. When we were two east-west trains in the station/Pulling apart, forever, forever. GOYP

September Midnight. Sara Teasdale. As those who part look long in the eyes they lean to,/Lest they forget them. PoA

September Song. Geoffrey Hill. This is plenty. This is more than enough. NoP; OBWP

September Sun: 1947. David Gascoyne. Of Chaos planted, all our trash to cinders bring. AtBAP

September, the First Day of School. Howard Nemerov. But may great kindness come of it in the end. GLGT; OxBC

The Sepulcher. Annie Johnson Flint. The place where the Lord once lay,/Is empty forevermore. STF

Sepulchral Imprecation. Crinagoras. Lie not light on the filth of your monstrous groom. LiTW

Sepulchre. George Herbert. Though it be cold, hard, foul, from loving man/Withhold thee. AnAnS 1

Sequaire. Godeschalk. ...that by it our devotion may with greater zeal prepare a/temple for the Lord. CTC

The Sequel. Theodore Roethke. I feel the autumn fail–all that slow fire/Denied in me, who has denied desire. NYBP

The Sequel. Delmore Schwartz. Try to die–to disappear/And hide. LiTM

Sequel to Finality. Patrick F. Kirby. ...by each one's side/Unseen One rode, Who had been crucified. GoBC

Sequence. George Barker. Eternally eternally bud and blossom/Evolve the particulars of doom. PoA

Sequence. Edgar Daniel Kramer. After the sleeping–God! BLRP

A Sequence. Leslie Scalapino. ...with a feeling of delay and retarding–/rather than out of nervousness. NPGG

Sequence for a Young Widow Passing. Deborah Munro. when at last they opened her/breast, no one dared touch/that red pulsing star IHMS

The Sequence of Generations. Hayim Be'er. Praise is comely VWA

A Sequence with Strophes in Paraphrase Thereof. Francis Burke. And with one light anointed of the Paraclete!/Unto all ages. CAW

The Seraph and the Snob. May Kendall. And lurid placards, orange, red,/Drive through his waking dreads. CenHV

Seraphion. James Keir Baxter. And between midnight and morning he taunts me still. AnNZ

Seravezza. Hoyt W. Fuller. I could not have endured it had he called my name PoBA

Serenade. *Anonymous.* And sang it for "Good-Night" beneath the moon. AWP

Serenade. Alan Britt. and places your skull/behind the moon. FAZ

Serenade. Jeremiah Joseph Callanan. Farewell, then, my dear one–/My Mary, farewell. IrPN; OnYI

Serenade. Emanuel Carnevali. Come on, open that window/or I'll go home. AnAmPo

Serenade. George Darley. The sweetest and sleepiest/Bird at this hour! HBV 1-2

Serenade. Aubrey Thomas De Vere. Leave warm 'mid the gray grass their dusky bed. HBV 1-2; OBEV

Serenade. Dorothy Donnelly. a transient, true, and treasured bliss. NCSH

Serenade. Bret (Francis Bret Harte) Harte. And sing, fal, la, la,/La, la, le. LBN

Serenade. Thomas Hood.
In patient love out watch the world. HBV 1-2
Who's that fallen–me or him? NLV

Serenade. John Gibson Lockhart. Nor chase from Zara's side/Dreams bright and pure as these. OBRV

Serenade. Henry Wadsworth Longfellow. My lady sleeps?/Sleeps! FaBoBe; HBV 1-2; LoBV; ViBoPo

Serenade. Richard Middleton. Beloved, can you hear? HBV 1-2

A Serenade. Edward Coate [(or Coote)] Pinkney. Of darker nights a day. AA; AmLP; AnFE; APA; HBV 1-2

Serenade. Kenneth Slessor. Personally, I have other things to do. PoL

Serenade. Henry Timrod. He watches in the lonely street. HBV 1-2

Serenade. Oscar Wilde. O loved for ever, evermore! HBV 1-2

Serenade for Strings. Dorothy Livesay. Behold–a man! NAs

A Serenade for Two Poplars. Esther Raab. quince fragrance in hedges,/ shadows on asphalt. VWA

Serenade of a Loyal Martyr. George Darley. Bleeds with its death-wound, but deeper yet for thee. NOBE; OBNC; OBRV; OnYI

Serenade of Angels. Rina Lasnier. You go off with the angels, but I...I remain. AMV-81

A Serendipity of Love. Richard Aldridge. A perfect halo of rich golden light. NePoAm-2

Serene Immediate Silliest and Whose. Edward Estlin Cummings. Awake, chaos: we have napped. MoVE

Serengeti Sunset. Andrew Oerke. except at sunset when it mingles milk with blood and urine. PoL

The Serenity in Stones. Simon J. Ortiz. I am happy as I hold this sky/in my hands, in my eyes, and in myself. CDW

The Serf. Roy Campbell. And ploughs down palaces, and thrones, and towers. GTBS-P; LiTB; MoBrPo; NAMP; OBMV

The Serf's Secret. William Vaughn Moody. The dew-damp daisies in the grass/Laugh up to greet me as I pass/To meet the upland sun. HBV 1-2

The Sergeant. Don Johnson. gathering the still-warm eggs with held breath. MAYP

Sergeant Champe. Anonymous. Arnold's to blame for Andre's fame,/And Andre's to be pitied. PAH

The Sergeant, He Is the Worst of All (with music). Anonymous. Then the slimy son of a gun, he gaives us double time. AS

Sergeant-Major Money. Robert Graves. In a New (bloody) Army he couldn't understand. MMM; OBWP

A Sergeant's Prayer. Hugh Brodie. Teach me the way that I should die. PGD

The Sergeant's Weddin'. Rudyard Kipling. An' a rogue is married to, etc. OxBTC

A Series 5.8. John Wieners. And the hand trembles/at the next word to put down. CoPo

A Serio-Comic Elegy. Richard Whately. Let him stand as a monument raised to himself. ShM

Serio-Comic History of Bridgwater. E. H. Burrington. Yet men have called thy swift return a bore! FaBoPP

A Serious and a Curious Night-Meditation. Thomas Traherne. sleep and Death differ, noe more, then a Carkasse/and a skeleton. SeCP

A Serious Danger. R. A. Davenport. May one day swear that he's my friend. PV

The Serious Merriment of Women. Patricia Goedicke. The superior lift of their wings lifts the heart. TAP

A Serious Poem. Ernest Walsh. To win one night in her bed ErPo

Serious Readers. Peter Redgrove. I let it be. Read and let read. OxBC

The Sermon. Richard Hughes. –Whether their hearts could break/How can I know? BoC; OBMV

Sermon. Bernadette Mayer. Next/the door is crumbling some-/thing flying in the dome/is tumbling forward. ANYP

A Sermon. Lady Margaret Sackville. For lake and village-pump and sea,/ For You–but also room for Me! HBMV

A Sermon at Clevedon. Thomas Edward Brown. And I can sit, and look upon the stones/That cover Hallam's grave. NOBV

Sermon in a Churchyard. Thomas Babington, Lord Macaulay. Must end in dust and silence here. OBRV

Sermon in a Stocking. Ellen A. Jewett. While in Grandma's lap, with a broken thread,/The finished stocking lies. BLPA

The Sermon in the Hospital (excerpt). Harriet Eleanor Hamilton King. May here be perfected and left behind. BoC

A Sermon on Swift. Austin Clarke. ...a voice proclaiming/The World's mad business–Eternal Absolution. BlrV; IPY

Sermon on the Mount. Jeff Wright. Then I'll leave/you in your tower/and over the world/will a glow spread. APU

The Sermon on the Warpland. Gwendolyn Brooks. luminously indiscreet;/ complete; continuous. BPo; LiTM; NOBA; PoBA

Sermonette. Ishmael Reed. gimmie dat ol time/religion/it's good enough/ for me! NIP; PoBA

The Serpent. Joseph Langland. Love dances, smiles. Oh, how he sings! MP

The Serpent. Theodore Roethke. As the Birds flew off to the End of Next Week. AmMo

Serpent Knowledge. Robert Pinsky. A new syllable buried in their name. NPGG

The Serpent Muses. Peggy Henderson. she lies long in the sun/slides among the roots/and muses NMM

The Serpent of God. Cerise Farallon. he was strong and of God! UnTE

The Serpent's Nature. Anonymous. Which is like to our head; let us protect it worthily. MeEV

Servant Girl and Grocer's Boy. Joyce Kilmer. Her soul spoke thus (I know it did). YaD

A Servant-Girl's Holiday. Anonymous. Durst I not my dame telle/What me betidde this holiday. OxBM

The Servant in Literature. Marjorie Welish. and my unspoken perturbations, even these. APU

The Servant Man (The Iron Door). Anonymous. Since love's broke through an iron door. AmFP

The Servant of Rosemary Lane. Anonymous. So I'll dry up my milk as you shall plainly see,/And pass for a maid in my own country.' OBSS

A Servant to Servants. Robert Frost. I'd rather you'd not go unless you must. CMoP

The Servants. Richard Wightman. Where the toiler turns to sod/Man beholds the living God. WGRP

Serve Her Right. John Barford. I decided to transfer/Affections to her brother;/And I did!... PeHV

Serve in Thy Post. Arthur Hugh Clough. Who serves her truly, sometimes serves the State. PGD

Service. Robert Browning. ...one deed/Power shall fall short in, or exceed! TrGrPo

The Service. Burges Johnson. I dreaded you two thundering behind! HBMV

Service. Georgia Douglas Johnson. Save the love we have shown to the children of men? CDC

Service Is No Heritage. Anonymous. And give us giftes most of prize,/ Heaven to be our heritage. CBEP; OxBM

The Service Man. Rudyard Kipling. 'Orse, foot an' guns, The Service Man/'Enceforward, evermore! Par

Service Supreme. Anonymous. I'm building for years to be–/That little chap who follows me. STF

The Serving Girl. Gladys May Casely Hayford. But who can guess, or even surmise/The countless things she served with her eyes? CDC; GoSl

The Serving Maid. Arthur Joseph Munby. Your rosy wrist peeps out between/And sends it home–and speeds it home. NOBV

A Serving Men's Song. John Lyly. Jove would leap down to surfeit here. ALV; NOBE; OBSC

Sesostris. Lloyd Mifflin. And dark thrones totter in the baleful air! AA; HBV 1-2

Sessions of Sweet Silent Thought. William Shakespeare. All losses are restored, and sorrows end. BoLiVe

A Sessions of the Poets. Sir John Suckling. When he lends any Poets about the Town. AnAnS 2; NCEP; SeCV 1-2

Sestina. Elizabeth Bishop. and the child draws another inscrutable house. LCAP; NoP; SM; WeW

Sestina. Donald Hall. About which, conversation is not dull. NePoEA

Sestina. Donald Justice. Why have they changed that way to wood? NePoEA

Sestina. Judith Kroll. beyond fixed sight, beyond nothing? AmPA; SM

Sestina. Algernon Charles Swinburne. Sing while he may, man hath no long delight. VLP

Sestina (after Dante). Dante Gabriel Rossetti. Under her summer-green the beautiful lady/Covers it, like a stone covered in grass. OAEL 1-2

Sestina: Altaforte. Ezra Pound. Hell blot black for alway the thought "Peace!" AmP; CMoP; CoBMV; FaBoTw; LiTA; MoAB; NOBA; SoSe; SOTW

Sestina d'Inverno. Anthony Hecht. Where to the natives destiny is snow/ That is neither to our mind nor of our making. NoP

A Sestina for Cynthia. David Lougee. ...know what love has known, this shifting image. NePA

Sestina from the Home Gardener. Diane Wakoski. ...the pointed mountain, far away, unfamiliar? NoAm

Sestina in Time of Winter. Patrick Anderson. and chateau childhoods prisoned in the bell/of dark, held back excited by the urns. PoA

Sestina: Of the Lady Pietra degli Scrovigni. Dante Alighieri. Under her summer-green the beautiful lady/Covers it, like a stone cover'd in grass. AWP; OBVE

Sestina of the Tramp-Royal. Rudyard Kipling. So write, before I die, "'E liked it all!" BrPo; FPL; LiTB; MoBrPo; PrIm

Sestina on Her Portrait. Howard Nemerov. The echo of the grave perfects desire. WaP

Sestina to the Common Glass of Beer: I Do Not Drink Beer. Diane Wakoski. each springtime when my friends, not I,/sit in some bar or outdoor cafe,/drinking beer. SM

Sestina with Refrain. Thomas W. Shapcott. ...the call for/water. CBAP

Set Down, Servant. Anonymous.
My soul's so happy,/Dat I cain' set down. ABF
Now, servent, please set down. FSW

Set Me whereas the Sun Doth Parch the Green. Henry Howard, Earl of Surrey. Yours will I be, and with this only thought/Comfort myself when that my hope is nought. AAS; CBEP; FCP; ForPo; HAP; SiPS; TEP

Seth Compton. Edgar Lee Masters. And no one knows what is true/Who knows not what is false. LiTA

Settin' on de Fence. Anonymous. Dat's de way you proves yo'se'f/An' shows yo'se'f a man. WBLP

The Setting of the Moon. Giacomo Leopardi. The gods have set a sign for us, the tomb. MOON

Setting/Slow Drag. Carolyn M. Rodgers. perhaps it should be clear why i am here. JB

The Setting Sun. George Moses Horton. Whilst weary creatures sleep. BALP

Setting the Table. Dorothy Aldis. And then I call them in to eat. TiPo

The Settled Men. George M. Brady. These men who through the centuries grew gaunt. NeIP

Settler. Stewart Lindh. And giving it a name: No No No PoA

The Settler. Alfred Billings Street. A Nation's freedom won. AA; FaBoBe; MC; PAH

The Settler's Lament. Anonymous. Don't go to the wilds of Australia. PoAu 1-2

The Settlers. Judith Hemschemeyer. In autumn we used maple leaves,/In winter, snow. SO

The Settlers. Laurence Housman. Out of the lives ye cast away/The coming race is born. HBV 1-2; OBVV

Settlers. Tom Paulin. Now snug in their oiled paper below the floors/Of sundry kirks and tabernacles in that county. FaBoIP

Settling In. Floyd C. Stuart. It is not a taunt. TAT

Settling Some Old Football Scores. Morris Bishop. Literature will make the ultimate touchdown. LiSp; SD

Seumas Beg. James Stephens. He was a real nice man. He liked me, too. EvOK; GrPl; OxBTC; RoGo

Seurat. Ira Sadoff. ...we are no more than tiny clusters of/dots, carefully placed together without touching. PoDr

Seven. Nicanor Parra. and the absolute marvel of a bunch of grapes. PoL

The Seven against Thebes. Aeschylus. Even to the bourne of all, to the unbeholden land. AWP

The Seven Ages of Elf-Hood. Rachel Field. But when he's a hundred and a day/He gets a little pipe to play! BiCB

The Seven Blessings of Mary. Anonymous. Father, Son and the Holy Ghost,/Through all eternity. FSW

Seven Cent Cotton and Forty Cent Meat. Anonymous. Forty cents a pound in a paper sack. FSW

The Seven Days, III: On First Knowing God. Reed Whittemore. God, God am I. GP

The Seven Days of the Sun (excerpt). Walter James Turner. And there's a poisonous cloud as dark as jet/Pouring from heaven. OBMV

Seven Dreams. John Bayliss. seeing the lake through the small doorway... EAS

The Seven Fiddlers. Sebastian Evans. And the winds be all asleep. OnMSP

The Seven Hells of the Jigoku Zoshi (excerpt). Jerome Rothenberg. They have left her NNaP

The Seven Houses. George Mackay Brown. This is the House of History. NAs

The Seven-League Boots. Ilarie Voronca. ..You sang/and the shadow was terrified, gone like a bird. VWA

Seven Long Years in State Prison (with music). Anonymous. I'd fly to the side of my mother/And there let me lay down and die. AS

Seven Mexican Children. Tom Schmidt. ...my sandaled/feet began to itch. NeAC

Seven of the Clock. Roy MacNab. And the definite stroke/Of Seven of the Clock. PeSA

The Seven Old Men. Charles Baudelaire. My soul like a dismasted wreck went driving/Over a monstrous sea without a bourn. OBVE

Seven Poems. Lorine Niedecker.
among birch. VGW
and town changed us, too. VGW
before goodbye/of all we know. VGW
the dragonfly. VGW
in a silent boat. VGW
nothing in it/but my hand. VGW
to ache/thru his arms. VGW

Seven Rainy Months. William Plomer. Blind as the gaze of a white blind eye. OxBTC

The Seven Sages. William Butler Yeats. They understood that wisdom comes of beggary. NOBI

Seven Sharp Propeller Blades. John Ciardi. Here come the jets. QQQ

Seven Sister Blues. Edward Thompson. Says I knowed by that/my gal was graveyard bound BluL

The Seven Sleepers. Sir Herbert Read. Beauty when we wake will be/a solitude on land and sea.' SeCePo

The Seven Sleepers. Mark Van Doren. The centuries are stars, and stud the way. FYAP

Seven South African Poems. David Wright.
Regret pour a poison in the ear of memory. PeSA
Time and the sea about Tristan da Cunha. PeSA

The Seven Spiritual Ages of Mrs. Marmaduke Moore. Ogden Nash. God knows what God is coming next. MoAmPo

Seven Stanzas at Easter. John Updike. and crushed by remonstrance. EaLo; EBCP; TrCP

Seven Times One Are Seven. Robert Hillyer. He chose a book called Storyland and lost himself in that. BiCB

Seven Times the Moon Came. Jessie B. Rittenhouse. That seven times the moon had come/And you were gone from me. HBMV

Seven Today. Ivy O. Eastwick. and they're all–for–ME! BiCB

The Seven Virgins. Anonymous.
Amen, Good Lord. Your charity/Is the ending of my song. GBP; OBET; OBEV; OxBoCh
I die, Mother dear, I die.".. CH

Seven Wealthy Towns. Anonymous. Through which the living Homer begged his bread. PP

The Seven Wonders of England. Sir Philip Sidney. A simple soul should breed so mixed woes. FaBoPP

The Seven Wonders of the Ancient World. Anonymous. Or the Palace of Cyrus, cemented with gold. EyDe; GoTF; TreFT

Seven Woodland Crows. Gerald Vizenor. marking the dead/landmen who ran the woodland/out of breath VoR

Seven Years. Robert, Marquess of Crewe. What if all you have learn'd but the more endears/Those seven years? OBVV

Seven Years at Sea. Anonymous. "And if I set my foot on land/I'll ask the fairest for her hand." OuSiCo

Seven Years Old. Algernon Charles Swinburne. Seven years since, of seven times seven. HBV 1-2

Seventeen. Jonathan Holden. ...ready/to be recruited by the night. Psk

Seventeen Come Sunday. Anonymous. And a merry man is mine O.' OBET

Seventeen Warnings in Search of a Feminist Poem. Erica Jong. Beware of the man who praises liberated women;/he is planning to quit his job. AmPA

Seventh Day. Kathleen Raine. This is the divine repose, that watches/The ever-changing light and shadow, rock and ksy and ocean. ChMP

Seventh Eclogue. Miklos Radnoti. since I can face neither death nor a life any longer without you. VWA

Seventh Georgic. George Economou. like all God's good animals/any time any place. PoL

The Seventh Hell... Jerome Rothenberg. And where will his eyes find rest CoPo; NMP

Seventh Son. Ed Roberson. has to carry evenings up the hill/to make it dark. PoBA

Seventh Station. Paul Claudel. Save us, Lord, from this second fall when the weary spirit crumbles! CAW

The Seventies. Tony Beyer. ...shouts/threats and obscenities at no one we know OCNZ

Seventy-Six. William Cullen Bryant. The footstep of a foreign lord/Profaned the soil no more. HBV 1-2; MC; PAH

Seventy Six Trombones. Meredith Wilson. And I oompahed, oompahed, oompahpahed, oompahed up and down the square. BLSo

Several Voices out of a Cloud. Louise Bogan. And it isn't for you. ExPo; MoVE

Seville. L. D'O. Walters. Breathe only roses,/Fallen at their feet. HBMV

The Sevin Seages: Epilogue. John Rolland. Pas on, and fend thy self amang thame. OxBS

Sex. Jean Valentine. And the thing itself not the thing itself,/But a metaphor. FaBoWP

Sex at thirty-one. Artie Gold. Sick of the tides of the heart. CaPN; NOBC

Sex Play in Four Acts. Doug Fetherling. yesterday i thot id die loving u/ or (be loving u when i die)? NeAC

Sex without Love. Sharon Olds. single body alone in the universe/against its own best time. MAYP

Sexsmith the Dentist. Edgar Lee Masters. ...a moral truth is a hollow tooth/Which must be propped with gold. NePA

Sextains. William Baylebridge.
But ah! to know that bliss shall fail not, and/Our hearts be dust! BoAV
Of all that waste me, no thrust as my own/Is half so dire. BoAV

The Sextant. A. M. Sullivan. Of steering home with a star/At the end of a golden stick. GoBC

Sextus Propertius: Turning Aside from Battles. Ezra Pound. Each man where he can, wearing out the day in his manner. WaaP

Sextus the Usurer. Martial (Marcus Valerius Martialis). But to refuse before you're asked displays/Inventive genius worthy of the bays! AWP

The Sexual Life of the Camel. Anonymous. Which accounts for the hump on the camel,/And the Sphinx's inscrutable smile. DBV

Sexual Privacy of Women on Welfare. Pinkie Gordon Lane. To follow the outline/of a city street whose perspective/darkens with the morning light?/ Document. BlSi

Sexual Soup. Erica Jong. "I lust for nothing." GP

Sexy Food Stamps. Jeffrey Miller. Each wave with a counterfeit shimmer. APU

Seymour and Chantelle or Un Peu de Vice. Stevie Smith. ...your tears/Are as nice as the sea, as icy and salt as it is. SBG

Seynt Steuyn and Herowdes. Anonymous. And perfore is his euyn/On Crystes owyn day. OxBB

Sgoran Dhu. Nan Shepherd. Nothing avails him here but the mind's own fineness. PoSH

Sgurr Nan Gillean. Sorley MacLean. Clearing of tenantry, exile, exploitation. PoSH

"Sh." James S. Tippett. "Can't you play a quiet game/Of some kind or other?" SUS; TiPo

Sh-Ta-Ra-Dah-Dey (Irish Lullaby). (with music). Anonymous. A dollar a day is all they pay/For work on the boulevard. AS

Shabbat Morning. Bradley R. Strahan. on an ancient wave/of dreams. AMV-81

Shabby Old Dad. Anne Campbell. Shabby old Dad! PoToHe

The Shack. Nellie Burget Miller. The car was gone and shifting sand/had drifted in so soon/and covered up its track. PoOW

Shack Bully Holler. Anonymous. Aincha gwine, ancha gwine, boys, aincha gwine? ABF

Shack Poem. Robert Bly. How marvelous to be a thought entirely surrounded by brains! CAPP

Shacked Up at the Ritz. Doug Fetherling. sheets like sacraments on a holiday. NeAC

Shackley-Hay. Anonymous. Thou shalt not live at Shackley-hay. GBP

Shadbush. Christina Rainsford. A tall candle burning/In a shadowy room. GoYe

Shade. Theodosia Garrison. And whoso rests beneath a tree/Hath cause to thank Him gratefully. OHIP

Shade. Charles Lynch. We reach out touch/All love CNA

The Shade-Seller. Josephine Jacobsen. ...O may he never/answer my one with three. TAP

The Shaded Pool. Norman Gale. And Laura's are the lips I sing. HBV 1-2; OBVV

The Shades of Night Were Falling Fast (parody). Alfred Edward Housman. But still he answered with a sigh:/"Unhappily I'm married." BXAP; FaBoNo; FiBHP; NLV; SpRo

Shadow. Guillaume Apollinaire. A god humbled WaaP

Shadow. Richard Bruce. I am a shadow in the light. CDC

The Shadow. Walter De la Mare. The wall will stand empty,/White as snow. OnUR

Shadow. Anthony Delius. ...he was his own/delight and solar system. PeSA

The Shadow. Ben Jonson. Say, are not women truly, then,/Styled but the shadows of us men? NOBE; OBEV

Shadow. Ann Mars. Starting from an unknown place/I fell into immortal space. GoYe

The Shadow. Richard Henry Stoddard. A wound that never will heal. AA

The Shadow. Arthur Symons. As those who see the far-off shadow of a fire/Gaze earnestly, and wonder if their roof-trees burn. OBVV

Shadow and Shade. Allen Tate. I said, lest we should die alone. InPo; LiTA; VGW; ViBoPo

The Shadow and the Light (excerpt). John Greenleaf Whittier. The white wings of the Holy Ghost/Stoop, seen or unseen, o'er the heads of all. TrPWD

A Shadow Boat. Arlo Bates. Whose deathless eyes once fixed on mine/Would draw me downward through the brine! HBV 1-2

Shadow-Bride. J. R. R. Tolkien. they dance together then till dawn/and a single shadow make. SO

The Shadow-Child. Harriet Monroe. Where green grass grows and roses gay,/There in the sun forever. HBV 1-2

Shadow Dance. Ivy O. Eastwick. And none else/At all. SoPo; TiPo

The Shadow Dance. Louise Chandler Moulton. She sees her image in the glass. AA; HBV 1-2

Shadow Dirge. R. P. Dexter. Slips silently down the river's winding way. LiSp

Shadow-Evidence. Mary Mapes Dodge. And guarded as my own,/All my life long. AA

The Shadow House of Lugh. Ethna (Anna Johnston MacManus) Carbery. And her arms make the rim of his rainbow world. AnIV

Shadow Life. Robert F. Reid, III. I have forgotten what. AMV-81

Shadow-Love. Heinrich Heine. Human eyes must fall asleep. TrJP

The Shadow of Cain. Edith Sitwell. He walks again on the Seas of Blood, He comes in the terrible Rain. CoBMV; OxBTC

Shadow of Darkness. Gladys May Casely Hayford. Come to me quickly—Shadow of Darkness. PBA

The Shadow of Himself. William Renton. And their muzzles meet/On the very tuft for which he contends. NOBV

The Shadow of Night. George Chapman.
So shall the wonders of thy power be seene,/And thou for euer live the Planets Queene. NCEP
Till vertue flourish in the light of light. PoEL 1-5

The Shadow of Night. Coventry Patmore. And call her crazed with wrong. CH

Shadow of Night: Hymnus in Noctem. George Chapman. There is thy glorie, riches, force, and Art. AtBAP

A Shadow of the Night. Thomas Bailey Aldrich. To be quite sure! AA

Shadow of the Old City. Yehuda Amichai. all crowded together, most of the pages/stuck like eyelids in the morning. VWA

The Shadow of the Rock. Frederick William Faber. Rest in the Shadow of the Rock. GoBC

The Shadow on the Stone. Thomas Hardy. My head unturned lest my dream should fade. QFR

The Shadow People. Francis Ledwidge. Oh! I would be wild and free/And with the shadow people be. MCCG

The Shadow Remains. Lynette Roberts. Two angels pinned to the wall—again two. NeBP

Shadow River. [(Emily)] Pauline Johnson. ...I only claim/The shadows and the dreaming. CaP

The Shadow Rose. Robert Cameron Rogers. To leave your shadow lingering/there? AA

The Shadow's Song. Yvor Winters. I am beside you, now. PoL

Shadow to Shadow. Hervey Allen. And with a web-like hand made salutation,/And went back to the Dead. HBMV

The Shadowgraphs. Richmond Lattimore. while the deft hand is sweeter than the eye. NYBP

Shadows. Anonymous. ...but/For all his clothes, his face, his face is black! WTO

Shadows. Paul Claudel. I must pray, for it is the hour of the Sovereign of the world. CAW

Shadows. D. H. Lawrence. to send me forth on a new morning, a/new man. OAEP; OxBTC

The Shadows. George Macdonald. For Thee, O Lord, the light. TRV

Shadows. Richard Monckton, Lord Houghton Milnes. Let fate and courage now conceal,/When truth could bring remorse alone. HBV 1-2

Shadows. Victor Plarr. The shadow of thy beauty over me. NOBV

The Shadows. Frank Dempster Sherman. And fill your eyes with sleep! AA

Shadows. Yehoash. My soul, my weary soul... TrJP

Shadows among the Ettrick Hills. William Addison. ...and hurries/Home to the light that floods the open door. PoSH

Shadows in the Water. Thomas Traherne. To which I shall, when that thin Skin/Is broken, be admitted in. AtBAP; EnLi 1-2; HAP; LiTB; MePo; NoP; OAEL 1-2; OBS; PoEL 1-5; SeCP

Shadows of Chrysanthemums. E. J. Scovell. ...and the florets more/Subtly crisp their bright profiles, or are lost in the flower. MoVE

Shadows of His Lady. Jacques Tahureau. The far-off splendid semblance of my maid. AWP

Shadows of Sails. John Anderson. I'll reach the dawn, and bind with faith your hope. EtS

The Shadows of the Evening Hours. Adelaide Anne Procter. O give us now repose. TreFS

Shadows To-Day. Christina Georgina Rossetti. In darkness for the city luminous. OxBoCh

Shadowy Swallows. Gustavo Adolfo Becquer. They will not love you so. LiTW

Shadrach. Anonymous. And to bed we go. FaBoNo

Shadwell Stair. Wilfred Owen. But when the crowing syrens blare/I with another ghost am lain. FaBoTw

A shady friend for torrid days. Emily Dickinson. The tapestries of paradise/So notelessly are made! NePA

Shady Grove. Anonymous. Don't wait till Judgment Day. FSW

Shady, Shady. T'ao Ch'ien. With a deep yearning I think of the Sages of Antiquity. AWP

Shaemus. Conrad Aiken. immortal dandy, towards an immortal star. OxBA

Shag Rookery. William Hart-Smith. and dry their wings in the light of the beacon lamp. AnNZ

Shaggy Dog Story. Frank Steele. wag what's left of my tail, and we/roll for a new view. Str

Shaka. Anonymous. Finisher off! Black Finisher off! WTO

Shaka, King of the Zulus. Anonymous. And old men shall drop by the wayside. PBA; TTY

Shake Hands with Your Bets, Friend. Lorenzo Thomas. But he doesn't know it may be the last time. APU

Shake, Mulleary and Go-ethe. Henry Cuyler Bunner. Shake, Mulleary and Go-ethe. ALV; AnAmPo; FiBHP; InMe

A Sheep Fair. Thomas Hardy. As he consigned to doom each meek, mewed band/At Pummery Fair. Prf

Sheep-Fuck Poem. Ed Sanders. she was,/as Hesiod says/a "lover of dicks" ANYP

The Sheep-Herder. Charles Badger Clark, Jr. Thank God! Here comes a man. BPAW

The Sheep-Herder's Lament. Arthur Chapman. And nary soul to help him/Watch the sheep feed on the hill. BPAW

Sheep in Fog. Sylvia Plath. Starless and fatherless, a dark water. FaBoWP; HaCAP; LCAP; NaP

Sheep in the Rain. James Wright. They have to be. AMV-80

Sheep in the Sheade. William Barnes. An' oh! that happy hours should glide/Away so soon, an' never bide. FM

Sheep in Winter. John Clare. And shun the hovel where they might be warm. BoAnP

Sheep Ranching. Owen Wister. But a collie, a pony and a gun. BPAW

Sheep Shearing. Anonymous. I'm afraid 'twill be past twelve o'clock. OBET

Sheepbells. Edmund Charles Blunden. In the dim and dewy loneness/Where the woodlark sings. BrPo

Sheepdog Trials in Hyde Park. C. Day-Lewis. Controlled woolgathering is my work too. NoAm; NoP; OxBTC

De Sheepfol'. Sarah Pratt McLean Greene. Dey all comes gadderin' in. AA; HBV 1-2

The Sheepherder. Lew Sarett. Are wandering over the hills of Heaven. AmFN

Sheepherder blues. Luci Tapahonso. then a 2-hour drive/to her sheep. STE

A Sheeprancher Named John. Gretel Ehrlich. Shy penis, mostly/swirled white. MAYP

Sheepstor. Leonard Alfred George Strong. How on the moor above it stand/Stone row and mound and pagan ring. HBMV

Sheer Joy. Ralph Spaulding Cushman. Lord of tomorrow,/Lover of me! TRV

Sheet Lightning. Edmund Charles Blunden. ...Joe beat its brain out on the wheel. HaMV

The Sheffield Apprentice. Anonymous.
Farewell to charming Mollie; I died for the love of you. AmFP; BFSS
My mistress said I'd robbed her. I was straightway sent to gaol. OBET

The Sheiling. Edward ("Edward Eastaway") Thomas. And the stone has taken the house/To its cold heart and is kind. PoSH

Shekhina and the Kiddushim. Edouard Roditi. And prayer must now replace the dance/To keep the world from stopping dead. VWA

Shekhinah. Karl Wolfskehl. And rest and work are one. TrJP; VWA

Shelby County, Ohio. November 1974. G. E. Murray. that cures like smoke. FAZ

Sheldonian Soliloquy. Siegfried Sassoon. And Benedictus sings my heart to Me. UnS

The Shell. James Stephens. To hear a cart go jolting down the street! BoNaP; CH; CMoP; MoAB; MoBrPo; MOS; MoShBr; MoVE

The Shell's Song. John Keats. And a wave fill'd it, as my sense was fill'd/With that new blissful golden melody. EtS

Shellbrook. William Barnes. With young offsunder'd from the young in/sleep. OBNC; VLP

Shelley. Robert Browning. ...–so/Wert thou to me–and art thou to the world. OBRV

Shelley's Arethusa Set to New Measures. Robert Duncan. seeking their way to love once more. CMoP

Shelley's Skylark. Thomas Hardy. For it inspired a bard to win/Ecstatic heights in thought and rhyme. CoBMV; FaBV; PBBP; VLP

The Shellpicker. Ronald Perry. This lady, curled like a shell. NePoEA-2

Shells. Medb Mahony. She flickers out to bone and calcium. AMV-80

Shells. Thomas Sturge Moore. Are formed art, virtue, truth. SeCePo

Shells. Kathleen Raine. "The world that you inhabit has not yet been created." ImOP

Shells in Rock. Elizabeth Madox Roberts. Suppose the sea should come back here/And gather up its shells. AnAmPo

Shelly. James McIntyre. So youthful, drowned and cremated. FiBHP

Shelly Beach. C. J. Koch. The boy believed the sound had made a curse,/Jarring on the piles of broken shells. NOAV

Shelter. Gene Derwood. We've come too quickly and too far. NePA

Sheltered Garden. Hilda ("H. D.") Doolittle. ...to find a new beauty/in some terrible/wind-tortured place. PG

Sheltering the Same Needs. Alex Kuo. our one prayer, improbable in the nearest/quarter-mile, killing us with all we've got. APU

Shema. Primo Levi. Your offspring avert their faces from you. VWA

Shemuel. Edward Ernest Bowen. All his fellows lived, and waited. HBV 1-2

Shenandoah. Anonymous.
'Cross the wide Missouri. ABF; AmFN
Hyah, bound away,/To the wild Missouri! ShS

Shenandoah: Let Us Consider Where the Great Men Are. Delmore Schwartz. Showing himself as such, among his friends. MoAB; MoAmPo

The Shepheard and the Milkmaid. Anonymous. Because she was cozen'd (in being too kind)/By three or four men before so. CoMu

The Shepheardes Calender. Edmund Spenser.
And when my Gotes shall han their bellies layd,/Cuddie shall have a Kidde to store his farme. EnPo; OAEL 1-2
Cease now my song, my woe now wasted is./O joyfull verse. AtBAP; PoEL 1-5

The Shepheards Hunting:. George Wither. And I more of this will say,/If thou come next Holy day. SeCV 1-2

Shepheards Sirena: Song to Sirena. Michael Drayton. Along let them bring her. AtBAP; FaBoPP; PoEL 1-5

The Shepherd. Anonymous. And thou shalt pipe and I'll come to thee. UnTE

Shepherd. Edmund Charles Blunden. And gently leads the yoes that are with young. HBMV

The Shepherd. Mary Gilmore. As they nibble the mound/That marks his sleep. ACV; PoAu 1-2

Shepherd. William Stafford. and according to the dark all wanderers are home. PoA

The Shepherd and His Flock. Mbuyiseni Oswald Mtshali. "O! Wise Sun above,/will you ever guide/me into school?" GrPI

Shepherd and Shepherdess. Nicholas Breton. In Aglaia's only eyes/All my worldly paradise. OBSC

Shepherd and Shepherdess. Thomas Hennell. Our flocks, upon the leas/May scatter far as wandering bees. FaBoTw

Shepherd and the Hawk. William Hart-Smith. himself into the air, straight up,/hand over hand. AnNZ

The Shepherd and the Milkmaid. Anonymous. By three or four men before so. UnTE

The Shepherd and the Shepherdess. Anonymous. For I can see that he loves me,/And that's as good as gold. OBET

The Shepherd Boy. John Clare. So looks and lyes the shepherd boy/The summer long his whole employ. NOBV

The Shepherd Boy. Edward J. O'Brien. Yet still I heard his joyous hymn come faintly down the wind. HBMV

The Shepherd-Boy and the Wolf. Aesop. Even when the liar speaks the truth. AWP

The Shepherd Boys. Nicolas Saboly. Good men/Go to your home again. OHIP

A Shepherd Kept Sheep on a Hill So High. Thomas D'Urfey. And he drew one Leg after a great way behind. CoMu; ErPo

The Shepherd Left Behind. Mildred Plew Merryman. To a Babe in Bethlehem. ChBR; TrCP

The Shepherd of King Admetus. James Russell Lowell. Till after-poets only knew/Their first-born brother as a god. HBVY

The Shepherd of Meriador. Wilfred Rowland Childe. And woke up on Meriador,/Drenched in the summer dew. HBMV

The Shepherd's Calendar. John Clare.
And croodling shepherds bend along/Crouching to the whizzing storms NCEP
And from the bosom's handkerchief/Bloom as it ne'er had lost a leaf. FaBoUs
As falling dews to thirsty flowers. OBRV
Longing for freedom on the moor. OBRV

A Shepherd's Coat. Lilian Bowes Lyon. A shepherd's coat drawn over me. ChMP

A Shepherd's Complaint. Richard Barnfield. Other help for him I know there's none. OBSC

The Shepherd's Despair. Thomas Dermody. Though the shadows still linger behind. OnYI

The Shepherd's Dirge. George Peele. And die for love as Colin died, as Colin died. OBSC

The Shepherd's Dochter. Anonymous. The Earl of Stamford's ae dochter/And the kind o' England's brither. OxBB

The Shepherd's Dog. Leslie Norris. The knowledge of peace,/True happiness. OBCP

Shepherd's Garland,. Michael Drayton. Let us to Daffadill. FaBoEn; ViBoPo

A Shepherd's Gift. Anyte [(or Anytes)]. And reached him sweetest water with their hands. AWP

Shepherd's Holiday. Elinor Wylie. Up among the rocks where the blueberries grow. CrMA; HBMV

The Shepherd's Home. William Shenstone. And I loved her the more when I heard/Such tenderness fall from her tongue. GN

The Shepherd's House. Alfred de Vigny. If you can see anything twice, it is not to be loved. NU

The Shepherd's Hut. Andrew Young. That ghosts are trying on her children's clothes. DTC; GrPI; OxBTC

The Shepherd's Lament. Johann Wolfgang von Goethe. The heart of the shepherd is sore. AWP

The Shepherd's Ode. Robert Greene. And go contented to their sheep. OBSC

The Shepherd's Pipe: Dawn of Day. William Browne. 'Tis but newly day. EIL

Shepherd's Play. *Anonymous.* And all in a yere. FaBoUs

The Shepherd's Praise of Diana. Sir Walter Ralegh. With Circes let them dwell that think not so. SiPS

The Shepherd's Song. John Bunyan. Is best from age to age. BoC; OxBoCh

Shepherd's Song at Christmas. Langston Hughes. I will bring my heart/To the Manger. PCh

The Shepherd's Star. Juan Ramon Jimenez. What fragrance the cool night bore/Along the country lane! LiTW

The Shepherd's Tale. Raoul Ponchon. Let's celebrate his birth! OBCP

The Shepherd's Week. John Gay.
   And Susan Blouzelinda's loss repairs. CEP; EiCP
   And till tomorrow comes defers her fate. EiCP; OAEL 1-2
   And turn me thrice around, around, around. PBBP
   Oh dear! I fall adown, adown, adown! CEP; PoEL 1-5
   Then saw the cow well served, and took a groat. NOEC

The Shepherd's Wife's Song. Robert Greene. What lady would not love a shepherd swain? EG; EIL; EnLit; HAP; HBV 1-2; LoBV; OBSC; PG; ViBoPo

Shepherd, Shepherd, Hark. Saint Theresa of Avila. Angels they are, and the day is dawning. AWP; CAW; LiTW

Shepherd, Show Me How to Go. Mary Baker Eddy. Shepherd, wash them clean. AH

The Shepherd Speaks. John Erskine. We started through the fields to find the Child. TrCP

The Shepherd upon a Hill. *Anonymous.* For in his pipe he made so much joy. GoBC; OxBoCh

The Shepherd Who Stayed. Theodosia Garrison. I ask no more–I stayed. OHIP; PCh

Shepherdess. Norman Cameron. Shepherdess, show me now where I may sleep. GBL; GTBS-P; OBSP; OxBS

The Shepherdess. Alice Meynell. She walks–the lady of my delight–/A shepherdess of sheep. ACP; AWP; GoBC; GoTF; HBV 1-2; HBVY; MoBrPo; NOBV; OBVV; PeD; SBG; TreFS

The Shepherdess and the Sailor. *Anonymous.* And the sailor your fortune he will make. OBET

Shepherdess' Valentine. Francis Andrewes. Come, be my valentine! OFD

The Shepherds. Beren Van Slyke. Bell them at dawn, tell them at evening/In what fold they must sleep. GoYe

The Shepherds. Henry Vaughan. Their day was dark, and dim. SBVL

Shepherds' Carol. Norman Nicholson. When the stars came out in the Christmas sky. OBCP

The Shepherds Had an Angel. Christina Georgina Rossetti. All Glory, glory, giv'n to Thee,/Thro' all the heav'nly height. OHIP

Sherburne. *Anonymous.* And glory shone around. AmFP

Sheridan at Cedar Creek. Herman Melville. But no knowledge in the grave/Where the nameless followers sleep. LiTA; PAH

Sheridan's Ride. Thomas Buchanan Read. From Winchester, twenty miles away! BBV; BeLS; FaBoBe; FaBV; FaFP; GN; HBV 1-2; HBVY; MC; OHFP; OHIP; PAH; TreF; WBLP; YaD

Sheriff. Ambrose Bierce. ...The affair/Was opened, it is said, with prayer. DBV

The Sheriff's Report. Arthur Chapman. We jest went out to git him, and we did. BPAW

Sherman. Richard Watson Gilder. Was the thought of duty done and the love/of his fellow-men. AA

The Sherman Cyclone. *Anonymous.*
   Now beneath the sod they're sleeping till the final Judgement Day. AmFP
   Will nurse the sad afflicted till health may be restored. BFSS

Sherman's in Savannah. Oliver Wendell Holmes. Till our banner flaps o'er all/As it crowns Savannah! MC; PAH

Sherman's March to the Sea. Samuel H. M. Byers. And the stars in our banner shone brighter/When Sherman marched down to the sea. MC; PAH

Sheskinbeg. Elizabeth Shane. An' not a one will lead me now to Sheskinbeg, or near it. HBMV

Shetland, Hill Dawn. Robin Munro. Before us, too, they found the hope/of islands, and the hope of dawns,/was of another day. PoSH

Shetland Pony. Maurice Lindsay. nuzzles confinement from my hand. BSV

Shew! Fly, Don't Bother Me. Billy Reeves. I feel, I feel, I feel, I feel like a morning star. PSoN

Shh! The Professor Is Sleeping. John N. Morris. An illustration of the snow. CABA

Shickered as He Could Be. *Anonymous* Spurs upon a chamber-pot I never saw before. NOAV

Shield. *Anonymous.* The marks of the war-blades double and deepen. AnOE

The Shield of Achilles. W. H. Auden. Iron-hearted man-slaying Achilles/Who would not live long. EBEV; FaBoMo; FaBoPV; GTBS-P; HAP; NePA; NOBE; NOCV; NoP; OAEP; PoA; WeW

The Shield of War. Thomas, Earl of Dorset Sackville. And from the soil great Troy, Neptunus' town. NOBE

Shifting Colors. Robert Lowell. like Mallarme who had the good fortune/to find a style that made writing impossible. HaCAP

Shih Ching. *Anonymous.* Take me with you in your coach! BoWoP

Shillin' a Day. Rudyard Kipling. GAWD SAVE THE/QUEEN! OAEP; ViBoPo

Shiloh, A Requiem. Herman Melville. And all is hushed at Shiloh. AmFN; AP; FF; LiTA; MAmP; NCEP; NOBA; NoP; OBWP; OxBA; PAL; SCV; ViBoPo; WiR

The Shimmer of Evil. Theodore Roethke. –There was no light; there was no light at all. NePoAm-2

Shimmering Pediment. John Yau. ...as I flew/Parallel to where I am now standing. APU

Shine Just Where You Are. *Anonymous.* So, fill, for the day, your mission/By shining just where you are. STF

Shine On. Luke Schoolcraft. Shine on, shine oh, Oh! Jerusalem. TrAS

Shine on Me, Secret Splendor. Edwin Markham. Yet be fastidious, and have such friends/That when I think of them my soul ascends! TrPWD

Shine Out, Fair Sun. *Anonymous.* Our beauty's Spring, our Prince of Light! ELP

Shine, Perishing Republic. Robinson Jeffers. God, when he walked on earth. AmLP; AnAmPo; CMoP; FF; LiTA; LiTM; MoAB; MoAmPo; NAMP; NePA; NOBA; NoP; OxBA; PrIm; TAP; TRV; UnPo; VGW; ViBoPo

Shine, Republic. Robinson Jeffers. and edge their love of freedom with contempt of/luxury. AmFN; FaBoPV; MoRP

Shining. Kathleen Spivack. in my haste, in my haste. AMV-81

A Shining Night; or, Dick Daring, the Poacher. *Anonymous.* From a shining night if 'tis our delight in the season of the year. CoMu

The Shiny Little House. Nancy M. Hayes. In this tweeny little, cosy little house of mine! SUS

The Ship. Louise A. Doran. Safely she takes her way and drops to rest,/Peace-filled and unafraid. EtS

The Ship. J. F. Hendry. To hide a cloud in a frame. NeBP

The Ship. Charles MacKay. And my name is Death!" quoth he. BLPA

The Ship. Lloyd Mifflin. And cast her anchors in the pools of gold. AA

The Ship. J. C. Squire. Or silks or gold. CH

The Ship A-Raging. *Anonymous.* She's sailed, and sailed, but she'll sail no more./She's a-sinking to the bottom of the sea. BFSS

A Ship, an Isle, a Sickle Moon. James Elroy Flecker. A crescent ship without a sail! BrPo; FaBoRV; SyP

The Ship and Her Makers. John Masefield. And know the thoughts of men in other/lands. CoBE

The Ship and the Sea. Blanche Edith Baughan. Bright shines the sun upon the shipless sea. AnNZ

Ship Bottom. Richmond Lattimore. ...climb/the arc of the world. NePoAm-2

Ship-Broken Men Whom Stormy Seas Sore Toss. William Fowler. Ye will me thole to anchor in your heaven. BSV; GoTS

The Ship-Builders. John Greenleaf Whittier. And glad hearts welcome back again/Her white sails from the sea! AnNE; EtS

Ship-Building Emperors Commanded... Peter Levi. let fall their heavy tears/gaunt music for lost ears. NePoEA-2

A Ship Burning and a Comet All in One Day. Richard Eberhart. A great comet appeared in the sky/With a star in its nether tail. NYBP

The Ship Canal from the Atlantic to the Pacific. Francis Lieber. "Make the ocean free." PAH

A Ship Comes in. Oliver Jenkins. So I will go down to the harbor soon/And stand around all afternoon. EtS

Ship from Thames. Rex Ingamells. a fiercer glitter in their eyes. PoAu 1-2

The Ship in Distress. *Anonymous.* May they never see no more such trials/And never know the like again. OBSS

The Ship in the Midst of the Sea. Christopher Wordsworth. When Christ is with us in the ship,/The ship is at the shore. BePJ

The Ship Is All Laden. *Anonymous.* And if they think fit they will court them next tide. OBSS

Ship near Shoals. Anna Wickham. Blow your shrill pipes, and I will follow after. HBMV

The Ship of Death. D. H. Lawrence.
   For the voyage of oblivion awaits you. CMoP; FaBoRV; FaBoTw; GTBS-P; LiTB; LoBV; MasP; MOS; NoP; OAEL 1-2; OAEP; PrIm
   Oh, nothing matters but the longest journey. DTC; MoAB; MoBrPo; NAMP; ViBoPo

The Ship of Earth. Sidney Lanier. And the best sailors in the ship lie there among the dead! MOS

The Ship of Fools. Alexander Barclay.
   Before he crow to cause others wake or rise. ACP

Sight Unseen. Kingsley Amis. It's galling, though, when girls omit/To switch the set on first. ErPo; NePoEA-2

Sightings I. Jerome Rothenberg. A pigeon dreaming of red flowers. CoPo

Sights and Sounds of the Night. Carlos Wilcox. To every finger's end from rapture deep and still. AnAmPo

Sightseers in a Courtyard. Nicolas Guillen. I'll sing you songs/Nobody can dance! TTY

Sigil. Hilda ("H. D.") Doolittle. and that song, heard,/will stifle out this note. FaBoWP; VGW

Sigismonda and Guiscardo. John Dryden. And Heav'n is double Heav'n, if thou art there. OBS

Sigismundo. Linda Gregg. for a chance to drown in that blue water of his./Sigismundo. AmPA

Sigmund Freud. Howard Nemerov. The towers of their most strategic lies. PoA

The Sign. Bhartrihari. And thou so fair–one fairest maid alone/Hath trod upon thy root. LiTW

The Sign. Paul Blackburn. more leaves on the surface of the pool than dixie cups/Fall is come TAT

Sign for My Father, Who Stressed the Bunt. David Bottoms. I'm getting a grip on the sacrifice. MAYP

The Sign of the Bonny Blue Bell. Anonymous. Goodnight, pretty maidens, till Wednesday morning.' OBET

The Sign of the Cross. John Henry, Cardinal Newman. Its source he cannot know. GoBC

The Sign-Post. Edward ("Edward Eastaway") Thomas. Wondering where he shall journey, O where? ViBoPo

The Signal. David Ignatow. ...I do not torture myself/with my shortcomings. NNaP

The Signal; or, A Satire against Modesty (excerpt). Francis Hawling. And ate out twelve months' labour at a meal. NOEC

Signals. Johari (Jewel C. Latimore) Amini. because you wont be/out/of/it/ when i need you PoBA

Signals. Keith Waldrop. My love makes death and death makes everything serious. AMV-81

Signature. Hannah Kahn. and I called it by its name. IHMS

Signature. Dorothy Livesay. ALIVE ON THIS AIR THESE LIVES ABIDE. OBCV

Signature. Larry Mollin. ...rings/stamped/from mattress buttons/all over/ my body NeAC

Signature. Carol Orlock. a map cut in my skin/on forehead, elbow, palm. AMV-81

Signature. Joseph Stroud.
Squabbling and laughing as they pushed/And pulled a cart full of dung. NPGG
...You knew more than any of us/That such is the Signature of all things. NPGG

Signature for Tempo. Archibald MacLeish. Out of deep time have shelved this shallow ledge/Where the waves break– MoVE; VGW

The Signature of All Things. Kenneth Rexroth. And all about were scattered chips/Of pale cold light that was alive. BoNaP; NNaP; NU

Signatures. Daniel Gerard Hoffman. In the confusions of our light. VGW

Signatures. Candace Thurber Stevenson. An elemental alphabet/Of splintered atom, stalking germs. AmFN

The Signboard. Robert Creeley. ...answers by/a being nothing there/where there was a man. ConAP

The Significance of a Veteran's Day. Simon J. Ortiz. I am talking about how we have been able/to survive insignificance. GP

Significant Fevers. Alison Fell. (the spiral deep in the storm,/the world turning over) BrRo

Signpost. Robinson Jeffers. But born of the rock and the air, not of a woman. GoYe; ViBoPo

Signs. Charles Martin. DAILY AT FIVE WEEKENDS AT NIGHTFALL. SM

Signs. Beatrice M. Murphy. She swept the heavy rugs today/And hung them on the line. GoSl

Signs. Gjertrud Schnackenberg. And a housefly's panicked scribbling on the air. PoA

Signs. William Soutar. Is ane in charity. ACV

Signs Everywhere of Birds Nesting, While. William Carlos Williams. He is led forward by their announcing wings. MoVE

Signs of Christmas. Edwin Lees. Then Christmas and his train are here. OHIP

Signs of Rain. Edward Jenner. Our jaunt must be put off to-morrow. BLPA; BoNaP; FaBoUs

The Signs of the Zodiac. Ebenezer Cobham Brewer. AQUARIUS rain, the FISH comes last. FaBoUs

Signs of Winter. John Clare. And laughing hurry in to keep them dry. BoNaP; ERoP 1-2; OAEL 1-2; PoSC; WiR

Signum Cui Contradicetur. Sister Mary Angelita. He bowed His head and, shuddering died,/Who was the Life. GoBC

Siilenboor. Anonymous. I'll grab my darling Siilenboor/As she goes to her wedding. WTO

Sila. Robert Penn Warren. Heart straining, to utter that cry?–But/Cannot, breath short. NoP

Silence. Bella Akhmadulina. You raise me now in song. BoWoP

Silence. Robert Bly. Moving at night like a diver among the bare branches/silently lying on the floor. NaP

Silence. Edward Estlin Cummings. (inquiry before snow CMoP

Silence. Samuel Miller Hageman. For to be alone with Silence/Is to be alone with God. TRV

Silence. Thomas Hood. There the true silence is, self-conscious and alone. CBEP; CH; EBEV; GTBS; NOBE; OBEV; OBRV; PoEL 1-5; ViBoPo

The Silence. Archibald MacLeish. We two shall follow through a world remote/The silence whereinto Love's music died. HBMV

Silence. Edgar Lee Masters.
The temple of our purest thoughts–Is silence. PoToHe
Their silence shall be interpreted/As we approach them. LaNeLa; MoAmPo

Silence. Marianne Moore. Inns are not residences. CMoP; FaBoMo; FaBoWP; InPS; LiTA; NOBA; PPoe; SBG; ViBoPo

Silence. James Herbert Morse. All earth, all life, all else pass by. AA

Silence. Gregory Orr. The black seed in its brain/parachuting toward earth. GeTw

Silence. John Lancaster Spalding. God cannot be expressed. AA

Silence. Charles Hanson Towne. the hills are mute: yet how they speak of God! TRV; WGRP

Silence. Walter James Turner. Let's make a noise, Hey!...Hey!...Hullo!/ Hullo! MoBrPo

Silence. Winifred Welles. In shiny bits like ribbons,/Sweet, like lavender. HBMV

Silence. John Hall Wheelock. Speak for the unreturning traveller. LiTM

Silence, an Eloquent Applause. Leona Gregory. Be still and know that I am God. TrCP

Silence and Stealth of Dayes! Henry Vaughan. And in the heart of Earth, and night/Find Heaven, and thee. JCP; MePo; SeCV 1-2; WHA

The Silence at Night. Edwin Denby. Roar when the pumping heart, bop, stops for a beat. ANYP

Silence Concerning an Ancient Stone. Rosario Castellânos. under which they buried my ancestor alive. PBWP

Silence Invoked. Richard Flecknoe. Seize this maid, and strike her dumb. GoBC

Silence Spoke with Your Voice. Ryah Tumarkin Goodman. Perched on your spray of speech. GoYe

Silences. Arthur William Edgar O'Shaughnessy. All would have answered had you answered then/With even a sigh. OBNC; VLP

Silences. Edwin John Pratt.
Away back before the emergence of fur or fether, back to the/unvocal sea and down deep... NOBC
...where the inhabitants slay in silence and are silently slain. OBCV; PoCh

Silences: A Dream of Governments. Jean Valentine. Listening for a human voice/our names. LCAP

The Silent. Jones Very. To tell of Him, the Unseen God. AmePo

The Silent Generation. Louis Simpson. She said, "it's history." CAPP; NePoAm-2

Silent Hill. Zilpha Keatley Snyder. About the child we saw pass by,/On Silent Hill. WSC

Silent Hour. Rainer Maria Rilke. Looks at me. AWP

Silent in America. Philip Levine. where the living are silent/in America. NaP

Silent Is the Night. Hirsch Glick. Proud of her small victory/For the new, free generation! FSW

Silent Love. Anonymous. Or it brings the heart/Smart/And pain. LiTW

Silent Love. John Clare. So lovers in their silence die. EnRP

The Silent Lover. Sir Walter Ralegh.
He smarteth most that hides his smart,/And sues for no compassion. EiL; PG; ViBoPo
They that are rich in words, in words discover/That they are poor in that which makes a lover. LiTB; OBEV

Silent Movies. Pedro Juan Pietri. the furniture will not move/unless you are there to move it yourself InW

Silent Night. Joseph Mohr.
Christ, the Saviour, is born! FaFP
Jesus, Lord, at thy birth, Jesus, Lord, at Thy birth. FSW; GoTF; TreF

The Silent One. Ivor Gurney. Again retreated–and a second time faced the screen. MMM; OBWP

The Silent Piano. Louis Simpson. This music was made entirely of silence. CAPP

Silent Poem. Robert Francis. weathercock snowfall starlight cockcrow. FiCP; LCAP

The Silent Pool. Harold Monro. And nothing that need trouble you. BrPo

The Silent Ranges. Stephen Moylan Bird. Let half-heard echoes of an Oread's song/Breathe on the drowsy lyre of my sleep. HBMV

The Silent Room.   Kingsley Amis.   Worm, with small-talk from hell.
OxBC

Silent, Silent Night.   William Blake.   But an honest joy/Does itself destroy/
For a harlot coy.   CBEP

The Silent Slain.   Archibald MacLeish.   The dead against the dead and on
the silent ground/The silent slain—   CMoP; CoBMV; ExPo; LiTM; MoVE;
NePA; PoL f10]; TiPo

Silent Testimony.   Catherine Parmenter.   Nothing is here of the life, the joy,
the loving,/Before a war was won.   PGD

The Silent Tower of Bottreaux.   Robert Stephen Hawker.   Come to thy God
at last!'   GoBC; OBRV

The Silent Town.   Richard Dehmel.   Begin a gentle hymn of praise.   AWP

The Silent Walls.   Ian Strachan.   and praise the land of silver snow frozen
on mossy bed.   PoSH

The Silent Woman: Clerimont's Song.   Ben Jonson.   That strike mine eyes,
but not my heart.   PoPle; TrGrPo

A Silent Wood.   Elizabeth Siddal.   Can God bring back the day when we
two stood/Beneath the clinging trees in that dark wood?   NOBV

Silent, You Say, I'm Grown of Late.   Walter Savage Landor.   Ah! that alone
is truly pain/Of which we never can complain.   GBL

Silentium.   Fyodor Tyutchev.   Heed that low music, and be mute.   LiTW;
PoPl

Silentium Altum.   Blanche Mary Kelly.   Like theirs that from an Ostian
window gazed/Beyond the bastions of eternity.   CAW

Silenus in Proteus.   Thomas Lovell Beddoes.   To suck the goatskin oftener
than the goat?   EnRP

Silet.   Ezra Pound.   To plague tomorrow with a testament!   MoAB;
MoAmPo

Silex Scintillans.   Henry Vaughan.
Alas, my God! Thy birth now here/Must not be numbred in the year.
AnAnS 1
And where thou mad'st an end, there I'le begin. AnAnS 1
And wind, and water to thy use/Both wash, and wing my soul. AnAnS 1;
FaBoPP
As a young Roe/Upon the mounts of spices. AnAnS 1
At whose dumbe urn/Thus all the year I mourn. AnAnS 1
Become both food, and Shepheard to thy sheep! AnAnS 1
Begge thou wouldst take thy Tenants Rent. AnAnS 1
But this later light they saw in him,/Their day was dark, and dim.
AnAnS 1
But who there weeping sits,/Hath got the Prize. AnAnS 1
come dear Lord/Upon the Clouds again to judge this world! AnAnS 1
A floud that drowns both tears, and grones,/My Saviours bloud. AnAnS 1
Fresh, spicie mornings; and eternal beams/These are his due. AnAnS 1
From this, unto the last of daies. AnAnS 1
I'le disapparell, and to buy/But one half glaunce, most gladly dye. AnAnS 1
If Saints, and Angels fal down, much more thou. AnAnS 1
Looke down great Master of the feast; O shine,/And turn once more our
Water into Wine! AnAnS 1
Lord, then said I, On me one breath,/And let me dye before my death!
AnAnS 1
My God would give a Sun-shine after raine. AnAnS 1
O for that night! where I in him/Might live invisible and dim. AnAnS 1
O let they power cleer/Thy gift once more, and grind this flint to dust!
AnAnS 1
O lose it not! look up, wilt Change those Lights/For Chains of Darkness,
and Eternal Nights? AnAnS 1
O my God, let it be thine! AnAnS 1
O thou, whom my soul Loves, and feares! AnAnS 1
On that water,/Which thy spirit blowes! AnAnS 1
so made,/Of their Red Sea, a Spring; I wash, they wade. AnAnS 1
So strengthen me, Lord, all the way,/That I may travel to thy Mount.
AnAnS 1
Strow at thy door/That one poor Blossome. AnAnS 1
Sure, thou wilt joy to see/Thy sheep with thee. AnAnS 1
That Curtain'd grave, though sleep, like ashes, hide/My lamp, and life, both
shall in thee abide. AnAnS 1
That God is true, as herbs unseen/Put on their youth and green. AnAnS 1
That these may be thy Praise, and my Joy too. AnAnS 1
That you'l Confess the Comfort such, as even/Brings to, and comes from
Heaven. AnAnS 1
Thou art the Channel my soul seeks,/Not this with Cataracts and Creeks.
AnAnS 1
Though life be dead, and my joys gone. AnAnS 1
Through thy Increase grow new, and quick. AnAnS 1
Thy God, thy life, thy Cure. AnAnS 1
who studies this,/Travels in Clouds, seekes Manna, where none is. AnAnS 1
Whose spittle only could restore the blind. AnAnS 1
Without Succession, and without a Sunne. AnAnS 1

Silhouette.   Annette M'Baye.   Two feet that erase the pattern on the sand.
PBWP

Silhouette in Sepia.   Robert V. Carr.   Their work is done–the camp's asleep.
PoOW

Les Silhouettes.   Oscar Wilde.   Like silhouettes against the sky.   BrPo;
MOS

Silica Carbonate Rock.   Fred Berry.   birds I never met before/act like this is
their home.   NU

The Silk Merchant's Daughter.   Anonymous.
And then they got married, this young man and maid.   OBSS
And when they got home to their own parents dear,/They had no objections
and married they were. BFSS 041

The Silk Merchant's Daughter (I).   Anonymous.   They boys they did dance
and the girls they did sing.   ShS

The Silk Merchant's Daughter (II).   Anonymous.   For venturing her sweet
life for the sake of her dear.   ShS

The Silk Weaver's Daughter.   Anonymous.   Here's adieu to my chains and
my cold strawy bed.   AmFP

The Silken Snake.   Robert Herrick.   But though it scared, it did not bite.
OBSP

The Silken Tent.   Robert Frost.   Is of the slightest bondage made aware.
AmPP; ExPo; InPo; MoPo; MP; NePA; NOBA

The Silkie O' Sule Skerrie.   Anonymous.   He'll shoot both my young son an'
me.   EtS

Silkweed.   Philip Henry Savage.   'T were not so grave a thing to bear/The
burden of a seed.   AA

The Silkworm.   Marco Girolamo Vida.   And the glad nations hailed the
long-sought "Golden Fleece."   CAW

The Silkworms.   Douglas Stewart.   Their soft wings whirr, they dream that
they are flying.   CBAP; PoAu 1-2

The Siller Croun.   Susanna Blamire.   And ere I'm forced to break my troth/
I'll lay me doun and dee.   HBV 1-2

Silly.   Anonymous.   And the miller gave it to Silly again.   OxNR

Silly Dog.   Myra Cohn Livingston.   And she'll bark and beg to go out
again/To try and outsmart the pouring rain.   GDP

The Silly Fool.   W. H. Auden.   And tales in tales/Where no one fails.
OBMV

The Silly Old Man.   Anonymous.   So go to your grave, you silly old man.
CoMu; TW

Silly Sweetheart.   Anonymous.   Dance thy dainty foot and straying/Come,
come away!   CH

Silly Willy.   R. L. B.   Damned if Willie didn't drown.   ShM

Silver.   Archie Randolph Ammons.   and dried to streaks of salt leaked white
from the hair.   NoP

Silver.   Walter De La Mare.   By silver reeds in a silver stream.   AnEnPo;
BoNaP; BrR; GoTF; GTBS; MoAB; MoBrPo; PoPl; SiSoSe; SUS; TiPo;
TreF

The Silver Dagger.   Anonymous.
Let this be a sad and woeful warning/To all true lovers that have to part.
BaBo
Saying, "Leave this as a dreadful token/To those that keep me and Julie
apart." AmFP

The Silver Flask.   John Montague.   so carefully hoarded by our mother/in
the cabin trunk of a Cunard liner.   FaBoIP

Silver in the Wind.   Ian Strachan.   there is silver in the wind.   PoSH

Silver Jack's Religion.   John P. Jones.   So the spread of infidelity was
checked in camp that day.   BPAW; CoSo

Silver Lamps.   W.C. Dix.   And heaven and earth through the spotless birth/
Are at peace on this night so fair.   BePJ

A Silver Lantern.   Karle Wilson Baker.   That picks out the climbing/
Hidden Way.   HBMV

The Silver Leaf.   John Hay.   His quick veins shying in the wind's war.
NePoAm

The Silver Moon.   Sappho.   I lie alone.   EnLi 1-2

The Silver Penny.   Walter de la Mare.   A bright silver penny.   CMoP;
ExPo; OBMV

The Silver Question.   Oliver Herford.   But, oh, I longed to ask the Fish/
Whence came their silver scales!   NA

The Silver Racer.   Joseph Colin Murphey.   across the rug to the mouse hole
AMV-80

Silver Sheep.   Anne Blackwell Payne.   And graze upon the sky.   SiSoSe

Silver Ships.   Mildred Plew Meigs.   But I'll let a rainbow ravel/Through the
wings of my silver plane.   TiPo

The Silver Tassie.   Robert Burns.   It's leaving thee, my bonnie Mary.
NOBE; OBEC

Silver Threads among the Gold.   Hart Pease and Eben E. Danks.   Life is
fading fast away.   BLSo; FaFP; FSW; GoTF; PSoN; TreF

Silver Wedding.   Ralph Hodgson.   I one time was,/And am no more," she
cried.   HBMV; OxBTC; TrGrPo

Silverthorn Bush.   Robert Finch.   Yet leaves me nourished by so many
roots/That I shall never cease ceasing to be.   NOBC

The Silvery Tide.   Anonymous.   And his last words were, "Poor Mary died
on the silvery tide."   AmFP

Fain would my Tongue adore my King/And pay the Worship due. TrPWD

In sweet Perfumes of Praise. CEP

Sindhi Woman. Jon Stallworthy. they stand most straight/who learn to walk beneath a weight. OxBC

The Sinew of Our Dreams. Edgar Jackson. Our life will be the same/held together by/the sinew of our dreams. LFAC

Sinfonia Domestica. Jean Starr Untermeyer. With ewer and basin, with clothing and with food? HBMV; MoAmPo

Sinfonia Eroica. Alice Archer (Sewall) James. And mine with longing that he might re-/main. AA

Sinful to Flirt (Willie down by the Pond). *Anonymous.* I'll always be faithful to you. AmFP

Sing a Song of Joy! Thomas Campion. Let us renown the King of Kings! UnS

Sing a Song of Juniper. Robert Francis. And gives me outdoor shadows/To haunt my indoor house. LOW; NCSH

Sing a Song of Moonlight. Ivy O. Eastwick. Asleep in bed? SiSoSe

Sing a Song of Sixpence. *Anonymous.* There came a little blackbird,/And snapped off her nose. HBV 1-2; OxNR; PoPl; SpRo

Sing a Song of Sixpence. Mother Goose. Along came a blackbird and pecked off her nose. FaBoBe; HBVY; SoPo; TiPo

Sing a Song of Sunshine. Ivy O. Eastwick. In Summertime? At school? SiSoSe

Sing a Song of the Cities. Morris Bishop. Dover Andover Depew! CAD

Sing Again. Marie Van Vorst. Sing again! AA

Sing, Brothers, Sing! W. R. Rodgers. War's dust-bin chariot drawing near. MoAB; MoBrPo

Sing for the Garish Eye. Sir William Schwenck Gilbert. For bratticed wrackers are singing aloud,/And the throngers croon in May! NA

Sing Heigh-Ho! Charles Kingsley. Young maids must marry. ALV; HBV 1-2

Sing Jigmijole. *Anonymous.* My master he did cudgel me,/For kissing of my dame. OxNR

Sing Little Bird. Maria Hastings. Sing for the world/has need of you. SoPo

Sing Me a New Song. John Henrik Clarke. Who will study war until they are free! PoBA

Sing, My Soul. *Anonymous.* Praise him till he calls thee home;/Trust his love for all to come. AH

Sing On, Blithe Bird! William Motherwell. It has been aching many a day with measures/full of sadness! GN; HBV 1-2; HBVY

Sing, Sing. *Anonymous.* The cat's run away/With the pudding too! OxNR

Sing, Sing for Christmas. J. H. Egar. On earth, good-will and peace. OHIP

Sing Song. Robert Creeley. who wouldn't even hear you if you asked her. NMP

Sing-Song: Is the Moon Tired? Christina Georgina Rossetti. Before the dawning of the day/She fades away. MOON

Sing-Song Rhyme. *Anonymous.* "Yes"–sh! sh! sh! SiSoSe

Sing Thou, My Soul. Theodosia Garrison. Sing thou, my Soul–Love's face–; yet this shall be! CAW

Sing to the Lord Most High. Timothy Dwight. O'er every sea and every land. AH

Sing We Yule. *Anonymous.* And therwith endeth Christmes. MeEL

Sing with Your Body. Janice Mirikitani. your mother swallows/what she has lost. WPOW

Sing, Woods and Rivers All. Claudian. crown her seven hills with flowers. HW

Singe We Alle and Say We Thus. *Anonymous.* I said: "God, what is al this?" EBEV

The Singer. Edward Dowden. Stir not the blissful quiet of the night. IrPN

The Singer. Anna Wickham. If it is sometimes swift and strong. HBMV; MoBrPo

A Singer Asleep. Thomas Hardy. I leave him, while the daylight gleam de-/clines/Upon the capes and chines. OAEP

The Singer in the Prison. Walt Whitman. O fearful thought–a convict soul. BeLS

The Singer of One Song. Henry Augustin Beers. "High over all the lonely bugle grieves." AA

The Singer's House. Seamus Heaney. Raise it again, man. We still believe what we hear. CIP; EBEV

The Singers. George Bruce. Where the winged instruments of celebration? OxBS

The Singers in a Cloud. Ridgely Torrence. Only lovely youth. AnAmPo; HBMV; UnS

The Singers in the Snow. *Anonymous.* Who did from death deliver us,/When we were left forlorn. OHIP

Singin' wid a Sword in Ma Han'. *Anonymous.* In ma han', Lord,/Shoutin' wid a sword in ma han'. BoAN 1-2

Singing. Robert Louis Stevenson. The organ with the organ man/Is singing in the rain. SUS

Singing Aloud. Carolyn Kizer. Or they'll lock us up like the apes, and control us forever. IHMS

The Singing Bones. Randolph Stow. ...to taste terrain their heirs need not draw near. CBAP

The Singing Bush. William Soutar. The singing leaves began to sing. ACV

The Singing Cat. Stevie Smith. In the love his beauty bringeth. BoC; OxBTC; PCat

Singing Death. Stan Rice. ...you leave/your shape on the lawn in the wet blades. Singing yet. FYAP

Singing in the Dark. Irma Wassall. singing in the darkness behind their own eyelids. PoNe

The Singing Leaves. James Russell Lowell. And he made her queen of the broader lands/He held of his lute in fee. GN

The Singing-Lesson. Jean Ingelow. And this tale has a moral, I know,/If you'll try to find it out. HBV 1-2

A Singing Lesson. Algernon Charles Swinburne. For the bounties of song are no jealous god's mercies,/Far-fetched and dear bought. HBV 1-2

The Singing Maid. *Anonymous.* Yiif I may, it shall him rewe/By this day!' MeEL

The Singing Man. Josephine Preston Peabody. "Give back the Singing Man!" HBV 1-2

Singing My Doubts Away. *Anonymous.* "Jesus, lover of my soul,/Let me to Thy bosom fly!" BePJ

Singing on the Moon. Ted Hughes. Then shudder away with cries of rapture diminishing/sadly. WSC

Singing the Reapers Homeward Come. *Anonymous.* Till they all appear'd on hill and plain/Like living gold. Io! Io! OHIP

Singing-Time. Rose Fyleman. And I sing and I sing and I sing. SiSoSe; TiPo

Singing Water. Rudolph Chambers Lehmann. A little water singing as litle waters do. HBMV

The Singing-Woman from the Wood's Edge. Edna St. Vincent Millay. And we watched him out of sight, and we conjured up the/devil! HBMV

Single Girl. *Anonymous.*
Oh, got her wedding band. FSW
When you are married, you've all to do. TrAS

A Single-Rhyme Alphabet. *Anonymous.* Z is the Zuyder Zee, dwelt in by coots. FaBoUs

Single Sonnet. Louise Bogan. To prove how stronger you are than my strength. AnEnPo

The Single Woman. Frances Cornford. Put out their coloured lights of comfort and of hope. ELU

Singles. Michael Waters. with such a beautiful stranger. GeTw; MAYP

Sings a Bird. John Nist. who will walk when he can dance? AMV-80

Singular Indeed. David McCord. ...One cold as ouse or ice/is not so nouse, is not so nice. OBCA

A Singular Metamorphosis. Howard Nemerov. Stars tangled with its mistletoe and ivy. ConAP

The Singular Sangfroid of Baby Bunting. Guy Wetmore Carryl. But he'll swallow with never a spasm/What ostriches couldn't digest. NA

Singular Singulars, Peculiar Plurals. Willard R. Espy. What's plural for hysteria? FaBoUs

Sinkholes. Janet Reed McFatter. the earth will silently open,/silently close. GrPl

The Sinking of the Graf Spee. *Anonymous.* She rusts beneath the rolling sea. OBSS

The Sinking of the Mendi. S. E. K. Mqhayi. So then, let it be. PeSA

The Sinking of the Merrimac. Lucy Larcom. Then sink them together–the ship and the name! MC; PAH

The Sinner. Margaret E. Bruner. It seemed as if she trod on holy ground. PoToHe

Sinner, Is Thy Heart at Rest? Jared B. Waterbury. Fly to Jesus, sinner, fly! AH

Sinner Man. *Anonymous.* All on that day? FSW

Sinner, Please Don't Let Dis Harves' Pass. *Anonymous.* Sinner, please, don't let dis harves' pass,/An' die, an' lose you' soul at las' yo' soul at las'. BoAN 1-2

A Sinner's Lament. Edward, Lord Herbert of Cherbury. Whil'st I do talk with my Creator thus. SeCP

The Sinner-Saint. Wilfrid Scawen Blunt. I was a saint of Heaven by right of birth. ACP; CAW

Sinners. D. H. Lawrence. ...and we were less lonely! ViBoPo

Sinners, Will You Scorn the Message? Jonathan Allen. Rebel sinners, rebel sinners,/Glad the message will obey. AH

Sinnes Heavie Loade. Robert Southwell. And eyther yeeld with me tin earth to lie,/Or else with thee to take me to the skie. AnAnS 1

Sins Loathed, and Yet Loved. Robert Herrick. Sins first disliked, are after that beloved. LiTB

The Sins of Kalamazoo. Carl Sandburg. a creeping mystic what-is-it. VGW

The Sins of Youth. Thomas, Lord Vaux. Forgive the guilt, that grew in youth's vain ways. ACP

Sins' Round. George Herbert. Sorry I am, my God, sorry I am. ExPo; LoBV

Sion. George Herbert. The note is sad, yet musick for a king. AnAnS 1

The Sioux. Eugene Field. And raised such a hellabelioux? FiBHP; GoJo

The Sioux Indians. Anonymous.
And we left them to rest in the green shady drill. AmFP; BFSS
Our journey is ended in the land of our dream. CoSo

Sipping Cider through a Straw. Anonymous. And now I've got/A mother-in-law/From sipping ci-/Der through a straw. FSW

Sir Aldingar. Anonymous.
And, if Arbattle's not enough,/To it we'll Fordoun join. ESPB
The lazar under the gallow tree,/Was made steward in King Henery's hall. BaBo; OxBB
"We'll doe ill deeds anew ere night,/Tho it were strucken twall." ESPB

Sir Andrew Barton. Anonymous. His men shall haue halfe a crowne a day/To bring them to my brother, King Iamye. BaBo; EnSB; ESPB; OxBB; ViBoFo

Sir Andrew Barton (Andrew Batann). Anonymous.
And tell my brothers as they pass by/I've done robbing around the salt sea. AmFP
While he remains king upon the dry land/I'll remain king of the sea. AmFP

Sir Beelzebub. Edith Sitwell. ...None of them come! BoWoP; CoBMV; FaBoWP; HoPM; MoAB; MoBrPo; OxBTC; PrIm

Sir Cawline. Anonymous. And fiftene sonnes this ladye beere/To Sir Cawline the knight. ESPB

Sir Colin. Anonymous. He wooed, he wooed that fair Janet/An' ca'd her Dear-Coft till her name. OxBB

Sir Dilberry Diddle, Captain of Militia. Anonymous. What havoc, ye gods, shall we have when he wakes? NOEC

Sir Eggnogg (parody). Bayard Taylor. And there found death, another death than hers. BXAP

Sir Eustace Grey. George Crabbe. I've dreaded all the guilty dread,/And done what they would fear to do. ELP; MyFE; PoEL 1-5

Sir Fopling Flutter. John Dryden. For no one fool is hunted from the herd. DiPo

Sir Francis Bacon. Ambrose Bierce. Buries the talent to manure the vice. DBV

Sir Francis Drake; or Eighty-Eight. Anonymous. Let 'em take heed, they do not speed as they did they know/when-a! GBP; OBSS

Sir Galahad: The Pure Heart. Alfred, Lord Tennyson. My strength is as the strength of ten,/Because my heart is pure. GoTF; TreF

Sir Gawain and the Green Knight. Anonymous.
Hony soyt qui mal pence. EnLi 1-2; OAEL 1-2
May He that was crowned with thorn/Bring all men to His bliss! Amen. MeEV; NAWM 1-2
On his axe hops across, and fiercely comes on.... FaBoPP

Sir Gawain and the Green Knight (excerpt). Anonymous.
And winter windes ayain,/as the worlde askes. PoEL 1-5
With lyppes smal laghande. EBEV

Sir Gawain and the Green Knight: Gawain and the Lady of the Castle. Anonymous. To soper thay yede as-swythe,/Wyth dayntes newe innowe. OxBM

Sir Gawaine and the Green Knight. Yvor Winters. And rested on a drying hill. AnFE; CoAnAm; MoVE; NoAm; QFR; VGW

Sir Halewyn. Anonymous. In the muckle ha' they birled the wine,/And glowered on the heid o' Sir Halewyn. OxBB

Sir Helmer Blaa and His Bride's Brothers. Anonymous. Gaily they drank their wedding feast,/Nor has their friendship ever ceas'd. BaBo

Sir Henry Clinton's Invitation to the Refugees. Philip Freneau. For 'tis true as the gospel, believe it or not,/Who are born to be hang'd, will never be shot. PAH

Sir Hugh; or, The Jew's Daughter (A vers.). Anonymous. And ne'er was such a burial/Sin Adam's days begun. BaBo; ESPB; FaBoBa; ViBoFo

Sir Hugh; or, The Jew's Daughter (B vers.). Anonymous. If my dear father should call for me,/Tell him that I am dead. ViBoFo

Sir Hugh; or, The Jew's Daughter (C version). Anonymous. Every mither had her son,/But sweet Sir Hew was dead. BaBo; CH; ESPB

Sir Hugh; or The Jew's Daughter (D vers.). Anonymous. And all the people that passed by/Thought the little boy was asleep. BaBo

Sir Hugh; or, The Jew's Daughter (N version). Anonymous. My little prayer-book at my right side,/And sound will be my sleep.' AmFP; ESPB

Sir Humphrey Gilbert. Henry Wadsworth Longfellow. And like a dream, in the Gulf-stream/Sinking, vanish all away. EtS; HBV 1-2; HBVY; MC; PAH

Sir Humphry Davy. Edmund Clerihew Bentley. Of having discovered sodium. FaBoCo; ImOP

Sir James the Rose. Anonymous. A traitor's end, you may depend,/Can be expect'd no better. ESPB

Sir John Barleycorn. Anonymous. And it will cause a man to drink/Till he neither can go nor stand. CBEP; FaBoBa

Sir John Butler. Anonymous. If thou wilt come to London, Lady But-/ler,/Thou shalt goe home Lady Gray.' ESPB

Sir Joshua Reynolds. William Blake. And all his pictures faded. ELU; FaBoCo; FiBHP

Sir Lark and King Sun: A Parable. George Macdonald. He popped his head under her wing, and lay/As still as a stone, till King Sun was away. GN; HBV 1-2; HBVY

Sir Launcelot and Queen Guinevere (excerpt). Alfred, Lord Tennyson. Upon her perfect lips. ACV

Sir Launfal. Thomas Chestre. Send us blessings free! ATP

Sir Launfal. John Moultrie. But have, at present, other fish to fry. OBRV

Sir Lionel. Anonymous.
And the norlan flowers spring bonny. ESPB
"But, lady, if you see that I must liue," BaBo; ESPB
For he was a jovial hunter. AmFP; ESPB

Sir Magnus and the Elf-Maid. Anonymous. "And thou canst answer 'nay' or 'no,'/"Or 'yea and yea and yea.'" BaBo

Sir Marmaduke's Musings. Theodore Tilton. O God, a sweet good-will/To all mankind. AA

Sir Menenius Agrippa, the Friend of the People. Robert Barnabas Brough. Sir Menenius Agrippa's the friend of the/people. VLP

Sir Ogey and Lady Elsey. Anonymous. And, ere that month was ended,/Was on her bier, and dead. BaBo

Sir Olaf. Johann Gottfried von Herder. Beneath, Sir Olaf was lyind dead. AWP

Sir Orfeo. Anonymous. God grant us all as well to fare. AtBAP; MeEV; OxBM

Sir Patient Fancy: Epilogue (excerpt). Aphra Behn. Since we no Provocation want from you. WPOW

Sir Patrick Spens. Anonymous.
Afore she see Sir Patrick Spens/Come drivin up the street. BaBo
Afore they see Sir Patrick Spence/Come sailing to Leith Sands. ESPB
And thair lies guid Sir Patrick Spence,/Wi the Scots lords at his feit. AnFE; AtBAP; AWP; BaBo; BiP; BSV; BuBa; CABA; CABL; CH; DiPo; EBEV; ELP; EnSB; ESPB; ExPo; FaBoBa; FaBoCh; FaPoR; FF; ForPo; GN; GoJo; GoTS; HAP; HBV 1-2; HoPM; InPK; InPo; InPS; InvP; LiTB; LoBV; LoGBV; MCCG; MOS; NIP; NOBE; NoP; OAEL 1-2; OAEP; OBEV; OxBB; OxBS; PAI; PoEL 1-5; PoRA; PPP; PrIm; SeCeV; TreF; TrGrPo; UnPo; ViBoFo; ViBoPo; WeW; WHA
Ere they see Sir Patrick and his men/Come sailing to the land. ESPB
"Oh, where can I get a good sailor/To sail this ship of mine?" AmFP

Sir Peter's Leman. Anonymous. And in that hour so sore/Died thirty knights and more. BaBo

Sir Rider Haggard. W. H. Auden. When his bride-to-be/Announced "I AM SHE!" FaBoCo

Sir Roderic's Song. Sir William Schwenck Gilbert. And ushers our next high holiday–the dead of the/night's high-noon! ShM

Sir Roland; a Fragment. Robert Merry. As spoke the anguish of severest woes,/And smote his heart–– NOEC

Sir, So Suspicious. Anonymous. No need to leave home,/sir, so suspicious. NOBI

Sir T. J.'s Speech to his Wife and Children. Anonymous. This it is to be Learned and Witty. CoMu

Sir Thomas Armstrong's Last Farewell to the World. Anonymous. But sure I shall find some friends where I go. APAS

Sir Toby Matthews. Sir John Suckling. Puts each minute such as you/A dozen dozen to disgrace. SeCV 1-2

Sir Tristrem: Tristrem and the Hunters. Thomas of Erceldoune. Marke, the king with croun,/Seyd that feir him thought. OxBS

Sir Turlough; or, The Churchyard Bride. William Carleton. By the bonnie green woods of Killeevy. IrPN

Sir Walter Ralegh to His Son. Sir Walter Ralegh. Then bless thee, and beware, and let us pray/We part not with thee at this meeting day. EnRePo

Sir Walter Ralegh to the Queen. Sir Walter Ralegh. Hee smarteth most that hides his smart,/And sues for no Compassion. AAS; OAEP

Sir Walter Raleigh Sailing in the Low-Lands. Anonymous. Wishing happiness to all Seamen, old or young,/in their sailing in the Low-lands. OBSS; OxBoLi

Sir Walter Rauleigh His Lamentation. Anonymous. Jesus receive me hence:/farewell sweet England. CoMu

Sir Walter Scott at the Tomb of the Stuarts in St. Peter's. Richard Monckton, Lord Houghton Milnes. ...I was sad that ancient head/Ever should pass those holy walls beyond. OBTV

Sir Walter Scott's Tribute. Sir Walter Scott. Who read to doubt, or read to scorn. WBLP

Sir William of Deloraine at the Wizard's Tomb. Sir Walter Scott. Before the cross was the body laid,/With hands clasped fast, as if still he prayed. OBNC

Six Variations. Denise Levertov. Is it a road at the world's edge? AmPP; ConAP; CoPo; LCAP

Six Variations (part iii). Denise Levertov. now and then to take breath in irregular/measure. HeIP; InPK

Six Week Old Blues. John Henry Barbee. Just so that my evil spirit won't be/hanging around your door no more BluL

Six Weeks Old. Christopher Morley. And does not care to learn the rest. BiCB

Six Winter Privacy Poems. Robert Bly. I am alone, yet someone else is with me,/drinking coffee, looking out at the snow. LCAP

Six Winters. Ruthven Todd. Disclosed the gentle hand grown horned and cruel. NeBP

Six-Year-Old Marjory Fleming Pens a Poem. Marjory Fleming. She did not give a single dam. TreFT

Six Years. Alice Bloch. every day/a new map of the same terrain. PeHV

Six Years Later. Joseph Brodsky. Somehow, it would appear, we drifted right/On through it into the future, into the night. AMV-80

Six Young Men. Ted Hughes. Smile from the single exposure and shoulder out/One's own body from its instant and heat. OBWP

Sixteen Dead Men. William Butler Yeats. That converse bone to bone? ACP; FaBoPV; OBWP; OnYI

The Sixth Day. Betty Adcock. the sure, small dream that kills,/that keeps. LiSp

Sixth-Month Song in the Foothills. Gary Snyder. ...and swallows/fly in to my shed. HaCAP

The Sixties. Thomas Listmann. crawling out of the water/and onto the tracks. AMV-80

Sixty-Eighth Birthday. James Russell Lowell. The milestones into headstones change,/'Neath every one a friend. OBSP; PCP; PoEL 1-5

The Skaian Gate (excerpt). Geoffrey Scott. What a stone you have builded, what bronze/You have moulded, blown out of death! OBMV

Skara Brae. Michael Longley. The table made of stone. FaBoIP

The Skater. Sir Charles G. D. Roberts. And I turned and fled, like a soul pursued,/From the white, inviolate solitude. NOBC

A Skater's Valentine. Arthur Guiterman. Your small hand warm in my big brown glove! SiSoSe

A Skater's Waltz. Gray Burr. Remain, O Dionysian, in our heart. CoPo

The Skaters. John Gould Fletcher. Is like the brushing together of thin wing-tips of silver. MoAmPo; SD

The Skaters. John Williams. Above the fragile ice they scrape and thin. LiSp; NePoAm-2; SD

Skating. Herbert Asquith. With the song of the lake/Beneath her feet. BrR; SoPo; SUS; TiPo

Skating. Rudyard Kipling. Now do I see in my head! SD

The Skein. Carolyn Kizer. without salutation, without close. PrIm; VGW

The Skeleton. Gilbert Keith Chesterton. Death was but the good King's jest,/It was hid so carefully. FaBoTw

The Skeleton at the Feast. James Jeffrey Roche. And dreaded him the least! AA

A Skeleton in Armor. Henry Wadsworth Longfellow Thus the tale ended. AA; AmePo; AnNE; AP; AWP; BeLS; BLPL; FaBoBe; HBV 1-2; HBVY; MaC; MCCG; PAH; TreF

The Skeleton in the Cupboard. Frederick Locker-Lampson. Stand by! Your humble servant owns/The Tenant of this Dark Apartment. HBV 1-2

Skeleton Key. John Hollander. Why not me/O let me/get in. AmC; NoP

The Skeleton of the Future. Hugh" (Christopher Murray Grieve) MacDiarmid. ...and behind them/The eternal lightning of Lenin's bones. GoTS; MoBrPo; OBMV; OBTV

Skeleton Parade. Jack Prelutsky. They march on Halloween. NTCP

Skelton Laureate, Defender, against Lusty Garnesche.... John Skelton. Till more matter may come./By the King's most noble commandment. TW

A Skeltoniad. Michael Drayton. How well to live, and not how long. PoEL 1-5; PP

The Skeptic. Robert W. Service. I don't know which loss hurt the worse–/My God or Santa Claus. PV

Skerryvore. Robert Louis Stevenson. I, on the lintel of this cot, inscribe/The name of a strong tower. EyDe

A Sketch. George Gordon, Lord Byron. And festering in the infamy of years. ERoP 1-2; OBRV

Sketch. Robert Farnsworth. ...You seem to have just fallen/into my heart at its dusk. GOYP

Sketch. Seumas (James Starkey) O'Sullivan. Under the quiet of the evening star. AnIV

A Sketch. Christina Georgina Rossetti. But, since your eyes are blind, you'd say,/"Where? What?' and turn away. GTBS-P

Sketch. Carl Sandburg. Are the shadows of the ships. AP

Sketch for a Job Application Blank. Jim Harrison. warmth, more warmth, I cry.) AmPA; NoAm

Sketch for a Morning in Muncie, Indiana. G. E. Murray. ...I pick up the tip he leaves, and pocket it. MAYP

Sketch of his Own Character. Thomas Gray. But left Church and State to Charles Townshend and Squire. CEP; EiCP; LAuP

Sketch of Lord Byron's Life. Julia A. Moore.
His career on earth, was marred/By his own misdeeds. FiBHP
Then closed the sad career,/Of the most celebrated "Englishman"/Of the nineteenth century. OBAL

Sketches of Harlem. David Henderson. "That's a moon." NNP; PoNe

The Skew-Ball Black. Anonymous. Whoa! skew, till I saddle you, whoa! CoSo

Ski Trail. Samuel ("Paul Vesey") Allen. He used to be swoopinaroundhere all–/of the time. FB

Skier. Robert Francis. Unfalling, trailing white foam, white fire. LiSp; NCSH; RFM; SD

Skiers. Robert Penn Warren. ...The human/Face has its own beauty. LiSp

The Skies Cant Keep Their Secret! Emily Dickinson. In your new-fashioned world! DiPo

Skiing on Russian Christmas. Nora Dauenhauer. Frosted alders:/shapes of coral/clawing outward. TWSS

The Skilful Listener. John Vance Cheney. Surprised by softer footfall of our dream. AA

A Skilful Spearman! Anonymous. He could hit an ant with his spear. WTO

Skimbleshanks: the Railway Cat. Thomas Stearns Eliot. You'll meet without fail on the Midnight Mail/The Cat of the Railway Train.' FaBoCh; FaBoCo; LoGBV; NOBL

Skimmers. Ted Walker. at a distance follows. NYBP

Skin. Philip K. Jason. And yet our skins hold the one and only life. AMV-81

The Skin-and-Bone Lady. Anonymous. You will look so when you are dead. AmFP

The Skin Divers. George Starbuck. throbs the dissolving call/of the beachball players. NYBP

Skin Diving in the Virgins. John Malcolm Brinnin. another floating off, his big pouch full. NYBP; TAP

Skin Man. Henry Brown. Well they sell your wife skins and/take her away from you BluL

Skin the Goat's Curse on Carey. Anonymous. And pick his bones as clean as stones,/Is the prayer of poor Skin the Goat. BIrV; TW

Skinning-the-Cat. Dennis Schmitz. the perfect animal, the group animal. NPGG

The Skinny Girl. Anne Hebert. And weird and childlike dreams/Sir/Like green water. BoWoP

Skins. Elizabeth Spires. ...gold stars stuck to its fin. MAYP

Skins (excerpt). Charles Wright. It comes to a point. It comes and it goes. HaCAP

Skip-Scoop-Anellie. Tom Prideaux. Pull up the jellyfish. You know the rest. FiBHP

Skip to My Lou. Anonymous. Skip to my Lou, my darling. ABF; AmFP; FSW; TrAS

The Skipper-Hermit. Hiram Rich. An' shet the shore out, an' the smell/Of sea-weed sweeter'n clover. EtS

Skipper Ireson's Ride. John Greenleaf Whittier. Tarred and feathered and carried in a cart/By the women of Marblehead! AA; AmP; AnNE; AP; BeLS; HBV 1-2; InMe; NOBA; OBAL; OBCA; OxBA; PAH; PoLf; StPo; TreFS; YaD

Skipping along Alone. Winifred Welles. I love to skip alone and play/Along the sand when mist is falling. SoPo; TiPo

Skirt Dance. Ishmael Reed. (that's all the spanish i know.) APU; FF

The Skull. Ian Young. Later, I half expected it/to peel off/in my mouth. NeAC

The Skull in the Desert. Alison A. Trimpi. and climb, to find,/Within, their nests. AMV-81

Skull of a Neandertal. Michael Cadnum. ginkgo leaves/the color of teeth. SUW

The Skunk. Dorothy Walter Baruch. ...But I won't... SoPo

The Skunk. Robert P. Tristram Coffin. He is a conscious black and white/Little symphony of night. TiPo

The Skunk. Seamus Heaney. Your head-down, tail-up hunt in a bottom drawer/For the black plunge-line nightdress. FaBoIP; OxBC

Skunk Hour. Robert Lowell. and will not scare. AmPP; AP; BiP; CAPP; CMoP; CoAP; ConAP; FaBoMo; HaCAP; HAP; HeIP; InPK; InPS; LCAP; MoAmPo; NIP; NMP; NoAm; NOBA; NoP; OxBC; PPP; PrIm; SCV; TAP; WeW

The Skunk (parody). Philip Dow. I awaken/on all fours. BXAP

Skunks (excerpt). Robinson Jeffers. quick trout dimple the pool.–Distance makes clean. BoAnP

The Sky. Anonymous. Everything knows its way. TTY

The Sky. Elizabeth Madox Roberts. The sky is always slipping back/And getting far away from me. MoAmPo

The Sky Clears. Anonymous. When my Mide drum/Sounds/For me. OBVE

Sky Diver. Adrien Stoutenburg. how deep the earth can be. LiSp

Sky Diving. Richmond Lattimore. Their little sky-time is over. LiSp

Sleet. Norman MacCaig. ...turning away/From the ill wind, the sky filthily weeping. OBCP

Sleet Storm. James S. Tippett. Caught on each glistening/Valley and hill. BrR; SiSoSe

Sleet Storm on the Merritt Parkway. Robert Bly. The slave systems of Rome and Greece, and no one agreed. ConAP; NOBA

Sleigh Bells at Night. Elizabeth Jane Coatsworth. that those who shook them must be dancing. SiSoSe

Sleighing Song. John Shaw. And the bells shall tinkle merrily. AA

Sleighride. Patrick Anderson. with a hallelujah hello from a nest of fur. CaP; OBCV

Slender Fingers. Chao Luan-luan. All their nails were painted scarlet. BoWoP

Slender Maid. Joseph Eliyia. And from the edge/Come pull me away. VWA

Slepynge Long in Greet Quiete is Eek a Greet Norice to Leccherie. John Hollander. With which the changing world outside peeped in. AmPC; ErPo

A Slice of Wedding Cake. Robert Graves. Do I?/It might be so. BoLoP; NOBE; OxBTC

Slick. Daniel Gerard Hoffman. An ocean of salt/Rubs in our wounds. SOTS

The Slide at the Empire Mine. Harriet L. Wason. Who living, loved, in death were not divided. PoOW

Slide, Kelly, Slide. J.W. Kelly. They'll take you to Australia! Slide, Kelly, slide! FaFP; TreFS

Slides. Jennifer Maiden. at rats & swallows burrowed warm/in antique porticos. CBAP

Sliding. Marchette Chute. Down we come again. TiPo

Sliding. Myra Cohn. and SLIDE/and SLIDE. SiSoSe

Sliding Trombone. Ribemont-Dessaignes George. To the loving turtle-doves who laugh like hell. EAS

Slievenamon. Anonymous. O the broken ranks and the trumpets ringing/On the sunny side of Slievenamon! KiLC

A Slight Confusion. James Reiss. you whisper, at last I've found you! AmPA

Slightly before the Middle of Congressman Pudd. Edward Estlin Cummings. and all the little school children sat down OBAL

Slightly Old. Bob Rosenthal. If I can only make twenty-eight. APU

Sligo and Mayo. Louis MacNeice. The coal-black turfstacks rose against the darkness/Like the tombs of nameless kings. FaBoPP

Slim Cunning Hands. Walter De la Mare. Nor all earth's flowers, how fair. ELU; FaBoEE; NIP; SeCePo

Slim Greer. Sterling A. Brown. Yes, indeed.... BALP; BANP

Slim in Hell. Sterling A. Brown. You'se a leetle too dumb,/Fo' to stay up here... BPo; FB

Slim Man Canyon. Leslie Marmon Silko. past cliffs with stories and songs/painted on rock./700 years ago. VoR

The Slip. Wendell Berry. Though death is in the healing, it will heal. NOCV

Slippery. Carl Sandburg. Give her a nickname: Slippery. BiCB; TiPo

Slipping out of Intensive Care. Florence Trefethen. out into traffic, dead or alive. AMV-80

The Sliprails and the Spur. Henry Lawson. Whose restless heart must rove for rest. PoAu 1-2

Slips. Mebdh McGuckian. My hair coming down in the middle of a conversation. FaBoIP

The Slithergadee Has Crawled out of the Sea. Shel Silverstein. You may catch all the others, but you wo— AmMo; NLV; OnUR; WSC

Sloe Gin. Seamus Heaney. I drink to you/in smoke-mirled, blue-black,/polished sloes, bitter/and dependable. FaBoIP

The Slogan. Paul Blackburn. DIG WE MUST/They dig . PoM

Sloops in the Bay. James Tate. Whispering like a garden of secrets. MAYP

The Sloth. Isabella Gardner. under branches in the zoo or in the subway under/town. BoAnP

The Sloth. Theodore Roethke. And you just know he knows he knows. FiBHP; NePA; NePoAm; OBAL; OBCA

The Sloth. George J. Romanes. What benefit arises in this sphere/By twisting all one's being towards the sky. FM

Slough. Sir John Betjeman. The earth exhales. DBV; MoBrPo

The Slough of Despond. Robert Lowell. All the bats of Babel flap about/The rising sun of hell. SyP

Slovenly Peter. Heinrich Hoffmann. Anything to me is sweeter/Than to see Shock-headed Peter. BBGG

Slow Dance. David St. John. & everyone simply dances away. AmPA; LCAP

Slow Dancer That No One Hears but You. Duane Niatum. River echoes of the women who fled. CDW

Slow Death. Lorri Martinez. I thought it was heavy–/& I liked the idea/before I came down/from my high. LFAC

Slow Drivers. Gerald William Barrax. seeing death/in their eyes/when they smirk/at you/as you/pass. AmC

Slow Mama Slow. Sam Collins. Look out your back door/see me leave this town BluL

Slow Me Down. Anonymous. Slow me down, Lord, so I can talk/With some of Your angels as they walk. STF

Slow Me Down, Lord! Orin L. Crane. That there is more to life/Than increasing its speed. GoTF; TreFT

Slow Movement. Louis MacNeice. Accelerando con forza, the sleeper open her eyes/And, so doing, open ours. FaBoIP

Slow Movement. William Carlos Williams. ...and not be/merely faint and sleepy/As they are now. PoA

Slow Oxen. Ilya Rubin. and the oxen's heavy bodies/draw His sad deeds,/and the road wails, stumbling. VWA

The Slow Pacific Swell. Yvor Winters. Or gathers seaward, ebbing out of mind. ForPo; HeIP; MOS; NoAm; NOBA; QFR

Slow Rain. Gabriela (Lucila Godoy Alcayaga) Mistral. this lethal water, sister/of death? PBWP

Slow Riff for Billy. James (Olumo) Cunningham. for huge ferocious stars. JB

Slow Summer Twilight. John Hall Wheelock. A face, once young, in age loved all the more. LiTM

Slow to Come, Quick A-Gone. William Barnes. That now do seem as in a reace/Wi' air-birds to ha' vled. NOBV; VLP

Slow Waker. Thom Gunn. so he can wait, and doze,/and get in nobody's way. Str

Slowly, By God's Hand Unfurled. William Henry Furness. And with light my being fill. AH

Slowly, Slowly. Anonymous. With a large heart, with a weary heart,/Today you go away. WeW

Slowly, Slowly Wisdom Gathers. Mark Van Doren. How ancient, and how full of grace. PoA

Slug. Gwen Head. holding me earthbound/by all that is at once/most vulnerable/most destructive. GP

Slug in Woods. Earle Birney. So spends a summer's jasper century. CaP; NOBC; OBCV; PeCV

The Sluggard. William Henry Davies. So I, dressed in my idle dreams,/Will think myself the king of men. OBMV

The Sluggard. Lucilius [(or Lucillius)]. and never went to sleep again in case– SD

The Sluggard. Isaac Watts.
But he scarce reads his Bible, and never loves thinking. OxBoLi; Par; TreFS
Who taught me betimes to love Working and Reading. CEP; CH; HAP; HBV 1-2; HBVY; MoShBr; NOEC; OBEC; OxBChV; PaPo; PoEL; 1-5; SpRo

A Slum Dwelling. George Crabbe. Doubling each look of Care, each token of Distress. OBNC

A Slumber Did My Spirt Seal. William Wordsworth. Rolled round in earth's diurnal course,/With rocks, and stones, and trees. ELP

Slumber Song. Louis V. Ledoux. Drowsily come the sheep. HBMV

Slumber Song. Siegfried Sassoon. And roses in the darkness; and my love. MCCG

Slump. Vassar Miller. staring from the socket of the darkness. BoWoP

The Slushy Snow Splashes and Sploshes. Mary Ann Hoberman. To keep out the ice and the sleet. TiPo

SM. Stanley Moss. and wearing sneakers, I sign with those/who have signed for me. AMV-81; NYP

The Smack in School. William Palmer. I thought she kind o' wished me to! HBV 1-2

The Smacksman. Anonymous. We ice them and keep them safely like an oyster in his shell. OBSS

The Small. Theodore Roethke. And all the stones have wings. GrPl; SO

The Small. Don Welch. an impulse of fish, dashed with light,/toward whatever intersections. WOLT

Small Aircraft. Bella Akhmadulina. Looking from their eyes like sad dachshunds/As their long bodies float by. BoWoP

Small and Early. Tudor Jenks. And I went to a real tea, and Dorothy to/bed. AA

A Small Bird's Nest Made of White Reed Fiber. Robert Bly. ...nearing/the shore where we will be reborn, ecstatic and black. CAPP; NNaP

Small Birds. Peter Quennell. Into a foam of riot–voices high/And tart as a sloe-berry. MoVE

Small Bones Ache. Moshe Dor. Candles are extinguished. Small bones/ache. VWA

A Small Boy, Dreaming. Albert Herzing. Nor Crusoe's raft nor any imploring gesture/Of thoughtful love shall ever find him here. NYBP

The Small Celandine. William Wordsworth. Age might but take the things Youth needed not! HBV 1-2; OBRV

Small Colored Boy in the Subway. Babette Deutsch. ...darkly your grace proffers/The grave accusation of innocence. PoNe

Small Comment. Sonia Sanchez. ˌbestial and natural of/any beast, you dig? NBP

Small Country. Claribel Alegría. I'll be in a position/to offer ten centavos to a beggar/and to feel compassion. BoWoP

Small Dark Song. Philip Dacey. For Wind's been everywhere today, and has an alibi. PPJ

A Small Dragon. Brian Patten. but I want instead to see/if you yourself will pass this way. AmMo

A Small Elegy. Jiri Orten. I will not live long. AMV-81

A Small Elegy. Richard Snyder. followed her bright vivacity. PCP

A Small Faculty Stag for the Visiting Poet. Earle Birney. grinning/& stoned/& desolate OxBC

A Small Farm. Michael Hartnett. the civil war of that household. CIP

Small Fountains. Lascelles Abercrombie. Spilt shattered gold about his back... CH

Small Frogs Killed on the Highway. James Wright. Not yet. HaCAP; NNaP

Small Game. Philip Levine. I do your work so why ask. AmPC

The Small Hotel. Michael Longley. Or the night-porter's knowledgeable smile. CIP

The Small Lady. Stevie Smith. Never will this poor lady come home. TEP

The Small Lizard. Linda Gregg. breathing in this stone room,/without evidence. MAYP

The Small Man Orders His Wedding. Clive Staples Lewis. ...while the mortal pair/Lie drowned in dreaming weariness. HW

Small Moon. Howard Nemerov. Developing someone else's negative. PCP

Small Park in East Germany: 1969. Gerda Mayer. and nymphs and satyrs breaking from weathered stone. OBTV

Small Paths. H. Roland-Holst. in the dull distress of our pitiful sphere. WPOW

Small Perfect Manhattan. Peter Viereck. Small perfect Manhattan. MiAP

Small Poem about the Hounds and the Hares. Lisel Mueller. how lovely their scared, gentle eyes. GP

Small Prayer. Weldon Kees. Whatever it is that a wound remembers/After the healing ends. PoA; VGW

Small Quiet Song. Robert Paul Smith. And I will not be the old man in the park/Who talks to his neighbor on the bench. CAD

A Small Registry of Births and Deaths: All Night It Bullied You. C. K. Stead. We had never been so nearly anonymous. NAs

Small Sad Song. Alastair Reid. nothing at all. NYBP

Small-Scale Reflections on a Great House. A. K. Ramanujan. on a perfectly good/chatty afternoon. OxBC

The Small Silver-Coloured Bookworm. Thomas Parnell. Myself the priest, my desk the shrine. OnYI

Small Song. Archie Randolph Ammons. ...and give/the wind away. NoP; PoL

Small Song. Luci Shaw. I know you'll see/the love that wings/to you from me. EBCP

The Small Square. Sophia de Mello Breyner Andresen. The fabric that death was weaving around you. WPOW

Small Talk. Don (Donald Robert Marquis) Marquis. small talk i said to myself/and went away from there. StPo

A Small Thought Speaks for the Flesh. Carleton Drewry. Think how our anguish must make/Some meaning for your sake. MoRP

Small Town. William Joyce. I teach this forsaken town to howl. FAZ

Small Town: The Friendly. Stephen P. Dunn. and they think I'm normal. PoL

Small Towns. Alejandro Murguia. as if in a movie FIA

The Small Towns of Ireland. Sir John Betjeman. Your murmuring waters and turf-scented air. OBTV

Small Woman on Swallow Street. William Stanley Merwin. ...God is/On High. He can see you. You will die. CoAP; ConAP

The Smallest Angel. Elsie Binns. You are the tidings that they bring! ChBR

Smell. William Carlos Williams. Must you have a part in everything? MoAB; MoAmPo; TAP; WeW

Smell My Fingers. David B. Axelrod. ...She tells me/it is spring and that means perfume. Str

The Smell of Coal Smoke. Les A. Murray. with our day-old Henholme chickens peeping in their box. NOAV

The Smell of Death Is So Powerful. Marguerite de Navarre. Since her heart was resurrected by/The smell of death. PBWP

The Smell of Fish. William Meissner. the faint odor of fish I couldn't quite/wash from my fingers. WOLT

The Smell of Old Newspapers Is Always Stronger... Mike Lowery. memories of old games/whose scores are lost forever. Psk

The Smell on the Landing. Peter Porter. ...once/More ourselves in ourselves alone. NMP

Smelling the End of Green July. Peter Yates. Under the blowlamp kisses of the sun. ChMP

Smells. Christopher Morley. She smells exactly like hot buttered toast! TiPo

Smells. Kathryn Worth. And everywhere the great green smell/Of grass the whole world over. BrR

A Smile. Anonymous.
As he or she who has no more smiles left to give. PoToHe
An' so, whatever is your lot,/Jes' smile, an' smile, an' smile. BLPA; WBLP
That man will win some other day,/Who loses with a smile. BLPA; WBLP

The Smile. William Blake. There's an end to all misery. OBRV

Smile. D. M. Thomas. some poems have no beginning and no end. AMV-81

Smile and Never Heed Me. Charles Swain. Then–thou then–mayst heed me! HBV 1-2

Smile at Me. Musa Moris Farhi. come/smile at me/with your breasts VWA

Smile, Death. Charlotte Mew. And we will not speak of life or believe in it or/remember it/as we go. WPOW

The Smile of the Goat. Oliver Herford. The Censor attending a risque Revue/And combining Stern Duty with pleasure. FiBHP

The Smile of the Walrus. Oliver Herford. And isn't quite sure what it means. FiBHP

Smiles. Peter Schjeldahl. Grimacing to break the seal ANYP

The Smiles of the Bathers. Weldon Kees. ...No death for you. You are/involved. NaP

A Smiling Demon of Notre Dame. Sophie Jewett. Serene, grotesque Olympian. AA

The Smiling Mouth and Laughing Eyen Grey. Charles, duc d' Orleans. The breastes round, and long small armes twain. HAP; NoP

Smith's Song. George Sigerson. Hammer at it brightly. OnYI

Smithereens. Dante Gabriel Rossetti. ...therein lies crushed/Thy heart–to smithereens. NOBV

Smithfield Ham. Dave Smith. I fill my cup again, drink, nod, listen. HaCAP

The Smiths. E. G. Murphy. And the maidens who were promised still await the absent Smith. NOAV

Smoke. Mebdh McGuckian. ...I run/Till the fawn smoke settles on the earth. FaBoIP

Smoke. Henry David Thoreau. And ask the gods to pardon this clear flame. AA; AmPP; AnNE; APA; AWP; HeIP; InPo; NoP; OxBA

Smoke. Charles Wright. ...the flames/Splash at the gunwales; and you/Are smoke, Nicky, you are smoke. NYBP

Smoke and Steel (excerpt). Carl Sandburg. Smoke and blood is the mix of steel.... MoAmPo

The Smoke-Blue Plains. Badger Clark. Coming up the canon from the smoke-blue plains! YaD

Smoke in Winter. Henry David Thoreau. As some refulgent cloud in the upper sky. AnNE

The Smoked Herring. Charles Cros. And to amuse children–so small, small, small. GrPl

The Smoker. Robert Huff. And will not stop to listen to my screams. GP; NePoEA-2

Smokestack Lightnin'. Howlin' Wolf. Little bitty boy/Derby on/Wooooo-ooooo..... BluL

Smokey the Bear Sutra. Anonymous. thus have we heard. MAT

Smoking Drugs with Strangers. George Bowering. That suits me, I'll do it for free. NeAC

Smoking Flax. Mary Josephine Benson. Clay of his mould and to his image prest! CaP

The Smoky Smirr o' Rain. George Campbell Hay. Aa was still an' saft an' silent in the smoky smirr o' rain. ACV

Smooth between Sea and Land. Alfred Edward Housman. Pours the confounding main. MoPo

The Smooth Divine. Timothy Dwight. Snug in my nest shall live, and snug shall/die. AA; AnAmPo; PPON; WGRP

Smothered Fires. Georgia Douglas Johnson. And with a sigh of victory/She breathed a soft–goodnight! BlSi

Smudging. Diane Wakoski. the golden orange every prince will fight/to own. AmPA; PrIm

A Smuggler's Song. Rudyard Kipling. Watch the wall, my darling, while the Gentlemen go by! OxBChV; PoPle

The Smuggler's Victory. Anonymous. Success to our wives and sweethearts and God save the king. OBSS

The Smugglers. Owen Wister. Pepe, Luis, Coyotito,/Ended not as they began. BPAW

The Snack (parody). L. L. Zeiger. Testicles, testicles, said Daddy. A Man gets tired of testicles. BXAP

Snacks. Ronald P. Tanaka. dashing, toward the sea. BrSi

Snagtooth Sal. Anonymous. Walking down through Laramie with Snagtooth Sal. ABF

The Snail. Anonymous. Run, tailors, run,/Or she'll kill you all e'en now. GBP

Snatches: "Maidenes of Engelande, sare may ye morne." *Anonymous.* Have y-gete Scotlande?/With rombylogh. OxBM

Snatches: "Marie, thou queen." *Anonymous.* In sinne, in sorwe, in nede us wisse. OxBM

Snatches: "Me thinketh thou art so lovely." *Anonymous.* That sikerly it were my deth,/Thy companie to lete. OxBM

Snatches: "Ne shalt thou never, levedy." *Anonymous.* That ich habbe in the bowre/Y-don almyn wille, wille. OxBM

Snatches: "So longe ich have, lavedy." *Anonymous.* "The while ich thrille me a thred,/Nu ich have ned." OxBM

Snatches: "Spende, and God shal sende." *Anonymous.* Go, peny, go! OxBM

Snatches: "Tax has teened us alle." *Anonymous.* Fuit in manibus cupidorum. OxBM

Snatches: "Tel thou never thy fomon." *Anonymous.* Er sith his lif, Quoth Hending. OxBM

Snatches: "The ax was sharp." *Anonymous.* In the fourthe yere of King Richarde. OxBM

Snatches: "The Cat, the Rat, and Lovel our dog." *Anonymous.* Ruleth all England under a Hog. OxBM

Snatches: "The formest of these bestes three." *Anonymous.* But some wille I save, and some wille I not.' OxBM

Snatches: "The lovedy Fortune is bothe frend and fo." *Anonymous.* No triste no man to his wele, the wheel it turneth so. OxBM

Snatches: "The nightingale singes." *Anonymous.* That the night is to long. OxBM

Snatches: "Thei thou the wulf hore hode to preste." *Anonymous.* Evere beeth his geres to the grove grene. OxBM

Snatches: "There is none so wise a man." *Anonymous.* But some man may hime greeve. OxBM

Snatches: "There was a man that hadde nought." *Anonymous.* Here is a tale of right nought. OxBM

Snatches: "This book is one." *Anonymous.* To see my book brought home again. OxBM

Snatches: "Two wimen in one house." *Anonymous.* Two dogges and one bone/May never accorde in one. OxBM

Snatches: "Wake wel, Annot." *Anonymous.* For he is lechoure. OxBM

Snatches: "Walterius Pollard non est but a dullard." *Anonymous.* I say that Pollard is none mery gollard. OxBM

Snatches: "Wel were him that wiste." *Anonymous.* Bet were him that knewe/The false fro the trewe. OxBM

Snatches: "Wela! qwa sal thir hornes blau." *Anonymous.* Now is he dede and lies law/Was wont to blaw thaim ay. OxBM

Snatches: "What shul these clothes thus manifold." *Anonymous.* Litel therof he shal distraine. OxBM

Snatches: "What! why didest thou wink." *Anonymous.* But he stare afterward, wonder me thinketh. OxBM

Snatches: "When Adam dalf and Eve span." *Anonymous.* Who was tho a gentelman? OxBM

Snatches: "When ye see the sunne amis." *Anonymous.* But if God of his goodnesse graunt us a trewe. OxBM

Snatches: "Whenne bloweth the brom." *Anonymous.* Thenne woweth he wurs. OxBM

Snatches: "Whenne I thenke thinges three." *Anonymous.* I ne wot whider I shal fare. OxBM

Snatches: "Whil that I was sobre." *Anonymous.* But in drunkeshipe I dide/The werste that mighten been thought. OxBM

Snatches: "Who so cometh to any hous." *Anonymous.* And say him sooth in his presence. OxBM

Snatches: "Who that lust for to looke." *Anonymous.* That this sette on youire booke behinde. OxBM

Snatches: "Winter alle etes." *Anonymous.* And ever bereth the fox the box of all good/thewes. OxBM

Snatches: "Wit hat wonder and kind ne can." *Anonymous.* For might hath maistry and skill goth under. OxBM

Sneeze on a Monday, You Sneeze for Danger. *Anonymous.* For you will have trouble the whole of the week. EvOK; HBV 1-2; HBVY; NLV

Sneezing. Marie Louise Allen. Ahh–CHOO!–Ahh–CHOO! SoPo

Sneezing. [James Henry] Leigh Hunt. Snuff is a delicous thing. HBV 1-2

Sniff. Frances Frost. and poke our noses into flowers! BrR; SiSoSe; TiPo

Snips and Snails and Puppydog Tails. *Anonymous.* That's what little boys are made of. TW

The Snitterjipe. James Reeves. Only his fearsome prints are seen. AmMo

Snoring. Aileen Fisher. with the noises they make. SoPo

The Snoring Bedmate. *Anonymous.* Would that one of us were dead! BIrV

Snow. Elizabeth Akers. Peace and I are at home, at home! HBV 1-2

Snow. Dorothy Aldis. And all the trees have silver skirts/And want to dance away. TiPo

Snow. *Anonymous.* White as allyblaster. GBP

Snow. Margaret Avison. The rest may ring our change, sad listener. NOBC

Snow. Fay Chiang. under lamplight in city streets. BrSi

Snow. Elizabeth Jane Coatsworth. and shouts, "Well, good-bye now! I'm going!" SiSoSe

Snow. Adelaide Crapsey. Of wintry wind...look up, and scent/The snow! QFR

The Snow. Robert Creeley. through the last echo of hurting,/brought now home. AP

Snow. Walter De la Mare. A robin shrills/His lonely tune. OnUR

The Snow. Clifford Dyment. And no way that I chose to go/Could lead me from the grief of snow. MoVE

Snow. Nan Fry. the scooped-out insides of waves. PPJ

The Snow. Donald Hall. and something will always be falling. NePoEA-2; NMP

Snow. John Kelleher. And hide Great Oak Hill from sight? ELU

The Snow. Sidney Keyes. Stumbles and cries like any lonely lover. NeBP

Snow. Archibald Lampman. Plod dumbly on, and dream. PeCV

Snow. Louis MacNeice. There is more than glass between the snow and the huge roses. BiP; CIP; CMoP; ExPo; FaBoIP; FaBoMo; FPL; LiTM; NoAm; NOBE; OBSP; OxBTC

Snow. David Malouf. ...Its brightness/creaks under our shoes. CBAP

Snow. Ralph Pomeroy. ...Hoses,/lax in their dreams of spring,/sleep deep. Psk

Snow. W. R. Rodgers. The bomb domanial in the dome of blue. LiTM

Snow. Ruth Stone. ...Still the old lady shakes her puff/In the well of the wind, and feathers fly from the rip. NYBP

Snow. Edward ("Edward Eastaway") Thomas. On the child crying for the bird of the snow. FaBoTw; MoVE

Snow. Alice Wilkins. But did not make a single sound! TiPo

Snow. Charles Wright. White ants, white ants and the little ribs. LCAP

Snow Anthology. Arthur Stanley Bourinot. The edition is limited/and will soon be out of print. GoYe

The Snow-Ball. Petronius Arbiter (Caius Petronius Arbiter). But not with water, ice, nor snow,/But with an equal fire. LiTW; OBVE

The Snow-Ball. Thomas Stanley. That by snow were set on fire. CavP

The Snow-Bird. Frank Dempster Sherman. Keeps him from walking on the snow/And printing it with stars. SiSoSe; SoPo; TiPo

Snow-Bound. John Greenleaf Whittier.
And down his querulous challenge sent. TrGrPo
And, pausing, takes with forehead bare/The benediction of the air. AmePo; AnNE; AP; MAmP; MCCG; NOBA; OxBA; TAP
Beneath the gray November cloud. AA; WiR
The great throat of the chimney laughed. OBCP
Of Pisa's leaning miracle. AA
To make the coldness visible. TrGrPo
The welcome of thy beckoning hand? AA
Whereof she dreams and prophesies! AA

Snow by Morning. May Swenson. a new loaf on every doorsill. NYBP

Snow Country. Dave Etter. Wyoming/ from the train/yesterday. AmFN

Snow Country Weavers. James Welch. those webs were filled with words/that tumbled meaning into wind. CDW

Snow Crystals on Meall Glas. Elizabeth A. Wilson. Nature's philosophy/in the snow. PoSH

The Snow Curlew. Vernon Watkins. To coax, where the cry fades, fires which cannot fall. NYBP

Snow-Dance for the Dead. Lola Ridge. quick, cool kisses. AnAmPo

The Snow Fall. Archibald MacLeish. Time in the snow is at last,/Is past. LOW; PoPl

Snow Fell with a Will. Richard Gillman. Nothing ours or what made earth seem ours to bless/Ever seemed ours less. NePoAm-2

Snow Fence. Ted Kooser. but neither has it/much to carry. PPJ

The Snow-Filled Nest. Rose Terry Cooke. The nest is full of snow. OBCA

Snow-Flakes. Mary Mapes Dodge. 'Tis summer!"–and it melts away. HBVY

Snow-Flakes. Henry Wadsworth Longfellow. Now whispered and revealed/To wood and field. `AnNE; AP; FaBoRV; FPL; MAmP; NOBA; PoEL 1-5; TAP; UnPo; WiR

Snow Geese in the Wind. Philip Dow. as scattered geese/suddenly weave a line of flight/from the wind's release. NPGG

Snow-Girl. Yunna Mortiz. And we are children. Grant us a little Spring! VWA

The Snow-Gum. Douglas Stewart. Flows where the green tree perfectly/Curves to its perfect shadow. PoAu 1-2

Snow Harvest. Andrew Young. While bushes weep loud tears to see it go. BoNaP

A Snow in Jerusalem. Hayim Naggid. And I went in the snow/That became mud/To the school/In the German Colony. VWA

Snow in New York. May Swenson. Hoses/were coming to whip back to water, wash to the sewers the/nuisance-freight. NYP

Snow in October. Alice Dunbar-Nelson. As a premature grief grays the strong head/Of a virile, red-haired man. BlSi; CDC

Snow in the City. Rachel Field. Can do a thing about the snow/But let it fall! TiPo

Snow in the City. Danny Siegel. like a wedding/of Heaven and Earth. VWA

Snow in the Suburbs. Thomas Hardy. A black cat comes, wide-eyed and thin;/And we take him in. BoNaP; CMoP; GoJo; MoAB; MoBrPo; OAEL 1-2; OBMV; OxBTC; PPP

The Snow-Leopard. Randall Jarrell. At all that he is: the heart of heartlessness. LiTM; MoPo; MP; TwCP

The Snow Lies Sprinkled on the Beach. Robert Bridges. The tossing of his mournful waves/Makes sweetest music evermore. NoAm

The Snow Light. May Sarton. Echoing the light/After you were gone/Of our white-on-white. NLV

The Snow-Man. Marian Douglas. Than be a man who walks with men,/But has a frozen heart! OBCA

The Snow Man. Wallace Stevens. Nothing that is not there and the nothing that is. AP; CMoP; CoBMV; CrMA; ForPo; GoJo; HaCAP; HAP; HeIP; MAT; NoP; NU; PrIm; QFR; SoSe

The Snow on Saddle Mountain. Gary Snyder. the only faint source of hope/is the snow on Kurakake mountain. NoAm; NOBA

The Snow Party. Derek Mahon. But there is silence/In the houses of Nagoya/And the hills of Ise. CIP; FaBoIP; FaBoPV; OxBC

Snow Queen's Portrait. Ruth Berman. Branching from the brilliant/Radiating cold. PoDr

The Snow-Shower. William Cullen Bryant. At rest in the dark and silent lake. AnNE; HBV 1-2

Snow, Snow. Marge Piercy. and the emerging earth drones bass. AMV-81

Snow, Snow Faster. Anonymous. Selling the feathers a penny a piece. PBBP

The Snow-Storm. Ralph Waldo Emerson The frolic architecture of the snow. AA; AnNE; AP; BLPL; DiPo; FaBoBe; GN; GoTF; LaNeLa; LiTA; MAmP; NePA; NOBA; OxBA; PoEL 1-5; PoLf; Prf; TreFT; UnPo; WiR

Snow Storm. Sister Mary Madeleva. Mine are white with swans from Galway. GoBC

The Snow Storm. Edna St. Vincent Millay. Where close to earth like mice we go/Under the horizontal snow. PoA

Snow Storm. Tu Fu. I brood on the uselessness of letters. NaP

Snow Toward Evening. Melville Cane. Fell with the falling night. SUS; TiPo

Snow Train. Louise Erdrich. Here is the bleak radiance that levels the world. TWSS

Snow White. Olga Broumas. Receive/me, Mother. DFT

Snow White. Robert M. Chute. but none-the-less a mirror for a life/that is less substantial than reflection. DFT

Snow White. Robert Gillespie. where the men on white horse DFT

Snow White. Ed Ochester. remodels the little cottage in the woods/with gingerbread. GP

Snow White and the Seven Dwarfs. Roald Dahl. Which shows that gambling's not a sin/Provided that you always win. DFT

Snow White and the Seven Dwarfs. Anne Sexton. and sometimes referring to her mirror/as women do. DFT; HaCAP

Snowbanks North of the House. Robert Bly. No one knows why he came, or why he turned away, and did not climb the hill. LCAP

The Snowbound City. John Haines. their faces glowing with disaster. EAS

The Snowdrop. Anna Bunston de Bary. Then you must, please,/Fall on your knees. HBMV

Snowdrop. Ted Hughes. Her pale head heavy as metal. FaBoMo

A Snowdrop. Harriet Prescott Spofford. It lifts again its spotless star. GN

Snowdrop. William Wetmore Story. And love me truly, just one minute. HBV 1-2

Snowdrops. George MacBeth. I feel its energy, its calm. OBCP

Snowfall. Artis Bernard. falling snow. NTCP

Snowfall. Giosue Carducci.
Down to the silence I come, in the shadow I will rest. AWP
Soon to the silence I come, soon in the shades to repose. PoPl

A Snowfall. Richard Eberhart. But to take this softness and this plenitude/As aesthetic, and control it as it falls. FiCP

Snowfall. "I. V. S. W." Do you think, perhaps, that some one/Would say that I was fair? InMe

The Snowfall. Donald Justice. Falling softly about our ears/In childhood, never believed till now. NePoEA-2; VGW

Snowfall. William Stanley Merwin. and a single footprint/brother NNaP

Snowfall. Hone Tuwhare. Why not...Oh, come in, Spring. OCNZ

Snowfall: A Poem about Spring. James Wright. We are not afraid of you, we will come out/And gather with you. LCAP

Snowfall: Four Variations. George Amabile. out of the dark ages of the sky. NYBP

Snowfall in the Afternoon. Robert Bly. All the sailors on deck have been blind for many years. CAPP; EAS; NMP; NOBA

The Snowfish. Edward Field. Today's the day when wise men see/The snowfish frisking in the snow. GrPl

The Snowflake. Walter De la Mare. Breathe, and I vanish/Instantly. NCSH

Snowflake on Asphodel. Conrad Aiken. love, these are you and I—enter this portal. CMoP

The Snowflake Which Is Now and Hence Forever. Archibald MacLeish. They also live/Who swerve and vanish in the river. NoP

Snowflakes. Alice Behrend. Earth holds her breath to hear/White silence on white silence, whirl. GoYe

Snowflakes. Henrietta Robins Eliot. 'T is summer!"—and it melts away. AA

Snowflakes. Howard Nemerov. Perfected in the moment of his fall. HaCAP; PCP

Snowflakes. Clive Sansom. And passes like a rhyme. OBCP

Snowgoose. Paula Gunn Allen. (North wind blowing.) TWSS

The Snowing of the Pines. Thomas Wentworth Higginson. The snow-flakes drop as lightly—snows on/snows. AA; GN

Snowman. Andrew McCord Jones. people tell/of the melting/man. LFAC

The Snowman. P.K. Page. in a landscape without love. NOBC

The Snowman's Resolution. Aileen Fisher. And it didn't mind the sun! SoPo

Snowstorm. John Clare. And little feel boys o'er their heads can stray. BoNaP; WiR

The Snowstorm. Pearl Riggs Crouch. Exultant shriek the demons of the gale! BPAW; PoOW

The Snowstorm. Frederick George Scott. And here is the long white winter road/And the silent woods. PeCV

Snowy Egret. Bruce Weigl. ...blasting/Such beauty into nothing. MAYP

Snowy Night. John Haines. the moon is anchored/like a ghost/in heavy chains. NCSH

The Snuff-Boxes. Anonymous. "Round, sir, on Sundays, square on other days." StPo

So? Alvin Greenberg. and that significance precedes us—me—through the night FAZ

So? James P. Vaughn. Then will such bright candles as these/Be not held hostages too soon. AmNP

So-and-So Reclining on Her Couch. Wallace Stevens. ...Good-bye,/Mrs. Pappadopoulos, and thanks. AmPP; LiTM; NOBA

So Be My Passing. William Ernest Henley. Death. HBVY

So Beautiful Is the Tree of Night. Pauline Hanson. I watch from century and from century. TAP

So Beautiful You Are, Indeed. Irene Rutherford McLeod. Each calling on the other's name! HBMV

So Big! Max Fatchen. I'm glad he lived so long ago/And didn't live in my day! AmMo

So Close Should Be Our Love. Anonymous. As near as seed to fruit,/So close should be our love. WTO

So Fair, So Sweet, Withal So Sensitive. William Wordsworth. Be Thou to love and praise alike impelled,/Whatever boon is granted or withheld. EnRP; NoP

So Far, So Near. Christopher Pearse Cranch. Silence only may adore thee! TrPWD

So Fast Entangled. Anonymous. Than break one hair to gain her liberty. EG; TrGrPo

So Fly by Night. Charles Osborne. and bless, promiscuous truth,/the day we meet. BoAV

So Graven. Josephine Miles. And there's the trick simplicity has to win. NoAm

So Handy. Anonymous. Oh, we'e the boys that'll do it once more!/Handy, me boys, so handy! ShS

So Handy, Me Boys, So Handy. Anonymous. And we'll make her go through frost and snow,/Handy, me boys, so handy. AmFP

So Have I Spent on the Banks of Ysca Many a Serious Hour. Thomas Vaughan. May every holy, happy, hearty tear/Help me to run to Heaven, as thou dost there. FaBoPP

So Help Me God. Caius Valerius Catullus. ...she'd fondle a diseased/Hangman and lick him anywhere he pleased. DBV

So I Let Her Go. Anonymous. I don't care a fig for her, so now let her go. AmFP

So I Said I Am Ezra. Archie Randolph Ammons. ...dunes/of unremembered seas NoAm; NOBA; NoP

So in Love. Cole Porter. So in love with you, my love am I. BLSo

So It Begins. James Agee. Adam is in this earth. So it begins. ATP

So it Happens. Irving Feldman. —and yearn indeed to become/those pure incalculable names. GP

So Late Removed from Him She Swore. Walter Savage Landor. These let her feel!...nor these too oft! OBRV

So Let Me Hence. William Ernest Henley. Accept the past, and be forever at rest. EnLit

So Little and So Much. John Oxenham. Only in hope of they redeeming grace/I live. BLRP

So Little Wanted. Cid Corman. And in the name of/God–abandon hope. GP

So Live, So Love, So Use That Fragile Hour. Robert Louis Stevenson. The poor survivor may not weep and wake. NOBV

So lonely am I. Ono no Komachi. I would follow it, I think. BoWoP; PBWP

So Long. Jayne Cortez. so long to love/so long BoWoP

So Long. William Stafford. ...and all that we'll have/to love may be what's near/in the cold, even then. PPJ

So Long! Walt Whitman. I am as one disembodied, triumphant, dead. AmP

So Long Ago. Morris Rosenfeld. It was so long ago... TrJP

So Long as Time & Space Are the Stars. Michael Silverton. I think you're great. PV

So Long Folks, Off to the War. Anthony Ostroff. With a glad, sad–I still don't know. NePoAm-2; PoPl

So Long Solon. Jack Myers. every inch of your life is like theirs, you move out. AmPA

So Look the Mornings. Robert Herrick. As Julia looks when she doth dress/Her either cheek with bashfulness. ELP

So, Man? Gene Derwood. Forget not the one potter and...the...lathe. NePA

So Many Feathers. Jayne Cortez. so many feathers i remember/Josephine Josephine BlSi

So Many Monkeys. Dorothy and Marion Edey Grider. You're a monkey, too! SoPo; TiPo

So Might It Be. John Galsworthy. Spring in the world when you fetch me/away! BLPL; PoLf

So Oft As I Her Beauty Do Behold. Edmund Spenser. Then sith to heaven ye lykened are the best,/Be lyke in mercy as in all the rest. BoLiVe

So proud she was to die. Emily Dickinson. Immediately–that Anguish stooped/Almost to Jealousy– NOBA

So Quicke, So Hot, So Mad Is Thy Fond Sute. Thomas Campion. But never, as you dreame, in bed, or grave. NCEP; PoEL 1-5

"So Quietly". Leslie Pinckney Hill. Stern truth will never write, "By hands unknown." BANP; IDB; PoBA

So Runs Our Song. Mary Eva Kitchel. Spit in his face, and pass him by. PGD

So Small Are the Flowers of Seamu. Anonymous. To see you, is more than food or drink. PBWP

So, So. William Clerke. Such is the sad disparity of time. ELP

So Sr. Henry Vane the Younger. John Milton. Therfore on thy firme hand religion leanes/In peace, and reck'ns thee her eldest son. OBS

So Sweet Love Seemed. Robert Bridges. How love so young could be so sweet. EnLit; FaBV; GTBS; HBV 1-2; LiTL

So That Even a Lover. Louis Zukofsky. 44 years to do. CoPo

So That's Who I Remind Me Of. Ogden Nash. Yet I write so much like me. BLPL; PoLf

So Then, I Feel Not Deeply! Walter Savage Landor. The Muse's mother, nurses, rears them up,/Informs, and keeps them with her all her days. EnRP

So They Went Deeper in the Forest. Roy Daniells. Unhindered, unresisted, unwithstood. WHW

So This Is Autumn. W. W. Watt. The colorings of autumn leaves. PoPl

So This Is Our Revolution. Sonia Sanchez. go to the moon/where they belong. GP

So through That Unripe Day You Bore Your Head. Philip Larkin. ...pastime of a provincial winter. NoAm

So Tir'd Are All My Thoughts. Thomas Campion. Virtue dies with too much rest. LoBV

So to Tell the Truth. Janet Dube. my silvery tail BrRo

So Touch Our Hearts with Loveliness. Gail Brook Burket. For all the love encompassing/Thy children constantly. AH

So unwarely was never no man caught. Sir Thomas Wyatt. This restless life I may not lead. FCP; SiPS

So Wags the World. Ellen Mackay Hutchinson Cortissoz. So wags the good old world away/Forever and a day. AA

So, We'll Go No More a Roving. George Gordon, Lord Byron. Yet we'll go no more a roving/By the light of the moon. AnFE; AtBAP; AWP; BLPL; BoLoP; ELP; ERoP 1-2; ExPo; FaFP; FF; FiP; HAP; HeIP; InPo; LiTB; LoBV; MBW 1-2; MyFE; NOBE; NoP; OAEL 1-2; OAEP; OBNC; OBRV; OBSP; OLR; OxBS; PoEL 1-5; PoPle; PoRA; PrIm; SeCeV; TreFS; ViBoPo; WeW; WHA

So We've Come at Last to Freud. Alice Walker. What we do have/Is Good. IHMS

So Well I Love Thee, as Without Thee I. Michael Drayton. As I therein no other's face but yours can view. EnRePo; GBL

So What (parody). Philip Appleman. We tasted, then chose ours. BXAP

So, When I Swim to the Shore. Molly Peacock. I own every blue day I'm not a part of. MAYP

So Young Ane King. Sir David Lindsay. I pray God let me never see ryng/Into this realm so young ane King. SeCePo

Soap (II). Jerome Rothenberg. There were always towns like that NNaP

Soap Suds. Louis MacNeice. Under the running tap that are not the hands of a child. FaBoIP; FaBoMo; NOBI; NoP; SCV

Soap, the Oppressor. Burges Johnson. And no one would complain about the parts of me that show. PoLf

Soaping Down for Saint Francis of Assisi: The Canticle of Sister Soap. Gibbons Ruark. In this room of the profane and holy bargain. MAYP

Soaps. Harold Witt. give me the bad new days. SOTS

Soaring. Cal Clothier. where a raven was soaring upside down/under the river, the rocks, the heather... PoSH

Sob, Heavy World. W. H. Auden. The grass that fades. DTC

Soccer. Andrei Voznesensky. "Well, so what–/it was a shot! A shot–/that's all that matters." LiSp

The Social Future. John Kells Ingram. And planned the work it will be yours to do. OnYI

Social Note. Dorothy Parker. Lady, lady, better run! FaBoUs; InMe

Social Science. Thomas Edward Brown. No carrack ever bore to Thames or Tiber. PeD

Social Studies. Mary Neville. "No," said Mother. PoL

The Society upon the Stanislow. Bret (Francis Bret Harte) Harte. That broke up our Society upon the Stanislow. AA; BeLS; BPAW; HBV 1-2; InMe; MaC; OBAL

Sockeye Salmon. Ronald Hambleton. In their prostituting mutual sight. CaP; OBCV

Socrates' Ghost Must Haunt Me Now. Delmore Schwartz. –Old Noumenon, come true, come true! AnFE; LiTM

Socrates Prays a Day and a Night. George O'Neil. His head sank, and a radiance flowed. AnAmPo

Socrates Snooks. Fitz Hugh Ludlow. "My dear, may we put on our new Sunday breeches?" BLPA

Socratic. Hilda ("H. D.") Doolittle. "Why,/the bees." AnEnPo; HoPM

The Sod-Breaker. Arthur Stringer. Like a thousand girls with golden hair/Are singing at his side! CaP

Sodom. Chaim Grade. The clouds hasten away from Sodom. TrJP

Sodom; or, The Quintessence of Debauchery (excerpt). John Wilmot, Earl of Rochester. She turns into corruption and disease. PeHV

Sodom's Sister City. Yehuda Amichai. the calm petals around the stem:/God! VWA

Soeur Marie Emilie. Caryll Houselander. and as clean and blue. BoC

The Sofa. Mebdh McGuckian. My books sleep, pretending to forget me. FaBoIP

Soft Answers. Robert Bagg. Like a giant heart toying with my bones. FF; UnTE

Soft-Boiled Egg. Russell Hoban. And I could do for many days/Without eggs. NTCP

A Soft Day. Winifred M. Letts. Drips, drips, drips from the leaves. AnIV; OnYI

Soft Falls the Sweet Evening. John Clare. I'm no longer weary/But happy and cheery/For in thee I meet all. NOBV

Soft Job. William C. Summers. To Jesus Christ our Lord, and God,/The hearts and souls of men. STF

Soft Landings. Howard Sergeant. To home and friends and everything/That gives your mission worth. OnUR

Soft-Man 1. Ed Sanders. & a man lurches out/coughing puke. ANYP

Soft-Man 3. Ed Sanders. The Board votes:/Turn control reset dials to Blob Culture. ANYP

Soft Snow. William Blake. And the winter called it a dreadful crime. AtBAP; FF; SoSe; WeW

Soft White. Lee Harwood. in winter grey as her eyes. EAS

Soft Wood. Robert Lowell. each drug that numbs alerts another nerve to pain. LiTM

Softened by time's consummate plush. Emily Dickinson. That devasted childhood's realm,/So easy to repair. NOBA

Softening to Heaven. Raymond Filip. A morning's work of carpentry,/A miracle enough for me. CaPN

Softly, Drowsily. Walter De la Mare. And out she tumbles/From her warm bed. SoPo; SUS

Softly Fades the Twilight Ray. Samuel Francis Smith. Where the Sabbath ne'er shall close. AH

Softly Softly. Richard Shelton. softly my friend/softly NPAW

Softly the Evening (parody). William Hurrell Mallock. With a little gift of sand.' BXAP

Softly through the Mellow Starlight. Charles L. Hutchins. Christ the Lord is ris'n to-day. OHIP

Softly, White and Pure. Dorothy R. Fulton. road and tree and house are one. AMV-80

Softly Woo Away Her Breath. Bryan Waller Procter. Take her, then, for evermore,–/For ever–evermore. HBV 1-2

LiTB; MaVP; NIP; NOBL; NOBV; NoP; OAEL 1-2; OAEP; SeCeV; TEP; TrGrPo; TW

Soliloquy on a Southern Strand. John Montague. Is it for this mild ending that I/Have carried, all this way, my cross? FaBoIP

Soliloquy on Death. F. K. Fiawoo. Death, are you come/To lay hands upon your prey? PBA

Soliloquy: South Africa. Arthur Nortje. It seems me speaking all the lonely time. WhB

Soliloquy I. Richard Aldington. Well, thank God for rum. BrPo

Soliloquy of a Tortoise on Revisiting the Lettuce Beds... Emile Victor Rieu. Of this delicious stuff! FiBHP

Solipsism. George Santayana. Is but the sum of dreams. AnFE; APA; CoAnAm

A Solis Ortus Cardine. Ford Madox Ford. Thro' your eternal or your finite day/Give us your prayers! ViBoPo

Solitaire. Amy Lowell. And the city is still! LaNeLa; MAPA; MoAmPo

The Solitary. Mary Barnard. bright wavelets unbroken/to the rim spread round him. FAZ

The Solitary. Friedrich Wilhelm Nietzsche. Woe unto him who has no home this night. AWP

Solitary. Sharon Olds. a witness, standing/alone/in a prison/courtyard/in Korea. SOTS

The Solitary. Rainer Maria Rilke. but here they hold their breath, as if/for shame. TrJP

The Solitary. Sara Teasdale. Who am self-complete as a flower or a stone? MoAmPo; WHA

A Solitary Canto to Chloris the Disdainful. John Smith. No, sweet Mrs. Chloris–pray excuse me for that. NOEC

Solitary Confinement. X. J. Kennedy. ...he'd nailed her fast/Between two thieves, him and herself. NePoEA-2

The Solitary-Hearted. Hartley Coleridge. She glides along–the solitary-hearted. HBV 1-2

A Solitary Life. William, of Hawthornden Drummond. Woods harmlesse Shades have only true Delights. OBS

The Solitary Lyre. George Darley. Impart it to my solitary lyre? LiTB; OBEV

The Solitary Reaper. William Wordsworth. The music in my heart I bore,/Long after it was heard no more. AnEnPo; AtBAP; AWP; BLPL; BoLiVe; DiPo; EnLit; ERoP 1-2; ExPo; FaBoCh; FaPoR; FiP; ForPo; GN; GoTF; HAP; HBV 1-2; InPo; InPS; LiTB; LiTL; LoBV; MBW 1-2; MCCG; NOBE; NoP; OAEL 1-2; OAEP; OBEV; OBNC; OBRV; PAI; PoEL 1-5; PoPle; PoRA; PPP; RoGo; SCV; SeCeV; SoSe; TEP; TreF; TrGrPo; UnPo; UnS; WeW; WHA

Solitary Song. Anonymous. Drive on and on,/On and on! WTO

Solitary Travel. Louis MacNeice. Where all tomorrows must be faced alone.... OBTV

Solitary Visions of a Kaufmanoid... James (Olumo) Cunningham. lost in a pale orbit/somewhere/(late at night) JB

The Solitary Woodsman. Sir Charles G. D. Roberts. Fellow to the falling leaves. CaP; OBCV

Solitude. James Beattie. For present pleasure soon is o'er,/And all the past is vain. OBEC

Solitude. John Clare.
And follow in thy steps to heaven. EnRP
Whose dark green oaks his noontide leisure shield. OBSP

Solitude. Walter De la Mare. Soft as its own may be, beyond the pale. CMoP

Solitude. Babette Deutsch. Yet I have known no loneliness like this,/Locked in your arms and bent beneath your kiss. HBMV

Solitude. James Grainger.
Allay the pangs of age, and smooth thy grave. CEP
Wake you with her solemn strain,/And teach pleas'd Echo to complain. OBEC

Solitude. John Keats. When to thy haunts two kindred spirits flee. EnRP

Solitude. Archibald Lampman. His five pure notes succeeding pensively. BoNaP; CBEP; ExPo; OBCV; PeCV

A Solitude. Denise Levertov. ...it is filled/with presences. He says, I am. NePoEA-2

Solitude. Mary Mollineux. The music of the morning stars/Here in their hearts did sound. CavP

Solitude. Harold Monro. Solitude walks one heavy step more near. BSV; MoBrPo; TrGrPo

Solitude. Hannah More. And angels point the way to peace. WBLP

Solitude. Frederick Peterson. The strange hereditary sigh/Of age on age of loneliness. AA

Solitude. Rainer Maria Rilke. then solitude flows onward with the/rivers... TrJP

Solitude. Philip Henry Savage. Shall see almost a forest. AA

Solitude. Edward Rowland Sill. God shall speak to thee out of the sky. AnNE

Solitude. Charles Simic. And setting out to visit you. GP

Solitude. Thomas Traherne. ...Oh, where/Shall I thee find to ease my Mind? Oh, where? OBS

Solitude. Ella Wheeler Wilcox. ...we must all file on/Through the narrow aisles of pain. AmePo; FaFP; FPL; HBV 1-2; OHFP; PaPo; PoLf; YaD

Solitude and the Lily. Richard Henry Horne. And, if illusion, feel it true. OBVV

Solitude Late at Night in the Woods. Robert Bly. Giving off the odor that partridges love. BiP; VGW

Solitudes. John Hall Wheelock. One thought soars like a hawk, in the heaven of my mind. MoLP

Solo for Bent Spoon. Donald. Finkel. Fixed by the needle in his bowels/Just as the literal sun went down. NePoEA-2

Solo for Ear-Trumpet. Edith Sitwell. Those boy-scouts practicing again! MoAB; MoBrPo

Solo Native. Thomas Lux. an awkward first audible/called language. LCAP

Solomon. Hermann Hagedorn. Only the steadfast and the true/Find that which is forever new. GoBC

Solomon. Heinrich Heine. But if thou love me not, I languish/and I die. TrJP

Solomon and Morolph, Their Last Encounter. Oscar Levertin. Who am the first-born of night's pain. VWA

Solomon and the Bees. John Godfrey Saxe. As Israel's King learned wisdom from the bees. GN

Solomon and the Witch. William Butler Yeats. O! Solomon! let us try again.' NoAm

Solomon Grundy. Mother Goose. This is the end of/Solomon Grundy. HBVY

Solomon: Inspiration. Anonymous. For everyone knew them in the Lord, and they lived by the/water of life forever./Hallelujah. WGRP

Solomon on the Vanity of the World. Matthew Prior.
For ever from that fatal tree debarred,/Which flaming swords and angry cherubs guard. EiCP
From Earth all came, to Earth must all return;/Frail as the Cord, and brittle as the Urn. NOEC; PoEL 1-5
If in the Schools or Porches should appear/The fierce Hyaena, or the foaming Bear? FM

Solomon to Sheba. William Butler Yeats. There's not a thing but love can make/The world a narrow pound. CMoP; ELP

Solomon: To Truth. Anonymous. And by the discovery of His planting and by the thought of/His mind./Hallelujah. WGRP

Solon's Song. Thomas D"Urfey. What Pleasure like Hunting can cherish the Soul. CEP

The Solsequium. Alexander Montgomerie. Farewell, with patience perforce till day. GoTS; NoP; OxBS

Solstice. Emery George. birth is its dying. HoAn

Solstice. Charles Weekes. The day is tired. OnYI

Solstitium Saeculare. Robert Fitzgerald. Peace to the heart's rage. MoVE

Soluble Noughts and Crosses; or, California, Here I Come. Roger Roughton. For love has grown up like a hair.' EAS

Solution. Ralph Waldo Emerson. So bloom the unfading petals five,/And verses that all verse outlive. OBAL

Solutions. David Barton. and wait for nothing to happen,/as nothing will. AMV-81

Solvitur Acris Hiems. Francis Sylvester ("Father Prout") Mahony. Who then, when thou art gone, will fire all bosoms/most! IrPN

Some Are Born. Stevie Smith. But only for a day as we/Shall not be here tomorrow. FaBoCo

Some Bird. Anonymous. They expect him to live/On the food of a canary. STF

Some Blesseds. John Oxenham. Blessed is the people whose heart is set on God,/It shall STAND. WGRP

Some Bombs (excerpt). Ron Padgett. The plays here at Mort author of News ANYP

Some Boys. Chuck Ortleb. masturbating in the twilight as though they were landing a 747. PeHV

Some Boys. John Penketman. Nothing but what is chaste becomes a child. OxBChV

Some Contemplations of the Poor, and Desolate State of the Church... John Williams. Thy Rich and Sovereign Grace, we will proclaim. SCAP

Some Day. Medora C. Addison. Then may I too find words to voice your praise–/But oh, not yet, not yet. HBMV

Some Day. Shel Silverstein. Today I've got the saddle. PH

Some Day or Days. Nora Perry. Its lonely, yearning years,/Shall vanish in the moment of that meeting. HBV 1-2

Some Day, Some Day. Cristobal de Castillejo. No more distressed,/Shalt thou find rest. AWP

Some Days. Maureen Owen. "And to think of the Grande Affaire I gave up for it! Lawdy! APU

Some Days/Out Walking above. De Leon Harrison. CREATION PoBA

Some Dreams They Forgot. Elizabeth Bishop. But their dreams are all inscrutable by eight or nine. NoAm

"God be kind to the noble boy,/Who is somebody's son, and pride and joy!" BeLS; BLPA; FaFP; TreF

Somebody Said That It Couldn't Be Done. *Anonymous.* And he couldn't do it. FiBHP

Somebody (with music). *Anonymous* Somebody asked me to marry him,/ 'Course I said, "All right." AS

Someday Baby. Big Joe Williams. You can steal my best woman/but you sure can't make her stay BluL

"Somedays now". Wendy G. Rickert. So I shook my head/and just didn't look around. NMM

Somehow, Somewhere, Sometime. Winifred M. Letts. The great surprise of death–sometime! HBMV

Somehow We Survive. Dennis Brutus. but somehow tenderness survives. WhB

Someone. John Ciardi. Right again: Eight...Nine...and...! BiCB

Someone. Walter De la Mare. So I know not who came knocking,/At all, at all, at all. MoBrPo

Someone Could Certainly Be Found. F. R. Scott. Forgot to close my hungry eyes/After giving them this wasted passion. CaP

Someone Gave Him Some Plastic Flowers Once. Dennis Shady. Grandson, he said, if that is true/then these flowers are like the whiteman. LFAC

Someone, I tell you. Sappho. yet are always saved/by judgment of good men. BoWoP

Someone Knocks. Peter Everwine. and your father sleeps in his own name. NNaP

Someone Like No One Else. Forugh Farrokhzad. And he'll give us all a share/I dreamed– WPOW

Someone Sits at the Harp. Jon Lang. ...And there are no words. AMV-81

Someone Talking. Joy Harjo. What voice/in the warm grass of her belly,/ What planet? TWSS

Someplace Else. Marge Piercy. in the sea that is salty like our blood. NeAC

Somersault. Dorothy Aldis. And every little buttercup/Looks down at me instead of up. SoPo

The Somerset Dam for Supper. John Holmes. I'm the father, and at fifty-six I know more, that's all. NYBP

Somerset Wassail. *Anonymous.* God bless all in this house till we do come again. OBET

Something. Robert Creeley. ...What/love might learn from such a sight. NaP

Something. Jared Smith. and that the earth will slide down farther down its swollen river. AMV-81

Something about It. John Hollander. A child will go on being tortured. GP

Something Else. Michael Brownstein. (When I am 28 I will be many) ANYP

Something for Jesus. Sylvanus D. Phelps. Through all eternity,/Something for Thee. BLRP

Something for My Russian Friends. Edmund Wilson. Or even a velvet-eyed lemur. OBAL
Transplanted her clear to Albania. OBAL

Something for Supper. Carroll Arnett. ...It/will be there/ahead of me, long/before I am. VoR

Something Has Fallen. Philip Levine. that turned all five fingers/to grease or black ink or ashes. LCAP

Something in Common. Richard Church. My way lies southward. Good day, brother. MoRP

Something Is Bound to Happen. W. H. Auden. Lucky with day approaching, with leaning dawn. CoBMV; OAEP; PoRA

Something Is Dying Here. Thomas McGrath. The poison of their own sweet country has brought them here. TAT

Something Is There. Lilian Moore. Something is coming and wants to get by. WSC

Something Starting Over. Thomas Hornsby Ferril. The old myth-makers, starting something over. AnAmPo

Something to Eat. Tom Veitch. No less true of course, no matter/how you look at it. ANYP

Something Told the Wild Geese. Rachel Field. Summer sun was on their wings,/Winter in their cry. BrR; NTCP; OBCA; OnUR; PoSC; SiSoSe; TiPo; YeAr

Something Very Elegant. Aileen Fisher. but something that is just my size:I'm eight. BiCB

Something You Can Do. *Anonymous.* "Here am I, send me, send me." STF

Sometime. May Riley Smith. I think that we will say, "God knew the best!" BLPA; HBV 1-2

Sometime during Eternity. Lawrence Ferlinghetti. from the usual unreliable sources/real dead CAPP; NoAm

Sometime I Loved. *Anonymous.* That they might sing with mery hert/This song with us in fere. OxBM

Sometime I sigh, sometime I sing. Sir Thomas Wyatt. And never to change you for no new. FCP; SiPS

Sometime It May Be. Arthur Colton. Else why these low graves laid so near,/In this forgotten place? HBV 1-2

Sometime Lively Gerald. Richard Stanyhurst. Thogh tumbd bee carcasse in towne of martyred Alban. NCEP

Sometime–Somewhere. Ophelia Guyon Browning. And cires, "It shall be done, sometime, somewhere!" BLRP; STF

Sometimes. Annie Johnson Flint. The peril that His care permits/Is our defence where'er we go. STF

Sometimes. Rose Fyleman. Anything might happen on a truly fairy night. SiSoSe

Sometimes. Herman Hesse. ...How should I reply? NU; WSC

Sometimes. Thomas S. Jones, Jr. I wonder if he hopes to see/The man I might have been. GoTF; HBV 1-2; TreFT; TRV

Sometimes a Little House Will Please. Elizabeth Jane Coatsworth. Creaks the small rocking chair. BrR

Sometimes Heaven Is a Mean Machine. William Pitt Root. It shines and you ride its shining. MAYP

Sometimes I Feel Like a Motherless Child. *Anonymous.* A long ways from home. BLSo; BoAN 1-2; FSW

Sometimes I Go to Camarillo & Sit in the Lounge. K. Curtis Lyle. the rivers of time/and/space PoBA

Sometimes I Think of Maryland... Jodi Braxton. and waits for a child/to burden with this heritage. CNA

Sometimes I Walk where the Deep Water Dips. Frederick Goddard Tuckerman. Hoar with salt-sleet and chalkings of the birds. NOBA

Sometimes I Want to Go Up. Rachel Korn. will bury only me/and my sorrow. VWA

Sometimes I Wish That I Were Helen-Fair. Lesbia Harford. And in this heavenly wife might deem himself/Not blest, but lonely. NOAV

A Sometimes Love Poem. George Leong. to eat my rice alone BrSi

Sometimes on My Way Back Down to the Block. Victor Hernandez Cruz. I Like to Fight/Sometimes on My Way Back to the Block. BOLo

Sometimes When I Sit Musing All Alone. Agnes Mary Frances (Mme Emile Duclaux) Robinson. The vision of eternity is strange. WHA

Sometimes when Night... Victoria Mary (Vita) Sackville-West. ...since the mark was not/Your heart or mine, not this time, my companion. SBG

Sometimes With One I Love. Walt Whitman. Yet out of that I have written these songs.) CBEP; GBL; OBSP

Somewhere. Mrs. Major Arnold. Lies open onward to eternal day. PoToHe

Somewhere. Robert Creeley. the inside he as me saw/in the dark there. NoAm

Somewhere. Walter De la Mare. The Somewhere meant for me! BrR; FaPON

Somewhere. Ezekiel Mphahlele. Somewhere a mother will rejoice. WhB

Somewhere Down below Me Is a Street. J. J. Maloney. Somewhere down below me is a street/Where faintly can be heard the sound of feet. LFAC

Somewhere Else. Paula Rankin. it's just beginning to be dark. MAYP

Somewhere Farm. Guy Rotella. Resisting, darkly, in the dark. AMV-81

Somewhere I Chanced to Read. Gustav Davidson. ...but say love died/Out of a cold and calculating pride. HBMV

Somewhere I Have Never Travelled, Gladly Beyond. Edward Estlin Cummings. nobody, not even the rain, has such small hands. AtBAP; BoLoP; CoBMV; InPS; LiTA; LiTL; LiTM; MoAB; MoAmPo; MoPo; MP; NoP; PAI; SOTW; TrGrPo; TwCP; VGW

Somewhere Is Such a Kingdom. John Crowe Ransom. And dare I think it is absurd/If no such beast were, no such bird? CMoP; LiTA

Somewhere Near Phu Bai. Yusef Komunyakaa. ...counting/sheep before I know it. MAYP

Somewhere or Other. Christina Georgina Rossetti. With just the last leaves of the dying year/Fallen on a turf grown green. NOBE; NOBV

Somewhere the Equation Breaks Down. Daniel Berrigan. decide. Oh, coincide! NYBP

Somewhere West. Andrew McCord Jones. And still drunk/Between Fort Worth and/Home,/Somewhere west. LFAC

Somewhere You Exist. Manfred Winkler. your velvety glances,/the glances of blind steel. VWA

Somnambulistic Ballad. Federico Garcia Lorca. The horses on the hill that browse. LiTW

Somtimes. Greg Kuzma. ...the lawn/sprinklers/spinning their little silver cornets. Psk

Son. James A. Emanuel. ...even you/Might close hands with this/crew? PoNe

The Son. R. S. Thomas. ...pain not yet become grief. NAs

The Son. Ridgely Torrence. The spring was late that year,/But the harvest early. HBMV; InvP; WHA

Son and Father. C. Day Lewis. And lift my maimed creations to beg rebirth. EaLo

Son and Surf. Julia Hurd Strong. ...And I,/Remembering, can almost feel/ The sea sand sucking at his heel. GoYe

The Son, Condemned.   Larry Rubin.   And now he'll spot the withered link, and strike.   GP

Son David.   *Anonymous.*   Whan the sun an' the moon meet in yon glen,/ 'Fore I'll return again.   OxBB

Son-Dayes.   Henry Vaughan.   Of a full feast; And the Out Courts of glory. AtBAP; SeCP

A Son Just Born.   Mary Britton Miller.   But who knows the name/of the new-born son/Of the beautiful swan?   TiPo

A Son Lit.   Samuel Johnson.   Of human bliss to human woe.   FaBoEE

The Son of a Gambolier (with music).   *Anonymous.*   I'm the son of a, son of a, son of a, son of a, son of a gambolier.   AS

Son of a Gun.   *Anonymous.*   And they're more happy than you'll ever know. CoSo

Son of Erebus and Night.   William Browne.   ...Then arise,/Sagest Greek... ViBoPo

The Son of God Goes Forth to War.   Reginald Heber.   O God! to us may grace be given/To follow in their train!   HBV 1-2; TreFS

The Son of Man.   Dorothy J. Langford.   The Firstborn He, and we shall heaven fill!   BePJ

Son of the King of May.   *Anonymous.*   She gave an armful of strawberries on rushes.   AnIL

A Son of the Romanovs.   Louis Simpson.   All of those Romanovs were a little bit crazy.'   OxBC

A Son of the Sea.   Bliss Carman.   Memories of the plunging sea.   EtS

Sonatina in Yellow.   Donald Justice.   And slowly the keys grow darker to the touch.   LCAP

A Sonet: "His Golden lockes, Time hath to Silver turn'd."   George Peele. Goddesse, allow this aged man his right,/To be your Beads-man now, that was your Knight.   PoEL 1-5

A Sonet Written in Prayse of the Browne Beautie.   George Gascoigne.   A lovely nutbrowne face is best of all.   AAS; EnPo

Sonet XXV.   William Alexander, Earl of Stirling.   But yet beware lest burning with desires,/That all thy waters cannot quench thy fires.   OxBS

Song.   *Anonymous.*
   Being at once the fuel and the fire.   CBEP
   Women like some other Fruit/Lose their relish when too Mellow. ErPo

A Song.   Joel Barlow.   And peace begin.   AmPP

A Song.   Laurence Binyon.   For the spirit, born to bless,/Lives but in its own excess.   HBMV; MoBrPo

Song.   John Clare.
   False love and folly I despise.   GBL
   I'll stop and take my rest;/And love as she loves me. OBRV
   I love the fond,/The faithful, and the true.   NoP; OBVV
   Who ever would love or be tied to a wife/When it makes a man mad all the days of his/life?   VLP

A Song.   Matthew Coppinger.   Or does in aught but Nature shine.   CavP

Song.   King of Portugal Dinis.   My friend, come speedily/To fare afield. CAW

The Song.   Edward Dorn.
   these cold blue hills/sometime.   ConAP
   the whole swelling difficulty.   CoPo; VGW

A Song.   Paul Laurence Dunbar.   Where shall we meet, who knows, who knows?   AmNP

The Song.   John Erskine.   I thought I loved the song; but no!/It was her singing of it!   AA

Song.   Gerald Griffin.   Oh, dearest, remember me.   BLPA

A Song.   Hildegarde Hawthorne.   Yet newest, and sweet to learn.   AA; FaBoBe; HBV 1-2

A Song.   Ralph Hodgson.   And O! the merry laughter/Across the hayfield after!   GoJo

The Song.   David Ignatow.   bowling or collecting coins,/writing about it. CAPP

Song.   Sophie Jewett.   The forest is mute.   AA

Song.   Henry Killigrew.   Knows not when we pass by.   CH

Song.   Maria White Lowell   To waken in the sky.   AA

Song.   Thomas Macdonagh.   Sweet is boldness, shyness, pain.   ACP

Song.   John Streeter Manifold.   And you tear me to pieces by being so kind. DTC

Song.   George Meredith.   The purer passion and the firmer faith.   EnLit

Song.   Alice Duer Miller.   What more is needed,/When both forget?   AA

Song.   Sir Henry Newbolt.   And joy thereby shall like a river/Wander from deep to deep for ever.   FaBoTw

Song.   Alfred Noyes.   Little child.   CH

Song.   John Boyle O'Reilly.   All he sought and gave/I am feeling.   ACP

Song.   Frances Sargent Osgood   My heart echoes to it "I love it!"   AA

Song.   Thomas Parnell.   I cannot wish it Less.   CEP

A Song.   Thomas Percy.   Where thou were fairest of the fair.   CEP

Song.   Ambrose Philips.   Would never see her more.   CEP

The Song.   Theodore Roethke.   My lips pressed upon stone.   AP; CrMA

The Song.   Hemda Roth.   unraveling in me like/dark water.   VWA

Song.   Harold C. Sandall.   The only things we ever keep/Are what we give away.   PoToHe

A Song.   Howard Schwartz.   That haunts my buds into blossoms/My voice/into song.   VWA

Song.   Richard Brinsley Sheridan.
   And brothers in the young.   CEP
   O, what a plague is an obstinate daughter. CEP

Song.   Florence Smith.   Heaven is older than you!   BLPA

Song.   Theodore Spencer.   But Oh, if you love me, forgive me,/And none of this is true.   AnFE

Song.   Stephen Spender.   Anything and everything/Which I know and do not know!   FaBoTw

Song.   Matthew Stevenson.   Why should we then with wrinkl'd care,/Deface what Nature made so fair?   CavP

Song.   Celia Thaxter.   Wave-cradled thus and wind-caressed.   AA

The Song.   Jones Very.   Forever playing where a boy I played,/By hill and grove, by field and stream delayed.   MAmP

Song.   Francis Howard Williams.   My heart groweth heavy, and whispereth/ –"Gone."   AA

Song (2).   Edwin Rolfe.   like imaged worlds and creatures–need/nurturing always.   TrJP

Song: "A lake and a fairy boat."   Thomas Hood.   But fairies have broke their wands,/And wishing has lost its power!   HBV 1-2

Song: "A little onion lay by the fireplace."   Nicholas Moore.   O that was me, said the madman.   EAS

Song: "A rowan like a lipsticked girl."   Seamus Heaney.   And that moment when the bird sings very close/To the music of what happens.   IPY

A Song: "A song of grass."   Yehoash.   If I but live/Enough millennial years. TrJP

Song: A Spirit Haunts the Year's Last Hours.   Alfred, Lord Tennyson. Heavily hangs the tiger-lily.   AtBAP; GTBS; GTBS-P; HeIP; OAEP; OBNC; PoEL 1-5; PoPle

Song: "A sunny shaft did I behold."   Samuel Taylor Coleridge.   Far, far away!/Today! today!'   PBBP; PoSC

Song: "A violet in her lovely hair."   Charles Swain.   That hallows e'en the very ground/Beneath her feet!   HBV 1-2

Song: ""A weary lot is thine, fair maid."   Sir Walter Scott.   And adieu for evermore.'   EnLoPo; OBNC

Song: "A widow bird sate mourning for her love."   Percy Bysshe Shelley. And little motion in the air/Except the mill-wheel's sound.   NOBE; OBNC; OBSP; PoPle

Song: "A woman's face is full of wiles."   Humfrey [(or Humphrey[) Gifford. But needs must call a spade a spade.   EIL

A Song About Charleston.   *Anonymous.*   Hearts of true British mould. PAH

A Song about Great Men.   Michael Hamburger.   who won or lost their game and died.   NePoEA

A Song about Major Eatherly.   John Wain.   say only "Eatherly, we have your message."   CABL; OxBTC

Song about My Father.   Elizabeth Smither.   Leaving the sleeping scaffolding in the port.   OCNZ

A Song About Myself, st. 4.   John Keats.   He stood in his/Shoes and he wonder'd.   CoBE; DiPo; FaBoCh; InvP; PoEL 1-5; PP

A Song About Singing.   Anne Reeve Aldrich.   Be sure it cares but little for/Thy wounded, bleeding breast!   AA

Song about Whiskers.   P. G. Wodehouse.   And three cheers for the U.S.A. FiBHP

Song: "Absent from thee, I languish still."   John Wilmot, Earl of Rochester. Faithless to thee, false, unforgiven,/And lose my everlasting rest.   BoLoP; ELP; EnLoPo; GBL; LoBV; MePo; OBS; SeCePo; SeCV 1-2; ViBoPo

Song–Across the Sea.   William Allingham.   And the water's bright in a still moonlight,/As I look across the sea.   IrPN

Song: "Afternoon cooking in the fall sun."   Robert Hass.   slices of green pepper/on a bone-white dish.   AmPA

Song: "Again rejoicing Nature sees."   Robert Burns.   Thy gloom will soothe my cheerless soul,/When nature all is sad like me!   BoNaP; HBV 1-2

The Song against Grocers.   Gilbert Keith Chesterton.   The Grocer trembles; for his time,/Just like his weight, is short.   CenHV; DBV; FaBoCo

The Song Against Songs.   Gilbert Keith Chesterton.   And damn your soul alive.   ALV

Song against Women.   Willard Huntington Wright.   And I'll sing of the sea and of battle/And of men's might.   HBV 1-2

Song: "Ah hate to see de evenin' sun go down."   *Anonymous.*   Or else he wouldn't have gone so far from me,/Dog-gone it!   NAMP

Song: Ah Stay.   William Congreve.   Nor casts one pitying Look behind. AtBAP; LoBV; OBEC

Song: "Ah, vale of woe, of gloom and darkness moulded."   Rachel Morpurgo. And who, ah, who can say how sweet/they are?   TrJP

Song: "All in green went my love riding."   Edward Estlin Cummings.   my heart fell dead before.   ViBoPo

Song: "All phantoms of the day."   Robert Mezey.   And the fiery brown earth/Speaks in tongues   SUW

Song: "And can the physician make sick men well?"   *Anonymous.*   And strawberry wire/And columbine.   EIL; LoBV

Song and Science. Millicent Washburn Shinn. Thy voice shall join its world-old notes/divine. AA

Song and Wine. Bacchylides. So is each man's spirit stirred by wine. LiTW

Song: "April, April." William Watson. Weep thy golden tears! GoTF; HBV 1-2; HBVY; OBEV; OBVV; PoSC; TreF; TrGrPo

Song: "As I walked out one evening." W. H. Auden. And the deep river ran on. MoAB; MoBrPo; OAEL 1-2

A Song as Yet Unsung. Yehoash. It was not given me to sing/The song as yet unsung. TrJP

A Song at Easter. Charles Hanson Towne. If flowers can wake,/Oh, why not He? BLRP

Song at Night. Norman Nicholson. Not I, my dear, not I. FaBoTw

Song at Santa Cruz. Francis Brett Young. There was no woman in all her mountains/Wonderful as thou! HBMV

Song: "At setting day and rising morn." Allan Ramsay. By vows you're mine, by love is yours/A heart that cannot wander. HBV 1-2

Song at Summer's End. A. R. D. Fairburn. Time speaks gravely, stroke on stroke. AnNZ

Song at the Beginning of Autumn. Elizabeth Jennings. When I said autumn, autumn broke. OxBTC

Song at the Feast of Brougham Castle. William Wordsworth. "The good Lord Clifford' was the name he bore. EnRP

Song at the Skirts of Heaven. Uri Z. Greenberg. He and she/Treading with naked foot/A running burning sea. VWA

Song (Attributed to the Earl of Pembroke). George Herbert. Our Bodyes, not wee move. AnAnS 1

Song: "Awake thee, my Bessy, the morning is fair." Jeremiah Joseph Callanan. Then awake from thy slumbers, my Bessy, awake. IrPN; OnYI

Song Ballet (I Was Sixteen Years of Age). Anonymous. When you meet a nagging man,/Pitch into him like me. AmFP

Song Be Delicate. John Shaw Neilson. Death is abroad...oh, the black season!/The deep–the dim! BoAV; PoAu 1-2

Song: "Because I know deep in my own heart." Pauli Murray. I will not cry "I Love You!"–but fain/Would say, "I want you always near." BlSi

Song: "Because the rose must fade." Richard Watson Gilder. Therefore, now is to me/Eternity! HBV 1-2

A Song Before Grief. Rose Hawthorne Lathrop. A flaming torch thrown to the golden sea/by your pale hand. AA; CAW

Song: "Beloved, it is morn!" Emily Henrietta Hickey. That I may be/Faithful to God and thee. OBVV

A Song: "Boast no more fond Love, thy Power." Thomas D'Urfey. Ah, hard Fate, that I must loose her. CavP

Song: "Bone-aged is my white horse." Brenda Chamberlain. Beautiful the youth who in green Spring/Broke earth with song. NeIP

Song: "Bring from the craggy haunts of birch and pine." John Todhunter. Thou blowest forgotten things into my mind,/From long ago. OBVV

Song by Mr. Cypress. Thomas Love Peacock. The soul is its own monument. ERoP 1-2; OAEL 1-2; OBNC; OBRV; Par

The Song Called "His Hide Is Covered with Hair.'. Hilaire Belloc. With his head like a wig, and the tuft on his knee,/His hide.... FaBoNo; FM

Song: "Can love be controll'd by advice?" John Gay. So I thought it both safest and best/To marry, for fear you should chide. LoBV; OBSP

Song: "Child, Is Thy Father Dead?" Ebenezer Elliott. We have no place of rest–/Yes, ye have one! SaC

Song: "Chloris, forbear a while." Henry Bold. And buckle now and then, and that's enough. GBL

A Song: "Chloris, when I to thee present." Anonymous. In that you'll all the treasures find/That can content a noble mind. OBS

Song: "Choose now among this fairest number." William Browne. Till lilies in their cheeks be turn'd to roses. GBL

Song: "Christ keep the Hollow Land." William Morris. Many green-lipped cavern mouths/Where the hills are blue. NBM

Song: "Closes and courts and lanes." John Davidson. A notable bit of the earth. HBV 1-2

Song: "Come at dawn, good friend." Anonymous. Come at light of dawn,/and bring no good friend. BoWoP

Song: "Come, Celia, let's agree at last." John, of Buckingham Sheffield. Sure to be grateful, to be kind,/Can never be too late. HBV 1-2

A Song: "Come, cheer up, my lads, like a true British band." Anonymous. Steady, boys, steady–/To give them our voices again and/again. PAH

Song: "Come, rest in this bosom, my own stricken deer." Thomas Moore. And shield thee, and save thee,–or perish there too! PG

Song: "Dark was de night an' col' was de groun'." Anonymous. An' in agony he prayed. NAMP

Song: "Day will rise and the sun from eastward." George Campbell Hay. brings to me thoughts of care and sorrow/out of the airt where dwells my lass. OxBS

Song: "Delicious beauty, that doth lie." John Marston. And bless his eyes, and bless his eyes with one kind glance. EiL

Song: "Desire for a woman took hold of me in the night." Anonymous. oo like madness. LLLT

Song: "Dew on the bamboos." Anonymous. Than be in love with you. LLLT

Song: "Distil not poison in mine ears." John Hall. Take journey and return again,/Yet on her crystal couch still lie. OBSP

Song: "Do I venture away too far." Keith Douglas. the one by day and one at night have charmed me. NePoEA

Song: "Don't Tell Me What You Dreamt Last Night." Franklin Pierce ("F.P.A.") Adams. Don't tell me what you dreamt last night, for I've been reading/Freud. FiBHP

Song: "Dorinda's sparkling wit, and eyes." Charles, Earl of Dorset Sackville. Her Cupid is a black-guard boy,/That runs his link full in your face. CavP; OBS; SeCV 1-2

Song: "Down the dimpled green-sward dancing." George Darley. Make your mocks and sly grimaces/At Love's self, and do not fear it. OnYI

Song: "Dress me in green." Anonymous. like the pear/when it grows ripe. BoWoP

Song: "Dressed up in my melancholy." M. Carl Holman. The image of my error. PoNe

Song: "Fain would I change that note." Anonymous. I serve thee with my heart,/And fall before thee. HBV 1-2

Song: "Fair is the night, and fair the day." William Morris. Break, break, because thou needs must part/From thine own Love, from thine own Sweet! HBV 1-2

A Song: "Fair, sweet and young, receive a prize." John Dryden. For after dying all reprieve's too late. LiTL; OBS

Song: "Farewell, adieu, that court-like life!" John Pickering. With hey trim and trixy too/Their banners they display. EiL

Song: Fie My Fum. Allen Ginsberg. Pit my plum. ErPo

Song: "Fire, fire." Henry Bold. Go hang thy self, and thy desire. GBL

Song: "Fish in the unruffled lakes." W. H. Auden. Last night should add/Your voluntary love. MoAB; MoBrPo

Song: "Flame at the core of the world." Arthur Upson. For out of the infinite past it came/With the love in the eyes of you! HBV 1-2

Song: "Follow thy fair sun, unhappy shadow." Thomas Campion. The sun still proved, the shadow still disdained. OBSC

Song: "Fond affection, hence, and leave me!" Robert Parry. Hence away, therefore, and leave me! EiL

Song: "Fond men! whose wretched care the life soon ending." Phineas Fletcher. Thou wilt not love to live, unless thou live to love. EiL

Song: "Fool, take up thy shaft again." Thomas Stanley. That disdains both me and you. EnLoPo

Song for a Birth or a Death. Elizabeth Jennings. And cries of love are cries of fear. EBEV

Song for a Blue Roadster. Rachel Field. Nothing is real/But Here and Now. TiPo

Song for a Camper. John Farrar. Down, boys, down for the morning swim! YeAr

Song for a Child. Helen Bayley Davis. To wake her, when she sleeps. SoPo

Song for a Country Wedding. William Jay Smith. And their love be enduring. GrPl

Song for a Cracked Voice. Wallace Irwin. (How strange you cannot see it in the corner of my eye!) InMe

Song for a Dance. Abraham Sutzkever. You struggle. I spank you with foam. And we both/are equal in our dance. VWA

Song for a Dancer. Kenneth Rexroth. Honeyed notes that never fail/Upon my lips they laid. TAP

Song for a Dark Girl. Langston Hughes. Love is a naked shadow/On a gnarled and naked tree. AmPP; CDC; IDB; PoBA

Song for a Day (excerpt). Francisco Arriví. here I feel/my wide forehead/a shore of eternity InW

Song for a Departure. Elizabeth Jennings. And haunt them when you depart. GOYP; NMP

Song for a Girl. John Dryden. I should long to be fifteen. ELP; ErPo

Song for a Girl on Her First Menstruation. Anonymous. kill the white eel. BoWoP

Song for a Jewess. Yvan Goll. Your heart is going to find its spring. TrJP

Song for a Little Cuckoo Clock. Elizabeth Jane Coatsworth. And slams his little door! SiSoSe

Song for a Little House. Christopher Morley. And in the phlox, the courteous bees/Are paying duty calls. TreF

Song for a Lost Art. Virginia Brasier. Kept the poison and lost the cure. AMV-81

Song for a Lyre. Louise Bogan. Night to your voice belongs. LiTA

Song for a Marriage. Vassar Miller. But how bone-masonry/Outweighs the skeleton. HW

Song for a New Generation. Gertrude May Lutz. wearing my name and face. AMV-80

Song for a Proud Relation. Patrick MacDonogh. And cock-a-doo, a-doodle-doo!/Will be his epitaph for you. OnYI

Song for a Slight Voice. Louise Bogan. Or on the struck tambour. AmLP

Song for a Suicide. Langston Hughes. They all bring rest in a nothingness/ From where no road returns. PoNe

Song for a Transformation (excerpt). Francisco Arrivi. it is the deep skin/ of an undeciphered presence InW

Song for All Seas, All Ships. Walt Whitman. All seas, all ships. CH; FaBoBe; HBV 1-2; HBVY; MCCG; MoRP; MOS; NePA

Song for an Allegorical Play. John Ciardi. in mercy, each by each set free. PoCh

Song for Autumn. Andrew Young. Come, love; come, love, for sweet love's sake. GBL

A Song for Beauty. P. Lal. supplicate with sweet gifts my heart your worshipper. ACV

Song for "Buvez les Vins du Postillon"–Advt. Jean Garrigue. And be drunk on the wines of the postilion. TAP

Song for December Thirty-First. Frances Frost. Look up! See, there he flies! YeAr

Song for Dov Shamir. Dannie Abse. You plant in your son the soul of the desert. VWA

Song for February. Tom Paulin. And the sugar hostess weeps/One year in four, but more and more. FaBoIP

Song for Healing. Roberta Hill. Live in a happy anonymous town, your lawn,/green, your hair, a bit grey. CDW

Song for Ireland. Phil and June Colclough. They twist and turn all in your air-blue sky. OBET

Song for Ishtar. Denise Levertov. In the black of desire/we rock and grunt, grunt and/shine NaP; NMM; NoAm; PoM

A Song for Lexington. Robert Kelley Weeks. Honor to Lexington,/Our first immortal name! AA

Song for Luanda. Luandino Vieira. –Luanda, you are here! WhB

Song: "For me the jasmine buds unfold." Florence Earle Coates. I love, and the world is mine! HBV 1-2

Song for Memorial Day. Clinton Scollard. Of peace and purity in all men's sight/For the unfolding age! OHIP

Song for Midsummer Night. Elizabeth Jane Coatsworth. When mortal eyes may glimpse the sight. YeAr

Song for Mother's Day. T. S. Matthews. But he came home again, with "Damaged Goods." ELU

Song for Music. G. S. Fraser. With these things of no note. ChMP

Song for My Father. Jessica Hagedorn. i even forget english. BrSi

Song for My Lady. A. Godwin. And that I may in her service/Ever to amend. OxBoLi

Song for My Little Friends. Leonard Adame. this poor poem that doesn't begin to give you/what i feel about you, my little friends... FIA

A Song for My Mother–Her Hands. Anna Hempstead Branch. Shaped happily beneath my cheek,/Hollow and beautiful. OHIP

A Song for My Mother–Her Stories. Anna Hempstead Branch. And they are sweet as rosemary/And dim as lavender. OHIP

A Song for My Mother–Her Words. Anna Hempstead Branch. And I am rich who learned from her/How beautiful they are. OHIP; YeAr

Song for My Name. Linda Hogan. It's the name that goes with me/back to earth/no one else can touch. STE; TWSS

Song for Naomi. Irving Layton. My gentle daughter. WHW

A Song for New Orleans. George Keithley. I can't whistle/you can't kiss/ eating salty fish. NPGG

A Song for Our Flag. Margaret E. Sangster. Our starry flag: red, white, and/blue. FaFP

Song for Past Midnight. Geoffrey Lehmann. Deep in the night dark shapes of cows are feeding. CBAP

Song for Peace. W. R. Rodgers. With rhythm that now is fallen utterly into rout. NeBP

Song for September. Robert Fitzgerald. Their hands in the dusk, their frail hair in the sun. VGW

Song for Seven Parts of the Body, 3. Maxine W. Kumin. The prince is again a frog. PoL

Song for Seven Parts of the Body, 5. Maxine W. Kumin. At times they whisper, touch me. PoL

Song for Seven Parts of the Body, 7. Maxine W. Kumin. make holes in theirs/to hang presents. PoL

A Song for Simeon. Thomas Stearns Eliot. Let thy servant depart,/Having seen thy salvation. BoLiVe; EaLo; EBCP; LiTB; NAs; NOCV; OxBoCh

Song for St. Cecilia's Day. W. H. Auden. O wear your tribulation like a rose. FaBoTw; MP

A Song For the Asking. Francis Orrery [(or Orray[) Ticknor. To thee, of thee! AA

Song for the Cattle. David Campbell. And ambling through mirage/With the squatter's daughter. NOAV

Song for the Clatter-Bones. Frederick Robert Higgins. There's music in the old bones yet. LiTB; OBMV; OnYI; OxBI

Song for the Dead, III. Anonymous. Dance all the colors of Life/For a lover of pleasure/Now dead. TTY

Song for the Divine Bride and Mother. Felix Lope de Vega Carpio. but she who carries the sun/has no fear of night. HW

Song for the Greenwood Fawn. I. L. Salomon. In the green green wood/Of the greenwood fawn, O lovely! GoYe

Song for the Heroes. Alex Comfort. nationless bones, under the still ground. MoBrPo; NeBP

Song for the Infant Judas. Thomas Blackburn. Lord, how much can we bear? NAs

Song for "The Jaquerie". Sidney Lanier.
U-lu-lo, howled the hound. AA
Was laid in a tomb without a mark,/Ah me! AA

Song for the Last Act. Louise Bogan. Now that I have your heart by heart, I see. AmLP; NePoAm; NoP; NYBP; UnPo

A Song for the Least of All Saints. Christina Georgina Rossetti. But love it is, is strong as death,/And I love Thee. BePJ

A Song for the Middle of the Night. James Wright. Legs up, la la, legs down, la la,/Back to sleep again. SM; WeW

Song for the New Year. W. H. Auden. It's good-bye, dear heart, good-bye to you all. EnLi 1-2

Song for the Newborn. Mary Austin. Newborn, on the naked sand/ Nakedly lay it. OFD

Song for the Old Ones. Maya Angelou. the lowly Uncle Tomming/and Aunt Jemimas' smiles. SaC

Song for the Passing of a Beautiful Woman. Anonymous. My blood is redder for your loveliness. LiTA

Song for the Pike's Peaker. Syntax". And with sluice, shovel and pick,/Fill our coffers mighty quick. PoOW

A Song for the Ragged Schools of London. Elizabeth Barrett Browning. Let us take them into pity. SBG

A Song for the Seasons. Bryan Waller Procter. Winter, Spring, Summer times! HBV 1-2

A Song for the Spanish Anarchists. Sir Herbert Read. Fifty men own the lemon grove/and no man is a slave. ChMP

Song for the Spinning Wheel. William Wordsworth. When the flocks are all at rest,/Sleeping on the mountain's breast. OBRV

Song for the Squeeze-Box. Theodore Roethke. –To help me eat up her money. NePoAm; NLV

Song for the Sun That Disappeared Behind the Rainclouds. Anonymous. until the basket overflows with light. TTY

Song: "For the tender beech and the sapling oak." Thomas Love Peacock. You can never teach either oak or beech/To be aught but a greenwood tree. OHIP

Song for the Third Marriage of Lucrezia Borgia (excerpt). Lodovico Ariosto. Come, O Hymenaeus. HW

A Song for the Virgin Mother. Felix Lope de Vega Carpio. Sith sleepeth my child here/Stay ye the branches. LiTW

Song for the Wandering Jew. William Wordsworth. Night and day, I feel the trouble/Of the Wanderer in my soul. ERoP 1-2

Song for These Days. Patrick F. Kirby. That shall be created from our chaos! GoBC

Song for Tomorrow. Lucia Trent. Raise your bewildered eyes to the luminous hills of tomorrow. PGD

Song for Unbound Hair. Genevieve Taggard. Marry another and prosper well,/But not, but never Ishmael. PG; PoRA

Song for War. W. R. Rodgers. ...and coldy mounts the moon/Of thought, and rules among the quorum of the dead. NeBP

Song Form. LeRoi (Imamu Amiri Baraka) Jones. ...Merely to be mere, ly to be CTBA; SOTW

Song: "Four arms, two necks, one wreathing." Anonymous. This "no' with griefs both prove/Report oft turns to love. EiL

Song from a Country Fair. Léonie Adams. But heavy like a bough in spring. GoJo; GrPl

Song from a Drama. Edmund Clarence Stedman. From the portionless king that would/wear it. AA

Song from a Two-Desk Office. Byron Buck. Why must I this short life share with/Randal Groveling? NYBP

A Song from Armenia. Geoffrey Hill. Your mouth, and your hand running over me/Deft as a lizard, like a sinew of water? FaBoMo

Song from "Chartivel." Marie de France. And warm wind stolen, part by part,/Your soul through faithless hours. AWP; EnLoPo; LiTW

Song from Fragment of an Eccentric Drama. Henry Kirke White. Where the green sod grows upon the grave. OBRV

A Song from Shakespeare's "Cymbeline". William Collins. And mourn'd, till Pity's self be dead. CEP; EiCP; ForPo; LAuP; NOEC; OAEP

A Song from Sylvan. Louise Imogen Guiney. Out in the fields with God. BLPA

Song from the Bride of Smithfield. Sylvia Townsend Warner. He is too skilled in bleeding hearts/To turn this way and pity mine. MoBrPo

A Song from the Coptic. James Clarence Mangan. Beetles were blind in the ages of yore. NOBI

A Song from the Gita Govinda. Jayadeva. Draw those dark braids lower, Lady!/But to Krishna go. LiTW

Song from the Gulf. Rolfe Humphries. By the same token,/Sustenance is. MoLP

A Song from the Italian. John Dryden. But cruel She I lov'd in vain. CEP; SeCV 1-2

Song from the Maker of Totems. Duane Niatum. The suicide stream inching its way to the breakers. STE

Song from the Story of Acontius and Cydippe. William Morris. Thou hast not kissed her silver feet. EG

Song from the Unfinished Man. Paul David Ashley. birds will not approach. LFAC

Song from the Waters. Thomas Lovell Beddoes. When a storm of ghosts shall shake/The dead, until they wake/In the grave. NOBE

Song: "From whence cometh song?–" Theodore Roethke. The wind shifting south. NCSH

Song: "Give her but a least excuse to love me!" Robert Browning. Fitting your hawks their jesses!") ViBoPo

Song: "Give Isaac the nymph who no beauty can boast." Richard Brinsley Sheridan. But I only desire she mayn't have a beard. NOBI

Song: "Give me leave to rail at you." John Wilmot, Earl of Rochester. And makes the slave grow pleas'd again. EG

Song: "Go, lovely rose!" Edmund Waller. How small a part of time they share/That are so wondrous sweet and fair! ForPo; JCP; LoBV; NIP; NoP; OAEL 1-2; PoEL 1-5; PrIm; SeCP; SeCV 1-2

Song: "Going down the old way." Margaret Widdemer. How he left my heart sore/And my eyes wet! HBMV

Song: "Gold wings across the sea!" William Morris. Gold wings across the sea. LoBV

A Song: "Good neighbour, why do you look awry?" Anonymous. You've tore my hood, you shall make it good/If it cost me forty pound! TW

Song: "Grace and beauty has the maid." Gil Vicente. Did you ever see/Cattle, vale, or mountain range/As beautiful as she? LiTW

Song: "Had I a heart for falsehood fram'd." Richard Brinsley Sheridan. For friends in all the ag'd you'll meet,/And brothers in the young. HBV 1-2; OBEC

Song: Hamlet. "When a man becomes tired of his life (parody). John Poole. Let us hope they'll go better to-morrow.–/Ri-tol-de-rol, etc. BXAP

Song: "Hang sorrow, cast away care." Anonymous. My Father hath made his Will. OBS

A Song: "Hark! 'tis Freedom that calls, come, patriots, awake!" Anonymous. It will smooth life's dull passage, 'twill slope/the descent,/And strew the way over with flowers. PAH

Song: "Has summer come without the rose." Arthur William Edgar O'Shaughnessy. Here, where she used to love me,/Here, where she loves me not. HBV 1-2

A Song: "Hast thou seen the Down in the Air." Sir John Suckling. Oh! so fickle, oh! so vain, oh! so false, so false, is she! EnLoPo

Song: "He found me sitting among flowers." Aubrey Thomas De Vere. A nook to cry in, and to die in,/'Mid the Ruin's gloom. IrPN

Song: "He that will court a Wench that is coy." Anonymous. Mad girls do love men. ErPo

Song: "Hears not my Phillis how the birds." Sir Charles Sedley. Phillis, without frown or smile,/Sat and knotted all the while! EnLoPo; SeCV 1-2

Song: "Help me now." Emmett Jarrett. Help me now! NeAC

Song: "Hence all you vaine Delights." Francis Beaumont and John Fletcher. Nothing so daintie sweet as lovely Melancholy. PoEL 1-5

Song: "Heron is harsh with despair." Brenda Chamberlain. When hawthorn and plum are/Brave with the blossom of Spring. NeBP; NeIP

Song: "Hither haste, and gently strew." Thomas Lovell Beddoes. Sprinkle here the twinkling shower/On each perfume-stifled flower. EG

Song: "Hold back thy hours, dark night, till we have done." Francis Beaumont and John Fletcher. But help not, though she call. OBSP

Song: "How can I care?" Robert Graves. Dear love, how can I care? GBL

Song: "How can that tree but withered be." Anonymous. But die, by whom each joy doth pass? EiL

Song: "How do I love you?" Irene Rutherford McLeod. Just where the world begins–/Under my eyes. HBV 1-2

Song: "How happy were my days, till now." Isaac Bickerstaffe. I wish I was a maid again,/And in my own country. OBEC

Song: "How many times do I love thee, dear?" Thomas Lovell Beddoes. So many times do I love again. ERoP 1-2; LiTB; LiTL; NBM; OBRV; PoEL 1-5; TrGrPo; ViBoPo

Song: "How pleas'd within my native bowers." William Shenstone. That verdant hill, and silver stream,/Divide my love and me. OBEC

Song: "I am weaving a song of waters." Gwendolyn B. Bennett. Sing a little faster,/Sing a little faster!/Sing! BlSi

Song: "I came to the door of the House of Love." Alfred Noyes. "Make room, make room for a faithful heart/In the House of Love, to-night." HBV 1-2

Song: "I can't be talkin' of love, dear." Esther Mathews. If there be one thing I can't talk of/That one thing do be love. NePA

Song: "I could make you songs." Dorothy Dow. How can I be happy/While you are not here? HBMV

Song: "I'd much rather sit there in the sun." Ruth Krauss. I'd much rather sit here in the sun. SO

Song: "I don't want to be a nun." Anonymous. I am a girl in pain./No! BoWoP

Song: "I kept neat my virginity." Glyn Jones. My sucking star-child dead./Lambleddian. NeBP

Song: "I know moon-rise. I know star-rise." Anonymous. When I lay dis body down. NAMP

Song: "I know that any weed can tell." Louis Ginsberg. I know the weed and moss too well,/To be afraid to sing. TrJP

Song: "I lately vow'd, but 'twas in haste." John Oldmixon. And break 'em when she's kind. PoL

A Song: "I'll sing you a song." Anonymous. And he must be hanged tomorrow. OxNR And the pin is mine. OxNR

Song: "I love my lady's eyes." Robert Bridges. And stray VLP

Song: "I made another garden, yea." Arthur William Edgar O'Shaughnessy. She turn'd back at the last to wait/And say farewell once more. HBV 1-2; OBEV; OBVV

Song: "I make my shroud but no one knows." Adelaide Crapsey. I make my shroud and no one knows,/So shimmering fine it is and fair. HBV 1-2

Song: "I placed my dream in a boat." Cecilia Meireles. my eyes dry like stones/and my two hands–broken. WPOW

Song: "I prithee let my heart alone." Thomas Stanley. I might thy scorn as justly move,/As now thou sufferest mine. ViBoPo

Song: "I prithee send me back my heart." Henry Hughes. For I'll believe I have her heart/As much as she hath mine. CavP; HBV 1-2; JCP; LiTL; ViBoPo

Song: "I promised Sylvia to be true." John Wilmot, Earl of Rochester. Away both leaf and promise flew. SeCePo

Song: "I saw the day's white rapture." Charles Hanson Towne. But you and I remember/Through every starlit night. HBV 1-2

A Song: I Thought No More Was Needed. William Butler Yeats. For who could have foretold/That the heart grows old? AtBAP

Song: "I've put some/ASHES in my sweet papa's bed." Anonymous. Mean Sundown Blues! NAMP

Song: "I've taught thee Love's sweet lesson o'er." George Darley. In Love there is society/She never yet could find with ye! OBRV

Song: "I walk'd in the lonesome evening." William Allingham. As I look across the sea. EnLoPo

Song: "I was so chill, and overworn, and sad." Anna Wickham. And happily I move/Forgetting weariness. MoBrPo

Song: "I went to her who loveth me no more." Arthur William Edgar O'Shaughnessy. Nor fetter for her lips, to make them cease/From saying still she loveth me no more. OBNC

Song: "I wrastled wid Satan, I wrastled wid sin." Anonymous. Dey'll git home bime-by. NAMP

A Song: "If for a woman I would die." Anne Finch, Countess of Winchilsea. Those melancholy thoughts we'll flee,/And cheerful lovers always be. ViBoPo

Song: "If I freely may discover." Ben Jonson. Neither her peevishness annoy me. EiL

Song: "If I had only loved your flesh." Victoria Mary (Vita) Sackville-West. Let my release be soon. HBMV

Song: "If love were but a little thing." Florence Earle Coates. One might not make of life and death/A pillow for love's feet! HBMV

Song: "If once I could gather in song." Wilfred Wilson Gibson. I bring from the shadow-world only/Pale blossoms that perish in air. OBVV

Song: "If she be not as kind as fair." Sir George Etherege. Her value is above the pearl,/That takes delight in sporting. CavP; CEP

Song: "If thou art sleeping." Gil Vicente. We shall have to pass through the dewy grass/And waters wide and fleet. AWP; LiTW

A Song: "If Wine and Musick have the Pow'r." Matthew Prior. And all the Day be Thine alone. LoBV

Song: "If you love God, take your mirror between your hands and look. Mahmud Djellaladin Pasha. How beautiful are your breasts with their two russet/berries. LiTW

Song II: "It Autumne was, and on our Hemispheare." William, of Hawthornden Drummond. Seem'd to have brought the Gold-smiths World againe. OBS

Song II. The Landskip. William Shenstone. Divide my love and me. CEP

Song: "In a maiden-time professed." Thomas Middleton. The middle's best, and that give me. OBSP

Song in a Siege. Robert Heath. And ourselves up to keep the town. CavP; OBS

Song: "In his last bin Sir Peter lies." Thomas Love Peacock. To hear no sound but three times three. OBRV; ViBoPo

A Song in Humility. Carleton Drewry. And nothing is too small/To thus accomplish all. MoRP

The Song in Making of the Arrows. John Lily. Holiday (boys), cry Holiday! LoBV; OBSC

Song: "O come, soft rest of cares! come, Night!" George Chapman. Lips his swords are,/The field his arms. ViBoPo

Song: "O, do not wanton with those eyes." Ben Jonson. Mine own enough betray me. HBV 1-2

Song: "O'er the waste of waters cruising." Philip Freneau. Till she ever, thus defeated,/Yields the sceptre of the main. PAH

Song: "O fair! O sweet! when I do look on thee." Sir Philip Sidney. Heart and soul do sing in me. SiPS

Song: "O faire sweet face, O eyes celestiall bright." Francis Beaumont and John Fletcher. While I in wonder sing this sacrifice,/To beauty sacred, and those Angell-eyes. PoEL 1-5

Song: "O harmless feast." Barten Holyday. And trip it in comely sort. EIL

Song: "O, it was out by Donncarney." James Joyce. But softer than the breath of summer/Was the kiss she gave to me. MoBrPo; OBVV

Song: "O lady, when the tipped cup of the moon blessed you." Ted Hughes. In my hands, and my hands full of dust,/O my lady. LLLT

Song: "O, like a queen's her happy tread." William Watson. Her woman's heart for me! HBV 1-2

Song: "O lovely April, rich and bright." Gustave Kahn. O lovely April rich and bright. TrJP

Song: "O memory! thou fond deceiver." Oliver Goldsmith. And he who wants each other blessing,/In these must ever find a foe. ViBoPo

Song: "O ruddier than the cherry!" John Gay. And fierce as storms that bluster! HBV 1-2; OBEC

Song: "O spirit of the Summertime!" William Allingham. Oh, bring again my heart's content,/Thou Spirit of the Summertime! IrPN

Song: "O, strew the way with rosy flowers." James Clarence Mangan. And—wreck of wrecks!–there lie the Fair/Whose beauty wins no more! IrPN

Song: "O, that joy so soon should waste!". Ben Jonson. It should be my wishing/That I might die kissing. LiTL; ViBoPo

Song: "O the month of May, the merry month of May." Thomas Dekker. Sweet Peg, thou shalt be my Summer's Queen. PBBP

Song (October 1969). Kathleen Fraser. I am serious Mrs Acorn, are you deaf? PeHV

Song of a Common Lover. Flavien Ranaivo. ...a calabash/intact, for drawing water;/in pieces, bridges for my guitar. TTY

Song of a Factory Girl. Marya Zaturenska. But it stirred in me as the seed in sod,/Or a broken rhyme. HBMV

The Song of a Factory Worker. Ruth Collins. Red brick building/With many windows. SaC

The Song of a Happy Rising. John Thewlis. Christ, send us happy rising! ACP

The Song of a Heathen. Richard Watson Gilder. The earth, the sea, and the air! AA; WGRP

Song of a Jewish Boy. J.M. I having no power over my shadow. TrJP

Song of a Man about to Die in a Strange Land. Anonymous. What does it matter, then,/If I die here in a strange land? DL

The Song of a Man Who Has Come Through. D. H. Lawrence. Admit them, admit them. CMoP; CoBMV; FaBoMo; GTBS-P; InPS; LiTM; MoPo; NoAm; PAI

Song of a Passionate Lover. Mary Austin. Lest from out my singing/Leaps my heart upon you! BPAW

Song of a Prison Guard. Lupenga Mphande. It's like a piece of thread on which our days hang,/To fall away, one after another, wasted. WhB

Song of a Rat. Ted Hughes. While it supplants Hell. CMoP; NoP

Song of a Second April. Edna St. Vincent Millay. You that alone I cared to keep. CMoP; OxBA

Song of a Shepherd Boy at Bethlehem. Josephine Preston Peabody. Smilest Thou? OHIP

Song of a Sick Child. Anonymous. And the basket I bear, its cords are broken. WTO

Song of a Train. John Davidson. Speeds through the land/The train. BrPo

Song of a Woman Abandoned by the Tribe... Mary Austin. Alas, that I should die,/Who know so much. BPAW

A Song of a Young Lady to Her Ancient Lover. John Wilmot, Earl of Rochester. Ancient Person of my Heart. BoLoP; CavP; EBEV; ErPo; GBL; MePo

Song of Abuse. Anonymous. He will become a monkey with one leg/And he will hop hop hop away. WTO

Song of Agony. Gouveia De Lemos. Which of us will die?/which of us?/which of us? WhB

A Song of Ale. Anonymous. God save the lives of them and their wives,/Whether they be young or old! AnFE; OBSC

Song of Allegiance. R. A. K. Mason. boldly bring I up the rear. AnNZ

Song of Amergin. Anonymous. I am the grave: of every hope. MOON

The Song of Ancient Ways. William Oandasan. the song of ancient ways/turns in our blood again STE

A Song of Angiola in Heaven. Henry Austin Dobson. And, in the holding of my dear Love's hand,/Forget the grieving and the misery. HBV 1-2

Song of Apollo. John Lyly. To the glittering Delian king. AtBAP; OBSC

A Song of Arno. Grace Ellery Channing-Stetson. And the deep-breathing heart grows faint/To be so near to Heaven. AA

A Song of Autumn. Joseph Ceravolo. Not even if the/flowers turn to moss and/loose sensations for their stems. ANYP

A Song of Autumn. Rennell Rodd. The dream had not been broken,/And love were with us yet. HBV 1-2

Song of Basket-Weaving. Constance Lindsay Skinner. Ere the Sunset and the Drooping Leaf! AnAmPo; BPAW

The Song of Bekotsidi. Anonymous. To form them fair, for them I labor. For them I make. OBVE

Song of Black Cubans. Federico Garcia Lorca. I'll go to Santiago. SOTW

The Song of Braddock's Men. Anonymous. 'Tis nobly done–the day's our own–huzzah, huzzah! MC; PAH

Song of Breath. Peire Vidal. Who turns the veriest sullen unto laughter. AWP

Song of Caribou, Musk Oxen, Women, and Men Who Would Be Manly. Anonymous. Glorious it is/When wandering time is come./Yayai–ya–yiya. WTO

The Song of Carroll's Sword. Dallan MacMore. Where Finn of the feasts is, they will hail thee with "welcome." OnYI

The Song of Chess. Abraham Ibn Ezra. For in death is resurrection. TrJP

Song of Coridon and Melampus. George Peele. When deeds win meeds, and words love's works/do prove. OBSC

The Song of Cove Creek Dam. Anonymous. He will gather us together some day. AmFP

Song of Cradle-Making. Constance Lindsay Skinner. Ah! never have I seen so much light/Through thy father's doorway. CaP

The Song of Crede. Anonymous. These are the arrows that murder sleep. BIrV; LiTW; OnYI

A Song of Dagger-Dancing (excerpt). Tu Fu. And ended like the shining calm of rivers and the sea. UnS

A Song of Dalliance. William Cartwright. The next conquest shall be thine. ALV; JCP

Song of Degrees. Paul Auster. ...Through the star-/mortared wall/that rises in our night, your soul/will not pass/again. VWA

A Song of Degrees. W. P. Ker. Where rocks of adamant understand/The secrets of the sky. PoSH

A Song of Derivations. Alice Meynell. Heavily on this little heart/Presses this immortality. WGRP

A Song of Desire. Frederic Lawrence Knowles. And touch my tongue with songs! HBV 1-2

Song of Despair. Rangiaho. Too many nights I have yearned/For one who would not return. WTO

A Song of Diana's Nymphs. John Lyly. Read his indictment, let him hear/What he's to trust to: Boy, give ear! OBSC

A Song of Diligence. Helen Frazee-Bower. What would a little kitchen maid/Be doing with romance? HBMV

A Song of Doubt. Josiah Gilbert Holland. God has fogotten the world! WGRP

Song of Duke William. Hilaire Belloc. Barbara stout and fine. FaBoNo

A Song of Dust. John Byrne Leicester Warren, Lord De Tabley One farewell kiss before we go. EnLoPo

A Song of Early Autumn. Richard Watson Gilder. And pile the wood by the barn-yard gate! HBV 1-2

Song of Egla. Maria Gowen Brooks. Come, and I will gaze on thee! AA; AnAmPo

A Song of Emptiness to Fill up the Empty Pages Following. Michael Wigglesworth. Delight thy self in that which worthless is. SCAP

A Song of Enchantment. Walter De la Mare. On the wood and the pool and the elder tree. GTBS

Song of Eros. George Edward Woodberry. The long-winged storm-gulls burning/Seaward when day is done,/Are like thee, young Desire. AA; HBV 1-2

Song of Exile. Antonio G. Dias. And the palm trees I would see/Where the "sabia" is singing. TTY

Song of Expectancy. George Hitchcock. And for the dark sad waters where legends swim backward like/squid EAS

Song of Fairies Robbing an Orchard (excerpt). [James Henry] Leigh Hunt. Yet the fruit were scarce worth peeling,/Were it not for stealing, stealing. OBRV

A Song of Faith. Josiah Gilbert Holland. God will remember the world! WGRP

Song of Farewell. Nellie Wong. and watch you dance playful as a baby girl? BrSi

The Song of Finis. Walter De la Mare. And quiet did quiet remain. MoBrPo

Song of Fionnuala. Thomas Moore. Call my spirit to the fields above. AnIL; BIrV; OnYI

The Song of Roland, CCXL. *Anonymous.* And go to strike, each with his trenchant lance. WaaP

The Song of Roland, CL. *Anonymous.* Nowhere on earth so sad a man you'd found. WaaP

The Song of Roland, CUV. *Anonymous.* No victory for glutton such as you. WaaP

The Song of Roland, LXXIX. *Anonymous.* Evil example will never come of me. WaaP

The Song of Roland: The Last Battle. *Anonymous.* So the count's soul they bare to Paradis. LiTW

The Song of Roland, XCIII. *Anonymous.* For we are right, but these gluttons are wrong. WaaP

The Song of Roland, XCIX. *Anonymous.* Then says Rollant: "Great power in that thrust." WaaP

The Song of Roland, XCVII. *Anonymous.* Say Oliver: "Now is our battle grand." WaaP

The Song of Roland, XCVIII. *Anonymous.* Says the Archbishop: "A baron's stroke, in truth." WaaP

A Song of Sack. *Anonymous.* Who drinks the deepest? Here's to him. OBS

The Song of Samuel Sweet. Charles Causley. I heard a horseman riding/ And the sound of running feet. OBNV

Song of Seyd Nimetollah of Kuhistan. Ralph Waldo Emerson. What men chatter know I not. NOBA

The Song of Shadows. Walter de la Mare. Music hath called them, dreaming,/Home once more. BoLiVe; MoBrPo; TrGrPo

The Song of Sherman's Army. Charles Graham Halpine. For Sherman and Grant, hurrah! MC; PAH

A Song of Sherwood. Alfred Noyes. In Sherwood, in Sherwood, about the break of day. BBV; HBV 1-2; HBVY; MCCG; TiPo

A Song of Sickness. Hine Tangikuku. I am dead weed cast upon the shore. WTO

Song of Sixpence. *Anonymous.* Up came a magpie/And bit off her nose. OxBoLi

Song of Slaves in the Desert. John Greenleaf Whittier. Where are we going, Rubee? AnAmPo; OxBA

Song of Snow-White Heads. Cho Wen-chun. Who will not leave her/Till her hair is white. BoWoP

The Song of Songs. Heinrich Heine. And though the task may break my back/I'll ask for no vacation! UnTE

Song of Songs. Wilfred Owen. Throbbing through you, and sobbing, unsubdued. NAMP

Song of Sukkaartik, the Assistant Spirit. *Anonymous.* I sang of these things,/Because they are so nice to think about. WTO

Song of Summer. Paul Laurence Dunbar. An' I'm a-layin' neah huh! MCCG

Song of Texas. William Henry Cuyler Hosmer. Have place in the flashing throng/That spangle your banner bright. PAH

A Song of Thanks. Edward Smyth Jones. Lord God of Hosts, we give Thee thanks! BANP

Song of Thanksgiving. John Richard Moreland. And give Thee thanks. PGD

Song of the All-Wool Shirt. Eugene Field. For if again that shirt is wet/ 'Twill vanish from our sight. StPo

The Song of the Ancient People. John Hay. For we are the Ancient People,/Born with the wind and rain. AA

Song of the Answerer (excerpt). Walt Whitman. To launch off with absolute faith, to sweep through the/ceaseless rings and never be quiet again. PP

Song of the Argonauts. William Morris. And half dried up thy waters be. EtS

The Song of the Arrow. Isabella Valancy Crawford. ...The gods know best. PeCV

Song of the Artesian Water. Andrew Barton ("Banjo") Paterson. It is flowing, ever flowing, further down. ACV

Song of the Ballet. J. B. Morton. Heave-ho! Away with her/Into the stalls. DBV; FiBHP

The Song of the Banjo. Rudyard Kipling. Yea, from Delos up to Limerick and back! FaBoCh; PrIm; VLP

Song of the Blue-Corn Dance. *Anonymous.* Onward, lo, they come,/Hither, hither bound! WTO

The Song of the Body Dreamed in the Spirit's Mad Behest. Brother Antoninus. When His great Godhead peels its stripping strength/In my red earth. ErPo

Song of the Border. Gordon W. Norris. For, south of the Border, I left her my heart! BPAW

The Song of the Borderguard. Robert Duncan. The borderlines of sense in the morning light/are naked as a line of poetry in a war. NeAP; PoM

The Song of the Bow. Arthur Conan Doyle. To the hearts that are true/ And the land where the true hearts dwell. HBV 1-2; MCCG

The Song of the Bower. Dante Gabriel Rossetti. Out of sight, beyond light, at what goal may we meet? HBV 1-2

Song of the Bowmen of Shu. *Anonymous.* Our mind is full of sorrow, who will know of our grief? OBVE

Song of the Brave. Laurence Altgood. Save your heart for the deathless brave. PAL

Song of the Breed. Carroll Arnett. damned road/and get hit. STE

Song of the Bride. Susan Mernit. The whole thing only a touch of the hand. VWA

Song of the Broad-Ax (excerpt). Walt Whitman. To be lean'd and to lean on. MoAmPo

Song of the Builders. Jessie Wilmore Murton. But the city's towers grow straight and high! AmFN

Song of the Bush-Shrike. *Anonymous.* totototo. PeSA

The Song of the Camp. Bayard Taylor. The loving are the daring. AA; BeLS; GN; HBV 1-2; HBVY; WBLP

Song of the Cape of Good Hope. Christian Schubart. And tears will mingle with the wine. NU

Song of the Captured Woman. James Devaney. The singing Murrawal, the Voice-that-does-not-cease. PoAu 1-2

Song of the Cauld Lad of Hylton. *Anonymous.* That's to grow to a man/ That's to lay me. GBP

Song of the Chattahoochee. Sidney Lanier. Calls through the valleys of Hall. AA; AmFN; AP; BoNaP; DiPo; FaBoBe; FaBV; HBV 1-2; LaNeLa; LiTA; MCCG; NePA; OHFP; TreF; YaD

The Song of the Christmas Tree. Blanche Elizabeth Wade. Oho, sing I, oho! OHIP

Song of the Closing Service. Aliza Shenhar. Its flowers are bluish. VWA

The Song of the Colorado. Sharlot M. Hall. Yet I keep the way of my will to the sea, when ye and your/race are not! HBV 1-2

Song of the Corsairs. George Gordon, Lord Byron. That thrills the wanderer of that trackless way? EtS

Song of the Dark Ages. Francis Brett Young. Poor savages who fought in France. HBMV

Song of the Darkness. John Bricuth. The sick never get well. SM

Song of the Darling River. Henry Lawson. To laugh at the rise of the Darling River. ACV

The Song of the Demented Priest. John Berryman. ...I am the king of the dead. MoPo

The Song of the Derelict. John McCrae. For ever at peace with the sea! EtS

Song of the Dew. *Anonymous.* Let fall this day Thy dew! TrJP

Song of the Elfin Steers - Man. George Hill. The blind bat flits - away! AA

Song of the Emigrants in Bermuda. Andrew Marvell. And all the way, to guide their chime,/With falling oars they kept the time. GTBS; GTBS-P; OxBoCh

Song of the Evil Spirit of the Woods. Thomas Moore. Till, beneath the solar fires,/Rankling all, the wretch expires! OBTV

Song of the Exposition (excerpt). Walt Whitman. She's here, installed amid the kitchen ware! PP

Song of the Factory Girls. *Anonymous.* Where "God save the "Queen" to cry are seen/The slaves of the British looms. SaC

Song of the Fairies. *Anonymous.* ...who/From the bridging of Lamrach shall gain, or rue? OnYI

Song of the Fallen Deer. *Anonymous.* The drunken butterflies sit/With opening and shutting wings. OBVE

Song of the Farmworker. T. R. Jahns. it won't go down. AMV-80

Song of the Fisherman's Lover. Roseann Lloyd. Say woman. WOLT

Song of the Fishes. *Anonymous.* Then blow ye winds westerly, westerly blow,/We're bound to the southward, so steady we go. AmSS

The Song of the Flags. Silas Weir Mitchell. "Forgive, but ah, never forget." PAH

Song of the Flea. Judah Al-Harizi. Be sure a murd'rer's malice to forestall. TrJP

The Song of the Flume. Anna M. Fitch. And there's wrath in my swelling tide. BPAW

The Song of the Forest Ranger. Herbert Bashford. I would seek the house of Quiet,/That the Master Workman made! HBV 1-2; OHIP

Song of the Forest Trees. *Anonymous.* To thy soul as to thy body, O man, 'twould work advantage. OnYI

A Song of the Four Seasons. Henry Austin Dobson. And my Love's heart. BoC; HBV 1-2

The Song of the Four Winds. Thomas Love Peacock. Swift feet the readiest aid supply. OBRV; WiR

Song of the Fucked Duck. Marge Piercy. rattling like dried leaves on a stunted tree. BoWoP; NMM

Song of the Full Catch. Constance Lindsay Skinner. Strong as love when my woman calls me! CaP

The Song of the Galley. *Anonymous.* If ye fetch him from the Moors! AWP

Song of the Galley-Slaves. Rudyard Kipling. Will you never let us go? GTBS-P; HAP; PoEL 1-5

The Song of the Ghost. Alfred Perceval Graves. They knew that sorrow her heart had broke. AnIV

The Song of the Good Samaritan. Vernon Watkins. Makes the world nothing, pouring in oil and wine.' LiTM

A Song of the GPO. Gerry Hamill. After five, then you deserve to go without. NOBL

The Song of the Graves. Ernest Rhys. Who seeks their kin, left naked now,/To dig in Gwanas' graves may go. OBMV

Song of the Gulf Stream. Francis Alan Ford. Give you welcome to the Glories with the Song of/the Gulf Stream. EtS

Song of the Hanged. Eleni Vakalo. Dark blue rings/Around our necks. PBWP

The Song of the Happy Shepherd. William Butler Yeats. Dream, dream, for this is also sooth. NoAm; VLP

Song of the Harper. Anonymous. ...and none that hath/gone may come again. LiTW

Song of the Harvest. Henry Stevenson Washburn. We will store it away gladly/In garner and bin. OHIP

A Song of the Hatteras Whale. Anonymous. Sing ho! for the Hatteras whale! EtS

The Song of the Heads. Anonymous. Back to where we belong/With the cold stones and the clay. KiLC

Song of the Hesitations. Paul Blackburn. But still I am not drunk enough/to dream us into Spring NMP

Song of the Highest Tower. Arthur Rimbaud. May they come, may they come/The days which enchant us. AWP

Song of the Hill. Edith Lodge. High on the hill/Here... GoYe

Song of the Horse. Anonymous. How joyous his neigh! AWP

Song of the Ill-Married. Anonymous. Without you I'll never know joy again. BoWoP

Song of the Intruder. Maria Jacobs. for all its giddy laughter/holds a smarting edge. AMV-81

Song of the Invisible Corpse in the Field. Gregory Orr. ...the pit/that opens, toothed with dew. LTB

The Song of the Jellicles. Thomas Stearns Eliot. They are resting and saving themselves to be right/For the Jellicle Moon and the Jellicle Ball. FaBoCh; FaBoNo; LoGBV; OxBChV; PCat; PoPle

The Song of the King's Minstrel. Richard Middleton. And sing no more. HBV 1-2

Song of the Last Jewish Child. Edmond Jabes. I am born to love them. VWA

Song of the Leadville Mine Boss. Don Cameron. I hope to see the day when you'll/Be working for a dollar. PoOW

The Song of the Lilies. Lucy Wheelock. They truly live who truly share!/Give, children, give. OHIP

Song of the Lioness for Her Cub. Anonymous. You water-drinker! BoWoP

Song of the Little Villages. James B. Dollard. God bless the little villages and guard them night and day! CAW

A Song of the Love of Jesus. Richard Rolle. Jesu, gif us grace as Thou wel may to luf Thee/withouten ending. PoEL 1-5

The Song of the Lower Classes. Ernest Charles Jones. We're not too low—to kill the foe,/But too low to touch the spoil. CoMu; OBVV; VLP

The Song of the Mad Prince. Walter De La Mare. That's what I said. AtBAP; EBEV; FaBoCh; GoJo; LoGBV; MoVE; NoAm; NOBE; OAEP; OxBChV

Song of the Mariner's Needle. C. R. Clarke. Ye love me, though, since mine is not/The mystery of wrath! EtS

The Song of the Mean Mary Jean Machine. James Baker Hall. ...the American/love song of the Mean Mary Jean Machine. FiCP; TAT

Song of the Mermaids and Mermen. Sir Walter Scott. Come to share the festal show. WSC

The Song of the MicMac. Joseph Howe. With triumph shall smile on the spots where they fell. CaP

The Song of the Militant Romance. Percy Wyndham Lewis. Return with me where I am crying out with the/gorilla and the bird! FaBoTw; OxBTC

Song of the Milkmaid. Alfred, Lord Tennyson. Come behind and kiss me milking the cow! HBV 1-2

The Song of the Mischievous Dog. Dylan Thomas. Let's hope you won't think me too vicious. FaFP; GrPl

Song of the Moderns. John Gould Fletcher. And think "These are the cast-off leavings of some star." AWP; InPo

A Song of the Moon. Claude McKay. To drink your wine mixed with sweet drafts of dews. PoNe

Song of the Murdered Child Whose Bones Grew into a Milk-white Dove. Anonymous. And I took to my wings/And away I flew. GBP

Song of the Navajo. Albert Pike. But when could their steeds, so mule-footed and slow,/Compare with the birds of the free Navajo? PoOW

Song of the Negro on the Ferry. Jose Craveirinha. And you would die/Bleeding.../Millions of times like me!!! WhB

Song of the New World. Angela Morgan. Man is facing the rising sun! HBMV; HBVY

Song of the Night at Day-Break. Alice Meynell. Sick with memories. CH

Song of the Old Love. Jean Ingelow. But perhaps I shall meet thee and know thee again/When the sea gives up her dead. HBV 1-2

Song of the Old Mother. William Butler Yeats. And the seed of the fire gets feeble and cold. AnIV; GTBS; LOW; MCCG; MoBrPo

Song of the Old Woman. Anonymous. and my hair my hair will have disappeared BoWoP

A Song of the Open Road. Anonymous. Brother to brother pressed,/Tara, tantara, teino! AWP

Song of the Open Road. Ogden Nash. I'll never see a tree at all. FaBoCo; FPL; GoTF; NAMP; OBAL; PPJ; TreFS

Song of the Open Road. Walt Whitman.
Let the paper remain on the desk unwritten, and the book on the shelf/unopen'd! FaFP
Shall we stick by each other as long as we live? MoAmPo; NePA; NOBA; TreFT; ViBoPo; WHA
Strong and content I travel the open road. HBVY; MCCG; RFM
Whoever accepts me he or she shall be blessed and shall bless me. AtBAP

Song of the Outlaws. Joanna Baillie. Uprouse ye, then, my merry men!/And use it as ye may. OBRV

The Song of the Owl. Richard Kendall Munkittrick. Tu-whit, tu-whit, tu-whit! OBCA

Song of the Palm. Tracy Robinson. Bereft of these and thee! AA

A Song of the Passion. Richard Rolle of Hampole. That thou be beryd in my brest and bryng me to blysse. OxBoCh

The Song of the Pen. Judah Al-Harizi. My pen, though frail and slim of figure,/Has a serpent's tooth and a lion's/vigour. TrJP

The Song of the Pilgrims. Rupert Brooke. Thine altar, wonderfully white,/Among the Forests of the Night. TrPWD

Song of the Pilgrims. Thomas Cogswell Upham. England's shores, adieu! adieu! MC; PAH

Song of the Poor Man. Anonymous. when a rich man is ill/to light a lamp/he must wait for a slave. TTY

Song of the Pop-Bottlers. Morris Bishop. When Pop bottles pop-bottles/Pop-bottles pop! FiBHP

Song of the Queen Bee. E. B. White. And I wish to state/That I'll always mate/With whatever drone I encounter. NYBP

Song of the Rabbits Outside the Tavern. Elizabeth Jane Coatsworth. Under a winter's moon. AnNE; OBCA

Song of the Rain. Hugh McCrae. And our children asleep in the attic above. BoAV; CBAP; PoAu 1-2

Song of the Rain Chant. Anonymous. Comes the rain with me. AWP

Song of the Redwood-Tree. Walt Whitman. To build a grander future. AmPP

The Song of the Reed Sparrow. Anonymous. I can sing about it still. OxBChV

Song of the Rejected Woman. Kibkarjuk. the earth turns white,/far inland./Ija-je-ja. WPOW

A Song of the Road. Robert Louis Stevenson. It is the tune to travel to. BrPo

The Song of the Robin. Beatrice Bergquist. But the robin's song is the best! SUS

Song of the Round Man. Michael Palmer. and we'll puff cigars from noon till night/as if we were alive. NPGG

Song of the Sabbath. (or Molodovski) Kadya, [(or Kadia) Molodovsky. And my heart's song/is an eternal Sabbath. PBWP; WPOW

Song of the Screw. Anonymous. All these and more, for motions small,/Have been discussed by Dr. Ball. NA

Song of the Sea. Richard E. Burton. Such is the song of the sea. EtS

Song of the Sea. Rumann MacColmain. ...the horrid/blast,/From Hell with furious tempest! OnYI

A Song of the Seamen and Land Soldiers. Anonymous. Pell-mell let's to the battle fall,/And lofty music sound, a.' OBSS

Song of the Seasons. Blanche De Good Lofton. The song of the seasons never grows old. YeAr

A Song of the Seasons. Cosmo Monkhouse. And a sexton in the churchyard/Digging in the cold. HBV 1-2

Song of the Seaweed. Eliza Cook. And some hot brains are beginning to think/Of a messmate's opened vein. FiBHP

The Song of the Seeress. Anonymous. The Dark Dragon from Darkfell,/bears on his pinions the bodies of men,/Soars overhead. I sink now. NAWM 1-2

The Song of the Shadows. Walter De la Mare. Home once more. CMoP

Song of the Sheet (parody). Anonymous. He sang the Song of the Sheet. BXAP

The Song of the Shirt. Thomas Hood. She sang this "Song of the Shirt!" CABL; CoBE; EnRP; FaPoR; HBV 1-2; MaC; MCCG; OBVV; PaPo; PPON; SaC; TEP; TreF; VLP; WBLP

Song of the Silent Land. Johann Gaudenz Salis-Seewis. Into the Silent Land! AWP; HBV 1-2

Song of the Sirens. William Browne. Where no joy dies till love hath gotten more. EiL; ViBoPo

Song of the Sky Loom. *Anonymous.* O our Mother the Earth, O our Father the Sky! WTO

The Song of the Smoke. William Edward Burghardt Du Bois. Hail to the black! OBVV; PoBA; UnPo

Song of the Son. Jean Toomer. Caroling softly souls of slavery. AmNP; BP; CDC; NIP; PoBA

The Song of the Sons of Esau. Bertha Brooks Runkle. To give us room to wander was the world/made wide! AA

The Song of the Spanish Main. John Bennett. Then hush, forevermore. HBV 1-2

The Song of the Spirits. Joseph Sheridan Lefanu. Stretched mazily this way and that in perspective. OnYI

Song of the Springbok Does. *Anonymous.* Wai! springbok child/sleep for me. PeSA

The Song of the Strange Ascetic. Gilbert Keith Chesterton. Of them that do not have the faith/And will not have the fun. HBMV

Song of the Strange Young Duckling. Deborah Munro. ...i tell you. you're singing. IHMS

Song of the Stygian Naiades. Thomas Lovell Beddoes. The bee of hearts, which mortals name/Cupid, Love, and Fie for shame. EnRP; ERoP 1-2; OAEL 1-2

Song of the Taste. Gary Snyder. Kissing the lover in the mouth of bread:/lip to lip. CAPP; LCAP

Song of the Three Angels. Gil Vicente. Upon the waters calm/No breath of wind may light. CAW

Song of the Three Hundred Thousand Drunkards...(excerpt). William B. Tappan. To glut the worm that never dies–/Hurrah! hurrah! hurrah! PeD

Song of the Thunder. *Anonymous.* You, O Xgoro/son of the Thundercloud. PeSA

Song of the Thunders. *Anonymous.* While I am carried by the wind/Across the sky. OBVE

The Song of the Tortured Girl. John Berryman. Minutes I lay awake to hear my joy. CoAP

Song of the Train. David McCord. Clickety, clickety,/Clackety/Clack. NTCP; SoPo

Song of the Trees. *Anonymous.* I am afraid of. OBVE

Song of the Trees of the Black Forest. Edmond Jabes. Now the forest is red/and the hanged men still laugh,/but do not burn. VWA

The Song of the Trout Fisher. Ikinilik. Who never inherited song/From the twittering birds of the sky. WTO

Song of the Truck. Doris Frankel. Coastline to coastline–/America moves! AmFN

Song of the Turkey Buzzard. Lew Welch. O SWEETEST WATER O GLORIOUS/WHEELING/BIRD PoM

The Song of the Turnkey. Harry Bache Smith. He is king of the donjon deeps. AA

Song of the Turtle and Flamingo. James Thomas Fields. The green, but a very mock-turtle! GN

The Song of the Ungirt Runners. Charles Hamilton Sorley. And we run because we like it/Through the broad bright land. EnLit; GoTF; HBMV; MoBrPo; OBEV; TreFT

Song of the Universal. Walt Whitman. Comprehending all,/All eligible to all. PGD

Song of the Unloved. *Anonymous.* Lovely with a high-bridged nose. PeSA

The Song of the Unsuccessful. Richard Burton. "God, give us another chance!" WGRP

The Song of the Valkyries. *Anonymous.* Start we swiftly with steeds unsaddled–/hence to battle with brandished swords! LiTW; WaaP

Song of the Vivandiere. Heinrich Heine. Come, let's be drunk together! UnTE

A Song of the Wave. George Cabot Lodge. And the end is death! AA; AmePo; EtS

Song of the Weaving Woman. Yuan Chen. They know how to spin a gossamer web in the void. SaC

The Song of the Western Men. Robert Stephen Hawker. But here's twenty thousand Cornish bold/Will know the reason why!' CBEP; EnRP; FaPoR; GoBC; HBV 1-2; OBNC; OBRV; OBVV; PaPo; RoGo

Song of the White Lady of Avenel. Sir Walter Scott. For seldom they land that go swimming with me. NBM

Song of the Wind and the Rain. Solomon Ibn Gabirol. And Thy blessing descends as the rain! TrJP

Song of the Wise Men. Edith Lovejoy Pierce. Do you not see the Christmas star/That we are guided by? PGD

The Song of the Woman-Drawer. Mary Gilmore. I am the root of life;/I am the chord. PoAu 1-2

Song: "Of thee, kind boy, I ask no red and white." Sir John Suckling. So to the height and nick/We up be wound,/No matter by what hand or trick. LoBV

The Song of This House. Stephen Vincent. It's November/and I'm waiting NeAC

Song of Three Smiles. William Stanley Merwin. And we all smile together. CoAP; VGW

Song of Thyrsis. Philip Freneau. I would advise you–and you might–/Love again to-morrow. AA; AnFE; APA; HBV 1-2; LiTA; ViBoPo

The Song of Troylus. Petrarch. For hete of cold, for cold of hete I dye. AWP

A Song of Twilight. *Anonymous.* "He couldn't stay awake for you, he had to go to bed!" HBV 1-2

A Song of Two Wanderers. Marguerite Wilkinson. Dear, we must go again/To where the town ends.... HBMV

A Song of Waking. Katharine Lee Bates. The Summer is begun. OHIP

The Song of Wandering Aengus. William Butler Yeats. The silver apples of the moon,/The golden apples of the sun. BoLiVe; BrPo; CMoP; DiPo; EnLi 1-2; FaBoCh; GoJo; LoGBV; LOW; MAT; MoAB; MoBrPo; PG; PoEL 1-5; PoRA; SOTW; TiPo; VLP; WSC

Song of Welcome. Hermia Fraser. Welcome, the journey is ended. CaP

A Song of White Snow. Ts'en Ts'an. Leaving behind him only foot-prints. LiTW

Song of Winter. *Anonymous.* That is why I say "cold"! AnIL; OnYI

A Song of Winter. Emily Davis. Bear witness to his human will. ACV

A Song off Clover. Saxe Holm. Oh! who knows what the Clover thinks?/No one! unless the Bob-o'-links! GN

A Song-Offering. Rabindranath Tagore. ...The heaven's river has/drowned its banks and the flood of joy is abroad. LiTW

Song: "Often I have heard it said." Walter Savage Landor. Will they be as bright again?/Not if kissed by other men. HBV 1-2

Song: "Oh, bid my tongue be still." Richard Watson Dixon. Or, if thou bid me yet,/Then dost thou bid me die. VLP

A Song: "Oh do not wanton with those eyes." Ben Jonson. Nor spread them as distract with feares,/Mine owne enough betray me. SeCP

Song: "Oh fly not, Pleasure, pleasant-hearted Pleasure." Wilfrid Scawen Blunt. Making thus my ditty/Of fair love lost for ever and a day. ViBoPo

Song: "Oh! Love," they said, "is King of Kings." Rupert Brooke. Love would be merely you. HBV 1-2

Song: "Oh roses for the flush of youth." Christina Georgina Rossetti. Give me the withered leaves I chose/Before in the old time. GTBS-P; LoBV; ViBoPo

Song: "Oh! say not woman's love is bought." Isaac Pocock. She loves, and loves for ever. HBV 1-2

Song: "Oh! that we two were Maying." Charles Kingsley. And our souls at home with God! HBV 1-2

Song: "Oh the charming month of May!" Joseph Addison. Who on her skimming-dish carves her name. NOEC

Song: "Old Farmer Oats and his son Ned." John Jay Chapman. Ye'll keep none when death's come, say I! PoEL 1-5

Song on a Young Lady Who Sung Finely. Wentworth Dillon, Earl of Roscommon. Let no ungentle cold destroy,/All taste we have of heavenly joy! CavP

Song on May Morning. John Milton. And welcome thee, and wish thee long. BoLiVe; BoNaP; GN; HBV 1-2; HBVY; TrGrPo

Song, on Reading That the Cyclotron has Produced Cosmic Rays... Samuel Hoffenstein. There's nothing to fear but life and death–as far as/we know today. ShM

A Song on the Duke's Late Glorious Success over the Dutch. *Anonymous.* And here's to all the captains' names,/And here's to the House of Stuart. OBSS

Song: "On the side of the road." Edmond Jabes. Will there be a spring/for the downtrodden Jews? VWA

A Song on the South Sea. Anne Finch, Countess of Winchilsea. Even love does now no longer find/A place in female souls. NOEC

Song on the Water. Thomas Lovell Beddoes. And quiet as its death/Upon a lady's breast. Are mirrored, and hover/Moonily. FaBoCh; LoGBV

The Song on the Way. *Anonymous.* Singin' all together! BrR

Song:"Once my heart was a summer rose." Edith Sitwell. All the bright summer long. ChMP

Song: "One day the god of fond desire." James (1700-48) Thomson. You drag him at your chariot-wheels. EnLoPo

Song: One Hard Look. Robert Graves. And one hard look/Can close the book/That lovers love to see. MoAB; MoBrPo

Song: "Only a little while since first we met." Brian Hooker. On that old self of yours that filled my heart/Only a little while! HBMV

Song: "Only tell her that I love." John, Lord Cutts. Why, O why should I despair? HBV 1-2

Song: "Only the wanderer." Ivor. Gurney. Do not forget me quite,/O Severn meadows. FaBoPP

Song: "Or love mee lesse, or love mee more." Sidney Godolphin. For I shall love the very scorne/which for my sake you do put on. CavP; JCP; MePo; OBS

Song: "Out upon it, I have lov'd." Sir John Suckling. There had been at least ere this/A dozen dozen in her place. MeLP; MePo; SeCP; WHA

Song: Paper. Keith Waldrop. ...and I can't see/Out my window anymore. MAT

Song: Phillis be Gentler. John Wilmot, Earl of Rochester. And never know the Joy. CavP

Song: "Phillis, for shame let us improve." Charles, Earl of Dorset Sackville. May I be dull enough to grow/Most miserably wise. SeCV 1-2

Song: "Phillis is my only joy." Sir Charles Sedley. What need lovers wish for more? EnLoPo; InMe; OBS; SeCV 1-2

Song: "Phillis, let's shun the common Fate." Sir Charles Sedley. Thus we will all the World excel/In Loving, and in Parting well. SeCV 1-2

Song: "Pious Selinda goes to prayers." William Congreve. Would she could make of me a saint,/Or I of her a sinner. BoLoP; FaBoCo; InMe; NIP; NLV; NOEC; OBSP

Song: "Poppies paramour the girls." Haniel Long. Past the solace of the shade/Or the rescue of the sun. HBMV

Song: "Rarely, rarely, comest thou." Percy Bysshe Shelley. Make once more my heart thy home. ERoP 1-2; HBV 1-2; OAEP; OBNC; OBRV; TrGrPo

Song: "Reading about the Wisconsin Weeping Willow." Ruth Krauss. I was thinking of you LLLT

Song: "Rose and grape, pear and bean." Anonymous. Rose and grape, pear and bean/are bad to keep. BoWoP

Song: "Roses and pinks will be strewn where you go." Sir William Davenant. I lie near a shade of willow, willow. ViBoPo

Song: "Rousing to rein his pad's head back." Geoffrey Taylor. Her rust-red autumn-beech-leaf hair. NeIP; OxBI

Song's Eternity. John Clare. Nature's glee/Is in every mood and tone/Eternity. CBEP; FaBoCh; LoGBV; NCEP; PG

A Song's Worth. Susan Marr Spalding. He hath his love; but I–I have my song. AA

Song: "Say, lovely dream! where couldst thou find." Edmund Waller. And, death resembling, equals all. CavP

Song: "See, see, she wakes! Sabina wakes!" William Congreve. How many will her coldness kill! HBV 1-2; NOEC; OBSP

Song: "Seek not the tree of silkiest bark." Aubrey Thomas De Vere. That love, or none, is fit for one/Man-shaped like thee. OBVV

Song: "Sergei's a flower." Ruth Herschberger. A stallion in the night. FF

Song Set by John Daniel: "Let not Chloris think, because." Anonymous. Why should not she/Still joy to reign in me? OBSC

Song Set by John Dowland: "Come, ye heavy states of night." Anonymous. Come, sorrow, come, her eyes that sings/By thee are turned into springs. OBSC

Song Set by John Dowland: "What poor astronomers are they." Anonymous. Till time too late we make them try/They study false astronomy. OBSC

Song Set by John Farmer: "Take Time while Time doth last." Anonymous. Friends fail and Love grow cold. OBSC

Song Set by Michael Cavendish: "Faustina hath the fairer face." Anonymous. My heart, alas! must be divided. OBSC

Song. Set by Mr. Coleman. Charles Cotton. Which with the Morn for Lustre strive,/That I may look on her, and live. OBS

Song Set by Nicholas Yonge. Anonymous. Yet have I seen despised/Dainty white lilies, and sad flowers well prized. CTC; OBSC

Song Set by Philip Rosseter: "And would you see my mistress' face?" Anonymous. And this is that my soul pursueth. OBSC

Song Set by Philip Rosseter: "What is a day.." Anonymous. But if we still in virtue delight, our souls are in heaven placed. OBSC

Song Set by Robert Jones: "A woman's looks." Anonymous. They think by this/Us men to overreach. OBSC

Song Set by Robert Jones: "In Sherwood lived stout Robin Hood." Anonymous. To follow me to the green wood. OBSC

Song Set by Robert Jones: "Life is a poet's fable." Anonymous. That I die, that I die, though my breath/Prolongs this space of lingering death. OBSC

Song Set by Robert Jones: "O! How my thoughts do beat me. Anonymous. Love did ever hoard up in his treasure. OBSC

Song Set by Robert Jones: "Once did I love and yet I live." Anonymous. I say no more, because I loved her. OBSC

Song Set by Robert Jones: "She whose matchless beauty staineth." Anonymous. Hope still lives on time depending,/By thy plagues my torments ending. OBSC

Song Set by Robert Jones: "The sea hath many thousand sands." Anonymous. Love's martyr, when his heat is past,/Proves Care's confessor at the last. OBSC

Song Set by Thomas Ford: "Unto the temple of thy Beauty." Anonymous. Duties which I thy pilgrim send/To Beauty living, Pity dead. OBSC

Song Set by Thomas Weelkes: "In pride of May." Anonymous. The birds that day/More cheerfully will sing. OBSC Anonymous. And dazzled Reason yields as quite undone. OBSC

Song Set by Thomas Weelkes: "Now is my Chloris fresh as May." Anonymous. August will come another day. OBSC

Song Set by Thomas Weelkes: "Three times a day my prayer is." Anonymous. But all the year my suit must be/That I may please, and she love me. OBSC

Song: "She has left me, my pretty." Sylvia Townsend Warner. How she lay against my side! MoAB; MoBrPo

Song: "She's somewhere in the sunlight strong." Richard Le Gallienne. Yea! sun and moon are sent by her,/And every wistful waiting star. HBV 1-2; OBEV; OBVV

Song: "She sat and sang alway." Christina Georgina Rossetti. Her songs died on the air. GBL

Song: "She spoke to me gently with words of sweet meaning." Patrick MacDonogh. So I left her alone at her door. NeIP

Song: "She was lyin face down in her face." Bill Knott. I looked in the mirror before I was born but I didn't see nothin MAT

Song: "Shephard loveth thow me vell?" Jean Passerat. Like to thee, faire cruell May. OBVE

Song: "Shepherd, who can pass such wrong." Bartholomew Young. As it is too short to weep. EIL

Song: "Shine out, fair Sun, with all your heat." Anonymous. Shine out, and make this winter night/Our beauty's Spring, our Prince of Light! EIL

Song: "Silly Boy, there is no cause." Thomas Pestel. As two true clocks together go. EIL

Song: "Since I'm a girl." Anonymous. It won't help God/for me to be a nun. BoWoP

Song: "Since the night is dark." Anonymous. Friend, why don't you come? BoWoP

Song: "Sing the old song, amid the sounds dispersing." Aubrey Thomas De Vere. Like some sweet singer's, when her sweetest strain/From the heaved heart is gradually dying! HBV 1-2

Song: "Singee songee sick a pence. (parody). Anonymous. Nipee off her nose! BXAP

Song: "Singer within the little streets." Monk Gibbon. Her eyes were kind. NeIP

A Song: "Smile, Massachusetts, smile." Anonymous. And glory will our valor crown. PAH

Song: "Smooth was the Water, calm the Air." Sir Charles Sedley. This Kiss, my Dear,/Is sweeter far/Than Strawberries, Cream and Sugar. SeCV 1-2

Song: "So large a morning, so itself, to lean." W. H. Auden. So lacks all picture of reproach it ends/Denying what it started up to say. NePoAm-2

Song: "Softly, O midnight Hours!" Aubrey Thomas De Vere. Ere yet the misty herds/Leave warm 'mid the gray grass their dusky bed. IrPN

Song: "Something calls and whispers, along the city street." Georgiana Goddard King. The still light of planets and the star-swarms whirled. HBV 1-2

Song: "Sometimes I feel like an eagle in de air." Anonymous. But I'll hear de trumpet sound/In-a dat mornin'. NAMP

Song: "Sometimes in the fast food kitchen." Randy Lane. almost every working day. FAZ

Song: "Song is so old." Hermann Hagedorn. Song is so fair,/Love is so new! HBV 1-2

Song: "Soules joy, now I am gone." George Herbert. This wonder to the vulgar prove,/Our bodyes, not wee move. OBS

Song: "Spring lights her candles everywhere." Fredegond Shove. And how, of all things vainest, he/Journeys above both land and sea. HBMV

Song: "Stay Phoebus, stay." Edmund Waller. Did not the rowling Earth snatch her away. SeCP

Song: Stop All the Clocks. W. H. Auden. For nothing now can ever come to any good. MoBrPo

Song: "Stop! Don't touch me." Anonymous. your hands are cold. BoWoP

Song: "Strew not earth with empty stars." Thomas Lovell Beddoes. 'Tis Bacchus' son who walks below. OBSP; ViBoPo

Song: "Sweet are the Charms of her I love." Barton Booth. Divine Abodes shall own his Pow'r,/When Time and Death shall be no more. OBEC

Song: "Sweet beast, I have gone prowling." W. D. Snodgrass. Sweet beast, cat of my own stripe,/come and take my milk. LLLT; NYBP; SM

Song: "Sweet in her green dell the flower of beauty slumbers." George Darley. Bleeds with its death-wound, its wound of love for thee! OBEV; OBVV

Song: "Take it, love!" Richard Le Gallienne. Take the laughter first of all. HBV 1-2

Song: "Take, oh take those Lips away." Francis Beaumont and John Fletcher. Bound in those Ivy Chains by thee. PoEL 1-5

Song–Talysarn. Brenda Chamberlain. Broke earth with song. NeBP

Song: "Tell me no more I am deceived." Sir George Etherege. The joy she gives it true. CavP

Song: "That women are but men's shadows." Ben Jonson. Stil'd but the shaddowes of us men? FaBoEn

Song: "The bee-keeper kissed me." Anonymous. By the taste of honey I knew it was he. BoWoP

Song: "The bee to the heather." Sir Henry Taylor. And whither shall I? OBVV

Song: "The bells of Sunday rang us down." John Ciardi. And all the seas were running late. WaP

Song: "The boat is chafing at our long delay." John Davidson. Our vessel, plunging deeper into night/To reach a land unknown. OBEV; OBVV; PoPle

Song the Eighth. Edward Moore. And let me deserve her, or still I say no. CEP

Song: "The engine screams and Murphy, isolate." Thomas Kinsella. Her pupils glow with pleasure all night long. FaBoIP

Song: "The feathers of the willow." Richard Watson Dixon. The robin pipeth low. GTBS-P; LoBV; LoGBV; NOBE; OBNC; OBVV; YeAr

Song: "The first month of his absence." Alun Lewis. The gradual self-effacement of the dead. LiTM; OBWP; WaaP

Song: "The fringed vallance of your eyes advance." Thomas Shadwell. And all those gems the ripening summer yields. ViBoPo

A Song the Grass Sings. Charles G. Blanden. I smiling at the buttercup,/ She smiling at the grass. HBV 1-2

Song: "The gross sun squats above." Dom Moraes. And dance and flute will cease. NePoEA-2

Song: The Hopeless Comfort. Robert Gould. Why shou'd I hope to shun? CEP

Song: "The little Black Rose shall be red at last!" Aubrey Thomas De Vere. –This song is secret. Mine ear it pass'd/In a wind o'er the stone plain of Athenry. IrPN

Song: "The merchant, to secure his treasure." Matthew Prior. Remarked how ill we all dissembled. HBV 1-2; LiTL; OBEV; TrGrPo

Song: "The moth's kiss, first!" Robert Browning. Over our head to sleep I bow. HBV 1-2; TrGrPo

Song: "The night is an ancient sorceress." Simeon S. Frug. And every little grass-blade/Wears a jewel all its own. LiTW

Song the Ninth. Edward moore. And I in my turn, may be taught to love too. CEP

A Song: "The nymph in vain bestows her pains." Anne Finch, Countess of Winchilsea. So inaccessible and cold,/That to be his is to be old. OBSP

The Song the Oriole Sings. William Dean Howells. So tenderly and sweetly dear/As my lost boyhood is to me? AmePo; HBV 1-2

Song: The Owl. Alfred, Lord Tennyson. The white owl in the belfry sits. GoJo; HBV 1-2; HBVY; MyFE; ORBV; SUS

Song: "The owl is abroad." Anonymous. And the Frog peeps out of the fountain. PoPle

Song: "The pints and the pistols, the pike-staves and pottles." Winthrop Mackworth Praed. And fire off a salvo for wine-cups and wars. SoSe

Song: "The primrose in the green forest." Thomas Deloney. Doth move the spirits with brave delights,/Who Beauty's darlings be. TiPo; ViBoPo

Song: The Railway Train. Anonymous. It blows like a spouting whale. NOAV

Song: "The shape alone let others prize." Mark Akenside. But go, behold Arpasia's face,/And read it perfect there. HBV 1-2

Song: "The streams that wind among the hills." George Darley. But I will never wend from thee! NBM

Song: "The sun is mine." Robert Hogg. Their voices upon the wind/are in my ear WHW

Song: "The world is full of loss." Muriel Rukeyser. Freedom to find to find to find/That nakedness. MiAP

Song: "There in the flower garden." Anonymous. There in the flower garden/they will kill me. BoWoP

Song: "There is many a love in the land, my love." Joaquin Miller. Deep in your heart to sleep, to sleep,/In the darlingest tomb of lovers. HBV 1-2

Song: "There is no joy in water apart from the sun." Ralph Nixon Currey. Walking alone in the valley of the shadow of death. PeSA

Song: "There's a barrel of porter at Tammany Hall." Fitz-Greene Halleck. For still dear to my soul, as 'twas then to my eyes,/Is that barrel of porter at Tammany Hall. OBAL

Song: "There's one great bunch of stars in hcaven." Theophile Marzials. Perhaps the lamp my love in heaven/Hangs out to light the way for me. OBVV

Song: "There stands a lonely pine-tree." Heinrich Heine. Lonely and silent longing/On her burning bank of sand. TrJP

Song: "Think of dress in every light." John Gay. Besides, when not a creature's by/'Tis inward satisfaction. OBEC; OBSP

Song: "This is the song." William Justema. pariahs and saints–this song is for you. NYBP

Song: "This peach is pink with such a pink." Norman Gale. My sweetheart keeps a warmer white. HBV 1-2

Song: "Those rivers run from that land." Robert Creeley. for the sake of the tree. VGW

Song: "Though I am dark." Anonymous. I lost my color/tending the flock. BoWoP

Song: "Three little maidens they have slain." Maurice Maeterlinck. Three seraphim watch three years through. AWP

Song: "Three Moorish girls I loved." Anonymous. Went apple-plucking there/In Jaen,/Axa and Fatima and Marien. LiTW

The Song-Throe. Dante Gabriel Rossetti. But if thy lips' loud cry leap to his smart,/The inspir'd recoil pierce thy brother's heart. MaVP

Song: "Thy fingers make early flowers." Edward Estlin Cummings. (though love be a day/and life be nothing, it shall not stop kissing). MoAmPo

Song: "Thyrsis, when we parted, swore." Thomas Gray. Cease, my doubts, my fears to move,/Spare the honour of my Love. OAEP

Song: Time Drawes Neere. Anne Waldman. I ride you unseene wave/wee rise together/under daddye's roof & hand. APU

Song: "'Tis affection but dissembled." Sidney Godolphin. Yet even these ne'er change their love. JCP

Song: "'Tis said that absence conquers love!" Frederick William Thomas. I've tried, alas! its power to prove,/But thou art not forgot. HBV 1-2

Song: "'Tis sweet to hear the merry lark." Hartley Coleridge. And woe may come to-morrow. HBV 1-2

Song: "'Tis true our life is but a long dis-ease." Katherine ("Orinda") Philips. Or else the object lost,/Ere we can call it ours. OBSP

Song to a Fair, Young Lady, Going out of the Town in the Spring. John Dryden. I only am by Love designed/To be the victim for mankind. CABA; HBV 1-2; LiTL; OBEV; OBS

Song to a Lover. Anonymous. Why am I in love/with him? BoWoP

Song to a Lute. Sir John Suckling. O so fickle, O so vain, O so false, so false is she! CaPo; TrGrPo

Song to a Negro Wash-Woman. Langston Hughes. Could I but find the words. GoSl

Song: "To all you ladies now at land." Charles, Earl of Dorset Sackville. We have too much of that at sea–/With a fa, la, la, la, la. CoMu; HBV 1-2; NOBE; OBEV; OBWP; SeCV 1-2

A Song to Amoret. Henry Vaughan. But with my soul had from above/This endless holy fire. HBV 1-2; LiTL; ViBoPo

Song to Be Sung by the Father of Infant Female Children. Ogden Nash. To marry somebody else's daughter! MoAmPo

Song to Beta. Michael Drayton. And thou under thy feet mayst tread that foul seven-headed/beast. OBSC

Song to Celia. Ben Jonson.
Since when it grows, and smells, I swear,/Not of itself but thee. AWP; CABA; DiPo; ELP; ForPo; GBL; GoTF; HeIP; InPo; NoP; OAEL 1-2; PoEL 1-5; PoPl; PrIm; SeCP; SeCV 1-2
These have crimes accounted been. InPS; JCP; OAEL 1-2

A Song to Celia. Sir Charles Sedley. When Change it self can give no more,/'Tis easie to be true. CavP; OBS; SeCePo

A Song to Cloris. John Wilmot, Earl of Rochester. Just in the happy Minute. ErPo

A Song to David. Christopher Smart. DETERMINED, DARED, and DONE AnFE; AtBAP; CEP; EaLo; EBEV; EiCP; EnPE; FaBoCh; GoTL; HAP; HBV 1-2; LaA; LAuP; LoBV; MasP; MyFE; NOBE; NOEC; OAEL 1-2; OBEC; OBEV; OxBoCh; PoEL 1-5; TrGrPo; TRV; UnS; ViBoPo; WGRP

Song to Death. Joan Escriva. My joy to see thee near/Will fill me with new breath. LiTW

Song to His Cynthia. Fulke, Lord Brooke Greville. ...you worthy be,/Yet without love naught worth to me. ViBoPo

A Song to His Purse for the King. Geoffrey Chaucer. And ye, that mowen alle mine harme amende,/Have minde upon my supplicacion. MeEL

Song to Imogen (parody). Richard Leighton Greene. My sweet respected woman, get up! BXAP

A Song to John, Christ's Friend. Anonymous. Thou be oure helpe we be not forsake,/Amice Christi, Johannes. MeEL

A Song to Mary. of Shoreham William. And thagh ich habbe ido thee wrange,/Thou graunte me amendinge. MeEL

Song to My Love. Laurence McKinney. The flowers are driving me wild. InMe

Song to Promote Growth. Anonymous. Thc voice of the bluebird is heard. OBVE

Song to the Evening Star. Thomas Campbell. Too delicious to be riven/By absence from the heart. GTBS; HBV 1-2

Song, to the Gods, is Sweetest Sacrifice. Annie Fields. And how our angels in the night-time/sing? AA

Song to the Masquers. James Shirley. Go kiss their hands and make your own/With every touch more white. OBSP

Song: To the Masquers Representing Stars. Thomas Campion. That every eye may here commend/The kind delights you breed. LoBV

Song to the Mountains. Anonymous. Resting there at last we sing our song. AWP

Song to the Runaway Slave. Anonymous. Dat you cain't git yo' lodgin' here. BPo

Song to the Tune of "Somebody Stole My Gal." X. J. Kennedy. Somebody stole my myths. CoPo

A Song to the Virgin. Anonymous. That havez hidut the fouled put,/ inferni. SeCePo

Song to the Virgin Mary. Pero Lopez de Ayala. Thy shrine in Guadalupe's tower/My pilgrim steps shall see. CAW

A Song to the Wind. Taliesin. Who exalt not the Father/Shall tunelessly sing! FaBoCh

Song: "Too late, alas! I must confess."   John Wilmot, Earl of Rochester. And give my tongue the glory/To boast, though my unfaithful eyes/Betray a tender story.   HBV 1-2

Song Tournament: New Style.   Louis Untermeyer.   At the shrine of the Poetry Contest in Kansas.   CrMA; OBAL

Song: "Trip it Gipsies, trip it fine."   William and Thomas Middleton Rowley. If Poet thou tosse not bowle for bowle/Thou shalt not kisse a Doxie.   OBS

Song: "Turn, turn thy beauteous face away."   Francis Beaumont and John Fletcher.   Let but their lids fall, and it will be night.   PoEL 1-5

The Song Turning Back into Itself 3.   Al Young.   blowing the right way/at just that moment in history   CNA; NPGG

Song: "Under a southern wind."   Theodore Roethke.   All things bring me to love.   CrMA

Song Under Shadow.   William Rose Benet.   A door stands open in the heart/And all good things are true.   MoRP

Song: Under the Bronze Leaves.   Saint-John Perse.   ..."Hail, daughter! robed in the loveliest robe of the/year."   AtBAP; PoPl

Song: "Under the lime-tree, on the daisied ground."   Walther von der Vogelweide.   She, I think, will tell no tale.   OBVE

Song: "Under the oak tree, oak tree."   *Anonymous.*   Very blessed be/every pilgrimage/under the oak tree.   BoWoP

Song: "Under the Winter, dear."   Eugene Lee-Hamilton.   Lo, thou shalt hear it.   OBVV

Song: "Virtue's branches wither, virtue pines."   Thomas Dekker.   Virtue's branches wither, virtue pines.   ElL; WHA

Song: "Wait but a little while."   Norman Gale.   A soul in her to match thine own,/Though yet ungrown.   HBV 1-2

Song: "We break the glass, whose sacred wine."   Edward Coate [(or Coote)] Pinkney.   Or that soft chain of spoken flowers/And airy gems,–thy words.   HBV 1-2

Song: "We came to Tamichi in 1880."   Judy. Scott Hammond.   "Doc"   We'll meet you again, when the snow melts away.   PoOW

Song: "We'll, placed in Love's triumphant chariot high."   William Cavendish, Duke of Newcastle.   Wretches, alas! that know not where we go.   OBSP

Song: "We only ask for sunshine."   Helen Hay Whitney.   But grief's redress is happiness,/Alternate through the years.   HBV 1-2

Song (We Sing).   Cosmo Pieterse.   And the birth from the dust that is green we sing.   WhB

Song: "Were I laid on Greenland's coast."   John Gay.   Over the hills and far away.   EnLoPo; OBEC; OxBoLi

Song: "Westron wynde when wyll thou blow."   *Anonymous.*   And I yn my bed agayne.   SeCePo

Song: "What binds the atom together."   Philip Dow.   or one cell's shadow/in the great body of growing/we grow in.   NPGG

Song: "What I took in my hand."   Robert Creeley.   ...What/I took in my hand/grows in weight.   NoP; PoA

Song: "What think you of this age now."   *Anonymous.*   'Tis a lie we all do know.   APAS

Song: "Whaur yon broken brig hings owre."   William Soutar.   Gang doun wi' a sang, gang doun.   GoTS; OxBS

Song: "When de golden trumpets sound."   *Anonymous.*   When de golden trumpets sound.   NAMP

Song: "When, dearest, I but think of".   Owen Felltham.   That flows not every day, but ever.   CavP; MePo; SeCeV

Song: "When I am dead, my dearest."   Christina Georgina Rossetti.   Haply I may remember,/And haply may forget.   BiP; BoLoP; DL; EBEV; FF; FPL; GBL; GoTF; GTBS; HBV 1-2; InPS; LiTL; NOBE; NoP; OAEL 1-2; OAEP; OBEV; OBVV; PoLf; PoRA; SCV; SoSe; TreFS; ViBoPo; VLP; WHA

Song: "When I lie burning in thine eye."   Thomas Stanley.   Since Phoenix-like I from this fire/Both life and youth receive.   ViBoPo

Song: "When I was a greenhorn and young."   Charles Kingsley.   'Tis no business of his where it goes.   NBM

Song: "When Love at first did move."   Ben Jonson.   Admit no shade. GoBC

A Song: "When lovely woman, prone to folly. (parody).   *Anonymous.*   To win fresh praises from her lover,/And make him offer–is to dye.   FaBoPa

Song: "When lovely woman stoops to folly."   Oliver Goldsmith.   To give repentance to her lover,/And wring his bosom–is to die.   AWP; BoLoP; LAuP; LiTL; NOBE; NOEC; OBEC; PoPl; SeCePo; TrGrPo; ViBoPo

Song: "When maidens are young, and in their spring."   Aphra Behn. There's nought but hum-drum, hum-drum, hum-drum.   FF

Song: "When the birds sang."   *Anonymous.*   come and ask him/what he dreamed?   BoWoP

Song: "When the echo of the last footstep dies."   E. W. Mandel.   Hanging isn't good enough for me.   OBCV

Song: "When the heart's feeling."   Thomas Moore.   Looks betray all that the heart would be at.   OBSP

Song: "When thy Beauty appears."   Thomas Parnell.   Still an Angel appear to each Lover beside,/But still be a Woman to you.   OBEC; OBEV; UnTE

Song: "When working blackguards come to blows."   Ebenezer Elliott.   Nap perished at Saint Helena.   EBEV; NBM

Song: "Whenever, Chloe, I begin."   Philip Stanhope, Earl of Chesterfield. Bless me, and by repentance make/A holy day in heaven.   NOEC

Song: "Where did you borrow that last sigh."   Sir William Berkeley.   Your eyes can only teach us love,/But cannot take it in.   OBSP

Song: "Where I walk out."   Yvor Winters.   quiver like a/heartbeat in the/air and are/no more   BoAnP; PoL

Song: "Where in blind files."   Eavan Boland.   He late that night/Followed the leaping tide.   CIP

Song: "Where is the nymph, whose azure eye."   Thomas Moore.   Come to me, love, the twilight star/Shall guide thee to my bower.   EnLoPo

Song:"Where shall Celia fly for shelter."   Christopher Smart.   Wear it on your knots and fans.   EnLoPo

Song: "Where shall the lover rest."   Sir Walter Scott.   Eleu loro!/Never, O never!   NBM

A Song: "While a thousand fine projects are planned ev'ry day."   *Anonymous.* Contrive that the poor may have something to eat.   NOEC

Song: "Whilst landmen wander, though controlled."   *Anonymous.*   No more will make mankind subdue/The work of devastation.   OBSS

Song: "Whipped by sorrow now."   Miklos Radnoti.   Above me, a pair of/hawks hang like wet rags.   VWA

Song: "Who can say."   Alfred, Lord Tennyson.   The cause is nowhere found in rhyme.   LoGBV

Song: "Who has robbed the ocean cave."   John Shaw.   Take, oh, take that heart from me.   HBV 1-2

Song: "Who hath his fancy pleased."   Sir Philip Sidney.   Let here his eyes be raised/On Nature's sweetest light!   OBEV; SiPS

Song: "Why canst thou not, as others do."   *Anonymous.*   O be as others are to me,/Or let me be more to thee.   LiTL

Song: "Why do the houses stand."   George Macdonald.   For the builders are not gone.   OBVV

Song: "Why, lovely charmer, tell me why."   Sir Richard Steele.   I cannot love thee less nor more.   LiTL; ViBoPo

Song: Wit and Beauty.   Robert Gould.   But what the Devil can be done/With Wit and Beauty too?   CavP

A Song with a Discord.   Arthur Colton.   For anything they'll buy.   AA

Song: "With my frailty don't upbraid me."   William Congreve.   I am Woman as Heaven made Me.   PoL

Song: "With whomsoever I share the spring."   Jan Burroway.   Imprison to spend all springs with you.   NePoAm-2

Song with Words.   James Agee.   And weave us one and wave us under/Where is neither faith nor wonder.   MoAmPo

Song: "Woman sits on her porch."   Earle Thompson.   Sudden splashing breaks/stillness of morning.   STE

Song: "Would you know what's soft?"   Thomas Carew.   Name my mistress, and 'tis done!   EG; EnLi 1-2

Song: "Ye happy swains, whose hearts are free."   Sir George Etherege.   The kind with falsehood to destroy,/The cruel with despair!   HBV 1-2; LiTL; ViBoPo

Song: "Yes, the book of Revelations will be brought forth dat/day."   *Anonymous.*   A-shoutin' "Hallelujah!" singing praises to de Lord.   NAMP

Song: "You are as gold."   Hilda ("H. D.") Doolittle.   so your hair on your brow/casts light for a shadow.   LiTA; LiTM; MAPA

Song: "You're wondering if I'm lonely."   Adrienne Rich.   but wood, with a gift for burning   PBWP

Song: "You wear the morning like your dress."   Hilaire Belloc.   With all her royal nymphs in train/Could so lead on the Spring.   OBEV; OBVV

Song: "You wrong me, Strephon."   Ephelia (Joan Philips).   And let her rival me.   CavP; LiTL

Song, Youth, and Sorrow.   William Cranston Lawton.   Grief, an untimely doom, fame that/eternal abides.   AA

Songe betwene the Quenes Majestie and Englande.   *Anonymous.*   thata by his powre & might/he may give them a right/For the welth of all christen landes.   CoMu

The Songe: "Drinke and be merry, merry, merry boyes."   Thomas Morton. Io to Hymen, &c.   SCAP

The Songs.   *Anonymous.*   In the mountains north of Zuni,/I heard their cry...   WTO

The Songs.   Martin Bell.   On the sunny side always, the sunny side of the/street.   FF

Songs.   Edward Estlin Cummings.   despair of violin.   APA

Songs.   Babette Deutsch.   Like love, wherefor I am so dumb to you. HBMV

Songs.   Richard Watson Gilder.
And thou art strange to me, Love, to-/night.   AA
For thou art the whole wide world to me.   AA

Songs.   Denis Glover.   Sings Harry in the wind-break.   AnNZ

Songs.   Richard Henry Stoddard.   Nature and the Poet's mind.   AA

Songs about Life and Brighter Things Yet.   Samuel Hoffenstein.
And, having swerved, no might or main/Can ever put her straight again. NLV
A checkered taxi runs him down. NLV

Sonnet: "They say that shadowes of deceased ghosts." Joshua Sylvester. Where I, alas dare not approach the cruell/Proud Monument, that doth inclose my Jewell. EIL; OBS

Sonnet: "This infant world has taken long to make." George Macdonald. Unfold a world that I, thy child, might see. OBVV

Sonnet: "This is the golden book of spirit and sense." Algernon Charles Swinburne. But see not twice unveiled the veiled God's face. SyP

Sonnet: "This virgin, beautiful and lively day." Stephane Mallarme. ...dream of contempt/Which clothes in his useless exile the Swan. PoPl

Sonnet: "Thou art indeed just, Lord, if I contend." Gerard Manley Hopkins. Mine, O thou Lord of life, send my roots rain. MoVE

Sonnet: "Three silences made him a single word." Richard P. Blackmur. ...we are/to this child's sun the silent morning star. PoA

Sonnet: "Time and the mortal will stand never fast." Luîs de Camoens. Not chequered with rare blessing as of yore. AWP

Sonnet to—. John Hamilton Reynolds. With Robin at their head, and Marian. OBRV

Sonnet: To–. William Wordsworth. Receiv'st the gift for more than mild content! ChRP

Sonnet to a Clam. John Godfrey Saxe. Declares, O clams, thy case is shocking hard! AnNE; BoAnP

Sonnet to a Friend... Samuel Taylor Coleridge. And dearer was the mother for the child. EnRP

Sonnet: To a Friend Who Does Not Pity His Love. Guido Cavalcanti. Come to behold the death of the poor heart. AWP

Sonnet to A Negro in Harlem. Helene Johnson. You are too splendid for this city street. BANP; CDC; NIP

Sonnet to a Tyrant. Mary Anne Ellis. I know that I would smile to see you dead. AMV-80

Sonnet to a Young Lady Who Sent Me a Laurel Crown. John Keats. Yet would I kneel and kiss thy gentle hand! EnRP

Sonnet to Be Written from Prison. Robert Adamson. The myth is torn apart and stashed away in books. CBAP

Sonnet to Britain. Ayton [(or Aytoun)] Sir Robert. Pounding them into mummy, Shoulder, hoop! FaBoCo

Sonnet: To Brunetto Latini. Dante Alighieri. Apply to Master Janus last of all. AWP

Sonnet to Byron. John Keats. The enchanting tale, the tale of pleasing woe. ERoP 1-2

Sonnet: To Certain Ladies. Dante Alighieri. If, when you speak, your words are of no worth. AWP

Sonnet to Chatterton. John Keats. On earth the good man base detraction bars/From thy fair name, and waters it with tears. ERoP 1-2

Sonnet: To Dante Alighieri (He Reports in a Feigned Vision). Guido Cavalcanti. If he believe not, let him note her eyes.' AWP

Sonnet: To Dante Alighieri (He Writes to Dante...). Cecco da Siena Angiolieri. For, Dante, I'm the goad and you're the bull. AWP

Sonnet: To Dante Alighieri (On the Last Sonnet of the Vita Nuova). Cecco da Siena Angiolieri. Of these your words the other's sense denies. AWP

Sonnet to Edgar Allan Poe. Sarah Helen Whitman. Sleep on my heart till Heaven the flower unfold. AnAmPo

Sonnet to Gath. Edna St. Vincent Millay. And cluck your children in about your knee? BoWoP; CMoP; MoAB; MoAmPo

Sonnet: To Guido Cavalcanti. Dante Alighieri. Our time, and each were as content and free/As I believe that thou and I should be. AWP

A Sonnet to Heavenly Beauty. Joachim Du Bellay. Behold the Very Beauty/Thou worshipest the shadow upon earth. AWP; CTC

Sonnet: To His Lady Joan, of Florence. Guido Cavalcanti. Because among them all thou art the best. AWP

Sonnet: To Homer. John Keats. Such seeing hadst thou, as it once befel/To Dian, Queen of Earth, and Heaven, and Hell. ChRP

Sonnet: To Love, in Great Bitterness. Cino da Pistoia. I must a little taste its opposite. AWP

Sonnet to My Friend, with an Identity Disc. Wilfred Owen. Until the name grow blurred and fade away. PeHV

Sonnet to My Mother. George Barker. That she will move from mourning into morning. FaFP; LiTB; MoAB; SeCePo; ViBoPo; WaP

A Sonnet to My Mother. Heinrich Heine. That is the precious, the/long-looked-for Love. TrJP

Sonnet to Negro Soldiers. Joseph Seaman Cotter, Jr. There breaks this day their dawn of liberty. PoBA

Sonnet: "To one who has been long in city pent." John Keats. E'en like the passage of an angel's tear/That falls through the clear ether silently. FaBoBe; FPL; LoBV

A Sonnet to Opium; Celebrating Its Virtues. Orestes". When madd'ning rapture goads to vice my throbbing sense. NOEC

Sonnet to Oxford. Thomas Russell. But most those Friends, whose much-lov'd converse gave/Thy gentle charms a tenfold power to please. OBEC

Sonnet: "To rail or jest, ye know I use it not." Sir Thomas Wyatt. That is to say, for service true and fast,/Too long delays, and changing at the last. SiPS

Sonnet–To Science. Edgar Allan Poe. The summer dream beneath the tamarind tree? AP; APA; MAmP; NePA; NoP; OxBA; TAP; TW

Sonnet to Seabrook. David Ray. Cranes hover over shale. Slow rivers shine. AMV-80

Sonnet–To Silence. Edgar Allan Poe. The Elfin from the green grass, and from me/The summer dream beneath the tamarind tree? PPON

Sonnet: To Tartar, a Terrier Beauty. Thomas Lovell Beddoes. Solicitudes canine, four-footed amities. NOBV; OBNC

Sonnet: To the Asshole. Arthur Rimbaud. It's a heavenly jam-pot, the Promised Land/Which with other milk and honey overflows! PeHV

Sonnet–To the Critic. Michael Drayton. I scorn all earthly dung-bred scarabies. LoBV

Sonnet to the Lady Beaumont. William Wordsworth. And all the mighty ravishment of spring. ChRP

A Sonnet, to the Noble Lady, the Lady Mary Worth. Ben Jonson. Her joyes, her smiles, her loves, as readers take/For Venus Ceston, every line you make. AnAnS 2

Sonnet to the Prince Regent. George Gordon, Lord Byron. A despot thou, and yet thy people free,/And by the heart, not hand, enslaving us. MBW 1-2

Sonnet, to the River Loddon. Thomas Warton, Jr.. Nor with the Muse's laurel unbestowed. CEP; NOEC; OBEC; ViBoPo

Sonnet: To the River Otter. Samuel Taylor Coleridge. Ah! that I were once more a careless child! ChRP; OAEL 1-2

Sonnet: To the Same Ladies; with Their Answer. Dante Alighieri. O weep no more; thou art all wan with sighs.' AWP

Sonnet to the Sea Serpent. John Gardiner Calkins Brainard. You are a great deal bigger than you are. EtS

Sonnet to the Virgin. William Wordsworth. Of high with low, celestial with terrene! ISi

Sonnet to Valclusa. Thomas Russell. Still Petrarch's Genius weeps o'er Laura's tomb. CEP; OBEC

Sonnet to Vauxhall. Thomas Hood. Back to the cold transparent ham again! PoEL 1-5

Sonnet to William Wilberforce, Esq. William Cowper. From all the Just on earth, and all the Blest above. CEP; OAEP

Sonnet–To Zante. Edgar Allan Poe. "Isola d'oro! Fior di Levante!" MAmP

Sonnet: True Ambition. Benjamin Stillingfleet. Who but the extremest . skirts of glory sees,/And hears celestial echoes with delight.' OBEC

A Sonnet: "Two voices are there." James Kenneth Stephen. Than write such hopeless rubbish as thy worst. DBV; FaBoCo; FaBoPa; NOBL; SpRo

Sonnet upon a Swedish Cottage. Sir John Carr. May such a spot, so wild, so sweet, be mine! OBTV

Sonnet: "We will not whisper, we have found the place." Hilaire Belloc. For us tired children, now our games are played. MoBrPo

A Sonnet: "Weeping, murmuring, complaining." Oliver Goldsmith. She long had wanted cause of fear. NOBI

Sonnet: "Were I as base as is the lowly plain." Joshua Sylvester. Wheresoe'er you are, my heart shall truly love you. EIL; OBSC; ViBoPo

Sonnet: "What doth it serve to see sun's burning face." William, of Hawthornden Drummond. No part of them can have now with me here? EIL

Sonnet: "When, from the tower whence I derive love's heaven." *Anonymous*. Mine heart, Zepheria, then became thy fee. EIL

Sonnet: "When I was marked for suffering, love forswore." Miguel de Cervantes Saarvedra. ...no witch hath brewed/The drug that might avert my martyrdom. AWP

Sonnet: "When Phoebe form'd a wanton smile." William Collins. The fabled queen of love. EnLoPo; OBSP

Sonnet: "When some men gather to talk of Love." Irene Rutherford McLeod. We lovers know ourselves the only wise! HBMV

Sonnet: "Where are we to go when this is done?" Alfred A. Duckett. We are the war-born. What are we to do? PoBA; PoNe

Sonnet: Where Lies the Land. William Wordsworth. Is with me at thy farewell, joyous Bark! ChRP

Sonnet: "Whilst thus my pen strives to eternise thee." Michael Drayton. My name shall mount upon eternity. ViBoPo

Sonnet with a Different Letter at the End of Every Line. George Starbuck. On voyage comme poisson, incog. OBAL

Sonnet: "Women have loved before as I love now." Edna St. Vincent Millay. Heedless and wilful, took their knights to bed. PoA

Sonnet Written after Seeing Wilton-House. Thomas Warton, Jr.. And in bright trophies cloath the twilight wall. OBEC

Sonnet: Written at Stonehenge. Thomas Warton, Jr.. We muse on many an ancient tale renown'd. CEP

Sonnet Written at the Close of Spring. Charlotte Smith. Ah! why has happiness–no second spring? OBEC

Sonnet Written at the End of "The Floure and the Lefe." John Keats. Were heard of none beside the mournful/robins. EnRP

Love is the hardest where all things are hard. HBMV

No more than bluets, blown when April takes/Millions of them to make one meadow blue. HBMV

Shall ask God's self, incredulous, some day,/Why in the name of Christ He let you come! HBMV

That came like lightning shattering my heart! HBMV

Sonnets.   John Masefield.   The sun will rise, the winds that ever move/Will blow our dust that once were men in love.   HBV 1-2

Sonnets.   Frederick Goddard Tuckerman.

And breaking hearts that hate the morning light!   AP

And in the angles of the fences found.   AP

And just awash, the low reef lifts its line.   AP

And left me listening to the sinking sound.   AP

And pore upon my verse, and court my grief,–.   AP

And, shattered on the roof like smallest snows,/The tiny petals of the mountain ash.   NoP

And shimmering suds of the sea!   AP

And with every gust of wind my heart goes by!   AP

A bird that shuts his wings for better speed.   NoP

Blackness, and scalding stench, for love and flowers.   HAP

Creation moveth, and the farmboy sleeps,/A still strong sleep till but the east is red.   MAmP

Dim bodings wherefore? Now indeed I know.   MAmP

Found us at tears and wept for company.   AP

Green diamond, or gem of girosol!   AP

Half-high, or tapering off at summer's end.   MAmP

Not to be left, but with the waste woodland.   AP

Now kept it flat, and raked the walks and shrubs.   AP

On flowers, until the vision and the glory came!   AP

Sideward, the River turning like a wheel.   AP

That Actia, Arlotte, and Mandane dreamed?   AP

To break the axe's edge of time and Fate!   AP

The wakeful bird that to the lighted window sings for dawn.   AP

Was it a thorn that touched the flesh, or did/The pokeberry spit purple on my hand?   MAmP

The wave broke fresher, flinging on my lip/Some drops of salt. I shuddered, and turned away.   MAmP

Will break anon: Lo! where the gray is white!   AP

Sonnets.   Sarah Helen Whitman.   Till God's great love, on both, one hopes one Heaven bestow.   AA

Sonnets.   George Edward Woodberry.   And ever round her shine the aureole/Of my sad verses, after I am dead!   HBMV

Sonnets: A Sequence on Profane Love.   George Henry Boker.

Ablaze to punish the presumptuous deed!   AmePo

And burn with fire whose source I cannot trace.   AmePo

And my world's mask lies empty at thy feet.   AmePo

And stain it with the dusty stir I make!   AmePo

And thy atonement my salvation win.   AmePo

Be what she thinks me, for her sweet thought's sake.   AmePo

But stony, death-like sleep, too deep for dreams.   AmePo

Ere her chaste will lay vanquished in my chains.   AmePo

For there is that which never should be known.   AmePo

I safely sheltered in thy heart at last.   AmePo

I would not give my loss for all his gain.   AmePo

Perhaps, alas, these prophet tears foretell.   AmePo

See God's own radiance in a tranquil star.   AmePo

To kiss and hug in God's insulted view.   AmePo

Which makes exhausted nature trip and fall/Just at the point where it becomes divine.   AmePo

While in God's patient hands his arrows rust!   AmePo

Sonnets–Actualities.   Edward Estlin Cummings.   and possibly i like the thrill/of under me you so quite new   UnTE

Sonnets after the Italian.   Richard Watson Gilder.   And every new day there is something new.   HBV 1-2

Sonnets at Christmas.   Allen Tate.

Punished by crimes of which I would be quit.   HAP; LiTM; NoAm; NOBA; OxBA; PoNe; VGW

Ring out the silence I am nourished by.   HAP; LiTA; NePA; NoAm; NOBA; OxBA; VGW

Sonnets, First Series.   Frederick Goddard Tuckerman.

And him, Ophion, earliest of the gods?   MAmP

And the catbird's silver song, the wakeful bird/That to the lighted window sings for dawn.   MAmP

God were not God, whom knowledge cannot know.   MAmP

Had Deborah fear? or was that vision vain/That Actia, Arlotte, and Mandane dreamed?   MAmP

Sonnets for a Dying Man.   Burns Singer.

And one storm petrel rises like a whip.   NePoEA-2

His eyes went slimy with the look of snails.   NePoEA-2

Those who deny it, though they cannot live,/Possess, but finally, a life to give.   NePoEA-2

A world found dying of the death you died.   NePoEA-2

...the world has grown so wide,/That we don't know which one of us has died.   NePoEA-2

Sonnets for Pictures: Our Lady of the Rocks.   Dante Gabriel Rossetti.   Amid the bitterness of things occult.   EBEV

Sonnets for Roseblush, XVIII.   John Hollander.   Because because because because because.   SM

Sonnets from a Sequence.   Shirley Barker.

I shall be still. The child may keep his toy.   AnAmPo

Seeking the thing no man has ever found.   AnAmPo

Sonnets from China (excerpt).   W. H. Auden.   Where life is evil now./Nanking. Dachau.   OBWP

Sonnets from Greece: Mount Lykaion.   Trumbull Stickney.   The great wind kill my little shell with sound.   TrGrPo

Sonnets from the Portuguese, I.   Elizabeth Barrett Browning.   The silver answer rang,–"Not Death, but Love."   AnFE; CoBE; EnLit; GBL; GTBS; HBV 1-2; NOBE; NoP; OAEP; OBEV; OBNC; TreFT; ViBoPo

Sonnets from the Portuguese, II.   Elizabeth Barrett Browning.   Go farther! let it serve to trample on.   OBVV

Sonnets from the Portuguese, III.   Elizabeth Barrett Browning.   And Death must dig the level where these agree.   GTBS; OAEP; OBEV; TrGrPo

Sonnets from the Portuguese, VI.   Elizabeth Barrett Browning.   And sees within my eyes the tears of two.   BLPL; GTBS; HBV 1-2; OBEV; TreFS; TrGrPo; ViBoPo

Sonnets from the Portuguese, VII.   Elizabeth Barrett Browning.   Because thy name moves right in what they say.   CTC; HBV 1-2; OAEP; VLP

Sonnets from the Portuguese, IX.   Elizabeth Barrett Browning.   Beloved, I only love thee! let it pass.   CTC; HBV 1-2

Sonnets from the Portuguese, X.   Elizabeth Barrett Browning.   ...and show/How that great work of Love enhances Nature's.   HBV 1-2

Sonnets from the Portuguese, XII.   Elizabeth Barrett Browning.   And that I love (O soul, we must be meek!)/Is by thee only, whom I love alone.   HBV 1-2

Sonnets from the Portuguese, XIII.   Elizabeth Barrett Browning.   Lest one touch of this heart convey its grief.   BrRo

Sonnets from the Portuguese, XIV.   Elizabeth Barrett Browning.   Thou mayst love on, through love's eternity.   CTC; GTBS; NOBE; OBEV; PG; UnPo; ViBoPo

Sonnets from the Portuguese, XVI.   Elizabeth Barrett Browning.   Make thy love larger to enlarge my worth.   OAEP

Sonnets from the Portuguese, XVII.   Elizabeth Barrett Browning.   A grave, on which to rest from singing?/Choose.   BrRo; HBV 1-2; VLP; WHA

Sonnets from the Portuguese, XVIII.   Elizabeth Barrett Browning.   The kiss my mother left there when she died.   HAP

Sonnets from the Portuguese, XX.   Elizabeth Barrett Browning.   Who cannot guess God's presence out of/sight.   CoBE

Sonnets from the Portuguese, XXI.   Elizabeth Barrett Browning.   To love me also in silence with thy soul.   HBV 1-2

Sonnets from the Portuguese, XXII.   Elizabeth Barrett Browning.   A place to stand and love in for a day,/With darkness and the death-hour rounding it.   AnFE; EnLi 1-2

Sonnets from the Portuguese, XXIV.   Elizabeth Barrett Browning.   God only, who made us rich, can make us poor.   NOBV; VLP

Sonnets from the Portuguese, XXVI.   Elizabeth Barrett Browning.   Because God's gifts put man's best dreams to shame.   EnLi 1-2

Sonnets from the Portuguese, XXVIII.   Elizabeth Barrett Browning.   If, what this said, I dared repeat at last!   CoBE

Sonnets from the Portuguese, XXXII.   Elizabeth Barrett Browning.   And great souls, at one stroke, may do and doat.   ViBoPo

Sonnets from the Portuguese, XXXV.   Elizabeth Barrett Browning.   And fold within the wet wings of thy dove.   EnLi 1-2; ViBoPo

Sonnets from the Portuguese, XXXVIII.   Elizabeth Barrett Browning.   I have been proud, and said, "My love, my own!"   BLPA; BLPL; CTC; FaBoBe; HBV 1-2; PoPl; ViBoPo

Sonnets from the Portuguese, XLI.   Elizabeth Barrett Browning.   Love that endures, from Life that disappears!   CoBE

Sonnets from the Portuguese, XLIII.   Elizabeth Barrett Browning.   I shall but love thee better after death.   BoLoP; CTC; FaBoBe; FaBV; FF; FPL; GoTF; GTBS; HBV 1-2; HeIP; HoPM; LiTB; LiTL; NIP; NoP; OAEP; OLR; PAI; PG; PoLf; PoPl; PoRA; TEP; TreF; TrGrPo; TRV; UnPo; WHA

Sonnets from the Portuguese, XLIV.   Elizabeth Barrett Browning.   Instruct thine eyes to keep their colours true,/And tell thy soul, their roots are left in mine.   OBNC

Sonnets from Walton's Life of Herbert, 1670.   George Herbert.   Than that, which one day, Worms, may chance refuse.   AnAnS 1

Sonnets of a Portrait Painter.   Arthur Davison Ficke

And I longed that my kiss should strike you dead at my feet.   AnAmPo

As when you came and swept me to your heart.   AnAmPo

For me, the world crumbles beneath my feet.   AnAmPo

That time's whole later hush would speak farewell?   AnAmPo

What can you say to me, or I to you?   AnAmPo

Sonnets of the Months.   Folgore da San Geminiano.

Sonnets, XII: "Some talke of Ganymede th' Idalian Boy." Richard Barnfield. They were (perhaps) lesse faire then Poets write./But he is fairer then I can indite. PeHV

Sonnets, XII: "When I do count the clock that tells the time." William Shakespeare. Save breed, to brave him when he takes thee hence. AWP; DiPo; InPo; InPS; OAEL 1-2; TEP

Sonnets, XIII: "I walk of grey noons by the old canal." Thomas Caulfield Irwin. Mossed gate, or farmyard hay-stacks tanned and/yellow. IrPN

Sonnets, XIII: "O! that you were yourself; but, love, you/are." William Shakespeare. You had a father: let your son say so. OAEP; TEP

Sonnets, XIV: "Here, hold this glove." Richard Barnfield. If thou from glove do'st take away the g,/Then glove is love: and so I send it thee. PeHV

Sonnets, XIV: "Not from the stars do I my judgement pluck." William Shakespeare. Or else of thee this I prognosticate:/"Thy end is truth's and beauty's doom and date." MasP

Sonnets, XIV: "Now, winter's dolorous days are o'er." Thomas Caulfield Irwin. Where grasses in sleek shallows waver dank,/Or drift in windy ripples greyly by. IrPN

Sonnets, XV: "When I consider every thing that grows." William Shakespeare. As he takes from you, I engraft you new. AWP; BLPL; DiPo; MasP; OAEP; OBSC; TEP; TrGrPo

Sonnets, XVI: "But wherefore do not you a mightier way." William Shakespeare. And you must live drawn by your own sweet skill. FaBoEn

Sonnets, XVI: "When I consider how my light is spent." John Milton. They also serve who only stand and wait. EBEV; JCP

Sonnets, XVII: "Cherry-Lipt Adonis in his snowie shape." Richard Barnfield. Oh how can such a body sinne-procuring,/Be slow to love, and quicke to hate, enduring? PeHV

Sonnets, XVII: "Who will believe my verse in time to come." William Shakespeare. But were some child of yours alive that time,/You should live twice–in it and in my rhyme. DiPo; OBSC

Sonnets, XVIII: "Shall I compare thee to a summer's day?" William Shakespeare. So long as men can breathe, or eyes can see,/So long lives this, and this gives life to thee. ATP; AWP; BoLoP; CTC; DiPo; ExPo; FaBoBe; FaBV; FaFP; FiP; FPL; GBL; GoTF; GTBS; GTBS-P; HAP; HBV 1-2; HeIP; InPK; InPS; InvP; LiTB; LiTL; LoBV; MasP; MAT; MBW 1-2; MCCG; NIP; NOBE; NoP; OAEL 1-2; OAEP; OBEV; OBSC; OLR; PAI; PoEL 1-5; PoLf; PoPl; PoRA; PPoe; PrIm; SCV; SeCePo; SeCeV; TEP; TreFT; TrGrPo; ViBoPo; WHA

Sonnets, XIX: "Ah no; nor I my selfe: though my pure love." Richard Barnfield. Even so of all the vowels, I and U,/Are dearest unto me, as doth ensue. PeHV

Sonnets, XIX: "Devouring Time, blunt thou the lion's paws." William Shakespeare. My love shall in my verse ever live young. AWP; DiPo; EBEV; InPo; MAT; OAEL 1-2; OBSC; PoEL 1-5; TrGrPo; WHA

Sonnets, XIX: "Methought I saw my late espoused Saint." John Milton. I wak'd, she fled, and day brought back my night. EBEV

Sonnets, XIX: "Those former loves wherein our lives have run." James Agee. Who for one time loved in them the truth concealed:/And now must leave them in the truth revealed. MoAmPo

Sonnets, XX: "A woman's face with nature's own hand painted." William Shakespeare. Mine be thy love, and thy love's use their treasure. InvP; MasP; OAEL 1-2; PeHV

Sonnets, XX: "But now my Muse toyled with continuall care." Richard Barnfield. But since that everie one cannot be wittie,/Pardon I crave of them, and of thee, pitty. PeHV

Sonnets, XX: "Now stands our love on that still verge of day." James Agee. As now, with earth outshone and earth's wide air,/Shows each to other as this morning fair. MoAmPo

Sonnets, XXI: "So is it not with me as with that Muse." William Shakespeare. Let them say more that like of hear-say well;/I will not praise that purpose not to sell. InvP; OBSC

Sonnets, XXII: "My glass shall not persuade me I am old." William Shakespeare. Presume not on thy heart when mine is slain;/Thou gavest me thine, not to give back again. OBSC

Sonnets, XXIII: "As an unperfect actor on the stage." William Shakespeare. O, learn to read what silent love hath writ:/To hear with eyes belongs to love's fine wit. BiP; HBV 1-2; InvP; OAEP

Sonnets, XXIV: "Mine eye hath play'd the painter, and hath steel'd." William Shakespeare. They draw but what they see, know not the heart. EyDe

Sonnets, XXV: "No more be grieved at that which thou hast done." William Shakespeare. To that sweet thief, which sourly robs from me. CBEP; OBSC; TEP; UnPo

Sonnets, XXVII: "Weary with toil, I haste me to my bed." William Shakespeare. For thee, and for myself, no quiet find. DiPo; OBSC

Sonnets, XXVIII: "How can I then return in happy plight." William Shakespeare. And night doth nightly make grief's strength seem/stronger. OBSC

Sonnets, XXIX: "When in disgrace with fortune and men's eyes." William Shakespeare. For thy sweet love remembered such wealth brings,/That then I scorn to change my state with Kings. ATP; AWP; CBEP; CTC; DiPo; EBEV; ExPo; FaBoEn; FaBoRV; FaBoWP; FaBV; GBL; GoTF; GTBS; GTBS-P; HAP; HBV 1-2; HeIP; InPK; InPo; InPS; InvP; LiTB; LiTL; LoBV; MasP; NOBE; NoP; OAEL 1-2; OAEP; OBEV; OBSC; PeHV; PG; PoEL 1-5; PoPl; PoRA; PPoe; PPP; Prf; PrIm; SCV; SeCeV; TEP; TreF; TrGrPo; TRV; ViBoPo; WHA

Sonnets, XXX: "When to the sessions of sweet silent thought." William Shakespeare. All losses are restored and sorrows end. ATP; AWP; BiP; CTC; DiPo; EBEV; ExPo; FaBoRV; FaBV; FaFP; FF; FPL; GBL; GoTF; GTBS; GTBS-P; HAP; HBV 1-2; InPo; InPS; LiTB; LoBV; MasP; NOBE; NoP; OAEL 1-2; OAEP; OBEV; OBSC; PAI; PoEL 1-5; PoLf; PoPle; PoRA; PPoe; PPP; PrIm; SeCeV; TEP; TreFS; TrGrPo; TRV; ViBoPo; WHA

Sonnets, XXXI: "Thy bosom is endeared with all hearts." William Shakespeare. Their images I loved I view in thee,/And thou, all they, hast all the all of me. NOBE; OBEV; OBSC; PoEL 1-5

Sonnets, XXXII: "If thou survive my well-contented day." William Shakespeare. But since he died, and poets better prove,/Theirs for their style I'll read, his for his love. CBEP; GTBS; GTBS-P; HBV 1-2; LiTL; OBSC; PP

Sonnets, XXXIII: "Full many a glorious morning have I seen." William Shakespeare. Suns of the world may stain when heaven's sun staineth. ATP; AWP; EBEV; FaFP; GoTF; HAP; HBV 1-2; InPo; LoBV; MBW 1-2; NoP; OAEL 1-2; OAEP; OBSC; OHFP; PoRA; PPP; SeCePo; SeCeV; TEP; TreFS; TrGrPo; ViBoPo

Sonnets, XXXIV: "Why didst thou promise such a beauteous day." William Shakespeare. Ah, but those tears are pearl which thy love sheds,/And they are rich, and ransom all ill deeds. CBEP; OBSC

Sonnets, XXXV: "No more be grieved at that which thou hast done." William Shakespeare. That I an accessary needs must be,/To that sweet thief which sourly robs from me. CBEP; PeHV

Sonnets, XXXVI: "Let me confess that we two must be twain." William Shakespeare. But do not so; I love thee in such sort/As thou being mine, mine is thy good/report. CBEP; OAEP; PeHV

Sonnets, XL: "Take all my loves my love, yea take them all." William Shakespeare. Lascivious grace, in whom all ill well shows,/Kill me with spites; yet we must not be foes. CBEP; InvP; OBSC

Sonnets, XLI: "Those pretty wrongs that liberty commits." William Shakespeare. Hers, by thy beauty tempting her to thee,/Thine, by thy beauty being false to me. CBEP; InvP

Sonnets, XLII: "Thou that last her, it is not all my grief." William Shakespeare. But here's the joy; my friend and I are one;/Sweet flattery! then she loves but me alone. CBEP; InvP

Sonnets, XLIII: "When most I wink, then do mine eyes best see." William Shakespeare. All days are nights to see till I see thee,/And nights bright days when dreams do show thee/me. CBEP

Sonnets, XLIV: "If the dull substance of my flesh were thought." William Shakespeare. Receiving naught by elements so slow/But heavy tears, badges of either's woe. CBEP

Sonnets, XLVI: "Mine eye and heart are at a mortal war." William Shakespeare. And my heart's right thine inward love of heart. EyDe

Sonnets, XLVII: "Betwixt mine eye and heart a league is took." William Shakespeare. Awakes my heart to heart's and eye's delight. EyDe

Sonnets, LII: "So am I as the rich, whose blessed key." William Shakespeare. Blessed are you, whose worthiness gives scope,/Being had, to triumph; being lacked, to hope. OBSC

Sonnets, LIII: "What is your substance, whereof are you made." William Shakespeare. In all external grace you have some part,/But you like none, none you, for constant heart. CTC; EBEV; FaFP; LiTB; LiTL; MasP; OAEL 1-2; OAEP; OBEV; OBSC; PeHV; ViBoPo

Sonnets, LIV: "O, how much more doth beauty beauteous seem." William Shakespeare. When that shall fade, my verse distils your truth. AWP; OBEV; OBSC; ViBoPo

Sonnets, LV: "Not marble, nor the gilded monuments." William Shakespeare. So, till the judgment that yourself arise,/You live in this, and dwell in lovers' eyes. AWP; BLPL; CBEP; CTC; DiPo; ExPo; FaBoEn; FaFP; FF; ForPo; HeIP; InPo; LiTB; LiTL; LoBV; MasP; MBW 1-2; NIP; NOBE; NoP; OAEL 1-2; OAEP; OBSC; PeHV; PoEL 1-5; PoRA; PP; PPoe; SeCeV; TEP; TrGrPo; ViBoPo

Sonnets, LVI: "Sweet love, renew thy force." William Shakespeare. Makes summer's welcome thrice more wish'd, more rare. CBEP; PoLf

Sonnets, LVII: "Being your slave, what should I do but tend." William Shakespeare. So true a fool is love, that in your will/Though you do anything, he thinks no ill. GTBS; GTBS-P; HAP; LiTL; OBEV; PeHV; PoEL 1-5; ViBoPo

Sonnets, LIX: "If there be. William Shakespeare. Oh sure I am the wits of former days,/To subjects worse have given admiring praise. FaBoEn

Sonnets, LX: "Like as the waves make towards the pebbled shore." William Shakespeare. And yet to times in hope, my verse shall stand/Praising thy worth, despite his cruel hand. ATP; CBEP; EBEV; ExPo; FaBoEn; FaFP; FPL; GTBS; GTBS-P; HBV 1-2; LiTB; LiTL; LoBV; NIP; NOBE; OBSC; PeHV; PoRA; SeCeV; TEP; UnPo; ViBoPo

Sonnets, LXI: "Is it thy wil, thy Image should keepe open." William Shakespeare. For thee watch I, whilst thou dost wake elsewhere,/From me farre off, with others all too neere. PoEL 1-5

Sonnets, LXII: "Sinne of selfe-love possesseth al mine eie." William Shakespeare. 'Tis thee (my selfe) that for my selfe I praise,/Painting my age with beauty of thy daies. EBEV; PoEL 1-5

Sonnets, LXIII: "Against my Love shall be, as I am now." William Shakespeare. His beauty shall in these black lines be seen,/And they shall live, and he in them still green. OBSC

Sonnets, LXIV: "When I have seen by Time's fell hand defaced." William Shakespeare. This thought is as a death, which cannot/choose/But weep to have that which it fears to lose. AWP; BLPL; FaFP; GTBS; GTBS-P; HAP; HeIP; InPo; LiTB; LiTL; MCCG; NOBE; NoP; OAEL 1-2; OBSC; PoRA; PPoe; SeCeV; ViBoPo

Sonnets, LXV: "Since brass, nor stone, nor earth, nor boundless sea." William Shakespeare. O, none, unless this miracle have might,/That in black ink my love may still shine bright. AWP; DiPo; FaFP; FF; FiP; GTBS; GTBS-P; HAP; InPS; LiTB; LiTL; MasP; MCCG; NOBE; NoP; PAI; PoRA; SeCeV; UnPo

Sonnets, LXVI: "Tired with all these, for restful death I cry." William Shakespeare. Tired with all these, from these would I be gone,/Save that to die, I leave my love alone. AWP; CTC; EBEV; ExPo; FaBoPV; FaFP; GTBS; GTBS-P; HAP; InPo; InPS; LiTB; MBW 1-2; MyFE; NOBE; OAEL 1-2; OBSC; PoEL 1-5; SeCeV; TrGrPo; ViBoPo; WeW; WHA

Sonnets, LXVII: "Ah wherefore with infection should he live." William Shakespeare. O him she stores, to show what wealth she had,/In days long since, before these last so bad. PeHV

Sonnets, LXVIII: "Thus is his cheek the map of days outworn." William Shakespeare. And him as for a map doth Nature store,/To show false Art what beauty was of yore. OBSC

Sonnets, LXXI: "No longer mourn for me when I am dead." William Shakespeare. Lest the wise world should look into your moan/And mock you with me after I am gone. AWP; CBEP; EBEV; FaBoRV; GBL; GoTF; GTBS; GTBS-P; HAP; HBV 1-2; InPo; LiTB; NoP; OAEP; OBSC; PoRA; PPoe; SeCeV; TEP; TreFT; TrGrPo; ViBoPo; WHA

Sonnets, LXXII: "O, lest your true love may seem false in this." William Shakespeare. And live no more to shame nore me nor you. LO

Sonnets, LXXIII: "That time of year thou mayst in me behold." William Shakespeare. To love that well which thou must leave ere long. AWP; BiP; BoLoP; CTC; DiPo; EBEV; ExPo; FaBoRV; FaBV; FF; FiP; ForPo; GBL; GTBS; GTBS-P; HAP; HBV 1-2; HeIP; HoPM; InPK; InPo; InPS; InvP; LiTB; LoBV; MasP; MBW 1-2; MyFE; NIP; NOBE; NoP; OAEL 1-2; OAEP; OBEV; OBSC; PAI; PoEL 1-5; PoPle; PoRA; PPoe; PPP; PrIm; QFR; SeCeV; SoSe; TEP; TrGrPo; UnPo; ViBoPo; WHA

Sonnets, LXXIV: "But be contented: when that fell arrest." William Shakespeare. The worth of that is that which it contains,/And that is this, and this with thee remains. OBSC

Sonnets, LXXVI: "Why is my verse so barren of new pride." William Shakespeare. So is my love still telling what is told. EBEV; PP

Sonnets, LXXXI: "Or I shall live your epitaph to make." William Shakespeare. Where breath most breathes,-/even in/the mouths of men. OAEP; OBSC

Sonnets, LXXXVI: "Was it the proud full sail of his great verse." William Shakespeare. But when your countenance filled up his line,/Then lacked I matter; that enfeebled mine. InvP; MBW 1-2; OAEL 1-2; OAEP; TEP

Sonnets, LXXXVII: "Farewell! thou art too dear for my possessing." William Shakespeare. Thus I had thee as a dream doth flatter,/In sleep, a king; but waking, no such matter. EBEV; GTBS; GTBS-P; InPS; InvP; LiTB; MasP; NOBE; OAEL 1-2; OAEP; OBEV; OBSC; PAI; PeHV; PoEL 1-5; QFR; TrGrPo; ViBoPo

Sonnets, LXXXIX: "Say that thou didst forsake me for some fault." William Shakespeare. For thee, against myself I'll vow debate,/For I must ne'er love him whom thou/dost hate. OAEP

Sonnets, XC: "Then hate me when thou wilt; if ever, now." William Shakespeare. And other strains of woe, which now seem woe,/Compared with loss of thee will not seem so. ATP; AWP; EBEV; NOBE; OBEV; OBSC; PG; PoEL 1-5; WHA

Sonnets, XCI: "Some glory in their birth, some in their skill." William Shakespeare. Wretched in this alone, that thou mayst take/All this away, and me most wretched make. CBEP

Sonnets, XCIII: "So shall I live, supposing thou art true." William Shakespeare. How like Eve's apple doth thy beauty grow,/If thy sweet virtue answer not thy show! InvP; MasP

Sonnets, XCIV: "They that have power to hurt, and will do none." William Shakespeare. Lilies that fester smell far worse than weeds. BLPL; ExPo; FaBoEn; GTBS; GTBS-P; InPS; LiTB; MasP; NOBE; NoP; OAEL 1-2; OBEV; PAI; PeHV; PoEL 1-5; PPoe; PPP; SCV; ViBoPo

Sonnets, XCV: "How sweet and lovely dost thou make the shame." William Shakespeare. The hardest knife ill-used doth lose his edge. CBEP 047; MasP; TrGrPo

Sonnets, XCVII: "How like a winter hath my absence been." William Shakespeare. Or, if they sing, 'tis with so dull a cheer,/That leaves look pale, dreading the winter's near. ATP; AWP; CBEP; DiPo; FaBoEn; GTBS; GTBS-P; NOBE; OAEL 1-2; OBEV; OBSC; PoRA; TEP; TrGrPo

Sonnets, XCVIII: "From you have I been absent in the spring." William Shakespeare. Yet seemed it winter still, and, you away,/As with your shadow I with these did play. AWP; DiPo; EBEV; InPo; LiTB; NOBE; OBEV; OBSC; PoPle; TEP; ViBoPo

Sonnets, XCIX: "The forward violet thus did I chide." William Shakespeare. More flowers I noted, yet I none could/see/But sweet or colour it had stol'n from/thee. OAEP; OBSC

Sonnets, C: "Where art thou, Muse, that thou forget'st so long." William Shakespeare. Give my Love fame faster than Time wastes life;/So thou prevent'st his scythe and crooked knife. OBSC

Sonnets, CII: "My love is strengthen'd." William Shakespeare. Therefore, like her, I sometime hold my tongue,/Because I would not dull you with my song. AWP; LiTL; OAEP; OBEV; OBSC; ViBoPo

Sonnets, CIV: "To me, fair friend, you never can be old." William Shakespeare. Ere you were born was beauty's summer dead. FaBoEn; FPL; GBL; GTBS; GTBS-P; HBV 1-2; HeIP; LiTL; OAEP; OBEV; OBSC; PeHV; Prf; ViBoPo

Sonnets, CVI: "When in the chronicle of wasted time." William Shakespeare. For we, which now behold these present/days,/Have eyes to wonder, but lack tongues to/praise. AWP; BLPL; CBEP; CTC; DiPo; EnRePo; ExPo; FaBV; FiP; GTBS; GTBS-P; HBV 1-2; InPo; LiTB; LiTL; LoBV; LoGBV; MasP; MBW 1-2; MCCG; NOBE; NoP; OAEL 1-2; OAEP; OBEV; OBSC; PoRA; PPoe; SeCeV; TEP; TreFT; TrGrPo; ViBoPo

Sonnets, CVII: "Not mine own fears, nor the prophetic soul." William Shakespeare. And thou in this shalt find thy monument/When tyrants' crests and tombs of brass are spent. AWP; CBEP; CTC; DiPo; EBEV; FiP; HAP; InPo; LiTB; LoBV; MasP; MBW 1-2; NoP; OAEL 1-2; OAEP; OBSC; PPoe; SeCeV

Sonnets, CIX: "O, never say that I was false of heart." William Shakespeare. For nothing this wide universe I call,/Save thou, my rose: in it thou art my all. GTBS; GTBS-P; HBV 1-2; LiTL; NOBE; OBEV; OBSC

Sonnets, CX: "Alas! 'tis true I have gone here and there." William Shakespeare. Then give me welcome, next my heaven the best,/Even to thy pure and most most loving breast. EBEV; OAEP; OBSC; PeHV; ViBoPo

Sonnets, CXIII: "Since I left you, mine eye is in my mind." William Shakespeare. My most true mind thus maketh mine eye untrue. WeW

Sonnets, CXVI: "Let me not to the marriage of true minds." William Shakespeare. If this be error, and upon me proved,/I never writ, nor no man ever loved. AWP; BoC; CBEP; DiPo; ExPo; FaBV; FaFP; FPL; GBL; GoBC; GoTF; GTBS; GTBS-P; HAP; HBV 1-2; HeIP; InPo; InPS; InvP; LiTB; LiTL; LoBV; MasP; MBW 1-2; MCCG; NIP; NOBE; NoP; OAEL 1-2; OAEP; OBEV; OBSC; PAI; PeHV; PG; PoEL 1-5; PoPl; PoRA; PPoe; PPP; PrIm; SCV; SeCeV; SoSe; TEP; TreF; TrGrPo; TRV; UnPo; ViBoPo; WHA

Sonnets, CXVIII: "Like as to make our appetites more keep". William Shakespeare. But thence I learn, and find the lesson true,/Drugs poison him that so fell sick of you. CBEP

Sonnets, CXIX: "What potions have I drunk of Siren Tears." William Shakespeare. So I return rebuked to my content,/And gain by ill thrice more than I have spent. CBEP; WHA

Sonnets, CXX: "That you were once unkind befriends me now." William Shakespeare. But that your trespass now becomes a fee;/Mine ransoms yours, and yours must ransom me. InvP

Sonnets, CXXI: "'Tis better to be vile than vile esteemed." William Shakespeare. All men are bad and in their badness reign. CBEP; InvP; OAEL 1-2; PoEL 1-5

Sonnets, CXXIII: "No, Time, thou shalt not boast that I do change." William Shakespeare. I will be true, despite thy scythe and/thee. OAEP; OBSC; TrGrPo

Sonnets, CXXVII: "In the ole age black was nor counted fair." William Shakespeare. Yet so they mourn, becoming of their woe,/That every tongue says beauty should look so. CBEP; DiPo

Sonnets, CXXIX: "Th' expense of spirit in a waste of shame." William Shakespeare. To shun the heaven that leads men to this hell. AWP; BiP; DiPo; EBEV; ExPo; FaBoEn; ForPo; GBL; HAP; HeIP; InPo; InPS; LiTB; LiTL; LoBV; MasP; MBW 1-2; NIP; NOBE; NoP; OAEL 1-2; OBEV; OBSC; PAI; PoEL 1-5; PPoe; PPP; QFR; SCV; SeCeV; TEP; TrGrPo; UnPo; ViBoPo; WeW; WHA

Sonnets, CXXX: "My mistress' eyes are nothing like the sun." William Shakespeare. And yet, by heaven, I think my love as rare/As any she belied with false compare. AWP; BiP; BoLoP; CBEP; DiPo; EBEV; ExPo; FF; HAP; HBV 1-2; HoPM; InPK; InPS; InvP; LiTB; LiTL; MBW 1-2; NIP; NoP; OAEL 1-2; OAEP; PAI; PoPle; PP; PPP; PrIm; SeCeV; SoSe; TEP; WeW

Sonnets, CXXXII: "Thine eyes I love, and they, as pitying me." William Shakespeare. Then will I swear beauty herself is/black,/And all they foul that thy complexion/lack. OAEP; OBSC

Sonnets, CXXXIII: "Beshrew that heart that makes my heart to groan." William Shakespeare. And yet thou wilt; for I, being pent in thee,/Perforce am thine, and all that is in me. CBEP; InvP

Sonnets, CXXXIV: "So, now I have confessed that he is thine." William Shakespeare. He pays the whole, and yet am I not free. CBEP; InvP

Sonnets, CXXXV: "Whoever hath her wish, thou hast thy Will." William Shakespeare. Let no unkind no fair beseechers kill;/Think all but one, and me in that one Will. OAEL 1-2

Sonnets, CXXXVII: "Thou blind fool, Love, what dost thou to mine eyes. William Shakespeare. And to this false plague are they now transferred. WeW

Sonnets, CXXXVIII: "When my love swears that she is made of truth." William Shakespeare. Therefore I lie with her and she with me,/And in our faults by lies we flattered be. AWP; BiP; EBEV; InPo; NoP; OAEL 1-2; OAEP; PoEL 1-5; PPP; SoSe; TEP; TrGrPo; ViBoPo

Sonnets, CXLI: "In faith, I do not love thee with mine eyes." William Shakespeare. That she that makes me sin awards me pain. PoEL 1-5; TrGrPo

Sonnets, CXLIII: "Lo, as a careful housewife runs to catch." William Shakespeare. So will I pray that thou mayst have thy Will,/If thou turn back and my loud crying still. BiP; CBEP; MBW 1-2

Sonnets, CXLIV: "Two loves I have of comfort and despair." William Shakespeare. Yet this shall I ne'er know, but live in doubt,/Till my bad angel fire my good one out. CBEP; EBEV; InvP; LoBV; NIP; OAEL 1-2; OAEP; PeHV; PoEL 1-5

Sonnets, CXLVI: "Poor soul, the centre of my sinful earth." William Shakespeare. And Death once dead, there's no more dying then. AWP; CAW; DiPo; ExPo; GoBC; GoTF; GTBS; GTBS-P; HBV 1-2; InPo; LiTB; MasP; MyFE; NIP; NOBE; NOCV; OAEL 1-2; OBEV; OBSC; OxBoCh; PoEL 1-5; TreFS; ViBoPo; WHA

Sonnets, CXLVII: "My love is as a feever longing still." William Shakespeare. For I have sworne thee faire, and thought thee bright,/Who art as black as hell, as darke as night. CBEP; DiPo; EBEV; HoPM; PoEL 1-5; TEP

Sonnets, CXLVIII: "O me! what eyes hath Love put in my head." William Shakespeare. Lest eyes well-seeing thy foul faults should find! GTBS; GTBS-P

Sonnets, CLI: "Love is too young to know what conscience is." William Shakespeare. No want of conscience hold it that I call/Her "love" for whose dear love I rise and fall. BiP; CBEP; EBEV; HeIP; PoEL 1-5

Sonnetto VII: "Who is she that comes." Guido Cavalcanti. That our thought may take her immediate in its embrace. CTC

Sonnetto XXXV: "My Lady's face it is they worship there." Guido Cavalcanti. For envy of her precious neighborhood. CTC

Sons. Jack Cope. ...time, unchanging blue/and winter frosts: Let the small day be. PeSA

Sons. Don Polson. He is my son. AMV-81

The Sons of Indolence. James (1700-48) Thomson. And court the vapoury God soft-breathing in the Wind. OBEC

The Sons of Levi. Anonymous. We're the root and branch of David,/The glorious bright and morning star. AmFP

The Sons of Martha. Rudyard Kipling. They have cast their burden upon the Lord, and–the/Lord He lays it on Martha's Sons! HBV 1-2; WGRP

The Sons of Our Sons. Ilya Ehrenburg. Far into the night, and into the ages,/we have scattered/The sparks of our extinguished life. TrJP

Sons of Promise. Thomas Curtis Clark. But has for Him some treasure chaste. PoToHe

Sons of the Kings. Joan Agnew. "When you and I are kings," he says,/ "Then we shall meet again." BiCB

Sonship. John C. Rezmerski. and wish I could stop ducking and watch/ them clap and laugh at our dancing and shouting. FAZ

Soon at Last My Sighs and Moans. Louis Ginsberg. While the moaning of a tree/Will be all my elegy... TrJP

Soon One Mornin' Death Come Creepin'. Anonymous. O my Lord, what shall I do to be saved? OuSiCo

Soon with the Lilac Fades Another Spring. Patrick MacDonogh. Bids the young eyes of spring witness eternal pain. OxBI

Sooner or Later. Sam Cornish. & your hands/are still/in your pockets CNA

Sooner or Later. John Digby. ...sunlight/hanging from the lips of the lightning. EAS

Soonest Mended. John Ashbery. Making ready to forget, and always coming back/To the mooring of starting out, that day so long ago HaCAP; Prf

"The soote season..." Henry Howard, Earl of Surrey. And thus I see among these pleasant things/Each care decays, and yet my sorrow springs. AAS; FCP; HeIP; InPS; NIP; NoP; SiPS

Sootie Joe. Melvin B. Tolson. But somebody hasta black hisself/For somebody else to stay white. FAZ

Sophia Nichols. Robin Blaser. there are birds summoned by words. CoPo

Sophisticate. Barbara Young. Now, I am four./ There's nothing more. BiCB; SiSoSe

Sophistication. Vassar Miller. with the trees before long dripping in sunlight/all in a sweat about nothing. NCSH

Sopolis. Callimachus. We find thy name and empty monument. AWP

Sopranosound, Memory of John. Sharon Bourke. Listen/To John. CNA

Sops of Light. Fredegond Shove. But the soul knows no time/Nor any sleep. ChMP

Soraidh Slan Don Oidhche Areir. Niall.Mor Mac Muireadach. Speed last night upon its way. BIrV

The Sorcerer. A.J.M. Smith. But kin of the trembling ocean, not of the dust. PeCV

The Sorcerer: Mr. Wells. Sir William Schwenck Gilbert. Number seventy, Simmery Axe! WSC

The Sorcerer! Vachel Lindsay. Aladdin's lamp is there. WSC

The Sorceress. Eugene Marais. and the wind mourns always/at being alone. PeSA

Sordello's Birth-Place. Robert Browning. The castle at its toils, the lapwings love/To glean among at grape-time. MyFE

Sorrow. Anonymous. I have driven, I have driven, the maiden into the damp/earth! AWP

Sorrow. Chu Shu-chen. And dream in the smoke, all alone. BoWoP

Sorrow. Samuel Daniel. Thou in my name/Must hold the same,/Until thou bring it to the grave. OBSC

Sorrow. Aubrey Thomas De Vere. And all night in rainy weather,/I hear his gentle breathings by me. WiR

Sorrow. Sir Aubrey De Vere. Great thoughts, grave thoughts lasting to the end. BLPA; GoBC; HBV 1-2; WGRP

Sorrow. Helen Parry Eden. Where, to my bliss, myself may meet/One hastening with pierced feet. CAW

Sorrow. D. H. Lawrence. I watched them float up the dark chimney. CMoP; GTBS-P; OBMV

Sorrow. Marie Tello Phillips. And find my solace following the Master's way. GoYe

Sorrow. George Santayana. Ay, and thy second slumber will be deep. WGRP

Sorrow. Katrina Trask. Great God, have mercy on my misery! AA

Sorrow Is the Only Faithful One. Owen Dodson. Sorrow is the only faithful one. AmNP; IDB; PoBA

The Sorrow of Kodio. Anonymous. How shall I tell it to her, I Kodio,/ When it is so hard/To hold back my own pain? PBA

The Sorrow of Love. William Butler Yeats. Are shaken with earth's old and weary cry. MoAB; MoBrPo; NoAm; NOBV; OAEL 1-2; PoEL 1-5; TEP; VLP

Sorrow of Mydath. John Masefield. Gently, dreamily, quietly over desolate sands! MoBrPo

The Sorrow of Unicume. Sir Herbert Read. evolved calmness,/my heart enfold. BrPo; ChMP

Sorrow's Ladder. Gertrude Callaghan. That I, though bruised, may fearlessly ascend/High sorrow's ladder, singing, to the end! CAW

Sorrow seldom killeth any. Francis Davison. Your only way is, in your arms to catch me. EG

Sorrow Shatters My Heart. Moses Ibn Ezra. That his heart may not be lifted up in pride. LiTW

Sorrows Humanize Our Race. Jean Ingelow. And when it shineth sometimes we shall know/That memory is possession. WGRP

The Sorrows of Sunday: An Elegy (excerpt). John Wolcot. Order their simple flocks to walk with God,/And ride themselves an airing with the Devil. NOEC

Sorrows of Werther. William Makepeace Thackeray. Like a well-conducted person,/Went on cutting bread and butter. ALV; BLPA; FaBoCo; FiBHP; FPL; HBV 1-2; InMe; LiTL; NA; NBM; NLV; NOBL; NOBV; PoPle; ShM; TreF; VLP

A Sort Hymne to Venus. Robert Herrick. I will promise there shall be/ Mirtles offer'd up to Thee. CavP

A Sort of a Song. William Carlos Williams. Saxifrage is my flower that splits/the rocks. BiP; FAZ; HoPM; NoP; OBSP; PP; SeCeV; TAP

A Sort of Elegy. Blanche Farley. Goodbye Elvis/Goodbye Groucho. SOTS

Sorting, Wrapping, Packing, Stuffing. James Schuyler. they never began and great hunks of the world will fit NoAm

SOS. LeRoi (Imamu Amiri Baraka) Jones. calling all black people, come in, black people, come/on in. BPo; CNA; PoBA

Sospetto d'Herode. Richard Crashaw. Of Dragons, Hydraes, Sphinxes, fill the Grove. SeCV 1-2

The Soul. Anonymous. Heaven stoops to give it life. STF

The Soul. George Barlow. –and she/Shall be queen of the wind and the night,/Stars, sun, and the sea. OBVV

Soul. Austin Black. wisdom of age is not facade!!! NBP

The Soul. Madison Cawein. Where Death stands knocking at the gate/To let him in. AA

The Soul. Abraham Cowley. May thy dear Body ne're be Mine. AnAnS 2

Soul. D. L. Graham. survival motion set to music. PoBA

A Soul. Randall Jarrell. My poor soul, forever. CMoP

A Soul. Christina Georgina Rossetti. Her face and will athirst against the light. WPOW

Soul and Body. Margaret Cavendish, Duchess of Newcastle. Fit for the soul to wear those clothes again. OBSP

Soul and Body. Samuel Waddington. In doubt we'll go together–thou and I. OBVV

The Soul and Body of John Brown. Muriel Rukeyser. part of our nation of our fanatic sun. MoAmPo

Soul and Sense. Hannah Parker Kimball. Looks on and marvels,–'t is the soul of/man. AA

The Soul and the Body. Sir John Davies. So from the eternal Light the soul doth spring,/Though in the body she her powers do show. CTC; NOBE; OBSC

Soul-Drift. Mathilde Blind. Go forth no longer as my body-slave,/But as the heir of all the Universe. SBG

The Soul Has Bandaged Moments. Emily Dickinson. The Horror welcomes her, again,/These, are not brayed of Tongue– MAmP

The Soul in the Body. Edith Matilda Thomas. Live somewhere yonder in the starlit/sphere? AA

Soul Lifted. Albert Durrant Watson. Push back the mountains and the stars. CaP

Soul-Light. Dante Gabriel Rossetti. Even so, through eyes and voice, your soul doth move/My soul with changeful light of infinite love. MaVP

The Soul Longs to Return Whence It Came. Richard Eberhart. Accept this humble servant evermore. AmP; CMoP; ExPo

The Soul of Dante. Buonarroti Michelangelo. His equal or his better ne'er was born. GoBC

The Soul of Jesus Is Restless. Cyprus R. Mitchell. The soul of Jesus is restless today,/But eternally undismayed. TrCP

The Soul of Lincoln. Chauncey R. Piety. Earth is enlarged to inherit/The soul of your Lincoln and mine. PGD

The Soul of Man. Dora Read Goodale. And then say brother–then say amn! AA

The Soul of the World. Ernest Crosby. but it is/to the heart universal, for the soul of/the world is abroad to-night. AA

The Soul of Time. Trumbull Stickney. A dizziness of the things I have not said. LiTA; NePA

The Soul, Reaching, Throwing Out for Love. Walt Whitman. You fathomless latent souls of love–you pent and unknown oceans of/love! InPK

The Soul's Bitter Cry. Anonymous. Weary of joyless life I've grown. WGRP

The Soul's Defiance. Lavinia Stoddard. Shall pass away. AA

The Soul's Desire. Eleanor Hull. To gain my soul's desire/And see Thy face, O Lord. OxBI

The Soul's Expression. Elizabeth Barrett Browning. ...my flesh would perish/there,/Before that dread apocalypse of soul. VLP

The Soul's Garment. Margaret Cavendish, Dutchess of Newcastre. Fit for the soul to wear those clothes again. OxBoCh; SeCePo

Soul's Kiss. Samuel Greenberg. The mingling serenade looks. LiTA

Soul's Liberty. Anna Wickham. We see God clear and high above the town. MoBrPo; OBSP

A Soul's Soliloquy. Wenonah Stevens Abbott. 'Tis but the beginning of life. BLPA

The Soul's Sphere. Dante Gabriel Rossetti. Wild pageant of the accumulated past/That clangs and flashes for a drowning man. MaVP

The Soul's Tendency Towards Its True Centre. John Byrom. Peace to ev'ry Christian Heart! CEP

The Soul's Travelling (excerpt). Elizabeth Barrett Browning. Forgets the rush and rapture of his wings. ILwL

The Soul Selects Her Own Society. Emily Dickinson. Then close the valves of her attention/Like stone. AmP; AnNE; APA; AWP; BLPL; BoWoP; CMoP; DiPo; GoTF; InPK; InPo; InPS; MAmP; MoAB; MoAmPo; NAWM 1-2; NePA; NoAm; NOBA; NoP; OxBA; PAI; PoEL 1-5; SBG; TAP; TreFT; TrGrPo; UnPo; WHA

Soul-Severance (parody). St. John Emile Clavering Hankin. And what on earth he means can no man say. FaBoPa

Soul-Sickness. Jones Very. Or plant of wondrous powers of which we dream! AP

The Soul Speaks. Edward H. Pfeiffer. Under the crust of things that die,/Living, unfathomed, here am I. HBMV

Soul, Wherefore Fret Thee? Gertrude Bloede. Ay, Soul, thy very Self is unto thee/Immortal pledge of Immortality. AA

The Soul Winner's Prayer. Eugene M. Harrison. Burn in my heart, burn evermore,/Till I burn out for Thee. STF

The Souldier Going to the Field. Sir William Davenant. My own seduced Heart to me,/Accompani'd with thine. MePo

The Souldiers Farewel to his Love. Anonymous. We will be wed, come Margaret let us go. CoMu

Souling Song. Anonymous. And we'll come no more a-souling/Till this time next year. OBET

Souls. Fannie Stearns Gifford. Your souls, that must be passionate,/Shining and swift, as mine? HBMV

Souls. Paul Wertheimer. And ever rustles yearning to and fro... TrJP

Souls Lake. Robert Fitzgerald. And infinite still the discourse of the night. MoPo; MP; TwCP

The Souls of the Slain. Thomas Hardy. And surceased on the sky, and but left in the gloaming/Sea-mutterings and me. CMoP; LiTB; PoEL 1-5

The Souls of Women at Night. Wallace Stevens. Of the loftiest amour, in a human midnight? CMoP

Sound. Jim Harrison. in the noise of the birds/as they burst from the trees. VGW

The Sound. Robert Kelly. but the thunder/was all over her mind. PoM

Sound Advice. Anonymous. Run in circles, scream and shout. FaBoUs; NLV

The Sound Country Lass. Anonymous. And freely give her Love. CoMu; ErPo

Sound from Leopardi. Bill Berkson. and out of plain talk spin/Truth and Falsehood, the greatest weapons in the world. ANYP

A Sound from the Earth. William Stafford. ...The whole/earthen bowl churned into foam. NNaP; RFM

The Sound of Afroamerican History Chapt I. S. E. Anderson. my high with fontella takin care of much business in the/rhythm of the blues PoBA

The Sound of Afroamerican History Chapt II. S. E. Anderson. becoming furious bitter rising up sounds PoBA

Sound of Breaking. Conrad Aiken. The sound of disaster and misery, the sound/of passionate heartbreak at the centre of the world. AnAmPo; AWP; InPo; MAPA

The Sound of Morning in New Mexico. Reeve Spencer Kelley. The coyotes and the bells. AmFN

The Sound of Night. Maxine W. Kumin. we lie, day creatures, overhearing night. BoNaP; DFF

The Sound of Rain. Bella Akhmadulina. I notice the surprise/of people who look at me as I pass. BoWoP

The Sound of Rain. David Allan Evans. The apron, bandana and knives/never did hide beauty from me. GOYP

The Sound of the Drum. Anonymous. And the villagers ran to the sound of the drum. OBET

The Sound of the Horn. Alfred de Vigny. The shade of the noble Roland is still forlorn! AWP

The Sound of the Sea. Henry Wadsworth Longfellow. Are some divine foreshadowing and foreseeing/Of things beyond our reason or control. AnFE; AP; APA; EtS; GoTF; MOS; TreFT

The Sound of the Sea. John Hall Wheelock. Beyond what glittering stars and in what ultimate re-/gions! EtS

The Sound of the Trees. Robert Frost. I shall have less to say,/But I shall be gone. AnFE; APA; AtBAP; MAPA; OxBA; PG

Sound of Water. Mary Devenport O'Neill. Flow,/Ice,/Snow. NTCP

Sound, Sound the Clarion. Thomas Osbert Mordaunt. One crowded hour of glorious life/Is worth an age without a name. FaPoR; NOBE

Sound the Loud Timbrel. Thomas Moore. Jehovah has triumphed–his people are free! GoBC

The Sounding. Conrad Aiken. man kills his children. But the birds endure. CrMA

Sounding. Doris Ferne. "overdue and must be considered lost..." CaP

Sounding. David Jauss. But still I find no bottom. Str

The Sounding Portage. Annie Charlotte Dalton. And the wind roars and the stream roars/As the tramping dead move on. CaP

Sounds. Paul David Ashley. behind us one death comes/and goes as it pleases/it is the one/we are. LFAC

Sounds. Robert Creeley. Tseet, tseet–/then chatter,/all the way home. GP

The Sounds Begin Again. Dennis Brutus. over the sirens, knuckles, boots;/my sounds begin again. WhB

The Sounds in the Morning. Eleanor Farjeon. As I jump out of bed/To the world of my eyes. SUS

The Sounds of Dawn. Efrain Huerta. Love is the pity that we feel for one another. LiTW

Soup. Carl Sandburg. Putting soup in his mouth with a spoon. NOBA; OBCA

The Soup of Venus. James Tate. lukewarm soup/is my second favorite. AmPA

Soup on a Cold Day. Nellie Hill. Mix them. Boil them. Swallow. AMV-81

Soup Song. Maurice Sugar. So-up, so-up, they gave me a bowl of soup. FSW

The Source. Jon Stallworthy. ...releasing now/loved women locked in you/and hungering to be found. NoP

Source of News. Anonymous. That she has a son, who has a friend/Who knows when the war is going to end! GoTF; TreF

Sources of Good Counsel. Peter Idley. And be not beaten with thine own rod. OxBChV

Space Shuttle. Diane Ackerman. ...Say again/how the cramped world turns, say again. MAYP; SUW

Space Travel. Jane W. Krows. Then make my reservation/On a rocket to the moon. SoPo

Space-Wanderer's Homecoming. Peter Viereck. Forgot it, I forgot it, the name "man." AMV-80

'Spacially Jim. Bessie Morgan. 'Twas the only way to git rid of 'em all,/ 'Spacially Jim. HBV 1-2

Spacin. Ronda Davis. anybody/can/get hi JB

The Spacious Firmament on High. Joseph Addison. The Hand that made us is Divine. EaLo; ELP; FaBoBe; FaPoR; GN; HBV 1-2; HBVY; MCCG; NIP; PoEL 1-5; TreFT

A Spade Is Just a Spade. Walter Everette Hawkins. When a spade is just a spade? PoBA

Spade Scharnweber. Don Welch. somehow thickening their grace. Psk

The Spaewife. Robert Louis Stevenson. –It's gey an' easy spierin', says the beggar-wife to me. BrPo; OxBS

Spain. Dorothy Livesay. Your sons to struggle for this grim, new heaven. NOBC

Spain. Arthur Symons. Flowers in her hair, castanets in her hands. OBTV

Spain, 1809. F. L. Lucas. But I remember one pale woman's face/In San Pedro. HaMV

Spain 1937. W. H. Auden. May say Alas but cannot help or pardon. CABL; FaBoPV; LiTB; OBWP; WaP

Spain's Last Armada. Wallace Rice. To shed their lurid lustre on the empire that/was Spain. PAH

The Span of Life. Robert Frost. I can remember when he was a pup. DiPo; GDP; HoPM; LiTM; SoSe

The Spangled Pandemonium. Palmer Brown. And since he nipped his keeper,/He would just as soon nip you! AmMo; TiPo

Spaniel's Sermon. Colin Ellis. And place our God in trust. PV

Spanish Blue. Herbert Morris. and where the dust is still, is still, is still. NYBP

The Spanish Curate. John Fletcher. And thou shalt be learned old Vicar. OBS

The Spanish Descent. Daniel Defoe. Saint Paul ne'er saw but one such day before. APAS; OBWP

Spanish Folk Songs. Anonymous. Fewer leaves and more fruit ever/We find on the little tree. AWP

The Spanish Friar. John Dryden. So we, grown penitent, on serious thinking,/Leave whoring, and devoutly fall to drinking. OBSV

The Spanish Girls. Ivan Arguelles. and with the wounds of bulls FIA

The Spanish Gypsy (excerpt). George Eliot.
...all save a trusty band/Who keep strict watch along the northern heights. OBTV
With mimicry as merry as the tasks/Of penance-working shades in Tartarus. OBTV

Spanish Is the Loving Tongue. Anonymous. "Adios, mi corazon!" FSW

Spanish Johnny. Willa Cather. The night before he swung, he sang/To his mandolin. ABF; BPAW; HBMV

Spanish Ladies. Anonymous.
But we hope in a short time to see you again. AmSS
From Ushant to Scilly is thirty-five leagues. FaBoCh; LoGBV
With a health to each jovial and true-hearted soul. OBSS

The Spanish Lions. Phyllis McGinley. Posed with his Knight astride, on the opposite wall. NYBP

The Spanish Needle. Claude McKay. In your far-off sunny southland/Do you dream of me tonight? GoSl

Spanish Song. Charles Divine. You can always sing to a copper pan. HBMV

The Spanish Student: Serenade. Henry Wadsworth Longfellow Sleeps! AA

The Spanish War. Hugh" (Christopher Murray Grieve) MacDiarmid. For a little while! CMoP; NMP

Spanish Waters. John Masefield. By the loud surf of Los Muertos which is beating in my ears. BeLS; FaBoBe; MCCG; OnMSP

Spare Us, O Lord, Aloud We Pray. Isaac Watts. And the dead saints be raised again. AH

The Spark. Joseph Mary Plunkett. And sail into the dark/With laughter on our lips. AnIV; AWP

A Spark of Laurel. Stanley Jasspon Kunitz. Mother and mistress, one. NoAm

Sparkles from the Wheel. Walt Whitman. Sparkles from the wheel. BiP; DiPo; InPS

Sparkling and Bright. Charles Fenno Hoffman And break on the lips while meeting. AA; HBV 1-2

The Sparkling Bowl. John Pierpont. And I will drink of you, and live. AnAmPo

Sparkling Water. Richard Schaaf. the best damn glass of water I ever had TAT

The Sparrow. William Carlos Williams. I did my best;/farewell. InPS; LCAP; PAI; PrIm; VGW

The Sparrow and Diamond. Matthew Green. A Venus kill her bird. FM; PBBP

A Sparrow-Hawk Proud. Anonymous. The hawk replied, "I will not lose my diet/To let a thousand such enjoy their quiet." CH; EBEV; OBSP

The Sparrow-Hawk's Complaint. Anonymous. Therfore this song sing I may,/Timor mortis conturbat me.' OxBM

Sparrow Hills. Boris Pasternak. the piebald clouds spill down on us like a country woman's house-dress. NaP

Sparrow on an Airport. Richard Snyder. cannot meet his eye. PPJ

A Sparrow in the Dust. Ruth Domino. until the bone will break. BoWoP

The Sparrow in the Zoo. Howard Nemerov. Though the cage fret kings, you may make free with it. NoAm

Sparrow in Winter. Takahashi Shinkichi. An atomic submarine nudges past your belly. NU

The Sparrow's Dirge. John Skelton. When I saw my sparrow die! FaBoCh; LoGBV; OBSC

A Sparrow's Feather. George Barker. I hope the whole unimportant affair is/soon forgotten. The analogies are too trite. NYBP

The Sparrow's Nest. William Wordsworth. And love, and thought, and joy. EnRP

The Sparrow's Skull. Ruth Pitter. ...and flee/Into the heart of terror, to find myself in thee. EaLo; FaBoWP

The Sparrow's Song. Anonymous. Perhaps it would make me vain. STF

Sparrows among Dry Leaves. William Carlos Williams. and love's/obscure and insatiable/appetite. NYBP

The Sparrows at the Airport. Anthony Ostroff. With quick indifferent nods/And rare understanding. NePoAm-2

Sparrows in College Ivy. Edgar Wolfe. ...vying and playing/and gossiping, trying hard to be heard. AMV-81

The Spartan Wrestler. Damagetus. But it's with strength alone that I prevail. LiSp

Spassky at Reykjavik. David Fisher. and we sat there/king to king/with the single pawn. AMV-81

Spate in Winter Midnight. Norman Maccaig. Curled neatly round his neat and evil head. BoC; GTBS-P; PoSH

The Spawn of Slums. James W. Thompson. and blast the bastard jackals/ lapping at my mother's heels. BPo

Spawning in Northern Minnesota. David McElroy. The Mesabi is young, my county an ocean. AmPA

Speak. Bea Opengart. of which you will not speak. AMV-80

Speak. James Wright. Come down. Come down. Why dost/thou hide thy face? HAP; SM; TAP; WeW

Speak Gently. David Bates. The good, the joy, that it may bring/Eternity shall tell. PaPo; SpRo

Speak Gently. G. W. Langford. The good, the joy that it may bring,/ Eternity shall tell. Par

Speak Like Rain. Jerred Metz. catches celestial wind in its sails/propelling the world through space. VWA

Speak Out for Jesus. Anonymous. If not, then live and speak for Jesus/And speak out like a man. STF

Speak, Parrot. John Skelton. Since Deucalion's flood in no chronicle is/ told. CoBE; PoEL 1-5; ViBoPo

Speak Roughly to Your Little Boy. Lewis (Charles Lutwidge Dodgson) Carroll. Wow! Wow! Wow! FaBoCh; FaBoCo; LoGBV; NLV; Par

Speak the Word. Charles Wesley. And perfect me in love. BePJ

Speak This Kindly to Her. Robert Bagg. "Your careless praise for it was my first despair." NePoAm-2

Speak Thou and Speed. Sir Thomas Wyatt. Of good and bad the tryers are these twain. EnRePo; FCP

Speak to the Sun. Dedie Huffman Wilson. Must be reborn and cradled in old skies/That fill with light his young and wondering eyes. GoYe

Speak when you're spoken to. Anonymous.
Good little kid. CenHV
Turn to the wall. OxNR

Speak With the Sun. David Campbell. Of such stuff the stars were made. ACV; SeCePo

The Speaker. Charles G. Ballard. Far in the forest dim they lie/Only for his eye VoR

Speakers, Columbus Circle. Raymond Souster. The farcical, tragic impotence of our world. CaP

Speaking. Michael Ryan. as if words enclosed the secret/in myself that lasts after death. AmPA

Speaking for Them. Hayden Carruth. crazy swallows/turn somersaults in the air. GP

Speaking of Cowboy's Home. Anonymous. It's then you will find that she's your best friend. CoSo

Speaking of Poetry. John Peale Bishop. until the torches deaden at the bedroom door. LiTA; OxBA; PP

Speaking of Television: Robin Hood. Phyllis McGinley. Here comes the man in the green flannel suit. OBSV

Speaking: The Hero. Felix Pollak. I died a coward./They called me a hero. CTBA

The Speaking Tree. Muriel Rukeyser. ...It tells us what we mean. VGW

Speaks the Whispering Grass. Jesse Stuart. The lamps of Heaven and earth's buried dream. FYAP

Special Bulletin. Langston Hughes. Peel peel/Peel off/The skin. PoBA

Special Delivery. John Montague. but blood seeps where/I sign before tearing/down the perforated line. CIP; IPY

A Special Moment. Frank Lamont Phillips. "Once we was slaves" FAZ

Special Pleading. Charles Bernstein. ...such/cackle as girls & boys will make/discomfit to their less demonstrative/fold. APU

Special Rider Blues. *Anonymous.* You know, I'm sorry today/That I ever knowed your name. AmFP

Special Starlight. Carl Sandburg. The Creator of night and of birth/was the Maker of the stars. MoRP

The Specialist. Anne S. Perlman. his whole territory/shut against trespassers. SUW

Specialist. Theodore Roethke. He could range like Paracelsus/Through his field and someone else's. PV

Specimen of an Induction to a Poem. Alan Bernheimer. Botanical calm slips from stills. APU

A Speck of Sand. Paul Celan. and I glide ahead as a leaf/that knows where the gates will open. VWA

Speckle-Black Toad and Freckle-Green Frog. George Darley. And mouths to their middles split down/with laughter!/Hu! hu! hex! EAS

The Speckled Horse... *Anonymous.* My heart, depressed and longing,/ Revives when I see you./O, my dearest Siilen. WTO

The Spectacle of Truth. John Hewitt. his old decaying mortal eye,/desiring it, despising it. CIP

Spectator Ab Extra. Arthur Hugh Clough. How pleasant it is to have money. ALV; FaBoCo; FiBHP; GTBS-P; NBM; NLV; OBSV; OxBoLi

Spectator's Guide to Contemporary Art. Phyllis McGinley. Nor are the titles any help. OBSV
Sibyl always answered,/"Dribble." OBSV

The Specter. Ernst Hardt. Which eats up nights and days and all our life. AWP

The Spectral Attitudes. Andre Breton. ...changed places with statues of wax/Banyans banyans. EAS

Spectral Lovers. John Crowe Ransom. Who touch quick fingers fluttering like a bird/Whose songs shall never be heard. GBL; HeIP

The Spectre Is on the Move. Gudam Ali Allana. And blacken the face of earth. ACV

The Spectre Ship. Thomas Stephen Collier. This blazoned flag and ghostly sail/Stream out upon a spectral gale. EtS

Spectrum. William Dickey. And then obscured, while the red blushes come. ELU

Spectrum. Mari E. Evans. ...blue/like midnight sometimes/or a robin's egg/sometimes BPo

Speculation. Howard Nemerov. ...as each star/Speeds outward, goes out, or goes out of sight. TAP

Speculative Evening. Marguerite Young. And harpers harping on a sea of glass. LiTA

The Speculators. William Makepeace Thackeray. For never a beggar need now despair, And every rogue has a/chance.' OBSV

Speech. Henry Taylor. I can hear them/making soft liquid sounds/of contentment. MAT; NLV

Speech for the Repeal of the McCarran Act. Richard Wilbur. ...the neural/ Web, the self-true mind, the trusty reflex. CMoP; NePoAm

The Speech of the Dead. Anne Ridler. And in that glory of love to learn/ Words of the dead through living lips a prayer. ChMP

Speech to a Crowd. Archibald MacLeish. The world was always yours: you will not take it. MoAB; MoAmPo; NePA

Speech to the Court. Walter Lowenfels. and we know we are moving/ towards the songs of others. PPON

Speech to Those Who Say Comrade. Archibald MacLeish. Not to be had for a word or a week's wishing. OxBA

Speeches at the Barriers (excerpt). Susan Howe. Reaching out alone in words oh/peerless poesy. APU

Speechless. Philip Bourke Marston. About their spirits, as they mix and meet/In passion-lighted silence, 'tranced and/sweet. VLP

Speed. William Henry Davies. Catch up with you at last. MoRP

The Speed of Darkness. Muriel Rukeyser. Who will speak these days,/if not I,/if not you? LCAP

The Spell. Medora C. Addison. How shall I sing of love again? HBMV

A Spell. John Dryden. Answer me, if this be done?/'Tis done. WiR

The Spell. Robert Herrick. Ring the saints'-bell to affright/Far from hence the evil sprite. CaPo; WSC

The Spell. Henry Martyn Hoyt. And thrice an elfin bugle blew/From the Gates of Faerie. HBMV

The Spell. Michelle Roberts. forge molten gold into the image of keys/one must surely fit this gate. LFAC

Spell against Sorrow. Kathleen Raine. Tear away grief. PBWP

The Spell Against Spelling. George Starbuck. But something. One finds out as one goes aughan. FYAP

A Spell before Winter. Howard Nemerov. The old hills hunch before the north wind blows. LiTM

The Spell o' the Hills. Douglas Fraser. Will ca' me and draw me/Until the day I dee. PoSH

Spell of Creation. Kathleen Raine. Lie like the seed within the flower. FaBoCh; LoGBV; OxBS

Spell of Sleep. Kathleen Raine. Where the troubled spirit grows wise/And the heart is comforted. HaMV

The Spell of the Yukon. Robert W. Service. It's the stillness that fills me with peace. BLPA; BLPL; FaBoBe; FaFP; PoPl; TreF

Spelling. Margaret Atwood. your first word. NoP

The Spelling Bee at Angels. Bret (Francis Bret Harte) Harte. ...dreamed of Angels' Spelling Bee and thought of/Truthful James. StPo

The Spelling of Elliot. *Anonymous.* But double L and Double T,/The de'il may ken wha they may be. FaBoUs

Spelt from Sibyl's Leaves. Gerard Manley Hopkins. Where, selfwrung selfstrung, sheathe-and-shelterless thoughts against/thoughts in groans grind. BrPo; CMoP; CoBMV; FaBoMo; LiTM; MoPo; NOBV; OAEL 1-2; PrIm

Spencer the Rover. *Anonymous.* I'll stay at home with my wife and go rambling no more. OBET

A Spending Hand That Alway Powreth Owte. Sir Thomas Wyatt. And coyne to kepe as water in a syve. AAS

Spendthrift. I. A. Richards. The possible/Our modicum/for this spent life at last. PoPl

Spenser's Ireland. Marianne Moore. I am troubled, I'm dissatisfied, I'm Irish. FaBoWP; LiTA; LiTM; MasP; NePA; NoAm; NOBA; OxBA; TAP

Sphere (excerpt). Archie Randolph Ammons. the return of the dream that will be only the arrival of/145/the nova:/..... HaCAP

The Sphere of Glass. John Lehmann. While through the bluebells and the fern/Sister and brother made their way. ChMP

The Sphinx. Henry Howard Brownell The Darling of the Nile. AA

The Sphinx. Ralph Waldo Emerson. "Who telleth one of my meanings/Is master of all I am." AP; DiPo; MAmP; NOBA; OxBA

Sphinx. Robert Earl Hayden. you would hardly find/it possible to live without/my joke and me. HaCAP

The Sphinx (excerpt). Oscar Wilde. And with your curved archaic smile you watched his passion come and go. MoBrPo; UnTE

The Sphinx Speaks. Francis Saltus Saltus. The Corsican, prophetic and renowned,/To whom I spake, one awful night alone! AA

Sphinxes Inclined to Be. Olga Orozco. ...two/hands in their duty of being just hands,/from beginning to end. WPOW

Spicewood. Lizette Woodworth Reese. And all familiar as a cup, a chair. MoAmPo

The Spider. Robert P. Tristram Coffin. This small son of Euclid's own. ImOP

Spider. Thomas Cole. A broom, a flame, a foot, a stronger mate. PoA

Spider. Padraic Colum. You're a wonderful fellow! RoGo

The Spider. Richard Eberhart. On ocean's long reach, on parables of God? PoA

The Spider. Loren C. Eiseley. Frail stairs the careless wind blows through. SUW

Spider. Norma Farber. Listen! my web is what you hear. PCh

The Spider. Hannah F. Gould. That leads him to the grave unblest,/And drops him, hopeless, in? OBCA

Spider. Richmond Lattimore. Spider does not sing,/only sits, sees, eats, and weaves. PP

The Spider. Edward Littleton. 'Tis ten to one but penury/Ends both the spider and the poet. NOEC

The Spider. Kenneth Mackenzie. towards the uncharted mountain of my shoulder. BoAnP

The Spider and the Fly. Mary Howitt. And take a lesson from this tale, of the Spider and the Fly. BeLS; FaFP; GoTF; HBV 1-2; HBVY; OHFP; OnUR; OxBChV; Par; TreFS; WBLP

The Spider and the Ghost of the Fly. Vachel Lindsay. I saw her eat my heart. VGW

Spider Crystal Ascension. Charles Wright. And when it does, we lie back in our watery hair and rock. GeTw; HaCAP; LCAP

A Spider Danced a Cosy Jig. Irving Layton. The poor man blessed the rich. WHW

The spider holds a silver ball. Emily Dickinson. Then dangle from the Housewife's Broom–/His Boundaries–forgot– FM; WPOW

Spider Reeves. Henry Carlile. You could have learned to live. Psk

The Spider's Nest. George MacBeth. ...Sleep comes. And with it my snails. NMP

Spiders. Diane Ackerman. ...at long last,/even their slack jaws quiver. MAYP

Spiel of the Three Mountebanks. John Crowe Ransom. Come, be instructed of my Lamb. MoAB; MoAmPo

Spike Driver Blues. Mississippi John Hurt. But he went down;/That's where I'm going. BluL

Spikenard. Laurence Housman. Near to Thine awful Feet let reach/This broken spikenard of my speech! TrPWD

Spilled Milk. John Haines. and this child stands/with a sopping sponge in his hand,/saying he never meant to do it. GP

Spilt Milk. William Butler Yeats. Must ramble, and thin out/Like milk spilt on a stone. OBSP

Spin Dame. *Anonymous* Spin, Dame, spin. OxNR

Spindrift. Galway Kinnell. Shining with time like any pilgrim? NaP; NYBP

The Spinner. Mary Ainge De Vere. Lo! where the toil of a lifetime lies/In a winding-sheet! AA

The Spinner. Charles L. O'Donnell. ...whispered Mary His Mother,/Her tears falling down on His hands. GoBC; ISi

Spinners at Willowsleigh. Marya Zaturenska. Now they are old and brown and all but dead! HBMV

Spinning. Helen Hunt Jackson. "Thou poor blind spinner, work is done." HBV 1-2

Spinning. Al Purdy. wait for me wait for me NOBC

The Spinning Girl. Nathan Alterman. And since then she is thief and beggar,/And sovereign queen and buffoon. VWA

Spinning in April. Josephine Preston Peabody. And leaves me at the spinning-wheel, with dark, unseeing/eyes. HBV 1-2

Spinning Song. *Anonymous.* My fingers are healing,/The pain is all gone. UnTE

A Spinning Song. John Francis O'Donnell. To the low, slow murmur of the brown round wheel. IrPN

Spinning Song. Edith Sitwell. If the spinning-wheel Time move slow or fast. MoAB; MoBrPo

The Spinning Wheel. Abraham Moses Klein. of their woven acres and their linen fields. CaP

The Spinning Wheel. John Francis Waller. Through the grove the young lovers by moonlight are rov-/ing. AnIV; StPo

The Spinning Woman. of Tarentum Leonidas. And in her eightieth year she saw the wave/Of Acaheron,–old Platthis,–kind and brave. AWP

Spinster. Sylvia Plath. As no mere insurgent man could hope to break/With curse, fist, threat/Or love, either. FaBoWP

Spinster's Lullaby. Vassar Miller. Trembling on the pulse of God. BoWoP; NMM

Spinster Song. Virginia Lyne Tunstall. Where is my lover? Where is my lover? HBMV

The Spiral. John Holmes. And worlds more in the grains that make mountains. MiAP

Spiral Landscape. Michael Brownstein. To satisfy your sight until you move ANYP

The Spire Cranes. Dylan Thomas. But do not travel down dumb wind like prodigals. PoA

The Spires of Oxford. Winifred M. Letts. God bring you to a fairer place/Than even Oxford town. EnLit; FaFP; HBV 1-2; MCCG; OHFP; OnYI; PoLf; PoRA; TreF; WGRP

The Spirit. Doug Turner. screaming defiance/all the way to the end AMV-81

The Spirit Craft. Charles G. Ballard. That always was from out of heaven's wall VoR

Spirit Flowers. Della Burt. Spirit flowers we are. BlSi

Spirit from Whom Our Lives Proceed. Howard Chandler Robbins. Until in our Redeemer's face/We read the meaning of our days. TrPWD

The Spirit in Our Hearts. Henry Ustic Onderdonk. Jesus, my Saviour, come. AH; BePJ

The Spirit-Land. Jones Very. That ne'er returns us to the fields of light. AmLP; HAP

Spirit-Like before Light. Arthur Gregor. calls home its own/and the children enter. VWA

The Spirit of 34th Street. Peggy Shriver. like folded dove wings,/his black leather gloves. AMV-80

Spirit of Freedom, Thou Dost Love the Sea. Henry Nehemiah Dodge. The diapason thunders shake the shore/And chant the song of freedom evermore. EtS

Spirit of Life, in This New Dawn. Earl Bowman Marlatt. ...eyes that see,/Beyond the dark, the dawn and thee. AH

The Spirit of Night. Thomas Rogers. For she is dead, and human flesh is frail. EIL

Spirit of Plato. *Anonymous.* ...;Athens doth inherit/His corpse below. AWP; EnLi 1-2; OBVE

The Spirit of Poetry. Henry Wadsworth Longfellow. Is the rich music of a summer bird/Heard in the still night, with its passionate cadence. PP

Spirit of Sadness. Richard Le Gallienne. Or is there still in those great eyes/That look of lonely hills and skies? HBV 1-2

The Spirit of the Birch. Arthur Ketchum. And evermore–I dance! I dance! OHIP

The Spirit of the "Bluenose." Claire Harris MacIntosh. My conquering spirit sails and will not die. CaP

The Spirit of the Cairngorms. Axel Firsoff. ...in terms/of shade and colour, without apprehension or regret. PoSH

The Spirit of the Fall. Danske Dandridge. There, on a winter dawn, thy corse I found,/Lone Spirit of the Fall. AA

The Spirit of the Maine. Tudor Jenks. Brave though her sons, how shall they meet/The spirit of the Maine! AA; MC; PAH

The Spirit of the Wheat. Edward A.U. Valentine. She fades into the wrinkling heat. AA

The Spirit of Wine. William Ernest Henley. His magnetic and mastering song. HBV 1-2

The Spirit of Wrath. William Heyen. the shark will swim away. AmPA; WOLT

The Spirit's Grace. Janie Screven Heyward. So would I that my Spirit's grace/Should beautify its dwelling place. HBMV

The Spirit's Light. William Cowper. It gives a light to every age–/It gives, but borrows none. BLRP

The Spirit's Odyssey. M. Krishnamurti. The waker, slumber-sooth'd! PeD

Spirit's Song. Louise Bogan. O far too long, and poisoned through! NYBP

Spirit, Silken Thread. Margot Ruddock. She is blind... OBMV

Spirit Song. *Anonymous.* Strength of soul brings health/To the place of feasting. WTO

Spirits. Robert Bridges. All the summer night/Threading dances light? OBEV; OBVV

Spirits. Victor Hernandez Cruz. they are our friends. PoBA; WSC

Spirits and Men (excerpt). Ebenezer Elliott. Dwelt in th' Almighty's form, and knew nor guilt, nor fear. OBRV

Spirits, Dancing. Arthur Gregor. ...Or you/would not have come this far. NYBP; VGW

Spirits Everywhere. Ludwig Uhland. Anear me Two from the Phantomland! AWP

Spirits of the Dead. Edgar Allan Poe. How it hangs upon the trees,/A mystery of mysteries! MAmP

Spirits Unchained. Keorapetse Kgositsile. to clarity to power/to the rebirth of real men PoBA

A Spiritual. Paul Laurence Dunbar. But lif' up yo' haid w'en de King go by! BPo

Spiritual Isolation. Isaac Rosenberg. Great awe to my sense is/Even in the rose time when all else is/well. TrJP

Spiritual Love. William Caldwell Roscoe. My devotion more secure/Woos thy spirit high and pure. OBVV

Spiritual Passion. George Barlow. Knowing her union holier and more fond. OBVV

Spirituality. Samuel Greenberg. Forgive our memory stain! e'er this might of love/Hath meekly found its room, so called immortality LiTA

The Spirk Troll-Derisive. James Whitcomb Riley. With a long piece of crape to her tail. LBN; NA

Spit. C. K. Williams. "Now therefore go," He said, "and I will be with thy mouth." VWA

Spit, Cat, Spit. Mother Goose. All the dogs in our town/Shall have a little bit! TW

Spitballer. Fred Chappell. Since while he pitches he waters the lawn. LiSp

Spite hath no power to make me sad. Sir Thomas Wyatt. It doth suffice she doth me wrong. FCP; SiPS

Spite of Thy Godhead, Powerful Love. Anne Wharton. And offer him my heart. CavP

Spitting on Ira Rosenblatt. Robert Hershon. ...high on a wall/spitting on Ira Rosenblatt NeAC

Spiv Song. Royston Ellis. and where are you off to, my son, my shadow,/with the bill unpaid, as the door swings shut? PeHV

Spleen. Charles Baudelaire.
he cannot warm up his shot corpse, whose food/is syrup-green Lethean ooze, not blood. NAWM 1-2
Set on my skull their black flags, in the wind's scope. SyP

Spleen. Ernest Christopher Dowson. With all my memories that could not sleep. BrPo; CBEP; MoBrPo; NCEP; NOBV; SyP

Spleen. John Gray. So, saving you, does everything. NOBV

The Spleen. Matthew Green. Own, by neglecting sorrow's wound,/The consanguinity of sound. NOEC

Spleen. Paul Verlaine. Of everything, alas, save thee. AWP; EnLi 1-2; SyP

Splendid and Terrible. Seumas (James Starkey) O'Sullivan. Deep in the heart whereto it came/Of old as some wind-wearied bird/Drops to its nest. HBMV

The Splendid Lover. John Richard Moreland. When your head lies on his breast. PGD

The Splendid Shilling (parody). John Phillips. The Ship sinks found'ring in the vast Abyss. BXAP; CEP; FaBoPa; NOEC; OAEL 1-2; Par

The Splendid Spur.   Sir Arthur Thomas ("Q") Quiller-Couch.   Count it the lists that God hath built/For haughty hearts to ride a-tilt.   HBV 1-2; HBVY

The Splendid Village.   Ebenezer Elliott.
He knows the Steward–he is known afar/To magistrats and bums–great man, John Marr!   NBM
Votes for my Lord, and hates the thankless poor.   NBM; OBSV

Splendor.   Shin Shalom.   against divine Light and the test/of transmitting the innermost Splendor.   VWA

Splinter.   Carl Sandburg.   It is so thin a splinter of singing.   OBCA; SoSe; SUS; TiPo

The Splinter.   James Kenneth Stephen.   And I, that noon in winter,/Forgot the cruel splinter.   CenHV

The Spoilers and the Spoils.   Judith Johnson Sherwin.   for our world was death without grief and all holds broken.   SM

Spoils.   Robert Graves.   For fear they burn a hole through two-foot steel.   HAP; MoLP; NYBP; WeW

The Spoils of War.   Vernon Watkins.   Look on her face; mine eyes dazzle; she died young.   WaP

Spokane Falls.   Phil George.   But, what a waste of rocks/For that "chapel," they called it.   VoR

Spoken by Venus on Seeing Her Statue Done by Praxiteles.   Anonymous.   But where has this Praxiteles been prying?   EyDe; FaBoEE

Spoken Extempore.   John Wilmot, Earl of Rochester.   And then to fall like Phaeton.   SeCePo

Spoken Extempore on the Death of Mr. Pope.   Anonymous.   And front the sun undaunted: Pope is dead!   NOEC

Spoken through Glass.   Eithne Wilkins.   all fall down.   NeBP

Spontaneous Me.   Walt Whitman.   It has done its work–I toss it carelessly to fall where/it may.   OxBA

Spontaneous Requiem for the American Indian.   Gregory Corso.   ...the vast black jacket brays in the full forced fell.   MAT; PoM

Spooks.   Nathalia Crane.   And you'll see them, one and all.   ShM

A Spool of Thread.   Sophie E. Eastman.   I was but a boy in war time, and I carried him/the thread.   PAH

The Spoon.   Charles Simic.   Just barely/Beginning to walk.   NNaP

Spoon River Anthology.   Edwin Meade Robinson.   When I lived/I was certainly rotten!   HBMV

The Spooniad.   Edgar Lee Masters.   Of running feet from every side was heard/Bent on the   OBAL

Sporting Acquaintances.   Siegfried Sassoon.   We backed The Tetrarch and got drunk together.   OxBTC

The Sporting Cowboy.   Anonymous.   So he won't forget his darling he's left so far behind.   OuSiCo

Sporting Life Blues.   Anonymous.   That old night life, that sportin' life is killin' me.   FSW

Sporting the Plaid.   Chris Wallace-Crabbe.   you were all huff and puff, a bolt of plaid/woven out of dropped names.   NOAV

Sports Field.   Judith Wright.   the night and the field glitter.   LiSp

The Sportsman.   David McCord.   He up and shot himself–well out of season.   LiSp

Spot-Check at Fifty.   Vernon Scannell.   But as I wave I see, appalled,/The new fast bowler's wicked grin.   NAs

The Spotless Maid.   Vincent McNabb.   ...And both shall be/Jesu's eternally.   ISi

Spots of Blood.   Phyllis Webb.   Breathing poppies. Thinking.   NOBC

The Spotted Flycatcher.   Walter De la Mare.   Sighs Nature an Alas? Or merely, Amen?   OBSP

Spouse.   Witter ("Emanuel Morgan") Bynner.   For this is Tuesday,–Wednesday is tomorrow.   AnFE

A Spouse I Do Hate.   William Wycherley.   Great wits and great braves,/Have always a punk to their mother.   OAEP

The Spouse to the Beloved.   William Baldwin.   All shadows dark and cause them slide,/According as his will is.   OBSC

The Spouse to the Younglings.   William Baldwin.   ...and cause them slide/According as his will is.   OBSP

Spray.   D.H. Lawrence.   with frustration how beautiful!   BoNaP

A Spray of Honeysuckle.   Mary Emily Bradley.   That thou hast sweetness to bestow!   AA

Spraying the Potatoes.   Patrick Kavanagh.   Or till blossomed stalks cannot weave a spell.   BIrV; FaBoIP; IPY; NoP; OxBI

The Sprig of Lime.   Robert Nichols.   Knowing, untold, he cannot need it now.   GTBS-P

A Sprig of Rosemary.   Amy Lowell.   And the soft brightness which is your soul.   PeHV

Sprin' Fevah.   Ray Garfield Dandridge.   To dat res'less, wretchit fevah evah Sprin'.   BANP

Spring.   William Allingham.   Around their lofty cradles, with the Spring's/Breath rocking slowly.   IrPN

Spring.   Anonymous.
And wight in wode be fleme.   AtBAP; OAEL 1-2
The nightingale sings.   SUS

The Spring.   William Barnes.   When God would gi'e woone zunsheen.   BoNaP; HBV 1-2

Spring.   Harry Behn.   Evening clouds are glowing/And dusk is full of song.   TiPo

Spring.   William Blake.   Merrily, merrily, to welcome in the Year.   FaBoCh; LoGBV; MoShBr; PoPl; SUS; YeAr

The Spring.   Thomas Carew.
June in her eyes, in her heart January.   AnAnS 2; CaPo; NoP; PoEL 1-5; PPoe; SeCV 1-2; TEP; TrGrPo; WiR
Welcome the coming of the longed-for May.   GN

Spring.   Caius Valerius Catullus.   Return by many a different road.   PoPl

Spring.   Marchette Chute.   And we can go barefoot/Whenever we like.   TiPo

Spring.   Carole Gregory Clemmons.   either way I'll be in.   PoBA

The Spring.   Abraham Cowley.   This is for beasts, and that for men the spring.   HAP; JCP; MeLP; OBS

Spring.   Charles d'Orleans.   The year lays down his mantle cold.   AWP; CTC

Spring.   Frederick Feirstein.   A glacial age demands a glacial heart.   AMV-81

The Spring.   Rose Fyleman.   I'm certain that he thought the place/Belonged by rights to him.   BrR; FaPON

Spring.   Caroline Giltinan.   The bird with the wisp of straw.   HBMV

Spring.   Giovanni Battista Guarini.   Am what I was no more, dear to another's eyes.   AWP

Spring.   Michael Hogan.   He imagines a speckled trout/coming up shining and raging with life.   LFAC; TAT

Spring.   Gerard Manley Hopkins.   Most, O maid's child, thy choice and worthy the winning.   ACV; BoLiVe; BoNaP; BrPo; DiPo; EBCP; FaBV; ForPo; HAP; InvP; LiTM; MoAB; MoBrPo; MoVE; NoAm; NOBE; NOBV; OAEL 1-2; OAEP; OBMV; OBNC; OxBoCh; SoSe; TrCP; VLP

Spring.   Richard Hovey.   And the slow clouds go by...   BBV

Spring.   Thomas Caulfield Irwin.   Until the limpid crescent of the moon/Lights the blue east above the evening trees.   IrPN

Spring.   Orrick Johns.   Show you the way? I will!   InMe

Spring.   Moishe Kulbak.   The world has surrendered to me.   VWA

Spring.   Philip Larkin.   Their visions mountain-clear, their needs immodest.   ACV; MoBrPo

Spring.   Robert Loveman.   Ah! surely now the virgin year/Is in her blushing maidenhood.   AA

Spring.   Vladimir Mayakovsky.   Sappy and gabby, just like a cadet,/Comes Spring.   CAD

Spring.   Linda McCarriston.   you imagine a rich man, maybe,/with his money.   AMV-81

Spring.   Hugh McCrae.   Two blocks and a half past the Bulletin office.   ACV

Spring.   Meleager.   Sing, poet, thou–and sing thy best for May!   AWP

Spring.   William Stanley Merwin.   Will have your answer.   NaP

Spring.   Edna St. Vincent Millay.   April/Comes like an idiot, babbling and strewing flowers.   BoWoP; MoAB; MoAmPo; NePA; NoP

The Spring.   John Francis O'Donnell.   Ah love, in sorrow, thou abid'st with me.   IrPN

Spring.   Boris Pasternak.   And let the thirsty paper drink its fill.   LiTW

Spring.   W.R. Rodgers.
It's all-containing cry.   AnIL
Waiting for a wedding, mobbing a bride.   OnYI

Spring.   Isaac Rosenberg.   But who could have woke them/While you were not near?   TrJP

Spring.   Christina Georgina Rossetti.   Now newly born, and now/Hastening to die.   OBNC

Spring.   Princess Shikishi.   You should have come/before the wind.   PBWP

Spring.   Edith Sitwell.   Like the leaping goat-footed waterfalls/Singing their cold, forlorn madrigals.   OAEP

Spring.   Christopher Smart.   And the rocks supply the coney/With a fortress and an home.   OBEC

Spring.   Andre Spire.   You silent lovers, wander hand in hand.   AWP

Spring.   Thomas Stanley.   Freshly bourgeons every bough.   AWP

Spring.   James Still.   To the grass, to the cows calving in the lot.   GrPl

Spring.   Thomas Nash.   Spring, the sweet Spring!   AtBAP; BoNaP; CBEP; ElL; GTBS; GTBS-P; HBV 1-2; MCCG; OBSC; OnUR; TrGrPo; WiR

Spring.   James (1700-48) Thomson.   Together freed, their gentle spirits fly/To scenes where love and bliss immortal reign.   EiCP; LAuP

Spring.   Henry Timrod.
"Behold me! I am May!"   HBV 1-2
Who turn her meads to graves.   AP

Spring.   Paul Verlaine.   And the wild sheets. O to your bed!   ErPo; PeHV

The Spring.   Ellen Bryant Voigt.   the last release, the rush,/the blunt completion   MAYP

Spring.   Ruth Whitman.   and rose up filling the sky blowsy with/fruit to come   IHMS

Spring.   Oscar Williams.   ...but God the performer/Is walking about with the bird in His hand.   LiTA

Spring 1940. W. H. Auden. O what weeps is the love that hears, an/ Accident occurring in his substance. OAEP

Spring 1942. Roy Fuller. O revolution in the whole/Of human use of man and nature! LiTM; NeBP; OxBTC; WaaP

Spring 1943. Roy Fuller. ...not believe that human art/Can fail to make reality its heart. LiTB; LiTM; WaP

Spring: a Formal Ode. Fyodor Tyutchev. Among these quickening joys participate. FaBoRV

Spring Again. Ronald Wallace. I ask to be taken in. PPJ

Spring Air. Gene Derwood. Is this my hand in yours? Am I/So close? Wait till the insinuant wind's gone by... FaFP; LiTL

Spring and All. Grace Bauer. Always counting on the odds/that April may be kind. PPJ

Spring and All. William Carlos Williams. rooted they/grip down and begin to awaken. AP; CABA; ExPo; ForPo; InPK; InPS; MoVE; NoAm; NOBA; QFR; TAP

Spring and Death. Gerard Manley Hopkins. Death, to mark them in the Spring. BrPo; SyP

Spring and Fall. Gerard Manley Hopkins. It is Margaret you mourn for. AnFE; BiP; BrPo; CMoP; DiPo; EBEV; ELP; ExPo; FaBoUs; FF; GoJo; GTBS-P; HAP; HeIP; HoPM; InPS; LiTB; LiTM; MAT; MoAB; MoPo; MoVE; NIP; NOBE; NoP; OAEP; PAI; PoEL 1-5; PoPl; PoPle; PoRA; PPoe; PPON; PPP; SCV; SeCeV; SOTW; TEP; VLP; WeW

Spring, and the Blind Children. Alfred Noyes. But O, Thy grief! For Thou canst see and hear. OxBTC

Spring Arithmetic. Anonymous. 1 privet bush,/1 ivy plant,/1 radish. FiBHP

Spring at Fort Okanogan. Ramona Wilson. The air will be sweet/as breath of new horses. VoR

The Spring Beauties. Helen Gray Cone. Young maids, beware of vanity! AA

Spring Bereaved. William, of Hawthornden Drummond.
But ah! what served it to be happy so?/Sith passed pleasures double but new woe? OBEV
But we, once dead, no more do see the sun. OBEV
Neglected virtue, seasons go and come,/While thine forgot lie closed in a tomb. OBEV

Spring Burning. Patrick Roland. And burn with fury through his age. PeSA

Spring Catch. Greg Keeler. ...something reminded/me of my own hand/at the other end of the line. WOLT

Spring Cellar. Gladys McKee. And one bewitched granddaughter. GoYe

Spring Cleaning. Phil George. I must air out the regalia. VoR

Spring Comes to Murray Hill. Ogden Nash. Instead of being confined on Madison Avenue I could/soar in a jiffy to Second or Third. FiBHP

Spring Coming. Archie Randolph Ammons. such nice machines. HeIP; InPK

Spring Cricket. Frances Rodman. That April's due to saunter by. SiSoSe

Spring Day. John Ashbery. We shall soon give all our attention to you. NOBA

A Spring Day on Campus. Gilbert Schedler. The love in my life. AMV-80

Spring Death. Russell Marano. In the year of many springs/my father was dead. AMV-81

Spring Doggerel. Rhoda Coghill. Comes pouring like sunlight the lark's noisiest music. NeIP

Spring Drawing II. Robert Hass. ...three jaguars are eating his entrails and he is/watching. MAYP

Spring Ease. Monty Reid. The men come in from the field/and don't notice. CaPN

Spring Ecstasy. Lizette Woodworth Reese. White thorn too much! MoAmPo

The Spring Equinox. Anne Ridler. Receiving a profit, before it holds a snare. NeBP

Spring (excerpt). Thomas Gisborne. Their pinions, in short flights their strength to prove,/And venturous, trust the bosom of the air. PBBP

Spring (excerpt). William Miller. Opening wi' gentle hand the bonnie green and yellow/buds... PoSC

The Spring Festival on the River. John Peck. Slabs of jasper, crystals of mica. AmPA

Spring Floods. Gregory Orr. laying her cool hand/on my forehead in the dark/room before sleep? GeTw

Spring Flowers. James (1700-48) Thomson. The Breath of Nature, and her endless Bloom. AtBAP; NOBE; OBEC

Spring Flowers from Ireland. Denis Florence McCarthy. And drink to days that yet may be. ACP; GoBC

Spring-Gazing Song. Hsueh T'ao. I see the future, and I will not see. BoWoP

Spring Goeth All in White. Robert Bridges. the cherry and hoary pear/ Scatter their snow around. BoNaP; HBMV

Spring Has Come to Town with Love. Anonymous. Ant wyght in wode be fleme. CABA

Spring Hath Her Own Bright Days of Calm and Peace. Robert Bridges. Will guady flies adventure in the air,/Nor any lizard sun his spotted skin. VLP

Spring Hawks. Jim Thomas. ...some part/of us forever gone on loan to hawks. AMV-81

Spring in England. Charles Buxton Going. The haunting stories of a thousand years/Waken to fragrance in the English Spring! HBMV

Spring in Hiding. Frances Frost. ...Spring in bud, in brook,/in small grass through the thaw! YeAr

Spring in New Hampshire. Claude McKay. Wearied, exhausted, dully sleeping. BANP; BPo; GoSl; PoNe

Spring in the Desert. Arthur Truman Merrill. And miles up there in the desert sky/A vulture specks the blue. BPAW

Spring in the Old World. Philip Levine. ...their skirts/flared out around them, open and burning. FAZ

Spring in the Students' Quarter. Henri Murger. She now may sit to Gavarni. AWP

Spring in These Hills. Archibald MacLeish. daffodils like drifting flaws/of sunlight on these winter hills. NCSH

Spring in Virginia. Ramona Wilson. the sun smooths and shines your mouth. VoR

Spring in War-Time. Sara Teasdale. But what of all the lovers now/Parted by Death,/Grey Death? OHIP

Spring in Washington. James Den Boer. ...as the republic accepts/the coup d'etat of spring. TAT

Spring Is a Looping-Free Time. Martin Robbins. Cleaner than Sunday, warmer than leaves. SD

Spring Is at Work with Beginnings of Things. Greta Leora Rose. Things that lie close to the earth. CaP

Spring Is Hard on Us. Anonymous. Winter, post-coital triste. ErPo; PV

Spring Is in the Making. Nona Keen Duffy. For spring is in the making! YeAr

The Spring Is Late. Louise Chandler Moulton. I am his own,–doth not my Father care? HBV 1-2

Spring Is Like a Perhaps Hand. Edward Estlin Cummings. without breaking anything. NePA; NoP; SOTW; TAP; VGW

Spring is short. Yosano Akiko. I grope for/my full breasts with my hands. BoWoP

Spring Is Showery, Flowery, Bowery. Mother Goose. Winter: slippy, drippy, nippy. TiPo

Spring is the Period. Emily Dickinson. Without a cordial interview/With God. TAP

A Spring Journey. Alice Freeman Palmer. Yet all the winters cannot blow its sweetness quite away. HBV 1-2

Spring-Joy Praising God. Praise of the Sun. C Greiffenberg. From out your bloom of light the Maker's beauty shines. WPOW

Spring Landscape. Arthur Davison Ficke. Spring's whole delight bloom like a marvel there! HBMV

Spring Landscape. Melvin Walker La Follette. A tulip like a red badge of courage. NePoEA-2

A Spring Lay. Oliver Opdyke. I could have went the beaten track/But I will lay quite here. InMe

A Spring Lilt. Anonymous. Repeat/The robins, nested over. HBV 1-2

Spring Market. Louise Driscoll. Or think you can bargain for/Wild flower grace. HBMV; HBVY

Spring MCMXL. David Gascoyne. Of one they can still recognise, though scarcely understand. MoVE

A Spring Memorandum. Robert Duncan. to force out each bud to the hungry day. PoA

A Spring Morning. John Clare. And every sound that meets the ear is Love. GBL

Spring Morning. D. H. Lawrence. See, how gorgeous the world is/Outside the door! BrPo; CMoP; MoAB; MoBrPo

Spring Morning–Santa Fe. Lynn Riggs. Words grew in the heart and clanged, the color of noon. BPAW

Spring Morning: Waking. Emily Seelbinder. the morning so early gone. AMV-81

Spring Mountain Climb. Richard Eberhart. And man fallen to his endless burden. GoYe; LiSp

Spring Night. Richard Aldridge. But I can't, you know; I have to keep on walking. NePoAm

Spring Night. Rana Mukerji. Till all my lips open, and you enter/All my dreams. UnTE

Spring Night. Su Tung-P'o. In the garden, a swing, where night is deep and still. Prf

Spring Night. Sara Teasdale. Why am I crying after love? BLPL; FaBoBe; HBMV; LiTA; LiTL; MoAmPo; PG

Spring Nocturne. Abraham Liessin. And the scented eve of springtime/ Greets my soul from silent bowers. TrJP

Spring Oak. Galway Kinnell. It shook itself and was all green. BoNaP; ELU; NePoAm

The Spring of Joy Is Dry. Anonymous. And love continue still. EIL

Spring of the Thief. John Logan. the white face and thigh of the thief. BiP; CAPP; NNaP

The Spring of the Year. Allan Cunningham. I'll meet them both in heaven/At the spring of the year. HBV 1-2

Spring of Work Storm. Joseph Ceravolo. I felt the oil/in the sand ANYP

Spring Offensive. Wilfred Owen. Why speak not they of comrades that went under? BrPo; GTBS-P; LiTB; MoVE

Spring Offensive, 1941. Maurice Biggs. ...let her alone/Bemoan those broken lips with kisses from her own. PoAu 1-2

The Spring Offensive of the Snail. Marge Piercy. ...the right place to be/where we start again. TAP

Spring Omnipotent Goddess. Edward Estlin Cummings. feet incorrigible/ragging the world, OxBA

Spring on the Ochils. James Logie Robertson. And Ochil brooks and Ochil braes/Grow classic in her smile! OBVV

Spring over the City. Anne Hebert. ...and the leprous stones in/the sun have the splendid shine of naked, victorious gods. PBWP

Spring Passion. Joel Elias Spingarn. And bask, a dreamer, in her dreamy smiles? HBV 1-2

Spring Pastoral. Elinor Wylie. Dipping their fingers in a stream. AnEnPo

Spring Poem. Bin Ramke. the certain taste and surer smell/of a dim-lit past when we slept well. AMV-81

Spring Poem. Julian Symons. You with the flowers and pigeons. NeBP

Spring Pools. Robert Frost. From snow that melted only yesterday AmPP; DiPo; MoAB; NoAm; NOBA; NoP; OxBA

Spring Quiet. Christina Georgina Rossetti. Though far off it be. BoNaP; CH; EG; GTBS-P; InPS; LoBV; PoEL 1-5

Spring Rain. Harry Behn. Ah me, she sighs, ah me! TiPo

Spring Rain. Marchette Chute. I fell into a river once/But this is even better. TiPo

The Spring Returns. Charles Leonard Moore. The Spring returns! O madness beyond sense,/Breed in bones thine own omnipotence! HBV 1-2

Spring Rites. Martin Robbins. Leather and wood by his side smell like/A summer he'll knock clear out of the park. AMV-81

Spring's Delights. Joseph Ashby Sterry. Sneeze and warble, Tra-la-la! CenHV

Spring's on the Curb. Hildegarde Flanner. The broad magnolia bud and wants the branch. AnAmPo

Spring Scene. Buson (Taniguchi Buso). ...and is fast asleep,/a butterfly. PoPl

Spring Sequence. Judith Minty. the burning left for another season. AMV-80

A Spring Serpent. Yvor Winters. Dips to the icy pool. ExPo

Spring Signs. Rachel Field. Now is the time when such as I/Must set down rhymes on sheets of paper! InMe

Spring Snow and Tui. Mary Ursula Bethell. a waking bugle it might be, a passing bell,/of life, death, life, life telling: it is all one. AnNZ

Spring Song. Anonymous.
I feel the summer in the spring. OBVE
She is looking so lovely today. PoLf

Spring Song. Bliss Carman. Make me anything but neuter/When the sap begins to stir! HBV 1-2

Spring Song. Hilda Conkling. Nobody must be sad or sorry/In the spring-time of flowers. PoSC

Spring Song. Aubrey Thomas De Vere. A random glance to see where next/Yon butterfly will go! IrPN

Spring Song. Donald Finkel. your foot is bruised against my head. NYBP

Spring Song. Rayner Heppenstall. If it were not so, I would have found another use for the/days of the year. NeBP

Spring Song. Hermann Hesse. Unto youth's land no more/Forever goes thy way. AWP

Spring Song. Rod McKuen. where were you/when I was growing up and needed somebody? CAD

Spring Song. Nahum. Hark! the redemption hour's/resounding stroke,/For him who bore with patient heart/the yoke! TrJP

Spring Song. Katharine O'Brien. the joy to be here/for one more spring. GoYe

Spring Song. George Brandon Saul. The rose forever doomed to globe but as it bleeds. GoYe

Spring Song. LeRoy Smith, Jr. I shall not walk the clover snows.) NePoAm

Spring Song. Theodore Spencer. I am here; we are dancing again. AnFE

Spring Song in the City. Robert Williams Buchanan. All is light and motion! HBV 1-2

Spring Song of a Super-Blake (parody). Louis Untermeyer. As long as two/And two are four. HBMV

Spring Song of Aspens. Lilian White Spencer. June's ecstacy are these/That men call aspen trees! PoOW

Spring Song of the Birds. King of Scotland James I Thank Lufe that list you to his merci call! OBEV

A Spring Song of Tzu-Yeh. Hsaio Yen. Love comes without bounds. LLLT

Spring, St. Stephen's Green. Leslie Daiken. Pleasantplash! OnYI

Spring Stops Me Suddenly. Valentin Iremonger. ...and freedom from my facile fears. OnYI

Spring Storm. Jim Wayne Miller. wisecracks and wonderment/spring up like dandelions. GOYP

Spring Street Bar. Mei-Mei Berssenbrugge. So she took some paper and began as she used to/when there had been a sky, to write about the sky. WPOW

Spring Street in '58. Derek Walcott. ...I/knew we'd all live as long as Hokusai. NYP

Spring Sunday on Quaker Street. Tom Bass. ...two country mechanics working/fast to beat a spring sunday. FAZ

Spring Thoughts. Huang-fu Jan. And his triumph will be carved on the rock of Yen-jan/Mountain! OFD

Spring Thoughts Sent to Tzu-an. Yu Hsuan-chi. In the pure light, my tears fall: a poem. BoWoP

The Spring Trip of the Schooner Ambition. Anonymous. And now the spring trip is ended/And everybody's feeling fine! ShS

The Spring Vacation. Derek Mahon. Exact more interest than my casual pity. FaBoIP

The Spring Waters. Ping Hsin (Hsieh Wang-ying).
Let mother be in a tiny boat,/And that boat float on a moonlit sea. WPOW
The north wind is tender after all. WPOW
That, braving the rain of bullets,/Comforts the fresh bones. PBWP

Spring Waters (excerpt). John Wolcot. Reflects the setting sun/And becomes the Sea of Gold. BoWoP

Spring Whistles. Lucy Larcom. Is sleeping a melody sweeter/Than ever on earth was made. OBCA

The Spring Will Come. Henry Dawson Lowry. You'll find once more the dreams you thought were dead. BoNaP

A Spring Wind. Bernard Spencer. Athens, and all the opening year on fire. GTBS-P

Spring Wind. Nancy Byrd Turner. It's Spring, Spring, Spring! SiSoSe

Spring Workman. Alan Creighton. And steel traffic flashing like swords/Along the highway. CaP

The Springboard. Louis MacNeice. And, like ten million others, dying for the people. ChMP; PoA

Springer Mountain. James Dickey. To hunt, under Springer Mountain,/Deer for the first and last time. CAPP

The Springfield Calibre Fifty. Joseph Mills Hanson. With the hard-fighting arm of the West! PoOW

Springfield Mountain. Anonymous.
Let this a warning be to all/to be prepared when God does call. AmFP
Too roo dee nay, Too roo dee noo, Too roo dee nay, Too roo dee noo. TrAS

Springfield Mountain (A vers.). Anonymous. the brightest Angels bowing round/Jehovah and his golden crown. ViBoFo

Springfield Mountain (B vers.). Anonymous. Out of the meadow he came to mow,/With nobody by to see him go.... ViBoFo

Springfield Mountain (C vers.). Anonymous. Now young and old, a warning take,/And shun the bite of a rattlesnake. ViBoFo

Springfield Mountain (D vers.). Anonymous. And mind when you're in love, don't pass/Too near to patches of high grass. ViBoFo

The Springfield of the Far Future. Vachel Lindsay. Bringing frankincense and praise/For her gift of the Infinite One. MoRP

The Springs. Wendell Berry. ...He bent and drank/in bondage to the ground. GP

Springtime. Alfred Kreymborg. She's nodding her head at me! MAPA

The Springtime. Denise Levertov. ...The rabbits/will bare their teeth at/the spring moon. CoAP; ConAP

Springtime in Cookham Dean. Cecil Roberts. He cannot know, he cannot tell/Where Spring performs her miracle. HBMV

The Springtime It Brings on the Shearing. E. J. Overbury. It is then you will see the flash shearers/Making johnny-cakes round in the bend. NOAV

The Springtime of the Earth. Isaiah Shembe. You people of Dingaan. WTO

Sprinkling. Dorothy Mason Pierce. And says, "Why, you need sprinkling,/You thirsty little rose!" SUS; TiPo

The Sprinters. Lee Murchison. And almost breaks the bands/Which lock us in. SD

Spruce. Phil George. And I wonder: Why? VoR

The Spruce and Limber Yellow-Hammer. Samuel Taylor Coleridge. With notes as of one who brass is filing FM; PBBP

The Spur. William Butler Yeats. What else have I to spur me into song? ELU

Squabbling Blues. Barefoot Bill. Said it's train time now/Hear that ring I do adore BluL

Squall. John Moore. A broken weathercock seeking/Its own north, its own lost/Bearings. NCSH

St. Valentine's Day. Wilfrid Scawen Blunt. My horse a thing of wings, myself a god. EnLoPo; NBM; OBVV; ViBoPo

St. Vincent's. William Stanley Merwin. who was St. Vincent NYP

The Stab. William Wallace Harney. That a dead man lay on the road. AA

Stabat Mater. Sam Hunt. To walk away and know there's no return. OCNZ

Stabat Mater. Jacopone da Todi.
And a purer love attaining,/May with Thee acceptance find. TreFS
Safe in Paradise with Thee. WGRP

Stabat Mater Dolorosa. Pope Innocent III. To the Paradisial place! CAW

Stabilities. Anne Stevenson. Child, love's flesh and bone. NCSH

The Stable. Jill Hoffman. the horses like hours standing hours in a row. PH

The Stable Cat. Leslie Norris. We look with joy/at Mary's boy,/Are safe in His love. PCh

Stable-Talk. Raymond Knister. We with the sun together/Tomorrow. CaP

The Stack. Stanley Snaith. Now that the marrying wrens are in/Setting up house? ChMP

Stack Arms! Joseph Blynth Alston. And it would be relief—to die! PAH

Stack o' Dollars. Sleepy John Estes. It weren't nothing that she knowed of/just something she had heard BluL

Stacking Up. Rita Rosenfeld. as you glow thanks. AMV-81

The Stadium. William Heyen. catching their difficult breath. LiSp

The Staff and Scrip. Dante Gabriel Rossetti. Here in His own abode,/Thy jealous God. OAEP

Staff-Nurse: New Style. William Ernest Henley. And gives at need (as one who understands)/Draft, counsel, diagnosis, exhortation. NBM

The Staff of Aesculapius. Marianne Moore. the symbol of medicine. ImOP

Stafford in Kansas (parody). James Baker Hall. And our side won, I think. BXAP

Stag-Hunt. Anonymous. We shall have game and sport ynow. OxBM

Stage Love. Algernon Charles Swinburne. When the play was played out so for one man's pleasure. NIP; PoEL 1-5

Stages. Roy Macnab. While a tubucular hunger/Slowly consumes him. ACV

Stages on a Journey Westward. James Wright. Plunged into the dark furrows/Of the sea again. AmPC; LCAP; NaP

Stagolee (A vers.). Anonymous. Took ole Stackolee to the cemetery/Never to bring him back./Oh poor, poor Stackolee! ViBoFo

Stagolee (B vers.). Anonymous. Carried po' man to cemetery but failed to bring him back,/Ev'ybody been dodgin' Stagolee. ViBoFo

Stags. William Montgomerie. Left only the cloven print of hooves/In mud beside a stream. PoSH

Stained Glass. Willis Barnstone. ...a stained glass of surprise. AMV-81

The Stained Glass Man. Cynthia Macdonald. ...with most cordial greetings to you and/Mrs. Ames,/Very sincerely yours,/MARY LEE WARE. FiCP

Stains. Theodosia Garrison. "Naked the soul goes up to God,/Brother, my brother." HBV 1-2; WGRP

The Staircase. Samuel (Paul Vesey) Allen. the twin goes exalted to his worms/hail cried "hail'. PoBA

The Staircase with a Hundred Steps. Benjamin Peret. Ah what a lovely voyage EAS

Stairs. Oliver Herford. So let his name go down to fame,/Whatever it may be. FiBHP; InMe

Stalagmites and Stalactites. Anonymous. And the tites come down. FaBoUs

Stalin. Robert Lowell. ...What raised him/was an unusual lust to break the icon,/joke cruelly, seriously, and be himself. HaCAP

The Stalin Epigram. Osip Mandelstam. He wishes he could hug them like big friends from home. FaBoPV

The Stallion. Boynton Merrill, Jr. Who would saddle me/Had better walk instead/In his quiet garden. PH

The Stallion. Alan Porter. But a bare hedge and bleak December. PH

Stallion. Walt Whitman. Even as I stand or sit passing faster than you. PH

The Stammerers. Margaret Kent. it is the tongue's easy wag that is deceptive. AMV-80

Stamp Blues. Tony Hollins. (Yeh/Play it a long time now boy) BluL

Stampede. Anonymous. A rod from the leader's nose. ABF

The Stampede. Earl Alonzo Brininstool. The stars peep forth through scudding clouds, and dawn/Finds wearied riders safe, the herd at rest. PoOW

The Stampede. Arthur I. Caldwell. When, helpless, he lay by his fallen bay, but cheered his/comrades on? BPAW

The Stampede. Wallace D. Coburn. Else I'd been riding in the clouds with angels long ago. PoOW

The Stampede. Freeman E. Miller. That he's the kind of a man it takes for the work here in the West. BPAW

Stan' Still Jordan. Anonymous Stan' still Jordan,/Lord, I can't stan' still. BoAN 1-2

Stance. Theodore Enslin. and this is where we came in. CoPo

Stand By. Anonymous. And it is all because/You're out of town. STF

Stand by the Flag. John Nichols Wilder. A guard celestial from Omnipotence. GN; PGD

Stand Fast, O My Heart. Anonymous Stand fast as often as thou recallest him,/O my heart, and do not flee. LiTW

Stand, Stately Tavie. Anonymous. Or by this hand I'll never draw thee, but against a post. ErPo; PV

The Stand-To. C. Day-Lewis. But pinned to the heart of darkness a tattered fire-flag flies. OBWP

Stand-To: Good Friday Morning. Siegfried Sassoon. And get my bloody old sins washed white! FaBoTw

Stand Up!–. D. H. Lawrence. bust in, and hold the ground! OxBTC

Stand Up for Jesus. George Duffield, Jr.. He with the King of glory/Shall reign eternally. AH; TreFS

Standard Forgings Plant. William Stephens. shake walls, floors, windows, brain and bone. NAMP

Standardization. A.D. Hope. Anonymous faces plastered with her smile. BoAV

Standin' on the Walls of Zion (with music). Anonymous. See my ship come sailin' home. AS

The Standing. Mebdh McGuckian. ...her dress unwrinkled/Like the Rhone passing through Geneva. FaBoIP

Standing on the Corner. Philip Levine. I can't hardly wait, he said. NNaP

Standing on the Streetcorner. Edwin Denby. Is more private than thought is, or upstairs sleeping. ANYP

Standing on Tiptoe. George Frederick Cameron. The clay grows less, and, leaving it, the mind/Dwells with the stars. CaP; OBCV; PeCV

Stanes. Duncan Glen. And the empty waitin yirth/–it talks loud enough? PoSH

Stanky. Bill Berkson. The space you see is all. ANYP

Stanley Matthews. Alan Ross. He rehearses steps, soloist in compulsions of a dream. LiSp; OxBTC

Stanley Meets Mutesa. James D. Rubadiri. The gate of polished reed closes behind them/And the West is let in. PBA

A Stanza Completed. William Lort Mansel. Cried "Damn it, how hot we shall be!" FaBoEE

Stanza from an Early Poem. Christopher Pearse Cranch What unto themselves was taught. AA; AmLP

A Stanza on Freedom. James Russell Lowell In the right with two or three. AA

A Stanza Put on Westminster Hall Gate. Anonymous. And perish by those laws ye have passed! APAS

Stanzas. John Gardiner Calkins Brainard. Feel–that it all is cold and gone. AnAmPo

Stanzas. Emily Bronte.
The earth that wakes one human heart to feeling/Can centre both the worlds of Heaven and Hell. ChRP; HBV 1-2; LiTB; LoBV; OAEL 1-2; OAEP; OBNC; PBWP
It is but that my soul is sighing,/To go and rest with thee. LoBV
Where the wild wind blows on the mountain side. OBVV

Stanzas. John Clare. Like voices on the gale. EnLoPo

Stanzas. Pierre Corneille. It should be courted, ne'ertheless/In one who must, like me, be feared. LiTW

Stanzas. Paul Goodman. and where the shadows fell, they lay. PoA

Stanzas. William Ernest Henley. Beyond the dark, into the dream/Over the hills and far away. HBV 1-2

Stanzas. Solomon Ibn Gabirol. The dew shines bright; I bide forlorn,/and shudder with the chill of morn. TrJP

Stanzas. Edgar Allan Poe. Wearing its own deep feeling as a crown. MAmP

Stanzas. Henry David Thoreau. Our rays united make one sun,/With fairest summer weather. AmLP

Stanzas. Richard Henry Wilde. But none, alas! shall mourn for me! AA

Stanzas–April, 1814. Percy Bysshe Shelley. From the music of two voices, and the light of one sweet smile. ChRP; EnRP; FiP; MBW 1-2; MyFE; OAEP; OBNC

Stanzas Cancelled from the Elegy. Thomas Gray. And little footsteps lightly print the ground. ViBoPo

Stanzas Concerning Love. Stefan George. When the cloudless morning rises cold. AWP

Stanzas (excerpt). Charles Newton. And I were pleased amid these bowers to stay/More than an evening's hour, or a long summer's day. NOEC

Stanzas for Music. George Gordon, Lord Byron.
Nor dare we think on what we are. ForPo
So, midst the withered waste of life, those/tears would flow to me. CoBE; EnLi 1-2; EnLit; HAP; HBV 1-2; OAEP

Starlings. Laura Jensen. ..:suet and seed are cool and good. AMV-81

Starlings. Norman MacCaig. bustling monks/tilling their green precincts. BoAnP

Starlings. Ted Olson. he squalls patrician goddamits from the magnolia. PV

The Starre. George Herbert. And garland-streams. AnAnS 1; AtBAP

The Starred Mother. Robert Whitaker. Bribing the Marys of the world to sell,/For tinseled star, their flesh and blood to hell! PGD

The Starry Frost Descends. Suibne Geilt. I would rather the bellowings/of a stag with forty prongs! NOBI

The Starry Host. John Lancaster Spalding. So that for them to be is to advance? AA; HBV 1-2

The Starry Night. Anne Sexton. no belly,/no cry. NMP; NoAm

The Starry Night. George Starbuck. of blackness, of blackness, of emptiness. NYBP

Starry Sky. Anonymous. My door shall close on none tonight. AnIL

Starry Sky. Charles Simic. All the convicts have their roaches lit. PoL

Stars. Rhoda Warner Bacmeister. Far, far away! BrR

Stars. George Mackay Brown. When Venus shook her hair/Owre the Soond. OxBS

The Stars. Mary Mapes Dodge. The eternal jewels of the short-lived night. AA

Stars. Robert Frost. Minerva's snow-white marble eyes/Without the gift of sight. MAmP

Stars. Robert Earl Hayden. following the stars/her mind a star CNA; LCAP

Stars. Howard Moss. Punchdrunk, against the carbon, seeing stars. HoAn

Stars. Alden Nowlan. alone through the woods and down to the frozen river. PoL

The Stars. Ping Hsin (Hsieh Wang-ying).
But the tiny grains of sand down beneath. WPOW
Only you so impartially adorn the entire world. WPOW

Stars. Kenneth Slessor. Infinity's trapdoor, eternal and merciless. BoAV

Stars. Sara Teasdale. Witness/Of so much majesty. HBMV; MoRP; TiPo

Stars and Planets. Norman MacCaig. Attended only by the loveless moon. OBSP

The Stars Are Lit. Hayim Nahman Bialik. It watches for the dawn. TrJP

The stars are old, that stood for me. Emily Dickinson. 'Twas Victory was slain. PeHV

The Stars Are Thundering. Anonymous. And the eagle dances across the sky. WTO

The Stars Are with the Voyager. Thomas Hood. And day is brighter day. EnRP

Stars Climb Girders of Light. Bert Meyers. Man made like his roads,/with somewhere to go. MAT

Stars Fade. Peretz Hirshbein. But human lives vanish/In dark night. TrJP

The Stars Go By. Lilian Bowes Lyon. Salt on the tongue I feel the smart/Of the blood of the fox that gnaws my heart. ChMP

The Stars Go over the Lonely Ocean. Robinson Jeffers. Said the gamey black-maned wild boar/Tusking the turf on Mal Paso Mountain. LiTA; LiTM; NePA; WaP

The Stars Have Given Me a Hard Fate. Gaspara Stampa. crushing the humble underfoot, indulging the cruel. PBWP

The Stars Have Not Dealt Me the Worst They Could Do. Alfred Edward Housman. With flint in the bosom and guts in the head. EBEV; ELU; EnLi 1-2; GTBS-P; OxBoLi; SeCeV

Stars, I Have Seen Them Fall. Alfred Edward Housman. And still the sea is salt. NoP; OBSP

Stars in Apple Cores. Luci Shaw. birth announcement/of Your/Day Star TrCP

The Stars on Shabbat. Avraham Schlonsky. The stars at their zenith, more tranquil than you– VWA

Stars over the Dordogne. Sylvia Plath. And drink the small night chill like news of home. PoA

Stars Shine So Faithfully. Jane Flanders. Over the static, light years away. AMV-80

The Stars Stand Up in the Air. Anonymous. 'Tis my grief that her ever I knew! AnIV; BIrV

Stars Wheel in Purple. Hilda ("H. D.") Doolittle. to freighted ships, baffled in wind and blast. NoAm; NOBA; TAP

Stars Which See, Stars Which Do Not See. Marvin Bell. to where a slight breeze broke the mirror/and then its promise, but never the water. LCAP

A Starscape. John Bellenden. And Lucifer left twinkling him alane. ACP

Starship. David McAleavey. ...yet still surrounded & pierced through with night. AMV-81

The Start. Anonymous. And three to go. SD

Start Where You Stand. Berton Braley. Start where you stand. PoToHe

Starting at Dawn. Sun Yun-feng. Only the sound of a stream/Through the misty trees. PBWP

Starting Early from the Ch'U-Ch'eng Inn. Po Chu-i. For ten miles, till day at last breaks. OBVE

Starting from Paumanok. Walt Whitman. O to haste firm holding–to haste, haste on with me. AtBAP; PAI; ViBoPo

Starting from San Francisco. Lawrence Ferlinghetti. Myself I saw in the window reflected. BiP; CAPP

Starting over. Shirley Kaufman. this is where you/begin VWA

Starting Rhymes for Hide-and-Seek: "Green lady, green lady." Anonymous. Thy tea is a'ready an' waiting for thee–/Coo-ee! GBP

Startled. Saigyo Hoshi. All the other birds are crying. AWP

Starvation Camp near Jaslo. Wislawa Szymborska. Write: about the stillness here./Yes. WPOW

Starvation Peak Evening. David O'Neil. Unpitied in its greatness. AnAmPo

Starving to Death on a Government Claim. Anonymous. And live on corn dodgers the rest of my life. AmFP; BPAW; FSW; OBAL

The State. Randall Jarrell. Now there's nothing. I'm dead, and I want to die. LiTM; MiAP

State Fair Pigs. Roger Pfingston. not even the knife-hot sun/that hangs overhead/like a spotlight on the fair. TAT

The State of Arkansas. Anonymous. It will be through a telescope from here to Arkansas. BFSS; CoSo; FSW; TrAS

The State of Innocence. John Dryden. And steal myself from life, and melt away. NOCV

A State of Nature. John Hollander. whose name/passes/for/a city. NIP

State Prison 4:00 p.m. Thomas G. Nickens. Fishing words dangle/untouched/as the hack fumbles through/our pocket-contents and his job. LFAC

State Prison 5:00 p.m. Thomas G. Nickens. forty years younger/and/twenty years freer. LFAC

State School. Paul D. Shiplett. and the cops keep the stash/for themselves. LFAC

The Stately Homes of England (parody). Noel Coward. We'll stand by the Stately Homes of England. FaBoPa

The Stately Structure of This Earth. Martha Brewster. Pronounce the sweet well done? AH

Stately Verse. Anonymous. She rode for exercise, and thus/Rhode Island every day. TiPo

Statement on Our Higher Education. W. M. Ransom. And to one old crippled bear/that neither of us will ever see. CDW

States. Tom Paulin. Polities that clock us safely/Over this dark; freighting us. FaBoIP

Statesboro Blues. Blind Willie McTell. I looked over in the corner: grandma and grandpa had 'em too. BluL

The Statesman. Hilaire Belloc. When he will be remembered for/A week, a month, or even more. NOBE

The Statesman in Retirement. William Cowper. Kneels, kisses hands, and shines again in place. OBEC

The Statesman's Holiday. William Butler Yeats. Tall dames go walking in grass/green Avalon. AtBAP; CMoP; OxBTC

Static. Rolfe Humphries. Who with intemperate crepitation sue/To keep sweet crooning sounds from me to you. UnS

Static. Barton Sutter. The blankets crackle with bright blue sparks. AMV-81

Static Autumn. Yvor Winters. With sunken head/In dropping leaves. PoA

Station Island (excerpt). Seamus Heaney. and he trembled like a heatwave and faded. FaBoIP; FaBoPV

The Stationed Scout. Lyman H. Sproull. Back down along the notched clift/To bid the world and him good-night. PoOW

The Stationmaster's Lament. Jerome Rothenberg. And the trains have been constant in death. CoPo

Stations. Ted Hughes. The head with its vocabulary useless/Among the flogged plantains. NoAm

The Stations of the Cross. Padraic Colum. Perfect, without wound nor mark! GoBC

Statistics. Stephen Spender. Despise all moderns, thinking more/Of Shakespeare and Praxiteles. MoBrPo

The Statue. Kenneth Allott. daylight and moonlight, all the fun in the world. EAS

The Statue. Hilaire Belloc. Which was your image), ride more slowly on. MoVE; PoL

The Statue. John Berryman. And salvaged less than the intolerable statue. NYP

The Statue. Robert Creeley. ...but by then/it will have returned to its place. LCAP

The Statue. Robert Finch. And the pigeon sitting awry on its carved curls. OBCV; PeCV

The Statue. John Fuller. Instead I see, and think I understand/The broken smile, whips in the missing hand. NePoEA-2

The Statue. Roy Fuller. And is what history is not. O love, O human fears! NOBE

The Stick. Bruce Bennett. He couldn't find the stick. LTB

The Stick. May O'Rourke. I hold thee and my thoughts arise/To Christ, His Cross! HBMV

The Stick in the Forest. William Stafford. "Be, be," Buddha said. CAPP

Stick to It. Edgar A. Guest. Victory's nearer, perhaps, than/you think it is! FaFP

Stigmata. Patrick Lane. I open my hand. The life leaps out. NOBC

Stigmata. Charles Warren Stoddard. Have mercy upon us, O Lord! TrPWD

Stiles. John Pudney. Or news of me cutting my throat/Would move you enough. NYBP

Still. Lucille Clifton. and our points/sharpening good as anybodys'. InPS; PAI

Still. Aila Meriluoto. there is life, still/unbelief is left. PBWP

Still. Lisa Zeidner. This snow, unsaying itself on the pavement. SM

Still and All. Burns Singer. Bell–that swings slowly and slowly over. NePoEA-2; OxBS

Still Barred Thy Doors. Aru Dutt. But where art thou? ACV

Still Birth. Catherine Rutan. flour the board for kneading. AMV-81

Still Century. Tom Paulin. Their dream of happiness is his smile/And his skilful way with the hardest rod. FaBoIP

Still, Citizen Sparrow. Richard Wilbur. all men are Noah's sons. AmPP; AP; CMoP; HoPM; LiTM; MiAP; MoAB; MoPo; NePA; NoAm

Still Do I Keep My Look, My Identity... Gwendolyn Brooks. ...What it showed in school. PoA

Still Falls the Rain. Edith Sitwell. "Still do I love, still shed my innocent light, my Blood, for thee." BoWoP; ChMP; CoBMV; DTC; EBCP; LiTM; MoAB; MoBrPo; MoPo; MoRP; MP; NoAm; NOBE; OBWP; SBVL; SeCePo; TEP; TrGrPo; TwCP; WaaP

Still Growing. Anonymous. So fare you well my own true love/For ever. FaBoBa

Still Gyte, Man? George Campbell Hay. Then, wheesht man. Sae it is wi me.' BSV

Still He Sings. Allan Taylor. Just for you the colours filter through,/Just for you. OBET

Still-Heart. Frank Pearce Sturm. Beautiful Still-heart rests/With the queens of old. OBMV

Still Here. Langston Hughes. But I don't care!/I'm still here! BPo

Still I Rise. Maya Angelou. I rise/I rise/I rise BlSi

Still Life. Regina M. Austin. a photograph of the real thing. AMV-80

Still Life. Betsy Bering. I will love you forever. PoDr

Still-Life. Elizabeth Daryush. that even the unopened future lies/like a love-letter, full of sweet surprise. FaBoWP; QFR

Still Life. Walter De la Mare. And engrossed, round-spectacled Chardin's/Passion for life. EyDe

Still-Life. Ted Hughes. The maker of the sea. NYBP

A Still Life. Jascha Kessler. we turn to our beginnings. HoAn

Still Life. Randolph Outlaw. In the background shades/of Eliot and Hughes. LFAC

Still-Life. Ronald Perry. Next winter, the oranges/Will bloom on another hill. NePoEA-2

Still Life. Kathleen Raine. Life-shaped and perfected,/So to remain. NeBP

Still Life. Vivian Smith. with something finished, something unfulfilled. AMV-80; AMV-81

Still Life. Reed Whittemore. A cough, a creaking stair. CoAP; ConAP

Still Life: Lady with Birds. Quandra Prettyman. Him, she brings in. CAD; PoBA

Still Lives. Emilie Buchwald. this horsefly hovering above the pear. PoDr

Still, O LORD, for Thee I Tarry. Charles Wesley. If Thou in my life hast pleasure,/Speak, and now my soul shall live. OxBoCh

Still Poem 9. Philip Lamantia. There is this look of love Throne Silent look of love NeAP

Still Pond, No More Moving. Howard Moss. The drunken sea bards come/to lounge on all its Capes. NYBP

The Still Pool. Kathleen Raine. True, though not here as they to themselves elsewhere are. MoAB

The Still Small Voice. Abraham Moses Klein. Jerusalem, next year! Next year, Jerusalem! OBCV; PeCV

Still, Still with Thee. Harriet Beecher Stowe. Shall rise the glorious thought–I am with Thee. AH; BLRP

Still the Mind Smiles. Robinson Jeffers. Antistrophe of desolation to the strophe multitude. CMoP

Still This, Still That I Would! William Lithgow. Thus leaving him, I with the consul bode,/Or went thence abroad. OBTV

Still Thou Art Question. Anonymous. O World–dost thou not know Me even yet? PGD

Still Though the One I Sing. Walt Whitman. I leave in him revolt, (latent right of insurrection! O quenchless, indispensable fire!). AA

Still Thy Sorrow, Magdalena! E. A. Washburn. Welcome love, and welcome gladness!/Hallelujah! BePJ

The Still Voice of Harlem. Conrad Kent Rivers. there shall be no more of you... CNA; IDB; NNP; PoBA

Still Wrestling. Phil Boiarski. Still wrestling with the father. AMV-81

Stillness. James Elroy Flecker. And only know I should drown if you laid not your hand on me. BrPo; CH; GoJo; MoBrPo; SyP

The Stillness of the Poem. Ron Loewinsohn. ...in the form of a sailor/with a shopping bag/whom nobody notices. NeAP; PoM

The stimulus beyond the grave. Emily Dickinson. Supports me like imperial drams/Afforded day by day. OBSP

The Sting of Death. Frederick George Scott. To sin as before/And more and more,/For evermore. OBCV; PeCV

Stinging Nettle. Gwen Head. Forgetful, you too may grasp it time and again/in an open field, among flowers. GP

Stings. Sylvia Plath. The mausoleum, the wax house. NaP

Stir Me. Anonymous. The night is past, our King is on His/way. STF

Stir the Wallaby Stew. Anonymous. So left him here to shepherd us and battled back to jail. FaBoBa

Stirling's Hotel. Anonymous. It revives all the boarders at Stirling's Hotel. AmFP

The Stirrup Cup. Douglas Ainslie. Here's to Prince Charlie and/Lochiel's granddaughter! GoTS

The Stirrup Cup. John Milton Hay. And at my door the Pale Horse stands,/To bear me forth to unknown lands. AA; HBV 1-2

The Stirrup Cup. Aline Kilmer. Only a cup of tears waits at the end. CAW

The Stirrup-Cup. Sidney Lanier. I'll drink it down right smilingly. AA; WHA

Stock Exchange Wisdom. Anonymous. Sell in May/And go away. FaBoUs

The Stockdove. Ruth Pitter. She brings the silver olive-leaf. HaMV; SeCePo

The Stockdoves. Andrew Young. To drop in trees, lover by lover. BoAnP

Stocking and Shirt. James Reeves. And only the handkerchiefs/Wave good-bye. OnUR

Stocking Fairy. Winifred Welles. I'll do what I said, now, and close you in neatly. SoPo; TiPo

Stocking Feet Blues. Blind Lemon Jefferson. Won't some good man/tell me some woman's name BluL

Stocking Song on Christmas Eve. Mary Mapes Dodge. Funny old Saint Nicholas. ChBR; OHIP

Stockton Lake; Stockton, Missouri. Mark Sanders. while all around me the walleyes/are pop-eyed at my feet. WOLT

The Stockyard. Sir John Collings Squire. Till it closed and again I resumed my life. OxBTC

Stoic. Lawrence Durrell. ...you see it so well/On the faces of the self-reliant dead. NYBP

The Stoic: for Laura von Courten. Edgar Bowers. Becomes at last no meaning and no place. CoAP; NePoEA; QFR

Stoklewath; or, The Cymbrian Village. Susanna Blamire. He feared but two things–to turn thief, and lie.' NOEC

The Stolen Child. William Butler Yeats. From a world more full of weeping than he can understand. CMoP; EnLi 1-2; NoP; OnYI; OxBI; WSC

The Stolen Fifer. Padraic Fiacc. Of the earth, which I do not believe/In, pulls me down, pulls me down. NeIP

A Stolen Kiss. George Wither. And twenty hundred thousand more for loan. HBV 1-2; LiTL

Stolen Pleasure. William, of Hawthornden Drummond. Prov'd here on earth the joys of paradise. EnLoPo

Stomach. Kathleen Norris. The ultimate/Stomach. OBAL

Stond Who So List upon the Slipper Toppe. Sir Thomas Wyatt. ...and of him self alas,/Doth dye unknowen, dazed with dreadfull face. AAS; PoEL 1-5

The Stone. Paul Blackburn.
He had been shaped like a drunken pyramid, ir-/regularly triangular. NYP
I liked him. NYBP

Stone. Juliet Chayat. who have broken down through/the surface. AMV-80

A Stone. Richard Eberhart. The eyes of lovers everywhere. NePoAm-2

The Stone. W. W. Gibson. Next night I labored late, alone,/To cut her name upon the stone. MoBrPo

Stone. E. L. Mayo. And all the stars fall down. FAZ

Stone. Charles Simic. The strange writings, the star-charts/On the inner walls. NU

The Stone. Thomas Vaughan. Shall move without all Night/Of Excentricity. OBS

Stone Age. Pat Nolan. for the big dog/at the end of the drive. APU

The Stone and the Blade of Grass in the Warsaw Ghetto. David Scheinert. ...a/blade of grass was then born, an immortal springtime! VWA

Stone and the Obliging Pond. Duane Ackerson. Bull's Eye: the water cries out. PoL

Storm on Fifth Avenue. Siegfried Sassoon. O Babylon! O Carthage! O New York! MoVE

Storm on the Island. Seamus Heaney. Strange, it is a huge nothing that we fear. NCSH

Storm Over Rockefeller Center. Raymond Holden. And finds it empty, the purse full. AnAmPo

Storm Song. Bayard Taylor. So, whether to harbor or ocean-grave,/Be it still with a cheery heart! EtS; HBV 1-2

Storm Tide on Mejit. *Anonymous.* Slaps, slaps, slaps/On the beach, and roars. RFM

Storm Warning. Alice Bardsley. Why? I saw deep in our woodland lot/A seagull sitting on a little hill. AMV-80

Storm Warnings. Adrienne Rich. These are the things that we have learned to do/Who live in troubled regions. GOYP; NIP

The Storm-Wind. William Barnes. So soft that a mother that's nigh/Her still cradle, may hear her babe sigh. NOBE

Storm Windows. Howard Nemerov. Runs on the standing windows and away. ConAP

Stormalong. *Anonymous.* To my aye, aye, aye, aye, Mister Stormalong! AmSS; ShS

Stormcock in Elder. Ruth Pitter. On elder-spray by broken tile. BoC

The Storming of Stony Point. Arthur Guiterman. Over the parapet, "spear in hand!" MC; PAH

Stormpetrel. Richard Murphy. It ends with a gasp. IPY

The Storms Are on the Ocean. *Anonymous.* This world may lose its motion, love/If I prove false to thee. FSW

A Stormy Day. *Anonymous.* This is a stormy day; yesterday was the calm day. WTO

Stormy Day. W. R. Rodgers. As behind him, perfectly timed, follows/The dumb shadow that mimes him all the way. LiTB

The Stormy Hebrides. William Collins. Nor ever vernal bee was heard to murmur there! NOBE

Stormy Night. W. R. Rodgers. Ah heart, heart, look! I throw myself at your feet. OxBI

Stormy Night in Autumn. Chu Shu-chen. Each beaten leaf contains/Ten thousand pains. BoWoP

Stormy Nights. Robert Louis Stevenson. And show you St. Francis of Assisi. BrPo

The Stormy Petrel. Bryan Waller Procter. Once more o'er the waves on thy stormy wing! EtS; HBV 1-2

The Stormy Scenes of Winter. *Anonymous.* And I'll drink a health to Flora, although she answers no. AmFP

Stormy Weather, Boys. *Anonymous.* So after all our fears and alarms/We all ended up in the Druid's Arms. OBSS

Story. Dorothy Parker. I hope/Her mother washed her mouth with soap. InMe; MaC

Story. Dennis Saleh. and it will beat for an answer. NeAC

The Story. Charles Simic. And caught/Its shadow/On the flypaper of my tongue. NNaP

A Story. William Stafford. I make my hole the deepest one/this high on the mountainside. NNaP; RFM

A Story about Chicken Soup. Louis Simpson. But to live in the tragic world forever. LCAP; NMP; NNaP; NoAm; TAP

A Story About the Body. Robert Hass. ...she must/have swept them from the corners of her studio–was full/of dead bees. GeTw; NPGG

A Story for a Child. Bayard Taylor. Father's house is a better place/When the stormy rain is pouring. HBV 1-2; HBVY

Story from Another World. Paul Petrie. No-one to touch. AMV-81

Story from Bear Country. Leslie Marmon Silko. not like other children. STE

Story from Russian Author. Peter Redgrove. "Unmelting wedged/Snow in her mouth." NePoEA-2

A Story from the Bushmen. Joseph Ceravolo. because they were even faster/than any cloud. ANYP

A Story in the Snow. Pearl Riggs Crouch. Shone Bunny's twinkling eye! SoPo; TiPo

Story of a Hotel Room. Rosemary Tonks. Follows the naked work, profoundly moved by it. OxBTC

The Story of a Stowaway. Clement Scott. "Manhood's stronger far than storms, and Love is mightier than Death!" PaPo

The Story of a Well-Made Shield. N. Scott Momaday. ...It is like the wind–nor is it quite like the/wind–but more powerful. CDW; GrPl

The Story of Abraham and Hagar. Edna Aphek. with a parched/pitcher and piece/of bread. VWA

The Story of Augustus Who Would Not Have Any Soup. Heinrich Hoffmann. And on the fifth day, he was–dead! BBGG; FaBoUs; GoJo; HBV 1-2; HBVY; MoShBr; NLV; OxBChV; ShM; SpRo; TiPo

The Story of Bamsi Beyrek of the Grey Horse. Dede Korkut. and forgive your sins for the honour of Muhammad the Chosen of/beautiful name, O my Khan! WTO

The Story of Cruel Psamtek. *Anonymous.* And man himself rewards our foes! NA

The Story of Fidgety Philip. Heinrich Hoffmann. Look quite cross, and wonder how/They shall have their dinner now. OxBChV

The Story of Flying Robert. Heinrich Hoffmann. Rob was never seen again! SpRo

The Story of Good. Phyllis Janik. come and play oh yes IHMS

A Story of How a Wall Stands. Simon J. Ortiz. the wall that stands a long, long time. MAYP

Story of Isaac. Leonard Cohen. The peacock spreads his fan. VWA

The Story of Johnny Head-in-Air. Heinrich Hoffmann. "Silly little Johnny look,/You have lost your writing-book!" BBGG; OxBChV; TiPo

The Story of Lava. David Allan Evans. ...a thin bar of Lava tumbling/over and over and over slowly in his cloudy hands. Psk

The Story of Life. John Godfrey Saxe. Then drop into his grave; and then;– PoToHe

The Story of Little Suck-a-Thumb. Heinrich Hoffmann. "Ah!" said mamma, "I knew he'd come/To naughty little Suck-a-Thumb." EvOK; HBV 1-2; HBVY

The Story of My Life. Carroll Arnett. will always be/a tenant and hold/as much as I can. VoR

The Story of Phoebus and Daphne Applied... Edmund Waller. He catched at love, and filled his arm with bays. InvP; OBS

The Story of Prince Agib. Sir William Schwenck Gilbert. When a yesterday has faded from its page! FaBoCo; InMe; LBN; NA

The Story of Pyramid Thothmes. *Anonymous.* A pyramid is strange to see,/Though only at its base you be. NA

The Story of Rimini. [James Henry] Leigh Hunt.
A moment, as for breath, and then with free/And usual tone said,–"O yes, certainly." EvOK
That day they read no more. EnRP

The Story of Samuel Jackson. Charles Godfrey Leland. One night he got upon the moon–and sailed away to Heaven! StPo

The Story of Sigurd the Volsung (excerpt). William Morris. And wends his ways through the twilight the Foe of the/Gods to meet. PoEL 1-5

The Story of the Baby Squirrel. Dorothy Aldis. For once a little looking down face/Seemed to be saying: "How do you do?" TiPo

Story of the Flowery Kingdom. James Branch Cabell. For these things occur...in the Flowery Land. HBMV; OnMSP

The Story of the Pot and the Kettle. Charles Montagu. For know that you are clay, and they are brass. APAS

The Story of the Rose. Alice". Say you'll be mine forever:/I love you. FSN

The Story of the Shepherd. *Anonymous.* O, who hath heard what I have heard, or seen what I/have seen? OHIP

The Story of the Wild Huntsman. Heinrich Hoffmann. "Oh dear," he cried, "what burns me so?"/And held up the spoon with his little toe. NA

The Story of Two Gentlemen and the Gardener. Christopher Logue. On your hands are four green thumbs. CABL

The Story of Ug. Edwin Meade Robinson. He became/A millionaire. HBMV; YaD

The Story of Uriah. Rudyard Kipling. I shouldn't like to be the man/Who sent Jack Barrett there. BrPo; NOBV; SCV

The Story of Vinland. Sidney Lanier. Across the sunset to their seaward isle/On solemn wings that wave but seldomwhile. PAH

The Story of Zeros. Victor Hernandez Cruz. & de museum started raining dollars & all de/zeros tried to get one. PoBA

The Story-Teller. Mark Van Doren. And nothing stood firm/Until day again. CTBA; LOW

Story Tellers Summer, 1980. Nia Francisco. being told on KWYK radio/in Navajo STE

A Story That Could Be True. William Stafford. "Maybe I'm a king." GOYP; NTCP

The Story We Know. Martha Collins. ...Hello,/Good-bye is the only story. We know, we know. SM

Stove. Ken Belford. I've been wondering about. NeAC

Stove. Philip Booth. ...the oven door says: it says/Queen Clarion/Wood & Bishop/Bangor, Maine 1911 FYAP

Stowaway. Bill Adams. They'll be fine ships on that eternal sea. EtS

Stradivarius: Working with God. George Eliot. Antonio Stradivari's violins/Without Antonio. TRV

Stragglers. Pietro Aretino. For a soldier always makes a perfect lover! ErPo

"The Straight Road. Ellen Hooper. The straightest path perhaps which may be sought,/Lies through the great highway men call "I ought. HBV 1-2

Strains of Sight. Robert Duncan. where the heart reflects. CMoP; NMP

The Strand. Louis MacNeice. Remains of face or feet when visitors have gone home. AnIV

The Strand at Lough Beg. Seamus Heaney. Green scapulars to wear over your shroud. NoP; OBWP

Strand on the Green. *Anonymous.* And never a house between. GBP

Strand-Thistle. Gustav Falke. And on the salt wind died away. AWP

Stranded in My Ontario. Ronald G. Everson. Madame Maynard has been ground down to a grey pebble/of strong Breton dignity NOBC

The Stranded Whales. Geoffrey Dutton. For as many days as they had taken to die. CBAP

Strange. Stanley Burnshaw. If we must live only in meeting and/parting/ The rest of our days. TrJP

Strange. Kirby Doyle. and then one day,/never look again. NeAP

Strange, All-Absorbing Love. Digby Mackworth Dolben. Some scarlet berries and a Christmas rose. GoBC; TrPWD

Strange Fits of Passion Have I Known. William Wordsworth. "O mercy!' to myself I cried,/"If Lucy should be dead!' CBEP; CoBE; EBEV; EnL; ERoP 1-2; FiP; GBL; LiTB; LiTL; MBW 1-2; OAEL 1-2; OAEP; OBNC; OBRV; PPP; TEP; ViBoPo

Strange Fruit. Randolph Stow. ...That cries: You shall try strange fruit. PoAu 1-2

The Strange Guest. Itzik Manger. The great and holy Baal Shem Tov awaits. VWA

Strange Hells. Ivor Gurney. The heart burns–but has to keep out of face how heart burns. OxBTC

Strange, Is It Not. Edward D. Kennedy. Or to be old, perhaps, is not to care. HBMV

Strange Kind (II). J. D. Reed. ...this Jason/of the vacuum MOON

Strange Lands. Laurence Alma-Tadema. "Mother's kiss–Mother's kiss." HBVY

Strange Legacies. Sterling A. Brown. Guess we'll give it one mo' try. CNA; PoBA; TTY

Strange Meeting. Wilfred Owen. Let us sleep now.... AnFE; AtBAP; BrPo; CMoP; CoBMV; DTC; EnLi 1-2; ExPo; FaBoMo; FaBoRV; GoTF; GTBS-P; HeIP; HoPM; LiTB; LoBV; MMM; MoAB; MoBrPo; MoPo; MoVE; NAMP; NoAm; NOBE; NoP; OAEL 1-2; OAEP; OBWP; SCV; SeCeV; TreFT; TrGrPo; WaaP; WaP

Strange Meetings. Harold Monro.
Difference between the living and the dead. PoA
I can't learn how to know men, or conceal/How strange they are to me. MoBrPo
They don't recognize each other. MoBrPo

Strange Monsters. Rowland Watkyns. Than rebels are without their head the King. FaBoEE

A Strange Passion of a Lover. George Gascoigne. I die to think to part from thee. EnLit

The Strange People. Louise Erdrich. Lope toward your own dark shelter. TWSS

Strange Tree. Elizabeth Madox Roberts. The tree was bending to the side/ And leaning out to look at me. BoNaP; GrPl; WSC

The Strange Visitor. Anonymous. "What do you come for?'/"For YOU!' FaBoCh; GBP

Strangeness of Heart. Siegfried Sassoon. ...I shall have/heard/Death; I shall know that I have lived/too long. MoRP; TrJP

The Stranger. Charles Baudelaire. "I love the clouds, the clouds that pass, eternally, the/marvellous clouds." SyP

The Stranger. John Clare. Yet without sin he suffered more/Than ever sinners did before. OxBoCh

The Stranger. Walter De la Mare. Its secret with the dead. BrPo; MoVE; OxBTC

The Stranger. William Everson. And shamble down time to doomsday? FF

The Stranger. Jean Garrigue. Is a stately thing. LiTA; LiTM; MP; NOBA; TwCP

The Stranger. Juan Gelman. he turned over and closed his eyes like a little bird. VWA

The Stranger. Daniel Henderson. Familiar, but for aye–the Stranger! HBMV

A Stranger. Lionel Pigot Johnson. With us, her passing image: but herself/ Far over the dark hills and the long sea. NOBV; VLP

Stranger. Thomas Merton. Our cleanest Light is One! EaLo

The Stranger. Adrienne Rich. ...how loose/ourselves from the disinterested/blaze of his wide pure eye? CoPo; NNaP

Stranger. Elizabeth Madox Roberts. Tum a-tum tum and danky dee-o! MoAmPo

Stranger Call This Not. Anonymous. To me it is a pleasant spot--/My husband's tomb. ShM

The Stranger in the Pumpkin. John Ciardi. Go and get your candle lit! NTCP

A Stranger in This Land. Cliff Ashby. For I am lonely/And a stranger in this land. NOCV

The Stranger Not Ourselves. William Stafford. stop there, wringing our hands this time. NNaP

The Stranger's Grave. Emily Lawless. Little faded grass-tufts, root and stalk. OnYI

The Stranger's Song. Thomas Hardy. And on his soul may God ha' mercy! BrPo

Stranger to Europe. Guy Butler. Brown hawthorne berry, red dog rose. ACV

Stranger, Why Do You Wonder So? K. B. Jones-Quartey. And would that make you wonder less,/O Stranger to our land? PBA

The Strangers. Audrey Alexandra Brown. "There goes the milk,"/As the hoofs went by! WHW

Strangers. William Stafford. ...I think better/lost back there in our old brown car. NNaP

Strangers. R. S. Thomas. Wrung with despair, profound/Audiences of the dead. NMP

The Strangers. Jones Very. For here my eye has seen but few,/Who in each act that act have done. CBEP; OxBA

Strangers Are We All upon the Earth. Franz Werfel. That to which we link ourselves must/die. TrJP

A Strappado for the Devil: Of Maids' Inconstancy. Richard Brathwaite. It is she shall be my bride. EIL

Stratagem. Allen Curnow. He told that story well. AnNZ

Strategies. Welton Smith. when words fail. NBP; PoBA

Stratfield. Anonymous. Or earth Thy humble footstool laid. AmFP

The Strath of Kildonan. Betty Morris. We turn and hurry on/Towards Dounreay. PoSH

Stratton Water. Anonymous. The night the mother should have died,/The young son shall be born. OxBB

Straus Park. Gerald Stern. Do not cry out again in clumsiness and shame. NYP

The Straw. Robert Graves. Have I undone her by my vehemence? MoVE; OxBTC

The Straw Men. Charles Culhane. and we must work hard to lose ourselves. LFAC

Strawberries. Judith Hemschemeyer. But they told me I had ruined my dress. DFF

Strawberries. Dorothy Hughes. unpacking parsley, and wet cress, on Second Avenue. AMV-81

Strawberries. Edwin Morgan. let the storm wash the plates BoLoP; LLLT

Strawberries in Mexico. Ron Padgett. It's just a very blue sky I'm looking at ANYP; EAS

Strawberries in November. Shaw Neilson. If you look at the crimson people/You look at the human heart. PoAu 1-2

Strawberries Mit Cream. Rochelle Owens. pass the pirogen/you/ communist! CoPo

Strawberry Blond. Bill Berkson. they went off socks ANYP

Strawberry Fair. Anonymous. That I should go to Strawberry Fair.' OBET

Strawberry Moon. Mary Oliver. ...when the white moon rises/women want to lash out/with a cutting edge? InPS

The Strawberry Roan. Anonymous. Oh, that Strawberry Roan. FSW

The Strawberry Roan. Curley W. Fletcher. Kin stay with that bronk when he makes/that high dive. BPAW

Strawberry Shortcake, Blueberry Pie. Anonymous. Central High School, yes, yes, yes! LoGBV

Straws. Elizabeth Jane Coatsworth. But a horse will stand always/Backed up to a gale. AmFN

Stray Animals. James Tate. This is a house of unwritten poems,/this is where I am unborn. NoAm

Stray Dog. Charlotte Mish. ...the one who bent/and petted you, and murmured–and went on. PoLf

Stray Dog, near Ecully. Margaret Avison. Deployed, they search, shouting "Sey-sahm, Sey-sahm." OBCV; PoA

The Strayed Reveller. Matthew Arnold. The bright procession/Of eddying forms,/Sweep through my soul! LoBV; OAEL 1-2; OBEV; VLP

The Straying Student. Austin Clarke. Must carry his own coffin and believe,/In dread, all that the clergy teach the young. AnIL; BIrV; CIP; IPY; MoAB; NeIP; NOBI; OxBI

The Stream. Lula Lowe Weeden. And just went arunning running on. CDC

The Stream of Life. William Cullen Bryant. The dust alone remains. AnNE

The Stream's Song. Lascelles Abercrombie. I shall have lost/Half my delight. OBMV

The Streams of Bunclody. Anonymous. When I think on Bunclody, I'm ready to die. BIrV

The Streams of Lovely Nancy. Anonymous. And an angel might direct us right, and where shall we go? FaBoBa; OBET; OxBoLi

The Street. Gene Baro. She is noiseless on the stones. NYBP

Street. George Oppen. So good, they expect to be so good... GP

The Street. Octavio Paz. Where I pursue, a man who trips and falls/Gets up and seeing me, keeps saying: "No one!" FF

The Street. Robert Pinsky. ...live, dangerous/Gray bark of the street. MAYP

The Street. Gary Soto. Eating only enough so as not to say good-bye. NPGG

Street Car Blues. Sleepy John Estes. Lord I'm gonna quit my bad way of living/And visit the Sunday school BluL

Street Chants: I should worry, I should care. *Anonymous.* I should marry another guy. ExPo

Street Chants: "Mother, mother what is that." *Anonymous.* That's the lady's corset string. ExPo

Street Chants; Old Daddy Witch. *Anonymous.* And thought he was rich. ExPo

Street Corner College. Kenneth Patchen. Cold stars and the whores. MoAmPo

Street Demonstration. Margaret Walker. We're Going to Miss Our Chance to go to Jail. BPo; CNA

Street Fight. Harold Monro. What comes into your mind when two men fight? FaBoTw

Street Fire. Daniel Halpern. bound with rubber that smolders into morning. AmPA; NYP

A Street in April. Louis Dudek. so April's without flower, and no song heard. OBCV

A Street in Bronzeville: Southeast Corner. Gwendolyn Brooks. While over her tan impassivity/Shot silk is shining. VGW

A Street in Bronzeville: The Ballad of Chocolate Mabbie. Gwendolyn Brooks. Mabbie or Mabbie to be. CAPP

A Street in Kaufman-Ville: or a Note Thrown to Carolyn... James (Olumo) Cunningham. ...a solitary broken hand or two upon the scales/like butchers do... JB

Street Kid. Duane Niatum. Reach my soul building a nest against the wall. STE

A Street Melody. Belle Cooper. Assisi lifts her towers to heaven again. GoBC

Street Musicians. John Ashbery. ...smeared/On the landscape, to make of us what we could. HaCAP

The Street of Named Houses. Robert David Cohen. My Love. NYBP

Street Performers, 1851. Terence Tiller. the paints are in their boxes: they have gone,/the fantoccini and the Chinese shades. GTBS-P

Street Preacher. Norman MacCaig. ...taking/His sensible underclothes off, rolls into bed? BSV

Street Scene. Robert Mezey. ...the small flakes/Inseparable from stars. LiTM

A Street Scene. Lizette Woodworth Reese. Turns back, and looks again. OBCA

Street Scene–1946. Kenneth Porter. Negro and a white man/picketing together! PoNe

Street Song. Thom Gunn. Keys lids acid and speed. HeIP; NoP; OxBC

Street Song. Edith Sitwell. Or the burden of Atlas falling? CMoP; CoBMV; MoPo; MoVE

The Street Sounds to the Soldiers' Tread. Alfred Edward Housman. Soldier, I wish you well. PPP

Street-Walker in March. Samuel L. Albert. This is a night to be out/Whoring with the wind. NePoAm-2

Street Window. Carl Sandburg. They tell stories. PCP

Streets. Douglas Goldring. For it's virtue and baths and good cooking go hand in/glove! HBMV

Streets. Amy Lowell. And the blood-red linings glow like sharp-toothed maple leaves/In Autumn. SBG

Streets of Baltimore. *Anonymous.* Fled, and left my shattered dwelling to the dust of Baltimore. BLPA

The Streets of Cairo. James Thornton. Lots of more men sorry will be,/If they dont try to keep away from this/Poor little country maid. FSN

The Streets of Forbes. Jack McGuire. And led him through the streets of Forbes to show the prize they/had. CBAP; NOAV

Streets of Glory. *Anonymous.* Walk and talk with Jesus one of these days. FSW

The Streets of Laredo. Louis MacNeice. Lay down the red carpet–My dowry is death. MoBS; OBWP

The Streets of New York. Henry Blossom. The queens you'll meet on any street in old New York. FSN

Strength, Love, Light. King of France Robert II. Sine on the path of right,/Show us the way! WGRP

Strength through Joy. Kenneth Rexroth. Standing sentry for the avalanche. FYAP; VGW

Strength to War. Stephen Stepanchev. A man earns strength to war only by dying. WaP

Strephon. John Smyth. The heedless virgin, unaware,/Plays with the dart that wounds her. UnTE

The Stricken Deer. William Cowper. And sound integrity not more, than famed/For sanctity of manners undefiled. LoBV

The Stricken South to the North. Paul Hamilton Hayne. But love, more potent than your haughtiest/anger,/Subdues the souls which hate could only/wound! PAH

Strictly for Posterity. Charles Simic. If I get through my 33rd year,/I'll live forever. NNaP

Strictly Germ-Proof. Arthur Guiterman. The Bunny and the Baby and the Prophylactic Pup. BLPA; HBV 1-2; TreF; TrJP; YaD

Strictures on the Economy of Nature. George Outram. By jingo, that's a deep ane! FaBoCo

The Strike. *Anonymous.* Let 'em find there's men meant te be men! OBET

A Strike among the Poets. *Anonymous.* "Shorter hours and better pay." FaBoCo; FiBHP; PP

Strike It up, Tabor. *Anonymous.* How now? fie fie fie! you dance false. NCEP

Strike the Bell. Anonymous. He's thinking more of shortening sail than striking the bell. OBSS

Strike the Blow. *Anonymous.* Strike the blow! PAH

Striking. Charles Stuart Calverley. "For indeed–the clocks have struck." CenHV

Striking Times. *Anonymous.* And swear they'll have their wages rose before they reap or sow. OBET

String. Dennis Schmitz. ..."privacy is only/contraction, heavy/body, dangle of shriveled nuts..." LCAP

The String of My Ancestors. Nina Nyhart. When you cut string/it crawls off/in two directions. Str

String Quartet. Babette Deutsch. Love sees how vilely it must live/And smiles? UnS

String Stars for Pearls. J. U. Nicolson. But love will lean to a smaller flame/Forever and forever. HBMV

The Stringer. James Brasfield. That so many rivers at once/Washed over you. AMV-81

The Strings' Excitement. W. H. Auden. Massive and taciturn years, the Age of Ice. MoAB; MoBrPo

Strings/Himo. Yuri Kageyama. streaming black hair BrSi

Strings in the Earth. James Joyce. And fingers straying/Upon an instrument. OnYI

The Stringybark Cockatoo. *Anonymous.* And he drove me off without a rap–the stringybark cockatoo. NOAV

Strip Me Naked, or Royal Gin for Ever. *Anonymous.* I was born naked, and I'll naked die. NOEC

Strip Mining Pit. Dan Gillespie. grab a handful of heart/and run like hell. TAT

A Strip of Blue. Lucy Larcom. Glad, when is opened unto my need/Some sea-like glimpse of thee. AA; HBV 1-2; WGRP

The Stripper. Anita Endrezze Probst. and the sound of its blue beat/matching the wine in my veins. CDW

Strive No More. George Peele. Lo, here they lie whom scorn defaced. CoBE

Strive Not, Vain Lover, to Be Fine. Richard Lovelace. She that a clinquant outside doth adore,/Dotes on a gilded statue, and no more. OAEP

Stroke. Mike Lowery. I ask for pillows/the nurse brings pudding. Psk

Strokes. William Stafford. The birthdays of the old require such candles. ConAP; PCP

The Strolling Player. Arthur Rimbaud. Like lyre strings I'd pluck the elastic laces/Of my battered shoes, one foot against my heart. GrPl

The Strong. John Vance Cheney. A look, a moan, like that on ocean's/shore. AA

The Strong Are Saying Nothing. Robert Frost. But the strong are saying nothing until they see. CMoP

Strong as Death. Henry Cuyler Bunner. And I will follow thee, O Death. HBV 1-2

The Strong Bond. Juana de Ibarbourou. And you will cry/and then...you will be mine as never before! PBWP

The Strong City. Alfred Noyes. And I drank Life through God's own death. GoBC

A Strong Hand. Aaron Hill. And the rogues obey you well. HBV 1-2

The Strong Heroic Line. Oliver Wendell Holmes And which Velasquez or Van Dyck refuse? AA

Strong Men. Sterling A. Brown. The strong men gittin' stronger./Strong men..../Stronger.... BANP; BPo; CNA; FB; PoBA; PPON; TTY

Strong Men, Riding Horses. Gwendolyn Brooks. I am not brave at all. PoBA

Strong Son of God. Alfred, Lord Tennyson. And in thy wisdom make me wise. OxBoCh

The Strong Swimmer. William Rose Benet. World without end–and not in vain–/Are rowing this world along! PoNe

A Strong Wind. Austin Clarke. The wind was telegraphing, hundreds/Of miles. All Ireland raced. BoNaP

The Strongest. Yehoash. That unseen, still, as from above,/Gives love. TrJP

Struck Was I, Nor Yet by Lightning. Emily Dickinson. Till the infinite aurora/In the other's eyes. AnNE

The Structural Study of Myth. Jerome Rothenberg. the Crow Indian had said about Coyote/hitting the nail at last PoM

Structure of Rime. Robert Duncan.
...Let me give you an illusion of not/grieving. CAPP

...This is the/meaning of the music of the spheres. CAPP

Struggle. Sidney Lanier. Each second I'm new-born from some new grave. CBEP; LiTA; OxBA

The Struggle. Sully Prudhomme. "Mother, I strove with God, and was hard prest." AWP; PoPl

The Struggle with the Angel. Claude Vigee. They breathe the wind of other nebulas... VWA

Strung out with Elgar on a Hill (excerpt). Jonathan Williams. clean sheets, again,/just in case GP

Stud Groom. John Glassco. As it sparks the impenetrable lives, like yours/ Whose year revolves around the county fair. OBCV

Student. *Anonymous.* And a straight deep furrow! AnIL; KiLC; OBMV

Student. Cheng Min. As if to tell me which is itself? PBWP

Student. Josephine Miles. Who, early in the alphabet, recited/More than I could learn until tonight? NoP

The Student. Marianne Moore. ...not because he/Has no feeling but because he has so much. MP; TwCP

A Student Courting. *Anonymous.* For holy wimman am I on. OxBM

Students. Haniel Long. and make little entries/in a ledger. AnAmPo

Students. Florence Wilkinson. Time waits for moments such as these. HBV 1-2

The Students of Justice. William Stanley Merwin. They leave me their keys which they never use. NaP

Studies at Delhi. Sir Alfred Comyn Lyall.
And the soul have rest, and the air be still? OBVV
"God smite their souls to the depths of hell." OBTV; OBVV

Studies from Life. Martha Dickey. they went inland to paint/the idea of storms. FAZ

The Studio. Derek Mahon. Its occasional cries of despair/A function of the furniture. FaBoIP

The Study in Aesthetics. Ezra Pound. And at this I was mildly abashed. CMoP; NOBA; NoP; PAI

A Study in Aesthetics (parody). Robert Peters. This is the end of good breeding. BXAP

Study in Blue. Evan Jones. It's me O Lord–or rather, it is I. NOAV

Study No. X. Pierre Coupey. flesh & dust PeCV

The Study of a Spider. John Byrne, Leicester Warren, Lord De Tabley. I break the toils around thy head/And from their gibbets take thy dead. NOBV; VLP

Study of an Elevation, in Indian Ink. Rudyard Kipling. Should I have riz to what Potiphar is,/Hadst thou been mated to Me? InMe

A Study of Reading Habits. Philip Larkin. Books are a load of crap. NOBL; SoSe; TW

Study of Two Pears. Wallace Stevens. The pears are not seen/As the observer wills. AP; InPK; InPS; NU; OxBA; PAI

Study Peace. LeRoi (Imamu Amiri Baraka) Jones. images cast against the eternally shifting/heavens. PoBA

Study War No More. *Anonymous.* I ain't gonna study war no more. FSW

Stuff. H. B. Johnson. But the lady gets in. AMV-80

The Stuffed Owl. William Wordsworth. Nor veil, with restless film, his staring eyes. Par

Stumbling. Dick Lourie. dance alone in the same place at the same time NeAC

The Stump Is Not the Tombstone. Ralph W. Seager. Some one may live in deeds we leave behind,/However unrecorded and unsigned. AMV-81

Stumpfoot on 42nd Street. Louis Simpson. Only to say, Here I am in person. NNaP; NYP; UnPo; VGW

Stumptown Attends the Picture Show. David Bottoms. moving in a cloud of dust toward the theater marquee. GP

Stun. James Schuyler. in prickle-green, speed-lashed/Massachusetts. ANYP; MAT

The Stupid Old Body. Edward Carpenter. Or fossilized into one set form–/ Which alone after all is death. WGRP

Stupidity. Mary Elizabeth ("E") Fullerton. No ill intent? CBAP

Stupidity Street. Ralph Hodgson. Nothing for sale in/Stupidity Street. AtBAP; BrPo; GoTF; HBV 1-2; LiTM; LOW; MoAB; MoBrPo; OxBTC; SiSoSe; TreFS

Stutterer. Alan Dugan. down to the old mill stream/where lies of love are fair. CAPP; NYBP

The Stwonen Steps. William Barnes. But who can ever tell what peairs/O' veet trod vu'st the steairs? NOBV

Style. Charles Bukowski. or you walking out of the bathroom naked/ without seeing/me. HoPM

Style. Howard Nemerov. That fire that eats what it illuminates. NoAm

Stylite. Louis MacNeice. And his eyes on the world. MoPo

Styro. Clark Coolidge. boreal armature. ANYP

Suave Mari Magno. Lucretius (Titus Lucretius Carus). Strike off your chains, and make your souls your own! AWP

The Sub-Average Time Reader. Ernest Wittenberg. My battered ego will reply/With (-1) subscription. FiBHP

Sub Rosa. Don Domanski. ...The/cold waters rising deep in labour. CaPN

Sub Specie Aeternitatis. Robert Earl Hayden. resonant with silence of/a conquered and/defiant god. AmPP

A Subaltern's Love-Song. Sir John Betjeman. And now I'm engaged to Miss Joan Hunter Dunn. BoLoP; HAP; LiSp; MP; NOBL; OxBTC; TwCP

Subalterns. Elizabeth Daryush. Now, life's so deadly slow.' OBWP

The Subalterns. Thomas Hardy. They owned their passiveness. CMoP; MoAB; MoBrPo; NoAm; NOBV; OAEL 1-2; PPP

Subject. Marie Ponsot. Do not spare. VGW

The Subject of the Bishop's Miracle. John Philip. and the deep song warming her lips. BoAV

Subject to All Pain. *Anonymous.* It is to me a verry dedly woo. MeEL

Subjectivity at Sestos. P. M. Hubbard. He had in fact been drowned the night before. NYBP

Sublimation. Alex Comfort. matches the fine content/of what we do together. ErPo; UnTE

The Submarine Bed. John Peale Bishop. It is not easy to adjust/The body to a severed head. LiTA

Submarine Mountains. Cale Young Rice. For only in Unmeaning Might is met/The intolerable thought none can ignore. EtS

Submission. *Anonymous.* A quiet small corner of your bedroom in which to hide. ErPo

Submission. George Herbert. Only do Thou lend me a hand,/Since thou hast both mine eyes. JCP

Submission in Affliction. *Anonymous.* My Health, my Life, my God! STF

Submission to Afflictive Providences. Isaac Watts. And we'll adore the Justice too/That strikes our comforts dead. NOCV

Substance and Shadow. John Henry, Cardinal Newman. Aided by Heaven, by earth unthwarted still. GoBC

Substantiations (excerpt). Vidya. will the champak think to blossom? PBWP

Substitution. Elizabeth Barrett Browning. Speak Thou, availing Christ!–and fill this pause. WGRP

Substitution. Anne Spencer. His All-Mind bids us keep this sacred place! BlSi; CDC

Subterranean Homesick Blues. Bob Dylan. The pump don't work/'Cause the vandals took the handles. InPK

Suburb. Harold Monro. In the little garden-square/Pampas grass will rustle there. HBV 1-2

The Suburb. Anne Stevenson. I am beyond blame. NMM

Suburb Hilltop. Richard Moore. what will we do/now? Flutter into butterflies? NYBP

Suburban. John Ciardi. when even these suburbs shall give up their dead. NLV

Suburban. H. R. Coursen. ...whether/Mrs. Haynes would have hanged herself/early one morning, while/we passed by to school. GOYP

Suburban Dream. Edwin Muir. And the masters come. OxBTC

Suburban Dusk. Bert Meyers. ...Each night, the city becomes a butterfly,/ trembling in its oil. EAS

Suburban Lovers. Bruce Dawe. All day it has been suspended there, above their heads. NOAV

Suburban Lullaby. John Streeter Manifold. Dare to hold or dare let go,/ What abysses gape below! BoAV

Suburban Song. Elizabeth Riddell. Close the door on love and hang/The key upon the nail. CBAP; NOAV

Suburban Sonnet. Gwen Harwood. She comforts them; and wraps it in a paper/featuring: Tasty dishes from stale bread. CBAP

Suburban Wife's Song. Robert Hutchinson. And do not know how far away you are. NYBP

Suburbia. Maurice Martinez. I've got.../WHAT? PoNe

The Suburbs Is a Fine Place. *Anonymous.* And having now no more to say, I think it fit to end. CoMu

Suburbs on a Hazy Day. D. H. Lawrence. to leave but only the merest possible taint! OBMV

Subversive. William Rose Benet. Yet still, throughout the world, there stands/His house, that is not made with hands. MoRP

The Subversive. Merle Woo. Let's just send her back right where she came from! BrSi

The Subverted Flower. Robert Frost. And drew her backward home. CMoP; HAP; NoAm; NOBA; OxBA; WeW

The Subway. Allen Tate. In the cold revery of an idiot. AP; NoAm; NOBA; NYP

The Subway from New Britain to the Bronx. Randall Jarrell. And peoples of the Bronx, their conquerors. NYP

The Subway Grating Fisher. Louis Simpson. ...Then winds up his line/and continues to walk, looking down. CAPP

Subway Psalm. Alden Nowlan. and everything is exactly as it should be. Str

The Subway Witnesses. Lorenzo Thomas. Our hands icepicks and soft blood/Blood in our pockets. PoBA

Success. *Anonymous.*

It is in giving, not in getting,/our lives are blest.   PoToHe
We find the thing we call success.   FaFP; PoToHe

Success.   Rupert Brooke.   And I'm alone; and you have not awoken.   OxBTC

Success.   C. C. Cameron.   Unless you're beaten there, you're bound to win.   PoToHe

Success.   William Empson.   You should be praised for taking them away.   OxBTC

Success.   Edgar A. Guest.   If but a few shall know my worth/And proudly call me friend.   TreF

Success.   Emma Lazarus.   The bold, significant, successful man.   SBG

Success is counted sweetest.   Emily Dickinson.   The distant strains of triumph/Burst agonized and clear!   AWP; CBEP; CMoP; DiPo; FPL; GoJo; InPo; InPS; LiTA; LiTM; MAmP; MCCG; MoAB; MoAmPo; NOBA; OxBA; PAI; PG; PoRA; SBG; TAP; TreFT; WaaP

Success Story.   Bruce Bennett.   It gave them something to write about.   LTB

Success Story.   Terence Winch.   ...I live a spine tingling life/of delirious sex & intense happiness.   APU

The Succession.   Frances Laughton Mace.   For his soul's peace his life to song has given.   AA

Succubi.   John Newlove.   ...As lustful/themselves as my schemes are/and as cruel   NeAC

The Succubus.   Robert Graves.   Yet is the fancy grosser than your lusts were gross?   OAEL 1-2

The Succubus.   Harriet Rose.   I am afraid of the name that you will name me.   BrRo

Succumbing.   Paul Eaton Reeve.   Thus the word assumed strange significance.   ErPo

Such a Parcel of Rogues in a Nation.   Robert Burns.   "We're bought and sold for English gold'–/Such a parcel of rogues in a nation!   OxBS

Such a Pleasant Familee.   Wallace Irwin.   Considering she came from such/A pleasant familee.   ShM

Such as in God the Lord Do Trust.   William Kethe.   Whose hearts are true and right.   AH

Such bitter fruit thy love doth yield.   Anonymous.   Fie upon Love and all his Laws.   EG

Such Comfort as the Night Can Bring to Us.   Peter Cooley.   ...shadows known to them/in parting only, and all flesh ravaging.   MAYP

Such Hap as I Am Happed in.   Sir Thomas Wyatt.   With hapless hand no man hath wraught/Such hap as I.   FCP; SiPS

Such is Holland!   Petrus Augustus de Genestet.   And, not at my request, extorted from the sea.   PoL

Such is the course that nature's kind hath wrought.   Sir Thomas Wyatt.   Nor furies that in hell be execrable,/For that they hate, are made most msierable.   FCP

Such Is the Death the Soldier Dies.   Robert Burns Wilson.   Such is the death the soldier dies.   AA; HBV 1-2

Such Is the Sickness of Many a Good Thing.   Robert Duncan.   to draw down the lover's hand/from its lightness to what's/underground.   CAPP

Such Love Is Like a Smoky Fire.   George Chapman.   'Twere better lose the fire, than find the smoke.   LO

Such Soft Ideas All My Pains Beguile.   Mary Wortley, Lady Montagu.   I only hear your voice, and see your eyes.   OBTV

Such Stuff as Dreams.   Franklin Pierce ("F.P.A.") Adams.   But don't say to Dr. Freud/Jenny kiss'd me.   FiBHP; SpRo

Such Stuff as Dreams Are Made Of.   Thomas Wentworth Higginson.   I drift in sweet enchantment back to rest.   AA

Such vain thought as wonted to mislead me.   Sir Thomas Wyatt.   But such it is I not how to begin.   FCP

Suche Waywarde Wais Hath Love.   Henry Howard, Earl of Surrey.   That doutfull hope, that certayne woo, and sure dispaire of/helthe.   AAS

Suckers for Truth.   Robyn Sarah.   and it's this we're after: without the risk/what would be possible?   CaPN

Sucking Cider Through a Straw.   Anonymous.   From sucking cider/Through a straw.   AS; GBP

Sudan.   Michael Jackson.   to draw water for any stranger.   OCNZ

The Sudbury Fight.   Wallace Rice.   That, fearing God's Wrath only, firm may/stand the State they made.   PAH

Sudden Assertion.   Kenneth Leslie.   you and the tender lambies,/now you know!   BoAnP; GDP; PoL

Sudden Frost.   David Wagoner.   ...the first snow falls too late.   PoPl

Sudden Shower.   John Clare.   Nor leaves his dry house though we come so near.   CBEP; OBRV; PoSC

Sudden Things.   Donald Hall.   we would put the animals back in their cages, and get to/the mainland.   EAS

Suddenly.   Robin Blaser.   the retired heart/where the wind glitters   PoM

Suddenly.   Leonora Speyer.   God, the slow withering!   PG

Suddenly Afraid.   Anonymous.   And with that word she vanished away.   CBEP; NCEP

Suenos.   James Reiss.   if I only knew the language to say it in.   FiCP

The Suet Dumpling (parody).   Anonymous.   He enjoys as full content, without his cares.   BXAP

The Suez Crisis.   Anonymous.   O God, the Powerful, save us from the roaring thunderbolts!   WTO

Suffer, Poor Negro.   David Diop.   Suffer, poor Negro/Negro black as Misery!   PBA

Suffering.   Albert Ehrenstein.   Grass sprang out of my skull,/My head was of black earth.   TrJP

Suffering in sorrow in hope to attain.   Sir Thomas Wyatt.   Content tô serve and suffer still I must.   FCP

Sufficed not, madam, tht you did tear.   Sir Thomas Wyatt.   And I no more such torments of the heart/Feel as I do. This shalt thou gain thereby.   FCP; SiPS

The Suffolk Miracle (A vers.).   Anonymous.   Your daughters' love, tgive them their way,/For force oft breeds their lives' decay.   BaBo; ESPB

The Suffolk Miracle (B vers.).   Anonymous.   He still wore the Holland handkerchief/Around his head.   BaBo

Sufi Quatrain.   Rabi'a bint Isma'il.   where then lies my hope of You, and where my/fear?   WPOW

Sugar Babe.   Anonymous.   'Cause your body's gonna swivel when you come to die, sugar babe.   ABF

A Sugar-Candy Bird.   Ian Young.   and spill/white sugar dust/over us both.   NeAC

The Sugar Cane.   James Grainger.
The blacks should cultivate the Cane-land isles.   NOEC
...for soon they seek/The neighbouring spring; and drink, and swell, and die.   FaBoUs

Sugar Daddy.   Elizabeth Smither.   Like an undiscovered new world.   OCNZ

Sugar in the Cane.   Tennessee Williams.   These winter nights are blue and cold!   OBAL

The Sugar-Plum Tree.   Eugene Field.   And I'll rock you away to that Sugar-Plum Tree/In the garden of Shut-Eye Town.   FaFP; GoTF; HBV 1-2; HBVY; NLV; OxBChV; SoPo; TreF

Sugar Weather.   Peter McArthur.   For the sap has commenced to run.   CaP

Sugarfields.   Barbara] Mahone.   this music cannot leave me.   CNA; PoBA

The Sugaring.   Abraham Moses Klein.   and blessing the sweetness of their sacrifice.   OBCV

Suggested by a Picture of the Bird of Paradise.   William Wordsworth.   That in the living Creature find on earth a/place.   VLP

Suggested Device of a New Western State.   John James Piatt.   Lighting the doorway of the pioneer!   AnAmPo

A Suggestion Made by the Posters of the "Globe."   J. E. Thorold Rogers.   The lowest savages on earth.   FaBoEE

Suggestions by Steam.   Thomas Hood.   To that small voice that crieth–"Stop her!"   NBM

Suicid/ing Indian Women.   Paula Gunn Allen.
and making joking fantasies/do for real   TWSS
Mother, so maybe they sent her away and made up the rest. TWSS
soft and comforting around this room? TWSS
They have taken your name. TWSS

A Suicide.   Tom Kryss.   The newness of it all had long since worn off.   NeAC

The Suicide.   V. R. Lang.   The spectres, the hawkers, the talkers, the damned are/all there.   PoA

The Suicide.   Louis MacNeice.
This man with the shy smile has left behind/Something that was intact.   FaBoIP
Walking on the crown of the road. DTC

The Suicide.   Joyce Carol Oates.   was that human?/Went where?   Psk

Suicide.   Anne Stevenson.   He was free as air when the girl's father found him,/returning from an evening out with friends.   FaBoWP

Suicide.   Alice Walker.   & tell if the days it/adds up to/is one.   FF

Suicide in Trenches.   Siegfried Sassoon.   The hell where youth and laughter go.   BrPo; MMM

Suicide off Egg Rock.   Sylvia Plath.   The forgetful surf creaming on those ledges.   NMP; PPP

Suicide Pond.   Kathy McLaughlin.   Grim suicides in bottom-rock and stone.   PoA

The Suicide's Grave.   Sir William Schwenck Gilbert.   "Oh willow, titwillow, titwillow!"   ALV; GoTF; LiTL; TreF; VLP

Suicide's Note.   Langston Hughes.   Asked me for a kiss.   CDC; DFF

The Suicides.   George Macbeth.   ...something that water blurs.   NoAm

The Suicides of the Rich.   Victor Contoski.   of the bodies of the rich/falling falling falling.   FAZ

Suilven.   Andrew Young.   As though I were the foul toad, said/To bear a precious jewel in his head.   OxBS

Suilven and the Eagle (excerpt).   Gordon Bottomley.   Come, light, now.   MoBrPo

The Suire.   Thomas Caulfield Irwin.   And, holding still the token, sunk to the sands/Of the deep river, and I breathed alone.   IrPN

A Suit of Nettles.   James Reaney.
...changed/Snow into grass and gave to all such powers.   OBCV
sicklestraw and all such glamourie. OBCV
...so you've done/Something for him by my bottle faith fiddle de dee you
have. PeCV
Suite for Celery and Blind Date (parody).   Philip Dow.   A saving grace and
its dividends.   BXAP
A Suite for Marriage.   David Ignatow.   a blessing for your life.   NNaP
Suite from Catullus.   Vincent McHugh.   he is a businessman,/and his
business is bad   ErPo
A Suite of Six Pieces for Siskind.   John Logan.   swims into the deep
humours of my eye/bringing this fish pale day.   LCAP
Suite to Fathers.   Jim Harrison.   Night stares down with her great bruised
eye.   AmPA
Sukey, You Shall Be My Wife.   *Anonymous.*   Say Yes, if you please.
OxNR
Sukkot.   Sol Lachman.   & even the birds are made joyful/by our shouts
VWA
Sulk when you're spoken to.   *Anonymous.*   Bad little kid.   CenHV
Sulky Sue.   *Anonymous.*   Turn her face to the wall/Till she comes to.
OxNR
Sulpicia's Rival.   Albius Tibullus.   So yield your zeal for hunting to your
elders/and run straight back into my encompassing heart.   LiTW
Sum.   James Nolan.   He never was married,/divided or touched.   Str
Sum, Es, Est.   *Anonymous.*   Sitting on a stool.   ChTr
The Sum of All Known Reverence.   Walt Whitman.   It is not they who give
the life, it is you who give the life.   MoRP
The Sumach Leaves.   Jones Very.   They gave its splendor to our fall.
NOBA
Sumburgh Heid.   George Bruce.   ...That an' mai's the dirdit/Word–
Sumburgh, Sumburgh Heid.   OxBS
Sumer Is Icumen In.   *Anonymous.*   Sing cuccu, sing cuccu, nu.   AWP; BiP;
EBEV; EnLi 1-2; FF; GBP; HeIP; InPo; InPS; InvP; MeEL; NIP; OAEL
1-2; OBEV; OxBM; PAI; PBBP; SeCePo; SeCeV; SpRo; TreFT; TrGrPo
Summa Contra Gentiles.   Paris Leary.   that I am guiltless of your innocent
blood.   CoPo
Summary.   Sonia Sanchez.   one night of words/will not change/all that.
BPo
Summary of the Distance between the Bomber and the Objective.   Walter
Benton.   bringing peace to many.   WaP
Summer.   Conrad Aiken.   formless ice on a formless plain/that was and is
and comes again.   NoAm
Summer.   Frank Asch.   I take my whole body off,/and throw it/in the river.
NTCP
Summer.   John Clare.
Summer sometime shall bless this spot, when I,/Hapt in the cold dark grave,
can heed it not.   BoNaP
That hides for shelter from the summer heat. CBEP
Summer.   Douglas Crase.   The wind arrives/With the flutter of something
really happening.   NoP
Summer.   John Davidson.   Hardly in the underwood/Russet pinions softly
whir.   BoNaP
Summer.   Edwin Denby.   They can suit whomever man's intestines can.
ANYP
Summer.   Moishe Kulbak.   here's where I lounge about–a splendid hard
steel.   VWA
Summer.   Bill Manhire.   ...I am fine thank/you.   OCNZ
Summer.   Tom Marshall.   the bruise of life burns outward.   NOBC
Summer.   Josephine Miles.   So they did, vanishing away off and shouting.
FaBoWP
Summer.   P. K. Page.   was sharp as a whistle of grass/in my green blood.
PeCV
Summer.   Christina Georgina Rossetti.   Of the dusty, musty, lag-last
fashion/That days drone elsewhere.   BoNaP; CBEP; ELP; NBM; PoPle
Summer.   James (1700-48) Thomson.
Hence rules the circling deep, and awes the/world.   CoBE
Will send you bounding to your hills again. EnLi 1-2
Summer.   Diane Wakoski.   and the fish/shouting/with their fins.   VGW
Summer.   Ramona Wilson.   the moon is so bright/the light bursts within
me.   VoR
Summer, 1960, Minnesota.   Robert Bly.   Into the Congo as if into a river,/
Or as wheat into open mills.   PAI
Summer, 1970.   Daniel Halpern.   near brandy, and my mouth that calls you,
calls you.   AmPA
Summer 1970.   Lindiwe Mabuza.   nerves pulled/like autumn/strings across/
an empty gourd.   WPOW
Summer Acres.   Anne Wilkinson.   I hail my fathers, sing their blood to the
leaf.   CaP
Summer Afternoon.   Basil Dowling.   While summer day to summer evening
passes.   AnNZ
Summer Afternoon.   Elizabeth B. Harrod.   Or in sea-song be drowned to
death.   NePoEA

Summer Afternoon.   Raymond Souster.   hot, naked, unashamed beauty!
BoNaP
Summer and Winter.   Percy Bysshe Shelley.   Alas, then, for the homeless
beggar old!   BoNaP
Summer Band Concert.   Vivian Smith.   and whispers darkness in her ear
CBAP
Summer Beach.   Frances Cornford.   Since first I laboured with a wooden
spade/Against the background of Etnity.   BrRo; ChMP
A Summer Christmas in Australia.   Douglas Brook Wheelton Sladen.   But
whence no messenger comes back.   OBCP
Summer Comes.   Edith Agnew.   Let me sit here by this adobe wall/And
lean against summer!   SiSoSe
A Summer Commentary.   Yvor Winters.   Smears brandy on the trampling
boot/And sends it sweeter on its way.   LiTM; QFR
Summer Concert.   Reed Whittemore.   And all we could do to be doing
would be to be Wednes/day.   AmFN
The Summer Countries.   Henry Rago.   ...It was/Both land and morning,
and the light/Was loud and everywhere, like bells.   VGW
Summer Dawn.   William Morris.   Over the tender, bowed locks of the corn.
AtBAP; CBEP; GTBS; LoBV; NOBE; NOBV; OAEL 1-2; OBEV; OBNC;
OBVV; ViBoPo
Summer Days.   Roy Daniells.   Such things my mind continually amaze.
CaP
The Summer Days Are Come Again.   Samuel Longfellow.   We lift our song
to Him.   TRV
The Summer Ending.   Glenway Wescott.   Now lover hits lover, in loathing,
in fright of criticism.   PoA
Summer Evening.   Walter De la Mare.   Gone is another summer's day.
FM; MoAB; MoBrPo; MoShBr; TiPo
A Summer Evening.   Archibald Lampman.   And sleep, dark sleep, so near,
so like to death.   PeCV
Summer Evening and Night.   James (1700-48) Thomson.   Unrival'd reigns,
the fairest Lamp of Night.   OBEC
Summer Farm.   Norman MacCaig.   Farm within farm and in the centre,
me.   ACV; BSV; OxBTC
Summer Garden.   Anna Akhmatova.   But the source of light is hidden in
the leaves.   BoWoP
A Summer Gone.   Howard Moss.   ...We'll have, someday,/That other
weather that we salt away.   NePoEA
The Summer Harvest Spreads the Fields.   Nathan Strong.   All heaven
approves the sovereign choice.   AH
Summer Has Come.   *Anonymous.*   Ravens flourish, summer has come!
LiTW; OnYI
Summer Has Two Beginnings.   Emily Dickinson.   Forever is deciduous/
Except to those who die.   InPo
Summer Holiday.   Robinson Jeffers.   In the rubbish dumps, a concrete dam
far off in the mountain....   CrMA; MoAmPo; MoVE; OxBA
Summer Holidays.   W. R. Rodgers.   Its acute and terrible attritions.   LiTB
Summer Home.   Seamus Heaney.   Our love calls tiny as a tuning fork.
FaBoIP; IPY
Summer Idyll.   George Barker.   And Summer, blowing over the
Mediterranean/Like swans, like perfect swans.   FaBoMo; MoPo
Summer Images.   John Clare.   He thinks the rain begun,/And hastes to
sheltering bowers.   CBEP; EG; OBNC; OBRV
Summer in a Small Town.   Linda Gregg.   loving the smell and the houses/
so completely it leaves my heart empty.   MAYP
Summer in England, 1914.   Alice Meynell.   The soldier dying dies upon a
kiss,/The very kiss of Christ.   BrRo; SBG
Summer Interlude.   Lionel Stevenson.   Till they and I dissolve in one.   CaP
Summer Is A-Coming In.   *Anonymous.*   Nor cease thou never now.   FSW
The Summer Is Coming.   Bryan Guinness.   Breathes like a flute/As he flits
high and low.   OxBI
Summer Is Ended.   Christina Georgina Rossetti.
An end locked fast,/Bent we cannot re-bend.   NOBV
A little while weep on,/Only a little while. HBV 1-2
Summer is Gone.   *Anonymous.*
Season of ice–these are my tidings.   FaBoCh; LoGBV; OnYI
Summer is gone. AnIL; PoPl
Summer Island.   William Logan.   ...Tomorrow we will separate.   MAYP
Summer Journey.   W. R. Rodgers.   May all your valleys be fat/With wine,
and full be every vat.   OBTV
The Summer Landscape; or, The Dragon's Teeth.   Rolfe Humphries.
Slaying and slain; and I am all of these.   NYBP
Summer Lightning.   Thomas Sturge Moore.   No girl had loved unless she
chose!   BrPo; SyP
Summer Longings.   Denis Florence MacCarthy.   Man is ever weary, weary,/
Waiting for the May!   HBV 1-2
Summer Magic.   Leslie Pinckney Hill.   And I was lord of life and death.
BANP
The Summer Malison.   Gerard Manley Hopkins.   And every heart think
loathingly/Its dearest changed to bores.   CMoP; NoAm; PoEL 1-5

Summer Mansions. Ruth Herschberger. The blue sky is accessible merriment to any, or we can try. HoAn

Summer Matures. Helene Johnson. This night was born for love, my Phaon./Come. BlSi; CDC; PoNe

Summer Morning. John Clare. And thinks he sees no beauties like the morn. CBEP; PoSC

A Summer Morning. Rachel Field. "Get up, my dear, it is to-day." SoPo; SUS; TiPo

Summer Morning. James (1700-48) Thomson. And from the crouded Fold, in Order, drives/His Flock, to taste the Verdure of the Morn. OBEC

A Summer Morning. Richard Wilbur. Possessing what the owners can but own. FaBoMo; NLV

Summer Music. May Sarton. As summer, lulling and so mild,/Goes golden-buttercup-wild. NCSH; NePoAm

Summer Near the River. Carolyn Kizer. It seems, for a moment, the river ceases flowing. CoAP; VGW

A Summer Night. Matthew Arnold. How fair a lot to fill/Is left to each man still. CBEP; ExPo; GTBS; MCCG; OAEP; SeCePo; SeCeV

A Summer Night. W. H. Auden. Tough in their patience to surpass/The tigress her swift motions. FaBoRV

Summer Night. Hayim Nahman Bialik. gleaming silver threads, making one garment/for high priest and swineherd. VWA

A Summer Night. Elizabeth Stoddard. That waiteth for me. AA

A Summer Night in the Beehive. Charles Tennyson Turner. Another day of honey has begun! FM

Summer Noon: 1941. Yvor Winters. Will repossess this ground. CrMA

A Summer Noon at Sea. Epes Sargent. As if the Power that chained the impatient wind/With the same fetter of respose had bound us! EtS

Summer on the Great American Desert. Rufus B. Sage. Thrice gladly will I turn away,/And bid these scenes adieu! BPAW; PoOW

Summer Oracle. Audre Lorde. under its cloak of lies. BlSi; PoBA

Summer Pogrom. Fay Zwicky. The dead lie deep in me. CBAP

Summer Rain. Hartley Coleridge. Joy fill'd the brook, and comfort cheer'd the/field. VLP

Summer Rain. Laurie Lee. The green hills break as our graves embrace. MoVE

Summer Rain. Sir Herbert Read. ...A warm breath/issues from the nostrils beneath/the mask of death. LiTM

Summer Rain. Henry David Thoreau. Who in a bearded coat does gayly go. AnNE

Summer Rain. Richard Tillinghast. and write these perishing words down/in the voice of summer rain. MAYP

The Summer Rentals. Daniel Halpern. I returned the handshake you taught me as a boy. MAYP

Summer Resort. P. K. Page. while pulse and leaf rustle and grow climatic. CaP

A Summer's Day. Alexander Hume. Na mair they move or steir... CH

A Summer's Dream. Elizabeth Bishop. still dreaming audibly. OxBC

Summer's Early End at Hudson Bay. Hayden Carruth. The long seas of Brazil. NYBP

Summer's Farewell. Nashe [(or Nash[) Thomas. Weepe heavens, mourne earth, here Summer ends. PoEL 1-5

Summer's Last Will and Testament: Adieu, Farewell Earths Blisse. Nashe [(or Nash[) Thomas. Lord, have mercy on us. AtBAP; DiPo; LO

Summer Sabbath. Jessie E. Sampter. Each life its task to do. TrJP

A Summer Santuary. John Hall Ingham. And, when I saw the flower at my feet,/I understood it all. AA

Summer Sky. Ruth McKee Gordon. I like the clouds up in the sky. TiPo

Summer Solstice. George Bowering. ...A visible/tyrant of light yanks their traces,demanding/they stride apart. NOBC

Summer Solstice. Diane Keating. shadowless, free, I'm lost/in these splinters. CaPN

Summer Song. Edith Nesbit. To be young before the heart grows old! PoSC

Summer Song. W. W. Watt. While my battered conscience tussles/With my thought-resistant brain. FiBHP; QQQ

Summer Song I. George Barker. Where all the love is true love, and/True love goes on for ever. ChMP

Summer Stars. Carl Sandburg. So lazy and hum-strumming. LOW; RFM; YeAr

Summer Storm. Lionel Pigot Johnson. Those be favourable hours/Hymned by Pan beneath the shepherd star. BrPo

Summer Storm. Richard B. Kent. Wielding a mighty hammer/Today. AMV-80

Summer Storm. John Montague. in obedience to/the pull & tug of your great tides. IPY

Summer Storm. Louis Simpson. Now they are married Nature breathes once more. ErPo; OxBC; WeW

Summer Storm. Louis Untermeyer. My eyes were closing and I may have dreamed. UnTE

A Summer Storm. Charles Whitehead. ...and sheds/Her lovely hues upon the flowers' dejected heads. OBRV

The Summer Story. John Lehmann. The dark Lieutenant from the sea. MP

Summer Street. Ana Ilce. And the stones. AMV-81

Summer Sun. Robert Louis Stevenson. The gardener of the World, he goes. MoBrPo

Summer Sunshine. Mary Artemisia ("Aunt Mary") Lathbury. Oh, come again! YeAr

A Summer Twilight. Charles Tennyson Turner. Wheeling the self-same circuit o'er and o'er. OBRV

Summer Visitors. Stephen Clark. I realize my life isn't going to turn out/the way I had planned. AMV-81

Summer Wind. William Cullen Bryant. ...and silver waters break/Into small waves and sparkle as he comes. AP; PoEL 1-5

Summer Wish. Louise Bogan. The stretched hawk fly. AnFE; CoAnAm

A Summer Wish. Christina Georgina Rossetti. I so might rest once more/Cool with refreshing dew. OBNC

A Summer Wooing. Louise Chandler Moulton. Does the free wind care? HBV 1-2

Summer Words for a Sister Addict. Sonia Sanchez. and we all sing. BlSi; BPo; UnPo

Summerhouse. Melvin Walker La Follette. ...the lost/Room is locked, my heart is attuned to frost. NePoEA

Summertime and the Living.... Robert Earl Hayden. with fantasies/of Ethiopia spreading her gorgeous wings. BPo; NCSH; PoBA; PPP; TwCP

The Summing-Up. Stanley Jasspon Kunitz. My sign: Mobility--and damn the cost! ELU; OBAL; PoPl

A Summing Up. Gabriel Preil. a broth of passion and boredom for the world. VWA

The Summing Up. James Simmons. and when those masters stir that slave will jump. PoL

Summing Up in Italy. Elizabeth Barrett Browning. The moral of every great deed is--/The virtue of slandering the doers. VLP

Summit Lake. Mark Thalman. I drop hook and worm, settle back,/wait for the pull. AMV-81

Summoned. Diana O Hehir. I care with my breasts. I care with my belly's blood./Come down. NPGG

Summoned by Bells: Cornwall in Childhood. Sir John Betjeman. Safe Cornish holidays before the storm! FaBoPP; OxBTC

The Summonee's Tale (parody). Stanley J. Sharpless. And this they found the beste game of alle. BXAP; FaBoPa

The Summons. James Dickey. Who summons him forth, and now/Pulls wide the great, thoughtful arrow. LiSp

Summons. Arthur Davison Ficke. But now the curtain lifts:--my soul's swift powers/Rise robed and crowned--for lo! the play is ours HBMV

The Summons. James Laughlin. and is mine/and endures. ExPo

The Summons. Elizabeth Roberts MacDonald. Heart of my heart, Hilaire! CaP

The Summons. W. W. Eustace Ross. Though your sleep be deeper/Than the depth of Night/Waken from your sleep! CaP

Summons for the Undead. Diane Keating. Robins on the roof, sing/Awaken the dead imprisoned in skin. CaPN

Summons to Love. William, of Hawthornden Drummond. And everything, save Her, who all should grace. GTBS

Summum Bonum. Abu-l-Ala al-Maarri. Then every voice of wisdom joins/To bid you leave them in your loins. LiTW

Summum Bonum. Robert Browning. Brightest truth, purest trust in the universe--all/were for me/In the kiss of one girl. ELU; EnLi 1-2; GTBS; HBV 1-2; LiTL; OHFP

Sumo Wrestlers. James Kirkup. Ten tons of rice-balls tumbling/Into a pleased ringside geisha's lap. OBTV

The Sums. Lauris Edmond. the disfigured legs that with a stolid/magnificence used to hold up the world. FaBoWP

Sumter. Henry Howard Brownell. We are all one to-day--/On with the cannon! MC; PAH

Sumter. Edmund Clarence Stedman. How shall Southern men be shriven/For the sin! MC; PAH

Sumter--A Ballad of 1861. Anonymous. "Our soil's redeemed from hateful yoke,/We'll keep it pure or die." PAH

Sumter's Band. J. W. Simmons. Their watchword is thy memory! PAH

The Sun. J. Davis. Will keep revolving in its orbit/Till heat and motion reabsorb it. NA

The Sun. John Drinkwater. ...I said/"I'm happy" to the Sun. NTCP; SoPo; TiPo

The Sun. Andrew Oerke. ...dissolving everything: Time,/Space and Fortune in its ferocious fashion. PoA

Sun. Henry Rowe. Thou, Lord of all within! OBEV

The Sun. Anne Sexton. a thin gray banner. NYBP; PBWP

The Sun. Walter James Turner. Startled to find itself in these dark lands. MoBrPo; NYBP; PBWP

Sun and Cloud. Melville Cane. The gradual shade is drawn. PoPl

Sun and I. Ken Mammone. To see what we have grown. AMV-81

Sun and Moon. Jay Macpherson. Shall the retreat/Of fierce brother from lost sister/End, and they meet. SoSe

The Sun and Moon So High and Bright. *Anonymous.* I'll joy in my salvation's God. AH

The Sun and the Moon and Fear of Loneliness. *Anonymous.* And yet, no more shall I see my uncle,/To whom my mind would fain be revealed. WTO

The Sun and Wind. Owen Felltham. So blowes me cool again. CavP

The Sun-Bather. Kim Kurt. Though gravity-held,/I lie unselved. NePoAm-2

The Sun Came. Etheridge Knight. (Though ain't no vision visited my cell). NeAC; PoBA

The Sun Came Out in April. C. Day-Lewis. Our tree will not light up for him/Another Christmas Day. MoBS

Sun Children. Leslie Marmon Silko. Spring grass/Deer fawn/sun children. VoR

A Sun-Day Hymn. Oliver Wendell Holmes. One holy light, one heavenly flame! AnNE; TrPWD; TRV; WGRP

The Sun-Dial. Thomas Love Peacock. But still flows on the eternal river. ERoP 1-2; OBNC; OBRV

The Sun Drops Red. Nellie Burget Miller. The sun drops red through a curtain of dust. PoOW

The Sun (excerpt). Vidya. an earring for the goddess of the east. PBWP

Sun Filters through My Window. Artie Gold. a yellow angel pedals about the world. CaPN

The Sun God. Aubrey Thomas De Vere. ..;and each passing cloud/Expanded, whitening like the ocean foam. ACP; OBVV

Sun Gonna Shine in My Door Some Day. *Anonymous.* Sun gonna shine in my door some day. OuSiCo

The Sun Has Long Been Set. William Wordsworth. On such a night as this is! YeAr

The Sun Has Set. Emily Bronte. Except the wind that far away/Comes sighing o'er the heathy sea. UnPo; ViBoPo; VLP

A Sun Heals. Johari (Jewel C. Latimore) Amini. control me for/i am and need JB

The Sun in Capricorn. Joyce Mansour. Sweat of taffeta beaches without shelter/Lunacy of my lost flesh. PBWP

Sun in the East. *Anonymous.* His foot is upon my threshold. LiTW

The Sun Men Call It. John Hall Wheelock. Fountain of light, the glory of a star. NePoAm-2

Sun Moon Kelp Flower or Goat. Linda Gregg. with windlessness, empty heat, or the taste of grapes. NPGG

The Sun Now Risen. Johann Conrad Beissel. His presence will my soul sustain/In days of deepest grief and pain. AH

The Sun of Grace. *Anonymous.* When our Lord God boren was/And to the herte stungen. OxBM

The Sun of My Perfection Is a Glass. Samar Attar. Return, and back into your Sun subside. ILwL

Sun of the Center. Robert Kelly. the corn is eaten, the animal howls, the sun flowers. CoPo

Sun of the Sleepless. George Gordon, Lord Byron. Distinct, but distant–clear–but, oh how cold! AtBAP; MOON

The Sun Rises Bright in France. Allan Cunningham. An' there I'll meet ye a' soon/Frae my ain countrie! BSV; HBV 1-2; OBRV

The Sun Rising. John Donne. This bed thy center is, these walls, thy sphere. BiP; BoLiVe; BoLoP; CABA; DiPo; ExPo; FF; GBL; HAP; HeIP; InvP; JCP; LiTB; LiTL; LoBV; NIP; NOBE; NoP; OAEL 1-2; OAEP; PAI; PoPle; PPP; SCV; SeCePo; SeCeV; SoSe; TEP; TrGrPo; UnTE

The Sun's Golden Bowl. Mimnermus. And rushing, rushing onward, gives us the day once/more. LiTW

The Sun's over the Foreyard. Christopher Morley. The yards are so much higher. EtS

The Sun's Shame. Dante Gabriel Rossetti. All soulless now, yet merry with the Spring! MaVP

Sun Set. Umberto Aridjis. I dazzle in blackness AMV-81

The Sun Shines over the Mountain. *Anonymous.* Who-ay hay-ay-hay, for yonder comes my beau. AmFP

Sun Song. Langston Hughes. I bring you my songs/To sing on the Georgia roads. CNA

The Sun Spirit. Ralph Chubb. swimming pupils gazing up seraphical at the azure vault... PeHV

Sun-Up in March. Abbie Huston Evans. ...Oh what/Of a century at one glance? What of that fury? NePoAm

The Sun upon the Weirdlaw Hill. Sir Walter Scott. Were barren as this moorland hill. BSV

The Sun Used to Shine. Edward ("Edward Eastaway") Thomas. Go talking and have easy hours. FaBoTw

The Sun Was Slumbering in the West. Thomas Hood. God bless you, dear, good night! FiBHP

The Sun Wields Mercy. Charles Bukowski. ...must we forever,/dear friends, die in our sleep? MAT

The Sun-Witch to the Sun. George Howe. Thou the bridegroom, I the bride! NYBP

The Sunbather. Vernon Watkins. The beat that consoles them most, his blood. MoPo; MoVE

The Sunbeam. *Anonymous.* "And bring fresh wine for my friend and me." NA

Sunday. Elizabeth Jane Coatsworth. the cats are keeping store! AmFN

Sunday. George Herbert. Till that we both, being toss'd from earth,/Flie hand in hand to heav'n. OBS; SeCV 1-2; TrCP

Sunday. Josephine Miles. Should aid the first created things/To meet upon their day of rest. PoA

Sunday. Lawrence R. Rungren. casting shadows without a sound. AMV-80

Sunday. Vern Rutsala. will anyone wake up today? DFF

Sunday Afternoon. Denise Levertov. ...wearing/other new dresses, of bloodred velvet. ConAP; IHMS

Sunday Afternoon. Philip Levine. the first great movies made flesh. NaP

Sunday Afternoon in Italy. D. H. Lawrence. Wreath and enlap and anoint them/Behind separate doors. BrPo

Sunday Afternoon Service in St. Enodoc Church, Cornwall. Sir John Betjeman. "The Second Evening and the Fourteenth Psalm." MoVE; NOCV

Sunday Afternoons. Anthony Thwaite. Passing the time away/Till the night begins. OxBTC

Sunday at Hampstead, X. James (1834-82) Thomson. For we carry the Heavens with us, Dear,/While the Earth slips from our feet! ViBoPo

Sunday at the End of Summer. Howard Nemerov. Being threshed at hip and thigh, against that trash/Of pale wild flowers and their drifting legs. BoNaP

Sunday at the State Hospital. David Ignatow. and trying with almost no success/to bring the present to its mouth. CAPP

Sunday Bells. William Allingham. Who like an alien sadly dwells/Within your chime, sweet Sunday Bells! IrPN

Sunday Crappies. Jim Thomas. a dripping stringer of night-caught crappies. WOLT

Sunday Evening. Barbara Guest. (as a pulse after the first September earthquake). NeAP

Sunday Evening in the Common. John Hall Wheelock. So tawdry and so dear! HBV 1-2; MoAmPo

Sunday Evenings. John Hollander. ...when the big, enlightening myths/Have sunk beyond the river and we are alone in the dark. NYBP; NYP

Sunday Funnies. Anne Keiter. my father would read on,/while we lay, listening, smiling/on either side. DFF

A Sunday in Cambridge. Eddie Linden. But a shadow hovering in our midst/Prevented a possible communion. PeHV

Sunday in Glastonbury. Robert Bly. Wealth is nothing but lack of people. ConAP

Sunday in South Carolina. Robert Parham. set in a cheap but perfect ring. AMV-80

Sunday in the Country. May Swenson. ...A black and/impudent Voltairean crow has spoiled/the sacrament. And I can rise and go. NePoAm-2

Sunday in the Park. William Carlos Williams. NO DOGS ALLOWED AT LARGE IN THIS PARK CrMA

Sunday, July 14th: A Fine Day at the Baths. Julian Symons. These events are intelligible. Interpret. You cannot enjoy. WaP

Sunday Morning. Judith Fitzgerald. that it blunt the edge of seeing. CaPN

Sunday Morning. James Grahame. His iron-armed hoofs gleam in the morning ray. OBRV

Sunday Morning. Christina Jenkins. Only I have enough insolence for that. BrRo

Sunday Morning. Louis MacNeice. Escape from the weekday time. Which deadens and/endures. CoBMV; FaBoIP; FaBoMo; HeIP; LiTB; MoAB; MoBrPo; MoVE; NIP

Sunday Morning. Wayne Moreland. how I love you for making things in the/morning. PoBA

Sunday Morning. Isidor Schneider. green fields call us on. AnAmPo

Sunday Morning. Wallace Stevens. Downward to darkness, on extended/wings. AmP; AP; BiP; BLPL; CMoP; CoBMV; CrMA; ForPo; HaCAP; HAP; HeIP; InPo; InPS; LiTA; LiTM; MasP; MoAB; MoAmPo; MoVE; NAWM 1-2; NePA; NIP; NOBA; NoP; OxBA; PPoe; QFR; SeCeV; TAP; WeW

Sunday Morning Apples. Hart Crane. The apples, Bill, the apples! NAMP

Sunday Morning, King's Cambridge. Sir John Betjeman. To praise Eternity contained in Time and coloured glass. BoC; EaLo

Sunday: New Guinea. Karl Shapiro. And your love's presence, snowy, beautiful, and kind. AmFN; PoPl

The Sunday News. Dana Gioia. A scrap I knew I wouldn't read again/Yet couldn't bear to lose. GOYP

Sunday Night in Santa Rosa. Dana Gioia. takes out a box, and peels away his face. GrPl

Sunday Night Walk. Raymond Souster. But then the world is tired, very tired of reality. CaP

Sunday on Hampstead Heath. George Woodcock. When the broken rise and the silent voices speak. NeBP

Sunday: Outskirts of Knoxville, Tennessee. James Agee. God show, God blind these children! ErPo; InPK

Sunday Rain. John Updike. but appears to know/only vertical words. DFF

Sunday Review Section. Baron Wormser. The living succeed, and the dead remain dead. MAYP

A Sunday School Teacher Speaks. *Anonymous.* Will you help him learn to use it/In your home and Sunday school? STF

Sunday Service (parody). Michael Heffernan. The only pontiff is the pontiff of candy bars. BXAP

Sunday Stroll. Michael Pettit. as the sun poured down its benediction. MAYP

Sunday up the River. James (1834-82) Thomson.
  At home, on land, on sea. GTBS
  He reeleth with his own heart,/That great rich Vine. ViBoPo
  O richest day of happy May,/My love will spend with me! ViBoPo
  This maiden is as young and pure and fair/As Eve agaze on Adam sleeping there. OAEP

Sundays. Marieve Rugo. unable to disguise the space between/what is and what should be. AMV-81

Sundays Visiting. Alberto Rios. whispering to fool the wind/which always carries a secret farther. Str

Sundered. John Barford. And the aching pain of that long, long night/Will last till my life is o'er! PeHV

Sundered. Israel Zangwill. Yet between us the Atlantic. TrJP

The Sundew. Algernon Charles Swinburne. O sundew, not remembering her. ELP; NoP; OBNC; VLP

The Sundial. Jane Cooper. Spent with sane joy beyond the bees' numb drone. AmPC

Sundown. Léonie Adams. And matter's sanctified, dipped in a gold stain. AmLP; MoAB; MoAmPo; TrGrPo

Sundown at Darlington 1878. Lance Henson. barking on and on/into the damp/fall wind VoR

The Sundowner. Shaw Neilson. The bunyip paddling in the dark. CBAP; PoAu 1-2

Sunflakes. Frank Asch. I wonder how they'd feel. NTCP

Sunflower. Andre Breton. Andre Breton he said may pass here. LiTW

Sunflower. Rolf Jacobsen. It's not all as evil as you think. NU

The Sunflower. Peter Quennell. To have the mastery? AtBAP

Sunflower. John Updike. ...we find/you wear a girl's/bonnet behind? BoNaP; GrPl

Sunflower Moccasins. Phil George. She changes my moccasins/as she pleases. VoR

Sunflower Rock. Paul Blackburn. feel the whiskey burn. NoAm

Sunflower Sonnet Number One. June Jordan. But don't you be the one to choose me: poor. SM

Sunflower Sonnet Number Two. June Jordan. And there are stars, but none of you, to spare. SM

Sunflower Sutra. Allen Ginsberg. Frisco hilly tincan evening sitdown vision. CoAP; HaCAP; InPS; MAT; NeAP; NOBA

The Sunflower to the Sun. Mary Elizabeth (DeWitt) Stebbins Take root like me, or give me life like thine! AA

Sunflowers. Clinton Scollard. You can hear their golden laughter/All the garden through! HBMV

The Sunflowers. Douglas Stewart. "Give me the knife. They move." BoAV; PoL

Sunflowers and Saturdays. Melba Joyce Boyd. of sunflowers/and saturdays,/yesterday/afternoon. BlSi

Sung on a Sunny Morning. Jean Starr Untermeyer. Keep me free/Eternally/As in this hour. TrPWD

Sunglasses. Tom Clark. Who cry "O Daughter!" ANYP

Sungrazer. Alvin Greenberg. and those orbits to cross again: this one and this one... FAZ

Sunk Lyonesse. Walter De La Mare. Caged in his stone-ribbed side. CoBMV; FaBoCh; LiTM

Sunken Evening. Laurie Lee. The slow night trawls its heavy net/And hauls the clerk to Surbiton. LiTM; NYBP

The Sunken Garden. Walter De La Mare. Stands with bowed and dewy head/That one little leaden Lad. HBMV

Sunken Gold. Eugene Lee-Hamilton. The gleam of irrecoverable gold. EtS; NCEP; NOBV

Sunlight. Joseph Bruchac. bubbling up through the earth all the way from the/other side. AMV-80

Sunlight. Seamus Heaney. And here is love/like a tinsmith's scoop/sunk past its gleam/in the meal-bin. NOBI; NoP

Sunlight and Sea. Alfred Noyes. Give me the sunlight and the sea/And who shall take my heaven from me? MOS

Sunlight in a Cafeteria. Criss E. Cannady. ...promising as the sunlight, carefully/arranged, cutting her right arm in half. PoDr

The Sunlight on the Garden. Louis MacNeice. And grateful too/For sunlight on the garden. BiP; CMoP; CoBMV; EBEV; GTBS-P; HAP; InPS; LiTB; MoPo; MP; NoAm; NOBE; NOBI; NoP; OAEP; OxBI; OxBTC; PPoe; PrIm; TwCP

The Sunlit Vale. Edmund Charles Blunden. That other does not smile. CBEP; MoVE

Sunning. James S. Tippett. But Old Dog happily lay in the sun/Much too lazy to rise and run. GDP; SiSoSe; SUS; TiPo

Sunny. Robert Vander Molen. Itself crumbled and became sand like salt and legends FAZ

Sunny Prestatyn. Philip Larkin. Now Fight Cancer is there. NoAm

Sunrise. Rowena Bastin Bennett. And sprays its gold on every tree. TiPo

Sunrise. Margaret E. Sangster. Thank God for every sunrise/In the circuit of the year. TRV

Sunrise. Jim Tollerud. The hunt for food/Brings glory to the/Warrior of knowledge VoR

Sunrise at Sea. Edwin Atherstone. Soars up! EtS

Sunrise at Sea. Epes Sargent. And every billow was his mirror splendid! EtS

Sunrise at Sea. Algernon Charles Swinburne. With motion as of one God's beating breast. EtS

The Sunrise Call. *Anonymous.* All arise, arise, arise!/Rise! arise, arise! WTO

Sunrise in Summer. John Clare. He turns the morning's earnest gaze away. FaBoPP

Sunrise in the Hills of Satsuma. Mary McNeil Fenollosa. Day has begun. AA

Sunrise on Mansfield Mountain. Alice Brown. And strikes out flame from the adoring hills. HBV 1-2

Sunrise on Rydal Water. John Drinkwater. And day/Comes up on Rydal mere. HBV 1-2; LiTM

Sunrise Sequence. *Anonymous.* Its shady branches spreading... NOAV

The Sunrise to the Poor. Robert Burns Wilson. It is the call to labor,–not to death. AA

Sunrise Trumpets. Joseph Auslander. Of sunrise-trumpets! Up! dawn is javelined! AnAmPo; TrJP

Sunset. Herbert Bashford. It lays a scarlet, outstretched wing. AA

Sunset. Arthur Bayldon. Reluctantly surrender every height. PoAu 1-2

Sunset. Hayim Nahman Bialik. As lost ones seek what's lost for/ever,/At some world's end. TrJP

The Sunset. Gelett Burgess. It should be better bred. FaBoNo; HBVY

A Sunset. Samuel Taylor Coleridge. And deep the cavern of the fountain mutters. ERoP 1-2; OBSP

Sunset. Edward Estlin Cummings. with/dream/-S. MoAmPo

Sunset. David Allan Evans. ...when it/met the silent current/burst into applause PPJ

Sunset. Mafika Pascal Gwala. fragments of cloudlets break/into light rain. WhB

A Sunset. Victor Hugo. If winter hue them like a pall, or if the summer night/Fantasy them starry brede. AWP

A Sunset. Robert Loveman. And, lo! her blushes crimson all the/west. AA

Sunset. William Julius Mickle. Glide on, and holy Peace assumes her woodland sway. OBEC

Sunset. John Montague. a redgold salmon/flowed into her/at full of evening. FaBoIP

Sunset after Rain. William Stanley Merwin. The darkness is cold/because the stars do not believe in each other PoA

A Sunset at Les Eboulements. Archibald Lampman. And the long line of golden villages. OBCV

The Sunset City. Henry Sylvester Cornwell. The silvery curtain is drawn, and he sees/The beautiful city no more! HBV 1-2

Sunset Horn. Myron O'Higgins. And borrow ransom from this bowel of violence. AmNP; PoNe

Sunset in the Sea. Tom (Thomas Hood, Jr.) Hood. Mixed with Soda's carbonate... FaBoNo

A Sunset of the City. Gwendolyn Brooks. Somebody muffed it? Somebody wanted to joke. FaBoWP; PBWP

Sunset over the Aegean. George Gordon, Lord Byron. Behind his Delphian rock he sinks to sleep. OBNC

Sunset Song. *Anonymous.* We thank thee for this day. WTO

Sunset Wings. Dante Gabriel Rossetti. And Sorrow fold such pinions on the heart/As will not fly away? FM; HBV 1-2

Sunsets. Carl Sandburg. ...And here sleep/Tosses a little with dreams. MoAmPo

The Sunshade. Thomas Hardy. The vain things thought when she flourished this? OxBTC

Sunshine and Music. *Anonymous.* A laugh is just like music/For making living sweet. PoToHe

The Sunshine of Paradise Alley. Walter H. Ford. She is the Sunshine of Paradise Alley. FSN

The Sunshine of the Gods (excerpt). Bayard Taylor. But give to the haughtiest question,/Smiling, a sweet reply. AA

The Sunshine of Thine Eyes. George Parsons Lathrop. I could turn to gold for thee. AA

A Sunshiny Shower. Anonymous. Won't last half an hour. FaBoBe; HBV 1-2; OxNR

Sunstrike. Douglas Livingstone. ...the choir/of assembled carrion crows. PeSA

Sunt Leones. Stevie Smith. And so our debt to Lionhood must never be forgotten. SBG

Sunthin' in the Pastoral Line. James Russell Lowell. An' give me sech a startle thet I woke. AP

Super Flumina Babylonis. Algernon Charles Swinburne. That the waters of Babylon should no longer flow,/And men see light. AnFE; MaVP; OBVV; PoEL 1-5; VLP

Superballs. Tom Clark. You replace your heart in your breast and go on your way ANYP; EAS

Superbull. Harold Witt. and robbed of his real function, like some men. FAZ

The Superfluous Saddle. Jean de La Fontaine. And him who saddled it, were both in Hell! UnTE

Superior Nonsense Verses. Anonymous. And in gray evening's emerald sea/The beauteous Star of Love is born. NA

Superman. John Updike. Super-super-superwho? LiSp

Supermarket. Felice Holman. and squashed the Chocolate Dreams. QQQ

A Supermarket in California. Allen Ginsberg. ...and stood watching/the boat disappear on the black waters of Lethe? AmPP; CoAP; ConAP; HaCAP; HAP; HeIP; InPS; LiTM; NaP; NeAP; NOBA; PoM; PrIm; SOTW; TAP; TwCP; UnPo

Supersensual. Evelyn Underhill. Because the King of Life is entered in. WGRP

Superstition. Minji Karibo. I know it–Yes I know it! WPOW

The Superstitious Ghost. Arthur Guiterman. And then–Oh, then I'll be one! ShM

Supervising Examinations. Sean Lucy. The river creeps, choked with weeds, through the lower/grounds. CIP

Supper. Walter De La Mare. Seemed as I dreamed the only things/That had ever stirred. NYBP

Supper. William Soutar. And be guid to beggar-bodies/When they come to your yett. OxBS

The Supper after the Last. Galway Kinnell. ...I breed the shape of your grave in the dirt. NOBA; PoCh

Supper Is Na Ready. Anonymous. But supper is na ready./Fal, lal, etc. GBP

Suppertime. Robert Burns. "My noble lord, just as ye please./But supper is na ready." UnTE

A Supplement. Benjamin Tompson. If these essayes shall raise some quainter pens/Twil to the Writer make a rich amends. SCAP

Suppliant. Florence Earle Coates. Reject me not! TrPWD

The Suppliant. Georgia Douglas Johnson. The strong demand, contend, prevail; the beggar is a fool! BALP; CDC; PoBA; PoNe

Suppliant. Alan Sullivan. That move unvexed to their mysterious end. CaP

A Supplication. Nicholas Breton. That Phillida with Love's content/Is sworn the shepherds' queen. OBSC

Supplication. Joseph Seamon, Jr Cotter. That I must journey on. BANP; CDC; PoNe

Supplication. Josephine Johnson. Holding them not in vain! TrPWD

Supplication. Edgar Lee Masters. To leave Thy own for long in hell–/Have mercy, Lord! TrCP; TrPWD

Supplication. Edith Lovejoy Pierce. For this I pray. For this alone I pray. TrPWD

Supplication. Louis Untermeyer. Turn away your eyes! HBMV

Supplication of the Black Aberdeen. Rudyard Kipling. That Cat awaits the Judgment. May I go? BLPA

Support Your Local Police Dog. Carter Revard. Or maybe, manager for some liquor chain. VoR

Suppose. Anne Reeve Aldrich. Smooth-visaged, while a seeming prude/Was marked for life. HBV 1-2

Suppose. Phoebe Cary. To do the best you can? BLPA; BLPL

Suppose... Lewis B. Horne. ...keys upon/which fingers recapitulate and learn. AMV-81

Suppose a Man. R. T. Smith. and will you testify? WOLT

Suppose in Perfect Reason. Howard Griffin. Recall the finished dead. CrMA

Suppose That Chris: Had Not Been Born. Martha Snell Nicholson. "Thanks be unto God for His unspeakable gift!" BePJ

Suppose This Moment Some Stupendous Question. Alden Nowlan. with every light gone out, the door blown open. NOBC

Suppose You Met a Witch (excerpt). Ian Serraillier. Yet there are witless folk will say/they don't exist. WSC

Supposed Confessions of a Second-Rate Sensitive Mind. Alfred, Lord Tennyson. O damned vacillating state! VLP

Suppositions. Margherita Faulkner. ...hold them gently/in the softness of my jaws. AMV-80

Supremacy. Edwin Arlington Robinson. I heard the dead men singing in the sun. NoAm

The Supremacy of Bacteria. Robert Frazier. To explore lunar dust and Martian clays/For their most distant of cousins. SUW

Supreme Death. Douglas Dunn. Too late, all the dead in the river are my friends. FaBoMo

Supreme Fiction. Howard Winn. Death would have been only/an abstraction,/evil only a rhyme. SOTS

Supreme Fortune Falls Soonest. Robert Herrick. The fattest ox the first must bleed. CaPo

The Supreme Sacrifice. John Stanhope Arkwright. In glorious hope their proud sorrowing Land/Commits her children to Thy gracious hand. WGRP

The Supreme Sacrifice. Furnley Maurice. I shall not know the sun is there/When next I see the sun. CBAP

Supreme Surrender. Dante Gabriel Rossetti. Lies the queen-heart in sovereign overthrow. MaVP

Sur le Pont d'Avignon. Anonymous. Then again bow that way. FSW

Sur Ma Guzzla Gracile. Wallace Stevens.
  And there I found myself more truly and more strange. PoA
  For answer from their icy Elysee. PoA
  Than mute bare splendors of the sun and moon. PoA

Surabaja. Bill Berkson. Later history will praise you/for being succinct. ANYP

Surcease. Patrick Lane. I could break so easily. NeAC

Sure a Poor Man. Anonymous. Just go on being a poor man. WTO

A Sure Sign. Nancy Byrd Turner. Someone's sent a valentine! SoPo; TiPo

Sure, There's a Tie of Bodies! Henry Vaughan. Because Incertainties we cannot know/Be sure, not to believe. NCEP

Sure You Can Ask Me a Personal Question. Diane Burns. This is my face. STE

Surely My Soul... Jacob Cohen. The mist looms and shines. TrJP

Surely You Remember. Dahlia Ravikovich. Sun and moon, winter and summer/come to you,/infinite treasures. VWA

Surf. Lillian Morrison. arms outstretched/foam fingers/reaching. NTCP

Surf-Casting. William Stanley Merwin. and the next night you will come back/to fish for the Hand NOBA

Surfaces. David Madden. Mystery is simply/a manipulation/of surfaces. AMV-80

Surfaces. Jane Mayhall. ...until darkness quenched/the vision, the traffic wild and stilled. NYP

Surfaces. Peter Meinke. if a cloud floated over it/I would hate the sky Str

Surfers at Santa Cruz. Paul Goodman. already sleek with narrow eyes. FF; LiSp

Surgeons Must Be Very Careful. Emily Dickinson. Stirs the culprit,–Life! CBEP; DiPo; ImOP; TAP

Surgery. Carol Burbank. And holds back, holds back, like a closed church door. SUW

Surgical Ward: Men. Robert Graves. Pain, that unpurposed, matchless elemental/Stronger than fear or grief, stranger than, love. FaBoMo

Surnames to Be Avoided in Marriage. Anonymous. Is a change for the worse, and not for the better. FaBoUs

The Surprise. Anonymous. This luck is something all of us must share. UnTE

Surprise. Harry Behn. All Plunky answered him was, Yes. BiCB; TiPo

Surprise. Anthony Cronin. Although we say I love you no one cares. CIP

Surprise. Harold Witt. and then the awful, truthful catching up. AMV-81

The Surprise at Ticonderoga. Mary A. P. Stansbury. Shine the names of Ethan Allen and his bold volunteers! MC; PAH

Surprised by Evening. Robert Bly. And our skin shall see far off, as it does under water. CAPP; NaP; VGW

Surprised by Me. Walter Darring. The arms of the outspread East/Receive/What I must give and give. NYBP

Surprises. Anonymous. Doubtless there'll be many/Surprised to see you there. STF

Surprises. Jean Conder Soule. I LIKE/SURPRISES! BiCB

The Surprising History of Aiken Drum. Anonymous. And his name was Aiken Drum. OxNR

Surrealism in the Middle Ages. Philip Lamantia. pulverable dunes of the Least Sandpiper. APU

Surrender. Amelia Josephine Burr. I am all yours. HBV 1-2

Surrender. Angelina Weld Grimke. We ask for peace. CDC

Surrender. Ruth Guthrie Harding. Once will I share thine ecstasy/With thee, O Death! HBMV

The Surrender. Henry, Bishop of Chichester King. As the divorc'd soul from her body parts. EBEV; TrGrPo

The Surrender at Appomattox. Herman Melville. All human tribes glad token see/In the close of the wars of Grant and/Lee. MC; PAH

The Surrender of Cornwallis. *Anonymous.* And with the arms of freedom cause the/wars they are all o'er. PAH

The Surrender of New Orleans. Marion Manville. A glory for one is another's Lost Cause. PAH

The Surrender of Spain. John Milton Hay. King over men who have learned all that it/costs to be free. AA

Surrender to Christ. Frederic William Henry Myers. Leap from the universe and plunge in Thee! OxBoCh

Sursum. Guillermo Valencia. And gaze on God, into His azure eyes CAW

Survey. Paul Lawson. or because we have fallen so far. GP

Survey of Cornwall. Richard Carew. Nor hills a bar; whereso he stray'th/Ensue loss, terror, ruin, death. FaBoPP

Survey of Literature. John Crowe Ransom. No belly and no bowels,/Only consonants and vowels. FaBoCh; LiTA; LoGBV; MP; NLV; OBAL; TAP; TwCP; VGW

A Survey of the Amphitheatre. Moses Browne. Who ne'er in those encounters fight/To die–but get their living by't. NOEC

Survey Our Progress from Our Birth. John Webster. As shadows wait upon the sun. LO

Surveyor. Guy Butler. The Commies are using it now. PeSA

Surview. Thomas Hardy. And my voice ceased talking to me. ChMP

The Survival. Edmund Charles Blunden. And even the dream's confusion can/Sustain to-morrow's road. OBEV; OBMV

Survival. Florence Earle Coates.
Still raised her yearning vision to the stars. AA
The winged Victory of Samothrace. AA

Survival in a Stone Maze. George Rachow. Now you bleed the desire to tear this maze down/and these segments of rock you know/own you. LFAC

Survival Kit. Robert Slater. These veins/And those latitudes. FAZ

The Survival of the Fittest. Sarah N. Cleghorn. So Booth of Lincoln thought: and so the High/Priests let Barabbas live, and Jesus die. HBMV

Survival This Way. Simon J. Ortiz. ..."We shall survive/this way." CDW; STE

Surviving. James Welch. ...To stay alive this way, it's hard.... CDW; STE

Surviving a Poetry Circuit. William Stafford. lest moss take all our names when Old Mortality's gone. FAZ

The Survivor. Robert Graves. Whispering in the dark: 'for ever and ever"? CMoP; MoVE

Survivor. Archibald MacLeish. I pull my pillow over my ear/but I hear. NCSH; PrIm

Survivor. Judy Dothard Simmons. no longer frightened because they don't care CNA

The Survivor. R. S. Thomas. From hard hearts huge tears are wrung. FaBoTw

Survivors. Elaine Feinstein. ...after so many lessons/to laugh in garrulous Sabbath on this pavement? VWA

The Survivors. S.S. Gardons. Nothing is different here. AmPC

The Survivors. Daryl Hine. Brightly shine our neighbours, Venus, Mars. TwCP

Survivors. Michael Hogan. gathering strength for flight. FAZ

Survivors. Mordecai Marcus. or a clean good-bye/to what can't be helped. AMV-81

The Survivors. Adrienne Rich. What else could we, what else could you, have done? NYBP

The Survivors. Robert Slater. We who in the beginning/were such an influence/are left to mind the fences. FAZ

The Survivors. Miriam Waddington. ...we move/to ancient Jewish law and strict command. VWA

Susan. *Anonymous.* And he said to Susan, "My dear, what next?" NA

Susan. Robin Magowan. In the sun of your white & laughing face. EAS

Susan to Diana. Frances Cornford. Your youth is like a water-wetted stone,/Bright with a beauty that is not its own. MoVE

Susan Van Dusan. *Anonymous.* That sticks to my bosom/Like you? ABF

Susanna and the Elders. Adelaide Crapsey. "For that/She is beautiful, delicate;/Therefore." AnAmPo

Susanna and the Elders. Jack Gilbert. And, sometimes, leaves. NPGG

Susannah and the Elders. *Anonymous.* Had the Elders been sprightly and able. ALV; OLR

Susannah Prout. Walter De la Mare. But for one hour/Come back to me. FaBoEE

The Susceptible Chancellor. Sir William Schwenck Gilbert. A highly susceptible Chancellor! ALV

Sushi-Okashi and Green Tea with Mitsu Yashima. Al Robles. in the spring rain. BrSi

Susiana. *Anonymous.* Away right over the mountain! ShS

Susie Asado. Gertrude Stein. Sweet sweet sweet sweet sweet tea. SOTW; TAP

Suspended Moment. Mariana B. Davenport. Suddenly into the arc a hummingbird flew/Miniature bird and bow–and the moment gone. GoYe

Suspense. D. H. Lawrence. To the lode of her agony. MoBrPo

Suspira. *Anonymous.* For where I am would I not be,/And where I would be I can not. OBEV

Suspiria. Henry Wadsworth Longfellow. And trails its blossoms in the dust! ViBoPo

The Suspition upon His Over-Much Familiarity with a Gentlewoman. Robert Herrick. ...:So live you free/From Fames black lips, as you from me. CavP

Sussyissfriin. Philip Dow. Persephoneous lutes/to be redeemed,/to swell the spring. NPGG

Sutcliffe and Whitby. William Logan. ...not/the sea exposing its fragile negatives. MAYP

Sutra Blues or, This Pain Is Bliss. Jody Aliesan. and we both know release from pain/comes from/letting/go. LTB

The Suttee. Thomas Skinner. Betrothed in life, in death to be allied. OBTV

Sutter's Fort, Sacramento. Lucius Harwood Foote. Dust and ashes and nothing more! BPAW

Suzanne Takes You Down. Leonard Cohen. because she's touched her perfect body/with her mind. BiP; NIP; NoP

Suzie's Enzyme Poem. Paul Zimmer. All the things that make my cork go pop. PPJ

Suzie's New Dog. John Ciardi. Fang, eh? Well, I must warn my cat. GDP

Suzie Wong Doesn't Live Here. Diane Mei Lin Mark. reaching righteously skyward! BrSi

Swahili Love Song. *Anonymous.* ...you would have known/if I am/the one for you. LLLT

The Swallow. Lucy Aiken. Till vernal gales should gently play/To waft us on our homeward way. OxBChV

The Swallow. Abraham Cowley. Nothing half so good can'st bring,/Though men say, Thou bring'st the Spring. CoBE; FM; PBBP

The Swallow. Thomas Stanley. Who Rodantha driv'st away/From my dreams by break of day. AWP

The Swallow (parody) (excerpt). J. C. Squire. If thou shouldst e'er forsake the spring/I should not wish to live. BXAP

The Swallow's Flight. Louis Levy. It's playing with your thought in/heaven's blue. TrJP

Swallow Song. Marjorie Pickthall. But in the cliff-grass Love builds deep/A place where wandering wings may sleep. CaP

Swallow the Lake. Clarence Major. I could not swallow the lake PoBA

Swallowing. Harold Bond. for the joy of feeling the thing inside. AMV-81

The Swallows. Agathias. That for a little space some wandering dream/May come and lock Rhodanthe's arms about me. LiTW

The Swallows. Patric Dickinson. Here is the place to wake. ChMP

Swallows. Thomas Hornsby Ferril. A treadmill of swallows almost holding their own. RFM

The Swallows: An Elegy. Richard Jago. But ever-smiling Spring, and Pleasure reign. CEP

Swallows over the Camp. Uys Krige. Give her, swallows,/my tenderness. PeSA

Swamp. Roberta Hill. A soft hot star hugged by the sea. VoR

The Swamp Fox. William Gilmore Simms. He fears, and flies from Marion's men. AA; AmePo; BeLS; FaBoBe; MC; PAH

The Swan. Charles Baudelaire. Of captives, vanquished...and of many more. SyP

The Swan. Sir Edmund Gosse. The awakened soul must sail or die. SyP

Swan. Donald Hall. the edges white/and sleek as a swan... LCAP

Swan. D. H. Lawrence. and stamps his black marsh-feet on their white and marshy flesh. CMoP

Swan. Edward Lowbury. For plotting Adam's fall. GTBS-P

The Swan. Jay Macpherson. "I am all that is and was and shall be,/My garment may no man put by." PeCV

The Swan. Stephane Mallarme. Icy cerecloth, exiled and useless Swan. SyP

The Swan. W. R. Rodgers. It held the heavens, shores, waters and all their brood. NeBP; NMP; NoAm

The Swan. Theodore Roethke. Or listen into silence, like a god. VGW

The Swan. Stephen Spender. Her hair that touched the ground, and, shown/Between her Swan's legs, feathers and white down. UnS

Swan and Shadow. John Hollander. sudden dark as/if a swan/sang. NoP; PoA; WeW

The Swan and the Goose. Aesop. And thus we see a proper tune/Is sometimes very opportune. AWP; LiTW; UnS

The Swan Bathing. Ruth Pitter. By him forgotten, and by her remembered. BoAnP; MoBrPo

Sweet 'n Sour.   Genny Lim.   The Chinese know all about/Sweet 'n sour   BrSi

The Sweet o' the Year.   George Meredith.   Welcome in the sweet o' the year.   BoNaP

Sweet Patuni.   Jesse James.   And I done told you two or three times/I don't want no junk   BluL

Sweet Peas.   John Keats.   Slowly across the chequer'd shadows pass.   GN

Sweet Peril.   George Macdonald.   Will be changed by the love into sunshine again.   BLPA; FaBoBe; TreFS

Sweet Pity, Wake.   Anonymous.   Because her glory in my death will die.   EIL

The Sweet, Red Rose.   Mary Mapes Dodge.   And that's what she must do.   BiCB

Sweet Riley.   Anonymous.   Anansi come up an' say, "God! a you love me, so med Stan'-up-stick/loss his t'ousan' pound!"   BaBo

Sweet Rivers of Redeeming Love.   John A. Granade.   Who bought me with his precious blood,/From endless misery.   AH

Sweet Robinette.   Anonymous.   You ne'er saw a girl like my sweet Robinette.   CoMu

Sweet Rosie O'Grady.   Maude Nugent.   I love sweet Rosie O'Grady,/And Rosie O'Grady, loves me.   FSN

Sweet September.   George Arnold.   And promise of exceeding joy hereafter.   GN

Sweet Silence after Bells!   Christopher John Brennan.   sweet silence after bells.   BoAV; NOAV

Sweet Slug-a-Bed.   Anonymous.   But when Myrtilla sleeps till ten,/Aurora steals them back agen.   FaBoCo

Sweet Spring Is Your.   Edward Estlin Cummings.   time for springtime is lovetime/and viva sweet love   NCSH

Sweet Stay-at-Home.   William Henry Davies.   Not for the knowledge in thy mind.   AtBAP; CH; HBMV

Sweet Thing.   Anonymous.   Let's go down to the crawfish hole.   OuSiCo

The Sweet Tooth.   Katharine Pyle.   Less greedy I will be.   BBGG

Sweet Trees Who Shade This Mould.   James Mabbe.   Do not my love detain.   GBL

Sweet Unsure.   Sir Walter Ralegh.   What hap, what heaven, what life, were like to love?   SiPS

Sweet Violets.   Anonymous.   Then may remorse, in pitying of my smart,/Dry up my tears, and dwell within her heart.   EIL; NoP

Sweet Voice of the Garb.   Suibne Geilt.   I hear it with longing/as they cry out the hours.   NOBI

Sweet Was the Song.   Walter Savage Landor.   "Come, let us talk of former days."   ViBoPo

Sweet Was the Song the Virgin Sung.   Anonymous.   And sweetly rocked him on her knee.   NOCV

Sweet Wild April.   William Force Stead.   Sing hi,/Sing hey,/Sing ho!   HBV 1-2; HBVY

Sweet William.   Anonymous.
And Fair Ellen, she died also.   OuSiCo
And out of Lydia Margaret's grave grows a rede, red rose,/Spread over Sweet William's breast.   BaBo
In her true love's arms she fell fast asleep.   OBET

Sweet William and May Marg'ret.   Anonymous   "'Tis time, 'tis time, my dear Marg'ret,/That you were gane awa'."   CH; HBV 1-2

Sweet William's Farewell to Black-Eyed Susan.   John Gay.   "Adieu!" she cries; and waved her lily hand.   BeLS; BoLoP; CEP; NOEC; OBEC

Sweet Willie's Ghost.   Anonymous.
Evanished in a cloud of mist,/And left her all alone.   BuBa
Wan grew her cheeks, she closd her een,/Stretched her soft limbs, and dy'd.   AWP; BaBo; InPo

Sweet William's Ghost (B vers.).   Anonymous.   But if you're dead and gone to hell in hell you must remain.   ViBoFo

Sweet William's Ghost (F version).   Anonymous.   For if ye were laid in your weel made/bed,/Your days will nae be lang.'   ESPB

Sweet Willie.   Anonymous.   And Willy's loos'd her left-foot shee,/And latten his lady lighter be.   OxBB

Sweeter Far Than the Harp, More Gold Than Gold.   Michael (Katherine Bradley and Edith Cooper) Field.   Who, in my youth, loved, as thou must, in vain.   OBMV

Sweetes' Li'l' Feller.   Frank Lebby Stanton.   But he mighty lak' a rose!   FaFP; TreFS

The Sweetest Home.   Anonymous.   And never shall ill befall you!   STF

Sweetest Love, I Do Not Go.   John Donne.   They who one another keep/Alive, ne'er parted be.   BiP; TEP; TreFT; TrGrPo

Sweetest of All.   Anonymous.   But sweeter still two lovers when one mantle covers both.   UnTE

The Sweetest Story Ever Told.   R. M. Stults.   Tell me that you love me,/For that's the sweetest story ever told.   BLSo; FSN; GoTF; TreFS

The Sweetest Thing.   Anonymous.   millions will find you asleep.   TTY

Sweethairt, Rejoice in Mind.   Alexander Montgomerie.   My awn true love she is,/That loves her paramours.   BSV

Sweetheart.   Phil Hey.   ...the shape/you had to leave behind/to grow away from here.   GOYP

A Sweetheart in the Army (A vers.).   Anonymous.   And now she is her rich sailor's wife.   BaBo

A Sweetheart in the Army (B vers.).   Anonymous.   Saying, "Is this my little single soldier,/Returning home to marry me?"   BaBo

Sweetly (My Dearest) I Left Thee Asleep.   John Saffin.   Your Ever loveing friend whilest Hee/Desolved is: or Cease to bee.   SCAP

Sweetness.   Anonymous.   Let me be severed/O Christ, from your sweetness!   BIrV

The Sweetness of Nature.   Anonymous.   Sever me not from Thy sweetness!   KiLC

Sweets That Die.   Langdon Elwyn Mitchell.   That they may have, in sweetly-breathed/air,/Their immortality!   AA

A Swell Idea.   Steve Kowit.   & bury my face in my hands.   APU

Swell My Net Full.   Anonymous   Sole is for Sunday, swell me net full.   OBSS

Swell People.   Carl Sandburg.   And they always say they are well met.   LOW

Swell's Soliloquy.   Anonymous.   Why don't the pawties compwamise?   FiBHP

Swell the Anthem, Raise the Song.   Nathan Strong.   Let us join the choral song,/And the heavenly notes prolong.   AH

The Swerve.   William Stafford.   any light. Oh, any light.   GP; SM

Swet Jesus.   Michael of Kildare.   Fram the schoure of pinis sure/Thou sild him her and thare! Amen.   NOBI

Swete Ihesu King of Blissc.   Anonymous.   And wite hit that hit springe mote.   OxBoCh

Swift.   Thomas Caulfield Irwin.
His horse's trampling echoes now.   BIrV
"Only a woman's hair."   IrPN

The Swift Bullets.   Carolyn Wells.   Gentle Jane felt shooting pains.   ShM

Swift Floods.   Kata S. Petroczi.   Draw them from my heart and from my eyes wipe/My constant flood of tears.   WPOW

Swift's Epitaph.   William Butler Yeats.   World-besotted traveler; he/Served human liberty.   CMoP; NAMP; OBVE

Swimmer.   Gladys Cardiff.   where their voices rise/as smoke from blue mountain.   CDW

Swimmer.   Robert Francis.
...The drowning sea/Is all he has between himself and drowning.   LiSp
...–The swimmer floats, the lover sleeps.   CrMA; DFF; NePoAm

The Swimmer.   Irving Layton.   And the last wave romping in/To throw its boyhood on the marble sand.   PeCV

The Swimmer.   Roden and Wriothesley Berkeley Noel.   Claim her impetuously!   OBVV

The Swimmer.   John Crowe Ransom.   Come to the top, O wicked swimmer!   SD

Swimmer in the Rain.   Robert Wallace.   no one but him.   FiCP; LiSp

The Swimmer of Nemi.   William Sharp.   Curv'd like a flower o'er the waters of Nemi.   SyP

The Swimmer's Moment.   Margaret Avison.   (The silver reaches of the estuary).   NOBC

Swimmers.   Paul D. Shiplett.   and evening/will camouflage the opening/to the bottomless pit.   LFAC

The Swimmers.   Allen Tate.   Though never claimed by us within my hearing.   AP; MoAmPo; MoVE; NOBA; PAI

Swimmers (excerpt).   Louis Untermeyer.   I felt the sea's vain pounding, and I grinned/Knowing I was its master, not its slave.   SD

Swimming by Night.   James Merrill.   ...the spinning globe/You wear, and the star running down his cheek.   NYBP; SM; VGW

Swimming Chenango Lake.   Charles Tomlinson.   The going-elsewhere of ripples incessantly shaping.   FaBoMo; NoAm

Swimming in the Pacific.   Robert Penn Warren.   Like a dream that all years had moved to.   AMV-80

The Swimming Lady.   Anonymous.   We'll both clasp Hands, in Wedlock Bands,/Marry, and to't again.   ErPo; UnTE

The Swimming Lesson.   Robert Hershon.   deep down green/they are told to let go   NeAC

The Swimming Pool.   Jonathan Holden.   all that he'd put into it.   MAYP

Swimming Pool.   Maria Teresa Horta.   enclosed in my/fruit/with breath inside   PBWP

Swinburne at Tea.   Barry Pain.   O hear us, our handmaid unheeding,/And take it away!   HBV 1-2

Swineherd.   Eilean Ni Chuilleanain.   And the apple-blossom is allowed to wither on the bough.'   BIrV; CIP; FaBoWP; WPOW

The Swing.   Robert Louis Stevenson.   Up in the air and down!   FaBoBe; FaFP; GoJo; NTCP; SoPo; SUS; TEP; TiPo; TreF

Swing Low, Sweet Chariot.   Anonymous.   Coming for to carry me home.   AA; ABF; AmFN; BLSo; BoAN 1-2; FSW; GBP; GoSl; LoGBV; UnPo

Swing One, Swing All.   George Bradley.   Avoids his grim act of participation.   AMV-80

A Swing Song. William Allingham. Slow-/slow-/slow-/slow. BrR; MoShBr; SUS

Swinging. *Anonymous.* With a good push-/Over the bowling green. OxNR

The Swiss Peasant. William Wordsworth. Well taught by that to feel his rights, prepar'd/With this "blessings he enjoys to guard." OBEC

The Switch Blade (or, John's Other Wife.). Jonathan Williams. (every man's woman and every/woman's man, said Suetonius NeAP

Switchback. Edith Sitwell. You with your regular,/Meaningless circles are!" PBWP

Switzerland. Matthew Arnold.
Ah, warn some more ambitious heart,/And let the peaceful be! OAEP; VLP
And bade betwixt their shores to be/The unplumb'd, salt, estranging sea. GTBS-P; OAEP; VLP
And Marguerite I shall see no more. MaVP; OAEP; VLP
In the stir of the forces/Whence issued the world. OAEP; VLP
...nor knew, although not less/Alone than thou, their loneliness. OAEP; VLP
Stay with me, Marguerite, still! OAEP
The thirst for peace a raving world/Would never let us satiate here. OAEP; VLP

Switzerland. Alfred Denis Godley. And the true delight of living, as you taste it only there! OBTV

Switzerland. Anthony Thwaite. The nimble piper and the strutting drummer/Putting the valley's herbivores to flight. OBTV

The Sword. Abu Bakr. It would have burned, or rolled/Away, I said.... TTY

A Sword. Karin Boye. a dancing sword of tempered steel. WPOW

The Sword and the Sickle. William Blake. But could not make the sickle yield. BoLiVe

A Sword in a Cloud of Light. Kenneth Rexroth. Who live by killing you and me. NMP

The Sword of Surprise. Gilbert Keith Chesterton. A stranger in the street. MoBrPo; MoRP

The Sword of Tethra. William Larminie. To stiffen through ages of pain/In the rock-rigid realms of death. OnYI

Swordy Well. John Clare. Who finds no reason to be proud at all. WHA

The Sycamore Tree. *Anonymous.* But I've not come to see you hang/Nor hung you shall not be. AmFP

The Sycophantic Fox and the Gullible Raven. Guy Wetmore Carryl. The fox is after dinner, too. AA; AnAmPo; BLPA; CenHV; FaFP; FiBHP; HBV 1-2; InMe; NLV; OBCA; TreFT

(The Syl La Ble Speaks En Erg y/Sound). Carol Lee Sanchez. we speak in/Now. TWSS

Les Sylphides. Louis MacNeice. And where were the white flowers. BoLoP; CoBMV

Sylvae, II (excerpt). Statius Publius Papinius. As he who with a joyous, loving art/Will teach the handsome lad to win your heart. PeHV

Sylvan Delights. Alexander Pope. And all things flourish where you turn your eyes. NOBE

Sylvester's Dying Bed. Langston Hughes. Then everything was darkness/In a great...big...night. NoAm; UnPo

Sylvia. Samuel Croxall. Let who would meet the beauty of the sky. NOEC

Sylvia. Alan Dienstag. The Spasm passed without detection. ErPo

Sylvia. Michael Drayton. These shepherds, and these nymphs do know,/Thy Sylvia is as chaste, as fair. LoBV

Sylvia. Giacomo Leopardi. you had always been pointing to/with such insistence/in the undistinguishable distance. NaP

Sylvia the Fair. John Dryden. And sighing and kissing so close. CBEP; UnTE

Sylvie and Bruno. Lewis (Charles Lutwidge Dodgson) Carroll. "The one thing I regret," he said,/"Is that it cannot speak!" NA

Sylvius, your hands near my mouth are heady flowers. Marguerite Burnat-Provins. ...and drink your life very very slowly, without raising/my head. BoWoP

Sylvoe: A Song. John Dryden. But ah! the Wretch the speechless lyes,/Attends but Death to close his Eyes. CavP

Symbol. David Morton. Comes beautifully back to me/In blossoms, everywhere. HBMV

Symbols. John Richard Moreland. ...a piercing cry/That tears my heart. "Eloi...lama/Sabachthani!" PGD

Symbols. Harry Roskolenko. Symbols, games, radiant, red, blonde, loving-so long ago. FAZ

Symbols. Christina Georgina Rossetti. Who waiteth for thy fruits in vain,/Should also take the rod? VLP

Symbols. Vance Thompson. She leaned her face, her thick hair shut/Her from the stars and trees. AA

Symbols. William Butler Yeats. Beauty and fool together laid. OBMV

Symbolum. Johann Wolfgang von Goethe. a pentagram/cut in packed soil,/the bricks stacked ready. FaBoPV

Symmetrical Poem. Michael Palmer. but the words will fail to come out. NPGG

Symon's Lesson of Wisdom for All Manner of Children... *Anonymous.* And therefore thou must learn fast/If thou wouldst be bishop when he is past. OxBChV

The Sympathizers. Josephine Miles. ...nor whether/To share, or to beware. CrMA

Sympathy. Emily Bronte. Then, journey on, if not elate,/Still never broken-hearted! OAEP

Sympathy. Paul Laurence Dunbar. I know why the caged bird sings! AmNP; CDC; IDB; PoBA; PoNe

Sympathy. Althea Gyles. Who know not any sorrow yet,/Call it the dew. HBV 1-2

Sympathy. Reginald Heber. Till then let us sorrow in company. BeLS

A Sympathy, a Welcome. John Berryman. whose wild bad father loves you well. GrPl; NYBP

Symphony. Alfred Dorn. Air is woven by orchestral looms/into a robe of color, touch and scent. AMV-80

Symphony. Frank Horne. of the symphony/of life? AmNP

The Symphony. Sidney Lanier. Music is Love in search of a word. AP; LiTA; ViBoPo

Symphony: First Movement. John Hall Wheelock. The violins begin their proud complaint/In the desert of the world. UnS

Symphony in Blue. Raymond F. Roseliep. Its torrent is immersing/The blue globe at her feet. ISi

Symphony in Gray Major. Ruben Dario. On the single cord of his violin/A cricket preludes his monotone. LiTW

Symphony in Yellow. Oscar Wilde. And at my feet the pale green Thames/Lies like a rod of rippled jade. FaBoPP; MoBrPo; NOBV; OBSP; SyP

A Symposium: Apples. Linda Pastan. like the skin of the old man/I have become,/from a single/bite. NIP

The Symposium (excerpt). Leah Goldberg. And the close sky spreads out. PBWP

Symptom Recital. Dorothy Parker. I'm due to fall in love again. SBG

Symptoms of Love. Robert Graves. Can you endure such grief/At any hand but hers? BoLoP

Synekdechestai. C. M. Schmid. I weep the dead. GoYe

Synge's Grave. Winifred M. Letts. And rose and took the windswept mountain road. AnIV

Synnove's Song. Bjornstjerne Bjornson. And made the pews go pair and pair/Along the aisle to the choir. LiTW; PoPl

Synthesizing Several Abstruse Concepts with an Experience (parody). Carol Poster. Existence, no doubt, precedes essence, but things/Became worse when the roof caved in. BXAP

The Syrian Lover in Exile Remembers Thee, Light of My Land. Ajan Syrian. Thus the exile lover remembers thee, Makhir Subatu! LiTL

Syringa. John Ashbery. Of what happened so long before that/In some small town, one indifferent summer. HaCAP

Syrinx. James Merrill. Or stop the four winds racing overhead/Nought/Waste/Eased/Sought HaCAP

System. Robert Louis Stevenson. Or else his dear papa is poor. TEP

Systole and Diastole. Conrad Aiken. ...the whisper/Of time to space. CrMA

T

T.A.H. Ambrose Bierce. And, having meanly lived, is grandly dead. AA; AnAmPo; YaD

T. B. Blues. Leadbelly. I want my body buried/In the deep blue sea BluL

T-Bar. P.K. Page. the spastic T-bars pivot and descend. NOBC; OBCV

T-Bone Steak Blues. Yank (James) Rachel. But you gonna want me some of these mornings/and poor James won't have you BluL

The T.E. Lawrence Poems: The Void. Gwendolyn MacEwen. I write this sad, left-handed poem. NOBC

T. R. Donald Hall. Chose to belaurel Robinson instead/Of famous men like Richard Watson Gilder. PoA

T. S. Eliot. W. H. Auden. "What, if you please,/Did you mean by The Mill on the Floss?" OBAL

T. S. Eliot. Robert Lowell. humor and boredom from the everlasting dross! NoAm; NOBA

T.V. (1). Anselm Hollo. the brain which takes that in its stride/is yours & mine & it is late. APU

T.V. (2). Anselm Hollo. then,/more funny nazis! APU

The T.V.A. *Anonymous.* Oh, things are up and comin', God bless the T.V.A. TrAS

Ta Wa Nee. Ronald James Dessus. his flowing mane protecting me always/ta wa nee ta wa nee ta wa nee LFAC

Tabernacle of Peace. Hayim Be'er. for in Salem also is His tabernacle. VWA

A Tabernacle Thought. Israel Zangwill. Only truth it lacks. TrJP

Tabernacles. Gerrit Lansing. god needs body and burns in unjust anger until the man is/faithful and his work be satisfied. CoPo

The Table. Michael Heffernan. ... ourselves arranged,/Oddly, in one room, at a stranger's table. PoA

The Table and the Chair. Edward Lear. Dined and danced upon their heads/Till they toddled to their beds. GoTF; HBVY; SoPo; TreFT

Table-Birds. Kenneth Mackenzie. under the olives, in whose night they sleep. NOAV; PoAu 1-2

Table Graces, or Prayers for Adults: Evening Meal. Anonymous. The bread of life sent down from Heaven. BLRP

Table Graces, or Prayers for Adults: Morning Meal. Anonymous. That each may have a blessing/From Thee to take away. Amen. BLRP

Table Graces, or Prayers for Adults: Noon Meal. Anonymous. These bounties bless and grant that we/May feast in Paradise with Thee. BLRP

Table Graces, or Prayers for Children. Anonymous. And keep us safe, whate'er befall./For Jesus' sake. Amen. BLRP

Table Manners. Gelett Burgess. So that is why I am glad that I/Am not a Goop. Are you? BBGG; OBCA

Table Manners for the Hostess (excerpt). Jean de Meung. And there repugnant it will shine. EnLi 1-2

A Table Richly Spread. John Milton. From their soft wings, and Flora's earliest smells. FaBoCh; LoGBV

Table Rules for Little Folk. Anonymous. And lift my heart to God above/ In praise for all His wondrous love. FaBoUs; OxBChV

Table Talk. William Cowper. I play with syllables, and sport in song. PP

Table Talk. Donald Mattam. After this interlude/He concentrates upon his food. FiBHP

Table Talk. Wallace Stevens. Happens to like is one/Of the ways things happen to fall. NoP

Tableau. Countee Cullen. ...lightning brilliant as a sword/Should blaze the path of thunder. AmFN; BANP; PoBA

Tableau. Judith Wright. We could have been desperate lovers met too late. CBAP

Tableau at Twilight. Ogden Nash. Alone, in the dusk, with the cleaning fluid. FiBHP

Tableau Vivant. Tess Gallagher. ...We leave them calling/after us, Sorry, Sorry, Sorry, and we don't/look back. GeTw

Tablerock. Darryl Wally. and see darkness falling/away from the self. AMV-81

Tables. Naomi Clark. I dream of axes. AMV-80

The Tables Turned. William Wordsworth. Come forth, and bring with you a heart/That watches and receives. CBEP; DiPo; ERoP 1-2; HBV 1-2; MBW 1-2; OAEL 1-2; OAEP; OBRV

Taboo to Boot. Ogden Nash. I bet she scratched/When she was itchy. FiBHP

The Taboo Woman. Anonymous. She is teck'wi:/Taboo. WTO

Tacita. James Benjamin Kenyon. Ne'er flee the hateful spell. AA

Tacking Ship Off Shore. Walter Mitchell. Eight bells have struck, and my watch is/below. AA; EtS; FaBoBe; GN; HBV 1-2

Tact. Harry Graham. As a masterpiece of Tact! ALV

Tact. Paul Pascal. ...Ya/Know what I mean? PV; WeW

Tact. Edwin Arlington Robinson. Alone below the stars. NoAm

Tadlow. Abel Evans. "God bless you, sir!' and lay their rammers by. FaBoCo

Tadoussac. Charles Bancroft. My heart is with them there. BLPA

Tae Titly. Anonymous. Ower the croon,/And awa' wi' it. OxNR

Taedium Vitae. Oscar Wilde. Where my white soul first kissed the mouth of sin. SyP

Taffy. Anonymous. I hung his coat and trousers to roast before a fire. BBGG

Taffy Was a Welshman. Anonymous. I hung his coat and trousers to roast before a fire. GBP; OxNR

Tagus, Fare Well, that Westward with Thy Stremes. Sir Thomas Wyatt. My Kyng, my Contry, alone for whome I lyve,/Of myghty love the winges for this me gyve. AAS

Tahola. Richard Hugo. long ago, riding a crude wave in. WOLT

A Tail of the See. Elizabeth T. Corbett. Say butt won word—"Neigh, let us weight/Until 'tis settled whether." OBCA

The Taill of the Foxe, That Begylit the Wolf... Robert Henryson. Christ keip all Christianis from that wickit well! OxBS

The Tailor. S, (Solomon Rapport) Ansky. No bread to eat! TrJP

Tailor. Eleanor Farjeon. And the knot the parson ties will be a tight, tight, tight one. OxBChV

The Tailor. Patricia Garfinkel. ...the thread rose and floated/through the open window. AMV-80

The Tailor. Joseph Leftwich. And he stitches, until he drops dead at/his work. TrJP

A Tailor Called Sorrow. Betti Alver. and mingled white basting thread/in their hair. BoWoP

Tailor of Bicester. Anonymous. He cannot cut a pair of green/galligaskins,/ If he were to die. OxNR

The Tailor's Wedding. Louis Simpson. Or a pair of scissors. NNaP

The Tailor That Came from Mayo. Denis A. McCarthy. Was the soul of the tailor that came from Mayo. OnYI

The Tain: Before the Last Battle. Anonymous. Woe to Ulster!/Hail men of Ireland!' NOBI

'Tain't Nobody's Business. Frank Stokes. Who in the world I do my business with/Said it ain't nobody's business but mine BluL

The Tain: The Armies Enter Cuailnge. Anonymous. death of kinsmen/ death death!' NOBI

Taisigh Agat Fein Do Phog. Anonymous. I ask no other till then. BIrV

The Taj. H. G. Keene. An aspiration fixed, a sigh made stone. OBTV

Tak for Sidst. Babette Deutsch. Your voice was an omen, an echo. PoA

Tak' Your Auld Cloak about Ye. Anonymous. Then I'll leave aff where I began,/And tak' my auld cloak about me. OxBS

Take a Drink on Me. Anonymous. Oh, Lord, honey, take a drink on me. FSW

Take a Walk around the Corner. Leroy Carr. I just love to hear my/baby call my name BluL

Take a Whiff on Me. Anonymous. An' a Hi, Hi, honey take a *! on me. FSW; NOBA

Take away. Margot Ruddock. Surging, sweetening, shaking,/Lapping. OBMV

Take Back the Heart. Charlotte Allington ("Claribel") Barnard. When on her world-weary pinion,/Flies back my lost love to me. TreFT

Take Back the Virgin Page. Thomas Moore. You still the unseen light/ Guiding my way. HBV 1-2; OBNC

Take Back Your Gold. Louis W. Paitzakow. Make me your wife, that's all I ask of you. FSN; GoTF; TreF

Take down the Fiddle, Karl! Shaw Neilson. ...the work is/all done for the day. CBAP

Take Heart. Edna Dean Proctor. Thy blossoms sleeping, tearful sown,/To greet thee in the immortal year! HBV 1-2

"Take heed betime lest ye be spied." Sir Thomas Wyatt. Therefore take heed! FCP; SiPS

Take Heed of Gazing Overmuch. Thomas Richardson. Becasue that he, sufficiently,/Hath tried the female kind. EIL

Take Home This Heart. John Holmes. And tell you love has led me to this place. LiTL

Take I, 4: II: 58. Philip Whalen. Invisible & in complete control of everything. NeAP

Take It from Me. Kenneth O. Hanson. Nothing like it in the British Museum. CoAP

Take Me Back to Old Montana. Anonymous. Let me die there when I'm old. CoSo

Take Me Out to the Ball Game. Jack Norworth. For it's one two three strikes, you're out/At the old ball game. OBAL

Take My Hand, O Blessed Master. Connie Calenberg. Lead me gently, lead me sweetly/To Thy home. Lead all the way! BePJ

Take My Heart. Saint Augustine. Keep it! for I cannot keep it for Thee. TRV

Take My Life and Let It Be. Frances Ridley Havergal. It shall be Thy royal throne. BLRP; GoTF; TreFT

Take My Song of Love to Heart. Anonymous. Don't pretend, and I won't,/ I ever looked at you before. NOBI

Take Nothing for Granite. Nate Salsbury. When they talk about the ilyoustrated press. InMe

Take Off Your Hat. Anonymous. We mourn for our country. WTO

Take One Home for the Kiddies. Philip Larkin. Mam, we're playing funerals now. ELU; OxBTC

Take the World as It Is (excerpt). Charles Swain. And the wisest and best take the world as it is. PoToHe

Take This Hammer. Anonymous. It hurts my pride. FSW; OuSiCo

Take Thou Our Minds, Dear Lord. William H. Foulkes. We hear, and henceforth heed, thy sovrign call. AH

Take Time to Be Holy. W. D. Longstaff. And, looking to Jesus,/Still trust to His word. BLRP

Take Time to Live. Thomas Curtis Clark. The world has much to give. PoToHe

Take Time to Talk with God. Helen Frazee-Bower. ...Not all our striving/ Can do as much as one small word with/Him. STF

Take Tools Our Strength... Gerald L. Simmons, Jr. We are beautiful,/ Winners. NBP

Take Two-O Coo, Taffy! Anonymous. Take two-o coo, Taffy! PBBP

Take Up the Pen... Anonymous. Our bodies twain shall be as one. WTO

Take Yo' Time, Miss Lucy Long. Anonymous. Take yo' time, Miss Lucy Long. GoSl

Take Your Accusation Back! Kittaararter. That I might know all things. WTO

Take Your Fingers off It. Anonymous. You know it don't belong to you. FSW

The Tapestry Weaver. Anson G. Chester. And God shall give him gold for his hire–not coin, but a crown! BLPA; BLRP; WBLP

Taps. Lizette Woodworth Reese. Sleep shall outlast them all./Sleep. OHIP

Tapwater. Laura Jensen. ...or wake without/breath, or without the familiar town,/or without the others. LCAP

Tar. C. K. Williams. ...every sidewalk on the block/was scribbled with obscenities and hearts. GeTw

Tara. *Anonymous.* He gave not protection to Temair. OnYI

Tara Is Grass. *Anonymous.* And even the English, perchance their hour will come. AnIL; AnIV; PoL

Tarantella. Hilaire Belloc. ...boom/Of the far waterfall like doom. GoBC

Tarantula. Diana O Hehir. In the middle of them/A creature with its terrified/Arms reaching out. NPGG

The Tarantula. Reed Whittemore. Should understand me, little me. My name is William/Too. CoAP

Tarantula or the Dance of Death. Anthony Hecht. That was the black winter when I came/Into my own. CoAP

Tardiness. Gelett Burgess. And she'll say that she's disgusted! BBGG

A Tardy Epithalamium for E. and N. Ralph Pomeroy. Grateful for you/all the same. PeHV

Tardy George. *Anonymous.* What are you waiting for, tardy George? PAH

Target Practice. Donald Finkel. ...the way you/Don't know me, or I know you. NePoEA-2

Tarpauling Jacket. *Anonymous.* Take me up in a tarpauling jacket,/And fiddle and dance to my grave. DTC; OxBoLi

Tarquin and Tullia. Arthur Mainwaring. These shine to aftertimes; each sacred name/Stands still recorded in the books of fame. APAS

Tarras Moon. James Keir Baxter. Moonstruck we staggered there. AnNZ

The Tarry Buccaneer. John Masefield. Like a fine old salt-sea scavenger, like a tarry Buccaneer. MCCG

Tarry Flynn (excerpt). Patrick Kavanagh. And I knew as I entered that I had come/Through fields that were part of no earthly estate. FaBoIP; IPY

Tarry with Me, O My Saviour. Caroline Sprague Smith. ...then awake me,/Morning of eternal rest! AH

Tarry Ye. *Anonymous.* The way to go and guide thee with mine eye. STF

The Tars of the Blanche. *Anonymous.* Drink success to the tars of the Blanche. OBSS

Tartar. Solyman Brown. Where health and purity should ever reign. FaBoUs

Tartary. Walter De La Mare. Her bird-delighting citron-trees/In every purple vale! HBMV; OxBChV

Tashkent Breaks into Blossom. Anna Akhmatova. and the small rolls of bread/in the young hands/of dark-haired mothers. BoWoP

The Task. Robert Bhain Campbell. May give us life before it gives us death. MoPo

The Task. William Cowper.
And find the total of their hopes and fears/Dreams, empty dreams.... CoBE; OAEP
And their inveterate habits, all forbid. TEP
And with Thee rich, take what Thou wilt away. EiCP
As bashful, yet impatient to be seen. CoBE
He seeks them headlong, and is seen no/more. CoBE
His horse and him, unconscious of them all. CoBE
A mutilated structure, soon to fall. FiP
Or all that we have left is empty talk/Of old achievements, and despair of new. OAEP
Proceeding soon a graduated dunce. CoBE
The sacramental host of God's elect. CoBE
...seize at once/The roving thought, and fix it on themselves. EnRP
So let us welcome peaceful ev'ning in. FiP
Then acts in Nature's office, brings to pass/The glad espousals, and ensures the crop. FaBoUs
There least amusement where he found the most. FiP
Thy joys and sorrows, with as true a heart/As any thund'rer there. FiP
A wish for ease and leisure, and ere/long/Found here that leisure and that ease I/wish'd. OAEP

The Task. Ruth Pitter. Was dead and is alive. Amen. MoBrPo

The Task That Is Given to You. Edwin Markham. To see what you do with your chance in the chamber of days. WBLP

Tasmania. Vivian Smith. the hills breathing like a horse's flank/with grasses combed and clean of the last snow. NOAV

Taste. John Updike. ...Go screw, taste–/itself a tasteless suggestion. AMV-81

The Taste of Prayer. Ralph W. Seager. Keep me in hunger through eternity. TrPWD

The Taste of Space. A. J. M. Smith. What a lovely smell, he said, we have here. PV

Tat for Tit. Walter De la Mare. Its wheels in need of grease. FM

Tatiana Kalatschova. William Logan. Quickly, she might say, unless she understands/that silence is itself a measure. SM

Tattle. Godfrey Turner. slippery sloppery, alumny calumny, raggery waggery, uttery/guttery trash! NOBL

Tattoo. Wallace Stevens. And in the edges of the snow. AnFE; APA; LiTA

Tattooed. William Plomer. The rose will die, and a skull/Gives back no caresses. ChMP

The Tattooed Man. Harry Bache Smith. Oh! it's perfectly true you can beat a tattoo,/But you can't beat a tattooed man. InMe

Tattoos. Charles Wright.
And we take it back. We give again... GP
Grains through the hourglass glint and spring. GP
You are him, and think yourself yourself. HaCAP

Taught to Be Polite. Virginia Brady Young. ...A farmer cursed/the mess his body made. AMV-81

Tauhid. Askia Muhammad Toure. in the Whirlwind of our Rising in the West! PoBA

Taunt. *Anonymous.* He can move a big ship–or p'raps win me. WTO

A Tawnymoor. *Anonymous.* Tawny petticoats,/Silver lace. OxNR

The Tax-Gatherer. John Banister Tabb. Have you nothing for me? GN

Tax Return. *Anonymous.* By this you see/I have children three/Depend on me. FaBoUs

Taxes. Don L. Lee. Black taxes,/on everything I do. BOLo

The Taxi. Amy Lowell. To wound myself upon the sharp edges of the night? BoWoP; MoAmPo; PBWP

Taxi Suite: After Anacreon. Lew Welch. When I drive a cab/I end the only lit and waitful thing in miles of/darkened houses. PoM

Taxis. Rachel Field. I wouldn't be a private car/In sober black, would you? SoPo; TiPo

The Taxis. Louis MacNeice. So many people, not to speak of the dog.' FaBoIP; OxBTC

The Tay Bridge Disaster. William McGonagall. The less chance we have of being killed. EvOK; PeD

Taylor's Travels from London to Prague (excerpt). John Taylor. And fill their ears (by word of mouth) with lies. OBTV

The Te Deum. *Anonymous.* We've hop'd in thee–let not our hope be vain. AWP

Te Deum. Gertrude von Le Fort. I will plunge with my song into the sea of Thy glory:/with shouts of joy into the waves of Thy power ILwL

Te Deum. Charles Reznikoff. not for a seat upon the dais/but at the common table. TrJP; VWA

Te Deum Laudamus. *Anonymous.* O Lord, in thee have I trusted; let me never be confounded. WGRP

Te Judice. Frederick George Scott. Thou wilt stand stark and dumb/At the first question asked. PeCV

Te Martyrum Candidatus. Lionel Pigot Johnson. White Horsemen with Christ their Captain: for ever He! ACP; BoC; CAW; HBV 1-2; OBMV; OxBoCh

Tea. Jacqueline Embry. (Poor, dear, fat Jane! And now–poor, dear, fat You!) HBMV; YaD

Tea. Ann Struthers. the sun of ancient dancers in my mouth. AMV-80

De Tea Fabula. Sir Arthur Thomas ("Q") Quiller-Couch. Is our CenHV

Tea for Two. Irving Caesar. Oh, can't you see how happy we will be. BLSo

Tea for Two. Pat Nolan. if I didn't hate gum/I wouldn't need valium. APU

Tea Poems: Afternoon Tea. George Mackay Brown. letters, trips and love in/every circling clay hollow. OxBC

Tea Poems: Chinaman. George Mackay Brown. Birds make all about those sippers and smilers ceremonies of/very sweet sound. OxBC

Tea Poems: Smugglers. George Mackay Brown. Noding but China tea. For silver. Fif box.' OxBC

The Tea Shop. Ezra Pound. She also will turn middle-aged. HeIP

Tea-Time. *Anonymous.* We'll all have tea. OxNR

Teach Us to Mark This, God. Franz Werfel. Death may not on its unmasked slope/Take you without all soul, all hope. TrJP

Teach Us to Serve Thee, Lord. Saint Ignatius Loyola. To labor and not ask for any reward/save that of knowing that we do Thy will. Amen. TRV

The Teacher. Helen Bevington. ...the teacher hides behind his fan. GLGT

Teacher. Sonya Dorman. a streamer of balloons/with faces like American children. GLGT

The Teacher. David Fisher. I hear the frosty clatter of goat hooves. NPGG

The Teacher. Leslie Pinckney Hill. Oh, let the little children see/A teacher leaning hard on Thee. BANP; PoNe; TrPWD

A Teacher. Reed Whittemore.
And g-rrr lumbered off to his eight o'clock/Gladly to teach. NCSH
Lumbered off to his eight o'clock/Gladly to teach– GLGT

The Teacher. Virginia Brady Young. but knows the taste of his meat. GoYe

The Teacher's Dream. William Henry Venable. He murmured, "After many days." BeLS

A Teacher's Prayer. Frances Ridley Havergal. Thy love to tell, Thy praise to show. BLRP; TRV

The Teacher Sees a Boy. Margaret Morningstar. O God, make this lively, mischievous boy/A power for Thee, to Thy heart a joy. STF

A Teacher Taught Me. Anna Walters. cousins and friends/laugh and say– "aye" VoR

The Teacher to Heloise (After Waddell). Daniel Burke. Tragedy as great. AMV-81

Teaching about Arthropods. Miroslav Holub. an absolute poet,/non-segmented,/non-antennated,/eightlegged. SUW

Teaching Poetry. Cyn. Zarco. You feel much better now. BrSi

Teaching Swift to Young Ladies. William Dickey. Safe in a world you do not need to know. PoA

Teaching the Ape to Write Poems. James Tate. Why don't you try writing something? GP

Teaching the Penguins to Fly. Barry Spacks. ...who/brought the revolution/uncramping their lives. GP

Teahouse. Nicholas Rinaldi. His monogram on the silver. AMV-81

The Teak Forest: For This Is Wisdom. Laurence Hope. To have,–to hold,–and,–in time,–let go! PoLf

The Team. Furnley Maurice. In death the whip lies in his sunburnt hands. CBAP

The Teams. Henry Lawson. And the lonely battle won. CBAP; PoAu 1-2

Teamster's Song. Anonymous. I hope I haven't offended you/If I've said anything wrong. TrAS

Teapots and Quails. Edward Lear. Set him a grinning/and see how he grins! GoJo

The Tear. Richard Crashaw. In th'heaven of Mary's eye, a tear. EnLi 1-2; LiTB; MasP; OAEP; SeCP

A Tear. Henry Austin Dobson. Such a clear little jewel! CenHV

Tear. Thomas Kinsella. unless like little Agnes/you vanish with early tears. IPY; NOBI

Tears. Anonymous. While she lies sleeping/Softly, now softly lies/Sleeping. NOBE; OBEV

Tears. Khansa. While pain sits ever closer to my heart. AWP

Tears. Lizette Woodworth Reese. Homer his sight, David his little lad. AA; GoTF; HBV 1-2; HBVY; MCCG; MoAmPo; TreFS; WGRP; WHA

Tears. Edith Sitwell. Hard diamond, infinite sun. CMoP; MoPo

Tears. Edward ("Edward Eastaway") Thomas. And have forgotten since their beauty passed. CBEP; GTBS-P; LiTB; PoPle

Tears. Walt Whitman. ...O then the unloosen'd ocean,/Of tears! tears! tears! AnAmPo; NePA

Tears against the Moon. Thomas Walsh. Tears on my pillow–tears against the moon. CAW

Tears at the Grave of Sir Albertus Morton. Sir Henry Wotton. While on this fluent globe my glasse shall role,/And run the rest of my remaining dust. SeCP

Tears, Flow No More. Edward, Lord Herbert of Cherbury. To dry those tears, and to blow out those fires? AnAnS 2; AtBAP; EIL; OBS; SeCP

Tears for Sale. Leonora Speyer. I sold the tear/That wept for you;/It's a thing that poets do. HBMV

Tears in My Heart That Weeps. Paul Verlaine. Too weary, not to know/Why thou hast all this woe. SyP

Tears in Spring. William Ellery Channing To the Spring that comes and kisses his feet. AA

The Tears of Scotland. Tobias George Smollett. "Mourn, hapless Caledonia, mourn/"Thy banish'd peace, thy laurels torn.' NOEC; OBEC

The Tears of Scotland Written in the Year MDCCXLVI. Tobias Smollett. "Thy banish'd peace, thy laurels torn." CEP

The Tears of the Poplars. Edith Matilda Thomas. Brother beloved, we are thy funeral trees! AA; AnAmPo

Tears of the World. King of Seville, Mu'tamid. A sea-wave full of sand and sound and foam. AWP

The Teasers. William Empson. Leave what you die for and be safe to die. OxBTC

Teasing. Anonymous. "Daddy, you haven't got it right!" OxNR

Teasing. Cecil Mack. Don't be angry, I was only, only teasing you. FSN

The Teasing Lovers. Horace. With all your faults I'd live and die with you,/You old deceiver! UnTE

Teasing Song. Princess Magogo. Little crooked-legs, gwenxe, gwenxe! WTO

Teatime Variations. Peter Titheradge.
And above all we have forgotten that this was supposed to/be/About tea... FaBoPa
And drank Alph's sacred stream like one athirst. FaBoPa
And had another lad concealed/Beneath the tablecloth. FaBoPa
At all events it's very old. FaBoPa
Drink deep and don't dribble for you are drinking my/dreams. FaBoPa
Too soon it will be carried away. FaBoPa

A Technical Supplement. Thomas Kinsella.

–delicate/as a flintflake–the knifed nous... CIP
...tiny crimson jets/poured from it everywhere. Transfused! IPY
When I laugh a black thing hovers. CIP

Technicalities for Jack Spicer. Philip Whalen. You will be known as Lump Skull Buddha! PoM

Technique. Burnham Eaton. some surfaces responded to your touch? GoYe

Technique. Philip Pierson. & eat & drink & wave their hands, clear at the top. AMV-80

The Technique of Laughter. Jascha Kessler. Soon we die, embracing and alone–remember we have/lost nothing. AmPC

The Technique of Love. Jascha Kessler. As if to understand, to accomplish ourselves, or become/happy! AmPC

The Technique of Power. Jascha Kessler. So that, iron ringing in our bones, we shall seem/admirable killers! AmPC

Technique on the Firing Line. Turner Cassity. An aim whose center can be seen no more? PoA

Technologies. George Starbuck. on Commonwealth, on Marlborough. NYBP

Tecumseh. Charles Mair.
And, for my people's welfare, banish love. NOBC
Great Nature's man content with Nature's food. OBCV
Here Peace has let her silvery tresses down,/And falls asleep beside the lapping wave. CaP
In countless myriads stretched for many a league. OBCV
To compass you, and light your souls to death! PeCV

Teddy Bear. A.(lan) A.(lexander) Milne. He's proud of being short and stout. OnUR

Teddy's Wonderings. John Kendrick Bangs. If I shall have the luck to be/The sort of man I like. BiCB

Tee Roo. Anonymous. She can whup out the devil and her husband too. OuSiCo

Tee-Vee Enigma. Selma Raskin. Is the joy of being/Rude to it! QQQ

A Teen-Ager. W. D. Snodgrass. ...Why add my barrel to her notch? TW

Teeth. Susan Griffin. And wipe your feet,/she adds. NPGG

Teeth. Miroslav Holub. Now close your mouths, children, and listen. SUW

The Teeth Mother Naked at Last. Robert Bly.
He is drifting sideways toward the dusty places. GP
...inside the drop of sweat/that falls/from the chin of the Protestant tied in the fire. NNaP

Teevee. Eve Merriam. But the set came suddenly right about,/and so they never did find out. QQQ

Telegram. Dick Lourie. stars beyond mist or through mist NeAC

Telegram. William Wise. But I'd like to get at least a million more! TiPo

Telegram One. Adrian Mitchell. SO UNCOY SOONEST ANDY PV

Telemachus and the Bow. Randall Colaizzi. ...I am another. AMV-81

The Telephone. Hilaire Belloc. ...So the sun/Peoples all heaven, although he be but one. MoVE

The Telephone. Edward Field. For the human voice and the good news of friends PPJ

The Telephone. Robert Frost. "Well, so I came." AnFE; APA; HBV 1-2; SO; SoSe

Telephone. Robin Shectman. ...gathering grasses/in the middle morning. AMV-81

Telephone Arguin' Blues. J. D. (Jelly Jaw) Short. Some woman that I used to have/gonna be my baby some day BluL

Telephone Conversation. Wole Soyinka. ..."Madam," I pleaded, "wouldn't you rather/See for yourself?" SoSe; TTY

Telephone Directory. Harry Crosby. Mad Queen Windmills and Weathervanes . Hurricane . 0164. EAS

Telephone Ghosts. Robert Frazier. with a tongue that is empty and heavy/as a cairn. SUW

Telephone Lineman. Ernest Kroll. And see the figure he is not. AMV-81

The Telephone Operator. Saint Francis of Assisi. like the candle the priest offers/for the sinner humming/in his ear. AMV-80

Telephone Poles. John Updike. These giants are more constant than evergreens/By being never green. FYAP; Psk; SaC

Telephoning It. Murray Edmond. someone is swimming to the surface/of our sleep. OCNZ

The Telescope. J. C. Hall. Oh devious miles/That stretch between! HaMV

Tell All the Truth but Tell It Slant. Emily Dickinson. The Truth must dazzle gradually/Or every man be blind– DiPo; HeIP; LiTA; LiTM; MAmP; NAWM 1-2; NePA; NoAm; NOBA; NoP; PPP; TAP; UnPo

Tell All the World. Harry Kemp. I fear that, otherwise they will not know! HBMV

Tell Forth His Fame. Anonymous. For He hath triumphed gloriously! BePJ

Tell Her So. Anonymous. She is worth her weight in gold/Tell her so! PoToHe

Tell Him So. *Anonymous.* Do not fail to tell men so! BLPA; BLPL; WBLP

Tell Jesus. *Anonymous.* Strength and calm for every crisis/Come–in telling Jesus all. BePJ; STF

Tell Me Again. Nigar Hanim. Tell me again. PBWP

Tell Me, Dearest. John Fletcher. Faith will be,/Never till they both believe. ElL; ViBoPo

Tell Me Man Blues. Henry Sims. I'm going to get me/A khaki suit BluL

Tell Me, My Heart, If This Be Love. George, Lord Lyttelton. Tell me, my heart, if this be love? HBV 1-2

Tell Me News. Sipho Sepamla. Tell me, tell me, sir/has the gruesome sight/of a mangled corpse/not begun to sit on your conscience WhB

Tell Me No More. William, of Hawthornden Drummond. He may, say we, but not well, be a lover. TrGrPo

Tell Me Not Here, It Needs Not Saying. Alfred Edward Housman. Nor ask amid the dews of morning/If they are mine or no. CBEP; CoBMV; ELP; GTBS-P; InPS; LiTM; MoPo; MoVE; NOBE; OAEL 1-2; OBNC; OxBTC; PoPle; SCV

Tell Me Not in Joyous Numbers. Stephen Crane. Dabbling much in rhyme. OBAL

Tell Me Now. Wang Chi. And, at the end, need no Paradise. FaBoCh; LoGBV

Tell Me, O Love. William Hammond. "Actions of women, by affection led,/Must backward, like the sacred tongue, be read." CBEP

Tell Me Pretty Maiden. Owen Hall. Yes, I must love some one, really/And it might as well be you! FSN

Tell Me Some Way. Lizette Woodworth Reese. Living, you break my heart, so would you dead! PG

Tell Me, Tell Me. Marianne Moore. it rescued a reader/from being driven mad by a scold. LiTM; NYBP

Tell Me, Tell Me, Smiling Child. Emily Bronte. A mighty, glorious, dazzling sea,/Stretching into infinity.' LoBV; OAEP; TEP; ViBoPo; VLP

Tell Me What Month Was My Jesus Born in. *Anonymous.* Last month of the year. FSW

Tell Me You Wandering Spirits. *Anonymous.* Fall downe, fall downe, and worship it, for that is shee. OBS

Tell Old Bill. *Anonymous.* This morning, this evening, so soon. FSW

Tell Our Daughters. Besmilr Brigham. big with tenderness IHMS

Tell Them I'm Struggling to Sing with Angels. David Meltzer. are merely metaphors for the void between/one pore & another VWA

Tell Us No More. *Anonymous.* That sang this song of ours/with pistols and grenades. FSW

Tell Us, Ye Servants of the Lord. William Staughton. Pour out with confidence their plaints,/And find celestial rest. AH

Tellers of Tales. Chester Kallman. May please his neighbors round a common fire. DFT

Telling It. Nancy Sullivan. I find what I mean/to tell myself the truth. TAP

Telling My Feelings. Yu Hsuan-chi. Wait for him. Why sweep them now? BoWoP

Telling the Bees. Lizette Woodworth Reese. Telling the bees. AA

Telling the Bees. John Greenleaf Whittier. Mistress Mary is dead and gone! AnNE; AP; AWP; BLPL; HBV 1-2; InPo; LaNeLa; NOBA; NoP; TAP

Telling the Cousins. Les A. Murray. ...But now it would hold even more/people who never in their lives have to know the score. AMV-81

Tellus. William Reed Huntington. Whose tranquil presence shames our dis-/content. AA

Tema con Variazioni. Lewis (Charles Lutwidge Dodgson) Carroll. Whilest one might trace, with half an eye,/The still triumphant carrot through. FaBoNo; SpRo

Temagami. Archibald Lampman. And saw at eve the broken sunset die/In crimson on the silent wilderness. OBCV

The Temeraire. Herman Melville. O, the Temeraire no more! WaaP

Temper. *Anonymous.* I never do a worthy thing, a decent deed or wise. PoToHe

Temper. Rose Fyleman. And now she's ever so good. OxBChV

The Temper. George Herbert. Thy power and love, my love and trust/Make one place ev'ry where. AnAnS 1; AtBAP; MePo; NOCV; OBS; OxBoCh; PoEL 1-5; WHA

The Temper of Aristippus. John Gilbert Cooper. Till time itself shall be no more. PBBP

Temperament. Martial (Marcus Valerius Martialis). There is no living with thee nor without thee. AWP; ELU

The Temperaments. Ezra Pound. He had to be four times cuckold. BoLoP; ErPo; NoAm; NOBA

Temperance. *Anonymous.* Vinum laetificat/Cor hominis. CAW

Temperance and Virginity. John Milton. Till all thy magick structures rear'd so high,/Were shatter'd into heaps o'er thy false head. OBS

The Temperance Billiards Rooms. P. J. Kavanagh. and for all I know men playing billiards temperately in there. OxBTC

Temperance or the Cheap Physitian upon the Translation of Lessius. Richard Crashaw. Hark hither; and thy selfe be HE. SeCV 1-2

Temperance Song. *Anonymous.* For every little boy like me/The temperance pledge should sign. FaBoUs

Temperature. Gerard Malanga. ...they/were neither necessary nor always present. NYBP

The Tempest. *Anonymous.* She rights! she rights! Boys, we're off shore! AmFP

The Tempest. Charles Cotton. And be as merciful as thou art chaste. SeCePo

A Tempest. Emily Dickinson. And peace was Paradise! MCCG

The Tempest. William Shakespeare.
Cry Cock-a-diddle-dow! AnFE; CH
Hark! now I hear them–Ding-dong, bell. BiP; EBEV; ELP; EnLi 1-2; ForPo; GTBS; HAP; HBV 1-2; HeIP; InPS; NoP; OAEP; OBEV; OBSC; OBSP; PAI; PoPle; PoRA; PPoe; SeCePo; SeCeV; TEP; ViBoPo; WHA
I cried to dream again. TrGrPo
...I not doubt/He came alive to land. MOS
That, if I then had wak'd after long sleep,/Will make me sleep again. UnS
Then to sea, boys, and let her go hang! FF; MOS; NOBL; OBSP; ViBoPo
Under the blossom that hangs on the bough. CTC; GTBS; HBV 1-2; HBVY; NLV; NoP; SeCeV; TreFT; ViBoPo; WHA
...We are such stuff/As dreams are made on, and our little life/Is rounded with a sleep. DiPo; FaBV; LiTB; PG; TreF; WHA

The Tempest. William Jay Smith. They might chart out that voyage to a shore/On which with confidence a nation would arise. MoAmPo

The Tempest. Marya Zaturenska. The unleashed tempest shakes the garden walls. BoLiVe; MoAmPo

Temple. John Donne. By miracles exceeding power of man. AnAnS 1; OBS

The Temple. Clifford Dyment. But no answer comes from stoat or bird or hill/Whether it is man's cross to kill, or die. ChMP

The Temple. George Herbert.
May at his perill further go. AnAnS 1
Theirs, who shall hurt themselves or me, refrain. AnAnS 1

The Temple. Josephine Winslow Johnson. –But the marble is not lost! MoRP

The Temple. Gustave Kahn. From the stones of Zion, a thousand temples are rebuilt. VWA

A Temple. Kenneth Patchen. Then the sky filled with tears of blood, and snakes sang. EAS

The Temple. Po Chu-i. Seventy being our span, then thirty years/Of idleness are still left to live. OBMV

The Temple. C. H. Sisson. What does not reply is the answer to prayer. OxBTC

The Temple at Segesta. Raymond Henri. ...in miniature, restages/The Vandal and Saracen outrages. GLGT

The Temple by the Sea. Geoffrey Dutton. Whose slender finger wears the sky for a ring. ACV

Temple Garlands. Agnes Mary Frances (Mme Emile Duclaux) Robinson. The roses of the Past! HBV 1-2

The Temple of Infamy (excerpt). Charles Harpur. To be the first name on his Faction's roll. PoAu 1-2

The Temple of Nature. Erasmus Darwin. And one great Slaughter-house the warring world! FM

The Temple of the Animals. Robert Duncan. Ah, bitterly I recall/the animals of last year. NOBA

Temple of the Muses. Beth Bentley. taut smiles stretched open as a hand. EyDe

The Temple of the Trees. J. D. C. Pellow. When I remember these/Fair sacramental trees! PGD

The Temple of Venus. Soame Jenyns. Let pilot Love the rudder guide,/And steer by Chloe's eyes. NOEC

A Temple to Friendship. Thomas Moore. Who came but for Friendship, and took away Love! BeLS; HBV 1-2

Templeogue. Blanaid Salkeld. Watches the slow, sweet slipping from the unlidded moon. NeIP

Tempora Acta. "Owen Meredith." And each man has, at most, but a noble need. OBVV

Tempora Mutantur. Charles Brasch. It is the physicians' love heals the patient. OCNZ

Tempora Mutantur. James Russell Lowell. And his too early tomb will not be dumb/To point a moral for our youth to come. HAP

Temporal. George Jonas. Which we both thought was yours/A comparatively short time ago. NOBC

Temporary Problems. Larry Rubin. That's very nice. He'll bless our enterprise. AMV-80

Tempt Me No More. C. Day-Lewis. Take it. It is well spent/Easing a savior's birth. AnFE; MoAB; MoBrPo; NAMP; OAEP; OBMV; PoPl

Temptation. William Cowper. Let neither winds nor stromy main,/Force back my shattered bark again. EiCP

Temptation. Robert Herrick. The devil tempts not least. LiTB

Temptation in Harvest. Patrick Kavanagh. I go to follow her who winked at me. FaBoIP

The Temptation of Saint Anthony. Arthur Symons. She smiles, she triumphs; but the Crucified/Falls off into the darkness with a cry. BrPo

The Temptation of Sir Gawain. *Anonymous.* As never he did but that day, to the dark night with bliss. ACP

The Temptations of Saint Anthony. Phyllis McGinley. Wrestling the Devil seemed to be/Quite a relief to Anthony. OBSP

Tempted. Edward Rowland Sill. Or to swear I will keep my soul/Clean for her kiss? AA

Ten Brothers. *Anonymous.* Come and play a little/In the middle of the square. MaC

The Ten Commandments. *Anonymous.*
Bless God for Christ, that kept them all. FaBoUs
These laws, O Lord, write in my heart, that I,/May in thy faithful service live and die. OxBChV

Ten Commandments, Seven Deadly Sins, and Five Wits. *Anonymous.* Rule well v and come to hevyn. FaBoEE

Ten Days Leave. W.D. Snodgrass. ...He wonders when/He'll grow into his sleep so sound again. MoAmPo; Psk; UnPo

Ten Definitions of Poetry. Carl Sandburg. ...leaving those who look through to/guess about what is seen during a moment. MoAmPo

The Ten-Fifteen Community Poems (excerpt). John Knoepfle. if I don't know who I am/the wind does MAT

Ten Little Indian Boys. M. M. Hutchinson. Captured another brave and then there were ten. SoPo

Ten Little Injuns. Septimus Winner. Six little, seven little, eight little,/nine little, ten little Injuns more. OBAL

Ten Little Nigger Boys. *Anonymous.* He got married, and then there were none. OxNR

Ten Poems. Stephen Crane. Roaming through a fenceless world. DBV

Ten Sonnets for Today. Phil Stanway. than still pursue a star as its light dims. AMV-80

Ten Thousand Cattle. Owen Wister. They've rustled my pile, my pile away. BPAW

Ten Thousand God-Damn Cattle. *Anonymous.* Lone man! Lone man!/Dead broke! CoSo

Ten Thousand Miles. *Anonymous.* Be true to me, my own sweetheart,/I'm bound to leave you here. AmFP

Ten Thousand Miles away. *Anonymous.* I'm taking a trip on a Government ship/Ten thousand miles away. FSW

Ten Thousand Miles Away from Home (with music). *Anonymous.* And I tucked my head and cried. AS

Ten Thousand Miles Away (with music). *Anonymous.* For I'm on the road to my own true love, ten thousand miles away! AS

Ten Thousand Miles From Home. *Anonymous.* On the Pennsylvania line! ABF

Ten Thousand Times Ten Thousand. Henry Alford. Thou Prince and Saviour, come. Amen. VLP

Ten Types of Hospital Visitor. Charles Causley. The tenth visitor/Is not usually named. OxBC

Ten Week Wife. Rhoda Donovan. growing smug, feeling like/a balloon in a world with no pins. Str

Ten Years and More. Miriam Waddington. and I was asking him/to forgive me too. NOBC

The Tenancy. Mary Gilmore. I shall pay no rust as rent/For the house that is mine. BoAV; CBAP; PoAu 1-2

Tenant at Number 9. John Blight. ...filling the room/like a flood and flushing me out. CBAP

Tenant Farmer. Robert Ward. He sleeps late, days before Christmas. AMV-81

Tenantry. George Scarbrough. For a little while. TAT

Tenants. Wilfred Wilson Gibson. The ghosts of lovers, who had lived and died/Within its walls, were sleeping in our bed. HBV 1-2

Tender Buttons: Objects. Gertrude Stein. Water astonishing and difficult altogether makes a meadow and a/stroke. PBWP

Tender, Slow. Wallace Rice. Who would not have it so? ErPo

Tending. Paula Rankin. The possibility alone keeps me reaching. AMV-81

Tenebrae. Paul Celan. Pray, Lord./We are near. VWA

Tenebrae. Austin Clarke. Darkness that man must dread at last. AnIL; BIrV; CIP; IPY; NeIP; NOBI

Tenebrae. Denise Levertov. ...They are/not listening, not listening. NoP

Tenebris. Angelina Weld Grimke. Is it a black hand,/Or is it a shadow? CDC; PoBA; PoNe

Tenebris Interlucentem. James Elroy Flecker. And someone there stole forth a hand/To draw a brother to his side. CBEP; MoBrPo

Tenement Room: Chicago. Frank Marshall Davis. The room sleeps dreamlessly... GoSl

Teneriffe (excerpt). Frederic William Henry Myers. Illumined Heaven, eternal Sea. OBVV

Tennesse Crickets. Randolph Outlaw. Therefore, I agree/night in the south/is different from the north/but silent/no. LFAC

Tennessee. *Anonymous.* Shoo, old lady, shoo, my love,/And I'm going to Tennessce. AmFP

Tennessee. Virginia Frazer Boyle. And the listening heart of the great world hears/The Paeans of Tennessee. PAH

Tennessee. Francis Brooks. In Tennessee. AA

Tennis. Margaret Avison. ...the pair/Score liquid Euclids in foolscaps of air. NoAm; PeCV

Tennis. Nina Nyhart. ...as if I loved games. AMV-81

The Tennis Court Oath. John Ashbery. lilacs blowing across his face .glad he brought you NoAm; TAP

Tennis in San Juan. Reuel Denney. So many ways they say death,/Up in the tennis tree, co-ki. SD

Tennis Pro. Lawrence Jay Dessner. A backhand explodes/Like a cloudburst. AMV-81

Tennyson. Thomas Bailey Aldrich. :it may chance that he/Will find no gift, where reverence is, unmeet. AA

Tennyson. Alan Ansen. Help us to break like oaks in the soughing bacterial wind. CoAP

Tennyson. Florence Earle Coates. At rest in all the best that love could give! AA

Tennyson. Thomas Henry Huxley. And whisper softly: All must fall asleep. HBV 1-2

Tennyson. Henry Van Dyke. Silence here–but, far beyond us, many/voices crying, Hail! AA

Tennyson at Tea. Barry Pain. O Hallelujah!...Kindly pass the milk. HBV 1-2

Tenson. Iselda Carenza. Beseech the glorious one/To keep me near you/At the Judgement. WPOW

Tentative Description of a Dinner to Promote the Impeachment... Lawrence Ferlinghetti. The President himself came in/Took one look around and said/We Resign. CoPo

Tenth Elegy. Elegy in Joy. Muriel Rukeyser. ...One life, or the faring stars. MiAP

Tenth Reunion. Edward Steese. And scorn the world's abuse–/As they dare not. GoYe

Tenth Symphony. John Ashbery. Hope to have more to tell you about/The latter in the foreseeable future. NOBA

Tenting on the Old Camp Ground. Walter Kittredge. Tenting on the old camp ground. FSW; PSoN

Tenuous and Precarious. Stevie Smith. One Roman,/Finis. FaBoNo; OxBTC

Tequila. Elizabeth Spires. ...so the regulars can make up/my story: Gone to find Tequila– MAYP

Terce. James McMichael. The air and the water go their ways. PoA

Tercets. Llywarch Hen. Without its genius, each exploit falls short. LiTW

Terence MacSwiney. George William Russell. Farewell, lightbringer, fly to thy heaven again! AnIV

Terence McDiddler. *Anonymous.* Can charm, if you please,/The fish from the seas. OxNR

Terenure. Blanaid Salkeld. I, solitary as one old horse, was standing/Alone in the meadows. NeIP

Teresa of Avila. Elizabeth Jennings. ...And the silences suffered no/shadows. NePoEA-2

The Teresian Contemplative. Robert Hugh Benson. And, one with Jesus, thirsts again. ACP; CAW

Teresina's Face. Margaret Widdemer. The patient, painted face of her, the little Tercsina,/With its cowed, all-knowing eyes! HBMV

Terly Terlow. *Anonymous.* The which was never defiled./Terly terlow. AtBAP; CBEP

The Term. William Carlos Williams. with the wind over/and over to be as/it was before. InvP; LiTA

The Term of Death. Sarah Piatt. The worm and butterfly–it is not long! AA

Terminal. Karl Shapiro. Distance is dead and light can only die. AmLP

Terminal Theater. Robert Sward. What is real? cried the oyster, glob of spit/In a pane of glass. CoPo

Terminal Version. Diana O Hehir. The clear blue California sun surrounds us. NPGG

Terminus. Ralph Waldo Emerson And every wave is charmed. AA; AmePo; AmPP; AnNE; AP; AWP; FPL; HBV 1-2; InPo; NOBA; OxBA; PoEL 1-5; PoLf; TAP

The Termite. Ogden Nash. And that is why your Cousin May/Fell through the parlor floor today. CenHV; NLV; OBCA; PoPl; ShM

Termites. Charles G. Bell. From this hot land where breeding is a curse? NePoAm-2

Termites. Eric Chock. picking off stragglers/with the garden hose. BrSi

A Ternarie of Littles, Upon a Pipkin of Jelly Sent to a Lady. Robert Herrick. This little Pipkin fits this little Jelly. ALV; FaBoCh; FaBoUs; GoJo; HBV 1-2; HBVY; LoGBV; PoEL 1-5; PoRA

Ternissa! You Are Fled.   Walter Savage Landor.   And your cool palm smoothes down stern Pluto's cheek.   ExPo; LoBV; NOBE; OBNC; PoEL 1-5; SeCeV

Terra Australis.   James Philip McAuley.   Stand the ecstatic solitary pyres/ Of unknown lovers, featureless with flame.   NOAV

Terra Australis.   Douglas Stewart.   And west went Captain Quiros, east went Lane.   NOAV

Terra Cotta.   K. Curtis Lyle.   ...a minuscule crack/in the great black wall/of the universe   CNA

The Terrace.   Richard Wilbur.   And we were the only part of the night that we/Couldn't believe.   MiAP

The Terrace in the Snow.   Su Tung-P'o.   The icicles on the eaves/Drone in the wind like the swords/Of murderers.   NaP

Terrain.   Archie Randolph Ammons.   ...the moon comes: terrain   ConAP

Terrapin War.   *Anonymous.*   And drive them headlong in the waters/Oh, this is great Terrapin war!   PAH

Terraplane Blues.   Robert Johnson.   And when I mash down on your little starter,/then your spark plug would give me fire   BluL

A Terre.   Wilfred Owen.   To do without what blood remained these wounds.   LiTM; MMM; OxBTC; WaP

Terre Promise.   Ernest Christopher Dowson.   But droop into mine arms, and understand!   NOBV

A Terrestrial Cuckoo.   Frank O'Hara.   go back when you're rich, behung with lice!   SOTW

Terrible Beauty.   Kingsley Amis.   When Dai touched Gwyneth up with his gloves on.   ErPo; NePoEA-2; PV

The Terrible Dead.   Mary Carolyn Davies.   We pity; we should dread/The terrible dead....   HBMV

The Terrible Door.   Harold Monro.   Who waits, at the terrible door, but I?   BoLoP; EnLoPo; FaBoTw

A Terrible Infant.   Frederick Locker-Lampson.   –And that's my earliest recollection.   ALV; FiBHP; GoTF; HBV 1-2; InMe; NOBV; TreFS

The Terrible People.   Ogden Nash.   Have you ever tried to buy them without money?   NePA; TAP

The Terrible Robber Men.   Padraic Colum.   The terrible robber men.   HBMV; LOW

The Terrible Sons.   Eleazar Ben Kalir.   The Lord is King, the Lord was King,/the Lord shall be King for ever and/ever.   TrJP

A Terrible Thought.   Eliezer Steinbarg.   It's dreadful your life to a dog to owe.   TrJP

Territory.   Susan Wood-Thompson.   believing in fire/for not knowing/my place.   AMV-81

Terror.   Thomas O'Brien.   It is the octopus in every soldier's eye/In still deep waters calm, O calm.   NeIP

Terror.   Robert Penn Warren.   Kisses the terror;/for you see an empty chair.   LiTA; MoPo; NePA; PoA; WaP

Terror.   Yehoash.   Nearer, nearer, oh, I fear/Murderous advances.   TrJP

The Terror by Night.   Giacomo Leopardi.   ...nobody/Has ever seen it fall, except in dreams...   MOON

Terror Conduction.   Philip Lamantia.   LIKE/RAINING/SWORDS!   NeAP

The Terror of Death.   John Keats.   Of the wide world I stand alone, and think/Till Love and Fame to nothingness do sink.   GTBS; GTBS-P

The Terrorist Smiles.   Anselm Hollo.   the single-minded/lovers of multiplication.   APU

Tess's Lament.   Thomas Hardy.   My doings be as they were not,/And gone all trace of me!   FaBoTw; TEP

The Test.   Ralph Waldo Emerson.   Have you eyes to find the five/Which five hundred did survive?   AA; OBAL; PP

The Test.   Robert Friend.   "Hamor, (donkey) he cried,/and proved the language living.   GP

The Test.   Walter Savage Landor.   Hers never was the heart for you.   HBV 1-2

The Test.   Rachel McAlpine.   o my sweet my sweet   OCNZ

The Test.   John Banister Tabb.   To love it is and love alone/That life or luxury is known.   AnAmPo

Test Drive.   Monty Reid.   ...A stupid panic/when we drive so noiselessly/ by.   CaPN

A Test of Competence.   Greg Forker.   but did wrap the thing in its rejection slip/that saw to it I am here.   LFAC

The Test of Manhood (excerpt).   George Meredith.   Will find them both an air that doth devour.   WGRP

A Testament.   *Anonymous.*   Go, ring out all the bells!   OBSC

Testament.   Lucille Clifton.   i/alone/in a room.   GeTw

Testament.   John Holmes.   Let us remember life, the salt, the sweet,/And make of that our tireless testament.   MoRP

Testament.   Langston Hughes.   I'll leave her more to nag about/Than she's got breath.   NePoAm-2

Testament.   Sister M. Therese.   In the sweat of his brow man lives and loves and sings/His ultimate hymn to God.   MoRP

Testament.   Bill Zavatsky.   Just a minute while I write that down!   APU

The Testament of a Man Forbid.   John Davidson.   The cliffed escarpment ends in stormclad strength.   BSV

The Testament of Beauty.   Robert Bridges.
...but ONE ETERNAL/in the love of Beauty and in the selfhood of Love.   OxBoCh
feel their glass canopies flutter in the heav'nward prayer.   MoVE
foldeth the sheep in pastures of eternal life.   OxBTC
the loss whereof leaveth the man's face shabby and dull.   EBEV
Seize me ere I die! I am the Life of Life.   MoVE
til sound and sight failing me they are lost in the clouds.   MoVE
untill our painters took their new fashion from France.   MoVE

The Testament of Cathaeir Mor.   *Anonymous.*   Here ends the Will of Cathaeir Mor, who was King of Ireland.   OnYI

The Testament of Cresseid.   Robert Henryson.   Sen scho is deid, I speik of hir no moir.   BSV; CABL; EBEV; GoTS; MeEV; OxBS; PoEL 1-5; SeCePo

The Testament of John Davidson: The Last Journey.   John Davidson. "Heel and toe from dawn to dusk,/Round the world and home again".   BSV; GoTS

The Testament of Mr. Andro Kennedy.   William Dunbar.   To fle the fendis, than hardely sing/De terra plasmasti me.   OxBS

Testimonies.   Weldon Kees.   Hung with the bloody calves' heads in the butcher shop.   NYP

A Testimony.   George Ella Lyon.   into the all of water, cold,/his hands bore me/down.   GOYP

Testimony.   Carolyn M. Rodgers.   ...hell needs its/teeth kicked out, here and now!   BPo

Testimony to an Inquisitor.   William Stafford.   The more suspicious you are, the longer I've known you.   NePoAm-2

Testing Ground.   Karla M. Hammond.   ...Someday I'm going to ask/him why poets just get by and/what it means to be a pangolin.   AMV-81

Testing, Testing.   Dan Dillon.   To come to the aid of their party.   PV

The Testing-Tree.   Stanley Jasspon Kunitz.   Give me back my stones!   FYAP; MAT; UnPo

Tete-a-Tete.   Edwin Honig.   as though a bolting tree trunk/had kicked some memory ajar?   AmC; NoAm

Tetelestai.   Conrad Aiken.   A fanfare of glory....And which of us dares to deny/him?   LiTA; LiTM; MAPA; MoAB; MoAmPo; PrIm

Tetrachordon (excerpt).   John Milton.   Sees his foule inside through his whited skin.   NCEP

Tewkesbury Road.   John Masefield.   At the noise of the lambs at play and the dear wild cry of the birds.   GoTF; MCCG; TreFT

Texas.   James Daugherty.   And just lately we've struck oil.   TiPo

Texas.   Amy Lowell.   And old sky and a long plain/Beyond, beyond, my bridle-rein.   AmFN; BPAW

Texas.   John Greenleaf Whittier.   Blessed of our fathers' God!   PAH

The Texas Cowboy.   *Anonymous.*
And you will never catch consumption by sleeping on the ground.   CoSo
I am bound to follow the F A steers until I am too old./Ho-loo-loo-loo-loo.   AmFP

The Texas Cowboys.   *Anonymous.*   To tell the fate of the cowboy that rode at his right hand.   CoSo

The Texas Ranger.   Margie B. Boswell.   For the trail he cut so long ago/ Runs straight through the heart of the West.   BPAW

Texas Rangers.   *Anonymous.*
And I tell you from experience you had better stay at home.   OuSiCo
But just to all the ladies,/I'm sure I wish you well.   BFSS

The Texas Song.   *Anonymous.*   But in that far-off cattle land/He sometimes acted like a man.   CoSo

Texas Trains and Trails.   Mary Austin.   Get a-long, get a-long,/Youpi-ya,/ Yo-o-u-u-p!   SoPo; TiPo

Texas Types–"The Bad Man."   William Lawrence Chittenden.   Texas has passed the pistol stage,/The law has come to stay.   PoOW

The Texian Boys.   *Anonymous.*   The devil is a-working in a Texian's head–/ In a Texian's head.   CoSo

Text.   Audrey Wurdemann.   The honeycomb, the holy land/Broken and bleeding in my hand.   FYAP

Text.   Aaron Zeitlin.   night comes and reads the stars.   VWA

A Text for These Distracted Times.   Rodney Hall.   Yet we are the most beautiful world of the world   CBAP

Textile Mills and Prison Reform.   George Rachow.   and hypocrisy never brought me pain before now.   LFAC

Th' Almighty Spake, and Gabriel Sped.   George Richards.   Glad tidings shout to all abroad,/So be it, Lord, Amen.   AH

Th Child's Purchase.   Coventry Patmore.   "Humility and greatness grace the task/Which he who does it deems impossible!"   CoBE

Th Church Bell at Night.   *Anonymous.*   With a woman foolish and light.   OnYI

Th Gypsy Countess.   *Anonymous.*   And then her red blood down did flow.   OBET

Th Unifying Principle.   Archie Randolph Ammons.   when it's found the people live the small wraths of ease.   NOBA

That Beauty I Ador'd Before.   Aphra Behn.   To kiss freely: if not, you may go spin.   UnTE

That Black Snake Mama.   Blind Lemon Jefferson.   Blake snake, mama, done/run my darling home   BluL

That Bright Chimeric Beast.   Countee Cullen.   The dead bird be reborn. AmNP

That Brings Us to the Woodstove in the Wilds, at Night.   Walter Hall.   Stay here; I'm warm; You're right.   AMV-81

That Corner.   Blanaid Salkeld.   From this inadequate night and day,/I would steal him away.   OnYI; OxBI

That "Craning of the Neck".   Isabella Gardner.   ...I shall never fly.   NePA

That Crawling Baby Blues.   Blind Lemon Jefferson.   My woman threw my clothes out doors/and now I got those crawling baby blues   BluL

That Crazy War.   Anonymous.   In that war, that crazy war.   FSW

That Dark Other Mountain.   Robert Francis.   And that dark other mountain.   LiSp; NCSH; SD

That Day.   David Kherdian.   that the lines of their lives/were sewn from a tougher fabric/than the son had previously known.   SaC

That Day.   John Leax.   until/my eyes boiled.   TrCP

That Day.   Anne Sexton.   and love is where yesterday is at.   BoWoP; ConAP

That Day.   Mark Van Doren.   On that day's children, armistice and all. WaP

That Day You Came.   Lizette Woodworth Reese.   But ever in my lavender/ I hear the brawling bees.   HBV 1-2

That Did in Luve So Lively Write.   Georgine M. Adams.   Them were the days, my fel-/Low bards!   InMe

That Distant Bliss.   Henry, Bishop of Chichester King.   In that it falls her sacrifice.   TrGrPo

That Each Thing Is Hurt of Itself.   Anonymous.   No outward harm need to be sough,/Where en'mies be within so near.   EIL

That English Weather: After Browning (parody).   Anonymous.   Despite the rhapsodies of Robert Browning.   Par

That English Weather: After Charles Kingsley (parody).   Anonymous.   All to have a Kingsley/Swear it does him good!   Par

That Ever I Saw.   Anonymous.   I shall have the best and fairest May/That ever I saw.   CBEP; TrGrPo

That Everything Moves Its Bowels (parody).   David R. Slavitt.   primitive, convincing, disgustingly real.   BXAP

That First Gulp of Air We All Took When First Born.   Nancy Paddock.   for the first time/she can breathe.   PoDr

That Harp You Play So Well.   Marianne Moore.   Must cure the harp's distress.   HBMV; MoAB; MoAmPo; PoA

That He Findeth Others as Fair, But Not So Faithful as His Friend.   George Turberville.   But fair and faithful few there be.   EIL

That Hill.   Blanche Taylor Dickinson.   And fleeing fast from Hell!   CDC

That Holy Thing.   George Macdonald.   That Thou mayst answer all my need–/Yea, every bygone prayer.   HBV 1-2; OBEV; OBVV; TrPWD; TRV

That Hypocrite.   Anonymous.   An' dat's de way dat hyporite 'ten'.   BPo

That Idiot, Wordsworth.   George Gordon, Lord Byron.   Conceive the bard the hero of the story.   DBV

That Is All I Heard.   Yehoash.   Gur-gur-gur and gur-gur-gur,/That is all I heard.   TrJP

That Is Not Indifference.   Howard G. Hanson.   extending your bleak shadow/into the bright web of song.   AMV-81

That it will never come again.   Emily Dickinson.   This instigates an appetite/Precisely opposite.   NOBA

That Little Black Cat.   D'Arcy Wentworth Thompson.   And that's the best cure for a little pussy cat.'   OxBChV

That Little Hatchet.   C. Butler-Andrews.   And "Little Hatchet."   PeD

That Little Lump of Coal.   Anonymous.   That takes those dangerous chances/For this little lump of coal.   AmFP

That Lonesome Train Took My Baby Away.   Charlie McCoy.   Gonna take my baby/And leave me lonesome here   BluL

That love is all there is.   Emily Dickinson.   Proportioned to the groove. NOBA

That Man in Manhattan.   Shannon Keith Kelley.   from a world not his. AMV-80

That Moment.   Ted Hughes.   Crow had to start searching for something to eat.   FF

That Morn Which Saw Me Made a Bride.   Meleager.   This epitaph which here you see,/Supplied the epithalamy.   NIP

That Mulberry Wine.   Janet Sylvester.   ...the tree shaken, and under it/ ground rooted with our new name.   MAYP

That Nature Is a Heraclitean Fire...   Gerard Manley Hopkins.   This Jack, joke, poor potsherd, patch, matchwood, immortal diamond,/Is immortal diamond.   AtBAP; BiP; BoW; CoBMV; DiPo; FaBoMo; GTBS-P; LiTB; MoAB; MoPo; MoVE; NoP; OAEL 1-2; OAEP; PoEL 1-5; TEP; VLP

That Night When Joy Began.   W. H. Auden.   And love's best glasses reach/ No fields but are his own.   OxBTC; SoSe

That No Man Should Write But Such as Do Excel.   George Turberville. ...to touch the highest degree/Is passing hard; to do the best, sufficing is for thee.   EnRePo

That Old Sauna High.   Anselm Hollo.   getting so clean/all clean inside PoM

That Poem.   Juan Saez Burgos.   Who can break down Wall Street with a poem?   InW

That Pure Place.   Daniel J. Moriarty.   memory that leads me now/and then back to that pure place.   WOLT

That Radio Religion.   William Ludlum.   No church on earth can be replaced/By "service"–on the air!   WBLP

That Reminds Me.   Ogden Nash.   ...it's just that at the Sacred/Moment they are always thinking of something else.   FiBHP

That Room.   John Montague.   To bind us together more: equal in adversity. CIP

That's All?   Anna Hajnal.   is my calmness to be a tight calmness?   PBWP

That's Faith.   S. N. Leitner.   Looking to Jesus and turning not back–/That's faith.   STF

That's Jesus.   Grace B. Renfrow.   My Song, my All in All,/That's JESUS. BePJ

That's July.   Mary Frances Butts.   Children out for holiday,–/That's July. YeAr

That's June.   Mary Frances Butts.   A blue sky, a soft breeze,–/That's June. YeAr

That's Life?   Alan Bold.   But he was bespoken for.   FF

That's No Way to Get Along.   Robert Wilkins.   And that'll be no way for me to get along.   BluL

That's Our Lot.   Moishe Leib Halpern.   Or else like scarecrows, that have been forgotten/In fields, when fall has preyed on everything.   VWA

That's Success!   Berton Braley.   It's doing your noblest–that's Success! PoToHe

That's What We'd Do.   Mary Mapes Dodge.   That's what we'd do,/When the moon came out.   OBCA

That Sharp Knife.   Thomas Wolfe.   He has been pierced by Spring,/That sharp knife.   NCSH

That spring night I spent.   Lady Suwo.   Unfortunately I am/Talked about anyway.   LiTW

That Strain Again.   Ronald Hambleton.   Outstripped by queenly sauntering. CaP

That such have died enable us.   Emily Dickinson.   That such have lived,/ Certificate for Immortality.   AA

That Summer.   Judith Hemschemeyer.   unable to let one more thing/one single blade of grass/die.   PPJ

That Summer.   Herbert Scott.   since, I ask, Ron, is that you?   PoL

That Summer.   Henry Treece.   ...for then I knew/It must break with as little warning.   NYBP

That Summer's Shore.   John Ciardi.   And I made this praise to your nakedness in the sea.   ErPo

That the Neighborhood Might Be Covered.   Larry Eigner.   After 3 days the air/empty from the rain   PoM

That the Night Come.   William Butler Yeats.   To bundle time away/That the night come.   CoBMV; PoEL 1-5

That There Are Powers above Us I Admit.   Arthur Hugh Clough.   I will not say they will not give us aid.   NOBV

That There Should Be Laughter.   Innocent Banda.   Where children wait/ For the carnival to break up.   WhB

That Things Are No Worse, Sire.   Helen Hunt Jackson.   "That things are xo worse, O my sire!"   OHIP

That Thou Art Nowhere to Be Found.   George Macdonald.   Eyes made for glory soon discover thee.   TrCP

That Time That Mirth Did Steer My Ship.   Sir Thomas Wyatt.   That she were mine, and might be sure/She should be while that life doth dure. FCP; SiPS

That Was Summer.   Marci Ridlon.   That was summer.   NTCP

That Was Then.   Isabella Gardner.   ...That was then.   GP

That Way.   Anne Welsh.   The shining of the morning is most marvellous. PeSA

That We Head Towards.   Stephany.   the sight,/the touch,/or memory/of You.   BPo

That Which Hath Wings Shall Tell.   Linda Lyon Van Voorhis.   Stronger their clasp upon the wind-swept bough/When the birds sleep.   GoBC

That Which We Call a Rose.   Michael Dransfield.   I dremt that madness passes like a dream   CBAP

That Which You Call "Love Me."   Luis Rosales.   ...and will make the same/life you surrrender to me impossible.   AMV-81

That Wind.   Emily Bronte.   Still beaming bright and fair.   CH

That Woman Down There beneath the Sea.   Anonymous.   Set matters right will I.   WSC

Thatcher.   Seamus Heaney.   And left them gaping at his Midas touch. FaBoIP; IPY

The Thatcher.   Brendan Kennelly.   "Let the wind rip and the rain pelt. This'll keep."   CIP

There is No Trumpet Like the Tomb. Emily Dickinson. For just one plaudit banishing/The might of human love. BoLiVe

There Is No Unbelief. Elizabeth York Case. The heart lives by the faith the lips deny,/God knoweth why. WBLP; WGRP

There Is No Unbelief. Lizzie York Case. God knoweth why. HBV 1-2; TreFS

There Is No Vacancy. Jessica Scarbrough. you dare to set up housekeeping/in my soul. LFAC

There Is No Word for Goodbye. Mary Tallmountain. There is no word for goodbye. STE

There Is None, O None But You. Thomas Campion. Or man a woman halfe so faire. AtBAP; ElL; HBV 1-2

There Is None to Help. Chad Walsh. "I wonder if God has a son." TrCP

There Is Nothin' Like a Dame. Oscar, II Hammerstein. A girly, womanly, female, feminine dame! OBAL

There Is Nothing False in Thee. Kenneth Patchen. What does not perish/Lives in thee. PoPl

There Is Nothing New in New York. Miguel Pinero. there is nothing new in new york. NYP

There Is Only One of Everything. Margaret Atwood. ...I want this. I want/this. NOBC

There Is Power. Joe Hill. One industrial union grand. FSW

There Is Snowdrift on the Mountain. W. P. Ker. Coming over by Ben Buy they have word of May,/O Donacha Ban! PoSH

There Is So Much of Loneliness. Anonymous. Yet we deny the brotherhood/The human heart demands. PoToHe

There Is Something. Deborah Pope. her hand on your sleeve. AMV-81

There Is Something I Want to Say. Alex Kuo. the ocean/with fierce courage? BrSi

There Is Strength in the Soil. Arthur Stringer. This ample and opulent bosom/That must some day nurse us all! OHIP

There Is Sweet Music Here. Alfred, Lord Tennyson. And from the craggy ledge the poppy hangs in sleep. FaBV

There Is Yet Time. Arvel Steece. There is yet time. PGD

There Isn't Enough Bread. Charles Culhane. with survival's bare wings/beating at the windows. LFAC

There Let Thy Bleeding Branch Atone. Emily Bronte. I once forgot the early days/That thou wouldst call to mind. SeCePo

There Lived a King. Sir William Schwenck Gilbert. When every one is somebodee,/Then no one's anybody! FiBHP; PoPle; StPo

There Lived a Lady in Milan. William Rose Benet. He never saw her from that day. HBMV

There Once Was a Puffin. Florence Page Jaques. And the puffin eats pancakes,/Like you/and/like/me. NTCP; SoPo; TiPo

There Once Was a Time. Anonymous. Now my hair has turned grey/and I'm not what I was.' NOBI

There Once Was a Wicked Young Minister. Conrad Aiken. except for one squeamish old spinster. OBAL

There Pipes the Wood-Lark. Thomas Gray. Scatters his loose notes in the waste of air. FM

There's a Certain Slant of Light. Emily Dickinson. When it goes, 'tis like the Distance/On the look of Death–. AmePo; AnFE; AP; APA; AtBAP; BLPL; BoWoP; CMoP; DiPo; ExPo; ForPo; HAP; HeIP; LiTM; LoGBV; MAmP; MasP; MoAB; MoAmPo; MoPo; NAWM 1-2; NePA; NoAm; NOBA; NoP; OxBA; PoEL 1-5; PPP; QFR; SBG; TreFT

There's a Feeling. Marcia Bullwinkle. And the rain is me. AMV-80

There's a Fire in the Forest. W. W. Eustace Ross. To reach the cool stream/For which they are yearning. WHW

There's a Grandfather's Clock in the Hall. Robert Penn Warren. ...Time thrusts through/the time of no-Time. NoP

There's a Light upon the Mountains. Henry K. Burton. And, my soul, be swift to bring/All thy sweetest and thy dearest/For the triumph of our King! TRV

There's a Man, I Really Believe.... Sappho. Well, endure is all I can do, reduced to.... WeW

There's A Regret. William Ernest Henley. His obscene victory vain. AnEnPo

There's an Unknown River in Soweto. Zindzi Mandela. the body/the blood/both unknown. WhB

There's been a death, in the opposite house. Emily Dickinson. The Intuition of the News–/In just a Country Town– BoLiVe; InPS; NCEP; PAI; SoSe

There's Been Some Sort of Mistake. Caroline Gilfillan. she dreams she writes this poem. PeHV

There's Gowd in the Breast. James Hogg. Oh, the world is all before us! HBV 1-2

There's Life in a Mussel. A Meditation. George Farewell. Patient, like thee, that prime of nature lies/T' imbibe the quintessence of flowing sweets. NOEC

There's Money in Mother and Father. Morris Bishop. But some little mite is learning how to write/To write a little book about you! FiBHP

There's More Pretty Girls Than One. Anonymous. There's more pretty girls than one. AmFP

There's Music in the Air. Fanny J. Crosby. Angelic voices greet us there,/In the music in the air. BLSo

There's Nae Place Like Otago Yet. John Barr. That money makes the man. AnNZ

There's No Lust Like to Poetry. Anonymous. Dying, should thrill through it! AWP

There's No Place to Sleep in This Bed, Tanguy. Charles Henri Ford. There are too many monuments of broken hearts. EAS

There's Nothing Like the Sun. Edward ("Edward Eastaway") Thomas. There's nothing like the sun till we are dead. FaBV

There's Nothing Polite about a Tank. John Paul Minarik. who don't really think at all/being rudely rusty inside. LFAC

There's Somethin'. Adam Small. ever stop me/loving/even you! PeSA

There's Wisdom in Women. Rupert Brooke. Have cried on love so bitterly, with so true a tongue? HBV 1-2

There Shall Always Be the Church. Thomas Stearns Eliot. And the Gates of Hell shall not prevail. TRV

There She Blows! Anonymous. Slowly he dies and the battle is o'er! EtS

There She Is. Linda Gregg. if paradise is to be here/it will have to include her. NPGG

There She Stands a Lovely Creature. Anonymous. Like a rose that blooms in the morning/And in evening dies away. AmFP; OLR

There Should Have Been. Sydney Lea. dazed as the couple I'd saved from the cake,/jacked in their tracks by the onrushing beams. SM

There Was a Boy. William Wordsworth.
...and that uncertain heaven received/Into the bosom of the steady lake. FaBoCh; LoGBV
A long half-hour together I have stood/Mute–looking at the grave in which he lies! ChRP; FaBoRV; MCCG; MyFE; OBRV; PoEL 1-5

There Was a Brisk Girle. Anonymous. Since fate has designed her to Ley alone. CoMu

There Was a Child Went Forth. Walt Whitman. and/who now goes, and will always go forth every day. AmePo; AmPP; AWP; BiP; InPo; LaNeLa; MAmP; OxBA; PAI; RFM; SoSe; TAP

There Was a Crimson Clash of War. Stephen Crane. That still the reason was not. UnPo

There Was a Crooked Man. Mother Goose. And they all lived together in a little crooked house. CBEP; FaBoBe; FaFP; HBV 1-2; HBVY; OxBoLi

There Was a Dance, Sweetheart. Joy Harjo. It was a dance. TWSS

There Was a Frog. Anonymous. If any do, it is not I. NA

There Was a King. Anonymous. If the basin had been stronger/My story would have been longer. NLV; OxBoLi; OxNR

There Was a Knight. Anonymous. You shall not when you will, sir."/Down, derry, down. UnTE

There Was a Knight and He Was Young. Anonymous. And I will have a special Care,/Of the rumpling of my Gown a. CoMu

There Was a Lady Loved a Swine. Anonymous. Hunc, hunc, hunc, he said./And away went he. GBP

There Was a Little Boy and a Little Girl. Anonymous. I will kiss you. OxNR

There Was a Little Girl. Henry Wadsworth Longfellow.
And when she was bad, she was horrid. BLPA; FaFP; OxBChV; YaD
She took and she did spank her most emphatic. GoTF; LBN; NA; TreF

There was a little man. Mother Goose. And knocked it right off his head,/head, head. FaFP; HBV 1-2; HBVY

There Was a Little Ship. Anonymous. As she sailed on the low land low,/As she sailed on the lonesome sea. BFSS

There Was a Little Woman. Mother Goose. "Lawk a mercy on me,/This is none of I!" InvP

There Was a Maid Went to the Mill. Anonymous. And he cherish'd his heart with a cup of old sack,/Oh ho! Oh ho! Oh ho! did he so? GBP

There Was a Man and He Was Mad. Anonymous. And there he cut his nose off/And flung it at the people. GBP

There Was a Man of Double Deed. Anonymous. 'Twas death and death and death/indeed. GBP; OxNR; WeW

There was a man of our town. Mother Goose. And scratched 'em in again. FaFP; HBV 1-2; HBVY

There Was a Man with a Tongue of Wood. Stephen Crane. And with that the singer was content. LiTA; NePA

There Was a Monkey. Anonymous. There was a navy went into Spain,/When it returned, it came again. NA; OxNR

There Was a Roaring in the Wind All Night. William Wordsworth. Raises a mist, that, glittering in the sun,/Runs with her all the way, wherever she doth run. GoTF; TreFT

There Was a Strife 'Twixt Man and Maid. Rudyard Kipling. And both were hard as the nether stone. PV

There Was a Time. Edward ("Edward Eastaway") Thomas. For what can neither ask nor heed his death. MMM

There Was a Wee Bit Mousikie. Anonymous. "Oh, cheetie-pussie-cattie, O!" MoShBr

There Was a Wyly Ladde. *Anonymous.* Let's kisse before you goe. ErPo

There Was a Young Lady of Rome. Ogden Nash. And blobs of gelatinous foam. QQQ

There Was a Young Man from Trinity. *Anonymous.* Dropped science, and took up divinity. ImOP

There Was an Indian. J.C. Squire. Columbus's doom-burdened caravels/ Slant to the shore, and all their seamen land. AmFN

There Was an Old Man Named Michael Finnegan. Mother Goose. Poor old Michael Finnegan. TiPo

There Was an Old Man, on Whose Nose. Edward Lear. Which relieved that Old Man and his nose. SoPo

There was an old owl lived in an oak. *Anonymous.* Oh, if men were all like that wise bird! CenHV

There Was an Old Soldier. *Anonymous.* And another wooden foot wouldn't do her any harm. FSW; TrAS

There Was an Old Woman. *Anonymous.*
And when she did die/She'd nothing to leave. OxNR
"You'll look that way when you are dead," hm,hm, hm. BFSS

There Was an Old Woman, and What Do You Think? Mother Goose.
And when she came back her husband was well. HBV 1-2
Yet this plaguey old woman would never keep quiet. FaBoCh

There Was an Old Woman, as I've Heard Tell. Mother Goose. "Oh! deary, deary me, this is none of I!" TiPo

There Was an Old Woman Who Lived in a Shoe. Mother Goose. Then whipped them all soundly and put them to bed. FaBoBe; FaFP; HBV 1-2; HBVY

There was Never Nothing More Me Pained. Sir Thomas Wyatt. Alas the while! AAS; CBEP; FCP; GBL; SiPS

There Was No Place Found. Mary Elizabeth Coleridge. There is no need of Hell, while Earth shall last.' OxBoCh

There Was No Room on the Cross. *Anonymous.* "Child, child, be not afraid. Your Cross/Is occupied by Me." GoBC

There Was One I Met upon the Road. Stephen Crane. "Poor soul," He said. EaLo

There Were an Old and Wealthy Man. *Anonymous.* If you love them, give them their way/For fear their love may lead astray. AmFP

There Were Fierce Animals in Africa. Alvin Aubert. ...a sundown/dance viewed from a cool veranda. GP

There Were Ninety and Nine. Elizabeth Cecilia Clephane. Rejoice! for the Lord brings back His own. VLP; WGRP

There Were Some Summers. Thomas Lux. in water cold enough to break your ankles. LCAP

There Were Three Jovial Welshmun. *Anonymous.* The third said 'twas an old man,/And his beard growing grey. GBP

There Were Two Blackbirds Sitting on a Hill. Mother Goose. Come again, Jack! Come again, Jill! HBV 1-2; HBVY

There Will Be No Peace. W. H. Auden. They hate for hate's sake. NePoAm-2

There Will Be Peace. Margaret Miller Pettengill. And yellow harvest when the wild geese fly. PGD

There Will Come Soft Rains. Sara Teasdale. And Spring herself, when she woke at dawn,/Would scarcely know that we were gone. LiTA

There Won't Be Another. Diane Glancy. He paddles the canoe-ark with deer and prairie hens/over the rabbiteye and red haw. STE

There You Sit. Shel Silverstein. Aren't you glad on Labor Day/There isn't any labor? PoSC

Therefore I Must Tell the Truth. Torlino. I hold my word tight to my breast. ExPo

Therefore Is the Name of It Called Babel. Osbert Sitwell. –And we are left to drink the less/Of Babel's direful prophecy. MMM

Therefore We Preserve Life. Shen Ch'uan. When living he was able to prevent/and abstain from killing (Isaac),/therefore we preserve life. TrJP

Therefore, We Thank Thee, God. Reuben Grossman. Together with those of a father and a/mother./We thank Thee... TrJP

Theresa. John Pass. beautiful mouth, murmurs/of pleasure. Theresa, you. AMV-81

Therese. Alden Nowlan. I could see/her white thighs/glistening with rain. NeAC

Theresienstadt Poem. Robert Mezey. thirteen years of life/and your heart on fire/Nely Silvinova! NaP; VWA

The Thermal Stair. W. S. Graham. It seems tonight all Closing bells are tolling/Across the Duchy shire wherever I turn. FaBoMo

Thermometer Wine. Robert Morgan. always chilled as snake or worm. SUW

Thermopylae. Robert Hillyer. The stark black cross against the setting sun. AnAmPo

Thermopylae. Michael Thwaites. Who died in the pass, and will not die again? PoAu 1-2

These. William Carlos Williams. and hears the sound of lakewater/ splashing–that is now stone. AP; CoBMV; MoAB; MoAmPo; NoAm; NOBA; NoP; OxBA

These Apple Trees. Valentin Iremonger. Or summer detonate in our heads. NeIP

These Are My People. Lucia Trent. Not slaves but masters of the earth! PGD

These Are Not Lost. Richard Metcalf. These are not lost. PoToHe

These Are the Chosen People. Robert Nathan. And guard the wells of pity of the/heart. TrJP

These are the days when birds come back. Emily Dickinson. Taste thine immortal wine! AmePo; FF; ForPo; HBV 1-2; MAmP; MoAmPo

These Are the Gifts I Ask. Henry Van Dyke. And discontent that casts a shadow gray/On all the brightness of the common day. FaBoBe; TreFT

"These are the live." Kenneth Fearing. Hey? Of what doth the noble poet brood/In a tragic mood? NAMP

These Crossings, These Words. Quincy Troupe. that continues to last LTB

These Damned Trees Crouch. Jim Barnes. Jim Barnes is crawling through the underbrush. CDW

These Days. Robert Jones. when the grass is green again/and bending and half grown. AMV-81

These Days. William Stafford. to crawl away over the horizon. NNaP

These Days the Papers in the Street. Charles Reznikoff. those for a moment lie still and sun themselves. VGW

These Green-Going-to-Yellow. Marvin Bell. which would not be our way/ if we truly thought we were gods. FYAP; LCAP

These Horses Came. Ray A. Young Bear. ...are you really afraid of children? CDW

These Images Remain. May Sarton. And those tears too expensive now that start/From radiant eyes and empty the whole heart. MoLP

These Labdanum Hours. Kathleen Fraser. Jade was never what I wanted. NPGG

These Lacustrine Cities. John Ashbery. Whose disappointment broke into a rainbow of tears. ANYP; CAPP; HaCAP; PoM; UnPo

These Leaves. William Stafford. We walk on, leaves blow past. NNaP

These Locusts by Day. Wallace Stevens. The honky-tonk out of the somnolent grasses/Is a memorizing, a trying out, to keep. PoA

These Magicians. Sarah Provost. and hearts of holy stone. AMV-81

These Men. Philip Booth. and measured for death by their words'/grave rise, sentence themselves to know. GLGT

These Men. Leon Gellert. Beyond some swinging open door/Into eternity. BoAV; PoAu 1-2

These Obituaries of Rattlesnakes Being Eaten by the Hogs. Roger Weingarten. off the tripes, he could pour us a sly drink, from the/cider jug. AmPA

These Past Years: Passages 10. Robert Duncan. "There is really no circumstance of human life,/in which He has not at times been our forerunner." PoM

These People. Howard McKinley Corning. That time frames miniatures on every hill. AnAmPo

These Plaintive Verse, the Postes of My Desire. Samuel Daniel. These lines I use, t'unburthen mine owne hart;/My love affects no fame, nor steemes of Art. AAS

These Poems, She Said. Robert Bringhurst. That is not love, she said rightly. NOBC

These Purists. William Carlos Williams. an organ grinder in Pine street. OBAL

These Stones. Menander. Stranger, look on these, and know. LiTW

These Things I Do Remember. Salaman Solomon ben Aaron. God, King, who sittest on a gracious/Throne. TrJP

These Things Shall Be. John Addington Symonds. For man shall be at one with God/In bonds of firm necessity. TRV

These Things to Come. Samuel (1835-1902) Butler. ...meet again,/Where dead men meet, on lips of living men. GLGT

These Trees Are. Susan Strayer Deal. like dipped, dark candy. AMV-81

These Trees Are No Forest of Mourners. D.G. Jones. ...They exist/Beyond your grief; they have their own/Quiet reality. NOBC

These Trees Stand... W. D. Snodgrass. Snodgrass is walking through the universe. NIP; NoAm; PPP

These Two. Howard Schwartz. We must learn how to read/The letters written/In the stars that circle/Our souls. VWA

These Women All. Heath. The beste may be amended:–/But I will nott say so. FaBoCo

These Words I Write on Crinkled Tin. Lynette Roberts. To the green wood now my love is gone. ChMP

Theseus: A Trilogy. Yvor Winters. To the cold perfection of unending peace. NOBA

Theseus and Ariadne. Robert Graves. Playing the queen to nobler company. HAP

Theseus and Ariadne. Lloyd Mifflin. Ye gods! he leaves me and my babe to be! AA

Thesis. William Walter De Bolt. Death is a useful comma/which punctuates, and labors to convince/of more to follow. AMV-80

The Thief. Stanley Jasspon Kunitz. And write this poem for money, rage, and love. MoAmPo; VGW

The Thief's Niece. George Keithley. drew down upon his heels to help him die. NPGG

Thiepval Wood. Edmund Charles Blunden. Nor the blue javelin-flame of thunderous noons strike fear. AnFE; MMM

Thieves. Perseus Adams. I listen to the summer expand. ACV

The Thieves. Robert Graves. For lost honour among thieves. BoLoP; CMoP; GTBS-P; LiTM; OAEL 1-2; OxBI; WeW

The Thieves' Anthology (excerpt) (parody). Sir Theodore Martin. "Our game is up, my covies, blow me tight!" FaBoPa

The Thieves of Love. R.A.D. Ford. And thieves of happiness,/Sodden in the underbrush. PeCV

A Thin Facade for Edith Sitwell. John Malcolm Brinnin. "Lunch is over!" says she. FiBHP; NYBP

Thin Ice. David McCord. Who's ill?/Me? A pill? TiPo

Thin Little Leaves of Wood Fern, Ribbed and Toothed. Frederick Goddard Tuckerman. Or the old grasshopper molasses-mouthed. TAP

The Thin Man. Donald Justice. ...Asleep, I/Am a horizon. SM

Thine Eyes Still Shined. Ralph Waldo Emerson. When the rosebud ripened to the rose,/In both I read thy name. NOBA

The Thing. Theodore Roethke. And the blue air darkened. CMoP

The Thing Is Violent. Gwendolyn MacEwen. appear and plot new zodiacs upon the flesh. NOBC; PeCV

The Thing Made Real. Ron Loewinsohn. like a White Rhinoceros. NeAP

Thing Poem. Petra von Morstein. I'd really like/a few things with/qualities of their own. BoWoP

A Thing Remembered. Anonymous. To see the stars of night hidden behind clouds. ErPo

A thing which fades. Ono no Komachi. Of the heart of man/In this world! AWP; BoWoP; PBWP

The Things. Conrad Aiken. so to deceive yourself until you move/into that house whose tenants do not love. HAP

Things. Walter De la Mare. And when I open the box, I know/What kind of self awaits me there. PoA

Things. Dorothy Dow. The hunger for lost arms.../Death. HBMV

Things. Aline Kilmer. And things have a terrible permanence/When people die. MCCG

Things. William Stanley Merwin. Depend on us. HAP

Things. Louis Simpson. Let there be a perpetual coming and going/Between your house and mine.' OxBC

Things. William Jay Smith. Poems for ending,/And sleeping's for bed. TiPo

Things About Comin' My Way. Anonymous. Now after all my hard trav'ling,/Things about comin' my way. FSW

Things Dead. Marcel Schwob. ...Cemeteries and all that is/dead breed pestilence. TrJP

Things Going out of My Life. Robert Adamson. the living things/that are going out of my life CBAP

Things I Didn't Know I Loved. Nazim Hikmet. ...as if on a journey/from which one does not return LLLT

The Things I Miss. Thomas Wentworth Higginson. To thank Thee for the things I miss. TrPWD

The Things I Prize. Henry Van Dyke. And best of all, along the way, friendship and mirth. GoTF; TreFT

The Things I Say Are True. Blanca Varela. I must have lunch alone forever. Terrible. BoWoP

Things I Used to Do (with music). Anonymous. There's been a great change since I been bohn. AS

Things Kept. William Dickey. pure peacock blue, brass glory, furious stone. NYBP

Things Known: Under the Hill. Richard Eberhart. Being earth, at last I knew/the vibrance under the hill. PoA

Things Lovelier. Humbert Wolfe. You cannot dream/Things lovelier. TrJP

Things Men Have Made–. D. H. Lawrence. warm still with the life of forgotten men who made them. NoAm; PCP

Things Not of This Union. Linda Gregg. ...Wanting a longer unity to go back home to. NPGG

Things of Late. David Phillips. nothing explains my eating alone NeAC

The Things of the North. Rennie McOwan. Let us give thanks for the things of the north. PoSH

Things of the Spirit. Mason Jordan Mason. As there seems to be/a plenty/more of gruel PoNe

The Things That Are More Excellent. William Watson. That nought which lives should wholly lack/The things that are more excellent. OHFP

Things That Are Worse Than Death. Sharon Olds. gracious and eternal death/who permits departure. MAYP

Things That Endure. Ted Olson. Is good for a million more! WBLP

Things That Happen. William Stafford. ...its blundering/stumbling days, again and again, to find my hand. NNaP

The Things That Make a Soldier Great. Edgar A. Guest. And only death can stop him now–he's fighting for them all. NIP

The Things That Matter. Edith Nesbit. Let me know something when I'm dead. OxBTC

Things That Might Have Been. Jorge Luis Borges. The son I did not have. AMV-80

Things to Come. James Reeves. This is the man whom I must get to know. OBSP

Things to Do around a Lookout. Gary Snyder. Get ready for the snow, get ready/To go down. CAPP; NaP; TAP

Things to Do around a Ship at Sea. Gary Snyder. Dreams of girls, about yr girl friend, writing letters, wanting children,/Making plans. CAPP

Things to Do around Kyoto. Gary Snyder. Going home. NaP

Things to Do in New York (City). Ted Berrigan. Make friends forever/& go away NoAm

Things to Do in Providence. Ted Berrigan. I can hear today's key sounds fading softly/& almost see opening sleep's epic novel. APU

Things We Dreamt We Died For. Marvin Bell. whose many fortunes are followed/by the many who have not one. CoAP

Think. Charles Weekes. And bethink thee thou art servant/To the same all-moving hand. AnIV; OnYI

Think as I Think. Stephen Crane. I said, "I will, then, be a toad." WeW

Think before You Act. Mary Elliott. And then, perhaps, regret the past,/When sorrow comes too late. HBVY

Think It Over. Anonymous. I'll help You some other day. STF

Think Naught a Trifle. Anonymous. and trifles–life. PoToHe

Think No More, Lad. Alfred Edward Housman. Think no more; 'tis only thinking/Lays lads underground. CABA; CMoP; InPo

Think Not When You Gather to Zion. Eliza R. Snow. Where freely the truth you may take. AH

Think of Eight Numbers. Shel Silverstein. And start all over again. BBGG

Think on Yesterday. Anonymous. When men beeth meriest at her mele/I rede ye thenk on yesterday. OxBM

Think Small. Elaine Equi. ...It doesn't mean I'm petty and it doesn't mean I want to/get caught. APU

Think'st Thou to Seduce Me Then. Thomas Campion. But, alas, who less could do, that found so good occasion? BiP; EiL; OBSP; SoSe

The Thinker. Berton Braley. Back of the Job–the Dreamer/Who's making the dream come true! BLPA; WBLP

The Thinker. Anthony Delius. it seems bloody queer. PeSA

The Thinker. William Carlos Williams. And I talk to them/in my secret mind/out of pure happiness. MoLP

Thinking. Walter D. Wintle. But soon or late the man who wins/Is the one who thinks he can. SoSe; WBLP

Thinking Happiness. Robert E. Farley. And in this you'll find your own! PoToHe

Thinking of a Master. Richard Church. That the grasshopper feeds on dew. HaMV

Thinking of Bookshops. James Liddy. "I love you I love you" again (never often enough)/"I love you" CIP

Thinking of Holderlin. Christopher Middleton. plucking the crowded vermin from their folds. NePoEA-2

Thinking of Iceland. Tom Paulin. was this coming-full-circle not the question they asked? FaBoIP

Thinking of Love. Elizabeth Jennings. As if the flesh were a house/With too many empty rooms. GOYP

Thinking of Tents. Reed Whittemore. War's end–/World's end–/Sullen Achilles. TAP

Thinking of "The Autumn Fields." Robert Bly. I bring my stocking feet close to the faint incense. NNaP

Thinking of the Lost World. Randall Jarrell. Nothing; the nothing for which there's no reward. NoAm; NOBA

Thinking of You. Dick Lourie. and the pumpkins dead in the roadside fields NeAC

Thinking Twice in the Laundromat. Harley Elliott.
I will help you fold/your gleaming sheets. NeAC
O la, o la. NeAC

Thinning out the Grove. Judith Neeld. ...will leave us/no shadows except our own. SOTS

Thir Lenterne Dayis ar Luvely Lang. William Stewart. As gud luve cumis as gais. OxBS

The Third Advice to a Painter. Andrew Marvell. To woods and groves, what once she painted, sings. APAS

Third Alley Blues. Iva Smith. All these women in Third Alley/won't let my rider alone BluL

Third and Fourth. Keidrych Rhys. I ponder too long the X-ray child in his mother's womb. NeBP

Third Avenue in Sunlight. Anthony Hecht. My bar is somewhat further down the street. CoAP; NePoEA-2; NYP; PPP

The Third Century. Thomas Traherne.

The Glorious Soul that was the King/Made to possess them, did appear/A Small and little thing! AnAnS 1

His Blood, thy Bane; my Balsam, Bliss, Joy, Wine;/Shall Thee Destroy; Heal, Feed, make me Divine. AnAnS 1

A Sin! Its Ugly face/More Terror, then its Dwelling Place,/Contains,(O Dreadfull Sin!)/Within! AnAnS 1

The Third Continent. Mary Erulkar. Before the apple-red and hungry mornings rise. ACV

The Third Day. Edith Lovejoy Pierce. Lord, we cannot guess or believe,/ We can only know. MoRP

Third Degree. Langston Hughes. I'll sign the/Paper... BPo

The Third Dimension. Denise Levertov. –a fiction, while I/breath and/ change pace. NeAP; NoAm

The Third Eclogue. Michael Drayton. And Albion on the Appenines advance her conquering Crest. AtBAP; PoEL 1-5

Third Enemy Speaks. C. Day Lewis. I'll show you face to face/Eugenics, Eupeptics and Euthanasia,/The clinic Trinity. EaLo

The Third Light. Michael Longley. ...did you imagine/A Woodbine passing to and fro, a face/That stabilizes like a smoke ring? FaBoIP

Third Limick. Ogden Nash. Were munched by a cow/When mistaken for clover. NePA

Third Madrigal. Gene Derwood. My clouds rain curtains, my vision's jewel is his. NePA

The Third Satire of Juvenal. John Dryden. One jail did all their criminals restrain,/Which, now, the walls of Rome can scarce contain. OAEL 1-2

Third Sunday in Lent. John Keble. There is no light but Thine: with Thee all/beauty glows. VLP

The Third Wonder. Edwin Markham. The long, long patience of the plundered poor. FYAP

Thirst. Musa Moris Farhi. you did not tell me/that one can never drink enough VWA

Thirst of the Dragon. Dianne Hai-Jew. wine vintage–long diluted. BrSi

Thirsty Island. Jim Tollerud. And depart the chilled island. VoR

The Thirsty Poet. John Philips. Nor Medlar, Fruit delicious in Decay. OBEC

Thirteen, Full of Life. Graham Everett. heat wove the air/and we smoked dime cigars. WOLT

Thirteen O'Clock. Kenneth Fearing. WHO? WHO? WHO? O WHO? ExPo

Thirteen Ways of Looking at a Blackbird. Wallace Stevens. The blackbird sat in the cedar-limbs. AP; BLPL; CABA; CMoP; CoBMV; DiPo; HaCAP; HeIP; InPK; LiTM; MAPA; NoAm; NOBA; NoP; SOTW; TAP

The Thirteenth Song. Michael Drayton. ...and by that mean the city clearly freed. SeCePo

Thirteenth Station. William A. Donaghy. And look to you for refuge and relief. ISi

Thirtieth Anniversary Report of the Class of '41. Howard Nemerov. There's nothing left for us to say of us. HaCAP

Thirty Bob a Week. John Davidson. and we fall, face forward, fighting, on the deck. BSV; CABL; EBEV; ELU; FaBoPV; FaBoTw; FaFP; LiTB; NBM; NoAm; NOBE; NOBV; OAEL 1-2; OBNC; OxBS; OxBTC; PAI; VLP

Thirty Childbirths. Millen Brand. giving me back to life. AMV-80

Thirty-Eight. Charlotte Smith. We'll not regret the stealing hours/That lead from Thirty–even to Forty-eight. SBG; WPOW

The thirty eighth year. Lucille Clifton. i had not expected to be/an ordinary woman. AmPA

The Thirty-One Camels. Rachel Korn. Thirty-one camels/make their way/ without a leader,/without a guide. VWA

This above All Is Precious and Remarkable. John Wain. That can happen at any time of the day or night. LiTM

This Afternoon... Juan Saez Burgos. from the two of us/from you/from many things InW

This Air That Blows in from the Sea. Elizabeth Jane Coatsworth. So coldly from the sea. BrR

This Alice. Herbert Morris. you wear the gold calypso Alice wore. PoRA

This Amber Sunstream. Mark Van Doren. No living man in any western room /But sits at amber sunset round a tomb. GoYe; LiTA; MoPo; MoVE

This and More. Glenn Siebert. Attend all this. HW

This Be Our Revenge. Saul Tchernichovsky. Which we have reared in asceticism/and chastity/And the yoke of the Ten/Commandments. TrJP

This Beach Can Be Dangerous. Allen Curnow. happy to the point of hopelessness. OCNZ

This Beast That Rends Me. Edna St. Vincent Millay. The scar of this encounter like a sword/Will lie between me and my troubled lord. PrIm

This blessed Christ of Calvary. Anonymous. This blessed Christ of Calvary! STF

This Blonde Girl. Kendrick Smithyman. grown up again to love. AnNZ

This Book Is Mine. Anonymous. My desk to find/And put it safe away. FaBoUs

This Book Is One Thing. Anonymous. Touch this one thing,/You'll sure feel the other. FaBoUs

This Bread I Break Was Once the Oat. Dylan Thomas. My wine you drink, my bread you snap. FaBoTw

This Child. Norman Rosten. though she look at us forever, silent,/from out of the cave of her eyes. TrJP

This Child Is the Mother. Gloria C. Oden. that soothing fountain/ outpouring/from her side. BlSi

This Cold Nothing Else. Dara Wier. ...nothing to do/but scald it with milk until it stops. MAYP

This Coloured Counterfeit That Thou Beholdest. Sister Juana Ines de la Cruz. is corpse and dust, shadow and nothingness. PBWP

This Compost. Walt Whitman. It gives such divine materials to men, and accepts such/leavings from them at last. AWP; CABA; LiTA; MAmP; MoAmPo

This Corruptible. Elinor Wylie. It is but for an hour," said the Spirit. AnFE; CoAnAm; MoAB; MoAmPo; MoRP

This Crosse-Tree Here. Robert Herrick. This Honour have,/to make my grave. OFD

This Darknight Speed. Eloise Klein Healy. I'd go absolutely right straight crazy to heaven. AmC

This Day. Lawrence Raab. ...the clouds/that cross my gaze with such terrible speed. NoP

This Day Be with Me. George Macdonald. And if he come, I shall be watching found. TrCP

This Day Is Thine. Verna Whinery. Hear in thy heart the Master's words, "Well done." BLRP

This Day, under My Hand. David Malouf. From the dark bay hissing/like crabs, red tropic suns. CBAP

This Decoration. Hayden Carruth. ...wordless,/as real things always are. NNaP

This Definition Poetry Doth Fit. Thomas Randolph. It is a witty madness, or mad wit. FaBoEE

This Dim and Ptolemaic Man. John Peale Bishop. He perishes toward Hercules. AmC; CrMA; ImOP; LiTA; LiTM; NePA

This dirty little heart. Emily Dickinson. The visage of the soul/And not the knees. PoEL 1-5

This Discord in the Pact of Things. Boethius. And seeks to bring the truth forgot/Again to that which he hath yet. LiTW

This Do in Remembrance of Me. Horatius Bonar. My strength is in Thy might, Thy might alone. STF; TrPWD

This Earth. Phillip Yellowhawk Minthorn. this arduous earth. STE

This Earthen Body. Anonymous. But no man can change/His earthen body. WTO

This Easter Day. Martha Snell Nicholson. Forevermore at home with Thee! BePJ

This Endris Night. Anonymous. And I shal sing/"Lullay, by-by, lullay".' EBEV; NOCV; NoP

This Englishwoman. Stevie Smith. She has no bosom and no behind. FaBoEE

This Ensuing Copy the Late Printer Hath been Pleased to Honour... Owen Felltham. As much, for that's an Ocean too,/That flows not every day, but ever. OBS

This Evening, My Love, Even as I Spoke Vainly. Sister Juana Ines de la Cruz. for even as water could you touch and behold/my heart, as through our hands it flowed. PBWP

This Evening, without Blinking. Pattiann Rogers. Before the dark. AMV-80

This Excellent Machine. John Lehmann. And very few are asking, Why not scrap it? OxBTC

This Fall. Jody Aliesan. call it autumn. AMV-81

This Feast of the Law. Anonymous. The Law is our Light and Defender. MoRP; TrJP

This Flock So Small. Anna Nitschmann. There is so much that shames me/Before Thy saints in radiant light. AH

This Form of Life Needs Sex. Allen Ginsberg. and that's my situation, Folks– NNaP

This Golden Summer. Robert Lowell. as if the walk/could cut bare feet. NoP

This Happy Day. Harry Behn. Thank you for this happy day,/This happy day! TiPo

This Heart That Flutters Near My Heart. James Joyce. Shall we not be as wise as they/Though love live but a day? AnIV

This Holy Night. Eleanor Farjeon. God bless you, brother. ChBR

This Hour. Oliver La Grone. Still crying out for life!! NNP; PoNe

This Hour Her Vigill. Valentin Iremonger. ...Suddenly, I thought/Of Elizabeth, frigidly stretched. CIP; NOBI; OxBI; OxBTC

This House. Ray A. Young Bear. encircles itself to a star/and dies in our place. CDW

This House, Where Once a Lawyer Dwelt. William Erskine. How rapidly the iron age/Succeeds the age of brass! GoTF; HBV 1-2; TreF

This Humanist Whom No Beliefs Constrained.   J. V. Cunningham.   Grew so broad-minded he was scatter-brained.   ELU; InPK

This I Can Do.   H. T. Lefevre.   Yet I with them may share/The King's "well done!"   STF

This Is a Photograph of Me.   Margaret Atwood.   but if you look long enough,/eventually/you will be able to see me.)   NoP

This Is a Poem for the Dead.   Michael Ryan.   you father stumbling through the door/calling to you Honey I'm home.   AmPA

This Is a Poem for the Fathers and for Michael Ryan.   Thomas Lux.   ...the termometers burning/in the mouths of the gone.   AmPA

This Is a Poem to My Son Peter.   Peter Meinke.   you, my oldest son Peter, age 10,/going on 11.   DFF; GP

This Is a Sin-Tryin' World.   Anonymous.   This is a sin-tryin' world.   TrAS

This Is after All Vacation.   Louis Zukofsky.   having contemplated without template to/flower so.   CoPo

This Is America.   Thomas Curtis Clark.   God keep our land forever free!   PGD

This Is an African Worm.   Margaret Danner.   Crawl, and wait.   BPo

This Is Halloween.   Dorothy Brown Thompson.   Shrieks and starts and laughter–/This is Halloween!   BrR; TiPo; YeAr

This Is Just to Say.   William Carlos Williams.   so sweet/and so cold.   AmP; FF; ForPo; GoJo; HoPM; InPK; InPS; NIP; NOBA; NoP; PAI; PPoe; SOTW; SpRo; TAP

This Is My Beloved (excerpt).   Walter Benton.   for my heart being yours released no blood to make ready for love.   UnTE

This Is My Carnac, Whose Unmeasured Dome.   Henry David Thoreau.   To enjoy our opportunities they remain.   EyDe

This Is My Death-Dream.   Ralph Salisbury.   myself in one/plane called "flying barn" teetering on an invisible thumb   STE

This Is My Father's World.   Maltbie Davenport Babcock.   God reigns, let the earth be glad!   AH; TRV

This Is My Hour.   Zoë Akins.   We sit in silence, while our thoughts go out–/Like treasure-seeking ships.   HBV 1-2

This Is My Letter to the World.   Emily Dickinson.   Judge tenderly–of Me   AmePo; AmPP; AnNE; GoTF; NoAm; NOBA; OxBA; SCV; TAP; TreFT

This Is My Love for You.   Grace Fallow Norton.   This is my love for you...   HBV 1-2

This Is My Rock.   David McCord.   I meet the evening face to face.   GeTw; NTCP; SiSoSe; SoPo; TiPo

This Is Not Death.   Humbert Wolfe.   "No, fool, this is not death."   MoBrPo

This Is Our Music.   George Leong.   and going on forever   BrSi

This Is Pioneer Weather.   William Carlos Williams.   down hill screaming/our heads off!   NePoAm-2

This Is the Garden.   Edward Estlin Cummings.   some silver-fingered fountain steals the world.   BoLiVe; MoAmPo

This Is the Hay That No Man Planted.   Elizabeth Jane Coatsworth.   Twined in the stalks of the wild salt hay.   BrR; OBCA

This Is the Horror That, Night after Night.   Gerald Gould.   And there's the price of sinning–and I'll pay.'   OxBTC

This Is the Key of the Kingdom.   Anonymous.
   Of the Kingdom this is the Key.   CH; FaBoCh; FaFP; LoGBV; MoShBr; OxBoLi; Prf; TreFS
   This is the key of the kingdom. OxNR

This Is the Last.   Gilbert Waterhouse.   "This is the last of wars–this is the last!"   PGD

This Is the Last Night.   Roo Borson.   ...A small purple cavern/that no one walks out of.   CaPN

This Is the Life.   Louis MacNeice.   ...a Pharaoh's portion of turkey and/ pumpkin pie.   NoAm

This Is the Non-Existent Beast.   Cid Corman.   and in her mirror was and in her.   GP

This Is the Place to Wait.   Horace Gregory.   You know again you have to wait.   MoAmPo

This Is the Time.   Josina Machel.   the time to give ourselves/to the Revolution.   WhB

This Is the Violin.   Trumbull Stickney.   I have it all thro' my heart, I tell you, crying/Childishly in the dark.   NCEP

This Is the Way the Ladies Ride.   Mother Goose.   This is the way the farmers ride,/Hobbledy-hobbledy-hoy!   FaBoUs; OxNR; TiPo f10]

This Is What the Watchbird Sings, Who Perches in the Lovetree.   Bruce Boyd.   For love is the kind of a tree whose fruit/Grows not on the branches, but at the root.   NeAP

This Is Willy Walker, and That's Tam Sim.   Anonymous.   And he owre him.../Till day brak.   OxNR

This Is Your Hour.   Herbert Kaufman.   You can force the world to cheer you.   PoToHe

This Island.   Archilochus.   like the backbone of an ass.   OBVE

This Journey.   Ingrid Jonker.   For the man of/whom you reminded me once   BoWoP

This Lady She Wears a Dark Green Shawl.   Anonymous.   Farewell to your lover, honey, my love,/I love her to my heart.   AmFP

This Land.   Ian Mudie.   strength and austerity/that this land has.   NOAV

This Landscape, These People.   Zulfikar Ghose.   Stranger or an inhabitant, this is my home.   ACV

This Last Pain.   William Empson.   And learn a style from a despair.   CMoP; CoBMV; EBEV; FaBoMo; GTBS-P; LiTM; MoAB; MoVE; NoAm; OAEL 1-2; SeCePo

This Life.   Anonymous.   With drede we wenden.   FaBoRV

This Life.   Rita Dove.   nursing the tough skin of figs.   AmPA

This Life a Theater.   Palladas.   Or learn to bear with grace his tragic part.   NIP

This Life Is All Chequer'd with Pleasures and Woes.   Thomas Moore.   From her fountain divine, 'tis sufficient for me.   ELP

This Life, Which Seems So Fair.   William, of Hawthornden Drummond.   Because it erst was nought, it turns to nought.   GTBS; GTBS-P

This Lime-Tree Bower My Prison.   Samuel Taylor Coleridge.   No sound is dissonant which tells of Life.   CBEP; ERoP 1-2; FaBoPP; HeIP; LoBV; NIP; PoEL 1-5

This little bride & groom are.   Edward Estlin Cummings.   nothing really exists   AmPP; HW

This Little House Is Sugar.   Langston Hughes.   And from its tiny window/ Peeps a maple-sugar child.   NTCP

This Little Light of Mine.   Anonymous.   Gonna let my little light shine.   FSW

This Little Pig Had a Rub-a-Dub.   Anonymous.   And this little pig had all the jam.   OxNR

This Little Pig Went to Market.   Anonymous.
   I can't find my way home.   OxNR; SoPo; TiPo
   This little pig cried wee, wee, all the way home. HBV 1-2; HBVY

This Little Vigil.   Charles G. Bell.   Lures to the longed-for and regretted joys.   MoLP; NePoAm

This Living Hand.   John Keats.   I hold it towards you.   BoLoP; CABA; HAP; InPK; InPS; MBW 1-2; NoP; OAEL 1-2; OBSP; PAI; SyP

This Loneliness for You Is Like the Wound.   Dunstan Thompson.   Who dares to say that love is like the war?   WaaP; WaP

This Love.   Judith Hemschemeyer.   Now let the pain I planned begin.   GOYP

This Lunar Beauty.   W. H. Auden.   Nor sorrow take/His endless look.   MoAB; MoBrPo; OBMV; OxBTC; SOTW

This Mad Carnival of Loving.   Heinrich Heine.   Woman, thou art dust– remember!   TrJP

This May Be Your Captain Speaking.   C. K. Stead.   pohutukawas endlessly/ varied endlessly the same.   OCNZ

This Measure.   Léonie Adams.   Rooted and blowing beyond sense or touch.   MoAB; MoAmPo

This Moment.   Annie Johnson Flint.   In ways that I know and know not,/ His labor of love I share.   BLRP

This Moment Yearning and Thoughtful.   Walt Whitman.   I know I should be happy with them.   MCCG

This Morning.   Lucille Clifton.   i survive/survive/survive   GLGT

This Morning.   Javier Galvez.   and came in laughing.   FF

This Morning.   Muriel Rukeyser.   this morning, waking the world away/in the violent day.   BoWoP; NMM

This Morning.   Jon Stallworthy.   as mine do this morning.   NoP

This Morning.   Jay Wright.   ...I don't think/I shall ever close my windows again.   NNP

This Morning I Wakened among Loud Cries of Seagulls.   Patrick MacDonogh.   Gathered the grey trunks as I stumbled homeward.   NeIP

This Morning Tom Child, the Painter, Died.   Samuel Sewall.   He paints it once; and paints no more.   SCAP

This My Emissary.   Christopher Dewdney.   In her misery we know it.   CaPN

This Narrow Stage.   Theodore Weiss.   ...Asia/on the one side, Afric on the other.   NoAm

This New Day.   Vail Read.   Walk the moon, but see thy light.   AH

This Night.   Nathan Alterman.   in the monstrous outstretched arms/of cranes and wagons.   VWA

This Night.   Dianne Hai-Jew.   You roll away.   BrSi

This Night.   William Heyen.   Which was our star this night?   MAYP

This Night.   Osip Mandelstam.   I awoke in my cradle/In the dark sun's light.   VWA

This Night of No Moon.   Ono no Komachi.   My heart is consumed in fire.   PBWP

This Night Sees Ireland Desolate.   Aindrais MacMarcuis.   ...With these/Our very souls pass overseas.   BIrV

This One Heart-Shaken.   Sister Maris Stella.   "I am afraid of silence. I am afraid."   GoBC

This One Is about the Others.   Dan Jaffe.   But no one took him home to dinner either.   FAZ

This One's on Me.   Phyllis Gotlieb.   See it at the Eastwood Theatre, friends,/next time 1930 rolls around.   NOBC

This Only Do I Know.   Anonymous.   Atoms, electrons–a kaleidoscope of worlds.   BePJ

This Only Grant Me. Abraham Cowley. Tomorrow let my sun his beams display,/Or in clouds hide them; I have lived today. TreFT

This Other Night. *Anonymous.* And ever among a Maiden sung,/"By by, Baby, lullay. ISi

This Page My Pigeon. Earle Birney. Windseed is barren takes no truehold/in heart tendrilled tight with éxistence of you PeCV

This Particular Christian. Louis Johnson. the broken-throated cry of the woman smashing the/near horizon. OCNZ

This Passion Is All Framed in Manner of a Dialogue. Thomas Watson. Why then despaire, goe packe thee hence away,/I live in hope to have a golden daie. AAS

This Pig Got in the Barn. *Anonymous.* I can't get over the barn door sill. OxNR

This Place in the Ways. Muriel Rukeyser. Poem in throat and hand, asleep,/and my storm beating strong! MiAP

This Place Rumord to Have Been Sodom. Robert Duncan. This place rumord to have been Sodom is blessd/in the Lord's eyes. NeAP; NOBA; PoM; PPP

This Poem Is for Nadine. Paul B. Janeczko. who this snowy night/rubs her small hands/wishing them lined with earth. GOYP

This Poem Will Never Be Finished. Raymond Souster. More beautiful songs as you climb/In splendour above the eternal rose. CaP

This Prayer I Make. William Wordsworth. Is full of blessings. PoToHe

This Pretty Woman. *Anonymous.* There were three wold be beten, three wold be/beten there were:/A myll, a stokfish, and a woman. OxBM

This Quiet Dust. John Hall Wheelock. Between two vigils fallen asleep. AnEnPo; MoAmPo; WHA

This quiet dust was gentlemen and ladies. Emily Dickinson. Then ceased, like these. CMoP; DL; EG; MoAB; MoAmPo; OxBA; ViBoPo

This Runner. Francis Webb. Here is your vicious, central shape/That has no need of cheer or tape. CBAP

This Shall Be Sufficient. Kenneth Rexroth. The air splotched with the gold,/Electric, coming day. CAD

This Shirt. Arturo Trias. meat and sweat: my/whole life. InW

This Solitude of Cataracts. Wallace Stevens. Breathing his bronzen breath at the azury centre of time. LCAP

This Song Shows Me Pictures: Morningside Drive, New York City... Richard Oyama. California. I have never been there. BrSi

This Stone. *Anonymous.* Oh, drink not thou forgetfulness of me. AWP

This Summer and Last. Thomas Hardy. Smiles your forerunner drew,/Know what it knew! OxBTC

This Sun Is Hot. *Anonymous.* I thinks I mus' 'a' been called to preach. BPo

This Tokyo. Gary Snyder. Peace war religion revolution/Will not help. NeAP

This, Too, Shall Pass Away. A. L. Alexander. Remember, even this, shall pass away! PoToHe

This, Too, Shall Pass Away. Lanta Wilson Smith. "This, too, shall pass away." BLPA

This Too Will Pass away. *Anonymous.* And bliss supreme shall never, never pass/away. STF

This Torch, Still Burning in My Hand. Crinagoras. I, Antiphanes,/The son of Antiphanes,/Dedicate to Hermes. SD

This Town. James Paul. ...In the hills/Beyond them, the pig farmers are ready for the kingdom. HoAn

This Town: Winter Morning. William Stafford. "I'm the girl who burned." NPAW

This Unimportant Morning. Lawrence Durrell. Like wings in waiting on the darkling lake. BoLoP; NeBP; OxBTC

This Version of Love. Dorothy Hewett. leaving no footprints. CBAP

This Very Hour. Lizette Woodworth Reese. His thirty coins held fast,/Goes dark Iscariot. AnAmPo; HBMV

This Was a Poet. Emily Dickinson. Himself–to Him–a Fortune–/Exterior–to Time– AmePo; MAmP; NOBA; PP

This Was My Brother. Mona Gould. And even death must have been a little ashamed/At his eagerness! CaP

This Way Only. Lesbia Harford. Lovely the dead tree lies. PoAu 1-2

This Way Out. Margaret Fishback. Continue to think that I really intend to forget you. ALV

This White and Slender Body. Heinrich Heine. And then, as usual, you'll betray me. UnTE

This Wind. Tom Kryss. and i listen to their footsteps in the wind/the wind/that only dead men do not hear. NeAC

This Winter's Weather It Waxeth Cold. *Anonymous.* And I'll have mine old cloak about me. InvP

This World. Abu-l-Ala al-Maarri. Some ill hap of Time is sure to meet him at morningtide. LiTW

This World. Abbie Huston Evans. Early and late the backdrop is for joy. NePoAm

This World and This Life Are So Scattered, They Try Me. Heinrich Heine. He'll stop up the chink of the wide Universe. ELU

This World Fares as a Fantasy. *Anonymous.* But Godes mercy is us alle beheeve,/For this world fareth as a fantasye. OxBM

This World Is All a Fleeting Show. Thomas Moore. There's nothing calm but Heaven! HBV 1-2

This world is amazingly flat. Natalya Gorbanyevskaya. Unfortunately,/we don't believe in it. BoWoP

This World Is Not Conclusion. Emily Dickinson. Narcotics cannot still the tooth/that nibbles at the soul–. AmePo; EaLo

This Year. Joseph Hutchison. ...Lowell/struck down in his cab. AmC; AMV-81

This Year, Before It Ends. Eve Langley. And the facade that we are; this year before it ends.' BoAV; NOAV

This Year I Intended Children. Margaret Atwood. and words fertilize each other/in the cold and with bulging eyes NeAC

This Year, Next Year... *Anonymous.* Barn. OxNR

This Yonder Night I Sawe a Sighte. *Anonymous.* This paine thu put away,/And if it possibil be may. NAs

Thisbe. Helen Gray Cone. For whose eyes, for whose lips, but mine! AA

Thistle-Down. Clara Doty Bates. It sails,–ah! quaint little bird indeed/Is the thistle-down. AA

Thistle, Yarrow, Clover. Kenneth Porter. I name them over and over. NePoAm

Thistledown. Denis Glover. He is only thistledown planted on the wind. AnNZ

Thistledown. James Merrill. Air at a breath blown! UnPo

Thistledown. Harold Monro. They almost try to dig, they need/So much to plant their thistle-seed. BrPo; OxBTC

Thistledown. Lizette Woodworth Reese. He drives them through the town. YeAr

Thistles. Ted Hughes. Stiff with weapons, fighting back over the same ground. NoAm; OBSP; OxBTC

Tho' I Can Not Your Cruelty Constrain. Sir Thomas Wyatt. This my poor and small request:/Rejoice not at my pain. SiPS

Tho We All Speak. Daniel Ort. where waters show/as much courtesy/to me as to/a speechless sky. AMV-80

Tho' You May Boast You're Fairer. *Anonymous.* We first must sin, before we can Repent. OBS

The Thocht. William Soutar. As hinny to a hungry ghaist/Maun be a thocht like yon. NeBP

Thomas a Kempis. Richard Rogers. Bowker. "Dear Lord, dear Lord, that I may be like/thee! AA

Thomas and Charlie. Peter Wild. they have slipped away into the mists... AmPA

Thomas at Chickamauga. Kate Brownlee Sherwood. They in the thickest fight shall stand and/proudly answer, "Here!" PAH

Thomas Carlyle. *Anonymous.* "Oh, stop your dodging, Mrs. C.!" FiBHP

Thomas Cromwell. *Anonymous.* "You shall neuer gett more from/mee." ESPB

Thomas Dudley Ah! Old Must Dye. *Anonymous.* When old in dust doe lye, it's best dye too. SCAP

Thomas Gray in Patterdale. Norman Nicholson. The wide-eyed stranger sky-line look at me? ACV

Thomas Hardy. Walter De la Mare. Yet thine, too, this solacing music, as we earthfolk stumble along.' NoAm

Thomas Hardy and A. E. Housman. Max Beerbohm. Housman the draught that's black. NLV

Thomas Hood. Edwin Arlington Robinson. As if the joys of time to dreams had fled,/Or sailed away with Ines to the West. HBMV

Thomas in the Fields. Lois Moyles. and separates out the wonder from the wet/and names its cause. NYBP

Thomas Iron-Eyes Born Circa 1840. Died 1919, Rosebud Agency, S.D. Marnie Walsh. To come and ride the starry road/Across the holy circle of the sky. WPOW

Thomas Jefferson. Rosemary and Stephen Vincent Benét. I lived past eighty,/I liked it, all, sir. TiPo

Thomas Logge. Walter De la Mare. Lest some fine canting pen/Should be at him again. FaBoEE

Thomas MacDonagh. Francis Ledwidge. Perhaps he'll hear her low at morn/Lifting her horn in pleasant meads. NOBI; OnYI; OxBI

Thomas More to Them That Seek Fortune. Sir Thomas More. As are the judgments of Astronomy. EnRePo

Thomas o Yonderdale. *Anonymous.* My brother's a knight o wealth and/might,/He'll wed nane but he will for me.' ESPB

Thomas of Erceldoune. *Anonymous.* On Huntly banks it is merry to be,/Where birds do sing both night and/day. MeEV

Thomas Rymer. *Anonymous.* And till seven years were past and gone/True Thomas on earth was never seen. FaBoBa; OAEP; ViBoFo

Thomas Shadwell the Poet. John Dryden. With this prophetic blessing–Be thou dull... ChTr

Thomas the Rhymer. *Anonymous.* True Thomas on earth was never seen. BSV; ELP; EnSB; FaBoCh; GoTS; HBV 1-2; InPS; LiTB; NOBE; OAEL 1-2; OBEV; OnMSP; OxBB; PAI; Prf; SeCeV; ViBoPo

Thomas Trevelyan.   Edgar Lee Masters.   To twitter amid cold winds and falling leaves!   AnFE; APA; MoPo

Thomas Winterbottom Hance.   Sir William Schwenck Gilbert.   And so, with undiminished pride,/Each went on his respective road.   InMe

Thomas Wolfe's Tombstone (excerpt).   Thomas Wolfe.   AND PUT THE SEAL OF HONOR ON HIM/WHEN HE DIED.   TRV

Thompson Street.   Samuel McCoy.   She smiles; she cannot quite forget/The mother overseas!   HBMV

Thoralf and Synnov.   Hjalmar Hjorth Boyeson.   And whispered, "Dearest Thoralf, you/promised something too."   AA

Thoreau.   Amos Bronson Alcott.   Be true as these, if ye would be more wise.   AA

Thoreau.   Rodney Jones.   and I am thinking of Thoreau's dry cow,/of his cornstalks splintered by hail.   AmC; MAYP

Thoreau's Flute.   Louisa May Alcott.   Seek not for him,–he is with thee.   AA; HBV 1-2

The Thorn.   William Wordsworth.
    And almost turned her brain to tinder.   EvOK; Par
    Oh woe is me! oh misery!""   EnRP

A Thorn Forever in the Breast.   Countee Cullen.   Between two wretched dying men, of whom/One doubts, and one for pity's sake believes.   BiP

Thorn Leaves in March.   William Stanley Merwin.   ...and the constellations/Sank nearer already, listing toward summer.   MP; TwCP

Thorn Piece.   Amy Lowell.   But the years–years–/Like leaves falling.   PeHV

Thorns Arm the Rose.   Claudian.   With license to indulge permitted jests.   HW

Those before Us.   Robert Lowell.   We have stopped watching them. They have stopped watching.   LCAP

Those Being Eaten by America.   Robert Bly.   The world will soon break up into small colonies of the saved   CoAP; NaP

Those Betrayed at Dawn.   Stanislaw Wygodski.   till dawn,/till noon,/till night,/were killed year by year.   VWA

Those Boys That Ran Together.   Lucille Clifton.   don't it make you want to cry?   CNA; PoBA

Those–Dying Then.   Emily Dickinson.   Better an ignis fatuus/Than no illume at all–.   AmePo; CABA; NAWM 1-2; NoP

Those Flapjacks of Brown's.   Bert Leston Taylor.   With his shirttails, in style Oriental,/Outside of his pants.   OBAL

Those Gambler's Blues (with music).   Anonymous.   O flowers on the coffin,/While the burial's carried on.   AS

Those Guyana Nights.   Richard Foerster.   ...Watch now, even the night's/a womb that swallows shooting stars.   SOTS

Those Hours When Happy Hours Were My Estate.   Edna St. Vincent Millay.   I feel its texture, though the gate is fast.   PrIm

Those I Love.   Victor Contoski.   and the sheep faces/of those that love me.   GP

Those Images.   William Butler Yeats.   Recognise the five/That make the Muses sing.   CMoP; PP

Those Last, Late Hours of Christmas Eve.   Lou Ann Welte.   Come those last, late, lingering hours before/Christmas Day.   PCh

Those Makheta Nights.   Frank Mkalawile Chipasula.   Out of those nights shall emerge/the blade of the flame that will rend the dark cloak!   WhB

Those Not Confused Are Prisoners of War....   Noah Mitchell.   Jailors and Jailees/Within us,/Struggling to disprove/Either/Position.   LFAC

Those Not Elect.   Léonie Adams.   Lest flesh at length lay waste the soul/In its sick heat.   MoVE

Those Not Live Yet.   Emily Dickinson.   Costumeless Consciousness–/That is he–   MAmP

Those of Pure Origin.   Roy Fuller.   Complexions marked with still unmalignant moles/Of the actual, scabs on unfolding leaves?   FaBoMo

Those Old Zen Blues.   James Richard Broughton.   It's where it is because it is/and not because it isn't.   GP

Those Rebel Flags.   John H. Jewett.   We are "Brothers-in-blood," and "Good/Hunting"/Is America's watchword to-day.   PAH

Those Trees That Line the Northway.   Ellen Perreault.   ...marry the long loved/and christen babies and the mended living into spring.   AMV-81

Those Troublesome Disguises.   Jonathan Williams.   We're Cooling it, Man, before the Fall'   NeAP

Those Two Boys.   Franklin Pierce ("F.P.A.") Adams.   You never can tell.   ALV; FiBHP; TrJP

Those Various Scalpels.   Marianne Moore.   are more highly specialised than the tissues of destiny/itself?   LoBV

Those We Love the Best.   Ella Wheeler Wilcox.   To those we love the best....   PoToHe

Those Wedding Bells Shall Not Ring Out.   Monroe F. Rosenfield.   She's mine till death shall set her free/Those bells shall not ring out!   FSN

Those Were the Days.   Anonymous.   Though our ancestors are dead we still remember/them.   WTO

Those Who Come What Will They Say of Us.   John Knoepfle.   how all things/cried out to share them   FAZ

Those Who Lost Everything.   David Diop.   Tom-toms of my nights,/Tom-toms of my fathers!   PBA

Those Who Love.   Sara Teasdale.   A light would pass over her face.   MoLP

Those Winter Sundays.   Robert Earl Hayden.   What did I know, what did I know/of love's austere and lonely offices?   BP; CNA; CTBA; DFF; FF; GP; GrPl; HaCAP; HAP; HoAn; IDB; LCAP; NoAm; NoP; PoBA; PPP; SoSe; UnPo

Those Zionists.   Crescenzo Del Monte.   ...When we do get there, when/that comes about, who shall we do business with?   VWA

Thou Alone Canst Save.   Amelia Wakeford.   For Thou alone canst save.   BePJ

Thou Art Coming!   Frances Ridley Havergal.   Unto earth's remotest end/Glorified, adored and owned!   WGRP

Thou Art Coming to a King.   John Newton.   For His grace and power are such/None can ever ask too much.   TRV

Thou Art Not Fair.   Thomas Campion.   Embrace and kiss and love me in despite.   AAS; AtBAP; EG; ElL; EnLoPo; EnRePo; InvP; ViBoPo

Thou Art Not Lovelier Than Lilacs.   Edna St.Vincent Millay.   I drink–and live–what has destroyed some men.   BoLiVe

Thou Art, O God, the God of Might.   Emily Swan Perkins.   Thy grace can wash away the stain,/And heaven receive us pardoned.   AH

Thou Art of All Created Things.   Pedro Calderon de la Barca.   To these the bounteous Godhead gave/These organs but to praise his name!   WGRP

Thou Art the Sky.   Rabindranath Tagore.   ...wherein is/neither day nor night, nor form nor colour, nor ever any/word.   OBMV

Thou Art the Source.   Jalal ed-Din or al-Din Rumi.   I was the magnet, and I gave them wings.'   ILwL

Thou Art the Tree of Life.   Edward Taylor.   The pleasant'st fruits in all God's Paradise.   AH

Thou Art the Way.   George Washington Doane.   That truth to keep, that life to win,/Whose joys eternal flow.   AH

Thou Beautiful Sabbath.   Anonymous.   All eager to greet thee with praise and/with song.   TrJP

Thou Blind Man's Mark.   Sir Philip Sidney.   Desiring nought but how to kill desire.   CABA; EnRePo; HeIP; PPP; ViBoPo

Thou Bounteous Giver of the Light.   Saint Hilary of Arles.   That this, our holy matin light,/May guide us thrugh the busy day.   BePJ

Thou Didst Delight My Eyes.   Robert Bridges.   A sail, that for a day/Has cheered the castaway.   ELP; MoAB; MoBrPo

Thou Didst Say Me.   Miriam Waddington.   ...and bitter/iron cuts and shapes/my death, I was so fool.   OBCV; PeCV

Thou Grace Divine, Encircling All.   Eliza Scudder.   To rise o'er sin and fear and death,/O love of God, to thee!   AH

Thou Great God.   Anonymous.   Thy blood that streameth for ever and ever/For the sake of us men was shed.   PBA

Thou Hast Diamonds.   Heinrich Heine.   My darling, what would'st thou/more?   TrJP

Thou Hast Made Us for Thyself.   Saint Augustine.   And our hearts are restless until they rest in Thee.   TRV

Thou Hast Wounded the Spirit That Loved Thee.   Mrs. David Porter.   All rudely and wildly dispelling/The love of the happiest home.   BLPA

Thou Joy'st, Fond Boy.   Thomas Campion.   'Tis far more conquest with one to live/true/Than every hour to triumph lord of/new.   OAEP

Thou Knowest.   Katharine Lee Bates.   And know that dim, wronged pattern for Thine own.   TrPWD

Thou Leanest to the Shell of Night.   James Joyce.   And all for some strange name he read/In Purchas or in Holinshed.   EBEV

Thou Light of Ages.   Rolland W. Schloerb.   Rekindle here the torch of love for Him.   TrPWD

Thou Lingering Star.   Robert Burns.   Hear'st thou the groans that rend his breast?   OBEC

Thou Long Disowned, Reviled, Oppressed.   Eliza Scudder.   And love be all in all!   AH

Thou, Lord, Hast Been Our Sure Defense.   John Hopkins.   And is cut down ere it be night/All withered, dead, and dry.   AH

Thou Lord of Hosts, Whose Guiding Hand.   Octavius Brooks Frothingham.   Thy truth, be that our firmest stay;/Our only rest to do thy will.   AH

Thou Mother with Thy Equal Brood.   Walt Whitman.   The FUTURE only holds thee and can hold thee.   AmePo

Thou Mother with Thy Equal Brood (excerpt).   Walt Whitman.   I merely thee ejaculate!   PeD

Thou One in All, Thou All in One.   Seth Curtis Beach.   The love that makes us one with thee.   AH

Thou, Our Elder Brother.   John Greenleaf Whittier.   If a blinder soul there be,/Let me guide him nearer Thee.   ILwL

Thou Remainest.   Annie Johnson Flint.   God of wisdom and of love.   BLRP

Thou Shalt Not.   Malka Tussman.   descended/into the abyss of secret self.   VWA

Thou Shalt Surely Die...: No Ghost Is True.   Leslie A. Fiedler.   In the evening you were still valid....   PoA

Thou should'st be living at this hour. Heathcote William Garrod. England hath need of thee, and not/Of Leavis and Eliot. CenHV

Thou Shouldst Be Living at This Hour! Kenyon West. And bring us back the glory that hath been! PGD

Thou Sleepest Fast. *Anonymous.* Thou dreamest still which way my life to wast. EIL; OBSP

Thou Strainest through the Mountain Fern. Robert Louis Stevenson. And William Wordsworth upon Tin-Tern! NOBV

An Thou Were My Ain Thing (excerpt). Allan Ramsay. And thou were my ain thing,/How dearly wou'd I love thee. ViBoPo

Thou Who Createdst Everything. *Anonymous.* Through all my wounds to thee I cry! NOCV

Thou Who Taught the Thronging People. Henry S. Minde. May o'ercome the bent to evil/By Thy purity. TRV

Though a Fool. Robert Francis. While the fool may well be jolly/Though why he cannot say. GP

Though a Soldier at Present. Thomas Moore. You but do with a sword what your pills did before. DBV

Though All the Fates Should Prove Unkind. Henry David Thoreau. Twine, wine, and hides, and China teas. AP; HAP; MAmP

Though Amaryllis Dance in Green. *Anonymous.* Heigh ho, heigh ho, 'chill love no more. NIP; OAEP

Though Bodies Are Apart. C. Day-Lewis. Come out into the sun! NAs

Though Fatherland Be Vast. Allen Eastman Cross. Thou hast a name, a name, a name,/To make the stars thine own. AH

Though He Slay Me. Vassar Miller. Resolves to music all Your negatives. NePoEA-2

Though He That Ever Kind and True. Robert Louis Stevenson. Waits on a stile. BBV

Though Here in Flesh I Be. Philip, Earl of Arundel Howard. That there my heart and joy may rest,/though here in flesh I be. CoBE

Though I am Laila of the Persian romance. Princess Zeb-un-Nissa. Even the moth is my disciple. BoWoP

Though I get home how late, how late! Emily Dickinson. And what itself will say to me,/Beguiles the centuries of way! MoAmPo

Though I Regarded Not. Henry Howard, Earl of Surrey. As I, in such desire,/Have once a thought to turn. AAS; SiPS

Though I Should Seek. Henry Ustic Onderdonk. In him thy righteousness be found. AH

Though I Thy Mithridates Were. James Joyce. Neither a love where may not be/Ever so little falsity. NoAm

Though I've a Clever Head. *Anonymous.* I can well say this of me:/Heavy hangs my sorrow. HAP

Though Mine Eye Sleep Not. *Anonymous.* Rather hast Thou braced his spirit/to withstand affliction. TrJP

Though My Thoughts. Francis Daniel Pastorius. And will never turn from me. AH

Though My Wanderings Are Many. Suibne Geilt. At Mo Ling's house, of endless angels,/by a horn point I shall die. NOBI

Though She Slumbers. Joseph Joel Keith. but heaven breathes softly/by her side. ISi

Though the Great Waters Sleep. Emily Dickinson. Ignited this Abode/To put it out– EaLo

Though this the port and I thy servant true. Sir Thomas Wyatt. Forget me not, en vogant la galere. FCP; SiPS

Though Ye Suppose. John Skelton. Ware of the lizard lieth lurking in the grass. CBEP; OBSP

Though You Are Young. Thomas Campion. "Thou fool, tomorrow thou must die." EnRePo

Though You Serve Richest Wines. Martial (Marcus Valerius Martialis). No, I really don't care for a drink. DBV

Though Your Strangenesse Frets My Hart. Thomas Campion. Is this faire excusing? O no, all is abusing. AAS

Thought. Christopher Pearse Cranch. Melting, flowing into one. WGRP

A Thought. William Henry Davies. But I see a wise man/When I look into a pool. GTBS; MoShBr

Thought. Ralph Waldo Emerson. But thought will glow when the sun grows cold,/And mix with Deity. AmePo

The Thought. Edward, Lord Herbert of Cherbury. If you do love as well as I. AnAnS 2; InvP

A Thought. Mikhail Yuryevich Lermontov. In bitter mockery the cheated son. AWP

The Thought. William Brighty ("Matthew Browne") Rands. Will that awful thing seem plain. OBEV; OBVV

A Thought. Margaret E. Sangster. Ever since, o'er all our loss/Shines the glory of the cross. TRV

A Thought. James Kenneth Stephen. To keep a small girl for the tenth of a year. FiBHP

Thought and the Poet. Peter Yates. We think, and thought corrupts love's image of the world. ChMP

The thought beneath so slight a film. Emily Dickinson. As laces just reveal the surge–/Or Mists–the Appenine. AmP; AmPP; OxBA

The Thought Eternal. Johann Wolfgang von Goethe. He is ever fair and great. AWP

Thought for a New Year. Gail Brook Burket. Who bears no useless burden from the past/Will find the miles ahead are always best. PGD

A Thought for My Love. Bruce Williamson. Quit me of stubborn death. NeIP

Thought for the Winter Season. Mary Elizabeth Osborn. Be reconciled to living things. NePoAm

The Thought-Fox. Ted Hughes. The page is printed. FaBoMo; HeIP; InPS; NCSH; NePoEA-2; NoAm; NoP; NYBP; SCV

A Thought from Cardinal Newman. Matthew Russell. And His own Mother as our nursing Mother. CAW

A Thought from Porpertius. William Butler Yeats. Or been fit spoil for a centaur/Drunk with the unmixed wine. OAEL 1-2; OBSP

A Thought in Time. Robert Hillyer. Edith Sitwell fell in love with Pope.) NYBP

Thought of a Briton on the Subjugation of Switzerland. William Wordsworth. And neither awful Voice be heard by thee! BoLiVe; MBW 1-2; SeCeV; SpRo

A Thought of Death. Thomas Flatman. That lies on th' other side Death's Rubicon. CEP; OBS

A Thought of Marigolds. Janice Farrar. I send a thought–of marigolds. GoYe

A Thought of the Nile. [James Henry] Leigh Hunt. Our own calm journey on for human sake. ERoP 1-2; NBM

A Thought on Human Life. *Anonymous.* And some in smoke of battle lost,/Whom drums, not lutes, delighted. OBSP

Thought on June 26. Raymond Mazisi Kunene. Was I wrong? Was I wrong? WhB

Thought's End. Léonie Adams. Stars that are worlds look out and see you not. MoAB; MoAmPo

A Thought Went Up My Mind. Emily Dickinson. And came my way no more. AmP; AnFE; APA; DiPo

Thoughts. Michael Benedikt. There is a spirit, shifting around from foot to foot. ConAP

Thoughts. David Ignatow. ...He is in my company,/with the first smashed bottle. FAZ

Thoughts. Duncan Campbell Scott. Or to the dull, intolerable bells/That beat the dawn/And will not let us rest! PeCV

Thoughts about the Person from Porlock. Stevie Smith. O Person from Porlock come quickly/And bring my thoughts to an end. FaBoCo; NoP

Thoughts after Ruskin. Elma Mitchell. And somehow find, in mirrors, colours, odours,/Their essences of lilies and of roses. FaBoWP

Thoughts after Work. David Rubadiri. Bringing back to me/Simple joys I once knew. WhB

Thoughts at the Museum. Eileen Brennan. for the like of the wan little fellow there? OnYI

Thoughts during an Air Raid. Stephen Spender. Which is all mystery or nothing. MoBrPo; ViBoPo

Thoughts for My Grandmother. Laya Firestone. How you boomed,/Vibrated, shouted/In utter self-restraint. VWA

Thoughts for St. Stephen. Christopher Morley. If Plymouth Rock/Had landed on the Puritans. ShM

Thoughts for You (when She Came back from the Mountains). Ranice Henderson Crosby. you are a mountain NMM

Thoughts from a Bottle. Carl Clark. I have paid your fee, whore,/And now I sing. JB

Thoughts from Abroad. Patrick Maybin. and smoke rising quietly to the evening sky. NeIP

Thoughts in Separation. Alice Meynell. Thou to thy crucifix, I to my mother. ACP; GoBC

Thoughts in the Gulf Stream. Christopher Morley. In clear summer midnight/Ever sees it alone. EtS

Thoughts of a Young Girl. John Ashbery. May you not be long on the way! ConAP; TAP; VGW

Thoughts of Chairman Mao. David Young. And the rulers ride the blue hills/holding their black whips high. AmPA

Thoughts of God. *Anonymous.* Trembling to be rejected/I turn to Thee again. WTO

Thoughts of Loved Ones. Margaret Fishback. But Mother...she must never know/That I have sunk to depths so low. FiBHP

Thoughts of Phena. Thomas Hardy. No mark of her late time as dame in her dwelling, whereby/I may picture her there. NOBV; NoP; OxBTC

Thoughts of Thomas Hardy. Edmund Charles Blunden. Your particular fate and experience, poor leaf. PoCh

Thoughts on Being Invited to Dinner. Christopher Morley. The hostess writes/B. Y. O. B. HBMV

Thoughts on Capital Punishment. Rod McKuen. But a cat too is an extension of God. InPK

Thoughts on One's Head. William Meredith. One dislikes it of course: it is the seat of Me. HAP

Thoughts on Pausing at a Cottage near the Paukataug River.   Sarah Kemble Knight.   When I reflect, my late fatigues do seem/Only a notion or forgotten Dreem.   SCAP

Thoughts on the Christian Doctrine of Eternal Hell.   Stevie Smith.   Oh oh have none of it,/Blow it away, have done with it.   PPON

Thoughts on the Commandments.   George Augustus Baker.   For her sweet eyes own that she/Also loves her neighbor.   AA; HBV 1-2

Thoughts on the Cosmos.   Franklin Pierce ("F.P.A.") Adams.   But how I hate the wabbly gink,/Like me, who knows not what to think!   HBMV

Thoughts on the Shape of the Human Body.   Rupert Brooke.   Patiently ever, through the eternal night!   BrPo

Thoughts on the Sight of the Moon.   Sarah Kemble Knight.   And pleasant prospects thou giv'st light to see.   SCAP

The Thoughts That Move the Heart of Man.   Ebenezer S. Oakley.   Thus shall our wills from hour to hour/Become not ours, but thine.   TrPWD

Thoughts upon a Walk with Natalie, My Niece, at Houghton Farm.   Harold Trowbridge Pulsifer.   Who knows what vagrant dreams may ride/On this frail ship forevermore?   HBMV   My heart is empty, O sons of Barmak.   AWP

The Thousand and One Nights: Birds.   Anonymous.   Wild pigeon of the leaves,/You are/Brother of lovers.   AWP; LiTW

The Thousand and One Nights: Dates.   Anonymous.   Shall hear us murmur ever above his sleep.   AWP; LiTW

The Thousand and One Nights: Death.   Anonymous.   But all's one level plain he hunts for flowers.   AWP

The Thousand and One Nights: Drinking Song.   Anonymous.   O night, O eyes of love!   LiTW

The Thousand and One Nights: Haroun's Favorite Song.   Anonymous.   Your mouth, dear child, is envied of the bees.   AWP

The Thousand and One Nights: Her Rival for Aziza.   Anonymous.   That they may weep.   AWP

The Thousand and One Nights: Inscriptions At the City of Brass.   Anonymous.
My jealous breast holds him for ever.   LiTW
Where are the lords of Ispahan,/O sons of men?   WaaP

The Thousand and One Nights: Love.   Anonymous.   Eating the green heart of the tree/Of man!   AWP; LiTW

The Thousand and One Nights: Pearls Seen through Amber.   Anonymous.   You'd smile through crying, if you knew/The cool sweetness of his strength.   LiTW

The Thousand and One Nights: Psalm of the Bottle.   Anonymous.   Beside an eternal river of scented honey.   AWP

The Thousand and One Nights: Tell Him, O Night.   Anonymous.   Tell him, O night.   AWP; LiTW

The Thousand and One Nights: The Beautiful Boy.   Anonymous.   No room for chains.   LiTW

The Thousand and One Nights: The Power of Love.   Anonymous.   And all the waters of the world are vain/To put them out again.   LiTW

The Thousand and One Nights: The Sleeper.   Anonymous.   Burst like a poppy in this solitude,/In this cool silence.   AWP; LiTW

The Thousand and One Nights: The Song of the Narcissus.   Anonymous.   As I hang my head above the waters.   AWP

The Thousand and One Nights: The Wazir Dandan for Prince Sharkan.   Anonymous.   Leads straightway to an old immortal wine/Pressed from God's vine.   AWP

The Thousand and One Nights: To Lighten My Darkness.   Anonymous.   You sit drinking the tulip-colored wine/In the midst of this green earth/With all her waters.   AWP

The Thousand and One Nights: Tumadir al-Khansa for Her Brother.   Anonymous.   Weep! Weep! Weep!   PG

The Thousand and Second Night.   James Merrill.   Too late to question what the tale had meant.   NYBP

A Thousand Hairy Savages.   Spike Milligan.   Munch munch munch.   NLV; OnUR; PV

A Thousand Killed.   Bernard Spencer.   ...With the lives, burned-off,/Of young men and boys.   OBWP

A Thousand Martyrs I Have Made.   Aphra Behn.   And while I thus at random rove/Despise the fools that whine for love.   CavP; SBG

The Thousand Things.   Christopher Middleton.   A naked child jumps over the threshold,/waving a green spray of leaves of vine.   NePoEA-2

A Thousand Years Have Come.   Thomas Toke Lynch.   Uprose the Light of man.   BLRP

A thousand years, you said.   Lady Heguri.   and the ache is hard to bear.   BoLoP

Thousands and Three.   Paul Verlaine.   Cherished ones without number and never enough!   PeHV

The Thracian Filly.   Anacreon.   But you frolic in the meadow, still in clover,/never having had a master ride astride you.   LiSp

The Thraldome.   Abraham Cowley.   Employ me, mighty Love, to dig the Mine.   SeCV 1-2

The Thre Prestis of Peblis: Prologue.   John, of Stobo Reid.   The thing begun, the soner it is endit.'   OxBS

Thread Suns.   Paul Celan.   still songs to be sung on the other side/of mankind.   OBVE

The Threat.   Andrei Codrescu.   And yet I want it out more than I want these words.   APU

Threatened.   Alice Walker.   it is this fear/that now devours/desire.   LTB

Three.   Marilyn Kitchell.   to sleep inside/the hollow of a bone.   APU

Three.   John N. Morris.   I keep me to myself.   GP

Three Acres of Land.   Anonymous.   Sing holly, go whistle, and ivy!   NA; OxNR

Three against One.   Anonymous.   Kicked Mrs. Kickabout/Round about our coal fire.   OxNR

Three American Women and a German Bayonet.   Winfield Townley Scott.   Lifts it heavy and wonderful in her hands and with triumphant/tenderness.   NMP

Three Around the Old Gentleman.   John Berryman.   sir,–taking cover.   AP

The Three Arrows.   Edward Fitzgerald.   That vainly weeping lovers call/Repentance, or Regret.   OBVV

Three Bad Ones.   Anonymous.   And they all grew ugly, and nobody cares.   BBGG

The Three Badgers.   Lewis (Charles Lutwidge Dodgson) Carroll.   Clear rang their voices through the ocean's roar,/"Hooray, hooray, hooray!"   FaBoNo

Three Ballate.   Angelo Poliziano.
For pastime in a field with blossoms strewn.   AWP
In a green garden in mid month of May.   AWP
Let him look fixedly on Myrrha's eyes.   AWP

Three Barrows Down.   Jocelyn Brooke.   The harsh and bitter seeding/Of the dragon-rooted flower.   ChMP

The Three Bells.   John Greenleaf Whittier.   The lights of God draw nigh!   EtS

Three Blessings (Parody on Dryden).   Anonymous.   The force of nature can no further go.   ALV

Three Blind Mice.   Anonymous.
Did ever you see such a sight in your life,/As three blind mice?   FSW; OxNR
She scrap'd her tripe, lick thou the knife.   FaBoNo; OBS

Three Brethren from Spain.   Anonymous.   Please to take my daughter in.   OxNR

Three Brown Girls Singing.   M. Carl Holman.   To mark the periphery/Of what shall be saved from calendars and decay.   NIP

The Three Bushes.   William Butler Yeats.   Know where its roots began./O my dear, O my dear.   DTC; LiTL

The Three Butchers.   Anonymous.   You have killed the bravest butcher boy/In North Amerikee!   BFSS

The Three Captains.   Anonymous.   That I might maiden come again/To my mother and to thee.   AWP

Three Car Poems, III.   Richard Jones.   in your brain will die/(1/2 a brain)   FAZ

Three Cezannes.   George Whipple.   –He always set his goals beyond the seen.   AMV-80

Three Cheers for the Black, White and Blue.   Ruth Pitter.   The Bruiser in his ritzy suit.   BoAnP

The Three Cherry Trees.   Walter de la Mare.   That happy and beautiful lady.   CMoP

Three Children.   Anonymous.   If you would have them safe abroad/Pray keep them safe at home.   NA; NOBL; OxNR

Three Children near Clonmel.   Eileen Shanahan.   The shadows of a king and queen/Will darken on the daffodils.   OnYI; OxBI

Three Christmas Carols: I.   Anonymous.   In the worship of that child,/Gloria tibi domine.   ACP

Three Christmas Carols: II.   Anonymous.   For He is made man for thy sake.   ACP

Three Christmas Carols: III.   Anonymous.   All our sorrow shall turn to game,/Verbum Caro factum est.   ACP

Three City Cantos.   Charles A. Wagner.   with song far too profound for words.   GoYe

Three Colts Exercising in a Six-Acre.   Joseph Campbell.   But I slacken my pace to watch them.   BoAnP; OnYI

Three Cooks.   Anonymous.   From the three cooks of Colebrook.   OxNR

The Three Cottage Girls.   William Wordsworth.   And that intrepid Nymph, on Uri's steep descried!   HBV 1-2

Three Crooked Cripples Went through Cripplegate.   Anonymous.   And through Cripplegate went three crooked cripples.   OxNR

Three Darks Come down Together.   Robert Francis.   Three future lights defend me.   LCAP

The Three Dead and the Three Living.   George Barker.   But questions were/asked.   LiTB

Three Dreams.   James Michie.   For spying to be done to death with sticks.   NePoEA-2

Three Elements.   Stephen Vincent Benét.   To drift between the cold forts of the stars.   EaLo

The Three Enemies.   Christina Georgina Rossetti.   My soul, oh, keep it by Thy Word.   CoBE; TrCP; VLP

Three Epigrams. J.V. Cunningham. If he could speak he would deny it. MoAmPo

Three Epigrams. Theodore Roethke.
But he was apprehended, bare,/By one who rose up from the dead. NLV
Some cannot praise him: I am one of those. NLV

Three Epitaphs. Francis Davison.
And now dead, thou dost enjoy/In high heaven an angel's place. OBSC
For base earth was far unfit/For thy beauty, grace, and wit. OBSC
For such loss in such young years. OBSC

Three Epitaphs: For a Virgin Lady. Countee Cullen. Death only was so amorous/I let him have his way. MoAmPo

Three Epitaphs on John Hewet and Sarah Drew. Alexander Pope. Here lie two poor lovers, who had the mishap/Though very chaste people, to die of a clap. NIP

The Three-Faced. Robert Graves. Once for an endless moment turned on me. FaBoEE

The Three Fates. Rosemary Dobson. the reel unrolling towards the river. BoWoP

Three Fields. Adolf Heyduk. Sparrows ate the half of it, the gentry will eat the rest. LiTW

The Three Fishers. Charles Kingsley. And good-by to the bar and its moaning. BBV; BeLS; EtS; FaPoR; HBV 1-2; MCCG; OnMSP; PoLf; TreF; WBLP

Three Fitts. Stewart Parker.
But he belly laughs. He's not wise. CIP
...Lovely day. CIP
Travelling on Rapid Sic Transit. CIP

Three Floors. Stanley Jasspon Kunitz. the windowpanes were crying. SM

The Three Foxes. A.(lan) A.(lexander) Milne. And they didn't wear stockings and they didn't wear sockses. GoJo; GrPl; MoShBr; OxBChV

Three Fragments. William Allingham. Fields, hills, and cots, and every forest brake/Slumber in dew. IrPN

Three Friends. Anonymous. And fruit killed them. BoWoP; PBA

Three Friends of Mine. Henry Wadsworth Longfellow. And summer is not summer, nor can be. MAmP

Three Gates. Beth Day. Then you may tell the tale, nor fear/What the result of speech may be. BLPA; GoTF; PoToHe; TreFS

Three Ghostesses. Anonymous. Oh, what beastesses/to make such feastesses! OxNR

Three Girls on a Buttress. Eilidh Nisbet. But too content at heart/To care. PoSH

Three Green Trees. Angela Morgan. While man—his hill is hardly crowned/Before another hill is found! HBMV

Three Green Windows. Anne Sexton. It is a time of water, a time of trees. NYBP

Three Grey Geese in a Green Field Grazing. Anonymous. Grey were the geese and green was the grazing. OxNR; PBBP

Three-Handed Fugue. Phyllis Gotlieb. pull down the house of cards. NOBC

Three Helpers in Battle. Mary Elizabeth Coleridge. But I, with Aaron, faint yet unafraid,/Held up the hands of Moses while he prayed. EaLo

The Three Hermits. William Butler Yeats. Sang unnoticed like a bird. AtBAP; CMoP

The Three Hills. J. C. Squire. And earth shall eat the stones, and we/Shall be alone again. HBMV

Three Holy Kings from Morgenland. Heinrich Heine. The kings raised their voices in song. PCh

Three Hours. Vachel Lindsay. To Heaven and Earth and men. ATP

Three Hundred Thousand More. James Sloan Gibbons. We are coming, Father Abraham, three hun-/dred thousand more! PAH

The Three Huntsmen. Anonymous. And a-hunting they did go. OnMSP; OxBoLi

Three in Transition. David Ignatow. out where the wind/is free/of the branches. CAPP

Three Jolly Fishermen. Anonymous. Mind how I sell them while the merry, merry bells do ring. OBSS

The Three Jolly Pigeons. Oliver Goldsmith. Toroddle, toroddle, toroll! PoRA

Three Jovial Gentlemen. Daniel Gerard Hoffman. Down, down the mountain/They hunt on, and on. MoBS

The Three Jovial Welshmen. Anonymous. And his beard growing grey. HBVY; OxNR

The Three Khalandeers. James Clarence Mangan. And slight luck or grace attends/Your boaters down the Bosphorus! OBVV

The Three Kingdoms of Nature. Gotthold Lessing. And, human, tell me, if you have neither/love nor wine–what are you? A stone. NU

The Three Kings. Ruben Dario. Christ, reborn, turns chaos into light,/and on His brow He wears the Crown of Life. PCh

The Three Kings. Eugene Field. My only tribute, Christ, my King. GN

The Three Kings. Henry Wadsworth Longfellow. And returned to their homes by another way. GN; HBV 1-2; HBVY; OnMSP

Three Kings. James P. Vaughn. Quietly Quietly Quietly NNP; PoNe

Three Kings Came. Thomas W. Shapcott. The child himself stayed fast asleep. PoAu 1-2

Three Knights from Spain. Anonymous. And adieu to you, my darlings. AtBAP; PoPle

The Three Ladies. Robert Creeley. Three old ladies sat in a tree. NeAP

Three Landscapes (excerpt). Jerome Rothenberg. be swallowed in its/darkness, like an eyelash. CoPo

Three little children sitting in the sand. Anonymous. Down in the green wood shady. ExPo

Three Little Girls. Richard Aldington. Marianne, Madeline, Alys. BrPo

The Three Little Kittens. Anonymous. We smell a rat/close by. OxNR; TreFS

Three Little Kittens. Eliza Cook. "We smell a rat near by."/"Mee-ow, mee-ow, mee-ow." OBCA; SoPo

The Three Little Pigs. Alfred Scott Gatty. For you only can say "Wee! wee!" OxBChV

Three Little Puffins. Eleanor Farjeon. All three/Were puffy as puffy can be. TiPo

Three Love Poems. Judah Halevi. A forecast 'tis of heav'nly bliss! TrJP

Three Loves. Lucy H. Hooper. Was the one of the three who loved him best. BeLS

Three Lyrics. Petronius Arbiter (Caius Petronius Arbiter).
And let what happened so suddenly,/Never suddenly stop. LiTW
If I could only die that way,/I'd say goodbye to the business of living. LiTW
Ruled by a mighty lust. LiTW

Three Maids a-Milking Would Go. Anonymous. For birds of a feather will all flock together,/Let their parents say little or much. CoMu

Three Memorial Sonnets. George Barker.
...paralysed with mere pity's peace? MasP
...pitches our pod/To the mouth of the death for which no one is ready. MasP

Three Men. Alice Moore. That's my best friend, my kid man,/the one that's kicking in my stall BluL

Three Migrations. Ralph Salisbury. three wars later, as well as I can. STE

Three Mile Island. Maureen Owen. O Rolling Rock! Goodbye! APU

The Three Mirrors. Edwin Muir. And you and myself there. NoAm

Three Modes of History and Culture. LeRoi (Imamu Amiri Baraka) Jones. ...my songs will be softer/and lightly weight the air. NoAm

Three Moments. Susan Sherman. Hidden behind the flower/of the moon DFF

Three Monkeys. Anonymous. They've descended from something, but/not from us. STF

The Three Movements. Donald Hall. ...It is/like himself, only visible. NePoEA-2

Three Movements. William Butler Yeats. What are all those fish that lie gasping on the strand? CMoP; ELU; FaBoEE

Three Moves. John Logan. and so all their multi-thousand-mile range/is too short for the hope of change. CAPP

The Three Musicians. Aubrey Beardsley. Red as his guide-book grows, moves on, and offers up a prayer for/France. NOBV; OBTV; VLP

Three Nights Drunk. Anonymous. Eyes and nose on a cabbage head I never did see before. OuSiCo

Three Old Brothers. Frank O'Connor. Like Paris and the Grecian chiefs/And the three Ulster brothers! OnYI

Three Part Invention. Paul Blackburn. ...Air moves thru'/the quiet stream of my wrist, moths/strike the screen. CoPo

Three Persons. Louise Townsend Nicholl. The trefoil of Divinity. CAW

Three Phases of Africa. Francis Ernest Kobina Parkes. The palm gives of its wine/At the sacramental font. PBA

Three Places Most Loved I Have Left. Colum Cille. I would choose to be buried in Gartan/out of all three. NOBI

Three Poems. Anonymous. Over the rushes/Of Inami Moor? LiTW

Three Poems. Basho (Matsuo Basho).
How quickly you must die. LiTW
Of twice ten thousand warriors slain. LiTW
Was eaten by the passing ass! LiTW

Three Poems. Stephen Crane.
–And the supple-souled men–. AP
A naked woman. AP

Three Poems. Hitomaro. I remember the past. LiTW

Three Poems. Jenny Mastoraki. The papers of the period/spoke of bloodless operations. PBWP

Three Poems. Ping Hsin (Hsieh Wang-ying). This silken thread of verse/Closely binds the departing sun and me. PBWP

Three Poems. Yakamochi.
and nothing touches the hand. LiTW
And we believed our love/Would last a thousand years. LiTW

Three Poems about Children. Austin Clarke.
How can we learn upon our knees,/That ironside unropes the bell? CIP
...one/But one, are thrown away. CIP

Those children, charred in Cavan,/Passed straight through Hell to Heaven. CIP

Three Poems for the Indian Steelworkers in a Bar... Joseph Bruchac. that this is a land/which has been bright with magic CDW

Three Poems for Women. Susan Griffin.
has trouble hearing. NPGG
Let us have a moment of silence/for the woman who cleans the floor. NPGG
and listen/to what you think/she might say. NPGG

Three Poems for Your Eyes. Rachel McAlpine. the harbour darkens above me OCNZ

Three Poems, I. Rosario Castellânos. and the world is newly freshly devoured. BoWoP

Three Poems, II. Rosario Castellânos. It stares beyond the glass. BoWoP

Three Poems, III. Rosario Castellânos. with no entrails, no force, nothing, cloud. BoWoP

Three Poems of the Atomic Age: Dirge for the New Sunrise. Edith Sitwell. Gone is the heart of Man. AtBAP

Three Poems on Morris Graves' Paintings. John Logan.
and pull and bend about these sweeps of light. PoDr
Moor Swan Moor Swan Moor Swan. PoDr
Morris Graves has given you/the sudden awful wings of a mirror! PoDr

The Three Poplars. Philip Francis Little. but upright as the staff of one who watcheth o'er his sheep. OxBI

Three Portraits. George Hitchcock. the Palo/Alto/bus schedule. VGW

Three Presidents: Andrew Jackson. Robert Bly. A horse that runs over wooden bridges, and sleeps/In abandoned barns... LCAP

Three Presidents: John F. Kennedy. Robert Bly. And when I ascend the third time, I will fall forever,/Missing the earth entirely. LCAP

Three Presidents: Theodore Roosevelt. Robert Bly. Carrying the robber down with him. LCAP

Three Prison Portraits: The Drug Addict. Miriam Waddington. And cries at the blood of his own life. ACV

Three Proverbs. James Clarence Mangan. Yet a little clay/Will fill it by and by. IrPN

The Three Ravens. Anonymous.
And pick his eyes out one by one. AmFP
God send every gentleman/Such hawks, such hounds, and such a leman. ExPo; FSW; InPK; NoP; OBET
She was dead herselfe ere even-song time. CABA

The Three Ravens (C vers.). Anonymous.
And they all flapped their wings and cried/Billy Magee Magar! BaBo
O maybe you think there's another verse,/But there isn't. ViBoFo

Three Rimas, 1. Gustavo Adolfo Becquer. O love is passing by! LiTW

Three Rimas, 2. Gustavo Adolfo Becquer. Woman, tell me, when love dies/Do you know where then it lies? LiTW

Three Rimas, 3. Gustavo Adolfo Becquer. And she: "If I had wept!" LiTW

Three Rounded Flanks I Loved. Anonymous. and the flank of Aed Mac Ainmirech. NOBI

Three Roundels of Love Unreturned. Geoffrey Chaucer.
For Danger halt your mercy in his chaine. MeEL
Sin I am free, I counte him not a bene! MeEL
So wondeth it thorowout my herte kene. MeEL

Three Sayings from Highlands, North Carolina. Jonathan Williams. and your timing's/a week off OBAL

Three Score and Ten. Anonymous.
Only one span is all the life we borrow. OBSP
There was many a hearty fisherlad did find a watery grave. OBSS

The Three Seamstresses. Isaac L. Peretz. Where undisturbed I may lie,/Sleeping, sleeping. TrJP

Three Seasons. Christina Georgina Rossetti. And memory for the evening gray/And solitary dove. HBV 1-2

Three Seasons. Francis Sparshott. holding to her thin breast his bald weeping head. NOBC

Three Sentences for a Dead Swan. James Wright. ...the/Ohio river, that is no tomb to/Rise from the dead/From. NaP; NoAm; NOBA

Three Sermons to the Dead. Laura Riding.
Aura of tattered hopes/Protesting as you dare not. LiTA
To each is given what defeat he will. LiTA
Toward which, as to later lives,/Young, later selves of you go futuring. LiTA

Three Shades of Light on the Windowsill. Susan Griffin. ...and delighted/by three shades of light/on the windowsill. NPGG

Three Shadows. Dante Gabriel Rossetti. "Ah! you can love, true girl, and is your love for me?" HBV 1-2; ViBoPo

Three Ships. Anonymous. On New-Year's day in the morning. OxNR

The Three Silences of Molinos. Henry Wadsworth Longfellow. And speakest only when thy soul is stirred! AnFE; APA

Three Sisters. Walter De la Mare. Sprightly Rebecca, Anne,/And Adelaide. FaBoEE

The Three Sisters. Arthur Davison Ficke. For one was wise and one was fair,/But one was mine. HBV 1-2

Three Songs. Francis Beaumont.
And all the Stars to follow! GoBC
And clip his wings, and break his glass,/And keep him ever by 'em. GoBC
And turn our blessing to a curse/By keeping you asunder. GoBC

Three Songs. Edgar Jackson. I will be like the arctic ice/that breaks from the shore/and drifts with the current. LFAC

The Three Songs. Bayard Taylor. Siegfried lies in his red, red blood! StPo

Three Songs from the Haida, II: Queen Charlotte's Island, B.C., 2. Anonymous. Like the snowbank/Behind which it blooms. BPAW

Three Songs from the Haida, III: Queen Charlotte's Island, B.C. Constance Lindsay Skinner. Hear us, hear us, O Good Sun! BPAW

Three Songs from the Temple. Don Domanski.
an ether/that muds its nose/and feet? NOBC
rising up in prayer/along the horizon. NOBC
whose reek of pleasure/hangs in the morning air? NOBC

Three Songs: Thessalian. Winifred Bryher. The fists of the wind are clenched. PoA

Three Songs to Mark the Night. Judith Mountain Leaf Volborth. And Coyote out collecting/dream chips along the shore. TWSS

Three Sonnets. [James Henry] Leigh Hunt.
And drinks, and stares, diversified with boggles? NOBL
Go by, linked fin by fin, most odiously. NOBL
Quickened with touches of transporting fear. NOBL

Three Sonnets on Oblivion. George Sterling.
And hears the blind sea chanting to the sun. HBV 1-2
Stricken at last Time's lonely Titans bend. HBV 1-2
–they leave/The skull of Pharaoh staring at the sky. HBV 1-2

Three Sonnets on The Divina Commedia. Henry Wadsworth Longfellow.
Proclaim the elevation of the Host! SeCeV
This medieval miracle of song! SeCeV
While the eternal ages watch and wait. SeCeV

Three Sorrowful Things. Anonymous. I know not whither I must fare. MeEV

Three Spring Notations on Bipeds. Carl Sandburg. She throws a stone and laughs at the clug-clug. AWP; InPo

Three Star Final. Conrad Aiken. and neon death at the end of the Avenue. OxBA

Three Streets. Umberto Saba. and his little son to rosier health. VWA

Three Sunrises from Amtrak. Florence Dolgorukov. the sun should choose those minutes to rise! AMV-81

Three Sweethearts. Heinrich Heine. I'll go and make love to Nature/In some more quiet spot. UnTE

The Three Tall Men. Anonymous. But nevermore the people spied/The tall men or the bull. OBET

Three Tanka, 1. Yosano Akiko. With this dream which obsesses me. LiTW

Three Tanka, 2. Yosano Akiko. A vague sorrow/Crossed my mind. LiTW

Three Tanka, 3. Yosano Akiko. Reflects the white Autumn/sky. LiTW

The Three Taverns: Out of Wisdom Has Come Love. Edwin Arlington Robinson. That measures and is of itself the measure/Of works and hope and faith. MoRP

Three Things. Joseph Auslander. The placid cows pensively/Wondering why they wondered. HBMV; TrJP

Three Things. May Sarton. When lovers, water, and leaves are wholly one. AMV-80

Three Things Jeame Lacks. Anonymous. Marke well this–that lovers will be/Must nedes have oone of thes thre. MeEL

Three Things to Remember. William Blake. He who shall hurt the little wren/Shall never be beloved by men. MoShBr

Three Thousand Dollar Death Song. Wendy Rose. ...coal/and uranium, children, a universe/of stolen things. TWSS

Three Tiny Songs. Cid Corman. ...The/contraction/of that is. HoAn

Three-Toed Sloth. Dorothy Donnelly. ...and he hangs with closed eyes/and the concentration of someone listening to music. HoAn

The Three Towns. Howard Nemerov. The road from Adonoi? I just don't know. AMV-81

The Three Travelers. Anonymous. Without ever a penny of money. UnTE

Three Trees. Charles Henry Crandall. But the Lord has need of all. OHIP

Three Trees at Solstice. Mary Finnin. Fails from sight,/Fails in the west. BoAV

The Three Troopers. George Walter Thornbury. "God send this Crumwell-down!" BeLS; HBV 1-2

Three Variations. Boris Pasternak. Like lips the hand has not wiped dry,/Are glistening, are glistening. TrJP

The Three Voices (parody). Lewis (Charles Lutwidge Dodgson) Carroll. And she, an avalanche of woe.' BXAP

The Three Warnings. Hester Thrale Piozzio. Yields to his fate–so ends my tale. BeLS; HBV 1-2

Three White Birds of Angus. Eleanor Rogers Cox. She chanted, till along the sea/The feet of Morn came whisperingly. HBMV

The Three Wise Couples. Elizabeth T. Corbett. And all the people said: "Let's go/To see the bear and the circus show!" BLPA

Three Wise Kings. William E. Brooks. And peace was born to abide alway,/In hearts that were long despairing. PGD

Three wise men of Gotham. Mother Goose. If the bowl had been stronger/My song had been longer. FaBoBe; FaFP; HBV 1-2; HBVY

The Three Wise Monkeys. Florence Boyce Davis. We might in time become as wise as they. WBLP

Three Wise Old Women. Elizabeth T. Corbett. You must find out, for I don't know. BLPA; OBCA; OxBChV

The Three Woes. Aubrey Thomas De Vere. Let God do that which He wills. Let his servants endure/and adore! AnIV

Three Women. Barry Dempster. ...her and the/bed: one quiet ache of white. CaPN

Three Women. Lauris Edmond. black, among the English newspapers. OCNZ

Three Women. Sylvia Plath. The little grasses/Crack through stone, and they are green with life. NAs

Three Women Blues. Blind Willie McTell. I'd-a been at home sleeping/in a doggone feather bed BluL

Three Years She Grew in Sun and Shower. William Wordsworth. The memory of what has been,/And never more will be. CBEP; ERoP 1-2; FiP; HAP; LoBV; MBW 1-2; NOBE; OAEL 1-2; OAEP; OBNC; PoEL 1-5

Three Young Rats. Mother Goose. And so they all went home again. FaBoNo; InvP; OxBoLi; OxNR; PoPle

Threes. Henry Chapin. Must everything resolve itself to two? FAZ

Threes. Carl Sandburg. –how much?–and–do you love me, kid? CMoP; OxBA; PoLf

Threescore and Ten. Richard Henry Stoddard. I have endured as best I could,/Threescore and ten! HBV 1-2

Threnody. Thomas Lovell Beddoes. His form unseen, his voice unheard– EnRP

Threnody. Waring Cuney. Are known beyond death's door. BANP

Threnody. Ralph Waldo Emerson Lost in God, in Godhead found. AA; AmePo; AnNE; AP; MAmP

Threnody. John Farrar. Across the far and lonely place/That airplanes know. BrR; SUS

Threnody. Denis Glover. But one dead albatross they found/At Karehana Bay. AnNZ

Threnody. Ruth Guthrie Harding. And never a road can reach him/Who lies so far from home. HBV 1-2

Threnody. Donald Jeffrey Hayes. Only the broken heart can sing/Not asking why...! AmNP

Threnody. David Ignatow. by your silence and acceptance of sorrow/as the bread itself. FAZ

Threnody. Alfred Kreymborg. "Love was dead all day." MAPA

A Threnody. George Thomas Lanigan. The great Ahkoond of Swat/Is not! AA; CBEP; CenHV; FiBHP; HBV 1-2; InMe; NA; NLV; PeCV; WHW

Threnody. Dorothy Parker. Let him wonder if I lie;/Let him half believe me. InMe

Threnody. I. O. Scherzo. I have seen truth and will no more despair. HoPM

Threnody for a Poet. Bliss Carman. For he was a blade of the April sod/That bowed and blew with the whisper of God. CaP

Threnos. J. R. Hervey. Ah, who will stand forever,/Out of this coil deliver. AnNZ

The Thresher's Labour. Stephen Duck. They cry their ink was faulty, and their pen;/We, "The corn threshes bad, 'twas cut too green." NOEC

The Threshing Machine. Alice Meynell. I knew the brain of Hercules! SeCePo

Threshold. Edmund Charles Blunden. And when time comes, for old time's sake/Primrosing in our earliest brake. HBMV

Threshold. Charles David Webb. But dark has not yet come. NePoAm-2

Thrice Blest the Man. John Barnard. But who his name and word abuse/Shall feel his wrath and melt away. AH

Thrice Happy He. William, of Hawthornden Drummond. Woods' silent shades have only true delights. BoNaP; HBV 1-2

Thrice Is He Armed That Hath His Quarrel Just. Josh Billings. And four times he who gets his fist in/fust. GoTF; TreFT

Thrice Toss These Oaken Ashes in the Air. Thomas Campion. She hath an art to break them with her eyes. AnFE; AtBAP; EBEV; ElL; EnLoPo; FaBoCh; HAP; LoBV; LoGBV; MAT; OAEL 1-2; OBSP; PoEL 1-5; PoRA; ViBoPo

Thrice Welcome First and Best of Days. Isaac Chanler. And fetch my longing soul on high,/That I may sing eternally. AH

The Thrifty Elephant. John Holmes. Red-eyed, foot-dragging, single-minded blunt-/Tusk, lugging his bones to the bones piled? NYBP

The Thrissil and the Rois. William Dunbar. Off lusty May upone the nynt morrow. HW

Thro' Grief and Thro' Danger. Thomas Moore. Than wed what I lov'd not, or turn one thought from thee. AnIV

Throbs the Night with Mystic Silence. Hayim Nahman Bialik. One world have I–yea, no other/Than the world which lives in me. TrJP

The Throstle. Alfred, Lord Tennyson. And all the winters are hidden. BoNaP; HBV 1-2; HBVY; MCCG; PBBP; PoSC

Through a Glass Eye, Lightly. Carolyn Kizer. Now she held on to Deborah, looked her steadily/in the empty eye. BoWoP

Through a Shop Window. Eleanor Farjeon. With longing eyes and flattened noses. ChBR

Through All the World. Anonymous. Since nature's works declare/God is there. TrAS

Through All Your Abstract Reasoning. Brian Patten. –always the light within you hooded by/your own protecting fingers. FaBoTw

Through Amaryllis Dance in Green. Anonymous. Hey ho! chill love no more. EIL

Through an Embrace. Paul Eluard. Our door is the door of man. LiTW

Through Baltimore. Bayard Taylor. Cleanse from thy skirts the slaughter shed,/Or make thyself an ashen bed,/O Baltimore! PAH

Through Binoculars. Charles Tomlinson. Like the retreat of water from sea-caves. OAEL 1-2

Through Fire in Mobile Bay. Anonymous. He waits to greet the gallant tars/Who fought in Mobile Bay. PAH

Through Storm and Wind. Anonymous. Groundsel in flower. OxNR

Through the Ages. Margaret Hope. The Christ-child knocks. PGD

Through the Barber Shop Window. Violet Anderson. of the day's/work/done. CaP

Through the Blowing Leaves. Glenn Ward Dresbach. With flower-like faces glowing. BoC

Through the Dark Aisles of the Wood. Henry Trecce. And the white skull grins in the fern. NeBP

Through the Dark the Dreamers Came. Earl Bowman Marlatt. Maxima, maxima,/Gloria Dei maxima AH

Through the Maze. Anonymous. And still He leads us on. BLRP

Through the Metidja to Abd-el-Kadr. Robert Browning. As I ride, as I ride! PeD

Through the Night of Doubt and Sorrow. Sabine Baring-Gould. Where the one almighty Father/Reigns in love for evermore. FaPoR

"Through the Open Door..." Patrick Kavanagh. What is the Virgin Mary now to do? AnIV

Through the Smoke Hole. Gary Snyder. plain men/come out of the ground. PoM

Through the Straight Pass of Suffering. Emily Dickinson. The needle to the north degree/Wades so, through polar air. MoRP

Through the thatched roof. Emperor Tenchi. Oh, and sleeves are drenched. LiTW

Through the Waters. Annie Johnson Flint. We shall not go down, or under,/For He saith, "Thou passest through." STF

Through the Whole Long Night. Halper Leivick. the morning apples clanged as they fell. VWA

Through the Year. Julian S. Cutler. God be with you in the Winter,/Just to guide you into rest. BLPA

Through These Pale Cold Days. Isaac Rosenberg. They see with living eyes/How long they have been dead. TrJP

Through Unknown Paths. Frederick Lucian Hosmer. Be thou, O God, our dwelling-place/And our eternal home! TrPWD

Through Warmth and Light of Summer Skies. Austin Faricy. With Holy Ghost in One. Amen. AH

Through Willing Heart and Helping Hand. Frederick Lucian Hosmer. And fire the souls that gather here! AH

Through You. Edwin Honig. Now walk through me TAP

Throughout the Day We Are Able to Ban the Voices. H. Roland-Holst. ...and we feel/each shuddering go through our depths. PBWP

Throughout the World. Sir Thomas Wyatt. That sweet accord is seldom seen. CBEP; ELU; FCP; MAT; OBSP

Throw away the Flowers. Elizabeth Daryush. have but hopeless, hard/rebellion for bard. PBWP

Throw Him Down, McCloskey. J. W. Kelly. Will read on hist'ry's pages of the great McCloskey fight. FSN; TreF

Throw out the Lifeline. Edward Smith Ufford. Someone is sinking today. TreF

Throwing the Racetrack Cats at Saratoga. David Ray. ...as I/absurdly seek and trust to find you still. SM

Thrown. Ralph Hodgson. A laughing child with feathered heels/Who shall outspeed our chariot wheels. HBMV

The Thrush. Alfred Austin. He is a better poet than us all. TEP

The Thrush. Laura Benet. Only the thrush, the thrush that never spoke,/Sang from her bursting heart. HBMV

The Thrush. Timothy Corsellis. Lord, pray forgive me–I did wrong. WaaP; WaP

A Thrush before Dawn.   Alice Meynell.   O innocent throat! O human ear! HBMV; MoBrPo

The Thrush in February.   George Meredith.   When lowly, with a broken neck,/The crocus lays her cheek to mire.   OBNC

The Thrush's Song.   W. Macgillivray.   Quiu, qui, qui.   CH

Thrushes.   Ted Hughes.   ...under what wilderness/Of black silent waters weep.   FaBoMo; GoYe; NePoEA-2

Thrustararorum.   Henry Nehemiah Dodge.   The brave old fisher from whom I came!   EtS

The Thrusting of It.   Robert Burns.   He's weary o' the thrusting of it. UnTE

Thule, the Period of Cosmography.   Anonymous.   Whose heart with fear doth freeze, with love doth fry.   HAP; NCEP; OBSP

Thumb.   Philip Dacey.   The odd, friendless boy raised by four aunts.   PoL; PPJ

The Thumb.   Dennis Saleh.   like the pages of a book coming together/for the last time.   MAT; NeAC

Thumb Bold.   Anonymous.   Mammie's wee man.   OxNR

Thumb He.   Anonymous.   Little Jack-a-Dandy.   OxNR

Thumbikin, Thumbikin, Broke the Barn.   Anonymous.   But Peesy-weesy paid for a'.   OxNR

Thumbing Old Magazines.   Gerald Vizenor.   wash themselves several times a day/washing after play   VoR

Thumbprint.   Celeste Turner Wright.   Leave but a filamentous line or two? Psk

Thunder.   Walter De la Mare.   Call the cows home!   BoNaP

Thunder in the Garden.   William Morris.   And in the dark house was I loved.   VLP

The Thunder Mutters Louder and More Loud.   John Clare.   In the sweet hay yet dry the hay folks cower/& some beneath the waggon shun the shower   NOBV

Thunder Pools.   Robert P. Tristram Coffin.   Poured from the hogsheads of the thunder.   LOW

A Thunder-Storm.   Emily Dickinson.   But overlooked my father's house/ Just quartering a tree.   BoNaP

The Thunderer.   Phyllis McGinley.   It takes all kinds/To make a Heaven. EaLo

A Thunderstorm.   Archibald Lampman.   Column on column comes the drenching rain.   CaP; NOBC

Thunderstorm.   Sam Mitchell.   Drenching all the trees between the two sandhills.   NOAV

A Thunderstorm in Town.   Thomas Hardy.   I should have kissed her if the rain/Had lasted a minute more.   BoLoP; EnLoPo; GBL; OBSP

Thunderstorms.   William Henry Davies.   My thoughts are dancing flowers/ And joyful singing birds.   HBV 1-2

Thursday.   Edna St. Vincent Millay.   I loved you Wednesday,–yes–but what/Is that to me?   InMe

Thus Bonny-Boots the Birthday Celebrated.   Anonymous.   Then sang the shepherds and Nymphs of Diana:/Long live fair Oriana.   NCEP

Thus Crosslegged on Round Pillow Sat in Space.   Allen Ginsberg.   a calm breath, a silent breath, a slow breath breathes outward from/the nostrils. NNaP

Thus I Resolve.   Thomas Campion.   Wild born be wild still, though by force made tame.   OBSP

Thus Lovely Sleep.   Richard Leigh.   A silent beauty half so fair.   ELP

Thus Saith My Chloris Bright.   Giovanni Battista Guarini.   For in her eyes I saw his torchlight blazing.   GBL

Thus Spake the Saviour.   Jeremy Belknap.   How rich, how full is their reward,/Reserved until the final day!   AH

Thus Speak the Slain.   Carl Holliday.   Thus speak the slain.   PGD

Thus Speaketh Christ Our Lord.   Anonymous.   If I condemn you, blame Me not.   PGD

Thus Spoke My Love.   Pieter Corneliszoon Hooft.   How like the dream is life, like life the dream.   LiTW

Thus Sung Orpheus to His Strings.   Anonymous.   Ah, dear Eurydice the echoing winds replied.   GBL; NCEP

Thus, When Soft Love Subdues the Heart.   Paul Scarron.   And speaks in moments more than years.   LO

Thy Beauty Fades.   Jones Very.   From virtue's changeless bloom that time and death defies.   AP

Thy Brother's Blood.   Jones Very.   that bloody stain/Shall not be seen upon thy hand again.   AP; MAmP; NOBA; PoEL 1-5; QFR; TAP

Thy Conquering Name.   Charles Wesley.   Faith in a dying Lord.   BePJ

Thy Faithful Sons.   Eleazar.   Crushed, drowned, or with harsh saws/asunder sawn.   TrJP

Thy Garden.   King of Seville, Mu'tamid.   My garden, full of fruits in harvest time.   AWP

Thy Garden, Orchard, Fields.   Francis Daniel Pastorius.   To him, to whom belongs/All Praise in Prose and Songs.   SCAP

Thy Glorious Face Above.   Charles Wesley.   And see Thy glorious face above.   BePJ

Thy Heart.   Anonymous.   That it may break beneath my feet/And let a lover in!   NA

Thy Kingdom Come.   Saint Bernard of Clairvaux   The longing world waits for Thee:/Arise, arise and shine!   CAW

Thy Kingdom Come.   Frederick Lucian Hosmer.   The day of perfect righteousnessThe promised day of God.   WGRP

Thy Kingdom Come.   A.B. Simpson.   Thy kingdom come.   BePJ

Thy Kingdom, Lord, We Long For.   Vida Scudder.   Thy Kingdom shall inherit,/The blessing of the just.   WGRP

Thy Mercies, Lord, to Heaven Reach.   William Kethe.   Thy righteousness to such men lend.   AH

Thy Nail-Pierced Hands.   Kathryn Bowsher.   Jesus, my Lord, sent from above.   STF

Thy Name We Bless and Magnify.   John Power.   Before Thine altar, Lord Most High,/Thy Name we bless and magnify.   BLRP

Thy Praise, O God, in Zion Waits.   Jacob Kimball.   And hills and vales rejoice and sing.   AH

Thy Rising Is Beautiful.   Akhnaton (Amenhotep IV).   Uplifted in adoration to the living Aton,/The maker...   ILwL

Thy Sea So Great.   Winfred Ernest Garrison.   Sweet silences abound, and all is peace.   TrPWD

Thy Way, Not Mine.   Horatius Bonar.   Be Thou my guide, my strength,/ My wisdom and my all.   OxBoCh; TrPWD; TRV

Thy Will Be Done.   Anonymous.   Lord of earth, and God of heaven,/ Evermore–Thy will be done.   BePJ

Thy Will Be Done.   Annie Johnson Flint.   His will shall yet be done.   STF

Thy Will Be Done.   Hugh Thomson Kerr.   Be Thou our master in the strife,/Until Thy will is done.   BLRP

Thy Will Be Done.   Albert Simpson Reitz.   Content to know, where'er He leads/That we can trust Him still.   STF

Thyestes, III: Chorus.   Seneca (Lucius Annaeus Seneca).   The God our things all tost and turned quight/Rolles with a whyrle wynde.   OBVE

Thyme.   Anonymous.   Let no man steal your thyme.   AmFP

Thyme Flowering among Rocks.   Richard Wilbur.   Not because that dream's/A falsehood, but because it's/Truer than it seems.   LCAP

Thyrsis.   Matthew Arnold.
   And the full moon, and the white evening-star.   PoPle
   Our scholar travels yet the loved hillside.   EnLit; NoP; OBEV; OBNC; OBVV
   They are all gone, and thou art gone as well!   FaBoPP

Thyrsis and Milla, Arm in Arm Together.   Anonymous.   And blush'd, and ran away, and he ran after.   GBL

Thyrsis, Sleep'st Thou?   Anonymous.   "Let me alone, alas, and drive him back to London."   InvP; OBSP

Thysia.   Morton Luce.
   And even in your grave, beauteous and free/From the cold grasp of mutability.   HBV 1-2
   Go then thy way with thine accustomed cheer,/Nor heed my churlish greeting, O New Year.   HBV 1-2
   Grant then, dear Lord, that all who love may be/Heirs of Thy glorious Immortality.   HBV 1-2
   Nor could that jubilant song of day prevail/Like thine of tender grief, O nightingale.   HBV 1-2
   Only in love can life's true path be trod;/Love is self-giving; therefore love is God.   HBV 1-2
   Say this, and her sweet pity will approve,/And bind yet closer her dead bond of love.   HBV 1-2
   "To prove thy love, live thou a nobler life."   HBV 1-2
   While here I cling, in life's short agony,/To God, and to your deathless memory.   HBV 1-2

Tiare Tahiti.   Rupert Brooke.   There's little comfort in the wise.   BrPo; SeCeV

Tick Picking in the Quetico.   Don Johnson.   ...night to crawl/into folds and crevices,/haired cracks,/to stay.   MAYP

The Ticket.   John Ashbery.   Automatically taking the things in, that had not been spoiled,/sordid.   ANYP

The Ticket Agent.   Edmund Leamy.   He deals in dreams, and calls it–work! HBMV

Ticking Clocks.   Rachel Field.   Hear how it booms out, Time and Tide,/ Solemnly, Time and Tide.   TiPo

The Tickle Rhyme.   Ian Serraillier.   ..."I'm learning/To crawl."   NTCP; OnUR; SoPo

Tickly, Tickly, on Your Knee.   Anonymous.   If you laugh you don't love me.   OxNR

Ticonderoga.   V. B. Wilson.   The chime of the silver bells.   PAL

Ticonderoga: A Legend of the West Highlands.   Robert Louis Stevenson. He sleeps in the place of the name/As it was doomed to be.   OBNV

The Tide in the River.   Eleanor Farjeon.   As the tide turned in its sleep. TiPo

The Tide of Faith.   George Eliot.   Sweeps in with every force that stirs our souls/To admiration, self-renouncing love.   TRV; WGRP

Time Long Past. Percy Bysshe Shelley. Beauty is like remembrance, cast/ From Time long past. HBV 1-2

A Time of Change. Egan O'Rahilly. Would make you swallow these Atlantic words. BIrV; FaBoPV

The Time of Creation Has Come. *Anonymous.* The time of creation has come. WTO

Time of Day. Selden Rodman. At the last silence cries for the unknown day. PoA

Time of fish dying. Gabriela Melinescu. he has not been seen since/not once BoWoP

A Time of Light, a Time of Shadow. Samuel Yellen. And heavy shadow pile up flake by flake. NePoAm-2

A Time of Night. David Ignatow. a time of morning,/a time of night. FAZ

The Time of the Barmacides. James Clarence Mangan. And I mourn for the time gone long ago,/The time of the Barmacides. EnRP; RoGo

Time of the Mad Atom. Virginia Brasier. Till the spring snaps–/And the fun's done! QQQ

A Time of Turquoise. Judith Mountain Leaf Volborth. born from a dark void/where Thunder sleeps. TWSS

Time of Turtles. Grace Perry. Slowly we lose our seabright colours/and wait to die. NOAV

Time of Waiting. Geoffrey Dutton. And words and minutes fall like clothing to the floor. CBAP

Time of Waiting in Amsterdam. Ingrid Jonker. with your own smile/ abandoned the world. BoWoP

Time; or, How the Line About Chagall's Lovers Disappears. Jane Miller. ...Speech is death/who can but laugh and pipe a flute,/who loves you. SM

Time Out. Frances Westgate Butterfield. What balance sheet can tot the hideous score/Of this, the least considered crime of war? GoYe

Time Out. Donald Finkel. April slides her long cool fingers/under his shirt. HoPM

Time Out. Oliver Jenkins. And the spell's over. GoYe

Time Out. John Montague. Sucking the sweet grass of stubbornness. BoAnP

Time Passes. R. P. Lister. While the hands of the rude, insatiate clock/Go tick, tock, tick, tock. NYBP

Time Passing, Beloved. Donald Davie. This siege of a shore that no misgivings have steeled,/No doubts defend? BoLoP; NePoEA-2

Time Piece. William Cole. each doing what it should be doing,/and ignoring you completely. ELU; GrPl; PPJ

Time Poem. Quentin Hill. ...inside two hundred white people hold/their annual convention. NBP

Time, Real and Imaginary. Samuel Taylor Coleridge. And knows not whether he be first or last. EnRP; ERoP 1-2; NOBE; OBEV; OBRV; OBSP

Time Recover'd. Girolamo Casone. Onely that of which Thou mak'st/Use in time, from time Thou tak'st. OBVE

Time Reminded Me. Julia Uceda. A time that is not mine/seems to rain inside my eyes. BoWoP

Time's Balm. Cuthbert Shaw. And my sad sighs are borne on ev'ry passing breeze. OBEC

Time's Bright Sand. Robert Finch. When, seeing its gleam,/We saw no time. CaP

Time's Changes. James Bramston. And Cibber's Opera from Johnny Gay's. OBEC

Time's Dedication. Delmore Schwartz. Moving together through time to all good. VGW

Time's Fool. Ruth Pitter. As then I had mine, in the place that was happy and poor. ChMP; MoBrPo; OxBTC; PoRA

Time's Fool. John Updike. "This was the time agreed upon?" DBV

Time's Hand is Kind. Margaret E. Bruner. And, in its stead, will come a strange new peace. PoToHe

Time's Mutability. Bertolt Brecht. It had better be soon. ELU

Time's Revenge. Walter Learned. She's really quite too old for me. HBV 1-2

Time's Revenges. Sir Owen Seaman. 'Tis my loyalty to Her,/To the Girl that once you were. FaBoUs

Time's Song. Winthrop Mackworth Praed. Where will rest my weary wings? Science turns/away! EnRP; NBM

Time's Times Again. Archie Randolph Ammons. having to do at times with love or in one time/the understanding of final pain, I go with that. SUW

Time-Servers. Judah Halevi. Seek God, my soul–God shall thy/portion be! TrJP

Time Stands Still, with Gazing on Her Face! *Anonymous.* And Fortune captive at her feet, condemned and conquered lies! EnLoPo

Time Time Said Old King Tut. Don (Donald Robert Marquis) Marquis. is something i ain t/got anything but FiBHP

Time to Be Wise. Walter Savage Landor. Upon her high-heeled Essex smiled/The brave Queen Bess. HBV 1-2; InMe

Time to Choose a Lover. Horace. 'Tis the time to choose a lover. UnTE

A Time to Dance: The Flight. C. Day-Lewis. That sours a doubtful earth,/ the stars commemorate. MoVE

Time To Die. Ray Garfield Dandridge. For something, ere in vain you die. BANP; PoBA

A Time to Eat. Gertrude Stein. ...This is not tardy. NMM

Time to Go. Susan (Sarah Chauncey Woolsey) Coolidge. That his sweet day augurs a sweeter morrow,/With smiles, not sorrow. GN

Time to Leave Her. *Anonymous.* It's time for us to leave her! AmSS

Time to Myself. Paulette Jiles. Bless the pine outside my window bless/the stranger in my midst. NOBC

Time to Rise. Robert Louis Stevenson. 'Ain't you 'shamed, you sleepy-head? OxBChV; SiSoSe

A Time to Talk. Robert Frost. ...I go up to the stone wall/For a friendly visit. LaNeLa; NCSH

The Time to Trust. *Anonymous.* That is just the time to trust. BLRP

Time-Travel. Sharon Olds. She does not know she is the one/survivor. AMV-80

Time Tryeth Truth. *Anonymous.* Thrice happy they that leaving mandring wayes/Sloe duely walk to their Creator's praise. SCAP

Time Was. Pati Hill. but hardly anyone feels/he has to be equal to his own fate FAZ

The Time We Climbed Snake Mountain. Leslie Marmon Silko. The mountain is his. VoR

Time! Where Dist Thou Those Years Inter. William Habington. ...There is no cure/Nor antidote but tears. OxBoCh

Time Will Not Grant. Sidney Keyes. That all my life must change and fall away. SeCePo

The Time Will Surely Come. Robert T. Daniel. And all thy chosen race shall sing/Thy free, redeeming love. AH

Time, You Old Gipsy Man. Ralph Hodgson. Put up your caravan/Just for one day? BoLiVe; BrPo; CH; GoTF; HBV 1-2; LiTM; MoAB; MoBrPo; MoShBr; PG; SiSoSe; TreF; TrGrPo; ViBoPo

Time Zones for Forty-Four. Donald A. Stauffer. Dead pilot adrift in raft. WaP

A Timepiece. James Merrill. For soon by what it tells the clock is stilled. HoPM; NePoEA-2; NoAm

Timers. Flora J. Arnstein. But unknown to the slim hands' betrayal. GoYe

The Times. *Anonymous.* But "Union forever,"/Shall be our last toast. PAH

The Times. Charles Churchill. A fine, fresh HYLAS, a delicious boy,/To serve our purposes of beastly joy. OBSV; PeHV

The Times. Charles Madge. For war is eating now. OBMV

The Times. Marcus Manilius. They form men's thoughts, and the obedient clay/Takes disagreeing tempers from their ray. LiTW

Times Are Getting Hard. *Anonymous.* Goin' to have the best old farm/ That you have ever seen. FSW

Times Gettin' Hard, Boys (with music). *Anonymous.* When she see dat yellow boy she almos' faint away. AS

The Times Have Altered. *Anonymous.* Oh! we might see as happy days as ever we did then. CoMu

Times o' Year. William Barnes. What ha' years in store for me? BoNaP

Times Square Parade. Robert Watson. What a wonderful piece of work is man. NYP

Times without Number Have I Pray'd. Charles Wesley. Forgive my vain repentances,/And bid me sin no more. OxBoCh

The Timid Gazelle. Kasmuneh. Accepting fate's decree with patient/heart. TrJP

Timid Hortense. Peter Newell. "And do fish bite? The horrid things! Indeed, I'll not catch/one!" NA

Timid Lover. Countee Cullen. Extends me holy fruit. BANP

Timocreon. Simonides (of Ceos). ...Lord, what a mess/Of beer and beef and bitterness. DBV

Timon of Archimedes. Charles Battell Loomis. "Might of the night, unfleeing, sight unseen." NA

Timon of Athens. William Shakespeare. And grant, as Timon grows, his hate may grow/To the whole race of mankind, high and low!/Amen. EBEV; TW

Timon's Epitaph. Callimachus. Pass by, and curse thy fill; but pass and stay not here/thy gait. AWP

Timon's Villa. Alexander Pope. ...What his hard Heart denies,/His charitable Vanity supplies. OBEC

Timon Speaks to a Dog. Philip Hobsbaum. Following my doggy ends to doggy end. TW

Timoshenko. Sidney Keyes. He made the pencilled map alive with war. OBWP

Timothy Boon. Ivy O. Eastwick. They have not come down yet! SoPo; TiPo

Timothy Titus Took Two Ties. *Anonymous.* How many T's in that? OxNR

Tin Cup Blues. Blind Lemon Jefferson. That tough luck has sunk me/and the rats is getting in my hat BluL

Tin-Ore. *Anonymous.* Do you float up to the surface of this my tank,/Or you shall be a rebel to God. WTO

The Tin-Whistle Player. Padraic Colum. That long face, in a place of graves/With nettles overgrown. UnS

The Tin Woodsman. Paulette Jiles. I will settle/in the shadow of this red rock/and be metal. NOBC

The Tinder. Thomas Carew. Flint and steel I'll ever name ye. CaPo

The Tinker. *Anonymous.* I'll swinge him if I may. CoMu

Tinker's Moon. Ewart Milne. I saw the stony, rocky road where the tinker's children bide. OnYI

Tinker's Wife. Patrick Kavanagh. And sharp-broken/Dinner plates. CIP; InPS; NoAm

Tinker, Tailor. *Anonymous.*
Church, Nobility,/Nothing at all. SaC
Thief. OxNR

The Tinkers. Joseph Campbell. ...—well, who knows that but God? OnYI

The Tint I Cannot Take Is Best. Emily Dickinson. Another way—to see— MAmP; MoAmPo

Tintern Abbey. William Wordsworth. More dear, both for themselves and for thy/sake! BLPL; LiTB; TRV; ViBoPo

Tintock. *Anonymous.* And set the caup on Tintock-Tap. GBP

Tiny Catullus. Steve Levine. so singularly among/the thundering numbers. APU

The Tip. Albert Goldbarth. ...Yes he's death's, he's/eternity's, one-tenth. HaCAP

Tip-of-the-Single-Feather. Velema. Go back so that Flight-of-the-Chiefs will be inhabited.'/Nabosulu/Nabusele WTO

Tip-Toe Tail. Dixie Willson. On the very tip-toe of his tail! NTCP

Tipperary Recruiting Song. *Anonymous.* Except for the green and Tipperary, boys. OnYI

Tiptoe Night. John Drinkwater. Hush! he's at the window-sill. SiSoSe

Tir-Nan-Og. J. F. Hendry. Whose hands rise up from feet and knees,/Encircle head and rub the eyes. NeBP

Tirade on Tea. Phyllis McGinley. But needn't expect me to drink it at their house. InMe

Tired. Fenton Johnson. I am tired of civilization. BANP; IDB; PoBA; PoLf; PoNe; TTY

Tired and Unhappy, You Think of Houses. Delmore Schwartz. Caught in an anger exact as a machine! LiTM; MoAB; MoAmPo; NePA

Tired as I Can Be. Bessie Jackson. And I'm going back south/To my used to be BluL

The Tired Man. Anna Wickham. And let us sit by the fire,/Patient until we die! HBMV

Tired Mothers. May Riley Smith. The little boy I used to kiss is dead. HBV 1-2

Tired of Eating Kisses. Edward Vincent Swart. Which way, which way, with hope hard as a boulder? PeSA

The Tired Petitioner (excerpt). George Wither. ...this life, I would not live,/For all, the King and Parliament could give. SeCV 1-2

Tired Tim. Walter De la Mare. Poor tired Tim! It's sad for him. ALV; MoShBr; NTCP; SoPo; TiPo

The Tired Woman. Anna Wickham. O Lover! drive me through a stilly land/With the compelling of your open hand. MoBrPo

The Tired Worker. Claude McKay. No! Once again the harsh, the ugly city. BANP; BPo

Tiresias. George Garrett. Blinder than you. NePoAm-2; SM

Tiresias. Alfred, Lord Tennyson. My close of earth's experience/May prove as peaceful as his own. VLP

Tiresias (excerpt). Austin Clarke. ...I longed for/Mortal or centaur to surprise me. CIP

Tiresias' Lament. Ellen de Young Kay. For this, which shall be lost/Before what is, is done. NePoEA

Tirocinium; or, A Review of Schools. William Cowper.
And some street-pacing harlot his first love. OBSV
As here and there a twinkling ray descried/Serves but to show how black is all beside. OBSV
The parson knows enough who knows a duke.' OBSV

'Tis a Little Journey. *Anonymous.* Do we need such shadows/Here in life? PoToHe

'Tis but a Little Faded Flower. Ellen Clementine Howarth. A faded flower, a broken ring,/A tress of golden hair. AA; HBV 1-2

'Tis but a Wanton Trick. *Anonymous.* 'Tis but a wanton trick. UnTE

'Tis Hard to Find God. Robert Herrick. ...but to comprehend/Him, as He is, is labour without end. LiTB

'Tis Highly Rational, We Can't Dispute. Richard Garnett. Whose fire's so oft extinguished by a match? HBV 1-2

'Tis Late and Cold. John Fletcher. And I shall smile, though under ground. ViBoPo

'Tis Merry in Greenwood. Sir Walter Scott. Like a chieftain's frowning tower. OHIP

'Tis Midnight. *Anonymous.* The pensive goat and sportive cow,/Hilarious, leap from bough to bough. NA; NTCP

'Tis Midnight and on Olive's Brow. William B. Tappan. That sweetly soothe the Saviour's woe. AH

'Tis not that dying hurts us so. Emily Dickinson. We stipulate–till pitying Snows/Persuade our Feathers Home. BoWoP; DiPo

'Tis Now Since I Sate Down. Sir John Suckling. I hate a fool that starves her love/Onely to feed her pride. AnAnS 2; CavP; PoEL 1-5; SeCV 1-2

'Tis Said That Some Have Died for Love. William Wordsworth. Such happiness as I have known today. EnRP

'Tis Said the Gods Lower Down That Chain Above. George Alsop. And dwelling so, you may for ever be/The only Emblem of Tranquility. SCAP

'Tis so much joy! Emily Dickinson. For Heaven is a different thing,/Conjectured and waked sudden in,/And might extinguish me. NOCV

'Tis Sorrow Builds the Shining Ladder Up. James Russell Lowell. Life is the jailer; Death the angel sent/To draw the unwilling bolts and set us free. WGRP

'Tis Summer Time on Bredon (parody). Hugh Kingsmill. The cattle then are sick. FaBoCo

'Tis Sweet to Rest in Lively Hope. *Anonymous.* O Lord, remember me. AmFP

'Tis Sweet to Roam. *Anonymous.* And the wolf rings out with a glittering shout,/To-whit, to-whit, to-whoo! NA

'Tis the Gift To Be Simple. *Anonymous.* Till by turning, turning we come round right. AH

'Tis the Last Rose of Summer. Thomas Moore. Oh! Who would inhabit/This bleak world alone? ATP; BLPA; BoNaP; ELP; FPL; GoTF; HBV 1-2; NOBI; PoEL 1-5; PoPl; TreF; WBLP; WHA

'Tis the White Plum Tree. John Shaw Neilson. As a bride goes combing/Her joy of hair. BoAV; PoAu 1-2

'Tis the Witching Hour of Night. John Keats. A poet now or never! TEP

'Tis Time, I Think. Alfred Edward Housman. Lie long, high snowdrifts in the hedge/That will not shower on me. PoPle

'Tis true–they shut me in the cold. Emily Dickinson. Forgive Them–Even as Myself–/Or else–forgive not me– SBG

'Tis Winter Now. Samuel Longfellow. And keep us through life's wintry days. AH

'Tis You That Makes My Friends My Foes. *Anonymous.* Before I'd part with you, my dear. YaD

Tissue. Susan Griffin. The old tissue goes outside./Into the fire, she says. NPGG

Tit for Tat: A Tale. John Aikin. Nor give an elephant a cuff,/To be repaid in kind. OxBChV

Tit, Tat, Toe. *Anonymous.* Stick one in the old man's crown. OxNR

The Titanic. *Anonymous.* It was sad when that great ship went down. AmFP; FSW

The Titanic (A vers.). *Anonymous.* While some were homeward bound,/Sixteen hundred had to drown. ViBoFo

The Titanic (B vers.). *Anonymous.* I was on de back of er mule singing "Alabama Bound." ViBoFo

Titanic Blues. Henry Brown. And the band all playing/Nearer Oh My God to Thee BluL

The Titanic (excerpt). Edwin John Pratt. The gray shape with the palaeolithic face/Was still the master of the longitudes. NOBC; PeCV

The Titans. Betti Alver. Yet some blazing hand will remake the chaos/of earth, people, and death. BoWoP

The Tithe: To the Bride. Robert Herrick. If children you have ten, Sir John/Won't for his tenth part ask you one. CaPo

Tithonus. Alfred, Lord Tennyson. And thee returning on thy silver wheels. CABA; CABL; DiPo; ForPo; HAP; LiTB; LoBV; MBW 1-2; NAWM 1-2; NOBE; NOBV; NoP; OAEL 1-2; OAEP; OBNC; PoEL 1-5; PoPle; PPP; TEP; VLP; WHA

Titian's "Bacchanal" in the Prado at Madrid (excerpt). Thomas Sturge Moore. While all their duty is to shine for love. QFR

Title divine–Is mine! Emily Dickinson. Stroking the Melody–/Is this–the way? NOBA; ViBoPo

Title of a Swift Horse. *Anonymous.* One from Ten Thousand! WTO

Titmouse. Walter De la Mare. And into time's enormous nought,/Sweet-fed, will flit away. BrPo

Tittery-Irie-Aye. *Anonymous.* Until we all get settled in some future day. AmFP

Titty Cum Tawtay. *Anonymous.* The geese follow after. OxNR

Titus and Berenice. John Heath-Stubbs. She the insect in his brain,/Nor he her angry God. GTBS-P

Titus, Son of Rembrandt: 1665. Richard J. Lyons. ...watch its tail/flip over and under the rocker. AMV-81

Tityrus to His Fair Phyllis. John Dickenson. Yet did love at last relieve him. EIL

Tlanusi'yi, the Leech Place. Gladys Cardiff. I am dressed in a whirlpool of leech skins. CDW; STE; TWSS

To —. William Stanley Braithwaite. My youth's dead fires of hope and love. BALP; PoBA

To * * * * *. Jeremiah Joseph Callanan. Then lady, by green Erin's wave,/I'll gladly wake my harp for thee. IrPN

To—? Richard Dehmel. Or–be shattered! AWP

To—. Thomas Hood. "The girl I love in England,'/I drink at Rotterdam! OBTV

To—. John Keats.
And grief unto my darling joys dost bring. SyP

To—. Katharine Morse. For this is true:–they need your eyes/To light the ways of Paradise. HBMV

To—. Robert Nichols. Whose face would greet me in hell's fiery way. HBMV

To —. Winthrop Mackworth Praed. Whose beauty was my vision! HBV 1-2

To—. Thomas Rymer. And spite of all your children seem a bride. OBSP

To—. Percy Bysshe Shelley.
And sky and sea, but two, which move/And form all others, life and love. EnRP
Dark as it is, all change would aggravate. ERoP 1-2
Love itself shall slumber on. AtBAP; AWP; ExPo; FiP; HeIP; InPo; NoP; OAEP; OBNC; OBSP; PoEL 1-5; SeCePo

To—. Alfred, Lord Tennyson.
As welcome to my crumbling bones. OBRV
Moulded by God, and temper'd with the tears/Of angels to the perfect shape of man. VLP

To. William Carlos Williams. which is the old back yard OBAL

To a Bad Heart. Tim Reynolds. What did I do to deserve a heart like you? TW

To a Baked Fish. Carolyn Wells. No matter how much they consume. FiBHP

To a Baseball. Anonymous. And, best of all, the eager silence there/When, swift from bat or hand, you hang in air. LiSp

To a Beautiful but Heartless Coquette. Francisco de Terrazas. To be ungrateful, cruel, vain, austere! LiTW

To a Bed of Tulips. Robert Herrick. For lost like these, 'twill be/As Time had never known ye. CaPo

To a Bicycle (parody). Anonymous. Moonshine'd not print me then, as it is printing now. BXAP

To a Bird after a Storm. Henry Vaughan. Thus praise and prayer here beneath the sun/Make lesser mornings, when the great are done. TRV

To a Blind Student Who Taught Me to See. Samuel Hazo. like magic to the tapping cane of thought. GOYP

To a Blossoming Pear Tree. James Wright. Blood in my body drags me/Down with my brother. HAP

To a Blue Flower. John Shaw Neilson. But I can give love-talk to you, you little blue flower of the/Spring! BoAV; PoAu 1-2

To a Blue Hippopotamus. Ellen de Young Kay. In such immobile art? ForPo; NePoEA

To a Book. Elinor Wylie. Remember that your birth was mortal. LiTA

To a Boon Companion. Oliver St. John Gogarty. And not Alcmena's chesty son/Have room to put your ribands on! OBMV

To a Boy. Anonymous. For the voice that speaks to the heart/Pleases the Master best. KiLC

To a Boy-Poet of the Decadence. Sir Owen Seaman. You were cast for a common or usual pig,/But you play the invincible bore. CenHV; FiBHP

To a Brown Girl. Ossie Davis. Hot suns of Africa are burning still! PoNe

To a Bull-Dog. J. C. Squire. And he won't be coming here any more. FM

To a Butterfly. William Henry Davies. I'd not move/Till you tired/Of my love. FM

To a Butterfly. L. Pearl Schuck. When you fly, I will follow. AMV-80

To a Butterfly. William Wordsworth. Sweet childish days, that were as long/As twenty days are now. EG; FM; HBV 1-2; SeCeV

To a Cactus Seller. Anwar Shaul. In word or deed deception abounds/Do not believe your eyes. VWA

To a Calvinist in Bali. Edna St. Vincent Millay. Earth is too harsh for Heaven to be/One little hour in jeopardy. NoAm

To a Candle. Walter De La Mare. Candle, I dream. Come, come away! ChMP; ELP

To a Captain in Sinai. Ada Aharoni. ending howls in sounds/of peace. AMV-81

To a Captious Critic. Paul Laurence Dunbar. But, sir, I may not, till you abdicate. BPo

To a Carmelite Postulant. Michael Earls. Love-of-God eternally/Keep your heart a-flower. CAW

To a Cat. Hartley Coleridge. Thou dost not know it, and I do. FM

To a Cat. John Keats. In youth thou enter'dst on glass-bottled wall. BoC; FaBoCh; PCat

To a Cat. Algernon Charles Swinburne. Just your foot upon my hand/Softly bids it understand. PCat

To a Caty-Did. Philip Freneau. With your song of Caty-did. AA; TAP

To a Certain Lady, in Her Garden. Sterling A. Brown. And that will be sufficient for my praise. CDC

To a Certain Most Certainly Certain Critic. David McCord. Or read the book. It's shorter. OBAL

To a Chameleon. Marianne Moore. could not snap the spectrum up for food/as you have done. GoYe; PoPl

To a Cherokee Rose. William Hamilton Hayne. A virgin dowered with a heart of gold. AA

To a Child. S. S. Gardons. I tell you love is possible./We have to try. NePoEA-2

To a Child. Robert Herrick. To spoil the first impression. EG

To a Child. David McCord. And things you never seem to find/In treatises and tracts. AnAmPo

To a Child. George Edgar Montgomery. Which dawns into a perfect star. AA

To A Child. Christopher Morley. But there were days, O tender elf,/When you were Poetry itself! BiCB; HBMV

To a Child. Norreys Jephson O'Conor. Learn, too, how God's own angels keep/Your ways by day, your dreams, asleep. DFT; HBMV

To a Child. William Wordsworth. Protects the lingering dewdrop from the sun. HBV 1-2; HBVY; OBSP

To a Child Before Birth. Norman Nicholson. So in her blood for you the bright bird sings. ChMP; NAs

To a Child Five Years Old. Nathaniel Cotton. Evergreens that ne'er decay. OxBChV

To a Child in Death. Charlotte Mew. Under the shadow of that wing. MoAB; MoBrPo

To a Child of Fancy. Sir Lewis Morris. The same dear winsome lass. HBV 1-2

To a Child of Quality. Matthew Prior. That I shall be past making love/When she begins to comprehend it. CBEP; CEP; CoBE; EiCP; ExPo; GN; HBV 1-2; LiTB; NIP; NOBE; NOEC; OBEC; OBEV; PoEL 1-5; SeCeV

To a Child Running with Outstretched Arms in Canyon de Chelly. N. Scott Momaday. ...You embrace/The spirit of this place. CDW

To a Child Trapped in a Barber Shop. Philip Levine. You think your life is over?/It's just begun. InPK; NoAm; NOBA; TAP; VGW

To a Child Who Inquires. Olga Petrova. And I snuggled you tight in my arms. BLPA

To a Child with Eyes. Mark Van Doren. There is more if there is any. LOW

To a Christmas Two-Year-Old. Luci Shaw. and died/in your place/so that you could. TrCP

To a Cloistress. Juan de Tassis. Now heaven's bright harbor opens to thy gaze! CAW

To a Cloud. Manuel Altolaguirre. and your love shall be clay. LiTW

To a Common Prostitute. Walt Whitman. Till then I salute you with a significant look that you do not/forget me. AnAmPo; MoAmPo; ViBoPo

To a Comrade in Arms. Alun Lewis. What vow shall we vow who love you/For the self that you did not value? FaBoTw; MoBrPo

To a Conscript of 1940. Sir Herbert Read. As he stood against the fretted hedge, which was like white/lace. ChMP; ExPo; LiTB; LiTM; OBWP; WaP

To a Contemporary Bunkshooter. Carl Sandburg. ...where the/spear of the Roman soldier rammed in between the ribs of/this Jesus of Nazareth. WGRP

To a Coquet Beauty. John, of Buckingham Sheffield. Unless you love, you please in vain. CEP

To a Courtesan a Thousand Years Dead. Paul Eldridge. Now you are a bit of foam that sizzles/Upon the peak of a wave in mid-ocean. PoA

To a Covetous Churl. Edward May. For all thy wealth, one penny is his fare. FaBoEE

To a Cricket. William C. Bennett. Prithee, haunt my fireside still,/Voice of Summer, keen and shrill! GN; HBV 1-2

To a Crow. Robert Burns Wilson. And her wide lap shall still provide for/thee. AA

To a Crucifix. Anna Wickham. Are most remembered for your wounds and grief. MoBrPo

To A. D. William Ernest Henley. We two have listened till he sang/Our hearts and lips together. AnFE; HoPM; ViBoPo

To a Daisy. Alice Meynell. From God's side even on such a simple thing? MoBrPo; WGRP

To A Dark Girl. Gwendolyn B. Bennett. And let your full lips laugh at Fate! BANP; BlSi; CDC; PoBA

To a Daughter with Artistic Talent. Peter Meinke. (while the birds change from green to blue to brown). Psk

To a Dead Elephant. Douglas Livingstone. ...not my will/wrought this antheap with flies and hamstrung thighs. PeSA

To a Dead Journalist. William Carlos Williams. beneath the lucid ripples/to have found so monstrous/an obscurity. QFR

To a Deaf and Dumb Little Girl. Hartley Coleridge. God must be with her in her solitude! PoEL 1-5; VLP

To a Defeated Saviour. James Wright. This dream, this drowning in your sleep. NePoEA

To a Departing Favorite. George Moses Horton. May rise when thou art gone. BALP

To a Depraved Lying Woman. Sorley MacLean. ...the sordidness/of your vicissitudes. NeBP

To a Detainee. Musaemura Bonus Zimunya. "Dogs, trucks and guns belong to them/but the soil, the spirit in the earth/is ours." WhB

To a Dictatorial Sultan. Anonymous. A small milking vessel, when filled to the brim, soon overflows. WTO

To a Dog. Josephine Preston Peabody. Can you forgive us, now?–/Your fallen gods? BLPA; WGRP

To a Dog Injured in the Street. William Carlos Williams. let all men believe it,/as you have taught me also/to believe it. LCAP; LiTM; MoAB; NePoAm; PP; SeCeV

To a Dog's Memory. Louise Imogen Guiney. And keep the watch for me. AnAmPo

To a Faithless Friend. Salaan Arrabey. Ah, friend, your memory is short as any woman's! WTO

To a Faithless Lover. Robert Greacen. With the gum of lips you stealing stormed to starve. OnYI

To a Fat Lady Seen from the Train. Frances Cornford. O why do you walk through the fields in gloves/Missing so much and so much? BLPA; ELU; FaBoWP; GoJo; MoBrPo; OBMV; SpRo; WeW

To a Field Mouse. Robert Burns. And forward, tho' I canna see,/I guess and fear. CBEP; GTBS-P

To a Fighter Killed in the Ring. Lou Lipsitz. roaring on under the tenements of Harlem. LiSp

To a Fine Young Woman. William Wycherley. By thy damned snake, which does about thee crawl/In reach of my bliss, to beget my fall. TW

To a Flea in a Glass of Water. D. A. Greig. On pavements Saul and David go. PeSA

To a Fly, Taken out of a Bowl of Punch. John Wolcot. Then, like an alligator, drags him in. NOEC

To a Foreign Friend. Leonard Nathan. I count the bars of his cage while we wait. GP

To a Friend. Matthew Arnold. Singer of sweet Colonus, and its child. EnLi 1-2; OAEP

To a Friend. Hartley Coleridge. The hills sleep on in their eternity. CBEP; HBV 1-2; OBRV; PoLf

To a Friend. James Fenimore Cooper, Jr. My star and my religion here! PeHV

To a Friend. Grace Stricker Dawson. But, after all, they didn't do it! BLPA

To a Friend. Charles Gullans. My own voice silent in the morning air. NePoEA

To a Friend. Amy Lowell. O stay your hand, and leave my heart its songs! FPL; PoLf

To a Friend Concerning Several Ladies. William Carlos Williams. ...the water/reflects the reeds and the reeds/move on their stalks and rattle drily. VGW

To a Friend Going on a Journey. Mahammed A. Hassan. Friend, yourself now say a last Amen. WTO

To a Friend in Love during the Riots. William Parsons. Glow at a smile and sicken at a frown! NOEC

To a Friend in the Country. Oliver St. John Gogarty. And wet young oak leaves fingering the pane. OnYI

To a Friend in the Wilderness (excerpt). A. R. D. Fairburn. that holds the summer in its green concave. AnNZ

To a Friend, Inviting Him to a Meeting upon Promise. William Habington. How good Castara is, how deare my friend. AnAnS 2

To a Friend, on Her Examination for the Doctorate in English. J. V. Cunningham. For you have learned, not what to say,/But how the saying must be said. EiCP; VGW

To a Friend on His Marriage. Frank Templeton Prince. ...and breathe/Contentment, savouring wine and wreath. LiTM

To a Friend on His Nuptials. Matthew Prior. He strong as Jove, she like Alcmena fair! HW

To a Friend's Child. Aliki Barnstone. Your baby smell could almost make me sleep. BoWoP

To a Friend Whose Work Has Come to Nothing. William Butler Yeats. Because of all things known/That is most difficult. AnFE; AWP; BiP; BoC; DiPo; ForPo; InPo; LiTM; MBW 1-2; MoAB; MoBrPo; OAEL 1-2; OBMV; PoA

To a Gardener. Robert Louis Stevenson. Of country wine, divinely sup. AnEnPo

To a Gentleman and Lady on the Death of the Lady's Brother and Sister. Phillis Wheatley. And seek beautitude beyond the skies. BlSi

To a Gentleman Objecting to Him His Grey Hairs. Robert Herrick. By those true tears y'are weeping. CaPo; JCP; MyFE

To a Gentleman, Who Desired Proper Materials for a Monody. Anonymous. Dodsley's your man–the poem's ended. NOEC

To a Gnat. Anonymous. And clothe thee in a lion's skin. UnTE

To a God Unknown. David Eller. Do you hear me, whispering/your name voicelessly,/tenderly?/Or must I shout? VWA

To a Golden-Haired Girl in a Louisiana Town. Vachel Lindsay. If your heart is as kind/As your young eyes now. MoAmPo; MoLP

To a Golden Heart, Worn Round His Neck. Johann Wolfgang von Goethe. They're stifled by the pressure of his chain. AWP; LiTW

To a Gone Era. Irma McClaurin. Their sorrow sings through the cracked tenement walls. BlSi

To a Good Physician. William Wycherley. Fate's King and not its Executioner. ACP

To a Goose. Robert Southey. Season'd with sage and onions, and port wine. BXAP; FM; NOBL

To a Greek Girl. Henry Austin Dobson. A dream,–a dream, Autonoe! HBV 1-2

To a Greek Ship in the Port of Dublin. W. B. Stanford. over whose unhungering marble there is no conquest. NeIP

To a Happy Warrior. Wilfrid Scawen Blunt. Who sleeps in Paradise. AnEnPo

To a Hedgehog. Samuel Thompson. For you, wi aa the pikes ye claim,/Wi him to battle. BIrV

To a Hero Dead at al-Safra. Hind bint Uthatha. the wayfarer lost/whom he made to feel at ease. WPOW

To a Highland Girl. William Wordsworth. And Thee, the Spirit of them all! CABL; GoTF; LoBV; TreFT

To a History Professor. Anonymous. Some other Paris does to your fair Helen. UnTE

To a Horse. Jill Hoffman. sweet mare: I never forget your name. PH

To a Humble Bug. Linda Lyon Van Voorhis. None cares if he is left upon a shelf. GoYe

To a Hurt Child. Grace Denio Litchfield. But no one knows. AA

To a Husband. Maya Angelou. I sit at home and see it all/Through you. IHMS

To a Jack Rabbit. Squire Omar Barker. Although you're useless, our old West/Would not be West without you! BPAW

To a Jilt. Martin Armstrong. ...you remain/As once, a creature singularly plain. FaBoEE

To a June Breeze. Henry Cuyler Bunner. Pray Her remember! AA

To a Junior Waiter. Sir Alan Patrick Herbert. If something doesn't happen soon. FiBHP

To a Kiss. John Wolcot. On Delia's blushing lips I see/A thousand full as sweet as thee. HBV 1-2

To A. L. Thomas Carew. Both bud and fade, both blow and wither. AnAnS 2; CaPo; SeCP

To a Lady. William Dunbar. So confortand his levis unto me bene. BSV; EG; GBL; GoBC; OBEV

To a Lady. John Gay. With ease they bear the loss of Delf. OBEV

To a Lady. J. B. Morton. Have not the slightest need of sorcery. PoL

To a Lady. John James Piatt. First let me see that you are growing old. AA

To a Lady. Sir Walter Scott. They but yield the passing stranger/Wild-flower wreaths for Beauty's hair. OAEP

To a Lady across the Way. E. B. White. Prithee know, my dear, that I've a/Scorn for him who watched Godiva. InMe; NLV

To a Lady Asking Him How Long He Would Love Her. Sir George Etherege. Were it not madness to deny/To live because we're sure to die? CEP; HBV 1-2; LiTL; LoBV; OBEV; ViBoPo

To a Lady Friend. William Henry Davies. Sticks, bones, or rags, or you! MoBrPo

To a Lady Holding the Floor. Mildred Weston. Of someone coming/To your aid. FiBHP

To a Lady in a Garden. Edmund Waller. Nor would I indulge my passion. NCEP

To a Lady on Her Marriage. William Bell. he has forgot to make me mad/to love your body and your mind.' NePoEA

To a Lady on Her Passion for Old China. John Gay. Then quickly choose the prudent/part,/Or else you break a faithful heart. FaFP; LiTB; LoBV; OBEC

To a Lady on Reading Sherlock upon Death. Philip Stanhope, Earl of Chesterfield. To me, at least, your Sherlock give,/'Tis I must learn to die. NOEC

To a Lady on the Death of Her Husband. Phillis Wheatley. ...pleasures more refin'd/And better suited to th' immortal mind. TAP

To a Lady: She Refusing to Continue a Dispute with Me... Matthew Prior. With cruel Skill the backward Reed/He sent; and as He fled, He slew. CEP; NoP; WHA

To a Lady Sitting before Her Glass. Elijah Fenton. But play'd so lightly on your Mind,/It left no lasting Print behind. OBEC

To a Lady That Desired I Would Love Her. Thomas Carew. You but unlock, so we each other bless. AnAnS 2; CaPo; LiTL; LoBV; MeLP; MePo; OBS; SeCV 1-2

To a Lady That Desired Me I Would Bear My Part with Her in a Song. Richard Lovelace. Not to be reached with human ears. CaPo

To a Lady That Forbad to Love before Company.   Sir John Suckling. Would they could find us both in bed together!   CaPo

To a Lady To Answer Directly with Yea or Nay.   Sir Thomas Wyatt.   And I mine own and yours no more.   ElL; EnLoPo

To a Lady Troubled by Insomnia.   Franklin Pierce ("F.P.A.") Adams.   If these fail to make thee weary,/Then I cannot help thee, dearie.   InMe

To a Lady Who Did Sing Excellently.   Edward, Lord Herbert of Cherbury. Or only the delights, which you did give?   AnAnS 2; OBS; SeCP

To a Lady Who Sent Me a Copy of Verses at My Going to Bed.   Henry, Bishop of Chichester King.   I, as the night invites me, fall asleep.   PP

To a Lady, with a Compass.   George Napier.   But touch'd with virtue's magnet force,/It trembles doing wrong.   FaBoUs

To a Lady: With a Head of Diana.   Thomas William Parsons   Thrice blest! in being seldom seen.   AA

To a Lady, with a Present of a Fan.   Charles Brandling.   To cool her passions, or to fan their flame.   FaBoUs; NOEC

To a Lady, with a Present of a Walking-Stick.   John Hookham Frere.   Its main utility and pride/To be your prop, support, and guide.   FaBoUs

To a Lark in War-Time.   Franz Werfel.   Thou art what thou art.   TrJP

To a Lily.   James Matthew Legare.   And make thy leaf a stain.   AA; AnAmPo

To a Linnet in a Cage.   Francis Ledwidge.   Across my eyelids, and my soul recall/From worlds of sleeping pain.   OnYI; RoGo

To a Little Boy Learning to Fish.   Robert D. Hoeft.   Casting your baited hook/Into the world of men.   AMV-81

To a Little Boy, Who Had Destroyed a Nest of Young Birds.   Anonymous. And mourn the ill thy cruel hand has done.   FaBoUs

To a Little Girl.   Helen Parry Eden.   You taught me here docility–and how to save my soul.   HBV 1-2

To a Little Girl.   Gustav Kobbe.   And, best of all, her little soul/Is, like a lily, white.   HBV 1-2

To a Little Girl, One Year Old, in a Ruined Fortress (excerpt).   Robert Penn Warren.   But defines for the fortunate, that joy in which all joys should/ rejoice.   MoVE

To a Little Sister, Aged Ten.   Alison Elizabeth Cummings.   For you, fairy music through all your days!   BiCB

To a Living Author.   Anonymous.   Take courage, man! and steal the rest.   NLV

To a Lock of Hair.   Sir Walter Scott.   Yes, God and man might now approve me/If thou hadst lived, and lived to love me!   GTBS-P

To a Lofty Beauty, from Her Poor Kinsman.   Hartley Coleridge.   Old times unqueen thee, and old loves endear thee.   OBVV

To a Lost Sweetheart.   Don (Donald Robert Marquis) Marquis.   To hold you to me, Sweet!   FiBHP; PoL

To a Loudmouth Pontificator.   Ray Mizer.   Ere I do thrum thee such a thwacking thump/As all the bawds of tizzy never twanged.   TW

To a Louse.   Robert Burns.   What airs in dress an' gait wad lea'e us,/And ev'n devotion!   BLPA; CEP; FaFP; InvP; LiTB; NOEC; OAEP; OxBS; PrIm; SeCeV; TreF; ViBoPo

To a Madonna.   Charles Baudelaire.   Deliberately plant them all where throbs/Thy bleeding heart, and stifling with its sobs.   SyP

To a Magnolia Flower in the Garden of the Armenian Convent in Venice. Silas Weir Mitchell.   Today is thine–tomorrow thou art/death's   AA

To a Man in a Picture Window Watching Television.   Mildred Weston. Watching me/Watching you/Watching it.   ELU

To a Maple Seed.   Lloyd Mifflin.   Under thy boughs, when I, alas! am dead. AA

To a Marsh Hawk in Spring.   Henry David Thoreau.   Thou dost waive disease and pain/And resume new life again.   PB; PoEL 1-5

To a Mayflower.   William E. Marshall.   And all thy fragrance saved for Love alone.   CaP

To a Midge.   Eilidh Nisbet.   At dusk they'll dance with desperation/On muirs and hills.   PoSH

To a Military Rifle.   Yvor Winters.   True shape of death and power. MoAmPo; WaP

To a Millionaire.   Archibald Lampman.   The griefs and hates, and all the meaner parts/That balance thy one grim misgotten pile.   NOBC

To a Mosquito.   William Cullen Bryant.   No angry hand shall rise to brush thy wings.   AnNE

To a Moth Crushed Within the Leaves of an Iliad.   Charles Edward Thomas. And roars the many-sounding main.   AA

To a Mountain Daisy.   Robert Burns.   Till crushed beneath the furrow's weight/Shall be thy doom!   AnEnPo; ATP; EnLi 1-2; EnLit; GN; HBV 1-2; OAEP; PoLf; WBLP

To a Mouse.   Robert Burns.   An' forward tho' I canna see,/I guess an' fear! AnEnPo; AnFE; ATP; BiP; BSV; DiPo; EiCP; EnL; FaFP; FF; FM; GoTS; GTBS; HAP; HBV 1-2; HBVY; HeIP; InPS; LAuP; LoBV; MCCG; NOEC; NoP; OAEL 1-2; OAEP; OBEC; OxBS; PAI; PoLf; PPP; PrIm; SeCeV; TEP; TreFS; TrGrPo; WHA

To a Musician.   William Austin.   I may aspire/When I this life forsake. OxBoCh

To a Negro Boy Graduating.   Eugene T. Maleska.   Remember where you walked you smoothed the way/That those who follow may discover day. PoNe

To a New-Born Baby Girl.   Grace Hazard Conkling.   The worship of thy mother's eyes.   HBV 1-2

To a New-Born Child.   Cosmo Monkhouse.   If we do what we should, may fly/Than Angels higher.   HBV 1-2

To a New Daughter-in-law.   Anonymous.   That him you love, is also loved by me.   PoToHe

To a New York Shop-Girl Dressed for Sunday.   Anna Hempstead Branch. God loves all prettiness, and on this/Surely his angels lay their kiss.   HBV 1-2

To a Nightingale.   William, of Hawthornden Drummond.   ...thou my Minde dost raise/To Ayres of Spheares, yes, and to Angels Layes.   OBS

To a Noisy Politician.   Philip Freneau.   That some have grown prodigious fat,/That were prodigious lean!   TAP

To a Nun.   Anonymous.   High in their other heaven, pardon love.   EBEV

To a Nun.   John Ormond.   For surely God and all his saints above,/High in their other heaven, pardon love.   FaBoTw

To a Painted Lady.   Alexander Brome.   Give me the pure, or none.   CavP

To a Pair of Egyptian Slippers.   Mrs. Major Arnold.   And wish that one game we might merrily play/At "Hunt the Slippers'–to see it all plain. HBV 1-2; OBTV; OBVV

To a Passer-By.   Charles Baudelaire.   We might have loved, and you knew this might be!   SyP

To a Persistent Phantom.   Frank Horne.   I buried you deeper last night. BANP; CDC

To a Pet Cobra.   Roy Campbell.   To sting these rotted wastes into a flower. AtBAP

To a Phoebe-Bird.   Witter ("Emanuel Morgan") Bynner.   O Phoebe, with so little noise,/What eloquence you teach!   HBMV

To a Photograph.   John Banister Tabb.   A memory of light removed,/ Behold in me!   AmP

To a Photograph.   Parker Tyler.   Immutable to rhyme,/Impossible to scan. NePA

To a Plagiarist.   Moses Ibn Ezra.   Every gem/Is perfect; and with care I polished/them!   TrJP

To a Poet.   Walter Conrad Arensberg.   Those moments when you say of beauty: "Be"?   AnAmPo

To a Poet.   Sister Mary Angelita.   ...words/Are flocks of singing birds? GoBC

To a Poet a Thousand Years Hence.   James Elroy Flecker.   I send my soul through time and space/To greet you. You will understand.   ChTr; FaBoRV; HBV 1-2; MoBrPo; PoRA

To a Poet a Thousand Years Hence.   John Heath-Stubbs.   There is no reason you should read,/And much less understand, this rhyme.   OxBC

To a Poet I Knew.   Johari (Jewel C. Latimore) Amini.   u split to becom/ one of th wasted ones   PoBA

To a Poet, Who Would Have Me Praise Certain Bad Poets...   William Butler Yeats.   But was there ever dog that praised his fleas?   CTC; DBV; FaBoEE; PV

To a Poetic Lover.   W. Hay.   For fear you should return the compliment. ALV

To A Polish Mother.   Adam Mickiewicz.   And fellow patriots' whispered words by night.   CAW; LiTW

To a Political Poet.   Heinrich Heine.   and the kids feel righteous–/righteous but cosy.   FaBoPV

To a Poor Old Woman.   William Carlos Williams.   They taste good to her OBAL; SOTW; TAP

To a Pope.   Pier Paolo Pasolini.   there has been no greater sinner than yourself.   PeHV

To a Portrait of Lermontov.   Margarita Aliger.   You don't answer, since you're dead/and I won't answer...I'm alive.   VWA

To a Portrait of Whistler in the Brooklyn Art Museum.   Eleanor Rogers Cox. I know, dear James–but then/It's I or none at all!   HBMV

To a Post-Office Inkwell.   Christopher Morley.   Put Heaven on a postal card.   PoLf

To a President.   Witter ("Emanuel Morgan") Bynner.   Which were our enemies, which were our friends!   OBAL

To a Pretty Girl.   Israel Zangwill.   And the sea is not so deep/As the soul in you asleep.   TrJP

To a Print of Queen Victoria.   James Keir Baxter.   ...The small rain spits/ today. You smile in your grave.   OxBC

To a Publisher...cut-out.   LeRoi (Imamu Amiri Baraka) Jones.   Day in, Day out, you just kept belching.   NeAP

To a Race Horse at Ascot.   Jennie M. Palen.   ...And kings come/in thousand horsepower Bentleys/to cheer.   PH

To a Recalcitrant Virgin.   Asclepiades.   We'll lie but dust and ashes there below.   LiTW

To a Red-Headed Do-Good Waitress.   Alan Dugan.   ...she has/a policeman and a wrong sonnet in fifteen lines.   CAPP

To a Republican. Philip Freneau. Without a king, to see the end of time. AmPP

To a Republican Friend. Matthew Arnold.
All difference with his fellow-mortal closed,/Shall be left standing face to face with God. VLP
Them am I yours, and what you feel, I share. VLP

To a Reviewer Who Admired My Book. John Ciardi. But never doubt your gift. You are right! You are right! OBAL

To a River in the South. Sir Henry Newbolt. Old love shall dwell with old delight. CH

To a Rogue. Joseph Addison. Should'st thou be honest, thou'rt a dev'lish cheat. PV

To a Roman. J. C. Squire. Perplexed, bewildered, languishing, an alien/Who was born to cherish all his world forgot. HBMV

To a Rose. Frank Dempster Sherman. Think what a lovely hand, O Rose,/Shall place your body in the tomb! AA

To a Rose. John Banister Tabb. Its shadow falls alike on thee and me! CAW

To a Sacred Cow. *Anonymous.* Let us have plenty of milk! WGRP

To a Sad Daughter. Michael Ondaatje. Your goalie/in his frightening mask/dreams perhaps/of gentleness. GOYP

To a Salesgirl, Weary of Artificial Holiday Trees. James Wright. And one more year's far gone. NYBP

To a Scarlatti Passepied. Robert Hillyer. Down the long lanes of the vanished years,/Echoing fraily and far away. HBMV

To a School-Girl. Shaw Neilson. Call that I love on the deep yellow/Between me and the Spring? PoAu 1-2

To a Scottish Poet. · G. S. Fraser. While we stand insolent, as poets stand. BSV

To a Sea-Bird. Bret (Francis Bret Harte) Harte. I on the shore and thou on the sea. EtS

To a Sea Eagle. Hugh" (Christopher Murray Grieve) MacDiarmid. And ootshines't like a turnin' wing. MoBrPo

To a Seaman Dead on Land. Kay Boyle. And the sea-mist coiled like silk about your bones. PoA

To a Seamew. Algernon Charles Swinburne. Ah, well were I for ever,/Wouldst thou change lives with me. EtS; VLP

To a Segar. Samuel Low. Till I, departing taper, light another. OBAL

To a Severe Nun. Thomas Merton. You most of all, are weak. CoPo

To a Shade. William Butler Yeats. Away, away! You are safer in the tomb. AnIL; LiTB; PoEL 1-5

To a Sicilian Boy. Theodore Wratislaw. and the dull ennui of a woman's kiss! PeHV

To a Single Shadow without Pity. Sam Cornish. and you/feel no more NBP; PoBA

To a Skeleton. Anna Jane Vardhill. And tread the palace of the sky! BLPA

To a Skull. Thomas Caulfield Irwin. And higher shapes reflect, as we do now,/Upon the structure of the Mastodon. IrPN

To A Skull. Joshua Henry Jones. Ere I pass life's sunset stile. BANP

To a Skylark. George Meredith. They tell of the heavens to me. EnLit

To a Skylark. Percy Bysshe Shelley. The world should listen then–as I am listening now. AtBAP; BoAnP; BoLiVe; DiPo; ERoP 1-2; FaBoBe; FaBV; FaFP; FPL; GN; GTBS; GTBS-P; HAP; HBV 1-2; HBVY; InPS; InvP; LiTB; LoBV; MCCG; MyFE; NoP; OAEL 1-2; OAEP; OBEV; OBNC; OBRV; OHFP; PAI; PB; PBBP; PoLf; RoGo; TEP; TreFS; TrGrPo; WHA

To a Skylark. William Wordsworth. True to the kindred points of Heaven and home! BoLiVe; HBV 1-2; HBVY; OAEP; PBBP; TrGrPo

To a Sleeping Friend. Jean Cocteau. I will not rouse your self-destructive wars/But let the sunlight quiet your harm. PeHV

To a Small Boy Standing on My Shoes While I Am Wearing Them. Ogden Nash. A happier man today I'd be/Had a visiting adult done it to me. ALV; DBV; FiBHP

To a Snail. Marianne Moore. in the curious phenomenon of your occipital horn. CMoP; FaBoMo; FaBoWP

To a Snowflake. Francis Thompson. With His hammer of wind,/And His graver of frost. BoLiVe; BoNaP; EBCP; FaBV; HBV 1-2; ImOP; LoBV; MoAB; MoBrPo; PoPl; SeCePo; TrGrPo

To a Solitary Disciple. William Carlos Williams. Observe/the jasmine lightness/of the moon. PP; VGW

To a Spaniel. Walter Savage Landor. And thou may'st whimper in thy sleep/These many days, and start and weep. FM

To a Spanish Poet. Stephen Spender. You stare through centrifugal bones/Of the revolving and dissolving world. OAEP

To a Sparrow. Francis Ledwidge. Though the wintry winds reprove you,/And the snow is on the hill. HBMV

To a Spider. Robert Southey. Thy bowels thou dost spin,/I spin my brains. FM

To a Squirrel at Kyle-Na-No. William Butler Yeats. When all I would do/Is to scratch your head/And let you go. FM

To a Steam Roller. Marianne Moore. the congruence of the complement is vain, if it exists. BoWoP; CMoP; FaBoMo; MoAB; MoAmPo; OxBA; PP; VGW

To a Stranger. Walt Whitman. I am to see to it that I do not lose you. NoAm; NOBA

To a Swallow. Bishop Euenos. For it is neither just nor fit/That poets should each other eat. OBVE

To a Swallow Building under Our Eaves. Jane Welsh Carlyle. While I–oh, ask not what I do with mine!/Would I were such! HBV 1-2; OBRV

To a Talkative Hairdresser. Phyllis McGinley. Which drones no windier than you/Or duller, nor expects an answer. DBV

To a Teacher of French. Donald Davie. Time and again I profit by your angers. OxBC

To a Tenting Boy. Charles Tennyson Turner. Methinks I owe thee much, my little boy,/For this new duty, and its quiet joy. OBNC

To a Thesaurus. Franklin Pierce ("F.P.A.") Adams. Farewell! adieu! good-by! so long! BLPL; NLV; PoPl

To a Thrush. Thomas Augustin Daly. O! prophet then, be prophet now/And paraclete! CAW

To a Town Poet. Lizette Woodworth Reese. The horns of morning sound above the/storm. AA

To a Traveler. Lionel Pigot Johnson. Earth, whom the vast stars crown. AnEnPo; MoBrPo; NBM

To a Traveler. Su Tung-P'o. And join us together with the chord of light/That reaches beneath the painted eaves of your home. HoPM

To a Tyrant. Joseph Brodsky. "Oh yes!" if only they could rise and be there. VWA

To a Vagabond. Constance Davies Woodrow. Since I renounced the whole wide world/For one beloved face. CaP

To a Very Beautiful Lady. Ruthven Todd. Or in your own breast place the suicidal blow. BSV; NeBP

To a Very Wise Man. Siegfried Sassoon. You soar...Is death so bad?...I wish you'd say. BrPo

To a Very Young Lady. Sir George Etherege. ...threatening eyes/When thou shalt to thy noon arise! CEP; ViBoPo

To a Very Young Lady. Edmund Waller.
All that was promis'd by the Spring. AnAnS 2; OBS; SeCP; TrGrPo; ViBoPo
Who shall abide its noon-tide hour? EG

To a Victim of Radiation. Arturo Vivante. Centuries will have to pass/before it will extinguish itself. FAZ

To a Vine-Clad Telegraph Pole. Louis Untermeyer. ...You dream. But you are dead. MoAmPo

To a Visiting Poet in a College Dormitiory. Carolyn Kizer. To father men and poems in your mind. PoA

To a Wall of Flame in a Steel Mill, Syracuse, New York, 1969. Larry Levis. And ride slowly out/Onto the thawing river. AMV-81; MAYP

To a Wanton. William Habington. And judge thee, witch, in thy owne flames to burne. AnAnS 2; SeCP

To a Wasp Caught in the Storm Sash... Peter Cooley. My soul against your song? MAYP

To a Waterfowl. William Cullen Bryant. In the long way that I must tread alone,/Will lead my steps aright. AA; AnFE; AnNE; AP; APA; AWP; BLPL; DiPo; EBCP; ExPo; FaBoBe; FaFP; ForPo; GN; GoTF; HBV 1-2; HBVY; HoPM; LiTA; MAmP; MCCG; NePA; NOBA; NoP; OBAL; OBRV; OHFP; OxBA; PB; PoEL 1-5; PoLf; PrIm; SeCeV; SoSe; TAP; TreF; TrGrPo; TRV; WBLP; WGRP

To a Weak Gamester in Poetry. Ben Jonson. There's no vexation that can make thee prime. JCP

To a Western Bard Still a Whoop and a Holler away from English Poetry. William Meredith. Containing passion still,/Who cared enough to sing. PP

To a Wild Rose Found in October. Ednah Proctor (Clarke) Hayes. I ope my curled petals to the sun. AA

To a Wind-Flower. Madison Cawein. For beauty born of beauty–that remains. AA; HBV 1-2

To a Withered Rose. John Kendrick Bangs. For was it not thy happy lot/To live and die a rose? AA

To a Witty Man of Wealth and Quality... William Wycherley. Which spares the lazy, Proud, yet Bashful Wit,/The Trouble, Pains, or Shame of asking it. SeCV 1-2

To a Woman. Denis Glover. And nowhere is there more despair/Than in the tangle of your hair. AnNZ

To a Woman Who Wants Darkness and Time. Gerald William Barrax. where light is the black taste of your body/between my savage teeth PoBA

To a Wood-Violet. John Banister Tabb. A moment's glance hath made/Our souls forever one. HBV 1-2

To a Worm Which the Author Accidentally Trode Upon. William Hawkins. Legions of worms (who knows how soon?)/Shall feast on me, and mine. FM

To a Writer of the Day. Langdon Elwyn Mitchell.
As now no poetaster dares to do! AA

For thoughts, like angels, wage eternal war. AA

To a Young Ass.   Samuel Taylor Coleridge.   The aching of pale Fashion's vacant breast!   EnRP; OBEC

To a Young Beauty.   William Butler Yeats.   And I may dine at journey's end/With Landor and with Donne.   CMoP

To a Young Brother.   Maria Jane Jewsbury.   If constant to your pets, I hold/You'll faithful be in friendships after.   OxBChV

To a Young Child.   Eliza Scudder.   Return unto they native land again. AA

To a Young Friend.   Samuel Taylor Coleridge.   Sleeps shelter'd there, scarce wrinkled by the gale!   ChRP

To a Young Gentle-Woman, Councel Concerning Her Choice.   Richard Crashaw.   May it not be amongst the sons of Men.   AtBAP; OBS

To a Young Gentleman in Love: A Tale.   Matthew Prior.   Love is a jest and vows are wind.   TEP

To a Young Girl.   D. Rosenmann-Taub.   Sunflower, swan, sandhill,/sprout hidden under the dress,/indescribable grave.   VWA

To a Young Girl.   William Butler Yeats.   Set all her blood astir/And glittered in her eyes.   EBEV; OLR

To a Young Girl Dying.   Thomas William Parsons   Pray that our pilgrimage may end like thine!   AA

To a Young Girl Leaving the Hill Country.   Arna Bontemps.   Come back to seek the girl she was in these familiar/stones.   CDC

To a Young Lady.   William Cowper.   And Heaven reflected in her face. GTBS; GTBS-P; HBV 1-2

To a Young Lady.   Richard Savage.   Some thought, much whim, and all a contradiction.   CBEP; OBEC

To a Young Lady.   William Wordsworth.   But an old age serene and bright,/And lovely as a Lapland night,/Shall lead thee to thy grave.   EG; EnRP

To a Young Lady Swinging Upside Down on a Birch Limb...   James H. Koch.   A rhythm's maker catch, by words uncaught.   GoYe

To a Young Lady, with Some Lampreys.   John Gay.   They have set my heart more cock-a-hoop,/Than could whole seas of crawfish soup.   FaBoUs; NOEC

To a Young Leader of the First World War.   Stefan George.   Hair become a ring first of rays around you/And then a crown.   WaaP

To a Young Lover.   Amur Mu'izzi.   I never heard of tulips amidst musk-shedding hya-/cinths.   LiTW

To a Young Poet.   Paula Bennett.   their power still to mar/known only from inside.   AMV-81

To a Young Poet.   Harry M. Meacham.   And let the doctor etherize. GoYe

To a Young Poet.   Edna St. Vincent Millay.   Not the lark, not you,/Can die as others do.   CrMA; OBSP

To a Young Poet Who Fled.   John Logan.   "I'd rather be a swineheard in the hut, understood/by swine, than a poet misunderstood by men."   SM

To a Young Woman on the World Staff.   Franklin Pierce ("F.P.A.") Adams.   But please don't sing while I work.   ALV

To a Young Wretch.   Robert Frost.   Help me accept its fate with Christmas feeling.   OFD

To Aaron Burr, under Trial for High Treason.   Sarah Wentworth Morton.   Here gives a prison, there a throne.   PAH

To Aberdein.   William Dunbar.   Be thankful to this burcht of Aberdein. FaBoPP

To Abraham Lincoln.   John James Piatt.   Made by God's providence the Anointed/One.   AA

To Adhiambo.   Gabriel Okara.   but she turned her eyes away.   PBA

To Aenone.   Robert Herrick.   Take me and mine together!   HBV 1-2

To Africa.   Raymond Mazisi Kunene.   Bring us the sacred sword!   WhB

To Age.   Walter Savage Landor.   He who hath braved Youth's dizzy heat/Dreads not the frost of Age.   EnRP; HBV 1-2; TreFS

To Ailsa Rock.   John Keats.   Another cannot wake thy giant size.   EnRP; MOS; OBNC

To Alan.   Douglas Fraser.   Until I scale that final peak/And view/The unimagined vistas of eternity.   PoSH

To Alexander Neville.   Barnabe Googe.   Feed on the bait, but yet beware the hooks.   EnRePo; NoP

To Alfred Tennyson.   Walter Savage Landor.   Come: among the sons of men is one/Welcomer than Alfred Tennyson?   FaBoUs; PoL

To All Angels and Saints.   George Herbert.   Since we are ever ready to disburse,/If any one our Masters hand can show.   SeCV 1-2

To All Brothers.   Sonia Sanchez.   this sister knows/and waits.   BPo

To All Sisters.   Sonia Sanchez.   and makes u/turn in/side out.   PoBA

To Allegra Florence in Heaven.   Thomas Holley Chivers.   For the sleep which now is thine!   BXAP; PeD

To Althea from Prison.   Richard Lovelace.   Angels alone, that soar above,/Enjoy such liberty.   AnAnS 2; AnEnPo; AnFE; AWP; BiP; BLPA; CaPo; CavP; EnLit; FaBoBe; FPL; GBL; GoTF; GTBS; GTBS-P; HAP; HBV 1-2; HeIP; InPo; InPS; JCP; LiTB; LiTL; LoBV; MCCG; MeLP; MePo; NOBE; NoP; OAEP; OBEV; OBS; PAI; PoPle; PoRA; SeCeV; SeCP; SeCV 1-2; SoSe; TEP; TreF; TrGrPo; ViBoPo; WHA

To Amanda.   James (1700-48) Thomson.   Thy beauties glow with full delight.   BSV

To Amarantha.   Richard Lovelace.   But shake your head, and scatter day! CaPo; HoPM; LiTL; MePo; NIP; NoP; OBEV; SeCP; SeCV 1-2; TrGrPo; UnTE; ViBoPo

To America.   Alfred Austin.   And our friendship last long as love doth last/and stronger than death is strong.   GN; HBV 1-2

To America, on Her First Sons Fallen in the Great War.   E. M. Walker.   Is not death but the door to life begun/To those who hear far Heaven cry, "Well/done!"   PAH

To Amine.   James Clarence Mangan.   The only eyes that, near or far,/Can gaze on thine without despair.   OBEV; OBVV

To Amoret.   Edmund Waller.   Wonder is shorter liv'd than Love.   SeCV 1-2

To Amoret Gone from Him.   Henry Vaughan.   Why, Amoret, why should not wee.   CBEP; MeLP; OBS

To Amy.   J. Gordon Coogler.   I'll toast you in Congaree mud.   OBAL

To an Acquaintance.   Anonymous.   The world believes nor one, nor/t'other. FaFP

To an Aging Charioteer.   Scholasticus.   If only you were immortal as your fame.   LiSp

To an Alcoholic.   Sandra McPherson.   ...to each his own/Piss-golden light. MAYP

To an Ambitious Friend.   Horace.   When dawns that day, that day.   AWP

To an American Poet Just Dead.   Richard Wilbur.   It's just as well that now you save your breath.   HaCAP; NLV; NoP

To an Anti-poetical Priest.   Giolla Brighde MacNamee.   For every Gael that shows so brave/Is nothing better than a slave!   AnIV

To an Artful Theatre Manager.   Lorenzo Da Ponte.   But you the cash must instant pay,/Or else Dorinda will not play.   TrJP

To an Artist.   Robert Burns.   You'll easy draw a lang-kent face,/But no sae weel a stranger.   EyDe

To an Artist, to Take Heart.   Louise Bogan.   Upon his bed, however, Shakespeare died,/Having endured them all.   GrPl; NYBP

To an Athlete Dying Young.   Alfred Edward Housman.   The garland briefer than a girl's.   ATP; BiP; BLPL; BrPo; CMoP; DL; ExPo; GoTF; HAP; HeIP; InPR; LiSp; LiTB; LiTM; MaC; MasP; MoAB; MoBrPo; NBM; NIP; NoAm; NoP; PoEL 1-5; PoPl; PoRA; PPoe; PrIm; SD; SeCeV; SoSe; TEP; TreF; TrGrPo; UnPo; VLP; WHA

To an Athlete Turned Poet.   Peter Meinke.   dogging with rage and joy over the broken backs/of words words words   LiSp

To an Author.   Philip Freneau.   She, only she, can please the taste! AmPP; MAmP; NOBA; OxBA

To an Autumn Leaf.   Albert Mathews.   "Dust unto dust," our roundelay. AA

To an Avenue Sport.   Helen Johnson Collins.   and you fell/scattering your winning hand!   PoNe

To an Early Primrose.   Henry Kirke White.   And hardens her to bear/Serene the ills of life.   HBV 1-2; OBNC; OBRV

To an Elder Poet.   William Carlos Williams.   Wait forever/shaken by the rain-/forever!   PoA

To an Elderly Virgin.   Mael Isu O Brolchain.   and the King's clear countenance shine upon us/when we have leaped from our bodies old. NOBI

To an Enemy.   Maxwell Bodenheim.   Showed me the virtues whose images/you destroyed.   TrJP

To an Estranged Wife.   Gary Young.   ...leaning gently/against the cupboard doors.   AMV-81

To an Icicle.   Blanche Taylor Dickinson.   And feel how tears can run. CDC

To an Imaginary Father.   Wendy Rose.   twenty-four years late.   CDW

To an Imperilled Traveller.   Nathan Haskell Dole.   Of pangs more grievous, sufferings more/fell,/Than Dante or his master dared rehearse!   AA

To an Indian Poet.   Patty L. Harjo.   This night you have given me much happiness to carry/within an empty heart.   VoR

To an Indian Skull (excerpt).   Alexander McLachlan.   With weary feet, to toil and plod/Through nature, back to nature's God...   CaP

To an Infant Daughter.   John Clare.   Child, it's a tender string to touch,/That sounds, "Thou'rt mine."   NAs

To an Infant Expiring the Second Day of its Birth.   Hetty Wright.   Hear a suppliant! Let me be/partner in thy destiny!   NOEC

To an Insect.   Oliver Wendell Holmes.   And then the child of future years/Shall hear what Katy did.   HBV 1-2; HBVY; TreF

To an Irish Blackbird.   James MacAlpine.   When the dew is on the fall. HBMV; HBVY

To an Island Princess.   Robert Louis Stevenson.   Gracious and helpful, wise and good,/The Fairy Princess Moe stood.   OBTV

To an Isle in the Water.   William Butler Yeats.   To an isle in the water/With her would I fly.   AWP

To an Oak Tree.   Sir Walter Scott.   Rome bound with oak her patriots' brows,/As Albyn shadows Wogan's tomb.   OBNC

To an Obscure Poet Who Lives on My Hearth. Charles Lotin Hildreth. Till thy rapt invocation still/My troubled dreams. AA

To an Old Danish Song-Book. Henry Wadsworth Longfellow. And recalling by their voices/Youth and travel. OBVV

To an Old Fraud. Martial (Marcus Valerius Martialis). A sponge would do a better job. LiTW

To an Old Lady. William Empson. And but in darkness is she visible. AtBAP; CoBMV; FaBoTw; GTBS-P; MoAB; MOON; NoAm; NOBE

To an Old Lady Dead. Siegfried Sassoon. With this, your semblance to a sculptured tomb/That clasps a rosary of nothingness. PoPle

To an Old Philosopher in Rome. Wallace Stevens. As if the design of all his words takes form/And frame from thinking and is realized. AP; NoAm; NOBA

To an Old Poet. Walter Savage Landor. And hammer it til cold and flat. DBV

To an Old San Francisco Poet. Keith Abbott. I think that's all you ever really wanted/Not jails pain or death. APU

To an Old Tune. William Alexander Percy. And if one turns to leave you/Or stab you–smile, lad, smile. HBMV

To an Old Venetian Wine-Glass. Lloyd Mifflin. Hath left it ever rosy round the rim! AA

To an Olde Gentlewoman, That Painted Hir Face. George Turberville. To other Trulles of tender yeares/Resigne the flagge of Fame. EnPo

To an Oriole. Edgar Fawcett. Yearning toward Heaven until its wish was heard,/Desire unspeakably to be a bird? HBV 1-2

To an Unborn Pauper Child. Thomas Hardy. Joys seldom yet attained by humankind! CoBMV; FaBoRV; GTBS-P; LiTB; NAs; ViBoPo

To an Ungentle Critic. Robert Graves. There are old-fashioned folk still like it. HBMV; InMe

To an Unknown Neighbor at the Circus. Rosemary Benet. When you're grown-up, you little blighter,/You'll be a typical first nighter. DBV; InMe

To and on Other Intellectual Poets.... Ramon Guthrie. Science is still/scratching its pretty head about. NMP

To Anne. William Stirling-Maxwell. I shall want just one kiss more. HBV 1-2

To Antenor. Katherine ("Orinda") Philips. Let him be still himself; and let him live. SBG

To Anthea, Who May Command Him Anything. Robert Herrick. And hast command of every part/To live and die for thee. BoC; CaPo; CBEP; EnLit; GTBS; GTBS-P; HBV 1-2; JCP; LoBV; NOBE; OAEL 1-2; OAEP; OBEV; OBS; SeCP; SeCV 1-2; TrGrPo; ViBoPo

To Any Daddy. Anonymous. For the little boy who's waiting to grow/up to be like you. STF

To Any M.F.H. Victoria Mary (Vita) Sackville-West. Shall come no scarlet-coated fool/To tease my foxes from their haunts. SBG

To Any Member of My Generation. George Barker. ...the whores of death/Whom we have found in our beds today, today? LiTM; ViBoPo; WaP

To Aphrodite: With a Mirror. Aline Kilmer. I would not see myself as I am now. HBMV

To Arcady. Charles Buxton Going. Here is the Land of Song! HBV 1-2

To Archinus. Callimachus. If this be crime, the crime's confessed. AWP

To Argos. Lawrence Durrell. And this is what breaks the heart. MoPo

To Ariake Kambara. Norman Rosten. As love is recalled to us, once/Having been so blinded. NYBP

To Arms. Park Benjamin. The first and foremost in the fight/Are sure to win the day! PAH

To Art. Dante Gabriel Rossetti. I loved thee ere I loved a woman, Love. PoL

To Ashtaroth and Bel. Saul Tchernichovsky. Arise, ascend, be bold, desire! TrJP

To Ask for All Thy Love. Anonymous. Let us so join our hearts that nothing may/Estrange them. EIL

To Atalanta. Dorothy Dow. Whisper to him that I will/Wait...beyond the farthest hill. HBMV

To Auden on His Fiftieth. Richard Eberhart. You flex a new twist to the spirit's feigning. GLGT; NAs

To Aunt Rose. Allen Ginsberg. the war in Spain has ended long ago/Aunt Rose LiTM; NoP; VGW

To Ausonius. Paulinus of Nola. Living, remembering, to eternity. PeHV

To Autumn. William Blake. Then rose, girded himself, and o'er the bleak/Hills fled from our sight; but left his golden load. BoNaP; ERoP 1-2; WiR

To Autumn. John Keats. And gathering swallows twitter in the skies. AnEnPo; AtBAP; AWP; BiP; BoNaP; DiPo; EBEV; ERoP 1-2; FaBoRV; FF; FiP; ForPo; FPL; GoTF; HAP; HBV 1-2; HBVY; InPK; InPo; InPS; InvP; LiTB; MBW 1-2; MyFE; NAWM 1-2; NIP; NOBE; NoP; NU; OAEL 1-2; OAEP; OBEV; OBNC; OBRV; PoEL 1-5; PoLf; PoPle; PPoe; PPP; Prf; PrIm; RoGo; SCV; SeCeV; SoSe; TEP; TreFS; UnPo; ViBoPo; WHA

To Avisa. Henry Willoby. Yet let me with the shadow play. EIL

To Azrael. Charles Baudelaire. Smile with those lips that never yet have spoken! SyP

To B. C. Sir John Suckling. Too late for me, the blind does lead the blind. CaPo

To Barba. Edward May. No more have I the power to enforce/Thy constancy, for lust will have its course. FaBoEE

To Bary Jade. Charles Follen Adams. Ck-thrash-ub! Ck-ck-tish-u!) OBAL

To Be a Jew in the Twentieth Century. Muriel Rukeyser. Daring to live for the impossible. TrJP

To Be a Master in Your House. Natan Zach. passing overhead at night/on their way to the sea. VWA

To be a mistress. Kiyoko Tsuda. I cut a watermelon. BoWoP

To Be a Nurse. A. H. Lawrence. The great Physician/Is working through you! PoToHe

To Be a Pilgrim. Robert Conquest. –Baptized? buried?–One of those. OxBC

To Be Black, To Be Lost. Hannah Kahn. Ask me how it feels to be both/Exposed and doubly denied. GoYe

To Be Carved on a Stone at Thoor Ballylee. William Butler Yeats. And may these characters remain/When all is ruin once again. FaBoEE; NoAm; NoP

To Be Continued. Jammes M. Flagg and Julian Street. Said E. P. Roe to Opie Read. FiBHP; InMc; PV

To Be Engraven on a Dial. Samuel Sewall. Tread sure, keep up with them, and All's your own. SCAP

To Be in Love. Gwendolyn Brooks. To see fall down, the Column of Gold,/Into the commonest ash. IHMS; OLR

To Be in Love While in Prison. John Paul Minarik. you're determined to float on your back/until you can stand on your feet. LFAC

To Be of Use. Marge Piercy. and a person for work that is real. GeTw; HoAn

To Be or Not to Be. Anonymous. It looks that way. But I dunno. FaBoCo; FaFP; MoShBr

To Be or Not to Be (parody). William H. Edmunds. Because, forsooth, "I'm married!" FaBoPa

To Be Quicker... Don L. Lee. jump forward into the past/to bring back/goodness. JB

To Be Recited to Flossie on Her Birthday. William Carlos Williams. you will believe me/a rose/to the end of time. VGW

To Be Said at the Seder. Karl Wolfskehl. A pillar of fire! TrJP

To Be Sung. Peter Viereck. To signal the falling,/"You're never alone"? FaBV

To Be Sung on the Water. Louise Bogan. Less than the sound of its blade/Dipping the stream once more. MoVE; PrIm; VGW

To Beachey, 1912. Carl Sandburg. With the cool, calm shadow at the wheel. TiPo

To Beatrice Stuart Wortley: Aetat 2. Alfred Austin. Patter, chatter everywhere. PeD

To Beauty. Charles Baudelaire. My eyes, my wide eyes of eternal light! EnLi 1-2

To Begin. Fran Winant. you have only to begin/again BrRo

To Begin the Day. Anonymous. And walk in heaven's pathway and the peacefulness thereof. BLRP

To Bellinus. Anonymous. No prick will bore your flabby arse again! PeHV

To Ben, at the Lake. Cilla McQueen. ...the world/is holding us up/very well, today. OCNZ

To Ben. Johnson. Upon Occasion of His Ode of Defiance. Thomas Carew. Then all men else, then Thy selfe onely lesse. AnAnS 2; CaPo; MePo

To Benjamin West. Washington Allston. E'en for itself to love thy soul-ennobling art. AnAmPo

To Bert Campaneris. Tom Clark. Which I guess just goes to show/how good you know English/don't count for everything LiSp

To Betsey-Jane, on Her Desiring to Go Incontinently to Heaven. Helen Parry Eden. In Heavenly leaves to play at tents/With all the Holy Innocents. HBMV

To Blossoms. Robert Herrick. Like you a while, they glide/Into the grave. BoNaP; CaPo; EG; GTBS; GTBS-P; HBV 1-2; JCP; LoBV; OBEV; OBS; SeCP; SeCV 1-2

To Bobby Seale. Lucille Clifton. was made for/men CNA; PoBA

To Borglum's Seated Statue of Abraham Lincoln. Charlotte B. Jordan. Thou war worn soul communing with thy God! OHIP

To Boris Pasternak. Alexander Kushner. You must remain silent. VWA

To Brander Matthews. Henry Austin Dobson. Alas! 'Tis all too clear I'm not/In vein today. ALV

To Bring Spring. George Keithley. ...The last girl/cradling several globes/in her bare arms/yellow and blue and rose. NPGG

To Bring the Dead to Life. Robert Graves. You in his spotted garments/Shall yourself lie wrapped. MoBrPo

To Brooklyn Bridge. Hart Crane. And of the curveship lend a myth to God. AP; BLPL; CrMA; DiPo; ExPo; EyDe; LiTM; NePA; OxBA; PoPl; PrIm; SeCeV

To Fine Lady Would-Be.　Ben Jonson.　...Write, then, on thy womb,/Of the not born, yet buried, here's the tomb.　FaBoEE; JCP; NoP; OBSP

To Flavia.　Edmund Waller.　Dissemble well, and win the field!　HBV 1-2

To Flaxman.　William Blake.　Thou call'st me madman, but I call thee blockhead.　FaBoEE

To flee from memory.　Emily Dickinson.　Of men escaping/From the mind of man.　FaBoEE

To Fletcher Reviv'd.　Richard Lovelace.　Yet all men henceforth be afraid to write.　OBS

To Flood Stage Again.　James Wright.　I open my eyes and gaze down/At the dark water.　NOBA; Prf

To Flossie.　William Carlos Williams.　but aren't they–/in wax/paper for the/moment–beautiful!　NePoAm-2

To Fool, or Knave.　Ben Jonson.　One doth not stroke me, nor the other strike.　FaBoEE; NoP; SoSe

To Ford Madox Ford in Heaven.　William Carlos Williams.　a part of that of which you were the known/part, Provence, he loved so well.　AmPP; NoAm; NOBA

To Forget Me.　Theodore Weiss.　...I am/flooded to that realm the lightnings/coil, I inmost far out in the world.　CoAP

To Fortune.　Robert Herrick.　Yet scarecrow-like I'll walk, as one/Neglecting thy derision.　OBSP; SeCV 1-2

To Fortune.　Sir Thomas More.　But in faith I bless you again a thousand times,/For lending me now some leisure to make rhymes.　ACP

To Fortune.　James (1700-48) Thomson.　Make but the dear Amanda mine!　BSV

To France.　Ralph Chaplin.　...The whole world holds its breath/To hear the crimson Gallic rooster crow!　HBMV

To Francelia.　Thomas Duffett.　And let me have my three daies' reign.　CavP

To Francis Beaumont.　Ben Jonson.　When even there, where most thou praisest/mee,/For writing better, I must envie thee.　OAEP; OBS

To Friend and Foe.　*Anonymous.*　But this is the sport in Country and Court,/Then let not these pastimes betray thee.　CoMu

To Friends Who Have Also Considered Suicide.　Phyllis Webb.　Decline, Fall, to futility and larks,/to the bright crustaceans of the oversky.　NOBC

To Frighten a Storm.　Gladys Cardiff.　You shall have her lying down/Upon the smoking mountains.　CDW; STE

To Fuscus Aristus.　Horace.　The horse doth with the horseman run away.　AWP

To G. K. Chesterton.　Joseph Mary Plunkett.　Then see us safe home to the boss.　OnYI

To G.R.　Samuel Elsworth Cottam.　A revelation! Just a speck/Of friendship, love and light!　PeHV

To Gabriel of the Annunciation.　Peter Abelard.　Unto the fatherland/Over the starry skies!　CAW

To George Barker.　Gene Derwood.　The burning grin of space, knelled hell, is sprung.　NePA

To George Pulling Buds.　Adelaide O'Keeffe.　Lest for a present paltry sport, you kill a future joy.　FaBoUs

To George Sand: A Desire.　Elizabeth Barrett Browning.　To kiss upon thy lips a stainless fame.　TEP

To Germany.　Charles Hamilton Sorley.　The darkness and the thunder and the rain.　MoBrPo

To Geron.　Hildebrand Jacob.　Unsettled yet by deed and free,/That you may leave to her–or me.　NOEC

To Giotto.　Wesley Trimpi.　And none can comprehend/What dissolution means.　NePoEA

To Giulia Grisi.　Nathaniel Parker Willis.　I die–for thou has poured to-night/The last drop into mine.　AA; AmLP

To Give One's Life.　Mary Carolyn Davies.　Than to give it in a moment, gloriously.　PoToHe

To God.　William Blake.　I should suspect that I worshiped the Devil/If I thanked my God for Worldly things　OAEL 1-2

To God.　Robert Herrick.　Tumble shall heaven, and so down will I.　TRV; WGRP

To God.　Furnley Maurice.
　　Earth and her vines may shroud our murderings,/But what shall kill immortal memory?　BoAV 030
　　Look on our broken hands, our withered wings,/And pity, Lord, our poor humanity.　BoAV
　　Redeem us by Thy hope, lest Thy disgust/Makes future empires violate our dust.　BoAV
　　Tears for such wrongs that only tears repair.　BoAV

To God Alone, the Only Donour.　Francis Daniel Pastorius.　To him belongs nought but the Foul.　SCAP

To God, on His Sickness.　Robert Herrick.　Yet I have hope, by thy great power,/to spring; though now a wither'd flower.　OxBoCh

To God Our Strength Shout Joyfully.　Henry Ainsworth.　And I, releasing, thee enlarged.　AH

To God the Father.　Henry Constable.　That it the temple of the Spirit may prove.　GoBC

To God the Son.　Henry Constable.　Made glory shine in her humility.　OBSC

To God, Ye Choir above.　Philip Skelton.　Adore the Wisdom, praise the Power,/That made and governs all.　OxBoCh

To Graecinus, on Loving Two Women at Once.　Ovid (Publius Ovidius Naso).　"Even as he led his life, so did he die."　EBEV

To Greet a Letter-Carrier.　William Carlos Williams.　Atta boy! Atta boy!　OBAL

To Grosphus.　Godfrey the Satirist　But on the turn, you're virile, true and straight!　PeHV

To Groves.　Robert Herrick.　That my poor name may have the glory/To live remembered in your story.　CaPo

To Guerdon.　John James Piatt.　Lo, her choice crown–its flowers are also/stone.　AA

To Guillaume Appollinaire.　Jim Brodey.　...and take/train into this wilderness of prisons & anthology.　APU

To Hafiz.　Thomas Bailey Aldrich.　Where she stands smiling, we kneel down/to her!　AA

To Hampstead.　[James Henry] Leigh Hunt.　And Love Domestic, smiling equally.　EnRP

To Harold Jacoby.　Irwin Edman.　Can make me, as it made you, Master of the Comic Spirit.　InMe

To Harriett.　John Clare.　Outshone the sun in summer skies.　AtBAP

To Hartley Coleridge.　William Wordsworth.　But, at the touch of wrong, without a strife,/Slips in a moment out of life.　HBV 1-2

To Hasekawa.　William Arensberg.　But life has told on you.　HBV 1-2

To Haydn.　Thomas Holcroft.　And consonance sublime amid confusion hears.　NOEC

To Hayley.　William Blake.　Do be my enemy for friendship's sake.　FaBoEE; TrGrPo

To Hear an Oriole Sing.　Emily Dickinson.　"No, sir! In thee!"　AnFE; APA; MAmP; PB; PoEL 1-5; UnS

To Hear My Head Roar.　Henry Taylor.　...reading some poetry/because he wants to have something to say.　MAYP

To Heaven.　Ben Jonson.　..or that these prayers be/For weariness of life, not love of thee.　AnAnS 2; EnRePo; ExPo; ForPo; HAP; ILwL; JCP; LiTB; LoBV; NOCV; OBS; PPoe; QFR; SeCeV; SeCP; TrPWD; UnPo

To Helen.　Edgar Allan Poe.　Ah, Psyche, from the regions which/Are Holy Land!　AA; AP; APA; AtBAP; ATP; AWP; BoLoP; EG; ExPo; FaBoBe; FaBV; FaFP; FaPo; FPL; GBL; GoTF; HAP; HBV 1-2; HBVY; HeIP; HoPM; InPo; InPS; InvP; LaNeLa; LiTA; LiTL; LoBV; MAmP; MCCG; NePA; NIP; NOBA; NoP; OBEV; OBRV; OBVV; OxBA; PAI; PoEL 1-5; PoLf; PoRA; PrIm; SeCeV; TAP; TreF; TrGrPo; ViBoPo

To Helen.　Winthrop Mackworth Praed.
　　Each of her tones and of her looks/Would have its four, not lines, but books.　LoBV
　　In sickness as in health, bless you, my Own! NOBV
　　The light her love o'er mine is throwing! HBV 1-2

To Helen Frankenthaler of Circe, 1974.　Anne Cherner.　I wind you to my weather.　PoDr

To Helen in a Huff.　Nathaniel Parker Willis.　Be laying up love, I should say!/Nay, lady, smile!　OBAL

To Heliodora: A Fretful Monody.　Meleager.　Suppose you just stay where you are:/I'll be your jailer!　LiTW

To Heliodora, Dead.　Meleager.　She who is dead brought sorrow to us all.　LiTW

To Hell with Commonsense.　Patrick Kavanagh.　We can fly to knowledge/Without ever going to college.　CIP; FaBoTw

To Hell with It.　Frank O'Hara.　as I make room for them, on one/after another filthy page of poetry.　NeAP

To Hell with Your Fertility Cult.　Gary Snyder.　–he had nothing to say.　NAs; TW

To Henrietta, on Her Departure for Calais.　Thomas Hood.　...that some delicious stew/Is cat instead of rabbit, you must answer, "Tant mi-eux"!　OBTV; OxBChV

To Henry Constable and Henry Keir.　Alexander Montgomerie.　I must perforce ga seik my fathers sword.　OxBS

To Henry Vaughan.　A. J. M. Smith.　Glad to be Nothing, to be All.　OBCV

To Henry Wright of Mobberley, Esq. on Buying the Picture...　John Byrom.　Huzza! Father Malebranche and shorthand for ever.　NOEC

To Her.　Robert Mezey.　and to her all sounds are music.　NaP

To Her Againe, She Burning in a Feaver.　Thomas Carew.　So shalt thou quench her fire, and mine.　AnAnS 2; SeCP

To Her Body, Against Time.　Robert Kelly.　rain against a hidden sun,/the form plain　CoPo

To Her Dead Mate: Montana, 1966.　Elizabeth Libbey.　Listen: the river, like riders, approaches from nowhere.　AmPA

To Her Eyes.　Edward, Lord Herbert of Cherbury.　That beams which pass/Through black cannot but be divine.　JCP; OBS

To Her in Absence.　Thomas Carew.　Where it for ever shall at anchor lie.　CaPo

To Her Love. Edward May. I am thy rose, my dear, and thou my tree. FaBoEE

To Her Lover's Complaint. Jane Barker. Or th' innocence of children's plays,/Or lamps in ancient urns. OBSP

To Her Portrait. Sister Juana Ines de la Cruz. It is a corpse; or dust; a shadow; naught. LiTW

To Her Questioning His Estate. William Hammond. The same then in our selves we are. JCP

To Her–Unspoken. Amelia Josephine Burr. Bid him judge me gently for the sake of long ago. HBV 1-2

To Him That Was Crucified. Walt Whitman. ...ages to come, may prove brethren and lovers, as/we are. AnEnPo; MoRP

To Him Who Is Feared. Eleazar Ben Kalir. And thrice shall the Shophar re-echo/your song/On mountain and altar to whom both/belong. TrJP

To Himself. Richard Aldridge. The rose, that draws the touch, and stings. NePoAm

To Himself. Anacreon. To-morrow–who can say? LiTW

To Himself. Caius Valerius Catullus. Catullus, still remember to be strong. AWP; LiTW

To Himselfe and the Harpe. Michael Drayton. To kindle, or to slake,/Although in SKELTON's Ryme. OBS

To His Book. Robert Herrick.
He's greedy of his life who will not fall,/Whenas a public ruin bears down all. CaPo; FaBoUs
May every ill that bites or smarts/Perplex him in his hinder parts. JCP
See, the fire's by: Farewell. CaPo
She'll run to all adulteries. OBSP

To His Book. Leon Stokesbury. Particularly, I let you go. Sink, or float, or fly now,/Bad child. SM

To His Book. William Walsh. What's built upon esteem, can ne'er decay. CEP

To His Books. Henry Vaughan. Then thank thyself, wild fool, that would'st not be/Content to know–what was too much for thee! QFR

To His Chi Mistress. George Starbuck. the Sooty Slut replaces/her defeated dead. NYBP

To His Child. William Bullokar. Old stems will rather break than yield. OxBChV

To His Conscience. Robert Herrick. So I'll not fear the judge or thee. AnAnS 2; NoP; OxBoCh; PoEL 1-5

To His Coy Love. Michael Drayton. I cannot live without thee. EIL; ErPo; HBV 1-2; LiTL; OBEV; OBS; ViBoPo

To His Coy Mistress. Andrew Marvell. Thus, though we cannot make our Sun/Stand still, yet we will make him run. AnAnS 1; AtBAP; ATP; AWP; BiP; BoLoP; DiPo; EBEV; ELP; EnLoPo; ExPo; FaBV; FaFP; FF; ForPo; FPL; GBL; GoTF; HAP; HBV 1-2; HeIP; HoPM; InPo; InPS; InvP; JCP; LiTB; LiTL; LoBV; MasP; MAT; MeLP; MePo; NIP; NOBE; NoP; OAEL 1-2; OAEP; OBEV; OBS; PAI; PoEL 1-5; PoLf; PoPl; PoPle; PoRA; PPoe; PPP; PrIm; SCV; SeCePo; SeCeV; SeCP; SeCV 1-2; SoSe; TEP; TreFT; TrGrPo; UnPo; UnTE; ViBoPo; WeW; WHA

To His Coy Mistress (parody). Edward Bird. Now, now, now, is the day we should be/Not waiting but mating. BXAP; FaBoPa

To His Coy Mistress (parody). John Flood. in the tiny world of lovers' arms and/challenge time. BXAP; FaBoPa

To His Coy Mistress (parody). Gerry Hamill. My mochiness tae ye wad thow an' get/Mair dwamin' than empires, an' mair switherin' yet. BXAP

To His Coy Mistress (parody). Peter Scupham. Veteran and novice hold their oath unbroken/Should trolls chumble and the rain strike upward. BXAP

To His Coy Mistress (parody). Stanley J. Sharpless. Stand still, I'll make Joan Hunter Dunn. BXAP

To His Coy Mistress (parody). W. J. Webster. It gives no pleasure–learn it now or later–/To be on heat in the incinerator. BXAP

To His Darrest Freind. of Baldynnis John Stewart. Thocht verse be vaine,/Composit heir. OxBS

To His Dead Body. Siegfried Sassoon. Dear, red-faced father God who lit your mind. NoAm

To His Dear Friend, Bones. Jay Parini. the only barrier which contrives/to keep us in our separate lives. MAYP

To His Dying Brother, Master William Herrick. Robert Herrick. To guard it so as nothing here shall be/Heavy, to hurt those sacred seeds of thee. CaPo; OAEP; PoPle; SeCV 1-2

To His Ever-Loving God. Robert Herrick. To leave this life, not loving it, but Thee. AnAnS 2; TrPWD

To His Excellency, General Washington. Phillis Wheatley. A crown, a mansion, and a throne that shine,/With gold unfading, Washington! be thine. OFD; SBG

To His Excellency Joseph Dudley Eqr Gover: &c. John Saffin. From him tho Aged, is not whimsey Pated,/Or prone to Dote, nor Superanuated. SCAP

To His Father on Praising the Honest Life of the Peasant. Parvin E'tesami. how can darkness look to our house for light? WPOW

To His Flocks. Henry Constable. From Woolfe and Foxe I will defend ye. FM

To His Forsaken Mistress. Ayton [(or Aytoun)] Sir Robert. To see thy love to every one/Hath brought thee to be loved by none. EIL; ErPo; HBV 1-2; OBEV; SeCePo

To His Friend–. Henry Vaughan. It matters not, we shall one day obtain/Our native and celestial scope again. OBS; PP

To his Friend Ben. Johnson, of his Horace made English. Edward, Lord Herbert of Cherbury. To be the Horace of our times and his. AnAnS 2

To His Friend in Absence. Wilafrid Strabo. Then for all time, O love, God give thee joy! LiTW; PeHV

To His Friend in Elysium. Joachim Du Bellay. About the gate, or labor at the oar. AWP

To His Friend J. H. Alexander Brome. Such as will drink, and drink again,/To treat about the matter. CavP

To His Friend Master R.L., in Praise of Music and Poetry. Richard Barnfield. One knight loves both, and both in thee remain. EIL; UnS

To His Friend, on the Untunable Times. Robert Herrick. Withered my hand, and palsy-struck my tongue. CaPo

To His Friend, Promising That Though Her Beauty Fade... George Turberville. Nor beauty's want my first good will remove. OBSC

To His Girl. Martial (Marcus Valerius Martialis). Oh, be less beautiful, or be/A little less available. UnTE

To His Heart. Sir Thomas Wyatt. Ah! my heart, ah! what aileth thee? OBSC

To His Honoured and Most Ingenious Friend, Master Charles Cotton. Robert Herrick. Long may I live so, and my wreath of bays/Be less another's laurel than thy praise. CaPo

To His Honoured Kinsman Sir William Soame. Robert Herrick. As Benjamin, and Storax, when they meet. AtBAP; BoW

To His Importunate Mistress. Peter De Vries. And that for paltry reasons given/His conscience may remain unriven. NLV

To His Inconstant Mistress. Thomas Carew. ...for thou shalt be/Damn'd for thy false apostasy. OBEV

To His Kinsman, Master Thomas Herrick, Who Desired to Be in His Book. Robert Herrick. It matters not, since thou art chosen one/Here of my great and good foundation. CaPo

To His Kinswoman, Mistress Penelope Wheeler. Robert Herrick. In chief, in this poetic liturgy. CaPo

To His Lady. Sir John Davies. So in the sun, some say, there is no heat,/Though his reflecting beams do fire beget. SiPS

To His Lady. King of England Henry VIII. Thus long to endure/Till that we meet again. CTC; EBEV; OBSC

To His Lady, Who Had Vowed Virginity. Walter Davison. For wisest conquerors do towns desire,/On honourable terms and not with fire. OBSC

To His Late Majesty Concerning the True Form of English Poetry. Sir John Beaumont. And be their wonder, as we were their scorn. JCP; OBS; PP

To His Little Son Benedict from the Tower of London. John Hoskyns. Imprison it or it will thee. OxBChV

To His Love. Ivor Gurney. Thing I must somehow forget. MMM; OBWP

To His Love in Middle-Age. Edwin Brock. ...and you have been/sixteen since it began. AMV-80

To His Love That Sent Him a Ring. George Turberville. Let Reason rule the hearts that she hath wonne. EnPo; EnRePo

To His Love When He Had Obtained Her. Sir Walter Ralegh. And show our plenty. They are poor/That count all they have and more. FCP

To His Lovely Mistresses. Robert Herrick. Though then I smile and speak no words at all. CaPo; CTC; OAEP; SeCP

To His Lute. William, of Hawthornden Drummond. Like widow'd turtle, still her loss complain. GTBS; GTBS-P; UnS

To His Maid Prew. Robert Herrick. Not two, but all the seasons of the yeare. OBS

To His Maistres. Alexander Montgomerie. Even in thyn armes, thair doutles had I deit. OxBS

To His Mistress. Abraham Cowley. She's fair, whose beauty only makes her gay. EG

To His Mistress. Robert Herrick. If you prove faithless thrice,/None then will woo ye. ViBoPo

To His Mistress. Ovid. Coax me to-morrow, by forswearing all. ErPo

To His Mistress. Ovid (Publius Ovidius Naso). And with my name shall thine be always sung. EBEV

To His Mistress. John Wilmot, Earl of Rochester.
My reason shall obey, my wings shall be/Stretch'd out no farther than from me to thee! OBEV
Without thee, love, I travel not, but stray. LiTL

To His Mistress. John, Duke of Buckingham Sheffield. Be kind, but kind to me alone. CavP

To His Mistress Desiring to Travel with Him as His Page. John Donne. ...except dread Jove/Think it enough for me to have had thy love. NOBE

To His Mistress for Her True Picture. Edward, Lord Herbert of Cherbury. Who from my mouth-grate, and eye-window bawl. AnAnS 2; SeCP

To Julius. Sir Charles Sedley. ...kind Heaven send/Me such a cook or coachman, but no friend. FaBoEE

To K. de M. Robert Louis Stevenson. The maiden jewels of the rain/Sit in your dabbled locks again. OBNC

To K. H. Thomas Edward Brown. Of water-pipes antiphonal, and the dome,/Round-arched, goes up to God in lapis lazuli? OBNC

To K.M. Walter De La Mare. Dark hair, dark eyes, slim shoulder.../God-speed, K.M.! BoC

To Kaaon. Ezra Pound. You have sent me only your handmaids. PoA

To Kate, Skating Better Than Her Date. David Daiches. And don't you want to hear him, Kate? CTBA; FiBHP; NYBP; SD

To Keep a True Lent. Robert Herrick. And that's to keep thy Lent. AnAnS 2; HBV 1-2; TrCP; TRV

To Keep the Cold Wind away. Anonymous. That we may love so with other mo/To kepe the cold wind away. OxBM

To Keep the Memory of Charlotte Forten Grimke. Angelina Weld Grimke. She came, she loved, and then she went away. BlSi

To King James. Ben Jonson. Whom should my Muse then flye to, but/the best/Of kings for grace; of poets, for my test? OAEP

To Know All Is to Forgive All. Nixon Waterman. If I knew you and you knew me. BLPA; GoTF; TreFT

To Know If It Be Leap Year. Anonymous. The cent'ries complete, or odd years beside. FaBoUs

To know just how he suffered would be dear. Emily Dickinson. Till love that was, and love too blest to be,/Meet—and the junction be Eternity? DiPo; InvP

To Know the Dark. Wendell Berry. and is traveled by dark feet and dark wings. GP

To know thy bent and then pursue. Ella Wheeler Wilcox. Holds half the secret of success. CenHV

To Know Whom One Shall Marry. Anonymous. And what he does, all days, and years. GBP

To Krishna Haunting the Hills. Andal. who lives on hills robed with the jungle. BoWoP

To Kurnos. Theognis. But wander, an imperishable name,/Kurnos, about the isles and shores of Greece! PeHV

To L–. D'Arcy Cresswell. Ah, heavy doubt! to doubt his dearest friend. AnNZ

To L. Julianne Perry. you weren't even a/revolutionary but/i loved you. PoBA

To L.B.S. Winfield Townley Scott. I am out of bed at midnight to beg this. DFF

To L. C. Lucy Hawkins. All sorrows in the loss of you, and turning/Your pretty head to me, set the old fires new burning. HBMV

To L.H.B. Katherine Mansfield. "These are my body. Sister, take and eat." AnNZ; HBMV

To Labienus. Martial (Marcus Valerius Martialis). But you've something behind, neatly shaven and shorn,/That's scarcely a mistress's toy. PeHV

To Labor. Charlotte Perkins Stetson Gilman. Believe, and Dare, and Do! PoLf

To Laddie. Anne Robinson. Whistle through the dark. SUS

To Ladies' Eyes. Thomas Moore. So drink them all! so drink them all! OxBoLi; PoEL 1-5

To Lady Eleanor Butler and the Honourable Miss Ponsonby... William Wordsworth. Sisters in love, a love allowed to climb/Ev'n on this earth, above the reach of time. PeHV

To Lady, When about Five Years Old, with a Present of Shells. Horace Walpole. –And some years hence he'll send the rest. NOEC

To Landrum Guy, Beginning to Write at Sixty. James Dickey. ...Here, where he begins. PP

To Lar. Robert Herrick. Go where I will, thou lucky Lar stay here,/Warm by a glittering chimney all the year. BoW; CaPo; SeCV 1-2

To Laura Phelan: 1880-1906. Leon Stokesbury. ...this stone/of yours, which is not you. Which is. MAYP

To Laura W—, Two Years Old. Nathaniel Parker Willis. With Him we trust thee, beautiful child! HBV 1-2

To Laurels. Robert Herrick. As the eternal monument of me. ExPo

To learn the transport by the pain. Emily Dickinson. To us, the duller scholars/Of the mysterious bard. NOCV

To Leave the World Serve God. Compiuta Donzella. ...to give me/in marriage to/I-know-not-who. WPOW

To Leigh Hunt, Esq. John Keats. A leafy luxury, seeing I could please/With these poor offerings, a man like thee. EnRP

To Lesbia. Caius Valerius Catullus.
And feel with torment that 'tis so. PoPl
Can work the unknown number harm. UnTE

To Lesbia. John Godfrey Saxe. Kiss me, then,/Every moment–and again! HBV 1-2; UnTE

To Leuconoe. Eugene Field. And, trusting not To-morrow, snatch To-/day for ease! AA; LoBV

To Leven Water. Tobias George Smollett. And hearts resolved and hands prepared/The blessings they enjoy to guard. OBEV

To Li Chien. Po Chu-i.
Of the sound of jade tinkling on your bridle-straps. AWP
Yet the sorrow of parting is still unsubdued. LiTW

To Li Po from Tu Fu. Carolyn Kizer. I, past saving, you, past praise. GP

To Licinius. Horace. Take half thy canvas in. AWP; EnLi 1-2

To Liebig–6. August von Platen. And unto them God calls: The world is thine. PeHV

To Liebig–7. August von Platen. On golden times to come our vision resting. PeHV

To Life I Said Yes. Chaim Grade. Like trees waiting for leaves in the/spring. TrJP

To Lighten My House. Alastair Reid. ...I wake in/the nowhere of the moment, single-willed/to love the world. NePoEA

To Lindsay. Allen Ginsberg. your shade falls over on the floor ConAP

To Little or No Purpose. Sir George Etherege. I cannot deny what I know would undo me! UnTE

To Little Renee on First Seeing Her Lying in Her Cradle. William Aspenwall Bradley. Only to coo their songs to thee. HBV 1-2

To Live and Die in Dixie (excerpt). John Beecher. but they made Spurgeon do. GP

To Live in Hell, and Heaven to Behold. Henry Constable. If this be love, if love in these be founded,/My hart is love, for these in it are grounded. AAS; InvP

To Live Merrily, and to Trust to Good Verses. Robert Herrick. Then only numbers sweet/With endless life are crowned. AnAnS 2; AWP; CaPo; InPo; InvP; LoBV; MyFE; OBS; PP; SeCP; SeCV 1-2

To Lizard Head. Clifford James Laube. Something within me shall tower/When you are talus and dust. CAW

To Lizbie Browne. Thomas Hardy. Yes, Lizbie Browne! DTC; ELP; EnLit; NOBV

To London the Train Gallops, Its Shrill Steel Hooves'. Clifford Dyment. I am the place and not the places me? HaMV

To Look at Any Thing. John Moffit. And touch the very peace/They issue from. RFM

To Lou Gehrig. John Kieran. Your pals of the Yankee team. SD

To Love A Sonnet. Philip Ayres. And as thou wound'st my Heart, inspire my Song. CEP

To Lovers of Earth: Fair Warning. Countee Cullen. And not a single star chime out of tune. CDC

To Lucasta. Richard Lovelace.
Raise her marble heart i' th' room,/And 'tis both her corse and tomb. CaPo
So you but with a touch from your fair Hand,/Turn all to Saraband. OBS

To Lucasta, from Prison. Richard Lovelace. To light me where I soon may see/How to serve you, and you trust me. AnAnS 2; CaPo

To Lucasta, Going to the Wars. Richard Lovelace. I could not love thee, dear, so much,/Loved I not Honour more. ALV; AnFE; AtBAP; CABA; CaPo; CoBE; ELP; EnLi 1-2; EnLoPo; ExPo; FaBV; FPL; GBL; GoTF; HAP; HBV 1-2; HeIP; InPS; LiTL; LoBV; MeLP; MePo; NIP; NOBE; NoP; OAEL 1-2; OAEP; OBEV; OBSP; OBWP; PAI; PoEL 1-5; PoRA; SCV; SeCeV; SeCP; SeCV 1-2; TreF; ViBoPo; WHA

To Lucasta: Her Reserved Looks. Richard Lovelace. So in one picture I have seen/An angel here, the Devil there. CaPo; SeCV 1-2

To Lucasta, on Going Beyond the Seas. Richard Lovelace. In Heaven, their earthy bodies left behind. GTBS-P; LiTB; TreFT

To Lucasta: The Rose. Richard Lovelace. Because her Cheekes are neere. SeCV 1-2

To Lucia at Birth. Robert Graves. Nothing will change them, let them not change you. NAs

To Lucy, Countesse of Bedford, with Mr. Donnes Satyres. Ben Jonson. Lucy, you brightnesse of our spheare, who are/The Muses evening, as their morning-starre. AnAnS 2; OBS; SeCV 1-2

To Luigi del Riccio, after the Death of Cecchino Bracci. Buonarroti Michelangelo. you must I carve to tell the world of him. PeHV

To Luve Unluvit. Alexander Scott. God gif him dolour and disease/That breaks their hairt, and nocht the better. GoTS; OxBS

To Lydia Languish. Henry Austin Dobson. Then, Lydia, then...I still shall stay,/And firmly answer–No. NBM; VLP

To Lydia, with a Coloured Egg, on Easter Monday. John Jones. The treasure within thy fair bosom enclose,/As eggs are enclosed in their shells. FaBoUs

To Lygdus. Martial (Marcus Valerius Martialis). May you ne'er stir from out your threshold's door,/Save at the heels of some damned one eye'd whore PeHV

To M. E. W. Gilbert Keith Chesterton. Beneath the burden of the years, and praise the earth/once more. HBV 1-2

To M.H. William Wordsworth. And therefore, my sweet Mary, this still nook,/With all its beeches, we have named from you! EiCP

To M.T. Bayard Taylor. The older, the dearer! AA

To Mackinnon of Strath. Iain Lom. swan of the waves, thin brow that will not bend/with gloom! GoTS

To Madame A. P. Kern. Alexander Pushkin. Life, love and tears to fill my eyes. LiTW

To Madame A. V. Pletneff. Karolina Pavlova. I have learned,/un-learned,/ nothing. PBWP

To Make a Bridge. Charles Madge. We have undertaken. NeBP

To Make a Pastoral: A Receipt. *Anonymous.* And they hie to their cottage–to eat bread and cheese. FaBoUs

To make a prairie it takes a clover and one bee. Emily Dickinson. The revery alone will do,/If bees are few. AmePo; BoWoP; DiPo; HBVY; HeIP; MAmP; NLV; OBCA; PoPl

To Make an Amblongus Pie. Edward Lear. Serve up in a clean dish, and throw the whole out of the/window as fast as possible. FaBoNo

"To make an end of all this strife." Sir Thomas Wyatt. From all mishap now hardily/This end to make. FCP

To Make the People Happy. Victor Hugo. Turns flabby and trembles; and– Peace! says War. PPON

To Make Your Candles Last for Aye. *Anonymous.* Says honest John Boldero. OxNR

To Man Who Goes Seeking Immortality, Bidding Him Look Nearer Home. Adelaide Crapsey. Thy double, and eternity is cupped/In the pale hollow of those ghostly hands. QFR

To Manon. Wilfrid Scawen Blunt. Like David with washed face who ceased to weep. NBM

To Manon, Comparing Her to a Falcon. Wilfrid Scawen Blunt. And thou shalt sail back heavenwards. Woe is me! OBVV

To Manon, on His Fortune in Loving Her. Wilfrid Scawen Blunt. ...inscribed in fire/Its dedication To the Unknown God. GTBS

To Maria Gisborne in England, from Italy. Percy Bysshe Shelley. Now– Italy or London, which you will! NOBE

To Marie. *Anonymous.* It is useless to say to the pulsating heart,/"Yankee-doodle ker-chuggety-chug!" NA

To Marie Osmond. Jack Skelley. ...now we wake up to mutual delight,/as priests and presidents wither into indefinite night. APU

To Mark Anthony in Heaven. William Carlos Williams. For then you are/ listening in heaven. NOBA

To Mark Rothko of Untitled (Blue, Green), 1969. Anne Cherner. the evergreen pricking its cool needles. PoDr

To market, to market. Mother Goose. Home again, home again, market is/ done. FaBoBe; FaFP; HBV 1-2; HBVY; OxNR; SoPo; TiPo

To Mars. George Chapman. Secure from violent and harmful fates. LoBV

To Mary. William Cowper. Thy worn-out heart will break at last,/My Mary! CBEP; EiCP; EnLoPo; FiP; LAuP; NOEC; OAEP; OBEC

To Mary. Gottfried von Strasburg. Thou dost all terrors quell. ISi

To Mary. Percy Bysshe Shelley. That burn from year to year with unextinguished/light. EnRP

To Mary. Charles Wolfe. As fancy never could have drawn,/And never can restore! GTBS; HBV 1-2; OBEV; OBRV; ViBoPo

To Mary at Christmas. John Gilland Brunini. We fly to covert of our Mother's wings. ISi

To Mary: At the Thirteenth Station. Raymond F. Roseliep. You are the priest tonight. ISi

To Mary: I Sleep with Thee, and Wake with Thee. John Clare. All sighing on, and will not hush,/Some pleasant tales of thee. GBL

To Mary: It Is the Evening Hour. John Clare. In the still hour when my mind was free/To walk alone–yet wish I walked with thee. BoLoP; GBL

To Mary Magdalen. Bartolome Leonardo de Argensola. Forever, to the skies! CAW

To Mary Unwin. William Cowper. And since thou own'st that praise, I spare/thee mine. CoBE; GTBS; GTBS-P; HBV 1-2; OBEV; TrGrPo

To Master Davenant for Absence. Sir John Suckling. Drinks wine i' th' very height o' th' fever. CaPo

To Master Denham, on His Prospective Poem. Robert Herrick. Lesse by their own jemms, then those beams of thine. AnAnS 2

To Master Edward Cobham. Barnabe Googe. And after many years to have a blessed end. EnRePo

To Master Henry Lawes, the Excellent Composr of Lyrics. Robert Herrick. Yet their Three praises praise but One; that's Lawes. CaPo

To Master Henrye Cobham, of the Most Blessed State of Lyfe. Barnabe Googe. This lyfe is best whan all is done. EnPo

To Maynard on the Long Road Home. W. D. Ehrhart. I think of you,/ and wonder if either of us/will ever come home. LTB

To Maystres Jane Blenner-Haiset. John Skelton. Therefore I render of her the memory/Unto the legend of fare Laodomi. AAS

To Me. William Barnes. Vor they be now my own, a-bound to me. NBM; PoEL 1-5

To me he seems like a god. Sappho. [but must suffer all, being poor.] BoWoP

To Meadows. Robert Herrick. Y'are left here to lament/Your poor estates, alone. AWP; CaPo; CBEP; HBV 1-2; InPo; JCP; LoBV; NOBE; OBEV; QFR; ViBoPo

To Meet, or Otherwise. Thomas Hardy. Somewhere afloat/Amid the spheres, as part of sick Life's antidote. OBNC

To Melite. Rufinus Domesticus. but a god, a god indeed/Is the man whose bed receives you as his bride! LiTW

To Melody. George Leonard Allen. The choicest is the gift of melody. CDC

To Memory. Mary Elizabeth Coleridge. And on my brow I feel a kiss/ That I would rather die than miss. CBEP

To Men. Anna Wickham. How well God works for you and me. MoBrPo

To Mercury. X. J. Kennedy. And stone her face with Nixon's signature. SOTS

To Midnight. *Anonymous.* If there is a hoss-heaven, please, God, rest his soul. BPAW; CoSo

To Midnight Nan at Leroy's. Langston Hughes. Wouldn't no good fellow/ Be your man. AnAmPo

To Miguel de Cervantes Saavadra. Richard Kendall Munkittrick. "There are no birds in last year's nests"? AA

To Milk in the Valley Below. *Anonymous.* Or to milk in the valley below. OBET

To Milton. Oscar Wilde. When Cromwell spake the word Democracy! BrPo

To Mind. Clark Coolidge. as if radar were likely or handy/as bedside/as cough drops or slang. APU

To Minerva. Thomas Hood. Then, Pallas, take away thine Owl,/And let us have a lark instead. FaBoCo; FaBoNo; FiBHP; HBV 1-2; InMe; NLV; NOBL; OxBoLi

To Miss–. Samuel Johnson. Thy music teach the nobler art/To tune the regulated heart. CABA

To Miss–. Thomas Moore. The thing's not worth inquiring! OBSP

To Miss Arundell. Walter Savage Landor. There's but one white violet. OBVV

To Miss B. John Clare. ...I neither love nor see/And cannot be a man. NOBV

To Miss Charlotte Pulteney in Her Mother's Arms. Ambrose Philips. This picture, once, resembled thee. CEP; ELP; NOEC; OBEC

To Miss Eleanor Ambrose... Philip Stanhope, Earl of Chesterfield. The whiteness of the rebel Rose? EnLoPo

To Miss Ferrier. Robert Burns. A' gude things may attend you! CBEP

To Miss L.F.... (parody). J. C. Squire. That I with more delight may share/My native meads again. BXAP

To Miss Lucy F—, with a New Watch. George, Lord Lyttelton. Then every minute count–as I do now. FaBoUs

To Miss Margaret Pulteney, Daughter of Daniel Pulteney, Esq. Ambrose Philips. Tender, and averse to killing. CEP

To Miss * * * * * on the Death of her Goldfish. Mr. Meredyth. ...no wriggling Eel/Expresses half the Pangs I feel. FM

To Mistress Anne. John Skelton. That I am your man. EnRePo

To Mistress Anne Cecil. William Cecil, Lord Burleigh. You, long years;/ and your father, health! EIL; OBSC

To Mistress Gertrude Statham. John Skelton. With womanhood endued,/ With virtue well renewed. OAEP

To Mistress Isabel Pennell. John Skelton. Good year and good luck,/With chuck, chuck, chuck, chuck! CBEP; LiTL; NOBE; OAEP; OBEV; OBSC; PoEL 1-5; SeCeV; TrGrPo

To Mistress Katherine Bradshaw, the Lovely, That Crowned Him... Robert Herrick. ...she must, of due,/Render for that a crown of life to you. CaPo

To Mistress Margaret Tilney. John Skelton. Madame, regent/I may you call/Of vertuows all. MeEL

To Mistress Margery Wentworth. John Skelton. Embroidered the mantle is/Of your maidenhead. CBEP; EBEV; EG; EnLoPo; LoBV; NOBE; OAEL 1-2; OBEV; OBSC; PoEL 1-5; TrGrPo; ViBoPo

To Modigliani to Prove to Him That I Am a Poet. Max Jacob. Who collapse the cloud to steal from it/our secret. TrJP

To Mollidusta. Planche. Oh, then, Mollidusta, I'll love thee no more. NA

To Monsieur de la Mothe le Vayer. Jean-Baptiste Poquelin Moliere. –Surely these claim eternity of tears! AWP

To Morfydd. Lionel Pigot Johnson. So mine be your eyes! AnIV; MoBrPo; OAEL 1-2; OBMV

To Morning. William Blake. Rouz'd like a huntsman to the chace, and, with/Thy buskin'd feet, appear upon our hills. EnRP; ERoP 1-2

To Morris Louis of the Blue Veil 1958-9. Anne Cherner. blending into pigments/and arching back again. PoDr

To-Morrow's the Fair. *Anonymous.* Stuffing my guts/With gingerbread nuts. GBP

To-Morrow Shall Be My Dancing Day. *Anonymous.* On the right hand of God, that man/May come unto the general dance. PoEL 1-5

To Mother and Steve. Mari E. Evans. I could not/mainline it/away.../was your/love BPo; PoBA

To Mother Fairie. Alice Cary. Now, have you such to spare? OBCA

To Mother Nature. Frederic Lawrence Knowles. And the impossible be done/When the Wish and Deed grow one! HBV 1-2

To Mr. Alexander Ross. James Beattie. If Ross wil be so kind as share in/Their pint at Drousty. OxBS

To Mr. ****, an Unlettered Poet, on Genius Unimproved. Ann Yearsley. And that be thine. NOEC

To Mr. Bays. Charles, Earl of Dorset Sackville. The honest Layman's Faith is still the same. APAS

To Mr C.B. John Donne. To melt all Ice, but that which walls her heart. AnAnS 1

To Mr. C, St. James's Place, London, October 22nd. Alexander Pope. Want nothing else, except your wife. OBSP

To Mr. Cyriack Skinner Upon His Blindness. John Milton. Content though blind, had I no better guide. DiPo; MBW 1-2; OBS

To Mr. E– on His Translation of and Commentaries on Martial. Robert Burns. 'Twas laurell'd Martial calling, Murther! FaBoEE

To Mr. Gay...On Finishing His House. Alexander Pope. Bleeds drop by drop, and pants his life away. NOEC

To Mr. George Herbert, with One of My Seals, of the Anchor and Christ. John Donne. To you, who bear his name, great bounties deal. OBVE

To Mr. Gray. David Garrick. Who humbly sips her learning from Reviews,/Or flutters in the Magazines. OBEC

To Mr. H. Lawes on His Airs. John Milton. Met in the milder shades of Purgatory. AWP; InPo; LoBV; NoP

To Mr. Henry Lawes. Katherine ("Orinda") Philips. Be it thy care our age to new-create:/What built a world may sure repair a state. SBG

To Mr. Henry Lawes. Edmund Waller. Let words, and sense, be set by thee. AnAnS 2; CTC; PP; SeCP; SeCV 1-2

To Mr. Hobbes. Abraham Cowley. And that which never is to die, for ever must be young. LoBV; SeCV 1-2

To Mr. I. L. John Donne. As thou telst her, and none but her, my paine. SeCP

To Mr. Izaak Walton. Charles Cotton. Contented live, and then contented die. ViBoPo

To Mr. Jervas, with Fresnoy's Art of Painting, Translated by Dryden. Alexander Pope. Thou but preserv'st a Form, and I a name. OBEC

To Mr. Murray. George Gordon, Lord Byron. And if you won't, you may be damn'd,/My Murray. FaBoCo

To Mr. Newton on His Return from Ramsgate. William Cowper. I, tempest-tossed, and wrecked at last,/Come home to port no more. NOEC

To Mr. Punchinello. Anonymous. To Mr. Punchinello. OxNR

To Mr. R.W. John Donne. I recreated, even by thy creature, live. AnAnS 1

To Mr. S. T. Coleridge. Anna Laetitia Barbauld. Now heaven conduct thee with a parent's love! NOEC

To Mr. T. W. John Donne. My verse, the strict map of my misery,/Shall live to see that, for whose want I die. PP

To Mr. Tilman after He Had Taken Orders. John Donne. And make thee now a blest Hermaphrodite. EBEV

To Mrs. Ann Flaxman. William Blake. "'Tis your own fault if you don't flourish now." OBRV

To Mrs. Anne Killigrew. John Dryden. As Harbinger of Heav'n, the Way to show,/The Way which thou so well hast learn'd below. SeCV 1-2

To Mrs. Diana Cecyll. Edward, Lord Herbert of Cherbury. When men might hope more then they understood. AnAnS 2

To Mrs. Leigh Upon Her Wedding Day. George Canning. Not wear herself, the breeches. ALV

To Mrs. M. B. on Her Birth-day. Alexander Pope. And wake to Raptures in a Life to come. CEP; EnLoPo; OBEC

To Mrs. Reynold's Cat. John Keats. Still is that fur as soft as when the lists/In youth thou enter'dst on glass-bottled wall. DiPo

To Mrs. Thrale on Her Thirty-Fifth Birthday. Samuel Johnson. And those who wisely wish to wive/Must look on Thrale at thirty-five. FaBoEE; NAs

To Mrs. Will H. Low. Robert Louis Stevenson. Nor find one jewel but the blazing log. NOBV

To Music. Robert Herrick. And make me smooth as balm and oil again. CaPo

To Music. William Kean Seymour. While in my Dream's despite/The minutes run to hours. HBMV

To Music: A Song. Robert Herrick. To charm our souls, as thou enchant'st our ears. CaPo

To Music, to Becalm a Sweet-Sick Youth. Robert Herrick. Like to a slumbering bride, awake again. CaPo

To Music, to Becalm His Fever. Robert Herrick. And take my flight/For heaven. ATP; CaPo; EG; HBV 1-2; OBEV; QFR

To Musicke Bent. Thomas Campion. Such heate they caste as lifts the Spirit high. AAS; CoBE; NOCV; OxBoCh; TrPWD; UnS

To My Auld Dog Dash. John Barr. Sae you and I maun tak the gate/Before it's lang. AnNZ

To My Blood Sister. Christine E. Hemp. Take the reins for me, will you? Str

To My Body. Nancy Sullivan. We're enough trouble to each other.' TAP

To My Booke. Ben Jonson. He that departs with his owne honesty/For vulgar praise, doth it too dearely buy. AnAnS 2; OAEP; SeCV 1-2

To My Brother. Louise Bogan. Save of peace alone. NYBP

To My Brother George. John Keats. 'Twas but to kiss my hand, dear George, to you! EnRP

To My Brothers. John Keats. From its fair face, shall bid our spirits fly. EnLi 1-2; NAs; TEP

To My Cat. Graham R. Tomson. Beholden still in blinking reveries,/With sombre sea-green gaze inscrutable. PCat

To My Child. Abraham Sutzkever. and bear greetings from me/to the small shoots beneath the cold. VWA

To My Child Carlino. Walter Savage Landor. Redder than coral round Calypso's cave? NoP; OBRV

To My Children, Fearing for Them. Wendell Berry. can I wish your lives unmade/though the pain of them is on me. Str

To My Children Unknown, Produced by Artificial Insemination. James Kirkup. By your ever-dying poet/Who remains/Your humble servant. NAs

To My Cosen Mrs. Ellinor Evins. George Alsop. Saint-like to Canonize you to the Sky. SCAP

To My Cousin, (C.R.) Marrying My Lady (A.). Thomas Carew. Strong perfumes, and glaring light,/Oft destroy both smell, and sight. AnAnS 2; SeCP

To My Cousin Mary, for Mending My Tobacco Pouch. Francis Scott Key. But here the stitches are–and I will take a quid. OBAL

To My Daughter. James Michie. And paddle in glee, my darling, while I drown. OBSP

To My Daughter. Hyam Plutzik. The messengers, of faces and names known/Or of forms familiar, are innocent. BiP

To My Daughter. Stephen Spender. Far from today as her eyes are far already. BoC; DFF

To My Daughter Betty, the Gift of God. Thomas Michael Kettle. And for the secret Scripture of the poor. CAW; HBMV; OnYI

To My Daughter Riding in the Circus Parade. Joan Labombard. that does not know it knows/there's an end to dreaming. GOYP

To My Daughter the Junkie on a Train. Audre Lorde. curse their children who became junk. CNA

To My Dead Friend Ben: Johnson. Henry, Bishop of Chichester King. A Relick fam'd by all Posterity. AnAnS 2; SeCP

To My Dear and Loving Husband. Anne Bradstreet. That when we live no more, we may live ever. AmPP; AP; BLPL; BoWoP; FF; ForPo; HAP; HeIP; HW; MAmP; NePA; NOBA; NOCV; OBSP; OxBA; PoEL 1-5; PoLf; PrIm; SBG; SCAP; TAP

To My Dear Friend Mr. Congreve, on His Comedy... John Dryden. You merit more; nor cou'd my Love do less. CEP; EBEV; FiP; OBS; PoEL 1-5; SeCV 1-2

To My Distant Beloved. Alois Jeitteles. Then return and linger not! TrJP

To My Dog Blanco. Josiah Gilbert Holland. My life would grow divine! PoLf

To My Excellent Lucasia, on Our Friendship. Katherine ("Orinda") Philips. As innocent as our design,/Immortal as our soul. CavP; MeLP; OBS; PeHV; SBG; WPOW

To My Father. James Keir Baxter. Who walked with Adam once in the green shade. AnNZ

To My Father. Tony Curtis. filling the hollow of my throat. AMV-81

To My Father. Susannah Fried. and you found me burst open/with memories, rotten memories. VWA

To My Father. W. S. Graham. Across the kindling skies/Takes over our bodies. FaBoTw

To My Father. Ralph Pomeroy. May darkness when it unfolds/presage only a field of stars. DFF

To My Father. Henrietta Cordelia Ray. Divine approval is thy sweetest praise. BlSi

To My Father. Iris Tree. The world is wearier, grown dark to grieve/Her child that was a pilgrim and a king. HBMV

To My Father Norman Alone in the Blue Mountains. Jack Lindsay. turn for a moment this way/your abstracted face. NOAV

To My Fellow-Mariners, March, '53. Thomas Whitbread. ...It still survives/Only in ashes, ashes of our lives. NYBP

To My First Love, My Mother. Christina Georgina Rossetti. Of time and change and mortal life and/death. OHIP

To My Friend. Anne Campbell. And wealth is mine! PoToHe

To My Friend. Francis Thompson. With the first light breaks the first thought–my Friend. PoA

To My Friend, behind Walls. Carolyn Kizer. ...Head in wings,/Or upside-down, they doze behind the walls. NePoAm-2

To My Friend Butts I Write. William Blake. Such a Vision to me/Appear'd on the sea. EnRP

To My Friend, Dr. Charleton, on His Learned and Useful Works. John Dryden. But, He Restor'd, 'tis now become a Throne. SeCV 1-2

To My Friend G. N. from Wrest. Thomas Carew. To keepe the memory of our Armes alive. AnAnS 2; CaPo

To Pile Like Thunder to Its Close.　Emily Dickinson.　For None see God and live–　MAmP

To Ping-Ku, Asleep.　Lawrence Durrell.　Made like fire by the rubbing of two sticks?　ChMP; NeBP

To Pius IX.　John Greenleaf Whittier.　If, roused thereby, the world shall tread/The twin-born vampires down!　TW

To Plautia.　Sir Aston Cokayne.　I'le not be won with all thy store.　CavP

To Pledge or Not to Pledge.　*Anonymous.*　And so I'll get the Gospel free,/You see!　STF

To Poem.　Lyn Lifshin.　the chance to/scares you off　NeAC

To Poesy.　Alfred, Lord Tennyson.　Tho' thou art all unconscious of thy Might.　VLP

To Poets.　Walter Savage Landor.
Cadets must envy every elder brother,/The little poet must the great. ViBoPo
The one that stinks the most infests the rose.　FaBoEE

To Poets and Airmen.　Stephen Spender.　...smile frozen at the North Pole/Might take pity on their tricks.　WaP

To Polycharmus.　Martial (Marcus Valerius Martialis).　But what do you do, Polycharmus, I pray,/When a lover's stiff prick stops your bum?　PeHV

To Postumus.　Horace.　Nectar more worthy of the halls/Where pontiffs hold high festivals.　LiTW

To Potapovitch.　Hart Crane.　Though silent as your sandals, danced undone.　UnS

To Primroses Fill'd with Morning-Dew.　Robert Herrick.　Conceiv'd with grief are, and with teares brought forth.　AnAnS 2; OBS; PoPl; SeCV 1-2; ViBoPo

To Promise Is One Thing, To Perform Is Another.　Jean de La Fontaine. Meanwhile, my sweet Perrette, adieu!　UnTE

To Prote.　Simmias.　In the pure light of ever-present Heaven.　AWP

To Psyche.　John Keats.　...a casement ope at night,/To let the warm Love in!　ViBoPo

To Puck.　Beatrice Llewellyn Thomas.　Give us laughter, Puck!　HBMV

To Purity and Truth.　*Anonymous.*　and solely attend to purity and/truth. TrJP

To Pyrrha.　William Browne.　And in freedom think of danger.　OAEL 1-2

To Pyrrha.　Horace.
And ne'er will tempt those seas again.　EnLi 1-2
To the stern god of sea.　AWP

To Queen Elizabeth.　Sir John Davies.　Which makest each place a heaven wherein thou art.　OBSC

To R. B.　Gerard Manley Hopkins.　Now, yields you, with some sighs, our explanation.　CBEP; CMoP; CoBMV; OAEL 1-2; VLP

To R. Hudson.　Alexander Montgomerie.　Let Christan Lyndesay wryt our epitaphis.　OxBS

To R. K. (parody).　James Kenneth Stephen.　When the Rudyards cease from Kipling/And the Haggards Ride no more?　BXAP; FaBoPa; Par

To R.W.E.　Ellen Hooper.　And find the peace which we had lost before. AnAmPo

To Redoute.　John Ashbery.　Tears that streak the dusty firmament.　PoA

To Remain.　Constantine P. Cavafy.　...and now returned/to remain in this poetry.　BoLoP; ErPo

To Retirement.　Luis Ponce de Leon.　'Mid such a sea of troubles blind and/dire!　TrJP

To Rich Givers.　Walt Whitman.　For I bestow upon any man or woman the entrance to all the/gifts of the universe.　AnAmPo

To Richard Wright.　Conrad Kent Rivers.　To live day by day/Is not to live at all.　AmNP; IDB; PoBA

To Robert Browning.　Walter Savage Landor.　The Siren waits thee, singing song for song.　EnLi 1-2; GTBS; MCCG; NoP; OAEP; ViBoPo

To Robert Earl of Oxford, and Earl Mortimer.　Alexander Pope.　Nor fears to tell, that MORTIMER is he.　CEP; OBEC

To Robert Louis Stevenson.　William Ernest Henley.　Of the old nurse, Death.　MoBrPo

To Robert Lowell and Osip Mandelstam.　Frederick Seidel.　The mailbox in which we'll mail this/Is slightly lighter than the sky.　AMV-81

To Robin Red-Breast.　Robert Herrick.　Here, here the Tomb of Robin Herrick is.　OBS; PBBP; TrGrPo

To Ronge.　John Greenleaf Whittier.　His hands for whom thou claim'st the freedom of the mind!　AnEnPo

To Rosamond.　Geoffrey Chaucer.　Though ye to me ne do no daliaunce. CBEP; NoP

To Rose.　Sara Teasdale.　Please be certain that it grows/Very, very much like Rose.　BiCB; HBV 1-2

To Rosemary.　Stephen Vincent Benét.　The fire that cried in pure crystal/Out of its cloud!　LaNeLa

To Roses in the Bosom of Castara.　William Habington.　There wants no marble for a tomb/Whose breast hath marble been to me.　AnAnS 2; EnLoPo; GoBC; HBV 1-2; LoBV; MeLP; NIP; OBEV; SeCP; UnTE; ViBoPo

To Rosina Pico.　William Wilberforce Lord　Lingered like incense from a censer/thrown.　AA

To Rotenham–3.　August von Platen.　Eternal beauty is for ever new. PeHV

To Ruin.　Robert Burns.　Enclasped and grasped/Within thy cold embrace! CoBE

To Rupert Brooke.　Wilfred Wilson Gibson.　And I was dazzled by a sunset glow,/And he was gone.　GTBS

To Russia.　Joaquin Miller.　Your Jew! Your Jew! Your hated Jew!　AA; AnAmPo

To S.A.　T. E. Lawrence.　The little things creep out to patch themselves hovels/in the marred shadow/Of your gift.　PeHV

To S. M. a Young African Painter, on Seeing His Work.　Phillis Wheatley. Cease, gentle muse! the solemn gloom of night/Now seals the fair creation from my sight.　BlSi

To S. T. C. on His 179th Birthday, October 12th, 1951.　Maurice Carpenter. In the roads outside a Jonah century/You paused, and smelled the darkness we know well.　FaBoTw

To Sabidius.　Martial (Marcus Valerius Martialis).　I do not love thee, I. DiPo

To Saffold's Customers.　John Case.　John Case yet lives, though Saffold's dead.　FaBoUs

To Saint Catherine.　Henry Constable.　And angels' hands thy body did entomb.　GoBC

To Saint Margaret.　Henry Constable.　And let my soul, made chaste, pass for a Maid.　ACP; GoBC

To Saint Mary Magdalen.　Henry Constable.　And in my spouses pallace gyve me place.　ACP; PoEL 1-5

To Sally.　John Quincy Adams.　Sweet smiling and sweet spoken.　AA; ALV; OBAL

To Sally.　Horace.　Nor stronger, eager for a feast,/The fell constrictor boa. AWP

To San Francisco.　S. J. Alexander.　And the East and the West at Her bidding/shall lie in a leash at Her feet.　PAH

To Satch.　Samuel ("Paul Vesey") Allen.　And look over at God and say/How about that!　AmNP; CTBA; LiSp; NIP; PoBA; PoNe; SD; SoSe; TTY

To Saxham.　Thomas Carew.　They cannot steal, thou giv'st so much. AnAnS 2; CaPo; JCP; NoP; OBS

To Schmidlein–2.　August von Platen.　Perchance an elfin choir is swarming nigh,/To whisper soft, sweet bridal melodies.　PeHV

To School!　Stevie Smith.　Why look already how far off she has flown, she is no fool.　FaBoEE

To Scilla.　Sir Charles Sedley.　For thy own Pox will they Revenge contrive. FaBoEE; PV

To Scott.　Winifred M. Letts.　That we commend your spirit to His care. PoLf

To Sea.　Thomas Lovell Beddoes.　The sails swell full: To sea, to sea!　CH; EtS

To Search Our Souls.　Jane McKay Lanning.　These are the things/God meant.　TRV

To See a World in a Grain of Sand.　William Blake.　Hold infinity in the palm of your hand/And eternity in an hour.　InPK

To See God's Bleeding Lam'.　*Anonymous.*　Yes, I want to go to heab'n when I die,/To see God's bleedin' Lam'.　BoAN 1-2

To see her is a picture.　Emily Dickinson.　A warmth as near as if the Sun/Were shining in your Hand.　PeHV

To See Him Again.　Gabriela (Lucila Godoy Alcayaga) Mistral.　...entwined in one anguished knot/around his blood-stained neck!　OLR

To See the Cross at Christmas.　Roger Cooper.　And cross the world–/To see the cross at Christmas.　TrCP

To seek each where, where man doth live.　Sir Thomas Wyatt.　Dare I well give, I say, my heart to year.　FCP; SiPS

To Seem the Stranger Lies My Lot.　Gerard Manley Hopkins.　Heard unheeded, leaves me a lonely began.　NOBV

To Sergius.　Sir Charles Sedley.　That she is thine, what can proclaim it more.　FaBoEE

To Sextus.　Pott and Wright.　True, no one ever thought that you would pay.　ALV

To Sextus.　Sir Charles Sedley.　None but has kill'd his man, or writ his play.　FaBoEE

To Shakespeare.　Richard Edwin Day.　Thou art, thyself, thy one unopened book.　AA

To Shelley.　Walter Savage Landor.　...thy weak child/Kneels at thy feet, and owns in shame a lie.　ViBoPo

To Shelley.　John Banister Tabb.　And the rekindling flame.　AA

To Sherrie.　Joseph Matuzak.　Things keep starting. They take their toll. AMV-81

To Shima sani.　Laura Tohe.　Now there is a memory on paper　STE

To Show How Humble.　*Anonymous.*　Like Jesus, humble, truly meek,/From self-applauses free.　AH

To Signora Cuzzoni.　Ambrose Philips.　Leave the Britons rough and free. CEP; LoBV; OBEC

To Silence.　Thomas Sturge Moore.　Still be to my fond hope a friend. BrPo

To the Child Jesus.   Henry Van Dyke.   Safe to its home in thy presence above.   TrPWD

To the Choice Bridegroom.   Judah Halevi   Their faces gleam through the marriage canopy/Like stars through a braiding of clouds.   HW

To the Christ.   John Banister Tabb.   Nor save together Thine are we.   TrPWD

To the Christians.   Francis Lauderdale Adams.   It's your "good taste' that prefers/A bastard God!   OxBS; WGRP

To the City of London.   William Dunbar.   London, thou art the flour of Cities all.   EBEV; FaBoPP

To the Colorado Desert.   Madge Morris.   God must have made thee in His anger, and/forgot.   BPAW

To the Contemporary Muse.   Edgar Bowers.   Your hands are cold, feeling me in the dark.   ELU

To the Countesee of Bedford.   John Donne.   Neither can reach you, great and innocent.   ATP; MeLP; OBS

To the Countesse of Salisbury.   Aurelian Townsend.   If all your servants prove not true,/May steale a heart or two from you.   AnAnS 2; MePo; OBS; SeCP

To the Cuckoo.   *Anonymous.*   In August away I must.   OxNR

To the Cuckoo.   F. H. Townsend.   With reasons for your choice.   FaBoNo

To the Cuckoo.   William Wordsworth.   That is fit home for thee!   BoLiVe; CBEP; CoBE; ELP; EnLit; FaFP; FiP; GTBS; GTBS-P; HBV 1-2; LoBV; MCCG; OBRV; PB; PBBP; PoLf; TreFT; TrGrPo

To the Daisy.   William Wordsworth.   ...repair/My heart with gladness, and a share/Of thy meek nature!   CoBE; EnRP; GTBS; GTBS-P; HBV 1-2

To the Dandelion.   James Russell Lowell.   On all these living pages of God's book.   AP; HBV 1-2; HBVY

To the Dead of '98.   Lionel Pigot Johnson.   Thy dead beseech thee: to Thy living give/In liberty to live!   HBV 1-2

To the Departing Spirit of an Alienated Friend.   Anna Seward.   Yet long must I lament thy hapless doom,/Thy lavish'd life and early hasten'd tomb.   PeHV

To the Divine Neighbor.   Teller. J. L.   and is at the same time/erased.   VWA

To the Driving Cloud.   Henry Wadsworth Longfellow.   Drifts evermore to the west the scanty smokes of thy/wigwams!   FaBoRV; PoEL 1-5

To the Earl of Dorset.   Ambrose Philips.   And, as he goes, the transient vision mourns.   LoBV

To the Earl of Warwick.   Thomas Tickell.   No chance could sever, nor the grave divide.   CEP; HBV 1-2; NOEC; OBEC

To the Elephants.   Nathan Alterman.   naked, it goes in search of you/to fall on the lap of light.   VWA

To the End.   John E. Bode.   If Thou wilt be my Guide.   BLRP

To the Eternal Feminine.   Tristan Corbiere.   when he snores—come kiss your Conqueror!   ErPo

To the Etruscan Poets.   Richard Wilbur.   Not reckoning that all could melt and go.   OxBC

To the Evening.   John Codrington Bampfylde.   So as my heart be pure and free my mind.   NOEC

To the Evening Star.   William Blake.   ...protect them with thine influence.   BoNaP; CEP; ChRP; EnRP; ERoP 1-2; FaBoRV; FaBV; FPL; HW; LAuP; LoBV; MCCG; NOEC; NoP; OAEL 1-2; OAEP; PoLf; PPP; TEP; TrGrPo; WiR

To the Evening Star: Central Minnesota.   James Wright.   Now they can see you, they know/The open meadows are safe.   NaP

To the Excellent Pattern of Beauty and Virtue, Lady Elizabeth...   James Shirley.   Die late, beloved of earth, and change for heaven.   GoBC

To the Fair Clarinda, Who Made Love to Me, Imagin'd More than Woman.   Aphra Behn.   While we the noblest Passions do extend/The Love to Hermes, Aphrodite the Friend.   SBG

To the Faithful.   Marcos Ana.   from the tree which was seeded by my blood.   BoC

To the Father of the Bride.   Torquato Tasso.   And in your seeds may live your name, and in each/A renewal be given to your life.   HW

To the Federal Convention.   Timothy Dwight.   And grant new scions from each friendly sky.   PAH

To the Field Mice.   Richard Eberhart.   And give you, white-footed field mice, my fidelity.   BoAnP

To the Film Industry in Crisis.   Frank O'Hara.   ...Roll on, reels of celluloid, as the great earth rolls on!   CAPP; NoAm; NOBA; OBAL; SOTW

To the First of August.   Ann Plato.   And teach the rising race the way/That they may not depart.   BlSi

To the Fly in My Drink.   David Wagoner.   In a garden where some cold-sober slug will celebrate/Your wake through the night.   DFF

To the Fountain of Bandusia.   Horace.   Posterity shall know/The cooling brooks that from thy nooks/Singing and dancing go.   AWP

To the Four Courts, Please.   James Stephens.   And the poor, when they're old, have little of peace!   BIrV; HBMV; MoAB; MoBrPo; UnPo

To the Fringed Gentian.   William Cullen Bryant.   Hope, blossoming within my heart,/May look to heaven as I depart.   AA; AnFE; AnNE; AP; APA; AWP; FaBoBe; FPL; GN; GoTF; HBV 1-2; NePA; NoP; OBRV; PoLf; TAP; TreFT

To the Frivolous Muse.   George Meason Whicher.   It would confirm, alas! those harsh opinions/Which some men think I always have deserved.   InMe

To the Gardener at Nuneham.   Horace Walpole.   And mix with Walter Clark's carnations.   FaBoEE

To the Generous Reader.   Robert Herrick.   Homer himself, in a long work, may sleep.   CaPo

To the Ghost of a Kite.   James Wright.   Some high magnificence to last as long/As the clear vision of the summer child.   NePoEA

To the Ghost of John Milton.   Carl Sandburg.   And God Himself and the rebels God threw into hell.   PP

To the Ghost of Martial.   Ben Jonson.   Thou flattered'st thine, mine cannot flat-/ter'd bee.   OAEP

To the Girls of My Graduating Class.   Irving Layton.   Who hobbles after you a little way/Fierce and ridiculous.   ErPo

To the God of Love.   E. G. V. Knox.   Any old sort will suit me.   ALV; HBMV; NOBL

To the Grasshopper and the Cricket.   [James Henry] Leigh Hunt.   In doors and out, summer and winter, Mirth.   EnLi 1-2; EnRP; GN; HBV 1-2; OBNC

To the Greek Anthologists.   George Rostrevor Hamilton.   And in sweet-vowelled English echo them along.   FaBoEE

To the Hand.   William Stanley Merwin.   and I am saying to the hand/turn/open the river.   EAS

To the Harbormaster.   Frank O'Hara.   the waves which have kept me from reaching you.   ANYP; CoAP; MOS; PoM

To the Harpies.   Arthur Davison Ficke.   Peace, since you know not love.   HBV 1-2

To the Heart.   Tadeusz Rozewicz.   yes sir/that was/a specialist   PoL

To the Holy Spirit.   Yvor Winters.   Quiet beyond recall,/Into irrelevance.   ForPo; MoAmPo; MoVE; QFR; VGW

To the Holy Trinity.   *Anonymous.*   Three Persons in God likewise, and but the one God.   NOBI

To the Honorable Charles Montague, Esq.   Matthew Prior.   I, Phillis but a perjured whore.   EiCP

To the Immortal Memory and Friendship of That Noble Pair...   Ben Jonson.   Who, ere the first down bloomed on the chin,/Had sowed these fruits, and got the harvest in.   NOBE; NoP; OAEL 1-2

To the Immortal Memory of the Halibut on Which I Dined This Day.   William Cowper.   To feed a bard, and to be praised in verse.   AnAnS 2; MOS; OBS; PoEL 1-5; SeCePo; SeCP; SeCV 1-2

To the Infant Martyrs.   Richard Crashaw.   The place that calls you hence is, at the worst,/Milk all the way.   NoP; OBSP; SeCV 1-2

To the Ingleezee Khafir, Calling Himself Djann Bool Djenkinzun.   James Clarence Mangan.   Thou dog, don at once/The grand Khizzilbash turban!   OnYI

To the Islands.   Howard Moss.   The beautiful scapegoats arrive by boat.   SM

To the Ivy.   John Clare.   With thy green darkness overshadowing me.   CBEP

To the Jews in Poland.   Jozef Wittlin.   Rustles the song of my pain—in the insomniac nights.   VWA

To the King, at His Entrance into Saxham.   Thomas Carew.   Should Jove descend, they could no more.   CaPo

To the King on His Navy.   Edmund Waller.   Dares trust such Power with so much Piety.   CEP

To the King's Most Excellent Majesty.   Phillis Wheatley.   A monarch's smile can set his subjects free!   TAP

To the King, Upon His Comming with His Army into the West.   Robert Herrick.   Ride on with all white Omens; so, that where/ Your Standard's up, we fix a Conquest there.   AnAnS 2

To the King, Upon his welcome to Hampton-Court.   Robert Herrick.   We'l from our owne, adde far more years to his.   AnAnS 2

To the Ladies.   Mary Lee, Lady Chudleigh.   You must be proud, if you'll be wise.   NOEC; WPOW

To the Ladies.   Arnold Kenseth.   Hearing her sister come, waiting the hiss/ To turn her to a Mrs. from a Miss...?   PPON

To the Lady-Bird.   *Anonymous.*   ...and harness you/fast,/With a cobweb, to Oberon's car.   PoPl

To the Lady in the Chemisette with Black Buttons.   Nathaniel Parker Willis.   My love shall hover round thee!   OBAL

To the Lady Lucy, Countess of Bedford.   Samuel Daniel.   By which, when all consumes, your fame shall live.   OBSC

To the Lady Margaret, Countess of Cumberland.   Samuel Daniel.   Than all the gold that leaden minds can frame.   FaBoEn; LoBV; OBSC

To the Lady Margaret Ley.   John Milton.   And to possess them, honour'd Margaret.   GTBS; GTBS-P; OBEV

To the Lady May.   Aurelian Townsend.   So smiles the spring, and so smiles lovely May.   GBL; MePo

To the Lady of Ch'i. *Anonymous.* Good love-sport to the lady of Ch'i! HW

To the Lady Portrayed by Margaret Dumont. John Hollander. Glimpse of that fierce green land of mink and henna. OBAL

To the Lady with a Book. *Anonymous.* When shall I hear that voice again? KiLC

To the Ladybird. *Anonymous.* And she has crept under/The warming pan. OxNR

To the Laggards. Joseph Bovshover. You throw off the weeds/Of the fled and the dead/For the now living creeds. TrJP

To the Landlord. Jonathan Swift. Hang up thy wife, and she'll make four. DBV

To the Last Wedding Guest. Horace Gregory. It is yours to take. NYBP

To the Leanan Shee. Thomas Boyd. And fares into the Night. OnYI

To the Learned and Reverend Mr. Cotton Mather... Grindall Rawson. Thy own Rich Pen (Peace, silly Momus, Peace!)/Hath given them a Lasting Writ of Ease. SCAP

To the Learned Critic. Ben Jonson. Shall outlive garlands, stol'n from the chaste tree. PP

To the Liffey with the Swans. Oliver St.John Gogarty. And the Twin Sportsmen were begotten! AnIL; OxBI

To the Lighted Lady Window. Marguerite Wilkinson. Jesus, little brother. CAW; ISi

To the Little House. Christopher Morley. Heaven is not built of country seats/But little queer suburban streets! HBMV

To the Looking-Glass World It Was Alice That Said (parody). Lewis (Charles Lutwidge Dodgson) Carroll. And welcome Queen Alice with ninety-times-nine! Par

To the Lord Chancellor (excerpt). Percy Bysshe Shelley. This curse should be a blessing. Fare thee well! DBV; ViBoPo

To the Lord General Cromwell. John Milton. Help us to save free conscience from the paw/Of hireling wolves, whose Gospel is their maw. AnEnPo; EnLit; FaBoPV; NoP; OBS; TrGrPo; ViBoPo

To the Lord Love. Michael (Katherine Bradley and Edith Cooper) Field. Keep me perpetual in grace and light! OBMV

To The Magpie. *Anonymous.* Turn up your tail and good luck/come to me. OxNR

To the Maiden in the East. Henry David Thoreau. And cardinal flowers/Stand in their sylvan bowers. OxBA

To the Maids Not to Walk in the Wind. Oliver St.John Gogarty. O walk not in the wind! AnIL

To the Man after the Harrow. Patrick Kavanagh. For you are driving your horses through/The mist where Genesis begins. CIP; FaBoIP; GTBS-P

To the Man I Live with. Ann Menebroker. I offer love to both. IHMS

To the Man-of-War Bird. Walt Whitman What joys! What joys were thine! AA; AmP; BoAnP; EtS; FaBoBe; FM; HBV 1-2; NePA

To the Man Who Sidled Up to Me and Asked: "How Long You in fer, Buddy?" Etheridge Knight. your eyes/sing/empty psalms NeAC

To the Man Who Watches Spiders. Siv Cedering Fox. that someone could love us,/seeing us. LTB

To the Marchesana of Pescara. Buonarroti Michelangelo. ...there blooms a deathless flower,/That breathes on earth the air of paradise. CTC

To the Marquis of Graham on His Marriage. *Anonymous.* A brood of goslings, cackling in debate. OBSV

To the Memory of a Lady. George, Lord Lyttelton. Was his most righteous will, and be that will obey'd. OBEC

To the Memory of Ben Johnson (excerpt). Jasper Mayne. That we both safely saw and lived thy Scene. OBS

To the Memory of Gavin Wilson (Boot, Leg and Arm Maker). George Galloway. Humming his elegy out o'er a flowing glass. NOEC

To the Memory of J. Horace Kimball. Ada Sister Mary. When slavery's galling chains are loosed, and all the oppressed are/free. BlSi

To the Memory of Lord Halifax (excerpt). Ambrose Philips. Ever elegant in woe. FaBoCo

To the Memory of Mr. Oldham. John Dryden. But Fate and gloomy Night encompass thee around. ATP; AWP; CABA; DiPo; EBEV; ExPo; FiP; ForPo; HAP; HeIP; InPK; InPo; InPS; LoBV; NIP; NOBE; NoP; OAEL 1-2; OBS; PAI; PoEL 1-5; PP; PPoe; PPP; Prf; SeCeV; SeCV 1-2; ViBoPo

To the Memory of My Beloved the Author Mr. William Shakespeare... Ben Jonson. And despairs day, but for thy volume's light. AnAnS 2; BoLiVe; EnRePo; GoTL; HAP; HBV 1-2; HeIP; JCP; LiTB; NOBE; NoP; OAEL 1-2; OAEP; OBS; PoEL 1-5; PP; SeCeV; SeCP; SeCV 1-2; TreFS; TrGrPo; ViBoPo; WHA

To the Memory of Sir Isaac Newton (excerpt). James (1700-48) Thomson. Forbear incessant to adore that Power/Who fills, sustains and actuates the whole? ImOP; NOEC

To the Memory of the Brave Americans. Philip Freneau. We trust they find a happier land,/A brighter sunshine of their own. AP; PAL; PoLf

To the Memory of the Learned and Reverend, Mr. Jonathan Mitchell... Francis Drake. Friendship in Him gain'd an Ubiquity. SCAP

To the Memory of Yale College. Howard Phelps (Phelps Putnam) Putnam. And so they came to us once, in our youth. AnAmPo

And then another cried,"More beer, more beer." AnAmPo

A dream of misty elms to plague the mind. AnAmPo

Leading him into friendship unawares. AnAmPo

That laughter sweeps across our pompous brains. AnAmPo

We clang the dull and sodden speech of men. AnAmPo

To the Men of Kent. William Wordsworth. Ye Men of Kent, 'tis victory or death! OBWP

To the Men Who Lose. George L. Scarborough. Here's to the men who lose. BLPA

To the Merchantis of Edinburgh. William Dunbar. That sum tyme ressoun may yow bind,/For to FaBoPP; OxBS

To the Mercy Killers. Dudley Randall. ...Let me still glow. DL

To the Milkweed. Lloyd Mifflin. Wild Weeds of Song—not all ungracious/things! AA

To the Minister Liu. Yu Hsuan-chi. Even small talents live at ease. BoWoP

To the Mocking-Bird. Albert Pike Over them pour thy song, like a rich flood/of light. AA

To the Mocking-Bird. Richard Henry Wilde. And sighing for thy motley coat again. AA; AnAmPo; BoAnP

To the Modern Man. John Hall Wheelock. All things are in yourself–/Love and Life and Death. HBMV

To the Moon. George Darley. And sweep thou on thy worldy way, O Moon! nor glance at mine! MOON

To the Moon. Johann Wolfgang von Goethe. Which, in mazes of the breast,/Wanders in the night. MOON

To the Moon. Thomas Hardy. God ought surely to shut up soon,/As I go. BoNaP

To the Moon. Pierre Ronsard. Bethink ye, now ye hold your heavenly place. AWP

To the Moon. Percy Bysshe Shelley.
That finds no object worth its constancy? AnFE; BoNaP; ERoP 1-2; GTBS; GTBS-P; MBW 1-2; MCCG; MOON; PPP; TrGrPo; ViBoPo
Thou chosen sister of the Spirit/That gazes on thee till in thee it pities... LoBV

To the Moon. Charlotte Smith. Poor wearied pilgrim–in this toiling scene! MOON

To the Moon. Yvor Winters. What is your pleasure now? HeIP

To the Moon, 1969. Babette Deutsch. The cruelty that the Universe feeds/while displaying its glories. MOON

To the Moon and Back. William Plomer. splashdown claptrap MOON

To the Moonflower. Craven Langstroth Betts. The proud, false queen should fealty take/ of thee! AA

To the Most Beautiful Lady, the Lady Bridget Manners. Barnabe Barnes. And is immortal, Time beguiling! EnLoPo

To the Most Fair and Lovely Mistris, Anne Soame, Now Lady Abdie. Robert Herrick. More lik'd by her, or lov'd by mee. AtBAP; CaPo; NOBE; ViBoPo

To the Most Learned, Wise, and Arch-Antiquary, M. John Selden. Robert Herrick. Live thou a Selden, that's a Demi-god. SeCV 1-2

To the Most Virtuous Mistress Pot, Who Many Times Entertained Him. Robert Herrick. He pays the half who does confess the debt. CaPo

To the Mother of Christ, the Son of Man. Alice Meynell. Thou innocent! He lingers in the breast/Of our humanity. ISi

To the Mothers. Ernst Toller. May be seed for ploughed up soil,/May help humanity/Grow. TrJP

To the Mountains. Henry David Thoreau. Who lingers in the purlieus of the towns/With unexplored grace and savage frowns. PoEL 1-5

To the Much Honoured R. F. Esq. Richard Chamberlain. And lead you to the source of Intellect'ual Light. SCAP

To the Muse. X. J. Kennedy. They, he and I know incense from dead ash. InPK; NoP

To the Muse. Robert Louis Stevenson. Leave unadorned by needless art/The picture as it came. EBEV

To the Muse. Philip Whalen. Who are the brilliance of that day/the glory of this night PoM

To the Muse. James Wright. ...or I will/Come down to you. NNaP

To the Muses. William Blake. The sound is forced, the notes are few! AnFE; BoLiVe; ChTr; ERoP 1-2; GTBS; HAP; HBV 1-2; HeIP; LAuP; LiTB; LoBV; NOBE; NOEC; NoP; OAEL 1-2; OAEP; OBEC; OBEV; SeCeV; TrGrPo; ViBoPo; WHA

To the Mutable Fair. Edmund Waller Not in the quarrey, but the flight. AnAnS 2; SeCP

To the Name Above Every Name, the Name of Jesus A Hymn. Richard Crashaw. Shall Then with Just Confusion, bow/And break before thee. SeCV 1-2

To the National Arts Council. Peter Schjeldahl. And if that isn't patriotism, America, what is? ANYP

To the New Annex to the Detroit County Jail. Richard W. Thomas. during the puberty rites in/the hallway. PoBA

To the New Owner. Lucile Hargrove Reynolds. Hoping to find a mislaid dream somewhere! PoToHe

To the New Year. Thomas Carew. Such a garland wreath'd shall be/As shall crown both her and thee. CaPo

To The New Yeere. Michael Drayton. The Diadem that beares. AtBAP; PoEL 1-5

To the Newborn. Judit Toth. in the still of this rose/he dreams his bright dream. WPOW

To the Nightingale. Philip Ayres. I ask but Silence whilst I dye. CEP

To the Nightingale. Sir John Davies. No country hath so short a night,/As England hath in summer. OBSC; PBBP; TrGrPo

To the Nightingale. Anne Finch, Countess of Wilchilsea. Or censure what we cannot reach. CEP; SBG

To the Nile. John Keats. And to the sea as happily dost haste. OBRV

To the Nile. Percy Bysshe Shelley. Beware, O Man–for knowledge must to thee,/Like the great flood to Egypt, ever be. OBRV

To the Noble Sir Francis Drake. Thomas Beedome. Phoebus forgets not his companion. OBSP

To the Noble Woman of Llanarth Hall. Evan Thomas. Why did you put her falsely in prison? PV; TW

To the Noblest and Best of Ladies, the Countess of Denbigh. Richard Crashaw. This fort of your fair self, if't be not won/He is repulsed indeed–but you are undone. JCP; MeLP

To the Oaks of Glencree. John Millington Synge. Then in Mount Jerome I will lie, poor wretch,/With worms eternally. ELU; MoBrPo; NOBI; OxBI

To the Old Masters. Wing Tek Lum. clothes, drying in the breeze. BrSi

To the One I Love Most. *Anonymous.* O! a Dieu, que vous gard;/Valete! MeEL

To the One of Fictive Music. Wallace Stevens. The imagination that we spurned and crave. AP; APA; CoBMV; MoAB; MoAmPo; MoVE; NoP

To the Painter Preparing to Draw M. M. H. James Shirley. Leave off, or paint her with a voice. CavP

To the Parted One. Johann Wolfgang von Goethe. O, come to me again, dear love. AWP

To the Pay Toilet. Marge Piercy. wait and wait and wait to do/what only the dead find unnecessary. GP

To the Pending Year. Walt Whitman. Crouch low thy neck to eleemosynary gifts. OBSP

To the Pines. *Anonymous.* Goin' to shiver when the cold winds blow. WTO

To the Pious Memory of the Accomplist Young Lady Mrs. Anne Killigrew. John Dryden. The Way which thou so well hast learn'd below. LoBV; OAEL 1-2; PoEL 1-5

To the Poem. Frank O'Hara. But be In a defiant land/of its own a real right thing. SM

To the Poet T. J. Mathias. Walter Savage Landor. Hand us a Sonnet cool and dry as/Your very best, and we shall freeze. PV

To the Poet Wordsworth. Felicia Dorothea Hemans. Bright healthful waves flow forth, to each glad wanderer/free! BrRo

To the Poets. John Keats. Ye have souls in heaven too,/Double-lived in regions new! HBV 1-2; ViBoPo

To the Polyandrous Lydia. Franklin Pierce ("F.P.A.") Adams. Thrice blessed they who cleave until/Death do them part! HBMV

To the Portrait of "A Gentleman." Oliver Wendell Holmes. Sure I can take my Bible oath/I've seen that face before. InMe

To the Postmaster General. Peter Redgrove. With energy and light on each leaf of the stacked flesh-pages. AMV-81

To the Prince. Sir John Davies. Than all the Muses with their pens can do. SiPS

To the Puss Moth. *Anonymous.* Hang the miller by his neck. OxNR

To the Queen. William Blake. The Blossoms of Eternal Life!' EnRP

To the Queen. Henry Stewart, Lord Darnley. Be bowsum ay to knaw thy God and Lord. OxBS

To the Queen, Entertain'd at Night by the Countess of Anglesey. Sir William Davenant. And t'ease the travailes of her beames to night,/In this small Lanthorn would contract her light. MeLP; MePo; OBS

To the Queen of Dolors. Sister Maura. remember the seed of my sires, Queen,/in this distress. ISi

To the Rainbow. Thomas Campbell. Nor lets the type grow pale with age,/That first spoke peace to man. HBV 1-2

To the Reader. Charles Baudelaire. –Hypocritical Reader–my co-equal–no, my Brother! SyP

To the Reader. J. V. Cunningham. The gain is gloss. NoAm; QFR

To the Reader. Samuel Daniel. I will ask nothing therein for my pain/But only to have in mine own again. PP

To the Reader. Ben Jonson.
But since he cannot, Reader, look/Not on his picture, but his book. EnRePo
To read it well: that is, to understand. NoP; OAEP; SeCV 1-2

To the Reader. Denise Levertov. turning/its dark pages. AmPP; CoPo; PoM; VGW

To the Reader. Urian Oakes. He wept his Friend in verse: then let us try,/Now Shepard's faln, to write his Elegy. SCAP

To the Reader of Master William Davenant's Play, The Wits. Thomas Carew. For men of better palate will by it/Take the just elevation of your wit. CaPo

To the Red Lory. John Shaw Neilson. Translate thy proud speech of the sunlight–O lory, come down! NOAV

To the Respective Judges. *Anonymous.* Your're downright rogues, they only knaves and fools. APAS

To the Returning Brave. Robert Underwood Johnson. That Liberty may greet you all, her shields of/land and wave. PAH

To the Rev'd Mr. Jno. Sparhawk on the Birth of His Son... Samuel Sewall. Omnia qui tua vult sua gaudia semper habes. SCAP

To the Rev. F. D. Maurice. Alfred, Lord Tennyson. Nor pay but one, but come for many,/Many and many a happy year. FaBoPP; GTBS-P; NOBV; VLP

To the Rev. Mr. Newton. William Cowper. A glimpse of joy that we have met/Shall shine, and dry the tear. LoBV

To the Revd. Mr.– on His Drinking Sea Water. John Winstanley. By bums venereal, ruefully discharged/By Ward's mysterious drop or magic pill. NOEC

To the Reverend Joseph Trapp, on the First Volume... Abel Evans. For it is written, That thou shalt not murther. FaBoEE

To the Reverend Mr. Murdoch. James (1700-48) Thomson. High bliss is only for a higher state. OBEC

To the Reverend Shade of His Religious Father. Robert Herrick. And take a life immortall from my Verse. AnAnS 2; CaPo; JCP; OBS; SeCV 1-2

To the Reverend W.L. Bowles. Samuel Taylor Coleridge. As the great Spirit erst with plastic sweep/Mov'd on the darkness of the unform'd deep. EnRP

To the Reviewers. Thomas Hood. Gives it a wipe,–and all is gone. TW

To the Right Hon. Henry Pelham... Edward Moore. And your Honour's petitioners ever shall pray. OBSV

To the Right Honourable Robert Walpole, Esq. Ambrose Philips. "Bless the toil of doing well! CEP

To the Right Honourable the Countesse of C. William Habington. It had turn'd wonder to Idolatry. AnAnS 2; SeCP

To the Right Honourable William, Earl of Dartmouth. Phillis Wheatley. And bear thee upwards to that blest abode,/Where, like the prophet, thou shalt find thy God. AmPP; SBG; WPOW

To the Right Noble, Valourous, and Learned Prince Henry... Sir John Davies. Who will to them more kind protection lend/Than He which did protect me in distress? SiPS

To the Right Person. Robert Frost. To make up for a lack of meditation. GLGT

To the Right Worthy Knight Sir Fulke Greville. Samuel Daniel. And have maintained your honor in the same,/Who herein holds an interest in my fame. EnRePo

To the River Beach: Stalks of Wild Hay. H. L. Davis. And for this trouble of spirit to come to an end. PoA

To the River Isca (the Usk). Henry Vaughan. Surround thee quite, and style thy borders/The land redeemed from all dissorders! FaBoPP

To the River Itchin, near Winton. William Lisle Bowles. From whom, in happier hours, we wept to part. OAEL 1-2

To the Rose. Sir John Davies. Now in this age should them succeed,/And reign in more sweet manner. OBSC

To the Rose. Robert Herrick. And burn thee' up, as well as I. HBV 1-2; OBS; SeCP

To the Rose upon the Rood of Time. William Butler Yeats. Red Rose, proud Rose, sad Rose of all my days. NoAm; OAEP; TEP; VLP

To the Rosella in the Poinsettia Tree. James Picot. And now there is but Light for Love to be! BoAV

To the Roving Pirate. George Turberville. Then brag not on thy cannon shot/as though there were no mo. EnRePo

To the Royal Society. Abraham Cowley. And all the comely Dress without the paint of Art. AnAnS 2; JCP

To the Rt. Hon. the Lady C. Tufton. Anne Finch, Countess of Winchilsea. To speak what in that tender age became/Your blooming Beauty then your cheifest Fame. SBG

To the Rulers. Howard Nemerov. If they all only had one neck...It's so/Unnecessary and out of date. We do. OxBC

To the Same. Ben Jonson. And the envious, when they find/What their number is, be pin'd. AnAnS 2; BiP; JCP; OAEL 1-2; SeCP; SeCV 1-2

To the Same Flower. William Wordsworth. Do thou, as thou art wont, repair/My heart with gladness, and a share/Of thy meek nature! EnRP

To the Same Man's Life. William Hammond. Since through a double mean nought right appears. OBS

To the Same Purpose. Thomas Traherne. 'Tis want of sense that makes us poor. NoP; SeCV 1-2

To the Ship in Which Virgil Sailed to Athens (Odes, I, 3). Horace. And pull the unwilling thunder down. AWP

To the Shore. May Swenson. their boredom real, and reassuring. NePoAm-2

To the Sister of Elia. Walter Savage Landor. Behold him! from the region of the blest/He speaks: he bids thee rest. HBV 1-2

To the Sistine Madonna. Cornelia Otis Skinner. You whom no one told her of. ISi

To the Skylark. William Wordsworth. True to the kindred points of Heaven and Home! FaFP; GTBS; GTBS-P

To the Small Celandine. William Wordsworth. I will sing, as doth behove,/ Hymns in praise of what I love! EnRP; HBV 1-2; OBRV

To the Snail. *Anonymous.* And I'll give you bread and barley/corns. OxNR

To the Snake. Denise Levertov. and I returned/smiling and haunted, to a dark morning. AmPP; LiTM; NePoEA-2; NMM; PoA

To the Snipe. John Clare. That in the dreariest places peace will be/A dweller and a joy. FaBoPV; NCEP; OBNC

To the Soul. Frederick Napier Broome. Shall climb their shining cars. ACV

To the Soul. John Collop. When angels needs must speak, shall man be mute? TrGrPo

To the Soure Reader. Robert Herrick. The Extreame Scabbe take thee, and thine, for me. AnAnS 2; NLV; NoP; OAEP; SeCP

To the South. Brewster Ghiselin. Of fruit boughs whitening, a foam of time. LiTA; NePA

To the Spirit Great and Good. [(James Henry[) Leigh Hunt. But with a face as towards a friend, and with thin sparkling tears. TrPWD

To the Spring. Sir John Davies. Now forever flourishing,/As long as heaven is lasting. EiL

To the Spring Sun. Freda Laughton. That all its folded hands may stretch with love. NeIP

To the State of Love. John Cleveland. Who would not die upon the spot. MePo; PeD

To the States. Walt Whitman. Once fully enslaved, no nation, state, city of this earth, ever after-/ward resumes its liberty. CTC

To the Statue. May Swenson. (I think of the flame carved like an asparagus tip.) NYP

To the Stone-Cutters. Robinson Jeffers. The honey of peace in old poems. AmP; MoAB; MoAmPo; MoVE; NIP; NOBA; NoP; OxBA; PoCh; PoPl; PP; PrIm; TrGrPo

To the Sun. Ingeborg Bachmann. I shall lament the inevitable loss of my sight. BoNaP

To the Sun. Roy Campbell. But rose snow-silver from the dead!) EaLo

To the Sun. Guido Gezelle. Come back, my Beloved, I am waiting/To rise up and be caressed! LiTW

To the (Supposed) Patron. Geoffrey Hill. Where fish at dawn ignite the powdery lake. NePoEA-2

To the Supreme Being. Buonarroti Michelangelo. That I may have the power to sing of thee,/And sound thy praises everlastingly. AWP; LiTW; TrPWD; TRV

To the Swallow. *Anonymous.* That a songster may be fed. OBVE

To the Swallows of Viterbo. Gibbons Ruark. The flawed hinges of our shoulders shine. SM

To the Terrestrial Globe. Sir William Schwenck Gilbert. Roll on!/It rolls on. FaBoNo; HBV 1-2; NLV; PoPl; TrGrPo

To the Thawing Wind. Robert Frost. Turn the poet out of door. LOW; OxBA

To the Thirty-Ninth Congress. John Greenleaf Whittier. Stretch hands, and bid ye welcome home! PAH

To the Thoughtful Reader. William Meredith. then which of us will not lie last at crossroads? NoAm

To the Translater of Lucan's Pharsalia (1614). Sir Walter Ralegh. Nature thy muse like Lucan's did create. SiPS

To the Translation of Palingenius. Barnabe Googe. Let some thee end that here remain behind. EnRePo

To the Trinity. Richard Stanyhurst. The sacred spirit, labourers refreshing,/Still be renowned. Amen. OxBoCh

To the Tune of, In Fayth I Cannot Keepe my Fathers Sheepe. Sidney Godolphin. Tis to be hop't I may remove/This scorne one day, one day by endless love. OBS

To the Tune of the Coventry Carol. Stevie Smith. Forget him and forget her. FaBoTw

To the Tune of "Ye Commons and Peers Pray Lend Me Your Ears..." *Anonymous.* The mob turns Tory/And preacheth up Passive Obedience. APAS

To the Tune "Red Embroiderd Shoes'. Huang O. Go and make somebody else/Unsatisfied. PBWP; WPOW

To the Tune "Soaring Clouds'. Huang O. You can make blossom in me/ Flowers of fire. PBWP; WPOW

To the Tune "The Fall of a Little Wild Goose." Huang O. This old witch can still/Make a furious scene! WPOW

To the Tune "The Phoenix Hairpin." T'ang Wan. Deceit. Deceit. Deceit. WPOW

To the Unconstant Cynthia. Sir Robert Howard. You what I am, I what you were before. CavP

To the United States of America. Robert Bridges. Freedom and Honor and sweet Loving-kind-/ness. HBV 1-2; PAH

To the University of Cambridge, in New-England. Phillis Wheatley. And in immense perdition sinks the soul. BALP; SBG; TAP

To the Unknown God. Friedrich Wilhelm Nietzsche. I will to know you, even serve you. ILwL

To the Unknown Light. Edward Shanks. Shine down, O Light,/Illumine this night. TrPWD

To the Unknown Warrior. Gilbert Keith Chesterton. That did alone defeat Publicity. MMM

To the Veld. Arthur Shearly Cripps. That gave me my lost manhood back! ACV

To the Veterans of the Abraham Lincoln Brigade. Genevieve Taggard. And what they dared, they dare. OFD

To the Virgin. John Lydgate. To thy five Joys that have devotion. ACP; CAW; GoBC

To the Virgin Mary. Petrarch. That my last sigh in peace may in His arms, be breathed! CAW

To the Virginian Voyage. Michael Drayton. And much commend/To after times thy wit. AtBAP; CBEP; HAP; HBV 1-2; MC; NOBE; OAEP; OBEV; OBS; PAH; PoEL 1-5; SeCePo; TEP; ViBoPo

To the Virgins, To Make Much of Time. Robert Herrick. For having lost but once your prime,/You may for ever tarry. ALV; AnAnS 2; AWP; BLPA; BoLiVe 026; BoLoP; CaPo; DiPo; ELP; EnLoPo; ExPo; FaBV; FaFP; FF; ForPo; FPL; GBL; GoTF; HAP; HBV 1-2; HeIP; InMe; InPK; InPo; InPS; JCP; LiTB; LiTL; LoBV; MasP; NIP; NLV; NOBE; NoP; OAEL 1-2; OAEP; OBEV; OBS; OLR; PAI; PG; PoEL 1-5; PoPl; PPoe; PrIm; QFR; SCV; SeCeV; SeCP; SeCV 1-2; SoSe; SpRo; TreFS; TrGrPo; ViBoPo; WHA

To the Water Nymphs, Drinking at the Fountain. Robert Herrick. And I shall see by that one kiss/The water turned to wine. AnAnS 2; CaPo; EG; ViBoPo

To the Wayfarer. *Anonymous.* Ye who pass by, listen to my prayer: harm/ me not. SiSoSe

To the Western Wind. Judah Halevi. O Maker of the hills and sea and wind! TrJP

To the Western Wind. Robert Herrick. Thy wings shall be embalm'd by me,/And all beset with flowers. CaPo; HBV 1-2; OBEV; SeCV 1-2

To the Western World. Louis Simpson. And grave by grave we civilize the ground. CAPP; CoAP; ConAP; LiTM; NePoAm-2; NePoEA-2; NOBA; PoPl; SM; TAP

To the White Fiends. Claude McKay. To show thy little lamp: go forth, go forth! BANP; PoBA

To the Wife of a Sick Friend. Edna St. Vincent Millay. And the sound of our tears, and the taste of my own. SBG

To the Willow Tree. Robert Herrick. The love-spent youth, and love-sick maid,/Come to weep out the night. CaPo; HBV 1-2; OBEV

To the Wind at Morn. William Henry Davies. Where is that child? ELU

To the Winds. A Song. Philip Ayres. Of lesser force, and less prevail. CEP

To the Woman in Bond Street Station. Edward Weismiller. Are not such furious boys with blood on their faces. NePA; WaP

To the World: a Farewell for a Gentlewoman, Virtuous and Noble. Ben Jonson. But make my strengths, such as they are,/Here in my bosom, and at home. EnRePo; JCP

To the World the Perfection of Love. William Habington. It may know age, but not decay. AnAnS 2; JCP

To the Yew and Cypress to Grace His Funeral. Robert Herrick. Thankful to you, or friends, for me. QFR

To the Young Man Jesus. Annie Charlotte Dalton. We have been fed with tales of bearded men. CaP

To the Young Rebels. E. L. Mayo. ...if you know/What you want, do, do, do, do, do. FAZ

To the Younger Lady Lucy Sydney. Edmund Waller. If such thy dawning beauty's power,/Who shall abide its noontide hour? CBEP

To Thee. *Anonymous.* To Thee, my Saviour and my King. BePJ

To Thee, Dear Henry Morison. Fynes Moryson. For monuments and all must die. OBTV

To Thee, Eternal Soul, Be Praise. Richard Watson Gilder. Send thou thy light, thy love, thy word. AH

To Thee, O God. Abiel Holmes. O may thy hand conduct me home! AH

To Thee, O God, the Shepherd Kings. John Gardiner Calkins Brainard. Our heritage is rich and fair,/And this thy chosen land. AH

To Thee the Tuneful Anthem Soars. Mather Byles. And beaming, wrap the globe around. AH

To Thee, Then, Let All Beings Bend. Nathaniel Evans. All nature to its God shall cry,/Who lives through vast eternity. AH

To Theodora. *Anonymous.* Where thou ever in heaven's spring/Shalt with saints and angels sing. OxBChV

To Theon from His Son Theon. C. A. Trypanis. There is an Alexandria for every age. NCSH

To Thine Eternal Arms, O God. Thomas Wentworth Higginson. And life still smile, like child-hood's hour. AH

To Think of Time. Walt Whitman.
And all preparation is for it–and identity is for it–and life/and materials are altogether for it MAmP
and he there takes no interest in them. AnFE; AP; APA; BLPL; CoAnAm; LiTA

To Think That Two and Two Are Four. Alfred Edward Housman. And long 'tis like to be. ImOP

To This Hill Again. James Macmillan. the dream peace/that would satisfy/as immortality. PoSH

To Thomas Lord Chancellor. Ben Jonson. The Virgin, long since fled from earth, I see,/T'our times return'd, hath made her heaven in thee. OBS

To Thomas Moore. George Gordon, Lord Byron. And a health to thee, Tom Moore. ATP; EnLit; EnRP; GoTF; MCCG; OAEP; TreFT

To Those Who Reproved the Author for Too Sanguine Patriotism. George Edward Woodberry. If I prove false, it is the future errs. AmePo

To Those Who Sing America. Frank Marshall Davis. Yu don't remember/The other verses/Anyway.... FB

To Time. A. W. All are in thee; thou, in thyself alone. EIL

To Tirzah. William Blake. Then what have I to do with thee? EnRP; NOBE; OxBoCh

To Tomas Costello at the Wars. Tomas O'Higgins. My love! Oh, God! Do not look back! AnIV; KiLC

To Tommaso de' Cavalieri. Buonarroti Michelangelo. ...and bare I go/an armed Knight's captive and slave confessed. PeHV

To Toussaint L'Ouverture. William Wordsworth. And love, and man's unconquerable mind. AnEnPo; EnLi 1-2; EnLit; ERoP 1-2; ExPo; FaBoPV; LoBV; MBW 1-2; NOBE; OAEP; OBNC; OBRV; PoNe; PoRA; PPP; TrGrPo; TRV

To Trust. Antonia Pozzi. listening to God/make the barley grow around his house. PBWP

To Turn Back. John Haines. and not be afraid. BoNaP; ConAP

To Turn from Love. Sarah Webster Fabio. gravedigger turning/daisy-filled clods/on a fresh made/bed. BlSi

To Two Bereaved. Thomas Ashe. Fair flowers thrive round the little grave, I pray. NOBV

To Ultima Thule. George Dangerfield. strides through the windows and the doors/and the stone floors CAW

To Urania on the Death of Her First and Only Child. Benjamin Colman. And means in tenderest Love, the Rod/To serve to thy eternal Good. SCAP

To Usward. Gwendolyn B. Bennett. For there is joy in long dried tears,/For whetted passions of a throng! BlSi

To Vanity. Darwin T. Turner. Will still be thought a pretty gem/When all your world of beauty's dim. PoNe

To Varus. Caius Valerius Catullus. In others the defect we find,/But cannot see our sack behind. AWP

To Venus. Horace. +Or Tiber's winding streams, I follow thee. AWP

To Vera Thompson. John Haines. and our years grow deep/in a snow of roses and stones. LCAP

To Vergil. Alfred, Lord Tennyson. Wielder of the stateliest measure ever molded by the lips/of man. AWP; InPo

To Victor Hugo. Algernon Charles Swinburne. Earth's loftiest head, found upright to the end. OBVV

To Vietnam. Charlie Cobb. Wind has never sung song of Nation/in my black face. PoBA

To Violet. Basil Bunting. And this unread memento be/The only lasting part of me. PoA

To Violets. Robert Herrick. Ye do lie,/Poor girls, neglected. CaPo; EG; FaBoMo; HBV 1-2; JCP; MBW 1-2; NoP; OBEV; OBS; SeCP; TrGrPo; ViBoPo

To Virgins. Robert Herrick. Gifts will get ye, or the man. CaPo; UnTE; ViBoPo

To Vittoria Colonna. Buonarroti Michelangelo. Except through death, a refuge and a crown. AWP

To Vulcan. Robert Herrick. Acceptance it might find of thee. CaPo

To W.B.Yeats Who Says That His Castle of Ballylee Is His Monument. Oliver St.John Gogarty. Their town first heard his babbling word. AnIL

To W. C. W. M. D. Alfred Kreymborg. If it lifts/And lowers/Common things,/It will do. PoA

To W.J.M. G. G. You shall not even hear me breathe your name. PeHV

To W.L.G. on Reading His Chosen Queen. Charlotte Forten. Than thee, thy chosen Queen shall never find/A truer subject nor a firmer friend. BlSi

To Waken a Small Person. Donald Justice. The puddles of parking lots/Cannot contain such rainbows NYBP

To Waken an Old Lady. William Carlos Williams. by a shrill/piping of plenty. HAP; InPK; InPo; NoP; QFR

To Walk on Hills. Robert Graves. Not thus from solitude/(solitude sobers only)/But from long hilltop striding. SD

To Walt Whitman. Tom MacInnes. Forever on their own! CaP

To Walt Whitman in America. Algernon Charles Swinburne. The earth-soul Freedom, that only/Lives, and that only is God. EnLi 1-2; VLP

To wet your eye withouten tear. Sir Thomas Wyatt. If I have the mock, ye shall have the loss. FCP; SiPS

To What Strangers, What Welcome. J. V. Cunningham. As luminous as love, lost as this place. NoAm

To Whistler, American. Ezra Pound. Show us there's chance at least of winning through. PoA

To White South Africa. Cosmo Pieterse. You're blind to, ten miles from your eyes, stark misery. WhB

To Whom Else? Robert Graves. Thankfully I consent/To my estrangement/From me in you. FaBoMo

To Whom It May Concern. J. V. Cunningham. A little wastefulness to end the day. FYAP

To Whom It May Concern. Adrian Mitchell. Tell me lies about Vietnam. OBWP

To Whom Shall the World Henceforth Belong? John Oxenham. We are here by God's help to redress it. WBLP

To Whom Shall They Go? *Anonymous.* O, help many of them to come unto You. STF

To William Allen White. Edna Ferber. I never want to see you in your new straw hat. InMe

To William Blake. Olive Dargan. Stones are tender, thorns are kind,/Where your piping goes before. HBMV

To William Camden. Ben Jonson. But for their powers, accept my piety. AnAnS 2; AWP; InPo; JCP; OBS; SeCV 1-2

To William Earle of Pembroke. Ben Jonson. The common-wealth still safe, must studie thee. SeCP

To William Lloyd Garrison. John Greenleaf Whittier. And God alone be Lord! PAH

To William Roe. Ben Jonson. ...This man hath travail'd well. OBS; SeCV 1-2

To William Sharp. Clinton Scollard. There lingering till time and tides/Shall surge no more. HBV 1-2

To William Shelley. Percy Bysshe Shelley. When we returned to gaze on thee– ChRP

To William Simpson, Ochiltree. Robert Burns. Count on a friend, in faith an' practice,/In ROBERT BURNS. MCCG; OxBS

To William Stanley Braithwaite. Georgia Douglas Johnson. Shall permeate the heavens at your feet! BALP

To William (Whom We Have Missed). P. G. Wodehouse. Looks on your feats with a pleasure that's genuine. NOBL

To William Wordsworth. Samuel Taylor Coleridge. And when I rose, I found myself in prayer. EnRP; ERoP 1-2; OAEL 1-2

To William Wordsworth from Virginia. Julia Randall. Run, Great Excursioner. Run if you can. NMM

To Winter. William Blake. Is driv'n yelling to his cares beneath Mount Hecla. AnEnPo; ERoP 1-2; WiR

To wish and want and not obtain. Sir Thomas Wyatt. To linger still alive as dead,/What may it avail me? FCP; SiPS

To––, with an Ivory Hand-Glass. Lord Alfred Bruce Douglas. I guess your face the shadow of your soul. FaBoUs

To Woman. George Gordon, Lord Byron. "Woman, thy vows are traced in sand." HBV 1-2; ViBoPo

To Women. Richard Hugo. My horse is not sure he can make it/to the next star. You are free. NIP

To Women, As Far As I'm Concerned. D. H. Lawrence. you'd better abandon all idea of feelings altogether. OBSP; PAI; WeW

To Women, to Hide Their Teeth, if They Be Rotten or Rusty. Robert Herrick. There in your teeth much Leprosie. FaBoUs

To Words. Ralph Pomeroy. Together, who knows?/we may last awhile. CoPo

To Wordsworth. John Clare. Merit will live, though parties disagree! ERoP 1-2; OAEL 1-2

To Wordsworth. Walter Savage Landor. When 'mid their light thy light appears. OAEL 1-2

To Wordsworth. Percy Bysshe Shelley. Thus having been, that thou shouldst cease to be. EnRP; ERoP 1-2; FiP; MCCG; NoP

To Wystan Auden. Geoffrey Grigson. ...by grike/and by fell, an extra fine light, though you/will disclaim that as well. NAs

To Xanadu, Which Is Beth Shaul. Arye Sivan. the mountain, wailing/in a terrible voice. VWA

To You. Kenneth Koch. ...the sun/Receives me in the questions which you always pose. CAPP

To You. Walt Whitman. And why should I not speak to you? BiP

To You Building the New House. Nelly Sachs. But don't weep the minutes away/Along with the dust/That cloaks the light. VWA

To You on the Broken Iceberg. Tess Gallagher. ...even this melting/lifts the sleepless ship toward grass. GP

To You Who Wait. John Pudney. Where force meets force under the sky's shocked arches. WaP

To Your Question. Duane Niatum. ...open your blossom/To the sun, blazing in the cattails. CDW

To Youth. Walter Savage Landor. And both, alas! take flight. EnRP; HBV 1-2

To Yvor Winters, 1955. Thom Gunn. Raise from the excellent the better still. GTBS-P

To Zion. Judah Halevi. And thy first youth in glory is renewed. AWP

A Toad. Elizabeth Akers Allen. He has never a story to tell! OBCA

The Toad. Tristan Corbiere. ...That toad you heard is I. SyP

Toad. John Cotton. and, as with us,/his warts are part of him. BoAnP

The Toad. Gerald Locklin. In May I lost her to a troll,/a recent arrival from Brooklyn. GP

The Toad-Eater. Robert Burns. Lord! an insect's an insect at most,/ Though it crawl on the curls of a Queen. PoL; TW

Toads. Philip Larkin. But I do say it's hard to lose either/ When you have both. CMoP; ForPo; NePoEA; NMP; NoAm; NOBL; OxBTC; SoSe

Toads Revisited. Philip Larkin. Help me down Cemetery Road. CMoP; NOBL; SaC

The Toadstool Wood. James Reeves. Yet you might think you saw at twilight/A little, crafty face. DuDa; WSC

A Toast. Anonymous.
He hasn't got far yet, but he's a damn good starter. PV
The health of other absent Lords. ALV

Toast. Frank Horne. Here's to your soul/as yet/unborn... BANP; PoNe

A Toast. Charles Stetler. and all three remained completely non-neurotic. GP

The Toast. Charles Warren Stoddard. The babes I've never dandled on my knee! CAW

Toast to a Departing Duchess. Clément Marot. And may the belt of your gown/Soon be too short. HW

A Toast to Our Native Land. Robert Bridges. Drink to Our Native Land! God Bless the State! MC; PAH; PAL

A Toast to the Flag. John Daly. Here's to the Soul of it,/Red, White, and Blue! PAL; PoLf

The Toaster. William Jay Smith. He hands them back when he sees they are done. GrPl; SoPo

Tobacco. Anonymous. That makes a chimney of your nose. FaBoEE

Tobacco. Philip Freneau. And sends me, reeling, home to bed! TAP

Tobacco. Graham Lee Hemminger. It's the worst darn stuff I've ever seen:/I like it. FPL; PoLf

Tobacco Hole. Mebdh McGuckian. ...like the coastguard's/windlight/In the tarted-up houses, widows' row. FaBoIP

Tobacco Plant. Ivor Gurney. And his man's friendliness so good to have, and lost so soon. OBTV

The Tobacconist of Eighth Street. Richard Eberhart. Such insight is one's own death rattling past. MiAP; NYP

Tobias and the Angel. John Gray. But meets the angel in the proper hour. NOBV

A Toccata of Galuppi's. Robert Browning. ...I feel chilly/and grown old. AnFE; EnLi 1-2; GTBS-P; HAP; HBV 1-2; LiTB; LoBV; MaVP; NCEP; NOBE; NOBV; NoP; OAEL 1-2; OAEP; TEP; WHA

The Tod's Hole. Anonymous. For ye'll be a' i' the tod's hole/In less than a hunner year. GBP

Today. John Kendrick Bangs. 'Twill be Today and Joy again! PoToHe

Today. Mary Frances Butts. God will help thee bear what comes/Of joy or sorrow. GoTF; TreFT; TRV

Today. Ethel Romig Fuller. I have lived a poem. PoToHe

Today. Langston Hughes. Walk lean/Together. VGW

Today. Angela Morgan. To be alive in such an age! BLPA

Today. James Schuyler. and the sun smites. ANYP

Today. Jones Very. The life today with me and mine to share. TAP

Today. Margaret Walker. beetle and locust and flies and lice and moth and rust/and mold. FB

Today Beneath Benignant Skies. Denis Wortman. From topmost peak to corner-stone! AH

Today I Am Envying the Glorious Mexicans. Michael C. Blumenthal. beside the rose, the sangria and the happy earth. MAYP

Today I Have Touched the Earth. William Jay Smith. The world was His word, the realm of His radiant mouth. WaP

Today in Bethlehem Hear I. St John Damascene. With angel words that pierce the sky/All earth with joy is ringing. BePJ

Today Is a Day of Great Joy. Victor Hernandez Cruz. it is a great day. TTY

Today Is Armistice, a Holiday. Delmore Schwartz. Loses each day what never will return/to us. TrJP

Today, Prison Won. Jessica Scarbrough. and bleed myself/into the sand. LFAC

Today's News. Ted Berrigan. ...Plus everything/else in the world/going on here. APU

Today: The Idea Market. Michael Nicholas. There is more of the same,/ Especially,/today... NBP

Todlen Butt, and Todlen Ben. Anonymous. When round as a neep ye come todlen hame. OBS

Todlin' Hame. Anonymous. When, round as a neep, ye come todlin' hame. HBV 1-2

Toe'osh: A Laguna Coyote Story. Leslie Marmon Silko. And the way Simon meant it/was for 300 or maybe 400 years. CDW; STE; VoR

Toe Queen Poems (excerpt). Ed Sanders. "I shall return dearies/and don't you motherfuck forget it!!!" ANYP

Toe Tipe. Anonymous. Billy Whistle,/Tripping-go. OxNR

Toe, Trip and Go. Anonymous. Tummy, trouble us,/trouble us. OxNR

Together. Maxine W. Kumin. It happens over/and over, me in/your body and you/in mine. BoWoP; NMM

Together. Ludwig Lewisohn. And this is marriage, this is love. HBMV; PoToHe; TrJP

Together. Siegfried Sassoon. But at the stable-door he'll say good-night. BrPo

Together Again. William Stafford. And drama enough, this time. LCAP

Tohub. Jakov van Hoddis. and earth and air were shattered. VWA

Toil Away. John Jay Chapman. Work, my friend, and so farewell. HBMV

The Toil of the Trail. Hamlin Garland. I have touched the most primitive wildness again. HBV 1-2

The Toiler (excerpt). Edwin Markham. How patient he has been with God! PGD

Toilet Bowl Congregation. Carolyn Baxter. Another slave's/blood christened cement...Again! LFAC

The Toilette. Chu Ching-Yu. "Have I penciled my eyebrows/sharply enough?" HW

The Toilette. A Town Eclogue. John Gay. And at the Play-house Harry keeps her box. CEP

Token. Peggy Bacon. love all the people they love. PV

A Token. Robert Creeley. as if all/worlds were there. VGW

The Token. Frank Templeton Prince. And here a group of women wanly quarrel/At a sale of Cupids. A hawk looks at them. FaBoTw; OxBTC

Tokens. William Barnes. An' every work her love ha' wrought/To eyezight's woone, but two to thought. NBM; PoEL 1-5; VLP

The Tokens of Love: I. Anonymous. She is with-out longing. GBP

The Tokens of Love: II. Anonymous. Perrie, merrie, dixi, domine. GBP

Tokyo West. Alfred Corn. ...They swim forward to greet me. NYP

Told by Seafareres. Galway Kinnell. As tell the seafarers, in the sea's disguises. NePoAm-2

Toledo. Roy Campbell. A sacred city of the mind. MoBrPo

Toledo. Antonio Gomez Restrepo. Fresh as the lips love's earliest sighs enthrall. CAW

Toledo. Jose Zorilla. Was adored of old the same/Through the Arab darkness then. CAW

Tolerance. Thomas Hardy. I had bent and broke, I should not dare/To linger in the shadows there. MoRP

Tolerance. Sir Lewis Morris. Let loose thy scorn on him, nor cease/Till thou hast cover'd him with shame. OBVV

The Tolerance of Crows. Charles Donnelly. Body awaits the tolerance of crows. CIP

Toleration. John Barford. Love–and let love. PeHV

The Toll-Gate Man. Wilson MacDonald. You can see his moonlit hair/ From the next far hill. CaP

The Toll of the Desert. Arthur W. Monroe. And the coyotes howl over you. BPAW; PoOW

Toll the Bell for Damon. Maxwell Anderson. His wife had never noticed that he died/His songs unsung. InMe

"Tollable Well." Frank Lebby Stanton. He allus felt "tollable well." FaFP

Tolling. Lucy Larcom. Slavery's curse went out. OHIP

The Tollund Man. Seamus Heaney. I will feel lost,/Unhappy and at home. BIrV; EBEV; FaBoIP; FaBoMo; IPY; NoP; TEP

Tom Agnew, Bill Agnew. Dante Gabriel Rossetti. Cries–"Go to it, Tom Agnew, Bill Agnew!" ChTr

Tom Ball's Barn. Ted Kooser. ...probably/dead (the doctor said)/before he hit that board pile. GP

Tom Bowling. Charles Dibdin. His soul has gone aloft. EtS; HBV 1-2

Tom Brown. Anonymous. Here's to you, Tom Brown, Here's to you, Tom Brown. FSW

The Tom-Cat. Don (Donald Robert Marquis) Marquis. With the swing of his demon's tail. BoAnP; PoRA

Tom Cat Blues. Anonymous. He goes out every night/With a new one by his side. FSW

Tom Dixon. Anonymous. Oh, Alice, good bye, I'm going! ShS

Tom Dooley. Anonymous.
If it hadn't been for Grayson/I'd-a-been in Tennessee. FSW
poor boy, you're bound to die. BLSo
That drinking and the women/Would be my ruin at last. AmFP; ViBoFo

Tom Dunstan, or, The Politician. Robert Williams Buchanan. O slave, pray still on thy knee–/"Freedom's ahead!" HBV 1-2

Tom Farley.   Colin Thiele.   And, nose to the ground, sink his teeth in a lagging hock.   NOAV; PoAu 1-2

Tom Fool at Jamaica.   Marianne Moore.   ...And you may have seen a monkey/on a greyhound, "But Tom Fool. . ."   AP; NYBP

Tom Gage's Proclamation...   Anonymous.   Thus graciously the war I wage,/ As witnesseth my hand,–TOM GAGE.   PAH

Tom, He Was a Piper's Son.   Anonymous.   The wind shall blow my topknot off.   GBP

Tom Joad.   Woody Guthrie.   That's where I'm a-goin' to be.   TrAS

Tom Jones's Plum Tree (The Juniper Tree).   Anonymous.   No harm in kisses, I know.   AmFP

Tom Long.   Anonymous.   Strike home thy pipe, Tom Long!   EBEV

Tom O'Bedlam.   Anonymous.   Methinks it is no journey.   CH; FaBoCh; LoGBV; PoPle; TrGrPo

Tom O'Bedlam's Song.   Anonymous.
   And the night-crow make/Me music; to my sorrow.   LO
   Poor Tom will injure nothing. AtBAP; EBEV; EvOK; InvP; LiTB; MOON; OAEL 1-2; OxBoLi; PoEL 1-5; SeCeV; ViBoPo

Tom O'Roughley.   William Butler Yeats.   I'd dance a measure on his grave.   CMoP

Tom on the Beach.   George Bruce.   I brood upon uncompleted tasks.   BSV

Tom Potts.   Anonymous.   Ffrom Thomas a Pott I'le turne his/name,/And the Lord of Arrundale hee shall/bee.'   ESPB

Tom Pringle.   Louis Simpson.   From perfect day to perfect night/And wonder what they mean.   NePoAm-2

Tom's Angel.   Walter De La Mare.   And we were safe again.   BoC

Tom's Garland.   Gerard Manley Hopkins.   Manwolf, worse; and their packs infest the age.   FaBoPV; VLP

Tom's Little Dog.   Walter De la Mare.   And down the sugar goes!   GDP; TiPo

Tom Southerne's Birth-Day Dinner at Ld. Orrery's.   Alexander Pope.   And scorn a rascal and a coach!   NAs

Tom Starr.   Robert J. Conley.   his hair had all turned white.   STE

Tom Tatter's Birthday Ode.   Thomas Hood.   Quoth Tom in Tatters.   LoBV

Tom the Lunatic.   William Butler Yeats.   In that faith I live or die.   OnYI

Tom, the Piper's Son.   Anonymous.   And Tom went howling down the/ street.   OxNR

Tom the Porter.   John Byrom.   Took up his Load, and trudg'd into the City.   CEP; NOEC

Tom Thomson.   Arthur Stanley Bourinot.   his spirit is awake.   CaP

Tom Thumb's Alphabet.   Anonymous.   Z was a Zany, a poor harmless fool.   HBV 1-2; HBVY; OxNR

Tom Thumbkin.   Anonymous.   And Little Dick.   OxNR

Tom Tiler; or,The Nurse.   Anonymous.   To swear and damn with a bonne grace.   APAS

Tom Tinker's Dog.   Anonymous.   Little Tom Tinker's dog,/Bow, wow, wow.   OxNR

Tom Tittlemouse.   Anonymous.   And Tom Tittlemouse woke.   OxNR

Tom, Tom, the Piper's Son.   John Crowe Ransom.   "Hush, hush, he is come!"   ViBoPo

Tom Wedgwood Tells.   Brian W. Aldiss.   Kissed her as the down was floating/On the phlogisticated air.   NOBL

Tomah Stream.   Anonymous.   A pox upon the devil, boys! Why didn't you skid the road?   ShS

The Tomb at Akr Caar.   Ezra Pound.   I do not go.   AnFE; APA; CoAnAm

The Tomb of Crethon.   of Tarentum Leonidas.   With lands, how narrow now, how ample then!   AWP

The Tomb of Diogenes.   Anonymous.   "Yes, but the stars are now his dwelling-place."   AWP

The Tomb of Honey Snaps Its Marble Chains.   Derek Stanford.   and bread shall be "a star upon the tongue."   NeBP

The Tomb of Lt. John Learmonth, A.I.F.   John Streeter Manifold.   ,I am filled/With queer affection for the human race.   BoAV; CBAP; PoAu 1-2; WaP

The Tomb of Michael Collins.   Denis Devlin.   And some, though mortal, have achieved their race.   OxBI

The Tomb of the Brave.   Joseph Hutton.   And glory thus bloom o'er the tomb of the/brave.   PAH

The Tomb of the Kings.   Anne Hebert.   And turn its punctured eyeballs/ Toward the morning?   BoWoP; PBWP

The Tombe.   Thomas Stanley.   Then to increase thy Triumph, let me rest,/ Since by thine Eye slain, buried in thy Breast.   OBS

Le Tombeau de Frank O'Hara.   Art Lange.   asking "What does anyone have that we/don"t?" eating March 21st lentil soup.   APU

A Tombless Epitaph.   Samuel Taylor Coleridge.   Yet docile, childlike, full of Life and Love!   OBRV

The Tomboy.   William Burford.   A boy is told to eat his meal in silence.   NePA

Tombstone Epitaphs.   Anonymous.
   Ah, Sidney! Sidney!   PeD

And of such/Is the kingdom of Heaven. PeD
Cut down our Lettuce/To make a salad. PeD
Mary Felton was her name. PeD
Now in another world he hops about. PeD
What will they do when soul and body meet? PeD
With earthworms creeping through my hair. PeD
Yet Jospeh Moodey's name continue must. PeD

The Tombstone Told When She Died.   Dylan Thomas.   A blazing red harsh head tear up/And the dear floods of his hair.   OxBTC

Tombstone with Cherubim.   Horace Gregory.   Disconnect the telephone;/cut the wires.   NAMP

Tombstones in the Starlight.   Dorothy Parker.
   And entertains the most exclusive worms.   NIP
   But, oh, dear friends, you should have seen/The one that got away! NIP

Tomlinson.   Rudyard Kipling.   And...the God that you took from a printed book be with you,/Tomlinson!   BeLS

Tommie Makes My Tail Toddle.   Robert Burns.   In and oot with diddle doddle/Tommie makes my tail toddle.   ErPo

Tommies in the Train.   D. H. Lawrence.   ...in one motion depart/From each other.   MMM

Tommy.   Rudyard Kipling.   An' Tommy ain't a bloomin' fool–you bet that Tommy sees!   BrPo; CABA; EBEV; FaBV; FaPoR; MoBrPo; NoP; OBWP; OxBTC; TreFS

Tommy and Bessy.   Anonymous.   Tomorrow will be Monday.   OxNR

Tommy O'Linn.   Anonymous.   We'll find ground at the bottom, said Tommy O'Linn.   OxNR

Tommy's Dead.   Sydney Thomas Dobell.   'Tis a poor world, this, boys,/And Tommy's dead.   HBV 1-2

Tommy's Gone to Hilo.   Anonymous.   Tommy's gone to Hilo.   AmSS; FSW; ShS

Tommy's Shop.   Anonymous.   That sent him out of the chandler's/shop.   OxNR

Tommy's Tears, and Mary's Fears.   Anonymous.   Will make them old before their years.   HBV 1-2; HBVY

Tommy Tacket.   Anonymous.   And if you will not have him,/You may let him be.   OxNR

Tommy Tibule.   Anonymous.   Little Wee-wee-wee.   OxNR

Tommy Tittlemouse.   Anonymous.   He caught fishes/In other men's ditches.   OxNR

Tommy Trot.   Anonymous.   To buy his wife a looking-glass.   OxNR

Tommy Tucker.   Anonymous.   How will he be married/Without e'er a wife?   OxNR

Tommy Was a Silly Boy.   Kate Greenway.   Full dearly Tom would rue it!   TiPo

Tomorrow.   Florence Earle Coates.   In death sings on–that days to come/ Are sweet as the days that are over!   AA

Tomorrow.   John Collins.   And this old worn-out stuff, which is threadbare Today,/May become everlasting Tomorrow.   GTBS-P; HBV 1-2

Tomorrow.   Kenneth Fearing.   to the wind, or to the sign that sways and creaks above the sta-/tioner's door.   CMoP

Tomorrow.   Della Adams Leitner.   In His hands I leave tomorrow/As I walk with Him today.   GTBS; GTBS-P; STF

Tomorrow.   Felix Lope de Vega Carpio.   And when the morrow came I answered still/"Tomorrow."   CAW

Tomorrow.   John Masefield.   By the living God, we'll try the game again!   MoBrPo; TrGrPo

Tomorrow.   Mark Strand.   ...Tomorrow they will come back and you/will invent an ending that comes out right.   GOYP; PPJ

Tomorrow Is a Birthday.   Gwendolen Haste.   The whirl will be marred. This I know.   GoYe

Tomorrow Is My Birthday: "The thing is sex, Ben."   Edgar Lee Masters.   Videlicet, was drunk." Well, where was I?–   NAs

Tomorrow Is the Marriage Day.   Anonymous.   For Love hath many loves in store.   NCEP

Tomorrow's Men.   Georgia Douglas Johnson.   For labor has her rugged peers/Who glorify the gown she wears!   GoSl

Tomorrow the Heroes.   A. B. Spellman.   there is no other hope.   CNA; PoBA

Tomorrow You Will Live.   Martial (Marcus Valerius Martialis).   Today itself's too late–the wise lived yesterday.   NIP

Tomorrows.   James Merrill.   These three times thirteen lines I'll write down for/Fun, some May morning between five and six.   OBAL

The Tomtit.   Walter De la Mare.   Yet not stay heedless when I heard/The tip-tap nothings of a tiny bird.   FM

Tone de Bell Easy.   Anonymous.   Jesus gonna make up my dyin' bed.   ABF

The Tone of Voice.   Anonymous.   Keep it out of your voice.   PoToHe

Tone's Grave.   Thomas Osborne Davis.   Till Ireland, a Nation, can build him a tomb.   OnYI

The Tongue.   Phillips Burrows Strong.   "Who keeps the tongue doth keep his soul."   PoToHe; TreFT; WBLP

Tongue River Psalm. Gary Gildner. where they rattle two pebbles to praise the moon. FAZ

Tongue-Tied in Black and White. Michael S. Harper. and our shared relatives in blacktown/on the outskirts of your tongue, tied still. HaCAP

Tongues. Sharon Berg. they stay puckered and promise to laugh again. AMV

Tongues. Philip Martin. "Ah yes. Of course I need not remind you, we/Are an old family. It was our forebears speaking." NOAV

Tongues. Thomas Sturge Moore. Wise men shun the tongues that rattle. HBMV

Tongues of Fire. Jorge Plescoff. I say moon, I see white,/a foam of sea of sky/over fire, consumed. VWA

Tonight. Franklin Pierce ("F.P.A.") Adams. Where shall you be at–well, say half-past seven/Tomorrow night? FiBHP

Tonight. Louise Chandler Moulton. Enfold me in your arms! AA

Tonight at Least, My Sinner. Anonymous. But at least, my sinner, we will spend tonight together. WTO

Tonight Everyone in the World Is Dreaming the Same Dream. Susan Litwack. the earth is created, and moves us/on our journey/towards remembering. VWA

Tonight I can write the saddest lines. Pablo Neruda. and these the last verses that I write for her BoLoP; OLR

Tonight I've Watched. Sappho. ...I am/in bed alone MOON

Tonight in Chicago... Anonymous ...a/Candlelight and spotlight/Kind of a place. AmFN

Tonight the City. R. L. Cook. Never can take the mask to be a face. AMV-81

Tonight the Famous Psychiatrist. Louis Simpson. For her the time passes slowly. OxBC

Tonight when You Leave... Gayle Elen Harvey. years from now, wanting to be remembered. AMV-81

Tonsilectomy. James W. Rivers. you press a hidden nerve in your wrist/and completely disappear. AMV-81

Tonto. Ronald Koertge. ..."Ugh," he/muttered to his black and white horse. "Get um up, Scout." GP

A Tonversaton with Baby. Morris Bishop. "You get in the baby carriage;/I'll push you home." FiBHP

Tony Get the Boys. D. L. Graham. the street lights are on/tony get the boys PoBA

Tony O! Colin Francis. And the poor have all the money. CH; FaBoCo; PV

Tony the Turtle. Emile Victor Rieu. For Tony was a Turtle/Delicately bred. SO

Too Anxious for Rivers. Robert Frost. To find 'twas the effort, the essay of love. CBEP

Too Bright a Day. Norman MacCaig. At the great conflagration there. GTBS-P

Too Busy. Anonymous.
Be ready to meet Jesus face to face. STF
My love for the Lord/Is about ready to die. STF

Too Candid by Half. John Godfrey Saxe. Quoth Tom, "So they said at our marriage." HBV 1-2

Too Dark. Mark McCloskey. ...it is too dark/to prove that I have ever seen him. PoA

"Too dearly had I bought my green and youthful years." Henry Howard, Earl of Surrey. On woman's word, but wisdom would mistrust it/to endure. FCP; SiPS

Too happy time dissolves itself. Emily Dickinson. 'Tis Anguish not a Feather hath/Or too much weight to fly– NOBA

Too Late. Dinah Maria Mulock Craik. Douglas, Douglas, tender and true! HBV 1-2

Too Late. Rachel Korn. and forms itself/into the letters of your name. VWA

Too Late. Fitz Hugh Ludlow. Had they only not come too late–too late! PoLf

Too Late. Philip Bourke Marston. Until I change them for the silent way. OBNC

Too Late. Nora Perry. Give consolation for the "might have been"? PoToHe

Too Late. R. S. Thomas. That will destroy you and your race? NMP

The Too-Late Born. Archibald MacLeish. The silent slain– AmP; APA; GoJo; MoAB; MoAmPo; NAMP; OxBA; SeCeV; WaP

The Too Literal Pupil. Martial (Marcus Valerius Martialis). I did not tell you to say "No" forever,/And to me. UnTE

Too Many Daves. Dr. Seuss. But she didn't do it. And now it's too late. OBCA

Too Many Miles of Sunlight between Us. Jack Myers. yellow space. The blackness, blank. AMV-80

Too Much. Edwin Muir. Threading my dazzling way within my night. LiTB

Too Much Coffee. Edwin Arlington Robinson. The Line that never was drawn. MoAmPo

Too Much Sex. Anonymous. But what that I shalle say, nowe herken me. MeEL

Too Solemn for Day, Too Sweet for Night. William Sidney Walker. When the gloom is soft, and the light is dim. OBEV

Too Soon the Lightest Feet. Amanda Benjamin Hall. Speechless, I hold love to my breast/And listen to the clock! HBMV

Too soon, too soon comes Death to show. Coventry Patmore. And love in life should strive to see/Sometimes what love in death would be. EG

Too Young for Love. Horace. ...smooth face might well perplex/A stranger to discern his sex. UnTE

The Tool of Fate. Yehoash. I am the open sesame,/And the unwitting tool of fate. TrJP

Tooten Out Blues. Ed Bell. And the blind man say told her that you/sure look good to me BluL

Top Hand. Anonymous. From the top to the bottom he's a bold Jackass. CoSo

Tophet. Thomas Gray. And Satan's self had thoughts of taking orders. MyFE; NCEP; NOEC; OBSP

Topsy-Turvy Land. H. E. Wilkinson. For when you go you're coming back,/In Topsy-Turvy Land. SoPo

Topsturvey-World. William Brighty ("Matthew Browne") Rands. The bird was on the brier! OxBChV

Tor House. Robinson Jeffers. With the mad wings and the day moon. AnAmPo; LoBV

Tora's Song. Knut Hamsun. And yet after all I have but one. PoPl

The Torch. Greg Forker. can't you see our shadows/when the light licks hard? LFAC

The Torch. Theodosia Garrison. Make me thy torch to burn out swiftly, Lord. BLPA

The Torch-Bearers: America. Arlo Bates. And none shall spare to mock thee in/thy fall. AA; PGD

Torch-Light in Autumn. John James Piatt. In Autumn's funeral train. AA

The Torch of Love Dispels the Gloom. Walter Savage Landor. Without it could not find his way. GBL

Tormenting Virgin. Anonymous. But oh, her lower half remains/Impenetrably pure. UnTE

The Torn Hat. Nathaniel Parker Willis As wandering and as lost as they! AA

The Torn Nightgown. Joel Oppenheimer. but the night is the day of my cock. CoPo

The Tornado. Charles De Kay. And strews for all impartially their grave. EtS

The Tornado. Norman H. Russell. from the death in the teeth of the tornado. STE

Tornado. William Stafford. and in the buried sound along the buried mouth of the creek. NaP

Tornado Soup. A. K. Redwing. "A bank president on his lunch break,"/I said. VoR

Tornado Watch. Paul Shuttleworth. A window flies across a pasture. AMV-80

Tornado Watch, Bloomington, Indiana. Gary Young. ...and I go on/living in the durable world. SUW

Toro. William Stanley Merwin. ...The light is different. And they are alone. NePA

Toroi Bandi. Anonymous. I'll be reborn upon this earth/Forever in the sun. WTO

The Torrent. Edwin Arlington Robinson. Were steps to the great place where trees and torrents go. NePA

The Torso: Passages 18. Robert Duncan. For my Other is not a woman but a man/the King upon whose bosom let me lie. CAPP; GP

The Tortoise. Cid Corman. the feeling is of/terrible slowness/overtaking haste. InPK; SM; VGW

Tortoise. Joanne De Longchamps. gravely accepts and eats my offering. BoAnP

Tortoise Family Connections. D. H. Lawrence. And biting the frail grass arrogantly,/Decidedly arrogantly. BrPo; ChMP; HaMV

Tortoise Gallantry. D. H. Lawrence. We will go on to the end. CMoP; NoAm

The Tortoise in Eternity. Elinor Wylie. I bear the rainbow bubble Earth/Square on my scornful back. ImOP

Tortoise-Shell. D. H. Lawrence. This slow one. CMoP; ExPo; FM; OAEL 1-2

Tortoise Shout. D. H. Lawrence. That which is in part, finding its whole again throughout the universe. LiTM; NoAm

The Tortoiseshell Cat. Patrick Reginald Chalmers. And every cat in the twilight's gray,/Every possible cat. BoAnP; CenHV; PCat

The Tortured Heart. Arthur Rimbaud. What can I do, my cheated heart? PeHV

Tory Pledges. Thomas Moore. "Long life to jobbing; may the days/Of Peculation shine again!" FaBoCo; OBSV

Tossed on a Sea of Trouble. Archilochus. How changeful are the ways of humankind. PoPl

The Total Influence or Outcome of the Matter: THE SUN. Marge Piercy. I know that now at last/it is beginning to grow light. WPOW

Totem. Nissim Ezekiel. And sundry decorations,/not without meaning. VWA

Tottel's Miscellany (excerpt). *Anonymous.* And brake her mould in great dispraise your like she could not frame. OAEL 1-2

Tottenham Court: Song: "What a dainty life the milkmaid leads." Thomas Nabbes. And merrily passeth her time away. EG

Tottingham Frolic. *Anonymous.* ...comfort/As lying with a man./To come down, down..... UnTE

The Toucan. Pyke Johnson, Jr. Another toucan in the/Zoo can. NTCP

Toucannery. Jack Prelutsky. in fact there is no toucan who can/do what four or three or two can. OnUR

Touch. Thom Gunn. walk with everyone. CMoP

Touch. Octavio Paz. ...My hands/Invent another body for your body. BoLoP

Touch It. Robert Mezey. ...Touch it. NaP

The Touch of Human Hands. Thomas Curtis Clark. And the warmth, the pulsing warmth/Of human hands.... PoToHe

The Touch of the Master's Hand. Myra Brooks Welch. By the touch of the Master's hand. BLPA; PoToHe; STF; TRV

Touch of zygosis. Judith Fitzgerald. so much film and conjugation/ depending on the angle CaPN

The Touch-Stone. Samuel Bishop. If she's a fool she'll wed the knave–/If she's a knave, the fool. HBV 1-2

Touch Thou Mine eyes. Marion Franklin Ham. To guard my steps, whatever may betide. AH

Touche. Jessie Redmond Fauset. Blue eyes he had and such waving gold hair! BlSi; CDC

Touches. William Stafford. I run my hand along those old grooves in the rock. CAPP

Touching. Christopher Gilbert. and I'll go forth and live with that. MAYP

Touching Shoulders. *Anonymous.* When once I rubbed shoulders with you. BLPA

Touching the River. Thomas Kinsella. the reeds are shivering (one clump of them/nestling a lark's eggs, I know, in a hoof-print). FaBoIP

Touchstone. James Worley. enlightened by the luster they inflict. AMV-80

A Tough Cuss from Bitter Creek. James Barton Adams. Was once the old original tough cuss from Bitter Creek. PoOW

A Tough Generation. David Gascoyne. Renounce its ragged petals one by one. LiTM

The Tough Ones. Errol Miller. feeling their bodies/for bruises. AMV-80

Toujours Amour. Edmund Clarence Stedman. But of Love I an't foretoken:/Ask some older sage than I! HBV 1-2

Toujours la Politesse. *Anonymous.* a huntsman not to be outdone in politeness. OBVE

Toulouse Lautrec. Astrid Tollefsen. before the thirst for red/has found a track to follow! PBWP

Tour 5. Robert Earl Hayden. its brightness harsh as bloodstained swords. PPP

Tour de Force. Peter Kane Dufault. Or is God a large rabbit? ErPo

Tour Guide: La Maison des Esclaves. Melvin Dixon. red empty rooms/to measure long journeys. LTB

The Tour of Dr. Syntax: In Search of the Picturesque. William Combe. "Which, when in happy contrast join'd,/Delights th'inform'd, well-judging mind." OBRV

Touring. David Morton. Always summer for my mind. TrPWD

Tourism. Lillie D. Chaffin. ...and go, believing they find us in the well-staged/parks. TAT

The Tourist. Garret Keizer. Aware I have begun to die. AMV-81

Tourist. Mark Van Doren. I still could tell you less of it/Than blind Homer may. NePoAm-2

The Tourist and the Town. Adrienne Rich. ...Your breath is on this air,/ And you are theirs and of their mystery. NePoEA-2

The Tourist from Syracuse. Donald Justice. You must not hope to arrive. TwCP

Tourist Guide: How You Can Tell for Sure When You're in South Dakota. Jim Heynen. The whole world stalls. GP

Tourist Time. F. R. Scott. O communication!/O rapid transit! PoPl

The Tourists. Cecil Day-Lewis. Forfeit through endless self-evasion/The estate of simple being. OBTV

Tourists. Howard Moss. Ending up tending shop up in Fiesole. FiBHP; NYBP

Tourists. Kizito Z. Muchemwa. Neither will it give out its rich sad secrets/To halfhearted tokens of transparent love. WhB

The Tournament of Man. Ernest Crosby. Away with your brutal disorder, and clear the field for/the tournament of Man. PGD

The Tournament of Tottenham. *Anonymous.* Was melody delycyus/For to here precyus/Of six menys song. OxBoLi

Tours. Stephen Shu Ning Liu. after our first tour by the Yangtze River. AMV-80

Toussaint l'Ouverture. Edwin Arlington Robinson. You are still there. And I know who is here. PoNe

Tow men wrote a lexicon. *Anonymous.* Which part wrote Scott, and which part wrote Liddell? CenHV

Toward a Theory of Instruction. Danny Rendleman. ...And talk about/ growing up in New England. SUW

Toward a True Peace. Ralph Cheyney. Make the will of the world your trumpet, the heart/of the world your drum! PGD

Toward Climax. Gary Snyder. A virgin/Forest/Is ancient; many-/ Breasted,/Stable; at/Climax. SUW

Toward Lesbos. Renee Vivien. And, see, we are landing on the island of magic...' PeHV

Toward Myself. Leah Goldberg. I go toward myself with a face/you looked for in vain/when I went toward you. VWA

Toward Tenses Two Moons. George Rachow. your death is his survival/ your dust is pure. LFAC

Toward the Solstice. Adrienne Rich. and my hand still suspended/as if above a letter/I long and dread to close. NoP

Toward the Splendid City. Ed Ochester. beneath the white ring of ice. LTB

Toward Winter. *Anonymous.* The pleasant wave has started muttering. NOBI

Towards a City That Sings. June Jordan. for your possible/discovery. NYP

Towards Democracy. Edward Carpenter. And I remain gazing into them. PeHV

Towards the Last Spike. Edwin John Pratt.
And wrap them cold in her pre-Cambrian folds. NOBC
The general of the patronymic march. OBCV
...had filled/Them up, would keep them filled until the end/Of Time. NOBC
Was this the thing Van Horne set out/To conquer? OBCV

Towards the Source: Let Us Go Down, the Long Dead Night Is Done. Christopher John Brennan. singing together in the eternal morn. PoAu 1-2

Towards the Vanishing Point. David Lehman. Our weather the invention of rain. SM

The Tower. Philip Booth. yes, not quite/the same. NePoEA-2

The Tower. Dan Pagis. the mass of my burnt bricks/crumbles/and turns back to clay. VWA

The Tower. Mark Van Doren. And round it, silent, silent,/Wheels the invisible flock. MoPo

The Tower. William Butler Yeats. Among the deepening shades. CMoP; CoBMV; LiTB; LiTM; MBW 1-2; MoPo; MoVE; NoAm; OAEP; SeCeV

The Tower of Babel. Nathaniel Crouch. They scatter all their stuff abroad,/And tumble down their tools. OxBChV

The Tower of the Dream (excerpt). Charles Harpur. Burning its sullen depths with one red blaze. PoAu 1-2

Towering O'er the Wrecks of Time. John Bowring. All the light of sacred story/Gathers round its head sublime. BePJ

The Town. David Rowbotham. Another camp-fire closer to its vision. PoAu 1-2

Town against Gown at Oxford. Robert of Gloucester Ne fort after Michelmasse hi ne come namore ther. OxBM

The Town Betrayed. Edwin Muir. Achilles, Siegfried, Lancelot/Have sworn to bring us low. CMoP

The Town Called Providence Its Fate. Benjamin Tompson. But know the dismal day draws neer wherein/The fire shall earth it self dissolve and sin. SCAP

The Town Clerk's Views. Sir John Betjeman. Until we've really got the country plann'd. CMoP

The Town Dump. Howard Nemerov. Their music marvelous, though sad, and strange. BiP; CMoP; MAT; NIP

Town Ghost. Lauris Edmond. Look lady just don't/you interfere. OCNZ

Town I Left. Helen Sorrells. among people sucked too dry/by their own all-day dying/to care about mine. IHMS

The Town I Was Born In. Yehuda Amichai. So don't pick me for a lover or son,/A crosser of bridges, a tenant or a citizen. VWA

Town Meeting. John Hay. Don't stop him saying what we knew before/we came. NePoAm

The Town Mouse and the Country Mouse (parody). Matthew Prior. Ten thousand Watchmen waited on this Mouse,/With Bills,and Halberds,to her Country-House. BXAP

The Town of Don't-You-Worry. I. Bartlett. On the banks of River Smile. BLPA

The Town of Hill. Donald Hall. door shuts/under dream water. FiCP; InPK; TAP

The Town of Nogood. W. E. Penny. Take this for your motto, "I can, will,"/And live up to it each day. BLPA

The Town of Passage. *Anonymous.* The shrimp and cockle, when the tide is out. OxBoLi

Town Owl. Laurie Lee. and plucks a quick mouse off the stair... PB

The Town-Rakes. Peter Anthony Motteux. What Death can compare with the jolly Town-Rakes. CoMu

The Town without a Market. James Elroy Flecker. Dark with no dream is hateful: let me live! MoBrPo

Towser Shall Be Tied Tonight. *Anonymous.* "Take her, boy, and make her happy. Towser shall be tied tonight. BLPA; BoAnP

The Toy. Cid Corman. and find myself with/my erector set. GP

The Toy Horse. Valentin Iremonger. He was so happy, I gave him also/ My vivid coloured crayons and my big glass marble. NOBI

The Toy Lamb Seller. *Anonymous.* I never would cry, Young lambs to sell! OxNR

The Toy-Maker. Padraic Colum. And coach and wheelbarrow I carve in my stall,/Making things with no troubles in them. SaC

Toyland. Glen MacDonough. Once you pass its borders, you can ne'er return again. BLSo; FSN

Toys. Abraham Sutzkever. seven little streets with dolls in each one,/and not one child in the town. VWA

The Toys Talk of the World. Katharine Pyle. But they did not speak; it was not worth while. OBCA

The Track. Nicholas Christopher. into a field which is always empty,/ where all the winners go. MAYP

Track. Tomas Transtromer. 2 o'clock: strong moonlight, few stars. EAS

The Track into the Swamp. Samuel French Morse. The wilderness it comprehends/It can explain, like summer snow. CrMA

Track-Lining Song. *Anonymous.* He, hi, he can tell time... AmFP

Tracking Rabbits: Night. Jim Barnes. call him brother,/semblance, prey. CDW

Tracking the Sled, Christmas 1951. Jeanne Murray Walker. It is the route you took through winter light/that falls across the pane again tonight. AMV-81

The Trackless Deeps. Percy Bysshe Shelley. Now to the sweet and many-mingling sounds/Of kindliest human impulses respond. EtS

Tracks. John Montague. giggling maids push/a trolley of fresh/linen down the corridor. FaBoIP

Tracks. Elaine Schwager. I'm still surprised/to see a cow/walking on the New York Central tracks. CAD

Tracks. Brad Lee Shurmantine. beautiful bruises on the crusted/glittering snow. AMV-81

Tracks. Joseph Torain. They are pregnant FAZ

Tracks in the Snow. Marchette Chute. I think was probably me. SiSoSe

Tract. William Carlos Williams. Go now/I think you are ready. AmP; AP; BiP; BLPL; CoBMV; DL; FF; LiTA; LiTM; MoAB; MoAmPo; MP; NePA; NoAm; NOBA; TAP; TrGrPo; TwCP; VGW

Tractatus. Derek Mahon. The steam rising wherever the edge may be? FaBoIP; OBSP

Traction: November 22,1963. Howard Moss. The end comes back. It always comes too soon. AmFN

Tractor. John L. Sellers. i guess they thought i was a farmer/going to work one of my fields/or on my way home. LFAC

Tractor Hour. Monty Reid. ...all we can do is look/at each other and hum the music/that's there. CaPN

"Trade" Rat. Eleanor Glenn. Till glitter calls to him and he succumbs. NePoAm

Trade Winds. John Masefield. ...the long low croon/Of the steady Trade Winds blowing. FaBoCh; OBMV

Trader. Jim Harrison. You've had your orange/now lie in it. NoAm

Trader's Return. Sylvia Lawson. islanders too who of necessity/made disconnectedness a daily act. PoAu 1-2

Trading Chicago. Charles O. Hartman. gleaming like a new promise, that silently carried you away. AMV-80

Tradition. Arthur Guiterman. With Homer chanting down the street. DBV

Traditional Charms for Finding the Identity of One's True Love. John Gay. For L is found in Lubberkin and Love! FaBoUs

Traditional Funeral Songs. *Anonymous.* I send the tears caught in my bandana. BoWoP

The Traditional Grammarian as Poet. Ted Hipple. Ku, they ku. Thang ku. PoL

Traditional Red. Robert Huff. Raking an iron rooster through the sky. HoPM; NePoEA-2

Traditional Tune. Robert D. Fitzgerald. the flash that hurtles/through upper night. BoAV

Traditions. Seamus Heaney. "I was born here. Ireland." FaBoMo

Trafalgar. Francis Turner Palgrave. And the hero of heroes was slain. BeLS; FaBoBe

Traffic Lights. Lina Kasdaglis. but you haven't made it across and never will. BoWoP

Trafique Is Earth's Great Atlas. George Alsop. And each years Trafique to thy self get more. SCAP

A Tragedy. Theophile Marzials.
But he's such a very great musician/Grimacing and fingering his fiddle-strings. HBV 1-2
Drop/Dead./Flip, flop./Plop. PeD

A Tragedy. Tom (Thomas Lansing Masson) Masson. I know it happened, just because/I was not there at all. OBAL

Tragedy. Howard Moss. When we fall from small hills/Into the common ground. NePoEA

A Tragedy. Edith Nesbit. Death will have gathered me. HBV 1-2

Tragedy. George William Russell. He turned him homeward sick and slow. MoBrPo

Tragedy. Jill Spargur. And I don't want one–now. BLPA

Tragedy. Mark Van Doren. the world is something I must try. NePoAm-2

The Tragedy of Pete. Joseph Seamon, Jr Cotter. And he welcomed death/ From his head to his feet. CDC

The Tragedy of Pompey the Great (excerpt). John Masefield. Death opens unknown doors. It is most grand to die. WGRP

The Tragedy of the Leaves. Charles Bukowski. because the world had failed us both. HoPM

The Tragi-Comedy of Titus Oates. *Anonymous.* No name can fit him, therefore, let him be/The grumbling ghost of old Presbytery. APAS

The Tragic Condition of the Statue of Liberty. Bernadette Mayer. This is the most generous contribution I can afford. APU

Tragic Guilt. Keidrych Rhys. Amid tremendous history, new pity. WaP

Tragic Love. Walter James Turner. But some pure lustre from their light/ All future worlds shall have. OBMV

The Tragic Mary Queen of Scots. Michael (Katherine Bradley and Edith Cooper) Field. As roses are by heaven designed/To bring the honey to the wind. EnLoPo; OBMV

A Tragic Story. William Makepeace Thackeray. Alas! still faithful to his back./The pigtail hangs behind him. HBV 1-2; HBVY; MoShBr; OnMSP

Tragic Verses. *Anonymous.* And, by the laws condemn'd ere long, most justly he will die. CoMu

The Tragical Death of A, Apple Pie. *Anonymous.* XYZ and &/All wished for/a piece in hand OxNR

The Trail. Edward Weismiller. Here: here is his trail. WaP

Trail All Your Pikes. Anne Finch, Countess of Winchilsea. To your mistaken shrine, to your false idol Honour. ExPo

Trail Breakers. James Daugherty. The terror and the splendor of the/ Atomic Age. AmFN

Trail Crew Camp at Bear Valley, 9000 Feet.... Gary Snyder. black coffee in a big tin can. HaCAP

Trail End. *Anonymous.* And a great, big puddle/Of blood on the ground. CoSo

The Trail Herd. *Anonymous.* Dreamin', dreamin' that you love me. BPAW

The Trail Horse. David Wagoner. No straddler of winged horses, no budding centaur,/But a man biting the dust. PH

The Trail of the Bird. W. J. Courthope. Were mad to fly forth from their nests in the north,/And follow the trail of the bird. HBVY

The Trail to Lillooet. [(Emily[) Pauline Johnson. And call across the canyon on the trail to Lillooet. CaP

Trail to Mexico. *Anonymous.*
And follow the cow trail till I die. FSW
I'll stay on the trail till the day I die. AmFP; AS; BPAW; CoSo

The Trail Up Wu Gorge. Sun Yun-feng. I am bound on a journey without end,/And can not bear the song of the cuckoo. BoWoP; PBWP

Trailer Park. Lewis MacAdams. And I still can't get a ride ANYP

The Trailing Arbutus. John Greenleaf Whittier. And make the sad earth happier for their bloom. AnAmPo

The Train. *Anonymous.* It comes from Pompi, the round-house, from Kgobola-diatla. TTY

The Train. Alan Brownjohn. As every devil thunders through. OxBTC

Train. Ken Smith. waving its little handkerchiefs of steam. EAS

Train Blues. Paul Zimmer. And no matter what we do, we'll never see one again. PPJ

The Train Butcher. Thomas Hornsby Ferril. And all love's wisdom that you left unsaid. GoYe

The Train Dogs. [(Emily[) Pauline Johnson. The wolfish blood in their veins. GDP; WHW

The Train Is off the Track. *Anonymous.* Oh I'd like for to change your name. AmFP

Train Journey. Judith Wright. I woke and saw the dark small trees that burn/suddenly into flowers more lovely than the white moon PBWP

The Train of Religion (excerpt). Martin Farquhar Tupper. How beautiful their feet, who follow in that train. FaBoCo

The Train Out. Sydney Lea. and the sun glows dull on the tracks. MAYP

Train Ride. John Wheelwright. the great grove leans to wind, past and to come. AnFE; MoPo; VGW

The Train Runs Late to Harlem.   Conrad Kent Rivers.   In her tiger's mouth/returning me, returning me.   IDB; PoBA

The Train Stops at Healy Fork.   John Haines.   In the starry gloom of the canyon.   TAT

Train to Dublin.   Louis MacNeice.   As you have perhaps, people at last attain/And find that they are rich and breathing gold.   FaBoIP

The Train to Glasgow.   Wilma Horsburgh.   Who drove the train to Glasgow.   OnUR

Train to Reflection.   Lawrence T. O'Neill.   somewhere under New York.   AMV-80

Train Tune.   Louise Bogan.   Back through midnight   NePoAm

The Train Will Fight to the Pass.   Ruth Pitter.   It is their triumph, and a true emblem of honour.   HaMV

Train Window.   Robert Finch.   to the running chalk-talk of powder-red/box-cars beyond, while our train waits here.   OBCV; PeCV

Training.   Demetrio Herrera.   Stray kids,/the sea-birds/sneak in through the roof.   TTY

Training for the Apocalypse.   Gloria Frym.   They sneak into your dreams/just before the world ends.   APU

Training on the Shore.   Shlomo Vinner.   Children/They teach to walk,/Soldiers/To fall.   VWA

Trains.   James S. Tippett.   Here come the trains.   SoPo; SUS; TiPo

Trains at Night.   Frances Frost.   ...stop to tuck/Each sleepy blinking town in bed!   BrR; TiPo

Trains Made of Stone.   Ray A. Young Bear.   knowing that it has not passed.   CDW

Trainwrecked Soldiers.   John Frederick Nims.   Crux in a savage tongue none of us know.   MiAP

Trala Trala La-Le-La.   William Carlos Williams.   to the end of time trala/trala trala la-le-la   OFD

Tramontana at Lerici.   Charles Tomlinson.   One is ignored/By so much cold suspended in so much night.   GTBS-P

The Tramp.   Joe Hill.   Keep on tramping, that's the best thing you can do.   FSW

Tramp.   Richard Hughes.   So many words to speak that the tongue cannot utter.   MoBrPo

Tramp Miner's Song.   *Anonymous.*   And the winter is over/And I'm rustling yet.   AmFP

The Tramp's Song.   Mary Devenport O'Neill.   Isn't it better have luck than gold?/As the man long ago said.   AnIV

Tramp! Tramp! Tramp!   George Frederick Root.   We shall breathe the air again,/Of the free land in our own beloved home.   BLSo; PSoN; TreFS

A Trampwoman's Tragedy.   Thomas Hardy.   –'Tis past! And here alone I stray/Haunting the Western Moor.   AtBAP; BeLS; HBMV; MoVE; OBNC; OBNV; VLP

The Trance.   Stephen Spender.   And their mutual terrors heal/Within our married miracle.   ChMP; CoBMV

Trance and Transformation.   Johann Wolfgang von Goethe.   You will be a sorry guest/On the sombre earth.   LiTW

The Trance of Time.   John Henry, Cardinal Newman.   Within to antedate/Heaven's Age of fearless rest.   OxBoCh

Tranquil Sea.   Claire Aven Thomson.   Always a ship...and pray the winds abate.   EtS

Trans Canada.   F. R. Scott.   And here is no shore, no intimacy,/Only the start of space, the road to suns.   PeCV

Transaction.   Archie Randolph Ammons.   shadows are bodiless shapes, yet they have a song.   HaCAP; PoA

The Transandean Railway.   Thomas Kretz.   ...Tracks/smile up ahead–for they/have been here before.   AMV-80

Transcendence.   Richard Hovey.   The sun doth not contain him nor the sea.   TRV; WGRP

Transcendentalism.   *Anonymous.*   And so plausibly fantastic,/That one gets enthusiastic/For a bit.   NA

Transcendentalism: A Poem in Twelve Books.   Robert Browning.   Bent, following the cherub at the top/That points to God with his paired half-moon wings.   DiPo; PP; VLP

Transducing.   George-Therese Dickenson.   ...Old theories of/seem to work again. At least for now.   APU

Transfiguration.   Djuna Barnes.   The unchained sun, in raging thirst,/Feeds the last day to the first.   EAS

The Transfiguration.   Robert Herrick.   That shin'st thus in thy counterfeit!   CaPo

The Transfiguration.   Edwin Muir.   ...and the betrayal/Be quite undone and never more be done.   MasP; OxBS

The Transfiguration of Beauty.   Buonarroti Michelangelo.   And this transfigured beauty wins thy love.   AWP

Transfigured.   Sarah Piatt.   One saw her with the Master's eyes.   AA

Transfigured Bird.   James Merrill.   And slept and would not till nearly dusk be woken.   MoAB

Transfigured Life.   Dante Gabriel Rossetti.   Then comes the sound as of abundant rain.   MaVP

Transformation.   Lewis Alexander.   For I wore the bitterness/From it long ago.   CDC; PoNe

Transformation.   Caius Valerius Catullus.   a paragon of virtue.   LiTW

Transformation.   Jessie B. Rittenhouse.   Not knowing that I walk in cloistered ways/Bearing within one rapt, still thought of you.   HBMV

Transformation.   Quincy Troupe.   ...and write/the love poem of your life.   CNA

Transformation Scene.   Constance Carrier.   her arm, her flesh, warm in the sun, and bleeding.   FYAP; GoYe

Transformations.   Thomas Hardy.   And the energy again/That made them what they were!   NoAm; PPoe; PPP; TEP

Transformed.   D. Weston Gates.   By simply looking toward the light.   STF

The Transformed Metamorphosis: Awake, Oh Heaven.   Cyril Tourneur.   To shake the strength of heaven's axletree.   MOON

Transience.   Sarojini Naidu.   And make your eyes unfaithful to their tears.   MCCG

Transit.   Margaret Avison.   Noon keeps swallowing.   FaBoWP

Transit.   Adrienne Rich.   ...where the skier/and the cripple must decide/to recognize each other?   NoP

Transit.   Richard Wilbur.   Leaving the stations of her body there/As a whip maps the countries of the air.   LCAP

Transition.   May Sarton.   The fierce wasp settle on a golden pear.   NePoAm

Transitional Poem.   Lewis, Cecil Day.   So I'll go bite the crust of things and thrive/While hedgerows still are sunny.   EnLit

The Translated Way.   Franklin Pierce ("F.P.A.") Adams.   So fine and clean and pure.   FiBHP

Translating.   Ruth Whitman.   rose in the morning/full of spermatic words.   VWA

Translation.   Roy Fuller.   Better to abdicate/From a material and spiritual terrain/Fit only for barbarians.   ChMP; NOBE; OxBTC

Translation.   Rika Lesser.   Unbidden, yours; a way to praise.   PoA

Translation.   Anne Spencer.   Stole my morning song!   BANP

A Translation from....   Fred Levinson.   no bow is strung forever   AmPA

A Translation from Petrarch.   John Millington Synge.   standing in her two eyes, and will not call me with a word.   MoBrPo

A Translation from Walter von der Vogelweide.   John Millington Synge.   ..I ask you can that behaviour have a good/end come to it?   MoBrPo

Translation into the Original.   Jack Gilbert.   He comes back through the dark singing/so quietly that you can hear nothing.   NPGG

Translation of Horace, Odes, IV, VII.   Horace.   Nor can the might of Theseus rend/The chains of hell that hold his friend.   LAuP

Translation of Lines by Benerade.   Samuel Johnson.   The near approach a bed may show/Of human bliss to human woe.   CABA

A Translation of the Cywdd to Morvydd....   *Anonymous.*   Behind me, the folly of my flight.   NOEC

The Translation of Verver.   Mei-mei Berssenbrugge.   as if the hue of the next feather were the shedding   LTB

Translations.   Patricia Y. Ikeda.   inventing translations.   BrSi

Translations.   Wing Tek Lum.   The difference/is obvious: the people/disappeared.   BrSi

Translations.   Adrienne Rich.   ignorant of the fact this way of grief/is shared, unnecessary/and political   WPOW

Translations from the Chinese.   Christopher Morley.
I myself am but little known in China.   EvOK
May I blow it out?   EvOK
O Buddha, when will he depart?   EvOK
There may emerge the green and tender shoots/Of two or three bright stanzas.   EvOK

Translations from the English.   George Starbuck.   I bet you somethin to eat.   VGW

Translator to Translated.   Ezra Pound.   Philista's pomp and Art's pomposities!   FaBoEE

Transmigration.   Seth D. Cudjoe.   And in the winged freedom of homing birds.   ACV

The Transparence of November.   Roo Borson.   Whatever small flowers/I may have mentioned in summer:/forget them.   CaPN; PPJ

The Transparent Man.   Anthony Hecht.   And sat here and let me rattle on this way.   FYAP

Transplantitis.   Lester A. Sobel.   With his demand "Lend me your ears."   QQQ

Transport.   Stefan George.   A thunder only of the holy tongue!   LiTW

Transport.   William Meredith.   ...But we shall prosper yet.   WaP

Transubstantiation.   Gary Geddes.   It has become meat.   NOBC

A Trapped Fly.   Robert Herrick.   The Urn was little, but the room/More rich than Cleopatra's Tomb.   WiR

Trapping Fairies in West Virginia.   Gelett Burgess.   I think I never saw fairies skinnier.   FaBoNo

The Trappist Abbey: Matins.   Thomas Merton.   And weep with Peter at the triple cock-crow.   PoPl

Traps.   Mary Carolyn Davies.   It is a trap to catch us two.   HBMV

Trash.   Earl Gene Box.   but I can't change it   LFAC

The Trash Men. Charles Bukowski. REX DISPOSAL CO. NoP

Trastevere. Edwin Denby. Then reading, then sinking into slumber, too does ANYP

Traumerei at Ostendorff's. William Laird. The waiter brought spaghetti; he looked up,/Hemmed, blinked, and fiddled with his coffee-cup. HBMV

The Travail of Passion. William Butler Yeats. Lilies of death-pale hope, roses of passionate dream. TrCP

Travel. Edna St. Vincent Millay. Yet there isn't a train I wouldn't take,/No matter where it's going. InMe; LaNeLa; MoShBr; OBCA; TiPo

Travel. Robert Louis Stevenson. And in a corner find the toys/Of the old Egyptian boys. BrPo; FaBoCh; MoShBr; TiPo

The Travel Bureau. Ruth Comfort Mitchell. The close, sequestered, colorless retreat/Where she was born, where she will always stay. HBMV

Travel Song. Hugo von Hofmannsthal. And the gentle breezes blow. TrJP

The Traveler. *Anonymous.* The last word I heard them say,/Was about Jerusalem, the saints' delightful home. AmFP

The Traveler. David Bottoms. no ticket for the body to travel on. AMV-80

The Traveler. Vachel Lindsay. O traveler, abiding not/Where he pretends to be! MoAmPo

Traveler's Curse after Misdirection. Robert Graves. But always, without fail THE NECK. DBV; FiBHP; HoPM; MoAB; MoBrPo; NLV; TW

Traveler's Rest. Ogden Nash. Because I'm sure it considers every knock a boost. DBV

The Travelers. James Reeves. And in the end account himself a bore. PoL

Travelin' Blues. Blind Willie McTell. I love you Emerald/Tell the world I do/Em BluL

Traveling America. Jan Struther. I shall stay here long. Strangeness, at last, brings peace. AmFN

Traveling Boy. William Meredith. He waits for the new commitments to be made. NoAm

Traveling North. John Woods. every compass is looking at you. PoL

Traveling on My Knees. Sandra Goodwin. I can go and heed Thy call/By traveling on my knees. STF

The Traveling Out. Lucile Adler. All alone as I am alone. IHMS

Traveling Riverside Blues. Robert Johnson. But I'm going back to Friar's Point if I be rocking/to my head BluL

Traveling through Ports That Begin with "M". Christy Sheffield Sanford. ...She adds a spring of/mint and bruises the leaves lightly against the rim of/the glass. APU

Traveling through the Dark. William Stafford. then pushed her over the edge into the river. AmC; BiP; BoAnP; CAPP; CoAP; GrPl; HAP; HeIP; InPK; LCAP; LiTM; NCSH; NMP; NoP; SM; SoSe; WeW

A Traveller. *Anonymous.*
I frightened a little mouse/Under her chair. OxNR
Into the dusk and snow! WGRP

The Traveller. W. H. Auden. As the earth has patience with the life of man. SyP

The Traveller. John Berryman. ...When the train stopped and they knew/The end of their journey, I descended too. VGW

The Traveller. C. J. Dennis. So I rode homeward, free of doubt. NOAV

A Traveller. J. R. Rowland. Sifting through hair as if through sand. CBAP

The Traveller. Allen Tate. Brings him the end he could not find. LiTM

The Traveller Has Regrets. G. S. Fraser. And that the bed was made/And that we could not stay. BSV; OBTV

The Traveller. Oliver Goldsmith.
And scholars, soldiers, kings unhonoured die. NOEC
As different good, by art or nature given,/To different nations makes their blessings even. GN

Traveller's Ditty. Miriam Allen DeFord. Oh, curious fate that makes us live,/But will not teach us how to do it! HBMV

Traveller's Guide to Antarctica. Adrien Stoutenburg. ...where the most re-/cent traveller/has pitched his blind, enduring tent. NYBP

Traveller's Hope. Charles Granville. And joy of sailors in their ships/When home's in sight at last. HBV 1-2; OBVV

The Travellers. Mark A. De Wolfe Howe. Where our blind eyes looked down on him/as dead. AA

Travellers Turning over Borders (parody). Basil Ransome. The view from the rocks burrowed by sensitive tunnels. BXAP

Travelling Backward. Gene Baro. in the crowd that has pressed beyond the gates. NYBP

Travelling Companions. Richard Armour. Reminding him that he is in it. GrPl

Travelling Light. David Wagoner. And knowing it by heart. NPAW

The Travelling Post Office. Andrew Barton ("Banjo") Paterson. My letter chases Conroy's sheep along the Castlereagh. CBAP; NOAV

Travelling Song. Thomas McGrath. How strange now is my face,/And how my life is rent. FAZ

A Travelogue: Clovelly. Carolyn Wells. And up that hill and down that dale/I'll curse Clovelly! InMe

Travelogue for Exiles. Karl Shapiro. The earth is taken: this is not your home. AnFE; MoAmPo; TrJP

Travels With the Band-Aid Army. Lance Henson. limp throatless words/dancing in shadows of snow VoR

Traverse City Zoo. Jim Harrison. ...He grew smaller and sputtered into sleep. BoAnP

Travis, the Kid Was All Heart. Terry Stokes. lying on her back waiting, fuck yes, waiting. AmPA

Tray. Robert Browning. How brain secretes dog's soul, we'll see! FM

The Tray. Thomas Cole. ...holds a season/Constant, green and perfect. NePoAm

Tray's Epitaph. Peter Pindar. Blush, Christians, if you can, and copy Tray. GoTF; TreFS

Treason. Lora Dunetz. should suddenly see a chicken devouring a worm.... NePoAm

Treason of Sand. Hemda Roth. in the quiet of your hands,/sparks of compassion,/in the stream, at night. VWA

Treason's Last Device. Edmund Clarence Stedman. But you–do you hear it, Yankee boys? PAH

Treasure. Elizabeth-Ellen Long. In pocket or by hand! BiCB

Treasure. Lucilius [(or Lucillius[). The treasure is not thine, but theirs. AWP; LiTW

A Treasure. Reed Whittemore. ...another treasure/For later scholars on generous grants to discover. NePoEA

Treasure Boat. Seiki Fujino. This is the ship of treasure,/laden with gold, silver, and jade. HW

Treasure Hunt. Robert Penn Warren. ...But hurry, for/The terror is, all promises are kept./Even happiness. NoP

Treasures. Mary Dixon Thayer. I will give him diamonds instead. SoPo

Treasures. Claire Richcreek Thomas. And I thrilled as I thought of the fun and the joy such/trivial things could give to a boy. PoToHe

Treat the Woman Tenderly, Tenderly. *Anonymous.* Let love be kind, or else ye'll break her. PoL

A Treatie of Human Learning. Fulke, Lord Brooke Greville. By which she yet must raise herself again,/Ere she can judge all other knowledge vain. FCP

Treaties. Archie Randolph Ammons. the black creek and/the small leaf slips in. HaCAP

Treaty-Trip from Shulus Reservation. Patrick Lane. to thump/on the flat red wall. NeAC

Trebetherick. Sir John Betjeman. Give to our children all the happy days you gave/To Ralph, Vasey, Alastair, Biddy, John and me. CMoP; EvOK; ExPo

The Tree. Dorothy Auchterlonie. Eve stretched her hand and plucked the fruit. NOAV

The Tree. Bjornstjerne Bjornson. Said the tree, while he bent down his laden boughs/low. OHIP; PoSC

The Tree. Ilya Ehrenburg. You died as gravely as a man. TrJP

The Tree. Alfred Kreymborg. How many monkeys are you? HBMV; PoPl

Tree. Harold LaMont Otey. the tree struggles to exist. LFAC

The Tree. Ezra Pound. And many a new thing understood/That was rank folly to my head before. AnFE; APA; CMoP; InPo

The Tree. Joel Sloman. Where is that voice coming from? VGW

The Tree. Jones Very. On stars that brighter beam when most we need their love. AnNE; GN; HBV 1-2; OHIP; PoSC

Tree. Pat Wilson. And made their huts and houses in the fir. AnNZ

The Tree. Anne Finch, Countess of Winchilsea. And some bright hearth be made thy urn. CoBE; OBEC

The Tree and the Lady. Thomas Hardy. Gone is she, scorning my bough! MoAB; MoBrPo

Tree at My Window. Robert Frost. Your head so much concerned with outer,/Mine with inner, weather. AnNE; BLPL; BoLiVe; BoNaP; FaBoBe; MoAB; MoAmPo; MoVE; NePA; NoAm; OxBA; TAP; TrGrPo

Tree Birthdays. Mary Carolyn Davies. Perhaps you have a birthday every week! BiCB; OHIP

Tree-Building. Franklin Cable. For him who hears, in soundless strains/The music of intangible things. PGD

A Tree Design. Arna Bontemps. A tree is something in me,/Very still and lonely now. CDC

Tree Feelings. Charlotte Perkins Stetson Gilman. And all those fringy leaves that flutter so. PGD

Tree Felling. George Woodcock. And its multitudinous summer under the whispering corn. NeBP

Tree Ferns. Stanley Plumly. Or break off what you can and cut it clean. SM

Tree in December. Melville Cane. The inner cry: "This is not death"? MoAmPo

The Tree in Pamela's Garden. Edwin Arlington Robinson. Could they have seen that she had overheard. MoLP

And may your happier wits grow lowd with fame/As you (my best of friends!) preserve my name. OBVE

But falsely called Euxine–its meaning is "hospitable"–/holds me. NAs

Which I believe (though fatall) will afford/An Endless name unto their ruin'd Lord. OBVE

Tristram and Isolt. Don (Donald Robert Marquis) Marquis. ...Death can never get true lovers' goats! HBMV

Tristram of Lyonesse. Algernon Charles Swinburne.
...and the land by Tristram's grace was free. WHA
Across the broad-backed rollers in to shore. GN

Tristram's End. Laurence Binyon. And the hand that lies in thine is not my hand. EnLit; OBMV

The Triumph. Sidney Lanier. God's, East–mine, West: good friends,/ behold my Land! PAH

Triumph. John Crowe Ransom. It is so far from these my Roman regions! HBMV

Triumph. L. D. Stearns. Grave is conquered! Christ is King! BLRP

A triumph may be of several kinds. Emily Dickinson. Acquitted from that naked bar,/Jehovah's countenance! NePA

Triumph of Bacchus and Ariadne. Lorenzo de Medici. ...How fair is youth that flies so fast! CTC

The Triumph of Beautie Song (excerpt). James Shirley. There is no hope to take it in. ErPo

The Triumph of Charis. Ben Jonson. O so white! O so soft! O so sweet is she! ELP; ExPo; GoBC; LiTB; LoBV; NOBE; NoP; PAI; PG; PoPle; SeCeV; WHA

The Triumph of Chastity. Barbara Howes. Each stares at his own self-love. NePoAm-2

The Triumph of Death. Barbara Howes. As we approach a new plateau of love. MoAmPo; NePoAm-2

The Triumph of Doubt. John Peale Bishop. That turns slowly, triumphantly, swiftly to God. EaLo

The Triumph of Forgotten Things. Edith Matilda Thomas. As, in the stranger's land, their native speech/Returns to dying lips! HBV 1-2

Triumph of His Grace. Charles Wesley. His blood availed for me. BePJ

The Triumph of Infidelity. Timothy Dwight. The oyster's churchyard, and the capon's tomb. NOCV

Triumph of Love. John Hall Wheelock. Whether he would or no, with love! MoAmPo

Triumph of Sensibility. Sylvia Townsend Warner. Woman, let me learn of you. MoAB; MoBrPo

The Triumph of the Whale. Charles Lamb. This should be the Prince of Whales. ImOP; OBRV

The Triumph of Time. Algernon Charles Swinburne.
From the first thou wert; in the end thou/art. GTBS; HBV 1-2; OAEP
I shall hate sweet music my whole life long. ViBoPo
If I cry to you then, will you hear or know? GTBS; MaVP; VLP
A vein in the heart of the streams of the sea. BoLiVe; TrGrPo

Triumphal March. Thomas Stearns Eliot. Et les soldats faisaient la haie? ILS LA FAISAIENT. MBW 1-2; OBWP

Triumphal Ode MCMXXXIX. George Barker. Further than New Zealand or a nebula. LiTB; WaP

Triumphalis. Bliss Carman. Never surrender! HBMV; PG

The Triumphs of Owen. Thomas Gray. Agony, that pants for breath,/Despair and honourable Death. CEP; PoEL 1-5

The Triumphs of Thy Conquering Power. William Hiley Bathurst. And fit us, by Thy grace, to share/The triumphs of Thy conquering power. BePJ

Trivial, Vulgar, and Exalted: 19. J. V. Cunningham. On a long shot at long odds, a black mare/By Hatred out of Envy by Despair. QFR

A Triviality. Waring Cuney. Not to dance with her/Was a trivial thing. CDC

Troas, II: Chorus (latter end). Seneca (Lucius Annaeus Seneca). Dreams, Whimseys, and no more. OBVE

Troia Fuit. Reginald Wright Kauffman. The world was wide and life was fair. HBV 1-2

The Troika. Louis Simpson. and the white bird, enchanted,/is flying through the world, across the sea. NoAm; NOBA

Troilus and Cressida. Aubrey Thomas De Vere. Which ratifies the deed that you have done/With plain approval. Other plea seek none. IrPN

Troilus and Cressida. John Dryden.
And Homer's angry Ghost repine in vain. SeCV 1-2
When we hope, when we hope to be happy again. NoP

Troilus and Cressida. William Shakespeare.
And give to dust that is a little gilt/More laud than gilt o'er-dusted. LiTB
The enterprise is sick. ImOP
For sluttish spoils of opportunity/And daughters of the game. TrGrPo
...grows to an envious fever/Of pale and bloodless emulation. NIP
Her bed is India; there she lies, a pearl. GBL

Troilus and Criseyde. Geoffrey Chaucer.
And farewel shrine of which the saint is oute!' OxBM
And kis the steppes where as thou seest pace/Virgile, Ovide, Omer, Lucan, and Stace. OxBM

and wex so mat, that joie nor penaunce/He feleth non, but lith forth in a traunce. LoBV

For love of maide and moder thyn benigne! ExPo; OxBM

My ship and me Caribdid wol devoure. DiPo

That to hirself she sayde: "Who yaf me drinke?" OxBM

The Trojan Horse. William, of Hawthornden Drummond. ...I captive raz'd a town. EyDe

The Trojan Women: Cassandra's Epithalamium. Euripides. Having destroyed the House of Atreus which has ruined/us utterly. HW

Troll Chanting. Anselm Hollo. I will hear/moom moom/moom moom/moom moom/moom WSC

The Troll's Nosegay. Robert Graves. Even yet, perhaps, a trifle piqued–who knows? PoCh

Troll the Bowl! Thomas Dekker. Nor help good hearts in need. ElL

Trombone Solo. Stoddard King. Strut your stuff, people–/I/won't/care! NLV

A Troop of the Guard. Hermann Hagedorn. On to the walls, and over! HBV 1-2; OHIP

Troop Train. Karl Shapiro. --Nightfall of nations brilliant after war. OxBA; WaaP; WaP

The Trooper and Maid. Anonymous. For the Highland hills are ill to climb,/And the bluidy swords woud fear ye. BaBo

Trooper and Maid, I. Anonymous. "When gray goose quills turn to silver pins, oh then, my dear, we'll marry." AmFP

Trooper and Maid, II. Anonymous. She cried out with a thrilling cry:/"O Lord, O Lord, I'm ruined." AmFP

The Trooper and the Maid. Anonymous. An' I'll har a' your ribbons reel/In the morn ere I leave ye. FSW

The Trooper's Horse. Anonymous. "He'll raise up his head and come knock at the door." OBET

The Troops. Siegfried Sassoon. The legions who have suffered and are dust. CMoP

Troopship for France, War II. George Bogin. of the olive drab dreamers/over the white wake. FAZ

Troopship in the Tropics. Alun Lewis. Time hardens. But the bitter Now grows gracious. WaP

The Trophy. Edwin Muir. Irreconcilables, their treaty signed. LiTM

Tropic Rain. Robert Louis Stevenson. And out of the cloud that smites, beneficent rivers of rain. OBTV

A Tropical Morning at Sea. Edward Rowland Sill. Blow, salt wind from the north upstarting,/Scatter such dreams away! EtS

Tropical Towns. Salomon de la Selva. ...to where/the lonely green trees and the white graves are. HBV 1-2

Tropical Weather. Epes Sargent. All, all is fair; and gazing round, we feel/Over the yielding sense the torrid languor steal. EtS

Tropics. Ellen Bryant Voigt. before the heavy drop/of the apples. SM

The Tropics in New York. Claude McKay. I turned aside and bowed my head and wept. AmNP; GoSl; NoAm; PoBA; PoNe; TTY

Tropisms on John Berryman. Gerald Vizenor. counting the common strokes of the empty swings VoR

The Trosachs. William Wordsworth. Lulling the year, with all its cares, to rest! EnLi 1-2; GTBS; HBV 1-2; OBEV; OBRV; SeCePo

Trot along Pony. Dorothy and Marion Edey Grider. So turn again, pony,/Turn again home. SoPo; TiPo

A Trot, and a Canter, a Gallop, and Over. Anonymous. Out of the saddle, and roll in the clover. OxNR

Trot, Trot! Mary Frances Butts. She buys a cotton gown. HBV 1-2; HBVY

Troubador. J. Edgar Simmons. He dredged forth the break-away tunes/Green from winter's bayous. TAT

Troubadour Alba. Anonymous. Alas! Alas! the dawn–it comes too soon! EnLi 1-2

The Troubadour of God. Charles Wharton Stork. And it fills my heart with song. WGRP

Troubadour Song. Bernard of Ventadour Forgive, if I have tarried long. EnLi 1-2

Troubadours. Arthur Davison Ficke. Here in the sun I put apart from me/Cassandra, Helen, and Persephone. HBMV

Trouble. Philip Brasfield. and tell him, "It'll be alright–/it'll be alright tomorrow..." LFAC

Trouble. David Keppel. May be nothing but a cipher/With its rim rubbed out. FaFP; FPL; GoTF; PoLf; TreF; WBLP

Trouble. James Wright. All that time she thought she was nothing/But skin and bones. FF

Trouble in the "Amen Corner." Thomas Chalmers Harbaugh. Where there are no church committees and no fashionable choirs! BLPA

Trouble Not the Maiden's Soul. Johan Ludvig Runeberg. For it never will be clear,/Never mirror heaven again.' LiTW

Trouble-Shooting. William Stafford. and the little brown bird steadfastly wanders on/pulling what counts wherever it goes. AMV-80

Trouble, Trouble. Anonymous. Well, I don't b'lieve I'd 'a' been here, wringin' my hand an' cryin'./Whoa dere! OuSiCo

The Trouble with Angels.   Ken Norris.   The trouble with angels is that the world/Has provided no place for them.   CaPN

The Trouble with Truck Drivers.   Margot Treitel.   as if he were a truckdriver, tree climber,/railroad mender, dealer in hard love.   AmC

Troubled Jesus.   Waring Cuney.   Po', good Jesus.   BANP; GoSl

The Troubled Soldier.   Anonymous.   I am a troubled soldier, no friend and no home.   AS

Troubled Woman.   Langston Hughes.   Like a/Wind-blown autumn flower/That never lifts its head/Again.   CTBA; PCP

Troubles of the Day.   William Barnes.   Come not along my way. I seek my rest.   GTBS-P

Trousers of Wind.   Anonymous.   Why am I in love with such a man as he?   PBA; TTY

Trout.   Seamus Heaney.   A volley of cold blood/ramrodding the current.   CIP

Trout.   Norman Hindley.   Warming their speckling bellies/On the turning, star-charged bottom.   WOLT

The Trout.   Daryl Hine.   I negotiate the steps of paradise/Leaping to measures that I cannot hear.   CoAP

The Trout.   John Montague.   ...To this day I can/Taste his terror on my hands.   BoAnP; FaBoIP; IPY; NMP

Trout Fisher.   George Mackay Brown.   And I betray the loch for a white coin.'   OxBC

Trout Fishing: A Sign.   Richard Behm.   then flap at last/in black circles sunward.   WOLT

Trout Fishing in Virginia.   Michael Beirne McMahon.   "Cash er charge?"   AMV-80

Trouvaille.   Richard Murphy.   ...a freak tide raised/The feathered stick she took to lure me home.   CIP; IPY

Troy.   Robin Flower.   The lovely vision of naked Helen.   SeCePo

Troy.   Edwin Muir.   Asking: "Where is the treasure?" till he died.   CMoP

Troy Town.   Dante Gabriel Rossetti.   (O Troy's down,/Tall Troy's on fire!)   MaVP

Troynovant.   Thomas Dekker.   For Jove dwells here: And 'tis no pity,/If Troynovant be now no more a City.   LoBV; OBSC

The Truant.   Edwin John Pratt.   No! by the Rood, we will not join your ballet.   NoAm; NOBC; NoP; OBCV

The Truants.   Walter De la Mare.   Magic hath stolen away.   MoBrPo

Truck Drivers.   Terri Haag.   Sad-eyed conquerors,/drink your coffee,/think of home.   CTBA

The Trucker.   Will Dyson.   ...and the fellow is a fool/Who cannot find some pleasure down below.   NOAV

A Trucker.   Thom Gunn.   a bright fountain of red eyes/tinkling sightless to the road.   PCP

Trudge, Body.   Robert Graves.   Trudge, body.   MoAB

A True Account of Talking to the Sun at Fire Island.   Frank O'Hara.   Darkly he rose, and then I slept.   ANYP; HaCAP; NNaP; SOTW

A True and Faithful Inventory of the Goods Belonging to Dr Swift...   Jonathan Swift.   Why not, as well as doctor Swift?   FaBoUs

True and False.   Isabella Valancy Crawford.   He sank in those white arms of guile/To seek the false moon in the sea.   PeCV

True and Joyful News.   Anonymous.   They, self-thought saints, a dissolution dread.   APAS

The True Apostolate.   Ruby T. Weyburn.   Till I fain would arise and follow, not them, not them,–/but their Lord!   BLRP

The True Aristocrat.   W. Stewart.   But win, as once their fathers won,/The laurel wreath of fame.   WBLP

The True Ballad of the Great Race to Gilmore City.   Phil Hey.   ...never be another like that great race between Ralph/and Peggy   Psk

True Beauty.   Francis Beaumont.   Happy he can compass it!   EiL; HBV 1-2

The True-Born Englishman.   Daniel Defoe.
And Lords whose parents the Lord knows who.   CEP; OBSV
For fame of families is all a cheat,/'Tis personal virtue only makes us great.   OBSV
Hard to be pleased at all, and never long.   OBSV
Will purge good manners and religion out.   OBSV

True Brotherhood.   Ella Wheeler Wilcox.   Rise to the meaning of True Brotherhood.   WBLP

A True Cat.   Anna Seward.   Qu-ow wow, quall, wawl, moon.   PCat

True Child.   Marion Hodge.   Go, True Child, heart of song, sing out, sing out!   AMV-81

The True Christmas.   Henry Vaughan.   And then you keep your Christmas right.   SBVL

A True Confession.   Jon Stallworthy.   ...But now and then our lies/betray us into truth.   NoAm

The True Confession of George Barker.   George Barker.
God Almighty sees we keep/Religiously to one another?   ErPo
I sent a letter to my love/On a sheet of stone.   FaBoTw

True Confessional.   Lawrence Ferlinghetti.   wherein I read/the poem that never ends.   NAs

The True Encounter.   Edna St. Vincent Millay.   I met the wolf alone/And was devoured in peace.   OBSP

True Enough: To the Physicist (1820).   Johann Wolfgang von Goethe.   It's yourself you should scrutinize to see/Whether you're center or periphery.   SUW

The True Facts of the Case.   Anthony Euwer.   His reply was the same as before.   OBAL

True Freedom.   Charles Mackay.   We join the cry "Fraternity!" We keep the march of Time.   PGD

True Happiness.   Morris Talpalar.   And neither wish nor fear to die.   PoToHe

The True Heaven.   Paul Hamilton Hayes.   But one unending NOW, to be/A boundless circle around us cast!   WGRP

A True Hymn.   George Herbert.   "O could I love!" and stops, God writeth "Loved."   InvP; NOCV; OxBoCh

The True Import of Present Dialogue: Black vs. Negro.   Nikki Giovanni.   Learn to be Black men   BPo; PoBA

The True Knight.   Stephen Hawes.
But for a truth, or for the common's sake.   AnEnPo; OBEV; TrGrPo
In stable love fixt, and not variant.   ACP

The True Knight.   Ella Wheeler Wilcox.   Give me, I say, our own American.   PeD

True Knowledge.   Panatattu.   An image made of lime or brass/That's cleaned with tamarind.   WGRP

True Love.   Anonymous.   The thinner she, the closer I/Can press against her heart.   UnTE

True Love.   Phoebe Cary.   And lo! I worship at his feet!   PoToHe

True Love.   Waring Cuney.   Her love is true I know.   CDC

True Love.   Joe Johnson.   I held Harriet until my lips burned   CNA

True Love.   James Russell Lowell.   Or the sweet coming of the evening star.   LiTL

True Love.   Percy Bysshe Shelley.   Tills for the promise of a later birth/The wilderness of this Elysian earth.   LoBV

A True Love Ditty.   Thomas Middleton.   That word begins that ends a true love ditty.   EiL

The True Lover.   Alfred Edward Housman.   The still air of the speechless night,/When lovers crown their vows.   ATP; BoLiVe; LiTL

The True Lover's Farewell.   Anonymous.   I'll love you till the day I die,/And then you know I'm done.   AS

The True Lovers Bold.   Anonymous.   Stay at home when the stormy winds do blow.   AmFP

A True Maid.   Matthew Prior.   Rose, were you not extremely sick?   ALV; FaBoCo; FaBoEE; NIP; NOEC; PV

The True Martyr.   Thomas Wade.   Perfect amid the flames, like Cranmer's heart.   OBVV

True Night.   Rene Char.   And we shall know it's true/When the glass goes black.   PoPl

The True Paddy's Song.   Anonymous.   Mushadoo, a-daddy doo-a-dum.   OuSiCo

A True Picture Restored.   Vernon Watkins.   Hard it must be, beyond this day,/For even the grass to rest.   NoAm

True Rest.   Johann Wolfgang von Goethe.   'Tis onward, unswerving,/And this is true rest.   TRV; WBLP

True Riches.   Bessie June Martin.   There are riches far greater/Than his he can know!   STF

True Riches.   Isaac Watts.   If her inward Worth were known/She might ever live alone.   OBEC

The True Romance.   Herbert Jones.   Far better to remember, in her stead,/Your fifteen years.   HBMV

True Son of God, Eternal Light.   P. J. Cormican.   To Father, Son, and Holy Ghost.   AII

A True Story.   Marvin Bell.   ...And so too everyone/who, when in Rome,/will do what the Romans do.   SV

The True Story of Mary and Her Little Lamb.   Anonymous.   And it went very well!   DBV

The True Story of Snow White.   Bruce Bennett.   To lie forever in unlovely sleep/Which not a prince on earth has power to break.   SM

The True, the Good and the Beautiful.   Delmore Schwartz.   Now in the last estrangement judge the truth!   MiAP

True to a Dream.   Donald Petersen.   He relinquished his hold/At the faraway call/Of a downstairs voice.   NePoEA-2

True to the Best.   Benjamin Keech.   We meet disloyal usage from a friend?   PoToHe

True Vine.   Elinor Wylie.   The earth again with honey sweet and salty.   AnFE; APA; LiTA

The True Weather for Women.   Louis Simpson.   How punctual death is, or else how slow.   NePoAm

True Woman.   Dante Gabriel Rossetti.   This test for love:–in every kiss sealed fast/To feel the first kiss and forbode the last.   MaVP

A Trueblue Gentleman.   Kenneth Patchen.   There's your fried egg   SO

Truelove.   Anonymous.   Sweetest mouth red as the rose.   AWP

A Truelove. Nicholas Grimald. With her so I may live and die, my weal cannot be told. OBSC

The Truest Poetry Is the Most Feigning; or, Ars Poetica for Hard Times. W. H. Auden. Like orthodoxy, is a reticence. NYBP

The Truisms. Louis MacNeice. And a tall tree sprouted from his father's grave. FaBoIP; NOBE; OBSV

Truly Great. William Henry Davies. Show me a man more great. HBV 1-2; OBMV; OBVV

The Trumpet. Ilya Ehrenburg. I glorify the victory/Of those by whom I was subdued? TrJP

The Trumpet. Edward ("Edward Eastaway") Thomas. Arise, arise! HBMV; MMM; MoBrPo; OHIP

Trumpet and Flute. Gunnar Hernaes. Then the hunger wakens in me–/For the glittering sensations of the night! LiTW

The Trumpet: Grass on the Cliff. Robinson Jeffers. ...and suck/The arteries and walk in triumph on the faces. PoA

The Trumpet of Liberty. John Taylor. Fall, tyrants, fall! NOEC

Trumpet Player. Langston Hughes. Trouble/Mellows to a golden note. TTY

The Trumpet Shall Sound. John V. Hicks. Make your own music. AMV-81

The Trumpet-Vine Arbour. Amy Lowell. And the smoke-tree puffs dun blossoms into/the blue air. MAPA

Trumpet Voluntary. Paul Hoover. It's the president of the country, scowling. APU

The Trumpeter. Anonymous. But whenever she goes to the play,/She never sits near to the trumpeter. CoMu

The Trumpeter of Fyvie. Anonymous. I come, my bonnie Annie! OxBB

The Truro Bear. Mary Oliver. ...and when has happiness ever/required much evidence to begin/its leaf-green breathing? SoSe

Trus' an' Smile. B.Y. Williams. Honey, trus' de Lawd a bit, an' doan' fohgit to smile! BLRP

Trust. Lizette Woodworth Reese. I die that after I may grow/As tall, as sweet again. AA

Trust and Obedience. Anonymous. The seeds of life and everlasting good. BLRP

Trust Him. Anonymous. And the trusting days are past. STF

Trust in Jesus. Josiah Conder. And Jesus is forever mine! BePJ

Trust in Me. Anonymous. A pillar of fire shall light the way/While you journey heavenward. AH

Trust in Women. Anonymous. Then put women in trust and confidence. NA

Trust Not the Treason. Edmund Spenser. O mighty charm! which makes men love theyr bane,/And thinck they dy with pleasure, live with payne. BoLiVe

Trust Only Yourself. Anonymous. Trust to thyselfe, and lerne to be wise. MeEL

A Trust-Song. Eben E. Rexford. Trust and let the sunshine of God's love shine through/Every overhanging cloud that darkens over you BLRP

Trust the Form of Airy Things. Henry Harington. Truth in woman, faith in men! LO

Trust the Great Artist. Thomas Curtis Clark. Trust the Great Artist, He/Who made the earth and sea. WBLP

Trust Thou Thy Love. John Ruskin. Fail, Sun and Breath!–yet, for thy peace, She shall endure. OBEV; OBVV

Trusting Jesus. Grace B. Renfrow. Let praise to Him arise. BePJ

Truth. Anonymous. He must him seeken esilye/In the bosom of Marye,/For ther he is, forsoothe, pardee! OxBM

Truth. Geoffrey Chaucer. And Trouthe shal delivere, it is no drede. AWP; CBEP; MyFE; NoP; OAEL 1-2; OxBM

Truth. William Cowper. That man is dead in sin, and life a gift.' NOCV

The Truth. William Henry Davies. The last strong rival for his food. FaBoTw

Truth. John Donne. Are like the sun, dazzling, yet plain to all eyes. SeCePo

The Truth. Randall Jarrell. She put her arms around me and we cried. OxBC

The Truth. Ted Joans. All god's SPADES got SHADES TTY

Truth. Ben Jonson. As gives a power to faith to tread/All falsehood under feet. PG

The Truth. Archibald Lampman. And thou shalt see thy thought another way. CaP

Truth. Cecil Francis Lloyd. For life, I give you love, that fears no death. CaP

Truth. John Masefield. The ship my striving made/May see night fade. WGRP

Truth. Claude McKay. Upon my knees, Oh Lord, for Truth I plead. BPo

A Truth... Noah Mitchell. victims/whom are angels/in disguise/questioning/their duties. LFAC

Truth. Howard Nemerov. But thought the deepening blue thought of the fly. HoPM; LiTM; MoVE

Truth. Jessica Nelson North. Like Chicken Little's, do not tumble down/And crash upon his crown. HBVY

Truth. Coventry Patmore. When none cares whether it prevail or not. TrGrPo

Truth. George William Russell. The fountain unbroken. AnIL; GTBS; MoBrPo

Truth. Susan Fromberg Schaeffer. Tree leaves clatter masses/For leaves. IHMS

The Truth about B. F. Albert Stillman. So Benjamin Franklin went to France. InMe

The Truth about Horace. Eugene Field. And Maecenas paid the freight! InMe

The Truth about My Sister and Me. Anita Endrezze Probst. I never saw a woman die/from living. CDW

Truth Brought to Light; or, Murder Will Out. Stephen College. There's nothing left but Lord, have mercy on us! APAS

Truth Doth Truth Deserve. Sir Philip Sidney. This done, thou hast no more, but leave the rest/To virtue, fortune, time, and woman's breast. HBV 1-2; LiTL

The Truth from Above. Anonymous. And if you want to know the way,/Be pleased to hear what He did say. OBET

Truth Has Perished. Ulma Seligman. Lord god, what will become of us! TrJP

Truth in Poetry. George Crabbe. Whose outward splendour is but folly's dress,/Exposing most, when most it gilds distress. OBEC; SeCePo

Truth Is a Native, Naked Beauty. Roger Williams. Repentance Teares may wash of all such Formes. SCAP

Truth is as old as god. Emily Dickinson. A lifeless Deity. MoAmPo

The Truth Is Blind. David Gascoyne. A sharp taste in the mouth. EAS

The Truth Is Quite Messy. William J. Harris. a wind blown room. BOLo

Truth Kills Everybody. Ted Hughes. He was blasted to nothing. PAI

The Truth Like the Belly of a Woman Turning. Gary Snyder. live oak and madrone. NNaP

The Truth Made Breakfast. Jeffrey Miller. ...We then commenced/to display our talent,/off into the astonished wild blue yonder. APU

Truth Never Dies. Anonymous. Truth never dies. WBLP

Truth's Complaint over England. Thomas Lodge. You banished me, before I fled from you. ACP

The Truth the Dead Know. Anne Sexton. ...They refuse/to be blessed, throat, eye and knucklebone. MoAmPo; NePoEA-2; NIP; NoAm; PBWP; TAP

Truth, the Invincible. William Cullen Bryant. But Error, wounded, writhes with pain,/And dies among his worshippers. GoTF; TreF

Truxton's Victory. Anonymous. To fight, and to conquer, to conquer or die. PAH

Try (parody). Philip Appleman. Tomorrow/I shall see it differently. BXAP

Try Smiling. Anonymous. The, it sort o' rests your face–/Just smiling. BLPA; FaFP; WBLP

Try the Uplook. Anonymous. His light will illumine the way. BLRP

Try This Once. Anonymous. When you get a lemon/Just make some lemonade. WBLP

Try Tropic. Genevieve Taggard. And not kill you. MoAmPo

Try, Try Again. Anonymous. Try, try again. FaFP; GoTF; TreF

Trying. Leonard Nathan. No one but him can see the good he's done. Str

Trying to Believe. Linda Gregg. ...Sit alone looking down at/evening on the ocean, drinking wine or not. NPGG

Trying to Sleep. Ralph Pomeroy. the cut of the moon/in my mind. ELU

Trying to Stay. Diana Chang. both of us trying to stay well/who move and crave. PoDr

Trying to Talk with a Man. Adrienne Rich. as if we were testing anything else. HaCAP; NIP

A Tryptych for Jan Bockelson. John Oliver Simon. the masked men are a spangle of leaves in the/suns crown NeAC

Tryst. Derek Butler. Let us lay down on it and rest. LFAC

The Tryst. Edward Valpy Knox. Trak-tak!...I must bury you, Kate my dear;/My bullet has gone through your head. CenHV

Tryst. Eve Merriam. I don't want/more responsibility. NMM

The Tryst. Christopher Morley. When I see Emma smiling/And twirling through the door! HBMV

A Tryst. Louise Chandler Moulton. When I shall pass the sundering bar/Our souls must still be wed. HBV 1-2

The Tryst. William Soutar. And wi' her a' my simmer days/Like they had never been. BoLoP; BSV; EBEV; GoTS; NeBP; OxBS

The Tryst. John Banister Tabb. And neither suspected a mutual love/Till they met in a Brunswick stew. OBAL

The Tryst after Death. Anonymous. Hush, woman, do not speak to me! LiTW

A Tryst in Brobdingnag. Adrienne Rich. Held Ministers in my palm and, laughing, blew/Confusion on the fleets of Blefuscu! NYBP

The Turncoat. LeRoi (Imamu Amiri Baraka) Jones. I become them, sometimes. Pure flight. Pure fantasy. Lean. NeAP

Turner's Camp on the Chippewa. *Anonymous.* They commenced to break their rollways and I knew it must be Spring. AmFP

Turner's Sunrise. Helen Bevington. "But," answered Turner, "don't you wish you could?" EyDe

Turners Dish of Lentten Stuffe. William Price Turner. And Turners turnd a gallant man,/at making of a Ballet. CoMu

Turning. Robert Finch. And wondered now whether to turn again. OBCV

The Turning. Philip Levine. The first Jew was God; the second/Denied him; I am alive. VGW

The Turning. Philip Murray. In that one moment I would have caught/ and held. NePoAm

Turning away from Lies. Robert Bly. The thieves are crying in the wild asparagus. LCAP

Turning Fifty. Judith Wright. to this new sun. NAs

The Turning of the Leaves. Vernon Watkins. Look up now, softly: break it with your eyes. NeBP

Turning on Daytime TV. Alex Kuo. we'll both stand in line/counting the coyotes howling in the hills/mountains apart. APU

Turning Point. W. L. Holshouser. a point on fire/with the friction of turning. AMV-81

Turning Thirty. W. D. Ehrhart. and when I will be old enough/to know. AMV-81

The Turnip Vender. *Anonymous.* Have a turnip than his father. OxNR

The Turnstile. William Barnes. His last white earms, an' they stood still. CH; NOBV; OBVV

Turris Eburnea. *Anonymous.* ...part/With earth for heaven, and climb, and reach God's feet. GoBC

The Turtle. *Anonymous.* For you are a cross/Of the old sea-hoss/And a regular terror-pin. PAH

Turtle. Robert Lowell. as it claws away pieces of my flesh/to make me small enough to swallow. LCAP

The Turtle. Ogden Nash. I think it clever of the turtle/In such a fix to be so fertile. FaFP; FiBHP; FPL; NePA; NIP; NoP; OBAL; SoSe; TAP

The Turtle and the Flamingo. James Thomas Fields. The green, but a very mock-turtle! HBV 1-2

The Turtle and the Sparrow (excerpt). Matthew Prior. Columbo and Adonis died. PBBP

Turtle Dove. *Anonymous.*
Or I a traitor turn. FSW
Till all my days are done!' OxBoLi

The Turtle Dove. Geoffrey Hill. As his lithe, fathoming heart absorbed and buried. FaBoTw; NePoEA

The Turtle-Doves' Nest. *Anonymous.* And they played together kindly/In the dark pine-tree. HBVY

Turtle Lake. Richard Hugo. ...the warm way/mountains call us citizens in debt. NPAW

Turtle Mountain Reservation. Louise Erdrich. Hands of earth, of this clay/ I'm also made from. TWSS

The Turtle's Belly. Ellen Pearce. He was nothing he had ever been and existed not/knowing how to do so. IHMS

The Turtle's Song. *Anonymous.* But you'd oughter git a liddle mo' pull in de head. BPo

Turtle Soup. Lewis (Charles Lutwidge Dodgson) Carroll. Beautiful, beauti-FUL SOUP! BrR; FaBoNo; InMe; NLV

The Turtle Thus with Plaintive Crying. John Gay. Paired in death, as paired in love. PBBP

Turvey Top. *Anonymous.* Is strangely like the folk in my dream,/And would flourish in Turvey Top. NA

Tuscaloosa Sam. Robert Henry Newell. Some whiskers, and four eyes! OBAL

Tuskegee. Leslie Pinckney Hill. The South will wear eternally a stain. BANP; PoNe

The Tusks of Blood. Samuel Greenberg. You, endless wretch of silver! MoPo

Tuslag. T. A. ("Vagaland") Robertson. Da colour an scent o a million flooers. OxBS

Tutankhamen. William Dickey. Steal what you want,/not what the catalogue/says you ought to. Psk

The Tutelage. Robert Mowry Bell. "Life ruled by Love nor dies nor dissi-/pates." AA

Tutivillus, the Devil. *Anonymous.* God bring us all to his in,/"Amen, amen,' dicentes. EBEV; MeEL

The Tutor. Carolyn Wells. Or to tutor two tooters to toot? MoShBr

Tutor's Dignity. Lewis (Charles Lutwidge Dodgson) Carroll. And so the lecture proceeds. FaBoNo

Tutto e Sciolto. James Joyce. When the dear love she yielded with a sigh/ Was all but thine? OBMV; OxBI

TV. John Forbes. green mould on its hand-made leather casing CBAP

TV Blooper Spotter. Jack Skelley. ...He takes/the old man's detonation device. He has a big plan. APU

Twa Bonny Lads. Robert Burns. So Jockie had siller, and Sandy had pleasure. OBSP

The Twa Books. Allan Ramsay. I'll thank the Gods for my Reward,/And smile at ilka Fop. OxBS

The Twa Corbies. *Anonymous.* O'er his white banes when they are bare,/ The wind sall blaw for evermair. AWP; BoLiVe; BSV; ELP; EnL; ESPB; ExPo; FaBoBa; FaBoCh; GoTS; GTBS; GTBS-P; HAP; HBV 1-2; InPK; InPo; LiTL; LoGBV; NoP; OBEV; OxBS; PBBP; PoPle; PPP; SeCePo; SeCeV; StPo; UnPo

The Twa Dogs. Robert Burns. An' each took aff his several way,/Resolv'd to meet some ither day. CABL; CEP

The Twa Knights. *Anonymous.* And a' the ladies who heard o it/Said she was a wise woman. ESPB

The Twa Magicians. *Anonymous.* The rusty smith her leman was,/For a' her muckle pride. BaBo; ESPB; GBP; OxBB

The Twa Mariit Wemen and the Wedo. William Dunbar. And with my pen did report their pastance most merry. BSV

The Twa Sisters of Binnorie. *Anonymous.* Bonny St. Johnstone stands on Tay. EnSB

'Twas an evening in November. *Anonymous.* At that the pig got up and walked away! CenHV

'Twas at the Matin Hour. *Anonymous.* And so lie down in peace. OHIP

'Twas Ever Thus. Henry Sambrooke Leigh. I would he were a young gazelle. FaBoCo; FaBoPa; HBV 1-2; SpRo

'Twas Ever Thus (parody). *Anonymous.* Invested money in a pet/That didn't misconduct itself. BXAP

'Twas Jolly, Jolly Wat. Charles William Stubbs. O merry, merry sing for joy,/Ut hoy! OHIP

'Twas Just This Time, Last Year, I Died. Emily Dickinson. Themself, should come to me– DiPo

'Twas Like a Maelstrom, with a Notch. Emily Dickinson. Which Anguish was the utterest–then–/To perish, or to live? AmePo; CMoP; ExPo; LiTA; LiTM; NePA; SeCeV

Twas Night. *Anonymous.* But on this Bank contented ever rest. OBS

'Twas Warm at First, Like Us. Emily Dickinson. It made no signal, nor demurred,/But dropped like adamant. CMoP; ExPo; ForPo; LiTA; NAWM 1-2; QFR; SoSe

'Twas When the Spousal Time of May. Coventry Patmore. Fit for their only listener, Heaven. GBL

Tweed and Till. *Anonymous.* For ae man that ye droon/I droon twa. BoNaP; FaBoCh; FaBoPP; GBP; PV

Tweedle-Dum and Tweedle-Dee. *Anonymous.* Which frightened both the heroes so/They quite forgot their quarrel. NA; NOBL

Twelfth Night. *Anonymous.* And our pockets full too. OxNR

Twelfth Night. Philip Booth. the burner is both burned and blessed. NePoEA

Twelfth Night. Elizabeth Jane Coatsworth. And then drifted away. ChBR

Twelfth Night. Laurie Lee. the sun of heaven, and the son of God. BoC

Twelfth Night. Peter Scupham. Whose brightness dies to image. And the snow. OBCP

Twelfth Night. William Shakespeare.
And we'll strive to please you every day. DiPo; EBEV; ElL; ExPo; FaBoCh; FiP; HBV 1-2; HeIP; InPo; LiTB; LoBV; LoGBV; NLV; NOBE; NoP; OAEL 1-2; OAEP; OBSC; OxBoLi; PoRA; PPoe; ViBoPo; WiR
Sad true lover never find my grave/To weep there! CBEP; CTC; DiPo; ElL; ELP; ExPo; FiP; GBL; GTBS; GTBS-P; InPo; NOBE; NoP; OBEV; OBSC; PoPle; PoRA; SeCeV; ViBoPo; WHA
...so full of shapes is fancy,/That it alone is high fantastical. TreFS
Youth's a stuff will not endure. AWP; BiP; BoLoP; CTC; ElL; ELP; ExPo; FaBV; FaFP; FiP; GBL; GTBS; GTBS-P; HAP; HBV 1-2; HeIP; InMe; InPo; InPS; LiTB; LiTL; MCCG; NLV; NOBE; OAEL 1-2; OAEP; OBEV; OBSC; OBSP; OLR; PAI; PoRA; SeCeV; ViBoPo; WHA

Twelfth Raga/for John Wieners. David Meltzer. dream thru the mind/like the beautiful words. NeAP

The Twelve. Alexander Blok. Jesus Christ is marching at their head. LiTW

The Twelve Days of Christmas. *Anonymous.* A partridge in a pear tree. FSW; GoTF; LiTL; OxBoLi; OxNR; PCh; TreFT

The Twelve-Elf. Christian Morgenstern. Sleep falls again on all the land. WSC

Twelve Lines About the Burning Bush. Melech Ravitch. moment I can't forget, eternity I can't comprehend. VWA

The Twelve Months. Gregory Gander. Breezy, Sneezy, Freezy. GoTF; TreFT

Twelve O'Clock Boat. J. A. R. McKellar. Though Scipio should wait upon Cremorne. BoAV

The Twelve Oxen. *Anonymous* Saweste not you mine oxen, you litill pretty boy? CH

Twelve P.M. William Dean Howells. ,and in one's naked soul/Confronted the eternal Verity. AmePo

The Twelve Properties or Conditions of a Lover. Sir Thomas More.
For body, soul, wit, cunning, mind and thought,/Part will He none, but either all or naught. EnRePo
or any thynge remove/His ardent mynde from God his hevenly/love. CoBE
Out break the tears again for pain and woe. EnRePo
The quick relics, the ministers of His Church. CoBE; EnRePo

The Twelve Weapons of Spiritual Battle. Sir Thomas More.
But fast it runneth on and passen shall/As doth a dream, or shadow on the wall. EnRePo
Thou shalt no pleasure comparable find/To the inward gladness of a virtuous mind. EnRePo

Twentieth-Century Blues. Kenneth Fearing. That stop, stop, go. CMoP

Twentieth Century Love-Song. Richard Church. Of what makes her remain/The one woman. HaMV

Twenty Below. R. A. D. Ford. ...and the woman takes her sadness/and thaws it before the flames. CaP; NOBC

The Twenty-Fifth Year of His Life. Constantine P. Cavafy. ...quite possibly this life of his/will land him in a devastating scandal. PeHV

Twenty Foolish Fairies. Nancy Byrd Turner. Twenty early robins/Chuckled at the joke. SUS

Twenty-Four Years. Dylan Thomas. I advance for as long as forever is. CMoP; DiPo; InPK; MAT; MoAB; NAs; NoAm; OBSP

Twenty Golden Years Ago. James Clarence Mangan. Curious anticlimax to thy dreams/Twenty golden years ago! IrPN; NOBV; OnYI

Twenty-One Love Poems. Adrienne Rich.
and soon I shall know I was talking to my own soul. BoWoP
and they still control the world, and you are not in my arms. BoWoP
our animal passion rooted in the city. PeHV
we were two women of one generation. PeHV
where grief and laughter sleep together. PeHV

Twenty-One Sonnets. C. K. Stead.
The children have scrawled it: BIG NORM IS DEAD. OCNZ
Fills the silence of God that has lasted forty-two years. OCNZ
He was third engineer, a Scotsman, a good neighbor/lost. OCNZ
Sanctuary against the malice of the world. OCNZ

Twenty-One Years. Anonymous. For twenty-one years, boys, is a mighty long time. AmFP

The Twenty-Second of December. William Cullen Bryant. The children of the Pilgrim sires/This hallowed day like us shall keep. GN

Twenty Stars to Match His Face. William Stanley Braithwaite. There is no wind can mark his place/Here, or hence. HBMV

Twenty-Third Flight. Earle Birney. And that I shall lie by the waters of Waikiki and want? HeIP; OxBC; SoSe

The Twenty-Third Psalm. George Herbert. And as it never shall remove,/So neither shall my praise. EBCP

Twenty-third Street Runs into Heaven. Kenneth Patchen. Our supper is plain but we are very wonderful. ErPo

Twenty-Two Minutes. Lorri Martinez. Twenty-two minutes/before eight o'clock/nothing ever changes. LFAC

Twenty-Year Marriage. Florence Anthony ("Ai"). old newspapers nobody's ever got to read again. BoWoP; GP; MAYP

Twenty Years After. Evan V. Shute. Dig in your heels against the slippery grave! CaP

Twenty Years Ago. Dill Armor Smith. I hope they'll lay us where we play'd, just twenty years ago. BFSS; BLPA

Twentyseven Bums. Edward Estlin Cummings. pink propaganda of annihilation. OBAL

Twice. Ian Hamilton Finlay. Sway again/And again, in the bright new clean rain. BSV

Twice. Christina Georgina Rossetti. Smile Thou and I shall sing,/But shall not question much. GBL; GTBS; NOBE; OBEV; OBNC; OBVV; TrCP; ViBoPo; VLP

Twice a Week the Winter Through. Alfred Edward Housman. Keeps the bones of man from lying/On the bed of earth. LiSp

Twice Fed. A. A. Bassett. For so God gives us twice our daily bread. HBV 1-2

Twice Shy. Seamus Heaney. Still waters running deep/Along the embankment walk. NCSH; TwCP

Twice Times Then Is Now. Ibn Hazm Al-Andalusi. how long or brief/it seems to be. OBVE

Twickenham Ferry. Theophile Marzials. There's danger in crossing to Twickenham Town. HBV 1-2

Twicknam Garden. John Donne. O perverse sex, where none is true but she,/Who's therefore true, because her truth kills me. AnAnS 1; EnLoPo; FaBoPP; MeLP; MePo; OBS; PoEL 1-5; SeCP

Twilight. Louisa S. Bevington. Acquiescence, acquiescence,/And the coming on of sleep. NOBV

Twilight. Ch'en Yun. The first hibiscus flower/falls. LiTW

Twilight. Olive Custance. Woman whom we call Twilight, when night's pall/You lift across our Earth to cover it. CAW; HBV 1-2

Twilight. Hazel Hall. My faith's frail candle/Before the night. AnAmPo; HBMV

Twilight. Heinrich Heine. Swiftly the darkness fell. AWP

Twilight. D. H. Lawrence. ...litter of day/Is gone from sight. OBMV

Twilight. Henry Wadsworth Longfellow. Drive the colour from her cheek? CH

Twilight. John Masefield. Beautiful souls who were gentle when I was a child. OxBTC

Twilight. Virginia McCormick. And set it rose-like in your tawny hair. HBMV

Twilight. Joaquin A. Pagaza. Enraptured by the sunset's charm divine. CAW

Twilight. Agnes Mary Frances (Mme Emile Duclaux) Robinson. And thrice more happy are the happy days/That live divinely in the lingering rays. HBV 1-2

Twilight at Sea. Amelia C. Welby. And held it trembling there. AA; HBV 1-2

Twilight at the Zoo. Alex Rodger. It is not manna/falls on them from these livid clouds. NCSH

Twilight Calm. Christina Georgina Rossetti. The quiet sands have run. BoNaP; OBNC

Twilight Comes. Hayden Carruth. I am not an old man. Not yet. NNaP

Twilight in California. Philip Dow. like buckshot, changing/wine to blood. AmPA

A Twilight in Middle March. Francis Ledwidge. From little knowledge where great sorrows brood. BIrV; OnYI; OxBI; WHA

The Twilight of Disquietude: The Years That Go to Make Me Man. Christopher John Brennan. a ghost upon this common earth. PoAu 1-2

Twilight of Freedom. Osip Mandelstam. this earth we possess has cost us ten heavens. VWA

Twilight of the Earth. George William Russell. Dominion and ancestral sway. AnIL

Twilight on Sumter. Richard Henry Stoddard. Hell shall rise in grim derision and make/room! PAH

Twilight on Tweed. Andrew Lang. You tell me that the voice is still/That should have welcomed me. BSV; OBVV

The Twilight People. Seumas (James Starkey) O'Sullivan. Sets the withered leaves fluttering to and fro. OnYI

Twilight's Last Gleaming. Arthur W. Monks. Propagandistically/Knew how to die. OFD

The Twilight Shadows Round Me Fall. Ernest Edwin Ryden. That with the morn I may awake/Unto the perfect day. AH

Twilight Song. John Hunter-Duvar. Sweet Mary, keep our souls from harm!/Good night! good night! WHW

Twilight Song. Edwin Arlington Robinson. Where the road leads along/Through the shine, through the rain. HBV 1-2

Twilight Thoughts in Israel. Melech Ravitch. that I was the one waiting for the miracle. VWA

Twilights. James Wright. A red shadow of steel mills. LCAP; NaP

Twilit Revelation. Léonie Adams. So space can pierce the crevice wide between/Fast hearts, skies deep-descended intervene. MoAB; MoAmPo

Twin. Phyllis Haring. Yet one exempts, and one of these redeems. PeSA

Twin Aces. Keith Wilson. ...looking/back over his shoulder, the quiet street/behind him. Psk

A "Twiner." J. A. Lindon. Good day to you, Pablo Picasso! DBV

Twinings Orange Pekoe. Judith Moffett. White white on white. PoA; SM

Twink Drives Back, in a Bad Mood, from a Party in Massachusetts. George Amabile. ...The sun outside/Has turned lead-colored lakes into pure gold. NYBP

Twinkle, Twinkle, Little Star (parody). Paul Dehn. What are you doing, twinkling there? SpRo

The Twinkling Earn. John Davidson. With the white world creaming over the rim.... PoSH

Twinkling Gown. Dorothy Vena Johnson. When dawn creeps from afar. GoSl

The Twins. Dorothy Aldis. A baby isn't twins! BiCB

Twins. Edward Bulwer-Lytton. The woman that I love leaps forth to me,/Naked and bold! ErPo

Twins. Robert Graves. And drank them both into the grave. FaBoEE; PV

The Twins. Kathryn Jackson. Excepting Paul and Peter. BiCB

The Twins. Henry Sambrooke Leigh. And when I died—the neighbors came/And buried brother John! BiCB; CenHV; HBV 1-2; HBVY; MaC; PoPl; ShM; TiPo

Twins. William Matthews. ...climbed my growing/body's staircase to the very tip of sleep. MAYP

The Twins. Elizabeth Madox Roberts. But now I always say it fast. BiCB; TiPo

The Twins. Karl Shapiro. And Dromio's denouement of tragic mirth. AnFE; MiAP; MoAmPo; TrJP

The Twins. Mona Van Duyn. my painted person crouched in his painted heart. GP

The Twins.   Judith Wright.   They move into the future and are gone. PoAu 1-2

Twirling.   *Anonymous.*   Turn, cheeses, turn.   OxNR

Twist-Rime on Spring.   Arthur Guiterman.   While poets sing in tripping rime/That Spring's a simply ripping time!   PoSC

'Twixt Cup and Lip.   Mark Hollis.   (With a Mene Tekel and otototoi). FiBHP; NLV

Two.   Margarita Aliger.   And have the time to sort things out and make up. VWA

Two.   Robert Canzoneri.   She wept and could not tell him why.   HoPM

Two.   Moishe Kulbak.   (in me, in me),/two people live side by side.   VWA

Two.   Winfield Townley Scott.   Which even to us were lost when we looked back.   NYBP

Two Against One.   *Anonymous.*   What can one mortal do against those two! UnTE

Two-An'-Six.   Claude McKay.   Was a princely two-an'-six.   BANP; GoSl

The Two Anchors.   Richard Henry Stoddard.   The great one on my right. BeLS

Two and One Are a Problem.   Ogden Nash.   Must I keep on buying lovebirds, Miss Dix, or do you think it would/be all right to buy a cat? FiBHP

Two Angels.   Richard Moncton, Lord Houghton Milnes.   Lulling him to downy slumbers/With remembrances of Heaven.   OBRV

The Two Angels.   John Greenleaf Whittier   Henceforth its sweetest song shall be the/song of sin forgiven!   AA

Two Animals, One Flood.   Diane Glancy.   Animals stand two by two, but there is only one/flood.   STE

The Two April Mornings.   William Wordsworth.   As at that moment, with a bough/Of wilding in his hand.   EBEV; EnRP; GTBS; GTBS-P; HBV 1-2

Two Are Together.   Geoffrey Grigson.   Together, then/After.   GBL

Two Argosies.   Wallace Bruce.   Her titled language crowned in high/entail. AA

Two Armies.   Stephen Spender.   The furious words and minerals which destroy.   ChMP; CoBMV; OBWP; OxBTC; SeCeV; WaP

Two at a Fireside.   Edwin Markham.   Yet all the day I glowed before the fire.   TRV

Two at Showtime.   Suzanne Brabant.   she pets the wet neck/of her horse! PH

Two Birds.   *Anonymous.*   And so the poor stone was left all alone,/Fa, la, la, la, lal, de.   OxNR

Two Birds.   Kathleen Linnell.   ...he rose upward like a stone.   AMV-81

Two Bits.   Sharlot M. Hall.   They buried him there on the Wingate Road. BPAW

The Two Boys.   Mary Ann Lamb.   No wonder if he wish he ne'er had learn'd to eat.   CBEP; OBRV

The Two Brothers.   *Anonymous.*
His bow and arrow across his breast/That he might sleep so sweet.   AmFP
"Oh tell her I lie in fair Kirk-land,/And home will never come." EBEV

Two Bums Walk out of Eden.   Robert Francis.   Where cool episcopal bells are calling, calling.   PPON

The Two Burdens.   Philip Bourke Marston.   What cry of longing the lips divide?   VLP

Two Campers in Cloud Country.   Sylvia Plath.   We'll wake blank-brained as water in the dawn.   NYBP

The Two Captains.   William Johnson Cory.   And treat some rescued Breton as a comrade and a guest.   FaPoR

Two Carols to Our Lady: II.   *Anonymous.*   Leave we all this worldly mirth,/And follow we this joyful birth/Transeamus.   ACP

Two-Cent Coal.   *Anonymous.*   That he never again shall commit/the crime/Of diggin' two-cent coal.   AmFP

Two Childhood Memories.   Al Zolynas.   What I remember about the tangerine/is how easily the skin came off.   LTB

The Two Children.   Emily Bronte.   And more unsleeping than angel's care. PoEL 1-5

Two Children.   Nicolas Guillen.   Two children, branches of the same tree of wretched-ness,/are in a doorway, beneath the torrid night   LiTW

Two Chorale-Preludes.   Geoffrey Hill.
BE FAITHFUL grows upon the mind/as lichen glimmers on the wood. OxBC
...the seven/dead stars in your sky.   OxBC

Two Clouds.   Lawrence Raab.   that sweeps the grass and is gone. AMV-80

Two Comical Folk.   *Anonymous.*   Helped, with drinking, to keep them alive. OxNR

Two Communist Poets.   Irving Layton.   Louder, Yanni, louder!   AMV-81

Two Countries.   Jose Marti.   Cuba, the widow, passes.   TTY

The Two Coyotes.   T. Walking Eagle Marietta.   giving a sense of someone, or something/being born/Hyeeeeee-a.   LFAC

Two Days.   William Ernest Henley.   ...when the ruined heart goes forth to/crave/Mercy of the high, austere, unpitying Grave.   VLP

Two Decisions.   Vernon Watkins.   Do not deny it.   OxBTC

Two Dedications, I: The Chicago Picasso.   Gwendolyn Brooks.   as meaningful and as meaningless as any/other flower in the western field. LiTM

Two Dedications: The Wall.   Gwendolyn Brooks.   And we sing.   PoBA; PoNe

The Two Deserts.   Coventry Patmore.   And out of obvious ways/Ne'er wandering far.   BoNaP

Two Dogs.   John Davidson.   What an unfathomable world it is!   FM

Two Dogs Have I.   Ogden Nash.   And her head was on his flank.   GDP

Two doves upon the selfsame branch.   Christina Georgina Rossetti.   And never give a thought to night.   EG

Two Drinking Songs.   Alcaeus.   For the fire of Sirius/Withers heads and knees.   LiTW

Two Drinking Songs.   Tao Yuan-Ming.   I walk around my study shouting and proud/because I can take up this life again.   NU

Two Egrets.   John Ciardi.   ...–a prayer/and the idea of prayer.   PoPl

Two Englishmen.   Douglas Stewart.   They understood each other pretty well.   CBAP

Two Families.   Charles G. Bell.   And his old wives and children–and look, how they smile!   FAZ

Two Fawns That Didn't See the Light This Spring.   Gary Snyder.   It had spots. And the little/hooves were soft and white.   HaCAP

Two Figures.   Molly Peacock.   And if they be broken, be sure they are dead.   AMV-81

Two Figures in Dense Violet Light.   Wallace Stevens.   That the moon shines.   MoAB; MoAmPo

The Two Fires.   Judith Wright.   The world's denied.   MoBrPo

Two Fishermen.   Stanley Moss.   The wrong angel takes over the lesson. CoAP; VWA

Two Folk Songs, 1.   *Anonymous.*   The deep forest, the bright heavens,/These comprehend my woe.   LiTW

Two Folk Songs, 2.   *Anonymous.*   Then my sorrow would never leave me,/Until the earth should cover me.   LiTW

The Two Foscari: Swimming.   George Gordon, Lord Byron.   –I was a boy then.   GN

The Two Friends.   Charles Godfrey Leland.   Or die in my bed, as a Christian should, is/all the same to me.   AA

Two Fusiliers.   Robert Graves.   In dead men breath.   MMM

Two Garden Scenes.   Charles Burgess.   Linked, than Death himself/With everything else....   NePoAm-2

Two Gardens.   Arlene De Bevoise.   Drink wine from quite extraordinary grapes.   AMV-80

Two Generations.   Leonard Alfred George Strong.   A gull above the ploughshare hears/The ironic song of our defeat.   OBMV

The Two Gentlemen of Verona.   William Shakespeare.
And by and by a cloud takes all away!   GBL
That they should harbour where their lord would be.'   CTC
To her let us garlands bring. BLPL; DiPo; EIL; FaFP; GN; HBV 1-2; InPo; LiTB; MCCG; OAEL 1-2; OBEV; SeCeV; TreF; TrGrPo; ViBoPo

Two Gifts.   *Anonymous.*   If they don't want them,/God rid me of both. BoWoP

Two Girls...   Charles Reznikoff.   in their shining innocence seeing/in him only another human being.   PCP

Two Girls Singing.   Iain Crichton Smith.   the unpredicted voices of our kind.   BSV

The Two Glasses.   Ella Wheeler Wilcox.   On the rich man's table, rim to rim.   BLPA; BLPL

Two Graces.   *Anonymous.*
For which the Lord be thankit!   FaBoCh
Hurly, hurly, AMEN.   FaBoCh

Two Graces.   Robert Herrick.
All are fragments from His dish.   PoPle
On our meat, and on us all. Amen.   PoPle

The Two Gretels.   Robin Morgan.   Those who would have the whole loaf,/let alone the house,/had better throw away their breadcrumbs.   DFT

Two Handfuls of Waka for Thelonious Sphere Monk (d. Feb. 1982).   Walter Lew.   Passed on: pure, round/Midnight   BrSi

Two Hangovers.   James Wright.
Ah, turn it off.   AmPC
...for he knows as well as I do/That the branch will not break. AmPC; LCAP

The Two-Headed Calf.   Laura Gilpin.   ...there are/twice as many stars as usual.   FYAP

Two Heavens.   [James Henry] Leigh Hunt.   The other, far on this side of the stars,/By men called home.   GN

Two Heroes.   Harriet Monroe.   The brave who, having fought, can never die.   OHIP

Two Hoboes.   *Anonymous.*   Oh, babes,/Oh, no-home babes.   WTO

Two Hookers.   A. K. Redwing.   A radio, a television set, and a bourgeois/prairie newspaper hang as accomplices   VoR

Two Hopper.   Ron Ikan.   My Dad he said a lot of things/you wouldn't tell your Mother.   Str

Two Travelers. Lewis, Cecil Day. And if either may carry on some reward or/regret for it/Whither he fares. EnLit

The Two Trees. William Butler Yeats. Gaze no more in the bitter glass. BrPo; OAEL 1-2; VLP

Two Trinities. Kenneth Mackenzie. Soul said, Now come with me. CBAP

Two Triolets. Harrison Robertson. What a poky poet! HBV 1-2

Two Variations. Denise Levertov.
...the rain that gave/my eyes their vigilance. NaP
she whose eyes are open forever. PPoe

Two Variations: All about Love. Philip Whalen. LOVE YOU NeAP

Two Vast Enjoyments Commemorated. John Danforth. Give, Lord! Their weakned Hearts strong Consolations./Amen. SCAP

Two Veterans. Walt Whitman. And my heart, O my soldiers, my veterans,/My heart gives you love. GN

Two Views of a Cadaver Room. Sylvia Plath. Foolish, delicate, in the lower right-hand corner. CMoP; GoYe; NMP

Two Views of Two Ghost Towns. Charles Tomlinson. ...How dry/the ghosts of dryness are. NoAm

The Two Villages. Rose Terry Cooke. "Patience! that village shall hold ye all!" HBV 1-2

Two Voices. Edmund Charles Blunden. And still "We're going South, man,' deadly near. OBWP

Two Voices. Alice Corbin. I know we grow more lovely/Growing wise. HBMV

The Two Voices. Alfred, Lord Tennyson. Than him that said, "Rejoice! rejoice!" MasP

Two Voices in a Meadow. Richard Wilbur.
I shall possess the field. NePoAm-2; UnPo
The sills of heaven would founder/Did such as I aspire. NePoAm-2; NLV; UnPo

Two-Volume Novel. Dorothy Parker. He didn't love back. InMe

Two Ways. John V. A. Weaver. Now you're gone for good...say,/Wasn't they no other way? HBMV

Two Weeks after an April Frost. Steven Helmling. The matron will not be a maiden, now. AMV-80

Two Went up to the Temple to Pray. Richard Crashaw. One nearer to God's altar trod,/The other to the altar's God. ALV; CAW; HAP; TRV

Two White Horses in a Line. Two Poor Boys. Then you know that the poor boy's in the ground BluL

Two White Horses (with music). Anonymous. Heb'n gate opened, and he rolled right in. AS

Two Windows by Magritte. Ruth Roston. God knows how many/lonely men the loaves/have eaten. PoDr

Two Wise Generals. Ted Hughes. ...Both/Have found their sleeping armies massacred. MoBS

The Two Witches. Robert Graves. And swallowed me down like a crumb of bread. SO

The Two Wives. Daniel Henderson. But–Lord ha'e mercy!–the ring was gone! ShM

The Two Wives. William Dean Howells. For love, that had made his friend's peace/ with Death,/ Alone could make his with life. AA

Two Women. Naomi Replansky. And still the clipped wing leans against/ Her eagle of experience. NMM

Two Women. Tania Van Zyl. or the stone heart probed of a Syrian tower. PeSA

Two Women. Nathaniel Parker Willis. But the sin forgiven by Christ in Heaven/By man is cursed alway! BeLS; OBVV

Two Women with Mangoes. Steven Cramer. as if she were about to speak, or had just spoken. AMV-80

Two Words: A Wedding. John Nichol. because you are wedded to the flux of life, because we are/words and our meanings change. NOBC

Two Wrestlers. Robert Francis. One wrestler challenging–oh how unsafe–/ Himself. LiSp

Two X "16 heures l'Etoile." Edward Estlin Cummings. (which stroll hither and thither through the/evening in bruised narrow questioning faces). FaBoMo

Two Years Later. John Wieners. The beauty of man never disappears/But drives a blue car through the parking lot. CoPo; PoM

Two Young Maids. Anonymous. When fruit is ripe the civet's there. WTO

Two Young Men, 23 to 24 Years Old. Constantine P. Cavafy. happy, they gave themselves to love. PeHV

Twoborn. Rokwaho. and glitters next/in the Eagle's twice born eyes... STE

The Ty Cobb Story. Tom Clark. "I don't care if I see another xerox as long as I live." LiSp

Tybrun and Westminster. John Heywood. At Tyburn half an hour's/ hanging endeth all. ACP

Tyin' a Knot in the Devil's Tail. Gail Gardner. You'll know it's nothin' but the Devil himself,/raisin' hell about the knots in his tail. ABF; FSW

Tymes Goe by Turnes. Robert Southwell. Who least hath some, who most hath never all. FaBoEn

Tymnes. Tymnes. Along those roads we cannot hear him bark. LoGBV

Tyne Dock. Francis Scarfe. Nor ever lose that child's despair. NeBP

The Typewriter Revolution. D. J. Enright. FACIT cry I!!! NoP

A Typical 6:00 P.M. in the Fun House. Daniel Berrigan. The small tree outside, unfit for a man's dead weight, breathes,/hang on! LFAC

Tyrannic Love. John Dryden.
Find out those faults, which they want wit to make. ViBoPo
Here Nelly lies, who, though she liv'd a Slater'n,/Yet dy'd a Princess acting in S. Cathar'n. SeCV 1-2; ViBoPo
If a flow in Age appear,/'Tis but rain, and runs not clear. CavP

Tyranny. Sidney Lanier. Stay: feed the worms. MAmP

Tyranny of Moths. Gerald Vizenor. we are drawn to another light/farther down the road VoR

The Tyrant Apple Is Eaten. Norman MacCaig. like a devil in a saint's book. NeBP

Tyson's Corner. Primus St. John. We made a promise. PoBA

Tywater. Richard Wilbur. Such violence. And such repose. CMoP; ConAP; LiTA; LiTM; MiAP; MoAB; NePA

Tzu Yeh Songs. Anonymous.
Because my silkworms were hungry. BoWoP
I thought the river stood still and did not flow. BoWoP
If it opens a little, I shall blame the spring wind. BoWoP
Out of Nowhere, Nothing answered "yes." BoWoP

U

U, Deux, Trois. Anonymous. Celui mo lais, celui mo prends. ABF

A, U, Hinny Burd. Anonymous. And Bedlington for nailers,/A, U, A. GBP

U is for Umbrellas. Phyllis McGinley. If a roof on stormy evenings/Isn't nicer to be under. TiPo

U Name This One. Carolyn M. Rodgers. couldn't be no action like what/i dun already seen. BlSi; NMM; PoBA

U.S. 1946 King's X. Robert Frost. King's X–no fairs to use it any more! NIP

The U.S. Coast and Geodetic Survey Ship Pioneer. Robert Hershon. I'm driving on NeAC

The U. S. Sailor with the Japanese Skull. Winfield Townley Scott. ..."Alas! I did not know him at all." LiTM; MiAP; NMP; WaP

The U-S-U Range. G. W. Barr. For I have been a cow-puncher on the U-S-U range. CoSo

Ubi Sunt Qui Ante Nos Fuerunt? Anonymous. Help us sin to flee,/That we may thy son see/In joy without end. CoBE; NoP; OAEP; OxBM; PrIm; SeCeV; WeW

Uccello. Gregory Corso. a golden prince of pictorial war NeAP; PoM

Uccello on the Heath. Geoffrey Grigson. Stab to the guts in a rich battle-scene. WaP

Uffia. Harriet R. White. Pangwangling was her pace. NA

Ugly Chile. Clarence Williams. You some ugly chile. TW

The Ugstabuggle. Peter Wesley-Smith. And when I sleep he goes, because/ I cannot see him then! AmMo

Uhuru. Mari E. Evans. Black unison/our heartbeats CNA

Ula Masondo's Dream. William Plomer. Are you lost in the hollow/Root of the city? MoBS

Ulalume. Edgar Allan Poe This ghoul-haunted woodland of/Weir. AA; AmP; AnEnPo; AP; APA; AWP; BLPL; DiPo; GoTF; LiTA; MAmP; NePA; NOBA; OxBA; TAP; TreF; ViBoPo; WHA

Ulf of Ireland. Charles De Kay. Horror, horror! AA

Ulinda. David Campbell. "Grandfather's dying. He's going to die,' I sang. CBAP

Ulric Dahlgren. Kate Brownlee Sherwood. A jewel set,/Unnumbered yet,/In our Republic's coronet! PAH

Ulster. Hans Adler. While surgeons rinsed their bitter gloves. AMV-81

Ulster. Rudyard Kipling. If England drive us forth/We shall not fall alone! FaBoPV

An Ulsterman. Lynn Doyle. I hope it's Michael Dan. OnYI

Ultima Ratio Regum. Stephen Spender. Lying under the olive trees, O world, O death? BBV; CMoP; FaFP; LiTB; LiTM; OAEL 1-2; OBWP; SeCePo; WaaP; WaP

Ultima Thule. Henry Wadsworth Longfellow. ...a while we rest/From the unending, endless quest. MOS; ViBoPo

Ultimate Anthology. Martin Bell. With X, and Y, and charming little Z. PoL

The Ultimate Antientropy. Theodore Weiss. Helen, it seems, is more/ herself the more she's reproduced. NoAm

Ultimate Equality. Ray Durem. That don't seem right, does it, Joe? PoNe

Under Ben Bulben. William Butler Yeats. Horseman, pass by! AnIV; CMoP; CoBMV; FaBoRV; HAP; LiTM; LoBV; NoAm; NoP; OxBI; OxBTC; WeW

Under Cancer. John Hollander. My shadow darkens without/Lengthening ever, ever. CoAP

Under Creag Mhor. Stewart Conn. Such monsters huddle yet. PoSH

Under Glass. Alfred Kreymborg. So clear to all my neighbours, so invisible–to/me. MAPA

Under Leafy Bowers. Judah Al-Harizi. And drink and drink old wine/At youth's eternal fount. TrJP

Under Milk Wood (excerpt). Dylan Thomas. Always used to say that stout and ale/Was good for a baby in a milking pail. FiBHP; LOW

Under My Window. Thomas Westwood. And I give her all my roses. HBV 1-2; HBVY

Under Our Own Wings. Nellie Wong. In love we work to live in America under our own wings. BrSi

Under Restless Clouds. Hanny Michaelis. which is unruly like the clouds/ and as homeless as the wind. VWA

Under Sirius. W. H. Auden. To whom these dull dog-days/Between event seem crowned with olive/And golden with self-praise. FaBoMo; NePA

Under Sorrow's Sign. Gofraidh Fionn O'Dalaigh. Sad every dungeon where earth's hosts/Lie hidden from the light of day. BIrV

Under Stars. Tess Gallagher. Again, I/am the found one, intimate, returned/by all I touch on the way. GeTw; MAYP

Under Stone. Elaine Feinstein. and the pain of our questions will melt like the/wax of our flesh/into silence. VWA

Under the Anheuser Bush. Andrew B. Sterling. Come down this ev'ning, I'll introduce you. OBAL

Under the Arc de Triomphe: October 17. Marilyn Hacker. nor what I thought. I slept and woke alone. PoA

Under the Bamboo Tree. Bob Cole. One live as two, two live as one,/ Under the bamboo tree. BLSo; FSN

Under the Blue. Francis Fisher Browne. But the sure light of sweet eyes bright/Shines on forever and forever. AA

Under the Boathouse. David Bottoms. I bobbed with a hook through the palm of my hand. MAYP

Under the Boughs. Gene Baro. Long ago there were white-trembling blossoms/upon the boughs where full fruit hangs now. BoNaP

Under the Casuarina. Elizabeth Riddell. What's left sleeps in a chair, and when it can/Babbles to strangers, such as you and I. PoAu 1-2

Under the Catalpa Trees. Gary Young. Then let them change. AMV-81

Under the Cliff. Geoffrey Grigson. And the caught bee dry and fade inside/The emptied room. WaP

Under the Drooping Willow Tree. Anonymous. Under the drooping willow tree. CBEP; OxBoLi

Under the Earth. Abraham Sutzkever. where words throb/hidden in violins. VWA

Under the Edge of February. Jayne Cortez. in your solitude of bruises in/ your arson of alert/beautiful BlSi

Under the Eildon Tree. Sydney Goodsir Smith. Deid for a ducat deid/By the crueltie o his ain maistress. OxBS

Under the Goal Posts. Arthur Guiterman. That balked our eager rushers beneath their very goal. BBV

Under the Greenwood Tree. Anonymous.
And a shaddaw for a windin' sheet/To row aboot his corse. OBVE
And then we did firk it, caper and jerk it/Under the greenwood tree. GBP

Under the Ladder to Heaven. Elizabeth Fenton. Later, I found/He told everyone that. NMM

Under the Leaves. Albert Laighton. God sees sweet flowers growing. HBV 1-2; OHIP

Under the Lindens. William Landor. Bees! bees! was it your hydromel/ Under the lindens? HBV 1-2

Under the Lindens. Walther von der Vogelweide Trust him not to breathe a word. CTC

Under the Locust Blossoms. Frederick Goddard Tuckerman. Oh that moment! Oh that breath of locust bloom! NOBA

Under the Mistletoe. Countee Cullen. Or else I'd never dared. GoSl; PCh

Under the Moon. William Butler Yeats. To dream of women whose beauty was folded in dismay,/Even in an old story, is a burden... EG

Under the Mountain. Louis MacNeice. The house is a maelstrom of loves and hates where you–/Having got down–belong. FaBoIP

Under the Old Elm. James Russell Lowell.
And learned to honor first, then love him, then revere. PGD
Who was all this and ours, and all men's,–/WASHINGTON. GN; PAL; PGD

Under the Pondweed. Anonymous. The King is drinking deep. AWP

Under the Pot. Robert Graves. On incandescent clouds of spirit or rage. FaBoEE

Under the Pyrenees. Alfred Noyes. ...among the lonely mountains/At Roncesvalles, in one last prayer for me.... GoBC

Under the Red Cross. Chauncey Hickox. Where healing hands were few. AA

Under the Rose. Anonymous. This grand conversation was under the rose. OBET

Under the Ruins of Poland. Itzik Manger. her dead face, my fallen city,/ are more real to me than love./My fate, my sorrow.) VWA

Under the Scub Oak, a Red Shoe. Dave Smith. ...the bruise/you might have kissed and might not yet refuse. GeTw

Under the Shade of the Trees. Margaret Junkin Preston. There to pass over the river and rest/Under the shade of the trees! MC; PAH

Under the Shawl. Rose Drachler. My bones feel small. I am lifted easily. VWA

Under the Sign of the Moth. David Wagoner. For what it came to find and will die for. AMV-81

Under the Snow. Robert Collyer. Fifty years syne come Christmas Day. AA

Under the Stars. Wallace Rice. Sweet the death she shall crown/Under the stars. AA; OHIP

Under the Umbrella of Blood. William Pitt Root. faster than the applauding coins of the world can ever fall. GeTw

Under the Violets. Oliver Wendell Holmes Lies withered where the violets blow. AA

Under the Violets. Edward Hilton Young. O grave! I would thy gates were wide. AA

Under the Waterfall. Thomas Hardy. No lip has touched it since his and mine/In turns therefrom sipped lovers' wine. BoLoP; CTC; LiTB

Under the Wattle. Douglas Brook Wheelton Sladen. I hardly know/Why Wattle should not do.' OBVV

Under the Williamsburg Bridge. Galway Kinnell. On an old spider wrapping a fly in spittle-strings. NYP

Under the Willow-Shades. Sir William Davenant. "We can supply you with a cradle too." BoLoP; ELP

Under the Window: Ouro Preto. Elizabeth Bishop. like tatters of the Morpho butterfly. NYBP

Under the Wood. Anonymous. Mary, I'm sad for your Son and you. HAP

Under the Woods. Edward ("Edward Eastaway") Thomas. And barely seen/On this shed wall. CH; LoBV

Under Which Heading Does All This Information Go? Mira Teru Kurka. I'd like you to meet/my daughter, Nebraska. APU

Under Which Lyre. W. H. Auden. Read the New Yorker; trust in God;/ and take short views. MoAB; MoBrPo; NOBL

Under Your Voice, among Legends. Phyllis Beauvais. I plant money in the asphalt/;I lunch on bitter apples NMM

An Underdeveloped Country. D. J. Enright. Still, we need that adult help/ If we are ever to develop. NOBL

Undergraduate. Merrill Moore. Were twisted sheets and feather-pillows instead. ErPo

The Underground. Guy Boas. For my part I/Am sitting in a bus. CenHV

Underground. Ian Mudie. ship-fed seas bring us/from colder waters. BoAV

The Underground Gardens. Robert Mezey. He is buried somewhere else. NaP

Underground Poetry. Pedro Juan Pietri. what is/stopping you? NYP

The Underground Stream. James Dickey. And then I smiled, and fell. NOBA

Underground System. Edna St. Vincent Millay. Small, and absurd, and hers: for once, not hers, unclassified. SBG

Underneath a Cypress Shade, The Queen of Love Sat Mourning. Anonymous. Then too late the scorn of youth by age shall be repented. GBL

Undersea Fever. William Cole. I'll sit in the rowboat, alone with my sinus.) FiBHP

The Underside of Trees. Charlotte De Clue. to become/other trees TWSS

The Undersong. Ralph Waldo Emerson Of Death and Fortune, Growth and Strife. AA

Undersong. Mark Van Doren. Has sung to such as me this undersong. PoCh

Understanding. Anonymous. How best these precious gifts to use/Thou hast bestowed on me. PoToHe

Understanding. H. W. Bliss. May it be with understanding that we live! PoToHe

Understanding. Pauline E. Soroka. I may not wish to seek your door again. PoLf

The Undertaker's Horse. Rudyard Kipling. "Sure to catch you sooner or later. Who's the next?" FaBoNo; FM

Undertakers. Ambrose Bierce. Of joy to his widow and pride to himself. DBV

The Undertakers' Club. Anonymous. The fav'rite grand march that is played in Black Beard. GBP

The Undertaking. John Donne. And a braver thence will spring,/Which is, to keepe that hid. AnFE; BoLiVe; MePo; NOBE

The Undertaking. Louise Gluck. everywhere you turn is luck. FaBoWP

The Undertaking. Gerrit Lansing. as men can have nothing more profit in their life than Me. CoPo

Undertone. W. B. Stanford. when the landfolk of Galway converse with a stranger. NeIP; OnYI

Undertones. George R. Sims. To-morrow succeeds to-day. NOBV

Undertow. Langston Hughes. Between Selma, Peking,/Westchester/And me. LiTM

Underwear. Lawrence Ferlinghetti. Don't shout. CoPo; OBAL

Underwood. Howard Moss. The marvellous animal blood go thin? MP; NePA; NePoEA-2; PP; TwCP

Underwoods. Ben Jonson. Safe from the wolves black jaw, and the dull Asses hoofe. AtBAP

Undine. Irving Layton. And all your wetness takes the form of tears. ErPo

The Undiscovered Country. Thomas Bailey Aldrich. That all beyond is not Oblivion. AA

The Undiscovered Planet. Norman Nicholson. The unknown is shown/ Only by a bend in the known. ChMP

Undo! Anonymous. Are all biweved with bloody drops/For thine sake.' NOCV; OxBM

Undo Your Heart. Anonymous. Undo thin herte, tell me thy thought,/Thy sennes grete and smale. MeEL

The Undreamed. Elaine V. Emans. Nor was your vision long enough to see US,/predators,/with disappearing prey. AMV-81

Undue significance. Emily Dickinson. ...It was the distance/Was savory. LiTA; LiTM

Undying Thirst. Antipater of Sidon. And, faith she thinks it very wrong/ This jug should stand unfilled so long. AWP

Unearth. Alfred Joseph Barrett. Gardener of Eden—and Gethsemane! GoBC

Unearthing. Betsy Rosenberg. And you will be jealous of our tombs. VWA

Uneasy Peace. Edmund Charles Blunden. While men were meditating war with which the world still bleeds. BrPo

Uneasy Rider. Diane Wakoski. finds blood spotting her legs/from the long ride. NIP

The Unemployed. LeVan Roberts. Symbols of Peace, now war is ended. PGD

Unemployment. William Mills. I feel like the road. HoPM

Unemployment/Monologue. June Jordan. you got it! WPOW

Unequal Distribution. Samuel Hoffenstein. Such unequal distribution/Is part of Heaven's constitution. TrJP

The Unerring Guide. Anna Shipton. He seeks with holy love to lure/The wanderer 'neath His wing. BLRP

An Unexpected Pleasure. Anonymous. Because the mother of my wife/Has come—and means to stay with me. FaBoCo

The Unexplorer. Edna St. Vincent Millay. (That's why I have not traveled more.) LOW; MoShBr; SUS

The Unexpress'd. Walt Whitman. (Who knows? the best yet unexpress'd and lacking.) NePA; PP

The Unfading. Madelaine Marie. The scarlet sin you planted there. PeHV

The Unfading Beauty. Thomas Carew. Where these are not, I despise/ Lovely cheeks or lips or eyes. AtBAP; EnLi 1-2; FaBV; LiTL; OBEV

The Unfailing Friend. Joseph Scriven. Thou wilt find a solace there. BLRP

The Unfailing One. Phillips Brooks. And carry away the song. BLRP

The Unfailing One. Frances Ridley Havergal. We rest on Him, today, forever! BLRP

Unfinished History. Archibald MacLeish. ...and the blood is/Thin in the throat and the time not come for death? NYBP; VGW

The Unfinished Race. Norman Cameron. Distinguished only from the ruck/By their impressive long run back. OxBS

An Unfinished Work (Excerpt). X. J. Kennedy. His heart lay down, took ether, and gave birth. PeD

Unfold! Unfold! Henry Vaughan. And here in dust and dirt, oh, here/The lilies of His love appear! ELP

The Unforeseen. Conrado Nale Roxlo. may my soul learn at the turn of a corner/that one step back it still lived. LiTW; MoRP

The Unforgiven. Edwin Arlington Robinson. There still would seem to be a way. CMoP

Unfortunate Coincidence. Dorothy Parker. One of you is lying. ALV; BXAP; FaBoUs; NoP; PoPl; SBG; TreF

An Unfortunate Lover. Anonymous. I thenche on hir that I ne see nought ofte. OxBM

The Unfortunate Male. Ben Kalonymos. "O Lord, I thank thee ('tis not scorn/That I was not a woman born." TrJP

The Unfortunate Man. Anonymous. I'm realyy a very unfortunate man. BFSS

The Unfortunate Miller. Alfred Edgar Coppard. And the sails, with the miller dying,/Went flying, flying. FaBoTw

The Unfortunate Miller; or, The Country Lasses Witty Invention. Anonymous. The damsel she laught, and was pleas'd in her mind,/And said he was very well serv'd in his kind. CoMu; OxBB

Unfortunate Miss Bailey. George the Younger Colman. Oh, Miss Bailey! unfortunate Miss Bailey! DTC; FiBHP; FSW; GBP; ViBoFo

The Unfortunate Mole. Mary Kennedy. The unfortunate mole! GoYe

The Unfortunate Reminder. William Pattison. 'Twas well you waked—we've slept too long. UnTE

Unfriendly Fortune. John Skelton. That where I love best I dare not discure. MeEL

Unfrocked Priest. Joseph Campbell. And he bled at the nose. AnIL; OnYI

Unfulfilment. Frances Louisa Bushnell. The harbor whither those were bound/Lieth, nor yet is found. AA

The Ungathered Apples. James Wright. Hidden in cellars when the boughs are bare. ErPo

Ungathered Love. Philip Bourke Marston. And which no heart had for gathering. OBNC

The Ungrateful Garden. Carolyn Kizer. "Nature is evil," Midas said. NePoEA-2

Ungrateful Jenny. Anonymous. Saying, Out upon you, fie/upon you,/Bold faced jig! OxNR

Unguarded. Ada Foster Murray. They dwell and dream together,/The kin of court and wild. HBV 1-2

Unguarded Gates. Thomas Bailey Aldrich. The lean wolf unmolested made her lair. AA; AnNE; MC; PAH

Unhappy Bella. Anonymous. "It's all the men, the dirty bastards!" ErPo

Unhappy Boston. Paul Revere. Keen execrations on this plate inscrib'd/ Shall reach a judge who nevr can be bribed. PAH

Unhappy Diary Days. Gerald Vizenor. she crashed through the glass VoR

The Unhappy Lover. Judah Al-Harizi. The folks will say, "Here's one by/ woman slain." TrJP

The Unhappy Schoolboy. Anonymous. What availeth it me though I say nay? OxBChV

Unharvested. Robert Frost. So smelling their sweetness would be no theft. BoNaP

The Unhistoric Story. Allen Curnow. It is something different, something/ Nobody counted on. AnNZ

Unholy Missions. Bob Kaufman. I want to prove once and for all that I am not crazy. CNA; TTY

The Unicorn. Ruth Pitter. And thou art with me there. MoBrPo; MoVE

The Unicorn. Emile Victor Rieu. When the hand of the fiddler surrenders the bow. AmMo

Unicorn. William Jay Smith. He lays his head in a lady's lap/As gently as a child. SO

The Unicorn. Ella Young. But he dared not stay/Over-long! SoPo; TiPo

The Unicorn and the Lady. Jean Garrigue. And the small heart sparkles amidst the leaves/Of the one thousand flowers, and flares. NYBP

Unidentified Flying Object. Robert Earl Hayden. The talk is getting mean. NCSH

The Unillumined Verge. Robert Bridges. Yes, I hear your faint voice: "This is/rest, and like sleeping!" AA

The Uninfected. E. L. Mayo. Eating what I like, sound as a bell. MiAP

An Uninscribed Monument on One of the Battle-Fields of the Wilderness. Herman Melville Silent as I, and lonesome as the land. AA; AmLP

Unintelligible Terms. Charles Simic. Listening to a child crying in the night/On a chance, the remote chance,/It will hush. NoP

The Uninvited. Dorothy Livesay. hear/another voice/singing under ice NOBC

The Uninvited. William D. Mundell. They move into the trackless cover of the night. NYBP

The Union Barge on Staten Island. Louis Simpson. And the drifting clouds/Are drifting over the Wilderness, over the still farm. NYP

Union Maid. Woody Guthrie. I'm sticking to the Union till the day I die. FSW

Union Man. Anonymous. AFL, CIO/Callin' strike, out she go! AmFP

Union Train. Millard and Lee Hays Lampell. Won't you get on board./Oh, get on board. FSW

Unique Among Girls. Anonymous. Never like this a lass of them all. WTO

Unison. John Hall Wheelock. No words are made for it. There is no way. MoRP

A Unison. William Carlos Williams. Hear the unison of their voices.... NOBA; SeCeV

Unit. Mary Elizabeth ("E") Fullerton. God keep us struggling shapes. BoAV; NOAV

Unitarian Easter. Sandra McPherson. ...—raindrops on the roof, no comment/On the matter of God. MAYP

United. Paulus Silentiarius. ...best that you and I/Should live together, or together die. AWP

United Front. Hans and Bertolt Brecht Eisler. March on in the worker's united front,/For you are a worker too. FSW

The United Fruit Co. Pablo Neruda. a cluster of dead fruit/thrown down on the dump. FaBoPV

United States. John Keble. Her towers, and lone sands heap her/crowned merchants' graves. CoBE

The United States and Macedonian. *Anonymous.*
Her motto is "Glory! we conquer or we die." PAH
Who 'fore they'd strike, will nobly sink/Our brave Yankee boys. PAH

The United States of America We. Sam Abrams. take drugs white men/are coming consciousness/& awareness are so different/you wouldn't believe. APU

The United States Prepare for the Permanent Revolution. George Hitchcock. Her tongue has been replaced by/a single mute camellia. EAS

Unity. Jakov De Haan. Do you think I know not God's law? VWA

Unity. Alfred Noyes. One, still one, while the world grows old. HBV 1-2

Unity. George William Russell. It shakes its wondrous plumes of thought/And trails the stars along with them. MoRP

The Unity of God. Panatattu. Impure and pure are all alike to him. WGRP

Univac to Univac. Louis B. Salomon. Men may take over the world! FF; QQQ

The Universal Favorite. Carolyn Wells. Incredible,/Inedible,/Salad of Greens! InMe; NLV

The Universal Prayer. Alexander Pope. All Nature's incense rise! BLPA; CEP; EnLit; FaBoBe; FPL; GoBC; HBV 1-2; ILwL; NoP; OAEP; TreFT; WGRP

The Universal Republic. Victor Hugo. The flag that rises ne'er to fall,/Republic of the World! PGD

The Universe. May Swenson. And what/about us? SUW

The Universe Is Closed and Has REMs. George Starbuck. And buck the odds, and hope, and give it my/Borrowed scratched-up happy hello-goodbye. SUW

University. Karl Shapiro. And shows us, rotted and endowed,/Its senile pleasure. LiTA; OxBA

University Curriculum. William Price Turner. there are courses in log-rolling/and a shortage of trees. OxBS; PoL

University Examinations in Egypt. D. J. Enright. And Goethe who never thought of Thought. MP; OxBTC; TwCP

Unkept Good Fridays. Thomas Hardy. As little of earth, earthy,/As his mankind proclaims. MoRP

Unkindness. George Herbert. Yet use I not my foes as I use Thee. HBV 1-2

Unkindness Has Killed Me. *Anonymous.* Behold this wreched body/That your unkindness haith slaine.' MeEL

The Unknown. John Davidson. Though the way with fire be strewn. MoBrPo

The Unknown. E. O. Laughlin. She won't forget. BLPA

The Unknown. Edward ("Edward Eastaway") Thomas. ...she/May not exist. GBL

The Unknown Beloved. John Hall Wheelock. White ribbons one was binding/About a flowery wreath. HBMV

The Unknown Bird. Edward ("Edward Eastaway") Thomas. Light as that bird wandering beyond my shore. ACV; DTC

The Unknown Child. Elizabeth Jennings. And birth and death close to us constantly. PBWP

The Unknown Citizen. W. H. Auden. Had anything been wrong, we should certainly have heard. BiP; CABA; FF; GoTF; HeIP; InPK; LiTA; LiTM; MoAB; MoRP; NePA; NIP; NLV; NOBL; NYBP; OBSV; PoRA; PPON; SoSe; TreFT; UnPo

The Unknown City. Sir Charles G. D. Roberts. And the great song that seemed to die unsung/Triumphs upon the tongue. CaP

The Unknown Color. Countee Cullen. "Poor little pigs, they see the wind." GoSI; OBCA

The Unknown Dead. Henry Timrod. Laughs gayly o'er their burial-place. AP; MAmP

The Unknown Eros. Coventry Patmore.
Hath less the characters of dark and cold/Than warmth and light asleep. LO
"I will be sorry for their childishness." SoSe

Unknown Girl in the Maternity Ward. Anne Sexton. Go child, who is my sin and nothing more. CoPo; NAs; NoAm

The Unknown God. Henry Francis Lyte. Grandeur has nothing so sublime,/Nor Beauty half so fair. TRV

The Unknown God. George William Russell. Our eyes could never see. GTBS; MoBrPo; WGRP

The Unknown God. William Watson. Above the cloud, beneath the clod:/The Unknown God, The Unknown God. WGRP

The Unknown Grave. Letitia Elizabeth Landon. While lingers in the heart one line/The nameless poet hath a shrine. VLP

Unknown Love. Lady Otomo of Sakanoe. Of the summer moor. AWP

Unknown Man in the Morgue. Merrill Moore. Will now be yours in your last loneliness. MoAmPo

The Unknown Soldier. Conrad Aiken. and know that this too needs heroes, and endurance, and ardor. WaP

Unknown Soldier. Alta Booth Dunn. With sons he's sent to fatal slumber! PGD

The Unknown Soldier. Alun Lewis. Velasquez, close those doglike dolorous eyes. MoBrPo

The Unknown Soldier. Billy Rose. I'd do it all over again. BLPA; FPL; PAL

The Unknown Soldier. Charles A. Wagner. To call each colored weed a flower. AnAmPo

Unknown Soldiers. Edgar Lee Masters. We should not be lying here! NoAm; TAP

Unlawful Assembly. D. J. Enright. Should one enter a caveat,/Or a monastery? OxBTC

Unless. Ella Dietz Glynes. For God is love, and His bright law/Should find our hearts without one flaw. AA

Unless We Guard Them Well. Jane Merchant. "Oh, I would give the moon if I had heard/A thrush, or ever seen a hummingbird!" QQQ

Unloading Rails. *Anonymous.* Now let's go back and get another one... AmFP

The Unloved to His Beloved. William Alexander Percy. More vainly turn and stretch to you my hands. HBMV

Unlucky Boat. George Mackay Brown. Tinkers, going past, make the sign of the cross. NePoEA-2

Unmanifest Destiny. Richard Hovey. I only know it shall be great. AA; AnAmPo; HBV 1-2; HBVY; PAL; TRV; WGRP

The Unnamed Lake. Frederick George Scott. We passed in silence, and the lake/We left without a name. CaP; NOBC

The Unpardonable Sin. Vachel Lindsay. To set the face, and make the heart a stone. BiP; CMoP; NePA

The Unpetalled Rose. Saint, of Lisieux Therese. That solace to Thy last, worn steps on Calvary/Gently to give. CAW

Unplanned Design. Neal Bowers. misery multiplied into infinity–and no door. AMV-80

The Unpossessed. Adele Naude. None has yet lost/The unpossessed. PeSA

Unposted Birthday Card. Norman MacCaig. that would add up only/to this one: that would be/without years. NAs

An Unpraised Picture. Richard Burton. Yet trembles forth a word of prayer and/praise. AA

Unpredictable but Providential. W. H. Auden. bewigged Descartes looks more outre than the painted wizard. SUW

The Unpredicted. John Heath-Stubbs. ...and blackbirds/Incontestably sang, and the people were beautiful. BoLoP; OxBC

Unprofitablenes. Henry Vaughan. And when th'hast done, a stench, or fog is all/The odour I bequeath. AtBAP; SeCV 1-2

The Unquiet Grave. *Anonymous.*
And he that was sae true to me,/Lies in the greenwood slain. CBEP
And wish my soul good rest.' EnSB
I'll set my sail before the wind/To waft me far away.' OBET
It's for my lips they're clay, clay-cold,/And my breath smells earthlye strong. AmFP
So make yourself content, my love,/Till God calls you away. AnFE; AtBAP; BaBo; DTC; ELP; ESPB; ExPo; GBP; HAP; HeIP; LoBV; NoP; OAEL 1-2; PoEL 1-5; PoPle; ViBoPo; WeW
"When the oaken leaves that fall from the trees/Are green and spring up again." FaBoBa; FSW; ViBoFo

The Unreal Song of the Old. James Koller. a song/yet to come PoM

The Unrealities. Friedrich von Schiller. ...from the vast Account/Of Time strike minutes, days, and years away. AWP

Unrecorded Speech. Anna Adams. proving that double negatives mean "No." BrRo

Unregenerate. Jacqueline Embry. She'll love to hear you mutter: "Damn that bird!" HBMV

Unrelenting Flood. William Matthews. tethering us all to our star. GeTw

The Unremarkable Year. Roy Fuller. Is also that of harmonies/That have made one's life and art for evermore off-key. OxBC

The Unremitting Voice of Nightly Streams. William Wordsworth. ...or hear the tinkling knell/Of water-breaks, with grateful heart could tell. NOBV

Unrest. Richard Watson Dixon. Ah, this thy emblem gives. OBNC

Unrest. Don (Donald Robert Marquis) Marquis. I sing the stinging discontent/That leaps from star to star! HBMV

The Unreturning. Wilfred Owen. I dreaded even a heaven with doors so chained. MoBrPo

The Unreturning. Clinton Scollard. Let not a whisper fall/That we have died in vain! PAH

Unreturning. Elizabeth Stoddard And the vast world beneath hides him/from me! AA

Unromantic Song. Anthony Brode. The first time they saw Paris they resolved to make the last? DBV; FiBHP

Unsaid. Archie Randolph Ammons. when I am/silent: gather the boundaried vacancies. NOBA

An Unsaid Word. Adrienne Rich. Knows this the hardest thing to learn. NMM

Unsatisfied. Oliver Wendell Holmes. Give her an Empire, she pines for a name! AnNE

Unsatisfied Yearning. Richard Kendall Munkittrick. To set up a doleful howling/In order to get in! GDP; InMe

The Unscarred Fighter Remembers France. Kenneth Slade Alling. Standing by an open grave. HBMV

The Unseaworthy Ship. *Anonymous.* And then we may boast of our ships and their crews. OBSS

Unseen. Fanny J. Crosby. We shall in righteousness behold Thy face. TrPWD

The Unseen Bridge. Gilbert Thomas. 'Tis the one pathway from Despair,/ And it is called the Bridge of Prayer. HBMV

An Unseen Deer. John Tagliabue. Blesses us with his power, and then the forest hides him and sings. Psk

An Unseen Fire. Michael G. Cooke. The burning secret of this mountain, that coal. AMV-81

Unseen Fire. Ralph Nixon Currey. Meets our bouquet of death–and turns sharp right. OBWP; OxBTC

Unseen Flight. Markos Georgeou. When the curse of death is upon your splendid dust. AMV-80

Unseen Horses. Joan Byers Grayston. Of a brave horse that could untie knots. PH

Unseen Spirits. Nathaniel Parker Willis By man is cursed alway! AA; AmePo; HBV 1-2

Unsent Message to My Brother in His Pain. Leon Stokesbury. Take a later flight,/a later train. Another look around. MAYP

An Unserer Beach. Kurt M. Stein. Er an sei Back muss floateh. InMe

The Unsettled Motorcyclist's Vision of His Death. Thom Gunn. And multiply in ignorance. ForPo; NePoEA-2; PoA

Unshrinking Faith. W.H. Balhurst. We'll tast e'en here the hallowed bliss/ Of an eternal home. BLRP

Unsleeping City. Federico Garcia Lorca. the perfidious goblets, the theater's skull, and the bane. NYP

Unsolicited Letters to Five Artists (parody). Clive James. But we'll find some action that fits your style./Can you drive? FaBoPa

Unspeakable. Margaret Avison. copious and new into the morning,/ celebrated. NOBC

Unsubdued. S. E. Kiser. Tomorrow again, I begin. PoToHe

The Unsung Heroes. Paul Laurence Dunbar. Who fought their way from night to day and struggled/up to God. BPo

An Unsuspected Fact. Edward Cannon. His tongue lay there by way of mat,/And he would wipe his feet on that! NA

The Unteaching. Carole Oles. picture of their teacher crumbling/before a blackboard spattered with lessons. SOTS

The Untended Field. Robert Hillyer. Where we who harvested the grain/ Lie buried under weeds. AnNE

Unter der Linde. George Ellenbogen. like a morning flower/before the first light. AMV-81

Until Death. Elizabeth Akers. But while I live, be true. HBV 1-2

Until I Reach-a Ma Home. *Anonymous.* I nevah inten' to give de journey ovah,/until I reach ma home. BoAN 1-2

Until I Saw the Sea. Lilian Moore. a sea breathes in and out/upon a shore. NTCP

Until the desert knows. Emily Dickinson. On the familiar road/Galloped in dreams. MoPo; NOBA

Until the Shadows Lengthen. John Henry, Cardinal Newman. Through Jesus Christ our Lord. Amen. TRV

Until They Have Stopped. Sarah E. Wright. Of the great man Robeson–nothing but a time for love. PoBA

Until We Built a Cabin. Aileen Fisher. I never knew how many/many/ stars there really are! TiPo

Untimely Thoughts. Thomas Bailey Aldrich. I wonder what month of the year. AnNE

Untitled. Peter Blue Cloud. and giggles the child awakened/into day. VoR

Untitled. Robert J. Conley. only insofar as it is honest–/no more–no less. STE

Untitled. John Crowne. Only to make a sound to last for ages. BoC

Untitled. Daryl Hine. The blood that we see shed, the tears that we/Shed, the wall, and the anonymous cross. NoAm; TwCP

Untitled. King D. Kuka. Gayle Marie, you're beautiful. VoR

Untitled. Lisel Mueller. I did not know/she was still there, my antilife,/ with her dark red wound. GP

Untitled. Dana Naone. A great bird rises from your chest/with wings that fill the room. CDW

Untitled. Herman Nibbelink. ...no/insurance, no brakes/the whole way! AMV-80

Untitled. Mark Rahschulte. We are just like you, except we got caught. AMV-80

Untitled. James A. Randall, Jr. This 300 year poem/To our suffering. For you, you this atheist. BPo

Untitled. Mah-do-ge Tohee. where/will we ride? STE

Untitled. Humbert Wolfe. They might as well. BoC

Untitled: "fisk is/a/negroid/institution..." Sharon Scott. a hundred and some odd years old. JB

Untitled: "Fivesucked the features of my girl by glory." Nicholas Moore. And save us God's inscription in the bone. PoA

Untitled (Hi Ronda). Sharon Scott. and/hold/their/hands. JB

Untitled I. Ishmael Reed. no matter what heavy/traffic was coming down/ on them CNA

Untitled Poem. Alan Dugan.
and come home to a woman saying honey. GP
So: First pleasures after hard times,/Hello in time for goodbye. GP

Untitled Poem. "A swim in Ohuira Bay." Robert Peterson. And overhead wild ducks soar like racers/into forms as delicious as life or money. NeAC

An Untitled Poem, about an Uncompleted Sonnet. Sanford Pinsker. Like the ugly duckling at a high school dance. AMV-81

Untitled Poem. "Hands folded like napkins in my lap." Robert Peterson. She's built. Does she or doesn't she? NeAC

Untitled Poem. "In the 2 A.M. Club, a working man's bar." Robert Peterson. and my life to this moment/cannot be totally explained. NeAC

Untitled Requiem for Tomorrow. Conyus. there is nothing/expected nor/ leaving PoBA

Untitled: "Words do not grow on the landscape." Jean Malley. Let us sit and not break the silence. PoA

Unto Adam, His Own Scriveyn. Geoffrey Chaucer. And all is through thy negligence and rape. OBSP

Unto Jehovah Sing Will I. Henry Ainsworth. The deeps them covered; they sank down/Into the bottoms as a stone. AH

Unto My Valentine. Margery Brews. ...And this letter was endited at Topcroft, with full/heavy heart, etc./By your own/Margery Brews. OFD

Unto Our God Most High We Sing. John Vance Cheney. Let earth wide with glory flame,/Forever, ever and amen. AH

Unto the Breach. Andrea Poliziano. ...or satisfy my itch/Upon some farmyard ass or common bitch. PeHV

Unto the Upright Praise: Chorus. Isaac Luzzatto. Our glorious beauty for the upright/heart. TrJP

Unto Us a Son Is Given. Alice Meynell. And he, too, whom we have by heart. EBCP; MoRP

The Untold Want. Walt Whitman. Now voyager sail thou forth to seek and find. MoAmPo

Untrodden Ways. Agnes Maule Machar. With ploughs and furrows left behind! CaP

The Untutored Giraffe. Oliver Herford. But really it's a funnier joke/To meet a head that's lost its folk! ShM

Unusual. Larry Eigner. some face and legs FAZ

Unusual Things. Tom Hennen. and can change/to an ugly stone/in the palm of your hand. FAZ

The Unutterable Beauty. G. Anketall "Woodbine Willie" Studdert-Kennedy. To guide men down the years,/Until they cross the last long bridge of sighs. TrPWD

The Unveiling. Suzanne Bernhardt. your mother weeps Yiddish/your father sneezes/ashes & gold. VWA

The Unwanted. C. Day-Lewis. Willy-nilly born it was, divinely formed and fair. PoPl

Unwanted. Edward Field. Responds to love, don't call him or he will come. CoPo; PPON; Psk

The Unwanted. Mary Gordon. Unbearable. Unborn. IHMS

Unwasted Days. James Russell Lowell. In work done squarely and unwasted days. MCCG

Unwelcome. Mary Elizabeth Coleridge. And a man with his back to the East. CH; OBEV; OBNC; OBVV; PoPle

Unwelcome. Irma Dovey. The day comes soon when I must let You in. AMV-80

The Unwilling Guest: An Urban Dialogue. Horace Gregory. It is excellent weather for a holiday. CrMA

The Unwilling Gypsy. Josephine Johnson. One clear fixed star forever is denied me.../The light of home! HBMV

Unwritten Poems. William Winter. Still lovely and still fugitive? AA

Up. Bill Kushner. ...thank you all for the best performance by a male APU

Up against the Wall. Cleve Phillips. and you going to/hell! AMV-81

Up against the Wall (parody). D. C. Berry. If you/want your wall/whole, get/rid of this. BXAP

Up and Down the City Road... *Anonymous.* Pop goes the weasel! EvOK

Up at a Villa–Down in the City. Robert Browning. Oh, a day in the city-square, there is no such pleasure/in life. CBEP; EnLit; FaBoPP; GTBS-P; HBV 1-2; InPS; MBW 1-2; NOBE; OBTV; PoRA; PPP; SeCeV

Up Early. Kit Robinson. rain glances off dots that divide the lanes/that contain the flow that issues from consummate waking APU

Up from the Egg: The Confessions of a Nuthatch Avoider. Ogden Nash. And I sometimes visualize in my gin/The Audubon that I audibin. BoAnP; FiBHP

Up from the Wheelbarrow. Ogden Nash. Because if you don't I shall starve or freeze. FaBoBe

Up, Helsum Hairt. Alexander Scott. Wissing all luvaris leill to haif sic chance,/That thay may haif us in remembrance. OxBS

Up-Hill. Christina Georgina Rossetti. Yea, beds for all who come. BLPA; FaBoBe; FaBoRV; FPL; GoTF; HAP; HBV 1-2; LoBV; MCCG; NoP; OAEL 1-2; OAEP; OBNC; PoRA; TrCP; TreFS; ViBoPo; VLP; WHA; WiR

Up I Arose in Verno Tempore. Anonymous. I shall lose God et vitam eternam. GBP

Up in the Air. Allan Ramsay. Dinna cheat, but drink fair,/Huzza, huzza, and huzza lads yet,/Up wi't, &c. NOEC

Up in the Air. James S. Tippett. Airplane,/Piloting you/Far in the blue? SoPo; SUS; TiPo

Up in the Lift Go We. Anonymous. Because my heel is as long as my toe! PBBP

Up in the Morning Early. Robert Burns. I'm sure it's winter fairly. PoSC

Up in the North. Anonymous. The donkey's got the whooping-cough. OxBoLi

Up on de Mountain. Anonymous. Chillun, an achin' heart Lord! BoAN 1-2

Up & out. Nila NorthSun. it doesn't look so bad. STE

Up out of the African. Ted Joans. ...these huge/animals of the ocean came. GP

Up Rising. Robert Duncan. now shines from the eyes of the President/in the swollen head of the nation. NNaP

Up Silver Stairsteps. Jesse Stuart. To coast from Heaven down where the world things are. AmFN; AmFN 005

Up Street and Down Street. Anonymous. Darling girl, do you love me? OxNR

Up-Tails All. Anonymous. There is no one but that will play/At up-tails all. UnTE

Up the Airy Mountain. William Allingham. Green jacket, red cap,/And white owl's feather. FaFP

Up the Barley Rows. Sora. a butterfly goes. SoPo

Up the Country. Henry Lawson. Drinking beer and lemon-squashes, taking baths and cooling down. CBAP

Up the Hill. Anonymous. Forget me not. PH

Up the Hill, Down the Hill. Eleanor Farjeon. Put best foot forward,/New Year, with a will. PoSC

Up the Mountain to Pick Mawu. Anonymous. The new—not quite as good as the old. HW

Up the Wooden Hill. Anonymous. Down Sheet Lane/to Blanket Fair. OxNR

Up There. W. H. Auden. Boy sails north or approaches coral islands. OxBTC

Up Time. Anonymous. Pull out your tongue,/And see what you can say. OxNR

Up to Date. Hugh" (Christopher Murray Grieve) MacDiarmid. And I'm no shair o' maist the sinners either. FaBoCo

Upanishads: Second Khanda. Anonymous. That radiance illumines all this world. ILwL

Upanishads: Seventh Brahmana. Anonymous. Then Uddalaka Aruni was silent. ILwL

Upanishads: Third Adhyaya. Anonymous. ...it stops for the one/who knows him whom the Brahman-knowers/call Eternal. ILwL

The Upas Tree. Alexander Pushkin. And they through every neighboring land/Death and disaster sped. LiTW

Upheld by His Hand. Grace B. Renfrow. He held me by His hand. BePJ

Upland. Archie Randolph Ammons. ...they are round and ready. NOBA

Upon a Black Twist, Rounding the Arm of the Countess of Carlisle. Robert Herrick. I beg of Love that ever I/May in like chains of darkness lie! CaPo

Upon a Braid of Hair in a Heart. Henry, Bishop of Chichester King. And if we never meet, think I/Bequeath'd it as my Legacy. EnLoPo

Upon a Child That Died. Robert Herrick. Give her strewings, but not stir/The earth that lightly covers her. CaPo; CavP; CH; ForPo; InPK; LoBV; NoP; OBS; SeCV 1-2; TrGrPo

Upon a Cock-Horse to Market I'll Trot. Anonymous. If it had not been killed, it would/surely have died. OxNR

Upon a Dainty Hill Sometime. Nicholas Breton. She made the little woods so ring,/They waked me from my sleep. PBBP

Upon a Dead Man's Head. John Skelton. Eternally/To behold and see/The Trinity!/Amen. CoBE; HAP; SeCePo

Upon a Delaying Lady. Robert Herrick. Or I shall quickly grow/To Frost or Snow. PoPle

Upon a Diamond Cut in Forme of a Heart... Ayton [(or Aytoun)] Sir Robert. Send mee it back as free from smart/As it was free from wrong. ElL; OBS

Upon a Dying Lady. William Butler Yeats. It is about to die. UnPo

Upon a Flie. Robert Herrick. Dead, and clos'd up in Yvorie. FM

Upon a Fool. John Hoskyns. Whether fools' souls go to heaven or to hell. FaBoEE

Upon a Funeral. Sir John Beaumont. Such is the end of all the sons of Earth. FaBoRV

Upon a Girl of Seven Years Old. Alexander Pope. And from those pretty things you speak have told/How Pallas talked when she was seven years old. OBSP

Upon a Gloomy Night. Roy Campbell. Threw them amongst the lilies there to fade. AtBAP; BoLoP; OBVE; PeSA

Upon a Great Shower of Snow That Fell on May-Day, 1654. Thomas Washbourne. A blessing on the Nation, and at last/A general pardon for all faults are past. NOCV

Upon a House Shaken by the Land Agitation. William Butler Yeats. Wrought of high laughter, loveliness and ease? CMoP

Upon A. M. Sir John Suckling. Men most of all enjoy, when least they do. CavP

Upon a Maid. Robert Herrick. Then depart, but see ye tread/Lightly, lightly, o'er the dead. CaPo; FaBoCh; FaBoEE; LoGBV; OxBoLi

Upon a Maid That Died the Day She Was Married. Meleager. This epitaph, which here you see,/Supplied the epithalamy. AWP; OBVE

Upon a Mole in Celia's Bosom. Thomas Carew. The sweet and smart from thence shall bring/Of the bee's honey and her sting. AnAnS 2; CaPo

Upon a Notorious Shrew. Anonymous. Methought I heard her very voice,/Rending the clouds asunder. FaBoEE

Upon a Passing Bell. Thomas Washbourne. This Bell bids thee, Beware! FaBoRV

Upon a Ribband. Thomas Carew. This makes my arm your prisoner, that my heart. AnAnS 2; CaPo; OAEL 1-2

Upon a Rich Country Gentleman. Anonymous. I need no more, I have no less. FaBoEE

Upon a Ring of Bells. John Bunyan. There's nothing to him like thy ding, dong, Bell. CH

Upon a Row of Old Boots and Shoes in a Pawnbroker's Window. Furnley Maurice. In paddocks of shadows and showers,/Far, far from here. CBAP

Upon a Second Marriage. James Merrill. ...those many marriages/That life on each live thing bestows. HW; NoP

Upon a Snail. John Bunyan. The herb, the flower, is eaten by the snail. OxBChV

Upon a Spider Catching a Fly. Edward Taylor. Yea, thankfully,/For joy. AmP; AmPP; AP; CBEP; MAmP; NePA; NOBA; NoP; OxBA; PoEL 1-5; SCAP; TAP

Upon a Virgin Kissing a Rose. Robert Herrick. Not so much Rose, as Wreathe. SeCP; SeCV 1-2

Upon a Wasp Chilled with Cold. Edward Taylor. Where all my pipes inspir'de upraise/An heavenly musick, furr'd with praise. AtBAP; CBEP; NOBA; NOCV; PoEL 1-5

Upon a Wife that Dyed Mad with Jealousie. Robert Herrick. And such spirits raise, 'twill then/Trouble Death to lay agen. CavP

Upon a Young Mother of Many Children. Robert Herrick. Pity me, too, who found so soon a tomb. CaPo

Upon Absence. Katherine ("Orinda") Philips. Love me no more! for I am grown/Too dead and dull for thee to own. PBWP

Upon an Hermaphrodite. John Cleveland. Coyning thee a Philip and Mary. AnAnS 2

Upon an Ingenious Friend, Over-Vain. Thomas Fitzgerald. Nor yet, whilst we his wit commend,/Despise his want of sense. OBSP

Upon an Obscure Night. Saint John of Damascus. How delicately thou teachest love to me! ILwL

Upon Appleton House, to My Lord Fairfax. Andrew Marvell. But I on it securely play,/And gall its horsemen all the day. JCP Let's in: for the dark Hemisphere/Does now like one of them appear. FaBoPV; SeCP; SeCV 1-2

Upon Batt. Robert Herrick. But out of hope his wife might die to bear 'em. AnAnS 2; FaBoEE

Upon Being Awakened at Night by My Four Year Old Daughter. Dachine Rainer. Those things which I most terrify/I neither can hear nor touch nor see. NePoAm-2

Upon Ben Johnson. Robert Herrick. That will speake what this can't tell/Of his glory. So farewell. CaPo; FaBoEE; NoP; OAEP; OBS; SeCV 1-2

Upon Ben. Johnson. Edmund Waller. Who was, nor this, nor that, but all we find,/And all we can imagine in mankind. SeCV 1-2

Upon Bishop Andrewes His Picture before His Sermons. Richard Crashaw. Looke on the following leaves, and see him breathe. OBS

Upon Boys Diverting Themselves in the River. Thomas Foxton. The greatest comforts, if abused,/Will torture and destroy. OxBChV

Upon Bunce: Epigram. Robert Herrick. Pay when th'art honest; let me have some hope. CaPo

Upon Castara's Absence. William Habington. My soule imparadis'd, for 'tis with her. AnAnS 2

Upon Christ His Birth. Sir John Suckling. Their hearts, as well as inn's, are made of clay. NCEP

Upon Christmas Eve. Sir John Suckling. And fancy then the Lord of Light is there/As he did once in Moses-bush appeare. NCEP

Upon de Mountain. *Anonymous.* Tired of starvin' won't starve no mo'. TrAS

Upon Drinking in a Bowl. John Wilmot, Earl of Rochester. With Wine I wash away my Cares,/And then to Love again. CEP; OBS; OxBoLi; SeCV 1-2

Upon Eckington Bridge, River Avon. Sir Arthur Thomas ("Q") Quiller-Couch. Turns in her sleep, and murmurs of the Spring. OBVV

Upon Faireford Windowes. Elizabeth T. Corbett. The Inside drosse, the Outside Saint. AnAnS 2; EyDe

Upon Fone a School-master. Epigram. Robert Herrick. that he do's whip with them. AnAnS 2

Upon Ford's Two Tragedies... Richard Crashaw. What is Loves Sacrifice but the Broken Heart. OBS

Upon Glass: Epigram. Robert Herrick. He'll turn a papist, ranker than before. JCP

Upon Groins: Epigram. Robert Herrick. Penance, and standing so, are both but one. CaPo

Upon Gryll. Robert Herrick. Gryll will not therefore say a Grace for it. AnAnS 2

Upon Hearing His High Sweet Tenor Again. Joseph Langland. such resonance, such love. AMV-81

Upon Her Feet. Robert Herrick. As if they started at bo-peep,/Did soon draw in again. CaPo; OBSP; ViBoPo

Upon Her Soothing Breast. Emily Bronte. A dreary glory smiled. BoWoP

Upon Her Voice. Robert Herrick. And angels will be born while thou dost sing. CaPo

Upon Himself. Robert Herrick. Rather than mend, put out the light. OBSP

Upon His Departure Hence. Robert Herrick. Where tell/I dwell,/Farewell. FaBoRV; QFR

Upon His Julia. Robert Herrick. The other parts will richly please. SpRo

Upon His Leaving His Mistress. John Wilmot, Earl of Rochester. No, live up to thy mighty Mind;/And be the Mistress of Mankind. EnLoPo; GBL; TEP; ViBoPo

Upon His Majesty's Being Made Free of the City. Andrew Marvell. You for slaves are decreed,/Until you all burn again, burn again. APAS

Upon His Picture. Thomas Randolph. Whose shadow is less given to change than he. CBEP; MePo; NOBE

Upon His Sister-in-Law, Mistress Elizabeth Herrick. Robert Herrick. Wherein thou liv'st for ever. Dear, farewell. CaPo

Upon His Spaniell Tracie. Robert Herrick. This shall my love doe, give thy sad death one/Teare, that deserves of me a million. FM

Upon His Timorous Silence in Her Presence. Francis Davison. To freeze the tongue, and fire the heart. EG

Upon Jack and Jill. Epigram. Robert Herrick. Let me feed full, till that I fart, sayes Jill. AnAnS 2; CaPo

Upon Jone and Jane. Robert Herrick. As so it doth? that's pittie. AnAnS 2

Upon Julia (parody). Ernest Radford. But in th' obverse/'Tis worse. BXAP

Upon Julia's Arctics. Bert Leston Taylor. Oh, how that flopping floppeth me! NLV; OBAL

Upon Julia's Breasts. Robert Herrick. Ravished in that fair Via Lactea. CaPo; NoP

Upon Julia's Clothes. Robert Herrick. O how that glittering taketh me! AnFE; AtBAP; AWP; CaPo; EnLi 1-2; EnLoPo; ExPo; FaBV; FaFP; FF; GBL; GoTF; GTBS; HAP; HBV 1-2; HeIP; HoPM; InPo; InPS; JCP; LiTB; LoBV; NIP; NLV; NOBE; NoP; OAEL 1-2; OAEP; OBEV; OBS; OBSP; PAI; PoEL 1-5; PoPle; PPP; PPoe; SeCeV; SeCP; SeCV 1-2; SpRo; TreF; TrGrPo; ViBoPo; WeW

Upon Julia's Clothes (parody). E. V. Knox ("Evoe"). Oh, how their likeness taketh me! BXAP

Upon Julia's Fall. Robert Herrick. And had told all, but did refrain/Because his tongue was tied again. UnTE

Upon Julia's Hair Filled with Dew. Robert Herrick. Danced by the streams. AtBAP; EG

Upon Julia's Petticoat. Robert Herrick. ...should it move/To life eternal, I could love. UnTE

Upon Julia's Recovery. Robert Herrick. As beames of Corrall, but more cleare. AtBAP

Upon Julia's Ribband. Robert Herrick. Wherein all pleasures of the world are wove. CaPo

Upon Julia's Voice. Robert Herrick. Melting melodious words, to Lutes of Amber. AtBAP; BoW; CABA; ExPo; JCP; MyFE; NOBE; SeCePo; SeCP; SoSe

Upon Julia Washing Herself in the River. Robert Herrick. Had not thy waves forbade the rest. CaPo

Upon Julia Weeping. Robert Herrick. She wept, and made it deeper by a tear. ExPo

Upon Kinde and True Love. Aurelian Townsend. Nor Pirate, though a Prince he be. CavP; EG; MeLP; MePo; OBS

Upon Lazarus His Teres. Richard Crashaw. He scornes them now, but o they'l sute full well/With th'Purple hee must weare in Hell. SeCV 1-2

Upon Leaving the Parole Board Hearing. Conyus. clinging/to lost/horizons/i PoBA

Upon Lesbia–Arguing. Alfred Cochrane. The voice is yours, whate'er you say. HBV 1-2

Upon Looking at a Book of Astrology. David McFadden. loops, billion-hookt principles undreamed-of. NeAC

Upon Love. Robert Herrick.
My desperate fears, in love, had seen/Mine execution. BoLiVe; TrGrPo
That joynt to ashes sho'd be burnt,/Ere I wo'd love at all. SeCV 1-2

Upon Love, by Way of Question and Answer. Robert Herrick. Kiss ye, to kill ye. CaPo

Upon Love Fondly Refus'd for Conscience Sake. Thomas Randolph. What youth and pleasure prompts us to. AnAnS 2; OAEL 1-2

Upon Lulls. Robert Herrick. By his proboscis that he is all nose. CaPo

Upon M. Ben Jonson–Epigram. Robert Herrick. Sleeping the lucklesse age out, till that she/Her resurrection ha's again with thee. CaPo; OAEP

Upon Master Edmund Spenser, the Famous Poet. Francis Beaumont. While Spenser is alive, it is no question. FaBoEE

Upon Master Fletchers Incomparable Playes. Robert Herrick. None writes love's passion in the world, like Thee. OBS

Upon Master Walter Montagu's Return from Travel. Thomas Carew. As laymen clasp their hands, we join our feet. CaPo

Upon Mistress Elizabeth Wheeler under the Name of Amarillis. Robert Herrick. He chirped for joy to see himself deceived. CaPo

Upon Mistress Susanna Southwell Her Feet. Robert Herrick. Did soon draw in again. EnLi 1-2

Upon Moon. Robert Herrick. That ebs from pittie lesse and lesse. MOON

Upon Mrs. Anne Bradstreet Her Poems, &c. John Rogers. What errors here be found, are in Errataes place. SCAP

Upon My Lady Carliles Walking in Hampton-Court Garden. Dialogue. Sir John Suckling. So lost a thing as thou hadst been. AnAnS 2; CaPo; NoP

Upon My Lord Brohall's Wedding. Sir John Suckling. Another, when they're ready, shows them game. CaPo

Upon My Lord Chief Justice's Election of My Lady Anne Wentworth... Thomas Carew. "I know no Heaven but fair Wentworth's eyes." CaPo

Upon New Year's Eve. Sir Arthur Thomas ("Q") Quiller-Couch. We, in our little home,/Sit unafraid. OBVV

Upon Nothing. John Wilmot, Earl of Rochester. Flow swiftly into thee, and in thee ever end. AtBAP; MePo; OBS; OBSV; PoEL 1-5; TrGrPo; ViBoPo

Upon One of the Maids of Honour to Queen Elizabeth. John Hoskyns. She died a maid, the more the pity. FaBoEE

Upon Pagget. Robert Herrick. Made him take up his shirt, lay down his sword. CaPo; FaBoCh

Upon Parson Beanes. Robert Herrick. That on the seaventh, he can nor preach, or pray. AnAnS 2

Upon Paul's Steeple Stands a Tree. *Anonymous.* Until they come to London Bridge. OxNR

Upon Phillis Walking in a Morning before Sun-rising. John Cleveland. But left the Sun her Curate-light. AnAnS 2; MeLP

Upon Prudence Baldwin Her Sickness. Robert Herrick. And a gallant cock shall be/Offer'd up by her, to thee. JCP; OAEP; SeCV 1-2

Upon Prue, His Maid. Robert Herrick. From whose happy spark here let/Spring the purple violet. ForPo; JCP; NoP; OAEP

Upon Rook: Epigram. Robert Herrick. He loves the gain that vanity brings in. CaPo

Upon Roses. Robert Herrick. Which as a warme, and moistned spring,/Gave them their ever flourishing. SeCP

Upon Saul Seeking His Father's Asses. Rowland Watkyns. Find out a hundred you in London may/Of Presbyterian asses in one day. FaBoEE

Upon Scarlet and Blush-Coloured Ribbands, Given by Two Ladies. James Shirley. I forfeit blush and scarlet back again. GoBC

Upon Scobble. Epigram. Robert Herrick. One slit's enough to let Adultry in. AnAnS 2; CaPo; FaBoEE; NoP; TW

Upon Shaving Off One's Beard. John Updike. Small-jawed, weak-chinned, big-eyed I stare/At the forgotten boy I was. OBSP

Upon Showbread: Epigram. Robert Herrick. And give me meat, or give me else thy plate. CaPo

Upon Sir Francis Drake's Return from his Voyage about the World...
Anonymous. And he ne'er came home again. God bless the Queen.
CoMu; EIL; FaBoCh; OBSS

Upon Sir John Lawrence's Bringing Water over the Hills... Sir John
Suckling. For love will creep where well it cannot go. CaPo

Upon Some Alterations in My Mistress, after My Departure into France.
Thomas Carew. In the deep flood she drowned her beamy face. CaPo

Upon Some Women. Robert Herrick. Onely true in shreds and stuffe.
AnAnS 2; CaPo; DBV

Upon Suddes a Laundresse. Robert Herrick. Both with her Husband's, and
her own tough fleame. AnAnS 2; DBV

Upon Sybilla. Robert Herrick. Then to the poor she freely gives the milk.
CaPo

Upon the Anonymous Author of Legion's Humble Address to the Lords.
Thomas (Tom) Brown. But 'tis in vermin that about thee throng. APAS

Upon the Author; by a Known Friend. Benjamin Woodbridge. And earthly
Fires, within their ashes shrink. SCAP

Upon the Author of a Play Called Sodom. John Oldham. And so thy book
itself turn Sodomite. TW

Upon the Author of the "Satire against Wit." Sir Charles Sedley. Go on
brave doctor, a third volume write,/And find us paper while you make us
sh–. APAS

Upon the Author's First Seven Years' Service. Thomas Tusser. And trust
to be so long as life shall last. EIL

Upon the Bankruptcy of a Physician. Henricus Selyns. Are rotten in the
box and mothy in the raiment. SCAP

Upon the Bleeding Crucifix. Richard Crashaw. N'ere wast thou in a sense
so sadly true,/The WELL of living WATERS, Lord, till now. SeCP

Upon the Crucifix. William Alabaster. Lord soe I am, if heare my thoughts
may rest. PoEL 1-5

Upon the Curtain of Lucasta's Picture It Was Thus Wrought. Richard
Lovelace. That you will swear her body by this law/Is but its shadow, as
this its–now draw. CaPo

Upon the Death of a Gentleman. Richard Crashaw. Weepe then, onely be
exprest/Thus much, Hee's Dead, and weepe the rest. CavP

Upon the Death of G: B. John Cotton. We have too many Divells still goe
loose. SCAP

Upon the Death of George Santayana. Anthony Hecht. "He whom I loved
for what he might have been/Freezes with traitors in the ultimate pit."
AmLP; CoPo; NePA

Upon the Death of His Late Highness the Lord Protector (excerpt). Andrew
Marvell. Always thy honour, praise, and name shall last. JCP

Upon the Death of His Much Esteemed Friend Mr Jno Saffin Junr....
Grindall Rawson. Maturior vis, quid moror alterna. ad Meunatem/Sicflevit
SCAP

Upon the Death of His Sparrow an Elegie. Robert Herrick. Not Virgil's
Gnat had such a Tomb. FM

Upon the Death of My Ever Desired Friend Doctor Donne Dean of Pauls.
Henry, Bishop of Chichester King. So Jewellers no Art or Metal trust/To
form the Diamond, but the Diamonds dust. AnAnS 2; SeCP

Upon the Death of Sir Albert Morton's Wife. Sir Henry Wootton. To live
without him, liked it not, and died. AnAnS 2; BoLoP; FaBoEE; NIP;
NoP; OBEV; OBS; PoPle; TreFT; ViBoPo; WeW

Upon the Death of Sir Antony Denny. Anonymous. Death brought him
blisse that ever shall endure. EnPo

Upon the Death of the Earl of Dundee. John Dryden. And couldst not fall
but with thy country's fate. ACP

Upon the Death of the Lord Hastings. John Dryden. Erect no
Mausoloeums: for his best/Monument is his Spouses Marble brest. CEP;
PeD; SeCV 1-2

Upon the Death of the Viscount of Dundee. John Dryden. Farewell! who
living didst support the State,/And coud'st not fall but with thy Country's
Fate. OBS

Upon the Decease of Mrs. Anne Griffin... John Fiske. That there Thou
hast more fully then requir'd/Or understood could bee whilst sin annoy
SCAP

Upon the Double Murther of King Charles I... Katherine ("Orinda") Philips.
O to what height of horror are they come/Who dare pull down a crown,
tear up a tomb! SBG

Upon the Downs. Sir George Etherege. ...forget/The nonsense and the
farce of what the fools call great? ViBoPo

Upon the Dramatick Poems of Mr. John Fletcher. William Cartwright.
That debt thou left'st to us, which none but he/Can truly pay, Fletcher, who
writes like thee. OBS

Upon the Ensignes of Christes Crucifyinge. William Alabaster. Thy bloode
the Inke, and with compassion/Write thus upon my soule: thy Jesu still.
MePo

Upon the Feast of St. Simon and St. Jude. Samuel Johnson. Those names
which in immortal strains/Angelic choirs have sung. EiCP

Upon the Heavenly Scarp. Abraham Moses Klein. Summoned the angels of
Sodom down to earth. PoA

Upon the Hill before Centreville. George Henry Boker. Strike for the
crown of victory! PAH

Upon the Holy Sepulchre. Richard Crashaw. Now the grave lies buried.
FaBoEE

Upon the Horse and Rider. John Bunyan. And by his going he may know
his rider. OxBChV

Upon the Image of Death. Robert Southwell. Oh! grant me grace, O God,
that I/My life may mend, sith I must die. CH; CoBE; EIL; NOBE; OBSC

Upon the Infant Martyrs. Richard Crashaw. Make me doubt if heaven will
gather/Roses hence, or lilies rather. NoP; OAEL 1-2

Upon the King's Return from Flanders. Henry Hall. Ring not your bells
ye fools, but wring your hands. APAS

Upon the King's Voyage to Chatham.... Anonymous. That the bishops, the
bishops did throw out the bill. APAS

Upon the Lake. Hayim Lenski. reeds whisper to the lake below. VWA

Upon the Lark and the Fowler. John Bunyan. And how it may this
fowler's net escape,/And not commit upon itself this rape. PBBP

Upon the Losse of His Little Finger. Thomas Randolph. How soone
mischance hath made a Hand of thee. AnAnS 2

Upon the Losse of His Mistresses. Robert Herrick. For to number sorrow
by/Their departures hence, and die. AnAnS 2; CaPo; OAEP; SeCV 1-2

Upon the Most Useful Knowledge, Craft or Cunning... William Wycherley.
Does in the World but more successful grow,/Than the True, which does
True Wits most undo. SeCV 1-2

Upon the Much-to-Be Lamented Desease of the Reverend Mr. John Cotton..
John Fiske. Lord unto thee: even so shall I./Jo: Fiske. SCAP

Upon the Nipples of Julia's Breast. Robert Herrick. So like to this, nay, all
the rest,/Is each neat niplet of her breast. CaPo; ErPo; LiTL; UnTE;
ViBoPo

Upon the Priory Grove, His Usual Retirement. Henry Vaughan. We'll kiss,
and smile, and walk agen. FaBoPP

Upon the Same. Robert Herrick. Then sure thou'lt like, or thou wilt envy
me. CaPo

Upon the Snail. John Bunyan. The prize they do aim at they do procure.
OBSP

Upon the Sudden Restraint of the Earle of Somerset. Sir Henry Wotton.
Vertue is the roughest way,/But proves at night a Bed of Downe. AnAnS
2; ELP; JCP; MePo; NOBE; NoP; OBS; SeCP

Upon the Swallow. John Bunyan. When I believe and sing, my doubtings
cease. OxBChV

Upon the Tomb of the Most Reverend Mr. John Cotton... Benjamin
Woodbridge. O happy Israel in America,/In such a Moses such a Joshua.
SCAP

Upon the Troublesome Times. Robert Herrick. Yet we must all/Down
fall,/And perish at the last. CaPo

Upon the Weathercock. John Bunyan. Face Antichrist in each disguise.
OxBChV

Upon the Works of Ben Jonson (excerpt). John Oldham. But all appeared
either the native ground,/Or twisted, wrought, and interwoven with the
piece. PP

Upon This Rock. Ruthven Todd. Lay in their fear of attitudes of stone.
PoA

Upon Thought Castara May Die. William Habington. A Heaven will
banish all corruption thence. ACP

Upon Time. Robert Herrick. And so away he flew. OBS

Upon Umber: Epigram. Robert Herrick. (As Umber swears) did make his
lion start. CaPo

Upon Venus Putting on Mars His Armes. Richard Crashaw. What need'st
thou put on armes against poore men? SeCP

Upon Visiting His Lady by Moonlight. A. W. Whose nights are clearer
than the days. CTC; MOON; OBSC

Upon Wedlock, and Death of Children. Edward Taylor. I joy, may I sweet
flowers for glory breed,/Whether thou getst them green, or let them seed.
AmPP; AP; NoP

Upon Your Leaving. Etheridge Knight. we are one./and are strong.
NeAC; NNaP

Upone Tabacco. Ayton [(or Aytoun)] Sir Robert. To live upon Tobacco
and on hope,/The ones but smoake, the other is but winde. OxBS

Upper Air. Frank Ernest Hill. That will not mix with our mortality.
AnAmPo

Upper Broadway. Adrienne Rich. I look at my face in the glass and see/a
halfborn woman. HaCAP; InPS

The Upper Canadian. James Reaney. That mind where thoughts float
round/As geese do round a pond/And never get out. NOBC

An Upper Chamber. Frances Bannerman. Shall I find that little chamber
as of old! HBV 1-2; OBEV

An Upper Chamber in a Darkened House. Frederick Goddard Tuckerman.
The tiny petals of the mountain-ash. AnNE; NOBA; TAP

Upper Family. Maxwell Bodenheim. And in nightmares they see him pull/
A rickshaw at the next World Fair. OBAL

The Upper Lake. Francis Stuart. At last to stand beside you and be dumb.
NeIP

Upper Lambourne. Sir John Betjeman. As to make the swelling downland,/Far surrounding, seem their own. FaBoTw

An Upper Room. D. L. Kelleher. Where still those generations, to and fro,/Mysteriously greet. NeIP

The Upper Skies Are Palest Blue. Robert Bridges. The whitened planking of the mill/Is now in shade and now in sun. VLP

Uppon the First Sight of New-England June 29, 1638. Thomas Tillam. Come yee my servants of my father Blessed SCAP

Uprising See the Fitful Lark. Anonymous. While fairy zephyrs deck each brow! NA

Upstairs Downstairs. Hervey Allen. Saying the black man living with the white/Had given more than white men could requite. HBMV; PoA; PoNe

Upstream. Carl Sandburg. The strong men keep coming on. HBMV; MoAB; MoAmPo; MoRP

Uptown. Allen Ginsberg. dapper Irishman. FF

Uptown. Paul Zweig. While cars and buses grunted by him on both sides. NYP

Ur Burial. Richard Eberhart. To serve the sun in a life beyond sleep. NePoAm

Urania. Robert Andrews. This cordial take.' I drank. Urania flew. NOEC

Urania. Matthew Arnold. Their pure, unwavering, deep disdain. HBV 1-2

Urania. Aubrey Thomas De Vere. ...The ocean's utmost rim/Burned yet a moment: then the world grew dim. IrPN

Urania. Ruth Pitter. now she advances: now she brings her vestal/lamp to the tomb, with nameless consolation. MoVE

An Urban Convalescence. James Merrill. But the dull need to make some kind of house/Out of the life lived, out of the love spent. CoAP; NOBA; NYP

Urban Dream. Victor Hernandez Cruz. alarm clock bursts. NBP

The Urban Experience. Lew Blockcolski.
He did not try. VoR
he dreamed the midnight dancers/buried him head down. VoR

Urban History. Chester Kallman. ...the sea, unstained,/Haunts what it cannot fill. CrMA

Urban Ode. Sandra McPherson. What do you think, Patron Happiness? MAYP

Urban Roses. Ted Isaac. Hold back the world from you and me. PoPl

Urceus Exit: Triolet. Henry Austin Dobson. I intended an Ode;/And it turn'd to a Sonnet. CenHV; GTBS; HBV 1-2; OBEV

Urgency. Betsy Sholl. ...O my husband, what is this/strange land I have no desire to explore? AMV-80

Urgency. Sarah E. Wright. We must/Make it–Now! PoNe

Uriel. Ralph Waldo Emerson. And the gods shook, they knew not why. AnNE; AP; APA; LiTA; MAmP; NePA; NOBA; OxBA

Uriel. William Force Stead.
All night Thy dedicated lamp burns on. OxBoCh
Here, for a moment, I am Thou. TrPWD

The Urn. Malcolm Cowley. Rumors of home like oceans in a shell. AnAmPo; MoVE

The Urn. Hart Crane.
And–backwards–is it thus the eagles fly? PoA
Here is the peace of the fathers. PoA
Return the mirage on a coin that spells/Something of sand and sun the Nile defends? PoA

Urn Burial. Ted Hughes. The aping shape of earth–sure/Of its weight now as in future. EBEV

Urn I: Silent for Twenty-Five Years, The Father of My Mother Advises.. Walter Lew. By the song of the crickets there./(...) BrSi

Ursa Major. James Kirkup. must lean out into time to catch, and die in seeing. ImOP

Ursula. Robert Underwood Johnson. She knows not I am beggar at her door. HBV 1-2

Ursula. David Ray. ...trees/Blazing with blackened apples. VGW

Uru-tu-sendo's Song. Anonymous. Upward going, upward going! WTO

The Urumbula Song. Anonymous. The great beam of The Milky Way/Unceasingly draws all men, wherever they may be. CBAP

Us. David Ignatow. Missles stand ready/to empty the world of us. PPJ

Us. Julius Lester. I cannot be destroyed. PoBA

Us. Anne Sexton. we harvested. CAPP

Us. Jiri Wyatt. it depends on us. LTB

Us Idle Wenches. Anonymous. And danced on earth again, O! PoPle

Us Potes. Franklin Pierce ("F.P.A.") Adams. Mine alone is made of stone–/Gotta work too hard. PoPl

Us Tasting the Air. David Shapiro. The best friends of the world. ANYP

Us Two. A.(lan) A.(lexander) Milne. "That's how it is,' says Pooh. OxBChV; TiPo

Usage. Sharon Thesen. Dear reader, take heed &/by the way, will you marry me? CaPN

The Use of Fiction. Naomi Shihab Nye. "Yes, Amigo"–hand on shoulder–/"It was I." MAYP

Useful Dates. Anonymous. George the Third said with a smile:/"Seventeen-sixty yards in a mile." FaBoUs

Useful for Avoiding Collisions at Sea. Anonymous. In danger with no room to turn,/Ease her, stop her, go astern. FaBoUs

The Useful Plow. Anonymous. Their days are spent, whose minds are bent/To follow the useful plow. HBV 1-2

A Useless Burden upon the Earth. Robert Bridges. What's left of me today will very soon be nothing. QFR

Useless Day. Rosario Castellânos. rising to the surface/without a single fish. WPOW

Uselessness. Ella Wheeler Wilcox. "She lives, but all her usefulness is past." TrPWD

The Uses of Ocean. Sir Owen Seaman. In which to take a dip. ALV; FiBHP

Uses of Poetry. Winfield Townley Scott. And they folded into each other. DFF; PoA

The Usk. C. H. Sisson. Come sleep, come lightning, comes the dove at last. NOCV

The Usual Exquisite Boredom of Patrols. Hugh Popham. ...Thank God,/the bar should be open when we land. OxBTC

Usually an Old Female Is the Leader. Tom Hennen. His shotgun pulls him into the sky. FAZ

Usufruct. Austin Clarke. ...Flash/Of inspiration makes thought rash. IPY

The Usurpers. Edwin Muir. These are imaginations. We are free. CMoP

Ut, Re, Mi, Fa, Mi, Re, Ut. Anonymous. Whip little David's bum. FaBoNo

Utah. Anne Stevenson. where the mountains are clouds, lightning, but no rain. NCSH

Utah Carl. Anonymous. "I know that Utah Carl won't be lost on that great day." BFSS

Utah Carroll. Anonymous.
And it was that very red blanket that brought him to his end. CoSo
And we'll meet him at the round up/on the plains beyond the sky. FSW

The Utah Iron Horse. Anonymous. For this great Union Railroad it will fetch the Devil through. AmFP

The Ute Lover. Hamlin Garland. And see the listening, longing maiden/Lit by the moon. AA

Ute Pass. Ernest Whitney. And wheresoe'er she stept, that spot transformed/Bears her soft smile amid his work of wrath. PoOW

A Utilitarian View of the Monitor's Fight. Herman Melville. And a singe runs through lace and feather. AP; UnPo

The Utmost in Friendship. John E. McCann. "I would go in." TreFT

Utopia. Johari (Jewel C. Latimore) Amini. not a one/for sale. BPo

The "Utopia'. Lee Harwood. ...the purpose of the total was obvious/& uncompromising. EAS

The Utopia of Lord Mayor Howard. Randolph Stow. And in truth, we half expect to see Lord Mayor Howard. PoAu 1-2

Utopia TV Store. Maxine Chernoff. CLICK CLICK, knowing we owe it our lives, more hazy and/blurred with each day. APU

Utrillo's World. John Glassco. We know they are prisons also, the thin walls/Between us and what cowers and shakes inside. PeCV

An Utter Passion Uttered Utterly (parody). John Todhunter. My starved lips play'd the vampyre with her hand. BXAP

Utterance. Emily Dickinson. Or noon in mazarin? AA

V

The V-a-s-e. James Jeffrey Roche. I was so entranced with that charming vaws! AmePo; HBV 1-2

V. B. Nimble, V. B. Quick. John Updike. And, by one o'clock, he's gone. CTBA; NYBP

V.D. Clinic. Adrien Stoutenburg. and then the noiseless skid/of beasts or angels skating down/into their nameless, cotton graves. GP

V.D.F. Anonymous Your star is steady over Oxford Town. HBV 1-2

V. Innocentia Veritas Viat Fides Circumdederunt Me Inimici Mei. Sir Thomas Wyatt. Ber low, therffor, geve god the sterne,/For sure, circa Regna tonat. AAS

V-J Day. John Ciardi. Wheels jammed, and flaming, on a metal sea. MiAP; PoPl

V-Letter. Karl Shapiro. ...because our love is whole/Whether I live or fail. AP; CoBMV; MiAP; MoLP; NoAm; TrJP; WaP

V-Letter to Karl Shapiro in Australia. Selden Rodman. Tuned to a prop's pitch on that terrible thinness. WaP

Vacancy in the Park. Wallace Stevens. Under its mattresses of vines. LCAP

The Vacant Cage. Charles Tennyson Turner. Yet the artist's kindly craft shall not retain/The filming eye, and beak that gasp'd with pain. FM

The Vacant Chair. Henry Stevenson Washburn. Dirges from the pine and cypress/Mingle with the tears we shed. TreFS

The Vacant Farm House.   Walter De La Mare.   Scared silent sparrows flew up out of the ivy there/Into an elder tree–for perching-place.   HaMV

The Vacant Lot.   Gwendolyn Brooks.   And letting them out again.   NoAm; NOBA

Vacation.   William Stafford.   I pour the cream.   AmFN; PoL; Psk

Vacation Exercise.   Michael Kennedy Joseph.   With satyrs dancing sarabands.   AnNZ

Vacation Song.   Edna St. Vincent Millay.   ...shadows leave the hills/And bring to the fields the quiet night.   YeAr

Vacation Time.   Rowena Bastin Bennett.   "There's magic, too, at home."   SiSoSe

Vacation Trip.   Donald Campbell Babcock.   Under the Trees of Paradise.   NePoAm

Vacation Trip.   William Stafford.   "I wish I hadn't come."   AmC; CTBA; PV

Vacationer.   Walker Gibson.   Except that old vacation boredom, and/A deep desire to be returned to land.   SD

Les Vaches.   Arthur Hugh Clough.   In, Rose, and in, Provence and La Palie.   OAEP; PeD

Vacillation.   William Butler Yeats.   So get you gone, Von Hugel, though with blessings/on your head.   MBW 1-2; MoVE; NoAm; OBMV

Vacuum.   Josephine Miles.   As moon on man the gold foil of his brain.   MOON

The Vacuum.   Howard Nemerov.   And still the hungry, angry heart/Hangs on and howls, biting at air.   NePoEA; NIP

The Vagabond.   Robert Louis Stevenson.   All I ask the heaven above,/And the road below me.   AnFE; BBV; BrPo; GTBS; HBV 1-2; HBVY; MCCG; TreFT; ViBoPo

Vagabond House.   Don Blanding.   Well–it's just a dream house, anyway.   BLPA

A Vagabond Song.   Bliss Carman.   She calls and calls each vagabond by name.   GN; HBV 1-2; HBVY; MCCG; PoSC

Vagabonds.   Langston Hughes.   The tearless/Who cannot/Weep.   SaC

Vagabonds.   Madelaine Marie.   For ever cursed–because mine eyes/Are fashioned so!   PeHV

The Vagabonds.   John Townsend Trowbridge.   The sooner, the better for Roger and me!   AA; BeLS; BLPA; TreFS

A Vagrant.   Erik Axel Karlfeldt.   But still I am glad I'm alive.   PoPl

The Vagrant.   Pauline Slender.   And a dream that the fairies spin from stars on the other/side of the moon.   HBMV

Vague Lyric by G.M.   Max Beerbohm.   Which was it?   FaBoEE

The Vaices That Be Gone.   William Barnes.   Down drough the orch'd, where my ears/Do miss the vaices gone.   NOBV

Vain Advice at the Year's End.   James Wright.   And darkening winter stars.   NYBP

Vain and Careless.   Robert Graves.   Water will not mix with oil,/Nor vain with careless heart.   LOW

Vain Finding.   Walter De la Mare.   Grey, and dear heart, how grey!   BrPo

Vain Gratuities.   Edwin Arlington Robinson.   Where there are none to listen or to care.   NePA

Vain Men, Whose Follies.   Thomas Campion.   Men must be men, and women women still.   NCEP

Vain Questioning.   Walter De la Mare.   There waits the peace thy spirit dwelleth in.   MoVE

Vain World Adieu.   Anonymous.   Vain world, adieu.   AmFP

Vainly.   Nelly Sachs.   It was/My beloved/It was–   NYBP

Vala; or, The Four Zoas.   William Blake.
And all his sorrows, till he reassumes his ancient bliss.   OBNC
And on the bed of silence sleep till thou awakest me. OBNC
...Awake, O/Hosts! ViBoPo
So careful wove & spread it out with sighs and weariness. OBNC
The weak remaining shadow of Vala that returns in sorrow/to thee. ViBoPo

Vale.   John Ciardi.   All we are sure of is goodbye, goodbye.   MiAP

Vale!   Roden and Wriothesley Berkeley Noel.   Remember us in our low dell,/Who love thee well!/Farewell!   OBVV

Vale from Carthage.   Peter Viereck.   What's left but this to say of any war?   LiTM; MiAP; MoAmPo

A Valediction.   Elizabeth Barrett Browning.   May God love thee, my beloved,–may God love thee!   HBV 1-2

A Valediction.   William Cartwright.
And Lovers live by thinking on their loss.   OBS
Nor would those fall, nor these shine forth to me. EG

A Valediction.   Ernest Christopher Dowson.   But words are weak.'   BoLoP

Valediction.   Seamus Heaney.   Until you resume command/Self is in mutiny.   PPJ

A Valediction.   Melvin Walker La Follette.   I prayed for grace, that I might love/The rain only.   CoPo

Valediction.   Louis MacNeice.   Your drums and your dolled-up Virgins and your ignorant/dead.   AnIL; FaBoIP; MoVE

Valediction.   Lawrence Raab.   featureless and alone.   AMV-81

Valediction.   John Hall Wheelock.   ...your cold Medusa stare/Has turned a heart to stone.   NePoAm

A Valediction Forbidding Mourning.   John Donne.   Thy firmness makes my circle just,/And makes me end where I begun.   AnAnS 1; BLPL; CABA; DiPo; EnL; ExPo; FaBoEn; FF; ForPo; HAP; HeIP; HoPM; InPK; InPS; JCP; LiTB; MasP; MBW 1-2; MeLP; MePo; NIP; NOBE; NoP; OAEL 1-2; OAEP; OBS; PAI; PoEL 1-5; PoPle; PPoe; PPP; PrIm; SeCeV; SeCP; SeCV 1-2; SoSe; TEP; TreFT; UnPo

A Valediction Forbidding Mourning.   Adrienne Rich.   To do something very common, in my own way.   NoAm; NoP

A Valediction (Liverpool Docks).   John Masefield.   So-long, my fancy man!   OBMV

A Valediction: Of My Name in the Window.   John Donne.   Impute this idle talk to that I go,/For dying men talk often so.   EnRePo; QFR

A Valediction: of Weeping.   John Donne.   Whoe'er sighs most is cruellest, and hastes the other's/death.   AtBAP; ATP; CBEP; EG; HAP; HeIP; InPS; MBW 1-2; MeLP; MePo; NoP; OAEL 1-2; OBS; SeCP

Valediction to Life.   Ignoto.   And if contentment be a stranger, then/I'l nere look for it, but in heaven again.   MeLP

Valediction to My Contemporaries.   Horace Gregory.   unwind the clock, empty the seasons down/rivers of memory–do not return!   MoAmPo

A Valedictory to Standard Oil of Indiana.   David Wagoner.   Which moved the suckers when they'd seen enough. Get out of town.   NYBP

A Valentine.   Matilda Betham-Edwards.   But hasten home, and I'll bespeak/Your services another day!   OBVV; PeHV

Valentine.   Len Gasparini.   you'll see a real valentine–/my heart in formaldehyde!   NeAC

A Valentine.   Jeannette Bliss Gillespy.   Dear heart, the wise forget.–/I am not wise!   AA

A Valentine.   Donald Hall.   Nothing else but/Us can matter.   GrPl; LLLT; NTCP; PCP

A Valentine.   Eleanor Hammond.   That is Outdoor's valentine!   TiPo; YeAr

A Valentine.   Ernest Hemingway.   stick them up your asses lads/My Valentine to you.   OBAL; TW

A Valentine.   Laura E. Richards.   Here is my heart for your valentine.   YeAr

Valentine.   Shel Silverstein.   But I didn't get none from you!   PoSC

A Valentine.   Hal Summers.   Each hour we are new souls: o love, each hour/Meet me the first time, say me last good-bye.   ChMP

Valentine.   Hollis Summers.   And food and the simple act of breathing.   GoYe

Valentine.   C. T.   My loving heart to thee would bear,/My Valentine.   YeAr

Valentine Browne.   Aogan O Rathaille.   Dwarf monsters have taken up the Blade of the Three/and hacked our dead across from heel to top.   NOBI

A Valentine for a Lady.   Lucilius [(or Lucillius)].   For a like amount you could just as well buy a face.   LiTW; OFD

Valentine for Earth.   Frances Frost.   But I'm wild in love/With the planet we've got!   QQQ

Valentine Promise.   Anonymous.   If ever I prove false/To my Love that loves me.   PoSC

Valentine's Day.   Aileen Fisher.   And listen! in the frosty pines/snowbirds twitter Valentines.   YeAr

Valentine to a Little Girl.   John Henry, Cardinal Newman.   Choose from out that company/Whom to serve, and whom to love.   GoBC

A Valentine to My Mother.   Christina Georgina Rossetti.   A lifelong love to this dear saint of mine.   OFD; OHIP

Valiant Love.   Richard Lovelace.   Since in your Hoast that Coward nere was fed/Who to his Prostrate ere was Prostrated.   SeCP

The Valiant Sailor.   Anonymous.   And here I lie a-bleeding on the deck/And it's all for her safety I shall die.   OBSS

The Valiant Seaman's Happy Return to His Love...   Anonymous.   Like nightingale in spring,/welcome my dearest.   GBP

The Valley.   Stanley Moss.   I am not sure that the hand of God/and the hand of man ever touch, even by chance.   NYBP; PCP

Valley Blood.   Barry Sternlieb.   No reason at all, he declares, just a fine/Jersey bull, such a beautiful bull, goddamn!   SM

Valley Forge.   Thomas Buchanan Read.   The hour when Liberty is born.   MC; PAH

The Valley of Decision.   John Oxenham.   Will it yield its soul unto the Heavenly Vision,/Or sink despairing into its own hell?   PGD

The Valley of Men.   Uri Z. Greenberg.   Red seamed are the ends of my days and nights.   VWA

The Valley of the Heavens.   Luis Ponce de Leon.   And stray no more, save paths Thou leadst them through.   CAW

Valley of the Shadow.   John Galsworthy.   Make my last breath a bugle call, carrying/Peace o'er the valleys and cold hills for ever!   OHIP; TrPWD

The Valley of the Shadow of Death.   William Cowper.   Nor let the pow'rs of darkness boast/That I am foiled, and thou art grieved!   EiCP

The Valley of Unrest.   Edgar Allan Poe.   Perennial tears descend in gems.   AP; PoEL 1-5; ViBoPo

The Valley of Vain Verses.   Henry Van Dyke.   And they crumble into dust.   HBV 1-2

The Valley's Singing Day.   Robert Frost.   That once you had opened the valley's singing day.   UnS

A Valley where I Don't Belong.   Marge Piercy.   I and my worn symbols see up the sun.   IHMS

The Valor of Ben Milam.   Clinton Scollard.   In song be praised, let a rouse be raised for the name of Ben/Milam!   HBV 1-2; MC; PAH

Valse Jeune.   Louise Imogen Guiney.   Be a kiss, be a ring with this posy:/ Aultre n'auray!   AA

Valse Oubliee.   John Heath-Stubbs.   Or are you hunting me, or I pursuing?   OxBTC

Valuable.   Stevie Smith.   If everybody says he is valuable/It will be comforting for him.   OxBTC

The Value of Dentistry.   Solyman Brown.   Where anarchy had else sustained alone/The undisputed title to his throne.   FaBoUs

The Value of Pi.   Anonymous.   How I wish I/Could calculate pie.   FaBoUs

Values in Use.   Marianne Moore.   Certainly the means must not defeat the end.   NePoAm-2

The Vamp Passes.   James J. Montague.   Just how hard I'd resist if a Vamp should insist,/On working the Vamp stuff on me!   HBMV

The Vampire.   Conrad Aiken.   All night long he ploughed.   HBMV

The Vampire.   Rudyard Kipling.   (Seeing, at last, she could never know why)/And never could understand!   BLPA; BLPL; EnLit; HBV 1-2; NOBV

Vampirella.   Elaine Equi.   I too make my excursions/into the land of the living/no different than anyone else.   APU

Van Amburgh's Menagerie.   Anonymous.   Those ladies giving those monkeys nuts will injure their constitution.   BLPA

Van Dieman's Land.   Anonymous.   I awoke all broken-hearted, lying in Van Dieman's Land.   BaBo

Van Dieman's Land (A vers.).   Anonymous.   Young men now all beware/ Lest you are drawn into a snare.   OBET

Van Dieman's Land (B vers.).   Anonymous.   For if you knew our hardships you'd never poach again.   CoMu; FaBoBa; NOAV; OBET

Van Elsen.   Frederick George Scott.   Praised Him with fervent breath/Who conquered death.   HBV 1-2

The Van Gogh Influence.   Shel Silverstein.   –You'd write me back for the one that matched it.   ELU

Van Winkle.   Hart Crane.   And hurry along, Van Winkle–it's get-/ting late!   AmP; CrMA

Vanbrug's House.   Jonathan Swift.   They from its ruins build their own.   PP

The Vance Song.   Anonymous.   I'll meet you in the world above/Where parting is no more.   OuSiCo

Vancouver Island.   Joan Swift.   Is it into, or out of, illusion?   DFT

Vancouver Lights.   Earle Birney.   Plutonian, descendant, or beast in the stretching night–/there was light.   CaP

The Vandals.   Jenny Mastoraki.   that history would ultimately justify/the Dorians   BoWoP

Vanessa Vanessa.   Ewart Milne.   Shade fading within the shadows, lost to me, to herself,/To the world: lost and looking back.   BIrV; NeIP

Vanguardia.   Sandra Maria Esteves.   for the dawn that only rises/in the heart of unity.   LTB

Vanished.   Steve Eng.   I find it at last, but still I can't see/Boyhood that used to be.   AMV-81

The Vanished Night.   Niall MacMurray.   God be with the night that's gone!   KiLC

The Vanishers.   John Greenleaf Whittier   Lost and found, in sunset land.   AA

Vanishing Point.   Peter Cooley.   already, masked, moving out.   AmPA

Vanitas Vanitatum.   John Webster.   And weave but nets to catch the wind.   NOBE; OBEV

Vanitas Vanitatum.   Israel Zangwill.   Wherein we glory while our eyes are/ wet.   TrJP

Vanity.   Robert Graves.   That fountains of the heart run dry.   GTBS-P

Vanity.   James (1834-82) Thomson.   "Vanity, my little man,/You're nothing of the kind."   BBV; DBV; FF; NOBV; PV; TreFS

Vanity.   Anna Wickham.   That I am lovelier without my dress/Gave me sweet wanton happiness.   FaBoTw

Vanity (I).   George Herbert.   Poor man, thou searchest round/To find out death, but missest life at hand.   NoP

The Vanity of All Worldly Things.   Anne Bradstreet.   And all the rest, but vanity we find.   NoP; SCAP

The Vanity of Existence.   Philip Freneau.   A bank of mud around me lay,/ And sea-weed on the river's bed.   AmPP; AP

The Vanity of Human Wishes.   Samuel Johnson.
Toil, envy, want, the patron, and the jail.   OBSV
With these celestial wisdom calms the mind,/And makes the happiness she does not find. ATP; CEP; EBEV; EiCP; EnPE; HeIP; LaA; LAuP; LoBV; MasP; NOEC; NoP; OAEL 1-2; PoEL 1-5; PrIm; TEP

The Vanity of Human Wishes.   Juvenal (Decimas Junius Juvenalis).   –be a purple patch/for schoolboys, and a theme for declamation!   OBVE

Vanity of Vanities.   Palladas.   Why should I labor for naught, seeing how naked the/end?   AWP; TRV

The Vanquished.   Charles Eglington.   May they advance defeated–as today.   AA; HBV 1-2; PeSA

The Vantage Point.   Robert Frost.   I look into the crater of the ant.   CoBMV; MAmP; OxBA

Vanzetti.   Charles Buckmaster.   Yet that purpose survives–/and is/love   CBAP

Vapor Trail Reflected in the Frog Pond.   Galway Kinnell.   seed dazzled over the footbattered blaze of the earth.   CAPP; NoP; OBWP; VGW

Vapor Trails.   Gary Snyder.   Watching for two-leaf pine/–spotting that design.   CAPP

Vapour and Blue.   Wilfred (William Wilfred Campbell) Campbell.   When the heart of the world was young.   CaP

Vaquero.   Edward Dorn.   Yi Yi, the cowboy's eyes/are blue. The top of the sky/is too.   NeAP; PoM

Vaquero.   Joaquin Miller.   The fallen, struggling monarch that has thrust/ His tongue in rage and roll'd his red eyes in/disgust   AA; BPAW

Variables of Green.   Robert Graves.   So love my loves of you.   FaBoEE

Variation.   Peter Wild.   toot, toot, they never came back.   GP

Variation on a Line by Emerson.   William Stanley Merwin.   Morning repeats the malice and the light.   NePA

Variation on a Sentence.   Louise Bogan.   Earth's bluish animals are few.   FM; ImOP

Variation on a Theme by Francis Kilvert.   Rolfe Humphries.   And tradesmen think they are surly/In spite of the wrinkled eyes/Scored by their years of smiling.   UnS

Variation on a Theme by John Lyly.   Sacheverell Sitwell.   ...he'll find me still a reed,/Though sighing at his breath, indeed.   ViBoPo

Variation on Heraclitus.   Louis MacNeice.   One cannot live in the same room twice.   NoAm

Variation on Ronsard.   Thomas Sturge Moore.   Be thou the Love, Love sees.   OBMV

Variation on the Gothic Spiral.   William Stanley Merwin.   For gazing at girls while I uncurl like greed.   PoA

Variation on the Word Sleep.   Margaret Atwood.   ...I would like to be that unnoticed/& that necessary.   NOBC

Variations.   Randall Jarrell.   Man is the judgment of the world.   MiAP; VGW

Variations, Calypso and Fugue on a Theme of Ella Wheeler Wilcox.   John Ashbery.   "I will tell you nothing! Nothing, do you hear?" he/shrieked. "Go away! Go away!"   ANYP; LCAP

Variations Done for Gerald Van de Wiele.   Charles Olson.   ...we salute you/ season of no bungling   NeAP; NoAm; NOBA; NoP

Variations (excerpt).   Conrad Aiken.   Quietly you possess me.   PG

Variations for Two Pianos.   Donald Justice.   There is no music now in all Arkansas.   NYBP

Variations of an Air.   Gilbert Keith Chesterton.   And the King slept beside the northern sea.   Par

Variations of Greek Themes.   Edwin Arlington Robinson.
He would have been eleventh.   OBAL
The raven dies.   OBAL
Where's a poor tortured soul to dwell?   OBAL

Variations on a Late October Day.   George, Jr Mosby.   control the rhythms of my soul.   LFAC

Variations on a Line from Shakespeare's Fifty-Sixth Sonnet.   E. L. Mayo.   Whose action is no stronger than a flower.   PoCh

Variations on a Medieval Theme.   Geoffrey Dutton.   She lies where I cannot be.   PoAu 1-2

Variations on a Still Morning.   Thomas Cole.   Amid the leafage of these breathless trees.   NePoAm .

Variations on a Theme.   John Hay.   Burns in their bones. The world is in their eyes.   NePoAm

Variations on a Theme.   Mark Vinz.   even though they cannot be heard.   LiTA; Psk

Variations on a Theme.   Oscar Whitman.   ...he couldn't move, the track was so deep.   NePA

Variations on a Theme.   Oscar Williams.
...but he couldn't move, the track was so deep.   LiTA
...he climbed our vines/and hid, on hands and knees, along our veins. LiTA
Hourly growing more haggard from the weight of the/grave. LiTA

Variations on a Theme by George Herbert.   Marya Zaturenska.   I praise the mortal wound that made me His!   TrPWD

Variations on a Theme by Sidney Keyes.   Eithne Wilkins.   through such snow falling, and so far from help.   NeBP

Variations on a Theme by William Carlos Williams.   Kenneth Koch.   I wanted you here in the wards, where I am the doctor!   BXAP; CAPP; FF; NIP; NLV; NoP; PoM; PV; SpRo

Variations on a Time Theme.   Edwin Muir.
The ark is borne unseen through the wilderness.   NoAm
As if it were all. This plain all. This journey all. MoVE

Set free, or outlawed, now I walk the sand/And search this rubble for the promised land. NoAm

While lost and empty lies Eternity. NoAm

Variations on an Air Composed on Having to Appear in a Pageant... Gilbert Keith Chesterton. I myself am a complete orchestra./So long. NLV

Variations on an Old Nursery Rhyme. Edith Sitwell. But neither sun nor moon, my dear,/Has yet caught me. HBMV

Variations on Sappho. Michael (Katherine Bradley and Edith Cooper) Field. And with your soft vitality/My weary bosom fill. PeHV

O foolish woman, dost thou set/Thy pride upon a ring? PeHV

Variations on Southern Themes. Donald Justice.

And the great wheels smash and pound beneath our feet. SV

Somewhere among the purpling wild verbena. SV

Variations: The Air Is Sweetest That a Thistle Guards. James Merrill. Became at once of pure pearl made. NePoEA

Varick Street. Elizabeth Bishop. And I shall sell you sell you/sell you of course, my dear, and you'll sell me. NYP

The Variety. John Dancer. 'Mongst all the earthly kings, there's none/Contented with one Crown alone. CavP

Variety: Why Do We Grumble? *Anonymous.* Wealth has a coat of many colours! WTO

Various Beasts. Hilaire Belloc. Child, if you have a rummy kind of name,/Remember to be thankful for the same. FaBoNo

Various Ends. Ruthven Todd. A widening of experience, for him it marked no end. NeBP; SeCePo

Various Wakings. Vincent Buckley. That under the enfeebled stars/They may feel happy and at home. PoAu 1-2

Varitalk. Weare Holbrook. A triple threat that makes me Very,/Very, very apprehensive. NYBP

Varium et Mutabile. Sir Thomas Wyatt. All is possible. OBSC; QFR

The Varuna. George Henry Boker. Oh! for the dead let us all kneel to pray! PAH

The Vase. Terence Tiller. of roses dying like Petronius/a seemly death. ChMP

A Vase of Flowers. John Ashbery. They mean absolutely nothing to me. ConAP

The Vase of Life. Dante Gabriel Rossetti. ...which now/Stands empty till his ashes fall in it. MaVP; SyP

The Vase of Tears. Stephen Spender. ...a glass vase which reflects/The world's grief weeping in its daughter. AtBAP

Vases. Nan Terrell Reed. Which do you think was broken? BLPA

Vashti. Lascelles Abercrombie. And woman's beauty is the flame therein. MoBrPo

Vashti. Frances E. W. Harper. A woman who could bend to grief/But would not bend to shame. BlSi

Vast Light. Richard Eberhart. It is the vague of the soul that I know. CMoP; NMP

Vastness. Alfred, Lord Tennyson. ...the dead are not dead but alive. VLP

Vaticide. Myron O'Higgins. And the seas return to their imagined homes. IDB; PoBA

Vaudeville. Lincoln Kirstein. And the performing dogs are led up from below. NoAm

Vaudeville Dancer. John Hall Wheelock. ...your reluctant beauty sways/In the old weary rhythms of unwearied love! UnS

Vaudracour and Julia (excerpt). William Wordsworth. Which, after a short time, by some mistake Or indiscretion of the Father, died. EvOK

A Vault inside the Castle at Goito. Robert Browning. The Arab's wisdom everywhere. MyFE

Vaunting Oak. John Crowe Ransom. Or the tears of a girl remembering her dread. OxBA; VGW

The Vedic Hymns: Forgive, Lord, Have Mercy. *Anonymous.* oh punish us not! ILwL

The Vedic Hymns: The Song of Creation. Anonymous. He surely knows–or maybe He does not! ILwL

The Vedic Hymns: To the One God. *Anonymous.* May we become the lords of many treasures! ILwL

The Vedic Hymns: Varuna. *Anonymous.* Loosen our bonds/that we may live! ILwL

The Veery. Henry Van Dyke. I fain would hear, before I go, the wood-/notes of the veery. AA

Vegas. Charles Bukowski. I kept my mouth/shut. NoP

Vegetable Destiny. Nina Cassian. oblivious to apricot-tree death. PBWP

Vegetable Loves. Erasmus Darwin. Aim their light shafts, and point their little stings. OBEC; SeCePo

Vegetables. Eleanor Farjeon. Miss half of the potato's joy,/And that's to dig it up. TiPo

Vegetables. Rachel Field. Where it's too dark to see? SoPo

A Vegetarian Sings. Audrey Conard. ...I'll taste your body/transmuted, and they'll proclaim my funghi marinati. AMV-81

A Veld Eclogue: The Pioneers. Roy Campbell. There would be far more goats on the Karroo/And far less in the Senate and the House. OBSV

The Velvet Hand. Phyllis McGinley. We don't debate./We just give in. TreFT

Velvet Shoes. Elinor Wylie. We shall walk in the snow. CH; FPL; GoJo; MoAB; MoAmPo; PG; PoPl; SiSoSe; SoPo; TreFS; TrGrPo; WHA

The Velvet Sonneteers. Tom MacInnes. Let sing again the velvet sonneteers! CaP

Vendor's Song. Adelaide Crapsey. I never would cry my songs to sell. AnFE; APA; HBV 1-2

The Venerable Bee. Abraham Moses Klein. Attend his Kiddush on/A flowercup of dew. TrJP

Veneris Venefica Agrestis. Lucio Piccolo. which shakes which unflowers unleafs/the bush and the forest rose. OBVE

Veneta. Mary Elizabeth Coleridge. In the city under the sea. CBEP

Venetian Air. Thomas Moore. Take day and night for woman's love, what angels we should/be! OBSP

A Venetian Night. Hugo von Hofmannsthal. That makes words empty and the senses dumb. AWP

Venetian Scene. Anne Ridler. And seaweed over the marble stairs. NMP

The Venetian Serenade. Richard Moncton, Lord Houghton Milnes. "I am coming–Sciar–and for you and to you!/Sciar–and to you!" OBRV

Venezuela. *Anonymous.* Unless he's drunk all the oil in Venezue.....la. FSW

Venga Jaleo. *Anonymous.* Y Franco se va paseo. FSW

Vengeance. Raymond Mazisi Kunene. Who will remain the ash-monuments/Witnessing the explosions of our revenge. WhB

The Vengeance of Finn: The Awakening of Dermuid. Austin Clarke. Lazily she lingered/Cradling a dream. AnIV

Veni,Coronaberis. *Anonymous.* Veni, coronaberis. AtBAP

Veni Coronaberis. Geoffrey Hill. Towers and steeples rise away/into the towering gulfs of air. NoP

Veni Crator Spiritus, Translated in Paraphrase. John Dryden. And equal Adoration be/Eternal Paraclete, to thee. AWP; CAW; CEP; CoBE; FaPoR; GoBC; HBV 1-2; ILwL; SeCV 1-2; WGRP

Veni Creator. Bliss Carman.

Or sink and merge forever/In that which bids them be. WGRP

Thou breath of things unseen! MoRP

Veni Creator. Alice Meynell. Come to our ignorant hearts and be forgiven. ILwL

Veni, Sancte Spiritus. King of France Robert II. And dwell with Thee in lasting bliss! HBV 1-2

Venice. Henry Wadsworth Longfellow. ...towers of cloud uplifting/In air their unsubstantial masonry. EyDe

Venice. Howard Moss. Lions to be golden must be painted gold. MoAB

Venice. John Addington Symonds. ...Loves that seize/Man's soul, and waft her on storm-melodies! HBV 1-2

Venice. Arthur Symons. A city without joy or weariness,/Itself beholding, from itself aloof. OBSP

Venice. James Wright. ...just just barely not wringing/The swan's neck. AMV-81

Venice Recalled. Bruce Boyd. that remarks the wider movement of its actual thought. NeAP

Venite Adoremus. Margery Cannon. He was the Flame eternal,/He was the Light. GoBC

Venom. James Dickey. Turn it, turn it,/Brother. PoA

Venomous thorns that are so sharp and keen. Sir Thomas Wyatt. Since every woe is joined with some wealth. FCP

The Ventriloquist. Robert Huff. Speak through the blighted chestnut: Was a lark. GP

Venus. Dante Gabriel Rossetti. And her grove glow with love-lit fires of Troy. MaVP

Venus Abandoned. William Shakespeare. Who doth the world so gloriously behold,/That cedar-tops and hills seem burnished gold. OBSC

Venus Accoutered as Mars. *Anonymous.* The god of war himself, and all mankind. UnTE

Venus and Cupide. Sir Thomas More. Now thou which erst despised children small/Shall wax a child again and be my thrall. EnRePo

Venus and the Rain. Mebdh McGuckian. ...and a waterfall/Unstitching itself down the front stairs. FaBoIP

The Venus of Bolsover Castle. Sacheverell Sitwell. while he who carved you burns with fiery blood. HBMV

Venus of the Louvre. Emma Lazarus. While mourns one ardent heart, one poet-brain,/For vanished Hellas and Hebraic pain. AA; AnAmPo; SBG

Venus of the Salty Shell. Denis Devlin. The doves, the hawthorn merge in the wrack and foam. BIrV; NOBI

Venus' Runaway. Ben Jonson. And that he's Venus' runaway. HBV 1-2

Venus Transiens. Amy Lowell. And the waves which precede you/Ripple and stir/The sands at my feet. PoA

Venus Victrix. Dante Gabriel Rossetti. And Venus Victrix to my heart doth bring/Herself, the Helen of thy guerdoning. MaVP

Venus Vigils (excerpt). *Anonymous.* Love he to morrow, who lov'd never;/To morrow, who hath lov'd, persever. OBVE

Venus, with Young Adonis.   Bartholomew Griffin.   To kiss and clip me till I run away!   ViBoPo

Veracruz.   Robert Earl Hayden.   light-years away, one farewell image/burns and fades and burns.   AmNP

Verandahs.   R. F. Brissenden.   Flooding level and bright along the verandah.   CBAP; NOAV

Veranius, My Dear Friend.   Caius Valerius Catullus.   Who is as happy as Catullus is?   PeHV

Verazzano.   Hezekiah Butterworth.   And the fairest name of the Eastern shore/Bears the fairest isle of the Western coast.   PAH

The Verb "To Think".   D. J. Enright.   To be reading a Japanese lexicon/ And to be unable to forget.   OxBC

Verbal Critics.   Alexander Pope.   The things, we know, are neither rich nor rare,/But wonder how the devil they got there.   OBEC

Verbatim from Boileau.   Alexander Pope.   'Twas a fat Oyster–Live in peace– Adieu.   DBV

Verbum Caro Factum Est.   Anonymous.   "Verbum caro factum est." SBVL

Verbum Supernum.   Saint Ambrose of Milan.   What praise hath been, so be it done/Through all eternity.   CAW

Verdancy.   Anonymous.   O'er the little green apple boy's green little grave. ShM

The Verdict.   Norman Cameron.   The first pressure on the trigger.   SeCePo

Vergidemiarum: Prologue: "I first adventure, with foolhardy might."   Richard Barnfield.   Truth be thy speed, and Truth thy patron be.   ViBoPo

Vergier.   Ezra Pound.   By God, how swift the night,/And day comes on! GBL

Vergissmeinicht.   Keith Douglas.   And death who had the soldier singled/ has done the lover mortal hurt.   ChMP; FaBoMo; GTBS-P; InPS; NePoEA; OBWP; OxBTC; PAI; SoSe

Verifying the Dead.   James Welch.   rubbed her hips and sang/of a country, like this, far off.   CDW

Verigin 3.   John Newlove.   ...and walked home alone, shoe full of blood. NeAC

Verigin, Moving in Alone.   John Newlove.   till everything breaks down. NeAC

Vermont.   Sarah N. Cleghorn.   High above them/Blinding crystal is the sunlit steep.   HBMV

Vermont Conversation.   Patricia Hubbell.   "Way o' the Lord."/"That's right."   CTBA

Vermont: Indian Summer.   Philip Booth.   in this other summer,/summer twice come.   NePoEA

Vern.   Gwendolyn Brooks.   Nor mock the tears you have to hide.   TiPo

Vernal Equinox.   Amy Lowell.   Why are you not here to overpower me with/your tense and urgent love?   MAPA

Vernal Equinox.   Ruth Stone.   Observe the tremble of the weeping willows. MoAmPo

Vernal Paradox.   Kim Kurt.   And turn again to telling time/By earth's uncertain seeds.   NePoAm-2

Vernal Sentiment.   Theodore Roethke.   I rejoice in the spring, as though no spring ever had been.   ELU; MiAP

Vernal Showers.   David O'Neil.   The flowers wince,/But drink.   AnAmPo

Vernon Castle.   Harriet Monroe.   Goodbye–perhaps your flight has just begun/Under the sun.   HBMV

Verona.   James Wright.   And a little peace.   NNaP

Vers de Societe.   Philip Larkin.   Whispering Dear Warlock-Williams: Why, of course–   InPK

Vers de Societe (parody).   Henry Duff Traill.   I trust you, James– to do your best/To save the soup at Grosvenor Gardens.   Par

Vers La Vie.   Arthur Upson.   Urges retreat to that Forgotten Land's/ Unthoughtful shores where thou and Silence are!   HBV 1-2

Vers Nonsensiques.   George Du Maurier.   "Scintellez, scintellez, petits astres!"   HBV 1-2; NA

Versailles (Petit Trianon).   Adrienne Rich.   And evening finds you in a restless town/Where each has back his old restricted face.   NePoEA

Verse.   Oliver St.John Gogarty.   All but the blithe/Hexameters.   AnIL; FaBoCh; HBV 1-2; LoGBV; OBEV; OBMV; PoRA

Verse.   Richmond Lattimore.   The process itself is too undignified to be worth description.   PP

Verse for a Certain Dog.   Dorothy Parker.   (Couldn't you wait until I took you out?)   GDP

Verse for Vestigials.   Elizabeth Allen.   The markings are for hope. AMV-80

Verse Written in the Album of Mademoiselle–.   Pierre Dalcour.   ...a glance of your eyes/Beneath their brown lashes.   PoNe; TTY

Verses.   Richard Bentley.   Great without patron, rich without South-Sea. ViBoPo

Verses.   James Russell Lowell.   Walk steady, dear, lest all be spilled.   AP

Verses.   Sir John Suckling.   Then hang me, Ladies, at your door,/If e'er I doat upon you more.   CavP

Verses Addressed to a Friend...   Samuel Henley.   And heaven's blest mansion be your last!   NOEC

Verses at Night.   Dannie Abse.   and across the darkness call.   MP

Verses Copied From the Window of an Obscure Lodging-House.   Anonymous. Her heart is empire, and her love is heaven.   LiTL; ViBoPo

Verses for a First Birthday.   George Barker.   And Nature renews it all. MoAB; MoBrPo

Verses for the 60th Birthday of T. S. Eliot.   George Barker.   Asseverations that tame/The great negations with his name.   ChMP

Verses Found in Thomas Dudley's Pocket after His Death.   Thomas Dudley. If men be left and otherwise combine,/Mine epitaph's–I did no hurt to thine. SCAP

Verses in the Style of the Druids (excerpt).   Sir Walter Scott.   Kindness fadeth away, but vengeance endureth.   TW

Verses Intended to Be Written below a Noble Earl's Picture.   Robert Burns. The noble ward he loves.   HoPM

Verses Made Sometime Since upon the Picture....   John Josselyn.   And such perfection here appears/It neither Wind nor Sun-shine fears.   SCAP

Verses Made the Night before He Died.   Michael Drayton.   ...makes a glass so true/As I therein no other's face but yours can view.   NOBE

Verses Occasioned by the Sudden Drying up...(excerpt).   Jonathan Swift.   A nauseous brood that fills your senate walls,/And in the chambers of your viceroy crawls.   OBSV

Verses on a Cat.   Charles Daubeny.   I'd drink in science at each look,/Nor fear the lapse of time.   HBV 1-2

Verses on Accepting the World.   Joseph Brodsky.   and generally our planet/ is like a recruit/sweating on a march.   VWA

Verses on Blenheim.   Martial (Marcus Valerius Martialis).   I find by all you have been telling/That 'tis a house, but not a dwelling.   AWP

Verses on Daniel Good.   Anonymous.   An we hope that his like we shall ne'er see again.   CoMu; OxBB

Verses on Sir Joshua Reynold's Painted Window at New College, Oxford. Thomas Warton, Jr..   With arts unknown before, to reconcile/The willing Graces to the Gothic pile.   CEP; NOEC; OBEC; PoEL 1-5

Verses on the Prospect of Planting Arts and Learning in America.   George Berkeley.   Time's noblest offspring is the last.   CEP; OBEC; OBTV; SeCePo; ViBoPo

Verses Pinn'd to a Sheet, in Which a Lady Stood to Do Penance... Anonymous.   You'd soon want one to lie on.   FaBoEE

Verses Placed Over the Door at the Entrance into the Apollo Room...   Ben Jonson.   Welcome all who lead or follow,/To the Oracle of Apollo.   HBV 1-2

Verses Said to Be Written on the Union.   Jonathan Swift.   So tossing faction will o'erwhelm/One crazy double-bottomed realm.   APAS

Verses Supposed to be Written by Alexander Selkirk.   William Cowper. And reconciles man to his lot.   CEP; NOEC; PoEL 1-5

Verses to Be Repeated by an Attorney...   John Willis.   Comb, Garters, Stockins, Gloves.   FaBoUs

Verses to Miss –.   J. Wilde.   Got a sound sleep, indeed, indeed I did,/ Though all this stuff laid somewhere in my head.   NOEC

Verses under a Peacock Portrayed in Her Left Hand.   Robert Greene.   Thus self-love, nursing up the pomp of pride,/Makes beauty wrack against an ebbing tide.   PBBP

Verses Written at Montauban in France, 1750.   Joseph Warton.   Be Albion still thy joy! with her remain,/Long as the surge shall lash her oak-crowned plain!   OBTV

Verses Written at The Hague. Ano 1696.   Matthew Prior.   That search all the province, you'd find no man there is/So blessed as the Englishen Heer SECRETARIS   OBTV

Verses Written During a Sleepless Night.   Alexander Pushkin.   I would study your dark tongue...   CBEP; OBEC; PoPI

Verses Written during the War 1756–1763.   Thomas Osbert Mordaunt.   Till death doth close the hapless scene,/And calls its angel home to rest. CBEP; OBEC

Verses Written In 1872.   Robert Louis Stevenson.   Or, whistling as he sees you through the brake,/Waits on a stile.   BLPA; BLPL

Verses Written in the Chiosk at Pera, Overlooking Constantinople.   Mary Wortley, Lady Montagu.   Who dares have virtue in a vicious age.   OBTV

Verses Written on Sand.   Melech, Ravitch.   and in the darkness trample on my poem written in the sand.   VWA

Verses Written upon Windows.   Jonathan Swift.   For me, you may hang 'em, or drown 'em.   DBV

Verses Wrote in a Lady's Ivory Table-Book.   Jonathan Swift.   He's a Gold Pencil tipt with Lead.   NCEP

A Version of a Song of Failure.   Larry Eigner.   now the owls hoot/at the fearful night   FAZ

Versions of Love.   Roy Fuller.   Yet aching almost as promptly as a boy. LiTM

Vert-Vert, the Parrot.   Louis Gresset.   He dwells, transformed into a tongue. CAW

Vertigo.   Brian Henderson.   ...Your floor, I/notice, is a roof of clouds. CaPN

Vertigos or Contemplation of Something That Is Over.   Alejandra Pizarnik. I'd die from these things.   VWA

Very Early. Karla Kuskin. And kissed the stars good night. SoPo

Very Fair My Lot. Jacob David Kamzon. a tiny lattice opens on the eternal/glory. TrJP

A Very Heroical Epistle in Answer to Ephelia. John Wilmot, Earl of Rochester. Disturbed by swords, like Damocles's feast. APAS

Very Like a Whale. Ogden Nash. What I mean by too much metaphor and/simile. BLPL; DTC; HAP; InPK; InPS; PoLf; TrGrPo; WeW

Very Lovely. Rose Fyleman. Wouldn't it be glorious? Wouldn't it be fun? SoPo; TiPo

A Very Minor Poet Speaks. Isabel Valle. God! Set me glowing! Let me shine! BLPA

Very Nearly. Queenie Scott-Hopper. I very, very nearly did! SoPo

A Very Odd Fish. D'Arcy Wentworth Thompson. Shrimps, periwinkles, and a most/Voracious appetite. OxBChV

The Very Old. Thomas Galloway. tissues already as withered as their autumn forerunners'. AMV-80

Very Old Man. James Henry. And from my view all objects shutting out. NOBV

A Very Old Song. William Laird. Mother, let me pass. HBV 1-2

A Very Old Woman. Clayton Eshleman. stemmed flower/at the cross's/foot MAT

A Very Phoenix. Thomas Lodge. O happy Love, where such delights consorteth! CBEP

The Very Pretty Maid of This Town... Anonymous. You're welcome, Sir, to this and more,/To quench your raging fire. CoMu

Vesper. Thomas Edward Brown. The blackbird saith. BoC

Vesperal. Ernest Christopher Dowson. "Sufficient for the day were the day's evil things!" OBMV

Vespers. W. H. Auden. ...no secular wall will safely stand. FaBoMo

Vespers. A.(lan) A.(lexander) Milne. Christopher Robin is saying his prayers. OxBChV; SpRo

Vespers. Silas Weir Mitchell. Brief be the twilight as I pass/From light to dark, from dark to light. WGRP

Vespers. Odell Shepard. Back to the grief and the toil/And the hopes and the homes of men. TrPWD

Vessels. Howard Schwartz. When you walk around me/Seven times/And I begin to glow. VWA

Vesta. John Greenleaf Whittier. Her setting star, like Bethlehem's,/To Thee shall point the way! TrPWD; WHA

The Vestal. Nathalia Crane. And a painted rainbow/Shone above her there. AnAmPo; TrJP

The Vestal. Alexander Pope. And melts in visions of eternal day. ACP; CAW

The Vestal in the Forum. James Wright. I can almost name. AMV-81

The Vestal Lady on Brattle. Gregory Corso. is up and about, as is her custom,/drunk with child. NoAm

The Vestal Virgin. John Plummer Derwent Llwyd. We never spoke, we simply looked and trembled/And we knew.... CaP

Vestigia. Bliss Carman. I knew God dwelt within my heart. CaP; WGRP

Vestigia Restrorsum: The Vales of the Medway. Arthur Joseph Munby. Till on the lucid sky loftier ridges appear. FaBoPP

The Vesture of the Soul. George William ("A.E.") Russell. I live and breath the joy of it.' ACV

The Vet. Guy Boas. Is to call yourself "Doctor," and so be allowed/To specialize only on Man. BoAnP

Vet's Rehabilitation. Ray Durem. I want a black artificial leg. PoBA

The Veteran. Edmund Charles Blunden. His bellman cockerel crying the first round. BrPo

The Veteran. Louis O. Coxe. The civil man to his lust/And the lookout to his mast. MoVE

A Veteran Cowboy's Ruminations. John M. Kuykendall. Whar the wicked cease from troublin' an' the weary are at rest. PoOW

The Veteran of Heaven. Francis Thompson. It is written "King of Kings, Lord of Lords.'" HBV 1-2

A Veteran of the Great War. John Bensko. ...children who believe/like he does, in today, and today, and today. MAYP

Veteran Sirens. Edwin Arlington Robinson. So far from Ninon and so near the grave. AnNE; NoAm; NOBA; QFR; SoSe

Veterans. George Johnston. Veterans of loving are wary-eyed and scarred/And they see into everything they see. NOBC

The Veterans. Donagh MacDonagh. Retouch in memory, with sentiment relive,/April and May. CIP; OnYI

Vetus Flamma. Robert Mezey. You only came to wrestle, and I lost. PoA

Vexilla Regis. Saint Venantius Fortunatus. Preserve and govern evermore! CAW

Via Crucis, Via Lucis. T. H. Hedge. Star, that points our high endeavor,/Whither Thou hast gone before! BePJ

Via Dolorosa. Phoebe Smith. And You there among them,/Staggering with the cross. PGD

Via Longa. Patrick MacDonogh. And sure it's not the going,/But that I find the way. HBMV

Via, Veritas, et Vita. Alice Meynell. "The way was He." WGRP

Viable. Archie Randolph Ammons. saying through the scary opposites to death. TAP

Viaticum. Ethna MacCarthy. but who knows what gay roisterer/before this dawn will pay their fare. NeIP

The Vicar. George Crabbe.
More like the Being that he enter'd in. OBNC
Whilst bishops may be damn'd the nearest way. AnFE

The Vicar of Bray. Anonymous.
And this is law... ALV
That whatsoever king shall reign,/I'll be the Vicar of Bray, Sir. CEP; DBV; FaBoPV; FSW; GBP; HBV 1-2; NOBE; NOBL; OBSV; OxBoLi; ViBoPo

The Vicar of Wakefield. Oliver Goldsmith. And wring his bosom–is, to die. EnLi 1-2

Vicarious Atonement. Richard Aldington. Take if thou canst this bitter cup from us. MoBrPo; WGRP

Vice. Anthony Hecht. Zeugmas, and rhymes he de-/Plored in his prose. OBAL

Vice. Alexander Pope. We first endure, then pity, then embrace. ELU; PoPl

Vicissitudes of the Creator. Archibald MacLeish. The small ironic silence of his claws. NePA

Vickery's Mountain. Edwin Arlington Robinson. And Vickery shall not know. MoAmPo

Vicksburg. Paul Hamilton Hayne. The people strode, with step of hope,/To the music in their hearts. AA; MC; PAH

The Victim. Lupenga Mphande. And started climbing the hillside back to the farm. WhB

The Victim. Ellen Bryant Voigt. she crawls toward him, not away,/bound by habits not yet broken. MAYP

The Victim of Aulis. Dannie Abse. as the tall slave sings why Father? why Father? NoAm

Victimae Paschali Laudes. Wipo. Hear the prayers our hearts are urging. CAW

The Victor. William Young. "Hail to the victor who passes by!" HBMV

The Victor Dog. James Merrill. The life it asks of us is a dog's life. NoP

Victor Galbraith. Henry Wadsworth Longfellow. "That is the wraith/Of Victor Galbraith!" PAH

The Victor of Antietam. Herman Melville. The one-armed lift the wine to you,/McClellan,/And great Antietam's cheers renew. MC; PAH

Victoria. Henry Van Dyke. To follow Thee, to fight for Thee,/Knights of the Holy Ghost. TRV

Victoria Market. Francis Brabazon. the highest spires were ablaze with the movement of feet. BoAV; NOAV

The Victoria Markets Recollected in Tranquillity. Furnley Maurice.
Apples, ripen for the dray! NOAV; PoAu 1-2
Stands in a drift of cabbage-leaves/And grieves. BoAV

Victorian Grandmother. Margo Lockwood. it carries your memory effortless–/like a sure thing. Psk

Victorian Song. John Farrar. Four kisses on his cheek! GoYe

The Victories of Love. Coventry Patmore.
Alas! 'tis everywhere her grave. FaBoRV
And, on the other, lions. FaBoRV; NBM
...Bright let be the air/About my lonely cloud of care. FaBoRV
Easier to love, we so should find,/It is than to be just and kind. GBL

The Victors. Denise Levertov. red-currant red, a graceful/ornament or a merry smile. NoP

Victory. Anonymous.
And my love was slain with Nelson upon that very day. CoMu
For Jesus Christ arose again/To everlasting life. STF
I saw the morning break. WGRP

Victory. Roger Axford. We too are fools and knaves. PGD

Victory. Eileen Duggan. Some may not be slain but live,/Forgotten in the thaw. AnNZ

Victory. Lionel Pigot Johnson. And went into the room of burning lights. NOBV

Victory Bells. Grace Hazard Conkling. And home-coming for weary men. HBV 1-2; MC; PAH

Victory comes late. Emily Dickinson. Who of little Love–know how to starve– InPK

A Victory Dance. Alfred Noyes. Watching the fun/Of the Victory Ball. EnLit; PoLf

Victory in Defeat. Edwin Markham. ...Sorrows come/To stretch out spaces in the heart for joy. BLPL; GoTF; PoLf; PoPl; TreFT

Victory in the Cabarets. Louis Untermeyer. While sixteen chorus men sang Over There. HBMV

Victory March. Michael Kennedy Joseph. And I shan't sleep so easy as the lads who march no more. AnNZ

The Victory of the Battle of Wounded Knee. Tom Parson. shaking the snow off his coat/his rifle glistening. SOTS

Victory Parade. George Edward Hoffman. And freedom from our vast ambitions' fears? PGD

The Victory Wreck. Will Carleton. And even our foemen cheer! PAH

Une Vie. Pentti Saarikoski. Grandma picked up her scissors and struck him through the/heart ELU

La Vie C'est La Vie. Jessie Redmond Fauset. I wish that I were dead. BANP; CDC; PoNe

The Vield Path. William Barnes. But you, broad woak, wi' ribby rind,/Wer here so long as I can mind. NOBV

Vienna. Peter Porter. The trivial is immortal. OBTV

"Vierge Ouvrante." Miriam Palmer. and the light/always followed her to mass. NMM

The Vierzide Chairs. William Barnes. All wold zights welcomer than new,/A-look'd on as I look'd on you. NOBV

A Viet Cong Sapper Dies. Stephen Sossaman. Let linger this reproach: behold the child. AMV-81

Vietnam. Clarence Major. & killing/like crazy PoBA

Vietnam #4. Clarence Major. you know, he said/two birds with one stone BOLo; FF; PoBA

The Vietnamese Girl in the Madhouse. David Fisher. and we are too poor for her madness. NPGG

Vieux Carre. Walter Adolphe Roberts. Framed in the midnight thicket of your hair. PoNe

View. Robin Munro. we make our pattern complete. PoSH

The View. Howard Nemerov. ...and every fall/Is once for all. NYBP

A View. Beverly Quint. ...And still my feet hold fast. NYBP

View. Christian J. Van Geel. ...Nothing more. AMV-81

View by Color Photography on a Commercial Calendar. William Carlos Williams. it has been accomplished. LCAP

The View from a Cab. Henry Taylor. fuck with the moon, the sun don't like it. NLV

View from a Window. Eldon Grier. mine is, that dozy flies can travel here without restraint/in the gentlest of hatchures. PeCV

View from an Apartment. Michael Palmer. You must stay awake until this ends. APU

The View from an Attic Window. Howard Nemerov. And a child I slept. CoAP; ConAP

View from an Institution. Franz Wright. You'll notice the library's books are all blank on the inside. AMV-81

The View from Father's Porch. Celeste Turner Wright. On Moosehead Lake I saw no boats except/The rented one that carried me away. Str

View from Heights. Arthur Davison Ficke. While youth is ours, turn to me for a space/The marvel of your rapture-lighted face! HBMV

The View from Here. William Stafford. We too stand and wait. ELU; RFM

View from My Window. Alasdair MacLean. something to roll up and stow in my mind/against those odd moments of happiness. PoSH

View from the Corner. Samuel ("Paul Vesey") Allen. Now the thing the Negro has GOT to do–! BP

View from the Gorge. Ben Belitt. and the spirit is willing. NYBP

View from the Planetarium. David Barker. ...From a million pinholes/the giant steel ant machine/pours forth galaxies. GP

View from the Window. Jane McCoy. The fall-out of our clinking/Brattling chains... AMV-80

The View from the Window. R.S. Thomas. This work and it was not finished? BoC

View Me, Lord, a Work of Thine. Thomas Campion. Though I am but clay and dust,/Yet thy grace can lift me high. OxBoCh; TrPWD

View of a Pig. Ted Hughes. Scald it and scour it like a doorstep. BoAnP; LiTM; MP; OxBTC; TwCP

A View of Jersey. Edward Field. Finding, if not the place, the way there. NeAP

View of Louisiana. Cleopatra Mathis. the white cluster of tombs. TAT

A View of Montreal (excerpt). Francis Webb. Legends and lights; and return is out of the question. BoAV

The View of Rangitoto. Charles Brasch. For it belongs to/A world of fire before the rocks and waters. AnNZ

A View of the Brooklyn Bridge. William Meredith. And put his chisel down for marvelling on that stone. MoVE

A View of the Burning. James Merrill. ...a succulence/On which to feast, grinning ourselves, I fear. NePoEA-2

View of the Capitol from the Library of Congress. Elizabeth Bishop. The gathered brasses want to go/boom—boom. AmFN

View of the Cathedral. Raymond Henri.
all combined in choired piety. EyDe
Whenever mortal enters Chartres, he/finds it thronged to its capacity. EyDe

A View of the Present State of Ireland. Edmund Charles Blunden. Betray what has been and what might have been. BrPo

A View of the Town (excerpt). Thomas Gilbert. Or else be banished to some desert place,/And perish in each other's foul embrace. NOEC

Viewing Russian Peasants from a Leningrad-Bound Train. Roger Gaess. blowing strong against our faces. LTB

Viewpoint. George Scarbrough. Which is only to say/That a poet needs to get under/His own light. AMV-81

Views. Harriet Susskind. the body outside the shadow moving/down once more. AMV-80

Views from the High Camp. William Stanley Merwin. When it is too late to save the harvest. ConAP

Views of Boston Common and Nearby. Richard P. Blackmur. you cannot rise, and we the living must. MoVE

Views of Our Sphere. Ernest Sandeen. ...our weather/vanish altogether (all together). MOON

Views of the Favorite Colleges. John Malcolm Brinnin. And a crazy child on roller skates skates through/The campus like a one-man thunderstorm. GLGT; LiTA; MoAB

Views of the Oxford Colleges. Barbara Howes. Oxford abounds in bird-watcher and fern. GLGT

Views of the Oxford Colleges. Paris Leary. how the age has scraped Christ's blood from everything. CoPo

Vigil. Marjorie Freeman Campbell. While I, upon an unknown, well-known shore,/Keep vigil. CaP

Vigil. Richard Dehmel. Oh, wert thou here,/Or still the crimson roses glow. AWP; LiTW

Vigil. William Ernest Henley. The unnatural, intolerable day. LoBV

Vigil. Michael Knoll. ...this brightness/which comes to us from across the world. LFAC

The Vigil. Denise Levertov. Chinese boxes, each containing/the World, and its shadow. NePoEA-2

The Vigil. Shlomo Reich. The clouds of hope/come to rest only in countries/where the calendar/has been abolished VWA

Vigil of the Assumption. Gertrude von Le Fort. What is to befall you, snow-pure one? You shall be taken up/into Heaven. ISi

Vigil of the Immaculate Conception. Maurice Francis Egan. For from all seasons shall we new jewels borrow/To deck the Mother born Immaculate. CAW

Vigil of the Wounded. Phillip Yellowhawk Minthorn. weeping from their pollen hearts/hunger for your return. STE

The Vigil of Venus. Anonymous. Tomorrow let loveless, let lover tomorrow make love. AWP; GBL; LiTW; UnTE

Vigil Strange I Kept on the Field One Night. Walt Whitman. And buried him where he fell. LoBV; MoAmPo; NOBA; NoP; OBWP; PeHV; TAP; WaaP; WHA

Vigilantius. Cotton Mather. And take their Deaths as Watch-words unto me. SCAP

Vigils. Siegfried Sassoon. Peace, remote in the morning star. CMoP

Vigils: Down the Glimmering Staircase. Siegfried Sassoon. Catching roach and gudgeon in the orchard pond. PoLf

Vignette: 1922. Lawrence P. Spingarn. He tucked a shrewd hand in his miser's vest. AMV-81

Vihio Images. Judith Mountain Leaf Volborth.
froth beneath the Peacock's tongue. TWSS
stark maple shadows emerge/ghost forest landscape. TWSS

The Viking. Whitley Stokes. Give him his sword, and set him free! OnYI

Viking 1 on Mars—July 20, 1976. Anne S. Perlman. A new Bible begins. SUW

Viking Dublin: Trial Pieces. Seamus Heaney. ...go hunting/lightly as pampooties/over the skull-capped ground. IPY

The Viking Terror. Anonymous.
I need not fear the hordes of Hell/Coursing the Irish Channel. KiLC
Will come over the water to me. AnIL; OnYI

The Vikings. Anonymous. ...no need to fear/the proud sea-coursing warrior. BIrV

Vilanelle. Walter H. Kerr. We lose because we fear to win. NePoAm-2

Vilikins and His Dinah. Edward Laman Blanchard. Else you'll be singing Too-ral-loo, etc. VLP

Villa d'Este Gardens. Siegfried Sassoon. I felt like that...and fumbled for my note-book. OBTV

Villa Sciarra: Rome. Christine Turner Curtis. walking, shaken, in its sighs and shadows. GoYe

Villa Thermidor. George Hitchcock. Cocktails are served from five/to seven at the bottom of the pool. GP

The Village. George Crabbe.
Still it flows on, and shall for ever flow. CEP; LAuP
To think a poor man's bones should lie unbles'd. NOEC; OAEL 1-2; PoEL 1-5

The Village. Marina Gashe. At dawn men ride away leaving the womenfolk/To fend for the bony goats and the crying children. PBA

The Village. Meridel Le Sueur. the same Village–our Village. GP

The Village. R. S. Thomas. By great Plato's solitary mind. HaMV

Village and Factory. A. Bezymensky. Life's pulse throbbing like a boy's. TrJP

The Village Atheist. Edgar Lee Masters. And only those who strive mightily/Shall possess it. AmP; EaLo; LiTA

Village before Sunset. Frances Cornford. Even the voices calling them to bed. BoNaP; LoGBV

The Village Blacksmith. *Anonymous.* And drops a conscience-stricken tear in case he is found out. FiBHP

The Village Blacksmith. Henry Wadsworth Longfellow. Thus on its sounding anvil shaped/Each burning deed and thought. AA; AmePo; AnNE; BLPL; FaBoBe; FaFP; FaPoR; GoTF; HBV 1-2; HBVY; OBAL; OBCA; PaPo; PoPl; TreF; WBLP

Village-Born Beauty. *Anonymous.* May hell seize the villain/That smiles to betray. PaPo

The Village Choir (parody). *Anonymous* Some tune they sang, but not,/Not the Old Hundred. FaBoPa

The Village Coddled in the Valley. George Barker. As, walking clouds, she keeps from harm/The whickering child and weeping lamb. OBSP

Village in Snowstorm. Norbert Krapf. filling up the night like a well. FAZ

Village Noon: Mid-Day Bells. Merrill Moore. And Time moved on a little way in Space. MoAmPo

The Village of Balmaquhapple. James Hogg. Of the great wicked village of Balmaquhapple!' FaBoCo; FaBoPP

The Village of Erith. *Anonymous.* ...a barge/That nobody roweth or steereth. WSC

The Village of Reason. Michael Palmer. This is a poppy,/this an epilogue NPGG

The Village of the Presents. James McMichael. turns with the river's leisure to the trees. AmPA

Village of Winter Carols. Laurie Lee. where I must try the blind/and final trick of youth. ChMP

A Village Tale. May Sarton. Together in guilt and mercy, world without end. BoAnP; GDP

The Village Tudda. Kenneth Patchen. She made me weep. VGW

The Villagers and Death. Robert Graves. Their groans and whispers down the village street/Soon soured his nature, which was never sweet. HeIP

Villages Demolis. Sir Herbert Read. In red and yellow/Heaps of rubble. BrPo

The Villain. William Henry Davies. Dragging the corn by her golden hair,/Into a dark and lonely wood. MoBrPo; OBSP; OxBTC; SoSe; WHA

Villancico. *Anonymous.* Axa, Fatima, Marien. AWP

Villanelle. W. H. Auden. If I could tell you, I would let you know. MoAB; MoBrPo

Villanelle. William Empson. Poise of my hands reminded me of yours. CMoP; EnLoPo; NoAm; OAEL 1-2

Villanelle. M. D. Feld. Unmask and be the sport of fate. SD

Villanelle. Marilyn Hacker. ...Every day we separate. AmPA; SM

The Villanelle. Donald Harington. Our couple have embraced and done it well. AMV-81; FAZ

Villanelle. Dilys Bennett Laing. proud inclination of the flesh/in honor of the secret wish. ErPo; NMP

Villanelle. John Nist. black with birds of carrion prey. AMV-81

Villanelle. Margaret Winefride Simpson. Simmer sall set thy sorrow free! OxBS

Villanelle. Walter William Skeat. You need not be an atom of a poet. FaBoCo; FiBHP

Villanelle of a Villaness. Edwin Meade Robinson. (She was the daughter of Glubstein the Glover,/I wooed with poems–a lyrical lover.) HBMV

Villanelle of Acheron. Ernest Christopher Dowson. By the pale marge of Acheron,/Beyond the scope of any sun. VLP

Villanelle of His Lady's Treasures. Ernest Christopher Dowson. And so I made a Villanelle. HBV 1-2

Villanelle of Marguerites. Ernest Christopher Dowson. And what care we how many petals fall! EnLi 1-2; MoBrPo

Villanelle of Sunset. Ernest Christopher Dowson. Behold, the weary West! BrPo

Villanelle of the Poet's Road. Ernest Christopher Dowson. Yet is day over long. OBMV; TrGrPo; UnPo

Villanelle of Washington Square. Walter Adolphe Roberts. The green-robed Spring has come to town tonight. PoNe

Villanelle: The Psychological Hour. Ezra Pound. "Dear Pound, I am leaving England." CTC

Villanelle with a Line by Yeats. Bruce Bennett. We'll rock together, dozing on the deep. AMV-80

Villeggiature. Edith Nesbit. Remember how you always bore me! NOBV

Villiers de L'Isle-Adam. Aldous Huxley. ...you bade the soul drink deep/Of infinite things, saying: "The rest is naught." HBMV

Villikins and His Dinah. *Anonymous.* Think of Villikins and Dinah and the cup of cold pizen./Singing tu la lol la rol lal to rol lal la. FSW

Villkins and His Dinah. *Anonymous.* Now Jimmy and Diana both lie in one grave. BaBo

Villkins and His Dinah (B vers.). *Anonymous.* Think of Hans and Katrina and the big bologna sausage. BaBo

Villon's Ballade. Andrew Lang. 'Tis all to taverns and to lasses! HBV 1-2

Villon's Good-night. William Ernest Henley. A mot's good-night to one and all! CenHV

Villon's Straight Tip to All Cross Coves. William Ernest Henley. Booze and the blowens cop the lot. AWP; CenHV; FaBoCo; HBV 1-2; InMe; InvP; NA; SeCePo

Vilna. Moishe Kulbak. Frozen, his beard tucked in–He stands and counts the stars. VWA

A Vilna Puzzle. Sasha Chorny. This crazy puzzle, even/Spinoza could not solve. VWA

Vincent Van Gogh. William Jay Smith. An intricate maze of thin-sown poppyheads. EyDe

The Vindictive Staircase or The Reward of Industry. Wilfred Wilson Gibson. While all night I lie awake and listen/In a damned and ghostly house in Houndsditch! AnFE

The Vine. Robert Herrick. More like a Stock than like a Vine. CaPo; CavP; ErPo; NoP; UnTE

The Vine. James (1834-82) Thomson. That great, rich Vine. HBV 1-2; OBVV

Vine and Fig Tree. Shalom Altman. Nations shall learn war no more. FSW

The Vine and the Goat. Aesop. To Dionysos, god of grapes. AWP

The Vine to the Goat. Bishop Euenos. When you are slaughtered for the sacrifice. LiTW

Vinegaroon. Witter ("Emanuel Morgan") Bynner. And almost as evil as I am. BPAW

The Vines. John Gray. Half-born tendrils, grasping, gasp. NOBV

The Vineyard. *Anonymous.* When the labor is done and the workers/Before Him, shall stand. STF

The Vineyard. William Stanley Merwin. where earliest the light/is seen that bids the cock crow NNaP

The Vintage. Belle Cooper. A fount of strength to brim earth's loving-cup. GoBC

The Vintage to the Dungeon. Richard Lovelace. And dance to th' music of your chains. CaPo; SeCV 1-2

Violence on Television. Louis Jenkins. ...The snow is piling up all around the/car. Are you coming? NU

The Violent Space. Etheridge Knight. (But the air can not stand my singing long.) BPo

Violent Storm. Mark Strand. And the dark brushes against our eyes. NYBP

Violet. John Hollander. ...burned not to lie/in the ashes of our dust, it will be to grow. FYAP

The Violet. Sir Walter Scott. Nor longer in my false love's eye/Remain'd the tear of parting sorrow. EnRP

The Violet. William Wetmore Story. ...as if a curse did stain/Thy velvet leaf. HBV 1-2

Violet. Arthur Symons. Because I have no heart to give you. BrPo

The Violet. Jane Taylor. That I may also learn to grow/In sweet humility. GoTF; HBV 1-2; HBVY; TreF

The Violet and the Rose. Joseph Skipsey. And I wept for the deed I had done! OBVV

The Violet and the Rose. Augusta Webster. Why dies one sweetness when another blows? HBV 1-2

Violet Star. Philip Lamantia. the timeless in time and the regional compass. APU

Violet Twilights. Edith Sodergran. tigerspots, taut strings, fearless stars. WPOW

Violets and Roses. *Anonymous.* Dry up my tears, and dwell within her heart. OBSC

Violets for Mother. Lonny Kaneko. whispers its pink flowers. BrSi

Violets in Thaumantia's Bosome. Sir Edward Sherburne. To find, like me, by Flames a sudden death? OBS

The Violin Calls. Florence Randal Livesay. To Ireland, on cloud-riven pinions/The Dead and the Fairies go. CaP

The Violin's Complaint. William Roscoe Thayer. I'm a soul–again confide me/To a lover, ere I perish. AA

The Violin Tree. Joel Rosenberg. when my father, restless,/is out breaking the cedars of Lebanon. VWA

A Violinist. Francis William Bourdillon. Thy thought is of thy failure; we/List raptured, and thank God for thee. OBVV

The Violinist. Archibald Lampman. A lady from her carriage leant,/And murmured softly, "It was Spohr." CaP

Violins in Repose. Jorge Plescoff. I prefer violins in repose/to some undefined yearning. VWA

The Viper. Ruth Pitter. And gazed when she had gone. FaBoTw

Virgidemiarum. Joseph Hall.
  All these observed, he would contented be/To give five marks and winter livery. ViBoPo

  Envy, ye monarchs with our proud excess,/At our low sail, and our high happiness. OBSV

  So robs the sheep, in favour's fair pretence. OBSV

  Sure will he Saint her in his Calendere. FaBoEn

  Thriving in ill, as it in age decays. OBSV

Virgil: Georgics, Book IV.   Dennis Schmitz.   such is their love/of flowers/& their pride/in honey-making   NPGG

Virgil's Aeneid, Book IV (excerpt).   Henry Howard, Earl of Surrey.   And laid her on her bed with tapets spread.   EnLit

Virgil's Farewell to Dante.   Laurence Binyon.   Over thyself I crown thee and mitre thee.'   FaBoTw

Virgil's Tomb.   Robert Cameron Rogers.   The tinkling of the bells.   AA

Virgilia (excerpt).   Edwin Markham.   She can ease the heart of the old, old aching,/And put away regret.   EtS

The Virgin.   Anonymous.   Whoso wol seche true love/In her it shall be found.   GBP

Virgin.   Padraic Fallon.   And blessed--to feel the whole earth quake.   OnYI

Virgin and Unicorn.   John Heath-Stubbs.   He was as full of tears and trust as a child.   NeBP

Virgin Country.   Roy McFadden.   Each hunger-striking for its daily bread.   NeIP

A Virgin Declares Her Beauties.   Francesco da Barberino.   Lo! this is she with whom are few on earth.   AWP; ErPo

The Virgin Martyr.   Ada Cambridge.   And possess the common heritage to which all flesh is heir?   NOAV

Virgin Martyrs.   John Heath-Stubbs.   Garlanded with blood-red lilies, for ever/And ever and ever, in love.   OxBC

The Virgin Mary.   Edgar Bowers.   Of carnal being, blind and glorified.   NePoEA; QFR

Virgin Mary Had One Son.   Anonymous.   Glory be to the new-born King.   FSW

The Virgin Mary to Christ on the Cross.   Robert Southwell.   Let Sorrow string my heavy lute.   ViBoPo

The Virgin Mary to the Child Jesus.   Elizabeth Barrett Browning.   Wak'st Thou, O loving One?--   ISi

The Virgin Mother (excerpt).   D. H. Lawrence.   I must go, but my soul lies helpless/Beside your bed.   ViBoPo

Virgin Pictured in Profile.   Rosanna Warren.   the full-throated kingdom of the truly dead.   AMV-81; MAYP

The Virgin's Slumber Song.   Francis Carlin.   His ear can hear/My Song of Sleep.)   ISi; YeAr

The Virgin's Song.   Anonymous.   And wite the from the colde.   AtBAP; NOBE; OxBM

The Virgin Sturgeon.   Anonymous.   Who fired the shot, the blue or the grey?   FSW

The Virgin Unspotted.   Anonymous.   Was the great God of mercy which proved our redeem.   OBET

The Virgin Warrior.   Gwendolyn MacEwen.   Thinking, in lines as long as a camel's stride, of Kipling.   FaBoWP

A Virginal.   Ezra Pound.   As white their bark, so white this lady's hours.   AP; APA; CMoP; CoBMV; MoAB; MoAmPo; NePA; NIP; NoAm; NOBA; OxBA; TAP

Virginia.   Elouise Loftin.   and having to understand/for real   PoBA

Virginia Beach.   Stanley Plumly.   ...sure that your voice/will carry, clear that it will all come back in another form.   AMV-81

Virginia Britannia.   Marianne Moore.   are to the child an intimation of what glory is.   MoVE

Virginia Capta.   Margaret Junkin Preston.   Superbly, like Zenobia, wear/Thy chains,--Virginia Victrix still!   PAH

Virginia's Bloody Soil.   Anonymous.   Thank God the Stars and Stripes still wave above Virginia's soil.   AmFP

The Virginia Song.   Anonymous.   Who always are ready, steady, boys, steady,/To fight for their freedom again and again.   PAH

Virginiana.   Mary Johnson.   Now the men will follow,/In Virginia,/In Virginia!   HBMV

The Virginians of the Valley.   Francis Orrery [(or Orray)] Ticknor.   but not a knight asleep.   AA; AnAmPo; HBV 1-2; PAH

Virgins.   Francis Carlin.   While the sunny beauty of blushing water/Came over the cheeks of MacSorley's daughter.   HBMV

The Virgins.   Derek Walcott.   heading for where the banks of silver thresh.   OxBC; SoSe

Virgo Descending.   Charles Wright.   ...It keeps on filling your room.   LCAP

A Virile Christ.   Rex Boundy.   Did he not bear the greatest pain of all,/Silent, upon the cross on Calvary?   TRV; WGRP

Virtual Particles.   Frank Wilczek.   Hamlet vacillated--so does this stuff.   NLV

Virtue.   Walter De la Mare.   Grant my son's ashes lie where these men are!   MMM

Virtue.   Immanuel Di Roma.   But in the wrinkled old crones with/silver-white hair.   TrJP

Virtue.   Nicholas Grimald.   Why tread you death? "I only cannot die."   OBSC

Virtue.   George Herbert.   But though the whole world turn to coal,/Then chiefly lives.   AWP; CH; ELP; EnLit; ExPo; ForPo; HAP; HBV 1-2; HeIP; InPo; InPS; InvP; JCP; LoBV; NOBE; NOCV; NoP; OAEL 1-2; OBEV; PoRA; PPP; SeCeV; SoSe; TEP; TreFT; TrGrPo; ViBoPo; WGRP; WHA

A Virtue of Shape.   Thomas Swiss.   ...meaning/Being a virtue of shape and order.   AMV-80

Virtue the Best Monument.   Sir Walter Ralegh.   With nature's harmony, which standing still,/Or faintly beating, show them dead or ill.   FCP

The Virtues of Carnation Milk.   Anonymous.   You just punch a hole in the son of a bitch.   OBAL

The Virtues of Sid Hamet, the Magician's Rod.   Jonathan Swift.   His next may be a rod in piss.   APAS

Virtuosa.   Mary Ashley Townsend.   A slave hr touch could quicken or benumb.   AA

The Virtuous Fox and the Self-Righteous Cat.   John Cunningham.   So ran to regale on a new-taken fly.   OnMSP

The Virtuous Wife.   Von Trimberg Susskind.   Her praise and worth I'll sing alway.   TrJP

The Virus.   Christian Morgenstern.   While Albert Pierce could but respond, "Hey,/Shoo!" and had him till next Monday.   PV

The Visible Baby.   Peter Redgrove.   What a closed book bound in wrinkled illustration his/father is to him!   NAs

Vision.   Delmira Augustini.   I saw you'd fallen back, you were wrapped/in some huge fold of darkness!   WPOW

The Vision.   Robert Burns.
She boasts a Race,/To ev'ry nobler virtue bred,/And polish'd grace.   OxBS
While here, half-mad, half-fed, half-sarkit,/Is a' th' amount.   BSV

A Vision.   John Clare.   I gave my name immortal birth/And kept my spirit with the free.   ERoP 1-2; FaBoRV; GTBS-P; NCEP; NOBV; OAEL 1-2; OBNC; PPP

The Vision.   Dante Alighieri.   "The love that moves the sun and the other stars."   BoC

A Vision.   Geoffrey Dearmer.   But in His still and shadowed face I saw/The agony of Man.   HBMV

The Vision.   Daniel Defoe.   But here's a more difficult matter remains,/To tell if he showed us less manners or brains.   APAS

Vision.   James Devaney.   The ever-imminent gleamed a space/Through the dull wear of commonplace.   NOAV

Vision.   Richard Eberhart.   Sing, sing with the hummingbirds.   NYBP

A Vision.   Michael (Katherine Bradley and Edith Cooper) Field.   And in tranquillity the vision knocks.   SyP

A Vision.   Edward, Lord Herbert of Cherbury.   Unless that he my Vision can unfold.   AnAnS 2; SeCP

The Vision.   Robert Herrick.
And I am wild and wanton like to him.   CaPo; CBEP
Herrick, thou art too coarse to love.'   AnAnS 2; CaPo; EAS; ErPo; JCP; SeCP

A Vision.   Hugo von Hofmannsthal.   With giant sails of yellow, strangely/shaped.   TrJP

Vision.   William Dean Howells.   The poor man's landlord leading down to/dine.   AA; AnAmPo

A Vision.   Maria Konopnicka.   ...I shall go/Thoughtfully toward the distant fields that show/Emptiness, white and endless.   WPOW

Vision.   William Stanley Merwin.   as long as there is day/and part of the night.   GP

The Vision.   Aogan O Rathaille.   that morning ere Titan had thought to stir his feet.   NOBI

Vision.   Frank Sidgwick.   He loans me eyes that look on heaven?   MMM

The Vision.   William Taylor.   But sceptres, scutcheons, mitres gold/Flew up and kicked the beam.   NOEC

The Vision.   Thomas Traherne.   Who All Things finds convey'd to him alone,/Must needs adore the Holy One.   ILwL

A Vision.   Henry Vaughan.   And all her train were hurl'd.   BBV; GTBS; ImOP

A Vision.   Yvor Winters.   ...the tremor of that scream/Shattered my being like an empty dream.   AnAnS 2; MoVE; SeCP

Vision.   Israel Zangwill.   And the strange, sweet tears!   TrJP

Vision and Prayer.   Dylan Thomas.   Now I am lost in the blinding/One./The sun roars at the prayer's end.   LiTM; MoPo

Vision by Sweetwater.   John Crowe Ransom.   From one of the white throats which it hid among?   AP; CMoP; CoBMV; FaBoMo; MoAB; NOBA; OxBA

A Vision (excerpt).   Bryan Waller Procter.   ...he played/('Fore Midas,) in the Phrygian shade,/With Pan, and to the Sylvan host.   OBRV

Vision of 400 Sunrises.   Ruth Lisa Schechter.   invading Vietnam like a woman/whose neck snaps and breaks/before rape.   SOTS

Vision of Belshazzar.   George Gordon, Lord Byron.   The Persian on his throne!   FaPo; GN; HBV 1-2

The Vision of Beulah.   William Blake.   Yet all in order sweet and lovely. Men are sick with love.   NOBE

Vision of Connaught in the Thirteenth Century.   James Clarence Mangan.   Of Cahal Mor of the Wine-red Hand!   AnIL; IrPN; NOBI

The Vision of Delight.   Ben Jonson.   Because the Morne, with Roses strew's the way.   SeCV 1-2

Vision of Ita.   Anonymous.   Though as Jesukin he sits at my breast.   AnIL

Voice in the Crowd. Ted Joans. You have nothing to fear/from the poet/ but the truth AmNP

Voice in the Dark. Avner Strauss. The whole of darkness rose in me and is. VWA

A Voice in the Garden. Selima Hill. Yoo-hoo, Gerald's here, yoo-hoo... FaBoWP

Voice of a Dissipated Woman inside a Tomb... Sor Violante do Ceu. ...the end which ends with no way out. BoWoP

The Voice of America 1961. James Liddy. let me steer close to touch YOUR BIG WHISKERS. CIP

The Voice of Ardent Zeal Speaks from the Lollard's Tower of St. Paul's. Henry Farley. There's little coin and less devotion. FaBoEE

The Voice of Christmas. Harry Kemp. The Master of the Centuries Who will not be denied! HBV 1-2

The Voice of Experience. Johann Wolfgang von Goethe. what response he may unloose/will offend and thus seduce. ErPo; PV

The Voice of God. Katherine R. Barnard. And His great works applaud. BLRP; WBLP

The Voice of God. Louis I. Newman. I dwell among the people. GoTF; PoToHe; TreF

The Voice of God. James Stephens. "We are the voice of God," I cried. WGRP

The Voice of God Is Calling. John Haynes Holmes. Command, and we obey! AH

Voice of the Crocus. Mildred N. Hoyer. To let the doubting see/ Resurrected life in me. AMV-80

The Voice of the Derwent. William Wordsworth. Half-heard and half-created. FaBoPP

The Voice of the Dove. Joaquin Miller. There is only one To-day. AA

The Voice of the Grass. Sarah Roberts Boyle Creeping, silently creeping everywhere. AA; HBV 1-2; HBVY

The Voice of the Lobster. Lewis (Charles Lutwidge Dodgson) Carroll. And concluded the banquet by--- EvOK

The Voice of the Power of This World. Gregory Hall. genital/faces/from the dark/mouth. NU

The Voice of the Void. George Parsons Lathrop. For I am Death! AA

Voice of the Western Wind. Edmund Clarence Stedman. And never shall I find the light/Of days forever flown! HBV 1-2

The Voice of Thought. Thomas Holley Chivers. In the Soul's sweet song to me. AnAmPo

The Voice of Toil. William Morris. And joy at last for thee and me. AnFE; HBV 1-2

The Voice of Webster (excerpt). Robert Underwood Johnson. His mighty frame was refuge, while his/mien/Did make dispute of stature with the/ gods. AA

A Voice Sings. Samuel Taylor Coleridge. Miserere Domine! CAW; CH

The Voice That Beautifies the Land. Anonymous. The voice that beautifies the land. AWP

The Voiceless. Oliver Wendell Holmes As sad as earth, as sweet as heaven! AA; ViBoPo

The Voices. Anonymous. Mutter the Voices–the Guns. MCCG

Voices. Nora Dauenhauer. blossoms/swaying in the wind. TWSS

Voices. Walter De la Mare. Sighs through the dews of evening peacefully/ Falling, "Dream!"? UnPo

The Voices. Janine Pommy-Vega. Hovering over the sound is a mother buried/inside me, her bare arms cover the sea. APU

Voices Answering Back: The Vampires. Lawrence Raab. if you stop believing in us/we inherit everything AmPA

Voices at the Window. Sir Philip Sidney.
　Never doth thy beauty flourish/More than in my reason's sight. OBEV; PoPle
　Which can make me thus to leave you,/And from louts to run away. NOBE

Voices from the Other World. James Merrill. Nor the full moon more quick to chill. GP; MP; TwCP

Voices from Things Growing in a Churchyard. Thomas Hardy. All day cheerily,/All night eerily! OxBTC

Voices in the Winter. Ken McCullough. I stand here in the rain and begin to weep. LTB

The Voices Inescapable. Ann Stanford. And the raped girl in the forest. IHMS

Voices of Heroes. Horace Gregory. And in a world at war, only the wars live on. OFD

The Voices of Nature. Thomas Edward Brown. And yet...I would go back. PeD

Voices of the Air. Katherine Mansfield. The shrill quick sound that the insect makes. HBMV

Voices That Have Filled My Day. Fay Chiang. I thank you for the sunrise BrSi

The Volatile Kerryman. Owen Roe O'Sullivan. and it's goodbye to Owen! BIrV

Volcanic Venus. D. H. Lawrence. and never knowing when you'll provoke an earthquake. InPS; PAI; PoL

Volcano. Derek Walcott. I must read more carefully. OxBC

Volcanoes. Bella Akhmadulina. ...Did he, didn't he,/Bellow. "Forgive me!"? PBWP

The Vole. Marvin Solomon. ..and build/A perfect freedom, though all else were foiled. NcPoAm-2

Volleyball Teacher Ends the Game. Jose Y., Jr. Teran. as though the train could think/reflecting no, no, no. LFAC

Volpone. Ben Jonson. ...transfuse our wandering souls/Out at our lips, and score up sums of pleasure. ViBoPo

Voltaire at Ferney. W. H. Auden. The uncomplaining stars composed their lucid song. LiTA; LiTM; NePA; PoA

Volto Sciolto e Pensieri Stretti. James Clarence Mangan. For there be more devouring beasts of prey/Than haunt the woods, among the human race. IrPN

Volubilis, North Africa. Ralph Nixon Currey. And argued city walls from uncut stone. PeSA

A Volume of Chopin. James Picot. Lady, I trust you come not to do harm. PoAu 1-2

Voluntaries. Ralph Waldo Emerson.
　All are ghosts beside. AmePo; WGRP
　When Duty whispers low, Thou must,/The youth replies, I can. FPL; PoLf; TRV

The Volunteer. Anonymous. And his crutches procure him permission to beg. NOEC

The Volunteer. Herbert Asquith. Who goes to join the men of Agincourt. MMM; OBWP; OxBTC

The Volunteer. Elbridge Jefferson Cutler. I follow, though I die! AA

A Volunteer's Grave. William Alexander Percy. Bequeathed us lovelier to recall/Than this dead boy! HBMV

The Volunteer's Thanksgiving. Lucy Larcom. For Peace will light the country on that Thanksgiving Day. OBCA

The Volunteers. William Haines Lytle. From storm-lashed Erie's wintry shore,/Shall spring the Volunteers once more. MC; PAH

Voluspo. Anonymous. The serpent bright: but now must I sink. AWP

Voodoo on the Un-Assing of Janis Joplin:Warning:To Ole Tom. Carolyn M. Rodgers. ZOT!!!!!! JB

The Voortrekker. Rudyard Kipling. Till on his last-won wilderness an Empire's outposts stand! HBV 1-2

Vor a Gauguin Picture zu Singen. Kurt M. Stein. Das iss doch kein Climate fur a mittelaged Mann. FiBHP

Voronezh. Anna Akhmatova. where every line has three stresses/and only the one word, dark. FaBoPV

Vota Amico Facta, Fol. 160. Gazaeus. God grant thee thine own wish, and grant thee mine. OBVE

Voting Machine. Norman Nathan. however miniatured/i will speak/me AMV-80

Votive Ode. Desiderius Erasmus. And free for aye from sin's foul tyranny./Erasmus, his vow. ISi

Votive Song. Edward Coate [(or Coote)] Pinkney. And fall these heavy tears. AA; APA

A Vow. Allen Ginsberg. over Puerto Rican agony lawyers' screams in slums. OBWP

The Vow. Anthony Hecht. Your younger brothers shall confirm in joy/ This that I swear. ConAP; InPK; NePoEA; PoCh; Prf

The Vow. Carl Rakosi. for I love/thee/more than Durer/loved a seaweed. FAZ

Vow. John Updike. From sopranino to contrabass. NYBP

The Vow-Breaker. Henry, Bishop of Chichester King. At length I feare thy perjur'd breath/Will blow out day, and waken death. OBS

A Vow for New Year's. Mary Carolyn Davies. That comes a model New Year's Day! PoToHe

The Vow of Washington. John Greenleaf Whittier.
　Repeat with us the pledge a century old! PAH
　The winds of heaven would sing the praise of him... MC

A Vow to Heavenly Venus. Joachim Du Bellay. Bound each to each, like flower to wedded flower. AWP

Vow to Love Faithfully, Howsoever He Be Rewarded. Henry Howard, Earl of Surrey. ...with this thought/Content myself, although my chance be nought. ElL; EnLi 1-2; EnPo; LiTL; TrGrPo; ViBoPo

Vowel Englyn to the Spider. Anonymous. And must its little liver all/The wondrous stuff supply? LiTW

Vowel Movements. Daryl Hine. Finally I tried to define why divine silence... PoA

Vowels. Arthur Rimbaud. O, Omega, violet ray of Her Eyes! SOTW

The Vowels of Another Language. Tom Disch. To ask why he felt for these strangers/Feelings for which he had no name PoA

The Vows. Andrew Marvell. And quack in their language still, Vive le Roy. TW

Vox Clero, Lilliburlero. Anonymous. Yet not find so much brain as in Oliver's porter. APAS

Vox Humana. Thom Gunn. ...For you bring,/to what you define now, all/ there is, ever, of future. NePoEA-2

Vox Oppressi to the Lady Phipps. Richard Henchman. And Typify, when Death hath clos'd her Eyes,/What she shall, at the Resurrection, rise. SCAP

Vox Populi. John Dryden. What fools our fathers were, if this be true! NOBE

Vox Populi, Vox Dei (excerpt). *Anonymous.*
All these men go to wrack,/That are the body and stay/Of your grace's realm alway. FaBoPV
O most noble king./Consider well this thing. FaBoPV

Vox Ultima Crucis. John Lydgate. For the I offered my blood in sacryfice. OBEV; OxBoCh

Voyage. John Lyle Donaghy. all but a few, mated, that lowered among the grasses/whom the gale, next morning, tried. OxBI

The Voyage. Heinrich Heine. ith woe too vast for being! AWP

Voyage. Josephine Miles. Seamews and curlews/In a brisk brine? LiTM

The Voyage. Edwin Muir. And knew the place to which we were sent. LiTM

Voyage. Donald G. H. Schramm. we race our protean bodies to the sea. AMV-81

The Voyage. Karl Shapiro. Uprooted abound in the water and choke in the air. MoLP

Voyage. Stanislaw Wygodski. and a damp, abandoned book/in the city morgue. VWA

Voyage a L'Infini. Walter Conrad Arensberg. The lake is a wide silence/Without imagination. AnAmPo

The Voyage of Jimmy Poo. James A. Emanuel. The next time you go sailing/Beyond enamel shore. AmNP; NNP

The Voyage of Life. Charles Bernstein. ...Or tossed in tune, emboss with gloss in-/Signias of air. APU

The Voyage of Maeldune. Alfred, Lord Tennyson. When I landed again with a tithe of my men, on the Isle/of Finn! PoEL 1-5

Voyage to Cythera. Charles Baudelaire. Give me, Lord God, to look upon that dung,/My body and my heart, without disgust. LiTW; NAWM 1-2; SyP

Voyage to the Moon. William Dickey. Which may serve as armament for the next expedition. MOON

Voyage to the Moon. Archibald MacLeish. Over us on these silent beaches the bright/earth,/presence among us. MOON

A Voyage to Tintern Abbey. Sneyd Davies. Weep o'er its ruins, at its follies laugh. NOEC

Voyage West. Archibald MacLeish. Steep from an ocean where no landfall can be. VGW

A Voyager's Prayer. *Anonymous.* Thou art able to make this water calm/Until we have safely passed over. WGRP

Voyager's Song. Clement Wood. But it was life to hear you speak,/And heaven to see your face. HBMV

Voyagers. Henry Van Dyke. Thy sea is great, our boats are small. TRV

Voyagers' Prayer. *Anonymous.* Thou art able to make this water calm/Until we have safely passed over. TRV

Voyages. Hart Crane.
The seal's wide spindrift gaze toward paradise. AmLP; CoBMV; DTC; ExPo; ForPo; HAP; LiTM; MoAB; MoAmPo; MoPo; NAMP; NePA; NU; PPP; UnPo; VGW; ViBoPo
Whose accent no farewell can know. AnFE; HAP; MoAB; MoAmPo; SeCeV; UnPo

The Voyages of Captain Cock. William Jay Smith. Not panting here, upended in the breech. ErPo; UnTE

Voyageur. R. E. Rashley. The coyote, lonely on the wind swept summit. CaP

Voyeur. John Edward Hardy. And own the betrayal of my unguarded heart. ErPo

The Voyeur. Deanna Louise Pickard. something like spoiled sweets. AMV-80

Vuillard: "The Mother and Sister of the Artist." W. D. Snodgrass. That merges into the empty twinkling/Of the air and of the bright wallpaper. CoAP

Vulcan begat me... Sir Thomas Wyatt. And if I be thine enemy I may thy life end. FCP

A Vulgar Error. J. E. Thorold Rogers. (Perhaps the parson) is self-interest. FaBoEE

A Vulnerary. Jonathan Williams. comely, comely, love trembles/and the sweet-shrub PoM

The Vulture. Hilaire Belloc. Oh, what a lesson for us all/To only eat at dinner. HBVY; OxBChV

The Vulture. Israel Kafu Hoh. And a king in my small village. ACV

Vulture. Robinson Jeffers. What a life after death. BoAnP; NOBA; NoP

Vulture. X. J. Kennedy. Thus making up in usefulness/For what he lacks in taste. GrPl

The Vulture and the Husbandman. Arthur Clement Hilton. And this was scarcely odd, because/They'd ploughed them every one! CenHV; FaBoCo

The Vulture of the Plains. Hamlin Garland. Monarch of cloudland—yet a ghoul at prey. BPAW

The Vultures. David Diop. Spring will be reborn under our bright steps. PBA; TTY

Vusumzi's Song. L. T. Manyase. So says the love-song of Vusumzi. PeSA

W

W. James Reeves. "I'm sorry," said he, "to trouble you." NTCP

W. C. W. David Ray. as all folks do,/walking along PoL

W'en you see a man in woe. Sam Walter Foss. How's the world a-usin' you? CenHV

W. H. Auden & Mantan Moreland. Al Young. For the same reason you probly stopped shufflin. NPGG

W. H. Eheu! Samuel Taylor Coleridge. He died like one who dared not hope to live. FaBoEE

W.L.M.K. F. R. Scott. Do nothing by halves/Which can be done by quarters. NOBC

W o m a n. Magda Portal. and the sea perhaps some way/and the sea so very far. WPOW

W's for Windows. Phyllis McGinley. When the dusk is coming down. TiPo

W. S. Landor. Marianne Moore. he could only say, "I'll/talk about them when I understand them." OBAL

W. W. LeRoi (Imamu Amiri Baraka) Jones. I mean. Like that. HeIP; NBP; NOBA; PoBA

The Wabash Cannonball. *Anonymous.* Riding through the jungles,/On the Wabash Cannonball. BLSo; FSW; TreFT

Wade in the Water. *Anonymous.* God's a-gonna trouble the water. FSW

Waders and Swimmers. Stanley Plumly. and water rising in a smoke of waters. GeTw

Wading at Wellfleet. Elizabeth Bishop. they try revolving,but the wheels/give way, they will not bear the weight. AmP

Wag a Leg, Wag a Leg. *Anonymous.* Two miles to Tong. OxNR

Wages. Alfred, Lord Tennyson. Give her the wages of going on, and not/to die. OAEP

The Waggon-Maker. John Masefield. Homing the bride, and harvest, and men dead. EBEV

The Waggoner. *Anonymous.* Tho' he's sair pock brocken,/And he's blind of an e'e. GBP

The Waggoner. Edmund Charles Blunden. As centuries past itself would do. AnFE

Wagner. Rupert Brooke. And all the while, in perfect time,/His pendulous stomach hangs a-shaking. FaBoTw; NAMP; NOBL

Wagon Full of Thunder. Louis (LittleCoon) Oliver. Words off Indian tongue/—from mind shell. STE

Wagon Train. E. L. Mayo. But drift to sleep where canvas hides the stars/Of the long, planetary wagon train. MiAP

The Wagon Train. Sam L. Simpson. "Ah, yes, I crossed the plains with him!" BPAW

Wagon Wheels. S. E. LaMoure. —a huge tractor wheels by/the edge of the sky. AMV-81

The Wagoner's Lad. *Anonymous.*
So fare you well darling, no longer to stand. FSW
Sweet instruments of music/And the firing of guns. AmFP
We will commence our music and the firing of guns. BaBo

Wagtail and Baby. Thomas Hardy. The baby fell a-thinking. HBMV

The Waif. Walter De la Mare. And silent slides the silver Brent, and mute is "Middlesex." FaBoNo

Waikiki. Rupert Brooke. Whose perplexed heart did evil, foolishly,/A long while since, and by some other sea. OBTV

The Wail of Archy (excerpt). Don (Donald Robert Marquis) Marquis. gods what a terrible tragedy/not to make good with the tragic/archy FiBHP

The Wail of Prometheus Bound. Aeschylus. And all life that approaches I wait for in fear. WGRP

The Wail of the Waiter. Marcus Clarke. "WAITER!!' "Yessir,' "Wake up, stupid! Biled calves' feet for/Number Two!' NOAV

Waillie. *Anonymous.* Waillie, Oh Waillie, but love it is bonnie/A little while when it is new. FSW

Waillie, Waillie! (with music). *Anonymous.* But it grows old and waxeth cold,/And fades away like evening dew. AS

A Waist. Gertrude Stein. ...A country climb is the best disgrace, a/couple of practices any of them in order is so left. NMM

The Waistcoat. Padraic Fallon. Ah, Padraic, I who tell the story/Cover my face and sigh. OxBI

The Wait. Phyllis Janowitz. Thumb in mouth it is laughing at you. AMV-80

Wait. Timothy Steele. And till then? Get some rest. Be patient. Wait. PoA

Wait for Me. Robert Creeley. home for herself./I said. NOBA; PPP

Wait for the Hour. William Soutar. To curb the fretful brain and trust the blood. NeBP

Wait for the Wagon. *Anonymous.* Wait till the Judgment-day. PAH

Wait for the Wagon. R. Bishop Buckley. Wait for the wagon,/And we'll all take a ride. BLSo; FSW; PSoN

Wait On! *Anonymous.* No time is lost–/Wait on! STF

Wait Till the Darkness is Deep. Wallada. full moon not come into view/ stars not journey by night. WPOW

Wait Till Then. Mark Van Doren. "Not as I do, not as I do. Wait."/"Till when?" SO

Waitaki Dam. Denis Glover. The river smoothly slides away to sea. AnNZ

Waiting. Harry Behn. When it is time to wake and grow. SiSoSe; TiPo

Waiting. John Burroughs. Can keep mine own away from me. AA; AnAmPo; APA; BLPA; FaBoBe; GoTF; HBV 1-2; OHFP; TreF; TRV; WGRP

Waiting. Jane Cooper. Let compassion breathe in and out of you/filling you with poems. TAP

Waiting. Hilary Corke. And her wind, her wind in my branches. ErPo

Waiting. Robert Creeley. That risk/is all there is. VGW

Waiting. John Davidson. ...a captain to command us,/And the word we must obey. ViBoPo

Waiting. John Freeman. Hiding her thoughts away. CH

Waiting. Ruth Apprich Jacob. Waiting to see if your wish comes true! BiCB

Waiting. Robert Pack. as I promise again I will wait here/for the rain, for you, to arrive. GOYP; PPJ

Waiting. Judith Skillman. to fall asleep under the influence/of a different gravity. SUW

Waiting. Liz Stout. like a gift/that explained the waiting. AMV-81

The Waiting. John Greenleaf Whittier. And good but wished with God is done! WGRP

Waiting. Yevgeny Yevtushenko. it will slide to the floor in a blue heap. LLLT

Waiting and Peeking. V. R. Lang. Maintains its own life and its powers, peeking at us as it does. NePA

Waiting at the Church; or, My Wife Won't Let Me. Fred W. Leigh. Can't get away to marry you today/My wife won't let me! FSN

Waiting Both. Thomas Hardy. So mean I. MoAB; MoBrPo; OxBoLi

Waiting Carefully. Nancy P. Kamm. And await some subtle invitation. AMV-80

The Waiting Chords. Stephen Henry Thayer. The secret that had wrought the spell. AA

Waiting for a Second Time. Frank LaPena. and wait for him/to tell me/a second time/for emphasis STE

Waiting for Breakfast, While She Brushed Her Hair. Philip Larkin. ...live/ Part invalid, part baby, and part saint? NoAm

Waiting for Death. Mordecai Gebirtig. Thus we pass our weary days/And our sleepless nights. TrJP

Waiting for E. gularis. Linda Pastan. binoculars/raised/like pistols. SUW

Waiting for God. Harry Roskolenko. To see her and a Healer named Placido. FAZ

Waiting for Her. Alden Nowlan. if she doesn't that I don't care. NeAC

Waiting for Icarus. Muriel Rukeyser. It would have been better than this. NNaP

Waiting for IT. May Swenson. ...It/is what is about to happen,/not/what is already here. BoAnP

Waiting for Lilith. Jascha Kessler. ...No laughters/of sons, no wife from my bone, can drown your voice. VWA

Waiting for Nighthawks in Illinois. Roger Pfingston. I believed him, and lit another cigar. FAZ

Waiting for the Bus. D. J. Enright. Then have we missed the bus? Or are we sure/which way the wind is blowing? OxBTC

Waiting for the Dawning. *Anonymous.* And my heart, my heart is longing/ To be His for evermore. BLRP

Waiting for the Doctor. Colette Inez. a 9-lb. load to cart in and out of next year's bed. IHMS

Waiting for the Fire. Philip Appleman. the path of the light comes to you. SOTS

Waiting for the Morning. *Anonymous.* O Sun of Righteousness, bring in/ The everlasting day. STF

Waiting for the Post. Dorothy Auchterlonie. The earth turns over, though the street is still. CBAP

Waiting for the Rain. Felix Mnthali. tired and sad/from praying for the rain. WhB

Waiting for Winter. George Keithley. Now it is coming, now it is here. NPGG

Waiting for You to Come By. Simon J. Ortiz. i have been waiting/for you to come by. CDW

The Waiting Harp. Gustavo Adolfo Becquer. To say its message,–"Soul, arise and walk." CAW

Waiting in Faith. Buonarroti Michelangelo. My heart's loved Lord to me desertless given! ILwL

Waiting in Front of the Columnar High School. Karl Shapiro. ...The horror of their years/stoned me to death. HAP

Waiting Inside. David Ignatow. with our arms around each other's waists,/ in support. CAPP

The Waiting-Room. Robin Fuller. I sit staring at a mirror. All it shows/is the reflection of a pale barred window. PoA

Waiting Rooms. Howard Nemerov. Where hope only remains. You wait and see. PoA

Waiting, the Hallways under Her Skin Thick with Dreamchildren. Lyn Lifshin. smiling, dying. NeAC

Waiting to Be Fed. Ray A. Young Bear. walking to the river. CDW

The Waiting Watchers. Henry Treece. Two and one, they shall be standing/At your door. NeBP

Waitress. Michael Brownstein. But you still have to wait ANYP

The Waits. Madeline Nightingale. We sang His birthday song, we did, upon His birthday/morn. SUS

Waiwera. Kendrick Smithyman. To the custom of such a world he offers himself. AnNZ

Wake. Langston Hughes. Cause there ain't no sense/In my bein' dead. OBAL; ShM

The Wake. Wyatt Prunty. That, cooling, moves from room to room. AMV-80

Wake. Elizabeth Spires. I am who you turn to when the world stops. AMV-80

Wake All the Dead. Sir William Davenant. Lie two in a grave, and to bed, to bed! CBEP; ELP; FaBoCh; HAP; LoGBV; SeCePo

The Wake at the Well. *Anonymous.* Withouten he find it milk and pap/A long while-ey. GBP

Wake, child. Mira Bai [(or Mirabai[). Handsome Girdhar, Mira's lord,/ saves those who come to be saved. BoWoP

Wake Cry. Waring Cuney. Made o' stone? BANP

Wake, Isles of the South. William B. Tappan. And the isles of the ocean shall wait for his law. AH

Wake, Lady! Joanna Baillie. Lo! while thou sleep'st they haste away! HBV 1-2

Wake Nicodemus. Henry Clay Work. And meet us at the gum-tree down in the swamp,/To wake Nicodemus today. FSW

Wake Not for the World-Heard Thunder. Alfred Edward Housman. Sleep away, lad; wake no more. CMoP; NoAm

The Wake of William Orr. William Drennan. Watch with us thro' dead of night–But expect the morning light. OnYI; OxBI

Wake the Song of Jubilee. Leonard Bacon. Joy, the whole creation sings,/ "Jesus is the King of Kings!" AH

Wake Up, Dear Boy That Holds the Flute! Mira Bai [(or Mirabai)]. The comely Girdhar, Mira's Lord,/saves those who for salvation come. WPOW

Wake Up, Jacob. *Anonymous.* If you don't come soon, gonna throw it all away. FSW

Wake-Up Niggers. Don L. Lee. that whi/te man with/that/cross on his back. PoBA

Wake Up! Wake Up! Basho (Matsuo Basho). sleeping butterfy! SoPo

Wake Up, You Drowsy Sleepers. *Anonymous.* Come back, come back, my own true lover,/And I will go away with you. BFSS

Waked by the Gospel's Powerful Sound. Samson Occom. The sinner now is born again,/To dwell with Christ above. AH

Wakeful in the Township. Elizabeth Riddell. Lost, lost, lost. NOAV; PoAu 1-2

The Wakening. *Anonymous.* Kiss me and take my soul in keeping,/Since I must go, now day is near.' OBEV

The Wakening. Sam Hamill. ...the morning/spreads over him like a stain. AMV-80

Wakepick I. Kristjana Gunnars. i disentangle sinew, hair/i turn to stone CaPN; NOBC

The Wakers. John Freeman. And there was the old scolding of the birds. HBMV

The Wakeupworld. Countee Cullen. They covered him, and none knew where/To find him when the storm was done. GoSl

Waking. Annie Higgins. You're going to be sorry, dear. ELU

Waking. Patrick MacDonogh. A wind among the grass and, sighing,/ Carries my spirit to hers. NeIP

Waking. Hugh Maxton. ...This has gone on ten years. BIrV; CIP

Waking. Katharine Pyle. And the little dream-child by the dreamland sea/ Will wait for me in vain. OBCA

The Waking. Theodore Roethke.
And see and suffer myself/In another being, at last. CoAP
I learn by going where I have to go. AP; BiP; CAPP; CoAP; CoBMV; CrMA; HaCAP; HAP; HeIP; InPK; InPS; LiTM; MoAmPo; MP; NIP; NoAm; NOBA; NoP; PAI; PoPl; PPP; PrIm; SM; SoSe; TAP; TwCP
Sang in my veins/That summer day. RFM

Waking Alone. *Anonymous.* For, when I awoke, ther was but I alone. MeEL

Waking an Angel. Philip Levine. like a raiment of victory. NaP

Waking Early. R. L. Barth. Then leave the room to you, my sleeping lover. AMV-81

Waking Early Sunday Morning. Robert Lowell. ...a ghost/orbiting forever lost/in our monotonous sublime. FaBoMo; HaCAP; NOBA; OxBC

Waking from a Nap on the Beach. May Swenson. The sea is/fat. NTCP; PCP; RFM

Waking from Sleep. Robert Bly. We know that our master has left us for the day. CAPP; EAS; NoAm; NOBA; NoP; PAI

Waking in New York. Allen Ginsberg. peek in the inky beauty of the roofs. NYP

Waking in Nice. Patricia Traxler. into the present tense. AMV-81

Waking in the Blue. Robert Lowell. We are all old-timers,/each of us holds a locked razor. CoAP; HaCAP; MoAmPo; PPP; UnPo

Waking in the Dark. Dorothy Livesay. in his right arm/he carries his head. NOBC

Waking in the Dark. Adrienne Rich. looking at the earth, the wildwood/ where the split began. FaBoWP

Waking on a Greyhound. Gordon Henry. from dead/on the side/of the road. STE

Waking, the Love Poem Sighs. Jim Hall. Never wake early enough to pull the/Words out of this dream and make/Them work for me in daylight. GOYP

Waking Time. Ivy O. Eastwick. And "I can't find my left shoe!" SiSoSe; TiPo

Waking Up. Edward Lense. bells, far off, very faint. AMV-80

Waking Up. Tom Schmidt. your brown and butter hair/drenching my face like/summer rain. GP

Walam Olum; or, Red Score (excerpt). Anonymous. At this time whites came on the Eastern sea. OBVE

Waldeinsamkeit. Ralph Waldo Emerson. For a proud idleness like this/ Crowns all thy mean affairs. AP; HBV 1-2; NOBA; WGRP

Walden. Henry David Thoreau.
And the host of airy quill-drivers/First dipped their pens in mist. MAmP
...The sun is but a morning star. NU

Walden in July. Donald Junkins. The night was opening/like a cotyledon. NYBP

Waldere 2. Anonymous. ,and attack me with swords/As ye have done. AnOE

Wales. Norman Nicholson. Aware that the mist will never lift to order. ChMP

Wales Visitation. Allen Ginsberg. upward in motion with wet wind. CAPP; NNaP; NOBA; NYBP; Prf

The Walk. Leonard Clark. And smoothed down my wild hair in the starred light of evening. AtBAP

The Walk. Thomas Hardy. Only that underlying sense/Of the look of a room on returning thence. CMoP; PoEL 1-5; PrIm

Walk. Frank Horne. and find the path/at your soft command. BPo

A Walk. Hedwig Lachmann. We have not lived but in a dream that/ wakes. TrJP

The Walk. W. W. Eustace Ross. the blue shimmering/of lake-water. PeCV; SD

A Walk. Gary Snyder. Stoppt and swam and ate my lunch. NoAm; NOBA

Walk about the Subway Station. Charles Reznikoff. a flat black fungus/that was chewing-gum. CAD; NYP

A Walk by the Charles. Adrienne Rich. Past innocence, beyond these aging bricks/To where the Charles flows in to join the Styx. NePoEA; NYBP

Walk, Damn You, Walk! William De Vere. "Walk, damn you, walk!" PoLf

The Walk Home. Reed Whittemore. The world doesn't oblige, and old pipes stink. ConAP

Walk in Jerusalem Jus' Like John. Anonymous. I want to be ready, to walk in Jerusalem jus' like John. BoAN 1-2; FSW

A Walk in Kyoto. Earle Birney. and higher into the endless winds of the world. GoYe

A Walk in March. Tim Reynolds. It is the darkest night of the year, and starless. MAT

A Walk in the Country. Galway Kinnell. That takes us all and under like that/grass. NePoAm

The Walk in the Garden. Conrad Aiken. a book that is never done, never done. PoCh

Walk in the Precepts. Moses Ibn Ezra. If worn and patched the garments that/men view. TrJP

A Walk in Wurzburg. William Plomer. And detect why the horde we are destroys itself. NYBP

Walk, Jaw-Bone. Silas S. Steele. Walk, jaw-bone, Jenny come along,/In come Sally wid de bootees on. TrAS

Walk on a Winter Day. Sara Van Alstyne Allen. Singing a winter song/ For you and me. YeAr

A Walk on Snow. Peter Viereck. ...the answer was/The only one earth ever got from sky. MiAP

Walk Past Those Houses on a Sunday Morning. Kendrick Smithyman. It will take shape in the end. AnNZ

Walk Slowly. Adelaide Love. And pause to hear if someone calls your name. BLPA

Walk Together Children. Anonymous. There's a great camp meeting in the Promised Land. BoAN 1-2; BPo

Walk-Up. William Stanley Merwin. His name/Would mean nothing to me, his questions are not/His own, but let my answers/Be mine. CoPo

Walk with De Mayor of Harlem. David Henderson. helicopters colliding with tenements/in orange surprise PoBA

Walken Hwome at Night. William Barnes. I'll lead ye right, you needen doubt. NOBV

The Walker. Arturo Giovannitti. it is not the key alone that can throw open the gate. AnAmPo

The Walker of the Snow. Charles Dawson Shanly. Before us lies the valley/Of the Walker of the Snow! OnYI

The Walker River Night. Adrian C. Louis. and tonight/we are returning together. STE

Walking. Grace Ellen Glaubitz. He doesn't stretch/At all! SoPo; TiPo

Walking. Frank O'Hara. and I see it rising there/New York/greater than the Rocky Mountains. TAT

Walking. Thomas Traherne. From viewing herbs and trees. TrGrPo

Walking. H. L. Van Brunt. singing blood's syllables. LTB

Walking against the Wind. Jon Stallworthy. whom God hath joined together/to have and not to hold. OxBC

Walking Along the Hudson. Donald Petersen. (Ah, see), we truly die. CoAP

Walking Along the Sea of Galilee. Dovid Knut. Who for a long time/ Waved a tanned hand after me. VWA

Walking Around. David Galler. Walking around should be its own excuse. AMV-81

Walking around. Pablo Neruda.
...shirts from which slow/dirty tears are falling. EAS
underdrawers, towels and shirts that weep/slow filthy tears. LiTW

Walking at Night. Anonymous. Stodole pumpa, pum, pum, pum. FSW

Walking at Night. Amory Hare. I travel the road, alone. PoLf

Walking at Night. Henry Treece. But thyme and parsley underneath the moon. WaP

Walking Blues. Robert Johnson. Lord she break in on a dollar/oh most anywhere she goes BluL

Walking down Jalan Thamrin. R. F. Brissenden. On his handlebars/a flower. CBAP

Walking for That Cake. Ed [(or Ned)] Harrigan. I feel so shy, I'll really die, A walking for that cake. BLSo

Walking Home at Night. Daniel Weissbort. I home on the lock/and my life explodes about me. VWA

Walking in a meadow green. Anonymous. Like a Trojan true she made a vow/she would have one should mend it. BoLoP; ErPo

Walking in a Swamp. David Wagoner. As upright as ever. HAP; NPAW

Walking in Beech Leaves. Andrew Young. But through how many years sinks down/My sullen heel. MoVE

Walking in Bush. Basil Dowling. I meet the sunlight flashing like a blade. AnNZ

Walking in London. Wrey Gardiner. Or the outstretched arms of the crucified man. NeBP

Walking in the Light. Bernard Barton. For God, by grace, shall dwell in Thee,/And God himself is Light! VLP

Walking in the Rain. Dan Saxon. soon i wear it as a wreath/around my neck and smile. DFF

Walking Late. John Montague. ...your/small, damp hand in mine,/no heavier than a leaf. CIP

Walking Milwaukee. Harold Witt. and think of Dante sweating through his hell. HoAn; TAT

The Walking of the Moon-Women. Shaw Neilson. Down in the barley gold. ACV

Walking on Sunday. Richard Murphy. And hawks nested there. IPY

Walking on the Green Grass. Anonymous. Oh, swing 'em 'round the green. AmFP

Walking on the Prayerstick. Wendy Rose. because touching ourselves/we touched everything. TWSS

Walking on Water. James Dickey. A huge, hammer-headed spirit/Shall pass, as if led by the nose into Heaven. NePoEA-2

Walking on Water. Mario Petaccia. ...Two/old players questioning the silence,/carressing the heaven in her. LFAC

Walking Parker Home. Bob Kaufman. That fierce dying of humans consumed/In raging fires of Love. PoBA

Walking Past Paul Blackburn's Apt. on 7th St. Diane Wakoski. Or maybe you have wisely moved to the country/in your old age? TAP

The Walking Road. Richard Hughes. Round twists old Earth, and round,/ Stillness not yet found. OBMV

Walking Song. William E. Hickson. In which there is no room for us. OxBChV

Walking-Sticks and Paperweights and Watermarks. Marianne Moore. ...part of a/bough of a juniper-tree,"/javelin-ed consecutively. PoA

Walking the Beach. Sarah Youngblood. Some creature on the waste sea-floor/Is spinning a heavenly city/From its dreaming shell. IHMS

Walking the Wilderness. William Stafford. ...till found by dawn he/reach out to God no trembling hand. NaP

Walking through a Cornfield in the Middle of Winter... (parody). Barbara Harr. with the droppings of last year's chickens/blazing into magazines under my feet. BXAP

Walking through the Door. Brian Henderson. ...gathers/all colour to itself/ and gives it to the sky CaPN

Walking through the Upper East Side. Erica Jong. Only our coats knew each other,/rubbing shoulders in the dark closet. NYP

Walking to Bellrock. Michael Ondaatje. following the easy fucking stupid plot to town. NOBC

Walking to Dedham. David Wright. Or grief may pierce, or falling, seem to fall. NeBP

Walking to Sleep. Richard Wilbur. Lay clear, unfathomed, taken as they came. LCAP; NYBP

Walking to the Mail. Alfred, Lord Tennyson. As you shall see—three pyebalds and a roan. VLP

The Walking Tour. W. H. Auden. Rock shutting out the sky, the old life done. CMoP

Walking Westward (excerpt). C. K. Stead. the caves of generation and the terraces of the stars OCNZ

Walking with God. Anonymous. The Lord holds fast my hand. BLRP

Walking with God. William Cowper. So purer light shall mark the road/ That leads me to the Lamb. EiCP; EnPE; NOCV; NOEC; OAEP; OBEC; PoEL 1-5; TEP; TRV

Walking with Him in White. Charles Wesley. For our glorious meeting there. BePJ

Walking with Lulu in the Wood. Naomi Lazard. the snow-dusted face of the god. NYBP

Walking with Your Eyes Shut. William Stafford. ...Today you know it,/a great rich room, a musical sky. GOYP

Walking Wounded. Vernon Scannell. And when recalled they must bear arms again. OBWP

Walky-Talky Jenny (with music). Anonymous. I'm a nigger from de state of Alabam! AS

The Wall. Ludvik Askenazy. "I must be here," she said,/"somewhere/ between John and Joseph." VWA

The Wall. David Jones. that's the new fatigue. PoA

The Wall. Eve Merriam. Shade for a sleeping child/Stirring in safety, smiling at being/a Jew. TrJP

The Wall. Arthur L. Phelps. "Here is beauty, here is hope, here is peace." CaP

The Wall. Henry Reed. We need not doubt, for such a wall/Is based in death, and does not fall. LiTB

The Wall. Isidor Schneider. our vast disfigures cast/immediate on the wall. PG

A Wall. Charles Simic. And no one else/As far as I know to verify. HaCAP

Wall, Cave, and Pillar Statements, After Asoka. Alan Dugan. other graffiti of the prisoners of this world. CoAP

The Wall-Flower. Henrik and Arnold Thaulov Wergeland. And, Wall-flower! do thou into Death's dark porch/Be its bridal torch! AWP

The Wall of China. Padraic Colum. Not many Tartars/With bow and arrow/The steps could mount/That were so narrow. GrPl; RoGo

Wall Shadows. Carl Sandburg. ...walls ever say, "When we try, we can remember/those shadows"? WSC

The Wall Test. Louis Simpson. In every case/you find yourself standing against the wall. GP

Wallace Stevens Gives a Reading. Harriet Zinnes. such tink and tank and tunk-a-tunk-tunk. AMV-81

Walleye. Allen Hoey. the first dull thunder stills the lake. WOLT

Wallflower to a Moonbeam (parody). Louis Untermeyer. But I am no longer thirsty. BXAP

The Walloping Window-Blind. Charles Edward Carryl. And we left the crew of the junk to chew/The bark of the rubagub tree. InMe; LBN; MoShBr; NA; NLV; OBCA

Walls. Hervey Allen. Till they had met great grandpapas/Twit-tittering on the seething coals. HBMV

Walls. Constantine P. Cavafy. Imperceptibly they shut me out of/the world. TrJP

Walls Breathe. Paul Mariah. ...A rite/Reflecting in the burning windows. LFAC

The Walls Do Not Fall. Hilda ("H. D.") Doolittle. the original great-mother,/who drove/harnessed scorpions/before her. PBWP
you are a mist/of snow: white, little flowers. PBWP

Walls of Ice. Janet Campbell Hale. And the words become/Slower,/And slower/Each time. STE

The Walls of Jericho. Blanche Taylor Dickinson. Thea very walls echo with cheer! CDC

Walnut. Jorge Carrera Andrade. Paralyzed for eternity. ELU

The Walnut Tree. David McCord. And a swing in the walnut tree is why. OBCA

The Walrus and the Carpenter. Lewis (Charles Lutwidge Dodgson) Carroll. And this was scarcely odd, because/They'd eaten every one. BeLS; BLPA; FaBoBe; FaBoCo; FaBoNo; FaBV; FaFP; FiBHP; FPL; GN; HBV 1-2; HBVY; InMe; LBN; LiTB; MaC; MCCG; NA; NOBL; OxBChV; PoRA; SoPo; TEP; TreF

Walrus Hunting. Aua. Now you can fill your lungs with song/Of another man's bold hunting. WTO

Walsinghame's Song (parody). James Hogg. Down for ever with Wat o' the Cleuch! BXAP

Walt Whitman. Emanuel Carnevali. All the shadows/Whisper of the sun. PoA

Walt Whitman. Edwin Honig. Below the ragged/Line he signed/His chummy name. NePA; TAP

Walt Whitman. Harrison Smith Morris. Till kind earth held him and he spake with/death. AA

Walt Whitman. Edwin Arlington Robinson. We write them there forever. AmePo; NePA; OxBA

Walt Whitman. Francis Howard Williams. Democracy's divine protagonist. AA

Walt Whitman at Bear Mountain. Louis Simpson. Dances like Italy, imagining red. CAPP; ConAP; LiTM; NePoEA-2; PoCh; PP

Walt Whitman at the Reburial of Poe. Nicholas Christopher. I wonder who he voted for./I wonder if he won. MAYP

Walter Jenks' Bath. William Meredith. This is me knowing, this is what I know. HoPM

Walter Lesly. Anonymous. For she'll go no more to Conland, this winter-time to lye. BaBo; ESPB

Walter Savage Landor. Dorothy Parker. But as for me, I never could. DBV

Walthena. Elisabeth Peck. A tall, smooth candle white,/Walthena. AmFN

The Waltz. Hilary Corke. Yes more than naked, dressed in not even skin. NYBP

Waltz. Heather Tosteson Reich. ...the movement of a prehistoric fish/ dredged up and exposed to light for the first time. AMV-80

Waltz. Edith Sitwell. Gone is the sweet swallow–/Gone, Philomel!' OAEP

Waltz against the Mountains. Thomas Hornsby Ferril. With lilacs when the hay is being cut. VGW

The Waltz: Hail, Spirit-Stirring Waltz. George Gordon, Lord Byron. Who sent us–so be pardoned all her faults–/A dozen dukes, some kings, a queen– and Waltz. OBSV

Waltz Me Around Again, Willie. Will D. Cobb. Oh, waltz me around again, Willie, a-round, a-round, a-round. FSN; GoTF; TreFT

The Waltzer in the House. Stanley Jasspon Kunitz. She laughs to see his bobbing dance. ErPo; NYBP

Waltzing It. William Thomas Moncrieff. And you make a thousand halts in it,/Giddily, Giddily, O! UnS

Waltzing Matilda. Anonymous. "Who'll come a-waltzing Matilda with me?" GBP

Waly, Waly. Anonymous. But when it's old, it groweth cold/And fades away like morning dew. AmFP

Wand'ring in This Place as in a Wilderness. Anonymous. Non est dolor, sicut dolor meus. GBL

A Wand'ring Minstrel. Sir William Schwenck Gilbert. And dreamy lulla-lullaby, lullaby! GoTF; TreFS

The Wander-Lovers. Richard Hovey. That's the Marna of my soul,/ Wander-bride of mine! AA; HBV 1-2

Wander-Thirst. Gerald Gould. You may put the blame on the stars and the sun and the/white road and the sky! HBV 1-2; TiPo

The Wanderer. Zoë Akins. That it will be a piteous thing/In one small grave to lie. HBMV

The Wanderer. Anonymous.
And happy the man who seeketh for mercy/From his heavenly Father, our Fortress and Strength. AnOE; LiTW; NAWM 1-2; OAEL 1-2
...And indeed there is mercy to him,/Solace from his Father in heaven, where all stability stands. TEP
Glory be to God on high, who grants us our/salvation! EnLi 1-2

The Wanderer. Christopher John Brennan.
and a clear dusk settle, somewhere, far in me. ACV; CBAP
and my heart be fill'd wholly with their old pitiless cry. PoAu 1-2

The Wanderer. Henry Austin Dobson. Love comes back to his vacant dwelling. HBV 1-2

The Wanderer. Eugene Field. Sing, O my home–sing, O my home, of thee. BPAW; PoOW; PoPl

The Wanderer.   Amanda Benjamin Hall.   Always, I am left at home,/Sitting in my mind...   HBMV

The Wanderer.   Seamus Heaney.   ...who could tell you now of flittings,/night-vigils, let-downs, women's cried-out eyes.   CIP

The "Wanderer."   John Masefield.   The meaning shows in the defeated thing.   BrPo; CABL; MCCG

Wanderer.   Jessica Powers.   oh, someone came and found me.   AMV-80

The Wanderer.   Claude Vigee.   Without watching for daylight.   VWA

The Wanderer.   William Carlos Williams.   In remembrance of me and my sorrow/And of the new wandering!   MAPA

The Wanderer.   Yehoash.   And he showed me–'twas a stone.   TrJP

The Wanderer (excerpt).   Roland Robinson.   above the mountains, trees, and plains of earth.   CBAP

The Wanderer from the Fold.   Emily Bronte.   A mourner still, though friend and lover/Have both forgotten thee!   EnLit

The Wanderer Recalls the Past.   William Wordsworth.   And she forgotten in the quiet grave.   OBNC

The Wanderer's Grave.   Rufus B. Sage.   Oh, let me 'mid my friends expire,/And with my fathers lie.   BPAW; PoOW

A Wanderer's Litany.   Arthur Stringer.   Then, on the anvil of Thy wrath, remake me, God, that day!   WGRP

Wanderer's Night Song.   Johann Wolfgang von Goethe.   Thou too shalt rest.   AWP; PoPl

A Wanderer's Song.   John Masefield.   For a wind's in the heart of me, a fire's in my heels.   MCCG; MoAB; MoBrPo

Wanderer's Song.   Arthur Symons.   Well, it's sound sleep and long sleep, and sleep too deep to/wake.   ViBoPo

Wanderers.   Charles Stuart Calverley.   That chickens had been miss'd at Syllabub Farm.   CenHV

Wanderers.   Thomas Curtis Clark.   Which feels in thee a Comrade strong,/In every soul a friend of thine.   TrPWD

Wanderin'(with music).   Anonymous.   And it looks like/I'm never gonna cease my wanderin'.   AS; FSW

Wandering.   Hortense Flexner.   My hand is at the door.   HBMV

Wandering Chorus.   B. (Eliezer Blum) Alquit.   And the West pours/red wine/on the white/banner/of silence.   VWA

The Wandering Cowboy.   Anonymous.   But now my pony's grazin' at the rancho I call home.   CoSo

The Wandering Gadling.   Sir Thomas Wyatt.   To sting that heart that would have my place.   CBEP

The Wandering Jew.   Benjamin Fondane.   Everywhere he wrote in sand/But in the language of Heaven.   VWA

The Wandering Jew.   Robert Mezey.   Live says the Law–I sit here doing my best,/Relishing meat, listening to music.   NePoEA-2; VWA

The Wandering Jew.   Edwin Arlington Robinson.   Those old, unyielding eyes may flash,/And flinch–and look the other way.   MAmP; QFR

The Wandering Jew Comes to the Wall.   Edmond Fleg.   "O lost Jerusalem."   TrJP

Wandering Jews.   Nancy Keesing.   Of Egyptian? Indian? Persian? Akkadian?/In Eighteen-hundred-and-forty-two...   VWA

The Wandering Knight's Song.   John Gibson Lockhart.   Some day more kind I fate may find,/Some night, kiss thee.   HBV 1-2

The Wandering Lunatic Mind.   Edward Carpenter.   For this were to give up your kingdom, and bow down your/neck to death.   WGRP

The Wandering Maiden; or, True Love at Length United.   Anonymous.   That beyond all expressing,/her joys did abound.   CoMu

The Wandering One Makes Music.   Mary Aldis.   Not one but every kind of song she found/In that great diapason of sweet sound.   HBMV

The Wandering Shepherdess.   Anonymous.   And lament for my shepherd all the days of my life.'   OBET

Wanderings: Champs d'Honneur.   Ernest Hemingway.   Choking through the whole attack.   PoA

The Wanderings of Oisin.   William Butler Yeats.
And laughed like murmurs of the sea.   SeCePo
To Fin, Caolte, and Conan, and Bran, Sgeolan, Lomair.   BrPo

Wandsworth Common.   David Bromwich.   ...nights/Are kept smooth for dark promenades.   PoA

Wang Peng's Recommendation for Improving the People.   Paul Eldridge.   To kill all the living/And resurrect the dead.   ShM

The Waning Moon.   Percy Bysshe Shelley.   A white and shapeless mass.   CH; MOON; OBSP; PoPle; TrGrPo

The Waning of Love.   Arthur Lyon Raile.   shall never compass, leaving thee behind.   PeHV

The Waning of the Harvest Moon.   John Wieners.   Speechless in the tide.   CoPo

Want of Want of.   Anne Szumigalski.   this sharp and sudden pain in the side/the compositor's error.   FaBoWP

The Want of You.   Ivan Leonard Wright.   God has forgotten, or he never knew–/This want of you.   BLPA; FaBoBe

Wanted.   Shel Silverstein.   I want to rid my house of cats.   PV

Wanted–A Man.   Edmund Clarence Stedman.   Abraham Lincoln, give us a MAN!   PAH

Wanted, a Minister's Wife.   Anonymous.   And we'll advertise: "Wanted/A minister and his wife!"   BLPA; TreFS

Wanting a Child.   Jorie Graham.   ...erosion/is its very face.   MAYP

Wanting a Mummy.   Sandra McPherson.   And my friend all/Shortbread and roots.   AmPA; LCAP

Wanting Out.   Gavin Ewart.   And a box in the British Museum for the last performance of/Hamlet.   EAS

Wanting to Die.   Anne Sexton.   and the love, whatever it was, an infection.   ConAP; IHMS; NoAm; TAP

The Wanton (excerpt).   Vidya.
and they grow old and hard.   PBWP
which knew our happy, graceful/unending bouts of love.   PBWP

The Wanton Seed.   Anonymous.   And she always commended me well for my seed.   OBET

The Wanton Trick.   Anonymous.   Whoop, 'tis but a Wanton Trick.   CoMu

Wants.   Philip Larkin.   Beneath it all, desire of oblivion runs,.   GTBS-P; NoP

The Wants of Man.   John Quincy Adams.
The Mercy of My God.   PoLf
That this thy WANT may be prepared/To meet the Judgment Day. OBAL

Wapentake.   Henry Wadsworth Longfellow   For thy allegiance to the poet's art.   AA

The Wapiti.   Ogden Nash.   Hippety-hoppity!   MoShBr

War.   Guillaume Apollinaire.   From the Beyond of this earth.   WaaP

War.   Michael Brownstein.   Except for that stifling thought.   ANYP

War.   Grace Ellery Channing-Stetson.   The great Republic comes from war! AA

War.   J. C. Hall.   "O Man! from tyrannous war release/Our troubled hearts and grant our children peace."   HaMV

War.   Georg Heym.   Sodom has collapsed upon its funeral pyre.   AMV-80

War.   Sulamith Ish-Kishor.   Two bloated bodies in rotted rags/Stare at the sun from island crags.   GoYe

A War.   Randall Jarrell.   –That's what they tell the eggs.   DFF; OBSP

War.   Chief Joseph.   From where the sun now stands I will fight no more forever!   PGD

War.   Joseph Langland.   Wash over their blood-hot feet with a springing crown of tears.   FF; MP; NePoEA; PoCh

War!   James Gilchrist Lawson.   Make tiger-like retaliation;/But 'tis true! WBLP

War.   William Alfred, Jr. McLean.   He suppose to die.   BOLo

The War.   William Stanley Merwin.   and wake with the war going on. LCAP

War.   Anthony Ostroff.   Let us try again!   FAZ

War.   Richard Shelton.   and trade our children/for the most expensive/versions of old lies.   PPJ

War.   Edgar Wallace.   But it's War! And–Orderly, clean this knife!   OBWP

The War against the Trees.   Stanley Jasspon Kunitz.   ...caught/In the rear-view mirrors of the passing cars.   HAP; NoAm; PPON

War and Silence.   Robert Bly.   The sheriff cuts off his black legs/And nails them to a tree   CAPP

War-Baby.   D. H. Lawrence.   Is it true that the little weed/Will flourish its branches in heaven when we/slumber beneath?   NAs

A War Bird's Burlesque (with music).   Anonymous.   And thought, "She's not hors do combat, 'tis part of an Officer's Pay."   AS

War Blinded.   Douglas Dunn.   Gripped on the shoulder of the man in front. OBWP

War Bride.   Douglas Worth.   ...he/was alive/his spit in the glue.   FF

War Comes.   Zalman Schneour.   The heavens are red.   TrJP

War Cry: To Mary.   Pope Leo XIII.   Where he may watch the serpents leave, as stars in flight.   ISi

The War Dance.   Robert V. Carr.   And to-morrow–to-morrow the women will wail.   PoOW

War Dance.   Miidhu.   I saw their emu feather tails sticking out behind them.   NOAV

The War God.   Stephen Spender.   Love's need does not cease.   MoRP

The War God's Horse Song.   Anonymous.   I stand for my horse.   LiTA; LoGBV

The War Horse.   Eavan Boland.   A cause ruined before, a world betrayed. BIrV; CIP

War Horses.   William Cole.   Instead, the cavalry ride tanks./No thanks. PH

War in Chang-An City.   Wang Tsan.   ...thinking of the good king/who lies there, long with a broken heart/for the sweet day of peace.   PPON

War Is Kind.   Stephen Crane.   There are no violets here.   AP

The War of the Secret Agents.   Henri Coulette.
marvelous to his marvelous eyes.   NePoEA-2
nor have the sad gift of tongues.   NePoEA-2
of Denise combing her hair.   AmPC; NePoEA-2
the publican is a cheat.   NePoEA-2

The War of the Worlds.   Vern Rutsala.   ...no invasion is worth/such tears and foolishness.   Psk

War on the Periphery. George Johnston. Guarding my family with guns. NOBC; PeCV

War Poem. Ilya Ehrenburg. but Summer, silence and sleep. AMV-81

War Poet. Roy Fuller. But the appearance of choice/In their sad and fatal voice. HoPM; PP

War Requiem. Del Marie Rogers. cut off, hurtling forward in the cold sky. LTB

War's Clown in the Proscenium. Gene Derwood. Natural as the veronica and the verbena,/In agricultural health. NePA

The War Ship of Peace. Samuel Lover. Let Erin's voice proclaim/In bardic praise on ev'ry hill/Columbia's glorious name. PAH

War Song. *Anonymous.* Told me to leave this country and go to Dixie's land. ABF
Where shall he now make war? WTO

A War Song. Bertrand. And closed in with lisses of strong piles. CTC

A War Song. William Blake. Prepare, O troops, that are to fall to-day!/ Prepare,prepare! OHIP

War Song. John Davidson. The race is to the swift,/The battle to the strong. NBM; OBNC

War Song of O'Driscol. Gerald Griffin. Hurry, hurry down to the shores of your island. OnYI

War Song of the Saracens. James Elroy Flecker. And the dead to the desert we gave, and the glory to God in/our song. FaBV; MoBrPo; OBVV; WHA

A War Song to Englishmen. William Blake. Prepare, prepare! CH; WaaP

War Story. Jon Stallworthy. And stubbed his fingers on a dead man's face. DFF; ELU; OxBC

War Swaggers. Emanuel Litvinoff. When gaunt men lie writhing in the night/Dreaming of their wives. WaP

War-Time. W. R. Rodgers. As an old tree, when lopped of every bough,/ Gathers the young leaves into itself, a frilled stump. OBSP

The War-Token. Henry Wadsworth Longfellow. Winding his sinuous way in the dark to the/depths of the forest. PAH

War Walking Near. Ray A. Young Bear. they say the spring air comes without much intention. CDW

War with the Weeds. Keith Sinclair. Will save the dandelion from hell AnNZ

The War Year. Ts'ao Sung. leaves/ten/thousand/corpses/to rot! PPON

The Waradgery Tribe. Mary Gilmore. Hunted, lonely, and spent,/Broken and dying. BoAV; PoAu 1-2

Waratah. Roland Robinson. ...the fierce flower from its steep/flamed upon the sounding deep. PoAu 1-2

Warblers. Marsden Hartley. But–how they fastened me. AnFE

Ward Two. Francis Webb.
　As a girl beleaguered by rain, and her yellow hair? CBAP
　As the Holy Spirit, travels the bubble of air. CBAP
　The decrepit persistent folly within this place/Will sow with itself the last paddock of space. CBAP
　Directing it to the house of no known address. CBAP
　Gape at your porridge, munch it like a dog! CBAP
　He is loving us now, he is loving all. CBAP
　Or Orange golden as the breast. CBAP
　Who said Let there be light? CBAP

Wardance. Phil George. They are really scared! VoR

Wardance Soup. Phil George. I could not add. VoR

The Warden of the Cinque Ports. Henry Wadsworth Longfellow. Nothing in Nature's aspect intimated/That a great man was dead. AA; HBV 1-2; WHA

Warden's Day. Carolyn Baxter. applauding in between/bites of watermelon/to their execution. LFAC

The Warden Said to Me the Other Day. Etheridge Knight. we ain't got no wheres to run to. FF

Wardour Street. Humbert Wolfe. They've no more use for us in Wardour Street. OxBTC

Wardrobe. Sister Mary Madeleva. Because He is my true love/He wore them instead. GoBC

Waring. Robert Browning. In Vishnu-land what Avatar? PoEL 1-5; VLP

Waring of Sonora-Town. Henry Herbert Knibbs. An'–a Chola lay a-chokin', an' a buzzard cut the blue. BPAW

Warm Babies. Keith Preston. An', far as Nebuchadnezzar could find,/Jes' as good as dey wuz behind. FiBHP; HBMV

Warm Hands. *Anonymous.* Wash your hands now. OxNR

The Warm of Heart Shall Never Lack a Fire. Elizabeth Jane Coatsworth. He cannot sit alone. TiPo

Warm rain, sunny wind. Li Ch'ing-chao. still/I/play,/trimming/the wick. BoWoP

Warm Tea. Lewis MacAdams. Awash with angels,/Reading alone in her chair. ANYP

A Warm Winter Day. Julian Cooper. Seed pods wait/With their sealed order. BoNaP

Warming Up for the Real Thing. Lee Rudolph. and die scratching it/with a coathanger. TW

Warmth. Barton Sutter. Who takes off his clothes/And holds out his hands to the stove. GOYP

A Warning. *Anonymous.* But if thou wilt amendes make. EnLit
You'll never thrive again. OxNR

Warning. Harold Lewis Cook. Your heel will measure a worm's girth. AnAmPo

The Warning. Adelaide Crapsey. ...Why am I grown/So cold? AnAmPo; WSC

The Warning. Robert Creeley. the virtues of an amulet/and quick surprise. NeAP; TAP; VGW

Warning. Robert Lee Frost. He will forget, he will forget. AmePo

Warning. Langston Hughes. Beware the hour/It uproots trees! BPo

Warning. Jenny Joseph. When suddenly I am old, and start to wear purple. FaBoWP; GOYP; OxBTC

The Warning. Henry Wadsworth Longfellow. A shapeless mass of wreck and rubbish lies. AmePo

A Warning. Alexander Nicolson. You had better not think of Skye. PoSH

A Warning. Coventry Patmore. Cities and their civilities,/And, on the other, lions. EnLoPo

Warning and Reply. Emily Bronte. But that heart was worthy thee! OBVV; OxBI

Warning of Winter. Mary Ursula Bethell. To the ice-fields: Let here spring thick bright lilies. FaBoWP

Warning to a Guest. John Holloway. Like you and me who, to sustain our pose,/Need wine and conversation, colour and light. NePoEA

A Warning to America. Philip Freneau. Nor slavish systems grant admittance here. TAP

A Warning to Beware. *Anonymous.* Of His gret goodnesse and His gras,/ Sende us such warning to be ware. OxBM

Warning to Children. Robert Graves. –he then unties the string. FaBoCh; FaFP; LoGBV; NoP; OAEL 1-2; SO

A Warning to Conquerors. Donagh MacDonagh. Only the faces and the names remain. CIP; OxBI

Warning to Cupid. *Anonymous.* She, too, has wings. UnTE

A Warning to My Love. David Wagoner. Less dead than deadly. Waiting for you, perhaps. NePoEA-2

Warning to One. Merrill Moore. And yours is the silly head it hangs above. MoAmPo; TrGrPo; YaD

A Warning to Those Who Serve Lords. *Anonymous.* Hevene to ben our heritage. MeEL

Warning to Travaillers Seeking Accomodations at Mr. Devills Inn. Sarah Kemble Knight. The Right hand keep, if Hell on Earth you fear! SCAP

The Warnings. Alice Furlong. Now must I rise and go to him, the Dead who calls on me. AnIV

Warp and Woof. Harry Halbisch. When he threads the golden warp of hope/Against the woof of gloom. BLRP

Warren Phinney. Bernadette Mayer. To give us time to make the little more love/We'd dreamed of before the tow truck came. APU

Warren's Address at Bunker Hill. John Pierpont. And the rocks shall raise their head,/Of his deeds to tell? AA; AnNE; FaBoBe; GN; GoTF; HBV 1-2; HBVY; MC; PAH; PAL; TreF

The Warrior Maid. Anna Hempstead Branch. I had borne thee savage daughters/And beautiful fierce sons. HBV 1-2

Warrior Nation Trilogy. Lance Henson. which grows near the full circle/of this/world VoR

The Warrior's Lament. Sir Owen Seaman. But Duty First is the rule and plan/Of a Prince who is also a family man. FiBHP

Warrior's Song. Mary Austin. Weep not for me, Loved Woman,/For yourself alone be weeping! BPAW

The Warrior to His Dead Bride. Adelaide Anne Procter. The heavens themselves look brighter, Love,/Since thy sweet soul is there. OBVV

Warrior with Shield. Michael Dennis Browne. ...As I am, as I will/never be, live with me. PoDr

Warriors. Douglas Dunn. ...In no war would I bleed. OxBC

Warriors. Michael Hogan. Old men speak of what they have to lose./ Young men of taking. LFAC

Warriors Prancing, Women Dancing... Niema Rashidd. first and/freedom. NBP

The Wars of Santa Fe. *Anonymous.* I married young Jack the farmer/And I brought him home again. AmFP

The Wars of the Roses. Anonymous. He was up and away at dawn of day/With the rose-bush under his arm. GBP

Wart Hog. Robin Skelton. through darkness/of the bald horn of the moon. NOBC

Wartime Blues. Blind Lemon Jefferson. You treat me like my trouble has just begun BluL

A Wartime Dawn. David Gascoyne. And one more day of War starts everywhere. LiTM; MoVE

A Wartime Exchange: As One Non-Combatant to Another. Alex Comfort. And spout your halo for a pint of bitter. OxBTC

A Wartime Exchange: Letter to an American Visitor. Alex Comfort. We send our best apologies to you. OxBTC

Warty Bliggins, the Toad. Don (Donald Robert Marquis) Marquis. lodged in the crinkles/of the human cerebrum. FiBHP

Warum Sind Denn Die Rosen So Blass. Heinrich Heine. And why it is, my heart of hearts/That thou forsakest me? AWP

Was a Man. Philip Booth. in final terror hung/the wrong face back. NCSH; NePoEA-2; VGW

A Was an Apple Pie, B Bit It, C Cut It. Anonymous. In equal parts the pye divide,/As you may see on t'other side. FaBoUs

A Was an Archer. Anonymous. Z was a zany, a silly old fool. FaBoUs; OxBChV

Was He Married? Stevie Smith. It will be a larger one. NoAm

Was, Is, and Yet-To-Be. Ella Wheeler Wilcox. And this alone," said practical Is. PoToHe

Was It a Dream. Edmund Spenser. My thoughts the guests, which would thereon have fed. NIP

Was It All Worth While? Anonymous. So we threw away our skins./Yiya wo! WTO

Was It Not Curious? Stevie Smith. It was not curious so much/As it was wicked of them. NoAm

Was It You? Stewart I. Long. This smile encouraged young and old—was it you? WBLP

Was She a Witch? Laura E. Richards. She never, no never, no never would tell. SoPo

Was Worm. May Swenson. to blue and green/Is queen BoAnP

Wash. Eilean Ni Chuilleanain. She begins to wash the water from the fish. BIrV; WPOW

Wash Day. Larry Mollin. like a wildman/kissing flowers NeAC

Wash-Day Wonder. Dorothy Faubion. It spins to a rest and sighs, "I'm done." QQQ

Wash Me Whiter Than Snow. Charles Wesley. Till all I am is lost in Thine. BePJ

Wash the Dishes, Wipe the Dishes. Mother Goose. I will give to thee. BrR; OxNR

Wash Well the Fresh Fish. Anonymous. Many a foul-footed thing/In the salt sea. PoPle

Washed in Silver. James Stephens. Clad in silver tissue, I/March magnificently by! ELU; MOON

The Washer-Woman. Otto Leland Bohanan. Where the light of her soul fell shining and clean. BANP

The Washers of the Shroud. James Russell Lowell. While waking I recalled my wandering brain. AP; HBV 1-2; PAH

Washing and Dressing. Ann Taylor. I thought you'd be good after this. FaBoUs

Washing between the Buildings. Larry Eigner. varying distance of wind. CoPo

Washing Day. Anonymous.
    For its thump thump scold scold/Thump thump away/The deil a bit of comfort is therre. CoMu
    She'll dress like a lady,/And dance on the green. OxNR

The Washing Machine. Jeffrey Davies. and the washing stops going round. PCP

Washing My Son. Jonathan Holden. ...All/the decals go on/perfectly. AMV-81

Washing the Coins. Douglas Dunn. And when the water settled I could see/Two English kings among their drowned Britannias. FaBoPV

Washing the Dishes. Christopher Morley. The Lord Himself will give you up/If you should drop a willow cup! PoLf

Washing Up. Anonymous. And pulled out golden fishes. OxNR

Washing Windows. Barry Spacks. They pause and smile, at peace,/each in his own condition. NCSH

Washing Windows. Peter Wild. that vagrant never so transparent staggering around the/neighborhood. Str

Washington. George Gordon, Lord Byron. To make men blush there was but one! MC; OHIP; PAH; PAL

Washington. Mae Winkler Goodman. We turn for strength and comfort to thy creed. PGD

Washington. Geraldine Meyrich. The way was straight because thou mad'st it so. OHIP

Washington. Denis O'Crowley. The beacon light of Liberty. OHIP

Washington. John A. Prentice. To gain Eternity, the goal you sought. OHIP

Washington. James Jeffrey Roche. While time endures, First Citizen of earth. MC; PAH

Washington. Nancy Byrd Turner. He loved America all his life! SoPo; TiPo; YeAr

Washington. B. Y. Williams. "First in the hearts of his countrymen." PGD

Washington. Mary Wingate. And loyal hearts in years to run/Shall turn to thee, O Washington. OHIP

Washington and Lincoln. Wendell Phillips Stafford. And the eternal sentinels shine on. PGD

Washington Cathedral. Karl Shapiro. He is only a good alien, nominally happy. MiAP

Washington Heights, 1959. Michael C. Blumenthal. ...we smiled, waited/for the ice truck, buried the dead, called it home. HaCAP

Washington in Love. John Berryman. Bring the wounded, Martha! Bring the wounded, men. LCAP

Washington Monument by Night. Carl Sandburg. It takes a long time to forget an iron man. CMoP; OFD; OHIP; PoSC

Washington's Birthday. Arthur J. Burdick. ...grander, build the edifice/Begun so long ago by Washington. OHIP

Washington's Monument. Anonymous. And may she ever rise in fame,/To honor thy immortal name! OHIP; PAH

Washington's Monument, February, 1885. Walt Whitman. Wherever Freedom, pois'd by Toleration, sway'd by/Law,/Stands or is rising thy true monument. OFD

Washington's Prayer for the Nation. George Washington. As He alone knows to be best. PGD

Washington's Statue. Henry Theodore Tuckerman Renew the patriot's vow! AA

Washington's Tomb. Ruth Lawrence. But 'neath thy much loved stars, a fitter tomb. OHIP

Washiri (Poet). Kattie M. Cumbo. Black/Angry/Proud BOLo

Washrags. Vern Rutsala. It was in the washrag I buried/For my father/To cure a wart. GP

Washyuma Motor Hotel. Simon J. Ortiz. The ancient spirits tell stories/and jokes and laugh and laugh. GP

Wasn't That a Mighty Storm? Anonymous. Isn't that a mighty storm/That blew the people away! AmFP

Wasn't your mother a woman? Honnamma. A noble daughter is blessed forever. BoWoP

The Wasp. John Davidson. Then soared away a captive queen set free. FM

The Wasp. Daryl Hine. It was a wasp. NYBP

Wasp. Alden Nowlan. I sit here, thinking of glass/and the jokes it plays in the world. BoAnP

The Wasp. Joyce Carol Oates. O don't flinch!—it is over./You are grateful. GeTw

The Wasp. William Sharp. A tiger-soul on elfin wings. FM

Wasp. William Welsh. he could have sent khomeini/the fish. SOTS

A Wasp Bite Nobi on Her Conch-Eye. Anonymous. Wasp bite Nobi on her conch-eye. OuSiCo

The Wasp's Frolic. Anonymous. We were taken by a seventy-four. PAH

The Wasp's Song. Lewis (Charles Lutwidge Dodgson) Carroll. Because I wear a yellow wig. FaBoNo

Wasp Sex Myth (One). Anselm Hollo. he'll never be on the prowl for other women/he has so many at home PoM

Wasp Sex Myth (Two). Anselm Hollo. ...let marge up only/long enough to get food & drink occasionally. PoM

Waspish. Robert Frost. But he's as good as anybody going. BoAnP

The Wasps' Nest. George Macbeth. Coming to no sure conclusion, nor anxious to come. OxBTC

The Wassail Song. Anonymous.
    And all the little children/That round the table go. OHIP; PoSC
    And come no more a wasselling/Until another year. GBP
    And 'tis joy come to our jolly wassail! OHIP

Wassailer's Song. Robert Southwell. Then, down fall butler, and bowl and all. OHIP

Waste. Harry Graham. Just too late to save the stamp. FaBoCo

Waste. G. A. Studdert Kennedy. War! EBCP

The Waste Land. Thomas Stearns Eliot.
    burning. FaBoMo
    Good night, ladies, good night, sweet ladies, good night, good night. CMoP; CoBMV; HAP; LiTA; LiTM; MasP; MoAmPo; MoPo; MoVE; NAWM 1-2; NoAm; NOBE; NoP; OxBA; OxBTC; PPoe; TAP
    Shantih shantih shantih CMoP; CoBMV; HAP; LiTA; LiTM; MasP; MoAB; MoAmPo; MoPo; NAWM 1-2; NePA; NoAm; NOBE; NoP; OAEL 1-2; OAEP; OxBA; PPoe; TAP; UnPo
    "You! hypocrite lecteur!–mon semblable,–mon frere!" CMoP; CoBMV; HAP; LiTA; LiTM; MasP; MoAB; MoAmPo; MoPo; MoVE; NAWM 1-2; NePA; NoAm; NOBE; NoP; OAEL 1-2; OxBA; OxBTC; TAP; UnPo

The Waste of War. William L. Stidger. "We call not your weak and your lame!" PGD

The Waste Places. James Stephens. And bear the demon with his prey/From the forest to the sun. HBV 1-2

Wasted Ammunition. Stoddard King. Come, what do you make of it, Watson?/By me! InMe

A Wasted Day. Frances Cornford. Whole as an apple,/Kind as a friend. HBMV; MoBrPo

Wasted Night. Anonymous. Unable to perform, unfit to play. UnTE

A Wasted Sympathy. Winifred Howells. Give your thanks that to a woman/Tears are given, and be at ease. AA

The Wastrel. Reginald Wright Kauffman. And I know your love will answer: "Here's my laddie/home from play!" HBV 1-2

The Watch. Frances Cornford. Come quick, come quick, come quick, come quick. DTC; HBMV; HeIP; InPK; MoBrPo; OxBTC

The Watch. Marge Piercy. red as dying, our quick bright blood. GeTw

The Watch. May Swenson. little face, quite as usual, in its place on my/wrist. HAP

Watch and Pray. Charlotte Elliott. All with one deep voice exclaim,/"Watch and pray." STF

Watch Any Day. W. H. Auden. With love's fidelity and with love's weakness. FaBoMo

Watch-Dog. Charles Brasch. Faithful guardian, would you destroy me? OCNZ

Watch Hill. Winfield Townley Scott. And all the while the sanded wind blew between us. ErPo

Watch Long Enough, and You Will See. Conrad Aiken. Throng the brief word. The maelstrom has us all. CMoP; NePA

The Watch of a Swan. Sarah Piatt. Had the love of a bird for a child. AA

The Watch on the Rhine. Max Schneckenburger. The Rhine, the Rhine, the German Rhine! HBV 1-2

The Watch on the Rhine. Gertrude Stein. In the midst of our happiness we were very pleased. AtBAP

Watch Repair. Charles Simic. We raise it/To the lips/Of the nearest/Ear. NoP

Watch the Lights Fade. Robinson Jeffers. ...be still while the/Sea-wind salts your head white. CMoP; NoAm; NOBA

Watch Yourself Go By. Strickland Gillilan. Have stood aside and watched yourself go by. BLPA; PoToHe

The Watcher. Sarah Josepha Hale. There's light for us above! AA

The Watcher. John Peck. The snow poised on that bough. AmPA

The Watcher. James Stephens. And the lips and the hair of the bride. HBV 1-2; MoBrPo; OBEV; OBVV

The Watcher. Ruth Stone. And snuffed the nighttime out around the bed. NYBP

The Watcher. Margaret Widdemer. Watching from Heaven's window,/Leaning from Heaven's gate. HBMV; OHIP

The Watchers. Arlo Bates. Loss were thrice loss that thus their faith/should mar. AA

The Watchers. Paul Blackburn. The leaves burgeon. NMP; NYBP

The Watchers. William Stanley Braithwaite. (And heaven on the long reach home.) PoNe

Watchers. William Stanley Merwin. With her reproach and her bony children/Before rain. NaP

The Watchers. Muriel Rukeyser. When I wake I will not weep. NMP

The Watchers. Charles Spear. And sink to the rhythms of El Chocolo. AnNZ

Watching. Emily Chubbuck Judson. Night deepens, and I sit in cheerless doubt, alone. AA

Watching a Cloud. Dannie Abse. sunny sunlight on stony stone returning. OxBC; TEP

Watching Clouds. John Farrar. I often wonder where they go. SoPo

Watching for Dolphins. David Constantine. With no admission of disappointment the company/Dispersed and prepared to land in the city. OBTV

Watching Gymnasts. Robert Francis. And flower-light, precise, and arabesque/Let their praise be. LiSp

Watching Jim Shoulders. Leo Connellan. ...looked like its spine would split through skin,/yet didn't in this master's hands. TAT

Watching My Daughter Sew. Katharine Privett. The whippoorwill is surer of her name/than we are sure of anything. AMV-81

Watching Salmon Jump. Simon J. Ortiz. so that my children may survive CDW

Watching Television. Robert Bly. Like a house in Nebraska that suddenly explodes. BiP; CoAP

Watching the Dance. James Merrill. A teenage plankton luminously twitch. NIP

Watching the Jets Lose to Buffalo at Shea. May Swenson. in a cradle of grass at the goalposts. LiSp

Watching the Moon. David McCord. Because the moon is coming down/Beyond the branches and will drown. YeAr

Watching the Out-Door Movie Show. Ann Struthers. Even now the horses of the stars/canter, early on Sunday mornings. FAZ

Watching the Sun Rise over Mount Zion. Ruth Whitman. The tower is on fire./It is today. VWA

Watching You Sleep under Monet's Water Lilies. Gibbons Ruark. ...and the too deep/Pool of desiring fill with sleep. SM

Watching You Walk. Ruthven Todd. Glad that, in loving you, the whole world lives afresh. LiTL; NeBP

Watching Your Gray Eyes. Morton Marcus. although the warmth on my back/flares from cities burning in the night. GP

Watchmaker God. Robert Lowell. but having perfected what He had to do,/stood off shrouded in his loneliness. HaCAP

The Watchman. Abraham Reisen. I cannot tell, I cannot see. TrJP

Watchman, Tell Me. Anonymous Soon the pilgrims will be there! AH

Watchman, Tell us of the Night. John Bowring. Lo! the Son of God is come! TreFS

Watchman, What of the Night? Algernon Charles Swinburne. Night is over and done. WiR

Water. Hilda Conkling. What is water,/That pours silver/And can hold the sky? ExPo; TiPo

Water. Ralph Waldo Emerson. With a face of golden pleasure/Elegantly destroy. AmPP; OBSP; PoEL 1-5

Water. Ted Hughes. An open-armed host, of poor cheer. OBSP

Water. Edmond Jabes. There is nothing but sand/where I go. VWA

Water. Philip Larkin. Where any-angled light/Would congregate endlessly. FaBoMo; OBSP

Water. Robert Lowell. the water was too cold for us. CMoP; HeIP; LCAP; NOBA; NoP; SM

Water. Judith McPheron. Waves, like the cool white hands/of my dreams, lift me, carry me home. AMV-81

Water. Anne Sexton. holding a lady's wornout shoe. CoPo

Water. Gary Snyder. Eyes open aching from the cold and faced a trout. LCAP

Water and Air. Robert Browning. Float with me there, Pauline, but not like air. OBRV; VLP

Water and Worship: An Open-Air Service on the Gatineau River. Margaret Avison. "Joyful, joyful, we adore Thee...." HAP

The Water Babies. Charles Kingsley. Play by me, bathe in me, mother and child. GN

Water-Boy. Anonymous. If you' don't-a come, I'm gwineter tell-a yo' Mammy./Oh, Water-Boy! TrGrPo

The Water Carrier. John Montague. Some living source, half-imagined and half-real/Pulses in the fictive water that I feel. FaBoIP

Water Color. Stephen Mooney. And a sheet of paper, solid gray, floats/On the water, which is also gray. NYBP

Water Color of Granchester Meadows. Sylvia Plath. the owl shall stoop from his turret, the rat cry out. NYBP

A Water-Colour of Venice. Lawrence Durrell. At the bottom of every soul a spoonful of sleep. MoBrPo

The Water-Drinker. Edward Johnson. Hurrah! for bright Water! hurrah, hurrah! BXAP; PeD

Water (excerpt). Kathleen Raine. In the ever-changing network woven between stars. ImOP

Water Fowl. William Wordsworth. As if they scorned both resting-place and rest! FM

Water-Front. Cecil Ffrench Salkeld. But everything passes... OnYI

Water-Girl. Anonymous. My heart is thirsty, water-girl. WTO

A Water Glass of Whisky. X. J. Kennedy. As though more than night or a hill/Had walled you in, back of its back. CoPo

The Water-Hole. Charles Erskine Scott Wood. The sky above and the desert flood/Of silence all around. BPAW

Water-Images. Mary Elizabeth Osborn. of one who, decision taken, darkly plunged/deep into water. NePoAm-2

The Water Is Wide. Anonymous. And fades away like the morning dew. FSW; OBET

Water Island. Howard Moss. Standing in a stillness that now is yours. CoAP; MP; NePoEA-2; NYBP; Prf

The Water Lady. Thomas Hood. But she's divine! CH; HBV 1-2

Water-Lilies. Sara Teasdale. And the shadow of mountains will not fall on your heart. MoAmPo

The Water-Lily. John Banister Tabb. Left her garment in the tide. AA; HBV 1-2; ViBoPo

The Water Lily. David Wagoner. To take nothing away but his mind's eye. PoDr

Water Music. Alun Lewis. This yearning, yearning, this ending/Of the heart and its ache. ChMP

Water Music. Hugh" (Christopher Murray Grieve) MacDiarmid. Singin' in the mornin',/Corrieneuchin' a' the nicht. GoTS

Water Noises. Elizabeth Madox Roberts. But when she goes I still can hear/The water say, "And do you think?" BoNaP

The Water-Nymph and the Boy. Roden and Wriothesley Berkeley Noel. Here in my breast! OBVV

The Water O Gamrie. Anonymous. There's neer a man lie by my side/Since Willie's drowned in Yarrow. BaBo

The Water of Kane. Anonymous. Life! O give us this life! WTO

Water on the Highway. Nancy Simpson. I will have to cross water to get there. AMV-80

The Water-Ousel. Mary Webb. With two small shadows following after it. CH

Water Ouzel. William H. Matchett. The rippling notes of his song, which are clear and sweet. CoAP; NePoEA; NYBP; PoCh

A Water-Party. Robert Bridges. O summer moon, shine bright! PoPle

Water Picture. May Swenson. tree-limbs tangle, the bridge/folds like a fan. BoNaP

Water Song. Solomon Ibn Gabirol. So my sad tears run/Like streams of Water, streams of/Water. TrJP

Water Tap. Norman MacCaig. And everything that was/Hoisting water/Suddenly spilled over. BSV

The Water Tower. James Paul. ...See–what thirst/We have we can quench from the sky. AMV-81

The Water-Truck. Patrick Lane. "Fuck you"/I said/"I quit" NeAC

Water under the Earth. Robert Bly. who can feel his children through all distance and time! NNaP

The Water-Wheel. Jack R. Clemo. Both wood and iron, to seal/The dream-world with the real. ChMP

Water Whirligigs. D. J. Opperman. the time goes by, the time goes by. PeSA

The Water-Witch. Martha Eugenie Perry. The gush of water from a thousand precious wells. CaP

Water Without Sound. Malka Tussman. What can be sadder/than water/without sound? VWA

Waterchew! Gregory Corso. ...O how deep into fear must I wedge/The strangeness I follow fools! VGW

Watercress & Ice. Chase Twichell. nor find, in cold, a home. MAYP

The Watercress Seller. Thomas Miller. For she can earn no other way/The bread which she doth eat. OxBChV

The Watered Lilies. Anonymous. And perhaps someday He may use me/To water His flowers again. BLPA

Waterfall. Seamus Heaney. Falls, yet records the tumult thus standing still. NoAm

The Waterfall. Henry Vaughan. Rise to a longer course more bright and brave. CoBE; FaBoPP; GoBC; NOBE; NOCV; NoP; OAEP; PrIm; ViBoPo; WiR

Waterfall. Anne Welsh. That life could stir in me/Like first free laughter. PeSA

Waterfalls. Vernon Watkins. ...the brook/Reminding the stones where, under a breath, it falls. NoAm

Waterfront. Oliver Jenkins. prowling along the desolate wharves/in the dead of night? EtS

Watergate. Ruth Herschberger. Those righteous unrueful ruthless men/On a May day in Washington. FAZ

The Watergaw. Hugh" (Christopher Murray Grieve) MacDiarmid. An' I think that mebbe at last I ken/What your look meant then. BSV; GoTS; NeBP; NoP

The Watering Place. Sextus Propertius. Off the map with Baiae, murderer of love–and waters/. LiTW

Watering the Horse. Robert Bly. The white flake of snow/That has just fallen in the horse's mane! CAPP; NaP

Waterloo. Aubrey Thomas De Vere. Persia's pale star: so empire passed away/From Harold's brow,–but He disdained to live! HBV 1-2

Watermelon. Ted Joans. ...Yeah watermelon is what I'm talking/about Watermelon. GP

Watermelons. Charles Simic. We eat the smile/And spit out the teeth. OBAL; PPJ

The waters chased him as he fled. Emily Dickinson. The object floating at his side/Made no distinct reply. PoEL 1-5

Waters of Babylon. Louis Untermeyer. Let the night be. Close the window, beloved...Come/here. AnAmPo

The Waters of Life. Humbert Wolfe. are but pale shadows of your dancing feet. MoBrPo

Waters of the Sea. Cecil Goldbeck. Potent armies of the peace/Love takes from me. EtS

The Waters of Tyne. Anonymous. Or scull him across that rough river to me! GBP

The Watershed. W. H. Auden. Ears poise before decision, scenting danger. OAEL 1-2

Watershed. Margaret Avison. Rain pastes the leather-black streets with large pale leaves. OBCV

The Watershed. Alice Meynell. And down a thousand vales I dropped,/I flowed to Italy. SBG

Watershed. Robert Penn Warren. ...no constant moon/Sustains the hill's lost granite surge. PoA

Waterspout. Luîs de Camoens. Oh! with what a fire your page had glow'd! EtS

Watertower. Albert Bellg. And you drift out with it through the trees/and into the evening. FAZ

Waterwall Blues. Howard Moss. Dumb sorrow rides the same old hulls/With his mad mariner. MoPo; NePA

The Waterwitch. Anonymous. Bound away in the Waterwitch to the west'ard we go. PoAu 1-2

Watkwenies. Duncan Campbell Scott. The lads playing snow-snake in the stinging cold. PeCV

Watt (excerpt). Samuel Beckett. ...then the whole bloody business starting all over/again. BIrV

Watt's Improvements to the Steam Engine. Thomas Baker. Such is the GREAT CREATOR'S glorious plan/Of veinous action in the frame of man! FaBoUs

Watts. Shirley Kaufman. loose skin over each/knuckle of my hand. NMM

Watts. Conrad Kent Rivers. to free the nigger/in his head? BOLo; PoBA

Watts. Alvin Saxon. while weeping Diogenes hurled his flame/to the barren soil. PoBA

Wave. Barbara Guest. Bountiful and Bare. AmPC

The Wave. Daryl Hine. God's interrupted wish-fulfillment, told/Some of the story. Prf

The Wave. David Phillips. waves we've loved in/and cannot claim NeAC

The.Wave. John Curtis Underwood. I am the pulse of the cosmos whose life is to God/as a wave. EtS

A Wave of Coldness. Yosano Akiko. And the distance of a foot/Becomes a thousand miles. WPOW

Wavelength. David St. John. As the moon & the wave remain individually one SUW

The Wavering Planet. Anonymous. Yet I know not where to find her. MOON

The Waverley Pen. Anonymous. The Pickwick, the Owl, and the Waverley Pen. FaBoUs

Waves. Ralph Waldo Emerson And breaks the glass of time. AA

The Waves Gleam in the Sunshine. Heinrich Heine. We were the best of friends. TrJP

Waving a Bough. Boris Pasternak. Wild horses won't tear them apart. TrJP

The Waving of the Corn. Sidney Lanier. Takes waving of the corn. AP

Wax. Winfield Townley Scott. The girls had not merely touched for future luck. ErPo

Waxwings. Robert Francis. ...for this I have abandoned/all my other lives. LCAP; NU

The Way. Leslie Savage Clark. Home to the heart of God! PGD

The Way. Robert Creeley. and love her as hard as you can. AP; BoLoP; LiTM; NeAP; PPP

The Way. Sidney Henry Morse. A victory worthy to be won,/Nor seek their gain with strife. HBV 1-2

The Way. Edwin Muir. The road leads on. LOW

The Way. Henry Van Dyke. But God will bring him where the Blessed are. TRV

The Way a Ghost Dissolves. Richard Hugo. the screaming face it was before it cracked/in wind from Asia and a wanton rain. NoP; SM

The Way Down. Philip Levine. and hold on and hold on. NOBA

'Way Down in Cuba. Anonymous. You can guess where she gives me a pain./'Way down in Cuba! AmSS

Way Down in Mexico. Anonymous. And never more we'll go and roam,/Way down in Mexico. CoSo

Way Down South... Anonymous. "Pick on somebody your own size." EvOK; SoPo

Way down the Ohio. Anonymous. And I'll turn my back on her and court who I please. TrAS

The Way Down: They Return. Jay Macpherson. They, returning, bring us back/Absence, winter, what we gave. PoA

The Way I Read a Letter's–This. Emily Dickinson. And sigh for lack of Heaven–but not/The Heaven God bestow–. AmePo; DiPo; InPS; PAI

The Way I Was... Carol Lee Sanchez. tengo que buscar/una linda mujer. TWSS

The Way It Happens. Philip Dacey. By now you are not thinking/at all/of what you are doing. LTB

The Way It Is. Gloria C. Oden. I am so pleased with myself. CNA

The Way My Ideas Think Me. Jose Garcia Villa. Brother."...This is the way we are. AnFE; EaLo

The Way of Cape Race. Edwin John Pratt. Lion-hunger, tiger-leap. CoBE; EtS; WHW

The Way of It. John Vance Cheney. But I know you will learn it too late, my dear. HBV 1-2

A Way of Keeping. Nancy Willard. the god in the forest of the heart. IHMS

The Way of Life. Joseph V. B. Danquah. Our true and only destiny. ACV

A Way of Life. Howard Nemerov. Still, I keep my weapons handy, sitting here/Smoking and shaving and drinking the dry beer. NIP

A Way of Looking. Elizabeth Jennings. Thought and reflection must begin again/To fit the image and to make it true. NePoEA; PP

The Way of Pain. Wendell Berry. too bright, unsparing, whole. AMV-80

A Way of Speaking. Gretel Ehrlich. or forward to what they might become. MAYP

The Way of the Cross. Joseph Ignatius Constantin Clarke. I drag the cross of sacrifice/To the top of the cruel hill! CAW

The Way of the World. James Jeffrey Roche. But Thy palms toil-worn by nails are torn,/O Christ, on Calvary. CAW

Way Out in Idaho. *Anonymous.* With a four-horse team, we'll soon be seen/Way out in Idaho. BPAW; CoSo; FSW; OuSiCo

Way-Out Morgan. Gwendolyn Brooks. to consider Ruin. BP

Way out West. LeRoi (Imamu Amiri Baraka) Jones. Closing the eyes. As/simple an act. You float NeAP; NMP; PoBA

Way Out West. Charles A. Siringo. But don't you fence it in. CoSo

Way Over in the Blooming Garden. *Anonymous.* Rise up an' choose de one dat's suitable to yo' min'. ABF

Way Over in the New Buryin' Groun' (with music). *Anonymous* Somebody's dying way over yonder,/Way over in the new buryin' groun'. AS

The Way-Side Well. Joseph Seamon, Jr Cotter. Fancies clog the way to Heaven, and saints miss/their crown. CDC; PoNe

The Way Sun Keeps Falling Away from Every Window. Lyn Lifshin. ...but almost certain that they can/never really come to be together. NeAC

The Way the Baby Woke. James Whitcomb Riley. And this is the way the baby woke. AA

The Way the Bird Sat. Ray A. Young Bear. he felt puzzled licking the rain/from the trees. CDW; VoR

The Way, the Truth, and the Life. Theodore Parker. To uplift their bleeding brothers rescued from the dust. TRV; WGRP Toil by the light, life, way, that thou hast given. HBV 1-2; TrPWD

The Way; The Truth; The Life. Samuel Judson Porter. Thou who art the Life, continue to live in us and love us. BLRP

The Way & the Way Things Are. Nila NorthSun. please/get me tobacco. GP

The Way Through. Denise Levertov. ...to career/up the plunge of the hill. AmC; NeAP; PoM

The Way Through the Woods. Rudyard Kipling. But there is no road through the woods! CH; FaBoCh; LoGBV; MCCG; MoVE; NOBE; OBEV; OBNC; OBVV; OxBChV; OxBTC; PoPle; RFM; SeCeV; VLP

The Way to Arcady. Henry Cuyler Bunner. Oh, yon's the way to Arcady,/Where all the leaves are merry. AA; InMe

The Way to Heaven. Charles Goodrich Whiting. He hath the watchword and the key,/In peace, or wars. AA

The Way to Hump a Cow. Edward Estlin Cummings. is hows to hump a cow AmP; NoAm; NOBA; OxBA

The Way to Jerusalem (excerpt). *Anonymous.* Upon a hull hit stondez on hee,/Where sent Jamez ferst schalt thou see. OBTV

The Way to Live. *Anonymous.* As we the world must now begin,/We will deal in every following thing. VLP

A Way to Make a Living. James Wright. ...That would have been a hell of/A way to make a living. NNaP

The Way to the River. William Stanley Merwin. But we/Will read it together CoAP; NYBP

The Way to the Sea. Laurence Lerner. The finished ships disturb it, and depart. NePoEA-2

The Way up Is the Way down. Charles Brasch. I am your elements, Lord,/In their nothingness. OCNZ

A Way Up on Clinch Mountain (A vers. with music). *Anonymous.* You rob my poor pockets, Of silver and gold. AS

A Way Up on Clinch Mountain (B vers. with music). *Anonymous.* I'd give the whole world if my Lulu was hyer. AS

Way Up on Old Smoky. *Anonymous.* Bury me on old Smoky, old Smoky so high,/Where the wild birds in heaven can hear my sad cry. TrAS

The Way We Live Now. Robert Patrick Dana. That this is the way/we live now AMV-80

The Way We Wonder. Robert Pack. What has become of our astonishment/We wonder, now our early gift is spent. NePoEA

The Wayfarer. Stephen Crane. "Doubtless there are other roads." AA; AmePo; LiTA; MoAmPo; NePA

The Wayfarer. Padraic Pearse. And I have gone upon my way/Sorrowful. OxBI

The Wayfarers. Rupert Brooke. Into the waste we know not, into the night? MoLP

Wayfarers. Dana Burnet. The third sat by the glowing hearth and smiled into/his glass. EtS

Wayfarers in the Wilderness. Alexander R. Thompson. O Christ our King, in mercy bring/Us thither we implore thee! AH

Wayman in Love. Tom Wayman. "I can see," he begins,/"that you two have problems..." NIP; NOBC

Wayne at Stony Point. Clinton Scollard. Than his charge on Stony Point in the heart of the murky/night. MC; PAH

The Ways. John Oxenham. And every man decideth/The Way his soul shall go. HBMV; PoLf; TRV

The Ways and the Peoples. Randall Jarrell. ...glittering virgin/Who is dying and glass on her marvelous bier. PoA

The Ways O' Men. Angelina Weld Grimke. Does it matter about the turnin's? CDC

Ways of Loving. Theodore Weiss. the teacher knows success. GP

Ways of Pronouncing "Ough". *Anonymous.* O'er life's dark lough my course I still pursue. FaBoUs

Ways of Seeing. William Stafford. the leaves move away/falling on all but the/unmarked path no one can find. SUW

The Ways of Trains. Elizabeth Jane Coatsworth. but leaves what you desire! SoPo; TiPo

Ways of War. Lionel Pigot Johnson. Of martial truth, that must prevail,/To lay on all the eternal law. AnIV

The Wayside. James Herbert Morse. Who only come for love. AA

The Wayside Station. Edwin Muir. Through the day and time and war and history. FaBoTw; MoVE

The Wayzgoose. Roy Campbell. Behold our Vegetable Athens rise/Where all the acres in the Land are wise! OBSV

We. Vladimir Kirillov. We are our own Deity and Judge and Law. LiTW

We All Have a Bench in the Park to Reach. George Jonas. He raised his eyes to follow my progress. NeAC

We Am Clim'in' Jacob's Ladder. *Anonymous.* Ev'ry roun' goes higher higher,/Soldiers of de cross. BoAN 1-2

We Are a People. Lance Henson. that pass through the cedars where/our old ones sleep/to tell us of their dreams VoR

We Are a Young Nation, Uncle. Marilyn Chin. Her pelvis may be ruined/For a thousand years. BrSi

We Are Acrobats. Jozef Habib Gerez. we fooled ourselves/with our false smiles. VWA

We Are All Workmen. Rainer Maria Rilke. God, you are vast. EaLo

We Are Brethren A'. Robert Nicoll. Come, gi'e me your hand,—we are brethren a'. HBV 1-2

We Are Building a Strong Union. *Anonymous.* Workers of the south. FSW

We Are Four Bums (with music). *Anonymous.* To hell with the man that works! AS

We Are God's Chosen Few. Jonathan Swift. We can't have heaven crammed! TRV

We Are Going. Kath Walker. The corroboree is gone./And we are going.' CBAP; NOAV

We Are Keeping an Eye on the Girls. Marina Tsvetayeva. ...is telling/to the very end a tale about Razin/and his most beautiful Persian girl. PBWP

We Are Leaning Away. Gayle Elen Harvey. something that can't breathe scratches/at the door. AMV-80

We Are Living, We Are Dwelling. Arthur Cleveland Coxe. Strike! let every blaze and sinew/Tell on ages, tell for God. TRV

We Are on Our Journey Home. *Anonymous.* And raise us up with thee/To the new,/To the new Jerusalem. AH

We Are Seven. William Wordsworth. And said, "Nay, we are seven!" BLPA; BLPL; EnRP; GN; GoTF; HBV 1-2; MBW 1-2; OxBChV; SpRo; TEP; TreF; WBLP

We Are Standing Facing Each Other. Margaret Atwood. which you won't let me see. NeAC

We Are Such Stuff As Dreams... Arbiter (Caius Petronius Arbiter) Petronius. So all night long endured, the wounds of day/Doubly are sorrow to the miserable. AWP

We Are the Burden-Bearers (excerpt). William L. Stidger. Who carry the brunt of the strife! PGD

We Are Transmitters–. D. H. Lawrence. even if it's only in the whiteness of a washed pocket-handkerchief. OxBTC

We Are Watching, We Are Waiting. William O. Cushing. Zion, shout, the Lord is here. AH

We Assume: On the Death of Our Son, Reuben Masai Harper. Michael S. Harper. We assume/you did not know we loved you. AmPA; GeTw; LCAP

We Be Soldiers Three. *Anonymous.* With never a penny of money. GBP

We Be Three Poor Mariners. *Anonymous.* Come, pledge me on this ground, aground, aground! AmSS

We Bear about No Cats' Skins. *Anonymous.* It makit maydenys wombys to swelle,/Thereof I have a quantyte. NCEP

We Bear the Strain of Earthly Care. Ozora S. Davis. And o'er the centuries still we hear/The Master's winsome call. TRV

We Become New. Marge Piercy. I am flying flying flying/in the trees of your eyes. TAP

We ben chapmen lyght of fote. *Anonymous.* Therof I have a quantyte. EnPo

We Bring No Glittering Treasures. Harriett C. Phillips. And, sweeter numbers swelling,/Forever praise thy name. AH

We Cannot Kindle. Matthew Arnold. But tasks, in hours of insight will'd,/May be through hours of gloom fulfilled. TRV

We Cared for Each Other. Heinrich Heine. That never again we could find each other. AWP

We Carry Eggshells. Hanny Michaelis. we wither away from the light/ without a trace. VWA

We Conquer or Die. James S. Pierpont. Ours, then, be the watchword, "We conquer or die." MC; PAH

We Continue. William Stanley Merwin. Charity, come home,/Begin. CAPP

We Dance Like Ella Riffs. Carolyn M. Rodgers. an infinite, essential note/ sounding down this world. CNA; PoBA

We Delighted, My Friend. Leopold Sedar Senghor. Black, white, and red, O red like the soil of Africa. PBA; TTY

We Did It. Yehuda Amichai. But the heavens/Were hard above us/Like the earth of the summer beneath. BoLoP

We Didn't Know. Tom Paxton. But what do you expect me to do? PPON

We do not play on graves. Emily Dickinson. Just looking round to see how far/It is–Occasionally– MoVE; NIP; PoEL 1-5

We Don't Get No Justice Here in Atlanta. *Anonymous.* You don't get no justice here in Atlanta. OuSiCo

We dream–it is good we are dreaming. Emily Dickinson. It's prudenter–to dream– BoWoP

We Dressed Each Other. Empress Eifuku. Our drowsy thighs touched and we/Were caught in bed by the dawn. WPOW

We Fooled Ourselves. Jozef Habib Gerez. a few minutes/only/for the sake of living VWA

We Give Thee but Thine Own. William Walsham How. To Thee our first fruits give. STF

We Go. Karl Wolfskehl. To go on,/To go on! TrJP; VWA

We Go out Together. Kenneth Patchen. We go together into town and buy wine and yellow candles. MoAmPo

We Greet Each Other in the Side (parody) (excerpt). *Anonymous.* Yes, yes, I will forever sit/There, where thy Side was split. BXAP; PeD

We Have Been Happy. Max Eastman. for you like a child's drawing on a piece of paper. AnEnPo

We Have Been Here Before. Morris Bishop. How long has this got to go on? EvOK; FiBHP; InMe; NYBP

We Have Lived and Loved Together. Charles Jefferys. And thou thy joys with me. BLPA; FaBoBe; GoTF; PoToHe; TreFT

We Have Seen Her. Hilda ("H. D.") Doolittle. at the turn of the palace stair. VGW

We Have Seen His Star in the East. Molly Anderson Haley. While our hearts remember Bethlehem,/And a cross on a far green hill. PGD

We have seen how the most amiable. Hilda ("H. D.") Doolittle. harnessed scorpions/before her. BoWoP

We Heart. Laura Chester. ...We brain–We heart–We will. NPGG

We Hurry On, Nor Passing Note. Digby Mackworth Dolben. The sprouting of the meadow grass,/But churchyard weeds about our head. OBNC

We Interrupt This Broadcast. Judith Hemschemeyer. Anyway, I'm a mouse. Str

We Laughed. Rochelle Kraut. and we laughed/and we laughed. APU

We Lay Un Down to Sleep. Louise Chandler Moulton. Whether to wake and weep,/Or wake no more, He knows. AA

We Let It Go That He Was a Perfect Man. Nicanor Parra. somehow or other we have to find it. PoL

We like March–his shoes are purple. Emily Dickinson. With the Blue Birds buccaneering/On his British sky– SOTW

We Live in a Cage. William J. Harris. and threaten to take our cage/away from us. PoBA

We Live in a Rickety House. Alexander McLachlan. Where the naked hide from day,/And thieves and drunkards meet. NOBC; OBCV

We'll All Feel Gay. Winfield Townley Scott. And he was running all the way to the door where my grandmother/stood. MiAP

We'll All Go A-Hunting Today. *Anonymous.* If they'll all go a-hunting today. OBET

We'll Go No More A-Roving. William Ernest Henley. We'll go no more a-roving, but weep at home, my dear. CBEP; DiPo; FaBV; FaPoR; HBV 1-2; MoBrPo; MOON; OBEV; PoLf; TrGrPo

We'll Have Another Drink before the Boat Shoves Off. *Anonymous.* And we'll have another drink before the boat shoves off! ShS

We'll Meet Again. J. Danson Smith. And to begin a fresh, but never-ending/story/Of life which shall endure forevermore. STF

We'll Never Know. Alma Hoellein. That with the Son of His dear love,/In heav'n we have a place. STF

We'll Roll the Golden Chariot Along. *Anonymous.* And we'll all hang on behind! ShS

We'll to the Woods No More. Alfred Edward Housman. And the bowers of bay no more. LOW; OAEL 1-2; PoRA

We Long to See Jesus. Anna E. Hamilton. Thy blessed promise, "I am with you always,"/Is ever faithful, O Immanuel! BePJ

We Love the Name of Texas. *Anonymous.* I will quit the trail of the longhorn and stay with my little wife. BFSS

We Love the Venerable House. Ralph Waldo Emerson. And in this fleeting lifetime trust/To find the narrow way. AH

We Love You the Way You Are. David McFadden. & Jennifer is the daughter of Willie Blake. NeAC

We Lying by Seasand. Dylan Thomas. Breaks, O my heart's blood, like a heart and hill. BiP; PoA; SyP

We Manage Most When We Manage Small. Linda Gregg. ...This touching/home goes far. This fishing in the air. AmPA; NPGG

We May Not Know. Cecil Frances Alexander. But we believe it was for us He hung and suffered there. TRV

We Meet in the Lives of Animals. Peter Everwine. And it is something like love. NNaP

We Men Are of Two Worlds. Mary Elizabeth Colman. with that other, unseen world,/our spirit's home. CaP

We Met on Roads of Laughter. Charles Divine. For I must hurry after/To overtake my heart. FaBoBe; HBMV

We miss a kinsman more. Emily Dickinson. Till we, who smiled at Pyrenees,/Of parishes complain. OBSP

We Must Make a Kingdom of It. Gregory Orr. like the shovelfull over/the gravedigger's shoulder. MAYP

We Must Not Part. *Anonymous.* To live on earth, as they in heaven. DiPo

We Need a King. Arthur R., Jr. Macdougall. I will demand to see his side/Before I make this King my own. PGD

We Need a Whole Lot More of Jesus. *Anonymous.* We need a whole lot more of Jesus,/And a lot less rock 'n roll. FSW

We Need Not Bid, for Cloistered Cell. John Keble. The secret this of Rest below. HBV 1-2

We Need the Tonic of Wildness. Henry David Thoreau. and the mink crawls on its belly close to the ground. RFM

We Needs Must Be Divided. George Santayana. And nothing of our heart to earth returned. ViBoPo

We Never Know How High We Are. Emily Dickinson. Did not ourselves the Cubits warp/For fear to be a King– AmP; AnFE; APA; TRV

We Never Said Farewell. Mary Elizabeth Coleridge. Two islands that the roaring seas divide/Are not more far apart. OBSP

We Never Speak as We Pass By. *Anonymous.* And in my heart her name shall live. GoTF; TreFS

We Object. *Anonymous.* Listen to the pen of the Commissioner/As it goes "hihi', scratch, scratch. WTO

We outgrow love, like other things. Emily Dickinson. Like Costumes Grandsires wore. NOBA

We Own the Night. LeRoi (Imamu Amiri Baraka) Jones. And we own the night BOLo; PoBA

We Passed by Green Closes. John Clare. Love from that days courting Burns my heart/to a coal. VLP

We Pity Our Bosses Five. *Anonymous.* The lousy son of a gun! FSW

We Play at Paste. Emily Dickinson. Practising sands. CBEP

We Plough the Fields. Jane M. Campbell. Then thank the Lord, O thank the Lord,/For all his love. FaPoR

We Poets Speak. Francis Thompson. It is not she! FaBV

We Praise Thee, God, for Harvests Earned. John Coleman Adams. But more for pledge of what remains/Past the horizon's utmost rim! AH

We Praise Thee, If One Rescued Soul. Lydia Huntley Sigourney. Till grateful to thy shrine we bring/The tribute of a ransomed land. AH

We Put the Urn Aboard Ship. Sappho. these curls of their soft hair. PBWP

We Raise de Wheat. *Anonymous.* And say dat's good enough for nigger. BPo; TAP

We're a' Dry wi' the Drinkin' o't. *Anonymous.* And he couldna preach for thinkin' o't. ELU; ErPo

We're All Bound to Go. *Anonymous.* And away, my Johnnie boys,/We're bound to go! AmSS

We're All Dry. *Anonymous.* And I can't sleep for thinking on't. NOBL

We're Gonna Move When the Spirit Says Move! *Anonymous.* We're gonna talk when the spirit says talk. FSW

We're OK. Gloria Fuertes. and I say, "Sure, just what we needed!" WPOW

We're Tenting To-Night. Walter Kittredge. Dying on the old camp-ground. PAL

We Reached Out Far. Peretz Markish. To the stars and skies above,/To our last longing, to our last love! TrJP

We Read of a People. *Anonymous.* The law has to answer us, Yea. AH

We Real Cool. Gwendolyn Brooks. Jazz June. We/Die soon. CAPP; FF; HAP; HeIP; HoPM; IDB; InPK; NoP; PoBA; PrIm; SM; SoSe; TAP; TTY; WeW

We Reason of These Things. Wallace Stevens. They were love's characters come face to face. CrMA

We Saw Three Boys. Dorothy Wordsworth. But when Coleridge began to inquire furthur,/Off they ran! GLGT

We See Jesus. Annie Johnson Flint. And perfect peace, and every hope fulfilled. BLRP

We Separate the Days. Henrik Nordbrandt. This way we experience both/ without knowing either of them. AMV-81

We Settled by the Lake. F. D. Reeve. The heart cries out like a conductor/On a morning train, "Change! All/change!" NYBP

We Shall Have Far to Go. James Wreford Watson. whose very map and compass are/the mortal hour? CaP

We Shall Not Be Moved. *Anonymous.* We shall not be moved. FSW

We Shall Not Escape Hell. Marina Tsvetayeva. we shall certainly find ourselves in Hell! BoWoP

We Shall Overcome. *Anonymous.*
I do believe/We shall build a new world some day. BLSo
The Lord will see us through some day. AH; EaLo
We shall overcome someday. FSW

We Shall Say. Miriam Allen DeFord. But a new earth healed, and a new sun rising. GoYe

We Shall Walk through the Valley. *Anonymous.* We shall meet our father over there. FSW

We Sit Solitary. *Anonymous.* Gather Thy dispersed children in/Jerusalem! TrJP

We Still Must Follow. E. L. Mayo. And damned be he who first cries "miracle." AMV-81

We Survive! Hirsch Glick. We survive! TrJP

We Thank Thee. Thomas Curtis Clark. Inspire our hearts and bless our native land. PGD

We Thank Thee. John Oxenham.
With equal mind/We thank Thee, Lord! PGD
With quickened hearts,/That find Thee everywhere,/We thank Thee, Lord. BLRP

We Thank Thee, Lord. Calvin W. Laufer. A splendor greater yet while serving thee. AH

We thirst at first. Emily Dickinson. Is that great water in the west/Termed Immortality. NOCV; WGRP

We Three Kings of Orient Are. John Henry Hopkins, Jr. Westward leading, still proceeding,/Guide us to thy perfect light! AH; OHIP; PCh

We Two Boys together Clinging. Walt Whitman. Cities wrenching, ease scorning, statutes mocking, feebleness/chasing,/Fulfilling our foray. PeHV

We Used to Play. Don Welch. ...he'd say, "Wanna play kick the can?" Psk

We've Done Our Hitch in Hell. *Anonymous.* For they've done their hitch in hell. ABF

We Walk the Way of the New World. Don L. Lee. & will want to be remembered/as realpeople. BPo; NeAC; PoBA

We Walked among the Whispering Pines. John Henry Boner. We walked among the whispering pines. AA

We Watch'd Her Breathing. Thomas Hood. Her quiet eyelids closed–she had/Another morn than ours! ELP

We Wear the Mask. Paul Laurence Dunbar. We wear the mask. AmePo; AmNP; CDC; FF; IDB; NoP; PoBA; TTY; UnPo

We Were Boys Together. George Pope Morris. When you and I were boys! AA

We Were in the 8th Grade. John Berryman. ...and/then, until now, she disappeared. GLGT

We Were Permitted to Meet Together in Prison to Prepare for Trial. Daniel Berrigan. I come to myself/a beast in a shoe box/sport/of the king of the cats. LFAC

We Who Are About to Die. Harold E. Fey. ...Lifting the lid on the/atom, He says: "Choose life or death, but choose!" PGD

We Who Are Dead. Paul L. Benjamin. ...to make an end/Of war and want; just this we ask,/We who are Dead. PGD

We Who Are Left. George Whalley. the long incredible anguish/of questioning childless arms. CaP

We Who Build Visions. Stanton A. Coblentz. And in man's spirit, where she comes by night/And shall remain when the last gunfires roll. PGD

We Who Were Born. Eiluned Lewis. Who walk by right/On the naked hills. BiCB; TiPo

We Whom the Dead Have Not Forgiven. Sara Bard Field. ...the invisible throng,/Beating the accent of their wrong. PGD

We Will Not Fear. David Diamond. Fearful though they be, fearful though they be. AH

We Will Speak Out. James Russell Lowell. While some faint gleamings we can see/Of Freedom's coming morn? GoTF; TreFT

We Will Watch the Northern Lights. *Anonymous.* ...small stars/in their sleepless flight. RFM

We Wish You a Merry Christmas. *Anonymous.* We Wish You a Merry Christmas,/And a Happy New Year! FSW

We Woke Together. Christopher John Brennan. of some blank world where dawn for ever wept. BoAV

We Women. Edith Sodergran. If my baby doesn't live, it's his... WPOW

We Won't Go Home Till Morning. *Anonymous.* We won't go home till morning,/Till day light does appear. BLSo; PSoN

We Would See Jesus. *Anonymous.*
And, saved by His redemption,/We'll spread the news abroad. STF

Then welcome day, and farewell mortal night! AH; BePJ

Weak Is the Will of Man, His Judgment Blind. William Wordsworth. And do not shrink from sorrow's keenest wind. EnRP

The Weak Monk. Stevie Smith. For this the monk is to blame. BoWoP; FaBoTw

The Weakest Thing. Elizabeth Barrett Browning. The strongest of the universe/Guarding the weakest! HBV 1-2

Weakness of Nature. Richard Hurrell Froude. Yet think not prayer and fast were given/To make one step 'twixt earth and Heaven. OBRV

Wealth. Ralph Waldo Emerson. Which bind the strengths of Nature wild/To the conscience of a child. ImOP

A Wealthy Man. William Allingham. Fair Idea his mistress,/Child of Eternity. IrPN

Weapons. Anna Wickham. In the house of my Love/I found a pen! MoBrPo

The Wearin' o' the Green. *Anonymous.* But till that day, plaise God, I'll stick to the Wearin' o' the/Green. AnIL; AnIV; HBV 1-2; NOBI; OnYI; PoSC; TreF

Wearing of the Green. Aileen Fisher. a green-all-over promise/of springtime just ahead! YeAr

The Weary Blues. Langston Hughes. He slept like a rock or a man that's dead. BALP; FaBV; NoAm; NOBA; NoP; PoNe; UnS

Weary in Well-Doing. Christina Georgina Rossetti. That I may let alone my toil/And rest with thee? SeCePo; TrPWD

A Weary Lot is Thine. Sir Walter Scott. And adieu for evermore. CH

A Weary Song to a Slow Sad Tune. Li Ch'ing-chao. How can I drive off this word–/Hopelessness? BoWoP

Weary Traveler. *Anonymous.* Let us cheer the weary traveler,/Along the heavenly way. BoAN 1-2

Weary Will. A. B. Paterson. And rigs a little swinging gate/To let Bill Wombat under. BoAnP

Wearyin' fer You. Frank Lebby Stanton. Jest a-wearyin' fer you! HBV 1-2

The Weasel. Robert Pack. If this goes on, I will believe in God. CoPo

Weather. Mary Ursula Bethell. Montana Rubens, wept for dead not long since,/Has turned herself into a delightful garland. AnNZ

Weather. Hilda Conkling. Hidden behind the hills of sky. TiPo

The Weather. Lorna Crozier. ...A hand moves across/a pencil drawing of the world/and smudges everything. CaPN

Weather. Archibald MacLeish. Blowing the oak leaves pale side out.... MoAmPo

Weather. William Meredith. Ours are the only natures/That you cannot give back. NYBP

Weather Ear. Norman Nicholson. "No wind at all, and the street stone-deaf with a cold in the/head." OBSP

The Weather Factory. Nancy Byrd Turner. In the weather factory/Things begin to hum. SUS

The Weather of Olympus. Robert Graves. By noting that the snake-tailed Chthonian winds/Were answerable to Fate alone, not Zeus. FaBoEE

The Weather of Six Mornings. Jane Cooper. why should I sign/my name? IHMS; NYBP

The Weather of the World. Howard Nemerov. As in the brilliant stillness of the sun. SUW

Weather Rhymes. Hamish Brown. Morning warning:/Red sun,/Rains come. PoSH

Weather Vanes. Frances Frost. knowing what autumn mischief lurks/ behind this April weather. SiSoSe

Weather Wisdom. *Anonymous.*
The earth's refreshed by frequent showers. GoTF; HBVY; TreF
Rainbow at morning,/Sailors, take warning. HBV 1-2

Weather Words. David McCord. Sirocco, monsoon, khamsin, and chinook. ImOP

Weathercock. Elizabeth Jennings. Could see my love's gold eye/And feel his fire. NePoEA

Weathergrams. Lloyd J. Reynolds. just call it weathergrams. FAZ

Weathering the Depths. Al Lee. To parachaute on the capitals of gaiety? AmPA

Weathers. Thomas Hardy. And rooks in families homeward go,/And so do I. ALV; BoLiVe; EvOK; FaBoCh; FaBV; GTBS; LoGBV; MoAB; MoBrPo; OBMV; PoPle; SeCePo

Weave Room Blues. *Anonymous.* I got the blues, the weave-room blues. FSW

The Weaver. *Anonymous.* I was judged not so much by my doing/As by what I had striven to do. BLRP

The Weaver. William Henry Burleigh. As he weaves our web of doom. BLPA

The Weaver. Fanny Forrester. May the stain of sorrow the deepest one,/ That I bear with me to Heaven. BLPA

The Weaver. Lisel Mueller. into doors that will not open. AMV-81

The Weaver and the Factory Maid. *Anonymous.* And trudge to the mill in the early morn. OBET

Weaver's Life. *Anonymous.* We will have to weave no more. FSW

The Weaver (with music). *Anonymous.* And the many, many times that I held her in my arms,/Just to shield her from the foggy, foggy dew. AS

Weavers. Heinrich Heine. We are weaving–still weaving. TrJP

Weaving at the Window. Wang Chien. Their ten fingers idle,/while clothes fill the hamper. SaC

Weaving Love-Knots. Hsueh T'ao. My fingers plait the same grasses, over and over. BoWoP

Weaving Love-Knots 2. Hsueh T'ao. But Spring hums everywhere: the nesting birds/Are stammering out their sympathy for me. BoWoP

The Weaving of the Wing. Ralph Hodgson. "Is done" I'll echo there/The Universal Voice. BrPo

The Web. Gregory O'Donoghue. In any drawingroom (in civil i/zation) an incred/ib/ly/long time... BIrV

The Web. Theodore Weiss. ...–and, last, its instruments. CoAP; NoAm

The Web of Eros. Edith Sitwell. Within your magic web of hair lies furled/The fire and splendor of the ancient world. HBMV

Webster: An Ode (excerpt). William Cleaver Wilkinson. This is a lonesome world, and WEBSTER/dead! AA

Weddase Maryam. *Anonymous.* of David Our Lord and Savior Jesus Christ was born of her. ISi

Wedded. Isaac Rosenberg. Dead, strayed, to love-strange lover. PoPle

Wedded Bliss. Charlotte Perkins Stetson Gilman. And the Clam sucked, the Salmon swam, alone. HBV 1-2

Wedded Memories. Philip Bourke Marston. Intense and sad, like changeless stars that/shine/On ruined towers of a predestined race. VLP

The Wedding. Conrad Aiken. Woke from the nap, forgetting him; and ate him. AnAmPo; CMoP; TAP

Wedding. *Anonymous.* Pussicat, wussicat, don't be too late. OxNR

Wedding. George Mackay Brown. At a white unbroken bed. BSV

The Wedding. Robert Graves. Through crowds of almost-men and almost women/Howl for their lost immediacy. HW

The Wedding. Tom (Thomas Hood, Jr.) Hood. Bound for the Dam of Rotter. InMe

The Wedding. Sandra Kohler. A light that loves them both. AMV-80

Wedding. Ewa Lipska. The world rocks/like a carriage with a baby in it. VWA

Wedding. Dorothy Livesay. on black curving thighs/thrusts love upward PeCV

The Wedding (1957). Boris Pasternak. Only a song, only a dream,/Only a blue dove. HW

Wedding and Funeral. *Anonymous.* An' blest is t' deead at t' rain rains on. GBP

Wedding Anniversary. Margaret E. Bruner. To us, for all the ills life chose to send. PoToHe

Wedding Celebration. Tenrai Kono. The newlyweds are in harmony,/and the family will prosper. HW

The Wedding Coat. Harriet Rose. It is the mute partner of her waltz. BrRo

Wedding Day at Nagasaki. Rodney Hall. This is today! Today! CBAP

The Wedding Gift. Minna Irving. Grandmother Granger's wedding gift/To every girl on her marriage day. BLPA

Wedding-Hymn. Sidney Lanier. Let an angel come and dwell to-night/In this dear double-heart, and teach! TrPWD

Wedding Morn. D. H. Lawrence. I shall weep, oh, I shall weep, I know/For joy or for misery. MoAB; MoBrPo

The Wedding Night. Johannes Secundus. O night! O doubly-happy night! UnTE

The Wedding Night. Anne Sexton. passed roughly through,/and before it was time. PoA

The Wedding of Alcmane and Mya. George Chapman. ...the turning of her back/Made them all shriek, it looked so ghastly black. OBSC

Wedding of the Clans. Aubrey Thomas De Vere. Because I never was married before! AnIL; IrPN

Wedding Party. Donald Hall. Above the crowd he holds his breathing box/That only empties, fills, empties, fills. LCAP

The Wedding Poem (excerpt). Lawrence Russ. And I longed to take shelter/in the forest of your hair. AMV-80

Wedding Procession. James A. Emanuel. And the tough young horns/Blared flippantly farewell. NNP

Wedding Signs. *Anonymous.* Married in pink, your fortune will sink. GoTF; TreFT

Wedding Song. *Anonymous.*
So if you wish to marry, boys, I'll tell you what to do. OBET
With his light he summons me to sport with him./Oh, the joy! LiTW

A Wedding-Song. John White Chadwick. And with a "Peace be with you!" go/my way. AA

Wedding Song. Johann Wolfgang von Goethe. He shyly turns and shields his eyes/And, smiling, gives his blessing. HW

Wedding Song. Conrad Ferninand Meyer. Go and love and suffer! HW

Wedding Wind. Philip Larkin. ...conclude/Our kneeling as cattle by all-generous waters? HW; MAT

A Wedgwood Bowl. Frances Beatrice Taylor. A circling wreath of little, dancing folk. CaP

Wedlock. *Anonymous.* Of every man and wife. ABF

Wedlock. Jenny Grahame. But nought is found, by sea or land,/That can a wayward wife withstand. LiTL

Wedlock. Bink Noll. ...my hand will want the exact/shape of his head, and my house will cry. GP

Wedlock. A Satire. Hetty Wright. May search successfully as well/For truth in whores and ease in hell. NOEC

Wednesbury Cocking. *Anonymous.* Jack Baker he whacked his own father,/And thus ended Wednesbury Cocking. FaBoBa

Wednesday at North Hatley. Ralph Gustafson. But softly the snow falls. NOBC

Wednesday Cocking. *Anonymous.* And thus ended Wednesday Cocking. EnSB

Wednesday in Holy Week. Christina Georgina Rossetti. Pointed at, mocked again/By men for whom He shed His Blood–in vain? PGD; TrCP

Wednesday, January 1, 1701. Samuel Sewall. All Four, in Consort join'd, shall Sing,/New Songs of Praise to Christ our King. SCAP

Wednesday Night Prayer Meeting. Jay Wright. unwilling to change their freedom for a god. PoBA

The Wee Cooper of Fife. *Anonymous.* Send ye for the wee cooper o' Fife. FSW

Wee Davie Daylicht. Robert Tennant. In amang the rosy clouds, far ayont the sea. OxBChV

Wee Hughie. Elizabeth Shane. God help him, he was cryin',/An', maybe, so was I. HBMV

The Wee May o'Caledon. Lewis Spence. Said her Pater Noster. ACV

The Wee Wee Man. *Anonymous.* But in the twinkling of an eye,/My wee, wee man was clean awa. BaBo; CH; EBEV; ELP; ESPB; FaBoCh; GBP; OAEL 1-2; OxBB

Wee Willie Gray. Robert Burns. Feathers of a flee wad feather up his bonnet. OxBChV

Wee Willie Winkie. Mother Goose. For it's now ten o'clock. SiSoSe; SoPo; TiPo

The Weed. Elizabeth Bishop. "but to divide your heart again." MoPo

Weed. Robert Hass. the bracts and bright white flowerets/of horse-parsnips. MAYP

Weed Puller. Theodore Roethke. Alive, in a slippery grave. AmPP; HaCAP

Weeding in January. Louis Daniel Brodsky. And snow clouds begin to form. AMV-80

Weeds. Ann Stanford. Spread the great round promises of green morning. GrPl

Week-End. Harold Munro. Week-end begins to merge itself in Week. SeCePo

Week-End by the Sea. Edgar Lee Masters. ...And where is the hand to 'gave/Words that tell so much for the lost on land? MoAmPo

The Week-End Indian. Anita Endrezze-Probst. thinking it to be only/the grave of an animal. VoR

Week-End Sonnet No. 1. Harold Monro. Purring and crooning:–"Lie in us, and dream." BSV

A Week of Birthdays. Mother Goose. Is bonny and blithe, and good and gay. SoPo

A Week of Doodle. Reed Whittemore. On those days of the week–just two, not counting/Sunday–when I was blank. NePoEA

Week-Seek. Jim Tollerud. To you I pray. VoR

A Weekday. Larry Eigner. though they were not always the same CoPo

Weekend Sonnets. Cilla McQueen. & all of the blue-lipped/hills in their eyes. OCNZ

Weekend Stroll. Frances Cornford. July is born. BoNaP

Weeksville Women. Elouise Loftin. they got so much/to be hot about PoBA

Weep Love's Losing. Imr el Kais. Yet, was I un-vanquished. Had I not happiness, I at/their hands in Daret, Daret of Juljuli? LiTW

Weep No More. John Fletcher. Gentlest fair, mourn, mourn no moe. EiL; OBEV; ViBoPo

Weep Not for a Warrior. Mbuyiseni Oswald Mtshali. Let him rest on the buffalo-hide bed,/where his forefathers repose. WhB

Weep Not To-Day. Robert Bridges. And the day will be to-day. OBMV; OBVV

Weep You No More. John Dowland. Softly, now softly lies/Sleeping. CH; EBEV; EiL; ELP; EnLoPo; ExPo; ForPo; GBL; HAP; LoBV; NoP; OAEP; PoPle; SoSe; TrGrPo; ViBoPo

Weepe O Mine Eyes. *Anonymous.* That I may drowne me in you? AtBAP; PoEL 1-5

The Weeper. Richard Crashaw. A worthy object; Our Lords Feet. AnAnS 1; MePo; OAEL 1-2; OBEV; SeCP; ViBoPo

The Weepers Tower in Amsterdam. Paul Goodman. all of them flow down into the sea. VGW

Weeping and Singing. Cesar Tiempo. and then, then we shall reap,/singing, brothers, singing. MoRP

The Weeping Cherry. Robert Herrick. For tincture, wonder at. AtBAP

Weeping Sad and Lonely. Henry and Charles C. Sawyer Ucker. (Yet praying) When this cruel war is over,/Praying that we meet again. FSW; TrAS

Weeping Sinner, Dry Your Tears. Oliver Holden. Flee, O flee to Jesus' arms. AH

Weeping Willow. Richard Aldridge. And drop her eyes, and turn home down the hill. NePoAm-2

The Weeping Willow. Anonymous. Perhaps some day he will weep for me. AmFP

Weevily Wheat. Anonymous. Charlie hugs and kisses the girls,/For he knows they taste like candy. ABF; AmFP; AS; FSW; TrAS

'Weh Down Souf. Daniel Webster Davis. 'Weh down Souf. BANP

Wei Wind. Confucius. and for the worse,/an end. CTC

Weighing the Baby. Ethel Lynn Beers. Its value in eternity... PoToHe

The Weight. William Aberg. I've been sitting here a long time/And always it feels like I'm falling. LFAC

The Weight Room. Thomas Rabbit. And not bloody your body or the tiles. MAYP

A Weightless Element. Gottfried Benn. go not the way lamenting goes. PoPl

Weir Bridge. Padraic Fallon. The tiny trickle of my birth/Dwindling back into the earth. CIP

A Welcome. William Browne. He that parteth from you never/Shall enjoy a spring for ever. HBV 1-2; LiTL; OBEV

The Welcome. Abraham Cowley. My dove, but once let loose, I doubt/Would ne'er return, had not the flood been out. BoLoP; SeCV 1-2

The Welcome. Thomas Osborne Davis.
And the linnets are singing,"True lovers don't sever!" HBV 1-2
And the oftener you come here the more I'll adore you. GoTF; TreFT

Welcome. Harvey Feinberg. cock of the morning/to you friends/cock o' the morning PoL

The Welcome. Freda Laughton. We shall be no older/Than the child and the animals. NeIP

Welcome. R. S. Thomas. You must travel back/to the cold bud of water/In the hard rock. NMP

Welcome. Rose Waldo. And we'll sing all the songs that we love to sing. SoPo

Welcome Every Guest. Anonymous. Softly swell the trembling air,/To complete our concert fair. TrAS

A Welcome for Etheridge. James (Olumo) Cunningham. cries out/for something like that... JB

Welcome, Fortune. Anonymous. Above all other I love her best,/Until I die, what wald sho more? BSV

Welcome Morning. Anne Sexton. The Joy that isn't shared, I've heard,/dies young. CAPP

Welcome My World. Denis Devlin. O my red phoenix from the south! AnIV

Welcome O Great Mary. Alice O'Gallagher. May the Father, the Son, and the Spirit all Three/Beneath thy protection praised be. WTO

Welcome! Our Messiah. Anonymous. The which hath sent,/By good assent,/To us his only Son. MeEL

Welcome over the Door of an Old Inn. Anonymous. If Foe, our love shall conquer thee. PoToHe

Welcome, Queen Sabbath. Zalman Schneour. Oh, come let us welcome sweet/Sabbath, the Queen! TrJP

Welcome, Summer. Geoffrey Chaucer. And drevine away the lange nightes blake. MeEL

Welcome, Sweet Rest. Michael Wigglesworth. Trusting through thee eternal life to inherit. AH

Welcome the Wrath. Stanley Jasspon Kunitz. With one wet match and all man's desolation. VGW

Welcome, Thou Safe Retreat! William Habington. We end our journey 'mong the dead. OxBoCh

A Welcome to Dr. Benjamin Apthorp Gould. Oliver Wendell Holmes. We bid thee welcome to thine earthly home! ImOP

Welcome to My Heart. Anonymous. I give it all to Thee. BePJ

Welcome to Prince of Ossory. James Clarence Mangan. Thousands this glad night, ere turning bedward,/Will, with us, drink "Victory to Charles Edward!" IrPN

The Welcome to Sack. Robert Herrick. Ne'r may Prophetique Daphne crown my Brow. AnAnS 2; CaPo; SeCP; SeCV 1-2

Welcome to the Moon. Anonymous. Excellency of stars, precious stone of the night. BoNaP; MOON

Welcome to the Nations. Oliver Wendell Holmes. Thrones of the continents! Isles of the sea! PAH

Welcome to the New Year. Eleanor Farjeon. See you sweep clean. YeAr

Welcome to the Sun. Gavin Douglas. Welcome celestial mirror and espy! ACP

Welcome to This House. Faye George. to warm the cold seepage of stone. AMV-80

Welcome, Ye Hopeful Heirs of Heaven. Phoebe Hinsdale Brown. Ere we exhaust the theme of love. AH

Welcome Yule. Anonymous. Welcome CAW; CH

A Welcoming Party. John Montague. And went home to my Christian school/To kick a football through the air. FaBoIP; IPY

The Welder. Frank Lima. A glacier suffocating a siren. ANYP

Weldon Kees. Larry Levis. Admiring the sun on Alcatraz. FAZ

Weldon Kees in Mexico, 1965. David Wojahn. ...walking across the bridge/for water to be blessed at vespers. MAYP

Welfare Store. Sonny Boy Williamson. I won't have to go down to that Welfare Store BluL

The Well. Thomas Edward Brown. Take me, and weep me on the desolate hills! NOBV

The Well. Denise Levertov. ...I feel the word"water'/spelled in my left palm. AP

The Well. Luis Palés Matos. filled with a remote sense of eternity. InW

The Well-Aimed Stare. Hugo Margenat. into your cup of always/oceanic water. InW

The Well Dressed Man with a Beard. Wallace Stevens. It can never be satisfied, the mind, never. BiP

Well, Honest John. John Clare. And Jack the Giant-killer's high renown. NCEP

Well I Never. Anonymous. Leather breeches to his toes. FaBoCh

The Well-intentioned question. Wendy Rose. for footsteps/stopping short of my door/then leaving forever. STE; TWSS

The Well of Life. Sir Herbert Read. God bless these wives and their strong/Men's endeavour. NoAm

The Well of Living Water. Charles Wesley. In streams of pure perennial peace. BePJ

The Well of St. Keyne. Robert Southey. For she took a bottle to church. BeLS; FaBoBe; HBV 1-2

The Well of Vertew and Flour of Womanheid. Anonymous. Ye beir the name of landis of lenth and breid,/The well of vertew and flour of womanheid. OxBS

Well Pleaseth Me the Sweet Time of Easter. Ezra Pound. Papiol, be glad to go speedily to "Yea and Nay," and tell him there's/too much peace about. InvP

The Well Rising. William Stafford. ...I place my feet/with care in such a world. NaP

The Well-Travelled Roadway. John Newlove. early, with my own name in mind. NeAC

The Well: Two Songs. Anonymous. You know the deep love of the heart. WTO

Well, Wanton Eye. Charles, duc d' Orleans. Your lookes nice ye let them run too wide. HAP

Well Water. Randall Jarrell. And gulp from them the dailiness of life. NOBA; NoP; OBSP; VGW

A Well-Wishing to a Place of Pleasure. Anonymous. When she in bed with Mars/By all the gods was seen. GBL

Well, World, You Have Kept Faith with Me. Thomas Hardy. Never, I own, expected I/That life would all be fair. SCV

Wellcome, to the Caves of Arta! Robert Graves. Wich deceased of thier emocion on a past excursion day. NLV; NOBL; NYBP

Wellfleet Harbor. Paul Goodman. though flaming like a werewolf in the night. CoAP

Wellington. Benjamin Disraeli. Yet sovereign of thyself, whate'er may speed. OBVV

Wellington. Charles Harpur. The pleading image of his native land. NOAV

Wellington. Bill Manhire. You haven't even got a window/and his is full of houses. OCNZ

Wellington Letter: XI. Lauris Edmond. that mortifies and saves us. OCNZ

Wells. Donald Hall. I drink from the well of cattle. NMP

The Wells of Jesus Wounds. Anonymous. Bowe thu down to the brinke,/And mekely taste of the welle. MeEL

Welsh Incident. Robert Graves. "I was coming to that." BoC; CMoP; NOBE; OxBTC; WSC

Welsh Landscape. R. S. Thomas. Worrying the carcase of an old song. FaBoMo

The Welsh Marches. Alfred Edward Housman. How long, how long, till spade and hearse/Put to sleep my mother's curse? FaBoTw

The Welsh Sea. James Elroy Flecker. And call across the years. BrPo

A Welshman to Any Tourist. R. S. Thomas. But shame has kept them late in bed. OxBC

The Welshmen of Tirawley. Sir Samuel Ferguson. Never taking/Further vengeance on his people of Tirawley. OBVV; OnYI

Welt. Georgia Douglas Johnson. Ere time has brushed cold fingers through my hair! BANP

Weltschmerz. Frank Yerby. And in your spirit flames your body's pyre. AmNP

Women's Wather. T. S. Law. I sayt an sayt again. OxBS

Wenberi's Song. *Anonymous.* rushing down singing inside this breast of mine. CBAP

The Wench in the Street. *Anonymous.* For when we have no money, we shall find chalk. CBEP

Wendell Phillips. Amos Bronson Alcott. Impartial History dare not leave thee/out. AA

Wendell Phillips (excerpt). John Boyle O'Reilly. Who dared to be traitor to Union when/Union was traitor to Right! AA

The Wendigo. Ogden Nash. The rest is merely gulps and gollops. AmMo

The Wensleydale Lad. *Anonymous.* So I clik'd hod o' my gret club stick an' went whistlin' oot/again. FaBoPP

Went up a year this evening! Emily Dickinson. A Difference–A Daisy–/Is all the rest I knew! HAP

Were I in Trouble. Robert Frost. For traveller there could do me no good/Were I in trouble with night tonight. OBSP

Were I to Choose. Gabriel Okara. ...And (O were I/To choose) I'd cheat the worms/And silence seek in stone. PBA

Were I to Mount beyond the Field. Sidney Keyes. ...the clamour of history/Will never deafen or decrease their glory. MoPo

Were I, Who to My Cost Already Am. John Wilmot, Earl of Rochester. Who is so proud of being Rational. SCV

Were My Hart as Some Mens Are. Thomas Campion. Hidden mischiefe to conceale in State and Love is treason. AAS; HBV 1-2

Were Not the Gael Fallen. Peadar O'Mulconry. And the man withered, strengthless, leprous, dead. AnIL

Were the Bright Day No More to Visit Us. *Anonymous.* As the first lovers in the garden were. LO

Were-Wolf. Julian Hawthorne. What gaunt, gray thing gallops on o'er/ the world? AA

Were You Ever in Dumbarton? *Anonymous.* Where they wear the tartan, little above the knee? ShS

Were You on the Mountain? *Anonymous.* And she was not pining in sorrow like thee. PV

Were You There. *Anonymous.* Were you there when they laid him in the tomb? AH

Werena My Heart Licht I Wad Dee. Lady Grizsel Baillie. And wow, gin I were but young for thee! OBEV

Wes Hardin: From a Photograph. Raymond Carver. through the slender, delicate-looking right hand. GeTw

Wesley in Heaven. Thomas Edward Brown. I heard the mighty bars/Of thunder-gusts that shook heaven's dome,/And moved the balanced stars. OBNC

Wessex Guidebook. Louis MacNeice. Since, though they fostered man, they never loved him. HaMV

Wessex Heights. Thomas Hardy. And ghosts then keep their distance; and I know some liberty. CMoP; FaBoPP; OAEL 1-2; OBNC; PoEL 1-5

The West. Edwin Muir. Say "Now" and "Here", and are in our own house. MoVE

The West-Country Damosel's Complaint. *Anonymous.* And warbled out their love-sick vows,/Whilst they both slept in their grave. ESPB

The West-Country Lover. Alice Brown. So I'll taste of joy, though I steal, beg, or borrow! HBV 1-2

West-Easterly Divan, IX (excerpt). Johann Wolfgang von Goethe. I will lie upon the threshold,/Watching lest thou slippest by. PeHV

West End Blues. John Hollander. In the treasonable night; by a kind of broken habit. NYP

West Fifty-Seventh Street. Byron Vazakas. like someone waiting at a rendezvous. FAZ

The West Forties: Morning, Noon, and Night. L. E. Sissman. To Stygian Forty-seventh Street below. CoAP; NYBP; NYP

West Helena Blues. Roosevelt Sykes. We have a real ball on a Saturdays and Sundays, Monday morning we'll rise and shine BluL

West Lake. Kenneth O. Hanson. Far off, the sound/of "Walkin' the Dog"/fading. CoAP

West London. Matthew Arnold. And points us to a better time than ours. FF; MCCG; OAEL

West of Alice. W. E. Harney. And I sing my song as we plunge along to the chatter of wheel and/steel. NOAV; PoAu 1-2

West of Chicago. John Dimoff. The bare winds/Moving across the great plains. RFM

West of Your City. William Stafford. Come west and see; touch these leaves. LiTM

West Paddocks. Arthur Davies. Since Grandad broke the council's regulation in the park.' NOAV

The West Palm Beach Storm. *Anonymous.* I'll meet the saints and chosen up in the heavenly skies. AmFP

The West Ridge Is Menthol-Cool. D. L. Graham. the cry–"uhuru" PoBA

West-Running Brook. Robert Frost. "Today will be the day of what we both said." AP; BLPL; DiPo; MoAB; MoAmPo; NOBA; NoP

The West's Asleep. Thomas Osborne Davis. We'll watch till death for Erin's sake! OnYI

West Sussex Drinking Song. Hilaire Belloc. I am singing the best song ever was sung,/And it has a rousing chorus. MoBrPo

West Texas. *Anonymous.* And the women get happy over some snuff. CoSo

West Wind. *Anonymous.* As she gangs tae the kirk,/With the sun on her side. PoPle

West Wind. Kenneth Koch. The intemperate climate of this double frame of the universe. CAPP

The West Wind. John Masefield. In the fine land, the west land, the land where I/belong. EnLi 1-2; FaFP; FPL; GoTF; GTBS; LiTB; LiTM; MoAB; MoBrPo; PG; PoPl; TreF

The West Wind's Secret. Mary Jane Carr. For the West Wind told me so. BrR

Wester Ross. Naomi Mitchison. And the bog creeps nearer/With the bog cotton for the fairies' flag. PoSH

Westering. Douglas V. Kane. Hover, phoenix-free, above the deep Edens of the valley. GoYe

The Western Approaches. Howard Nemerov. There lived a certain man and he had three sons. HaCAP; TAP

Western Civilization. Agostinho Neto. A reed mat on dark nights/enough for him to die on/thankfully/and of hunger. WhB

Western Emigration. David Humphreys. The seat of bliss, and last retreat of man. AnAmPo

Western Formula. *Anonymous.* And there's your sure-fire Western Thriller. PoOW

Western Lines. Walt Whitman. –I stand and look at the stars, which I think/now I never realized before. BPAW

Western Magic. Mary Austin. Of older things than fairy-folk will talk. AmFN

Western Movies. Jeffry Jensen. Just as the screening room door slams shut. AMV-80

The Western Rebel. *Anonymous.* Whilst our hands, hearts, and swords are all true to the crown. APAS

Western Star (excerpt). Stephen Vincent Benét. And every girl on Natchez bluff/Will cry as we go by-o! AmFN

Western Town. David Wadsworth Cannon, Jr.. One sun, one moon, and called it heaven. PoNe

Western Town. Karl Shapiro. Somewhere, a city will take the train apart. NYBP

The Western Trail. Robert V. Carr. In time the wound healed, but a scar was left–a long, white scar/across the prairie's breast. PoOW

Western Wagons. Rosemary and Stephen Vincent Benét. But we're going West tomorrow, with our fortune in our hands. BPAW

Western Ways. Richmond Lattimore. Sometimes in the great desert the Greeks imagined/Atlantis. AMV-80

Western Wind. *Anonymous.* Christ, if my love were in my arms/And I in my bed again! AnFE; AtBAP; BiP; BoLoP; CABA; CTC; DiPo; EBEV; EnLoPo; EnPo; ExPo; FaBoCh; FF; ForPo; GBL; GBP; HAP; HeIP; InPK; InPS; InvP; LiTL; LLLT; LoGBV; MAT; MeEL; NIP; NOBE; NoP; OAEL 1-2; OBSP; OBTV; OLR; PAI; PoEL 1-5; PPoe; PPP; SeCeV; TEP; UnPo; ViBoPo

Westgate-on-Sea. Sir John Betjeman. "Plimsolls, plimsolls in the summer,/Oh goloshes in the wet!" OxBoLi

Westland Row. Thomas Kinsella. Daughterwife, look upon me. NoAm

Westland Row. James Stephens. And such other grave affairs/As they thought of during prayers. HBMV

Westminster Drollery, 1671. Aphra Behn. Let's both to kiss begin;/To kiss freely: if not, you may go spin. SBG

A Westminster Wedding. *Anonymous.* Tom come tickle me once again CoMu

Westphalian Song. *Anonymous.* Say, I come to-morrow. AWP; LiTW; OBVE

Westward Ho. *Anonymous.* And I'll build a cot on a corner lot/And get rich as soon as I can. CoSo

Westward Ho! Joaquin Miller. Of bluff, bold men who dared and died/In foremost battle, quite aside. AA; FaBoBe

Westward on the High-Hilled Plains. Alfred Edward Housman. And the youth at morning shine/Makes the vow he will not keep. MCCG

A Wet August. Thomas Hardy. Were wrought more bright than brightest skies today. PPP

Wet Casements. John Ashbery. I shall not repeat others' comments about me. PoM

A Wet Night. Richard Ryan. Shores aglow under/Its receding inches. CIP

Wet or Fine. Amory Hare. Why could I think of nothing/But–"What darling eyes he has!" HBMV

A Wet Sheet. Allan Cunningham. While the hollow oak our palace is,/Our heritage the sea. BSV; EG; EtS; GoTF; GoTS; GTBS; GTBS-P; HBV 1-2; HBVY; MCCG; OBRV; PaPo; RoGo; TiPo; TreFS

Wet Summer. May Williams Ward. Blessed be water! GoYe

Wet Summer: Botanic Gardens. Nan McDonald. Seeing this season of the world's despair. BoAV

Wet Through. Hal Summers. ...even the sun/Seems washed, and with adored heat burns my back. HaMV

Wet Thursday. Weldon Kees. The cat sleeps like an old campaigner/ During this season of the long rains. NaP; NYBP

Wet Weather. Patricia Low. A sun, in this wash, would run and fade on the sky. VGW

The Wexford Girl. *Anonymous.* You'll hang like me, a murderer,/All on the gallows high. AmFP; ShS; ViBoFo

The Wexford Girl (I). *Anonymous.* But I will never marry you/Nor to you will I be tied! ShS

Wha Is Perfyte. Alexander Scott. And everilk grief is gane for evermair. GoTS

Wha Is That at My Bower-Door? Robert Burns. Indeed will I, quo' Findlay! ErPo; InvP; UnTE

Wha Lies Here? *Anonymous.* Ay, man, but a'm dead now. FiBHP

Whack Fol the Diddle. Peadar Kearney. Come and listen while we pray/ Whack fol the diddle lol the dido day. FiBHP; OnYI

Whaddaya Do for Action in This Place? George Starbuck. I too must worship blindly, Jonathan. NePoEA-2

Whalan of Waitin' a While. James William Gordon. And she doesn't mind Waitin' a While. PoAu 1-2

The Whale. *Anonymous.*
And for sea they bore away. AmSS
And have His bliss and blessedness for ever! AnOE
And locks drowning in the hall of death/Both ships and souls! EBEV
And that's the truth," said he. EtS

Whale. William Rose Benet. For the Lord said, "Let Whale Be!'/And there was Whale!" EtS; MoAmPo

The Whale. (Taniguchi Buso) Buson. up goes its tail! SoPo

The Whale and the Essex. A. M. Sullivan. Men are each other. The whale was Moby Dick... EtS

Whale at Twilight. Elizabeth Jane Coatsworth. tranquil as a fountain in a garden where no/wind blows. BoAnP

The Whale, His Bulwark. Derek Walcott. The tale apocryphal. OxBC; TTY

The Whale's Nature. *Anonymous.* Whoso fasteneth hope on him/Shall follow him to hell so dim. MeEV

Whale Song. Francis Maguire. PLEASE... BoAnP; PoL

Whalefeathers. Paul Violi. I'm not even moving my lips. APU

The Whaleman's Song. *Anonymous.* Nor sweeter they'll slumber the green sod beneath,/Than we in the boisterous wave! EtS

Whalen's Fate (George Whalen). *Anonymous.* The pride of many a father, likewise a mother's joy. ShS

The Whaler's Pig. Edwin James Brady. First whale, then pig, then man, some day/The worm will make it square. NOAV

Whaler's Rhyme. *Anonymous.* Sixteen thousand miles I've come,/To march along with a blanket drum. NOAV

Whales. Scott Bates. They would skip off lightly across the green water/ And soar without a sound BoAnP

The Whales off Wales. X. J. Kennedy. They move like melting mountains. OBCA

Whales Weep Not! D. H. Lawrence. and dense with happy blood, dark rainbow bliss in the sea. CMoP; MOS; NU; PPoe

Whan netilles in wynter bere rosis rede. *Anonymous.* Than put in a woman your trust and confidence. EnPo

Whan the Hert Is Laich. Sidney Goodsir Smith. That mock yir thrawan with their peace. NeBP

The Whango Tree. *Anonymous.* As he chirps, "I am blammed and corruptibly jammed,/In this cuggerdom whango tree. NA

The Wharf, May 1978. Carolyn Foster Segal. Our words/beat the air/like tarpaulins. WOLT

The Wharf of Dreams. Edwin Markham. And bales of fantasy from No-Man's Land. HBV 1-2

What? Langston Hughes. So what would you do? NLV; OBAL

What a Court Hath Old England. *Anonymous.* And we'll die in defense of the rights of the land./Derry down, down, down derry down. TrAS

What a Friend We Have in Cheeses! William Cole. So bring on a whole caboosley/Of the stuff of life! The cheeses of the gourmet! OBAL

What a Friend We Have in Jesus. Joseph Scriven. In his arms he'll take and shield thee,/Thou wilt find a solace there. FSW; TreFT

What a Friend We Have in Mother. Charles E. Roat. Love is always waiting there. FSW

What A Grand and Glorious Feeling. Bill Wolff. Peace on earth, peace on earth, peace on earth. FSW

What a Proud Dreamhorse. Edward Estlin Cummings. almost walk air). now who stops. Smiles.he/stamps. InvP; VGW

What about You? (parody). Edward Pygge. Thinking barbed thoughts in stanza form/after shafting's a right sweat. Time for a nap. BXAP; FaBoPa

What Am I? Abo Stoltzenberg. an ox/bound to God's yoke. VWA

What Am I, Life? John Masefield. ...this myriad I/Tingles, not knowing how, yet wondering why. ImOP

What Am I to Do With My Sister? Prince Yuhara. But not touch with my hands? AWP

What Am I Who Dare. William Habington. But who th' Almightie feare, deride/Pale death, and meete with triumph in the tombe. OxBoCh; TrPWD

What Are Outward Forms. Isaac Bickerstaffe. Virtues of more sovereign power/Than the garden's gayest pride. OnYI

What Are They Thinking... Bryan Guinness. To the sheep on the hills and the church and the steeple. OxBI

What Are We Playing At? Andree Chedid. and nearby–/the real collison. BoWoP

What Are Years? Marianne Moore. This is mortality,/this is eternity. AmP; AP; BLPL; CMoP; CoBMV; EaLo; ForPo; LiTA; MoAB; MoAmPo; MoPo; NoAm; NOBA; OxBA; TrGrPo

What Are You Doing for Jesus? Martha Snell Nicholson. What can you say? BePJ

What Are You Thinking About? James Macmillan. for they sped, first swallows,/and passed me by/to star the sky. PoSH

What Became of Them? *Anonymous.* But what befell them I never can tell,/For they never came back again. OBCA; OxBChV

What Bids Me Leave. Herbert Trench. And I must dream what taught our dreamless dead/To save Man, by a thread. HBMV

What Birds Were There. Brother Antoninus. Birthmarked that dawn! NoAm

What Black Elk Said. R. T. Smith. A song was singing me. LTB

What Bright Pushbutton? Samuel ("Paul Vesey") Allen. And reaches down/And calls His children home? PoNe

What Called Me to the Heights? Lawrence Pilkington. And resting there behold/Across unmeasured space/The Majesty of God? PoSH

What Can I Tell My Bones? Theodore Roethke. Unprayed-for,/And final. AmPP; NOBA

What Can the Matter Be? *Anonymous.* That tie up my bonny brown hair. OxNR

What Can You Expect. Maryam bint Abi. she walks like a captive/in fetters. WPOW

What Care I? *Anonymous.* For I'm my mother's bouncing girl. OxNR

What Changes, My Love. Edwin Honig. What stays me, my love,/is your hand dripping honey/out of my skinflint heart. PPJ

What Cheer? *Anonymous.* Be merry and glad this good New Year. SBVL

What Child Is This? William Chatterton Dix. The Babe, the Son of Mary. FSW

What Christ Is to Us. *Anonymous.* The Best of All to find–is Jesus! BLRP

What Color Is Lonely. Carolyn M. Rodgers. Tell me sister,/What color is lonely? BPo

What Constitutes a State? William, Sir Jones. These constitute a State... BLPA; MCCG; PGD

What Could Be. John Gill. we leap again and again and again. NeAC

What Could Be Lovelier Than to Hear. Elizabeth Jane Coatsworth. And hear the thunder cross the sky/With elephant tread. BrR; SiSoSe

What Could It Be? William Cole. I really do not like that cat! BoAnP

What Counsel Has the Hooded Moon. James Joyce. No more be tears in moon or mist/For thee, sweet sentimentalist. MOON; OnYI; OxBI

What Curious Dresses All Men Wear. Delmore Schwartz. Hide private parts which I disclose/To those who know what a poem knows. ELU

What death is worse than this." Sir Thomas Wyatt. A deadly life in woe? FCP; SiPS

What Did I Dream? Robert Graves. The finest entertainment known,/And given rag-cheap? DuDa

What Dim Arcadian Pastures. Alice Corbin. And under your hair the faun's eyes/Look out on me? HBMV

What Do I Care. Sara Teasdale. It is my heart that makes my songs, not I. VGW

What Do I Care for Morning. Helene Johnson. What do I care for dawn! CDC

What Do I Know? Christopher John Brennan. and stars begotten on their night. BoAV

What Do They Say. Gary Snyder. a garden full of weeds. NNaP

What Do We Plant? Henry Abbey. We plant all these when we plant the tree. HBV 1-2; HBVY; OHIP; PGD; TiPo; WBLP

What Do You Do when It's Spring? John Woods. What do you do when you're born? ConAP

What Do You Say When a Man Tells You, You Have the Softest Skin. Mary Mackey. I'm still fishing for my body. FF

What Do You Want? John Newlove. I want a lover/who suffers indignities. NOBC

What Does a Man Think About. John Holmes. Like speaking of his love too little, or of love too much. CrMA

What Does Easter Mean to You? May Ricker Conrad. Dear friend, of Easter when it means all this. PGD

What Does It Mean to Be American? Roselle Mercier Montgomery. A worthy daughter, or a noble son... MC

What Does Little Birdie Say? Alfred, Lord Tennyson. Baby too shall fly away. HBV 1-2; HBVY

What Does the Bee Do? Christina Georgina Rossetti. Eat up the honey. OxBChV; SUS; TiPo

What Does This Mean. Sir Thomas Wyatt. What menys thys? EnPo; MeEL

What Dreamed I? *Anonymous.* Since for my truth she needeth no witness. CBEP

What Fair Pomp Have I Spied of Glittering Ladies. Thomas Campion. Come, we'll associate this jolly pilgrimage! AtBAP; GBL; PoEL 1-5; Prf

What Far Kingdom. Arthur Stanley Bourinot. To what far kingdom have they gone/The men whose dust we walk upon? CaP

What Fifty Said. Robert Frost. I go to school to youth to learn the future. NAs

What Finer Hills? J. K. Annand. Or fail to satisfy the urge/To hansel their untrodden snaw. PoSH

What Five Books Would You Pick To Be Marooned with... Paris Leary. the deaf and mute may feel where I have failed. CoPo

What Folks Are Made Of. *Anonymous.* And that's what old men are made of. ABF; GoTF; TreF

What For. Garrett Kaoru Hongo. and chant him a blessing, a sutra. MAYP

What Form or Shape to Describe? Kabir. I offer myself to a being/based/on nothing. ILwL

What Form the World Has. William Bronk. and never see it, believing the form were there. AMV-80

What Frenzy Has of Late Possess'd the Brain! Sir Samuel Garth. Though few can write, yet fewer can refrain. NLV

What Glorious Vision. Thomas Cradock. And scorn to fix thy views on aught beside. AH

What God Has Promised. Annie Johnson Flint. Unfailing sympathy,/Undying Love. BLRP; STF; TRV; WBLP

What Good Poems Are For. Tom Wayman. in a small container/on the ledge where the light enters. NoP

What Grandma Knew. Edward Field. She was glad to be alone. CoPo; Psk

What Guardian Counsels? Auzias March. My soul awaits–imprisoned here on earth. CAW

What Guile Is This. Edmund Spenser. Fondness it were for any being free,/To covet fetters, though they golden be. ForPo; LiTL

What Habacuck Once Spake, Mine Eyes. Roger Williams. And eate up those which now a while/Their fierce devourers be. SCAP

What Happened? John Wieners. Better not lock it/up again. PoM

What Happened Here before. Gary Snyder. Bluejay screeches from a pine. NNaP; PoM

What Happens. June Jordan. ...children leave the greatest/show on earth/and see the circus? BPo

What Happiness Can Equal Mine. John David. I lie secure in Jesus' arms. AH

What Harvest Half So Sweet Is. Thomas Campion. That which kind and harmless is,/None can deny us. EG; PBBP; UnTE

What Has Happened. Charles Angoff. ...the sturdy indifference of whatever/there is that rules us all? AMV-81

What Hath Man Wrought Exclamation Point. Morris Bishop. Exclamation line of dots close quote. NYBP

What, Have I Thus Betrayed My Liberty? Sir Philip Sidney. Unkind, I love you not! O me, that eye/Doth make my heart give to my tongue the lie! NIP

What Have They Done to the Rain. Malvina Reynolds. What have they done to the rain? FSW

What Have We Done Today? Nixon Waterman. Yet, this is the thing our souls must ask,/What have we done today? WBLP

What He Saw. Robert Currie. Even when he looks away/he sees his uncle's body fall Str

What He Took. *Anonymous.* He took her father's silver spoons,/And after that he took his leave. CoMu

What Helps It If of Love I Sing. Hadewijch. Love bridled me so forcefully/What good is now my reining in? PBWP

What Her Girl-Friend Said to Her. Okkur Macatti. with young archers driving by his side. BoWoP; PBWP

What hundred books are best. John Kendrick Bangs. "I hardly know–I've only written ten." CenHV

What I Did Last Summer. Ron Ikan. to warn the Crow who rode with Custer I had taken sides. AMV-80

What I Expected. Stephen Spender. Like the created poem,/Or faceted crystal. CoBMV; MoAB; MoBrPo; MoPo; NoAm; NOBE; OAEP

What I Have. Susan North. all the does had twins; have you found something better? AMV-81

What I Have Done. Gerard Malanga. I want to re-set the slab in its/proper place but cannot scrape/off my name. FAZ

What I Have Written I Have Written. Peter Porter. What I have written I have written. NOAV

What I Live For. George Linnaeus Banks. And the good that I can do. BLPA; FaBoBe; GoTF; TreFS

What I'm Doing Here. Leonard Cohen. I wait/for each one of you to confess. PeCV

What I Saw in October. Warren Carrier. perhaps a building, and whatever is holy. PoDr

What I Saw Passages 3. Robert Duncan. time/vertical to the horizon NoAm; NOBA

What I See in Me. *Anonymous.* Let each "I" look at "Me." STF

What I Tell Him. Simon J. Ortiz. Tht's what I tell him. CDW

What I Think of Hiawatha (parody). J. W. Morris. Honour paid to Mudjekeewis,/But no honour to the muse. Par; SpRo

What If a Day. Thomas Campion. Secret fates guide our states,/Both in mirth and mourning. AAS; BiP; EBEV; ElL; EnRePo; PrIm

What If a Much of a Which of a Wind. Edward Estlin Cummings. the most who die, the more we live. AP; BLPL; FaFP; LiTA; LiTM; MasP; MoAMpo; MoPo; MoVE; NePA; NoP; OxBA; PoA; PoRA; PPP; SoSe; ViBoPo; WaP

What If Jealousy... Miriam Palmer. ...Our laughs are/belts of Indian bells as we walk. NMM

What If the Saint Must Die. John Peck. The angels join, and all combine/To spread their anthems round. AH

What inn is this. Emily Dickinson. Who are these below? MasP; NePA

What Invisible Rat. Jean-J. Rebearivelo. The rat will have dragged it into his hole. TTY

What Is. Edward Estlin Cummings. CriesWhichAreWings. MOS

What Is a Jewish Poem? Myra Sklarew. little Jewish poem/come sing to me. VWA

What Is a Sonnet? Edward Watkins. And you should ask, I'd say "It's just a sonnet." AMV-80

What Is an Epigram? Samuel Taylor Coleridge. Its body brevity, and wit its soul. HBV 1-2; NIP; PV

What Is Being Forgotten. Eloise Klein Healy. ...That every shirt needed/ironing is being forgotten. GP

What Is Black? Mary Devenport O'Neill. If they couldn't lean against/Black.... NTCP

What Is Charm? Louisa Carroll Thomas. And rules alike the cottage and the throne. BLPA

What Is Good. John Boyle O'Reilly. "Each heart holds the secret;/Kindness is the word." GoTF; HBV 1-2; HBVY; PoToHe; TreF; WBLP

What Is It? Marie Louise Allen. And–hop, he goes! TiPo

What Is Left? Assata Shakur. What is left? AMV-80

What Is Left? Istvan Vas. And their bodies' gold...their bodies' gold... VWA

What is Life? Samuel Taylor Coleridge. A war-embrace of wrestling life and death? ERoP 1-2; FiP

What Is Liquid. Margaret Cavendish, Duchess of Newcastle. But 'tis the wet that makes it die, no doubt. FaBoUs

What Is Lived. Carmen Valle. You are my eternal guests. InW

What Is Love? John Clare. It centres, Mary, still with thee. NCEP

What Is Needed. Marcos Rodriguez Frese. as in Che. And so forth. InW

What Is Our Life? Sir Walter Ralegh. And then we die, in earnest, not in jest. EBEV; EnRePo; ForPo; MePo; NIP; OBSP; SiPS

What Is–"Paradise". Emily Dickinson. Maybe–"Eden" a'nt so lonesome/As New England used to be! CMoP; DiPo

What Is Pink? Christina Georgina Rossetti. Just an orange! GoJo; OnUR; OxBChV; SUS; TiPo

What Is Poetry. John Ashbery. It might give us–what?–some flowers soon? LCAP

What Is Poetry. James Scully. but if you don't know/shut up, we'll understand FYAP

What Is Prayer? James Montgomery. Lord! teach us how to pray! BLRP; STF; TRV; WGRP

What Is't to Us? Charles Churchill. No tribute's laid on Castles in the Air. SeCePo

What Is Terrible. Roy Fuller. It must be for them and changed by them all. WaP

What Is That in Thine Hand? Eva Gray. We see His will and work well done/Yoked with our impotence. STF

What Is That Music High in the Air? A.J.M. Smith. Unlaurelled, unlamented, vain. NMP

What Is the Case in Point? Abraham Reisen. Waiting for the life to come.... VWA

What Is the Opposite of a Prince? Richard Wilbur. He always ends up green and sad/And sitting on a lily pad. WSC

What Is the Rhyme for Porringer? *Anonymous.* And gave the Prince of Orange her. OxNR

What Is the Use? (excerpt). Erastus Wolcott Ellsworth. Let us not use them ill. AA

What Is the World? John Dryden. No Atoms casually together hurl'd/Could e'er produce so beautiful a world. TRV

What Is There. Marvin Bell. until we accept what is written there. GP

What Is This Why? *Anonymous.* Why, why, what is this why/But virtus verbi Domini? OxBM

What Is to Come. William Ernest Henley. And we can conquer, though we may not share/In the rich quiet of the after-glow/What is to come. HBV 1-2; TreFT

What Is Truth? (excerpt). James Harold Manning. Revenge and pride shall spur them? CaP

What Is Veal? *Anonymous.* Its mother was a cow. FaBoUs

What Is White? Thomas Macdonagh. The Voice of Youth/Singing before her throne. CAW

What Is Winter? Edmund Charles Blunden. And death is no more dead than this/Flower-haunted haze. ChMP

What Is Young Passion. Hartley Coleridge. For morn nor eve can change that fiery gloom/That glares within the spirit's living tomb. NCEP

What It Means, Living in the City. William Dickey. camping with quick hands. PoL

What It Was. Robert Sward. In her window, in her sky. CoPo

What Jenner Said on Hearing in Elysium That Complaints Had Been Made.. Shirley Brooks. And now you grudge a spot to me. EyDe; FaBoEE

What Kin' O Pants Does the Gambler Wear (with music). *Anonymous.* I'll be blamed ef I can see/How all my money got away from me./For sometime. AS

What Kind of a Guy Was He? Howard Nemerov. You can say that again, he'd say it again. PCP

What Kind of Mistress He Would Have. Robert Herrick. Be she such as neither will/Famish me, nor over-fill. CaPo; TrGrPo; UnTE

What Kind of War? Larry Rottman. and you cheer inside? PoL

What'll Be the Title? Justin Richardson. I guess I'd settle/For somewhere ethical and practical like Bootle. FiBHP

What'll We Do with the Baby-O? *Anonymous.* That's what we'll do with the baby-o. FSW

What Maisie Know She Don't Want No/Anger Game at Shinkolobwe. Judith Johnson Sherwin. ...don't shake/your shinkolobwe at me NoAm

What Makes a Happy Life. Martial (Marcus Valerius Martialis). Wish not for death, and fear it not. AWP

What Makes a Home? *Anonymous.* And a few plain household treasures are. PoToHe

What Makes a Nation Great. Alexander Blackburn. Be God's delight–man's best estate. WBLP

What Matter? *Anonymous.* What matter if the Congress ignores us? WTO

What Meanest Thou, My Fortune. *Anonymous.* To love did first apply. EnLoPo

What Music. Joy Harjo. You sweat in the winter in the north,/and you are afraid,/sweetheart. TWSS

What Must I Do to Be Saved? *Anonymous* Stand "in HIm," in Him alone,/Gloriously "complete!" STF

What Must (iii). Archibald MacLeish. The green cove below the light. MoLP

What My Child Learns of the Sea. Audre Lorde. I stand already condemned. NBP; PoBA

What My Lover Said. Homer Greene. As they fell from the lips of my lover. AA; HBV 1-2; TreFS

What Mystery Pervades a Well! Emily Dickinson. That those who know her, know her less/The nearer her they get. MAmP

What Nedeth These Thretning Wordes and Wasted Wynde?" Serafino. Let us se nowe, if th'one be wourth th'othre. OBVE

What Need Have I for Memory? Georgia Douglas Johnson. Winding the trail regret? CDC

What need I travel, since I may. John Hall. That who would travel here might know/The little world in folio. EG

What Needeth All This Travail. *Anonymous.* Or either Indies, East or West, do send us. EIL

What News. Walter Savage Landor. And tears are longer ere they dry. BoLoP

What No Man Knoweth. Hugh Francis Blunt. O Jesu, Jesu, will it be/That Thou wilt turn away from me? CAW

What of the Darkness? Richard Le Gallienne. What of the Darkness? Is it very fair? HBV 1-2

What Once I Was. Sir Thomas Wyatt. In your remembrance let it lie/That ons I was. EnPo; MeEL

What One May and May Not Call a Woman. *Anonymous.* You may call her a vision, but you must not call her a sight. GoTF; TreF

What Pablo Picasso Did in "Les Demoiselles d'Avignon'. John Robert Colombo. this way he settled us into a savagery PeCV

What Price. Lulu Minerva Schultz. But O the lure of chancing winds/Outriding rain! GoYe

What Profit? Immanuel Di Roma. ...which I shall forget on the/day of my death for the long sleep/within my tomb? TrJP

What rage Is this? Sir Thomas Wyatt. So wrathful love with spites of just disdain/May threat thy cruel heart. AAS; EnLoPo; FCP; SiPS

What Riches Have You. George Santayana. I walk contented to the peopled grave. HBV 1-2; TrGrPo

What Riddle Asked the Sphinx. Archibald MacLeish. What riddle is it has for answer, Man? IIoPM

What Rider Spurs Him from the Darkening East? Edna St. Vincent Millay. Listen; it has a faint voice even so. TrCP

"What? Rise Again with All One's Bones." Samuel Taylor Coleridge. To go without my rib. HBV 1-2

What Robin Told. George Cooper. That's what Robin told me. TiPo

What's Going to Happen to the Tots? Noel Coward. What's, what's, what's going to happen to the tots? NLV

What's Good for the Soul Is Good for Sales. Richard Wilbur. All hangs together if you take it hard. NLV

What's Hard. Laurence Lerner. Because I love you, and I know you're right. NePoEA-2

What's in a Name? Helen F. More. He was Revere and I was Dawes. PAH

What's in a Name? Richard Kendall Munkittrick. "They little think my real name's/V. Stuyvesant De Vere!" InMe

What's In It For Me? Edgar A. Guest. That money was all he had ever earned. PoToHe

What's in the Cupboard. *Anonymous.* And away they all flew. GBP; OxNR

What's in There? *Anonymous.* High, high up in the air. CH; OxNR

What's Living? Linda Hogan. struggling to death and birth. AMV-81

What's My Thought Like? Thomas Moore. In one weak, washy, everlasting flood! CBEP; FaBoEE; OBRV

What's That Smell in the Kitchen? Marge Piercy. Burning dinner is not incompetence but war. NLV

What's the Life of a Man? *Anonymous.* Like the green life it did wither and down it did fall. OBET

What's the News? *Anonymous.* They say the balloon/Is gone up to the moon. OxNR

What's the Plural? *Anonymous.* The plural's what one damn well pleases. FaBoUs

What's the Railroad. Henry David Thoreau. It sets the sand a-blowing,/And the blackberries a-growing. ELU; MAmP; PoEL 1-5; TAP

What's the Use. Ogden Nash. Have you seen yourself retreating? PoPl

What's This of Death. Edna St.Vincent Millay. Make known him Master, and for what good reason. BoLiVe

What's worse than this past century? Anna Akhmatova. ravens crying out, ravens flying in. BoWoP

What's Wrong, Little Blonde. *Anonymous.* I go for the blonde, and the brune I pass by. OuSiCo

What's Your Fancy. *Anonymous.* And kiss with two guineas, and all's your own. UnTE

What's Your Name? *Anonymous.* What's your number?/Cucumber. FaBoNo

What Sanguine Beast? LeRoy Smith, Jr. Dreamt as a prelude to realities.) NePoAm

What Schoolmasters Say. Martin Seymour-Smith. ...Head up, and watch for talking: we're not/Expected to pray!' OxBTC

What Secret Desires of the Blood. Nelly Sachs. Colossal the star of death/Standing like the clock of the times. VWA

What Semiramis Said. Vachel Lindsay. To-morrow night 'tis full again,/Golden, and foaming red. MAPA; MOON

What Shall I Give? Edward ("Edward Eastaway") Thomas. Wanting a thousand little things/That time without contentment brings. FaBoCh; LoGBV; OxBChV

What Shall I Give My Children? Gwendolyn Brooks. ...my little halves who bear/Across an autumn freezing everywhere. BPo

What Shall It Profit? William Dean Howells. What do I gain by that I have undone? AA

What Shall We Do with a Drunken Sailor? *Anonymous.* Way, hey, and up she rises,/Early in the morning. FSW

What Shall We Render. *Anonymous.* In Jesus we receive the best we have. BLRP

What Shame Forbids to Speak. Robert Herrick. The rest I'll speak, when we meet both in bed. UnTE

What She Said. Maturai Eruttalan Centamputan. my forehead was mistaken for the moon./But now BoLoP

What She Said. Okkur Macatti. He left me and went in search/of wealth. PBWP

What She Said to Her Girl-Friend. Venmanipputi. What shall I make of this? PBWP

What She Wanted. Ronald Koertge. "Look at yourself," she said,/"You're disgusting." GP

What She Wished. Marilyn Throne. under brand new stars toward home. AMV-81

What Shines in Winter Burns. T. R. Hummer. ...Touch me. This is the body. I know. MAYP

What Ship Is This? Samuel Hauser. 'Tis the old ship of Zion, hallelujah. AH

What Should I Say. Sir Thomas Wyatt. Farewell, unkissed! EnRePo; FCP; GBL; NoP; SiPS

What soft–cherubic creatures. Emily Dickinson. Redemption–Brittle Lady– /Be so–ashamed of Thee– AnNE; HAP; MoAB; MoAmPo; PPON; SoSe

What Splendid Rays. Christian Gregor. Fixed in him may I abide,/Kept from ever turning. AH

What, Still Alive. Hugh Kingsmill. Lads whose job is still to do/Shall whet their knives, and think of you. BXAP; DBV; FaBoCo; InPK; NLV; SpRo

What Sugred Termes, What All-Perswading Arte. Richard Lynche. Love looketh faire, but Lovers are accurst. AAS

"What tears, dear prince, can serve to water all." Sir Walter Ralegh. The world would die that thou shouldst be no more. FCP

What the Animals Said. Peter Serchuk. Let us bury her alongside all other lovers. HoAn

What the Birds Said. John Greenleaf Whittier. And in the evening there was light. NOBA

What the Bones Know. Carolyn Kizer. I do not waste my breath. NePoAm-2

What the Bullet Sang. Bret (Francis Bret Harte) Harte. O sweetheart! waht is this/Lieth there so cold? AA; CBEP; OBEV; OBVV; PeD

What the Chairman Told Tom. Basil Bunting. Go and find work. OxBTC

What the Choir Sang about the New Bonnet. M.T. Morrison. Will never get a blessing from sermons or from prayers. BLPA

What the Devil Said. James Stephens. Satan's deep voice–O thou unhappy God! CMoP

What the Donkey Saw. U. A. Fanthorpe. I could see the baby and I/ Would be going places together. OBCP

What the Earth Asked Me. James Wright. No good to me, no good to me. NYBP

What the Engines Said. Bret (Francis Bret Harte) Harte. Spoken slightly through the nose,/With a whistle at the close. BPAW

What the Gray Cat Sings. Arthur Guiterman. Thr-ree thr-reads in the thr-rum,/Pr-rrum! MoShBr

What the King Has. Ethel Romig Fuller. Once to live,/Once to die. PoToHe

What the Light Was Like. Amy Clampitt. ...this year we haven't/seen the hummingbird. FaBoWP

What the Lord High Chamberlain Said. Virginia Woodward Cloud. And the cockatoo's head went under its wing. BBGG

What the Moon Saw. Vachel Lindsay. Next day, the deadlock broke. CrMA; FaBoEE; OBSP

What the Motorcycle Said. Mona Van Duyn. Am, the world's my smilebutton. NIP

What the Old Man Said. C. Fox Smith. But–don't you take no sail off 'er," said the Ol' Man,/said 'e. EtS

What the Orderly Dog Saw. Ford Madox Ford. And you,/Sitting in the firelight. CTC

What the Prince of I Dreamt. Henry Cholmondeley-Pennell. I s'pose no man before or since/Dreamt such a funny thing? NA

What the Red-haired Bo'sun Said. Charles H. Souter. As the red-haired bo'sun said. PoAu 1-2

What the Rooster Does before Mounting. Cyn. Zarco. carrots bell pepper onions APU; BrSi

What the Serpent Said to Adam. Archibald MacLeish. Now two are one and one is you:–/Which one? Which one? NePA

What the Sixties Were Really Like. Sam Abrams. they'll have something to think about. APU

What the Sonnet Is. Eugene Lee Hamilton. The dark deep emerald that Rossetti wrought/For his own soul, to wear for ever more. HoPM; OBVV

What the Stone Dreams. James B. Hathaway. imagining that I was one of those peaceful stones. GOYP

What the Thrush Said. John Keats. And he's awake who thinks himself asleep. DiPo; EBEV; NIP

What the Toys Are Thinking. ffrida Wolfe. Well, next time you're passing through/You'll remember what to do. TiPo

What the Violins Sing in Their Baconfat Bed. Jean Arp. and on his left foot jumps over his right ear WeW

What Then? Anonymous. And we stand up before Him–what/then? STF

What Then? William Butler Yeats. But louder sang that ghost, "What then?" CMoP

What Then, Dancer? Kay Smith. when you stop pirouetting on the gilded lawn,/what then, dancer? CaP

What Then Is Love But Mourning. Thomas Campion. Come away, come away, my darling. EnRePo

What There Is. Kenneth Patchen. O there's love all day LLLT

What They Are For. Dorothy Aldis. Puddles are to plop. SoPo

What They Do to You in Distant Places. Marvin Bell. Perhaps she's with you now. Psk

What Thing Is Love. George Peele. Since Mars and she played even and odd. ElL; ELP; EnRePo; NOBE; OAEP; SeCePo; UnTE

What Thomas an Buile Said in a Pub. James Stephens. And stayed His hand. MoAB; MoBrPo; TrGrPo

What Thou Lovest Well, Remains American. Richard Hugo. you are welcome in the secret club they have formed. GP; NIP; NPAW

What Though the Dark! Archie Edwards. Ours is to watch, with a living faith in Him–the victorious One! BePJ

What though the Green Leaf Grow? Maybury Fleming. What though the red leaf fall? AA

What Tidings? John Audelay. That Lord us grant now our prayere,/To dwel in heven that we may.' OxBM

What to Do. William Wise. When the sun is out. TiPo

What to Say to the Pasha. George Hitchcock. I surrender myself OBAL

What Trinkets? Thomas Hornsby Ferril. Flicker in the embers on the hill. NePoAm-2

What Triumph Moves on the Billows So Blue? Matthew Gregory Lewis. Low sinks the sun–and all is gone! OBTV

What Ulysses Said to Circe on the Beach of Aeaea. Irving Layton. Should you want, O lovely and divine Circe,/Another erection. ErPo

What Vaileth Trouth? Sir Thomas Wyatt. What vaileth trouth? AAS; FCP

What Voice at Moth-Hour. Robert Penn Warren. ...and as I/Once heard, hear the voice: It's late! Come home. SM

What Was a Cure for Love? Thomas Godfrey. And death were ease to lay their ashes there. AnAmPo

What Was My Dream? Joseph O'Connor. Love's sigh its harginber? What was/my dream? AA

What Was Solomon's Mind? Geoffrey Scott. Quivering, quiet, dumb,/ Drinks up the lighted room. OBMV

What Was Your Dream, Doctor Murricombe? Osbert Sitwell. For one day/You'll die! AtBAP

What Was Your Name in The States? (with music). Anonymous. Say, what was your name in the States? AS

What We Can. Ray A. Young Bear. feeling everything that/we are it's not enough. VoR

What We Listened for in Music. Gray Burr. Then we knew that earth to earth had called. HW

What We May Live Without. Owen Meredith. But where is the man that can live without dining? GoTF; TreF

What We Said. W. D. Snodgrass. Surely. That's what we said. GP

What We See Is What We Think. Wallace Stevens. Since what we think is never what we see. SyP

What Were They Like? Denise Levertov. It is silent now. HeIP; NIP; OBWP; PPON; VGW

What Wild Dawns There Were. Denise Levertov. We have not spoken of these tired/risings of the sun. NOBA

What Will Remain after Me? Mendel Naigreshel. A sunbeam/flickering at twilight/on a wall in a courtyard. VWA

What Will We Do for Linen? Anonymous. And we'll wear his skin for linen,/Says the Shan Van Vocht. GBP

What Will You Do, Love? Samuel Lover. That's what I'd do! OnYI

What Will You Learn about the Brobinyak. John Ciardi. In the Land of the Pshah of Psham. EvOK

What Winter Floods, What Showers of Spring. Emily Bronte. It comes at last to cancel time,/And waken unavailing tears. NOBV

What Women Are Not. Anonymous. For, God wot, ther hartes wold be wo/To spende ther husbondes money so. MeEL

What Would I Do White? June Jordan. I would do nothing./That would be enough. NMM

What Would I Do without This World Faceless Incurious. Samuel Beckett. among the voices voiceless/that throng my hiddenness NoAm; NOBI

What Would I Give? Christina Georgina Rossetti. To wash the stain ingrain and to make me clean again. OBSP

What Would You Fight For? D. H. Lawrence. And I must say, I am often worsted. OBSP

What Wourde Is That That Chaungeth Not. Sir Thomas Wyatt. It is my helth eke and my sore. AAS

What Yo' Gwine to Do When Yo' Lamp Burn Down? Anonymous. What yo' gwine to do when yo' lamp burn down. BoAN 1-2; BPo

What You Goin' to Do When the Rent Comes 'Round? Andrew B. Sterling. Guess that's sifficient, "Good-night." OBAL

What You Need. Kathleen Fraser. You are brave. But you need to be touched. AmPA

What You See Is Me. Barbara Gibbs. Right then we'd be in heaven. NYBP

What You Should Know to Be a Poet. Gary Snyder. real danger. gambles. and the edge of death. NNaP; PoM

What Zimmer Would Be. Paul Zimmer. Fix and fix, you're all better. Psk

Whate'er You Dream with Doubt Possest. Arthur Hugh Clough. The wind it blows, the ship it goes,/Though where and whither, no one/knows. OAEP

Whatever Comes. William Stafford. ...all over fashionable people,/comes the wide gray, forgiving rain. NPAW

Whatever Is–Is Best. Ella Wheeler Wilcox. Whatever is–is best. BLPA; GoTF; PoToHe; TreFS

Whatever Is, Is Right. Frank Gaik. ...Nothing/is perfect in the world. AMV-81

Whatever It Was I Was Saving for My Old Age. Ann Darr. ...and what I seem to have saved for my/old age is science fiction. SUW

Whatever You Say Say Nothing. Seamus Heaney. We hug our little destiny again. OBWP; OxBC

Whatsoever I Do. Mary Louise Hector. ...with eagerly, utterly offering heart/All things whatsoever I do. GoBC

Whaup o' the Rede: The Blades of Harden. Will H. Ogilvie. "There will be moonlight again!" GoTS

Wheat Metropolis. Alfred Starr Hamilton. On a nickel or a dime/Or hitchhiking or nonetheless FAZ

Wheatlet Son of Milklet. MacConglinne. His halter and his traces all/Of fresh butter. OnYI

The Wheel. Wendell Berry. ...and timeless/is the wheel that brings it round. GeTw

The Wheel. James Cole. Bottles, rags, gelignite. FAZ

The Wheel. Robert Earl Hayden. and curse the moon and fear the rising of the sun. BPo

The Wheel. Edwin Muir. And take/From that which made us that which will make us again. NoAm

The Wheel. Rene Sully-Prudhomme. With a speed which even thou didst not discover! ImOP

The Wheel. William Butler Yeats. nor know that what disturbs our blood/Is but its longing for the tomb. GTBS-P; MoVE

The Wheel Change. Bertolt Brecht. Why am I watching the wheel change/With impatience? ELU

Wheel of Fortune. Anonymous. Eleven, nine, seven, five, three and one. FSW

The Wheel of Fortune. Thom Gunn. And Lambert Simnel stirs the under-footman's porridge. OxBC

The Wheel Revolves. Kenneth Rexroth. All this will never be again. NoAm

Wheel Turning on the Hub of the Sun. William Pitt Root. I found myself alone. MAYP

The Wheelbarrow. Russell Edson. ...then turning they/drift out like heavy clouds into the meadow. LCAP

Wheelbarrow. Eleanor Farjeon. Down he stumbled! down she tumbled!/Right at the Parson's feet! FiBHP

The Wheelchair Butterfly. James Tate. Beware the Warden of Light has married/an old piece of string! NoAm

Wheeler at Santiago. James Lindsay Gordon. As, wan and white, to the heart of the fight/rode little old Fighting Joe! PAH

Wheeler's Brigade at Santiago. Wallace Rice. Kept time to the tune of "Dixie." MC; PAH

Wheels. Dorothy Donnelly. ...distant/cousin to the floating traffic of uncrowded stars. HoAn

Wheesht, Wheesht. Hugh" (Christopher Murray Grieve) MacDiarmid. Wheesht, wheesht, ye fule! BSV; ELU; ErPo; HAP; InPK

When. Susan (Sarah Chauncey Woolsey) Coolidge. Thou canst not come too soon; and I can wait/If Thou come late. HBV 1-2

When. Hitomaro. It gives me the impression of meeting/An unknown old gentleman. AWP

When. George William ("A.E.") Russell. Breathe a gay goodnight. ATP; OnYI

When a Beau Goes In. Gavin Ewart. It's just a Beau going in. OBWP; OxBTC; WaP

When a Body. Gene Dawson. in a luminous sea of sense. AMV-80

When a Feller's Itchin' to Be Spanked. Paul Laurence Dunbar. W'en a feller's itchin' to be spanked. BALP

When a Fellow's Four. Mary Jane Carr. And we both play I'm only three. BiCB

When a Girl Looks Down. Kay Smith. Gathers me nearer to be born. OBCV

When a Goose Meets a Moose. Zhenya Gay. I wonder if all three/Sit down and drink tea. TiPo

When a Man Has Married a Wife. William Blake. Her Knees and elbows are only/glued together. ErPo; FF

When a Man Hath No Freedom to Fight for at Home. George Gordon, Lord Byron. And, if not shot or hanged, you'll get knighted. EnRP; NIP; NLV; PoLf; PPoe; TrGrPd

When a Man Turns Homeward. Daniel Whitehead Hicky. Leaving the world like a kitten outside! PoToHe

When a People Reach the Top of a Hill. Stephen Crane. These new battalions/–The blue battalions–. AmePo

When a Ring's Around the Moon. Mary Jane Carr. And you will hear the music/Of the wee folks' dancing tune. BrR; TiPo

When a Twister, A-Twisting, Will Twist Him a Twist. John Wallis. The twine that untwisteth, untwisteth the twist. FaBoNo; OxNR

When a Warlock Dies. Isabella Gardner. ...a surfing shout of love,/and blasts of flowers. NePA

When a Woman Blue (with music). Anonymous. And dat'll pacify my min.' AS

When Adam Day by Day. Alfred Edward Housman. The more I think of this/The more I beat my wife. ELU; FiBHP; PoPl

When Adam Delved. Anonymous. Who was then a gentleman? SaC

When Adam Was Created. Anonymous. As is the solemn duty of every man and wife. TrAS

When Adam Was First Created. Anonymous. His happiness was not completed/Until that a helpmate was found. OBET

When Alexander Our King Was Dead. Anonymous. That is stade in perplexite. GoTS

When Alexander Pope. Edmund Clerihew Bentley. Never mind what he said. FiBHP

When All Is Done. Paul Laurence Dunbar. I greet the dawn and not a setting sun,/When all is done. TRV

When All My Five and Country Senses See. Dylan Thomas. The heart is sensual, though five eyes break. MoAB; MoBrPo; NoAm; PoA; SeCePo

When All of Tem Ran Off. John Hollander. we /finally contrived to/move/into the chilling,/sad, September night. AmPC

When All the Young Were Dying. Edmund Wilson. What doubt, what draining of the spirit's blood,/Were ended where you lay. AnAmPo

When All This All Doth Pass from Age to Age. Fulke, Lord Brooke Greville. To do me harm, content to do amiss? EBEV

When All Thy Mercies. Joseph Addison. Thine arm unseen convey'd me safe/And led me up to man. OxBoCh

When Almonds Bloom. Millicent Washburn Shinn. When almond buds unclose,/Who doubts of May's red rose? AA

When Any Mortal. Edward Estlin Cummings. ...mortals can/not justify the ways of God to man PoPl

When as a Lad. Isabel Ecclestone Mackay. Those thoughts too fleet/For any save the soul's swift feet! HBV 1-2

When as I Do Record. Anonymous. I would drink a whole carrouse/That Jenny were here again. EBEV

When at Night. Mark M. Perlberg. The wind blew away his name. AMV-80

When Aurelia First I Courted. Anonymous. Only kind and am'rous Spirits,/Kindle and maintain a flame. OBS

When Banners Are Waving. Anonymous. They were smote, they were fallen,/And had melted for ever. GN; HBV 1-2

When before those eyes, my life and light. Gaspara Stampa. ...one beauty alone,/can give me life and deprive me of wits. BoWoP

When Billy the Kid Rides Again. Squire Omar Barker. Look! Billy the Kid comes a-galloping down! BPAW

When Black People Are. A. B. Spellman. back & forth between us like/borrowed breath. BPo; CNA; PoBA

When Both My Fathers Die. Robert Gillespie. the white blossoms of the apple trees/wet to knee high. FAZ

When Boys Go A-Courting. Anonymous. How happy this young man keeps bachelor hall./Larey-wo, wo, larey wo. TrAS

When Brothers Forget. Jill Witherspoon Boyer. like mama leaning out the window/calling her children home CNA

When Cats Run Home. Alfred, Lord Tennyson. The white owl in the belfry sits. CH

When Charlie Bowdre Married Manuela. Michael Ondaatje. until I get used to it./HAWHAWHAW PoL

When Christ Was Born of Mary Free. Anonymous. Where we may sing to thy solace:/In excelsis gloria. MeEV

When Daddy Died. Duane Ackerson. seemed almost a personal loss. PoL

When Damon First Began to Love. Aphra Behn. To yield what all his sighs could never do. . UnTE

When Dawn Comes to the City: New York. Claude McKay. There I would be at dawn. GoSl

When de Co'n Pone's Hot. Paul Laurence Dunbar. An' de co'n pone's hot. BANP

When de Good Lord Sets You Free. Anonymous. When de good Lord sets you free. ABF

When de Saints Go Ma'chin' Home. Sterling A. Brown. Or to his dances in old Tinbridge flat. AmNP

When De Whale Get Strike. Anonymous. No more, no more green land for you. OuSiCo

When, Dearest, I but Think of Thee. Sir John Suckling. Which flows not every day, but ever! HBV 1-2; JCP; OBEV

When Death Came April Twelve 1945. Carl Sandburg. Commander, sweet good night. AP

When Death Comes. *Anonymous.* And of alle ben lot that her thee were ilewe.' MeEL

When Death to Either Shall Come. Robert Bridges. Or read to thyself alone/The songs that I made for thee. HBV 1-2; OBEV; PoPl

When Dey 'Listed Colored Soldiers. Paul Laurence Dunbar. W'en dey 'listed colo'ed sojers an' my 'Lias went to wah. BPo

When Diamonds, Nibbling in my Ears. William Henry Davies. What joy to see those diamonds burn/Their own clear space to dance and turn! BrPo

When Did the World Begin. Robert Clairmont. And I copied all the answers too,/A quack, a honk, an oink, a moo. GrPl

When Doctrines Meet with General Approbation. David Garrick. It is not heresy, but reformation. HBV 1-2

When Doris Danced. Richard Eberhart. Doris lay down, all out of pity. CMoP

When Dutchy Plays the Mouth Harp. Robert V. Carr. When Dutchy plays th' mouth harp,/In a way to beat th' band. PoOW

When Each Bright Star Is Clouded. Jeremiah Joseph Callanan. How welcome will the last blast be that lays me low. IrPN

When Eve upon the First of Men. Thomas Moore. That Adam was not Adam-ant! HBV 1-2

When Evening Comes. Yakamochi. To meet me in my dreams. AWP

When Faces Called Flowers. Edward Estlin Cummings. (all the mountains are dancing are dancing) BoNaP; PrIm

When Father Came Home for Lunch. Jim Mitsui. soaking his long-sleeved workshirt. BrSi

When Father Carves the Duck. Ernest Vincent Wright. He couldn't carve a duck. FaBV

When Father Slept. James Anderson. where one by one they became/the promises he made us. AMV-80

When First. Edward ("Edward Eastaway") Thomas. ...and louder the heart's dance/At parting than at meeting be. NoAm

When First Mine Eyes Did View and Mark. Sir Thomas Wyatt. I would my heart had been as thine,/Or else thy heart had been as mine. FCP; SiPS

When First to This Country a Stranger I Came. *Anonymous.* With my coat of many colors, like Jacob's of old. FSW; OuSiCo

When Fishes Set Umbrellas Up. Christina Georgina Rossetti. Lizards will want their parasols/To shade them from the sun. FM

When Flora Had O'erfret the Firth. *Anonymous.* –Quhom I luve I dare nocht assay!' NoP; OBEV

When Fog Come Creepin' over Beccles (parody). Molly Fitton. The wife'll drop 'un mighty soon. BXAP

When from the Calyx-Canopy of Night. Freda Laughton. Across their shadowy forests into sleep. NeIP

When Geometric Diagrams... Novalis (George Friedrich Philipp von Hardenerg). Then our entire twisted nature will turn/And run when a single secret word is spoken. NU

When God Descends with Men to Dwell. Hosea Ballou I. To dwell with men on earth again. AH

When God First Said. Natan Zach. But they were multitudes. VWA

When God Lets My Body Be. Edward Estlin Cummings. With the bulge and nuzzle of the sea MoAB; MoAmPo; NOBA

When Green Buds Hang. Alfred Edward Housman. Are lying about the world. ACV

When he sailed into the harbor. Korinna. while the wind like a nightingale/sang with its whirling war axe. BoWoP

When He Spoke to Me of Love. M. A. Mokhomo. And my tongue, unstrung, confessed to him. PeSA

When He Thought Himself Contemned. Thomas Howell. Now hate returns no news, O heart, now die! EiL

When He Who Adores Thee. Thomas Moore. But the next dearest blessing that Heaven can give/Is the pride of thus dying for thee. HoPM; OBRV

When He Would Have His Verses Read. Robert Herrick. Let rigid Cato read these lines of mine. CaPo; EnL; NOBE; OAEP; OBS; SeCV 1-2

When Heaven Would Strive to Do the Best She Can. Michael Drayton. When she a Poet to the world doth send. LO

When Helen First Saw Wrinkles in Her Face. Walter Savage Landor. Well, and what matters it...while you are too! EnLoPo

When Helen Lived. William Butler Yeats. A word and a jest. CMoP; ViBoPo

When Howitzers Began. Hayden Carruth. ...spreading/a darker darkness/over the river. Psk

When I Admire the Greatness. Jacob Steendam. We pray they may be in/Every heart enthroned. AH

When I am Big, I Mean to Buy. Mary Mapes Dodge. And sit up late whenever I choose. BiCB

When I Am Dead. *Anonymous.* And flowers, I want flowers on my coffin/While my burial is carried on. OxBoLi

When I Am Dead. Hugh Barrie. And I shall see the sunset and anon/Shall know the velvet kindness of the night/And see the stars. PoSH

When I Am Dead. Georgia Douglas Johnson. O, it would grieve me utterly, to find me on my bier! CDC

When I Am Dead. George Macbeth. This is my will. OxBTC

When I Am Dead. John G. Neihardt. I will be lightning if you dare forget! HBMV

When I Am Dead. Albert Stillman. I'll get no notions in my head/Beginning with: "When I am dead." InMe

When I Am Dead. James Edward Wilson. A mound of earth and naught beside,/There let me lie. PoLf

When I Am Dead and Sister to the Dust. Elsa Barker. And faring out for regions unexplored,/Went singing down the River of the Dead. HBV 1-2

When I am grown to man's estate. Robert Louis Stevenson. Not to meddle with my toys. CenHV

When I Am Not With You. Sara Teasdale. There is nothing/To comfort me but you. MoLP

When I Am Old. Caroline Atherton Briggs Mason. By God's sweet peace—when I am old. BLPA

When I Awoke. Raymond Richard Patterson. I have to see,/I said. NNP; PoBA

When I Buy Pictures. Marianne Moore. it must acknowledge the spiritual forces which have made it. EyDe; OxBA

When I Came from Colchis. William Stanley Merwin. What fable should I tell them,/That they should believe me? AP; NePoEA; VGW

When I Came to Israel. Bert Meyers. proudly, under the lights/of Jerusalem. AMV-80; VWA

When I Came to London. Rachael Castelete. And I cannot even buy a little bottle/of wine or raki. VWA

When I Consider. Margaret Griffith. And I, too, am in danger, sir. AMV-80

When I Cut My Hair. Rayna Green. I touched center/and forgave myself TWSS

When I Die. Fenton Johnson. And the moonbeams thousand strong/Past my grave each night shall file. CDC; PoNe

When I Die. Brenda G. Macrow. And I may move again/with the great tides of cloud and wind/that cover me. PoSH

When I First Came to This Land. *Anonymous* Son...my work's done. FSW

When I Get Time. Tom (Thomas Lansing Masson) Masson. I've no more time. BLPA; FPL

When I Grow Up. Rupert Sargent Holland. I don't see why grown people stay/At home when they could be away. BiCB

When I Grow Up. William Wise. I think I'll be all of them/By taking turns. BiCB

When I Had Need of Him. S.E. Kiser. My faith in God was sure and strong/When I had need of Him. BLRP

When I have gone away. Sugawara Michizane. don't forget to bloom each spring! LiTW

When I Have Gone Weird Ways. John G. Neihardt. And Oh, how oft with new life shalt thou lift/Out of the atom-drift! HBV 1-2

When I Hear Your Name. Gloria Fuertes. God will sentence me to repeating it endlessly and forever. AMV-81

When I Heard at the Close of the Day. Walt Whitman. And his arm lay lightly around my breast-and that night I/was happy. AP; GBL; NePA; OxBA

When I Heard Dat White Man Say. Zack Gilbert. An' you better believe it. PoBA

When I Heard the Learn'd Astronomer. Walt Whitman. Look'd up in perfect silence at the stars. AmePo; BoLiVe; DiPo; FF; FPL; GoTF; HAP; HeIP; InPK; LoGBV; MCCG; MoAmPo; NoP; OxBA; SoSe; SUW; TAP; TreFT; TrGrPo; TRV; WHA

When I Held You to My Chest, You Fit. Jack Myers. When I see the big view, you see/how it hides its thousand hearts. AmPA

When I Loved Thee. Thomas Stanley. Any thy despis'd disdain too late shall find/That none are fair but who are kind. LiTL

When I Loved You. Thomas Moore. And oh! 'tis delicious to hate you! ALV; HBV 1-2

When I Loved You. Charles A. Wagner. And trees are brown/And they are trees. InMe

When I'm Going Well. Ronald G. Everson. A girl walking by along the platform/explodes the whole Glen area. PeCV

When I Peruse the Conquer'd Fame. Walt Whitman. –I hastily walk away fill'd with the/bitterest envy. ELU; MCCG; PoEL 1-5

When I Read Shakespeare–. D. H. Lawrence. Yet the language so lovely! like the dyes from gas-tar. NoAm

When I Saw You Last, Rose. Henry Austin Dobson. How fast the time goes! HBV 1-2

When I See Another's Pain. Mani Leib. Like the tree apples, from me/I cast my songs around. TrJP

When I See Old Men. Raymond Souster. And the cries echoing around the hoarse arena. CaP

When I See on Rood. *Anonymous.* If I of love can. OBSP

When I See the Earth Ornate and Lovely. Veronica Gambara. nor can such happy fate be given us/as will make death pity us. PBWP

When I Set out for Lyonnesse. Thomas Hardy. When I came back from Lyonnesse/With magic in my eyes! BrPo; InPS; MoBrPo; PAI; SeCePo; VLP

When I Solidly Do Ponder. Francis Daniel Pastorius. Vagrants, Fugitives and Rogues,/That deserve the Stocks and Strokes. SCAP

When I strip. Anne-Marie Kegels. I think of you/restless,/journeying. BoWoP

When I Think of the Hungry People. O-Shi-O. I am ashamed of my fortune in the presence of God. TRV

When I Thy Parts Run O'er. Robert Herrick. There's still more cause why I the more should love. UnTE

When I Vexed You. Robert Browning. Crushed eggs whence snakes could crawl! OBSP

When I Want to Speak. Rav Abraham I. Kook. And seeds of light/Fill the world, my whole being. VWA

When I Was a Bachelor. Anonymous. Down came wheelbarrow,/Little wife and all. HBV 1-2

When I Was a Brave Cowboy. Anonymous. We're the brave cowboys on the western trail. CoSo

When I Was a Cowboy. Anonymous. Coma-cow-cow, coma-cow-cow, yicky-yicky-yee. ABF

When I was a good and quick little girl. Anonymous. What is the good of grieving/if nobody will listen/oh heart! BoWoP

When I Was a Lad. Anonymous. And I got an egg that day for my tay. OxNR

When I Was a Little Boy. Anonymous. And I can kiss a bonny girl/At twelve o'clock at night. OxNR

When I Was a Little Girl. Alice Milligan. God, if they prayed to Him,/Would give fine weather. OnYI; OxBI

When I Was a Young Maid. Anonymous. Catch him who you can! AmFP

When I Was Conceived. Michael Ryan. arm in arm, without saying anything. MAYP

When I Was Dying. William Hathaway. ...What did/I care, bobbing off in dark/blue sea, under light blue sky? APU

When I Was Fair and Young. Queen of England, Elizabeth I. Importune me no more!' BoLoP; CBEP; CTC; EnLi 1-2; NIP; NoP; PoRA

When I Was Growing Up. David Vogel. Then we shall turn to the evening,/We two on our own,/To rest. VWA

When I Was Lost. Dorothy Aldis. And hollow./and Alone. SoPo

When I Was Nine. Raymond F. Roseliep. No garlic wreath can catch me,/nor your cold, cold cross. FAZ

When I Was Otherwise Than Now I Am. Anonymous. A toy by fitts to play withall at leasure. NCEP

When I Was Single. Anonymous.
And I wish I was single again. ABF
I'll go with him wherever he goes. FSW

When I Was Six. Zora Cross. For all the world belonged to me/When I was six years old. BiCB; HBVY

When I Was Small. Andre Marie de Chenier. "O wasted kisses! O too happy child!" ErPo

When I Was Still a Child. Lesbia Harford. All my life I'll learn/How to love as long. NOAV

When I Was Well into Being Savored. Joanne Kyger. ...Oh Lord, the possible/bells ringing, to bring me out of here. PoM

When I Was Young and Foolish (with music). Anonymous. "There goes another girlie,/That's being led astray." AS

When I Was Young I Tried to Sing. Donald Finkel. the mares drinking it in drinking it in. GP

When I went into my garden. Sister Bertken. His love is sweetest breath,/beyond all things on earth. BoWoP

When I Went Off to Prospect. Anonymous. And whiskey bills at me they poke–but I'll make it right in the morning! AmFP

When I Went out. Karla Kuskin. And where the rain and river met/The water got completely wet. NTCP

When I Went to the Circus. D. H. Lawrence. in the bright wild circus flesh. CMoP; LiTB; NoAm

When I Would Image. George Meredith. My soul basks on for hours. NOBV

When in My Arms. Alexander Pushkin. Their tears, their late regrets I curse. ErPo

When in Rome. Mari E. Evans. I'm tired of eatin'/what they eats in Rome...). AmNP; SoSe

When in the Chronicle. William Shakespeare. Have eyes to wonder, but lack tongues to praise. BoLiVe

When in the Crowd I Suddenly Behold. Robert Nathan. Dwindle to silence like the sound of birds. MoLP

When in the Woods I Wander All Alone. Edward Hovell-Thurlow. I with the deer, and with the nightingale! HBV 1-2; HBVY

When Indians Heare That Some There Are. Roger Williams. Or men have mixt with Beasts and so,/Brought forth that monstrous Race. SCAP

When Israel out of Egypt Came. Alfred Edward Housman. To my inheritance amid/The nation that is not. LiTB

When Israel Was In Egypt's Land. Anonymous. Tell ole Pharoh,/Let my people go. AH

When It Burns before the Harps and Freezes behind the Easels. Hans Arp. a wowl is the ultimate substance. FaBoNo

When It Rains. H. A. Maxson. certainly as apples, around me. AMV-80

When Jacky's a Very Good Boy. Mother Goose. He shall have nothing but mustard. BrR; EvOK

When Jesus Wept. William Billings. When Jesus groan'd, a trembling fear/Seiz'd all ye guilty world a round. TrAS

When Johnny Comes Marching Home. Patrick Sarsfield (Louis Lambert) Gilmore. When Johnny comes marching home. BLSo; FSW; PAH; PAL; PoSC; PSoN; TrAS; TreF

When Klopstock England Defied. William Blake. What might he not do if he sat down to write OAEL 1-2

When Lads Have Done (parody). Humbert Wolfe. the hangman mutters: "Plenty/even for Housman's verse." BXAP; Par; SpRo

When Land Is Gone and Money Spent. Anonymous. Then learning is most excellent. OxNR

When Last Seen. Hortense Flexner. A nice little star, but not very bright. QQQ

When Let By Rain. Edward Taylor. Burns up the building: Lord forbid the same. MAmP

When Life Is Quite Through With. Edward Estlin Cummings. lies her head/by oaks and roses/deliberated.) CrMA

When, Like a Running Grave. Dylan Thomas. Happy Cadaver's hunger as you take/The kissproof world. OAEL 1-2

When London Calls. Victor J. Daley. Death in her heart! CBAP

When Love Comes Knocking. William Henry Gardner. And vow 't was sweet to wait. AA

When Love Meets Love. Thomas Edward Brown. O, where is all our love? OBVV; PeD; UnPo

When Lovely Woman. Phoebe Cary. Whether a husband or a lover,/If he have a feeling is–to cry. ALV; FaBoBe; GoTF; HBV 1-2; TreFS

When Lovely Woman Stoops to Folly (parody). Mary Demetriadis. The evening can be awfully jolly. FaBoPa

When Mahalia Sings. Quandra Prettyman. He finds no worship alien or odd. IDB; PoBA

When Malindy Sings. Paul Laurence Dunbar. Sof' an' sweet, "Swing Low, Sweet Chariot,"/Ez Malindy sings. MCCG; PoBA; PoNe

When Mary Goes Walking. Patrick Reginald Chalmers. To make her a carpet,/To make her a crown. HBVY

When Men Shall Find. Samuel Daniel. Thou may'st repent that thou hast scorned my tears,/When Winter snows upon thy golden hairs. LiTL

When Molly Smiles. Anonymous. A good fat goose shall thank you well. HBV 1-2

When Moonlike Ore the Hazure Seas. William Makepeace Thackeray. Dost thou remember Jeames? InMe; NA

When My Beloved Appears. Ibn al-Arabi. In my knowing Him, I create Him. ILwL

When My Beloved Sleeping Lies. Irene Rutherford McLeod. I take his head upon my breast,/And hold my dearest till he wakes. HBV 1-2

When My Blood Runs Chilly and Col'. Anonymous. Oh, do, Lord, remember me. ABF

When My Brothers Come Home. Aires de A. Santos. DON'T WAIT, MOTHER/THEY ARE COMING, SWIFTLY... WhB

When My Dog Died. Freya Littledale. and then I cried/and made his collar wet. NTCP

When My Grandmother Died. Sam Cornish. lost/inside/the/house. Psk

When My Love Becomes. Ono no Komachi. Night dark as leopard-flower. PBWP

When My Love Was Away. Robert Bridges. If thou wert longer away. BrPo

When My Ship Comes In. Robert Jones Burdette. When my ship comes in. FaFP

When My Uncle Willie Saw. Carol [(or Carole[) Freeman. i seen uncle willie cry some. NMM

When Nature Hath Betrayed the Heart That Loved Her. Sophie Jewett. I cannot bear the still grief of the sky. AA

When night is almost done. Emily Dickinson. For that old faded midnight/That frightened but an hour. TRV

When Nobody Prays. Merl A. Clapper. "Nobody prays for me." STF

When None Shall Rail. David Lewis. That day (for come it will) that day/Shall I lament to see. CBEP; OBEC

When Oats Were Reaped. Thomas Hardy. Nor a bill of any bird; and no response accorded she. OxBTC

When Ol' Sis' Judy Pray. James Edwin Campbell. When ol' Sis' Judy pray.... BANP

When 'omer Smote 'is Bloomin' Lyre. Rudyard Kipling. An' 'e winked back–the same as us! Par

When One or Other Rambles. Francis Daniel Pastorius. Short Follies are the best. SCAP

When Orpheus Went Down. Samuel Lisle. Such merit had music in hell. ALV

When Other Lips and Other Hearts. Alfred Bunn. In such a moment I but ask/That you'll remember me. TreF

When Our Earthly Sun Is Setting. Edwin H. Nevin. Oh! 'tis glorious,/To know we'll meet again. AH

When (parody). Philip Appleman. they'll call you/a minor poet. BXAP

When Poor Mary Came Wandering Home (with music). Anonymous. And the wind blew across the wild moor. AS

"When reckless youth in an unquiet breast." Henry Howard, Earl of Surrey. Had not David, the perfect warrior, taught/That of my fault thus pardon should be sought. FCP

When Sadness Fills a Journey. John Waller. When limbs and charm and favour/Are warm but worn away. NeBP

When Santa Claus Comes. Anonymous. For it brings the time nearer when Santa Claus comes. ChBR

When Satan Fell. D. H. Lawrence. And hell and heaven are the scales of the balance of life/which swing against each other. MoRP

When Senses Fled. John Woods. To name the kneeling animals. CoPo

When Serpents Bargain for the Right to Squirm. Edward Estlin Cummings. then we'll believe in that incredible/unanimal mankind(and not until) MP; PrIm; SoSe; TwCP

When Shall My Pilgrimage, Jesus My Saviour, Be Ended? Andrew Rudman. Join in their anthems immortal. AH

When Shall We All Meet Again? Anonymous. Where immortal spirits reign,/There may we all meet again. AH

When Shall We See Thy Like Again? Mary Wingate. When shall we see thy like again? PGD

When She a Maiden Slim. Maurice Hewlett. ...made her heart rejoice/That she was almoner. OHIP

When She Comes Home. James Whitcomb Riley. Again is hidden in the old embrace. AA; BLPL; FaBoBe; HBV 1-2

When Silence Divests Me. Henry Birnbaum. ...more like clouds/than those which farmers see. GoYe

When Sir Beelzebub. Edith Sitwell. Took them in charge while Beelzebub roared for his rum./...None of them come! FaBoMo

When Slavery Seems Sweet. Ed Bullins. singing/daddy/daddy/daddy NBP

When Smoke Stood Up from Ludlow. Alfred Edward Housman. And that will be the best. EnLit; MoBrPo

When Something Happens. James A. Randall, Jr. who are, with the Indians,/the first Americans. BPo

When Spring Came. Anonymous. Making love to everything/Before it moves on/Yet returning. RFM

When Spring Comes Back to England. Alfred Noyes. And tell the heart of England/The Spring is here again! HBV 1-2

When Stars Are Shrouded. I. T. They do it bind/In cloudy errors. EiL

When Statesmen Gravely Say "We Must Be Realistic." W. H. Auden. Their generals are already poring over maps. FaBoCo; PV

When Structure Fails Rhyme Attempts to Come to the Rescue. William Carlos Williams. by far all pace and every/refuge of his dreams. PP

When Sue Wears Red. Langston Hughes. Sweet silver trumpets,/Jesus! CNA; GoSl; TTY

When Summer's End Is Nighing. Alfred Edward Housman. And then the heart replies. MoVE

When Sun Came to Riverwoman. Leslie Marmon Silko. for rainsmell on pale blue winds/from China VoR

When Sun Doth Rise. Roger Williams. Who gives these stars their names/More bright ten thousand fold. AH

When that I call unto my mind. Sir Thomas Wyatt. I ask but right for my redress. FCP

When the Ambulance Came. Robert Morgan. when he slammed the spattered door/on her seventy years/of staying home. Str

When the Angels Are Exhausted. Yona Wallach. and wound them/until dew floods the earth. VWA

When the Assault Was Intended to the City. John Milton. To save the Athenian walls from ruin bare. GTBS; GTBS-P; NoP; RoGo

When the Bells Justle in the Tower. Alfred Edward Housman. Then on my tongue the taste is sour/Of all I ever did. NOBV

When the Christ Child Came. Frederic Edward Weatherly. "The Christ Child hath been here." OHIP

When the Clouds Are upon the Hills. Anonymous. They'll come down by the mills. OxNR

When the Cows Come down to Drink. Allen Hoey. ...The planet spins/and tips these acres further into night. WOLT

When the Curtains of Night Are Pinned Back (with music). Anonymous. I remember you,/Love,/In my prayers. AS

When the Dawn Comes. Anonymous. How sad the helping each other to put on/our clothes! AWP

When the Day. Thomas Sessler. grinds up/flaming graves/and gives birth/to ashes. VWA

When the Days Grow Long. Hayim Nahman Bialik. Has no one heard the sound of his horn? TrJP; VWA

When the Dead Men Die. Rose O'Neill. And kings may call in vain for strength/When the dead men die. HBMV

When the Dew Is on the Grass. Anonymous. Rain will never come to pass. OxNR

When the Dews Are Earliest Falling. Arthur Hugh Clough. I return, return, return. OAEP

When the Drive Goes Down. Douglas Malloch. There's logs to run, there's peavy fun/To break the timber loose! AmFN

When the Dumb Speak. Robert Bly. And the dumb shall speak. CAPP; NoAm; NOBA

When the Eye of Day Is Shut. Alfred Edward Housman. Lie you must, and not with me. NOBV; OAEL 1-2

When the Fairies. Edward Dorn. guessing what color and raiment. NeAP; TAT

When the fifth month comes. Lady Ise. It is now I long to hear you,/before the summer begins. BoWoP

When the Five Prominent Poets. Josephine Jacobsen. ...and not a sound/came from the savage carpet. TAP

When the Frost Is on the Punkin. James Whitcomb Riley. When the frost is on the punkin and the fodder's in the shock! AmePo; BoNaP; FaBoBe; FaBV; FaFP; FPL; HBV 1-2; HBVY; MCCG; OBAL; PoLf; TreF

When the God Returns. Russell Edson. They must obey... GP

When the Great Gray Ships Come in. Guy Wetmore Carryl. Thank God for peace! Thank God for peace, when/the great gray ships come in! AA; EtS; FaBoBe; HBV 1-2; MC; PAH

When the Green Lies over the Earth. Angelina Weld Grimke. Yours is the face, my dear. CDC; PoNe

When the Hounds of Spring. Algernon Charles Swinburne. The wolf that follows, the fawn that flies. FaBoBe; LiTB; PrIm; TreF

When the Iceworms Nest Again. Robert W. Service. We'll be married when the iceworms nest again. FSW

When the King Enjoys His Own Again. Martin Parker. That the king enjoys his own again. FaBoCh; OxBoLi

When the Kye Comes Hame. James Hogg. 'Tween the gloamin' and the mirk,/When the kye comes hame! HBV 1-2; OxBS

When the Lamp Is Shattered. Percy Bysshe Shelley. When leaves fall and cold winds come. BoLiVe; CBEP; FiP; MCCG; OBRV; PG; PPP; TEP; TreFT; TrGrPo; ViBoPo; WHA

When the Last Riders. Natan Zach. The gate must be closed, logic tells me. At night/the dark is darkest. VWA

When the Light Falls. Stanley Jasspon Kunitz. Whose ceremonial art/Is dying into light. MoAmPo

When the Loneliness of the Tomb Went down into the Marketplace. Mona Sa'udi. I take on shapes like water. WPOW

When the Mint Is in the Liquor. Clarence Ousley. And lingered at the julep in the ever-brimming glass. PoLf

When the Mississippi Flowed in Indiana. Vachel Lindsay. The cave by the Mississippi/Where Tom and Becky strayed. CMoP

When the Most Is Said. Mary Ainge De Vere. While death waits on either side,–before/and behind us, Death! AA; HBV 1-2

When the Nightingale Sings. Anonymous.
I wile mone my song/On whom that it is on y-long. EnLit; OxBM
So much I think upon thee, that I wax all green. CBEP

When the Orient Is Lit by the Great Light. Vittoria da Colonna. ...the door is opened/to sleep which brings me to my sun. WPOW

When the Rain Raineth. Anonymous. Little wotteth the Gosling/What the Goose thinketh. GBP

When the Ripe Fruit Falls. D. H. Lawrence. silky with oil of distilled experience. CMoP

When the Roll Is Called up Yonder. James M. Black. And the roll is called up yonder, I'll be there. TreFT

When the Saints Come Marching In. Audre Lorde. I only know she will be terrible/and very busy/and very old. NYP

When the Saints Come Marching In. Edward C. Redding. When the saints come marching in. BLSo; EaLo; FSW

When the Seed of Thy Word Is Cast. Cotton Mather. With fruits of thy good spirit filled,/More than a hundred-fold. AH

When the Sleepy Man Comes. Sir Charles G. D. Roberts. (So hush-a-by, weary my Dearie!) HBV 1-2; HBVY

When the spent day begins to frail. Edward Estlin Cummings. buttons his coat against the wind ErPo

When the Storms Come. Lupenga Mphande. I am the blank between the colors/the interspace between tongues/the one who foresees the end. WhB

When the Sultan Goes to Ispahan. Thomas Bailey Aldrich. Has gone to the city Ispahan. AA; BeLS; FaBoBe; HBV 1-2

When the Sword of Sixty Comes Nigh His Head. Firdausi. think of that only when they think of me. 'NAs; OBVE

When the Tree Bares. Conrad Aiken. Move slowly, turn, return, and bring once more/Your lights and music. It will be good to talk. MoAmPo

When the Troubled Sea Swells and Surrounds. Vittoria da Colonna. Jesus, live rock, so that whenever I wish/I can return to port. PBWP

When the Turf Is Thy Tower. Anonymous. Can all the world's bliss/Save thee from this? MeEV; SeCePo

When the Vacation Is Over for Good. Mark Strand. We are dying. NYBP

When the War Is Over. William Stanley Merwin. And we will all enlist again. OBSP

When the Wind Blows. Anonymous. Then the mill stops. OxNR

When the Wind Is in the East. Anonymous. Then 'tis at the very best. OxNR

When the Wine Was Gone. Alvin Aubert. ...break, brother,/sister, and die. CNA

When the Work's All Done This Fall. Anonymous. And he'll not see his mother/When the work is done this fall. AS; BFSS; BPAW; CoSo; FSW

When the World Ends. Mark Van Doren. This indolent, this all but evermore/October such as never came before. GoYe

When the World is Burning. Ebenezer Jones. Crocus in the shade. ACV; OBEV; OBVV; PoPle; VLP

When the World Was in Building. Ford Madox Ford. The trout will be rising.... CTC

When There Is Music. David Morton. When in this hush of strings you draw more near/Than any sound of music that I hear. HBMV

When There Is Peace. Henry Austin Dobson. And, like men waking from a spell,/Grow stronger, nobler, than before,/When there is Peace. PAH

When There Were Trees. Nancy Willard. and I can remember when there were trees. HoAn

When These Old Barns Lost Their Inhabitants.... David Kherdian. They wish again to be a/falling tree TAT

When They Found Giotto. Allan M. Laing. to see Nell Gwynn beckoned/by Charles the Second. FiBHP

When They Grow Old. Nathan Ralph. They are teased/By fear/And snickering death. CaP

When They Have Lost. C. Day-Lewis. To warm men's hearts again and light the land. EnLit; MoAB; MoBrPo

When Thickly Beat the Storms of Life. Gurdon Robins. The shelter of th' eternal Rock. AH

When Things Go Wrong. Anonymous. Just find something good to do. STF

When Things Go Wrong with You. Anonymous. Well, it hurts me too. FSW

When This Carnival Finally Closes. Jack A. Mapanje. What did he think he would become, a God? The devil! WhB

When This Cruel War Is Over. Anonymous. How we love the starry banner,/The emblem of the free! AmFP

When This Old Hat Was New. Anonymous. It was not so when Bess did reign and this old hat was new. OBET

When This Tide Ebbs. Verna Loveday Harden. The gold of dreams we fashioned long ago. CaP

When Thou Didst Think I Did Not Love. Ayton [(or Aytoun)] Sir Robert. Men do not so. EiL

When Thou Must Home. Thomas Campion. Then tell, O tell, how thou didst murder me. AWP; InPo; LoBV; OBSP; SeCeV; ViBoPo

When through the Whirl of Wheels. G. A. Studdert Kennedy. Sweeping the shavings from his work-shop floor. EBCP

When Thy Heart with Joy O'erflowing. Theodore Chickering Williams. When thy heart enfolds a brother,/God is there. AH

When Thy King Is a Boy (excerpt). Ed Roberson. ...you/been home been home PoBA

When to Her Lute Corinna Sings. Thomas Campion. But if she doth of sorrow speak,/E'en from my heart the strings do break. AAS; AtBAP; CABA; EnLi 1-2; ExPo; NoP; OAEL 1-2; SeCeV

When To My Deadlie Pleasure. Sir Philip Sidney. All what I am, it is you. AtBAP; EnLoPo; PoEL 1-5

When to My Serene Body. Freda Laughton. Along belly and thigh and breast,/Sinks in its long caress. NeIP

When Two Are Parted. Heinrich Heine. The tears, the sighs, the anguish/Came later–and to me. AWP

When Two Suns Do Appear. Sir Philip Sidney. Hurt not the face which nothing can amend. EnRePo; MOON; SiPS

When Was It That the Particles Became. Wallace Stevens. The total of human shadows bright as glass. PoA

When We Are Like Two Drunken Suns. Yvonne Caroutch. ...marriage/of the river's dark soul/with our endless thirst LLLT

When We Are Parted. Hamilton Aïdé. At thy heart's door I stand and beat,/Though we are parted. HBV 1-2

When We Court and Kiss. Thomas Campion. She never will say "No!" UnTE

When We Drive at Night. Katha Pollitt. of small black shadows on roads/that trail off into the back country and are lost. AmC

When We Hear the Eye Open... Bob Kaufman. The sun burns at love's two ends,/On the eternal launching pad. CNA

When We in Kind Embracements Had Agre'd. Anonymous. But now (old man) flye on, as swift as thought,/Sith eyes from love and hope from heart is wrought. AAS

When We Looked Back. William Stafford. ...And the camp we left/was a little spot in the trees when we looked back. NYBP

When We That Now Ha' Childern Wer Childern. William Barnes. An' leave our litty childern's tooes/To leap an' run in play. NOBV

When We Two Parted. George Gordon,Lord Byron. How should I greet thee?–/With silence and tears. AnFE; BoLiVe; BoLoP; CBEP; DiPo; FiP; ForPo; FPL; GTBS; GTBS-P; HBV 1-2; HoPM; LiTL; LoBV; NOBE; NoP; OAEP; OBEV; OBNC; OBRV; OLR; PG; PoLf; TreFS; TrGrPo; ViBoPo; WHA

When We Were Very Silly. J. B. Morton.
Christopher Robin/Has/Fallen/Down-Stairs. FaBoPa
That many people nowadays/Like hugaboo/To read. FaBoPa
You little/Prig,/You/ARE! FaBoPa

When West Comes East. Corey Ford. For I can never collect my self-respect/When I use a revolving door. InMe

When What Hugs Stopping Earth Than Silent Is. Edward Estlin Cummings. only one snowflake(and we speak our names PoA

When Wild Confusion Wrecks the Air. Mather Byles. All hallelujah on my tongue,/All rapture in my heart. AH

When Will He Come? Anonymous. And feel no alarm at His coming,/But hasten His heralds to greet. STF

When Will Love Come? Pakenham Beatty. Will it be summer when we meet,/Or autumn ere you come? HBV 1-2

When Wilt Thou Save the People? Ebenezer Elliott. From vice, oppression, and despair,/God, save the people! BLPA; EaLo

When Wilt Thou Teach the People—? D. H. Lawrence. God of justice, when wilt thou teach them to save themselves? OBSV

When Windsor Walles Sustain'd My Wearied Arme. Henry Howard, Earl of Surrey. And I have bent to throwe me downe withall. AAS; EnPo; FCP; SiPS

When Winds Are Raging. Harriet Beecher Stowe. And in the secret of thy presence dwelleth/Fullness of joy, for ever and for ever. AH

When Winds That Move Not Its Calm Surface Sweep. Moschus. Moves the calm spirit, but disturbs it not. OBVE

When Winter Fringes Every Bough. Henry David Thoreau. Resounds the rare domestic sound/Along the forest path. MAmP

When Yon Full Moon. William Henry Davies. Raves in his windy heights above a cloud. MoBrPo; MOON

When You and I Must Part. Anonymous. I'd set my foot on some fine ship/And sail the ocean around. AmFP

When You and I Were Young, Maggie. James, and George W. Johnson Butterfield. But to me you're as fair as you were, Maggie,/When you and I were young. BLSo; FSW; PSoN; TreF

When You Are Gone. Nance Van Winckel. airing the closet and/drawers of love. AMV-81

When You Are Old. William Butler Yeats. And hid his face amid a crowd of stars. AWP; BoLiVe; BoLoP; CMoP; CTC; DiPo; FaBV; FaFP; FPL; GBL; GoJo; GoTF; GTBS; HBV 1-2; HeIP; InvP; LiTL; LiTM; MoAB; MoBrPo; MoLP; NAWM 1-2; NoAm; NOBV; NoP; OBEV; OBVV; OxBTC; PCP; PoLf; PoPl; PP; PrIm; TEP; TreFS

When You Go Away. William Stanley Merwin. Like the tucked sleeve of a one-armed boy. LCAP

When You Have Forgotten Sunday: The Love Story. Gwendolyn Brooks. You have forgotten me well. BPo; FF; WPOW

When You Laugh. Ingrid Jonker. so I can hear how pomegranates laugh. WPOW

When You Leave. Kimiko Hahn. and she, the one who opened the color forever. BrSi

When you Love, or speak of it. Aphra Behn. 'Tis by wanton play and sport/Heedless Virgins you will gain. BoWoP

When You're Away. Samuel Hoffenstein. I feel the same when you are near. FiBHP; PoL

When You Reach the Hilltop the Sky Is on Top of You. Etta Blum. contain my heart's/merry-making. GoYe

When You See Millions of the Mouthless Dead. Charles Hamilton Sorley. Great death has made all his for evermore. MMM; OBWP

When You Send Out Invitations, Don't Ask Me. Palladas. and, for some fine piece to goggle at, forego/all hope of eating, if the hallmarks show. OBVE

When You Speak to Me. Tess Gallagher. they fall apart. LTB

When You Touch. William Hart-Smith. and hand on heart/is hand on every heart. BoAV

When You've Been Here Long Enough. Lawrence Joseph. as the doors open and no one comes on. HoAn

When You Were Sweet Sixteen. James Cooper and George Thornton. When you were sweet sixteen. FSW

When You Will Walk in the Field. Leah Goldberg. And in purity once again be meek,/and submissive,/As is a blade of grass, as is mere man? TrJP

When You with Hogh Dutch Heeren Dine. Matthew Prior. They always talk, who never think. OBTV

When You Write Again. Ingrid Jonker. The sun that I now cover for always/With black butterflies PBWP

When Young Hearts Break. Heinrich Heine. And hence we stars are deathless. AWP

When Young Ladies Get Married. Anonymous. And it's hard times, boys. AmFP

When Young Melissa Sweeps. Nancy Byrd Turner. Just watch Melissa sweep a room! NTCP

When Your Cheap Divorce Is Granted. Robert Henry Newell. Tell me, mother, which the best? OBAL

When Your Eyes. Anonymous. In the court of heaven, your only comfort/Must come from her that day. WTO

When Your Pants Begin to Go. Henry Lawson. ...and I'll swear there's nothing/low,/In the pride of Human Nature when its pants begin to go. NOAV

When Your Parents Grow Old. Joanne Hart. as you were and as/you too will be AMV-80

When Youth and Beauty Meet Together. Anonymous. For when their work begins to wither/Their worth decays. EIL

When Youth Had Fled. Henry Howard, Earl of Surrey. And nourisheth his sacred flame/From whence no blazing sparks do fly. EnRePo; SiPS

Whenas in Jeans. Paul Dehn. The lacquefaction of her toes. FiBHP

Whenas the Nightingale. John Cleveland. Dallied more wantonly/With the fair Egyptian Queen. LiTL; UnTE

Whence and Whither. Hayim Nahman Bialik. And the dullness is awful! TrJP

Whence Had They Come? William Butler Yeats. What sacred drama through her body heaved/When world-transforming Charlemagne was conceived? BoLoP

Whenever a Little Child Born. Agnes Carter Mason. Somewhere, somewhere. AA; BiCB

Whenever I Go There. William Stanley Merwin. Today belongs to few and tomorrow to no one. NaP

Whenever I Have. Furnley Maurice. The uncapturable, the indefinable thing, the unlearned. NOAV

Whenever I Say "America." Nancy Byrd Turner. Whenever I say "America"/So many things I say! YeAr

Whenever the Snakes Come. Hedva Harkavi. A king. I know he is a king. VWA

Where. Walter De La Mare. Honey in a beehive,/And me in bed. NYBP

Where? Kenneth Patchen. There must be some such place somewhere/But I never heard of it LiTM

Where? Arthur Seymour John Tessimond. But if you can see it, though no one else can, it will yours. OBTV

Where a Roman Villa Stood, above Freiburg. Mary Elizabeth Coleridge. Crying aloud, "How beautiful they are,/But not our English hills!" OBNC; OBTV

Where Are All Thy Beauties Now, All Hearts Enchaining? Thomas Campion. None ever liv'd more just, none more abused. GBL

Where Are the Hebrew Children? Peter Cartwright. Safe in the promised land. AH

Where Are the Men Seized in This Wind of Madness? Alda Espírito Santo. where liberty/is the fatherland of men... TTY; WPOW

Where Are the Ones Who Lived Before? Anonymous. And when do they leave there? Never... HAP

Where Are the War Poets? C. Day-Lewis. Defend the bad against the worse. OBWP

Where Are the Waters of Childhood? Mark Strand. Now you look down. The waters of childhood are there. HaCAP; LCAP

Where Are You Going. Eliza Lee Follen. Who ever yet saw a pig in a wig? SoPo

Where Are You Going, Greatheart? John Oxenham. God goeth with you, Greatheart! BLPA; PAL; PGD

Where Are You Going, My Good Old Man? Anonymous. Meanest old devil in the world. FSW

Where Are You Going, My Pretty Maid. Anonymous. "Nobody asked you, sir," she said. HBVY; NLV

Where Are You Now Superman? Brian Patten. To attract the attention of passing solutions.... FF

Where Art Is a Midwife. Tom Paulin. ...Is it possible/That none of you can understand? FaBoIP

Where Avalanches Wail. Anonymous. The Poet's heart shall quiver in the brine. NA

Where Babylon Ends. Nathaniel Tarn. and speak to you in those provinces/she has in every nook and cranny of your countries. VWA

Where Be You Going, You Devon Maid? John Keats. And kiss on a grass-green pillow. ErPo; HBV 1-2; LiTL; UnTE

Where Beeth They Biforen Us Weren. Anonymous. In joye withouten ende. EBEV

Where Children Live. Naomi Shihab Nye. the roots of the tiniest grasses curl toward one another/like secret smiles. MAYP

Where Cross the Crowded Ways of Life. Frank Mason North. Shall come the city of our God. AH

Where Did He Run To? Mark Van Doren. Where is the boy? SO

Where Did You Get That Hat? Joseph J. Sullivan. Where'er I go they shout: "Hello! Where did you get that hat?" FSN; TreF

Where Didst Thou Find, Young Bard. John Keats. Yea unto thee beldams drink metheglin,/And anises, and caraway, and gin. CBEP

Where Do I Love You, Lovely Maid? Raymond F. Roseliep. Before my altar's dark rose tree. ISi

Where Do the Gipsies Come From? Sir Henry Howarth Bashford. Or look in a gipsy's eye. ALV

Where-e'er My Flatt'ring Passions Rove. Isaac Watts. God in himself is bliss enough,/For we have all in Thee. NOCV; OxBoCh

Where Fire Burns. Gladys Cardiff. da nita'ga, "They are standing/together as one." TWSS

Where Fled. John Wieners. The moon? She shines through the blood/& clouds. CoPo

Where Go the Boats? Robert Louis Stevenson. Other little children/Shall bring my boats ashore. FaBoBe; FaBoCh; GoJo; NTCP; OxBChV; SoPo; SUS; TiPo; TreFT

Where Have All the Flowers Gone? (excerpt). Pete Seeger. O when will they ever learn?... WeW

Where Have All the Indians Gone? Janet Campbell Hale. more Indian that we are it makes my stomach want/to turn. STE

Where Have You Been Dear? Karla Kuskin. There are some thoughts that are my own/I do not wish to share. NTCP

Where Have You Been, My Good Old Man? Anonymous. Don't care if I do,/So long as I'm near you. OuSiCo

Where Have You Gone. Mari E. Evans. rent money/in one pocket and/my heart/in another... BPo; NNP; PoNe; TTY

Where Have You Gone, Little Boy. Patty L. Harjo. If i should see you again, will you give me more/Yesterdays from your tomorrows? VoR

Where He Hangs His Hat. Deborah Lee. Where the falling is soft. BrSi

Where He Takes Tea with Cromwell. Anonymous. No doubt he's at home in hell. DBV

Where His Lady Keeps His Heart. A. W. Then, Lady, take your own,/That lives for you alone. CTC; EiL; OBSC

Where Hudson's Wave. George Pope Morris. Me onward to my home! AA

Where I Am. Marcelin Dos Santos. from the end of the night/and from the beginning of the day. WhB

Where I Am Now. Harvey Shapiro. And chairs of the office, should/It come between nine and five. GP

Where I Hang My Hat. Dick Gallup. Second Avenue or any other/blueprint of the future. APU

Where I'll Be Good. Michael Ryan. where my bones will shut up, where I'll be good. SM

Where I Took Hold of Life. Robert P. Tristram Coffin. It made its man, and it may rest/Forever from the plow. BiCB

Where I Walk in Nebraska. Nancy G. Westerfield. Walking out in all weathers to these parts. AMV-80

Where Is He? Anonymous. Oh where, oh where is he? OxNR

Where Is Heaven? Bliss Carman. And His voice has talked to me/In the sunlit apple tree. TRV

Where Is Justice? Eliezer Steinbarg. And I the noble cat am poor/And left to crouch beside the door! VWA

Where Is My Butterfly Net? David McCord. Give me an extra set of wings. FiBHP

Where Is My Wandering Boy Tonight? Robert Lowry. O where is my boy tonight? FaFP; FSW; TreF

Where Is Our Holy Church? Edwin H. Wilson. Wherever strong men truly seek/With character the goal. AH

Where Is Paris and Helene? Thomas of Hales. Fol he is the on hire is bold. OxBM

Where Is She Now? Anonymous. A mind more pure, a form more fair. LO

Where Is the Black Community? Joyce Carol Thomas. and swilling Old Crow/out of a crystal flask. CNA

Where Is the Fruit. Innocent Banda. Where is the fruit/in this land you promised? WhB

Where Is the Sea? Felicia Dorothea Hemans. –Where is my own blue sea? EtS

Where Is Your Boy Tonight? Anonymous. Watch ere watching is wholly vain–/Where is your boy tonight? PaPo

Where It Is Winter. George O'Neil. Where there is little left to die/And no more Spring. HBMV

Where Knock Is Open Wide. Theodore Roethke. Maybe God has a house./But not here. HAP; VGW

Where Lies the Land? Arthur Hugh Clough. Far, far behind, is all that they can say. AWP; EtS; FaBoBe; FaBoCh; FaBoRV; GN; GoTF; GTBS; HBV 1-2; LoGBV; MCCG; NOBE; OBVV; TreFT; WGRP

Where Lies the Truth? Has Man, in Wisdom's Creed. William Wordsworth. A happier, brighter, purer Heaven than theirs. TrCP

Where Love Is. Amelia Josephine Burr. Ah Love, my country in your arms—my home upon your/heart! HBV 1-2

Where Love Is King. Hilda ("H. D.") Doolittle. (Ah, love is come indeed!) HBMV

Where Mountain Lion Lay down with Deer February 1973. Leslie Marmon Silko. the memory/spilling out/into the world. STE; VoR; WPOW

Where My Books Go. William Butler Yeats. Storm-darken'd or starry bright. OBEV; OBVV

Where Nothing Dwelt But Beasts of Prey. Isaac Watts. And bids the dying churches live. AH

Where Now Are the Hebrew Children? Anonymous. While all heaven is beaming o'er us,/Safe in the promised land. AH

Where, O Where? Milton Bracker. And Harry (The Cat) Brecheen? LiSp; SD

Where O Where Is Old Elijah? (with music). Anonymous. Way over in the promised land. AS

Where, Oh Where Are the Hebrew Children? Anonymous. Safe now in the Promised Land. BLPA

Where One Would Be. Sir Edward Dyer. Eche lovings harte would see his frynde,/And soe woulde I doe mine. PoEL 1-5

Where or When. Philip Whalen. The city running to weed patch right on time. PoM

Where Runs the River? Francis William Bourdillon. And I, and you. HBV 1-2; WGRP

Where's Mary? Ivy O. Eastwick. She's sitting on the garden bench/Listening to a bird! TiPo

Where's the Poet? John Keats. And to him the Tiger's yell/Comes articulate and presseth/On his ear like mother-tongue. DiPo

Where Shall I Be when de Firs' Trumpet Soun'? Anonymous. Where shall I be when it soun'. O, Bretheren. BoAN 1-2

Where shall I have at mine own will. Sir Thomas Wyatt. For I am gone for evermore. FCP; SiPS

Where Shall the Baby's Dimple Be? Josiah Gilbert Holland. And my baby the angel's seal shall keep. BLPA

Where Shall the Lover Rest. Sir Walter Scott. Never, O never! CH; GTBS; GTBS-P

Where Shall Wisdom Be Found. Euripides. ...Shall our white feet gleam/In the dim expanses? UnS

Where She Told Her Love. John Clare. Yet stood the fair maid nigh me and told me all/her love. VLP

Where She Was Not Born. Yvonne. where she could hardly root,/let alone glorify her wings. CNA

Where Ships of Purple–Gently Toss. Emily Dickinson. And then–the Wharf is still! AmP

Where the Blessed Feet Have Trod. Michael (Katherine Bradley and Edith Cooper) Field. Jesu, Thou art found: my God I hail,/My Lord, my God! OxBoCh

Where the Cedars. Jacob Glatstein. Who have escaped the dispersion,/And have got rid of the damned/Yiddish. TrJP

Where the Dead Men Lie. Barcroft Henry Boake. Too long lying in grave-mould, camped with/Death where the dead men lie. BoAV; CBAP; PoAu 1-2

Where the Dropwort Springs up Lithe and Tall. John Lyle Donaghy. She will feel his heartbeats in sun and air. NeIP

Where the Fight Was. Alice Corbin. The women go wailing/To pick up the dead. BPAW

Where the Hayfields Were. Archibald MacLeish. Dancing in the meadows where the hayfields were. DuDa; LOW

Where the Lilies Used to Spring. David Gray. Then bleak and cold is the silent spot/Where the lilies used to spring! OxBS

Where the Picnic Was. Thomas Hardy. And one–has shut her eyes/For evermore. OxBTC

Where the Rainbow Ends. Robert Lowell. The dove has brought an olive branch to eat. AnNE; CoBMV; HaCAP; MoAB; MoAmPo; NePoEA; TrGrPo

Where the Rainbow Ends. Richard Rive. And it's music we're going to sing/Where the rainbow ends. ·PBA; TTY

Where the River Shannon Flows. James I. Russell. For there's not a colleen sweeter,/Where the River Shannon flows. FSN

Where the Single Men Go in Summer. Nina Bourne. Who might, but never does, arrive on the next train. FiBHP

Where the Slow Fig's Purple Sloth. Robert Penn Warren. It fills/The darkening room with light. NoP

Where There's a Will There's a Way. Eliza Cook. For "Where there's a will there's a way." BLPA; FaFP; GoTF; TreF

Where to Seek Love. William Blake. In the naked and outcast, seek Love there. TRV

Where Two O'Clock Came From. Kenneth Patchen. And upsetting the table in their eagerness to find it. SO

Where Unimaginably Bright. Oliver Hale. and are returned upon your hand. GoYe

Where Wards Are Weak. Robert Southwell. Yet grasse is greene, when flowers doe fade away. NCEP

Where We Must Look for Help. Robert Bly. The crow shall find new mud to walk upon. ConAP; NePoEA

Where? When? Which? Langston Hughes. With old and not too gentle/Colorless apartheid? BPo; NePoAm-2

Where You Go When She Sleeps. T. R. Hummer. Into itself if you love enough, and will not, will never let you go. MAYP

Where You Passed. Amelia Josephine Burr. But where you passed there is a trail/Of blossoms in my heart. HBMV

Whereat Erewhile I Wept, I Laugh. Robert Greene. Through her I weep, at her I smile. EIL

Wherefore Peep'st Thou, Envious Day? Anonymous. Darkness only gives us leisure/Our stol'n joys to number. GBL

Wherefore, Unlaurelled Boy. George Darley. Fated of grief to die,/Impart it to a solitary lyre? ERoP 1-2; FaBoRV; NOBE; OBRV

Wherein Consists the High Estate. Ebenezer Dayton. His godhead shines through clay. AH

Wherelings Whenlings. Edward Estlin Cummings. with north/over/the barn HAP; WeW

Wherever Beauty Has Been Quick in Clay. John Masefield. But the still grass, the leaves, the trembling flower/Keep, through dead time, that everlasting hour MoRP

Wherever God Erects a House of Prayer. Daniel Defoe. The latter has the largest congregation. GoTF; TreF

Whether Men Do Laugh or Weep. Thomas Campion. No ill can be felt but pain,/And that happy men disdain. EnRePo; NCEP

Whether or Not. D. H. Lawrence. So good-by, an' let's be let! MoBrPo

Whether There Is Sorrow in the Demons. John Berryman. ...their will/Grinds on their fate. So was, so shall be still. LiTM

Which Are You? Anonymous. Or am I a wrecker, who walks the town,/Content with the labor of tearing down. FPL; PoLf

Which Is the Bow? Anonymous. (The cuckoo who singeth it all day long). GBP

Which Loved Best? Joy (Mary A. Cragin) Allison. Which of them really loved her best? OHIP; WBLP

Which Road? William Barnes. An' a maid, wi' her head a-borne on in a proud/Gait o' walken, so smooth as an air-zwimmin cloud. NOBV

Which Shall It Be? Ethel Lynn Beers. Thankful to work for all the seven,/Trusting the rest to One in heaven! BLPA; TreF

Which Side Are You On? Florence Reese. Which side are you on? FSW

Which Sword? Jason Noble Pierce. 'Tis the sword of love, my Son. PGD

Which Washington. Eve Merriam. Though all of them were George. NTCP

Whichever Way the Wind Doth Blow. Caroline Atherton Briggs Mason. The wind that blows, that wind is best. GoTF; TreFS

A Whigmaleerie. William Soutar. Vermin are ill to thole. OxBS

The Whigs' Lamentation for the Death of Their Dear Brother College.... Anonymous. And make the proud Tories resign us the nation. APAS

While April Rain Went By. Shaemas O'Sheel. And coaxed all growing things to greet/With gracious garb the May. HBMV

While Cecil Snores: Mom Drinks Cold Milk. James (Olumo) Cunningham. look/among the oppressors for his dad. JB

While Dissecting Frogs in Biology Class Scrut Discovers... George Roberts. you have nothing on me today. GOYP

While I Am Young. Silas Ballou. My mansion and my crown. AH

While I Have Vision. Peter Quennell. This finger's length above reality. ChMP

While I walked in the moonlight. Lady Murasaki Shibiku. I heard only the sigh of the wind. LiTW

While O'er Our Guilty Land, O Lord. Samuel Davies. Let them prevail to save us too! AH

While O'er the Deep Thy Servants Sail. George Burgess. Abroad, at home, or in the deep. AH

While on Those Lovely Looks I Gaze. John Wilmot, Earl of Rochester. The vanquished die with pleasure. CBEP

While Shepherds Watched. Margaret Deland. Because the longed-for Christ looked up/In Mary's happy eyes! GN; HBVY

While Shepherds Watched Their Flocks by Night. Nahum Tate. Good will henceforth from Heaven to men/Begin and never cease. GN; HBV 1-2; HBVY; NOCV; OnYI; OxBI; TreFS

While Someone Telephones. Elizabeth Bishop. might they not be his green gay eyes. NMP

While Stars of Christmas Shine. Emilie Poulsson. Gladden the poor and sad/For love's dear sake. OHIP

While Strolling through the Park. Ed Haley. I met her at the fountain in the park. BLSo; FSW

While the Bells Ring. Lora Dunetz. To Superman,/While the bells ring praises. NePoAm

While the Billy Boils. David McKee Wright. But I somehow fancy we'll all be pen-mates on the day when/they callthe Roll of the Sky. AnNZ

While the Days Are Going By. George Cooper. And will keep our hearts aglow,/While the days are going by. BLRP; STF; WBLP

While the leaves of the bamboo rustle. Anonymous. Are not so warm, not so warm/As the body of my wife. BoLoP

While the Summer Trees Were Crying. Valentin Iremonger. I only knew the pity and the pain. AnIV

While to Bethlehem We Are Going. Sister Violante Do Ceo. For of all heaven's gifts the sweetest/Sure is peace,–the sweetest, best. CAW

While Waiting for Kohoutek. Christopher Erb. No one will herald our return. SOTS

While We Lowly Bow Before Thee. Daniel C. Colesworthy. Blessed Saviour, Blessed Saviour,/Hear and answer from above. AH

While We Slept. David Wolff. universal, and the abolition of the poor. AnAmPo; TrJP

While we were fearing it. Emily Dickinson. Is terribler than wearing it/A whole existence through. NCEP; NIP; PPP

Whilst Adam Slept. Anonymous. Strange! his first sleep should be his last repose! HBV 1-2

Whilst Alexis Lay Prest. John Dryden. The nymph died more quick, and the shepherd more slow. ErPo; FF; PrIm; UnTE

Whilst Eccho Cryes, What Shall Become of Mee. Henry Constable. And hee, in ruth of my distressed cry,/Plants mee a weeping starre within mine eye. AAS

Whilst I Beheld the Neck o' th' Dove. Patrick Cary. This was I taught by th' swan. JCP

Whilst in This World I Stay. Philip Pain. ...Lord, before I die/Let me a better kingdom far espy. AH

Whilst It Is Prime. Edmund Spenser. Make hast, therefore, sweet love, whilest it is prime;/For none can call again the passed time. OBEV

Whim Alley. Hervey Allen. And only shadows dwell in Danger Court. AnAmPo

A Whim of Time. Stephen Spender. Sod lifted, turned, slapped back again with spade. MoAB; MoBrPo

Whimper of Awakening Passion. Ebenezer Jones. You must either prevent all these whims,/Or a way, love, to humour them find. NOBV

The Whip. Robert Creeley. ...for which act/I think to say this/wrongly. NaP; NeAP; NoAm; PoM

Whip Jamboree. Anonymous. Oh Jenny get your oat cake done. OBSS

Whiplash. William Matthews. ...but a force/that water welcomes and displays. AmC; MAYP

Whippet. Prudence Andrew. How such a freak can be so beautiful. GDP

The Whipping. Robert Earl Hayden. avenged in part for lifelong hidings/she has had to bear. BP; GP; GrPl; IDB; NCSH; PoBA; TW

Whipping Cheare. Anonymous. Ther's hemp, and flax and tow to to to,/Tow to to to to tero. FaBoBa

The Whirlpool. Anonymous. The changeable Whirlpool of Life. PoToHe

Whirlwinds of Danger. Anonymous. March, march you toilers, the world will be free. FSW

Whirring Wheels. John Oxenham. I will turn to sleep again. TRV

Whiskey Bill,–A Fragment. Anonymous. How are things on the Great Divide,/O Whiskey Bill? BPAW

The Whisperer. Arthur Bullen. The visionary gold/That in my heart I hold/Doth far in worth outshine/All metal from the mine. HBMV

The Whisperer. James Stephens. Deep anger unto me was lent/To write this strain. WGRP

The Whisperer. Mark Van Doren. And do not mind it if I cry/Passing my mother's bed. AnFE; CoAnAm; MoAmPo; UnTE

The Whisperers. Wilfred Wilson Gibson. And his shadow walks alone. HBV 1-2

Whisperin' Bill. Irving Bacheller. So ye best be kind o' careful down there in Washington. PoLf

Whispering Clouds. Mariquita Platov. come with a rattle, a jingle, a tone and a word. AMV-80

Whispering Ghosts of the West. Anonymous Stand up and depart! WTO

Whispering Hope. Alice Hawthorne. Making my heart in its sorrow rejoice. PSoN

Whisperings in Wattle-Boughs. Adam Lindsay Gordon. CAN NEVER BE DISTURB'D BY SUCH AS THOU!' OBVV

Whispers. Roberta Hill. to see that storm of riches in your sudden gaze. CDW

Whispers of Heavenly Death. Walt Whitman. On the frontiers to eyes impenetrable,/Some soul is passing over.) AnFE; APA; LiTA; NePA; NoAm

Whispers of Immortality. Thomas Stearns Eliot. But our lot crawls between dry ribs/To keep our metaphysics warm. ATP; CMoP; CTC; LiTA; MAPA; NePA; NoAm; NOBA; NoP; OBMV

Whist. Eugene Fitch Ware. Play what I get until the break of day. PoLf

The Whistle. Charles Murray. For the maister brunt the whistle that the wee herd/made! GoTS; OxBS

Whistle Aloud, Too Weedy Wren. Wallace Stevens. But he that of repetition is most master. LiTA

Whistle an' I'll Come to Ye, My Lad. Robert Burns. For fear that she wile your fancy frae me. BoLiVe; LiTL; OxBoLi; UnTE; ViBoPo

Whistle, Daughter, Whistle. Anonymous. I'd rather whistle for a man than for a sheep or cow. FSW

Whistle O'er the Lave o't. Robert Burns. Whistle o'er the lave o't. BSV; CEP; GBP; OxBS

Whistles. Rachel Field. To tell the sleepy folk on land/All's well at sea. TiPo

The Whistling Boy. George Crabbe. And, oh! how taught shall I return? TrGrPo

Whistling Boy. John Robert Quinn. If he didn't set/To whistling first. BiCB

Whistling Boy. Nixon Waterman. Like the boy who goes whistling by. PoLf

Whistling Willie. Kaye Starbird. The thing I keep on wondering, though,/Is: where did Whistling Willie go? QQQ

Whit Sunday. Joseph Beaumont. And in the shelter of Thy wing/Obtain Thy leave and grace to sing. OxBoCh

White. Marguerite Bouvard. knowing only the moment. AMV-81

White. Karl Krolow. until it melts. AMV-81

White. George Woodcock. You are white's evening nature of my thought. NeBP

White an' Blue. William Barnes. But gi'e her my breast-knot, white an' blue? GBL; GTBS-P

White and Red. Edward, Earl of Oxford De Vere. These beauties make me die. OBSC

The White and the Black. N. M. Khaketla. The fleeing partridge finds the forbidden grain. PeSA

The White Anemone. "Owen Meredith." Each virgin flowerest faint and wan/With the bliss of her own sweet breath so pure. GN

White Apples. Donald Hall. I would put on my coat and galoshes TAP

White as a Paper A-Sail in the Air. Anonymous. And I feel when in love with my fair,/Like a ship that is breasting the sea. WTO

White as Snow. Anonymous. I chose death to save my honor. OuSiCo

White Attic. Kenward Elmslie. where I reach out at night/and bat the far air. ANYP

White Autumn. Robert Morgan. and the sun just appearing at her elbow. Str

White Azaleas. Harriet McEwen Kimball. Nay, white as the angel of a child/That looks into God's own eyes! AA; HBV 1-2

White Bear. Susan Griffin. What else she learns,/I am afraid to/name. GP

The White Beauty. Anonymous. Betwene hire kurtle and hire smok/I wolde ben hid. MeEL; OxBM

The White Bird. Anna Akhmatova. I hear my sweet bird sing. LiTW

The White Bird. Roy McFadden. I'd silence all those cries/That desolate the land. ACV; NeIP

White Bird. Matti Megged. Only the wind continued/To call. VWA

The White Birds. William Butler Yeats. Were we only white birds, my beloved,/buoyed out on the foam of the sea! EnL

A White Blossom. D. H. Lawrence. She shines, the first white love of my youth, passionless and in vain. MoBrPo

White Blossoms. Robert Mezey. ...The blossoms are/white, and I am almost there. NaP; VWA

The White Canoe. Alan Sullivan. When there's trouble on shore, there's peace on the wave,/Afloat in the White Canoe. CaP

White-Capped Waves. James Freeman Clarke. With sharp observance of law divine. EtS

White Cat. Raymond Knister. And it thinks we're awfully slow/Coming with the milk. WHW

The White Cat of Trenarren. A. L. Rowse. My cat and I grow old together. OxBTC; PCat

White Center. Richard Hugo. and why do I feel no shame kicking the loose gravel home? NoP

White Christmas. William Robert Rogers. Of repentance for the false day that's fled. ChMP; LiTM; MoAB; MoBrPo; PPON; SeCePo

The white chrysanthemum. Mitsune (Oshikochi no Mitsune). I could find it only by chance. LiTW

The White City. Richard Watson Gilder. Beauty walks forth to light the world for-/ever! PAH

The White City. Claude McKay. The tides, the wharves, the dens I contemplate,/Are sweet like wanton loves because I hate. BPo; NoAm; TAP; TW

A White City. James Schuyler. and find it has snowed. ANYP

The White Cliffs. Alice Duer Miller.
I stayed many weeks in England/Instead of just one. PoLf
Only the English are really her own. BLPL

The White Cockade. *Anonymous.* Huzza for the right and the white cockade! OnYI

White Conduit House. William Woty. While rival beaux and jealous belles exist,/So long, White Conduit House, shall be thy fame.' NOEC

White Country. Peter Schjeldahl. Chase the little the etc. it's 10 a.m. ANYP

The White Devil, V, iv: "Call for the Robin Redbreast." John Webster. For with his nails he'll dig them up again. AnFE; EBEV; FaBoCh; FaBoEn; GTBS; GTBS-P; HAP; HBV 1-2; HeIP; LiTB; LoBV; LoGBV; NoP; OBEV; OBS; PAI; PoEL 1-5; PoRA; PrIm; SeCePo; TrGrPo; ViBoPo

White Dove of the Wild Dark Eyes. Joseph Mary Plunkett. They miss your flashing wings,/Your splendorous flying. HBMV

The White Dove Sat on the Castle Wall. W. Wager. If you will any more, sing it yourself. FaBoNo

The White Dream. May Doney. I greet you when I wake. HBMV

The White Dress. Roberta Spear. when you've forgotten how I look in white. MAYP

The White Dress. Marya Zaturenska. And on her lap, the clasped, closed, iron book. MoAmPo

White Dusk. Marion M. Boyd. Like white thoughts smiling through gray memory. HBMV

The White Dust. W. W. Gibson. To wipe the dust from my mahogany. MoBrPo

The White Eagle. Nan McDonald. All his white beauty warm in the eye of the sun. PoAu 1-2

White Earth Reservation 1980. Gerald Vizenor. tribal touchwood at the seams STE

White Fear. Winifred Welles. I would find my hair silver,/And feel my heart cold. HBMV

White Fields. James Stephens. Where it is the children go. BoNaP; MoShBr; PoSC; SiSoSe; SoPo; SUS

The White Fisher. *Anonymous.* If it hadna come o yoursell, my lord,/'T would neer hae come o me.' ESPB

The White Flag. John Milton Hay. The white rose meant surrender. HBV 1-2

The White-footed Deer. William Cullen Bryant. And prowls the fox at night. AnNE

White Fox. Elizabeth Alsop Shepard. there is life. GoYe

White Goat, White Ram. William Stanley Merwin. ...the covering of our feet/Offends, for the ground where we find we stand is holy NePoEA

The White Goddess. Robert Graves. Heedless of where the next bright bold may fall. MoBrPo; OAEL 1-2

White Guardians of the Universe of Sleep. Edward Estlin Cummings. sing more will wonderfully birds than are NYBP

White-Haired Lover (excerpt). Karl Shapiro. I'd say I love you but I don't know how. PoA

The White-Haired Man. May Sarton. Love not transcending the person but incarnate/As in his own hand given you in greeting. MoRP

The White Hare. Lilian Bowes Lyon. Time rings a snow-change. OxBTC; PoPle

White Heliotrope. Arthur Symons. Ever again my handkerchief/Is scented with White Heliotrope. BoLoP; EBEV; PAI

The White Horse. William Henry Davies. When you come up behind, to mount? OxBTC

The White Horse. D. H. Lawrence. They are so silent they are in another world. SOTW

The White Horse. Mary Mills. driven to smash the blank unsilvered mirror. NePoAm

White Horse of the Father, White Horse of the Son. William Pitt Root. That I rode on. Am still riding. MAYP

The White Horse of Westbury. Charles Tennyson Turner. He floated upwards, and regain'd the steep. EBEV; VLP

White Horses. Eleanor Farjeon. Wish on the ninth horse, your wish will come true. PH

White Horses. Winifred Howard. On Little White Horses all speckled with foam. BrR; SoPo; SUS

The White House. Claude McKay. Against the potent poison of your hate. AmNP; AmPP; NIP; PoBA; PoNe

White House Blues. *Anonymous.* He's gone a long, old time. FSW; OuSiCo

White in the Moon. Alfred Edward housman. White in the moon the long road lies,/That leads me from my love. AWP; CMoP; ELP; LiTB

A White Iris. Pauline B. Barrington. As it did for her/In a garden? PoLf

The White Island. Robert Herrick. And fresh joys, as never too/Have ending. AnAnS 2; HBV 1-2; JCP; NoP; OAEL 1-2; OBS; OxBoCh; WiR

The White Isle of Leuce. Sir Herbert Read. and tremble for the limbs of Helen and the secrets of/the sacred isle. FaBoTw

The White Jessamine. John Banister Tabb. When, lo! a paler flower than mine/Had blossomed in the gloom! HBV 1-2

The White Kite. *Anonymous.* As they, ever looking upward,/Watched it fly across the heavens. LiTW

The White Knight's Song. Lewis (Charles Lutwidge Dodgson) Carroll. That summer evening long ago/A-sitting on a gate. EnLi 1-2; FaBoCh; FaBoCo; FaBoNo; HAP; InPS; LoGBV; NOBE; NOBL; NoP; OAEL 1-2; PAI; VLP

White Magic: An Ode. William Stanley Braithwaite. Up the steep road of life to Heaven's gate. PoNe

The White Man Pressed the Locks. James C. Kilgore. in the white arms/hugging the black city. InPK

The White Man's Burden. Rudyard Kipling. The judgment of your peers! EnLi 1-2; FaBoPV

The White Monster. William Henry Davies. A big, fat, lazy slug that, even then,/Killed women, children, and defenceless men. AmMo; LiTB

White Notes. Donald Justice. Then, in another time. LCAP

The White, Orphaned Camel Kid. *Anonymous.* From amongst the fifty/Camels on the slopes? WTO

White Pass Ski Patrol. John Logan. something has just flown over the mountain! BiP; CAPP

The White Peace. William Sharp. The moonlight of a perfect peace/Floods heart and brain. FaBoBe; HBV 1-2

The White Peacock. Mary Mills. But nobody sees, nobody hears. NePoAm

White People. David Henderson. some baked some fried/some burned/some blue PoBA

White Pines. Barry Silesky. ...down highway and river/to the deaf and hungry cities. AMV-80

White Queen. John Fuller. Ashen and wailing scattering veils and pins? NePoEA-2

The White Rainbow. Starr Nelson. "Let him who may sight glory before death." GoYe

The White Rat. Marguerite Young. For the purposes of what intrinsic studies? MoPo

A White Rose. John Boyle O'Reilly. For the love that is purest and sweetest/Has a kiss of desire on the lips. AA; AnAmPo; HBV 1-2; OBEV; OBVV; OnYI; PoPl; SoSe

White Roses. John Ashbery. The new white flowers that are beginning to shoot up/around now. TAP

White Roses. Cora Fabbri. And while the others wept I smiled. AA

The White Sand. Edmund Wilson. Printing white sand, the fair skin–blue-veined and/curved, has pressed. NePoAm

White Sand and Grey Sand. *Anonymous.* Who'll buy my white sand? CBEP

White Season. Frances Frost. Like puffs of snow. TiPo

White Serpent. Nelly Sachs. And the snail/with the ticking luggage of God's time. BoWoP

The White Ship. Geoffrey Hill. Creatures passed through the wet sieve/Without enrichment or decay. OxBC

The White Ship. Dante Gabriel Rossetti. (The sea hath no King but God alone.) OBNV; VLP

The White Ships and the Red. Joyce Kilmer. But one–shall be like blood. MC; PAH

The White Skirt. Stephen Dobyns. grips his arm, draws him down to his own dark home. MAYP

White Spider. Marita Garin. ...a negative print/of a spider, a stopped moment. AMV-80

The White Stag. Ezra Pound. Bid the world's hounds come to horn! LOW

The White Stallion. Guy Owen. To read the rage the stallion spent. InPK

The White Steed of the Prairies. J. Barber. And his gallant heart swells with the pride of the free. BPAW; CoSo

White Summer Flower. William Stanley Merwin. and why should they DFF

White Swan. Glanz-Leyeles. A. Pecks at my heart/With pink and tender bill. VWA

The White-Tailed Hornet. Robert Frost. And this day's work made even that seem doubtful. OxBA

A White-Throat Sings. Walter Prichard Eaton. Until the smallest sparrow's song/Is louder than the drums! HBMV

A White Tree in Bloom. John Richard Moreland. Anything lovelier/Than a white tree? PGD

White Violet. Marian Osborne. And now...I dare not live. CaP

White Violets. Benjamin R. C. Low. Love that never quite touched earth,–/They...and thou and I. HBMV

A White Wall under the Wallpaper. Brian Henderson. ...It obliterates all tracks/leaving, clearly, nothing to go on. CaPN

White Was His Naked Breast. *Anonymous.* On fif stedes on His body/The stremes ran o blode. OxBM

White Weekend. Quincy Troupe. the stock market went up 18 points... NBP

White Whales Specked Black. Randolph Outlaw. clouds drift across the sky gracefully, like white whales/specked black. LFAC

The White Window. James Stephens. And it never makes a sound. TiPo

The White Witch. James Weldon Johnson. And in her smile there is a blight. BANP; CDC

The White Women. Mary Elizabeth Coleridge. Saw with his human eyes a wild white maid,/And gazing, died. BrRo

White World. Hilda ("H. D.") Doolittle. and the blush of the rose-petal,/ lifted, of the flower. LLLT

White Zombie. Harrison Fisher. ...clear mental image, against/the lingering headache of sky. APU

Whitebeard on Videotape. James Merrill. Along with being holy, life was hell. NoP

Whitehall Stairs. Aaron Hill. I, rapt in your dear heav'n, my loss describe. NOEC

Whiteness. Isobel Hume. And the bridegroom, taking her home at evening,/Will think he weds the Spring. HBMV

Whiteness. Yunna Moritz. And I refuse to let my mother past. VWA

Whiteness, or Chastity. Joseph Beaumont. Cast on the name of genuine whiteness, which/Doth thee alone, for chastity, enrich. LiTL; LoBV

Whither. John Vance Cheney. To the white quiet of the churchyar/fold. AA

Whither. Philip Becker Goetz. Or, art thou on fair angel lips a song? AA

Whither? Wilhelm Muller. The wheels of a mill are going/In every brooklet clear. AWP

Whither Away? Mary Elizabeth Coleridge. Sat with you there. CH

Whither Is Gone the Wisdom and the Power. Hartley Coleridge. Then might our pretty modern Philomels/Sustain our spirits with their roundelays. HBV 1-2

Whither Shall I Go. Anonymous. And my poor heart hath felt it,/Heigh, heigho. GBL

Whitley at Three O'Clock. Jeff Worley. ...the white/lie already forming/ like a blister on his lips. GOYP

Whitman. Larry Levis. To find me now will cost you everything. MAYP

Whitman in Black. Ted Berrigan. Whitman's walk unchanged after its fashion. APU

Whitman's Ride for Oregon. Hezekiah Butterworth. And round them mountain-castled lie/The hundred states of Oregon. PAH

Whitmonday. Louis MacNeice. The quiet (Thames' or Don's or Salween's) waters by. NYBP

The Whitsun Weddings. Philip Larkin. ...an arrow-shower/Sent out of sight, somewhere becoming rain. FaBoMo; NePoEA-2; NoAm; NoP; OxBTC

Whitsunday. George Herbert. Unto his ancient and miraculous right. AtBAP

Whitsunday. John Keble. Save, Lord, by Love or Fear. OBRV

Whitsuntide an' Club Walken. William Barnes. Zoo in the dusk ov evenen, zome/Went back to drink, an' zome went hwome. VLP

Whittier. Margaret E. Sangster. It was not time to go! AA

Whittingham Fair. Anonymous. For once he was a true love of mine. GBP

Whittling. John Pierpont. For, when his hand's upon it, you may know/ That there's go in it, and he'll make it go. GN

Who. Moishe-Leib Halpern. I am the rider, it is I. TrJP

Who. Edwin Honig. all water without earth or sky a water all over water gone over for-/ever TAP

Who? Dan Jaffe. Who is the source of soul?/ADONAI FAZ

Who Am I? Felice Holman. But a piece/of/it/all. RFM

Who among You Knows the Essence of Garlic? Garrett Kaoru Hongo. and pale blue rice wine simmering/in the stomach of a big red fish? HoAn

Who Are My People? Rosa Zagnoni Marinoni. I met his eyes...And then I knew... BLPA; PoToHe

Who Are They? Anonymous. They are peaceful; they have great things; who are they? NIP

"Who Are You?" Asked the Cat of the Bear. Elizabeth Jane Coatsworth. My spirit is great," said the cat. TiPo

Who Are You, Little I. Edward Estlin Cummings. this is a beautiful way) NYBP

Who Be Kind To. Allen Ginsberg. since the days of the snake. NNaP

Who Bids Us Sing? Rhys Carpenter. Who else? Under the earth the blossoms hide. WGRP

Who but the Lord? Langston Hughes. So who but the Lord/Can protect me?/We'll see. BPo

Who Calls. Frances Clarke Sayers. "I am the Spring, the Spring, the Spring with laughter on my lips. SiSoSe

"Who can make a poem of the depths of weariness." Carl Sandburg. And if so, who?? NAMP

Who Can Tell? Anonymous. But who can tell the sorrow of her heart? WTO

Who Can Tell When He Is Awake. James Tate. Honestly I don't know why/everybody's looking at me like this. MAYP

Who'd Be a Hero (Fictional)? Morris Bishop. I murmur with a sour grimace,/""Where's me?" FiBHP; OBAL

Who Dat A-Comin' ovah Yondah? Anonymous. O, who dat a comin' ovah yonder, Hallelu. BoAN 1-2

Who Did Swallow Jonah? Anonymous. David killed Goliath–dead! FSW

Who Does Not Love True Poetry. Henry Clay Hall. He has not known his God. PoToHe

Who Does Not Love Wine, Women and Song. J. H. Voss. Remains a fool his whole life/long. FaFP

Who Doth Not See the Measure of the Moon? Sir John Davies. And doth consumer, waste, spoil, disorder all.... MOON

Who Drags the Fiery Artist Down? Clarence Day. It is the wife, it is the home. FaBoCo

Who Folds a Leafe Downe. Anonymous. Who stealeth thise boke/Ye divel shall cooke. FaBoUs

Who Follows in His Train? Reginald Heber. Oh God, to us may grace be given/To follow in their train! WGRP

Who Goes Round My Pinfold Wall. Anonymous. Nip, Johnny Ringo. GBP

Who Goes with Fergus? William Butler Yeats. And all dishevelled wandering stars. CMoP; FaBoCh; GoJo; InPK; LoGBV; MBW 1-2; NoAm; NOBE; NOBV

Who Has Known Heights. Mary Brent Whiteside. Who once has trodden stars seeks peace no more. BLPA

Who Has Not Walked Upon the Shore. Robert Bridges. Dapple in France the fertile plains. CMoP; MOS

Who Has Our Redeemer Heard. Stephen Collins Foster. Every prayer is heard in heaven/That is breathed from a truthful mind. AH

Who Has Seen the Wind? Christina Georgina Rossetti. The wind is passing by. BrR; GoJo; HBVY; NTCP; SUS

Who Hath a Book. Wilbur D. Nesbit. All this is his/Who hath a book. BLPA; SiSoSe; TiPo; TreFS

Who Here Can Cast His Eyes Abroad. Abiel Holmes. To thee I consecrate my praise. AH

Who I Am. Luis Da Gama. We are all members of the goatherd TTY

Who Is at My Window. Anonymous. But in at my dure thou go. EG; TrGrPo

Who Is It Talks of Ebony? Manmohan Ghose. There from the burning light of you/The world and I am laid. OBMV

Who Is My Brother? Pinkie Gordon Lane. The sun has always been red BlSi

Who Is Not a Stranger Still. Stephany. I understand my clinging/to the thought of you. BPo

Who Is Tapping at My Window. A. G. Deming. "Tapping at your windowpane." SoPo

Who Is That A-Walking in the Corn? Fenton Johnson. But nowhere could I find Him who walks/Master's cornfield in the morning. GoSl; PoNe

Who Is the Man? Anonymous. And they shall not be judged unjust,/All that in him for safety trust. TrAS

Who Is This That Cometh from Edom? William Herebert. Adreint al with shennesse, y-drawe down with shame.' OxBM

Who Is This Who Howls and Mutters? Stevie Smith. Howling much worse, and oh the door is open. OxBC

Who Kill'd John Keats? George Gordon, Lord Byron. Or Southey, or Barrow.' EnRP

Who Killed Cock Robin? Anonymous. When they heard the bell toll/For poor Cock Robin. PBBP

Who Killed Kildare? Jonathan Swift. Death killed Kildare–who dare kill whom he will. GoTF; HBV 1-2

Who Killed Lawless Lean? Stevie Smith. He should be glad they did not wring his neck. TEP

Who Killed Poor Robin? Anonymous. It was I, it was I. AmFP

Who Knows? Titus Munson Coan. To the new, strange world that lies/ Outstretched to its wondering eyes! AA

Who Knows? A. L. Milner-Brown. The Prince of Peace may found His home/In Africa at last. Who knows? Who knows? PBA; TTY

Who knows if the moon's. Edward Estlin Cummings. in love and flowers pick themselves LOW

Who Knows Where. Detlev Freiherr von Liliencron. Who knows where! AWP

Who Likes the Rain? Clara Doty Bates. In the soft, cool mud. Quack! Quack! Quack! TiPo

Who'll Be a Witness for My Lord? Anonymous. My soul is a witness for my Lord. BoAN 1-2

Who'll Buy My Valley Lilies? Eleanor Farjeon. Who'll buy my daffydillies? BrR

Who Loves a Garden. Louise Seymour Jones. And sees beyond his little sphere/The waving fronds of heaven, clear. BLPA

Who Loves the Rain. Frances Shaw. And looks on life with quiet eyes. BrR; HBMV; PoToHe

Who lyst his welthe and eas retayne. Sir Thomas Wyatt. For sure, circa Regna tonat. EnPo

Who Makes the Journey. Cathy Song. History moves like an old woman/ crossing the street. BrSi

Who Misses or Who Wins. William Makepeace Thackeray. Be each, pray God, a gentleman. SD

Who Needs Charlie Manson? Raymond Thompson. Even the Viet Cong were called Charlie. LFAC

Who Never Ate with Tears His Bread. Johann Wolfgang von Goethe. For guilt must all be compensated. WGRP

Who of Those Coming After. Darcy Gottlieb. we tried to make of love/a celebration? AMV-81

Who Pilots Ships. Daniel Whitehead Hicky. Has drained the cup of beauty drop by drop. BrR

Who Prayed? *Anonymous.* Tell us: Was it you who prayed? STF

Who Reigns? Percy Bysshe Shelley. Who is his master? Is he too a slave? SeCePo

Who's Gonna Shoe Your Pretty Little Foot? *Anonymous.* The only girl I ever did love,/Was on that train and gone. FSW

Who's In. Elizabeth Fleming. "What, everyone's out?/Why, everyone's in!" BrR

Who's in Charge Here? Marvin Bell. Then he became his truck again, and I my car/to cross a river–that's where the highway was going. AmC

Who's in the Next Room? Thomas Hardy. "Yea he; and he brought such; and you'll know him/anon." PoEL 1-5; PoPle; QFR; WSC

Who's Most Afraid of Death? Edward Estlin Cummings. my mouth, steer our lost bodies carefully downward) CMoP; SeCeV; VGW

Who's That at My Bedroom Window? *Anonymous.* I'll die with the one that loves me best." W ShS

Who's That Ringing At My Door Bell? *Anonymous.* For that's the best cure for a little pussy cat. FaBoCh; LoGBV

Who's Who. W.H. Auden. answered some/Of his long marvellous letters but kept none. CABA; CoBMV; MoAB; MoBrPo; NoAm

Who Says. Musa Moris Farhi. the dead/but who hears them VWA

Who Shall Die? James A. Randall, Jr. Pulls out a long blade,/Who slit his throat... BPo

Who Shall Have My Fair Lady? *Anonymous.* Under the leaves green! AtBAP; CBEP; EG; EnLoPo; PoEL 1-5

Who Shall Speak for the People? Carl Sandburg. ...hopeful as a/rainwashed hill of moonlit pines. OxBA

Who Shapes a Balustrade? Conrad Aiken. earth's wish, and the sun's prayer, in granite kept. EyDe

Who Shined Shoes in Times Square. Lance Jeffers. Through the majesty of his/melody, I see a nation rise... CNA

Who Sleeps by Day and Walks by Night. Henry David Thoreau. Will meet no spirit but some sprite. PoEL 1-5

Who Taught Caddies to Count? or; A Burnt Golfer Fears the Child. Ogden Nash. In such an unhumble, contemptful gamie/How anyone plays together. LiSp

Who Taught Thee First to Sigh? Edward, Earl of Oxford De Vere. As nought but death may ever change thy/mind. CoBE

Who Then Is Crazy? Barry Spacks. they fuck for their lives/in heatless rooms. GP

Who Threw the Overalls in Mistress Murphy's Chowder. George L. Geifer. I can lick the mick that threw the overalls in Mistress Murphy's chowder. FSN

Who Translates a Poet Badly. Gonzalez Prada. Grotesquely garbed/In his master's clothes. ELU

Who Walks with Beauty. David Morton. The wine of Beauty and the bread he breaks. BLPA; FaBoBe; GoTF; HBMV; TreFT

Who Wants a Birthday? David McCord. ("Hello!" says my own.) BiCB

Who Was It Came. Daniel Gerard Hoffman. Inexorable gaffer in an old hat/Croaking our names. CoAP

Who Was It, Tell Me. Heinrich Heine. The sun brightly beam'd, the birds/sweetly sang. TrJP

Who Were before Me. John Drinkwater. While the slow mosses weave an end of my forgotten name. OBMV

Who Wert and Art and Evermore Shalt Be. William Channing Gannett. Who wert and art and evermore shalt be! TrPWD

Who? Who? *Anonymous.* I not the bride can be! CH

Who Will Buy a Poem? Mahon O'Heffernan. It is a vain matter about which I ask. AnIL

Who Will Endure. W. H. Auden. Where gaitered gamekeeper with dog and gun/will shout "Turn back'. FaBoPV

Who Will Shoe Your Pretty Little Foot? (with music). *Anonymous.* And who will kiss your ruby lips/When I've gone to the foreign land? AS

Who Will Stop His Hand from Giving Warmth. Alejandra Pizarnik. She dies of a distant death/she who loves the wind. VWA

Who Wot Nowe That Ys Here. *Anonymous.* Cryste may send sich a yere. InPS; PAI

Who Would Have Thought? George Herbert. It cannot be/That I am he/On whom thy tempests fell all night. EG

Who Would Have Thought. Thomas Howell. Who would have thought so full of change? EIL; PoL

Whoa Back, Buck. *Anonymous.* Who made the back-band? Whoa, goddam! FSW

Whoe'er This Book, if Lost, Doth Find. *Anonymous.* Whole name they'll see page fifty-three. FaBoUs

Whoever You Are Holding Me Now in Hand. Walt Whitman. Therefore release me and depart on your way. InvP; PoEL 1-5

Whole and Without Blessing. Linda Gregg. ...the center,/where there are no clues except pleasure. MAYP; NPGG

The Whole Armour of God. Charles Wesley. Till Christ the Lord descends from High/And takes the Conqu'rors Home. NOCV

The Whole Duty of a Poem. Arthur Guiterman. That which is felt but may never be told. PoToHe

The Whole Duty of Berkshire Brooks. Grace Hazard Conkling. And whisper sorrow into sleep! HBMV; HBVY

Whole Duty of Children. Robert Louis Stevenson. And behave mannerly at table;/At least as far as he is able. EvOK; FaBoUs; GoTF; HBV 1-2; HBVY; NLV; OxBChV; TreFS

"Whole gulfs of red and fleets of red". Emily Dickinson. That bows and disappears. AmLP

The Whole Story. William Stafford. ...I will be waiting to go/with you to the end of the story. NNaP

The Whole Universe Is Full of God. Yunus Emre. for we will not live here forever LLLT

The Whole World Now Is but the Minister. Robert Bridges. But quite forgets her frowns and antics rude,/So kindly hath she grown to her new use. VLP

The Whole Year Christmas. Angela Morgan. If only a magic way were found/To make us children the whole year round! TRV

Wholesome. William Meredith. ...But it doesn't bear dwelling on. TAP

Whom Do You Visualize as Your Reader? Linda Pastan. reads my poems by his locker/instead of the sports page PPJ

Whom Jesus Loved. John Barford. You the divinity of it have proved,/"Whom Jesus loved." PeHV

Whom Lesbia Loved. Caius Valerius Catullus. fathered centuries ago by the noble Remus. LiTW

Whom the Gods Love. Margaret E. Bruner. Old age is something they can never know. PoLf

Whom the Gods Love. Mark A. De Wolfe Howe. One youth we loved as tenderly as ye. AA

Whoopee Blues. King Solomon Hill. Then I got 300 miles to go/traveling through the mud and clay/Mmmmmmmmmmmmmmm BluL

Whore. Linda King. I like to pick and choose/and who knows someone/like you might arrive... GP

The Whore That Rides in Us Abides. *Anonymous.* Needs not to feare that engineer/Whose bottoms on the sand. SCAP

Whoroscope. Samuel Beckett. and grant me my second/starless inscrutable hour. NoAm

Whose Hand. *Anonymous.* And all believe that his work is perfect. TrJP

Whose Little Pigs. *Anonymous.* I dearly love his wife. OxNR

Whose Old Cow? *Anonymous.* So old Nigger Add'll just brand her now. CoSo

Whose Scene? Ruth Stone. I go behind the baseboard to fornicate and spread/Myself, ancient as the ovulum and sperm. BoWoP

Whose Voice. Barney Bush. I think I am/alone and I will/still shiver. STE

Whoso Draws Nigh to God. *Anonymous.* God will advance a mile in blazing light to him. TRV

Whoso liest to hunt, I know where is an hind.. Petrarch (Francesco Petrarca). And wild for to hold, though I seem tame. BoLoP

Whoso Would See This Song of Heavenly Choice. John Wilson. A joyful, blessed life for aye to last. AH

The Whummil Bore. *Anonymous.* Her neck and breast was like the snow,/Then from the bore I was forced to go. ESPB

Why? Melba Joyce Boyd. and why/do teardrops/dry in/the pockets/of my/cracked/smile? BlSi

Why. Bliss Carman. And the old, old love/So long ago. OBVV

Why? Richard Augustine Chima. Workers and peasants/Stop displaying your ribs;/Eat cakes. WhB

Why? Stephen Crane. If the spirit was just,/Why did the maid weep? AA

Why? Walter De La Mare. But when these eyes encountered Tim's/Mine was the emptier stare. FiBHP

Why. Robert Freeman. The Savior of men, he answered, "Why?" PGD

Why? Talmud. I only did the Will of my Father in/Heaven! TrJP

Why Adam Sinned. Alex Rogers. But Adam nevuh had no dear old Ma-am-my. BANP

Why Are Our Summer Sports So Brittle? *Anonymous.* No pleasure could be tasted/If flowery sommer always lasted. NCEP

Why Art Thou Silent! William Wordsworth. Speak, that my torturing doubts their end may know! CBEP; HBV 1-2; OBRV

Why Can't I Leave You? Ai. and let me laugh for you from my second mouth. AmPA; GP

Why Come Ye Not to Court (excerpt). John Skelton. I would he were gone. OBSV

Why Did I Laugh To-night? John Keats. Verse, fame, and beauty are intense indeed,/But death intenser–death is life's high meed. CBEP; TEP

A Wicker Basket. Robert Creeley. I make it/in my wicker basket. AmPC; CAPP; HAP; NoAm; NoP; SM

Widcombe Churchyard. Walter Savage Landor. But the rich odor some fine day/Shall (what I can not do) repay/That little care. FaBoPP

Widdecombe Fair. Anonymous. Old Uncle Tom Cobley and all. BBV; CH; MoShBr; PH

Wide Empty Landscape with a Death in the Foreground. N. Scott Momaday. He was always here. CDW

Wide, Ho? Anonymous. (did I not venerate/Sung's line and state.) OBVE

The Wide Land. Archie Randolph Ammons. Blind in the wide land I/turned and risked my feet/to loose stones and sudden/alterations of height TwCP

The Wide Mizzoura (with music). Anonymous. Ah-hah, I'm bound away 'cross the wide Mizzoura. AS

Wide Open Are Thy Hands. Saint Bernard of Clairvaux Dying, alone am Thine. AH; TRV

The Wide Open Spaces. Oscar H. Lear. As long as he makes his meters mete and a fairly passable/rhyme. InMe

Wide Walls. Anonymous. Give me wide walls to build my house of Life. PoToHe

Widgeon. Seamus Heaney. unexpectedly/his own small widgeon cries. FaBoIP

The Widow. Mariana B. Davenport. I hear the autumn winds; and it is cold. AMV-80

The Widow. Susan Ludvigson. to turn off the lights/that burned all night/in the kitchen. MAYP

The Widow. William Stanley Merwin. Invisible invisible invisible NYBP; UnPo; VGW

Widow. Felix Pollak. ..."Remember our life together," she whispers,/as she falls asleep. FAZ

The Widow. Allan Ramsay. Unfit for the widow, my laddie. HBV 1-2

The Widow. Robert Southey. God had released her. NOEC; OBEC

The Widow at Windsor. Rudyard Kipling. (Poor beggars!–they'll never see 'ome!) BrPo; NoP; OAEP

Widow Brown's Christmas. John Townsend Trowbridge. There's tew ways o' remittin'? BeLS

A Widow in Wintertime. Carolyn Kizer. Or waken in a caterwaul of dying. NMP

Widow Machree. Samuel Lover. When you'd me near your heart,/Och hone! Widow Machree! HBV 1-2

The Widow Malone. Charles James Lever. O they're all like sweet Mistress Malone! HBV 1-2; TreFS

The Widow of Drynam. Patrick MacDonogh. The two of us laughing together or stepping in silence. NeIP; OnYI; OxBI

The Widow Perez. Gary Soto. ...The floor ticked/And she turned to listen. MAYP

The Widow's Curse. Anonymous. Your heir, Gerald, may he never inherit! NOBI

A Widow's Hymn. George Wither. Yet neither life nor death should end/The being of a faithful friend. OBEV

Widow's Lament. Anonymous. Year after year of them must pass/Till I go to his home. BoWoP

The Widow's Lament in Springtime. William Carlos Williams. and sink into the marsh near them. AP; CMoP; CoBMV; ForPo; HAP; LiTM; MoLP; NoAm; NOBA; TAP

The Widow's Mite. Frederick Locker-Lampson. Much faith; and, carefully laid by,/A little crutch. HBV 1-2

The Widow's Mites. Richard Crashaw. The other cast away, she only gave. OxBoCh

The Widow's Old Broom. Anonymous. And carry the marks of the widow's old broom. AmFP

The Widow's Party. Rudyard Kipling. And the river's clean where the raw blood/flowed/When the Widow give the party. VLP

The Widow's Plot; or, She Got What Was Coming to Her. William Plomer. It's justifiable matricide,/Isn't it, Bess?' NoAm

Widow's Walk. Elizabeth Spires. a cutout, a fancy French silhouette. MAYP

A Widow's Weeds. Walter De La Mare. A poor old Widow in her weeds. AtBAP; FaBV

The Widow That Keeps the Cock Inn. Anonymous. I'll marry the widow, and keep the Cock Inn. CoMu

Widow to Her Son. R. T. Smith. Listen. You can hear the river rising. Str

The Widowed Heart. Albert Pike And see thy face in Heaven, Isadore! AA

The Widower. Royall Tyler. Steal from the world, without a wife/To LAUGH–or CRY! OBAL

Widows. Edgar Lee Masters. Patience and the withered hands of toil. MoAmPo

Widsith, the Minstrel. Anonymous. He who earns praise/Has under heaven the greatest glory. AnOE

Wie Langsam Kriechet Sie Dahin. Heinrich Heine. And my bony fingers write/What daylight must not see. AWP

The Wife. Robert Creeley. and watch the other die. AmPC; AP; VGW

The Wife. Anna Peyre Dinnies I could not live alone. AA

The Wife. Theodosia Garrison. Through some closed corner of my heart,/Should laugh to find you there. HBV 1-2

A Wife. Matthew Gregory Lewis. That's the fault of the puppy to whom it is tied. DBV; PV

The Wife A-Lost. William Barnes. An' be a-waiten vor me now,/To come vor evermwore. BoLoP; ELP; EnLoPo; HAP; OBEV; OBVV

A Wife–at Daybreak I Shall Be. Emily Dickinson. Savior–I've seen the face–before! AmePo

The Wife from Fairyland. Richard Le Gallienne. Home through the greenwood–home. HBV 1-2

The Wife-Hater. Anonymous. Confess no trouble like unto a Wife. CoMu

A Wife in London. Thomas Hardy. And of new love that they would learn. NOBV; OBWP

Wife of Aed mac Ainmirech, King of Ireland, Laments Her Husband. Anonymous. And the side of Aed son of Ainmire. AnIL

The Wife of Auchtermuchty. Anonymous. For I and this house will never do weil.' BSV; GoTS

The Wife of Bath Her Prologue, from Chaucer (excerpt). Alexander Pope. And all the woman glares in open day. OBSV

The Wife of Kelso (The Wily Auld Carle). Anonymous. "Now, wasn't she a darned old fool, to think that I was blin'." ShS

Wife of Kohelet. Shlomit Cohen. your eyes burn to see/a dove turn blue/or seem to. VWA

The Wife of Usher's Well. Anonymous. And fare ye weel, the bonny lass/That kindles my mother's fire! AWP; BoLiVe; BSV; CBEP; DiPo; EBEV; FaBoBa; GoTS; HBV 1-2; InPo; LiTB; NOBE; NoP; OAEL 1-2; OAEP; OBEV; OnMSP; OxBB; OxBS; PoEL 1-5; PrIm; TreF; TrGrPo

The Wife of Winter's Tale. Michael Dennis Browne. where she and her glistening lover race/over a murderous snow. SM

The Wife's Complaint. Anonymous. ...Sorrow follows/this too long wait for one who is estranged. BoLoP

The Wife's Lament. Anonymous.
...Grief for them/who wait longing for love. BoWoP
...Hard is the lot/of one that longs for love in vain. PBWP
Woeful his fate whose doom is to wait/With longing heart for an absent love. AnOE; LiTW

A Wife's Song. William C. Bennett. For the roaring wind and the blessed time/That brings him home again. HBV 1-2

The Wife's Tale. Seamus Heaney. Spread out, unbuttoned, grateful, under the trees. IPY

The Wife Speaks. Mary Stanley. for a bloody death. AnNZ

The Wife Takes a Child. Ellen Bryant Voigt. I carry the offense of my flat belly,/the silent red loss of monthly bleeding. SM

A Wife Talks to Herself. Stephen Berg. in the tiny person/looking at me out of his eyes. NaP

The Wife to Her Husband. Anonymous. Flies to its haven of securest rest! HBV 1-2

The Wife Who Would a Wanton Be. Anonymous. Wo worth marriage for evermair! FaBoCo

The Wife-Woman. Anne Spencer. And you, glory-clad, reach down. BANP; NoAm

Wight in the Broom. Anonymous. "Hold thine tunge stille/And have al thine wille." OxBM

Wigs and Beards. Robert Graves. As they, in the same sense, call themselves artists. NOBL

Wihelmina Mergenthaler. Harry P. Taber. Ate her lovely ermine collar. BBGG

Wil the Merry Weaver, and Charity the Chamber-Maid. Anonymous. Though I'm a Weaver of low degree,/Ile teach them to read their A.B.C. CoMu

The Wild. Wendell Berry. ...They are/its remembrance of what it is. VGW

Wild Ass. Padraic Colum. The only being that bears a heart/Not recreant to the wild. MoBrPo

Wild Beasts. Evaleen Stein. And I will roar some more! SoPo

Wild Bees. James Keir Baxter. ...preaching the truth of winter/To the fallen heart that does not cease to fall. AnNZ; NoP

Wild Bill Jones. Anonymous. Just push back the coffin lid,/Look down on a gambling man. AmFP

The Wild Boar and the Ram. John Gay. And well revenge may rest contented,/Since drums and parchment were invented. PPON

Wild Bronc Peeler. Anonymous. Why, what the hell's the matter–have I lost my nerve? CoSo

Wild Cherry. Louise Townsend Nicholl. And do not weep a woodland-in-the-little. NePoAm

Wild Cherry. Lizette Woodworth Reese. Let all else go to roof within your heart. AnAmPo

Wild Cherry Tree. Edmund Charles Blunden. A long long sigh to the darling tree. BrPo

The Wild Colonial Boy. *Anonymous.* And that's the way they captured him–the wild Colonial boy. AmFP; FaBoBa; FSW; OuSiCo; PoAu 1-2; ViBoFo

The Wild Common. D. H. Lawrence. In confirmation, I hear sevenfold lark-songs pealing. CoBMV

Wild Crab. Mary Ellen Solt. [concrete poem] BoWoP

The Wild Dog Rose. John Montague. at the rim/of each bruised and heart-/shaped petal. BIrV; CIP; IPY

Wild Dreams of a New Beginning. Lawrence Ferlinghetti. as the Hudson retakes its thickets/and Indians reclaim their canoes. GP

Wild Dreams of Summer What Is Your Grief? George Barker. And we can take, but not keep. OxBTC

The Wild Duck. John Masefield. In a land that no man knows. BrPo

Wild Eden. George Edward Woodberry.
And the cords that no man breaketh are/bound about my feet. AA
But silence steals the song. AA
Fly to Wild Eden! HBV 1-2
Hail Earth, the Rose of Stars. AA
If one sweet maid is true. AA
It hath made the whole day sweet. AA
My spirit follows her, and loves. AA
So will deep love deplore. AA
Then fling me back to the battle where/men labor the peace of God! AA
This world should wake and be a soul AA
We are sailing westward, homeward;/our western home is near. AA

The Wild Flower Man. Lu Yu. Only give you a drunken/Smile from under his tousled hair. NaP

The Wild Flower's Song. William Blake. But, oh! met with scorn.' CBEP

Wild Flowers. Peter Newell. "Oh, sir! the flowers, they are wild," replied the timid/creature. NA

The Wild Garden. Alexander Pope. But vindicate the ways of God to Man. PrIm

Wild Geese. Elinor Chipp. I heard the wild geese flying/In the dead of the night. HBMV; TiPo

Wild Geese. William Hart-Smith. I can remember/nothing about it now/but the geese. BoAnP

The Wild Geese. Violet Jacob. "O Wind, hae maircy, haud yer whisht, for I daurna listen mair!" BSV

The Wild Geese. John Masefield. And be (if God should please),/Almost as wise as geese. NoAm

The Wild Geese. James Herbert Morse. 'T is we who dread the thunder, and not/they. AA

Wild Geese. Frederick Peterson. Symbol of coming Springs! HBV 1-2; HBVY

Wild Geese, Wild Geese, Ganging to the Sea. *Anonymous.* The weather it will spill. PBBP

The Wild Goat. Claude McKay. But the wild goat bounding on the barren hill/Droops in the grassy pen. CDC

Wild Honey. Maurice Thompson. The pollen-dust of centuries! AnFE; APA; HBV 1-2

The Wild Honey Suckle. Philip Freneau. The frail duration of a flower. AmLP; AP; BLPL; CBEP; HBV 1-2; LITA; MAmP; NOBA; OxBA; PoEL 1-5; PoLf; TAP; TrGrPo

Wild Horse. Elder Olson. Or if it must be ridden at last, let it bear a hero on its back. GrPl

Wild Horse Jerry's Story. Sarah Elizabeth Howard. A victim of man's cruelty and greed. PoOW

Wild Iron. Allen Curnow. And the foundering shriek of the gale. AnNZ

The Wild Knight. Gilbert Keith Chesterton. Burning forever in consuming fire. WGRP

Wild March. Constance Fenimore Woolson. Inbringing, inbringing the March's wild weather. YeAr

Wild Miz-zou-rye. *Anonymous.* I'm bound away for ther wild Miz-zou-rye. ABF

The Wild Montana Boy. *Anonymous.* And that's the way they captured him, that wild Montana boy. CoSo

The Wild Mushroom. Gary Snyder. For food, for fun, for poison/They are a help to man. NoP

The Wild Mustard River. *Anonymous.* While the Lord holds his soul in command. AmFP

Wild Negro Bill. *Anonymous.* But ole Mosser hain't cotch me, an' he never will! BPo

Wild nights–wild nights! Emily Dickinson. Might I but moor–Tonight–/In Thee! NIP; NOBA; NoP; OLR; OxBA; PBWP; SBG; TAP; UnTE; WeW

Wild Oats. William Henry Davies. Are there no more wild oats to sow? ACV

Wild Oats. Philip Larkin. Unlucky charms, perhaps. InPS; PAI

Wild Oats. Norman MacCaig. and went dowdily on with whatever/pigeons do when they're knitting. OxBTC

Wild Old Wicked Man. William Butler Yeats. Daybreak and a candle-end. AnIL; AtBAP; CMoP; MBW 1-2

Wild Peaches. Elinor Wylie. And sleepy winter, like the sleep of death. AmP; FaBoWP; LiTA; LiTM; NAMP; OxBA; SBG

Wild Pigs. Ted Kooser. They're up there now, if anybody'd look. SM; TAT

Wild Plum. Orrick Johns. Who love, better than the earth,/Wild plum at night. HBMV; PG

Wild Provoke of the Endurance Sky. Joseph Ceravolo. wild provoke of the endurance sky! ANYP

A Wild Rattling Cowboy. *Anonymous.* I'll shun all bad company/And every girl forsake. CoSo

The Wild Ride. Louise Imogen Guiney. Thou leadest, O God! All's well with/Thy troopers that follow. AA; CAW; HBV 1-2

The Wild Rippling Water. *Anonymous.* Leave you to rock cradles, sing "Bye-o-babee.'" CoSo; FaBoBa

A Wild Romantic Dell. William Julius Mickle. And calls her wanderd young, the call each banck replies. OBEC

Wild Rose. William Allingham. For mirthful, gentle, delicate, and warm. GN

Wild Roses. Edgar Fawcett. Like rustic maids that meekly stand/Below the ladies of their land! HBV 1-2

Wild Roses. Mary Effie Lee Newsome. Of daddy's big rough cows. CDC

Wild Rover. *Anonymous.* And I never will play the wild rover no more. FSW

Wild Sports of the West. John Montague. Patrols for God His private grounds. CIP

Wild Strawberries. Robert Graves. And glory for all time/Keep the boy Tom who tending geese/First made the nursery rhyme. FaBoCh; LoGBV

Wild Strawberry. Maurice Kenny. January snow falls, listen... STE

Wild Swan. *Anonymous.* But soar in air, a wandering spirit. AnOE

The Wild Swan. D. S. Savage. my mood was shattered with its calm explosion. NeBP

Wild Swans. Edna St. Vincent Millay. The town again, trailing your legs and crying! CMoP; PBWP; UnPo

The Wild Swans at Coole. William Butler Yeats. To find they have flown away? ACV; BoAnP; CMoP; DiPo; FaBoPP; FaBoRV; FM; HeIP; InPS; MBW 1-2; MoAB; MoBrPo; MoVE; NoAm; NoP; OnYI; PB; PBBP; PPP; SoSe; SOTW; TEP; UnPo; WHA

Wild Thyme. Eleanor Farjeon. I'll stay where I am," said Alice. SiSoSe

Wild Weather. Katharine Lee Bates. His quiet hand will lead the sunshine in. PGD

Wild West. Mark Vinz. ...along the windy Interstates,/where our shadows stretch for miles. Psk

Wild Wishes. Ethel M. Hewitt. But most of all, I wish, my dearest darling,/To be the Blessed Morning when you wake! HBV 1-2

The Wilderness. Gyula Juhasz. Or seekest thou, in mouldering realms of night,/Rest, by the crumbling comrades, out of sight? LiTW

The Wilderness. Sidney Keyes. Flesh is fire in this wilderness of fire/Which is our dwelling. LiTB

The Wilderness. Kathleen Raine. Drunk water cold and clear from an inexhaustible hidden fountain. BoWoP; PoSH

Wilderness. Carl Sandburg. I came from the wilderness. AP

The Wilderness. Maura Stanton. Trying to interpose God's perfect details/Between history and his own unready eyes. MAYP

Wilderness Gothic. Alfred W. Purdy. Perhaps he will fall. NOBC; NoP; PeCV

Wilderness Rivers. Elizabeth Jane Coatsworth. No will, no purpose/But their own. AmFN

Wilderness Sacred Wilderness. Philip Lamantia. as the Buffalo Bill Follies autodestruct by 1916. APU

Wilderness Theme. Ian Mudie. ...that all my days/with that persistent search were full. PoAu 1-2

Wildfire. Judit Toth. already the sense/of the stone's inscription if final. VWA

Wildflower. Stanley Plumly. her face lily-white, kissed and dry and cold. LCAP

The Wilding. Philip Booth. ...this wood/is for you. NePoEA

Wildness. Blanche Shoemaker Wagstaff. To be as forest things are, free,/Lonely, and strange and wild! HBMV

Wildtrack: "Lie easy in your secret cradle." John Wain. I in my deanery, she in her booth. NAs

Wildwood Flower. *Anonymous.* When he won and neglected this frail wildwood flower. BLSo; FSW

Wilfred Owen's Photographs. Ted Hughes. The motion was passed. FaBoPV; OxBC

Wilful Waste Brings Woeful Want. *Anonymous.* How I wish I had that crust/That once I threw away. OxNR

Wili Woyi, Shaman, also known as Billy Pigeon. Robert J. Conley. never caught him/and never/understood. STE

The Will. John Donne. To invent, and practise this one way, to annihilate all three. EBEV; LiTB; MePo; OAEP

The Will   Sipho Sepamla.   The cat spotted black and white/you will have to divide/for that you'll need God's guidance.   WhB

Will.   Ella Wheeler Wilcox.   And waits an hour sometimes for such a will.   BLPA; FPL; PoToHe

Will Beauty Come.   Robert Nathan.   –Oh, will I hear her calling/Over the sea again, over the hill?   HBMV

Will God's Patience Hold Out for You?   Edythe Johnson.   While His patience holds out for you!   STF

Will he always love me?   Lady Horikawa.   Are as disordered/As my black hair.   BoWoP; LiTW; OLR

Will He No Come Back Again?   Anonymous.   And will you no come back again?   OBEC; OBEV

The Will's Love.   Besmilr Brigham.   I am/love me   IHMS

Will Stewart and John.   Anonymous.   And William Stewart is Erle of Marr,/And his father-in-law dwells with/him indeed.   ESPB

Will the Weaver.   Anonymous.   And what was black she turned it red.   AmFP

Will there really be a morning?   Emily Dickinson.   Where the place called morning lies!   AA; OBCA; SiSoSe; SoPo; WGRP

The Will to Change.   Adrienne Rich.   the artists talking of freedom/in their chains   NMM

The Will to Live.   Mekeel McBride.   it is not from human grief, or any other.   MAYP

Will to Win.   F. R. Scott.   I ride like Joan to conquer my whole man.   OBCV

Will Waterproof's Lyrical Monologue.   Alfred, Lord Tennyson.   But carved cross-pipes, and, underneath,/A pint-pot neatly graven.   VLP

Will Ye No Come Back Again?   Lady Nairn.   Will Ye No Come Back Again?   BSV

Will ye see what wonders love hath wrought?   Sir Thomas Wyatt.   The flame whereof doth aye repair/My life when it is gone.   FCP; SiPS

Will Yer Write It Down for Me?   Henry Lawson.   Takes his pen in tears and triumph, and he writes it down for them.   CBAP

Will You Be as Hard?   Augusta Gregory, Lady Gregory.   The little road that has led/Thousands to sleep.   OBMV

Will You Be My Little Wife.   Kate Greenaway.   And green sage cheese.   MoShBr

Will You Come?   Edward ("Edward Eastaway") Thomas.   Beloved, beautiful, come!   CH; GoJo; GrPl; LoBV

Will You Come Out Now?   Valerie Sinason.   WILL YOU COME OUT NOW?   BrRo

Will You Go, Lassie, Go?   Anonymous.   Will you go, lassie, go?   FSW

Will You Love Me in December as You Do in May?   James J. Walker.   That you love me in December as you do in May?   FSN; GoTF; TreFT

Will You Love Me When I'm Old?   Anonymous.   It is only this, my darling,/That you'll love me when I'm old.   BLPA; BLPL; FaBoBe

Will You, One Day.   Marian Ramie.   Is love that ever seems of life a part,/And understand?/Try to.–One day?   HBMV

Will you sleep forever.   Korinna.   There was a time/when you were not a loafer.   BoWoP

Will You, Won't You?   Mark Van Doren.   ...Two/Minds about it–mine. Yours, a third.   NCSH

William and Helen.   Sir Walter Scott.   Her soul is from her body reft;/Her spirit be forgiven!'   EnRP; OAEP

William and Margaret.   David Mallet.   And word spake never more!   CEP; NOEC; OBEC

William and Mary.   Anonymous.   And he made little Mary his bride.   AmFP

William and Phyllis.   Anonymous.   The young Phyllis and William all from the greenwood tree.   OBET

William Blake.   James (1834-82) Thomson.   Perhaps he was found at the Throne.   CBEP; HBV 1-2; OAEP; OBVV

William Blake Sees God.   Roy McFadden.   The strangler in the dark.   NeIP

William Brown.   Joaquin Miller.   And dream sweet dreams of Mary Jane...   BPAW

William Gifford.   Walter Savage Landor.   Kneel, and thank Heaven they are not yours.   GTBS-P

William Glen.   Anonymous.   Then all young sailors pray beware,/And never sail with a murderer!   BaBo

William Hall.   Anonymous.   And there this couple were lawfully married,/Whe'r their parents were willing or no.   AmFP; BFSS

William I–1066.   Eleanor Farjeon.   They jumped BONG into bed like a bull at a gate.   BBV

William Jones.   Edgar Lee Masters.   I have passed on the march eternal of endless life.   ImOP

William Lisle Bowles.   George Gordon, Lord Byron.   And link'd thee to the Dunciad for thy pains.   OBNC

William of Orange.   Anonymous.   With Orange flags flying and on God relying,such music will lead us to conquer or die.   BFSS

The William P. Frye.   Jeanne Robert Foster.   To make the harbor glad because she's come.   MC; PAH

William Shakespeare.   Algernon Charles Swinburne.   All stars are angels; but the sun is God.   TrGrPo

William Shakespeare to Mrs. Anne,...   Thomas Gray.   While Nancy earns the praise to Shakespeare due,/For glorious puddings and immortal pies.   CEP

William Street.   Kenneth Slessor.   You find it ugly, I find it lovely.   CBAP

William Taylor.   Anonymous.   It was only three weeks after/Sarah became the captain's wife.   OBET

William the Bastard.   Lakon".   In a manner unbecoming to the successor/Of Edward the Confessor.   FiBHP

William Wallace.   Francis Lauderdale Adams.   The robber rich, a yet more hateful band!   OxBS

William Was a Royal Lover.   Anonymous   Soon, soon he sickened and then died.   AmFP

William Wilson.   Malcolm Cowley.   true love lay strangled by Othello.   AnAmPo; MoVE

William Wordsworth.   Sidney Keyes.   Blank through the dalehead and the bony face.   ChMP; OxBTC; SeCePo

William Yeats in Limbo.   Sidney Keyes.   Silent be the singer who thinks of me/And how I was defeated.   MoBrPo

Williams: An Essay.   Denise Levertov.   and the long stem of connection.   InPS

Willie and Helen.   Hew Ainslie.   An' his luik was like the luik o' man/Wha's heart in twa is riven.   HBV 1-2; LO

Willie and Lady Margerie.   Anonymous.   And with a deep and heavy sich/Her heart it brak in twa O.   OxBB

Willie Brew'd a Peck o' Maut.   Robert Burns.   Wha first beside his chair shall fa',/He is the King amang us three!   CEP; InPo; OxBS; ViBoPo

Willie Leonard.   Anonymous.   With his pinks and red roses and fine garden fruit.   AmFP; BaBo

Willie Macintosh.   Anonymous.   "I left them in the Stapler,/Sleeping in their sheen."   CBEP; ESPB; OxBoLi; ViBoFo

Willie Macintosh (B version).   Anonymous.   I lost the best feather i my wing/For my crowse crawing.   ESPB

Willie O Douglas Dale.   Anonymous.   He's haild her lady of Douglassdale,/Himsel the lord within.   BaBo; ESPB

Willie O Winsbury.   Anonymous.   And there's as much corn in each o them/As they can grind in a year.   BaBo; ESPB

Willie o Winsbury (D version).   Anonymous.   "Come, let us all now mery be,/Since she has made such a happy/choice."   ESPB

Willie of Winsbury.   Anonymous.   And for every pound that you give her,/I'll give her ten thousand pounds.   AmFP

Willie Riley.   Anonymous.   May her honor bright gain high estate and her offspring rise to fame.   BaBo

Willie's and Nellie's Wish.   Julia A. Moore.   If it is her, I sincerely wish/Her papa won't drink any more.   FiBHP

Willie's Fatal Visit.   Anonymous.   But Meggie reave her yellow hair.   BaBo; ESPB

Willie's Lady.   Anonymous.   And now he's gotten a bonny young son,/And mickle grace be him upon.   BaBo; ESPB; ViBoFo

Willie's Lyke-Wake.   Anonymous.   But ye shall gae hame a wedded wife with child.   BaBo; ESPB

Willie the Poisoner.   Anonymous.   "Really, Will," said he, "what next?"   NTCP

Willie the Weeper.   Anonymous.   And dreaming he's dead, he'll forget to awake.   ABF; BeLS; BLPA; OBAL; TrAS; YaD

Willie Winkie.   William Miller.   Hey, Willie Winkie!–See, there he comes!   FaFP; HBV 1-2; HBVY; OxBChV; OxNR

The Willing Mistress.   Aphra Behn.   Ah! who can guess the rest?   SBG; UnTE; ViBoPo

The Willing Prisoner to His Mistress.   Thomas Carew.   Survey the pains my sick heart feels,/And wounds themselves have made discover.   CaPo

A Willing Suspension.   John Holmes.   I feel safe from my own or even Milton's hell?   PoCh

The Willis.   Samuel Willoughby Duffield.   And I at the oars, our course to hold.   AA

Willis Beggs.   Edgar Lee Masters.   Dedicated to the canning works!   SaC

The Willow.   Tu Fu.   Wind broke its longest bough.   NaP

Willow Bend and Weep.   Herbert Clark Johnson.   Bend down and weep. I have not tears.   PoNe

The Willow Cats.   Margaret Widdemer.   Those willow cats that ran away/And left their toes behind!   BrR

The Willow Garland.   Robert Herrick.   Will, with my willow-wreath also,/Come forth and sweetly dye.   OAEP

The Willow-Man.   Juliana Horatia Ewing.   And chuckled in his wooden heart, that ancient Willow tree.   OxBChV

Willow Poem.   William Carlos Williams.   the last to let go and fall/into the water and on the ground.   NCSH

The Willow Tree.   Anonymous.   If I only had that one I love,/How happy, happy should I be.   OBET

The Willow-Tree.   William Makepeace Thackeray.   And always remember to take the door-key.   CenHV; HBV 1-2; InMe

The Willows. Walter Prichard Eaton. Weeping water maidens/That were once so fair. HBMV; OHIP

The Willows. Bret (Francis Bret Harte) Harte. And this Nightingale, kept by one Shear. BXAP; InMe

Willows. Joseph Langland. Dreaming toward natural grace in a green town. NePoEA

Willows. Laura Schreiber. It stirs the willow trees. AMV-81

The Willows by the Water Side. Anonymous. O, my little breath, now I go there alone in sorrow. WTO

Willows in Alma-Ata. Aleksander Wat. if I forget Thee/if I forget You VWA

Willows in the Snow. Tsuru. The freshly fallen snow. SUS

Willowware Cup. James Merrill. Tilted honeycombs, thunderhead blue. NoP

Willy. Richard Moore. —deftly you've caught it–that carton/of–ice cream! MAT

Willy and the Lady. Gelett Burgess. Come and talk the Man-Talk, that's the cure for you! HBMV

Willy Boy. Anonymous. I am going to help them/Turn the new hay. OxNR

Willy Lyons. James Wright. Willy, and John, whose life and art, if any,/I never knew. HaCAP; NNaP

Willy the Weeper. Anonymous. BIM BAM BOO!–an' the dope gave out. AS; GBP

Willy to Jinny. Joseph Skipsey. Nothing dark could Jinny see/A-coming from the colliree. VLP

Willy Wet-Leg. D. H. Lawrence. He's resigned, and when you hit him/he lets you hit him twice. CMoP; TW

Willy, Willy Wilkin. Anonymous. He set them all a-laughing,/Ha, ha, ha! OxNR

Willy Wood. Anonymous. And that ended Willy Wood. OxNR

Wilt Thou Lend Me Thy Mare? Anonymous. Money will make the mare to go. CBEP; ELU; OBS

Wilt Thou Not Visit Me? Jones Very. Man's spirit comes with thine in peace to dwell. AH

Wiltshire Downs. Andrew Young. Lying like broken sticks among the stones. ChMP; GTBS-P; OxBTC

Win at First and Lose at Last; or, A New Game at Cards. Laurence Price. We wish'd the Cards had all been burn'd. OxBoLi

Winchester. Lionel Pigot Johnson. Mother mine: loved Winchester! OBVV

The Winchester Wedding. Thomas D'Urfey. Scarce Five of the Fifty was left ye,/That so did return again. CavP

The Wind. Anonymous.
The King o' Scots, and a' his power/Canna turn Arthur O'Bower. FaBoCh; LoGBV
Who it is stays me when again I'm still. AnOE
Wind that levels all before it. WTO

Wind. Hamish Brown. ...By nature we'll have sinned/If, in the lairig bothy, we do not fear the wind. PoSH

The Wind. Alice Corbin. The wind is carrying me round the sky. BPAW

The Wind. Robert Creeley. But as love is long-winded,/the moving wind/describes its moving colors of sound and flight. AmPC

The Wind. William Henry Davies. And all who saw and heard him were amazed. SeCePo

Wind. Sydney Thomas Dobell. Oh the wold, the wold, the wold! PeD

The Wind. Dorothy Graddon. Now, Mr. Wind, just come along/And blow me if you dare. OnUR

Wind. Ted Hughes. Hearing the stones cry out under the horizons. SoSe

The Wind. Betty Miller. Who? oooh/The wind. BrR

The Wind. Harold Monro. Wind, overturn the goblet, spill/On me the everlasting skies! OBVV

The Wind. William Morris. Yet still thou wanderest the lily-seed to find. NBM

The Wind. Elizabeth Rendall. Why does he want so much to be/Here in my little room with me? HBVY

The Wind. Christina Georgina Rossetti. But when the trees bow down their heads,/The wind is passing by. BLPL; FaBoBe; OxBChV

Wind. James Stephens. And so he will! And so he will! AnIL; BoNaP; ELU; HeIP; InPK; NoAm

The Wind. Robert Louis Stevenson. O wind, that sings so loud a song! GN; HBVY; SoPo; SUS; TiPo

The Wind. John Banister Tabb. A blind, demented giant. AnAmPo

Wind and Impulse. Duane Big Eagle. piercing the darkness/for the slightest/wind and impulse. STE

Wind and Lyre. Edwin Markham. Shine to the trembling heart of me,/Light my soul to the mother-sea. TRV

Wind and Mist. Edward ("Edward Eastaway") Thomas. As I should like to try being young again. BrPo

Wind and Rain. Anonymous. How can I any more be sad? HW

Wind and Silver. Amy Lowell. As she passes over them. BoWoP; HeIP; MoAmPo

The Wind and the Bird. Anonymous. "I am he who arouses the Wind." PeSA

The Wind and the Moon. George Macdonald. She had never heard the great Wind blare. GoJo; HBV 1-2; HBVY; MoShBr; OnMSP; SUS; TreFS

Wind and Wave. Coventry Patmore. Laugh and fling pebbles on the rainbowed crest/Of its untired unrest. NBM

Wind and Wave. Charles Warren Stoddard. I seem to hear the rushing wave/I heard far out at sea. AA

The Wind at Penistone. Donald Davie. To find in Art no fellow but the wind. LiTM; NePoEA-2; NMP

The Wind at the Door. William Barnes. An' nwone o' comely height like her/Went by; but all my grief agean awoke. AtBAP; CBEP; ELP; GBL; GTBS-P; NBM; PoEL 1-5

The Wind at Your Door. Robert D. FitzGerald. ...I've my own faults to face. NOAV; PoAu 1-2

The wind begun to knead the grass. Emily Dickinson. Just Quartering a Tree– HAP

The Wind Blow East. Anonymous. Oh, the wind blow the China/Right down in town. OuSiCo

The Wind Bloweth Where It Listeth. Susan L. Mitchell. Not the old wayward child to see/But some bright-haired divinity. AnIV

The Wind Blows. Donagh MacDonagh. I fail for breath and cannot keep that pace. NeIP

The Wind Carol. Lewis Turco. The black snow falls, and the wind blows. SM

The Wind Carries Me Free. Dennis Shady. is carried across/the sky. LFAC

The Wind-Flower. Jones Very. A lesson taught by Him who loved all humankind. AnNE

Wind Flowers. Margo Lockwood. and feel like a fossil/in a burning museum. DFF

Wind Force. Bernadette Mayer. Visibility very/seriously affected. ANYP

A Wind from the West. Lauchlan MacLean Watt. None, living or dying, like those dead hearts that are/lying/Away in the West in the rain! PoSH

Wind Gardens (parody). Louis Untermeyer. shower us with breath of pine/and freesia buds. BXAP

Wind, Gentle Evergreen. Anonymous. Prove grateful emblems of the lays he sung. CBEP

The Wind Has Such a Rainy Sound. Christina Georgina Rossetti. Oh will the ships go down, go down,/In the windy sea? BrR; TiPo

The Wind Has Wings. Anonymous. And children must fear them–ahe, ahe, ee, ee, iee. GrPl; WHW

The Wind in a Frolic. William Howitt. Laughing to think, in its fearful fun,/How little of mischief it had done. MoShBr; OxBChV

Wind in the Alleys. Lola Ridge. Wind rising out of the alleys/Carrying stuff of flame. OnYI

The Wind in the Elms. J. Corson Miller. And every leaf is exquisite with song. HBMV

Wind in the Grass. Mark Van Doren. Are you so tired? Unfasten your mind/And follow it hence. FaBV

Wind in the Pine. Lew Sarett. Wash over me, God, with your wind and night,/And leave me clean and cool. TrPWD; TRV

The Wind in the Pines. Madison Cawein. Meseems I hear sonorous lines/Of Iliads that the woods are dreaming. AA

The Wind in the Tree. Frank Templeton Prince. ..."Do I know/Whether my motion makes the wind that moves me?" OBSP

Wind in the Willows (excerpt). Kenneth Grahame. Joy shall be theirs in the morning!' PCh

Wind Is a Cat. Ethel Romig Fuller. Curls down for a nap/And purrs and purrs. SoPo

The Wind Is Blind. Alice Meynell. From those blind uses of the slave. MoBrPo; SeCePo

The Wind Is Blowing West. Joseph Ceravolo. I am just coming/Just going in ANYP

The Wind Is Ill. John Malcolm Brinnin. Here, there, and everywhere. LiTA

The Wind Is Wild Tonight. Anonymous. ...It is calm seas/bring the sharp warriors from the North. NOBI

The Wind It Blew Up the Railroad Track (with music). Anonymous. And the wind it blew,/Holy Jiminy! how it blew! AS

The Wind Like an Ocean. Larry Eigner. (o shut your eyes against the wind PoM

Wind Me a Summer Crown. Menella Bute Smedley. There is a face which you shall see/And wish for nothing more. HBV 1-2; OBVV

The Wind of January. Christina Georgina Rossetti. Let him in to feel your fire,/And toss him of your crumbs. YeAr

The Wind of Our Enemy (excerpt). Anne Marriott. No rain, no crop, no feed, no faith, only/wind. CaP

The Wind of the Cliff Ka Hea. Phyllis Thompson. At the base of the cliff. FAZ

Wind of the Prairie. Grace Clementine Howes. The will of the wind for my pilot only, the stardrift/my compass and guide. GoYe

The Wind on the Hills. Dora Sigerson Shorter. When the wind is out in Erinn/And the sun is in the west. HBMV; NOBV

Wind on the Lyre. George Meredith. The blood of us a lighted dew. EG; NBM

A Wind Rose in the Night. Aline Kilmer. She lay before me small and still/And did not care at all. HBMV

The Wind's Song. (Thomas Nicoll Hepburn) "Setoun. Gabriel" For father's ship is coming home/With wondrous things from foreign lands. HBV 1-2; HBVY

The Wind's Way. Grace Hazard Conkling. Who would follow the wind must go/The wind's way. HBV 1-2

The Wind's Way. Richard Le Gallienne. Shall we ever again be heart to heart? HBMV

Wind's Work. Thomas Sturge Moore. But the wind knows! BrPo; HBMV; HBVY

Wind Secrets. Diane Wakoski. There was nothing I could do. AmPA

Wind-Song. Anonymous. To and fro, the blossoms swaying, swaying. SUS

Wind Song. Carl Sandburg. counting its money/and throwing it away? MoAB; MoAmPo; MoShBr

Wind Song. Zoe A. Tilghman. But these are they who have conquer'd and kept, the People/of Eighty-Nine. BPAW

The Wind Sou'West. Anonymous. And the ruffling seas rolled mountains high. AmFP

The Wind Sprang up at Four O'Clock. Thomas Stearns Eliot. The Tartar horsemen shake their spears. NePA

The Wind Suffers. Laura Riding. By my further dying. AnAmPo

The Wind-Swept.Wheat. Mary Ainge De Vere. Life's chords all answer from the wind-/swept wheat! AA

The wind tapped like a tired man. Emily Dickinson. And I became alone. MoAB; MoAmPo; NePA

The Wind, the Clock, the We. Laura Riding. The script not altered by a breath/Of perhaps meaning otherwise? LiTA

"The wind took up the northern things". Emily Dickinson. The transport of the bird! AmLP; SOTW

The Wind Was There. Bravig Imbs. and all my body's flight become a strange return. EAS

Wind-Wolves. William D. Sargent. ...bands of cloud-deer flee/In scattered groups of two and three. TiPo

Windfall. Joel Arsenault. and marbled by shadows/clocking around his face. AMV-81

Windfall. David Mitchell. a/mars/bar? OCNZ

Windfall. F. R. Scott. And lay down gently now my poem is over. CaP

Windham. Anonymous. Nature must call her gold but dross,/If she would gain this heav'nly land. AmFP

Windharp. John Montague. like the pile upon/a mountain pony's coat. CIP; FaBoIP

The Windhover. Gerard Manley Hopkins. Fall, gall themselves, and gash gold-vermilion. AtBAP; BiP; BrPo; CAW; CMoP; CoBMV; DiPo; EaLo; EBCP; ExPo; FaBoMo; ForPo; GTBS-P; HAP; InPK; InPS; InvP; LiTB; LiTM; LoBV; MoAB; MoBrPo; MoPo; MoVE; NIP; NoAm; NOBE; NOBV; NoP; OAEL 1-2; OAEP; OBNC; PAI; PBBP; PoEL 1-5; PoPl; PoPle; PoRA; PPoe; PPP; PrIm; SCV; SeCeV; SyP; TEP; TreFT; UnPo; VLP; WeW

Windigo. Paulette Jiles. People shoot the Windigo, they/do not pray for him, or it. NOBC

The Winding Banks of Erne. William Allingham. ...I surely will return/To my native Ballyshannon, and the winding banks of/Erne. AnIV; IrPN; NBM

Winding down the War. Philip Appleman. ...the pause,/hand over eyes, the glare,/the desert sea. SOTS

Windlass Song. William Allingham. Next year we'll come back with some more,/Heave O! GN

Windle-Straws. Edward Dowden. –Then died before her feet. HBV 1-2

The Windmill. John Byrne Leicester Warren, Lord De Tabley. Life, as a windmill grinds the bread of Life. NBM

The Windmill. Geoffrey Johnson. And the sadder time when mill and man/Will be both as if they never began. HaMV

The Windmill. Henry Wadsworth Longfellow. I cross my arms on my breast,/And all is peace within. MoShBr

Windmill in March. Katharine Privett. the power to bring birds and wheat/and gentle rain again. AMV-80

The Windmill of Evening. Shlomo Reich. of spheres with lead/under their wings. VWA

Windmill on the Cape. William Vincent Sieller. But wind, quixotic in its dance,/Has tried for conquest more than once. GoYe

The Windmills. John Gould Fletcher. And the choking gurgle of tepid water. CrMA

The Window. Conrad Aiken. and sees a whole world. CMoP

Window. Anne Cherner. longing for women in windows. AMV-80

The Window. Robert Creeley. ...I can/feel my eye breaking. CAPP; NoAm; NOBA; TAP; VGW

The Window. Stephen Dobyns. Look, they say, see how gracefully we are dancing. MAYP

The Window. Edwin Muir. Across the towering window fled/Disasters, victories, festivals. LiTM

The Window. Francis Scarfe. Cannot be lived again, yet has not died. NeBP

The Window. Iain Crichton Smith. · and it was all our searching spirits lacked. NePoEA-2

The Window (excerpt). Alfred, Lord Tennyson. Why?/For it's ay ay, ay ay. PBBP

The Window Frames the Moon. Laureen Mar. taking my place among the small things of the world. BrSi

The Window-Glance. Heinrich Heine. When wanders each churchyard spirit. AWP

The Window Has Four Little Panes. Gelett Burgess. I wonder why! HBV 1-2

Window Ledge in the Atom Age. E. B. White. (The tranquil heart may yet outrun/The rocket and the car.) NLV; OBAL

The Window of the Tobacco Shop. Constantine P. Cavafy. the sensitive approach of body to body,/hands joined, lips meeting. PeHV

The Window Sill. Robert Graves. A white and cankered rose. AtBAP; EnLoPo

Window to the East. Virginia Moran Evans. A boy with a window to the east/is a boy with an extra eye! AMV-80

Windowed Habitations. Charles G. Bell. That is one of the soul's windowed habitations. NePoAm-2

The Windows. George Herbert. And in the ear, not conscience, ring. AnAnS 1; CABA; MeLP; NOCV; NoP; OAEP; SeCP; SeCV 1-2; TrCP

Windows. Mordechai Husid. God, how have we led ourselves astray and gone wrong? VWA

The Windows. Ron Loewinsohn. ...all night spilling into/the dark house, all night they are there. GP

The Windows. William Stanley Merwin. and without moving he flies DFF

Windows in Providence. Aliki Barnstone. We are both an indifferent ocean and people shouting. BoWoP

The Windows of Waltham. John Wieners. Two met and made a first. CoPo

The Winds. Jack R. Clemo. The Christ renews his vows. EBCP

The Winds. John (William Kirkpatrick Magee) Eglinton. And ships are wreck'd, and shores are strewn. OnYI

Winds. Hugh McCrae. Red Rahab and white Maid! CBAP

The Winds. Thomas Tusser. It is an ill wind turns none to good. WiR

The Winds. William Carlos Williams. from scabby eyes,scales from/the mind and husbands from wives. AnAmPo

Winds A-Blowing. May Justus. The Spring Wind is a gay lad/Who blows a silver whistle. BrR

Winds of Africa. Dorothy S. Obi. They are speaking of you at home. WPOW

The Winds of Change. Charles G. Ballard. Pass, then, into oblivion, sweet word VoR

Winds of Eros. George William Russell. And keep for lovers yet to be/All the enchantment of our hearts. HBMV

The Winds of Fate. Ella Wheeler Wilcox. And not the calm or the strife. BLPA; FPL; TRV; WBLP

Winds of the West, Arise! George Darley. Over the ocean blown! AtBAP

Windshield. Robert Fitzgerald. A child's wish to do something simply superb. AmC; CrMA

Windshield Wipers. Dennis Lee. Please bring the sunshine/Back again. WHW

Windsor-Forest To the Right Honourable George Lord Lansdown. Alexander Pope. First in these fields I sung the sylvan strains. CEP

Windy Bill. Anonymous. And you'll never see your old rim-fire/Go drifting down the draw. CoSo

The Windy Bishop. Wilfred Watson. Of the windy bishop who'd preach our dust home. OBCV

Windy Morning. Harry Behn. With paper and paste and trains and toys. TiPo

The Windy Night. Thomas Buchanan Read. And dreams he is ringing a funeral knell! GN

Windy Nights. Robert Louis Stevenson. By at the gallop he goes, and then/By he comes back at the gallop again. GoJo; OxBChV; PH; PoRA; SiSoSe; TiPo

The Windy Planet. Annie Dillard. ar easterlies polar easterlies pol/pole SUW

Windy Trees. Archie Randolph Ammons. there's also no place comfortable to sit. PPJ

Windy Wash Day. Dorothy Aldis. Upside down/And skipping. TiPo

Wine. Daqiqi. But ever rises on the cheeks again. LiTW

Wine. Micah Joseph Lebensohn. Makes glad the life,/And brings Death low! LiTW; TrJP

Wine and Cakes for Gentlemen. *Anonymous.* And kisses for young lasses. OxNR

Wine and Dew. Richard Henry Stoddard. And drink her in dew! AA

Wine and Grief. Solomon Ibn Gabirol. Ye cannot stifle her sincere lament. LiTW; TrJP

Wine and Love and Lyre. *Anonymous.* Woe should I turn traitor to/Wine and love and lyre! UnTE

Wine and Water. Gilbert Keith Chesterton. But I don't care where the water goes if it doesn't get into/the wine. ACP; CenHV; FaBoCo; FiBHP; GoBC; HBMV; InMe; MoBrPo; ViBoPo

Wine Bowl. Hilda ("H. D.") Doolittle. I will chisel a bowl for the wine,/for the white wine/and red. NoP

The Wine Cup. Meleager. Deep draught drink down my soul! OLR

Wine from the Cape. Turner Cassity. Inside the glass repeats its four, its five. AMV-81

The Wine Menagerie. Hart Crane. Petrushka's valentine pivots on its pin. AP; NoAm; NOBA; OxBA; VGW

Wine O Living. Matt Marshall. Never lipped the wine o Living to the lees! PoSH

The Wing Factory. Dona Stein. all feather and fire. AMV-80

The Wing of Separation. al Andalusi Ibn Darraj And that I was worthy of the favor of Ibn Aamir. AWP

Winged Hours. Dante Gabriel Rossetti. Sees through the untuneful bough the wingless skies? MaVP

Winged Man. Stephen Vincent Benét. Mounting, mounting still, triumphant, on his torn and broken wings! MoAmPo

Winged Mariner. Grace Clementine Howes. Furling his wings at last to rock and rest/In the green hollow of the the stormy wave. EtS

The Winged Worshippers. Charles Sprague. And Nature's own great God adore. AA; HBV 1-2

Wings. Miroslav Holub. This/gives us/wings. SUW

Wings. Victor Hugo. Knowing that he has wings. TRV

The Wings. Denise Levertov. could I go/on one wing,/the white one? CAPP

Wings. Judith Wright. they blow beyond the headland, to the sea. CBAP; NOAV

Wings and Seeds. Sandra McPherson. For the long wait till our meeting. GeTw

Wings and Wheels. Nancy Byrd Turner. You know, birds! SoPo; SUS; TiPo

Wings at Dawn. Joseph Auslander. And their wings are split silver as they pass. HBMV

Wings in the Dark. John Gray. The fishers mumble, waiting till the night/Urge on the clouds, and cover up the moon. NOBV

The Wings of Love. James H. Cousins. For the Heart of all hearts, through the fire of love, and the/wine of love, and the wings. AnIV

Wingtip. Carl Sandburg. When will man know what birds know? PCP

Wingwalking in Oregon. Robert Peterson. ...& to whom/will I complain? NeAC

Winifred Waters. William Brighty ("Matthew Browne") Rands. Winifred will come back cured,/Let us hope, of crying. OxBChV

Winifreda. *Anonymous.* And I'll go wooing in my boys. HBV 1-2; OBEV

The Winners. Rudyard Kipling. He travels the fastest who travels alone! BLPA; FaPoR; FPL

The Winning of Cales. *Anonymous.* And when the town burnt in a flame,/With tan ra ra, tan ta ra ra, from thence we came. CoMu; OBSS; OBTV

The Winning of the TV West. John T. Alexander. The West is won again. AmFN

Winnipeg at Christmas. Rose Fyleman. You'd like it there, I know. ChBR

The Winnowers. Robert Bridges. 'Tis merry winnowing. OAEP

Winnsboro Cotton Mill Blues. *Anonymous.* I got the Winnsboro Cotton Mill Blues. FSW

Wino. Ted Hughes. ...I'm found/Feeble as a babe, but renewed. NoAm

Winslow Homer, Prisoners from the Front. Roger Blakely. who, like us, has yet to know,/if ever,/the losers from the winners. PoDr

Winter. Bella Akhmadulina. not my shadow, but light,/direct, not blocked by me. BoWoP

Winter. *Anonymous.*
And the word I chose is "chill." KiLC
On the fire the cauldron bubbles/All the long dark day. KiLC

Winter. Robert Burns. Assist me to resign. EiCP

Winter. John Clare. And hoarse loud bellows puffing up the blaze. ATP

Winter. Maurice James Craig. There crackles in the hearth/The holly's fusillade. OnYI

Winter. Walter De la Mare. Over that sea of frozen foam/Floats the white moon. OAEL 1-2; OBMV

Winter. Aubrey Thomas De Vere. Be still this night. The rite proceeds! IrPN

Winter. John Lyle Donaghy. How shall my feet then stay? BIrV

Winter. Gavin Douglas. So busteously Boreas his bugle blew. SeCePo

Winter. Richard Hughes. Old Thomas Kelly/Thrusts his bit hands, for warmth,/'Twixt waistcoat and belly. OBMV

Winter. James Hurnard. And thus the year goes round, and round, and round. PoSC

Winter. Jean Jaszi. Wearing mittens/Like my hand. SoPo

Winter. Mani Leib. Smoke curls even higher/Like silvery doves. VWA

Winter. Charles Mair. Then, winter, do I cry, "Thy greed/Is great, ay, thou art cold indeed!" OBCV; PeCV

Winter. Samuel Menashe. I am where I go GrPl

Winter. Dante Gabriel Rossetti. And leave memorial forest-kings o'erthrown. CBEP

Winter. Thomas, Earl of Dorset Sackville. The summer's beauty yields to winter's blast. EiL; SeCePo

Winter. Princess Shikishi. ...The moon/bares the garden. PBWP

Winter. Edmund Spenser. That scarce his loosed limbs he able was to weld. GN

Winter. Ruth Stone. I feel thir entire histories ravish me. BoWoP

Winter. John Millington Synge. For I go walking night and noon/To spare my sack of coals. NOBI; OBMV; OxBTC

Winter. James (1700-48) Thomson.
Pure flowing Joy, and Happiness sincere. CABL; EnLit; NOEC
Tipt with a wreath high-curling in the sky. CoBE

Winter. William Carlos Williams. ...leaves/spearshaped/in the falling snow NCSH

Winter. Sheila Wingfield. Our love which had a thousand leaves. EnLoPo

Winter and Red Berries. Nicholas Moore. The bouquet of your flesh turn sad by mine. NeBP

Winter and Summer. Stephen Spender. ...garden, falsified by snow/Waiting to melt, and become real again. MoAB; MoBrPo; MoPo

Winter Anemones. Charles Brasch. To lamp me through inscrutable dusk/And down the catacombs of death. OCNZ

Winter Apples. Winifred Welles. To lift one like a lantern in her hands. AnAmPo

Winter at Tomi. Ovid. And horses' hoofs ring loud where once their oarsmen/plied. AWP

Winter Burn. Roberta Hill. you burn into the yellow grass of winter,/into one reed, trembling on the plain. VoR

Winter Central. Christopher Dewdney. ...of the countless passing fry the ice into a fissile brocade/of tormented hydrogen CaPN

Winter Circus. Aileen Fisher. there's a circus in the sky/every snowy winter day! YeAr

Winter Climb. Beinn Eunaich. ...Dissonance/Is far below, where man is. PoSH

Winter Coming On. Martin Bell. Join in the chorus, sound the right sour note. FaBoMo; OxBTC

Winter Count of Sean Spotted Wolf. Earle Thompson. Even then, yes–they will behold another sunrise. STE

Winter Crickets. John Heath-Stubbs. And spring will come. OBCP

Winter Dawn. D. H. Lawrence. Of all feeling bereft. BrPo

Winter Day. Susannah Fried. your winter gnaws at my bones with the strength/of your unceasing melancholy... VWA

A Winter Daybreak above Vence. James Wright. ...Now we are all sitting here strangely/On top of the sunlight. InPS; LCAP

Winter Days. Henry Abbey. De Rohan staked a name to gain. AA

Winter Days. Gareth Owen. Nipped by winter/Stay in bed. OBCP

Winter Developing. Nora Dauenhauer. Dissolve inversion,/positive appears. TWSS

Winter Drive. James Philip McAuley. What is left to make us try? PoA

Winter Dusk. Walter De La Mare. Leaned close and drew them near. AnEnPo

Winter: East Anglia. Edmund Charles Blunden. And hard as winter dies. LiSp; OxBTC

Winter Encounters. Charles Tomlinson. Calmness within the wind, the warmth in cold. LiTM

Winter Evening. Archibald Lampman. Glittering and still shall come the awful night. OBCV; PeCV

Winter Evening Poem. Laura Jensen. from a place that will not mend for you? LCAP

Winter Fairyland in Vermont. Francis P. Osgood. Sends rich aroma through the house. WeW

Winter Feast. Frances Frost. we'll fly like brown leaves through/the cold! YeAr

The Winter Galaxy. Charles Heavysege. And forms more bright than diamond diadems. NOBC; OBCV

Winter Garden. David Gascoyne. A savage sun consumes its hidden day. ChMP; GTBS-P

The Winter Glass. Charles Cotton. His zeal may freeze, whilst we, kept warm/With love and wine, can know no harm. HBV 1-2

Winter Has At Last Come. Minamoto-No- Shigeyuki. Among the rush-leaves. AWP

Winter Has Come. *Anonymous.* The merry wave mutters. AnIL

Winter Heavens.   George Meredith.   And this is the soul's haven to have felt.   BoLiVe; NoP

Winter Holding Off the Coast of North America.   N. Scott Momaday.   The polar currents close,/And stiffen, and remain.   CDW

Winter Homily on the Calton Hill.   Douglas Young.   The culture of Athens was a nation's awaking.   OxBS

The Winter House.   Norman Cameron.   And comes to put my native fire to proof.   CBEP

A Winter Hymn–to the Snow.   Ebenezer Jones.   ...and bless the Powers/ That let thy loveliness to my soul be known!   OBNC

Winter in Another Country.   Florence Anthony ("Ai").   God carry her to Paradise/and dance there with her immortal soul.   AMV-81

Winter in Durnover Field.   Thomas Hardy.   The cruel frost encrusts the cornland!   MoBrPo

Winter in Etienburgh.   Stephen Parker.   Here, for just a season,/Among these clever citizens.   NYBP

Winter in the Fens.   John Clare.   I watch for spring–and there's the crocus come!   BoNaP

Winter in the Sierras.   Mary Austin.   And the snow wreaths drift/To the canons deep and still.   BPAW

Winter in the Wood.   Ivy O. Eastwick.   Only Robin/still is here!   YeAr

Winter is Another Country.   Archibald MacLeish.   I could endure this all/If autumn ended and the cold light came.   NCSH

Winter is Coming.   Waverly Turner Carmichael.   Like it done in days of old.   BANP

Winter Is Gone, and Spring Is Over.   Alfred Austin.   The cuckoo-flowers grow mauver and mauver.   FaBoCo

Winter Is Here.   Katri Vala.   But the berries of the rowan-tree/are burning like beacon fires.   PBWP

Winter Is Icumen In.   Bradford Smith.   Snort kerchoo!   PoSC

Winter Journey.   Stanislaw Wygodski.   Come, rains,/come,/come again/and again.   VWA

Winter Juniper.   Joseph Langland.   Caught in that alien axis, grown immense/In that green will.   NePoEA

The Winter Lakes.   Wilfred (William Wilfred Campbell) Campbell.   Death and hate on the rocks, as sandward and landward it/roars.   BoNaP; NOBC; OBCV

Winter Landscape.   John Berryman.   Descend, while three birds watch and the fourth flies.   AP; LiTA; LiTM; MoAmPo; MP; PoPl; TwCP

Winter Landscape.   Stephen Spender.   And our thin dying souls against Eternity pressed.   MoAB; MoBrPo

Winter Life and Scenery.   Thomas Caulfield Irwin.   We sighed for one sweet temperate breeze/To freshen earth with norland cold.   IrPN

The Winter Lightning for Paul.   Howard Nemerov.   Illuminate this dream/ With a cold art.   MoVE

Winter Love.   Hilda ("H. D.") Doolittle.   there was a Helen before there was a War,/but who remembers her?   FaBoWP

Winter Love.   Elizabeth Jennings.   The white skin shaken like a white snowflake.   BoLoP; NePoEA; PPJ

Winter Love Song.   Anonymous.   Yea, even the bitterness of love/Is bitter-sweet.   LiTW

A Winter Madrigal.   Morris Bishop.   My beauty broke her ankle:/Hey nonny, nonny, etc.   InMe

Winter Mask.   Allen Tate.   The sea worth living for.   AmLP; NePA; OxBA; Prf

Winter Memories.   Henry David Thoreau.   So by God's cheap economy made rich/To go upon my winter's task again.   AmLP; AmPP; NePA; OxBA

Winter Moon.   Langston Hughes.   Is the slim curved crook of the moon tonight!   DuDa

The Winter Moon.   Tagaki Kyozo.   The moon like a thousand lanterns.   LLLT

Winter Moon.   Maria Spaziani.   that an empty, cruel burst of wind rubs out.   PBWP

Winter Morning.   William Jay Smith.   A harbor of bone.   BoNaP; NCSH

Winter: My Secret.   Christina Georgina Rossetti.   Or you may guess.   BrRo; NOBV; TEP

Winter, New Hampshire.   David Kherdian.   to hear first/bear hoots/of spring   TAT

Winter News.   John Haines.   the voice of the snowman/calls the white-/ haired children home.   PPJ

A Winter Night.   William Barnes.   And I alone of all mankind/Were left in loneliness behind.   FaBoRV; NOBE; OBNC

A Winter Night.   Robert Burns.   While pitiless the tempest wild/Sore on you beats.   BSV; MCCG

Winter Night.   Louis O. Coxe.   Standing with held breath in the hall.   NYBP

Winter Night.   Cecil Day-Lewis.   But does not need to know/Why spirit was flesh-bound.   PoA

Winter Night.   A. R. D. Fairburn.   like young leaves in a forest place.   AnNZ

Winter Night.   Robert Fitzgerald.   ...The dead/Sleep light this wind being overhead.   PoPl

Winter Night.   Roy Fuller.   The world men made were man's no more.   NeBP

Winter Night.   Boris Pasternak.   A candle flamed upon a table;/A candle flamed.   PoPl

Winter Night.   Charles Simic.   An iceberg is a large, drifting/Piece of ice, broken off a glacier.   HaCAP

A Winter Night.   James (1700-48) Thomson.   Lifts her pale eye unjoyous.   NOBE

Winter Night, Cold Spell.   Howard Nelson.   and the icy sprays of stars.   AMV-81

Winter Nightfall.   Robert Bridges.   And braves as he may the night/Of darkness and tears.   MoAB; MoBrPo; OBEV

Winter Nightfall.   Sir John Collings Squire.   In this desolate country's/ Cadaverous clay.   OxBTC

Winter Nights.   Thomas Campion.   Though love and all his pleasures are but toys,/They shorten tedious nights.   CBEP; NOBE; OBEV

Winter Nights.   Lora Dunetz.   Call us to shelter, hearth, and fireside chair.   AMV-80

Winter Noon.   Sara Teasdale.   Chipmunk, do you like the sun,/The blowing snow and me?   YeAr

Winter Noon in the Woods.   Thomas Caulfield Irwin.   So bitter keen the sky/These dark December days.   IrPN

Winter Ocean.   John Updike.   portly pusher of waves, wind-slave.   ELU; InPK; MOS; SoSe

The Winter of '73.   Anonymous.   That was my first experience on the Miramichi.   ShS

Winter Offering.   D. S. Savage.   Poverty's fixed, archaic physiognomy/ Projects only through masks where nothing else extrudes.   LiTB; NeBP

Winter on Black Mingo (excerpt).   Anonymous.   Winter has a place/No season can erase.   FiBHP

Winter over Nothing.   Elliott Coleman.   Snow us Under/Winter Over Nothing   FAZ

A Winter Piece.   William Cullen Bryant.   ,and the loud North again/Shall buffet the vexed forest in his rage.   AmPP; AP; OxBA

A Winter-Piece to a Friend Away.   John Berryman.   Your letter came!   NOBA

Winter Ploughing.   William Everson.   And the thin cries of the gleaming, bent-winged birds.   NU

Winter Pond.   Ben Belitt.   and the swimmer arose in his nakedness and called from the opposite shore.   NYBP

Winter Portrait.   Robert Southey.   Watching children at their Christmas mirth.   BoNaP

Winter Rain.   Christina Georgina Rossetti.   Not a lily on the land,/Or lily on the water.   BoNaP; WiR

Winter Rains: Cataluna.   Philip Levine.   and spreads their darkness like a sigh.   NaP

Winter Remembered.   John Crowe Ransom.   Ten frozen parsnips hanging in the weather.   AP; HAP; MoAB; NOBA; OxBA; PrIm; UnPo; VGW

Winter Report.   Ben Howard.   ...And the thing which only a moment ago/ I'd thought to say, is already fled and gone.   PoA

Winter Rune.   Elizabeth Jane Coatsworth.   And pleases dogs and children/ And the philosopher!   SUS

Winter's Dregs.   George Bowering.   though now we muffle our souls/our very darkling selves ourselves   PeCV

Winter's Edge.   P. R. Roberts.   five belated addresses/to the Lord.   SOTS

Winter's End.   Howard Moss.   I saw the heart of summer start.   NePoEA

Winter's Onset from an Alienated Point of View.   Alan Dugan.   so I do none of this/in offices away from weather.   FF

The Winter's Spring.   John Clare.   Nature's white spirits of the spring.   AtBAP

A Winter's Tale.   Robert Patrick Dana.   And the blue snow melts about us as it falls.   NYBP

A Winter's Tale.   D. H. Lawrence.   Why does she come, when she knows what I have to tell?   MoAB; MoBrPo

The Winter's Tale.   William Shakespeare.   ...these are flowers/Of middle summer.   YeAr
Your sad tires in a mile-a.   TrGrPo

A Winter's Tale.   Dylan Thomas.   And she rose with him flowering in her melting snow.   AtBAP; CMoP; LiTB; SeCeV

The Winter's Walk.   Samuel Johnson.   And hide me from the sight of life.   CBEP; EiCP

Winter Saint.   Archie Randolph Ammons.   I'm for ice and shutters/and the miles and miles/winter clears between us.   TW

Winter Scene.   Archie Randolph Ammons.   quivers and/breaks out in blue leaves.   WeW

A Winter Scene.   Reed Whittemore.   ...noses/have stopped their incessant running and it is quiet here.   NCSH

Winter Scene.   Marguerite Young.   And the white ptarmigan treads in the snow among the low hills.   NU

The Winter Shore. Thomas Wade. In gloomy grandeur o'er the hills and seas/Reigneth omnipotent. ERoP 1-2; NBM; OAEL 1-2

Winter Sign. Loren C. Eiseley. ...It will last through the autumn days. SUW

Winter Sketch. Arthur Stanley Bourinot. And then the silence of the dead/ Is held within the listening wood. CaP

Winter Sketches. Charles Reznikoff. on these honeycombs of light, the buildings of Manhattan. PoA

Winter Sleep. Edith Matilda Thomas. And turf-bound silence, in the frosty year. AA

Winter Sleep. Elinor Wylie. Soft, soft, soft, and deep, deep, deep! NePA

Winter-Solitude. Archibald Lampman. So deathly silent–I so utterly alone. PeCV

Winter Solstice–For Frank. Asphodel. And will expect me one day. BrRo

Winter Solstice Poem. Diana Scott. that the lady of light is lovely and returns/regardless, uncaring, like the grass. BrRo

Winter Song. David Daiches. "I keep my nerve, I keep my nerve!" NYBP

Winter Song. Juan Ramon Jimenez. The birds that are singing. WSC

Winter Song. George Macdonald. A gaze in the eyes, a kiss–/Why will it not go by! NOBV

Winter Song. Elizabeth Tollet. While faithful love the watch should keep,/ To banish danger from thy sleep. NOEC

Winter Stars. Larry Levis. Cold enough to reconcile/Even a father, even a son. MAYP

The Winter Storm at Sea. George Crabbe. A seaman's body! There'll be more tonight! EtS

Winter Streams. Bliss Carman. Slip their snowy bands and run/Sparkling in the welcome sun. YeAr

Winter Sunrise (excerpt). Laurence Binyon. A memory floating up from a dark water,/Can be more beautiful than the thing remembered. ChMP

Winter Sunset. Jules Laforgue. ...may there be nothing known/Of this rotten Brain which was the Earth, one day. SyP

Winter Swan. Louise Bogan. Bird, the long throat bent back, and the eyes in hiding. AnAmPo

A Winter Talent. Donald Davie. ...Better still to burn/Upon that gloom where all have felt a chill. NePoEA-2; OAEL 1-2

Winter Term. John Malcolm Brinnin. These are the features only futures know. GLGT

Winter: The Abandoned Nest. Ron Baxter. Far-out voice calls, "Look, no moon!" WeW

Winter the Huntsman. Osbert Sitwell. Cracking his cruel whip/To the gathering shades? AtBAP; BoW

Winter Time. Robert Louis Stevenson. And tree and house, and hill and lake,/Are frosted like a wedding-cake. MoBrPo; OxBChV

Winter to Spring. Horace. And whom tomorrow girls will find a fire. LiTW

Winter Trees. Conrad Diekmann. ...Fools like me/Should never try to shave a tree. LiSp; SD

Winter Trees. Sylvia Plath. The shadows of ringdoves chanting, but easing nothing. CAPP; HaCAP; LCAP; NMM; SBG

Winter Trout. James Dickey. And the thing seen right,/For once, that winter bought. LiSp

Winter Tryst. Mark Van Doren. Yet it was hers. And time's result/Is love's most fair, most speechless fable. LiTA

A Winter Twilight. Arlo Bates. That takes at last the bitter sting/Of day's keen pain away. AA

A Winter Twilight. Angelina Weld Grimke. One star that I loved ere the fields went brown. CDC; PoBA; PoNe

Winter Twilight. Lou Lipsitz. When I see them I feel like a hundred men/ who know they have slipped out of prison/without a trace. GOYP

Winter Twilight. George Tracy Rlliot. The peace of heaven within thy tranquil/breast. AA

Winter Twilight. Jeff Schiff. Let them speak. AMV-81

The Winter Twilight, Glowing Black and Gold. Delmore Schwartz. But once more, as before, accepted and refused. NoAm

Winter Verse for His Sister. William Meredith. And the field tilting always toward day. NYBP; TAP

Winter Wakens All My Care. Anonymous. –Don't know the place I'm for. Don't know the day. HAP; OxBM

Winter Warfare. Edgell Rickword. stabbing those who lingered there/torn by screaming steel. OBWP; OxBTC

Winter Watch. Jeff Daniel Marion. our stories grow too dark to tell. AMV-80

Winter Westerlies. James Devaney. Ceaseless, changeless, malign, searching into the very soul/The rushing desolation reigns. BoAV

Winter Will Follow. Richard Watson Dixon. Take fright in his bewildering bower, and die. GTBS-P

Winter Winds Cold and Blea. John Clare. Where my head droops to rest,/ Leave its bed bare. GBL; OBNC

A Winter Wish. Robert Hinckley Messinger. If these I tine,/Can books, or fire, or wine be good? AA; ViBoPo

Winter with the Gulf Stream. Gerard Manley Hopkins. Into the flat blue mist the sun/Drops out and all our day is done. CMoP; ExPo; NoAm; SyP; VLP

A Winter without Snow. J. D. McClatchy. On the house, on a world of possibilities. FYAP

Wintered Sunflowers. Richard Snyder. ...They've snowed their gold/to Ikhnaton and stand/tracking stations with nothing to behold. PPJ

Winterfall. Anonymous.. And ich with wel michel wrong/Sorow and murne and fast. OxBM

Wintering. Sylvia Plath. The bees are flying. They taste the spring. NMM

A Wintering Moon. R. Wayne Hardy. i grow quiet as a sleeping child/in a moon-dripping winter. LFAC

Winterscape. Jess Perlman. but now...oh now the moon comes shining through! AMV-80

Winterward. William Stafford. Oh winter, oh snowy interior,/rocks and hurt birds, we come. SM

Winwick, Lancashire. Anonymous. The steeple gives a nod. GBP

Wire Monkey. Paul D. Shiplett. Mockingbirds do not kill/they mock... LFAC

Wires. Lee Bassett. High above the world of talk/he slips honestly, falls/ into the wind. SOTS

The Wisconsin Soldier Boy. Anonymous. With his knapsack for a pillow/ And his musket on his breast. BFSS

Wisdom. Padraic Fallon. That the crown of love is...to be in at the death. OnYI

Wisdom. Ford Madox Ford. "We do not know," he said,/"Nor may till we be dead." HBV 1-2

Wisdom. Phyllis Hanson. fold ancient pity/over new-turned earth. GoYe

Wisdom. Daniel Whitehead Hicky. And kiss your love and latch the door/ And let the world go by! BiCB

Wisdom. Langston Hughes. And make earth happy/As the dreamed of skies. TiPo

Wisdom. Scudder Middleton. One must go trustful through the dark/To earn the friendship of the stars. HBMV

Wisdom. Linda Peavy. An equal wisdom, I'd surmise. PH

Wisdom. Christina Georgina Rossetti. Seated alone and in peace till God bids it arise. OBVV

Wisdom. Hy Sobiloff. Prayers to be said/With no sacrifice. VGW

Wisdom. Sara Teasdale. It is the things we have that go. AmLP; MoAmPo

Wisdom. William Butler Yeats. Considering what wild infancy/Drove horror from His Mother's/breast. TrCP

Wisdom. Frank Yerby. And, in a month, to be at peace again.! AmNP

Wisdom Is the Finest Beauty of a Person. Anonymous. Come and sacrifice, that you may have rest in your body,/Inside and outside. WTO

The Wisdom of Folly. Ellen Thorneycroft Fowler. A merry heart goes twice the way/That tires a sad one. HBV 1-2

The Wisdom of Insecurity. Richard Eberhart. An infant, the soul, springing from its head. NePA

The Wisdom of Merlyn. Wilfrid Scawen Blunt. To gather the daisies, and drop them, and sleep on the/nursing knees of the Fates. OBMV; ViBoPo

The Wisdom of Old Jelly Roll. A.J.M. Smith. Being on whiskey, ragtime, chicken, and the scriptures fed. PeCV

Wisdom of the Gazelle. George P. Solomos. The wisdom of the gazelle/ Remains in my head. GoYe

The Wisdom of the World. Siegfried Sassoon. Companioned by those powers who keep me unafraid. MoBrPo

The Wise. Countee Cullen. Or think me strange who long to be/Wrapped in their cool immunity. PoNe

Wise. Lizette Woodworth Reese. But you are dead and gone. HBV 1-2

Wise Johnny. Edwina Fallis. I just saw a lady-bug/And heard a robin sing. SiSoSe; SUS; TiPo

The Wise Men. Edgar Bowers. ...They wait upon a sign/That promises no future but their name. NePoEA

The Wise Men Ask the Children the Way. Heinrich Heine. And the kings began to sing. OBCP

Wise Men in Their Bad Hours. Robinson Jeffers. And a few dead men's thoughts have the same temper. AnAmPo

A Wise Old Owl. Edward Hersey Richards. Why can't we all be like that bird? BLPA; FaBoBe; FaFP; GoTF; TreF; YaD

A Wise Old Owl Sat in an Oak. Anonymous. Why aren't we all like that wise old/bird? OxNR

Wise Owl. Patricia Goedicke. Ahead is the home light. SM

The Wise Woman. Louis Untermeyer. Who understands him. ALV; HBMV

Wiser Than the Children of Light. Monk Gibbon. But men prefer to take the cash/And let such fragile credit go. NeIP

Wisga. Lew Blockcolski. But no one blames Wisga/anymore. VoR

A Wish. *Anonymous.* Yea, Jesus be Himself to thee the Same/As that He is declared by His Name. CAW

A Wish. Matthew Arnold.
...and give/The ill he cannot cure a name. DBV
Then willing let my spirit go/To work or wait elsewhere or here! HBV 1-2

The Wish. Abraham Cowley. And so make a city here. BoC; CavP; HBV 1-2; LiTB; NOBE; NoP; OAEP; OBEV; OBS; SeCV 1-2; TrGrPo; ViBoPo; WHA

A Wish. Hamlin Garland. Lit by the sky's unfailing grace. AA

Wish. Lance Henson. repeat the only/word you know CDW

A Wish. Laurence Lerner. ...nothing on earth is free. FF

A Wish. Vidal de Nicolas. filling the songs of poets everywhere. BoC

A Wish. Samuel Rogers. And point with taper spire to Heaven. FaPoR; GTBS; HBV 1-2; MCCG; NOBE; OBEC; OBEV; OBVV; TreFS

The Wish. Thomas Stanley. That thou might'st but tread on me. AWP

A Wish. John Millington Synge. Sorrow's sauce for every kiss. FaBoEE

The Wish. Rowland Watkyns. This is the summe of my desire,/Until I come unto heaven's quire. CavP

Wish for a Young Wife. Theodore Roethke. When I am undone,/When I am no one. NoAm; NoP; OBSP; TAP

A Wish for the New Year. Phillips Brooks. That makes life blessed. STF

A Wish for Waving Goodbye. Roberta Hill. ...grace, the largest space we know,/may be just across the threshold. AMV-80

Wish of Manchin of Liath. *Anonymous.* and for me to be sitting for a while praying to God in every/place. AnIL

The Wish to Be Believed. Mona Van Duyn. "Believe. Believe this is what I see." PoA

Wishes. Norman Ault. Only the king of the land and the sea. HBMV; HBVY

Wishes. A. C. Child. God granting these, before I die, I'd ask no more of life. PoToHe

Wishes. Patty L. Harjo. Forever in beauty/Always VoR

Wishes for a Bridal Couple and Their Unborn Child. Statius Publius Papinius. And your loveliness be slow to fade. HW

Wishes for Her. Denis Devlin. I wish you well, wish/Tall angels whose rib-freezing/Beauty attend you. CIP; NOBI

Wishes for My Son. Thomas Macdonagh. These for you, so small and young,/In your hand and heart and tongue. AnIV; GoBC; HBMV

Wishes for William. Winifred M. Letts. Saying: "He's late–he's late." OnYI

Wishes of an Elderly Man. Sir Walter Ralegh. I wish I thought What Jolly Fun! DBV; FaBoCh; FaBoCo; FaBoEE; FiBHP; FPL; LoGBV; NLV; NOBL; PV

Wishes to His Supposed Mistress. Richard Crashaw. Be ye my fictions–but her story. AnFE; ATP; BoLoP; EBEV; HBV 1-2; LiTL; MePo; OBEV; OBS; TreFT; ViBoPo

Wishful Thinking. Michael C. Blumenthal. ...a bird rising over the ashes, a dream. HaCAP

The Wishin' Well. Helen B. Cruickshank. But–Losh keep me,/What did I speir?' BSV

Wishing. William Allingham. For Mother's kiss,–sweeter this/Than any other thing! HBV 1-2; HBVY; OHIP; OxBChV

Wishing Africa. Marilyn Bowering. and remember how it hurt/to be greedy and eat. CaPN; NOBC

Wishing Poem. *Anonymous.* Wish I may, wish I might,/Have this wish I wish tonight. NTCP

Wishmakers' Town. William Young.
Awake! Awake! AA
Deign to forget not Peter and his pence. AA
Pity us, pray for us, ye that will! AA
Though he stand in the shambles of death. AA

The Wistful Days. Robert Underwood Johnson. We have not truly known the Spring. AA

The Wit. Elizabeth Bishop. the glinting birthday of a fractious star. NePoAm-2

Wit's-End Corner. *Anonymous.* But only at Wit's-End Corner/Is the "God who is able" proved. BLRP; STF

Wit, Whither Wilt Thou? *Anonymous.* And never more say "Woe is me!" EIL

Wit Wonders. *Anonymous.* Beleeve and leave to wonder. MeEL

A Witch. William Barnes. Did meake the hag bewitch em woo'se. VLP

Witch. Patricia Beer. I shall see justice done. OxBC

The Witch. Mary Elizabeth Coleridge. To lift her over the threshold, and let her in/at the door! BrRo; NCEP

The Witch. Lord Alfred Bruce Douglas. Poor fool! be not deceived, God is not mocked. HBMV

The Witch. Wilfrid Gibson. Spinning, she swathes herself again/In a fresh web of mist and rain. PoSH

The Witch. Katharine Tynan Hinkson. I do forgive her, with hate and scorn. NOBV; OnYI

The Witch. Robert Southey. Started, and scream'd with fear. WiR

Witch. Jean Tepperman. We are screaming,/we are flying,/laughing, and won't stop. NMM

The Witch. William Butler Yeats. To the chamber where/Lies one long sought/With despair? ELU

The Witch-Bride. William Allingham. Weary day!–the foul Witch-Bride. NOBV

Witch Cat. Rowena Bastin Bennett. And which cat is a witch cat,/I really cannot tell. SiSoSe

Witch Doctor. Robert Earl Hayden. And of himself as God. AmNP; MAT; NoAm

The Witch Doctor's Magic Flight. Smiler Narautjarri. So you travel, Pararuru. NOAV

A Witch Going Down to Egypt. Raquel Chalfi. and my roasted body/my skull. VWA

Witch Hazel. Theodore Enslin. Cut me a switch to whip old ghosts/through sunsets to the morning. CoPo

The Witch in the Glass. Sarah Piatt. They found his wayward wife's sweet hair. AA

The Witch o' Fife. James Hogg. For he sees thee yet, he sees thee yet! BSV

The Witch of Atlas. Percy Bysshe Shelley. Scarcely believe much more than we can see. ERoP 1-2; PBBP

The Witch of Coos. Robert Frost. The rural letter box said Toffile Lajway. AP; AtBAP; CMoP; CoBMV; DiPo; ExPo; InPK; InPS; MoAB; NePA; NoAm; NOBA; ViBoPo

The Witch of East Seventy-Second Street. Morris Bishop. And I took her charred contract/And signed in triplicate. NYBP; NYP

The Witch's Ballad. William Bell Scott. We'll dance again the saraband! AnFE; EvOK; NBM; NOBV; OBEV; OBVV; VLP

Witch's Broomstick Spell. *Anonymous.* Horse and pelatis, Ho, ho! GBP

The Witch's Cat. Ian Serraillier. "But planet-and-space-ship,/Rocket or race-ship/Never shall part me from that." SO; WSC

Witch's Milking Charm. *Anonymous.* Come a' to me, come a' to me. GBP

The Witch's Whelp. Richard Henry Stoddard. And hear, as now, the voices of the sea. AA; AnAmPo

The Witch's Work Song. T. H. White. With a hey-nonny-nonny and I don't mean maybe. FaBoNo

The Witch, V, i. Thomas Middleton. All ill come running in, all good keep out! WSC

Witchcraft by a Picture. John Donne. Being in thine owne heart, from all malice free. EyDe

Witchcraft: New Style. Lascelles Abercrombie. –"The law should have a say to that, by God!" MoBrPo

Witchcraft was hung, in history. Emily Dickinson. Find all the witchcraft that we need/Around us, every day– WSC

Witches. Ted Hughes. Over our harms, who's to know/Where their feet dance while their heads sleep? GoYe

The Witches' Charm. Ben Jonson. Let all be dumb. EIL; FaBoCh; LoBV; LoGBV; NOBE

The Witches' Song. Ben Jonson. And now our orgies let's begin. CH

Witches' Spells. Madeleine Edmondson. To your natural shape return! NTCP

The Witches' Wood. Mary Elizabeth Coleridge. Had frightened off the eye of day/And kept the Moon reflected there. PBWP

The Witching Song. James (1700-48) Thomson. To toil for what you here untoiling may obtain. OBEC

Witchwood. May Justus. A witch makes her broom from a sassafras stick. SiSoSe

With a Book at Twilight. Jakov Steinberg. And your fearful gaze embraces only the shadows of emptiness. VWA

With a Bottle of Blue Nun to All My Friends. Madeline De Frees. That's what happens when Blue Nuns/bail out./It's that simple. GP

With a China Chamberpot, to the Countess of Hillsborough. Henry Fox, Lord Holland. My warm imagination should proceed/To what you must not write, she must not read. FaBoUs

With a Coin from Syracuse. Oliver St. John Gogarty. And blood that, tamed and mild,/Can suddenly go wild. OBMV

With a First Reader. Rupert Hughes. For all things trite shall leap alight/And bloom again for you! HBMV

With a Flower. Emily Dickinson. You, unsuspecting, feel for me/Almost a loneliness. LiTL

With a Gift of Rings. Robert Graves. But, naked on your couch, wear them for me. GBL

With a Guitar, to Jane. Percy Bysshe Shelley. It keeps its highest, holiest tone/For our beloved Jane alone. ERoP 1-2; HBV 1-2; OAEL 1-2

With a Lifting of the Head. Hugh" (Christopher Murray Grieve) MacDiarmid. Above the poor slut's face/Another woman's name. MoBrPo

With a Little Bit of Luck. Alan Jay Lerner. With a little bit of bloomin' luck! FaFP

With a Nantucket Shell. Charles Henry ("John Paul") Webb. Of Christian should more have been wrecked/on shore/Than ever lost at sea! AA

With a Posthumous Medal. John Malcolm Brinnin. Though this was but a death among ruined stones/Of one who knew them with the intimacy of children. SaC

With a rocking. Prince Yuke. Because of a child of man. LiTW

With a Rod No Man Alive. Walther von der Vogelweide. Have good care of all the three. AWP

With a Rose from Conway Castle. Julia Caroline Ripley Dorr. Fair Conway sends this sweet wild rose to/thee! AA

With a Sliver of Marble from Carrara. James Wright. Even he/Could not live long enough. EyDe

With a Spray of Apple Blossoms. Walter Learned. And sent this snowy spray to thee. AA

With All Deliberate Speed. Don L. Lee. went home to alabama/to brag about/it. JB

With All My Heart, Jehovah, I'll Confess. Henry Ainsworth. Let heathens know weak men they be. Selah. AH

With Child. Genevieve Taggard. To be untangled from these mother's bones. AnEnPo; MoAmPo

With Christ and All His Shining Train. Thomas Prince. And filled with joy, we'll ever praise. AH

With Cindy at Vallecito. Walter McDonald. ...and then/like losers in a poker game will cast/their own lines far, far out. WOLT

With Corse at Allatoona. Samuel H. M. Byers. As if there had not been a battle/This morning up there on the hill. PAH

With Cortez in Mexico. Wilfred (William Wilfred Campbell) Campbell. Trolling an old Moorish song. PAH

With Due Deference to Thomas Wolfe. Joanne Townsend. —heedless of Sabbath/and immune to echoes. AMV-81

With every note. Anonymous. how sad to hear/day turn dark BoWoP

With Every Rising of the Sun. Ella Wheeler Wilcox. Go forth I say—attain–attain. GoTF; TreFT

With Eyes at the Back of Our Heads. Denise Levertov. mountain/of short grass and subtle shadows. AmPP

With Flowers. Emily Dickinson. That gathered these today! AA

With Fragrant Flowers We Strew the Way. Thomas Watson. Accept of our unfeigned joy! EIL

With Freedom's Seed. Alexander Pushkin. Their dower the yoke their sires have worn/Through snug and sheeplike generations. TTY

With Garments Flowing. John Clare. Thou with the spring wouldst wander there. GBL

With God and His Mercy. Carl Olof Rosenius. Our thanks and our praises we'll render to thee. AH

With God Conversing. Gene Derwood. We-you? Post-suicides, shall we awaken? LiTA; LiTM; MoRP; NePA

With Hands Like Leaves. James Still. He seeks a hill where living day shall stand. GrPl

With Happiness Stretched Across the Hills. William Blake. ...May God us keep/From Single vision & Newton's sleep! EnRP

With Him. Julia E. Martin. He giveth His beloved rest,/To the weary one. STF

With How Sad Steps, O Moon, Thou Climb'st the Sky. William Wordsworth. Queen both for beauty and for majesty. MBW 1-2

With I and E. Anonymous. Of all thy kith dare sleep thee with a night under thy/shete. OxBM

...With Its Quiet Tongue. Kamala Das. With its quiet tongue... ACV

With Kathy at Wisdom. Richard Hugo. Morning Wisdom, Kathy. It is no dream. FAZ

With Kit, Age 7, at the Beach. William Stafford. and as I talked, I swam. RFM

With Lilacs. Charles Henry Crandall. A heart less perfect, needing cure/By Love's own music, softly played. AA

With Lilacs in My Eye. Lucile Coleman. So I'm a next-door beggar/With lilacs in my eye. GoYe

With Long Black Wings. Trumbull Stickney. I knew your brow was cooled, you well again. NCEP

With Lullay, Lullay. John Skelton. I wys, powle hachet, she bleryd thyne I. AAS; InvP; NCEP

With Me My Lover Makes. Cecil Day-Lewis. In a green melancholy/Of overblown summer. OBMV

With Mercy for the Greedy. Anne Sexton. they are the tongue's wrangle,/the world's pottage, the rat's star. CAPP; HaCAP

With Metaphor. Sarah Wingate Taylor. still master in his pyramid. GoYe

With My Breath I Cut My Way through the Six Forests. Lalleswari. At that very instant, Siva was there with me. WPOW

With My Crowbar Key. William Stafford. myself at work with this crowbar key. ConAP

With My God, the Smith. Uri Z. Greenberg. Now it is night; come, let us both rest. VWA

With My Grandfather. Zelda. And in the shambles of his room/angels sang/of the Heavenly Jerusalem. VWA

With Pipe and Flute. Henry Austin Dobson. Not so it fared, when time began,/With pipe and flute! VLP

With Poems Already Begun. Rachel Korn. and the promise of May/to my frost-silvered lines. VWA

With Roses. Beatrix Demarest Lloyd. For love: each petal of each rose a kiss! AA

With Rue My Heart Is Laden. Alfred Edward Housman. The rose-lipt girls are sleeping/In fields where roses fade. AWP; BLPL; CMoP; EnL; FaFP; GoTF; GTBS; HAP; HeIP; HoPM; InPK; LiTB; LiTL; LiTM; MasP; MoAB; MoBrPo; NoAm; NoP; PG; PrIm; SoSe; TreFT; TrGrPo; UnPo

With Rue My Heart Is Laden (parody). Samuel Hoffenstein. While richer boys are keeping/The girls that do not fade. UnPo

With Schoolchildren. Willis Barnstone. ...I hope/you always remember our pact. I will. GLGT

With Seed the Sowers Scatter. Alfred Edward Housman. And touch it and it stings. EnLi 1-2

With Self Dissatisfied. Frederick Lucian Hosmer. The discipline of thy rebuke/Shall be refining fire! TrPWD

With Serving Still. Sir Thomas Wyatt. Thus for her sake/To be undone! EG; EiL; FCP; InPK; LoBV; SiPS; WHA

With Ships the Sea Was Sprinkled. William Wordsworth. On went She, and due north her journey took. EnRP; HBV 1-2; MOS

With Snow White Veil. Henry Wadsworth Longfellow. ...bring at last/That perfect pardon which is perfect peace. TreFT

With Strawberries. William Ernest Henley. Can sweethearts all their thirst allay/With strawberries? HBV 1-2

With Tendrils of Poems. Michael McClure. SEPTEMBER BLACKBERRIES! PoM

With the Bait of Bread. Helene Pilibosian. If not already, Armenian will/ring in one of your ears someday. AMV-81

With the Dawn. Thomas Caulfield Irwin. To be alive, and suffer not, is sleep. BIrV; EnLoPo; IrPN

With the Door Open. David Ignatow. I am happy only/with the door open between us. CTBA

With the Face. Laura Riding. With such faint brightnesses. NoAm

With the Herring Fishers. Hugh" (Christopher Murray Grieve) MacDiarmid. Singin': "Come, shove in your heids and growl!" BSV; LiTM

With the Most Susceptible Element, the Mind, Already Turned... Walter Benton. ...a better way of killing a louse/than by destroying the body it feeds on. WaP

With the Nuns at Cape May Point. David Earle Anderson. and I, a ship melting in the night. AMV-81

With the Shell of a Hermit Crab. James Wright. So far away, so delicate,/Stars in a wilderness of stars. NoP; SM

With the Sun's Fire. David Ignatow. air, with dirt, with food/and with the sun's fire. FAZ

With Thee. Cora M. Pinkham. Peace will be yours, the greatest known. STF

With Thee Conversing. John Milton. ...nor walk by moon,/Or glittering starling, without thee is sweet. WiR

With Thee to Soar to the Skies. Anonymous. In life or death we still may be. BePJ

With Timrels. Anonymous. And they shall weep and feel their pain/for ever. TrJP

With Two Fair Girls. Robert C. MacGregor. Alas! alike is punishment to me. ALV

With What Conviction the Young Man Spoke. W. H. Auden. No one believes the booming old bore. PV

With Whom Is No Variableness, Neither Shadow of Turning. Arthur Hugh Clough. I steadier step when I recall/That, if I slip, Thou dost not fall. EnLi 1-2; GoTF; TreFS; TRV; WGRP

With Wordsworth at Rydal. James Thomas Fields When, winged for heaven, thy soul ascended? AA

With You a Part of Me. George Santayana. What I keep of you, or you rob from me. TrGrPo

With you first shown to me. William Barnes. Seem'd that which fell along your flow'ry ways. EnLoPo

With You Here at Mertu. Anonymous. With your arms around me/I feel as if I belong to the Pharoah. PBWP

The Withdrawal. Robert Lowell. until the wristwatch is taken from the wrist. NoP

A Withered Rose. Yehoash. Long, long ago someone had loved./Oh, whom? and who? TrJP

Within a Greenwood Sweet of Myrtle Savour. Anonymous. She kindly kissed his cheek with lips of roses. GBL

Within and Without. George Macdonald. And found myself in Thee–the Father then/Will come with Thee, and will abide with me. TRV; WGRP

Within My Breast. Sir Thomas Wyatt. Nor I am not in number one of those/That list to blow retreat to every train. EnRePo; FCP

Within my Garden, rides a Bird. Emily Dickinson. An Exquisite Reply! AmPP

Within My Heart. Judah Al-Harizi. The woe that tell-tale tears confess. TrJP

Within the Dream You Said. Philip Larkin. As cold as my heart. InPS; PAI

Within the Shelter of Our Walls. Elinor Lennen. Our daily strength for thee be spent/With thought and loving care. AH

Within the Veil. Margaret E. Sangster. When, soft as zephyr, his touch shall fall. BLRP

Within These Doors Assembled Now. Oliver Holden. If Satan fright our trembling souls,/Thy mercy may appear. AH

Within This Grave Do Lie. Anonymous. If she gets up, I'll just lie still. ShM

Within Us, Too. R. H. Grenville. a yearning, upward burning/spirit-fire. AMV-80

Without, and Within. James Russell Lowell. ...will he/Think me the happier, or I him? HBV 1-2

Without Benefit of Declaration. Langston Hughes. Mama, don't cry. AmNP; TTY

Without Benefit of Tape. Dorothy Livesay. speech echoes from the canyon's wall/resonant/indubitable. NOBC

Without Ceremony. Vassar Miller. When we have not a prayer except ourselves. CoPo; MoAmPo; SM

Without Her. Dante Gabriel Rossetti. Where the long cloud, the long wood's counterpart,/Sheds doubled darkness up the labouring hill. CBEP; GBL; MaVP; NCEP

Without Me You Won't Be Able to See Yourself. Chaim Grade. Now you're a fading woman–and not a goddess. VWA

Without More Weight. Giuseppe Ungaretti. Who still would fear, who judge? PoPl

Without My Friends the Day Is Dark. Moses Ibn Ezra. But in their company the night is/luminous. TrJP

Without Name. Pauli Murray. But our lips shall be silent, uncommitted. AmNP; PoBA; PoNe

Without Names. Jeff Tagami. I forget my name. BrSi

Without Regret. Lilith Lorraine. And what it covers...let all men forget. PGD

Without That Once Clear Aim. Stephen Spender. The writings are my only wings away. CMoP

Without the Herdsman. Diotimus. Sent to his slumber by the lightning's stroke. AWP

Without the Moon. Jules Laforgue. Come now–appease me just a little/With the why-and-wherefore of your sex! LiTW

Without You. Cid Corman. ...to see/heaven one/wants a star. GP

Withstanders. William Barnes. An' vind that helplessness, wi' right,/Is strong beyond all e'thly might. OxBoCh

The Witness. Ananda Acharya. blessedness, all encompassed–within, without, above,/below – by Me, the Witnessing One. ACV

Witness. Jon Anderson. It is night & already there are stars. MAYP

Witness. Josephine Miles. But how to tell without dying/Is not told by the dying trees. GP

Witness to Death. Richmond Lattimore. and it does no good. VGW

The Witnesses. X.J. Kennedy.
And whir, His personal star. PCh
Not with a bleat, but with a human voice. PCh
That he may choose which are the pure in heart. PCh
Who are those kings? Why do the oxen kneel? PCh

The Witnesses. Henry Wadsworth Longfellow. "We are the Witnesses!" AtBAP

Witnesses. William Stanley Merwin. As for us, we enter your country/With our eyes closed. AmPC; LCAP

The Witnesses: The Innkeeper's Wife. Clive Sansom. In the chaff-strewn light of the stable lantern/Was something beautiful and new and strange. PCh

The Wits. Sir John Suckling. But sure they were out, for he forfeits his crown/When he lends any poet about the Town. CaPo

The Wives. Donald Hall. on the white sidewalks. CoAP

Wives in the Sere. Thomas Hardy. Time again subdues her. BrPo; NOBE; NOBV; VLP

The Wives of Mafiosi. Erica Jong. We imagine we are different/from the wives of Mafiosi. AmPA

The Wives of Spittal. Anonymous. That makes their broo' baith thick and fat. GBP

Wizard Frost. Frank Dempster Sherman. Quick! and see what he has done/Ere 'tis stolen by the Sun. YeAr

The Wizard of Alderley Edge. Peter Coe. But most say that she stricken was, with the March Hare as her mate. OBET

Wizard Oil (with music). Anonymous. I'll take another bottle of Wizard Oil,/I'll take another bottle or two. AS

The Wizard's Funeral. Richard Watson Dixon. Shall turn and welcome me at the door. ELP; LoBV; NOBV; VLP

Wm. Brazier. Robert Graves. But good enough for them, the suckers. NOBL

Wmffre the Sweep. Rolfe Humphries. Left a great poem, praise of his God. EaLo

Woak Hill. William Barnes. I wanted to think that I guided/My guide vrom Woak Hill. GTBS

Wobbly Rock. Lew Welch. I am/Rocked by the sea PoM

Wodwo. Ted Hughes. again very queer but I'll go on looking NoAm

Woe Be Unto You. Anonymous. But it's woe be unto you. ABF

Woe Is Me, My Soul Says, How Bitter Is My Fate. Rahel Morpurgo. The wisdom of woman to the distaff is bound. PBWP

Woe to Him Who Slanders Women. Gearoid Iarla Mac Gearailt. Woe to him who slanders women! NOBI

Woefully Arrayed. John Skelton. My body blue and wan,/Woefully arrayed. CABA; CBEP; LoBV; OxBoCh

Wofully Araide. Anonymous. I have purvaide a place full clere/For mankinde, whom I have bought dere. MeEL

Woke Up This Morning with My Mind on Freedom. Anonymous. Doin' the twist with my mind stayed on freedom,/Hallelu, hallelu, hallelu, hallelujah! FSW

Wolf. Peter Blue Cloud. now you are dancing. VoR

The Wolf. Donald Davidson. The breath that should go howling to the moon/Blows out the lamp and wheezes off to bed. AnAmPo

The Wolf and the Dog. Jean de La Fontaine. So ran Sir Wolf, and runneth yet. LiTW; OBVE

The Wolf and the Stork. Jean de La Fontaine. Shun my paws if you care to live.' FM; OBVE

Wolf-Boy. David Malouf. ...its shadow/on all fours, shaggy, limping at his heel. CBAP

Wolf Dream. Edward Lense. as a lover, as a great wolf. AMV-81

Wolf Hunting near Nashoba. Jim Barnes. ...At your/feet the fire you forgot you ever lit is out. STE

The Wolf in the Kennels. Ivan Andreyevich Krylov. With that he let the whole pack loose. LiTW

Wolfhound. Richard Murphy. By turf embers she gives tongue/When the choirs are silenced in wood and stone. NOBI

The Wolfman. Greg Kuzma. moon rising without him/might be its suitable title. GP

Wolfram's Dirge. Thomas Lovell Beddoes. ...thou'lt meet her/In eastern sky. NOBE; OBEV

Wolfram's Song. Thomas Lovell Beddoes. In the ghosts' moonshine. CBEP; OBVV

Wolves. John Haines. blown by the night wind/with the moon for an icy sail. BoAnP; LCAP

The Wolves. Galway Kinnell. ...His tobacco pouch,/I observed, was already missing from beside his bed. NePoEA-2

Wolves. Louis MacNeice. ...no one hears them among the talk and laughter. NoAm; OxBTC

The Wolves. Allen Tate. ...–and man can never be alone. LiTA; LiTM; NoAm; NOBA; OxBA; PoA

Wolves for Company. Anonymous. running with the red stag through fields. BIrV

Woman. Ai. the last man couldn't, can you? GP

Woman. Anonymous.
Among those who cannot be trained or taught/Are women and eunuchs. AWP; LiTW
And fawn-like eyes still tremble as they glow. HBV 1-2
We weep, and curse, and smack our lips. UnTE

Woman. Eaton Stannard Barrett. Last at the cross and earliest at the grave. HBV 1-2; OnYI; OxBI

Woman. Jane Chambers. She wraps me in her belly/From/Across the room. IHMS

Woman. Randall Jarrell. The heavens' sun perfected in your eyes. NoAm; NOBA

A Woman. Denis Johnson. ...climate where how swiftly/the dark grows, and the time comes. MAYP

The Woman. George Keithley. downstream where the yolk of the sun breaks,/bleeding in the water. NPGG

Woman. Irving Layton. I roar like a sick lion/between her breasts. ErPo

The Woman. Frank Lima. I ran off with it, as happy as a faggot/in boy's town. ANYP

Woman. Elouise Loftin. you cant see me/see you PoBA

Woman. Valente Malangatana. and woman's glance shall watch me/as I go up to Heaven. PBA; TTY

Woman. Thomas O'Hagan. Kindred to angels on high. CAW

Woman. Coventry Patmore. And partly sound its Polity. OBVV

Woman. Carl Rakosi. Man rises/from the kiss/and answers Yes. TAP

Woman. Umberto Saba. ...I'm no longer afraid/of the little white pointed demon ear. AMV-81

A Woman. Mary Dixon Thayer. This is your plan. HBMV

The Woman. R. S. Thomas. ...They shall come to you for ever/with their desire, and you shall bleed for them in return. OxBC

Woman Alone. Denise Levertov. O blessed Solitude. WPOW

Woman and Nature. Susan Griffin.
And they stand there forever that way, locked in silence. NPGG
But we bear. NPGG
...that in such places little/girls must be afraid. NPGG
...that we survive by hearing. NPGG

The Woman and the Aloe. Perseus Adams. A neighbour to stones am I, a sister to a priceless gift. PeSA

Woman and Tree. Robert Graves. Or a sole woman's fatefulness? ErPo

Woman Asleep on a Banana Leaf. Katha Pollitt. When she wakes up she will be completely happy. PoDr

Woman at the Piano. Marya Zaturenska. Two voices ring in the dawn, the morning enters. MoAmPo

The Woman at the Washington Zoo. Randall Jarrell. You see what I am: change me, change me! AP; CoAP; HaCAP; HAP; InPK; LiTM; MP; NMP; OxBC; TAP; TwCP; UnPo

The Woman at the Washtub. Victor J. Daley. I claim his soul and body,/And I will share his doom.' NOAV

Woman Blue. Anonymous. De win' gwine rise, baby, an' blow my blues away. ABF

Woman Blues. Anonymous. In this wide world I ain't got no place at all. OuSiCo

A Woman Came to Me. Michael Silverton. it was terrible for me all over again PoL

A Woman Defending Herself Examines Her Own Character Witness. Susan Griffin. A. And that is what they require of us. NPGG

Woman, Don't Be Troublesome. Augustus Young. the milkwhite tooth of passion/is between us–or should be. CIP

The Woman Driving the Country Squire. David Dayton. I'm really not like that. Really I'm not. AMV-81

Woman (excerpt). Alexander McLachlan. Nursing flowers of sweet affection/In the valleys of the heart.... CaP

Woman Free (excerpt). Elizabeth Wolstenholme-Elmy. Regent of Nature's will, in heart, in head, in hand. BrRo

A Woman from the Book of Genesis. Dovid Knut. ...A peculiar Jewish-Russian air.../Blessed be he who has breathed it. VWA

Woman from the West Coast. Lorna Crozier. I wonder what/she'll call the wind. CaPN

Woman, Gallup, N.M. Karen Swenson. She shattered on the pavement. NYBP

A Woman Grows Soon Old. Larin Paraske. Often am I by my husband/Always in the arms of man. PBWP

Woman Guard. Pancho Aguila. just a small break,/from this war/on earth. LFAC

The Woman Hanging from the 13th Floor Window. Joy Harjo. climbs back up to claim herself again. TWSS

The Woman I Am. Glen Allen. Her beneath the woman/I seem to be! BLPA

The Woman I Met. Thomas Hardy. She turned and thinned away. AtBAP

A Woman I Mix Men Up... Bernadette Mayer. In what they used to call Man, now not. APU

Woman in an Abandoned House. Michael Bily-Hurd. let your breath fill my crumbled walls. AMV-81

The Woman in My Notebook. Lorna Dee Cervantes. The woman I have always tried/to keep subdued/under lock/and ink. WPOW

The Woman in Sunshine. Wallace Stevens. Invisibly clear, the only love. BiP; MoVE

The Woman in the. Marge Piercy. like a handgrenade set to explode,/like goldenrod ready to bloom. NMM

The Woman in the Wagon. Clyde Robertson. Without the woman in the wagon,/Would you have won the West? PoOW

A Woman Is a Branchy Tree. James Stephens. While wind and man woo in the glade/Another tree, another maid. ErPo

A Woman Is a Worthy Thing. Anonymous. And yet she hath but care and wo. FaBoCo; GBP; OxBM

Woman Looking at a Vase of Flowers. Wallace Stevens. Without clairvoyance, close to her. CrMA

Woman Made of Stars. Earle Thompson. My lover's skin forms/stars in the morning. STE

A Woman Making Advances Publicly. Judith Kazantzis. I did not look so strange. BrRo

Woman Me. Maya Angelou. A stomp of feet. A bevy of swift hands. BlSi

A Woman Mourned by Daughters. Adrienne Rich. ...save exactly/as you would wish it done. IHMS; NCSH

The Woman of Beare. Anonymous. And far and farther from me/Ebbs the wave of the sea. AnIV

The Woman of the House. Richard Murphy. Only to think of her, now warms my mind. IPY

Woman of This Earth (excerpt). Frances Frost. none knows if his death will be hard or his flesh desire it. AnAmPo

The Woman of Three Cows. James Clarence Mangan. I'd thwack you well to cure your pride, my Woman of/Three Cows! AnIL; IrPN; NOBI; OnYI; OxBI

A Woman of Words. Amanda Benjamin Hall. They know a softer, stranger thing–/That there are children to be borne. HBMV

Woman Painter of Mithila. Erika Mumford. ...Then we will dance/to the music/of his flute. PoDr

Woman Par Excellence. Rochelle Owens. like a cat's tongue tastes/its whiskers/matter-of-factly. CoPo

Woman Poem. Nikki Giovanni. cause its the only/for real thing/i/know BlSi; NMM; NoAm

The Woman Poet. Gertrud Kolmar. You hear me speak. But do you hear me feel? VWA

A Woman's Answer to the Vampire. Felicia Blake. For one who could not understand. BLPA

Woman's Arms. Anacreon. Cap-a-pie with nakedness. UnTE

Woman's Constancy. John Donne. For by tomorrow I may think so too. EnLit; LiTL; MBW 1-2; NLV; NoP

Woman's Constancy. Sir John Suckling. Till all their sweets are gone, and all again refuse them. CaPo

The Woman's Dream. Frances Horovitz. She does not turn to watch/where he, unmoving now,/is drowned, subsumed, in light. BrRo

A Woman's Execution. Edward King. Vve la Commune! AA

Woman's Faith. Sir Walter Scott. And I believed them again ere night. ViBoPo

The Woman's Labour. Mary Collier. For all our pains, no prospect can we see/Attend us, but old age and poverty. NOEC

A Woman's Last Word. Robert Browning. And so fall asleep, Love,/Loved by thee. BLPA; BLPL; BoLiVe; FaBoBe; FaFP; HBV 1-2; InPo; LiTL; OAEP; TreFS; TrGrPo; UnTE; ViBoPo

Woman's Liberation. Sister Maura. coming and coming and coming. She screamed. AMV-81

Woman's Love. Anonymous. 'Tis shed upon the tomb of him she loves. WBLP

A Woman's Love. John Milton Hay. To be deceived in your true heart's desire/Was bitterer than a thousand years of fire! HBV 1-2

A Woman's Pride. Helen Hay. Ah, love, thine eyes!–Nay, love–Thy/heart, thy heart! AA

A Woman's Question. Lena Lathrop. Are not to be won that way. BLPA; PoToHe; WBLP

A Woman's Question. Adelaide Anne Procter. Whatever on my heart may fall–remember, I would risk it/all! HBV 1-2; LiTL

A Woman's Reason. Gelett Burgess. But I don't like the sound of the moddle. FaBoNo

Woman's Ruling Passions. Alexander Pope. ...by Man's oppression curst,/They seek the second not to lose the first. OBEC

A Woman's Shortcomings. Elizabeth Barrett Browning. Oh never call it loving! BLPA; HBV 1-2

A Woman's Song. Colleen J. McElroy. ...I am the/egg, the sperm. BlSi

Woman's Song. Judith Wright. Pain and the dark must claim you,/and passion and the day. BoAV

A Woman's Sorrow (excerpt). Ho Nansorhon. I know not whether I shall live or die. PBWP

A Woman's Thought. Richard Watson Gilder. Pity me, lean to me,/Thou God above me! HBV 1-2

Woman's Will. Anonymous. And if she won't, she won't–and there's an end on't. HBV 1-2

Woman's Will. John Godfrey Saxe. Why should they make what all/their lives/The gentle dames have had? FaFP; GoTF; HBV 1-2; TreFT

The Woman's Wish. Matthew Prior. O had thou suck'd thy thumb! FaBoEE

Woman Seed Player. Roberta Hill Whiteman. the dark dust already fallen for tomorrow/from long since gentle stars. STE

A Woman Shaman's Song. Uvavnuk. It carries me with it,/so I shake with joy. WPOW

A Woman Sings of Her Love. Anonymous. Will I ever find your like, you who have been shown to me only/once? WTO

Woman Skating. Margaret Atwood. Over all I place/a glass bell. FaBoWP; IHMS

The Woman That Had More Babies Than That. Wallace Stevens. On her lips familiar words become the words/Of an elevation, an elixir of the whole. LiTA

The Woman Thing. Audre Lorde. bakes off its covering of snow/like a rising blackening sun. BlSi; NMM

Woman through the Window. Marcia Falk. Which one will soon be wearing/the darkly woven patterns/of her dress? VWA

Woman to Child. Judith Wright. I am the stem that fed the fruit/the link that joins you to the night. PBWP

A Woman to Her Lover. Christina Walsh. Until we reach the very heart of God. BrRo

Woman to Man. Ai. For a while, I'll let it make you strong,/make your heart lion,/then I'll take it back. GP

Wondrous Love. Alex Means. And through eternity I'll sing on. AmFP; BLSo; FSW; TrAS

Wondrous Love. Mary Herbert, Countess of Pembroke. Lord, who can live to see such love again? BePJ

Wondrous Motherhood. *Anonymous.* Dearest of all God's creations,/Great and wondrous motherhood. PGD

A Wondrous Show. James (1700-48) Thomson. Then all at once in Air dissolves the wondrous Show. OBEC

Wondrous Son of God. Berniece Goertz. Someday we'll behold His face–/Wondrous Son of God. STF

Wonga Vine. Judith Wright. O twilight bell,/flower of the wonga vine. PoAu 1-2

Woo'd and Married and A'. Alexander Ross. Folk need not on frets to be standing/That's wooed and married and a'. OxBS

Woo Not the World. King of Seville Mu'tamid. And put on wisdom with the robe of dust. AWP; LiTW

Wood. Thomas Hornsby Ferril. And seven wondrous stags that I/Could not believe walked slowly by. PoRA

Wood and Hill. Andrew Young. That made of wood and hill a market-square. HaMV

Wood Butcher. Norman Hindley. That it's your disappointment that drives me. AMV-81

Wood-cut. Victoria Mary (Vita) Sackville-West. And rungs of ladders reared against the sky. ChMP

The Wood-Cutter's Night Song. John Clare. Bill and mittens, lie ye there! EnRP; OBRV

The Wood-Dove's Note. Emily Huntington Miller. "Soul of the vanished years,/O where! where! where! HBV 1-2

Wood Floor Dreams. Lance Henson. leaving their names/on our mantles/at waking VoR

Wood Flower. Richard Le Gallienne. And now, alas, what voice shall wake her! HBMV

Wood Music. Ethel King. As tree-born instrument's soft discipline/Releases all the pent-up harmony. GoYe

The Wood of the Self-Destroyers. Samuel Yellen. Snuffle No! No! to proffered hand and heart. NePoAm-2

Wood-Pigeons. John Masefield. That Dread can darken not, nor Death destroy. ChMP

The Wood-Pile. Robert Frost. With the slow smokeless burning of decay. AmP; CABA; CoBMV; LiTA; MAmP; MAPA; NoAm; NoP; SeCeV; VGW

A Wood Song. Ralph Hodgson. And listen while you may. GoJo; HBV 1-2

Wood-Song. Eugene Lee-Hamilton. "Only a day, love,'/Murmurs the bee. OBVV

Wood-Song. Josephine Preston Peabody. Speed you, and good-morrow! AA

The Wood, the Weed, the Wag. Sir Walter Ralegh. God bless the child! CBEP; SiPS; TrGrPo

Wood-Thrush. John Hall Wheelock. Closing the door upon/Those half-remembered things– NePoAm

Wood Witchery. Richard Burton. Unaging beauty by another name. AnAmPo

Woodbines in October. Charlotte Fiske Bates. And poured its treasure out upon the/leaves. AA

Woodbird. Charles G. Bell. And lose the sun. NePoAm

The Woodchuck Who Lives on Top of Mt. Ritter. John Oliver Simon. ...in the timehonored/tradition of what they are trying/to do to the universe NeAC

Woodchucks. Maxine W. Kumin. gassed underground the quiet Nazi way. HoPM; InPK; NIP

Woodcut. R. N. D. Wilson. and a rider and horse/the woods have laid siege to. OxBI

The Woodcutter's Wife. William Rose Benet. That grows full glory when she comes again. AnAmPo; AWP; InPo

The Wooden Chamber. Anne Hebert. I am naked and all black under a bitter tree. WPOW

The Wooden Fence. Christian Morgenstern. The architect, though, ran away/To Afri- or Americay. LiTW

The Wooden Horse then said. Jenny Mastoraki. he'd worked as a pony on a merry-go-round. BoWoP

Wooden Ships. David Morton. Or dreamed among the stars on some tall hill. EtS

The Wooden Tiger. Samuel Yellen. But it prowls forever powerless, cut off from its jungle. NePoAm

A Woodland Revel. Clarence Urmy. Hey for home! Lo, for our guiding,/Hesper in the dusk abiding! HBMV

Woodland Worship. Ethelwyn Wetherald. And dizzy height/Of utmost worship, where it seems/Too still for dreams. CaP

The Woodlanders: In a Wood. Thomas Hardy. There, now and then, are found/Life-loyalties. PoPl

The Woodlands. William Barnes. Though you've a-lost em, zunny woodlands. BoNaP; OBVV

Woodlands. Sir Herbert Read. Cleaving the green/Twilight like a rhythmic sword. BrPo

Woodlore. Kim Kurt. The thinnest deer-track prints,/Or a midwood trail ahead. NePoAm-2

The Woodlot. Amy Clampitt. I/you, whatever that conundrum may yet/prove to be, amounts to nothing. HaCAP

The Woodman's Dog. William Cowper. Then shakes his powdered coat and barks for joy. ELU; GDP

Woodman, Spare That Tree. George Pope Morris. Thy axe shall harm it not. AA; BLPA; BLSo; FaBoBe; FaFP; FPL; FSW; HBV 1-2; OHIP; PaPo; PSoN; TreF; WBLP

Woodnotes. Ralph Waldo Emerson. Than all it holds more deep, more high.' NOBA; WGRP

The Woodpecker. Richard Church. With his prod, prod, prod,/And jerk. HaMV

The Woodpecker. Elizabeth Madox Roberts. He can snuggle back in the telephone pole. OBCA; TiPo

Woodpigeons at Raheny. Donald Davie. ...I know the dove/Outsang me down the afternoon. PP

Woodrow Wilson. Robinson Jeffers. "This is my last/Worst pain, the bitter enlightenment that buys peace." FaBoPV

Woods. W. H. Auden. A culture is no better than its woods. NePA; NePoAm

Woods. Louis MacNeice. And cow pats–and inconsequent wild roses. FaBoIP

The Woods. Derek Mahon. while we, released/from that pale paradise,/ponder the darkness in another place. NOBI

Woods and Kestrel. Julian Bell. And swirling up the blue weald landscape shifts/To the forest ridge's pine-wood darkened crest. ChMP

The Woods Are Still. Michael (Katherine Bradley and Edith Cooper) Field. I sing to the echo of my own voice crying. OBVV

The Woods at Night. May Swenson. repeats, repeats, repeats its plea/for cruelty. DuDa

Woods Gets Religion. John Woods. ...and your sweet tongue/was the only wafer I could not wash down. GP

Woods in Winter. Henry Wadsworth Longfellow. I listen, and it cheers me long. CBEP; MAmP

Woods Night. Tom Hennen. The last thing/I want to hear before going to sleep/Is that man/Splashing ashore. GP

The Woods No More. Jay Macpherson. –But make no bones. PeCV

The Woodspurge. Dante Gabriel Rossetti. The woodspurge has a cup of three. AtBAP; EBEV; ELP; GTBS-P; HAP; HeIP; LoBV; NBM; NOBE; NOBV; NoP; OAEL 1-2; OAEP; OBEV; OBNC; PoEL 1-5; PrIm; TreFT; UnPo; VLP; WeW; WHA

Woodstock. Joni Mitchell. And we've got to get ourselves/Back to the garden NIP

Woodtown Manor. John Montague. Their dual disciplines of tenderness. IPY

Woodworker's Ballad. Herbert Palmer. But the things that are honour'd of Zion/Are most of them made from wood. HaMV; OBEV

Woodyards in the Rain. Anne Marriott. smallpocks the oil-green water with a hurled/ten million wire nails. CaP

Wooed and Married and A'. Alexander Ross. I dinna ken what I should want,/If I could get but a man! HBV 1-2

Woof of the Sun, Ethereal Gauze. Henry David Thoreau. Establish thy serenity o'er the fields. AnNE; AP; TAP; ViBoPo

The Wooing. *Anonymous.* Now I'm on fire too! UnTE

The Wooing Frog. James Reeves. Now what had chanced, to spoil the tale? SO

The Wooing Lady. William Jay Smith. As he awakens, beautifully deceived. NePoEA

The Wooing Maid. Martin Parker. O let me not die a maid, take me for pitty. CoMu

The Wooing of Etain. *Anonymous.* We shall share, O Lady Fair! BIrV

The Wooing Rogue. *Anonymous.* And leave our old ones for a pledge. CoMu

Wooing Song. Giles the Younger Fletcher. Thy wooing shall thy winning be. EiL; HBV 1-2; OBEV

The Wool Trade. John Dyer. ...let the sounding loom/Mix with the melody of ev'ry vale. OBEC; SeCePo

Woolly Words. Robert N. Feinstein. So hiero the glyphics and poly the glot. NLV

The Woolworth Philodendron. Stephen Sandy. Mesh with dark plots implicit in the sun. CoPo

Woolworth's. Donald Hall. I followed this vision to Boston. WeW

The Wooyeo Ball. *Anonymous.* And many there were who may blush to recall/The polkas they danced at the Wooyeo Ball. NOAV

The Word. Basil Bunting. rusty ingot, bleak paralyzed blob! PoA

The Word. Gustave Kahn. To the smiling angels it sounds heavy, uncouth. VWA

The Word. Richard Realf. The fringes of the sunsets and the hills. AA; AmLP

Word. Stephen Spender. Or shall I pull it in/To rhyme upon a dish? NYBP; PP

The Word. Neil Weiss. some word huge and black in my mouth. NYBP

A Word about Freedom and Identity in Tel Aviv. Jon Silkin. ...The Torah is:/suffering begets suffering, that is. VWA

A Word About Woodpiles. Nancy Byrd Turner. There's nothing like a woodpile/At one's back door! BrR

A Word in Edgeways. Charles Tomlinson. pleasure and I yes I did enjoy our/conversation goodnightthankyou NOBL

The Word Made Flesh? Walter James Turner. And agony is their making-kiss. OBMV

A Word Made Flesh Is Seldom. e d. This loved Philology. MAmP

The Word Man. Larry Moffi. I will sell him my name. AMV-80

The "Word" of a Watch-Dog. Sandag. And grow old faithfully/With my master/Whom I was predestined to find. WTO

The "Word" of a Wolf Encircled by the Hunt. Sandag. Now may my lord spare me! WTO

The "Word" of an Antelope Caught in a Trap. Sandag. May I find a peaceful new birth,/Transcending the state of the wild beast. WTO

Word of Art. Alan Bernheimer. But it wasn't the stars that thrilled me. APU

A Word of Encouragement. J. R. Pope. How vastly we improve our style! ELU; FiBHP; FPL; NLV; NOBL; PV

The Word of God. Annie Johnson Flint. I rest upon Thy word alone. BLRP

The Word of God. J. Harold Gwynne. Till earth's dark night of sin shall turn/To God's own perfect day. STF

The Word of God. Einar Skjaeraasen. —For you were a lover in the world. HW

Word of God, Across the Ages. Ferdinand Q. Blanchard. And thy knowledge fills the earth. AH

The Word of God to Leyden Came. Jeremiah Eames Rankin. And where they cast their anchor down,/Rose Freedom's realm to be. AA; HBV 1-2; MC; PAH; PAL

The Word of the Lord from Havana. Richard Hovey. Remember the Maine! HBV 1-2; PAH

A Word of Warning. Anonymous. The Master that you seek in Rome/You find at home, or seek in vain. KiLC

The Word of Water. E. L. Mayo. ...uttering a word/That no man living has interpreted. PoA

Word over All. Cecil Day Lewis. Flooded by dawn's pale courage, rapt in/eve's/Rich acquiescence. OAEP

The Word Plum. Helen Chasin. and reply, lip and tongue/of pleasure. NIP

Word Poem. Nikki Giovanni. what we become/when we dream BOLo; PoBA

A Word to Husbands. Ogden Nash. Whenever you're right, shut up. PoL

A Word to New England. William Bradford. That God's presence may with you dwell. SCAP

A Word to Peter Olds. Charles Brasch. With yellow robe and begging bowl. OCNZ

A Word to the Wise. Caroline Duer. That wisdom is the folly of the wise. AA

Words. Anonymous. But God himself can't kill them when they're said! PoLf

Words. Helen Morgan Brooks. Even tho, I must remember this, I have forgotten you. NNP; PoNe

Words. Jean Burden. nothing, window,/weep. AMV-81

Words. Richard Eberhart. It was the world-memory alone/When I was dead and gone. NePA

Words. Robert Finch. ...words that are left unsaid/And the undetectable words used in their stead. PoA

Words. Ulalume Gonzales De Leon. Words mean whatever one wants AMV-81

Words. Charles Harpur. A nobler feat than Inkerman. PoAu 1-2

The Words. Lee Harwood. This apparent clumsiness is far from true. EAS

Words. Philip Levine. ...the ache/I feel to be no/longer only myself. VWA

Words. David Phillips. the wounds/perfectly/cut NeAC

Words. Sylvia Plath. From the bottom of the pool, fixed stars/Govern a life. ConAP; HaCAP

Words. Ernest Rhys. And see the blue steel redden at the word. HBMV

Words. W. R. Rodgers. And speak for me–their most astonished host. OBSP

Words. Vern Rutsala. And this way we came to love/the double negative. GP

The Words. David Wagoner. As I set loose, like birds/In a landscape, the old words. PoA

Words. Miller Williams. "Tower, we're going down. This is PSA." AMV-81

Words and Monsters. Vernon Scannell. The Abysmal Brute was grunting in the hot/Dark outside, would follow him to bed. OxBC

Words and Music (excerpt). Samuel Beckett. That old starlight/On the earth again. BIrV

Words Are Never Enough. Charles Bruce. These are the fellows who keep the salt in the blood. CaP; OBCV

Words at Farewell. Vahan Derian. Pluck the sun down/and go. AMV-81

Words for a Picture of Newlyweds. T'ang Yin. "Tonight, go sleep with your flowers alone!" HW

Words for a Resurrection. Leo Kennedy. With laughter in His blessed bones,/And lilies on His brow. OBCV; PeCV

Words for Hart Crane. Robert Lowell. must lay his heart out for my bed and board. AP; CABA; CMoP; NMP

Words for Love. Ted Berrigan. my heart still loves, will break. ANYP

Words for Music Perhaps. William Butler Yeats.
  All things remain in God. AtBAP
  A bone wave-whitened and dried in the wind. AtBAP
  Fol de rol, fol de rol. AtBAP
  Love is like the lion's tooth. AtBAP
  Mad as the mist and snow. AtBAP
  Mine would walk being dead. AtBAP
  The moon in a silver bag. AtBAP
  The solid man and the coxcomb. AtBAP
  That has not been rent. AtBAP
  "That's certainly the case," said he. AtBAP

Words for the Raker of Leaves. Léonie Adams. As it were a vista upon/The suffered and fordone. PoCh

Words for the Wind. Theodore Roethke. In another being, at last. AP; NoAm; NOBA; PoCh

Words from a Bottle. Deborah Lee. me with only one word left;/survive. BrSi

Words from an Old Spanish Carol. Ruth Sawyer. Who will kneel them gently down/before the Lord, new-born? BrR; ChBR; PCh

Words from Hell. David Helwig. I was eighteen when I came in these gates. NOBC

Words from the Window of a Railway Car. Anatoly Steiger. They're said to us in consolation/From the window of a railroad car)... VWA

Words in the Mourning Time. Robert Earl Hayden. oh dreadfully, our humanness must be achieved. CNA

Words in Time. Archibald MacLeish. The poet with a beat of words/Flings into time for time to keep. CrMA; NePA; PoCh; PoRA

Words Like Freedom. Langston Hughes. If you had known what I know/You would know why. BPo

Words, Like Spiders. P. Wolny. and wake me with their screams. PCP

Words Made of Water. Burns Singer. On thoughts like these no man ever grew fat. NePoEA-2

Words Most Often Mispronounced in Poetry. Alex Kuo. Whatever happens, I am ready. APU

The Words of Jesus. William Rose Benet. The dark, the horrible pain, the anguish, the bloody sweat.... MoRP

Words of Oblivion and Peace. Gabriel Preil. and I saw Jenny, the villages of her peaceful words in flower. VWA

The Words of the All-Wise (excerpt). Anonymous. Dawn has broken, Dwarf,/Stiffen now to stone. OBVE

Words on the Windowpane. Dante Gabriel Rossetti. Rebelled not, loathing from the trodden heart/That thing which she had found man's love to be. SyP

Words Spoken Alone. Dannie Abse. till music be my body. NYBP

Words Spoken by Pasternak during a Bombing. Bella Akhmadulina. A mountain stone–clear, like water. BoWoP

Words That Speak of Death. Anadad Eldan. Wind in the reeds:/it is not words that speak of death. VWA

The Words, the Words, the Words. William Carlos Williams. Rise and shake your skirts/to the buttercups, yellow as polished/gold BiP

Words to a Song. Agnes Nemes Nagy. the falling fruits' uneven spastic/extrasystolic beats. BoWoP

Words to My Friend. Renee Vivien. ...since we are/Pure before life and since we love one another?... PeHV

Words to My Mother. Alfonsina Storni. To watch the great birds that pass without destination. AMV-80

Words to Remind Me of Grandmother. Andres Castro Rios. "Andres, my poet, I love you so much..." InW

Words to the Wind. Pier Giorgio Di Cicco. ...I want you to understand what keeps/your shadow growing. AMV-80

Words Wherein Stinging Bees Lurk. Judah Halevi. And forsake the mother of paths? TrJP

The Words Will Resurrect. Jorge De Lima. You will not understand me, brother! TTY

Words without Music. Irving Layton. And the goats leap into their faces shrieking. CaP

Words! Words! Jessie Redmond Fauset. Think of the things we used to say! CDC

Words Words Words. Marilyn Krysl. and I love you!" You don't say. Well, I don't believe you. AMV-80

Wordspinning. Olga Kirsch. That God's the God of children who are white? PeSA

Wordsworth at Tea. Barry Pain. I called that milk"—she blushed with pride—/"You bade me speak the truth." HBV 1-2

Wordsworth's Grave. William Watson. In rest, in peace, his labor nobly done. EnLit; GoTL; HBV 1-2; OBNC; VLP

Work. Louis James Block. The limitless sun of Truth shines more and/ more. AA

Work. Andrei Codrescu. i have a great desire to move elsewhere. EAS

Work. Kenyon Cox. That these things shall/Be added unto thee. PGD

Work. G. A. Studdert Kennedy Take me, and brand me with thy cross,/ Thy slave's proud sign. EBCP

Work. D. H. Lawrence. he will cancel the machines we have got. OBMV

Work. James Russell Lowell. And he who waits to have his task marked out,/Shall die and leaves his errand unfulfilled. PoSC

Work. Alexander Pushkin. Friend of the golden-haired Dawn, friend of the gods/of the hearth? AWP

Work. James W. Thompson. So that's why God invented work. PoToHe

Work. Henry Van Dyke. Because I know for me my work is best. TRV

Work: A Song of Triumph. Angela Morgan. Thank God for the splendor of work! PoLf

Work and Play. Martial (Marcus Valerius Martialis). That handsome boy does not do your wife's work./He does yours. UnTE

Work for Small Men (excerpt). Sam Walter Foss. Then leave all this for smaller men to do. PoToHe

Work, for the Night Is Coming. Annie L. Walker. Work, while the night is dark'ning,/When man's work is o'er. SaC

Work Gangs. Carl Sandburg. ...people whose song/hearts break if there is no song mouth; these are my people. SaC

Work Horses. Edith Newlin Chase. Eat oats, eating hay, munch! munch! munch! SoPo

A Work of Artiface. Marge Piercy. the hands you/love to touch. IHMS; Psk

The Work of Happiness. May Sarton. Windows look out on mountains and the walls are kind. MoRP

The Work of Love. Margaret Sangster. Oh, it's Love, Love, Love, LOVE,/ That makes the world go 'round! BLRP

The Work of the Weavers. Anonymous. We wouldna' have a coat, neither black nor blue,/If it wasna' for the work of the weavers. FSW

The Work-Out. Geoffrey Movius. the plunge forward, the awful/crashing and surging of the new. MAT

Work Room. Kenward Elmslie. good weather for work. ANYP

Work Song. Raymond Mazisi Kunene. He handles us severely,/That despicable White man! WTO

The Work Song. Sipho Sepamla. abelungu goddamn! WhB

The Work That Saves! Horatius Bonar. The blood divine invites us near. BePJ

Work to Do Toward Town. Gary Snyder. all roads descend toward town. VGW

Work without Hope. Samuel Taylor Coleridge. And Hope without an object cannot live. BiP; BoNaP; EnLi 1-2; ERoP 1-2; FiP; HBV 1-2; LoBV; NOBE; NoP; OBEV; OBRV; PG; SaC; TEP

The Workbox. Thomas Hardy. As if she had known not only John,/But known of what he died. UnP

Workday Morning. Astrid Tollefsen. the unfeeling/immovable ones/draw imperceptibly closer PBWP

The Worker. Richard Thomas. Lapping up his dripping iron. PoBA; PoNe

The Workers Rose on May Day or Postscript to Karl Marx. Audre Lorde. securing Wall Street/against the striking students. GP

The Workhouse Boy. Anonymous. Oh the Poor Workhouse Boy. GBP; VLP

Working against Time. David Wagoner. ...Two green/survivors/Are tangled under the biting rain as I say this. MAT

Working at a Service Station, I Think of Shinkichi Takahashi. Dennis Finnell. and when a car pulls up a bell/rings and I say, "Fill 'er up?" FAZ

Working Class. Bertram Warr. And on the bleached bones, in clean sunlight, we shall begin to build. NOBC; OBCV; WaP

Working Girls. Carl Sandburg. So the green and the grey move in the early morning on the/downtown streets. SaC

The Working Man. Gregory Donovan. until someone comes to take me/to the place where I belong. AMV-81

Working Man Blues. Sleepy John Estes. You know the children can go in the daytime/oooo boy, and the old folks have it at night BluL

Working near Lake Traverse. Tom Hennen. I look just like/That dark/ Bunch of woods/Over there. FAZ

A Working Party. Siegfried Sassoon. And as he dropped his head the instant split/His startled life with lead, and all went out. CMoP; MMM

Working Song. Anonymous. Scales, drop off my carved snake. CBAP

Working the Rain Shift at Flanagan's. Gibbons Ruark. As if we had died and gone to Dublin. MAYP

Working the Skeet House. Jon Eastman. the one who is going to die in my place. AMV-80

Working with Tools. Archie Randolph Ammons. ...I understand/and won't give assertion up. NoAm

Workmen. Herbert Morris. ...and this first/sheer pain that drinking means to be alive. NePoAm-2

Works and Days. Hesiod. ...and/leave/evil too great to resist, and mortals who grieve. LiTW
Thine is the ev'n of life before the noon. FaBoUs

The Works of God. Moses Ibn Ezra. May His praise be fitly sung! TrJP

The Workshop. Aileen Fisher. and Father seems to know the minute anything/is gone! SoPo

The World. Francis Bacon. –What then remains, but that we still should cry/For being born, or, being born, to die? HBV 1-2

The World. Robert Creeley. and the light then/of the sun coming/for another morning/in the world. NaP; NoAm; NoP

The World. George Herbert. But Love and Grace took Glorie by the hand,/And built a braver Palace than before. OBS; SeCV 1-2

The World. Thomas Love Peacock. And scramble for what we can get. PV

The World. Kathleen Raine. A burning void/Upheld by stillness. OxBTC

The World. Christina Georgina Rossetti. Till my feet, cloven too, take hold on hell? BoWoP

The World. Vern Rutsala. ...safe in the arc cut/by the rope swing/thirty years ago. Psk

The World. Henry Vaughan. "This Ring the Bridegroom did for none provide,/But for his bride." AtBAP; ATP; AWP; CABA; CoBE; DiPo; EnL; ExPo; FaBV; GoTL; HAP; HBV 1-2; HeIP; ILwL; InPo; JCP; LiTB; LoBV; MasP; MePo; NOBE; NOCV; OAEL 1-2; OAEP; OBS; OxBoCh; PoEL 1-5; PPoe; PPP; SeCeV; SeCP; SeCV 1-2; TEP; TrCP; TreFS; TrGrPo; ViBoPo; WGRP

The World: a Ghazel. James Clarence Mangan. All came, all went; but never man/Knew whence they came, or where they went to! OBVV

The World a Hunt. William, of Hawthornden Drummond. Old Age with stealing pace/Casts up his nets, and there we panting die. NOBE; OBS

The World an Illusion. Anonymous. For this world is but fantasy. MeEL

The World as Meditation. Wallace Stevens. Never forgetting him that kept coming constantly so near. AP; HeIP; LCAP; MoAB; NIP; PPP

The World As Wave and Idea. Louis O. Coxe. the beast was beauty and what we hide/is how it came from and where it goes. SOTS

"The world below the brine". Walt Whitman. The change onward from ours to that of beings who walk/other spheres. AmLP; BiP; BoNaP; FM; MAT; NePA; NoP; PAI

A World Beyond. Nathaniel Ingersoll Bowditch God's perfect wisdom, power, and love. AA

World, Defined. Edward Weismiller. Shared with the adder and the mole. AnAmPo

World Enough. Jeanine Hathaway. where God, surprised, blooms/like a white peacock. AMV-80

The world feels dusty. Emily Dickinson. Dews of thyself to fetch/And holy balms. MoAmPo

A World for Love. John Clare. Herself grow Eden once again, possest of Love and/thee. PG

"The world goes turning". George Dillon. And the world goes turning. AmLP

The World Hymn. James Gilchrist Lawson. With equal measures, weights and coins,/And just and righteous laws. WBLP

The World I Am Passing Through. Lydia Maria Child. God help us all to kindly view/The world that we are passing through! AA; HBV 1-2

World I Have Not Made. Elizabeth Jennings. and the taut mind turns to its own requirings. ACV

The World in Making. Sir Gilbert Parker. (Glad is the wind and tall is the fire). CaP

The World Is a Bundle of Hay. George Gordon, Lord Byron. And the greatest of all is John Bull. EnRP; FF

The World Is a Mighty Ogre. Fenton Johnson. Have mercy on a humble bard, O Lord! AmNP

The World Is Full of Remarkable Things. LeRoi (Imamu Amiri Baraka) Jones. into dreams BP

The World Is Full of Wonderful Smells. Zhenya Gay. Wouldn't it be dreadful if you'd no nose to tell/Of every wonderful, wonderful smell? TiPo

The World Is Mine. Florence Earle Coates. I love, and the world is mine! AA

The World Is Not a Fenced-Off Garden. Jakov Steinberg. Sees the grave and is silent and restrains himself within his heavens. VWA

The World Is Really a Sugarplum House in the Forest. Aram Boyajian. But the forest–I sometimes wonder about the forest! NeAC

The World Is with Me Just Enough. Sam Abrams. & of all these/the greatest is the last/by far. APU

The World Is Young Today. Digby Mackworth Dolben. We see them not, but Death/Is palpable–and Love. NOBV

The World Looks On. Louis I. Newman. Lighting up the ridge of the world. PoNe

World Music. Frances Louisa Bushnell. Pipe of Pan was once its naming, now it/hath a name diviner. AA

The World Narrowed to a Point. William Carlos Williams. give it a home. MoLP

The World Needs. Anonymous. And fewer on graves at the end of the strife. PoToHe

World of Bacteria. Sakutaro Hagiwara. Everywhere bacteria swim. AMV-80

World of Darkness. Robert Chatain. ...We enter the world of daylight/ Blind and unable to find home. PoA

The World of Expectations. Albert Goldbarth. ...And it came/long, red and clamorous. Firetruck. HaCAP

The World of Fools Has Such a Store. Anonymous. And even break his looking-glass. DBV

A World of Light. Elizabeth Jennings. ...a sudden homage/To peace that penetrates and is not feared. NePoEA-2

The World Outside. Denise Levertov. ...and silences/are dark windows? ConAP

World Planners. Arvel Steece. They seek a solution; they have it,/And they know it not. PGD

The World's a Well Strung Fidle, Mans Tongue the Quill. Nathaniel Ward. The universall song goes smooth and sweet. SCAP

The World's Bible. Annie Johnson Flint. How can we hope to help Him/ And hasten His return? STF; TRV

World's Bliss. Alice Notley. ...oh each poet's a/beautiful human girl who must die. APU

World's Bliss, Have Good Day! Anonymous. Tech herte myn right love thee/Whos herte-blood was shed for me. OxBM

World's Centre. Ruth Dallas. That only children listen to and ponder. AnNZ

The World's Desire. William Rose Benet. And yet we feel–what pain–in the intense/Desire for thee to end thy long seclusion! TrPWD

World's End. G. K. Chettur. He gave it up, and scuttled to his hole. ACV

The World's End. William Empson. This place's curvature precludes its end. CoBMV; MoVE

World's Fare. Charles Stetler. unfortunately we're all stuck/with what's between our legs. GP

The World's Great Age Begins Anew. Percy Bysshe Shelley. And leave, if naught so bright may live,/All earth can take or Heaven can give. GoTF; TEP

The World's Greatest Tricycle Rider. C. K. Williams. and drives him again and again on the same block. NYBP

The World's Illusion. Moses Ibn Ezra. If any seek her favor, deeming it/A garden of delights–such are its/fruits. TrJP

The World's Justice. Emma Lazarus. Still on Israel's head forlorn,/Every nation heaps its scorn. HBV 1-2

The World's Last Unnamed Poem. A. K. Redwing. there is someone who understands why.../we do the things we do. VoR

The World's Miser. Theodore Maynard. To show in every spot and place/ The living glory of His face. CAW

The World's Music. (Thomas Nicoll Hepburn) "Setoun. Gabriel" And never, never sulk at all. FaBoBe; HBV 1-2; HBVY

The World's So Big. Aileen Fisher. And Mother's calling me! SoPo

The World's Wanderers. Percy Bysshe Shelley. Hast thou still some secret nest/On the tree or billow? EnLit; ViBoPo

The World's Way. Thomas Bailey Aldrich. You get beheaded when your skill is gone. HBV 1-2

The World's Wonders. Robinson Jeffers. ...and a tortured Jew became God. NePA

The World's Worst Boxer. Lucilius [(or Lucillius)]. ...grateful that you/ never hit one of them, erect this statue. SD

World's Worth. Dante Gabriel Rossetti. He said: "O God, my world in Thee!" GoBC; VLP

World-Secret. Hugo von Hofmannsthal. Now but a vague dream, circling, flies. LiTW; TrJP

The World So Wide. Anonymous. Though I go loose, tied am I with a lune. OxBM

The World-Soul. Ralph Waldo Emerson. The warm rosebuds below. AmePo

The World State. Gilbert Keith Chesterton. And hate my next-door neighbor. CoBE; DBV

The World, the Devil, and Tom Paine. Anonymous. I'm bound to march in endless bliss,/And die a shouting Methodist. AH

The World Turned Upside Down. Anonymous. "But thanks to my friend here, I've hum-/bled your pride." PAH

World War. Richard Eberhart. Cold Dreadful Mass Destruction. WaP

World War I. Anonymous. And the son of a gun was never there. FaFP

World War II. Anonymous. So what the hell are we fighting for? FaFP

World War II. Langston Hughes. Did/Somebody/Die? HaCAP

World War III. Anonymous. The verses written on World War III. FaFP

The World Was Never Real to Me. George Randall Griffin. and ride far away. AMV-81

The World We Make. Alfred Grant Walton. We make our world–and there we live. PoToHe

The World Well Lost. Edmund Clarence Stedman. All after-life compressed within the span/Of that one year,–the year I met with/Rose! AA

World Winter. Earle Birney. this your one wrynecked woedealing/world GrPl

A World within a War. Sir Herbert Read. In a house beneath a beechwood/In an acre of wild land. MoPo

World within a World. Debra Woolard Bender. Within a world. AMV-80

World without End. Caius Valerius Catullus. And his slow-spoken word: Farewell for ever,/Farewell, farewell. LiTW

A World without Objects Is a Sensible Emptiness. Richard Wilbur. Lampshine blurred in the steam of beasts, the spirit's right/Oasis, light incarnate. ConAP; LiTM; NoAm; NOBA; PoA

World without Peculiarity. Wallace Stevens. Become a single being, sure and true. HaCAP

World Youth Song. Anonymous. Freedom's song, freedom's song. FSW

Worldly Wealth. Rowland Watkyns. To wait at rich mens' tables, or their door. FaBoEE

Worldly Wisdom. Omar Khayyam. Make game of that which makes as much of Thee. EG

Worlds on Worlds Are Rolling Ever. Percy Bysshe Shelley. Wailed for the golden years. TEP

The Worm. Willis Barnstone. ...With no God or fear I am/a free son–with the worm eating my heart. FAZ; VWA

The Worm. Ralph W. Bergengren. Because she thinks I ate that worm! SiSoSe

The Worm. Raymond Souster. in that dark morning street/of early April. WHW

A Worm Fed on the Heart of Corinth. Isaac Rosenberg. More amorous than Solomon. AtBAP; BrPo; MoPo; OAEL 1-2

The Worm in the Whirling Cross. John Malcolm Brinnin. Wherever I walk now, I wake not here. MoPo

The Worms of History. Robert Graves. The ages of a putrefying corpse. MoPo

Wormwood. Thomas Kinsella. I will dream it again. CIP; FaBoIP

Worried Life Blues. Anonymous. You ain't gonna worry my life anymore. AmFP

Worried Man Blues. Anonymous. Tell 'em it was me, and I sing it all day long. FSW

The Worried Skipper. Wallace Irwin. "The trouble's with yer liver." BLPA

Worry. Anonymous. Have pictured in our mind. PoToHe

Worry. George W. Swarberg. Then substitute a little hope/And lots of faith in God. STF

Worry about Money. Kathleen Raine. From the little there is in the bin of flour and the/cruse of oil. FaBoTw

Worsening Situation. John Ashbery. ..My wife/Thinks I'm in Oslo–Oslo, France, that is. NOBA

Worship. Bob Jones, Jr. And at morn I meet the Saviour,/In the glory of the dawn! BePJ

Worship. William Wilberforce Lord A human soul knows and adores its God! AA

Worship. Robert Whitaker. Thine all the ministries of natural power? TrPWD

Worship. John Greenleaf Whittier. And in its ashes plant the tree of peace! NOCV

The Worshiper. Vassar Miller. Turn from her, being also pitiful. NePoEA-2

The Worst. Shel Silverstein. The Glurpy Slurpy Skakagrall–/Who's standing right behind you. WSC

The Worst Horror. Euripides. ...he was for men the artist/Of woes unnumbered, and their deadly foe. DBV

Worth While. Ella Wheeler Wilcox. For we find them but once in a while. BLPA; FPL; GoTF; PoToHe; TreF

The Worthless Heart. Immanuel Di Roma. You shall perish in the nether furnace. TrJP

Would a circling surface vulture. Mahadevi (Mahadeviyakka). these/ mosquitoes/on the buffalo's hide? BoWoP

Would God That It Were Holiday! Thomas Deloney. Hey derry down, down adown. EiL

Would I Be Called a Christian? Mrs. J. F. Moser. Unselfish, kind, forgiving/To others every day? STF

Would I Be Shrived? John D. Swain. They are the things which I regret! BLPA

Would I Might Go Far Over Sea.   Marie de France.   And too fond loving of thy hair.   AWP; PoRA

Would I Might Rouse the Lincoln in You All.   Vachel Lindsay.   Fire that freed the slave.   PoSC

Would I Were Chang'd into That Golden Shower.   Sir Arthur Gorges.   To end my life in that I loved best.   GBL

Would That I Were.   Arthur Hugh Clough.   Would I could wish my wishes all away,/And learn to wish the wishes that I ought.   TrPWD

Would You Be a Man of Fashion?   *Anonymous*.   Wine will do the work alone.   ALV

Would you come back if I said the earth.   Nadia Tueni.   would you come back if I said the earth/was at the tip of my fingers?   BoWoP

Would You in Venus' Wars Succeed.   *Anonymous*.   But boldly march up sword in hand/And that's the way to win her.   ErPo

Would You Like to Sin.   *Anonymous*.   To err with her/On some other fur?   PV

Wouldn't You Like to Know.   John Godfrey Saxe.   Wouldn't you like to know?   HBV 1-2

The Wound.   Thom Gunn.   I had to let those storm-lit valleys heal.   NePoEA

The Wounded.   Louise Louis.   but far down the road a tall stone stood...   GoYe

The Wounded Breakfast.   Russell Edson.   The man turns to his breakfast again, but sees it's been wounded, the yolk of/one of his eggs...   LCAP

The Wounded Cupid.   Robert Herrick.   Come, tell me then how great's the smart/Of those thou woundest with thy dart!   AWP; OFD

A wounded deer leaps highest.   Emily Dickinson.   Lest anybody spy the blood/And "You're hurt" exclaim!   AWP; InPo; TAP

The Wounded Hawk.   Herbert Palmer.   And one with word–birds, knaves, fools, fish.   FaBoTw; HaMV

The Wounded Man and the Swarm of Flies.   William Somervile.   Seizes the prey with more voracious bite,/To satisfy his hungry appetite?   FM

Wounds.   Michael Longley.   I think "Sorry Missus' was what he said.   FaBoIP; FaBoPV

Wounds.   Judith Minty.   ..There is no one/to hear. The water is red.   GeTw

The Woyi.   Lew Blockcolski.   Tribal elders tell of some/who ran for a mile before/they fell.   VoR

Wprroes/.   *Anonymous*.   For once out of the woods, all the fears are forgot.   PoToHe

Wrack.   Irving Feldman.   And the wind came on as before.   AmPC

Wraith.   Edna St. Vincent Millay.   Wonder just what sort of people/Could have had this house before...   WSC

The Wraith-Friend.   George Barker.   But in whose dust all brighter dust must lie.   OBMV

The Wrangler Kid.   *Anonymous*.   To-day the Kid bears scars, 'tis true,/Brands of the Red God's own.   BPAW

Wrap Me in Blankets of Momentary Winds.   Harold Littlebird.   together our spirits will make love and give birth/to the seasons   VoR

Wrap Me Up in My Tarpaulin Jacket.   *Anonymous*.   Oh, ain't there some place in between them/Where this poor buffer can go?   AS

Wrapped Hair Bundles.   Frank LaPena.   how death takes/gifts of hair/and makes/itself a shawl   STE

"Wrapt in my careless cloak..."   Henry Howard, Earl of Surrey.   What will she do when hoary hairs are powdered/in her head!   FCP; SiPS

Wrath.   John Hollander.   Pianississississimo/Notes for the horn.   PV

Wrath to Sadness.   Robert Grenier.   and the "archaic smile' opens/again finally/to recite my doom.   APU

The Wreath.   Robert Graves.   You shall be punished with a deathless crown/For your dark head, resist it how you may.   BoLoP

A Wreath.   George Herbert.   For this poor wreath, give thee a crown of praise.   OBSP; SeCP

Wreathe the Bowl.   Thomas Moore.   And leave dull earth behind us!   HBV 1-2

Wreathmakertraining.   Karl Patten.   Could it be that we neither celebrate nor mourn?   FAZ

Wreaths.   Geoffrey Hill.   What hurts appeased by the sea's handsomeness!   PoA

The Wreck.   Walter De la Mare.   And, sipping of contrast, finds the day more fair.   MOS

Wreck.   Noel Polk.   to cool the conflagration in my head.   AmC; AMV-81

The Wreck of Number Nine.   *Anonymous*.   For I know you will be true/Till we meet at the golden gate.   BFSS

Wreck of the Deutschland.   Gerard Manley Hopkins.
   Mastery, but be adored, but be adored King.   BoC
   Our hearts' charity's hearth's fire, our thoughts' chivalry's throng's Lord.
   AtBAP; BoC; BrPo; CMoP; CoBMV; DiPo; FaBoMo; LiTB; LiTM; MasP; MoVE; NoAm; NOBE; NOBV; OAEP; OBNC; OxBoCh; PoEL 1-5; SeCePo; SeCeV; TEP; VLP

The Wreck of the Deutschland (parody).   David Annett.   The dead were the fortunate ones.   BXAP

The Wreck of the Great Northern.   Robert Hedin.   ...the wind was rattling/The dry husks of corn.   AMV-81

The Wreck of the Hesperus.   Henry Wadsworth Longfellow.   Christ save us all from a death like this,/On the reef of Norman's Woe!   AnNE; BeLS; BLPA; EtS; FaBoBe; FaFP; FaPoR; FPL; GN; GoTF; HBV 1-2; HBVY; MOS; OBCA; OBNV; PAH; PaPo; TreF; WBLP

The Wreck of the Northfleet.   *Anonymous*.   May God in heaven above protect them from all the perils of the sea.   OBSS

The Wreck of the Old 97.   *Anonymous*.   He may leave you and never return.   FSW; ViBoFo

The Wreck of the Rambler.   *Anonymous*.   For Plymouth Town it flowed with tears/When they heard of the sad and dread affair.   OBSS

The Wreck of the Royal Charter.   *Anonymous*.   Likewise the parents of the seamen brave/Who in the Royal Charter met a watery grave.   OBSS

The Wreck of the Royal Palm.   *Anonymous*.   For if we get our orders mixed/It'll surely be too late.   AmFP

The Wreck of Walsingham.   *Anonymous*.   Walsingham, oh, farewell.   ACP

Wreck on the C. and O.(Or) Death of Jack Hinton.   *Anonymous*.   And laid in his lonesome grave.   ABF

The Wreck on the Somerset Road.   *Anonymous*.   And for hours and hours, well, that brakeman waited/For a train that will never pull in.   OuSiCo

The Wrecker Driver Foresees Your Death.   David Baker.   each of these a promise you could never keep.   MAYP

The Wrecker's Prayer.   Theodore Goodridge Roberts.   Heave us a wrack to beguile our grief. Amen.   OBCV; PeCV

The Wren.   *Anonymous*.   For none would use with disrespect,/Whom Heaven thinks proper to protect.   OxBChV

The Wren.   Issa.   "Dropped something?"   NTCP

The Wren Hunt.   *Anonymous*.   In the brewer's big pan, says everyone.   OxNR

The Wren She Lies in Care's Bed.   *Anonymous*.   A kind sweetheart o' mine, O.   PBBP

Wrens and Robins in the Hedge.   Christina Georgina Rossetti.   Building, perching, pecking, fluttering,/Everywhere!   SUS; TiPo

Wrestlers.   Michael Drayton.   Within a spacious ring, by the beholders made,/According to law.   SD

The Wrestling.   Abbie Huston Evans.   The touched thew bearing witness.   GP

Wrestling Angels.   David Bottoms.   leaning over graves like old men lamenting their age.   MAYP

Wrestling Jacob.   Charles Wesley.   Thy Nature, and thy Name is LOVE.   CEP; NOBE; NOCV; NOEC; OBEC; OBEV; PoEL 1-5; SeCePo

The Wrestling Match.   Robert Penn Warren.   That forever we would keep if but we could.   AnAmPo

Wretched Man.   John Wilmot, Earl of Rochester.   Is only who's a knave of the first rate.   SeCePo

Writ on the Eve of My 32nd Birthday.   Gregory Corso.   but it does tell me my soul has a shadow.   NAs

Write, Do Write.   Marilyn Chin.   write, do write.   BrSi

The Writer.   Hildebrand Jacob.   He writes himself; he has no time.   FaBoCo

The Writer.   Richard Wilbur.   ...I wish/What I wished you before, but harder.   CAPP; HaCAP; OxBC; Str

The Writer to His Book.   Thomas Campion.   Thy lightness can not help or hurt my/fame.'   OAEP

Writing.   William Allingham.   Most books, indeed, are records less/Of fulness than of emptiness.   NOBV

Writing.   Howard Nemerov.   ...which long/remembers nothing, neither wind nor wake.   NYBP

Writing for Money.   Edward Field.   That's why I'm writing this poem,/to sell for money.   PPJ

Writing in England Now.   Philip O'Connor.   to teach the reader what I know about writing in England today.   OxBTC

Writing on Napkins at the Sunshine Club Macon, Georgia 1971.   David Bottoms.   even the low belch of the brunette behind the flippers.   TAT

Writing on the Wall.   Padraic Fallon.   Wondering how belly-hunger with this quill of spray and storm/Could forge such a dazzling signature   NeIP

Writing to Aaron.   Denise Levertov.   ...each leaf/imprinted, syllables in our lives.   FAZ

Writing While My Father Dies.   Linda Pastan.   and shivering I rub these words/together, hoping for a spark.   PCP

Written.   Mary Ruelfe.   hands have opened doors/to let the dead wind in.   AMV-81

Written After Swimming From Sestos to Abydos.   George Gordon, Lord Byron.   For he was drown'd and I've the ague.   ALV; ERoP 1-2; InMe; LiSp; MBW 1-2; MOS; NLV; NoP; OBRV; OBTV

Written after the Death of Charles Lamb (excerpt).   William Wordsworth.   O, he was good, if e'er a good man lived!   CoBE

A Written Answer.   Tom Paulin.   and the critics yonder say his work is alright.   FaBoIP

Written at an Inn at Henley. William Shenstone. May sigh to think he still has found,/The warmest welcome, at an inn. AWP; CEP; HBV 1-2; LoBV; NOBE; NOEC; OBEC; OBEV; ViBoPo

Written at Cambridge. Charles Lamb. And half had stagger'd that stout Stagirite! EnRP; OBRV

Written at Florence. Wilfrid Scawen Blunt. No sudden weariness that thou art young? OBVV

Written at Mr. Pope's House at Twickenham. George, Lord Lyttelton. G—lle, whose eyes have power to make/A Pope of every swain. CEP

Written at the End of a Book. Langdon Elwyn Mitchell. I blew as he said! AA

Written at the White Sulphur Springs. Francis Scott Key. If you wish to fare well, say farewell to the springs. OBAL

Written for My Son...at His First Putting on Breeches. Mary Barber. We yield to his despotic sway,/The only monarch all obey. NOEC

Written Forty Miles South of a Spreading City. Robert Bly. half soul and half body. NNaP

Written in a Copy of Swift's Poems, for Wayne Burns. James Wright. Nobilities, light, light and air. NOBA

Written in a Copy of The Earthly Paradise. William Morris. Life is a waste and windless Sea. VLP

Written in a Lady's Prayer Book. John Wilmot, Earl of Rochester. That we by easy steps may rise/Through all the joys on earth to those above. BoLoP

Written in a Little Lady's Little Album. Frederick William Faber. But little things/On little wings/Bear little souls to heaven. HBV 1-2; HBVY

Written in a Thunder Storm July 15th 1841. John Clare. Bid earth and its delusions pass away/But leave the mind as its creator free. ERoP 1-2; VLP

Written in a Time of Crisis. Stephen Vincent Benét. Say it and speak it loud, United, free... PAL

Written in an Ovid. Matthew Prior. To any woman, maid or bride,/Who resolves to go astray. FaBoEE; FaBoUs

Written in Butler's Sermons. Matthew Arnold. Whereo'er the chariot wheels of life are roll'd/In cloudy circles to eternity. VLP

Written in Dejection near Rome. Robert Bly. piercing through rotting bark for their food. NaP

Written in Exile. Kathleen Raine. Your love's great realm, my separation measures. TrCP

Written in Flight from His Royal Patron. Al Mutanabbi. The great white bulls at moments fail to rise/To the occasion, eunuchs can't do otherwise. LiTW

Written in Her French Psalter. Queen of England, Elizabeth I. Nor yet so ugly half can be/As is the inward suspicious mind. PBWP

Written in Ireland. Mary Alcock. No more shall wars thy land divide,/Wert thou as good as great. NOEC; OBTV

Written in Juice of Lemmon. Abraham Cowley. The Gods, though beasts they do not Love,/Yet like them when they'r burnt in Sacrifice. AnAnS 2; SeCP; SeCV 1-2

Written in July, 1824. Mary Russell Mitford. Echoes!–Oh, wintery cricket, welcome thou! OBRV

Written in March. William Wordsworth. The rain is over and gone! BoNaP; EnRP; GoJo; HBV 1-2; HBVY; NTCP; SUS; TiPo; UnPo; YeAr

Written in My Lady Speke's Singing-Book. Edmund Waller. But the image of her graces/Fills my heart and leaves no spaces. CavP

Written in Prison. John Clare. The fly I envy settling in the sun/On the green leaf, and wish my goal was won. OAEL 1-2

Written in the Beginning of Mezeray's History of France. Matthew Prior. Unwilling to retire, though weary. CEP; EiCP; NOBE; OBEC; PoEL 1-5

Written in the Visitors' Book at the Birthplace of Robert Burns. George Washington Cable. Whose thorns are in his hands. AA

Written in Unbridled Repugnance near Sioux Falls, Alabama... A. K. Redwing. Adam weeps... VoR

Written in Very Early Youth. William Wordsworth. The officious touch that makes me droop again. EnRP

Written on a Fly-Leaf of Theocritus. Maurice Thompson. And with his goat-hoof keeping time! AA

Written on a Girl's Table-Napkin at Wiesbaden. Ronald Duncan. ...take off that crucifix around your neck/And hang a corkscrew there? WeW

Written on a Leaf. Anonymous. I write this poem on a fallen leaf and send it out to a wandering man. BoWoP

Written on a Looking-Glass. Anonymous. But I reflect–which women never do. FaBoEE; HBV 1-2

Written on a Paper Napkin. Len Gasparini. contained my hate in embryo. NeAC

Written on a Sunday Morning. Robert Southey. She woos Reflection in the silent gloom,/And ponders on the world to come. OBEC

Written on a Wall at Woodstock. Queen of England, Elizabeth I. So God send to my foes all they have thought. PBWP

Written on an Island off the Breton Coast. Saint Venantius Fortunatus. So dark, O love, my spirit without thee. PeHV

Written on Seeing the Flowers, and Remembering My Daughter. Kao Ch'i. The wind makes desolate sounds in the night curtains. DL

Written on the Banks of Wastwater during a Calm. John Wilson. ...the gentle Lake/Lies like a sleeping child too blest to wake! OBRV

Written on the Plain of Thebes. John William Burgon. Will still flow on in strain sublime/When stones, and even men, are mute. OBTV

Written on the Raod. Mary Mapes Dodge. Till all thy birthdays are come to thee. BiCB

Written on the Sense of Isolation in Contemporary Ireland. Robert Greacen. So now in days of fevered fret and stress/Let Europe measure out our Irishness! NeIP

Written on the Wall at Chang's Hermitage. Tu Fu. An empty boat, floating, adrift. HoPM; NaP

Written on the Walls of His Dungeon. Luis Ponce de Leon. Envying none, and envied not. TrJP

Written over a Gate. John, Duke of Buckingham Sheffield. For how could such a wretch succeed,/But that, alas, it was decreed? NIP

Written to a Young Lady. Jeremiah Joseph Callanan. And give all thy blushes/And sweets to thy God. IrPN

Written upon the Top of Ben Nevis. John Keats. But in the world of thought and mental might! ERoP 1-2; PoSH

Written with a Diamond on Her Window at Woodstock. Queen of England, Elizabeth I. Nothing proved can be,/Quoth Elizabeth prisoner. PBWP

The Wrong Kind of Insurance. John Ashbery. Each night/Is trifoliate, strange to the touch. NYP

The Wry Rowan. Anonymous. we brought in no prey to Fionn/but the berries of the tree and two swine./Swineherd. OnYI

A Wry Smile. Roy Fuller. Outside my perfect knowledge or my fate. WaaP; WaP

Wulf. Bill Manhire. you & I, Wulf, the one/with the other/& singing OCNZ

Wulf and Eadwacer. Richard Ryan. Easily stopped what/had hardly started,/our song together. BoWoP; CIP; TrGrPo

Wunst I Had an Old Gray Mare. Anonymous. Taddle diddle dink dink, taddle diddle day. OuSiCo

Wyat Resteth Here, that Quicke Coulde Never Rest. Henry Howard, Earl of Surrey. The earth his bones, the heavens possesse his goost. AAS; EnPo; FCP; NCEP; NoP

A Wykehamist's Address to Learning. P. N. Shuttleworth. A Bishop or at least a Dean. FaBoCo

Wyncote, Pennsylvania: A Gloss. Thomas Kinsella. And over them I will take/ever more painstaking care. NOBI

Wynken, Blynken, and Nod. Eugene Field. Wynken/Blynken,/And Nod. BeLS; FaFP; HBVY; MOON

Wynken De Worde. Frederick von Ende. 'Tis tyme that the worlde heard the worde about Wynken. PoL

Wynter Wakeneth. Anonymous. For y not whider y shal, ne hou longe her duelle. OxBoCh; SeCePo

Wynyard Sailor. Ray Mathew. have never, will never/face death having known. CBAP

The Wyoming Massacre. Uriah Terry. To help our cause and break the jaws/Of cruel tyranny. PAH

Wyvern. Charles Connell. And maybe that's why it's extinct! AmMo

X

X Minus X. Kenneth Fearing. spoken;even when your friend, the magnate, is/gone. AmLP

The X of the Unknown. Tom Clark. For he seemed like a man leaving his mind behind him/Somewhere there on the ground LiSp

X, Oh X. Mark Simpson. the prize I have/given you for travelling/so closely with me. GOYP

X-Ray. David Ray. Oh he is out of hiding now/and is drumming drumming/drumming my heart. NePoEA-2

X-Ray. Leonora Speyer. Into that house of bone/I entered–and alone. ImOP

Xantippe. Amy Levy. ...now sent back/Swift to their sources, never more to rise;... BrRo

Xenophanes. Ralph Waldo Emerson. Repeats one note. AnNE; NOBA

Xerox. Ben Belitt. ...And the original man on the/plate/stands and steps down, unassisted. NYP

Xmas for the Boys. Gavin Ewart. But Shakespeare's extra, as you ought to know. OBSV

Xmas Time. Walta Karsner. And all the Xmas that she had/Was in her little head. ELU

XXXVI. Ted Berrigan. feminine marvelous and tough. ANYP

Y

D-Y Bar. James Welch. the dormant bear. CDW; STE

Y M & V Blues. Lost John Hunter. Yeah, I'll find you baby/'cause you rode that old YM & V BluL

Ya Se Van Los Pastores. Dudley Fitts. Eastward, into sunrise. FYAP

The Yacht. Caius Valerius Catullus. As a free gift and offering she devotes/Herself, as long as she survives and floats. AWP

The Yacht. Walter Savage Landor. There may be still one left for you. OBVV

Yachting in Arkansas. Craig Weeden. ...I climb aboard/my tractor and sail. AMV-80; PPP

The Yachts. William Carlos Williams. in waves still as the skillful yachts pass over. AmPP; BiP; CMoP; CoBMV; ExPo; HeIP; InPo; LiSp; LiTA; LiTM; MasP; MoAB; MoAmPo; MoPo; MOS; MoVE; NAMP; NePA; NoAm; NOBA; NoP; OxBA; SeCeV; ViBoPo

Yachts on the Nile. Bernard Spencer. to make the migration of sails/and wings a crying matter. ChMP

Yaddo. Ruth Herschberger. For words, and birds, not apples/On the tongue, nor roast in the gut. FAZ

Yahrzeit. Dan Jaffe. knowing his tears/will turn to dew. VWA

Yahrzeit. Susan Fromberg Schaeffer. And wore it well, and wore it long,/And did not die. VWA

Yahrzeit Candle. Jean Nordhaus. to burn forever with a clear flame/and not be taken. AMV-81

The Yak. Hilaire Belloc. (I cannot be positive which). ALV; FaBV; HBVY; InMe; NA; NLV; NOBL; OxBChV; TreFS

The Yak. Virna Sheard. While for the princess? She went back to play!/Tra-rill-a-la-lo! CaP; PeCV; WHW

Yak. William Jay Smith. Would look when perched in a barber chair! TiPo

Yale Boola March. Charles H. Loomis.
"For God, for Country and for Yale!" FSN
Oh, Yale, Eli Yale! FSN

Yang-Se-Fu. Yehoash. "Who is there as small as you?" TrJP

Yankee Cradle. Robert P. Tristram Coffin. And the fog rolled high on Cranberryhorn. EvOK

Yankee Doodle. Anonymous. And called it macaroni. OxNR

Yankee Doodle. Edward Bangs. And with the girls be handy. ABF; AmFP; BLSo; ExPo; FaFP; FSW; HBV 1-2; OBAL; PAL; TrAS; TreF; YaD

The Yankee Doodle Boy. George M. Cohan. I am the Yankee Doodle Boy. BLSo; FSN

Yankee Doodle's Expedition to Rhode Island. Anonymous. And made him stir his stumps, sir. GBP; PAH

The Yankee Man-of-War. Anonymous. Down the North Channel Paul Jones did/steer just at the break of day. AA; EtS; FaBoBe; LaNeLa; OBSS; PAH; PaPo

The Yankee Man-of-War or The Stately Southerner. Anonymous. On an autumn night we raised the light on the old head of Kinsale. AmSS

Yankee Poet. Robley Wilson, Jr. Tradition sets the straightest line to sense. AMV-81

The Yankee Privateer. Arthur Hale. Here is three times three/For the Yankee Privateer! PAH

The Yankee's Return from Camp. Edward Bangs. Locked up in mother's chamber. MC; PAH

Yankee Thunders. Anonymous. And her Yankee thunders roar. PAH

A Yankee View. Anonymous. No soldier could sniff it without having an erection. OBAL

The Yankeys' Return from Camp. Anonymous. Mind the music and the step./And with the girls be handy. OxBoLi

Yaqui Women: Three Generations. Rick Casillas. and the sons of her sons/will let the metate grow cold on the porch. GP

Yardbird's Skull. Owen Dodson. Come sing, come sing, come sing sing/And sing. AmNP; CNA; IDB; PoBA; VGW

Yardley-Oak. William Cowper. ...History, not wanted yet,/Lean'd on her elbow, watching Time... LaA; NCEP; NOEC

The Yarn of the Loch Achray. John Masefield. Hear the yarn of a sailor,/An old yarn learned at sea. SeCeV; StPo

The Yarn of the "Nancy Bell'. Sir William Schwenck Gilbert. And a bosun tight, and a midshipmite,/And the crew of the captain's gig!' BeLS; BLPA; CenHV; EtS; EvOK; FaBoBe; FaBoCh; FaBoCo; FaBV; FaFP; GoTF; HBV 1-2; HoPM; InMe; LoGBV; MCCG; MOS; MoShBr; NOBL; OnMSP; TreFS; TrGrPo; VLP

Yarrow Revisited. William Wordsworth. And dearer still, as now I feel,/To memory's shadowy moonshine! EnLi 1-2; VLP

Yarrow Unvisited. William Wordsworth. The bonny holms of Yarrow! EnLi 1-2; EnRP; GTBS; GTBS-P; HBV 1-2; PoRA

Yarrow Visited. William Wordsworth. And cheer my mind in sorrow. EnLi 1-2; GTBS; GTBS-P; HBV 1-2

Yattendon. Sir Henry Newbolt. Hither, by singer's magic,/The pilgrim world must come. HBMV

Yaw, Dot Is So! Charles Follen Adams. Dot's pest as anydings I know;/Yaw, dot is so! HBV 1-2

Yawcob Strauss. Charles Follen Adams. I prays der Lord, "Dake anyding,/But leaf dot Yawcob Strauss." PaPo

The Yawn. Paul Blackburn. I have only to think of her and I/o-oh-aaaww–hm/wow! CTBA; ELU

Ye Ballade of Ivan Petrofsky Skevar. Anonymous. Of Abdullah Boul Boul Ameer. ABF

Ye Beauties, Beaux, Ye Pleaders at the Bar. Anonymous. He'll so supply, you'll think you've got your own. FaBoUs

Ye Bruthers Dogg. Jon Anderson. O'Toole, Hodain, ye Bruthers Dogg. NLV

Ye Clerke of Ye Wethere (parody). Anonymous. Let non don him offence, lest ille befalle. BXAP

Ye Flowery Banks. Robert Burns. And left the thorn wi' me. AWP; CEP; EnRP; InPo; OAEP; OBEC; PoEL 1-5; UnPo

Ye Golden Lamps of Heaven. Philip Doddridge. Nor the meridian sun decline/Amidst those brighter skies. OxBoCh

Ye Heavens, Uplift Your Voice. Anonymous. Jesus, as He foresaid,/Is risen from the dead. OHIP

Ye know my heart... Sir Thomas Wyatt. Why are ye then so cruel foe,/Unto your own that loveth you so? FCP; LoBV; SiPS

Ye Little Birds That Sit and Sing. Thomas Heywood. Return with pleasant warblings. EiL; ViBoPo

Ye Mariners of England. Thomas Campbell. And the storm has ceased to blow. BLPA; CBEP; EtS; FaPoR; GN; GTBS; GTBS-P; HBV 1-2; NOBE; OBEV; OBRV; OBWP; TreF

Ye Mongers Aye Need Masks for Cheatrie. Sydney Goodsir Smith. The bluid ye drave til ilka airt/Sall feed its ain reid sleepan hert. OxBS

Ye Old Mule. Sir Thomas Wyatt. To pourchase it by payement and by prayer,/Ye old mule! AAS

Ye Parliament of England. Anonymous. The flag she waves at her masthead–"Free Trade and Sailors' Rights!" AmFP; AmSS; PAH

Ye Realms Below the Skies. Hosea Ballou II. Through all the universal frame. AH

Ye Scattered Nations. Thomas Cradock. (And be the God that hears our prayers adored.) AH

Ye Shall Live Also. Arthur Cleveland Coxe. Thou wilt be my confidence! BePJ

Ye Simple Men. John Stuart Blackie. While Law, that still should help the weak,/Gave spurs to aid the strong. PoSH

Ye Sons of Columbia. Anonymous. Bad women to a certainty are the downfall of men,/As Adam was beguiled by Eve. BFSS

Ye Sons of Columbia. Thomas Green Fessenden. Till the continent sinks, and the ocean is dry! PAH

Ye Sorrowers. Franz Werfel. Into the kingdom of my strong arm. TrJP

Ye Spier Me. Sydney Goodsir Smith. Frae the burst craters o the hert. AtBAP; BSV

Ye Tourists and Travellers, Bound to the Rhine. Thomas Hood. Take care of your pocket!–take care of your pocket! OBTV

Ye Walls! Sole Witnesses of Happy Sighs. Walter Savage Landor. All you have seen and heard. EnLoPo

Ye Wearie Wayfarer: Sun and Rain and Dew from Heaven. Adam Lindsay Gordon. With its moral drifting leeward,/Ends the wanderer's lay. PoLf

The Year 1812. Adam Mickiewicz. Spring of the war, Spring of the mighty yield,/That promised corn but ripened into men. OBVE; OBWP

Year after year I have watched. Li Ch'ing-chao. The gates of Heaven are nearer/Than the body of my beloved. BoWoP

The Year Ahead. Horatio Nelson Powers. This is the Year that for you waits/Beyond To-morrow's mystic gates. WBLP

A Year of Sorrow. Aubrey Thomas De Vere. And minister the last sad Rite,/Where altar there is none, nor priest. ACP; IrPN

Year of the Bird. Brian Swann. a feather from their breasts AmPA

The Year of the Foxes. David Malouf. ...old foxes, rusty red like dried-up wounds,/and a G.I. escort. NOAV

The Year of Winter. Frank LaPena. The earth was covered/with the bones of winter/for as far as the eye could see STE

A Year Passes. Amy Lowell. But the sword-shaped moon/Has cut my heart in two. MOON

The Year's at the Spring. Robert Browning. God's in his heaven–/All's right with the world! BLPA; FaBoBe; FaBV; YeAr

The Year's Awakening. Thomas Hardy. How do you know? CMoP; OxBTC

A Year's Burden. Algernon Charles Swinburne. Cry wellaway, but well befall the right. VLP

Year's End. Brother Antoninus. ...the death of a year,/And watch it go down in thunder. NoAm

Year's End. Nathaniel A. Benson. We have done more than make the seas divide. CaP

The Year's End.   Timothy Cole.   Contentedly he glides away, serene.   HBV 1-2

Year's End.   Richard Wilbur.   The New-year bells are wrangling with the snow.   CAPP; CoAP; HeIP; SM

The Year's Ending.   St. J. Page Yako.   ...not to return again,/Never until the uttermost end of time.   PeSA

The Year That's Awa'.   John Dunlop.   Nor depart like the year tha's awa'.   HBV 1-2

A Year without Seasons.   Mance Williams.   ...Strangulation/Could occur with one slip of the tongue.   NNP

The Yearbook.   Tom Clark.   And the other, whose role never/Came clear to me till tonight; even/Now I do not know his name.   ANYP

Yearning.   Alfred Kreymborg.   A bright yellow nut, so they say!   MAPA

Years.   Jon Anderson.   Slept, & woke alone, awhile serene.   AmPA

Years.   Walter Savage Landor.   I see it not, nor hear Adieu.   CBEP; HBV 1-2; OBEV

Years.   Anna Margolin.   and seek you, not believing in you.   VWA

The Years.   John Hall Wheelock.   ...I/Stare back, with a still face, but not of stone.   CrMA

Years and Years I Have Loved You.   Gabriel Gillett.   Our love can despise the world.)   PeHV

Years Later.   Laurence Lerner.
The dying sound of laughter in the dark.   NAs
They were the helpless lips that long ago/Kept me from being born. PeSA

Years Later.   Ruth Stone.   ...their delicate mouse-like tread/printed in tracks of snow over my mind.   BoWoP

Years of Indiscretion.   John Ashbery.   And yesterday the place where we left off a little while ago.   NOBA

Years of the Modern.   Walt Whitman.   The unperform'd, more gigantic than ever, advance, advance upon me.   AmePo

Yeats in Dublin (excerpt).   Vernon Watkins.   All is rewarded on a breath/By an accident.   PP

Yeats' Tower.   Vernon Watkins.   O under grass, O under grass, the secret.   NeBP

Yee Shall Not Misse of a Few Lines in Remembrance of Thomas Hooker.   Edward Johnson.   Thy Head's in Heaven, and hath a crown for thee.   SCAP

Yehuda Amichai.   Seymour Mayne.   Your fatigue/is an elegy etched/for a moment/on disappearing flesh   VWA

Yellow.   De Leon Harrison.   words/3poets   PoBA

Yellow.   Josephine Jacobsen.   Outside the madhouse hung the yellow sun. GP

Yellow.   Kenton Kilmer.   Looks up into the yellow sun each mirror-yellow flake.   GoYe

Yellow.   Charles Wright.   The yellow of sulfur, the finger, the road home. AmPA

The Yellow Bird Sings.   Rabindranath Tagore.   My name is known to all the village, and her name is/Ranjana.   OBMV

The Yellow Bittern.   Thomas Macdonagh.   And a dram won't stop our thirst this night.   OnYI; OxBI

The Yellow Bittern.   Cathal Bui Mac Giolla Ghunna.   There won't be a drop when you're dead and gone.   NOBI

The Yellow Bittern.   Tom MacIntyre.   Warm them worms waitin' undergroun'.   CIP

Yellow Butterflies.   Koianimptiwa.   All day shall come the rushing rain. WTO

Yellow Cloud.   Liagarang.   Wide cloud with hands extended, and black girdle.   WTO

Yellow Dusk: Messenger Fails to Appear.   Anonymous.   Averting face–sob in darkness.   OBVE

The Yellow Flower.   William Carlos Williams.   for me to naturalize/and acclimate/and choose it for my own.   HAP

The Yellow-haired Laddie.   Anonymous.   For the yellow-hair'd laddie my gudeman shall be.   GBP

Yellow Jessamine.   Constance Fenimore Woolson.   The spring has come–has come to Florida,/With yellow jessamine.   AA; HBV 1-2

Yellow Light.   Garrett Kaoru Hongo.   in a heavy light like yellow onions. HoAn; MAYP

Yellow Meal.   Anonymous.   Where I'll get lashings of corned meat, and none of your yellow meal.   ShS

A Yellow Pansy.   Helen Gray Cone.   For the butterfly-soul that is in it/Longs for the winds again!   HBMV

The Yellow Rose of Texas.   Anonymous.   But the Yellow Rose of Texas/beat the belles of Tennessee.   BLSo; FSW; PSoN; TreFT

The Yellow Season.   William Carlos Williams.   beyond the crackle/of death's stinking certainty.   MoAB; MoAmPo

The Yellow Violet.   William Cullen Bryant.   I'll not o'erlook the modest flower/That made the woods of April bright.   AnNE; AP; BLPL; MAmP; PoLf; TAP

The Yellow Witch of Caribou.   Clyde Robertson.   At dawn, Selina found him there/Strangled by a golden hair.   BPAW; PoOW

Yellow Woman Speaks.   Merle Woo.   keep house, make love, wreak vengeance.   BrSi

The Yellowhammer.   John Clare.   To fix a place and choose a near early home/With yellow breast and head of solid gold.   NOBV

The Yeoman of the Guard (excerpt).   Sir William Schwenck Gilbert.   But every Jack/He must study the knack/If he wants to make sure of his Jill. FaBoUs

Yes.   Richard Doddridge Blackmore.   When young eyes look upon it/Through a slender wedding ring.   HBV 1-2

Yes?   Henry Cuyler Bunner.   Love, don't give me up!   HBV 1-2

Yes, But...   Theodore Weiss.   can I lean/on it, lean more than on all/his accomplishments, those greeny/asphodel triumphs.   TAP

Yes, I Could Love if I Could Find.   Anonymous.   She is a mistress to my mind.   ALV

Yes, I Have Been to Calvary.   Avis B. Christiansen.   And I shall go with Him to dwell/For all eternity!   STF

Yes: I Write Verses.   Walter Savage Landor.   The brave Queen Bess.   EnLi 1-2; EnRP

Yes, It Was the Mountain Echo.   William Wordsworth.   For of God,–of God they are.   EnRP

Yes Please Gentlemen.   A. R. D. Fairburn.   said he wouldn't have another drink, he couldn't take it.   ACV

Yes, the Agency Can Handle That.   Kenneth Fearing.   ...fall upon corroded monuments and the/graves of the forgotten dead.   WeW

Yes, the Secret Mind Whispers.   Al Young.   into your mouth/&/swallow for dear life   PoBA

Yes, What?   Robert Francis.   her goofs her goons her big galoots/under the red-face moon?   LCAP

Yesterday.   Hugh Chesterman.   Nor call you back again?   SiSoSe

Yesterday.   William Stanley Merwin.   though there was nowhere I had to go/and nothing I had to do   FYAP

Yesterday.   Carol Lee Sanchez.   He'll tell us/Why/we are.   TWSS

Yesterday Evening I Saw Your Corpse.   Joyce Mansour.   Yet I preferred you so/My flower   WPOW

Yesterday in Oxford Street.   Rose Fyleman.   That she should come to Oxford Street, and I be there to see!   TiPo

Yet Another Song.   David Rubadiri.   Today/I sing yet another song,/A song of exile.   WhB

Yet Dish.   Gertrude Stein.   ...Open so mister soil in to close not a see/wind not seat glass.   SOTW

Yet Do I Marvel.   Countee Cullen.   To make a poet black and bid him sing! AmNP; AnAmPo; BANP; BP; BPo; CDC; FF; IDB; MAPA; MOON; NoAm; PoBA; PoNe; TAP; TTY

Yet Listen Now.   Amy Carmichael.   Can we accept the unexplained, the loss,/The crushing agony, and hold us still.   TRV

Yet Love Was Born.   Charles Hannibal Voss.   To the Holy Child who came to stay,/On Christmas Eve.   BePJ

Yet Vain, Perhaps, the Fruits.   Frederick Goddard Tuckerman.   In the great flight of stars across the earth?   AnNE

Yetzer ha Ra.   Edward Codish.   My ears fill and empty with the hiss! of snake.   VWA

The Yew-Tree.   Anonymous.   Dear heart, you lay above the ground.   GBL

The Yew-Tree.   Vernon Watkins.   That word kills grief, and through the dark-boughed tree/Gives to each dead his resurrection day.   EaLo; LiTB

Yew-Trees.   William Wordsworth.   Murmuring from Glaramara's inmost caves.   CABA; EnRP; UnPo

Yiddish.   Judith Herzberg.   It no longer needs you/but it misses you. VWA

Yiddish.   Abraham Sutzkever.   and wake the coming generations with a roar like thunder.   VWA

Yiddish Poet.   A. C. Jacobs.   His dreams led nowhere–yet alive he sang. VWA

Yiddish Speaking Socialists of the Lower East Side.   Ed Sanders.   They were the Yiddish speaking socialists/of the Lower East Side.   APU

Yield.   Ronald Gross.   Merging Traffic Ahead/Yield./Yield.   InPK

The Yielded Life.   G. W.A..   Lays all with gladness at the feet/Of God's most Holy Son.   BLRP

Yielding.   Shellie Keir Robbins.   and then–/to give way.   AMV-80

Yo Soy de la Tierra.   Anonymous.   Sabe Dios si volvere.   OuSiCo

Yogi, don't go away.   Mira Bai [(or Mirabai)].   Mira says: Lord Girdhar Nagar,/let our fires unite.   BoWoP

The Yoke.   Ben Kalonymos.   And death soon brings a swift relief!   TrJP

The Yoke of Tyranny.   Sir Philip Sidney.   ...O me, that eye/Doth make my heart give to my tongue the lie.   TrGrPo

Yoke Soft and Dear.   John C. Kunze.   Send from above harmonious love/And joy and consolation.   AH

Yolp, Yolp, Yolp, Yolp.   Anonymous.   Yolp, yolp, yolp, yolp.   EIL

Yom Kippur.   Chana Bloch.   raising their braided heads,/their gold tongues whetted.   VWA

Yom Kippur.   Eric Chaet.   I am trying to operate/from the fire that is the bush.   VWA

You Kicked and Stomped and Beat Me. *Anonymous.* Goin' to make you run, sir. OuSiCo

You Kissed Me. Josephine Slocum Hunt. And if you were here, would you kiss me again? BLPA; FaBoBe; FPL

You Know. Jean Garrigue. And we get on the bus,/Taking the last of it down with us. NYBP; UnPo

You Know, Joe. Ray Durem. Ought to have a separate bomb for colored! BOLo

You Know Not How Deep Was the Love Your Eyes Did Kindle. Ibn al-Abbar. Did it not know that she was sleeping on my arm? PeHV

You Know the Place. Sappho. Fill our gold cups with love/stirred into clear nectar PBWP

You Laughed and Laughed and Laughed. Gabriel Okara. "Because my fathers and I/are owned by the living/warmth of the earth/through our naked feet." PBA

You lay in wait. Sappho. and suddenly: beauty/of your garments. BoWoP

You, Letting the Trees Stand as My Betrayer. Diane Wakoski. the man who stomps into the heart of this/forest. NoAm

You Lingering Sparse Leaves of Me. Walt Whitman. The faithfulest–hardiest–last. CBEP

You Little Stars That Live in Skies. Fulke, Lord Brooke Greville. To love and never seek compassion. EiL; NCEP

You'll Love Me Yet! Robert Browning. What's death? You'll love me yet! OLR

You'll Never Miss Your Jelly. Lil Johnson. You sure won't miss your jelly/till your jelly roller's gone BluL

You Lovely People. Virginia Cerenio. within each crack/a story BrSi

You Made It Rain. Fareedah Allah. Because of you, Madame Moon/It rains. BlSi

You Masks of the Masquerade. Gustave Kahn. and cradle me my Destiny. TrJP

You May Bury Me in de Eas'. *Anonymous.* How I long to go,/For to hear de trumpet soun',/In dat mornin'. BoAN 1-2

You Move Forward. Thomas Sessler. in the unatonable guilt/of the executioner. VWA

You Must Have Been a Sensational Baby (excerpt). Harold Norse. the whole place trembled with lust. GP

You Naughty, Naughty Men. T. Kennick. And when kind we'll say, oh, bless you, oh! you naughty, dear, delightful men. BLSo

You, Neighbor God. Rainer Maria Rilke. And then my senses, which too soon grow lame,/exiled from you, must go their homeless ways. MoRP

You Never Can Tell. Ella Wheeler Wilcox. Whatever went out from your mind. BLPA; BLPL; PoToHe

You Never Miss the Water. L. C. Williams. Yes, she's a good little girl/but she just won't be true. BluL

You never touch. Yosano Akiko. Are you not bored,/Expounding the Way? BoWoP; PBWP

You Northern Girl. Charles G. Ballard. Toward the fires of our Indian world. VoR

You on the Tower. Thomas Hardy. He brushed you by as he flew. SaC

You Owe Them Everything. John Allman. ...They smoke Lucky Strikes. They buy Wonder Bread. SaC

You Preach to Me of Laws. Iris Tree. Pity your littleness from all my passion,/Leave you my sins to weep and whine away! HBMV

You're. Sylvia Plath. A clean slate, with your own face on. FaBoTw; FaBoWP; NAs; NCSH

You're a Grand Old Flag. George M. Cohan. Keep your eye on the grand old flag. FSN

You're a poet. *Anonymous.* LONGFELLOW! FaFP

You're Going to Reap Just What You Sow. *Anonymous.* You're going to reap just what you sow. AmFP

You're in the Army Now. *Anonymous.* You'll never get rich/On the salary which/You get in the Army now. BLSo

You're Not Alone. Michael Drayton. You do bewitch me...O that I could fly/From my self you, or from your own self I! LiTL

You're Not the Only Pebble on the Beach. Harry Braisted. But he's not the only pebble on the beach! FSN

You're Nothing but a Spanish Colored Kid. Felipe Luciano. Get real nigger/And stop making gestures. PoBA

You're Sorry, Your Mother Is Crazy, & I'm a Chinese Shiksa. Deborah Lee. three-legged stray? BrSi

You're the Top. Cole Porter. But if, Baby, I'm the bottom,/You're the top! FSN; NLV; OBAL; UnPo

You Read Us Your Verse. Martial (Marcus Valerius Martialis). That some wool in our ears/Would really be more apropos. DBV

You Refuse to Own. Margaret Atwood. only the eyes show through. NeAC

You Rise Up. Paul Eluard. Woman you put into the world a body always the same/Yours/You are resemblance. PoP1

You Say, "I Will Come." Lady Otomo of Sakanoe. Have I learned to understand you? LiTW; OLR

You Say You Love Me. Robert Heath. I'll not believe you, I. PoL

You See the Worst of Love, but Not the Best. Walter Savage Landor. In the heart's temple his pure torch abides. GBL

You Serve the Best Wines Always, My Dear Sir. Martial (Marcus Valerius Martialis). They say...A drink? I don't believe I would. InPK

You Shall. Frank Stokes. Now when the good Lord set me free BluL

You Shall Above All Things Be Glad and Young. Edward Estlin Cummings. than teach ten thousand stars how not to dance NePA; NoAm; NOBA; OxBA

You Shall Be Queen. *Anonymous.* Sugar is sweet/And so are you. OxNR

You Simple Bostonians. *Anonymous.* And if that will not please you, you shall have half a score,/Derry down, down, down derry down. TrAS

You smiled, you spoke, and I believed. Walter Savage Landor. Deceive, deceive me once again! BoLoP; GBL; OAEP

You Stand and Hold the Post of My Small House. Auvaiyar. It is on the battlefield that you will find him. WPOW

You Take My Hand And. Margaret Atwood. the smell of popcorn and worn plush/lingers for weeks. HAP

You Take the Pilgrims, Just Give Me the Progress. Loyd Rosenfield. A tribute to our matriarch/And our digestive juices. QQQ

You Tell Me to Sit Quiet. A. C. Jordan. Tell the darkness/Never to flee/When smitten at dawn/By the shafts of the sun. PBA

You Tell Me Your Dream, I'll Tell You Mine. Rice. Seymour Brown. Albert H. You tell me your dream,/I'll tell you mine. FSN

You Tell On Yourself. *Anonymous.* In these ways, and more, you tell on yourself. PoToHe

You That Are Jealous and Have a Wife. *Anonymous.* If you can't manage that, for honour's sake/outclimb all idiots to the peak of madness. NOBI

You That Have Been Often Invited. *Anonymous.* O bow to his scepter while it's called today. AH

You That Love England. C. Day-Lewis. Wielders of power and welders of a new world. FaBoMo

You That Sing in the Blackthorn. Alfred Noyes. Pour through the lifted/Throat of a bird. GoBC

You, the Young Rainbow. Edith Sitwell. From the flowering earth and darkness of my heart. MoVE

You told me: "I am not worthy of you." Marguerite Burnat-Provins. You don't know anything, so shut up. BoWoP

You Too? Me Too–Why Not? Soda Pop. Robert Hollander. that is to say which makes/soda pop. NIP

You Turn for Sugar an' Tea. *Anonymous.* You turn, I turn. OuSiCo

You Understand the Requirements. Lyn Lifshin. please don't call us. NeAC

You've Been a Good Old Wagon, But You've Done Broke Down. Ben Harney. You have kill'd three Niggers in the first degree,/No bail. OBAL

You've Got to be Carefully Taught. Oscar, II Hammerstein. You've got to be carefully taught! AmFN

You want the summer lightning, throw the knives. Ingeborg Bachmann. The bell rings, and it is enough. BoWoP

You Want to Go Back. Margaret Atwood. This is the way it is, get used to it. NeAC

You Went to the Verge, You Say, and Came Back Safely? Conrad Aiken. It is the answer that no question asked. LiTA

You Were Wearing. Kenneth Koch. ...a/garbage can lid smashed into a likeness of the mad English/king, George the Third. ANYP; CoAP; EAS; NIP; NNaP; NoAm; NoP

You Who Dog My Footsteps. Leib Kwitko. Hide from me my dead pages/Against the black wall oblivion. TrJP

You Who Occupy Our Land. Manuela Margarido. barely empty ghosts of men/you who occupy our land? WPOW

You Who Were Made for This Music. Louis Zukofsky. only glory restores. CoPo

You, Whoever You Are. Walt Whitman. Each of us here as divinely as any is here. AmFN

You, Whose Mother's Lover Was Grass. Gregory Corso. his jealousy makes bastards of us all. NoAm

You Will Die. *Anonymous.* And another will take your place. AWP

You Will Find a Joy in Service. Dorothy Conant Stroud. You will find a joy in service/That will bless the world and you! STF

You Will Know When You Get There. Allen Curnow. Down you go alone, so late, into the surge-black/fissure. OCNZ

You Will See Your Lord A-Coming. *Anonymous.* While the band of music/Shall be sounding through the air. AH

You within Love. Norman MacCaig. ...rise with passion/in an echoing spring burn every day. NeBP

You would have understood me, had you waited. Paul Verlaine. Here we who loved so, were so cold and bitter,/Hardly can disagree. BoLoP

Youghall Harbor. *Anonymous.* ...maybe, a little baby,/By and by to nestle within your arm. OnYI

Young. Anne Sexton. elbows, knees, dreams, goodnight. NCSH

The Young Acacia. Hayim Nahman Bialik. All her young admirers, whither/have they gone? TrJP

Young Africa's Resolve. Dennis C. Osadebay. I'll go forward and do and dare. ACV

Young Allan. *Anonymous.*
I hae but only ae daughter,/And wedded to her ye'se be. BaBo
An ther came never on back/Bat Young Allan alive. ESPB

The Young American. Alexander H. Everett. Happy if it be thy call/In the holy cause to fall. PaPo

Young and Radiant, He Is Standing. Allen Eastman Cross. He must wear a crown of sorrow/Who would be a Son of Man. AH

Young and Simple Though I Am. Thomas Campion. Love he must, or flatter me. EnL; FaBoEn; SeCeV

Young Andrew. *Anonymous.* For ther as the wolfe devoured him,/There lyes all this great erles gold. ESPB

Young Argonauts. Sheila Wingfield. Row on, row on, to catch the gold/In dripping fleece, as they of old. SD

The Young Author. Samuel Johnson. Glad to be hid, and proud to be forgot. EiCP; LAuP

Young Barnswell. *Anonymous.* It lay in your power to slay me/All on the mountains high.' OBET

The Young Bather. *Anonymous.* And archly looks to see if someone sees. UnTE

Young Bearwell. *Anonymous.* And Young Bearwell was the first man/In all that companie. ESPB

Young Beichan and Susie Pye. *Anonymous.* And called her his bonny love, Lady Jane. OnMSP

Young Benjie. *Anonymous.*
"The ae best man about your house/Maun wait young Boonjie on." ESPB
For that's the penance he maun drie,/To scug his deadly sin. BaBo; OxBB

Young Billy Crane. *Anonymous.* I mean to ride the swells and tides till I gain young Billy Crane. ShS

A Young Birch. Robert Frost. It was a thing of beauty and was sent/To live its life out as an ornament. BoNaP; LiTA

Young Blondes. Gavin Ewart. Into such sinful thoughts about young blondes! ErPo

The young bloods come round less often now. Horace. As a gift to the east wind, winter's friend. BoLoP

The Young Bride's Dream. Rhoda Coghill. But the words may be true ones: "Obedience is ice to the wine." OxBI

The Young Calves. Robert P. Tristram Coffin. The three of them went down the road/and never glanced behind. TiPo

Young Charlottie. William Lorenzo Carter. Till at last he died with the bitter grief—now they both lie in one tomb. BeLS; BLPA

Young Charlottie. Seba ("Major Jack Downing") Smith. And his thoughts turned back to the place where she said, "I'm growing/warmer now." AmFP

Young Companions. *Anonymous.* You may forget the singer,/But don't forget the song. CoSo

The Young Conquistador. Robert Peterson. ...His mother's/last hope: that he'll give up vice for art. GP

The Young Cordwainer. Robert Graves. With wine at my elbow,/And sword beneath the pillow,/I shall perfect all. MoBS

Young Couples Strolling By. Carl Rakosi. and Italians become lizards/and Diogenes goes sailing. PAI

A Young David: Birmingham. Helen Morgan Brooks. I am a boy. PoNe

The Young Dead Soldiers. Archibald MacLeish. We have died./Remember us. OFD; WaP

A Young Deer/Dust. Hemda Roth. so that many would come back/to me, come back/one by one. VWA

Young Democracy (excerpt). Bernard O'Dowd. That man is God, however low—/Is man, however high. PoAu 1-2

The Young Dove. Moses Ibn Ezra. And rejoice in the dust of their/land! TrJP

The Young Earl of Essex's Victory over the Emperor of Germany. *Anonymous.* For Essex's sake they would fight all. ESPB; OBET

Young Edmondale. *Anonymous.* Whose body, stabbed and bleeding, was plunged into the Low Lands Low. BFSS

Young Edwin in the Lowlands Low. *Anonymous.* Her shrieks were for Young Edwin that ploughed the Lowlands low. BaBo; OBET

Young Edwin in the Lowlands Low (B vers.). *Anonymous.* His body is in motion,/I hope his soul's at rest. BaBo

The Young Fellow Walks About. Charles Reznikoff. a stranger he has just met; hesitates;/and offers me a cigarette. CTBA

The Young Fenians. Padraic Fallon. A country rising from its knees/To upset all the histories. BIrV

A Young Fir-Wood. Dante Gabriel Rossetti. Upon the earth and elder stands. GN

Young Forbest. *Anonymous.* Here ends the days of a faithful youth. ShS

Young Girl. Ricarda Huch. What crown will be yours one day/O Amazon— WPOW

The Young Girl. Theodore Roethke. A bird my body,/My bird-blood ready. NoAm

Young Girl. Thomas Waltner. "How do you spell your last name?" LFAC

The Young Girl and the Beach. Sophia de Mello Breyner Andresen. And the wind scatters all with its hands WPOW

Young Girl: Annam. Padraic Colum. I am one separated,/But from whom I do not know. LOW

A Young Girl's Song. Paul Heyse. Advise me well, but don't dissuade me! PoPl

Young Girls. Raymond Souster. We whistle after them, then laugh, for they/stiffen, not knowing what to do or say. HeIP

The Young Glass-Stainer. Thomas Hardy. Martha I paint, and dream of Hera's brow,/Mary, and think of Aphrodite's form. CTC; EyDe; SaC

The Young Gray Head. Caroline Bowles Southey. There was an empty place,—they were but three. BeLS

Young Heroes. Frank Horne.
I like to see you living in the world. BPo
This Foreign Country speaks to You. BPo

Young Heroes, III: Walter Bradford. Gwendolyn Brooks. Not overmuch for a/Tree-planting Man./Stay. BPo

A Young Highland Girl Studying Poetry. Iain Crichton Smith. but he by many deaths will bless her days. NePoEA-2; PP

The Young Housewife. William Carlos Williams. ...as I bow and pass smiling. HeIP; NoAm; NoP; TAP

Young Hunting. *Anonymous.*
And I'd sing on as I fly. OxBoLi
An' it took on her fair body;/She burnt like holly gren. BaBo; OxBB; ViBoFo
You could always hear me sing. FaBoBa

Young Hunting (Loving Henry). *Anonymous.* I'd fly away to some tall tree/And there I'd sit and sing. AmFP

Young John. *Anonymous.* And made her lady of halls and towers,/Into sweet Berwick town. BuBa

Young Johnny. *Anonymous.* Without any exceptions, you'll be turned out-of-doors. BFSS

Young Johnstone (A version). *Anonymous.* See you not where my red heart's blood/Runs trickling down my knee? ESPB

Young Johnstone (B version). *Anonymous.* Till four and twenty broad arrows/Were thrilling in his heart. ESPB

The Young Laird and Edinburgh Katy. Allan Ramsay. And love and kiss, and kiss and love. CEP

Young Lambs. John Clare. With legs stretch'd out as though he could not rise. EG; TrGrPo

Young Lincoln. Edwin Markham. To bend the law to let his mercy out. OHIP

Young Lochinvar. Sir Walter Scott. Have ye e'er heard of gallant like young Lochinvar? FiBHP; HBVY; InMe; OBNV

Young Love. Gerald Massey. Not I, sweet soul, not I! OBVV

The Young Man. Lewis MacAdams. the sorrow in my head/will wrench it through the roof. ANYP

The Young Man and the Young Nun. A. D. Mackie. I'll pray for ye,' said the young nun/To the man at the convent yett. OxBS

Young Man Cut Down in His Prime. *Anonymous.* Saying, "There goes an unfortunate lad to his home.'" FSW

Young Man of Alien Beauty. Muireadhach Albanach O Dalaigh. a swift steed–gift of the stranger–/or the lipped and lidded goblet! NOBI

A Young Man's Epigram on Existence. Thomas Hardy. Lessons that leave no time for prizes. BrPo; NoAm

Young Man's Fancy. Ray Mathew. I won't spend two nights/waiting for a lover. BoAV

A Young Man's Song. William Bell. Ask me nothing you can guess. FaBoTw; NePoEA

The Young Man Thinks of Sons. R. A. K. Mason. and what I left undone. AnNZ

A Young Man to an Old Woman Courting Him. John Cleveland. I'l never be 'stead of a Lover,/An aged Chronicle's new Cover. AnAnS 2

The Young Man Who Loved the Girl Who Took Care of Her Aging Father. Greg Kuzma. and blew softly into the turned/down wick of his mouth, and the/room went dark. AmPA

Young Man Who Wouldn't Hoe Corn. *Anonymous.* All because he wouldn't hoe corn. FSW

The Young Martins. Andrew Young. And from their nests of clay/Like disembodied spirits suddenly fly away. FM

Young Master's Account of a Puppet Show. John Marchant. Yet I could lug him by the ears/For beating honest Cherry. OxBChV

The Young May Moon. Thomas Moore. He might happen to take thee for one, my dear. ELP; EnRP; HBV 1-2; MOON; OAEP; OBEV

The Young Men Come Less Often–Isn't It So? Horace. Consigning dry leaves to the winter sea. ErPo

Young Men You Are So Beautiful up There. Patricia Goedicke. Who is waiting and waiting for you to come down/Out of the heaven into her arms. GP

Young Molly Ban. *Anonymous*. Molly Ban she shone above them like a mountain of snow. FaBoBa

Young Monroe at Gerry's Rock. *Anonymous*. The bravest of all shanty-boys, the foreman, Young Monroe. AmSS

The Young Neophyte. Alice Meynell. And lay the crucifix on this silent heart. ACP; CAW; GoBC

The Young Ones. Elizabeth Jennings. So many ways to be unsure or bold. OxBTC

The Young Ones, Flip Side. James A. Emanuel. Youth hurts. And then/ It's gone. PCP

Young Paris. George Crabbe. Oh! think me not a Prince of Troy,/By whom such treacherous deeds are done. OBRV

Young Peggy. *Anonymous*. But ere they wan to the tap o the hill/The wedding was a' bye. BaBo; ESPB

Young People Who Delight in Sin. *Anonymous*. Though I am doomed to endless flames. AmFP

Young Poet. Myron O'Higgins. And kiss his young mouth into wisdom/ And healing. PoBA; PoNe

Young Poets. Nicanor Parra. You have to improve the blank page. PoL

The Young Price and the Young Princess. John Ashbery. You will say, "That is how we lived, you and I." ConAP

The Young Priest to His Hands. Edward F. Garesche. O happy hands–an angel's fee!/That clasp the Lord of Majesty! CAW

The Young Recruit. Arthur Davison Fiche. He has escaped the private wars of peace. ELU

Young Reynard. George Meredith. Haply you live a day longer in verse. HoPM

The Young Rhymer Snubbed. William Barnes. My heart a pleasure that do leave noo sting. VLP

Young Ronald. *Anonymous*. Gaed hame and married that lady,/And heird her father's land. ESPB

The Young Sailor Cut down in His Prime. Anonymous. He's a young sailor cut down in his prime. OBSS

Young Sammy Watkins. *Anonymous*. She hopes that he never will do it again. BBGG

Young Sea. Carl Sandburg. Where storms and stars come from. MOS

Young Shepherd Bathing His Feet. Peter Clarke. Then opened wide.../In ecstasy. PBA

Young Soul. LeRoi (Imamu Amiri Baraka) Jones. Make some muscle/in your head, but/use the muscle/in yr heart BPo; CNA

Young Stock. Victoria Mary (Vita) Sackville-West. Well-uddered heifers, bullocks strong and stout. OxBTC

Young Strephon and Phillis. *Anonymous*. For oh! Thou'rt all kind, and all soft at the bottom. UnTE

Young Sycamore. William Carlos Williams. bending forward/hornlike at the top TAP

Young Training. Lawrence McGaugh. "When shall we three meet again?" PoBA

Young Virgins Plucked Suddenly. Berl Pomerantz. Young virgins, plucked suddenly,/on a spring night, when the ice breaks up on the rivers– VWA

Young Washington. Arthur Guiterman. That's the life for a man! OHIP; PoSC

Young Waters. *Anonymous*. And for the words the queen had spoke/ Young Waters he did die. EnLit; ESPB; OxBB

A Young Wife. D. H. Lawrence. The pain of loving you/Is almost more than I can bear. BrPo; ChMP; ELP; MoBrPo

The Young Wife. C. K. Stead. every night the same stew. OCNZ

Young Windebank. Margaret Louisa Woods. To give us honor strong as death/And loyal love as sure. HBV 1-2; HBVY

Young Woman. Geoffrey Chaucer. My faire bryd, my sweete cynamone. BoW

Young Woman. Howard Nemerov. There is no pity in the flesh. ErPo

Young Woman at a Window. Mark Van Doren. And still the dreamless body stands. LiTA; MoPo; MoVE

The Young Woman from Aenos. *Anonymous*. And we brought her a leaf from the green-h'us. OBAL

The Young Woman of Beare. Austin Clarke. That dreams, the eye has known,/May trouble souls to-night. NoAm

Young Woman's Neo-Aramaic Jewish Persian Blues. Jerome Rothenberg. because you wouldn't/let it just be BoWoP

The Young Workman. Mary Dillingham Frear. Let us ever honor Thee as Thou/Didst ever honor toil. TrCP

A Young Poet. Peter Schjeldahl. He pokes at it obsessively/With the instrument of his chastened line PoA

The Younger Van Eyck. Edmund Clerihew Bentley. The thought of this curious mistake/Often kept him awake. FiBHP

The Youngest Daughter. Cathy Song. a thousand cranes curtain the window,/fly up in a sudden breeze. MAYP

Your Absence Has Not Taught Me. Doug Fetherling. ...truths men/ thought of years ago without/telling me. NeAC

Your Air of My Air. Hugo Margenat. of a ride on horseback over the forehead. InW

Your Animal. Gerald Stern. It is my victory over meanness. AMV-81

Your Attention Please. Peter Porter. Now go quickly to your shelters. OBWP; OxBTC

Your Back Is Rough. Margaret Atwood. there is something in your throat that wants/to get out and you won't let it. NeAC

Your Beauty and My Reason. *Anonymous*. And dazzled Reason yields as quite undone. TrGrPo

Your Birds Build Sun-Castles with Song. Daniel Sloate. As the rain was falling. AMV-81

Your Birthday Comes to Tell Me This. Edward Estlin Cummings. and will be and my birthday is. NAs

Your Birthday in Wisconsin You Are 140. John Berryman. Hot diggity! NAs

Your Body Is Stars. Stephen Spender. And then there comes the shutting of a door. FaBoTw; MoLP

Your Burnt-Out Body. Peretz Markish. A wayside hamlet on your twilit field... VWA

Your Catullus Is Depressed. Caius Valerius Catullus. Send me only some little line of comfort/Though it be as sad as Simonides' tears. PeHV

Your Chase Had a Beast in View. John Peale Bishop. One syllable of ecstasy/Confusing shame, confounding bone. LiTA

Your cheeks flat on the sand. Venus Khoury-Gata. get up/only men erect bind heavens to the earth BoWoP

Your Church and Mine. Phillips H. Lord. But let's walk along together. BLPA

Your Dog Dies. Raymond Carver. you wonder how long this can go on. GeTw

Your Eyes. Kosrof Chantikian. your eyes are/the sound of morning becoming the wind AMV-81

Your Eyes Have Their Silence. Gerald William Barrax. ...and my reason/ crawls into the silence of your eyes. Spring CNA; PoBA

Your Fair Looks Inflame My Desire. Thomas Campion. O farewell, my life's treasure! UnTE

Your Flag and My Flag. Wilbur D. Nesbit. Glorified all else beside–the Red and White and Blue! FaFP; WBLP

Your Friend. *Anonymous*. Cling to what's divine in him. GoTF; TreFT

Your Friends Come and Go. Jeffrey Miller. (Someday when Whatchmacallit and Whathisface are "out of/town.") APU

Your Glory, Lincoln. Mae Winkler Goodman. You cannot sleep till man has understood/That peace is Universal Brotherhood! PGD

Your Hand Full of Hours. Paul Celan. The leafage of years is brown, our hair is not brown. OBVE

Your Hands. Ernest Christopher Dowson. The hands of a girl, and most, your hands. UnTE

Your Hands. Angelina Weld Grimke. ....Even if you forgot. CDC; PoBA

Your House. *Anonymous*. The maker of a house, of a real human house, is God him-/self, the same who made the stars and ... PoToHe

Your Lad, and My Lad. Randall Parrish. As your dear lad, and my dear lad, go on their way to France. MC; PAH

Your Last Drive. Thomas Hardy. You are past love, praise, indifference, blame. OBNC

Your Light. Ann Lee. ...I wonder, wait the day/of your return, wrestling with heavy night. AMV-80

Your Little Voice. Edward Estlin Cummings. leaping/Sweetly/your voice LLLT; OLR

Your Looks So Often Cast. Sir Thomas Wyatt. There will be found no stays/To stop a thing so clear. EnRePo; FCP; SiPS

Your lynx-eyes, Asia. Anna Akhmatova. from the cupped palms of a stranger's hands. BoWoP

Your Mission. Ellen M. Huntington Gates. If you want a field of labor,/ You can find it anywhere. BLPA; BLRP; GoTF; TreFT

Your Money and Mine. *Anonymous*. And grow rich toward your God. STF

Your Mother. Sam Cornish. flies/even in the winter/live here CNA

Your Mouth. Jenab Shehabuddin. ...for your mouth has wrapped my life in a/thin gauze of hope. LiTW

Your Name in Arezzo. James Wright. I leave it to the sunlight, like the one/Landor the master left his voice upon. SM

Your Need Is Greater Than Mine. Theodore Enslin. I need so much more than you do. CoPo

Your Neighbor. H. Howard Biggar. If you'll stop with this neighbor and visit awhile. PoToHe

Your Own Version. Paul Gilbert. Say, what is the gospel/According to you? BLRP

Your Pain. Armando Guebuza. My blood/yet more your blood/shall irrigate our victory. WhB

Your Passing, Fleet Passing. Joseph Eliyia. Some soul, poor soul, in its mute weeping,/Drags the specter of pain to asphodel prairies. VWA

Your Phone Call at Eight A.M. Joy Harjo. this poem isn't for you/but for me/after all TWSS

Your Place. John Oxenham. Not yours alone, but His/Who set you there. BLRP; TRV

Your Presence. David Diop. And necklaces of laughter hung around our days/Days sparkling with new joys. PBA

Your Presence. Mordecai Temkin. You also will cease to be,/my Lord. VWA

Your Snow-White Shoulder. Heinrich Heine. Closer your arms shall twine. UnTE

Your Songs. Gwendolyn B. Bennett. For silence is a sounding thing/To one who listens hungrily. CDC

Your Tears. Edwin Markham. Bring me your tears! HBMV

Your Thoughts Don't Have Words Every Day. Emily Dickinson. You cannot comprehend its price/Nor its infrequency. DiPo; MAmP

Your Voice on the Telephone. Donald Hall. in the cell/of matter-of-fact. FF

Your Woods. Margaret Holley. ...so tentatively kneading/its claws into my temples. AMV-80

Your World. Georgia Douglas Johnson. With rapture, with power, with ease! AmNP

Yours. Rabindranath Tagore. Yours is the heaven that lies in the common dust,/and you are there for me, you are there for all. MoRP

Yours Truly. Leonard Nathan. and this is a judgment. AMV-80

Yourself. Jones Very. But he who speaks, or him who's spoken to,/Must both remain as strangers still to you. AA; AmLP; MAmP; NePA; NOBA; OxBA; PoEL 1-5

Yourself and Myself. Anonymous. Have pity on me/lying here by myself/in the feather bed. NOBI

Youth. Anonymous. It is for youth the meetest play. OBSC

Youth. Katharine Lee Bates. Build a world where life rejoices,/Generous Youth. PGD

Youth. Preston Clark. And in our castles others come and go,/Dreaming our dreams and watching from our towers. HBMV

Youth. Virginia Woodward Cloud. Though the bird were long since slain,/though the song had died in the/ dark. AA

Youth. Frances Cornford. Magnificently unprepared/For the long littleness of life. ELU; PCP

Youth. Bartholomew Griffin. But after all, my comfort rests in this,/That for thy sake my youth decayed is. OBSC

Youth. Laurence Hope. Could he plead guilty in a lovelier way?/His judges acquitted him. WeW

Youth. Langston Hughes. We march! AmFN; GoSl

Youth. George Cabot Lodge. Let it but be the tarrying of the sun. AA

Youth. Jessie B. Rittenhouse. When I walked alone in a wooded lane/With perfect peace of heart. HBMV

Youth. Blanaid Salkeld. Not to be bought back the wealth I betrayed for it. OxBI

Youth. Richard Shelton. when I tell the truth/there is so little to say. DFF

Youth. Barend Toerien. ...Oh noble/Ulysses! Oh Zeus! before the tumble. PeSA

Youth. James Wright. The waters flow past, older, younger/Than he is, or I am. NaP; NoP

Youth and Age. George Arnold. And then–and then–I'll bless/This twain that gives me happiness! HBV 1-2

Youth and Age. George Gordon, Lord Byron. So midst the wither'd waste of life, those tears would flow to me! GTBS; GTBS-P

Youth and Age. Samuel Taylor Coleridge. And tells the jest without the smile. BLPL; EnLi 1-2; ERoP 1-2; FiP; GTBS; GTBS-P; HBV 1-2; OBEV; OBNC; OBRV; PoLf

Youth and Age. Mimnermus. So hard a lot God lays upon the old. AWP

Youth and Age. William Shakespeare. Age, I do defy thee. O! sweet shepherd, hie thee,/For methinks thou stays too long. OBSC

Youth and Age. William Butler Yeats. It speeds the parting guest. ELU; FaBoEE

Youth and Age on Beaulieu River, Hants. Sir John Betjeman. But the older woman only/Knows the ebb tide leaves her lonely/With the shining fields of mud. ChMP; FaBoTw; MP; TwCP

Youth and Art. Robert Browning. And we missed it, lost it for ever. BoLiVe; CTC; HBV 1-2; MBW 1-2; NOBV; ViBoPo

Youth and Beauty. Aurelian Townsend. For fear my Cradle prove my Urn. AnAnS 2; GBL; MePo; SeCP

Youth and Cupid. Queen of England Elizabeth I. "Go, go, go, seek some otherwhere,/Importune me no more!" OBSC

Youth and Maidenhood. Sarah Williams. When it comes my heart breaks forth and sings. OBVV

The Youth and the Northwind. John Godfrey Saxe. A cudgel for his enemies,/And money for his friends. StPo

Youth, Day, Old Age, and Night. Walt Whitman. The Night follows close with millions of suns, and sleep and/restoring darkness. AnAmPo

The Youth Dreams. Rainer Maria Rilke. And still our horses rustle like the rain. AWP; TrJP

A Youth in Apparel That Glittered. Stephen Crane. And died, content. LiTA; NePA

Youth in Arms: IV. Carrion. Harold Monro. I can hardly think you will not turn over and creep/Along the furrows trenchward as if to die. MMM

A Youth Mowing. D. H. Lawrence. Yea, though I'm sorry for thee. InPK; MoAB; MoBrPo; NoAm; TrGrPo

The Youth of Nature: Wordsworth's Country. Matthew Arnold. And darkness returns to our eyes. FaBoPP

Youth of the Mountain. Walter Hand. I ain't nothin' but a yearlin'. AnNE

Youth's Agitations. Matthew Arnold. To youth and age in common–discontent. CBEP

Youth's Progress. John Updike. At twenty-one, I was elected Zeus. FiBHP

Youth's Spring-Tribute. Dante Gabriel Rossetti. With whom cold hearts are counted castaway. MaVP

Youth's Thankfulness. Edgar Daniel Kramer. Into communion, Lord, with Thee and God. PGD

Youth Sings a Song of Rosebuds. Countee Cullen. Can fan into a fire. BANP; PoLf

Youth! Thou Wear'st to Manhood Now. Sir Walter Scott. Graver follies must thou follow,/But as senseless, false, and hollow. OBSP

The Youth with Red-Gold Hair. Edith Sitwell. Sighed over the fields of wheat, "He is gone.../Forlorn." FaBoTw; MoVE

Youthful Age. Thomas Stanley. For his heart belies his hairs. AWP

Ypres. Laurence Binyon. ...toward her, each alone,/Glide the dark dreams that seek an English grave. MMM

Ys Yt Possyble. Sir Thomas Wyatt. As men wedd ladyes by lycence and leve,/All ys possyble. AAS; PoEL 1-5

Yucca in the Moonlight. Glenn Ward Dresbach. It takes a shadowy stand/That shames a groping hand. BPAW

Yucca Is Yellowing. William Haskel Simpson. It is for beauty only. BPAW

The Yucca Moth. Archie Randolph Ammons. the radiant, white, hanging day? NOBA

Yugoslav Cemetery. Celeste Turner Wright. These large-eyed mournful lovers in the rain. DFF

Yuh Lookin GOOD. Carolyn M. Rodgers. the brothas, the beautiful brothas/sho will! BPo

Yuki. Mary McNeil Fenollosa. 'T is all I know of weather. AA

The Yule Days. Anonymous. Who learns my carol and carries it away? GBP

The Yule Log. William Hamilton Hayne. Yet trembling on the verge of speech. AA

Yule's Come, and Yule's Gane. Anonymous. Sae Jock maun to his flail again,/And Jenny to her wheel. GBP

Yuma. Charles Henry Phelps. And the dread mirage are there. AA

Yung Wind. Confucius.
All your hundred plans come to naught,/none matched my thought. CTC
A man without courtesy/might quite as well cease to be. CTC

Yussouf. James Russell Lowell. Thou art avenged, my first-born, sleep in peace! BBV; BeLS; BLPA; BLPL; FaBoBe

Yves Tanguy. David Gascoyne. Whose feet are so deep in the sand. EAS

Z

Z Is for Zoroaster. Eleanor Farjeon. The ABRACADABRA/Of old Zoroaster!' WSC

Zachary Zed. James Reeves. And never a person lived to tell/If ever Zachary died. QQQ

Zagonyi. George Henry Boker. Whene'er you lead your well-known way/to death or victory! PAH

Zalinka. Tom MacInnes. A girl in pyjamas and bangles/Slept with her hands in my hair. PeCV

Zalka Peetruza. Ray Garfield Dandridge. That, though we saw–we saw not her. BANP; PoBA

The Zambra Dance. John Dryden. Asleep or waking, you must ease my pain. CEP; SeCV 1-2

Zapata & the Landlord. A. B. Spellman. & he has never fought/a thief. NNP; PoBA

Zarathustra. Thomas S. Jones, Jr. And from the stars still falls the answering fire. AnAmPo

Zaydee. Philip Levine. the long streets were still and the snow/swirled where I lay down to rest. NNaP; VWA

Zeal and Love. John Henry, Cardinal Newman. Book-lore ne'er served, when trial came,/Nor gifts, when faith was dead. TW

The Zeal of Jehu. John Henry, Cardinal Newman. For a soul that thou slightest–/Thine own. OBRV

The Zealless Xylographer. Mary Mapes Dodge. And the end of it was he never again/In a Xanthic Xebec went sailing the main. OBAL

Zealot Without a Face. Charles Dobzynski. Zealot without a face VWA

Zealots of Yearning. David Rokeah. Desolation will not vanish out of the/Negev/Ere it vanishes out of the hearts. TrJP

The Zealous Puritan. Anonymous. You would sink into Perdition. OBS

Zebaoth. Else Lasker-Schüler. The gold of Thy gate is melting/in my yearning. TrJP

Zebra. Isak (Karen Blixen) Dinesen. And to wander to the water-hole. GoJo; RFM

Zebra. William Jay Smith. And a green-and-yellow jumping jack. TiPo

The Zebra Dun. Anonymous. That every educated feller ain't a plumb greenhorn. AmFP; CoSo; FSW; PH; StPo; ViBoFo

The Zebras. Roy Campbell. To roll his mare among the trampled lilies. AnFE; LiTB; MoBrPo; PoPle; PrIm; ViBoPo

Zechariah. Earl Bowman Marlatt. "For we have heard/"That the Lord, our God, is with you." MoRP

Zeimbekiko. Robin Magowan. Moving over all the floor/moving/threshing/sowing. EAS

Zek'l Weep (with music). Anonymous. Chillun, I know you go'n to miss me/When I'm gone. AS

Zeke. Leonard Alfred George Strong. An' 'oller in ees yerole. MoBrPo

'Zekiel Saw de Wheel. Anonymous. Wheel, oh, wheel,/Wheel in de middle of a wheel. BoAN 1-2

The Zen Archer. James Kirkup. Lets fly the shaft that is/Himself, and splits/The first arrow at the centre of the gold. EaLo

Zen Buddhism and Psychoanalysis Psychoanalysis and Zen Buddhism. Jackson MacLow. ...Statements made/speak PoM

The Zen of Housework. Al Zolynas. Ah, grey sacrament of the mundane! LTB

Zennor. Anne Ridler. But all life here is carried on/Against the crash and cry of the moving tides. MoVE

Zephyr. Eugene Fitch Ware. It will land you, without doubt,/Upside down and wrong side out. PoLf

Zeppelin. Andrew Glaze. I mean so I will know if I should/feel resentful or honored. WeW

Zermatt. Thomas Hardy. ...yea, even that Noon/When darkness filled the earth till the ninth hour. OBNC

The Zest of Life. Henry Van Dyke. Because the road's last turn will be the best. WBLP

Zeyde. Roberta Metz. humming softly, something ancient. AMV-81

Zillebeke Brook. Edmund Charles Blunden. On my way up to Sanctuary Wood. MMM

The Zilver-Weed. William Barnes. Now woone by woone the trees do die,/An' vew of all the row do stand. NOBV

Zimbabwe. F. D. Sinclair. Deeper than thought, earthed in the feeling heart. PeSA

Zimmer and His Turtle Sink the House. Paul Zimmer. ...ready to snap/My digits off if I gave him/Half a chance. Psk

Zimmer Drunk and Alone, Dreaming of Old Football Games. Paul Zimmer. With my bottle tucked up high away from fumbles. MAT

Zimmer Envying Elephants. Paul Zimmer. Everybody loose and at a distance. GP

Zimmer in Fall. Paul Zimmer. Let it all stand as it is. PPJ

Zimmer in Grade School. Paul Zimmer. And sits all day in shame/Outside the office of the principal. GP

Zimmer's Hard Dream. Paul Zimmer. I raise the human race within my loins/And fire it off to home! GP

Zimmer's Head Thudding against the Blackboard. Paul Zimmer. And curse her yellow teeth with this. PCP

Zimmer's Last Gig. Paul Zimmer. Her ear, she never/Would have bounced. AMV-80

A Zimmershire Lad. Paul Zimmer. Beware the ale foam in your way/Or you will end like Zimmer. SM

Zimri. John Dryden. He left not Faction, but of that was left. AnFE

Zinnias. Valerie Worth. ...I wish/I were like zinnias. NTCP

Zion; or, the City of God. John Newton. Solid joys and lasting treasure/None but Zion's children know. NOEC

Zion's Sons and Daughters. Anonymous. Jesus gave him leave to drink,/He drank and fled to glory. AmFP

Zionist Marching Song. Naphtali Imber. In Jordan now set we our watch. TrJP

Zip Coon. Anonymous. Zip a duden duden duden zip a duden day. PSoN

Zippora Returns to Moses at Rephidim. Rose Drachler. You jealous/Bridegroom of blood VWA

Zito the Magician. Miroslav Holub. through the throng of courtiers, to his home/in a nutshell. SUW

The Ziz. John Hollander. We are blind to, a birdhood/to cover the head of the sky. VWA

Zizi's Lament. Gregory Corso. will I ever get it? NeAP; VGW

Zlotchev, My Home. Moishe Leib Halpern. My home, my Zlotchev. VWA

The Zobo Bird. Frank A. Collymore. O Zobo bird! AmMo; GoJo

The Zodiac Rhyme. Anonymous. The Fish with glittering tails. GBP

The Zodiac Song. John Ruskin. Daisies round the dish and a pearl on every/scale. NOBV

The Zodiac: The Valley of Sleep. Hendrik Marsman. An unfathomed oblivion. LiTW

The Zodiac, X. James Dickey. Too much light. Too much love. TAP

Zoe and the Ghosts. Dieter Weslowski. thrashing back and forth, a swimmer/going under. PPJ

Zohara. Jack Hirschman. who keeps her secret in the leaves Who is You Her dark Her/green outspreading VWA

Zola. Edwin Arlington Robinson. Throbbing, the pulse, the divine heart of man. AmePo; MoVE; NePA; OxBA

Zolgotz. Anonymous. "That was Theodore Roosevelt..." AmFP

Zollicoffer. Henry Lynden Flash. And fame to shout with immortal voice/Dead on the field of Glory! PAH

Zone. Guillaume Apollinaire. Sun throat cut SOTW

Zone. Louise Bogan. We have learned how to bear. PoCh

Zone of Death. William Everson. Opens his executing eye/And gibbets me. VGW

A Zong. William Barnes. The zwell o' thy bosom, thy eyes' sparklen light. BoLoP

Zong Belegt Baatar. Anonymous. He drank his kumis and wine,/Ate his pure food,/And lived happily ever after. WTO

The Zonnebeke Road. Edmund Charles Blunden. And freeze you back with that one hope, disdain. MMM; OBWP

The Zoo. John Logan. how much an animal death. LCAP

The Zoo. Gilbert Sorrentino. goliathus was better and he/not a native. NeAP

The Zoo. Humbert Wolfe. And yet I can-/not like the Zoo/as much as other/people do. MoShBr

Zoo Dream. David Barker. Gamey snorting of hot breath/on the back of my neck. GP

The Zoo in the City. Sara Van Alstyne Allen. Keeping to round his holiday/The netted bird, the futile beast. GoYe

The Zoo of You. Arthur Freeman. Unlock, unlock! Let's feed thy zoo. ErPo

Zoo You Too! Ted Joans. WHY DO Third World animals/have to pay...such heavy/lifetime dues? GP

Zophiel: Palace of the Gnomes. Maria Gowen Brooks. And thought upon the music of the spheres. AA

Zoroaster Devoutly Questions Ormazd. Zoroaster. Who in the morning, noon, and evening did decree/As reminders to the wise, of duty's call? AWP; WGRP

The Zucca (excerpt). Percy Bysshe Shelley. Adore thee present or lament thee lost. ERoP 1-2

The Zulu Girl. Roy Campbell. Or the first cloud so terrible and still/That bears the coming harvest in its breast. AtBAP; MoVE; OBMV; PoPl

The Zulu King: New Orleans. Josephine Copeland. Africa called to her own again. GoSl

Zummer Stream. William Barnes. My zummer-brighten'd years do pass. BoNaP

Zummer Thoughts in Winter Time. William Barnes. Be zummer thoughts in winter-tide. VLP

The Zun A-Lighten Eyes A-Shut. William Barnes. Wi' you, my fancy's ev'ry pleace/Wer ever fay, vor you wer there. VLP

Zun-Zet. William Barnes. An' while the gossamer's light netten/Sparkled to the zun a-zetten. PoEL 1-5

Zurich, zum Storchen. Paul Celan. We/simply do not know, you know,/we/simply do not know/what/counts. VWA